HAMMOND®
WORLD ATLAS

HAMMOND® MEDALLION

WORLD

ATLAS

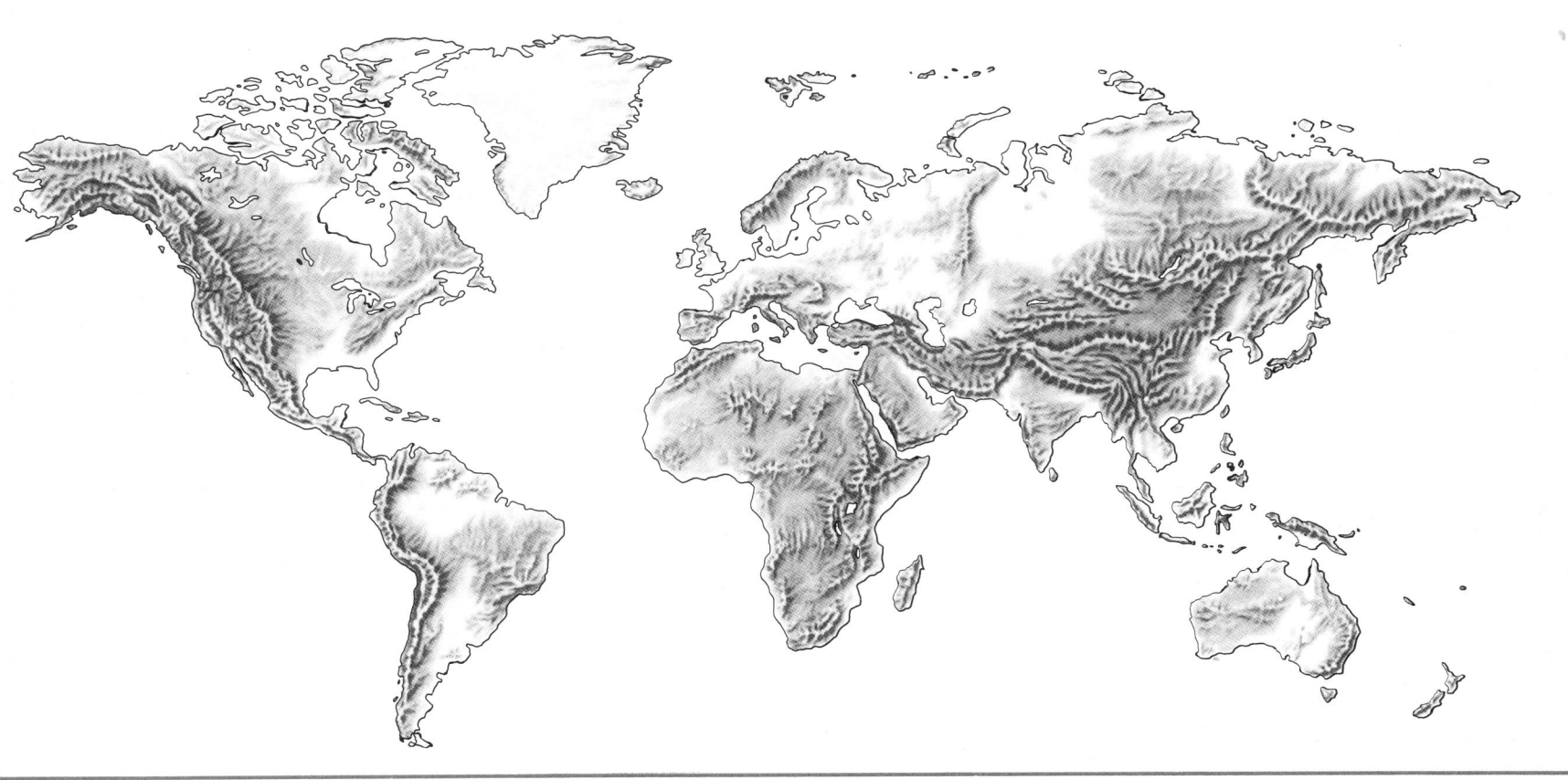

HAMMOND INCORPORATED   MAPLEWOOD, NEW JERSEY 07040

Library of Congress Cataloging in Publication Data

Hammond Incorporated.
    Hammond medallion world atlas.

    Includes glossary and indexes.
    1. Atlases.   2. Zip code—United States.   I. Title.
II. Title: Medallion world atlas.
G1021.H273   1984   912   84-675070
ISBN 0-8437-1250-3

Hammond Publications Advisory Board

Contents

Part IV—World History Map Collection

Part V—United States History Map Collection

Introduction to the World Atlas

As in previous editions, this Hammond World Atlas is organized to make the retrieval of information as simple and quick as possible. The guiding principle in organizing the atlas material has been to present separate subjects on *separate* maps. In this way, each individual map topic is shown with the greatest degree of clarity, unencumbered with extraneous information that is best revealed on separate maps. Of equal importance from the standpoint of good atlas design is the treatment of all current information on a given country or state as a single atlas unit. Thus, the basic reference map of an area is accompanied on adjacent pages by all supplementary information pertaining to that area. For example, the detailed index for a given map always appears on the same page as, or on the pages immediately following, the reference map. This same map index provides population data for the many cities, towns and villages shown on the map. Highlight information on the area, i.e., the total population and area, the capital, the highest point, is listed in the summary fact listings accompanying each unit. An adjacent locator map relates the subject area to the larger world beyond. A three-dimensional picture of the area is exhibited by means of the accompanying full-color topographic map. A separate economic map defines the vital agricultural, industrial and mineral resources of the area. In the case of the foreign maps, the flag of each independent nation appears on the appropriate page. Finally, certain country units contain special subject maps dealing with the history, climate, demography and vegetation of the area.

An outstanding feature of the atlas is the addition of ZIP codes to the index entries for each of the legion of communities shown on the state maps. With the exception of the U.S. Postal Service directories of limited availability, the ZIP code listings herein are the most extensive published. In addition to listing ZIP codes for the communities possessing post offices, ZIP codes of the nearest post offices are listed for communities without postal facilities. It may be said with a fair degree of certainty that this innovation in atlas content doubles the value of the work for home, office and school.

The back of the book contains a second type of index. This is a multi-paged "A-to-Z" index of all the world's places that appear on the maps. The use of this map index is essential when the name of a place is known but its country, state, or province is unknown. ZIP codes also are given here for each U.S. city, town, or community entry.

The numerous geographical changes of the decade are all recorded in the Hammond World Atlas. Over 8,000 changes, which occurred throughout the world since the last major revision, were entered on the maps. The state maps now reveal the many new towns and cities that have developed in the recent past. The majority of these are burgeoning suburbs on the fringes of our larger cities. On the other hand, large numbers of abandoned and defunct rural hamlets have been removed from the maps and map indexes. Hundreds of other changes are also recorded on the state maps: new national parks and monuments, new dams, new reservoirs, name changes, etc.

Of course, the maps of foreign areas have been thoroughly updated. These revisions echo the new nations, shifting boundaries and the fluid internal divisions of many countries. New communities generated by the opening up of resources in the developing nations are also noted.

In closing it may be said that the atlas has truly been designed for contemporary use. Just as the information presented on the following pages is as current and up to date as the editors and cartographers could issue it, so the design and organization has been as well planned as possible to create a work useful to present generations.

President
HAMMOND INCORPORATED

Gazetteer-Index of the World

This alphabetical list of continents, countries, states, colonial possessions and other major geographical areas provides a quick reference to their area in square miles and square kilometers, population, capital or chief town, map page number and index key thereon. The last name indicates the square on the respective page in which the name may be found. An indication of the population sources used is also included, and refers both to the total figures given in this Gazetteer-Index and to the populations appearing in greater detail with the maps throughout the atlas. The population figures used in each case are the latest reliable figures obtainable. A glance at the sources will show that the dates vary considerably throughout the world. In certain areas where no census has ever been taken, we must rely on official estimates. In other areas where censuses have been taken at infrequent intervals, we again rely on estimates. The key to the abbreviations used in the Gazetteer-Index follows:

aut = autonomous	est = estimates	reg = regions
boro = boroughs	excl = excluding	rep = republics
cap = capital	FC = final census	S.S.R. = Soviet Socialist Republic
CE = census (undetermined)	gov = governorates	terr = territories; territory
CIA = U.S. Central Intelligence Agency	incl = including	TP = total population
	isl = islands	U.K. = United Kingdom
cit = cities	met = metropolitan	UN = United Nations
co = counties	OE = official estimate	U.S.A. = United States of America
com = communes	oth = other populations	U.S.S.R. = Union of Soviet Socialist Republics
dept = departments	par = parishes	
dist = districts	PC = preliminary census	ws = with suburbs
div = divisions	prov = provinces; provincial	

Country	Area Square Miles	Area Square Kilometers	Population	Capital or Chief Town	Page and Index Ref.	Sources of Population Data
*Afghanistan	250,775	649,507	15,540,000	Kabul	68/A 2	79 PC
Africa	11,707,000	30,321,130	469,000,000		102/.....	80 UN est
Alabama, U.S.A.	51,705	133,916	3,893,888	Montgomery	195/.....	80 FC & OE
Alaska, U.S.A.	591,004	1,530,700	401,851	Juneau	196/.....	80 FC & OE
*Albania	11,100	28,749	2,590,600	Tiranë	45/E 5	TP—79 PC; cit over 6,000—70 OE; oth—63 OE
Alberta, Canada	255,285	661,185	2,237,724	Edmonton	182/.....	81 FC
*Algeria	919,591	2,381,740	17,422,000	Algiers	106/D 3	77 PC
American Samoa	77	199	32,297	Pago Pago	87/J 7; 86/.....	80 FC
Andorra	188	487	31,000	Andorra la Vella	33/G 1	TP—79 OE; cap—75 OE
*Angola	481,351	1,246,700	7,078,000	Luanda	114/C 6	TP—80 UN est; oth—70 FC
Anguilla	35	91	6,519	The Valley	156/F 3	74 FC
Antarctica	5,500,000	14,245,000	....	....	5/.....	....
*Antigua and Barbuda	171	443	75,000	St. John's	161/E11; 156/G 3	TP—80 OE; oth—70 FC
*Argentina	1,072,070	2,776,661	28,438,000	Buenos Aires	143/.....	TP—82 OE; oth—80 PC
Arizona, U.S.A.	114,000	295,260	2,718,425	Phoenix	198/.....	80 FC & OE
Arkansas, U.S.A.	53,187	137,754	2,286,435	Little Rock	202/.....	80 FC & OE
Armenian S.S.R., U.S.S.R.	11,506	29,800	3,031,000	Erivan	52/F 6	TP, cit over 50,000—79 PC; oth—70 FC
Aruba, Neth. Antilles	70	181	55,148	Oranjestad	161/E 9	TP—71 FC; cap—72 est
Ascension Island, St. Helena	34	88	719	Georgetown	102/A 5	76 FC
Ashmore & Cartier Islands, Australia	61	159		(Canberra, Austr.)	88/C 2	....
Asia	17,128,500	44,362,815	2,633,000,000	....	54/.....	80 est
*Australia	2,966,136	7,682,300	14,576,330	Canberra	88/.....	81 FC
Australian Capital Territory	927	2,400	221,609	Canberra	96/E 4	81 FC
*Austria	32,375	83,851	7,507,000	Vienna	40/B 3	TP—80 OE; cap, cit over 100,000—73 OE; oth—71 FC
Azerbaidzhan S.S.R., U.S.S.R.	33,436	86,600	6,028,000	Baku	52/G 6	TP, cit over 50,000—79 PC; oth—70 FC
Azores Islands, Portugal	902	2,335	264,400	Ponta Delgada; Angra do Heroísmo; Horta	32/.....	TP—77 OE; oth—70 FC & PC
*Bahamas	5,382	13,939	209,505	Nassau	156/C 1	80 PC
*Bahrain	240	622	358,857	Manama	58/F 4	TP—81 PC; oth—71 FC
Baker Island, U.S.A.	1	2.6	....	....	87/J 5	....
Balearic Islands, Spain	1,936	5,014	558,287	Palma	33/H 3	70 FC
*Bangladesh	55,126	142,776	87,052,024	Dhaka	68/G 4	TP—81 PC; oth—74 FC
*Barbados	166	430	248,983	Bridgetown	161/B 8	80 PC
Belau (Palau)	188	487	12,116	Koror	86/D 5	80 FC
*Belgium	11,781	30,513	9,855,110	Brussels	27/E 7	TP—80 OE; oth—70 FC (com)
*Belize	8,867	22,966	144,857	Belmopan	154/C 2	TP, cap, cit over 1,000—80 PC; oth—70 PC
*Benin	43,483	112,620	3,338,240	Porto-Novo	106/E 6	TP—79 PC; cap, Cotonou—75 OE; oth—73 OE
Bermuda	21	54	67,761	Hamilton	156/H 3	80 PC
*Bhutan	18,147	47,000	1,298,000	Thimphu	68/G 3	TP—80 UN est; oth—70 OE
*Bolivia	424,163	1,098,582	5,600,000	La Paz; Sucre	136/.....	TP—80 OE; cap, dept, dept cap—76 FC; oth—50 FC
Bonaire, Neth. Antilles	112	291	8,087	Kralendijk	161/E 9	TP—71 FC; cap—72 est
Bophuthatswana (rep.), South Africa	15,570	40,326	1,200,000	Mmabatho	119/D 5	TP—78 est; oth—70 FC
*Botswana	224,764	582,139	819,000	Gaborone	119/C 4	TP—80 OE; cap, Francistown—74 OE; Selebi-Pikwe—75 FC; oth—71 FC
Bouvet Island	22	57	....	....	5/D 1	....
*Brazil	3,284,426	8,506,663	119,098,992	Brasília	132/.....	80 PC
British Columbia, Canada	366,253	948,596	2,744,467	Victoria	184/.....	81 FC
British Indian Ocean Terr.	29	75	2,000	(London, U.K.)	54/L10	78 est
British Virgin Islands	59	153	11,006	Road Town	157/H 1	TP—80 FC; oth—70 FC
Brunei	2,226	5,765	192,832	Bandar Seri Begawan	85/E 4	81 PC
*Bulgaria	42,823	110,912	8,862,000	Sofia	45/F 4	TP—80 OE; oth—75 PC
*Burma	261,789	678,034	32,913,000	Rangoon	72/B 2	TP—79 OE; states, div. cit over 100,000—73 PC; oth—53 FC
*Burundi	10,747	27,835	4,021,910	Bujumbura	114/E 4	79 PC
*Byelorussian S.S.R. (White Russian S.S.R.), U.S.S.R.	80,154	207,600	9,560,000	Minsk	52/C 4	TP, cit over 50,000—79 PC; oth—70 FC
California, U.S.A.	158,706	411,049	23,667,565	Sacramento	204/.....	80 FC & OE
*Cambodia (Kampuchea)	69,898	181,036	5,200,000	Phnom Penh	72/E 4	TP—79 CIA est; cap—80 est
*Cameroon	183,568	475,441	8,503,000	Yaoundé	114/B 2	TP—80 OE; cit over 21,000—76 FC; Ebolowa, oth—70 OE
*Canada	3,851,787	9,976,139	24,343,181	Ottawa	162/.....	81 FC
Canary Islands, Spain	2,808	7,273	1,170,224	Las Palmas; Santa Cruz	32/B 4	70 FC
Cape of Good Hope, South Africa	261,705	677,816	5,543,506	Cape Town	118/C 6	TP—80 PC; oth—70 FC
*Cape Verde	1,557	4,033	324,000	Praia	106/B 8	TP—80 UN est; oth—70 PC
Cayman Islands	100	259	18,000	Georgetown	156/B 3	TP—81 OE; oth—79 FC

*Member of the United Nations.

Gazetteer-Index of the World

Country	Area Square Miles	Area Square Kilometers	Population	Capital or Chief Town	Page and Index Ref.	Sources of Population Data
Celebes, Indonesia	72,986	189,034	7,732,383	Ujung Pandang	**85/G 6**	71 PC
*Central African Republic	242,000	626,780	2,284,000	Bangui	114/C 2	TP—79 est; oth—75 FC
Central America	197,480	511,475	21,000,000	....	154/......	79 OE
Ceylon, see Sri Lanka						
*Chad	495,752	1,283,998	4,309,000	N'Djamena	111/C 4	TP—78 OE; oth—72 OE
Channel Islands	75	194	133,000	St. Helier; St. Peter Port	13/E 8	TP—81 OE; oth—71 FC
*Chile	292,257	756,946	11,275,440	Santiago	138/......	TP—82 PC; cit (part)—79 OE; oth—70 FC & PC
*China, People's Rep. of	3,691,000	9,559,690	958,090,000	Peking (Beijing)	77/......	TP, prov, Peking, Shanghai, Tianjin—78 OE; oth—70 est
China, Republic of (Taiwan)	13,971	36,185	16,609,961	Taipei	77/K 7	TP, cap, Penghu Isl., cit over 300,000—77 OE; oth—70 OE
Christmas Island, Australia	52	135	3,184	Flying Fish Cove	54/O11	80 OE
Ciskei (rep.), S. Africa	2,988	7,740	635,631	Bisho	119/D 6	80 PC
Clipperton Island	2	5.2	....	....	146/H 8	....
Cocos (Keeling) Islands, Australia	5.4	14	555	West Island	54/N11	81 PC
*Colombia	439,513	1,138,339	27,520,000	Bogotá	126/......	TP—80 OE; oth—73 PC
Colorado, U.S.A.	104,091	269,596	2,889,735	Denver	208/......	80 FC & OE
*Comoros	719	1,862	290,000	Moroni	119/G 2	TP—78 est; cap—75 OE; oth—66 FC
*Congo	132,046	342,000	1,537,000	Brazzaville	114/B 4	TP—80 UN est; cap—74 FC; oth—74 PC
Connecticut, U.S.A.	5,018	12,997	3,107,576	Hartford	210/......	80 FC & OE
Cook Islands	91	236	17,695	Avarua	87/K 7	81 PC
Coral Sea Islands, Australia	8.5	22	....	....	88/J 3	....
Corsica, France	3,352	8,682	289,842	Ajaccio; Bastia	28/B 6	75 FC
*Costa Rica	19,575	50,700	2,245,000	San José	**154/E 5**	TP—80 OE; oth—73 FC
*Cuba	44,206	114,494	9,706,369	Havana	158/......	TP—81 PC; prov, cap—81 PC; oth—81 & 70 PC
Curaçao, Neth. Antilles	178	462	145,430	Willemstad	161/G 7	TP—71 FC; cap—75 OE
*Cyprus	3,473	8,995	629,000	Nicosia	62/E 5	TP—80 OE; oth—73 FC, 72 OE
*Czechoslovakia	49,373	127,876	15,276,799	Prague	41/C 2	TP—80 PC; cap, cit over 100,000—75 OE; rep, reg—74 OE; oth—75 OE, 70 FC
Delaware, U.S.A.	2,044	5,294	594,317	Dover	245/R 3	80 FC & OE
*Denmark	16,629	43,069	5,124,000	Copenhagen	21/......	TP—80 OE; oth—75 OE, 71 OE, 70 FC
District of Columbia, U.S.A.	69	179	638,432	Washington	244/F 5	80 FC
*Djibouti	8,880	23,000	386,000	Djibouti	111/H 5	TP—79 est; cap—73 OE
*Dominica	290	751	74,089	Roseau	161/E 7	TP—80 PC; oth—70 FC
*Dominican Republic	18,704	48,443	5,647,977	Santo Domingo	158/D 6	81 PC
*East Germany (German Democratic Republic)	41,768	108,179	16,737,000	Berlin (East)	22/......	TP—80 OE; oth—75 OE
*Ecuador	109,483	283,561	8,644,000	Quito	128/C 3	TP—81 OE; oth—74 OE
*Egypt	386,659	1,001,447	41,572,000	Cairo	110/E 2	TP—79 OE; oth—76 PC
*El Salvador	8,260	21,393	4,813,000	San Salvador	154/C 4	TP—80 OE; oth—71 FC
England, U.K.	50,516	130,836	46,220,955	London	13/......	TP—81 PC; co, cap (boro & ws)—76 OE; cit—76 & 73 OE; oth—71 FC
*Equatorial Guinea	10,831	28,052	244,000	Malabo	114/A 3	TP—79 est; terr—68 OE; oth—60 FC
Estonian S.S.R., U.S.S.R.	17,413	45,100	1,466,000	Tallinn	**52/C 3;** 53/......	TP, cit over 50,000—79 PC; oth—70 FC
*Ethiopia	471,776	1,221,900	31,065,000	Addis Ababa	110/G 5	TP—80 OE; cap, Asmara—78 OE; prov—72 OE; oth—72 & 71 OE
Europe	4,057,000	10,507,630	676,000,000	....	7/......	80 est
Faeroe Islands, Denmark	540	1,399	41,969	Tórshavn	21/B 2	77 FC
Falkland Islands & Dependencies	6,198	16,053	1,813	**Stanley**	**120/E 8;** 143/D 7	80 FC
*Fiji	7,055	18,272	588,068	**Suva**	**87/H 8;** 86/......	80 FC
*Finland	130,128	337,032	4,788,000	Helsinki	18/O 6	TP—80 OE; prov—75 OE; oth—75 OE, 70 FC
Florida, U.S.A.	58,664	151,940	9,746,342	Tallahassee	212/......	80 FC & OE
*France	210,038	543,998	53,788,000	Paris	28/......	TP—80 OE; oth—75 FC
French Guiana	35,135	91,000	73,022	Cayenne	131/E 3	82 FC
French Polynesia	1,544	4,000	137,382	Papeete	87/L 8	77 FC
*Gabon	103,346	267,666	551,000	Libreville	114/B 4	TP—80 UN est; oth—70 FC
*Gambia	4,127	10,689	601,000	Banjul	106/A 6	TP—80 OE; oth—73 FC
Gaza Strip	139	360	400,000	Gaza	65/A 4	TP—76 OE; oth—67 CE
Georgia, U.S.A.	58,910	152,577	5,463,105	Atlanta	217/......	80 FC & OE
Georgian S.S.R., U.S.S.R.	26,911	69,700	5,015,000	Tbilisi	52/F 6	TP, cit over 50,000—79 PC; oth—70 FC
*Germany, East (German Democratic Republic)	41,768	108,179	16,737,000	Berlin (East)	22/......	TP—80 OE; oth—75 OE
*Germany, West (Federal Republic)	95,985	248,601	61,658,000	Bonn	22/......	TP—80 OE; states, cap—76 OE; oth—76 OE, 70 FC
*Ghana	92,099	238,536	11,450,000	Accra	106/D 7	TP—80 OE; oth—70 FC
Gibraltar	2.28	5.91	29,760	Gibraltar	33/D 4	79 OE
*Great Britain & Northern Ireland (United Kingdom)	94,399	244,493	55,672,000	London	10/......	TP—81 OE (see England, Wales, Scotland, Northern Ireland)
*Greece	50,944	131,945	9,599,000	Athens	45/F 6	TP—80 OE; oth—71 OE
Greenland	840,000	2,175,600	49,773	Nuuk (Godthåb)	4/B12	TP—80 OE
*Grenada	133	344	103,103	**St. George's**	**161/D 9;** 156/G 4	TP, cap—81 OE; oth—70 FC
Guadeloupe & Dependencies	687	1,779	328,400	**Basse-Terre**	**161/A 5;** 156/F 4	82 FC
Guam	209	541	105,979	**Agaña**	**87/E 4;** 86/......	80 FC
*Guatemala	42,042	108,889	7,262,419	Guatemala	154/B 3	TP—80 OE; oth—73 FC
*Guinea	94,925	245,856	5,143,284	Conakry	106/B 6	TP, cap (ws), Kankan, Kindia, Labé—**72 FC**; oth—67 OE
*Guinea-Bissau	13,948	36,125	777,214	Bissau	106/A 6	79 PC
*Guyana	83,000	214,970	793,000	Georgetown	131/B 3	TP—80 OE; cap, cit over 10,000—70 FC; oth—60 FC
*Haiti	10,694	27,697	5,053,792	Port-au-Prince	158/C 5	82 PC
Hawaii, U.S.A.	6,471	16,760	964,691	Honolulu	218/......	80 FC & OE
Heard & McDonald Islands, Australia	113	293	....	....	2/N 8	....
Holland, see Netherlands						
*Honduras	43,277	112,087	3,691,000	Tegucigalpa	154/D 3	TP—80 OE; oth—74 FC
Hong Kong	403	1,044	5,022,000	**Victoria**	**77/H 7;** 78/......	TP—81 PC; oth—76 OE
Howland Island, U.S.A.	1	2.6	....	....	87/J 5	....
*Hungary	35,919	93,030	10,709,536	Budapest	41/D 3	TP, cap, co—80 PC; oth—80 PC, 70 FC
*Iceland	39,768	103,000	228,785	Reykjavík	21/B 1	TP—80 PC; oth—70 FC
Idaho, U.S.A.	83,564	216,431	944,038	Boise	220/......	80 FC & OE

Country	Area Square Miles	Square Kilometers	Population	Capital or Chief Town	Page and Index Ref.	Sources of Population Data
Illinois, U.S.A.	56,345	145,934	11,426,596	Springfield	222/......	80 FC & OE
*India	1,269,339	3,287,588	683,810,051	New Delhi	68/D 4	TP & states—81 PC; oth—71 FC
Indiana, U.S.A.	36,185	93,719	5,490,260	Indianapolis	227/......	80 FC & OE
*Indonesia	788,430	2,042,034	147,490,298	Jakarta	85/D 7	TP—80 PC; cit—80 PC & 71 PC; isls.—71 PC
Iowa, U.S.A.	56,275	145,752	2,913,808	Des Moines	229/......	80 FC & OE
*Iran	636,293	1,648,000	37,447,000	Tehran	66/F 4	TP—80 OE; div, cit over 50,000—76 PC; oth—66 FC & PC, 56 FC
*Iraq	172,476	446,713	12,767,000	Baghdad	66/C 4	TP—79 OE; oth—65 & 57 FC
*Ireland	27,136	70,282	3,440,427	Dublin	17/......	TP—81 PC; oth—71 FC
Ireland, Northern, U.K.	5,452	14,121	1,543,000	Belfast	17/F 2	TP—81 OE; dist—76 OE; cap, Londonderry—73 OE; oth—71 FC
Isle of Man	227	588	64,000	Douglas	13/C 3	TP—80 OE; oth—71 FC
*Israel	7,847	20,324	3,878,000	Jerusalem	65/B 4	TP—80 OE; cap, cit over 100,000—77 OE; dist, cit over 5,000—72 PC; oth—61 FC
*Italy	116,303	301,225	57,140,000	Rome	34/......	TP—80 OE; oth—71 FC
*Ivory Coast	124,504	322,465	7,920,000	Abidjan	106/C 7	TP—79 OE; oth—75 PC
*Jamaica	4,411	11,424	2,184,000	Kingston	158/......	TP—80 OE; oth—70 & 60 FC
Jan Mayen	144	373	....		6/D 1	
*Japan	145,730	377,441	117,057,485	Tokyo	81/......	TP—80 PC; oth—75 FC
Jarvis Island, U.S.A.	1	2.6	....		87/K 6	....
Java, Indonesia	48,842	126,500	73,712,411	Jakarta	85/J 2	71 PC
Johnston Atoll	.91	2.4	327		87/K 4	80 FC
*Jordan	35,000	90,650	2,152,273	Amman	65/D 3	TP—79 PC; cap, cit over 100,000—77 OE; gov, cit 9,000-100,000—73 OE; oth—61 FC
*Kampuchea (Cambodia)	69,898	181,036	5,200,000	Phnom Penh	72/E 4	TP—79 CIA est; cap—80 est
Kansas, U.S.A.	82,277	213,097	2,364,236	Topeka	232/......	80 FC & OE
Kazakh S.S.R., U.S.S.R.	1,048,300	2,715,100	14,684,000	Alma-Ata	48/G 5	TP, cit over 50,000—79 PC; oth—70 FC
Kentucky, U.S.A.	40,409	104,659	3,660,257	Frankfort	237/......	80 FC & OE
*Kenya	224,960	582,646	15,327,061	Nairobi	115/G 3	TP—79 PC; oth—69 FC
Kermadec Islands	13	33	5	....	87/J 9	81 FC
Kingman Reef	0.1	0.26	....		87/K 5	
Kirgiz S.S.R., U.S.S.R.	76,641	198,500	3,529,000	Frunze	48/H 5	TP, cit over 50,000—79 PC; oth—70 FC
Kiribati	291	754	56,213	Bairiki	87/J 6	TP—78 FC; oth—73 FC
Korea, North	46,540	120,539	17,914,000	P'yŏngyang	80/D 3	TP—80 UN est; cap—76 OE; Hamhŭng—72 OE; oth—70 OE
Korea, South	38,175	98,873	37,448,836	Seoul	80/D 5	TP—80 PC; oth—75 FC & PC
*Kuwait	6,532	16,918	1,355,827	Al Kuwait	58/E 4	80 PC
*Laos	91,428	236,800	3,721,000	Vientiane	72/D 3	TP—80 UN est; cap—66 FC; oth—58 OE
Latvian S.S.R., U.S.S.R.	24,595	63,700	2,521,000	Riga	52/B 3; 53/......	TP, cit over 50,000—79 PC; oth—70 FC
*Lebanon	4,015	10,399	3,161,000	Beirut	62/F 6	TP—80 UN est; cap—70 FC; Tarabulus—64 OE; oth—61 OE
*Lesotho	11,720	30,355	1,339,000	Maseru	119/D 5	TP—80 OE; oth—80 est
*Liberia	43,000	111,370	1,873,000	Monrovia	106/C 7	TP—80 OE; oth—74 FC
*Libya	679,358	1,759,537	2,856,000	Tripoli	110/B 2	TP—79 OE; oth—73 FC & PC
Liechtenstein	61	158	25,220	Vaduz	39/J 2	80 PC
Lithuanian S.S.R., U.S.S.R.	25,174	65,200	3,398,000	Vilna	52/B 3; 53/......	TP, cit over 50,000—79 PC; oth—70 FC
Louisiana, U.S.A.	47,752	123,678	4,206,312	Baton Rouge	238/......	80 FC & OE
*Luxembourg	999	2,587	364,000	Luxembourg	27/J 9	TP—79 OE; cap—74 OE; oth—70 FC
Macau	6	16	271,000	Macau	77/H 7	TP—78 OE; cap—70 FC
*Madagascar	226,657	587,041	8,742,000	Antananarivo	119/H 3	TP—80 UN est; prov, cap, cit over 40,000—75 PC; oth—71 OE
Madeira Islands, Portugal	307	796	262,800	Funchal	32/A 2	TP—77 OE; oth—70 FC & PC
Maine, U.S.A.	33,265	86,156	1,125,027	Augusta	243/......	80 FC & OE
*Malawi	45,747	118,485	5,968,000	Lilongwe	114/F 6	TP—80 OE; oth—77 PC
Malaya, Malaysia	50,806	131,588	11,138,227	Kuala Lumpur	72/D 6	TP, states, Kuala Lumpur—80 PC; cit over 100,000—70 FC; oth—70 PC
*Malaysia	128,308	332,318	13,435,588	Kuala Lumpur	72/D 6; 85/E 4	TP, states, Kuala Lumpur—80 PC; Kuching, Kota Kinabalu, cit over 100,000—70 FC; oth—70 PC
*Maldives	115	298	143,046	Male	54/L 9	78 FC
*Mali	464,873	1,204,021	6,906,000	Bamako	106/C 6	TP—80 OE; oth—76 PC
*Malta	122	316	343,970	Valletta	34/E 7	TP, cit—79 OE; oth—73 OE
Man, Isle of	227	588	64,000	Douglas	13/C 3	TP—80 OE; oth—71 FC
Manitoba, Canada	250,999	650,087	1,026,241	Winnipeg	179/......	81 FC
Marquesas Islands, French Polynesia	492	1,274	5,419	Atuona	87/N 6	77 FC
Marshall Islands	70	181	30,873	Majuro	87/G 4	80 FC
Martinique	425	1,101	328,566	Fort-de-France	161/D 5	82 FC
Maryland, U.S.A.	10,460	27,091	4,216,975	Annapolis	245/......	80 FC & OE
Massachusetts, U.S.A.	8,284	21,456	5,737,037	Boston	249/......	80 FC & OE
*Mauritania	419,229	1,085,803	1,634,000	Nouakchott	106/B 5	TP—80 UN est; oth—76 PC
*Mauritius	790	2,046	959,000	Port Louis	119/G 5	TP—80 OE; cap—77 OE; Curepipe, Quatre Bornes—74 OE; oth—72 PC
Mayotte	144	373	47,300	Dzaoudzi	119/G 2	TP—78 CE; cap—66 FC
*Mexico	761,601	1,972,546	67,395,826	Mexico City	150/......	TP, states, cap—80 PC; cap (ws), Guadalajara (ws), Monterrey (ws)—78 OE; oth—70 FC
Michigan, U.S.A.	58,527	151,585	9,262,078	Lansing	250/......	80 FC & OE
Micronesia, Federated States of	....	....	73,160	Kolonia	87/E 5	TP—80 FC
Midway Islands	1.9	4.9	453	....	87/J 3	80 FC
Minnesota, U.S.A.	84,402	218,601	4,075,970	St. Paul	255/......	80 FC & OE
Mississippi, U.S.A.	47,689	123,515	2,520,638	Jackson	256/......	80 FC & OE
Missouri, U.S.A.	69,697	180,515	4,916,759	Jefferson City	261/......	80 FC & OE
Moldavian S.S.R., U.S.S.R.	13,012	33,700	3,947,000	Kishinev	52/C 5	TP, cit over 50,000—79 PC; oth—70 FC
Monaco	368 acres	149 hectares	25,029	Monaco	28/G 6	75 FC
*Mongolia	606,163	1,569,962	1,594,800	Ulaanbaatar	77/E 2	TP—79 PC; prov, cap, Darhan—77 OE; oth—69 FC
Montana, U.S.A.	147,046	380,849	786,690	Helena	262/......	80 FC & OE
Montserrat	40	104	12,073	Plymouth	157/G 3	80 PC
*Morocco	172,414	446,550	20,242,000	Rabat	106/C 2	TP—80 OE; oth—71 FC
*Mozambique	303,769	786,762	12,130,000	Maputo	119/E 4	TP, prov, cap—80 OE; oth—70 FC
Namibia (South-West Africa)	317,827	823,172	1,200,000	Windhoek	118/B 3	TP—74 est; oth—70 PC
Natal, South Africa	33,578	86,967	5,722,215	Pietermaritzburg	119/E 5	TP—80 PC; oth—70 PC
Nauru	7.7	20	7,254	Yaren (district)	87/G 6	77 PC
Navassa Island	2	5	....		156/C 3	....
Nebraska, U.S.A.	77,355	200,349	1,569,825	Lincoln	264/......	80 FC & OE
*Nepal	54,663	141,577	14,179,301	Kathmandu	68/E 3	TP—81 PC; oth—71 FC
*Netherlands	15,892	41,160	14,227,000	The Hague; Amsterdam	27/F 5	TP—81 OE; oth—76 OE (com)

Gazetteer-Index of the World

Country	Area Square Miles	Area Square Kilometers	Population	Capital or Chief Town	Page and Index Ref.	Sources of Population Data
Netherlands Antilles	390	1,010	246,000	Willemstad	156/E 4	TP—78 OE; Willemsted—75 OE; oth—72 est.
Nevada, U.S.A.	110,561	286,353	800,493	Carson City	266/......	80 FC & OE
New Brunswick, Canada	28,354	73,437	696,403	Fredericton	170/......	81 FC
New Caledonia & Dependencies	7,335	18,998	133,233	Nouméa	87/G 8	76 FC
Newfoundland, Canada	156,184	404,517	567,681	St. John's	166/......	81 FC
New Hampshire, U.S.A.	9,279	24,033	920,610	Concord	268/......	80 FC & OE
New Hebrides, see Vanuatu						
New Jersey, U.S.A.	7,787	20,168	7,364,823	Trenton	273/......	80 FC & OE
New Mexico, U.S.A.	121,593	314,926	1,302,981	Santa Fe	274/......	80 FC & OE
New South Wales, Australia	309,498	801,600	5.126,217	Sydney	96/B 2	81 FC
New York, U.S.A.	49,108	127,190	17,558,072	Albany	276/......	80 FC & OE
*New Zealand	103,736	268,676	3,175,737	Wellington	100/......	TP, inc. places, isls.—81 FC; oth—76 FC
*Nicaragua	45,698	118,358	2,703,000	Managua	154/D 4	TP—80 OE; oth—71 FC
*Niger	489,189	1,267,000	5,098,427	Niamey	106/F 5	TP, cap, Maradi, Tahoua, Zinder—77 PC; oth—72 OE
*Nigeria	357,000	924,630	82,643,000	Lagos	106/F 6	TP—79 OE; prov—63 FC; oth—75 & 71 OE
Niue	100	259	3,578	Alofi	87/K 7	79 OE
Norfolk Island, Australia	13.4	34.6	2,175	Kingston	88/L 5	81 FC
North America	9,363,000	24,250,170	370,000,000	....	146/......	80 UN est
North Carolina, U.S.A.	52,669	136,413	5,881,813	Raleigh	281/......	80 FC & OE
North Dakota, U.S.A.	70,702	183,118	652,717	Bismarck	282/......	80 FC & OE
Northern Ireland, U.K.	5,452	14,121	1,543,000	Belfast	17/F 2	TP—81 OE; dist—76 OE; cap, Londonderry—73 OE; oth—71 FC
Northern Marianas	184	477	16,780	Capitol Hill	87/E 4	80 FC
Northern Territory, Australia	519,768	1,346,200	123,324	Darwin	93/......	81 FC
North Korea	46,540	120,539	17,914,000	P'yŏngyang	80/D 3	TP—80 UN est; cap—76 OE; Hamhŭng—72 OE; oth—70 OE
Northwest Territories, Canada	1,304,896	3,379,683	45,741	Yellowknife	187/G 3	81 FC
*Norway	125,053	323,887	4,092,000	Oslo	18/F 7	TP—80 OE; co, Svalbard—76 OE; oth—76 OE, 70 FC
Nova Scotia, Canada	21,425	55,491	847,442	Halifax	168/......	81 FC
Oceania	3,292,000	8,526,280	23,000,000		87/......	80 UN est
Ohio, U.S.A.	41,330	107,045	10,797,624	Columbus	284/......	80 FC & OE
Oklahoma, U.S.A.	69,956	181,186	3,025,290	Oklahoma City	288/......	80 FC & OE
*Oman	120,000	310,800	891,000	Muscat	58/G 6	TP—80 UN est; cap, Matrah—66 OE; Salala—68 OE
Ontario, Canada	412,580	1,068,582	8,625,107	Toronto	175, 177/......	81 FC
Orange Free State, South Africa	49,866	129,153	1,833,216	Bloemfontein	119/D 5	TP—80 PC; oth—70 FC
Oregon, U.S.A.	97,073	251,419	2,633,149	Salem	291/......	80 FC & OE
Orkney Islands, Scotland	376	974	17,675	Kirkwall	15/E 1	TP—76 OE; oth—71 FC
Pacific Islands, Territory of the	533	1,380	132,929	Saipan	87/F 5	80 FC
*Pakistan	310,403	803,944	83,782,000	Islamabad	68/B 3	TP—81 PC; Abbottabad, Bannu, cit over 50,000—72 PC; oth—61 FC
Palau (Belau)	188	487	12,116	Koror	86/D 5	80 FC
Palmyra Atoll	3.85	1			87/K 5	....
*Panama	29,761	77,082	1,830,175	Panamá	154/G 6	TP, cit over 1,600—80 PC; oth—70 PC
*Papua New Guinea	183,540	475,369	3,010,727	Port Moresby	85/B 7; 87/E 6	80 PC
Paracel Islands	....	....			85/E 2	
*Paraguay	157,047	406,752	2,973,000	Asunción	144/......	TP—79 OE; oth—72 PC
Pennsylvania, U.S.A.	45,308	117,348	11,863,895	Harrisburg	294/......	80 FC & OE
Persia, see Iran						
*Peru	496,222	1,285,215	17,031,221	Lima	128/......	81 PC
*Philippines	115,707	299,681	48,098,460	Manila	82/......	80 FC
Pitcairn Islands	18	47	54	Adamstown	87/O 8	81 FC
*Poland	120,725	312,678	35,815,000	Warsaw	47/......	TP—81 OE; prov, cap, Cracow, Łódź—75 OE; oth—70 FC
*Portugal	35,549	92,072	9,933,000	Lisbon	32/B 3	TP—80 OE; cap (ws)—76 OE; oth—70 FC & PC
Prince Edward Island, Canada	2,184	5,657	122,506	Charlottetown	168/E 2	81 FC
Puerto Rico	3,515	9,104	3,196,520	San Juan	161/......	80 FC
*Qatar	4,247	11,000	220,000	Doha	58/F 4	TP—80 UN est; cap—79 OE
Québec, Canada	594,857	1,540,680	6,438,403	Québec	172, 174/......	81 FC
Queensland, Australia	666,872	1,727,200	2,295,123	Brisbane	95/......	81 FC
Réunion	969	2,510	491,000	St-Denis	119/F 5	TP—80 OE; oth—74 FC
Rhode Island, U.S.A.	1,212	3,139	947,154	Providence	249/H 5	80 FC & OE
Rhodesia, see Zimbabwe						
*Romania	91,699	237,500	22,048,305	Bucharest	45/F 3	79 OE
Russian S.F.S.R., U.S.S.R.	6,592,812	17,075,400	137,551,000	Moscow	48/D 4	TP, cit over 50,000—79 PC; oth—70 FC
*Rwanda	10,169	26,337	4,819,317	Kigali	114/E 4	78 PC
Sabah, Malaysia	29,300	75,887	1,002,608	Kota Kinabalu	85/F 4	TP—80 PC; Kota Kinabalu—70 FC; oth—70 PC
*Saint Christopher and Nevis	104	269	44,404	Basseterre	156/F 3; 161/C11	TP, isl, cap—80 PC; oth—70 FC
Saint Helena & Dependencies	162	420	5,147	Jamestown	102/B 6	76 FC
*Saint Lucia	238	616	115,783	Castries	161/G 6	80 PC
Saint Pierre & Miquelon	93.5	242	6,034	Saint-Pierre	166/C 4	82 FC
*Saint Vincent & the Grenadines	150	388	124,000	Kingstown	161/A 8; 157/G 4	TP—80 OE; oth—70 FC
Sakhalin, U.S.S.R.	29,500	76,405	655,000	Yuzhno-Sakhalinsk	48/P 4	TP, cit over 50,000—79 PC; oth—70 FC
*Salvador, El	8,260	21,393	4,813,000	San Salvador	154/C 4	TP—80 OE; oth—71 FC
San Marino	23.4	60.6	19,149	San Marino	34/D 3	TP—76 FC; oth—77 OE
*São Tomé e Príncipe	372	963	85,000	São Tomé	106/F 8	TP—80 UN est; oth—70 PC
Sarawak, Malaysia	48,202	124,843	1,294,753	Kuching	85/E 5	TP—80 PC; Kuching—70 FC; oth—70 PC
Sardinia, Italy	9,301	24,090	1,450,483	Cagliari	34/B 4	71 FC
Saskatchewan, Canada	251,699	651,900	968,313	Regina	181/......	81 FC
*Saudi Arabia	829,995	2,149,687	8,367,000	Riyadh	58/D 4	TP—80 UN est; oth—74 PC
Scotland, U.K.	30,414	78,772	5,117,146	Edinburgh	15/......	TP—81 PC; reg—75 OE; cit—75 & 73 OE, 71 FC; oth—71 FC
*Senegal	75,954	196,720	5,508,000	Dakar	106/A 5	TP—79 OE; oth—76 PC
*Seychelles	145	375	63,000	Victoria	119/H 5	TP—79 OE; oth—77 FC
Shetland Islands, Scotland	552	1,430	18,494	Lerwick	15/G 2	TP—76 OE; oth—73 OE & 71 FC
Siam, see Thailand						
Sicily, Italy	9,926	25,708	4,628,918	Palermo	34/D 6	71 FC
*Sierra Leone	27,925	72,325	3,470,000	Freetown	106/B 7	TP—80 UN est; cap, Bo, Kenema, Makeni—74 PC; oth—63 FC
*Singapore	226	585	2,413,945	Singapore	72/F 6	80 FC
Society Islands, French Polynesia	677	1,753	117,703	Papeete	87/L 7	77 FC
*Solomon Islands	11,500	29,785	221,000	Honiara	87/G 6; 86/......	TP—79 OE; oth—76 FC
*Somalia	246,200	637,658	3,645,000	Mogadishu	115/H 3	TP—80 UN est; prov, cap—75 PC; oth—69, 68, 67, 63 & 62 OE

Gazetteer-Index of the World

Country	Area Square Miles	Area Square Kilometers	Population	Capital or Chief Town	Page and Index Ref.	Sources of Population Data
*South Africa	455,318	1,179,274	23,771,970	Cape Town; Pretoria	118/C 5	TP (excl Transkei, Bophuthatswana, Venda), prov—80 PC; Transkei, Bophuthatswana—78 est; Venda—79 est; oth—70 FC
South America	6,875,000	17,806,250	245,000,000	....	120/......	80 UN est
South Australia, Australia	379,922	984,000	1,285,033	Adelaide	94/......	81 FC
South Carolina, U.S.A.	31,113	80,583	3,121,833	Columbia	296/......	80 FC & OE
South Dakota, U.S.A.	77,116	199,730	690,768	Pierre	298/......	80 FC & OE
South Korea	38,175	98,873	37,448,836	Seoul	80/D 5	TP—80 PC; oth—75 FC & PC
South-West Africa (Namibia)	317,827	823,172	1,200,000	Windhoek	118/B 3	TP—74 est; oth—70 PC
*Spain	194,881	504,742	37,430,000	Madrid	33/......	TP—80 OE; met areas—75 OE; oth—70 FC
Spratly Island	....	....		....	85/E 4	....
*Sri Lanka	25,332	65,610	14,850,001	Colombo	68/E 7	TP—81 PC; cap, Jaffna—73 OE; oth—71 FC
*Sudan	967,494	2,505,809	18,691,000	Khartoum	110/E 4	TP—80 OE; cap, prov, prov cap—73 PC; oth—73 PC, 72 OE
Sumatra, Indonesia	164,000	424,760	19,360,400	Medan	84/B 5	71 PC
*Suriname	55,144	142,823	354,860	Paramaribo	131/C 3	TP, cap—80 PC; dist—71 PC; oth—64 FC
Svalbard, Norway	23,957	62,049	3,431	Longyearbyen	18/C 2	76 OE
*Swaziland	6,705	17,366	547,000	Mbabane	119/E 5	TP—80 OE; oth—76 FC
*Sweden	173,665	449,792	8,320,000	Stockholm	18/J 8	TP—81 OE; oth—75 FC
Switzerland	15,943	41,292	6,365,960	Bern	39/......	TP—80 FC; cantons—78 OE; cap, cit over 100,000 (& ws)—74 OE; cit (com) over 30,000 (& ws)—73 OE; oth—70 FC
*Syria	71,498	185,180	8,979,000	Damascus	62/G 5	TP—80 OE; oth—70 FC
Tadzhik S.S.R., U.S.S.R.	55,251	143,100	3,801,000	Dushanbe	48/G 6	TP, cit over 50,000—79 PC; oth—70 FC
Tahiti, French Polynesia	402	1,041	95,604	Papeete	87/L 7	77 FC
Taiwan	13,971	36,185	16,609,961	Taipei	77/K 7	TP, cap, Penghu Isl., cit over 300,000—77 OE; oth—70 OE
*Tanzania	363,708	942,003	17,527,560	Dar es Salaam	114/F 5	TP—78 PC; div, cap, cit over 17,000—78 PC; oth—67 FC
Tasmania, Australia	26,178	67,800	418,957	Hobart	99/......	81 FC
Tennessee, U.S.A.	42,144	109,153	4,591,120	Nashville	237/......	80 FC & OE
Texas, U.S.A.	266,807	691,030	14,229,288	Austin	303/......	80 FC & OE
*Thailand	198,455	513,998	46,455,000	Bangkok	72/D 3	TP—80 OE; oth—70 FC
Tibet, China	463,320	1,200,000	1,790,000	Lhasa	76/C 5	TP—78 OE; oth—70 est
*Togo	21,622	56,000	2,472,000	Lomé	106/E 7	TP—79 OE; oth—70 FC
Tokelau	3.9	10	1,575	Fakaofo	87/J 6	TP—76 FC; oth—72 FC
Tonga	270	699	90,128	Nuku'alofa	87/J 8	76 PC
Transkei (rep.), South Africa	16,910	43,797	2,000,000	Umtata	119/D 6	TP—80 est; oth—70 FC
Transvaal, South Africa	109,621	283,918	10,673,033	Pretoria	119/D 4	TP—80 PC; oth—70 FC
*Trinidad and Tobago	1,980	5,128	1,067,108	Port-of-Spain	157/G 5; 161/A10	80 PC
Tristan da Cunha, St. Helena	38	98	251	Edinburgh	2/J 7	79 OE
Tuamotu Archipelago, French Polynesia	341	883	9,052	Apataki	87/M 7	77 FC
*Tunisia	63,378	164,149	6,367,000	Tunis	106/F 1	TP—79 OE; oth—75 FC
*Turkey	300,946	779,450	45,217,556	Ankara	62/D 3	TP—80 PC; oth—75 FC
Turkmen S.S.R., U.S.S.R.	188,455	488,100	2,759,000	Ashkhabad	48/F 6	TP, cit over 50,000—79 PC; oth—70 FC
Turks and Caicos Islands	166	430	7,436	Cockburn Town, Grand Turk	156/D 2	80 PC
Tuvalu	9.78	25.33	7,349	Fongafale, Funafuti	87/H 6	79 FC
*Uganda	91,076	235,887	12,630,076	Kampala	114/F 3	TP, cap—80 PC; oth—69 FC
*Ukrainian S.S.R., U.S.S.R.	233,089	603,700	49,755,000	Kiev	52/D 5	TP, cit over 50,000—79 PC; oth—70 FC
*Union of Soviet Socialist Republics	8,649,490	22,402,179	262,436,227	Moscow	48/......	TP, S.S.R., cit over 50,000—79 PC; oth—70 FC
*United Arab Emirates	32,278	83,600	1,040,275	Abu Dhabi	58/F 5	TP—80 PC; oth—79 OE
*United Kingdom	94,399	244,493	55,672,000	London	10/......	TP—81 OE (see England, Wales, Scotland, Northern Ireland)
*United States of America	3,623,420	9,384,658	226,504,825	Washington	188/......	80 FC & OE
*Upper Volta	105,869	274,200	6,908,000	Ouagadougou	106/D 6	TP—80 UN est; oth—75 FC, 73 OE
*Uruguay	72,172	186,925	2,899,000	Montevideo	145/......	TP—80 OE; oth—75 PC
Utah, U.S.A.	84,899	219,888	1,461,037	Salt Lake City	304/......	80 FC & OE
Uzbek S.S.R., U.S.S.R.	173,591	449,600	15,391,000	Tashkent	48/G 5	TP, cit over 50,000—79 PC; oth—70 FC
*Vanuatu	5,700	14,763	112,596	Vila	87/G 7	79 FC
Vatican City	108.7 acres	44 hectares	728	....	34/B 6	78 OE
Venda (rep.), South Africa	2,510	6,501	450,000	Thohoyandou	119/E 4	79 est
*Venezuela	352,143	912,050	14,313,000	Caracas	124/......	TP—81 OE; oth—71 FC
Vermont U.S.A.	9,614	24,900	511,456	Montpelier	268/......	80 FC & OE
Victoria, Australia	87,876	227,600	3,832,443	Melbourne	96/B 5	81 FC
*Vietnam	128,405	332,569	52,741,766	Hanoi	72/E 3	TP—79 FC; cap, Haiphong, Ho Chi Minh City—79 PC; oth cit over 100,000 (north)—70 est, (south)—73 & 71 OE; oth—69 OE, 60 FC
Virginia, U.S.A.	40,767	105,587	5,346,818	Richmond	307/......	80 FC & OE
Virgin Islands, British	59	153	11,006	Road Town	157/H 1	TP—80 FC; oth—70 FC
Virgin Islands, U.S.A.	132	342	96,569	Charlotte Amalie	161/A 4	80 FC
Wake Island	2.5	6.5	302	Wake Islet	87/G 4	80 FC
Wales, U.K.	8,017	20,764	2,790,462	Cardiff	13/D 5	TP—81 PC; co—76 OE; cit—76 & 73 OE; par—71 FC
Wallis and Futuna	106	275	9,192	Mata Utu	87/J 7	76 FC
Washington, U.S.A.	68,139	176,480	4,132,180	Olympia	310/......	80 FC & OE
West Bank	2,100	5,439	c. 800,000	....	65/C 3	TP—81 est; oth—67 CE & 61 FC
Western Australia, Australia	975,096	2,525,500	1,273,624	Perth	92/......	81 FC
Western Sahara	102,703	266,000	76,425	....	106/B 3	70 FC
*Western Samoa	1,133	2,934	158,130	Apia	87/J 7	81 PC
*West Germany (Federal Republic)	95,985	248,601	61,658,000	Bonn	22/......	TP—80 OE; states, cap—76 OE; oth—76 OE, 70 FC
West Virginia, U.S.A.	24,231	62,758	1,950,279	Charleston	312/......	80 FC & OE
*White Russian S.S.R. (Byelorussian S.S.R.), U.S.S.R.	80,154	207,600	9,560,000	Minsk	52/C 4	TP, cit over 50,000—79 PC; oth—70 FC
Wisconsin, U.S.A.	56,153	145,436	4,705,521	Madison	317/......	80 FC & OE
World	(land) 57,970,000	150,142,300	4,415,000,000	....	1, 2/......	80 UN est
Wyoming, U.S.A.	97,809	253,325	469,557	Cheyenne	319/......	80 FC & OE
*Yemen, People's Democratic Republic of	111,101	287,752	1,969,000	Aden	58/E 7	TP—81 PC; oth—75 FC
*Yemen Arab Republic	77,220	200,000	6,456,189	San a	58/D 6	TP—80 OE; Mukalla, Seiyun—76 OE; cap—73 OE; Saihut—60 OE
*Yugoslavia	98,766	255,804	22,471,000	Belgrade	45/C 3	TP—81 OE; oth—71 FC
Yukon Territory, Canada	207,075	536,324	23,153	Whitehorse	186/E 3	81 FC
*Zaire	905,063	2,344,113	28,291,000	Kinshasa	114/D 4	TP—80 OE; prov, cap—70 FC; oth—70 FC & PC
*Zambia	290,586	752,618	5,679,808	Lusaka	114/E 7	80 PC
*Zimbabwe	150,803	390,580	7,360,000	Harare (Salisbury)	119/D 3	TP—80 OE; cap, cit over 12,000—77 OE; oth—69 FC

Introduction to the Maps and Indexes

The following notes have been added to aid the reader in making the best use of this atlas. Though he may be familiar with maps and map indexes, the publisher believes that a quick review of the material below will add to his enjoyment of this reference work.

Arrangement — The Plan of the Atlas. The atlas has been designed with maximum convenience for the user as its objective. All geographically related information pertaining to a country or region appears on adjacent pages, eliminating the task of searching throughout the entire volume for data on a given area. Thus, the reader will find, conveniently assembled, political, topographic, economic and special maps of a political area or region, accompanied by detailed map indexes, statistical data, and illustrations of the national flags of the area.

The sequence of country units in this American-designed atlas is international in arrangement. Units on the world as a whole are followed by a section on the polar regions which, in turn, is followed by pages devoted to Europe and its countries. Every continent map is accompanied by special population distribution, climatic and vegetation maps of that continent. Following the maps of the European continent and its countries, the geographic sequence plan proceeds as follows: Asia, the Pacific and Australia, Africa, South America, North America, and ends with detailed coverage on the United States.

Political Maps — The Primary Reference Tool. The most detailed maps in each country unit are the *political maps.* It is our feeling that the reader is likely to refer to these maps more often than to any other in the book when confronted by such questions as — Where? How big? What is it near? Answering these common queries is the function of the political maps. Each political map stresses *political* phenomena — countries, internal political divisions, boundaries, cities and towns. The major political unit or units, shown on the map, are banded in distinctive colors for easy identification and delineation. First-order political subdivisions (states, provinces, counties on the state maps) are shown, scale permitting.

The reader is advised to make use of the *legend* appearing under the title on each political map. Map *symbols,* the special "language" of maps, are explained in the legend. Each variety of dot, circle, star or interrupted line has a special meaning which should be clearly understood by the user so that he may interpret the map data correctly.

Each country has been portrayed at a *scale* commensurate with its political, areal, economic or tourist importance. In certain cases, a whole map unit may be devoted to a single nation if that nation is considered to be of prime interest to most atlas users. In other cases, several nations will be shown on a single map if, as separate entities, they are of lesser relative importance. Areas of dense settlement and important significance within a country have been enlarged and portrayed in inset maps inserted on the margins of the main map. The scale of each map is indicated as a fractional representation (1:1,000,000). The reader is advised to refer to the linear or "bar" scale appearing on each map or map inset in order to determine the distance between points.

The *projection* system used for each map is noted near the title of the map. Map projections are the special graphic systems used by cartographers to render the curved three-dimensional surface of the globe on a flat surface. Optimum map projections determined by the attributes of the area have been used by the publishers for each map in the atlas.

A word here as to the choice of place names on the maps. Throughout the atlas names appear, with a few exceptions, in their local official spellings. However, conventional Anglicized spellings are used for major geographical divisions and for towns and topographic features for which English forms exist; i.e., "Spain" instead of "España" or "Munich" instead of "München." Names of this type are normally followed by the local official spelling in parentheses. As an aid to the user the indexes are cross-referenced for all current and most former spellings of such names.

Names of cities and towns in the United States follow the forms listed in the *Post Office Directory* of the United States Postal Service. Domestic physical names follow the decisions of the Board on Geographic Names, U.S. Department of the Interior, and of various state geographic name boards.

It is the belief of the publishers that the boundaries shown in a general reference atlas should reflect current geographic and political realities. This policy has been followed consistently in the atlas. The presentation of *de facto* boundaries in cases of territorial dispute between various nations does not imply the political endorsement of such boundaries by the publisher, but simply the honest representation of boundaries as they exist at the time of the printing of the atlas maps.

Indexes — Pinpointing a Location. Each political map is accompanied by a comprehensive index of the place names appearing on the map. If you are unfamiliar with the location of a particular geographical place and wish to find its position within the confines of the subject area of the map, consult the map index as your first step. The name of the feature sought will be found in its proper alphabetical sequence with a key reference letter-number combination corresponding to its location on the map. After noting the key reference letter-number combination for the place name, turn to the map. The place name will be found within the square formed by the two lines of latitude and the two lines of longitude which enclose the co-ordinates — i.e., the marginal letters and numbers. The diagram below illustrates the system of indexing.

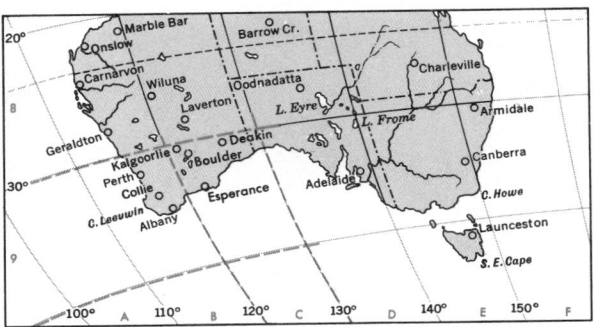

In the case of maps consisting entirely of insets, the place name is found near the intersection point of the imaginary lines connecting the co-ordinates at right angles. See below.

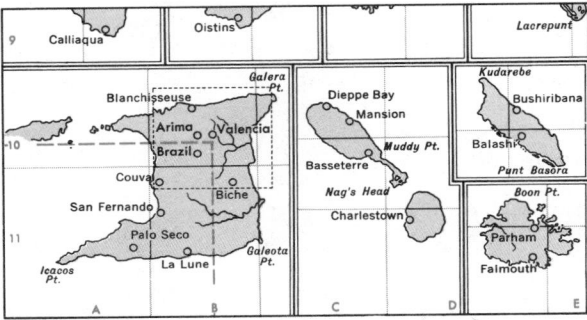

Where space on the map has not permitted giving the complete form of the place name, the complete form is shown in the index. Where a place is known by more than one name or by various spellings of the same name, the different forms have been included in the index. Physical features are listed under their proper names and not according to their generic terms; that is to say, Rio Negro will be found under Negro and not under Rio Negro. On the other hand, Rio Grande will be found under Rio Grande. Accompanying most index entries for cities and towns, and for other political units, are *population figures* for the particular entries. The large number of population figures in the atlas makes this work one of the most comprehensive statistical sources available to the public today. The population figures have been taken from the latest official censuses and estimates of the various nations. Dates and sources for the population figures are listed in the Gazetteer-Index of the World preceding this section.

Population and area figures for countries and major political units are listed in bold type *fact lists* on the margins of the indexes. In addition, the capital, largest city, highest point, monetary unit, principal languages and the prevailing religions of the country concerned are also listed. The Gazetteer-Index of the World on the preceding pages provides a quick reference index for countries and other important areas. Though population and area figures for each major unit area also found in the map section, the Gazetteer-Index provides a conveniently arranged statistical comparison contained in five pages. As mentioned, dates and sources of the population figures appearing in the country indexes are also listed in this section.

All index entries for cities and towns in the United States are preceded by a five-digit postal ZIP code number applying to the community. This useful feature permits the reader to address his mail so that it will be routed and delivered more efficiently and quickly by the U.S. Postal Service. A dagger (†) designates those places that do not possess a post office. The ZIP code number listed in such cases refers to that of the nearest post office. An asterisk (*) marks those larger cities which are divided into multiple ZIP code areas. Using the single ZIP code number listed in such cases will direct your letter to the proper city with dispatch. However, if the precise ZIP code number of the address within the city is needed, it is suggested that the reader refer to the latest National ZIP Code Directory at his local post office. This detailed guide lists every street in a multiple ZIP code city with the proper ZIP code for the street.

Relief Maps. Accompanying each political map is a relief map of the area. The purpose of the relief map is to illustrate the surface configuration (TOPOGRAPHY) of the region. A shading technique in color simulates the relative ruggedness of the terrain — plains, plateaus, valleys, hills and mountains. Graded colors, ranging from greens for lowlands, yellows for intermediate elevations to browns in the highlands, indicate the height above sea level of each part of the land. A vertical scale at the margin of the map shows the approximate height in meters and feet represented by each color.

Economic Maps — Agriculture, Industry and Resources. One of the most interesting features that will be found in each country unit is the economic map. From this map one can determine the basic activities of a nation as expressed through its economy. A perusal of the map yields a full understanding of the area's economic geography and natural resources.

The agricultural economy is manifested in two ways: color bands and commodity names. The color bands express broad categories of *dominant land use,* such as, cereal belts, forest lands, livestock range lands, nonagricultural wastes. The red commodity names, on the other hand, pinpoint the areas of production of *specific* crops; i.e., wheat, cotton, sugar beets, etc.

Major mineral occurrences are denoted by standard letter symbols appearing in blue. The relative size of the letter symbols signifies the relative importance of the deposit.

The manufacturing sector of the economy is presented by means of diagonal line patterns expressing the various *industrial areas* of consequence within a country.

The fishing industry is represented by names of commercial fish species appearing offshore in blue letters. Major waterpower sites are designated by blue symbols.

The publishers have tried to make this work the most comprehensive and useful atlas available, and it is hoped that it will prove a valuable reference work. Any constructive suggestions from the reader will be welcomed.

Sources and Acknowledgments

A multitude of sources goes into the making of a large-scale reference work such as this. To list them all would take many pages and would consume space better devoted to the maps and reference materials themselves. However, certain general sources were very useful in preparing this work and are listed below.

STATISTICAL OFFICE OF THE UNITED NATIONS.
Demographic Yearbook. New York. Issued annually.

STATISTICAL OFFICE OF THE UNITED NATIONS.
Statistical Yearbook. New York. Issued annually.

THE GEOGRAPHER, U.S. DEPARTMENT OF STATE.
International Boundary Study papers. Washington. Various dates.

THE GEOGRAPHER, U.S. DEPARTMENT OF STATE.
Geographic Notes. Washington. Various dates.

UNITED STATES BOARD ON GEOGRAPHIC NAMES.
Decisions on Geographic Names in the United States. Washington. Various dates.

UNITED STATES BOARD ON GEOGRAPHIC NAMES.
Official Standard Names Gazetteers. Washington. Various dates.

CANADIAN PERMANENT COMMITTEE ON GEOGRAPHICAL NAMES.
Gazetteer of Canada series. Ottawa. Various dates.

UNITED STATES POSTAL SERVICE.
National Five Digit ZIP Code and Post Office Directory. Washington. 1983.

UNITED STATES POSTAL SERVICE.
Postal Bulletin. Washington. Issued weekly.

UNITED STATES DEPARTMENT OF THE INTERIOR. BUREAU OF MINES.
Minerals Yearbook. 4 vols. Washington. Various dates.

UNITED STATES GEOLOGICAL SURVEY.
Elevations and distances in the United States. Reston, Va. 1980.

CARTACTUAL.
Cartactual — Topical Map Service. Budapest. Issued bi-monthly.

AMERICAN GEOGRAPHICAL SOCIETY.
Focus. New York. Issued ten times a year.

THE AMERICAN UNIVERSITY.
Foreign Area Studies. Washington. Various dates.

CENTRAL INTELLIGENCE AGENCY.
General reference maps. Washington. Various dates.

A sample list of sources used for specific countries follows:

Afghanistan
CENTRAL STATISTICS OFFICE.
Preliminary Results of the First Afghan Population Census 1979. Kabul.

Albania
DREJTORIA E STATISTIKES.
1979 Census. Tiranë.

Argentina
INSTITUTO NACIONAL DE ESTADISTICA Y CENSOS.
Censo Nacional de Población y Vivienda 1980. Buenos Aires.

Australia
AUSTRALIAN BUREAU OF STATISTICS.
Census of Population and Housing 1981. Canberra.

Brazil
FUNDAÇAO INSTITUTO BRASILEIRO DE GEOGRAFIA E ESTATISTICA.
IX Recenseamento Geral do Brasil 1980. Rio de Janeiro.

Canada
STATISTICS CANADA.
1981 Census of Canada. Ottawa.

Cuba
COMITE ESTATAL DE ESTADISTICAS.
Censo de Población y Viviendas 1981. Havana.

Hungary
HUNGARIAN CENTRAL STATISTICAL OFFICE.
1980 Census. Budapest.

Indonesia
BIRO PUSAT STATISTIK.
Sensus Penduduk 1980. Jakarta.

Kuwait
CENTRAL OFFICE OF STATISTICS.
1980 Census. Al Kuwait.

New Zealand
DEPARTMENT OF STATISTICS.
New Zealand Census of Population and Dwellings 1981. Wellington.

Panama
DIRECCIÓN DE ESTADISTICA Y CENSO.
Censos Nacionales de 1980. Panamá.

Papua New Guinea
BUREAU OF STATISTICS.
National Population Census 1980. Port Moresby.

Philippines
NATIONAL CENSUS AND STATISTICS OFFICE.
1980 Census of Population. Manila.

Saint Lucia
CENSUS OFFICE.
1980 Population Census. Castries.

Singapore
DEPARTMENT OF STATISTICS.
Census of Population 1980. Singapore.

U.S.S.R.
CENTRAL STATISTICAL ADMINISTRATION.
1979 Census. Moscow.

United States
BUREAU OF THE CENSUS.
1980 Census of Population. Washington.

Vanuatu
CENSUS OFFICE.
1979 Population Census. Port Vila.

Zambia
CENTRAL STATISTICAL OFFICE.
1980 Census of Population and Housing. Lusaka.

Glossary of Abbreviations

A

A. A. F. — Army Air Field
Acad. — Academy
A. C. T. — Australian Capital Territory
adm. — administration; administrative
A. F. B. — Air Force Base
Afgh., Afghan. — Afghanistan
Afr. — Africa
Ala. — Alabama
Alb. — Albania
Alg. — Algeria
Alta. — Alberta
Amer. — American
Amer. Samoa — American Samoa
And. — Andorra
Ant., Antarc. — Antarctica
Ant. & Bar. — Antigua and Barbuda
Ar. — Arabia
arch. — archipelago
Arg. — Argentina
Ariz. — Arizona
Ark. — Arkansas
A. S. S. R. — Autonomous Soviet
    Socialist Republic
Aust. — Austria
Aust. Cap. Terr. — Australian Capital
    Territory
Austr., Austral. — Australian, Australia
aut. — autonomous
Aut. Obl. — Autonomous Oblast

B

B. — bay
Bah. — Bahamas
Barb. — Barbados
Battlef. — Battlefield
Bch. — Beach
Belg. — Belgium
Berm. — Bermuda
Bol. — Bolivia
Bots. — Botswana
Br. — Branch
Br. — British
Braz. — Brazil
Br. Col. — British Columbia
Br. Ind. Oc. Terr. — British Indian
    Ocean Territory
Bulg. — Bulgaria

C

C. — cape
Calif. — California
Can. — Canada
can. — canal
cap. — capital
Cent. Afr. Rep. — Central African
    Republic
Cent. Amer. — Central America
C. G. Sta. — Coast Guard Station
C. H. — Court House
chan. — channel
Chan. Is. — Channel Islands
Chem. Ctr. — Chemical Center
co. — county
C. of G. H. — Cape of Good Hope
Col. — Colombia
Colo. — Colorado
comm. — commissary
Conn. — Connecticut
cont. — continent
cord. — cordillera (mountain range)
C. Rica — Costa Rica
C. S. — County Seat
C. Verde — Cape Verde
Czech. — Czechoslovakia

D

D. C. — District of Columbia
Del. — Delaware
Dem. — Democratic
Den. — Denmark
depr. — depression
dept. — department
des. — desert
dist., dist's — district, districts
div. — division
Dom. Rep. — Dominican Republic

E

E. — East
Ec., Ecua. — Ecuador
E. Ger. — East Germany
elec. div. — electoral division
El Salv. — El Salvador
Eng. — England
Equat. Guinea, Eq. Guin — Equatorial
    Guinea

escarp. — escarpment
est. — estuary
Eth. — Ethiopia

F

Falk. Is. — Falkland Islands
Fin. — Finland
Fk., Fks. — Fork, Forks
Fla. — Florida
for. — forest
Fr. — France, French
Fr. Gui. — French Guiana
Fr. Poly. — French Polynesia
Ft. — Fort

G

G. — gulf
Ga. — Georgia
Game Res. — Game Reserve
Ger. — Germany
geys. — geyser
Gibr. — Gibraltar
glac. — glacier
gov. — governorate
Gr. — Group
Greenl. — Greenland
Gren. — Grenada
Gt. Brit. — Great Britain
Guad. — Guadeloupe
Guat. — Guatemala
Guinea-Biss. — Guinea-Bissau
Guy. — Guyana

H

har., harb., hbr. — harbor
hd. — head
highl. — highland, highlands
Hist. — Historic, Historical
Hond. — Honduras
Hts. — Heights
Hung. — Hungary

I

i., isl. — island, isle
I. C. — independent city
Ice., Icel. — Iceland
Ida. — Idaho
Ill. — Illinois
Ind. — Indiana
ind. city — independent city
Indon. — Indonesia
Ind. Res. — Indian Reservation
int. div. — internal division
inten. — intendency
Int'l — International
Ire. — Ireland
is., isls. — islands
Isr. — Israel
isth. — isthmus
Iv. Coast — Ivory Coast

J

Jam. — Jamaica
Jct. — Junction

K

Kans. — Kansas
Ky. — Kentucky

L

L. — Lake, Loch, Lough
La. — Louisiana
Lab. — Laboratory
lag. — lagoon
Ld. — Land
Leb. — Lebanon
Les. — Lesotho
Liecht. — Liechtenstein
Lux. — Luxembourg

M

Mad., Madag. — Madagascar
Man. — Manitoba
Mart. — Martinique
Mass. — Massachusetts
Maur. — Mauritania
Md. — Maryland
met. area — metropolitan area
Mex. — Mexico
Mich. — Michigan
Minn. — Minnesota
Miss. — Mississippi
Mo. — Missouri
Mon. — Monument
Mong. — Mongolia
Mont. — Montana
Mor. — Morocco

Moz., Mozamb. — Mozambique
mt. — mount
mtn. — mountain

N

N., No., North. — North, Northern
N. Amer. — North America
Nam., Namib. — Namibia
N. A. S. — Naval Air Station
Nat'l — National
Nat'l Cem. — National Cemetery
Nat'l Mem. Park — National Memorial
    Park
Nat'l Mil. Park — National Military
    Park
Nat'l Pkwy. — National Parkway
Nav. Base — Naval Base
Nav. Sta. — Naval Station
N. B., N. Br. — New Brunswick
N. C. — North Carolina
N. Dak. — North Dakota
Nebr. — Nebraska
Neth. — Netherlands
Neth. Ant. — Netherlands Antilles
Nev. — Nevada
New Bruns. — New Brunswick
New Cal., New Caled. — New Caledonia
Newf. — Newfoundland
New Hebr. — New Hebrides
N. H. — New Hampshire
Nic. — Nicaragua
N. Ire. — Northern Ireland
N. J. — New Jersey
N. Mex. — New Mexico
Nor. — Norway, Norwegian
North. — Northern
North. Terr., No. Terr. — Northern
    Territory
    (Australia)
N. S. — Nova Scotia
N. S. W., N.S. Wales — New South Wales
N. W. T., N. W. Terrs. — Northwest
    Territories
    (Canada)
N. Y. — New York
N. Z., N. Zealand — New Zealand

O

Obl. — Oblast
O. F. S. — Orange Free State
Okla. — Oklahoma
Okr. — Okrug
Ont. — Ontario
Ord. Depot — Ordnance Depot
Oreg. — Oregon

P

Pa. — Pennsylvania
Pac. Is. — Pacific Islands,
    Territory of the
Pak. — Pakistan
Pan. — Panama
Papua N. G. —Papua New Guinea
Par. — Paraguay
par. — parish
passg. — passage
P.D.R. Yemen — People's Democratic
    Republic of Yemen
P. E. I. — Prince Edward Island
pen. — peninsula
Phil., Phil. Is. — Philippines
Pk. — Park
pk. — peak
plat. — plateau
P. N. G. — Papua New Guinea
Pol. — Poland
Port. — Portugal, Portuguese
Pr. Edward I. — Prince Edward Island
pref. — prefecture
P. Rico — Puerto Rico
prom. — promontory
prov. — province, provincial
pt. — point

Q

Que. — Quebec
Queens. — Queensland

R

R. — River
ra. — range
Rec., Recr. — Recreation, Recreational
reg. — region
Rep. — Republic
res. — reservoir
Res. — Reservation, Reserve
R. I. — Rhode Island

riv. — river
Rom. — Romania

S

S. — South
Sa. — Sierra, Serra
S. Afr., S. Africa — South Africa
salt dep. — salt deposit
salt des. — salt desert
S. Amer. — South America
São T. & Pr. — São Tomé
    and Príncipe
Sask. — Saskatchewan
Saudi Ar. — Saudi Arabia
S. Aust., S. Austral. — South Australia
S. C. — South Carolina
Scot. — Scotland
Sd. — Sound
S. Dak. — South Dakota
Sen. — Senegal
sen. dist. — senatorial district
Seych. — Seychelles
S. F. S. R. — Soviet Federated Socialist
    Republic
Sing. — Singapore
S. Leone — Sierra Leone
S. Marino — San Marino
Sol. Is. — Solomon Islands
Sp. — Spanish
Spr., Sprs. — Spring, Springs
S. S. R. — Soviet Socialist Republic
St., Ste. — Saint, Sainte
Sta. — Station
St. Chris.-Nevis — Saint Christopher-
    Nevis
St. P. & M. — Saint Pierre and
    Miquelon
St. Vin. & Grens. — St. Vincent & The
    Grenadines
str., strs. — strait, straits
Sur. — Suriname
S. W. Afr. — South-West Africa
Swaz. — Swaziland
Switz. — Switzerland

T

Tanz. — Tanzania
Tas. — Tasmania
Tenn. — Tennessee
terr., terrs. — territory, territories
Tex. — Texas
Thai. — Thailand
trad. — traditional
Trin. & Tob. — Trinidad and Tobago
Tun. — Tunisia
twp. — township

U

U. A. E. — United
    Arab Emirates
U. K. — United Kingdom
Upp. Volta — Upper Volta
urb. area — urban area
Urug. — Uruguay
U. S. — United States
U. S. S. R. — Union of Soviet Socialist
    Republics

V

Va. — Virginia
Ven., Venez. — Venezuela
V. I. (Br.) — Virgin Islands (British)
V. I. (U. S.) — Virgin Islands (U. S.)
Vic. — Victoria
Viet. — Vietnam
Vill. — Village
vol. — volcano
Vt. — Vermont

W

W. — West, Western
Wash. — Washington
W. Aust., W. Austral. — Western
    Australia
W. Ger. — West Germany
W. Indies — West Indies
Wis. — Wisconsin
W. Samoa — Western Samoa
W. Va. — West Virginia
Wyo. — Wyoming

Y

Yugo. — Yugoslavia
Yukon — Yukon Territory

Z

Zim. — Zimbabwe

Environment & life

The Sun: *Energy Source of the Solar System*

*For longer than the memory of man, a
glowing furnace of nuclear activity has held our solar
system within its gravitational orbit and,
deep within its interior, fused the nuclei of
hydrogen and helium, dispensing them as heat, light and the
other forms of radiation which nurture the very elements of
life on earth. The sun—with radiant energy so fierce that
it was deified by ancient man—still dominates the
lives of laymen and the minds of
scientists who seek to comprehend its nature
and utilize its mighty force.*

The Biosphere: Realm of Living Things

Polar and mountainous regions of perpetual **ice and snow** cover one-tenth of the earth's land areas. Windswept, always below freezing, it can support life only peripherally, if at all.

A place of mosses, lichens and stunted flowering plants and trees, the **tundra** is an area so marginal that only specially adapted life-forms, such as reindeer, can live there.

As favorable climates produce and sustain an abundance of vegetation, the **mid-latitude forest** regions of the world continue to serve as home for a majority of the world's population.

Ranging from the luxuriant vegetation of the rainforest to scrub-like woodlands in drier areas, the **tropical forest** is noted for containing a wide variety of insects, birds and small animals.

The **savanna** or tropical grassland is a land of tall grass interspersed with trees. A place of winter droughts and summer rainfall, it is the true jungle home of big-game animals.

On the **mid-latitude grasslands** are found many of the sheep and cattle ranches of the earth, and, where the land has been successfully cultivated, the great grain fields.

Except in scattered oases and irrigated lands, the **deserts** of the world are inhabited only by livestock-herding nomads and wildlife capable of surviving in moisture-deficient areas.

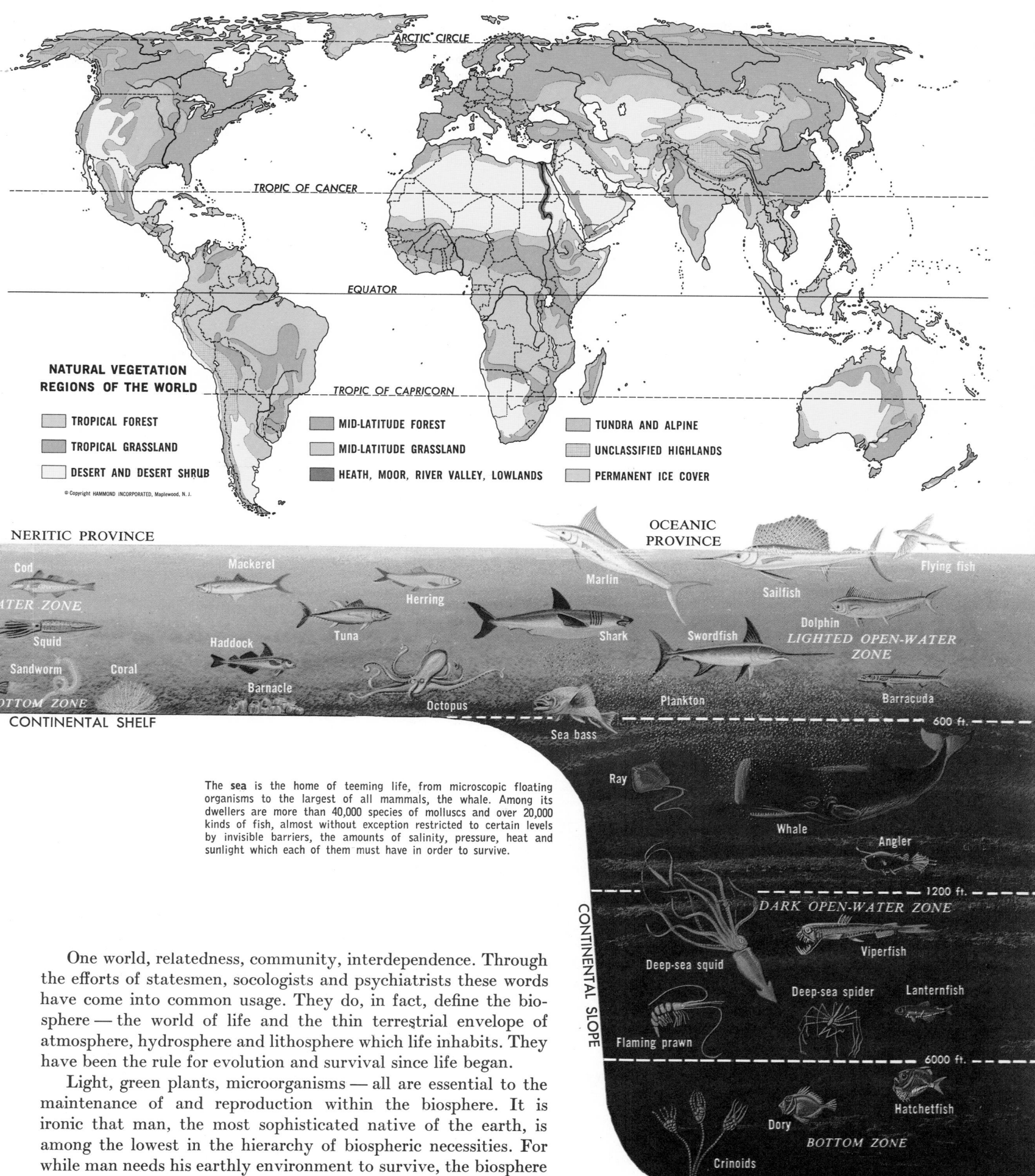

NATURAL VEGETATION REGIONS OF THE WORLD

- TROPICAL FOREST
- TROPICAL GRASSLAND
- DESERT AND DESERT SHRUB
- MID-LATITUDE FOREST
- MID-LATITUDE GRASSLAND
- HEATH, MOOR, RIVER VALLEY, LOWLANDS
- TUNDRA AND ALPINE
- UNCLASSIFIED HIGHLANDS
- PERMANENT ICE COVER

ARCTIC CIRCLE

TROPIC OF CANCER

EQUATOR

TROPIC OF CAPRICORN

© Copyright HAMMOND INCORPORATED, Maplewood, N. J.

NERITIC PROVINCE

OCEANIC PROVINCE

WATER ZONE

LIGHTED OPEN-WATER ZONE

BOTTOM ZONE

CONTINENTAL SHELF

Cod, Squid, Sandworm, Coral, Haddock, Barnacle, Mackerel, Herring, Tuna, Octopus, Sea bass, Marlin, Shark, Swordfish, Plankton, Sailfish, Dolphin, Flying fish, Barracuda

600 ft.

Ray, Whale, Angler

1200 ft.

DARK OPEN-WATER ZONE

Deep-sea squid, Flaming prawn, Deep-sea spider, Viperfish, Lanternfish

6000 ft.

Crinoids, Dory, Hatchetfish

BOTTOM ZONE

CONTINENTAL SLOPE

OCEAN FLOOR

The **sea** is the home of teeming life, from microscopic floating organisms to the largest of all mammals, the whale. Among its dwellers are more than 40,000 species of molluscs and over 20,000 kinds of fish, almost without exception restricted to certain levels by invisible barriers, the amounts of salinity, pressure, heat and sunlight which each of them must have in order to survive.

One world, relatedness, community, interdependence. Through the efforts of statesmen, socologists and psychiatrists these words have come into common usage. They do, in fact, define the biosphere — the world of life and the thin terrestrial envelope of atmosphere, hydrosphere and lithosphere which life inhabits. They have been the rule for evolution and survival since life began.

Light, green plants, microorganisms — all are essential to the maintenance of and reproduction within the biosphere. It is ironic that man, the most sophisticated native of the earth, is among the lowest in the hierarchy of biospheric necessities. For while man needs his earthly environment to survive, the biosphere could exist very well without him.

© Copyright HAMMOND INCORPORATED, Maplewood, N. J.

Environmental Controls

Primitive man worshiped the sun, danced for rain, and trembled when the angry gods unleashed the force of hurricane or hid the face of the sun in clouds. Modern man curses the drought, hides from the wind and snow and builds walls against the onslaught of flood.

Little has changed in the impact of climate and environment on the life of man. There are no vegetarians in the desert or in the ice-bound regions of the far north. Houses exposing vast expanses of glass to the burning fingers of the sun are not found in the Sahara, at the Equator or near the Poles. Man does not die of malaria in regions too dry or too cold to support the larvae of mosquitoes; swollen goiterous necks are never seen in areas where local water is naturally supplied with iodine.

Men who live near lakes or seas build boats while those near mountains climb or ski. The plainsman nurtures cattle or grain; the farmer in the valley cultivates tomatoes or legumes. In work, in play, in sickness and varying degrees of health — even in the formation of national traditions — the world of man is subject to the force of nature.

By a variety of adaptations man wrestles with the problems of his environment. He can air-condition or heat his home, refrigerate his food, quench parts of the thirsty deserts with irrigated water, drain the swamps and navigate the seas. He has developed intricate technologies to forecast earthquakes, blizzards, floods and hurricanes.

But the ancient sun still governs the movements of the earth within its orbit, determining heat and cold, the progress of the winds and ocean currents, the levels of the seas — the glacier's trail. Man continues to bow before the "god of day."

The interactions of sun, rain and wind are so closely related that they function as a single entity which is, perhaps, the most dominant force in creating man's environment.

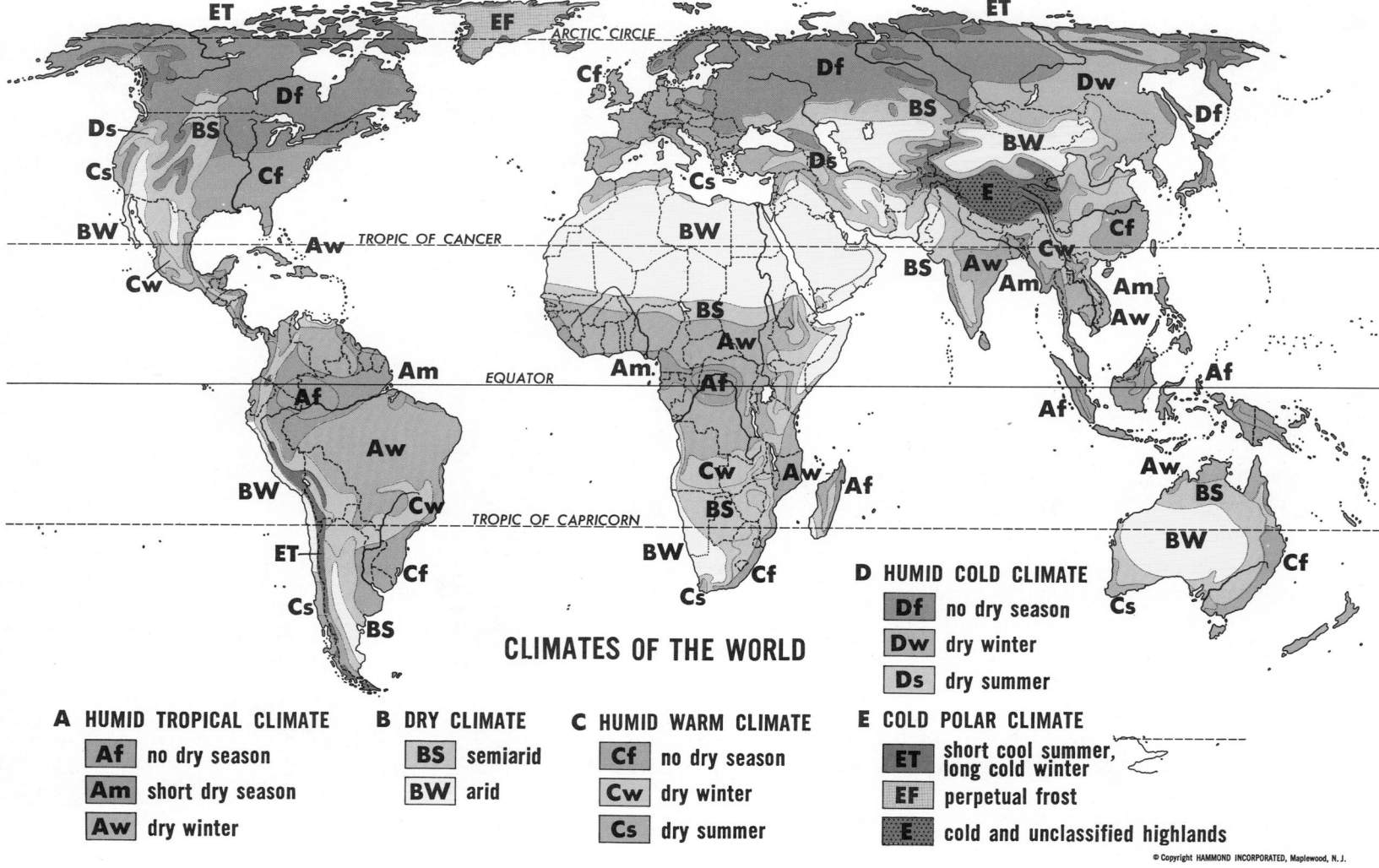

CLIMATES OF THE WORLD

A HUMID TROPICAL CLIMATE
- **Af** no dry season
- **Am** short dry season
- **Aw** dry winter

B DRY CLIMATE
- **BS** semiarid
- **BW** arid

C HUMID WARM CLIMATE
- **Cf** no dry season
- **Cw** dry winter
- **Cs** dry summer

D HUMID COLD CLIMATE
- **Df** no dry season
- **Dw** dry winter
- **Ds** dry summer

E COLD POLAR CLIMATE
- **ET** short cool summer, long cold winter
- **EF** perpetual frost
- **E** cold and unclassified highlands

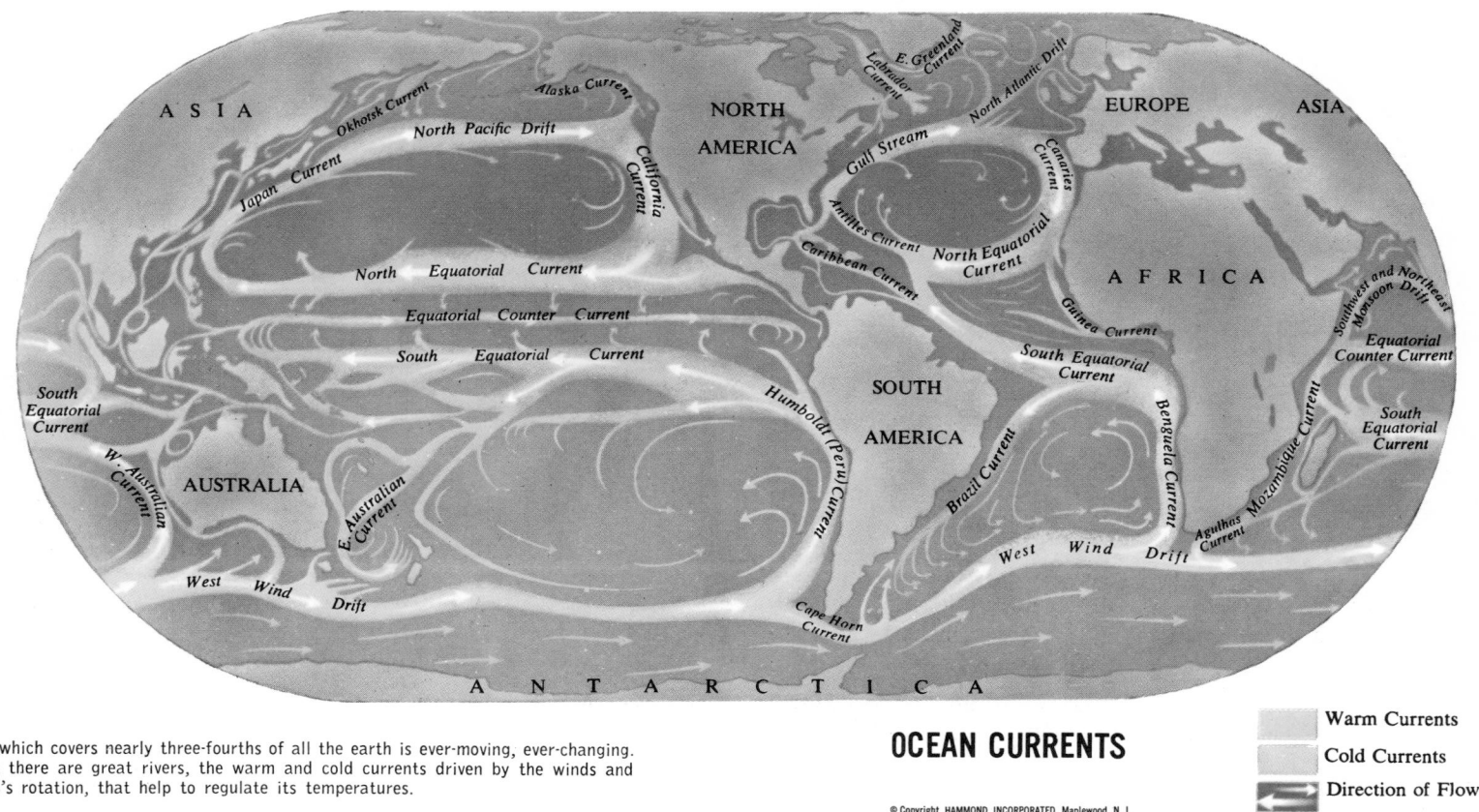

OCEAN CURRENTS

The sea, which covers nearly three-fourths of all the earth is ever-moving, ever-changing. Within it there are great rivers, the warm and cold currents driven by the winds and the earth's rotation, that help to regulate its temperatures.

Warm Currents
Cold Currents
Direction of Flow

© Copyright HAMMOND INCORPORATED, Maplewood, N. J.

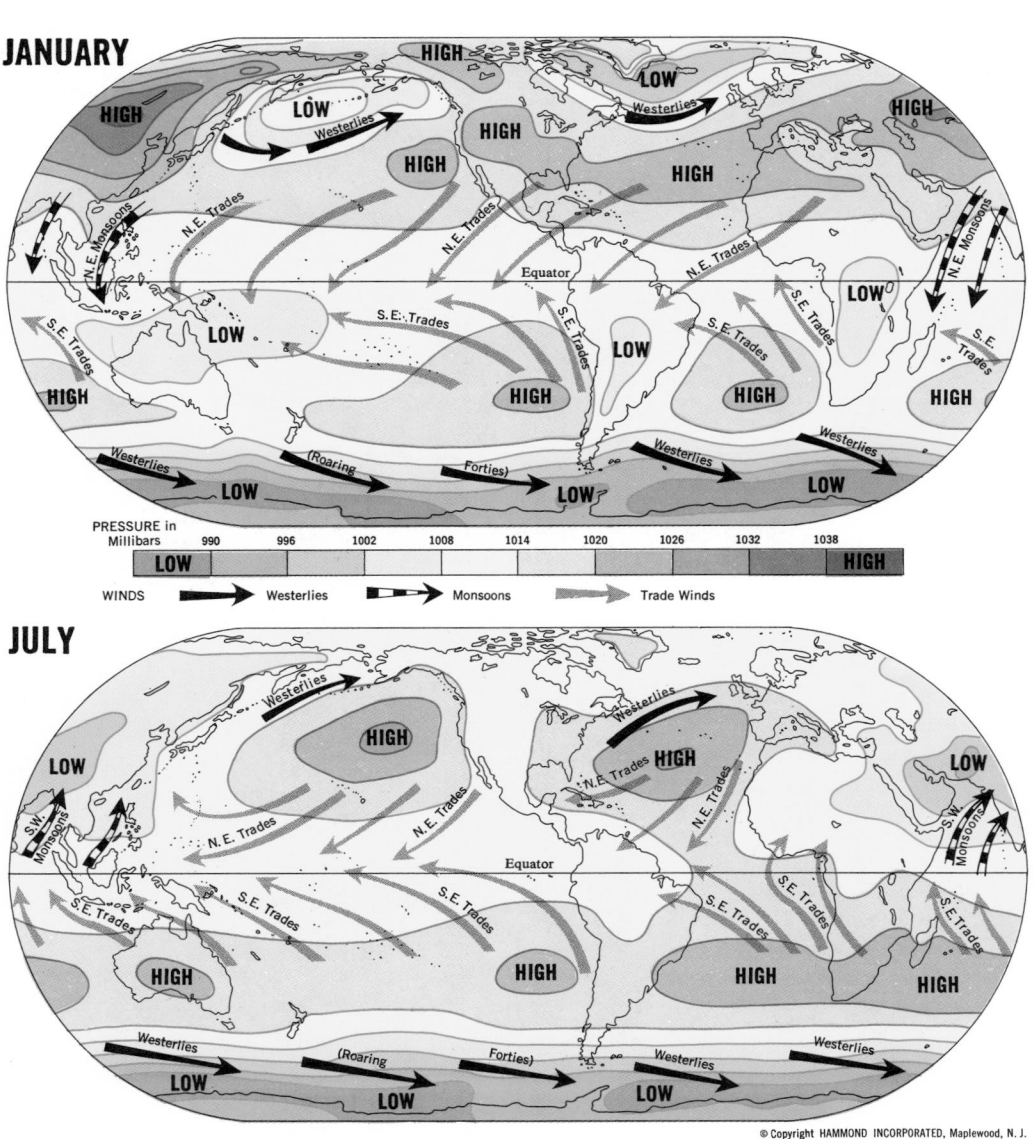

PRESSURE in Millibars

| LOW | 990 | 996 | 1002 | 1008 | 1014 | 1020 | 1026 | 1032 | 1038 | HIGH |

WINDS   → Westerlies   ▷ Monsoons   → Trade Winds

AIR PRESSURE AND WINDS

Just as the atmosphere tends to equalize heat distribution, it tends to maintain equal pressure over the earth. Whenever this equilibrium, or balance, is disturbed, air flows from areas of higher pressure to areas of lower pressure. In the Northern Hemisphere winds flow clockwise around a high pressure area (high) and counterclockwise around the center of a low pressure area (low). These movements are reversed in the Southern Hemisphere.

© Copyright HAMMOND INCORPORATED, Maplewood, N. J.

Life Support Cycles

With an intuition clearly beyond their scientific knowledge, the ancients of India developed a theory of reincarnation which, in some philosophic ways, parallels what science has learned of the workings of the biosphere. In the remarkable thrift of nature nothing is lost — in tremendous complex cycles atoms from the first life on earth still move through the biosphere.

The miracle of energy is constantly performed in the cycles of the "life-giving" elements. Carbon, hydrogen, oxygen, nitrogen, sulfur and phosphorus act together to produce all living matter. While many other elements such as calcium, iodine and iron are also found in living things, they are not absolute essentials in all cases. Carbon, hydrogen and oxygen are vital for photosynthesis and are the components of the basic food substances — carbohydrates and fats. Carbon, in its common gaseous form, carbon dioxide, is absorbed by green plants and triggers

the production of carbohydrate compounds by reacting with molecules of water.

Some "energy" is stored within the plant in the form of new tissue; other "energy," in the form of oxygen is released into the air to be used by other organisms. The seemingly inexhaustible supply of carbon dioxide available for use is replenished in the atmosphere through the respiration of all living things, and in the soil as bacteria and fungi break down plant and animal cells,

Nitrogen, sulfur and phosphorus are essential to animals and plants for the production and maintenance of protein. Nitrogen, with carbon, hydrogen and oxygen, is used for the growth and repair of tissue. Sulfur acts as a "stiffening" agent in all protein. To perform their functions proteins must be folded and shaped in a particular way, and their structure is maintained by bonds between sulfur atoms. While phosphorus is not a constituent of protein,

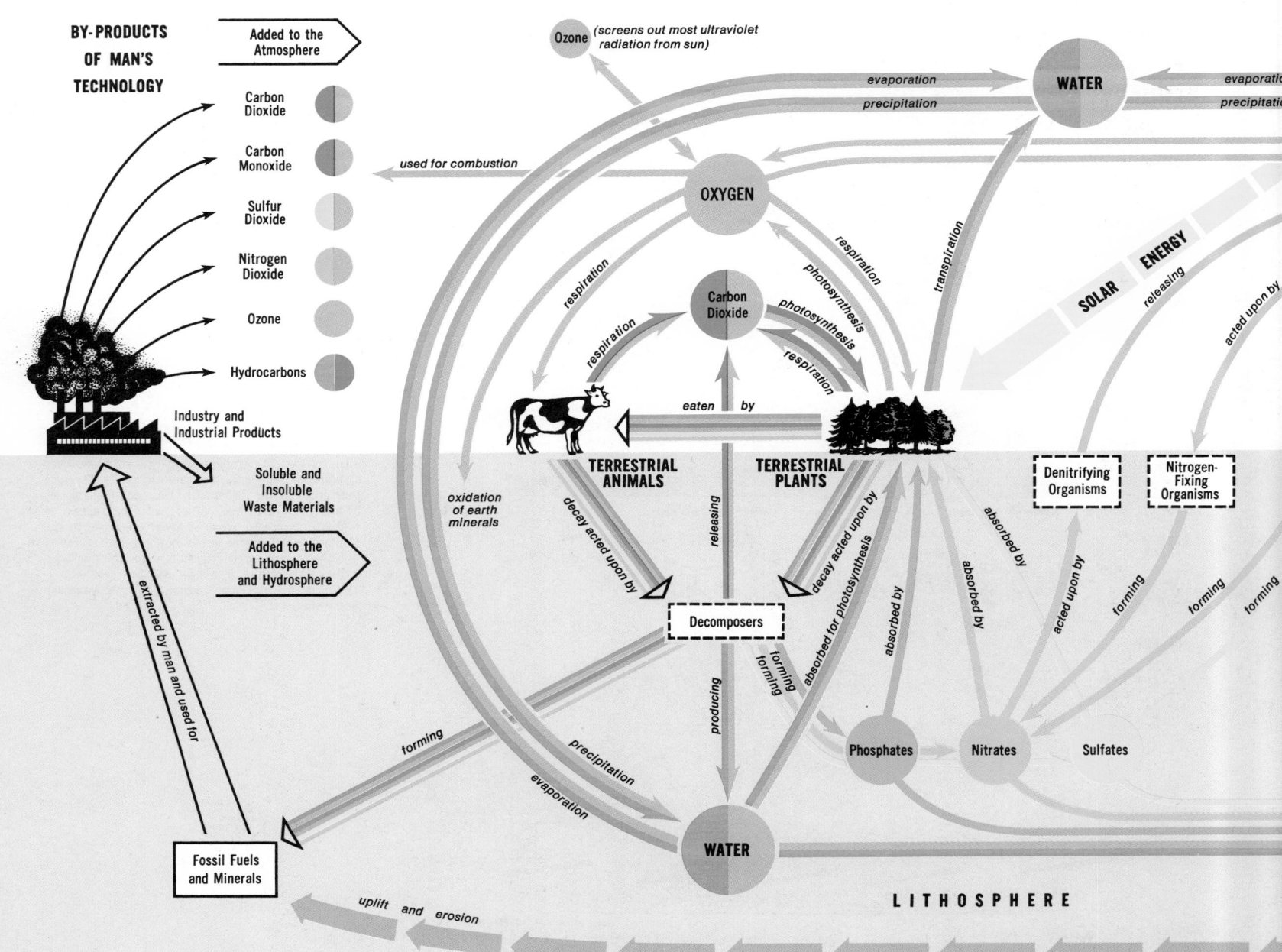

no protein can be made without it. Special phosphate compounds are the "fuel" for all biochemical work within the cell.

Although about four-fifths of the atmosphere is nitrogen, higher forms of life cannot make use of it in its "free" state and must absorb it at one or more points in its biospheric cycle. The decomposers — bacteria and fungi — act on waste matter, breaking down complex compounds into simpler usable forms including nitrogen. Some nitrogen-fixing bacteria are able to utilize atmospheric nitrogen in their own metabolism, while others convert it to those nitrogen-enriched substances necessary for all plant growth.

In nature, no part is greater than the whole and almost every element is dependent on another for some essential part of its cycle. Water, which is incorporated into every organism, is essential in the formation of free oxygen which in turn sustains the life of that organism. Water is also

the principal "carrier" in the cycling of all elements. When it evaporates, water returns certain elements to the atmosphere; when it seeps through the soil on its return to the sea, water distributes nutrients to plant roots.

Carbon monoxide, sulfur and nitrogen oxides, hydrocarbons — by-products of man's industry — are being injected into the biosphere in ever-increasing amounts. There, as the "new compounds," they must in some way co-exist with the life-support cycles established throughout millions of years of evolution. Their compatability with these cycles and the organisms they nurture will determine the future of life on our planet.

Already man has learned one thing. Although the question of reincarnation or any form of life after death remains unanswered for many, science has proved that there is no natural end to the raw materials of nature or to the "new compounds" man has made from them.

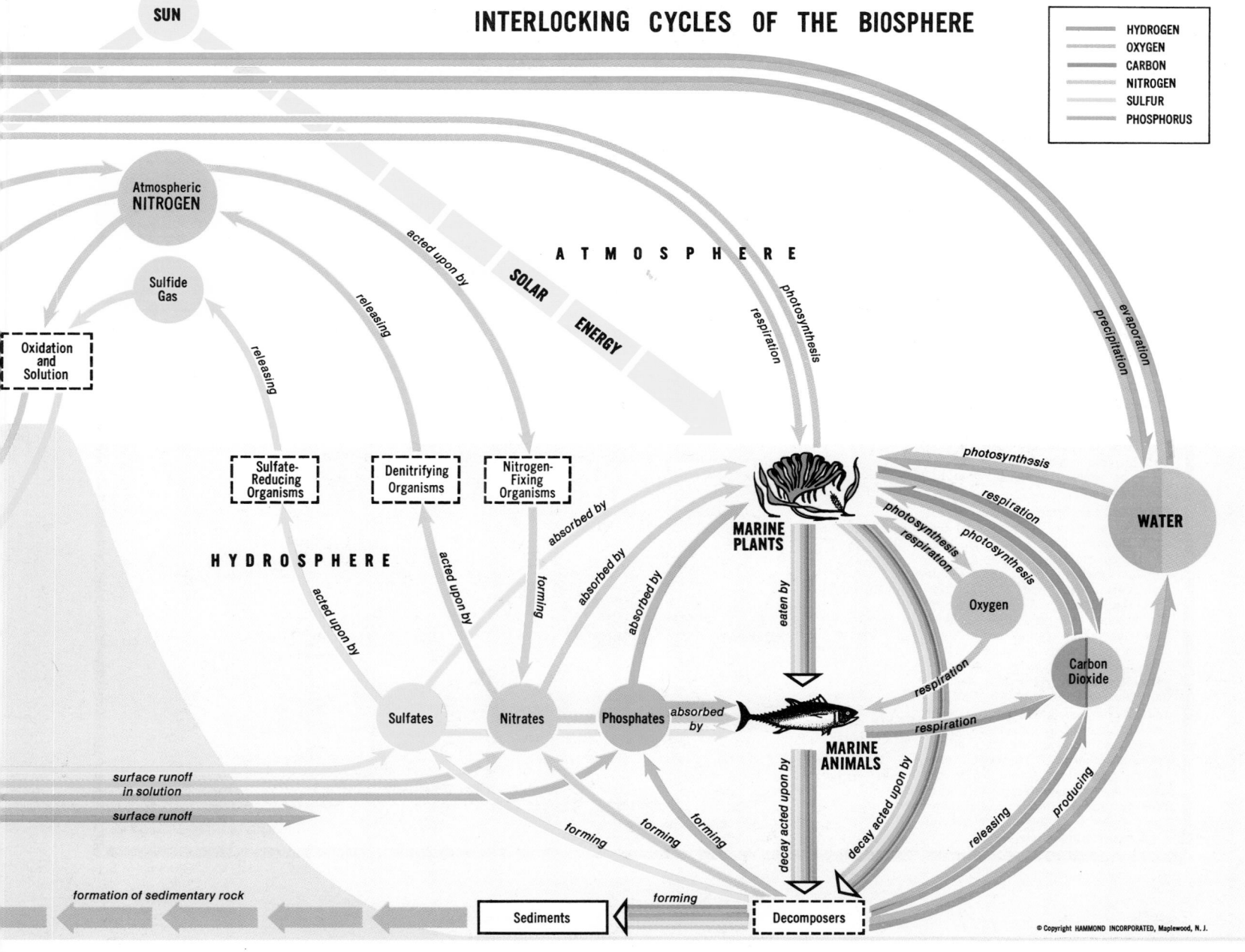

INTERLOCKING CYCLES OF THE BIOSPHERE

PHOTOSYNTHESIS: Converting the sun's energy

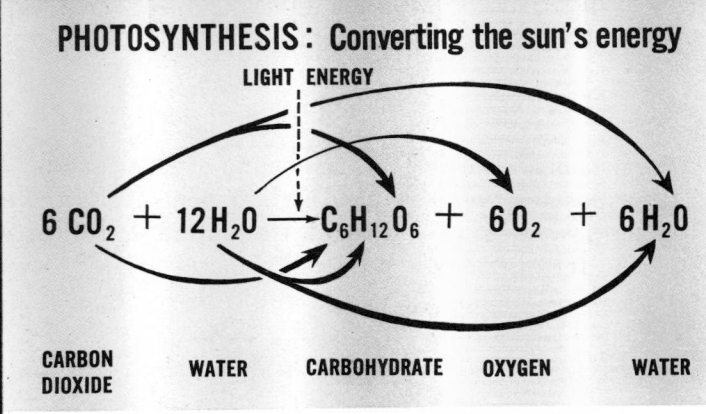

LIGHT ENERGY

$$6\,CO_2 + 12H_2O \rightarrow C_6H_{12}O_6 + 6\,O_2 + 6\,H_2O$$

| CARBON DIOXIDE | WATER | CARBOHYDRATE | OXYGEN | WATER |

Using light energy, green plants build up organic foods such as carbohydrates — stored chemical energy to be used by the entire community — from the simple inorganic substances of carbon dioxide and water. The important by-product of this reaction is the release of oxygen, an element vital to the respiration of all living things.

THE LEAF: An organ of photosynthesis
CROSS SECTION

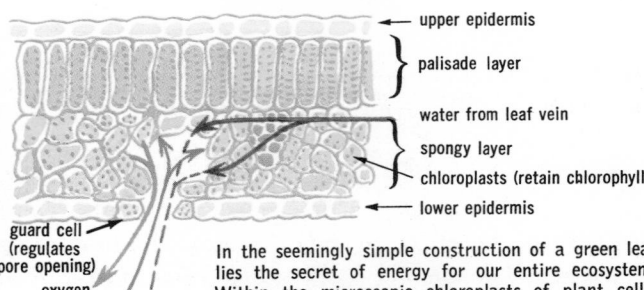

- upper epidermis
- palisade layer
- water from leaf vein
- spongy layer
- chloroplasts (retain chlorophyll)
- lower epidermis

guard cell (regulates pore opening)
oxygen
carbon dioxide
water vapor

In the seemingly simple construction of a green leaf lies the secret of energy for our entire ecosystem. Within the microscopic chloroplasts of plant cells, which contain the vital green pigment known as chlorophyll, carbon dioxide and water are absorbed, decomposed and converted into carbohydrate and oxygen molecules. Special "guard cells" control the surface pore openings to regulate the intake and output of materials.

PRODUCER - CONSUMER FOOD WEB

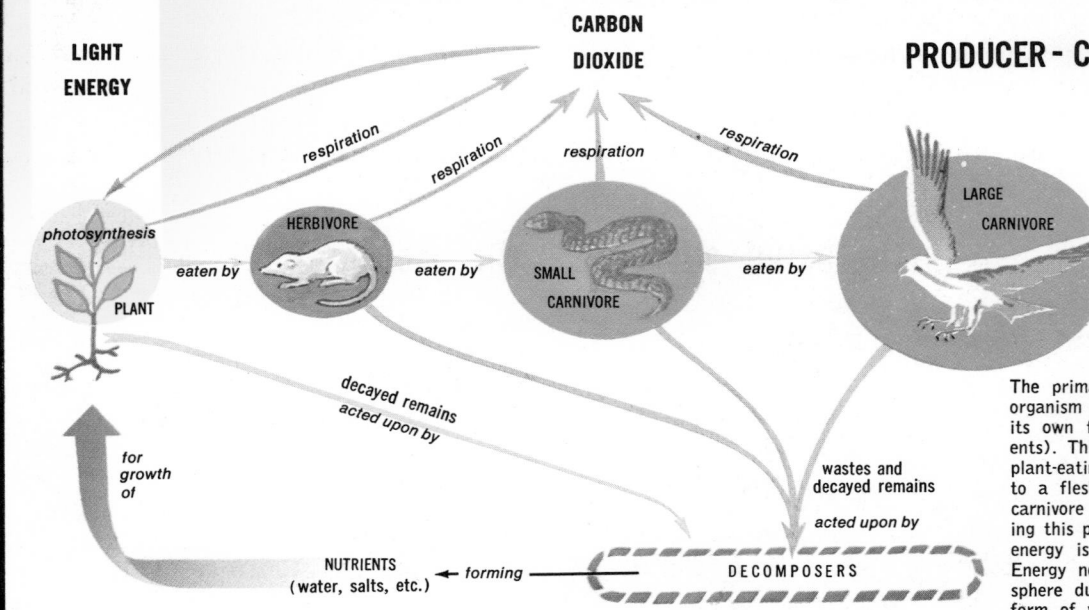

LIGHT ENERGY

CARBON DIOXIDE

respiration

photosynthesis

PLANT — eaten by — HERBIVORE — eaten by — SMALL CARNIVORE — eaten by — LARGE CARNIVORE

decayed remains acted upon by

for growth of

wastes and decayed remains

acted upon by

NUTRIENTS (water, salts, etc.) ← forming — DECOMPOSERS

Some of the complex relationships of life in an ecological system can be described by tracing the passage of energy through a simplified community in what is called a food chain or web.

The primary food source is the producer, that organism which uses light energy to manufacture its own food from inorganic substances (nutrients). This producer or plant is consumed by a plant-eating animal which in turn may fall prey to a flesh-eating animal or carnivore. A larger carnivore may extend the food chain further. During this process part of the consumed organism's energy is passed on to the consuming animal. Energy not passed on is released to the atmosphere during respiration or to the soil in the form of waste materials. Eventually, death and decay of all organisms lead to a recycling of nutrient compounds to be used by the producers.

CHAIN OF LIFE IN THE SEA

Although community members are constructed to adapt to their watery habitat, the chain of life in the sea is quite similar to the chain of life on land.

The most important members of the oceanic community are those that contain chlorophyll or a chlorophyll-like substance and thus are able to make organic matter from inorganic ingredients. Algae and phytoplankton are the ocean's principal producers. In the open seas the initial consumers are tiny crustacea only a few centimeters long, while in coastal waters these consumers include the more familiar starfish, sea urchins, molluscs and some worms.

Just as on land, where the smaller or weaker animal is consumed by the larger and stronger, members of the oceanic community feed upon each other. Nutrients are returned to the atmosphere through respiration and to the hydrosphere through a breakdown of complex organisms by the work of decomposing organisms.

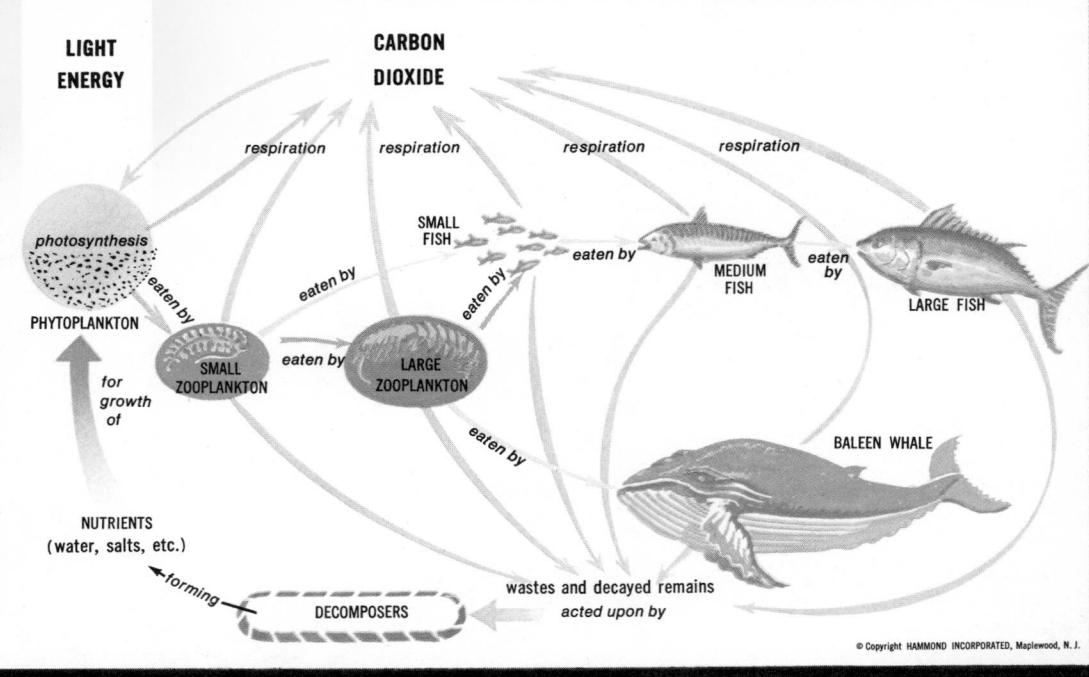

LIGHT ENERGY

CARBON DIOXIDE

respiration   respiration   respiration   respiration

photosynthesis

PHYTOPLANKTON — eaten by — SMALL ZOOPLANKTON — eaten by — LARGE ZOOPLANKTON

SMALL FISH — eaten by — MEDIUM FISH — eaten by — LARGE FISH

BALEEN WHALE

for growth of

NUTRIENTS (water, salts, etc.) ← forming — DECOMPOSERS — acted upon by — wastes and decayed remains

Ecology:
INTERRELATION OF LIVING THINGS AND THEIR SURROUNDINGS

Freedom and independence do not exist in the universe except in the creative reaches of man's intellect which distinguishes him from the other living organisms with which he shares a portion of the biosphere.

Dependent on the sun for its creation, the earth is dependent on it still for solar energy to sustain and move all living things. The amount and types of earthly life are determined by the amounts and patterns of flow of this energy which is fixed by green plants and converted into the organic compounds to maintain the plants themselves and every other organism.

In a seemingly tangled web of forces — in competition, cooperation, neutrality — in a constantly changing and more or less suitable climate, and in the processes of evolution continually in flux throughout the thin layers of atmosphere, earth and sea, strands of mutual dependence have been woven. Each form of life, from the simple one-celled organism to the complexity of man, is subject to the same laws of nature, depending one upon the other for energy and food — creating it as they destroy it and are destroyed themselves.

The word "ecology" comes from two Greek words meaning "the study of the home," and in modern times has signified the study of all living things in relation to their environments — or homes — and to each other. Western man, particularly, has romanticised his notion of a home and often chose to think of it as a solitary fortress snug against intrusion by other men and the forces of nature. But the making and maintaining of a home for man as for other forms of life is a subtle combination and balance of light, heat, moisture and food any one of which may be disturbed or destroyed by natural calamity or inadvertent act.

Through a closer study of ecology and ecological systems man is learning, hopefully not too late, that even the "lilies of the field," which neither sow nor reap, are as essential to him as are the insects clinging to their leaves, the rodents burrowing at their feet, and the soil and air that they enrich.

A TYPICAL FOOD CHAIN

1. Through the process of photosynthesis a green plant or primary producer begins the food chain.

2. A cricket, feeding upon the plant, becomes a primary consumer.

3. A secondary consumer is the frog who devours the cricket.

4. It is the fate of the frog to turn into a meal for the snake, the third or tertiary consumer.

5. The food chain ends with a snake-eating hawk, the fourth consumer, who has no predator other than man.

Photos: Ernst G. Hofmann

Man's Impact Upon Nature

Since he could think man has been at war with death. He has fought his battles against destruction with science and technology as his weapons, virtually eliminating his own annihilation by predatory animals and from diseases such as leprosy, tuberculosis and diphtheria. He has walked into many valleys of death to fight malaria and yellow fever, and he has resolved that each year more of his own kind will live to finish out their threescore years and ten.

However, the victory over nature, which had balanced population with food supply and space, is bitter, for the population has "exploded" leaving man with the seemingly insolvable problem of providing more food and space for himself or reducing his numbers by starvation or by war.

Man outsmarted himself in many ways as he worked toward creating a more perfect world for himself without understanding that natural laws go beyond human manipulation. He has destroyed forests and meadows, polluted the water and air, eliminated organisms that tried to share his bread. However, he has yet to learn to recreate the wood and brush or the interdependent communities of bacteria, insects and animals that he learned — too late — enrich the air, the soil and the water and without which he cannot function.

Modern man knows how to manufacture "miraculous" materials to work for his pleasure or his seemingly insatiable needs, but the sophistications of technology have yet to control effectively the by-products. These new materials, still subject to the order of nature's cycles, penetrate the biosphere and eventually come to roost in his own vulnerable body.

New battles are being fought throughout the world and new standards bearing the slogans of ecology float in the "unsafe" air. It is somehow ironic to find that many people now believe that man has been fighting the wrong fight in his gigantic struggle with nature. That, after all, nature never was his enemy.

Man cannot turn back to his beginnings when he lived with, and not against, the natural world. But a compromise between technology and nature must take place for our "plundered planet" cries out for the day of reckoning.

Conservation Problems

Wastes from our industrial society and air and water pollution levels have increased to the point where some of our cities are approaching disaster conditions. Unwise use of rural land is eroding the soil and contributing to silt build-up in our reservoirs. The great dust storms of the 1930's should be grim reminders of what occurs when nature's balance is upset.

- ● METROPOLITAN CENTERS WITH SEVERE AIR POLLUTION
- ━ MAJOR POLLUTED RIVERS & WATERWAYS
- AREAS WITH SEVERE SOIL EROSION
- "DUST BOWL" OF THE GREAT PLAINS (1931–38)

A sloping barnyard provides a convenient runoff for chemical and organic fertilizers, causing overenrichment (eutrophication) of the pond.

Trash burning billows clouds of air pollution over the nation's capital.

A forest stripped of trees reduces the supply of oxygen-producing greenery and inhibits good soil development and maintenance.

Poor drainage procedures near a housing development produce unstable soil, resulting in earth slides.

Unauthorized dumping affects the beauty of the countryside and later will pollute the nearby river.

Photos: U.S. Department of Agriculture

This stream is rapidly becoming polluted because of the direct discharge of soap and detergent suds into it.

POLLUTION CIRCLE
TYPES OF POLLUTION AND THEIR EFFECT ON THE TOTAL ENVIRONMENT

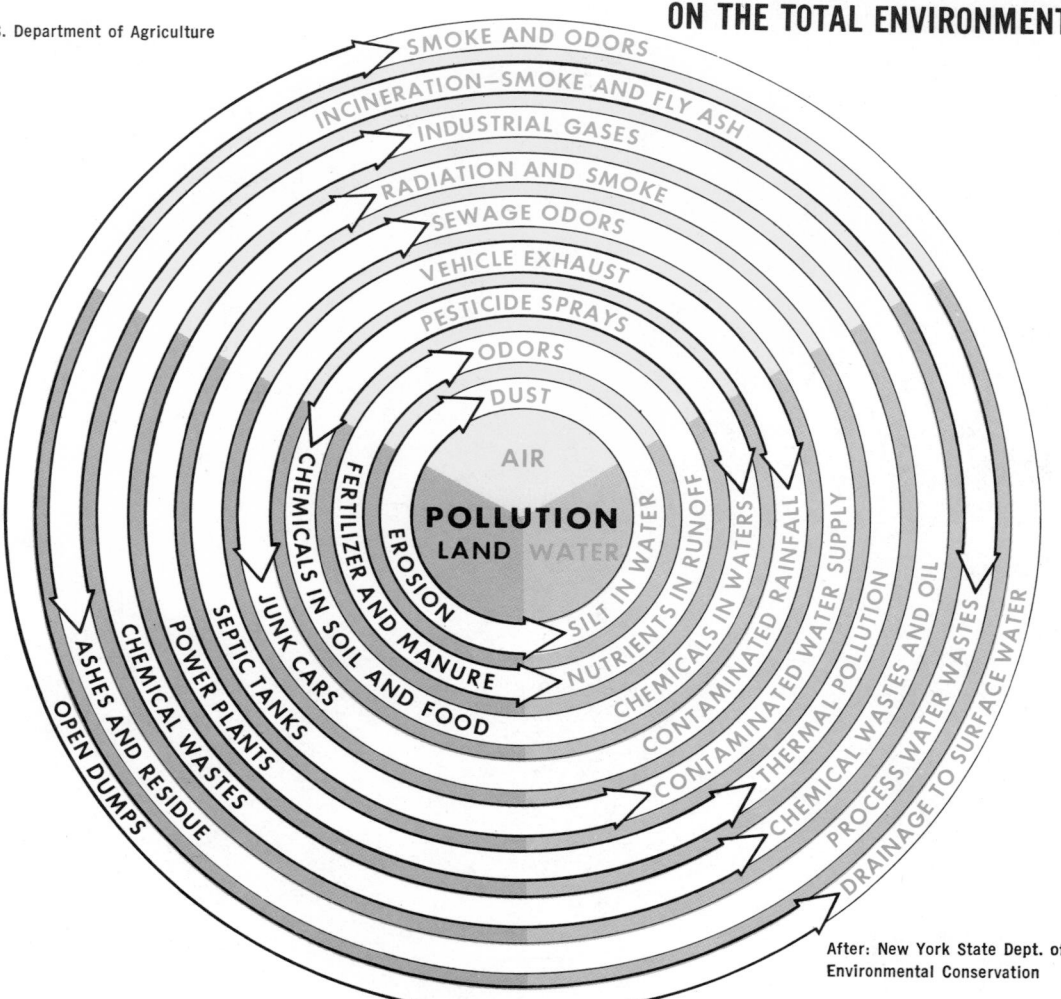

After: New York State Dept. of Environmental Conservation

In soaring cities, in golden plains of wheat, in the meanderings of highways, in the warmth of firesides — in homes, factories, forests, farms and seasides — we see the tracings of man's intellect and imagination. Unlike other creatures man's energies are not directed merely toward survival but to the challenge of creating his own environment.

For too many years man has played games with his environment without knowing nature's ground rules and it has become apparent, even to children, that the tools that mold the stuffs of nature to man's liking are double-edged.

It is unlikely that man will turn his wits and his technology toward a return to a simple and primitive way of life. It is also unlikely that man can stand still and survive.

Now man must begin to grapple with causes that have more than one effect. It is time for man to meditate on his heritage and to act, remembering that "knowledge is a fountain of life to him who possesses it."

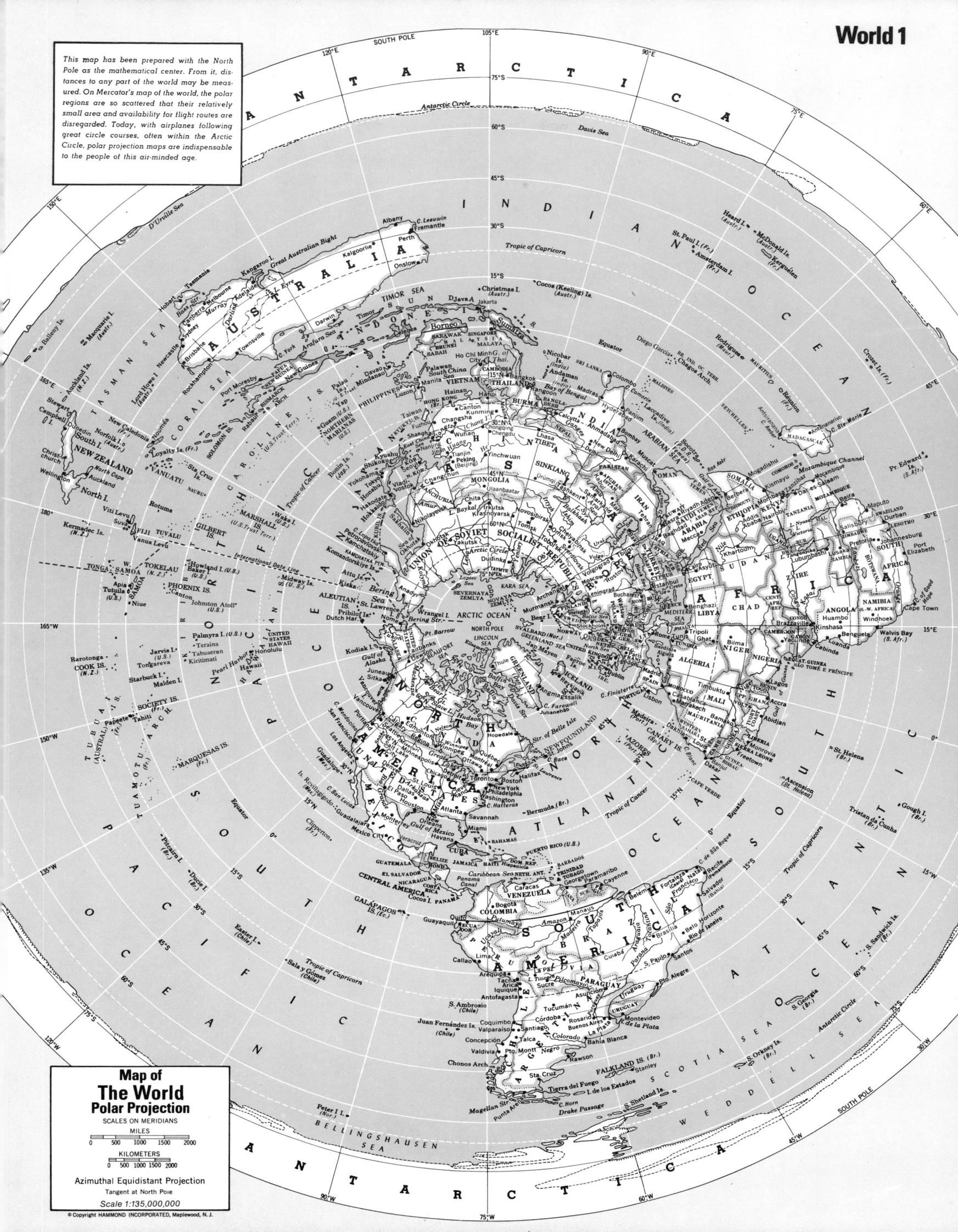

This map has been prepared with the North Pole as the mathematical center. From it, distances to any part of the world may be measured. On Mercator's map of the world, the polar regions are so scattered that their relatively small area and availability for flight routes are disregarded. Today, with airplanes following great circle courses, often within the Arctic Circle, polar projection maps are indispensable to the people of this air-minded age.

Map of The World Polar Projection

SCALES ON MERIDIANS

MILES
0 500 1000 1500 2000

KILOMETERS
0 500 1000 1500 2000

Azimuthal Equidistant Projection
Tangent at North Pole
Scale 1:135,000,000

© Copyright HAMMOND INCORPORATED, Maplewood, N.J.

The World

BRIESEMEISTER ELLIPTICAL
EQUAL-AREA PROJECTION

Capitals of Countries ....⊛
Other Capitals.........................◉
International Boundaries.....– – –

Scale 1:80,000,000

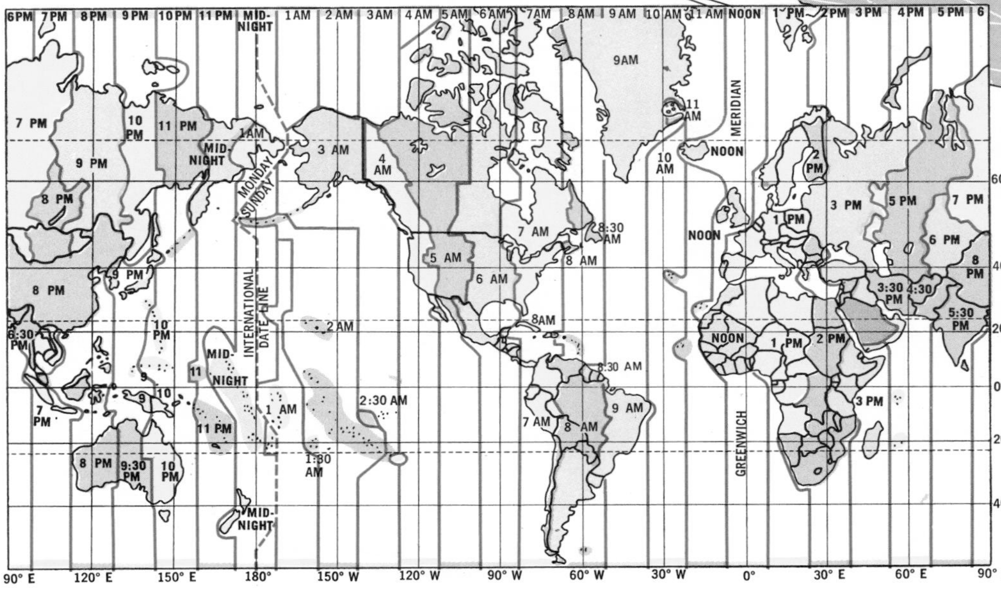

Time Zones

STANDARD	Areas using half hour deviations.
TIME	Areas not using zone system.
ZONES	

NOTE: Standard time zones in the U.S.S.R. are always advanced one hour.

LAND AREA 57,970,000 sq. mi.
        (150,142,300 sq. km.)
WATER AREA 139,781,000 sq. mi.
        (362,032,790 sq. km.)
TOTAL SURFACE AREA 197,751,000 sq.mi.
        (512,175,090 sq. km.)
POPULATION 4,415,000,000

Antarctica
AZIMUTHAL EQUIDISTANT PROJECTION
Scale 1:62,000,000

© Copyright HAMMOND INCORPORATED, Maplewood, N.J.

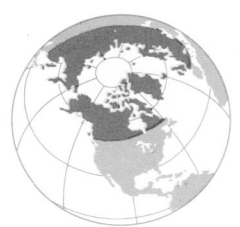

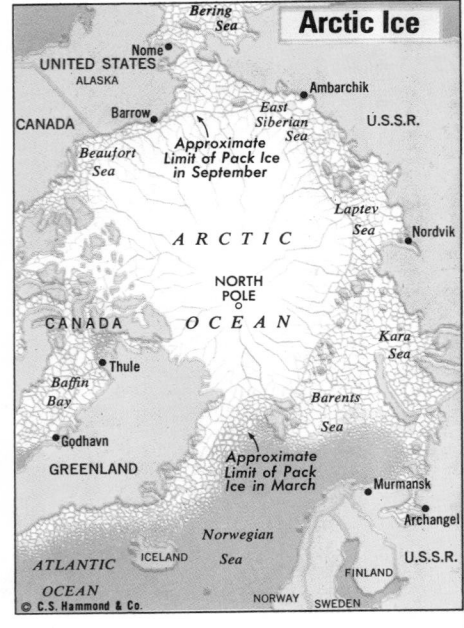

Arctic Ice
Bering Sea
Nome
UNITED STATES
ALASKA
Barrow
CANADA
Ambarchik
East Siberian Sea
U.S.S.R.
Beaufort Sea
Approximate Limit of Pack Ice in September
Laptev Sea
Nordvik
ARCTIC
NORTH POLE
OCEAN
CANADA
Kara Sea
Thule
Baffin Bay
Barents Sea
Godhavn
GREENLAND
Approximate Limit of Pack Ice in March
Murmansk
Archangel
Norwegian Sea
ICELAND
ATLANTIC OCEAN
FINLAND
U.S.S.R.
NORWAY
SWEDEN
© C.S. Hammond & Co.

Longitude 17 West of 160° Greenwich 18
180° 1 Longitude 160° East of 2 Greenwich
Arctic Ocean
AZIMUTHAL EQUIDISTANT PROJECTION
SCALE OF MILES
0 100 200 400 600
SCALE OF KILOMETERS
0 200 400 600 800 1000
Scale 1:41,000,000
BERING SEA
SEA OF OKHOTSK
GULF OF ALASKA
UNITED STATES
ALASKA
CANADA
BEAUFORT SEA
EAST SIBERIAN SEA
LAPTEV SEA
ARCTIC OCEAN
KARA SEA
BARENTS SEA
GREENLAND SEA
NORWEGIAN SEA
GREENLAND
(KALÂTDLIT-NUNÂT)
(Denmark)
BAFFIN BAY
UNION OF SOVIET SOCIALIST REPUBLICS
EUROPE
ATLANTIC OCEAN
NORTH SEA
NORTH POLE
Peary Apr. 6, 1909
Byrd May 9, 1926 (airplane)
Amundsen-Ellsworth-Nobile May 12, 1926 (dirigible)
Anderson in U.S.S. Nautilus Aug. 3, 1958
International Date Line
Arctic Circle
EXPLORERS' ROUTES
Peary 1909
Byrd 1926
Amundsen, Ellsworth & Nobile 1926
Anderson in U. S. S. Nautilus 1958
By ship
By sledge
By airplane
By dirigible
By nuclear submarine
Longitude 11 West of 20° Greenwich 10
0° Longitude 20° East of 8 Greenwich

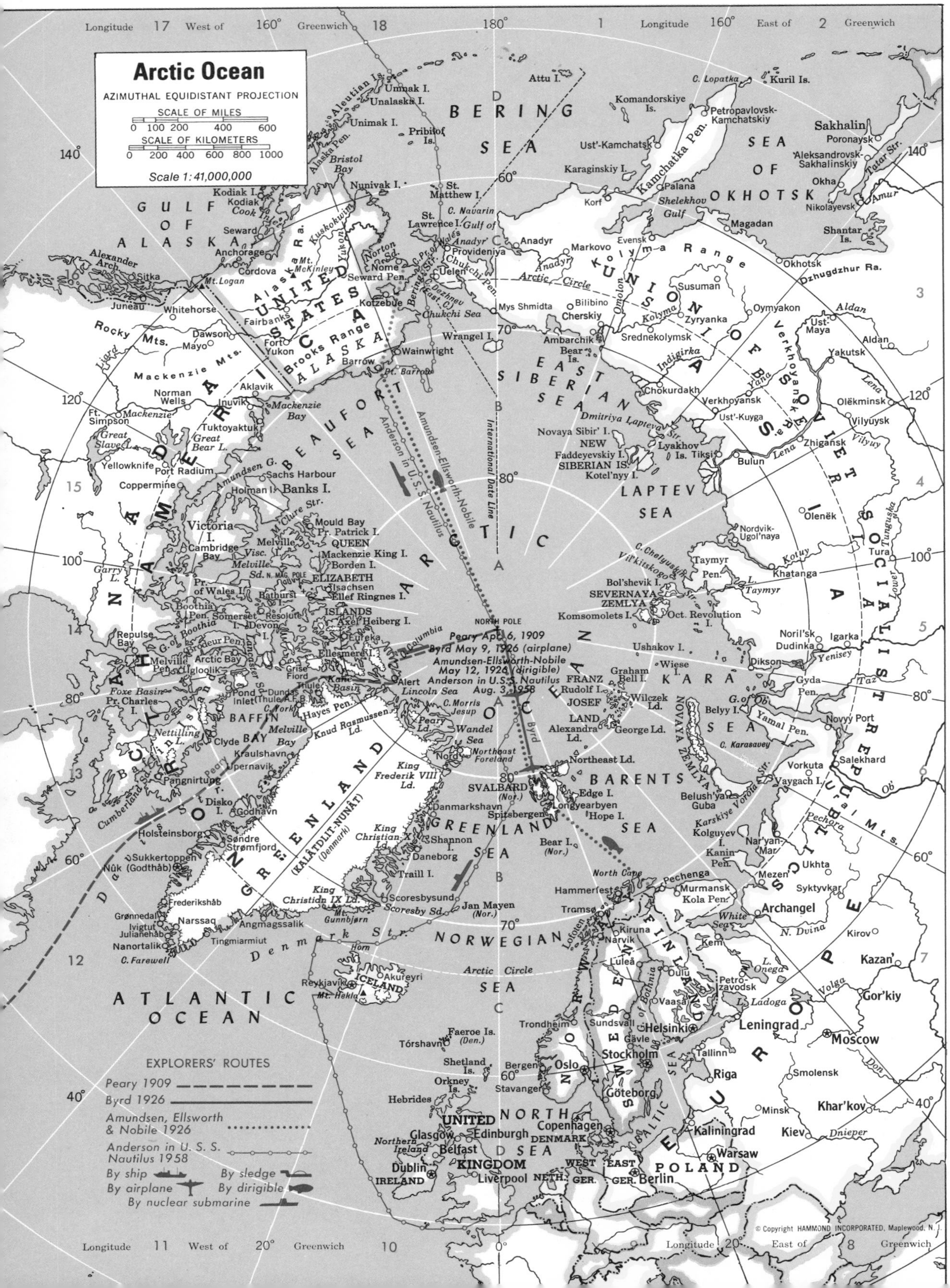

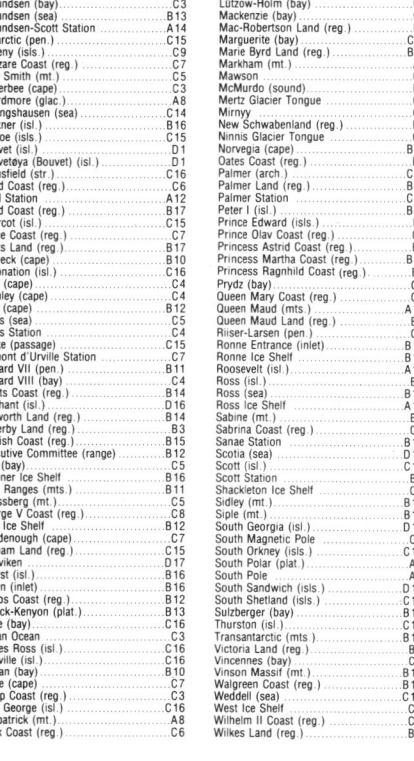

Antarctica
AZIMUTHAL EQUIDISTANT PROJECTION
SCALE OF MILES
0   200   400   600   800
KILOMETERS
0   200   400   600   800   1000
Scale 1:52,000,000
© Copyright HAMMOND INCORPORATED, Maplewood, N.J.
Prince Edward Is.° (S. Afr.)

EXPLORERS' ROUTES

Palmer 1820
Amundsen 1910-12
Scott 1910-13
Byrd 1928-30
Fuchs 1957-58
By ship   By sledge   By airplane
By snow tractor

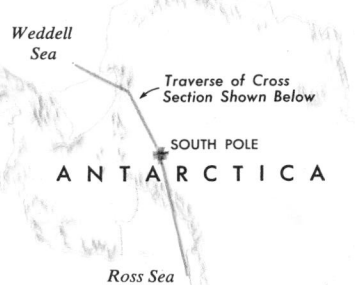

Weddell Sea
Traverse of Cross Section Shown Below
SOUTH POLE
ANTARCTICA
Ross Sea

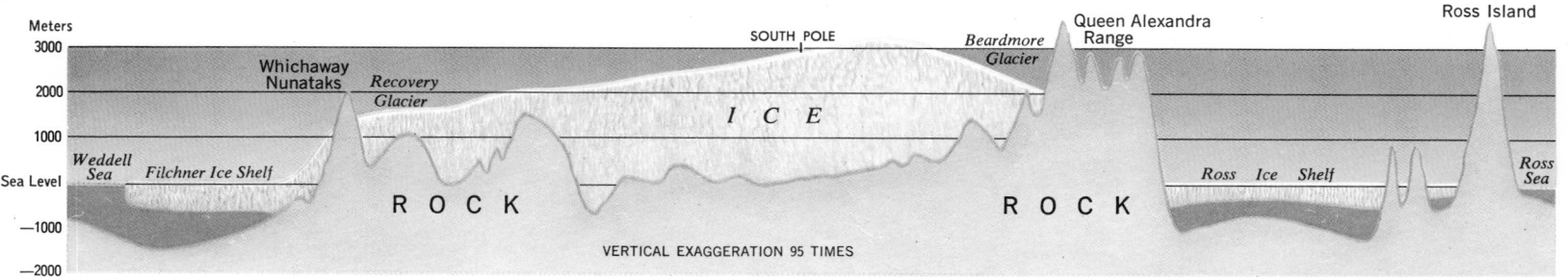

Antarctic Cross Section: Weddell Sea to Ross Sea

Meters
3000
2000
1000
Sea Level
−1000
−2000

Whichaway Nunataks
Recovery Glacier
SOUTH POLE
Beardmore Glacier
Queen Alexandra Range
Ross Island
ICE
Weddell Sea   Filchner Ice Shelf
ROCK
ROCK
Ross Ice Shelf
Ross Sea

VERTICAL EXAGGERATION 95 TIMES

Information Based on American Geographical Society's "Antarctic Map Folio Series"

Europe

POLYCONIC PROJECTION

SCALE OF MILES

0   100   200   300   400

KILOMETERS

0 100 200 300 400

Capitals of Countries.....................⊛

Other Capitals.............................⊛

International Boundaries..........—··—··—

Internal Boundaries................—···—···—

Canals..............................—·—·—·—

Scale 1:20,800,000

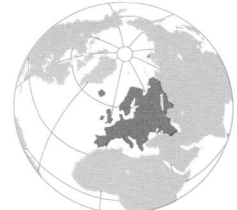

AREA 4,057,000 sq. mi.
(10,507,630 sq. km.)
POPULATION 676,000,000
LARGEST CITY Paris
HIGHEST POINT El'brus 18,510 ft.
(5,642 m.)
LOWEST POINT Caspian Sea -92 ft.
(-28 m.)

© Copyright HAMMOND INCORPORATED, Maplewood, N.J.

Population Distribution

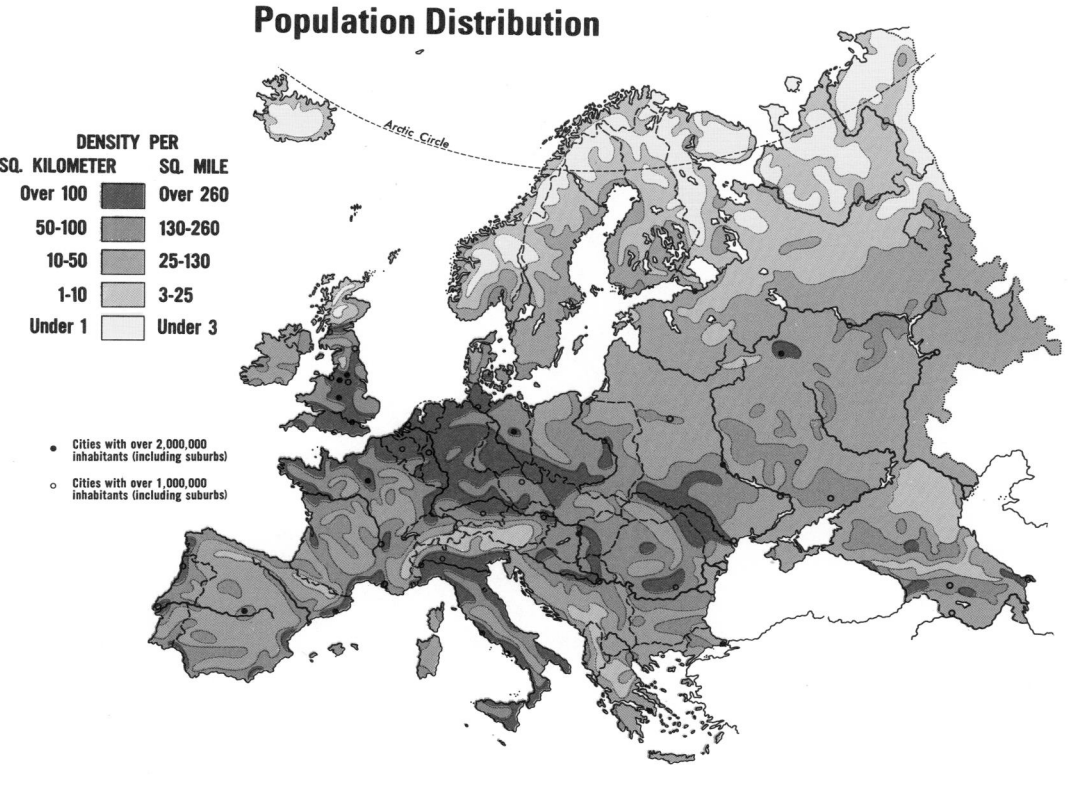

DENSITY PER

SQ. KILOMETER	SQ. MILE
Over 100	Over 260
50-100	130-260
10-50	25-130
1-10	3-25
Under 1	Under 3

● Cities with over 2,000,000
inhabitants (including suburbs)

○ Cities with over 1,000,000
inhabitants (including suburbs)

Vegetation

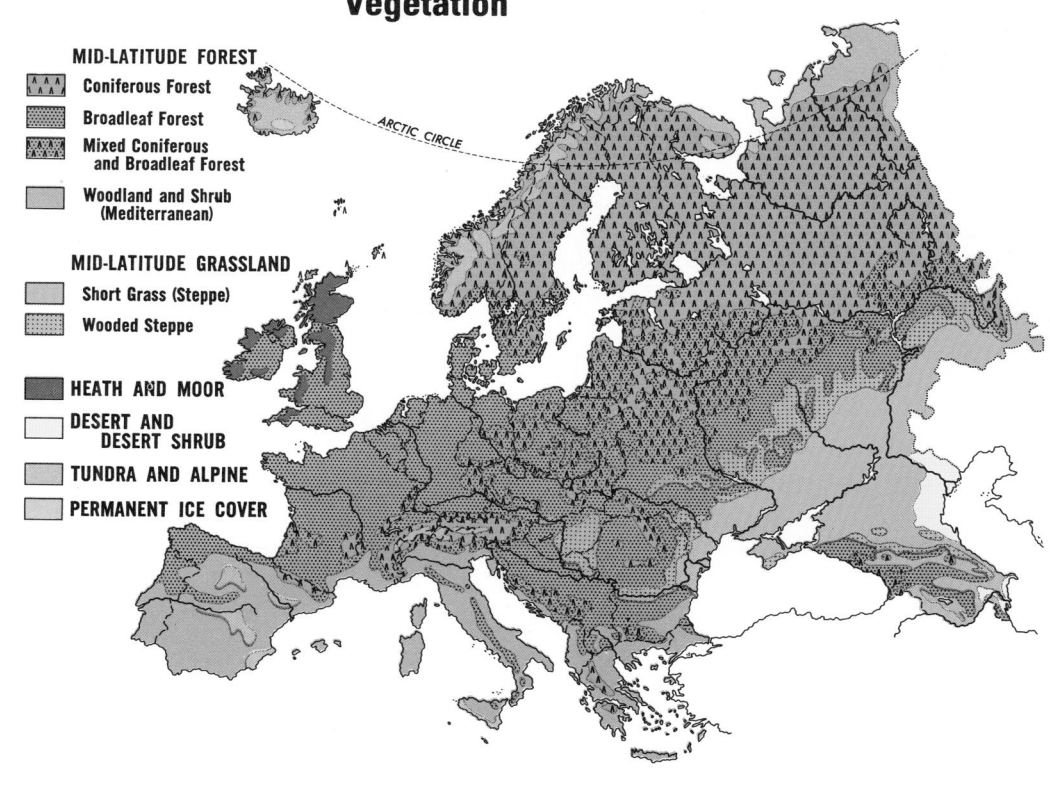

MID-LATITUDE FOREST

Coniferous Forest

Broadleaf Forest

Mixed Coniferous
and Broadleaf Forest

Woodland and Shrub
(Mediterranean)

MID-LATITUDE GRASSLAND

Short Grass (Steppe)

Wooded Steppe

HEATH AND MOOR

**DESERT AND
DESERT SHRUB**

TUNDRA AND ALPINE

PERMANENT ICE COVER

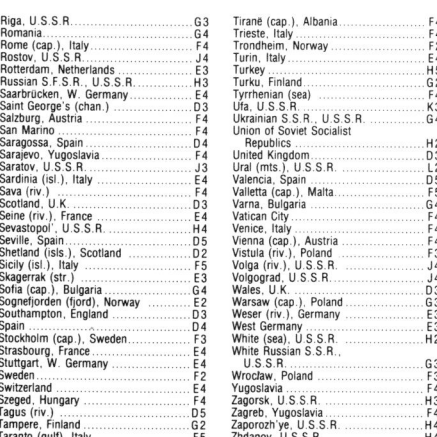

Vegetation/Relief

SCALE OF MILES
0   100   200   300   400   500   600   700   800   900   1000

SCALE OF KILOMETERS
0   100   200   300   400   500   600   700   800   900   1000

Capitals of Countries .... ⊛
International Boundaries .... —·—·—
Canals ....
Depths in Fathoms

Map labels:

NORWEGIAN SEA
BARENTS SEA
WHITE SEA
ICELAND
Reykjavik
Arctic Circle
Horn
Fontur
Faeroe Is. (Den.)
Shetland Is.
Nordkapp
Serøy
Hammerfest
Murmansk
Kola Pen.
Kolguyev I.
Kanin Pen.
Chesha Bay
Pechora
Vesterålen
Lofoten
Vestfjord
Kiruna
NORWAY
SWEDEN
FINLAND
Oulu
Glittertind 8,110 ft. (2,472 m.)
Trondheim
Sundsvall
Bergen
Oslo
Tampere
Helsinki
Åland Is.
Lake Onega
Lake Ladoga
Gulf of Bothnia
Gulf of Finland
Leningrad
Northern Dvina
Archangel
UNION OF
SOCIAL
Volga
Gor'kiy
Kuy...
Moscow
Western Dvina
Minsk
Riga
Gotland
Stockholm
Västerås
Göteborg
Vänern
Hiiumaa
Saaremaa
BALTIC SEA
Lindesnes
Skagerrak
Kattegat
NORTH SEA
Hebrides
Orkney Is.
Moray Firth
Ben Nevis 4,406 ft. (1,343 m.)
Aberdeen
Glasgow
Belfast
U.K.
UNITED KINGDOM
IRELAND
Dublin
IRISH SEA
C. Clear
St. Georges Chan.
Birmingham
Liverpool
London
Land's End
ATLANTIC OCEAN
English Channel
Channel Is. (U.K.)
DENMARK
Copenhagen
Bornholm
Rügen
Gdańsk
NETHERLANDS
Amsterdam
Frisian Is.
Hamburg
EAST
WEST
GERMANY
Berlin
Elbe
Weser
Leipzig
POLAND
Vistula
Warsaw
Łódź
Oder
Bug
Kiev
Khar'kov
Don
Dnieper
BELGIUM
Brussels
Cologne
Bonn
LUX.
GERMANY
Prague
Cracow
CZECHOSLOVAKIA
Brno
L'vov
Le Havre
Seine
Paris
Nantes
Loire
FRANCE
Bordeaux
Dordogne
Garonne
Bay of Biscay
Finisterre
C.
Lyon
Rhône
Stuttgart
Munich
Danube
Bern
SWITZ.
Mt. Blanc 15,771 ft. (4,807 m.)
LIECH.
AUSTRIA
Vienna
Graz
Budapest
HUNGARY
Cluj-Napoca
ROMANIA
Bucharest
Carpathian Mts.
Prut
Odessa
Moldova
Turin
Milan
Genoa
Venice
SAN MARINO
Sava
Zagreb
YUGOSLAVIA
Belgrade
Danube
Balkan Mts.
SEA OF AZOV
Crimea
Krasnodar
BLACK SEA
PORTUGAL
Lisbon
Porto
Douro
Tagus
Guadiana
C. de São Vicente
SPAIN
Madrid
Ebro
Saragossa
ANDORRA
Pyrenees
Gulf of Lions
Marseille
MONACO
Barcelona
Valencia
Bilbao
Málaga
Cádiz
Str. of Gibraltar
GIBRALTAR (U.K.)
Tangier
Rabat
Casablanca
MOROCCO
Oran
Algiers
ALGERIA
Constantine
TUNISIA
Tunis
C. Bon
Balearic Is.
Minorca
Majorca
Ibiza
C. Teulada
Corsica
Sardinia
APENNINES
Rome
VATICAN CITY
Naples
Palermo
Sicily
Etna 11,053 ft. (3,369 m.)
C. Passero
MALTA
Valletta
TYRRHENIAN SEA
IONIAN SEA
ADRIATIC SEA
MEDITERRANEAN SEA
Skopje
Tirane
ALBANIA
Sofia
BULGARIA
Istanbul
Bosporus
Sea of Marmara
Dardanelles
GREECE
Thessaloniki
Lésvos
Athens
C. Tainaron
Crete
Rhodes
TURKEY
Ankara
Izmir
CYPRUS
Nicosia
LEBANON
Beirut
Damascus
SY...
AFRICA
Longitude West of Greenwich
Longitude East of Greenwich

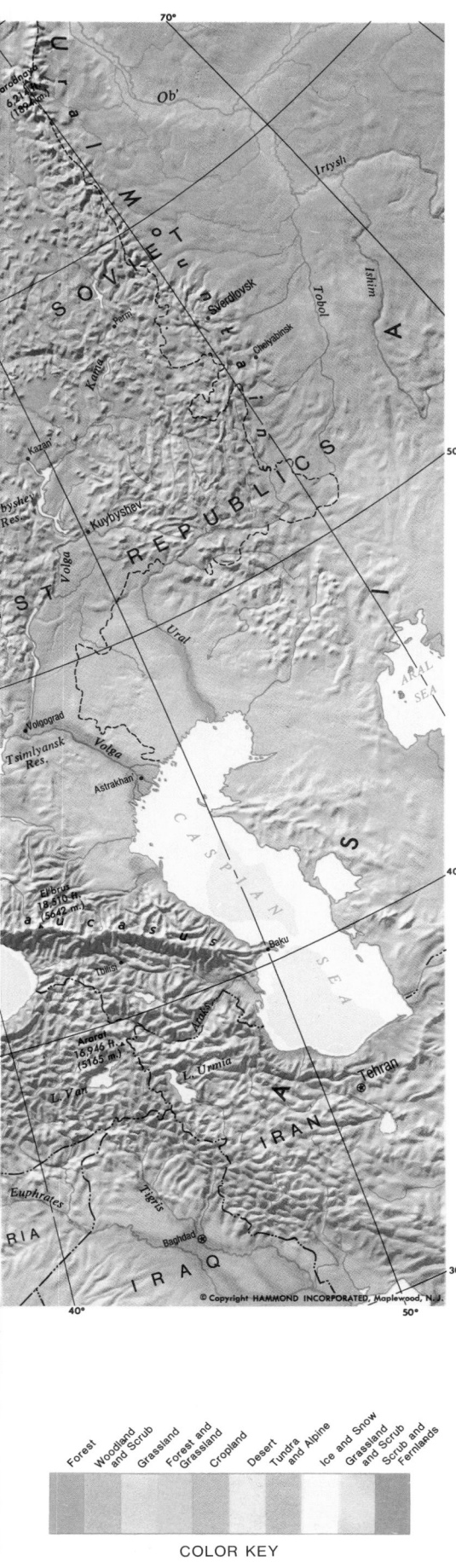

COLOR KEY

Forest | Woodland and Scrub | Grassland | Forest and Grassland | Cropland | Desert | Tundra and Alpine | Ice and Snow | Grassland and Scrub | Scrub and Fernlands

Rainfall

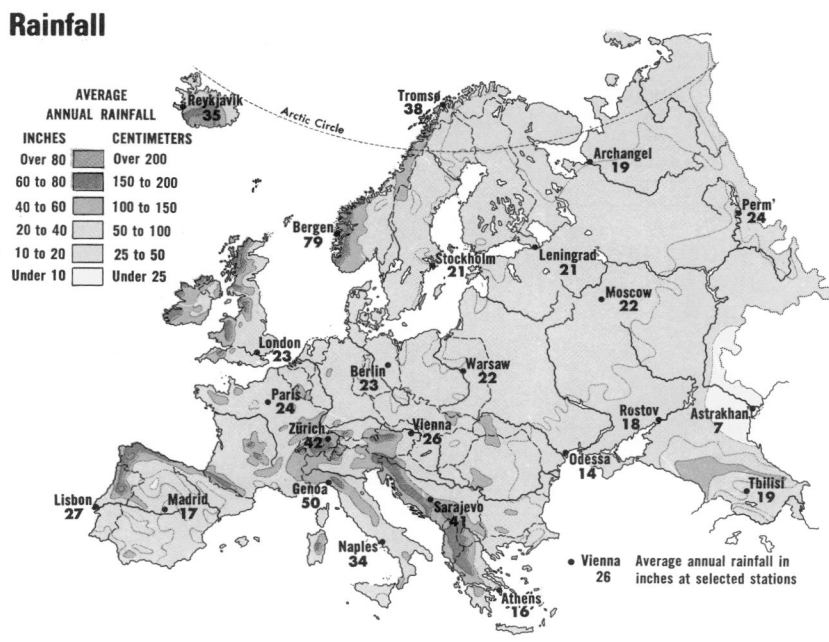

AVERAGE ANNUAL RAINFALL

INCHES	CENTIMETERS
Over 80	Over 200
60 to 80	150 to 200
40 to 60	100 to 150
20 to 40	50 to 100
10 to 20	25 to 50
Under 10	Under 25

Reykjavík 35 — Arctic Circle — Tromsø 38 — Archangel 19 — Perm' 24 — Bergen 79 — Stockholm 21 — Leningrad 21 — Moscow 22 — London 23 — Berlin 23 — Warsaw 22 — Paris 24 — Zürich 32 — Vienna 26 — Rostov 18 — Astrakhan 7 — Odessa 14 — Tbilisi 19 — Lisbon 27 — Madrid 17 — Genoa 50 — Sarajevo 41 — Naples 34 — Athens 16

• Vienna 26   Average annual rainfall in inches at selected stations

Average January Temperature

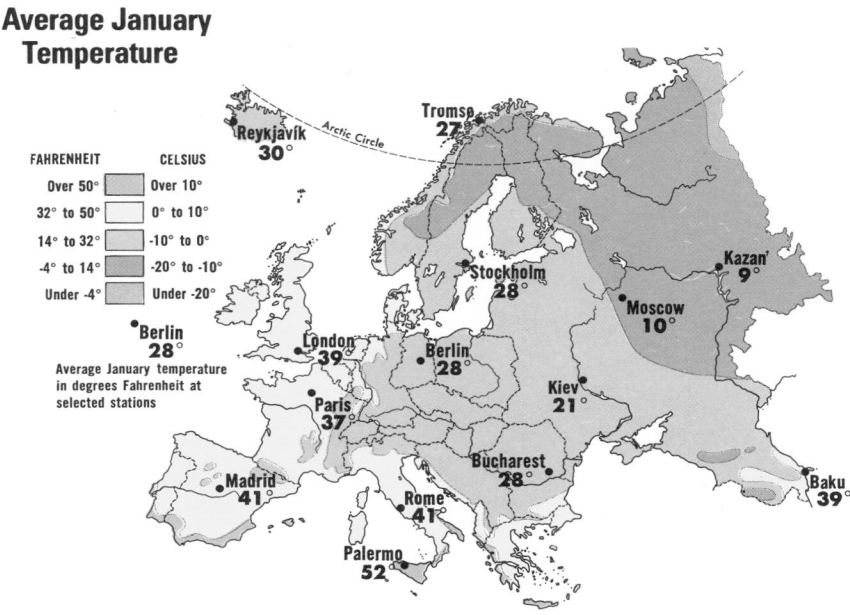

FAHRENHEIT	CELSIUS
Over 50°	Over 10°
32° to 50°	0° to 10°
14° to 32°	-10° to 0°
-4° to 14°	-20° to -10°
Under -4°	Under -20°

Reykjavík 30° — Arctic Circle — Tromsø 27 — Stockholm 28 — Kazan' 9 — Moscow 10 — • Berlin 28°

Average January temperature in degrees Fahrenheit at selected stations

London 39 — Berlin 28 — Kiev 21 — Paris 37 — Bucharest 28 — Baku 39 — Madrid 41 — Rome 41 — Palermo 52

Average July Temperature

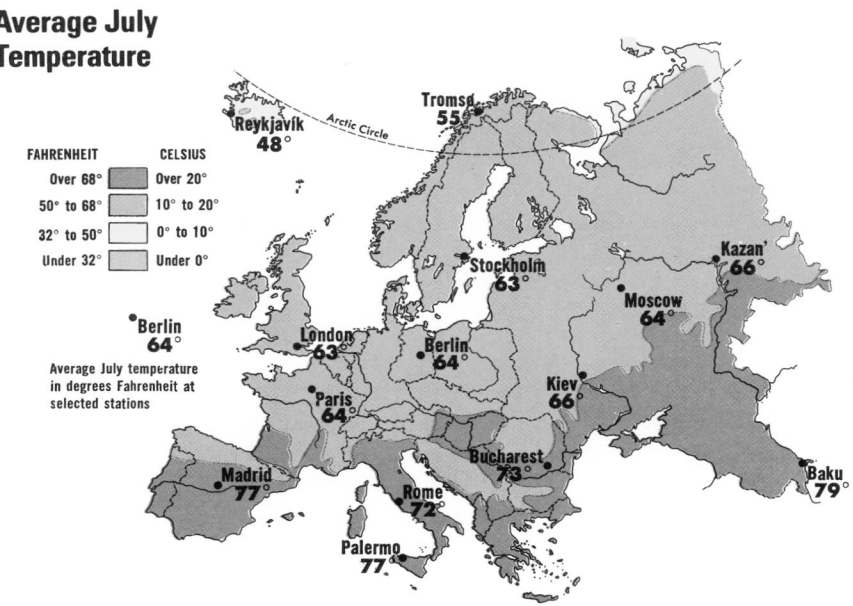

FAHRENHEIT	CELSIUS
Over 68°	Over 20°
50° to 68°	10° to 20°
32° to 50°	0° to 10°
Under 32°	Under 0°

Reykjavík 48° — Arctic Circle — Tromsø 55 — Stockholm 63 — Kazan' 66 — Moscow 64 — • Berlin 64°

Average July temperature in degrees Fahrenheit at selected stations

London 63 — Berlin 64 — Kiev 66 — Paris 64 — Bucharest 73 — Baku 79 — Madrid 77 — Rome 72 — Palermo 77

UNITED KINGDOM

AREA 94,399 sq. mi. (244,493 sq. km.)
POPULATION 55,672,000
CAPITAL London
LARGEST CITY London
HIGHEST POINT Ben Nevis 4,406 ft. (1,343 m.)
MONETARY UNIT pound sterling
MAJOR LANGUAGES English, Gaelic, Welsh
MAJOR RELIGIONS Protestantism, Roman Catholicism

IRELAND

AREA 27,136 sq. mi. (70,282 sq. km.)
POPULATION 3,440,427
CAPITAL Dublin
LARGEST CITY Dublin
HIGHEST POINT Carrantuohill 3,415 ft. (1,041 m.)
MONETARY UNIT Irish pound
MAJOR LANGUAGES English, Gaelic (Irish)
MAJOR RELIGION Roman Catholicism

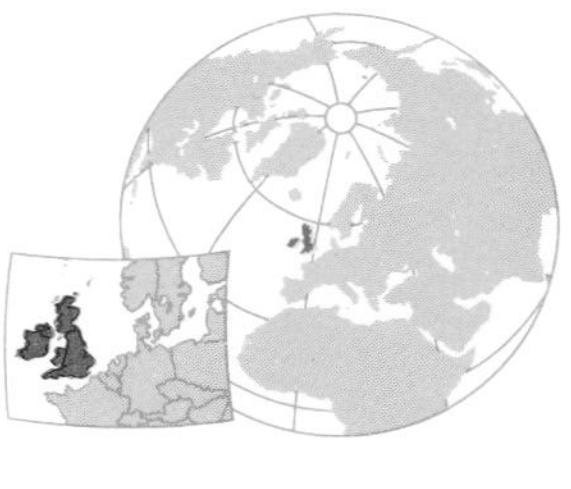

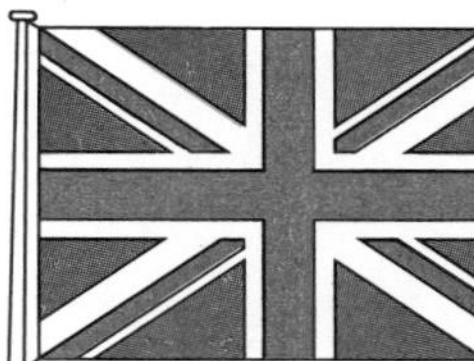

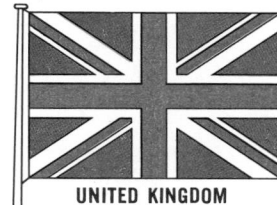

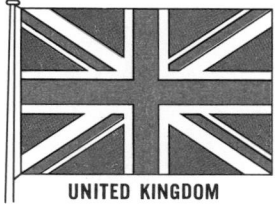

UNITED KINGDOM

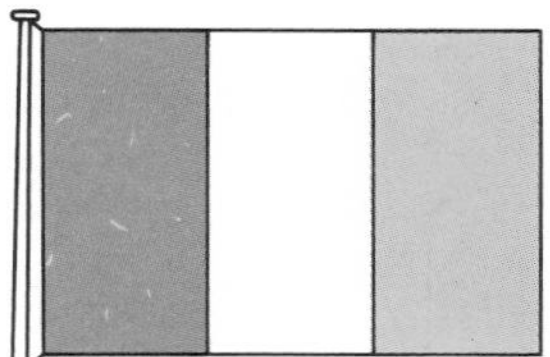

IRELAND

ENGLAND

ENGLAND

AREA 50,516 sq. mi. (130,836 sq. km.)
POPULATION 46,220,955
CAPITAL London
LARGEST CITY London
HIGHEST POINT Scafell Pike 3,210 ft. (978 m.)

WALES

AREA 8,017 sq. mi. (20,764 sq. km.)
POPULATION 2,790,462
CAPITAL Cardiff
LARGEST CITY Cardiff
HIGHEST POINT Snowdon 3,560 ft. (1,085 m.)

SCOTLAND

AREA 30,414 sq. mi. (78,772 sq. km.)
POPULATION 5,117,146
CAPITAL Edinburgh
LARGEST CITY Glasgow
HIGHEST POINT Ben Nevis 4,406 ft. (1,343 m.)

NORTHERN IRELAND

AREA 5,452 sq. mi. (14,121 sq. km.)
POPULATION 1,543,000
CAPITAL Belfast
LARGEST CITY Belfast
HIGHEST POINT Slieve Donard 2,796 ft. (852 m.)

ENGLAND

COUNTIES

Avon, 920,200	E 6
Bedfordshire, 491,700	G 5
Berkshire, 659,000	F 6
Buckinghamshire, 512,000	G 6
Cambridgeshire, 563,000	G 5
Cheshire, 916,400	E 4
Cleveland, 567,900	F 3
Cornwall, 405,200	C 7
Cumbria, 473,600	D 3
Derbyshire, 887,600	F 5
Devon, 942,100	D 7
Dorset, 575,800	E 7
Durham, 610,400	F 3
East Sussex, 655,600	H 7
Essex, 1,426,200	H 6
Gloucestershire, 491,500	E 6
Greater London, 7,028,200	H 8
Greater Manchester, 2,684,100	H 2
Hampshire, 1,456,100	F 6
Hereford and Worcester, 594,200	E 5
Hertfordshire, 937,300	G 6
Humberside, 848,600	G 4
Isle of Wight, 111,300	F 7
Isles of Scilly, 1,900	A 7
Kent, 1,448,100	H 6
Lancashire, 1,375,500	E 4
Leicestershire, 837,900	F 5
Lincolnshire, 524,500	G 4
London, Greater, 7,028,200	H 8
Manchester, Greater, 2,684,100	H 2
Merseyside, 1,578,000	G 2
Norfolk, 662,500	H 5
Northamptonshire, 505,900	G 5
Northumberland, 287,300	E 2
North Yorkshire, 653,000	F 3
Nottinghamshire, 977,500	F 4
Oxfordshire 541,800	F6
Shropshire (Salop) 359,000	E5
Somerset 404,400	E6
South Yorkshire 1,318,300	F4
Staffordshire 997,600	E5
Suffolk 577,600	H5
Surrey 1,002,900	G6
Sussex, East 655,600	H7
Sussex, West 623,400	G7
Tyne and Wear 1,182,900	H3
Warwickshire 471,000	F5
West Midlands 2,743,300	F5
West Sussex 623,400	G7
West Yorkshire 2,072,500	J1
Wiltshire 512,800	E6
Yorkshire, North 653,000	F3
Yorkshire, South 1,318,300	F4
Yorkshire, West 2,072,500	J1

CITIES and TOWNS

Abingdon, 20,130	F 6
Accrington, 36,470	H 1
Adwick le Street, 17,650	K 2
Aldeburgh, 2,750	J 5
Aldershot, 33,750	G 8
Aldridge Brownhills, 89,370	E 5
Alfreton, 21,560	F 4
Alnwick, 7,300	F 2
Altrincham, 40,800	H 2
Amersham, ⊙17,254	G 7
Andover, 27,620	F 6
Appleby, 2,240	E 3
Arnold, 35,090	F 4
Arundel, 2,390	G 7
Ashford, 36,380	H 6
Ashington, 24,720	F 2
Ashton-under-Lyne, 48,500	H 2
Axminster, ⊙4,515	D 7
Aycliffe, ⊙20,203	F 3
Aylesbury, 41,420	G 7
Bacup, 14,990	H 1
Bakewell, 4,100	J 2
Banbury, 31,060	F 5
Banstead, 44,100	H 8
Barking, 153,800	H 8
Barnet, 305,200	H 7
Barnsley, 74,730	J 2
Barnstaple, 17,820	D 6
Barrow-in-Furness, 73,400	D 3
Barton-upon-Humber, 7,750	G 4
Basildon, 135,720	J 8
Basingstoke, 60,910	F 6
Bath, 83,100	E 6
Batley, 41,630	J 1
Battle, ⊙4,987	H 7
Bebington, 62,500	G 2
Bedford, 74,390	G 5
Bedlington, 27,200	F 2
Bedworth, 41,600	F 5
Beeston and Stapleford, 65,360	F 5
Benfleet, 49,180	J 8
Bentley with Arksey, 22,320	F 4
Berkhamsted, 15,920	G 7
Beverley, 16,920	G 4
Bexhill, 34,680	H 7
Bexley, 213,500	H 8
Biddulph, 18,720	H 2
Birkenhead, 135,750	G 2
Birmingham, 1,058,800	F 5
Bishop Auckland, 32,940	E 3
Bishop's Stortford, 21,720	H 6
Blackburn, 101,670	H 1
Blackpool, 149,000	G 1
Blaydon, 31,940	H 3
Blyth, 35,390	F 2
Bodmin, 10,430	C 7
Bognor Regis, 34,620	G 7
Boldon, 24,430	J 3
Bolton, 154,480	H 2
Bootle 71,160	G2
Boston 26,700	G5
Bournemouth 144,100	F7
Bracknell† 34,067	G8
Bradford 458,900	J1
Braintree and Bocking 26,300	H6
Brent 256,500	H8
Brentwood 58,690	J8
Bridgwater 26,700	E6
Bridlington 26,920	G3
Bridport 6,660	E7
Brigg 4,870	G4
Brighouse 35,320	J1
Brightlingsea 7,170	J6
Brighton 156,500	G7
Bristol 416,300	E6
Broadstairs and Saint Peter's 21,670	J6
Bromley 299,100	H8
Bromsgrove 41,430	E5
Buckfastleigh 2,870	C7
Buckingham 5,290	G6
Bude-Stratton 5,750	C7
Bungay 4,120	J5
Burgess Hill 20,030	G7
Burnham-on-Crouch 4,920	H6
Burnley 74,300	H1
Burntwood† 23,088	F5
Burton upon Trent 49,480	F5
Bury 69,550	H2
Bury Saint Edmunds 26,800	H5
Bushey 24,500	H7
Buxton 20,050	J2
Caister-on-Sea† 6,287	J5
Camborne-Redruth 43,970	B7
Cambridge 106,400	G5
Camden 185,800	H8
Cannock 56,440	E5
Canterbury 115,600	H6
Canvey Island 29,550	J8
Carlisle, 99,600	D 3
Carlton, 46,690	F 5
Caterham and Warlingham, 35,840	H 8
Chatham, 59,550	J 8
Cheadle and Gatley, 62,460	H 2
Chelmsford, 58,320	J 7
Cheltenham, 75,910	E 6
Chertsey, 45,070	G 8
Chesham, 20,830	G 7
Cheshunt, 45,750	H 7
Chester, 117,200	G 2
Chesterfield, 69,480	J 2
Chester-le-Street, 20,720	J 3
Chichester, 20,940	G 7
Chigwell, 54,220	H 8
Chippenham, 18,550	E 6
Chorley, 31,800	G 2
Christchurch, 31,610	F 7
Cirencester, 14,500	E 6
Clacton, 39,380	J 6
Clay Cross, 9,630	J 2
Cleator Moor, ⊙7,686	D 3
Cleethorpes, 37,200	H 4
Clevedon, 15,140	D 6
Clun, ⊙1,261	D 6
Coalville, 28,740	F 5
Cockermouth, 6,480	D 3
Colchester, 79,600	H 6
Colne, 19,030	H 1
Colne Valley, 21,190	J 2
Congleton, 21,500	H 2
Consett, 35,080	H 3
Corby, 48,850	G 5
Coventry, 336,800	F 5
Cowes, 19,190	F 7
Crawley, 72,600	G 6
Crewe and Nantwich, 98,100	E 4
Cromer, 5,720	J 5
Crook and Willington, 21,120	E 3
Crosby, 56,750	G 2
Croydon, 330,600	H 8
Cuckfield, 26,500	G 6
Darlington, 85,120	F 3
Dartford, 44,130	J 8
Darton, 15,710	J 2
Darwen, 29,290	H 1
Deal, 26,840	J 6
Dearne, 24,780	K 2
Denton, 38,110	H 2
Derby, 213,700	F 5
Dewsbury, 50,560	J 1
Didcot, ⊙14,277	F 6
Doncaster, 81,530	F 4
Dorking, 22,410	G 8
Dover, 34,160	J 6
Downham Market, 4,120	H 5
Droitwich, 13,950	E 5
Dronfield, 20,000	J 2
Dudley, 187,110	E 5
Dunstable, 32,090	G 6
Durham, 88,800	J 3
Ealing, 293,800	H 8
Eastbourne, 73,200	H 7
East Grinstead, 19,420	G 6
Eastleigh, 46,340	F 7
East Retford, 18,260	G 4
Egham, 30,320	G 8
Egremont, ⊙7,253	D 3
Eling, ⊙20,006	F 7
Ellesmere, ⊙2,630	E 5
Ellesmere Port, 63,870	G 2
Enfield, 260,900	H 7
Epsom and Ewell, 70,700	G 8
Esher, 63,970	H 8
Eston, ⊙46,219	F 3
Eton, 4,950	G 8
Evesham, 14,090	F 5
Exeter, 93,300	D 7
Exminster, ⊙3,181	D 7
Exmouth, 26,840	D 7
Falmouth, 17,530	B 7
Fareham, 86,300	F 7
Farnborough, 43,520	G 8
Farnham, 33,140	G 8
Farnworth, 26,110	H 2
Faversham, 15,010	H 6
Felixstowe, 19,460	J 6
Felling, 38,990	J 3
Filey, 5,660	G 3
Fleet, 22,930	G 8
Fleetwood, 30,070	D 4
Folkestone, 45,610	J 6
Formby, 24,850	G 2
Framlingham, ⊙2,258	J 5
Frimley and Camberley, 47,390	G 8
Fulwood, 22,910	G 1
Gainsborough, 17,440	G 4
Gateshead, 91,230	J 3
Gillingham, Dorset, ⊙4,050	E 6
Gillingham, Kent, 93,900	J 8
Glastonbury, 6,580	E 6
Glossop, 24,820	J 2
Gloucester, 91,600	E 6
Godalming, 18,840	G 8
Golborne, 28,720	G 2
Goole, 17,920	G 4
Gosport, 82,300	F 7
Grange, 3,520	E 3
Grantham 27,830	G5
Gravesend 53,500	J8
Great Grimsby 93,800	G4
Great Torrington 3,430	C7
Great Yarmouth 49,410	J5
Greenwich 207,200	H8
Guildford 58,470	G8
Guisborough 14,860	F3
Hackney 192,500	H8
Hale 17,080	H2
Halesowen 54,120	E5
Halifax 88,580	J1
Haltemprice 54,850	G4
Haltwhistle† 3,511	E2
Hammersmith 170,000	H8
Haringey 228,200	H8
Harlow 79,160	H7
Harrogate 64,620	F4
Harrow 200,200	B5
Hartlepool 97,100	F3
Harwich 15,280	J6
Haslingden 15,140	H1
Hastings 74,600	H7
Hatfield† 25,359	H7
Havant and Waterloo 112,430	G7
Haverhill 14,550	H5
Havering 239,200	J8
Hayle† 5,378	B7
Hazel Grove and Bramhall 40,400	H2
Heanor 24,590	F4
Hebburn 23,150	J3
Hedon 3,010	G4
Hemel Hempstead 71,150	G7
Hereford 47,800	E5
Hertford 20,760	H7
Hetton 16,810	J3
Hexham 9,820	E3
Heywood 31,720	H2
High Wycombe 61,190	G8
Hillingdon 230,800	G8
Hinckley 49,310	F5
Hinderwell† 2,551	G3
Hitchin 29,190	G6
Hoddesdon 27,510	H7
Holmfirth 19,790	J2
Horley† 18,593	H8
Hornsea 7,280	G4
Horsham 26,770	G6
Horwich 16,670	G2
Houghton-le-Spring 33,150	J3
Hounslow, 199,100	G 8
Hove, 72,000	G 7
Hoylake, 32,000	G 2
Hoyland Nether, 15,500	J 2
Hucknall, 27,110	F 4
Huddersfield, 130,060	J 2
Hugh Town, ⊙1,958	A 8
Hull, 276,600	G 4
Hunstanton, 4,140	H 5
Huntingdon and Godmanchester, 17,200	G 5
Huyton-with-Roby, 65,950	G 2
Hyde, 37,040	H 2
Ilfracombe, 9,350	C 6
Ilkeston, 33,690	F 5
Immingham, ⊙10,259	G 4
Ipswich, 121,500	J 5
Islington, 171,600	H 8
Jarrow, 28,510	J 3
Kendal, 22,440	E 3
Kenilworth, 19,730	F 5
Kensington and Chelsea, 161,400	G 8
Keswick, 4,790	D 3
Kettering, 44,480	G 5
Keynsham, 18,970	E 6
Kidderminster, 49,960	E 5
Kidsgrove, 22,690	E 4
King's Lynn, 29,990	H 5
Kingston upon Thames, 135,600	H 8
Kingswood, 30,450	E 6
Kirkburton, 20,320	J 2
Kirkby, 59,100	G 2
Kirkby Lonsdale, ⊙1,506	E 3
Kirkby Stephen, ⊙1,539	E 3
Knutsford, 14,840	H 2
Lambeth, 290,300	H 8
Lancaster, 126,300	E 3
Leatherhead, 40,830	G 8
Leeds, 744,500	J 1
Leek, 19,460	H 2
Leicester, 289,400	F 5
Leigh, 46,390	H 2
Leighton-Linslade, 22,590	F 7
Letchworth, 31,520	G 6
Lewes, 14,170	H 7
Lewisham, 237,300	H 8
Leyland, 23,690	G 1
Lichfield, 23,690	F 5
Lincoln, 73,700	G 4
Liskeard, 5,360	C 7
Litherland, 23,530	G 2
Littlehampton, 20,320	G 7

(continued on following page)

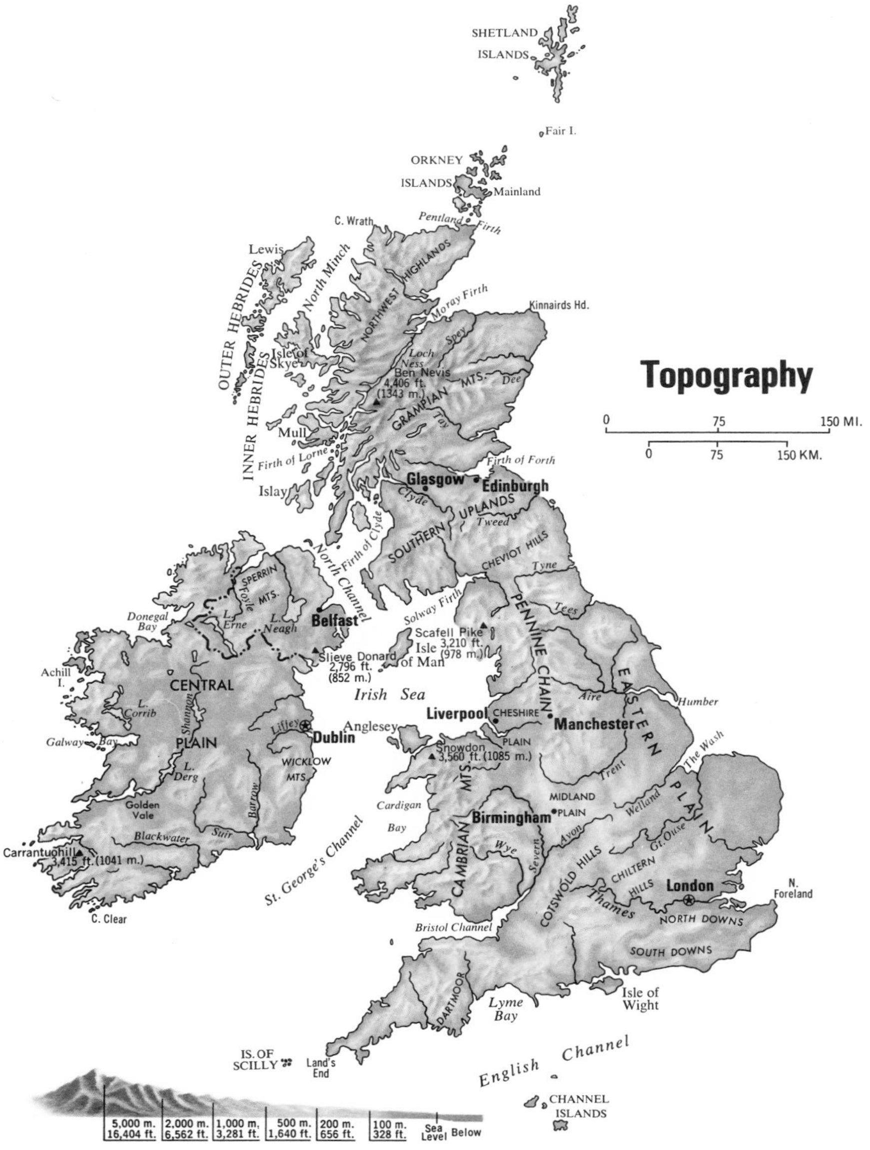
Topography
0 75 150 MI.
0 75 150 KM.
SHETLAND ISLANDS
Fair I.
ORKNEY ISLANDS
Mainland
C. Wrath
Pentland Firth
Lewis
OUTER HEBRIDES
North Minch
NORTHWEST HIGHLANDS
Moray Firth
Kinnairds Hd.
Isle of Skye
Loch Ness
Ben Nevis 4,406 ft. (1343 m.)
GRAMPIAN MTS.
Dee
Spey
INNER HEBRIDES
Mull
Firth of Lorne
Islay
Firth of Forth
Glasgow
Edinburgh
Clyde
SOUTHERN UPLANDS
Tweed
CHEVIOT HILLS
Tyne
Firth of Clyde
North Channel
SPERRIN MTS.
Donegal Bay
L. Erne
L. Neagh
Belfast
Solway Firth
Scafell Pike 3,210 ft. (978 m.)
Isle of Man
Slieve Donard 2,796 ft. (852 m.)
PENNINE CHAIN
Tees
Achill I.
CENTRAL PLAIN
L. Corrib
Shannon
Irish Sea
Anglesey
Dublin
Liffey
WICKLOW MTS.
Galway Bay
L. Derg
Liverpool
CHESHIRE PLAIN
Manchester
Aire
EASTERN PLAIN
Humber
Snowdon 3,560 ft. (1085 m.)
Trent
The Wash
Golden Vale
Barrow
Suir
Blackwater
Cardigan Bay
CAMBRIAN MTS.
MIDLAND PLAIN
Birmingham
Welland
Gt. Ouse
Severn
Avon
Wye
COTSWOLD HILLS
CHILTERN HILLS
Carrantuohill 3,415 ft. (1041 m.)
St. George's Channel
London
Thames
N. Foreland
NORTH DOWNS
C. Clear
Bristol Channel
SOUTH DOWNS
DARTMOOR
Isle of Wight
Lyme Bay
IS. OF SCILLY
Land's End
English Channel
CHANNEL ISLANDS
5,000 m. 16,404 ft.
2,000 m. 6,562 ft.
1,000 m. 3,281 ft.
500 m. 1,640 ft.
200 m. 656 ft.
100 m. 328 ft.
Sea Level
Below

★Population of met. area.
⊙Population of parish.

(continued)

England and Wales

CONIC PROJECTION

MILES

KILOMETERS

Capitals of Countries.......... ⊛
Administrative Centers.......... ⊛
Other Capitals.......... ⊙
Canals.......... ·········

International Boundaries.......... — · —
County Boundaries.......... — — —
Other Boundaries.......... — — — —

Scale 1 : 2,886,000

The administrative centers for MID GLAMORGAN, NORTHUMBERLAND and SURREY are Cardiff, Newcastle upon Tyne and Kingston upon Thames, respectively.

© Copyright HAMMOND INCORPORATED, Maplewood, N.J.

Longitude West of Greenwich   Longitude East of Greenwich

Lennoxtown, 3,070 .....B 1
Lerwick, 6,195 .....G 2
Leslie, 3,303 .....E 4
Lesmahagow, 3,906 .....E 5
Leswalt, 237 .....C 6
Letham, 804 .....F 4
Leuchars, 2,482 .....F 4
Leurbost, 461 .....B 2
Leven, 9,507 .....F 4
Leverburgh, 223 .....B 3
Lhanbryde, 1,184 .....E 3
Lilliesleaf, 212 .....F 5
Limekilns, 812 .....D 1
Linlithgow, 6,098 .....C 1
Linwood, 10,510 .....B 2
Lionel, 187 .....B 2
Livingston, 21,900 .....C 2
Loanhead, 5,971 .....D 2
Lochailort, ⊙673 .....C 4
Lochaline, 213 .....C 4
Lochans, 355 .....D 6
Locharbriggs, 2,561 .....E 5
Lochawe, 200 .....C 4
Lochboisdale, 382 .....A 3
Lochcarron, 204 .....C 3
Lochgelly, 7,754 .....D 1
Lochgilphead, 1,217 .....C 4
Lochgoilhead, 216 .....D 4
Lochinver, 283 .....C 2
Lochmaben, 1,304 .....E 5
Lochmaddy, 307 .....A 3
Lochore, 2,994 .....D 1
Lochwinnoch, 2,064 .....A 2
Lockerbie, 3,135 .....E 5
Lossiemouth and Branderburgh, 5,817 .....E 3
Lumsden, 248 .....F 3
Luncarty, 584 .....E 4
Lybster, 554 .....E 2
Lyness, ⊙454 .....E 2
Macduff, 3,682 .....F 3
Machrihanish, 212 .....C 5
Maidens, 536 .....D 5
Mallaig, 903 .....C 4
Markinch, 2,366 .....E 4
Mauchline, 3,612 .....D 5
Maud, 634 .....F 3
Maybole, 4,703 .....D 5
Mayfield, 8,232 .....D 2
Meigle, 357 .....E 4
Melrose, 2,197 .....F 5
Melvaig, ⊙1,794 .....C 3
Methlick, 315 .....F 3
Methven, 806 .....E 4
Mid Yell, 220 .....G 2
Millport, 1,161 .....A 2
Milnathort, 1,099 .....E 4
Milngavie, 10,846 .....B 1
Minnigaff, 658 .....D 6
Mintlaw, 657 .....F 3
Moffat, 2,041 .....E 5
Moniaive, 342 .....E 5
Monifieth, 7,100 .....F 4
Montrose, 4,704 .....F 4
Morar, 184 .....C 4
Motherwell and Wishaw, 72,991 .....C 2
Muirkirk, 2,607 .....E 5
Muir of Ord, 1,339 .....D 3
Musselburgh, 17,045 .....D 2
Muthill, 672 .....E 4
Nairn, 5,821 .....E 3
Neilston, 4,358 .....B 2
Nethy Bridge, 431 .....E 3
New Abbey, 339 .....E 6
Newarthill, 7,003 .....C 2
Newburgh, Fife, 2,124 .....E 4
Newburgh, Grampian, 447 .....G 3
Newcastleton, 903 .....F 5
New Cumnock, 5,077 .....D 5
New Deer, 601 .....F 3
New Galloway, 337 .....D 5
Newmains, 6,847 .....C 2
Newmarket, 613 .....B 2
Newmill, 449 .....E 3
Newmilns and Greenholm, 3,509 .....D 5
New Pitsligo, 1,125 .....F 3
Newport-on-Tay, 3,762 .....F 4
New Scone, 3,830 .....E 4
Newtongrange, 4,555 .....D 2
Newton Mearns, 6,901 .....B 2
Newtonmore, 894 .....D 3
Newton Stewart, 1,983 .....D 6
Newtown Saint Boswells, 1,101 .....F 5
Newtyle, 664 .....E 4
North Berwick, 4,317 .....F 4
North Tolsta, 527 .....B 2
Oakley, 3,499 .....C 1
Oban, 6,515 .....C 4
Old Kilpatrick, 3,256 .....B 2
Oldmeldrum, 1,103 .....F 3
Oykel Bridge, ⊙742 .....D 3
Paisley, 94,833 .....B 2
Palnackie, 225 .....E 6
Patna, 2,867 .....D 5
Peebles, 6,049 .....E 5
Penicuik, 10,476 .....D 2
Penpont, 364 .....E 5
Perth, 43,098 .....E 4
Peterculter, 3,226 .....F 3
Peterhead, 14,846 .....G 3
Pierowall, ⊙735 .....E 1
Pitlochry, 2,468 .....E 4
Pitmedden, 313 .....F 3
Pittenweem, 1,548 .....F 4
Plockton, 288 .....C 3
Poolewe, ⊙1,794 .....C 3
Port Appin, ⊙2,172 .....C 4
Port Askaig, ⊙1,795 .....B 5
Port Bannatyne, 730 .....A 2
Port Charlotte, 240 .....B 5
Port Ellen, 932 .....B 5
Port Glasgow, 22,189 .....A 2
Portgordon, 814 .....F 3
Portknockie, 1,217 .....F 3
Portmahomack, 226 .....E 3
Portpatrick, 643 .....C 6
Portree, 1,374 .....B 3
Portsoy, 1,717 .....F 3
Port William, 517 .....D 6
Prestonpans, 3,272 .....D 1
Prestwick, 13,218 .....D 5
Queensferry, 5,339 .....D 1
Reay, 283 .....E 2
Renfrew, 18,880 .....B 2
Renton, 3,443 .....A 1
Rhu, 1,540 .....A 1
Rhynie, 333 .....F 3
Rigside, 1,195 .....E 5
Rosehearty, 1,220 .....F 3
Rosneath, 946 .....A 1
Rothes, 1,240 .....E 3
Rothesay, 6,285 .....A 2
Rutherglen, 24,091 .....B 2
Saint Abbs, 203 .....F 5
Saint Andrews, 12,837 .....F 4
Saint Combs, 738 .....G 3
Saint Cyrus, 340 .....F 4
Saint Margaret's Hope, 210 .....F 2
Saint Monance, 1,205 .....F 4
Saline, 831 .....C 1
Saltcoats, 14,861 .....D 5
Sandbank, 850 .....A 1
Sandhead, 248 .....D 6
Sandwick, 603 .....B 2
Sanquhar, 2,030 .....D 5
Sauchie, 6,082 .....C 1
Scalasaig, ⊙137 .....B 4
Scalloway, 896 .....G 2
Scarinish, ⊙875 .....B 4
Scourie, ⊙745 .....C 2
Scrabster, 273 .....E 2
Selkirk, 5,635 .....F 5
Shader, 258 .....B 2
Shawbost, 458 .....B 2
Shieldaig, ⊙550 .....C 3
Shotts, 9,512 .....C 2
Skateraw, 674 .....F 3
Skelmorlie, 1,535 .....A 2
Skipness, ⊙765 .....C 5
Slamannan, 1,584 .....C 2
Spean Bridge, 235 .....D 4
Springholm, 340 .....E 5
Stanley, 1,385 .....E 4
Stenhousemuir, 8,203 .....C 1
Stevenston, 11,786 .....D 5
Stewarton, 5,165 .....D 5
Stirling, 29,799 .....C 1
Stonehaven, 4,837 .....F 4
Stonehouse, 7,900 .....D 5
Stornoway, 5,371 .....B 2
Stow, 485 .....F 5
Strachan, ⊙390 .....F 3
Strachur Bay, ⊙678 .....C 4
Stranraer, 10,174 .....C 6
Strathaven, 5,464 .....D 5
Strathpeffer, 874 .....D 3
Strichen, 962 .....F 3
Stromeferry, ⊙1,724 .....C 3
Stromness, 1,680 .....E 2
Strontian, ⊙764 .....C 4
Struan, ⊙772 .....B 3
Swinton, 235 .....F 5
Tain, 2,057 .....D 3
Tarbert, Strathclyde, 1,391 .....C 5
Tarbert, W. Isles, 479 .....B 3
Tarbolton, 2,224 .....D 5
Tarland, 452 .....F 3
Tayport, 2,848 .....F 4
Thornhill, Central, 443 .....D 4
Thornhill, Dumf. & Gall., 1,510 .....E 5
Thurso, 9,113 .....E 2
Tillicoultry, 4,320 .....C 1
Tobermory, 652 .....B 4
Tolob, ⊙2,033 .....G 2
Tomatin, 214 .....D 3
Tomintoul, 306 .....E 3
Torphins, 499 .....F 3
Tradespark, 425 .....E 3
Tranent, 7,212 .....F 5
Troon, 11,656 .....D 5
Tullibody, 6,082 .....C 1
Turriff, 3,051 .....F 3
Tweedsmuir, ⊙105 .....E 5
Twynholm, 274 .....D 6
Tyndrum, ⊙1,153 .....D 4
Uddingston, 5,278 .....B 2
Uig, Highland, 103 .....B 3
Uig, W. Isles, ⊙1,948 .....A 2
Ullapool, 807 .....C 3
Uphall, 3,035 .....C 1
Viewpark, 9,812 .....C 2
Walkerburn, 842 .....F 5
Watten, 347 .....E 2
Wemyss Bay, 323 .....A 2
West Barns, 659 .....F 5
West Calder, 2,005 .....C 2
West Kilbride, 3,883 .....D 5
West Linton, 705 .....D 2
Whitburn, 11,647 .....C 2
Whitehills, 875 .....F 3
Whithorn, 990 .....D 6
Whiting Bay, 352 .....C 5
Wick, 7,804 .....E 2
Wigtown, 1,118 .....D 6
Winchburgh, 2,409 .....D 1
Yetholm, 435 .....F 5

OTHER FEATURES

A'Chralaig (mt.) .....C 3
Ailsa Craig (isl.), 3 .....C 5
Almond (riv.) .....E 4
Annan (riv.) .....E 5
Appin (dist.), 2,006 .....C 4
Ardgour (dist.), 315 .....C 4
Ardle (riv.) .....E 4
Ardnamurchan (pen.), 764 .....B 4
Argyll (dist.), 4,940 .....C 4
Arkaig, Loch (lake) .....C 4
Arran (isl.), 3,564 .....C 5
Askival (mt.) .....B 4
Assynt (dist.), 833 .....C 2
Athol (dist.), 1,082 .....D 4
Atlantic Ocean .....B 2
Avon (riv.) .....C 1
Avon (riv.) .....E 3
Awe, Loch (lake) .....C 4
Ayr (riv.) .....D 5
Ayr, Heads of (cape) .....D 5
Badenoch (dist.), 2,717 .....D 4
Baleshare (isl.), 64 .....A 3
Balmoral Castle .....E 3
Barra (sound) .....A 3
Barra (isl.), 1,005 .....A 4
Barra (head) .....A 4
Barra Isles (isls.), 1,092 .....A 4
Battock (mt.) .....F 4
Beauly (riv.) .....D 3
Beinn Dearg (mt.) .....D 3
Beinn a Ghlo (mt.) .....E 4
Bell Rock (isl.), 3 .....F 4
Ben Alder (mt.) .....D 4
Ben Avon (mt.) .....E 3
Benbecula (isl.), 1,355 .....A 3
Ben Cruachan (mt.) .....C 4
Ben Lawers (mt.) .....D 4
Ben Lui (mt.) .....D 4
Ben Macdhui (mt.) .....E 3
Ben Mhor (mt.) .....A 3
Ben More (mt.) .....B 4
Ben More (mt.) .....D 4
Ben More Assynt (mt.) .....D 2
Ben Nevis (mt.) .....D 4
Bernera (isl.), 276 .....B 2
Berneray (isl.), 131 .....A 3
Berneray (isl.), 6 .....A 4
Bidean nam Bian (mt.) .....D 4
Black Isle (pen.), 7,209 .....D 3
Blackwater (res.) .....D 4
Boisdale, Loch (inlet) .....A 3
Bracadale, Loch (inlet) .....B 3
Braemar (dist.), 7,624 .....E 3
Breadalbane (dist.), 3,649 .....D 4
Bressay (isl.), 248 .....G 2
Broad (bay) .....B 2
Broad Law (mt.) .....E 5
Broom, Loch (inlet) .....C 3
Brough Ness (prom.) .....F 2
Buchan (dist.), 40,089 .....F 3
Buddon Ness (prom.) .....F 4
Burray (isl.), 209 .....F 2
Burrow (head) .....D 6
Bute (isl.), 8,423 .....C 5
Bute (sound) .....C 5
Butt of Lewis (prom.) .....B 2
Cairn Gorm (mt.) .....E 3
Cairngorm (mts.) .....E 3
Cairn Toul (mt.) .....E 3
Caledonian (canal) .....D 3
Canna (isl.), 22 .....B 3
Carn Ban (mt.) .....D 3
Carn Eige (mt.) .....C 3
Carrick (dist.), 21,425 .....D 5
Carron (riv.) .....C 1
Carron (riv.) .....C 3
Cheviot (hills) .....F 5
Cheviot, The (mt.) .....F 5
Clisham (mt.) .....B 3
Clyde (riv.) .....D 5
Clyde (firth) .....D 5
Coll (isl.), 144 .....B 4
Colonsay (isl.), 137 .....B 4
Copinsay (isl.), 3 .....F 2
Cowal (dist.), 15,548 .....C 4
Creag Meagaidh (mt.) .....D 4
Cromarty (firth) .....D 3
Cuillin (hills) .....B 3
Cuillin (sound) .....B 3
Dee (riv.) .....D 5
Dee (riv.) .....F 3
Dennis (head) .....F 1
Deveron (riv.) .....F 3
Don (riv.) .....F 3
Doon (riv.) .....D 5
Dornoch (firth) .....E 3
Duirinish (dist.), 1,085 .....B 3
Duncansby (head) .....F 2
Dunnet (head) .....E 2
Earn (riv.) .....E 4
Earn, Loch (lake) .....D 4
Eday (isl.), 179 .....F 1
Eddrachillis (bay) .....C 2
Eden (riv.) .....F 4
Egilsay (isl.), 39 .....F 1
Eigg (isl.), 69 .....B 4
Eil, Loch (lake) .....C 4
Eishort, Loch (inlet) .....B 3
Enard (bay) .....C 2
Eriboll, Loch (inlet) .....D 2
Ericht, Loch (lake) .....D 4
Eriskay (isl.), 219 .....A 3
Erisort, Loch (inlet) .....B 2
Esk (riv.) .....F 5
Etive, Loch (inlet) .....C 4
Ewe, Loch (inlet) .....C 3
Eye (pen.), 850 .....B 2
Fair Isle (isl.), 65 .....F 3
Fetlar (isl.), 88 .....G 2
Fife Ness (prom.) .....F 4
Findhorn (riv.) .....E 3
Flannan (isls.), 3 .....A 2
Formartine (dist.), 10,768 .....F 3
Forth (riv.) .....B 1
Forth (firth) .....F 4
Forth and Clyde (canal) .....B 2
Foula (isl.), 33 .....F 2
Fyne, Loch (inlet) .....C 5
Galloway (dist.), 54,972 .....D 5
Galloway, Mull of (prom.) .....D 6
Gare Loch (inlet) .....A 1
Garioch (dist.), 6,863 .....F 3
Garry, Loch (lake) .....D 3
Gigha (isl.), 174 .....C 5
Girdle Ness (prom.) .....G 3
Glass (riv.) .....D 3
Glen More (dist.), 55,035 .....D 3
Goat Fell (mt.) .....C 5
Gometra (isl.), 10 .....B 4
Grampian (mts.) .....D 4
Great Cumbrae (isl.), 1,296 .....A 2
Gruinard (bay) .....C 3
Hallandale (riv.) .....E 2
Harris (sound) .....A 3
Harris (dist.), 2,175 .....B 3
Hebrides (sea) .....B 3
Hebrides, Inner (isls.), 14,881 .....B 4
Hebrides, Outer (isls.), 29,615 .....A 3
Helmsdale (riv.) .....E 2
Herma Ness (prom.) .....G 2
Holy (isl.), 10 .....C 5
Holy Loch (inlet) .....A 1
Hoy (isl.), 419 .....E 2
Inchcape (Bell Rock) (isl.), 3 .....F 4
Inchkeith (isl.), 3 .....D 1
Indaal, Loch (inlet) .....B 5
Inner (sound) .....C 3
Inner Hebrides (isls.), 14,881 .....B 4
Iona (isl.), 145 .....B 4
Isla (riv.) .....E 4
Islay (isl.), 3,816 .....B 5
Jura (isl.), 210 .....C 5
Jura (sound) .....C 5
Katrine, Loch (lake) .....D 4
Kerrera (isl.), 27 .....C 4
Kilbrannan (sound) .....C 5
Kinnairds (head) .....G 3
Kintyre (pen.), 10,077 .....C 5
Kintyre, Mull of (prom.) .....C 5
Knapdale (dist.), 4,082 .....C 5
Kyle of Tongue (inlet) .....D 2
Laggan (bay) .....B 5
Lammermuir (hills) .....F 5
Lennox (hills) .....B 1
Leven (lake) .....E 4
Leven, Loch (inlet) .....D 4
Lewis (dist.), 20,047 .....B 2
Liddel Water (riv.) .....F 5
Linnhe, Loch (inlet) .....C 4
Lismore (isl.), 166 .....C 4
Little Minch (sound) .....B 3
Lochaber (dist.), 13,813 .....D 4
Lochnagar (mt.) .....E 4
Lochy, Loch (lake) .....D 3
Lomond, Loch (lake) .....D 4
Long, Loch (inlet) .....D 4
Lorne (dist.), 12,162 .....C 4
Lorne (firth) .....C 4
Loyal, Loch (lake) .....D 2
Luce (bay) .....D 6
Luing (isl.), 151 .....C 4
Lyon (riv.) .....D 4
Machers, The (pen.), 6,192 .....D 6
Mainland (isl.), 12,747 .....E 1
Mainland (isl.), 12,944 .....G 2
Mar (dist.), 23,931 .....F 3
Maree, Loch (lake) .....C 3
May, Isle of (isl.), 10 .....F 4
Merrick (mt.) .....D 5
Minginish (dist.), 772 .....B 3
Moidart (dist.), 155 .....C 4
Monach (sound) .....A 3
Monadhliath (mts.) .....D 3
Moorfoot (hills) .....E 5
Moray (firth) .....E 3
Moriston (riv.) .....D 3
Morven (dist.), 398 .....C 4
Morven (mt.) .....E 2
Muck (isl.), 24 .....B 4
Muckle Flugga (isl.), 3 .....G 2
Mull (isl.), 2,024 .....C 4
Mull (head) .....F 1
Mull (sound) .....C 4
Nairn (riv.) .....D 3
na Keal, Loch (inlet) .....B 4
Naver (riv.) .....D 2
Ness, Loch (lake) .....D 3
Nevis, Loch (inlet) .....C 3
Nith (riv.) .....E 5
North (chan.) .....C 5
North (sound) .....F 1
North (sound) .....G 4
North Esk (riv.) .....F 4
North Minch (sound) .....B 3
North Ronaldsay (isl.), 134 .....F 1
North Uist (isl.), 1,469 .....A 3
Oa, Mull of (prom.) .....B 5
Ochil (hills) .....E 4
Oich (riv.) .....D 3
Orchy (riv.) .....D 4
Orkney (isls.), 17,675 .....F 1
Oronsay (isl.), 2 .....B 4
Outer Hebrides (isls.), 29,615 .....A 3
Oykel (riv.) .....D 3
Pabbay (isl.), 4 .....A 3
Papa Stour (isl.), 24 .....F 2
Papa Westray (isl.), 106 .....F 1
Paps of Jura (mt.) .....C 5
Park (dist.), 210 .....B 2
Peel Fell (mt.) .....F 5
Pentland (hills) .....D 2
Pentland (firth) .....E 2
Pladda (isl.), 2 .....C 5
Quoich, Loch (lake) .....C 3
Raasay (isl.), 163 .....C 3
Rannoch (dist.), 1,177 .....D 4
Rannoch, Loch (lake) .....D 4
Rhinns, The (pen.), 8,295 .....C 6
Roag, Loch (inlet) .....B 2
Rona (isl.), 3 .....B 3
Ross of Mull (pen.), 585 .....B 4
Rousay (isl.), 181 .....E 1
Rudha Hunish (cape) .....B 3
Rudh Re (cape) .....C 3
Rum (isl.), 40 .....B 3
Ryan, Loch (inlet) .....C 5
Saint Kilda (isl.), 65 .....A 2
Saint Magnus (bay) .....F 2
Sanda (isl.), 9 .....C 5
Sanday (isl.), 11 .....B 3
Sanday (isl.), 592 .....F 1
Scalpay (isl.), 483 .....B 3
Scalpay (isl.), 5 .....C 3
Scapa Flow (chan.) .....E 2
Scarp (isl.), 12 .....A 2
Scridain, Loch (inlet) .....B 4
Scurdie Ness (prom.) .....F 4
Seaforth, Loch (inlet) .....B 3
Seil (isl.), 326 .....C 4
Sgurr a Choire Ghlais (mt.) .....D 3
Sgurr Alasdair (mt.) .....B 3
Sgurr Mor (mt.) .....C 3
Sgurr na Lapaich (mt.) .....C 3
Shapinsay (isl.), 346 .....F 1
Shetland (isls.), 18,494 .....G 2
Shiant (sound) .....B 3
Shiel, Loch (lake) .....C 4
Shin (falls) .....D 3
Shin, Loch (lake) .....D 2
Shona (isl.), 17 .....C 4
Sidlaw (hills) .....E 4
Sinclair's (bay) .....E 2
Skye, Isle of (isl.), 7,183 .....B 3
Sleat (pt.) .....B 4
Sleat (dist.), 449 .....C 3
Small Isles (isls.), 171 .....B 4
Snizort, Loch (inlet) .....B 3
Soay (isl.), 5 .....B 3
Solway (firth) .....E 6
South Esk (riv.) .....F 4
South Ronaldsay (isl.), 776 .....F 2
South Uist (isl.), 2,281 .....A 3
Spean (riv.) .....D 4
Spey (riv.) .....E 3
Start (pt.) .....F 1
Stinchar (riv.) .....D 5
Strathbogie (dist.), 7,959 .....F 3
Strathmore (valley) .....E 4
Strathspey (dist.), 6,668 .....E 3
Strathy (pt.) .....E 2
Stroma (isl.), 8 .....E 2
Stronsay (isl.), 436 .....F 1
Sumburgh (head) .....G 2
Sunart, Loch (inlet) .....C 4
Swona (isl.), 3 .....E 2
Taransay (isl.), 5 .....A 3
Tarbat Ness (prom.) .....E 3
Tarbert, East Loch (inlet) .....B 3
Tarbert, Loch (inlet) .....B 5
Tarbert, West Loch (inlet) .....A 3
Tay (riv.) .....E 4
Tay (firth) .....F 4
Tay, Loch (lake) .....D 4
Teith (riv.) .....D 4
Teviot (riv.) .....F 5
Thurso (riv.) .....E 2
Tiree (isl.), 875 .....B 4
Tolsta (head) .....B 2
Tor Ness (prom.) .....E 2
Torridon, Loch (inlet) .....C 3
Trossachs, The (valley) .....D 4
Trotternish (dist.), 1,948 .....B 3
Tweed (riv.) .....F 5
Tyne (riv.) .....F 5
Ulva (isl.), 23 .....B 4
Unst (isl.), 1,124 .....G 2
Vaternish (dist.), 162 .....B 3
Vatersay (isl.), 77 .....A 4
West Burra (isl.), 501 .....G 2
Westray (firth) .....E 1
Westray (isl.), 735 .....E 1
Whalsay (isl.), 870 .....G 2
White Coomb (mt.) .....E 5
Wigtown (bay) .....D 6
Wrath (cape) .....C 2
Wyre (isl.), 36 .....F 1
Yarrow (riv.) .....E 5
Yell (isl.), 1,143 .....G 2
Ythan (riv.) .....F 3

★Population of met. area
⊙Population of parish.

Agriculture, Industry and Resources

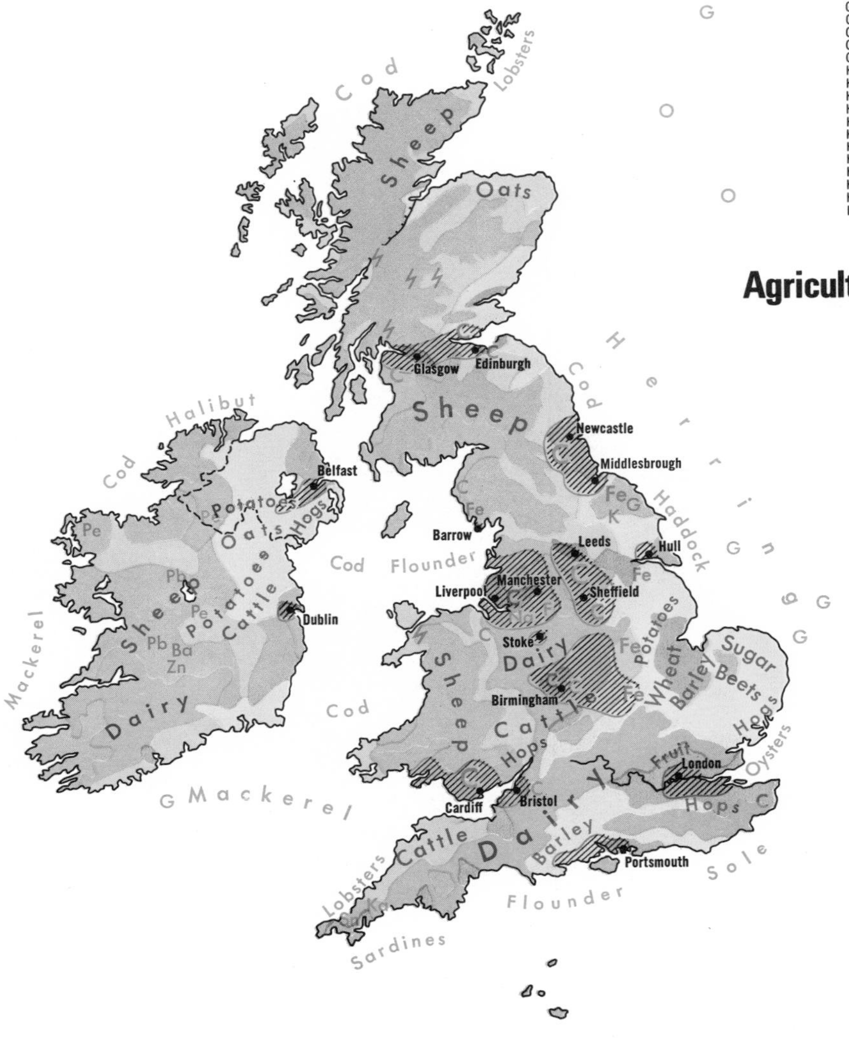

DOMINANT LAND USE

- Cereals (chiefly oats, barley)
- Truck Farming, Horticulture
- Dairy, Mixed Farming
- Livestock, Mixed Farming
- Pasture Livestock

MAJOR MINERAL OCCURRENCES

Ba	Barite	Na	Salt
C	Coal	O	Petroleum
F	Fluorspar	Pb	Lead
Fe	Iron Ore	Pe	Peat
G	Natural Gas	Sn	Tin
K	Potash	Zn	Zinc
Ka	Kaolin (china clay)		

Water Power

Major Industrial Areas

Scotland

CONIC PROJECTION

MILES

KILOMETERS

Capital.................... ⊛
Regional Centers......... ⊙
Canals....................

International Boundaries —·—·—
Regional Boundaries —–—–—
Other Boundaries ············

Scale 1:1,850,000

© Copyright HAMMOND INCORPORATED, Maplewood, N.J.

Former Counties

1 CLACKMANNAN
2 DUNBARTON
3 KINROSS
4 MIDLOTHIAN
5 PEEBLES
6 RENFREW
7 SELKIRK
8 STIRLING
9 W. LOTHIAN

Shetland Islands

16 United Kingdom and Ireland
(continued)

IRELAND

Carlow 34,237 H6
Cavan 52,618 G4
Clare 75,008 D6
Cork 352,883 D7
Donegal 108,344 K2
Dublin 852,219 J5
Galway 149,223 D5
Kerry 112,772 B7
Kildare 71,977 H5
Kilkenny 61,473 G6
Laois 45,259 G6
Leitrim 28,360 E3
Leix (Laois) 45,259 G6
Limerick 140,459 D7
Longford 28,250 F4
Louth 74,951 J4
Mayo 109,525 C4
Meath 71,729 H4
Monaghan 46,242 H3
Offaly 51,829 F5
Roscommon 53,519 E4
Sligo 50,275 D3
Tipperary 123,565 F6
Waterford 77,315 F7
Westmeath 53,570 G5
Wexford 86,351 H7
Wicklow 66,295 J5

CITIES and TOWNS

Abbeydorney, 188 B 7
Abbeyfeale, 1,337 C 7
Abbeylara, ‡290 F 4
Abbeyleix, 1,033 G 6
Achill Sound, ‡1,163 B 4
Aclare, ‡336 D 3
Adare, 545 D 6
Aghada-Farsid-Rostellan, 461 E 8
Aghadoe, ‡497 B 7
Aghagower, ‡693 C 4
Ahascragh, 221 E 5
Annagry, 201 E 1
Annascaul, 236 B 7
An Uaimh, 4,605 H 4
An Uaimh, *6,665 H 4
Ardagh, Limerick, 213 C 7
Ardagh, Longford, ‡974 F 4
Ardara, 683 E 2
Ardee, *3,183 H 4
Ardee, 3,096 H 4
Ardfert, 286 B 7
Ardfinnan, 510 F 7
Ardmore, 233 F 8
Ardrahan, ‡239 D 5
Arklow, 6,948 J 6
Arthurstown, 1,188 H 7
Arva, 370 F 4
Ashford, 341 J 5
Askeaton, 844 D 6
Athboy, 705 H 4
Athea, 328 C 7
Athenry, 1,240 D 5
Athleague, ‡955 E 4
Athlone, 9,825 F 5
Athlone, *11,611 F 5
Athy, 4,270 H 6
Athy, *4,654 H 6
Aughrim, 451 J 6
Avoca, ‡620 J 6
Bagenalstown (Muinebeag), 2,321 H 6
Baile Átha Cliath (Dublin) (cap.), 567,866 K 5
Bailieborough, 1,293 G 4
Balbriggan, 3,741 J 4
Balla, 293 C 4
Ballaghaderreen, 1,121 E 4
Ballina, Mayo, 6,063 C 3
Ballina, *6,369 C 3
Ballina, Tipperary, 336 E 6
Ballinagh, 459 G 4
Ballinakill, 300 G 6
Ballineen D 8
Ballinamore, 808 F 3
Ballinasloe, 5,969 E 5
Ballincollig-Carrigrohane, 2,110 D 8
Ballindine, 232 C 4
Ballingarry, Limerick, 422 D 7
Ballingarry, Tipperary, ‡574 F 6
Ballinlough, 242 D 4
Ballinrobe, 1,272 C 4
Ballintober, ‡867 E 4
Ballintra, 197 E 2
Ballisodare, 486 E 3
Ballivor, 287 H 4
Ballybay, 754 G 3
Ballybay, *1,159 G 3
Ballybofey-Stranorlar, 2,214 F 2
Ballybunion, 1,287 B 7
Ballycanew, ‡460 J 6
Ballycarney, ‡294 J 6
Ballycastle, ‡724 C 3
Ballyconnell, 421 F 3
Ballycotton, 389 F 8
Ballydehob, 253 C 8
Ballyduff, 406 B 7
Ballygar, 359 E 4
Ballygeary, 725 J 7
Ballyhaise, 274 G 3
Ballyhaunis, 1,093 D 4
Ballyheigue, 450 B 7
Ballyjamesduff, 673 G 4
Ballylanders, 266 E 7
Ballylongford, 504 B 6
Ballymahon, 707 F 4
Ballymakeery, 272 C 8
Ballymore, ‡447 F 5
Ballymore Eustace, 433 J 5
Ballymote, 952 D 3
Ballyporeen, ‡810 E 7
Ballyragget, 519 G 6
Ballyroan, ‡478 G 6
Ballyshannon, 2,325 E 3
Ballytore, ‡580 H 5
Baltimore, 200 C 9
Baltinglass, 909 H 6
Baltray, 236 J 4
Banagher, 1,052 F 5
Bandon, 2,257 D 8
Bandon, *4,071 D 8
Bannow, ‡798 H 7
Bansha, 184 E 7
Bantry, 2,579 C 8
Barna, ‡1,734 C 5
Belmullet, 744 B 3
Belturbet, 1,092 G 3
Bennettsbridge, 367 G 6
Birr, 3,319 F 5
Birr, *3,881 F 5
Blanchardstown, 3,279 H 5
Blarney, 1,128 D 8
Blessington, 637 J 5
Boherbue, 372 C 7
Borris, 430 H 6
Borris-in-Ossory, 276 F 6
Borrisokane, 769 E 6
Borrisoleigh, 471 E 6
Boyle, 1,727 E 4
Boyle, *1,939 E 4
Bray, 14,467 K 5
Bray, *15,841 K 5
Brí Chualann (Bray), 14,467 K 5
Broadford, 226 C 7
Brosna, 250 C 7
Bruff, 547 D 7
Bruree, 243 D 7
Bunbeg-Derrybeg, 878 E 1
Bunclody-Carrickduff, 929 H 6
Buncrana, 2,955 G 1
Buncrana, *3,334 G 1
Bundoran, 1,337 E 3
Burtonport, ‡1,288 E 2
Buttevant, 1,045 D 7
Cahir, 1,747 F 7
Cahirciveen, 1,547 A 8
Callan, 1,283 G 7
Camolin, 306 J 6
Campile, 231 H 7
Cappamore, 567 E 6
Cappawhite, 305 E 6
Cappoquin, 872 F 7
Carbury, ‡894 H 5
Carlingford, 559 J 3
Carlow, 9,588 H 6
Carlow, *10,399 H 6
Carndonagh, 1,146 G 1
Carnew, 570 H 6
Carrickmacross, 2,100 H 4
Carrickmacross, *2,475 H 4
Carrick-on-Shannon, 1,854 F 4
Carrick-on-Suir, 5,006 F 7
Carrigaholt, ‡493 B 6
Carrigaline, 951 E 8
Carrigallen, 230 F 4
Carrigart, ‡753 F 1
Carrigtwohill, 622 E 8
Carrowkeel, ‡326 G 1
Cashel, 2,692 F 7
Castlebar, 5,979 C 4
Castlebar, *6,476 C 4
Castlebellingham, 407 J 4
Castleblayney, 2,118 H 3
Castleblayney, *2,395 H 3
Castlecomer-Donaguile, 1,244 G 6
Castledermot, 583 H 6
Castlefin, 610 F 2
Castlegregory, 216 A 7
Castleisland, 1,929 B 7
Castlemartyr, 491 E 8
Castlepollard, 693 G 4
Castlerea, 1,752 D 4
Castletown, ‡504 F 6
Castletownbere, 812 B 8
Castletownroche, 399 D 7
Castletownshend, 170 C 9
Causeway, 215 B 7
Cavan, 3,273 G 3
Cavan, *4,312 G 3
Ceanannus Mór, 2,391 G 4
Ceanannus Mór, *2,653 G 4
Celbridge, 1,568 H 5
Charlestown-Bellahy, 677 D 4
Charleville (Rathluirc), 2,232 D 7
Clara, 2,156 F 5
Claregalway, ‡594 D 5
Claremorris, 1,718 C 4
Clashmore, ‡379 F 8
Clifden, 790 B 5
Cloghan, 404 F 5
Clogh-Chatsworth, 324 G 6
Clogheen, 530 F 7
Clogherhead, 649 J 4
Clonakilty, 2,430 D 8
Clonaslee, 285 F 5
Clondalkin, 7,009 J 5
Clonegal, 202 H 6
Clones, 2,164 G 3
Clonfert, ‡430 E 5
Clonmany, ‡936 G 1
Clonmel, 11,622 F 7
Clonmel, *12,291 F 7
Clonmellon, 328 H 4
Clonroche, 222 H 7
Clontuskert, 351 E 4
Cloone, ‡460 F 4
Cloughjordan, 480 E 6
Cloyne, 654 E 8
Coachford, 290 D 8
Cóbh, 6,076 E 8
Cóbh, *7,141 E 8
Coill Dubh, 920 H 5
Collon, 262 J 4
Collooney, 546 E 3
Cong, 233 C 4
Convoy, 654 F 2
Coolaney, ‡352 D 3
Coolgreany, ‡603 J 6
Cootehill, 1,415 G 3
Cootehill, *1,542 G 3
Cork, 128,645 E 8
Cork, *134,430 E 8
Corofin, 342 C 6
Courtmacsherry, 210 D 8
Courtown Harbour, 291 J 6
Creeslough, 269 F 1
Crookhaven, ‡400 B 9
Croom, 756 D 6
Crosshaven, 1,222 E 8
Crossmolina, 1,077 C 3
Crusheen, ‡405 D 6
Culdaff, ‡621 G 1
Daingean, 492 G 5
Delvin, 223 G 4
Dingle, 1,401 A 7
Doaghbeg, ‡701 F 1
Donabate, 426 J 5
Donegal, 1,725 F 2
Doneraile, 799 D 7
Dooagh-Keel, 649 A 4
Doon, 387 E 6
Douglas, ‡4,448 D 8
Drimoleague, 415 C 8
Drishane, ‡1,548 C 7
Drogheda, 19,762 J 4
Drogheda, *20,095 J 4
Droichead Nua, 5,053 H 5
Droichead Nua, *6,444 H 5
Dromahair, 177 E 3
Drumcar, ‡1,215 J 4
Drumconrath, ‡1,044 H 4
Drumkeerin, ‡467 E 3
Drumlish, 205 F 4
Drumshanbo, 576 E 3
Dublin (cap.), 567,866 K 5
Dublin, *679,748 K 5
Duleek, 658 J 4
Duncannon, 228 H 7
Dundalk, 21,672 H 3
Dundalk, *23,816 H 3
Dunfanaghy, 303 F 1
Dungarvan, 5,583 F 7
Dungloe, 940 E 2
Dunkineely, 288 E 2
Dún Laoghaire, 53,171 K 5
Dún Laoghaire, *98,379 K 5
Dunlavin, 423 H 5
Dunleer 855 J4
Dunmanway 1,392 C8
Dunmore 522 D4
Dunmore East 656 G7
Dunshaughlin⊙ 283 H5
Durrow, Laois 596 G6
Durrow, Offaly⊙ 441 F5
Easky 184 D3
Edenderry 2,953 G5
Edenderry* 3,116 G5
Elphin 489 E4
Emyvale 281 G3
Ennis 5,972 D6
Ennis* 10,840 D6
Enniscorthy 5,704 J7
Enniscorthy* 6,642 J7
Enniskerry 772 J5
Ennistymon 1,013 C6
Eyrecourt 314 E5
Fahan⊙ 1,023 G1
Falcarragh 506 E1
Feakle⊙ 398 D6
Fenit 360 B7
Ferbane 1,064 F5
Fermoy 3,237 E7
Fermoy* 4,033 E7
Ferns 712 J6
Fethard, Tipperary 1,064 F7
Fethard, Wexford⊙ 637 H7
Foxford 868 C4
Foynes 624 C6
Frankford (Kilcormac) 1,089 F5
Frenchpark⊙ 693 E4
Freshford 585 G6
Galbally 258 E7
Galway 27,726 C5
Galway* 29,375 C5
Geashill⊙ 751 G5
Glandore⊙ 695 C8
Glanmire-Riverstown 1,113 E8
Glanworth 335 E7
Glenamaddy 315 D4
Glenbeigh 266 B7
Glencolumbkille⊙ 787 D2
Glengarriff 244 C8
Glenties 734 E2
Glenville⊙ 264 D7
Glin 623 C6
Golden⊙ 640 F7
Gorey 2,946 J6
Gorey* 3,024 J6
Gormanston⊙ 1,384 J4
Gort 975 D5
Gowran 402 G6
Graiguenamanagh-Tinnahinch 1,303 H6
Granard 1,054 F4
Greencastle 322 H1
Greenore 882 J4
Greystones-Delgany 4,517 K5
Gurteen 165 D3
Hacketstown 574 H6
Headford 673 C5
Holycross⊙ 902 F6
Hospital 525 E7
Inchigeelagh⊙ 516 C8
Inishannon 190 D8
Inistioge 179 G7
Inniscrone 582 C3
Johnstown 303 G6
Kanturk 2,063 D7
Keel-Dooagh 649 A4
Kells⊙ 423 G6
Kells (Ceanannus Mór) 2,391 G4
Kenmare 903 B8
Kilbaha⊙ 471 B6
Kilbeggan 635 G5
Kilcar 273 D2
Kilcock 827 H5
Kilconnell⊙ 629 E5
Kilcoole 679 K5
Kilcormac 1,089 F5
Kilcullen 880 H5
Kildare 3,137 H5
Kildysart 239 C6
Kilfenora⊙ 441 C6
Kilfinane 561 D7
Kilgarvan 228 B8
Kilkee 1,287 B6
Kilkelly 225 D4
Kilkenny 9,838 G6
Kilkenny* 13,306 G6
Killala 368 C3
Killaloe 871 D6
Killarney 7,184 C7
Killarney* 7,541 C7
Killavullen 221 D7
Killenaule 592 F6
Killeshandra 432 F3
Killimor 221 E5
Killinaboy⊙ 297 C6
Killorglin 1,150 B7
Killucan-Rathwire 290 G4
Killybegs 1,094 E2
Kilmacrennan 274 F1
Kilmacthomas 396 G7
Kilmallock 1,170 D7
Kilmeadan⊙ 262 G7
Kilmihill 284 C6
Kilmoganny 181 G7
Kilmore Quay 273 H7
Kilmurry⊙ 387 C6
Kilnaleck 273 G4
Kilronan 243 B5
Kilrush 2,671 C6
Kilsheelan⊙ 665 F7
Kiltimagh 978 C4
Kilworth 360 E7
Kingscourt 1,016 H4
Kingstown (Dún Laoghaire) 53,171 K5
Kinlough 160 E3
Kinnegad 362 G5
Kinnitty⊙ 420 F5
Kinsale 1,622 D8
Kinsale* 1,989 D8
Kinvara 293 D5
Knightstown 236 A8
Knock⊙ 1,202 D4
Knocklong 248 D7
Knocknagashel 168 C7
Labasheeda⊙ 468 C6
Laghy⊙ 625 E2
Lahinch 455 C6
Lanesborough-Ballyleague 906 E4
Laracor⊙ 404 H4
Laytown-Bettystown-Mornington 1,882 J4
Leenane⊙ 271 B4
Leighlindridge 379 H6
Leitrim⊙ 544 F3
Leixlip 2,402 H5
Letterkenny 4,930 F2
Letterkenny* 5,207 F2
Lifford 1,121 F2
Limerick 57,161 D6
Limerick* 63,002 D6
Liscarroll 231 D7
Lisdoonvarna 459 C5
Lismore 884 F7
Lismore⊙ 1,041 F7
Listowel 3,021 C7
Littleton 322 F6
Longford 3,876 F4
Longford* 4,791 F4
Lorrha⊙ 685 E5
Loughrea 3,075 E5
Louisburgh 310 B4
Louth 208 J4
Lucan-Doddsborough 4,245 J5
Luimneach (Limerick) 57,161 D6
Lusk 553 J4
Macroom 2,256 C8
Malahide 3,834 J5
Malin⊙ 552 G1
Mallow 5,901 D7
Mallow* 6,506 D7
Manorhamilton 858 E3
Manulla⊙ 660 C4
Maryborough (Portlaoise) 3,902 G5
Maynooth 1,296 H5
Meathas Truim 546 G4
Midleton 3,075 E8
Midleton* 4,666 E8
Milford 763 F1
Millstreet 1,319 D7
Milltown 260 A7
Miltown-Malbay 677 C6
Minard⊙ 397 A7
Mitchelstown 2,783 E7
Moate 1,378 F5
Mohill 868 F4
Monaghan 5,256 G3
Monasterevan 1,619 H5
Moneygall 282 F6
Monivea⊙ 405 D5
Mooncoin 413 G7
Mount Bellew 275 D5
Mountcharles 445 E2
Mountmellick 2,595 G5
Mountmellick* 2,864 G5
Mountrath 1,098 F5
Moville 1,089 G1
Moycullen⊙ 498 C5
Moynalty⊙ 583 H4
Muff 240 G1
Muinebeag 2,321 H6
Mullagh 293 H4
Mullaghmore⊙ 629 D3
Mullinahone 262 F7
Mullinavat 343 G7
Mullingar 6,790 G4
Mullingar* 9,245 G4
Naas 5,078 H5
Navan (An Uaimh) 4,605 H4
Nenagh 5,085 E6
Nenagh* 5,174 E6
Newbliss⊙ 547 G3
Newbridge (Droichead Nua) 5,053 H5
Newcastle 2,549 D7
Newcastle* 2,680 D7
Newmarket 886 C7
Newmarket-on-Fergus 1,052 D6
New Pallas⊙ 1,271 E6
Newport, Mayo 420 C4
Newport, Tipperary 582 E6
New Ross 4,775 H7
New Ross* 5,153 H7
Newtown Forbes⊙ 495 F4
Newtownmountkennedy 882 J5
Newtownsandes 268 C6
O'Briensbridge-Montpelier 237 D6
Oldcastle 759 G4
Old Leighlin⊙ 309 G6
Oola 348 E6
Oranmore 440 D5
Oughterard 628 C5
Passage East 408 G7
Passage West 2,709 E8
Patrickswell 415 D6
Pettigo 332 F2
Piltown 456 G7
Portarlington 3,117 G5
Portlaoise 3,902 G5
Portlaoise* 6,470 G5
Portlaw 1,166 G7
Portmarnock 1,726 J5
Portumna 913 E5
Queenstown (Cóbh) 6,076 E8
Rahan⊙ 531 F5
Ramelton 807 F1
Raphoe 945 F2
Rathangan 868 G5
Rathcoole 1,740 J5
Rathcormac 191 E7
Rathdowney 892 F6
Rathdrum 1,141 J6
Rathgormuck⊙ 231 F7
Rathkeale 1,543 D7
Rathluirc 2,232 D7
Rathmore 437 J5
Rathmullen 486 F1
Rathnew-Merrymeeting 954 J6
Rathowen⊙ 294 F4
Rathvilly 230 H6
Ratoath 300 J5
Riverstown 236 E3
Rockcorry 233 H3
Rosapenna⊙ 822 F1
Roscommon 1,556 E4
Roscommon* 2,821 E4
Roscrea 3,855 F6
Rosscarbery 309 C8
Rosses Point 464 D3
Rosslare 588 J7
Rosslare Harbour (Ballygeary) 725 J7
Roundstone 204 A5
Roundwood 260 J5
Rush 2,633 J4
Saint Johnston 463 F2
Scarriff 619 E6
Schull 457 B8
Scotstown 264 H3
Shanagolden 231 C6
Shannon Airport 3,657 D6
Shannon Bridge 188 F5
Shercock 313 G4
Shillelagh 246 J6
Shinrone 365 F5
Shrule 288 C4
Sixmilebridge 567 D6
Skerries 3,044 J4
Skibbereen 2,104 C8
Slane 483 H4
Sligo 14,080 E3
Sligo* 14,456 E3
Sneem 285 B8
Spiddal⊙ 819 C5
Stepaside 748 J5
Stradbally, Laois 891 G5
Stradbally, Waterford 158 F7
Strokestown 563 E4
Swanlinbar 257 F3
Swinford 1,105 C4
Swords 4,133 J5
Taghmon 369 H7
Tallaght 6,174 J5
Tallow, 883 F 7
Tarbert, 485 C 6
Teltown, ‡739 H 4
Templemore, 2,174 F 6
Templetuohy, 197 F 6
Termonfeckin, 328 J 4
Thomastown, 1,270 G 7
Thurles, 6,840 F 6
Thurles, *7,087 F 6
Timoleague, 257 D 8
Tinahely, 450 H 6
Tipperary, 4,631 E 7
Tipperary, *4,717 E 7
Toomevara, 272 E 6
Tralee, 12,287 B 7
Tralee, *13,263 B 7
Tramore, 3,792 G 7
Trim, 1,700 H 4
Trim, *2,255 H 4
Tuam, 3,808 D 4
Tuam, *4,952 D 4
Tubbercurry, 959 D 3
Tulla, 415 D 6
Tullamore, 6,809 G 5
Tullamore, *7,474 G 5
Tullaroan, ‡301 G 6
Tullow, 1,838 H 6
Tullow, *1,945 H 6
Tynagh, ‡452 E 5
Tyrrellspass, 289 G 5
Urlingford, 652 F 6
Virginia, 583 G 4
Waterford, 31,968 G 7
Waterford, *33,676 G 7
Waterville, 547 A 8
Westport, 3,023 C 4
Wexford, 11,849 H 7
Wexford, *13,293 H 7
Whitegate, 370 E 8
Wicklow, 3,786 K 6
Wicklow, *3,915 K 6
Woodenbridge, ‡620 J 6
Woodford, 198 E 5
Youghal, 5,445 F 8
Youghal, *5,626 F 8

OTHER FEATURES

Achill (isl.), 3,129 A 4
Allen (lake) E 3
Allen, Bog of (marsh) H 5
Aran (isl.), 773 D 2
Aran (isls.), 1,499 B 5
Arklow (bank) K 6
Arrow (lake) E 3
Awbeg (riv.) D 7
Ballinskelligs (bay) A 8
Ballycotton (bay) F 8
Ballyheige (bay) B 7
Ballyhoura (hills) E 7
Ballyteige (bay) H 7
Bandon (riv.) D 8
Bann (riv.) J 6
Bantry (bay) B 8
Barrow (riv.) H 7
Baurtregaum (mt.) A 7
Bear (isl.), 288 B 8
Blacksod (bay) A 3
Blackstairs (mt.) H 6
Blackwater (riv.) D 7
Blackwater (riv.) H 4
Blasket (isls.) A 7
Bloody Foreland (prom.) E 1
Blue Stack (mts.) E 2
Boderg (lake) E 4
Boggeragh (mts.) D 7
Boyne (riv.) J 4
Brandon (head) A 7
Bride (riv.) E 7
Broad Haven (harb.) B 3
Brosna (riv.) F 5
Bull, The (isl.), 5 A 8
Caha (mts.) B 8
Carlingford (inlet) J 3
Carnsore (pt.) J 7
Carrantuohill (mt.) B 7
Clare (riv.) D 5
Clare (isls.), 168 A 4
Clear (cape) B 9
Clear (isl.), 192 C 9
Clew (bay) B 4
Comeragh (mts.) F 7
Conn (lake) C 3
Connacht (prov.), 390,902 C 4
Connemara (dist.), 7,599 B 5
Cork (harb.) E 8
Corrib (lake) C 5
Courtmacsherry (bay) D 8
Curragh, The H 5
Dee (riv.) H 4
Deel (riv.) D 7
Deele (riv.) F 2
Derg (lake) E 6
Derravaragh (lake) G 4
Derryveagh (mts.) E 2
Dingle (bay) A 7
Donegal (bay) D 3
Drum (hills) F 7
Dublin (bay) J 5
Dundalk (bay) J 4
Dunmanus (bay) B 8
Dursey (isl.), 38 A 8
Ennell (lake) G 5
Erne (riv.) E 3
Errigal (mt.) E 1
Erris (head) A 3
Fanad (head) F 1
Fastnet Rock (isl.), 3 B 9
Feale (riv.) C 7
Fergus (riv.) D 6
Finn (riv.) F 2
Finn (riv.) G 3
Flesk (riv.) C 7
Foyle (inlet) G 1
Foyle (riv.) G 2
Galley (head) D 9
Galtee (mts.) E 7
Galtymore (mt.) E 7
Galway (bay) C 5
Gara (lake) D 4
Garadice (lake) F 3
Gill (lake) E 3
Glyde (riv.) H 4
Golden Vale (plain) E 7
Gorumna (isl.), 1,108 B 5
Gowna (lake) G 4
Grand (canal) G 5
Greenore (pt.) J 7
Gweebarra (bay) D 2
Hags (head) B 6
Helvick (head) G 7
Hook (head) H 7
Horn (head) E 1
Iar Connacht (dist.), 10,774 C 5
Inishbofin (isl.), 236 A 4
Inishbofin (isl.), 103 E 1
Inisheer (isl.), 313 B 5
Inishmaan (isl.), 319 C 5
Inishmore (isl.), 864 B 5
Inishowen (head) H 1
Inishowen (pen.), 24,109 G 1
Inishtrahull (isl.), 3 G 1
Inishturk (isls.), 83 A 4
Inny (riv.) A 8
Inny (riv.) F 4
Inver (bay) E 2
Ireland's Eye (isl.) K 5
Irish (sea) K 4
Joyce's Country (dist.), 2,021 B 4
Kenmare (riv.) A 8
Kerry (head) A 7
Key (lake) E 3
Kilkieran (bay) B 5
Killala (bay) C 3
Killary (harb.) A 4
Kinsale (harb.) E 8
Kippure (mt.) J 5
Knockboy (mt.) B 8
Knockmealdown (mts.) F 7
Lady's Island Lake (inlet) J 7
Lambay (isl.), 24 K 4
Laune (riv.) B 7
Leane (lake) B 7
Leane (lake) G 4
Lee (riv.) D 8
Leinster (mt.) H 6
Leinster (prov.), 1,498,140 G 5
Lettermullan (isl.), 221 B 5
Liffey (riv.) H 5
Liscannor (bay) B 6
Long Island (bay) B 9
Loop (head) A 6
Lugnaquillia (mt.) J 5
Macgillicuddy's Reeks (mts.) B 7
Macnean (lake) F 3
Maigue (riv.) D 6
Maine (riv.) C 7
Malin (head) F 1
Mask (lake) C 4
Maumturk (mts.) B 5
Melvin (lake) E 3
Mizen (head) B 9
Moher (cliffs) B 6
Monavullagh (mts.) F 7
Moy (riv.) C 3
Mulkear (riv.) E 6
Mullaghareirk (mts.) C 7
Mulroy (bay) F 1
Munster (prov.), 882,002 D 7
Mweelrea (mt.) B 4
Mweenish (isl.), 198 B 5
Nagles (mts.) E 7
Nenagh (riv.) E 6
Nephin (mt.) C 3
Nore (riv.) G 7
North (sound) B 5
Omey (isl.), 34 A 5
Oughter (lake) G 3
Ovoca (riv.) J 6
Owenmore (riv.) D 3
Owey (isl.), 51 D 1
Paps, The (mt.) C 7
Partry (mts.) C 4
Pollaphuca (res.) J 5
Punchestown H 5
Rathlin O'Birne (isl.), 3 C 2
Ree (lake) F 5
Roaringwater (bay) B 9
Rosses (bay) D 1
Rosskeeragh (pt.) D 3
Royal (canal) G 4
Saint Finan's (bay) A 8
Saint George's (chan.) K 7
Saint John's (pt.) D 2
Saltee (isls.) H 7
Seven (heads) D 8
Seven Hogs, The (isls.) A 7
Shannon (riv.) E 6
Sheeffry (hills) B 4
Sheelin (lake) G 4
Sheep Haven (harb.) F 1
Sheeps (head) B 8
Sherkin (isl.), 82 C 9
Silvermine (mts.) E 6
Slaney (riv.) H 7
Slieve Aughty (mts.) D 5
Slieve Bloom (mts.) F 5
Slieve Gamph (mts.) D 3
Slievenaman (mt.) F 7
Sligo (bay) D 3
Slyne (head) A 5
South (sound) C 5
Stacks (mts.) B 7
Suck (riv.) E 5
Suir (riv.) G 7
Swilly (inlet) F 1
Tara (hill) H 4
Tory (isl.), 273 E 1
Tory (sound) E 1
Tralee (bay) B 7
Trawbreaga (bay) F 1
Ulster (part) (prov.), 207,204 G 2
Valencia (Valentia) (isl.), 770 A 8
Valentia (isl.), 770 A 8
Waterford (harb.) G 7
Wexford (bay) J 7
Wicklow (head) K 6
Wicklow (mts.) J 6
Youghal (bay) F 8

NORTHERN IRELAND

DISTRICTS

Antrim, 37,600 J 2
Ards, 52,100 K 2
Armagh, 47,500 H 3
Ballymena, 52,200 J 2
Ballymoney, 22,700 J 1
Bainbridge, 28,800 J 3
Belfast, 368,200 J 2
Carrickfergus, 27,500 K 2
Castlereagh, 63,600 K 2
Coleraine, 44,900 H 1
Cookstown, 27,500 H 2
Craigavon, 71,200 J 3
Down, 48,800 K 3
Dungannon, 43,000 H 3
Fermanagh, 50,900 F 3
Larne, 29,000 K 2
Limavady, 25,000 H 1
Lisburn, 80,800 J 2
Londonderry, 86,600 G 2
Magherafelt, 32,200 H 2
Mourne (Newry and Mourne), 75,300 J 3
Moyle, 13,400 J 1
Newtownabbey, 71,500 J 2
North Down, 59,600 K 2
Omagh, 41,800 G 2
Strabane, 35,500 G 2

CITIES and TOWNS

Ahoghill, ‡1,929 J 2
Annalong, 1,001 K 3
Antrim, 8,351 J 2
Ardglass, 1,052 K 3
Armagh, 13,606 H 3
Armoy, ‡1,051 J 1
Augher, ‡1,986 G 3
Aughnacloy, ‡1,885 H 3
Ballycastle, 2,899 J 1
Ballyclare, 5,155 J 2
Ballygawley, ‡2,165 G 3
Ballykelly, 1,116 G 1
Ballymena, 23,386 J 2
Ballymoney, 5,697 J 1
Ballynahinch, 3,485 J 3
Banbridge, 7,968 J 3
Bangor, 35,260 K 2
Belfast (cap.), 353,700 J 2
Belfast, *551,940 J 2
Bellaghy, ‡2,265 H 2
Belleek, ‡2,487 E 3
Beragh, ‡2,137 G 2
Bessbrook, 2,619 J 3
Brookeborough, ‡2,534 G 3
Broughshane, 1,288 J 2
Bushmills, 1,288 J 1
Caledon, ‡1,828 H 3
Carnlough, 1,416 J 2
Carrickfergus, 16,603 K 2
Carrowdore, 2,548 K 2
Castledawson, 1,162 H 2
Castlederg, 1,766 F 2
Castlewellan, 1,488 K 3
Claudy, ‡2,507 G 2
Clogher, ‡1,888 G 3
Coalisland, 3,614 H 2
Coleraine, 16,354 H 1
Comber, 5,575 K 2
Cookstown, 6,965 H 2
Craigavon, 12,740 J 3
Crossgar, 1,098 K 3
Crossmaglen, 1,085 H 3
Crumlin, 1,450 J 2
Cullybackey, 1,649 J 2
Derrygonnelly, ‡2,539 F 3
Dervock, ‡1,191 J 1
Donaghadee, 4,008 K 2
Downpatrick, 7,918 K 3
Draperstown, ‡2,247 H 2
Dromore, Bainbridge, 2,848 J 3
Dromore, Omagh, ‡2,224 G 3
Drumquin, ‡1,982 F 2
Dundrum, ‡2,245 K 3
Dungannon, 8,190 H 3
Dungiven, 1,536 H 2
Dunnamanagh, ‡2,242 G 2
Ederny and Kesh, ‡2,497 F 2
Enniskillen, 9,679 F 3
Feeny, ‡1,459 H 2
Fintona, 1,190 G 3
Fivemiletown, ‡1,649 G 3
Garvagh, ‡2,363 H 2
Gilford, 1,592 J 3
Glenarm, ‡1,728 J 2
Glenavy, ‡2,360 J 2
Glynn, ‡1,872 K 2
Gortin, ‡2,033 G 2
Greyabbey, ‡2,646 K 2
Hillsborough, 1,021 J 3
Holywood, 9,892 K 2
Irvinestown, 1,457 F 3
Keady, 2,145 H 3
Kells, ‡2,560 J 2
Kesh, ‡2,497 F 3
Kilkeel, 4,090 K 3
Killough, ‡3,295 K 3
Killyleagh, 2,359 K 3
Kilrea, 1,196 H 2
Kircubbin, 1,075 K 3
Larne, 18,482 K 2
Limavady, 6,004 H 1
Lisburn, 31,836 J 2
Lisnaskea, 1,443 G 3
Londonderry, 51,200 G 2
Loughbrickland, ‡2,056 J 3
Maghera, 2,085 H 2
Magherafelt, 4,704 H 2
Markethill, ‡2,352 H 3
Millisle, 1,172 K 2
Moneymore, 1,178 H 2
Moy, ‡2,349 H 3
Moygashel, 1,086 H 3
Newcastle, 4,647 J 3
Newry, 20,279 J 3
Newtownabbey, 58,114 K 2
Newtownards, 15,484 K 2
Newtownbutler, ‡2,663 G 3
Newtownhamilton, ‡1,936 H 3
Newtownstewart, 1,433 G 2
Omagh, 14,594 G 2
Pomeroy, ‡1,786 H 2
Portaferry, 1,730 K 3
Portavogie, 1,310 K 3
Portglenone, ‡2,061 H 2
Portrush, 5,376 H 1
Portstewart, 5,085 H 1
Randalstown, 2,799 J 2
Rathfriland, 1,886 J 3
Rostrevor, 1,617 J 3
Saintfield, ‡2,198 K 3
Sion Mills, 1,588 G 2
Sixmilecross, ‡1,980 G 2
Stewartstown, ‡1,759 H 2
Strabane, 9,413 G 2
Strangford, ‡1,987 K 3
Tandragee, 1,725 J 3
Tempo, ‡2,282 G 3
Trillick, ‡2,167 G 3
Warrenpoint, 4,291 J 3
Whitehead, 2,642 K 2

OTHER FEATURES

Bann (riv.) H 2
Belfast (inlet) K 2
Blackwater (riv.) H 3
Bush (riv.) H 1
Derg (riv.) F 2
Divis (mt.) J 2
Dundrum (bay) K 3
Erne (lake) F 3
Foyle (inlet) G 1
Foyle (riv.) G 2
Giant's Causeway H 1
Lagan (riv.) K 2
Larne (inlet) K 2
Magee, Island (pen.), 1,581 K 2
Magilligan (pt.) H 1
Main (riv.) J 2
Mourne (mts.) J 3
Mourne (riv.) G 2
Neagh (lake) J 2
North (chan.) K 1
Rathlin (isl.), 109 J 1
Red (bay) K 1
Roe (riv.) H 1
Saint John's (pt.) K 3
Slieve Donard (mt.) K 3
Sperrin (mts.) G 2
Strangford (inlet) K 3
Torr (head) K 1
Ulster (part) (prov.), 1,537,200 G 2
Upper Lough Erne (lake) F 3

*City and suburbs.
‡Population of district.

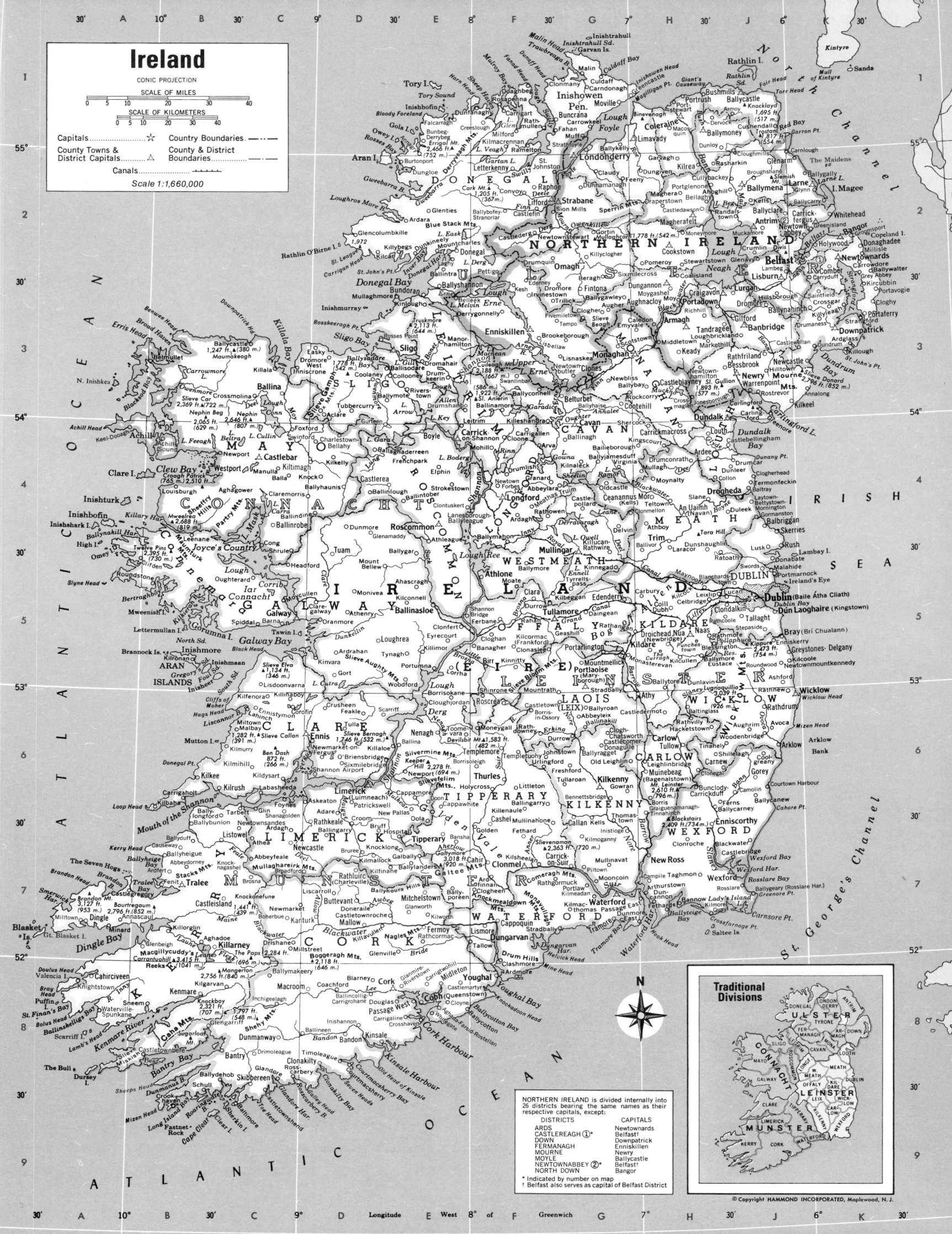

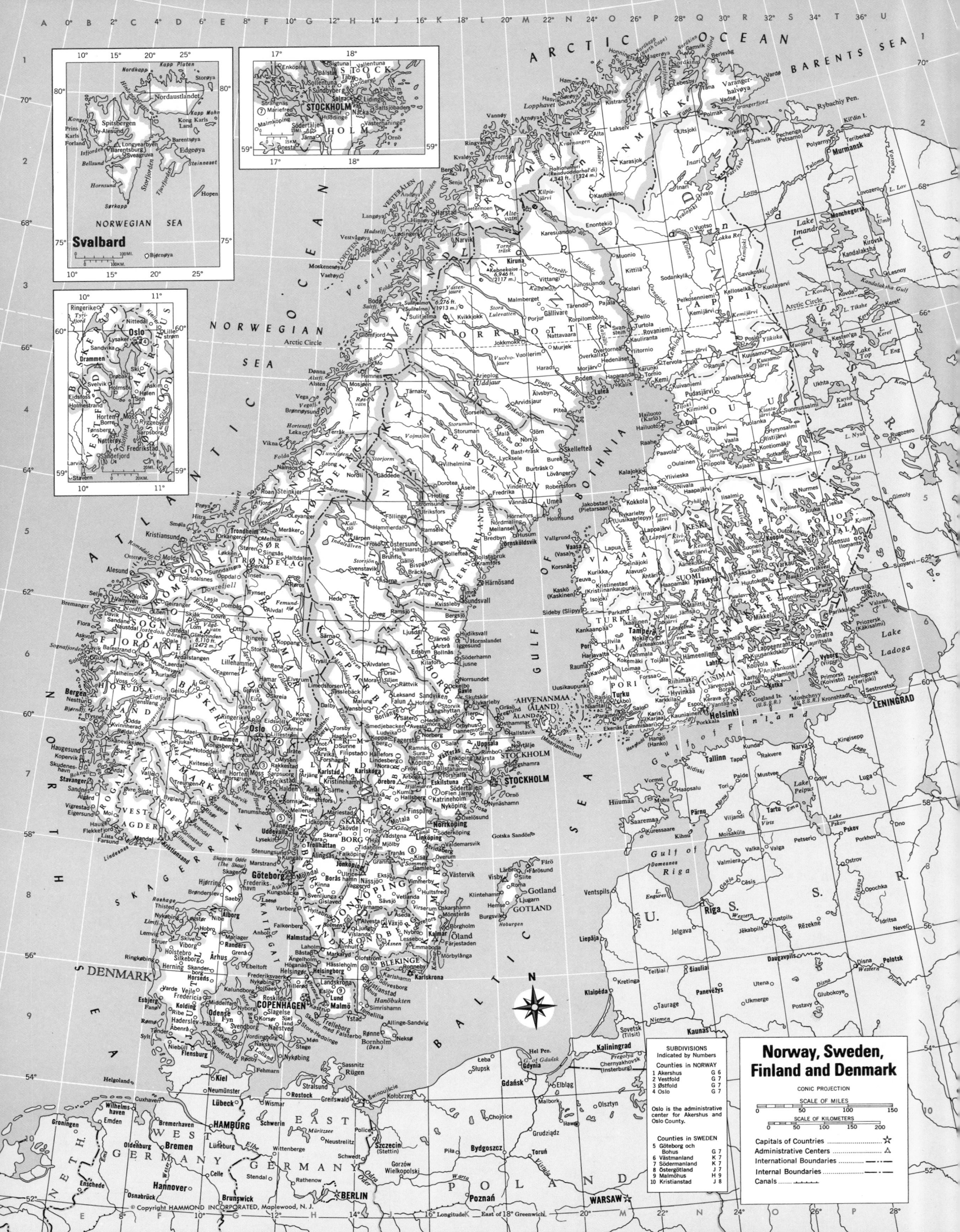

Svalbard

NORWEGIAN SEA

Norway, Sweden, Finland and Denmark

CONIC PROJECTION

SCALE OF MILES
0   50   100   150

SCALE OF KILOMETERS
0   50   100   150   200

SUBDIVISIONS
Indicated by Numbers

Counties in NORWAY
1 Akershus   G 6
2 Vestfold   G 7
3 Østfold   G 7
4 Oslo   G 7

Oslo is the administrative
center for Akershus and
Oslo County.

Counties in SWEDEN
5 Göteborg och
   Bohus   G 7
6 Västmanland   K 7
7 Södermanland   K 7
8 Östergötland   J 7
9 Malmöhus   H 9
10 Kristianstad   J 8

Capitals of Countries .... ☆
Administrative Centers .... ▲
International Boundaries .... ▬▬▬
Internal Boundaries .... ▬·▬·▬
Canals .... ▬▬▬

AREA 125,053 sq. mi. (323,887 sq. km.)
POPULATION 4,092,000
CAPITAL Oslo
LARGEST CITY Oslo
HIGHEST POINT Glittertinden 8,110 ft. (2,472 m.)
MONETARY UNIT krone
MAJOR LANGUAGE Norwegian
MAJOR RELIGION Protestantism

AREA 173,665 sq. mi. (449,792 sq. km.)
POPULATION 8,320,000
CAPITAL Stockholm
LARGEST CITY Stockholm
HIGHEST POINT Kebnekaise 6,946 ft. (2,117 m.)
MONETARY UNIT krona
MAJOR LANGUAGE Swedish
MAJOR RELIGION Protestantism

AREA 130,128 sq. mi. (337,032 sq. km.)
POPULATION 4,788,000
CAPITAL Helsinki
LARGEST CITY Helsinki
HIGHEST POINT Haltiatunturi 4,343 ft. (1,324 m.)
MONETARY UNIT markka
MAJOR LANGUAGES Finnish, Swedish
MAJOR RELIGION Protestantism

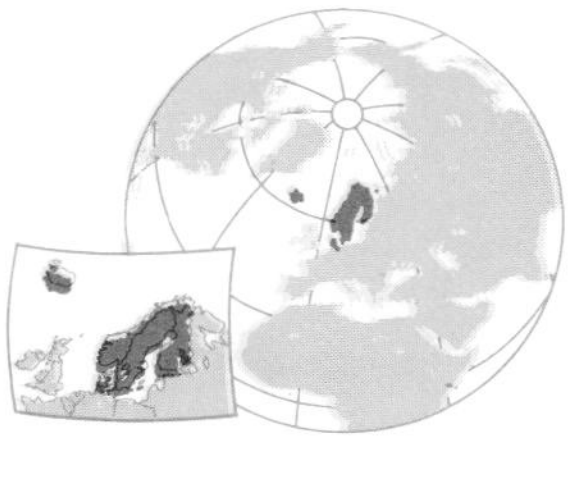

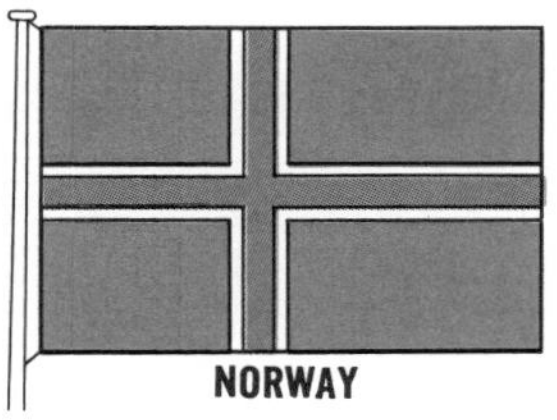
NORWAY

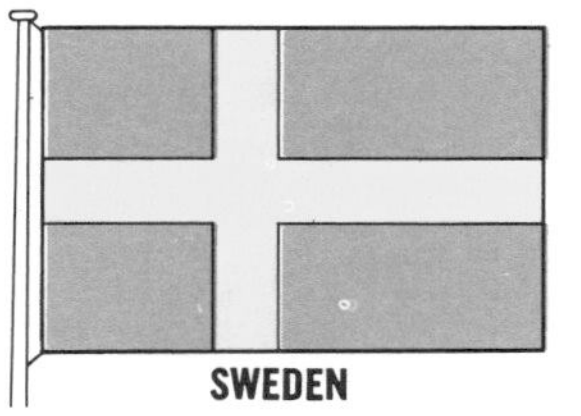
SWEDEN

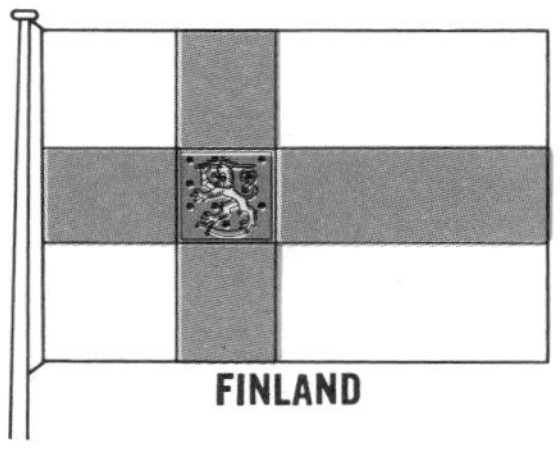
FINLAND

FINLAND

PROVINCES

Ahvenanmaa 22,380 ..... L6
Åland (Ahvenanmaa) 22,380 ..... L6
Häme 662,500 ..... O6
Keski-Suomi 241,770 ..... O5
Kuopio 252,023 ..... P5
Kymi 346,478 ..... Q6
Lappi 196,792 ..... P3
Mikkeli 211,453 ..... P6
Oulu 406,309 ..... P4
Pohjois-Karjala 179,065 ..... Q5
Turku ja Pori 697,988 ..... N6
Uusimaa 1,085,625 ..... O6
Vaasa 425,283 ..... N5

CITIES and TOWNS

Äänekoski 10,725 ..... O5
Åbo (Turku) 164,857 ..... N6
Alavus 10,285 ..... N5
Borgaå 18,740 ..... O6
Ekenäs 7,391 ..... N6
Espoo 117,090 ..... O6
Forssa 18,442 ..... N6
Haapajärvi 7,791 ..... O5
Hämeenlinna 40,761 ..... O6
Hamina 11,055 ..... P6
Hangö 10,374 ..... N7
Hanko (Hangö) 10,374 ..... N7
Harjavalta 8,445 ..... M6
Heinola 15,350 ..... P6
Helsinki (cap.) 502,961 ..... O6
Helsinki* 794,746 ..... O6
Huutokoski† 6,458 ..... P5
Hyvinkää 35,865 ..... O6
Iisalmi 21,159 ..... P5
Ikaalinen 8,364 ..... N6
Imatra 35,590 ..... Q6
Ivalo 2,661 ..... P2
Jakobstad 20,397 ..... N5
Jämsä 12,526 ..... O6
Järvenpää 16,259 ..... O6
Joensuu 41,429 ..... R5
Jyväskylä 61,209 ..... O5
Jyväskylä* 84,185 ..... O5
Kajaani 20,583 ..... P4
Kalajoki 3,624 ..... N4
Kankaanpää 12,564 ..... M6
Karhula 21,834 ..... P6
Karis 8,152 ..... N6
Karjaa (Karis) 8,152 ..... N6
Karkkila 8,678 ..... N6
Kauniainien 6,219 ..... O6
Kauttua 3,297 ..... M6
Kelloselkä† 8,200 ..... Q3
Kemi 27,893 ..... O4
Kemijärvi 12,951 ..... P3
Kerava 19,966 ..... O6
Kokemäki 10,188 ..... N6
Kokkola 22,096 ..... N5
Kotka 34,026 ..... P6
Kotka* 60,235 ..... P6
Kouvola 29,383 ..... P6
Kouvola* 59,507 ..... P6
Kristiinankaupunki (Kristinestad) 9,331 ..... N5
Kristinestad 9,331 ..... N5
Kuhmo 4,150 ..... Q4
Kuopio 71,684 ..... Q5
Kurikka 11,177 ..... M5
Kuusamo 4,449 ..... Q4
Kuusankoski 22,342 ..... P6
Lahti 94,864 ..... O6
Lahti* 112,129 ..... O6
Lappeenranta 52,682 ..... P6
Lapua 15,189 ..... N5
Lieksa 20,274 ..... R5
Loimaa 6,575 ..... N6
Lovisa 8,674 ..... P6
Maarianhamina (Mariehamn) 9,574 ..... M7
Mänttä 7,910 ..... O6
Mariehamn 9,574 ..... M7
Mikkeli 27,112 ..... P6
Naantali 7,814 ..... M6
Nokia 22,308 ..... N6
Nurmes 11,721 ..... Q5
Nykarleby 7,408 ..... N5
Oulainen 7,322 ..... O4
Oulu 93,707 ..... O4
Oulu* 103,044 ..... O4
Outokumpu 10,736 ..... Q5
Parainen 10,170 ..... M6
Parkano 8,518 ..... N6
Pieksämäki 12,923 ..... P5
Pietarsaari (Jakobstad) 20,397 ..... N5
Pori 80,343 ..... M6
Pori* 86,635 ..... M6
Posio† 6,205 ..... Q3
Pudasjärvi† 12,594 ..... P4
Raahe 15,379 ..... O4
Raisio 14,271 ..... M6
Rauma 29,081 ..... M6
Riihimäki 24,106 ..... O6
Rovaniemi 28,411 ..... O3
Saarijärvi 2,714 ..... O5
Salo 19,176 ..... N6
Savonlinna 28,336 ..... Q6
Seinäjoki 22,123 ..... N5
Sodankylä 3,304 ..... P3
Sotkamo 2,316 ..... Q4
Suolahti 5,936 ..... O5
Suonenjoki 9,286 ..... P5
Tammisaari (Ekenäs) 7,391 ..... N6
Tampere 168,118 ..... N6
Tampere* 220,920 ..... N6
Toijala 8,080 ..... N6
Tornio 19,971 ..... O4
Turku 164,857 ..... N6
Turku* 217,423 ..... N6
Turtola† 5,852 ..... O3
Ulvila† 8,040 ..... N6
Uusikaarlepyy (Nykarleby) 7,408 ..... N5
Uusikaupunki 11,915 ..... M6
Vaasa 54,402 ..... M5
Vaasa* 58,224 ..... M5
Valkeakoski 22,588 ..... N6
Vammala 16,363 ..... N6
Varkaus 24,450 ..... Q5
Vasa (Vaasa) 54,402 ..... M5
Vuotso† 10,186 ..... P2
Ylivieska 10,827 ..... O4

OTHER FEATURES

Åland (isls.) L6
Baltic (sea) K9
Bothnia (gulf) M5
Finland (gulf) P7
Hailuoto (isl.) O4
Haltiatunturi (mt.) M2
Hangöudd (prom.) N7
Haukivesi (lake) Q5
Iijoki (riv.) O4
Inari (lake) P2
Ivalojoki (riv.) P2
Juojärvi (lake) Q5
Kalajoki (riv.) O4
Kallavesi (lake) P5
Karlö (Hailuoto) (isl.) O4
Keitele (lake) O5
Kemijärvi (lake) Q3
Kemijoki (riv.) O3
Kiantajärvi (lake) Q4
Kilpisjärvi (lake) M2
Kitinen (riv.) P3
Kivijärvi (lake) O5
Koitere (lake) R5
Kuusamojärvi (lake) Q4
Längelmävesi (lake) O6
Lapland (reg.) O2
Lappajärvi (lake) O5
Lapuanjoki (riv.) N5
Lestijärvi (lake) O5
Lokka (res.) Q3
Muojärvi (lake) R4
Muonio (riv.) M2
Näsijärvi (lake) O6
Onkivesi (lake) P5
Orihvesi (lake) Q5
Oulujärvi (lake) P4
Oulujoki (riv.) O4
Ounasjoki (riv.) O3
Päijänne (lake) O6
Pielinen (lake) Q5
Puruvesi (lake) Q6
Puulavesi (lake) P5
Pyhäjärvi (lake) O5
Pyhäjärvi (lake) M6
Saimaa (lake) Q6
Siikajoki (riv.) O4
Simojärvi (lake) P3
Simojoki (riv.) O4
Tana (riv.) P2
Tornio (riv.) O3
Vallgrund (isl.) M5
Ylikitka (lake) Q3

NORWAY

COUNTIES

Akershus 355,196 ..... G6
Aust-Agder 86,216 ..... E7
Buskerud 209,684 ..... F6
Finnmark 79,373 ..... O2
Hedmark 183,465 ..... G6
Hordaland 386,492 ..... E6
Møre og Romsdal 231,944 ..... E5
Nordland 243,233 ..... J3
Nord-Trøndelag 122,886 ..... H4
Oppland 178,259 ..... F6
Oslo (city) 462,732 ..... D3
Østfold 228,546 ..... G7
Rogaland 287,653 ..... E7
Sogn og Fjordane 103,135 ..... E6
Sør-Trøndelag 241,361 ..... G5
Telemark 158,853 ..... F7
Troms 144,111 ..... L2
Vest-Agder 131,659 ..... E7
Vestfold 182,433 ..... G7

CITIES and TOWNS

Ålesund 40,868 ..... D5
Ålgård 2,322 ..... D7
Alta 5,582 ..... N2
Åndalsnes 2,574 ..... F5
Årdalstangen 2,360 ..... F6
Arendal 11,701 ..... F7
Arendal* 21,228 ..... F7
Årnes 2,267 ..... G6
Askim 8,413 ..... E4
Bamble† 7,031 ..... F7
Barentsburg C2
Bergen 213,434 ..... D6
Bodø 31,077 ..... J3
Borge† 3,294 ..... H2
Brønnøysund 3,130 ..... G4
Dombås 1,114 ..... F5
Drammen 50,777 ..... C4
Drammen* 56,521 ..... C4
Drøbak 4,538 ..... D4
Eidsvoll 2,906 ..... G6
Eigersund 11,379 ..... D7
Elverum 7,391 ..... G6
Farsund 8,908 ..... E7
Flekkefjord 8,750 ..... E7
Flora 8,822 ..... D6
Fredrikstad 29,024 ..... D4
Fredrikstad* 51,141 ..... D4
Gjøvik 25,963 ..... G6
Grimstad 13,091 ..... F7
Halden 27,087 ..... G7
Hamar 16,418 ..... G6
Hamar* 25,138 ..... G6
Hammerfest 7,610 ..... N1
Hammerfest* 8,005 ..... N1
Harstad 21,125 ..... K2
Haugesund 27,386 ..... D7
Haugesund* 29,277 ..... D7
Hermansverk 706 ..... E6
Holmestrand 8,246 ..... C4
Holmsbu 273 ..... D4
Honningsvag 3,780 ..... O1
Horten 13,746 ..... D4
Horten* 17,246 ..... D4
Kirkenes 4,466 ..... Q2
Kongsberg 19,854 ..... F7
Kongsvinger 16,146 ..... H6
Kopervik 4,221 ..... D7
Kornsjø† 6,079 ..... G7
Kragerø 5,249 ..... F7
Kristiansand 59,488 ..... F8
Kristiansund 18,847 ..... E5
Kvinnherad† 2,898 ..... E6
Larvik 9,097 ..... C4
Larvik* 19,202 ..... C4
Lenvik† 11,098 ..... L2
Levanger 5,066 ..... G5
Lillehammer 21,248 ..... F6
Lillesand 3,028 ..... F7
Lillestrøm† 11,550 ..... E3
Longyearbyen D2
Lysaker† 81,612 ..... D3
Mandal 11,579 ..... E7
Meråker† 2,907 ..... G5
Mo 21,033 ..... J3
Molde 20,334 ..... E5
Mosjøen 9,341 ..... H4
Moss 25,786 ..... D4
Moss* 27,430 ..... D4
Mysen 3,760 ..... G7
Namsos 11,452 ..... G4
Narvik 19,582 ..... K2
Nesttun† 11,519 ..... D6
Nittedal† 8,889 ..... D3
Notodden 12,970 ..... F7
Nøtterøy 11,944 ..... D4
Ny-Ålesund C2
Odda 7,401 ..... E6
Oppdal 2,173 ..... F5
Orkanger 3,685 ..... F5
Oslo (cap.) 462,732 ..... D3
Oslo* 645,413 ..... D3
Porsgrunn 31,709 ..... G7
Rakkestad 2,392 ..... G7
Ringerike 30,156 ..... C3
Risør 6,560 ..... F7
Rjukan 5,334 ..... F7
Røros 3,041 ..... G5
Sandefjord 33,350 ..... C4
Sandnes 33,934 ..... D7
Sandvika† 34,337 ..... C3
Sarpsborg 12,889 ..... D4
Sarpsborg* 36,449 ..... D4
Selje† 3,386 ..... D5
Ski 9,081 ..... D4
Skien 47,105 ..... F7
Stavanger 86,639 ..... D7
Stavern 2,604 ..... D4
Steinkjer 20,553 ..... G4
Stor-Elvdal† 2,993 ..... G6
Sunndalsøra 5,114 ..... F5
Sveagruva D2
Svolvaer 3,942 ..... J2
Tønsberg 9,964 ..... D4
Tønsberg* 36,374 ..... D4
Tromsø 43,830 ..... L2
Trondheim 134,910 ..... F5
Ullensvang† 2,326 ..... E6
Vadsø 6,019 ..... Q1
Vardø 3,875 ..... R1
Vik 1,019 ..... E6
Volda 3,511 ..... E5
Voss 5,944 ..... E6

OTHER FEATURES

Alsten (isl.) H4
Andøya (isl.) J2
Barduelv (riv.) L2
Bellsund C2
Bjørnafjorden (fjord) D6
Bjornøya (isl.) D3
Boknafjord (fjord) D7
Bremanger (isl.) D6
Dønna (isl.) H3
Dovrefjell (hills) F5
Edgeøya (isl.) E2
Femundsjø (lake) G5
Folda (fjord) G4
Folda (fjord) J3
Frohavet (bay) F5
Frøya (isl.) F5
Glittertinden (mt.) F6
Hardangervidda (plat.) E6
Hardangerfjord (fjord) D7
Hinlopenstreten (str.) C1
Hinnøya (isl.) K2
Hitra (isl.) F5
Hopen (isl.) E2
Isfjorden (fjord) C2
Jostedalsbreen (glac.) E6
Kjölen (mts.) K3
Kongsfjorden (fjord) B2
Kvaløya (isl.) O1
Lågen (riv.) G6
Laksefjorden (fjord) P1
Langøy (isl.) J2
Lapland (reg.) K2
Leka (isl.) G4
Lindesnes (cape) E8
Lista (pen.) E7
Lofoten (isls.) H2
Lopphavet (bay) M1
Magerøya (isl.) P1
Moskenesøya (isl.) H3
Namsen (riv.) H4
Nordaustlandet (isl.) D1
Nordfjord (fjord) E6
Nordkapp (pt.) C1
Nordkinn (headland) Q1
Nordkinn (pen.) P1
North Cape (Nordkapp) (pt.) P1
Norwegian (sea) F3
Ofotfjorden (fjord) K2
Oslofjord (fjord) D4
Otra (riv.) E7
Otterøya (isl.) E5
Pasvikelv (riv.) Q2
Platen, Kapp (pt.) D1
Porsangen (fjord) O1
Rana (fjord) H3
Rauma (riv.) F5
Ringvassøy (isl.) L2
Romsdalsfjorden (fjord) E5
Saltfjorden (fjord) J3
Seiland (isl.) N1
Senja (isl.) K2
Skagerrak (str.) F8
Smøla (isl.) E5
Sognafjorden (fjord) D6
Sørkapp (pt.) C2
Sorøya (isl.) N1
Spitsbergen (isl.) C2
Storfjorden (fjord) D2
Sulitjelma (mt.) J3
Svalbard (isls.) C3
Tana (riv.) P1
Tanafjord (fjord) Q1
Tokke (riv.) F7
Trondheimsfjorden (fjord) G5
Tyrifjord (lake) C3
Vaerøy (isl.) H3
Vagåvatn (lake) F6
Vannøy (isl.) L1
Varangerhalvøya (pen.) Q1
Varangerfjord (fjord) Q2
Vega (isl.) G4
Vesterålen (isls.) J2
Vestfjord (fjord) H3
Vestvågøya (isl.) H3
Vikna (isls.) G4

SWEDEN

COUNTIES

Älvsborg 418,150 ..... H7
Blekinge 155,391 ..... J8
Gävleborg 294,595 ..... K6
Göteborg och Bohus 714,660 ..... G7
Gotland 54,447 ..... L8
Halland 219,767 ..... H8
Jämtland 133,559 ..... J5
Jönköping 301,905 ..... H8
Kalmar 240,768 ..... K8
Kopparberg 281,082 ..... J6
Kristianstad 272,090 ..... J8

(continued on following page)

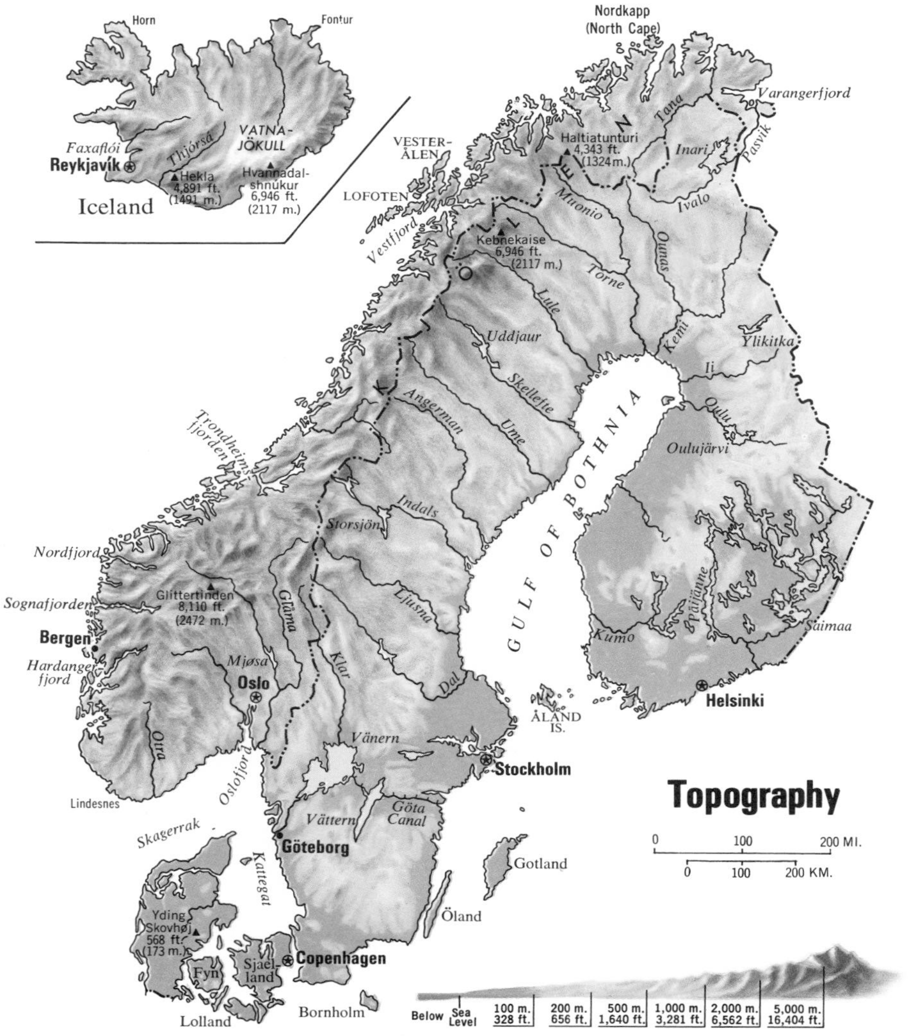

Horn
Fontur
Faxaflói
Reykjavík
Thjórsá
VATNA-JÖKULL
Hekla 4,891 ft. (1491 m.)
Hvannadal-shnukur 6,946 ft. (2117 m.)
Iceland
Nordkapp (North Cape)
Varangerfjord
VESTER-ÅLEN
LOFOTEN
Haltiatunturi 4,343 ft. (1324 m.)
Inari
Pasvik
Tana
Ivalo
Vestfjord
Kebnekaise 6,946 ft. (2117 m.)
Muonio
Ounas
Torne
Lule
Uddjaur
Kemi
Ylikitka
Ii
Skellefte
Ångerman
Ume
Oulu
Oulujärvi
Trondheimsfjorden
GULF OF BOTHNIA
Indals
Storsjön
Nordfjord
Sognafjorden
Glittertinden 8,110 ft. (2472 m.)
Ljusna
Glåma
Päijänne
Kumo
Saimaa
Bergen
Hardanger fjord
Mjøsa
Oslo
Klar
Dal
Helsinki
ÅLAND IS.
Otra
Vänern
Oslofjord
Stockholm
Lindesnes
Vättern
Göta Canal
Skagerrak
Göteborg
Kattegat
Gotland
Yding Skovhøj 568 ft. (173 m.)
Öland
Fyn
Sjælland
Copenhagen
Lolland
Bornholm
Topography
0 100 200 MI.
0 100 200 KM.
Below
Sea Level
100 m. 328 ft.
200 m. 656 ft.
500 m. 1,640 ft.
1,000 m. 3,281 ft.
2,000 m. 6,562 ft.
5,000 m. 16,404 ft.

20 Norway, Sweden, Finland, Denmark and Iceland

(continued)

Kronoberg 169,454 J8
Malmöhus 740,137 H9
Norrbotten 264,215 L3
Örebro 273,994 J7
Östergötland 387,104 J7
Skaraborg 263,382 H7
Södermanland 252,030 K7
Stockholm 1,493,052 L7
Uppsala 229,879 K7
Värmland 284,442 H7
Västerbotten 236,367 K4
Västernorrland 268,202 K5
Västmanland 259,872 K7

CITIES and TOWNS

Åhus 6,125 J9
Alingsås 18,892 H7
Älmhult 7,390 H8
Alvesta 7,261 J8
Älvsbyn 4,707 M4
Åmål 9,556 H7
Ånge 3,760 J5
Ängelholm 16,016 H8
Arboga 11,819 J7
Arbrå 2,734 K6
Årjäng† 2,596 H7
Arvidsjaur 4,194 L4
Arvika 13,934 H7
Åseda 2,465 J8
Askim 17,609 G8
Åtvidaberg 8,436 K7
Avesta 19,095 J6
Bålsta 8,243 G1
Båstad 2,452 H8
Bengtsfors 3,535 H7
Boden 19,590 M4
Bollnäs 13,305 K6
Bollstabruk 3,548 L5
Borås 67,537 H8
Borås* 187,710 H8
Borgholm 2,789 K8
Borlänge 40,158 J6
Brunflo 3,460 J5
Dalby† 4,013 H6
Danderyd† 36,596 H1
Dannemora 291 K6
Edsbyn 4,388 J6
Eksjö 9,686 J8
Emmaboda 5,652 J8
Enköping 18,541 G1
Eskilstuna 66,409 K7
Eslöv 13,629 H9
Fagersta† 14,778 J6
Falkenberg 14,148 H8
Falköping 15,126 H7
Falun 30,073 J6
Färjestaden 2,995 K8
Filipstad 7,835 H7
Finspång 16,346 J7
Flen 6,770 K7
Forshaga 6,000 H7
Frösö 10,274 J5
Frövi 2,583 J7
Gällivare 8,669 M3
Gamleby 3,666 J8
Gävle 67,454 K6
Gimo 3,154 K6
Gislaved 8,564 H8
Gnesta 3,835 G2
Göteborg 444,540 G8
Göteborg* 690,767 G8
Hagfors 8,060 H6
Hällefors 7,862 J7
Hallsberg 6,799 J7
Hallstahammar 13,583 K7
Hallstavik 5,162 L6
Halmstad 49,558 H8
Haparanda 5,031 N4
Härnösand 18,971 L5
Hässleholm 16,813 H8
Hedemora 7,039 K6
Helsingborg 80,986 H8
Helsingborg* 215,894 H8
Hjo 4,615 J7
Hofors 11,459 K6
Höganäs 10,866 H8
Holmsund 5,467 M5
Hörnefors 2,441 L5
Huddinge 48,339 H1
Hudiksvall 15,004 K6
Hultsfred 5,763 K8
Husum 2,517 L5
Hyltebruk 3,469 H8
Iggesund 4,448 K6
Järna 6,237 G2
Jokkmokk 3,186 L3
Jönköping 78,650 H8
Jönköping* 131,499 H8
Kalix 7,668 N4
Kalmar 32,049 K8
Karlshamn 17,447 J8
Karlskoga† 35,425 J7
Karlskrona 33,414 J8
Karlstad 51,243 H7
Katrineholm 22,884 K7
Kinna 13,676 H8
Kiruna 25,410 L3
Kisa 4,323 J7
Köping 20,059 J7
Kopparberg 3,942 J7
Kramfors 7,719 L5
Kristianstad 30,780 J9
Kristinehamn 21,146 H7
Kumla 11,451 J7
Kungälv† 12,764 G8
Kungsbacka† 11,986 G8
Kvissleby 3,413 K5
Laholm 3,898 H8
Landskrona 29,486 H9
Långshyttan 2,744 K6
Laxå 5,166 J7
Leksand 4,410 J6
Lessebo 2,991 J8
Lidingö 30,098 H1
Lidköping 21,001 H7
Lindesberg 8,247 J7
Linköping 80,274 K7
Linköping* 132,839 K7
Ljungby 12,969 J8
Ljusdal 7,075 J6
Ljusne 3,578 K6
Ludvika 18,217 J6
Luleå 42,139 N4
Lund 55,047 H9
Lycksele 8,586 L4
Lysekil 7,815 G7
Malmberget 10,239 M3
Malmö 241,191 H9
Malmö* 453,339 H9
Malung 6,211 H6
Mariefred 2,553 F1
Mariestad 16,454 H7
Markaryd 4,266 H8
Märsta 17,066 K7
Marstrand 1,168 G8
Mellerud 3,579 H7
Mjölby 12,488 J7
Mölndal† 47,248 H8
Mönsterås 5,005 K8
Mora 8,772 J6
Motala 29,454 J7
Nacka 19,708 H1
Nässjö 18,634 J8
Nora 5,515 J7
Norberg 5,438 K6
Norrköping 85,244 K7
Norrköping* 163,206 K7
Norrtälje 12,784 L7
Nybro 13,010 J8
Nyköping 30,352 K7
Nynäshamn 11,070 L7
Ockelbo 2,810 K6
Olofström 10,096 J8
Örebro 117,877 J7
Örebro* 171,440 J7
Örnsköldsvik 29,514 L5
Orrefors 919 J8
Orsa 5,099 J6
Oskarshamn 19,021 K8
Östersund 40,056 J5
Östhammar 1,783 L6
Oxelösund 13,862 K7
Piteå 16,169 M4
Rättvik 4,087 J6
Rimbo 3,404 L7
Ronneby 12,086 J8
Säffle 11,428 H7
Sala 11,216 K7
Saltsjöbaden 8,113 J1
Sandviken 27,994 K6
Säter 4,297 J6
Sävsjö 4,913 J8
Sigtuna 4,780 H1
Simrishamn 5,834 J9
Skanör med Falsterbo 4,909 H9
Skara 10,138 H7
Skellefteå 29,353 M4
Skövde 29,945 H7
Skutskär 7,174 K6
Smedjebacken 8,418 J6
Söderhamn 14,673 K6
Söderköping 5,310 K7
Södertälje 58,408 G1
Sollefteå 8,923 K5
Sollentuna† 40,905 H1
Solna† 53,992 H1
Sölvesborg 7,292 J9
Stenungsund 8,361 G7
Stockholm (cap.) 665,550 G1
Stockholm* 1,357,183 G1
Storuman 2,587 K4
Storvik 2,748 K6
Strängnäs 10,255 F1
Strömstad 4,735 G7
Strömsund 4,119 K5
Sundbyberg† 27,058 G1
Sundsvall 52,268 K5
Sunne 4,273 H7
Surahammar 6,509 J7
Sveg 2,608 J5
Svenljunga 3,189 H8
Täby† 41,285 H1
Tibro 8,476 J7
Tidaholm 8,039 J7
Tierp 5,005 K6
Timrå 11,416 K5
Tomelilla 5,371 J9
Torsby 3,632 H6
Torshälla 8,231 K7
Tranås 14,854 J7
Trelleborg 22,559 H9
Trollhättan 42,499 H7
Trosa 3,128 K7
Uddevalla 32,700 G7
Ulricehamn 7,827 H8
Umeå 49,715 M5
Uppsala 101,850 K7
Uppsala* 157,202 L7
Vadstena 5,294 J7
Vaggeryd 3,974 J8
Valdemarsvik 3,558 K7
Vallentuna 10,477 H1
Vänersborg 20,510 G7
Vännäs 3,876 L5
Vansbro 2,708 H6
Vara 3,049 H7
Varberg 19,467 G8
Värnamo 15,726 J8
Västerås 98,858 K7
Västerås* 147,508 K7
Västerhaninge 14,125 H1
Västervik 21,239 K8
Vaxholm† 3,744 J1
Växjö 40,328 J8
Vetlanda 12,358 J8
Vilhelmina 4,060 K4
Vimmerby 7,405 J8
Virserum 2,495 J8
Visby 19,886 L8
Ystad 14,286 H9

OTHER FEATURES

Ångermanälven (riv.) K5
Åsnen (lake) J8
Baltic (sea) K9
Bolmen (lake) H8
Bothnia (gulf) N4
Dalälven (riv.) K6
Fårö (isl.) L8
Göta (canal) J7
Göta (riv.) H7
Gotland (isl.) L8
Gräsö (isl.) L6
Hanöbukten (bay) J9
Hjälmaren (lake) J7
Hoburgen (cliff) L8
Hornslandet (pen.) K6
Indalsälven (riv.) H5
Kalixälv (riv.) N3
Kalmarsund (sound) K8
Kattegat (str.) G8
Kebnekaise (mt.) L3
Kölen (mts.) K3
Klarälv (riv.) H6
Lapland (reg.) M2
Ljusnan (riv.) H5
Luleälv (riv.) M4
Mälaren (lake) G1
Muonioälv (riv.) M2
Öland (isl.) K8
Öresund (sound) H9
Ornö (isl.) J2
Österdalälven (riv.) H6
Piteälv (riv.) M4
Siljan (lake) J6
Skagerrak (str.) F8
Sommen (lake) J8
Stora Lulevatten (lake) L3
Storsjön (lake) J5
Sulitelma (mt.) K3
Torneälv (riv.) M3
Uddjaur (lake) L4
Umeälv (riv.) L4
Vänern (lake) H7
Västerdalälven (riv.) H6
Vättern (lake) J7

*City and suburbs.
†Population of commune.
†Population of parish.

DENMARK

COUNTIES

Århus 534,333 D5
Bornholm 47,241 F9
Copenhagen (commune) 622,612 F6
Faerøe Islands 41,969 B2
Frederiksberg (commune) 101,874 F6
Frederiksborg 260,825 E5
Fyn 433,765 D7
København (Copenhagen) (commune) 622,612 F6
Københaven 616,571 F6
Nordjylland 457,165 D4
Ribe 198,153 B7
Ringkøbing 242,006 B5
Roskilde 154,314 E6
Sønderjylland 238,502 C7
Storstrøm 252,780 E7
Vejle 306,809 C6
Vestsjaelland 259,484 E6
Viborg 221,002 C4

CITIES and TOWNS

Åbenrå 15,196 C7
Åbybro 2,897 C3
Åkirkeby 2,001 F9
Ålborg 154,582 D4
Ålestrup 1,926 C4
Århus 245,941 D5
Års 4,266 C4
Årup 1,675 D7
AErøskøbing 1,223 D8
Agerbaek 935 B6
Allingaåbro 1,385 D5
Allinge-Sandvig 1,991 F8
Ansager 1,157 B6
Arden 1,303 C4
Asaå 1,344 D3
Askov 904 C7
Asnaes 1,413 E6
Assens, Århus 1,341 D4
Assens, Fyn 5,139 D7
Augustenborg 2,628 D8
Auning 1,516 D5
Avlum 1,729 B5
Baelum 1,169 D4
Bagenkop 776 D8
Ballerup 50,673 F6
Bandholm 693 E8
Bedsted 965 B4
Birkerød 13,663 F6
Bjerringbro 4,761 C5
Bogense 2,861 D6
Bolderslev 774 C8
Børkop 1,410 C6
Borup 1,591 E7
Braedstrup 2,163 C6
Bramming 3,678 B7
Brande 4,784 B6
Bredebro 1,173 B7
Broager 2,143 C8
Brønderslev 10,247 C3
Brørup 2,584 C7
Brovst 4,200 C3
Bryrup 579 C5
Christiansfeld 1,994 C7
Copenhagen (cap.) 603,368 F6
Copenhagen* 1,327,940 F6
Dronninglund 4,661 D3
Dybvad 805 D3
Ebeltoft 3,017 D5
Egernsund 1,323 C8
Egtved 1,311 C6
Ejby 1,372 C7
Esbjerg 68,097 B7
Faåborg 6,495 D7
Fakse 2,720 F7
Fakse Ladeplads 1,799 F7
Farsø 2,821 C4
Farum 9,936 F6
Fjerritslev 2,134 C3
Fredensborg 4,709 F6
Fredericia 36,157 C6
Frederiksberg 101,874 F6
Frederikshavn 24,846 D3
Frederikssund 11,272 E6
Frederiksvaerk 8,903 E6
Fuglebjerg 1,094 E7
Gedser 1,200 F8
Gedsted 1,006 C4
Gelsted 1,307 C7
Gentofte 77,744 F6
Gilleleje 2,943 F5
Give 2,366 C6
Glamsbjerg 2,226 D7
Glostrup 28,326 F6
Glumsø 1,027 E7
Glyngøre 1,071 C4
Gørding 1,261 B7
Gørlev 1,542 E7
Graested 1,654 F5
Gram 2,061 C7
Graåsten 2,947 C8
Grenaå 12,569 D5
Grindsted 7,558 B6
Haårby 1,506 D7
Haderslev 20,042 C7
Hadsten 3,914 C5
Hadsund 3,652 D4
Hals 1,654 D3
Hammel 3,247 C5
Hammerum 3,227 C5
Hanstholm 1,716 B3
Harboør 1,359 B4
Haårlev 1,228 F7
Hasle 18
Haslev 6,925 E7
Havdrup 1,833 F6
Hedensted 2,659 C6
Hellebaek 2,911 F5
Helsinge 3,613 F6
Helsingør 42,425 F6
Herning 32,973 B5
Hillerød 23,963 F6
Hinnerup 2,061 D5
Hirtshals 6,861 C2
Hjallerup 1,573 C3
Hjerm 647 B5
Hjørring 19,692 C3
Hobro 8,737 C4
Højer 1,416 B8
Højslev 1,641 C4
Holbaek 19,485 E6
Holeby 1,434 E8
Holstebro 25,006 B5
Holsted 1,390 B6
Høng 2,488 E7
Hornslet 2,561 D5
Horsens 44,120 C6
Hørsholm 19,346 F6
Hørve 1,139 E6
Hov 635 D6
Humlum 546 B4
Hundested 5,443 E6
Hurup 2,287 B4
Hvidbjerg 994 B4
Hvide Sande 2,129 A6
Ikast 9,222 C5
Jelling 1,540 C6
Jerslev 798 D3
Juelsminde 1,991 D6
Jyderup 2,901 E6
Kalundborg 12,248 D6
Karise 1,184 F7
Karup 1,694 C5
Kastrup† 17,391 F6
Kerteminde 5,007 D7
Kibaek 1,279 B5
Kjellerup 3,245 C5
Klitmøller 542 B3
København (Copenhagen) (cap.) 603,368 F6
Køge 18,608 F7
Kolding 41,602 C7
Kolind 1,036 D5
Korsør 15,502 E7
Kvaerndrup 891 D7
Langaå 2,320 C5
Lem 1,026 B5
Lemvig 6,448 B4
Løgstør 3,633 C4
Løgumkloster 2,091 B7
Lohals 580 D7
Løjt Kirkeby 1,203 C7
Løkken 1,345 C3
Løsning 1,967 C6
Lundby 747 E7
Lunderskov 1,494 C7
Lyngby 61,516 F6
Malling 1,584 D5
Mariager 1,692 D4
Maribo 5,287 E8
Marstal 4,124 D8
Middelfart 13,315 C7

Agriculture, Industry and Resources

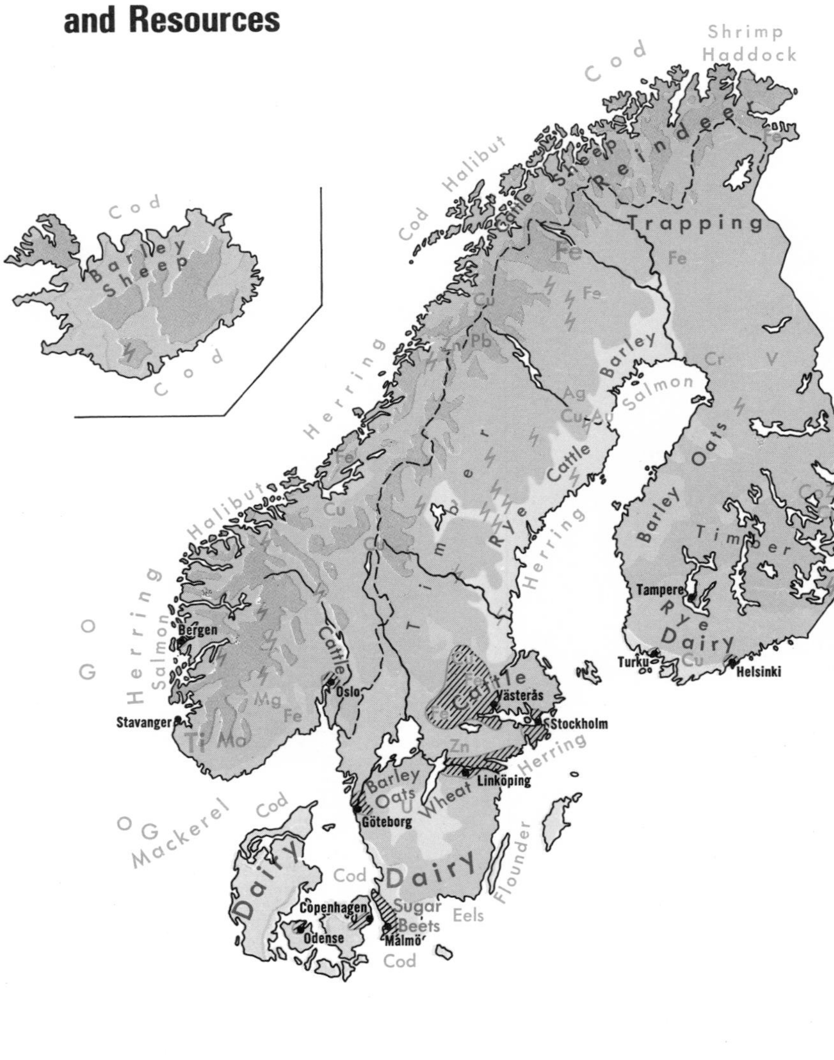

DOMINANT LAND USE

- Cash Cereals, Dairy
- Dairy, Cattle, Hogs
- Dairy, General Farming
- General Farming (chiefly cereals)
- Nomadic Sheep Herding
- Forests, Limited Mixed Farming
- Nonagricultural Land

MAJOR MINERAL OCCURRENCES

Ag	Silver	Ni	Nickel
Au	Gold	O	Petroleum
Co	Cobalt	Pb	Lead
Cr	Chromium	Ti	Titanium
Cu	Copper	U	Uranium
Fe	Iron Ore	V	Vanadium
Mg	Magnesium	Zn	Zinc
Mo	Molybdenum		

Water Power
Major Industrial Areas

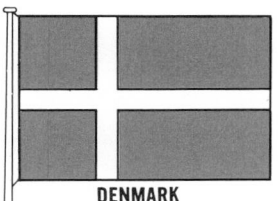

DENMARK

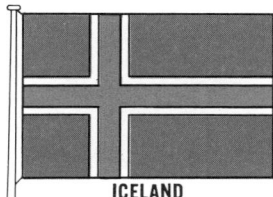

ICELAND

DENMARK

AREA 16,629 sq. mi. (43,069 sq. km.)
POPULATION 5,124,000
CAPITAL Copenhagen
LARGEST CITY Copenhagen
HIGHEST POINT Yding Skovhøj
568 ft. (173 m.)
MONETARY UNIT krone
MAJOR LANGUAGE Danish
MAJOR RELIGION Protestantism

ICELAND

AREA 39,768 sq. mi. (103,000 sq. km.)
POPULATION 228,785
CAPITAL Reykjavík
LARGEST CITY Reykjavík
HIGHEST POINT Hvannadalshnúkur
6,952 ft. (2,119 m.)
MONETARY UNIT króna
MAJOR LANGUAGE Icelandic
MAJOR RELIGION Protestantism

Denmark and Iceland

CONIC PROJECTION

SCALE OF MILES

SCALE OF KILOMETERS

Capitals of Countries _____ ★
Capitals of Counties (amter) ____ △
International Boundaries ____ _____
Internal Boundaries ____ _____

Scale 1:2,300,000

Denmark is divided into fourteen Counties plus Copenhagen and Frederiksberg communes.

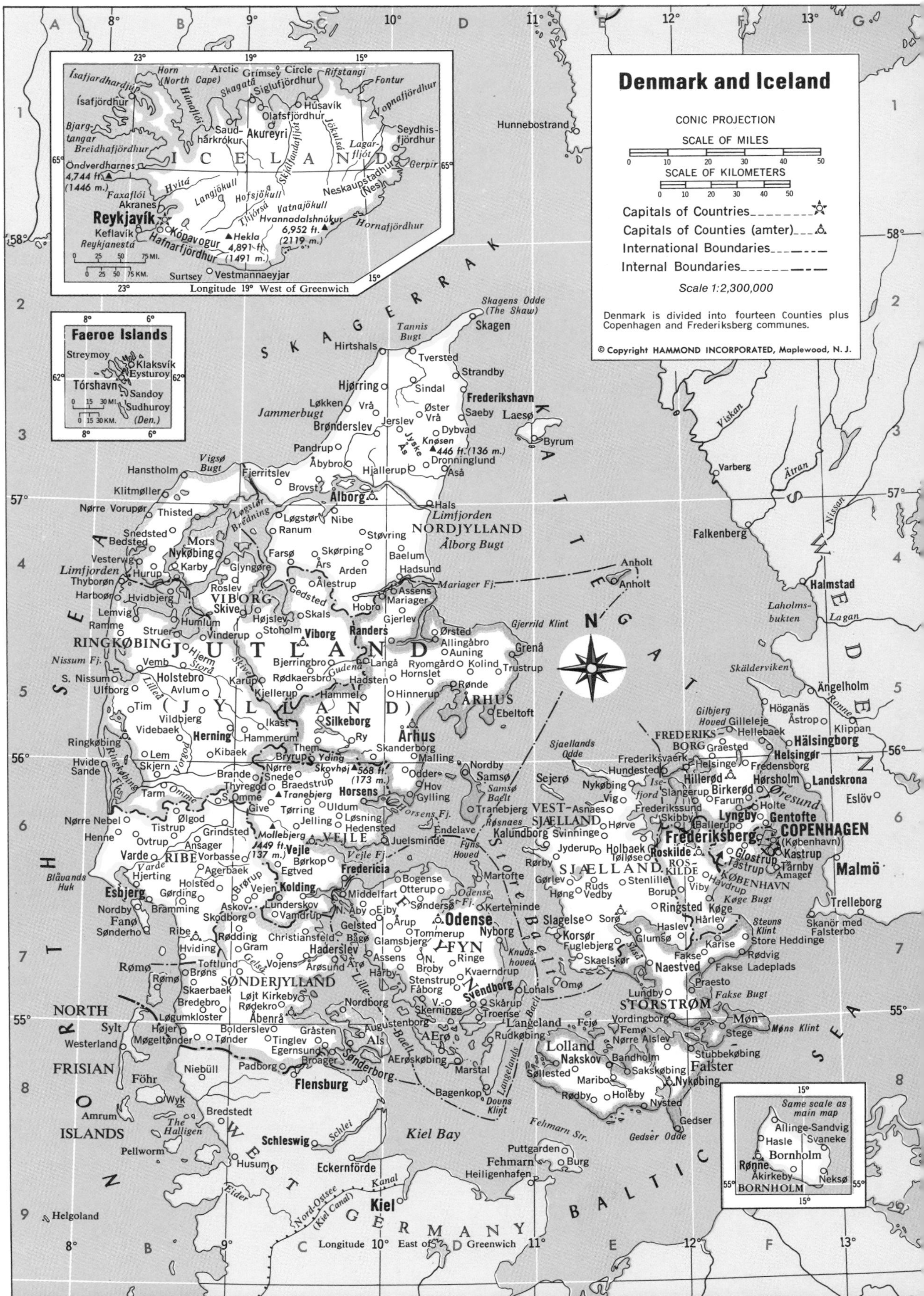

Germany

CONIC PROJECTION

SCALE OF MILES

SCALE OF KILOMETERS

Capitals of Countries .... ☆
State and District Capitals .... ◉
International Boundaries ....
State and District Boundaries ....
Canals ....

Scale 1:3,040,000

East Germany is divided into districts bearing the same name as their respective capitals.

© Copyright HAMMOND INCORPORATED, Maplewood, N.J.

Berlin

AREA 95,985 sq. mi. (248,601 sq. km.)
POPULATION 61,658,000
CAPITAL Bonn
LARGEST CITY Berlin (West)
HIGHEST POINT Zugspitze 9,718 ft. (2,962 m.)
MONETARY UNIT Deutsche mark
MAJOR LANGUAGE German
MAJOR RELIGIONS Protestantism, Roman Catholicism

AREA 41,768 sq. mi. (108,179 sq. km.)
POPULATION 16,737,000
CAPITAL Berlin (East)
LARGEST CITY Berlin (East)
HIGHEST POINT Fichtelberg 3,983 ft. (1,214 m.)
MONETARY UNIT East German mark
MAJOR LANGUAGE German
MAJOR RELIGIONS Protestantism, Roman Catholicism

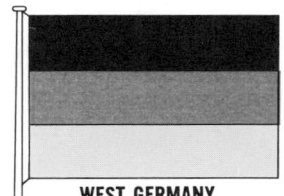

WEST GERMANY

EAST GERMANY

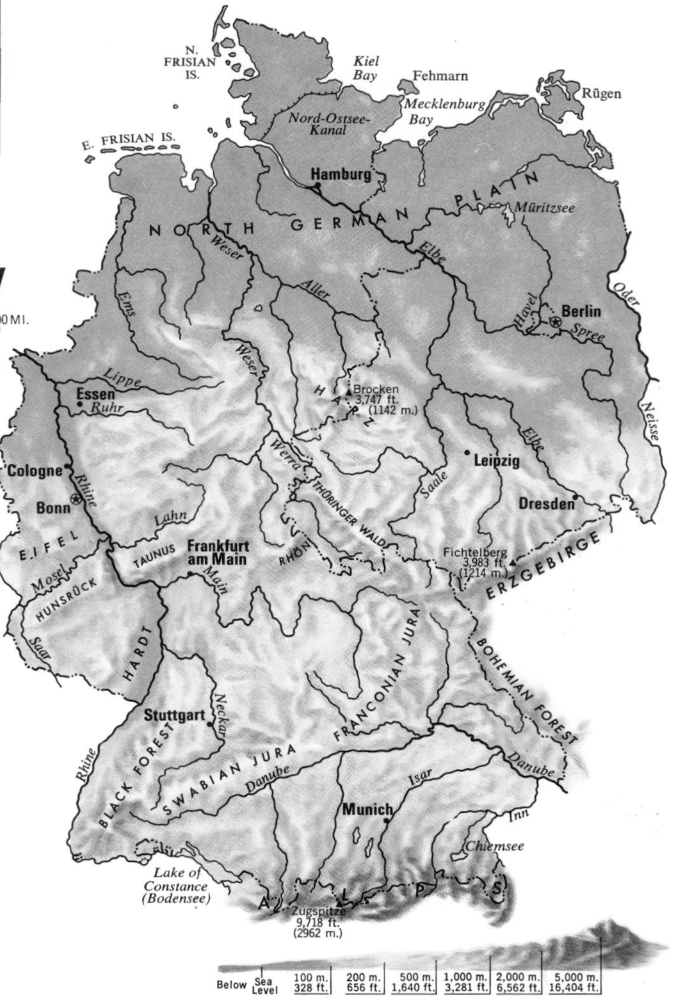

EAST GERMANY

DISTRICTS

Berlin 1,094,147	F4
Cottbus 872,242	F3
Dresden 1,845,459	E3
Erfurt 1,247,213	D3
Frankfurt 688,637	F2
Gera 738,847	D3
Halle 1,890,187	D3
Karl-Marx-Stadt 1,994,115	E3
Leipzig 1,457,817	E3
Magdeburg 1,297,881	D2
Neubrandenburg 628,686	E2
Potsdam 1,124,892	E2
Rostock 867,806	E1
Schwerin 592,334	D2
Suhl 550,497	D3

CITIES and TOWNS

Aken 11,742	D3
Altenburg 51,193	E3
Angermünde 11,786	E2
Anklam 19,099	E2
Annaberg-Buchholz 26,561	E3
Apolda 28,649	D3
Arnstadt 29,462	D3
Aschersleben 36,674	D3
Aue 32,622	E3
Auerbach 18,168	E3
Bad Doberan 12,541	D1
Bad Dürrenberg 15,192	D3
Bad Langensalza 166,282	D3
Bad Salzungen 17,277	C3
Barth 12,069	E1
Bautzen 45,851	F3
Bergen 13,244	E1
Berlin, East (cap.) 1,094,147	F4
Bernau bei Berlin 15,749	E2
Bernburg 44,428	D3
Bischofswerda 11,540	F3
Bitterfeld 27,062	D3
Blankenburg am Harz 18,784	D3
Boizenburg an der Elbe 12,428	D2
Borna 21,807	E3
Brandenburg 94,071	E2
Burg bei Magdeburg 29,027	D2
Calbe 15,976	D3
Chemnitz (Karl-Marx-Stadt) 303,811	E3
Coswig, Dresden 22,149	E3
Coswig, Halle 12,473	D3
Cottbus 94,293	F3
Crimmitschau 28,845	E3
Delitzsch 24,076	E3
Demmin 17,270	E2
Dessau 100,820	D3
Döbeln 27,624	E3
Dresden 507,692	E3
Ebersbach 12,694	F3
Eberswalde-Finow 47,141	E2
Eilenburg 22,245	E3
Eisenach 49,954	C3
Eisenberg 13,450	D3
Eisenhüttenstadt 46,455	F2
Eisleben 29,293	D3
Erfurt 202,979	D3
Falkensee 25,295	E2
Falkenstein 14,367	E3
Finsterwalde 22,316	E3
Forst 28,084	F3
Frankfurt an der Oder 70,817	F2
Freiberg 50,815	E3
Freital 46,061	E3
Friedland	F2
Fürstenwalde 31,065	F2
Gardelegen 12,987	D2
Genthin 15,916	E2
Gera 113,108	E3
Glauchau 30,927	E3
Görlitz 84,658	F3
Gotha 59,243	D3
Greifswald 53,940	E1
Greiz 37,612	E3
Grevesmühlen 12,005	D2
Grimma 17,100	E3
Grimmen 14,011	E1
Grossenhain 18,712	E3
Grossräschen 12,889	F3
Guben (Wilhelm-Pieck-Stadt) 32,731	F3
Güstrow 36,824	E2
Halberstadt 46,669	D3
Haldensleben 19,194	D2
Halle 241,425	D3
Halle-Neustadt 67,956	D3
Havelberg	E2
Heidenau 21,315	E3
Heiligenstadt 13,931	C3
Hennigsdorf bei Berlin 24,853	E2
Hettstedt 20,291	D3
Hildburghausen 11,372	D3
Hoyerswerda 64,904	F3
Ilmenau 22,021	D3
Jena 99,431	D3
Johanngeorgenstadt 10,328	E3
Jüterbog 13,477	E3
Kamenz 18,221	F3
Karl-Marx-Stadt 303,811	E3
Klingenthal 13,614	E3
Königs Wusterhausen 11,825	F4
Köpenick 130,987	F4
Köthen 35,451	D3
Kühlungsborn	D1
Lauchhammer 26,939	F3
Leipzig 570,972	E3
Lichtenberg 192,063	F4
Limbach-Oberfrohna 25,706	E3
Löbau 18,077	F3
Lübben 14,224	F3
Lübbenau 22,350	F3
Luckenwalde 28,544	E3
Ludwigslust 13,280	D2
Magdeburg 276,089	D2
Markkleeberg 22,380	E3
Meerane 25,037	E3
Meiningen 26,134	D3
Meissen 43,561	E3
Merseburg 54,269	D3
Meuselwitz 13,585	E3
Mittweida 19,259	E3
Mühlhausen (Thomas-Müntzer-Stadt) 44,106	D3
Nauen 11,940	E2
Naumburg 36,358	D3
Neubrandenburg 59,971	E2
Neuenhagen bei Berlin 12,603	F4
Neuruppin 24,888	E2
Neustrelitz 27,074	E2
Nordhausen 44,442	D3
Oelsnitz 15,084	D3
Oelsnitz im Erzgebirge 16,063	E3
Olbernhau 13,479	E3
Oranienburg 24,452	E2
Oschatz 18,974	E3
Oschersleben 17,377	D3
Pankow 136,527	F3
Parchim 22,927	D2
Pasewalk 15,099	E2
Peenemünde	E1
Perleberg 15,029	D2
Pirna 49,771	E3
Plauen 80,353	E3
Pössneck 18,648	D3
Potsdam 117,236	E2
Prenzlau 22,738	E2
Pritzwalk 11,887	E2
Quedlinburg 29,796	D3
Radeberg 18,528	E3
Radebeul 38,383	E3
Rathenow 32,011	E2
Reichenbach 27,440	E3
Ribnitz-Damgarten 17,254	E1
Riesa 49,989	E3
Rosslau 16,520	D3
Rostock 210,167	E1
Rudolstadt 31,698	D3
Saalfeld 33,648	D3
Salzwedel 21,741	D2
Sangerhausen 32,721	D3
Sassnitz 13,857	E1
Schkeuditz 15,585	D3
Schmalkalden 15,017	D3
Schmölln 13,406	E3
Schneeberg 20,376	E3
Schönebeck 45,197	D2
Schwedt 45,729	F2
Schwerin 104,984	D2
Sebnitz 13,470	F3
Senftenberg 29,953	F3
Sömmerda 20,712	D3
Sondershausen 23,383	D3
Sonneberg 29,193	D3
Spremberg 22,862	F3
Stassfurt 26,225	D3
Stendal 39,647	D2
Stralsund 72,167	E1
Strausberg 21,334	F2
Suhl 36,642	D3
Tangermünde 12,898	D2
Teltow 16,171	E4
Templin 11,718	E2
Thale 17,248	D3
Thomas-Müntzer-Stadt 44,106	D3
Torgau 21,813	E3
Torgelow 14,320	F2
Treptow 127,448	F4
Ueckermünde 11,423	F2
Waldheim 11,925	E3
Waltershausen 13,893	D3
Waren 22,921	E2
Weida 11,016	E3
Weimar 63,144	D3
Weissenfels 43,191	D3
Weissensee 78,451	F4
Weisswasser 25,910	F3
Werdau 22,249	E3
Wernigerode 34,658	D3
Wilhelm-Pieck-Stadt 32,731	F3
Wismar 56,765	D2
Wittenberg 51,364	E3
Wittenberge 32,907	D2
Wolfen 27,570	D3
Wolgast 16,384	E1
Wurzen 20,501	E3
Zehdenick 12,651	E2
Zeitz 44,582	D3
Zella-Mehlis 16,301	D3
Zerbst 19,136	D3
Zeulenroda 13,452	D3
Zittau 42,278	F3
Zwickau 123,069	E3

OTHER FEATURES

Altmark (reg.)	D2
Arkona (cape)	E1
Baltic (sea)	E1
Black Elster (riv.)	E3
Brandenburg (reg.)	E2
Elbe (riv.)	D2
Elde (riv.)	D2
Elster, Black (riv.)	E3
Elster, White (riv.)	E3
Erzgebirge (mts.)	E3
Fichtelberg (mt.)	E3
Harz (mts.)	D3
Havel (riv.)	E2
Lusatia (reg.)	F3
Mecklenburg (bay)	D1
Mecklenburg (reg.)	E2
Mulde (riv.)	E3
Neisse (riv.)	F3
Oder (riv.)	F2
Peene (riv.)	E2
Pomerania (reg.)	E2
Pomeranian (bay)	F1
Rhön (mts.)	D3
Rügen (isl.)	E1
Saale (riv.)	D3
Saxony (reg.)	E3
Spree (riv.)	F3
Spreewald (for.)	F3
Thüringer Wald (for.)	D3
Thuringia (reg.)	C3
Ücker (riv.)	E2
Unstrut (riv.)	D3
Usedom (isl.)	F1
Warnow (riv.)	D2
Werra (riv.)	C3
White Elster (riv.)	E3

WEST GERMANY

STATES

Baden-Württemberg 9,152,700	C4
Bavaria 10,810,400	D4
Berlin (West) (free city) 1,984,800	E4
Bremen 716,800	C2
Hamburg 1,717,400	D2
Hesse 5,549,800	C3
Lower Saxony 7,238,500	C2
North Rhine-Westphalia 17,129,600	B3
Rhineland-Palatinate 3,665,800	B4
Saarland 1,096,300	B4
Schleswig-Holstein 2,582,400	C1

CITIES and TOWNS

Aachen 242,453	B3
Aalen 64,735	D4
Ahaus 27,126	B2
Ahlen 54,214	B3
Ahrensburg 24,964	D2
Alfeld 24,506	C3
Alsdorf 47,473	B3
Alsfeld 18,091	C3
Altena 26,753	B3
Altona	C2
Alzey 15,190	C4
Amberg 46,934	D4
Andernach 27,132	B3
Ansbach 39,117	D4
Arnsberg 80,287	C3
Arolsen 15,619	C3
Aschaffenburg 55,398	C4
Augsburg 249,943	D4
Aurich 34,194	B2
Backnang 29,614	C4
Bad Berleburg 20,415	C3
Bad Driburg 17,478	C3
Bad Dürkheim 16,133	C4
Bad Ems 10,487	B3
Baden-Baden 49,718	C4
Bad Gandersheim 11,614	D3
Bad Harzburg 25,786	D3
Bad Hersfeld 29,248	C3
Bad Homburg vor der Höhe 51,196	C3
Bad Honnef 20,903	B3
Bad Kissingen 22,279	C3
Bad Kreuznach 42,588	B4
Bad Lauterberg im Harz 14,715	D3
Bad Mergentheim 19,895	C4
Bad Münstereifel 14,340	B3
Bad Nauheim 25,916	C3
Bad Neuenahr-Ahrweiler 26,371	B3
Bad Oldesloe 19,640	D2
Bad Pyrmont 21,896	C3
Bad Reichenhall 13,048	E5
Bad Salzuflen 50,924	C2
Bad Schwartau 18,696	D2
Bad Segeberg 13,320	D2
Bad Tölz 12,458	D5
Bad Vilbel 25,012	C3
Bad Waldsee 14,296	C5
Bad Wildungen 15,418	C3
Bad Wimpfen 5,536	C4
Baiersbronn 14,845	C4
Balingen 29,310	C4
Bamberg 74,236	D4
Barsinghausen 32,873	C2
Bassum 14,113	C2
Baumholder 4,837	B4
Bayreuth 67,035	D4
Bayrischzell 1,639	D5
Bebra 15,740	C3
Bendorf 15,943	B3
Bensheim 32,653	C4
Bentheim 13,681	B2
Berchtesgaden 8,558	E5
Bergisch Gladbach 99,517	B3
Berleburg (Bad Berleburg) 20,415	C3
Berlin (West) 1,984,837	E4
Biberach an der Riss 28,891	C4
Bielefeld 316,058	C2
Bietigheim-Bissingen 34,042	C4
Bingen 24,341	B4
Birkenfeld 5,883	B4
Blaubeuren 11,652	C4
Böblingen 40,547	C4
Bocholt 65,460	B3
Bochum 414,842	B3
Bonn (cap.) 283,711	B3
Boppard 16,888	B3
Borken 30,212	B3
Bornheim 32,847	B3
Bottrop 101,495	B3
Brake 18,089	C2
Bramsche 24,119	B2
Braunschweig (Brunswick) 268,519	D2
Breisach am Rhein 9,230	B4
Bremen 572,969	C2
Bremerhaven 143,836	C2
Bremervörde 17,565	C2
Bretten 22,140	C4
Brilon 24,595	C3
Bruchsal 38,929	C4
Brühl 44,305	B3
Brunsbüttel 11,451	C2
Brunswick 268,519	D2
Buchholz in der Nordheide 25,713	C2
Bückeburg 21,393	C2
Büdingen 16,845	C3
Bühl 21,596	C4
Bünde 40,021	C2
Büren 17,352	C3
Burg auf Fehmarn 5,874	D1
Burghausen 16,892	E4
Butzbach 20,592	C3
Buxtehude 30,249	C2
Castrop-Rauxel 82,373	B3
Celle 74,347	D2
Cham 22,539	E4
Charlottenburg 201,732	E4
Clausthal-Zellerfeld 16,690	D3
Cloppenburg 19,757	B2
Coburg 46,244	D3
Coesfeld 30,617	B3
Cologne 1,013,771	B3
Crailsheim 60,353	C4
Dachau 33,207	D4
Dahlem	E4
Darmstadt 137,018	C4
Deggendorf 25,188	E4
Delmenhorst 71,488	C2
Detmold 65,629	C3
Dietzenbach 18,528	C3
Dillenburg 14,068	C3
Dillingen 21,925	C3
Dillingen an der Donau 11,601	D4
Dingolfing 13,325	D4
Dinkelsbühl 10,034	D4
Donaueschingen 17,578	C5
Donauwörth 17,077	D4
Dorsten 65,718	B3
Dortmund 630,609	B3
Duderstadt 23,255	D3
Dudweiler 27,877	B4
Duisburg 591,635	B3
Dülmen 37,013	B3
Düren 87,774	B3
Düsseldorf 664,336	B3
Eberbach 15,834	C4
Ebingen 22,594	C4
Eckernförde 22,938	C1
Ehingen 21,600	C4
Eichstätt 13,080	D4
Einbeck 29,821	C3
Eiserfeld 22,346	C5
Ellwangen 21,994	D4
Elmshorn 41,355	C2
Emden 53,509	B2
Emmendingen 24,722	B4
Emmerich 29,411	B3
Emsdetten 30,195	B2
Erlangen 100,671	D4
Eschwege 24,882	C3
Eschweiler 53,603	B3
Espelkamp 22,670	C2
Essen 677,568	B3
Esslingen am Neckar 95,298	C4
Ettlingen 35,159	C4
Euskirchen 43,558	B3
Eutin 17,701	D1
Fellbach 42,501	C4
Flensburg 93,213	C1
Forchheim 23,430	D4
Frankenberg-Eder 15,337	C3
Frankenthal 43,684	C4
Frankfurt am Main 636,157	C3
Frechen 41,453	B3
Freiburg im Breisgau 175,371	B4
Freising 31,563	D4
Freudenstadt 19,454	C4
Friedberg 24,082	C3
Friedrichshafen 51,544	C5
Fritzlar 15,079	C3
Fulda 58,916	C3
Fürstenfeldbruck 27,194	D4
Fürth 101,639	D4
Füssen 10,506	D5
Gaggenau 28,846	C4
Garbsen 56,337	C2
Garmisch-Partenkirchen 26,831	D5
Gatow	E4
Geesthacht 24,745	D2
Geislingen an der Steige 28,693	C4
Geldern 24,062	B3
Gelnhausen 17,889	C3
Gelsenkirchen 322,584	B3
Georgsmarienhütte 30,259	B2
Geretsried 17,330	D5
Germersheim 12,041	C4
Gerolstein 6,857	B3
Gersthofen 16,857	D4
Gevelsberg 33,650	B3
Gifhorn 31,635	D2
Glückstadt 12,159	C2
Goch 28,213	B3
Göggingen 15,980	D4
Göppingen 54,365	C4
Goslar 53,957	D3
Göttingen 123,797	C3
Greven 27,479	B2
Grevenbroich 56,392	B3
Griesheim 18,548	C4
Gronau 40,527	B2
Gummersbach 49,316	B3
Günzburg 13,528	D4
Gunzenhausen 13,565	D4
Gütersloh 77,128	C3
Hagen 229,224	B3
Haltern 29,750	B3
Hamburg 1,717,383	D2
Hameln 61,063	C2
Hamm 172,210	B3
Hammelburg 12,350	C3
Hanau 86,676	C3
Hannover 552,955	C2
Harburg-Wilhelmsburg	D2
Hassloch 17,752	C4
Haunstetten 21,810	D4
Hechingen 15,926	C4
Heide 21,918	C1
Heidenheim 129,368	D4
Heidenheim an der Brenz 49,943	D4
Heilbronn 113,177	C4
Helmstedt 28,095	D2
Hennef 27,815	B3
Herford 64,385	C2
Herne 190,561	B3
Herten 69,842	B3
Hildesheim 105,290	D2
Hockenheim 16,890	C4
Hof 54,357	D3
Hofgeismar 13,380	C3
Holzminden 23,650	C3
Homburg 41,861	B4
Horn-Bad Meinberg 16,927	C3
Höxter 32,759	C3
Hückelhoven 34,865	B3
Hückeswagen 11,873	B3
Hürth 51,692	B3
Husum 24,984	C1
Hüttental 38,272	C3
Ibbenbüren 42,202	B2
Idar-Oberstein 37,179	B4
Immenstadt im Allgäu 13,720	D5
Ingolstadt 88,500	D4
Iserlohn 96,174	B3
Isny im Allgäu 12,367	D5
Itzehoe 35,077	C2
Jever 12,096	B2
Jülich 31,564	B3
Kaiserslautern 100,886	B4
Karlsruhe 280,448	C4
Kassel 205,534	C3
Kaufbeuren 42,224	D5
Kehl 29,861	B4
Kelheim 11,996	D4
Kempten 56,944	D5
Kevelaer 20,971	B3
Kiel 262,164	D1
Kirchheim unter Teck 31,666	C4
Kitzingen 19,116	D4
Kleve 44,043	B3
Koblenz 118,394	B3
Köln (Cologne) 1,013,771	B3
Königswinter 34,586	B3
Konstanz 70,152	C5
Korbach 22,998	C3
Kornwestheim 27,771	C4
Krefeld 228,463	B3
Kreuztal 30,473	C3
Kulmbach 25,711	D3
Lage 31,724	C3
Lahnstein 19,725	B3
Lahr 35,570	B4
Lampertheim 31,993	C4
Landau in der Pfalz 37,661	C4
Landsberg am Lech 15,862	D4
Landshut 55,858	D4
Langen 30,473	C4
Langenhagen 47,092	C2
Lauenburg an der Elbe 11,077	D2
Lauf an der Pegnitz 19,443	D4
Lauingen 8,778	D4
Lauterbach 15,007	C3
Leer 32,785	B2
Lehrte 38,272	D2
Lemgo 39,664	C2
Lengerich 20,836	B2
Leverkusen 165,947	B3
Lichtenfels 13,719	D3
Limburg an der Lahn 28,606	C3
Lindau 23,930	C5

(continued on following page)

Topography

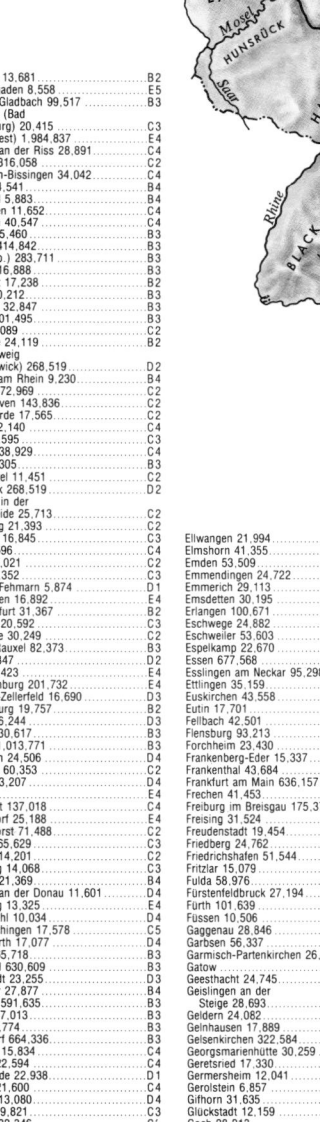

0 50 100 MI.
0 50 100 KM.

Below Sea Level	100 m. 328 ft.	200 m. 656 ft.	500 m. 1,640 ft.	1,000 m. 3,281 ft.	2,000 m. 6,562 ft.	5,000 m. 16,404 ft.

Germany Before World War I 1871-1914

Germany Between Wars 1919-1937

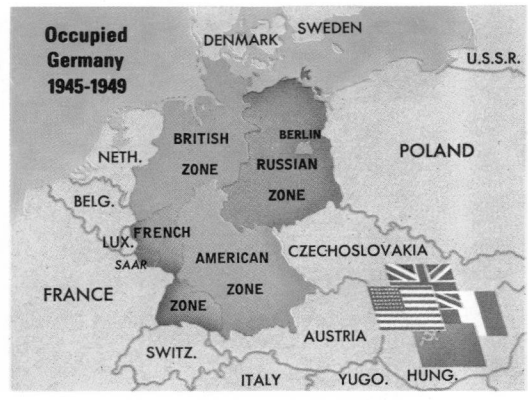

Occupied Germany 1945-1949

Agriculture, Industry and Resources

DOMINANT LAND USE

- Wheat, Sugar Beets
- Cereals (chiefly rye, oats, barley)
- Potatoes, Rye
- Dairy, Livestock
- Mixed Cereals, Dairy
- Truck Farming
- Grapes, Fruit
- Forests

MAJOR MINERAL OCCURRENCES

Ag	Silver	K	Potash
Ba	Barite	Lg	Lignite
C	Coal	Na	Salt
Cu	Copper	O	Petroleum
Fe	Iron Ore	Pb	Lead
G	Natural Gas	U	Uranium
Gr	Graphite	Zn	Zinc

⚡ Water Power

▨ Major Industrial Areas

AREA 15,892 sq. mi. (41,160 sq. km.)
POPULATION 14,227,000
CAPITALS The Hague, Amsterdam
LARGEST CITY Amsterdam
HIGHEST POINT Vaalserberg 1,056 ft. (322 m.)
MONETARY UNIT guilder (florin)
MAJOR LANGUAGE Dutch
MAJOR RELIGIONS Protestantism, Roman Catholicism

AREA 11,781 sq. mi. (30,513 sq. km.)
POPULATION 9,855,110
CAPITAL Brussels
LARGEST CITY Brussels (greater)
HIGHEST POINT Botrange 2,277 ft. (694 m.)
MONETARY UNIT Belgian franc
MAJOR LANGUAGES French (Walloon), Flemish
MAJOR RELIGION Roman Catholicism

AREA 999 sq. mi. (2,587 sq. km.)
POPULATION 364,000
CAPITAL Luxembourg
LARGEST CITY Luxembourg
HIGHEST POINT Ardennes Plateau 1,825 ft. (556 m.)
MONETARY UNIT Luxembourg franc
MAJOR LANGUAGES Luxembourgeois (Letzeburgisch), French, German
MAJOR RELIGION Roman Catholicism

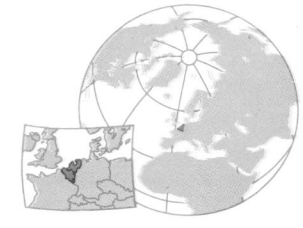

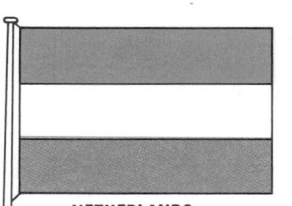

NETHERLANDS

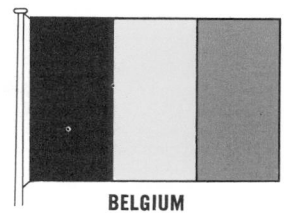

BELGIUM

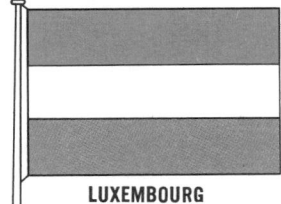

LUXEMBOURG

Agriculture, Industry and Resources

DOMINANT LAND USE

- Dairy, Truck Farming
- Cash Crops, Livestock
- Mixed Cereals, Dairy
- Specialized Horticulture
- Grapes, Wine
- Forests
- Sand Dunes

MAJOR MINERAL OCCURRENCES

C	Coal	Na	Salt
Fe	Iron Ore	O	Petroleum
G	Natural Gas		

///// Major Industrial Areas

Land from the Sea

Reclaimed Land and Dates of Completion
Future Polders
□ =10 Square Miles

For centuries the Dutch have been renowned for the drainage of marshes and the construction of polders, i.e., arable land reclaimed from the sea. Future projects will convert much of the present IJsselmeer to agricultural land.

Topography

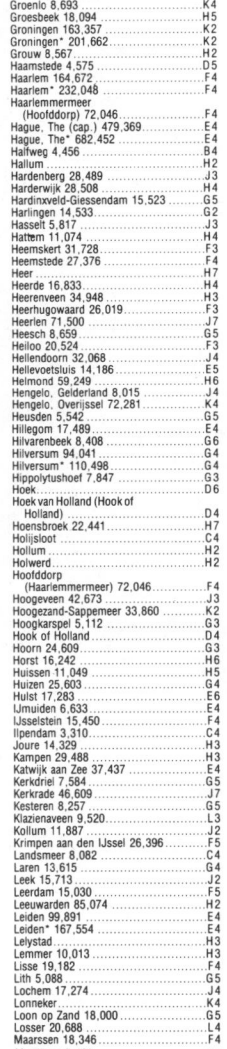

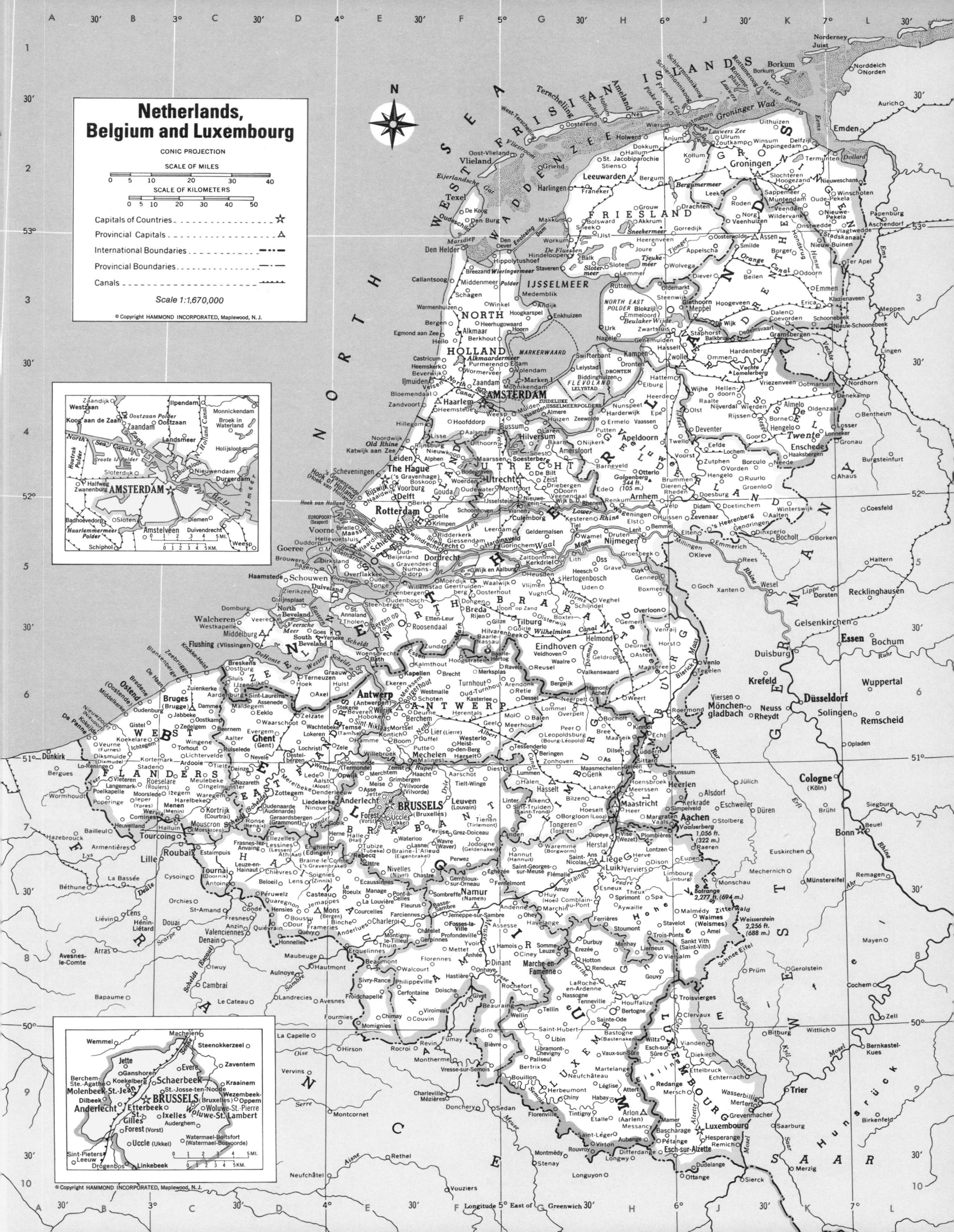

Netherlands, Belgium and Luxembourg

CONIC PROJECTION

SCALE OF MILES

0 5 10   20   30   40

SCALE OF KILOMETERS

0 5 10   20   30   40   50

Capitals of Countries .... ☆
Provincial Capitals .... △
International Boundaries .... ▬ ▪ ▬ ▪
Provincial Boundaries .... ▬ ▪ ▬ ▪
Canals .... ═══

Scale 1:1,670,000

© Copyright HAMMOND INCORPORATED, Maplewood, N.J.

DEPARTMENTS

Ain 376,477 ..... F4
Aisne 533,862 ..... E3
Allier 378,406 ..... E4
Alpes-de-Haute-Provence 112,178 ..... G5
Alpes-Maritimes 816,681 ..... G6
Ardèche 257,065 ..... F5
Ardennes 309,306 ..... F3
Ariège 137,857 ..... D6
Aube 284,823 ..... E3
Aude 272,366 ..... E6
Aveyron 278,306 ..... E5
Bas-Rhin 882,121 ..... G3
Belfort (terr.) 128,125 ..... G4
Bouches-du-Rhône 1,632,974 ..... F6
Calvados 560,967 ..... C3
Cantal 166,549 ..... E5
Charente 337,064 ..... D5
Charente-Maritime 497,859 ..... C5
Cher 316,350 ..... E4
Corrèze 240,363 ..... D5
Corse du Sud 128,634 ..... B6
Côte-d'Or 456,070 ..... F4
Côtes-du-Nord 525,556 ..... B3
Creuse 146,214 ..... D4
Deux-Sèvres 335,829 ..... C4
Dordogne 373,179 ..... D5
Doubs 471,082 ..... G4
Drôme 361,847 ..... F5
Essonne 923,063 ..... E3
Eure 422,952 ..... D3
Eure-et-Loir 335,151 ..... D3
Finistère 804,088 ..... A3
Gard 494,575 ..... F6
Gers 175,366 ..... D6
Gironde 1,061,480 ..... C5
Haute-Corse 161,208 ..... B6
Haute-Garonne 777,431 ..... D6
Haute-Loire 205,491 ..... E5
Haute-Marne 212,304 ..... F3
Hautes-Alpes 97,358 ..... G5
Haute-Saône 222,254 ..... G4
Haute-Savoie 447,795 ..... G5
Hautes-Pyrénées 227,222 ..... D6
Haute-Vienne 352,149 ..... D5
Haut-Rhin 635,209 ..... G4
Hauts-de-Seine 1,438,930 ..... A2
Hérault 648,202 ..... E6
Ille-et-Vilaine 702,199 ..... C3
Indre 248,523 ..... D4
Indre-et-Loire 478,601 ..... D4
Isère 860,339 ..... F5
Jura 238,856 ..... F4
Landes 288,323 ..... C5
Loire 742,396 ..... F5
Loire-Atlantique 934,499 ..... C4
Loiret 490,189 ..... E4
Loir-et-Cher 283,686 ..... D4
Lot 150,778 ..... D5
Lot-et-Garonne 292,616 ..... D5
Lozère 74,825 ..... E5
Maine-et-Loire 629,849 ..... C4
Manche 451,662 ..... C3
Marne 530,399 ..... F3
Mayenne 261,789 ..... C3
Meurthe-et-Moselle 722,588 ..... G3
Meuse 203,904 ..... F3
Morbihan 563,588 ..... B4
Moselle 1,006,373 ..... G3
Nièvre 245,212 ..... E4
Nord 2,510,738 ..... E2
Oise 606,320 ..... E3
Orne 293,523 ..... C3
Paris (city) 2,299,830 ..... B2
Pas-de-Calais 1,403,035 ..... E2
Puy-de-Dôme 580,033 ..... E5
Pyrénées-Atlantiques 534,748 ..... C6
Pyrénées-Orientales 299,506 ..... E6
Rhône 1,429,647 ..... F5
Saône-et-Loire 569,810 ..... F4
Sarthe 490,385 ..... D3
Savoie 305,118 ..... G5
Seine-et-Marne 755,762 ..... E3
Seine-Saint-Denis 1,322,127 ..... C1
Somme 538,462 ..... E3
Tarn 338,024 ..... E6
Tarn-et-Garonne 183,314 ..... D5
Val-de-Marne 1,215,713 ..... C1
Val-d'Oise 840,885 ..... E3
Var 626,093 ..... G6
Vaucluse 390,446 ..... F6
Vendée 450,641 ..... C4
Vienne 357,366 ..... D4
Vosges 397,957 ..... G3
Yonne 299,851 ..... E4
Yvelines 1,082,255 ..... D3

CITIES and TOWNS

Abbeville 25,252 ..... D2
Agde 9,856 ..... E6
Agen 33,763 ..... D5
Aix-en-Provence 91,665 ..... F6
Aix-les-Bains 21,884 ..... G5
Ajaccio 47,065 ..... B7
Albert 11,746 ..... E2
Albertville 16,630 ..... G5
Albi 43,942 ..... E6
Alençon 32,917 ..... D3
Alès 33,315 ..... E5
Ambérieu-en-Bugey 9,294 ..... F5
Amboise 10,498 ..... D4
Amiens 129,453 ..... D3
Ancenis 6,689 ..... C4
Angers 136,603 ..... C4
Angoulême 46,293 ..... D5
Annecy 53,058 ..... G5
Annonay 19,234 ..... F5
Antibes 44,226 ..... G6
Antony 57,450 ..... B2
Apt 9,735 ..... F6
Arcachon 13,856 ..... C5
Argentan 16,063 ..... D3
Argenteuil 101,542 ..... A1
Arles 37,337 ..... F6
Armentières 23,850 ..... E2
Arras 45,804 ..... E2
Asnières-sur-Seine 75,328 ..... A1
Aubagne 26,145 ..... F6
Aubenas 11,967 ..... F5
Aubervilliers 72,859 ..... B1
Auch 18,767 ..... D6
Audincourt 18,570 ..... G4
Aulnay-sous-Bois 77,982 ..... B1
Auray 10,006 ..... B4
Aurignac 744 ..... D6
Aurillac 29,458 ..... E5
Autun 19,441 ..... F4
Auxerre 36,039 ..... E4
Auxonne 6,414 ..... F4
Avallon 8,518 ..... E4
Avignon 73,482 ..... F6
Avion 22,860 ..... E2
Avranches 10,128 ..... C3
Ax-les-Thermes 1,456 ..... D6
Bagnères-de-Bigorre 9,080 ..... D6
Bagnolet 35,858 ..... B2
Bagnols-sur-Cèze 13,111 ..... F5
Barbizon 1,189 ..... E3
Barcelonnette 2,523 ..... G5
Barfleur 701 ..... C3
Bar-le-Duc 19,188 ..... F3
Bar-sur-Aube 7,227 ..... F3
Bastia 45,387 ..... B6
Bayeux 13,381 ..... C3
Bayonne 41,281 ..... C6
Beaucaire 10,189 ..... F6
Beaune 16,386 ..... F4
Beauvais 53,493 ..... E3
Belfort 54,469 ..... G4
Belley 6,612 ..... F5
Berck 14,104 ..... D2
Bergerac 25,488 ..... D5
Bernay 9,928 ..... D3
Besançon 119,803 ..... G4
Béthune 26,208 ..... E2
Béziers 79,213 ..... E6
Biarritz 27,453 ..... C6
Blois 49,134 ..... D4
Bobigny 43,041 ..... B1
Bogny-sur-Meuse 6,845 ..... F3
Bolbec 12,347 ..... D3
Bondy 48,285 ..... B1
Bonneville 6,717 ..... G4
Bordeaux 220,830 ..... C5
Boulogne-Billancourt 103,527 ..... A2
Boulogne-sur-Mer 48,309 ..... D2
Bourg-en-Bresse 40,052 ..... F4
Bourges 75,200 ..... E4
Bourgoin-Jallieu 18,504 ..... F5
Bressuire 9,778 ..... C4
Brest 163,940 ..... A3
Briançon 8,523 ..... G5

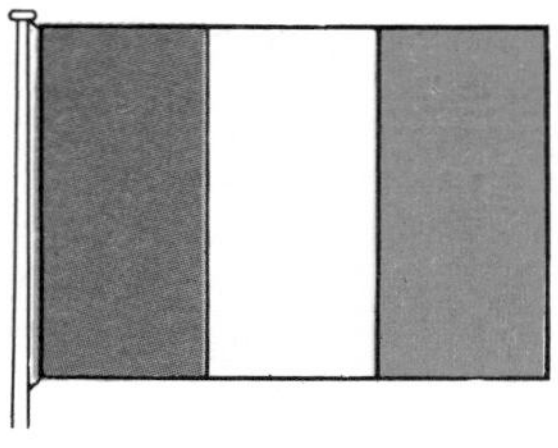

AREA 210,038 sq. mi. (543,998 sq. km.)
POPULATION 53,788,000
CAPITAL Paris
LARGEST CITY Paris
HIGHEST POINT Mont Blanc 15,771 ft. (4,807 m.)
MONETARY UNIT franc
MAJOR LANGUAGE French
MAJOR RELIGION Roman Catholicism

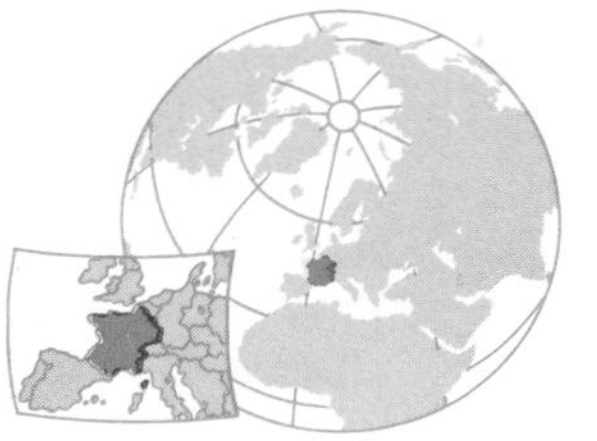

Brignoles 8,784 ..... G6
Brioude 7,756 ..... E5
Brive-la-Gaillarde 49,276 ..... D5
Bruay-en-Artois 25,544 ..... E2
Caen 116,987 ..... C3
Cahors 19,288 ..... D5
Calais 73,009 ..... D2
Caluire-et-Cuire 43,024 ..... F5
Cambrai 38,706 ..... E2
Cannes 70,226 ..... G6
Carcassonne 38,887 ..... D6
Carmaux 11,970 ..... E5
Carpentras 20,169 ..... F5
Castelnaudary 8,947 ..... E6
Castelsarrasin 6,562 ..... D6
Castres 41,037 ..... E6
Cavaillon 17,383 ..... F6
Châlons-sur-Marne 50,870 ..... F3
Chalon-sur-Saône 55,495 ..... F4
Chambéry 52,286 ..... F5
Chambord 166 ..... D4
Chamonix-Mont-Blanc 6,246 ..... G5
Champigny-sur-Marne 80,189 ..... C2
Chantilly 10,517 ..... E3
Charenton-le-Pont 20,383 ..... B2
Charleville-Mézières 59,513 ..... F3
Chartres 38,574 ..... D3
Châteaubriant 12,417 ..... C4
Château-du-Loir 5,598 ..... D4
Châteaudun 14,634 ..... D3
Château-Gontier 8,301 ..... C4
Châteauroux 53,166 ..... D4
Château-Thierry 13,379 ..... E3
Châtellerault 33,811 ..... D4
Châtillon 26,562 ..... B2
Châtillon-sur-Seine 7,367 ..... F4
Chatou 26,415 ..... A1
Chaumont 26,568 ..... F3
Chauny 14,324 ..... E3
Chelles 24,192 ..... C1
Cherbourg 31,333 ..... C3
Chinon 5,378 ..... D4
Choisy-le-Roi 38,629 ..... B2
Cholet 49,887 ..... C4
Clamart 52,881 ..... A2
Clermont 7,834 ..... E3
Clermont-Ferrand 153,379 ..... E5
Clichy 47,731 ..... B1
Cluny 4,335 ..... F4
Cluses 12,713 ..... G4
Cognac 21,567 ..... C5
Colmar 58,585 ..... G3
Colombes 83,241 ..... A1
Commentry 8,074 ..... E4
Commercy 6,918 ..... F3
Compiègne 37,009 ..... E3
Concarneau 15,096 ..... A4
Cosne-Cours-sur-Loire 9,768 ..... E4
Coudekerque-Branche 24,702 ..... E2
Coulommiers 11,363 ..... E3
Courbevoie 54,391 ..... A1
Coutances 8,286 ..... C3
Creil 31,893 ..... E3
Crépy-en-Valois 10,661 ..... E3
Créteil 58,665 ..... B2
Cusset 13,672 ..... E4
Dax 18,019 ..... C6
Deauville 5,655 ..... C3
Decazeville 9,318 ..... E5
Decize 6,853 ..... E4
Denain 26,096 ..... E2
Dieppe 25,607 ..... D3

Topography

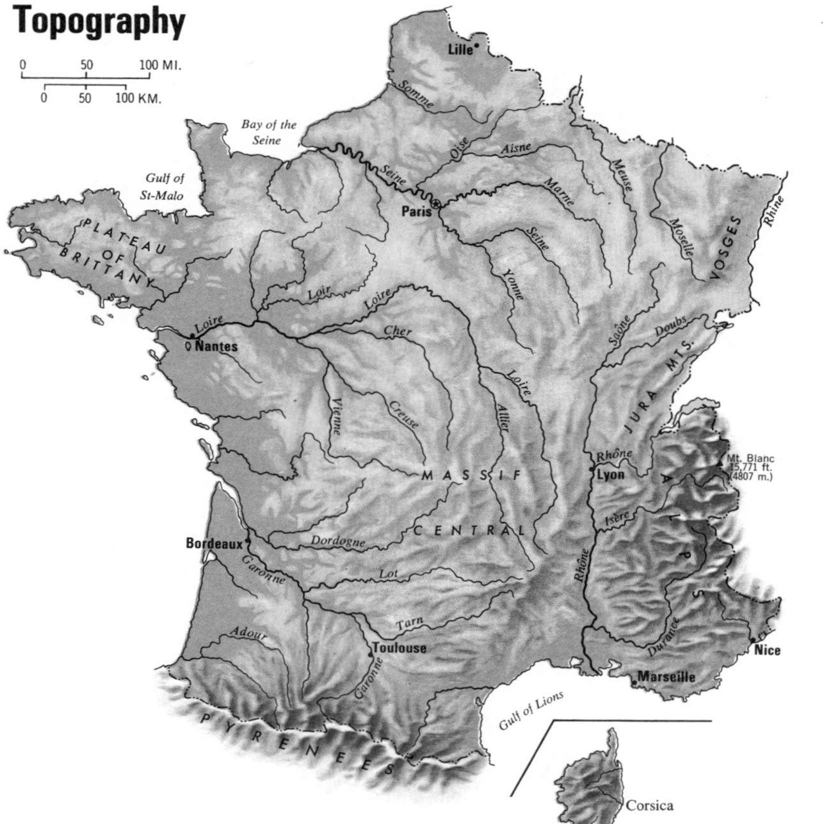

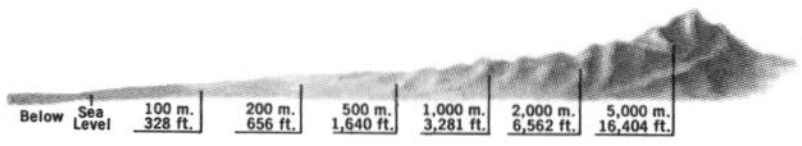

Historic Provinces

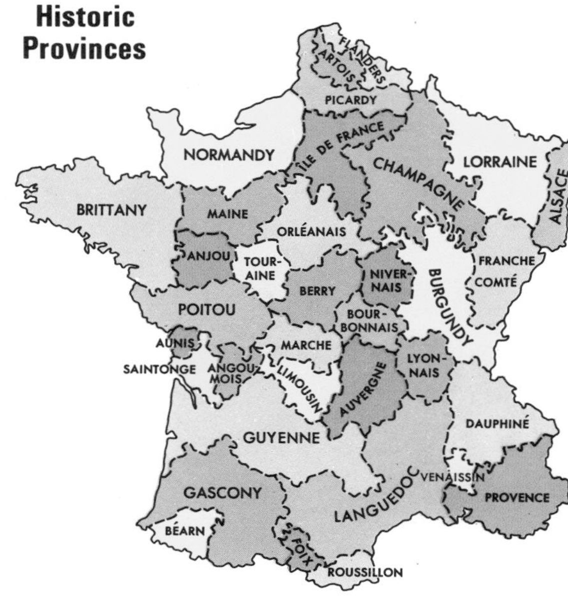

A resident of the city of Caen thinks of himself as a Norman rather than as a citizen of the modern department of Calvados. In spite of the passing of nearly two centuries, the historic provinces which existed before 1790 command the local patriotism of most Frenchmen.

Digne 13,140 ..... G5
Digoin 10,449 ..... F4
Dijon 149,899 ..... F4
Dinan 13,303 ..... B3
Dinard 9,211 ..... B3
Dôle 28,109 ..... F4
Domrémy-la-Pucelle 190 ..... F3
Douai 43,954 ..... E2
Douarnenez 17,851 ..... A3
Doullens 6,806 ..... E2
Draguignan 19,653 ..... G6
Drancy 64,258 ..... B1
Dreux 31,503 ..... D3
Dunkirk (Dunkerque) 78,171 ..... E2
Elbeuf 18,642 ..... D3
Épernay 29,286 ..... E3
Épinal 39,000 ..... G3
Épinay-sur-Seine 46,458 ..... B1
Erstein 6,494 ..... G3
Étampes 18,810 ..... E3
Étaples 10,423 ..... D2
Eu 8,349 ..... D3
Évreux 46,181 ..... D3
Évry 15,300 ..... E3
Falaise 8,133 ..... C3
Fécamp 20,835 ..... D3
Figeac 8,675 ..... D5
Firminy 23,776 ..... F5
Flers 18,590 ..... C3
Foix 9,569 ..... D6
Fontainebleau 16,436 ..... E3
Fontenay-le-Comte 12,301 ..... C4
Fontenay-sous-Bois 46,200 ..... C2
Forbach 24,812 ..... G3
Fougères 26,260 ..... C3
Fourmies 15,318 ..... F2
Fréjus 27,805 ..... G6
Gagny 36,714 ..... C1
Gaillac 7,653 ..... D6
Gap 24,962 ..... G5
Gardanne 8,175 ..... F6
Gennevillers 50,154 ..... B1
Gentilly 16,843 ..... B2
Gex 3,959 ..... G4
Gien 13,817 ..... E4
Gif 10,866 ..... E3
Gisors 7,591 ..... D3
Givet 7,787 ..... F2
Givors 19,356 ..... F5
Granville 12,869 ..... C3
Grasse 24,260 ..... G6
Graulhet 11,099 ..... E6
Gray 8,718 ..... F4
Grenoble 165,431 ..... F5
Guebwiller 10,477 ..... G4
Guéret 14,418 ..... D4
Guingamp 9,269 ..... B3
Guise 6,642 ..... E3
Haguenau 23,023 ..... G3
Harfleur 9,857 ..... D3
Hautmont 19,130 ..... F2
Hayange 8,479 ..... F3
Hazebrouck 18,867 ..... E2
Hendaye 9,404 ..... C6
Hénin-Beaumont 26,296 ..... E2
Hennebont 8,978 ..... B4
Héricourt 8,481 ..... G4
Hirson 11,909 ..... F3
Honfleur 8,995 ..... D3
Hyères 29,366 ..... G6
Issoire 13,560 ..... E5
Issoudun 15,065 ..... D4
Issy-les-Moulineaux 47,355 ..... A2
Istres 10,127 ..... F6
Ivry-sur-Seine 62,804 ..... B2
Joigny 10,825 ..... E3
La Baule-Escoublac 13,854 ..... B4
La Ciotat 29,290 ..... F6
La Courneuve 37,917 ..... B1
La Flèche 12,743 ..... C4
La Grand-Combe 9,406 ..... E5
L'Aigle 9,198 ..... D3
Landerneau 13,983 ..... B3
Langres 10,745 ..... F4
Lannion 13,692 ..... B3
Laon 27,420 ..... E3
La Pallice C4
La Rochelle 72,936 ..... C4
La Roche-sur-Yon 40,789 ..... C4
La Seyne-sur-Mer 50,059 ..... F6
Laval 50,734 ..... C3
Lavelanet 9,278 ..... E6
Le Blanc 7,431 ..... D4
Le Blanc-Mesnil 49,062 ..... B1
Le Bourget 10,520 ..... B1
Le Cateau 8,680 ..... E2
Le Chesnay 24,590 ..... A2
Le Creusot 31,643 ..... F4
Le Havre 216,917 ..... C3
Le Mans 150,289 ..... C3
Lens 39,973 ..... E2
Le Puy 24,793 ..... F5
Les Andelys 7,524 ..... D3
Les Sables-d'Olonne 17,157 ..... B4
Le Teil 7,993 ..... F5
Le Tréport 6,463 ..... D2
Levallois-Perret 52,460 ..... A1
Lézignan-Corbières 6,929 ..... E6
Libourne 21,265 ..... C5
Liévin 33,040 ..... E2
Lille 171,010 ..... E2
Limoges 136,059 ..... D5
Limoux 9,595 ..... E6
Lisieux 24,972 ..... D3
Livry-Gargan 32,879 ..... C1
Lodève 7,131 ..... E6
Longwy 20,107 ..... F3
Lons-le-Saunier 20,897 ..... F4
Lorient 68,655 ..... B4
Loudéac 7,173 ..... B3
Loudun 7,060 ..... D4
Lourdes 17,685 ..... C6
Louviers 17,919 ..... D3
Luçon 8,834 ..... C4
Lunel 12,392 ..... E6
Lunéville 22,438 ..... G3
Lure 8,538 ..... G4
Luxeuil-les-Bains 10,061 ..... G4
Lyon 454,265 ..... F5
Mâcon 39,130 ..... F4
Maisons-Alfort 53,963 ..... B2
Maisons-Laffitte 23,465 ..... A1
Malakoff 34,100 ..... A2
Manosque 17,256 ..... G6
Mantes-la-Jolie 42,408 ..... D3
Marmande 13,223 ..... C5
Marseille 901,421 ..... F6
Martigues 26,850 ..... F6
Maubeuge 34,152 ..... F2
Mayenne 11,278 ..... C3
Mazamet 13,148 ..... E6
Meaux 41,831 ..... E3
Mehun-sur-Yèvre 6,533 ..... E4
Melun 36,913 ..... E3
Mende 10,040 ..... E5
Menton 24,736 ..... G6
Metz 110,939 ..... G3
Meudon 31,294 ..... A2
Millau 20,401 ..... E5
Mimizan 6,826 ..... C5
Mirecourt 7,160 ..... G3
Moissac 7,403 ..... D5
Montargis 18,021 ..... E3
Montauban 35,344 ..... D5
Montbard 7,477 ..... F4
Montbéliard 29,968 ..... G4
Montbrison 9,945 ..... E5
Montceau-les-Mines 28,093 ..... F4
Mont-de-Marsan 24,812 ..... C6
Mont-Dore 2,074 ..... E5
Montélimar 25,422 ..... F5
Montfort 2,701 ..... C3
Montigny-les-Metz 24,208 ..... G3
Montluçon 56,337 ..... E4
Montmédy 1,859 ..... F3
Montpellier 178,136 ..... E6
Montreuil,
Seine-Saint-Denis 96,441 ..... B2
Montrouge 40,189 ..... B2
Mont-Saint-Michel 88 ..... C3
Morlaix 15,919 ..... B3
Morteau 6,515 ..... G4
Moulins 25,856 ..... E4
Moyeuvre-Grande 12,448 ..... G3
Mulhouse 116,494 ..... G4
Muret 13,041 ..... D6
Nancy 106,906 ..... G3
Nanterre 94,441 ..... A1
Nantes 252,537 ..... C4
Narbonne 36,525 ..... E6
Nemours 11,159 ..... E3
Neufchâteau 8,582 ..... F3
Neuilly-sur-Seine 65,941 ..... A1
Nevers 45,122 ..... E4
Nice 331,002 ..... G6
Nîmes 123,914 ..... F6
Niort 59,297 ..... C4
Nogent-le-Rotrou 12,284 ..... D3
Noisy-le-Sec 37,674 ..... B1
Noyon 13,784 ..... E3
Oloron-Sainte-Marie 11,616 ..... C6
Orange 19,847 ..... F5
Orléans 88,503 ..... D3
Orly 26,090 ..... B2
Orthez 9,639 ..... C6
Oullins 27,731 ..... F5
Oyonnax 22,548 ..... F4
Pamiers 12,906 ..... D6
Pantin 42,651 ..... B1
Paray-le-Monial 11,523 ..... F4
Paris (cap.) 2,291,554 ..... B2
Parthenay 12,549 ..... C4
Pau 81,560 ..... C6
Périgueux 34,779 ..... D5
Péronne 8,358 ..... E3
Perpignan 101,198 ..... E6
Pessac 50,333 ..... C5
Pézenas 6,768 ..... E6
Pithiviers 9,976 ..... E3
Poitiers 78,739 ..... D4
Pont-à-Mousson 14,461 ..... G3
Pontarlier 17,778 ..... G4
Pontivy 9,478 ..... B3
Pont-l'Abbe 6,618 ..... A4
Pontoise 26,702 ..... E3
Port-de-Bouc 20,448 ..... F6
Port-Saint-Louis-du-Rhône 9,649 ..... F6
Port-Vendres 5,448 ..... E6
Privas 9,385 ..... F5
Provins 12,281 ..... E3
Puteau 35,366 ..... A2
Quimper 50,856 ..... A4
Quimperlé 9,783 ..... B4
Rambouillet 18,446 ..... D3
Redon 9,528 ..... C4
Reims 177,320 ..... E3
Remiremont 10,250 ..... G3
Rennes 194,094 ..... C3

(continued on following page)

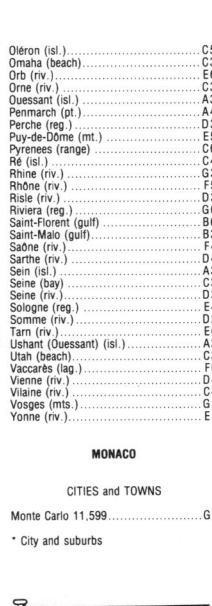

Wine Regions

Climate, soil and variety of grape planted determine the quality of wine. Long, hot and fairly dry summers with cool, humid nights constitute an ideal climate. The nature of the soil is such a determining influence that identical grapes planted in Bordeaux, Burgundy and Champagne, will yield wines of widely different types.

MONACO

AREA 368 acres (149 hectares)
POPULATION 25,029

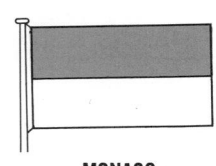

Agriculture, Industry and Resources

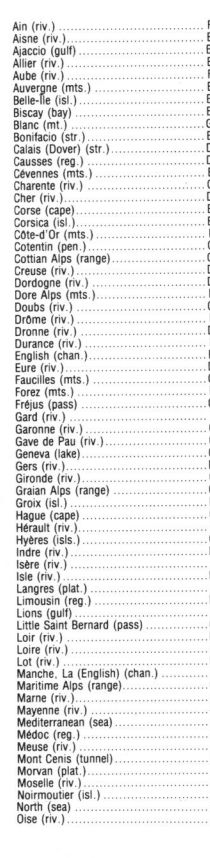

DOMINANT LAND USE

- Cereals (chiefly wheat)
- Cereals (chiefly rye, oats, barley)
- Dairy
- Pasture Livestock
- Truck Farming, Horticulture
- Grapes, Wine
- Forests

MAJOR MINERAL OCCURRENCES

Ab	Asbestos	Na	Salt
Al	Bauxite	O	Petroleum
C	Coal	Pb	Lead
F	Fluorspar	U	Uranium
Fe	Iron Ore	W	Tungsten
G	Natural Gas	Zn	Zinc
K	Potash		

- ⚡ Water Power
- ▨ Major Industrial Areas

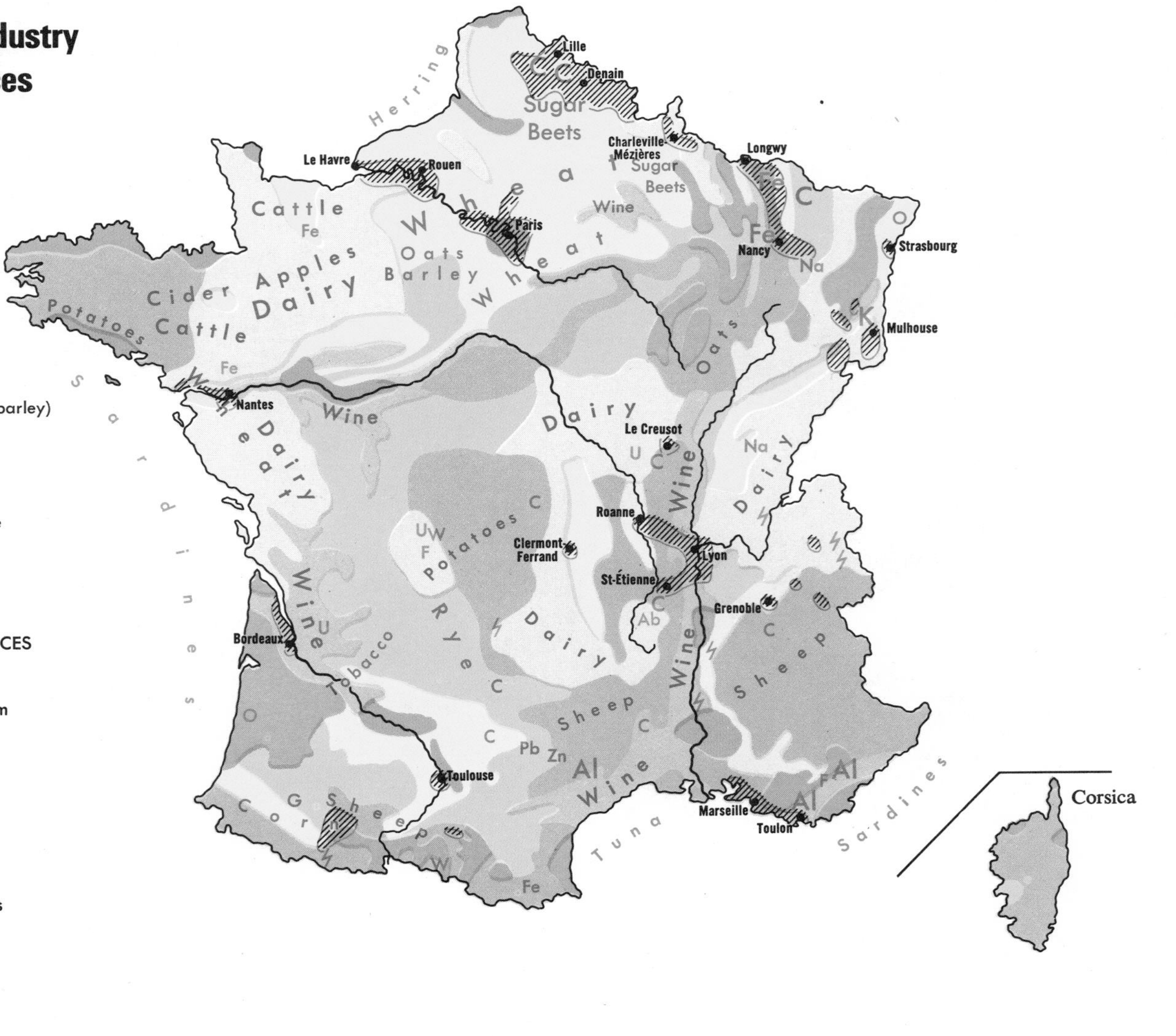

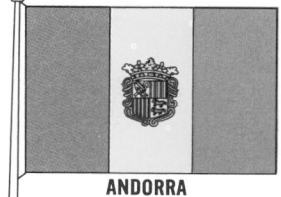

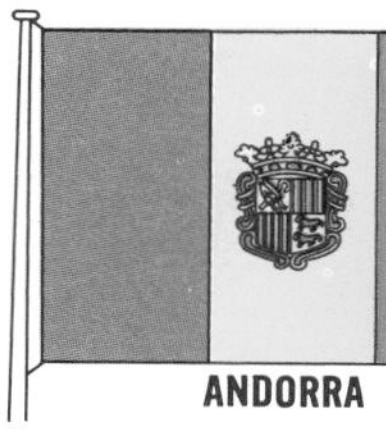
ANDORRA

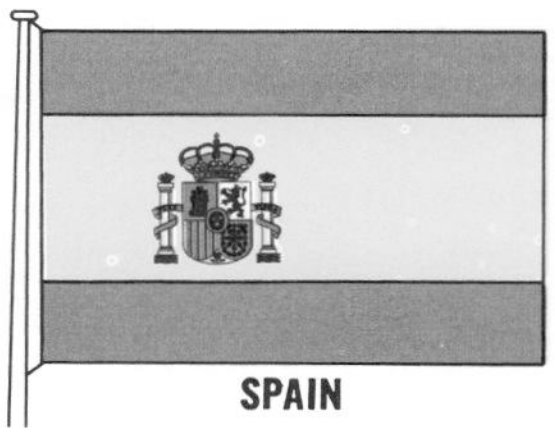
SPAIN

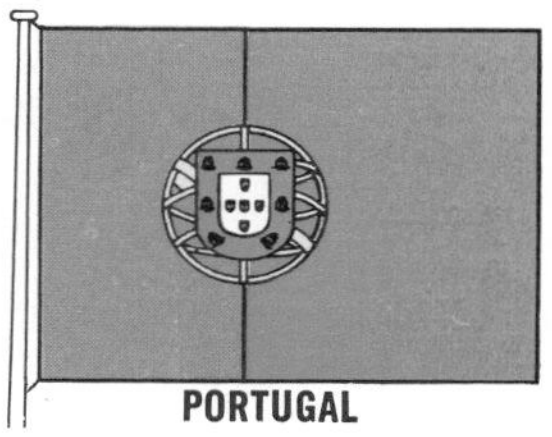
PORTUGAL

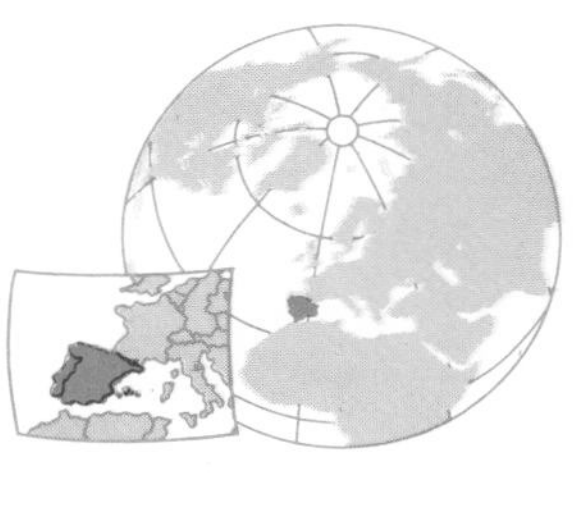

SPAIN

AREA 194,881 sq. mi. (504,742 sq. km.)
POPULATION 37,430,000
CAPITAL Madrid
LARGEST CITY Madrid
HIGHEST POINT Pico de Teide 12,172 ft. (3,710 m.) (Canary Is.); Mulhacén 11,411 ft. (3,478 m.) (mainland)
MONETARY UNIT peseta
MAJOR LANGUAGES Spanish, Catalan, Basque, Galician, Valencian
MAJOR RELIGION Roman Catholicism

ANDORRA

AREA 188 sq. mi. (487 sq. km.)
POPULATION 31,000
CAPITAL Andorra la Vella
MONETARY UNITS French franc, Spanish peseta
MAJOR LANGUAGE Catalan
MAJOR RELIGION Roman Catholicism

PORTUGAL

AREA 35,549 sq. mi. (92,072 sq. km.)
POPULATION 9,933,000
CAPITAL Lisbon
LARGEST CITY Lisbon
HIGHEST POINT Malhão da Estrela 6,532 ft. (1,991 m.)
MONETARY UNIT escudo
MAJOR LANGUAGE Portuguese
MAJOR RELIGION Roman Catholicism

GIBRALTAR

AREA 2.28 sq. mi. (5.91 sq. km.)
POPULATION 29,760
CAPITAL Gibraltar
MONETARY UNIT pound sterling
MAJOR LANGUAGES English, Spanish
MAJOR RELIGION Roman Catholicism

SPAIN

PROVINCES

Álava 204,323	E1
Albacete 335,026	E3
Alicante 920,105	F3
Almería 375,004	E4
Ávila 203,798	D2
Badajoz 687,599	C3
Baleares 558,287	H3
Barcelona 3,929,194	G2
Burgos 358,075	E1
Cáceres 457,777	C3
Cádiz 885,433	D4
Castellón 385,823	G2
Ciudad Real 507,650	D3
Córdoba 724,116	D3
Cuenca 247,158	E2
Gerona 414,397	H1
Granada 733,375	E4
Guadalajara 147,732	E2
Guipúzcoa 631,003	E1
Huelva 397,683	C4
Huesca 222,238	F1
Jaén 661,146	E4
La Coruña 1,004,188	B1
Las Palmas 579,710	C4
León 548,721	C1
Lérida 347,015	G2
Logroño 235,713	E1
Lugo 415,052	C1
Madrid 3,792,561	E2
Málaga 867,330	D4
Murcia 832,313	F4
Navarra 464,867	F1
Orense 413,733	C1
Oviedo 1,045,635	C1
Palencia 198,763	D1
Pontevedra 750,701	B1
Salamanca 371,607	C2
Santa Cruz de Tenerife 590,514	B5
Santander 467,138	D1
Segovia 162,770	D2
Sevilla 1,327,190	D4
Soria 114,956	E2
Tarragona 431,961	G2
Teruel 170,284	F2
Toledo 468,925	D3
Valencia 1,767,327	F3
Valladolid 412,572	D2
Vizcaya 1,043,310	E1
Zamora 251,934	D2
Zaragoza 760,186	F2

CITIES and TOWNS

Adra 10,851	E4
Aguilar 12,893	D4
Aguilas 15,525	F4
Alagón 5,114	F2
Alayor 5,124	J3
Albacete 82,607	F3
Albox 5,072	E4
Alburquerque 7,530	C3
Alcalá de Guadaira 28,781	D4
Alcalá de Henares 59,783	G4
Alcalá de los Gazules 5,262	D4
Alcalá la Real 9,849	E4
Alcanar 5,961	G2
Alcañiz 10,229	F2
Alcantarilla 19,895	F4
Alcaudete 8,557	E4
Alcázar de San Juan 24,620	E3
Alcira 30,493	F3
Alcora 6,711	F2
Alcoy 61,371	F3
Alfaro 8,766	F1
Algeciras 74,754	D4
Algemesí 21,158	F3
Alhama de Granada 6,148	E4
Alhama de Murcia 9,274	F4
Alicante 177,918	F3
Almadén 10,713	D3
Almagro 9,066	E3
Almansa 16,965	F3
Almendralejo 21,929	C3
Almería 104,008	E4
Almodóvar del Campo 7,310	D3
Almonte 9,960	C4
Almuñécar 7,812	E4
Álora 8,209	D4
Altea 7,262	G3
Amposta 11,767	G2
Andorra 6,485	F2
Andújar 25,962	D3
Antequera 28,039	D4
Aracena 5,390	C4
Aranda de Duero 18,183	E2
Aranjuez 28,559	E2
Archena 7,118	F3
Archidona 6,084	D4
Arcos de la Frontera 16,217	D4
Arenas de San Pedro 5,225	D2
Arenys de Mar 8,325	H2
Arévalo 5,807	D2
Argamasilla de Alba 6,192	E3
Arganda 11,876	G4
Arnedo 9,809	E1
Arrecife 21,310	C4
Arroyo de la Luz 8,130	C3
Artá 5,284	H3
Arucas 9,095	B5
Aspe 13,229	F3
Astorga 11,794	C1
Ávila de los Caballeros 30,958	D2
Avilés 67,186	C1
Ayamonte 9,897	C4
Ayora 5,249	F3
Azpeitia 7,835	E1
Azuaga 10,719	D3
Badajoz 80,793	C3
Badalona 162,888	H2
Baena 16,496	D4
Baeza 12,607	E4
Bailén 13,207	E3
Balaguer 11,676	G2
Bañolas 9,807	H1
Baracaldo 108,757	E1
Barbastro 13,243	F1
Barcarrota 5,012	C3
Barcelona 1,741,144	H2
Barcelona‡ 2,000,000	H2
Baza 14,290	E4
Beas de Segura 6,592	E3
Béjar 16,804	D2
Bélmez 5,161	D3
Benavente 11,779	D1
Benicarló 12,831	G2
Berga 11,163	G1
Berja 7,081	E4
Bermeo 16,714	E1
Betanzos 7,283	B1
Bilbao 393,179	E1
Bilbao‡ 450,000	E1
Binéfar 6,821	G2
Blanes 15,810	H2
Borjas Blancas 4,991	G2
Bujalance 8,236	D4
Bullas 8,131	F4
Burgos 118,366	E1
Burriana 21,298	G3
Cabeza del Buey 8,704	D3
Cabra 16,177	D4
Cáceres 53,108	C3
Cádiz 135,743	C4
Calahorra 16,315	E1
Calasparra 7,238	F3
Calatayud 16,524	F2
Calella 9,696	H2
Callosa de Ensarriá 5,701	G3
Calzada de Calatrava 5,751	E3
Campanario 7,722	D3
Campillos 7,014	D4
Campo de Criptana 12,604	E3
Candás 5,517	D1
Candeleda 5,153	D2
Cangas de Narcea 4,826	C1
Caniles 5,099	E4
Caravaca de le Cruz 10,411	E3
Carballo 5,542	B1
Carcagente 18,223	F3
Carmona 22,832	D4
Cartagena 52,312	F4
Caspe 8,766	G2
Cassá de la Selva 5,248	H2
Castellón de la Plana 79,773	G2
Castro del Río 10,087	D4
Castro-Urdiales 8,369	E1
Castuera 8,060	D3
Caudete 7,332	F3
Cazalla de la Sierra 5,382	D4
Cazorla 6,938	E4
Cehegín 9,661	F3
Cervera 5,693	G2
Ceuta 60,639	D5
Chiclana de la Frontera 22,986	C4
Chiva 5,394	F3
Ciempozuelos 9,185	F5
Cieza 22,929	F3
Ciudadela 13,701	H2
Ciudad Real 39,931	D3
Ciudad-Rodrigo 11,694	C2
Cocentaina 8,375	F3
Coín 14,190	D4
Colmenar de Oreja 4,930	G5
Colmenar Viejo 12,886	F4
Constantina 10,227	D4
Consuegra 10,026	E3
Córdoba 216,049	D4
Corella 5,850	F1
Coria 8,083	C3
Coria del Río 18,085	C4
Corral de Almaguer 8,006	E3
Crevillente 15,749	F3
Cuéllar 6,118	D2
Cuenca 33,980	E2
Cullera 15,128	F3
Daimiel 17,710	E3
Denia 14,514	G3
Dolores 5,420	F3
Don Benito 21,351	C3
Dos Hermanas 36,921	D4
Durango 20,403	E1
Écija 27,295	D4
Eibar 36,729	E1
Ejea de los Caballeros 9,766	F1
El Arahal 14,703	D4
Elche 101,271	F3
Elda 41,404	F3
Elizondo 2,516	F1
El Puerto de Santa María 36,451	C4
Espejo 5,925	D4
Estella 10,371	E1
Estepa 9,376	D4
Estepona 18,560	D4
Felanitx 9,100	H3
Ferrol del Caudillo 75,464	B1
Figueras 22,087	H1
Fraga 9,665	G2
Fregenal de la Sierra 6,826	C3
Fuengirola 20,597	D4
Fuente de Cantos 5,967	C3
Fuenterrabiá 2,350	E1
Fuentes de Andalucía 8,257	D4
Gandía 30,702	F3
Gerona 37,095	H2
Getafe 68,680	F4
Gijón 159,806	D1
Granada 185,799	E4
Granollers 30,066	H2
Guadalajara 30,924	E2
Guadix 15,311	E4
Guareña 7,706	C3
Guernica y Luno 12,046	E1
Haro 8,393	E1
Hellín 15,934	F3
Herencia 8,212	E3
Hinojosa del Duque 9,873	D3
Hortaleza	G4
Hospitalet 241,978	H2
Huelma 5,260	E4
Huelva 96,689	C4
Huercal-Overa 5,158	F4
Huesca 33,076	F1
Huéscar 6,384	E4
Ibiza 16,943	G3
Igualada 27,941	G2
Inca 16,930	H3
Irún 38,014	F1
Iscar 5,192	D2
Isla Cristina 11,402	C4
Iznalloz 4,814	E4
Jaca 9,936	F1
Jaén 71,145	E4
Jaraíz de la Vera 6,379	D2
Játiva 20,934	F3
Jávea 6,228	G3
Jerez de la Frontera 112,411	C4
Jerez de los Caballeros 8,607	C3
Jijona 8,117	F3
Jódar 11,973	E4
Jumilla 16,407	F3
La Almunia de Doña Godina 4,835	F2
La Bañeza 8,480	C1
La Bisbal 6,374	H1
La Carolina 13,138	E3
La Coruña 184,372	B1
La Granja (San Ildefonso) 3,198	E2
La Guardia 4,967	B2
La Línea de la Concepción 51,021	D4
La Orotava 8,246	B4
La Palma del Condado 9,256	C4
La Puebla 9,923	H3
La Puebla de Montalbán 6,629	D3
La Rambla 6,525	D4
Laredo 9,114	E1
La Roda 11,460	E3
La Solana 13,894	E3
Las Palmas de Gran Canaria 260,368	B4
Las Pedroñeras 5,846	E3
La Unión 9,998	F4
Lebrija 15,081	D4
Leganés 57,537	F4
León 99,702	D1
Lérida 73,148	G2
Linares 45,330	E3
Liria 11,323	F3
Llerena 5,728	C3
Llivia 801	G1
Llodio 15,587	E1
Lluctmayor 9,630	H3
Logroño 83,117	E1
Loja 11,549	D4
Lora del Río 15,741	D4
Lorca 25,208	F4
Los Santos de Maimona 7,899	C3
Los Yébenes 5,477	E3
Lucena 21,527	D4
Lugo 53,504	C1
Madrid (cap.) 3,146,071	F4
Madrid‡ 3,500,000	F4
Madridejos 9,948	E3
Madroñera 5,397	D3
Mahón 17,802	J3
Málaga 334,988	D4
Málaga‡ 400,000	D4
Malagón 7,732	E3
Malpartida de Cáceres 5,054	C3
Manacor 20,266	H3
Mancha Real 7,547	E4
Manlleu 13,169	H1
Manresa 52,526	G2
Manzanares 15,024	E3
Marbella 19,648	D4
Marchena 16,227	D4
Marín 10,948	B1
Martos 16,395	E4
Mataró 73,129	H2
Medina del Campo 16,345	D2
Medina de Rioseco 4,874	D2
Medina-Sidonia 7,523	D4
Mérida 36,916	C3
Miajadas 8,042	D3
Mieres 22,790	D1
Minas de Ríotinto 3,939	C4
Miranda de Ebro 29,355	E1
Moguér 7,629	C4
Mollerusa 6,685	G2
Monesterio 5,923	C3
Monforte 14,002	C1
Monóvar 9,071	F3
Montehermoso 5,952	C2
Montellano 6,658	D4
Montijo 11,931	C3
Montilla 18,670	D4
Montoro 9,295	D3
Monzón 14,089	G2
Mora 10,523	E3
Moratalla 5,101	E3
Morón de la Frontera 25,662	D4
Mota del Cuervo 5,130	E3
Motril 25,121	E4
Mula 9,168	F3
Munera 5,003	E3
Murcia 102,242	F4
Navalcarnero 6,212	F4
Navalmoral de la Mata 9,650	D3
Nerja 7,413	E4
Nerva 10,830	C4
Novelda 16,867	F3
Nules 9,027	F3
Ocaña 5,603	E3
Oliva 16,717	F3
Oliva de la Frontera 8,560	C3
Olivenza 7,616	C3
Olot 18,062	H1
Olvera 9,825	D4
Onda 13,012	F3
Onteniente 23,685	F3
Orense 63,542	C1
Orihuela 17,610	F3
Osuna 17,384	D4
Oviedo 130,021	C1
Padul 6,377	E4
Palafrugell 10,421	H2
Palamós 7,679	H2
Palencia 58,327	D2
Palma 191,416	H3
Palma del Río 15,075	D4
Pamplona 142,686	F1
Pego 8,861	F3
Peñafiel 4,794	E2
Peñaranda de Bracamonte 6,094	D2
Peñarroya-Pueblonuevo 15,649	D3
Pinos-Puente 7,634	E4
Plasencia 26,897	C2
Pola de Lena 5,760	D1
Pollensa 7,625	H3
Ponferrada 22,838	C1
Pontevedra 27,118	B1
Porcuna 8,169	D4
Port-Bou 2,230	H1
Portugalete 45,589	E1
Posadas 7,245	D4
Pozoblanco 13,280	D3
Pozuelo de Alarcón 14,041	D2
Priego de Córdoba 12,676	D4
Puente-Genil 22,888	D4
Puertollano 50,609	D3
Puerto Real 13,993	D4
Puigcerdá 4,418	G1
Quesada 6,965	E4
Quintana de la Serena 5,171	D3
Quintanar de la Orden 7,764	E3
Reinosa 10,863	D1
Requena 9,836	F3
Reus 47,240	G2
Ripoll 9,283	H1
Ronda 22,094	D4
Roquetas 5,617	G2
Rosas 5,448	H1
Rota 20,021	C4
Rute 8,294	D4
Sabadell 148,223	H2
Sagunto 17,052	F3
Salamanca 125,132	D2
Sallent 7,118	H2
Salobreña 5,961	E4
Salt 5,572	H1
Sama 9,863	D1
San Carlos de la Rápita 8,946	G2
San Clemente 6,016	E3
San Felíu de Guíxols 12,006	H2
San Fernando 59,309	C4
San Ildefonso 3,198	E2

Agriculture, Industry and Resources

DOMINANT LAND USE

- Cereals (chiefly wheat)
- Livestock (chiefly sheep, goats)
- Mixed Cereals, Livestock
- Olives, Fruit
- Grapes, Fruit, Nuts, Mixed Cereals
- Forests
- Nonagricultural Land

MAJOR MINERAL OCCURRENCES

Ag	Silver	Na	Salt
C	Coal	O	Petroleum
Cu	Copper	Pb	Lead
Fe	Iron Ore	Py	Pyrites
G	Natural Gas	Sb	Antimony
Hg	Mercury	Sn	Tin
K	Potash	U	Uranium
Lg	Lignite	W	Tungsten
Mg	Magnesium	Zn	Zinc

Water Power
Major Industrial Areas

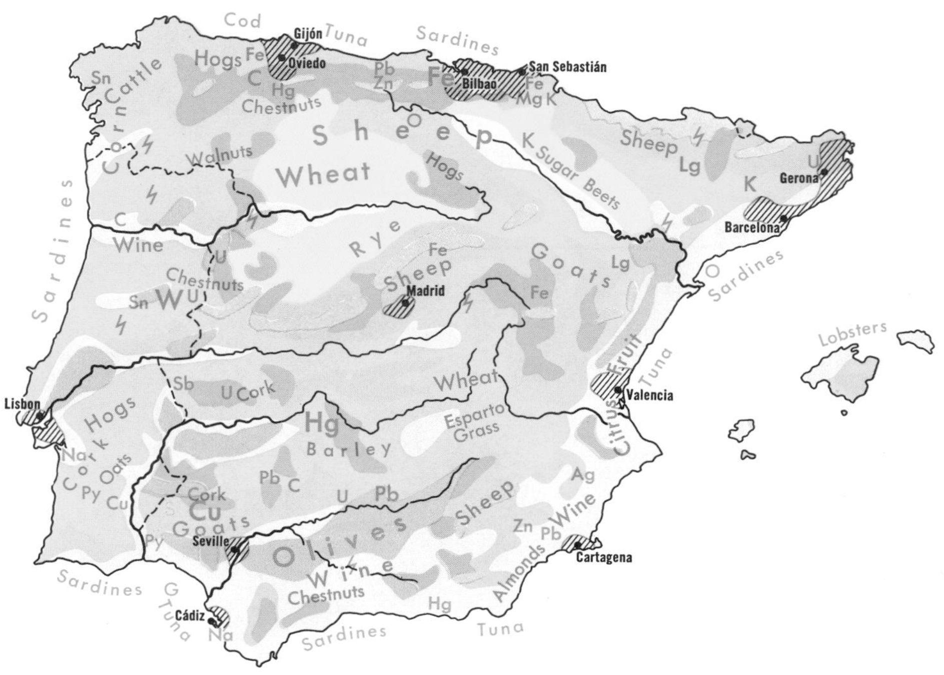

(continued on following page)

Topography

0   50   100 MI.
0   50   100 KM.

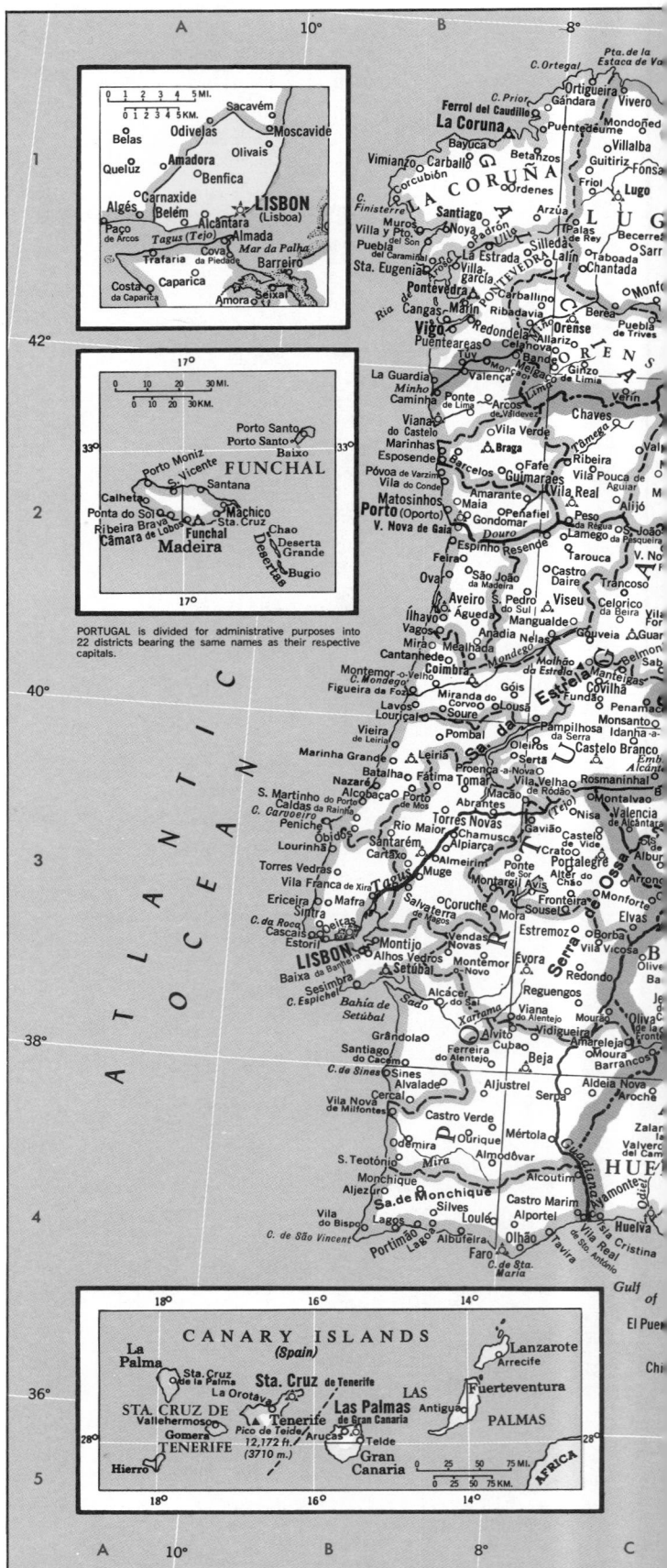

PORTUGAL is divided for administrative purposes into 22 districts bearing the same names as their respective capitals.

Below Sea Level	100 m. 328 ft.	200 m. 656 ft.	500 m. 1,640 ft.	1,000 m. 3,281 ft.	2,000 m. 6,562 ft.	5,000 m. 16,404 ft.

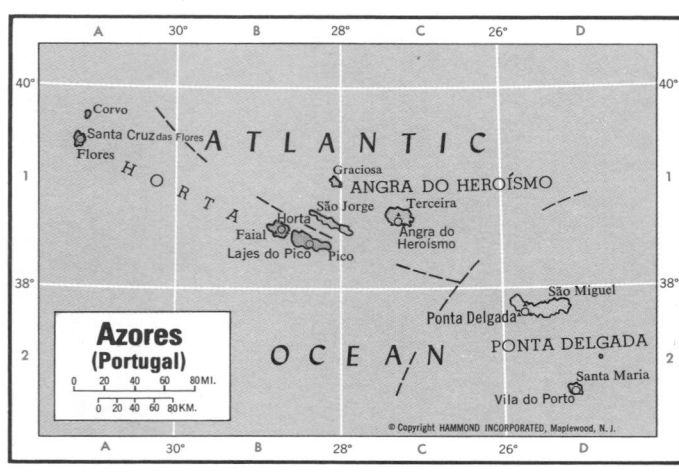

Azores
(Portugal)

0 20 40 60 80 MI.
0 20 40 60 80 KM.

© Copyright HAMMOND INCORPORATED, Maplewood, N.J.

Italy

CONIC PROJECTION

SCALE OF MILES

SCALE OF KILOMETERS

Capitals of Countries	_____☆
Regional Capitals	_____⌖
Provincial Capitals	_____△
International Boundaries	__.__.__
Regional Boundaries	__.__.__

Scale 1:4,710,000

The regions are subdivided into provinces bearing
the same names as their respective capitals, except:

PROVINCE	CAPITAL
MASSA-CARRARA	Massa
PESARO-URBINO	Pesaro

Vatican City

Rome and Environs

© Copyright HAMMOND INCORPORATED, Maplewood, N.J.

VATICAN CITY

AREA 108.7 acres (44 hectares)
POPULATION 728

SAN MARINO

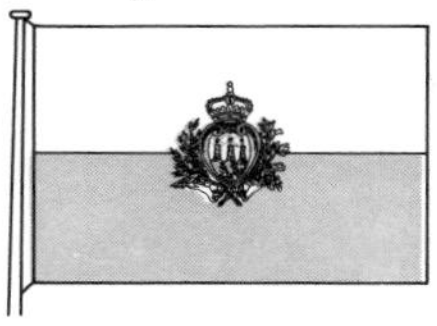

AREA 23.4 sq. mi. (60.6 sq. km.)
POPULATION 19,149

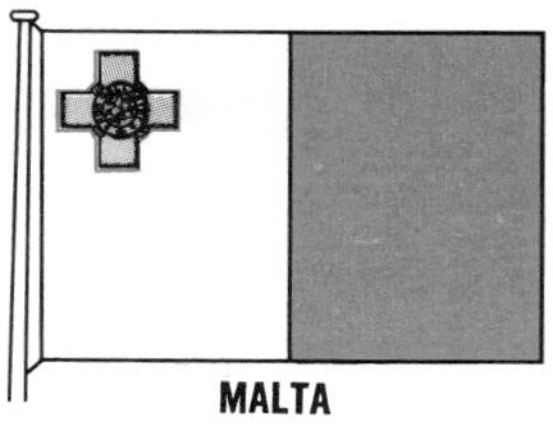

MALTA

AREA 122 sq. mi. (316 sq. km.)
POPULATION 343,970
CAPITAL Valletta
LARGEST CITY Sliema
HIGHEST POINT 787 ft. (240 m.)
MONETARY UNIT Maltese pound
MAJOR LANGUAGES Maltese, English
MAJOR RELIGION Roman Catholicism

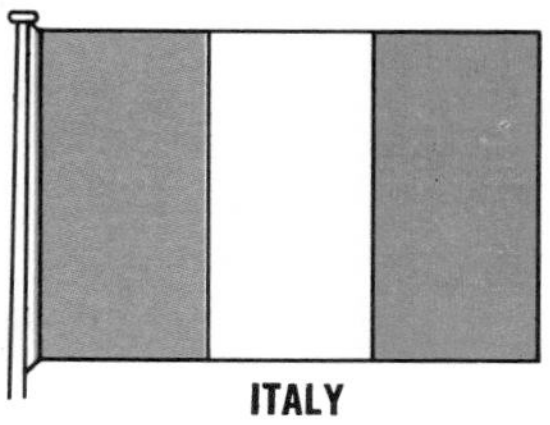

ITALY

AREA 116,303 sq. mi. (301,225 sq. km.)
POPULATION 57,140,000
CAPITAL Rome
LARGEST CITY Rome
HIGHEST POINT Dufourspitze (Mte. Rosa) 15,203 ft. (4,634 m.)
MONETARY UNIT lira
MAJOR LANGUAGE Italian
MAJOR RELIGION Roman Catholicism

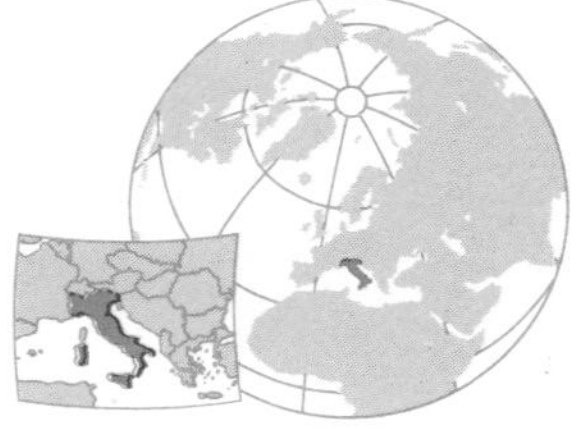

ITALY

REGIONS

Abruzzi 1,166,664 D3
Aosta 109,150 A2
Apulia (Puglia) 3,582,787 F4
Basilicata 603,064 F4
Calabria 1,988,051 F5
Campania 5,059,348 E4
Emilia-Romagna 3,846,755 C2
Friuli-Venezia Giulia 1,213,532 D1
Latium (Lazio) 4,689,482 D3
Liguria 1,853,578 B2
Lombardy 8,543,657 B2
Marche 1,359,907 D3
Molise 319,807 E4
Piedmont 4,432,313 A2
Sardinia 1,473,800 B4
Sicily 4,680,715 D6
Trentino-Alto Adige 841,886 C1
Tuscany 3,473,097 C3
Umbria 775,783 D3
Veneto 2,109,502 D3

PROVINCES

Agrigento 454,045 D6
Alessandria 483,183 B2
Ancona 416,611 D3
Aosta 109,150 A2
Arezzo 306,340 C3
Ascoli Piceno 340,758 D3
Asti 218,547 B2
Avellino 427,509 E4
Bari 1,351,288 F4
Belluno 221,155 D1
Benevento 286,499 E4
Bergamo 829,019 B2
Bologna 918,844 C2
Bolzano-Bozen 414,041 C1
Brescia 957,686 C2
Brindisi 366,027 G4
Cagliari 802,888 B5
Caltanissetta 282,069 D6
Campobasso 227,641 E4
Caserta 677,959 E4
Catania 938,273 E6
Catanzaro 718,069 F5
Chieti 351,567 E3
Como 720,463 B2
Cosenza 691,659 F5
Cremona 334,281 B2
Cuneo 540,504 A2
Enna 202,131 E6
Ferrara 383,639 C2
Florence 1,146,367 C3
Foggia 657,292 E4
Forlì 565,470 D2
Frosinone 422,630 D4
Genoa 1,087,973 B2
Gorizia 142,412 D2
Grosseto 216,315 C3
Imperia 225,127 B3
Isernia 92,166 E4
L'Aquila 293,066 D3
La Spezia 244,435 B2
Latina 376,238 D4
Lecce 696,503 G4
Leghorn 335,265 C3
Lucca 380,356 C3
Macerata 286,155 D3
Mantua 376,892 C2
Massa-Carrara 200,955 C2
Matera 194,629 F4
Messina 654,703 E5
Milan 3,903,685 B2
Modena 553,852 C2
Naples 2,709,929 E4
Novara 496,811 B2
Nuoro 273,021 B4
Padua 762,998 C2
Palermo 1,124,015 D5
Parma 395,497 C2
Pavia 526,389 B2
Perugia 552,936 D3
Pesaro e Urbino 316,383 D3
Pescara 264,981 E3
Piacenza 284,881 B2
Pisa 375,933 C3
Pistoia 254,335 C2
Pordenone 253,906 D2
Potenza 408,435 E4
Ragusa 255,047 E6
Ravenna 351,876 D2
Reggio di Calabria 578,323 E5
Reggio nell'Emilia 392,696 C2
Rieti 143,162 D3
Rome 3,490,377 F6
Rovigo 251,908 C2
Salerno 957,452 E4
Sassari 397,891 B4
Savona 296,043 B2
Siena 257,221 C3
Sondrio 169,149 B1
Syracuse 365,039 E6
Taranto 511,677 F4
Teramo 257,080 D3
Terni 222,847 D3
Trapani 405,393 D5
Trento 427,845 C1
Treviso 668,620 D2
Trieste 300,304 E2
Turin 2,287,016 A2
Udine 516,910 D1
Varese 725,823 B2
Venice 807,251 D2
Vercelli 406,252 B2
Verona 733,595 C2
Vicenza 677,884 C2
Viterbo 257,075 C3

CITIES and TOWNS

Acireale 34,081 E6
Acqui Terme 20,099 B2
Acri 8,150 F5
Adrano 31,988 E6
Adria 11,951 D2
Agira 11,262 E6
Agnone 3,965 E4
Agrigento 40,513 D6
Agropoli 9,413 E4
Alassio 13,512 A2
Alatri 5,710 D4
Alba 23,522 B2
Albano Laziale 15,561 F7
Albenga 13,397 B3
Albino 8,837 B2
Alcamo 41,448 D6
Alessandria 78,644 B2
Alghero 28,454 B4
Altamura 44,879 F4
Amalfi 4,205 E4
Amantea 6,132 E5
Amelia 4,331 D3
Ancona 88,427 D3
Andria 76,405 F4
Anguillara Sabazia 3,241 F6
Anzio 14,966 D4
Aosta 35,053 A2
Aprilia 18,412 D4
Aragona 11,213 D6
Arezzo 56,693 C3
Argenta 6,682 D2
Ariano Irpino 9,796 E4
Ariccia 7,287 F7
Artena 5,034 F7
Ascoli Piceno 43,041 D3
Assisi 4,630 D3
Asti 62,277 B2
Atessa 3,079 E3
Atri 4,686 D3
Augusta 32,501 E6
Avellino 44,750 E4
Aversa 46,536 E4
Avezzano 26,456 D3
Avigliano 5,400 E4
Avola 29,089 E6
Bagheria 32,465 D5
Barcellona Pozzo di Gotto 25,280 E5
Bari 339,110 F4
Barletta 75,116 F4
Bassano del Grappa 33,002 C2
Bellagio 3,258 B2
Belluno 22,180 D1
Benevento 48,523 E4
Bergamo 127,553 B2
Biancavilla 18,743 E6
Biella 46,453 B2
Bisceglie 45,014 F4
Bitonto 39,714 F4
Bitti 4,606 B4
Bologna 493,282 C2
Bolzano (Bolzen) 102,806 C1
Bondeno 7,451 C2
Bonorva 5,232 B4
Bordighera 8,994 A3
Borgo 4,013 C1
Borgomanero 16,655 B2
Bôrgo San Lorenzo 7,699 C2
Bosa 8,045 B4
Boves 3,896 A2
Bra 18,399 A2
Bracciano 7,681 C3
Brescia 189,092 C2
Bressanone 12,261 C1
Brindisi 76,612 G4
Bronte 17,823 E6
Brunico 5,175 D1
Budrio 5,635 C2
Busto Arsizio 72,400 B2
Cagli 4,356 D3
Cagliari 211,015 B5
Caltagirone 34,444 E6
Caltanissetta 52,838 D6
Camaiore 8,578 C3
Camerino 4,644 D3
Campobasso 35,551 E4
Campo Tures 1,325 C1
Canicatti 28,761 E6
Canosa di Puglia 30,263 E4
Cantù 28,617 B2
Capua 13,938 E4
Caravaggio 11,298 B2
Carbonia 23,031 B5
Carini 14,255 D5
Carloforte 6,671 B5
Carmagnola 16,469 A2
Carpi 41,789 C2
Carrara 56,236 C2
Casale Monferrato 35,156 B2
Casalmaggiore 6,374 C2
Cascina-Navacchio 28,263 C3
Caserta 51,621 E4
Cassano allo Ionio 9,661 F5
Cassino 14,747 D4
Castelfranco Veneto 16,042 D2
Castel Gandolfo 2,965 F7
Castellammare del Golfo 13,144 D5
Castellammare di Stabia 64,341 E4
Castel San Pietro Terme 6,985 C2
Castelvetrano 29,167 D6
Castiglion Fiorentino 3,797 C3
Castrovillari 15,207 F5
Catania 403,390 E6
Catanzaro 52,054 F5
Caulonia 3,402 F5
Cava de'Tirreni 33,868 E4
Cavarzere 7,917 D2
Cecina 19,415 C3
Cefalù 11,043 E5
Ceglie Messapico 17,512 F4
Celano 9,531 D3
Cerignola 44,648 E4
Cernobbio 8,026 B2
Cerveteri 5,239 E6
Cesano 2,883 F6
Cesena 49,915 D2
Cesenatico 12,805 D2
Chiari 12,017 C2
Chiavari 29,950 B2
Chieri 27,548 A2
Chieti 31,895 E3
Chioggia 24,044 D2
Chivasso 21,369 A2
Ciampino 36,728 F7
Cittadella 9,321 C2
Città di Castello 18,880 C3
Cittanova 11,045 F5
Cividale del Friuli 8,345 D1
Civitavecchia 41,305 C3
Clusone-Fiorine 6,428 C2
Codroipo 6,117 D2
Colle di Val d'Elsa 8,657 C3
Comacchio 10,437 D2
Comiso 24,508 E6
Como 73,257 B2
Conegliano 28,635 D2
Conversano 16,805 F4
Corato 38,163 F4
Cori 6,829 F7
Corigliano Calabro 14,518 F5
Corleone 11,057 D6
Correggio 11,415 C2
Cortina d'Ampezzo 7,285 D1
Cortona 3,482 C3
Cosenza 94,565 F5
Courmayeur 1,401 A2
Crema 26,061 B2
Cremona 75,988 B2
Crotone 44,081 F5
Cuneo 41,633 A2
Cuorgnè 6,752 A2
Desenzano del Garda 14,624 C2
Diano Marina 6,001 B3
Domodossola 18,562 A1
Dorgali 6,714 B4
Eboli 19,787 E4
Edolo 3,707 C1
Empoli 30,526 C3
Enna 27,351 E6
Este 12,992 C2
Fabriano 18,355 D3
Faenza 36,241 D2
Fano 31,238 D3
Fasano 21,247 F4
Favara 27,940 D6
Feltre 11,806 C1
Fermo 17,521 D3
Ferrandina 8,372 F4
Ferrara 97,507 C2
Fidenza 18,064 B2
Fiesole 3,772 C3
Finale Emilia 7,474 C2
Finale Ligure 11,461 B2
Firenze (Florence) 441,654 C3
Fiumicino 13,180 F7
Florence 441,654 C3
Floridia 16,562 E6
Foggia 136,436 E4
Foligno 26,887 D3
Fondi 16,472 D4
Forlì 83,303 D2
Formia 18,978 D4
Fossano 15,857 A2
Fossombrone 5,882 D3
Francavilla Fontana 30,347 F4
Frascati 14,217 F7
Frosinone 34,066 D4
Gaeta 21,973 D4
Galatina 22,137 G4
Galatone 13,880 F4
Gallarate 43,773 B2
Gallipoli 16,878 F4
Garessio 3,359 A2
Gela 66,845 E6
Gemona 6,863 D1
Genoa 787,011 B2
Genova (Genoa) 787,011 B2
Genzano di Roma 14,147 F7
Giarre 18,233 E6
Gioia del Colle 23,299 F4
Gioiosa Ionica 3,811 F5
Giovinazzo 17,768 F4
Giulianova 17,926 E3
Gorizia 35,912 D2
Gravina in Puglia 32,006 F4
Grosseto 48,309 C3
Grottaferrata 10,639 F7
Grottaglie 23,556 F4
Guardiagrele 4,122 E3
Guastalla 7,639 C2
Gubbio 12,371 D3
Guidonia 8,413 F6
Iglesias 24,472 B5
Imola 42,111 C2
Imperia 37,585 B3
Isernia 12,290 E4
Ivrea 26,530 B2
Jesi 33,011 D3
Ladispoli 6,625 E6
Lagonegro 5,613 E4
La Maddalena 10,405 B4
Lanciano 19,652 E3
Lanusei 5,508 B5
Lanuvio 2,970 F7
L'Aquila 36,233 D3
Larino 5,166 E4
La Spezia 121,254 B2
Latina 53,003 D4
Lauria 4,927 E4
Lavello 11,486 E4
Lecce 80,114 G4
Lecco 53,165 B2
Leghorn 170,369 C3
Legnago 15,534 C2
Lendinara 7,079 C2
Lentini 31,429 E6
Leonforte 16,317 E6
Lerici 5,407 B2
Licata 40,997 D6
Lido di Ostia 61,492 F7
Lido di Venezia 18,794 D2
Lipari 3,886 E5
Livigno 2,135 C1
Livorno (Leghorn) 170,369 C3
Lodi 42,489 B2
Lonigo 6,368 C2
Lucca 54,280 C3
Lucera 29,355 E4
Lugo 19,497 D2
Macerata 33,470 D3
Macomer 9,433 B4
Maglie 13,326 G4
Manduria 25,194 F4
Manfredonia 44,463 F4
Mantua 59,529 C2
Marino 12,135 F7
Marsala 34,150 D6
Marsciano 5,372 D3
Martina Franca 31,811 F4
Massa 56,591 C2
Massafra 22,610 F4
Massa Marittima 6,438 C3
Matera 43,026 F4
Mazara del Vallo 37,441 D6
Mazzarino 14,981 E6
Melfi 13,355 E4
Menfi 12,386 D6
Merano 30,951 C1
Mesagne 26,955 G4
Messina 203,937 E5
Mestre 184,818 D2
Milan 1,724,557 B2
Milazzo 18,576 E5
Minturno 2,428 D4
Mirandola 11,551 C2
Mira Taglio 10,194 D2
Mistretta 6,631 E6
Modena 149,029 C2
Modica 31,074 E6
Mola di Bari 23,778 F4
Molfetta 63,250 F4
Moncalieri 49,953 A2
Mondovì Breo 12,524 A2
Monfalcone 29,589 D2
Monopoli 29,776 F4
Monreale 19,348 D5
Monselice 9,047 C2
Montalto Uffugo 3,173 E5
Montebelluna 9,573 D2
Montefiascone 6,885 D3
Montepulciano 4,069 C3
Monterotondo 15,869 F6
Monte Sant'Angelo 17,756 F4
Montevarchi 16,849 C3
Monza 110,735 B2
Mortara 13,929 B2
Naples 1,214,775 E4
Nardò 24,142 F4
Narni 6,213 D3
Naro 13,171 D6
Nettuno 20,927 D4
Nicastro 27,206 F5
Nicosia 13,982 E6
Niscemi 23,925 E6
Nizza Monferrato 7,532 B2
Nocera Inferiore 44,415 E4
Noto 21,606 E6
Novara 92,634 B2
Novi Ligure 29,944 B2
Nuoro 30,551 B4
Olbia 20,998 B4
Oliena 7,030 B4
Orbetello 6,884 C3
Oristano 20,966 B5
Ortona 11,966 E3
Orvieto 8,813 D3
Osimo 12,034 D3
Ostia Antica 2,583 F7
Ostuni 27,241 F4
Otranto 3,707 G4
Ozieri 9,149 B4
Pachino 20,427 E6
Padua 210,950 C2
Palazzolo Acreide 8,981 E6
Palermo 556,374 D5
Palestrina 9,239 F7
Palma di Montechiaro 22,381 D6
Palmi 14,405 E5
Palombara Sabina 5,292 F6
Pantelleria 3,116 C6
Paola 11,330 E5
Parma 151,967 C2
Partanna 10,303 D6
Partinico 25,447 D6
Paterno 41,504 E6
Patti 7,500 E5
Pavia 80,639 B2
Pavullo nel Frignano 5,026 C2
Penne 5,889 D3
Pergine Valsugana 6,248 C1
Pergola 3,866 D3
Perugia 65,975 D3
Pesaro 72,104 D3
Pescara 125,391 E3
Pescia 9,918 C3
Piacenza 100,001 B2
Piazza Armerina 21,754 E6
Pietrasanta 6,620 B3
Pinerolo 33,935 A2
Piombino 35,641 C3
Piove di Sacco 7,035 C2
Pisa 91,156 C3
Pisticci 11,239 F4
Pistoia 55,403 C2
Poggibonsi 21,271 C3
Pomezia 11,915 F7
Pont Canavese 4,075 A2
Pontecorvo 5,986 D4
Pontinia 3,166 D4
Pontremoli 5,222 B2
Popoli 5,372 E3
Pordenone 43,230 D2
Portocivitanova 25,773 D3
Porto Empedocle 15,986 D6
Portoferraio 7,579 C3
Portofino 720 B2
Portogruaro 12,258 D2
Portomaggiore 6,343 C2
Porto Recanati 5,389 D3
Porto Torres 15,422 B4
Potenza 46,869 E4
Pozzallo 12,199 E6
Pozzuoli 53,546 D4
Prato 108,385 C3
Prima Porta 11,393 F6
Priverno 9,950 D4
Putignano 19,290 F4
Quartu Sant'Elena 29,715 B5
Ragusa 55,751 E6
Rapallo 22,272 B2
Ravenna 75,153 D2
Recanati 10,176 D3
Reggio di Calabria 110,291 E5
Reggio nell'Emilia 102,337 C2
Rho 39,206 B2
Riesi 15,855 E6
Rieti 26,775 D3
Rimini 101,579 D2
Rionero in Vulture 11,230 E4
Riva del Garda 8,513 C2
Roccastrada 2,629 C3
Rome (cap.) 2,535,018 F6
Ronciglione 5,900 C3
Rossano 12,119 F5
Rovereto 26,827 C2
Rovigo 31,124 C2
Ruvo di Puglia 23,133 F4

(continued on following page)

Topography

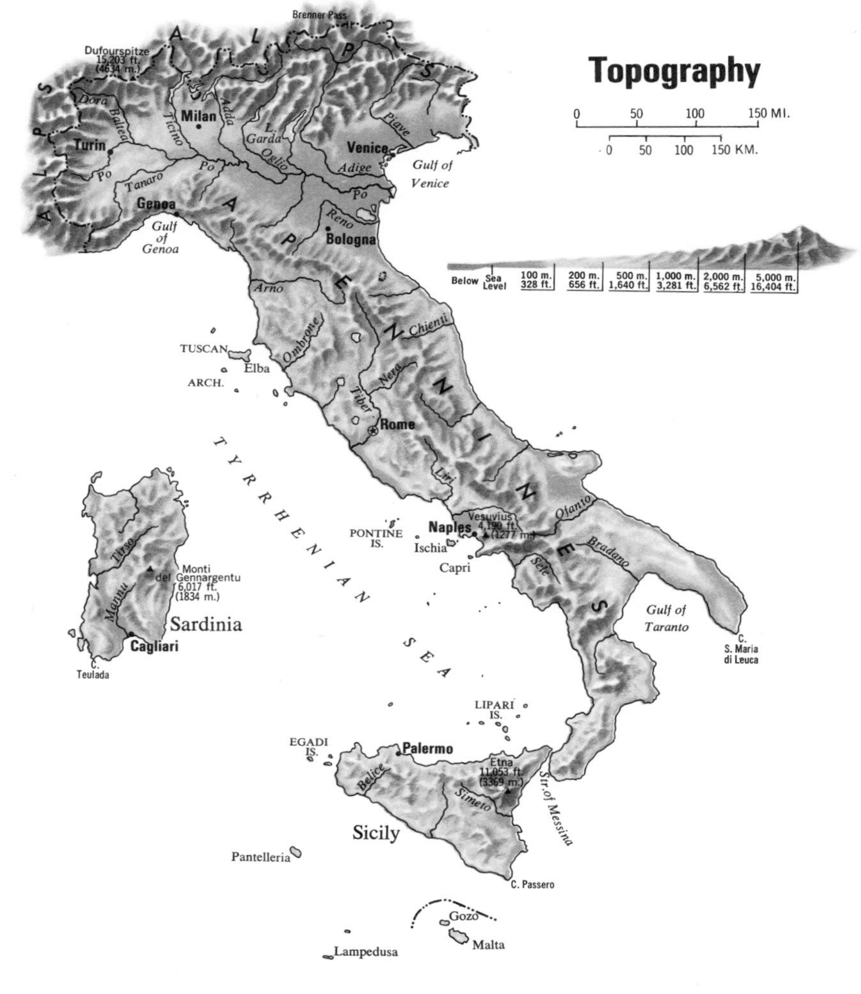

0 50 100 150 MI.
0 50 100 150 KM.
Below Sea Level
100 m. 328 ft.
200 m. 656 ft.
500 m. 1,640 ft.
1,000 m. 3,281 ft.
2,000 m. 6,562 ft.
5,000 m. 16,404 ft.
Brenner Pass
Dufourspitze 15,203 ft. (4634 m.)
ALPS
Milan
Turin
Venice
Gulf of Venice
Genoa
Gulf of Genoa
Bologna
Po
Tanaro
Ticino
Adda
Oglio
Garda
Adige
Piave
Reno
Arno
Ombrone
Tiber
Chienti
Nera
APENNINES
TUSCAN ARCH.
Elba
Rome
Liri
PONTINE IS.
Naples
Vesuvius
Ischia
Capri
Ofanto
Bradano
Sele
Gulf of Taranto
C. S. Maria di Leuca
TYRRHENIAN SEA
Sardinia
Cagliari
Teulada
Monti del Gennargentu 6,017 ft. (1834 m.)
Tirso
Flumendosa
LIPARI IS.
EGADI IS.
Palermo
Etna 11,053 ft. (3369 m.)
Simeto
Belice
Str. of Messina
Sicily
C. Passero
Pantelleria
Gozo
Malta
Lampedusa

Agriculture, Industry and Resources

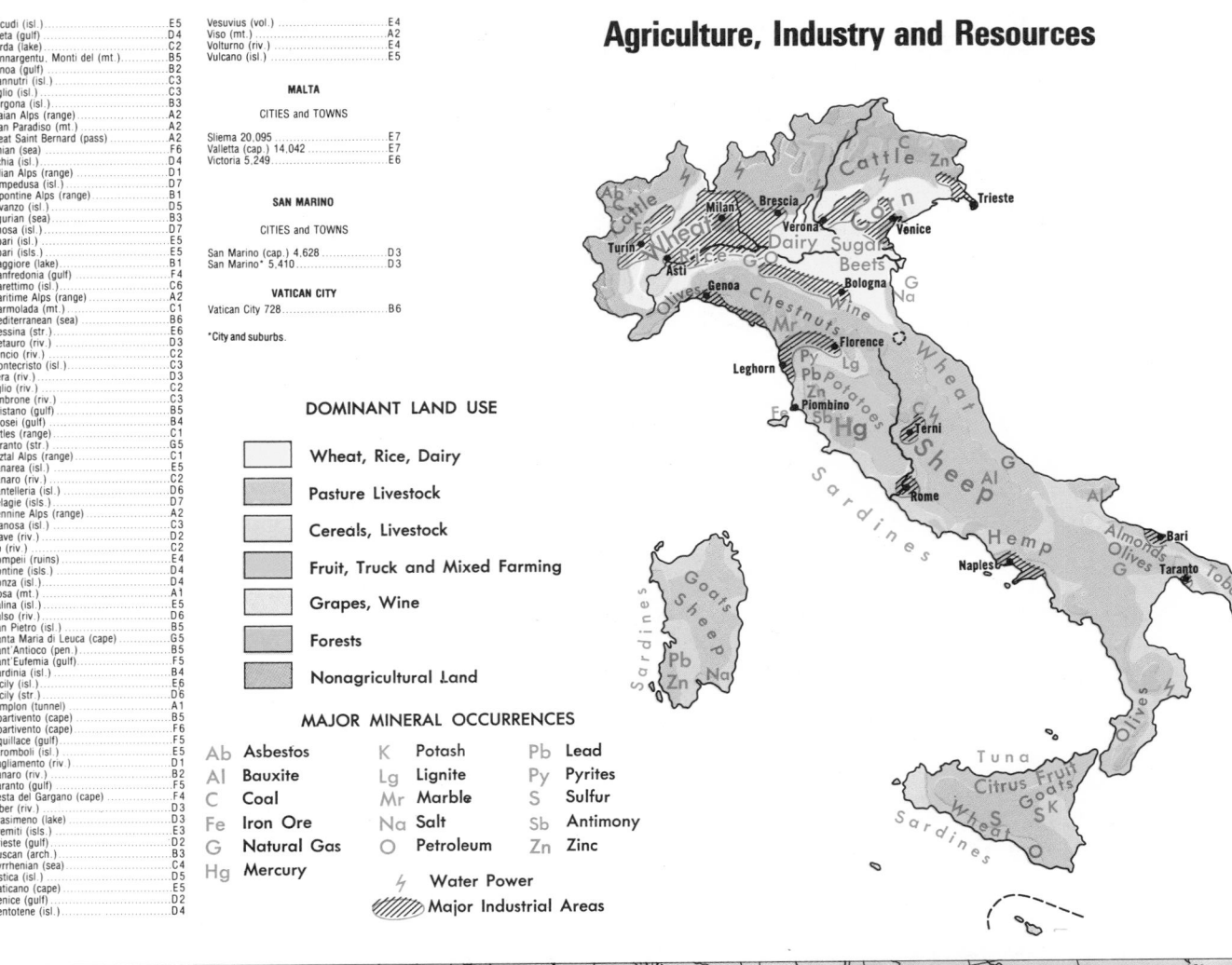

DOMINANT LAND USE

Wheat, Rice, Dairy

Pasture Livestock

Cereals, Livestock

Fruit, Truck and Mixed Farming

Grapes, Wine

Forests

Nonagricultural Land

MAJOR MINERAL OCCURRENCES

Ab Asbestos
Al Bauxite
C Coal
Fe Iron Ore
G Natural Gas
Hg Mercury

K Potash
Lg Lignite
Mr Marble
Na Salt
O Petroleum

Pb Lead
Py Pyrites
S Sulfur
Sb Antimony
Zn Zinc

⚡ Water Power

Major Industrial Areas

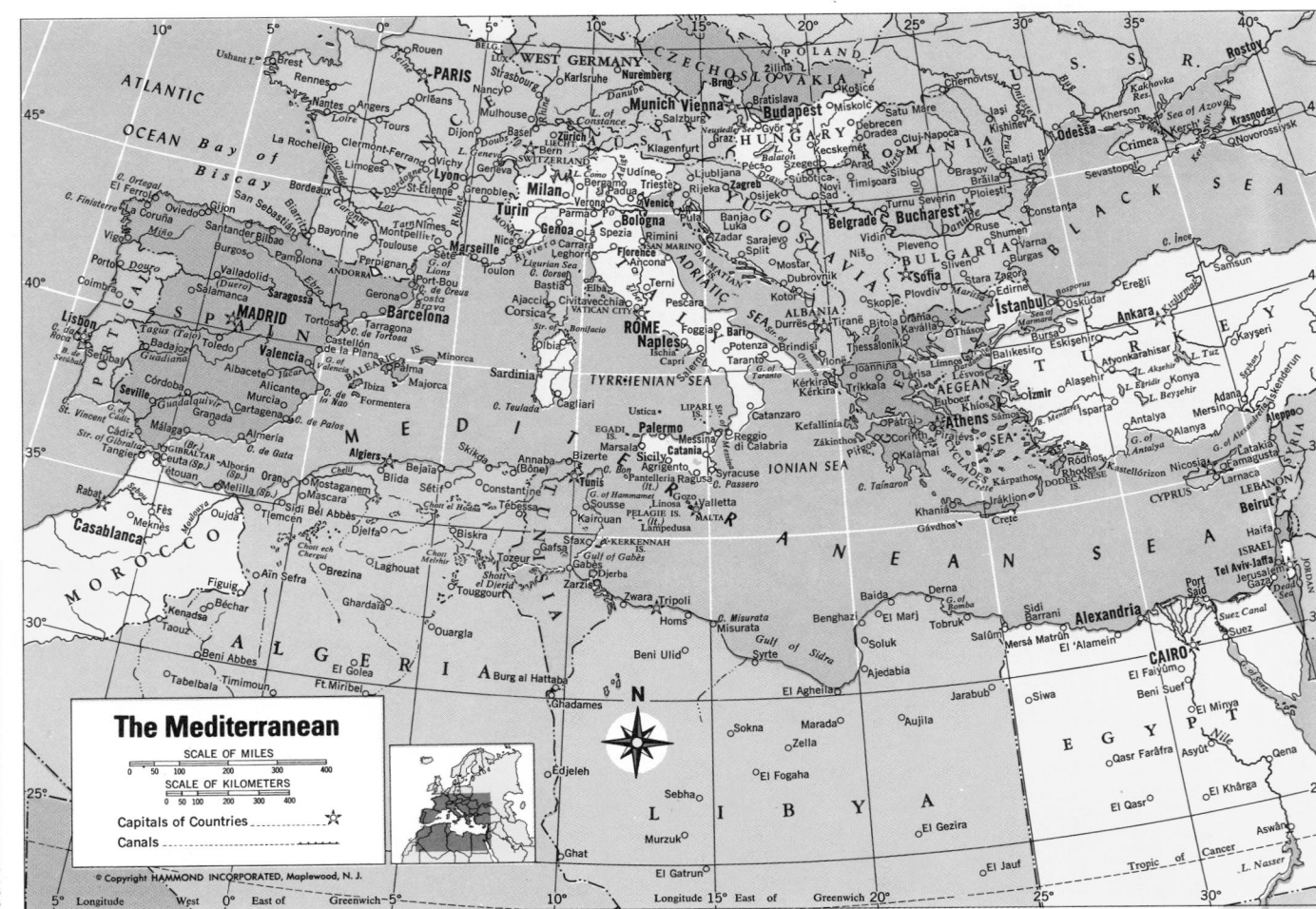

The Mediterranean

SCALE OF MILES
0 50 100   200   300   400

SCALE OF KILOMETERS
0 50 100   200   300   400

Capitals of Countries .... ☆
Canals ....

© Copyright HAMMOND INCORPORATED, Maplewood, N.J.

SWITZERLAND

AREA 15,943 sq. mi. (41,292 sq. km.)
POPULATION 6,365,960
CAPITAL Bern
LARGEST CITY Zürich
HIGHEST POINT Dufourspitze
   (Mte. Rosa) 15,203 ft. (4,634 m.)
MONETARY UNIT Swiss franc
MAJOR LANGUAGES German, French,
   Italian, Romansch
MAJOR RELIGIONS Protestantism,
   Roman Catholicism

LIECHTENSTEIN

AREA 61 sq. mi. (158 sq. km.)
POPULATION 25,220
CAPITAL Vaduz
LARGEST CITY Vaduz
HIGHEST POINT Grauspitze 8,527 ft.
   (2,599 m.)
MONETARY UNIT Swiss franc
MAJOR LANGUAGE German
MAJOR RELIGION Roman Catholicism

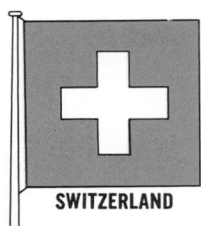

SWITZERLAND

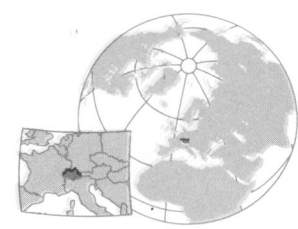

LIECHTENSTEIN

Languages

Basel
Zürich
St. Gallen
Biel
Lucerne
★ Bern
Chur
Fribourg
Lausanne
St. Moritz
Geneva
Sion
Bellinzona

- German
- French
- Italian
- Romansch

Switzerland is a multilingual nation with four
official languages. 70% of the people speak
German, 19% French, 10% Italian and 1% Romansch.

SWITZERLAND

CANTONS

Aargau 442,400	F2
Appenzell, Ausser	
Rhoden 46,700	H2
Baselland 219,500	E2
Baselstadt 209,700	E1
Bern 920,900	D2
Fribourg 181,600	D3
Geneva (Genève) 338,600	B4
Glarus 35,700	H3
Graubünden (Grisons) 164,300	H3
Grisons (Graubünden) 164,300	H3
Jura 67,200	D2
Lucerne (Luzern) 292,900	F2
Luzern 292,900	F2
Neuchâtel 162,200	C3
Nidwalden 26,900	F3
Obwalden 25,400	F3
Sankt Gallen 385,000	H2
Schaffhausen 69,300	G1
Schwyz 93,100	G2
Soleure (Solothurn) 221,800	E2
Solothurn 221,800	E2
Thurgau 183,500	H1
Ticino 264,400	G4
Uri 34,000	G3
Valais 214,000	D4
Vaud 523,500	B3
Zug 73,600	G2
Zürich 1,117,300	G2

CITIES and TOWNS

Aadorf 3,022	G2
Aarau 16,881	F2
Aarau* 51,800	F2
Aarberg 3,122	D2
Aarburg 5,943	E2
Adelboden 3,326	E3
Adliswil 15,920	F2
Aeschi bei Spiez 1,402	E3
Affoltern am Albis 7,363	F2
Affoltern im Emmental 1,223	E2
Aigle 6,532	C4
Airolo 2,140	G3
Aile 1,615	D2
Allschwil 17,638	D1
Alpnach 3,277	F3
Altdorf 8,647	G3
Altstätten 9,084	J2
Amriswil 7,601	H1
Andelfingen 1,453	G1
Andermatt 1,589	G3
Ardon 1,498	D4
Arosa 2,717	J3
Arth 7,580	F2
Ascona 4,086	G4
Attalens 1,116	C3
Au 4,944	J2
Aubonne 1,983	B4
Avenches 2,235	D3
Baar 14,074	F2
Baden 14,115	F2
Baden* 66,800	F2
Bad Ragaz 3,713	H2
Balerna 3,885	G5
Balsthal 5,607	E2
Bäretswil 2,733	G2
Basel 199,600	E1
Basel* 379,700	E1
Bassecourt 2,985	D2
Bätterkinden 1,757	E2

Bauma 3,159	G2
Beatenberg 1,263	E3
Beinwil am See 2,520	F2
Belfaux 1,075	D3
Bellinzona 16,979	H4
Bellinzona* 31,000	H4
Belp 6,981	D3
Berg 1,039	H1
Bern (cap.) 154,700	D3
Bern* 285,300	D3
Beromünster 1,552	F2
Bettlach 4,046	D2
Bex 5,069	D4
Biasca 4,696	H4
Biberist 7,769	D2
Biel 63,400	D2
Biel**89,900	D2
Bière 1,252	B3
Binningen 15,344	D1
Bischofszell 4,233	H1
Blumenstein 1,049	E3
Bodio 1,425	G4
Bolligen 26,121	E3
Boltigen 1,519	D3
Bonaduz 1,289	H3
Boncourt 1,528	C2
Bönigen 1,738	E3
Boswil 1,904	F2
Boudry 4,372	C3
Bourg Saint-Pierre 236	D5
Breil-Brigels 1,215	H3
Breitenbach 2,455	E2
Bremgarten 4,873	F2
Brienz 2,796	F3
Brig 5,191	F4
Brissago 2,120	G4
Brittnau 2,888	F2
Broc 1,842	D3
Brugg 8,635	F2
Brusio 1,344	K4
Bubendorf 2,070	E2
Bubikon 3,244	G2
Buchs 8,454	H2
Bülach 11,043	G1
Bulle 7,556	D3
Buochs 3,232	F3
Büren an der Aare 3,085	D2
Burgdorf 15,888	E2
Burgdorf* 18,400	E2
Bürglen, Thurgau 1,920	H1
Bürglen, Uri 3,401	G3
Bussigny-près-Lausanne 4,509	B3
Bütschwil 3,270	H2
Carouge 14,055	B4
Castagnola 4,430	G4
Cazis 1,687	H3
Cernier 1,717	C2
Chalais 1,651	E4
Cham 8,209	F2
Chamoson 2,049	D4
Charmey 1,155	D3
Château-d'Oex 3,203	D4
Châtel-Saint-Denis 2,842	C3
Chêne-Bougeries 8,670	B4
Chavornay 1,521	C3
Chexbres 1,607	C3
Chiasso 8,868	G5
Chippis 1,561	E4
Chur 32,400	J3
Churwalden 1,052	J3
Claro 1,143	G4
Collombey-Muraz 2,279	C4
Collonge-Bellerive 3,541	B4
Conthey 4,259	D4
Coppet 1,097	B4
Corcelles-près-Payerne 1,256	C3
Corgémont 1,645	D2
Cossonay 1,529	B3
Courgenay 1,954	D2
Courrendlin 2,656	D2
Courroux 1,788	D2
Courtelary 1,462	D2
Courtételle 1,864	D2
Couvet 3,481	C3
Cully 1,535	C4
Davos 10,238	J3
Degersheim 3,400	H2
Delémont 11,797	D2
Derendingen 4,917	E2
Dielsdorf 2,691	F1
Diemtigen 1,913	D3
Diepoldsau 3,311	J2
Diessenhofen 2,532	G1
Dietikon 22,705	F2
Disentis-Muster 2,319	G3
Domat-Ems 5,701	H3
Dombresson 1,109	C2
Dornach 5,258	E2
Döttingen 3,380	F1
Dübendorf 19,639	G2
Düdingen 4,932	D3
Dürnten 4,620	G2
Dürrenroth 1,084	E2
Ebnat-Kappel 5,131	H2
Echallens 1,643	C3
Ecublens 6,379	B3
Egg 5,250	G2
Eggiwil 2,391	E3
Eglisau 2,160	G1
Egnach 3,466	H1

(continued on following page)

Agriculture, Industry and Resources

DOMINANT LAND USE

- Cereals, Dairy
- Pasture Livestock
- General Farming, Livestock
- Fruit, Truck, Mixed Farming
- Forests
- Nonagricultural Land

⚡ Water Power
///// Major Industrial Areas

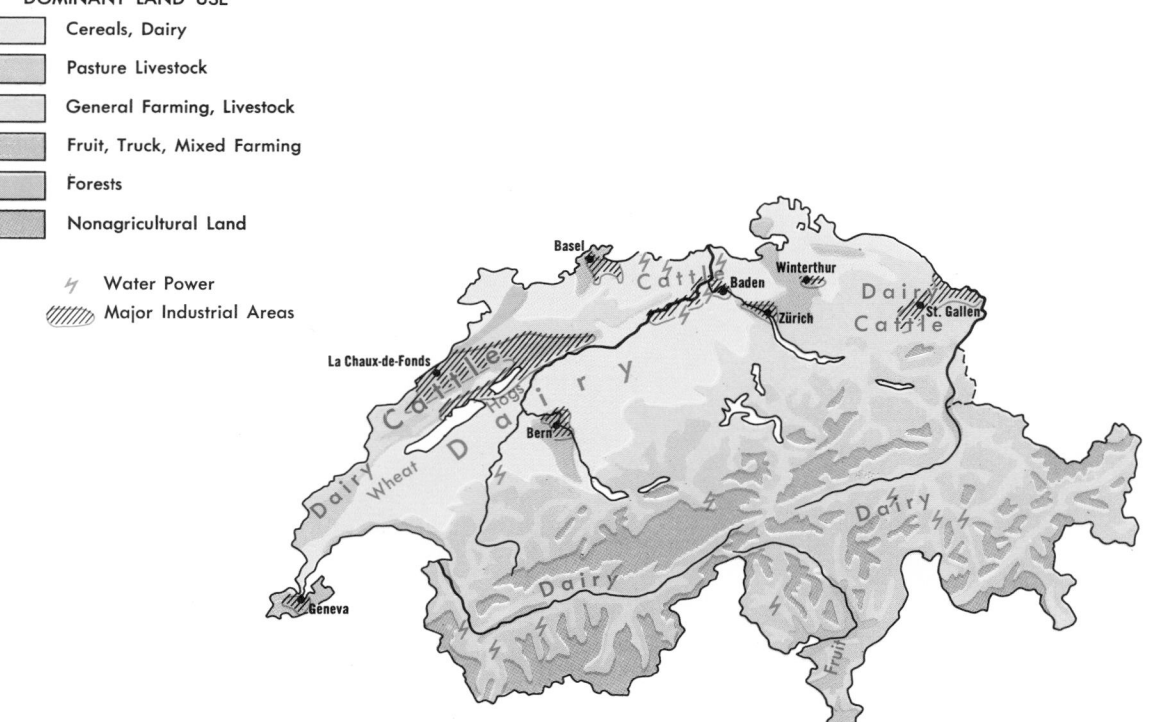

Basel
Winterthur
Baden
Zürich
St. Gallen
La Chaux-de-Fonds
Bern
Geneva
Cattle
Dairy
Wheat
Hogs
Dairy
Dairy
Dairy
Fruit

Topography

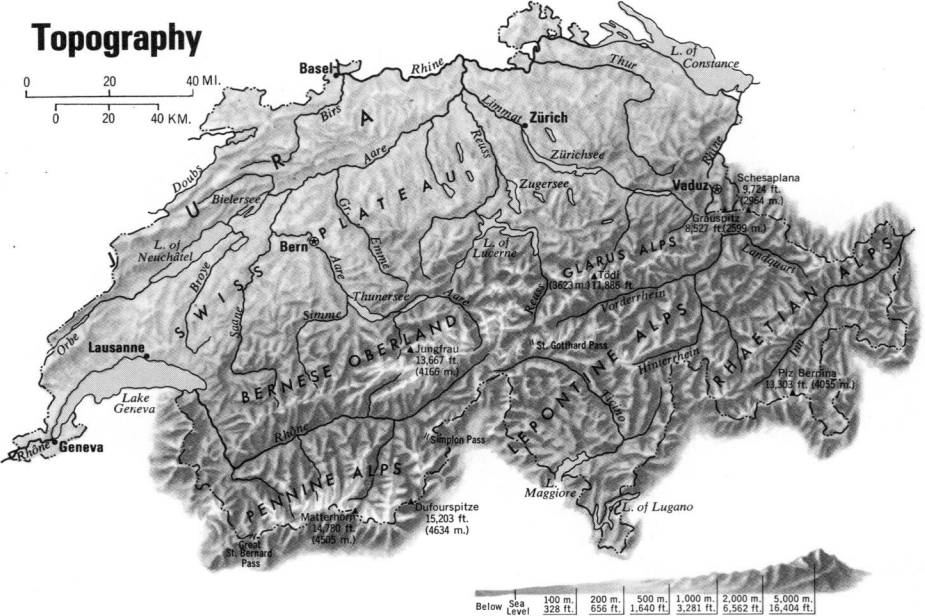

Scale: 0 20 40 MI. / 0 20 40 KM.

Elevation legend:
Below Sea Level | 100 m. 328 ft. | 200 m. 656 ft. | 500 m. 1,640 ft. | 1,000 m. 3,281 ft. | 2,000 m. 6,562 ft. | 5,000 m. 16,404 ft.

Place	Ref
Einsiedeln 10,020	G2
Elgg 2,970	G2
Emmen 22,040	F2
Engelberg 2,841	F3
Ennenda 2,762	H2
Entlebuch 3,310	E2
Erlach 1,052	D2
Erlenbach im Simmental 1,436	E3
Ermatingen 1,787	H1
Erstfeld 4,516	G3
Eschenbach 3,387	G2
Escholzmatt 3,161	E3
Estavayer-le-Lac 3,439	C3
Evolène 1,403	D4
Faido 1,866	G4
Felsberg 1,321	H3
Feuerthalen 3,118	G1
Flawil 8,474	H2
Fleurier 4,124	C2
Flims 1,936	H3
Flüelen 1,731	G3
Flums 4,474	H2
Frauenfeld 17,576	G1
Freienbach 8,429	G2
Fribourg 41,600	D3
Fribourg* 53,500	D3
Frick 3,112	E1
Frutigen 5,796	E3
Fully 3,643	D4
Gais 2,344	H2
Gelterkinden 5,157	E2
Geneva (Genève) 163,100	B4
Geneva (Genève)* 320,200	B4
Gersau 1,753	F3
Gimel 1,205	B3
Giornico 1,389	G4
Giswil 2,760	F3
Giubiasco 5,796	H4
Gland 2,404	B4
Glarus 6,189	H2
Glattfelden 2,887	F1
Glis 3,389	E4
Gordola 2,586	G4
Gossau 12,793	H2
Grabs 4,245	H2
Grächen 1,063	E4
Grandson 2,135	C3
Grenchen 20,051	D2
Grenchen* 28,300	D2
Grindelwald 3,511	F3
Grosswangen 2,213	E2
Gruyères 1,234	D3
Gstaad	D4
Gsteig 865	D4
Guggisberg 1,739	D3
Gurtnellen 1,048	G3
Guttingen 1,060	H1
Hallau 1,836	F1
Heiden 3,716	H2
Heimberg 3,046	E2
Hérémence 1,484	D4
Hergiswil 4,364	F3
Herisau 14,597	H2
Herzogenbuchsee 5,140	E2
Hilterfingen 3,647	E3
Hinwil 6,547	G2
Hitzkirch 1,468	F2
Hochdorf 5,222	F2
Horgen 15,691	G2
Huttwil 4,800	E2
Igis 5,283	J3
Ilanz 1,866	H3
Illnau 13,693	G2
Ingenbohl 5,111	F2
Innertkirchen 1,064	F3
Ins 2,435	D2
Interlaken 4,735	E3
Jegenstorf 2,858	D2
Jenaz 1,124	J3
Jona 9,286	G2
Jungfraujoch	E3
Kaltbrunn 2,751	G2
Kandersteg 957	E4
Kerns 3,807	F3
Kerzers 2,688	D2
Kirchberg, Bern 3,595	E2
Kirchberg, St. Gallen 6,309	H2
Kleinlützel 1,271	D2
Klingnau 2,545	F1
Klosters Dorf 3,534	J3
Kloten 16,388	G1
Koblenz 1,439	F1
Kölliken 3,219	E2
Köniz 33,800	D3
Konolfingen 4,137	E3
Kreuzlingen 15,760	H1
Kriens 20,409	F2
Krummenau 1,904	H2
Küsnacht 12,193	F2
Küssnacht am Rigi 7,956	F2

Place	Ref
Küttigen 4,181	F2
L'Abbaye 1,319	B3
La Chaux-de-Fonds 42,500	C2
Lachen 4,914	G2
Lancy 20,523	B4
La Neuveville 3,917	D2
Langenthal 13,077	E2
Langenthal* 22,100	E2
Langnau am Albis 4,879	G2
Langnau in Emmental 8,950	E3
La Roche 1,069	D3
La Sarraz 1,190	C3
La Tour-de-Peilz 8,864	D4
Läufelfingen 1,243	E2
Laufen 4,723	D2
Laufenburg 2,128	F1
Laupen 2,139	D3
Lauperswil 2,542	E3
Lausanne 136,100	C4
Lausanne* 228,700	C3
Lauterbrunnen 3,431	E3
Le Brassus 5,465	B3
Lenk 1,876	E4
Le Noirmont 1,516	C2
Lens 2,052	D4
Lenzburg 7,594	F2
Les Bois 1,110	C2
Les Ponts-de-Martel 1,327	C2
Leuk 2,796	E4
Leukerbad 1,056	E4
Leysin 2,752	D4
Lengau 4,736	D2
Liestal 12,500	E2
Liestal-Sissach* 40,800	E2
Linthal 1,458	H3
Littau 13,495	F2
Locarno 14,143	G4
Locarno* 39,200	G4
Lodrino 1,075	G4
Lotzwil 2,323	E2
Lucens 2,144	C3
Lucerne 70,200	F2
Lucerne* 158,600	F2
Lugano 22,280	G4
Lugano* 64,200	G4
Lungern 1,813	F3
Luthern 1,706	E2
Lutry 4,994	C3
Lützelflüh 3,842	E3
Luzern (Lucerne) 70,200	F2
Lyss 8,131	D2
Maienfeld 1,542	J2
Malans 1,294	J3
Malleray 1,969	D2
Malters 5,100	F2
Malvaglia 1,099	H4
Männedorf 7,419	G2
Marbach 1,265	E3
Martigny 10,478	D4
Meilen 9,881	G2
Meiringen 3,759	F3
Melide 1 315	G5
Mellingen 3,211	F2
Mels 5,969	H2
Mendrisio 6,223	G5
Menzingen 3,483	G2
Menznau 2,185	E2
Mesocco 1,376	H4
Meyrin 15,627	B4
Minusio 5,027	G4
Möhlin 6,003	E1
Mollis 2,628	H2
Montana 1,725	D4
Monthey 10,114	C4
Montreux 20,421	C4
Morges 11,931	C3
Morges* 17,200	C3
Moudon 3,773	C3
Moutier 8,794	D2
Müllheim 1,620	G1
Mümliswil-Ramiswil 2,702	E2
Münchenbuchsee 6,459	D2
Münsingen 8,350	E3
Muotathal 2,763	G3
Muri 4,853	F2
Muri bei Bern 3,057	E3
Mürren 4,226	E3
Murten 4,226	D3
Muttenz 15,518	E1
Näfels 3,739	H2
Naters 5,517	E4
Nebikon 1,378	E2
Nendaz 4,051	D4
Nesslau 1,934	H2

Place	Ref
Netstal 2,771	H2
Neuchâtel 38,400	C3
Neuchâtel* 61,700	C3
Neuenegg 3,452	D2
Neuhausen am Rheinfall 12,103	G1
Neunkirch 1,239	F1
Nidau 7,962	D2
Niederbipp 3,293	E2
Niederurnen 3,354	H2
Nunningen 1,450	E2
Nyon 11,424	B4
Oberägeri 2,992	G2
Oberburg 3,015	E3
Oberdiessbach 2,145	E3
Oberdorf 1,953	E2
Oberriet 6,123	J2
Obersiggenthal 6,623	F1
Oberwil 4,659	H2
Oensingen 3,387	E2
Oftringen 9,189	E2
Ollon 4,470	D4
Olten 21,200	E2
Olten* 49,000	E2
Opfikon 11,115	G2
Orbe 4,327	C3
Orsières 2,470	D4
Ouchy	C4
Paradiso 3,101	G5
Payerne 6,891	C3
Penthalaz 1,701	C3
Péry 1,486	D2
Peseux 5,578	C3
Pfaffnau 2,584	E2
Pieterlen 3,485	D2
Pfäffeln 1,448	D3
Pontresina 1,646	J3
Porrentruy 7,827	C2
Port-Valais 1,363	C4
Poschiavo 3,563	J4
Prangins 1,466	B4
Pratteln 15,127	E1
Pully 15,917	C4
Quinto 1,490	G3
Rafz 1,925	G1
Ramsen 1,217	G1
Rapperswil 8,713	G2
Raron 1,257	E4
Regensdorf 8,566	F2
Reichenbach im Kandertal 2,900	E3
Reiden 3,275	E2
Reinach in Aargau 5,862	F2
Reinach in Baselland 13,419	E2
Renan 1,094	C2
Renens 17,391	C3
Rheinau 2,075	G1
Rheineck 3,275	J2
Rheinfelden 6,866	E1
Richterswil 7,380	G2
Riehen 21,026	E1
Riggisberg 2,193	E3
Riva San Vitale 1,607	G5
Rivera 1,146	G4
Roggwil 3,403	E2
Rolle 3,658	B4
Romanshorn 8,329	H1
Romont 3,276	C3
Rorschach 11,963	H1
Rorschach* 24,200	H1
Rosenlaui	F3
Rothrist 5,883	E2
Roveredo 2,037	H4
Rüeggisberg 1,857	E3
Rumlang 5,677	G1
Rüschegg 1,346	D3
Ruswil 4,756	E2
Rüthi 1,493	J2
Rüti, Zürich 9,546	G2
Saanen 5,840	D4
Sachseln 3,059	F3
Saignelégier 1,745	C2
Saint-Aubin-Sauges 2,058	C3
Saint-Blaise 2,586	D2
Sainte-Croix 6,240	C3
Saint-Imier 5,677	C2
Saint-Légier-La
Chiésaz 2,230	C4
Saint-Martin 1,120	D4
Saint-Maurice 3,808	C4
Saint Moritz 5,699	J3
Saint Niklaus 2,043	E4
Saint Stephan 1,213	E3
Saint-Ursanne 1,073	D2
Samedan 2,574	J3
Sankt Gallen 81,900	H2
Sankt Gallen* 90,400	H2
Sankt Margrethen 5,101	J2
Sargans 4,058	H2
Sarnen 6,952	F3
Satigny 1,877	A4

Place	Ref
Savièse 3,585	D4
Saxon 2,409	D4
Schaffhausen 36,800	G1
Schaffhausen* 55,800	G1
Schänis 2,355	H2
Schattdorf 3,292	G3
Scherzingen 1,420	H1
Schiers 2,342	J3
Schinznach-Dorf 1,154	F2
Schleitheim 1,544	G1
Schlieren 11,869	F2
Schönenwerd 4,793	E2
Schübelbach 4,395	G2
Schüpfheim 3,773	F3
Schwanden 2,823	H2
Schwyz 12,194	G2
Scuol 1,686	K3
Sempach 1,619	F2
Seon 3,628	F2
Seuzach 3,258	G2
Sevelen 2,742	H2
Sierre 11,017	E3
Signau 2,642	E3
Signigni 3,540	E3
Sileren 2,338	D3
Sils im Domleschg 762	H3
Silvaplana 714	J4
Sins 2,435	F2
Sion 21,925	D4
Sirnach 3,706	G2
Sissach 4,938	E2
Solothurn (Soleure) 17,708	E2
Solothurn* 35,600	E2
Somvix 1,555	G3
Sonvico 1,129	G4
Spiez 9,911	E3
Stäfa 9,937	G2
Stalden 1,121	E4
Stans 5,180	F3
Steckborn 3,752	G1
Steffisburg 12,621	E3
Stein 1,763	E1
Stein am Rhein 2,751	G1
Suhr 7,223	F2
Sulgen 1,834	H1
Sumiswald 5,334	E2
Sursee 7,052	F2
Tafers 2,021	D3
Täuffelen 1,761	D2
Tavannes 3,869	D2
Tavetsch 1,273	G3
Teufen 5,300	H2
Thal 4,919	J2
Thalwil 13,591	G2
Thayngen 3,640	G1
Therwil 5,412	E1
Thun 37,000	E3
Thun* 63,600	E3
Thunstetten 2,483	E2
Thusis 2,381	H3
Trachselwald 1,199	E2
Tramelan 5,549	D2
Trimmis 1,109	J3
Troistorrents 2,208	C4
Trub 1,833	E3
Trun 1,607	G3
Turbenthal 2,939	G2
Uetendorf 3,132	E3
Unterägeri 4,671	G2
Unteriberg 1,344	G2
Unterkulm 2,596	F2
Unterseen 4,192	E3
Untervaz 1,230	H3
Urnäsch 2,313	H2
Uster 21,819	G2
Utzenstorf 3,193	E2
Uznach 3,984	G2
Uzwil 9,133	H2
Vallorbe 4,028	B3
Vaz/Obervaz 2,003	J3
Vechigen 3,595	E3
Vernayaz 1,356	D4
Versoix 5,627	B4
Vevey 17,957	C4
Vevey-Montreux* 62,300	C4
Villeneuve 3,705	C4
Visp 5,290	E4
Vouvry 1,851	C4
Vuadens 1,278	D3
Wädenswil 15,695	G2
Wald 8,185	G2
Waldenburg 1,449	E2
Waldkirch 2,869	H2
Walenstadt 3,446	H2
Wallisellen 10,415	G2
Walzenhausen 2,082	J2
Wangen an der Aare 2,013	E2
Wängi 2,730	G2
Wartau 3,604	H2

Place	Ref		Place	Ref		Place	Ref
Wattwil 8,508	H2		Zell, Luzern 1,590	E2		Bernina (peak)	J4
Weesen 1,308	H2		Zell, Zürich 4,008	G2		Bernina (pass)	K4
Weggis 2,517	F2		Zermatt 3,101	E4		Bielersee (lake)	D2
Weinfelden 8,621	H1		Zizers 1,913	J3		Bietschhorn (mt.)	E4
Wettingen 19,900	F2		Zofingen 9,292	F2		Birs (riv.)	D2
Wetzikon 13,469	G2		Zollikofen 9,069	D2		Blinnenhorn (mt.)	F4
Wil 14,646	H2		Zollikon 12,117	G2		Blümlisalp (mt.)	E4
Wil* 20,500	H2		Zug 22,972	G2		Bodensee (Constance) (lake)	H1
Wilchingen 1,066	G1		Zug* 51,300	G2		Borgne (riv.)	D4
Wildberg 1,666	G2		Zuoz 1,165	J3		Breithorn (mt.)	E5
Wildhaus 1,104	H2		Zürich 401,600	G2		Breithorn (mt.)	F4
Wilisau 2,728	E2		Zürich* 718,100	G2		Brienzer Rothorn (mt.)	F3
Wimmis 1,833	E3		Zurzach 3,098	F1		Brienzersee (lake)	E3
Windisch 7,444	F1		Zweisimmen 2,738	D3		Broye (riv.)	C3
Winterthur 86,200	G2					Buchegg (mts.)	E2
Winterthur* 110,100	G1		OTHER FEATURES			Buin (peak)	K3
Wohlen 12,024	F2					Campo Tencia (peak)	G4
Wohlen* 16,000	F2		Aa (riv.)	F3		Chasseron (mt.)	C3
Wohlen bei Bern 4,190	D3		Aare (riv.)	E2		Churfirsten (mt.)	H2
Wolfenschiessen 1,470	F3		Ägerisee (lake)	G2		Clariden (mt.)	G3
Wohlusen 3,556	F2		Aiguille d'Argentière (mt.)	D4		Constance (lake)	H1
Worb 9,526	E3		Aletschhorn (mt.)	E4		Cornettes de Bise (mts.)	C4
Wünnewil 3,652	D3		Aroser Rothorn (mt.)	J3		Dammastock (mt.)	F3
Wigen 1,986	E2		Ault (peak)	H3		Davos (valley)	J3
Yverdon 20,538	C3		Balmhorn (mt.)	E4		Dent Blanche (mt.)	D4
Yvonand 1,321	C3		Bernese Oberland (reg.)	E3		Dent de Lys (mt.)	D4

Switzerland and Liechtenstein

CONIC PROJECTION

SCALE OF MILES

SCALE OF KILOMETERS

Capitals of Countries .... ☆
Capitals of Cantons .... ◉
International Boundaries .... —··—··—
Canals .... ········

Scale 1:1,140,000

© Copyright HAMMOND INCORPORATED, Maplewood, N.J.

Dent de Ruth (mt.)	D3	
Dent d'Hérens (mt.)	E5	
Dents du Midi (mt.)	C4	
Diablerets (mt.)	D4	
Doldenhorn (mt.)	D4	
Dolent (mt.)	C5	
Dom (mt.)	E4	
Doubs (riv.)	C3	
Drance (riv.)	D5	
Dufourspitze (mt.)	E5	
Emmental (valley)	E3	
Err (peak)	J3	
Finsteraarhorn (mt.)	E3	
Finstermünz (pass)	K3	
Fletschhorn (mt.)	F4	
Fluela (pass)	J3	
Furka (pass)	F3	
Generoso (mt.)	H5	
Geneva (mt.)	C4	
Glärnisch (mt.)	H2	
Glarus Alps (mts.)	G3	
Grand Combin (mt.)	D5	
Grand Muveran (mt.)	D4	
Grande Dixence (dam)	D4	

Grauehörner (mts.)	H3
Great Saint Bernard (mt.)	D5
Great Saint Bernard (pass)	D5
Greifensee (lake)	G2
Greina (pass)	G3
Grimsel (pass)	F3
Gross Emme (riv.)	E2
Gross Litzner (mt.)	K3
Hinterrhein (riv.)	H3
Hochwang (mt.)	J3
Hohenstollen (mt.)	F3
Horn (mt.)	G2
Inn (riv.)	K3
Jorat (mt.)	C3
Jungfrau (mt.)	E3
Jura (mts.)	B3
Kaiseregg (mt.)	D3
Kesch (peak)	J3
La Dôle (mt.)	B4
Landquart (riv.)	J3
Le Chasseral (mt.)	C3
Le Gros Crêt (mt.)	B3
Léman (Geneva) (lake)	C4
Lepontine Alps (range)	F4

Linard (peak)	K3
Linden (mts.)	F2
Linth (riv.)	G2
Lötschberg (tunnel)	E4
Lower Engadine (valley)	K3
Lucerne (lake)	F2
Lugano (lake)	H5
Madrisahorn (mt.)	J3
Maggia (riv.)	G4
Maggiore (lake)	G5
Marmontana (mt.)	H4
Matterhorn (mt.)	E4
Mauvoisin (dam)	D5
Moësa (riv.)	H4
Morat (lake)	C3
Muota (riv.)	G3
Murg (riv.)	G2
Murtaröl (mt.)	K3
Muttler (mt.)	K3
Naafkopf (mt.)	J2
Napf (mt.)	E3
National Park	K3
Neuchâtel (lake)	C3
Noirmont (mt.)	B3
Oberalp (pass)	G3

Oberalpstock (mt.)	G3
Ochsen (mt.)	D3
Ofen (pass)	K3
Ofenhorn (mt.)	F4
Orbe (riv.)	C3
Pennine Alps (range)	E4
Pilatus (mt.)	F2
Plessur (riv.)	J3
Poschiavo (valley)	K4
Pragel (pass)	G2
Quatervals (peak)	K3
Reuss (riv.)	F2
Rhaetian Alps (range)	J3
Rhätikon (mts.)	J2
Rheinwaldhorn (mt.)	H4
Rhine (riv.)	D4
Rhône (riv.)	D4
Rigi (mt.)	F2
Rimpfischhorn (mt.)	E4
Ringelspitz (mt.)	H3
Risoux (mt.)	B3
Rosa (mt.)	E5
Rosstock (mt.)	F3
Rothorn (mt.)	J3
Saane (Sarine) (riv.)	D3
Saint Gotthard (pass)	G4

Saint Gotthard (tunnel)	G3
San Bernardino (pass)	H3
Säntis (mt.)	H2
Sarine (Saane) (riv.)	D3
Sarnen (lake)	F3
Schesaplana (mt.)	J2
Scherhorn (mt.)	G3
Schreckhorn (mt.)	E3
Schwarzhorn (mt.)	E4
Schwarzhorn (mt.)	E4
Seez (riv.)	H2
Sempach (lake)	F2
Septimer (pass)	J4
Sesvenna (peak)	K3
Sihlsee (lake)	G2
Simplon (pass)	F4
Simplon (tunnel)	F4
Sonnenhorn (mt.)	F4
Splügen (pass)	H3
Stockhorn (mt.)	D3
Sulzfluh (mt.)	J2
Susten (pass)	F3
Tamaro (mt.)	G4

Tamina (riv.)	H3
Tendre (peak)	B3
Terri (peak)	G3
Thunersee (lake)	E3
Thur (riv.)	G1
Ticino (riv.)	G4
Titlis (mt.)	F3
Tödi (mt.)	G3
Toggenburg (dist.)	H2
Töss (riv.)	G2
Tour d'Aï (mt.)	D4
Umbrail (peak)	K3
Untersee (lake)	H1
Unterwalden (reg.)	F3
Upper Engadine (valley)	J4
Urirotstock (mt.)	G3
Vadret (peak)	J3
Valserrhein (riv.)	H3
Vanil Noir (mt.)	D3
Velan (mt.)	D5
Visp (riv.)	E4
Vorab (mt.)	H3
Vorderrhein (riv.)	G4
Wandfluhhorn (mt.)	G4
Weissenstein (mt.)	D2
Weisshorn (mt.)	E4

Weisshorn (mt.)	J3
Weissmies (mt.)	F4
Wetterhorn (mt.)	F3
Wildhorn (mt.)	D4
Wildstrubel (mt.)	E4
Zellersee (lake)	G1
Zugersee (lake)	F2
Zürichsee (lake)	G2

LIECHTENSTEIN

CITIES and TOWNS

Schaan 4,552	H2
Triesen 2,971	H2
Vaduz (cap.) 4,614	H2

OTHER FEATURES

Grauspitz (mt.)	J2
Ochsenkopf (mt.)	J2
Rhätikon (mts.)	J2
Rhine (riv.)	J2

*City and suburbs

AUSTRIA

PROVINCES

Burgenland 272,119 ....D3
Carinthia 525,728 ....B3
Lower Austria 1,414,161 ....C2
Salzburg 401,766 ....B3
Styria 1,192,442 ....B3
Tirol 540,771 ....A3
Upper Austria 1,223,444 ....B2
Vienna (city) 1,614,841 ....D2
Vorarlberg 271,473 ....A3

CITIES and TOWNS†

Admont 3,126 ....C3
Allentsteig 2,783 ....C2
Altheim 4,766 ....B2
Althofen 3,886 ....C3
Amstetten 13,330 ....C2
Andau 3,058 ....D3
Arnoldstein 6,740 ....B3
Aspang Markt 2,316 ....D3
Attnang-Puchheim 7,837 ....B2
Bad Aussee 5,039 ....B3
Baden 22,631 ....D2
Badgastein 5,228 ....B3
Bad Goisern 6,360 ....B3
Bad Hofgastein 5,525 ....B3
Bad Ischl 12,740 ....B3
Bad Leonfelden 2,712 ....C2
Bad Sankt-Leonhard im
  Lavanttal 4,882 ....C3
Berndorf 8,371 ....D2
Bischofshofen 9,417 ....B3
Bludenz 12,050 ....A3
Bramberg am Wildkogel 3,129 ...B3
Braunau am Inn 16,432 ....B2
Bregenz 22,839 ....A3
Bruck an der Leitha 7,506 .....D2
Bruck an der Mur 16,359 ....C3
Deutsch Feistritz 3,820 ....C3
Deutschkreutz 3,673 ....D3
Deutsch Landsberg 6,614 ....C3
Deutsch Wagram 4,481 ....D2
Dornbirn 33,810 ....A3
Ebenfurth 2,272 ....D2
Ebensee 9,413 ....B3
Eferding 3,014 ....B2
Eggenburg 3,730 ....C2
Ehrwald 2,198 ....A3

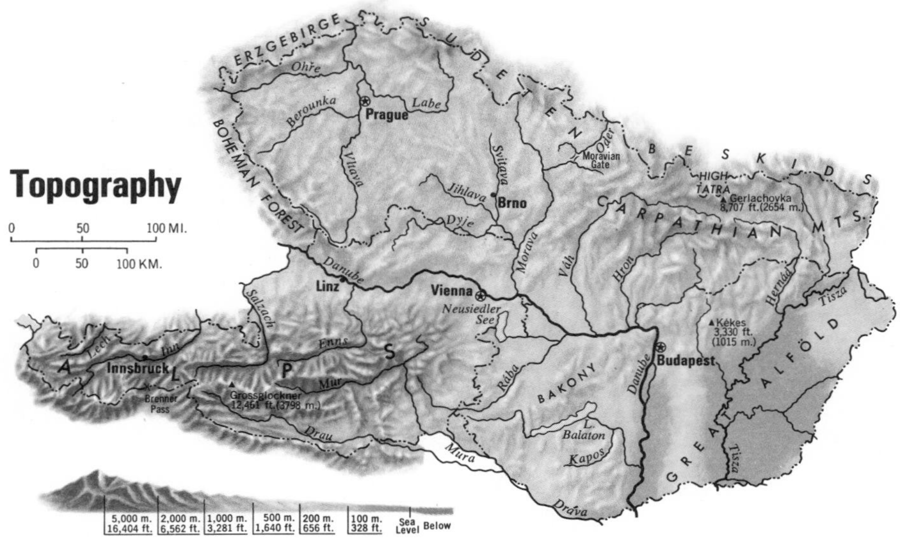

Eisenerz 11,563 ....C3
Eisenkappel-Vellach 3,761 .....C3
Eisenstadt 10,059 ....D3
Enns 9,622 ....C2
Feldbach 3,887 ....C3
Feldkirch 21,214 ....A3
Feldkirchen in
  Kärnten 11,188 ....B3
Ferlach 7,621 ....B3
Fieberbrunn 3,651 ....B3
Fohnsdorf 11,169 ....C3
Frankenmarkt 2,960 ....B3
Frauenkirchen 2,749 ....D3
Freistadt 5,956 ....C2
Freidberg 2,504 ....D3
Friesach 7,257 ....C3
Frohnleiten 5,081 ....C3
Fulpmes 2,553 ....A3
Fürstenfeld 6,054 ....C3
Gaming 4,181 ....C2
Gänserndorf 4,211 ....D2
Gleisdorf 4,921 ....C3
Gloggnitz 7,078 ....D3
Gmünd, Carinthia 2,267 ....B3
Gmünd, Lower Austria 6,323 ....C2
Gmunden 12,270 ....B3
Golling an der Salzach 3,089 ..B3
Götzis 7,931 ....A3
Gratwein 2,747 ....C3
Graz 251,900 ....C3
Graz* 314,200 ....C3
Grein 2,767 ....C2
f21Grieskirchen 4,519 ....B2
Grosssiegharts 3,288 ....C2
Grünburg 3,775 ....C3
Güssing 3,675 ....D3
Haag 5,060 ....C2
Hainburg an der Donau 6,009 ...D2
Hainfeld 3,897 ....C2
Hallein 14,371 ....B3
Hallstatt 1,303 ....B3
Hartberg 5,702 ....C3
Haslach an der Mühl 2,636 .....C2
Heidenreichstein 4,361 ....C2
Heiligenblut 1,324 ....B3
Hermagor-Pressegger 7,531 .....B3
Herzogenburg 7,299 ....C2
Hohenau an der March 3,591 ....D2
Hohenberg 2,016 ....C2
Hohenems 11,487 ....A3
Hollabrunn 6,563 ....C2
Hopfgarten in Nordtirol 4,784 .B3

Horn 6,264 ....C2
Hüttenberg 3,251 ....C3
Imst 5,855 ....A3
Innsbruck 115,800 ....A3
Innsbruck* 167,200 ....A3
Jenbach 5,868 ....A3
Jennersdorf 4,210 ....C3
Judenburg 11,346 ....C3
Kapfenberg 26,001 ....C3
Kappl 2,156 ....A3
Kaprun 2,604 ....B3
Kindberg 6,128 ....C3
Kirchdorf an der Krems 3,471 ..C2
Kitzbühel 7,995 ....B3
Klagenfurt 74,326 ....C3
Klagenfurt* 112,600 ....C3
Klosterneuburg 21,912 ....D2
Knittelfeld 14,517 ....C3
Köflach 12,612 ....C3
Königswiesen 2,921 ....C2
Korneuburg 8,892 ....D2
Kössen 2,764 ....B3
Kötschach-Mauthen 3,740 ....B3
Krems an der Donau 21,733 .....C2
Kufstein 12,766 ....A3
Kundl 3,020 ....A3
Laa an der Thaya 5,455 ....C2
Laakirchen 7,664 ....B3
Lambach 3,301 ....C2
Landeck 7,388 ....A3
Längenfeld 2,838 ....A3
Langenlois 4,957 ....C2
Langenwang 4,071 ....C3
Lavamünd 4,120 ....C3
Leibnitz 6,646 ....C3
Lenzing 5,385 ....B3
Leoben 35,153 ....C3
Lienz 11,696 ....B3
Liezen 6,244 ....C3
Lilienfeld 3,126 ....C2
Linz 205,700 ....C2
Linz* 356,500 ....C2
Lustenau 15,239 ....A3
Mannersdorf am
  Leithagebirge 4,012 ....D3
Marchegg 2,678 ....D2
Mariazell 2,298 ....C3
Matrei in Osttirol 4,003 ......B3
Mattersburg 5,417 ....D3
Mattighofen 4,344 ....B2
Mauerkirchen 2,237 ....B2
Mautern in Steiermark 2,536 ...C3

Mauthausen 4,419 ....C2
Mauthen-Kötschach 3,750 ....B3
Mayrhofen 3,174 ....A3
Melk 5,108 ....C2
Mistelbach an der Zaya 6,306 ..D2
Mittersill 4,361 ....B3
Mödling 18,712 ....D2
Mondsee 2,941 ....B3
Murau 2,710 ....C3
Mürzzuschlag 11,564 ....C3
Neuberg an der Mürz 2,183 .....C3
Neumarkt am Wallersee 3,267 ...B3
Neunkirchen 10,922 ....C2
Neusiedl am See 3,999 ....D3
Neustift im Stubaital 2,789 ...A3
Ober Grafendorf 4,109 ....C2
Oberndorf bei Salzburg 3,293 ..B3
Obervellach 2,420 ....B3
Oberwart 5,661 ....D3
Paternion 5,805 ....B3
Perg 4,872 ....C2
Peuerbach 2,161 ....B2
Pfunds 2,043 ....A3
Pinkafeld 4,610 ....C3
Pöchlarn 3,199 ....C2
Pörtschach am
  Wörthersee 2,511 ....C3
Poysdorf 5,774 ....D2
Pregarten 3,249 ....C2
Raabs an der Thaya 4,194 ......C2
Radenthein 6,847 ....B3
Radkersburg 2,000 ....C3
Radstadt 3,585 ....B3
Rankweil 8,440 ....A3
Rechnitz 3,412 ....D3
Reichenau an der Rax 4,053 ....C3
Retz 4,198 ....C2
Ried im Innkreis 10,534 ....B2
Rottenmann 4,781 ....C3
Saalfelden am Steinernen
  Meer 10,172 ....B3
Salzburg 122,100 ....B3
Salzburg* 213,430 ....B3
Sankt Aegyd am Neuwalde 3,165 .C3
Sankt Anton am Arlberg 2,086 ..A3
Sankt Johann in Tirol 5,942 ...A3
Sankt Michael im Lungau 2,839 .B3
Sankt Michael in
  Obersteiermark 3,717 ....C3
Sankt Michael im Lungau 2,839 .B3
Sankt Paul im Lavanttal 6,721 .C3
Sankt Pölten 43,300 ....C2

Sankt Valentin 8,715 ....C2
Sankt Veit an der Glan 11,047 .C3
Sankt Wolfgang im
  Salzkammergut 2,746 ....B3
Schärding 5,874 ....C2
Scheibbs 4,419 ....C2
Schladming 3,460 ....B3
Schrems 3,393 ....C2
Schruns 3,607 ....A3
Schwarzach im Pongau 3,616 ....B3
Schwaz 10,253 ....A3
Schwechat 14,997 ....D2
Schwertberg 3,881 ....C2
Sillian 1,988 ....B3
Solbad Hall in Tirol 12,335 ...A3
Spital am Pyhrn 2,315 ....C3
Spittal an der Drau 13,690 ....B3
Steinach 2,698 ....A3
Steyr 40,578 ....C2
Stockerau 12,634 ....C2
Strassburg 2,850 ....C3
Tamsweg 5,060 ....B3
Telfs 6,589 ....A3
Ternitz 10,287 ....D3
Traiskirchen 8,878 ....D2
Traun 20,843 ....C2
Trieben 4,639 ....C3
Trofaiach 8,731 ....C3
Tulln 7,705 ....D2
Velden am Wörthersee 7,306 ....C3
Vienna (cap.) 1,700,000 ....D2
Vienna* 1,858,700 ....D2
Villach 50,979 ....B3
Vöcklabruck 10,627 ....B2
Voitsberg 11,094 ....C3
Völkermarkt 10,772 ....C3
Vordernberg 2,508 ....C3
Waidhofen an der Thaya 4,200 ..C2
Waidhofen an der Ybbs 5,218 ...C3
Weitensfeld-Flattnitz 5,206 ...C3
Weitra 3,250 ....C2
Weiz 8,241 ....C3
Wels 47,279 ....C2
Weyer Markt 2,518 ....C2
Wien (Vienna) (cap.) 1,700,000 D2
Wiener Neustadt 34,774 ....D3
Wildon 2,002 ....C3
Wilhelmsburg 6,307 ....C2
Wolfsberg 31,176 ....C3
Wörgl 7,811 ....A3
Ybbs an der Donau 6,422 ....C2

Zams 3,120 ....A3
Zell am See 7,456 ....B3
Zell am Ziller 1,882 ....A3
Zeltweg 6,431 ....C3
Zistersdorf 3,412 ....D2
Zwettl-Niederösterreich 11,624 C2

OTHER FEATURES

AllgäU Alps (mts.) A3
Bavarian Alps (mts.) A3
Bodensee (Constance) (lake) ...A3
Brenner (pass) A3
Carnic Alps (mts.) B3
Constance (lake) A3
Danube (riv.) D2
Donau (Danube) (riv.) D2
Drau (riv.) B3
Enns (riv.) C3
Grossglockner (mt.) B3
Hohe Tauern (range) B3
Inn (riv.) B2
Karawanken (range) C3
March (riv.) D2
Mühlviertel (reg.) C2
Mur (riv.) C3
Neusiedler See (lake) D3
Niedere Tauern (range) C3
Ötztal Alps (mts.) A3
Raab (riv.) C3
Rhine (riv.) A3
Salzach (riv.) B2
Salzkammergut (reg.) C3
Semmering (pass) C3
Thaya (riv.) C2
Traun (riv.) C2
Wildspitze (mt.) A3
Zugspitze (mt.) A3

CZECHOSLOVAKIA

REPUBLICS

Czech Socialist Rep. 9,964,338 B1
Slovak Socialist Rep. 4,670,409 E2

REGIONS

Bratislava (city) 333,000 .....D2
Jihočeský 662,002 ....D2
Jihomoravský 1,966,850 ....D2
Praha (city) 1,161,200 ....C1

Severočeský 1,122,035 ....C1
Severomoravský 1,849,286 ......D2
Středočeský 1,193,041 ....C2
Středoslovenský 1,436,351 .....E2
Východočeský 1,214,581 ....C2
Východoslovenský 1,298,481 ....F2
Západočeský 865,094 ....B2
Západoslovenský 1,610,542 .....D2

CITIES and TOWNS

Aš 120,000 ....B1
Austerlitz (Slavkov) D2
Bánovce nad Bebravou 11,400 ...E2
Banská Bystrica 53,000 ....E2
Banská Štiavnica 7,486 ....E2
Bardejov 17,400 ....F2
Benešov 11,100 ....C2
Beroun 17,600 ....B2
Bílina 17,800 ....B1
Blansko 13,800 ....D2
Boskovice 8,531 ....D2
Brandýs nad Labem-Stará
  Boleslav 333,000 ....C1
Bratislava 333,000 ....D2
Břeclav 21,100 ....D2
Brezno 14,800 ....E2
Brno 335,700 ....D2
Broumov 7,782 ....C1
Bruntál 12,300 ....D2
Bystřice nad
  Pernštejnem 6,471 ....D2
Bystřice pod
  Hostýnem 6,681 ....D2
Bytča 6,922 ....E2

Čadca 16,800 ....E2
Čalovo 6,591 ....D3
Galanta 12,300 ....D2
Gottwaldov 84,300 ....D2
Handlová 16,200 ....D2
Hanušovce 14,700 ....E2
České Budějovice 80,800 ....C2
České Třebová 14,700 ....C2
Český Brod 6,640 ....C1
Český Krumlov 12,000 ....C2
Český Těšín 17,200 ....E2
Cheb 27,000 ....B1
Chocen 8,198 ....C1
Chodov 14,400 ....B1
Chomutov 44,200 ....B1
Chotěboř 6,692 ....C2
Chrudim 18,800 ....C2
Čierny Balog 6,435 ....E2
Děčín 46,500 ....B1
Detva 13,100 ....E2
Dobříš 6,378 ....C2
Dobruška 5,778 ....C1
Dolný Kubín 9,900 ....E2
Domažlice 9,100 ....B2
Dubnica nad Váhom 11,300 ......E2
Duchcov 9,712 ....B1
Dunajská Streda 13,000 ....D2
Dvory nad Žitavou 5,847 ....E3
Děčín Králové nad
  Labem 16,800 ....C1
Falknov (Sokolov) 23,900 ......B1
Fiľakovo 7,822 ....E2
Frenštát pod
  Radhoštěm 8,516 ....E2
Frýdek-Místek 43,800 ....E2
Frýdlant v.
  Čechách 5,948 ....C1

Frýdlant nad
  Ostravicí 6,250 ....E2
Galanta 12,300 ....D2
Gottwaldov 84,300 ....D2
Handlová 16,200 ....D2
Havlíčkův Brod 19,200 ....C2
Hlinsko 8,890 ....C2
Hlohovec 15,200 ....D2
Hlučín 15,300 ....E2
Hnúšťa-Likier E2
Hodonín 22,600 ....D2
Holešov 9,091 ....D2
Holíč 7,602 ....D2
Holice 6,715 ....C1
Horažďovice B2
Hořice C1
Podkrkonoší 7,715 ....C1
Horná Štubňa D2
Hornl Benešov D2
Hornl Libina D2
Hořovice 5,665 ....C2
Hosušovský Týn C1
Hostinné C1
Hradec Králové 85,600 ....C1
Hranice 13,300 ....D2
Hrinova 7,800 ....E2
Hronov 9,767 ....D1
Hrušov D2
Humenné 22,200 ....F2
Humpolec 7,810 ....C2
Hurbanovo D2
Hustopeče D2
Ilava D2
Ivančice 7,314 ....D2

AREA 32,375 sq. mi. (83,851 sq. km.)
POPULATION 7,507,000
CAPITAL Vienna
LARGEST CITY Vienna
HIGHEST POINT Grossglockner
12,457 ft. (3,797 m.)
MONETARY UNIT schilling
MAJOR LANGUAGE German
MAJOR RELIGION Roman Catholicism

AREA 49,373 sq. mi. (127,876 sq. km.)
POPULATION 15,276,799
CAPITAL Prague
LARGEST CITY Prague
HIGHEST POINT Gerlachovka 8,707 ft.
(2,654 m.)
MONETARY UNIT koruna
MAJOR LANGUAGES Czech, Slovak
MAJOR RELIGIONS Roman Catholicism,
Protestantism

AREA 35,919 sq. mi. (93,030 sq. km.)
POPULATION 10,709,536
CAPITAL Budapest
LARGEST CITY Budapest
HIGHEST POINT Kékes 3,330 ft.
(1,015 m.)
MONETARY UNIT forint
MAJOR LANGUAGE Hungarian
MAJOR RELIGIONS Roman Catholicism,
Protestantism

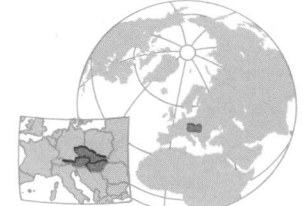

AUSTRIA

CZECHOSLOVAKIA

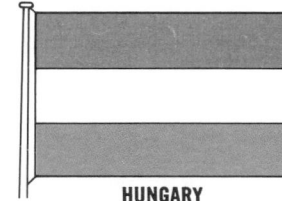

HUNGARY

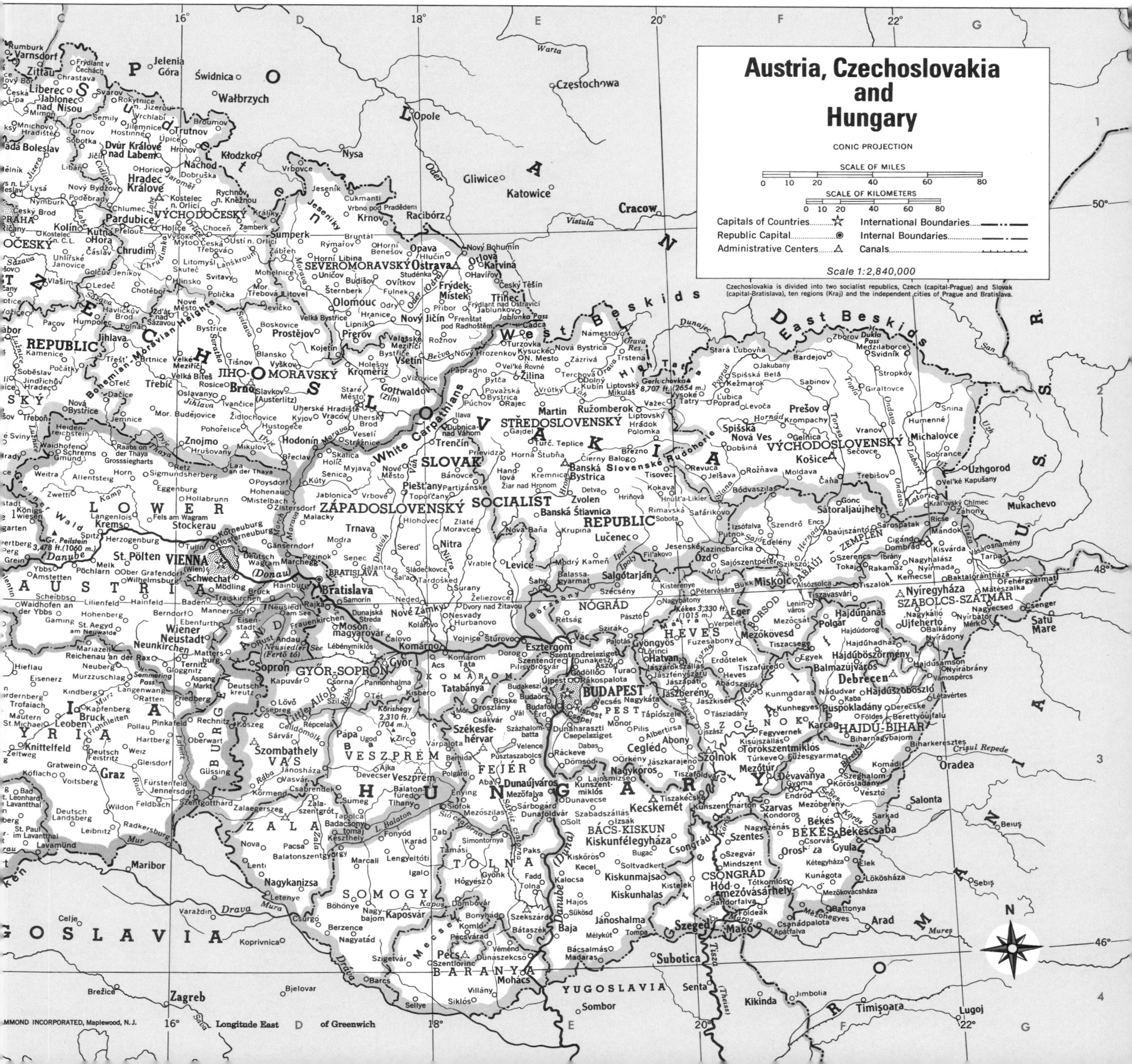

Austria, Czechoslovakia and Hungary

CONIC PROJECTION

SCALE OF MILES
0 10 20   40   60   80

SCALE OF KILOMETERS
0 10 20   40   60   80

Capitals of Countries........☆   International Boundaries.........
Republic Capital...............◉   Internal Boundaries..........
Administrative Centers.......△   Canals............................

Scale 1:2,840,000

Czechoslovakia is divided into two socialist republics, Czech (capital-Prague) and Slovak (capital-Bratislava), ten regions (Kraj) and the independent cities of Prague and Bratislava.

Jablonec nad Nisou 36,300 C1
Jablonica D2
Jablunkov 9,405 E2
Jáchymov B1
Jakubany F2
Jaroměř 11,600 C1
Jelšava F2
Jemnice C2
Jeseník 10,900 D1
Jesenské F2
Jevíčko D2
Jičín 13,200 C1
Jihlava 44,500 C2
Jilemnice C1
Jindřichův Hradec 15,700 C2
Jiřkov 11,400 B1
Kadaň 18,100 B1
Kamenice C2
Kaplice C2
Karlovy Vary 43,300 B1
Karviná 79,100 E2
Kdyně B2
Kežmarok 11,000 F2
Kladno 61,200 B1
Klatovy 18,500 B2
Kojetín 5,852 D2
Kokava nad Rimavicou 5,391 E2
Kolárovo 10,500 D3
Kolín 29,100 C1
Komárno 28,200 D3
Košice 169,100 F2
Kostelec nad Orlicí 5,575 D1
Král'ovský Chlmec 5,329 G2
Kralupy nad Vltavou 16,900 C1
Kraslice 6,733 B1
Kremnica 5,941 E2
Krnov 25,000 D1
Kroměříž 23,200 D2
Krompachy 6,332 F2
Krupina 6,627 E2
Krupka 8,301 B1
Kutná Hora 19,200 C2
Kyjov 10,700 D2
Kynšperk 5,524 B1
Kysucké Nové Mesto 11,700 E2
Lanškroun 8,683 D2
Levice 19,000 E2
Levoča 10,100 F2
Libáň C1
Liberec 75,600 C1

Moravě 6,581 D2
Nové Město nad
Váhom 15,900 D2
Nové Strašecí B1
Nové Zámky 27,300 D3
Nový Bohumín 16,700 E2
Nový Bor 7,621 C1
Nový Bydžov 6,824 C1
Nový Hrozenkov E2
Nový Jičín 21,400 E2
Nymburk 13,600 C1
Nýřany 6,204 B2
Nýrsko B2
Odry D2
Olomouc 82,800 D2
Opava 53,800 E2
Orlová 25,500 E2
Ostrava 293,500 E2
Ostrov 18,200 B1
Pardubice 78,500 C1
Partizánske 15,100 E2
Pelhřimov 11,900 C2
Pezinok 13,100 D2
Piešt'any 25,400 D2
Písek 25,100 C2
Plzeň 155,000 B2
Počátky C2
Podbořany B1
Poděbrady 13,400 C1
Pohořelice D2
Polička 6,529 D2
Polná C2
Polomka E2
Poprad 25,800 F2
Považská Bystrica 19,300 E2
Prachatice 7,900 B2
Prague (Praha) (cap.) 1,161,200 C1
Přelouč 6,251 C1
Přerov 43,500 D2
Prešov 61,000 F2
Přeštice B2
Příbor 7,726 E2
Příbram 31,300 B2
Prievidza 30,900 E2
Prostějov 44,200 D2
Protivín C2
Púchov 9,306 E2
Radnice B2
Rajec E2
Rakovník 14,200 B1

Štúrovo 8,287 E3
Šumperk 25,900 D1
Šurany 6,693 E2
Sušice 10,300 B2
Svárov C1
Svidník 4,600 F2
Svitavy 15,000 D2
Tábor 28,100 C2
Tachov 11,400 B2
Telč 5,285 C2
Teplice 52,300 B1
Tišnov 8,263 D2
Topol'čany 17,500 D2
Třebíč 23,900 C2
Trebišov 13,700 F2
Třeboň 6,068 C2
Trenčín 38,800 E2
Třešť 5,053 C2
Třinec 32,000 E2
Trnava 48,600 D2
Trutnov 24,500 D1
Turnov 13,600 C1
Turzovka 6,107 E2
Uherské Hradiště 32,100 D2
Uherský Brod 12,800 D2
Uničov 10,800 D2
Úpice 6,323 C1
Ústí nad Labem 74,900 C1
Ústí nad Orlicí 13,700 D2
Valašské
Meziříčí 19,400 D2
Varnsdorf 14,700 C1
Važec E2
Vejprty B1
Velká Bíteš D2
Velká Bystřice D2
Vel'ké Kapušany G2
Velké Meziříčí 7,590 D2
Vel'ké Rovné E2
Veselí nad Lužnicí C2
Veselí nad Moravou 11,500 D2
Vimperk 5,749 B2
Vítkov 5,138 D2
Vizovice D2
Vlašim 8,873 C2
Vodňany 5,620 C2
Vojnice E3
Volary B2
Volyně B2
Votice C2

Jablunka (pass) E2
Jeseníky (mts.) D1
Jihlava (riv.) D2
Krušné Hory (Erzgebirge)
(mts.) B1
Labe (riv.) C1
Lipno (res.) C2
Lužnice (riv.) C2
Moldau (Vltava) (riv.) C2
Morava (riv.) D2
Nitra (riv.) E2
Oder (Odra) (riv.) D2
Ohře (riv.) B1
Ondava (riv.) F2
Orava (riv.) E2
Orlická (res.) C2
Sázava (riv.) C2
Slovenské Rudohorie (mts.) E2
Sudeten (mts.) C1
Svitava (riv.) D2
Svratka (riv.) D2
Tatra, High (mts.) E2
Torysa (riv.) F2
Úhlava (riv.) B2
Váh (riv.) D2
Vltava (riv.) C2
White Carpathians (mts.) E2

HUNGARY

COUNTIES

Bács-Kiskun 568,532 E3
Baranya 434,030 E4
Békés 436,987 F3
Borsod-Abaúj-Zemplén 808,924 F2
Budapest (city) 2,060,170 E3
Csongrád 456,862 F3
Fejér 421,568 E3
Győr-Sopron 428,476 D3
Hajdú-Bihar 552,417 F3
Heves 350,874 F3
Komárom 321,579 E3
Nógrád 239,907 E3
Pest 973,486 E3
Somogy 360,308 D3
Szabolcs-Szatmár 593,746 G3
Szolnok 446,379 F3
Tolna 266,414 E3
Vas 285,527 D3

Csenger 4,792 G3
Csepel 71,693 E3
Csepreg 4,079 D3
Csongrád 22,202 E3
Csorna 12,131 D3
Csorvás 6,826 F3
Csurgó 5,463 D3
Dabas 13,075 E3
Debrecen 192,484 F3
Derecske 9,579 F3
Dévaványa 11,208 F3
Devecser 5,482 D3
Dombóvár 19,917 E3
Dombrád 6,328 F2
Dömsöd 6,545 E3
Dorog 10,754 E3
Dunaföldvár 10,318 E3
Dunaharaszti 15,788 E3
Dunakeszi 25,187 E3
Dunaszekcső 2,999 E3
Dunaújváros 60,694 E3
Dunavecse 4,521 E3
Edelény 9,559 F2
Eger 61,283 F3
Egyek 7,956 F3
Elek 6,032 F3
Enes 2,565 F2
Endrőd 8,136 F3
Enying 7,518 E3
Érd 41,210 E3
Erdőtelek 4,250 F3
Esztergom 30,476 E3
Fadd 4,805 E3
Fegyvernek 8,421 F3
Fehérgyarmat 6,729 G3
Földeák 3,855 F3
Földes 5,293 F2
Fonyód 3,957 D3
Füzesabony 6,965 F3
Füzesgyarmat 7,097 F3
Gödöllő 28,057 E3
Gönc 2,875 F2
Gyoma 10,392 F3
Gyöngyös 36,927 E3
Gyönk 2,507 E3
Győr 123,618 D3
Gyula 34,514 F3
Hajdúböszörmény 32,145 F3
Hajdúdorog 10,118 F3
Hajdúhadház 13,626 F3

Körmend 11,787 D3
Körösladány 6,565 F3
Kőszeg 12,705 D3
Kunágota 4,622 F3
Kunhegyes 10,116 F3
Kunmadaras 7,343 F3
Kunszentmárton 11,103 F3
Kunszentmiklós 7,952 E3
Lajosmizse 12,872 E3
Lébénymiklós 6,190 D3
Lengyeltóti 3,389 D3
Leninváros 18,667 F3
Lenti 8,106 D3
Létavértes 9,106 G3
Letenye 4,395 D3
Lőkösháza 2,514 F3
Lőrinci 10,679 E3
Madaras 4,519 E3
Makó 29,943 F3
Mándok 5,093 G2
Marcali 12,485 D3
Mátészalka 17,709 G3
Mélykút 7,640 E3
Mérk 3,211 G3
Mezőberény 12,702 F3
Mezőcsát 6,729 F3
Mezőfalva 5,008 E3
Mezőhegyes 8,631 F3
Mezőkovácsháza 7,473 F3
Mezőkövesd 18,435 F3
Mezőszilas 2,792 E3
Mezőtúr 22,018 F3
Mindszent 8,730 F3
Miskolc 206,727 F2
Mohács 21,385 E4
Monor 16,838 E3
Mór 12,066 E3
Mosonmagyaróvár 29,732 D3
Nádudvar 9,447 F3
Nagyatád 12,946 D3
Nagybajom 4,402 D3
Nagyecsed 8,225 G3
Nagyhalász 6,437 F2
Nagykálló 11,282 F3
Nagykanizsa 48,494 D3
Nagykáta 11,922 E3
Nagykőrös 27,900 E3
Nagyszénás 7,124 F3
Nyírábrány 4,509 G3
Nyíradony 7,146 G3

Szarvas 20,598 F3
Szécsény 5,690 E2
Százhalombatta 13,963 E3
Szeged 171,342 E3
Szeghalom 9,736 F3
Szegvár 6,395 F3
Székesfehérvár 103,197 E3
Szekszárd 34,592 E3
Szendrő 4,098 F2
Szentendre 16,844 E3
Szentes 35,326 F3
Szentgotthárd 5,837 D3
Szentlőrinc 3,926 E3
Szerencs 8,612 F2
Szigetvár 12,114 D3
Szikszó 6,419 F2
Szil 2,073 D3
Szolnok 75,203 F3
Szombathely 82,830 D3
Tab 3,922 E3
Tamási 7,602 E3
Tápiószele 5,575 E3
Tapolca 17,161 D3
Tarpa 3,436 G2
Tata 24,114 E3
Tatabánya 75,942 E3
Tét 4,441 D3
Tiszacsege 6,263 F3
Tiszaföldvár 12,560 F3
Tiszafüred 12,259 F3
Tiszakécske 12,378 E3
Tiszalök 6,230 F2
Tiszavasvári 13,292 F3
Tokaj 4,845 F2
Tolna 8,997 E3
Tompa 5,365 E3
Törökszentmiklós 25,551 F3
Tótkomlós 8,803 F3
Tura 8,235 E3
Túrkeve 11,393 F3
Újfehértó 14,412 F3
Újpest 80,384 E3
Újszász 7,098 F2
Vác 34,837 E3
Vál 2,488 E3
Vámospércs 5,213 F3
Várpalota 28,293 E3
Vásárosnamény 8,637 G2
Vasvár 4,275 D3
Vecsés 19,193 E3

Agriculture, Industry and Resources

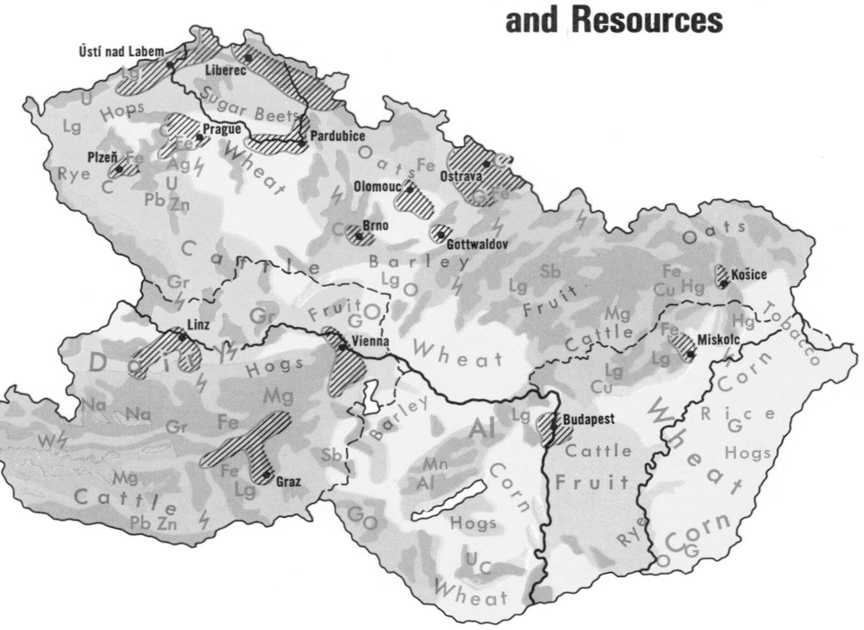

DOMINANT LAND USE

- Cereals (chiefly wheat, corn)
- Other Cereals, Livestock, Dairy
- General Farming, Livestock
- General Farming, Truck Farming
- Pasture Livestock
- Grapes, Wine
- Forests
- Nonagricultural Land

MAJOR MINERAL OCCURRENCES

Ag	Silver	Mg	Magnesium
Al	Bauxite	Mn	Manganese
C	Coal	Na	Salt
Cu	Copper	O	Petroleum
Fe	Iron Ore	Pb	Lead
G	Natural Gas	Sb	Antimony
Gr	Graphite	U	Uranium
Hg	Mercury	W	Tungsten
Lg	Lignite	Zn	Zinc

Water Power
Major Industrial Areas

Lidice C1
Lipník nad Bečvou 7,358 D2
Liptovský Mikuláš 19,400 E2
Litoměřice 19,700 C1
Litomyšl 8,112 D2
Litovel 5,805 D2
Litvínov 23,300 B1
Lomnice C2
Louny 15,200 B1
Lovosice 9,323 C1
L'ubica F2
Lučenec 23,300 E2
Lysá nad Labem 9,920 C1
Malacky 13,200 D2
Mariánské Lázně 14,600 B2
Martin 47,800 E2
Medzilaborce F2
Mělník 17,800 C1
Michalovce 23,600 G2
Mikulov 6,267 D2
Milevsko 7,091 C2
Mimoň 6,773 C1
Mladá Boleslav 36,900 C1
Mladá Vožice C2
Mnichovo Hradiště 5,239 C1
Modra 7,219 D2
Modrý Kameň 6,200 E2
Mohelnice 6,050 D2
Moldava nad Bodvou 5,397 F2
Moravská Třebová 9,052 D2
Moravské Budějovice 5,576 D2
Most 59,400 B1
Myjava 6,657 D2
Náchod 19,300 D1
Námestovo E2
Neded D2
Nejdek 8,187 B1
Nepomuk B2
Nesvady 5,453 E3
Netolice C2
Nitra 50,000 E2
Nová Baňá 6,218 E2
Nová Bystrica E2
Nová Bystřice C2
Nové Hrady C2
Nové Město na Moravě 6,581 D2

Revúca 5,901 F2
Říčany u Prahy 8,407 C2
Rimavská Sobota 5,800 E2
Rokycany 12,800 B2
Rokytnice nad Jizerou C1
Rosice D2
Roudnice nad Labem 11,800 C1
Rožňava 12,400 F2
Rožnov pod
Radhoštěm 11,600 E2
Rumburk C1
Ružomberok 22,600 E2
Rychnov nad Kněžnou 7,500 D1
Rýmařov 7,522 D2
Sabinov 5,473 F2
Šafárikovo F2
Šahy 5,049 E2
Šal'a 15,200 D2
Samorín 8,287 D2
Sečovce 5,744 F2
Sedlčany C2
Semily 8,200 C1
Senec 8,544 D2
Senica 12,300 D2
Sereď 12,500 D2
Skalica 11,100 D2
Skuteč D2
Sládečkovce 5,598 D2
Slaný 13,200 C1
Slavkov D2
Snina 10,900 G2
Soběslav 6,140 C2
Sobotka C1
Sobrance G2
Sokolov 23,900 B1
Spišská Belá F2
Spišská Nová Ves 26,100 F2
Stará L'ubovňa 5,800 F2
Staré Město 6,293 D2
Šternberk 13,700 D2
Stod B2
Strakonice 19,000 B2
Strážnice 5,482 D2
Stříbro B2
Stropkov 5,645 F2
Studénka 9,744 D2

Vráble E2
Vracov D2
Vranov nad Teplou 14,700 F2
Vrbno pod Pradědem 5,594 D1
Vrbovce D1
Vrbové D2
Vrchlabí 11,700 C1
Vrútky 5,756 E2
Vsetín 24,100 D2
Vyškov 15,100 D2
Vysoké Mýto 8,830 D2
Vysoké Tatry F2
Vyšší Brod C2
Zábřeh 11,300 D2
Žamberk 5,040 D1
Žatec 17,400 B1
Zázrivá E2
Zbiroh B2
Zborov F2
Žd'ár nad Sázavou 17,800 C2
Želiezovce 5,478 E2
Žiar nad Hronom 14,800 E2
Židlochovice D2
Žilina 56,000 E2
Zlaté Moravce 10,300 E2
Zlín (Gottwaldov) 84,300 D2
Žlutice B1
Znojmo 28,500 D2
Zvolen 29,000 E2

OTHER FEATURES

Berounka (riv.) C2
Beskids, East (mts.) F1
Beskids, West (mts.) E2
Bohemian (for.) B2
Bohemian-Moravian Heights
(hills) C2
Danube (riv.) C2
Dunajec (riv.) F2
Dyje (riv.) D2
Erzgebirge (mts.) B1
Gerlachovka (mt.) E2
Hornád (riv.) F2
Hron (riv.) E2
Ipel' (riv.) E2

Veszprém 386,740 D3
Zala 316,610 D3

CITIES and TOWNS

Aba 4,271 E3
Abádszalók 6,386 F3
Abaújszántó 4,209 F2
Abony 15,624 E3
Ács 8,423 E3
Ajka 29,601 D3
Albertirsa 11,252 E3
Alsózsolca 5,045 F2
Arló 4,203 F2
Aszód 6,218 E3
Bácsalmás 9,025 E3
Badacsonytomaj 2,933 D3
Baja 38,456 E3
Baktalórántháza 3,736 G2
Balassagyarmat 18,534 E2
Balatonfüred 12,599 D3
Balkány 7,667 G3
Balmazújváros 17,371 F3
Barcs 11,448 D4
Bátaszék 7,274 E3
Battonya 9,324 F3
Békés 22,287 F3
Békéscsaba 67,266 F3
Berettyóújfalu 16,406 F3
Berzence 3,406 D3
Bicske 10,720 E3
Biharkeresztes 4,788 F3
Biharnagybajom 4,093 F3
Böhönye 3,215 D3
Bonyhád 14,841 E3
Budafok 40,623 E3
Budaörs 13,958 E3
Budakeszi 10,429 E3
Budapest (cap.) 2,060,170 E3
Bugak 4,989 E3
Cegléd 40,567 E3
Celldömölk 12,533 D3
Cigánd 4,767 F2
Csabrendek 3,045 D3
Csákvár 5,238 E3
Csanádpalota 4,642 F3

Hajdúnánás 18,146 F3
Hajdúsámson 7,492 F3
Hajdúszoboszló 23,374 F3
Hajós 5,113 E3
Hatvan 24,790 E3
Heves 10,943 F3
Hódmezővásárhely 54,481 F3
Högyész 3,534 E3
Ibrány 7,037 F2
Izsák 7,686 E3
Izsófalva 6,816 F2
Jánoshalma 12,534 E3
Jánosháza 3,274 D3
Jászapáti 10,424 E3
Jászárokszállás 10,139 E3
Jászberény 31,347 E3
Jászfényszaru 6,869 E3
Jászkarajenő 4,101 E3
Jászkisér 6,816 F3
Jászladány 7,823 F3
Kaba 6,654 F2
Kalocsa 18,613 E3
Kaposvár 72,330 D3
Kapuvár 11,243 D3
Karád 2,754 D3
Karcag 25,264 F3
Kazincbarcika 37,481 F2
Kecel 10,493 E3
Kecskemét 91,929 E3
Kemecse 4,583 F2
Keszthely 21,671 D3
Kétegyháza 4,728 F3
Kisbér 4,562 D3
Kiskőrös 15,499 E3
Kiskunfélegyháza 35,339 E3
Kiskunhalas 30,552 E3
Kiskunmajsa 14,439 E3
Kispest 65,106 E3
Kistelek 8,544 E3
Kisterenye 6,844 E2
Kisújszállás 13,699 F3
Kisvárda 17,828 G2
Komádi 8,765 F3
Komárom 19,955 E3
Komló 30,301 E3
Kondoros 7,319 F3

Nyírbátor 13,388 G3
Nyíregyháza 108,156 F3
Nyírmada 4,744 F2
Örkény 5,013 E3
Orosháza 36,243 F3
Oroszlány 20,604 E3
Ózd 48,521 F2
Pacsa 1,984 D3
Paks 19,514 E3
Pannonhalma 3,731 D3
Pápa 32,202 D3
Pásztó 7,962 E3
Pécs 168,788 E3
Pécsvárad 3,672 E3
Pétervására 2,753 F3
Pilis 9,055 E3
Pilisvörösvár 10,217 E3
Polgár 9,429 F3
Polgárdi 5,767 E3
Püspökladány 15,730 F3
Pusztaszabolcs 5,794 E3
Putnok 7,103 F2
Ráckeve 7,534 E3
Rajka 2,448 D3
Rakamaz 5,407 F2
Rákospalota 60,983 E3
Répcelak 1,997 D3
Ricse 2,992 G2
Sajószentpéter 13,992 F2
Salgótarján 49,320 E2
Sándorfalva 5,949 F3
Sárbogárd 11,178 E3
Sarkad 11,937 F3
Sárospatak 15,316 F2
Sárvár 15,126 D3
Sátoraljaújhely 19,252 F2
Sellye 2,804 D4
Siklós 10,567 E4
Simontornya 4,892 E3
Siófok 20,084 E3
Solt 6,911 E3
Soltvadkert 7,934 E3
Sopron 53,930 D3
Sükösd 4,430 E3
Sümeg 6,229 D3
Szabadszállás 8,223 E3

Velence 3,463 E3
Vémend 2,293 E3
Verpelét 4,622 F2
Veszprém 54,898 D3
Vésztő 9,815 F3
Villány 2,764 E4
Záhony 3,049 G2
Zalaegerszeg 39,671 D3
Zalaszentgrót 5,346 D3
Zirc 5,980 D3

OTHER FEATURES

Bakony (mts.) D3
Balaton (lake) D3
Berettyó (riv.) F3
Bükk (mts.) F2
Csepelsziget (isl.) E3
Danube (riv.) E3
Dráva (riv.) D3
Duna (Danube) (riv.) E3
Fertő tó (Neusiedler See)
(lake) D3
Great Alföld (plain) F3
Hernád (riv.) F2
Kapos (riv.) D3
Kékes (mt.) E3
Körös (riv.) F3
Maros (riv.) F3
Mátra (mts.) E3
Mecsek (mts.) D3
Mura (riv.) D3
Rába (riv.) D3
Sajó (riv.) F2
Sárviz csatorna (canal) E3
Sió csatorna (canal) E3
Szentendreisziget (isl.) E3
Tisza (riv.) F3
Zala (riv.) D3

*City and suburbs.
†Population of Austrian cities
are communes.

YUGOSLAVIA

AREA 98,766 sq. mi. (255,804 sq. km.)
POPULATION 22,471,000
CAPITAL Belgrade
LARGEST CITY Belgrade
HIGHEST POINT Triglav 9,393 ft. (2,863 m.)
MONETARY UNIT Yugoslav dinar
MAJOR LANGUAGES Serbo-Croatian, Slovenian, Macedonian, Montenegrin, Albanian
MAJOR RELIGIONS Eastern Orthodoxy, Roman Catholicism, Islam

ALBANIA

AREA 11,100 sq. mi. (28,749 sq. km.)
POPULATION 2,590,600
CAPITAL Tiranë
LARGEST CITY Tiranë
HIGHEST POINT Korab 9,026 ft. (2,751 m.)
MONETARY UNIT lek
MAJOR LANGUAGE Albanian
MAJOR RELIGIONS Islam, Eastern Orthodoxy, Roman Catholicism

ROMANIA

AREA 91,699 sq. mi. (237,500 sq. km.)
POPULATION 22,048,305
CAPITAL Bucharest
LARGEST CITY Bucharest
HIGHEST POINT Moldoveanul 8,343 ft. (2,543 m.)
MONETARY UNIT leu
MAJOR LANGUAGES Romanian, Hungarian
MAJOR RELIGION Eastern Orthodoxy

BULGARIA

AREA 42,823 sq. mi. (110,912 sq. km.)
POPULATION 8,862,000
CAPITAL Sofia
LARGEST CITY Sofia
HIGHEST POINT Musala 9,597 ft. (2,925 m.)
MONETARY UNIT lev
MAJOR LANGUAGE Bulgarian
MAJOR RELIGION Eastern Orthodoxy

GREECE

AREA 50,944 sq. mi. (131,945 sq. km.)
POPULATION 9,599,000
CAPITAL Athens
LARGEST CITY Athens
HIGHEST POINT Olympus 9,570 ft. (2,917 m.)
MONETARY UNIT drachma
MAJOR LANGUAGE Greek
MAJOR RELIGION Eastern (Greek) Orthodoxy

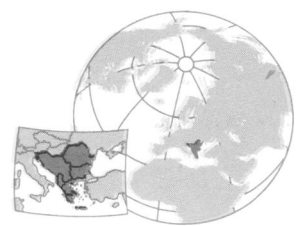

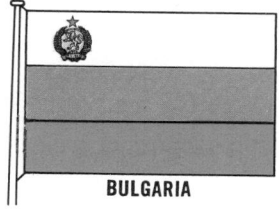

BULGARIA

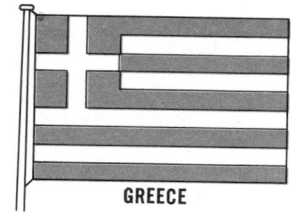

GREECE

YUGOSLAVIA

ALBANIA

ROMANIA

Agriculture, Industry and Resources

DOMINANT LAND USE

- Cereals (chiefly wheat, corn)
- Mixed Farming, Horticulture
- Pasture Livestock
- Tobacco, Cotton
- Grapes, Wine
- Forests
- Nonagricultural Land

MAJOR MINERAL OCCURRENCES

Ab	Asbestos	Mg	Magnesium
Ag	Silver	Mn	Manganese
Al	Bauxite	Mr	Marble
C	Coal	Na	Salt
Cr	Chromium	Ni	Nickel
Cu	Copper	O	Petroleum
Fe	Iron Ore	Pb	Lead
G	Natural Gas	Sb	Antimony
Hg	Mercury	U	Uranium
Lg	Lignite	Zn	Zinc

⚡ Water Power
Major Industrial Areas

ALBANIA

CITIES and TOWNS

Berat 25,700 ... D5
Çorovode ... E5
Burrel ... D5
Delvine 6,000 ... D6
Durrës (Durazzo) 53,800 ... D5
Elbasan 41,700 ... E5
Erseke ... E5
Fier 23,000 ... D5
Gjirokastër 17,100 ... D5
Kavajë 18,700 ... D5
Korçë 47,300 ... E5
Krujë 7,900 ... D5
Kuçovë (Stalin) 14,000 ... D5
Kukës 6,100 ... E4
Leskovik ... E5
Lezhë ... D5
Lushnjë 18,900 ... D5
Memaliaj ... D5
Peqin ... E5
Përmet ... E5
Peshkopi 6,600 ... E5
Pogradec 10,100 ... E5
Pukë ... E4
Sarandë 8,700 ... E6
Shëngjin ... D5
Shijak 8,000 ... D5
Shkodër 55,300 ... D5
Stalin 14,000 ... D5
Tepelenë ... D5
Tiranë (Tirana) (cap.) 171,300 ... E5
Vlorë 50,000 ... D5

OTHER FEATURES

Adriatic (sea) ... B4
Drin (riv.) ... E4
Korab (mt.) ... E5
Ohrid (lake) ... E5
Otranto (str.) ... D5
Prespa (lake) ... E5
Sazan (isl.) ... D5
Scutari (lake) ... D5
Vijosë (riv.) ... D5

BULGARIA

CITIES and TOWNS

Akhtopol 938 ... H4
Alfatar 3,249 ... H4
Ardino 5,080 ... G5
Asenovgrad 43,049 ... G5
Aytos 20,967 ... H4
Balchik 11,070 ... H4
Bansko 10,011 ... F5
Belogradchik 6,892 ... F4
Berkovitsa 16,253 ... F4
Blagoevgrad 50,043 ... F5
Botevgrad 17,789 ... F4
Bregovo 5,567 ... F4
Breznik 4,699 ... F4
Burgas 144,449 ... H4
Byala 10,564 ... G4
Byala Slatina 15,788 ... F4
Chirpan 20,595 ... G4
Devin 7,120 ... G5
Dimitrovgrad 45,596 ... G4
Dobrich (Tolbukhin) 86,184 ... H4
Dryanovo 9,804 ... G4
Elena 7,008 ... G4
Elin Pelin 5,499 ... F4
Elkhovo 12,397 ... H4
Gabrovo 75,034 ... G4
General-Toshevo 8,928 ... H4
Godech 5,225 ... F4
Gorna Oryakhovitsa 34,157 ... G4
Gotse Delchev 17,015 ... F5
Grudovo 9,871 ... H4
Ikhtiman 11,482 ... F4
Isperikh 10,500 ... H4
Ivaylovgrad 3,900 ... H5
Karapelit ... H4
Karlovo 25,472 ... G4
Karnobat 21,480 ... H4
Kavarna 10,872 ... H4
Kazanlük 53,607 ... G4
Kharmanli 19,240 ... H5
Khaskovo 75,031 ... G4
Kotel 8,229 ... H4
Krumovgrad 5,211 ... H5
Kubrat 9,826 ... H4
Kula 5,667 ... F4
Kürdzhali 47,757 ... G5
Kyustendil 48,239 ... F4
Lom 39,453 ... F4
Lovech 43,858 ... G4

Lukovit 10,400 ... G4
Malko Tŭrnovo 4,233 ... H4
Maritsa 8,664 ... H4
Michurin 4,434 ... H4
Mikhaylovgrad 40,064 ... F4
Momchilgrad 8,185 ... G5
Nesebŭr 6,768 ... H4
Nikopol 5,563 ... G4
Nova Zagora 21,872 ... H4
Novi Pazar 15,751 ... H4
Omurtag 9,067 ... H4
Oryakhovo 14,012 ... F4
Panagyurishte 20,649 ... F4
Pazardzhik 65,577 ... G4
Pernik 87,432 ... F4
Peshtera 16,882 ... G4
Petrich 24,381 ... F5
Pirdop 8,248 ... G4
Pleven 107,567 ... G4
Plovdiv 300,242 ... G4
Pomorie 11,960 ... H4
Popina ... H3
Popovo 19,428 ... H4
Provadiya 15,143 ... H4
Radomir 10,436 ... F4
Razgrad 42,486 ... H4
Razlog 13,690 ... F5
Rositsa ... H4
Ruse 160,351 ... G4
Samokov 25,763 ... F4
Sandanski 19,003 ... F5
Sevlievo 24,421 ... G4
Shabla 4,471 ... J4
Shumen 83,525 ... H4
Silistra 58,270 ... H3
Simeonovgrad (Maritsa) 8,664 ... H4
Sliven 90,137 ... H4
Smolyan 29,032 ... G5
Smyadovo 5,020 ... H4
Sofia (cap.) 965,728 ... F4
Sozopol 3,877 ... H4
Stanke Dimitrov 42,034 ... F4
Stara Zagora 122,200 ... G4
Svilengrad 15,150 ... G5
Svishtov 29,412 ... G4
Teteven 12,555 ... G4
Tolbukhin 86,184 ... H4
Topolovgrad 7,230 ... H4
Troyan 23,692 ... G4
Trŭn 3,435 ... F4
Tŭrgovishte 38,796 ... H4
Tutrakan 11,447 ... H4
Varna 251,654 ... J4
Veliko Tŭrnovo 56,497 ... G4
Vidin 53,030 ... F4
Vratsa 61,265 ... F4
Yambol 75,861 ... H4
Zimnitsa ... H4
Zlatograd 7,732 ... G5

OTHER FEATURES

Balkan (mts.) ... G4
Black (sea) ... J4
Danube (riv.) ... H4
Dunav (Danube) (riv.) ... H4
Emine (cape) ... J4
Iskŭr (riv.) ... G4
Kaliakra (cape) ... J4
Maritsa (riv.) ... G4
Mesta (riv.) ... F5
Midzhur (mt.) ... F4
Musala (mt.) ... F4
Osŭm (riv.) ... G4
Rhodope (mts.) ... G5
Rujen (mt.) ... F4
Struma (riv.) ... F5
Timok (riv.) ... F3
Tundzha (riv.) ... G4
Vit (riv.) ... G4

GREECE

REGIONS

Aegean Islands 417,813 ... G6
Athens, Greater 2,566,775 ... F7
Áyion Óros (aut. dist.) 1,732 ... G5
Central Greece and Euboea 966,543 ... F6
Crete 456,642 ... G8
Epirus 310,334 ... E6
Ionian Islands 184,443 ... D6
Macedonia 1,888,952 ... F5
Pelopónnisos 986,912 ... F7
Thessaly 659,913 ... F6
Thrace 329,582 ... G5

CITIES and TOWNS

Agrínion 30,973 ... E6
Aíyina 5,704 ... F7

Aíyion 18,829 ... F6
Alexandroúpolis 22,995 ... H5
Alivérion 4,414 ... G6
Almirós 5,680 ... F6
Amaliás 14,177 ... E7
Amfilokhía 4,668 ... E6
Amfissa 6,605 ... F6
Andíssa 1,762 ... H6
Andravídha 3,046 ... E6
Ándros 1,827 ... G7
Áno Viánnos 1,431 ... G8
Anóyia 2,750 ... G8
Ardhéa 3,555 ... F5
Areópolis 674 ... F7
Argalastí 1,621 ... F6
Árgos 18,890 ... F7
Argostólion 7,060 ... E6
Arkhángelos 3,016 ... J7
Árnaia 2,424 ... F5
Árta 19,498 ... E6
Astipálaia 787 ... H7
Atalándi 4,581 ... F6
Athens (cap.) 867,023 ... F7
Athens, Greater 2,566,775 ... F7
Ayía 3,241 ... F6
Áyios Kírikos 1,083 ... H7
Áyios Matthaíos 1,596 ... D6
Áyios Nikólaos 5,002 ... G8
Candia (Iráklion) 77,506 ... G8
Canea (Khaniá) 40,564 ... F8
Corinth 20,773 ... F7
Delfí 1,185 ... F6
Delvinákion 1,067 ... E6
Dhidhimótikhon 8,388 ... H5
Dhílaia 1,222 ... F6
Dhimitsána 996 ... F7
Dhomokós 1,991 ... F6
Dráma 29,692 ... G5
Édhessa 13,967 ... F5
Elassón 7,200 ... F6
Elevtheroúpolis 4,888 ... G5
Ermoúpolis 13,502 ... G7
Fársala 6,967 ... F6
Filiátes 2,579 ... E6
Filiatrá 5,919 ... E7
Filíppias 3,248 ... E6
Flórina 11,164 ... E5
Gargaliánoi 5,888 ... E7
Grevená 8,106 ... E5
Ídhra 2,381 ... F7
Ierápetra 7,055 ... G8
Igoumenítsa 4,109 ... E6
Ioánnina 40,130 ... E6
Íos 1,270 ... G7
Iráklion 77,506 ... G8
Istiaía 4,059 ... F6
Itháki 2,293 ... E6
Kalámai 39,133 ... F7
Kalampáka 5,453 ... E6
Kálimnos 6,492 ... H7
Kándanos 403 ... F8
Kardhítsa 25,685 ... E6
Karía 1,350 ... E6
Karíaí 301 ... G5
Káristos 3,550 ... G6
Kárpathos 1,363 ... H8
Karpenísion 4,414 ... E6
Kastéllion (Kíssamos) 2,996 ... F8
Kastéllion 1,152 ... G8
Kastoría 15,407 ... E5
Katákolon 690 ... E7
Kateríni 28,808 ... F5
Kaválla 46,234 ... G5
Kéa 693 ... G7
Kérkira 28,630 ... D6
Khalkís 36,300 ... F6
Khaniá 40,564 ... F8
Khíos 24,084 ... G6
Kiáton 7,392 ... F7
Kílkis 10,538 ... F5
Kími 2,772 ... F6
Kiparissía 3,882 ... E7
Kíssamos 2,996 ... F8
Kíthira 349 ... F7
Komotiní 28,896 ... G5
Kónitsa 3,150 ... E5
Koropí 9,367 ... F7
Kos 7,828 ... H7
Kozáni 23,240 ... E5
Kranídhion 3,363 ... F7
Lagkadás 1,350 ... F5
Lamía 37,872 ... F6
Langadhás 6,707 ... F5
Langádhia ... F7
Lárisa 72,336 ... F6
Lávrion 8,283 ... G7
Leonídhion 3,181 ... F7
Levádhia 15,445 ... F6
Levkás 6,818 ... E6
Limenária 1,507 ... G5

(continued on following page)

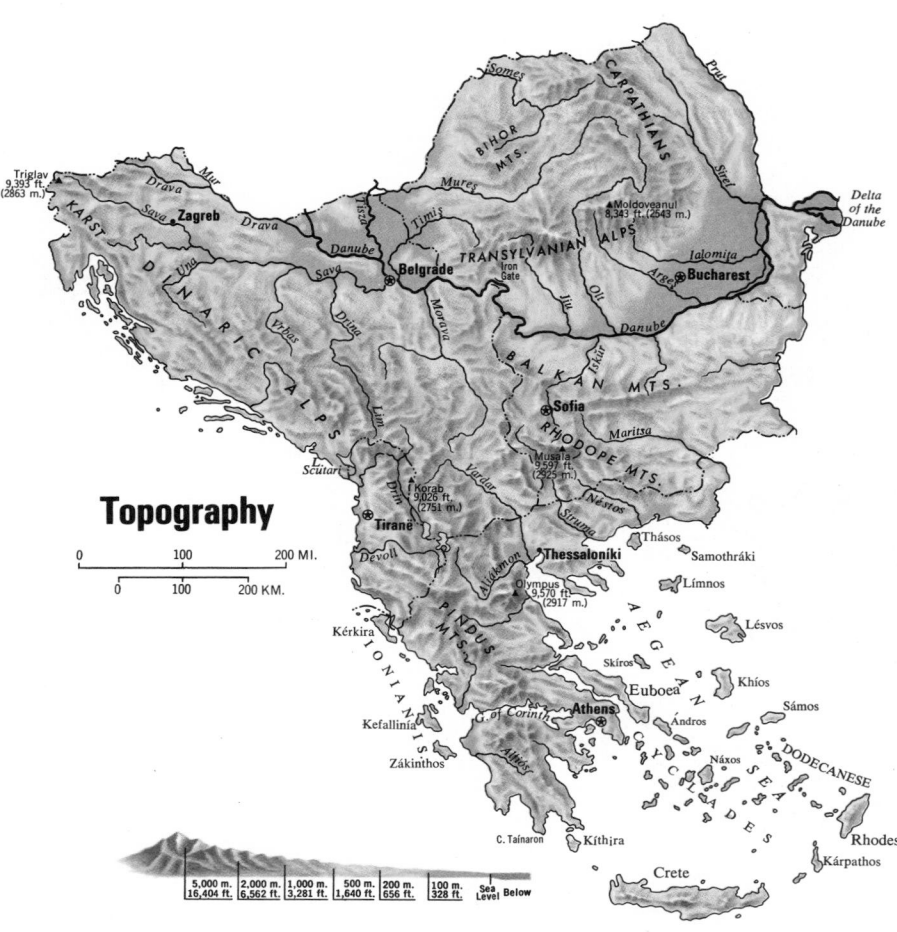

Topography

```
0      100      200 MI.
0      100      200 KM.
```

Triglav 9,393 ft. (2863 m.)

```
5,000 m.   2,000 m.   1,000 m.   500 m.   200 m.   100 m.   Sea
16,404 ft.  6,562 ft.  3,281 ft. 1,640 ft. 656 ft.  328 ft.  Level Below
```

The Balkan States

CONIC PROJECTION

SCALE OF MILES

0 25 50 75 100 125 150 175

SCALE OF KILOMETERS

0 25 50 75 100 125 150 175

Scale 1:6,150,000

Capitals of Countries .... ☆
Administrative Centers .... △
International Boundaries .... — — —
Major Internal Boundaries .... — ᛫ —
Minor Internal Boundaries .... ᛫᛫᛫᛫᛫᛫
Canals .... —

BULGARIA and GREECE are divided into counties and
departments, respectively. Because of the scale no
attempt has been made to delimit and name these subdivisions; their administrative centers have, however,
been designated.
   The larger divisions named in Greece are well-known
geographical regions, without administrative function.
ROMANIA consists of thirty-nine counties and
three cities of regional status, Bucharest, Constanţa
and Petroşeni. Scale does not permit delimiting
these counties.
   ALBANIA is divided into twenty-seven districts. Scale
does not permit the delimitation of these divisions.
   YUGOSLAVIA is a federation of six republics. The
Serbian republic includes an autonomous province
(Vojvodina), and an autonomous region (Kosovo).

© Copyright HAMMOND INCORPORATED, Maplewood, N.J.

Topography

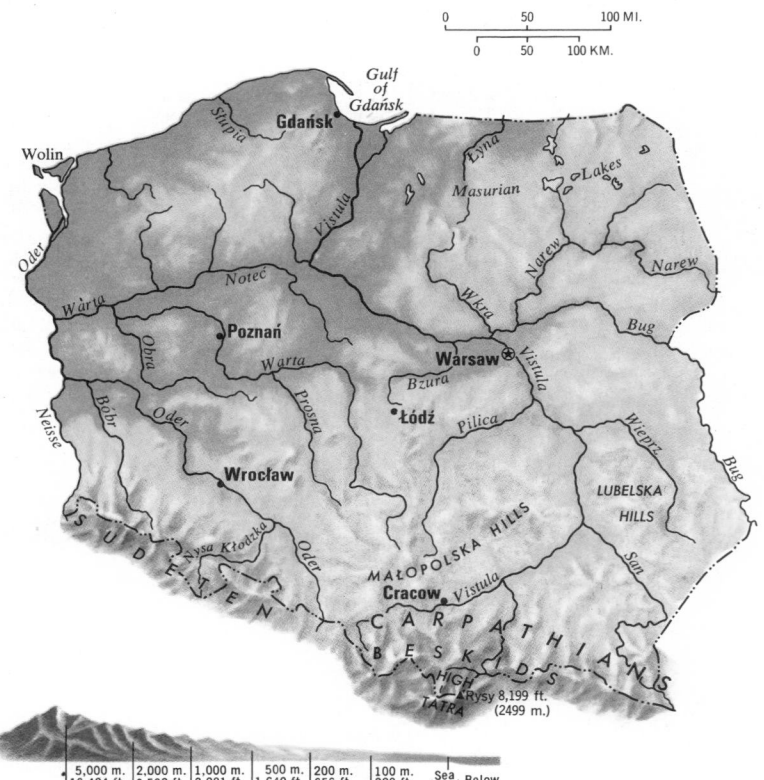

Scale:
0 — 50 — 100 MI.
0 — 50 — 100 KM.

5,000 m. 16,404 ft. | 2,000 m. 6,562 ft. | 1,000 m. 3,281 ft. | 500 m. 1,640 ft. | 200 m. 656 ft. | 100 m. 328 ft. | Sea Level | Below

Agriculture, Industry and Resources

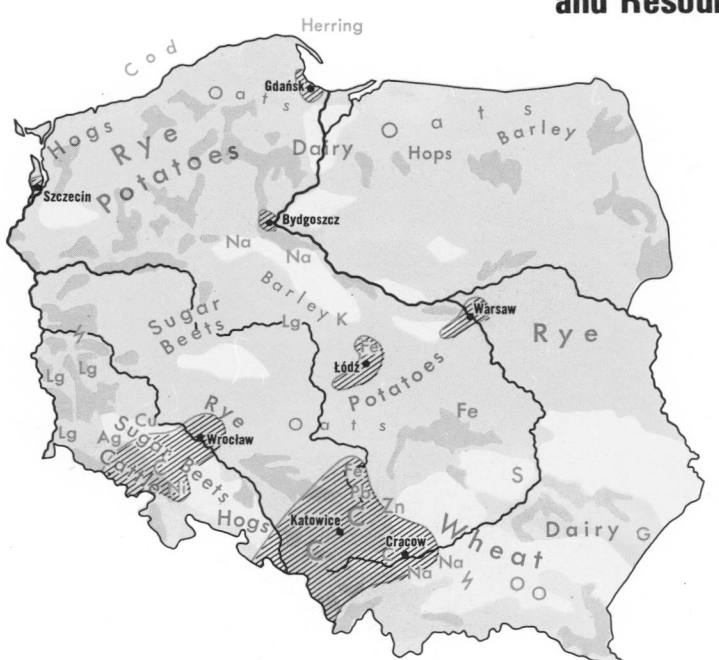

MAJOR MINERAL OCCURRENCES

Ag	Silver	Na	Salt
C	Coal	Ni	Nickel
Cu	Copper	O	Petroleum
Fe	Iron Ore	Pb	Lead
G	Natural Gas	S	Sulfur
K	Potash	Zn	Zinc
Lg	Lignite		

⚡ Water Power
▨ Major Industrial Areas

DOMINANT LAND USE

☐ Cereals (chiefly wheat)

☐ Rye, Oats, Barley, Potatoes

☐ General Farming, Livestock

☐ Forests

Poland 1938

0 — 50 — 100 MILES

Poland 1945

0 — 50 — 100 MILES

Braniewo 12,100	D1
Breslau (Wrocław) 461,900	C3
Brieg (Brzeg) 30,780	C3
Brodnica 17,300	D2
Brzeg 30,780	C3
Brzeg Dolny 10,800	C3
Brzesko 9,701	E3
Busko Zdrój 11,100	E3
Bydgoszcz 280,460	C2
Bytom 186,993	A3
Bytów 10,642	C1
Chełm 38,789	F3
Chełmno 17,906	D2
Chełmza 14,200	D2
Chodziez 14,100	C2
Chojnice 23,500	C2
Chojnów 11,000	B3
Chorzów 151,338	B4
Choszczno 9,800	B2
Chrzanów 29,300	B4
Ciechanów 28,500	E2
Cieplice Śląskie-Zdrój 15,400	B3
Cieszyn 25,234	D4
Cracow 651,300	E4
Czechowice-Dziedzice 25,400	D4
Czeladź 31,843	B4
Częstochowa 187,613	D3
Dąbrowa Górnicza 61,660	B3
Danzig (Gdańsk) 364,285	D1
Darłowo 11,200	C1
Dębica 22,900	E3
Dęblin 14,600	E3
Dębno 10,700	B2
Działdowo 10,100	E2
Dzierzoniów 32,800	C3
Elbing (Elblag) 89,835	D1
Ełk 27,188	F2
Gdańsk 364,285	D1
Gdynia 190,125	D1
Gizycko 18,200	E1
Gleiwitz (Gliwice) 170,912	A4
Głogów (Glogau) 20,226	C3
Głowno 12,800	D2
Głubczyce 11,300	C3
Głuchołazy 13,200	C3
Gniezno 50,643	C2
Goleniów 14,600	B2
Gorlice 15,200	E4
Gorzów Wielkopolski 74,267	B2
Gostyń 13,000	C3
Gostynin 12,000	D2
Grajewo 11,200	F2
Grodzisk Mazowiecki 20,400	E2
Grójec 10,300	E3
Grudziądz 75,511	D2
Grünberg (Zielona Góra) 59,700	B3
Gryfice 13,200	B2
Guben (Gubin) 14,600	B3
Hajnowka m4,345	F2
Hindenburg (Zabrze) 199,400	A4
Hirschberg (Jelenia Góra) 55,720	B3
Hrubieszów 14,999	F3
Iława 16,400	D2
Inowrocław 54,817	D2
Jarocin 18,100	C3
Jarosław 29,000	F4
Jasło 17,025	E4
Jastrzębie Zdroj 34,400	D3
Jaworzno 63,271	B4
Jędrzejów 13,264	E3
Jelenia Góra 55,720	B3
Kalisz 81,227	D3
Kamienna Góra 21,000	B3
Kartuzy 10,558	C1
Katowice 303,264	B4
Kedzierzyn-Koźle 45,600	C3
Kępno 10,151	C3
Kętrzyn 19,300	E1
Kielce 125,952	E3
Kłobuck 12,600	D3
Kłodzko 26,000	C3
Kluczbork 18,000	D3
Knurów 28,400	A4
Kolberg (Kołobrzeg) 25,419	B1
Koło 13,100	D2
Kołobrzeg 25,419	B1
Konin 40,600	D2
Końskie 13,100	E3
Konstantynów Łódzki 12,800	D3
Kościan 18,700	C2
Kościerzyna 18,914	C1
Köslin (Koszalin) 64,414	C1
Kostrzyń 11,200	B2
Koszalin 64,414	C1
Kraków (Cracow) 651,300	E4
Krapkowice 13,800	D3
Kraśnik Fabryczny 14,600	F3
Krasnystaw 12,495	F3
Krosno 26,500	E4
Krotoszyn 21,900	C3
Krynica 10,200	E4
Küstrin 11,200	B2
Kutno 30,000	D2
Kwidzin 23,104	D2
Łancut 12,049	F3
Landsberg (Gorzów Wielkepolski) 74,267	B2
Łaziska Górne 10,800	A4
Lębork 25,000	C1
Łęczyca 13,900	D2
Legionowo 20,800	E2
Legnica 75,843	C3
Leszcyny 12,200	A4
Leszno 33,890	C3
Libiaz 10,600	D3
Lidzbark Warmiński 12,900	E1
Liegnitz (Legnica) 75,843	C3
Lipno 10,900	D2
Łódź 777,800	D3
Łomza 25,500	F2
Łowicz 20,400	D2
Lubań 17,200	B3
Lubartów 10,000	F3
Lubin 28,400	C3
Lublin 235,937	F3
Lubliniec 19,800	D3
Luboń 16,400	C2
Lubsko 12,600	B3
Łuków 15,500	F3
Malbork (Marienburg) 30,900	D1
Międzyrzec Podlaski 13,500	F3
Międzyrzecz 14,900	B2
Mielec 26,800	E3
Mikłów 21,300	B4
Mińsk Mazowiecki 24,200	E2
Mława 20,007	E2
Mońki 9,560	F2
Morąg 9,681	E2
Mrągowo 13,400	E2
Myślenice 12,100	E4
Mysłowice 44,737	C4
Myszków 18,000	D3
Nakło nad Notecia 16,800	C2
Namysłów 11,076	C3
Neisse (Nysa) 31,837	C3
Nidzica 9,642	E2
Nisko 10,000	E3
Nowa Ruda 18,100	C3
Nowa Sól 33,300	B3
Nowy Dwór Mazowiecki 16,900	E2
Nowy Sącz 41,103	E4
Nowy Targ 21,900	E4
Nysa 31,837	C3
Oborniki 10,200	C2
Oława 17,746	C3
Oleśnica 27,500	C3
Olkusz 15,800	D3
Olsztyn 94,119	E2
Opoczno 12,168	E3
Opole 86,510	C3
Oppeln 86,510	C3
Orzesze 9,600	A4
Ostróda 21,300	D2
Ostrołęka 21,981	E2
Ostrów Mazowiecka 15,000	E2
Ostrów Wielkopolski 49,530	C3
Ostrowiec Świętokrzyski 49,958	E3
Oświęcim 39,600	D3
Otwock 39,863	E2
Ozorków 18,200	D3
Pabianice 62,275	D3
Piekary Śląskie 36,300	B4
Piła 43,778	C2
Pionki 13,600	E3
Piotrków Trybunalski 59,683	D3
Pisz 11,100	E2
Pleszew 13,348	C3
Płock 71,727	D2
Płońsk 11,619	E2
Police 12,700	B2
Poznań 469,085	C2
Prudnik 20,300	C3
Pruszcz Gdanski 13,000	D1
Pruszków 42,961	E2
Przasnysz 11,100	E2
Przemyśl 53,228	F4
Puck 9,500	D1
Puławy 34,800	F3
Pułtusk 12,600	E2
Rabka 10,700	D4
Racibórz 40,418	C3
Radom 158,640	E3
Radomsko 31,179	D3
Ratibor (Racibórz) 40,418	C3
Rawa Mazowiecka 9,800	E3
Rawicz 14,100	C3
Ruda Śląska 142,407	B4
Rumia 23,300	D1
Rybnik 43,415	D3
Rypin 10,029	D2
Rzeszów 82,192	F4
Sandomierz 16,800	E3
Sanok 21,600	F4
Schneidemühl (Piła) 36,600	C2
Schweidnitz (Świdnica) 47,542	C3
Siedlce 38,983	F2
Siemianowice Śląskie 67,278	B4
Sieradz 18,500	D3
Sierpc 12,700	D2
Skarzysko-Kamienna 39,194	E3
Skawina 15,900	D4
Skierniewice 25,590	E2
Sławno 10,700	C1
Słubice 12,000	B2
Słupsk 68,311	C1
Sochaczew 20,500	E2
Sokółka 10,023	F2
Sokołów Podlaski 9,569	F2
Sopot 47,573	D1
Sosnowiec 144,652	B4
Śrem 15,600	C2
Środa Śląska 10,259	C3
Środa Wielkopolska 14,800	C2
Stalowa Wola 29,768	F3
Starachowice 42,807	E3
Stargard Szceciński 44,400	B2
Starogard Gdański 33,400	D2
Stary Sacz 57,400	E4
Stettin (Szczecin) 337,294	B2
Stolp (Słupsk) 68,311	C1
Strzegom 14,000	C3
Strzelce Opolskie 14,700	D3
Strzelin 9,800	C3
Sulechów 10,200	B2
Suwałki 25,360	F1
Swarzędz 12,100	C2
Świdnica 47,542	C3
Świdnik 21,900	F3
Świdwin 12,500	B2
Świebodzice 18,500	C3
Świebodzin 14,900	B2
Świecie 17,900	D2
Świętochłowice 57,633	A4
Świnoujście (Swinemünde) 27,900	B1
Szamotuły 14,600	C2
Szczecin 337,204	B2
Szczecinek 28,600	C2
Szczytno 17,371	E2
Szprotawa 11,200	B3
Tarnobrzeg 18,800	E3
Tarnów 85,514	E4
Tarnowskie Góry 34,200	A3
Tczew 40,794	D1
Tomaszów Lubelski 12,329	F3
Tomaszów Mazowiecki 54,911	E3
Toruń 129,152	D2
Trzcianka 10,900	C2
Trzebinia-Siersza	C4
Turek 18,500	D2
Tychy 71,384	B4
Ustka 9,900	C1
Wąbrzeźno 11,800	D2
Wadowice 11,700	D4
Wągrowiec 15,600	C2
Wałbrzych 125,048	C3
Wałcz 18,900	C2
Waldenburg (Wałbrzych) 125,048	C3
Warsaw (Warszawa) (cap.) 1,377,100	E2
Wejherowo 33,600	D1
Wieliczka 13,600	E3
Wieluń 14,300	D3
Wisła 9,800	D4
Włocławek 77,169	D2
Wodzisław Śląski 25,600	D4
Wolin 35,458	B2
Wołomin 24,000	E2
Wołów 10,500	C3
Wrocław 523,318	C3
Września 17,800	C2
Wschowa 10,000	C3
Wyszków	E2
Ząbki 16,000	E2
Ząbkowice Śląskie 13,800	C3
Zabrze 197,214	A4
Zagań 21,400	B3
Zakopane 27,039	D4
Zambrów 14,082	E2
Zamość 34,734	F3
Zary 28,300	B3
Zawiercie 39,410	D3
Zduńska Wola 29,066	D3
Zgierz 42,838	D3
Zgorzelec 28,400	B3
Ziębice 9,700	C3
Zielona Góra 73,156	B3
Złocieniec 10,100	C2
Złotoryja 12,200	C3
Złotów 11,600	C2
Znin 9,600	C2
Zyrardów 33,196	E2
Zywiec 22,400	D4

OTHER FEATURES

Baltic (sea)	B1
Beskids (range)	D4
Brda (riv.)	C2
Brynica (riv.)	B4
Bug (riv.)	F2
Danzig (Gdańsk) (gulf)	D1
Dukla (pass)	E4
Dunajec (riv.)	E4
Gwda (riv.)	C2
Hel (pen.)	D1
High Tatra (range)	D4
Kłodnica (riv.)	A4
Łyna (riv.)	E1
Mamry, Jezioro (lake)	E1
Masurian (lkes)	E2
Narew (riv.)	E2
Neisse (riv.)	B3
Noteć (riv.)	B2
Nysa Kłodzka (riv.)	C3
Nysa Łuzycka (Neisse) (riv.)	B3
Oder (riv.)	B2
Orava (res.)	D4
Pilica (riv.)	D3
Pomeranian (bay)	B1
Prosna (riv.)	C3
Przemsza (riv.)	B4
Rysy (mt.)	D4
San (riv.)	F3
Słupia (riv.)	C1
Śniardwy, Jezioro (lake)	E2
Sudeten (range)	B3
Uznam (Usedom) (isl.)	B1
Vistula (riv.)	D2
Warmia (reg.)	D1
Warta (riv.)	B2
Wieprz (riv.)	F3
Wisła (Vistula) (riv.)	D2
Wkra (riv.)	E2
Wolin (Wollin) (isl.)	B2

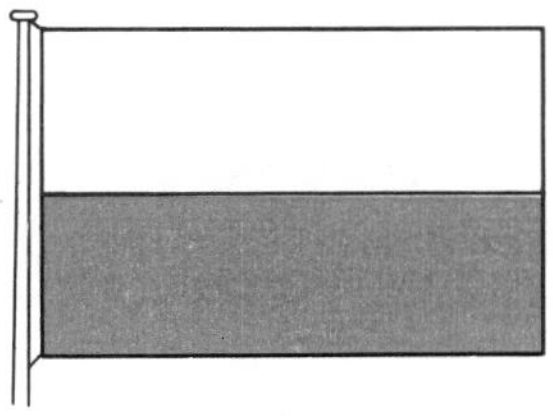

AREA 120,725 sq. mi. (312,678 sq. km.)
POPULATION 35,815,000
CAPITAL Warsaw
LARGEST CITY Warsaw
HIGHEST POINT Rysy 8,199 ft. (2,499 m.)
MONETARY UNIT zloty
MAJOR LANGUAGE Polish
MAJOR RELIGION Roman Catholicism

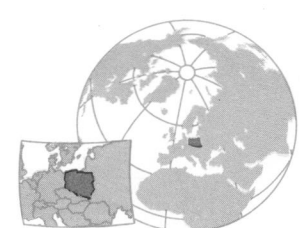

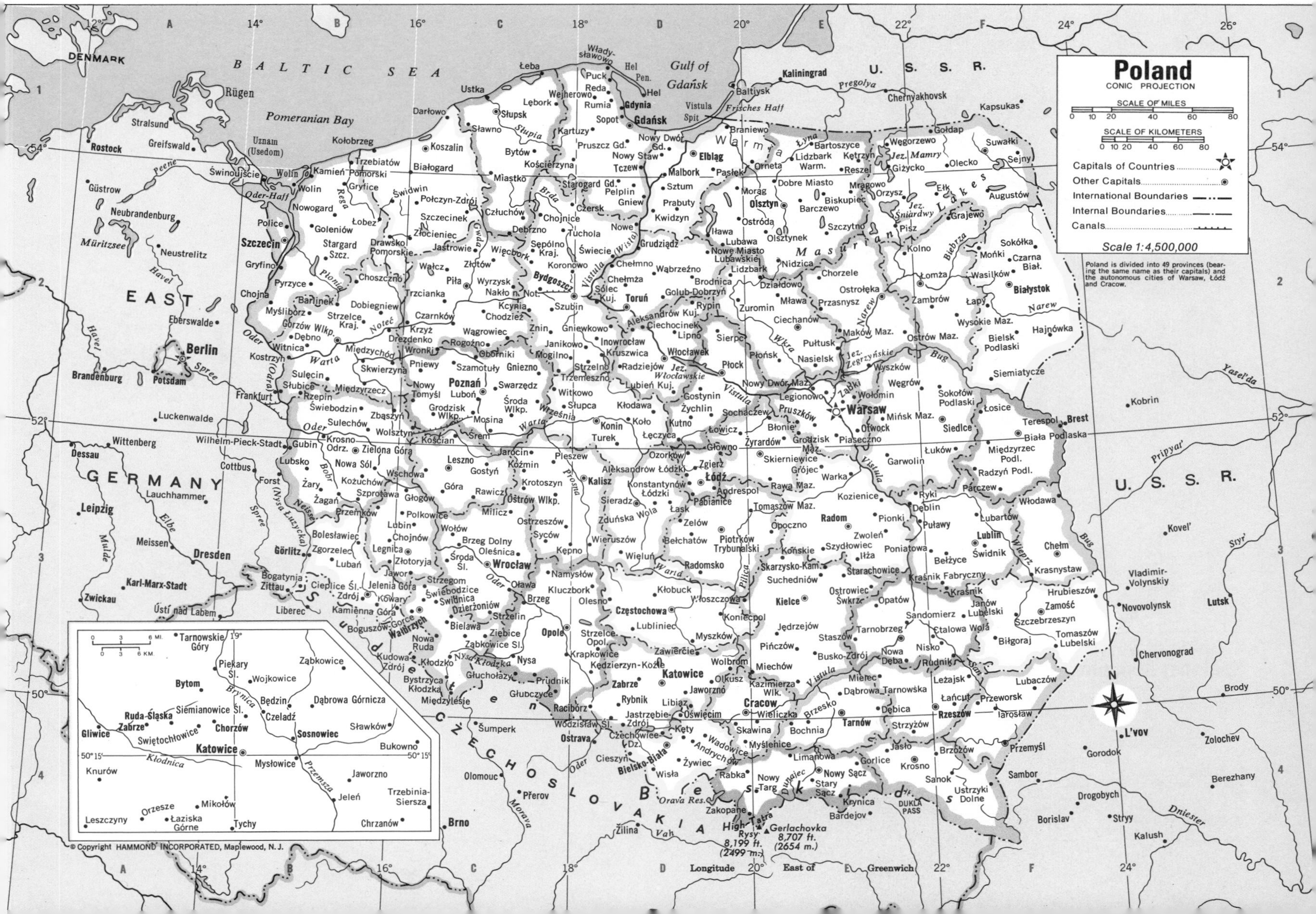

Poland
CONIC PROJECTION
SCALE OF MILES
SCALE OF KILOMETERS
Capitals of Countries
Other Capitals
International Boundaries
Internal Boundaries
Canals
Scale 1:4,500,000
Poland is divided into 49 provinces (bearing the same name as their capitals) and the autonomous cities of Warsaw, Łódź and Cracow.
BALTIC SEA
Gulf of Gdańsk
Pomeranian Bay
DENMARK
EAST GERMANY
U.S.S.R.
CZECHOSLOVAKIA
Warsaw
Gdańsk
Poznań
Wrocław
Łódź
Cracow
Katowice
Szczecin
Berlin
Longitude East of Greenwich
© Copyright HAMMOND INCORPORATED, Maplewood, N.J.

Union of Soviet Socialist Republics

UNION REPUBLICS

Armenian S.S.R. 3,031,000 ..... E6
Azerbaidzhan S.S.R. 6,028,000 ..... E5
Estonian S.S.R. 1,466,000 ..... C4
Georgian S.S.R. 5,015,000 ..... D5
Kazakh S.S.R. 14,684,000 ..... G5
Kirgiz S.S.R. 3,529,000 ..... H5
Latvian S.S.R. 2,521,000 ..... C4
Lithuanian S.S.R. 3,398,000 ..... C4
Moldavian S.S.R. 3,947,000 ..... C5
Russian S.F.S.R. 137,551,000 ..... D4
Tadzhik S.S.R. 3,801,000 ..... H6
Turkmen S.S.R. 2,759,000 ..... F6
Ukrainian S.S.R. 49,755,000 ..... C5
Uzbek S.S.R. 15,391,000 ..... G5
White Russian S.S.R. 9,560,000 ..... C4

INTERNAL DIVISIONS

Abkhaz A.S.S.R. 505,000 ..... E5
Adygey Aut. Obl. 405,000 ..... D5
Adzhar A.S.S.R. 354,000 ..... E5
Aginsk Buryat Aut. Okr. 69,000 ..... M4
Bashkir A.S.S.R. 3,849,000 ..... F4
Buryat A.S.S.R. 900,000 ..... M4
Chechen-Ingush A.S.S.R. 1,154,000 ..... E5
Chukchi Aut. Okr. 133,000 ..... R3
Chuvash A.S.S.R. 1,292,000 ..... E4
Dagestan A.S.S.R. 1,628,000 ..... E5
Evenki Aut. Okr. 16,000 ..... K3
Gorno-Altay Aut. Obl. 172,000 ..... J4
Gorno-Badakhshan Aut. Obl. 127,000 ..... H6
Jewish Aut. Obl. 190,000 ..... O5
Kabardin-Balkar A.S.S.R. 674,000 ..... E5
Kalmuck A.S.S.R. 294,000 ..... E5
Karachay-Cherkess Aut. Obl. 368,000 ..... E5
Karakalpak A.S.S.R. 904,000 ..... G5
Karelian A.S.S.R. 736,000 ..... D3
Khakass Aut. Obl. 500,000 ..... J4
Khanty-Mansi Aut. Okr. 569,000 ..... H3
Komi A.S.S.R. 1,119,000 ..... F3
Komi-Permyak Aut. Okr. 173,000 ..... F4
Koryak Aut. Okr. 34,000 ..... R3
Mari A.S.S.R. 703,000 ..... E4
Mordvinian A.S.S.R. 991,000 ..... E4
Nagorno-Karabakh Aut. Obl. 161,000 ..... E5
Nakhichevan' A.S.S.R. 239,000 ..... E6
Nenets Aut. Okr. 47,000 ..... F3
North Ossetian A.S.S.R. 597,000 ..... E5
South Ossetian Aut. Obl. 98,000 ..... E5
Tatar A.S.S.R. 3,436,000 ..... F4
Taymyr Aut. Okr. 44,000 ..... K2
Tuvinian A.S.S.R. 267,000 ..... K4
Udmurt A.S.S.R. 1,494,000 ..... F4
Ust'-Ordynskiy Buryat Aut. Okr. 133,000 ..... L4
Yakut A.S.S.R. 839,000 ..... N3
Yamal-Nenets Aut. Okr. 158,000 ..... H3

CITIES and TOWNS

Abakan 128,000 ..... K4
Abay 34,245 ..... H5
Abaza 15,202 ..... J4
Achinsk 117,000 ..... K4
Agata K3
Aginskoye 7,922 ..... M4
Akmolinsk (Tselinograd) 234,000 ..... H4
Aksay 10,010 ..... F4
Aktas G5
Aktash J4
Aktyubinsk 191,000 ..... F4
Aldan 17,689 ..... N4
Aleksandrovsk-Sakhalinskiy 20,342 ..... P5
Alekseyevka 18,041 ..... H4
Aleysk 32,487 ..... J4
Alga 12,000 ..... F5
Aliskerovo R3
Allakh-Yun' O3
Alma-Ata 910,000 ..... H5
Almaznyy M3
Ambarchik R3
Amderma F3
Amursk 24,010 ..... O4
Anadyr' 7,703 ..... S3
Andizhan 230,000 ..... H5
Angarsk 239,000 ..... L4
Angren H5
Anzhero-Sudzhensk 105,000 ..... J4
Aral'sk 37,722 ..... G5
Archangel (Arkhangel'sk) 385,000 ..... E3
Arkalyk 15,108 ..... G4
Armavir 162,000 ..... E5
Arsen'yev 60,000 ..... O5
Artem 69,000 ..... O5
Artemovskiy M4
Arys' 26,414 ..... G5
Arzamas 93,000 ..... E4
Asbest 79,000 ..... G4
Ashkhabad 312,000 ..... F6
Asino 29,395 ..... J4
Astrakhan' 461,000 ..... E5
Atbasar 37,228 ..... G4
Atka Q3
Ayaguz 35,827 ..... J5
Ayan O4
Aykhal M3
Bagdarin M4
Baku 1,022,000 ..... F5
Baku* 1,550,000 ..... F5
Balakovo 152,000 ..... E4
Balashov 93,000 ..... E4
Baley 27,215 ..... M4
Balkhash 78,000 ..... H5
Balykshi 22,397 ..... F5
Bam N4
Barabinsk 37,274 ..... H4
Baranovichi 131,000 ..... C4
Barnaul 533,000 ..... J4
Batagay 10,000 ..... O3
Batumi 123,000 ..... E5
Baykit K3
Baykonyr G5
Bayram-Ali 31,987 ..... G6
Belgorod 240,000 ..... D4
Belogorsk 63,000 ..... N4
Belomorsk 16,595 ..... D3
Beloretsk 71,000 ..... F4
Belovo 112,000 ..... J4
Berdichev 80,000 ..... C5
Berdsk 67,000 ..... J4
Berezniki 185,000 ..... F4
Berezovo 6,000 ..... G3
Beringovskiy T3
Bikin 17,473 ..... O5
Bira O5
Birobidzhan 69,000 ..... O5
Biruni G5
Biysk 212,000 ..... J4
Blagoveshchensk 172,000 ..... N4
Bobruysk 192,000 ..... C4
Bodaybo 19,000 ..... M4
Borisoglebsk 68,000 ..... E4
Borzya 27,815 ..... M4
Bratsk 214,000 ..... L4
Brest 177,000 ..... C4
Brindakit O4
Bryansk 394,000 ..... D4
Bugul'ma 80,000 ..... F4
Bukachacha 10,000 ..... M4
Bukhara 185,000 ..... G5
Bulun N2
Buzuluk 76,000 ..... F4
Chadan K4
Chapayevsk 85,000 ..... F4
Chara M4
Chardzhou 140,000 ..... G6
Charsk 10,100 ..... J5
Cheboksary 308,000 ..... E4
Chegdomyn 16,499 ..... O4
Chelkar 19,377 ..... F5
Chelyabinsk 1,030,000 ..... G4
Cheremkhovo 77,000 ..... L4
Cherepovets 266,000 ..... D4
Cherkessk 91,000 ..... E5
Chernigov 238,000 ..... D4
Chernogorsk 71,000 ..... K4
Chernovtsy 219,000 ..... C5
Chernyshevsk 10,000 ..... M4
Cherskiy Q3
Chimbay 18,899 ..... F5
Chimkent 322,000 ..... H5
Chirchik 132,000 ..... H5
Chita 303,000 ..... M4
Chokurdakh P2
Chumikan O4
Dal'negorsk 33,506 ..... O5
Dal'nerechensk 28,224 ..... O5
Daugavpils 116,000 ..... C4
Denau G6
Dikson J2
Dimitrovgrad 106,000 ..... F4
Dnepropetrovsk 1,066,000 ..... D5
Donetsk 1,021,000 ..... D5
Drogobych 66,000 ..... C5
Druzhba J5
Druzhina P3
Dudinka 19,701 ..... J3
Dushanbe 494,000 ..... G6
Dzerzhinsk 257,000 ..... E4
Dzhalal-Abad 55,000 ..... H5
Dzhalinda N4
Dzhambul 264,000 ..... H5
Dzhelinda M2
Dzhetygara 32,169 ..... G4
Dzhezkazgan 89,000 ..... G5
Dzhusaly 20,658 ..... G5
Egvekinot S3
Ekibastuz 66,000 ..... H4
Ekimchan O4
El'dikan O3
Elista 70,000 ..... E5
Emba 17,820 ..... F5
Engel's 161,000 ..... E4
Erivan 1,019,000 ..... E6
Evensk Q3
Fergana 176,000 ..... H5
Fort-Shevchenko 12,000 ..... F5
Frolovo 33,398 ..... E5
Frunze 533,000 ..... H5
Gasan-Kuli F6
Gol'chikha J2
Gomel' 383,000 ..... D4
Gor'kiy 1,344,000 ..... E4
Gorno-Altaysk 34,413 ..... J4
Gornyak 16,643 ..... J4
Grodno 195,000 ..... C4
Groznyy 375,000 ..... E5
Gubakha 33,243 ..... F4
Gulistan 30,879 ..... G5
Gur'yev 131,000 ..... F5
Gusinoozersk 10,000 ..... L4
Gyda H2
Igarka 15,624 ..... J3
Igrim G3
Ilanskiy 22,852 ..... K4
Indiga E3
Inta 51,000 ..... G3
Iolotan' 10,000 ..... G6
Irkutsk 550,000 ..... L4
Ishim 63,000 ..... H4
Isil'kul' 25,958 ..... H4
Iul'tin T3
Ivano-Frankovsk 150,000 ..... C5
Ivanovo 465,000 ..... E4
Ivdel 15,308 ..... G3
Izhevsk 549,000 ..... F4
Izmail 83,000 ..... C5
Kachug L4
Kagan 34,117 ..... G6
Kalachinsk 20,809 ..... H4
Kalakan M4
Kalinin 412,000 ..... D4
Kaliningrad 355,000 ..... B4
Kalmykovo F5
Kaluga 265,000 ..... D4
Kamen'-na-Obi 35,604 ..... H4

Division	Ref.	Division	Ref.
1. Abkhaz A.S.S.R.	E5	13. Khakass Aut. Oblast	J4
2. Adygey Aut. Oblast	D5	14. Komi-Permyak Aut. Okrug	F4
3. Adzhar A.S.S.R.	E5	15. Mari A.S.S.R.	E4
4. Aginsk Buryat Autonomous Okrug	M4	16. Mordivian A.S.S.R.	E4
5. Chechen-Ingush A.S.S.R.	E5	17. Nagorno-Karabakh Aut. Oblast	E5
6. Chuvash A.S.S.R.	E4	18. Nakhichevan' A.S.S.R.	E6
7. Gorno-Altay Aut. Oblast	J4	19. North Ossetian A.S.S.R.	E5
8. Gorno-Badakhshan Aut. Oblast	H6	20. South Ossetian Aut. Oblast	E5
9. Jewish Aut. Oblast	O5	21. Tatar A.S.S.R.	F4
10. Kabardin-Balkar A.S.S.R.	E5	22. Tuvinian A.S.S.R.	K4
11. Karachay-Cherkess Aut. Oblast	E5	23. Udmurt A.S.S.R.	F4
12. Karakalpak A.S.S.R.	G5	24. Ust'-Ordynsk Buryat Autonomous Okrug	L4

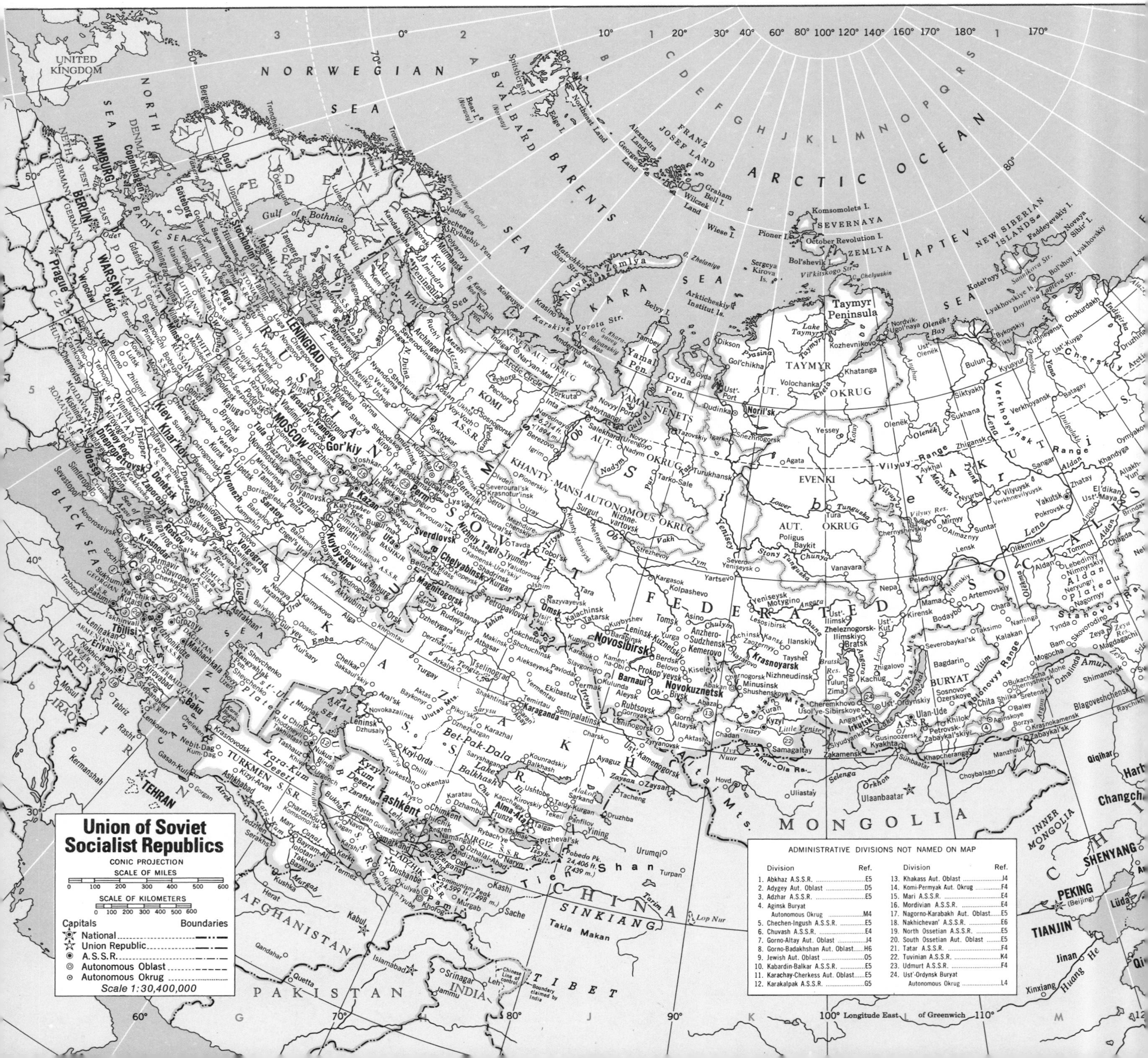

AREA 8,649,490 sq. mi. (22,402,179 sq. km.)
POPULATION 262,436,227
CAPITAL Moscow
LARGEST CITY Moscow
HIGHEST POINT Communism Peak 24,599 ft. (7,498 m.)
MONETARY UNIT ruble
MAJOR LANGUAGES Russian, Ukrainian, White Russian, Uzbek, Azerbaidzhani, Tatar, Georgian, Lithuanian, Armenian, Yiddish, Latvian, Mordvinian, Kirgiz, Tadzhik, Estonian, Kazakh, Moldavian (Romanian), German, Chuvash, Turkmenian, Bashkir
MAJOR RELIGIONS Eastern (Russian) Orthodoxy, Islam, Judaism, Protestantism (Baltic States)

UNION REPUBLICS

	AREA (sq. mi.)	AREA (sq. km.)	POPULATION	CAPITAL and LARGEST CITY
RUSSIAN S.F.S.R.	6,592,812	17,075,400	137,551,000	Moscow 7,831,000
KAZAKH S.S.R.	1,048,300	2,715,100	14,684,000	Alma-Ata 910,000
UKRAINIAN S.S.R.	233,089	603,700	49,755,000	Kiev 2,144,000
TURKMEN S.S.R.	188,455	488,100	2,759,000	Ashkhabad 312,000
UZBEK S.S.R.	173,591	449,600	15,391,000	Tashkent 1,780,000
WHITE RUSSIAN S.S.R.	80,154	207,600	9,560,000	Minsk 1,262,000
KIRGIZ S.S.R.	76,641	198,500	3,529,000	Frunze 533,000
TADZHIK S.S.R.	55,251	143,100	3,801,000	Dushanbe 494,000
AZERBAIDZHAN S.S.R.	33,436	86,600	6,028,000	Baku 1,022,000
GEORGIAN S.S.R.	26,911	69,700	5,015,000	Tbilisi 1,066,000
LITHUANIAN S.S.R.	25,174	65,200	3,398,000	Vilna 481,000
LATVIAN S.S.R.	24,595	63,700	2,521,000	Riga 835,000
ESTONIAN S.S.R.	17,413	45,100	1,466,000	Tallinn 430,000
MOLDAVIAN S.S.R.	13,012	33,700	3,947,000	Kishinev 503,000
ARMENIAN S.S.R.	11,506	29,800	3,031,000	Erivan 1,019,000

Topography

Agriculture, Industry and Resources

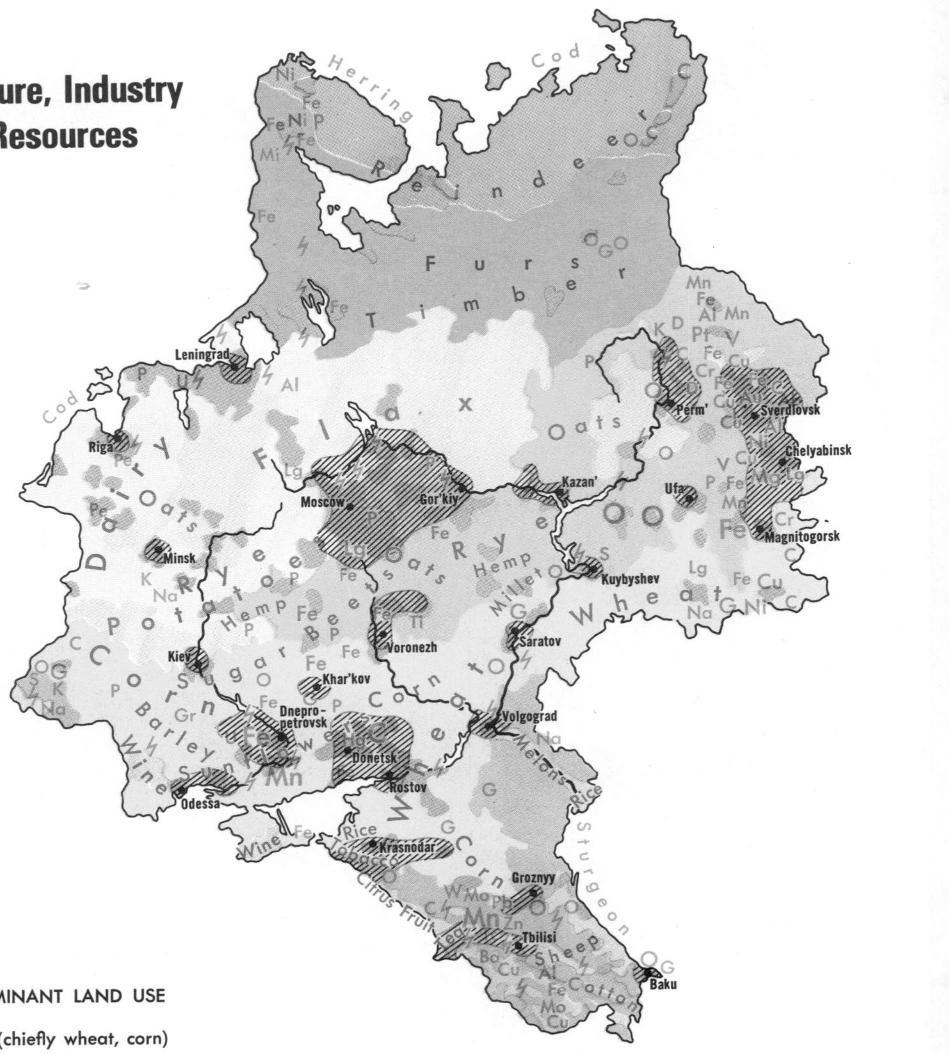

DOMINANT LAND USE

- Cereals (chiefly wheat, corn)
- Cereals (chiefly wheat, rye, oats)
- Dairy, Hogs, Livestock
- Livestock, Dairy
- Pasture Livestock
- Truck Farming, Potatoes, Vegetables, Dairy
- Flax, Dairy, Potatoes
- Cotton
- Vineyards, Orchards, Horticulture
- Sheep Herding, Limited Agriculture
- Forests
- Nonagricultural Land

MAJOR MINERAL OCCURRENCES

Ab	Asbestos	Hg	Mercury	Pb	Lead
Al	Bauxite	K	Potash	Pe	Peat
Au	Gold	Lg	Lignite	Pt	Platinum
Ba	Barite	Mg	Magnesium	S	Sulfur, Pyrites
C	Coal	Mi	Mica	Tc	Talc
Cr	Chromium	Mn	Manganese	Ti	Titanium
Cu	Copper	Mo	Molybdenum	U	Uranium
D	Diamonds	Na	Salt	V	Vanadium
Fe	Iron Ore	Ni	Nickel	W	Tungsten
G	Natural Gas	O	Petroleum	Zn	Zinc
Gr	Graphite	P	Phosphates		

⚡ Water Power   ▨ Major Industrial Areas

Agriculture, Industry and Resources

DOMINANT LAND USE

- Cereals (chiefly wheat, corn)
- Livestock, Dairy
- Truck Farming, Potatoes, Vegetables, Dairy
- Cotton
- Sheep Herding, Limited Agriculture
- Forests
- Nonagricultural Land

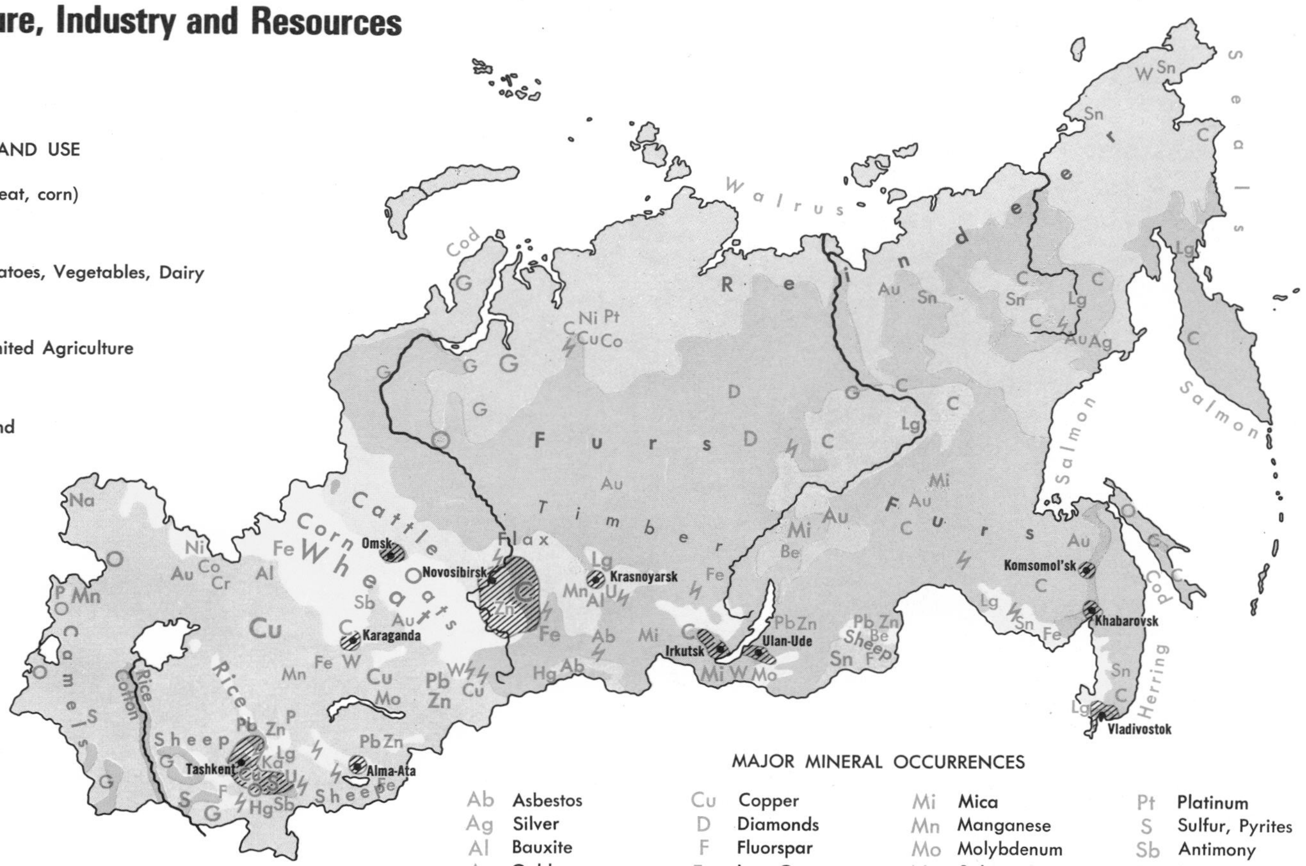

MAJOR MINERAL OCCURRENCES

Ab	Asbestos	Cu	Copper	Mi	Mica	Pt	Platinum
Ag	Silver	D	Diamonds	Mn	Manganese	S	Sulfur, Pyrites
Al	Bauxite	F	Fluorspar	Mo	Molybdenum	Sb	Antimony
Au	Gold	Fe	Iron Ore	Na	Salt	Sn	Tin
Be	Beryl	G	Natural Gas	Ni	Nickel	U	Uranium
C	Coal	Hg	Mercury	O	Petroleum	W	Tungsten
Co	Cobalt	Ka	Kaolin	P	Phosphates	Zn	Zinc
Cr	Chromium	Lg	Lignite	Pb	Lead		

⚡ Water Power ▨ Major Industrial Areas

Map labels: Omsk, Novosibirsk, Krasnoyarsk, Karaganda, Irkutsk, Ulan-Ude, Komsomol'sk, Khabarovsk, Vladivostok, Tashkent, Alma-Ata. Cattle, Corn, Wheat, Oats, Rice, Sheep, Camels, Cotton, Flax, Timber, Furs, Reindeer, Cod, Walrus, Salmon, Herring, Seals.

U.S.S.R.—Railroads and Navigation

Legend:
- Principal Railroads
- Navigable Rivers
- Canals
- Main Sea Routes
- Major Russian Ports ⚓

Countries: FRANCE, W.GERMANY, E.GER., SW., NORWAY, SWEDEN, DEN., FINLAND, POLAND, AUST., CZ., HUN., YUGO., RUMANIA, BULG., TURKEY, SYRIA, IRAQ, IRAN, AFGHANISTAN, CHINA, MONGOLIA, N. KOREA, S. KOREA, JAPAN.

Cities/features: Berlin, Stockholm, Vienna, Kaliningrad, Riga, Kandalaksha, Murmansk, Leningrad, Archangel, Brest, L'vov, Minsk, Kiev, Moscow, Vologda, Nar'yan-Mar, Vorkuta, Ukhta, Dudinka, Noril'sk, Salekhard, Pevek, Anadyr', Ambarchik, Nordvik, Tiksi, Ust'-Kamchatsk, Magadan, Okhotsk, Petropavlovsk-Kamchatskiy, Odessa, Khar'kov, Kazan', Gor'kiy, Kirov, Serginy, Surgut, Tobol'sk, Sverdlovsk, Kuybyshev, Ural'sk, Chelyabinsk, Ayan, Rostov, Novorossiysk, Volgograd, Astrakhan', Gur'yev, Orsk, Omsk, Chul'man, Ust'-Kut, Bam, Svobodnyy, Vanino, Korsakov, Batumi, Tbilisi, Shevchenko, Baku, Krasnovodsk, Kungrad, Aral'sk, Tselinograd, Karaganda, Dzhezkazgan, Semipalatinsk, Novosibirsk, Novokuznetsk, Krasnoyarsk, Bratsk, Irkutsk, Chita, Zabaykal'sk, Harbin, Khabarovsk, Nakhodka, Vladivostok, Tehran, Mary, Tashkent, Alma-Ata, Dushanbe, Osh, Ulaanbaatar, Peking. Trans-Siberian Railroad, Baykal-Amur Mainline, L. Baykal, Volga, Kama, Ob', Irtysh, Yenisey, Lena, Amur, Black Sea, Caspian Sea, Aral Sea, Baltic Sea, Arctic Ocean, Pacific Ocean, Sea of Okhotsk, Sea of Japan. Approximate Limit of Permanent Ice.

(continued on following page)

Union of Soviet Socialist Republics
European Part

CONIC PROJECTION
SCALE OF MILES

| | 50 | 100 | 200 | 300 |

SCALE OF KILOMETERS

| | 50 | 100 | 200 | 300 |

National Capitals	☆
Capitals of Union Republics	⬠
Administrative Centers	△
International boundaries	
Union Republic boundaries	
A.S.S.R., Oblast, Kray boundaries	
Autonomous Oblast boundaries	
Autonomous Okrug boundaries	

Scale 1:13,250,000

The government of the United States has not recognized the incorporation of Estonia, Latvia and Lithuania into the Soviet Union, nor does it recognize as final the de facto western limit of Polish administration in Germany (the Oder-Neisse line).

Administrative Divisions bear same names as their respective Capitals or Centers, except:

Abkhaz A.S.S.R.	Sukhumi	F6
Adygey Aut. Oblast	Maykop	F6
Adzhar A.S.S.R.	Batumi	F6
Bashkir A.S.S.R.	Ufa	J4
Chechen-Ingush A.S.S.R.	Groznyy	G6
Chuvash A.S.S.R.	Cheboksary	G3
Crimean Oblast	Simferopol'	D6
Dagestan A.S.S.R.	Makhachkala	G6
Kabardin-Balkar A.S.S.R.	Nal'chik	F6
Kalmuck A.S.S.R.	Elista	F5
Karachay-Cherkess Aut. Obl.	Cherkessk	F6
Karelian A.S.S.R.	Petrozavodsk	D2
Komi A.S.S.R.	Syktyvkar	H2
Komi-Permyak Aut. Okrug	Kudymkar	H3
Mari A.S.S.R.	Yoshkar-Ola	G3
Mordvinian A.S.S.R.	Saransk	G4
Nagorno-Karabakh Aut. Obl.	Stepanakert	G7
Nenets Aut. Okrug	Nar'yan-Mar	H1
North Ossetian A.S.S.R.	Ordzhonikidze	F6
South Ossetian Aut. Obl.	Tskhinvali	F6
Tatar A.S.S.R.	Kazan'	G3
Trans-Carpathian Oblast	Uzhgorod	B5
Udmurt A.S.S.R.	Izhevsk	H3
Volyn Oblast	Lutsk	C4

© Copyright HAMMOND INCORPORATED, Maplewood, N.J.

U.S.S.R. — EUROPEAN

UNION REPUBLICS

Armenian S.S.R. 3,031,000 ... F6
Azerbaidzhan S.S.R. 6,028,000 ... G6
Estonian S.S.R 1,466,000 ... C3
Georgian S.S.R. 5,015,000 ... F6
Latvian S.S.R 2,521,000 ... B3
Lithuanian S.S.R. 3,398,000 ... B3
Moldavian S.S.R. 3,947,000 ... C5
Russian S.F.S.R. 137,551,000 ... F3
Ukrainian S.S.R. 49,755,000 ... D5
White Russian S.S.R. 9.560.000 ... C4

INTERNAL DIVISIONS

Abkhaz A.S.S.R. 505,000 ... F6
Adygey Aut. Obl. 405,000 ... F6
Adzhar A.S.S.R. 354,000 ... F6
Bashkir A.S.S.R. 3,849,000 ... J4
Chechen-Ingush
A.S.S.R. 1,154,000 ... G6
Chuvash A.S.S.R. 1,292,000 ... G3
Crimean Oblast 2,183,000 ... D6
Dagestan A.S.S.R. 1,628,000 ... G6
Kabardin-Balkar
A.S.S.R. 674,000 ... F6
Kalmuck A.S.S.R. 294,000 ... F5
Karachay-Cherkess Aut. Obl. 368,000 ... F6
Karelian A.S.S.R. 736,000 ... D2
Komi A.S.S.R. 1,119,000 ... H2
Komi-Permyak Aut. Okr. 173,000 ... H3
Mari A.S.S.R. 703,000 ... G3
Mordvinian A.S.S.R. 991,000 ... G4
Nagorno-Karabakh Aut.
Obl. 161,000 ... G7
Nakhichevan' A.S.S.R. 239,000 ... F7
Nenets Aut. Okr. 47,000 ... H1
North Ossetian
A.S.S.R. 597,000 ... F6
South Ossetian Aut.
Obl. 98,000 ... F6
Tatar A.S.S.R. 3,436,000 ... G3
Trans-Carpathian
Oblast 1,155,000 ... B5
Udmurt A.S.S.R. 1,494,000 ... H3
Volyn Oblast 1,015,000 ... C4

CITIES and TOWNS

Abdulino 26,010 ... H4
Agdam 21,277 ... G6
Agryz 19,267 ... H3
Akhaltsikhe 18,972 ... F6
Akhtubinsk 43,466 ... G5
Akhty ... G6
Akhtyrka 41,354 ... E4
Akkerman
(Belgorod-Dnestrovskiy) 32,928 ... D5
Alagir 18,161 ... F6
Alatyr' 43,499 ... G4
Alaverdi 21,311 ... F6
Aleksandriya 82,000 ... D5
Aleksandrovsk 18,286 ... J3
Alekseyevka 25,562 ... E4
Aleksin 67,000 ... E4
Ali-Bayramly 33,828 ... G7
Al'met'yevsk 110,000 ... H3
Alushta 22,016 ... D6
Amderma ... K1
Anapa 29,900 ... E6
Apatity 62,000 ... D1
Apsheronsk 32,867 ... F6
Archangel
(Arkhangel'sk) 385,000 ... F2
Armavir 162,000 ... F5
Arzamas 93,000 ... F3
Astara ... G7
Astrakhan' 461,000 ... G5
Atkarsk 28,881 ... G4
Azov 75,000 ... E5
Bakhchisaray 15,912 ... D6
Baku 1,022,000 ... H6
Baku* 1,550,000 ... H6
Balakhna 36,542 ... F3
Balaklava ... D6
Balakovo 152,000 ... G4
Balashov 93,000 ... F4
Baltiysk 20,300 ... A4
Baranovichi 131,000 ... C4
Barysh 20,792 ... G4
Bataysk 90,000 ... E5
Batumi 123,000 ... F6
Belaya Tserkov' 151,000 ... C5
Belebey 32,460 ... H4
Belev 17,733 ... E4
Belgorod 240,000 ... E4
Belgorod-Dnestrovskiy 32,928 ... D5
Belomorsk 16,595 ... D2
Belorechensk 35,970 ... E6
Beloretsk 71,000 ... J4
Belozersk ... E3
Bel'tsy 125,000 ... C5
Belush'ya Guba ... H1
Bendery 101,000 ... C5
Berdichev 80,000 ... C5
Berdyansk 122,000 ... E5
Beregovo 27,308 ... B5
Berezniki 185,000 ... J3
Beslan 26,893 ... F6
Bezhetsk 30,030 ... E3
Birsk 29,607 ... J3
Bobrov 17,977 ... F4
Bobruysk 192,000 ... C4
Bologoye 33,949 ... D3
Bor 63,000 ... F3
Borislav 33,800 ... B5
Borisoglebsk 68,000 ... F4
Borisov 112,000 ... C4
Borovichi 60,000 ... D3
Brest 177,000 ... B4
Brezhnev 301,000 ... H3
Bryansk 394,000 ... D4
Bugul'ma 80,000 ... H4
Buguruslan 54,000 ... H4
Buturlinovka 21,643 ... F4
Buy 29,946 ... F3
Buynaksk 37,946 ... G6
Buzuluk 76,000 ... H4
Bykhov 17,371 ... C4
Cēsis 17,696 ... C3
Chadyr-Lunga 20,474 ... C5
Chapayevsk 85,000 ... G4
Chaykovskiy 48,034 ... H3
Cheboksary 308,000 ... G3
Cherepovets 266,000 ... E3
Cherkassy 228,000 ... D5
Cherkessk 91,000 ... F6
Chernigov 238,000 ... D4
Chernovtsy 219,000 ... C5
Chernushka 21,106 ... J3
Chervonograd 55,000 ... B4
Chiatura 25,474 ... F6
Chistopol' 64,000 ... H3
Chortkov 19,183 ... B5
Chudovo ... D3
Chusovoy 56,000 ... J3
Danilov 17,500 ... E3
Dankov 20,030 ... E4
Daugavpils 116,000 ... C3
Davlekanovo 20,123 ... H4
Derbent 70,000 ... G6
Dimitrovgrad 106,000 ... G4
Dneprodzerzhinsk 250,000 ... D5
Dnepropetrovsk 1,066,000 ... D5
Dobrush 16,809 ... D4
Dobryanka 18,349 ... J3
Donetsk 1,021,000 ... E5
Drogobych 66,000 ... B5
Dubna 55,000 ... E3
Dubna ... E4
Dubno 25,442 ... C4
Dvinsk (Daugavpils) 116,000 ... C3
Dyat'kovo 26,825 ... D4
Dzerzhinsk 257,000 ... F3
Dzhankoy 43,459 ... D5
Dzhul'fa ... G7
Echmiadzin 31,819 ... F6
Elektrostal' 139,000 ... E3
Elista 70,000 ... F5
El'ton ... G5
Engel's 161,000 ... G4
Erivan 1,019,000 ... F6
Fastov 51,000 ... C4
Feodosiya 76,000 ... D5
Frolovo 33,398 ... F5
Furmanov 40,155 ... F3
Gagra 23,025 ... E6
Galich 19,374 ... F3
Gandzha (Kirovabad) 232,000 ... G6
Gatchina 75,000 ... C3
Gay 28,250 ... J4
Gaysin 23,741 ... C5
Gdov ... C3
Gelendzhik 29,086 ... E6
Genichesk 20,031 ... E5
Georgiu-Dezh 52,000 ... E4
Glazov 81,000 ... H3
Glubokoye ... C3
Glukhov 27,096 ... D4
Gomel' 383,000 ... D4
Gori 56,000 ... F6
Gorki 22,117 ... D4
Gor'kiy 1,344,000 ... F3
Gorlovka 336,000 ... E5
Gorodets 34,229 ... F3
Gremikha ... E1
Gremyachinsk 29,975 ... J3
Grodno 195,000 ... B4
Groznyy 375,000 ... G6
Gryazi 41,292 ... F4
Gubakha 33,243 ... J3
Gubkin 65,000 ... E4
Gudauta ... F6
Gudermes 32,445 ... G6
Gukovo 68,000 ... F5
Gus'-Khrustal'nyy 72,000 ... F3
Imishli 17,839 ... G7
Inta 51,000 ... K1
Inza 19,060 ... G4
Ishimbay 57,000 ... J4
Ivano-Frankovsk 150,000 ... B5
Ivanovo 465,000 ... E3
Izberbash 17,299 ... G6
Izhevsk 549,000 ... H3
Izmail 83,000 ... C5
Izyum 61,000 ... E5
Jēkabpils 22,440 ... C3
Jelgava 68,000 ... B3
Jurmala 61,000 ... B3
Kadiyevka (Stakhanov) 108,000 ... E5
Kafan 29,916 ... G7
Kagul 26,249 ... C5
Kakhovka 28,472 ... D5
Kalach 18,475 ... F4
Kalach-na-Donu 20,795 ... F5
Kalinin 412,000 ... E3
Kaliningrad,
Kaliningrad 355,000 ... B4
Kaliningrad, Moscow
Oblast 133,000 ... E3
Kalinkovichi 23,918 ... C4
Kaluga 265,000 ... E4
Kalush 60,000 ... B5
Kamenets-Podol'skiy 81,000 ... C5
Kamenka, Penza 30,067 ... F4
Kamensk-Shakhtinskiy 72,000 ... F5
Kamyshin 112,000 ... F4
Kanash 40,682 ... G3
Kandalaksha 42,656 ... D1
Kapsukas 28,763 ... B4
Karachayevsk ... F6
Karachev 15,972 ... E4
Kashin 17,678 ... E3
Kasimov 33,066 ... F4
Kaspiysk 38,990 ... G6
Kaunas 370,000 ... B4
Kazan' 993,000 ... G3
Kazatin 26,649 ... C5
Kem' 21,025 ... D2
Kerch' 157,000 ... E5
Keret' ... D1
Khachmas 22,313 ... G6
Khadyzhensk 17,856 ... E6
Khar'kov 1,444,000 ... E5
Khasavyurt 65,000 ... G6
Khashuri 24,469 ... F6
Kherson 319,000 ... D5
Khmel'nitskiy 172,000 ... C5
Khotin ... C5
Khust 23,810 ... B5
Khvalynsk 16,249 ... G4
Kiev 2,144,000 ... D4
Kiliya 24,276 ... C5
Kimovsk 44,490 ... E4
Kimry 58,000 ... E3
Kinel' 39,373 ... H4
Kineshma 101,000 ... F3
Kirishi 27,252 ... D3
Kirov, Kaluga 29,355 ... D4
Kirov, Kirov 390,000 ... G3
Kirovabad 232,000 ... G6
Kirovakan 146,000 ... G6
Kirovo-Chepetsk 71,000 ... H3
Kirovograd 237,000 ... D5
Kirovsk 38,484 ... D1
Kirsanov 21,795 ... F4
Kishinev 503,000 ... C5
Kislovodsk 101,000 ... F6
Kizel 46,264 ... J3
Kizlyar 29,745 ... G6
Klaipeda 176,000 ... B3
Klintsy 67,000 ... D4
Kobrin 24,935 ... B4
Kobuleti 18,051 ... F6
Kohtla-Järve 73,000 ... C3
Kolomiya 52,000 ... B5
Kolomna 147,000 ... E4
Kolpino 114,000 ... D3
Kommunarsk 120,000 ... E5
Komrat 21,369 ... C5
Komsomol'skiy 17,078 ... K1
Kondopoga 27,908 ... D2
Königsberg
(Kaliningrad) 355,000 ... B4
Konotop 82,000 ... D4
Konstantinovka 112,000 ... E5
Korenovsk 26,323 ... E5
Korosten' 65,000 ... C4
Korostyshev 21,153 ... C4
Koryazhma 33,230 ... G2
Kostopol' 17,548 ... C4
Kostroma 255,000 ... F3
Kotel'nich 29,196 ... G3
Kotel'nikovo 19,063 ... F5
Kotlas 61,000 ... G2
Kotovo 20,553 ... G4
Kotovsk, Odessa 36,463 ... C5
Kotovsk, Tambov 33,347 ... F4
Kovel' 33,351 ... C4
Kovrov 143,000 ... F3
Kovylkino 17,300 ... F4
Kramatorsk 178,000 ... E5
Krasnoarmeysk 60,000 ... G4
Krasnodar 560,000 ... E6
Krasnograd 18,386 ... E5
Krasnokamsk 56,000 ... H3
Krasnoslobodsk 17,749 ... G5
Krasnovishersk ... J2
Krasnyy Kut 17,087 ... G4
Krasnyy Luch 106,000 ... E5

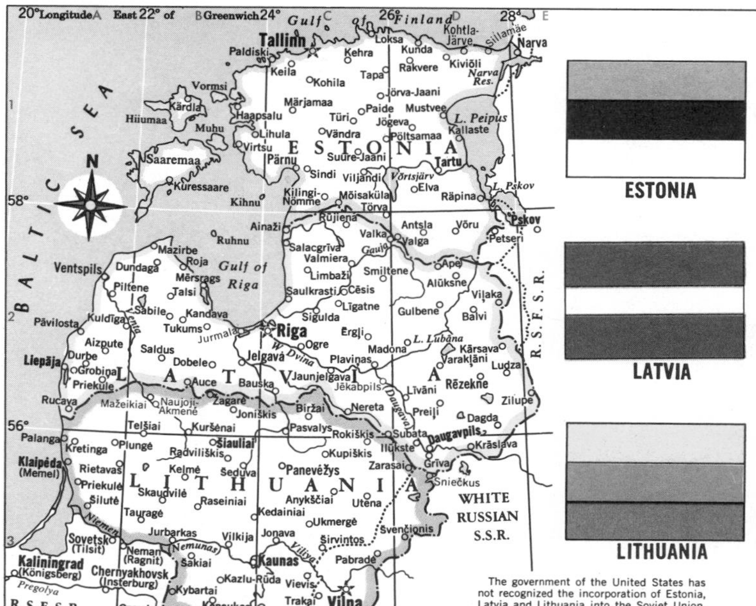

The government of the United States has not recognized the incorporation of Estonia, Latvia and Lithuania into the Soviet Union, nor does it recognize other post-war territorial changes shown on this map. The flags shown here were the official flags of the independent Baltic States prior to 1939.

© Copyright HAMMOND INCORPORATED, Maplewood, N. J.

SCALE OF MILES 0 25 50 75 100
SCALE OF KILOMETERS 0 30 60 90 120 150 180

Capitals ... ☆
International Boundaries ... —·—
Union Republic Boundaries ... —·—
Prewar boundaries of the Baltic States where divergent from present boundaries ... .

BALTIC STATES

Alytus 55,000 ... C3
Biržai 11,400 ... C2
Cēsis 17,696 ... C2
Daugava (Western Dvina)
(riv.) ... D2
Daugavpils 116,000 ... D3
Dobele 10,100 ... B2
Druskininkai 11,200 ... C3
Dvina Western (riv.) ... C2
Finland (gulf) ... D1
Gauja (riv.) ... C2
Haapsalu 11,483 ... B1
Hiiumaa (isl.) ... B1
Jēkabpils 22,400 ... C2
Jelgava 68,000 ... B2
Jonava 14,400 ... C3
Jurmala 61,000 ... B2
Kapsukas 28,763 ... B3
Kaunas 370,000 ... C3
Kedainiai 19,677 ... C3
Kihnu (isl.) ... B1
Kingisepp (Kuressaare) 12,140 ... B1
Kiviõli 11,153 ... D1
Klaipeda 176,000 ... A3
Kohtla-Järve 73,000 ... D1
Kretinga 13,000 ... A3
Kuldīga 12,300 ... A2
Kuressaare 12,140 ... B1
Kuršenai 11,500 ... B2
Liepāja 108,000 ... A2
Lubāna (lake) ... D2
Mažeikiai 13,400 ... A2
Memel (Klaipeda) 176,000 ... A3
Muhu (isl.) ... B1
Narva 73,000 ... E1
Naujoji-Akmene 10,200 ... B2
Niemen (riv.) ... A3
Ogre 15,708 ... C2
Panevežys 102,000 ... C3
Pärnu 51,000 ... C1
Peipus (lake) ... D1
Plunge 13,600 ... B3
Radviliškis 16,841 ... B3
Rakvere 17,891 ... D1
Rēzekne 30,803 ... D2
Riga (cap.), Latvia 835,000 ... C2
Riga (gulf) ... B2
Saaremaa (isl.) ... B1
Saldus 10,000 ... B2
Šiauliai 118,000 ... B3
Sillamäe 13,505 ... D1
Šilute 12,400 ... A3
Tallinn (cap.),
Estonia 430,000 ... C1
Tapa 10,037 ... C1
Tartu 105,000 ... D1
Taurage 19,461 ... B3
Telšiai 20,220 ... B2
Tukums 14,800 ... B2
Ukmerge 21,663 ... C3
Utena 13,300 ... C3
Valga 16,795 ... D2
Valmiera 20,331 ... C2
Venta (riv.) ... B2
Ventspils 40,467 ... A2
Viliya (riv.) ... C3
Viljandi 20,814 ... C1
Vilna (Vilnius) (cap.),
Lithuania 481,000 ... C3
Vormosi (isl.) ... B1
Võrtsjärv (lake) ... D1
Võru 15,398 ... D2
Western Dvina (riv.) ... C2

Krasnyy Sulin 41,684 ... F5
Kremenchug 210,000 ... D5
Krichev 25,682 ... D4
Krivoy Rog 650,000 ... D5
Krolevets 18,307 ... D4
Kronshtadt 39,477 ... C3
Kropotkin 70,000 ... F5
Krymsk 41,430 ... E5
Kuba 18,871 ... G6
Kudymkar 26,350 ... H3
Kulebaki 46,252 ... F3
Kumertau 52,000 ... J4
Kunda ... C3
Kungur 80,000 ... J3
Kupyansk 30,055 ... E5
Kuressaare 12,140 ... B3
Kursk 375,000 ... E4
Kutaisi 194,000 ... F6
Kuvandyk 22,914 ... J4
Kuybyshev 1,216,000 ... H4
Kuznetsk 94,000 ... G4
Kuzomen' ... E1
Labinsk 54,000 ... F6
Lakhdenpokh'ya ... C2
Lebedin 29,240 ... D4
Leninakan 207,000 ... F6
Leningrad 4,073,000 ... C3
Leningrad* 4,588,000 ... C3
Leninogorsk 54,000 ... H4
Lenkoran' 35,505 ... G7
L'gov 25,110 ... E4
Lida 66,000 ... C4
Liepāja 108,000 ... B3
Likhoslavl' ... E3
Lipetsk 396,000 ... E4
Lisichansk 119,000 ... E5
Livny 37,290 ... E4
Lodeynoye Pole 19,632 ... D2
Lozovaya 53,000 ... E5
Lubny 54,000 ... D4
Luga 31,905 ... C3
Lutsk 137,000 ... B4
L'vov (Lwów) 667,000 ... B5
Lys'va 75,000 ... J3
Lyubertsy 160,000 ... E3
Lyubotin 33,324 ... E4
Lyudinovo 33,871 ... D4
Makeyevka 436,000 ... E5
Makhachkala 251,000 ... G6
Makharadze 21,679 ... F6
Malaya Vishera 15,381 ... D3
Malgobek 20,548 ... F6
Manturovo 21,510 ... F3
Marganets 50,000 ... E5
Mariupol' (Zhdanov) 503,000 ... E5
Marks 17,132 ... G4
Maykop 128,000 ... F6
Mednogorsk 38,024 ... J4
Medvezh'yegorsk 17,465 ... D2
Melenki 18,545 ... F3
Meleuz 24,851 ... J4
Melitopol' 161,000 ... D5
Memel (Klaipeda) 176,000 ... B3
Merefa 29,985 ... E5
Mezen' ... F1
Michurinsk 101,000 ... F4
Mikhaylovka 58,000 ... F4
Millerovo 34,627 ... F5
Mineral'nye Vody 67,000 ... F6
Mingechaur 60,000 ... G6
Minsk 1,262,000 ... C4
Minsk* 1,276,000 ... C4
Mirgorod 28,407 ... D5
Mogilev 290,000 ... C4
Mogilev-Podol'skiy 26,051 ... C5
Molodechno 73,000 ... C4
Molotov (Perm') 999,000 ... J3
Monchegorsk 51,000 ... D1
Morshansk 44,245 ... F4
Moscow (Moskva)
(cap.) 7,831,000 ... E3
Moscow* 8,011,000 ... E3
Mozhaysk 20,321 ... E3
Mozhga 38,930 ... H3
Mozyr' 73,000 ... C4
Mtsensk 27,833 ... E4
Mukachevo 72,000 ... B5
Murmansk 381,000 ... D1
Murom 114,000 ... F3
Mytishchi 141,000 ... E3
Nakhichevan' 33,279 ... F7
Nal'chik 207,000 ... F6
Narva 73,000 ... C3
Nar'yan-Mar 16,864 ... H1
Neftekamsk 70,000 ... J3
Nelidovo 29,813 ... D3
Nerekhta 25,722 ... F3
Nevel' 17,804 ... D3
Nevinnomyssk 104,000 ... F6
Nezhin 70,000 ... D4
Nikel' 21,299 ... C1
Nikolayev 440,000 ... D5
Nikol'sk 20,740 ... G4
Nikopol' 146,000 ... D5
Nizhnekamsk 134,000 ... H3
Nizhniy Lomov 17,460 ... F4
Nizhniy Novgorod
(Gor'kiy) 1,344,000 ... F3
Nosovka 19,430 ... D4
Novaya Kakhovka 52,000 ... D5
Novgorod 186,000 ... D3
Novgorod-Severskiy ... D4
Novoanninskiy 20,461 ... F4
Novocherkassk 183,000 ... F5
Novograd-Volynskiy 41,194 ... C4
Novogrudok 19,374 ... C4
Novokuybyshevsk 109,000 ... G4
Novomoskovsk 147,000 ... E4
Novopolotsk 67,000 ... C3
Novorossiysk 159,000 ... E6
Novoshakhtinsk 104,000 ... E5
Novotroitsk 95,000 ... J4
Novoukrainka 19,554 ... D5
Novouzensk ... G4
Novovolynsk 41,187 ... B4
Novovyatsk 26,408 ... G3
Novozybkov 34,433 ... D4
Nurlat 17,533 ... H4
Nyandoma 23,366 ... F2
Nytva 17,491 ... H3
Nyuvchim ... H2
Obninsk 73,000 ... E3
Ochamchira 18,718 ... F6
Odessa 1,046,000 ... D5
Oktyabr'sk 33,981 ... G4
Oktyabr'skiy 88,000 ... H4
Okulovka 19,194 ... D3
Olenegorsk 21,485 ... D1
Olonets ... D2
Omutninsk 28,777 ... H3
Onega 25,047 ... E2
Ordzhonikidze 279,000 ... F6
Orel 305,000 ... E4
Orenburg 459,000 ... J4
Orgeyev 25,798 ... C5
Orsha 112,000 ... C4
Orsk 247,000 ... J4
Osa 15,038 ... J3
Osipenko (Berdyansk) 122,000 ... E5
Osipovichi 19,705 ... C4
Ostashkov 23,419 ... D3
Ostrogozhsk 29,921 ... E4
Ostrov 22,369 ... C3
Otradnyy 44,426 ... H4
Panevežys 102,000 ... B3
Pärnu 51,000 ... C3
Pavlograd 107,000 ... E5
Pavlovo 68,000 ... F3
Pechenga ... D1
Pechora 56,000 ... J1
Penza 483,000 ... G4
Perm' 999,000 ... J3
Pervomaysk 72,000 ... D5
Petrokrepost' ... D3
Petrovsk 30,953 ... G4
Petrozavodsk 234,000 ... D2
Petsamo (Pechenga) ... D1
Pinsk 90,000 ... C4
Podol'sk 202,000 ... E3
Podporozh'ye 21,545 ... D2
Pokhvistnevo 26,125 ... H4
Polonnoye 22,484 ... C4
Polotsk 71,000 ... C3
Poltava 279,000 ... D5
Polyarnyy 15,321 ... D1
Ponoy ... F1
Poti 45,979 ... F6
Povenets ... E2
Povorino 20,591 ... F4
Prikumsk 35,768 ... F6
Priluki 65,000 ... D4
Primorsk ... C2
Primorsko-Akhtarsk 25,981 ... E5
Priozersk 16,652 ... D2
Privolzhskiy 23,041 ... G4
Priyutovo 21,051 ... H4
Prokhladnyy 40,074 ... F6
Pskov 176,000 ... C3
Pugachev 33,963 ... G4
Pushkin 90,000 ... C3
Pyatigorsk 110,000 ... F6
Rabocheostrovsk ... D1
Rakhov ... B5
Rakvere 17,891 ... C3
Rasskazovo 40,038 ... F4
Razdan 26,833 ... G6
Rechitsa 60,000 ... C4
Reni 19,625 ... C5
Revel (Tallinn) 430,000 ... B3
Rēzekne 30,803 ... C3
Riga 835,000 ... B3
Romny 53,000 ... D4
Roslavl' 56,000 ... D4
Rossosh' 36,438 ... E4
Rostov 30,815 ... E3
Rostov-na-Donu 934,000 ... F5
Rovno 179,000 ... C4
Rtishchevo 37,146 ... F4
Rubezhnoye 66,000 ... E5
Rustavi 129,000 ... G6
Ruzayevka 41,084 ... F4
Ryazan' 453,000 ... E4
Ryazhsk 25,425 ... F4
Rybinsk 239,000 ... E3
Rybnitsa 32,266 ... C5
Rzhev 69,000 ... D3
Safonovo 53,000 ... D3
Saki 24,208 ... D5
Salavat 137,000 ... H4
Sal'sk 57,000 ... F5
Sal'yany 24,228 ... G7
Samara (Kuybyshev) 1,216,000 ... H4
Sambor 29,253 ... B5
Saransk 263,000 ... G4
Sarapul 107,000 ... H3
Saratov 856,000 ... G4
Sasovo 27,228 ... F4
Segezha 28,810 ... D2
Semenov 23,633 ... F3
Semiluki 18,221 ... E4
Sengiley ... G4
Serdobol (Sortavala) 22,188 ... D2
Serdobsk 33,783 ... F4
Sergach 22,509 ... F3
Serpukhov 140,000 ... E4
Sevastopol' 301,000 ... D6
Severodonetsk 113,000 ... E5
Severodvinsk 197,000 ... E2
Severomorsk 50,000 ... D1
Shakhty 209,000 ... F5
Shakhun'ya 20,009 ... G3
Shar'ya 25,788 ... G3
Shchekino 70,000 ... E4
Shchigry 17,133 ... E4
Sheki 43,158 ... G6
Shemakha 17,986 ... G6
Shepetovka 38,707 ... C4
Shostka 82,000 ... D4
Shpola 19,806 ... D5
Shumerlya 33,816 ... G3
Shuya 72,000 ... F3
Šiauliai 118,000 ... B3
Sibay 37,656 ... J4
Simferopol' 302,000 ... D6
Skadovsk ... D5
Skopin 24,429 ... F4
Slantsy 41,146 ... C3
Slavuta 25,573 ... C4
Slavyansk 140,000 ... E5
Slavyansk-na-Kubani 54,000 ... E5
Slobodskoy 34,374 ... H3
Slonim 30,279 ... B4
Slutsk 35,609 ... C4
Smela 62,000 ... D5
Smolensk 276,000 ... D4
Sochi 287,000 ... E6
Sokol 48,243 ... F3
Soligorsk 65,000 ... C4
Solikamsk 101,000 ... J3
Sol'-Iletsk 22,227 ... J4
Sorochinsk 23,235 ... H4
Soroki 21,924 ... C5
Sortavala 22,188 ... D2
Sosnogorsk 24,688 ... H2
Sovetsk (Tilsit) 38,456 ... B4
Sovetsk 17,027 ... G3
Stakhanov 108,000 ... E5
Stalingrad (Volgograd) 929,000 ... F5
Staraya Russa 34,577 ... D3
Staryy Oskol 115,000 ... E4
Stavropol' 258,000 ... F5
Stepanakert 30,293 ... G7
Sterlitamak 220,000 ... J4
Stupino 70,000 ... E4
Sudak ... E6
Sukhumi 114,000 ... F6
Sumgait 190,000 ... G6
Sumy 228,000 ... E4
Svetlogorsk 55,000 ... C4
Svetlograd 40,265 ... F5
Syktyvkar 171,000 ... H2
Syzran' 178,000 ... G4
Taganrog 276,000 ... E5
Tallinn 430,000 ... B3
Tambov 270,000 ... F4
Tartu 105,000 ... C3
Taurage 19,461 ... B3
Tbilisi 1,066,000 ... F6
Telavi 21,179 ... G6
Telšiai 20,220 ... B3
Temryuk 23,172 ... E5
Ternopol' 144,000 ... C5
Teykovo 41,607 ... E3
Tiflis (Tbilisi) 1,066,000 ... F6
Tighina (Bendery) 101,000 ... C5
Tikhoretsk 64,000 ... F5
Tikhvin 59,000 ... D3
Tilsit (Sovetsk) 38,456 ... B4
Timashevsk 29,055 ... E5
Tiraspol' 139,000 ... D5
Togliatti (Tol'yatti) 502,000 ... G4
Tokmak 59,000 ... E5
Toropets 16,863 ... D3
Torzhok 45,443 ... D3
Troitsko-Pechorsk ... J2
Tskhinvali 30,311 ... F6
Tuapse 60,000 ... E6
Tukums 14,800 ... B3
Tula 514,000 ... E4
Tutayev 16,839 ... E3
Tuymazy 37,021 ... H4
Tver (Kalinin) 412,000 ... E3
Tyrnyauz 18,253 ... F6
Uchaly 21,808 ... J4
Ufa 969,000 ... J4
Uglich 35,463 ... E3
Ukmerge 21,663 ... C3
Ul'yanovsk 464,000 ... G4
Uman' 79,000 ... D5
Unecha 21,749 ... D4
Ungeny 17,228 ... C5
Uryupinsk 38,192 ... F4
Usinsk ... J1
Usman' 20,150 ... E4
Uvarovo 24,946 ... F4
Uzhgorod 91,000 ... B5
Uzlovaya 65,000 ... E4
Valga 16,795 ... C3
Valmiera 20,331 ... C3
Valuyki 29,093 ... E4
Vasil'kov 26,741 ... D4
Velikiye Luki 102,000 ... D3
Velikiy Ustyug 36,737 ... F2
Vel'sk 21,899 ... F2
Ventspils 40,467 ... B3
Vereshchagino 23,585 ... H3
Vichuga 52,000 ... F3
Viipuri (Vyborg) 76,000 ... C2
Vileyka ... C4
Vilna (Vilnius) 481,000 ... C4
Vinnitsa 314,000 ... C5
Vinogradov 20,580 ... B5
Vitebsk 297,000 ... C3
Vladimir 296,000 ... F3
Vladimir-Volynskiy 28,412 ... B4
Volgodonsk 91,000 ... F5
Volgograd 929,000 ... F5
Volkhov 47,025 ... D3
Volkovysk 28,266 ... B4
Vologda 237,000 ... F3
Vol'sk 66,000 ... G4
Volzhsk 52,000 ... G3
Volzhskiy 209,000 ... G5
Vorkuta 100,000 ... K1
Voronezh 783,000 ... E4
Voroshilovgrad 463,000 ... E5
Voskresensk 76,000 ... E3
Votkinsk 90,000 ... H3
Voznesensk 36,457 ... D5
Vyatskiye Polyany 32,729 ... H3
Vyaz'ma 52,000 ... D3
Vyborg 76,000 ... C2
Vyksa 54,000 ... F3
Vyshniy Volochek 72,000 ... D3
Yalta 80,000 ... D6
Yanaul 20,115 ... J3
Yaroslavl' 597,000 ... E3
Yartsevo 36,662 ... D3
Yefremov 53,000 ... E4
Yelabuga 31,728 ... H3
Yelets 112,000 ... E4
Yenakiyevo 114,000 ... E5
Yershov 21,731 ... G4
Yessentuki 78,000 ... F6
Yevlakh 29,462 ... G6
Yevpatoria 93,000 ... D5
Yeysk 71,000 ... E5
Yoshkar-Ola 201,000 ... G3
Yur'yevets 20,144 ... F3
Zagorsk 107,000 ... E3
Zapolyarnyy 22,084 ... D1
Zaporozh'ye 781,000 ... E5
Zelenodol'sk 85,000 ... G3
Zelenokumsk 29,691 ... F6
Zernograd 20,324 ... F5
Zhdanov 503,000 ... E5
Zheleznodorozhnyy 76,000 ... H2
Zheleznogorsk 65,000 ... E4
Zhigulevsk 52,130 ... G4
Zhitomir 244,000 ... C4
Zhlobin 25,359 ... D4
Zhmerinka 36,195 ... C5
Zhodino 22,083 ... C4
Zhovtnevoye 31,102 ... D5
Znamenka 27,393 ... D5
Zolotonosha 27,639 ... D5
Zugdidi 39,896 ... F6
Zuyevka 17,001 ... H3

OTHER FEATURES

Apsheron (pen.) ... H6
Araks (riv.) ... G7
Azov (sea) ... E5
Baltic (sea) ... B3
Barents (sea) ... E1
Belaya (riv.) ... H3
Beloye (lake) ... E2
Black (sea) ... D6
Bug (riv.) ... B4
Bug (riv.) ... D5
Caspian (sea) ... G6
Caucasus (mts.) ... F6
Crimea (pen.) ... D5
Desna (riv.) ... D4
Dnieper (riv.) ... D5
Dniester (riv.) ... C5
Don (riv.) ... F5
Donets (riv.) ... E5
Dvina (bay) ... E2
Dvina, Northern (riv.) ... F2
Dvina, Western (riv.) ... C3
Dykh-Tau (mt.) ... F6
El'brus (mt.) ... F6
Finland (gulf) ... C3
Hiiumaa (isl.) ... B3
Il'men' (lake) ... D3
Imandra (lake) ... D1
Kakhovka (res.) ... D5
Kama (riv.) ... H2
Kandalaksha (gulf) ... D1
Kanin (pen.) ... G1
Kara (sea) ... K1
Karskiye Vorota (str.) ... J1
Kazbek (mt.) ... F6
Khoper (riv.) ... F4
Kola (pen.) ... E1
Kolguyev (isl.) ... G1
Kuban' (riv.) ... E5
Kura (riv.) ... G6
Kuybyshev (res.) ... G4
Ladoga (lake) ... D2
Lapland (reg.) ... D1
Mezen' (riv.) ... G1
Moksha (riv.) ... F4
Narodnaya (mt.) ... J1
Niemen (riv.) ... B4
Novaya Zemlya (isls.) ... H1
Oka (riv.) ... F4
Onega (bay) ... E2
Onega (lake) ... E2
Onega (riv.) ... E2
Pechora (riv.) ... H1
Peipus (lake) ... C3
Pripet (marshes) ... C4
Pripyat' (riv.) ... C4
Prut (riv.) ... C5
Riga (gulf) ... B3
Rybachiy (pen.) ... D1
Rybinsk (res.) ... E3
Saaremaa (isl.) ... B3
Samara (riv.) ... H4
Sevan (lake) ... G6
Seym (riv.) ... D4
Sura (riv.) ... G4
Svir' (riv.) ... D2
Timan (ridge) ... G1
Tsil'ma (riv.) ... H1
Tsimlyansk (res.) ... F5
Tuloma (riv.) ... D1
Ural (mts.) ... J2
Ural (riv.) ... J4
Usa (riv.) ... K1
Valday (hills) ... D3
Vaygach (isl.) ... K1
Velikaya (riv.) ... C3
Volga (riv.) ... G5
Volga-Don (canal) ... F5
Volgograd (res.) ... G5
Volkhov (riv.) ... D3
Vorskla (riv.) ... E4
Vyatka (riv.) ... H3
Vychegda (riv.) ... G2
Vyg (lake) ... E2
White (sea) ... E1
Yamantau (mt.) ... J4
Yugorskiy (pen.) ... K1

*City and suburbs.

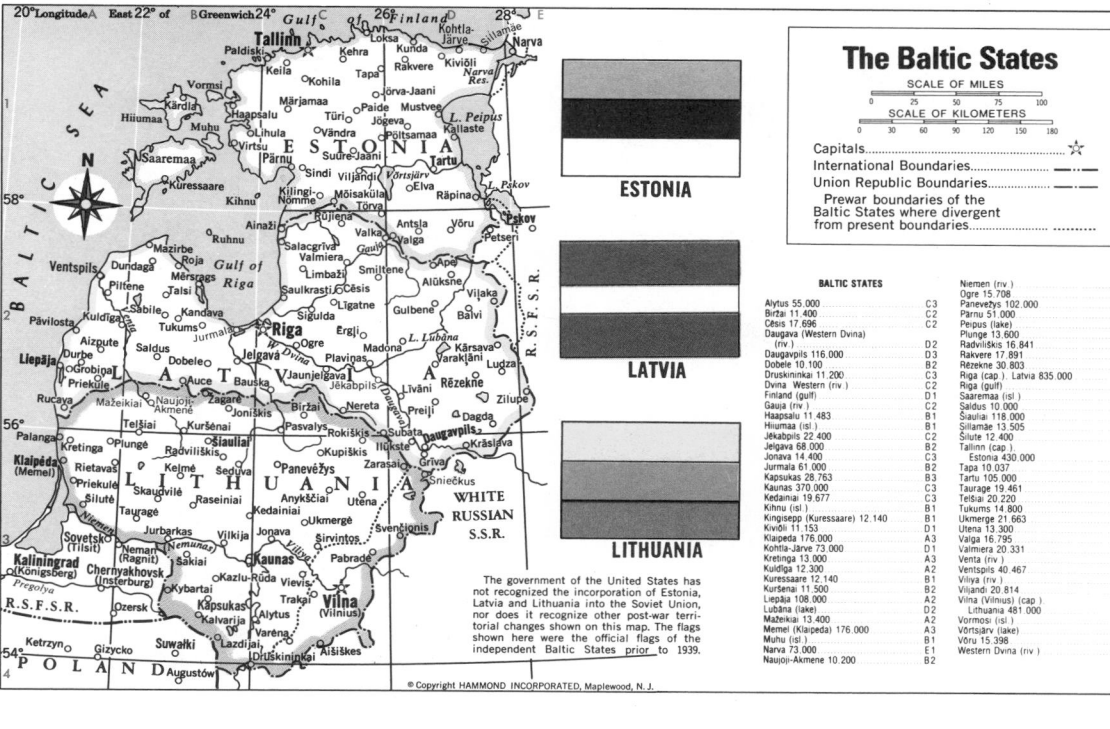

Asia

LAMBERT AZIMUTHAL EQUAL-AREA PROJECTION

SCALE OF MILES
0   100 200   400   600   800   1000   1200

SCALE OF KILOMETERS
0 200 400 600 800 1000 1200

Capitals of Countries .... ⊛
Other Capitals .... ⊛
International Boundaries ....
Other Boundaries ....
Canals ....

Scale 1: 46,500,000

© Copyright HAMMOND INCORPORATED, Maplewood, N.J.

Population Distribution

AREA 17,128,500 sq. mi.
(44,362,815 sq. km.)
POPULATION 2,633,000,000
LARGEST CITY Tokyo
HIGHEST POINT Mt. Everest 29,028 ft.
(8,848 m.)
LOWEST POINT Dead Sea -1,296 ft.
(-395 m.)

Vegetation

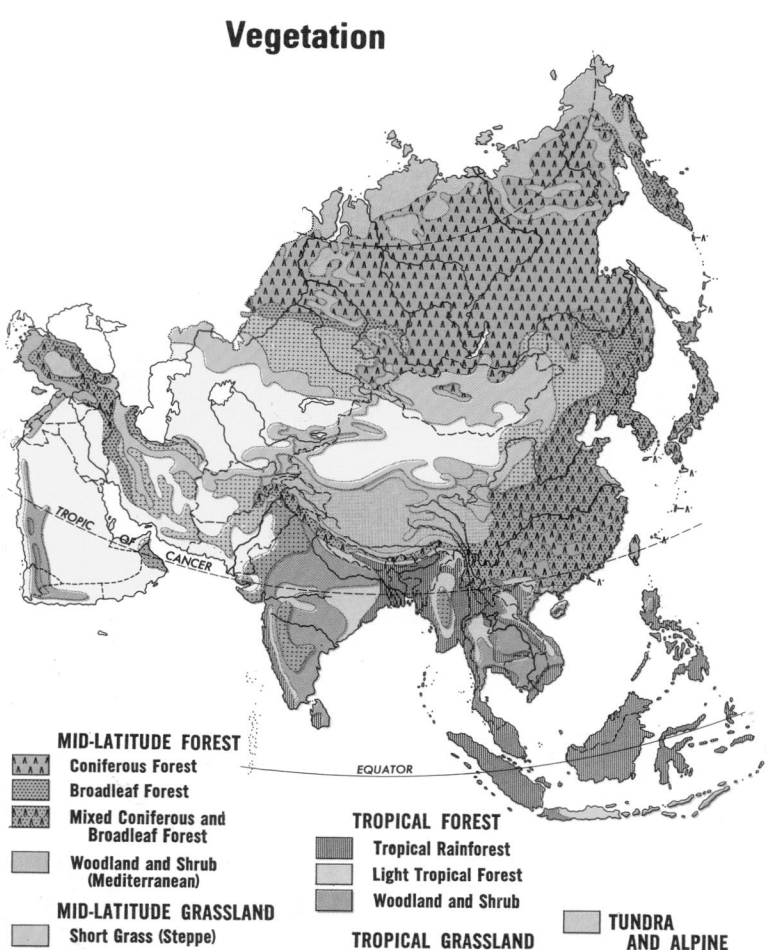

DENSITY PER

SQ. KILOMETER	SQ. MILE
Over 100	Over 260
50-100	130-260
10-50	25-130
1-10	3-25
Under 1	Under 3

• Cities with over 2,000,000 inhabitants (including suburbs)

○ Cities with over 1,000,000 inhabitants (including suburbs)

MID-LATITUDE FOREST
Coniferous Forest
Broadleaf Forest
Mixed Coniferous and Broadleaf Forest
Woodland and Shrub (Mediterranean)

MID-LATITUDE GRASSLAND
Short Grass (Steppe)
Wooded Steppe

DESERT AND DESERT SHRUB

TROPICAL FOREST
Tropical Rainforest
Light Tropical Forest
Woodland and Shrub

TROPICAL GRASSLAND
Grass and Shrub (Savanna)
Wooded Savanna

TUNDRA AND ALPINE

UNCLASSIFIED HIGHLANDS

Average January Temperature

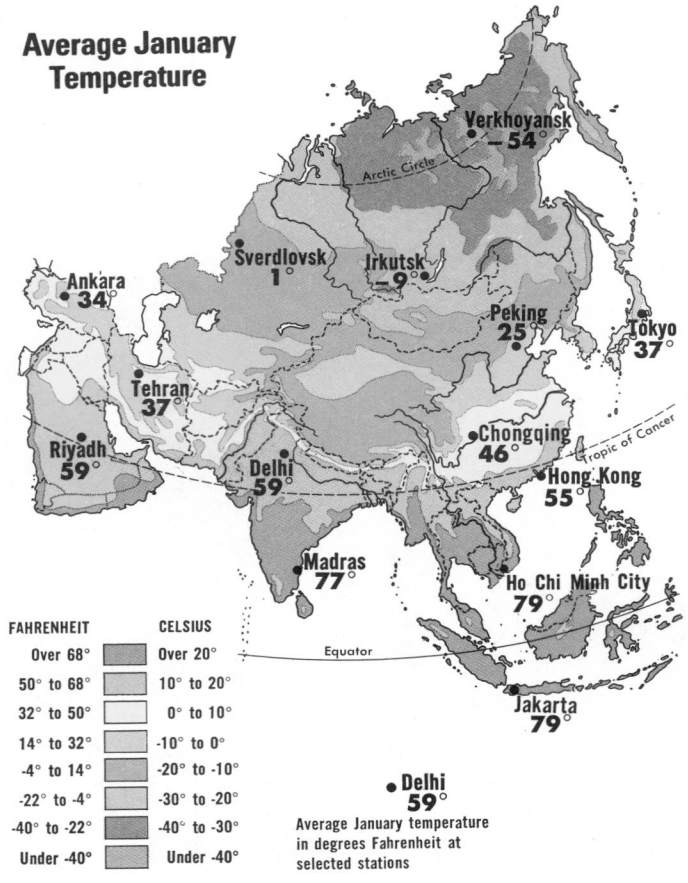

Verkhoyansk −54°

Sverdlovsk 1°
Irkutsk −9°
Ankara 34°
Peking 25°
Tokyo 37°
Tehran 37°
Chongqing 46°
Riyadh 59°
Delhi 59°
Hong Kong 55°
Madras 77°
Ho Chi Minh City 79°
Jakarta 79°

Arctic Circle
Tropic of Cancer
Equator

FAHRENHEIT		CELSIUS
Over 68°		Over 20°
50° to 68°		10° to 20°
32° to 50°		0° to 10°
14° to 32°		−10° to 0°
−4° to 14°		−20° to −10°
−22° to −4°		−30° to −20°
−40° to −22°		−40° to −30°
Under −40°		Under −40°

• Delhi 59°
Average January temperature in degrees Fahrenheit at selected stations

Average July Temperature

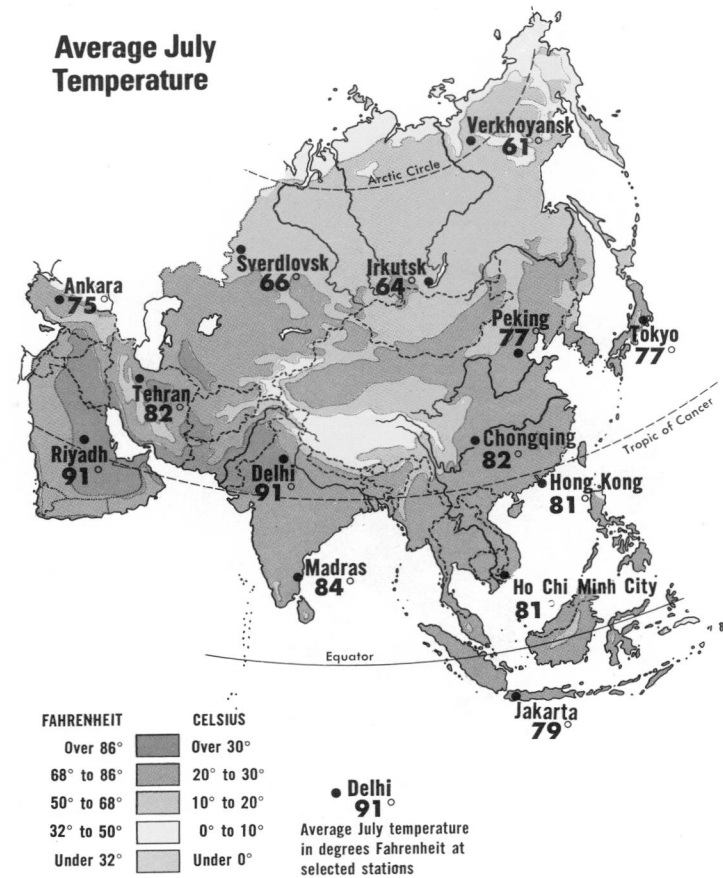

Verkhoyansk 61°

Sverdlovsk 66°
Irkutsk 64°
Ankara 75°
Peking 77°
Tokyo 77°
Tehran 82°
Riyadh 91°
Chongqing 82°
Delhi 91°
Hong Kong 81°
Madras 84°
Ho Chi Minh City 81°
Jakarta 79°

Arctic Circle
Tropic of Cancer
Equator

FAHRENHEIT		CELSIUS
Over 86°		Over 30°
68° to 86°		20° to 30°
50° to 68°		10° to 20°
32° to 50°		0° to 10°
Under 32°		Under 0°

• Delhi 91°
Average July temperature in degrees Fahrenheit at selected stations

Rainfall

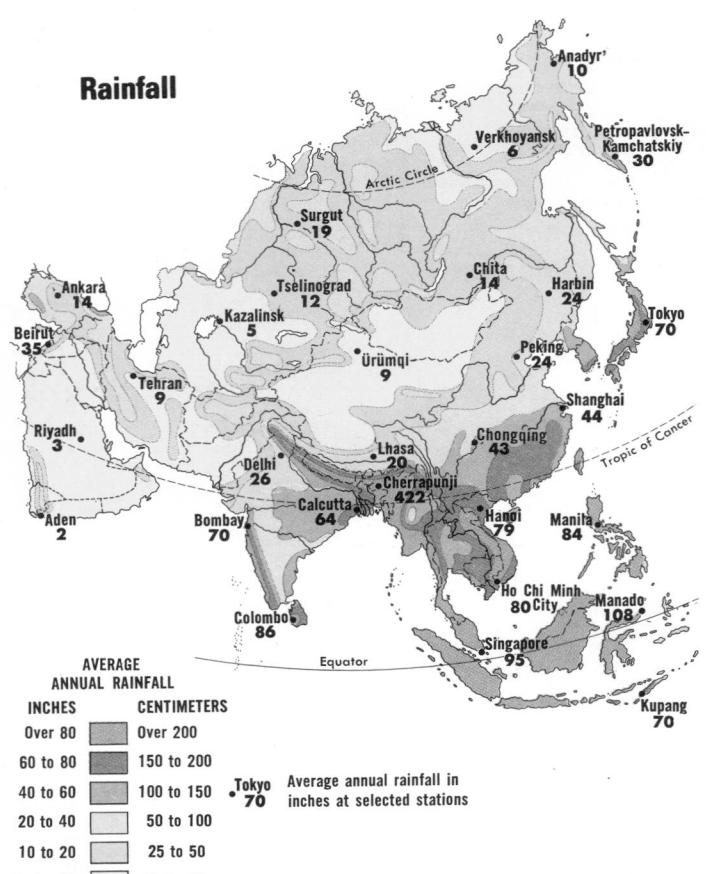

Anadyr' 10
Verkhoyansk 6
Petropavlovsk-Kamchatskiy 30
Surgut 19
Chita 14
Harbin 24
Tselinograd 12
Tokyo 70
Ankara 14
Kazalinsk 5
Beirut 35
Peking 24
Ürümqi 9
Tehran 9
Shanghai 44
Riyadh 3
Lhasa 20
Chongqing 43
Delhi 26
Cherrapunji 422
Aden 2
Bombay 70
Calcutta 64
Hanoi 79
Manila 84
Ho Chi Minh City 80
Manado 108
Colombo 86
Singapore 95
Kupang 70

Arctic Circle
Tropic of Cancer
Equator

AVERAGE ANNUAL RAINFALL

INCHES		CENTIMETERS
Over 80		Over 200
60 to 80		150 to 200
40 to 60		100 to 150
20 to 40		50 to 100
10 to 20		25 to 50
Under 10		Under 25

• Tokyo 70
Average annual rainfall in inches at selected stations

Vegetation/Relief

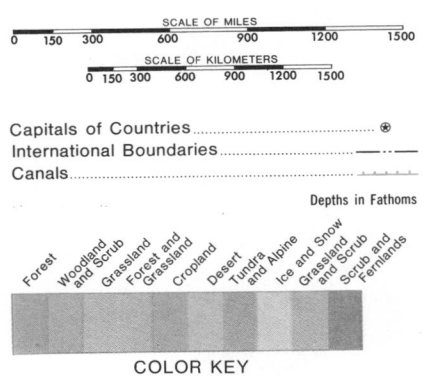

SCALE OF MILES
0 150 300 600 900 1200 1500

SCALE OF KILOMETERS
0 150 300 600 900 1200 1500

Capitals of Countries .... ⊛
International Boundaries ....
Canals ....

Depths in Fathoms

Forest | Woodland and Scrub | Grassland | Forest and Grassland | Cropland | Desert | Tundra and Alpine | Ice and Snow | Grassland and Scrub | Scrub and Fernlands

COLOR KEY

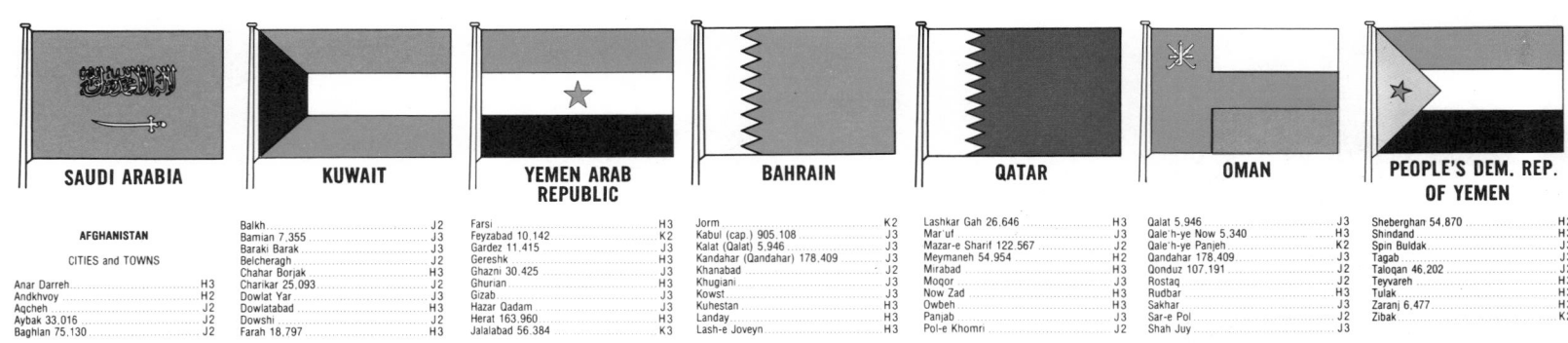

| SAUDI ARABIA | KUWAIT | YEMEN ARAB REPUBLIC | BAHRAIN | QATAR | OMAN | PEOPLE'S DEM. REP. OF YEMEN |

AFGHANISTAN

CITIES and TOWNS

Anar Darreh	H3	Balkh	J2	Farsi	H3	Jorm	K2	Lashkar Gah 26,646	H3	Qalat 5,946	J3	Sheberghan 54,870	H2
Andkhvoy	H2	Bamian 7,355	J3	Feyzabad 10,142	K2	Kabul (cap.) 905,108	J3	Mar'uf	J3	Qale'h-ye Now 5,340	H3	Shindand	H3
Aqcheh	J2	Baraki Barak	J3	Gardez 11,415	J3	Kalat (Qalat) 5,946	J3	Mazar-e Sharif 122,567	J2	Qale'h-ye Panjeh	K2	Spin Buldak	J3
Aybak 33,016	J2	Belcheragh	J2	Gereshk	H3	Kandahar (Qandahar) 178,409	J3	Meymaneh 54,954	H2	Qandahar 178,409	J3	Taqab	J3
Baghlan 75,130	J2	Chahar Borjak	H3	Ghazni 30,425	J3	Khanabad	J3	Mirabad	H3	Moqor	J3	Taloqan 46,202	J2
		Charikar 25,093	J3	Ghurian	H3	Khugiani	J3	Now Zad	H3	Rostaq	J2	Teyvareh	H3
		Dowlat Yar	J3	Gizab	J3	Kowst	J3	Owbeh	H3	Rudbar	H3	Tulak	H3
		Dowlatabad	J2	Hazar Qadam	J3	Kuhestan	H3	Panjab	J3	Sar-e Pol	J2	Zaranj 6,477	H3
		Dowshi	J2	Herat 163,960	H3	Landay	J3	Pol-e Khomri	J2	Shah Juy	J3	Zibak	K2
		Farah 18,797	H3	Jalalabad 56,384	K3	Lash-e Joveyn	H3					

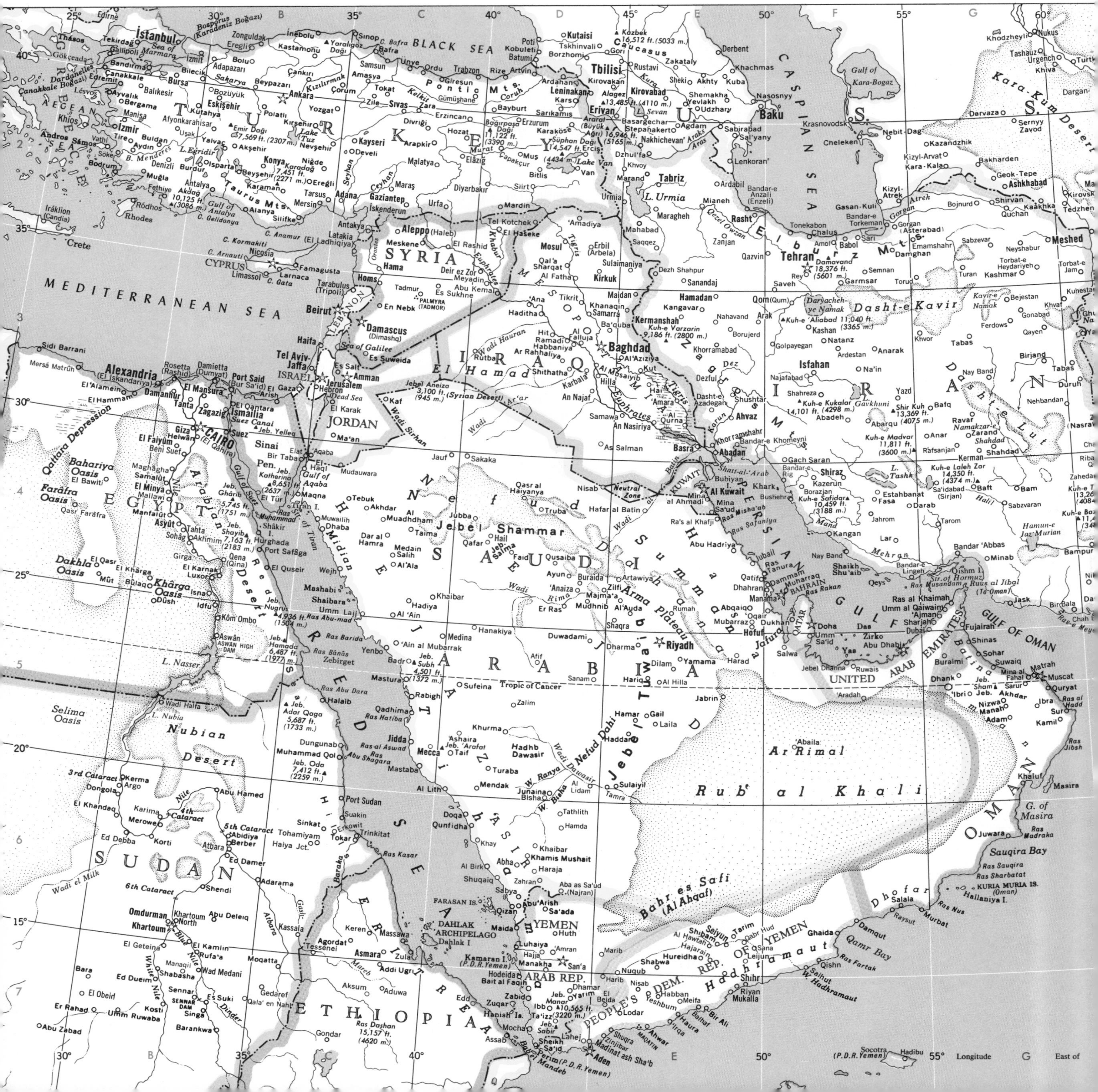

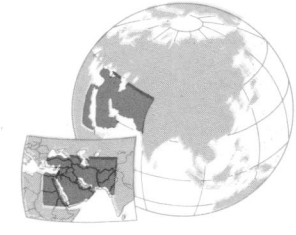

UNITED ARAB EMIRATES

(continued on following page)

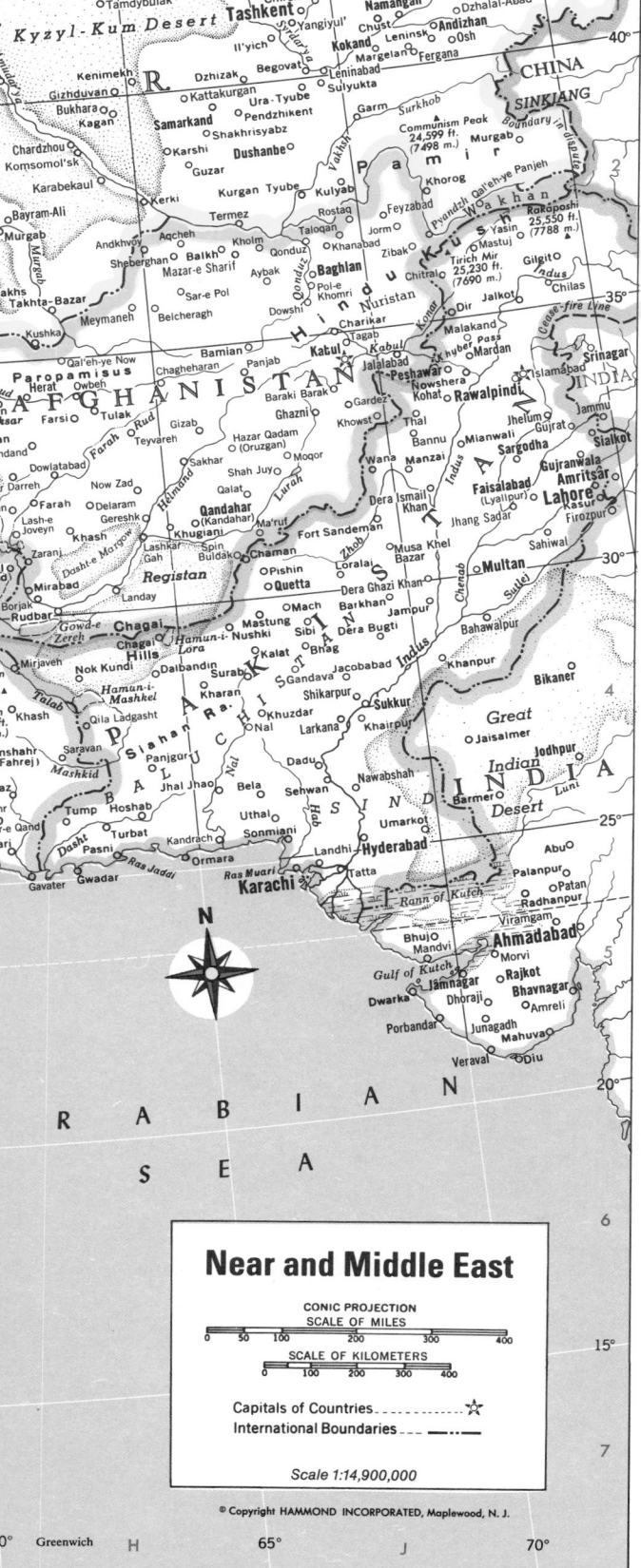

SAUDI ARABIA

AREA 829,995 sq. mi.
(2,149,687 sq. km.)
POPULATION 8,367,000
CAPITAL Riyadh
MONETARY UNIT Saudi riyal
MAJOR LANGUAGE Arabic
MAJOR RELIGION Islam

YEMEN ARAB REPUBLIC

AREA 77,220 sq. mi. (200,000 sq. km.)
POPULATION 6,456,189
CAPITAL San'a
MONETARY UNIT Yemeni rial
MAJOR LANGUAGE Arabic
MAJOR RELIGION Islam

QATAR

AREA 4,247 sq. mi. (11,000 sq. km.)
POPULATION 220,000
CAPITAL Doha
MONETARY UNIT Qatari riyal
MAJOR LANGUAGE Arabic
MAJOR RELIGION Islam

PEOPLE'S DEM. REP. OF YEMEN

AREA 111,101 sq. mi. (287,752 sq. km.)
POPULATION 1,969,000
CAPITAL Aden
MONETARY UNIT Yemeni dinar
MAJOR LANGUAGE Arabic
MAJOR RELIGION Islam

KUWAIT

AREA 6,532 sq. mi. (16,918 sq. km.)
POPULATION 1,355,827
CAPITAL Al Kuwait
MONETARY UNIT Kuwaiti dinar
MAJOR LANGUAGE Arabic
MAJOR RELIGION Islam

BAHRAIN

AREA 240 sq. mi. (622 sq. km.)
POPULATION 358,857
CAPITAL Manama
MONETARY UNIT Bahraini dinar
MAJOR LANGUAGE Arabic
MAJOR RELIGION Islam

OMAN

AREA 120,000 sq. mi. (310,800 sq. km.)
POPULATION 891,000
CAPITAL Muscat
MONETARY UNIT Omani rial
MAJOR LANGUAGE Arabic
MAJOR RELIGION Islam

UNITED ARAB EMIRATES

AREA 32,278 sq. mi. (83,600 sq. km.)
POPULATION 1,040,275
CAPITAL Abu Dhabi
MONETARY UNIT dirham
MAJOR LANGUAGE Arabic
MAJOR RELIGION Islam

Near and Middle East

CONIC PROJECTION
SCALE OF MILES
0 50 100   200   300   400

SCALE OF KILOMETERS
0 100 200   300   400

Capitals of Countries .... ☆
International Boundaries _____

Scale 1:14,900,000

© Copyright HAMMOND INCORPORATED, Maplewood, N. J.

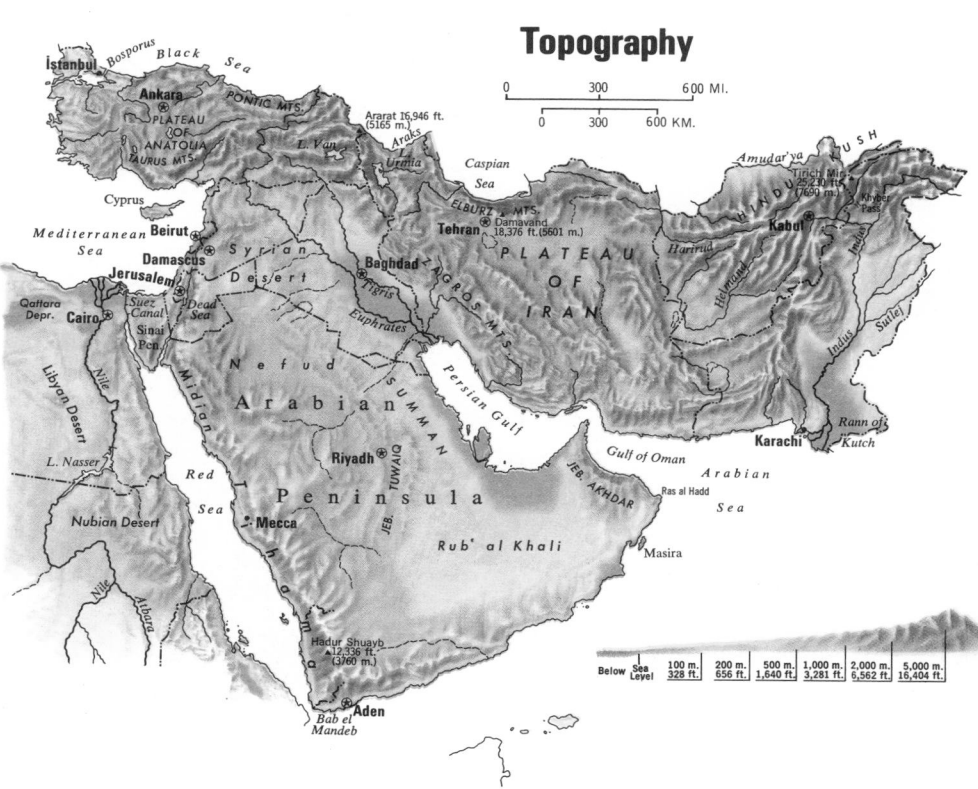

Topography

0   300   600 MI.
0   300   600 KM.

| Below Sea Level | 100 m. 328 ft. | 200 m. 656 ft. | 500 m. 1,640 ft. | 1,000 m. 3,281 ft. | 2,000 m. 6,562 ft. | 5,000 m. 16,404 ft. |

Agriculture, Industry and Resources

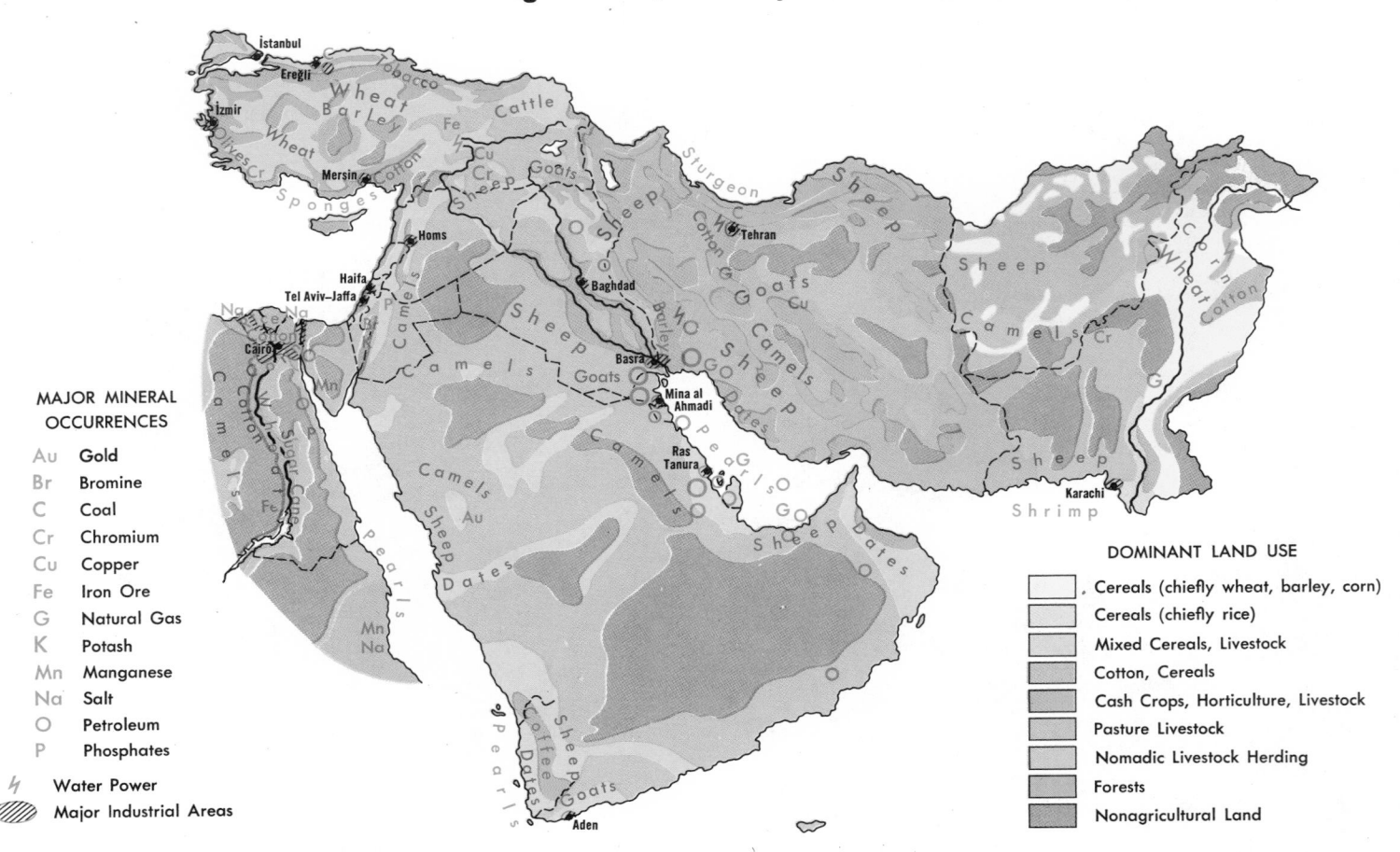

MAJOR MINERAL OCCURRENCES

Au Gold
Br Bromine
C   Coal
Cr Chromium
Cu Copper
Fe Iron Ore
G   Natural Gas
K   Potash
Mn Manganese
Na Salt
O   Petroleum
P   Phosphates

⚡ Water Power
▨ Major Industrial Areas

DOMINANT LAND USE

Cereals (chiefly wheat, barley, corn)
Cereals (chiefly rice)
Mixed Cereals, Livestock
Cotton, Cereals
Cash Crops, Horticulture, Livestock
Pasture Livestock
Nomadic Livestock Herding
Forests
Nonagricultural Land

TURKEY

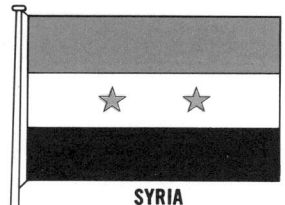

SYRIA

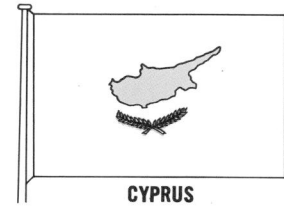

LEBANON

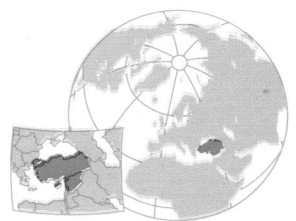

CYPRUS

AREA 300,946 sq. mi.
(779,450 sq. km.)
POPULATION 45,217,556
CAPITAL Ankara
LARGEST CITY Istanbul
HIGHEST POINT Ararat 16,946 ft.
(5,165 m.)
MONETARY UNIT Turkish lira
MAJOR LANGUAGE Turkish
MAJOR RELIGION Islam

AREA 71,498 sq. mi. (185,180 sq. km.)
POPULATION 8,979,000
CAPITAL Damascus
LARGEST CITY Damascus
HIGHEST POINT Hermon 9,232 ft.
(2,814 m.)
MONETARY UNIT Syrian pound
MAJOR LANGUAGES Arabic, French,
Kurdish, Armenian
MAJOR RELIGIONS Islam, Christianity

AREA 4,015 sq. mi. (10,399 sq. km.)
POPULATION 3,161,000
CAPITAL Beirut
LARGEST CITY Beirut
HIGHEST POINT Qurnet es Sauda
10,131 ft. (3,088 m.)
MONETARY UNIT Lebanese pound
MAJOR LANGUAGES Arabic, French
MAJOR RELIGIONS Christianity, Islam

AREA 3,473 sq. mi. (8,995 sq. km.)
POPULATION 629,000
CAPITAL Nicosia
LARGEST CITY Nicosia
HIGHEST POINT Troödos 6,406 ft. (1,953 m.)
MONETARY UNIT Cypriot pound
MAJOR LANGUAGES Greek, Turkish, English
MAJOR RELIGIONS Eastern (Greek) Orthodoxy,
Islam

CYPRUS

CITIES and TOWNS

Dhali 2,970	E5
Episkopi 2,150	E5
Famagusta 38,960	E5
Ktima	E5
Kyrenia 3,892	E5
Kythrea 3,400	E5
Lapithos 3,600	E5
Larnaca 19,608	E5
Lefka 3,650	E5
Limassol 79,641	E5
Morphou 9,040	E5
Nicosia (cap.) 115,718	E5
Paphos 8,984	E5
Polis 2,200	E5
Rizokarpasso 3,600	E5
Yialousa 2,750	E5

OTHER FEATURES

Andreas (cape)	F5
Arnauti (cape)	E5
Gata (cape)	E5
Greco (cape)	F5
Kormakiti (cape)	E5
Troodos (mt.)	E5

LEBANON

CITIES and TOWNS

A'leih 18,630	F6
Amyun 7,926	F6
Baa'lbek 15,560	G5
Batrun 5,976	F6
Beirut (cap.) 474,870	F6
Beirut* 938,940	F6
Hermil 2,652	G5
Merj U'yun 9,318	F6
Rasheiya 6,731	F6
Rayak 1,480	G6
Saida 32,200	F6
Sidon (Saida) 32,200	F6
Sur 16,483	F6
Tripoli (Tarabulus) 127,611	F5

Tyre (Sur) 16,483	F6
Zahle 53,121	G6
Zegharta 18,210	G5

OTHER FEATURES

Lebanon (mts.)	F6
Leontes (Litani) (riv.)	F6
Litani (riv.)	F6
Sauda, Qurnet es (mt.)	G5

SYRIA

PROVINCES

Aleppo 1,316,872	G4
Damascus 1,457,934	G6
Deir ez Zor 292,780	H5
Dera' 230,481	G6
El Quneitra 16,490	F6
Es Suweida 139,650	G6
Hama 514,748	G5
Haseke 468,506	J4
Homs 546,176	G5
Idlib 383,695	G5
Latakia 389,552	F5
Rashid 243,736	H5
Tartus 302,065	G5

CITIES and TOWNS

Abu Kemal 6,907	J5
A'in el A'rab 4,529	H4
Aleppo 639,428	G4
Azaz 13,923	G4
Baniyas 8,537	F5
Busra	G6
Damascus (cap.) 836,668	G6
Damascus* 923,253	G6
Deir ez Zor 66,164	H5
Dera' 27,651	G6
Duma 30,050	G6
El Bab 27,366	G4
El Haseke 32,746	J4
El Ladhiqiya (Latakia) 125,716	F5
El Qurayetin	G5
El Quneitra 17,752	F6
El Rashid 37,151	H5

En Nebk 16,334	G5
Es Suweide 29,524	G6
Et Tell el Abyad	H4
Haffe 4,656	G5
Haleb (Aleppo) 639,428	G4
Hama 137,421	G5
Harim 6,837	G4
Homs 215,423	G5
Idlib 34,515	G5
Izra 3,226	G6
Jeble 15,715	F5
Jerablus 8,610	G4
Jisr esh Shughur 13,131	G5
Khan Sheikhun	G5
Latakia 125,716	F5
Masyaf 7,058	G5
Membij 13,796	G4
Meskene	H5
Meyadin 12,515	J5
Qala't es Salihiye	J5
Qamishliye 31,448	J4
Quteife 4,993	G6
Ragqa (El Rashid) 37,151	H5
Sabkha 3,375	H5
Safita 9,650	G5
Selemiya 21,677	G5
Tadmur 10,670	H5
Tartus 29,842	F5
Telkalakh 6,242	G5
Zebdani 10,010	G6

OTHER FEATURES

A'mrit (ruins)	F5
Arwad (Ruad) (isl.)	F5
A'si (Orontes) (riv.)	G5
Druz, Jebel ed (mts.)	G6
El Furat (riv.)	H4
Euphrates (El Furat) (riv.)	H4
Hermon (mt.)	F6
Khabur (riv.)	J5
Orontes (riv.)	G5
Palmyra (Tadmor) (ruins)	H5
Ruwaq, Jebel er (mts.)	G5

TURKEY

PROVINCES

Adana 1,240,475	F4

Adiyaman 346,892	H4
Afyonkarahisar 579,171	D3
Ağri 330,201	K3
Amasya 322,806	F2
Ankara 2,585,293	E3
Antalya 669,357	D4
Artvin 228,026	J2
Aydin 609,869	B4
Balikesir 789,255	B3
Bilecik 137,120	C2
Bingöl 210,804	J3
Bitlis 218,305	J3
Bolu 428,704	D2
Burdur 222,896	C4
Bursa 961,639	C2
Çanakkale 369,385	B2
Çankiri 265,468	E2
Çorum 547,580	F2
Denizli 560,916	C4
Diyarbakir 651,233	H4
Edirne 340,732	B2
Elâziğ 417,924	H3
Erzincan 283,683	H3
Erzurum 746,666	J3
Eskişehir 495,097	D3
Gaziantep 715,939	G4
Giresun 463,587	H2
Gümüşhane 293,673	H2
Hakkâri 126,036	K4
Hatay 744,113	F4
İçel 714,817	F4
Isparta 322,685	D4
Istanbul 3,904,588	C2
Izmir 1,673,966	B3
Kahramanmaraş 641,480	G4
Kars 707,398	K2
Kastamonu 438,243	E2
Kayseri 676,809	F3
Kirklareli 266,399	B2
Kirşehir 232,853	F3
Kocaeli 477,736	C2
Konya 1,422,461	E4
Kütahya 470,423	C3
Malatya 574,558	H3
Manisa 873,375	B3
Mardin 519,687	J4
Muğla 400,796	C4
Muş 267,203	J3
Nevşehir 249,308	F3
Niğde 463,121	F4

Ordu 664,290	G2
Rize 336,278	J2
Sakarya 495,649	D2
Samsun 906,381	F2
Siirt 381,503	J4
Sinop 267,605	F2
Sivas 741,713	G3
Tekirdağ 319,987	B2
Tokat 599,166	G2
Trabzon 719,008	H2
Tunceli 164,591	H3
Urfa 597,277	H4
Uşak 229,679	C3
Van 386,314	K3
Yozgat 500,371	F3
Zonguldak 836,156	D2

CITIES and TOWNS

Acigöl 3,934	F3
Acipayam 5,916	C4
Adalia (Antalya) 130,774	D4
Adana 475,384	F4
Adapazari 114,130	D2
Adilcevaz 9,022	K3
Adiyaman 43,782	H4
Afşin 18,231	G3
Afyonkarahisar 60,150	D3
Ağlasun 4,288	D4
Ağli 3,399	E2
Ağri (Karaköse) 35,284	K3
Ahlat 7,995	J3
Akçaabat 10,756	H2
Akçadağ 7,366	G3
Akçakoca 9,066	D2
Akdağmadeni 7,909	F3
Akhisar 53,357	B3
Aksaray 45,564	F3
Akşehir 35,544	D3
Akseki 5,141	D4
Akviran 3,799	E4
Akyazi 12,438	D2
Alaca 12,552	F2
Alaçam 2,321	G3
Alaçam 10,013	F2
Alanya 18,520	D4
Alaşehir 23,243	C3
Alexandretta (İskenderun) 107,437	G4
Aliağa 5,727	B3

Alibeyköyü 33,387	D6
Almus 4,225	G2
Alpu 3,718	D3
Altindağ 512,392	D2
Altinova 6,980	B3
Altintaş 3,386	C3
Altinözü 5,158	G4
Alucra 7,070	H2
Amasra 4,369	E2
Amasya 41,496	G2
Anamur 21,475	E4
Andirin 5,018	G4
Ankara (cap.) 1,701,004	E3
Antakya 77,518	G4
Antakya 130,774	G4
Antioch (Antakya) 77,518	G4
Araç 3,594	E2
Aralik 4,155	L3
Arapkir 8,436	H3
Ardahan 16,285	K2
Ardeşen 7,980	J2
Ardanuç 2,942	J2
Arguvan 2,461	H3
Arhavi 6,311	J2
Arpaçay 2,651	K2
Arsin 6,557	H2
Artova 2,813	G2
Artvin 13,390	J2
Aşkale 10,817	J3
Avanos 8,635	F3
Ayancik 7,202	F2
Ayaş 4,575	E2
Aydin 13,180	C4
Aydin 59,579	B4
Aydincik 6,739	E4
Ayranci 2,664	E4
Ayvacik 3,120	B3
Ayvalik 18,041	B3
Babadağ 5,890	C4
Babaeski 17,090	B2
Bafra 34,288	F2
Bahçe 10,212	G4
Bakirköy 200,942	D6
Baklan 3,327	C4
Balâ 4,107	E3
Balikesir 99,443	B3
Balya 2,362	B3
Banaz 6,264	C3
Bandirma 45,752	B2
Bartin 18,409	E2

Başkale 8,558	K3
Başmakçi 5,925	C4
Batman 64,384	J4
Bayat 4,671	F2
Bayburt 20,156	J2
Bayindir 14,078	B3
Baykan 2,690	J3
Bayramiç 6,385	B3
Bergama 29,749	B3
Beşiktaş 174,931	D6
Beşiri 4,165	J4
Besni 16,313	G4
Beykoz 76,804	D5
Beyoğlu 230,532	D6
Beypazari 14,963	D2
Beyşehir 15,060	D4
Beytüşşebap 2,766	K4
Biga 15,188	B2
Bigadiç 7,535	C3
Bilecik 11,269	D2
Bingöl (Çapakçur) 22,047	J3
Birecik 20,104	H4
Bismil 12,775	J4
Bitlis 25,054	J3
Bodrum 7,858	B4
Boğazliyan 10,329	F3
Bolu 32,812	D2
Bolvadin 29,218	D3
Bor 16,560	F4
Borçka 4,636	J2
Bornova 45,096	B3
Boyabat 13,139	F2
Bozdoğan 7,218	C4
Bozkir 5,294	E4
Bozova 2,948	F2
Bozova 5,462	H4
Bozüyük 15,197	C3
Bucak 15,090	D4
Bulancak 14,153	H2
Bulanik 8,296	K3
Buldan 11,115	C3
Bünyan 12,277	G3
Burdur 36,633	D4
Bursa 346,103	C2
Büyükada	D6
Büyükdere	D5
Çal 3,274	C3
Çala 2,450	K2
Çaldiran 3,366	K3

(continued on following page)

Agriculture, Industry and Resources

DOMINANT LAND USE

- Cereals (chiefly wheat, barley), Livestock
- Cash Crops, Horticulture, Livestock
- Pasture Livestock
- Nomadic Livestock Herding
- Forests
- Nonagricultural Land

MAJOR MINERAL OCCURRENCES

Ab	Asbestos	Na	Salt	
Al	Bauxite	O	Petroleum	
C	Coal	P	Phosphates	
Cr	Chromium	Pb	Lead	
Cu	Copper	Py	Pyrites	
Fe	Iron Ore	Sb	Antimony	
Hg	Mercury	Zn	Zinc	
Mg	Magnesium			

⚡ Water Power

Major Industrial Areas

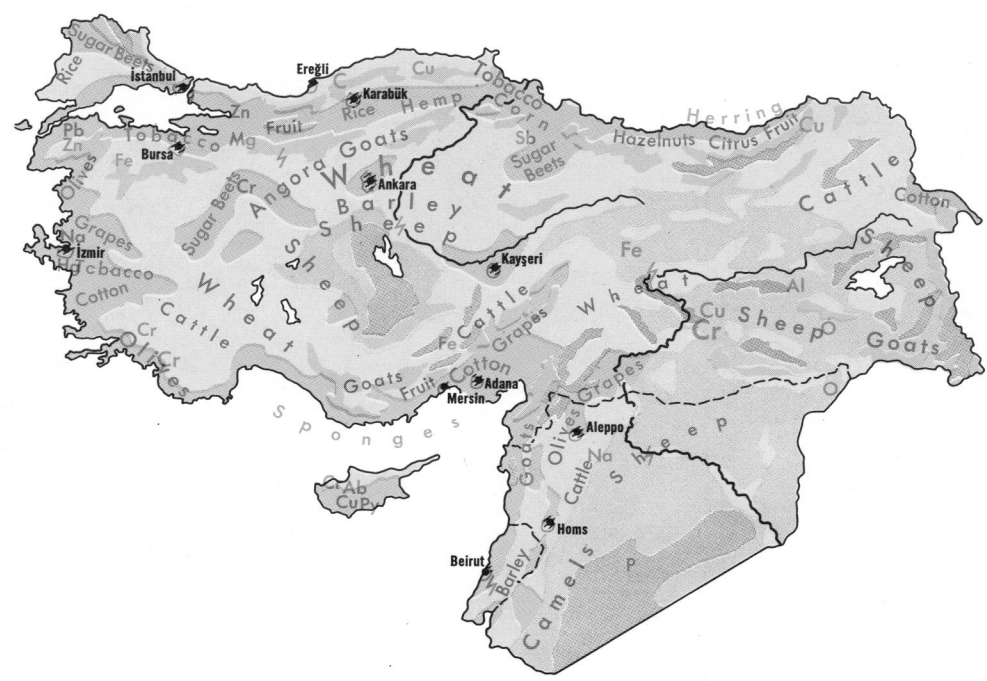

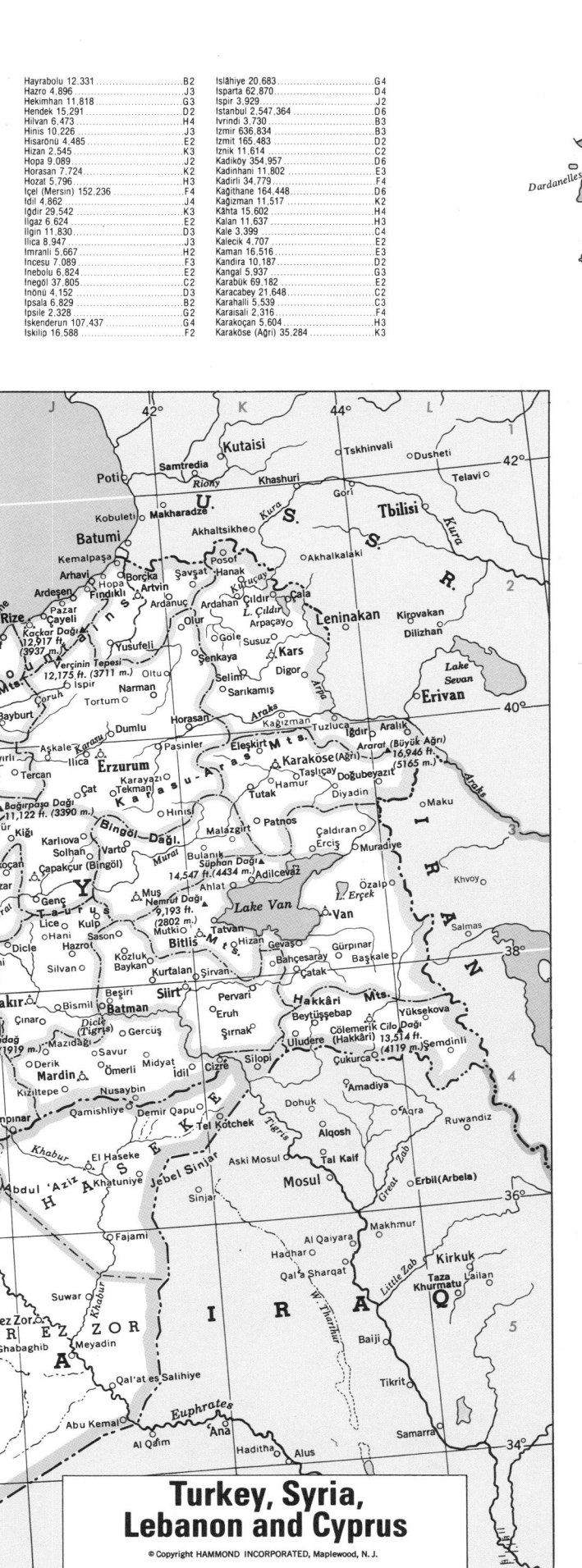

Topography

0   100   200 MI.
0   100   200 KM.

| Below Sea Level | 100 m. 328 ft. | 200 m. 656 ft. | 500 m. 1,640 ft. | 1,000 m. 3,281 ft. | 2,000 m. 6,562 ft. | 5,000 m. 16,404 ft. |

Turkey, Syria, Lebanon and Cyprus

© Copyright HAMMOND INCORPORATED, Maplewood, N.J.

SCALE OF MILES
0 25 50 75 100 125 150

SCALE OF KILOMETERS
0 25 50 75 100 125 150

Capitals of Countries .... ★
Capitals of Provinces .... △
Provincial Boundaries .... _____

Scale 1:5,440,000

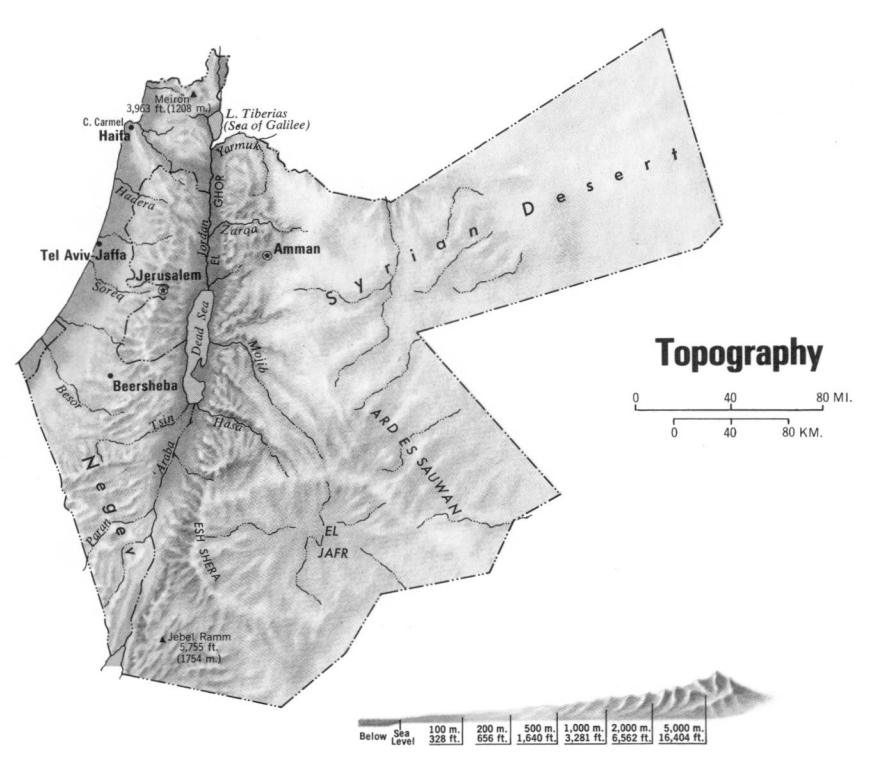

Topography

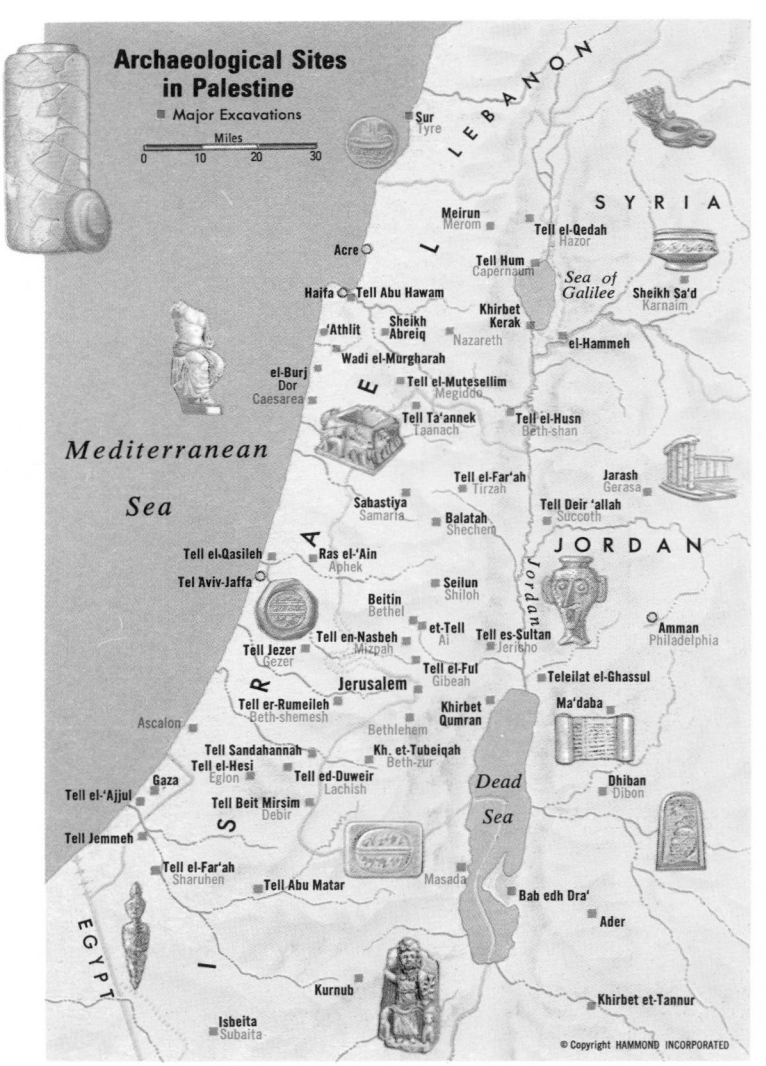

Archaeological Sites in Palestine
■ Major Excavations

Agriculture, Industry and Resources

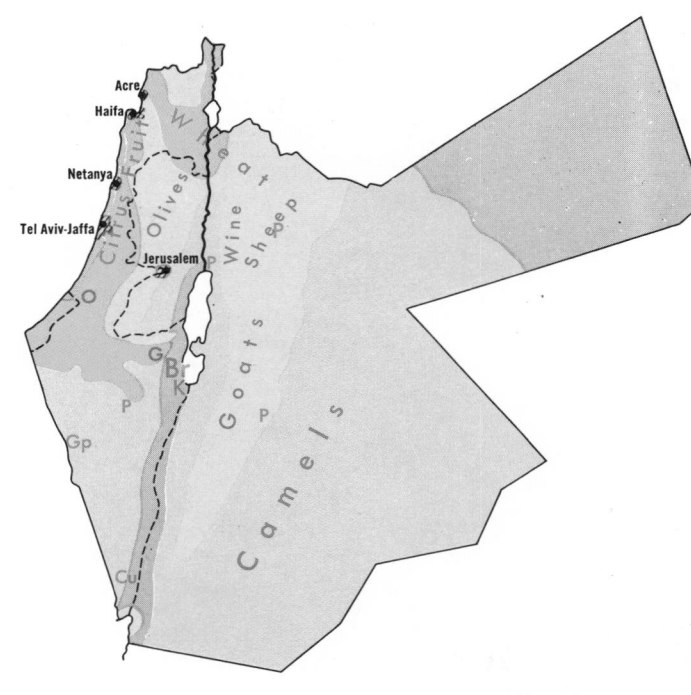

DOMINANT LAND USE

Cereals, Livestock

Cash Crops, Horticulture

Nomadic Livestock Herding

Nonagricultural Land

MAJOR MINERAL OCCURRENCES

Br Bromine
Cu Copper
G Natural Gas
Gp Gypsum

K Potash
O Petroleum
P Phosphates

▨ Major Industrial Areas

© Copyright HAMMOND INCORPORATED

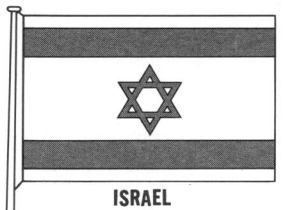

ISRAEL

JORDAN

ISRAEL

AREA 7,847 sq. mi. (20,324 sq. km.)
POPULATION 3,878,000
CAPITAL Jerusalem
LARGEST CITY Tel Aviv-Jaffa
HIGHEST POINT Meiran 3,963 ft. (1,208 m.)
MONETARY UNIT shekel
MAJOR LANGUAGES Hebrew, Arabic
MAJOR RELIGIONS Judaism, Islam, Christianity

JORDAN

AREA (East Bank) 35,000 sq. mi. (90,650 sq. km.)
POPULATION 2,152,273
CAPITAL Amman
LARGEST CITY Amman
HIGHEST POINT Jeb. Ramm 5,755 ft. (1,754 m.)
MONETARY UNIT Jordanian dinar
MAJOR LANGUAGE Arabic
MAJOR RELIGION Islam

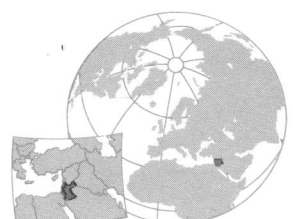

Israel and Jordan

CYLINDRICAL PROJECTION

© Copyright HAMMOND INCORPORATED, Maplewood, N.J.

SCALE OF MILES
0   5   10   15   20   25   30

SCALE OF KILOMETERS
0   5   10 15 20 25 30

Capitals of Countries .... ☆
Internal Capitals .... ⊙
International Boundaries .... — —
Internal Boundaries .... · · ·

Scale 1:1,325,000

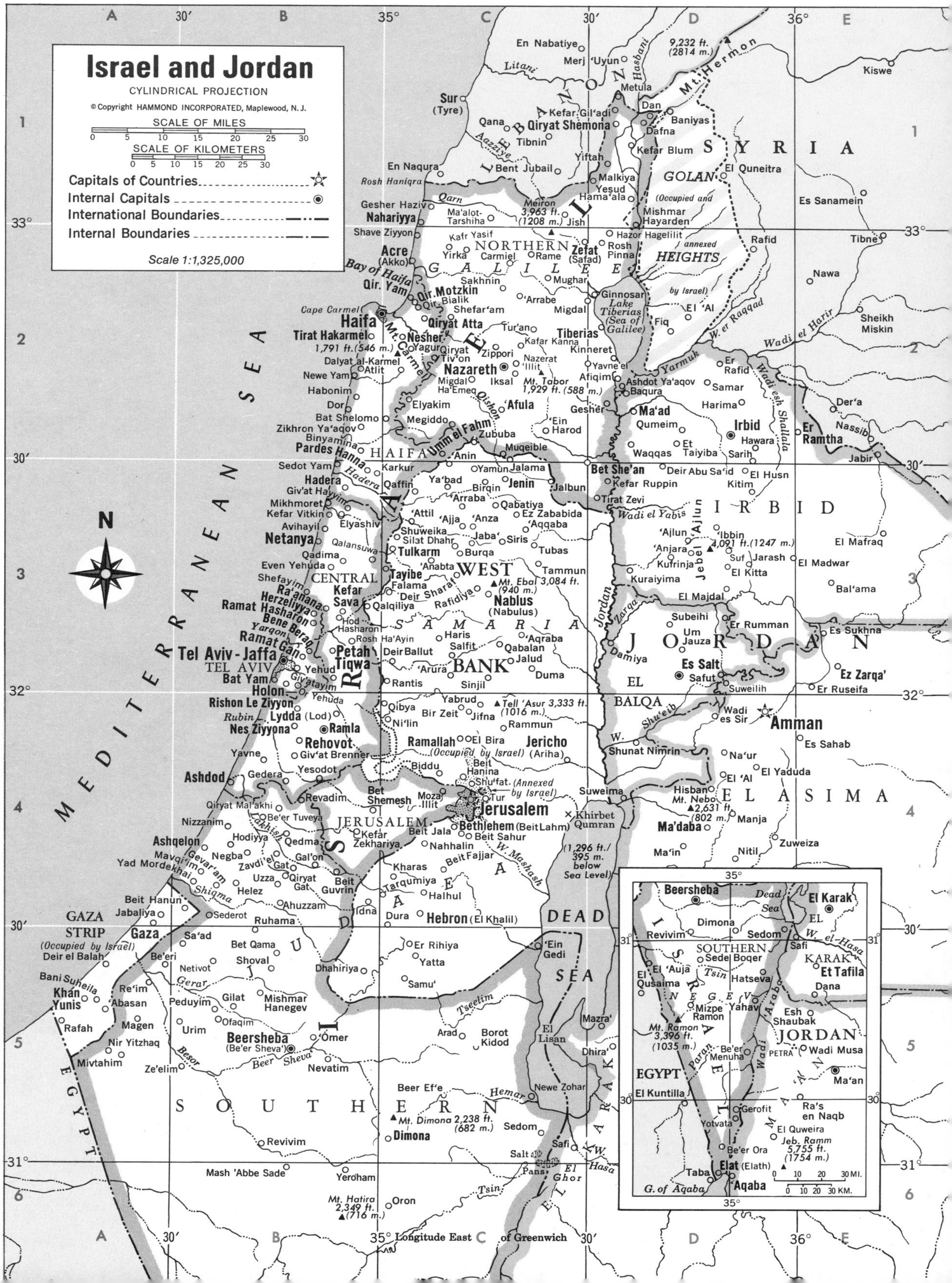

IRAN

INTERNAL DIVISIONS

Azerbaijan, East (prov.) 3,194,543 ... E1
Azerbaijan, West (prov.) 1,404,875 ... D1
Bakhtiari (governorate) 394,300 ... F4
Boyer Ahmediyeh and Kohkiluyeh (governor) 244,750 ... G5
Bushehr (prov.) 345,427 ... G6
Central (Markazi) 6,921,283 ... G3
Esfahan (Isfahan) (prov.) 1,974,938 ... H4
Fars (prov.) 2,020,947 ... H6
Gilan (prov.) 1,577,800 ... F2
Hamadan (governorate) 1,086,512 ... F3
Hormozgan (prov.) 463,419 ... J7
Ilam (governorate) 244,222 ... E4
Isfahan (prov.) 1,974,938 ... H4
Kerman (prov.) 1,088,045 ... K6
Kermanshahan (prov.) 1,016,199 ... E3
Khorasan (prov.) 3,266,650 ... K3
Khuzestan (prov.) 2,176,612 ... F5
Kordestan (Kurdistan) (prov.) 781,889 ... E3
Lorestan (Luristan) (governorate) 924,848 ... F4
Mazandaran (prov.) 2,384,226 ... H2
Semnan (governorate) 485,875 ... J3
Sistan and Baluchestan (prov.) 659,297 ... M6
Yazd (governorate) 356,218 ... J5
Zanjan (governorate) 579,000 ... F2

CITIES and TOWNS

Abadan 296,081 ... F5
Abadeh 16,000 ... H5
Abarqu 8,000 ... H5
Abhar 24,000 ... F2
Ahar 24,000 ... E1
Ahvaz (Ahwaz) 329,006 ... F5
Amol 68,782 ... H2
Anarak 2,038 ... H4
Aradan 8,978 ... H3
Arak 114,507 ... F3
Ardabil 147,404 ... F1
Ardestan 5,868 ... H4
Asadabad 7,000 ... F3
Asterabad (Gorgan) 88,348 ... J2
Azaran 3,153 ... E1
Babol 67,790 ... H2
Babol Sar 7,237 ... H2
Baft 6,000 ... J6
Bajgiran 1,151 ... L2
Bam 22,000 ... K6
Bampur 1,585 ... M7
Bandar A'bbas 89,103 ... J7
Bandar-e Anzali ... F2
Bandar-e Deylam 3,691 ... G5
Bandar Khomeyni 6,000 ... F5
Bandar-e Lengeh 4,920 ... J7
Bandar-e Mas'hur 17,000 ... F5
Bandar-e Rig 1,889 ... G6
Bandar-e Torkeman 13,000 ... H2
Bandar Shahpuri 6,000 ... F5
Bastak 2,473 ... J7
Bastam 3,296 ... J2
Behbehan 39,874 ... G5

Behshahr 26,032 ... H2
Bejestan 3,823 ... K3
Bijar 12,000 ... E3
Birjand 25,854 ... L4
Bojnurd 31,248 ... K2
Borazjan 20,000 ... G6
Borujerd 100,103 ... F4
Bostan 4,619 ... F5
Bowkan 9,000 ... E2
Bushehr (Bushire) 57,681 ... F5
Chah Bahar 16,000 ... M8
Chalus 15,000 ... G2
Damavand 5,319 ... H3
Damghan 13,000 ... J2
Darab 13,000 ... J6
Daran 4,609 ... H4
Darreh Gaz 11,000 ... L2
Dasht-e-Azadegan 21,000 ... F5
Dehkhvareqan 6,000 ... D2
Delijan 6,000 ... H4
Dezful (Dezfuli) 110,287 ... F4
Duzdab (Zahedan) 92,628 ... M6
Emamshahr 30,767 ... J2
Enzeli 55,978 ... F2
Esfahan (Isfahan) 671,820 ... G4
Elamabad 12,000 ... F4
Estahbanat 18,187 ... J6
Ezna 5,000 ... F4
Fariman 4,000 ... L3
Farrashband 3,532 ... H6
Fasa 19,000 ... H6
Ferdows 11,000 ... K3
Firuzabad 8,718 ... H6
Firuzkuh 4,684 ... H3
Fowman 9,000 ... F2
Gach Saran 5,000 ... G5

Ganaveh 9,000 ... G6
Garmsar 4,723 ... H3
Gavater ... M8
Ghaemshahr 63,289 ... H2
Golpayegan 20,515 ... G4
Golshan (Tabas) 10,000 ... K4
Gonabad 8,000 ... L3
Gonbad-e Kavus 59,868 ... J2
Gonbadli 531 ... M2
Gorgan (Gurgan) 88,348 ... J2
Haft Gel 10,000 ... F5
Hamada 155,846 ... F3
Hashtpar 5,000 ... F2
Hormoz 2,569 ... J7
Huzgan 4,722 ... F5
Ilam 15,000 ... E4
Iranshahr 5,000 ... M7
Isfahan 671,825 ... G4
Izeh 1,983 ... F5
Jahrom 38,236 ... H6
Jajarm 3,641 ... K2
Jask 1,078 ... K8
Kakhk 4,043 ... L3
Kangan 2,682 ... G6
Kangavar 9,414 ... F3
Karaj 138,774 ... G3
Kashan 84,545 ... G3
Kazeroon 51,309 ... G6
Kazerun 51,309 ... G6
Kazvin (Qazvin) 138,527 ... F2
Kerman 140,309 ... K6
Kermanshah 290,861 ... E3
Khaf 5,000 ... L3
Khalkhal 5,422 ... F2
Khash 7,439 ... M6
Khiyav 9,000 ... E1
Khoman 3,054 ... F2
Khomeinishar 46,836 ... G4

Khorramabad 104,928 ... F4
Khorramshahr 146,709 ... F5
Khvaf 5,000 ... L3
Khvonsar 16,000 ... F4
Khvoy (Khoi) 70,040 ... D1
Kord Kuy 9,855 ... J2
Lahijan 25,725 ... G2
Lar 22,000 ... J7
Mahabad 28,610 ... D2
Mahallat 12,000 ... G4
Mahan 8,000 ... K5
Maku 7,000 ... D1
Malamir (Izeh) 1,983 ... F5
Malayer 28,434 ... F3
Maragheh 60,820 ... E2
Mianeh 28,447 ... E2
Mehran 664 ... E4
Meshed 670,180 ... L2
Masjed Soleyman 77,161 ... F5
Medishahr 9,000 ... J2
Mehrabad ... D1
Marv Dasht 25,498 ... H6
Mashhad (Meshed) 670,180 ... L2
Meybod 15,000 ... J4
Miandoab 19,000 ... D2
Mianeh 28,447 ... E2
Minab 4,028 ... K7
Mirjaveh 11,000 ... M6
Naft-e Shah 3,043 ... D4
Nahavand 24,000 ... F3
Na'in 5,925 ... H4
Najafabad 76,236 ... G4
Naraq 2,725 ... G3
Nasratabad (Zabol) 20,000 ... M5
Natanz 4,370 ... H4
Neyriz 16,114 ... J6
Neyshabur 59,101 ... L2

Nishapur (Neyshabur) 59,101 ... L2
Nosratabad 20,000 ... L6
Now Shahr 8,000 ... G2
Orumiyeh (Urmia) 163,991 ... D2
Oshnoviyeh 5,000 ... D2
Oshnoviyeh (Urmia) 163,991 ... D2
Mehran 2,912 ... E4
Pahlevi (Enzeli) 55,978 ... F2
Pazanan 81 ... G5
Qasr-e-Shirin 15,094 ... D3
Qayen 6,000 ... L4
Qazvin 138,527 ... F2
Qom 246,831 ... G3
Qom (Qum) 246,831 ... G3
Quchan 29,133 ... L2
Rafsanjan 21,000 ... K5
Ramhormoz 9,000 ... F5
Rasht 187,203 ... F2
Ravar 5,074 ... K5
Resht (Rasht) 187,203 ... F2
Rey 102,825 ... G3
Reza 'iyeh (Urmia) 163,991 ... D2
Rud Sar 7,460 ... G2
Sabzevar 69,174 ... K2
Sabzvaran 7,000 ... K6
Saeendey 4,195 ... E2
Sai'dabad 20,000 ... J6
Sakht-Sar 12,000 ... G2
Salmas 13,161 ... D1
Sanandaj 95,834 ... E3
Sarab 16,000 ... E2
Sarakhs 3,461 ... M2
Saravan 4,012 ... N7
Sari 70,936 ... H2
Savanat (Estahbanat) 18,187 ... J6
Saveh 17,565 ... G3
Semnan 31,058 ... H3

Shadegan 6,000 ... F5
Shahdad 2,777 ... K5
Shahistan (Saravan) 4,012 ... N7
Shahr Kord 24,000 ... H4
Shahreza 34,222 ... G4
Shahr Kord 24,000 ... H4
Shahrud (Emamshahr) 30,767 ... J2
Sharafkhaneh 1,260 ... D1
Shiraz 416,408 ... H6
Shush 1,433 ... F5
Shushtar 24,000 ... F5
Sinneh (Sanandaj) 95,834 ... E3
Sirjan (Sai'dabad) 20,000 ... J6
Sivand 1,811 ... H5
Songor 10,433 ... E3
Sufian 2,914 ... E1
Sultanabad (Kashmar) 17,000 ... L3
Tabas 10,000 ... K4
Tabriz 598,576 ... D1
Taft 7,000 ... J5
Tajrish 157,486 ... G3
Takestan 13,485 ... F2
Tehran (cap.) 4,496,159 ... G3
Tonekabon 12,000 ... G2
Torbat-e-Heydariyeh 30,106 ... L3
Torbat-e Jam 13,000 ... M3
Tun (Ferdows) 11,000 ... K3
Tuyserkan 12,000 ... F3
Urmia 163,991 ... D2
Yazd (Yezd) 135,978 ... J5
Yazd-e Khvasat 3,544 ... H5
Zabol 20,000 ... M5
Zahedan 92,628 ... M6
Zanjan 99,967 ... F2
Zarand 5,000 ... K5
Zarqam 7,000 ... H6
Zenjan (Zanjan) 99,967 ... F2

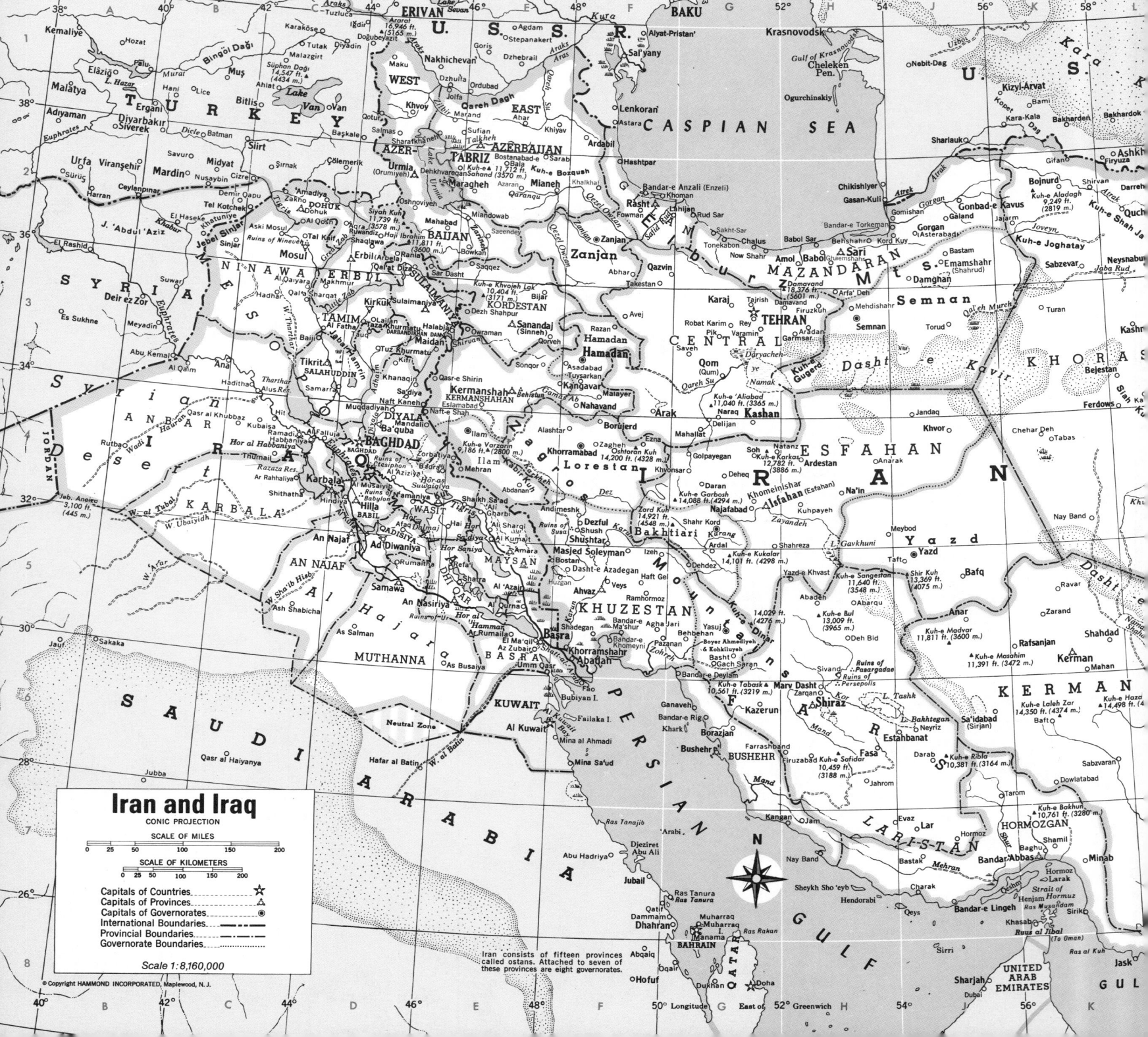

Iran and Iraq

CONIC PROJECTION

SCALE OF MILES
0 25 50 100 150 200

SCALE OF KILOMETERS
0 25 50 100 150 200

Capitals of Countries .... ★
Capitals of Provinces .... △
Capitals of Governorates .... ⊙
International Boundaries ....
Provincial Boundaries ....
Governorate Boundaries ....

Scale 1:8,160,000

© Copyright HAMMOND INCORPORATED, Maplewood, N.J.

Iran consists of fifteen provinces called ostans. Attached to seven of these provinces are eight governorates.

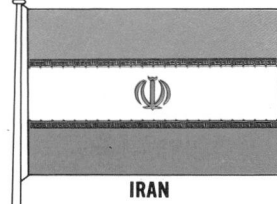

IRAN

IRAQ

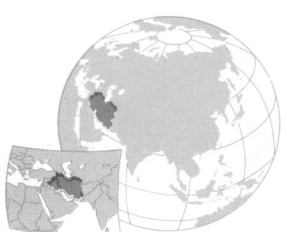

AREA 636,293 sq. mi. (1,648,000 sq. km.)
POPULATION 37,447,000
CAPITAL Tehran
LARGEST CITY Tehran
HIGHEST POINT Damavand 18,376 ft. (5,601 m.)
MONETARY UNIT Iranian rial
MAJOR LANGUAGES Persian, Azerbaijani, Kurdish
MAJOR RELIGION Islam

AREA 172,476 sq. mi. (446,713 sq. km.)
POPULATION 12,767,000
CAPITAL Baghdad
LARGEST CITY Baghdad
HIGHEST POINT Haji Ibrahim 11,811 ft. (3,600 m.)
MONETARY UNIT Iraqi dinar
MAJOR LANGUAGES Arabic, Kurdish
MAJOR RELIGION Islam

Topography

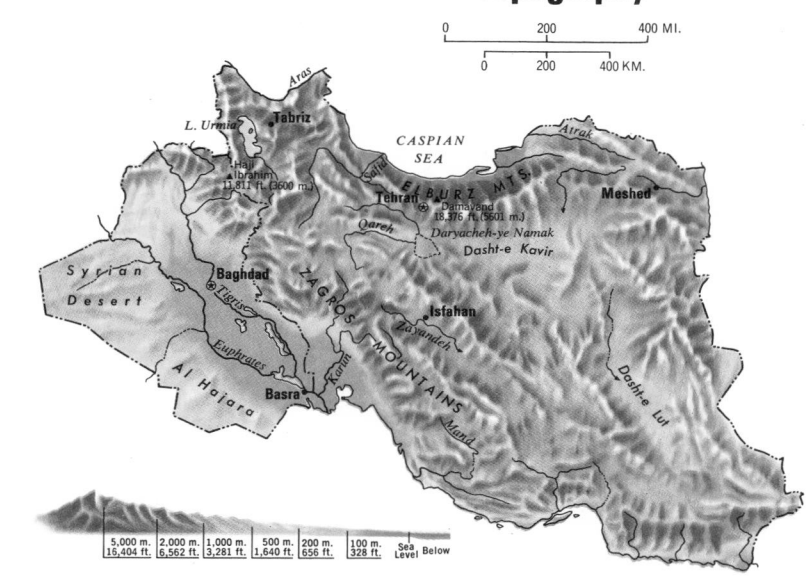

Agriculture, Industry and Resources

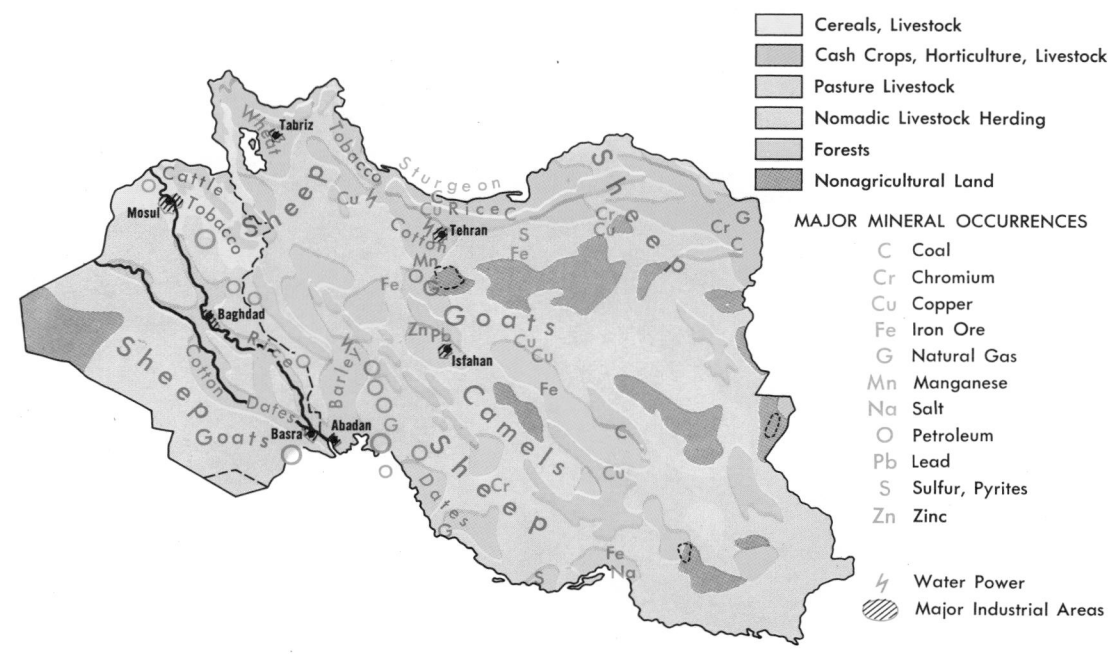

DOMINANT LAND USE

- Cereals, Livestock
- Cash Crops, Horticulture, Livestock
- Pasture Livestock
- Nomadic Livestock Herding
- Forests
- Nonagricultural Land

MAJOR MINERAL OCCURRENCES

C	Coal
Cr	Chromium
Cu	Copper
Fe	Iron Ore
G	Natural Gas
Mn	Manganese
Na	Salt
O	Petroleum
Pb	Lead
S	Sulfur, Pyrites
Zn	Zinc

⚡ Water Power
▨ Major Industrial Areas

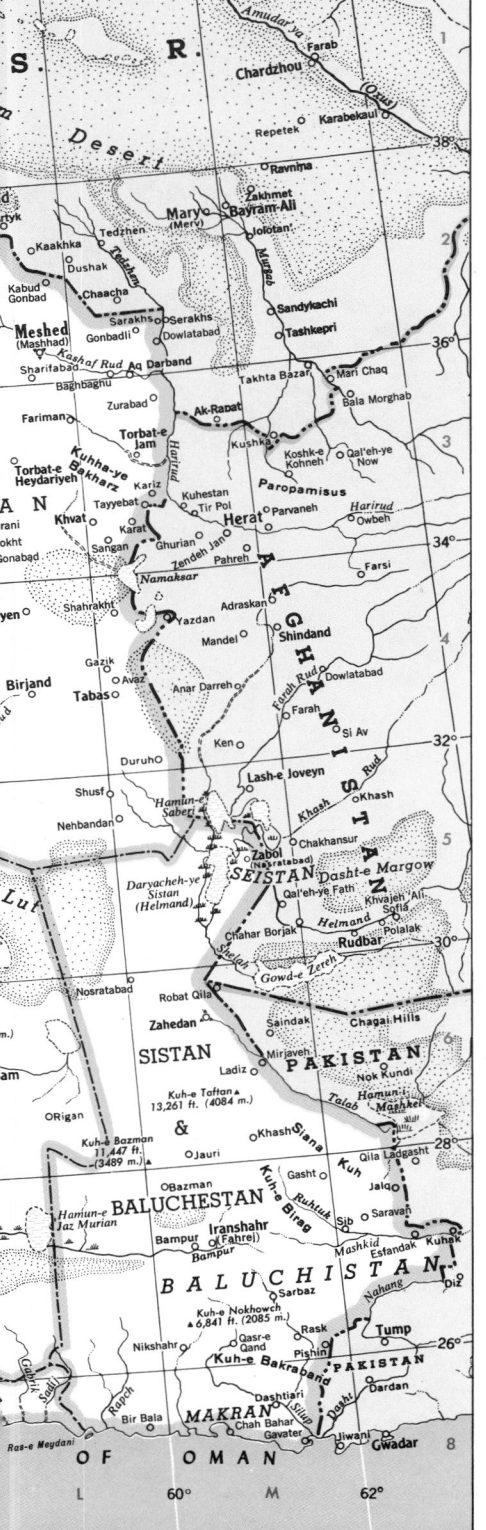

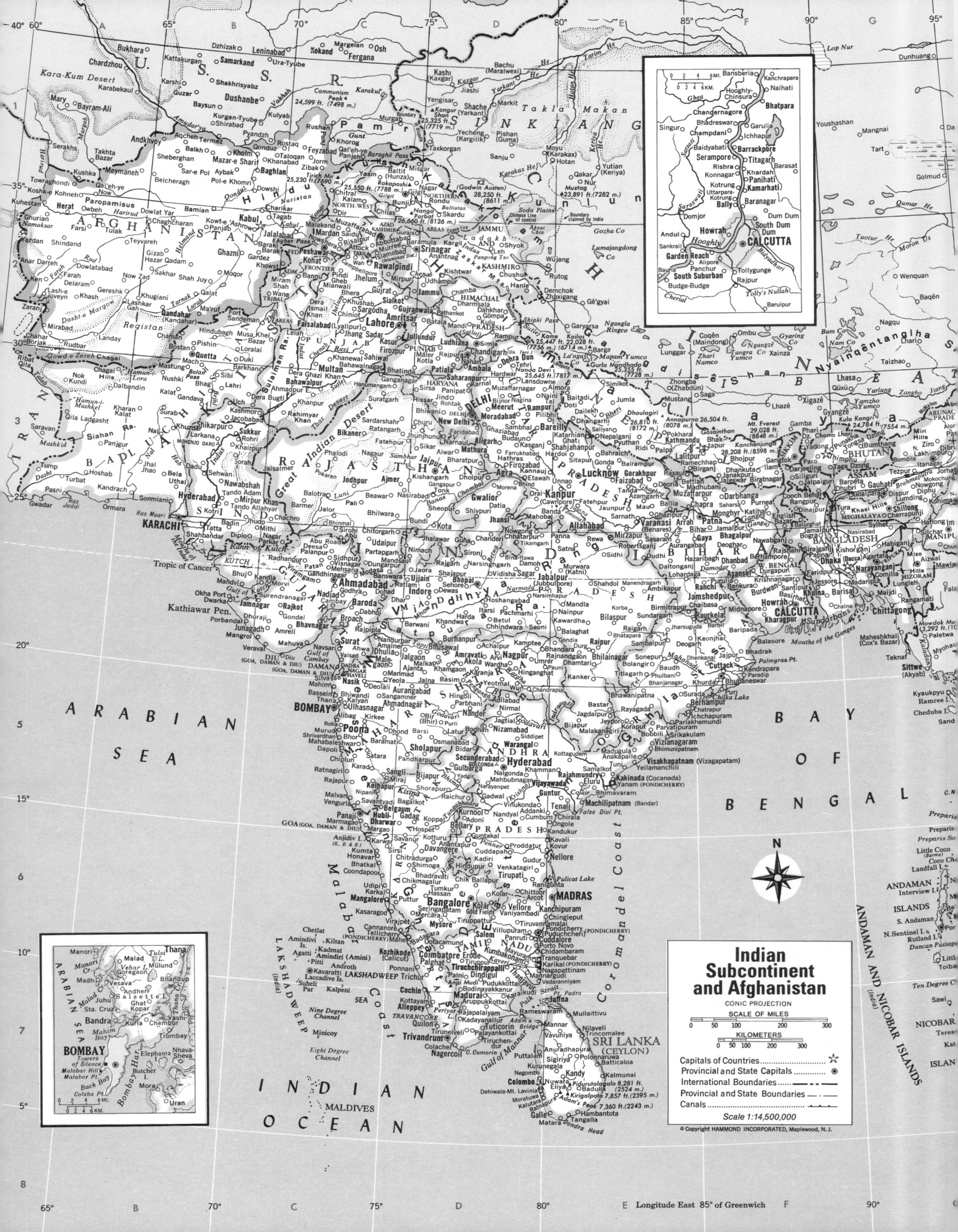

Indian Subcontinent and Afghanistan

CONIC PROJECTION

SCALE OF MILES

KILOMETERS

Capitals of Countries............☆
Provincial and State Capitals...........◉
International Boundaries..........
Provincial and State Boundaries.......
Canals..........

Scale 1:14,500,000

© Copyright HAMMOND INCORPORATED, Maplewood, N.J.

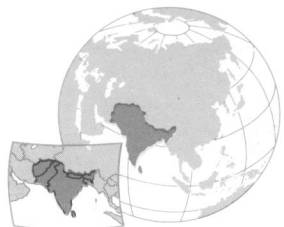

INDIA

AREA 1,269,339 sq. mi. (3,287,588 sq. km.)
POPULATION 683,810,051
CAPITAL New Delhi
LARGEST CITY Calcutta (greater)
HIGHEST POINT Nanda Devi 25,645 ft. (7,817 m.)
MONETARY UNIT Indian rupee
MAJOR LANGUAGES Hindi, English, Bihari, Telugu, Marathi, Bengali, Tamil, Gujarati, Rajasthani, Kanarese, Malayalam, Oriya, Punjabi, Assamese, Kashmiri, Urdu
MAJOR RELIGIONS Hinduism, Islam, Christianity, Sikhism, Buddhism, Jainism, Zoroastrianism, Animism

PAKISTAN

AREA 310,403 sq. mi. (803,944 sq. km.)
POPULATION 83,782,000
CAPITAL Islamabad
LARGEST CITY Karachi
HIGHEST POINT K2 (Godwin Austen) 28,250 ft. (8,611 m.)
MONETARY UNIT Pakistani rupee
MAJOR LANGUAGES Urdu, English, Punjabi, Pushtu, Sindhi, Baluchi, Brahui
MAJOR RELIGIONS Islam, Hinduism, Sikhism, Christianity, Buddhism

SRI LANKA (CEYLON)

AREA 25,332 sq. mi. (65,610 sq. km.)
POPULATION 14,850,001
CAPITAL Colombo
LARGEST CITY Colombo
HIGHEST POINT Pidurutalagala 8,281 ft. (2,524 m.)
MONETARY UNIT Sri Lanka rupee
MAJOR LANGUAGES Sinhala, Tamil, English
MAJOR RELIGIONS Buddhism, Hinduism, Christianity, Islam

AFGHANISTAN

AREA 250,775 sq. mi. (649,507 sq. km.)
POPULATION 15,540,000
CAPITAL Kabul
LARGEST CITY Kabul
HIGHEST POINT Nowshak 24,557 ft. (7,485 m.)
MONETARY UNIT afghani
MAJOR LANGUAGES Pushtu, Dari, Uzbek
MAJOR RELIGION Islam

NEPAL

AREA 54,663 sq. mi. (141,577 sq. km.)
POPULATION 14,179,301
CAPITAL Kathmandu
LARGEST CITY Kathmandu
HIGHEST POINT Mt. Everest 29,028 ft. (8,848 m.)
MONETARY UNIT Nepalese rupee
MAJOR LANGUAGES Nepali, Maithili, Tamang, Newari, Tharu
MAJOR RELIGIONS Hinduism, Buddhism

MALDIVES

AREA 115 sq. mi. (298 sq. km.)
POPULATION 143,046
CAPITAL Male
LARGEST CITY Male
HIGHEST POINT 20 ft. (6 m.)
MONETARY UNIT Maldivian rupee
MAJOR LANGUAGE Divehi
MAJOR RELIGION Islam

BHUTAN

AREA 18,147 sq. mi. (47,000 sq. km.)
POPULATION 1,298,000
CAPITAL Thimphu
LARGEST CITY Thimphu
HIGHEST POINT Kula Kangri 24,784 ft. (7,554 m.)
MONETARY UNIT ngultrum
MAJOR LANGUAGES Dzongka, Nepali
MAJOR RELIGIONS Buddhism, Hinduism

BANGLADESH

AREA 55,126 sq. mi. (142,776 sq. km.)
POPULATION 87,052,02
CAPITAL Dhaka
LARGEST CITY Dhaka
HIGHEST POINT Keokra 4,034 ft. (1,230 m.)
MONETARY UNIT taka
MAJOR LANGUAGES Benga English
MAJOR RELIGIONS Islam, Hinduism Christianity

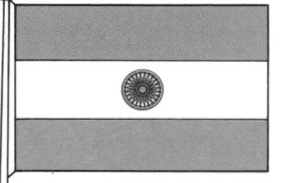
INDIA

PAKISTAN

SRI LANKA (CEYLON)

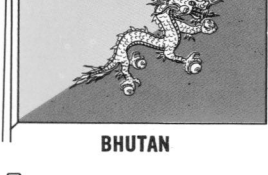
BHUTAN

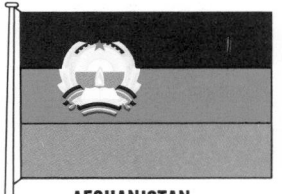
AFGHANISTAN

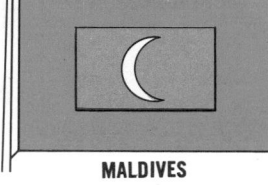
MALDIVES

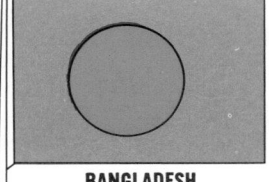
BANGLADESH

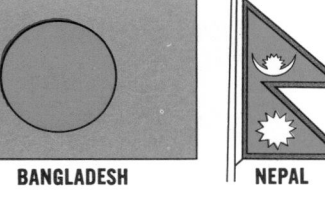
NEPAL

AFGHANISTAN

CITIES and TOWNS

Andkhvoy	A1
Aqcheh	B1
Aybak 33,016	B1
Baghlan 75,130	B1
Balkh	B1
Bamian 7,355	B2
Belcheragh	B1
Chaghcharan 2,974	B2
Chahar Borjak	A2
Charikar 25,093	B1
Delaram	A2
Dowlatabad	A1
Dowlat Yar	B2
Dowshi	B1
Farah 18,797	A2
Farsi	A2
Feyzabad 10,142	C1
Gardez 11,415	B2
Gereshk	A2
Ghazni 30,425	B2
Ghurian	A2
Gizab	B2
Hazar Qadam	B2
Herat 163,960	A2
Jalalabad 56,384	C2
Jorm	C1
Kabul (cap.) 905,108	B2
Kalat (Qalat) 5,946	B2
Kandahar (Qandahar) 178,409	B2
Ken	B2
Khanabad	B1
Khash	A2
Kholm	B1
Khowst	B2
Khugiani	B2
Koshke-e Kohneh	A2
Kowt-e 'Ashrow	B2
Kuhestan	A2
Landay	A2
Lash-e Joveyn	A2
Lashkar Gah 26,646	A2
Mar'uf	B2
Mazar-e Sharif 122,567	B1
Meymaneh 54,954	A1
Mirabad	A2
Moqor	B2
Now Zad	A2
Oruzgan (Hazar Qadam)	B2
Owbeh	A2
Panjab	B2
Pol-e Khomri	B1
Qalat 5,946	B2
Qale'h-ye Now 5,340	A1
Qale'h-ye Panjeh	C1
Qandahar 178,409	B2
Qonduz 107,191	B1
Rostaq	B1
Rudbar	A2
Sakhar	B2
Sar-e Pol	B1
Shay Juy	B2
Sheberghan 54,870	B1
Shindand	A2
Spin Buldak	B2
Tagab	B1
Taloqan 46,202	B1
Teyvareh	B2
Towraghondi	A1
Tulak	A2
Zaranj 6,477	A2
Zibak	C1

OTHER FEATURES

Farah Rud (riv.)	A2

Harirud (riv.)	A1
Helmand (riv.)	B2
Hindu Kush (mts.)	B1
Kabul (riv.)	C2
Konar (riv.)	C1
Lurah (riv.)	B2
Margow, Dasht-e (des.)	A2
Namaksar (salt lake)	A2
Paropamisus (range)	A2
Tarnak (riv.)	B2

BANGLADESH

CITIES and TOWNS

Barisal 98,127	G4
Bogra 47,154	F4
Chalna Port 14,590	F4
Chittagong 889,760	G4
Comilla 86,446	G4
Cox's Bazar (Maheshkhali) 15,720	G4
Dhaka (Dacca) (cap.) 1,679,572	G4
Dinajpur 61,866	F3
Faridpur 46,232	F4
Habiganj 16,281	G4
Jamalpur 60,261	F4
Jessore 76,168	F4
Khulna 437,304	F4
Kishorganj 35,605	G4
Madaripur 32,488	G4
Maheshkhali 15,720	G4
Mymensingh (Nasirabad) 182,153	G4
Narayanganj 270,680	G4
Nasirabad 182,153	G4
Nawabganj 46,059	F4
Noakhali 32,490	G4
Pabna 62,254	F4
Rajshahi 132,909	F4
Rangamati 26,473	G4
Rangpur 72,829	F3
Sirajganj 74,457	F4
Sylhet 59,546	G4
Teknaf	G4

OTHER FEATURES

Bengal, Bay of (sea)	F5
Brahmaputra (riv.)	G3
Ganges (riv.)	F3
Sundarbans (reg.)	F4

BHUTAN

CITIES and TOWNS

Bumthang 10,000	G3
Paro 35,000	F3
Punakha 12,000	G3
Taga Dzong 18,000	G3
Thimphu (cap.) 50,000	G3
Tongsa Dzong 2,500	G3

OTHER FEATURES

Chomo Lhari (mt.)	F3
Himalaya (mts.)	E2
Kula Kangri (mt.)	G3

INDIA

INTERNAL DIVISIONS

Andaman and Nicobar Isls. (terr.) 188,254	G6
Andhra Pradesh (state) 53,403,619	D5
Arunachal Pradesh (terr.) 628,050	G3

(continued on following page)

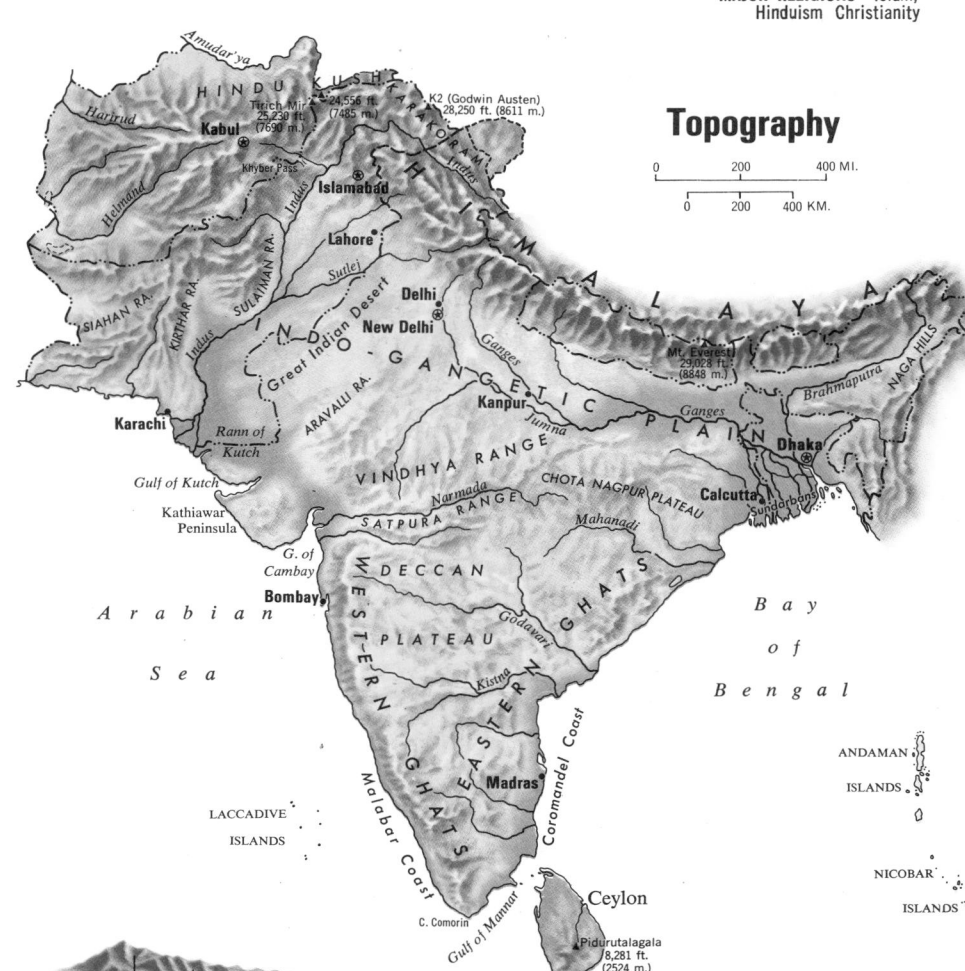

Topography

0 — 200 — 400 MI.
0 — 200 — 400 KM.

| 5,000 m. 16,404 ft. | 2,000 m. 6,562 ft. | 1,000 m. 3,281 ft. | 500 m. 1,640 ft. | 200 m. 656 ft. | 100 m. 328 ft. | Sea Level | Below |

70 Indian Subcontinent and Afghanistan

(continued)

Assam (state) 19,902,826 G3
Bihar (state) 69,823,154 F4
Chandigarh (terr.) 450,061 D2
Dadra and Nagar Haveli (terr.) 103,677 C4
Delhi (terr.) 6,196,414 D3
Goa, Daman and Diu (terr.) 1,082,117 C4
Gujarat (state) 33,960,905 C4
Haryana (state) 12,850,902 D3
Himachal Pradesh (state) 4,237,569 D2
Jammu and Kashmir (state) 5,981,600 D2
Karnataka (state) 37,043,451 D6
Kerala (state) 25,403,217 D6
Lakshadweep (terr.) 40,237 C6
Madhya Pradesh (state) 52,131,717 D4
Maharashtra (state) 62,693,898 C5
Manipur (state) 1,433,691 G4
Meghalaya (state) 1,327,874 G3
Mizoram (terr.) 487,774 G4
Nagaland (state) 773,281 G3
Orissa (state) 26,272,054 E5
Pondicherry (terr.) 604,136 E6
Punjab (state) 16,669,755 D2
Rajasthan (state) 34,102,912 C3
Sikkim (state) 315,682 F3
Tamil Nadu (state) 48,297,456 D6
Tripura (state) 2,060,189 G4
Uttar Pradesh (state) 110,858,019 D3
West Bengal (state) 54,485,560 F4

CITIES and TOWNS

Abu 9,840 C4
Abu Road 25,331 C4
Achalpur 42,326 D4
Addanki 10,223 D5
Adilabad 30,368 D5
Adoni 85,311 D5
Agartala 59,625 G4
Agartala□ 100,264 G4
Agra 591,917 D3
Agra□ 634,622 D3
Ahmadabad 1,591,832 C4
Ahmadabad□ 1,741,522 C4
Ahmadnagar 118,236 C5
Ahmadnagar□ 148,405 C5
Aizwal 31,740 G4
Ajanta D4
Ajmer 262,851 C3
Akola 168,438 D4
Alibag 11,913 C5
Aligarh 252,314 D3
Alipore F2
Allahabad 490,622 E3
Allahabad□ 513,036 E3
Alleppey-Cochin 160,166 D7
Almora 19,671 D3
Along 3,524 G3
Alwar 100,378 D3
Amalner 55,544 C4
Ambala 83,633 D2
Ambala□ 186,168 D2
Ambikapur 23,087 E4
Amravati 193,800 D4
Amreli 39,520 C4
Amritsar 407,628 C2
Amritsar□ 458,029 C2
Anakapalle 57,273 E5
Anantapur 80,069 D6
Anantnag 27,643 D2
Andheri B7
Andul 3,602 F2
Arcot 30,230 D6
Arrah 92,919 E3
Aruppukkottai 62,223 D7
Arvi 26,494 D4
Asansol 155,968 F4
Asansol□ 241,792 F4
Aurangabad, Bihar 18,714 E4
Aurangabad, Maharashtra 150,483 D5
Aurangabad□ 165,253 D5
Azamgarh 40,963 E3
Badagara 53,938 D6
Bagalkot 51,746 D5
Bahraich 73,931 E3
Baidyabati 54,130 F1
Balaghat 27,872 E4
Balasore 46,239 F4
Ballia 47,101 E3
Bally 38,892 F1
Balotra 17,595 C3
Balrampur 36,191 E3
Balurghat 67,088 F3
Banda 50,575 D3
Bandar (Machilipatnam) 112,612 E5
Bandra B7
Bangalore 1,540,741 D6
Bangalore□ 1,653,779 D6
Bankura 79,129 F4
Bansberia 61,748 F1
Banswara 27,363 C4
Baramati 27,912 C5
Baramula 26,334 C2
Baranagar 136,842 F1
Barasat 42,642 F1
Barbil 24,342 F4
Bareilly 296,248 D3
Bareilly□ 326,106 D3
Baripada 28,725 F4
Barmer 38,630 C3
Baroda (Vadodara) 466,696 C4
Barpeta 26,479 G3
Barrackpore 96,889 F1
Barrackpore□ 198,255 F1
Barsi 62,374 D5
Baruipur 20,501 F2
Barwani 22,099 D4
Basim 32,496 D4
Basirhat 63,816 F4
Bassein 30,594 C5
Bastar E5
Batala 58,200 D2
Baudh 8,891 E4
Bauria 10,610 E2
Beawar 66,114 C3
Belgaum 192,427 C5
Belgaum□ 213,872 C5
Bellary 125,183 D5
Benares (Varanasi) 583,856 E3
Berhampore 72,605 F4
Berhampur 117,662 F5
Bettiah 51,018 E3
Betul 30,862 D4
Bhadrak 40,487 F4
Bhadravati 40,203 D6
Bhadravati□ 101,358 D6
Bhadreswar 45,586 F1
Bhagalpur 172,202 F4
Bhandara 39,423 E4
Bhandup B7
Bhanjanagar 12,353 E4
Bharatpur 68,036 D3
Bharuch 91,589 C4
Bhatapara 20,980 E4
Bhatinda 53,684 C2
Bhatkal 18,732 C6
Bhatpara 204,750 F1
Bhavnagar 225,358 C4
Bhavnagar□ 225,974 C4
Bhawanipatna 22,808 E5
Bhilai 157,173 E4
Bhilwara 82,155 C3
Bhimavaram 63,762 E5
Bhimunipatnam 14,291 E5
Bhind 42,371 D3
Bhinmal 14,050 C3
Bhir (Bir) 49,965 D5
Bhiwandi 79,576 C5
Bhiwani 73,086 D3
Bhopal 298,022 D4
Bhor 10,708 C5
Bhubaneswar 105,491 F4
Bhuj 52,177 B4
Bhusawal 96,800 D4
Bhusawal□ 104,708 D4
Bidar 50,670 D5
Bihar 100,046 F3
Bijapur, Karnataka 103,931 D5
Bijapur, Madhya Pradesh 5,289 E5
Bijnor 43,290 D3
Bikaner 188,518 C3
Bikaner□ 208,894 C3
Bilaspur 98,410 E4
Bina-Itawa 33,106 D4
Bir 49,965 D5
Birmitrapur 28,063 E4
Bobbili 30,649 E5
Bodhan 37,589 D5
Bodinayakkanur 54,176 D6
Bolangir 35,748 E4
Bombay (Greater)* 5,970,575 B7
Bomdila 2,264 G3
Broach (Bharuch) 91,589 C4
Budaun 72,204 D3
Budge-Budge 51,039 F2
Bundi 34,279 D3
Burdwan 143,318 F4
Burhanpur 105,246 D4
Calcutta 3,148,746 F2
Calcutta□ 7,031,382 F2
Calicut (Kozhikode) 333,979 D6
Cambay 62,097 C4
Cannanore 55,162 C6
Cawnpore (Kanpur) 1,154,388 E3
Chaibasa 35,386 F4
Chamba 11,814 D2
Champdani 58,596 F1
Chanderi 10,294 D4
Chandernagore 75,238 F1
Chandigarh 218,743 D2
Chandigarh□ 232,940 D2
Chandrapur 75,134 D5
Chapra 83,101 F3
Chatrapur 10,835 F5
Chembur B7
Cherrapunji⊙ 83,987 G3
Chhatarpur 32,271 D4
Chhindwara 53,492 D4
Chidambaram 48,811 E6
Chik Ballapur 29,227 D6
Chikmagalur 41,639 D6
Chingleput 38,419 E6
Chiplun 20,942 C5
Chirala 54,487 E5
Chitorgarh 25,917 C4
Chitradurga 50,254 D6
Chittoor 63,035 D6
Churachandpur 8,706 G4
Churu 52,502 D3
Chushul D2
Cocanada (Kakinada) 164,200 E5
Cochin-Alleppey 439,066 D6
Coimbatore 356,368 D6
Coimbatore□ 736,203 D6
Colachel 18,819 D7
Cooch Behar 53,684 F3
Coondapoor 23,831 C6
Cuddalore 101,335 E6
Cuddapah 66,195 D6
Cumbum 9,745 D5
Cuttack 194,068 F4
Cuttack□ 205,759 F4
Dabhoi 37,892 C4
Daltonganj 32,367 E4
Damoh 59,489 D4
Dapoli 6,296 C5
Darbhanga 132,059 F3
Darjeeling 42,873 F3
Datia 36,439 D3
Davangere 121,110 D6
Deesa 28,324 C4
Dehra Dun 166,073 D2
Dehra Dun□ 203,464 D2
Delhi 3,287,883 D3
Delhi□ 3,647,023 D3
Demchok D2
Deogarh, Orissa 8,906 E4
Deoghar, Bihar 40,356 F4
Deolali 55,436 C5
Deoria 38,161 E3
Dewas 51,545 D4
Dhamtari 34,546 E4
Dhanbad 79,838 F4
Dhanbad□ 434,031 F4
Dhar 36,172 C4
Dharmsala 10,939 D2
Dharwar-Hubli 379,166 C5
Dhenkanal 19,615 E4
Dholpur 31,865 D3
Dhond 16,583 C5
Dhoraji 59,773 C4
Dhubri 36,503 G3
Dhulia 137,129 C4
Dibrugarh 80,348 G3
Digboi 16,538 H3
Dindigul 128,429 D6
Diphu 10,200 G3
Dispur 1,725 G3
Diu 6,214 C4
Dohad 44,506 C4
Domjor 10,896 F1
Dudhi 5,084 E4
Dum Dum 31,363 F1
Dum Dum□ 273,812 F1
Dungarpur 19,773 C4
Durg 67,892 E4
Durgapur 206,638 F4
Dwarka 17,801 B4
Eluru 127,023 E5
English Bazar 61,335 F3
Erode 105,111 D6
Etawah 85,894 D3
Faizabad-cum-Ayodhya 102,835 E3
Faridabad 85,762 D3
Farrukhabad-cum-Fatehgarh 102,768 D3
Farrukhabad-cum-Fatehgarh□ 110,835 D3
Fatehpur, Rajasthan 34,929 C3
Fatehpur, Uttar Pradesh 54,665 E3
Firozabad 133,863 D3
Firozpur 49,545 C2
Gadag-Betgeri 95,426 D5
Gadwal 21,828 D5
Gandhinagar 24,055 C4
Ganganagar 90,042 C3
Gangapur 27,453 D3
Gangtok 12,000 F3
Garden Reach 154,913 F2
Garulia 44,271 F1
Gauhati 123,783 G3
Gauhati□ 200,377 G3
Gaya 179,884 F4
Ghat Kopar 34,256 B7
Ghaziabad 118,836 D3
Ghaziabad□ 127,700 D3
Ghazipur 45,635 E3
Goalpara 16,703 G3
Godhra 66,403 C4
Gonda 52,662 E3
Gondal 54,928 C4
Gondia 77,992 E4
Gorakhpur 230,911 E3
Goregaon B7
Gudur 33,778 D6
Gulbarga 145,588 D5
Guna 40,006 D4
Guntakal 66,320 D5
Guntur 269,991 D5
Gurais D2
Gwalior 384,772 D3
Gwalior□ 406,140 D3
Haflong 5,197 G3
Hanle D2
Hanumangarh 30,017 C3
Harda 28,504 D4
Hardoi 46,639 E3
Hardwar 77,864 D2
Hassan 51,325 D6
Hathras 74,349 D3
Hazaribagh 54,818 F4
Hindupur 42,959 D6
Hinganghat 44,349 D4
Hingoli 31,948 D5
Hissar 89,437 D3
Honavar 12,444 C6
Hooghly-Chinsura 105,241 F1
Hoshangabad 27,011 D4
Hospet 65,196 D5
Howrah 737,877 F2
Hubli-Dharwar 379,166 C5
Hyderabad 1,607,396 D5
Hyderabad□ 1,796,339 D5
Ichchapuram 15,850 F5
Ichhapur 11,975 F1
Imphal 100,366 G4
Indore 543,381 D4
Indore□ 560,936 D4
Itanagar⊙ 18,787 G3
Itarsi 44,191 D4
Jabalpur 426,224 D4
Jabalpur□ 534,845 D4
Jagdalpur 31,344 E5
Jagtial 30,900 D5
Jaipur 615,258 D3
Jaipur□ 636,768 D3
Jaisalmer 16,578 C3
Jajpur 16,707 F4
Jalgaon 106,711 D4
Jalna 91,099 D4
Jalor 15,478 C3
Jalpaiguri 55,159 F3
Jamalpur 61,731 F3
Jammu 155,338 D2
Jammu□ 164,207 D2
Jamnagar 214,816 B4
Jamnagar□ 227,640 B4
Jamshedpur 341,576 F4
Jamshedpur□ 456,146 F4
Jaora 37,235 D4
Jaunpur 80,737 E3
Jeypore 34,319 E5
Jhalawar 20,035 D4
Jhansi 173,292 D3
Jhansi□ 198,135 D3
Jharsuguda 24,727 E4
Jhunjhunu 32,024 D3
Jind 38,161 D3
Jodhpur 317,612 C3
Jorhat 30,247 G3
Jubbulpore (Jabalpur) 426,224 D4
Juhu B7
Jullundur 296,106 D2
Jullundur□ 329,830 D2
Junagadh 95,485 B4
Kadayanallur 50,295 D7
Kadiri 33,810 D6
Kakinada 164,200 E5
Kalyan 99,547 C5
Kamarhati 169,404 F1
Kamptee 53,412 D4
Kanchipuram 110,657 E6
Kanchrapara 78,768 F1
Kandla 17,995 C4
Kandukur 16,654 E5
Kanker 9,278 E4
Kannauj 28,187 D3
Kanpur 1,154,388 E3
Kanpur□ 1,275,242 E3
Karad 42,329 C5
Karaikudi 55,449 D7
Karanja 31,150 D4
Kargil 2,390 D2
Karikal 26,080 E6
Karkal 18,593 C6
Karnal 92,784 D3
Karwar 27,770 C6
Kasaragod 34,984 C6
Kasganj 46,467 D3
Katarnian Ghat E3
Katihar 67,014 F3
Katni (Murwara) 54,864 E4
Kavali 29,616 E6
Kavaratti 4,420 C6
Kawardha 11,226 E4
Kendrapara 20,079 F4
Keonjhar 19,340 F4
Khamgaon 53,692 D4
Khamman 56,919 D5
Khandwa 84,517 D4
Kharagpur 61,783 F4
Khardah 32,302 F1
Khurda 15,879 F4
Kirkee 65,497 C5
Kishangarh 37,405 D3
Kishtwar 5,276 D2
Kohima 21,545 G3
Kolar 43,418 D6
Kolar Gold Fields 76,112 D6
Kolhapur 259,050 C5
Konnagar 34,424 F1
Koppal 27,277 D5
Koraput 21,505 E5
Korba 30,963 E4
Kota 212,991 D3
Kottaguden 75,542 E5
Kottayam 59,714 D7
Kotturu 12,873 D6
Kovur 16,846 E6
Kozhikode 333,979 D6
Krishnanagar 85,923 F4
Kulu 8,958 D2
Kumbakonam 113,130 D6
Kumta 19,112 C6
Kurla B7
Kurnool 136,710 D5
Laful⊙ 8,161 G7
Lansdowne 6,670 D3
Latur 70,156 D5
Leh 5,519 D2
Lohardaga 17,087 E4
Lucknow 749,239 E3
Lucknow□ 813,982 E3
Ludhiana 397,850 D2
Ludhiana□ 401,176 D2
Lumding 29,253 G3
Lungleh 6,019 G4
Machilipatnam 112,612 E5
Madh B7
Madhubani 32,919 F3
Madras 2,469,449 E6
Madras□ 3,169,930 E6
Madugula 8,376 E5
Madurai 549,114 D7
Madurai□ 711,501 D7
Mahabaleshwar 7,318 C5
Mahbubnagar 51,756 D5
Mahe 8,972 D6
Mahim 11,344 C5
Mahoba 29,707 D3
Mahuva 39,497 C4
Malad B6
Malakanagiri 7,494 E5
Malegaon 191,847 C4
Maler Kotla 48,536 D2
Malkapur 35,476 D4
Malvan 17,579 C5
Mandi 16,849 D2
Mandla 24,406 E4
Mandsaur 52,347 C4
Mandvi 27,849 B4
Manendragarh 11,936 E4
Mangalore 165,174 C6
Mangrol 27,183 B4
Manmad 29,571 C4
Mannargudi 42,783 E6
Manori B6
Margao 41,655 C5
Marmagao 44,065 C5
Mathura 132,028 D3
Mau 64,058 E3
Mayuram 60,195 D6
Meerut 270,993 D3
Mehsana 51,598 C4
Mercara 19,357 D6
Mhow 59,037 D4
Midnapore 71,326 F4
Miraj 77,606 D5
Mirzapur-cum-Vindhyachal 105,939 E4
Modasa 22,483 C4
Mokokchung 17,423 G3
Monghyr 102,474 F3
Mora B7
Moradabad 258,590 D3
Morena 44,901 D3
Morvi 60,976 C4
Mulund B6
Murud 11,210 C5
Murwara 54,864 E4
Muzaffarnagar 114,783 D3
Muzaffarpur 126,379 E3
Mysore 355,685 D6
Nadiad 108,269 C4
Nagapattinam 68,026 E6
Nagaur 36,448 C3
Nagercoil 141,288 D7
Nagina 37,066 D3
Nagpur 866,076 D4
Nagpur□ 930,459 D4
Nahan 16,017 D2
Naihati 82,080 F1
Naini Tal 23,986 D3
Nainpur 14,683 E4
Nalgonda 33,126 D5
Nander 126,538 D5
Nandurbar 54,070 C4
Nandyal 63,193 D5
Narayanpet 21,744 D5
Narnaul 31,875 D3
Narsimhapur 25,552 D4
Narsinghgarh 13,814 D4
Nasik 176,091 C5
Nasirabad 25,732 C3
Navsari 72,979 C4
Nellore 133,590 E6
New Delhi (cap.) 301,801 D3
Nhava-Sheva B7
Nimach 47,113 D4
Nipani 35,116 C5
Nirmal 28,529 D5
Nizamabad 115,640 D5
North Lakhimpur 20,094 G3
Nova Goa (Panaji) 34,953 C5
Nowgong, Assam 56,537 G3
Nowgong, Madhya Pradesh 10,248 D3
Okha Port 10,687 B4
Ongole 53,330 E5
Ootacamund 63,310 D6
Orai 42,513 D3
Osmanabad 27,279 D5
Pachmarhi 1,212 D4
Palanpur 42,114 C4
Palayankottai 70,070 D7
Palghat 95,788 D6
Pali 49,834 C3
Palni 49,575 D6
Panaji 34,953 C5
Panchur 59,021 F2
Pandharpur 53,638 D5
Panihati 148,046 F1
Panipat 87,981 D3
Panna 22,316 E4
Panruti 34,065 D6
Paradip F4
Parbhani 61,570 D5
Parlakhemundi 26,917 E5
Partapgarh 17,402 C4
Parvatipuram 30,025 E5
Pasighat 5,116 G3
Patan 64,519 C4
Pathankot 76,355 D2
Patiala 148,686 D2
Patiala□ D2
Patna 473,001 F3
Patna□ F3
Pauni 17,781 E4
Phalodi 17,379 C3
Phulbani 10,677 E4
Pilibhit 68,273 D3
Pokaran 7,769 C3
Pondicherry 90,537 E6
Ponnani 35,723 D6
Poona (Pune)□ C5
Porbandar 96,881 B4
Porbandar□ B4
Port Blair 26,218 G6
Porto Novo 17,412 E6
Proddatur 70,822 D6
Puduchcheri (Pondicherry) 90,537 E6
Pudukkottai 66,384 D6
Pune 856,105 C5
Puri 72,674 F5
Purli 31,078 D5
Purnea 56,484 F3
Purulia 57,708 F4
Puttur 17,483 D6
Quilon 124,208 D7
Radhanpur 18,360 C4
Raichur 79,831 D5
Raigarh 46,745 E4
Raipur 174,518 E4
Raipur□ E4
Rajahmundry 165,912 E5
Rajahmundry□ E5
Rajapalaiyam 86,952 D7
Rajapur 9,017 C5
Rajgarh 11,475 D4
Rajkot 300,612 C4
Rajnandgaon 41,183 E4
Rajpipla 25,769 C4
Rajpur 34,393 F2
Rajpura 14,840 D2
Rameswarem 16,755 D7
Rampur, Him. Pradesh 2,623 D2
Rampur, Uttar Pradesh 161,417 D3
Ranchi 175,934 F4
Ratangarh 31,506 C3
Ratlam 106,666 C4
Ratnagiri 37,551 C5
Raurkela 47,076 F4
Raxaul 12,064 E3
Rayagada 25,064 E5
Renigunta 8,567 E6
Rewa 69,182 E4
Rishra 63,486 F1
Robertsganj 7,093 E4
Roha 8,631 C5
Rohtak 124,783 C5
Sadiya⊙ 64,252 H3

British India
U.S.S.R.
GILGIT AGENCY
KASHMIR & JAMMU
AFGHANISTAN
N.W. FRONTIER PROV.
PUNJAB
BALUCHISTAN
Indus
PUNJAB STATES
TIBET
CHINA
IRAN
BAHAWALPUR (PUNJ. ST.)
DELHI
RAMPUR
UNITED PROVINCES
NEPAL
SIKKIM
BHUTAN
Brahmaputra
ASSAM
PUNJ. ST.
RAJPUTANA
SIND
AJMER-MERWARA
E. ST.
KHASI HILLS
Gwadar (Oman)
Ganges
BENARES
BIHAR
MANIPUR
GWALIOR
INDIA
WESTERN INDIA
CENTRAL INDIA
EASTERN STATES
BENGAL
TRIPURA (E. ST.)
Arabian Sea
GUJARAT ST.
Chandernagore (Fr.)
BURMA
CENTRAL PROVINCES
BERAR
E. ST.
ORISSA
Diu (Port.)
Damão (Port.)
BOMBAY
EASTERN STATES
Bay of Bengal
HYDERABAD
DECCAN STATES
ORISSA
Yanaon (Fr.)
Gôa (Port.)
MADRAS
MYSORE
Bangalore (Br.)
COORG
Mahé (Fr.)
Pondichéry (Fr.)
Karikal (Fr.)
M. ST.
Laccadive Islands (Madras)
Cochin (Br.)
MADRAS STATES
CEYLON
Andaman Islands (Br.)
Nicobar Islands (Br.)
British India. The provinces of British India were directly administered by Britain. A few areas were leased from the Indian princes.
Indian States. The Indian States, sometimes referred to as the "Native" or "Princely States," were under the nominal control of maharajas or other hereditary princes.
Possessions of Other Countries in India
State or Provincial Boundaries
Other Internal Boundaries

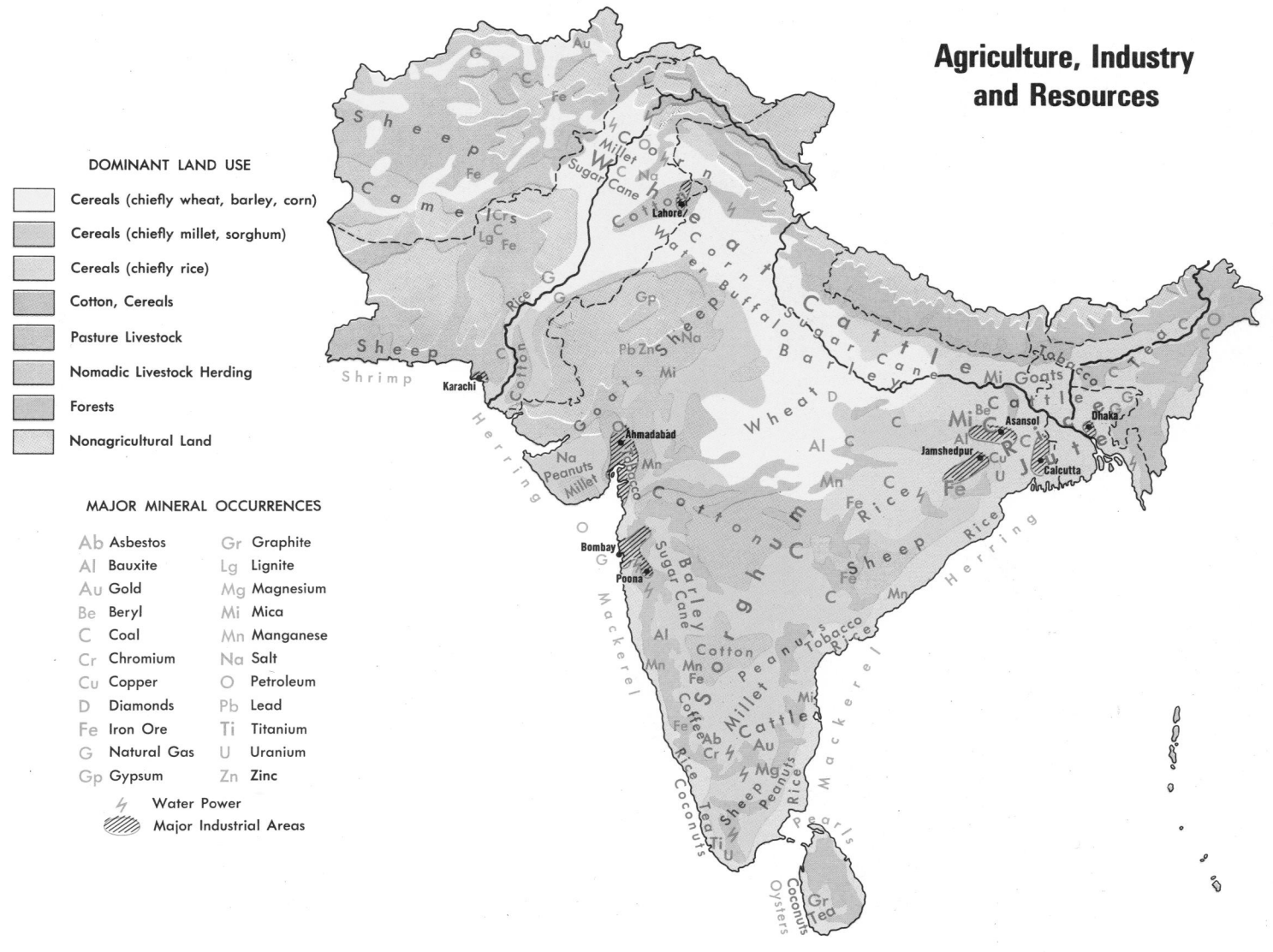

Agriculture, Industry and Resources

DOMINANT LAND USE

Cereals (chiefly wheat, barley, corn)
Cereals (chiefly millet, sorghum)
Cereals (chiefly rice)
Cotton, Cereals
Pasture Livestock
Nomadic Livestock Herding
Forests
Nonagricultural Land

MAJOR MINERAL OCCURRENCES

Ab	Asbestos	Gr	Graphite
Al	Bauxite	Lg	Lignite
Au	Gold	Mg	Magnesium
Be	Beryl	Mi	Mica
C	Coal	Mn	Manganese
Cr	Chromium	Na	Salt
Cu	Copper	O	Petroleum
D	Diamonds	Pb	Lead
Fe	Iron Ore	Ti	Titanium
G	Natural Gas	U	Uranium
Gp	Gypsum	Zn	Zinc

⚡ Water Power
▨ Major Industrial Areas

Burma, Thailand, Indochina and Malaya

CONIC PROJECTION

SCALE OF MILES

SCALE OF KILOMETERS

International Boundaries	_._._._
Division and State Boundaries	_.._.._
Capitals of Countries	☆
Division and State Capitals	◉

Scale 1:10,000,000

© Copyright HAMMOND INCORPORATED, Maplewood, N.J.

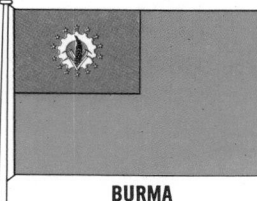

BURMA

THAILAND

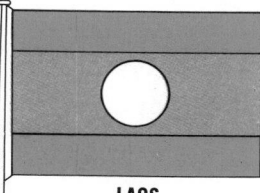

LAOS

CAMBODIA

VIETNAM

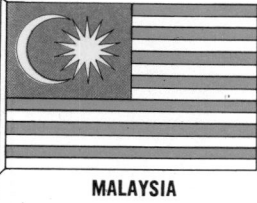

MALAYSIA

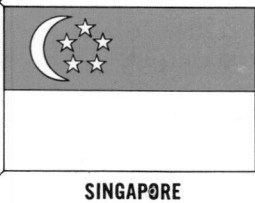

SINGAPORE

BURMA

AREA 261,789 sq. mi. (678,034 sq. km.)
POPULATION 32,913,000
CAPITAL Rangoon
LARGEST CITY Rangoon
HIGHEST POINT Hkakabo Razi 19,296 ft.
(5,881 m.)
MONETARY UNIT kyat
MAJOR LANGUAGES Burmese, Karen, Shan,
Kachin, Chin, Kayah, English
MAJOR RELIGIONS Buddhism, tribal religions

THAILAND

AREA 198,455 sq. mi. (513,998 sq. km.)
POPULATION 46,455,000
CAPITAL Bangkok
LARGEST CITY Bangkok
HIGHEST POINT Doi Inthanon 8,452 ft.
(2,576 m.)
MONETARY UNIT baht
MAJOR LANGUAGES Thai, Lao, Chinese,
Khmer, Malay
MAJOR RELIGIONS Buddhism, tribal religions

LAOS

AREA 91,428 sq. mi. (236,800 sq. km.)
POPULATION 3,721,000
CAPITAL Vientiane
LARGEST CITY Vientiane
HIGHEST POINT Phou Bia 9,252 ft. (2,820 m.)
MONETARY UNIT kip
MAJOR LANGUAGE Lao
MAJOR RELIGIONS Buddhism, tribal religions

CAMBODIA

AREA 69,898 sq. mi. (181,036 sq. km.)
POPULATION 5,200,000
CAPITAL Phnom Penh
LARGEST CITY Phnom Penh
HIGHEST POINT 5,948 ft. (1,813 m.)
MONETARY UNIT riel
MAJOR LANGUAGE Khmer (Cambodian)
MAJOR RELIGION Buddhism

VIETNAM

AREA 128,405 sq. mi. (332,569 sq. km.)
POPULATION 52,741,766
CAPITAL Hanoi
LARGEST CITY Ho Chi Minh City (Saigon)
HIGHEST POINT Fan Si Pan 10,308 ft.
(3,142 m.)
MONETARY UNIT dong
MAJOR LANGUAGES Vietnamese, Thai,
Muong, Meo, Yao, Khmer, French,
Chinese, Cham
MAJOR RELIGIONS Buddhism, Taoism,
Confucianism, Roman Catholicism,
Cao-Dai

MALAYSIA

AREA 128,308 sq. mi. (332,318 sq. km.)
POPULATION 13,435,588
CAPITAL Kuala Lumpur
LARGEST CITY Kuala Lumpur
HIGHEST POINT Mt. Kinabalu 13,455 ft.
(4,101 m.)
MONETARY UNIT ringgit
MAJOR LANGUAGES Malay, Chinese, English,
Tamil, Dayak, Kadazan
MAJOR RELIGIONS Islam, Confucianism,
Buddhism, tribal religions, Hinduism,
Taoism, Christianity, Sikhism

SINGAPORE

AREA 226 sq. mi. (585 sq. km.)
POPULATION 2,413,945
CAPITAL Singapore
LARGEST CITY Singapore
HIGHEST POINT Bukit Timah 581 ft. (177 m.)
MONETARY UNIT Singapore dollar
MAJOR LANGUAGES Chinese, Malay, Tamil,
English, Hindi
MAJOR RELIGIONS Confucianism, Buddhism,
Taoism, Hinduism, Islam, Christianity

Topography

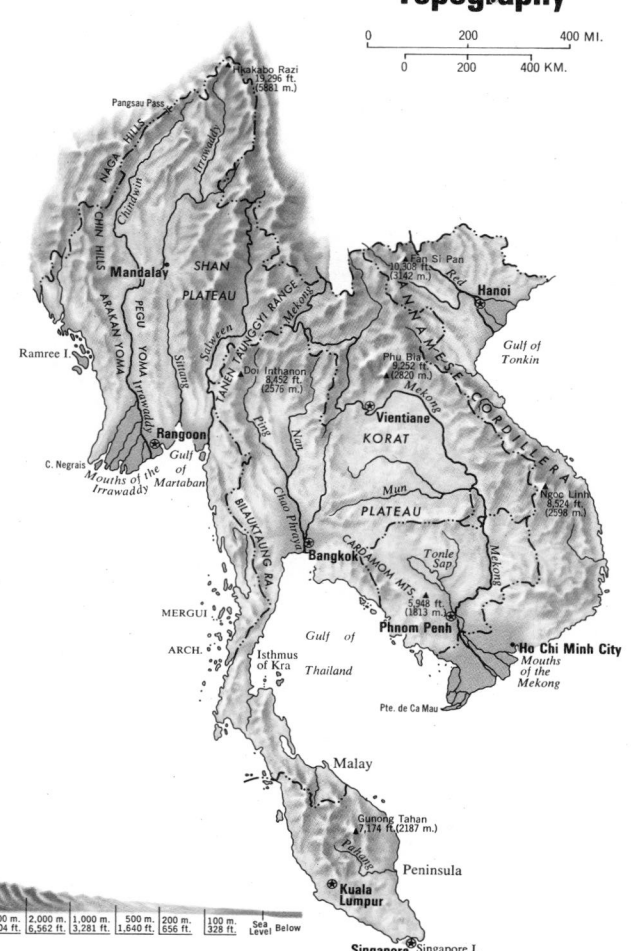

0   200   400 MI.
0   200   400 KM.

5,000 m. | 2,000 m. | 1,000 m. | 500 m. | 200 m. | 100 m. | Sea
16,404 ft. | 6,562 ft. | 3,281 ft. | 1,640 ft. | 656 ft. | 328 ft. | Level | Below

(continued on following page)

(continued)

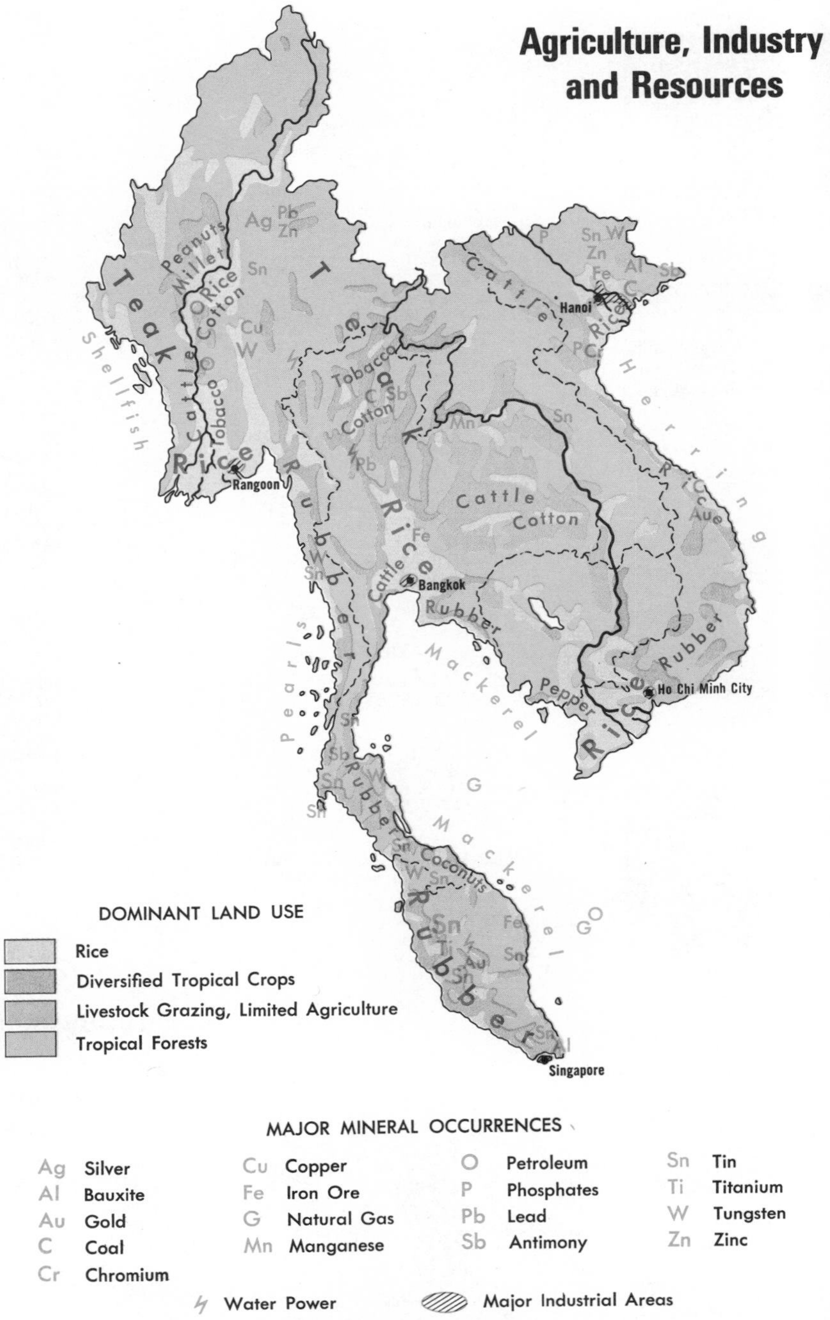
Agriculture, Industry and Resources
Hanoi
Rangoon
Bangkok
Ho Chi Minh City
Singapore
Teak
Cattle
Rice
Rubber
Tobacco
Cotton
Peanuts
Millet
Shellfish
Pearls
Mackerel
Herring
Pepper
Coconuts
DOMINANT LAND USE
Rice
Diversified Tropical Crops
Livestock Grazing, Limited Agriculture
Tropical Forests
MAJOR MINERAL OCCURRENCES
Ag Silver
Al Bauxite
Au Gold
C Coal
Cr Chromium
Cu Copper
Fe Iron Ore
G Natural Gas
Mn Manganese
O Petroleum
P Phosphates
Pb Lead
Sb Antimony
Sn Tin
Ti Titanium
W Tungsten
Zn Zinc
Water Power
Major Industrial Areas

Bilauktaung (range) C4
Chaukan (pass) C1
Cheduba (isl.) B3
Chin (hills) B2
Chindwin (riv.) B2
Coco (chan.) B4
Combermere (bay) B3
Daung Kyun (isl.) C4
Dawna (range) C3
Great Coco (isl.) B4
Great Tenasserim (riv.) C4
Heinze Chaung (bay) C4
Heywood (chan.) B3
Hka, Nam (riv.) C2
Hkakabo Razi (mt.) C1
Indawgyi (lake) C1
Inle (lake) C2
Irrawaddy (riv.) B3
Irrawaddy, Mouths of the (delta) B4
Kadan Kyun (isl.) C4
Kaladan (riv.) B2
Kalegauk (isl.) C4
Khao Luang (mt.) C5
Lanbi Kyun (isl.) C5
Launglon Bok (isls.) C4
Loi Leng (mt.) C2
Manipur (riv.) B2
Martaban (gulf) C4
Mekong (riv.) D2
Mergui (arch.) C5
Mon (riv.) B2
Mu (riv.) B2
Negrais (cape) B3
Pakchan (riv.) C5
Pangsau (pass) C1
Pawn, Nam (riv.) C2
Pegu Yoma (mts.) B3
Preparis (isl.) B4
Ramree (isl.) B3
Salween (riv.) C3
Shan (plat.) C2
Sittang (riv.) C3
Taungthonton (mt.) B1
Tavoy (pt.) C4
Tenasserim (isl.) C4
Teng, Nam (riv.) C2
Three Pagodas (pass) C4
Victoria (mt.) B2

CAMBODIA (KAMPUCHEA)

CITIES and TOWNS

Batdambang (Battambang) D4
Choam Khsant E4
Kampong Cham E4
Kampong Chhnang D4
Kampong Khleang E4
Kampong Saom D5
Kampong Spoe E5
Kampong Thum E4
Kampong Trabek E5
Kampot E5
Kaoh Nhek E4
Kracheh E4
Krong Kaoh Kong D4
Krong Keb E5
Kulen E4
Lumphat E4
Moung Roessei D4
Pailin D4
Paoy Pet D4
Phnom Penh (cap.) c. 300,000 E5
Phnum Tbeng Meanchey E4
Phsar Ream D5
Phumi Banam E5
Phumi Phsar E4
Phumi Prek Kak E4
Phumi Samraong D4
Pouthisat D4
Prek Pouthi E5
Prey Veng E5
Pursat (Pouthisat) D4
Rovieng Tbong E4
Sambor E4
Senmonoron E4
Siempang E4
Siemreab D4
Sisophon D4
Sre Ambel D5
Sre Khtum E4
Stoeng Treng E4
Suong E5
Svay Rieng E5
Takev E5
Virochey E4

OTHER FEATURES

Angkor Wat (ruins) E4
Dangrek (mts.) D4
Drang, la (riv.) E4
Joncs (plain) E5
Khong, Se (riv.) E4
Kong, Kaoh (isl.) D5
Mekong (riv.) E4
Rung, Kaoh (isl.) D5
San, Se (riv.) E4
Sen, Stoeng (riv.) E4
Srepok (riv.) E4
Tang, Kaoh (isl.) D5
Thailand (gulf) D5
Tonle Sap (lake) D4
Wai, Poulo (isls.) D5

LAOS

CITIES and TOWNS

Attapu 2,750 E4
Ban Khon E4
Ban Lahanam E3
Borikan D3
Champasak 3,500 E4
Dônghén E3
Khamkeut⊙ 31,206 E3
Louang Namtha 1,459 D2
Louangphrabang 7,596 D3
Muang Hinboun 1,750 E3
Muang Kènthao D3
Muang Khammoun 5,500 E3
Muang Không 1,750 E4
Muang Khôngxédôn 2,000 E4
Muang Khoua D2
Muang May E4
Muang Ou Tai D2
Muang Paktha D2
Muang Phin E3
Muang Tahoi E3
Muang Vapi E4
Muang Xaignabouri (Sayaboury) 2,500 D3
Mounlapamôk E4
Napè E3
Nong Het E3
Pakxé 8,000 E4
Phiafai⊙ 17,216 E4
Phôngsali 2,500 D2
San Nua (Sam Neua) 3,000 E2
Saravan 2,350 E4
Savannakhét 8,500 E3
Sayaboury (Muang Xaignabouri) 2,500 D3
Thakhek (Muang Khammouan) 5,500 E3
Tourakom D3
Viangchan (Vientiane) 132,253 D3
Vientiane (cap.) 132,253 D3
Xiangkhoang 3,500 D3

OTHER FEATURES

Bolovens (plat.) E4
Hou, Nam (riv.) D2
Jars (plain) D3
Mekong (riv.) D3
Ou, Nam (riv.) D2
Phou Bia (mt.) D3
Phou Cô Pi (mt.) E3
Phou Loi (mt.) D2
Rao Co (mt.) E3
Se Khong (riv.) E4
Tha, Nam (riv.) D2
Xianghoang (plat.) D3

MALAYA, MALAYSIA*

STATES

Federal Territory 937,875 D7
Johor (Johore) 1,601,504 D7
Kedah 1,102,200 D6
Kelantan 877,575 D6
Melaka 453,153 D7
Negeri Sembilan 563,955 D7
Pahang 770,644 D7
Perak 1,762,288 D6
Perlis 147,726 D6
Pinang (Penang) 911,586 D6
Selangor 1,467,441 D7
Terengganu 542,280 D6

CITIES and TOWNS

Alor Gajah 2,222 D7
Alor Setar 66,260 D6
Bandar Maharani (Muar) 61,218 D7
Bandar Penggaram (Batu Pahat) 53,291 D7
Batu Gajah 10,692 D6
Batu Pahat 53,291 D7
Bentong 22,683 D7
Butterworth 61,187 D6
Chukai 12,514 D6
Gemas 5,214 D7
George Town (Pinang) 269,603 C6
Ipoh 247,953 D6
Johor Baharu (Johore Bharu) 136,234 F5
Kampar 26,591 D6
Kangar 8,758 D6
Kelang 113,611 D7
Keluang 43,272 D7
Kota Baharu 55,124 D6
Kota Tinggi 8,725 F5
Kuala Dungun 17,560 D6
Kuala Lipis 9,270 D6
Kuala Lumpur (cap.) 451,977 D7
Kuala Lumpur* 937,875 D7
Kuala Pilah 12,508 D7
Kuala Rompin 1,384 D7
Kuala Selangor 3,132 D7
Kuala Terengganu 53,320 D6
Kuantan 43,358 D7
Kulai 11,841 F5
Lumut 3,255 D6
Malacca (Melaka) 87,160 D7
Mawai F5
Melaka 87,160 D7
Mersing 18,246 E7
Muar 61,218 D7
Pekan 4,682 D7
Pekan Nanas 9,003 E5
Pinang (George Town) 269,603 C6
Pontian Kechil 8,349 E5
Port Dickson 10,300 D7
Port Kelang D7
Port Weld 3,233 D6
Raub 18,433 D7
Segamat 17,796 D7
Seremban 80,921 D7
Sungai Petani 35,959 C6
Taiping 54,645 D6
Tanah Merah 7,012 D6
Telok Anson 44,524 D6
Tumpat 10,673 D6

OTHER FEATURES

Aur, Pulau (isl.) E7
Belumut, Gunong (mt.) D7
Gelang, Tanjong (pt.) D6
Johor, Sungai (riv.) F5
Johore (str.) E6
Kelantan, Sungai (riv.) D6
Langkawi, Pulau (isl.) C6
Ledang, Gunong (mt.) D7
Lima, Pulau (isl.) F6
Malacca (str.) D7
Malay (pen.) D6
Pahang, Sungai (riv.) D7
Pangkor, Pulau (isl.) D6
Perak, Gunong (mt.) D6
Perhentian, Kepulauan (isls.) D6
Pulai, Sungai (riv.) E5
Ramunia, Tanjong (pt.) F6
Redang, Pulau (isl.) D6
Sedili Kechil, Tanjong (pt.) F5
Tahan, Gunong (mt.) D6
Temiang, Bukit (mt.) D6
Tenggol, Pulau (isl.) D6
Tinggi, Pulau (isl.) E7

SINGAPORE

CITIES and TOWNS

Jurong 50,974 E6
Nee Soon 37,641 F6
Serangoon 89,558 F6
Singapore (cap.) 2,413,945 F6

OTHER FEATURES

Keppel (harb.) F6
Main (str.) F6
Singapore (str.) F6
Tekong Besar, Pulau (isl.) F6

THAILAND (SIAM)

CITIES and TOWNS

Ang Thong 7,267 C4
Ayutthaya (Phra Nakhon Si Ayutthaya) 37,213 D4
Ban Aranyaprathet 12,276 D4
Bangkok (cap.) 1,867,297 D4
Bangkok* 2,495,312 D4
Bang Lamung D4
Bang Saphan C5
Ban Kantang 9,247 C6
Ban Kapong C5
Ban Khlong Yai D5
Ban Kui Nua D4
Ban Ngon D3
Ban Pak Phanang 13,590 D5
Banphot Phisai C3
Ban Pua D3
Ban Sattahip D4
Ban Tha Uthen D3
Bua Chum D4
Buriram 16,431 D4
Chachoengsao 22,106 D4
Chai Badan D4
Chai Buri D3
Chainat 9,944 D4
Chaiya C5
Chaiyaphum 12,540 D4
Chang Khoeng C3
Chanthaburi 15,479 D4
Chiang Dao C3
Chiang Khan D3
Chiang Mai 83,729 C3
Chiang Rai 13,927 C3
Chiang Saen C2
Chon Buri 39,367 D4
Chumphon 11,643 C5
Den Chai C3
Hat Yai 47,953 C6
Hot C3
Hua Hin 21,426 D4
Kalasin 14,960 D3
Kamphaeng Phet 12,378 C3
Kanchanaburi 16,397 C4
Khanu C3
Khemmarat E4
Khon Kaen 29,431 D3
Khorat (Nakhon Ratchasima) 66,071 D4
Krabi 8,764 C5
Krung Thep (Bangkok) (cap.) 1,867,297 D4
Kumphawapi D3
Lae D3
Lampang 40,100 C3
Lamphun 11,309 C3
Lang Suan 4,020 C5
Loei 10,137 D3
Lom Sak 10,597 D3
Lop Buri 23,112 D4
Mae Hong Son 3,981 C3
Maha Sarakham 19,707 D3
Mukdahan E3
Nakhon Nayok 8,185 D4
Nakhon Pathom 34,300 C4
Nakhon Phanom 20,385 D3
Nakhon Ratchasima 66,071 D4
Nakhon Sawan 46,853 D4
Nakhon Si Thammarat 40,671 D5
Nan 17,738 D3
Nang Rong D4
Narathiwat 21,256 D6
Ngao D3
Nong Khai 21,150 D3
Pattani 21,938 D6
Phanat Nikhom 10,514 D4
Phangnga 5,738 C5
Phatthalung 13,336 D6
Phayao 20,346 C3
Phet Buri 27,755 C4
Phetchabun 6,240 D3
Phichai D3
Phichit 10,814 D3
Phitsanulok 33,883 D3
Phon Phisai D3
Phrae 17,555 D3
Phra Nakhon Si Ayutthaya 37,213 D4
Phuket 34,362 C6
Phutthaisong D4
Prachin Buri 14,167 D4
Prachuap Khiri Khan 9,075 D5
Pran Buri D4
Rahaeng (Tak) 16,317 C3
Ranong 10,301 C5
Rat Buri 32,271 C4
Rayong 14,846 D4
Roi Et 20,242 D4
Rong Kwang D3
Sakon Nakhon 18,943 E3
Samut Prakan 46,632 D4
Samut Sakhon 33,619 D4
Samut Songkhram 23,574 C4
Sara Buri 25,025 D4
Satun 7,315 C6
Sawankhalok 8,387 C3
Selaphum E3
Sing Buri 9,050 D4
Singora (Songkhla) 41,193 D6
Sisaket 13,662 E4
Songkhla 41,193 D6
Sukhothai 15,488 D3
Suphan Buri 18,768 C4
Surat Thani 24,923 C5
Surin 16,342 D4
Suwannaphum D4
Tak 16,317 C3
Takua Pa 7,825 C5
Thoen C3
Thon Buri 628,015 D4
To Mo D6
Trang 32,985 C6
Trat 7,917 D4
Ubon 40,650 E4
Udon Thani 56,218 D3
Uthai Thani 10,525 C4
Uttaradit 12,022 D3
Warin Chamrap 21,520 E4
Yala 30,051 D6
Yasothon 12,079 D4

OTHER FEATURES

Amya (pass) C4
Bilauktaung (range) C4
Chang, Ko (isl.) D4
Chao Phraya, Mae Nam (riv.) D4
Chi, Mae Nam (riv.) D3
Dangrek (Dong Rak) (mts.) D4
Doi Inthanon (mt.) C3
Doi Pha Hom Pok (mt.) C2
Doi Pia Fai (mt.) D4
Kao Prawa (mt.) C3
Khao Luang (mt.) C5
Khwae Noi, Mae Nam (riv.) C4
Kra (isth.) C5
Kut, Ko (isl.) D5
Laem Pho (cape) D6
Laem Talumphuk (cape) D5
Lanta, Ko (isl.) C6
Luang (mt.) C5
Mae Klong, Mae Nam (riv.) C4
Mekong (riv.) E3
Mun, Mae Nam (riv.) D4
Nan, Mae Nam (riv.) D3
Nong Lahan (lake) D3
Pakchan (riv.) C5
Pa Sak, Mae Nam (riv.) D4
Phangan, Ko (isl.) D5
Phuket, Ko (isl.) C5
Ping, Mae Nam (riv.) C3
Samui (str.) D5
Samui, Ko (isl.) D5
Siam (Thailand) (gulf) D5
Tao, Ko (isl.) C5
Tapi, Mae Nam (riv.) C5
Terutao, Ko (isl.) C6
Tha Chin, Mae Nam (riv.) C4
Thale Luang (lag.) D6
Thalu, Ko (isls.) C5
Three Pagodas (pass) C4
Wang, Mae Nam (riv.) C3

VIETNAM

CITIES and TOWNS

An Loc (Binh Long) 15,276 E5
An Nhon F4
An Tuc (An Khe) F4
Ap Long Ha F5
Ap Vinh Hao F5
Bac Can E2
Bac Giang E2
Bac Lieu 53,841 E5
Bac Ninh 22,560 E2
Ba Don E3
Bai Thuong E3
Ban Me Thuot 68,771 F4
Bao Ha D2
Bao Lac E2
Bien Hoa 87,135 E5
Binh Long (An Loc) 15,276 E5
Binh Son F4
Bo Duc E4
Bong Son (Hoai Nhon) F4
Cam Ranh 118,111 F5
Can Tho 182,424 E5
Cao Bang E2
Cao Lanh 16,482 E5
Chau Phu 37,175 E5
Chu Lai F4
Con Cuong E3
Cua Rao E3
Da Lat 105,072 F5
Dam Doi E5
Da Nang 492,194 E3
Dien Bien Phu D2
Dong Hoi E3
Duong Dong D5
Gia Dinh E5
Go Cong 33,191 E5
Ha Giang E2
Haiphong* 1,279,067 E2
Hanoi (cap.)* 2,570,905 E2
Ha Tien E5
Ha Tinh E3
Hau Bon E4
Hoa Binh E2
Hoa Da F5
Hoai Nhon F4
Ho Chi Minh City (Saigon)* 3,419,678 E5
Hoi An 45,059 F4
Hoi Xuan E2
Hon Chong E5
Hon Gai 100,000 E2
Hue 209,043 E3
Huong Khe E3
Ke Bao E2
Khanh Hoa F4
Khanh Hung 59,015 E5
Khe Sanh E3
Kien Hung E5
Kontum 33,554 E4
Lac Giao (Ban Me Thuot) 68,771 E4
Lai Chau D2
Lang Son 15,071 E2
Lao Cai E2
Loc Ninh E5
Long Xuyen 72,658 E5
Mo Duc F4
Mong Cai E2
Muong Khuong E2
My Tho 119,892 E5
Nam Dinh E2
Nghia Lo D2
Nha Trang 216,227 F4
Ninh Binh E3
Phan Rang 33,377 F5
Phan Thiet 80,122 F5
Phu Cuong 28,267 E5
Phu Lang Thuong (Bac Giang) E2
Phuc Loi E3
Phu Dien E3
Phu Ly E2
Phu My F4
Phu Qui E3
Phu Rieng E5
Phu Tho 10,888 E2
Phu Vinh 48,485 E5
Pleiku 23,720 E4
Quang Nam E4
Quang Ngai 14,119 F4
Quang Tri 15,874 E3
Quang Yen E2
Quan Long 59,331 E5
Qui Nhon 213,757 F4
Rach Gia 104,161 E5
Ron E3
Sa Dec 51,867 E5
Saigon (Ho Chi Minh City)* 3,419,678 E5
Song Cau F4
Son Ha F4
Son La D2
Son Tay 19,213 E2
Tam Ky 38,532 F4
Tam Quan F4
Tan An 38,082 E5
Tay Ninh 22,957 E5
Thai Binh 14,739 E2
Thai Nguyen E2
Thanh Hoa 31,211 E3
Thanh Tri E5
That Khe E2
Tien Yen E2
Tra Vinh (Phu Vinh) 48,485 E5
Truc Giang 68,629 E5
Trung Khanh Phu E2
Tuyen Quang E2
Tuy Hoa 63,552 F4
Van Hoa E2
Van Ninh F4
Van Yen E2
Vinh 43,954 E3
Vinh Long 30,667 E5
Vinh Yen E2
Vu Liet E3
Vung Tau 108,436 E5
Xuan Loc E5
Yen Bai E2

OTHER FEATURES

Bach Long Vi, Dao (isl.) F2
Ba Den, Nui (mt.) E5
Bai Bung, Mui (Ca Mau) (pt.) E5
Black (riv.) D2
Ca Mau (Mui Bai Bung) (pt.) E5
Cam Ranh, Vinh (bay) F5
Cat Ba, Dao (isl.) E2
Chon May, Vung (bay) F3
Cu Lao, Hon (isls.) F5
Deux Frères, Les (isls.) E5
Dinh, Mui (cape) F5
Fan Si Pan (mt.) D2
la Drang (riv.) E4
Joncs (plain) E5
Kontum (plat.) E4
Khoai, Hon (isl.) E5
Lang Bian, Nui (mts.) E4
Lay, Mui (cape) E3
Mekong, Mouths of the (delta) E5
Nam Tram, Mui (cape) F4
Nightingale (Bach Long Vi) (isl.) F2
Panjang, Hon (Hon Tho Chau) (isl.) D5
Phu Quoc, Dao (isl.) D5
Rao Co (mt.) E3
Red (riv.) E2
Se San (riv.) E4
Sip Song Chau Thai (mts.) D2
Song Ba (riv.) F4
Song Ca (riv.) E3
Song Cai (riv.) E4
South China (sea) F4
Tonkin (gulf) E3
Varella, Mui (cape) F4
Wai, Poulo (isls.) E4
Yang Sin, Chu (mt.) F4

*See Southeast Asia, p. 85 for other part of Malaysia.

*City and suburbs.

⊙Population of district.

CHINA (MAINLAND)

AREA 3,691,000 sq. mi. (9,559,690 sq. km.)
POPULATION 958,090,000
CAPITAL Peking (Beijing)
LARGEST CITY Shanghai
HIGHEST POINT Mt. Everest 29,028 ft. (8,848 m.)
MONETARY UNIT yuan
MAJOR LANGUAGES Chinese, Chuang, Uigur, Yi, Tibetan, Miao, Mongol, Kazakh
MAJOR RELIGIONS Confucianism, Buddhism, Taoism, Islam

CHINA (TAIWAN)

AREA 13,971 sq. mi. (36,185 sq. km.)
POPULATION 16,609,961
CAPITAL Taipei
LARGEST CITY Taipei
HIGHEST POINT Yü Shan 13,113 ft. (3,997 m.)
MONETARY UNIT new Taiwan yüan (dollar)
MAJOR LANGUAGES Chinese, Formosan
MAJOR RELIGIONS Confucianism, Buddhism, Taoism, Christianity, tribal religions

MONGOLIA

AREA 606,163 sq. mi. (1,569,962 sq. km.)
POPULATION 1,594,800
CAPITAL Ulaanbaatar
LARGEST CITY Ulaanbaatar
HIGHEST POINT Tabun Bogdo 14,288 ft. (4,355 m.)
MONETARY UNIT tughrik
MAJOR LANGUAGES Khalkha Mongolian, Kazakh (Turkic)
MAJOR RELIGION Buddhism

HONG KONG

AREA 403 sq. mi. (1,044 sq. km.)
POPULATION 5,022,000
CAPITAL Victoria
MONETARY UNIT Hong Kong dollar
MAJOR LANGUAGES Chinese, English
MAJOR RELIGIONS Confucianism, Buddhism, Christianity

MACAU

AREA 6 sq. mi. (16 sq. km.)
POPULATION 271,000
CAPITAL Macau
MONETARY UNIT pataca
MAJOR LANGUAGES Chinese, Portuguese
MAJOR RELIGIONS Confucianism, Buddhism, Taoism, Christianity

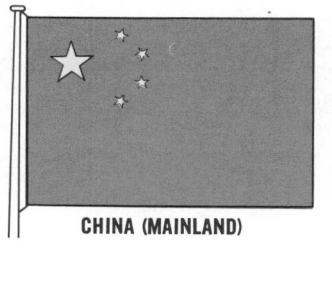

CHINA (MAINLAND)

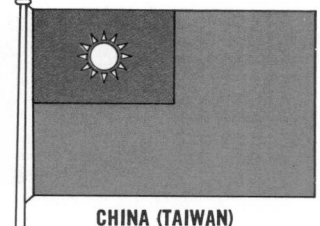

CHINA (TAIWAN)

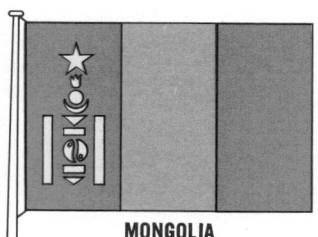

MONGOLIA

CHINA

PROVINCES

Anhui (Anhwei) 47,130,000 .... J5
Chekiang (Zhejiang) 37,510,000 .... K6
Fujian (Fukien) 24,500,000 .... J6
Gansu (Kansu) 18,730,000 .... E3
Guangdong (Kwangtung) 55,930,000 ..... H7
Guangxi Zhuangzu (Kwangsi Chuang Aut. Reg.) 34,020,000 ... G7
Guizhou (Kweichow) 26,860,000 .... G6
Heilongjiang (Heilungkiang) 33,760,000 .. K2
Hebei (Hopei) 50,570,000 .... J4
Henan (Honan) 70,660,000 .... H5
Hubei (Hupei) 45,750,000 .... H5
Hunan 51,660,000 .... H6
Inner Mongolian Aut. Reg. (Nei Monggol) 8,900,000 ... H3
Jiangxi (Kiangsi) 31,830,000 .... J6
Jiangsu (Kiangsu) 58,340,000 .... K5
Jilin (Kirin) 24,740,000 .... L3
Kansu (Gansu) 18,730,000 .... E3
Kiangsi (Jiangxi) 31,830,000 .... J6
Kiangsu (Jiangsu) 58,340,000 .... K5
Kirin (Jilin) 24,740,000 .... L3
Kwangsi Chuang Aut. Reg. (Guangxi Zhuang) 34,020,000 ... G7
Kwangtung (Guangdong) 55,930,000 ..... H7
Kweichow (Guizhou) 26,860,000 .... G6
Liaoning 37,430,000 .... K3
Nei Monggol (Inner Mongolian Aut. Reg.) 8,900,000 ... H3
Ningxia Huizu (Ningsia Hui Aut. Reg.) 3,660,000 ... F3
Qinghai (Tsinghai) 3,650,000 .... E4
Shaanxi (Shensi) 27,790,000 .... G5
Shanxi (Shansi) 24,340,000 .... H4
Shandong (Shantung) 71,600,000 .... J4
Sichuan (Szechwan) 97,070,000 .... F5
Sinkiang-Uigur Aut. Reg. (Xinjiang Uygur) 12,330,000 ... B3
Taiwan 16,609,961 .... K7
Tibet Aut. Reg. (Xizang) 1,790,000 .... B5
Tsinghai (Qinghai) 3,650,000 .... E4
Xinjiang Uygur (Sinkiang-Uigur Aut. Reg.) 12,330,000 ... B3
Xizang (Tibet Aut. Reg.) 1,790,000 .... B5
Yunnan 30,920,000 .... F7
Zhejiang (Chekiang) 37,510,000 .... K6

CITIES AND TOWNS†

(continued on following page)

China and Mongolia Transportation

Railroads	————
Under Construction	– – –
Connecting Roads	————
Navigable Rivers	~~~~
Canals	~~~~
Major Seaports	⚓

© Copyright HAMMOND INCORPORATED, Maplewood, N.J.

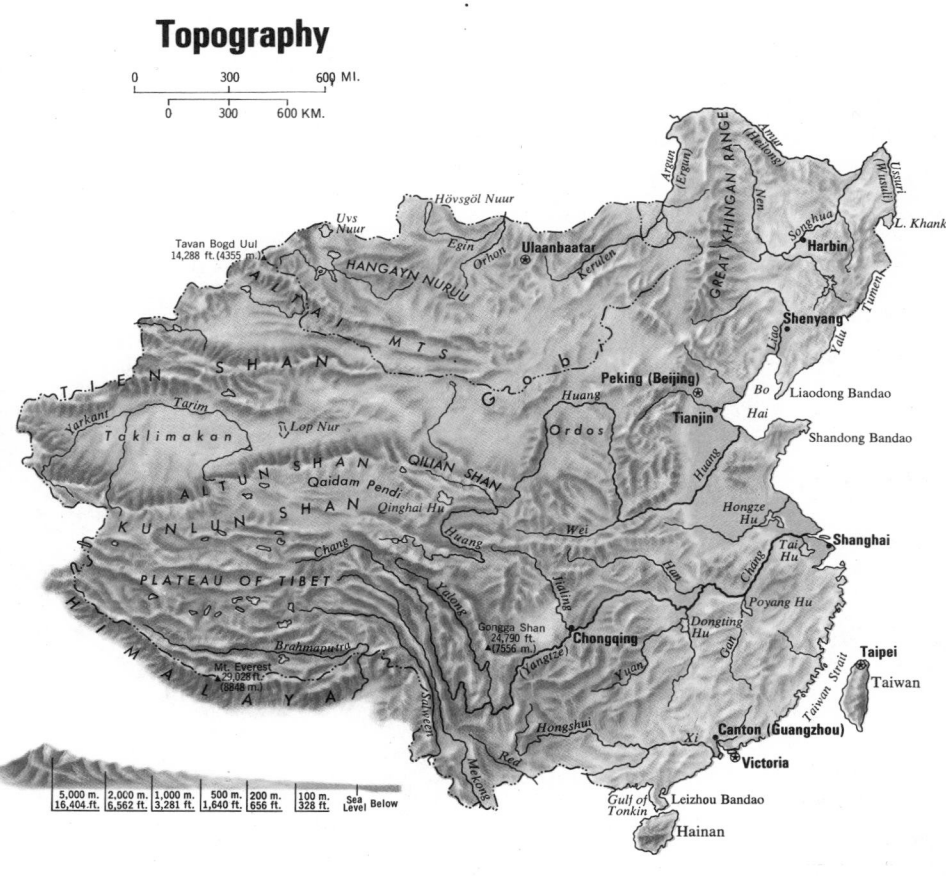

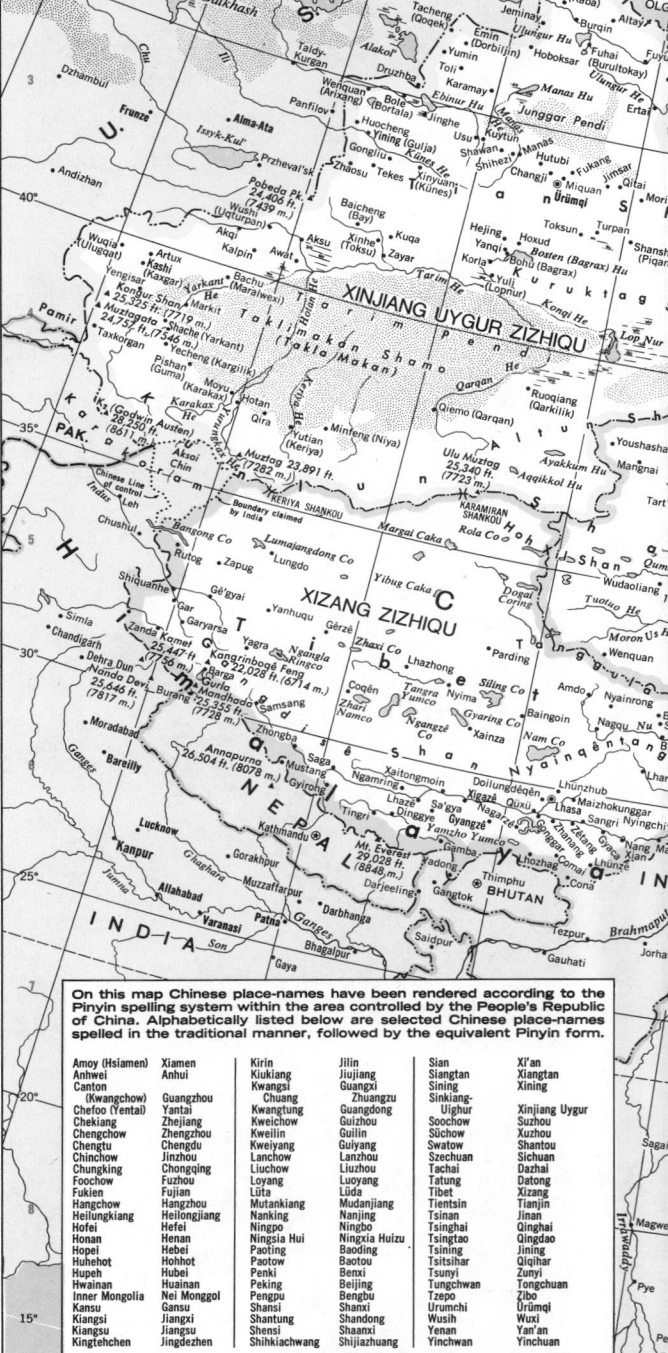

On this map Chinese place-names have been rendered according to the Pinyin spelling system within the area controlled by the People's Republic of China. Alphabetically listed below are selected Chinese place-names spelled in the traditional manner, followed by the equivalent Pinyin form.

Amoy (Hsiamen)	Xiamen	Kirin	Jilin	Sian	Xi'an
Anhwei	Anhui	Kiukiang	Jiujiang	Siangtan	Xiangtan
Canton		Kwangsi	Guangxi	Sining	Xining
(Kwangchow)	Guangzhou	Chuang	Zhuangzu	Sinkiang-	
Chefoo (Yentai)	Yantai	Kwangtung	Guangdong	Uighur	Xinjiang Uygur
Chekiang	Zhejiang	Kweichow	Guizhou	Soochow	Suzhou
Chengchow	Zhengzhou	Kweilin	Guilin	Süchow	Xuzhou
Chengtu	Chengdu	Kweiyang	Guiyang	Swatow	Shantou
Chinchow	Jinzhou	Lanchow	Lanzhou	Szechuan	Sichuan
Chungking	Chongqing	Liuchow	Liuzhou	Tachai	Dazhai
Foochow	Fuzhou	Loyang	Luoyang	Tatung	Datong
Fukien	Fujian	Lüta	Lüda	Tibet	Xizang
Hangchow	Hangzhou	Mutankiang	Mudanjiang	Tientsin	Tianjin
Heilungkiang	Heilongjiang	Nanking	Nanjing	Tsinan	Jinan
Hofei	Hefei	Ningpo	Ningbo	Tsinghai	Qinghai
Honan	Henan	Ningsia Hui	Ningxia Huizu	Tsingtao	Qingdao
Hopei	Hebei	Paoting	Baoding	Tsining	Jining
Hupeh	Hubei	Paotow	Baotou	Tsitsihar	Qiqihar
Hwainan	Huainan	Peking	Beijing	Tsunyi	Zunyi
Huhehot	Hohhot	Pengpu	Bengbu	Tungchwan	Tongchuan
Inner Mongolia	Nei Monggol	Shansi	Shanxi	Tzepo	Zibo
Kansu	Gansu	Shantung	Shandong	Urumchi	Ürümqi
Kiangsi	Jiangxi	Shensi	Shaanxi	Wusih	Wuxi
Kiangsu	Jiangsu	Shihkiachwang	Shijiazhuang	Yenan	Yan'an
Kingtehchen	Jingdezhen			Yinchwan	Yinchuan

Tsining (Jining), Shandong J4
Tsitsihar (Qiqihar) 1,500,000 ......K2
Tsunyi (Zunyi) 275,000 ....G6
Tumen M3
Tungchwan (Tongchuan) G5
Tunghwa (Tonghua) 275,000 ....L3
Tungkiao (Tongliao) M2
Tungliao (Tongjiao) ....
Tunhwa (Dunhua) L3
Tunki (Tunki) J6
Turpan (Turfan) C3
Tzekung (Zigong) 350,000 ....G6
Tzepo (Zibo) 1,750,000 ....J4
Uch Turfan (Wushi) A3
Ulanhot (Horqiun Youyi)
  Qianqi) 100,000 ....K2
Ulughchat (Wuqia) A4
Ürümqi (Urumchi) 500,000 ....C3
Usu B3
Wanning H8
Wanxian (Wanhsien) 175,000 ......G5
Weichang J3
Weifang 260,000 ....J4
Weihai (Weihaiwei) E6
Weixin E6
Wenchow (Wenzhou) 250,000 ......J6
Wenquan, Qinghai D5
Wenquan, Xinjiang Uygur B3

Wenzhou 250,000 ....J6
Wuchang L3
Wuchow (Wuzhou) 150,000 ....H7
Wuchuan, Guizhou G6
Wuchuan, Nei Monggol H3
Wuchung (Wuzhong) G4
Wuda ....
Wuhai ....
Wuhan 4,250,000 ....H5
Wuhing (Wuxing) 160,000 ....K5
Wuhu 300,000 ....J5
Wuqi G4
Wushi A4
Wusih (Wuxi) 900,000 ....J5
Wutai H4
Wuwei F4
Wuxi (Wusih) 900,000 ....K5
Wuxing (Wuhing) 160,000 ....K5
Wuyuan G3
Wuzhong (Wuchung) G4
Wuzhou (Wuchow) 150,000 ....H7
Xiaguan (Siakwan) E6
Xiamen (Amoy) J77 ....J7
Xi'an (Sian) 1,900,000 ....G5
Xiangtan (Siangtan) 150,000 ......H5
Xiangtan (Siangtan) 300,000 ......H4
Xianyang (Sienyang) 125,000 .....G5
Xiapu (Siapu) K6
Xichang (Sichang) F6

Xigazê (Shigatse) C6
Ximiao F3
Xin Barag Youqi J2
Xingtai (Singtai) H4
Xinhe (Toksu) B3
Xining (Sining) 250,000 ....F4
Xinxiang (Sinsiang) 300,000 ......H4
Xinyang (Sinyang) 125,000 ....H5
Xinyuan (Künes) B3
Xuchang (Hsüchang) H5
Xuguit K2
Xuzhou (Süchow) 1,500,000 ....J5
Ya'an 100,000 ....F6
Yadong C6
Yan'an (Yenan) G4
Yancheng K5
Yangchow (Yangzhou) 210,000 ....J5
Yangchün (Yangquan) 350,000 ....H4
Yangjiang H7
Yanji (Yenki) 130,000 ....L3
Yangquan (Yangchün) 350,000 ....H4
Yangzhou (Yangchow) 210,000 ....J5
Yanqi C3
Yantai (Chefoo) 180,000 ....K4
Yarkant (Shache) A4
Ya Xian G8
Yecheng A4
Yenan (Yan'an) G4
Yenki (Yanji) 130,000 ....L3
Yibin (Ipin) 275,000 ....F6

Yichang (Ichang) 150,000 ....H5
Yichun, Jiangxi H6
Yichun, Heilongjiang 200,000 .....H2
Yidu, Hubei H5
Yidu, Shandong J4
Yinchuan (Ningsia) 175,000 ......G4
Yingkou 215,000 ....K3
Yingtan J6
Yiwu (Aratürük) D3
Yiyang H6
Yongxin H6
Yuci (Yütze) H4
Yueyang H6
Yuli (Lopnur) C3
Yulin, Guangxi Zhuangzu G7
Yulin, Shanxi G5
Yumen 325,000 ....E4
Yuncheng H4
Yungkia (Wenzhou) 250,000 ......J6
Yushu, Jilin L3
Yushu, Qinghai E5
Yutian, Hebei J4
Yutian, Xinjiang Uygur B4
Yütze (Yuci) H4
Zaozhuang J5
Zayü E6
Zêtang D6
Zhanghei ....
Zhangjiakou (Kalgan) 1,000,000 ..J3
Zhangye (Changyeh) F4

Zhangzhou (Changchow) J7
Zhanjiang (Chankiang) 220,000 ...H7
Zhaodong K2
Zhaojue F6
Zhaoqing H7
Zhaotong (Chaotung) F6
Zhengzhou (Chengchow) 1,500,000 .H5
Zhenjiang (Chinkiang) 250,000 ....J5
Zhenyuan G6
Zhongba B6
Zhongshan (Chungshan) 135,000 ..H7
Zhongwei F4
Zhumadian (Chumatien) H5
Zhuzhou (Chuchow) 350,000 ......H6
Zibo (Tzepo) 1,750,000 ....J4
Zigong (Tzekung) 350,000 ....F6
Zinhui H7
Zunhua J3
Zunyi (Tsunyi) 275,000 ....G6

OTHER FEATURES

Altun Shan (range) C4
Alxa Shamo (des.) F4
Amur (Heilong Jiang) (riv.) L2
A'nyêmaqên Shan (mts.) E5
Aqqikkol Hu (lake) C4
Argun' (Ergun He) (riv.) K1

Bagrax (Bosten Hu) (lake) C3
Bangong Co (lake) A5
Bashi (chan.) K7
Bayan Har Shan (range) E4
Bo Hai (gulf) J4
Bosten (Bagrax) Hu (lake) C3
Chang Jiang (Yangtze) (riv.) K5
Da Hinggan Ling (range) J3
Dian Chi (lake) F7
Dongsha (isl.) K7
Dongting Hu (riv.) H6
East China (sea) L6
Ebinur Hu (lake) B2
Ergun He (Argun') (riv.) K1
Er Hai (lake) F6
Everest (mt.) C5
Fen He (riv.) H4
Formosa (Taiwan) (str.) J7
Formosa (Taiwan)
  (isl.) K7
Gangdisê Shan (range) B5
Gaoyou Hu (lake) J5
Ghenghis Khan Wall (ruin) H2
Gobi (des.) G3
Gongga Shan (mt.) F6
Grand (canal) J4
Great Wall (ruins) G4,J
Gurla Mandhata (mt.) B5
Hailar He (riv.) K2
Hainan (isl.) H8

Hangzhou Wan (bay) K5
Han Shui (riv.) H5
Heilong Jiang (Amur) (riv.) L2
Himalaya (mts.) C6
Hongshui He (riv.) G7
Hongze Hu (lake) J5
Hotan He (riv.) B4
Huang He (Yellow) (riv.) J4
Hulun Nur (lake) J2
Hungtze (isl.) K7
Inner Mongolia (reg.) H3
Jinmen (Quemoy) (isl.) J7
Jinsha Jiang (Yangtze) (riv.) E5
Junggar Pendi (desert basin) C2
Kangrinboqê Feng (mt.) B5
Karakhoto (ruins) F3
Karamiran Shankou (pass) C4
Keriya Shankou (pass) B4
Khanka (lake) M3
Kongur Shan (mt.) A4
Künes He (riv.) B3
Kunlun Shan (range) B4
Kuruktag Shan (range) C3
Lancang Jiang (riv.) F7
Leizhou Bandao (pen.) G7
Liaodong Bandao (pen.) K3
Liao He (riv.) K3
Lop Nor (Lop Nur) (lake) D3
Manas He (riv.) C3
Manas (lake) C2

(continued on following page)

China and Mongolia

SCALE OF MILES

0   100   200   300   400   500

SCALE OF KILOMETERS

0 100 200 300 400 500

Capitals of Countries ......⊛   International Boundaries _____
Provincial Capitals ....⊙   Provincial Boundaries _ . _ . _
Canals ....   Walls ....

Scale 1:19,100,000

© Copyright HAMMOND INCORPORATED, Maplewood, N.J.

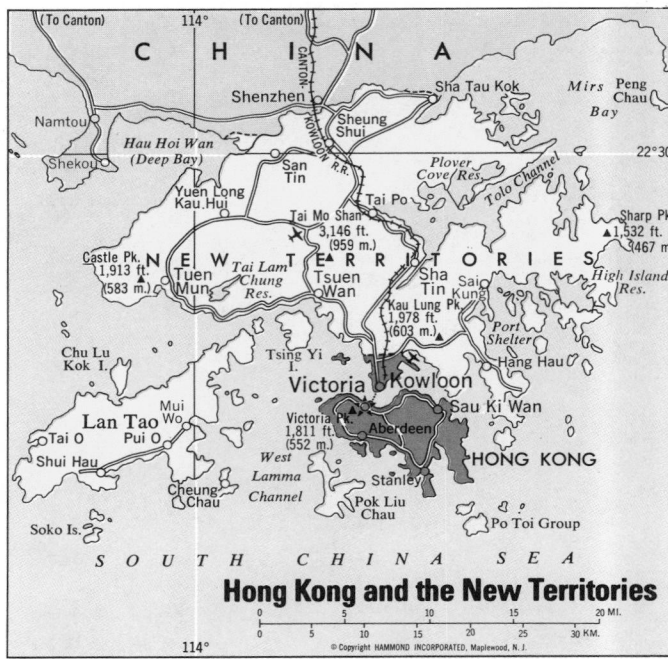

Hong Kong and the New Territories

Agriculture, Industry and Resources

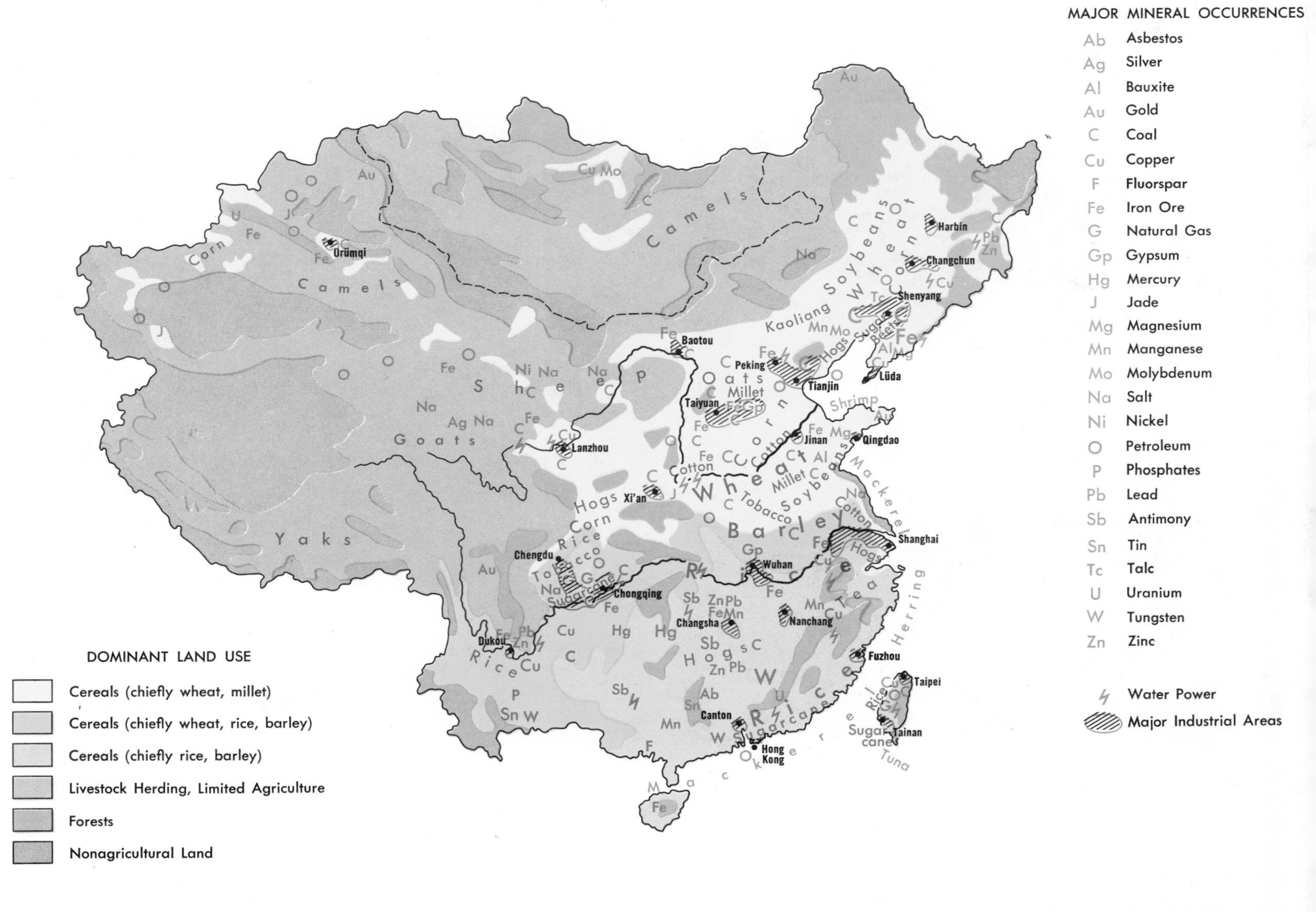

DOMINANT LAND USE

Cereals (chiefly wheat, millet)

Cereals (chiefly wheat, rice, barley)

Cereals (chiefly rice, barley)

Livestock Herding, Limited Agriculture

Forests

Nonagricultural Land

MAJOR MINERAL OCCURRENCES

Ab	Asbestos
Ag	Silver
Al	Bauxite
Au	Gold
C	Coal
Cu	Copper
F	Fluorspar
Fe	Iron Ore
G	Natural Gas
Gp	Gypsum
Hg	Mercury
J	Jade
Mg	Magnesium
Mn	Manganese
Mo	Molybdenum
Na	Salt
Ni	Nickel
O	Petroleum
P	Phosphates
Pb	Lead
Sb	Antimony
Sn	Tin
Tc	Talc
U	Uranium
W	Tungsten
Zn	Zinc

⚡ Water Power

▨ Major Industrial Areas

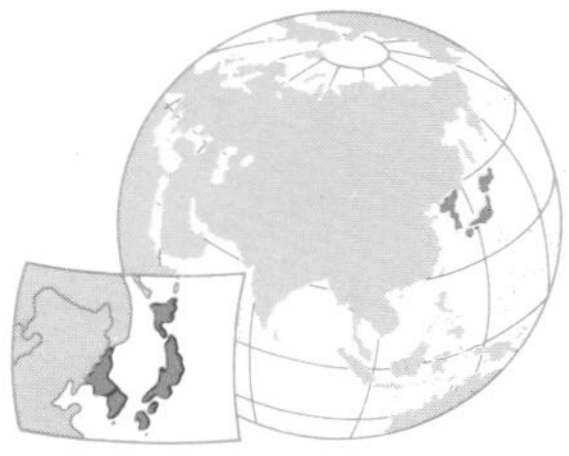

AREA 145,730 sq. mi. (377,441 sq. km.)
POPULATION 117,057,485
CAPITAL Tokyo
LARGEST CITY Tokyo
HIGHEST POINT Fuji 12,389 ft. (3,776 m.)
MONETARY UNIT yen
MAJOR LANGUAGE Japanese
MAJOR RELIGIONS Buddhism, Shintoism

AREA 46,540 sq. mi. (120,539 sq. km.)
POPULATION 17,914,000
CAPITAL P'yŏngyang
LARGEST CITY P'yŏngyang
HIGHEST POINT Paektu 9,003 ft. (2,744 m.)
MONETARY UNIT won
MAJOR LANGUAGE Korean
MAJOR RELIGIONS Confucianism, Buddhism, Ch'ondogyo

AREA 38,175 sq. mi. (98,873 sq. km.)
POPULATION 37,448,836
CAPITAL Seoul
LARGEST CITY Seoul
HIGHEST POINT Halla 6,398 ft. (1,950 m.)
MONETARY UNIT won
MAJOR LANGUAGE Korean
MAJOR RELIGIONS Confucianism, Buddhism, Ch'ondogyo, Christianity

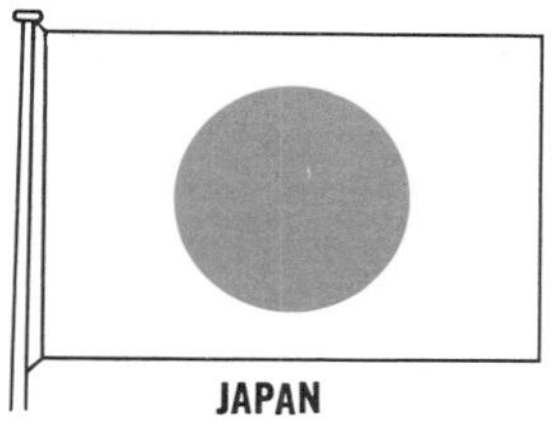

JAPAN

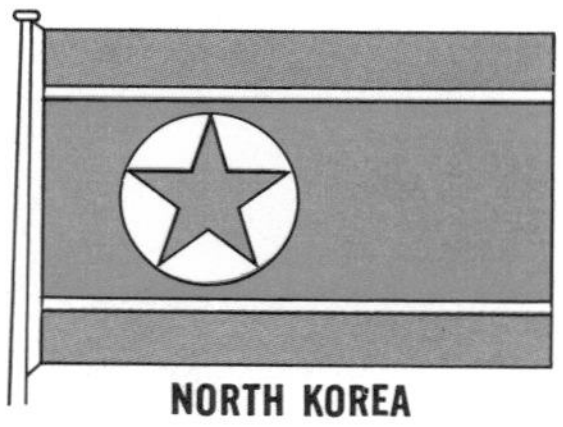

NORTH KOREA

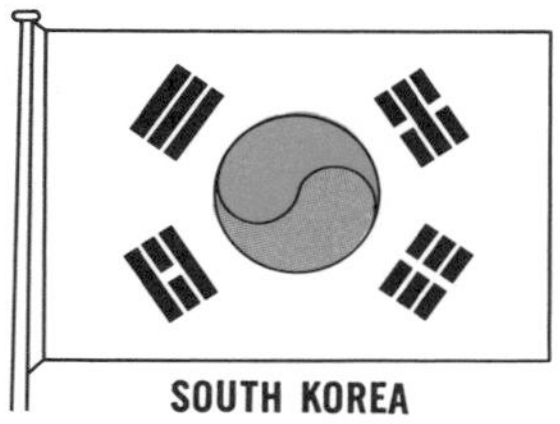

SOUTH KOREA

JAPAN

PREFECTURES

Aichi 5,923,569 ..... H6
Akita 1,232,481 ..... J4
Aomori 1,468,646 ..... K3
Chiba 4,149,147 ..... P2
Ehime 1,465,215 ..... F7
Fukui 773,599 ..... G5
Fukuoka 4,292,963 ..... D7
Fukushima 1,970,616 ..... K5
Gifu 1,867,978 ..... H6
Gumma 1,756,480 ..... J5
Hiroshima 2,646,324 ..... E6
Hokkaido 5,338,206 ..... K2
Hyogo 4,992,140 ..... H7
Ibaraki 2,342,198 ..... K5
Ishikawa 1,069,872 ..... H5
Iwate 1,385,563 ..... K4
Kagawa 961,292 ..... G6
Kagoshima 1,723,902 ..... E8
Kanagawa 6,397,748 ..... O2
Kochi 808,397 ..... F7
Kumamoto 1,715,273 ..... E7
Kyoto 2,424,856 ..... J7
Mie 1,626,002 ..... H6
Miyagi 1,955,267 ..... K4
Miyazaki 1,085,055 ..... E8
Nagano 2,017,564 ..... J5
Nagasaki 1,571,912 ..... D7
Nara 1,077,491 ..... J8
Niigata 2,391,938 ..... J5
Oita 1,190,314 ..... E7
Okayama 1,814,305 ..... F6
Okinawa 1,042,572 ..... N6
Osaka 8,278,925 ..... J8
Saga 837,674 ..... E7
Saitama 4,821,340 ..... O2
Shiga 985,621 ..... J7
Shimane 768,886 ..... F6
Shizuoka 3,308,799 ..... H6
Tochigi 1,698,003 ..... K5
Tokushima 805,166 ..... G7
Tokyo 11,673,554 ..... O2
Tottori 581,311 ..... G6
Toyama 1,070,791 ..... H5
Wakayama 1,072,118 ..... G6
Yamagata 1,220,302 ..... K4
Yamaguchi 1,555,218 ..... E6
Yamanashi 783,050 ..... J6

CITIES and TOWNS

Abashiri 43,825 ..... M1
Ageo 146,358 ..... O2
Aikawa 13,546 ..... H4
Aizuwakamatsu 108,650 ..... J5
Ajigasawa 18,086 ..... J3
Akashi 234,905 ..... H8
Aki 24,480 ..... F7
Akita 261,246 ..... J4
Akkeshi 16,778 ..... M2
Akune 30,295 ..... E7
Amagasaki 545,783 ..... H8
Amagi 42,725 ..... E7
Anan 60,439 ..... G7
Aomori 264,222 ..... K3
Asahi 34,028 ..... K6
Asahikawa 320,526 ..... L2
Ashibetsu 36,520 ..... L2
Ashikaga 162,359 ..... J5
Ashiya 76,211 ..... H8
Atami 51,437 ..... J6
Atsugi 108,955 ..... O2
Awaji 9,623 ..... H8
Ayabe 43,490 ..... G6
Beppu 133,894 ..... E7
Bibai 38,416 ..... L2
Biratori 9,331 ..... L2
Chiba 659,356 ..... P2
Chichibu 61,798 ..... J5
Chigasaki 152,023 ..... O3
Chitose 61,031 ..... K2
Chofu 175,924 ..... O2
Choshi 90,374 ..... K6
Daito 110,829 ..... J8
Ebetsu 77,624 ..... K2
Eniwa 39,884 ..... K2
Esashi, Hokkaido 10,172 ..... L1
Esashi, Hokkaido 14,409 ..... J3
Esashi, Iwate 36,336 ..... K4
Fuchu, Hiroshima 50,217 ..... F6
Fuchu, Tokyo 182,474 ..... O2
Fuji 199,195 ..... J6
Fujieda 90,358 ..... J6
Fujisawa 265,975 ..... O3
Fukagawa 36,000 ..... L2
Fukuchiyama 60,003 ..... G6
Fukue 32,018 ..... D7
Fukui 231,364 ..... G5
Fukuoka 1,002,201 ..... D7
Fukushima 246,531 ..... K5
Fukuyama 329,714 ..... F6
Funabashi 423,101 ..... P2
Furukawa 54,356 ..... K4
Gifu 408,707 ..... H6
Gobo 30,272 ..... G7
Gose 37,554 ..... J8
Gosen 39,376 ..... J5
Goshogawara 49,040 ..... K3
Gotsu 27,992 ..... F6
Habikino 94,160 ..... J8
Haboro 13,624 ..... K1
Hachinohe 224,366 ..... K3
Hachioji 322,580 ..... O2
Hadano 103,663 ..... O3
Hagi 52,724 ..... E6
Hakodate 307,453 ..... K3
Hakui 28,726 ..... H5
Hamada 50,316 ..... E6
Hamamatsu 468,884 ..... H6
Hanamaki 65,826 ..... K4
Hanno 55,926 ..... O2
Haramachi 43,483 ..... K5
Hayama 24,026 ..... O3
Higashiosaka 524,750 ..... J8
Hikone 85,066 ..... H6
Himeji 436,086 ..... G6
Himi 61,789 ..... H5
Hino 126,847 ..... O2
Hirakata 297,618 ..... J7
Hirara 29,301 ..... L7
Hirata 30,942 ..... F6
Hiratsuka 195,635 ..... O3
Hiroo 11,399 ..... L2
Hirosaki 164,911 ..... K3
Hiroshima 852,611 ..... E6
Hitachi 202,383 ..... K5
Hitachiota 35,322 ..... K5
Hitoyoshi 41,118 ..... E7
Hofu 105,540 ..... E6
Hondo 40,432 ..... E7
Honjo 40,488 ..... J4
Hyuga 53,448 ..... E7
Ibaraki 210,286 ..... J7
Ibusuki 32,339 ..... E8
Ichihara 194,068 ..... P3
Ichikawa 319,291 ..... P2
Ichinohe 21,433 ..... K3
Ichinomiya 238,463 ..... H6
Ichinoseki 59,122 ..... K4
Ide 9,112 ..... J7
Iida 77,112 ..... H6
Iizuka 75,417 ..... E7
Ikeda, Hokkaido 12,306 ..... L2
Ikeda, Osaka 100,268 ..... H7
Ikoma 48,848 ..... J8
Ikuno 6,658 ..... G6
Imabari 119,726 ..... F6
Imari 60,913 ..... D7
Imazu 11,519 ..... G6
Ina 54,468 ..... H6
Isahaya 73,341 ..... D7
Ise 104,957 ..... H6
Ishigaki 34,657 ..... L7
Ishige 19,220 ..... P2
Ishinomaki 115,085 ..... K4
Ishioka 43,679 ..... K5
Itami 171,978 ..... H7
Ito 68,072 ..... J6
Itoigawa 36,646 ..... H5
Itoman 39,363 ..... N6
Iwaizumi 20,219 ..... K4
Iwaki 330,213 ..... K5
Iwakuni 111,069 ..... E6
Iwami 16,063 ..... G6
Iwamizawa 72,305 ..... L2
Iwanai 25,823 ..... K2
Iwasaki 4,437 ..... J3
Iwata 67,665 ..... H6
Iwatsuki 83,825 ..... O2
Iyo 27,805 ..... F7
Izuhara 18,460 ..... D6
Izumi 118,237 ..... J8
Izumiotsu 66,250 ..... J8
Izumisano 86,139 ..... G6
Izumo 71,568 ..... F6
Joetsu 123,418 ..... H5
Joyo 58,923 ..... J7
Kadoma 143,238 ..... J7
Kaga 61,599 ..... H5
Kagoshima 456,827 ..... E8
Kaizuka 79,506 ..... H8
Kakogawa 169,293 ..... G6
Kamaishi 68,981 ..... L4
Kamakura 165,552 ..... O3
Kameoka 58,184 ..... J7
Kamiisco 27,229 ..... K3
Kaminoyama 37,858 ..... J4
Kamiyaku 8,668 ..... E8
Kamo 8,953 ..... J7
Kanazawa 395,263 ..... H5
Kanonji 44,131 ..... F6
Kanoya 67,951 ..... E8
Kanuma 81,799 ..... J5
Karatsu 75,224 ..... D7
Kaseda 24,969 ..... D8
Kashihara 95,701 ..... J8
Kashiwa 203,065 ..... P2
Kashiwara 63,586 ..... J8
Kashiwazaki 80,351 ..... J5
Kasugai 213,857 ..... H6
Kasukabe 121,639 ..... O2
Katsuta 79,996 ..... K5
Katsuura 26,755 ..... K6
Kawachinagano 66,936 ..... J8
Kawagoe 225,465 ..... O2
Kawaguchi 345,538 ..... J6
Kawanishi 115,773 ..... H7
Kawasaki 1,014,951 ..... O2
Kesennuma 66,616 ..... K4
Kikonai 10,034 ..... K3
Kimitsu 76,016 ..... O3
Kiryu 134,239 ..... J5
Kisarazu 96,840 ..... P3
Kishiwada 174,952 ..... J8
Kitaibaraki 44,332 ..... K5
Kitakami 48,759 ..... K4
Kitakata 37,471 ..... J5
Kitakyushu 1,058,058 ..... E6
Kitami 91,519 ..... L2
Kizu 11,890 ..... J7
Kobayashi 38,325 ..... E8
Kobe 1,360,605 ..... H7
Kochi 280,962 ..... F7
Kodaira 156,181 ..... O2
Kofu 193,879 ..... J6
Koga 55,973 ..... J5
Koganei 102,714 ..... O2
Kokubu 31,660 ..... E8
Komagane 30,318 ..... H6
Komatsu 100,273 ..... H5
Koriyama 264,628 ..... K5
Koshigaya 195,917 ..... P2
Koyama 16,394 ..... E8
Kubohama 17,817 ..... F7
Kuji 38,122 ..... K3
Kuki 45,797 ..... O2
Kumagaya 131,485 ..... J5
Kumamoto 488,166 ..... E7
Kumano 27,026 ..... G7
Kumiyama 11,540 ..... J7
Kurashiki 392,755 ..... F6
Kurayoshi 50,785 ..... F6
Kure 242,655 ..... F6
Kuroiso 42,349 ..... K5
Kurume 204,474 ..... E7
Kushikino 30,456 ..... E8
Kushima 30,038 ..... E8
Kushimoto 18,997 ..... G7
Kushiro 206,840 ..... M2
Kyonan 13,067 ..... O3
Kyoto 1,461,059 ..... J7
Machida 255,305 ..... O2
Maebashi 250,241 ..... J5
Maihara 12,845 ..... G6
Maizuru 97,780 ..... G6
Makubetsu 18,444 ..... L2
Makurazaki 29,685 ..... O3
Mashike 9,312 ..... K2
Masuda 50,734 ..... E6
Matsubara 132,662 ..... H8
Matsue 127,440 ..... F6
Matsumae 18,307 ..... J3
Matsumoto 185,595 ..... H5
Matsusaka 108,893 ..... H6
Matsuto 36,170 ..... H5
Matsuyama 367,323 ..... F7
Mihara 83,679 ..... F6
Miki 53,731 ..... H7
Mikuni 21,602 ..... G5
Minamata 36,782 ..... E7
Minobu 10,345 ..... J6
Minoo 79,621 ..... J7
Misawa 37,437 ..... K3
Mitaka 164,950 ..... O2
Mito 197,953 ..... K5
Mitsukaido 38,820 ..... P2
Miura 47,888 ..... O3
Miyako 61,912 ..... L4
Miyakonojo 118,289 ..... E8
Miyazaki 234,347 ..... E8
Miyazu 30,194 ..... G6
Miyoshi 37,193 ..... F6
Mizusawa 52,266 ..... K4
Mobara 64,942 ..... K6
Mombetsu 32,825 ..... L1
Monbetsu 15,029 ..... L2
Mooka 47,345 ..... K5
Mori 17,030 ..... K2
Moriguchi 178,383 ..... J7
Morioka 216,223 ..... K4
Motobu 17,823 ..... N6
Muko 45,886 ..... J7
Murakami 32,939 ..... J4
Muroran 158,715 ..... K2
Muroto 26,660 ..... G7
Musashino 139,508 ..... O2
Mutsu 44,646 ..... K3
Nachikatsuura 23,596 ..... H7
Nagahama, Ehime 13,144 ..... F7
Nagahama, Shiga 54,064 ..... H6
Nagano 306,637 ..... J5
Nagaoka, Kyoto 65,557 ..... J7
Nagaoka, Niigata 171,742 ..... J5
Nagaokakyo 65,557 ..... J7
Nagasaki 450,194 ..... D7
Nagato 27,327 ..... E6
Nago 45,210 ..... N6
Nagoya 2,079,740 ..... H6
Naha 295,006 ..... N6
Nakaminato 33,147 ..... K5
Nakamura 34,437 ..... F7
Nakasato 14,248 ..... K3
Nakatsu 59,111 ..... E7
Nanao 49,493 ..... H5
Nankoku 42,832 ..... F7
Nara 257,538 ..... J8
Narashino 117,852 ..... P2
Nayoro 35,145 ..... L1
Naze 46,359 ..... O5
Nemuro 45,817 ..... M2
Neyagawa 254,311 ..... J7
Nichinan 52,171 ..... E8
Niigata 423,188 ..... J5
Niihama 131,712 ..... F6
Niimi 30,014 ..... F6
Niitsu 58,970 ..... J5
Nishinomiya 400,622 ..... H8

(continued on following page)

Agriculture, Industry and Resources

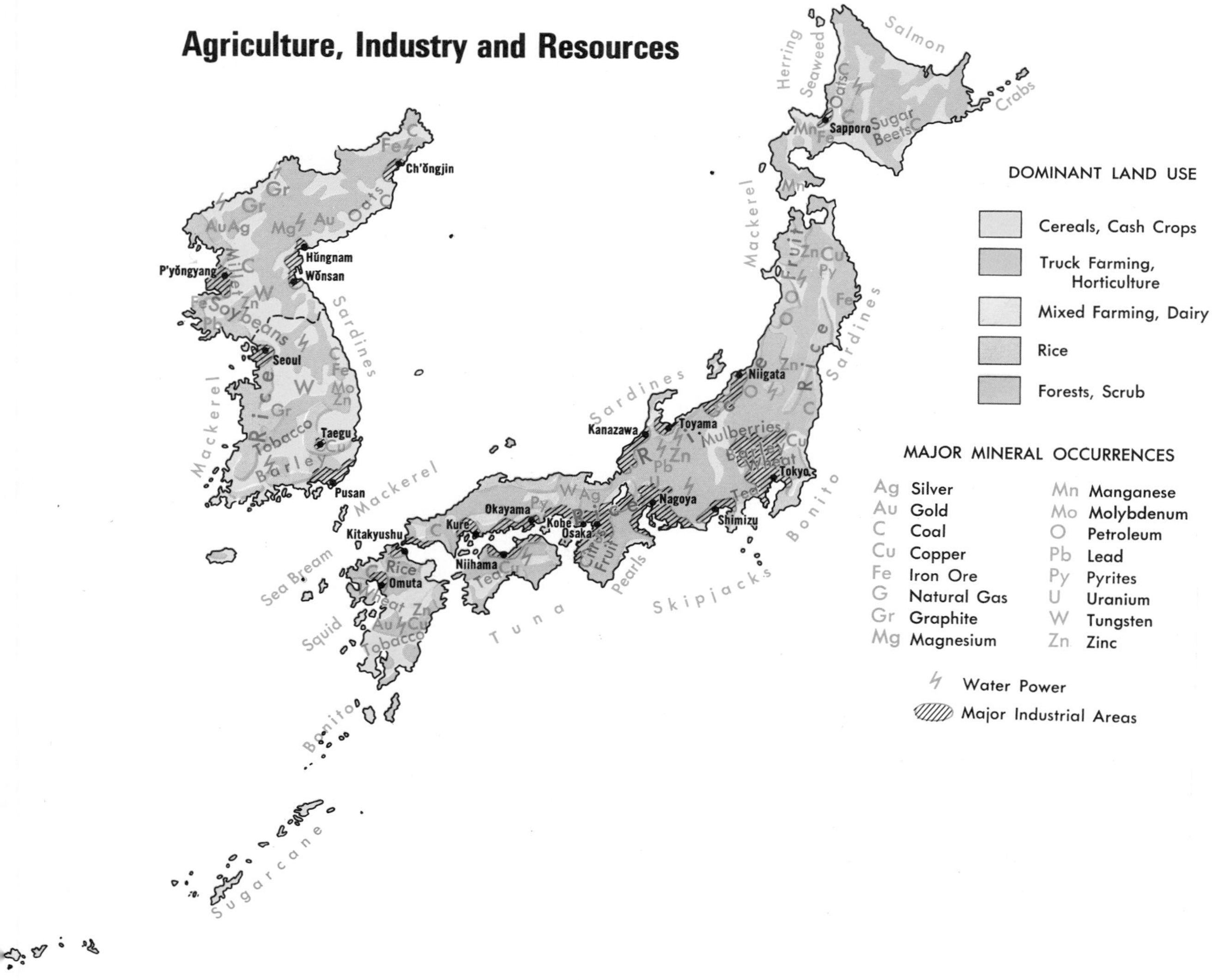
Ch'ŏngjin
P'yŏngyang
Hŭngnam
Wŏnsan
Seoul
Taegu
Pusan
Sapporo
Niigata
Kanazawa
Toyama
Tokyo
Nagoya
Shimizu
Okayama
Kure
Kobe
Osaka
Kitakyushu
Niihama
Omuta
Herring
Seaweed
Salmon
Crabs
Oats
Sugar Beets
Mackerel
Sardines
Fruit
Rice
Millet
Soybeans
Tobacco
Barley
Mulberries
Wheat
Tea
Citrus Fruit
Pearls
Bonito
Skipjacks
Tuna
Sea Bream
Squid
Sugarcane
DOMINANT LAND USE
Cereals, Cash Crops
Truck Farming, Horticulture
Mixed Farming, Dairy
Rice
Forests, Scrub
MAJOR MINERAL OCCURRENCES
Ag Silver
Au Gold
C Coal
Cu Copper
Fe Iron Ore
G Natural Gas
Gr Graphite
Mg Magnesium
Mn Manganese
Mo Molybdenum
O Petroleum
Pb Lead
Py Pyrites
U Uranium
W Tungsten
Zn Zinc
Water Power
Major Industrial Areas

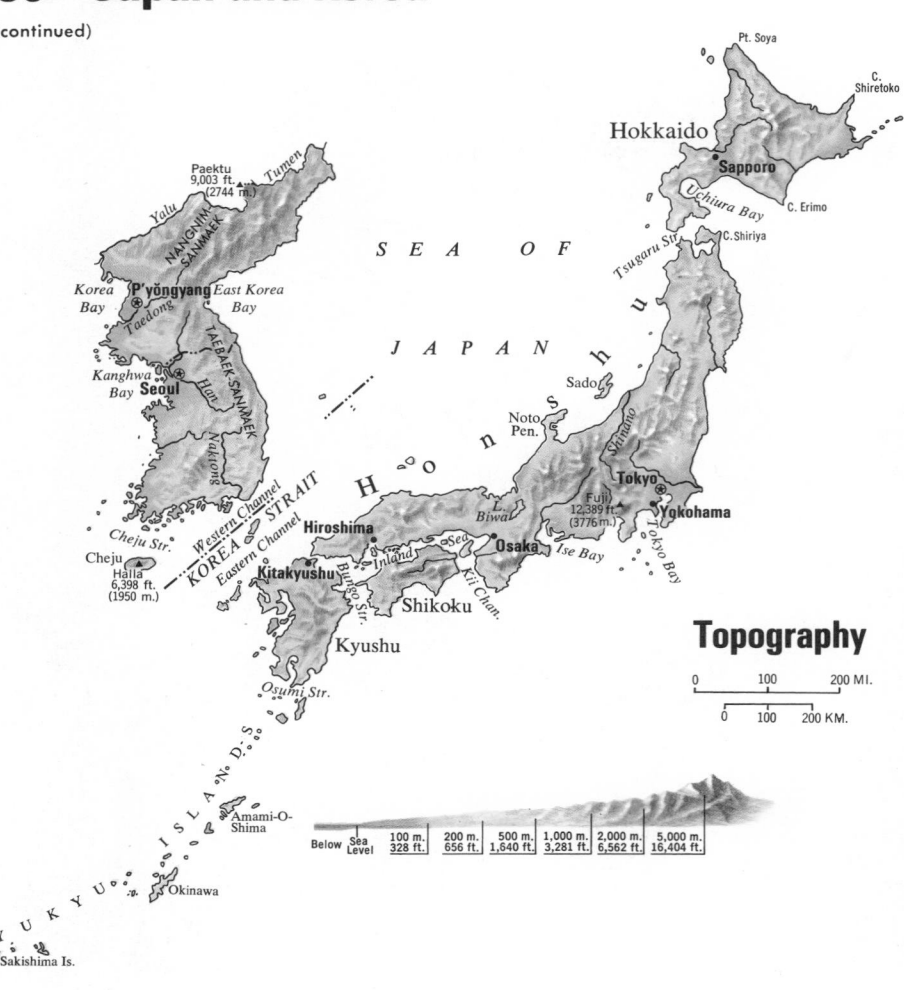

Topography

JAPAN is divided into prefectures bearing the same names as their capitals except:

Prefecture	Capital	Ref.
AICHI	NAGOYA	H 6
EHIME	MATSUYAMA	F 7
GUMMA	MAEBASHI	J 5
HOKKAIDO	SAPPORO	K 2
HYOGO	KOBE	H 7
IBARAKI	MITO	K 5
ISHIKAWA	KANAZAWA	H 5
IWATE	MORIOKA	K 4
KAGAWA	TAKAMATSU	G 6
KANAGAWA	YOKOHAMA	O 3
MIE	TSU	H 6
MIYAGI	SENDAI	K 4
OKINAWA	NAHA	N 6
SAITAMA	URAWA	O 2
SHIGA	OTSU	J 7
SHIMANE	MATSUE	F 6
TOCHIGI	UTSUNOMIYA	K 5
YAMANASHI	KOFU	J 6

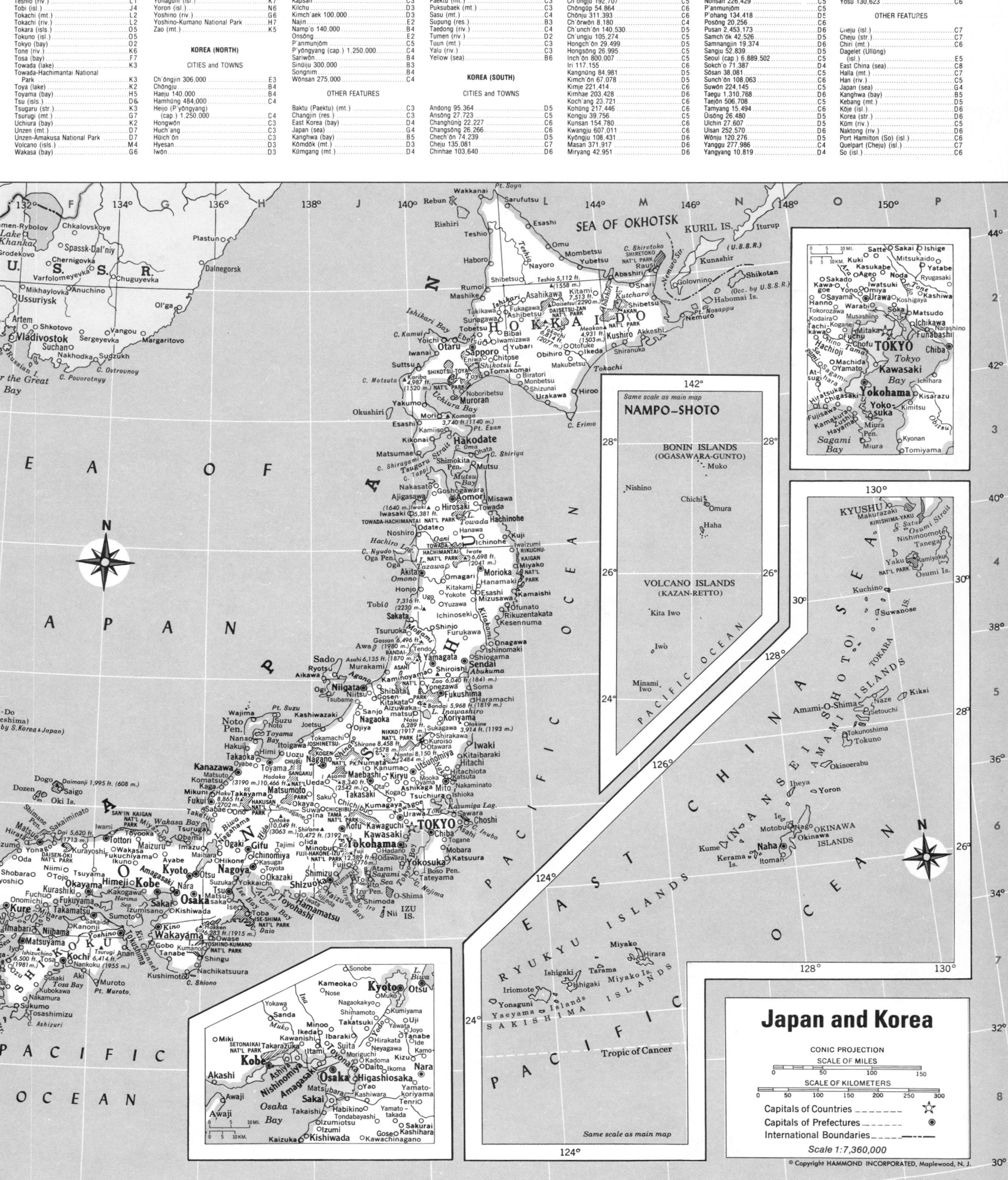

Japan and Korea

CONIC PROJECTION

SCALE OF MILES

SCALE OF KILOMETERS

Capitals of Countries
Capitals of Prefectures
International Boundaries

Scale 1:7,360,000

© Copyright HAMMOND INCORPORATED, Maplewood, N.J.

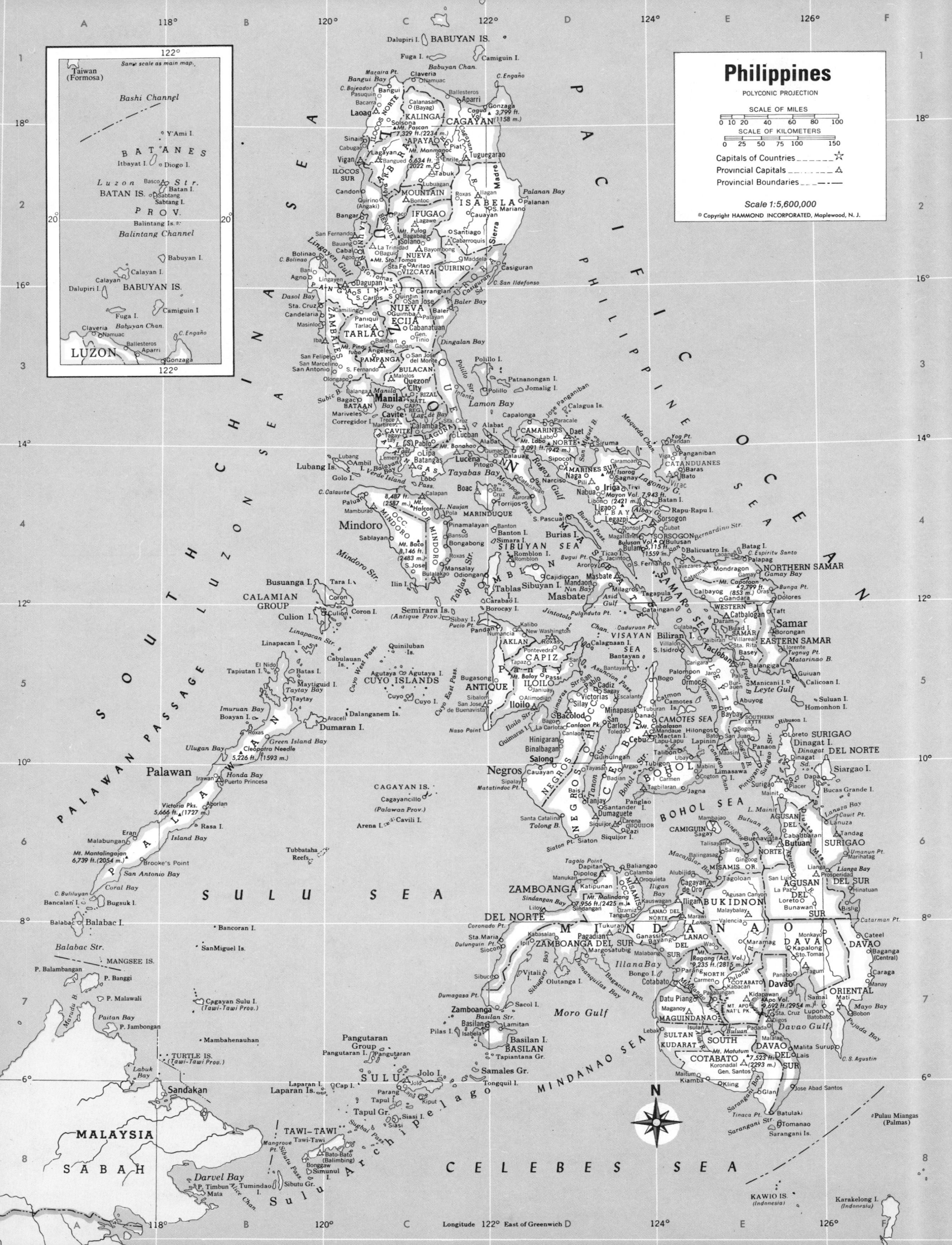

Philippines

POLYCONIC PROJECTION

SCALE OF MILES

0 10 20 40 60 80 100

SCALE OF KILOMETERS

0 25 50 75 100 150

Capitals of Countries _____ ☆
Provincial Capitals _____ △
Provincial Boundaries _____

Scale 1:5,600,000

© Copyright HAMMOND INCORPORATED, Maplewood, N.J.

Philippines 83

PROVINCES

Abra 160,198 . . . . C2
Agusan del Norte 365,421 . . E6
Agusan del Sur 631,634 . . . . E6
Aklan 324,563 . . . . D5
Albay 809,177 . . . . D4
Antique 344,879 . . . . D5
Aurora 107,145 . . . . C3
Basilan 201,407 . . . . D7
Bataan 323,254 . . . . C3
Batanes 12,091 . . . . A2
Batangas 1,174,201 . . . . C4
Benguet 354,751 . . . . C2
Bohol 806,031 . . . . E6
Bukidnon 631,634 . . . . E6
Bulacan 1,098,046 . . . . C3
Cagayan 711,476 . . . . C1
Camarines Norte 368,007 . . . D3
Camarines Sur 1,099,346 . . D4
Camiguin 57,126 . . . . E6
Capiz 492,231 . . . . D5
Catanduanes 175,247 . . . . . . E4
Cavite 771,320 . . . . C3
Cebu 2,091,602 . . . . D5
Davao 725,153 . . . . E7
Davao del Sur 1,133,599 . . . E7
Davao Oriental 339,931 . . . . . F7
Eastern Samar 320,637 . . . . E5
Ifugao 111,368 . . . . C2
Ilocos Norte 390,666 . . . . . . C1
Ilocos Sur 443,591 . . . . C2
Iloilo 1,433,641 . . . . D5
Isabela 870,604 . . . . C2
Kalinga-Apayao 185,063 . . . . C1
Laguna 973,104 . . . . C3
Lanao del Norte 461,049 . . . E6
Lanao del Sur 404,971 . . . . . E7
La Union 452,578 . . . . C2
Leyte 1,302,648 . . . . E5
Maguindanao 536,546 . . . . . E7
Manila 5,925,884 . . . . C3
Marinduque 173,715 . . . . . . C4
Masbate 584,526 . . . . D4
Misamis Occidental 386,328 D6
Misamis Oriental 690,032 . . . E6
Mountain 103,052 . . . . C2
National Capital Region (Manila) 5,925,884 . . . . . . C3
Negros Occidental 1,930,301 . . . . D6
Negros Oriental 819,399 . . . D6
North Cotabato 564,599 . . . . E7
Northern Samar 378,516 . . . E4
Nueva Ecija 1,069,409 . . . . . C3
Nueva Vizcaya 241,690 . . . . . C2
Occidental Mindoro 222,431 C4
Oriental Mindoro 448,938 . . . C4
Palawan 371,782 . . . . B6
Pampanga 1,181,590 . . . . C3
Pangasinan 1,636,057 . . . . . C3
Quezon 1,129,277 . . . . C3
Quirino 83,230 . . . . C2
Rizal 555,533 . . . . C3
Romblon 193,174 . . . . D4
Siquijor 70,300 . . . . D6
Sorsogon 500,685 . . . . E4
South Cotabato 770,473 . . . . E7
Southern Leyte 298,294 . . . . E5
Sultan Kudarat 303,784 . . . . E7
Sulu 360,588 . . . . C7
Surigao del Norte 363,414 . . F5
Surigao del Sur 377,647 . . . . F6
Tarlac 638,457 . . . . C3
Tawi-Tawi 194,651 . . . . B8
Western Samar 501,439 . . . . E5
Zambales 444,037 . . . . C3
Zamboanga del Norte 588,015 . . . . D6
Zamboanga del Sur 1,183,845 . . . . D7

CITIES and TOWNS

Angeles 188,834 . . . . C3
Aparri 45,070 . . . . C1
Bacolod 262,415 . . . . D5
Bagac 13,109 . . . . C3
Bago 99,631 . . . . D5
Baguio 119,009 . . . . C2
Balanga 39,132 . . . . C3
Baler 18,349 . . . . C3
Balimbing (Bato-Bato) 22,189 . . . . C8
Bamban 26,072 . . . . C3
Basco 4,341 . . . . A2
Batangas 143,570 . . . . C4
Bato-Bato 22,189 . . . . C8
Baybay 74,640 . . . . E5
Bislig 81,615 . . . . F6
Boac 37,005 . . . . C4
Bontoc 17,091 . . . . C2
Burauen 48,058 . . . . E5
Butuan 172,489 . . . . E6
Cabanatuan 138,298 . . . . C3
Cabarroquis 17,450 . . . . C2
Cadiz 129,632 . . . . D5
Cagayan de Oro 227,312 . . . E6
Calamba 121,175 . . . . C3
Calbayog 106,719 . . . . E4
Carigara 34,377 . . . . E5
Cauayan 70,017 . . . . D6
Cavite 87,666 . . . . C3
Cebu 490,281 . . . . D5
Cotabato 83,871 . . . . D7
Dagupan 98,344 . . . . C2
Davao 610,375 . . . . E7
Digos 70,065 . . . . E7
Escalante 71,293 . . . . D5
General Santos 149,396 . . . . E7
Gingoog 79,937 . . . . E6
Guihulngan 84,156 . . . . D5
Guimba 58,847 . . . . C3
Iba 22,791 . . . . B3
Ilagan 79,336 . . . . C2
Iligan 167,358 . . . . E6
Iloilo 244,827 . . . . D5
Infanta 27,914 . . . . C3
Jaro 29,739 . . . . E5
Jolo 52,429 . . . . C8
Koronadal 80,566 . . . . E7
Lagawe 15,075 . . . . C2
Lapu-Lapu 98,723 . . . . E5
Legazpi 99,766 . . . . D4
Ligao 69,860 . . . . D4
Lingayen 65,187 . . . . C2
Lipa 121,166 . . . . C4
Lucena 107,880 . . . . C4
Maganoy 45,845 . . . . E7
Mainit 18,078 . . . . E6
Malabang 18,955 . . . . D7
Malolos 95,699 . . . . C3
Mandaue 110,590 . . . . E5
Manila (cap.) 1,630,485 . . . . C3
Mariveles 48,594 . . . . C3
Mati 78,178 . . . . F7
Naga 90,712 . . . . D4
Olongapo 156,430 . . . . C3
Ormoc 104,978 . . . . E5
Ozamiz 77,832 . . . . D6
Pagadian 80,861 . . . . D7
Palo 31,124 . . . . E5
Palompon 40,242 . . . . E5
Panabo 71,098 . . . . E7
Prosperidad 33,824 . . . . F6
Puerto Princesa 60,234 . . . . B6
Quezon City 1,165,865 . . . . . C3
Romblon 24,251 . . . . D4
Roxas 81,183 . . . . D5
Sagay 99,118 . . . . D5
San Antonio 42,969 . . . . B3
San Carlos, Negros Occ. 91,627 . . . . D5
San Carlos, Pangasinan 101,243 . . . . C3
San Fernando, La Union 68,410 . . . . C2
San Fernando, Pampanga 110,891 . . . . C3
San Jose 64,254 . . . . C3
San Jose del Monte 90,732 . C3
San Pablo 131,655 . . . . C3
Santa Fe 6,338 . . . . C2
Santiago 69,877 . . . . C2
Silay 111,131 . . . . D5
Siquijor 17,533 . . . . D6
Surigao 79,745 . . . . E6
Tacloban 102,523 . . . . E5
Tagaytay 16,322 . . . . C3
Tagum 86,201 . . . . E7
Tarlac 175,691 . . . . C3
Toledo 91,668 . . . . D5
Tuguegarao 73,507 . . . . C2
Zamboanga 343,722 . . . . C7

OTHER FEATURES

Agusan (riv.) E6
Alabat (isl.) D3
Apo (vol.) E7
Babuyan (isl.) B2
Balabac (isl.) A7
Balayan (bay) C4
Balintang (chan.) A2
Baloy (mt.) D5
Bantayan (isl.) D5
Banton (isl.) D4
Bashi (chan.) A1
Basilan (isl.) D7
Batan, Albay (isl.) E4
Batan, Batanes (isl.) B2
Batan (isls.) A2
Bay, Laguna de (lake) C3
Biliran (isl.) E5
Bohol (isl.) E6
Bojeador (cape) C1
Borocay (isl.) D5
Bucas Grande (isl.) F6
Bugsuk (isl.) A6
Buliluyan (cape) A6
Bunga (pt.) E4
Burias (isl.) D4
Busuanga (isl.) B4
Cabalasan (mt.) E5
Cabulauan (isls.) C5
Cagayan (isls.) C6
Cagayan (riv.) C2
Cagayan Sulu (isl.) B7
Cagua (vol.) D1
Calagua (isls.) D3
Calamian Group (isls.) B4
Calayan (isl.) A2
Calicoan (isl.) E5
Camiguin, Cagayan (isl.) . . . B3
Camiguin, Camiguin (isl.) . . . E6
Camotes (isls.) E5
Camotes (sea) E5
Canigao (chan.) E5
Canlaon (peak) D5
Capotoan (mt.) E4
Carabao (isl.) D4
Catanduanes (isl.) E4
Cebu (isl.) D5
Celebes (sea) D8
Cleopatra Needle (mt.) B5
Coron (isl.) C5

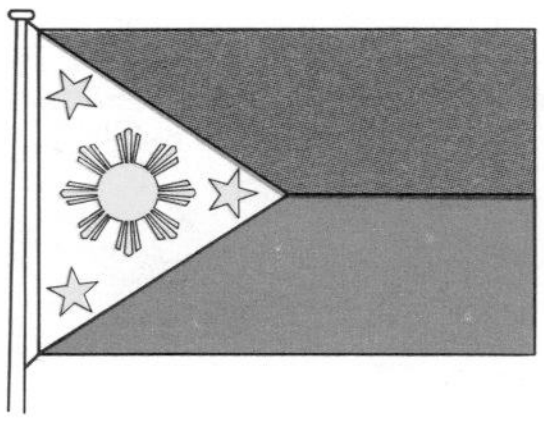

AREA 115,707 sq. mi. (299,681 sq. km.)
POPULATION 48,098,460
CAPITAL Manila
LARGEST CITY Manila
HIGHEST POINT Apo 9,692 ft. (2,954 m.)
MONETARY UNIT piso
MAJOR LANGUAGES Pilipino (Tagalog), English, Spanish, Bisayan, Ilocano, Bikol
MAJOR RELIGIONS Roman Catholicism, Islam, Protestantism, tribal religions

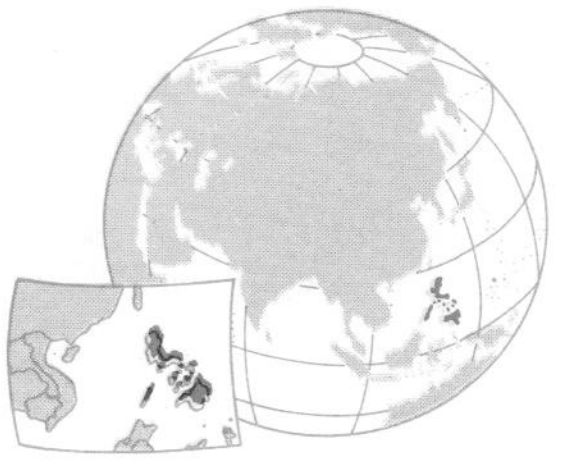

Topography

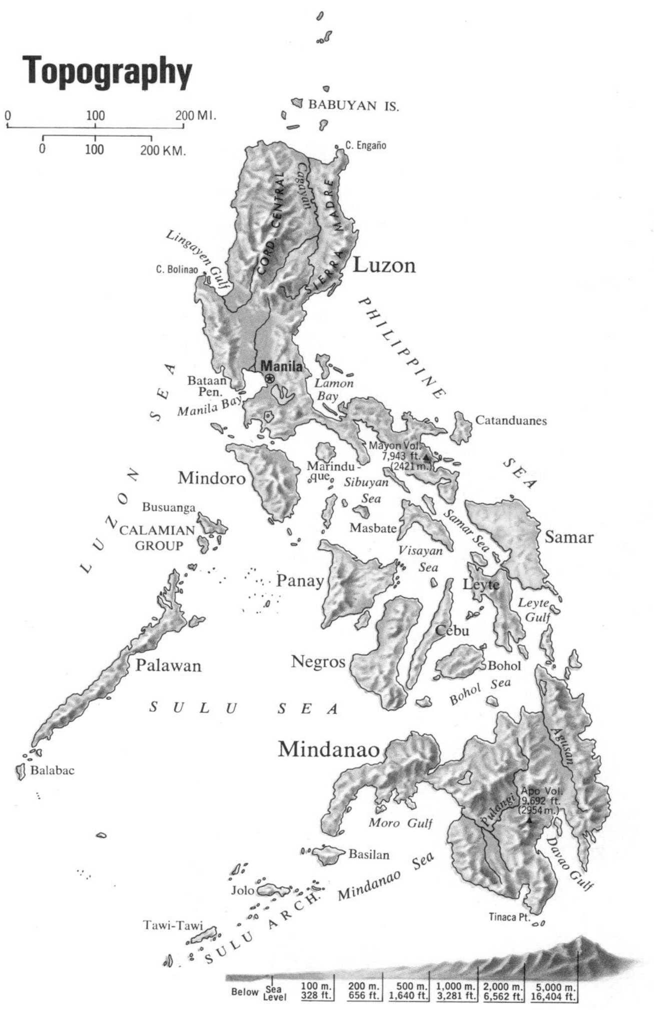

0
100
200 MI.
0
100
200 KM.
BABUYAN IS.
C. Engaño
CORD. CENTRAL
SIERRA MADRE
Lingayen Gulf
C. Bolinao
Luzon
PHILIPPINE
Bataan Pen.
Manila
Manila Bay
Lamon Bay
Catanduanes
Mayon Vol. 7,943 ft. (2421 m.)
Marinduque
Sibuyan Sea
Mindoro
Masbate
Samar Sea
Samar
Busuanga
CALAMIAN GROUP
LUZON
SEA
Visayan Sea
Panay
Leyte
Leyte Gulf
Cebu
Negros
Palawan
Bohol
Bohol Sea
S U L U S E A
Mindanao
Agusan
Pulangi
Apo Vol. 9,692 ft. (2954 m.)
Balabac
Moro Gulf
Davao Gulf
Basilan
Jolo
Mindanao Sea
SULU ARCH.
Tawi-Tawi
Tinaca Pt.
Below
Sea Level
100 m. 328 ft.
200 m. 656 ft.
500 m. 1,640 ft.
1,000 m. 3,281 ft.
2,000 m. 6,562 ft.
5,000 m. 16,404 ft.

Agriculture, Industry and Resources

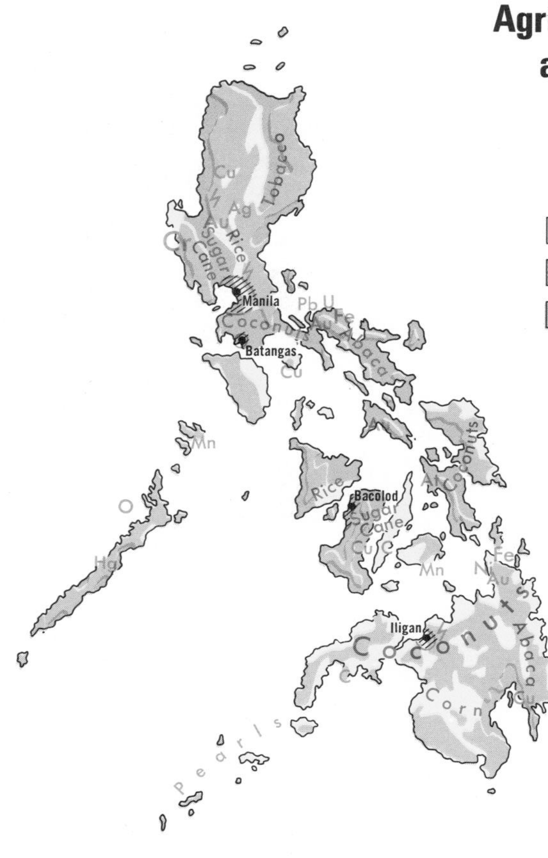

Cu
Tobacco
Ag
Rice
Sugar Cane
Manila
Pb
Fe
Batangas
Cu
Mn
O
Hg
Rice
Bacolod
Sugar Cane
Cu
Mn
Ni
Fe
Au
Iligan
Coconuts
Abaca
Corn
Pearls

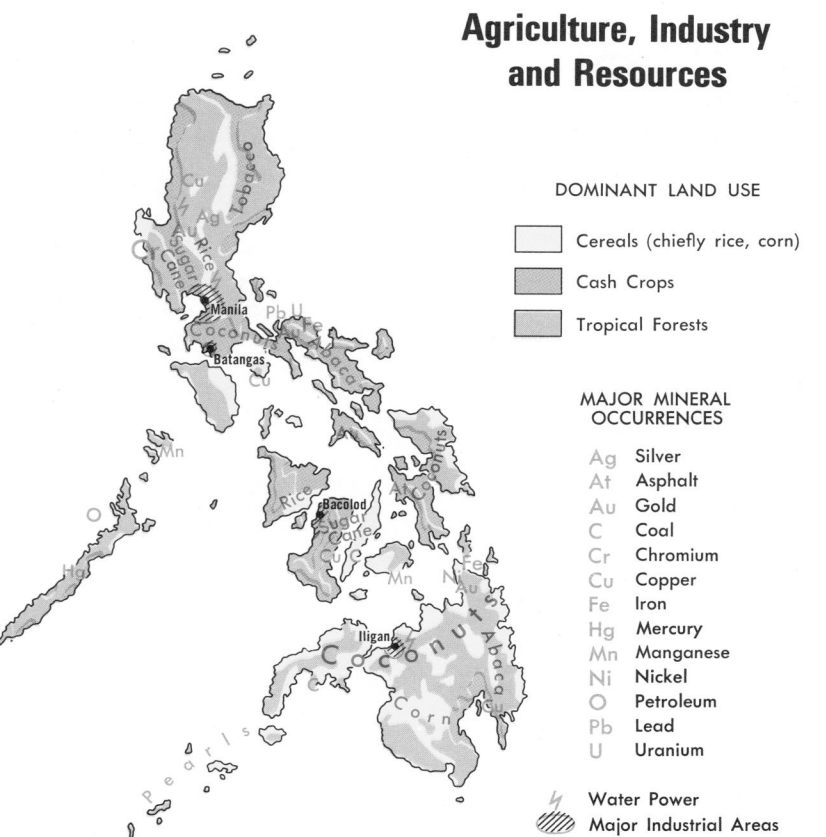

DOMINANT LAND USE

- Cereals (chiefly rice, corn)
- Cash Crops
- Tropical Forests

MAJOR MINERAL OCCURRENCES

- Ag Silver
- At Asphalt
- Au Gold
- C Coal
- Cr Chromium
- Cu Copper
- Fe Iron
- Hg Mercury
- Mn Manganese
- Ni Nickel
- O Petroleum
- Pb Lead
- U Uranium

- Water Power
- Major Industrial Areas

Corregidor (isl.) C3
Culion (isl.) B5
Cuyo (isl.) C5
Cuyo (isls.) C5
Daram (isl.) E5
Davao (gulf) E7
Dinagat (isl.) E5
Diuata (mts.) E6
Dumanquilas (bay) D7
Dumaran (isl.) C5
Engaño (cape) D1
Espiritu Santo (cape) E4
Fuga (isl.) A3
Guimaras (isl.) D5
Halcon (mt.) C4
Hibuson (isl.) E5
Homonhon (isl.) E5
Honda (bay) B6
Iligan (bay) E6
Ilin (isl.) C4
Illana (bay) D7
Imuruan (bay) B5
Island (bay) B6
Itbayat (isl.) A2
Jintotolo (chan.) D5
Jolo (isl.) C7
Jomalig (isl.) D3
Lagonoy (gulf) E4
Lamon (bay) C3
Lanao (lake) E7
Laparan (isls.) B8
Lapinin (isl.) E5
Leyte (gulf) E5
Leyte (isl.) E5
Limasawa (isl.) E6
Linapacan (isl.) B5
Lingayen (gulf) C2
Lubang (isls.) B4
Luzon (isl.) C3
Luzon (str.) A2
Macajalar (bay) E6
Malindang (mt.) D6
Mangsee (isls.) A7
Manila (bay) C3
Mantalingajan (mt.) A6
Maqueda (chan.) D3
Maraira (pt.) C1
Marinduque (isl.) C4
Masbate (isl.) D4
Mayon (vol.) D4
Maytiguid (isl.) B5
Mindanao (isl.) D7
Mindanao (riv.) E7
Mindoro (isl.) C4
Mindoro (str.) C4
Mompog (passg.) D4
Moro (gulf) D7
Mount Apo National Park . . . E7
Naso (pt.) C5
Negros (isl.) D6
Olutanga (isl.) D7
Pacsan (mt.) C2
Palawan (isl.) B6
Palawan (passg.) A6
Panaon (isl.) E5
Panay (isl.) D5
Panglao (isl.) D6
Pangutaran (isl.) C7
Pangutaran Group (isls.) . . . C7
Patnanongan (isl.) D3
Philippine (sea) D3
Pilas (isl.) C7
Pinatubo (mt.) C3
Polillo (isl.) C3
Pujada (bay) F7
Pulangi (riv.) E7
Ragang (vol.) E7
Ragay (gulf) D4
Rapu-Rapu (isl.) E4
Romblon (isl.) D4
Sabtang (isl.) B2
Sacol (isl.) D7
Samal (isl.) E7
Samales Group (isls.) D7
Samar (isl.) E5
Samar (sea) E4
San Agustin (cape) F7
San Bernardino (str.) E4
San Miguel (bay) D3
San Pedro (bay) E5
Santo Tomas (mt.) C2
Semirara (isls.) C5
Siargao (isl.) F6
Sibay (isl.) C5
Sibuguey (bay) D7
Sibutu Group (isls.) B8
Sibuyan (isl.) D4
Sibuyan (sea) D4
Sierra Madre (mt.) D2
Simunul (isl.) B8
Siquijor (isl.) D6
South China (sea) B3
Subic (bay) C3
Sulu (arch.) B8
Sulu (sea) B6
Suluan (isl.) F5
Surigao (str.) E6
Taal (lake) C4
Tablas (isl.) D4
Tablas (str.) C4
Tagapula (isl.) E4
Tagolo (pt.) D6
Tanon (str.) D6
Tapul (isl.) C8
Tapul Group (isls.) C8
Tara (isl.) C4
Tawi-Tawi (isl.) B8
Tayabas (bay) C4
Ticao (isl.) D4
Tinaca (pt.) E8
Tongquil (isl.) D8
Tumindao (isl.) B8
Turtle (isls.) B7
Verde Island (passg.) C4
Victoria (peaks) B6
Visayan (sea) D5

BRUNEI

CITIES and TOWNS

Bandar Seri Begawan 63,868 E4
Seria 23,511 E5

INDONESIA

CITIES and TOWNS

Adaut J7
Agats K7
Ambon (Amboina) 208,898 H6
Amuntai F6
Amurang G5
Atambua G7
Baa G8
Bagansiapiapi C5
Balikpapan 280,675 F6
Banda Aceh 72,090 A4
Bandanaira H6
Bandung 1,462,637 H2
Banggai G6
Banjarmasin 381,286 E6
Banyumas J2
Batang J2
Batavia (Jakarta) (cap.) 6,503,449 H1
Bekasi H2
Belawan B5
Bengkulu 64,783 C6
Beo H5
Biak K6
Binjai 76,464 B5
Bintuhan C6
Blitar 78,503 K2
Bogor 247,409 H2
Bojonegoro J2
Bukittinggi 70,771 B6
Bula J6
Bulukumba G7
Buntok F6
Cianjur H2
Cimahi H2
Cirebon 223,776 H2
Demta L6
Denpasar E7
Dili H7
Djambi (Jambi) 230,373 C6
Djokjakarta (Yogyakarta) 398,727 J2
Dobo J7
Donggala F6
Enaratoli K6
Ende G7
Fakfak J6
Garut H2
Gorontalo 97,628 G5
Hollandia (Jayapura) K6
Indramayu H2
Jailolo H5
Jakarta (cap.) 6,503,449 H1
Jambi 230,373 C6
Jayapura (Hollandia) K6
Jogjakarta (Yogyakarta) 398,727 J2
Jombang K2
Kaimana J6
Kampung Baru (Tolitoli) G5
Kediri 221,830 K2
Kendari G6
Kepi K7
Ketapang E6
Kokonau K6
Kolonodale G6
Kotabaharu E6
Kotabaru F6
Kotawaringin E6
Kragen K2
Kupang G8
Kutaraja (Banda Aceh) 72,090 A4
Labuha H6
Labuhan G2
Laiwui H6
Larantuka G7
Lekitobi G6
Longiram F5
Madiun 150,562 K2
Magelang 123,484 J2
Majalengka H2
Makassar (Ujung Pandang) 709,038 F7
Malang 511,780 K2
Malili G6
Manado 217,159 G5
Manokwari J6
Maumere G7
Medan 1,378,955 B5
Menggala D6
Merauke K7
Mindiptana L7
Mojokerto 68,849 K2
Muarasiberut B6
Nangatayap E6
Pacitan J2
Padang 480,922 B6
Padangpanjang 34,517 B6
Padangsidempuan B5
Pakanbaru 186,262 C5
Palangkaraya 60,447 E6
Palembang 787,187 D6
Pangkalanbuun E6
Pangkalpinang 90,096 D6
Parepare 86,450 F6
Pasangkayu F6
Pasuruan 95,864 K2
Payakumbuh 78,836 C6
Pekalongan 132,558 J2
Pemalang J2
Pematangsiantar 150,376 B5
Pinrang F6
Plaju D6
Pontianak 304,778 D6
Probolinggo 100,296 K2
Purbolinggo J2
Raha G6
Rantauprapat C5
Rembang K2
Sabang, Celebes F5
Sabang, Weh 23,821 B4
Salatiga 85,849 J2
Samarinda 264,718 F6
Sampit E6
Sarmi K6
Sawahlunto 13,561 C6
Seba G8
Semarang 1,026,671 J2
Semitau E5
Serui K6
Sibolga 59,897 B5
Sigli B4
Sinabang B5
Singaraja F7
Solo (Surakarta) 469,888 J2
Solok 31,724 C6
Sorong J6
Sragen J2
Subang H2
Sukabumi 109,994 H2
Sumbawa Besar F7
Sumedang H2
Surabaya 2,027,913 K2
Surakarta 469,888 J2
Tanahmerah K7
Tanjungbalai 41,894 C5
Tanjungkarang 284,275 D7
Tanjungpinang C5
Tanjungselor F5
Tarakan F5
Tebingtinggi 92,087 B5
Tegal 131,728 J2
Telukbayur C6
Tepa H7
Terempa D5
Tjilatjap (Cilicap) H2
Tjirebon (Cirebon) 223,776 H2
Tolitoli G5
Tuban K2
Ujung Pandang 709,038 F7
Vila Arminda Monteiro H7
Vila Salazar H7
Viquique H7
Wahai H6
Waigama H6
Wajabula H5
Waren K6
Weda H5
Wonreli H7
Yogyakarta 398,727 J2

OTHER FEATURES

Anambas (isls.) 29,572 D5
Arafura (sea) J8
Aru (isls.) 34,195 K7
Babar (isl.) H7
Bali (isl.) 2,074,438 F7
Banda (sea) H7
Banggai (arch.) 169,025 G6
Bangka (isl.) 298,017 D6
Banyak (isls.) 1,980 B5
Barisan (mts.) C6
Barito (riv.) E6
Batu (isls.) 16,390 B6
Bawean (isl.) 64,551 K1
Belitung (Billiton) (isl.) 128,694 D6
Berau (bay) J6
Biak (isl.) K6
Billiton (isl.) 128,694 D6
Binongko (isl.) 11,549 G7
Bone (gulf) G7
Borneo (isl.) E5
Bosch, van den (cape) J6
Bunguran (Great Natuna) (isl.) D5
Buru (isl.) 23,034 H6
Butung (isl.) 188,173 G6
Celebes (Sulawesi) (isl.) 7,732,383 G5
Celebes (sea) G5
Cenderawasih (bay) K6
Dampier (str.) J6
Digul (riv.) K7
Doberai (pen.) J6
Enggano (isl.) 1,082 C7
Ewab (Kai) (isls.) 108,328 J7
Flores (isl.) 860,328 G7
Flores (sea) F7
Frederik Hendrik (Kolepom) (isl.) K7
Geelvink (Cenderawasih) (bay) K6
Great Kai (isl.) 38,748 J7
Halmahera (isl.) 122,521 H5
Irian Jaya (reg.) 923,440 J6
Jambuair (cape) B4
Jamursba (cape) J5
Java (head) C7
Java (isl.) 73,712,411 J2
Java (sea) D6
Jaya, Puncak (mt.) K6
Jayawijaya (range) K6
Jemaja (isl.) 5,628 D5
Kabaena (isl.) G7
Kai (isls.) 108,328 J7
Kalao (isl.) G7
Kalaotoa (isl.) G5
Kalimantan (reg.) 4,956,865 E5
Kangean (isl.) F7
Kapuas (riv.) D6
Karakelong (isl.) H5
Karimata (arch.) 9,398 D6
Karimunjawa (isls.) 5,025 J1
Kerinci (mt.) C6
Kisar (isl.) H7
Komodo (isl.) 30,407 F7
Krakatau (Rakata) (isl.) C7
Laut (isl.) 55,711 F6
Leuser (mt.) B5
Lingga (arch.) 46,658 D5
Lingga (isl.) 18,027 D6
Lombok (isl.) 1,581,193 F7
Madura (isl.) 1,509,774 K2
Mahakam (riv.) F6
Makassar (str.) F6
Malacca (str.) C5
Mamberamo (riv.) K6
Maoke (mts.) K6
Mapia (isls.) J5
Mentawai (isls.) 30,107 B6
Misool (isl.) J6
Molucca (sea) H6
Moluccas (isls.) 944,240 H6
Morotai (isl.) 27,333 H5
Muli (str.) K7
Müller (mts.) E5
Muna (isl.) 156,186 G7
Musi (riv.) C6
Natuna (isls.) 23,893 D5
Ngunju (cape) F8
Nias (isl.) 356,093 B5
Numfoor (isl.) J6
Obi (isls.) 12,437 H6
Ombai (str.) H7
Pantar (isl.) 28,259 G7
Perkam (cape) K6
Puting, Borneo (cape) E6
Puting, Sumatra (cape) C7
Raja Ampat Group (isls.) H6
Rakata (isl.) C7
Rantekombola (mt.) F6
Raya (mt.) E6
Riau (arch.) 483,230 C5
Rokan (riv.) C5
Roti (isl.) 76,270 G8
Salawati (isl.) J6
Sangihe (isl.) H5
Sangihe (isls.) 183,000 G5
Sawu (isls.) 51,002 G8
Sawu (sea) G7
Schouten (isls.) 110,148 K6
Schwaner (mts.) E6
Sebuku (bay) F5
Selatan (cape) E6
Selayar (isl.) 92,342 G7
Semeru (mt.) K2
Siau (isl.) 46,801 H5
Siberut (str.) B6
Simeulue (isl.) 29,147 A5
Singkep (isl.) 28,631 D6
Sipura (isl.) 6,051 B6
Slamet (mt.) J2
Sorikmerapi (mt.) B5
South Natuna (isls.) D5
Sudirman (range) K6
Sula (isls.) 36,922 H6
Sulawesi (isl.) 7,732,383 G6
Sumatra (isl.) 19,360,400 B5
Sumba (isl.) 291,190 F7
Sumba (str.) F7
Sumbawa (isl.) 621,140 F7
Sunda (str.) C7
Tahulandang (isl.) 21,493 H5
Talaud (isls.) 46,395 H5
Taliabu (isl.) 18,303 G6
Tambelan (isls.) 4,032 D5
Tanimbar (isls.) 55,405 J7
Tariku (riv.) K6
Tidore (isl.) 28,655 H5
Timor (reg.) 1,435,527 H7
Timor (sea) H7
Toba (lake) B5
Tolo (gulf) G6
Tomini (gulf) G6
Tukangbesi (isls.) 73,106 G7
Vals (cape) K7
Vogelkop (Doberai) (pen.) J6
Waigeo (isl.) J5
Wakde (isl.) K6
Wangiwangi (isl.) 28,469 G7
We (isl.) B4
Wetar (isl.) H7
Yapen (isl.) 50,888 K6

MALAYSIA

STATES

North Borneo (Sabah) 1,002,608 F3
Sarawak 1,294,753 E5

CITIES and TOWNS

Beaufort 2,709 F4
Bintulu 4,424 E5
Kabong E5
Kampong Sibuti E5
Kapit 1,929 E5
Keningau 2,037 F4
Kota Kinabalu 40,939 F4
Kuching 63,535 E5
Kudat 5,089 F4
Labuan 7,216 E4
Lahad Datu 5,169 F5
Lamag F4
Marudi 4,700 E5
Miri 35,702 E5
Mukah 1,717 E5

Topography

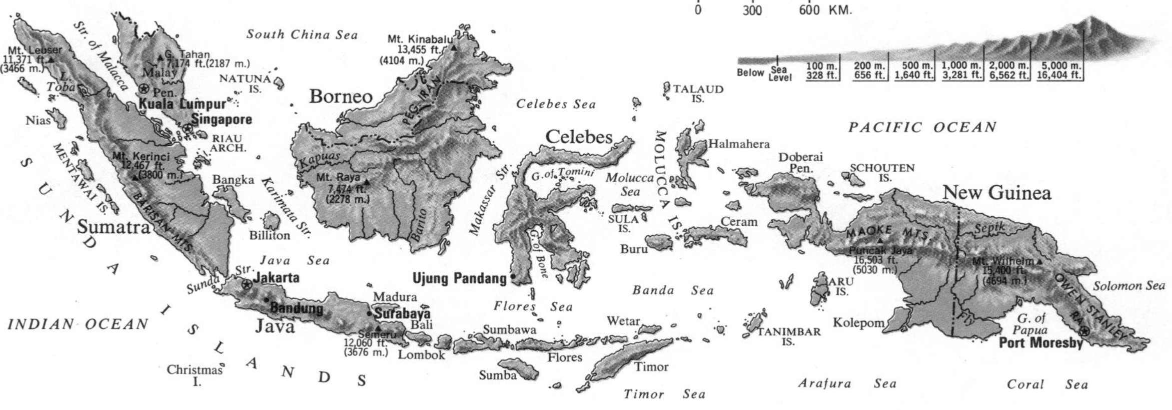

Agriculture, Industry and Resources

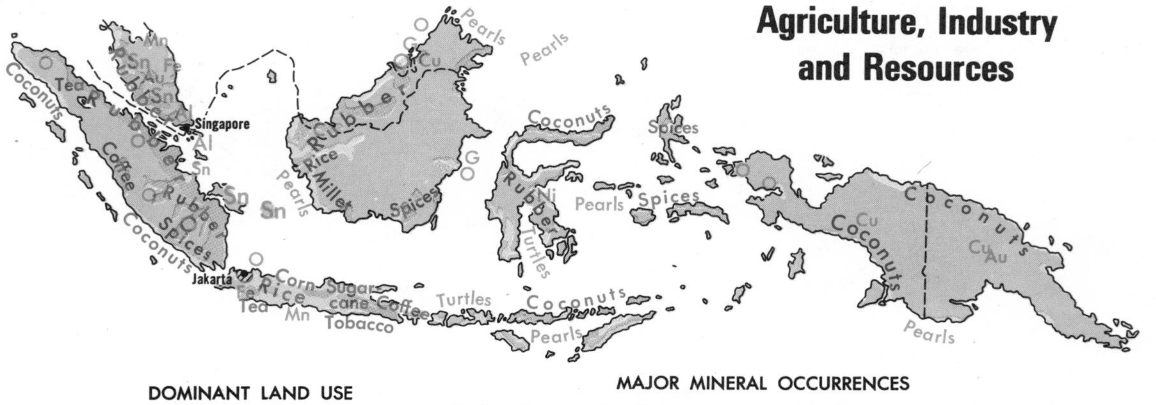

DOMINANT LAND USE

- Cereals (chiefly rice, corn)
- Diversified Tropical Crops
- Forests

MAJOR MINERAL OCCURRENCES

Al	Bauxite	Cu	Copper	Mn	Manganese	O	Petroleum
Au	Gold	Fe	Iron Ore	Ni	Nickel	Sn	Tin
C	Coal	G	Natural Gas				

Major Industrial Areas

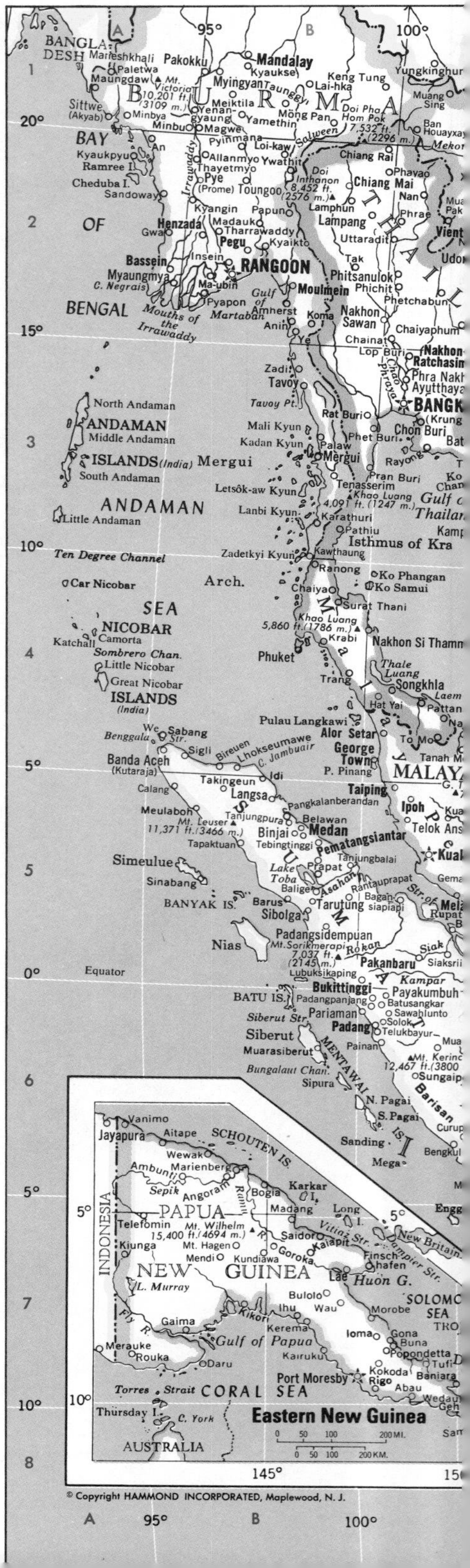

INDONESIA

AREA 788,430 sq. mi. (2,042,034 sq. km.)
POPULATION 147,490,298
CAPITAL Jakarta
LARGEST CITY Jakarta
HIGHEST POINT Puncak Jaya 16,503 ft. (5,030 m.)
MONETARY UNIT rupiah
MAJOR LANGUAGES Bahasa Indonesia, Indonesian and Papuan languages, English
MAJOR RELIGIONS Islam, tribal religions, Christianity, Hinduism

PAPUA NEW GUINEA

AREA 183,540 sq. mi. (475,369 sq. km.)
POPULATION 3,010,727
CAPITAL Port Moresby
LARGEST CITY Port Moresby
HIGHEST POINT Mt. Wilhelm 15,400 ft. (4,694 m.)
MONETARY UNIT kina
MAJOR LANGUAGES pidgin English, Hiri Motu, English
MAJOR RELIGIONS Tribal religions, Christianity

BRUNEI

AREA 2,226 sq. mi. (5,765 sq. km.)
POPULATION 192,832
CAPITAL Bandar Seri Begawan
LARGEST CITY Bandar Seri Begawan
HIGHEST POINT Pagon 6,070 ft. (1,850 m.)
MONETARY UNIT Brunei Dollar
MAJOR LANGUAGES Malay, English, Chinese
MAJOR RELIGIONS Islam, Buddhism, Christianity, tribal religions

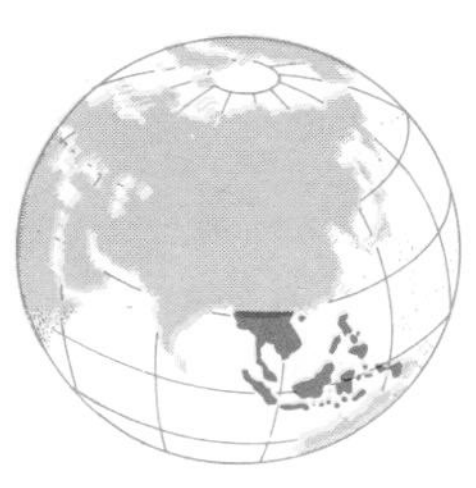

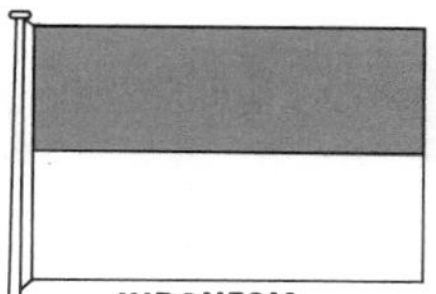

INDONESIA **PAPUA NEW GUINEA** **BRUNEI**

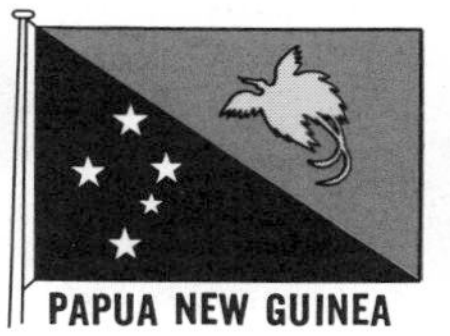

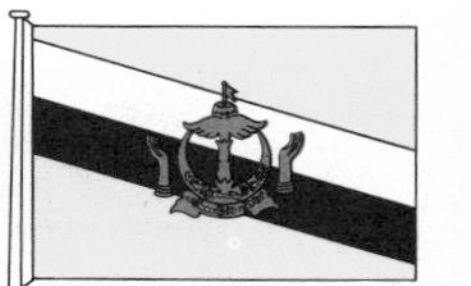

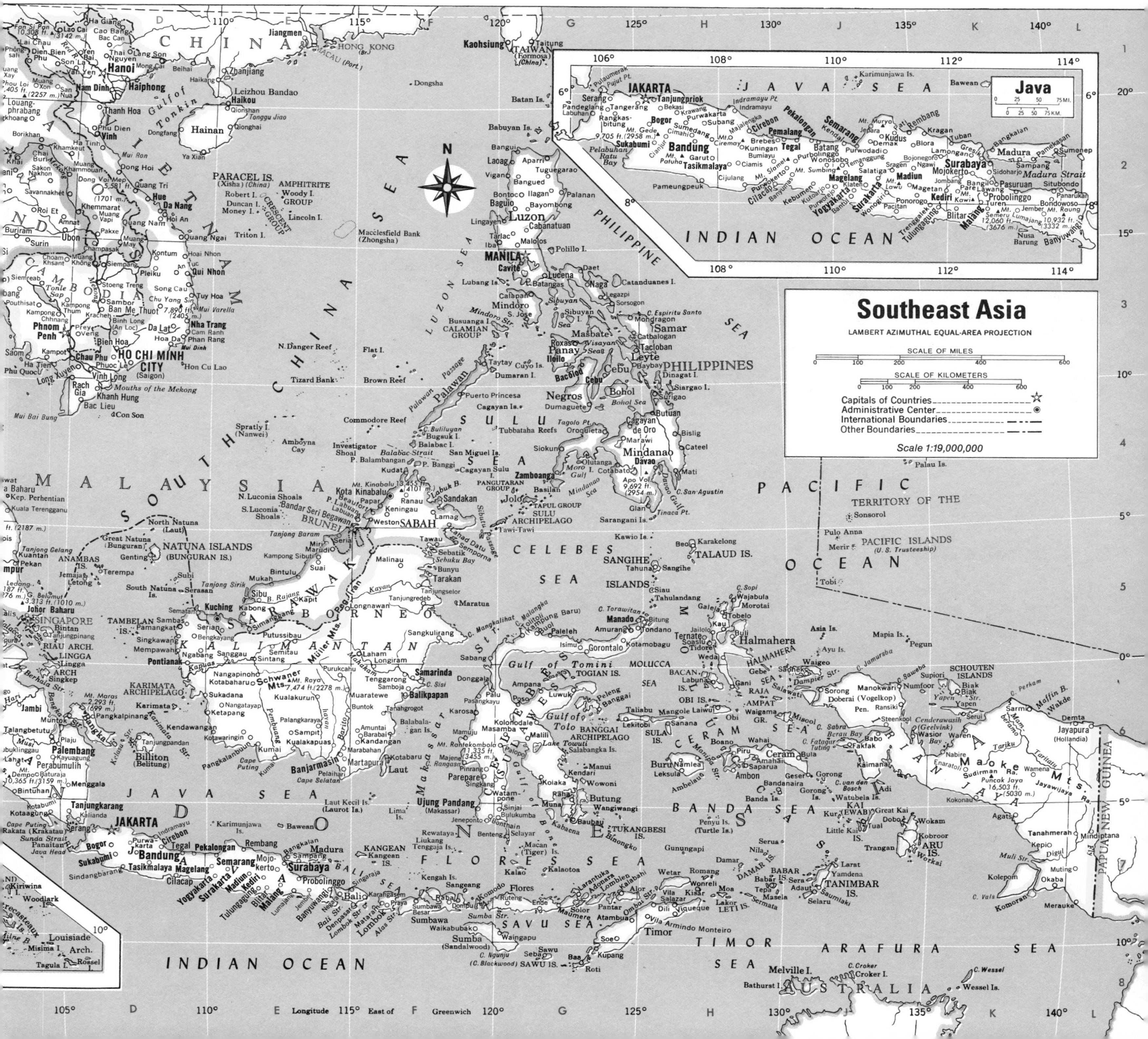

FIJI

AREA 7,055 sq. mi. (18,272 sq. km.)
POPULATION 588,068
CAPITAL Suva
LARGEST CITY Suva
HIGHEST POINT Tomaniivi 4,341 ft. (1,323 m.)
MONETARY UNIT Fijian dollar
MAJOR LANGUAGES Fijian, Hindi, English
MAJOR RELIGIONS Protestantism, Hinduism

KIRIBATI

AREA 291 sq. mi. (754 sq. km.)
POPULATION 56,213
CAPITAL Bairiki (Tarawa)
HIGHEST POINT (on Banaba I.) 285 ft. (87 m.)
MONETARY UNIT Australian dollar
MAJOR LANGUAGES I-Kiribati, English
MAJOR RELIGIONS Protestantism, Roman Catholicism

NAURU

AREA 7.7 sq. mi. (20 sq. km.)
POPULATION 7,254
CAPITAL Yaren (district)
MONETARY UNIT Australian dollar
MAJOR LANGUAGES Nauruan, English
MAJOR RELIGION Protestantism

SOLOMON ISLANDS

AREA 11,500 sq. mi. (29,785 sq. km.)
POPULATION 221,000
CAPITAL Honiara
HIGHEST POINT Mount Popomanatseu 7,647 ft. (2,331 m.)
MONETARY UNIT Solomon Islands dollar
MAJOR LANGUAGES English, pidgin English, Melanesian dialects
MAJOR RELIGIONS Tribal religions, Protestantism, Roman Catholicism

TONGA

AREA 270 sq. mi. (699 sq. km.)
POPULATION 90,128
CAPITAL Nuku'alofa
LARGEST CITY Nuku'alofa
HIGHEST POINT 3,389 ft. (1,033 m.)
MONETARY UNIT pa'anga
MAJOR LANGUAGES Tongan, English
MAJOR RELIGION Protestantism

TUVALU

AREA 9.78 sq. mi. (25.33 sq. km.)
POPULATION 7,349
CAPITAL Fongafale (Funafuti)
HIGHEST POINT 15 ft. (4.6 m.)
MONETARY UNIT Australian dollar
MAJOR LANGUAGES English, Tuvaluan
MAJOR RELIGION Protestantism

Abaiang (atoll) 3,296	H 5
Abemama (atoll) 2,300	H 5
Adamstown (cap.), Pitcairn Is. 54	N 8
Admiralty (isls.)	E 6
Agaña (cap.), Guam 896	E 4
Agrihan (isl.)	E 4
Ailinglapalap (atoll) 1,385	G 5
Ailuk (atoll) 413	H 4
Aitutaki (atoll) 2,348	K 7
Alofi (cap.), Niue 960	K 7
Alotau 4,310	E 7
Ambrym (isl.) 6,324	G 7
Anaa (atoll) 444	M 7
Angaur (isl.) 243	D 5
Apataki (atoll)	M 7
Apia (cap.), W. Samoa 33,100	J 7
Arno (atoll) 1,487	H 5
Arorae (atoll) 1,626	H 6
Atafu (atoll) 577	J 6
Atiu (isl.) 1,225	L 8
Austral (isls.) 5,208	L 8
Avarua (cap.), Cook Is.	L 8
Babelthuap (isl.) 10,391	D 5
Bairiki (cap.), Kiribati 1,777	H 5
Baker (isl.)	J 5
Banaba (isl.) 2,314	G 6
Banks (isls.) 3,158	G 7
Belau (Palau) 12,116	D 5
Belep (isls.) 624	G 7
Bellona (reefs)	G 8
Beru (atoll) 2,318	H 6
Bikini (atoll)	G 4
Bismarck (arch.) 218,339	E 6
Bonin (isls.) 1,879	E 3
Bora-Bora (isl.) 2,572	L 7
Bougainville (isl.) 71,761	F 6
Bounty (isls.)	H 10
Bourail 3,149	G 8
Butaritari (atoll) 2,971	H 5
Canton (isl.)	J 6
Capitol Hill (cap.), No. Marianas 592	E 4
Caroline (isl.)	M 7
Caroline (isls.)	E 5
Chichi (isl.) 1,879	E 3
Choiseul (isl.) 10,349	F 6
Christmas (Kiritmati) (isl.) 674	L 5
Cook (isls.) 17,695	K 7
Coral (sea)	F 6
Danger (Pukapuka) (atoll) 797	K 7
Daru 7,127	E 6
Disappointment (isls.) 373	N 7
Ducie (isl.)	O 8
Easter (isl.) 1,598	Q 8
Ebon (atoll) 887	G 5
Efate (isl.) 18,038	G 7
Enderbury (isl.)	J 6
Enewetak (Eniwetok) (atoll) 542	G 4
Erromanga (isl.) 945	H 7
Espiritu Santo (isl.) 16,220	G 7
Fais (isl.) 207	E 5
Fakaofo (atoll) 654	J 6
Fanning (Tabuaeron) (isl.) 340	L 5
Faraulep (atoll) 132	E 5
Fatuhiva (isl.) 386	N 7
Fiji 588,068	H 8
Flint (isl.)	L 7
Fly (riv.)	E 6
Fongafale (cap.), Tuvalu	H 6
French Polynesia 137,382	L 8
Funafuti (atoll) 2,120	H 6
Futuna (Hoorn) (isls.) 3,173	J 7
Gambier (isls.) 556	N 8
Gardner (isl.)	J 6
Gilbert (isls.) 47,711	H 6
Greenwich (Kapingamarangi) (atoll) 508	F 5
Guadalcanal (isl.) 46,619	F 7
Guam (isl.) 105,979	E 4
Hall (isls.) 647	F 5
Hawaiian (isls.) 964,691	J 3
Henderson (isl.)	O 8
Hivaoa (isl.) 1,159	N 6
Honiara (cap.), Solomon Is. 14,942	F 6
Hoorn (isls.) 3,173	J 7
Howland (isl.)	J 5
Huahine (isl.) 3,140	L 7
Hull (isl.)	J 6
Huon (gulf)	E 6
Ifalik (atoll) 389	E 5
Iwo (isl.)	E 3
Jaluit (atoll) 1,450	G 5
Jarvis (isl.)	K 6
Johnston (atoll) 327	K 4
Kadavu (Kandavu) (isl.) 8,699	H 7
Kapingamarangi (atoll) 508	F 5
Kavieng 4,633	E 6
Kermadec (isls.) 5	J 9
Kieta 3,491	F 6
Kimbe 4,662	F 6
Kingman (reef)	K 5
Kiribati 57,500	J 6
Kirimati (isl.) 674	L 5
Kolonia (cap.), Micronesia 5,549	F 5
Koror (cap.), Belau 6,222	D 5
Kosrae (isl.) 5,491	G 5
Kwajalein (atoll) 6,624	G 5
Lae 61,617	E 6
Lau Group (isls.) 14,452	J 7
Lavongai (isl.)	E 6
Lifu (isl.) 7,585	G 8
Line (isls.)	K 5
Little Makin (atoll) 1,445	H 5
Lord Howe (Ontong Java) (isl.) 1,082	G 6
Lord Howe (isl.) 287	G 9
Lorengau 3,986	E 6
Louisiade (arch.)	F 7
Loyalty (isls.) 14,518	G 8
Luganville 4,935	G 7
Madang 21,335	E 6

Majuro (atoll) (cap.), Marshall Is. 8,583	H 5
Makin (Butaritari) (atoll) 2,971	H 5
Malaita (isl.) 50,912	G 6
Malden (isl.)	L 6
Malekula (isl.) 15,931	G 7
Maloelap (atoll) 763	H 5
Mangaia (isl.) 1,364	L 8
Mangareva (isl.) 556	N 8
Manihiki (atoll) 405	K 7
Manua (isls.) 1,459	K 7
Manus (isl.) 25,844	E 6
Marcus (isl.)	F 3
Maré (isl.) 4,156	G 8
Marianas, Northern 16,780	E 4
Mariana Trench	E 4
Marquesas (isls.) 5,419	N 6
Marshall Islands 30,873	G 4
Marutea (atoll)	N 8
Mata Utu (cap.), Wallis and Futuna 558	J 7
Mauke (isl.) 684	L 8
Melanesia (reg.)	E 5
Micronesia (reg.)	E 4
Micronesia, Federated States of 73,160	F 5
Midway (isls.) 453	J 3
Mili (atoll) 763	H 5
Moen (isl.) 10,351	F 5
Moorea (isl.) 5,788	L 7
Mururoa (isl.)	M 8
Nadi 6,938	H 7
Namonuito (atoll) 783	E 5
Namorik (atoll) 617	G 5
Nanumea (atoll) 844	H 6
Nauru 7,254	G 6
Ndeni (isl.) 4,854	G 7
New Britain (isl.) 148,773	F 6
New Caledonia 133,233	G 8
New Caledonia (isl.) 118,715	G 8
New Georgia (isl.) 16,472	F 6
New Guinea (isl.)	E 6
New Ireland (isl.) 65,657	F 6
Ngatik (atoll) 560	F 5
Ngulu (atoll) 21	D 5
Niuatoputapu (isl.) 1,650	J 7
Niue (isl.) 3,578	K 7
Niutao (atoll) 866	H 6
Nomoi (isls.) 1,879	F 5
Nonouti (atoll) 2,223	H 6
Norfolk Island (terr.) 2,175	G 8
Northern Marianas 16,780	E 4
Nouméa (cap.), New Caled. 56,078	G 8
Nouméa '74,335	G 8
Nui (atoll) 603	H 6
Nuku'alofa (cap.), Tonga 18,356	J 8
Nukuhiva (isl.) 1,484	M 6
Ocean (Banaba) (isl.) 2,314	G 6

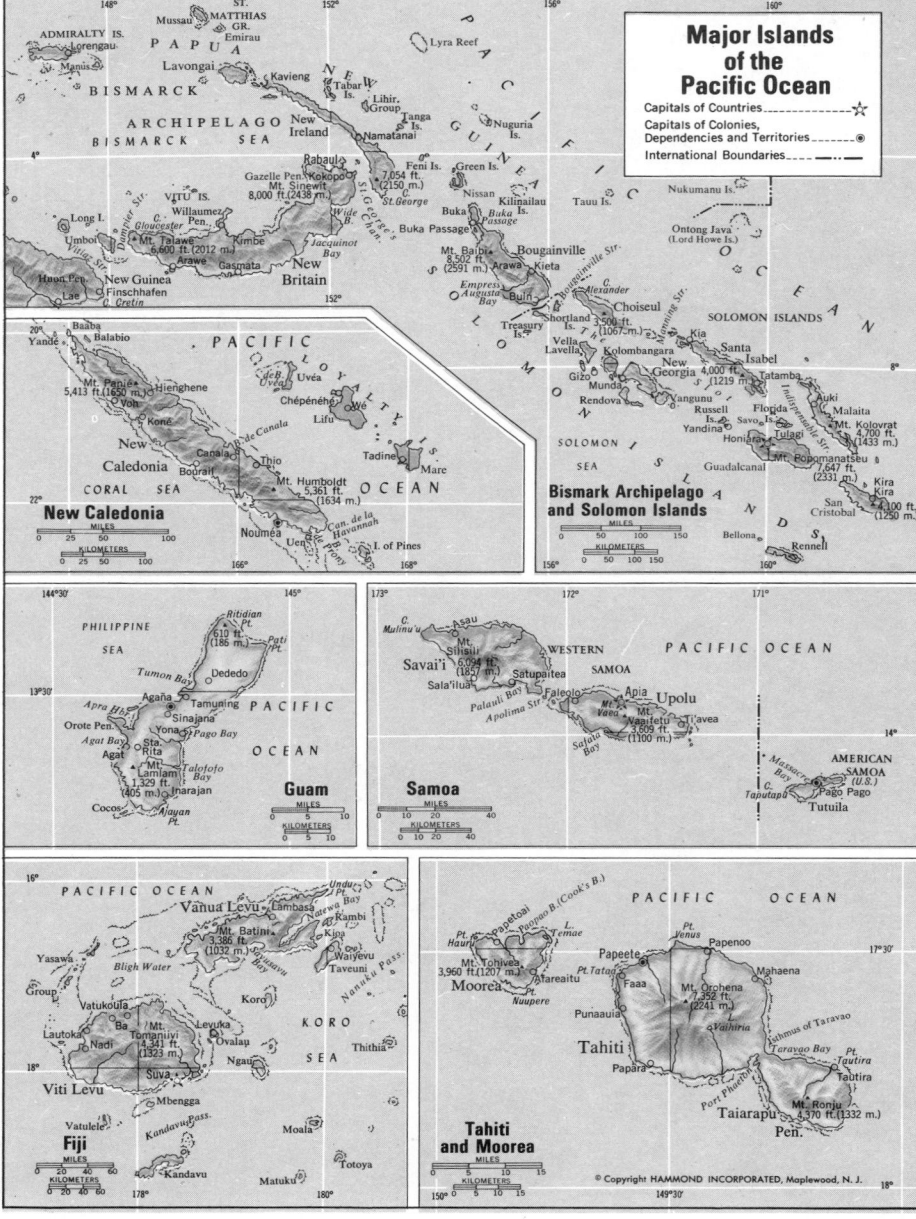

Major Islands of the Pacific Ocean
Capitals of Countries .... ☆
Capitals of Colonies, Dependencies and Territories ...... ⊛
International Boundaries .... — — —

New Caledonia

Bismark Archipelago and Solomon Islands

Guam

Samoa

Fiji

Tahiti and Moorea

© Copyright HAMMOND INCORPORATED, Maplewood, N. J.

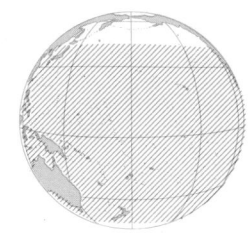

VANUATU

AREA 5,700 sq. mi. (14,763 sq. km.)
POPULATION 112,596
CAPITAL Vila
HIGHEST POINT Mt. Tabwemasana
6,165 ft. (1,879 m.)
MONETARY UNIT vatu
MAJOR LANGUAGES Bislama, English, French
MAJOR RELIGIONS Christian, animist

WESTERN SAMOA

AREA 1,133 sq. mi. (2,934 sq. km.)
POPULATION 158,130
CAPITAL Apia
LARGEST CITY Apia
HIGHEST POINT Mt. Silisili 6,094 ft.
(1,857 m.)
MONETARY UNIT tala
MAJOR LANGUAGES Samoan, English
MAJOR RELIGIONS Protestantism,
Roman Catholicism

FIJI — TONGA — KIRIBATI — TUVALU — NAURU — VANUATU — SOLOMON ISLANDS — WESTERN SAMOA

Pacific Ocean

LAMBERT AZIMUTHAL EQUAL-AREA PROJECTION

©Copyright HAMMOND INCORPORATED, Maplewood, N.J.

NAUTICAL MILES
0 200 400 600 800 1000 1200
STATUTE MILES
0 200 400 600 800 1000 1200
KILOMETERS
0 200 400 600 800 1000 1200

Capitals of Countries . . . . ☆
Capitals of Colonies,
Dependencies, States and Territories . ★
Administrative Centers . . . . ◉
International Boundaries . . . .
Internal Boundaries . . . .
Railroads . . . .
Distances Between Points . . . 5444
(nautical miles)

Scale 1:50,000,000

Australia

CONIC PROJECTION

MILES
0 50 100 200 300 400 500

KILOMETERS
0 50 100 200 300 400 500

Capital of Country .... ⊛   State & Territorial Capitals ..... ◉

International Boundaries ....— ·· —   State & Territorial Boundaries .... ———

Scale 1:19,000,000

© Copyright HAMMOND INCORPORATED, Maplewood, N.J.

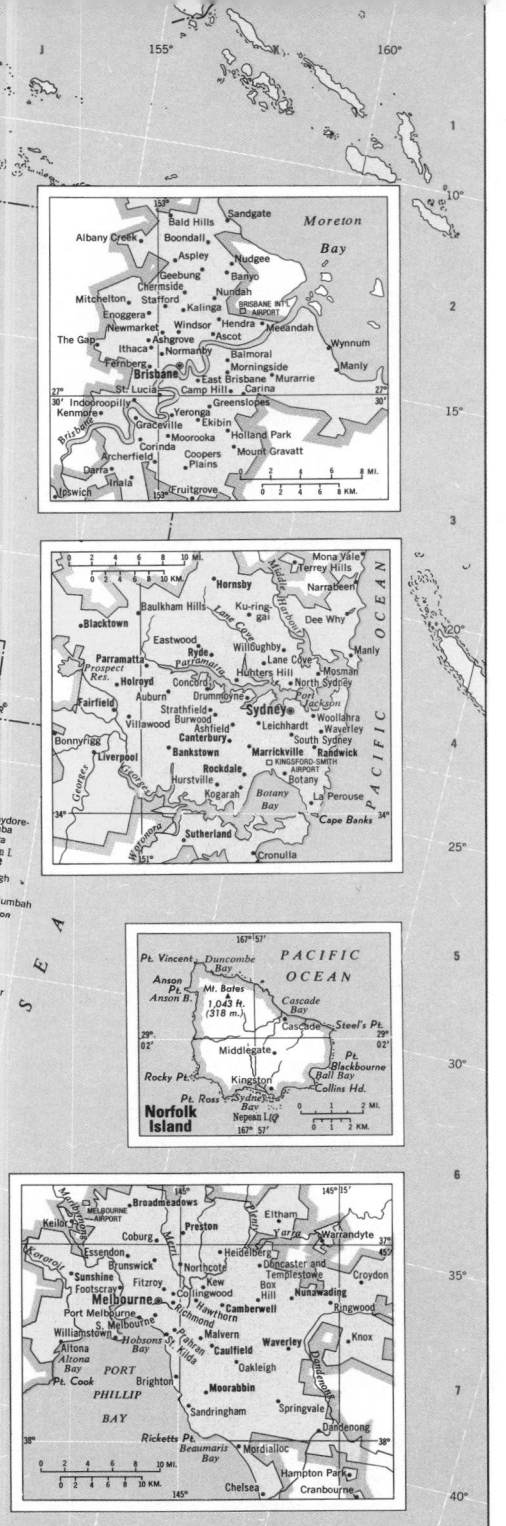

AREA 2,966,136 sq. mi. (7,682,300 sq. km.)
POPULATION 14,576,330
CAPITAL Canberra
LARGEST CITY Sydney
HIGHEST POINT Mt. Kosciusko 7,310 ft.
 (2,228 m.)
LOWEST POINT Lake Eyre -39 ft. (-12 m.)
MONETARY UNIT Australian dollar
MAJOR LANGUAGE English
MAJOR RELIGIONS Protestantism,
Roman Catholicism

Population Distribution

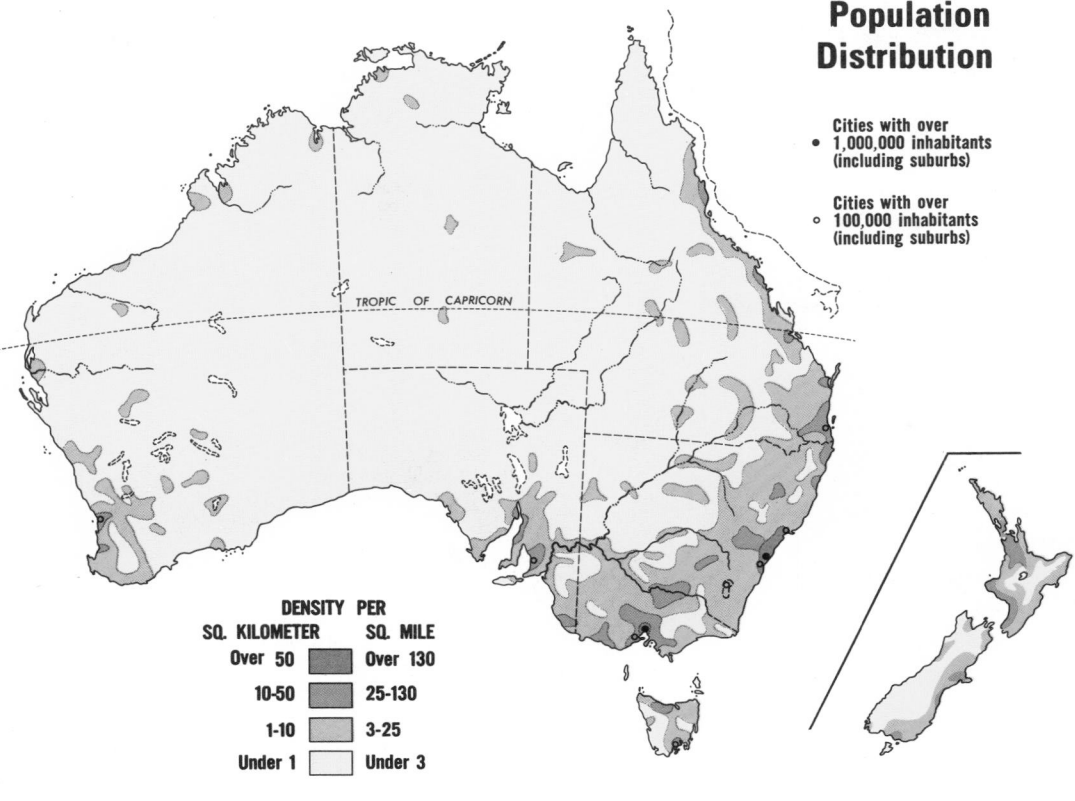

● Cities with over
 1,000,000 inhabitants
 (including suburbs)

○ Cities with over
 100,000 inhabitants
 (including suburbs)

DENSITY PER	
SQ. KILOMETER	SQ. MILE
Over 50	Over 130
10-50	25-130
1-10	3-25
Under 1	Under 3

Vegetation

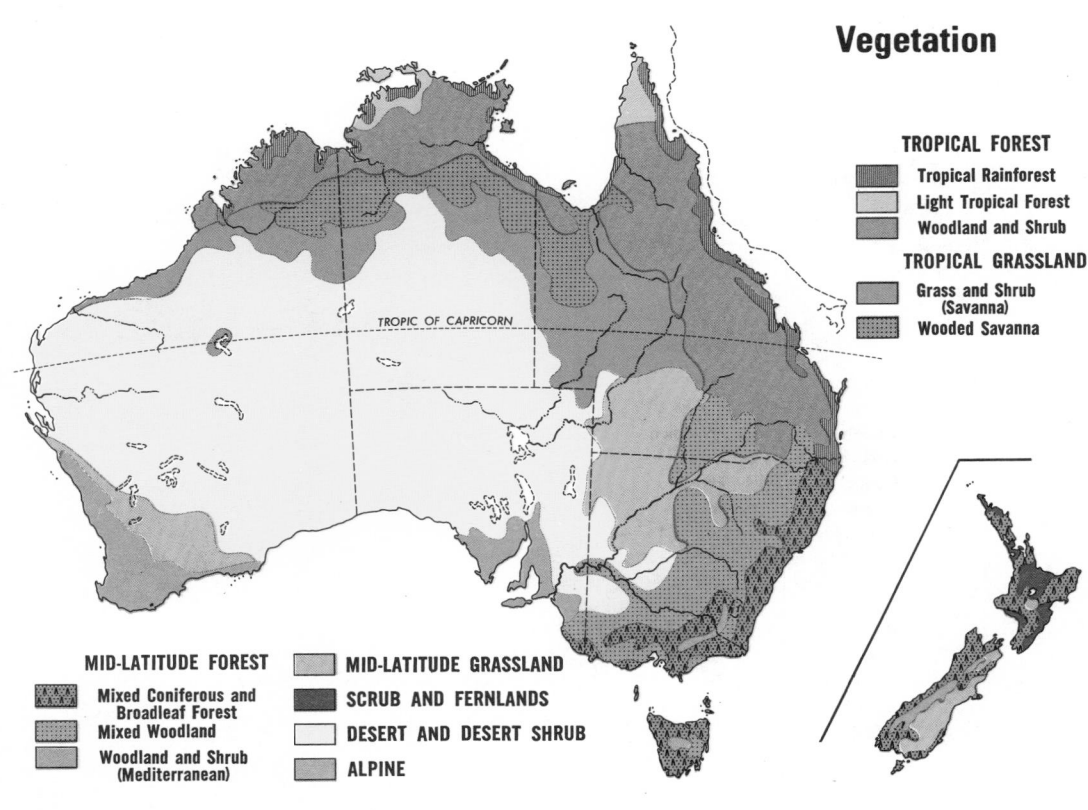

TROPICAL FOREST
Tropical Rainforest
Light Tropical Forest
Woodland and Shrub

TROPICAL GRASSLAND
Grass and Shrub (Savanna)
Wooded Savanna

MID-LATITUDE FOREST
Mixed Coniferous and Broadleaf Forest
Mixed Woodland
Woodland and Shrub (Mediterranean)

MID-LATITUDE GRASSLAND

SCRUB AND FERNLANDS

DESERT AND DESERT SHRUB

ALPINE

*City and suburbs.
†Population of met. area.
‡Population of urban area.

Average January Temperature

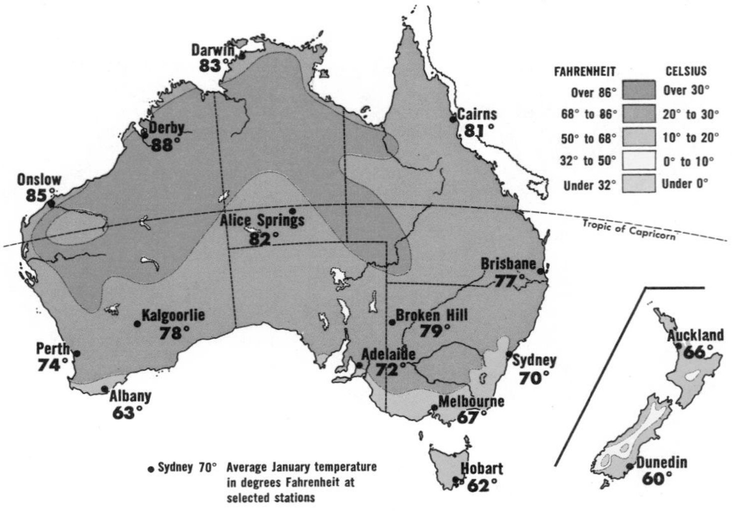
Darwin 83°
Derby 88°
Onslow 85°
Alice Springs 82°
Cairns 81°
Brisbane 77°
Kalgoorlie 78°
Broken Hill 79°
Perth 74°
Adelaide 72°
Sydney 70°
Albany 63°
Melbourne 67°
Hobart 62°
Auckland 66°
Dunedin 60°
Tropic of Capricorn
FAHRENHEIT
CELSIUS
Over 86° Over 30°
68° to 86° 20° to 30°
50° to 68° 10° to 20°
32° to 50° 0° to 10°
Under 32° Under 0°
• Sydney 70° Average January temperature in degrees Fahrenheit at selected stations

Average July Temperature

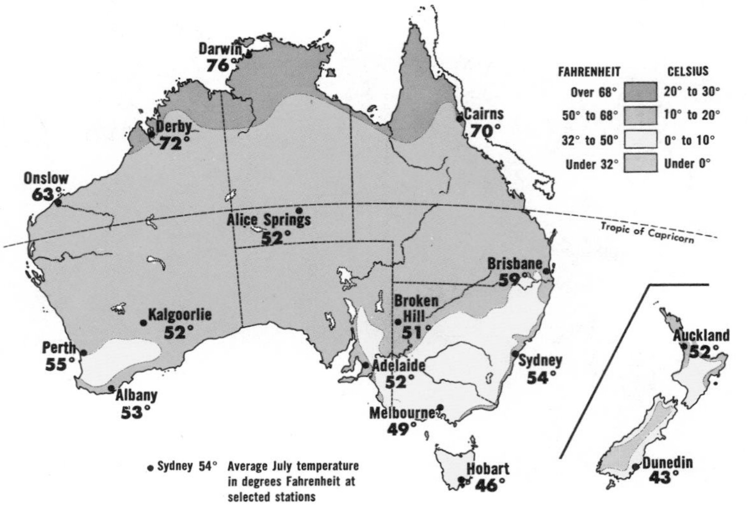
Darwin 76°
Derby 72°
Onslow 63°
Alice Springs 52°
Cairns 70°
Brisbane 59°
Kalgoorlie 52°
Broken Hill 51°
Perth 55°
Adelaide 52°
Sydney 54°
Albany 53°
Melbourne 49°
Hobart 46°
Auckland 52°
Dunedin 43°
Tropic of Capricorn
FAHRENHEIT
CELSIUS
Over 68° 20° to 30°
50° to 68° 10° to 20°
32° to 50° 0° to 10°
Under 32° Under 0°
• Sydney 54° Average July temperature in degrees Fahrenheit at selected stations

Rainfall

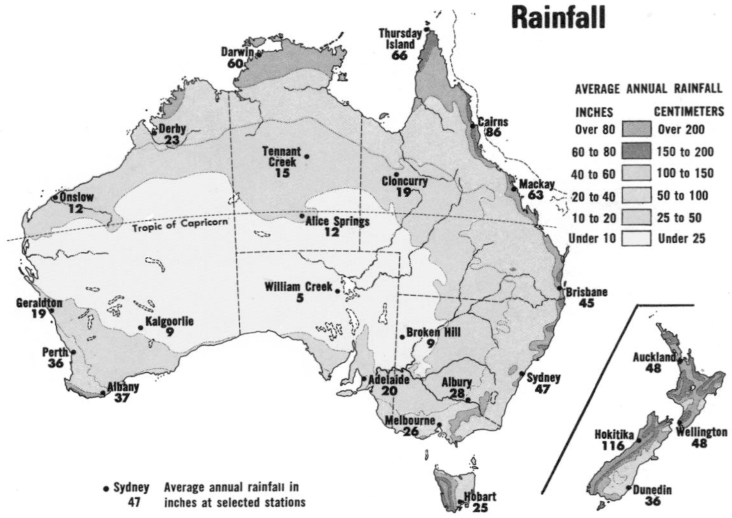
Thursday Island 66
Darwin 60
Derby 23
Cairns 86
Tennant Creek 15
Cloncurry 19
Mackay 63
Onslow 12
Tropic of Capricorn
Alice Springs 12
Brisbane 45
William Creek 5
Geraldton 19
Kalgoorlie 9
Broken Hill 9
Perth 36
Albany 37
Adelaide 20
Albury 28
Sydney 47
Melbourne 26
Hobart 25
Auckland 48
Hokitika 116
Wellington 48
Dunedin 36
AVERAGE ANNUAL RAINFALL
INCHES
CENTIMETERS
Over 80 Over 200
60 to 80 150 to 200
40 to 60 100 to 150
20 to 40 50 to 100
10 to 20 25 to 50
Under 10 Under 25
• Sydney 47 Average annual rainfall in inches at selected stations

DOMINANT LAND USE

- Cereals (chiefly wheat), Livestock
- Dairy, Truck Farming
- Cash Crops, Horticulture, Fruit
- Pasture Livestock
- Range Livestock
- Forests
- Nonagricultural Land

MAJOR MINERAL OCCURRENCES

Ab	Asbestos	Na	Salt
Ag	Silver	Ni	Nickel
Al	Bauxite	O	Petroleum
Au	Gold	Op	Opals
C	Coal	P	Phosphates
Cu	Copper	Pb	Lead
D	Diamonds	S	Sulfur, Pyrites
Fe	Iron Ore	Sb	Antimony
G	Natural Gas	Sn	Tin
Gp	Gypsum	Ti	Titanium
Lg	Lignite	U	Uranium
Ls	Limestone	W	Tungsten
Mg	Magnesium	Zn	Zinc
Mi	Mica	Zr	Zirconium
Mn	Manganese		

Water Power

Major Industrial Areas

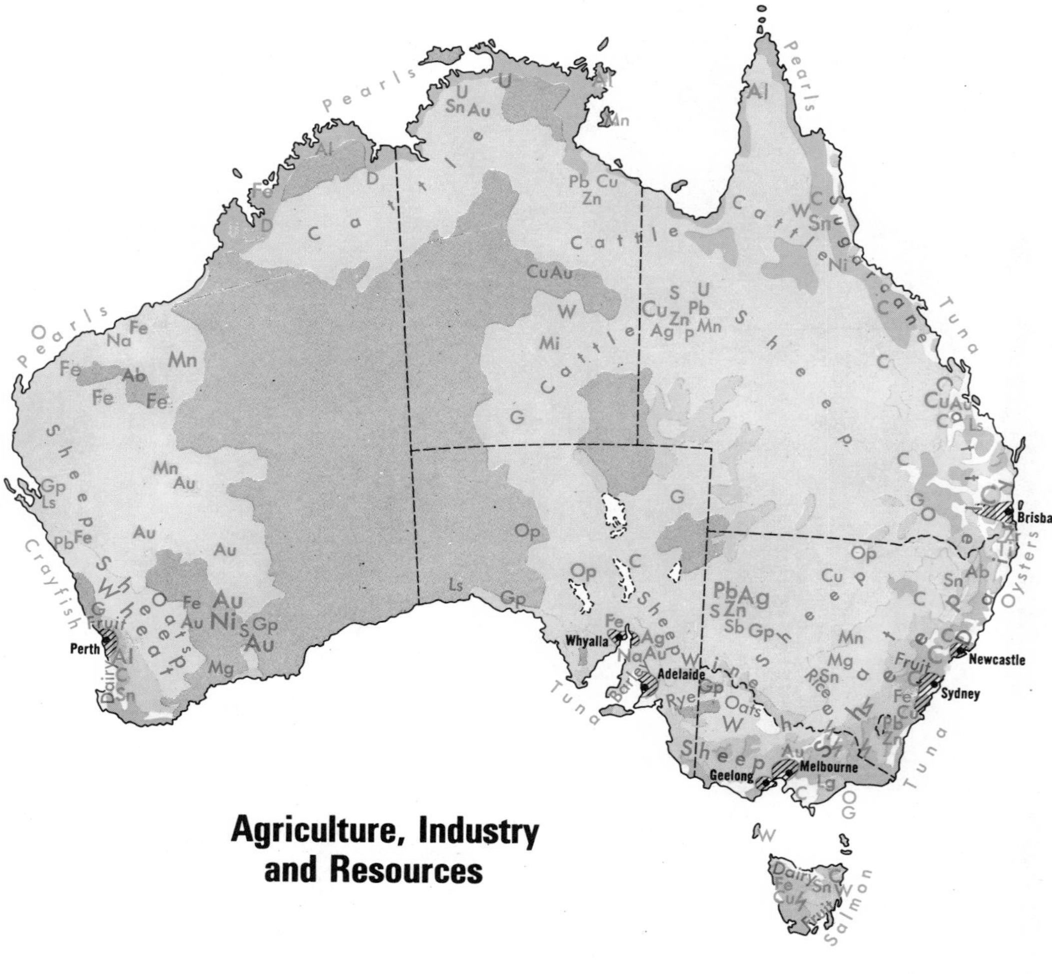
Pearls
Cattle
Sheep
Wheat
Oats
Fruit
Dairy
Crayfish
Tuna
Sugar cane
Oysters
Wine
Rice
Barley
Rye
Salmon
Perth
Whyalla
Adelaide
Geelong
Melbourne
Sydney
Newcastle
Brisbane

Agriculture, Industry and Resources

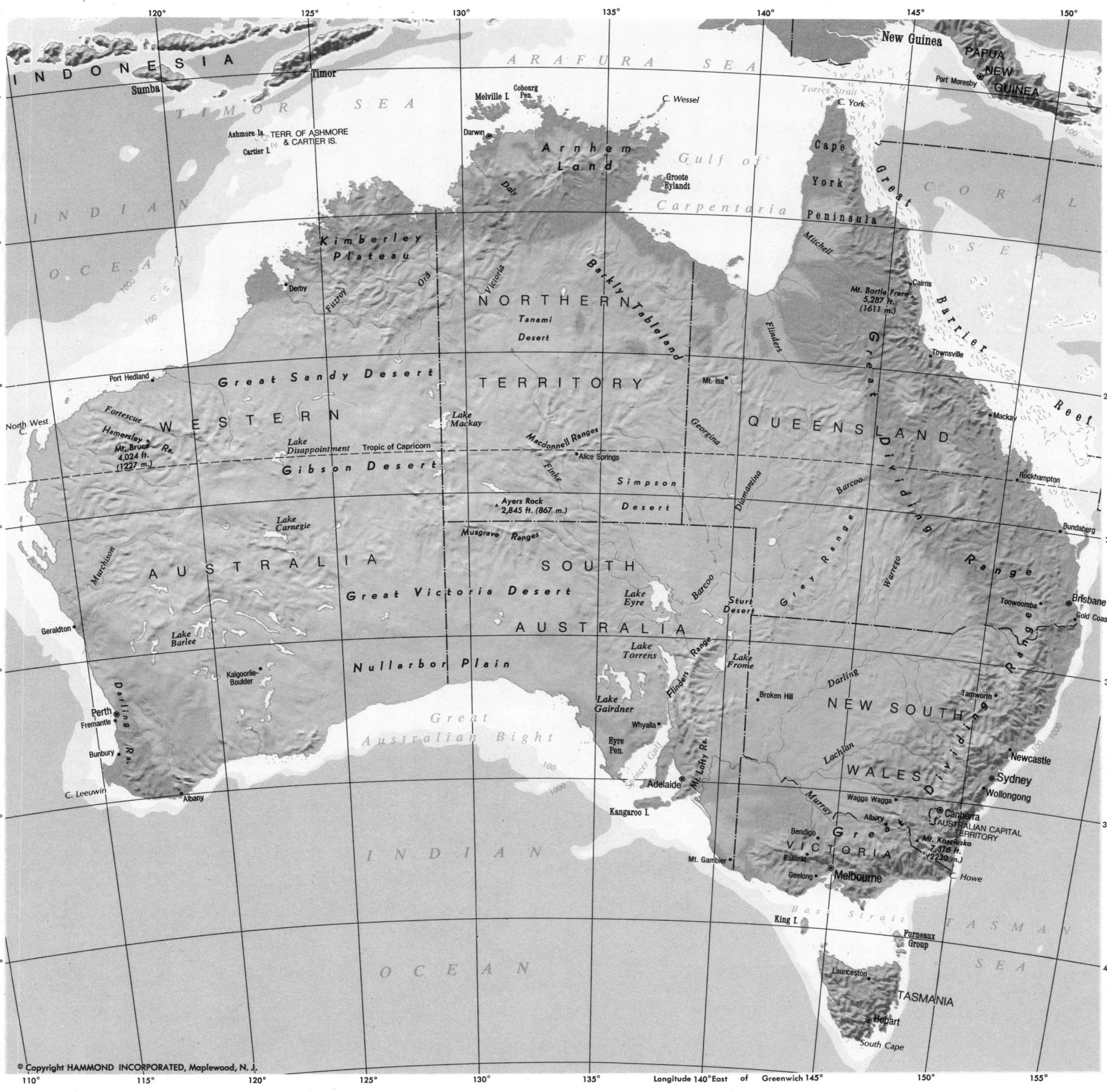

INDONESIA
Sumba
Timor
TIMOR SEA
ARAFURA SEA
New Guinea
PAPUA NEW GUINEA
Port Moresby
Torres Strait
C. York
C. Wessel
Melville I.
Cobourg Pen.
Darwin
Ashmore Is.
TERR. OF ASHMORE & CARTIER IS.
Cartier I.
Arnhem Land
Gulf of Carpentaria
Groote Eylandt
Cape York Peninsula
Great Barrier Reef
CORAL SEA
INDIAN OCEAN
Kimberley Plateau
Derby
Fitzroy
Ord
Victoria
Daly
NORTHERN TERRITORY
Tanami Desert
Barkly Tableland
Mitchell
Mt. Bartle Frere 5,287 ft. (1611 m.)
Cairns
Townsville
Mackay
Rockhampton
Bundaberg
Flinders
Port Hedland
Great Sandy Desert
Mt. Isa
North West C.
Fortescue
Hamersley Ra.
Mt. Bruce 4,024 ft. (1227 m.)
WESTERN AUSTRALIA
Lake Mackay
Lake Disappointment
Tropic of Capricorn
Gibson Desert
Macdonnell Ranges
Alice Springs
Finke
Simpson Desert
Georgina
Diamantina
QUEENSLAND
Barcoo
Great Dividing Range
Ayers Rock 2,845 ft. (867 m.)
Musgrave Ranges
Lake Carnegie
Murchison
SOUTH AUSTRALIA
Great Victoria Desert
Lake Eyre
Sturt Desert
Grey Range
Warrego
Toowoomba
Brisbane
Gold Coast
Geraldton
Lake Barlee
Lake Torrens
Lake Frome
Nullarbor Plain
Kalgoorlie-Boulder
Flinders Range
Darling Ra.
Perth
Fremantle
Bunbury
Lake Gairdner
Broken Hill
Darling
NEW SOUTH WALES
Tamworth
Great Australian Bight
Whyalla
Eyre Pen.
Spencer Gulf
Mt. Lofty Ra.
Lachlan
Newcastle
Sydney
Wollongong
C. Leeuwin
Albany
Adelaide
Kangaroo I.
Wagga Wagga
Murray
Canberra
AUSTRALIAN CAPITAL TERRITORY
Albury
Bendigo
Ballarat
VICTORIA
Mt. Kosciusko 7,316 ft. (2230 m.)
Mt. Gambier
Geelong
Melbourne
C. Howe
Bass Strait
King I.
TASMAN SEA
Furneaux Group
Launceston
TASMANIA
Hobart
South Cape
© Copyright HAMMOND INCORPORATED, Maplewood, N. J.
Longitude 140° East of Greenwich

Vegetation/Relief

SCALE OF MILES
0 100 200 300 400 500 600
SCALE OF KILOMETERS
0 100 200 300 400 500 600

Capital of Country ⊛
State and Territorial Capitals ◉
International Boundaries —·—
State and Territorial Boundaries —·—

Depths in Fathoms

Forest
Woodland and Scrub
Grassland
Forest and Grassland
Cropland
Desert
Tundra and Alpine
Ice and Snow
Grassland and Scrub
Scrub and Fernlands

COLOR KEY

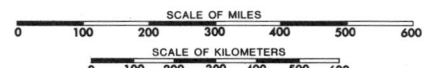

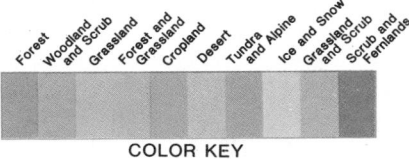

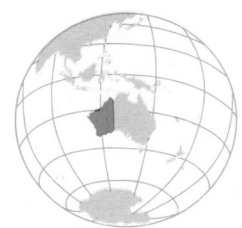

AREA 975,096 sq. mi.
(2,525,500 sq. km.)
POPULATION 1,273,624
CAPITAL Perth
LARGEST CITY Perth
HIGHEST POINT Mt. Bruce 4,024 ft.
(1,227 m.)

CITIES and TOWNS

Albany 15,222 . . . . B6
Augusta 588 . . . . A6
Australind 1,681 . . . . A2
Balladonia D6
Beverley 756 . . . . B1
Boddington 367 . . . . B2
Boulder-Kalgoorlie 19,848 . . C5
Boyanup 365 . . . . A2
Bridgetown 1,521 . . . . B6
Brookton 595 . . . . B2
Broome 3,666 . . . . C2
Bruce Rock 565 . . . . B5
Brunswick Junction 889 . . . A2
Bunbury 21,749 . . . . A2
Busselton 6,463 . . . . A6
Canning 52,816 . . . . A1
Capel 680 . . . . A2
Carnamah 422 . . . . A5
Carnarvon 5,053 . . . . A4
Collie 7,667 . . . . B2
Coolgardie 891 . . . . C5

Coorow 226 . . . . B5
Corrigin 841 . . . . B6
Cranbrook 316 . . . . B6
Cuballing ○647 . . . . B2
Cue 320 . . . . B4
Cunderdin 731 . . . . B5
Dalwallinu 639 . . . . B5
Dampier 2,471 . . . . B3
Dandaragan ○1,748 . . . . . . A5
Darkan 242 . . . . B2
Denham 402 . . . . A4
Denmark 985 . . . . B6
Derby 2,933 . . . . C2
Dongara-Port Denison 1,155 . A5
Donnybrook 1,197 . . . . A2
Dwellingup 453 . . . . B2
Esperance 6,375 . . . . C6
Eucla E5
Exmouth 2,583 . . . . A3
Fitzroy Crossing D2
Fremantle 22,484 . . . . A1
Geraldton 20,895 . . . . A5
Gingin 382 . . . . A1
Gnowangerup 872 . . . . B6

Goldsworthy 923 . . . . B3
Goomalling 600 . . . . B1
Halls Creek 966 . . . . D2
Harvey 2,479 . . . . A2
Hopetoun C6
Hyden B6
Jarrahdale 315 . . . . B2
Kalbarri 820 . . . . A4
Kalgoorlie 9,145 . . . . C5
Kalgoorlie-Boulder 19,848 . . C5
Kambalda 4,463 . . . . C5
Karratha 8,341 . . . . B3
Katanning 4,413 . . . . B6
Kellerberrin 1,091 . . . . B5
Kojonup 544 . . . . B6
Koolyanobbing 277 . . . . . . B5
Kununurra 2,081 . . . . E2
Kwinana New Town 12,355 . . A1
Lake Grace 575 . . . . B6
Laverton 872 . . . . C5
Learmonth A3
Leonora 524 . . . . C5
Madura D5
Mandurah 10,978 . . . . A2

Manjimup 4,150 . . . . B6
Marble Bar 357 . . . . C3
Margaret River 798 . . . . . . A6
Meekatharra 989 . . . . B4
Melville 61,211 . . . . A1
Menzies 232 . . . . C5
Merredin 3,520 . . . . B5
Mingenew 368 . . . . A5
Moora 1,677 . . . . B5
Morawa 694 . . . . B5
Mount Barker 1,519 . . . . . . B6
Mount Magnet 618 . . . . . . B5
Mukinbudin 370 . . . . B5
Mullewa 918 . . . . A5
Mundijong 356 . . . . A2
Nannup 552 . . . . B6
Narrogin 4,969 . . . . B2
Nedlands 20,257 . . . . A1
Newman 5,466 . . . . B3
New Norcia A5
Northam 1,895 . . . . C6
Northam 6,791 . . . . B1
Northampton 750 . . . . A5
Northcliffe B6
Nungarin ○332 . . . . B5
Onslow 594 . . . . A3
Pannawonica 1,170 . . . . . . B3
Paraburdoo 2,357 . . . . B3
Pardoo B3
Pemberton 871 . . . . A6
Perenjori 257 . . . . B5
Perth (cap.) 809,035 . . . . . A1
Perth *898,918 . . . . A1
Pingelly 937 . . . . B2
Pinjarra 1,336 . . . . A2
Port Denison-Dongara 1,155 . A5
Port Hedland 12,948 . . . . . B3
Quairading 741 . . . . B1
Ravensthorpe 327 . . . . B6
Rockingham 24,932 . . . . . . A2
Roebourne 1,688 . . . . B3

Sandstone ○133 . . . . B4
Shay Gap 853 . . . . C3
Southern Cross 798 . . . . . . B5
South Perth 31,524 . . . . . . A1
Stirling 161,858 . . . . A1
Three Springs 638 . . . . B5
Tom Price 3,540 . . . . B3
Toodyay 560 . . . . B1
Turkey Creek 212 . . . . E2
Wagin 1,488 . . . . B2
Walpole 291 . . . . B6
Wandering ○470 . . . . B2
Wanneroo 6,745 . . . . A1
Waroona 1,462 . . . . A2
Wickepin 267 . . . . B2
Wickham 2,387 . . . . B3
Williams 453 . . . . B2
Wiluna 221 . . . . C4
Wittenoom 247 . . . . B3
Wongan Hills 947 . . . . B5
Wundowie 720 . . . . B1
Wyalkatchem 453 . . . . B5
Wyndham 1,509 . . . . E1
Yalgoo ○315 . . . . B5
Yampi Sound C2
York 1,136 . . . . B1

OTHER FEATURES

Adele (isl.) C1
Admiralty (gulf) D1
Aloysius (mt.) E4
Argyle (lake) E2
Arid (cape) C6
Ashburton (riv.) A3
Augustus (mt.) B4
Austin (lake) B4
Australia Aboriginal Res. . . . E4
Bald (head) B6
Balwina Aboriginal Res. . . . E3
Barlee (lake) B5
Barrow (isl.) A3
Beaglebay Aboriginal Res. . . C2
Bluff Knoll (mt.) B6
Bonaparte (arch.) D1
Bougainville (cape) D1
Brassey (range) C4
Bruce (mt.) B3
Brunswick (bay) D1
Buccaneer (arch.) C2
Carey (lake) C5
Carnegie (lake) C4
Central Aboriginal Res. E3
Churchman (mt.) B5
Collier (bay) C1
Cosmo Newbery Aboriginal
   Res. C5
Cowan (lake) C5
Cundeelee Aboriginal Res. . . C5
Dale (mt.) B1
Dampier (arch.) B3
Dampier Land (reg.) C2
Darling (range) A1
De Grey (riv.) B3
D'Entrecasteaux (pt.) A6
Dirk Hartogs (isl.) A4
Disappointment (lake) C3
Drysdale (riv.) D1
Dundas (lake) C6
Egerton (mt.) B4
Eighty Mile (beach) C2
Enid (mt.) B3
Esperance (bay) C6

Exmouth (gulf) A3
Fitzroy (riv.) D2
Flinders (bay) A6
Forrest River Aboriginal Res. . D1
Fortescue (riv.) B3
Garden (isl.) A1
Gascoyne (riv.) B4
Geelvink (chan.) A5
Geographe (bay) A6
Geographe (chan.) A4
Gibson (des.) D3
Great Australian (bight) E6
Great Sandy (des.) C3
Great Victoria (des.) D5
Hamersley (range) B3
Hann (mt.) D1
Hopkins (lake) E4
Houtman Abrolhos (isls.) . . . A5
Indian Ocean A5
Johnston, The (lakes) C6
Joseph Bonaparte (gulf) . . . E1
Kimberley (plat.) D2
King (sound) C2
King Leopold (range) C2
Koolan (isl.) C1
Leeuwin (cape) A6
Le Grand (cape) C6
Lévêque (cape) C2
Londonderry (cape) D1
Lyons (riv.) A4
Macdonald (lake) E3
Mackay (lake) E3
McLeod (lake) A4
Minigwal (lake) C5
Monte Bello (isls.) A3
Moore (lake) B5
Murchison (riv.) B4
Murray (riv.) A2
Naturaliste (cape) A6
Naturaliste (chan.) A4
North West (cape) A3
North-West Aboriginal Res. . . E4
Nullarbor (plain) D5
Oakover (riv.) C3
Ord (mt.) D2
Ord (riv.) E2
Percival (lakes) D3
Peron (pen.) A4
Petermann (ranges) E4
Rason (lake) D5
Rebecca (lake) C5
Recherche (lake) C6
Robinson (ranges) B4
Roebuck (bay) C2
Rottnest (isl.) A1
Saint George (ranges) D2
Shark (bay) A4
Southesk Tablelands D3
Sturt (creek) D2
Swan (riv.) A1
Timor (sea) D1
Tomkinson (ranges) E4
Wanna (lakes) C4
Warburton Aboriginal Res. . . D4
Way (lake) C4
Weld (range) B4
Wells (lake) C4
Whaleback (mt.) B3
Wooramel (riv.) A4
York (sound) D1

○ Population of district.
*Population of met. area.

Topography

Below Sea Level | 100 m. 328 ft. | 200 m. 656 ft. | 500 m. 1,640 ft. | 1,000 m. 3,281 ft. | 2,000 m. 6,562 ft. | 5,000 m. 16,404 ft.

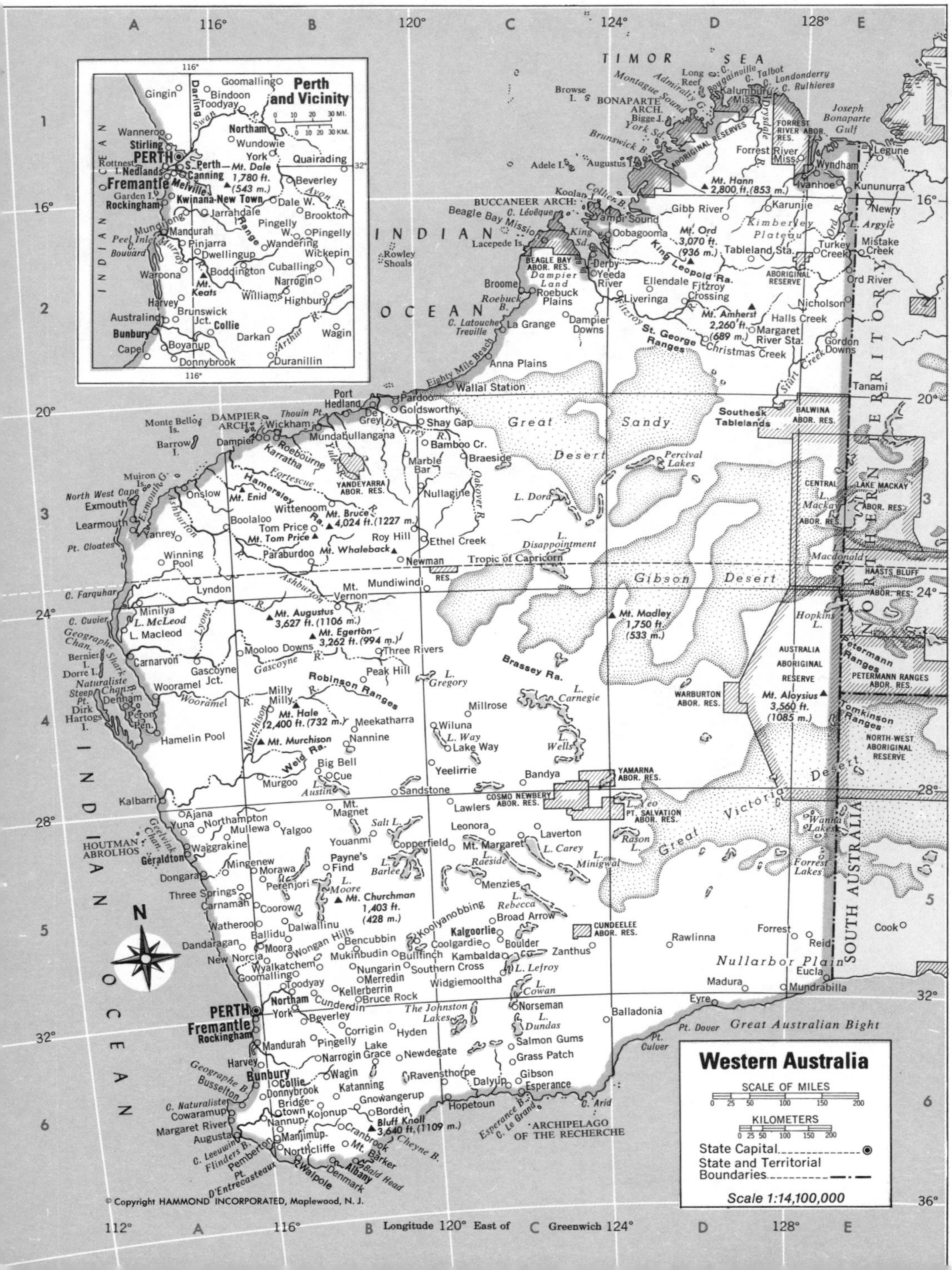

Western Australia

SCALE OF MILES

KILOMETERS

State Capital ◉
State and Territorial Boundaries ▬ ▬ ▬

Scale 1:14,100,000

© Copyright HAMMOND INCORPORATED, Maplewood, N.J.

CITIES and TOWNS

Adelaide River	B2
Aileron	C7
Alice Springs 18,395	D7
Alyangula 1,181	E2
Angurugu 597	E3
Anthony Lagoon	D4
Areyonga	C8
Arltunga	D7
Avon Downs	E5
Bamyili-Beswick 685	C3
Banka Banka	C5
Barrow Creek	D6
Batchelor	B2
Bathurst Island 1,032	B1
Birdum	C3
Birrimbah	C3
Birrindudu	A5
Borroloola 420	E4
Bundooma	D8
Burramurra	E6
Charlotte Waters	D8
Claravale	B3
Coniston	C7
Coolibah	B3
Creswell Downs	E4
Croker Island Mission	C1
Daly River	B2
Daly Waters	C3
Darwin (cap.) 56,482	B2
Docker River 217	A8
Elliott	C4
Epenarra	D6
Erldunda	C8
Eva Downs	D5

Ewaninga	D7
Goulburn Island 277	C1
Gove (Nhulunbuy) 3,879	E2
Harts Range	D7
Hatches Creek	D6
Helen Springs	C5
Henbury	C8
Hermannsburg 541	C7
Hooker Creek 671	B5
Humpty Doo	B2
Katherine 3,737	B3
Kildurk	A4
Koolpinyah	B2
Kulgera	C8
Kurundi	D6
Lake Nash	E6
Larrimah	C3
Legune	A3
Limbunya	B4
Lucy Creek	E7
Mainoru	C3
Maningrida 702	C2
Mataranka	C3
Milingimbi 564	D2
Mistake Creek	A4
Montejinnie	C4
Mount Cavenagh	C8
Mount Doreen	B7
Murray Downs	D6
Napperby	C7
Newcastle Waters	C4
Nhulunbuy 3,879	E2
Numbulwar 422	D3
Oenpelli 452	C2
O. T. Downs	D4
Papunya 635	B7
Pine Creek 214	C2

Plenty River Mine	D7
Port Keats 819	A3
Powell Creek	C5
Rankine Store	E5
Robinson River	E4
Rockhampton Downs	D5
Rodinga	C7
Rum Jungle	B2
Santa Teresa 479	D7
Soudan	E6
Stirling Station	D3
Tanami	A4
Tarlton Downs	E7
Tea Tree Well	C7
Tempe Downs	C8
Tennant Creek 3,118	C5
The Granites	B6
Top Springs	C4
Ucharonidge	D4
Umbakumba 247	E3
Umbeara	C8
Urapunga	D3
Utopia	D7
Victoria River Downs	B4
Warrabri 459	C7
Warrego 991	C5
Wave Hill	B4
White Quartz Hill	D7
Willeroo	B3
Willowra	C6
Wollogorang	F4
Yambah	D7
Yirrkala 543	E2
Yuendumu 687	B7

OTHER FEATURES

Amadeus (lake)	B8

Arafura (sea)	D1
Arnhem (cape)	E2
Arnhem Land (reg.)	D2
Arnhem Land Aboriginal Res.	C2
Arnold (riv.)	D3
Ayers Rock Nat'l Park	B8
Barkly Tableland	D4
Bathurst (isl.)	A1
Beagle (gulf)	A2
Beatrice (cape)	E3
Bennett (lake)	B7
Beswick Aboriginal Res.	C3
Bickerton (isl.)	E2
Blaze (pt.)	A2
Carpentaria (gulf)	E3
Central Wedge (mt.)	C7
Clarence (str.)	B2
Cobourg (pen.)	C1
Conner (mt.)	C8
Hopkins (lake)	A8
Joseph Bonaparte (gulf)	A3
Katherine (riv.)	C3
Daly (riv.)	B2
Daly River Aboriginal Res.	A2
Davenport (mt.)	B7
Dundas (str.)	B1
East Alligator (riv.)	C2
Ehrenberg (range)	A7
Elcho (isl.)	D1
Finke (riv.)	C7
Fitzmaurice (riv.)	A3
Ford (cape)	A2
Georgina (riv.)	E6
Goulburn (isls.)	C1
Goyder (riv.)	D2
Groote Eylandt (isl.) 2,230	E3
Haasts Bluff Aboriginal Res.	B7
Hale (riv.)	D8

Hanson (riv.)	C6
Hay (dry riv.)	E7
Hogarth (mt.)	E6
Hopkins (mt.)	A8
Joseph Bonaparte (gulf)	A3
Katherine (riv.)	C3
Lake MacKay Aboriginal Res.	A6
Lander (riv.)	C6
Leisler (mt.)	A7
Limmen (bight)	D3
Limmen Bight (riv.)	D4
Macdonald (lake)	B7
Macdonald (ranges)	C7
MacKay (lake)	A7
Mann (riv.)	D2
Marshall (riv.)	D7
Melville (bay)	E2
Melville (isl.)	B1
Mount Olga Nat'l Park	B8

Murchison (range)	D6
Napier (mt.)	A4
Neale (lake)	A8
Newcastle (creek)	C4
Nicholson (riv.)	E5
Olga (mt.)	B8
Peron (isls.)	A2
Petermann (ranges)	A8
Petermann Ranges Aboriginal Res.	A8
Port Darwin (inlet)	B2
Ranken (riv.)	E6
Robinson (riv.)	E4
Roper (riv.)	C3
Sandover (riv.)	D6
Simpson (des.)	E8
Singleton (mt.)	B6
Sir Edward Pellew Group (isls.)	E3
South Alligator (riv.)	C2

Stanley (mt.)	B7
Stewart (cape)	D1
Stirling (creek)	A4
Sturt (plain)	C4
Tanami (des.)	C5
Timor (sea)	A2
Todd (riv.)	D8
Vanderlin (isl.)	E3
Van Diemen (cape)	A1
Van Diemen (gulf)	B1
Victoria (riv.)	B3
Wagait Aboriginal Res.	B2
Warwick (chan.)	E2
Wessel (cape)	E1
Wessel (isls.)	E1
West Baines (riv.)	A4
White (lake)	A6
Woods (lake)	C4
Young (mt.)	D3
Ziel (mt.)	C7

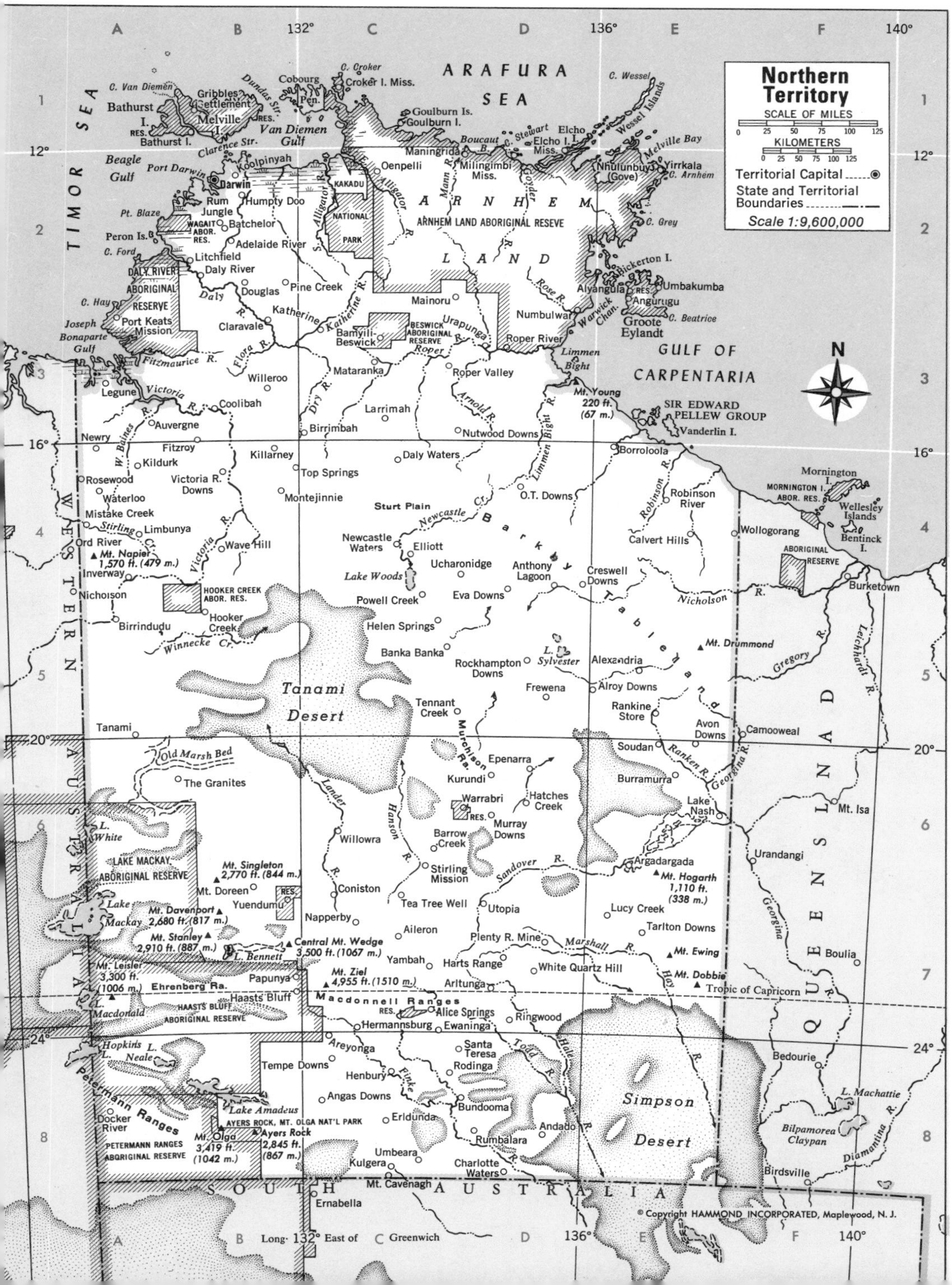

AREA 519,768 sq. mi.
(1,346,200 sq. km.)
POPULATION 123,324
CAPITAL Darwin
LARGEST CITY Darwin
HIGHEST POINT Mt. Ziel 4,955 ft.
(1,510 m.)

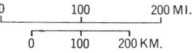

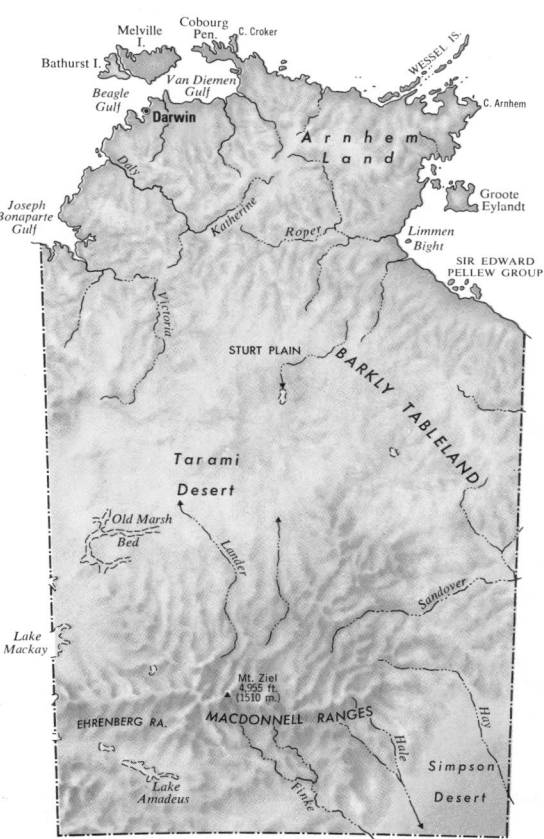

Topography

© Copyright HAMMOND INCORPORATED, Maplewood, N.J.

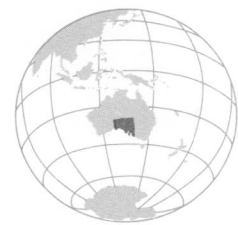

AREA 379,922 sq. mi. (984,000 sq. km.)
POPULATION 1,285,033
CAPITAL Adelaide
LARGEST CITY Adelaide
HIGHEST POINT Mt. Woodroffe 4,970 ft. (1,515 m.)

CITIES and TOWNS

Adelaide (cap.) 882,520 ....B6
Adelaide *931,886 ....B6
Andamooka 402 ....E4
Angaston 1,753 ....F6
Balaklava 1,306 ....F6
Barmera 2,014 ....G6
Beachport 357 ....F7
Berri 3,419 ....G6
Birdwood 397 ....C7
Blinman F4
Bordertown 2,138 ....G7
Brighton 19,441 ....A8
Burnside 37,593 ....B8
Burra 1,222 ....F5
Campbelltown 43,084 ....B7
Ceduna 2,794 ....D5
Clare 2,381 ....F5
Cleve 827 ....E5
Coober Pedy 2,078 ....D3
Cowell 626 ....E5
Crafters-Bridgewater 9,764 ..B8
Crystal Brook 1,240 ....E5
Cummins 767 ....D6
Edithburgh 359 ....E6
Elizabeth 32,608 ....B7
Elliston ○1,345 ....D5
Enfield 66,797 ....B7
Gawler 9,433 ....B6
Gladstone 680 ....F5
Glenelg 13,306 ....A8
Gumeracha 387 ....C7
Hahndorf 1,274 ....C8
Hawker 351 ....F4
Hindmarsh 7,593 ....A7
Iron Knob 398 ....E5
Jamestown 1,384 ....F5
Kadina 2,943 ....F5
Kapunda 1,340 ....F6
Keith 1,147 ....G7
Kensington and Norwood 8,950 ....B8
Kimba 862 ....E5
Kingscote 1,236 ....E6
Kingston 1,325 ....G7
Lameroo 599 ....G6
Laura 504 ....F5
Leigh Creek 1,635 ....F4
Lobethal 1,522 ....C7
Lock 213 ....D5
Loxton 3,100 ....G6
Lyndoch 539 ....C6
Maitland 1,085 ....E6
Mannum 1,984 ....F6
Marion 66,580 ....A8
Marree E3
Meadows 388 ....B8
Meningie 807 ....F6
Millicent 5,255 ....F7
Minlaton 865 ....E6
Mitcham 60,309 ....B8
Moonta 1,751 ....E5
Mount Barker 4,190 ....C8
Mount Gambier 18,193 ....G7
Murray Bridge 8,664 ....F6
Nairne 706 ....C8
Nangwarry 758 ....G7

Topography

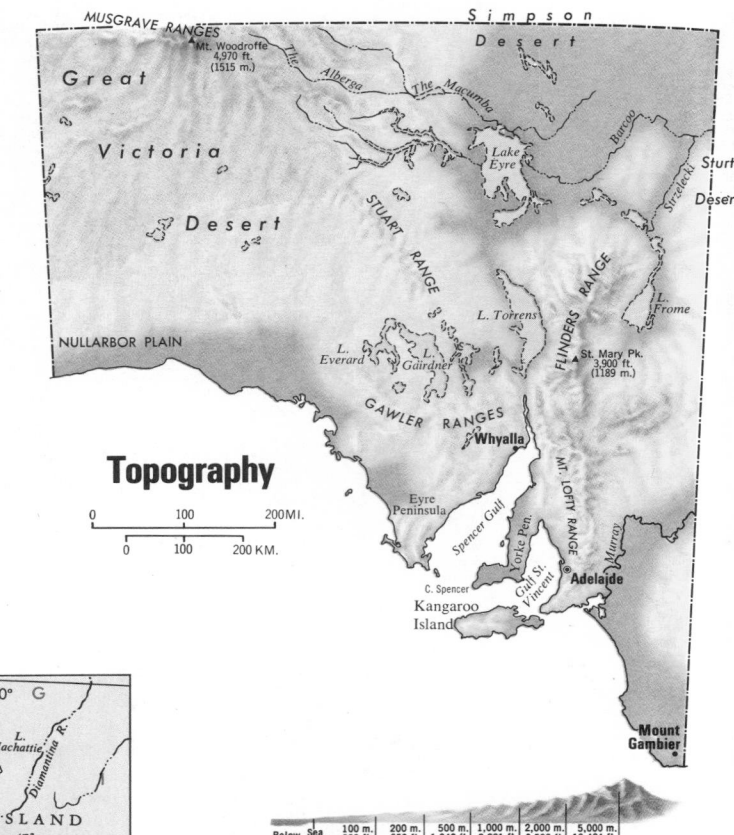

Below Sea Level	100 m. 328 ft.	200 m. 656 ft.	500 m. 1,640 ft.	1,000 m. 3,281 ft.	2,000 m. 6,562 ft.	5,000 m. 16,404 ft.

Naracoorte 4,758 ....G7
Noarlunga 60,928 ....A8
Nuriootpa 2,851 ....F6
Oodnadatta D2
Orroroo 604 ....F5
Payneham 16,502 ....B7
Penola 1,205 ....G7
Peterborough 2,575 ....F5
Pinnaroo 731 ....G6
Port Adelaide 35,407 ....A7
Port Augusta 15,566 ....E5
Port Broughton 587 ....E5
Port Lincoln 9,846 ....E6
Port Pirie 14,695 ....E5
Prospect 18,591 ....B7
Quorn 1,049 ....F5
Renmark 3,475 ....G5
Robe 590 ....F7
Salisbury 86,451 ....B7
Snowtown 492 ....E5
Strathalbyn 1,756 ....F6
Streaky Bay 985 ....D5
Tailem Bend 1,677 ....F6
Tanunda 2,621 ....C6
Tea Tree Gully 67,237 ....B7
Thebarton 9,208 ....A7
Tumby Bay 933 ....E6
Unley 35,844 ....B8
Uraidla 303 ....B8
Victor Harbor 4,522 ....F6
Virginia 353 ....B7
Waikerie 1,629 ....F6
Wallaroo 2,043 ....E5
West Torrens 45,099 ....A8
Whyalla 30,518 ....E5
Williamstown 495 ....C7
Willunga 667 ....F6
Wilmington 227 ....F6
Woodside 724 ....C8
Woodville 77,634 ....A7
Woomera 1,658 ....E4
Wudinna 572 ....D5
Yorketown 713 ....E6

OTHER FEATURES

Acraman (lake) D5
Alberga, The (riv.) D2
Alexandrina (lake) F6
Anxious (bay) D5
Arckaringa (creek) F3
Barcoo (creek) F3
Birksgate (range) A2
Blanche (lake) F3
Brady (mt.) D3
Cadibarrawirracanna (lake) D3
Callabonna (lake) F3
Catastrophe (cape) D6
Coffin (bay) D6
Coffin Bay (pen.) D6
Coopers (Barcoo) (creek) F3
Coorong, The (lag.) F6
Dey Dey (lake) B3
Encounter (bay) F6
Everard (lake) B3
Everard (ranges) C2
Eyre (pen.) D5
Eyre North (lake) E3
Eyre South (lake) E3
Finke (riv.) C1
Flinders (range) F4
Frome (lake) G4
Gairdner (lake) D4
Gawler (ranges) E5
Gawler (riv.) B6
Gilles (lake) E5
Goyders (lag.) F2
Great Australian (bight) A5
Great Victoria (des.) B3
Gregory (lake) F3
Hack (mt.) D2
Hamilton, The (riv.) D2
Harris (lake) D4
Head of Bight (bay) B4
Indian Ocean E7
Investigator (str.) E6
Investigator Group (isls.) D5
Island (lag.) E4
Jaffa (cape) F7
Kangaroo (isl.) 3,515 ....E7
Lacepede (bay) F7
Lofty (mt.) B8
Macfarlane (lake) E5
Macumba, The (riv.) D2
Maurice (lake) B3
Meramangye (lake) C3
Morris (mt.) B2
Murray (res.) F6
Musgrave (ranges) B2
Neales, The (riv.) E3
Northumberland (cape) F8
Nukey Bluff (mt.) D5
Nullarbor (plain) A4
Nuyts (arch.) C5
Nuyts (cape) C5
Peera Peera Poolanna (lake) F2
Saint Mary (peak) F4
Saint Vincent (gulf) F6
Serpentine (lakes) A3
Simpson (des.) E1
Sir Joseph Banks Group (isls.) E6
Spencer (cape) E6
Spencer (gulf) E6
Stevenson, The (riv.) D2
Streaky (bay) C5
Strzelecki (creek) G3
Stuart (range) D3
Sturt (des.) E2
The Alberga (riv.) D2
The Coorong (lag.) F6
The Hamilton (riv.) D2
The Macumba (riv.) D2
The Neales (riv.) E3
The Stevenson (riv.) D2
The Warburton (riv.) F2
Thistle (isl.) E6
Torrens (lake) E4
Torrens (riv.) C7
Warburton, The (riv.) F2
Wilkinson (lakes) C3
Woodroffe (mt.) B2
Yalata Aboriginal Res. B4
Yarle (lakes) B4
Yorke (pen.) E6

Adelaide and Vicinity

South Australia

SCALE OF MILES

KILOMETERS

State Capital ....◉

State and Territorial Boundaries ....

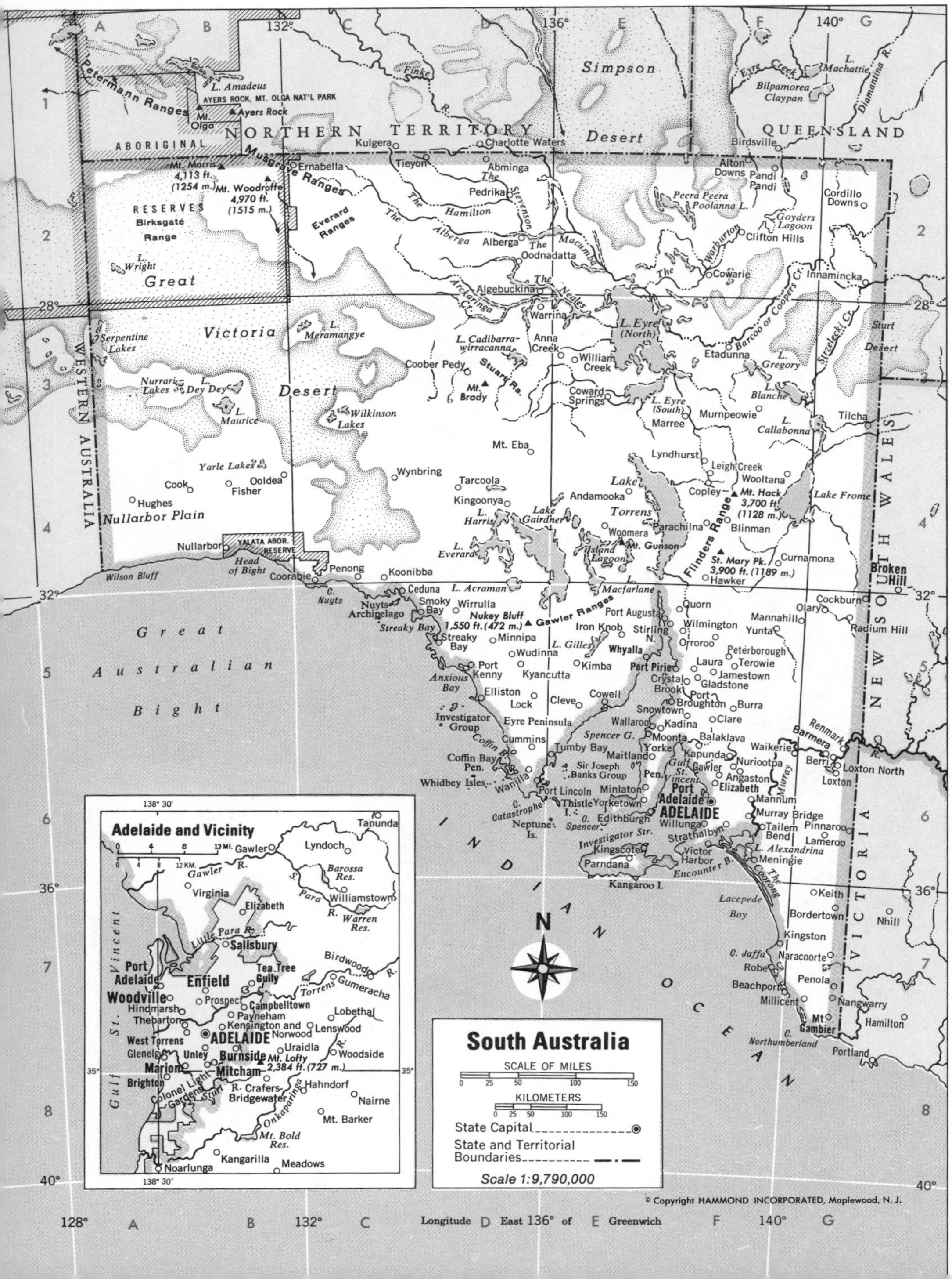

Scale 1:9,790,000

CITIES and TOWNS

Aramac 428 . . . . C4
Archerfield 785 . . . . D3
Ascot 4,298 . . . . E2
Atherton 4,196 . . . . C3
Ayr 8,787 . . . . C3
Balmoral 2,915 . . . . E2
Barcaldine 1,432 . . . . C4
Beaudesert 3,780 . . . . E6
Biloela 4,643 . . . . D5
Birdsville A5
Blackall 1,609 . . . . C5
Blackwater 5,434 . . . . D4
Boulia 292 . . . . A4
Bowen 7,663 . . . . D3
Brisbane (cap.) 689,378 . . . . . D2
Brisbane *1,028,527 . . . . D2
Bucasia 1,356 . . . . D4
Bundaberg 32,560 . . . . D5
Burketown 210 . . . . A3
Cairns 48,557 . . . . C3
Caloundra 16,758 . . . . E5
Camooweal 251 . . . . A3
Camp Hill 8,999 . . . . E3
Capella 660 . . . . D4
Cardwell 1,249 . . . . C3
Charleville 3,523 . . . . C5
Charters Towers 6,823 . . . . . . C4
Cherbourg 963 . . . . D5
Chermside 6,892 . . . . D2
Clermont 1,659 . . . . C4
Cloncurry 1,961 . . . . B4
Collinsville 2,756 . . . . C4
Cooktown 913 . . . . C2
Coopers Plains 4,492 . . . . D3
Corinda 4,894 . . . . D3
Croydon ○255 . . . . B3
Cunnamulla 1,627 . . . . C5
Dalby 8,784 . . . . D5
Dirranbandi 480 . . . . D6
East Brisbane 4,853 . . . . E3
Eidsvold 613 . . . . D5
Emerald 4,628 . . . . C4
Esk 676 . . . . E5
Gatton 4,190 . . . . E5
Gayndah 1,708 . . . . D5
Geebung 4,850 . . . . E2
Georgetown 319 . . . . B3
Gladstone 22,083 . . . . D4
Gold Coast 135,437 . . . . E6
Goondiwindi 3,576 . . . . D6
Gordonvale 2,375 . . . . C3
Greenslopes 7,219 . . . . E3
Gympie 10,768 . . . . E5

Hervey Bay 13,569 . . . . E5
Holland Park 7,363 . . . . E3
Home Hill 3,138 . . . . C3
Hughenden 1,657 . . . . B4
Inala 17,383 . . . . D3
Indooroopilly 7,959 . . . . D3
Ingham 5,598 . . . . C3
Injune 407 . . . . D5
Innisfail 7,933 . . . . C3
Ipswich 68,297 . . . . E5
Isisford ○605 . . . . C5
Jandowae 781 . . . . D5
Jericho ○1,177 . . . . C4
Julia Creek 602 . . . . B4
Karumba 670 . . . . B3
Kilcoy 1,257 . . . . E5
Kingaroy 5,134 . . . . D5
Longreach 2,971 . . . . B4
Mackay 35,361 . . . . D4
Mareeba 6,309 . . . . C3
Marian 796 . . . . D4
Maroochydore-Mooloolaba
  17,460 . . . . E5
Maryborough 20,111 . . . . E5
Mary Kathleen 830 . . . . A4
McKinlay ○1,477 . . . . B4
Millmerran 1,107 . . . . D5
Mitchell 1,171 . . . . C5
Mitchelton 5,810 . . . . D2
Monto 1,397 . . . . D5
Moorooka 8,740 . . . . D3
Moranbah 4,362 . . . . C9
Mossman 1,614 . . . . C3
Mount Isa 23,679 . . . . A4
Moura 2,871 . . . . D5
Murgon 2,327 . . . . D5
Nambour 7,965 . . . . E5
Newmarket 3,520 . . . . D2
Normanton 926 . . . . B3
Nundah 7,358 . . . . E2
Proserpine 3,058 . . . . D4
Quilpie 694 . . . . C5
Ravenshoe 915 . . . . C3
Redcliffe 42,223 . . . . E5
Richmond 784 . . . . B4
Rockhampton 50,146 . . . . . . D4
Roma 5,706 . . . . D5
Saint George 2,204 . . . . D5
Saint Lucia 6,075 . . . . D3
Sandgate 6,776 . . . . D2
Sarina 2,815 . . . . D4
Springsure 774 . . . . D5
Stafford (Stafford Heights)
  13,731 . . . . D2
Stanthorpe 3,966 . . . . D6
Tara 864 . . . . D5

Taroom 688 . . . . D5
Tewantin-Noosa 9,965 . . . . . E5
Theodore 643 . . . . D5
Thursday Island 2,283 . . . . . . B1
Toowoomba 63,401 . . . . D5
Townsville 86,112 . . . . C3
Tully 2,728 . . . . C3
Walkerston 1,277 . . . . D4
Warwick 8,853 . . . . D6
Weipa 2,433 . . . . B2
Windsor 6,119 . . . . D2
Winton 1,259 . . . . B4
Wynnum 10,794 . . . . E5
Yeppoon 6,447 . . . . D4
Yeronga 4,579 . . . . D3

OTHER FEATURES

Albatross (bay) B2
Archer (riv.) B2
Balonne (riv.) D6
Banks (isl.) B1
Barcoo (creek) B5
Barkly Tableland A4
Bartle Frere (mt.) C3
Beal (range) B5

Belyando (riv.) C4
Broad (sound) D4
Bulloo (lake) B6
Bulloo (riv.) B6
Bunker Group (isls.) E4
Burdekin (riv.) C3
Cape York (pen.) B2
Capricorn (chan.) D4
Capricorn Group (isls.) D4
Carnarvon (range) D5
Carpentaria (gulf) A3
Cloncurry (riv.) B4
Coopers (Barcoo) (creek) B5
Coral (sea) C1
Culgoa (riv.) C6
Cumberland (isls.) D4
Curtis (isl.) D4
Darling Downs D5
Dawson (riv.) D5
Diamantina (riv.) B4
Drummond (range) C5
Duifken (pt.) B2
Endeavour (str.) B1

Fitzroy (riv.) D4
Flinders (riv.) B3
Fraser (isl.) E5
Georgina (riv.) A4
Gilbert (riv.) B3
Great Dividing (range) C4
Gregory (range) B3
Gregory (riv.) A3
Grey (range) B5
Hamilton (riv.) B4
Hervey (bay) E5
Hinchinbrook (isl.) C3
Hook (isl.) D4
Leichhardt (riv.) A3
Machattie (lake) A4
Macintyre (riv.) D6
Maranoa (riv.) C5
Mary (riv.) E5
Melville (cape) C2
Mitchell (riv.) B2
Moreton (bay) E5
Moreton (isl.) E5
Mornington (isl.) A3

Norman (riv.) B3
Northern Peninsula
  Aboriginal Res. B1
Prince of Wales (isl.) B1
Princess Charlotte (bay) C2
Sandy (cape) E5
Selwyn (range) B4
Simpson (des.) A5
Sturt (des.) B5
Suttor (riv.) C4
Swain (reefs) E4
Thompson (riv.) B5
Torres (str.) B1
Warrego (range) C5
Warrego (riv.) C5
Wellesley (isls.) A3
Whitsunday (isl.) D4
Willies (range) C6
Yamma Yamma (lake) B5
York (cape) B1

○ Population of district.
* Population of met. area.

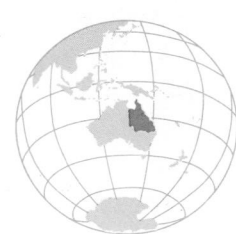

AREA 666,872 sq. mi. (1,727,200 sq. km.)
POPULATION 2,295,123
CAPITAL Brisbane
LARGEST CITY Brisbane
HIGHEST POINT Mt. Bartle Frere 5,287 ft.
  (1,611 m.)

Topography

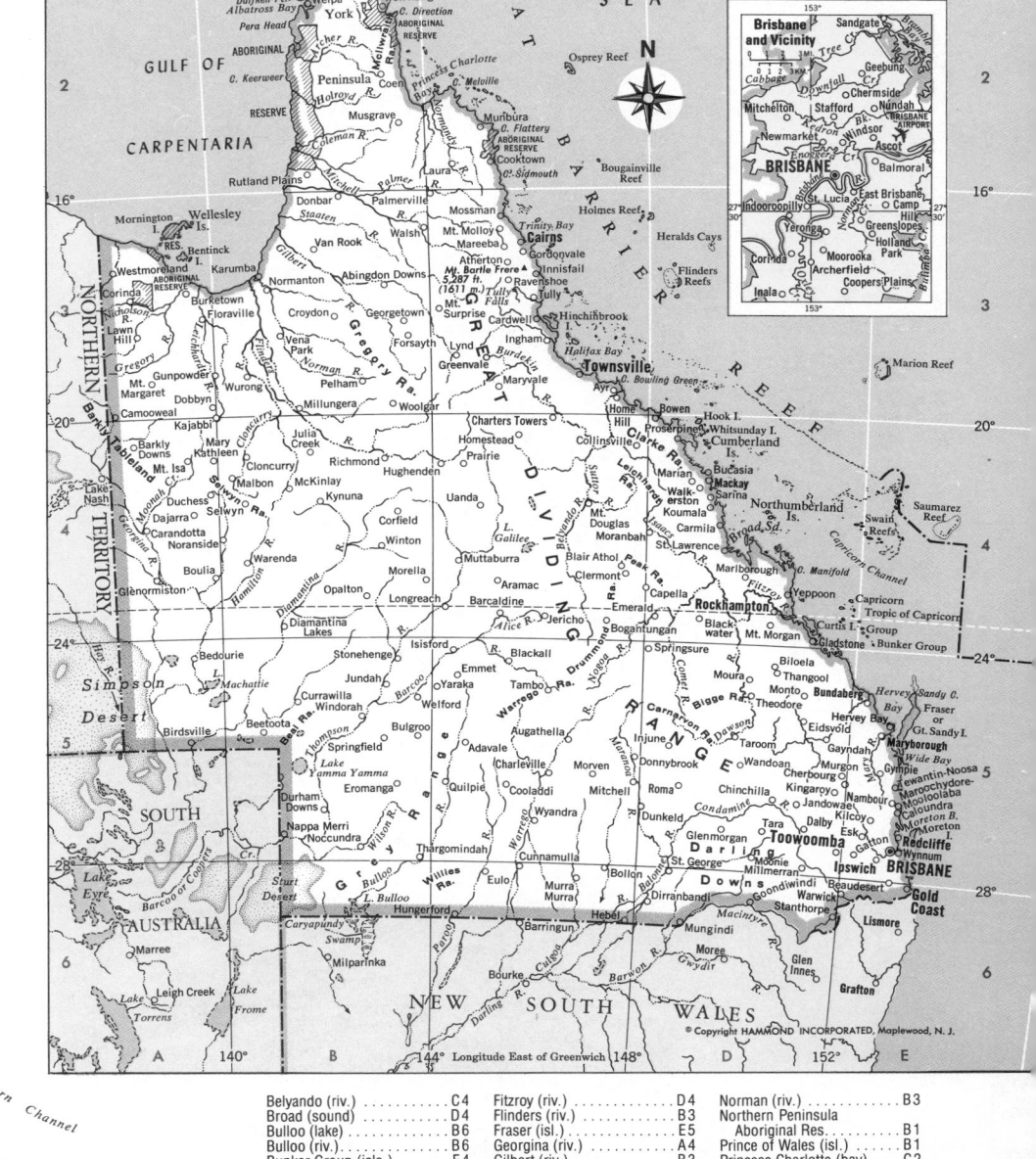

96 New South Wales and Victoria

NEW SOUTH WALES

AREA 309,498 sq. mi.
(801,600 sq. km.)
POPULATION 5,126,217
CAPITAL Sydney
LARGEST CITY Sydney
HIGHEST POINT Mt. Kosciusko
7,310 ft. (2,228 m.)

VICTORIA

AREA 87,876 sq. mi.
(227,600 sq. km.)
POPULATION 3,832,443
CAPITAL Melbourne
LARGEST CITY Melbourne
HIGHEST POINT Mt. Bogong
6,508 ft. (1,984 m.)

Topography

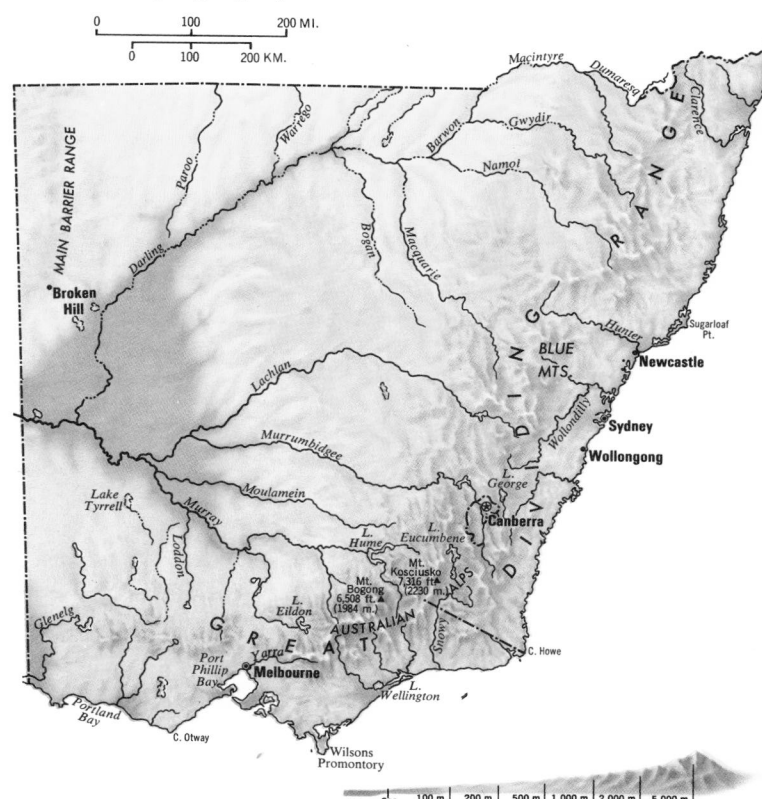

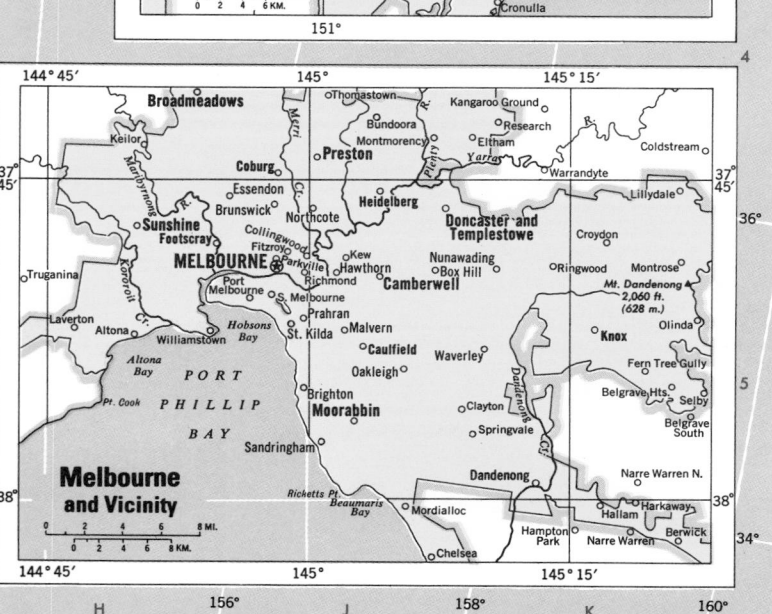

New South Wales and Victoria

SCALE OF MILES

SCALE OF KILOMETERS

Capital of Country _____ ⊛
State Capitals _____ ⊛
State and Territorial Boundaries _____

Scale 1:5,280,000

Lord Howe I.

Sydney and Vicinity

Melbourne and Vicinity

(continued)

OTHER FEATURES

VICTORIA

CITIES and TOWNS

OTHER FEATURES

*City and suburbs.
○ Population of district.
†Population of met. area.
‡Population of urban area.

Irrigation Areas and Artesian Basins in Australia

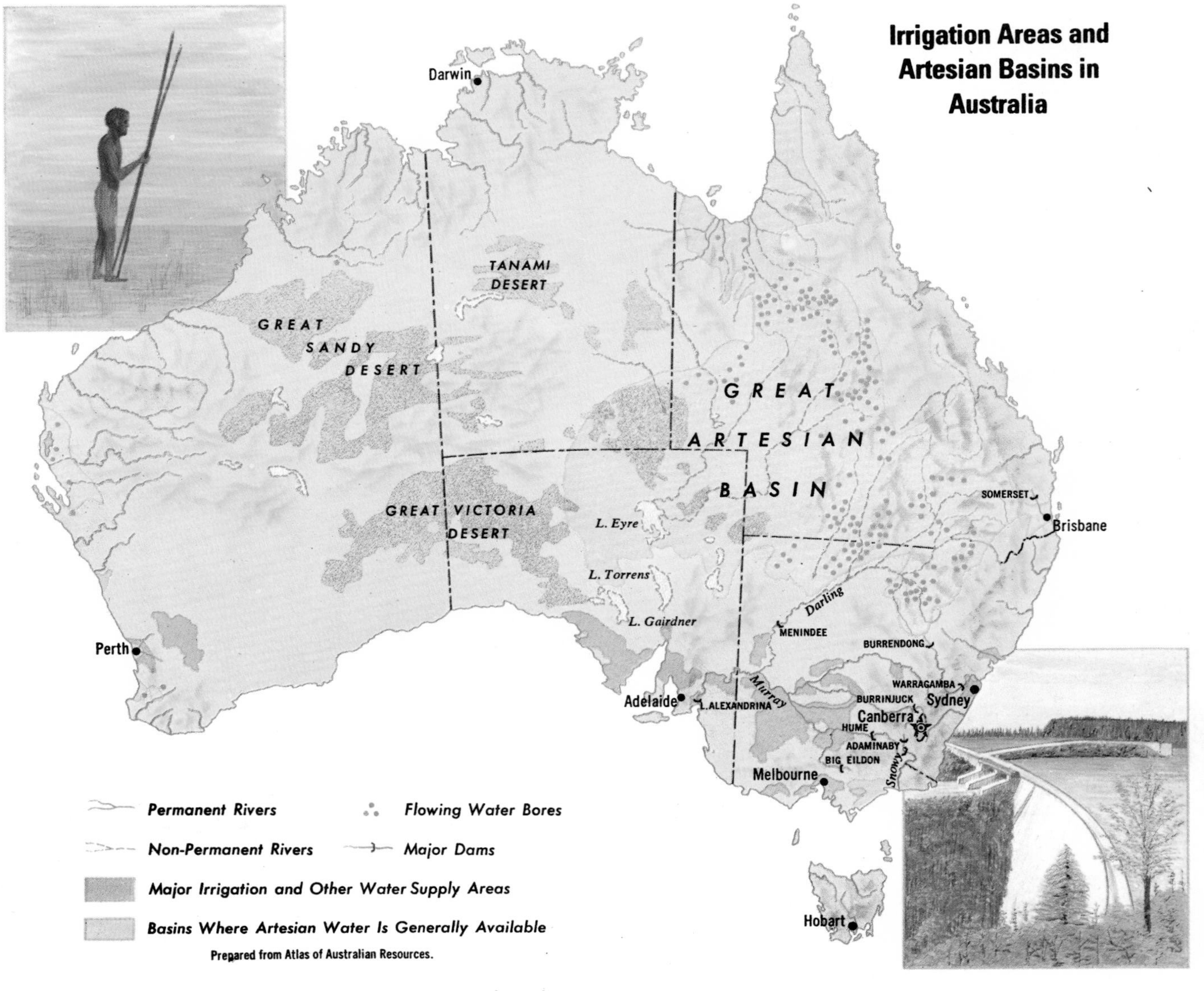

Darwin
TANAMI DESERT
GREAT SANDY DESERT
GREAT ARTESIAN BASIN
GREAT VICTORIA DESERT
L. Eyre
L. Torrens
L. Gairdner
Darling
MENINDEE
BURRENDONG
SOMERSET
Brisbane
Perth
Adelaide
L. ALEXANDRINA
Murray
WARRAGAMBA
BURRINJUCK
Sydney
Canberra
HUME
ADAMINABY
BIG EILDON
Snowy
Melbourne
Hobart
Permanent Rivers
Flowing Water Bores
Non-Permanent Rivers
Major Dams
Major Irrigation and Other Water Supply Areas
Basins Where Artesian Water Is Generally Available

Prepared from Atlas of Australian Resources.

Topography

0 30 60 MI.
0 30 60 KM.

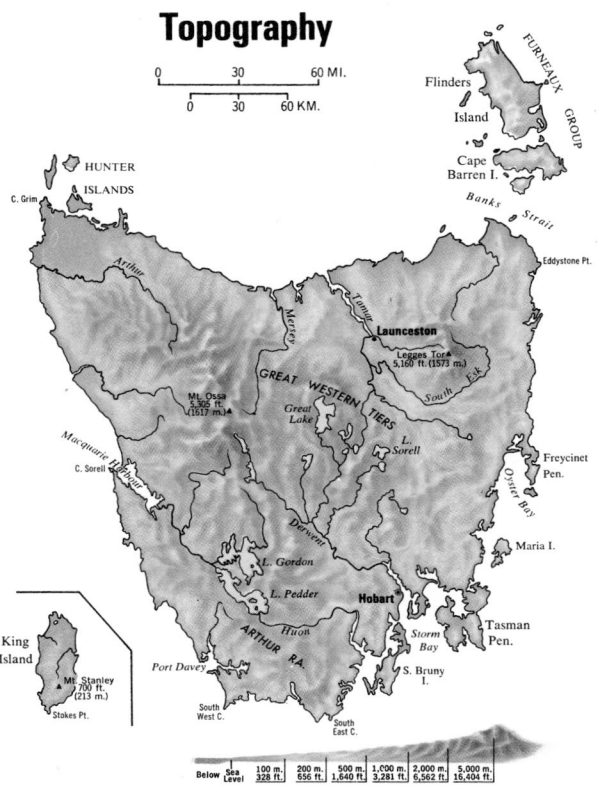

Below Sea Level | 100 m. 328 ft. | 200 m. 656 ft. | 500 m. 1,640 ft. | 1,000 m. 3,281 ft. | 2,000 m. 6,562 ft. | 5,000 m. 16,404 ft.

TASMANIA
AREA 26,178 sq. mi. (67,800 sq. km.)
POPULATION 418,957
CAPITAL Hobart
LARGEST CITY Hobart
HIGHEST POINT Mt. Ossa 5,305 ft.
(1,617 m.)

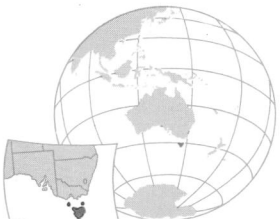

Main map labels

VICTORIA

BASS STRAIT

KING I.
Same Scale as Main Map

INDIAN OCEAN

TASMAN SEA

FURNEAUX GROUP

Banks Strait

N

Tasmania

MILES
0 10 20 30
KILOMETERS
0 10 20 30

State Capital .... ◉
State Boundaries _._._.
Scale 1:3,000,000

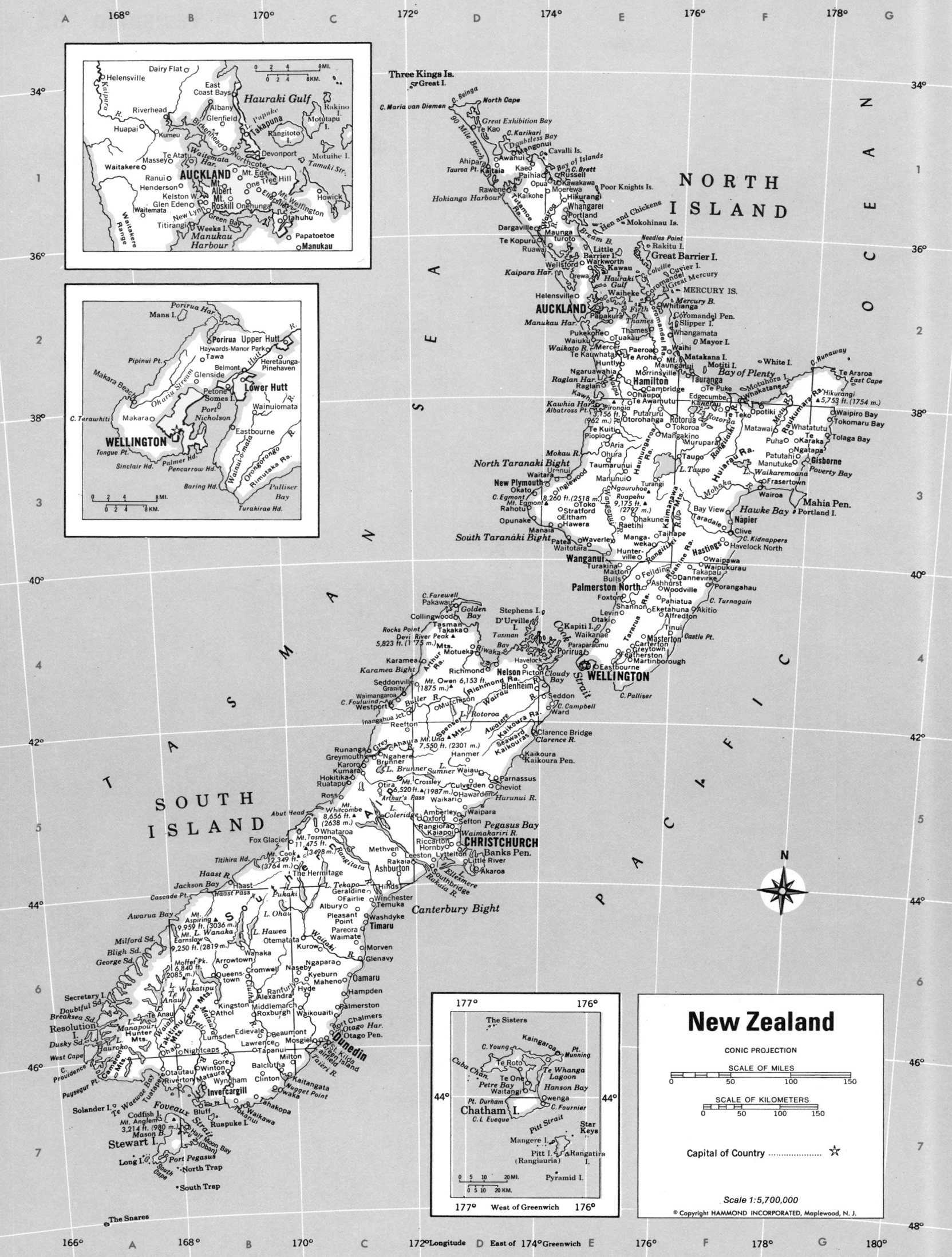

New Zealand

CONIC PROJECTION

SCALE OF MILES

SCALE OF KILOMETERS

Capital of Country .... ☆

Scale 1:5,700,000

® Copyright HAMMOND INCORPORATED, Maplewood, N.J.

NORTH ISLAND

SOUTH ISLAND

Chatham I.

Three Kings Is.

Topography

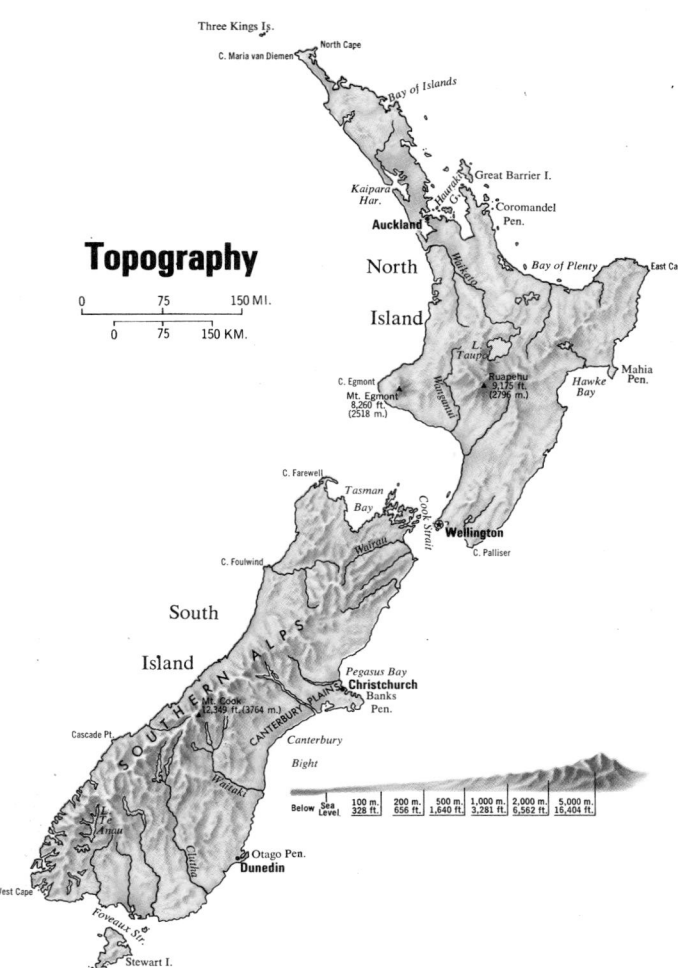

Three Kings Is.
C. Maria van Diemen
North Cape
Bay of Islands
Great Barrier I.
Kaipara Har.
Coromandel Pen.
Auckland
North
Island
Bay of Plenty
East Cape
L. Taupo
Ruapehu 9,175 ft. (2796 m.)
Mahia Pen.
C. Egmont
Mt. Egmont 8,260 ft. (2518 m.)
Hawke Bay
C. Farewell
Tasman Bay
Cook Strait
Wellington
C. Foulwind
C. Palliser
South
Island
SOUTHERN ALPS
Pegasus Bay
Mt. Cook 12,349 ft. (3764 m.)
Christchurch
Banks Pen.
Cascade Pt.
Canterbury Bight
Otago Pen.
Dunedin
West Cape
Foveaux Str.
Stewart I.

0 75 150 MI.
0 75 150 KM.

Below Sea Level | 100 m. 328 ft. | 200 m. 656 ft. | 500 m. 1,640 ft. | 1,000 m. 3,281 ft. | 2,000 m. 6,562 ft. | 5,000 m. 16,404 ft.

AREA 103,736 sq. mi. (268,676 sq. km.)
POPULATION 3,175,737
CAPITAL Wellington
LARGEST CITY Auckland
HIGHEST POINT Mt. Cook 12,349 ft. (3,764 m.)
MONETARY UNIT New Zealand dollar
MAJOR LANGUAGES English, Maori
MAJOR RELIGIONS Protestantism, Roman Catholicism

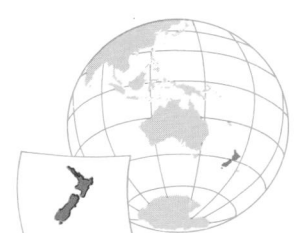

CITIES and TOWNS

Albany 2,001 .... B1
Alexandra 4,348 .... B6
Ashburton 14,151 .... C5
Ashhurst 1,906 .... E4
Auckland 144,963 .... B1
Auckland †769,558 .... B1
Balclutha 4,495 .... B7
Belmont 2,402 .... B2
Birkenhead 21,324 .... B1
Blenheim 17,849 .... D4
Bluff 2,720 .... B7
Bulls 1,839 .... E4
Cambridge 8,514 .... E2
Carterton 3,971 .... E4
Christchurch 164,680 .... D5
Christchurch †289,959 .... D5
Cromwell 2,364 .... B6
Dannevirke 5,663 .... F4
Dargaville 4,747 .... D1
Devonport 10,410 .... C1
Dunedin 77,176 .... C6
Dunedin †107,445 .... C6
Eastbourne 4,561 .... B3
East Coast Bays 28,866 .... B1
Edgecumbe 1,929 .... F2
Ellerslie 5,404 .... C1
Eltham 2,411 .... E3
Fairfield 1,849 .... C6
Featherston 2,458 .... E4
Feilding 11,522 .... E4
Foxton 2,719 .... E4
Geraldine 2,128 .... C6
Gisborne 29,986 .... G3
Gisborne †32,062 .... G3
Glen Eden 9,406 .... B1
Glenfield 3,691 .... B1
Gore 9,185 .... B7
Green Bay 3,035 .... B1
Green Island 6,899 .... C7
Greymouth 8,103 .... C5
Greytown 1,797 .... E4
Half Moon Bay (Oban) 2,448 .... B7
Hamilton 91,109 .... E2
Hamilton †97,907 .... E2
Hastings 36,083 .... F3
Hastings †52,563 .... F3
Havelock North 8,507 .... F3
Hawera 8,400 .... E3
Helensville 1,360 .... B1
Henderson 6,645 .... B1
Heretaunga-Pinehaven 6,171 .... C2
Hokitika 3,414 .... C5
Hornby 8,215 .... D5
Howick 13,866 .... C1
Huntly 6,534 .... E2
Hutt (Upper and Lower) †131,257 .... B2
Inglewood 2,839 .... E3

Invercargill 49,446 .... B7
Invercargill †53,868 .... B7
Kaiapoi 4,894 .... D5
Kaikohe 3,663 .... D1
Kaikoura 2,180 .... D5
Kaitaia 4,737 .... D1
Kawerau 8,593 .... F3
Kumeu 3,414 .... B1
Levin 14,652 .... E4
Lower Hutt 63,245 .... B2
Lyttelton 3,184 .... D5
Manukau 159,362 .... C1
Marton 4,858 .... E4
Masterton 18,785 .... E4
Mataura 2,345 .... B7
Milton 2,193 .... B7
Morrinsville 5,080 .... E2
Mosgiel 9,264 .... C6
Motueka 4,693 .... D4
Mount Albert 26,462 .... B1
Mount Eden 18,305 .... B1
Mount Maunganui 11,391 .... E2
Mount Roskill 33,577 .... B1
Mount Wellington 19,528 .... C1
Murupara 2,964 .... F3
Napier 48,314 .... F3
Napier †51,330 .... F3
Nelson 33,304 .... D4
Nelson †43,121 .... D4
New Lynn 10,445 .... B1
New Plymouth 36,048 .... D3
New Plymouth †44,095 .... D3
Ngaruawahia 4,435 .... E2
Northcote 10,061 .... B1
Oamaru 13,043 .... C6
Oban (Half Moon Bay) 2,448 .... B7
Onehunga 15,386 .... B1
One Tree Hill 11,078 .... B1
Opotiki 3,388 .... F3
Orewa 5,552 .... E2
Otahuhu 10,298 .... C1
Otaki 4,301 .... E4
Otorohanga 2,574 .... E2
Paeroa 3,702 .... E2
Pahiatua 2,599 .... F4
Paihia 1,740 .... D1
Palmerston North 60,105 .... E4
Palmerston North †66,691 .... E4
Papakura 22,473 .... E2
Papatoetoe 21,700 .... C1
Patea 1,938 .... E3
Petone 8,113 .... B2
Picton 3,220 .... D4
Pinehaven (Heretaunga-Pinehaven) 6,171 .... C2
Porirua 41,104 .... B2
Port Chalmers 2,917 .... C6
Pukekohe 9,070 .... E2
Putaruru 4,222 .... E3
Queenstown 3,367 .... B6

Raetihi 1,247 .... E3
Raglan 1,414 .... E2
Rangiora 6,385 .... D5
Reefton 1,200 .... C5
Riccarton 6,709 .... D5
Richmond 6,847 .... D4
Riverton 1,479 .... B7
Rotorua 38,157 .... F3
Rotorua †48,314 .... F3
Runanga 1,264 .... C5
Saint Kilda 6,147 .... C7
Shannon 1,465 .... E4
Stratford 5,518 .... E3
Taihape 2,586 .... E3
Takapuna 64,844 .... B1
Tapanui 1,042 .... B6
Taradale 4,681 .... F3
Taumarunui 6,541 .... E3
Taupo 13,651 .... F3
Tauranga 37,099 .... F2
Tauranga †53,097 .... F2
Tawa 12,216 .... B2
Te Anau 2,610 .... A6
Te Atatu 14,713 .... B1
Te Aroha 3,331 .... E2
Te Awamutu 7,922 .... E3
Te Kauwhata 842 .... E2
Te Kuiti 4,795 .... E3
Te Puke 4,577 .... F2
Temuka 3,771 .... C6
Thames 6,456 .... E2
The Hermitage C5
Timaru 28,412 .... C6
Timaru †29,225 .... C6
Titirangi 8,426 .... B1
Tokoroa 18,713 .... F3
Tuakau 1,982 .... E2
Tuatapere 884 .... A7
Turangi 5,517 .... E3
Upper Hutt 31,405 .... B2
Waihi 3,538 .... E2
Waikanae 4,818 .... E4
Waikouaiti 858 .... C6
Waimate 3,393 .... C6
Wainuiomata 19,192 .... B3
Waipawa 1,732 .... F3
Waipukurau 3,648 .... F4
Wairoa 5,439 .... F3
Waitangi D7
Waitara 6,012 .... E3
Waitemata 87,452 .... B1
Waiuku 3,654 .... E2
Wanaka 1,155 .... B6
Wanganui 37,012 .... E3
Wanganui †39,595 .... E3
Warkworth 1,734 .... E2
Washdyke 949 .... C6
Waverley 1,239 .... E3
Wellington (cap.) 135,688 .... A3

Wellington †321,004 .... A3
Wellsford 1,621 .... E2
Westport 4,686 .... C4
Whakatane 12,286 .... F2
Whangamata 1,566 .... F2
Whangarei 36,550 .... E1
Whangarei †40,212 .... E1
Whitianga 1,960 .... E2
Winton 2,035 .... B7
Woodville 1,647 .... F4

OTHER FEATURES

Arthur's (pass) C5
Aspiring (mt.) B6
Banks (pen.) D5
Bream (bay) E1
Brett (cape) E1
Buller (riv.) D4
Campbell (cape) E4
Canterbury (bight) D6
Cascade (pt.) B6
Chatham (isls.) 751 .... D7
Cloudy (bay) E4
Clutha (riv.) B6
Coleridge (lake) C5
Colville (cape) E2
Cook (mt.) C5
Cook (str.) E4
Coromandel (pen.) F2
Devil River (peak) D4
D'Urville (isl.) D4
Dusky (sound) A6
East (cape) G2
Egmont (cape) D3
Egmont (mt.) D3
Ellesmere (lake) D5
Farewell (cape) D4
Foulwind (cape) C4
Fournier (cape) E7
Foveaaux (str.) A7
Golden (bay) D4
Great Barrier (isl.) 572 .... E2
Hauraki (gulf) C1
Hawke (bay) F3
Hikurangi (mt.) G2
Hokianga (harb.) D1
Huiarau (range) F3
Hutt (riv.) C2
Islands (bay) E1
Jackson (bay) B5
Kaikoura (range) D5
Kaimanawa (range) E3
Kaipara (harb.) D2
Karamea (bight) C4
Kawhia (harb.) E3
Kidnappers (cape) F3
Mahia (pen.) G3
Manapouri (lake) A6
Manukau (harb.) B1
Maria van Diemen (cape) D1
Mataura (riv.) B6
Mercury (isls.) F2
Milford (sound) A6
Needles (pt.) E2
Nicholson, Port (inlet) B3
Ninety Mile (beach) D1
North (cape) D1
North (isl.) 2,322,989 .... F1
North Taranaki (bight) D3
Otago (pen.) C6
Owen (mt.) D4
Palliser (cape) E4
Pegasus (bay) D5
Pitt (isl.) E7
Plenty (bay) F2
Port Nicholson (inlet) B3
Port Pegasus (inlet) B7
Pukaki (lake) B6
Puysegur (pt.) A7
Rakaia (riv.) C5
Rangitata (riv.) C5
Rangitikei (riv.) E3
Raukumara (range) F3
Reinga (cape) D1
Resolution (isl.) A6
Richmond (range) D4
Rocks (pt.) C4
Rotorua (lake) F3
Ruahine (range) F4
Ruapehu (mt.) E3
Ruapuke (isl.) B7
South (cape) A7
South (isl.) 852,748 .... B5
Southern Alps (range) C5
South Taranaki (bight) D3
Spenser (mts.) D5
Stewart (isl.) 600 .... A7
Tararua (range) E4
Tasman (bay) D4
Tasman (mt.) C5
Tasman (mts.) D4
Tasman (sea) B4
Taupo (lake) F3
Tauroa (pt.) D1

Te Anau (lake) A6
Tekapo (lake) C5
Terawhiti (cape) A3
Thames (firth) E2
Three Kings (isls.) D1
Turakirae (head) B3
Una (mt.) D5
Waiheke (isl.) 3,223 .... E2
Waikato (riv.) E2
Waimakariri (riv.) D5
Waipa (riv.) E2
Wairau (riv.) D4
Waitaki (riv.) C6
Waitemata (harb.) B1
Wakatipu (lake) B6
Wanaka (lake) B6
Wanganui (riv.) E3
West (cape) A6
Whitcombe (mt.) C5

†Population of urban area.

Agriculture, Industry and Resources

DOMINANT LAND USE

Mixed Farming, Livestock
Dairy
Truck Farming, Horticulture
Pasture Livestock (chiefly sheep)
Livestock Herding
Forests
Nonagricultural Land

MAJOR MINERAL OCCURRENCES

C Coal
G Natural Gas
J Jade
Ka Kaolin
Lg Lignite
O Petroleum
U Uranium

Water Power
Major Industrial Areas

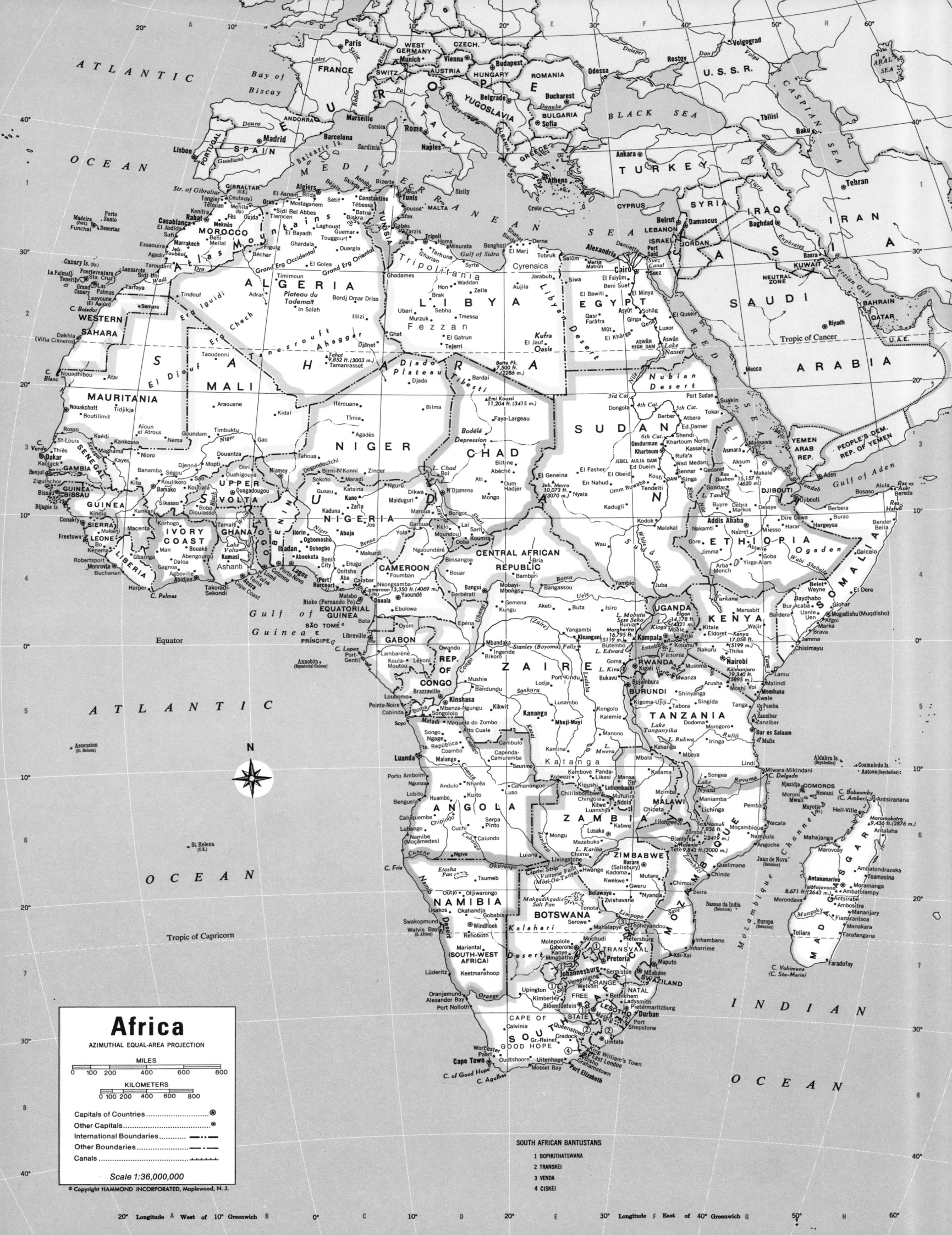

AREA 11,707,000 sq. mi. (30,321,130 sq. km.)
POPULATION 469,000,000
LARGEST CITY Cairo
HIGHEST POINT Kilimanjaro 19,340 ft. (5,895 m.)
LOWEST POINT Lake Assal, Djibouti -512 ft. (-156 m.)

Population Distribution

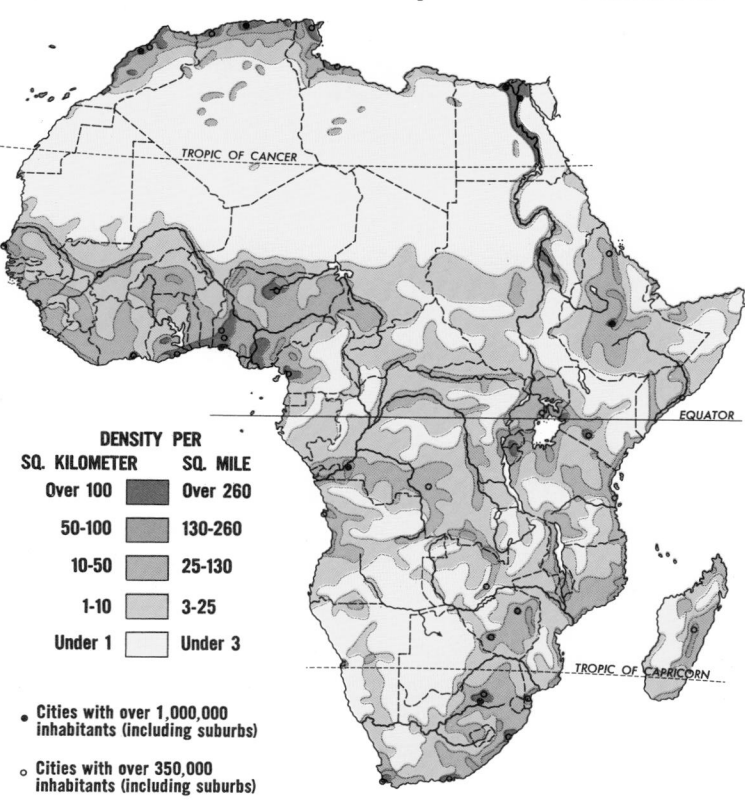

DENSITY PER

SQ. KILOMETER	SQ. MILE
Over 100	Over 260
50-100	130-260
10-50	25-130
1-10	3-25
Under 1	Under 3

● Cities with over 1,000,000 inhabitants (including suburbs)

○ Cities with over 350,000 inhabitants (including suburbs)

Vegetation

TROPICAL FOREST
- Tropical Rainforest
- Light Tropical Forest
- Woodland and Shrub

TROPICAL GRASSLAND
- Grass and Shrub (Savanna)
- Wooded Savanna

MID-LATITUDE FOREST
- Mixed Coniferous and Broadleaf Forest
- Woodland and Shrub (Mediterranean)

MID-LATITUDE GRASSLAND
- Short Grass (Steppe)

RIVER VALLEY AND OASIS

DESERT AND DESERT SHRUB

UNCLASSIFIED HIGHLANDS

Average January Temperature

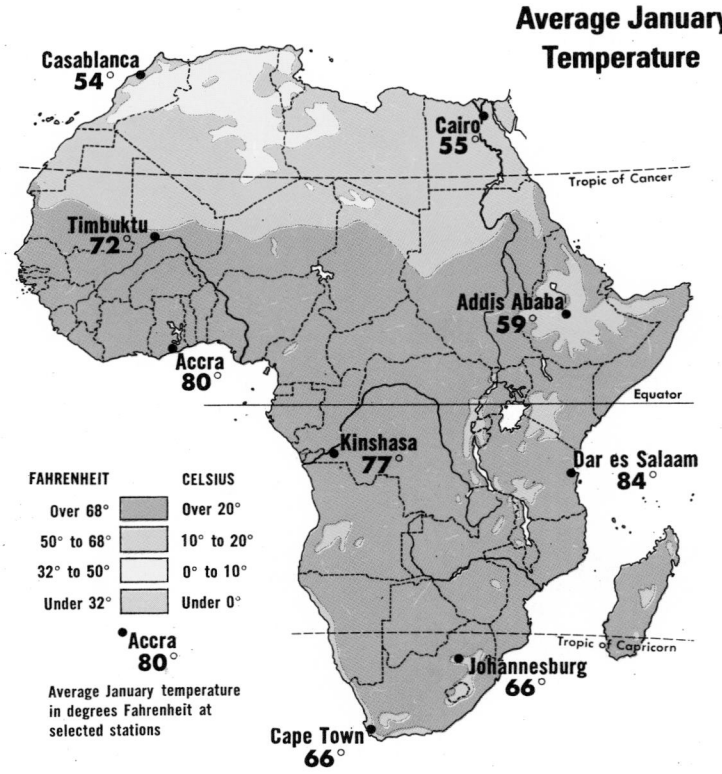

Casablanca 54°
Cairo 55°
Timbuktu 72°
Addis Ababa 59°
Accra 80°
Kinshasa 77°
Dar es Salaam 84°
Johannesburg 66°
Cape Town 66°

Tropic of Cancer
Equator
Tropic of Capricorn

FAHRENHEIT
Over 68°
50° to 68°
32° to 50°
Under 32°

CELSIUS
Over 20°
10° to 20°
0° to 10°
Under 0°

• Accra 80°
Average January temperature in degrees Fahrenheit at selected stations

Average July Temperature

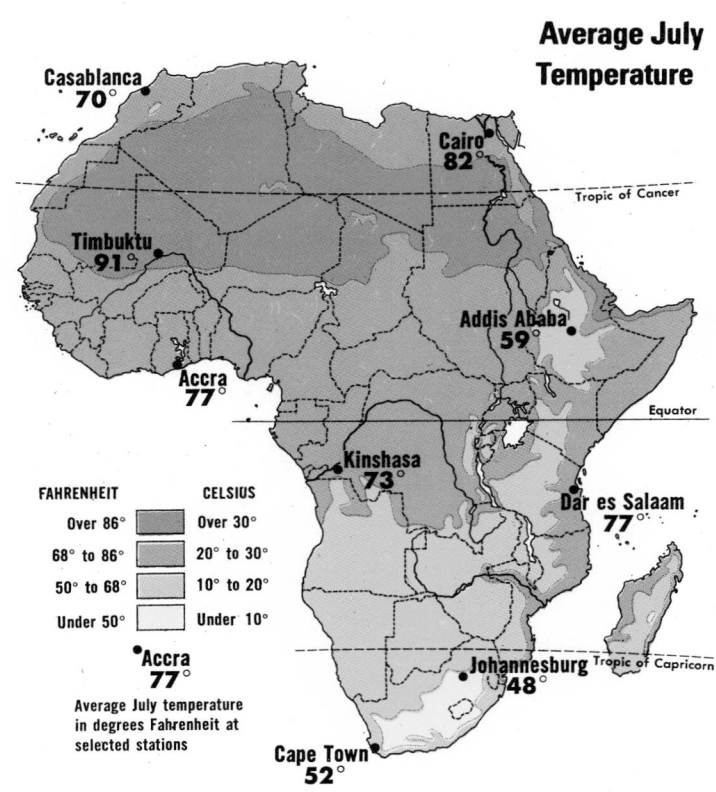

Casablanca 70°
Cairo 82°
Timbuktu 91°
Addis Ababa 59°
Accra 77°
Kinshasa 73°
Dar es Salaam 77°
Johannesburg 48°
Cape Town 52°

Tropic of Cancer
Equator
Tropic of Capricorn

FAHRENHEIT
Over 86°
68° to 86°
50° to 68°
Under 50°

CELSIUS
Over 30°
20° to 30°
10° to 20°
Under 10°

• Accra 77°
Average July temperature in degrees Fahrenheit at selected stations

Rainfall

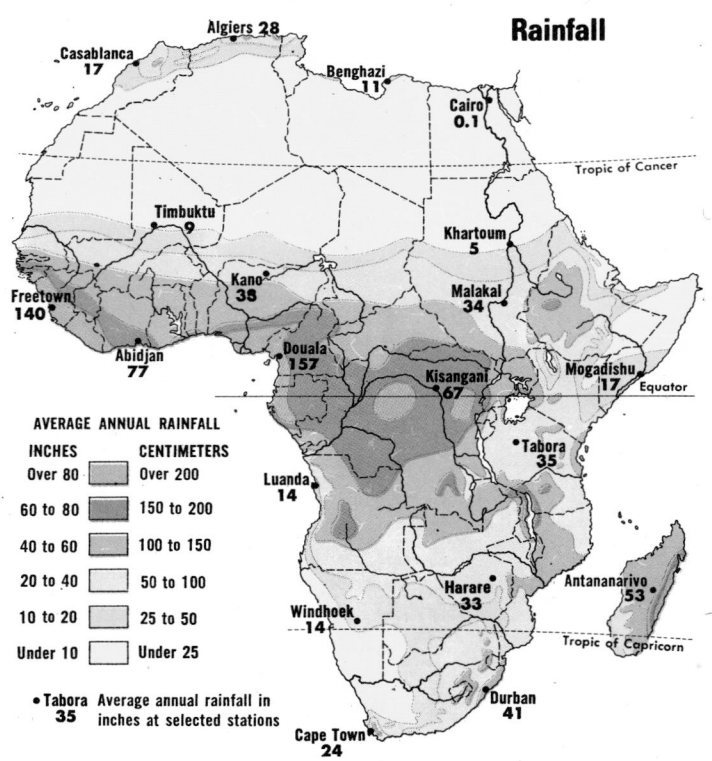

Algiers 28
Casablanca 17
Benghazi 11
Cairo 0.1
Timbuktu 9
Khartoum 5
Kano 35
Malakal 34
Freetown 140
Douala 157
Mogadishu 17
Abidjan 77
Kisangani 67
Tabora 35
Luanda 14
Harare 33
Antananarivo 53
Windhoek 14
Durban 41
Cape Town 24

Tropic of Cancer
Equator
Tropic of Capricorn

AVERAGE ANNUAL RAINFALL

INCHES	CENTIMETERS
Over 80	Over 200
60 to 80	150 to 200
40 to 60	100 to 150
20 to 40	50 to 100
10 to 20	25 to 50
Under 10	Under 25

• Tabora 35 Average annual rainfall in inches at selected stations

Vegetation/Relief

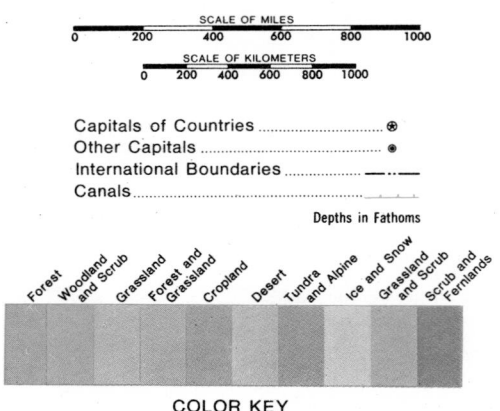

SCALE OF MILES
0 200 400 600 800 1000

SCALE OF KILOMETERS
0 200 400 600 800 1000

Capitals of Countries .... ⊛
Other Capitals .... ⊛
International Boundaries .... – – –
Canals ....

Depths in Fathoms

Forest
Woodland and Scrub
Grassland
Forest and Grassland
Cropland
Desert
Tundra and Alpine
Ice and Snow
Grassland and Scrub
Scrub and Fernlands

COLOR KEY

Longitude 10° West of Greenwich Longitude 10° East of Greenwich

Western Africa

CONIC EQUAL-AREA PROJECTION

SCALE OF MILES

0   100   200   400

SCALE OF KILOMETERS

0   100   200   400

Capitals of Countries ___ ☆   International Boundaries ___
Other Capitals ___ ◉   Internal Boundaries ___

Scale 1:15,200,000

© Copyright HAMMOND INCORPORATED, Maplewood, N.J.

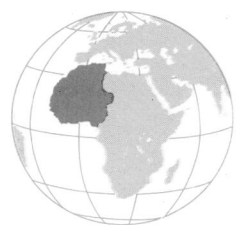

ALGERIA

AREA 919,591 sq. mi. (2,381,740 sq. km.)
POPULATION 17,422,000
CAPITAL Algiers
LARGEST CITY Algiers
HIGHEST POINT Tahat 9,852 ft. (3,003 m.)
MONETARY UNIT Algerian dinar
MAJOR LANGUAGES Arabic, Berber, French
MAJOR RELIGION Islam

BENIN

AREA 43,483 sq. mi. (112,620 sq. km.)
POPULATION 3,338,240
CAPITAL Porto-Novo
LARGEST CITY Cotonou
HIGHEST POINT Atakora Mts. 2,083 ft. (635 m.)
MONETARY UNIT CFA franc
MAJOR LANGUAGES Fon, Somba, Yoruba, Bariba, French, Mina, Dendi
MAJOR RELIGIONS Tribal religions, Islam, Roman Catholicism

CAPE VERDE

AREA 1,557 sq. mi. (4,033 sq. km.)
POPULATION 324,000
CAPITAL Praia
LARGEST CITY Praia
HIGHEST POINT 9,281 ft. (2,829 m.)
MONETARY UNIT Cape Verde escudo
MAJOR LANGUAGE Portuguese
MAJOR RELIGION Roman Catholicism

GAMBIA

AREA 4,127 sq. mi. (10,689 sq. km.)
POPULATION 601,000
CAPITAL Banjul
LARGEST CITY Banjul
HIGHEST POINT 100 ft. (30 m.)
MONETARY UNIT dalasi
MAJOR LANGUAGES Mandingo, Fulani, Wolof, English, Malinke
MAJOR RELIGIONS Islam, tribal religions, Christianity

GHANA

AREA 92,099 sq. mi. (238,536 sq. km.)
POPULATION 11,450,000
CAPITAL Accra
LARGEST CITY Accra
HIGHEST POINT Togo Hills 2,900 ft. (884 m.)
MONETARY UNIT cedi
MAJOR LANGUAGES Twi, Fante, Dagbani, Ewe, Ga, English, Hausa, Akan
MAJOR RELIGIONS Tribal religions, Christianity, Islam

GUINEA

AREA 94,925 sq. mi. (245,856 sq. km.)
POPULATION 5,143,284
CAPITAL Conakry
LARGEST CITY Conakry
HIGHEST POINT Nimba Mts. 6,070 ft. (1,850 m.)
MONETARY UNIT syli
MAJOR LANGUAGES Fulani, Mandingo, Susu, French
MAJOR RELIGIONS Islam, tribal religions

GUINEA-BISSAU

AREA 13,948 sq. mi. (36,125 sq. km.)
POPULATION 777,214
CAPITAL Bissau
LARGEST CITY Bissau
HIGHEST POINT 689 ft. (210 m.)
MONETARY UNIT Guinea-Bissau escudo
MAJOR LANGUAGES Balante, Fulani, Crioulo, Mandingo, Portuguese
MAJOR RELIGIONS Islam, tribal religions, Roman Catholicism

IVORY COAST

AREA 124,504 sq. mi. (322,465 sq. km.)
POPULATION 7,920,000
CAPITAL Abidjan
LARGEST CITY Abidjan
HIGHEST POINT 5,745 ft. (1,751 m.)
MONETARY UNIT CFA franc
MAJOR LANGUAGES Bale, Bete, Senufu, French, Dioula
MAJOR RELIGIONS Tribal religions, Islam

LIBERIA

AREA 43,000 sq. mi. (111,370 sq. km.)
POPULATION 1,873,000
CAPITAL Monrovia
LARGEST CITY Monrovia
HIGHEST POINT Wutivi 5,584 ft. (1,702 m.)
MONETARY UNIT Liberian dollar
MAJOR LANGUAGES Kru, Kpelle, Bassa, Vai, English
MAJOR RELIGIONS Christianity, tribal religions, Islam

MALI

AREA 464,873 sq. mi. (1,204,021 sq. km.)
POPULATION 6,906,000
CAPITAL Bamako
LARGEST CITY Bamako
HIGHEST POINT Hombori Mts. 3,789 ft. (1,155 m.)
MONETARY UNIT Mali franc
MAJOR LANGUAGES Bambara, Senufu, Fulani, Soninke, French
MAJOR RELIGIONS Islam, tribal religions

MAURITANIA

AREA 419,229 sq. mi. (1,085,803 sq. km.)
POPULATION 1,634,000
CAPITAL Nouakchott
LARGEST CITY Nouakchott
HIGHEST POINT 2,972 ft. (906 m.)
MONETARY UNIT ouguiya
MAJOR LANGUAGES Arabic, Wolof, Tukolor, French
MAJOR RELIGION Islam

MOROCCO

AREA 172,414 sq. mi. (446,550 sq. km.)
POPULATION 20,242,000
CAPITAL Rabat
LARGEST CITY Casablanca
HIGHEST POINT Jeb. Toubkal 13,665 ft. (4,165 m.)
MONETARY UNIT dirham
MAJOR LANGUAGES Arabic, Berber, French
MAJOR RELIGIONS Islam, Judaism, Christianity

NIGER

AREA 489,189 sq. mi. (1,267,000 sq. km.)
POPULATION 5,098,427
CAPITAL Niamey
LARGEST CITY Niamey
HIGHEST POINT Banguezane 6,234 ft. (1,900 m.)
MONETARY UNIT CFA franc
MAJOR LANGUAGES Hausa, Songhai, Fulani, French, Tamashek, Djerma
MAJOR RELIGIONS Islam, tribal religions

NIGERIA

AREA 357,000 sq. mi. (924,630 sq. km.)
POPULATION 82,643,000
CAPITAL Lagos
LARGEST CITY Lagos
HIGHEST POINT Dimlang 6,700 ft. (2,042 m.)
MONETARY UNIT naira
MAJOR LANGUAGES Hausa, Yoruba, Ibo, Ijaw, Fulani, Tiv, Kanuri, Ibibio, English, Edo
MAJOR RELIGIONS Islam, Christianity, tribal religions

SÃO TOMÉ E PRÍNCIPE

AREA 372 sq. mi. (963 sq. km.)
POPULATION 85,000
CAPITAL São Tomé
LARGEST CITY São Tomé
HIGHEST POINT Pico 6,640 ft. (2,024 m.)
MONETARY UNIT dobra
MAJOR LANGUAGES Bantu languages, Portuguese
MAJOR RELIGIONS Tribal religions, Roman Catholicism

SENEGAL

AREA 75,954 sq. mi. (196,720 sq. km.)
POPULATION 5,508,000
CAPITAL Dakar
LARGEST CITY Dakar
HIGHEST POINT Futa Jallon 1,640 ft. (500 m.)
MONETARY UNIT CFA franc
MAJOR LANGUAGES Wolof, Peul (Fulani), French, Mende, Mandingo, Dida
MAJOR RELIGIONS Islam, tribal religions, Roman Catholicism

SIERRA LEONE

AREA 27,925 sq. mi. (72,325 sq. km.)
POPULATION 3,470,000
CAPITAL Freetown
LARGEST CITY Freetown
HIGHEST POINT Loma Mts. 6,390 ft. (1,947 m.)
MONETARY UNIT leone
MAJOR LANGUAGES Mende, Temne, Vai, English, Krio (pidgin)
MAJOR RELIGIONS Tribal religions, Islam, Christianity

TOGO

AREA 21,622 sq. mi. (56,000 sq. km.)
POPULATION 2,472,000
CAPITAL Lomé
LARGEST CITY Lomé
HIGHEST POINT Agou 3,445 ft. (1,050 m.)
MONETARY UNIT CFA franc
MAJOR LANGUAGES Ewe, French, Twi, Hausa
MAJOR RELIGIONS Tribal religions, Roman Catholicism, Islam

TUNISIA

AREA 63,378 sq. mi. (164,149 sq. km.)
POPULATION 6,367,000
CAPITAL Tunis
LARGEST CITY Tunis
HIGHEST POINT Jeb. Chambi 5,066 ft. (1,544 m.)
MONETARY UNIT Tunisian dinar
MAJOR LANGUAGES Arabic, French
MAJOR RELIGION Islam

UPPER VOLTA

AREA 105,869 sq. mi. (274,200 sq. km.)
POPULATION 6,908,000
CAPITAL Ouagadougou
LARGEST CITY Ouagadougou
HIGHEST POINT 2,352 ft. (717 m.)
MONETARY UNIT CFA franc
MAJOR LANGUAGES Mossi, Lobi, French, Samo, Gourounsi
MAJOR RELIGIONS Islam, tribal religions, Roman Catholicism

WESTERN SAHARA

AREA 102,703 sq. mi. (266,000 sq. km.)
POPULATION 76,425
HIGHEST POINT 2,700 ft. (823 m.)
MAJOR LANGUAGE Arabic
MAJOR RELIGION Islam

Topography

0	200	400	600 MI.
0	200	400	600 KM.

5,000 m. / 16,404 ft.   2,000 m. / 6,562 ft.   1,000 m. / 3,281 ft.   500 m. / 1,640 ft.   200 m. / 656 ft.   100 m. / 328 ft.   Sea Level   Below

ALGERIA
CITIES and TOWNS

Abadla 12,200 ...D2
Adrar 22,800 ...D3
Aïn Belda 26,976 ...F1
Aïn Sefra 22,400 ...D2
Aïn Temouchent 42,000 ...D1
Algiers (cap.) 1,365,400 ...E1
Amguid ...F3
Annaba 255,900 ...F1
Aoulet 17,200 ...E3
Arak ...E3
Batna 112,100 ...F1
Béchar 72,800 ...D2
Bejaia 89,500 ...F1
Beni Abbès 5,000 ...D2
Beni Ounif 7,500 ...D2
Beni Saf 30,700 ...D1
Berga ...E3
Bidon 5 (Poste Maurice Cordier) ...E4
Biskra 90,500 ...F1
Blida 160,900 ...E1
Bône (Annaba) 255,900 ...F1
Bordj Bou Arreridj 65,000 ...E1
Bordj Fly Sainte Marie ...D3
Bordj Omar Driss 1,900 ...F3
Boufarik 50,000 ...E1
Bougie (Bejaïa) 89,500 ...E1
Bou Sada 50,000 ...E1
Brezina 10,000 ...E2
Charouine ...D3
Chenachane ...D3
Cherchell 36,800 ...E1
Constantine 335,100 ...F1
Deldoul ...E3
Dellys 29,700 ...E1
Djanet 5,300 ...F4
Djelfa 51,000 ...E2
Djemaa 34,600 ...F2
Edjeleh ...F4
El Abiod Sidi Cheikh 15,300 ...E2
El Asnam 106,100 ...E1
El Bayadh 38,500 ...E2
El Djezair (Algiers) (cap.) 1,365,400 ...E1
El Goléa 24,400 ...E2
El Oued 72,100 ...F2
Fort Lallemand ...F2
Fort MacMahon ...E3
Fort Miribel ...E3
Fort Tarat ...F3
Ghardaïa 70,500 ...E2
Ghazaouet 25,900 ...D2
Guelma 60,100 ...F1
Guemar ...F2
Guerara 22,300 ...E2
Guerzim ...D3
Hassi Messaoud ...F2
Hassi R'Mel ...E2
Ideles ...F4
Igli 3,400 ...D2
Illizi 4,600 ...F3
In Amenas 4,200 ...F3
In Amguel ...F4
In Eker ...E4
In Guezzam ...F5
In Rhar ...E3
In Salah 18,800 ...E3
Jijel 49,800 ...F1
Kenadsa 7,600 ...D2
Kerzaz 2,900 ...D3
Khemis Miliana 57,800 ...E1
Ksar el Boukhari 41,200 ...E1
Laghouat 59,200 ...E2
Mascara 62,300 ...D1
Mecheria 22,600 ...E2
Médéa 72,300 ...E1
Metlili Chaamba 21,300 ...E2
Miliana 36,400 ...E1
Mohammadia 53,700 ...D1
Mostaganem 101,600 ...D1
M'Sila 49,100 ...E1
Oran 491,900 ...D1
Orléansville (El Asnam) 106,100 ...E1
Ouallene ...E4
Ouargla 77,400 ...F2
Ouled Djellal 22,700 ...F2
Philippeville (Skikda) 107,700 ...F1
Poste Maurice Cortier ...E4
Poste Weygand ...D4
Reggane 11,300 ...D3
Relizane 60,000 ...E1
Saïda 62,100 ...E2
Sbaa ...D3
Sétif 144,200 ...F1
Sidi Bel-Abbes 116,000 ...D1
Silet ...E4
Skikda 107,700 ...F1
Souk Ahras 60,200 ...F1
Tabelbala 3,100 ...D3
Taghit 3,500 ...D2
Tamanrasset 23,200 ...F4
Tamentit ...D3
Taourirt ...E3
Tébessa 67,200 ...F1
Temacine ...F2
Tenès 30,100 ...E1
Tiaret 62,900 ...E1
Tiguentourine ...F3
Timgad 9,800 ...F1
Timimoun 20,500 ...E3
Tindouf 6,500 ...C3
Tinzouatine ...E5
Tizi Ouzou 73,100 ...E1
Tlemcen 109,400 ...D2
Touggourt 75,600 ...F2
Zaouiet Kounta 13,800 ...D3

OTHER FEATURES

Adrar des Iforas (plat.) ...E5
Ahaggar (range) ...F4
Anaï (well) ...G4
Aouinet Bel Egra (well) ...C3
Atlas (mts.) ...E1
Aurès (reg.) ...F1
Azzel Mati, Sebkha (lake) ...E3
Bougaroun (cape) ...E1
Chech, Erg (des.) ...D3
Chelia (mt.) ...F1
Chelif (riv.) ...E1
Chergui, Chott Ech (salt lake) ...E2
Gourara (oasis) ...E3
Grand Erg Occidental (des.) ...E2
Grand Erg Oriental (des.) ...F2
Guir Hamada (des.) ...D2
High Plateaus (ranges) ...D2
Iguidi, Erg (des.) ...C3
In Ezzane (well) ...G4
Irharhar, Wadi (dry riv.) ...F3
Issaouane Erg (des.) ...F3
Kabylia (reg.) ...F1
Mediterranean (sea) ...E1
Medjerda (riv.) ...F1
Melrhir, Chott (salt lake) ...F2
Mouydir (mts.) ...E3
Mya, Wadi (dry riv.) ...E2
M'zab (oasis) ...E2
Raoui, Erg er (des.) ...D3
Rhir, Wadi (dry riv.) ...F2
Sahara (des.) ...E4
Saharan Atlas (ranges) ...E2
Saoura, Wadi (dry riv.) ...D3
Souf (oasis) ...F2
Tademaït, Plateau du (plat.) ...E3
Tafassasset, Wadi (dry riv.) ...F4
Tahat (mt.) ...F4
Tamanrasset, Wadi (dry riv.) ...E4
Tanezrouft (des.) ...E4
Tassili N'Ahagger (plat.) ...E4
Tassili N'Ajjer (plat.) ...F3
Tidikelt (oasis) ...E3
Timmissao (well) ...E4
Tindouf, Sebkha de (salt lake) ...C3
Tinrhert, Hamada de (des.) ...F3
Tni Hala (well) ...D4
Touat (oasis) ...E3
Touila (well) ...C3

BENIN
CITIES and TOWNS

Abomey 38,000 ...E7
Cotonou 178,000 ...E7
Djougou ...E7
Grand-Popo ...E7
Kandi ...E6
Lokossa 6,000 ...E7
Malanville ...E6
Natitingou 49,000 ...E6
Nikki ...E7
Ouidah ...E7
Parakou 21,000 ...E7
Porto-Novo (cap.) 104,000 ...E7
Savalou ...E7
Savé ...E7

OTHER FEATURES

Atakora (mts.) ...E6
Benin (bight) ...E8
Guinea (gulf) ...E8
Mono (riv.) ...E7
Niger (riv.) ...E6
Ouémé (riv.) ...E7
Slave Coast (reg.) ...E7
Sudan (reg.) ...E6

CAPE VERDE
CITIES and TOWNS

Mindelo 28,797 ...A7
Praia (cap.) 21,494 ...B8
Ribeira Grande 1,892 ...B7
Sal Rei 1,296 ...B8
Santa Maria 956 ...B8

OTHER FEATURES

Boa Vista (isl.) ...B8
Brava (isl.) ...B8
Fogo (isl.) ...B8
Maio (isl.) ...B8
Sal (isl.) ...B7
Santa Luzia (isl.) ...B7
Santo Antão (isl.) ...A7
São Nicolau (isl.) ...B8
São Tiago (isl.) ...B8
São Vicente (isl.) ...B7

GAMBIA
CITIES and TOWNS

Banjul (cap.) 39,476 ...A6
Basse Santa Su 2,899 ...B6
Brikama 9,483 ...A6
Georgetown 2,510 ...A6

GHANA
CITIES and TOWNS

Accra (cap.) 564,194 ...D7
Accra* 738,498 ...D7
Ada 4,285 ...E7
Akuse 3,791 ...E7
Attebubu 6,630 ...D7
Awaso 5,449 ...D7
Axim 8,107 ...D8
Bawku 20,567 ...D6
Bekwai 11,287 ...D7
Berekum 14,296 ...D7
Bole 4,772 ...D7
Bolgatanga 18,896 ...D6
Cape Coast 51,653 ...D7
Daboya 1,872 ...D7
Damongo 7,760 ...D7
Dunkwa 15,437 ...D7
Elmina 11,401 ...D8
Enchi 4,382 ...D7
Gambaga 3,730 ...D6
Gyaskan 6,403 ...D7
Half Assini 5,429 ...D8
Ho 24,199 ...E7
Keta 14,446 ...E7
Kete Krachi 5,097 ...E7
Kintampo 7,149 ...D7
Koforidua 46,235 ...D7
Kpandu 12,842 ...D7
Kumasi 260,286 ...D7
Kumasi* 345,117 ...D7
Lawra 2,709 ...D6
Mampong 13,895 ...D7
Mpraeso 5,908 ...D7
Navrongo ...D6
Nsawam 25,518 ...D7
Nsuta 3,854 ...D7
Obuasi 31,005 ...D7
Oda 20,957 ...D7
Prestea 15,143 ...D7
Salaga 6,413 ...D7
Sekondi 33,713 ...D8
Sekondi-Takoradi* 160,868 ...D8
Sunyani 23,780 ...D7
Takoradi 58,161 ...D8
Tamale 83,653 ...D7
Tarkwa 14,702 ...D7
Tema 60,767 ...E7
Tumu 4,366 ...D6
Wa 21,374 ...D6
Wenchi 13,836 ...D7
Wiawso 5,558 ...D7
Winneba 30,778 ...D7
Yapei 1,203 ...D7
Yendi 22,072 ...D7

OTHER FEATURES

Ashanti (reg.) ...D7
Benin (bight) ...E8
Black Volta (riv.) ...D6
Gold Coast (reg.) ...D8
Guinea (gulf) ...D8
Oti (riv.) ...E7
Red Volta (riv.) ...D6
Saint Paul (cape) ...E7
Three Points (cape) ...D8
Volta (lake) ...D7
Volta (riv.) ...E7
White Volta (riv.) ...D6

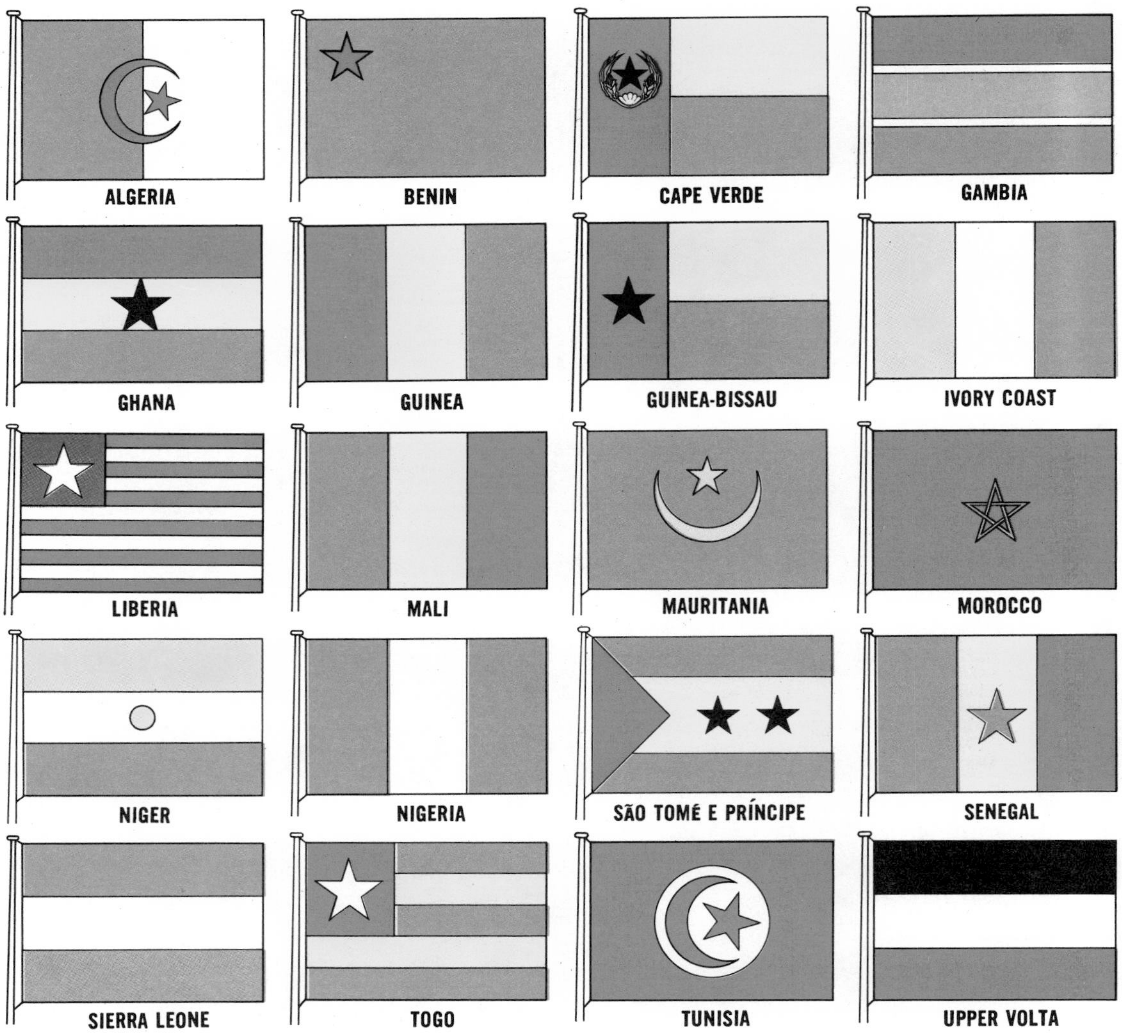

GUINEA
CITIES and TOWNS

Beyla ...C7
Boffa ...B6
Boke ...B6
Conakry (cap.)* 525,671 ...B7
Dabola ...B6
Dalaba ...B6
Dinguiraye ...B6
Dubréka ...B7
Faranah ...B7
Forécariah ...B7
Fria ...B6
Gaoual ...B6
Guéckédou ...B7
Kamsar ...B6
Kankan 85,310 ...C6
Kérouane ...C7
Kindia 79,861 ...B6
Kissidougou ...B7
Koundara 6,000 ...B6
Kouroussa ...C6
Labé 79,670 ...B6
Macenta ...C7
Mali ...B6
Mamou ...B6
N'Zérékoré 23,000 ...C7
Sangaredyi ...B6
Siguiri ...C6
Télimélé 12,000 ...B6
Tougué ...B6
Victoria ...B6

OTHER FEATURES

Bafing (riv.) ...B6
Bakoy (riv.) ...B6
Futa Jallon (lag.) ...B6
Los (isls.) ...B7
Milo (riv.) ...C7
Moa (riv.) ...B7
Niger (riv.) ...C6
Nimba (lag.) ...C7
Verga (cape) ...B6

GUINEA-BISSAU
CITIES and TOWNS

Bissau (cap.) 109,486 ...A6
Bolama 9,133 ...A6
Bubaque 6,706 ...B6
Bubaque* 8,441 ...A6
Cacheu 15,194 ...A6

OTHER FEATURES

Bijagós (isls.) ...A6

IVORY COAST
CITIES and TOWNS

Abengourou 31,239 ...D7
Abidjan (cap.) 685,828 ...D7
Aboisso 14,272 ...D7
Agboville 27,192 ...D7
Bingerville 18,218 ...D7
Bondoukou 19,111 ...D7
Bouaflé 15,917 ...C7
Bouaké 173,248 ...C7
Boundiali 9,869 ...C7
Dabakala 3,272 ...C7
Dabou 23,870 ...D7
Daloa 60,958 ...C7
Danané 19,872 ...C7
Dimbokro 30,986 ...D7
Divo 37,896 ...C7
Ferkessédougou 25,307 ...D7
Fresco 1,865 ...C7
Gagnoa 42,362 ...C7
Grand-Bassam 25,808 ...D7
Grand-Lahou 4,070 ...C8
Guiglo 10,441 ...C7
Issia 11,143 ...C7
Katiola 21,559 ...C7
Kong 2,551 ...C7
Korhogo 47,657 ...C7
Man 50,315 ...C7
Mankono 6,570 ...C7
Odienné 13,864 ...C7
Port-Bouet 72,616 ...D7
San Pedro 27,616 ...C8
Sassandra 9,404 ...C7
Séguéla 12,587 ...C7
Sinfra 16,399 ...C7
Tabou 7,255 ...C8
Touba 5,256 ...C7
Toumodi 12,983 ...D7

OTHER FEATURES

Aby (lag.) ...D8
Bagoé (riv.) ...C6
Bandama (riv.) ...C7
Baoulé (riv.) ...C7
Black Volta (riv.) ...D6
Cavally (riv.) ...C7
Comoe (riv.) ...C7
Ebrié (lag.) ...D7
Guinea (gulf) ...C8
Ivory Coast (reg.) ...C8
Kossou, Lac de (lake) ...C7
Nimba (lag.) ...C7
Sassandra (riv.) ...C7

LIBERIA
CITIES and TOWNS

Buchanan 23,999 ...B7
Gbarnga 6,896 ...B7
Grand Cess ...C8
Greenville 8,462 ...B7
Harbel 11,445 ...B7
Harper 10,627 ...C8
Kolahun ...B7
Marshall ...B7
Monrovia (cap.) 166,507 ...B7
Plahn ...B7
River Cess 2,041 ...C7
Robertsport 2,562 ...B7
Sasstown ...C8
Tapeta 3,927 ...C7
Tchien 6,094 ...C7
Tubmanburg 14,089 ...B7

OTHER FEATURES

Bong (range) ...B7
Cavalla (riv.) ...C7
Cestos (riv.) ...B7
Grain Coast (reg.) ...B8
Kru Coast (reg.) ...C8
Mano (riv.) ...B7
Mount (cape) ...B7
Nimba (lag.) ...C7
Palmas (cape) ...C8
Roberts Field Int'l Airport ...C7

MALI
CITIES and TOWNS

Anéfis ...E5
Ansongo 3,485 ...E5
Araouane ...D5
Bafoulabé 2,163 ...B6
Bamako (cap.) 404,022 ...C6
Bamba ...D5
Bananba 6,776 ...C6
Bandiagara 8,920 ...D6
Bankass 3,229 ...D6
Bou Djebeha ...D5
Bougouni 17,246 ...C6
Bourem 4,538 ...D5
Dioïla 4,563 ...C6
Dire 8,941 ...D5
Djenné 10,251 ...D6
Douentza 6,746 ...D6
Gao 30,714 ...E5
Goundam 10,262 ...D5
Gourma-Rharous 4,671 ...D5
Hombori ...D6
Kadiolo 3,991 ...C6
Kangaba 3,184 ...C6
Kati 24,991 ...C6
Kayes 44,736 ...B6
Ké-Macina 5,426 ...C6
Kénieba 4,510 ...B6
Kerrchoual ...E5
Kidal 3,308 ...E5
Kita 17,538 ...B6
Kolokani 8,923 ...C6
Kolondiéba 5,849 ...C6
Koulikoro 16,376 ...C6
Kourouba ...B6
Koutiala 27,497 ...D6
Mabrouk ...D5
Ménaka 3,693 ...E5
Mopti 53,885 ...D6
Nampala ...C5
Nara 6,091 ...C5
Niafunké 6,399 ...D5
Nioro 12,290 ...C5
Nioro 11,617 ...C5
San 22,962 ...D6
Satadougou ...B6
Ségou 64,890 ...C6
Sikasso 47,030 ...C6
Sokolo ...C6
Taoudenni ...D4
Ténenkou 4,708 ...D6
Tessalit ...E4
Timbuktu (Tombouctou) 20,483 ...D5
Toukoto ...C6
Yanfolila 3,809 ...C6
Yélimané 1,481 ...B5
Yorosso 2,390 ...C6

OTHER FEATURES

Achourat (well) ...D4
Adrar des Iforas (plat.) ...E5
Asselar (well) ...D5
Azaouad (reg.) ...D5
Azaouak (dry riv.) ...E5
Bafing (riv.) ...B6
Bagoé (riv.) ...C6
Bakoy (riv.) ...C6
Bani (riv.) ...C6
Baoulé (dry riv.) ...B6
Baoulé (riv.) ...C6
Bir Ounane (well) ...D4
Chech, Erg (des.) ...D4
Debo (lake) ...D5
El Mraïti (well) ...D4
Faguibine (lake) ...D5
Falémé (riv.) ...B6
Haricha Hamada (des.) ...D4
Hombori (mts.) ...D5
In Dagouber (well) ...D4
Macina (dépr.) ...D6
Niger (riv.) ...D5
Oum el Asel (well) ...D4
Sahara (des.) ...D4
Sekkane, Erg (des.) ...D4
Sénégal (riv.) ...B5
Sudan (reg.) ...D4
Tadjnout Hagguerete (well) ...C5
Terhazza (ruins) ...C4
Tilemsi (valley) ...E5
Toufourine (well) ...C4

MAURITANIA
CITIES and TOWNS

Aloun el Atrous ...C5
Akjoujt 8,044 ...B5
Akreïbt ...C5
Aleg 6,415 ...B5
Atar 16,326 ...B4
Bassikounou ...C5
Bir Mogreïn ...B3
Boutilimit 7,261 ...B5
Bogué 8,056 ...B5
Chinguetti ...B4
Fderik (Fort-Gouraud) 2,160 ...B4
Kaédi 20,848 ...B5
Kankossa ...C5
Kiffa 10,629 ...B5
M'Bout ...B5
Méderdra ...A5
Néma 8,232 ...C5
Nouakchott (cap.) 134,986 ...A5
Nouadhibou 21,961 ...A4
Ouadane ...B4
Oualata ...C5
Oujaft ...B4
Rosso 16,466 ...A5
Sélibaby 5,994 ...B5
Tamsagout ...C4
Tazadit ...B4
Tichitt ...C5
Tidjikja 7,870 ...B5
Timbédra 5,317 ...C5
Zouîrât 17,474 ...B4

OTHER FEATURES

Adafer (reg.) ...B5
Adrar (reg.) ...B4
Affolé (reg.) ...B5
Agueraktem (well) ...C4
Aïn ben Tili (well) ...C3
Arguin (bay) ...A4
Assaba (reg.) ...B5
Atoui, Wadi (dry riv.) ...B4
Ben Guerdane (well) ...B3
Bir el Khzaïm (well) ...C4
Blanc (cape) ...A4
Brakna (reg.) ...B5
Chegga (well) ...C3
Djouf, El (des.) ...C4
El Krayer (well) ...C4
El Mreïti (well) ...C4
Gorgol (reg.) ...B5
Hodh (reg.) ...C5
Iguidi, Erg (des.) ...C3
Inchiri (reg.) ...A5
Koumbi Saleh (ruins) ...C5
Lévrier (bay) ...A4
Maktelr (des.) ...B4
Meraïa (reg.) ...C5
Mirik (Timiris) (cape) ...A5
Ouarane (reg.) ...B4
Sahara (des.) ...C4
Sénégal (riv.) ...B5
Tagant (reg.) ...B5
Tidra (isl.) ...A5
Timiris (cape) ...A5
Touila (well) ...C3
Trarza (reg.) ...A5

MOROCCO
CITIES and TOWNS

Agadir 61,192 ...C2
Al Hoceima 18,686 ...D1
Asilah 14,074 ...C1
Azemmour 17,182 ...C2
Azrou 20,756 ...C2
Beni Mellal 53,826 ...C2
Berguent 3,356 ...D2
Bou Arfa ...D2
Bou Izakarn 2,342 ...C3
Boujad 18,838 ...C2
Casablanca 1,506,373 ...C2
Chechaouene 15,362 ...D1
Dar-el-Beida (Casablanca) 1,506,373 ...C2
El Jadida 55,501 ...C2
El Kelaa des Srarhna 17,163 ...C2
Erfoud 5,400 ...D2
Er Rachidia 16,775 ...D2
Essaouira 30,061 ...B2
Fedala (Mohammedia) 70,392 ...C2
Fès (Fez) 325,327 ...D1
Figuig 13,660 ...D2
Goulmima 4,056 ...C2
Inezgane 11,495 ...C2

ALGERIA

BENIN
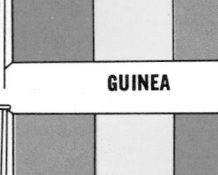

CAPE VERDE

GAMBIA

GHANA

GUINEA
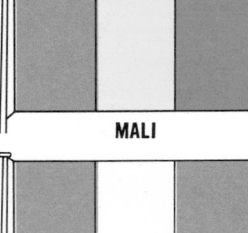

GUINEA-BISSAU

IVORY COAST

LIBERIA

MALI
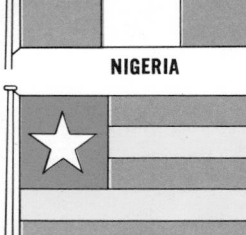

MAURITANIA

MOROCCO

NIGER

NIGERIA
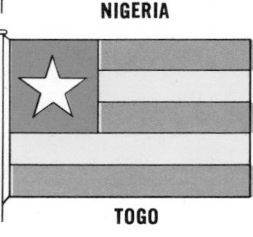

SÃO TOMÉ E PRÍNCIPE

SENEGAL

SIERRA LEONE

TOGO

TUNISIA

UPPER VOLTA

Agriculture, Industry and Resources

DOMINANT LAND USE

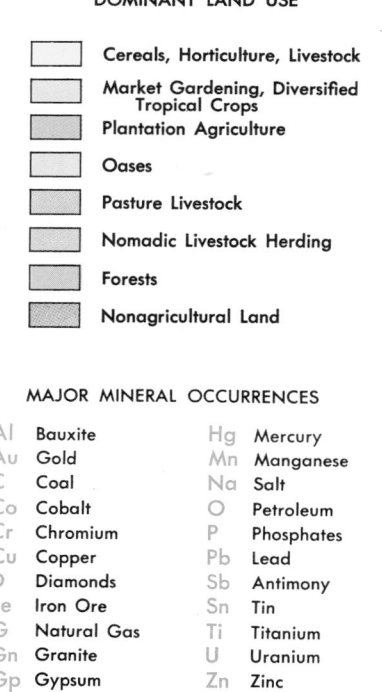

- Cereals, Horticulture, Livestock
- Market Gardening, Diversified Tropical Crops
- Plantation Agriculture
- Oases
- Pasture Livestock
- Nomadic Livestock Herding
- Forests
- Nonagricultural Land

MAJOR MINERAL OCCURRENCES

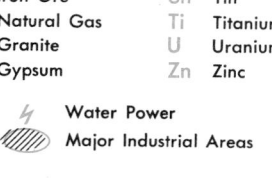

Al	Bauxite	Hg	Mercury
Au	Gold	Mn	Manganese
C	Coal	Na	Salt
Co	Cobalt	O	Petroleum
Cr	Chromium	P	Phosphates
Cu	Copper	Pb	Lead
D	Diamonds	Sb	Antimony
Fe	Iron Ore	Sn	Tin
G	Natural Gas	Ti	Titanium
Gn	Granite	U	Uranium
Gp	Gypsum	Zn	Zinc

⚡ Water Power

▨ Major Industrial Areas

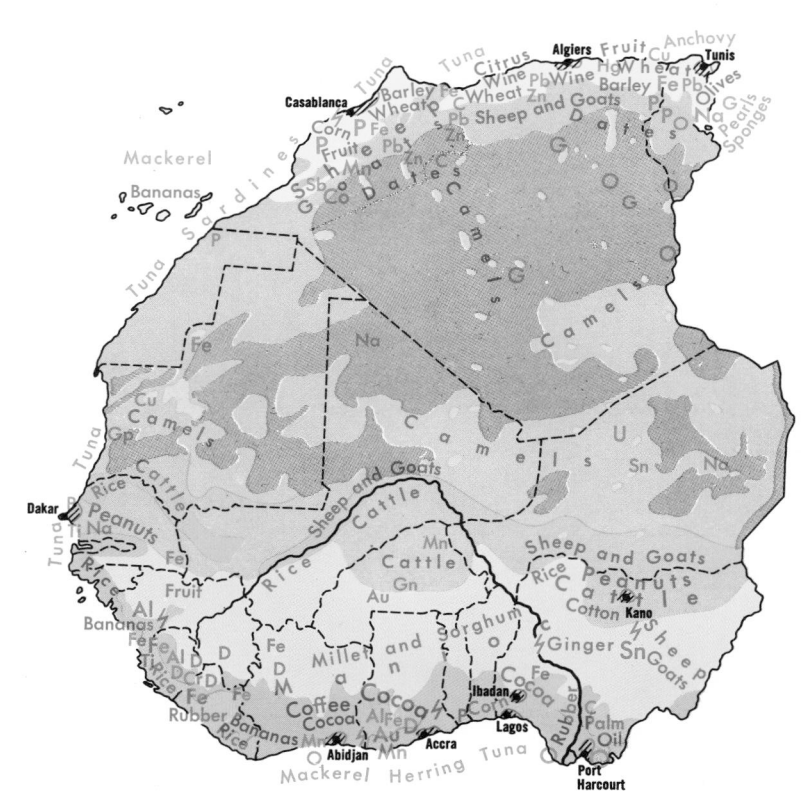

LIBYA

AREA 679,358 sq. mi. (1,759,537 sq. km.)
POPULATION 2,856,000
CAPITAL Tripoli
LARGEST CITY Tripoli
HIGHEST POINT Bette Pk. 7,500 ft. (2,286 m.)
MONETARY UNIT Libyan dinar
MAJOR LANGUAGES Arabic, Berber
MAJOR RELIGION Islam

EGYPT

AREA 386,659 sq. mi. (1,001,447 sq. km.)
POPULATION 41,572,000
CAPITAL Cairo
LARGEST CITY Cairo
HIGHEST POINT Jeb. Katherina 8,651 ft. (2,637 m.)
MONETARY UNIT Egyptian pound
MAJOR LANGUAGE Arabic
MAJOR RELIGIONS Islam, Coptic Christianity

CHAD

AREA 495,752 sq. mi. (1,283,998 sq. km.)
POPULATION 4,309,000
CAPITAL N'Djamena
LARGEST CITY N'Djamena
HIGHEST POINT Emi Koussi 11,204 ft. (3,415 m.)
MONETARY UNIT CFA franc
MAJOR LANGUAGES Arabic, Bagirmi, French, Sara, Massa, Moudang
MAJOR RELIGIONS Islam, tribal religions

SUDAN

AREA 967,494 sq. mi. (2,505,809 sq. km.)
POPULATION 18,691,000
CAPITAL Khartoum
LARGEST CITY Khartoum
HIGHEST POINT Jeb. Marra 10,073 ft. (3,070 m.)
MONETARY UNIT Sudanese pound
MAJOR LANGUAGES Arabic, Dinka, Nubian, Beja, Nuer
MAJOR RELIGIONS Islam, tribal religions

ETHIOPIA

AREA 471,776 sq. mi. (1,221,900 sq. km.)
POPULATION 31,065,000
CAPITAL Addis Ababa
LARGEST CITY Addis Ababa
HIGHEST POINT Ras Dashan 15,157 ft. (4,620 m.)
MONETARY UNIT birr
MAJOR LANGUAGES Amharic, Gallinya, Tigrinya, Somali, Sidamo, Arabic, Ge'ez
MAJOR RELIGIONS Coptic Christianity, Islam

DJIBOUTI

AREA 8,880 sq. mi. (23,000 sq. km.)
POPULATION 386,000
CAPITAL Djibouti
LARGEST CITY Djibouti
HIGHEST POINT Moussa Ali 6,768 ft. (2,063 m.)
MONETARY UNIT Djibouti franc
MAJOR LANGUAGES Arabic, Somali, Afar, French
MAJOR RELIGIONS Islam, Roman Catholicism

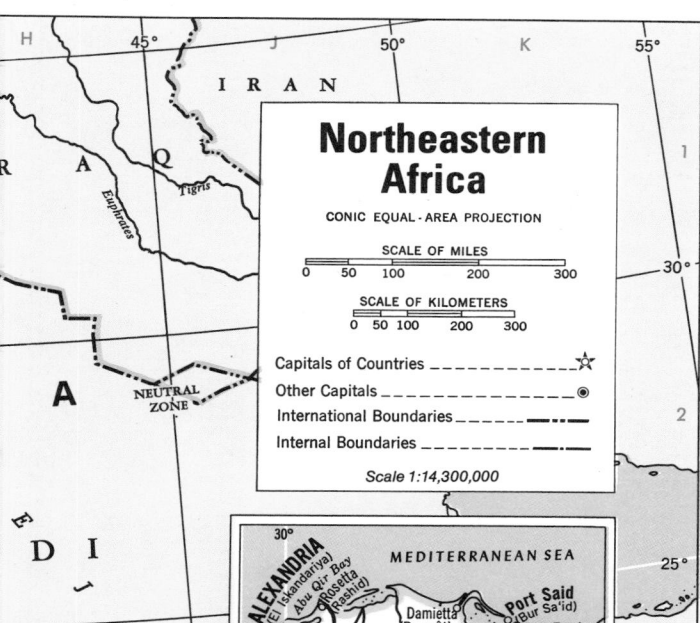

Northeastern Africa

CONIC EQUAL-AREA PROJECTION

SCALE OF MILES
0   50   100   200   300

SCALE OF KILOMETERS
0 50 100   200   300

Capitals of Countries _____ ☆
Other Capitals _____ ◉
International Boundaries _____
Internal Boundaries _____

Scale 1:14,300,000

© Copyright HAMMOND INCORPORATED, Maplewood, N.J.

CHAD

CITIES and TOWNS

Abéché 28,100	D5
Abou Dela	D5
Adré	D5
Ain-Galakka	C4
Am-Dam	D5
Am-Timan 4,200	D5
Arada	D4
Ati 7,500	C5
Baibokoum 5,500	C6
Bardai	C3
Biltine 3,900	D5
Bitkine 5,000	C5
Bokoro 6,500	C5
Bol 2,500	B5
Bongor 14,300	C5
Bousso 4,500	C5
Doba 13,300	C6
Fada	D4
Faya-Largeau 6,800	C4
Fianga 10,000	C6
Goré	C6
Gouro	C4
Goz Belda	D5
Guéréda	D5
Ham	C5

Haraz	C5
Iriba	D4
Kélo 16,800	C6
Koro Toro	C4
Koumra 17,000	C6
Kouno	C6
Kyabé 5,000	C6
Lal 10,400	C6
Léré	B6
Madadi	D4
Mangueigne	D5
Mao 4,900	C5
Massakory	C5
Massénya	C5
Melfi	C5
Mogororo	D5
Moïssala 5,100	C6
Mongo 8,300	C5
Moundou 39,600	C6
Moussoro 7,700	C5
N'Djamena (cap.) 179,000	C5
Nokou	B5
Oum Chalouba	D4
Oum Hadjer 5,600	D5
Ounianga-Kébir	D4
Pala 13,200	C6
Rig Rig	B5
Sarh 43,700	C6
Wour	C3
Yarda	C4

Yebbi-Bou	C3
Ziguei	C5
Zouar	C3

OTHER FEATURES

Azoum, Bahr	D5
Baguirmi (reg.)	C5
Bahr el Ghazal (dry riv.)	C5
Batha (riv.)	C5
Bodélé (depr.)	C4
Borku 72	C4
Chad (lake)	C5
Domar (dry riv.)	C4
Emi Koussi (mt.)	C4
Ennedi (plat.)	D4
Fittri (lake)	C5
Haouach, Wadi (dry riv.)	C4
Jef Jef es Seghin (plat.)	D3
Kanem (reg.)	C5
Logone (riv.)	C6
Maro (dry riv.)	C6
Mbéré (riv.)	C6
Mourdi (depr.)	D4
Ouham (riv.)	C6
Pendé (riv.)	C6
Sahara (des.)	C3
Salamat, Bahr (riv.)	C6
Sara (riv.)	C5
Shari (riv.)	C6

SUDAN

Sudan (reg.)	C5
Tibesti (mts.)	C3
Wadai (reg.)	D5

DJIBOUTI

CITIES and TOWNS

Ali Sabieh	H5
Dikhil	H5
Djibouti (cap.) 96,000	H5
Obock	H5
Tadjoura	H5

OTHER FEATURES

Abbe (lake)	H5
Aden (gulf)	J5
Bab el Mandeb (str.)	H5

EGYPT

CITIES and TOWNS

Abnûb 39,343	J4
Abu Qurqâs	J4
Akhmim 53,234	F2
Alexandria 2,318,655	J2

(continued on following page)

Topography

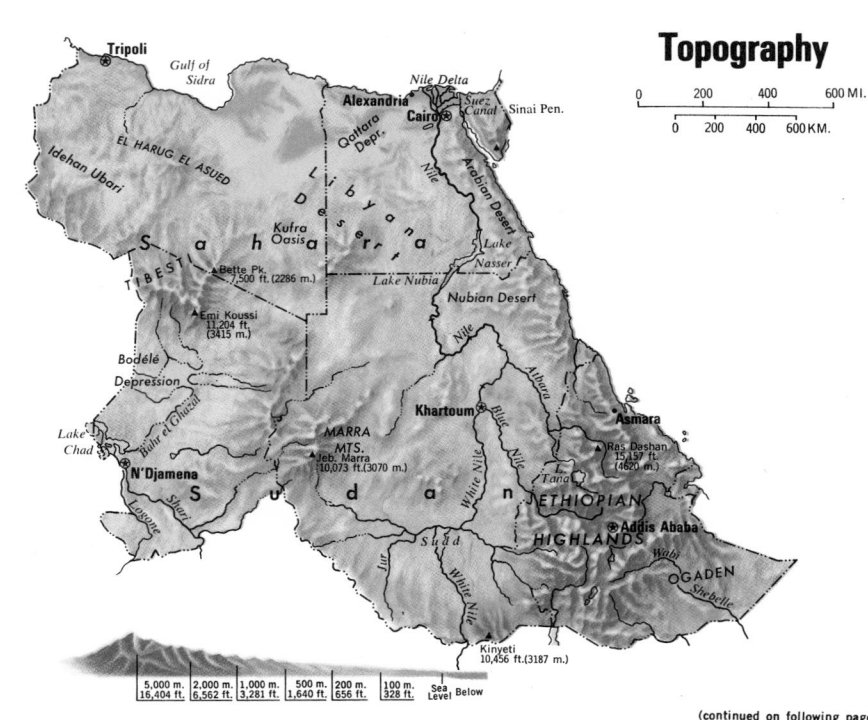

0   200   400   600 MI.

0   200   400   600 KM.

| 5,000 m. | 2,000 m. | 1,000 m. | 500 m. | 200 m. | 100 m. | Sea |
| 16,404 ft. | 6,562 ft. | 3,281 ft. | 1,640 ft. | 656 ft. | 328 ft. | Level | Below |

(continued on following page)

Agriculture, Industry and Resources

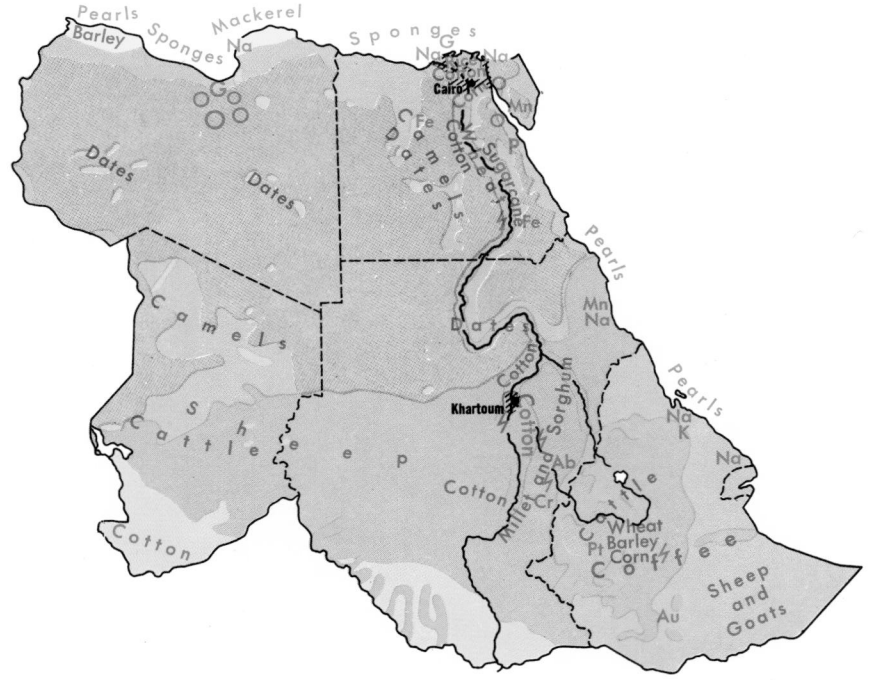

DOMINANT LAND USE

Cereals, Horticulture, Livestock
Cash Crops, Mixed Cereals
Cotton, Cereals
Market Gardening, Diversified Tropical Crops
Plantation Agriculture
Oases
Pasture Livestock
Nomadic Livestock Herding
Forests
Nonagricultural Land

MAJOR MINERAL OCCURRENCES

Ab Asbestos
Au Gold
Cr Chromium
Fe Iron Ore
G   Natural Gas
K   Potash

Mn Manganese
Na Salt
O   Petroleum
P   Phosphates
Pt Platinum

⚡ Water Power
▨ Major Industrial Areas

ANGOLA

AREA 481,351 sq. mi. (1,246,700 sq. km.)
POPULATION 7,078,000
CAPITAL Luanda
LARGEST CITY Luanda
HIGHEST POINT Mt. Moco 8,593 ft. (2,620 m.)
MONETARY UNIT kwanza
MAJOR LANGUAGES Mbundu, Kongo, Lunda, Portuguese
MAJOR RELIGIONS Tribal religions, Roman Catholicism

BURUNDI

AREA 10,747 sq. mi. (27,835 sq. km.)
POPULATION 4,021,910
CAPITAL Bujumbura
LARGEST CITY Bujumbura
HIGHEST POINT 8,858 ft. (2,700 m.)
MONETARY UNIT Burundi franc
MAJOR LANGUAGES Kirundi, French, Swahili
MAJOR RELIGIONS Tribal religions, Roman Catholicism, Islam

CAMEROON

AREA 183,568 sq. mi. (475,441 sq. km.)
POPULATION 8,503,000
CAPITAL Yaoundé
LARGEST CITY Douala
HIGHEST POINT Cameroon 13,350 ft. (4,069 m.)
MONETARY UNIT CFA franc
MAJOR LANGUAGES Fang, Bamileke, Fulani, Duala, French, English
MAJOR RELIGIONS Tribal religions, Christianity, Islam

CENTRAL AFRICAN REP.

AREA 242,000 sq. mi. (626,780 sq. km.)
POPULATION 2,284,000
CAPITAL Bangui
LARGEST CITY Bangui
HIGHEST POINT Gao 4,659 ft. (1,420 m.)
MONETARY UNIT CFA franc
MAJOR LANGUAGES Banda, Gbaya, Sangho, French
MAJOR RELIGIONS Tribal religions, Christianity, Islam

CONGO

AREA 132,046 sq. mi. (342,000 sq. km.)
POPULATION 1,537,000
CAPITAL Brazzaville
LARGEST CITY Brazzaville
HIGHEST POINT Leketi Mts. 3,412 ft. (1,040 m.)
MONETARY UNIT CFA franc
MAJOR LANGUAGES Kikongo, Bateke, Lingala, French
MAJOR RELIGIONS Christianity, tribal religions, Islam

EQUATORIAL GUINEA

AREA 10,831 sq. mi. (28,052 sq. km.)
POPULATION 244,000
CAPITAL Malabo
LARGEST CITY Malabo
HIGHEST POINT 9,868 ft. (3,008 m.)
MONETARY UNIT ekuele
MAJOR LANGUAGES Fang, Bubi, Spanish
MAJOR RELIGIONS Tribal religions, Christianity

GABON

AREA 103,346 sq. mi. (267,666 sq. km.)
POPULATION 551,000
CAPITAL Libreville
LARGEST CITY Libreville
HIGHEST POINT Ibounzi 5,165 ft. (1,574 m.)
MONETARY UNIT CFA franc
MAJOR LANGUAGES Fang and other Bantu languages, French
MAJOR RELIGIONS Tribal religions, Christianity, Islam

KENYA

AREA 224,960 sq. mi. (582,646 sq. km.)
POPULATION 15,327,061
CAPITAL Nairobi
LARGEST CITY Nairobi
HIGHEST POINT Kenya 17,058 ft. (5,199 m.)
MONETARY UNIT Kenya shilling
MAJOR LANGUAGES Kikuyu, Luo, Kavirondo, Kamba, Swahili, English
MAJOR RELIGIONS Tribal religions, Christianity, Hinduism, Islam

MALAWI

AREA 45,747 sq. mi. (118,485 sq. km.)
POPULATION 5,968,000
CAPITAL Lilongwe
LARGEST CITY Blantyre
HIGHEST POINT Mulanje 9,843 ft. (3,000 m.)
MONETARY UNIT Malawi kwacha
MAJOR LANGUAGES Chichewa, Yao, English, Nyanja, Tumbuka, Tonga, Ngoni
MAJOR RELIGIONS Tribal religions, Islam, Christianity

RWANDA

AREA 10,169 sq. mi. (26,337 sq. km.)
POPULATION 4,819,317
CAPITAL Kigali
LARGEST CITY Kigali
HIGHEST POINT Karisimbi 14,780 ft. (4,505 m.)
MONETARY UNIT Rwanda franc
MAJOR LANGUAGES Kinyarwanda, French, Swahili
MAJOR RELIGIONS Tribal religions, Roman Catholicism, Islam

SOMALIA

AREA 246,200 sq. mi. (637,658 sq. km.)
POPULATION 3,645,000
CAPITAL Mogadishu
LARGEST CITY Mogadishu
HIGHEST POINT Surud Ad 7,900 ft. (2,408 m.)
MONETARY UNIT Somali shilling
MAJOR LANGUAGES Somali, Arabic, Italian, English
MAJOR RELIGION Islam

TANZANIA

AREA 363,708 sq. mi. (942,003 sq. km.)
POPULATION 17,527,560
CAPITAL Dar es Salaam
LARGEST CITY Dar es Salaam
HIGHEST POINT Kilimanjaro 19,340 ft. (5,895 m.)
MONETARY UNIT Tanzanian shilling
MAJOR LANGUAGES Nyamwezi-Sukuma, Swahili, English
MAJOR RELIGIONS Tribal religions, Christianity, Islam

UGANDA

AREA 91,076 sq. mi. (235,887 sq. km.)
POPULATION 12,630,076
CAPITAL Kampala
LARGEST CITY Kampala
HIGHEST POINT Margherita 16,795 ft. (5,119 m.)
MONETARY UNIT Ugandan shilling
MAJOR LANGUAGES Luganda, Acholi, Teso, Nyoro, Soga, Nkole, English, Swahili
MAJOR RELIGIONS Tribal religions, Christianity, Islam

ZAIRE

AREA 905,063 sq. mi. (2,344,113 sq. km.)
POPULATION 28,291,000
CAPITAL Kinshasa
LARGEST CITY Kinshasa
HIGHEST POINT Margherita 16,795 ft. (5,119 m.)
MONETARY UNIT zaire
MAJOR LANGUAGES Tshiluba, Mongo, Kikongo, Kingwana, Zande, Lingala, Swahili, French
MAJOR RELIGIONS Tribal religions, Christianity

ZAMBIA

AREA 290,586 sq. mi. (752,618 sq. km.)
POPULATION 5,679,808
CAPITAL Lusaka
LARGEST CITY Lusaka
HIGHEST POINT Sunzu 6,782 ft. (2,067 m.)
MONETARY UNIT Zambian kwacha
MAJOR LANGUAGES Bemba, Tonga, Lozi, Luvale, Nyanja, English
MAJOR RELIGIONS Tribal religions

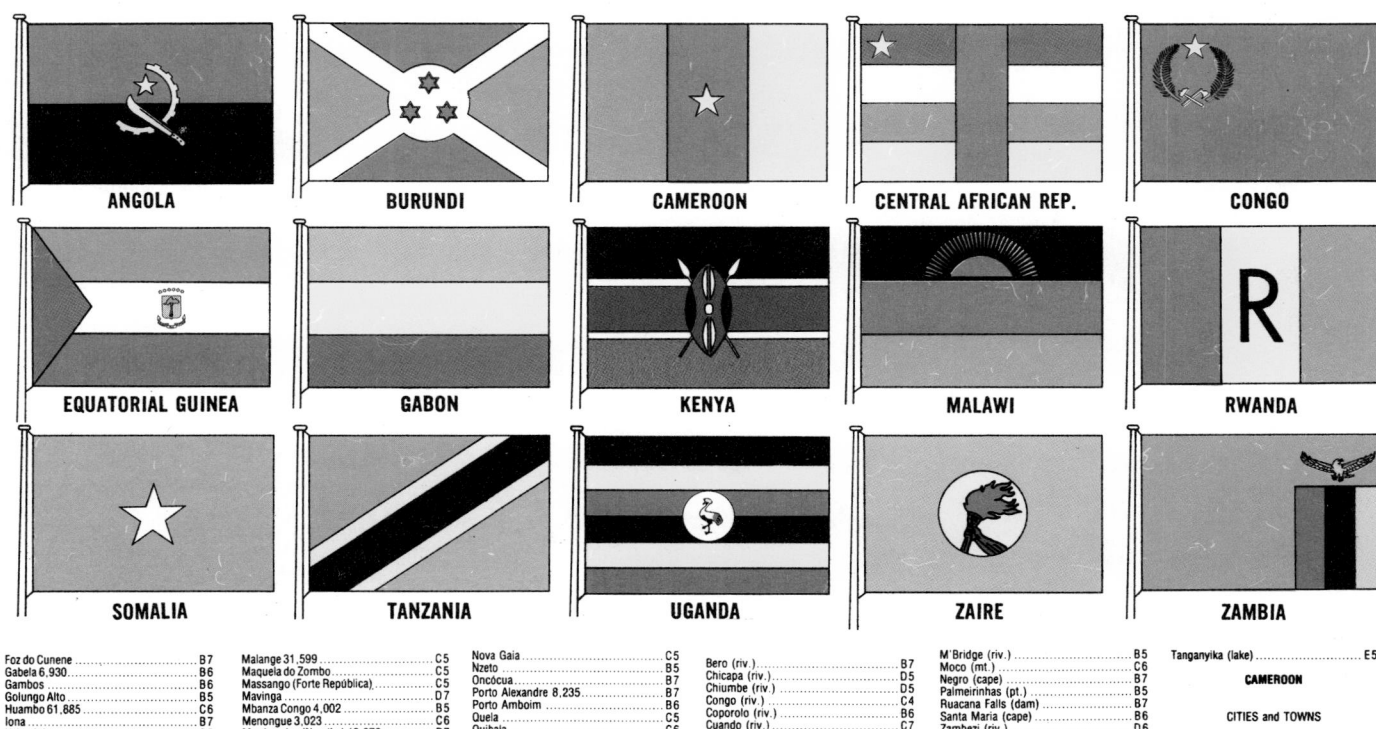

Flags: ANGOLA, BURUNDI, CAMEROON, CENTRAL AFRICAN REP., CONGO, EQUATORIAL GUINEA, GABON, KENYA, MALAWI, RWANDA, SOMALIA, TANZANIA, UGANDA, ZAIRE, ZAMBIA

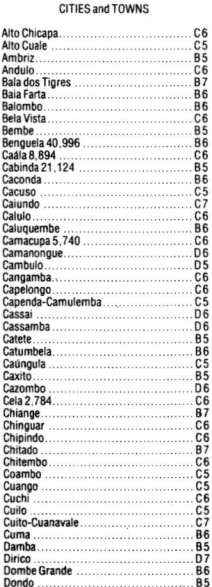
(continued on following page)

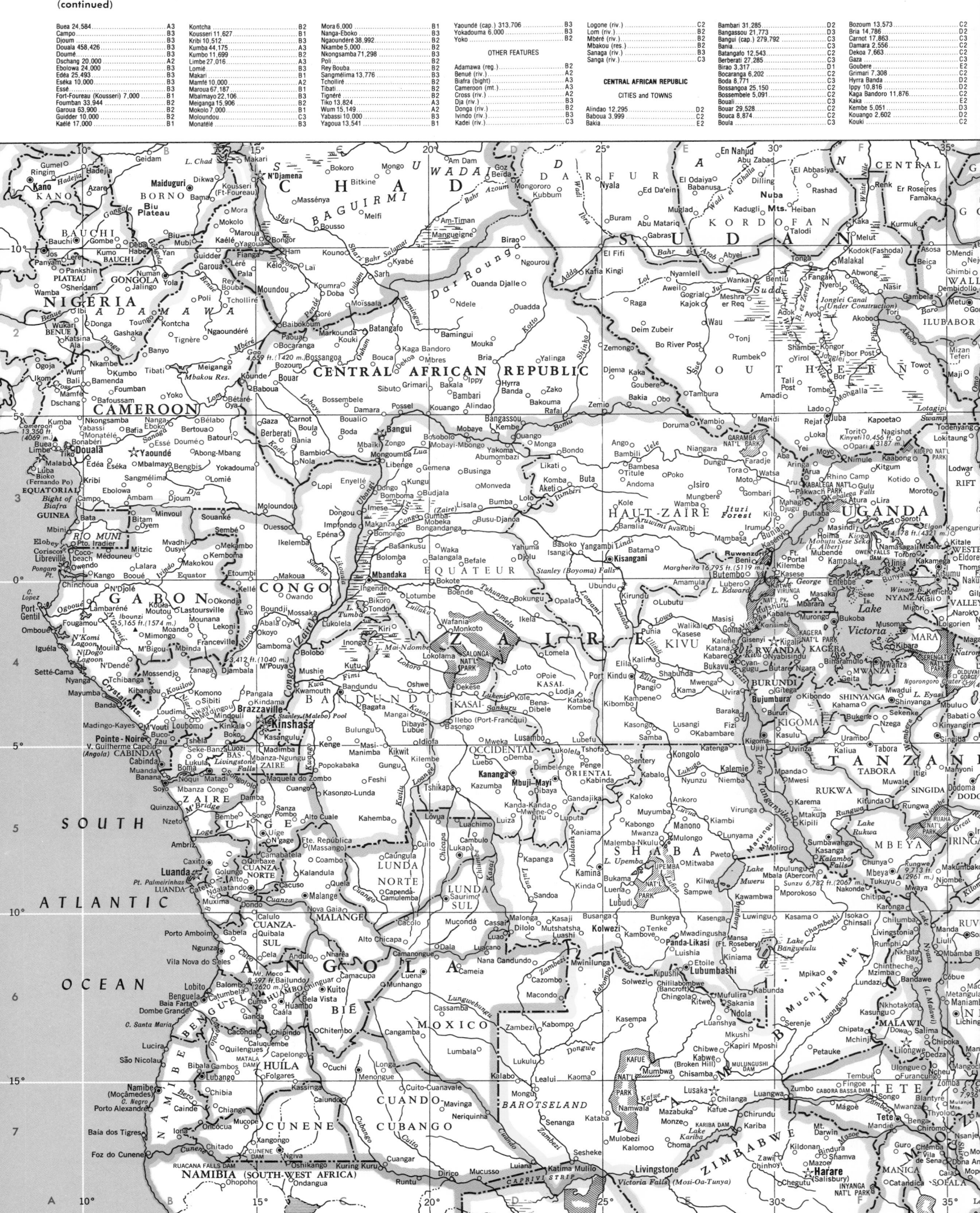

Kounde B2
Mbaîki 12,346 .... C3
Mbres 2,622 .... D2
Mobaye 4,220 .... D3
Mouka D2
Ndele 5,858 .... D2
Ngourou D2
Nola 6,703 .... C3
Obo 3,978 .... E2
Ouadda 3,009 .... D2
Paoua 7,052 .... C2
Possel C2
Sibut 13,341 .... C2
Zako D2
Zemio 3,259 .... D2
Zemongo E2

OTHER FEATURES

Bamingui (riv.) C2
Bomu (riv.) D3
Dar Rounga (reg.) D2
Gao (mt.) C2
Kadei (riv.) C3
Kotto (riv.) D2
Lobaye (riv.) C2
Mbéré (riv.) B2
Ouham (riv.) C2
Pendé (riv.) C2
Sanga (riv.) C3
Sara (riv.) C2
Shari (riv.) C2
Shinko (riv.) D2
Ubangi (riv.) C3

CONGO

CITIES and TOWNS

Abala C4
Boko B4
Brazzaville (cap.) 298,967 .... C4
Boundji C4
Djambala B4
Dongou C3
Enyellé C3
Epéna C3
Etoumbi B3
Ewo B4
Gamboma C4
Ikelemba C3
Impfondo C3
Kellé B4
Kibangou B4
Kindama C4
Kinkala B4
Komono B4
Loubomo 29,600 .... B4
Loudima B4
Madingo-Kayes B4
Madingou B4
Makoua C3
Mbinda B4
Mindouli B4
Mossaka C4
Mossendjo B4
M'Pouya C4
M'Vouti B4
Nkayi 30,600 .... B4
Okoyo C4
Ouesso C3
Owando C4
Oyo C4
Pangala B4
Pointe-Noire 141,700 .... B4
Sembé B3
Sibiti B4
Souanké B3
Zanaga B4

OTHER FEATURES

Alima (riv.) B4
Congo (riv.) C4
Crystal (mts.) B4
Dja (riv.) B3
Ivindo (riv.) B3
Kadei (riv.) C3
Kouilou (riv.) B4
Likouala (riv.) C3
N'Gounié (riv.) B4
Niari (riv.) B4
Ogooué (riv.) A4
Sangha (riv.) C3
Ubangi (riv.) C3

EQUATORIAL GUINEA

TERRITORIES

Bioko 78,000 .... A3
Río Muni 203,000 .... B3

CITIES and TOWNS

Bata 27,024 .... B3
Luba 19,933 .... A3
Malabo (cap.) 37,237 .... A3
Mbini 14,503 .... A3

OTHER FEATURES

Biafra (bight) A3
Bioko (isl.) A3
Corisco (isl.) A3
Elobey (isls.) A3
Fernando Po (Bioko) (isl.) A3

GABON

CITIES and TOWNS

Banda B4
Bitam 5,936 .... B3
Booué B3
Chinchoua A4
Cocobeach B3
Fougamou A4
Franceville 9,345 .... B4
Iguéla A4
Kango B3
Kemboma B3
Koula-Moutou 8,032 .... B4
Lalara B3
Lambaréné 17,770 .... B4
Lastoursville B4
Lekoni B4
Libreville (cap.) 105,080 .... A3
Makokou 5,005 .... B3
Mayumba A4
M'Bigou B4
Médouneu B3
Mekambo B3
Mimongo B4
Minvoul B3
Mitzic B3
Moanda 10,709 .... B4
Mouila 15,016 .... B4
Mounana 4,000 .... B4
N'Dendé B4
N'Djolé B4
Nyanga A4
Okondja B4
Omboué A4
Owendo A3
Oyem 12,455 .... B3
Port-Gentil 48,190 .... A4
Setté-Cama A4
Tchibanga 14,001 .... B4

OTHER FEATURES

Crystal (mts.) B4
Ibounzi (mt.) B4
Ivindo (riv.) B3
Lopez (cape) A4
N'Dogo (lag.) B4
N'Gounié (riv.) B4
N'Komi (lag.) A4
Ogooué (riv.) A4
Onangué (lake) A4
Pongara (pt.) A3

KENYA

PROVINCES

Central 1,675,647 .... G4
Coast 944,082 .... G4
Eastern 1,907,301 .... G4
Nairobi 509,286 .... G4
North-Eastern 245,757 .... G3
Nyanza 2,122,045 .... F4
Rift Valley 2,210,289 .... G3
Western 1,328,298 .... G3

CITIES and TOWNS

Buna G3
Bunyala F3
Bura H4
Eldoret 18,196 .... G3
El Wak H3
Embu 3,928 .... G4
Fort Hall 4,750 .... G4
Galole 3,609 .... G4
Garba Tula G3
Garissa G4
Garsen G4
Gilgil 4,178 .... G4
Isiolo 8,201 .... G3
Kakamega 6,244 .... F3
Kaningo G4
Kericho 10,144 .... F4
Kiambu 2,776 .... G4
Kilifi 2,662 .... G4
Kipini H4
Kisii 6,080 .... F4
Kisumu 32,431 .... F3
Kitale 11,573 .... G3
Kitui 3,071 .... G4
Kolbio H4
Konza G4
Laisamis G3
Lamu 7,403 .... H4
Lodwar G3
Lokitaung 4,090 .... G3
Lolgorien G4
Machakos 6,312 .... G4
Magadi G4
Malindi 10,757 .... H4
Mambrui H4
Maralal 3,878 .... G3
Marsabit 6,635 .... G3
Meru 4,475 .... G3
Mombasa 247,073 .... G4
Moyale G3
Nairobi (cap.) 509,286 .... G4
Naivasha 6,920 .... G4
Nakuru 47,151 .... G4
Namanga G4
Nanyuki 11,624 .... G3
Narok 2,608 .... G4
North Horr G3
South Horr G3
Taveta G4
Thika 18,387 .... G4
Thomson's Falls 7,602 .... G3
Todenyang G3
Tsavo G4
Vanga G4
Voi 5,313 .... G4
Wajir H3
Wamba 2,650 .... G3

OTHER FEATURES

Daua (riv.) H3
Elgon (mt.) F3
Formosa (bay) H4
Galana (riv.) G4
Gedi (ruins) G4
Kavirondo (gulf) F4
Kenya (mt.) G4
Lak Dera (dry riv.) H3
Lorian (swamp) G3
Natron (lake) G4
Nyiru (mt.) G3
Patta (isl.) H4
Rudolf (Turkana) (lake) G3
Tana (riv.) G4
Tsavo Nat'l Park G4
Turkana (lake) G3
Victoria (lake) F4
Winam (bay) F4

MALAWI

CITIES and TOWNS

Bandawe F6
Blantyre 222,153 .... F7
Chilumba F6
Chipoka F6
Chiromo F7
Chitipa 3,079 .... F5
Dedza 5,448 .... F6
Karonga 11,873 .... F5
Kasungu F6
Lilongwe (cap.) 102,924 .... F6
Livingstonia F6
Mangochi 3,341 .... G6
Mzimba 4,962 .... F6
Nkhata Bay 4,024 .... F6
Nkhotakota 10,312 .... F6
Nsanje 6,091 .... G7
Rumphi 3,998 .... F6
Salima 4,646 .... F6
Thyolo 4,186 .... F7
Zomba 21,000 .... G7

OTHER FEATURES

Chilwa (lake) G7
Malawi (Nyasa) (lake) F6
Mulanje (mts.) G7
Nyasa (lake) F6
Shire (riv.) G7

RWANDA

CITIES and TOWNS

Butare 21,691 .... E4
Cyangugu 7,042 .... E4
Gisenyi 12,436 .... E4
Kigali (cap.) 117,749 .... F4
Nyabisindu 8,587 .... F4

OTHER FEATURES

Kagera Nat'l Park F4
Karisimbi (mt.) E4
Kivu (lake) E4
Ruzizi (riv.) E4
Virunga (range) E4

SOMALIA

PROVINCES

Bakool 100,000 .... H3
Bari 155,000 .... J1
Bay 302,000 .... H3
Galguduud 182,000 .... J2
Gedo 212,000 .... H3
Hiiraan 147,000 .... J3
Jubbada Hoose 246,000 .... H3
Mogadiscio 371,000 .... J3
Mudug 215,000 .... J2
Nugaal 85,000 .... J2
Sanaag 146,000 .... J1
Shabeellaha Dhexe 237,000 .... J3
Shabeellaha Hoose 398,000 .... H3
Togdheer 258,000 .... J2
Woqooyi Galbeed 440,000 .... H1

CITIES and TOWNS

Adadle H2
Afgoi J3
Afmadu 2,580 .... H3
Alula K1
Ankhor J1
Audegle J3
Baduen J2
Barawa (Brava) H3
Bardera H3
Bargal K1
Baydhabo 14,962 .... H3
Belet Weyne 11,426 .... J3
Bender Beila K2
Bender Cassim (Bosaso) J1
Berbera 12,219 .... J1
Bereda K1
Bircao H4
Bohodleh J2
Borama 3,244 .... H1

(continued on following page)

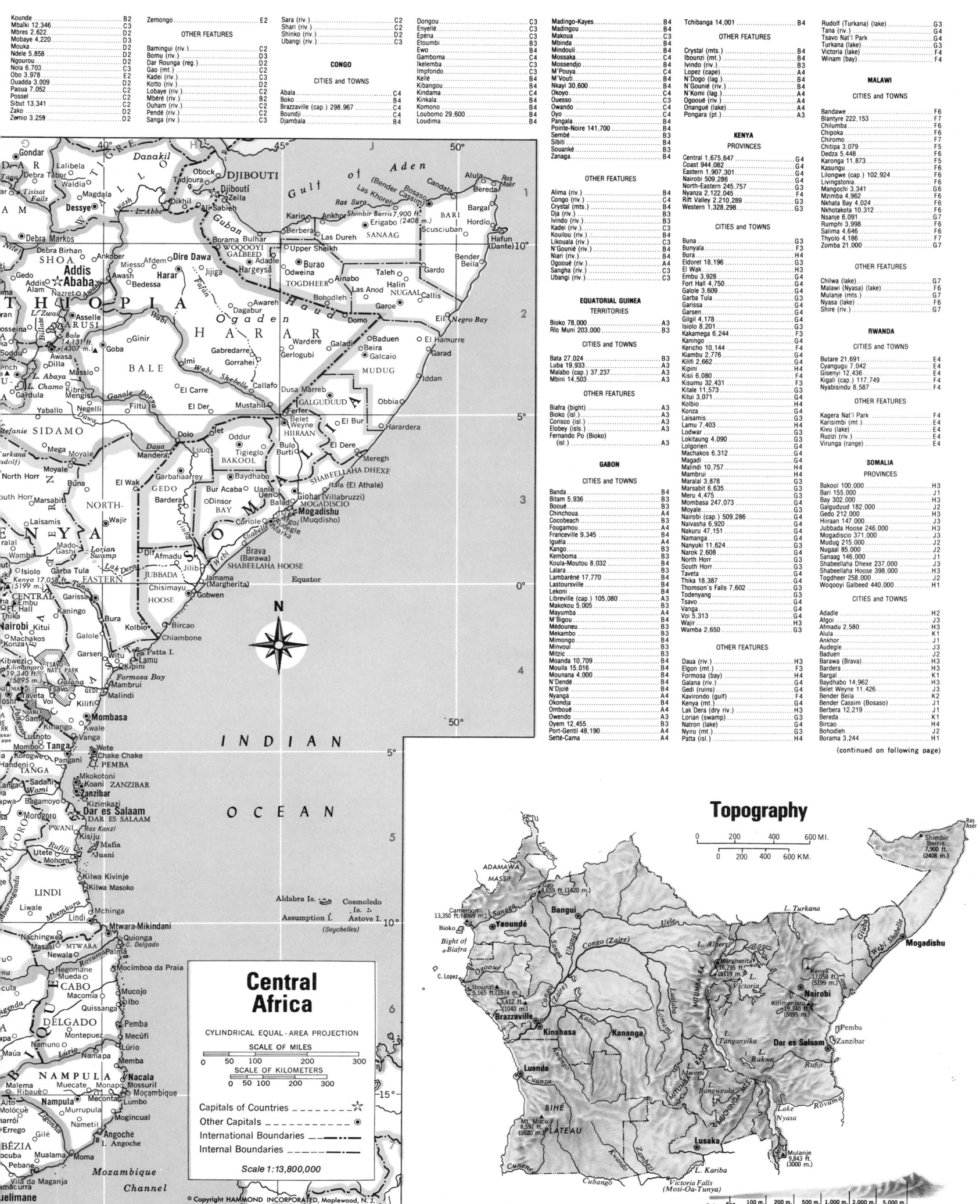

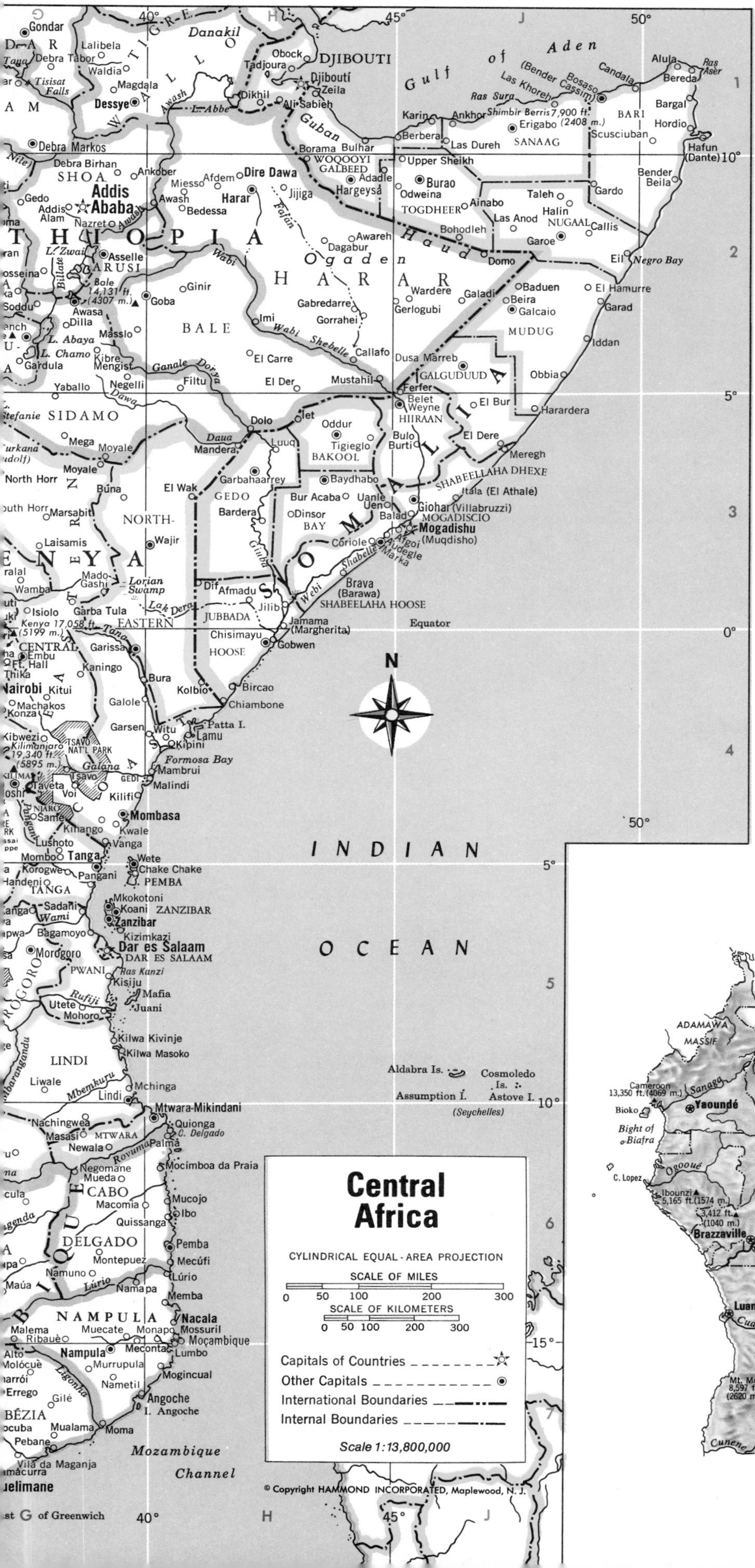
Central Africa
CYLINDRICAL EQUAL-AREA PROJECTION
SCALE OF MILES
0 50 100 200 300
SCALE OF KILOMETERS
0 50 100 200 300
Capitals of Countries
Other Capitals
International Boundaries
Internal Boundaries
Scale 1:13,800,000
Gulf of Aden
DJIBOUTI
Djibouti
Addis Ababa
Mogadishu
Nairobi
Mombasa
Dar es Salaam
Zanzibar
INDIAN OCEAN
Mozambique Channel
Equator
© Copyright HAMMOND INCORPORATED, Maplewood, N. J.

Topography

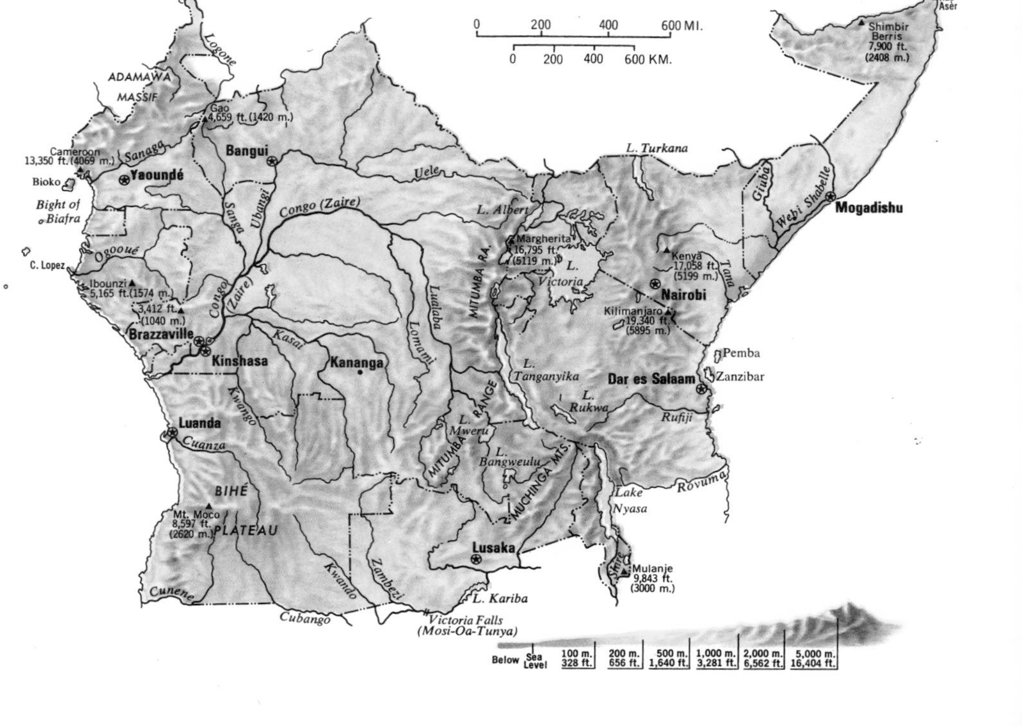
0 200 400 600 MI.
0 200 400 600 KM.
Bangui
Yaoundé
Brazzaville
Kinshasa
Kananga
Luanda
Lusaka
Nairobi
Dar es Salaam
Mogadishu
L. Turkana
L. Albert
L. Victoria
L. Tanganyika
L. Rukwa
L. Mweru
L. Bangweulu
Lake Nyasa
L. Kariba
Victoria Falls (Mosi-Oa-Tunya)
Below Sea Level
100 m. 328 ft.
200 m. 656 ft.
500 m. 1,640 ft.
1,000 m. 3,281 ft.
2,000 m. 6,562 ft.
5,000 m. 16,404 ft.

(continued)

Bosaso J1
Brava 6,167 H3
Bulhar H1
Bulo Burti 5,247 J3
Bur Acaba H3
Burao 12,617 J2
Callis J2
Candala J1
Chisimayu 17,872 H4
Chiambone H4
Coriole 4,341 H3
Dante (Hafun) K1
Dif H3
Dinsor H3
Dusa Marreb J2
Eil J2
El Athale (Itala) J3
El Bur J3
El Dere J3
El Hamurre J2
Erigabo 4,279 J1
Ferfer J2
Galcaio J2
Garad J2
Garbahaarrey H3
Gardo J2
Garoe J2
Giohar 13,156 J3
Gobwen H4
Hafun K1
Halin J2
Harardera J3
Hargeysa 40,254 H2
Hordio K1
Iddan J2
Iet H3
Itala J3
Jamama 5,408 H3
Jilib 3,232 H3
Karin J1
Kismayu (Chisimayu) 17,872 H4
Las Dureh J1
Luuq H3
Margherita (Jamama) H3
Marka (Merka) 17,708 H3
Mogadishu (cap.) 371,000 J3
Muqdisho (Mogadishu) (cap.) 371,000 J3
Obbia J2
Oddur H3
Taleh J2
Uanle Uen H3
Upper Sheikh J2
Villabruzzi (Johar) J3
Zeila 1,226 H1

OTHER FEATURES

Aden (gulf) J1
Asèr, Ras (cape) K1
Giuba (riv.) H3
Guban (reg.) H1
Hafun, Ras (cape) K1
Haud (plat.) J2
Lak Dera (dry riv.) H3
Negro (bay) J2
Nogal (reg.) J2
Shimbir Berris (mt.) J1
Sura, Ras (cape) J1
Surud Ad (mt.) J1
Webi Shabelle (riv.) H3

TANZANIA

REGIONS

Arusha 928,478 G4
Dodoma 971,921 G5
Iringa 922,801 G5
Kigoma 648,950 F4
Kilimanjaro 902,394 G4
Lindi 527,902 G5
Mara 723,295 F4
Mbeya 1,080,241 F5
Morogoro 939,190 G5
Mtwara 771,726 G5
Mwanza 1,443,418 F4
Pemba 205,870 H5
Pwani (Coast) 516,949 G5
Rukwa 451,897 F5
Ruvuma 564,113 G6
Shinyanga 1,323,482 F4
Singida 614,030 F5
Tabora 818,049 F5
Tanga 1,088,592 G5
Zanzibar Mjini 143,616 G5
Zanzibar Shambani North 77,424 G5
Zanzibar Shambani South 52,325 G5
Ziwa Magharibi (West Lake) 1,009,379 F4

CITIES and TOWNS

Arusha 55,281 G4
Babati G4
Bagamoyo 5,112 G5
Bukoba 20,430 F4
Chake Chake 4,862 H5
Dar es Salaam (cap.) 757,346 G5
Dodoma 45,703 G5
Geita 3,066 F4
Handeni G5
Ifakara G5
Iringa 57,182 G5
Itigi F5
Kahama 3,211 F4
Kaliua F5
Kanga G5
Karema F5
Kasanga F5
Kasulu F4
Kibara F4
Kibaya G5
Kibondo F4
Kigoma-Ujiji 50,044 E4
Kilosa 4,458 G5
Kilwa Kivinje 2,790 G5
Kilwa Masoko G5
Kinyangiri G4
Kipili F5
Kisiju G5
Kitunda F5
Kizimkazi G5
Kondoa 4,514 G4
Kongwa G5
Korogwe 6,675 G5
Lindi 27,308 G5
Liuli F6
Liwale G5
Longido G4
Mahenge G5
Makumbako G5
Manda F6
Manyoni G5
Masasi G6
Mbamba Bay G6
Mbeya 76,606 F5
Mbulu G4
Mchinga H5
Mohoro G5
Mombo G4
Morogoro 61,890 G5
Moshi 52,223 G4
Mpanda F5
Mtakuja F5
Mtwara-Mikindani 48,510 H6
Murongo F4
Musoma 32,658 F4
Muwale F5
Mwadui 7,383 F4
Mwanza 110,611 F4
Mwaya F5
Mwesi F5
Nachingwea 3,751 G6
Newala G6
Ngara F4
Njombe F5
Pangani 2,955 G5
Rungwa F5
Sadani G5
Same G4
Sekenke F4
Shinyanga 21,703 F4
Singida 29,252 F4
Songea 17,954 G6
Sumbawanga 28,586 F5
Tabora 67,392 F5
Tanga 103,409 G4
Tukuyu 4,089 F5
Tunduru G6
Urambo F4
Utete G5
Uvinza F5
Wete 8,469 G4
Zanzibar 110,669 G5

OTHER FEATURES

Eyasi (lake) F4
Great Ruaha (riv.) G5
Juani (isl.) G5
Kalambo (falls) F5
Kanzi (cape) G5
Kilimanjaro (mt.) G4
Kilombero (riv.) G5
Mafia (isl.) H5
Manyara (lake) G4
Masai (steppe) G4
Mbarangandu (riv.) G5
Mbemkuru (riv.) G5
Meru (mt.) G4
Mikumi Nat'l Park G5
Natron (lake) G4
Ngorongoro (crater) F4
Njombe (riv.) F5
Nyasa (lake) F6
Olduvai Gorge (canyon) G4
Pangani (riv.) G4
Pemba (isl.) H5
Rovuma (riv.) G6
Rufiji (riv.) G5
Ruaha Nat'l Park F5
Rukwa (lake) F5
Rungwa (riv.) F5
Rungwe (mt.) F5
Serengeti Nat'l Park F4
Tanganyika (lake) E5
Tarangire Nat'l Park G4
Victoria (lake) F4
Wami (riv.) G5
Wembere (riv.) F4
Zanzibar (isl.) G5

UGANDA

CITIES and TOWNS

Arua 10,837 F3
Atura F3
Butiaba 261 F3
Entebbe 21,096 F4
Fort Portal 7,947 F3
Gulu 18,170 F3
Hoima 2,339 F3
Jinja 52,509 F3
Kabale 8,234 E4
Kampala (cap.) 478,895 F3
Kasese 7,213 F3
Kilembe F3
Kitgum 3,242 F3
Lira 7,340 F3
Masaka 12,987 F4
Masindi 2,100 F3
Mbale 23,544 F3
Mbarara 16,078 F4
Moroto 5,488 F3
Moyo 2,656 F3
Mubende 6,004 F3
Rhino Camp 198 F3
Soroti 8,130 F3
Tororo 15,977 F3

OTHER FEATURES

Albert (Mobuto Sese Seko) (lake) F3
Edward (lake) E4
Elgon (mt.) F3
George (lake) F4
Kabalega (falls) F3
Kagalega Nat'l Park F3
Kidepo Nat'l Park F3
Kioga (lake) F3
Margherita (mt.) E3
Mobuto Sese Seko (lake) F3
Owen Falls (dam) F3
Ruwenzori (range) E3
Sese (isls.) F4
Victoria (lake) F4
Virunga (range) E4
Virunga Nat'l Park F4

ZAIRE

PRUVINCES

Bandundu 2,600,556 C4
Bas-Zaïre 1,504,361 B4
Equateur 2,431,812 D3
Haut-Zaïre 3,356,419 E3
Kasai-Occidental 2,433,861 D4
Kasai-Oriental 1,872,231 D5
Kinshasa 1,323,039 C4
Kivu 3,361,883 E4
Shaba 2,753,714 E5

CITIES and TOWNS

Aba 7,600 F3
Abumombazi D3
Aketi 17,200 D3
Andoma E3
Ango E3
Ankoro E5
Bagata C4
Balangala D3
Bambesa E3
Bambili E3
Banalia E3
Banana B5
Bandundu 74,467 C4
Baraka E4
Basankusu C3
Basoko 9,100 D3
Basongo D4
Befale D3
Bena-Dibele D4
Beni 22,800 E3
Bikoro C4
Boende 12,800 D4
Bokote D4
Bokungu D4
Bolobo 10,300 C4
Bolomba 7,200 C3
Boma 61,100 B5
Bomboma C3
Bomongo C3
Bondo 10,000 D3
Bongandanga 12,900 D3
Bosobolo 11,100 D3
Budjala C3
Bukama E5
Bukavu 134,861 E4
Bulungu 16,300 C4
Bumba 34,700 D3
Bunia 28,800 E3
Bunkeya 5,100 E6
Businga 11,000 D3
Busu-Djanoa D3
Buta 19,800 D3
Butembo 27,800 E3
Dekese D4
Demba 22,000 D5
Dibaya 11,400 D5
Dibaya-Lubue 7,900 C4
Dilolo 14,000 D6
Dimbelenge D5
Djolu D3
Djugu F3
Dongo C3
Doruma E3
Dungu 9,100 E3
Etoile E6
Faradje 10,400 E3
Feshi C5
Fizi E4
Gandajika 60,100 D5
Gemena 37,300 D3
Goma 48,600 E4
Gungu C5
Idiofa C4
Ikela D4
Ilebo 32,200 D4
Imese C3
Ingende C4
Inongo 14,800 C4
Irumu 9,300 E3
Isangi D3
Isiro 49,300 E3
Kabalo 22,600 E5
Kabambare E4
Kabare 12,600 E4
Kabinda 60,500 D5
Kabongo 6,500 E5
Kahemba C5
Kalehe E4
Kalemie 62,300 E5
Kalima 27,500 E4
Kama 17,700 E4
Kambove 18,900 E6
Kamina 56,300 D5
Kampene 14,600 E4
Kananga 428,960 D5
Kanda-Kanda D5
Kaniama D5
Kapanga D5
Kasaji D6
Kasangulu 11,900 C4
Kasenga E6
Kasenyi E3
Kasese E4
Kasongo 37,800 E4
Kasongo-Lunda C5
Katako-Kombe D4
Katenga E5
Kazumba D5
Kenge 17,500 C4
Kiambi E5
Kibombo E4
Kikwit 111,960 C5
Kilembe C5
Kilwa E5
Kilo E3
Kinda D5
Kiniama E6
Kinshasa (cap.) 1,323,039 C4
Kipushi 32,900 E6
Kiri C4
Kirundu E4
Kisangani 229,596 E3
Kole, Kasai-Oriental D4
Kole, Haut-Zaïre E3
Kolwezi 81,600 E6
Komba D3
Kongolo 14,800 E5
Kungu C3
Kutu 10,000 C4
Kwamouth C4
Libenge 12,500 C3
Likasi, Panda- 146,394 E6
Likati D3
Lisala D3
Lodja 20,300 D4
Lokolama D4
Lomela D4
Loto D4
Luashi D6
Lubefu D4
Lubero E4
Lubudi 6,000 E5
Lubumbashi 318,000 E6
Lubutu E4
Luebo 21,800 D5
Luishia E6
Luiza D5
Lukolela, Equateur C4
Lukolela, Kasai-Oriental D5
Lukula 9,400 B5
Luozi 7,000 B5
Lusambo 13,100 D4
Makanza C3
Malemba-Nkulu E5
Mambasa 7,400 E3
Mangai 15,200 C4
Manono 44,500 E5
Masi-Manimba 6,300 C4
Masisi E4
Matadi 110,436 B5
Mbandaka 107,910 C3
Mbanza-Ngungu 55,800 C5
Mbuji-Mayi 256,154 D5
Mitwaba E5
Moanda 6,400 B5
Mobayi-Mbongo D3
Moliro E5
Monga D3
Monkoto D4
Mulongo E5
Mungbere E3
Mushie 13,700 C4
Mutshatsha D6
Muyumba E5
Mwadingusha E6
Mwanza E5
Mweka 24,900 D4
Mwene-Ditu 71,200 D5
Mwenga E4
Niangara 9,200 E3
Niemba E5
Nyunzu 11,300 E5
Opala D4
Oshwe C4
Panda-Likasi 146,394 E6
Pangi E4
Penge D5
Poko E3
Popokabaka C5
Port Kindu 42,800 E4
Punia E4
Pweto E5
Rutshuru E4
Sakania E6
Sampwe E5
Sandoa D5
Seke-Banza B5
Sentery 24,300 E5
Shabunda 6,900 E4
Songololo 4,600 B5
Tenke E6
Titule E3
Tshela 10,700 B4
Tshikapa 38,900 D5
Tshofa D5
Ubundu 6,300 E4
Uvira 15,900 E4
Virunga 21,900 E5
Waka D3
Walikale E4
Wamba 11,500 E3
Watsa 21,300 E3
Yahuma D3
Yakoma D3
Yangambi 22,600 D3
Zongo C3

OTHER FEATURES

Albert (Mobuto Sese Seko) (lake) F3
Aruwimi (riv.) E3
Bomu (riv.) D3
Boyoma (Stanley) (falls) D3
Chicapa (riv.) D5
Congo (riv.) C4
Edward (lake) E4
Elila (riv.) E4
Fimi (riv.) C4
Garamba Nat'l Park E3
Giri (riv.) C3
Itimbiri (riv.) D3
Ituri (for.) E3
Karisimbi (mt.) E4
Kasai (riv.) C4
Kivu (lake) E4
Kwa (riv.) C4
Kwango (riv.) C5
Kwilu (riv.) C5
Lindi (riv.) E3
Livingstone (falls) B5
Loange (riv.) C5
Lokoro (riv.) C4
Lomami (riv.) D4
Lomela (riv.) D4
Lowa (riv.) E4
Lua (riv.) C3
Lualaba (riv.) E4
Luapula (riv.) E6
Lubilash (riv.) D5
Lufira (riv.) E5
Luilaka (riv.) C4
Lukenie (riv.) D4
Lukuga (riv.) E5
Lulua (riv.) D5
Luvua (riv.) E5
Mai-Ndombe (lake) C4
Malebo (Stanley Pool) (lake) C4
Margherita (mt.) E3
Marungu (mts.) E5
Mobuto Sese Seko (lake) F3
Mweru (lake) E5
Ruwenzori (range) E3
Ruzizi (riv.) E4
Salonga Nat'l Park D4
Sankuru (riv.) D4
Stanley (falls) D3
Stanley Pool (lake) C4
Tanganyika (lake) E5
Tshuapa (riv.) D4
Tumba (lake) C4
Ubangi (riv.) C3
Uele (riv.) E3
Ulindi (riv.) E4
Upemba (lake) E5
Upemba Nat'l Park E5
Virunga (range) E4
Virunga Nat'l Park E4
Zaire (Congo) (riv.) C4

ZAMBIA

CITIES and TOWNS

Abercorn (Mbala) 11,179 F5
Bancroft (Chililabombwe) 61,928 E6
Broken Hill (Kabwe) 143,635 E6
Chibwe E6
Chilanga 12,503 E7
Chililabombwe 61,928 E6
Chingola 145,869 E6
Chinsali 4,211 F6
Chipata 32,291 F6
Choma 17,943 E7
Fort Rosebery (Mansa) 34,801 E6
Isoka 6,832 F6
Kabompo 5,357 D6
Kabwe 143,635 E6
Kafue 29,794 E7
Kalabo 7,398 D6
Kalomo 5,878 E7
Kaoma 6,731 D6
Kapiri Mposhi 13,677 E6
Kasama 38,093 F6
Kasempa 3,063 E6
Kataba D7
Kawambwa 7,235 E5
Kitwe 314,794 E6
Lealui D6
Livingstone 71,987 E7
Luanshya 132,164 E6
Lundazi 4,083 F6
Lusaka (cap.) 538,469 E7
Luwingu 3,763 E6
Mansa 34,801 E6
Mazabuka 29,602 E7
Mbala 11,179 F5
Mkushi 4,104 E6
Mongu 24,919 D7
Monze 13,141 E7
Mpika 25,880 F6
Mporokoso 6,008 F5
Mpulungu 6,354 F5
Mufulira 149,778 E6
Mulobezi 2,589 E7
Mumbwa 7,570 E6
Mwinilunga 3,169 D6
Nakonde 4,599 F5
Namwala 3,008 E7
Ndola 282,439 E6
Petauke 7,531 F6
Senanga 7,204 D7
Serenje 6,008 F6
Sesheke 3,500 D7
Solwezi 15,032 E6
Zambezi 8,166 D6

OTHER FEATURES

Bangweulu (lake) F6
Barotseland (reg.) D7
Chambeshi (riv.) F6
Cuando (riv.) D7
Dongwe (riv.) D6
Kabompo (riv.) D6
Kafue (riv.) E7
Kafue Nat'l Park E6
Kalambo (falls) F5
Kariba (dam) E7
Kariba (lake) E7
Luangwa (riv.) F6
Luapula (riv.) E6
Lungwebungu (riv.) D6
Mosi-Oa-Tunya (Victoria) (falls) E7
Mulungushi (dam) E6
Mweru (lake) E5
Sunzu (mt.) F5
Tanganyika (lake) E5
Victoria (falls) E7
Zambezi (riv.) D7

Agriculture, Industry and Resources

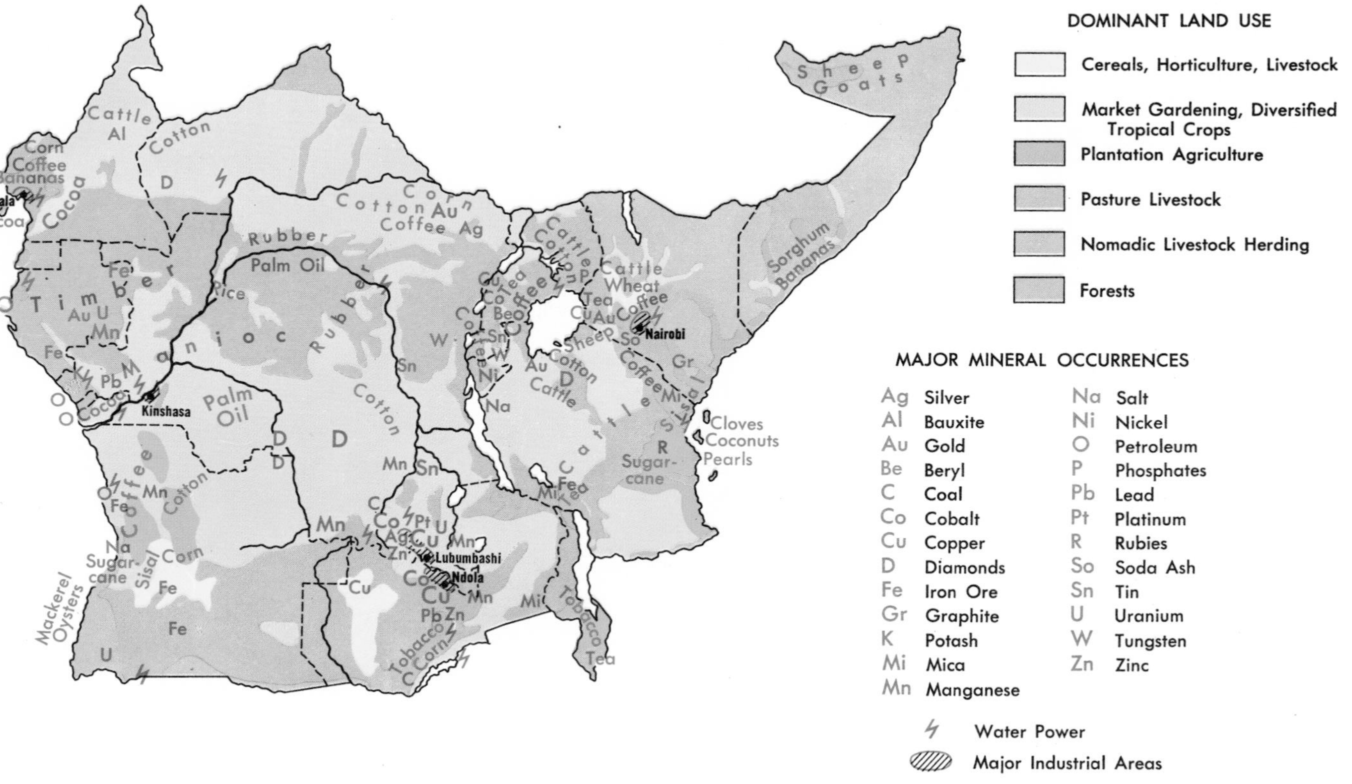
Sheep
Goats
Cattle
Al
Cotton
Corn
Coffee
Bananas
Douala
Cocoa
Cocoa
D
Cotton
Corn
Au
Coffee
Ag
Rubber
Palm Oil
Timber
Au U
Mn
Fe
Rice
Manioc
Rubber
Pb
Kinshasa
Palm Oil
Cotton
D
D
Sn
W
Cattle
Cotton
Wheat
Coffee
Tea
Cu Au
Coffee
Nairobi
Sheep
So
Cotton
Cattle
Gr
Coffee
Mi
Sisal
Cattle
Na
Sorghum
Bananas
Cloves
Coconuts
Pearls
R
Sugar-cane
Mn
Sn
Fe
Mn
Co Pt U
Ag Cu
Zn
Lubumbashi
Ndola
Cu
Mn
Mi
Pb Zn
Tobacco
Corn
Tobacco
Tea
Coffee
Fe
Mn
Cotton
Na
Sugar-cane
Sisal
Corn
Fe
Mackerel
Oysters
Fe
U
Cu
DOMINANT LAND USE
Cereals, Horticulture, Livestock
Market Gardening, Diversified Tropical Crops
Plantation Agriculture
Pasture Livestock
Nomadic Livestock Herding
Forests
MAJOR MINERAL OCCURRENCES
Ag Silver
Al Bauxite
Au Gold
Be Beryl
C Coal
Co Cobalt
Cu Copper
D Diamonds
Fe Iron Ore
Gr Graphite
K Potash
Mi Mica
Mn Manganese
Na Salt
Ni Nickel
O Petroleum
P Phosphates
Pb Lead
Pt Platinum
R Rubies
So Soda Ash
Sn Tin
U Uranium
W Tungsten
Zn Zinc
Water Power
Major Industrial Areas

NAMIBIA (SOUTH-WEST AFRICA)

AREA 317,827 sq. mi. (823,172 sq. km.)
POPULATION 1,200,000
CAPITAL Windhoek
LARGEST CITY Windhoek
HIGHEST POINT Brandberg 8,550 ft.
(2,606 m.)
MONETARY UNIT rand
MAJOR LANGUAGES Ovambo, Hottentot,
Herero, Afrikaans, English
MAJOR RELIGIONS Tribal religions,
Protestantism

SOUTH AFRICA

AREA 455,318 sq. mi. (1,179,274 sq. km.)
POPULATION 23,771,970
CAPITALS Cape Town, Pretoria
LARGEST CITY Johannesburg
HIGHEST POINT Injasuti 11,182 ft. (3,408 m.)
MONETARY UNIT rand
MAJOR LANGUAGES Afrikaans, English,
Xhosa, Zulu, Sesotho
MAJOR RELIGIONS Protestantism,
Roman Catholicism, Islam, Hinduism,
tribal religions

LESOTHO

AREA 11,720 sq. mi. (30,355 sq. km.)
POPULATION 1,339,000
CAPITAL Maseru
LARGEST CITY Maseru
HIGHEST POINT 11,425 ft. (3,482 m.)
MONETARY UNIT loti
MAJOR LANGUAGES Sesotho, English
MAJOR RELIGIONS Tribal religions,
Christianity

BOTSWANA

AREA 224,764 sq. mi. (582,139 sq. km.)
POPULATION 819,000
CAPITAL Gaborone
LARGEST CITY Francistown
HIGHEST POINT Tsodilo Hill 5,922 ft.
(1,805 m.)
MONETARY UNIT pula
MAJOR LANGUAGES Setswana, Shona,
Bushman, English, Afrikaans
MAJOR RELIGIONS Tribal religions,
Protestantism

MOZAMBIQUE

AREA 303,769 sq. mi. (786,762 sq. km.)
POPULATION 12,130,000
CAPITAL Maputo
LARGEST CITY Maputo
HIGHEST POINT Mt. Binga 7,992 ft.
(2,436 m.)
MONETARY UNIT metical
MAJOR LANGUAGES Makua, Thonga,
Shona, Portuguese
MAJOR RELIGIONS Tribal religions,
Roman Catholicism, Islam

SWAZILAND

AREA 6,705 sq. mi. (17,366 sq. km.)
POPULATION 547,000
CAPITAL Mbabane
LARGEST CITY Manzini
HIGHEST POINT Emlembe 6,109 ft.
(1,862 m.)
MONETARY UNIT lilangeni
MAJOR LANGUAGES siSwati, English
MAJOR RELIGIONS Tribal religions,
Christianity

ZIMBABWE

AREA 150,803 sq. mi. (390,580 sq. km.)
POPULATION 7,360,000
CAPITAL Harare
LARGEST CITY Harare
HIGHEST POINT Mt. Inyangani 8,517 ft.
(2,596 m.)
MONETARY UNIT Zimbabwe dollar
MAJOR LANGUAGES English, Shona,
Ndebele
MAJOR RELIGIONS Tribal religions,
Protestantism

MADAGASCAR

AREA 226,657 sq. mi. (587,041 sq. km.)
POPULATION 8,742,000
CAPITAL Antananarivo
LARGEST CITY Antananarivo
HIGHEST POINT Maromokotro 9,436 ft.
(2,876 m.)
MONETARY UNIT Madagascar franc
MAJOR LANGUAGES Malagasy, French
MAJOR RELIGIONS Tribal religions,
Roman Catholicism, Protestantism

COMOROS

AREA 719 sq. mi. (1,862 sq. km.)
POPULATION 290,000
CAPITAL Moroni
LARGEST CITY Moroni
HIGHEST POINT Karthala 7,746 ft.
(2,361 m.)
MONETARY UNIT CFA franc
MAJOR LANGUAGES Arabic, French,
Swahili
MAJOR RELIGION Islam

MAURITIUS

AREA 790 sq. mi. (2,046 sq. km.)
POPULATION 959,000
CAPITAL Port Louis
LARGEST CITY Port Louis
HIGHEST POINT 2,711 ft. (826 m.)
MONETARY UNIT Mauritian rupee
MAJOR LANGUAGES English, French,
French Creole, Hindi, Urdu
MAJOR RELIGIONS Hinduism, Christianity,
Islam

SEYCHELLES

AREA 145 sq. mi. (375 sq. km.)
POPULATION 63,000
CAPITAL Victoria
LARGEST CITY Victoria
HIGHEST POINT Morne Seychellois
2,993 ft. (912 m.)
MONETARY UNIT Seychellois rupee
MAJOR LANGUAGES English, French,
Creole
MAJOR RELIGION Roman Catholicism

RÉUNION

AREA 969 sq. mi. (2,510 sq. km.)
POPULATION 491,000
CAPITAL St-Denis

MAYOTTE

AREA 144 sq. mi. (373 sq. km.)
POPULATION 47,300
CAPITAL Dzaoudzi

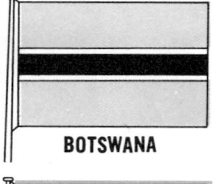

ZIMBABWE

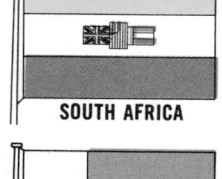

BOTSWANA

SOUTH AFRICA

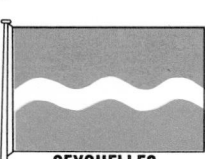

LESOTHO

SWAZILAND

MOZAMBIQUE

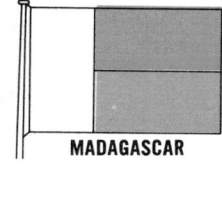

COMOROS

MADAGASCAR

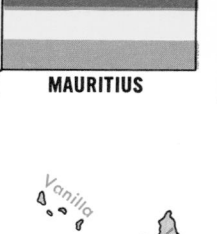

MAURITIUS

SEYCHELLES

Agriculture, Industry and Resources

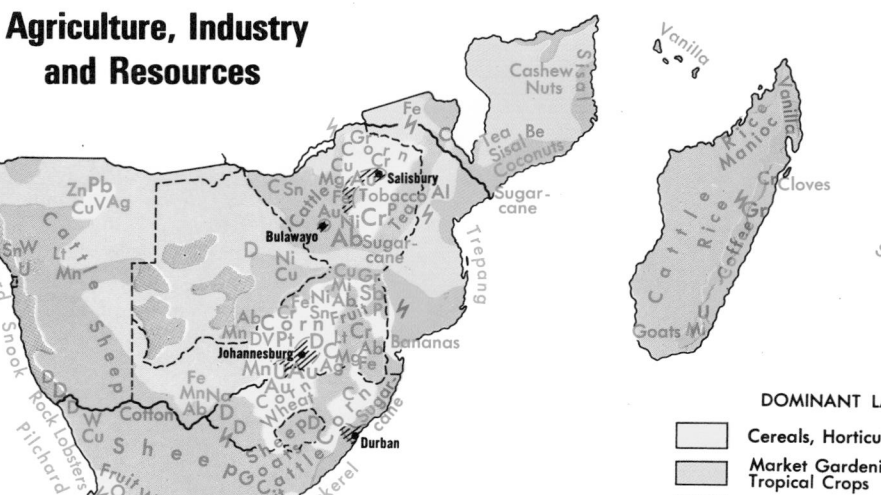

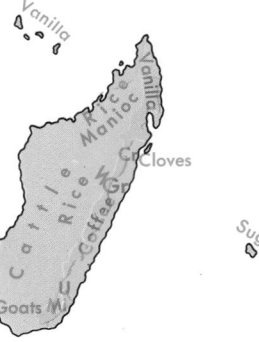

DOMINANT LAND USE

Cereals, Horticulture, Livestock
Market Gardening, Diversified Tropical Crops
Plantation Agriculture
Pasture Livestock
Nomadic Livestock Herding
Forests
Nonagricultural Land

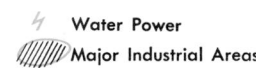

Water Power
Major Industrial Areas

MAJOR MINERAL OCCURRENCES

Ab	Asbestos	Cu	Copper
Ag	Silver	D	Diamonds
Al	Bauxite	Fe	Iron Ore
Au	Gold	Gr	Graphite
Be	Beryl	Lt	Lithium
C	Coal	Mg	Magnesium
Cr	Chromium	Mi	Mica
Pb	Manganese	Sb	Antimony
Pt	Salt	Sn	Tin
Mn	Nickel	U	Uranium
Na	Phosphates	V	Vanadium
Ni	Lead	W	Tungsten
P	Platinum	Zn	Zinc

BOTSWANA

CITIES and TOWNS

Bobonong 2,184 .... D4
Dibete 1,599 .... D4
Dinokwe 560 .... D4
Francistown 22,000 .... D4
Gaborone (cap.) 21,000 .... D4
Ghanzi 1,198 .... C4
Gumare 689 .... C3
Kalkfontein 1,532 .... C4
Kang 1,151 .... C4
Kanye 10,664 .... C5
Kasane 1,476 .... D3
Lehututu 988 .... C4
Lephepe 1,355 .... D4
Lobatse 11,936 .... D5
Machaneng 725 .... D4
Mahalapye 12,056 .... D4
Maun 9,614 .... C4
Mochudi 6,945 .... D4
Molepolole 9,448 .... C4
Nata 873 .... D4
Orapa 1,269 .... D4
Palapye 5,217 .... D4
Ramotswa 7,991 .... D4
Selebi-Pikwe 20,572 .... D4
Serowe 15,723 .... D4
Serule 1,718 .... D4
Shakawe 1,767 .... C3
Shashe 1,337 .... D4
Shoshong 3,132 .... D4
Tonota 4,494 .... D4
Tsau 427 .... C4
Tshabong 983 .... C5
Tshane 604 .... C4

OTHER FEATURES

Chobe (riv.) C3
Kalahari (des.) C4
Limpopo (riv.) D4
Makgadikgadi (salt pan) D3
Molopo (riv.) B5
Ngami (lake) C4
Ngamiland (reg.) C3
Nossob (riv.) B4
Okovango (swamps) C3
Orange (riv.) B5
Shashe (riv.) D4
Tati (riv.) D4

COMOROS

CITIES and TOWNS

Fomboni 3,229 .... G2
Mitsamiouli 3,196 .... G2
Moroni (cap.) 12,000 .... G2
Mutsamudu 7,652 .... G2

OTHER FEATURES

Anjouan (Nzwani) (isl.) 83,486 .... G2
Grand Comoro (Njazidja) (isl.) 118,443 .. G2
Mohéli (Mwali) (isl.) 9,525 .... G2

LESOTHO

CITIES and TOWNS

Leribe 5,200 .... D5
Mafeteng 4,600 .... D5
Maseru (cap.) 71,500 .... D5
Mohaleshoek 3,600 .... D6

MADAGASCAR

PROVINCES

Antananarivo 2,167,973 .... H3
Antsiranana 597,982 .... H2
Fianarantsoa 1,804,365 .... H4
Mahajanga 819,750 .... H3
Toamasina 1,179,660 .... H3
Toliara 1,034,114 .... G4

CITIES and TOWNS

Ambalavao 6,988 .... H4
Ambanja 12,258 .... H2
Ambato Boeny 3,317 .... H3
Ambatofinandrahana 2,161 .... H4
Ambatolampy 11,539 .... H3
Ambatomainty 1,276 .... H3
Ambatondrazaka 18,044 .... H3
Ambilobe 9,415 .... H2
Amboasary 2,420 .... H4
Ambodifototra 1,112 .... J3
Ambohimahasoa 5,851 .... H4
Ambositra 16,780 .... H4
Ambovombe 1,375 .... H5
Ampanihy 2,262 .... G4
Analalava 5,184 .... H2
Andapa 6,275 .... H2
Andilamena 3,512 .... H3
Androka 1,068 .... G5
Ankazoabo 1,677 .... G4
Antalaha 17,541 .... J2
Antananarivo (cap.) 451,808 ...... H3
Antsalova 2,202 .... G3
Antsirabe 32,979 .... H3
Antsiranana 40,443 .... H2
Antsohihy 8,721 .... H2
Arivonimamo 8,497 .... H3
Bealanana 2,299 .... H2
Befandriana 3,004 .... H3
Bekily 1,933 .... G4
Belo-Tsiribihina 4,403 .... G3
Beroroha 1,742 .... G4
Besalampy 2,874 .... G3
Betioky 3,964 .... G4
Betroka 3,943 .... H4
Brickaville (Vohibinany) 1,741 ... H3
Diégo-Suarez
  (Antsiranana) 40,443 .... H2
Fandriana 4,139 .... H4
Faradofay 13,805 .... H5
Farafangana 10,817 .... H4
Fenoarivo, Toamasina 7,696 ...... H3
Fianarantsoa 68,054 .... H4
Fort-Dauphin
  (Faradofay) 13,805 .... H5
Foulpointe H3
Hell-Ville 6,183 .... H2
Ifanadiana 1,111 .... H4
Ihosy 4,521 .... H4
Ivohibe 1,254 .... H4
Madirovalo 3,991 .... H3
Maevatanana 7,197 .... H3
Mahabo 4,941 .... G4
Mahanoro 5,041 .... H3
Maintirano 6,375 .... G3
Majunga 65,864 .... H3
Manakara 19,768 .... H4
Manananjary 14,638 .... H4
Mandabe 1,757 .... G4
Mandritsara 6,826 .... H3
Manja 4,151 .... G4
Manombo 2,908 .... G4
Maroantsetra 6,645 .... J3
Marovoay 20,253 .... H3

(continued on following page)

(continued)

Topography

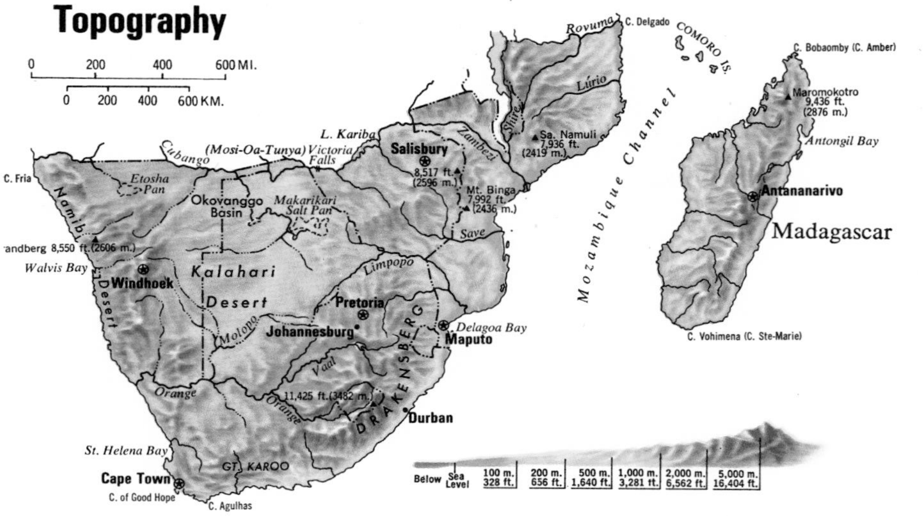
0 200 400 600 MI.
0 200 400 600 KM.
C. Delgado
COMORO IS.
C. Bobaomby (C. Amber)
Rovuma
Lúrio
Maromokotro 9,436 ft. (2876 m.)
Antongil Bay
Sa. Namuli 7,936 ft. (2419 m.)
L. Kariba
Salisbury
(Mosi-Oa-Tunya) Victoria Falls
Cubango
C. Fria
Etosha Pan
Okovanggo Basin
Makarikari Salt Pan
8,517 ft. (2596 m.)
Mt. Binga 7,992 ft. (2436 m.)
Antananarivo
Madagascar
Mozambique Channel
Save
Brandberg 8,550 ft. (2606 m.)
Walvis Bay
Windhoek
Kalahari Desert
Limpopo
Pretoria
Johannesburg
Delagoa Bay
Maputo
C. Vohimena (C. Ste-Marie)
Molopo
Vaal
Orange
11,425 ft. (3482 m.)
DRAKENSBERG
Durban
St. Helena Bay
Cape Town
C. of Good Hope
GT. KAROO
C. Agulhas
Below Sea Level 100 m. 328 ft. 200 m. 656 ft. 500 m. 1,640 ft. 1,000 m. 3,281 ft. 2,000 m. 6,562 ft. 5,000 m. 16,404 ft.

Miandrivazo 2,371 .... G3
Midongy Atsimo 1,068 .... H4
Mitsinjo 3,118 .... H3
Moramanga 10,806 .... H3
Morombe 6,967 .... G4
Morondava 19,061 .... G3
Nosy-Varika 1,252 .... H4
Port-Bergé 4,734 .... H3
Sambava 6,215 .... J2
Soanierana-Ivongo 2,876 .... H3
Sosumav 10,946 .... H2
Tamatave (Toamasina) 77,395 .... H3
Tambohorano 1,383 .... G3
Tananarive (Antananarivo) (cap.) 451,808 .... H3
Tangainony 6,952 .... H4
Toamasina 77,395 .... H3
Toliara (Tuléar) 45,676 .... G4
Tsihombe 1,008 .... H5
Tsiroanomandidy 11,444 .... H3
Tsivory 1,036 .... H4
Vangaindrano 3,249 .... H4
Vatomandry 4,202 .... H3
Vohibinany 1,741 .... H3
Vohimarina (Vohémar) 4,289 .... J2
Vohipeno 2,736 .... H4

OTHER FEATURES

Alaotra (lake) H3
Amber (Bobaomby) (cape) H2
Antongil (bay) J3
Betsiboka (riv.) H3
Bobaomby (Amber) (cape) H2
Mangoky (riv.) G4
Mangoro (riv.) H3
Maromokotro (mt.) H2
Masoala (pen.) J3
Mozambique (chan.) G3
Nosy Be (isl.) H2
Nosy Boraha (isl.) J3
Onilahy (riv.) G4
Saint-André (cape) G3
Sainte-Marie (Vohimena) (cape) G5
Sainte-Marie (Nosy Boraha) (isl.) J3
Tsiafajavona (mt.) H3
Tsiribihina (riv.) G3
Vohimena (cape) G5

MAURITIUS

CITIES and TOWNS

Curepipe 52,709 .... G5
Mahébourg 15,463 .... G5
Port Louis (cap.) 141,022 .... G5
Poudre d'Or 1,799 .... G5
Quatre Bornes 51,638 .... G5
Souillac 3,361 .... G5

OTHER FEATURES

Mascarene (isls.) F5

MAYOTTE

CITIES and TOWNS

Dzaoudzi (cap.) 196 .... H2

MOZAMBIQUE

PROVINCES

Cabo Delgado 940,000 .... F2
Gaza 999,900 .... E4
Inhambane 977,000 .... E4
Manica 541,200 .... E4
Maputo 491,800 .... E5
Maputo (city) 755,300 .... E5
Nampula 2,402,700 .... F2
Niassa 514,100 .... F2
Sofala 1,055,200 .... E3
Tete 831,000 .... E3
Zambézia 2,500,000 .... F3

CITIES and TOWNS

Alto Molócuè 415 .... F3
Angoche 1,714 .... G3
Bartolomeu Dias○ 6,102 .... F4
Beira 46,293 .... F3
Beira* 130,398 .... F3
Bela Vista 851 .... E5
Benga 1,398 .... E3
Caia 1,363 .... E3
Catandica 663 .... E3
Chemba 588 .... E3
Chibuto 23,763 .... E4
Chicualacuala 2,050 .... E4
Chimoio 4,507 .... E3
Chinde 742 .... F3
Cóbuè○ 770 .... F2
Cuamba 1,416 .... F2
Dona Ana (Mutarara) 686 .... F3
Dondo 2,112 .... F3
Errego 418 .... F3
Espungabera 405 .... E4
Fíngoè 1,137 .... E2
Funhalouro○ 42,366 .... E4
Gorongoza 435 .... E3
Guija 530 .... E4
Homoíne 1,122 .... E4
Ibo 1,015 .... G2
Inhambane 4,975 .... F4
Inhaminga 1,607 .... F3
Inharrime 856 .... F4
Lichinga 3,011 .... F2
Lumbo○ 11,080 .... G3
Lúrio○ 13,417 .... G2
Mabalane○ 13,158 .... E4
Mabote○ 28,970 .... E4
Machanga○ 15,754 .... F4
Machaze○ 42,255 .... E4
Macia 1,203 .... E4
Macomia 730 .... F2
Magude 1,502 .... E5
Malema 430 .... F2
Mandié○ 24,382 .... E3
Mandimba○ 7,634 .... F2
Manhiça 1,680 .... E5
Maniamba○ 2,045 .... F2
Manica 1,529 .... E3
Manjacaze 641 .... E5
Maputo (cap.) 755,300 .... E5
Marracuene 1,342 .... E5
Marromeu 1,330 .... F3
Marrupa 824 .... F2
Massangena○ 3,301 .... E4
Massinga 517 .... F4
Maxixe 902 .... F4
Meconta 1,051 .... F3
Memba 379 .... G2
Metangula 1,502 .... F2
Milanje 1,048 .... F3
Moamba 643 .... E5
Moçambique 1,730 .... G3
Mocímboa da Praia 935 .... G2
Mocuba 2,293 .... F3
Moma 433 .... F3
Monapo 902 .... G2
Montepuez 2,837 .... F2
Morrumbala 415 .... F3
Morrumbene 1,121 .... F4
Mualama○ 34,992 .... F3
Mucojo○ 15,867 .... G2
Mueda 1,583 .... F2
Murrupula 444 .... F3
Mutarara (Dona Ana) 686 .... F3
Nacala 4,601 .... G2
Namacurra 399 .... F3
Namapa 440 .... F2
Nametil 453 .... F3
Nampula 23,072 .... F3
Negomane○ 656 .... F2
Nova Lusitânia 1,363 .... E3
Nova Mambone 883 .... F4
Nova Sofala 274 .... F4
Pafúrio○ 2,599 .... E4
Pemba 3,629 .... G2
Quelimane 10,522 .... F3
Quionga○ 3,181 .... G2
Quissico 2,615 .... F4
Ribáuè 437 .... F3
Songo 1,350 .... E3
Tete 4,549 .... E3
Ulongue 451 .... E2
Vila de Sena○ 21,074 .... E3
Vilanculos 887 .... E4
Xai-Xai 5,234 .... E5

OTHER FEATURES

Angoche (isl.) G3
Bazaruto, Ilha do (isl.) F4
Binga (mt.) E3
Changane (riv.) E4
Chilwa (lake) F3
Delagoa (bay) E5
Delgado (cape) G2
Ligonha (riv.) F3
Limpopo (riv.) E4
Lugenda (riv.) F2
Lúrio (riv.) F2
Mazoe (riv.) E3
Mozambique (chan.) G3
Namuli, Serra (mt.) F3
Nyasa (lake) E2
Olifants (riv.) D4
Rovuma (riv.) F2
São Sebastião (pt.) F4
Save (riv.) E4
Shire (riv.) E3
Zambezi (riv.) E3

NAMIBIA (SOUTH-WEST AFRICA)

CITIES and TOWNS

Aroab 783 .... B5
Aus 767 .... B5
Berseba B5
Bethanie 1,207 .... B5
Gibeon B5
Gobabis 4,428 .... B4
Grootfontein 4,627 .... B3
Kalkfeld 587 .... B4
Kamanjab 713 .... A3
Karasburg 2,693 .... B5
Karibib 1,653 .... B4
Katima Mulilo C3
Keetmanshoop 10,297 .... B5
Khorixas 1,299 .... A4
Koes 514 .... B5
Lüderitz 6,642 .... A5
Maltahöhe 1,313 .... B4
Mariental 4,629 .... B4
Ohopoho A3
Okahandja 1,688 .... B4
Omaruru 2,783 .... B4
Ondangua B3
Ongwediva B3
Oranjemund 2,594 .... B5
Otavi 1,814 .... B3
Otjiwarongo 8,018 .... B4
Outjo 2,545 .... B4
Rehoboth 5,363 .... B4
Runtu 521 .... B3
Stampriet 271 .... B4
Swakopmund 5,681 .... A4
Tsumeb 12,338 .... B3
Usakos 2,334 .... B4
Warmbad 810 .... B5
Windhoek (cap.) 61,369 .... B4
Witvlei 303 .... B4

OTHER FEATURES

Brandberg (mt.) A4
Caprivi Strip (reg.) C3
Chobe (riv.) C3
Cubango (riv.) B3
Damaraland (reg.) B4
Diamond Coast (reg.) A5
Elephant (riv.) B5
Etosha Pan (salt pan) B3
Fish (riv.) B5
Great Namaland (reg.) B4
Hottentot (bay) A5
Kalahari (des.) C4
Kaokoveld (reg.) A3
Kaukauveld (mts.) C3
Namib (des.) A3
Nossob (riv.) B4
Okovango (riv.) C3
Ovamboland (reg.) B3
Skeleton Coast (reg.) A3
Swakop (riv.) B4
Zambezi (riv.) C3

REUNION

CITIES and TOWNS

Le Port 21,564 .... F5
Saint-André 6,584 .... G5
Saint-Benoît 7,778 .... G5
Saint-Denis (cap.) 80,075 .... F5
Saint-Denis* 104,603 .... F5
Saint-Joseph 8,928 .... G6
Saint-Louis 10,252 .... F5
Saint-Pierre 21,817 .... F6

OTHER FEATURES

Bassas da India (isl.) F4
Europa (isl.) G4
Glorioso (isls.) H2
Juan de Nova (isl.) G3
Piton des Neiges (mt.) G5

SEYCHELLES

CITIES and TOWNS

Anse Boileau† 3,420 .... H5
Anse Royale† 3,182 .... H5
Cascade† 2,600 .... H5
Victoria (cap.) 15,559 .... H5
Victoria* 23,012 .... H5

OTHER FEATURES

Aldabra (isls.) H1
Assumption (isl.) H1
Astove (isl.) H2
Cosmoledo (isls.) H1
Frigate (isl.) J5
La Digue (isl.) J5
Mahé (isl.) H5
North (isl.) H5
Praslin (isl.) H5
Silhouette (isl.) H5

SOUTH AFRICA

PROVINCES

Cape of Good Hope 5,543,506 .... C6
Natal 5,722,215 .... E5
Orange Free State 1,833,216 .... D5
Transvaal 10,673,033 .... D4

AUTONOMOUS REPUBLICS

Bophuthatswana 1,200,000 .... D5
Ciskei 345,191 .... D6
Transkei 2,000,000 .... D6
Venda 450,000 .... E4

CITIES and TOWNS

Aberdeen 4,968 .... C6
Adelaide 7,227 .... D6
Alberton 23,988 .... H6
Alexandra 57,040 .... H6
Alexander Bay 2,675 .... B5
Aliwal North 12,311 .... D6
Barberton 12,382 .... E5
Barkly East 4,023 .... D6
Beaufort West 17,862 .... C6
Bellville 49,026 .... F6
Benoni 151,294 .... J6
Benoni□ 164,543 .... J6
Bethlehem 29,918 .... D5
Bethulie 4,918 .... D6
Bloemfontein 149,836 .... C5
Bloemfontein□ 182,329 .... C5
Bloubergstrand 378 .... E6
Boksburg 106,126 .... J6
Botrivier 743 .... F7
Brakpan 73,210 .... J6
Brandvlei 1,337 .... B6
Bredasdorp 5,264 .... B6
Brentwood Park 5,296 .... J6
Brits 12,182 .... D5
Britstown 3,039 .... C6
Burgersdorp 8,340 .... D6
Butterworth (Gcuwa) 2,769 .... D6
Caledon 5,406 .... G7
Calvinia 6,386 .... B6
Cape Town (cap.) 697,514 .... E6
Cape Town□ 833,731 .... E6
Carltonville 40,641 .... G7
Carnarvon 5,199 .... C6
Ceres 9,230 .... B6
Christiana 6,882 .... D5
Clanwilliam 2,724 .... B6
Clayville 3,994 .... H6
Colesberg 7,088 .... D6
Constantia 7,220 .... E6
Cradock 20,822 .... D6
De Aar 18,057 .... C6
Delmas 6,424 .... J6
Dibeng 945 .... C5
Douglas 4,335 .... C5
Dundee 17,162 .... E5
Dunnottar 3,089 .... J6
Durban 736,852 .... E5
Durban□ 975,494 .... E5
Durbanville 7,438 .... F6
East London 119,727 .... D6
East London□ 126,671 .... D6
Edenburg 3,710 .... D5
Edendale 41,194 .... D5
Edenvale 25,126 .... H6
Eersterivier 1,459 .... F6
Elliot 3,739 .... D6
Eloff 1,134 .... J6
Elsburg 3,501 .... H6
Elsiesrivier 63,706 .... F6
Empangeni 7,532 .... E5
Ermelo 19,036 .... E5
Eshowe 4,552 .... E5
Estcourt 10,922 .... D5
Ficksburg 9,504 .... D5
Firgrove 2,551 .... F6
Fort Beaufort 11,640 .... D6
Franschhoek 1,216 .... F6
Garies 1,339 .... B6
Gcuwa 2,769 .... D6
George 24,625 .... C6
Germiston 221,972 .... H6
Germiston□ 293,257 .... H6
Glencoe 10,513 .... E5
Goodwood 31,592 .... F6
Gordon's Bay 1,112 .... F7
Graaff-Reinet 22,392 .... C6
Grabouw 4,286 .... F7
Grahamstown 41,302 .... D6
Grassy Park 32,709 .... E6
Greytown 9,028 .... E5
Griquatown 2,996 .... C5
Halfway House 3,639 .... H6
Harrismith 16,082 .... D5
Hawston 2,501 .... G7
Heidelberg 12,521 .... J7
Heilbron 8,258 .... D5
Hermanus 4,956 .... G7
Hopetown 3,273 .... C5
Houtbaai 5,691 .... E6
Howick 12,429 .... E5
Humansdorp 4,215 .... C6
Ingwavuma 718 .... E5
Jagersfontein 4,142 .... D5
Jameson Park 2,280 .... J7
Johannesburg 654,232 .... H6
Johannesburg□ 1,417,818 .... H6
Keimoes 4,534 .... C5
Kempton Park 37,205 .... J6
Kenhardt 3,230 .... C5
Kimberley 105,258 .... C5
Kimberley□ 108,609 .... C5
King William's Town 15,798 .... D6
Kirkwood 5,151 .... D6
Kleinmond 1,115 .... F7
Klerksdorp 63,558 .... D5
Knysna 13,479 .... C6
Koffiefontein 3,672 .... D5
Kokstad 10,227 .... D6
Kraaifontein 10,286 .... F6
Kroonstad 51,988 .... D5
Krugersdorp 92,725 .... H6
Kuilsrivier 8,132 .... F6
Kuruman 5,758 .... C5
Ladybrand 8,757 .... D5
Ladysmith 28,920 .... D5
Lambert's Bay 3,247 .... B6
Lombardy 3,395 .... H6
Louis Trichardt 8,906 .... E4
Lydenburg 7,427 .... E4
Macassar 882 .... F6
Maclear 3,279 .... D6
Mafikeng (Mafeking) 6,515 .... C5
Malmesbury 9,314 .... B6
Margate 4,410 .... E6
Matatiele 3,853 .... D6
Melkbosstrand 453 .... E6
Messina 12,121 .... D4
Meyerton 8,654 .... H7
Middelburg, C. of Good Hope 11,121 .... D6
Middelburg, Transvaal 26,942 .... D5
Milnerton 10,893 .... F6
Modderfontein 8,538 .... H6
Molteno 5,825 .... D6
Montagu 5,504 .... C6
Moorreesburg 4,945 .... B6
Mossel Bay 17,574 .... C6
Nababeep 8,293 .... B5
Nelspruit 25,092 .... E5
Newcastle 14,407 .... E5
Nigel 41,179 .... J7
Noupoort 7,403 .... C6
Nyanga 15,655 .... F6
Nylstroom 6,906 .... D4
Odendaalsrus 15,603 .... D5
Okiep 4,983 .... B5
Oudtshoorn 26,907 .... C6
Paarl 49,244 .... F6
Parow 60,768 .... F6
Parys 17,447 .... D5
Phalaborwa 7,543 .... E4
Pietermaritzburg 114,822 .... E5
Pietermaritzburg□ 174,179 .... E5
Pietersburg 27,174 .... D4
Piet Retief 10,056 .... D5
Piketberg 3,638 .... B6
Pinelands 11,769 .... F6
Pinetown 22,721 .... E6
Pniel 1,596 .... F6
Port Alfred 8,640 .... D6
Port Elizabeth 392,231 .... D6
Port Elizabeth□ 413,961 .... D6
Port Nolloth 2,893 .... B5
Port Saint Johns (Umzimbuvu) 1,817 .... D6
Port Shepstone 5,581 .... E6
Postmasburg 9,020 .... C5

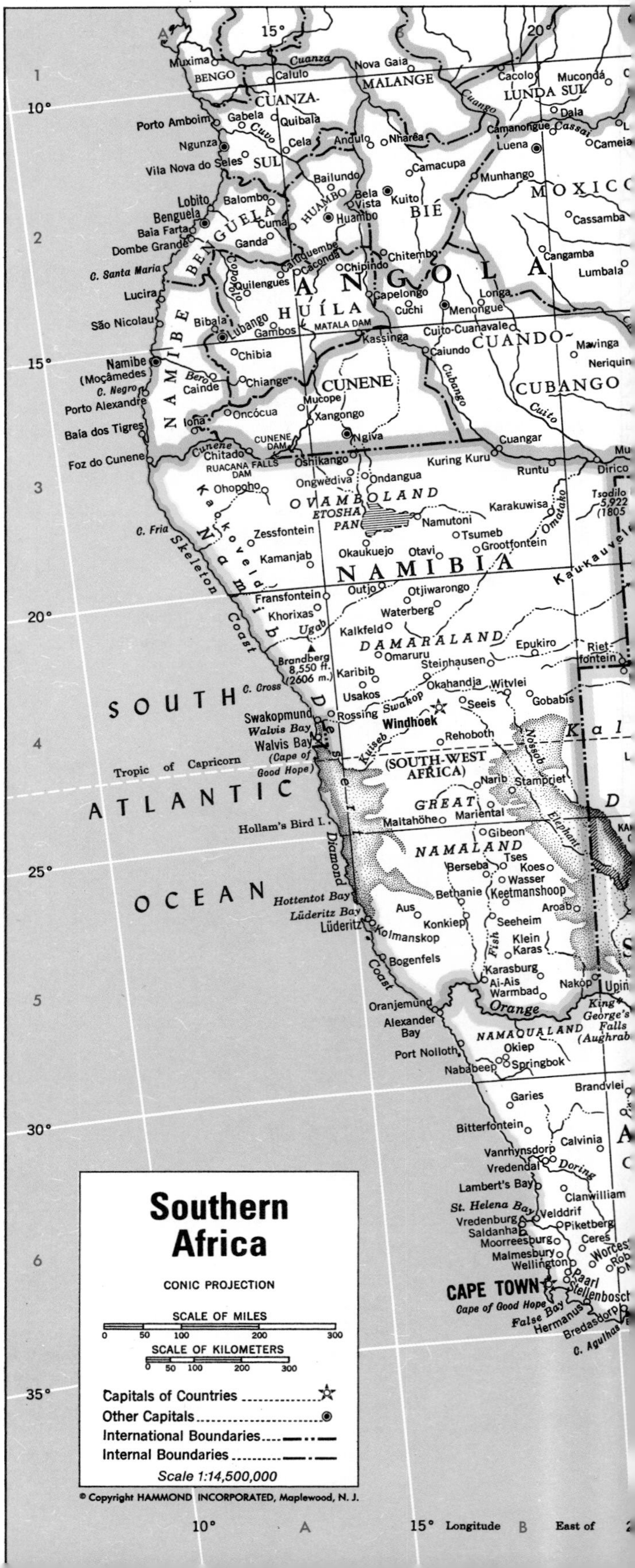
Southern Africa
CONIC PROJECTION
SCALE OF MILES
0 50 100 200 300
SCALE OF KILOMETERS
0 50 100 200 300
Capitals of Countries
Other Capitals
International Boundaries
Internal Boundaries
Scale 1:14,500,000
© Copyright HAMMOND INCORPORATED, Maplewood, N. J.
SOUTH ATLANTIC OCEAN
ANGOLA
NAMIBIA
(SOUTH-WEST AFRICA)
Windhoek
Walvis Bay
Lüderitz
CAPE TOWN
Tropic of Capricorn
10° 15° Longitude East of

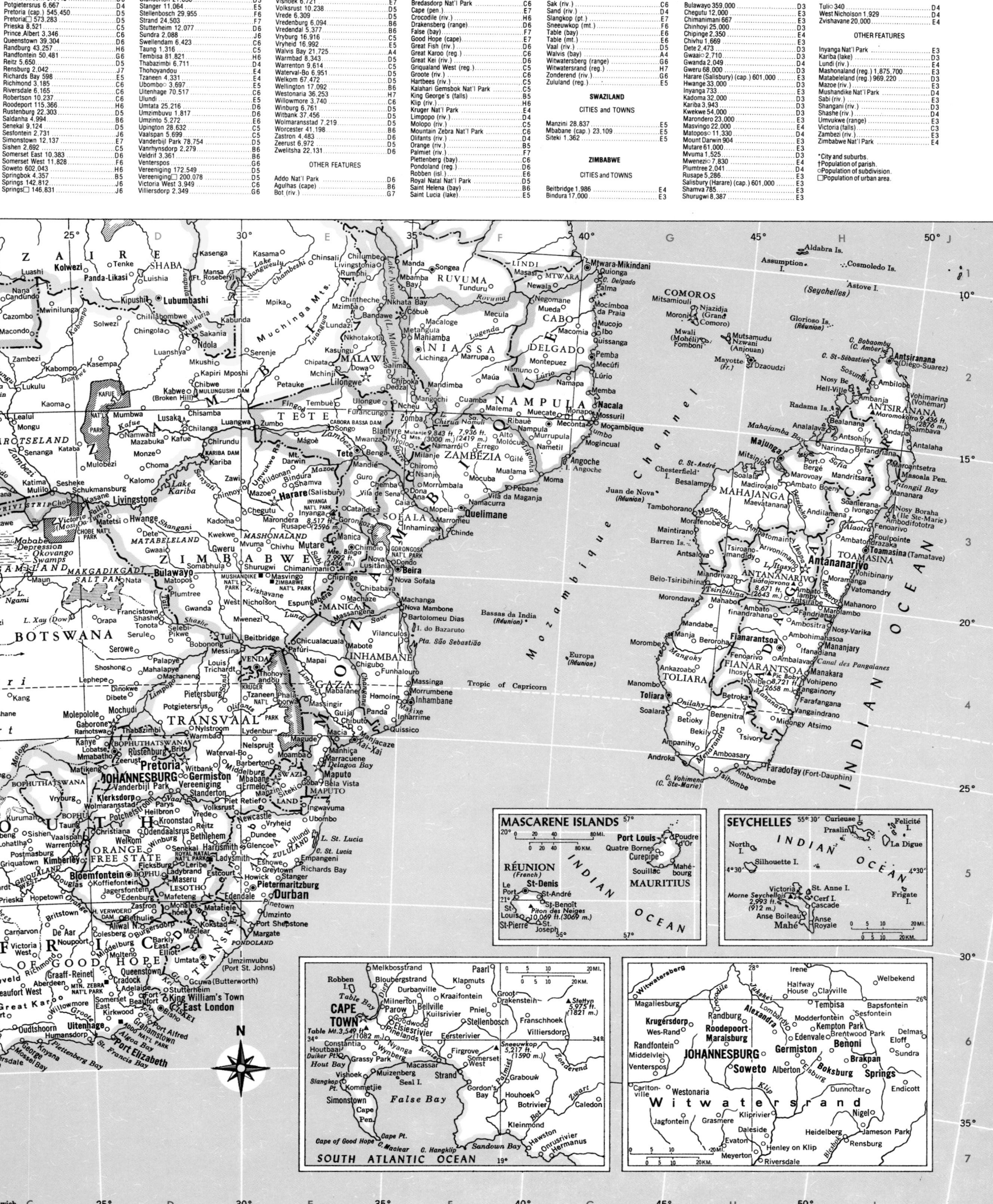

South America

AZIMUTHAL EQUAL-AREA PROJECTION

MILES

0   100   200   400   600

KILOMETERS

0   100 200   400   600

Capitals of Countries .... ⊛

Other Capitals .... ⊛

International Boundaries ....

Canals ....

Scale 1:27,000,000

© Copyright HAMMOND INCORPORATED, Maplewood, N.J.

Population Distribution

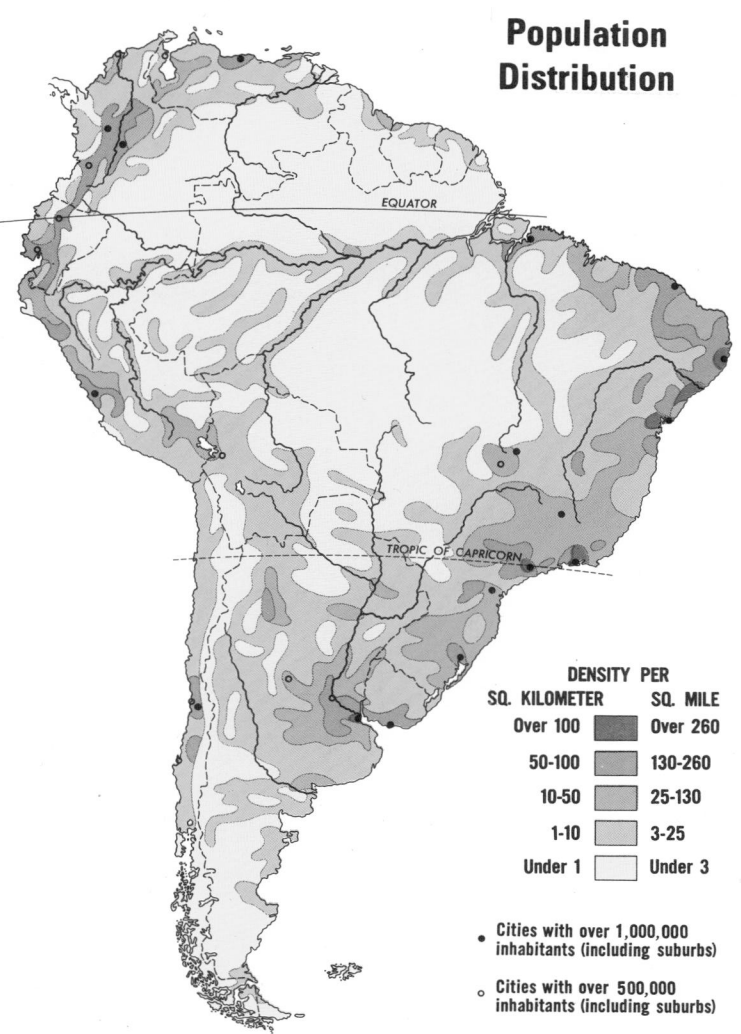

EQUATOR

TROPIC OF CAPRICORN

AREA 6,875,000 sq. mi. (17,806,250 sq. km.)
POPULATION 245,000,000
LARGEST CITY São Paulo
HIGHEST POINT Cerro Aconcagua 22,831 ft.
  (6,959 m.)
LOWEST POINT Salina Grande -131 ft. (-40 m.)

Vegetation

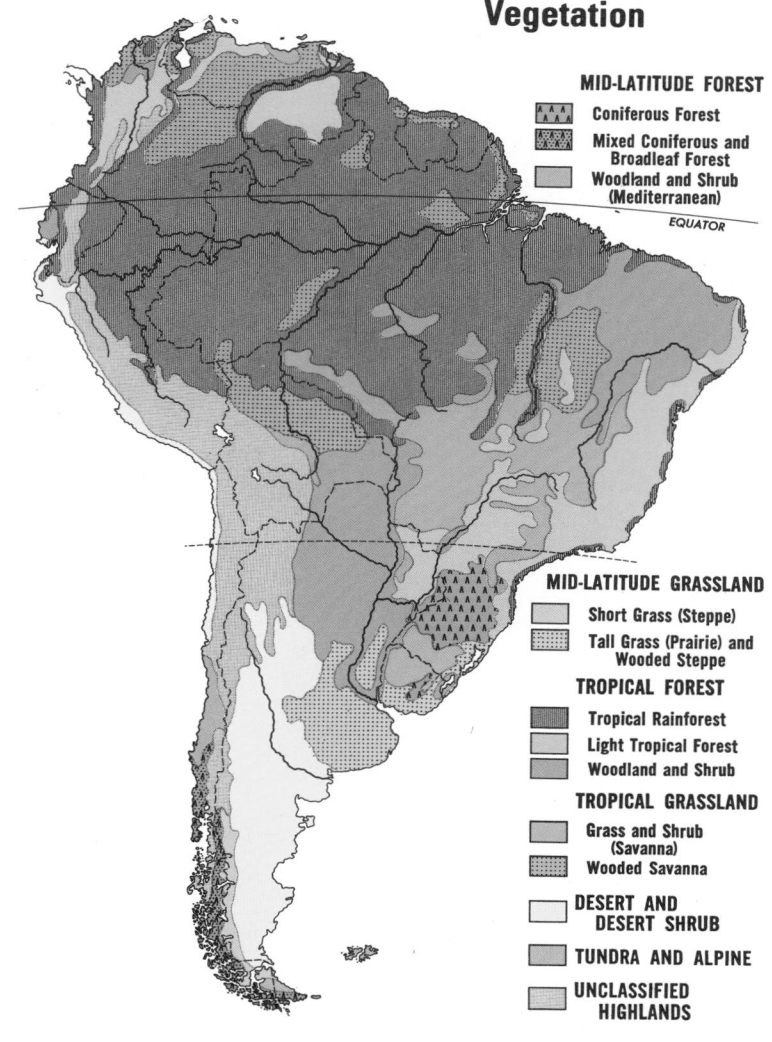

EQUATOR

DENSITY PER

SQ. KILOMETER	SQ. MILE
Over 100	Over 260
50-100	130-260
10-50	25-130
1-10	3-25
Under 1	Under 3

• Cities with over 1,000,000 inhabitants (including suburbs)

○ Cities with over 500,000 inhabitants (including suburbs)

MID-LATITUDE FOREST
- Coniferous Forest
- Mixed Coniferous and Broadleaf Forest
- Woodland and Shrub (Mediterranean)

MID-LATITUDE GRASSLAND
- Short Grass (Steppe)
- Tall Grass (Prairie) and Wooded Steppe

TROPICAL FOREST
- Tropical Rainforest
- Light Tropical Forest
- Woodland and Shrub

TROPICAL GRASSLAND
- Grass and Shrub (Savanna)
- Wooded Savanna

DESERT AND DESERT SHRUB

TUNDRA AND ALPINE

UNCLASSIFIED HIGHLANDS

Average January Temperature

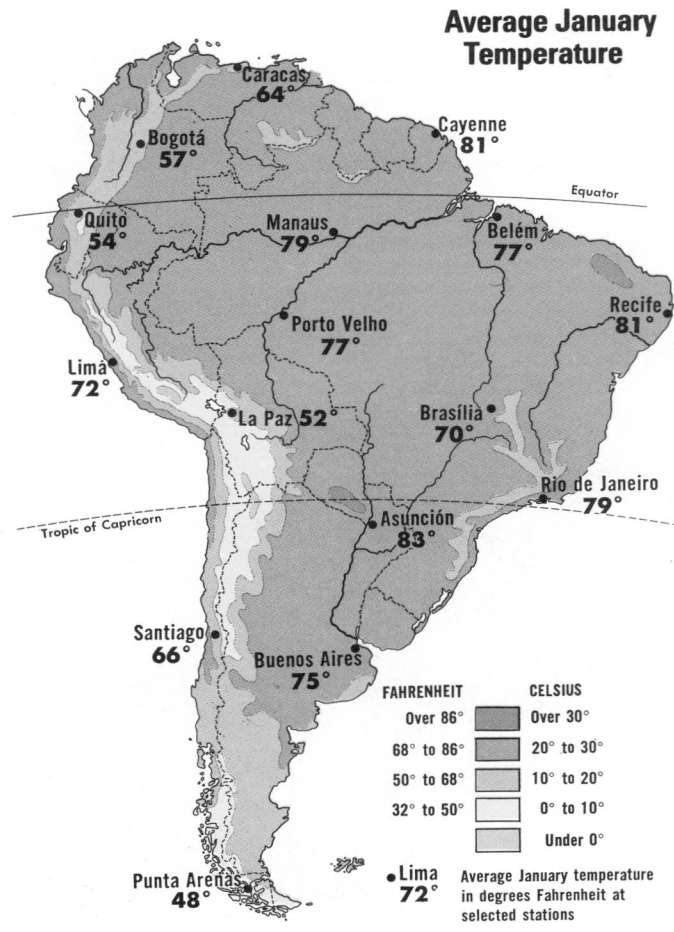

Caracas 64°
Cayenne 81°
Bogotá 57°
Equator
Quito 54°
Manaus 79°
Belém 77°
Lima 72°
Porto Velho 77°
Recife 81°
La Paz 52°
Brasília 70°
Rio de Janeiro 79°
Asunción 83°
Tropic of Capricorn
Santiago 66°
Buenos Aires 75°
Punta Arenas 48°

FAHRENHEIT	CELSIUS
Over 86°	Over 30°
68° to 86°	20° to 30°
50° to 68°	10° to 20°
32° to 50°	0° to 10°
	Under 0°

• Lima 72° Average January temperature in degrees Fahrenheit at selected stations

Average July Temperature

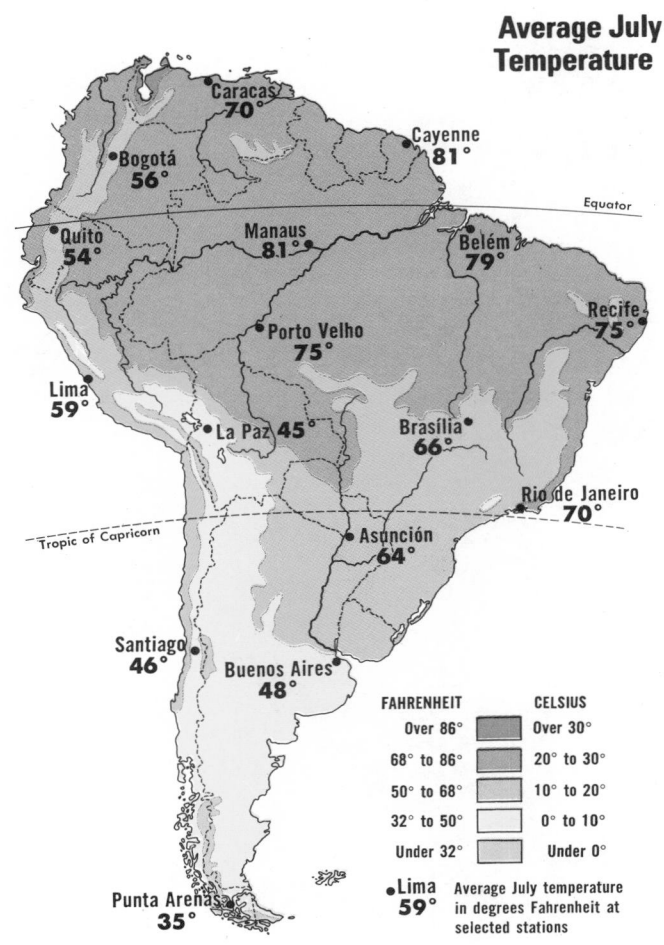

Caracas 70°
Cayenne 81°
Bogotá 56°
Equator
Quito 54°
Manaus 81°
Belém 79°
Lima 59°
Porto Velho 75°
Recife 75°
La Paz 45°
Brasília 66°
Rio de Janeiro 70°
Asunción 64°
Tropic of Capricorn
Santiago 46°
Buenos Aires 48°
Punta Arenas 35°

FAHRENHEIT	CELSIUS
Over 86°	Over 30°
68° to 86°	20° to 30°
50° to 68°	10° to 20°
32° to 50°	0° to 10°
Under 32°	Under 0°

• Lima 59° Average July temperature in degrees Fahrenheit at selected stations

Rainfall

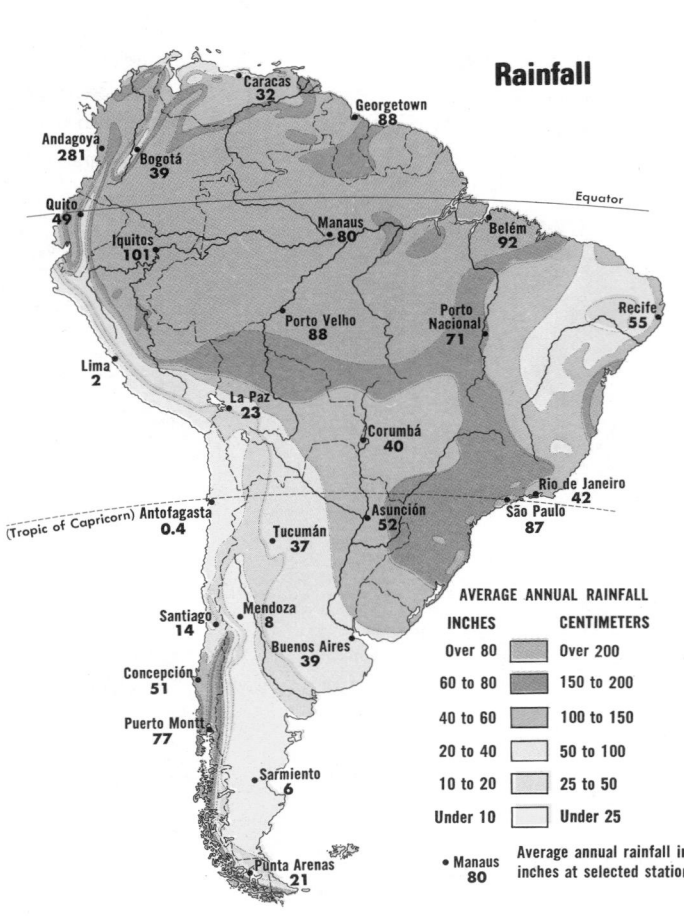

Caracas 32
Georgetown 88
Andagoya 281
Bogotá 39
Quito 49
Equator
Iquitos 101
Manaus 80
Belém 92
Porto Velho 88
Porto Nacional 71
Recife 55
Lima 2
La Paz 23
Corumbá 40
Rio de Janeiro 42
Antofagasta 0.4
Asunción 52
São Paulo 87
(Tropic of Capricorn)
Tucumán 37
Mendoza 8
Santiago 14
Buenos Aires 39
Concepción 51
Puerto Montt 77
Sarmiento 6
Punta Arenas 21

AVERAGE ANNUAL RAINFALL

INCHES	CENTIMETERS
Over 80	Over 200
60 to 80	150 to 200
40 to 60	100 to 150
20 to 40	50 to 100
10 to 20	25 to 50
Under 10	Under 25

• Manaus 80 Average annual rainfall in inches at selected stations

Vegetation/Relief

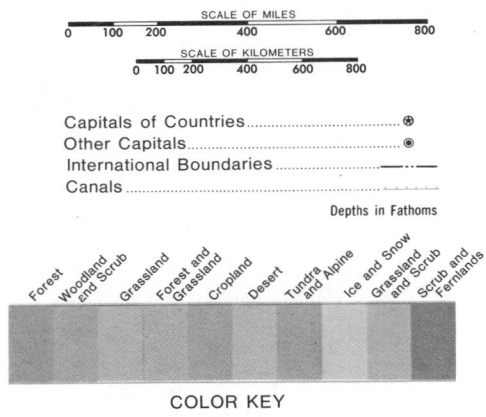

SCALE OF MILES
0 100 200 400 600 800

SCALE OF KILOMETERS
0 100 200 400 600 800

Capitals of Countries .... ⊕
Other Capitals .... ⊚
International Boundaries ....———
Canals ....

Depths in Fathoms

Forest | Woodland and Scrub | Grassland | Forest and Grassland | Cropland | Desert | Tundra and Alpine | Ice and Snow | Grassland and Scrub | Scrub and Fernlands

COLOR KEY

30° Longitude West of Greenwich 20°

STATES

Amazonas (terr.) 21,696	E5
Anzoátegui 506,297	F3
Apure 164,705	D4
Aragua 543,170	E2
Barinas 231,046	C3
Bolívar 391,665	F7
Carabobo 659,339	D2
Cojedes 94,351	D3
Delta Amacuro (terr.) 48,139	H3
Dependencias Federales (terr.) 463	E2
Distrito Federal 1,860,637	E2
Falcón 407,957	D2
Guárico 318,905	E3
Lara 671,410	C2
Mérida 347,095	C3
Miranda 856,272	E2
Monagas 298,239	G2
Nueva Esparta 118,830	G2
Portuguesa 297,047	D3
Sucre 469,004	G2
Táchira 511,346	C3
Trujillo 381,334	C3
Yaracuy 223,545	D2
Zulia 1,299,030	B2

CITIES and TOWNS

Acarigua 56,743	D3
Achaguas 4,633	D4
Adícora 707	D2
Aguada Grande 2,901	D2
Agua Frla	E5
Agua Linda	E5
Aguasay 1,752	G3
Altagracia 11,116	C2
Altagracia de Orituco 18,717	E3
Amuay	D2
Anaco 29,487	F3
Aparurén	G5
Apurito 740	D4
Aragua de Barcelona 9,107	F3
Aragua de Maturín 4,051	G3
Araure 22,466	D3
Aricagua 231	C3
Arichuna 1,204	E4
Aripao 296	F3
Arismendi 1,257	D3
Aroa 5,418	D2
Atapirire 337	F3
Bachaquero	C3
Baragua 659	C3
Barbacoas 2,513	E3
Barcelona 78,201	F2
Barinas 56,329	C3
Barinitas 5,849	C3
Barquisimeto 330,815	D2
Barrancas, Barinas 4,489	C3
Barrancas, Monagas 5,738	G3
Betijoque 5,851	C3
Biruaca 2,266	E4

Biscucuy 6,114	D3
Bobare 1,204	D2
Bobures 2,468	C3
Boca de Aroa 2,756	D2
Boca del Mangle	F3
Boca del Pao 403	F3
Bocono 15,915	C3
Borbón	F3
Borojó 423	C2
Bruzual 941	D4
Buena Vista, Anzoátegui	F3
Buena Vista, Apure	D4
Buena Vista, Falcón 944	D2
Cabimas 118,037	C2
Cabruta 1,927	E4
Cabudare 14,593	D2
Cabure 1,673	D2
Cachipo	F5
Cacuri	E5
Cagua 29,601	E2
Caicara 6,092	E3
Caicara de Orinoco 6,867	E3
Calabozo 37,282	E3
Calderas 1,195	C3
Camaguán 4,143	E3
Camatagua 3,335	E3
Campo Claro 1,832	F4
Candelaria	C2
Cantaura 15,839	F3
Capatárida 1,375	C2
Capibara	E6
Carabobo, Bollvar	H4

Carabobo, Carabobo	D3
Caracas (cap.) 1,035,499	E2
Caracas* 2,183,935	E2
Carache 3,966	C3
Carapa 119	G3
Cariaco 6,549	G2
Caribén	E4
Caripe 4,729	G2
Caripito 19,053	G2
Carirubana 15,701	C2
Carmelo 2,556	C2
Carora 36,115	C2
Carrasquero 2,193	B2
Carúpano 50,935	G2
Casanay 4,985	G2
Casigua, Falcón 460	C2
Casigua, Zulia 3,665	B3
Caucagua 6,218	E2
Cazorla 700	E3
Chaguaramas 2,748	E3
Chichiriviche 3,236	D2
Chivacoa 19,210	D2
Choroní 534	E2
Churuguara 6,636	D2
Ciudad Bolívar 103,728	G3
Ciudad Bolivia 4,864	C3
Ciudad Guayana 143,540	G3
Ciudad de Nutrias 769	D3
Ciudad Ojeda 83,083	C2
Ciudad Piar 3,965	G3
Clarines 2,099	F3
Cojoro	C2

Colón	E6
Comunidad	E6
Coporito	H3
Coro 68,701	D2
Corozo Pando	D3
Cúa 9,953	E2
Cubiro 1,988	D2
Cuchivero	E3
Cumaná 119,751	F2
Cumanacoa 9,179	G2
Cunaviche 795	E4
Curiapo	H3
Dabajuro 4,516	C2
Delicias 1,616	B4
Democracia	D3
Dolores 1,454	D3
Duaca 7,519	D2
Ejido 11,170	C3
El Almacén	G4
El Amparo de Apure 2,015	C4
El Baúl 1,715	D3
El Callao 4,270	H4
El Calvario 384	E3
El Chaparro 3,768	F3
El Cristo	G4
El Dorado 1,888	H4
El Empedrado 1,788	C3
El Guapo 1,231	F2
El Manteco 1,962	H4
El Miamo 335	H4
Elorza 3,184	D4
El Oso	H5

El Palmar 2,758	G4
El Pao, Anzoátegui 761	F3
El Pao, Bollvar 1,259	G3
El Pao, Cojedes 1,715	D3
El Perú	H4
El Pilar 3,278	G2
El Rastro 903	E3
El Roque	G4
El Samán de Apure 1,399	C4
El Socorro	E3
El Sombrero 8,373	F3
El Tigre 49,801	F3
El Tocuyo 19,351	C3
El Toro	H3
El Vigia 20,970	C3
El Vínculo	D1
El Yagual 699	D4
Encontrados 5,607	B3
Espino 559	F3
Garcitas	D3
Guacara 35,111	D2
Guachara 577	D4
Guadarrama 334	D3
Guana	G5
Guanare 34,148	D3
Guanarito 3,150	D3
Guanoco	G2
Guanta 9,017	F2
Guardatinajas 1,206	E3
Guarero	B2

Guárico 3,259	D3
Guariquén 619	G2
Guasdualito 7,793	C4
Guasimal 582	D4
Guasipati 4,807	H4
Guayabal, Amazonas	E6
Guayabal, Anzoátegui	E3
Guayabal, Guárico 1,403	E3
Guayabo 13,905	C3
Guiria 8,134	G2
Guri	G4
Guzmán Blanco	D3
Higuerote 5,008	E2
Icabarú	H5
Independencia 4,897	B4
Irapa 4,470	G2
Juangriego 6,062	G2
Judibana	C2
Jusepln	G3
Kavanayen	H5
La Aduana	D3
La Asunción 6,381	G2
La Canoa	G3
La Ceiba, Apure	C4
La Ceiba, Trujillo 212	C3
La Concepción	B2
La Concepción 13,885	F6
La Esmeralda	E6
La Esperanza	H3
La Frla 8,134	B3
La Grita 9,954	C3
Laguna 20,344	E2
Lagunetas	C3
Lagunillas	C2

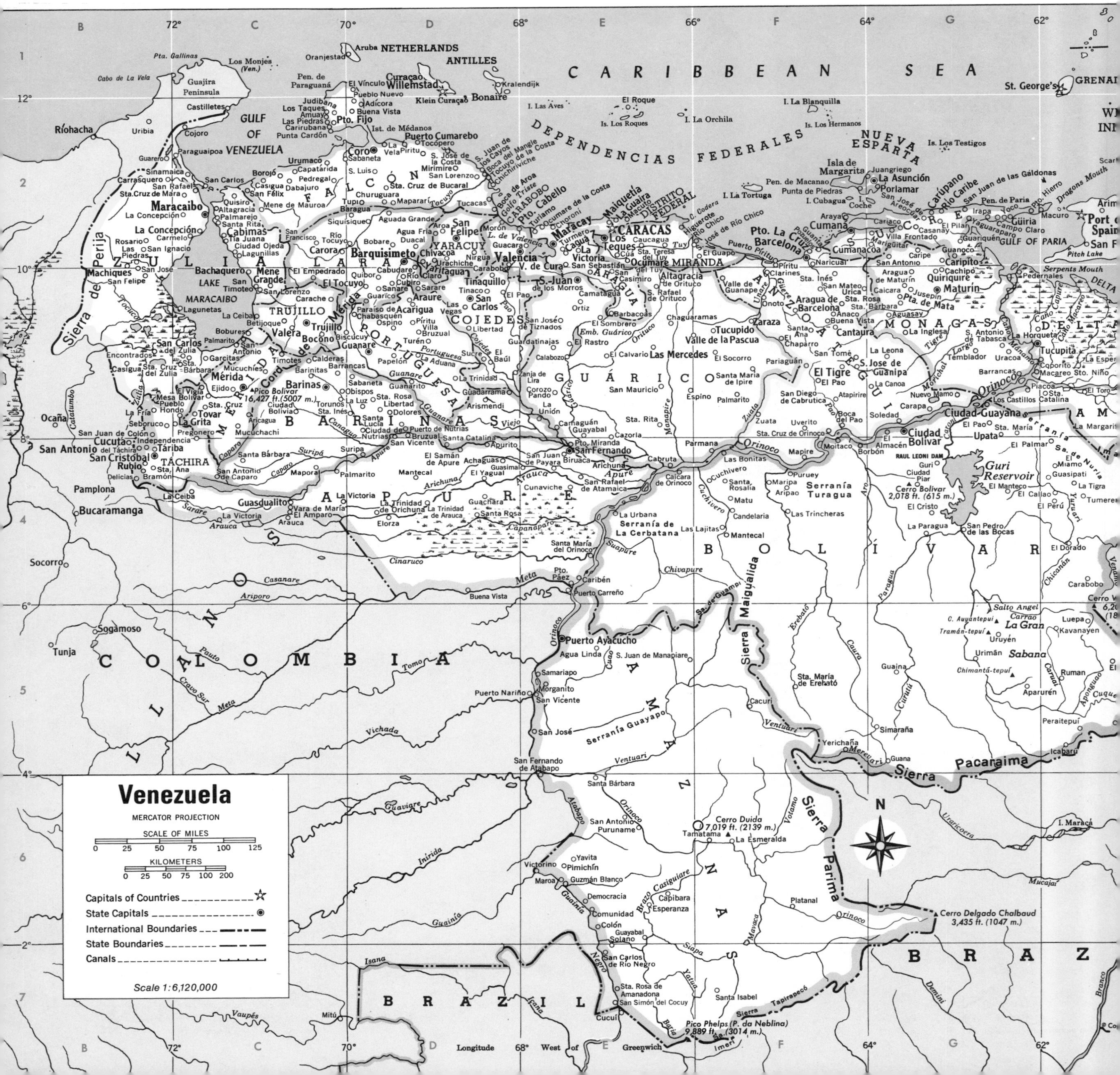

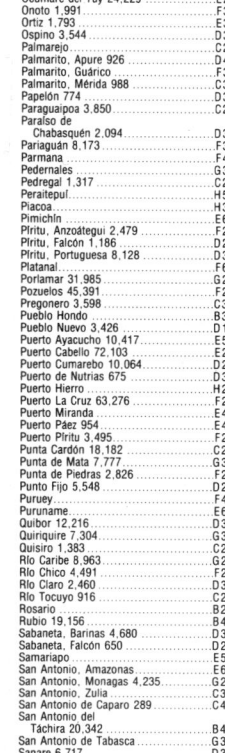

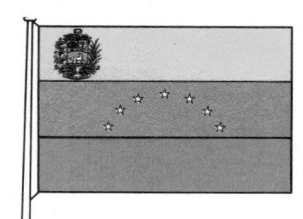

AREA 352,143 sq. mi. (912,050 sq. km.)
POPULATION 14,313,000
CAPITAL Caracas
LARGEST CITY Caracas
HIGHEST POINT Pico Bolívar 16,427 ft.
   (5,007 m.)
MONETARY UNIT Bolívar
MAJOR LANGUAGE Spanish
MAJOR RELIGION Roman Catholicism

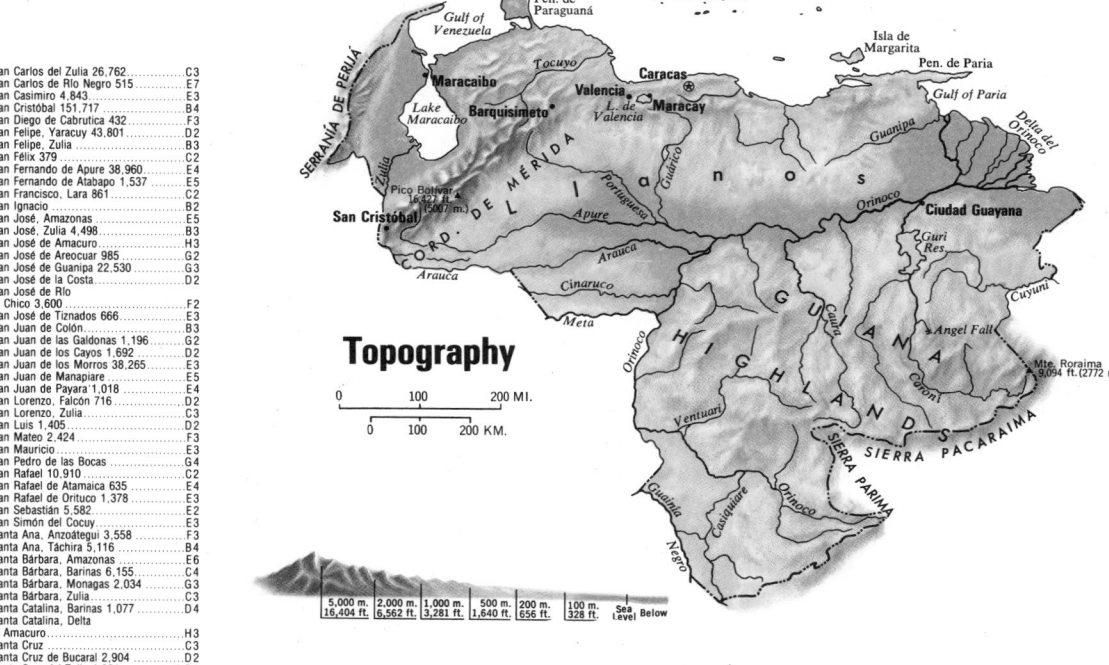

Topography

0   100   200 MI.
0   100   200 KM.

5,000 m. | 2,000 m. | 1,000 m. | 500 m. | 200 m. | 100 m. | Sea | Below
16,404 ft. | 6,562 ft. | 3,281 ft. | 1,640 ft. | 656 ft. | 328 ft. | Level

Agriculture, Industry and Resources

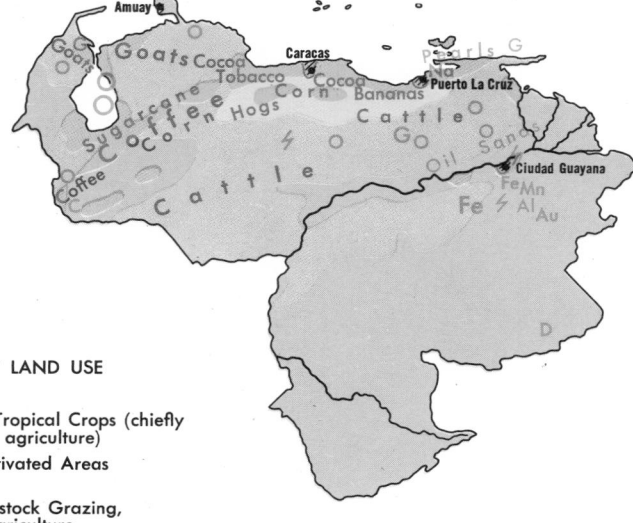

MAJOR MINERAL
OCCURRENCES

Al   Bauxite
Au   Gold
C   Coal
D   Diamonds
Fe   Iron Ore
G   Natural Gas
Mn   Manganese
Na   Salt
O   Petroleum

⚡   Water Power
▨   Major Industrial
     Areas

DOMINANT LAND USE

Diversified Tropical Crops (chiefly
   plantation agriculture)

Upland Cultivated Areas

Upland Livestock Grazing,
   Limited Agriculture

Extensive Livestock Ranching

Forests

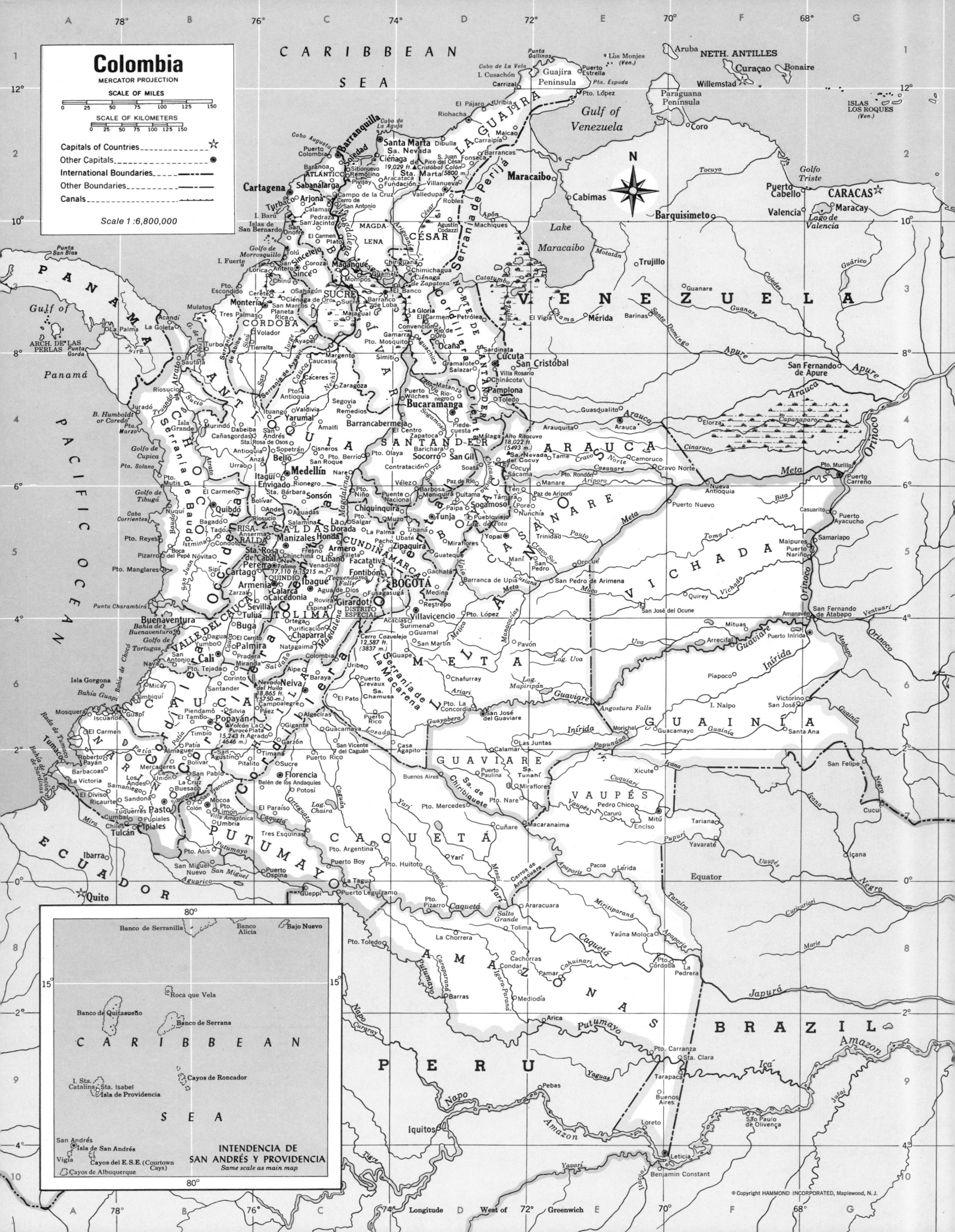

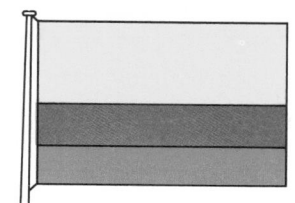

AREA 439,513 sq. mi. (1,138,339 sq. km.)
POPULATION 27,520,000
CAPITAL Bogotá
LARGEST CITY Bogotá
HIGHEST POINT Pico Cristóbal Colón
19,029 ft. (5,800 m.)
MONETARY UNIT Colombian peso
MAJOR LANGUAGE Spanish
MAJOR RELIGION Roman Catholicism

INTERNAL DIVISIONS

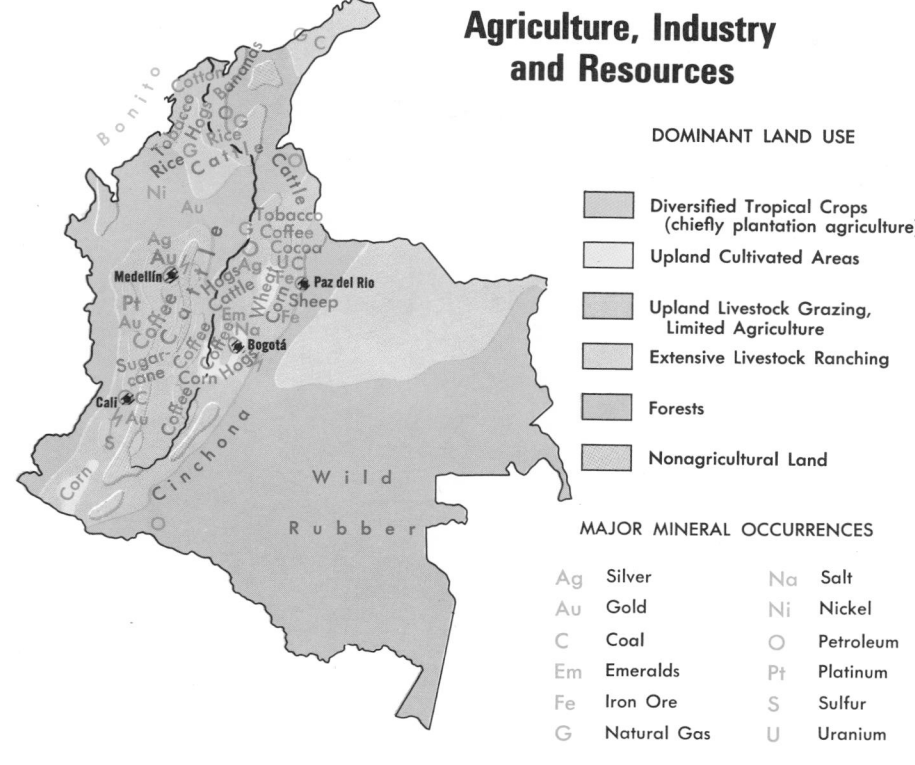

Agriculture, Industry and Resources

DOMINANT LAND USE

Diversified Tropical Crops (chiefly plantation agriculture)

Upland Cultivated Areas

Upland Livestock Grazing, Limited Agriculture

Extensive Livestock Ranching

Forests

Nonagricultural Land

MAJOR MINERAL OCCURRENCES

Ag	Silver	Na	Salt
Au	Gold	Ni	Nickel
C	Coal	O	Petroleum
Em	Emeralds	Pt	Platinum
Fe	Iron Ore	S	Sulfur
G	Natural Gas	U	Uranium

⚡ Water Power

▨ Major Industrial Areas

Topography

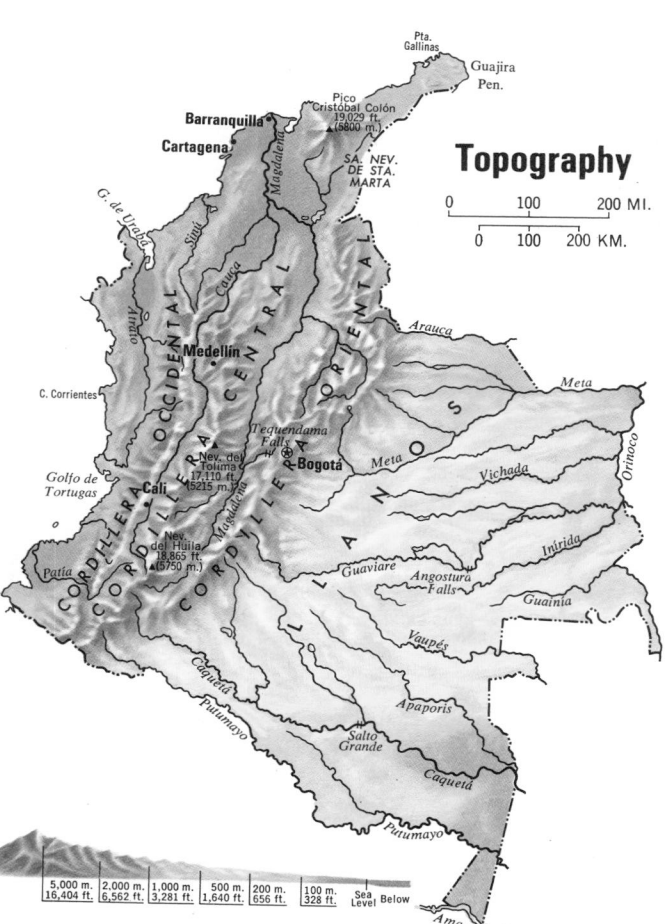

0   100   200 MI.
0   100   200 KM.

5,000 m. / 2,000 m. / 1,000 m. / 500 m. / 200 m. / 100 m. / Sea Level / Below
16,404 ft. / 6,562 ft. / 3,281 ft. / 1,640 ft. / 656 ft. / 328 ft.

Peru and Ecuador

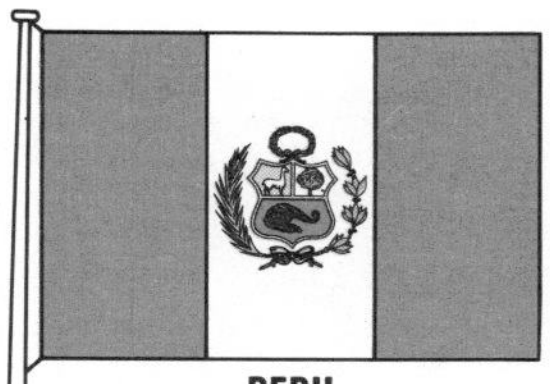

PERU

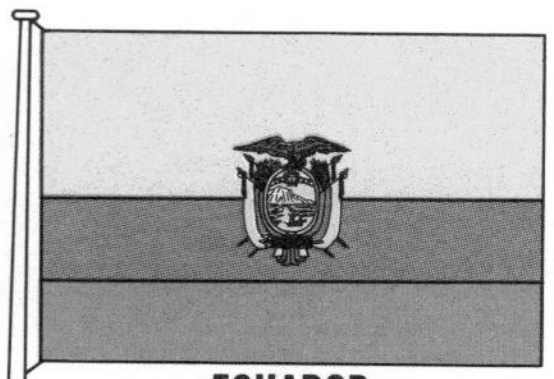

ECUADOR

PERU

AREA 496,222 sq. mi. (1,285,215 sq. km.)
POPULATION 17,031,221
CAPITAL Lima
LARGEST CITY Lima
HIGHEST POINT Huascarán 22,205 ft. (6,768 m.)
MONETARY UNIT sol
MAJOR LANGUAGES Spanish, Quechua, Aymara
MAJOR RELIGION Roman Catholicism

ECUADOR

AREA 109,483 sq. mi. (283,561 sq. km.)
POPULATION 8,644,000
CAPITAL Quito
LARGEST CITY Guayaquil
HIGHEST POINT Chimborazo 20,561 ft. (6,267 m.)
MONETARY UNIT sucre
MAJOR LANGUAGES Spanish, Quechua
MAJOR RELIGION Roman Catholicism

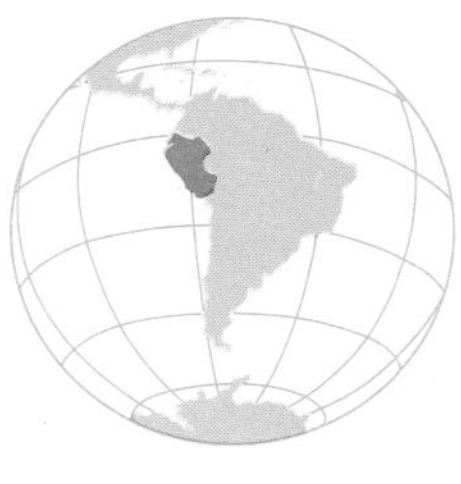

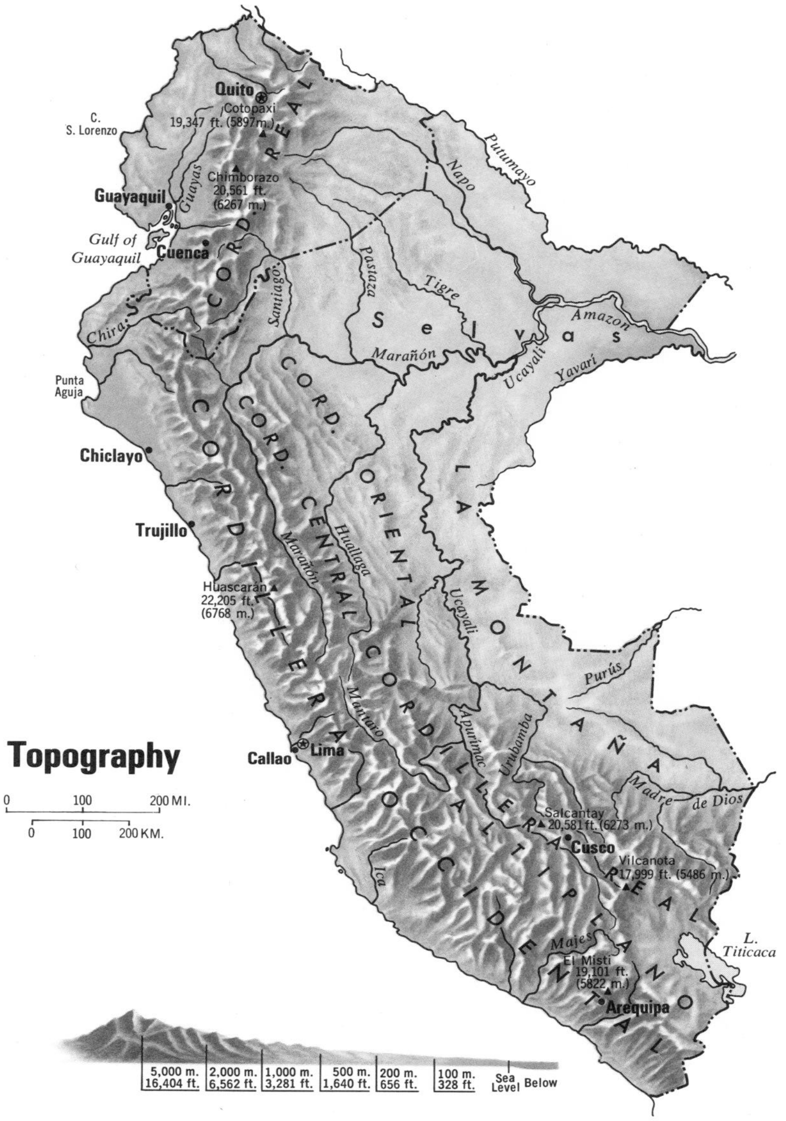

PERU

DEPARTMENTS

Amazonas 256,460 ..... C5
Ancash 815,646 ..... D7
Apurímac 321,936 ..... F10
Arequipa 702,308 ..... F10
Ayacucho 500,732 ..... E9
Cajamarca 1,044,689 ..... C6
Callao (prov.) 446,730 ..... D9
Cusco 829,294 ..... F9
Huancavelica 346,460 ..... E9
Huánuco 481,924 ..... D7
Ica 431,442 ..... E10
Junín 848,993 ..... E8
La Libertad 960,537 ..... C6
Lambayeque 683,425 ..... B6
Lima 4,738,266 ..... D8
Loreto 446,316 ..... E5
Madre de Dios 36,555 ..... G8
Moquegua 99,287 ..... G11
Pasco 221,219 ..... E8
Piura 1,168,442 ..... B5
Puno 893,586 ..... G10
San Martín 319,670 ..... D6
Tacna 133,240 ..... G11
Tumbes 103,979 ..... B4
Ucayali 200,085 ..... E6

CITIES and TOWNS

Abancay 19,807 ..... F9
Acarí 4,907 ..... E10
Acobamba 2,156 ..... E9
Acolla 5,717 ..... E8
Acomayo, Cusco 1,419 ..... G9
Acomayo, Huánuco 2,883 ..... E7
Acora 1,910 ..... H11
Acuracay 1,282 ..... F5
Aija 1,843 ..... D7
Alca 755 ..... F10
Ambo 3,060 ..... D8
Ananea 668 ..... H10
Ancón 8,610 ..... D8
Andahuaylas 7,654 ..... F9
Andamarca 470 ..... E8
Anta 3,703 ..... F9
Antabamba 2,223 ..... F10
Aplao 1,941 ..... F11
Aquia 970 ..... D8
Arequipa 107,858 ..... G11
Arequipa* 447,431 ..... G11
Ascope 12,070 ..... C6
Astillero H9
Atalaya 2,229 ..... E8
Atico 2,316 ..... F11
Ayabaca 4,543 ..... C5
Ayacucho 68,535 ..... F9
Ayaviri 11,067 ..... G10
Azángaro 7,658 ..... H10
Bagua 9,735 ..... C5
Balsapuerto 164 ..... D5
Bambamarca 6,867 ..... C6
Barranca, Lima 31,312 ..... C8
Barranca, Loreto 1,351 ..... D5
Bartra Antiguo E4
Bartra Nuevo E4
Bayóvar B5
Bellavista 4,906 ..... C5
Bolívar 1,106 ..... D6
Bolognesi F6
Bolognesi 661 ..... F8
Borja 215 ..... D5
Bretaña 1,035 ..... E5
Buldibuyo 582 ..... D7
Cabana 1,804 ..... C7
Cabo Blanco B5
Cahuapanas 304 ..... D5
Cailloma 1,187 ..... G10
Cajabamba 7,282 ..... C6
Cajacay 668 ..... D8
Cajamarca 60,280 ..... C6
Cajatambo 1,721 ..... D8
Calca 6,112 ..... G9
Callalli 819 ..... G10
Callao 260,581 ..... D9
Callao* 441,374 ..... D9
Camaná 11,386 ..... F11
Candarave 1,207 ..... G11
Cangallo 1,584 ..... E9
Canta 3,431 ..... D8
Capachica 307 ..... H10
Caraz 6,376 ..... D7
Caravelí 1,827 ..... F10
Carhuás 3,147 ..... D7
Carumás 1,031 ..... G11
Cascas 2,638 ..... C6
Casma 12,725 ..... C7
Castrovirreyna 1,749 ..... E9
Catacaos 30,927 ..... B5
Celendín 8,538 ..... D6
Cerro Azul 2,314 ..... D9
Cerro de Pasco 71,558 ..... D8
Chachapoyas 11,919 ..... D6
Chala 1,646 ..... E10
Chalhuanca 3,071 ..... F10
Chancay 18,993 ..... D8
Chao C7
Chepén 29,919 ..... C6
Chicama 11,160 ..... C6
Chiclayo 280,244 ..... C6
Chilca (Pucusana) 3,329 ..... D9
Chilete 2,537 ..... C6
Chimbote 216,406 ..... C7
Chincha Alta 237,475 ..... D9
Chiquián 3,521 ..... D8
Chirinos 1,061 ..... C5
Chivay 3,296 ..... G10
Chosica D8
Chota 8,299 ..... C6
Chulucanas 34,977 ..... B5
Chupaca 5,422 ..... E9
Chuquibamba 2,630 ..... F10
Chuquibambilla 2,147 ..... F9
Churín 1,801 ..... D8
Cocachacra 5,985 ..... G11
Cocama G8
Cojata 888 ..... H10
Colasay 721 ..... C5
Colcamar 1,216 ..... D6
Conaica 1,154 ..... E9
Concepción 7,129 ..... E8
Concordia 1,372 ..... E5
Contamana 5,718 ..... E6
Contumazá 2,491 ..... C6
Coracora 4,598 ..... F10
Córdova 453 ..... E10
Corongo 1,762 ..... D7
Cotahuasi 1,301 ..... F10
Culebras C7
Cumaría F7
Cusco (Cuzco) 85,044 ..... F9
Cusco* 181,604 ..... F9
Cutervo 6,890 ..... C6
Cuyocuyo 1,101 ..... H10
Desaguadero 2,682 ..... H11
Deustua 544 ..... G10
Dos de Mayo 574 ..... E6
Echarate 1,071 ..... F9
El Portugués C7
Esperanza 375 ..... G7
Espinar 6,381 ..... G10
Ferreñafe 22,200 ..... C6
Francisco de Orellana 445 ..... F4
Guadalupe 7,613 ..... E9
Güeppi E3
Huacho 43,402 ..... D8
Huacrachuco 1,210 ..... D7
Hualgayoc 1,691 ..... C6
Hualla 4,042 ..... F9
Huallanca, Ancash 930 ..... D7
Huallanca, Huánuco 4,806 ..... D7
Huamachuco 8,273 ..... D6
Huancabamba 4,393 ..... C5
Huancané 5,227 ..... H10
Huancapi 2,539 ..... E9
Huancavelica 20,889 ..... E9
Huancayo 165,132 ..... E9
Huanchaco 6,005 ..... C7
Huanta 11,213 ..... E9
Huánuco 52,628 ..... E7
Huaral 34,235 ..... D8
Huaráz 45,116 ..... D7
Huari 2,344 ..... D7
Huariaca 2,671 ..... E8
Huarmey 11,094 ..... C8
Huarochirí 1,828 ..... D9
Huarocondo 2,498 ..... F9
Huaura 9,338 ..... D8
Huaylas 1,344 ..... C7
Iberia 2,307 ..... F5
Ica 111,087 ..... E10
Ichuña 277 ..... G11
Ilave 9,891 ..... H11
Ilo 31,549 ..... G11
Imperial 20,894 ..... D9
Iñapari 188 ..... H8
Intutu 746 ..... E4
Iparia 278 ..... E7
Iquitos 173,629 ..... F4
Jaén 24,356 ..... C5
Jauja 14,630 ..... E8
Jayanca 6,401 ..... B6
Jeberos 1,493 ..... D5
Juanjuí 9,324 ..... D6
Juli 5,575 ..... H11
Juliaca 77,976 ..... G10
Jumbilla 1,035 ..... C5
Junín 8,988 ..... E8
Lagunas 4,601 ..... E5
La Huaca 5,161 ..... B5
La Jalca 1,769 ..... D6
La Joya 5,000 ..... G11
Lamas 8,937 ..... D6
Lambayeque 23,746 ..... B6
Lampa 4,319 ..... G10
Lamud 2,405 ..... C6
Lanlacuni Bajo 405 ..... G9
La Oroya 33,305 ..... D8
Las Piedras H9
Las Yaras 759 ..... G11
La Unión 2,828 ..... D7
Leimebamba 1,957 ..... D6
Lima (cap.) 375,957 ..... D8
Lima* 3,968,972 ..... D8
Limbani 728 ..... H10
Lircay 5,213 ..... E9
Llata 2,922 ..... D7
Lobitos 2,975 ..... B5
Locumba 369 ..... G11
Lomas 287 ..... E10
Lucerna H9
Lurín 14,405 ..... D9
Machupicchu 544 ..... F9
Macusani 3,389 ..... G10
Madre de Dios 660 ..... G9
Máncora 5,358 ..... B5
Manú 234 ..... G9
Marcapata 369 ..... G9
Marcona 25,962 ..... E10
Margos 1,622 ..... D8
Masisea 1,586 ..... E7
Matarani F11
Matucana 4,196 ..... D8
Mavila H8
Mazán 281 ..... F4
Mazocruz 1,580 ..... H11
Mendoza 1,902 ..... D6
Mishagua F8
Moho 2,560 ..... H10
Mollendo 21,206 ..... F11
Monsefú 17,186 ..... C6
Moquegua 21,488 ..... G11
Morales 4,370 ..... D6
Morococha 11,234 ..... D8
Morropón 7,611 ..... C5
Motupe 3,411 ..... C6
Moyobamba 14,319 ..... D6
Nauta 4,083 ..... F5
Nazca 22,756 ..... E10
Negritos 12,476 ..... B5
Nuñoa 3,613 ..... G10
Ocoña 1,062 ..... F11
Ocros 1,037 ..... D8
Ollachea 1,308 ..... G9
Ollantaytambo 1,500 ..... F9
Olmos 7,946 ..... C5
Omaguas F5
Omas 249 ..... D9
Omate 1,131 ..... G11
Orcotuna 3,359 ..... E8
Orellana 2,886 ..... E6
Otuzco 5,765 ..... C6
Oxapampa 5,233 ..... E8
Oyón 6,279 ..... D8
Pacasmayo 17,588 ..... C6
Pachiza 889 ..... D6
Paiján 12,699 ..... C6
Paita 18,749 ..... B5
Palpa 3,393 ..... E10
Pampachiri 428 ..... F10
Pampacolca 2,010 ..... F10
Pampas 3,850 ..... E9
Panao 1,363 ..... E7
Pantoja 457 ..... E3
Parinari 375 ..... E5
Paruro 1,727 ..... F9
Pataz 759 ..... D6
Paucarbamba 534 ..... E9
Paucartambo, Cusco 1,620 ..... G9
Paucartambo, Pasco 3,497 ..... E8
Pevas 1,325 ..... G4
Picota 2,288 ..... D6
Pimentel 9,129 ..... B6
Pinquén G9
Pisac 1,566 ..... G9
Pisco 53,414 ..... D9
Piura 186,354 ..... B5
Pizacoma 400 ..... H11
Pomabamba 2,489 ..... D7
Porvenir E5
Pozuzo 326 ..... E8
Puca Barranca E4
Pucallpa 91,953 ..... E7
Pucará 2,268 ..... G10
Pucaurco 628 ..... G4
Pucusana 3,329 ..... D9
Puerto Alianza D5
Puerto América 240 ..... D5
Puerto Arturo F3
Puerto Bermúdez 1,133 ..... E8
Puerto Caballas E10
Puerto Chicama 3,136 ..... C6
Puerto Eten 2,575 ..... B6
Puerto Inca 1,286 ..... E7
Puerto José Pardo D4
Puerto Leguía, Loreto D4
Puerto Leguía, Puno G9
Puerto Maldonado 12,609 ..... H9
Puerto Morín C7
Puerto Ocopa 1,088 ..... E8
Puerto Pardo F7
Puerto Pizarro B4
Puerto Portillo 86 ..... F7
Puerto Prado 328 ..... E8
Puerto Samanco 1,435 ..... C7
Puerto Tahuantinsuyo G9
Puerto Victoria E7
Puno 66,477 ..... G10
Punta de Bombón 4,647 ..... F11
Punta Moreno C6
Puquina 1,026 ..... G11
Puquio 8,099 ..... F10
Putina 5,414 ..... H10
Querecotillo 10,637 ..... B5
Quicacha 255 ..... F10
Quilca 235 ..... F11
Quillabamba 16,837 ..... F9
Quince Mil G9
Ramón Castilla 1,811 ..... G5
Recuay 2,764 ..... D7
Requena 8,270 ..... F5
Reventazón B6
Rioja 9,876 ..... D6
Salaverry 5,539 ..... C7
Saña 40,144 ..... C6
Sandia 1,682 ..... H10
San José 4,070 ..... B6
San José de Sisa 3,782 ..... D6
San Juan E10
San Lorenzo 124 ..... H8
San Martín E3
San Miguel, Ayacucho 1,440 ..... F9
San Miguel, Cajamarca 1,798 ..... C6
San Pedro de Lloc 11,463 ..... C6
San Ramón 7,145 ..... E8
Santa 20,490 ..... C7
Santa Clotilde 1,068 ..... E4
Santa Cruz, Cajamarca 2,739 ..... C6
Santa Cruz, Loreto 449 ..... E5
Santa Elena 368 ..... F5
Santa María de Nanay 294 ..... F4
Santiago 5,092 ..... E10
Santiago de Cao 22,119 ..... C6
Santiago de Chocorvos 525 ..... E9
Santiago de Chuco 5,189 ..... C7
Santo Tomás, Amazonas 1,093 ..... C6
Santo Tomás, Cusco 2,755 ..... G10
Santo Tomás de Andoas 272 ..... D4
San Vicente de Cañete 15,277 ..... D9
Saposoa 4,541 ..... D6
Saquena 2,755 ..... F5
Satipo 9,208 ..... E8
Sauce 2,263 ..... D6
Sayán 5,129 ..... D8
Sechura 11,724 ..... B5
Sicuani 21,176 ..... G10
Sihuas 2,178 ..... D7
Sullana 80,947 ..... B5
Sumbay G10
Sumbilca 1,155 ..... D8
Supe 10,061 ..... D8
Tacna 92,640 ..... G11
Tahuamanu 2,619 ..... H8
Talara 55,122 ..... B5
Tambo de Mora 2,790 ..... D9
Tambo Grande 10,087 ..... B5
Tamshiyacu 2,040 ..... F5
Tarapoto 33,429 ..... D6
Tarata 2,624 ..... H11
Tarma 34,369 ..... E8
Tarqui E3
Tayabamba 1,649 ..... D7
Ticaco 781 ..... H11
Tingo María 25,030 ..... D7
Tiruntán 723 ..... E6
Tocache 5,940 ..... D7
Tonegrama D4
Topará D9
Toquepala G11
Torata 6,320 ..... G11
Tournavista E7
Trujillo 354,557 ..... C7
Tumbes 48,187 ..... B4
Ubinas 422 ..... G11
Uchiza 2,471 ..... D7
Unini F8
Urcos 4,155 ..... G9
Urubamba 4,686 ..... F9
Vinchos 735 ..... E9
Virú 6,587 ..... C7
Vitor 416 ..... G11
Yambrasbamba 277 ..... D5
Yanahuanca 5,109 ..... D8
Yanaoca 1,152 ..... G10
Yauca 1,805 ..... E10
Yauli 1,020 ..... D8
Yauyos 1,296 ..... E9
Yunguyo 7,253 ..... H11
Yurimaguas 22,858 ..... E5
Zarumilla 9,713 ..... B4
Zorritos 4,497 ..... B4

OTHER FEATURES

Acarí (riv.) E10
Aguaytía (riv.) E7
Aguja (pt.) B5
Amazon (riv.) F4
Andes, Cordillera de los (mts.) F10
Apurímac (riv.) F9
Azángaro (riv.) G10
Azul, Cordillera (mts.) E7
Blanca, Cordillera (mts.) D7
Blanco (cape) B5
Blanco (riv.) F6
Boquerón, El (pass) E7
Cañete (riv.) D9
Casma (riv.) C7
Chimbote (bay) C7
Chincha (isls.) D9
Coles (pt.) G11
Cóndor, Cordillera del (range) C5
Coropuna, Nudo (mt.) F10
Corrientes (riv.) E4
El Boquerón (pass) E7
El Misti (mt.) G11
Ene (riv.) E8
Ferrol (pen.) C7
Grande (riv.) E10
Guañape (isls.) C7
Heath (riv.) H9
Huallaga (riv.) D5
Huasaga (riv.) D4
Huascarán (mt.) D7
Huayabamba (riv.) D6
Ica (riv.) E10
Inambari (riv.) H9
Independencia (bay) D10
Independencia (isl.) D10
Junín (lake) E8
Juruá (riv.) F7
Lachay (pt.) D8
Lobos de Afuera (isls.) B6
Lobos de Tierra (isl.) B6
Locumba (riv.) G11
Madre de Dios (riv.) G9
Majes (riv.) F11
Mantaro (riv.) E8
Manú (riv.) G8
Marañón (riv.) E5
Mayo (riv.) D6
Misti, El (mt.) G11
Montaña, La (reg.) F8
Morona (riv.) D5
Nanay (riv.) E4
Napo (riv.) F4
Negra, Cordillera (mts.) D7
Negra (pt.) B6
Ñermete (pt.) B5
Occidental, Cordillera (range) F10
Ocoña (riv.) F11
Oriental, Cordillera (range) H10
Pachitea (riv.) E7
Paita (bay) B5
Pampas (riv.) E9
Paracas (pen.) D9
Parinacochas (lake) F10
Pariñas (pt.) B5
Pastaza (riv.) D5
Pativilca (riv.) D8
Perené (riv.) E8
Pichis (riv.) E8
Piedras, Las (riv.) G8
Pisco (bay) D9
Pisco (riv.) D9
Piura (riv.) B5
Puinagua, Canal de (riv.) E5
Purús (riv.) G8
Putumayo (riv.) G4
Rímac (riv.) D9
Salcantay (mt.) F9
Sama (riv.) G11
San Gallán (isl.) D9
San Lorenzo (isl.) D9
San Nicolás (bay) E10
Santa (riv.) C7
Santiago (riv.) D4
Sechura (bay) B5
Tahuamanu (riv.) H8
Tambo (riv.) G11
Tambopata (riv.) H9
Tapiche (riv.) E6
Tigre (riv.) E4
Titicaca (lake) H10
Tumbes (riv.) B4
Ucayali (riv.) F5

(continued on following page)

Agriculture, Industry and Resources

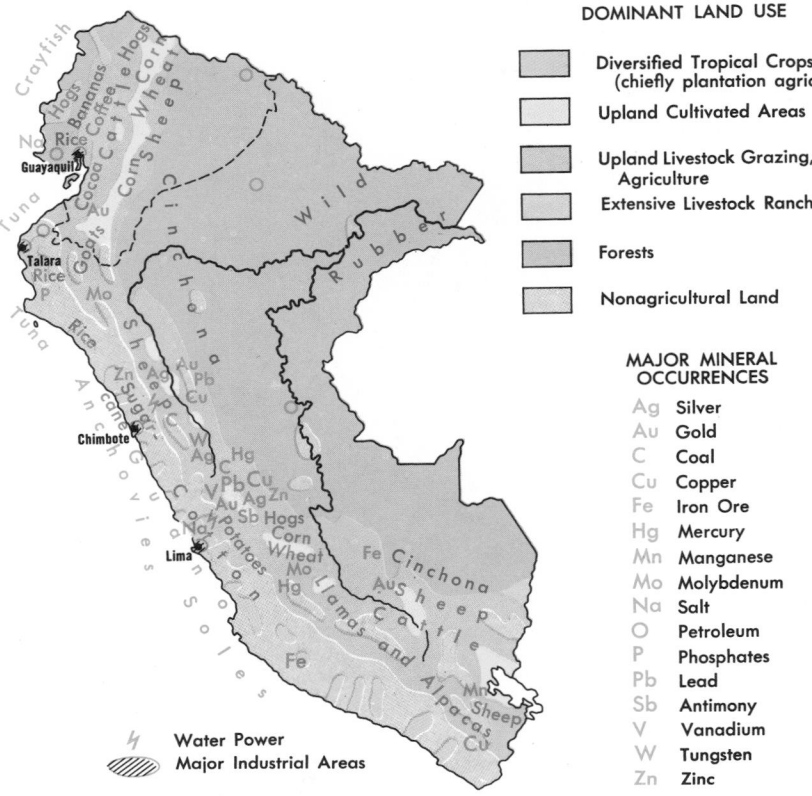

DOMINANT LAND USE

- Diversified Tropical Crops (chiefly plantation agriculture)
- Upland Cultivated Areas
- Upland Livestock Grazing, Limited Agriculture
- Extensive Livestock Ranching
- Forests
- Nonagricultural Land

MAJOR MINERAL OCCURRENCES

Ag	Silver
Au	Gold
C	Coal
Cu	Copper
Fe	Iron Ore
Hg	Mercury
Mn	Manganese
Mo	Molybdenum
Na	Salt
O	Petroleum
P	Phosphates
Pb	Lead
Sb	Antimony
V	Vanadium
W	Tungsten
Zn	Zinc

⚡ Water Power
▨ Major Industrial Areas

Agriculture, Industry and Resources

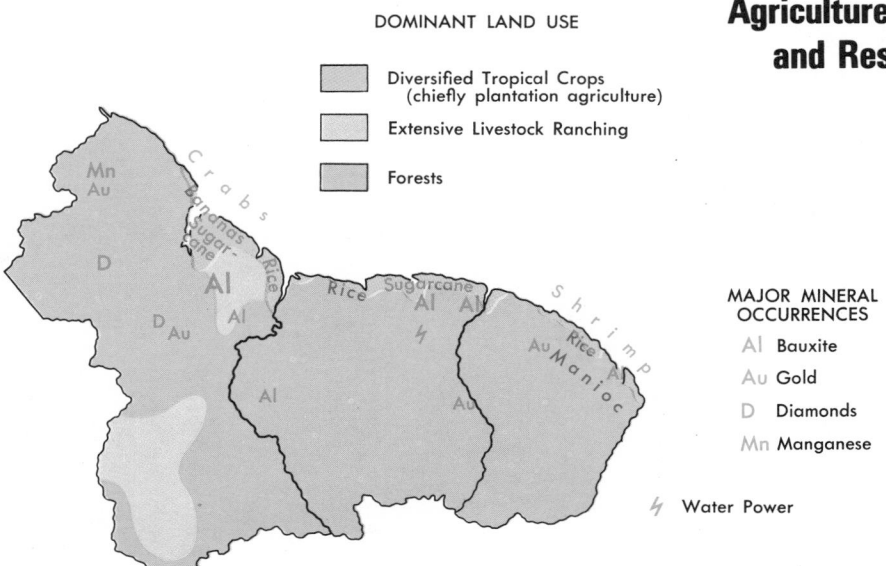

DOMINANT LAND USE

- Diversified Tropical Crops (chiefly plantation agriculture)
- Extensive Livestock Ranching
- Forests

MAJOR MINERAL OCCURRENCES

Al	Bauxite
Au	Gold
D	Diamonds
Mn	Manganese

⚡ Water Power

GUYANA

AREA 83,000 sq. mi. (214,970 sq. km.)
POPULATION 793,000
CAPITAL Georgetown
LARGEST CITY Georgetown
HIGHEST POINT Mt. Roraima 9,094 ft. (2,772 m.)
MONETARY UNIT Guyana dollar
MAJOR LANGUAGES English, Hindi
MAJOR RELIGIONS Christianity, Hinduism, Islam

SURINAME

AREA 55,144 sq. mi. (142,823 sq. km.)
POPULATION 354,860
CAPITAL Paramaribo
LARGEST CITY Paramaribo
HIGHEST POINT Julianatop 4,200 ft. (1,280 m.)
MONETARY UNIT Suriname guilder
MAJOR LANGUAGES Dutch, Hindi, Indonesian
MAJOR RELIGIONS Christianity, Islam, Hinduism

FRENCH GUIANA

AREA 35,135 sq. mi. (91,000 sq. km.)
POPULATION 73,022
CAPITAL Cayenne
LARGEST CITY Cayenne
HIGHEST POINT 2,723 ft. (830 m.)
MONETARY UNIT French franc
MAJOR LANGUAGE French
MAJOR RELIGIONS Roman Catholicism, Protestantism

Courantyne (riv.)	C3
Cuyuni (riv.)	B2
Demerara (riv.)	B3
Enwarak (mt.)	B3
Essequibo (riv.)	B3
Great (fall)	B3
Ireng (riv.)	B3
Kaieteur (fall)	B3
Kamaria (falls)	B2
Kuyuwini (riv.)	B4
Kwitaro (riv.)	B4
Leguan (isl.)	B2
Marudi (mts.)	B5
Mazaruni (riv.)	A2
Moruka (riv.)	B2
New (riv.)	C4
Pakaraima (mts.)	A3
Playa (pt.)	B1
Pomeroon (riv.)	B2
Potaro (riv.)	B2
Puruni (riv.)	B2
Roraima (mt.)	A3
Rupununi (riv.)	B4
Sororieng (mt.)	B2
Surwakwima (fall)	A2
Takutu (riv.)	B4
Venamo (mt.)	A3
Waini (riv.)	B2
Wenamu (riv.)	A2

Albina 1,000	D3
Asidonhoppo	D4
Berg en Dal	D3
Bitagron	C3
Brokopondo	D3
Burnside	C2
Calcutta 1,100	C3
Cottica	D4
Domburg 1,200	D3
Groningen 600	D2
Huwelijkszorg	C2
Kwakoegron	D3
Lelydorp 300	D3
Majoli	D4
Mariënburg 3,500	D3
Moengo 2,100	D3
Nieuw-Amsterdam 1,400	D2
Nieuw-Nickerie 7,400	C2
Paramaribo (cap.) ⊙ 167,905	D2
Paranam	D3
Totness 1,300	C3
Uitkijk	D3
Wageningen 800	C3
Zanderij	D3

OTHER FEATURES

Bakhuys (mts.)	C3
Coeroeni (riv.)	C4
Commewijne (riv.)	D3
Coppename (riv.)	C3
Corantijn (riv.)	C3
Cottica (riv.)	D3
Eilerts de Haan (mts.)	C4
Frederik Willem IV (falls)	C4
Julianatop (mt.)	C4
Kayser (mts.)	C4
Lely (mts.)	D3
Litani (riv.)	D4
Marowijne (riv.)	D3
Nickerie (riv.)	C3
Orange (mts.) . j.	D4
Saramacca (riv.)	D3
Sipwliwini (riv.)	C3
Suriname (riv.)	D3
Tapanahoni (riv.)	D4
Toekomstig (res.)	C3
Van Blommestein (lake)	D3
Wilhelmina (mts.)	C4

SURINAME

DISTRICTS

Brokopondo 17,763	D4
Commewijne 18,740	D3
Coronie 3,251	C3
Marowijne 25,911	D4
Nickerie 35,178	C3
Para 16,635	D3
Paramaribo 102,297	D2
Saramacca 13,554	C3
Suriname 151,585	D3

CITIES and TOWNS

Ajoewa	C4
Alalapadu	C4

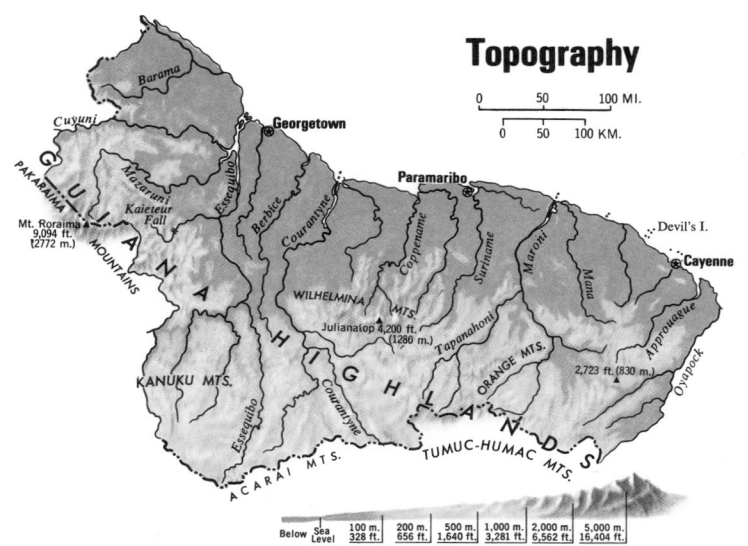

Topography

Topography scale: 0 50 100 MI. / 0 50 100 KM.

Georgetown, Paramaribo, Cayenne, Devil's I.

Mt. Roraima 9,094 ft. (2772 m.)

GUIANA HIGHLANDS

PAKARAIMA MOUNTAINS, Kaieteur Fall

WILHELMINA MTS., Julianatop 4,200 ft. (1280 m.)

ORANGE MTS. 2,723 ft. (830 m.)

KANUKU MTS., ACARAI MTS., TUMUC-HUMAC MTS.

Below Sea Level	100 m. 328 ft.	200 m. 656 ft.	500 m. 1,640 ft.	1,000 m. 3,281 ft.	2,000 m. 6,562 ft.	5,000 m. 16,404 ft.

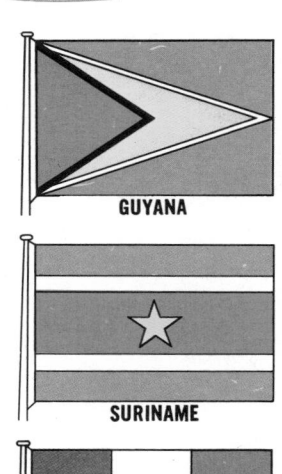

GUYANA

SURINAME

FRENCH GUIANA

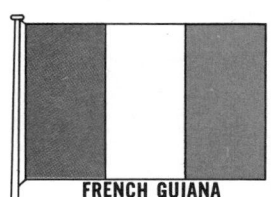

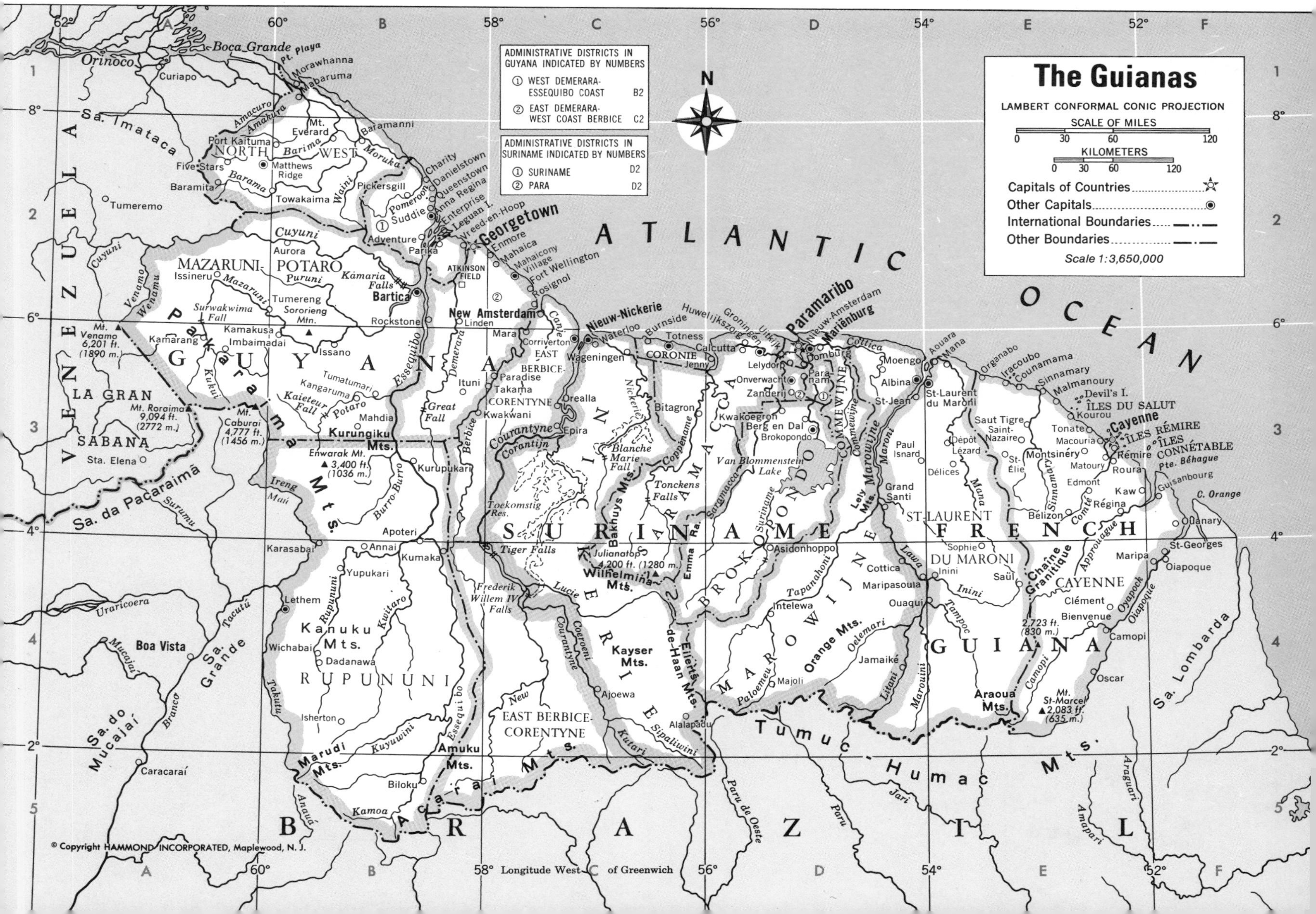

The Guianas

LAMBERT CONFORMAL CONIC PROJECTION

SCALE OF MILES
0 30 60 120
KILOMETERS
0 30 60 120

Capitals of Countries .... ☆
Other Capitals .... ⊙
International Boundaries ......
Other Boundaries ......

Scale 1:3,650,000

ADMINISTRATIVE DISTRICTS IN GUYANA INDICATED BY NUMBERS
① WEST DEMERARA-ESSEQUIBO COAST B2
② EAST DEMERARA-WEST COAST BERBICE C2

ADMINISTRATIVE DISTRICTS IN SURINAME INDICATED BY NUMBERS
① SURINAME D2
② PARA D2

© Copyright HAMMOND INCORPORATED, Maplewood, N.J.

58° Longitude West of Greenwich

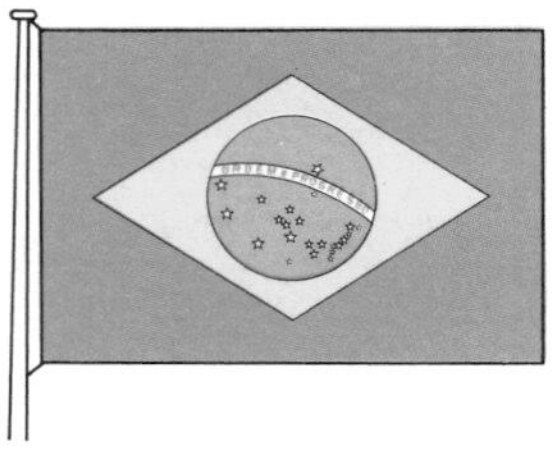

AREA 3,284,426 sq. mi. (8,506,663 sq. km.)
POPULATION 119,098,992
CAPITAL Brasília
LARGEST CITY São Paulo (greater)
HIGHEST POINT Pico da Neblina 9,889 ft. (3,014 m.)
MONETARY UNIT cruzeiro
MAJOR LANGUAGE Portuguese
MAJOR RELIGION Roman Catholicism

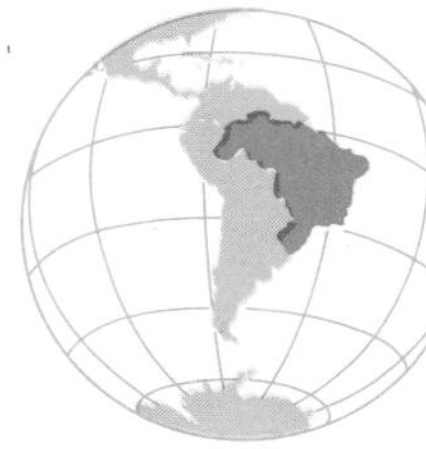

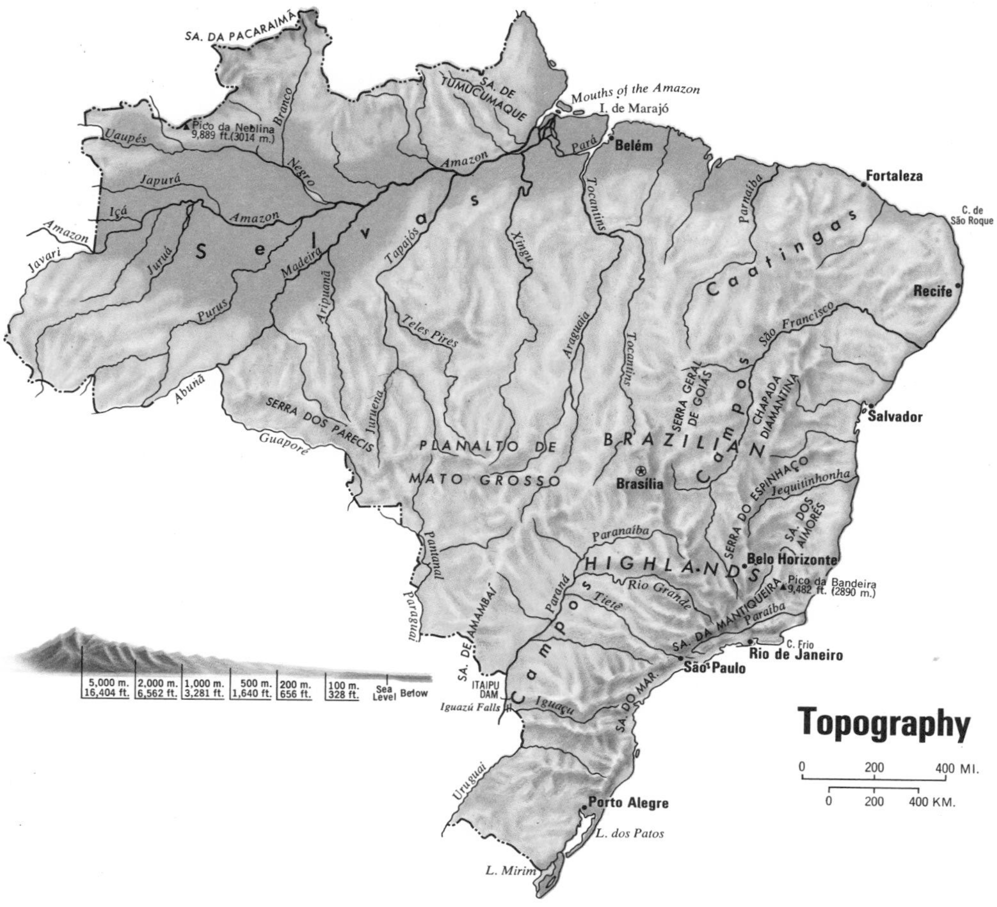

Topography

STATES and TERRITORIES

Acre 301,605 .... G10
Alagoas 1,987,581 .... G5
Amapá (terr.) 175,634 .... D2
Amazonas 1,432,066 .... G9
Bahia 9,474,263 .... F6
Ceará 5,294,876 .... G4
Espírito Santo 2,023,821 .... F7
Federal District 1,177,393 .... E6
Goiás 3,865,482 .... D6
Maranhão 4,002,599 .... E4
Mato Grosso 1,141,661 .... B6
Mato Grosso do Sul 1,370,333 .... C7
Minas Gerais 13,390,805 .... E7
Pará 3,411,868 .... C4
Paraíba 2,772,600 .... G4
Paraná 7,630,466 .... D9
Pernambuco 6,147,102 .... G5
Piauí 2,140,066 .... F4
Rio de Janeiro 11,297,327 .... F8
Rio Grande do Norte 1,899,720 .... G4
Rio Grande do Sul 7,777,212 .... C10
Rondônia (terr.) 492,810 .... H10
Roraima (terr.) 79,153 .... H8
Santa Catarina 3,628,751 .... D9
São Paulo 25,040,698 .... D8
Sergipe 1,141,834 .... G5

CITIES and TOWNS

Abaeté 12,861 .... E7
Abaetetuba 33,031 .... D3
Acaraú 7,144 .... F3
Acopiara 10,747 .... G4
Açu 20,544 .... G4
Agudos 18,790 .... *B3
Alagoa Grande 14,204 .... H4
Alagoinhas 76,377 .... G6
Alcobaça 3,430 .... G7
Alegre 9,441 .... *F2
Alegrete 54,786 .... B10
Além Paraíba 23,028 .... *E2
Alenquer 16,477 .... C3
Alfenas 31,815 .... *D2
Altamira 24,846 .... C3
Altos 13,621 .... F4
Amambaí 12,507 .... C8
Amapá 2,676 .... D2
Amarante 6,848 .... F4
Amargosa 11,118 .... F6
Americana 121,794 .... *C3
Amparo 26,970 .... *C3
Anápolis 160,520 .... D7
Anchieta 5,741 .... F8
Andaraí 2,476 .... F6
Andradina 42,036 .... D8
Andrelândia 8,737 .... *D2
Angra dos Reis 24,894 .... *D3
Antonina 11,950 .... *B4
Aparecida 27,265 .... *D3
Apiaí 7,809 .... *B4
Aquidauana 21,514 .... C8
Aracaju 288,106 .... G5
Aracati 20,282 .... G4
Araçatuba 113,486 .... *A2
Araçuaí 12,292 .... F7
Araguari 73,302 .... D7
Araranguá 22,468 .... D10
Araraquara 77,202 .... *B2
Araras 54,323 .... *C3
Araxá 51,339 .... E7
Arcoverde 40,646 .... G5
Areia Branca 12,979 .... G4
Assis 57,217 .... *A3
Avaré 40,716 .... *B3
Bacabal 43,229 .... E4
Bagé 66,743 .... C10
Bahia (Salvador) 1,496,276 .... G6
Baixo Guandu 13,714 .... F7
Balsas 13,566 .... E4
Bambuí 14,172 .... *C2
Barão de Cocais 11,950 .... *E1
Barbacena 69,675 .... *E2
Barcelos 1,846 .... H9
Bariri 15,372 .... *B3
Barra 10,809 .... F5
Barra do Corda 19,280 .... E4
Barra do Piraí 51,214 .... *E3
Barra Mansa 123,421 .... *D3
Barras 8,904 .... F4
Barreiras 30,355 .... E6
Barreiros 19,419 .... H5
Barretos 65,294 .... *B2
Batatais 30,478 .... *C2
Baturité 12,388 .... G4
Bauru 178,861 .... *B3
Bebedouro 39,070 .... *B2
Bela Vista 11,936 .... C8
Belém 758,117 .... E3
Belém †1,000,349 .... E3
Belo Horizonte 1,442,483 .... *D1
Belo Horizonte †2,541,788 .... *D1
Benjamin Constant 6,563 .... G9
Bento Gonçalves 40,323 .... C10
Betim 71,599 .... *D2
Bicas 8,611 .... *E2
Birigui 45,348 .... *A2
Blumenau 144,819 .... D9
Boa Esperança 17,394 .... *D2
Boa Vista 43,131 .... H8
Bocaiúva 16,616 .... E7
Bom Conselho 13,196 .... G5
Bom Despacho 22,941 .... *D1
Bom Jesus da Lapa 19,978 .... F6
Bom Sucesso 10,331 .... *D2
Borba 5,366 .... H9
Bragança Paulista 61,021 .... *C3
Brasiléia 4,835 .... G10
Brasília (cap.) 411,305 .... E6
Brasília de Minas 10,171 .... F7
Brejo 5,859 .... F3
Breves 31,452 .... D3
Brumado 24,663 .... F6
Brusque 37,898 .... D9
Cabedelo 18,581 .... H4
Cabo Frio 40,668 .... *F3
Caçador 25,287 .... D9
Caçapava 45,258 .... *D3
Caçapava do Sul 15,180 .... C10
Cáceres 33,472 .... B7
Cachoeira 11,520 .... G6
Cachoeira do Sul 59,967 .... C10
Cachoeiro de Itapemirim 84,994 .... G8
Caeté 23,331 .... *E1
Caetité 8,823 .... F6
Caiapônia 9,358 .... C7
Caicó 30,777 .... G4
Cajazeiras 30,834 .... G4
Cajuru 9,670 .... *C2
Camaquã 28,078 .... C10
Cambará 13,218 .... *A3
Cambuí 8,552 .... *C3
Cametá 15,539 .... D3
Camocim 19,921 .... F3
Campina Grande 222,229 .... G4
Campinas 566,517 .... *C3
Campo Belo 30,392 .... *D2
Campo Formoso 10,324 .... F5
Campo Grande 282,844 .... C8
Campo Largo 34,506 .... *B4
Campo Maior 24,009 .... F4
Campos 174,218 .... *F2
Cananéia 5,581 .... *C4
Canavieiras 14,076 .... G6
Canindé 18,573 .... G4
Canoas 214,115 .... D10
Canoinhas 25,880 .... D9
Capanema 28,272 .... E3
Capão Bonito 24,081 .... *B4
Caraguatatuba 22,932 .... *D3
Carangola 15,621 .... *E2
Caratinga 39,621 .... *E1
Caravelas 3,704 .... G7
Carazinho 41,913 .... C10
Carolina 10,136 .... E4
Caruaru 137,636 .... G5
Casa Branca 13,739 .... *C2
Cascavel 16,238 .... G4
Cássia 10,701 .... *C2
Castanhal 51,797 .... E3
Castelo 9,162 .... F8
Castro 21,079 .... *B4
Castro Alves 11,286 .... G6
Cataguases 40,659 .... *E2
Catalão 30,516 .... E7
Catanduva 64,813 .... *B2
Catolé do Rocha 12,165 .... G4
Caxambu 16,221 .... *D2
Caxias 56,755 .... F4
Caxias do Sul 198,824 .... D10
Ceará (Fortaleza) 648,815 .... G3
Ceará-Mirim 17,097 .... H4
Ceres 13,671 .... D6
Chapecó 53,198 .... C9
Coari 14,841 .... H9
Codajás 4,923 .... H9
Codó 11,593 .... E4
Colatina 61,057 .... F7
Conceição do Araguaia 18,143 .... D5
Concórdia 17,973 .... D9
Conselheiro Lafaiete 66,262 .... *E2
Corinto 17,056 .... E7
Cornélio Procópio 31,201 .... D8
Coroatá 16,070 .... F3
Coromandel 11,604 .... E7
Corumbá 66,014 .... B7
Coxim 14,876 .... C7
Crateús 29,905 .... F4
Crato 49,244 .... G4
Criciúma 74,003 .... D10
Cristalina 10,521 .... E7
Cruz Alta 53,315 .... C10
Cruzeiro 55,175 .... *D3
Cruzeiro do Sul 11,189 .... G10
Cubatão 78,327 .... *C3
Cuiabá 167,894 .... C6
Curitiba 843,733 .... *B4
Curitiba †1,441,743 .... *B4
Currais Novos 25,663 .... G4
Cururupu 10,358 .... E3
Curvelo 37,734 .... E7
Diamantina 20,197 .... F7
Divinópolis 108,344 .... *D2
Dois Córregos 11,811 .... *B3
Dom Pedrito 25,773 .... C10
Dores do Indaiá 13,058 .... E7
Dourados 76,838 .... C8
Duque de Caxias 306,057 .... *E3
Erexim 46,927 .... C9
Esperança 12,964 .... G4
Esplanada 9,822 .... G5
Estância 28,250 .... G5
Feira de Santana 225,003 .... G5
Fernandópolis 39,737 .... *A2
Floriano 35,761 .... F4
Florianópolis 153,547 .... E9
Fonte Boa 3,278 .... G9
Formiga 36,681 .... *D2
Formosa 29,304 .... E6
Fortaleza 648,815 .... G3
Fortaleza †1,581,588 .... G3
Foz do Iguaçu 93,619 .... C9
Franca 143,630 .... *C2
Frutal 22,955 .... *B2
Garanhuns 64,854 .... G5
Garça 26,527 .... *B3
Goiana 30,108 .... H4
Goiânia 703,263 .... D7
Goiás 15,768 .... D6
Governador Valadares 173,699 .... F7
Grajaú 11,147 .... E4
Guacuí 12,715 .... *F2
Guajará-Mirim 19,992 .... H10
Guarapuava 17,189 .... C9
Guaratinguetá 68,370 .... *D3
Guarujá 67,730 .... *C4
Guarulhos 395,117 .... *C3
Guaxupé 23,637 .... *C2
Guiratinga 8,981 .... C7
Gurupi 27,319 .... D5
Humaitá 10,004 .... H10
Ibaiti 11,352 .... *A3
Ibiá 11,161 .... E7
Ibicaraí 18,202 .... G6
Ibitinga 23,359 .... *B2
Icó 13,007 .... G4
Igarapava 15,342 .... *C2
Igarapé-Miri 12,172 .... D3
Iguape 16,827 .... *C4
Iguatu 39,611 .... G4
Ijuí 51,925 .... C10
Ilhéus 71,240 .... G6
Imbituba 9,998 .... D10
Imperatriz 111,818 .... E4
Inhumas 23,455 .... D7
Ipameri 14,163 .... E7
Ipu 12,787 .... F4
Irati 21,956 .... *A4
Itabaiana, Paraíba 17,843 .... H4
Itabaiana, Sergipe 26,055 .... G5
Itaberaba 27,590 .... F6
Itabira 57,691 .... F7
Itabirito 22,978 .... *E2
Itabuna 129,938 .... G6
Itacoatiara 26,737 .... B3
Itaituba 19,644 .... C4
Itajaí 78,867 .... D9
Itajubá 53,506 .... *D3
Itanhaem 26,181 .... *C4
Itapecerica 10,234 .... *D2
Itapecuru-Mirim 12,216 .... F3
Itapemirim 16,829 .... F8
Itaperuna 34,644 .... *F2
Itapetinga 36,897 .... G6
Itapetininga 61,344 .... *B3
Itapeva 36,551 .... *B3
Itapipoca 19,463 .... G3
Itapira 36,308 .... *C3
Itápolis 13,750 .... *B2
Itaporanga 8,988 .... G4
Itaqui 23,136 .... B10
Itararé 24,368 .... *B4
Itatiba 35,537 .... *C3
Itaúna 49,372 .... *D2
Itu 62,211 .... *C3
Ituaçu 1,749 .... F6
Ituiutaba 65,178 .... D7
Itumbiara 56,602 .... D7
Iturama 12,363 .... *A1
Ituverava 21,323 .... *C2
Jaboatão 67,120 .... H5
Jaboticabal 40,276 .... *B2
Jacareí 103,652 .... *D3
Jacarezinho 23,684 .... *A3
Jacobina 26,723 .... F5
Jacupiranga 7,044 .... *B4
Jaguaquara 11,336 .... F6
Jaguarão 18,165 .... C11
Jaguariaíva 8,566 .... *B4
Januária 20,484 .... E6
Jataí 40,957 .... D7
Jaú 59,522 .... *B3
Jequié 84,792 .... F6
Jequitinhonha 10,900 .... F7
Ji-Paraná 31,724 .... H10
Joaçaba 16,195 .... D9
João Pessoa 290,424 .... H4
João Pinheiro 17,013 .... E7
Joinvile 217,074 .... D9
Juazeiro 60,940 .... G5
Juazeiro do Norte 125,248 .... F4
Juiz de Fora 299,728 .... *E2
Jundiaí 210,015 .... *C3
Lages 108,768 .... D9
Laguna 27,743 .... D10
Lambari 9,722 .... *D2
Lapa 13,314 .... D9
Laranjeiras do Sul 19,329 .... C9
Lavras 35,345 .... *D2
Leme 40,155 .... *C3
Leopoldina 28,554 .... *E2
Limeira 137,812 .... *C3
Limoeiro 36,088 .... H4
Limoeiro do Norte 13,112 .... G4
Linhares 51,575 .... F7
Lins 44,633 .... *B2
Londrina 258,054 .... D8
Lorena 51,276 .... *D3
Luís Correia 3,576 .... F3
Luz 10,068 .... *D1
Luziânia 67,284 .... E7
Macaé 39,644 .... *F3
Macaíba 17,036 .... H4
Macapá 89,081 .... D2
Macau 17,543 .... G4
Maceió 376,479 .... H5
Machado 16,164 .... *C2
Mafra 26,226 .... D9
Magé 37,597 .... *E3
Mamanguape 16,321 .... H4
Manacapuru 17,016 .... H9
Manaus 613,068 .... H9
Manhuaçu 22,678 .... *E2
Manhumirim 11,085 .... *E2
Manicoré 9,532 .... H9
Marabá 41,564 .... D4
Maracaju 9,699 .... C8
Maragogipe 13,512 .... G6
Maranguape 20,098 .... G3
Marechal Deodoro 9,400 .... H5
Mariana 11,785 .... *E2
Marília 103,904 .... *A3
Maringá 158,047 .... D8
Mata de São João 23,741 .... G6
Mato Grosso (Vila Bela da Santissima Trindade) 1,401 .... B6
Maués 10,846 .... B3
Mazagão 1,824 .... D3
Mineiros 16,844 .... C7
Miracema 15,545 .... *E2
Mirassol 25,173 .... *B2
Mococa 33,682 .... *C2
Mogi das Cruzes 122,265 .... *C3
Mogi-Mirim 41,827 .... *C3
Monte Alegre 10,646 .... C3
Monte Aprazível 9,767 .... *A2
Monteiro 11,051 .... G4
Montenegro 27,246 .... D10
Montes Claros 151,881 .... E7
Morrinhos 20,154 .... D7
Mossoró 118,007 .... G4
Muriaé 50,040 .... *E2
Muzambinho 8,803 .... *C2
Nanuque 34,445 .... F7
Natal 376,552 .... H4
Nazaré 18,068 .... G6
Niquelândia 8,828 .... D6
Niterói 386,185 .... *E3
Nova Cruz 12,824 .... H4
Nova Era 11,126 .... *E1
Nova Friburgo 88,943 .... *E3
Nova Iguaçu 491,802 .... *E3
Nova Lima 35,035 .... *E2
Nova Russas 10,021 .... F4
Novo Hamburgo 132,066 .... D10
Novo Horizonte 18,439 .... *B2
Óbidos 17,143 .... C3
Oeiras 12,406 .... F4
Olímpia 24,376 .... *B2
Olinda 266,392 .... H4
Oliveira 22,642 .... *D2
Oriximiná 12,078 .... C3
Orlândia 22,924 .... *C2
Osasco 376,689 .... *C3
Ourinhos 52,698 .... *B3
Ouro Preto 27,821 .... *E2
Palmares 40,624 .... H5
Palmas 15,823 .... C9
Palmeira 11,521 .... *B4
Palmeira das Missões 23,943 .... C9
Pará (Belém) 758,117 .... E3
Paracatu 29,911 .... E7
Pará de Minas 37,127 .... *D1
Paraguaçu Paulista 17,399 .... D8
Paraíba do Sul 13,510 .... *E3
Paranaíba 21,305 .... D7
Paranaguá 68,366 .... *B4
Parati 8,684 .... *D3
Parintins 29,369 .... B3
Parnaíba 78,718 .... F3
Passo Fundo 103,121 .... D10
Passos 56,998 .... *C2
Patos 58,735 .... G4
Patos de Minas 59,896 .... E7
Patrocínio 29,520 .... E7
Pau dos Ferros 12,985 .... G4
Paulo Afonso 62,066 .... G5
Pederneiras 18,864 .... *B3
Pedra Azul 13,615 .... F6
Pedreiras 30,843 .... E4
Pedro Segundo 9,693 .... F4
Pelotas 197,092 .... C10
Penápolis 32,168 .... *A2
Penedo 27,064 .... G5
Pernambuco (Recife) 1,184,215 .... H5
Petrolina 73,436 .... G5
Petrópolis 149,427 .... *E3
Picos 33,098 .... F4
Piedade 13,054 .... *C3
Pilar 14,778 .... H5
Pindamonhangaba 51,174 .... *D3

(continued on following page)

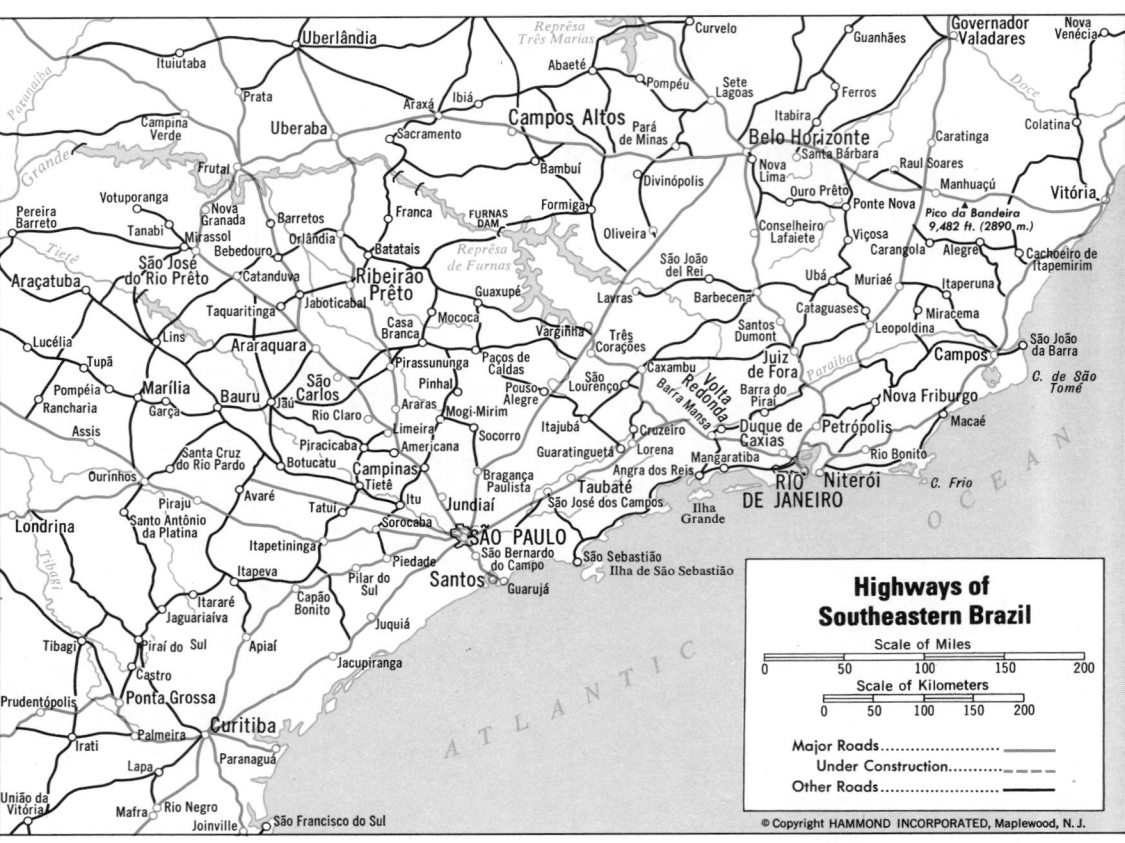

Highways of Southeastern Brazil

Scale of Miles
0 — 50 — 100 — 150 — 200

Scale of Kilometers
0 — 50 — 100 — 150 — 200

Major Roads . . . .
Under Construction . . . .
Other Roads . . . .

© Copyright HAMMOND INCORPORATED, Maplewood, N.J.

Agriculture, Industry and Resources

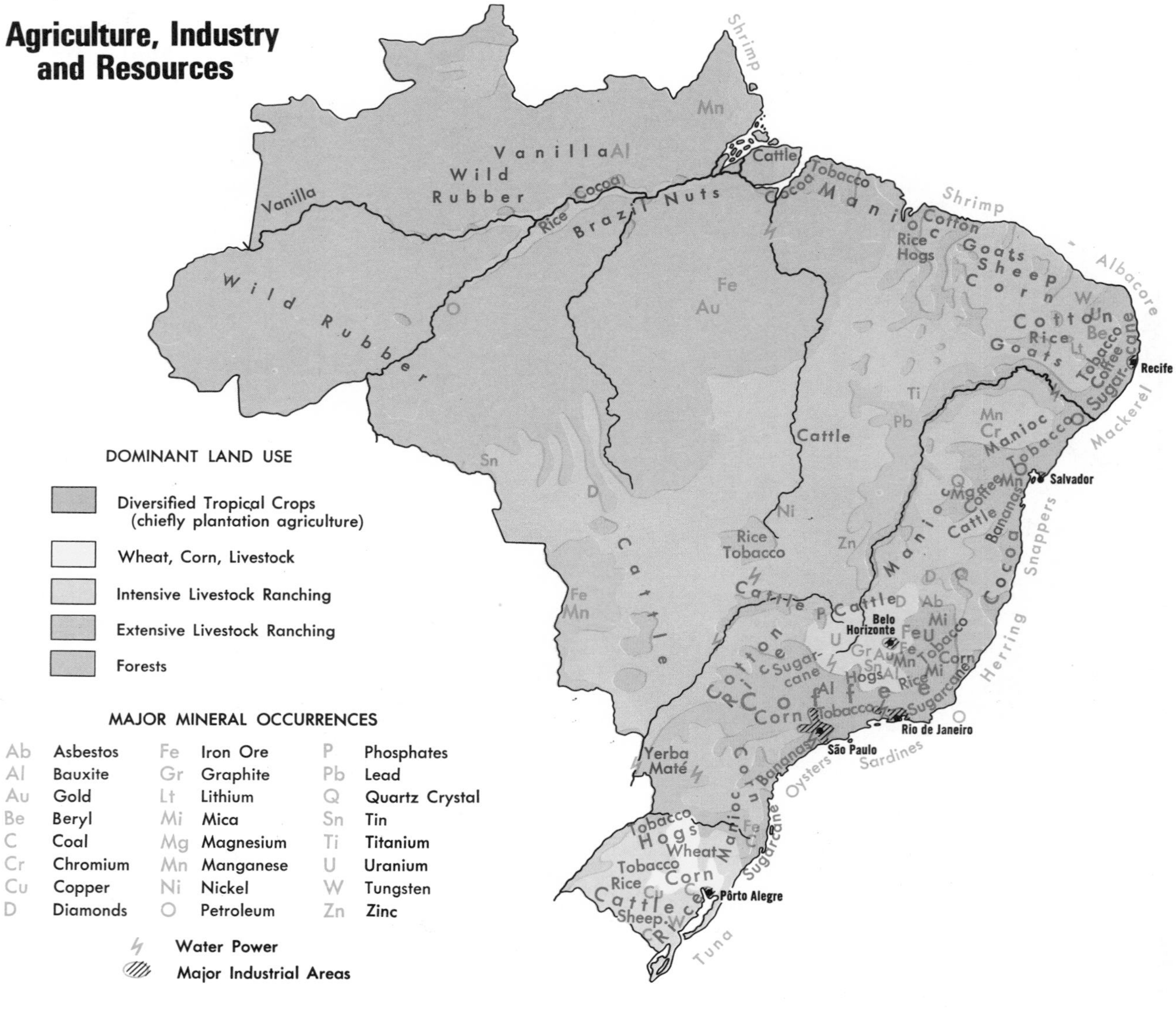

DOMINANT LAND USE

- Diversified Tropical Crops (chiefly plantation agriculture)
- Wheat, Corn, Livestock
- Intensive Livestock Ranching
- Extensive Livestock Ranching
- Forests

MAJOR MINERAL OCCURRENCES

Ab	Asbestos	Fe	Iron Ore	P	Phosphates
Al	Bauxite	Gr	Graphite	Pb	Lead
Au	Gold	Lt	Lithium	Q	Quartz Crystal
Be	Beryl	Mi	Mica	Sn	Tin
C	Coal	Mg	Magnesium	Ti	Titanium
Cr	Chromium	Mn	Manganese	U	Uranium
Cu	Copper	Ni	Nickel	W	Tungsten
D	Diamonds	O	Petroleum	Zn	Zinc

⚡ Water Power

🏭 Major Industrial Areas

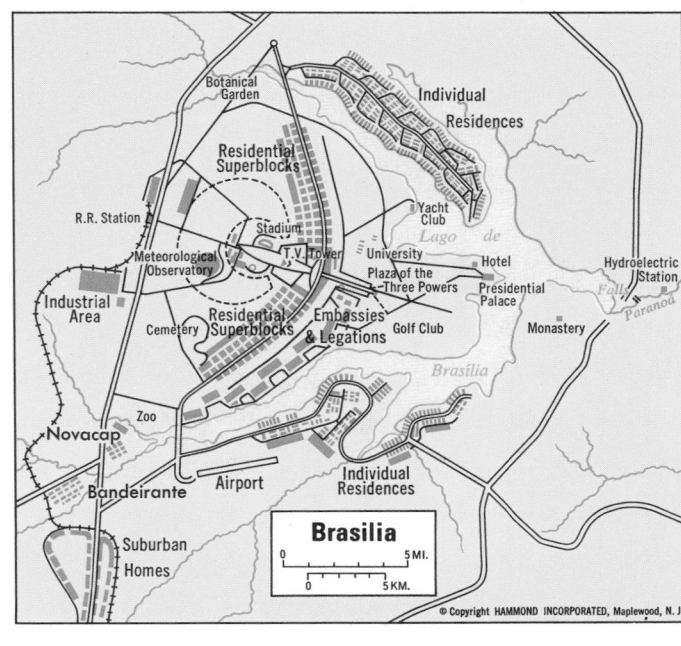

Brasilia

0   5 MI.

0   5 KM.

© Copyright HAMMOND INCORPORATED, Maplewood, N.J.

Southeastern Brazil

POLYCONIC PROJECTION

SCALE OF MILES

0   25   50   100   150

SCALE OF KILOMETERS

0 25 50   100   150

State Capitals . . . . ◉

State Boundaries . . . . —

Scale 1:4,480,000

© Copyright HAMMOND INCORPORATED, Maplewood, N.J.

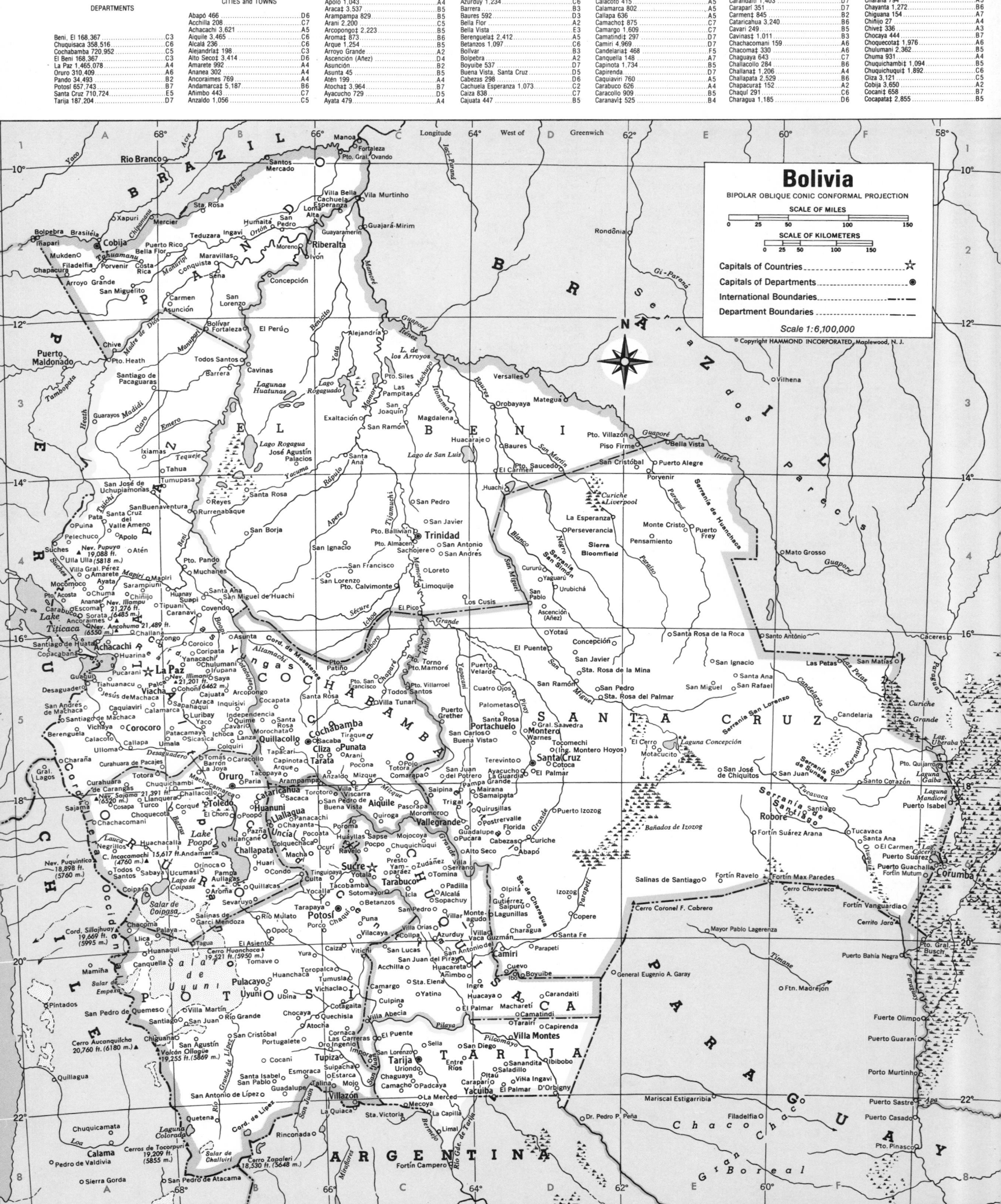

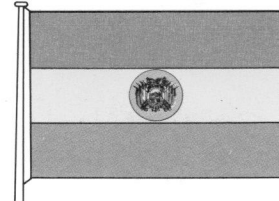

AREA 424,163 sq. mi. (1,098,582 sq. km.)
POPULATION 5,600,000
CAPITALS La Paz, Sucre
LARGEST CITY La Paz
HIGHEST POINT Nevada Ancohuma 21,489 ft. (6,550 m.)
MONETARY UNIT Bolivian peso
MAJOR LANGUAGES Spanish, Quechua, Aymara
MAJOR RELIGION Roman Catholicism

Topography

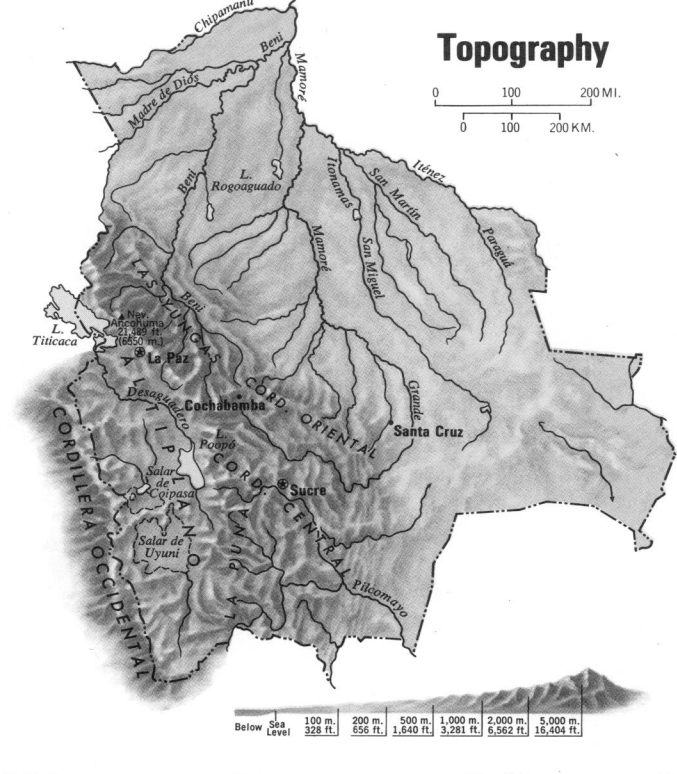

	Below Sea Level	100 m. 328 ft.	200 m. 656 ft.	500 m. 1,640 ft.	1,000 m. 3,281 ft.	2,000 m. 6,562 ft.	5,000 m. 16,404 ft.

Agriculture, Industry and Resources

DOMINANT LAND USE

- Diversified Tropical Crops (chiefly plantation agriculture)
- Upland Cultivated Areas
- Upland Livestock Grazing, Limited Agriculture
- Extensive Livestock Ranching
- Forests
- Nonagricultural Land

MAJOR MINERAL OCCURRENCES

Ag	Silver	G	Natural Gas	Sb	Antimony
Au	Gold	O	Petroleum	Sn	Tin
Cu	Copper	Pb	Lead	W	Tungsten
Fe	Iron Ore	S	Sulfur	Zn	Zinc

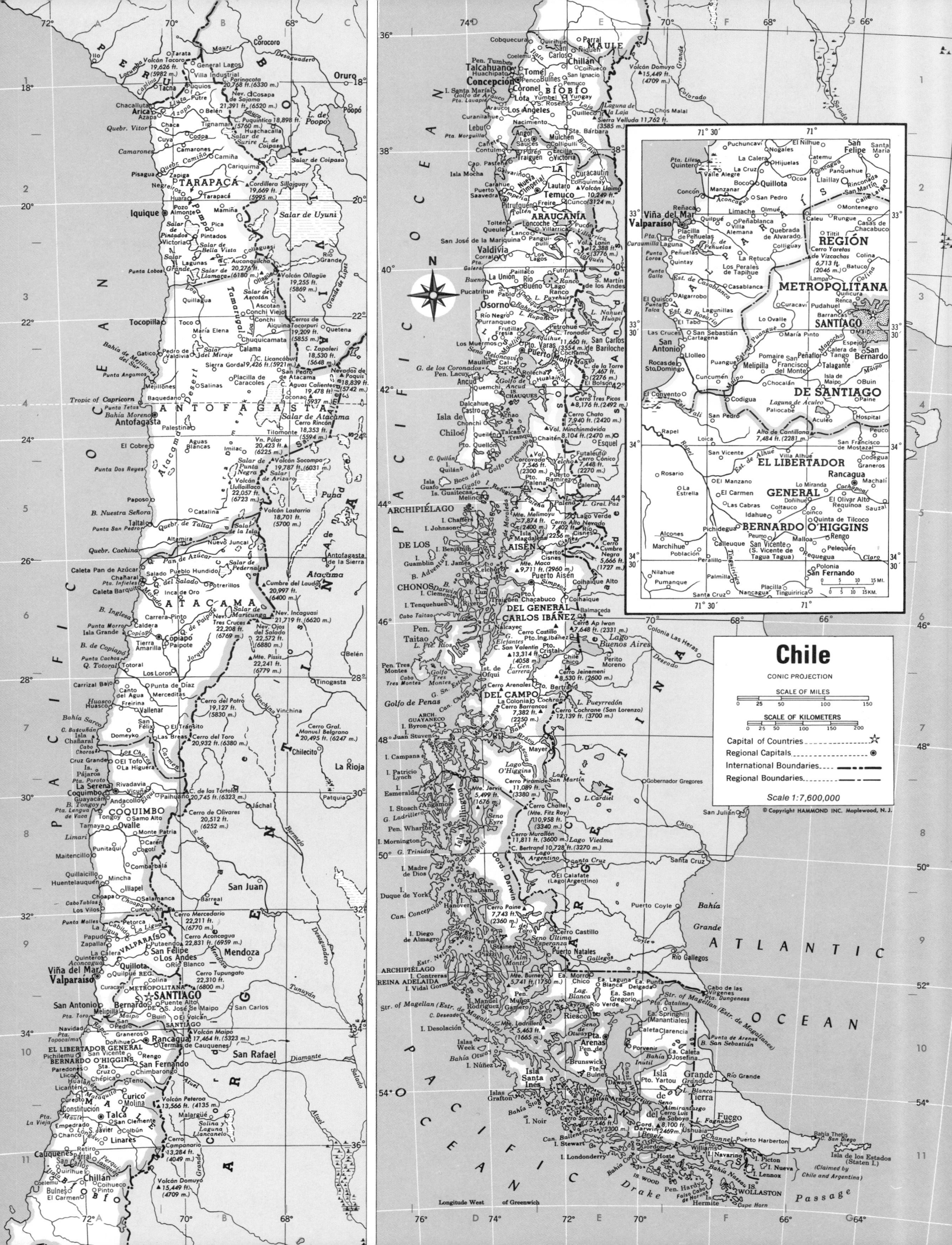

Chile

CONIC PROJECTION

SCALE OF MILES

25   50   100   150

SCALE OF KILOMETERS

25 50   100   150   200

Capital of Countries .... ★

Regional Capitals .... ◉

International Boundaries ....

Regional Boundaries ....

Scale 1:7,600,000

© Copyright HAMMOND INC. Maplewood, N.J.

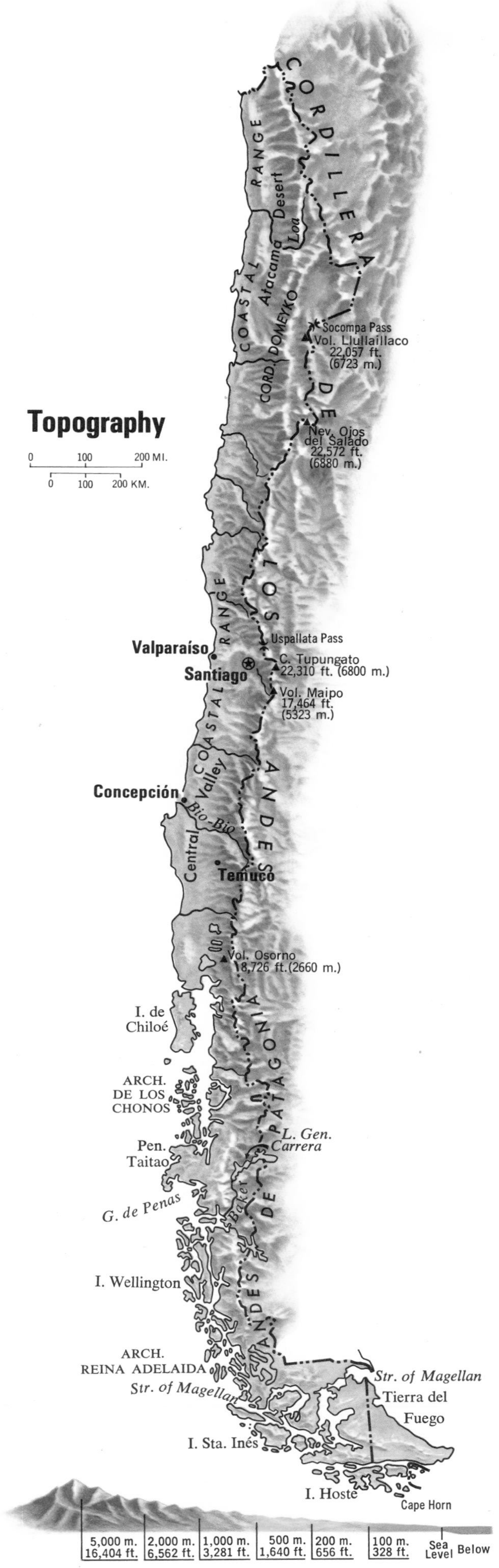
Topography
0 100 200 MI.
0 100 200 KM.
CORDILLERA DE LOS ANDES
COASTAL RANGE
Atacama Desert
Loa
CORD. DOMEYKO
Socompa Pass
Vol. Llullaillaco 22,057 ft. (6723 m.)
Nev. Ojos del Salado 22,572 ft. (6880 m.)
Valparaíso
Santiago
Uspallata Pass
C. Tupungato 22,310 ft. (6800 m.)
Vol. Maipo 17,464 ft. (5323 m.)
COASTAL RANGE
Central Valley
Concepción
Bío-Bío
Temuco
Vol. Osorno 8,726 ft. (2660 m.)
I. de Chiloé
ARCH. DE LOS CHONOS
L. Gen. Carrera
Pen. Taitao
G. de Penas
Baker
ANDES DE PATAGONIA
I. Wellington
ARCH. REINA ADELAIDA
Str. of Magellan
Str. of Magellan
Tierra del Fuego
I. Sta. Inés
I. Hoste
Cape Horn
5,000 m. 16,404 ft.
2,000 m. 6,562 ft.
1,000 m. 3,281 ft.
500 m. 1,640 ft.
200 m. 656 ft.
100 m. 328 ft.
Sea Level
Below

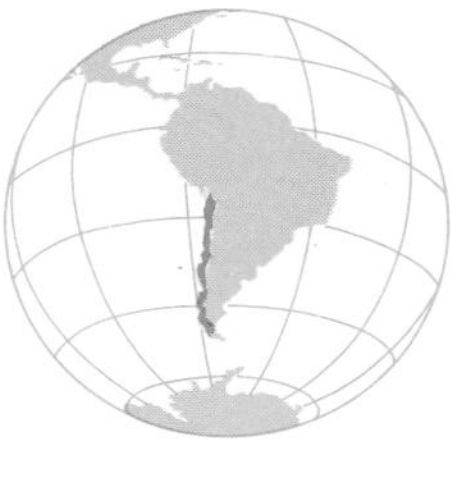

AREA 292,257 sq. mi. (756,946 sq. km.)
POPULATION 11,275,440
CAPITAL Santiago
LARGEST CITY Santiago
HIGHEST POINT Ojos del Salado 22,572 ft. (6,880 m.)
MONETARY UNIT Chilean escudo
MAJOR LANGUAGE Spanish
MAJOR RELIGION Roman Catholicism

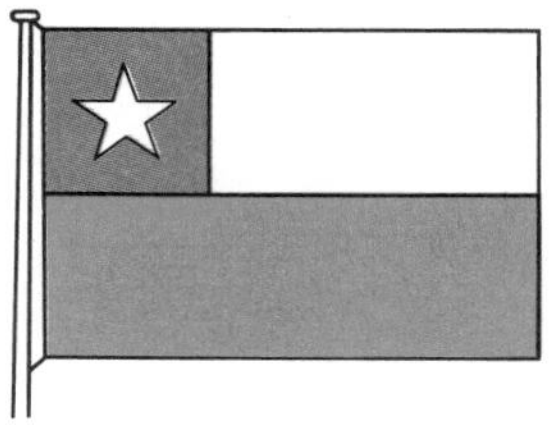

REGIONS

Aisén del General Carlos Ibáñez del Campo 65,478 . . . . E6
Antofagasta 341,203 . . . . B4
Atacama 183,071 . . . . B6
Bíobío 1,516,552 . . . . E1
Coquimbo 419,178 . . . . A8
El Libertador General Bernardo O'Higgins 584,989 . . . . A10
La Araucanía 692,924 . . . . E2
Los Lagos 843,430 . . . . D3
Magallanes 132,333 . . . . E10
Maule 723,224 . . . . A11
Santiago, Región Metropolitana de (Santiago Metropolitan Region) 4,294,938 . . . . A9
Tarapacá 273,427 . . . . B2
Valparaíso 1,204,693 . . . . A9

CITIES and TOWNS

Achao ○11,501 . . . . D4
Aguas Blancas ○203 . . . . B4
Algarrobo ○3,941 . . . . F3
Ancud 11,900 . . . . D4
Andacollo 6,000 . . . . A8
Angol 42,670 . . . . D1
Antofagasta 125,100 . . . . A4
Arauco 5,400 . . . . D1
Arica 87,700 . . . . A1
Ascotán B3
Barrancas ○184,241 . . . . G3
Belén ○925 . . . . B1
Buin 11,800 . . . . G4
Bulnes 6,900 . . . . E1
Cabildo 5,800 . . . . A9
Calama 45,900 . . . . B3
Calbuco ○21,673 . . . . D4
Caldera ○3,268 . . . . A6
Calera de Tango ○6,198 . . . . G4
Calle Larga ○7,172 . . . . G2
Cañete 7,900 . . . . D2
Carahue ○12,733 . . . . D2
Cartagena ○7,124 . . . . F3
Casablanca 5,500 . . . . F3
Casas de Chacabuco G2
Castro 11,200 . . . . D4
Catalina ○1,637 . . . . B5
Catemu ○8,728 . . . . G2
Cauquenes 20,200 . . . . A11
Cerro Castillo ○537 . . . . E9
Cerro Manantiales F10
Chaitén ○4,067 . . . . E4
Chañaral ○36,949 . . . . A6
Chanco ○12,433 . . . . A11
Chépica ○11,199 . . . . A10
Chillán 128,515 . . . . A11
Chimbarongo 5,300 . . . . A10
Chonchi ○8,911 . . . . D4
Chuquicamata 22,100 . . . . B3
Cobquecura ○6,298 . . . . D1
Cochamó ○5,042 . . . . E3
Codegua ○6,757 . . . . G4
Codpa ○950 . . . . B1
Coelemu 5,400 . . . . D1
Coihaique 32,129 . . . . E6
Coihueco ○17,276 . . . . A11
Coinco ○4,942 . . . . G5
Colbún ○12,924 . . . . A11
Colina 7,400 . . . . G3
Collipulli 7,200 . . . . E2
Coltauco ○11,857 . . . . F5
Combarbalá ○17,332 . . . . A8
Concepción 206,226 . . . . D1
Constitución 11,500 . . . . A11
Contulmo ○13,987 . . . . D2
Copiapó 45,200 . . . . B6
Coquimbo 73,953 . . . . A8
Coronel 37,300 . . . . D1
Corral ○5,533 . . . . D3
Cunco ○18,836 . . . . E2
Curacautín 9,800 . . . . E2
Curacaví 5,800 . . . . G3
Curanilahue 13,200 . . . . D1
Curepto ○13,020 . . . . A10
Curicó 41,300 . . . . A10
Dalcahue ○7,084 . . . . D4
Domeiko A7
Doñihue ○8,837 . . . . G5
El Carmen ○13,226 . . . . A11
El Monte 7,000 . . . . G4
El Quisco ○2,152 . . . . E3
El Tabo ○2,180 . . . . F3
El Tofo A7
Empedrado ○7,887 . . . . A11
Ercilla ○8,061 . . . . E2
Estancia Caleta Josefina ○1,042 . . . . F10
Estancia Morro Chico ○785 . E9
Estancia San Gregorio ○1,156 . . . . E9
Estancia Springhill (Cerro Manantiales) F10
Freire ○23,313 . . . . E2
Freirina ○5,523 . . . . A7
Fresia ○15,359 . . . . D3
Frutillar ○12,721 . . . . D3
Futaleufú ○2,366 . . . . E4
Futrono ○7,109 . . . . E3
Galvarino ○9,495 . . . . D2
General Lagos ○810 . . . . B1
Graneros 8,900 . . . . G5
Guayacán A8
Hijuelas ○7,128 . . . . F2
Hualañé ○6,912 . . . . A10
Huara ○1,934 . . . . B2
Huasco ○4,971 . . . . A7
Illapel 12,200 . . . . A8
Inca de Oro 1,406 . . . . B6
Iquique 64,500 . . . . A2
Isla de Maipo ○12,903 . . . . G4
La Calera 24,600 . . . . F2
La Cruz ○8,907 . . . . F2
La Estrella ○3,707 . . . . F5
Lago Ranco ○12,767 . . . . E3
Lagunas ○5,653 . . . . B3
La Higuera ○6,991 . . . . A7
La Ligua 7,500 . . . . A9
Lampa ○10,220 . . . . G3
Lanco 5,200 . . . . D2
Las Cabras ○12,119 . . . . F5
La Serena 99,908 . . . . A8
La Unión 15,200 . . . . D3
Lautaro 11,900 . . . . E2
Lebu 12,500 . . . . D1
Licantén ○6,354 . . . . A10
Limache 15,200 . . . . F2
Linares 37,900 . . . . A11
Llay-Llay 9,700 . . . . G2
Loica F4
Loncoche ○17,539 . . . . D2
Longaví ○15,909 . . . . A11
Lonquimay ○9,524 . . . . E2
Los Andes 23,500 . . . . B9
Los Ángeles 49,500 . . . . D1
Los Lagos ○14,934 . . . . D3
Los Muermos ○9,296 . . . . D3
Los Sauces ○7,613 . . . . D2
Los Vilos ○10,453 . . . . A9
Lota 48,100 . . . . D1
Machall 5,800 . . . . G5
Maipú ○117,872 . . . . G3
Malloa ○9,742 . . . . G5
Marchigüe ○4,451 . . . . F5
Marla Elena 5,900 . . . . B3
Marla Pinto ○5,980 . . . . G3
Maullln ○14,544 . . . . D4
Mejillones ○3,333 . . . . A4
Melipilla 23,900 . . . . F4
Mincha ○11,329 . . . . A8
Molina 9,400 . . . . A10
Monte Patria ○18,927 . . . . A8
Mulchén 13,700 . . . . E1
Nacimiento ○17,651 . . . . D1
Nancagua ○11,076 . . . . F6
Navidad ○6,618 . . . . A10
Negreiros ○1,144 . . . . B2
Ñiquén ○13,640 . . . . E1
Nogales ○18,529 . . . . F2
Nueva Imperial 8,000 . . . . D2
Olivar Alto ○5,414 . . . . G5
Ollagüe B3
Olmué ○8,804 . . . . F2
Osorno 68,800 . . . . D3
Ovalle 31,700 . . . . A8
Paihuano ○6,048 . . . . B8
Paillaco 5,200 . . . . D3
Paine ○21,876 . . . . G4
Palena ○2,508 . . . . E5
Palmilla ○7,965 . . . . F6
Panguipulli 5,700 . . . . E2
Panquehue ○4,230 . . . . G2
Papudo ○2,594 . . . . A9
Paredones ○7,404 . . . . A10
Parral 17,000 . . . . A11
Pedro de Valdivia 6,200 . . . . B4
Pemuco ○7,577 . . . . E1
Peñaflor 15,500 . . . . G4
Penco ○33,962 . . . . D1
Peñuelas F3
Petorca ○8,343 . . . . A9
Petrohué E3
Peumo ○11,308 . . . . F5
Pica ○1,487 . . . . B2
Pichidegua ○13,550 . . . . F5
Pichilemu ○8,042 . . . . A10
Pinto ○8,687 . . . . A11
Pisagua ○1,880 . . . . A2
Pitrufquén 7,800 . . . . D2
Placilla ○6,441 . . . . F6
Porvenir ○4,000 . . . . E10
Potrerillos 5,800 . . . . B6
Pozo Almonte ○1,798 . . . . B2
Puchuncaví ○7,542 . . . . F2
Pucón 18,000 . . . . E2
Pudahuel G3
Pueblo Hundido 6,200 . . . . B6
Puente Alto 65,100 . . . . B10
Puerto Aisén 17,848 . . . . E6
Puerto Cisnes ○2,800 . . . . E5
Puerto Ingeniero Ibáñez ○1,900 . . . . E6
Puerto Montt 119,059 . . . . E4
Puerto Natales 17,280 . . . . E9
Puerto Quellón ○7,734 . . . . D4
Puerto Varas 10,900 . . . . E3
Puerto Williams ○949 . . . . F11
Pumanque ○3,137 . . . . F6
Punitaqui ○16,167 . . . . A8
Punta Arenas 2,140 . . . . E10
Purén ○11,604 . . . . D2
Purranque 5,900 . . . . D3
Putaendo ○12,806 . . . . A9
Putre ○855 . . . . B1
Puyehue E3
Queilén ○6,055 . . . . D4
Quemchi ○6,707 . . . . D4
Quilicura 8,100 . . . . G3
Quillagua B3
Quilleco ○16,043 . . . . E1
Quillota 36,500 . . . . F2
Quilpué 40,600 . . . . F2
Quinta de Tilcoco ○6,513 . . G5
Quintero 9,900 . . . . F2
Quirihue ○11,178 . . . . E1
Rancagua 140,589 . . . . G5
Renca ○67,168 . . . . G3
Rengo 12,400 . . . . G5
Requlnoa ○10,730 . . . . G5
Retiro ○15,146 . . . . A11
Rinconada San Martín ○4,118 . . . . G2
Río Blanco B9
Río Bueno 9,600 . . . . D3
Río Negro 5,100 . . . . D3
Río Verde ○554 . . . . E10
Rocas de Santo Domingo ○4,114 . . . . F4
Rosario ○3,383 . . . . F5
Salamanca ○18,741 . . . . A9
Samo Alto ○5,689 . . . . A8
San Antonio 46,700 . . . . F3
San Bernardo ○117,766 . . . G4
San Carlos 17,000 . . . . E1
San Clemente ○23,273 . . . A11
San Felipe 26,100 . . . . G2
San Fernando 23,600 . . . . G6
San Francisco de Mostazal ○11,439 . . . . G4
San Ignacio ○13,523 . . . . E1
San Javier 10,800 . . . . A11
San José de Maipo ○9,601 . . . . B10
San Pablo ○7,978 . . . . D3
San Pedro ○8,255 . . . . F4
San Pedro de Atacama C4
San Rosendo ○14,337 . . . . E1
Santa Bárbara ○14,345 . . . . E1
Santa Cruz 8,600 . . . . F6
Santa María ○8,162 . . . . G2
Santiago (cap.) 3,614,947 . . G3
Santiago *3,672,374 . . . . G3
San Vicente F4
San Vicente (San Vicente de Tagua Tagua) ○28,333 F5
Sierra Gorda ○8,805 . . . . B4
Talagante 16,500 . . . . G4
Talca 133,160 . . . . A11
Talcahuano 148,300 . . . . D1
Taltal 6,400 . . . . A5
Tamaya A8
Tarapacá B2
Temuco 197,232 . . . . E2
Teno ○17,675 . . . . A10
Termas de Cauquenes B10
Tierra Amarilla ○7,899 . . . . A6
Tiltil ○9,198 . . . . G2
Toco ○8,734 . . . . B3
Toconao C4
Tocopilla 22,000 . . . . A3
Toltén ○16,265 . . . . D2
Tomé 29,600 . . . . D1
Traiguén 11,400 . . . . D2
Valdivia 115,536 . . . . D3
Vallenar 26,800 . . . . A7
Valparaíso 271,580 . . . . E2
Victoria 16,500 . . . . D2
Vicuña 5,100 . . . . A8
Villa Alemana 29,600 . . . . F2
Villa Alhué ○5,078 . . . . G4
Villarrica 25,091 . . . . E2
Viña del Mar 281,361 . . . . F2
Yumbel ○21,858 . . . . E1
Yungay ○10,725 . . . . E1
Zapallar ○2,894 . . . . A9
Zapiga B2

OTHER FEATURES

Aconcagua (riv.) F2
Aculeo (lag.) G4
Adventure (bay) D5
Aguas Calientes, Cerro (mt.) C4
Almirantazgo (bay) F11
Almirante Montt (gulf) D9
Ancud (gulf) D4
Angamos (isl.) D8
Angamos (pt.) A4
Ap Iwan, Cerro (mt.) E6
Arauco (gulf) D1
Arenales, Cerro (mt.) D7
Atacama (des.) B4
Atacama, Salar de (salt dep.) C4
Aucanquilcha, Cerro (mt.) . . B3
Azapa, Quebrada (riv.) B1
Baker (riv.) D7
Ballenero (chan.) E11
Bascuñán (cape) A7
Beagle (chan.) E11
Bella Vista, Salar de (salt dep.) B3
Benjamín (isl.) D5
Bío-Bío (riv.) E2
Blanca (lag.) E10
Blanco (lake) F10
Bravo (riv.) D7
Brunswick (pen.) E10
Bueno (riv.) D3
Buenos Aires (lake) E6
Byron (isl.) D7
Cachapoal (riv.) G5
Cachina, Quebrada (riv.) A5
Cachos (pt.) A6
Calafquén (lake) E3
Camarones (riv.) A2
Camiña, Quebrada (riv.) B2
Campana (isl.) D7
Campanario, Cerro (mt.) . . A10
Capitán Aracena (isl.) E10
Carmen (riv.) B7
Castillo, Cerro (mt.) E6
Catalina (pt.) F10
Chaffers (isl.) D5
Chaltel, Cerro (mt.) E8
Chañaral (isl.) A7
Chatham (isl.) D9
Chauques (isls.) D4
Cheap (chan.) D7
Chiloé (isl.) 119,286 . . . . D4
Choapa (riv.) A9
Chonos (arch.) D6
Choros (cape) A7
Cisnes (riv.) E5
Clarence (isl.) E10
Clemente (isl.) D6
Cochrane (lake) E7
Cochrane, Cerro (mt.) E7
Cockburn (chan.) E11
Concepción (chan.) D9
Cónico, Cerro (mt.) E4
Contreras (isl.) D9
Cook (bay) E11
Copiapó (bay) A6
Copiapó (riv.) A6
Corcovado (gulf) D4
Corcovado (vol.) D5
Coronados (gulf) D4
Curaumilla (pt.) E2
Darwin (bay) D6
Darwin, Cordillera (mts.) . . . D8
Darwin, Cordillera (mts.) . . E11

(continued on following page)

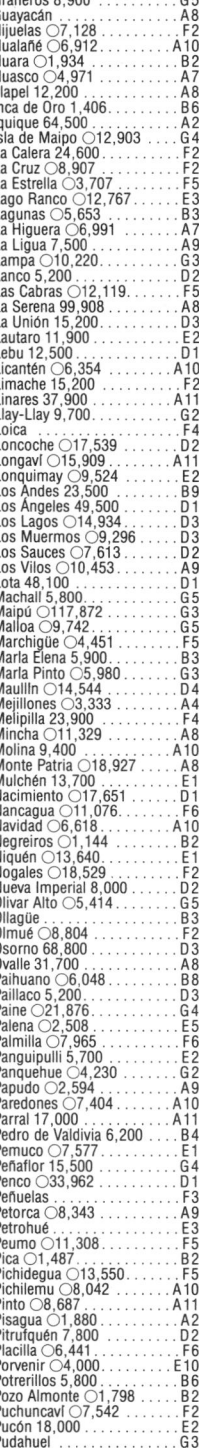

Agriculture, Industry and Resources

DOMINANT LAND USE

- Cereals, Livestock
- Mediterranean Agriculture (cereals, fruit, livestock)
- Pasture Livestock
- Extensive Livestock Ranching
- Limited Seasonal Grazing
- Forests
- Nonagricultural Land

MAJOR MINERAL OCCURRENCES

Ag	Silver		Hg	Mercury
Au	Gold		Id	Iodine
C	Coal		Mn	Manganese
Cu	Copper		Mo	Molybdenum
Fe	Iron Ore		N	Nitrates
G	Natural Gas		Na	Salt
Gp	Gypsum		O	Petroleum
			S	Sulfur

⚡ Water Power   ▨ Major Industrial Areas

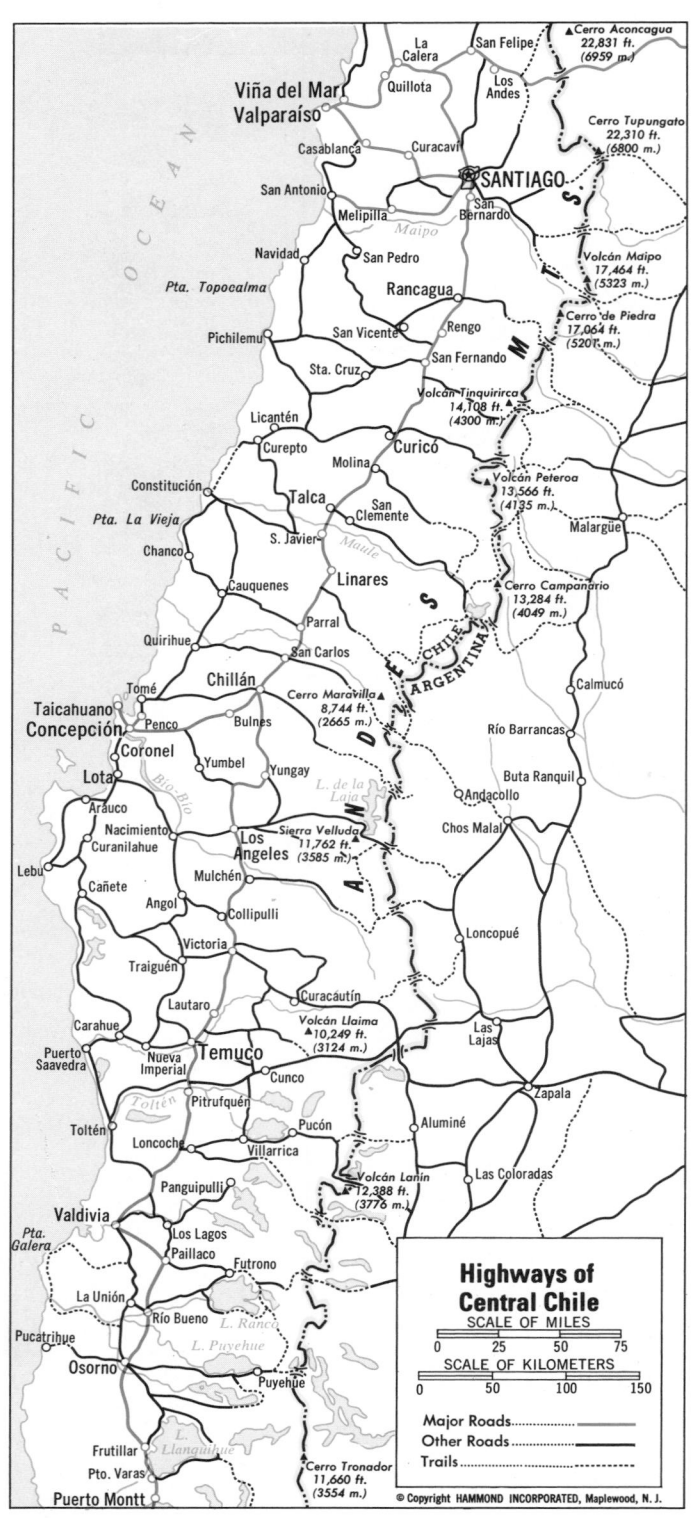

Highways of Central Chile

SCALE OF MILES
0   25   50   75
SCALE OF KILOMETERS
0   50   100   150

Major Roads ——————
Other Roads ——————
Trails -----------

© Copyright HAMMOND INCORPORATED, Maplewood, N.J.

*City and suburbs.
○ Population of commune.

PROVINCES

Buenos Aires 10,796,036 . . . D4
Catamarca 206,204 . . . . C2
Chaco 692,410 . . . . D2
Chubut 262,196 . . . . C5
Córdoba 2,407,135 . . . . . . D3
Corrientes 657,716 . . . . . . E2
Distrito Federal 2,908,001 . . H7
Entre Ríos 902,241 . . . . . . E3
Formosa 292,479 . . . . D1
Jujuy 408,514 . . . . C1
La Pampa 207,132 . . . . C4
La Rioja 163,342 . . . . C2
Mendoza 1,187,305 . . . . . . C4
Misiones 579,579 . . . . F2
Neuquén 241,904 . . . . C4
Río Negro 383,896 . . . . . . C4
Salta 662,369 . . . . D1
San Juan 469,973 . . . . C3
San Luis 212,837 . . . . C4
Santa Cruz 114,479 . . . . . . C6
Santa Fe 2,457,188 . . . . . . D3
Santiago del Estero 652,318 . D2
Tierra del Fuego, Antártida,
  e Islas del Atlántico
  Sur 29,451 . . . . C7
Tucumán 968,066 . . . . C2

CITIES and TOWNS

Abra Pampa 2,929 . . . . C1
Adolfo Alsina 7,707 . . . . . . D4

Aguaray 4,802 . . . . D1
Aguilares 20,286 . . . . C2
Aimogasta 4,640 . . . . C2
Alberti 6,440 . . . . G7
Alcorta 5,818 . . . . F6
Algarrobo del Águila C4
Allen 14,041 . . . . C4
Alpachiri 1,657 . . . . D4
Alta Gracia 30,628 . . . . . . D3
Aluminé 1,560 . . . . B4
Alvear 5,419 . . . . E2
Ameghino 2,775 . . . . D3
Añatuya 15,025 . . . . D2
Andalgalá 6,853 . . . . C2
Antofagasta de la Sierra . . . C2
Apóstoles 11,252 . . . . E2
Arrecifes 17,719 . . . . F7
Arroyo Seco 12,886 . . . . . . F6
Ascensión 3,031 . . . . F7
Avellaneda 330,654 . . . . . . G7
Ayacucho 12,363 . . . . E4
Azul 43,582 . . . . E4
Bahía Blanca 220,765 . . . . . D4
Bahía Bustamante C6
Bahía Thetis C7
Balcarce 28,985 . . . . E4
Balnearia 4,531 . . . . D3
Baradero 20,103 . . . . G6
Barrancas 3,602 . . . . F6
Barranqueras E2
Barreal 2,739 . . . . C3
Basavilbaso 7,657 . . . . G6
Belén 7,411 . . . . C2

Bella Vista, Corrientes
  14,229 . . . . E2
Bella Vista, Tucumán 9,177 . D2
Bell Ville 26,559 . . . . D3
Bolívar 16,382 . . . . D4
Bovril 4,735 . . . . G5
Bragado 27,101 . . . . F7
Buenos Aires (cap.)
  2,908,001 . . . . H7
Buenos Aires *9,927,404 . . . H7
Cafayate 5,048 . . . . C2
Calafate B7
Calchaquí 5,958 . . . . F5
Caleta Olivia 20,141 . . . . . C6
Camarones C6
Campana 51,498 . . . . G6
Cañada de Gómez 24,706 . . F6
Canals 6,627 . . . . D3
Cañuelas 14,831 . . . . G7
Carcarañá 11,121 . . . . F6
Carlos Casares 13,286 . . . . F7
Carlos Tejedor 4,421 . . . . . D4
Carmen de Areco 7,882 . . . . G7
Carmen de Patagones
  13,981 . . . . D5
Casilda 23,492 . . . . F6
Castelli 4,507 . . . . H7
Catamarca 88,432 . . . . C2
Caucete 14,512 . . . . C3
Ceres 10,743 . . . . D2
Chabás 5,156 . . . . F6
Chacabuco 26,492 . . . . F7
Chajarí 15,242 . . . . G5

Chamical 6,333 . . . . C3
Charadai 1,078 . . . . D2
Charata 13,070 . . . . D2
Chascomús 21,864 . . . . H7
Chepes 4,775 . . . . C3
Chicoana 1,844 . . . . C2
Chilecito 14,010 . . . . C2
Chivilcoy 43,779 . . . . F7
Choele-Choel 6,191 . . . . . . C4
Chos-Malal 4,823 . . . . C4
Cinco Saltos 15,094 . . . . . . C4
Cipolletti 40,123 . . . . C4
Clorinda 21,008 . . . . D1
Colón, Buenos Aires 16,070 . F6
Colón, Entre Ríos 11,648 . . . G6
Colonia Las Heras 3,176 . . . C6
Comandante Fontana 4,468 . D2
Comandante Luis Piedrabuena
  2,492 . . . . C6
Comodoro Rivadavia 96,865 . C6
Concepción 29,359 . . . . . . C2
Concepción de
  la Sierra 2,778 . . . . E2
Concepción del
  Uruguay 46,065 . . . . . . G6
Concordia 93,618 . . . . G5
Constanza 1,313 . . . . D3
Córdoba 982,018 . . . . D3
Coronda 11,554 . . . . F6
Coronel Brandsen 10,484 . . . H7
Coronel Dorrego 10,661 . . . . D4
Coronel Pringles 16,592 . . . . D4
Coronel Suárez 16,359 . . . . D4

AREA 1,072,070 sq. mi. (2,776,661 sq. km.)
POPULATION 28,438,000
CAPITAL Buenos Aires
LARGEST CITY Buenos Aires
HIGHEST POINT Cerro Aconcagua 22,831 ft.
  (6,959 m.)
MONETARY UNIT Argentine peso
MAJOR LANGUAGE Spanish
MAJOR RELIGION Roman Catholicism

Agriculture, Industry and Resources

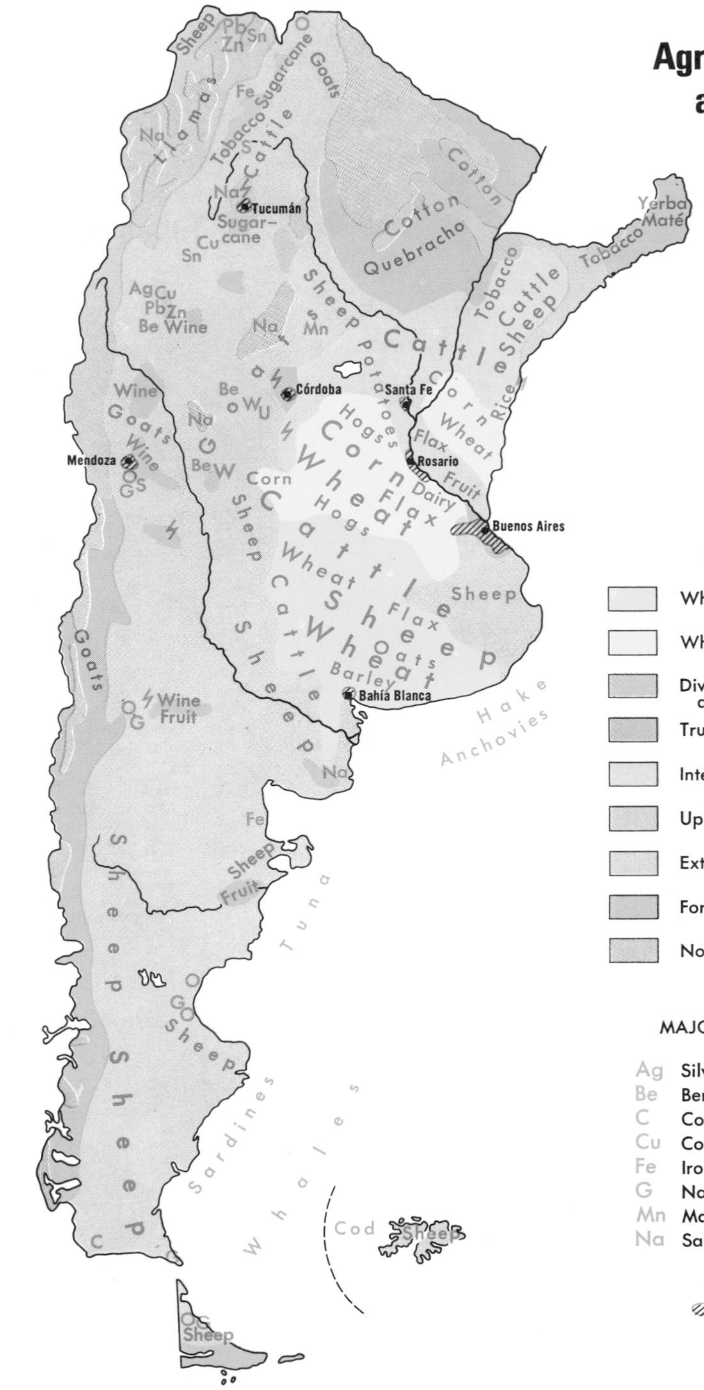

DOMINANT LAND USE

	Wheat, Livestock
	Wheat, Corn, Livestock
	Diversified Tropical Crops (chiefly plantation agriculture)
	Truck Farming, Horticulture, Special Crops
	Intensive Livestock Ranching
	Upland Livestock Grazing, Limited Agriculture
	Extensive Livestock Ranching
	Forests
	Nonagricultural Land

MAJOR MINERAL OCCURRENCES

Ag Silver   O   Petroleum
Be Beryl   Pb Lead
C   Coal   S   Sulfur
Cu Copper   Sn Tin
Fe Iron Ore   U   Uranium
G   Natural Gas   W   Tungsten
Mn Manganese   Zn Zinc
Na Salt

⚡ Water Power
▨ Major Industrial Areas

Coronel Vidal 4,774 . . . . . . E4
Corral de Bustos 8,613 . . . . D3
Corrientes 179,590 . . . . . . E2
Cosquín 13,929 . . . . D3
Crespo 10,668 . . . . F6
Cruz del Eje 23,473 . . . . . . C3
Curuzú Cuatiá 24,955 . . . . . G5
Cutral-Có 25,870 . . . . C4
Daireaux 8,150 . . . . D4
Deán Funes 16,306 . . . . . . D3
Diamante 13,464 . . . . F6
Dolavon 1,778 . . . . C5
Dolores 19,307 . . . . E4
Eduardo Castex 5,397 . . . . D4
El Bolsón 5,001 . . . . B5
Eldorado 22,821 . . . . F2
El Maitén 2,350 . . . . B5
Elortondo 4,939 . . . . F6
El Quebrachal 2,202 . . . . . . D2
Embarcación 9,016 . . . . . . D1
Empedrado 4,732 . . . . E2
Escobar 70,829 . . . . G7
Esperanza 22,838 . . . . F5
Esquel 17,228 . . . . B5
Esquina 10,380 . . . . G5
Famatina 1,237 . . . . C2
Federación 7,259 . . . . G5
Felipe Yofré 1,140 . . . . G4
Fernández 6,062 . . . . D2
Fiambalá 1,201 . . . . C2
Firmat 13,588 . . . . F6
Formosa 95,067 . . . . E2
Fortín Olmos 1,101 . . . . . . F4
Frías 20,901 . . . . C2
Gaiman 2,651 . . . . C5
Gálvez 14,711 . . . . F6
General Acha 7,647 . . . . . . C4
General Alvear, Buenos Aires
  5,481 . . . . F7
General Alvear,
  Mendoza 21,250 . . . . . . C3
General Arenales 3,332 . . . . F7
General Belgrano 10,909 . . . G7
General Conesa 3,566 . . . . . C5
General Galarza 3,057 . . . . . C6
General Güemes 15,534 . . . D1
General José de
  San Martín 16,296 . . . . . E2
General Juan Madariaga
  13,409 . . . . E4
General La Madrid 5,154 . . . D4
General Las Heras 6,005 . . . G7
General Paz 5,127 . . . . H7
General Pico 30,180 . . . . . . D4
General Ramírez 5,393 . . . . F6
General Roca 38,296 . . . . . C4
General San Martín, Buenos
  Aires 384,306 . . . . G7
General San Martín,
  La Pampa 2,168 . . . . . . D4
General Viamonte 10,112 . . . F7
General Villegas 11,307 . . . . D4
Gobernador Crespo 2,972 . . F5
Godoy Cruz 141,553 . . . . . . C3
Goya 47,357 . . . . G4
Gualeguay 24,883 . . . . G6
Gualeguaychú 51,057 . . . . . G6
Guandacol 1,351 . . . . C2
Hasenkamp 2,804 . . . . F5
Helvecia 3,927 . . . . F5
Hernandarias 3,002 . . . . . . F5
Hernando 8,619 . . . . D3
Huinca Renancó 7,187 . . . . D4
Humahuaca 3,963 . . . . C1
Humberto (Humberto
  Primo) 4,163 . . . . F5
Ibarreta 5,262 . . . . D2
Ibicuy 3,082 . . . . G6
Ingeniero Huergo 3,385 . . . . C4
Ingeniero Jacobacci 4,045 . . C5
Ingeniero Luiggi 3,002 . . . . D4
Intendente Alvear 3,640 . . . D4
Itatí 3,269 . . . . E2

Ituzaingó 8,687 . . . . E2
Jáchal 8,832 . . . . C3
Jesús María 17,594 . . . . . . D3
Joaquín V. González 6,054 . . D2
Juárez 11,798 . . . . E4
Jujuy 124,487 . . . . C1
Junín 62,080 . . . . F7
Junín de los Andes 5,638 . . . B4
La Banda 46,994 . . . . D2
Laboulaye 16,883 . . . . D3
La Carlota 8,614 . . . . D3
La Cruz 4,132 . . . . E2
La Cumbre 6,110 . . . . C3
La Falda 12,502 . . . . D3
Laguna Paiva 11,129 . . . . . F5
Lanús 465,891 . . . . H7
La Paz, Entre Ríos 14,920 . . G5
La Paz, Mendoza 4,604 . . . . C3
La Plata 560,341 . . . . H7
Laprida 6,495 . . . . D4
La Quiaca 8,289 . . . . C1
La Rioja 66,826 . . . . C2
Larroque 3,147 . . . . F5
Las Flores 18,287 . . . . E4
Las Lomitas 4,047 . . . . D1
Las Palmas 5,061 . . . . E2
Las Parejas 7,430 . . . . F6
Las Rosas 9,725 . . . . F6
Las Varillas 10,605 . . . . . . D3
La Toma 4,325 . . . . C3
Lincoln 19,009 . . . . F7
Loberia 8,898 . . . . E4
Lobos 20,798 . . . . G7
Lomas de Zamora 508,620 . . G7
Lucas González 3,015 . . . . . G6
Luján 38,919 . . . . G7
Lules 11,391 . . . . C2
Maciel 4,066 . . . . F6
Magdalena 7,135 . . . . H7
Maipú 7,269 . . . . E4
Malabrigo 3,294 . . . . F4
Malargüe 9,496 . . . . C4
Maquinchao 1,299 . . . . C5
Marcos Juárez 19,827 . . . . . D3
Mar del Plata 407,024 . . . . . E4
Máximo Paz 3,216 . . . . F6
Mburucuyá 3,044 . . . . E2
Médanos 4,511 . . . . D4
Mendoza 596,796 . . . . C3
Mercedes, Buenos Aires
  46,581 . . . . G7
Mercedes, Corrientes
  20,603 . . . . G4
Mercedes, San Luis 50,856 . . C3
Merlo 293,059 . . . . G7
Metán 18,928 . . . . D2
Miramar 15,473 . . . . E4
Monte Caseros 18,247 . . . . G5
Monte Quemado 4,707 . . . . D2
Monteros 15,832 . . . . C2
Morón 596,769 . . . . G7
Moreteros 11,456 . . . . D3
Navarro 7,176 . . . . G7
Necochea 50,939 . . . . E4
Neuquén 90,037 . . . . C4
Nogoyá 15,862 . . . . F6
Ñorquincó B5
Nueve de Julio 26,608 . . . . . F7
Oberá 27,311 . . . . F2
Olavarría 63,686 . . . . D4
Oliva 9,231 . . . . D3
Palo Santo 3,088 . . . . E2
Paraná 159,581 . . . . F5
Paso de Los Libres 24,112 . . E2
Pedro Luro 3,142 . . . . D4
Pehuajó 25,613 . . . . D4
Pellegrini 3,940 . . . . D4
Pergamino 68,989 . . . . F6
Pico Truncado 9,626 . . . . . . C6
Pigüé 10,793 . . . . D4
Pilar 3,805 . . . . F5
Pirané 9,039 . . . . E2
Plaza Huincul 7,988 . . . . . . B4

(continued on following page)

Topography

0 150 300 MI.
0 150 300 KM.

| 5,000 m. | 2,000 m. | 1,000 m. | 500 m. | 200 m. | 100 m. | Sea | Below |
| 16,404 ft. | 6,562 ft. | 3,281 ft. | 1,640 ft. | 656 ft. | 328 ft. | Level | |

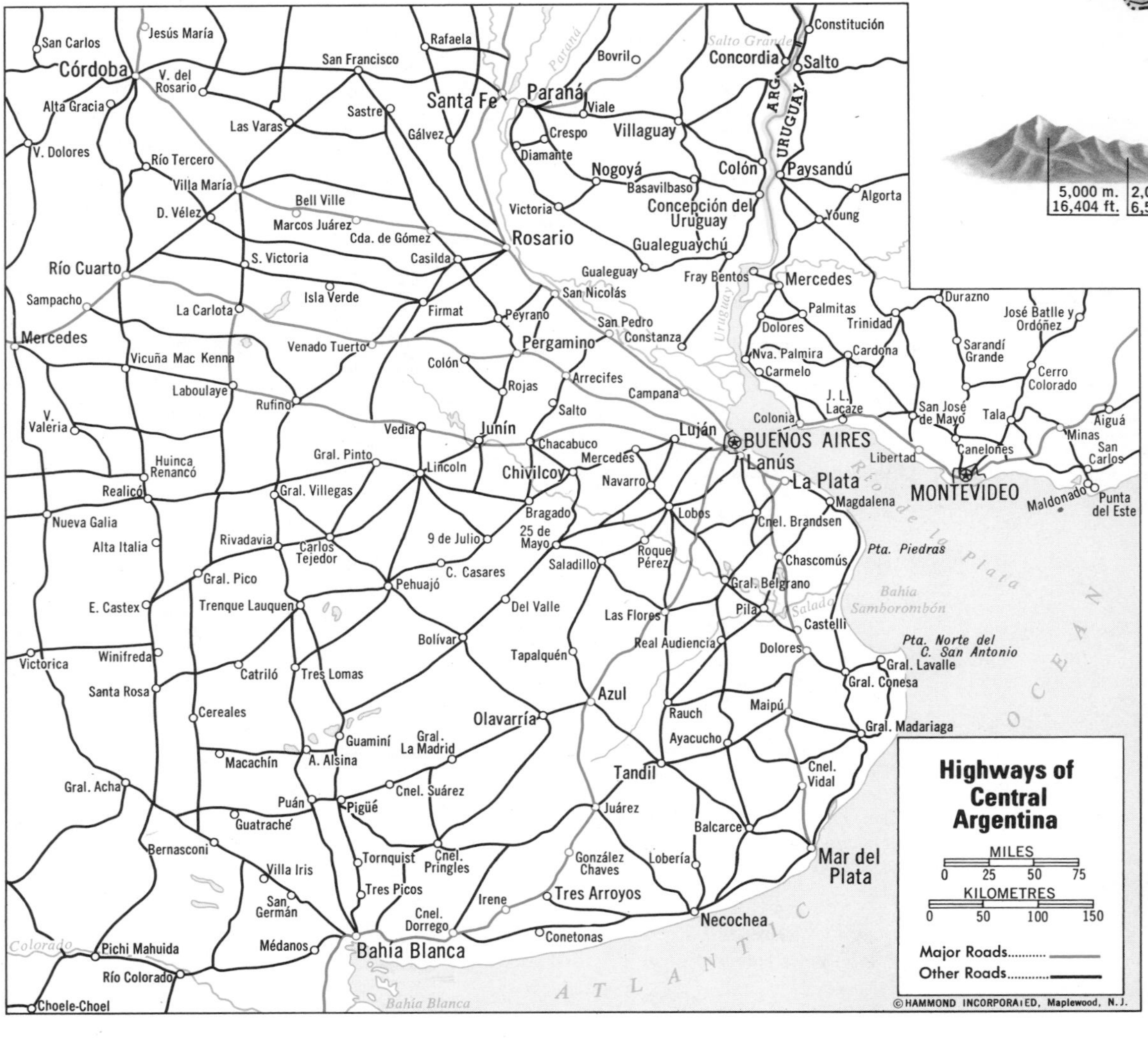

Highways of Central Argentina

MILES
0 25 50 75
KILOMETRES
0 50 100 150

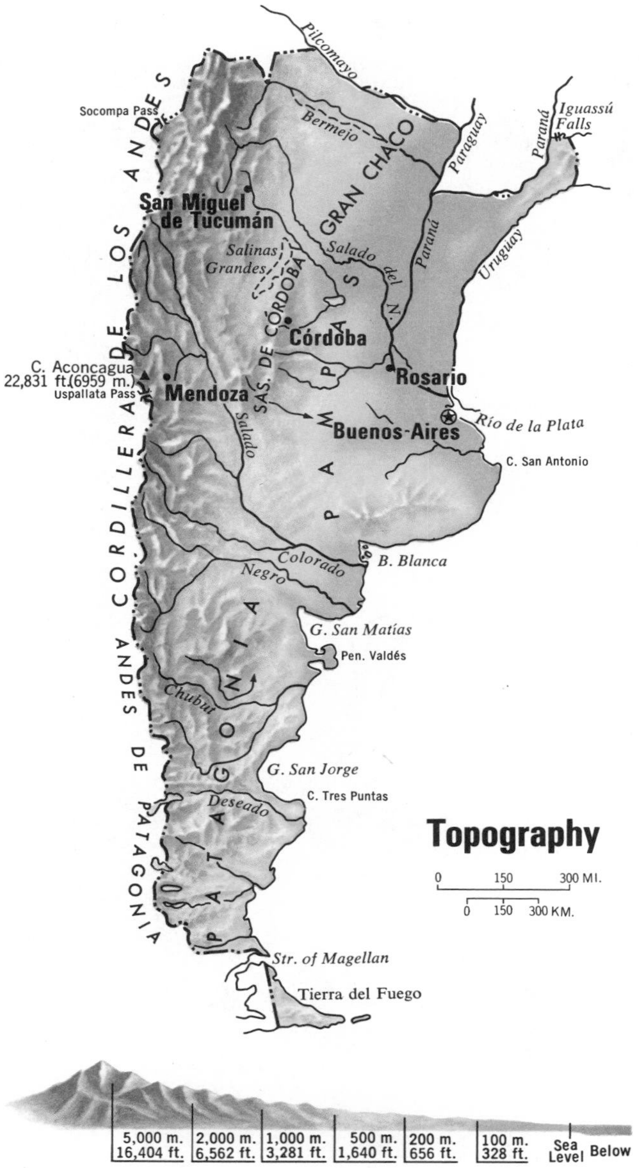

Major Roads
Other Roads

© HAMMOND INCORPORATED, Maplewood, N.J.

Argentina

CONIC PROJECTION

SCALE OF MILES

0 50 100 200 300

SCALE OF KILOMETERS

0 50 100 200 300

Capitals of Countries	☆
Capitals of Provinces	◉
International Boundaries	·—··—··—
Boundaries of Provinces	·—·—·—

Scale 1:13,000,000

FALKLAND ISLANDS
(ISLAS MALVINAS)
(Br., claimed by Arg.)

BUENOS AIRES
(DISTRITO FEDERAL)

® Copyright HAMMOND INCORPORATED, Maplewood, N.J.

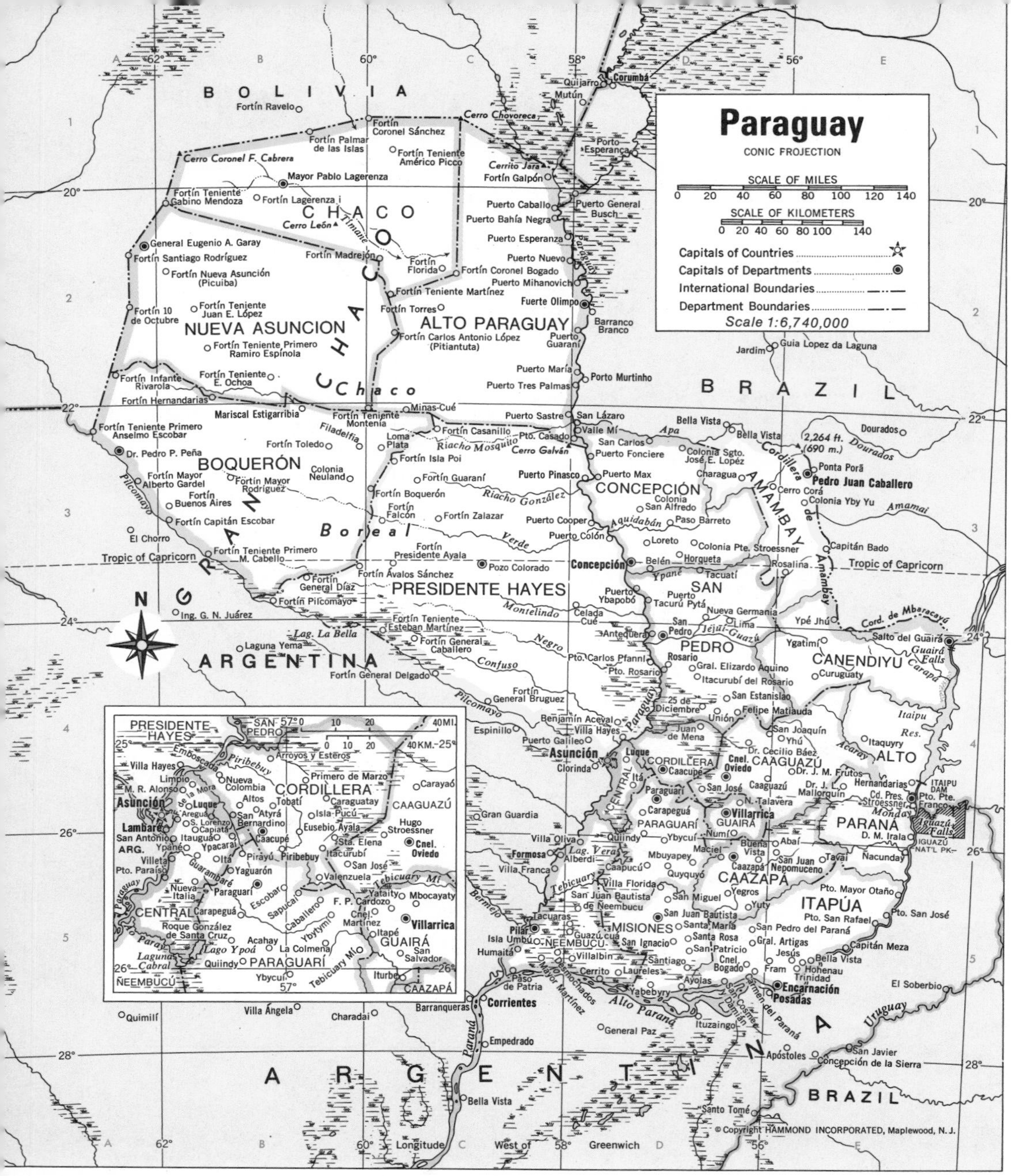

Paraguay

CONIC PROJECTION

SCALE OF MILES

0 20 40 60 80 100 120 140

SCALE OF KILOMETERS

0 20 40 60 80 100 120 140

Capitals of Countries .... ★
Capitals of Departments .... ◉
International Boundaries .... —··—··—
Department Boundaries .... —·—·—

Scale 1:6,740,000

© Copyright HAMMOND INCORPORATED, Maplewood, N.J.

PARAGUAY

DEPARTMENTS

Alto Paraguay	C2
Alto Paraná	E4
Amambay	D3
Asunción	A4
Boquerón	B3
Caaguazú	D-E4
Caazapá	E5
Canendiyu	E4
Central	D4
Chaco	B-C2
Concepción	D3
Cordillera	D4
Guairá	D4
Itapúa	E5
Misiones	D5
Ñeembucú	C-D5
Nueva Asunción	B2
Paraguarí	D4-5
Presidente Hayes	C3
San Pedro	D4-5

CITIES and TOWNS

Abaí 1,507	E4
Acahay 1,937	B5
Alberdi 2,346	D5
Altos 1,441	B4
Antequera 1,281	D4
Aregua 3,941	B4
Arroyos y Esteros 1,253	B4
Asunción (cap.) 387,676	A4
Atyrá 1,427	B4
Ayolas 309	D5
Belén 1,219	D3
Bella Vista 3,101	D3
Bella Vista 1,421	E5
Benjamín Aceval 2,877	C4
Buena Vista 1,353	D5
Caacupé 7,278	B5
Caaguazú 7,950	D4
Caapucú 1,400	D5
Caazapá 3,132	D5
Caballero 1,225	B5
Capiatá 2,827	B4
Capitán Bado 915	E3
Capitán Meza 375	E5
Caraguatay 1,439	B5
Carapeguá 3,416	D5
Carayaó 1,190	C4
Carmen del Paraná 1,980	D5
Cerrito 958	C5
Ciudad Presidente Stroessner 7,085	E4
Concepción 19,392	D3
Coronel Bogado 3,973	D5
Coronel Martínez 1,598	B5
Coronel Oviedo 13,786	C5
Curuguaty 1,112	E4
Desmochados 551	D5
Doctor Cecilio Báez 1,300	C5
Doctor Juan L. Mallorquín 1,913	E4
Doctor Juan Manuel Frutos 1,494	E4
Doctor M. Irala 468	E4
Emboscada 1,222	B4
Encarnación 23,343	E5
Escobar 548	B5
Eusebio Ayala 4,328	B4
Fernando de la Mora 36,834	B4
Filadelfia 1,438	B3
Fram 1,090	E5
Fuerte Olimpo 3,063	C2
General Aquino 3,542	D5
General Artigas 3,542	D5
General Elizardo Aquino 1,304	D4
General Eugenio A. Garay 740	A2
Guarambaré 3,640	B5
Hernandarias 3,898	E4
Hohenau 1,121	E5
Horqueta 4,328	D3
Hugo Stroessner 536	C4
Humaitá 938	C5
Isla Pucú 1,766	B4
Isla Umbú 236	C5
Itá 7,041	B4
Itacurubí 1,997	B5
Itacurubí del Rosario 2,467	D4
Itapé 1,376	C5
Itaquyry	E4
Itauguá 3,767	B5
Iturbe 3,413	C5
Jesús 1,495	E5
Juan de Mena 1,027	D4
La Colmena 1,804	B5
Lambaré 31,656	A4
Laureles 435	D5
Lima 1,098	D4
Limpio 2,219	B4
Loreto 1,258	D3
Luque 13,921	B4
Maciel 376	D5
Mariano Roque Alonso 1,492	A4
Mariscal Estigarribia 3,150	B3
Mayor Martínez 324	C5
Mayor Pablo Lagerenza	B1
Mbocayaty 925	C5
Mbuyapey 1,560	D5
Ñacunday 380	E5
Natalicio Talavera 1,228	D4
Nueva Germania 572	D5
Nueva Italia 1,517	D5
Numí 941	D4
Paraguarí 5,036	B5
Paso de Patria 698	C5
Pedro Juan Caballero 21,033	E3
Pilar 12,506	C5
Pirayú 2,698	B5
Piribebuy 4,497	B5
Primero de Marzo 696	D4
Puerto Casado 4,078	C3
Puerto Guaraní 302	C2
Puerto Pinasco 5,477	C3
Puerto Presidente Franco 4,152	E4
Puerto Sastre 160	C3
Quiindy 2,664	B5
Quyquyó 928	D5
Roque González de Santa Cruz 1,375	B5
Rosario 4,165	D4
Salto del Guairá	E4
San Antonio 4,906	A5
San Bernardino 949	B4
San Cosme y Damián 602	D5
San Estanislao 4,753	D4
San Ignacio 6,116	D5
San Joaquín 536	E4
San José 3,102	B5
San Juan Bautista 6,457	D5
San Juan Bautista de Ñeembucú 688	
San Juan Nepomuceno 2,974	D5
San Lázaro 1,767	C3
San Lorenzo 11,616	B4
San Miguel 1,030	D5
San Patricio 1,130	D5
San Pedro 3,186	D3
San Pedro del Paraná 2,723	D5
San Salvador 1,393	C5
Santa Elena 1,439	B5
Santa María 793	D5
Santa Rosa 3,736	D5
Santiago 1,265	D5
Sapucaí 1,864	B5
Tacuaras 193	C5
Tacuatí 836	D3
Tavaí 472	E5
Tebicuary Mí 183	B5
Tobatí 4,983	B4
Trinidad 837	E5
Unión 1,286	D5
Valenzuela 1,108	D5
Valle Mí 1,318	D3
25 de Diciembre 439	D5
Villa Florida 1,261	D5
Villa Franca 359	C5
Villa Hayes 4,749	C4
Villa Oliva 564	C5
Villarrica 17,687	C5
Villeta 3,156	A5
Yabebyry 797	C5
Yaguarón 3,368	B5
Yataity 1,159	C5
Ybycuí 1,736	B5
Ybytymí 816	B5
Yegros 1,051	D5
Ygatimí 396	E4
Yhú 964	D4
Ypacaraí 5,195	B5
Ypané 1,474	B5
Ype Jhú 645	E3
Yuty 2,392	D5

OTHER FEATURES

Acaray (riv.)	E4
Alto Paraná (riv.)	D5
Amambay, Cordillera de (mts.)	D-E3
Apa (riv.)	D3
Aquidabán (riv.)	D3
Chaco Boreal (reg.)	B2-3
Chovoreca (mt.)	C1
Confuso (riv.)	C4
Coronel F. Cabrera (mt.)	B1
González, Riacho (riv.)	C3
Gran Chaco (reg.)	B2-3
Iguazú (falls)	E4
Itaipú (res.)	E4
Jara (hill)	C1
Mbaracayú, Cordillera de (mts.)	E3
Monday (riv.)	E4
Montelindo (riv.)	C3
Mosquito, Riacho (riv.)	C2
Negro (riv.)	C4
Paraguay (riv.)	D4
Pilcomayo (riv.)	C4
Tebicuary (riv.)	C5
Timane (riv.)	B2
Vera (lag.)	D5
Verde (riv.)	C3

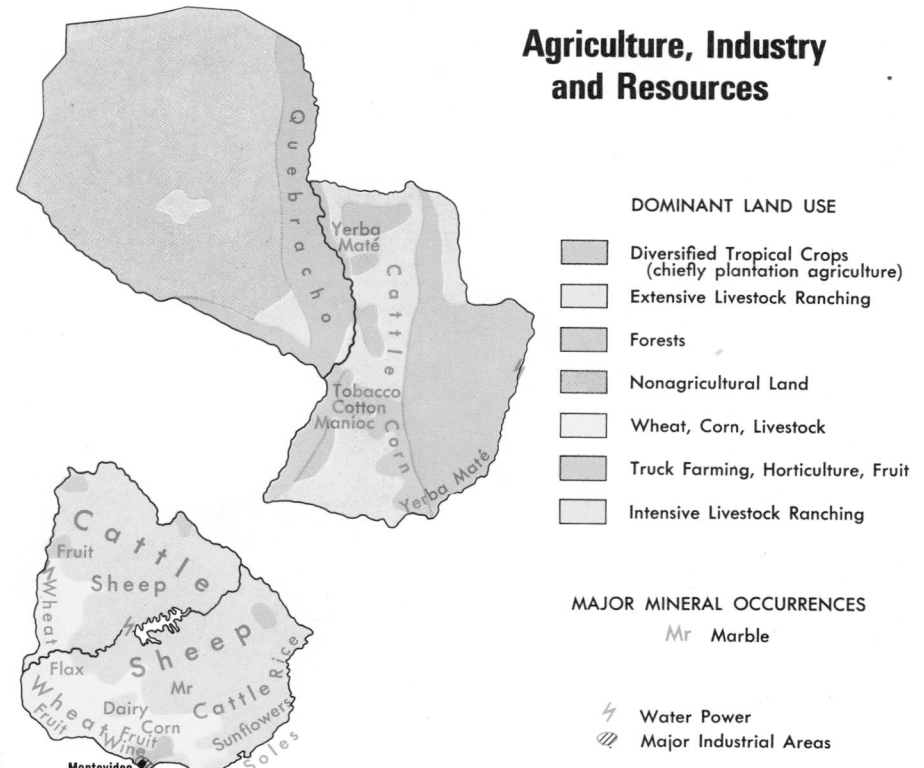

Agriculture, Industry and Resources

DOMINANT LAND USE

- Diversified Tropical Crops (chiefly plantation agriculture)
- Extensive Livestock Ranching
- Forests
- Nonagricultural Land
- Wheat, Corn, Livestock
- Truck Farming, Horticulture, Fruit
- Intensive Livestock Ranching

MAJOR MINERAL OCCURRENCES

Mr Marble

⚡ Water Power

▨ Major Industrial Areas

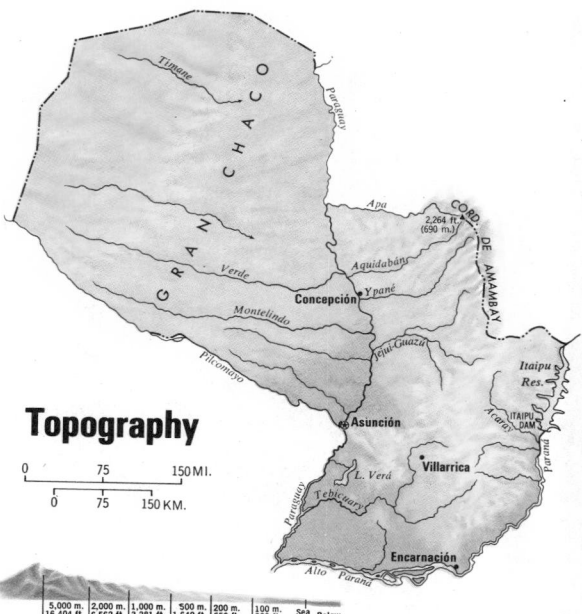

Topography

0 75 150 MI.

0 75 150 KM.

5,000 m. / 16,404 ft. 2,000 m. / 6,562 ft. 1,000 m. / 3,281 ft. 500 m. / 1,640 ft. 200 m. / 656 ft. 100 m. / 328 ft. Sea Level Below

URUGUAY

DEPARTMENTS

PARAGUAY

AREA 157,047 sq. mi. (406,752 sq. km.)
POPULATION 2,973,000
CAPITAL Asunción
LARGEST CITY Asunción
HIGHEST POINT Amambay Range
  2,264 ft. (690 m.)
MONETARY UNIT guaraní
MAJOR LANGUAGES Spanish, Guaraní
MAJOR RELIGION Roman Catholicism

URUGUAY

AREA 72,172 sq. mi. (186,925 sq. km.)
POPULATION 2,899,000
CAPITAL Montevideo
LARGEST CITY Montevideo
HIGHEST POINT Mirador Nacional 1,644 ft.
  (501 m.)
MONETARY UNIT Uruguayan peso
MAJOR LANGUAGE Spanish
MAJOR RELIGION Roman Catholicism

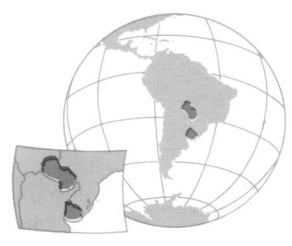

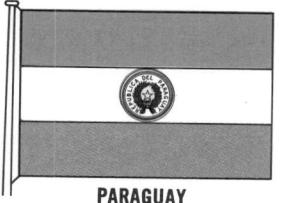

PARAGUAY

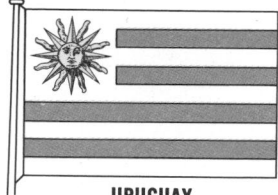

URUGUAY

Topography

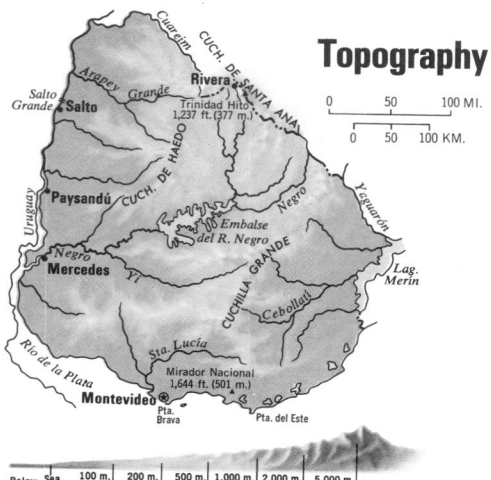

| Below Sea Level | 100 m. 328 ft. | 200 m. 656 ft. | 500 m. 1,640 ft. | 1,000 m. 3,281 ft. | 2,000 m. 6,562 ft. | 5,000 m. 16,404 ft. |

0   50   100 MI.
0   50   100 KM.

Uruguay

CONIC PROJECTION

SCALE OF MILES
0   20   40   60

SCALE OF KILOMETERS
0   20   40   60

Capitals of Countries ....☆
Department Capitals ....●
International Boundaries ....━ ━ ━
Department Boundaries ....─ ─ ─

Scale 1:3,800,000

© Copyright HAMMOND INCORPORATED, Maplewood, N.J.

Longitude 56° West of Greenwich 55°

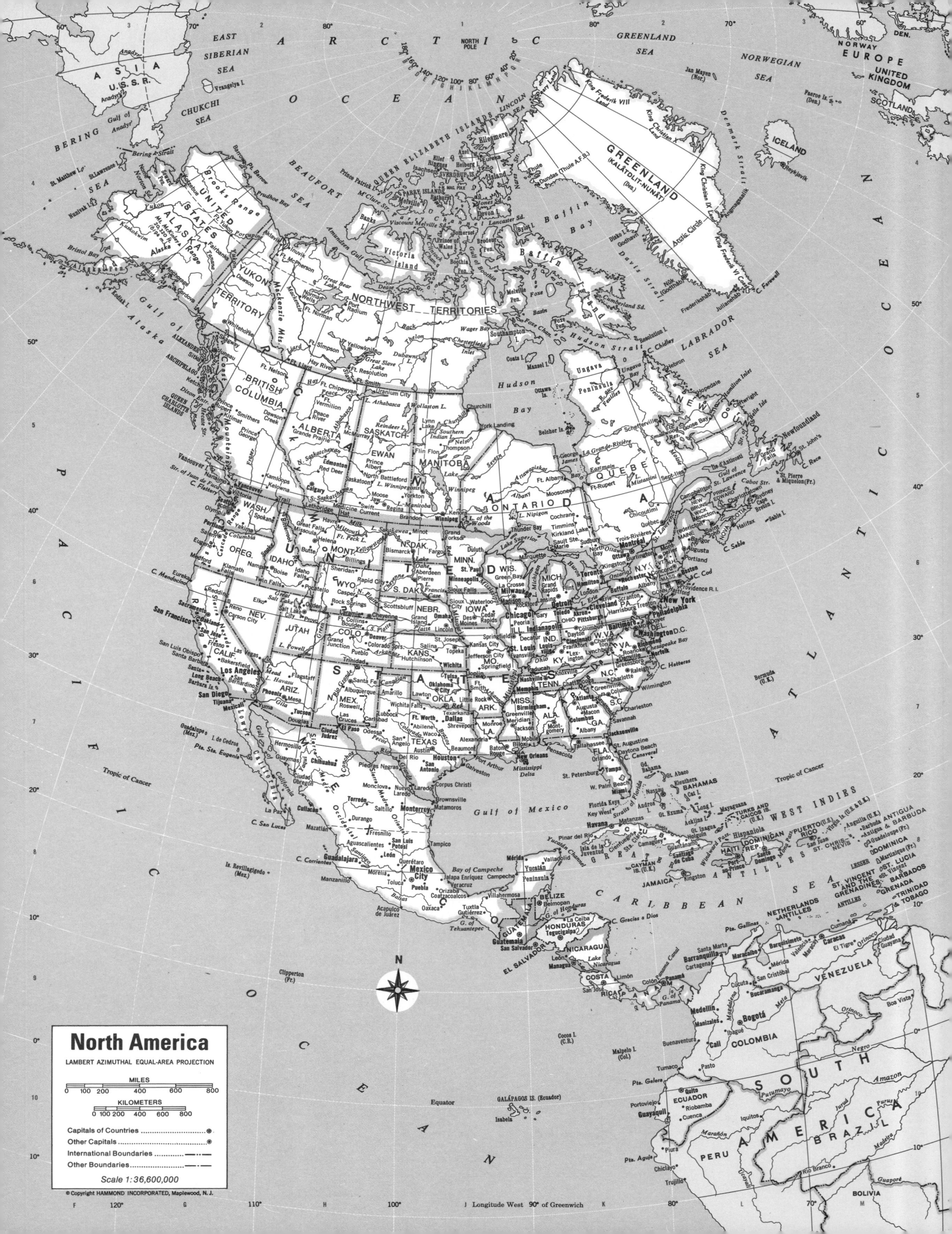

North America

LAMBERT AZIMUTHAL EQUAL-AREA PROJECTION

MILES
0 100 200 400 600 800

KILOMETERS
0 100 200 400 600 800

Capitals of Countries	⊛
Other Capitals	⊛
International Boundaries	— ·· — ··
Other Boundaries	— · — ·

Scale 1:36,600,000

© Copyright HAMMOND INCORPORATED, Maplewood, N.J.

Population Distribution

AREA 9,363,000 sq. mi.
(24,250,170 sq. km.)
POPULATION 370,000,000
LARGEST CITY New York
HIGHEST POINT Mt. McKinley 20,320 ft.
(6,194 m.)
LOWEST POINT Death Valley -282 ft.
(-86 m.)

Vegetation

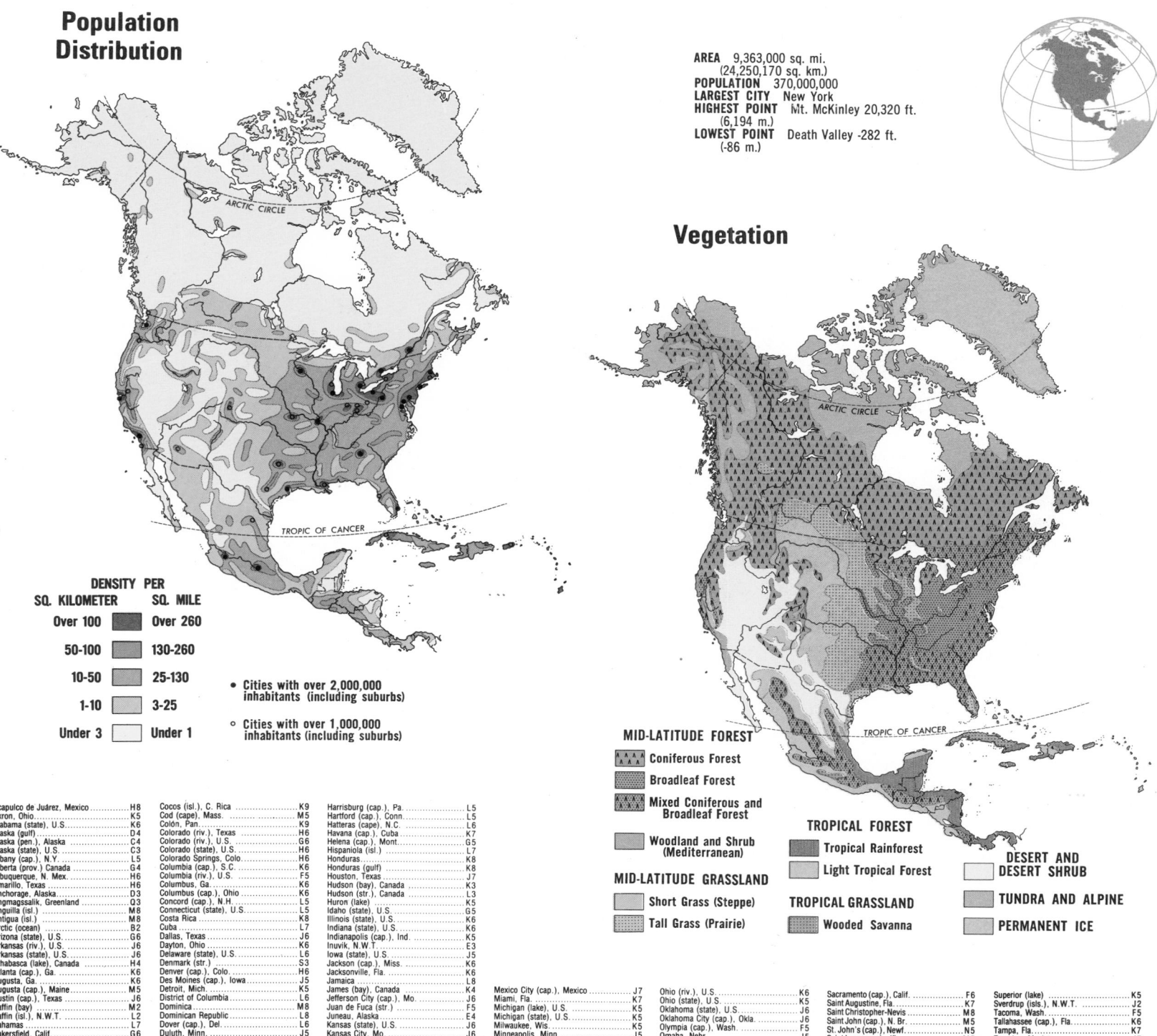

DENSITY PER

SQ. KILOMETER	SQ. MILE
Over 100	Over 260
50-100	130-260
10-50	25-130
1-10	3-25
Under 3	Under 1

• Cities with over 2,000,000 inhabitants (including suburbs)

○ Cities with over 1,000,000 inhabitants (including suburbs)

MID-LATITUDE FOREST

- Coniferous Forest
- Broadleaf Forest
- Mixed Coniferous and Broadleaf Forest
- Woodland and Shrub (Mediterranean)

MID-LATITUDE GRASSLAND

- Short Grass (Steppe)
- Tall Grass (Prairie)

TROPICAL FOREST

- Tropical Rainforest
- Light Tropical Forest

TROPICAL GRASSLAND

- Wooded Savanna

DESERT AND DESERT SHRUB

TUNDRA AND ALPINE

PERMANENT ICE

Average January Temperature

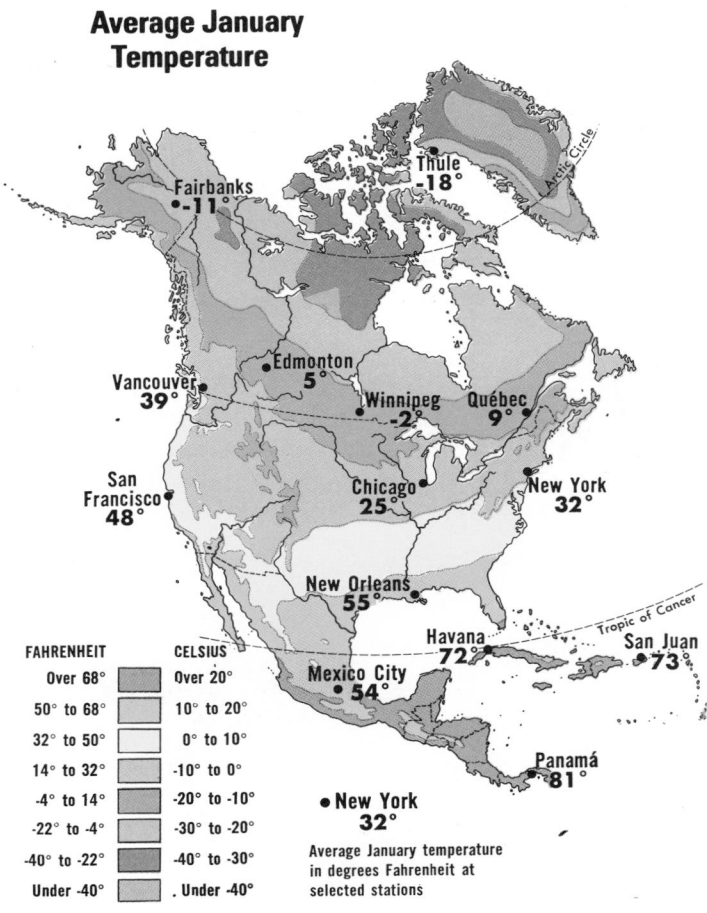

Fairbanks -11°
Thule -18°
Edmonton 5°
Vancouver 39°
Winnipeg -2°
Québec 9°
San Francisco 48°
Chicago 25°
New York 32°
New Orleans 55°
Havana 72°
San Juan 73°
Mexico City 54°
Panamá 81°

FAHRENHEIT		CELSIUS
Over 68°		Over 20°
50° to 68°		10° to 20°
32° to 50°		0° to 10°
14° to 32°		-10° to 0°
-4° to 14°		-20° to -10°
-22° to -4°		-30° to -20°
-40° to -22°		-40° to -30°
Under -40°		Under -40°

● New York 32°

Average January temperature in degrees Fahrenheit at selected stations

Average July Temperature

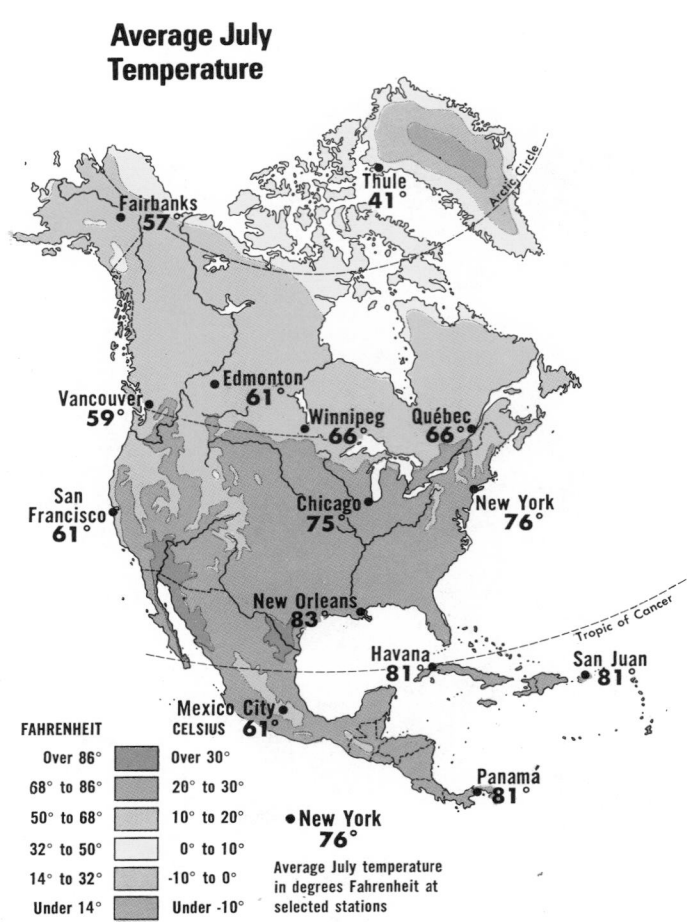

Thule 41°
Fairbanks 57°
Edmonton 61°
Vancouver 59°
Winnipeg 66°
Québec 66°
San Francisco 61°
Chicago 75°
New York 76°
New Orleans 83°
Havana 81°
San Juan 81°
Mexico City 61°
Panamá 81°

FAHRENHEIT		CELSIUS
Over 86°		Over 30°
68° to 86°		20° to 30°
50° to 68°		10° to 20°
32° to 50°		0° to 10°
14° to 32°		-10° to 0°
Under 14°		Under -10°

● New York 76°

Average July temperature in degrees Fahrenheit at selected stations

Rainfall

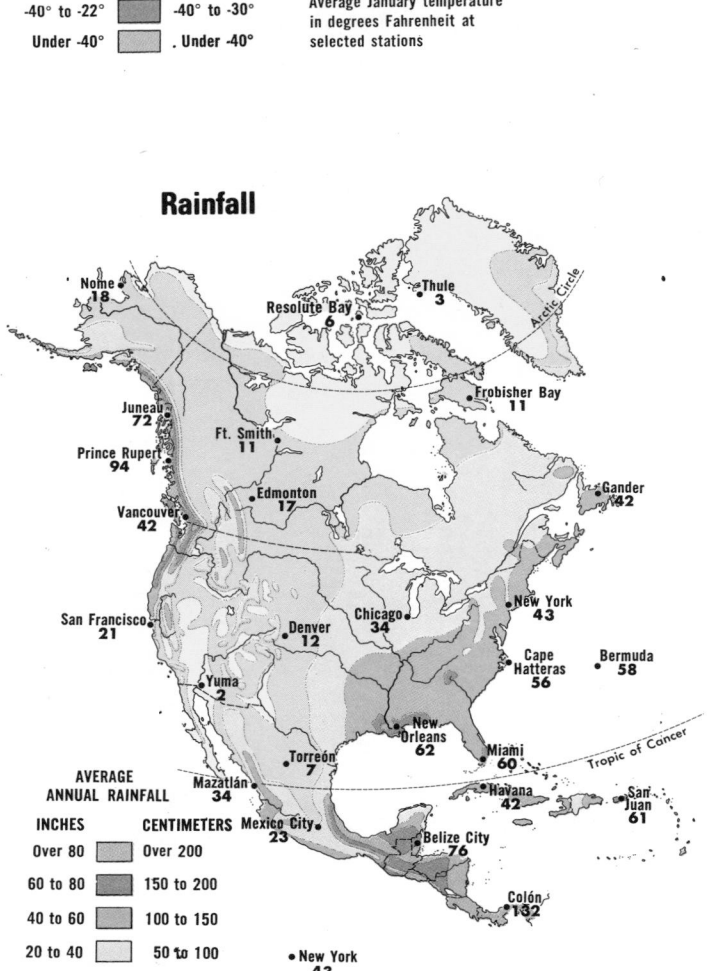

Nome 18
Thule 3
Resolute Bay 6
Frobisher Bay 11
Juneau 72
Ft. Smith 11
Prince Rupert 94
Edmonton 17
Gander 42
Vancouver 42
San Francisco 21
Denver 12
Chicago 34
New York 43
Yuma 2
Cape Hatteras 56
Bermuda 58
Torreón 7
New Orleans 62
Miami 60
Mazatlán 34
Havana 42
San Juan 61
Mexico City 23
Belize City 76
Colón 132

AVERAGE ANNUAL RAINFALL

INCHES		CENTIMETERS
Over 80		Over 200
60 to 80		150 to 200
40 to 60		100 to 150
20 to 40		50 to 100
10 to 20		25 to 50
Under 10		Under 25

● New York 43

Average annual rainfall in inches at selected stations

Vegetation/Relief

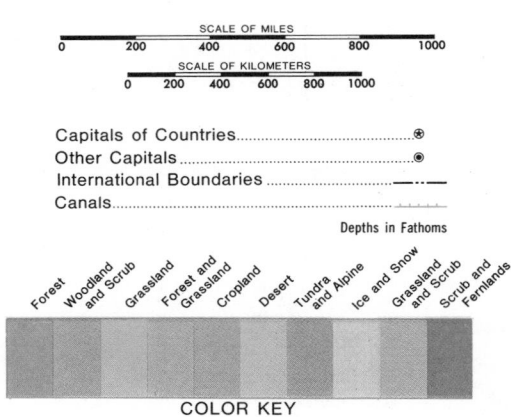

SCALE OF MILES
0   200   400   600   800   1000

SCALE OF KILOMETERS
0   200   400   600   800   1000

Capitals of Countries............................⊛
Other Capitals..◉
International Boundaries .... —·—
Canals..

Depths in Fathoms

Forest | Woodland and Scrub | Grassland | Forest and Grassland | Cropland | Desert | Tundra and Alpine | Ice and Snow | Grassland and Scrub | Scrub and Farmlands

COLOR KEY

Longitude 90° West of Greenwich

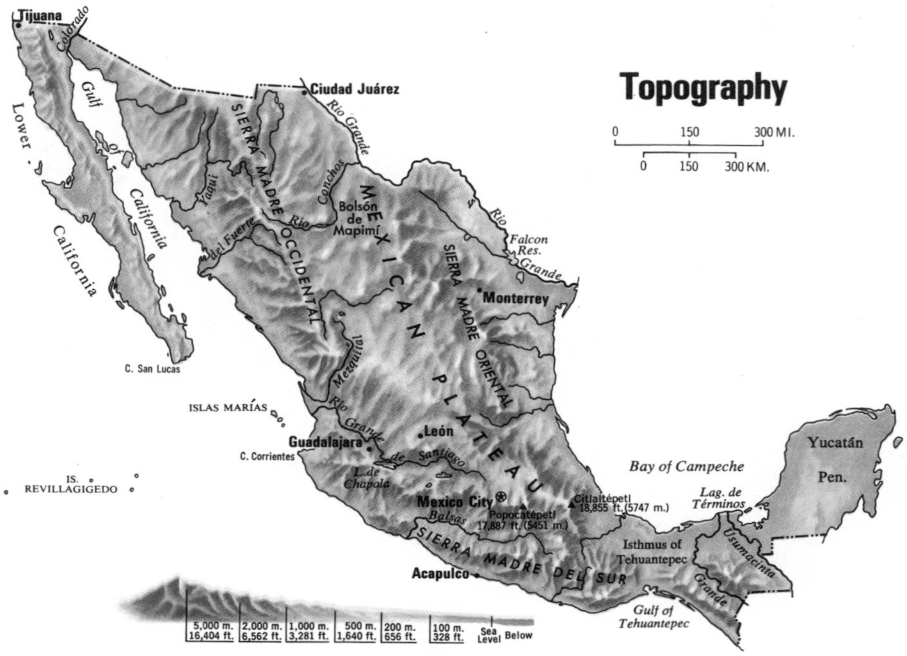

Topography
0 150 300 MI.
0 150 300 KM.
Tijuana
Colorado
Lower California
Gulf of California
Ciudad Juárez
Rio Grande
SIERRA MADRE OCCIDENTAL
Conchos
Bolsón de Mapimí
MEXICAN PLATEAU
Falcon Res.
Monterrey
SIERRA MADRE ORIENTAL
C. San Lucas
ISLAS MARÍAS
IS. REVILLAGIGEDO
C. Corrientes
Guadalajara
León
L. de Chapala
Mexico City
Popocatépetl 17,887 ft. (5451 m.)
Citlaltépetl 18,855 ft. (5747 m.)
Balsas
SIERRA MADRE DEL SUR
Acapulco
Bay of Campeche
Lag. de Términos
Isthmus of Tehuantepec
Gulf of Tehuantepec
Yucatán Pen.
5,000 m. 16,404 ft.
2,000 m. 6,562 ft.
1,000 m. 3,281 ft.
500 m. 1,640 ft.
200 m. 656 ft.
100 m. 328 ft.
Sea Level
Below

STATES

Aguascalientes 504,300 H6
Baja California 1,227,400 B1
Baja California Sur 221,000 C3
Campeche 371,800 O7
Chiapas 2,097,500 N8
Chihuahua 1,935,100 F2
Coahuila 1,561,000 H3
Colima 339,400 G7
Distrito Federal 9,377,300 L1
Durango 1,160,300 G4
Guanajuato 3,045,600 J6
Guerrero 2,174,200 J8
Hidalgo 1,518,200 K6
Jalisco 4,296,500 H6
México 7,542,300 K7
Michoacán 3,049,400 H7
Morelos 931,400 K7
Nayarit 729,500 G6
Nuevo León 2,463,500 K4
Oaxaca 2,517,500 L8
Puebla 3,285,300 L7
Querétaro 730,900 J6
Quintana Roo 209,900 P7
San Luis Potosí 1,669,900 J5
Sinaloa 1,882,200 F4
Sonora 1,498,100 D2
Tabasco 1,150,000 N7
Tamaulipas 1,924,900 K4
Tlaxcala 548,500 N1
Veracruz 5,263,800 L7
Yucatán 1,034,300 P6
Zacatecas 1,144,700 H5

CITIES and TOWNS

Acala 11,483 N8
Acámbaro 32,257 J7
Acaponeta 11,844 G5
Acapulco de Juárez 309,254 K8
Acatlán de Osorio 7,624 K7
Acatzingo de Hidalgo 6,905 N2
Acayucan 21,173 M8
Aconchi 1,596 D2
Actopan, Hidalgo 11,037 K6
Actopan, Veracruz 2,265 Q1
Agua Dulce 21,060 M7
Agualeguas 2,502 J3
Agua Prieta 20,754 E1
Aguascalientes 181,277 H6
Aguililla 5,715 H7
Ahome 4,182 E4
Ahuacatitlán 6,436 L1
Ahuacatlán 5,350 G6
Ahumada 6,466 F1
Ajalpan 8,238 L7
Alamo 9,954 L6
Álamos 4,269 E3
Aldama, Chihuahua 6,047 G2
Aldama, Tamaulipas 3,033 L5
Aljojuca 3,204 O1
Allende, Coahuila 11,076 J2
Allende, Nuevo León 9,914 J4
Almoloya del Río 3,714 K1
Altamira 6,053 L5
Altar 2,519 D1
Altepexi 6,661 L7
Alto Lucero 3,698 P1
Altotonga 6,754 P1
Alvarado 15,592 M7
Amatlán de los Reyes 3,664 P2
Amealco 2,960 K6
Ameca 21,018 H6
Amecameca de Juárez 16,276 L1
Amozoc de Mota 9,203 N2
Anáhuac, Chihuahua 10,886 F2
Anáhuac, Nuevo León 8,168 J3
Angostura 2,663 E4
Antiguo Morelos 1,569 K5
Apan 13,705 M1
Apatzingán de la Constitución 44,849 H7
Apizaco 21,189 N1
Aquiles Serdán 2,565 G2
Aramberri 1,786 J5
Arandas 18,934 H6
Arcelia 10,024 J7
Ario de Rosales 8,774 J7
Arizpe 1,736 D1
Armería 10,616 G7
Arriaga 13,193 N8
Arteaga 5,324 H7
Ascensión 4,104 E1
Asunción Nochixtlán 3,235 L8
Atlixco 41,967 M2
Atotonilco el Alto 16,271 H6
Atoyac de Álvarez 8,874 J8
Autlán de Navarro 20,398 G7
Axochiapan 8,283 M2
Ayutla de los Libres 3,618 K8
Azcapotzalco 534,554 L1
Azoyú 3,446 K8
Bacadéhuachi 1,514 E2
Bacalar 2,121 P7
Bachíniva 1,809 F2
Bácum 2,668 D3
Bahía Tortugas 1,457 B3
Balancán de Domínguez 3,669 O8
Bamoa 5,866 E4
Banderilla 3,488 P1
Baviácora 2,049 E2
Benjamín Hill 5,366 D1
Bernardino de Sahagún 12,327 M1
Boca del Río 2,354 Q2
Bolonchén de Rejón 2,342 O7
Buenaventura 3,924 F2
Burgos 673 K4
Cabo San Lucas 1,534 E5
Cacahoatán 5,079 N9
Cadereyta Jiménez 13,586 K4
Calkiní 6,870 O6
Calnali 3,318 K6
Calpulálpan 8,659 M1
Calvillo 6,453 H6
Campeche 69,506 O7
Cananea 17,518 D1
Canatlán 5,983 G4
Cancún 326 Q6
Candela 1,689 J3
Candelaria 1,982 O7
Cañitas de Felipe Pescador 4,885 H5
Capulhuac de Mirafuentes 8,289 K1
Carbo 2,804 D2
Cárdenas, San Luis Potosí 12,020 K6
Cárdenas, Tabasco 15,643 N8
Carichic 1,520 F2
Castaños 8,996 J3
Catemaco 11,786 M7
Ceballos 2,937 H3
Cedral 4,057 J5
Celaya 79,977 J6
Celestún 1,490 O6
Cerritos 10,421 J5
Cerro Azul 20,259 L6
Chahuites 5,218 M8
Chalchihuites 1,894 G5
Chalco de Díaz Covarrubias 12,172 M1
Champotón 6,606 O7
Charcas 10,491 J5
Chetumal 23,685 Q7
Chiapa de Corzo 8,571 N8
Chiautempan 12,327 N1
Chietla 4,602 M2
Chignahuapan 3,805 N1
Chihuahua 327,313 F2
Chilapa de Álvarez 9,204 K8
Chilpancingo de los Bravos 36,193 K8
China, Nuevo León 4,958 K4
Chocomán 5,114 P2
Choix 2,503 E3
Cholula de Rivadavia 15,399 M1
Cihuatlán 9,451 G7
Cintalapa de Figueroa 12,036 N8
Ciudad Acuña (Villa Acuña) 30,276 J2
Ciudad Altamirano 8,694 J7
Ciudad Camargo, Chihuahua 24,030 G3
Ciudad Camargo, Tamaulipas 5,953 K3
Ciudad del Carmen 34,656 N7
Ciudad Delicias 52,446 G2
Ciudad del Maíz 5,241 K5
Ciudad de Río Grande 11,651 H5
Ciudad Guerrero 3,110 F2
Ciudad Guzmán 48,166 H7
Ciudad Hidalgo, Chiapas 4,105 N9
Ciudad Hidalgo, Michoacán 24,692 J7
Ciudad Juárez 424,135 F1
Ciudad Lerdo 19,803 H4
Ciudad Madero 115,302 L5
Ciudad Mante 51,247 K5
Ciudad Mendoza 18,696 O2
Ciudad Miguel Alemán 11,259 K3
Ciudad Obregón 144,795 E3
Ciudad Río Bravo 39,018 K4
Ciudad Satélite 35,083 L1
Ciudad Serdán 9,581 O2
Ciudad Valles 47,587 K5
Ciudad Victoria 83,897 K5
Coalcomán de Matamoros 4,875 H7
Coatepec 21,542 P1
Coatetelco 5,268 L2
Coatzacoalcos 69,753 M7
Coatzingo 3,038 N2
Cocorit 4,478 E3
Colima 58,450 H7
Colón 3,346 K6
Colotlán 6,135 H5
Comala 5,592 H7
Comalcalco 14,963 N7
Comitán de Domínguez 21,249 O8
Compostela 9,801 G6
Concepción del Oro 8,144 J4
Concordia 3,947 G5
Contla 7,517 N1
Copala 3,783 K8
Coquimatlán 6,212 G7
Córdoba 78,495 P2
Cosalá 2,279 F4
Cosamaloapan de Carpio 19,766 M7
Cosautlán de Carvajal 2,039 P1
Coscomatepec de Bravo 6,023 P2
Cosío 2,680 H5
Costa Rica 11,795 F4
Cotija de la Paz 9,178 H7
Coyoacán 339,446 L1
Coyotepec 8,888 L1
Coyuca de Benítez 6,328 J8
Coyuca de Catalán 2,926 J7
Coyutla 3,726 L6
Cozumel 5,858 Q6
Creel 2,449 E3
Cuatrociénagas de Carranza 5,523 H3
Cuauhtémoc 26,598 F2
Cuautepec de Hinojosa 5,501 K6
Cuautitlán de Romero Rubio 11,439 L1
Cuautla Morelos 13,946 L2
Cuencamé de Ceniceros 3,774 H4
Cuernavaca 239,813 L2
Cuicatlán 2,733 L8
Cuitlahuac 4,813 P2
Culiacán 228,001 F4
Cumpas 2,395 E1
Cunduacán 4,397 N7
Dimas 2,194 F5
Doctor Arroyo 4,290 K5
Dolores Hidalgo de la Independencia Naci 16,849 J6
Durango 182,633 G1
Dzibalchén 1,917 P7
Dzidzantún 7,064 P6
Dzitbalché 4,393 P6
Ebano 17,489 K5
Ecatepec de Morelos 11,899 L1
Ejutla de Crespo 5,263 L8
Eldorado 8,115 E4
El Fuerte 7,179 E3
El Porvenir 3,030 G1
El Potosí 2,032 J4
El Salto 7,818 G5
El Zacatón 2,686 J5
Empalme 24,927 D2
Encarnación de Díaz 10,474 H6
Ensenada 77,687 A1
Escalón 2,998 G3
Escarcega 7,248 O7
Escuinapa de Hidalgo 16,442 G5
Escuintla 4,111 N9
Esperanza, Puebla 4,258 O2
Esperanza, Sonora 11,762 E3
Espita 5,394 Q6
Esqueda 1,458 E1
Etchojoa 4,398 E3
Ezequiel Montes 3,139 K6
Fortín de las Flores 9,358 P2
Francisco I. Madero 12,613 H4
Fresnillo de González Echererría 44,475 H5
Frontera 10,066 N7
Galeana, Nuevo León 3,429 J4
General Bravo 2,894 K4
General Cepeda 3,486 J4
General Terán 5,354 K4
Gómez Farías 3,030 F2
Gómez Palacio 79,650 G4
González 6,440 K5
Guadalajara 1,478,383 H6
Guadalajara* 2,343,034 H6
Guadalupe, Nuevo León 51,899 K4
Guadalupe, Zacatecas 13,246 H5
Guadalupe Bravo 3,333 F1
Guadalupe Victoria, Durango 7,931 H4
Guadalupe Victoria, Puebla 3,946 O1
Guamúchil 17,151 E4
Guanajuato 36,809 J6
Guasave 26,080 E4
Guaymas 57,492 D3
Gustavo Díaz Ordaz 10,154 K3
Gutiérrez Zamora 9,099 L6
Halachó 4,804 O6
Hecelchakán 4,279 O6
Hermosillo 232,691 D2
Heroica Caborca 20,771 C1
Heroica Nogales 52,108 D1
Hidalgo, Tamaulipas 2,450 K4
Hidalgo del Parral (Parral) 57,619 G3
Hopelchén 3,699 P7
Huajuapan de León 13,822 L8
Huamantla 15,565 N1
Huaquechula 2,294 M2
Huatabampo 18,506 D3
Huatusco de Chicuellar 9,501 P2
Huauchinango 16,826 L6
Huautla de Jiménez 6,132 L7
Huehuetlán el Chico 2,667 M2
Huejotzingo 8,552 M1
Huejutla 6,854 K6
Huetamo 9,333 J7
Hueyotlipan de Hidalgo 2,353 M1
Huimanguillo 7,075 N8
Huitzilán 3,573 O1
Huitzuco de los Figueroa 9,406 K7
Huixcolotla 4,039 N2
Huixtepec 5,927 L8
Huixtla 15,737 N9
Hunucmá 8,020 O6
Ignacio de la Llave 3,962 Q2
Iguala de la Independencia 45,355 K7
Imuris 1,958 D1
Irapuato 135,596 J6
Isla Mujeres 2,663 Q6
Isla, Veracruz 8,075 M7
Ixmiquilpan 6,048 K6
Ixtapa J8
Ixtapalapa 522,095 L1
Ixtenco 5,035 N1
Ixtepec 14,025 M8
Ixtlán del Río 10,986 G6
Izamal 9,749 P6
Izúcar de Matamoros 21,164 M2
Jala 4,535 G6
Jalacingo 3,427 P1
Jalapa Enríquez 161,352 P1
Jalpa 9,904 H6
Jalpa de Méndez 4,785 N7
Jalpan 1,878 K6
Jáltipan de Morelos 15,170 M8
Jantetelco 2,015 L2
Jaumave 3,072 K5
Jerez de García Salinas 20,325 H5
Jico 7,269 P1
Jilotepec de Abasolo 4,252 K7
Jiménez, Chihuahua 18,095 G3
Joachín 3,918 Q2
Jojutla de Juárez 14,438 L2
Jonacatepec 3,868 M2
Jonuta 2,746 N7
José Cardel 5,396 Q1
Juan Aldama 9,667 H4
Juchipila 6,328 H6
Juchitán de Zaragoza 30,218 M8
Kantunilkin 1,970 Q6
La Barca 18,055 H6
La Barra de Navidad 1,829 G7
La Concordia 3,559 N9
La Cruz, Sinaloa 4,218 F5
Lagos de Moreno 33,782 J6
La Huerta 4,328 G7
La Paz, Baja California Sur 46,011 D5
La Paz, San Luis Potosí 3,735 J5
La Piedad Cavadas 34,963 H6
Las Choapas 20,166 M7
Las Hadas G7
Las Nieves 2,262 G3
Las Rosas 7,658 N8
León 468,887 J6
Lerdo de Tejada 11,628 M8
Lerma 4,158 O7
Libres 4,830 O1
Linares 24,456 K4
Llera de Canales 3,564 K5
Loma Bonita 15,804 M7
Loreto, Baja California 2,570 D4
Loreto, Zacatecas 7,132 J5
Los Mochis 67,953 E4
Los Reyes de Salgado 19,452 H7
Macuspana 12,293 N8
Madera 9,759 F2
Magdalena de Kino 10,281 D1
Maltrata 5,457 O2
Manzanillo 20,777 G7
Mapastepec 5,907 N9
Mapimí 2,737 G4
Martínez de la Torre 17,203 L6
Mascota 5,674 G6
Matamoros, Coahuila 15,125 H4
Matamoros, Tamaulipas 165,124 L4
Matehuala 28,799 J5
Matías Romero 13,200 M8
Maxcanú 6,505 O6
Mazatlán 147,010 F5
Melchor Múzquiz 18,868 H3
Melchor Ocampo del Balsas 4,766 H8
Meoquí 12,308 G2
Mérida 233,912 P6
Metepec 4,625 M2
Metlatonoc 1,870 K8
Mexicali 317,228 B1
Mexico City (cap.) 9,377,300 L1
Mexico City* 13,993,866 L1
Miacatlán 3,980 K2
Mier 5,636 K3
Miguel Auza 9,303 H4
Minatitlán 68,397 M8
Mineral del Monte 8,887 K6
Miquihuana 1,971 J5
Misantla 8,799 P1
Miahuatlán de Porfirio Díaz 5,714 L8
Mocorito 3,993 F4
Moctezuma, San Luis Potosí 1,734 J5
Moctezuma, Sonora 2,700 E2
Monclova 78,134 J3
Montemorelos 18,642 K4
Monterrey 1,006,221 J4
Monterrey* 1,923,402 J4
Morelia 199,099 J7
Morelos 4,241 J2
Morelos Cañada 2,288 O2
Moroleón 25,620 J6
Motozintla de Mendoza 4,682 N9
Motul de Felipe Carillo Puerto 12,949 P6
Muna 5,491 P6
Naco 3,580 D1
Nacozari 2,976 E1
Nadadores 2,461 H3
Naica 7,190 G2
Namiquipa 4,875 F2
Nanacamilpa 6,356 M1
Naolinco de Victoria 4,365 P1
Naranjos 14,732 L6
Naucalpan de Juárez 9,425 L1
Nautla 1,935 L6
Nava 4,097 J2
Navojoa 43,817 E3
Navolato 12,799 E4
Nazas 2,881 G4
Netzahualcóyotl 580,436 L1
Nieves 3,966 H5
Nochistlán 8,780 H6
Nogales 14,254 P2
Nombre de Dios 3,188 G5
Nopalucan de la Granja 3,002 O1
Nueva Casas Grandes 20,023 F1
Nueva Ciudad Guerrero 3,300 K3
Nueva Italia de Ruiz 14,718 J7
Nueva Rosita 34,706 J2
Nuevo Ideal 5,252 G4
Nuevo Laredo 184,622 J3
Oaxaca de Juárez 114,948 L8
Ocampo, Coahuila 1,613 H3
Ocampo, Tamaulipas 4,801 K5
Ocosingo 2,946 O8
Ocotlán 35,361 H6
Ocotlán de Morelos 5,882 L8
Ojinaga 12,757 G2
Ojocaliente 7,582 H5
Ometepec 7,342 K8
Oriental 6,009 O1
Orizaba 105,150 P2
Otumba de Gómez Farías 3,198 M1
Oxkutzcab 8,182 P6
Ozuluama 2,851 L6
Ozumba de Alzate 6,876 M1
Pachuca de Soto 83,892 K6
Padilla 4,581 K5
Palenque 2,595 O8
Palizada 2,332 O7
Palomas 2,129 F1

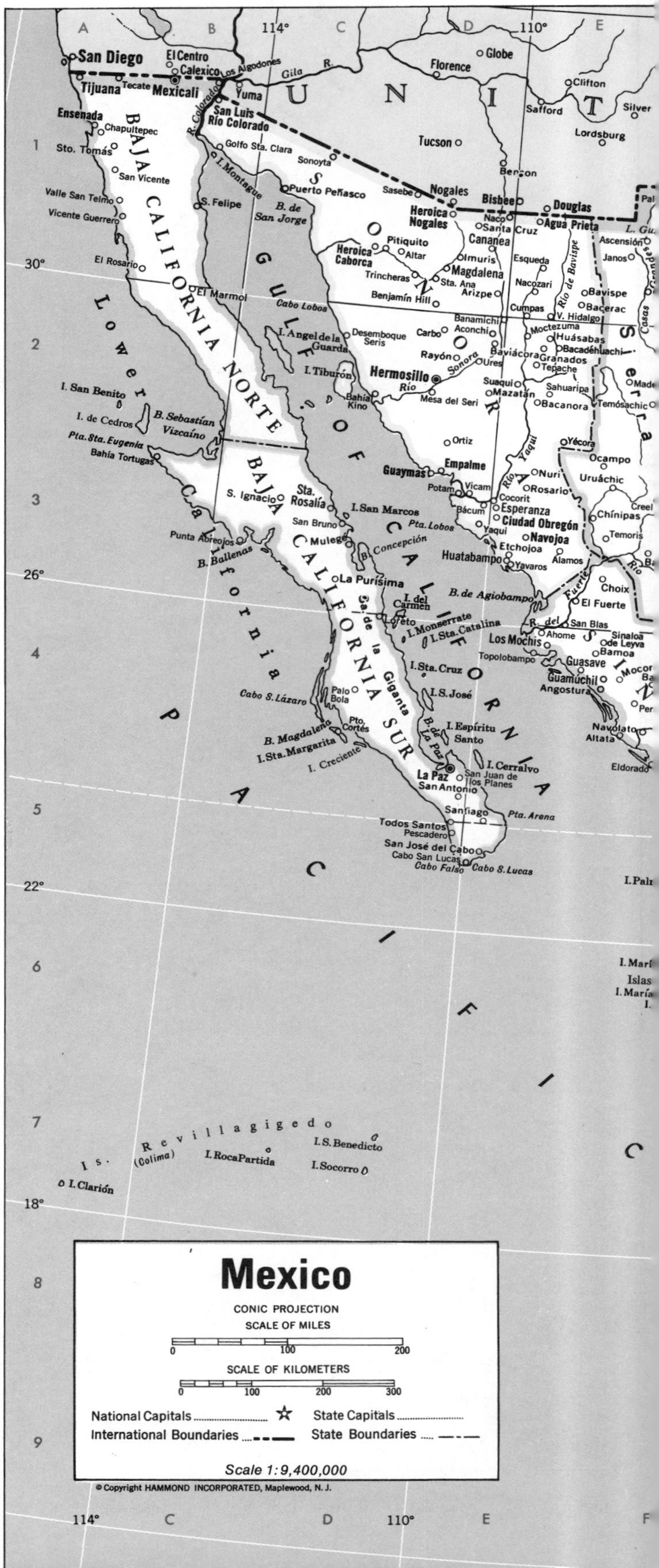

San Diego
El Centro
Calexico
Tijuana
Tecate
Mexicali
Yuma
San Luis Río Colorado
Ensenada
Gila R.
Florence
Globe
Tucson
Nogales
Heroica Nogales
Bisbee
Douglas
Agua Prieta
Cananea
Hermosillo
Guaymas
Empalme
Ciudad Obregón
Navojoa
Huatabampo
Los Mochis
BAJA CALIFORNIA NORTE
BAJA CALIFORNIA SUR
GULF OF CALIFORNIA
Lower California
PACIFIC
Santa Rosalía
Mulegé
La Purísima
La Paz
Todos Santos
San José del Cabo
Cabo San Lucas
Cabo Falso
I. Tiburón
I. Ángel de la Guarda
I. de Cedros
I. Sta. Margarita
I. Cerralvo
Is. Revillagigedo
I. Clarión
I. Socorro
I. S. Benedicto
I. Roca Partida
Mexico
CONIC PROJECTION
SCALE OF MILES
0 100 200
SCALE OF KILOMETERS
0 100 200 300
National Capitals
State Capitals
International Boundaries
State Boundaries
Scale 1:9,400,000
© Copyright HAMMOND INCORPORATED, Maplewood, N. J.

(continued on following page)

AREA 761,601 sq. mi. (1,972,546 sq. km.)
POPULATION 67,395,826
CAPITAL Mexico City
LARGEST CITY Mexico City
HIGHEST POINT Citlaltépetl 18,855 ft.
  (5,747 m.)
MONETARY UNIT Mexican peso
MAJOR LANGUAGE Spanish
MAJOR RELIGION Roman Catholicism

States Indicated by Numbers

1	Tlaxcala	6	Querétaro
2	Morelos	7	Guanajuato
3	Distrito Federal	8	Aguascalientes
4	México	9	Nayarit
5	Hidalgo	10	Colima

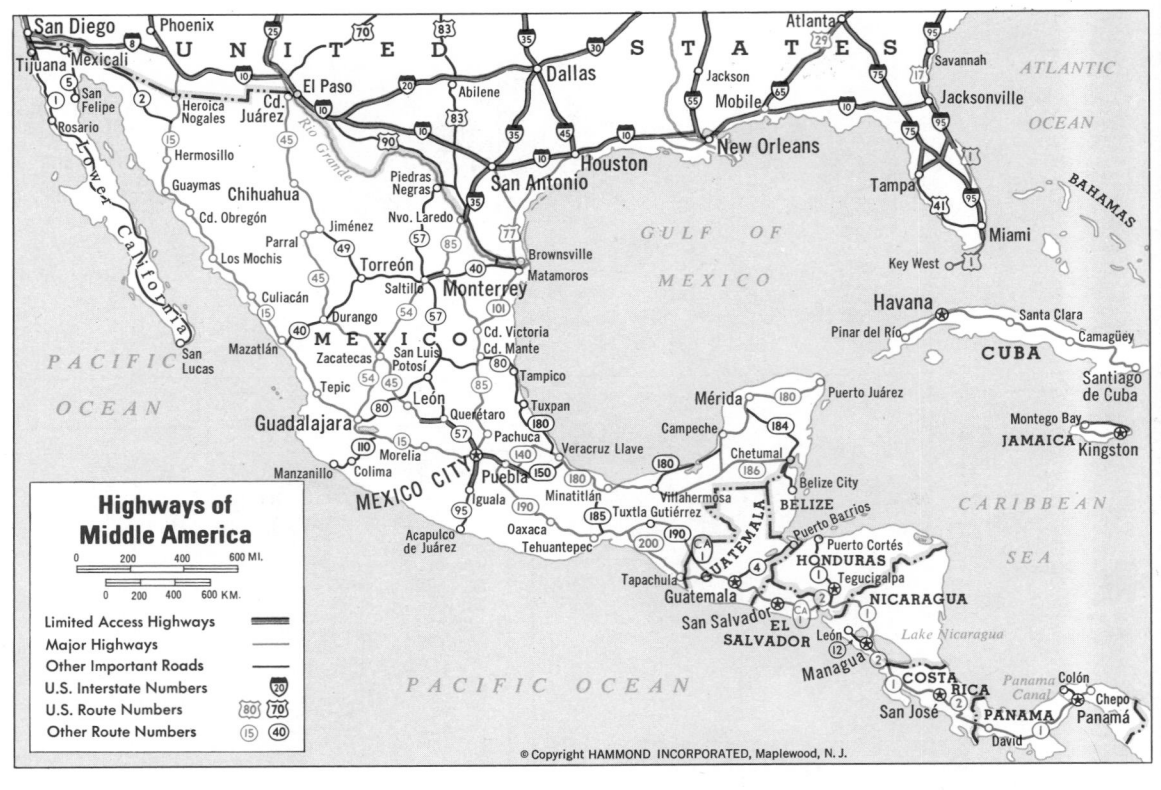

Highways of Middle America

0 200 400 600 MI.		
0 200 400 600 KM.		

Limited Access Highways
Major Highways
Other Important Roads
U.S. Interstate Numbers
U.S. Route Numbers
Other Route Numbers

© Copyright HAMMOND INCORPORATED, Maplewood, N.J.

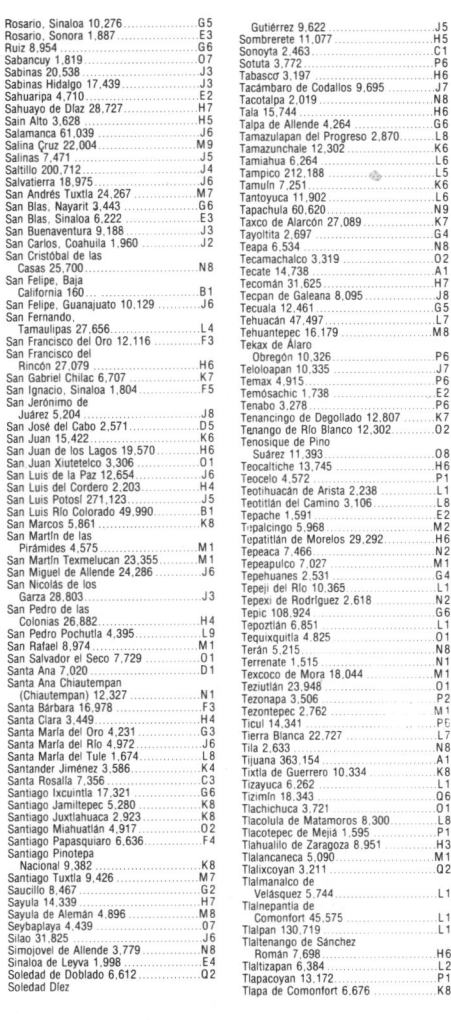

Agriculture, Industry and Resources

DOMINANT LAND USE

- Wheat, Livestock
- Cereals (chiefly corn), Livestock
- Diversified Tropical Cash Crops
- Cotton, Mixed Cereals
- Livestock, Limited Agriculture
- Range Livestock
- Forests
- Nonagricultural Land

Water Power
Major Industrial Areas

MAJOR MINERAL OCCURRENCES

Ag	Silver	G	Natural Gas	O	Petroleum		
Au	Gold	Gr	Graphite	Pb	Lead		
C	Coal	Hg	Mercury	S	Sulfur		
Cu	Copper	Mn	Manganese	Sb	Antimony		
F	Fluorspar	Mo	Molybdenum	Sn	Tin		
Fe	Iron Ore	Na	Salt	W	Tungsten		
				Zn	Zinc		

GUATEMALA

AREA 42,042 sq. mi. (108,889 sq. km.)
POPULATION 7,262,419
CAPITAL Guatemala
LARGEST CITY Guatemala
HIGHEST POINT Tajumulco 13,845 ft. (4,220 m.)
MONETARY UNIT quetzal
MAJOR LANGUAGES Spanish, Quiché
MAJOR RELIGION Roman Catholicism

BELIZE

AREA 8,867 sq. mi. (22,966 sq. km.)
POPULATION 144,857
CAPITAL Belmopan
LARGEST CITY Belize City
HIGHEST POINT Victoria Peak 3,681 ft. (1,122 m.)
MONETARY UNIT Belize dollar
MAJOR LANGUAGES English, Spanish, Mayan
MAJOR RELIGIONS Roman Catholicism, Protestantism

EL SALVADOR

AREA 8,260 sq. mi. (21,393 sq. km.)
POPULATION 4,813,000
CAPITAL San Salvador
LARGEST CITY San Salvador
HIGHEST POINT Santa Ana 7,825 ft. (2,385 m.)
MONETARY UNIT colón
MAJOR LANGUAGE Spanish
MAJOR RELIGION Roman Catholicism

HONDURAS

AREA 43,277 sq. mi. (112,087 sq. km.)
POPULATION 3,691,000
CAPITAL Tegucigalpa
LARGEST CITY Tegucigalpa
HIGHEST POINT Las Minas 9,347 ft. (2,849 m.)
MONETARY UNIT lempira
MAJOR LANGUAGE Spanish
MAJOR RELIGION Roman Catholicism

NICARAGUA

AREA 45,698 sq. mi. (118,358 sq. km.)
POPULATION 2,703,000
CAPITAL Managua
LARGEST CITY Managua
HIGHEST POINT Cerro Mocotón 6,913 ft. (2,107 m.)
MONETARY UNIT córdoba
MAJOR LANGUAGE Spanish
MAJOR RELIGION Roman Catholicism

COSTA RICA

AREA 19,575 sq. mi. (50,700 sq. km.)
POPULATION 2,245,000
CAPITAL San José
LARGEST CITY San José
HIGHEST POINT Chirripó Grande 12,530 ft. (3,819 m.)
MONETARY UNIT colón
MAJOR LANGUAGE Spanish
MAJOR RELIGION Roman Catholicism

PANAMA

AREA 29,761 sq. mi. (77,082 sq. km.)
POPULATION 1,830,175
CAPITAL Panamá
LARGEST CITY Panamá
HIGHEST POINT Vol. Baru 11,401 ft. (3,475 m.)
MONETARY UNIT balboa
MAJOR LANGUAGE Spanish
MAJOR RELIGION Roman Catholicism

Agriculture, Industry and Resources

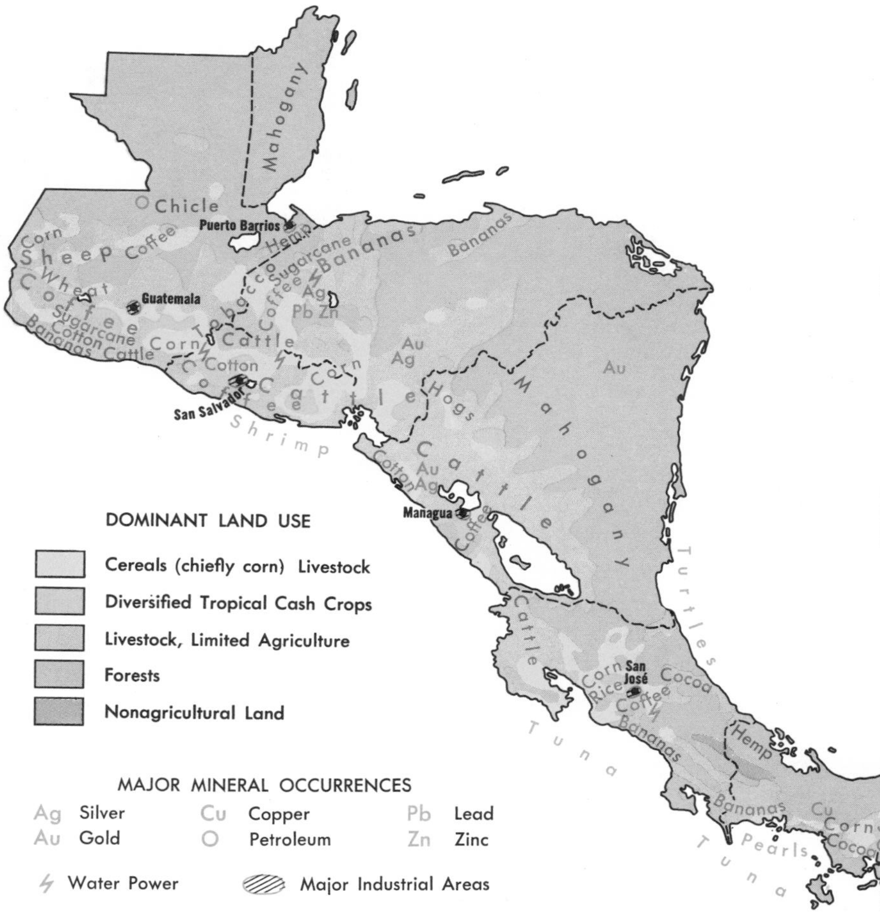

DOMINANT LAND USE

- Cereals (chiefly corn) Livestock
- Diversified Tropical Cash Crops
- Livestock, Limited Agriculture
- Forests
- Nonagricultural Land

MAJOR MINERAL OCCURRENCES

Ag Silver   Cu Copper   Pb Lead
Au Gold   O Petroleum   Zn Zinc

⚡ Water Power   ▨ Major Industrial Areas

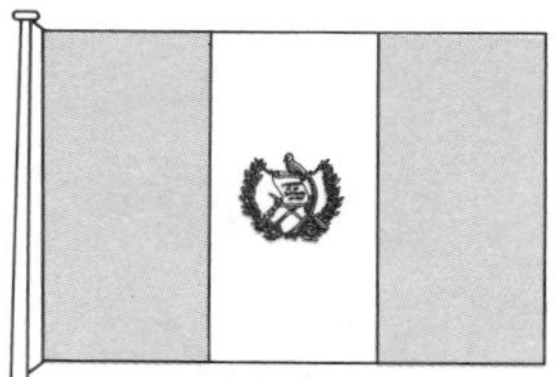

GUATEMALA

HONDURAS

BELIZE

NICARAGUA

EL SALVADOR

COSTA RICA

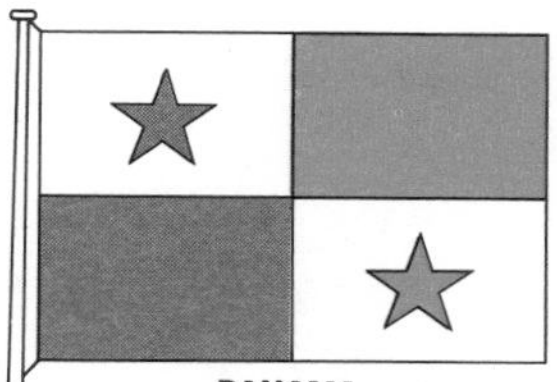

PANAMA

(continued on following page)

Central America

CONIC PROJECTION

SCALE OF MILES

SCALE OF KILOMETERS

Capitals of Countries .... ☆

International Boundaries .... — · —

Canals .... ┼┼┼┼

Scale 1:5,780,000

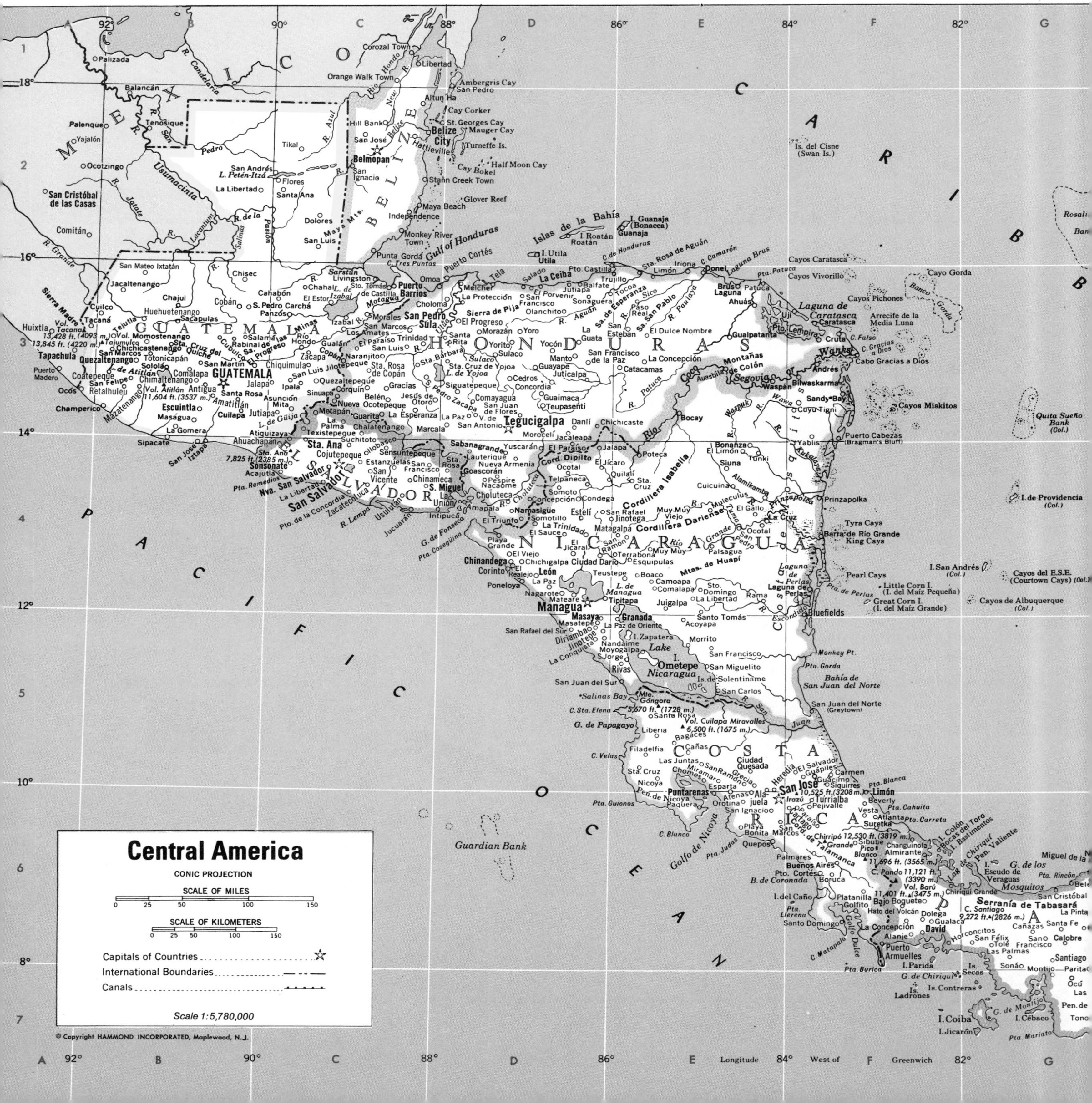

© Copyright HAMMOND INCORPORATED, Maplewood, N.J.

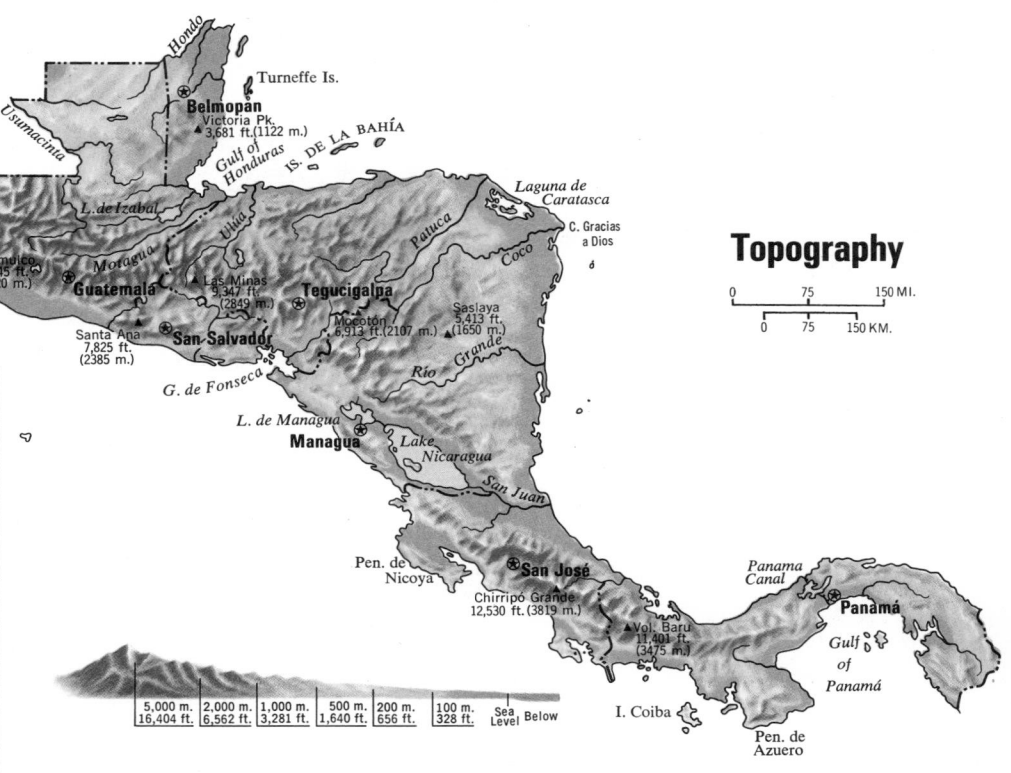

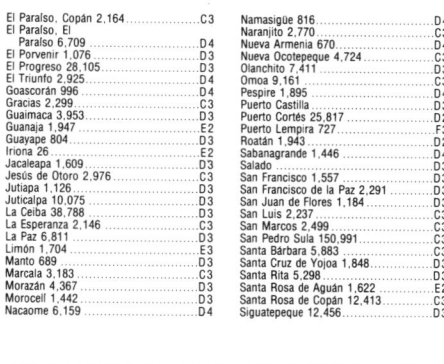

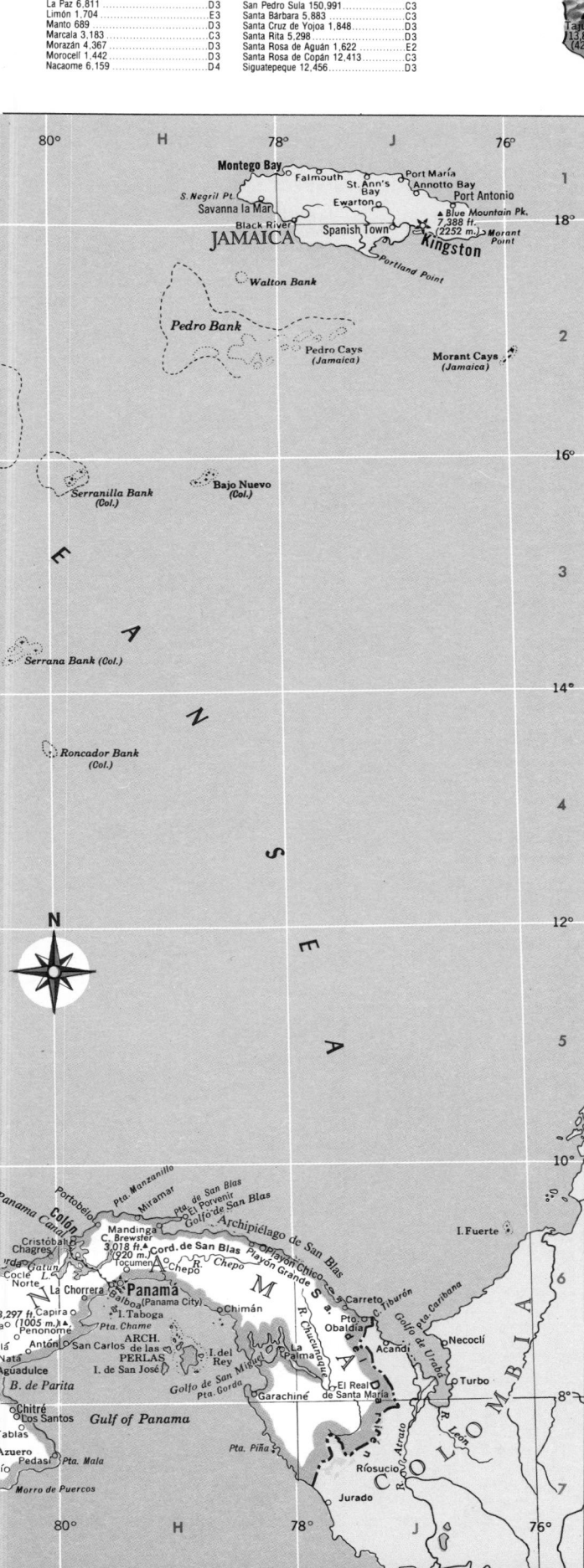

CUBA

HAITI

DOMINICAN REPUBLIC

JAMAICA

TRINIDAD AND TOBAGO

BARBADOS

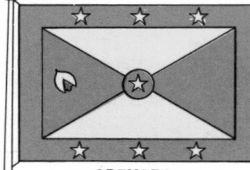
GRENADA

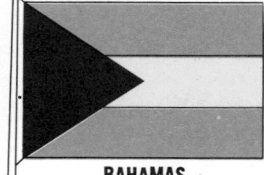
BAHAMAS

DOMINICA

ST. LUCIA

ST. VINC. & GRENS.

ANTIGUA AND BARBUDA

CUBA

AREA 44,206 sq. mi. (114,494 sq. km.)
POPULATION 9,706,369
CAPITAL Havana
LARGEST CITY Havana
HIGHEST POINT Pico Turquino
6,561 ft. (2,000 m.)
MONETARY UNIT Cuban peso
MAJOR LANGUAGE Spanish
MAJOR RELIGION Roman Catholicism

HAITI

AREA 10,694 sq. mi. (27,697 sq. km.)
POPULATION 5,053,792
CAPITAL Port-au-Prince
LARGEST CITY Port-au-Prince
HIGHEST POINT Pic La Selle 8,793 ft. (2,680 m.)
MONETARY UNIT gourde
MAJOR LANGUAGES Creole French, French
MAJOR RELIGION Roman Catholicism

DOMINICAN REPUBLIC

AREA 18,704 sq. mi. (48,443 sq. km.)
POPULATION 5,647,977
CAPITAL Santo Domingo
LARGEST CITY Santo Domingo
HIGHEST POINT Pico Duarte
10,417 ft. (3,175 m.)
MONETARY UNIT Dominican peso
MAJOR LANGUAGE Spanish
MAJOR RELIGION Roman Catholicism

JAMAICA

AREA 4,411 sq. mi. (11,424 sq. km.)
POPULATION 2,184,000
CAPITAL Kingston
LARGEST CITY Kingston
HIGHEST POINT Blue Mountain Peak
7,402 ft. (2,256 m.)
MONETARY UNIT Jamaican dollar
MAJOR LANGUAGE English
MAJOR RELIGIONS Protestantism,
Roman Catholicism

PUERTO RICO

AREA 3,515 sq. mi. (9,104 sq. km.)
POPULATION 3,196,520
CAPITAL San Juan
MONETARY UNIT U.S. dollar
MAJOR LANGUAGES Spanish, English
MAJOR RELIGION Roman Catholicism

NETHERLANDS ANTILLES

AREA 390 sq. mi. (1,010 sq. km.)
POPULATION 246,000
CAPITAL Willemstad
MONETARY UNIT Antilles guilder
MAJOR LANGUAGES Dutch, Papiamento, English
MAJOR RELIGIONS Roman Catholicism,
Protestantism

BERMUDA

AREA 21 sq. mi. (54 sq. km.)
POPULATION 67,761
CAPITAL Hamilton
MONETARY UNIT Bermuda dollar
MAJOR LANGUAGE English
MAJOR RELIGION Protestantism

ANGUILLA

Anguilla (isl.) 6,519 . . . . F3

ANTIGUA and BARBUDA

Antigua (isl.) 76,213 . . . . G3
Barbuda (isl.) 1,071 . . . . G3
Caribbean (sea) B4
Codrington 1,071 . . . . G3
Falmouth 1,134 . . . . F3
Redonda (isl.) F3
Saint John's (cap.) 21,814 . . . . G3

BAHAMAS

Acklins (isl.) 616 . . . . C2
Andros (isl.) 8,397 . . . . B1
Atwood (Samana) (cay) D2
Berry (isls.) 509 . . . . B1
Biminis, The (isls.) 1,432 . . . . . B1
Caicos (passg.) D2
Cat (isl.) 2,143 . . . . C1
Cay Sal (bank) B2
Crooked (isl.) 517 . . . . D2
Crooked Island (passg.) C2
Eleuthera (isl.) 8,326 . . . . C1
Exuma (cays) C1
Exuma (sound) C1
Flamingo (cay) B1
Freeport 22,301 . . . . B1
Grand Bahama (isl.) 33,102 . . . B1
Great Abaco (isl.) 7,324 . . . . . . B1
Great Bahama (bank) B2
Great Exuma (isl.) 939 . . . . D2
Great Inagua (isl.) D2
Great Isaac (isl.) B1
Gun (cay) B1
Harbour (isl.) C1
Little Inagua (isl.) D2

Long (cay) 33 . . . . C2
Long (isl.) 3,353 . . . . C2
Mayaguana (isl.) 476 . . . . D2
Mayaguana (passg.) D2
Mira Por Vos (cays) C2
Nassau (cap.) 135,437 . . . . C1
New Providence (isl.) 135,437 . . C1
North East Providence (chan.) . . C1
North West Providence (chan.) . . B1
Old Bahama (chan.) B2
Plana (cays) D2
Ragged (cays) 146 . . . . C2
Rum (cay) C2
Samana (cay) D2
San Salvador (isl.) D1
Santaren (chan.) B1
Tongue of the Ocean (chan.) . . . C1
Verde (cay) C2
Watling (San Salvador) (isl.) . . . C1

BARBADOS

Bridgetown (cap.) 7,552 . . . . . . G4
Speightstown G4

BERMUDA

Bermuda (isl.) H3
Castle (harb.) H2
Great (sound) G3
Hamilton (cap.) 1,617 . . . . G3
Harrington (sound) H3
Ireland (isl.) G3
North (rapid) H2
Saint Davids (isl.) H2
Saint George 1,647 . . . . H2
Saint George's (isl.) H2
Somerset (isl.) G3

CAYMAN ISLANDS

Bartlett Deep B3
Cayman Brac (isl.) 1,603 . . . . . . B3
George Town (cap.) 7,617 . . . . . B3
Grand Cayman (isl.) 15,000 . . . . B3
Little Cayman (isl.) 74 . . . . B3
Misteriosa (bank) A3

CUBA

Bayamo 109,201 . . . . C2
Camagüey 245,235 . . . . B2
Cienfuegos 107,396 . . . . B2
Florida (str.) B1
Guanabacoa 81,741 . . . . B2
Guantánamo 178,129 . . . . C2
Havana (cap.) 1,924,886 . . . . . . A2
Holguín 190,155 . . . . C2
Juventud (Pines) (isl.) 57,879 . . A2
Manzanillo 95,420 . . . . C2
Marianao ○127,563 . . . . A2
Matanzas 103,302 . . . . B2
Pinar del Río 104,598 . . . . A2
San Felipe (cays) A2
Santa Clara 175,113 . . . . B2
Santiago de Cuba 362,432 . . . . C3
Windward (passg.) C3

DOMINICA

Portsmouth 2,329 . . . . G4
Roseau (cap.) 9,968 . . . . G4

DOMINICAN REPUBLIC

La Romana 91,571 . . . . E3
San Francisco de Macorís 64,906 . E3
San Pedro de Macorís 78,562 . . E3
Santiago 278,638 . . . . E3
Santo Domingo (cap.) 1,313,172 . E3

GRENADA

Carriacou (isl.) 6,052 . . . . G4
Gouyave 2,498 . . . . F4
Grenadines (isls.) G4
Saint George's (cap.) 6,463 . . . . F5

GUADELOUPE

Basse-Terre (cap.) 13,397 . . . . . F4
Saint-Barthélemy 3,059 . . . . F3
Saint Martin 8,072 . . . . F3

HAITI

Cap-Haïtien 64,406 . . . . D3
Gonaïves 34,209 . . . . D3
Port-au-Prince (cap.) 449,831 . . D3
Gonâve (isl.) D3
Jamaica (chan.) C3
Tortuga (isl.) D2

JAMAICA

Blue Mountain (peak) C3
Jamaica (chan.) C3
Kingston (cap.) 106,791 . . . . . . C3
Montego Bay 43,521 . . . . B3
Pedro (cays) C3
Savanna-la-Mar 11,759 . . . . B3

MARTINIQUE

Fort-de-France (cap.) 96,649 . . . G4
Saint-Pierre 4,923 . . . . G4
Pelée (vol.) G4

MONTSERRAT

Plymouth (cap.) 1,623 . . . . F3

NETHERLANDS ANTILLES

Aruba (isl.) E4
Bonaire (isl.) E4
Curaçao (isl.) E4
Oranjestad 10,100 . . . . D4
Saba (isl.) F3
Saint Eustatius (isl.) F3
Saint Martin (Sint Maarten) (isl.) . F3
Willemstad (cap.) 95,000 . . . . . . E4

PUERTO RICO

Bayamón 185,087 . . . . G1
Caguas 87,214 . . . . G1
Culebra (isl.) 1,265 . . . . G1
Mayagüez 82,968 . . . . F1
Mona (passg.) E3
Ponce 161,739 . . . . F1

San Juan (cap.) 424,600 . . . . . . G1
Vieques (isl.) 7,662 . . . . G1

SAINT CHRISTOPHER and NEVIS

Basseterre (cap.) 14,725 . . . . . . F3
Nevis (isl.) 9,300 . . . . F3
Saint Christopher (isl.) 35,104 . . F3

SAINT LUCIA

Castries (cap.) •42,770 . . . . G4
Vieux Fort •10,675 . . . . G4

SAINT VINCENT and THE GRENADINES

Bequia (isl.) G4
Georgetown 1,100 . . . . G4
Grenadines (isls.) 8,371 . . . . G4
Kingstown (cap.) 17,117 . . . . . . G4

TRINIDAD and TOBAGO

Port-of-Spain (cap.) 67,978 . . . . G5
Scarborough 6,057 . . . . G5
Tobago (isl.) 39,695 . . . . G5
Trinidad (isl.) 1,020,130 . . . . G5

TURKS and CAICOS ISLANDS

Caicos (isls.) 4,008 . . . . D2
Cockburn Harbour D2
Grand Caicos (isl.) 371 . . . . D2
Grand Turk (isl.) 3,146 . . . . D2
Providenciales (isl.) 979 . . . . . . D2
Turks (isls.) 3,348 . . . . D2

VIRGIN ISLANDS (British)

Anegada (isl.) 89 . . . . H1
Jost Van Dyke (isl.) 135 . . . . . . G1
Road Town (cap.) 2,200 . . . . H1
Tortola (isl.) 9,257 . . . . H1
Virgin Gorda (isl.) 1,443 . . . . . . H1

VIRGIN ISLANDS (U.S.)

Charlotte Amalie (cap.) 11,842 . . H1
Christiansted 2,914 . . . . H2
Fredriksted 1,046 . . . . G2
Saint Croix 49,725 . . . . H2
Saint John (isl.) 2,472 . . . . H1
Saint Thomas (isl.) 44,372 . . . . . G1

WEST INDIES

Antilles, Greater (isls.) B2
Antilles, Lesser (isls.) E4
Aves (Bird) (isl.) F4
Hispaniola (isl.) D2
Leeward (isls.) F3
Navassa (isl.) C3
Windward (isls.) G4

• Population of district.
○ Population of municipality.

Topography

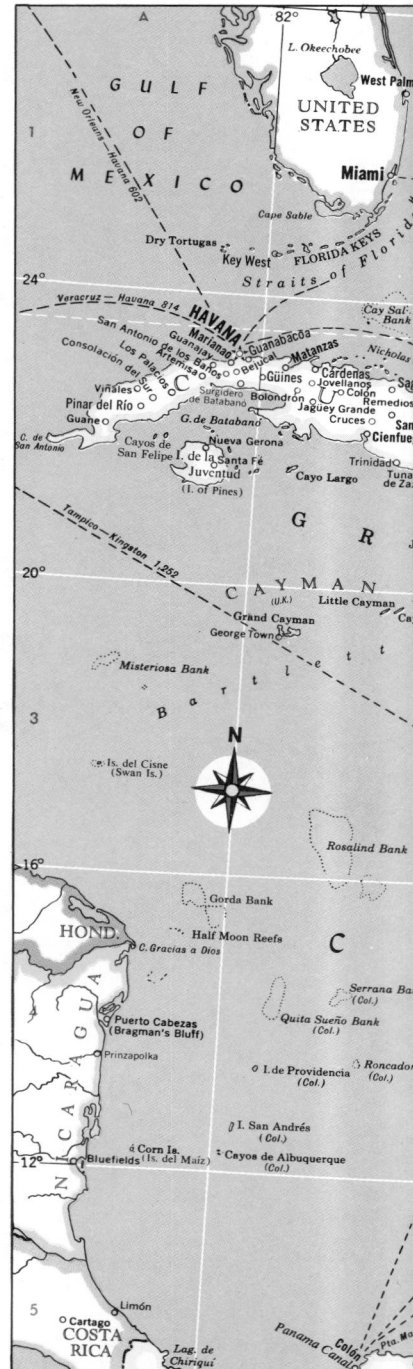

TRINIDAD AND TOBAGO

AREA 1,980 sq. mi. (5,128 sq. km.)
POPULATION 1,067,108
CAPITAL Port of Spain
LARGEST CITY Port of Spain
HIGHEST POINT Mt. Aripo 3,084 ft. (940 m.)
MONETARY UNIT Trinidad and Tobago dollar
MAJOR LANGUAGES English, Hindi
MAJOR RELIGIONS Roman Catholicism, Protestantism, Hinduism, Islam

SAINT CHRISTOPHER-NEVIS

BARBADOS

AREA 166 sq. mi. (430 sq. km.)
POPULATION 248,983
CAPITAL Bridgetown
LARGEST CITY Bridgetown
HIGHEST POINT Mt. Hillaby 1,104 ft. (336 m.)
MONETARY UNIT Barbadian dollar
MAJOR LANGUAGE English
MAJOR RELIGION Protestantism

BAHAMAS

AREA 5,382 sq. mi. (13,939 sq. km.)
POPULATION 209,505
CAPITAL Nassau
LARGEST CITY Nassau
HIGHEST POINT Mt. Alvernia 206 ft. (63 m.)
MONETARY UNIT Bahamian dollar
MAJOR LANGUAGE English
MAJOR RELIGIONS Roman Catholicism, Protestantism

GRENADA

AREA 133 sq. mi. (344 sq. km.)
POPULATION 103,103
CAPITAL St. George's
LARGEST CITY St. George's
HIGHEST POINT Mt. St. Catherine 2,757 ft. (840 m.)
MONETARY UNIT East Caribbean dollar
MAJOR LANGUAGES English, French patois
MAJOR RELIGIONS Roman Catholicism, Protestantism

DOMINICA

AREA 290 sq. mi. (751 sq. km.)
POPULATION 74,089
CAPITAL Roseau
HIGHEST POINT Morne Diablotin 4,747 ft. (1,447 m.)
MONETARY UNIT Dominican dollar
MAJOR LANGUAGES English, French patois
MAJOR RELIGIONS Roman Catholicism, Protestantism

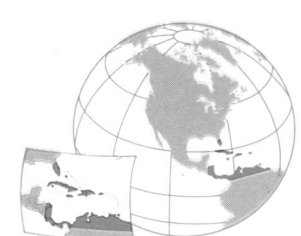

SAINT LUCIA

AREA 238 sq. mi. (616 sq. km.)
POPULATION 115,783
CAPITAL Castries
HIGHEST POINT Mt. Gimie 3,117 ft. (950 m.)
MONETARY UNIT East Caribbean dollar
MAJOR LANGUAGES English, French patois
MAJOR RELIGIONS Roman Catholicism, Protestantism

SAINT VINCENT AND THE GRENADINES

AREA 150 sq. mi. (388 sq. km.)
POPULATION 124,000
CAPITAL Kingstown
HIGHEST POINT Soufrière 4,000 ft. (1,219 m.)
MONETARY UNIT East Caribbean dollar
MAJOR LANGUAGE English
MAJOR RELIGIONS Protestantism, Roman Catholicism

ANTIGUA AND BARBUDA

AREA 171 sq. mi. (443 sq. km.)
POPULATION 75,000
CAPITAL St. John's
HIGHEST POINT Boggy Peak 1,319 ft. (402 m.)
MONETARY UNIT East Caribbean dollar
MAJOR LANGUAGE English
MAJOR RELIGION Protestantism

SAINT CHRISTOPHER-NEVIS

AREA 104 sq. mi. (269 sq. km.)
POPULATION 44,404
CAPITAL Basseterre
HIGHEST POINT Mt. Misery 4,314 ft. (1,315 m.)
MONETARY UNIT East Caribbean dollar
MAJOR LANGUAGE English
MAJOR RELIGIONS Protestantism, Roman Catholicism

The West Indies

CONIC PROJECTION

SCALE OF MILES
0 50 100 150 200

SCALE OF KILOMETERS
0 50 100 200 300

Capitals ⎯⎯⎯⎯⎯ ☆

Scale 1:11,200,000
Distances are given in Nautical Miles

Puerto Rico

Bermuda Islands

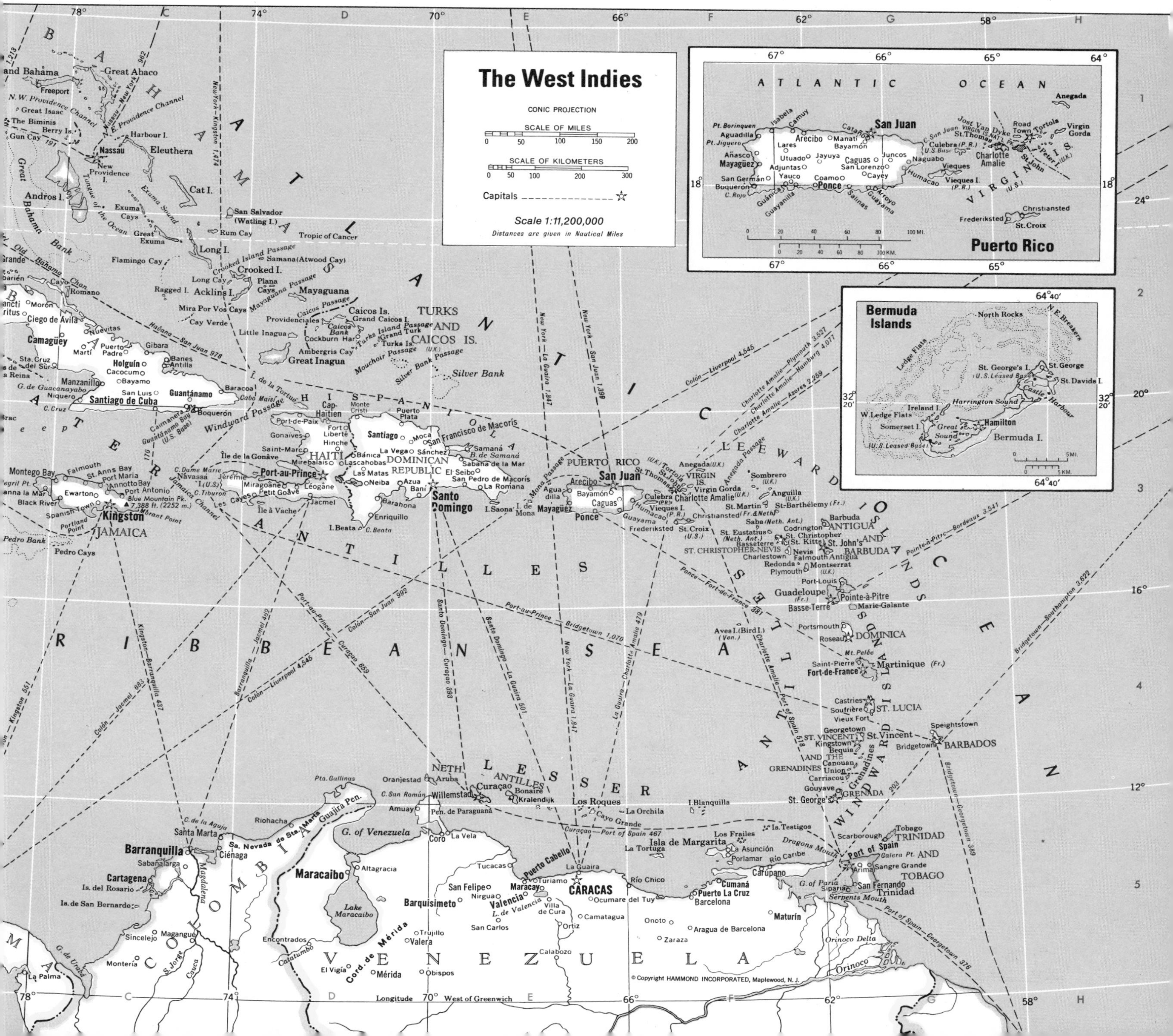

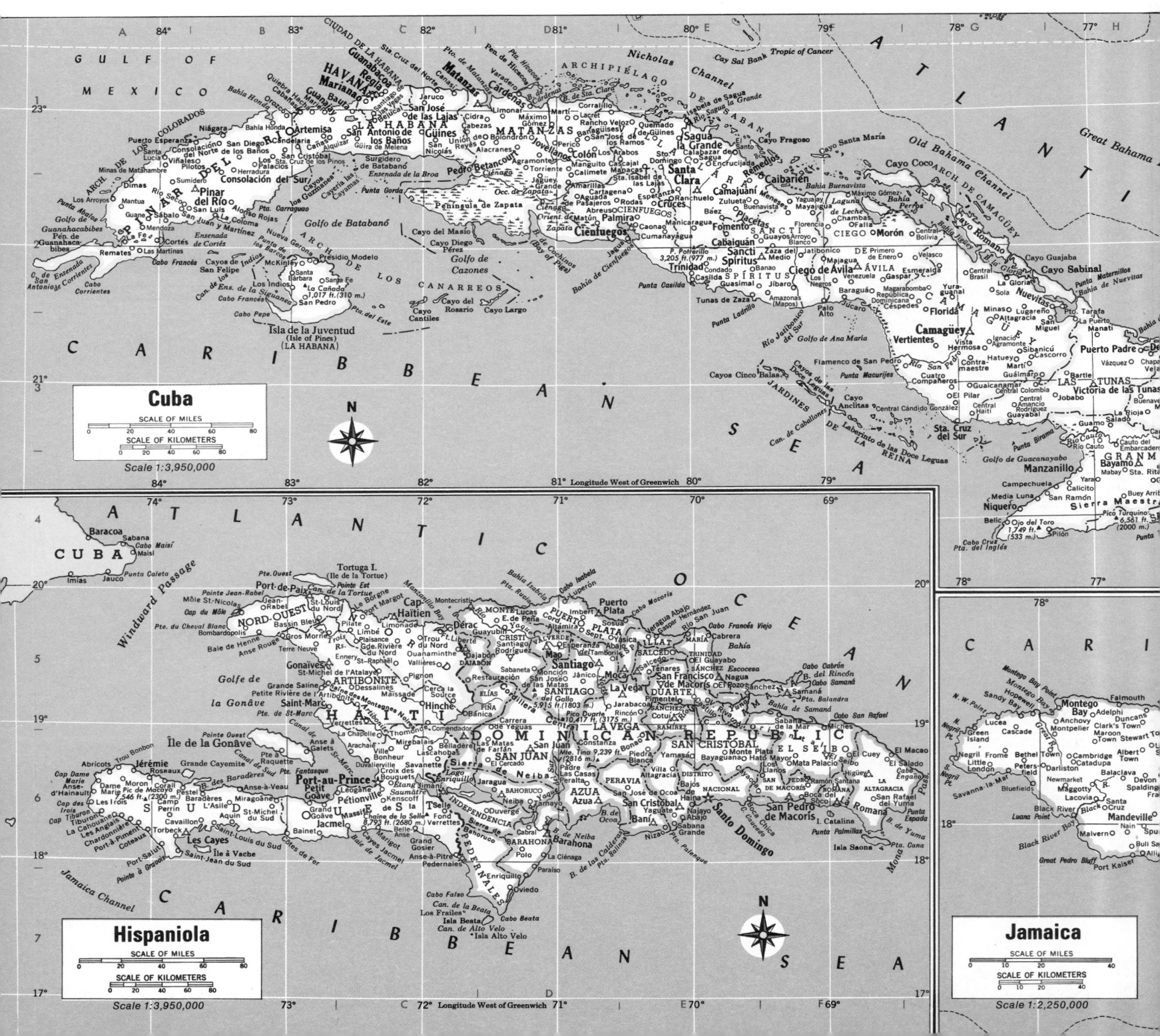

Cuba
SCALE OF MILES
0 20 40 80
SCALE OF KILOMETERS
0 20 40 60 80
Scale 1:3,950,000

Hispaniola
SCALE OF MILES
0 20 40 80
SCALE OF KILOMETERS
0 20 40 60 80
Scale 1:3,950,000

Jamaica
SCALE OF MILES
0 10 20 40
SCALE OF KILOMETERS
0 10 20 40
Scale 1:2,250,000

Santa Cruz de los Pinos
3,545 ....B1
Santa Cruz del Sur 27,142 . G3
Santa Fe 3,925 ....B2
Santa Isabel de las Lajas
7,279 ....E2
Santa Lucía 3,734 ....J3
Santa Rita 6,358 ....H4
Santiago de Cuba 362,432 . J4
Santiago de las Vegas
29,325 ....C1
Santo Domingo 32,950 ... E1
Sibanicú 14,252 ....G3
Sola 2,436 ....G2
Sumidero 980 ....A2
Surgidero de Batabanó
11,533 ....C1
Tacajó 4,469 ....G3
Torriente 1,759 ....D11
Trinidad 42,080 ....E2
Unión de Reyes 28,422 . . C1
Varadero 14,737 ....D1
Vázquez 3,851 ....H3
Velasco 5,618 ....H3
Venezuela 13,744 ....F2
Vertientes 25,178 ....G3
Victoria de las Tunas 87,522 H3
Viñales 2,049 ....A1
Yaguajay 30,720 ....F2
Yara 238,879 ....H4
Zaza del Medio 7,495 . . . F2
Zulueta 5,425 ....E2

OTHER FEATURES

Abalos (pt.) A2
Ana María (gulf) F3
Anclitas (cay) F3
Batabanó (gulf) C2
Birama (pt.) G4
Broa (inlet) C1
Buenavista (bay) F2
Caballones (chan.) F3
Camagüey (arch.) G2
Cantiles (cay) C3
Cárdenas (bay) D1
Carraguao (pt.) B2
Casilda (bay) E2
Cauto (riv.) H3
Cayamas (cays) C2
Cazones (gulf) C2
Cienfuegos (bay) D2
Cinco Balas (cays) E3
Cochinos (bay) D2
Coco (cay) G1
Corrientes (cape) A2
Corrientes (inlet) A2
Cortés (inlet) B2
Cristal, Sierra del (mts.) . J3
Cruz (cape) G4
Diego Pérez (cay) C2
Doce Leguas (cays) F3
Este (cay) C3
Fragoso (cay) F1
Francés (cape) A2

Gorda (pt.) C2
Gran Piedra (mt.) J4
Guacanayabo (gulf) G4
Guajaba (cay) G2
Guanahacabibes (gulf) . . A2
Guanahacabibes (pen.) . . A2
Guantánamo (bay) J4
Guantánamo Bay U.S. Nav.
Reserve K4
Guarico (cay) K3
Guzmanes (cays) B2
Hicacos (pen.) D1
Hicacos (pt.) D1
Honda (bay) B1
Indios (chan.) B2
Inglés (pt.) G4
Jardines de la Reina (arch.) . F3
Jatibonico del Sur (riv.) . . F3
Jigüey (bay) G2
Jiguey (bay) G2
Juventud, Isla de (la Pines)
(isl.) 57,879 ....B3
Laberinto de las Doce
Leguas (cays) F3
Ladrillo (pt.) E3
Largo (cay) D2
Leche (lag.) F2
Los Barcos (pt.) B2
Los Canarreos (arch.) . . . C2
Los Colorados (arch.) . . . A1
Lucrecia (cape) J3
Macuríges (pt.) F3
Maestra, Sierra (mts.) . . . H4
Maisí (cape) K4
Mangle (pt.) J3
Masío (cay) C2
Matanzas (bay) D1
Nicholas (chan.) E1
Nipe (bay) J3
Nuevitas (bay) H2
Ojo del Toro (mt.) G4
Old Bahama (chan.) G1
Pepe (cape) B3
Perros (bay) G2
Pigs (Cochinos) (bay) . . . D2
Pines (Isla de la Juventud)
(isl.) 57,879 ....B3
Potrerillo (peak) E2
Quemado (pt.) K4
Romano (cay) G2
Rosario (cay) C2
Sabana (arch.) E1
Sabinal (cay) H2
Sagua la Grande (riv.) . . . E1
San Antonio (cape) A2
San Felipe (cays) B2
San Pedro (riv.) G3
Santa Clara (bay) D1
Santa María (cay) F1
Siguanea (bay) B2
Tabacal (pt.) H4
Toa, Cuchillas de (mts.) . . K4
Tortuguilla (pt.) K4
Turquino (peak) H4
Zapata (pen.) C2
Zapata Occidental (swamp) . D2
Zapata Oriental (swamp) . . D2

DOMINICAN REPUBLIC

PROVINCES

Azua 142,770 ....D6

Bahoruco 78,636 ....D6
Barahona 137,160 ......D6
Dajabón 57,709 ....D5
Distrito Nacional 1,550,739 . E6
Duarte 235,544 ....E5
El Seibo 157,866 ....F6
Espaillat 164,017 ......E5
Independencia 38,768 . . . D6
La Altagracia 100,112 . . . F6
La Romana 109,769 .....F6
La Vega 385,043 ....E5
María Trinidad Sánchez
112,629 ....E5
Monte Cristi 83,407 ....D5
Pedernales 17,006 .....D7
Peravia 168,123 ....E6
Puerto Plata 206,757 . . . D5
Salcedo 99,191 ....E5
Samaná 65,699 ....E5
Sánchez Ramírez 126,567 . E5
San Cristóbal 446,132 . . . E6
San Juan 239,957 ......D6
San Pedro de Macorís
152,890 ....F6
Santiago 550,372 ....D5
Santiago Rodríguez 55,411 . D5
Valverde 100,319 ......D5

CITIES and TOWNS

Altamira 2,759 ....D5
Azua 31,481 ....D6
Bajos de Haina 33,135 . . . E6
Baní 36,705 ....E6
Barahona 49,334 ....D6
Bonao 44,486 ....E6
Cabrera 2,542 ....E5
Comendador 5,962 .....C6
Constanza 15,141 ......D6
Cotuí 16,688 ....E5
Dajabón 8,808 ....D5
El Seibo 13,511 ....F6
Hato Mayor 17,859 .....F6
Higüey 33,501 ....F6
Imbert 5,315 ....D5
Jarabacoa 13,416 ......E5
Jimaní 3,327 ....C6
La Romana 91,571 ......F6
La Vega 52,432 ....E5
Luperón 2,500 ....D5
Mao 33,527 ....D5
Moca 31,176 ....E5
Monción 3,344 ....D5
Nagua 20,912 ....E5
Puerto Plata 45,348 ....D5
Sabana de la Mar 9,983 . . F5
Sabaneta 9,170 ....D5
Samaná 5,023 ....F5
Sánchez 7,919 ....E5
San Cristóbal 58,520 . . . E6
San Francisco de Macorís
64,906 ....E5
San Juan 49,764 ....D6
San Pedro de Macorís
78,562 ....F6
Santiago 278,638 ......D5
Santo Domingo (cap.)
1,313,172 ....E6
Tenares 4,065 ....E5
Villa Altagracia 20,890 . . . E6

OTHER FEATURES

Alto Velo (chan.) C7
Alto Velo (isl.) D7
Balandra (pt.) F5
Beata (cape) D7
Beata (chan.) C7
Beata (isl.) C7
Cabrón (cape) F5
Calderas (bay) D6
Cana (pt.) F6
Catalina (isl.) F6
Caucedo (cape) E6
Central, Cordillera (range) . D5
Duarte (peak) E5
Engaño (cape) F6
Enriquillo (lake) C6
Escocesa (bay) F5
Espada (pt.) F5
Falso (cape) C7
Francés Viejo (cape) E5
Gallo (mt.) D5
Isabela (bay) D5
Isabela (cape) D5
Los Frailes (isl.) C7
Macorís (cape) F5
Manzanillo (bay) C5
Mona (passg.) F6
Neiba (bay) D6
Neiba, Sierra de (mts.) . . . D6
Ocoa (bay) E6
Oriental, Cordillera (range) . F6
Palenque (pt.) E6
Palmillas (pt.) E6
Rincón (bay) F5
Rucia (pt.) D5
Salinas (pt.) E6
Samaná (bay) F5
Samaná (cape) F5
San Rafael (cape) F5
Saona (isl.) F6
Septentrional, Cordillera
(range) D5
Tina (mt.) D6
Yaque del Norte (riv.) . . . D5
Yaque del Sur (riv.) D6
Yuma (bay) F6
Yuna (riv.) E5

HAITI

DEPARTMENTS

Artibonite C5
Nord C5
Nord-Ouest B5
Ouest C6
Sud A6

CITIES and TOWNS

Anse-à-Galets 3,623 . . . . B6
Anse-d'Hainault 5,220 . . . A6
Aquin 3,820 ....B6
Cap-Haïtien 64,406 .....C5
Croix des Bouquets 4,365 . C6
Dame Marie 4,320 ......A6
Dérac 1,300 ....C5

Dessalines 7,984 ....C5
Fort Liberté 5,012 ......C5
Gonaïves 34,209 ....B5
Grande Rivière du Nord
6,007 ....C5
Gros Morne 4,739 ......B5
Hinche 10,070 ....C5
Jacmel 13,730 ....C6
Jérémie 18,493 ....A6
Kenscoff 2,605 ....C6
Lascahobas 3,805 ......C6
Léogâne 5,782 ....C6
Les Cayes 34,090 ......B6
Limbé 10,476 ....C5
Mirebalais 6,069 ....C6
Miragoâne 4,327 ....B6
Ouanaminthe 7,276 .....C5
Pétionville 35,333 ......C6
Petite Rivière de l'Artibonite
10,099 ....B5
Petit Goâve 7,310 ......B6
Pignon 4,576 ....C5
Port-au-Prince (cap.)
449,831 ....C6
Port-de-Paix 15,540 ....B5
Saint-Louis du Nord 7,203 . B5
Saint-Marc 24,165 .....B5
Saint-Michel de l'Atalaye
7,559 ....C5
Saint-Raaphaël 3,889 . . . C5
Trou du Nord 7,637 .....C5
Verrettes 3,670 ....C5

OTHER FEATURES

Artibonite (riv.) C5
Baradères (bay) B6
Cheval Blanc (pt.) B5
Dame Marie (cape) A6
Est (pt.) C4
Fantasque (pt.) C4
Gonâve (gulf) B5
Gonâve (isl.) B6
Grande Cayemite (isl.) . . . A7
Gravois (pt.) A6
Irois (cape) A6
Jean-Rabel (pt.) B5
Macaya (mt.) A6
Manzanillo (bay) C5
Môle (pt.) B5
Noires (mts.) C5
Ouest (pt.) B4
Ouest (pt.) B6
Saint-Marc (chan.) B6
Saint-Marc (pt.) B5
Saumâtre (lake) C6
Selle (peak) C6
Sud (chan.) A6
Tortue (chan.) C5
Tortue (Tortuga) (isl.) . . . C4
Tortuga (isl.) C4
Trois-Rivières (riv.) B5
Vache (isl.) B6
Windward (passg.) A5

JAMAICA

CITIES and TOWNS

Alley J7

Alligator Pond H6
Anchovy 2,558 ....H5
Annotto Bay K6
Bamboo 2,971 ....J6
Bath K6
Black River 2,701 ......H6
Bog Walk J6
Bowden J6
Browns Town 5,479 .....J6
Bull Savanna-Junction
5,110 ....H6
Cambridge 2,449 ......H6
Catadupa H6
Christiana H6
Discovery Bay 1,814 . . . . J5
Falmouth 3,937 ....H5
Green Island G6
Hope Bay K6
Kingston (cap.) 106,791 . . K6
Kingston *516,865 .....J7
Linstead J6
Lucea 3,635 ....G5
Mandeville 14,421 .....H6
Maroon Town 2,717 .....H6
May Pen 26,074 ....J6
Montego Bay 43,521 ....H5
Montpelier H6
Morant Bay 7,465 ......K7
Negril G6
Ocho Rios 5,851 ....J6
Oracabessa J5
Port Antonio 10,538 ....K6
Port Kaiser H7
Port Maria 5,259 ......J6
Port Morant K6
Saint Ann's Bay 7,101 . . . J5
Saint Margaret's Bay K6
Savanna-la-Mar 11,759 . . G6
Spanish Town 40,731 . . . J6
Williamsfield H6

OTHER FEATURES

Black (riv.) H6
Black River (bay) G6
Blue (mts.) J6
Blue Mountain (peak) . . . K6
Galina (pt.) J6
Grande (riv.) K6
Great (riv.) H6
Great Pedro Bluff (prom.) . H6
Long (bay) H7
Luana (pt.) G6
Minho (riv.) J6
Montego (bay) G5
Montego Bay (pt.) G5
North East (pt.) K6
North Negril (pt.) G6
North West (pt.) G5
Old Harbour (bay) J6
Portland (pt.) J7
Sir John's (peak) K6
South East (pt.) K6
South Negril (pt.) G6

*City and Suburbs.
○ Population of municipality.

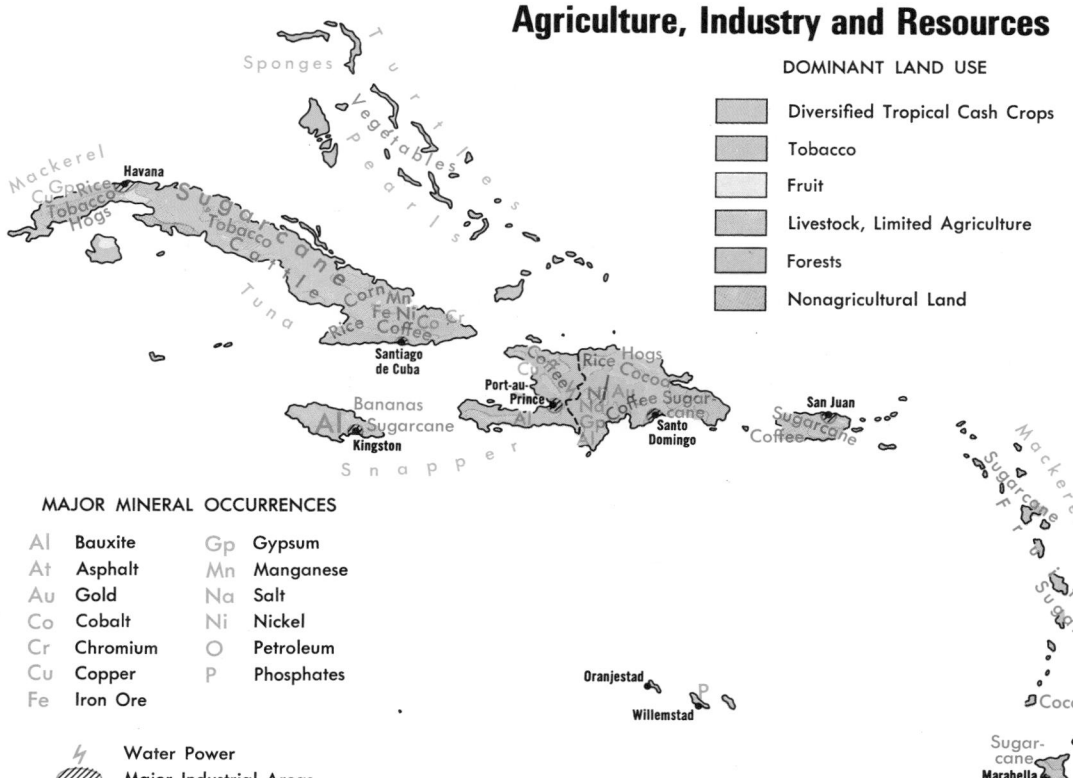

Agriculture, Industry and Resources

DOMINANT LAND USE

- Diversified Tropical Cash Crops
- Tobacco
- Fruit
- Livestock, Limited Agriculture
- Forests
- Nonagricultural Land

MAJOR MINERAL OCCURRENCES

Al	Bauxite	Gp	Gypsum
At	Asphalt	Mn	Manganese
Au	Gold	Na	Salt
Co	Cobalt	Ni	Nickel
Cr	Chromium	O	Petroleum
Cu	Copper	P	Phosphates
Fe	Iron Ore		

⚡ Water Power
▨ Major Industrial Areas

(continued)

PUERTO RICO

DISTRICTS

Aguadilla . . . A1
Arecibo . . . C1
Bayamón . . . D1
Guayama . . . D2
Humacao . . . E2
Mayagüez . . . B2
Ponce . . . C2
San Juan . . . D1

CITIES and TOWNS

Adjuntas 5,239 . . . B2
Aguada 5,025 . . . A1
Aguadilla 22,039 . . . A1
Aguas Buenas 3,766 . . . E2
Aibonito 9,331 . . . D2
Añasco 5,646 . . . A1
Angeles ○2,817 . . . B2
Arecibo 48,779 . . . B1
Arroyo 8,435 . . . E3
Bahomamey . . . A1
Bajadero 3,678 . . . C1
Barceloneta 4,502 . . . C1
Barranquitas 3,618 . . . D2
Bayamón 185,087 . . . D1
Boquerón ○3,675 . . . A3
Cabo Rojo 10,292 . . . A2
Caguas 87,214 . . . E2
Caguas †156,819 . . . E2
Camuy 3,834 . . . B1
Carolina 147,835 . . . E1
Cataño 26,243 . . . D1
Cayey 23,305 . . . D2
Ceiba 4,973 . . . F2
Central Aguirre 1,049 . . . D3
Ciales 3,582 . . . C1
Cidra 6,069 . . . D2
Coamo 12,851 . . . D2
Comerío 5,736 . . . D2
Coquí 3,018 . . . D3
Corozal 5,889 . . . D1
Coto Laurel ○5,192 . . . C2
Culebra (Dewey) 938 . . . G1
Dorado 10,203 . . . D1
Ensenada . . . B3
Esperanza 1,130 . . . G2
Fajardo 26,928 . . . F1
Florida 3,641 . . . C1
Guánica 9,628 . . . B3
Guayama 21,097 . . . E3
Guayanilla 6,163 . . . B3
Guaynabo 65,075 . . . D1
Gurabo 7,645 . . . E2
Hatillo 5,019 . . . B1
Hato Rey . . . E1
Hormigüeros 12,031 . . . A2
Humacao 19,147 . . . E2
Isabela 12,087 . . . A1
Isabel Segunda 2,330 . . . G2
Jayuya 3,588 . . . C2
Jobos 4,194 . . . D3
Juana Díaz 10,469 . . . C2
Juncos 7,851 . . . E2
Lajas 4,275 . . . A2
Lares 5,224 . . . B2
Las Piedras 4,857 . . . E2
Levittown 31,613 . . . D1
Loíza 3,932 . . . E1
Loíza Aldea . . . E1
Luquillo 4,531 . . . F1
Manatí 17,347 . . . C1
Maricao 1,390 . . . B2
Mayagüez 82,968 . . . A2
Mayagüez †98,155 . . . A2
Moca 3,960 . . . A1
Naguabo 4,135 . . . F2
Naranjito 2,849 . . . D1
Palmer 1,566 . . . F1
Palo Seco 1,172 . . . D1
Parguera . . . A3
Patillas 3,172 . . . E2
Peñuelas 4,235 . . . B2
Playa de Fajardo . . . F1
Playa de Humacao ○5,573 . . F2
Ponce 161,739 . . . C3
Ponce †168,272 . . . C3
Puerto Nuevo . . . D1
Puerto Real 2,390 . . . A2
Puerto Real (Playa de Fajardo) . . . F1
Punta Santiago (Playa de Humacao) ○5,573 . . . F2
Quebradillas 3,770 . . . B1
Río Blanco 1,433 . . . F2
Río Grande 12,047 . . . E1
Río Piedras . . . E1
Rosario . . . A2
Sabana Grande 7,435 . . . B2
Sabana Seca 11,431 . . . D1
Salinas 6,220 . . . D3
San Antonio 2,681 . . . A1
San Germán 13,054 . . . A2
San Juan (cap.) 424,600 . . . E1
San Juan †1,081,193 . . . E1
San Lorenzo 8,880 . . . E2
San Sebastián 10,619 . . . B1
Santa Isabel 6,948 . . . C3
Santurce . . . E1
Tallaboa 1,059 . . . B3
Toa Alta 4,427 . . . D1
Toa Baja 1,992 . . . D1
Trujillo Alto 41,141 . . . E1
Utuado 11,113 . . . B2
Vega Alta 10,582 . . . D1
Vega Baja 18,233 . . . D1
Vieques (Isabel Segunda) 2,330 . . . G2
Villalba 3,469 . . . C2
Yabucoa 6,797 . . . E2
Yauco 14,594 . . . B2

OTHER FEATURES

Aguadilla (bay) . . . A1
Algarrobo (pt.) . . . A2
Añasco (bay) . . . A1
Arenas (pt.) . . . F2
Bauta (riv.) . . . C2
Bayamón (riv.) . . . D1
Boquerón (bay) . . . A3
Borinquen (pt.) . . . A1
Cabullones (pt.) . . . C3
Caja de Muertos (isl.) . . . C3
Camuy (riv.) . . . B1
Canovanas (riv.) . . . E1
Caonillas (lake) . . . C2
Carite (lake) . . . E2
Carraízo (lake) . . . E1
Cayey, Sierra de (mts.) . . . D2
Central, Cordillera (range) . . C2
Cerro Gordo (pt.) . . . D1
Coamo (res.) . . . D3
Coamo (riv.) . . . D3
Culebra (isl.) 1,265 . . . G1
Culebrinas (riv.) . . . A1
Culebrita (isl.) . . . G2
El Toro (mt.) . . . F2
El Yunque (mt.) . . . F1
Este (pt.) . . . G2
Fajardo (riv.) . . . F1
Figuras (pt.) . . . E3
Fosforescente (bay) . . . A3
Grande de Añasco (riv.) . . . B2
Grande de Arecibo (riv.) . . . C1
Grande de Loíza (riv.) . . . E1
Grande de Manatí (riv.) . . . C1
Guajataca (lake) . . . B1
Guanajibo (pt.) . . . A2
Guanajibo (riv.) . . . A2
Guánica (lake) . . . B3
Guaniquilla (pt.) . . . A2
Guayabal (lake) . . . C2
Guayanés (pt.) . . . F2
Guayanés (riv.) . . . E2
Guayanilla (bay) . . . B3
Guayo (lake) . . . B2
Guilarte (mt.) . . . B2
Honda (bay) . . . F2
Jacaguas (riv.) . . . C2
Jaicoa, Cordillera (mts.) . . . B1
Jiguero (pt.) . . . A1
Jobos (bay) . . . D3
Lima (pt.) . . . F2
Luquillo, Sierra de (mts.) . . . E2
Manglillo (pt.) . . . B3
Mayagüez (bay) . . . A2
Miquillo (pt.) . . . F1
Molinos (pt.) . . . G1
Mona (passg.) . . . A2
Negra (pt.) . . . G2
Nigua (riv.) . . . D2
Ola Grande (pt.) . . . D3
Palmas Altas (pt.) . . . C1
Patillas (lake) . . . E2
Petrona (pt.) . . . D3
Pirata (mt.) . . . F2
Plata (riv.) . . . D2
Puerca (pt.) . . . F2
Puerto Medio Mundo (bay) . . F2
Punta, Cerro de (mt.) . . . C2
Ramey A.F.B. . . . A1
Rincón (bay) . . . D3
Rojo (cape) . . . A3
Roosevelt Road Naval Res. . . F2
Salinas (pt.) . . . D1
San José (lag.) . . . E1
San Juan, Cabezas de (prom.) . . . F1
San Juan Nat'l Hist. Site . . . D1
Soldado (pt.) . . . G2
Sucia (bay) . . . A3
Tanamá (riv.) . . . B1
Toro, El (mt.) . . . F2
Torrecilla (lag.) . . . E1
Tortuguero (lag.) . . . D1
Tuna (pt.) . . . E3
Vacía Talega (pt.) . . . E1
Vieques (isl.) 7,662 . . . G2
Vieques (passg.) . . . F2
Vieques (sound) . . . G2
Yagüez (riv.) . . . A2
Yauco (lake) . . . B2
Yeguas ((pt.) . . . F3

ANTIGUA

CITIES and TOWNS

All Saints 1,796 . . . E11
Cedar Grove 1,460 . . . E11
Falmouth 1,134 . . . E11
Freetown 1,250 . . . E11
Jennings 1,370 . . . D11
Liberta 2,394 . . . E11
Old Road 1,244 . . . D11
Parham 1,570 . . . E11
Saint John's (cap.) 21,814 . E11
Willikies 1,843 . . . E11

OTHER FEATURES

Antigua (isl.) 76,213 . . . E11
Boggy (peak) . . . D11
Boon (pt.) . . . E11
Green (isl.) . . . E11
Guiana (isl.) . . . E11
Long (isl.) . . . E11
Saint John's (harb.) . . . C11
Standfast (pt.) . . . E11
Willoughby (bay) . . . E11

BARBADOS

CITIES and TOWNS

Bathsheba . . . B8
Belleplaine . . . B8
Bridgetown (cap.) 7,552 . . . B9
Carlton . . . B8
Cave Hill . . . B9
Checker Hall . . . B8
Codrington . . . B8
Crab Hill . . . B8
Crane . . . C9
Drax Hall . . . B8
Ellerton . . . B9
Greenland . . . B8
Holetown . . . B8
Kendal . . . B8
Lodge Hill . . . B8
Marchfield . . . B9
Mount Standfast . . . B8
Oistins . . . B9
Rose Hill . . . B8
Rouen . . . B9
Saint Lawrence . . . B9
Saint Martins . . . C9
Scarboro . . . B9
Seawell . . . B9
Six Mens . . . B8
Speightstown . . . B8
Spring Hall . . . B8
Welchman Hall . . . B8

OTHER FEATURES

Carlisle (bay) . . . B9
Hillaby (mt.) . . . B8
Long (bay) . . . B9
North (pt.) . . . B8
Oistins (bay) . . . B9
Pelican (isl.) . . . B9
Ragged (pt.) . . . C8
Sam Lord's Castle . . . C9
South (pt.) . . . B9

DOMINICA

CITIES and TOWNS

Barroui 1,480 . . . E6
Castle Bruce 1,975 . . . F6
Coulihaut 1,735 . . . E6
Delice . . . F7
Grand Bay 3,152 . . . F7
Hampstead . . . E5
La Plaine . . . F6
Mahout 2,095 . . . E6
Marigot 3,183 . . . F6
Petit Soufrière . . . F6
Portsmouth 2,329 . . . E5
Rosalie . . . F6
Roseau (cap.) 9,968 . . . E7
Roseau *16,035 . . . E7
Saint Joseph 2,643 . . . E6
Salybia . . . F6
Soufrière . . . E7
Vieille Case . . . E5
Wesley 2,002 . . . F5

OTHER FEATURES

Capuchin (cape) . . . E5
Carib Reserve . . . F6
Clyde (riv.) . . . F6
Crumpton (pt.) . . . F5
Diablotin, Morne (mt.) . . . E6
Dominica (passg.) . . . E5
Douglas (bay) . . . E5
Grand (bay) . . . F7
Jaquet (pt.) . . . E5
Layou (riv.) . . . E6
Martinique (passg.) . . . E7
Micotrin (mt.) . . . F6
Pagoua (bay) . . . F6
Prince Rupert (bay) . . . E5
Scotts (head) . . . E7
Soufrière (bay) . . . E7
Trois Pitons, Morne (mt.) . . E6

GRENADA

CITIES and TOWNS

Gouyave 2,498 . . . C8
Grand Roy . . . C8
Grenville 1,723 . . . D8
Hermitage . . . D8
La Taste . . . D8
Marquis . . . D8
Mount Tivoli . . . D8
Saint George's (cap.) 6,463 . C9
Saint George's *34,624 . . . C9
Sauteurs 605 . . . D8
Victoria 1,673 . . . D8
Woodford . . . C8

OTHER FEATURES

Bedford (pt.) . . . D8
David (pt.) . . . D8
Great Bacolet (pt.) . . . D8
Green (isl.) . . . D8
Grenville (bay) . . . D8
Gros (pt.) . . . C8
Halifax (harb.) . . . C8
Irvin's (bay) . . . D8
Les Tantes (isls.) . . . D7
Molinière (pt.) . . . C8
Prickly (pt.) . . . C9
Ronde (isl.) . . . D7
Saint Catherine (mt.) . . . D8
Saline (pt.) . . . C9
Sinai (mt.) . . . D8
Telescope (pt.) . . . D8

GUADELOUPE

Total Population 329,017

CITIES and TOWNS

Anse-Bertrand 1,921 . . . A5
Baie-Mahault 5,874 . . . A6
Baillif 3,844 . . . A7
Bananier . . . A7
Basse-Terre (cap.) 13,397 . . A7
Bouillante 1,821 . . . A6
Bourg-des-Saintes 907 . . . A7
Capesterre 7,541 . . . A7
Ferry . . . A6
Gosier 13,741 . . . B6
Gourbeyre 5,637 . . . A7
Goyave 1,709 . . . A6
Grand-Bourg 3,249 . . . B7
Lamentin 2,319 . . . A6
Les Abymes 51,837 . . . B6
Morne-à-l'Eau 9,457 . . . A6
Moule 9,800 . . . B6
Petit-Bourg 5,097 . . . A6
Petit-Canal 1,581 . . . A6
Pigeon . . . A6
Pointe-à-Pitre 25,151 . . . B6
Pointe-Noire 2,180 . . . A6
Port-Louis 4,517 . . . B5
Saint-Claude 6,755 . . . A7
Sainte-Anne 11,527 . . . B6
Sainte-Marguerite . . . B6
Sainte-Marie . . . A6
Sainte-Rose 4,805 . . . A6
Saint-François 3,141 . . . B6
Trois-Rivières 7,881 . . . A7
Vieux-Fort 1,073 . . . B7
Vieux-Habitants 4,065 . . . A7

OTHER FEATURES

Allègre (pt.) . . . A6
Antigues (pt.) . . . A5
Basse-Terre (isl.) 138,777 . . A6
Châteaux (pt.) . . . B6
Constant, Morne (hill) . . . B7
Désirade, La (isl.) 1,602 . . . B6
Fajou (isl.) . . . A6
Grand Cul-de-Sac Marin (bay) . . . A6
Grande-Terre (isl.) . . . B6
Grande Vigie (pt.) . . . B5
Grand-Îlet (isl.) . . . A7
Guadeloupe (isl.) 167,896 . . B6
Guadeloupe (passg.) . . . A5
Guadeloupe Nat'l Park . . . A6
Kahouanne (isl.) . . . A6
Marie-Galante (isl.) 13,757 . . B7
Nord (pt.) . . . B7
Nord-Est (bay) . . . B6
Petit Cul-de-Sac Marin (bay) . A6
Petite-Terre (isls.) . . . B6
Saintes (chan.) . . . A7
Saintes (isls.) 2,901 . . . A7
Salée (riv.) . . . A6
Sans Toucher (mt.) . . . A6
Soufrière (mt.) . . . A7
Terre-de-Bas (isl.) 1,427 . . . A7
Terre-de-Haut (isl.) 1,453 . . A7
Vieux-Fort (pt.) . . . A7

MARTINIQUE

Total Population 330,220

CITIES and TOWNS

Ajoupa-Bouillon 1,569 . . . C5
Basse-Pointe 2,163 . . . C5
Bellefontaine 818 . . . C6
Case-Pilote 1,776 . . . C6
Ducos 4,429 . . . D6
Fond-Saint-Denis 962 . . . C6
Fort-de-France (cap.) 96,649 C6
Grand' Rivière 1,053 . . . C5
Gros-Morne 1,976 . . . D6
La Trinité 3,380 . . . D6
Le Carbet 2,321 . . . C6
Le François 2,940 . . . D6
Le Lamentin 6,872 . . . D6
Le Lorrain 2,024 . . . D6
Le Marin 2,651 . . . D7
Le Morne-Rouge 2,650 . . . C5
Le Prêcheur 1,350 . . . C5
Le Robert 3,610 . . . D6
Le Saint-Esprit 3,947 . . . D6
Les Trois-Îlets 1,484 . . . D6
Le Vauclin 3,054 . . . D6
Macouba 1,142 . . . C5
Marigot 1,765 . . . D5
Rivière-Pilote 1,587 . . . D7
Rivière-Salée 1,859 . . . D7
Sainte-Luce 1,502 . . . D7
Sainte-Marie 3,966 . . . D5
Saint-Joseph 2,052 . . . D6
Saint-Pierre 4,923 . . . C6
Schoelcher 16,412 . . . C6

OTHER FEATURES

Cabet, Pitons du (mt.) . . . C6
Cabrits (isl.) . . . D7
Caravelle (pen.) . . . D6
Cul-de-Sac du Marin (bay) . . D7
Diable (pt.) . . . D5
Ferré (cape) . . . E7
Fort-de-France (bay) . . . C6
Galion (bay) . . . D6
Lézarde (riv.) . . . D6
Long (isl.) . . . D6
Lorrain (riv.) . . . D5
Martinique (passg.) . . . C5
Pelée (vol.) . . . C5
Pilote (riv.) . . . D7
Ramiers (isl.) . . . C6
Ramville (isl.) . . . D6
Robert (harb.) . . . D6
Rose (pt.) . . . D6
Saint-Martin (cape) . . . C5
Saint-Pierre (bay) . . . C6
Salines (pt.) . . . D7
Salomon (pt.) . . . C7
Vauclin (mt.) . . . D6

NETHERLANDS ANTILLES

CITIES and TOWNS

Aresji . . . D9
Ascension . . . F8
Bacuna . . . E8
Balashi . . . E10
Boven Bolivia . . . E8
Bubali . . . D10
Bushiribana . . . E10
Dokterstuin . . . F8
Druif . . . D1
Emmastad . . . F9
Entrejo . . . E8
Fontein . . . E8
Fuik . . . G9
Groot Sint Joris . . . G9
Hato . . . G8
Kralendijk (cap.), Bonaire 2,500 . . . E8
Lago . . . E10
Lagoen . . . F8
Montanja di Reij . . . G9
New Port . . . G9
Noord di Salinja . . . E8
Onima . . . E8
Oranjestad (cap.), Aruba 10,100 . . . D10
Otrabanda . . . F9
Patrick . . . F8
Rincon . . . E8
Rooi . . . E8
Santa Barbara . . . G9
Santa Catharina . . . G9
Savaneta . . . E10
Savonet . . . F8
Sint Anna . . . D1
Sint Jan . . . D8
Sint Kruis . . . F8
Sint Martha . . . F8
Sint Michiel . . . F9
Sint Nicolaas . . . E10
Sint Willebrordus . . . F8
Terra Corra . . . E8
Westpunt, Aruba . . . D10
Westpunt, Curaçao . . . F8
Willemstad (cap.) 95,000 . . F9
Willemstad *130,000 . . . F9

OTHER FEATURES

Aruba (isl.) 55,148 . . . E9
Basora (pt.) . . . E10
Bonaire (isl.) 8,087 . . . E9
Bullen (bay) . . . F8
Caracas (bay) . . . G9
Curaçao (isl.) 145,430 . . . G7
Goto (lake) . . . D8
Jamanota (mt.) . . . E10
Kanon (pt.) . . . G9
Klein Bonaire (isl.) . . . E8
Kudarebe (pt.) . . . D9
Lac (bay) . . . D9
Lacre (pt.) . . . E9
Malmok (mt.) . . . E8
Noord (pt.) . . . D8
Noord (pt.) . . . F8
Paarden (bay) . . . D10
Palm (beach) . . . D10
Pekelmeer (lake) . . . E9
Piscadera (bay) . . . F9
Schottegat (bay) . . . G9
Sint Anna (bay) . . . F9
Sint Christoffel (mt.) . . . F8
Sint Joris (bay) . . . G9
Slag (bay) . . . D8
Vierkant (pt.) . . . E8

SAINT CHRISTOPHER and NEVIS

CITIES and TOWNS

Basseterre (cap.) 14,725 . . C10
Cayon . . . C10
Charlestown 1,326 . . . C11
Cotton Ground 471 . . . C11
Dieppe Bay . . . C10
Frigate Bay . . . C10
Gingerland . . . D11
Golden Rock . . . C10
Newcastle . . . D11
Old Road Town . . . C10
Sadlers Village . . . C10
Sandy Point 862 . . . C10
Tabernacle . . . C10
Zion Hill . . . D11

OTHER FEATURES

Brimstone (hill) . . . C10
Dogwood (pt.) . . . D11
Fort (pt.) . . . C11
Great Salt (pond) . . . D10
Heldens (pt.) . . . C10
Horse Shoe (pt.) . . . C11
Misery (mt.) . . . C10
Monkey (hill) . . . C10
Narrows, The (str.) . . . D11
Nevis (isl.) 9,300 . . . D11
Nevis (peak) . . . D11
North Friars (bay) . . . D10
Pinney's (beach) . . . D11
Saint Christopher (Saint Kitts) (isl.) 35,104 . . . D10
South Friars (bay) . . . C10

SAINT LUCIA

CITIES and TOWNS

Anse la Raye •5,007 . . . F6
Canaries •2,075 . . . G6
Castries (cap.) •42,770 . . . G6
Choc . . . G5
Choiseul •6,382 . . . F7
Dauphin . . . G5
Dennery •9,654 . . . G6
Gros Islet •10,329 . . . G5
Laborie •6,944 . . . G7
Marigot . . . G6
Marquis . . . G6
Micoud •12,264 . . . G6
Preslin . . . G6
Soufrière •7,456 . . . F6
Vieux Fort •10,675 . . . G7

OTHER FEATURES

Beaumont (pt.) . . . F6
Canaries, Piton (mt.) . . . G6
Cannelles (pt.) . . . G7
Cannelles (riv.) . . . G6
Cap (pt.) . . . G5
Choc (bay) . . . G5
Fond d'Or (bay) . . . G6
Gimie (mt.) . . . G6
Grand Caille (pt.) . . . F6
Grand Cul de Sac (riv.) . . . G6
Gros Islet (bay) . . . G5
Gros Piton (mt.) . . . G6
La Sorcière (mt.) . . . G6
Maria (isls.) . . . G7
Ministre (pt.) . . . G7
Moule-à-Chique (cape) . . . G7
Petit Piton (mt.) . . . G6
Pigeon (isl.) . . . G5
Port Castries (harb.) . . . G6
Port Praslin (bay) . . . G6
Roseau (riv.) . . . G6
Saint Lucia (chan.) . . . G5
Saint Vincent (chan.) . . . G7
Savannes (bay) . . . G7
Sorcière, La (mt.) . . . G6
Soufrière (bay) . . . F6
Vierge (pt.) . . . G6

SAINT VINCENT and THE GRENADINES

CITIES and TOWNS

Barrouallie 1,298 . . . A9
Calliaqua 627 . . . A9
Camden Park . . . A9
Colonarie . . . A9
Georgetown 1,100 . . . A8
Kingstown (cap.) 17,117 . . . A9
Kingstown *23,330 . . . A9
Layou 1,147 . . . A9
Wallibu . . . A8

OTHER FEATURES

Colonarie (pt.) . . . A9
Cumberland (bay) . . . A8
Dark (head) . . . A8
De Volet (pt.) . . . A8
Espagnol (pt.) . . . A8
Greathead (bay) . . . A9
Kingstown (bay) . . . A9
Owia (bay) . . . A8
Porter (pt.) . . . A8
Richmond (peak) . . . A8
Saint Andrew (mt.) . . . A9
Saint Vincent (passg.) . . . A8
Soufrière (mt.) . . . A8
Yambou (head) . . . A9

TRINIDAD and TOBAGO

CITIES and TOWNS

Arima 11,390 . . . B10
Arouca . . . B10
Basse Terre . . . B11
Biche . . . B10
Blanchisseuse . . . B10
California . . . A11
Carapichaima . . . B10
Caroni . . . B10
Cedros . . . A11
Chaguanas 6,122 . . . B10
Chaguaramas . . . A10
Couva 3,635 . . . B10
Cunapo . . . B10
Ecclesville . . . B11
Flanagin Town . . . B10
Fullarton . . . A11
Fyzabad 1,564 . . . A11
Grande Rivière . . . B10
Guaico . . . B10
Guayaguayare . . . B11
La Brea 1,487 . . . A11
Marabella 18,158 . . . A11
Matelot . . . B10
Matura . . . B10
Mayaro 2,638 . . . B11
Moruga . . . B11
Mucurapo . . . A10
Palo Seco . . . A11
Peñal 3,606 . . . B11
Point Fortin 6,538 . . . A11
Port-of-Spain (cap.) 67,978 . . . A10
Princes Town 8,288 . . . B11
Redhead . . . B10
Rio Claro 2,423 . . . B11
Saint Joseph 4,132 . . . B10
Saint Joseph . . . B11
San Fernando 33,490 . . . A11
San Francique . . . A11
Sangre Grande 8,948 . . . B1
San Juan . . . A10
Sans Souci . . . B10
Siparia 5,773 . . . B11
Tabaquite 2,309 . . . B11
Tacarigua . . . B10
Talparo . . . B10
Toco 1,287 . . . B10
Tunapuna 10,251 . . . B10
Upper Manzanilla . . . B1
Valencia . . . B10
Waterloo . . . A10

OTHER FEATURES

Aripo, El Cerro del (mt.) . . B10
Boca Grande (passg.) . . . A10
Chacachacare (isl.) . . . A10
Chupara (pt.) . . . B10
Cocos (bay) . . . B10
Dragons Mouth (str.) . . . A10
El Tucuche (mt.) . . . B10
Erin (bay) . . . A11
Galeota (pt.) . . . B11
Galera (pt.) . . . C10
Guapo (bay) . . . A11
Guatuaro (pt.) . . . B11
Icacos (pt.) . . . A11
Maracas (bay) . . . C10
Pitch (lake) . . . A11

VIRGIN ISLANDS (Br.)

CITIES and TOWNS

Road Town (cap.) 2,200 . . . D3
West End . . . C4

OTHER FEATURES

Flanagan (passg.) . . . D4
Frenchman (cay) . . . C4
Great Thatch (isl.) . . . C4
Great Tobago (isl.) . . . B3
Jost Van Dyke (isl.) 135 . . . C3
Little Tobago (isl.) . . . B3
Narrows, The (str.) . . . C4
Norman (isl.) . . . D4
Peter (isl.) . . . D4
Road (bay) . . . D3
Sage (mt.) . . . D4
Sir Francis Drake (chan.) . . . D4
Tortola (isl.) 9,257 . . . D3

VIRGIN ISLANDS (U.S.)

CITIES and TOWNS

Bethlehem . . . E4
Canebay . . . E3
Charlotte Amalie (cap.) 11,842 . . . B4
Christiansted 2,914 . . . F4
Cruz Bay 1,928 . . . C4
Diamond . . . F4
Eastend . . . D4
Emmaus . . . C4
Fredensdal . . . F4
Frederiksted 1,046 . . . E4
Grove Place 3,599 . . . E4
Kingshill . . . F4
Longford . . . F4
Negro Bay . . . E4

OTHER FEATURES

Altona (lag.) . . . F4
Annaly (bay) . . . E3
Baron Bluff (prom.) . . . E3
Bordeaux (mt.) . . . C4
Brass (isls.) . . . A4
Buck (isl.) . . . G3
Buck Island (chan.) . . . F3
Buck Island Reef Nat'l Mon. . G3
Butler (bay) . . . E4
Caneel (bay) . . . B4
Capella (isls.) . . . B5
Christiansted Nat'l Hist. Site . F4
Coral (bay) . . . C4
Crown (mt.) . . . A4
Dutch Cap (cay) . . . A4
Eagle (mt.) . . . E4
East (pt.) . . . G4
Flanagan (passg.) . . . D4
Flat (cays) . . . A4
Grass (pt.) . . . G4
Great (pond) . . . F4
Great Pond (bay) . . . F4
Green (cay) . . . F4
Hams Bluff (prom.) . . . E3
Hans Lollik (isls.) . . . B4
Hassel (isl.) . . . B4
Jersey (bay) . . . B4
Krause Lagoon (chan.) . . . F4
Leeward (passg.) . . . B4
Long (pt.) . . . B4
Long (pt.) . . . E4
Lovango (cay) . . . C4
Magens (bay) . . . B4
Maho (bay) . . . C4
Narrows, The (str.) . . . C4
Nulliberg (mt.) . . . B4
Perseverance (bay) . . . A4
Picara (pt.) . . . B4
Pillsbury (sound) . . . B4
Privateer (pt.) . . . D4
Pull (pt.) . . . F3
Ram (head) . . . C5
Red (pt.) . . . D4
Reef (bay) . . . C4
Saba (isl.) . . . A4
Saint Croix (isl.) 49,725 . . . G4
Saint James (isls.) . . . B4
Saint John (isl.) 2,472 . . . C4
Saint Thomas (harb.) . . . B4
Saint Thomas (isl.) 44,372 . . A4
Salt (cay) . . . A4
Salt (riv.) . . . F4
Salt River (bay) . . . F3
Sandy (pt.) . . . D4
Savana (isl.) . . . A4
Southwest (cape) . . . E4
Tague (bay) . . . G4
Thatch (cay) . . . B4
Turner Hole (bay) . . . G4
U.S. Nav. Air Sta. . . . A4
Virgin (str.) . . . A4
Virgin Isls. Nat'l Park . . . C4
Water (isl.) . . . A4
Westend Saltpond (lag.) . . . E4

*City and suburbs.
• Population of district.
†Population of met. area.
○ Population of municipality.

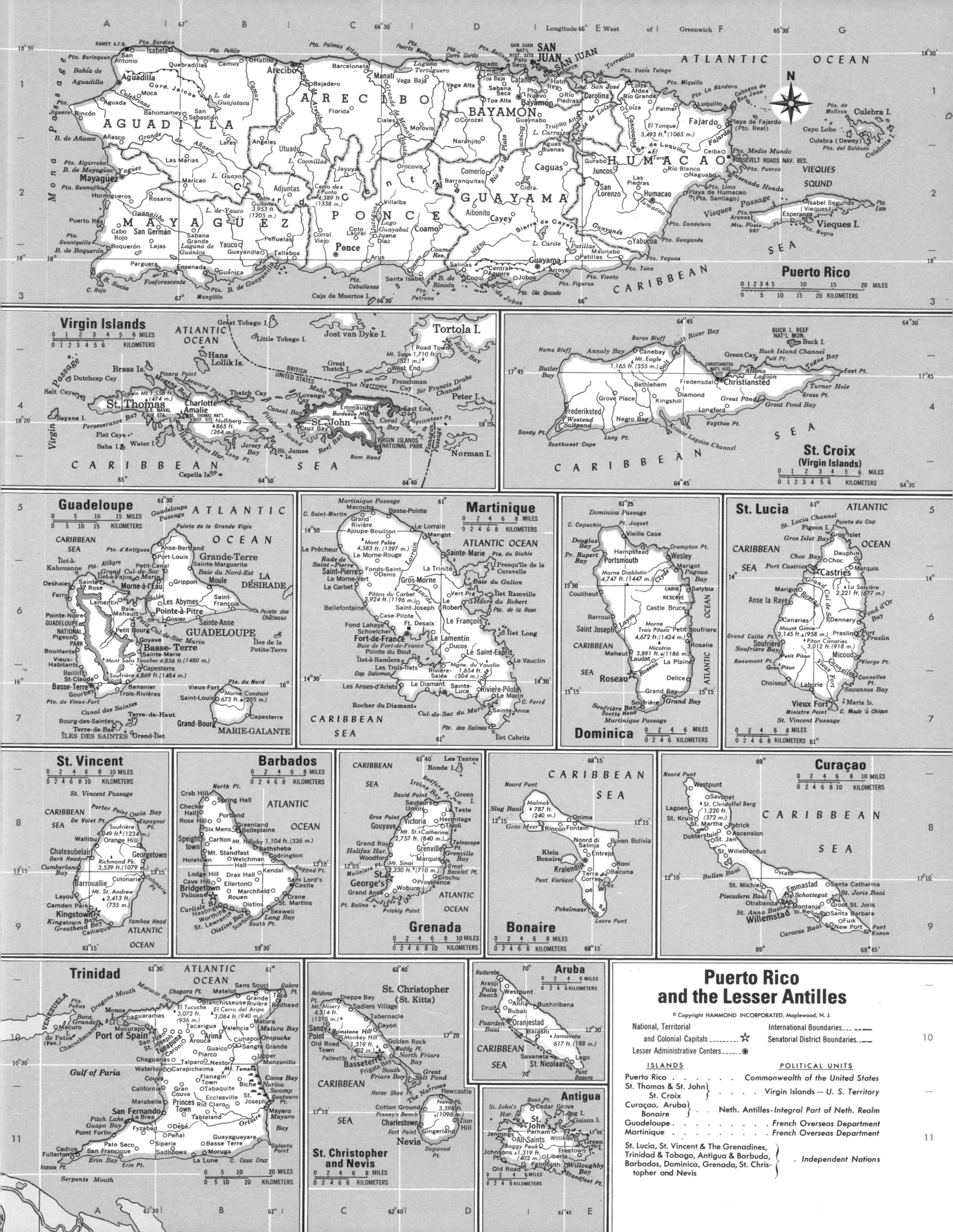

Puerto Rico and the Lesser Antilles

© Copyright HAMMOND INCORPORATED, Maplewood, N.J.

National, Territorial and Colonial Capitals ☆

Lesser Administrative Centers ◉

International Boundaries

Senatorial District Boundaries

ISLANDS	POLITICAL UNITS
Puerto Rico	Commonwealth of the United States
St. Thomas & St. John	Virgin Islands — U. S. Territory
St. Croix	
Curaçao, Aruba Bonaire	Neth. Antilles-Integral Part of Neth. Realm
Guadeloupe	French Overseas Department
Martinique	French Overseas Department
St. Lucia, St. Vincent & The Grenadines, Trinidad & Tobago, Antigua & Barbuda, Barbados, Dominica, Grenada, St. Christopher and Nevis	Independent Nations

Canada

CONIC PROJECTION

SCALE OF MILES
0 50 100 300

SCALE OF KILOMETERS
0 50 100 200 300 500

Capitals of Countries .... ☆
Provincial & Territorial Capitals .... △
Administrative Centers .... ◉
International Boundaries .... —··—··—
Provincial Boundaries .... —·—·—
Regional Boundaries .... —— ——

Scale 1:19,600,000

© Copyright HAMMOND INCORPORATED, Maplewood, N.J.

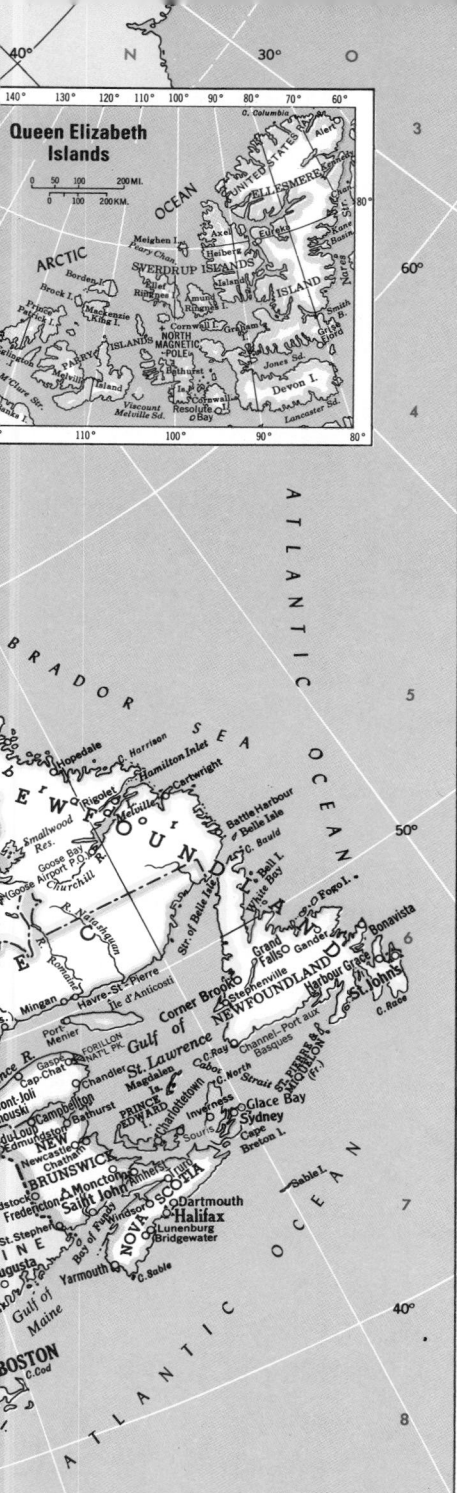

AREA   3,851,787 sq. mi. (9,976,139 sq. km.)
POPULATION   24,343,181
CAPITAL   Ottawa
LARGEST CITY   Montréal
HIGHEST POINT   Mt. Logan 19,524 ft. (5,951 m.)
MONETARY UNIT   Canadian dollar
MAJOR LANGUAGES   English, French
MAJOR RELIGIONS   Protestantism, Roman Catholicism

Population Distribution

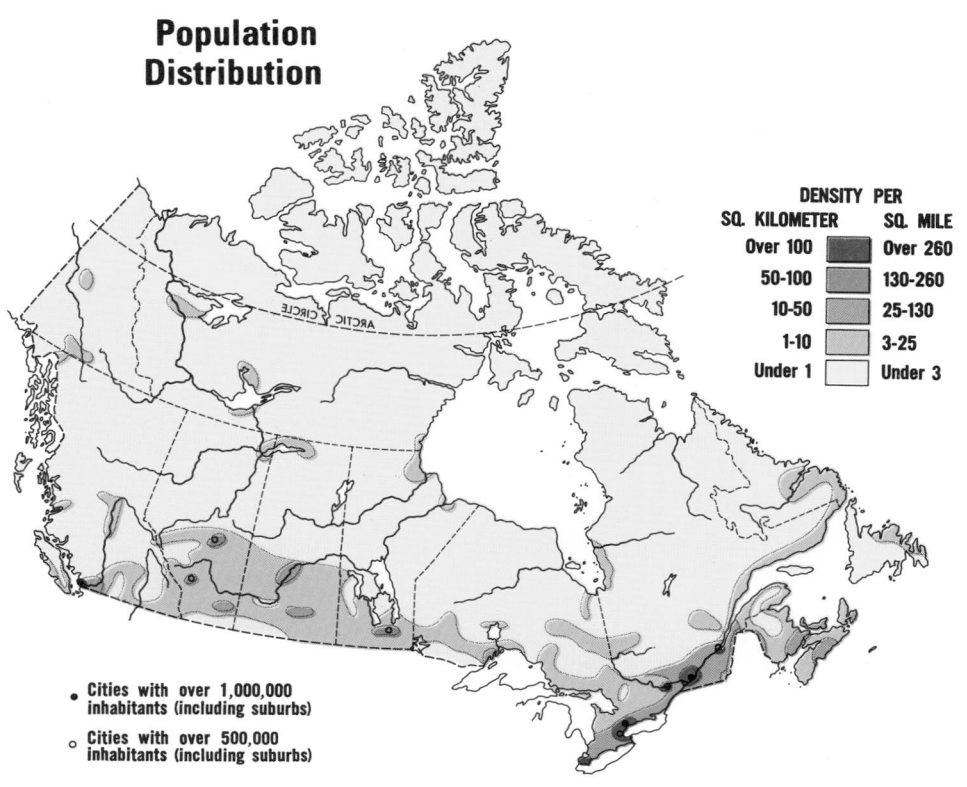

DENSITY PER

SQ. KILOMETER		SQ. MILE
Over 100		Over 260
50-100		130-260
10-50		25-130
1-10		3-25
Under 1		Under 3

● Cities with over 1,000,000 inhabitants (including suburbs)

○ Cities with over 500,000 inhabitants (including suburbs)

Vegetation

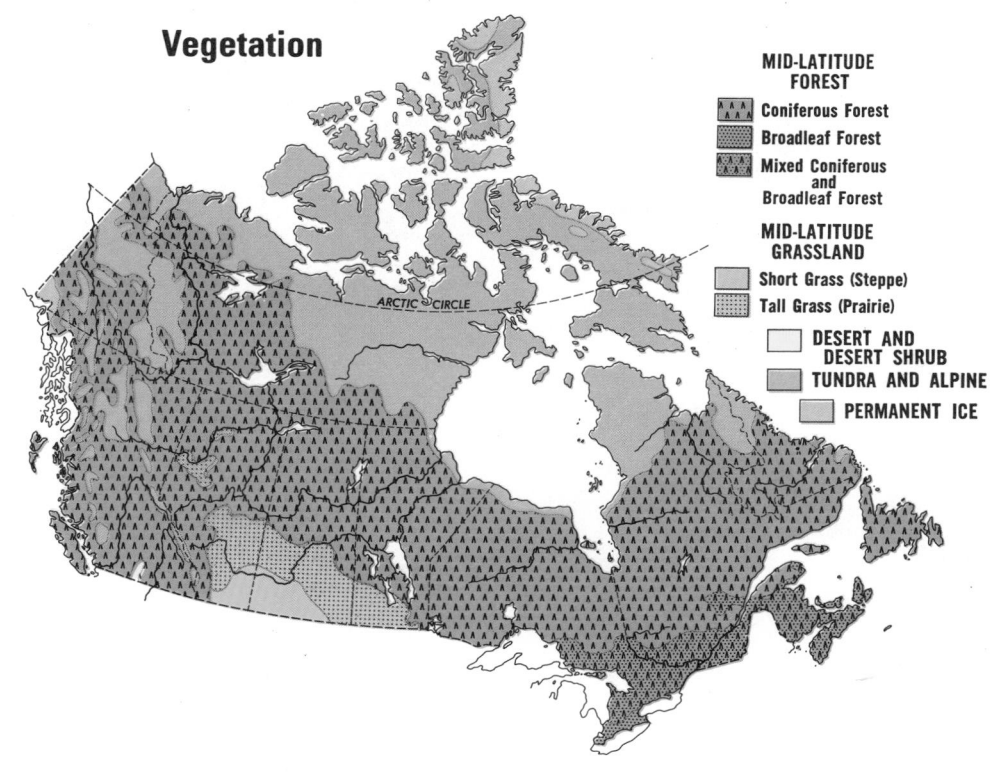

MID-LATITUDE FOREST

Coniferous Forest

Broadleaf Forest

Mixed Coniferous and Broadleaf Forest

MID-LATITUDE GRASSLAND

Short Grass (Steppe)

Tall Grass (Prairie)

DESERT AND DESERT SHRUB

TUNDRA AND ALPINE

PERMANENT ICE

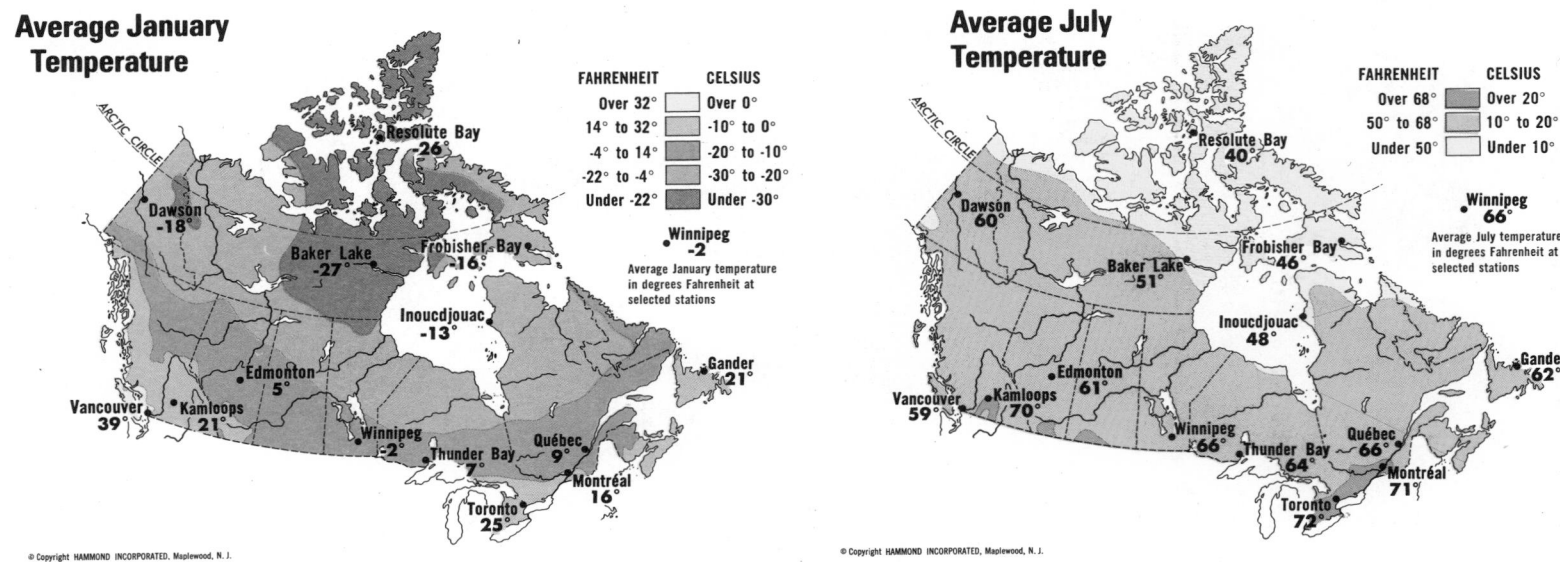

Average January Temperature

FAHRENHEIT	CELSIUS
Over 32°	Over 0°
14° to 32°	-10° to 0°
-4° to 14°	-20° to -10°
-22° to -4°	-30° to -20°
Under -22°	Under -30°

Average January temperature in degrees Fahrenheit at selected stations

ARCTIC CIRCLE

Resolute Bay -26
Dawson -18
Baker Lake -27
Frobisher Bay -16
Inoucdjouac -13
Edmonton 5°
Gander 21°
Vancouver 39
Kamloops 21°
Winnipeg -2
Thunder Bay 7°
Québec 9°
Montréal 16°
Toronto 25°

© Copyright HAMMOND INCORPORATED, Maplewood, N. J.

Average July Temperature

FAHRENHEIT	CELSIUS
Over 68°	Over 20°
50° to 68°	10° to 20°
Under 50°	Under 10°

Average July temperature in degrees Fahrenheit at selected stations

ARCTIC CIRCLE

Resolute Bay 40
Dawson 60°
Baker Lake 51°
Frobisher Bay 46°
Winnipeg 66°
Inoucdjouac 48°
Edmonton 61°
Gander 62°
Vancouver 59°
Kamloops 70°
Winnipeg 66°
Thunder Bay 64
Québec 66°
Montréal 71°
Toronto 72°

© Copyright HAMMOND INCORPORATED, Maplewood, N. J.

Agriculture, Industry and Resources

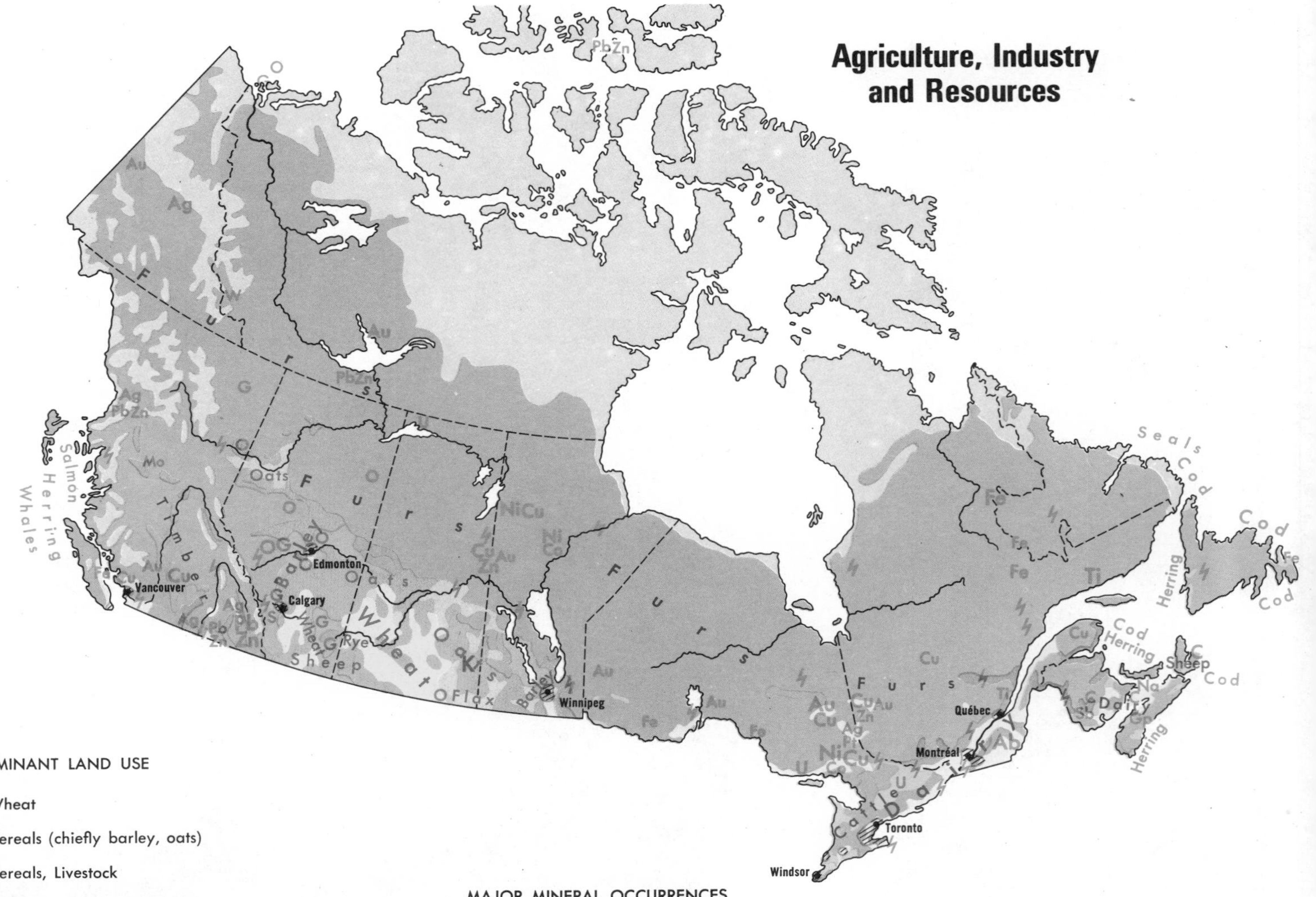

Edmonton
Calgary
Vancouver
Winnipeg
Québec
Montréal
Toronto
Windsor

DOMINANT LAND USE

- Wheat
- Cereals (chiefly barley, oats)
- Cereals, Livestock
- General Farming, Livestock
- Dairy
- Fruit, Vegetables
- Pasture Livestock
- Range Livestock
- Forests
- Nonagricultural Land

MAJOR MINERAL OCCURRENCES

Ab	Asbestos	Fe	Iron Ore	Ni	Nickel	Sb	Antimony
Ag	Silver	G	Natural Gas	O	Petroleum	Ti	Titanium
Au	Gold	Gp	Gypsum	Pb	Lead	U	Uranium
C	Coal	K	Potash	Pt	Platinum	W	Tungsten
Co	Cobalt	Mo	Molybdenum	S	Sulfur	Zn	Zinc
Cu	Copper	Na	Salt				

⚡ Water Power

▨ Major Industrial Areas

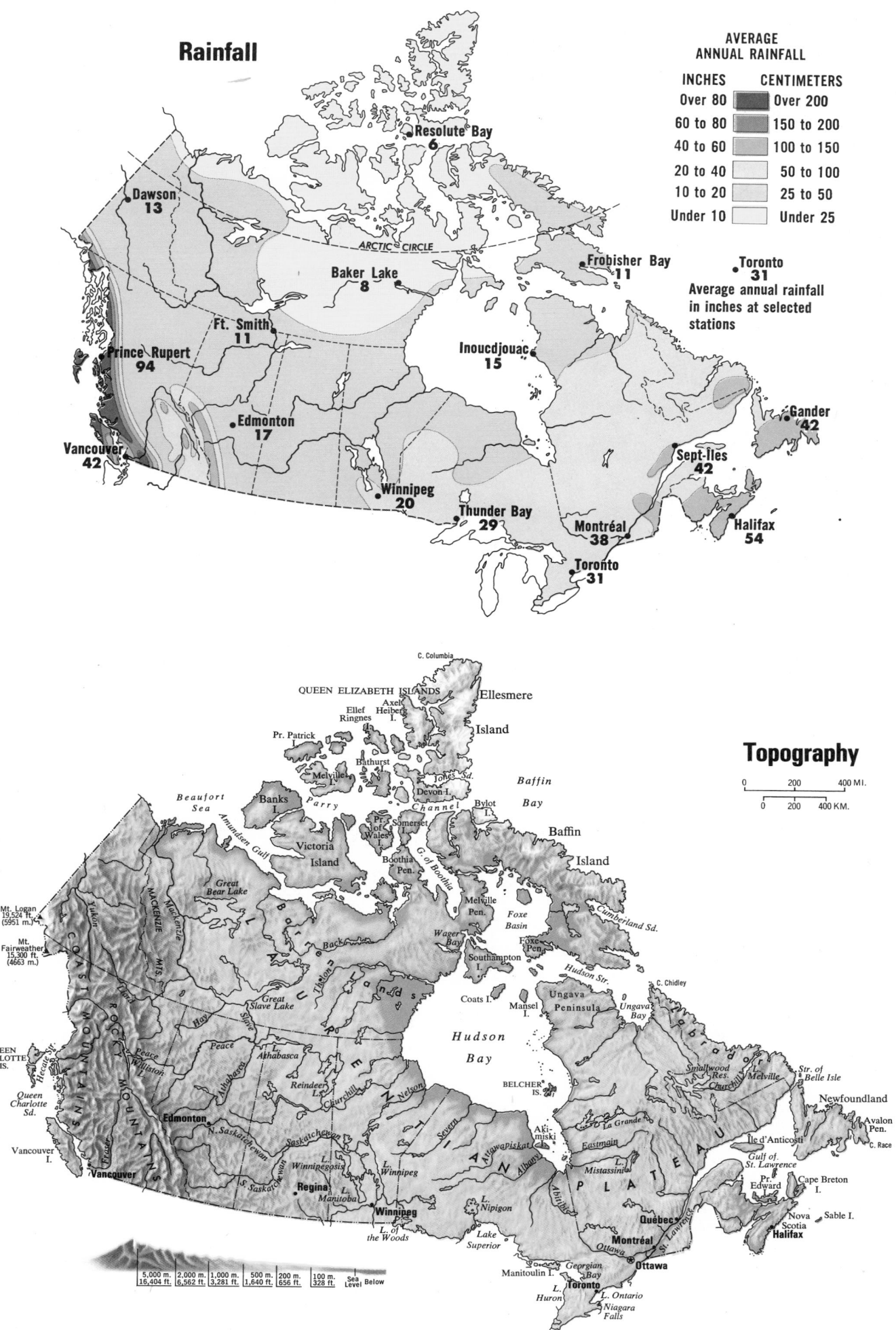

Rainfall

AVERAGE
ANNUAL RAINFALL

INCHES	CENTIMETERS
Over 80	Over 200
60 to 80	150 to 200
40 to 60	100 to 150
20 to 40	50 to 100
10 to 20	25 to 50
Under 10	Under 25

Resolute Bay
6

Dawson
13

ARCTIC CIRCLE

Baker Lake
8

Frobisher Bay
11

Toronto
31

Average annual rainfall
in inches at selected
stations

Ft. Smith
11

Prince Rupert
94

Inoucdjouac
15

Gander
42

Edmonton
17

Vancouver
42

Sept-Îles
42

Winnipeg
20

Thunder Bay
29

Montréal
38

Halifax
54

Toronto
31

Topography

0   200   400 MI.
0   200   400 KM.

C. Columbia

QUEEN ELIZABETH ISLANDS   Ellesmere

Ellef
Ringnes   Axel
Heiberg
I.   Island

Pr. Patrick

Bathurst

Melville   Jones Sd.   Baffin
Bay

Beaufort
Sea   Banks
I.   Parry   Devon I.

Channel   Bylot
I.

Amundsen Gulf   Pr.
of
Wales   Somerset
I.   Baffin

Victoria
Island   Boothia
Pen.   Island

G. of Boothia

Mt. Logan
19,524 ft.
(5951 m.)   Great
Bear Lake   Melville
Pen.   Cumberland Sd.

Foxe
Basin

Mt.
Fairweather
15,300 ft.
(4663 m.)   Great
Slave Lake   Wager
Bay   Foxe
Pen.

Southampton
I.   Hudson Str.

C. Chidley

QUEEN
CHARLOTTE
IS.   Peace   Coats I.   Mansel
I.   Ungava
Peninsula   Ungava
Bay

Queen
Charlotte
Sd.   Williston   Hudson
Bay   Smallwood
Res.   Melville   Str. of
Belle Isle

Edmonton   N. Saskatchewan   BELCHER
IS.   Churchill   Newfoundland

Reindeer
L.   Churchill   La Grande   Avalon
Pen.

Vancouver
I.   Saskatchewan   Severn   Eastmain   Île d'Anticosti   C. Race

Vancouver   S. Sask.   Winnipegosis   Albany   Mistassini   Gulf of
St. Lawrence   Pr.
Edward   Cape Breton
I.

Regina   L.
Manitoba   L.
Winnipeg   Nipigon   Abitibi   Québec   Sable I.

Winnipeg   Lake
Superior   Montréal   Nova
Scotia   Halifax

L. of
the Woods   Georgian
Bay   Ottawa

Manitoulin I.   Toronto
L.
Huron   L. Ontario
Niagara
Falls

5,000 m. | 2,000 m. | 1,000 m. | 500 m. | 200 m. | 100 m. | Sea
16,404 ft. | 6,562 ft. | 3,281 ft. | 1,640 ft. | 656 ft. | 328 ft. | Level   Below

Newfoundland
including Labrador

SCALE

0   25   50   100   150 MI.

0   25   50   100   150 KM.

Capitals of Provinces .... ⊛
Provincial Boundaries ....
Provincial Boundary according to
Imperial Privy Council decision, 1927 ......

Scale 1:5,200,000

© Copyright HAMMOND INCORPORATED, Maplewood, N.J.

Longitude West of Greenwich

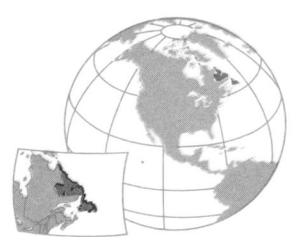

AREA 156,184 sq. mi. (404,517 sq. km.)
POPULATION 567,681
CAPITAL St. John's
LARGEST CITY St. John's
HIGHEST POINT in Torngat Mountains 5,420 ft. (1,652 m.)
SETTLED IN 1610
ADMITTED TO CONFEDERATION 1949
PROVINCIAL FLOWER Pitcher Plant

Agriculture, Industry and Resources

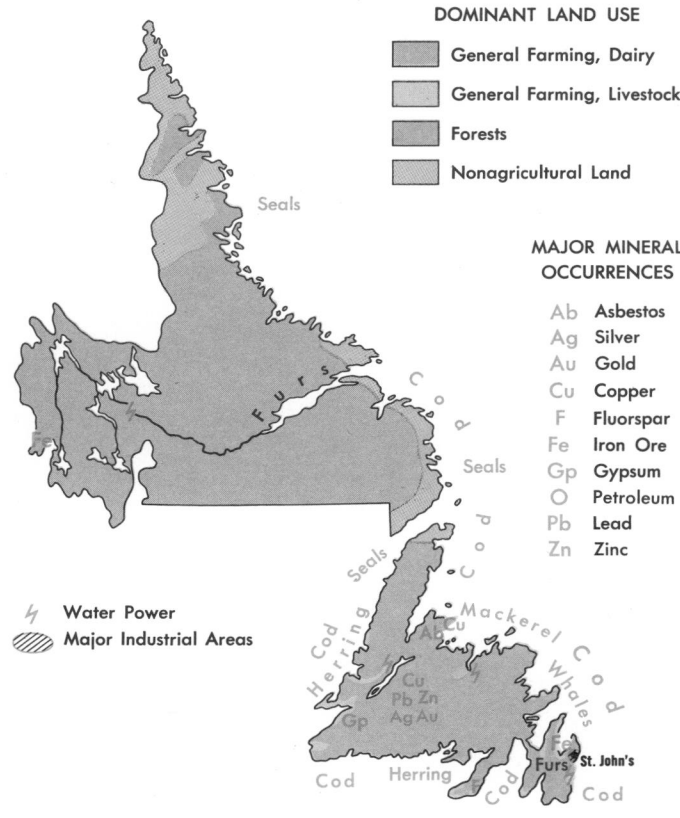

DOMINANT LAND USE

- General Farming, Dairy
- General Farming, Livestock
- Forests
- Nonagricultural Land

MAJOR MINERAL OCCURRENCES

Ab	Asbestos
Ag	Silver
Au	Gold
Cu	Copper
F	Fluorspar
Fe	Iron Ore
Gp	Gypsum
O	Petroleum
Pb	Lead
Zn	Zinc

⚡ Water Power
▨ Major Industrial Areas

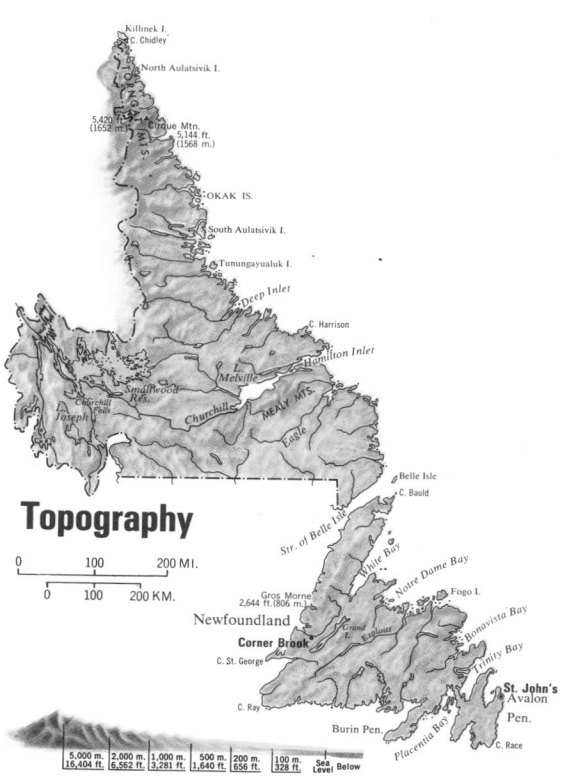

Topography

0   100   200 MI.
0   100   200 KM.

| 5,000 m. 16,404 ft. | 2,000 m. 6,562 ft. | 1,000 m. 3,281 ft. | 500 m. 1,640 ft. | 200 m. 656 ft. | 100 m. 328 ft. | Sea Level | Below |

NOVA SCOTIA

COUNTIES

Annapolis 22,522 .... C 4
Antigonish 18,110 .... F 3
Cape Breton 127,035 .... H 3
Colchester 43,224 .... E 3
Cumberland 35,231 .... D 3
Digby 21,689 .... C 4
Guysborough 12,752 .... F 3
Halifax 288,126 .... E 4
Hants 33,121 .... D 4
Inverness 22,337 .... G 2
Kings 49,739 .... D 4
Lunenburg 45,746 .... D 4
Pictou 50,350 .... F 3
Queens 13,126 .... C 4
Richmond 12,284 .... H 3
Shelburne 17,328 .... C 5
Victoria 8,432 .... H 2
Yarmouth 26,290 .... C 5

CITIES and TOWNS

Alder Point 651 .... H 2
Aldershot .... D 3
Amherst◉ 9,684 .... D 3
Annapolis Royal◉ 631 .... C 4
Antigonish◉ 5,205 .... F 3
Arichat 824 .... H 3
Aylesford 744 .... D 3
Baddeck◉ 972 .... H 2
Barrington Passage 722 .... C 5
Bear River-Sissiboo 854 .... C 4
Beaverbank 1,322 .... E 4
Berwick 1,691 .... D 4
Bridgetown 1,047 .... C 4
Bridgewater 6,669 .... D 4
Brookfield 619 .... E 3
Brooklyn 1,269 .... D 4
Cambridge Station 799 .... D 3
Canning 763 .... D 3
Canso 1,255 .... H 3
Centreville 765 .... D 3
Chéticamp 1,022 .... G 2

Chester 1,131 .... D 4
Chester Basin 639 .... D 4
Church Point 318 .... B 4
Clark's Harbour 1,059 .... C 5
Coldbrook Station 617 .... D 3
Cow Bay 670 .... E 4
Dartmouth 62,277 .... E 4
Debert 618 .... E 3
Digby◉ 2,558 .... C 4
Dominion 2,856 .... J 2
Donkin 873 .... J 2
Ellershouse-Hartville 662 .... D 4
Elmsdale 1,172 .... E 4
Enfield 1,510 .... E 4
Fall River 1,897 .... E 4
Falmouth 1,110 .... D 3
Glace Bay 21,466 .... J 2
Guysborough◉ 496 .... G 3
Halifax (cap.)◉ 114,594 .... E 4
Halifax◉ 277,727 .... E 4
Hantsport 1,395 .... D 3
Herring Cove 1,323 .... E 4
Hilden 1,262 .... E 3

Ingonish 471 .... H 2
Inverness 2,013 .... G 2
Judique 925 .... G 3
Kentville◉ 4,974 .... D 3
Kingston 1,612 .... D 4
Lakeside 936 .... E 4
Lantz 1,172 .... E 4
Liverpool◉ 3,304 .... D 4
Lockeport 929 .... C 5
Louisbourg 1,410 .... J 3
Louisdale 979 .... G 3
Lower West Pubnico 790 .... C 5
Lunenburg◉ 3,014 .... D 4
Mahone Bay 1,228 .... D 4
Meteghan 890 .... B 4
Middleton 1,834 .... D 4
Milford Station 748 .... E 3
Milton 1,678 .... D 4
Mount Uniacke 1,145 .... D 4
Mulgrave 1,099 .... G 3
Musquodoboit Harbour 936 .... E 4
New Glasgow 10,464 .... F 3
New Victoria 1,374 .... H 2

New Waterford 8,808 .... J 2
North Sydney 7,820 .... H 2
Oxford 1,470 .... E 3
Parrsboro 1,799 .... D 3
Pictou◉ 4,628 .... F 3
Porters Lake 893 .... E 4
Port Hastings 312 .... G 3
Port Hawkesbury 3,850 .... G 3
Port Hood◉ 701 .... G 2
Port Morien 717 .... J 2
Port Williams 1,227 .... D 3
Prospect 693 .... E 4
Pugwash 648 .... E 3
Reserve Mines 2,472 .... H 2
River Hébert 835 .... D 3
Saint Peters 669 .... H 3
Sandy Point 691 .... C 5
Scotchtown 2,037 .... H 2
Sheet Harbour 819 .... F 4
Shelburne◉ 2,303 .... C 5
Shubenacadie 984 .... E 3
Springhill 4,896 .... E 3
Stellarton 5,435 .... F 3

Stewiacke 1,174 .... E 3
Sydney◉ 29,444 .... H 2
Sydney Mines 8,501 .... H 2
Terence Bay 960 .... E 4
Thorburn 1,014 .... F 3
Three Mile Plains 1,355 .... D 4
Timberlea 1,159 .... E 4
Trenton 3,154 .... F 3
Truro◉ 12,552 .... E 3
Waterville 687 .... D 3
Waverley 1,699 .... E 4
Wedgeport 827 .... C 5
Western Shore 1,712 .... D 4
Westmount 3,097 .... H 2
Westville 4,522 .... F 3
Wileville 746 .... D 4
Windsor◉ 3,646 .... D 3
Wolfville 3,235 .... D 3
Yarmouth◉ 7,475 .... B 5

OTHER FEATURES

Advocate (bay) .... D 3

Ainslie (lake) .... G 2
Amet (sound) .... E 3
Andrew (pt.) .... H 3
Annapolis (basin) .... C 4
Annapolis (riv.) .... C 4
Antigonish (harb.) .... F 3
Argos (cape) .... G 3
Aspy (bay) .... H 2
Avon (riv.) .... D 4
Baccaro (pt.) .... C 5
Baddeck (riv.) .... H 2
Barachois (pt.) .... H 3
Barren (isl.) .... H 3
Barrington (bay) .... C 5
Bedford (basin) .... E 4
Berry (head) .... G 3
Boularderie (isl.) .... H 2
Bras d'Or (lake) .... H 3
Breton (cape) .... J 3
Brier (isl.) .... B 4
Canso (cape) .... H 3
Canso (str.) .... G 3
Cap d'Or (cape) .... D 3

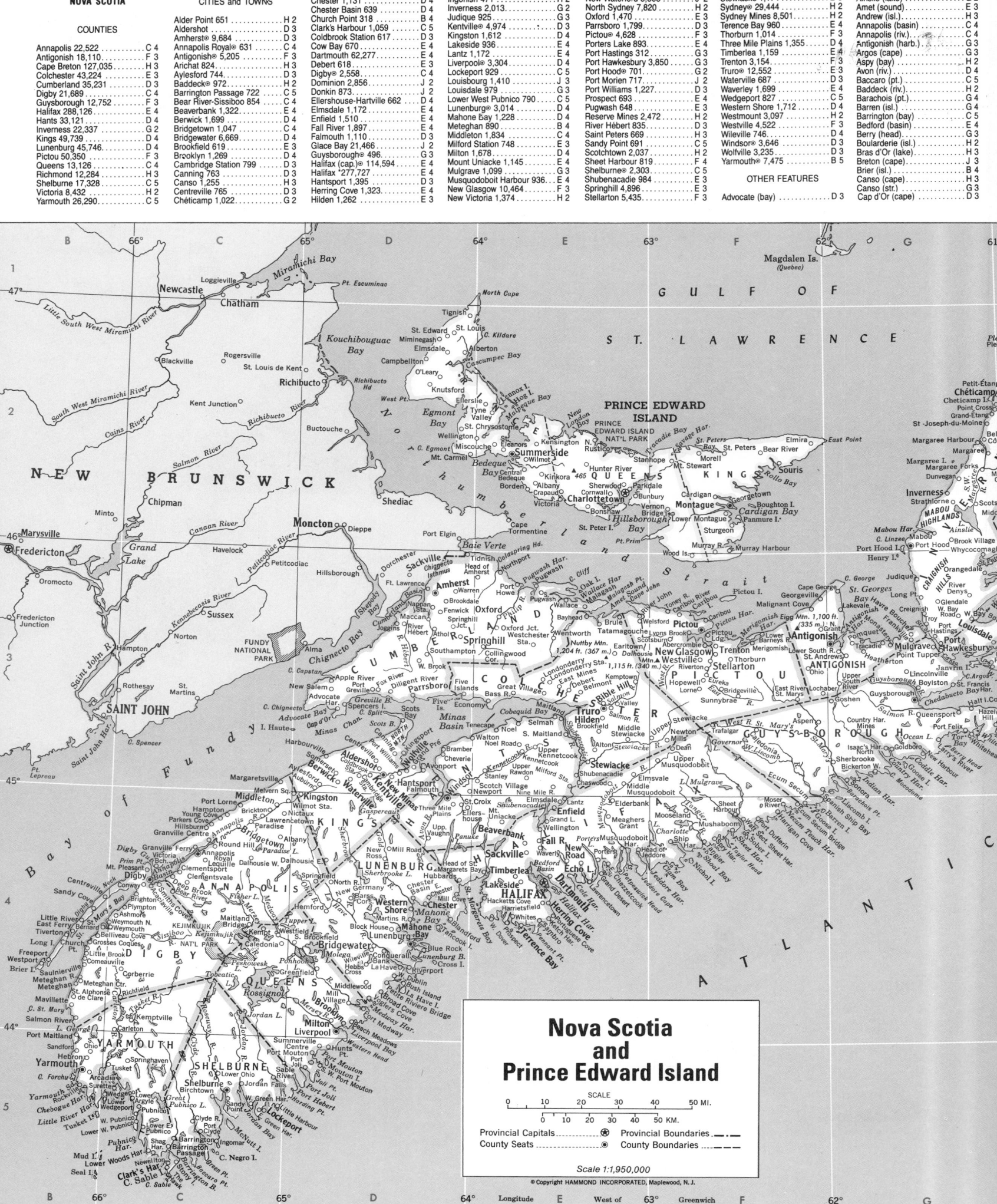

Nova Scotia and Prince Edward Island

SCALE
0 10 20 30 40 50 MI.
0 10 20 30 40 50 KM.

Provincial Capitals .... ⊛
County Seats .... ◉
Provincial Boundaries .... — ·· —
County Boundaries .... — — —

Scale 1:1,950,000

© Copyright HAMMOND INCORPORATED, Maplewood, N.J.

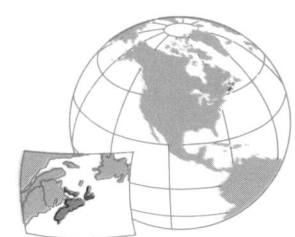

Cape Breton (isl.) .... J 2	Craignish (hills) .... G 3
Cape Breton Highlands Nat'l	Cross (isl.) .... D 4
Park .... H 2	Cumberland (basin) .... D 3
Cape Negro (riv.) .... C 5	Dalhousie (mt.) .... E 3
Cape Sable (isl.) .... C 5	Dauphin (cape) .... H 2
Capstan (cape) .... D 3	Digby Gut (chan.) .... C 4
Caribou (isl.) .... F 3	Digby Neck (pen.) .... B 4
Carleton (riv.) .... C 4	East (bay) .... H 3
Charlotte (lake) .... F 4	East (riv.) .... F 3
Chebogue (harb.) .... B 5	East Bay (hills) .... H 3
Chedabucto (bay) .... G 3	Egmont (cape) .... H 2
Chéticamp (isl.) .... G 2	Eigg (mt.) .... F 3
Chignecto (bay) .... D 3	Fisher (lake) .... C 4
Chignecto (cape) .... D 3	Five (isls.) .... D 3
Chignecto (isth.) .... D 3	Forchu (bay) .... H 3
Clam (bay) .... F 4	Forchu (cape) .... B 5
Cliff (cape) .... E 3	Framboise Cove (bay) .... H 3
Clyde (riv.) .... C 5	Fundy (bay) .... C 3
Cobequid (bay) .... E 3	Gabarus (bay) .... H 3
Coddle (harb.) .... G 3	Gabarus (cape) .... J 3
Coldspring (head) .... G 3	Gaspereau (lake) .... D 4
Cole (harb.) .... E 4	George (cape) .... G 3
Country (harb.) .... G 3	George (lake) .... B 5

Gold (riv.) .... D 4	Salmon (riv.) .... E 3
Goose (isl.) .... F 4	Salmon (riv.) .... G 3
Goose (isl.) .... G 3	Scatarie (isl.) .... J 2
Governor (lake) .... F 3	Scots (bay) .... D 3
Great Bras d'Or (chan.) ..... H 2	Seall (isl.) .... B 5
Great Pubnico (lake) .... C 5	Sheet (harb.) .... F 4
Green (pt.) .... C 5	Sherbrooke (lake) .... D 4
Greville (bay) .... D 3	Sherbrooke (riv.) .... G 3
Guysborough (riv.) .... G 3	Shoal (bay) .... F 4
Halifax (harb.) .... E 4	Shubenacadie (lake) .... E 4
Harding (pt.) .... D 5	Shubenacadie (riv.) .... E 3
Haute (isl.) .... C 3	Sissiboo (riv.) .... C 4
Hébert (riv.) .... D 3	Smoky (cape) .... H 2
Henry (isl.) .... G 3	Sober (isl.) .... F 4
Indian (harb.) .... H 3	South West Margaree (riv.) .. G 2
Ingonish North (bay) .... H 2	Split (cape) .... D 3
Janvrin (isl.) .... G 3	Spry (harb.) .... F 4
Jeddore (harb.) .... F 4	Stewiacke (riv.) .... E 3
John (cape) .... D 3	Sydney (harb.) .... H 2
Joli (pt.) .... D 5	Tangier (riv.) .... F 4
Jordan (bay) .... C 5	Taylor (head) .... F 4
Jordan (lake) .... C 4	Tobeatic (lake) .... C 4
Jordan (riv.) .... C 5	Tor (bay) .... G 3
Kejimkujik (lake) .... C 4	Tupper (lake) .... D 4
Kejimkujik Nat'l Park .... C 4	Tusket (isl.) .... B 5
Kennetcook (riv.) .... E 3	Tusket (riv.) .... C 4
La Have (isl.) .... D 4	Verte (bay) .... D 2
La Have (riv.) .... D 4	Wallace (harb.) .... E 3
Linzee (cape) .... G 2	West (bay) .... G 3
Liscomb (isl.) .... G 4	West (pt.) .... H 5
Little River (harb.) .... B 5	West (riv.) .... F 3
Liverpool (harb.) .... D 5	Western (head) .... D 5
Lomond, Loch (lake) .... H 3	West Liscomb (riv.) .... G 3
Long (isl.) .... C 3	West Saint Mary's (riv.) .... F 3
Louisbourg Nat'l Hist. Park .. J 3	Whitehaven (harb.) .... G 3
Lunenburg (bay) .... D 4	Yarmouth (sound) .... B 5
Mabou (harb.) .... G 2	
Mabou Highlands (hills) ..... G 2	**PRINCE EDWARD ISLAND**
Madame (isl.) .... H 3	
Mahone (bay) .... D 4	**COUNTIES**
Malagash (pt.) .... E 3	
Margaree (isl.) .... F 4	Kings 19,215 .... F 2
McNutt (isl.) .... C 5	Prince 42,821 .... D 2
Medway (harb.) .... D 4	Queens 60,470 .... E 2
Medway (riv.) .... C 4	
Merigomish (harb.) .... F 3	**CITIES and TOWNS**
Mersey (riv.) .... C 4	
Michaud (pt.) .... H 3	Alberton 1,020 .... E 2
Minas (basin) .... D 3	Bunbury 1,024 .... F 2
Minas (chan.) .... D 3	Charlottetown (cap.)⊚ 15,282 . E 2
Mira (bay) .... J 2	
Mira (riv.) .... H 3	
Mocodome (cape) .... G 3	
Molega (lake) .... D 4	
Morien (cape) .... J 2	
Mouton (isl.) .... D 5	
Mud (isl.) .... B 5	
Mulgrave (lake) .... F 3	
Musquodoboit (riv.) .... E 4	
Necum Teuch (harb.) .... F 4	
Nichol (isl.) .... F 4	
North (cape) .... H 1	
North (mt.) .... D 3	
North Aspy (riv.) .... H 1	
North Bay Ingonish (bay) .... H 2	
North East Margaree (riv.) ... H 2	
Northumberland (str.) ...... E 2	
Nuttby (mt.) .... E 3	
Oak (isl.) .... E 3	
Ocean (lake) .... G 3	
Ohio (riv.) .... D 4	
Panuke (lake) .... D 4	
Paradise (lake) .... C 4	
Pennant (pt.) .... E 4	
Percé (cape) .... J 2	
Peskowesk (lake) .... C 4	
Petit-de-Grat (isl.) .... H 3	
Petpeswick (head) .... E 4	
Philip (riv.) .... E 3	
Pictou (harb.) .... F 3	
Pictou (isl.) .... F 3	
Pleasant (bay) .... H 2	
Ponhook (lake) .... D 4	
Porters (lake) .... E 4	
Port Hebert (harb.) .... D 5	
Port Hood (isl.) .... G 2	
Port Joli (harb.) .... D 5	
Port Mouton (harb.) .... D 5	
Poulet Cove (bay) .... H 2	
Prim (pt.) .... C 4	
Pubnico (harb.) .... C 5	
Pugwash (harb.) .... E 3	
Roseway (riv.) .... C 4	
Rossignol (lake) .... C 4	
Sable (cape) .... C 5	
Sable (isl.) .... J 5	
Saint Andrews (chan.) ...... H 2	
Saint Anns (bay) .... H 2	
Saint Georges (bay) .... G 3	
Saint Lawrence (bay) .... H 1	
Saint Lawrence (cape) ...... H 1	
Saint Margarets (bay) ...... E 4	
Saint Mary (cape) .... B 4	
Saint Marys (bay) .... B 4	
Saint Mary's (riv.) .... F 3	
Saint Patrick (chan.) .... G 3	
Saint Paul (isl.) .... H 1	
Saint Peters (bay) .... H 3	

PRINCE EDWARD ISLAND

AREA 2,184 sq. mi. (5,657 sq. km.)
POPULATION 122,506
CAPITAL Charlottetown
LARGEST CITY Charlottetown
HIGHEST POINT 465 ft. (142 m.)
SETTLED IN 1720
ADMITTED TO CONFEDERATION 1873
PROVINCIAL FLOWER Lady's Slipper

NOVA SCOTIA

AREA 21,425 sq. mi. (55,491 sq. km.)
POPULATION 847,442
CAPITAL Halifax
LARGEST CITY Halifax
HIGHEST POINT Cape Breton Highlands 1,747 ft. (532 m.)
SETTLED IN 1605
ADMITTED TO CONFEDERATION 1867
PROVINCIAL FLOWER Trailing Arbutus or Mayflower

Topography

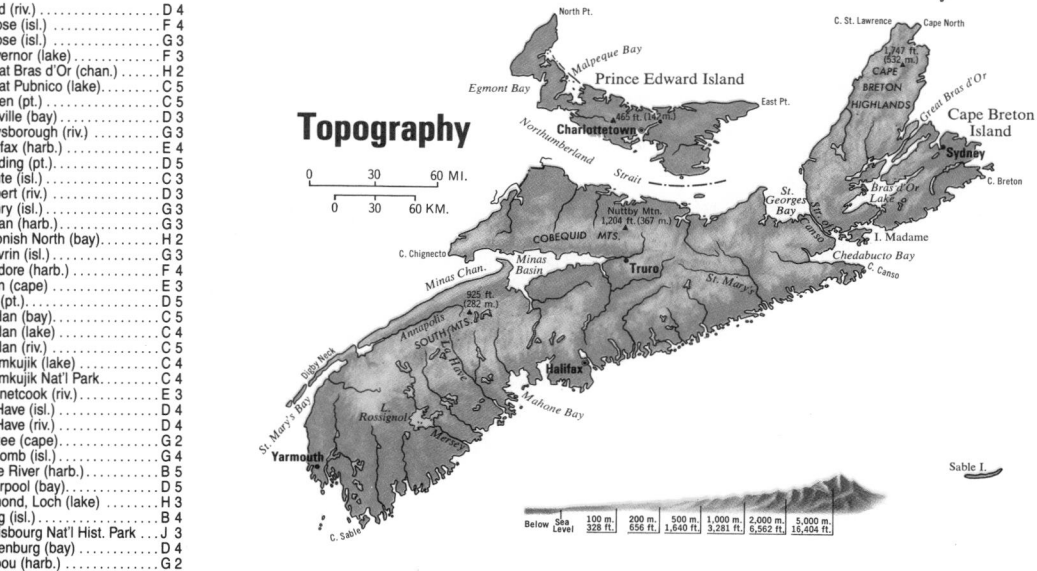

Cornwall, 1,838 .... E 2	Egmont (cape) .... D 2
Georgetown⊚ 737 .... F 2	Hillsborough (bay) .... E 2
Kensington 1,143 .... E 2	Hog (isl.) .... E 2
Miscouche 752 .... D 2	Kildare (cape) .... E 2
Montague 1,957 .... F 2	Lennox (isl.) .... D 2
Murray Harbour 443 .... F 2	Malpeque (bay) .... E 2
North Rustico 688 .... E 2	New London (bay) .... E 2
O'Leary 736 .... D 2	North (pt.) .... E 1
Parkdale 2,018 .... E 2	Northumberland (str.) ...... D 2
Saint Edward 650 .... D 2	Panmure (isl.) .... F 2
Saint Eleanors 2,716 .... E 2	Prim (pt.) .... E 2
Sherwood 5,681 .... E 2	Prince Edward Island Nat'l
Souris 1,413 .... F 2	Park .... E 2
Summerside* 7,828 .... E 2	Rollo (bay) .... F 2
Tignish 982 .... D 2	Saint Lawrence (gulf) ...... F 2
Wilmot 1,563 .... E 2	Saint Peters (bay) .... F 2
	Saint Peters (isl.) .... E 2
OTHER FEATURES	Savage (harb.) .... F 2
	Tracadie (bay) .... F 2
Bedeque (bay) .... E 2	West (pt.) .... D 2
Boughton (isl.) .... F 2	Wood (isls.) .... F 3
Cardigan (bay) .... F 2	
Cascumpeque (bay) .... E 2	⊚County seat.
East (pt.) .... G 2	*Population of metropolitan area.
Egmont (bay) .... D 2	

Agriculture, Industry and Resources

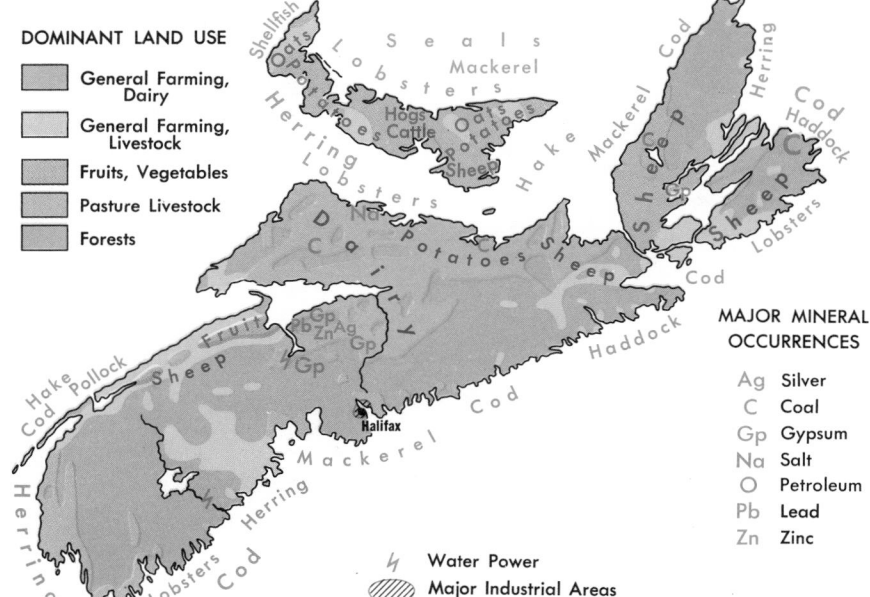

DOMINANT LAND USE

General Farming, Dairy
General Farming, Livestock
Fruits, Vegetables
Pasture Livestock
Forests

MAJOR MINERAL OCCURRENCES

Ag   Silver
C   Coal
Gp   Gypsum
Na   Salt
O   Petroleum
Pb   Lead
Zn   Zinc

⚡ Water Power
▨ Major Industrial Areas

New Brunswick

SCALE
0 5 10   20   30   40 MI.
0 5 10   20   30   40 KM.

Provincial Capitals ....⊕
County Seats ....⊙
International Boundaries .... — —
Provincial Boundaries .... — · —
County Boundaries .... — — —

Scale 1:1,900,000

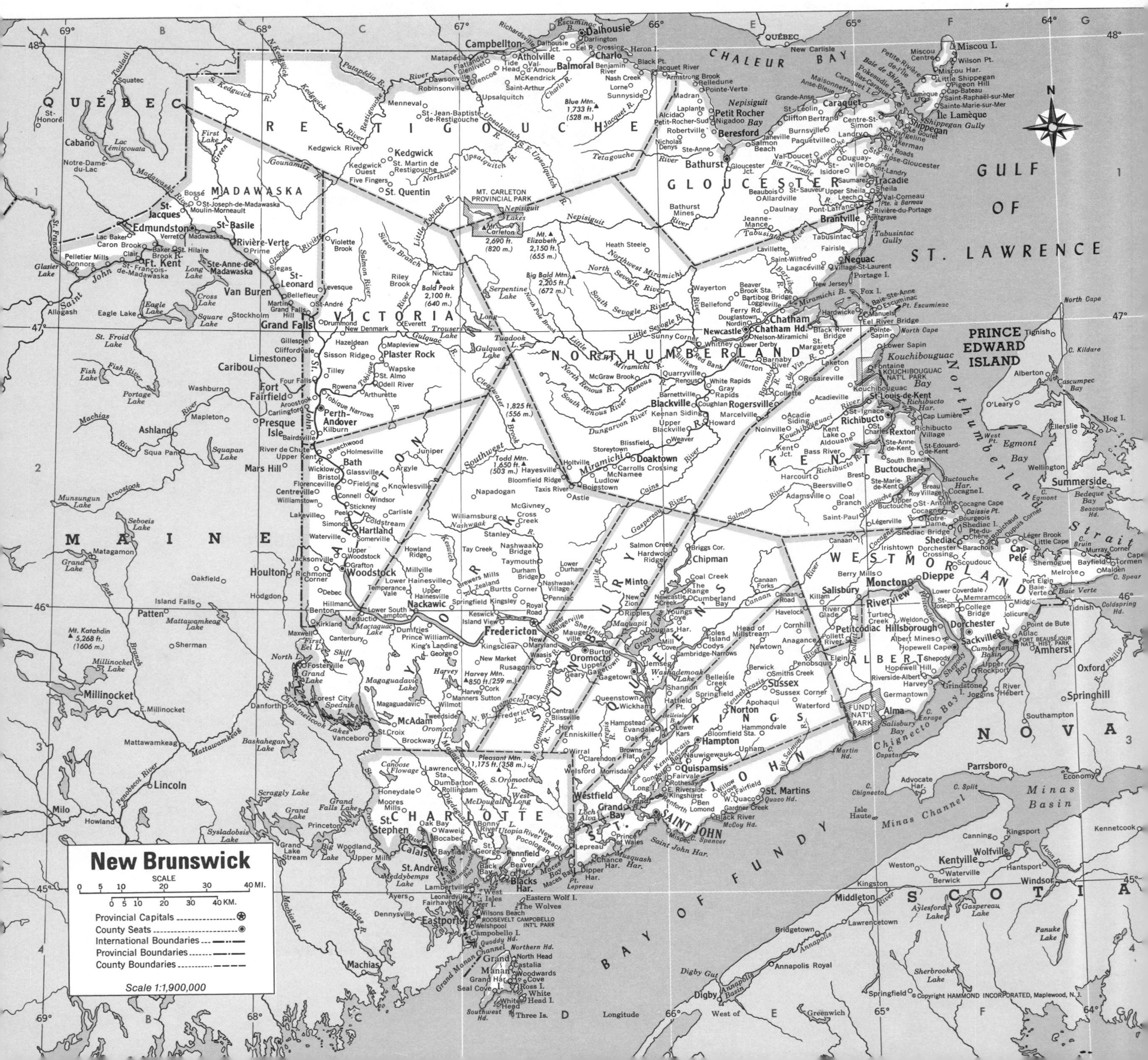

AREA 28,354 sq. mi. (73,437 sq. km.)
POPULATION 696,403
CAPITAL Fredericton
LARGEST CITY Saint John
HIGHEST POINT Mt. Carleton 2,690 ft.
    (820 m.)
SETTLED IN 1611
ADMITTED TO CONFEDERATION 1867
PROVINCIAL FLOWER Purple Violet

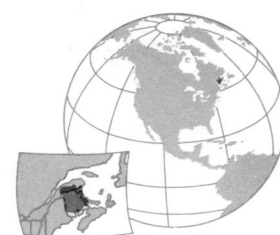

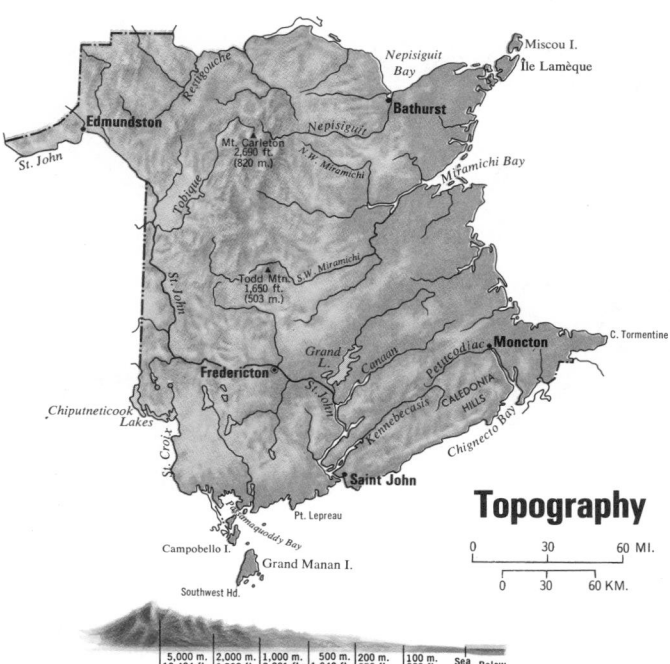

Topography

0   30   60 MI.
0   30   60 KM.

| 5,000 m. | 2,000 m. | 1,000 m. | 500 m. | 200 m. | 100 m. | Sea |
| 16,404 ft. | 6,562 ft. | 3,281 ft. | 1,640 ft. | 656 ft. | 328 ft. | Level Below |

Agriculture, Industry and Resources

DOMINANT LAND USE

- Cereals, Livestock
- Dairy
- Potatoes
- General Farming, Livestock
- Pasture Livestock
- Forests

MAJOR MINERAL OCCURRENCES

Ag Silver
C Coal
Cu Copper
Pb Lead
Sb Antimony
Zn Zinc

⚡ Water Power
▨ Major Industrial Areas

Topography

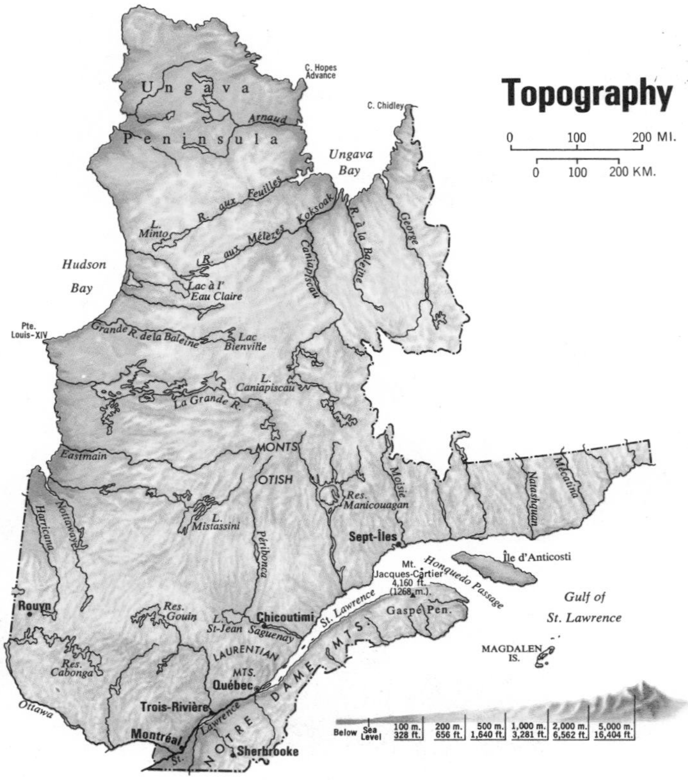
Ungava Peninsula
Ungava Bay
Hudson Bay
C. Hopes Advance
C. Chidley
Pte. Louis-XIV
Lac à l'Eau Claire
Lac Bienville
L. Caniapiscau
La Grande R.
Eastmain
MONTS OTISH
Res. Manicouagan
L. Mistassini
Sept-Îles
Île d'Anticosti
Mt. Jacques-Cartier 4,160 ft. (1268 m.)
Honguedo Passage
Gulf of St. Lawrence
Gaspé Pen.
MAGDALEN IS.
Rouyn
Res. Gouin
Chicoutimi
L. St-Jean
Saguenay
Res. Cabonga
Trois-Rivières
Québec
Montréal
Sherbrooke
Ottawa
LAURENTIAN MTS.
NOTRE DAME MTS.
Below Sea Level
100 m. 328 ft.
200 m. 656 ft.
500 m. 1,640 ft.
1,000 m. 3,281 ft.
2,000 m. 6,562 ft.
5,000 m. 16,404 ft.

0 100 200 MI.
0 100 200 KM.

COUNTIES

Argenteuil 32,454 . . . . . C 4
Arthabaska 59,277 . . . . . E 4
Bagot 26,840 . . . . . E 4
Beauce 73,427 . . . . . G 3
Beauharnois 54,034 . . . . . C 4
Bellechasse 23,559 . . . . . G 3
Berthier 31,096 . . . . . C 3
Bonaventure 40,487 . . . . . C 2
Brome 17,436 . . . . . E 4
Chambly 307,090 . . . . . J 4
Champlain 119,595 . . . . . E 2
Charlevoix-Est 17,448 . . . . . G 2
Charlevoix-Ouest 14,172 . . . . . G 2
Châteauguay 59,968 . . . . . D 4
Chicoutimi 174,441 . . . . . G 1
Compton 20,536 . . . . . F 4
Deux-Montagnes 71,252 . . . . . C 4
Dorchester 33,949 . . . . . C 3
Drummond 69,770 . . . . . E 4
Frontenac 26,814 . . . . . G 4
Gaspé-Est 41,173 . . . . . D 1
Gaspé-Ouest 18,943 . . . . . C 1
Gatineau 54,229 . . . . . B 3
Hull 131,213 . . . . . B 4
Huntingdon 16,953 . . . . . C 4
Iberville 23,180 . . . . . D 4
Île-de-Montréal 1,760,122 . . . . . H 4
Île-Jésus 268,335 . . . . . H 4
Joliette 60,384 . . . . . C 3
Kamouraska 28,642 . . . . . H 2
Labelle 34,395 . . . . . B 3
Lac-Saint-Jean-Est 47,891 . . . F 1
Lac-Saint-Jean-Ouest 62,952 . E 1
Laprairie 105,962 . . . . . H 4
L'Assomption 109,705 . . . . . D 4
Lévis 94,104 . . . . . J 3
L'Islet 22,062 . . . . . G 2
Lotbinière 29,653 . . . . . F 3
Maskinongé 20,763 . . . . . D 3
Matane 29,955 . . . . . B 1
Matapédia 23,715 . . . . . B 2
Mégantic 57,892 . . . . . F 3
Missisquoi 36,161 . . . . . D 4
Montcalm 27,557 . . . . . C 3
Montmagny 25,622 . . . . . G 3
Montmorency No. 1 23,048 . . . F 2
Montmorency No. 2 6,436 . . . . G 3
Napierville 13,562 . . . . . D 4
Nicolet 33,513 . . . . . E 3
Papineau 37,975 . . . . . B 4
Pontiac 20,283 . . . . . A 3
Portneuf 58,843 . . . . . E 3
Québec 458,980 . . . . . F 3
Richelieu 53,058 . . . . . D 4
Richmond 40,871 . . . . . E 4
Rimouski 69,099 . . . . . J 1
Rivière-du-Loup 41,250 . . . . . H 2
Rouville 42,391 . . . . . D 4
Saguenay 115,881 . . . . . H 1
Saint-Hyacinthe 55,888 . . . . . D 4
Saint-Jean 55,576 . . . . . D 4
Saint-Maurice 107,703 . . . . . D 3
Shefford 70,733 . . . . . E 4
Sherbrooke 115,983 . . . . . E 4
Soulanges 15,429 . . . . . C 4
Stanstead 38,186 . . . . . F 4
Témiscouata 52,570 . . . . . J 2
Terrebonne 193,865 . . . . . H 4
Vaudreuil 50,043 . . . . . C 4
Verchères 63,353 . . . . . J 4
Wolfe 15,635 . . . . . F 4
Yamaska 14,797 . . . . . E 3

CITIES and TOWNS

Acton Vale 4,371 . . . . . E 4
Albanel 992 . . . . . E 1
Alma⊙ 26,322 . . . . . F 1
Amqui⊙ 4,048 . . . . . B 2
Ancienne-Lorette 12,935 . . . . . H 3
Angers . . . . . B 4
Anjou 37,346 . . . . . H 4
Annaville 712 . . . . . E 3
Armagh 878 . . . . . G 3
Arthabaska⊙ 6,827 . . . . . F 3
Arvida . . . . . F 1
Asbestos 7,967 . . . . . F 4
Ascot Corner 847 . . . . . F 4
Audet 760 . . . . . G 4
Ayer's Cliff⊙ 810 . . . . . E 4
Aylmer 26,695 . . . . . B 4
Baie-Comeau 12,866 . . . . . A 1
Baie-d'Urfé 3,674 . . . . . G 4
Baie-Saint-Paul⊙ 3,961 . . . . . G 2
Baie-Trinité 749 . . . . . B 1
Beaconsfield 19,613 . . . . . H 4
Beauceville 4,302 . . . . . G 3
Beauharnois⊙ 7,025 . . . . . D 4
Beaumont 791 . . . . . F 3
Beauport 60,447 . . . . . J 3
Beaupré 2,740 . . . . . G 2
Bécancour⊙ 10,247 . . . . . E 3
Bedford⊙ 2,832 . . . . . E 4
Beebe Plain 1,072 . . . . . E 4
Bélair (Val-Bélair) 12,695 . . . . . H 3
Beloeil 17,540 . . . . . D 4
Bernierville 2,120 . . . . . F 3
Berthier-en-Bas 562 . . . . . G 3
Berthierville⊙ 4,049 . . . . . D 3
Bic 2,994 . . . . . J 1
Biencourt 824 . . . . . J 2
Black Lake 5,148 . . . . . F 3
Blainville 14,682 . . . . . H 4
Boischatel 3,345 . . . . . J 3
Bois-des-Filion 4,943 . . . . . H 4
Bolduc 1,565 . . . . . G 4
Bonaventure 1,371 . . . . . C 2
Boucherville 29,704 . . . . . J 4
Bromont 2,731 . . . . . E 4
Bromptonville 3,035 . . . . . F 4
Brossard 52,232 . . . . . H 4
Brownsburg 2,875 . . . . . C 4
Buckingham 7,992 . . . . . B 4
Cabano 3,291 . . . . . J 2
Cacouna 1,160 . . . . . H 2
Calumet 729 . . . . . C 4
Candiac 8,502 . . . . . J 4
Cap-à-l'Aigle 819 . . . . . G 2
Cap-Chat 3,464 . . . . . B 1
Cap-de-la-Madeleine 32,626 . E 3
Caplan-Rivière Caplan 1,139 . C 2
Cap-Saint-Ignace 1,485 . . . . . G 2
Cap-Santé⊙ 671 . . . . . F 3
Carignan 4,544 . . . . . J 4
Carleton 2,710 . . . . . C 2
Causapscal 2,501 . . . . . B 2
Chambly 12,190 . . . . . J 4
Chambord 961 . . . . . E 1
Chandler 3,946 . . . . . D 2
Charlemagne 4,827 . . . . . H 4
Charlesbourg 68,326 . . . . . J 3
Charny 8,240 . . . . . J 3
Châteauguay 36,928 . . . . . H 4
Château-Richer⊙ 3,628 . . . . . F 3
Chénéville 633 . . . . . B 4
Chicoutimi⊙ 60,064 . . . . . G 1
Chicoutimi-Jonquière *135,172 . . . . . G 1
Chute-aux-Outardes 2,280 . . . A 1
Clermont 3,621 . . . . . G 2
Coaticook 6,271 . . . . . F 4
Coleraine 1,660 . . . . . F 4
Compton 728 . . . . . F 4
Contrecoeur 5,449 . . . . . D 4
Cookshire⊙ 1,480 . . . . . F 4
Coteau-du-Lac 1,247 . . . . . C 4
Coteau-Landing⊙ 1,386 . . . . . C 4
Côte-Saint-Luc 27,531 . . . . . H 4
Courcelles 608 . . . . . G 4
Courville . . . . . J 3
Cowansville 12,240 . . . . . E 4
Crabtree 1,950 . . . . . D 4
Danville 2,200 . . . . . E 4
Daveluyville 1,257 . . . . . E 3
Deauville 942 . . . . . E 4
Dégelis 3,477 . . . . . J 2
Delisle 4,011 . . . . . F 1
Delson 4,935 . . . . . H 4
Desbiens 1,541 . . . . . E 1
Deschaillons-sur-Saint-Laurent 950 . . . . . E 3
Deschambault 977 . . . . . E 3
Deschênes . . . . . B 4
Deux-Montagnes 9,944 . . . . . H 4
Didyme 667 . . . . . E 1
Disraëli 3,181 . . . . . F 4
Dolbeau 8,766 . . . . . E 1
Dollard-des-Ormeaux 39,940 . H 4
Donnacona 5,731 . . . . . F 3
Dorion 5,749 . . . . . C 4
Dorval 17,727 . . . . . H 4
Dosquet 703 . . . . . F 3
Douville . . . . . D 4
Drummondville⊙ 27,347 . . . . . E 4
Drummondville-Sud 9,220 . . . . . E 4
Dunham 2,887 . . . . . E 4
Durham-Sud 1,045 . . . . . E 4
East Angus 4,016 . . . . . F 4
East Broughton 1,397 . . . . . F 3
East Broughton Station 1,302 . F 3
Eastman 612 . . . . . E 4
Entrelacs 1,735 . . . . . C 3
Farnham 6,498 . . . . . E 4
Ferme-Neuve 2,266 . . . . . B 3
Forestville 4,271 . . . . . H 1
Frampton 684 . . . . . G 3
Francoeur 1,422 . . . . . F 3
Gaspé 17,261 . . . . . D 1
Gatineau 74,988 . . . . . B 4
Giffard . . . . . J 3
Girardville 1,128 . . . . . E 1
Gracefield 869 . . . . . A 3
Granby 38,069 . . . . . E 4
Grand'Mère 15,442 . . . . . E 3
Grande-Rivière 4,420 . . . . . D 2
Grandes-Bergeronnes 748 . . . . . H 1
Grande-Vallée 700 . . . . . D 1
Greenfield Park 18,527 . . . . . J 4
Grenville 1,417 . . . . . C 4
Gros-Morne 672 . . . . . C 1
Hampstead 7,598 . . . . . H 4
Ham-Sud⊙ 62 . . . . . F 4
Hauterive 13,995 . . . . . A 1
Hébertville 2,515 . . . . . F 1
Hébertville-Station 1,442 . . . . . F 1
Hemmingford 737 . . . . . D 4
Henryville 595 . . . . . D 4
Howick 639 . . . . . D 4
Hudson 4,414 . . . . . C 4
Hull⊙ 56,225 . . . . . B 4
Huntingdon⊙ 3,018 . . . . . C 4
Île-Perrot 5,945 . . . . . G 4
Iberville⊙ 8,587 . . . . . D 4
Inverness⊙ 329 . . . . . F 3
Joliette⊙ 16,987 . . . . . D 3
Jonquière 60,354 . . . . . F 1
Jonquière-Chicoutimi *135,172 . . . . . F 1
Kingsey Falls 818 . . . . . E 4
Kirkland 10,476 . . . . . H 4
Knowlton (Lac-Brome)⊙ 4,316 . . . . . E 4
La Baie 20,935 . . . . . G 1
Labelle 1,534 . . . . . C 3
Lac-à-la-Croix 1,017 . . . . . F 1
Lac-Alouette-Lac-Brière 1,356 D 4
Lac-au-Saumon 1,332 . . . . . B 2
Lac-aux-Sables 838 . . . . . E 3
Lac-Beaufort . . . . . F 3
Lac-Bouchette 1,703 . . . . . E 1
Lac-Carré 717 . . . . . C 3
Lac-des-Écorces 766 . . . . . B 3
Lac-Drolet 1,120 . . . . . G 4
Lac-Etchemin 2,729 . . . . . G 3
Lachenaie 8,631 . . . . . D 4
Lachine 37,521 . . . . . H 4
Lachute⊙ 11,729 . . . . . C 4
Lac-Mégantic⊙ 6,119 . . . . . G 4
Lacolle 1,319 . . . . . D 4
Lac-Saint-Charles 5,837 . . . . . H 3
Lafontaine 4,799 . . . . . C 4
La Guadeloupe 1,692 . . . . . F 4
La Malbaie⊙ 4,030 . . . . . G 2
Lambton 1,559 . . . . . F 4
L'Annonciation 2,384 . . . . . C 3
Lanoraie (Lanoraie-d'Autry) 1,613 . . . . . D 4
La Pêche 4,977 . . . . . B 4
La Pérade 1,039 . . . . . E 3
La Pocatière 4,560 . . . . . H 2
La Prairie⊙ 10,627 . . . . . J 4
La Providence . . . . . E 4
Larouche 662 . . . . . F 1
La Salle 76,299 . . . . . H 4
L'Ascension 1,287 . . . . . F 1
L'Assomption⊙ 4,844 . . . . . D 4
La Station-du-Coteau 892 . . . C 4
Laterrière 788 . . . . . F 1
La Tuque 11,556 . . . . . E 2
Laurentides 1,947 . . . . . D 4
Laurier-Station 1,123 . . . . . F 3
Laurierville 939 . . . . . F 3
Lauzon 13,362 . . . . . J 3
Laval 268,335 . . . . . H 4
Lavaltrie 2,053 . . . . . D 4
L'Avenir 1,116 . . . . . E 4
Lawrenceville 562 . . . . . E 4
Le Moyne 6,137 . . . . . J 4
L'Épiphanie 2,971 . . . . . D 4
Léry 2,239 . . . . . H 4
Lévis 17,895 . . . . . J 3
Lennoxville 3,922 . . . . . F 4
Les Méchins 803 . . . . . B 1
Linière 1,168 . . . . . G 3
L'Islet 1,070 . . . . . G 2
L'Islet-sur-Mer 774 . . . . . G 2
L'Isle-Verte 1,142 . . . . . G 1
Longueuil⊙ 124,320 . . . . . J 4
Loretteville⊙ 15,060 . . . . . H 3
Lorraine 6,881 . . . . . H 4
Louiseville⊙ 3,735 . . . . . E 3
Luceville 1,524 . . . . . J 1
Lyster 830 . . . . . F 3
Magog 13,604 . . . . . E 4
Maniwaki⊙ 5,424 . . . . . B 3
Manseau 626 . . . . . E 3
Maple Grove 2,009 . . . . . H 4
Maria 1,178 . . . . . C 2
Marieville⊙ 4,877 . . . . . D 4
Mascouche 20,345 . . . . . H 4
Maskinongé 1,005 . . . . . E 3
Masson 4,264 . . . . . B 4
Massueville 671 . . . . . E 4
Matane⊙ 13,612 . . . . . B 1
Matapédia 586 . . . . . B 2
Melocheville 1,892 . . . . . C 4
Mercier 6,352 . . . . . H 4
Metabetchouan 3,406 . . . . . F 1
Mirabel⊙ 14,080 . . . . . H 4
Mistassini 6,682 . . . . . E 1
Montauban 557 . . . . . E 3
Mont-Carmel 807 . . . . . H 2
Montcerf 570 . . . . . A 3
Montebello 1,229 . . . . . B 4
Mont-Joli 6,359 . . . . . J 1
Mont-Laurier⊙ 8,405 . . . . . B 3
Mont-Louis 756 . . . . . C 1
Montmagny⊙ 12,405 . . . . . G 3
Montréal⊙ 980,354 . . . . . H 4
Montréal *2,828,349 . . . . . H 4
Montréal-Est 3,778 . . . . . J 4
Montréal-Nord 94,914 . . . . . H 4
Mont-Rolland 1,517 . . . . . C 4
Mont-Royal 19,247 . . . . . H 4
Mont-Saint-Hilaire 10,066 . . . D 4
Morin Heights 592 . . . . . C 4
Murdochville 3,396 . . . . . C 1
Nantes 1,167 . . . . . F 4

Agriculture, Industry and Resources

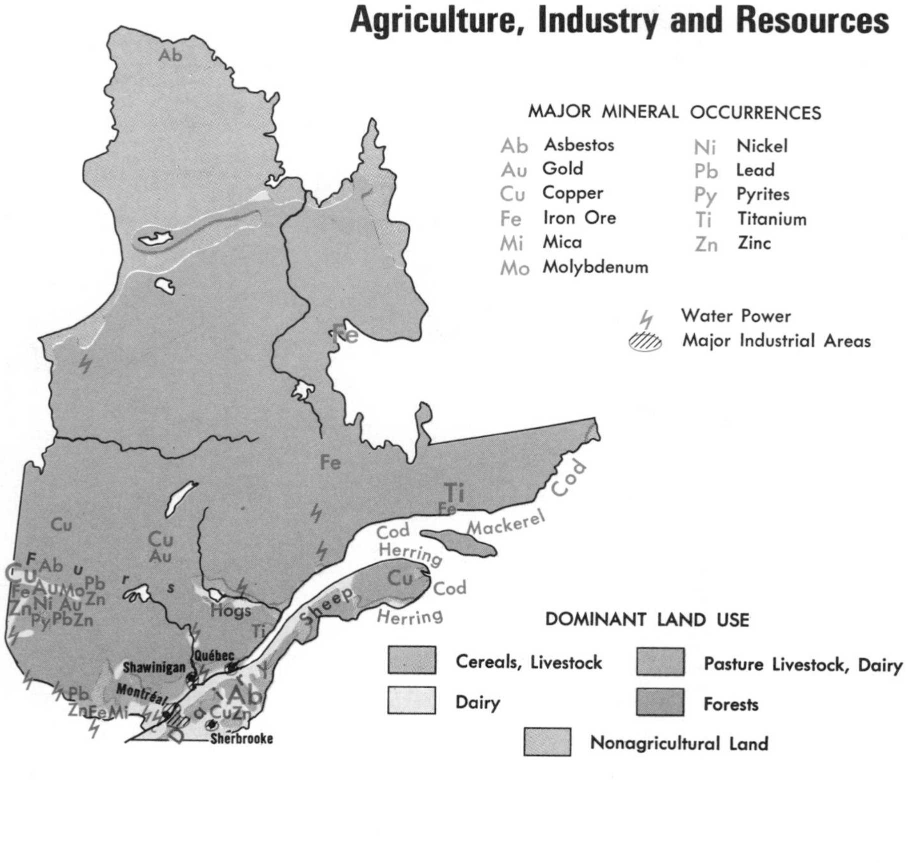
MAJOR MINERAL OCCURRENCES
Ab Asbestos
Au Gold
Cu Copper
Fe Iron Ore
Mi Mica
Mo Molybdenum
Ni Nickel
Pb Lead
Py Pyrites
Ti Titanium
Zn Zinc
Water Power
Major Industrial Areas
DOMINANT LAND USE
Cereals, Livestock
Dairy
Pasture Livestock, Dairy
Forests
Nonagricultural Land
Cod
Herring
Mackerel
Hogs
Sheep
Shawinigan
Québec
Montréal
Sherbrooke

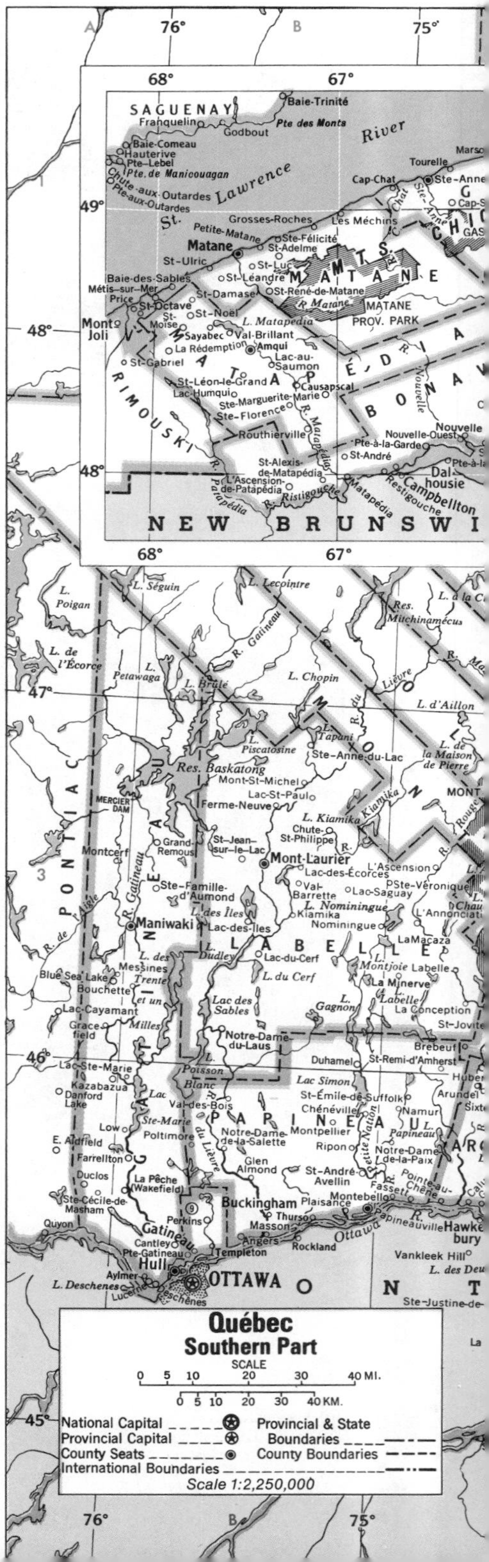
Québec
Southern Part
SCALE
0 5 10 20 30 40 MI.
0 5 10 20 30 40 KM.
National Capital
Provincial Capital
County Seats
International Boundaries
Provincial & State Boundaries
County Boundaries
Scale 1:2,250,000
OTTAWA
NEW BRUNSWICK
SAGUENAY
MATANE
RIMOUSKI
BONAVENTURE
PONTIAC
LABELLE
PAPINEAU
GATINEAU

Napierville⊙ 2,343 .... D 4
Neuville 996.................. F 3
New Carlisle⊙ 1,292........ D 2
New Richmond 4,257......... C 2
Nicolet 4,880 .... E 3
Nominingue 881 .... B 3
Normandin 4,041 .... E 1
North Hatley 689............. F 4
Notre-Dame-de-la-Doré 1,064 E 1
Notre-Dame-des-Laurentides . H 3
Notre-Dame-des-Prairies
6,150 .... D 3
Notre-Dame-du-Bon-Conseil
1,089 .... E 4
Notre-Dame-du-Lac⊙ 2,258 .. J 2
Nouvelle 669 .... C 2
Oka 1,538...................... C 4
Omerville 1,398.............. E 4
Ormstown 1,659 .... D 4
Orsainville .... H 3
Otis 673 .... G 1
Otterburn Park 4,268 .... D 4
Outremont 24,338............ H 4
Pabos 1,295................... D 2
Pabos-Mills 1,565 .... D 2
Papineauville⊙ 1,481 .... C 4
Paspébiac 1,914 .... D 2
Percé⊙ 4,839................. D 2
Petit-Cap 1,023 .... D 1
Petite-Matane 1,065.......... B 1
Petit-Saguenay (Saint-
François-d'Assise) 804 .... G 1
Pierrefonds 38,390........... H 4
Pierreville 1,212 .... E 3
Pincourt 8,750................. D 4
Pintendre 1,849................ J 3
Plaisance 748 .... B 4
Plessisville 7,249 .... F 3
Pohénégamook 3,702 .... H 2
Pointe-à-la-Croix 1,481 ...... C 2
Pointe-au-Père 796........... J 1
Pointe-au-Pic 1,054 .... G 2
Pointe-aux-Outardes 1,056 ... A 1
Pointe-aux-Trembles 36,270 .. J 4
Pointe-Calumet 2,935 .... G 4
Pointe-Claire 24,571.......... H 4
Pointe-du-Lac 5,359.......... E 3
Pointe-Gatineau .... B 4
Pointe-Lebel 1,573 .... A 1
Pont-Rouge 3,580............. F 3
Port-Alfred 8,621.............. G 1
Portneuf 1,333................ F 3
Portneuf-sur-Mer (Rivière-
Portneuf-sur-Mer) 1,255 ... H 1
Price 2,273.................... A 1
Princeville 4,023 .... F 3
Proulxville 588................ E 3
Québec (cap.) 166,474 ...... H 3
Québec *576,075 .... H 3
Quyon 744 .... A 4
Rawdon 2,958 .... D 3
Repentigny 34,419........... J 4
Richelieu 1,832................ D 4
Richmond⊙ 3,568............ E 4
Rigaud 2,268 .... C 4
Rimouski⊙ 29,120 .... J 1
Rimouski-Est 2,506 .... J 1
Ripon 620...................... B 4
Rivière-à-Pierre 615 .... E 3
Rivière-au-Renard 2,211 ..... D 1
Rivière-Bleue 1,690 .... J 2
Rivière-Bois-Clair 604 .... F 3
Rivière-du-Loup⊙ 13,459..... H 2
Rivière-du-Moulin .... G 1
Rivière-Éternité 659 .... G 1
Rivière-Portneuf-Portneuf-sur-
Mer 1,255 .... H 1
Robertsonville 1,987 .... F 3
Roberval⊙ 11,429............. E 1
Rock Island 1,179............. E 4
Rosemère 7,778 .... H 4
Rougemont 972................ D 4
Roxboro 6,292................. H 4
Roxton Falls 1,245 .... E 4
Sacré-Coeur-de-Saguenay
1,678 .... H 1
Saint-Adelme 618............. B 1
Saint-Adelphe 1,159.......... E 3
Saint-Adolphe-d'Howard
1,686........................... C 4
Saint-Adrien 597.............. F 4
Saint-Agapitville 2,954....... F 3
Saint-Aimé-des-Lacs 861 ..... G 2
Saint-Alban 673............... E 3
Saint-Alexandre-de-
Kamouraska 1,048........... H 2
Saint-Alexis-des-Monts 1,984. D 3
Saint-Amable 2,424 .... J 4
Saint-Ambroise 3,606.......... F 1
Saint-Anaclet 1,377 .... J 1
Saint-André-Avellin 1,312 .... B 4
Saint-André-Est 1,293 .... C 4
Saint-Anselme 1,808 .... F 3
Saint-Antoine 7,012 .... H 4
Saint-Antonin 941.............. H 2
Saint-Aubert 884............... G 2
Saint-Augustin-de-Québec
2,475 .... E 3
Saint-Basile-Sud 1,719 .... F 3
Saint-Basile-le-Grand 7,658 .. J 4
Saint-Benjamin 1,027.......... G 3
Saint-Bernard 585 .... F 3
Saint-Bernard-sur-Mer 711 ... G 2
Saint-Boniface-de-Shawinigan
3,164 .... D 3
Saint-Bruno 2,580.............. F 1
Saint-Bruno-de-Montarville
22,880 .... J 4
Saint-Camille-de-Bellechasse
1,744 .... G 3
Saint-Casimir 1,133 .... E 3
Saint-Césaire 2,935 .... D 4
Saint-Charles 1,019 .... G 3
Saint-Charles-de-Mandeville
1,392 .... D 3
Saint-Chrysostome 1,018 ..... D 4
Saint-Côme 660 .... D 3
Saint-Constant 9,938 .... H 4
Saint-Cyprien 860.............. J 2
Saint-Cyrille 1,041 .... E 4
Saint-Damien-de-Buckland
1,522 .... G 3
Saint-David 5,380 .... J 3
Saint-David-de-Falardeau
1,876 .... F 1
Saint-Denis 861 .... D 4

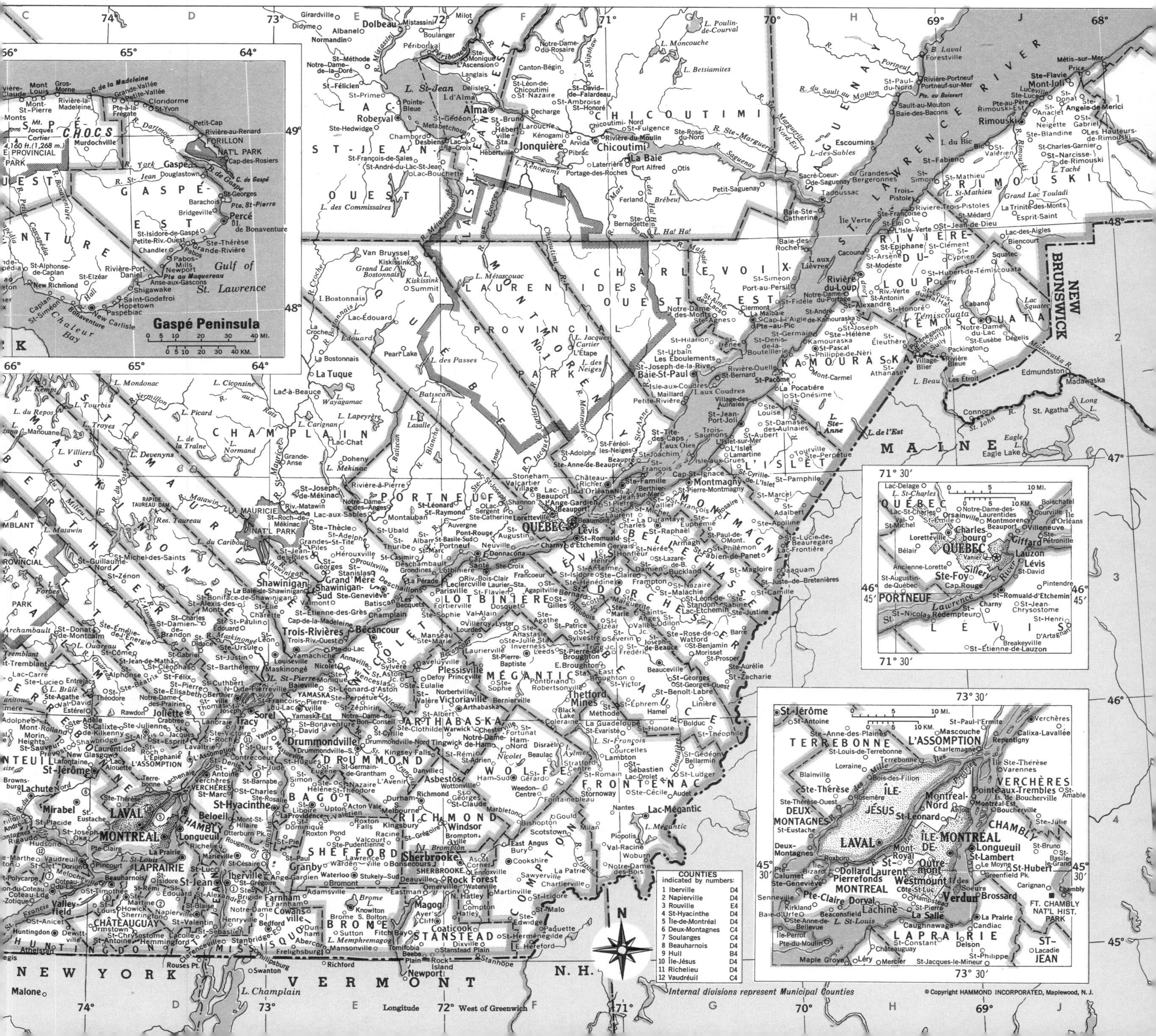

AREA 594,857 sq. mi. (1,540,680 sq. km.)
POPULATION 6,438,403
CAPITAL Québec
LARGEST CITY Montréal
HIGHEST POINT Mont D'Iberville 5,420 ft. (1,652 m.)
SETTLED IN 1608
ADMITTED TO CONFEDERATION 1867
PROVINCIAL FLOWER White Garden Lily

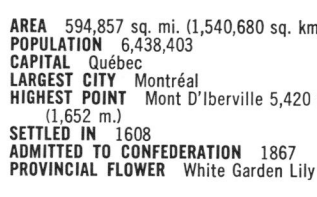

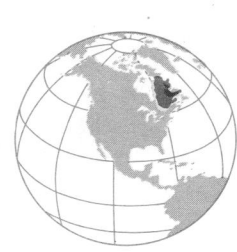

Saint-Dominique 2,068 .... E 4
Saint-Donat-de-Montcalm
1,521 .... C 3
Sainte-Adèle 4,675............ C 4
Sainte-Agathe 709 .... F 3
Sainte-Agathe-des-Monts
5,641 .... C 3
Sainte-Anne-de-Beaupré
3,292 .... F 2
Sainte-Anne-de-Bellevue
3,981 .... H 4
Sainte-Anne-des-Monts⊙
6,062 .... C 1
Sainte-Anne-des-Plaines
4,258 .... H 4
Sainte-Anne-du-Lac 686 ...... B 3
Sainte-Aurélie 1,045........... G 3
Sainte-Blandine 849........... J 1
Sainte-Catherine 1,474 .... F 3
Sainte-Claire 1,566............ G 3
Sainte-Croix⊙ 1,814........... F 3
Sainte-Félicité 711 .... B 1
Sainte-Foy 68,883 .... H 3
Sainte-Geneviève 2,573 ...... H 4
Sainte-Geneviève-de-
Batiscan⊙ 356 .... E 3
Sainte-Hélène-de-Bagot
1,328............................ E 4
Sainte-Hénédine⊙ 639......... F 3
Sainte-Julie-de-Verchères
14,243 .... J 4
Sainte-Julienne⊙ 750.......... D 4
Sainte-Justine 1,080 .... G 3
Saint-Élie 639 .... E 3
Saint-Elzéar 743................. F 3
Sainte-Marie 8,937.............. G 3
Sainte-Martine⊙ 2,196......... D 4
Saint-Émile 5,216............... H 3
Sainte-Monique 705............. F 1
Sainte-Pétronille 982 .... J 3
Sainte-Perpétue-de-L'Islet
1,232 .... H 2
Saint-Éphrem-de-Tring 973... G 3
Saint-Épiphane 647 .... H 2
Sainte-Pudentienne 866 .... E 4
Sainte-Rosalie 2,862 .... E 4
Saint-Esprit 1,068............... D 4
Sainte-Thérèse 18,750......... H 4
Sainte-Thérèse-Ouest
(Boisbriand) 13,471 .... H 4
Saint-Thècle 1,703 .... E 3
Saint-Étienne-de-Grès 845.... E 3
Saint-Étienne-de-Lauzon
1,218 .... J 3

Gaspé Peninsula
Gulf of St. Lawrence
CHICOUTIMI
CHARLEVOIX EST
LAURENTIDES PROVINCIAL PARK
MONTMORENCY No. 1
ST-JEAN OUEST
QUÉBEC
MONTRÉAL
LAVAL
Trois-Rivières
Sherbrooke
MAINE
NEW BRUNSWICK
NEW YORK
VERMONT
N.H.
COUNTIES indicated by numbers:
1 Iberville D4
2 Napierville D4
3 Rouville E4
4 St-Hyacinthe D4
5 Île-de-Montréal D4
6 Deux-Montagnes C4
7 Soulanges C4
8 Beauharnois D4
9 Hull B4
10 Île-Jésus D4
11 Richelieu D4
12 Vaudreuil C4
Internal divisions represent Municipal Counties
Longitude 72° West of Greenwich
© Copyright HAMMOND INCORPORATED, Maplewood, N. J.

OTHER FEATURES

® County seat.
*Population of metropolitan area.

QUÉBEC, NORTHERN
INTERNAL DIVISIONS

CITIES and TOWNS

OTHER FEATURES

®County seat.
*Population of metropolitan area.

© Copyright HAMMOND INCORPORATED, Maplewood, N.J.

Northern Québec

SCALE
0 50 100 150 200 MI.
0 50 100 150 200 KM.

Provincial Capital......⊛ Provincial Boundaries ——·——
County Seats......◉ County Boundaries ————
International Boundaries ——·—— Territorial Boundaries ········

Scale 1:8,400,000

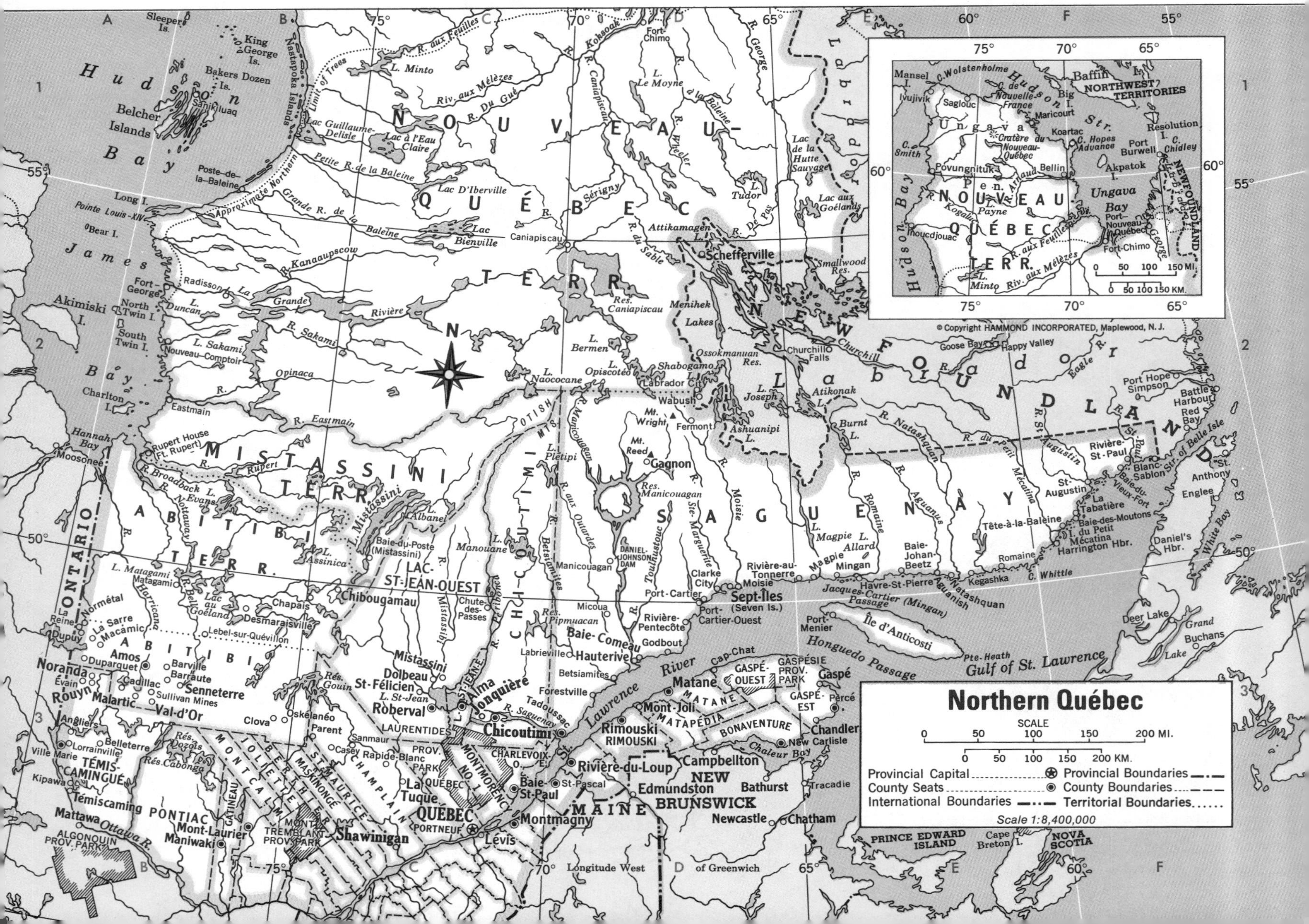

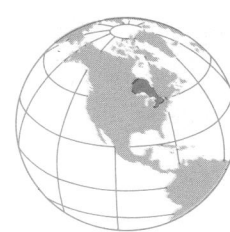

(continued on following page)

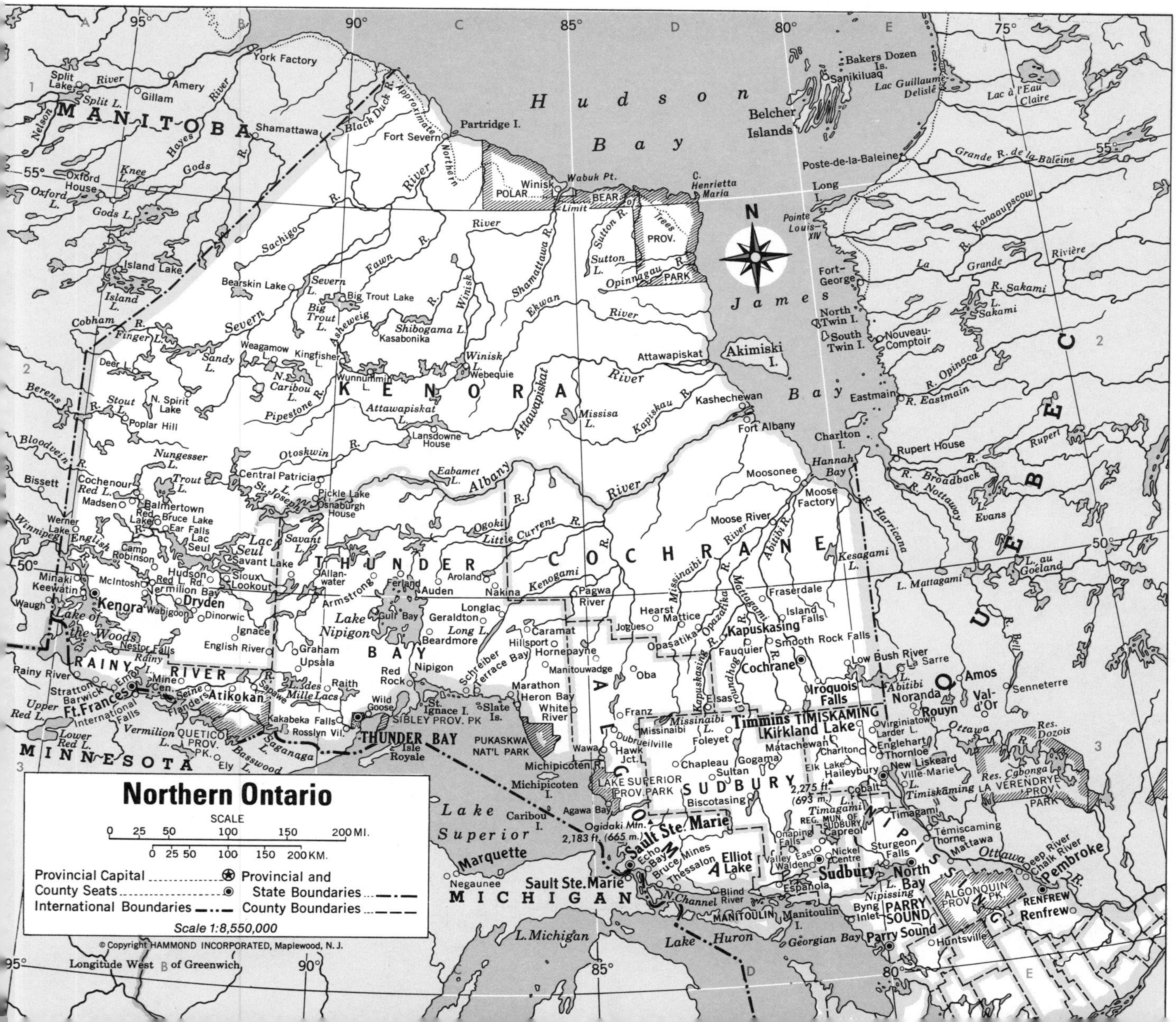

AREA 412,580 sq. mi. (1,068,582 sq. km.)
POPULATION 8,625,107
CAPITAL Toronto
LARGEST CITY Toronto
HIGHEST POINT in Timiskaming Dist.
  2,275 ft. (693 m.)
SETTLED IN 1749
ADMITTED TO CONFEDERATION 1867
PROVINCIAL FLOWER White Trillium

Northern Ontario

SCALE
0   25 50   100   150   200 MI.
0 25 50   100   150   200 KM.

Provincial Capital .... ⊛
County Seats .... ⊚   Provincial and
International Boundaries ___   State Boundaries ___
                               County Boundaries ___

Scale 1:8,550,000

© Copyright HAMMOND INCORPORATED, Maplewood, N.J.

Longitude West of Greenwich

Ontario Central Part

Saint Jacobs 1,189 . . . . D 4
Saint Mary's 4,883 . . . . C 4
Saint Thomas⊛ 28,165 . . . . C 5
Saint Williams 442 . . . . D 5
Salem 825 . . . . D 4
Sarnia⊛ 50,892 . . . . B 5
Sauble Beach 729 . . . . C 3
Sault Sainte Marie⊛ 82,697 . . . . J 5
Scarborough 443,353 . . . . K 4
Schomberg 923 . . . . J 3
Schreiber 1,968 . . . . H 5
Scotland 600 . . . . D 4
Seaforth 2,114 . . . . C 4
Searchmont 384 . . . . J 5
Sebringville 579 . . . . C 4
Seeleys Bay 503 . . . . H 3
Shakespeare 602 . . . . D 4
Shallow Lake 418 . . . . C 3
Shannonville 314 . . . . G 3
Shanty Bay 358 . . . . E 3
Sharbot Lake 495 . . . . H 3
Shedden 292 . . . . C 5
Shelburne 2,862 . . . . D 3
Simcoe⊛ 14,326 . . . . D 5
Sioux Lookout 3,074 . . . . G 4
Sioux Narrows 394 . . . . F 5
Smithfield 349 . . . . G 3
Smiths Falls 8,831 . . . . H 3
Smithville 1,936 . . . . E 4
Smooth Rock Falls 2,352 . . . . . . J 5
Sombra 420 . . . . B 5
Southampton 2,830 . . . . C 3
South Mountain 285 . . . . J 3
South River 1,109 . . . . E 2
Spanish 1,063 . . . . J 5
Sparta 283 . . . . C 5

Spencerville 438 . . . . J 3
Springfield 555 . . . . C 5
Springford 309 . . . . D 5
Stayner 2,530 . . . . E 3
Stirling 1,638 . . . . G 3
Stittsville 2,652 . . . . J 2
Stoney Creek 36,762 . . . . E 4
Stoney Point 1,090 . . . . B 5
Straffordville 752 . . . . D 5
Stratford⊛ 26,262 . . . . C 4
Strathroy 8,748 . . . . C 5
Sturgeon Falls 6,045 . . . . E 1
Sudbury⊛ 91,829 . . . . K 5
Sudbury *149,923 . . . . K 5
Sunderland 703 . . . . E 3
Sundridge 734 . . . . E 2
Sydenham 595 . . . . H 3
Tamworth 402 . . . . H 3
Tara 687 . . . . C 3
Tavistock 1,885 . . . . D 4
Tecumseh 6,364 . . . . B 5
Teeswater 1,026 . . . . C 3
Terrace Bay 2,639 . . . . H 5
Thamesford 1,920 . . . . C 4
Thamesville 961 . . . . C 5
Thedford 694 . . . . C 4
Thessalon 1,620 . . . . J 5
Thornbury 1,435 . . . . D 3
Thorndale 581 . . . . C 4
Thornton 414 . . . . E 3
Thorold 15,412 . . . . E 4
Thunder Bay⊛ 112,486 . . . . H 5
Thunder Bay *121,379 . . . . H 5
Tilbury 4,298 . . . . B 5
Tillsonburg 10,487 . . . . D 5
Timmins 46,114 . . . . J 5

Tiverton 806 . . . . C 3
Tobermory 282 . . . . C 2
Toronto (cap.)⊛ 599,217 . . . . . . K 4
Toronto *2,998,947 . . . . K 4
Tottenham 3,022 . . . . E 3
Trenton 15,085 . . . . G 3
Trout Creek 652 . . . . E 2
Turkey Point 407 . . . . D 5
Tweed 1,574 . . . . G 3
Udora 375 . . . . E 3
Union 485 . . . . C 5
Uxbridge 4,209 . . . . E 3
Valley East 20,433 . . . . J 5
Vanier 18,792 . . . . J 2
Vankleek Hill 1,774 . . . . K 2
Vars 527 . . . . J 2
Vaughan 29,674 . . . . J 4
Verner 1,076 . . . . D 1
Vernon 303 . . . . J 2
Verona 754 . . . . H 3
Victoria Harbour 1,125 . . . . E 3
Vienna 369 . . . . D 5
Virginiatown 1,010 . . . . K 5
Vittoria 420 . . . . D 5
Wabigoon 268 . . . . G 5
Walden 10,139 . . . . J 5
Walkerton⊛ 4,682 . . . . C 3
Wallaceburg 11,506 . . . . B 5
Wardsville 450 . . . . C 5
Warkworth 618 . . . . G 3
Warren 579 . . . . D 1
Warsaw 314 . . . . F 3
Wasaga Beach 4,705 . . . . D 3
Washago 569 . . . . E 3
Waterloo 49,428 . . . . D 4
Watford 1,402 . . . . C 5
Waubaushene 878 . . . . E 3
Wawa 4,206 . . . . J 5
Webbwood 519 . . . . C 1
Welcome 293 . . . . F 4
Welland 454,448 . . . . E 5
Wellesley 997 . . . . D 4
Wellington 1,082 . . . . G 4
Wendover 326 . . . . J 2
West Lorne 1,258 . . . . C 5
Westmeath 262 . . . . H 2
Westport 621 . . . . H 3
Wheatley 1,638 . . . . B 5
Whitby⊛ 36,698 . . . . F 4
Whitchurch-Stouffville 13,557 . . J 3
White River △1,006 . . . . J 5
Whitney 766 . . . . F 2
Wiarton 2,074 . . . . C 3
Wikwemikong 1,030 . . . . C 2
Williamsburg 407 . . . . J 3
Williamsford 256 . . . . D 3
Williamstown 328 . . . . K 2
Winchester 2,001 . . . . J 2
Windsor⊛ 192,083 . . . . B 5
Windsor *246,110 . . . . B 5
Wingham 2,897 . . . . C 4
Wolfe Island 271 . . . . H 3
Woodstock⊛ 26,603 . . . . D 4
Woodville 575 . . . . F 3
Wroxeter 350 . . . . C 4
Wyoming 1,682 . . . . B 5
Yarker 319 . . . . H 3
York 134,617 . . . . J 4
Zephyr 330 . . . . E 3
Zurich 795 . . . . C 4

OTHER FEATURES

Abitibi (riv.) . . . . J 5
Algonquin Prov. Park . . . . F 2
Amherst (isl.) . . . . H 3
Balsam (lake) . . . . F 3
Barrie (isl.) . . . . B 1
Bays (lake) . . . . F 2
Big Rideau (lake) . . . . H 3
Black (riv.) . . . . E 3
Bruce (pen.) . . . . C 2
Buckhorn (lake) . . . . F 3
Cabot (head) . . . . C 2
Charleston (lake) . . . . J 3
Christian (isl.) . . . . D 3
Clear (lake) . . . . F 3
Cockburn (isl.) . . . . A 2
Couchiching (lake) . . . . E 3
Croker (cape) . . . . D 3

Don (riv.) . . . . J 4
Doré (lake) . . . . G 2
Douglas (pt.) . . . . C 3
Erie (lake) . . . . E 5
Flowerpot (isl.) . . . . C 2
French (riv.) . . . . D 1
Georgian (bay) . . . . D 2
Georgian Bay Is.
 Nat'l Park . . . . C 2, D 3
Georgina (isl.) . . . . E 3
Grand (riv.) . . . . D 4
Humber (riv.) . . . . J 3
Hurd (cape) . . . . C 2
Huron (lake) . . . . B 3
Ipperwash Prov. Park . . . . C 4
Joseph (lake) . . . . E 2
Killarney Prov. Park . . . . C 1
Killbear Point Prov. Park . . . . . D 2
Lake of the Woods (lake) . . . . . F 5

Lake Superior Prov. Park . . . . . J 5
Lonely (isl.) . . . . C 2
Long (pt.) . . . . D 5
Long Point (bay) . . . . D 5
Madawaska (riv.) . . . . G 2
Magnetawan (riv.) . . . . D 2
Main (chan.) . . . . C 2
Manitou (lake) . . . . C 2
Manitoulin (isl.) . . . . B 2
Mattagami (riv.) . . . . J 5
Michipicoten (isl.) . . . . H 5
Missinaibi (riv.) . . . . J 5
Mississagi (riv.) . . . . A 1
Mississippi (lake) . . . . H 2
Muskoka (lake) . . . . E 2
Niagara (riv.) . . . . E 4
Nipigon (lake) . . . . H 5
Nipissing (lake) . . . . E 1
North (chan.) . . . . A 1
Nottawasaga (bay) . . . . D 3
Ogidaki (mt.) . . . . J 5
Ontario (lake) . . . . G 4
Opeongo (lake) . . . . F 2
Ottawa (riv.) . . . . H 2
Owen (sound) . . . . D 3
Panache (lake) . . . . C 1
Parry (isl.) . . . . D 2
Parry (sound) . . . . D 2
Pelee (pt.) . . . . B 6
Petre (pt.) . . . . G 4
Point Pelee Nat'l Park . . . . . . B 5
Presqu'ile Prov. Park . . . . G 4
Pukaskwa Prov. Park . . . . H 5
Quetico Prov. Park . . . . G 5

Rainy (lake) . . . . G 5
Rice (lake) . . . . F 3
Rideau (lake) . . . . H 3
Rondeau Prov. Park . . . . C 5
Rosseau (lake) . . . . E 2
Saint Clair (lake) . . . . B 5
Saint Clair (riv.) . . . . B 5
Saint Lawrence (lake) . . . . K 3
Saint Lawrence (riv.) . . . . J 3
Saint Lawrence Is. Nat'l Park . . . J 3
Saugeen (riv.) . . . . C 3
Scugog (lake) . . . . F 3
Seul (lake) . . . . G 4
Severn (riv.) . . . . E 3
Sibley Prov. Park . . . . H 5
Simcoe (lake) . . . . E 3
South (bay) . . . . C 2
Spanish (riv.) . . . . C 1
Stony (lake) . . . . G 3
Superior (lake) . . . . H 5
Sydenham (riv.) . . . . B 5
Thames (riv.) . . . . B 5
Theano (pt.) . . . . J 5
Thousand (isls.) . . . . H 3
Timagami (lake) . . . . K 5
Trout (lake) . . . . E 1
Vernon (lake) . . . . E 2
Walpole (isl.) . . . . B 5
Welland (canal) . . . . E 5
Woods (lake) . . . . F 5

⊛County seat.
*Population of metropolitan area.
△Population of town or township.

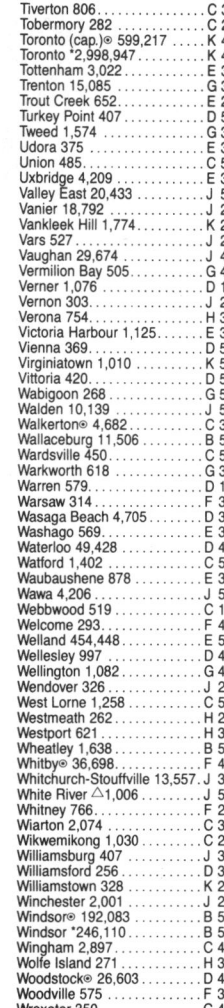

Ontario
Southern Part

SCALE
0 10 20 30 40 50 MI.
0 10 20 30 40 50 KM.

National Capital	⊛
Provincial Capital	⊛
County Seats	⊛
International Boundaries	

Provincial & State Boundaries
County Boundaries
Canals

Scale 1:2,620,000

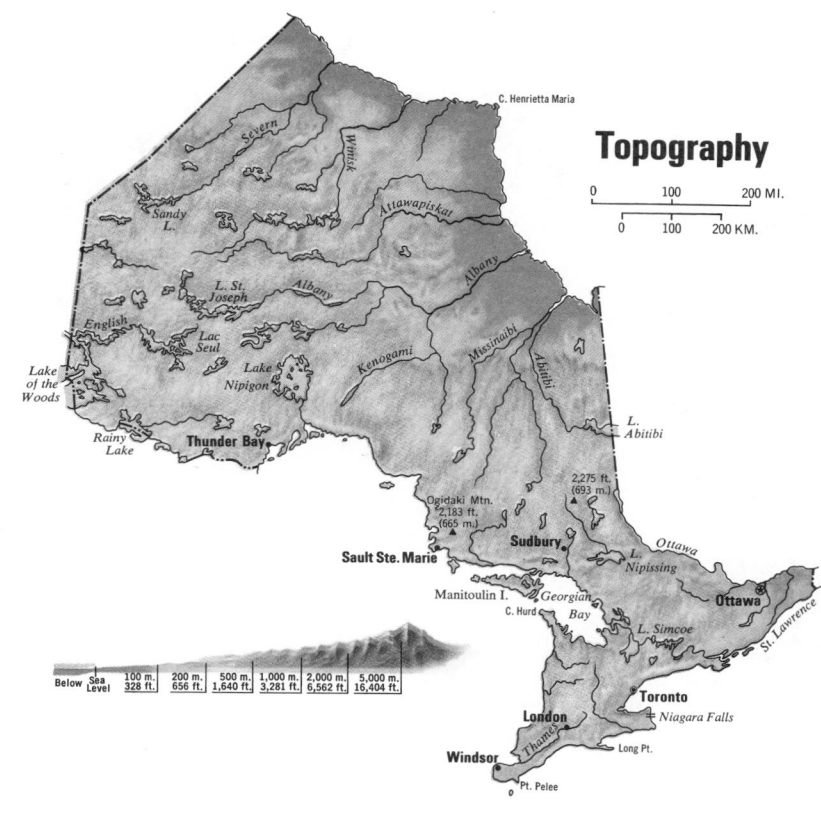

Topography

0 100 200 MI.
0 100 200 KM.

Below Sea Level | 100 m. 328 ft. | 200 m. 656 ft. | 500 m. 1,640 ft. | 1,000 m. 3,281 ft. | 2,000 m. 6,562 ft. | 5,000 m. 16,404 ft.

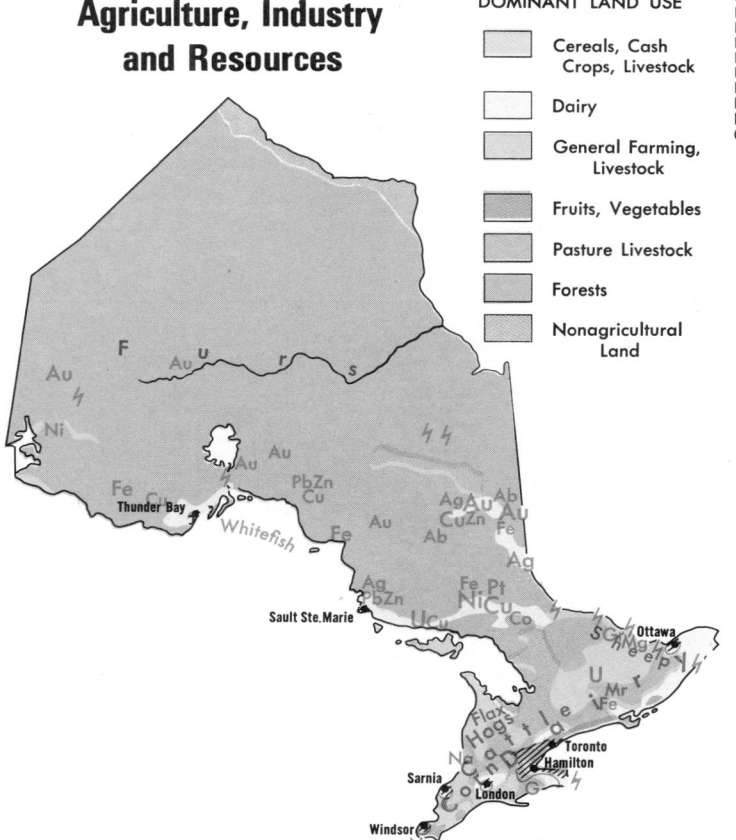

Agriculture, Industry and Resources

DOMINANT LAND USE

Cereals, Cash Crops, Livestock
Dairy
General Farming, Livestock
Fruits, Vegetables
Pasture Livestock
Forests
Nonagricultural Land

MAJOR MINERAL OCCURRENCES

Ab Asbestos
Ag Silver
Au Gold
Co Cobalt
Cu Copper
Fe Iron Ore
G Natural Gas
Gr Graphite

Mg Magnesium
Mr Marble
Na Salt
Ni Nickel
Pb Lead
Pt Platinum
U Uranium
Zn Zinc

⚡ Water Power
░ Major Industrial Areas

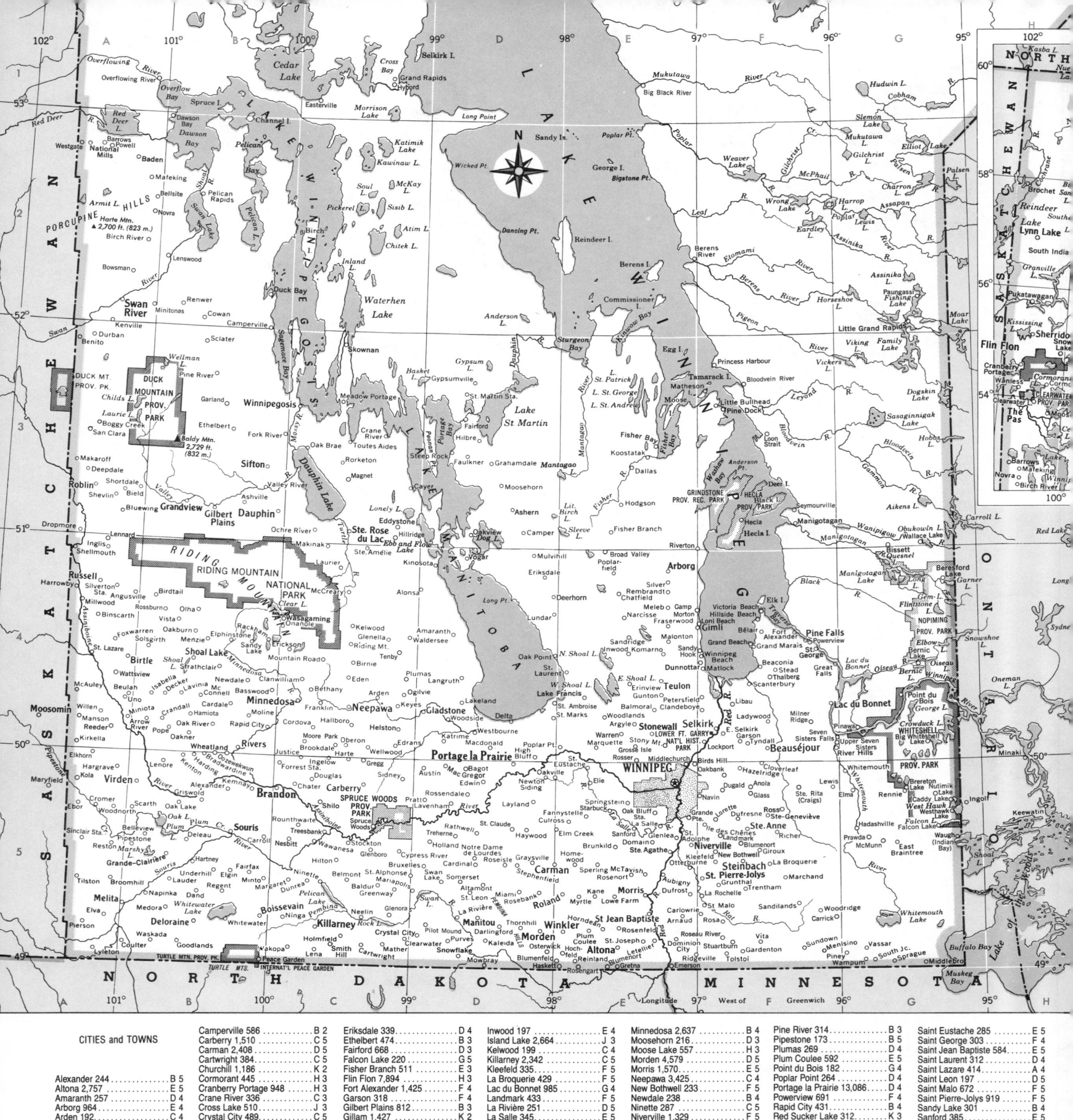

Manitoba
Northern Part

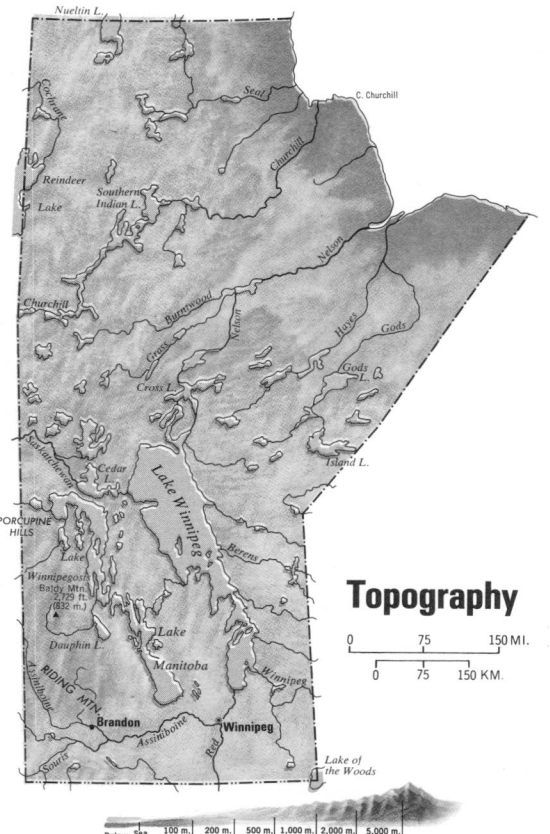

WEST TERRS

HUDSON BAY

Manitoba
Southern Part
SCALE

0 5 10 20 40 60 MI.

0 5 10 20 40 60 KM.

Provincial Capital .... ⊛
International Boundaries ...—..—..—
Provincial Boundaries ...———

Scale 1:2,340,000

© Copyright HAMMOND INCORPORATED, Maplewood, N.J.

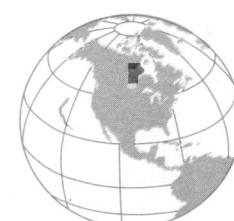

The Pas 6,390 .... H 3
Thicket Portage 195 .... J 3
Thompson 14,288 .... J 2
Treherne 743 .... D 5
Tyndall 421 .... F 4
Virden 2,940 .... A 5
Vita 364 .... F 5
Wabowden 655 .... J 3
Wallace Lake •2,044 .... G 3
Wanless 193 .... H 3
Warren 459 .... E 4
Waskada 239 .... B 5
Wawanesa 492 .... C 5
Whitemouth 320 .... E 5
Whitewater •856 .... B 5
Winkler 5,046 .... E 5
Winnipeg (cap.) 564,473 .... E 5
Winnipeg *584,842 .... E 5
Winnipeg Beach 565 .... F 4
Winnipegosis 855 .... B 3
Woodlands 185 .... E 4
Wooodridge 170 .... G 5
York Landing 229 .... J 2

AREA 250,999 sq. mi. (650,087 sq. km.)
POPULATION 1,026,241
CAPITAL Winnipeg
LARGEST CITY Winnipeg
HIGHEST POINT Baldy Mtn. 2,729 ft.
(832 m.)
SETTLED IN 1812
ADMITTED TO CONFEDERATION 1870
PROVINCIAL FLOWER Prairie Crocus

OTHER FEATURES

Aikens (lake) .... G 3
Anderson (lake) .... D 2
Anderson (pt.) .... F 3
Armit (lake) .... A 2
Assapan (riv.) .... C 2
Assiniboine (riv.) .... C 5
Assinika (lake) .... G 2
Assinika (riv.) .... G 2
Atim (lake) .... C 2
Baldy (mt.) .... B 3
Basket (lake) .... C 3
Beaverhill (lake) .... J 3
Berens (isl.) .... E 2
Berens (riv.) .... F 2
Bernic (lake) .... G 4
Big Sand (lake) .... H 2
Bigstone (lake) .... J 3
Bigstone (pt.) .... E 2
Bigstone (riv.) .... J 3
Birch (lake) .... C 2
Black (isl.) .... F 3
Black (riv.) .... F 4
Bloodvein (riv.) .... F 3
Bonnet (lake) .... G 4
Buffalo (bay) .... G 5
Burntwood (riv.) .... J 2
Caribou (riv.) .... J 1
Carroll (lake) .... G 3
Cedar (lake) .... B 1
Channel (isl.) .... B 2
Charron (lake) .... G 2
Childs (lake) .... A 3
Chitek (lake) .... C 2
Churchill (cape) ...... K 2
Churchill (riv.) ...... J 2
Clear (lake) .... C 4
Clearwater Lake Prov. Park .. H 3
Cobham (riv.) .... G 1
Cochrane (riv.) .... H 2
Commissioner (isl.) .... E 2
Cormorant (lake) ...... H 3
Cross (bay) .... C 1
Cross (lake) .... J 3
Crowduck (lake) ...... G 4
Dancing (pt.) .... D 2
Dauphin (lake) .... C 3
Dauphin (riv.) .... D 3
Dawson (bay) .... B 2
Dog (lake) .... D 3
Dogskin (lake) .... G 3
Duck Mountain Prov. Park .. B 3
Eardley (lake) .... F 2

East Shoal (lake) .... E 4
Ebb and Flow (lake) ...... C 3
Egg (isl.) .... E 3
Elbow (lake) .... G 4
Elk (isl.) .... F 4
Elliot (lake) .... G 2
Etawney (lake) .... J 2
Etomami (riv.) .... F 2
Falcon (lake) .... G 5
Family (lake) .... G 3
Fisher (bay) .... E 3
Fisher (riv.) .... E 3
Fishing (lake) .... G 2
Flintstone (lake) ..... G 2
Fox (riv.) .... K 2
Gammon (riv.) .... G 3
Garner (lake) .... G 4
Gem (lake) .... G 4
George (isl.) .... E 2
George (lake) .... G 3
Gilchrist (creek) ..... F 2
Gilchrist (lake) ...... G 2
Gods (lake) .... K 3
Gods (riv.) .... K 3
Granville (lake) ..... H 2
Grass (riv.) .... H 2
Grass River Prov. Park .. H 3
Grindstone Prov. Rec. Park .. F 3
Gunisao (lake) ...... G 3
Gypsum (lake) ...... D 3
Harrop (lake) .... G 2
Harte (mt.) .... A 2
Hayes (riv.) .... K 3
Hecla (isl.) .... F 3
Hecla Prov. Park .... F 3
Hobbs (lake) ...... G 3
Horseshoe (lake) ... G 2
Hubbart (pt.) ...... K 2
Hudson (bay) ...... K 2
Hudwin (lake) ..... G 1
Inland (lake) ...... C 2
International Peace Garden .. B 5
Island (lake) ...... K 3
Katimik (lake) ..... C 2
Kawinaw (lake) .... C 2
Kinwow (bay) ..... E 2
Kississing (lake) ... H 2
Knee (lake) ...... J 3
Lake of the Woods (lake) .. H 5
La Salle (riv.) ..... E 5
Laurie (lake) ..... A 3
Leaf (riv.) .... F 2
Lewis (lake) ..... A 2
Leyond (riv.) .... F 3
Little Birch (lake) .. E 3
Lonely (lake) .... C 3
Long (lake) ..... G 4
Long (pt.) ...... D 1
Long (pt.) ...... D 4
Manigotagan (lake) .. G 4

Manigotagan (riv.) ..... G 3
Manitoba (lake) ...... D 4
Mantagao (riv.) ...... E 3
Marshy (lake) .... B 5
McKay (lake) .... C 2
McPhail (riv.) ...... F 2
Minnedosa (riv.) .... B 4
Moar (lake) .... G 2
Molson (lake) ...... J 3
Moose (isl.) .... E 3
Morrison (lake) ..... C 1
Mossy (riv.) .... C 3
Mukutawa (lake) ... G 3
Mukutawa (riv.) .... E 1
Muskeg (bay) ..... G 6
Nejanilini (lake) ... J 1
Nelson (riv.) ..... J 2
Nopiming Prov. Park .. G 4
Northern Indian (lake) .. J 2
North Knife (lake) .. J 2
North Seal (riv.) ... H 2
North Shoal (lake) .. E 4
Nueltin (lake) ..... H 1
Oak (lake) .... B 5
Obukowin (lake) ... G 3
Oiseau (lake) ..... G 4
Oiseau (riv.) ..... G 4
Overflow (bay) .... A 1
Overflowing (riv.) .. A 1
Owl (riv.) .... K 2
Oxford (lake) .... J 3
Paint (lake) ..... J 2
Palsen (riv.) .... G 2
Pelican (bay) .... B 2
Pelican (lake) ... B 2
Pelican (lake) ... C 5
Pembina (hills) .. D 5
Pembina (riv.) .. C 5
Peonan (pt.) ... D 3
Pickerel (lake) .. C 2
Pigeon (riv.) ... F 2
Pipestone (creek) .. A 5
Plum (creek) ... B 5
Plum (lake) .... B 5
Poplar (riv.) ... E 2
Porcupine (hills) .. A 2
Portage (bay) ... D 3
Punk (isl.) ..... F 3
Quesnel (lake) .. G 4
Rat (riv.) ...... F 5
Red (riv.) ..... F 4
Red Deer (lake) .. A 2
Red Deer (riv.) .. A 2
Reindeer (isl.) .. E 2
Reindeer (lake) .. H 2
Riding (mt.) .... B 4
Riding Mountain Nat'l Park .. B 4
Rock (lake) ..... C 5
Ross (isl.) ..... J 3
Sagemace (bay) .. B 3

Saint Andrew (lake) ..... E 3
Saint George (lake) ..... E 3
Saint Martin (lake) ..... D 3
Saint Patrick (lake) .... E 3
Sale (riv.) .... E 5
Sandy (isls.) .... D 2
Sasaginnigak (lake) ... G 3
Seal (riv.) .... J 2
Selkirk (isl.) ...... C 1
Setting (lake) ..... H 3
Shoal (lake) ..... G 5
Shoal (riv.) ..... B 2
Sipiwesk (lake) ... J 3
Sisib (lake) ..... C 2
Sleeve (lake) .... E 3
Slemon (lake) ... G 1
Snowshoe (lake) .. G 4
Soul (lake) ..... C 2
Souris (riv.) .... B 5
Southern Indian (lake) .. H 2
South Knife (riv.) ... J 2
South Seal (riv.) ... J 2
Split (lake) ..... J 2
Spruce (isl.) .... B 1
Spruce Woods Prov. Park .. C 5
Stevenson (lake) .. J 3
Sturgeon (bay) ... E 3
Swan (lake) ..... D 5
Swan (lake) ..... B 2
Swan (riv.) ..... A 3
Tadoule (lake) ... J 2
Tamarack (isl.) .. F 3
Tatnam (cape) ... K 2
Traverse (bay) ... F 4
Turtle (mts.) .... B 5
Turtle (riv.) ..... C 3
Turtle Mountain Prov. Park .. B 5
Valley (lake) .... B 3
Vickers (lake) ... F 3
Viking (lake) .... G 3
Wanipigow (riv.) .. G 3
Washow (bay) ... F 3
Waterhen (lake) .. C 2
Weaver (lake) ... F 2
Wellman (lake) .. B 3
West Hawk (lake) .. G 5
West Shoal (lake) . E 4
Whitemouth (lake) .. G 5
Whitemouth (riv.) .. G 5
Whiteshell Prov. Park .. G 4
Whitewater (lake) .. B 5
Wicked (pt.) .... D 2
Winnipeg (lake) .. E 2
Winnipeg (riv.) .. G 4
Winnipegosis (lake) .. C 2
Woods (lake) ... H 5
Wrong (lake) ... F 2

*Population of metropolitan area.
•Population of rural municipality.

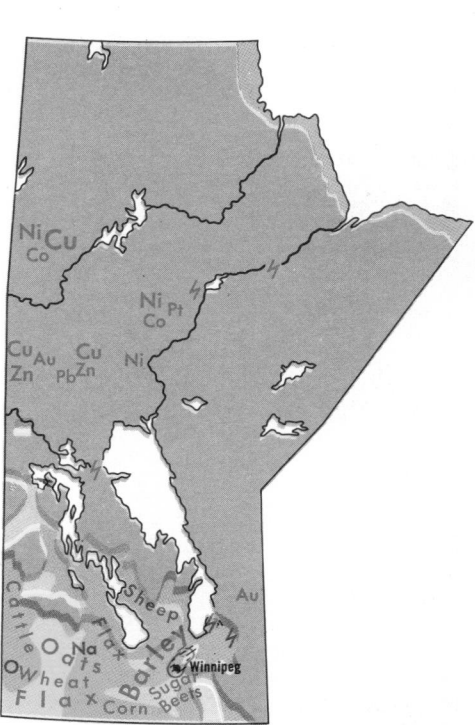

Agriculture, Industry and Resources

DOMINANT LAND USE

Cereals (chiefly barley, oats)
Cereals, Livestock
Dairy
Livestock
Forests
Nonagricultural Land

MAJOR MINERAL OCCURRENCES

Au Gold
Co Cobalt
Cu Copper
Na Salt

Ni Nickel
O   Petroleum
Pb Lead
Pt Platinum
Zn Zinc

⚡ Water Power
⚡ Major Industrial Areas

Topography

0 75 150 MI.

0 75 150 KM.

Below Sea Level | 100 m. 328 ft. | 200 m. 656 ft. | 500 m. 1,640 ft. | 1,000 m. 3,281 ft. | 2,000 m. 6,562 ft. | 5,000 m. 16,404 ft.

Topography

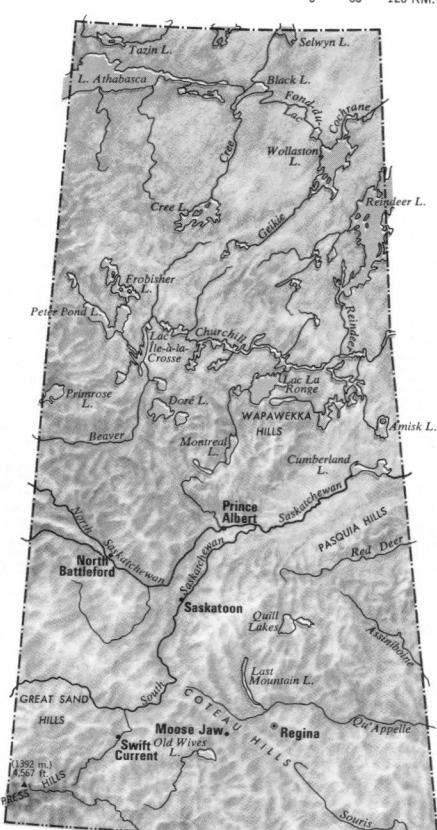

0 60 120 MI.
0 60 120 KM.

5,000 m. 2,000 m. 1,000 m. 500 m. 200 m. 100 m. Sea Level Below
16,404 ft. 6,562 ft. 3,281 ft. 1,640 ft. 656 ft. 328 ft.

CITIES and TOWNS

Abbey 218	E 5
Aberdeen 496	E 3
Abernethy 300	H 5
Air Ronge 557	M 3
Alameda 318	J 6
Alida 169	K 6
Allan 871	E 4
Alsask 652	B 4
Annaheim 209	G 3
Antelope ●231	C 5
Arborfield 439	H 2
Archerwill 286	H 3
Arcola 493	J 6
Arlington Beach ●432	F 4
Asquith 507	D 3
Assiniboia 2,924	E 6
Avonlea 442	G 5
Baildon ●799	F 5
Balcarres 739	H 5
Balgonie 777	G 5
Batoche	E 3
Battleford 3,565	C 3
Beauval 606	L 3
Beechy 279	D 5
Bengough 536	F 6
Bethune 369	F 5
Bienfait 801	J 6
Biggar 2,561	C 3
Big River 819	D 2
Birch Hills 957	F 3
Bjorkdale 269	H 3
Blaine Lake 653	D 3
Borden 197	D 3
Brabant Lake 245	M 3
Bradwell 168	E 4
Bredenbury 467	K 5
Briercrest 151	F 5
Broadview 840	J 5
Brock 184	C 4
Browning ●687	J 6
Bruno 772	F 3
Buchanan 392	J 4
Buffalo Gap ●598	F 6
Buffalo Narrows 1,088	L 3
Burstall 550	B 5
Cabri 632	C 5
Cadillac 173	D 6
Calder 164	K 5
Cana ●1,238	J 5
Candle Lake 219	F 2
Cando 163	C 3
Canoe Lake 182	L 3
Canora 2,667	J 4
Canwood 340	E 2
Carievale 246	K 6
Carlyle 1,074	J 6
Carnduff 1,043	K 6
Carrot River 1,169	H 2
Central Butte 548	E 5
Ceylon 184	G 6
Chaplin 389	E 5
Chitek Lake 170	D 2
Choiceland 543	G 2
Christopher Lake 227	F 2
Churchbridge 972	J 5
Clavet 234	E 4
Climax 293	C 6
Cochin 221	C 2
Codette 236	G 2
Coleville 383	B 4
Colonsay 594	F 4
Connaught Heights ●982	G 3
Conquest 256	D 4
Consul 153	B 6
Coronach 1,032	F 6
Craik 565	F 4
Craven 206	G 5
Creelman 184	H 5
Creighton 1,636	N 4
Cudworth 947	F 3
Cumberland House 831	J 2
Cupar 669	G 5
Cut Knife 624	B 3
Dalmeny 1,064	E 3
Davidson 1,166	E 4
Debden 403	E 2
Delisle 980	D 4
Denare Beach 592	M 4
Denzil 199	B 3
Deschambault Lake 386	M 3
Dinsmore 398	D 4
Dodsland 272	C 4
Domremy 209	F 3
Drake 211	G 4
Duck Lake 699	E 3
Dundurn 531	E 4
Dysart 199	H 5
Earl Grey 303	G 5
Eastend 723	C 6
Eatonia 528	B 4
Ebenezer 164	J 4
Edam 384	C 2
Edenwold 143	G 5
Elbow 313	E 4
Eldorado 229	L 2
Elfros 199	H 4
Elrose 624	D 4
Elstow 143	E 4
Endeavour 199	J 3
Englefeld 271	G 3
Erwood 149	J 3
Esterhazy 3,065	K 5
Estevan 9,174	J 6
Eston 1,413	C 4
Eyebrow 168	E 5
Fillmore 396	H 6
Fleming 141	K 5
Flin Flon 367	N 4
Foam Lake 1,452	H 4
Fond du Lac 494	L 2
Fort Qu'Appelle 1,827	H 5
Fox Valley 380	B 5
Francis 182	H 5
Frobisher 166	J 6
Frontier 619	C 6
Gainsborough 308	K 6
Gerald 197	K 5
Glaslyn 430	D 2
Glenavon 284	J 5
Glen Ewen 168	K 6
Goodsoil 263	L 4
Govan 394	G 4
Grand Coulee 208	G 5
Gravelbourg 1,338	E 6
Grayson 264	J 5
Green Acres 139	F 2
Green Lake 634	L 4
Grenfell 1,307	J 5
Guernsey 198	G 4
Gull Lake 1,095	C 5
Hafford 557	D 3
Hague 625	E 3
Hanley 484	E 4
Harris 259	D 4
Hawarden 187	E 4
Hearts Hill ●552	B 3
Hepburn 411	E 3
Herbert 1,019	D 5
Hodgeville 329	E 5
Holdfast 297	F 5
Hudson Bay 2,361	J 3
Humboldt 4,705	F 3
Hyas 165	J 4
Ile-à-la-Crosse 1,035	L 3
Imperial 501	F 4
Indian Head 1,889	H 5
Invermay 353	J 4
Ituna 870	H 4
Jansen 223	G 4
Jasmin ●14	H 4
Kamsack 2,688	K 4
Kelliher 397	H 4
Kelvington 1,054	H 3
Kenaston 345	E 4
Kennedy 275	J 5
Kerrobert 1,141	C 4
Kincaid 256	D 6
Kindersley 3,969	B 4
Kinistino 783	F 3
Kipling 1,016	J 5
Kisbey 228	J 6
Kronau 154	G 5
Kyle 516	C 5
Lac Pelletier ●586	C 5
Lafleche 583	E 6
Laird 233	E 3
Lake Lenore 361	G 3
Lampman 651	J 6
Lancer 156	C 5
Landis 277	C 3
Lang 219	G 6
Langenburg 1,324	K 5
Langham 1,151	E 3
Lanigan 1,732	F 4
La Ronge 2,579	L 3
Lashburn 813	B 2
Leader 1,108	B 5
Leask 478	E 2
Lebret 274	H 5
Lemberg 414	H 5
Leoville 393	D 2
Leroy 504	G 4
Lestock 402	G 4
Limerick 164	E 6
Lintlaw 234	H 3
Lipton 364	H 5
Lloydminster 6,034	A 2
Loon Lake 369	B 1
Loreburn 201	E 4
Lucky Lake 333	D 5
Lumsden 1,303	G 5
Luseland 704	B 3
Macdowall 171	E 2
Macklin 976	A 3
Macoun 190	H 6
Maidstone 1,001	B 2
Mankota 375	D 6
Manor 368	K 6
Maple Creek 2,470	B 6
Marcelin 238	E 3
Margo 153	H 4
Marriott ●627	D 4
Marsden 229	B 3
Marshall 453	B 2
Martensville 1,966	E 3
Maryfield 431	K 6
Maymont 212	D 3
McLean 189	G 5
Meacham 178	F 3
Meadow Lake 3,857	C 1
Meath Park 262	F 2
Medstead 163	D 2
Melfort 6,010	G 3
Melville 5,092	J 5
Meota 235	C 2
Mervin 155	C 2
Midale 564	H 6
Middle Lake 275	F 3
Milden 251	D 4
Milestone 602	G 5
Montmartre 544	H 5
Montreal Lake 448	F 1
Moose Jaw 33,941	F 5
Moose Range ●679	H 2
Moosomin 2,579	K 5
Morse 416	D 5
Mortlach 293	E 5
Mossbank 464	E 6
Muenster 385	F 3
Naicam 886	G 3
Neilburg 354	B 3
Neuanlage 144	E 3
Neudorf 425	J 5
Neuhorst 146	E 3
Nipawin 4,376	H 2
Nokomis 524	F 4
Norquay 552	J 4
North Battleford 14,030	C 3
North Portal 164	J 6
Odessa 232	H 5
Ogema 441	G 6
Osler 527	E 3
Outlook 1,976	E 4
Oxbow 1,191	J 6
Paddockwood 211	F 2
Pangman 227	G 6
Paradise Hill 421	B 2
Patuanak 173	L 3
Paynton 210	B 2
Pelican Narrows 331	N 3
Pelly 391	K 4
Pennant 202	C 5
Pense 472	G 5
Perdue 407	D 3
Pierceland 425	K 4
Pilger 150	F 3
Pilot Butte 1,255	G 5
Pine House 612	M 3
Plenty 175	C 4
Plunkett 150	F 4
Ponteix 769	D 6
Porcupine Plain 937	H 3
Preeceville 1,243	J 4
Prelate 317	B 5
Prince Albert 31,380	F 2
Prud'homme 222	F 3
Punnichy 394	H 4
Qu'Appelle 653	H 5
Quill Lake 514	G 3
Quinton 169	G 4
Rabbit Lake 159	D 2
Radisson 439	D 3
Radville 1,012	G 6
Rama 133	H 4
Raymore 635	G 4
Redvers 859	K 6
Regina (cap.) 162,613	G 5
Regina ●164,313	G 5
Regina Beach 603	F 5
Rhein 211	J 4
Richmound 188	B 5
Riverhurst 193	E 5
Rocanville 934	K 5
Roche Percé 142	J 6
Rockglen 511	F 6
Rosetown 2,664	D 4
Rose Valley 538	H 3
Rosthern 1,609	E 3
Rouleau 443	G 5
Saint Benedict 157	F 3
Saint Brieux 401	G 3
Saint Louis 448	F 3
Saint Philips ●538	K 4
Saint Walburg 802	B 2
Saltcoats 549	J 4
Sandy Bay 756	N 3
Saskatoon 154,210	E 3
Saskatoon *154,210	E 3
Sceptre 169	B 5
Scott 203	C 3
Sedley 373	H 5
Semans 344	G 4
Shaunavon 2,112	C 6
Sheho 285	H 4
Shell Lake 220	D 2
Shellbrook 1,228	E 2
Simpson 231	F 4
Sintaluta 215	H 5
Smeaton 246	G 2
Southey 697	G 5
Spalding 337	G 3
Spiritwood 926	D 2
Springside 533	J 4
Spy Hill 354	K 5
Star City 527	G 3
Stenen 143	J 4
Stockholm 391	J 5
Stonehenge ●701	F 6
Storthoaks 142	K 6
Stoughton 716	J 6
Strasbourg 842	G 4
Sturgis 789	J 4
Swift Current 14,747	D 5
Tantallon 196	K 5
Theodore 473	J 4
Timber Bay 152	F 1
Tisdale 3,107	H 3
Togo 181	K 4
Tompkins 255	C 5
Torch River ●2,440	G 2
Torquay 311	H 6
Tramping Lake 178	B 3
Tugaske 175	E 5
Turnor Lake 166	L 3
Turtleford 505	B 2
Unity 2,408	B 3
Uranium City 2,507	L 2
Val Marie 236	D 6
Vanguard 292	D 6
Vanscoy 298	D 4
Vibank 369	H 5
Viscount 386	F 4
Vonda 313	F 3
Wadena 1,495	H 4
Wakaw 1,030	F 3
Waldeck 292	D 5
Waldheim 758	E 3
Walpole ●711	K 6
Wapella 487	K 5
Warman 2,076	E 3
Waseca 169	B 2
Waskesiu Lake 176	E 1
Watrous 1,830	F 4
Watson 901	G 3
Wawota 622	J 6
Weldon 279	F 2
Welwyn 170	K 5
Weyburn 9,523	H 6
White City 602	G 5
White Fox 394	G 2
Whitewood 1,003	J 5
Wilcox 202	G 5
Wilkie 1,501	C 3
Willow Bunch 494	F 6
Willow Creek ●1,218	B 6
Windthorst 254	J 5
Wiseton 195	D 4
Wishart 212	H 4
Wolseley 904	H 5
Wymark 162	D 5
Wynyard 2,147	G 4
Yarbo 158	K 5
Yellow Grass 477	H 6
Yorkton 15,339	J 4
Young 456	F 4
Zenon Park 273	H 2

OTHER FEATURES

Allan (hills)	E 4
Amisk (lake)	M 4
Antelope (lake)	B 2
Antler (riv.)	K 6
Arm (riv.)	F 5
Assiniboine (riv.)	J 3
Athabasca (lake)	L 2
Bad (lake)	C 4
Bad (hills)	C 4
Basin (lake)	F 3
Batoche Nat'l Hist. Site	E 3
Battle (creek)	B 6
Battle (riv.)	B 3
Bear (hills)	C 4
Beaver (hills)	H 4
Beaver (riv.)	L 4
Beaverlodge (lake)	L 2
Big Muddy (lake)	G 6
Bigstick (lake)	B 5
Birch (lake)	C 2
Bitter (lake)	B 5
Black (lake)	M 2
Boundary (plat.)	B 6
Brightsand (lake)	B 2
Bronson (lake)	B 2

Agriculture, Industry and Resources

DOMINANT LAND USE

- Wheat
- Cereals (chiefly barley, oats)
- Cereals, Livestock
- Livestock
- Forests

MAJOR MINERAL OCCURRENCES

Au	Gold	Na	Salt
Cu	Copper	O	Petroleum
G	Natural Gas	S	Sulfur
He	Helium	U	Uranium
K	Potash	Zn	Zinc
Lg	Lignite		

⚡ Water Power

▨ Major Industrial Areas

Buffalo Pound Prov. Park . . . . F 5
Cabri (lake) . . . . B 4
Cactus (hills) . . . . F 5
Candle (lake) . . . . F 2
Cannington Manon Hist. Park . J 6
Canoe (lake) . . . . L 3
Carrot (riv.) . . . . J 2
Chaplin (lake) . . . . E 5
Chipman (riv.) . . . . M 2
Chitek (lake) . . . . D 2
Churchill (riv.) . . . . M 3
Clearwater (riv.) . . . . L 3
Cochrane (riv.) . . . . N 2
Coteau (hills) . . . . D 4
Cowan (lake) . . . . D 2
Crane (lake) . . . . B 5
Crean (lake) . . . . E 1
Cree (lake) . . . . L 3
Cree (riv.) . . . . M 2
Cumberland (lake) . . . . J 1
Cypress (hills) . . . . B 6
Cypress (lake) . . . . B 6
Cypress Hills Prov. Park . . . . B 6
Danielson Prov. Park . . . . . . E 4
Delaronde (lake) . . . . E 1
Diefenbaker (lake) . . . . E 4
Doré (lake) . . . . L 3
Douglas Prov. Park . . . . E 4
Duck Lake Hist. Park . . . . . . E 3
Duck Mountain Prov. Park . . . K 4
Eagle (hills) . . . . C 3
Eaglehill (creek) . . . . D 4
Ear (lake) . . . . B 3
Echo Valley Prov. Park . . . . . G 5
Etomami (riv.) . . . . J 3
Eyebrow (lake) . . . . E 5
Eyehill (creek) . . . . B 3
Fife (lake) . . . . E 6
File (hills) . . . . H 5
Fir (riv.) . . . . J 2
Fond du Lac (riv.) . . . . M 2
Forrest (lake) . . . . L 3
Fort Battleford Nat'l Hist. Park C 3
Fort Carlton Hist. Park . . . . . E 3
Fort Pitt Hist. Park . . . . B 2
Fort Walsh Nat'l Hist. Park . . . A 6
Foster (riv.) . . . . M 3
Frenchman (riv.) . . . . C 6
Frobisher (lake) . . . . L 3
Gap (creek) . . . . B 6
Gardiner (dam) . . . . D 4
Geikie (riv.) . . . . M 3
Good Spirit (lake) . . . . J 4
Goodspirit Lake Prov. Park . . J 4
Great Sand (hills) . . . . B 5
Green (lake) . . . . D 1
Greenwater Lake Prov. Park . . H 3
Haultain (riv.) . . . . L 3
Île-à-la-Crosse (lake) . . . . . L 3
Ironspring (creek) . . . . G 3
Jackfish (lake) . . . . C 2
Katepwa Prov. Park . . . . H 5
Kingsmere (lake) . . . . E 1
Kiyiu (lake) . . . . C 4
Lac La Ronge Prov. Park . . . . M 3
Lanigan (creek) . . . . F 4
Last Mountain (lake) . . . . . . F 4
Leaf (lake) . . . . J 2
Leech (lake) . . . . J 4
Lenore (lake) . . . . G 3
Little Manitou (lake) . . . . . . F 4
Lodge (creek) . . . . B 6
Long (creek) . . . . H 6
Loon (creek) . . . . G 4
Makwa (lake) . . . . B 1
Makwa (riv.) . . . . B 1
Manito (lake) . . . . B 3
Maple (creek) . . . . B 5
McFarlane (riv.) . . . . L 2
Meadow (lake) . . . . C 1
Meadow Lake Prov. Park . . . . K 4
Meeting (lake) . . . . D 2
Midnight (lake) . . . . C 2
Ministikwan (lake) . . . . B 1
Missouri Coteau (hills) . . . . . F 5
Montreal (lake) . . . . F 1
Moose (mt.) . . . . J 6
Moose Jaw (riv.) . . . . G 5
Moose Mountain (creek) . . . . J 6
Moose Mountain Prov. Park . . . J 6
Mossy (riv.) . . . . H 1
Muddy (lake) . . . . B 4
Mudjatik (riv.) . . . . L 3
Nipawin Prov. Park . . . . G 1
North Saskatchewan (riv.) . . . D 3
Notukeu (creek) . . . . D 6
Oldman (riv.) . . . . L 2
Old Wives (lake) . . . . E 5
Opuntia (lake) . . . . C 4
Overflowing (riv.) . . . . K 2
Pasquia (hills) . . . . J 2
Pasquia (riv.) . . . . K 2
Pelican (lake) . . . . E 5
Peter Pond (lake) . . . . L 3
Pheasant (hills) . . . . J 5
Pine Lake Prov. Park . . . . . . E 4
Pinto (creek) . . . . D 6
Pipestone (creek) . . . . K 6
Pipestone (riv.) . . . . L 2
Ponass (lakes) . . . . H 3
Poplar (riv.) . . . . E 6
Porcupine (hills) . . . . K 3
Primrose (lake) . . . . L 3
Primrose Lake Air Weapons Range . . . . L 3
Prince Albert Nat'l Park . . . . E 1
Qu'Appelle (riv.) . . . . J 5
Quill (lakes) . . . . G 4
Red Deer (riv.) . . . . A 5
Red Deer (riv.) . . . . K 3
Reindeer (lake) . . . . N 3
Reindeer (riv.) . . . . M 3
Riou (lake) . . . . M 2
Rivers (lake) . . . . F 6
Ronge, La (lake) . . . . M 3
Rowans Ravine Prov. Park . . . F 4
St. Victor Petroglyphs Hist. Park . . . . E 6
Saskatchewan (riv.) . . . . H 2
Saskatchewan Landing Prov. Park . . . . C 5
Saskeram (riv.) . . . . K 2
Scott (lake) . . . . M 2
Selwyn (lake) . . . . M 2
Souris (riv.) . . . . H 6
South Saskatchewan (riv.) . . . C 5
Steele Narrows Hist. Park . . . . B 2
Stripe (lake) . . . . C 4
Sturgeon (riv.) . . . . E 2
Swan (riv.) . . . . J 3
Swift Current (creek) . . . . . . D 5
Tazin (lake) . . . . L 2
The Battlefords Prov. Park . . . C 2
Thickwood (hills) . . . . D 2
Thunder (hills) . . . . L 4
Tobin (lake) . . . . H 2
Torch (riv.) . . . . H 2
Touchwood (hills) . . . . G 4
Tramping (lake) . . . . C 3
Trout (riv.) . . . . L 3
Turtle (lake) . . . . C 2
Twelvemile (lake) . . . . E 6
Vermilion (hills) . . . . E 5
Wapawekka (hills) . . . . M 4
Waskana (creek) . . . . G 5
Waskesiu (lake) . . . . E 2
Wathaman (riv.) . . . . M 3
Weed (hills) . . . . J 5
White Fox (riv.) . . . . G 2
White Gull (creek) . . . . G 2
Whiteshore (lake) . . . . C 3
Whiteswan (lakes) . . . . F 1
William (riv.) . . . . L 2
Willow Bunch (lake) . . . . F 6
Witchekan (lake) . . . . D 2
Wollaston (lake) . . . . N 2
Wood (mt.) . . . . E 6
Wood (riv.) . . . . E 6
Wood Mountain Hist. Park . . . . E 6

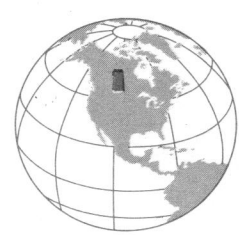

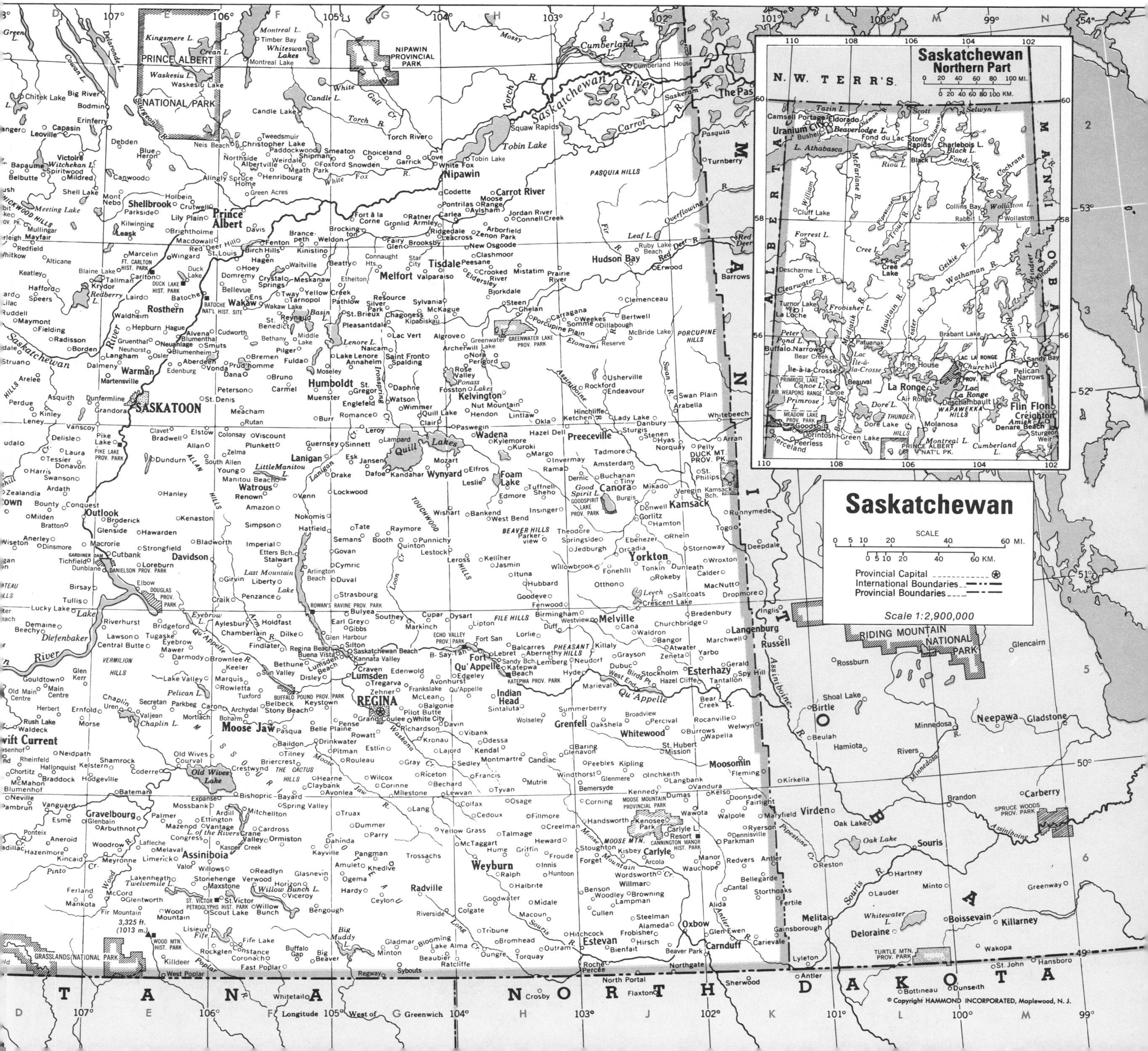

*Population of metropolitan area.
•Population of rural municipality.

AREA 251,699 sq. mi. (651,900 sq. km.)
POPULATION 968,313
CAPITAL Regina
LARGEST CITY Regina
HIGHEST POINT Cypress Hills 4,567 ft. (1,392 m.)
SETTLED IN 1774
ADMITTED TO CONFEDERATION 1905
PROVINCIAL FLOWER Prairie Lily

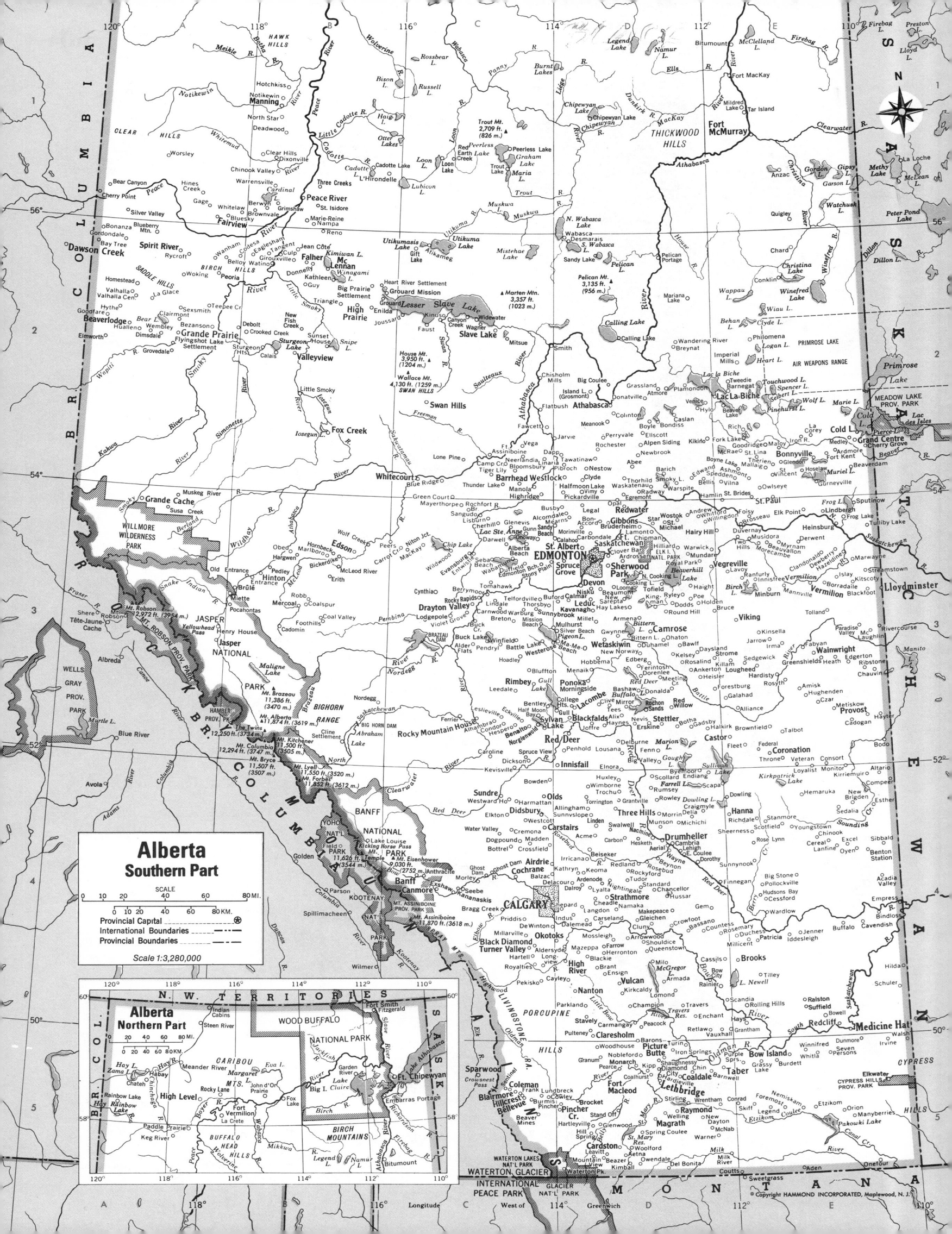

Alberta
Southern Part

SCALE
0 10 20 40 60 80 MI.
0 10 20 40 60 80 KM. ⊕
Provincial Capital ⊛
International Boundaries
Provincial Boundaries

Scale 1:3,280,000

Alberta
Northern Part

0   20   40   60   80 MI.
0 20 40 60 80 KM.

N. W. T E R R I T O R I E S

WOOD BUFFALO

NATIONAL PARK

CARIBOU

MTS.

BUFFALO

HEAD

HILLS

BIRCH MOUNTAINS

© Copyright HAMMOND INCORPORATED, Maplewood, N.J.

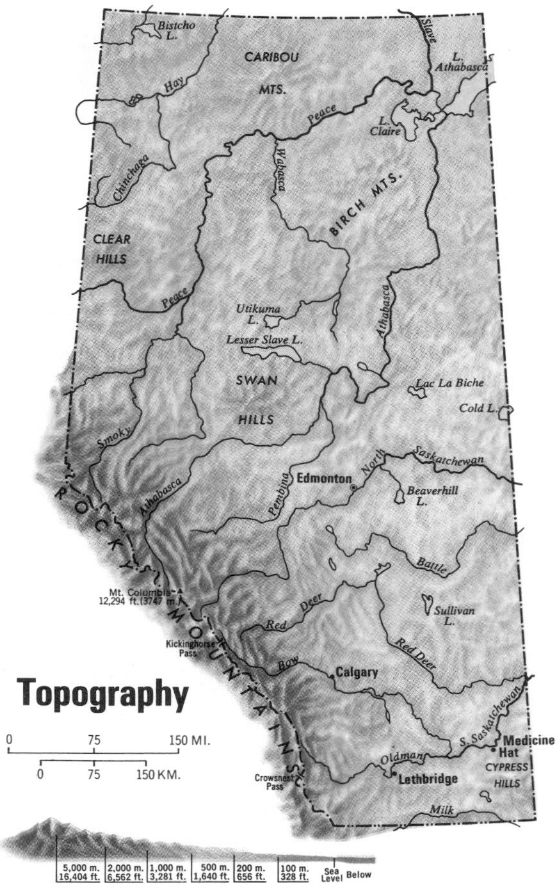
Bistcho L.
CARIBOU MTS.
Hay
Slave
L. Athabasca
Peace
L. Claire
Chinchaga
Wabasca
BIRCH MTS.
CLEAR HILLS
Utikuma L.
Lesser Slave L.
Athabasca
SWAN HILLS
Lac La Biche
Cold L.
Smoky
North
Saskatchewan
Pembina
Edmonton
Beaverhill L.
Battle
ROCKY MOUNTAINS
Mt. Columbia 12,294 ft. (3747 m.)
Kickinghorse Pass
Red Deer
Sullivan L.
Bow
Calgary
S. Saskatchewan
Medicine Hat
Oldman
Lethbridge
CYPRESS HILLS
Crowsnest Pass
Milk
0 75 150 MI.
0 75 150 KM.
5,000 m. 16,404 ft.
2,000 m. 6,562 ft.
1,000 m. 3,281 ft.
500 m. 1,640 ft.
200 m. 656 ft.
100 m. 328 ft.
Sea Level
Below

Topography

AREA 255,285 sq. mi. (661,185 sq. km.)
POPULATION 2,237,724
CAPITAL Edmonton
LARGEST CITY Edmonton
HIGHEST POINT Mt. Columbia 12,294 ft. (3,747 m.)
SETTLED IN 1861
ADMITTED TO CONFEDERATION 1905
PROVINCIAL FLOWER Wild Rose

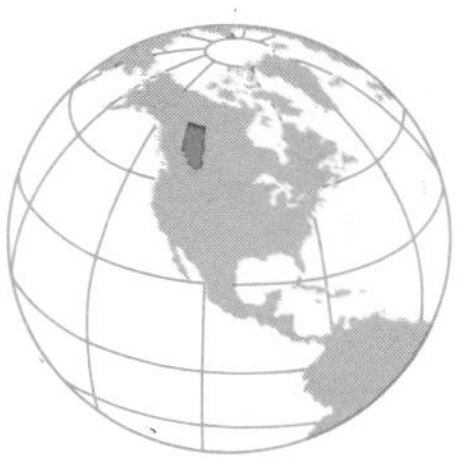

CITIES and TOWNS

Acme 457 D 4
Airdrie 8,414 C 4
Alberta Beach 485 C 3
Alix 837 D 3
Andrew 548 D 3
Antler Lake 334 D 3
Ardmore 224 E 2
Arrowwood 156 D 4
Athabasca 1,731 D 2
Banff 4,208 C 4
Barnwell 359 D 5
Barons 315 D 4
Barrhead 3,736 C 2
Bashaw 875 D 3
Bassano 1,200 D 4
Bawlf 350 D 3
Beaumont 2,638 D 3
Beaverlodge 1,937 A 2
Beiseker 580 D 4
Bentley 823 C 3
Berwyn 557 B 1
Big Valley 360 D 3
Black Diamond 1,444 C 4
Blackfalds 1,488 D 3
Blackfoot 220 E 3
Blackie 298 D 4
Bon Accord 1,376 D 3
Bonnyville 4,454 E 2
Bowden 989 C 4
Bow Island 1,491 E 5
Boyle 638 D 2
Bragg Creek 505 C 4
Breton 552 C 3
Brooks 9,421 E 4
Bruce 88 E 3
Bruderheim 1,136 D 3
Burdett 220 E 5
Calgary 592,743 C 4
Calgary *592,743 C 4
Calmar 1,003 D 3
Camrose 12,570 D 3
Canmore 3,484 C 4
Carbon 434 D 4
Cardston 3,267 D 5
Carmangay 266 D 4
Caroline 436 C 3
Carseland 484 D 4
Carstairs 1,587 D 4
Castor 1,123 D 3
Cereal 249 E 4
Champion 339 D 4
Chauvin 298 E 3
Chipman 266 D 3
Clairmont 469 A 2
Claresholm 3,493 D 4
Clive 364 D 3
Clyde 364 D 2
Coaldale 4,579 D 5
Coalhurst 882 D 5
Cochrane 3,544 C 4
Cold Lake 2,110 E 2
College Heights 267 D 3
Consort 632 E 3
Cooking Lake 218 D 3
Coronation 1,309 E 3
Coutts 400 D 5
Cowley 304 D 5
Cremona 382 C 4
Crossfield 1,217 C 4
Daysland 679 D 3
Delburne 574 D 3
Desmarais 260 D 2
Devon 3,885 D 3
Didsbury 3,095 C 4
Donalda 280 D 3
Donnelly 336 B 2
Drayton Valley 5,042 C 3
Drumheller 6,508 D 4
Duchess 429 E 4
East Coulee 218 D 4
Eckville 870 C 3
Edgerton 387 E 3
Edmonton (cap.) 532,246 D 3
Edmonton *657,057 D 3
Edmonton Beach 280 C 3
Edson 5,835 B 3
Elk Point 1,022 E 3
Elnora 249 D 3
Entwistle 462 C 3
Erskine 259 D 3
Evansburg 779 C 3
Exshaw 353 C 4
Fairview 2,869 A 1
Falher 1,102 B 2
Faust 399 C 2
Foremost 568 E 5
Forestburg 924 E 3
Fort Assiniboine 207 C 2
Fort Chipewyan 944 C 5
Fort Macleod 3,139 D 5
Fort McKay 267 E 1
Fort McMurray 31,000 E 1
Fort Saskatchewan 12,169 D 3
Fort Vermilion 752 B 5
Fox Creek 1,978 B 2
Fox Lake 634 B 5
Gibbons 2,276 D 3
Gift Lake 428 C 2
Girouxville 325 B 2
Gleichen 381 D 4
Glendon 430 E 2
Glenwood 259 D 5
Grand Centre 3,146 E 2
Grande Cache 4,523 A 3
Grande Prairie 24,263 A 2
Granum 399 D 5
Grimshaw 2,316 B 1
Grouard Mission 221 C 2
Hanna 2,806 E 4
Hardisty 641 E 3
Hay Lakes 302 D 3
Heisler 212 D 3
High Level 2,194 A 5
High Prairie 2,506 B 2
High River 4,792 D 4
Hines Creek 575 A 1
Hinton 8,342 B 3
Holden 430 D 3
Hughenden 267 E 3
Hythe 639 A 2
Innisfail 5,247 D 3
Innisfree 255 E 3
Irma 474 E 3
Irricana 558 D 4
Irvine 360 E 5
Jasper 3,269 B 3
John d'Or Prairie 437 B 5
Joussard 330 B 2
Killam 1,005 E 3
Kinuso 285 C 2
Kitscoty 497 E 3
Lac La Biche 2,007 E 2
Lacombe 5,591 D 3
La Crete 479 B 5
Lake Louise 355 B 4
Lamont 1,563 D 3
Leduc 12,471 D 3
Legal 1,022 D 3
Lethbridge 54,072 D 5
Linden 407 D 4
Little Buffalo Lake 253 B 1
Lloydminster 8,997 E 3
Longview 301 C 4
Lougheed 226 E 3
Lundbreck 244 C 5
Magrath 1,576 D 5
Manning 1,173 B 1
Mannville 788 E 3
Marlboro 211 B 3
Marwayne 500 E 3
Mayerthorpe 1,475 C 3
McLennan 1,125 B 2
Medicine Hat 40,380 E 4
Milk River 894 D 5
Millet 1,120 D 3
Mirror 507 D 3
Monarch 212 D 5
Morinville 4,657 D 3
Morrin 244 D 4
Mundare 604 D 3
Myrnam 397 E 3
Nacmine 369 D 4
Nampa 334 B 1
Nanton 1,641 D 4
New Norway 291 D 3
New Sarepta 417 D 3
Nobleford 534 D 5
North Calling Lake 234 D 2
Okotoks 3,847 C 4
Olds 4,813 D 4
Onoway 621 C 3
Oyen 975 E 4
Peace River 5,907 B 1
Penhold 1,531 D 3
Picture Butte 1,404 D 5
Pincher Creek 3,757 D 5
Plamondon 259 D 2
Pollockville 19 E 4
Ponoka 5,221 D 3
Provost 1,645 E 3
Rainbow Lake 504 A 5
Ralston 357 E 4
Raymond 2,837 D 5
Redcliff 3,876 E 4
Red Deer 46,393 D 3
Redwater 1,932 D 3
Rimbey 1,685 C 3
Robb 230 B 3
Rockyford 329 D 4
Rocky Mountain House 4,698 C 3
Rosemary 328 E 4
Rycroft 649 A 2
Ryley 483 D 3
Saint Albert 31,996 D 3
Saint Paul 4,884 E 3
Sangudo 398 C 3
Sedgewick 879 E 3
Sexsmith 1,180 A 2
Shaughnessy 270 D 5
Sherwood Park 29,285 D 3
Slave Lake 4,506 C 2
Smith 216 D 2
Smoky Lake 1,074 D 2
Spirit River 1,104 A 2
Spruce Grove 10,326 D 3
Standard 379 D 4
Stavely 504 D 4
Stettler 5,136 D 3
Stirling 688 D 5
Stony Plain 4,839 C 3
Strathmore 2,986 D 4
Strome 281 E 3
Sundre 1,742 C 4
Swan Hills 2,497 C 2
Sylvan Lake 3,779 C 3
Taber 5,988 E 5
Thorhild 576 D 2
Thorsby 737 C 3
Three Hills 1,787 D 4
Tilley 345 E 4
Tofield 1,504 D 3
Trochu 880 D 4
Turner Valley 1,311 C 4
Two Hills 1,193 E 3
Valleyview 2,061 B 2
Vauxhall 1,049 D 4
Vegreville 5,251 E 3
Vermilion 3,766 E 3
Veteran 314 E 3
Viking 1,232 E 3
Vilna 345 E 2
Vulcan 1,489 D 4
Wabamun 662 C 3
Wabasca 701 D 2
Wainwright 4,266 E 3
Warburg 501 C 3
Warner 477 D 5
Waskatenau 290 D 2
Wembley 1,169 A 2
Westlock 4,424 C 2
Wetaskiwin 9,597 D 3
Whitecourt 5,585 C 2
Wildwood 441 C 3
Willingdon 366 E 3
Youngstown 297 E 4

OTHER FEATURES

Abraham (lake) B 3
Alberta (mt.) B 3
Assiniboine (mt.) C 4
Athabasca (lake) C 5
Athabasca (riv.) D 1
Banff Nat'l Park B 4
Battle (riv.) D 3
Bear (lake) A 2
Beaver (riv.) E 2
Beaverhill (lake) D 3
Behan (lake) E 2
Belly (riv.) D 5
Berland (riv.) A 3
Berry (creek) E 4
Biche (lake) E 2
Big (isl.) B 5
Big Horn (dam) B 3
Bighorn (range) B 3
Birch (hills) A 2
Birch (lake) E 3
Birch (mts.) B 5
Birch (riv.) B 5
Bison (lake) B 1
Bittern (lake) D 3
Botha (riv.) B 1
Bow (riv.) D 4
Boyer (riv.) A 5
Brazeau (mt.) B 3
Brazeau (riv.) B 3
Buffalo (lake) D 3
Buffalo Head (hills) B 5
Burnt (lakes) C 1
Cadotte (lake) B 1
Cadotte (riv.) B 1
Calling (lake) D 2
Canal (creek) E 5
Cardinal (lake) B 1
Caribou (mts.) B 5
Chinchaga (riv.) A 5
Chip (lake) C 3
Chipewyan (lake) D 1
Chipewyan (riv.) D 1
Christina (lake) E 2
Christina (riv.) E 1
Claire (lake) B 5
Clear (hills) A 1
Clearwater (riv.) C 4
Clearwater (riv.) E 1
Clyde (lake) E 2
Cold (lake) E 2
Columbia (mt.) B 3
Crowsnest (pass) C 5
Cypress (hills) E 5
Cypress Hills Prov. Park E 5
Dillon (riv.) E 2
Dowling (lake) D 4
Dunkirk (riv.) D 1
Eisenhower (mt.) C 4
Elbow (riv.) C 4
Elk Island Nat'l Park D 3
Ells (riv.) D 1
Etzikom Coulee (riv.) E 5
Eva (lake) B 5
Farrell (lake) D 4
Firebag (riv.) E 1
Forbes (mt.) B 4
Freeman (riv.) C 2
Frog (lake) E 3
Garson (lake) E 1
Gipsy (lake) E 1
Gordon (lake) E 1
Gough (lake) D 3
Graham (lake) C 1
Gull (lake) C 3
Haig (lake) B 1
Hawk (hills) B 1
Hay (lake) A 5
Hay (riv.) A 5
Heart (lake) E 2
Highwood (riv.) C 4
House (mt.) C 2
House (riv.) D 2
Iosegun (lake) B 2
Iosegun (riv.) B 2
Jackfish (riv.) B 5
Jasper Nat'l Park A 3
Kakwa (riv.) A 2
Kickinghorse (pass) B 4
Kimiwan (lake) B 2
Kirkpatrick (lake) E 4
Kitchener (mt.) B 3
Legend (lake) D 1
Lesser Slave (lake) C 2
Liége (riv.) D 1
Little Bow (riv.) D 4
Little Cadotte (riv.) B 1
Little Smoky (riv.) B 2
Livingstone (range) C 4
Logan (lake) E 2
Loon (lake) C 1
Loon (riv.) C 1
Lubicon (lake) C 1
Lyell (mt.) B 4
MacKay (riv.) D 1
Maligne (lake) B 3
Margaret (lake) B 5
Marie (lake) E 2
Marion (lake) D 3
Marten (mt.) C 2
McClelland (lake) E 1
McGregor (lake) D 4
McLeod (riv.) B 3
Meikle (riv.) A 1
Mikkwa (riv.) B 5
Milk (riv.) D 5
Mistehae (lake) C 2
Muriel (lake) E 2
Muskwa (lake) C 1
Muskwa (riv.) C 1
Namur (lake) D 1
Newell (lake) E 4
Nordegg (riv.) C 3
North Saskatchewan (riv.) E 3
North Wabasca (lake) D 1
Notikewin (riv.) A 1
Oldman (riv.) D 5
Otter (lakes) B 1
Pakowki (lake) E 5
Panny (riv.) C 1
Peace (riv.) B 1
Peerless (lake) C 1
Pelican (lake) D 2
Pelican (mts.) D 2
Pembina (riv.) C 3
Pigeon (lake) D 3
Pinehurst (lake) E 2
Porcupine (hills) C 4
Primrose (lake) E 2
Rainbow (lake) A 5
Red Deer (lake) D 3
Red Deer (riv.) D 4
Richardson (riv.) C 5
Rocky (mts.) B-C 4
Rosebud (riv.) D 4
Russell (lake) C 1
Saddle (hills) A 2
Sainte Anne (lake) C 3
Saint Mary (res.) D 5
Saint Mary (riv.) D 5
Saulteaux (riv.) C 2
Seibert (lake) E 2
Simonette (riv.) A 2
Slave (riv.) C 5
Smoky (riv.) A 2
Snake Indian (riv.) A 3
Snipe (lake) B 2
Sounding (creek) E 4
South Saskatchewan (riv.) E 4
South Wabasca (lake) D 2
Spencer (lake) E 2
Spray (mts.) C 4
Sturgeon (lake) B 2
Sullivan (lake) D 3
Swan (hills) C 2
Swan (riv.) C 2
Temple (mt.) B 4
The Twins (mt.) B 3
Thickwood (hills) D 1
Touchwood (lake) E 2
Travers (res.) D 4
Trout (mt.) C 1
Trout (riv.) C 1
Utikuma (lake) C 2
Utikuma (riv.) C 1
Utikumasis (lake) C 2
Vermilion (riv.) E 3
Wabasca (riv.) C 1
Wallace (mt.) C 2
Wapiti (riv.) A 2
Wappau (lake) E 2
Watchusk (lake) E 1
Waterton-Glacier Int'l Peace Park C 5
Waterton Lakes Nat'l Park C 5
Whitemud (riv.) A 1
Wildhay (riv.) B 3
Willmore Wilderness Prov. Park A 3
Winagami (lake) B 2
Winefred (lake) E 2
Winefred (riv.) E 2
Wolf (lake) E 2
Wolverine (riv.) B 1
Wood Buffalo Nat'l Park B 5
Yellowhead (pass) A 3
Zama (lake) A 5

*Population of metropolitan area.

Agriculture, Industry and Resources

DOMINANT LAND USE

- Wheat
- Cereals (chiefly barley, oats)
- Cereals, Livestock
- Dairy
- Pasture Livestock
- Range Livestock
- Forests
- Nonagricultural Land

MAJOR MINERAL OCCURRENCES

- C Coal
- G Natural Gas
- Na Salt
- O Petroleum
- S Sulfur

- Water Power
- Major Industrial Areas

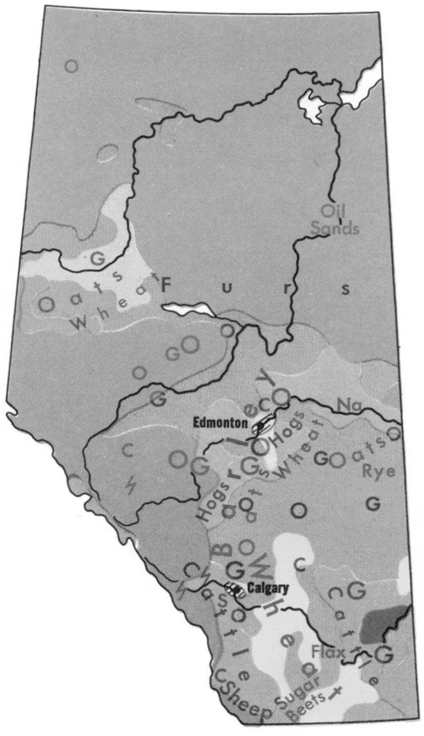
Oil Sands
Oats
Wheat
Furs
Edmonton
Hogs
Rye
Calgary
Flax
Sheep
Sugar Beets

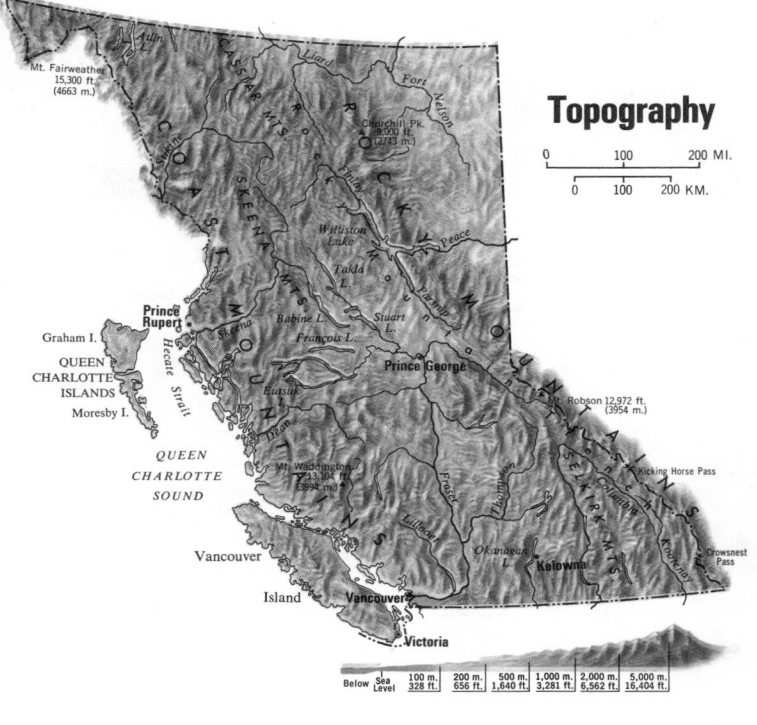

Topography

0   100   200 MI.

0   100   200 KM.

| Below Sea Level | 100 m. 328 ft. | 200 m. 656 ft. | 500 m. 1,640 ft. | 1,000 m. 3,281 ft. | 2,000 m. 6,562 ft. | 5,000 m. 16,404 ft. |

Agriculture, Industry and Resources

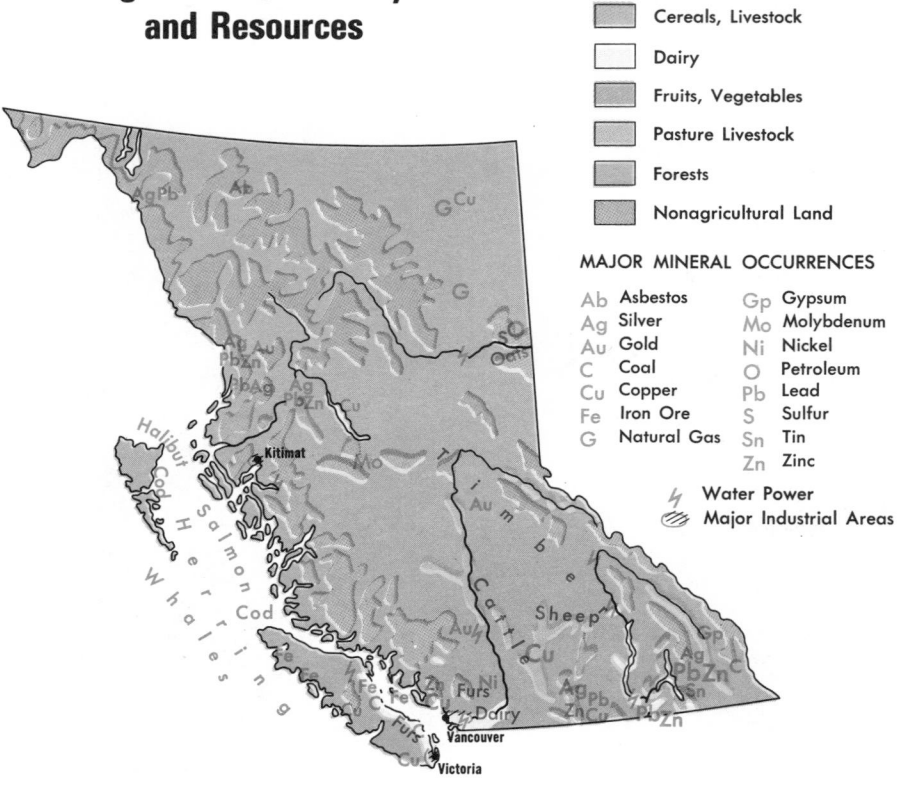

DOMINANT LAND USE

- Cereals, Livestock
- Dairy
- Fruits, Vegetables
- Pasture Livestock
- Forests
- Nonagricultural Land

MAJOR MINERAL OCCURRENCES

Ab	Asbestos	Gp	Gypsum
Ag	Silver	Mo	Molybdenum
Au	Gold	Ni	Nickel
C	Coal	O	Petroleum
Cu	Copper	Pb	Lead
Fe	Iron Ore	S	Sulfur
G	Natural Gas	Sn	Tin
		Zn	Zinc

⚡ Water Power
〰 Major Industrial Areas

CITIES and TOWNS

Abbotsford 12,745 .... L 3
Alert Bay 626 .... D 5
Armstrong 2,683 .... H 5
Ashcroft 2,156 .... G 5
Ashton Creek 452 .... H 5
Balfour 472 .... J 5
Barlow 441 .... F 3
Barrière 1,370 .... H 4
Blueberry Creek 635 .... J 5
Blue River 384 .... H 4
Boston Bar 498 .... G 5
Bowen Island 1,125 .... K 3
Brackendale 1,719 .... F 5
Burnaby ○136,494 .... K 3
Burns Lake 1,777 .... D 3
Cache Creek 1,308 .... G 5
Campbell River 15,370 .... E 5
Canal Flats 919 .... K 5
Canyon 698 .... J 5
Cassiar 1,045 .... K 2
Castlegar 6,902 .... J 5
Cawston 785 .... H 5
Central Saanich ○9,890 .... K 3
Chase 1,777 .... H 5
Chemainus 2,069 .... J 3
Cherry Creek 450 .... G 5
Chetwynd 2,553 .... G 2
Chilliwack ○40,642 .... M 3
Clearwater 1,461 .... G 4
Clinton 804 .... G 4
Coldstream ○6,450 .... H 5
Comox 6,607 .... H 2
Coquitlam ○61,077 .... K 3
Courtenay 8,992 .... E 5
Cranbrook 15,915 .... K 5
Creston 4,190 .... J 5
Crofton 1,303 .... J 3
Cultus Lake 481 .... M 3
Cumberland 1,947 .... E 5
Dawson Creek 11,373 .... G 2
Delta ○74,692 .... K 3
Duncan 4,228 .... J 3
Elkford 3,126 .... K 5
Enderby 1,816 .... H 5
Erickson 972 .... J 5
Errington 609 .... J 3
Esquimalt ○15,870 .... K 4
Falkland 478 .... H 5
Fernie 5,444 .... K 5
Forest Grove 444 .... G 4
Fort Fraser 574 .... E 3
Fort Langley 2,326 .... L 3
Fort Nelson 3,724 .... M 2
Fort Saint James 2,284 .... E 3
Fort Saint John 13,891 .... G 2
Fraser Lake 1,543 .... E 3
Fruitvale 1,904 .... J 5
Gabriola 1,627 .... J 3
Galiano 669 .... K 3
Ganges 1,118 .... K 3
Gibsons 2,594 .... K 3
Gold River 2,225 .... D 5
Golden 3,476 .... J 4
Grand Forks 3,486 .... H 6
Granisle 1,430 .... D 3
Greenwood 856 .... H 5
Hagensborg 350 .... D 4
Harrison Hot Springs 569 .... M 3
Hatzic 1,055 .... L 3
Hazelton 393 .... D 2
Hedley 426 .... G 5
Holberg 444 .... C 5
Honeymoon Bay 474 .... J 3
Hope 3,205 .... M 3
Hornby Island 474 .... H 2
Horsefly 430 .... G 4
Houston 1,714 .... D 3
Hudson Hope 984 .... F 2
Invermere 1,969 .... J 4
Kaleden 998 .... H 5
Kamloops 64,048 .... G 5
Kaslo 854 .... J 5
Kelowna 59,196 .... H 5
Kent ○3,394 .... M 3
Keremeos 830 .... G 5
Kimberley 7,375 .... K 5
Kitimat 12,462 .... C 3
Kitsault 554 .... C 2
Kitwanga 369 .... D 2
Lac La Hache 647 .... G 4
Ladysmith 4,558 .... J 3
Langley 15,124 .... L 3
Lantzville 969 .... J 3
Likely 425 .... G 4
Lillooet 1,725 .... G 5
Lion's Bay 1,078 .... K 3
Logan Lake 2,637 .... G 5
Lumby 1,266 .... H 5
Lytton 428 .... G 5
Mackenzie 5,797 .... F 2
Mackenzie ○5,890 .... F 2
Malakwa 392 .... H 5
Maple Bay 393 .... K 3
Maple Ridge ○32,232 .... L 3
Masset 1,569 .... B 3
Matsqui ○42,001 .... L 3
Mayne 546 .... K 3
McBride 641 .... G 3
Merritt 6,110 .... G 5
Midway 633 .... H 6
Mill Bay 583 .... K 3
Mission ○20,056 .... L 3
Mission City 9,948 .... L 3
Montrose 1,229 .... J 5
Nakusp 1,495 .... J 5
Nanaimo 47,069 .... J 3
Nanaimo 876 .... H 5
Nelson 9,143 .... J 5
New Denver 642 .... J 5
New Hazelton 792 .... D 2
New Westminster 38,550 .... K 3
Nicomen Island 360 .... L 3
Nootka .... D 5
North Cowichan ○18,210 .... J 3
North Pender Island 906 .... K 3
North Saanich ○6,117 .... K 3
North Vancouver 33,952 .... K 3
North Vancouver ○65,367 .... K 3
Oak Bay ○16,990 .... K 4
Okanagan Falls 1,030 .... H 5
Okanagan Landing 834 .... H 5
Okanagan Mission .... H 5
Old Barkerville 11 .... G 3
Oliver 1,893 .... H 5
One Hundred Mile House
   1,925 .... G 4
Osoyoos 2,738 .... H 5
Oyama 430 .... H 5
Parksville 5,216 .... J 3
Peachland ○2,865 .... G 5
Penticton 23,181 .... H 5
Pitt Meadows ○6,209 .... L 3
Port Alberni 19,892 .... H 3
Port Alice 1,668 .... D 5
Port Clements 380 .... B 3
Port Coquitlam 27,535 .... L 3
Port Edward 989 .... B 3
Port Hardy ○3,778 .... D 5
Port McNeill 2,474 .... D 5
Port Moody 14,917 .... L 3
Pouce-Coupé 821 .... G 2
Powell River ○13,423 .... E 5
Prince George 67,559 .... F 3
Prince Rupert 16,197 .... B 3
Princeton 3,051 .... H 5
Qualicum Beach 2,844 .... J 3
Queen Charlotte 1,070 .... A 3
Quesnel 8,240 .... F 4
Radium Hot Springs 419 .... J 5
Revelstoke 5,544 .... J 5
Richmond ○96,154 .... K 3
Roberts Creek 926 .... J 3
Robson 1,008 .... J 5
Rossland 3,967 .... H 6
Royston 754 .... H 2
Saanich ○78,710 .... K 3
Salmo 1,169 .... J 5
Salmon Arm 1,946 .... H 5
Salmon Arm ○10,780 .... H 5
Saltair 1,356 .... J 3
Sandspit 794 .... B 3
Sayward 482 .... D 5
Sechelt 1,096 .... J 2
Shawnigan Lake 419 .... J 3
Shoreacres 555 .... J 5
Sicamous 1,057 .... H 5
Sidney 7,946 .... K 3
Slocan 351 .... J 5
Slocan Park 414 .... J 5
Smithers 4,570 .... D 3
Sointula 567 .... D 5
Sooke 852 .... J 4
Sorrento 659 .... H 5
South Hazelton 500 .... D 2
South Wellington 620 .... J 3
Spallumcheen 4,213 .... H 5
Sparwood 3,476 .... K 5
Sproat Lake 440 .... H 3
Squamish 1,590 .... F 5
Stewart ○1,456 .... C 2
Summerland ○7,473 .... G 5
Surrey ○147,138 .... K 3
Tahsis 1,739 .... D 5
Taylor 966 .... G 2
Telkwa 840 .... D 3
Terrace 8,893 .... C 3
Terrace ○10,914 .... C 3
Thornhill 4,281 .... C 3
Thrums 360 .... J 5
Tofino 705 .... E 5
Trail 9,599 .... J 6
Ucluelet 1,593 .... E 6
Union Bay 601 .... H 2
Valemount 1,130 .... H 4
Vancouver 414,281 .... K 3
Vancouver (Greater)
   *1,169,831 .... K 3
Vanderhoof 2,323 .... E 3
Vavenby 479 .... H 4
Vernon 19,987 .... H 5
Victoria (cap.) 64,379 .... K 4
Victoria *233,481 .... K 4
Warfield 1,969 .... J 5
Wasa 345 .... K 5
Wells 417 .... G 3
Westbank 1,271 .... H 5
West Vancouver ○35,728 .... K 3
Westwold 409 .... H 5
Whistler ○1,365 .... F 5
White Rock 13,550 .... K 3
Williams Lake 8,362 .... F 4
Wilson Creek 611 .... J 2
Windermere 611 .... K 5
Winlaw 435 .... J 5
Woss Lake 395 .... D 5
Wynndel 566 .... J 5
Yarrow 1,201 .... M 3
Youbou 965 .... J 3

OTHER FEATURES

Adams (lake) .... H 4
Adams (riv.) .... H 4
Alberni (inlet) .... H 3
Alsek (riv.) .... H 1
Aristazabal (isl.) .... C 4
Assiniboine (mt.) .... K 5
Atlin (lake) .... J 1
Azure (lake) .... G 4
Babine (lake) .... E 3
Babine (riv.) .... D 2
Banks (isl.) .... B 3
Barkley (sound) .... E 6
Beale (cape) .... E 6
Beatton (riv.) .... G 1
Bella Coola (riv.) .... D 4
Bennett, W.A.C. (dam) .... F 2
Birkenhead Lake Prov. Park . F 5
Bowron Lake Prov. Park .... G 3
Bowser (lake) .... C 2
Brooks (pen.) .... D 5
Browning Entrance (str.) .... B 3
Bryce (mt.) .... J 4
Bugaboo Glacier Prov. Park . J 5
Bulkley (riv.) .... D 2
Burke (chan.) .... D 4
Burnaby (isl.) .... B 4
Bute (inlet) .... E 5
Caamaño (sound) .... C 4
Calvert (isl.) .... C 4
Canim (lake) .... G 4
Canoe (riv.) .... H 4
Cariboo (mts.) .... G 3
Carpenter (lake) .... F 5
Carp Lake Prov. Park .... F 3
Cassiar (mts.) .... K 2
Castle (mt.) .... A 2
Cathedral Prov. Park .... H 5
Chatham (sound) .... B 3
Chehalis (lake) .... L 3
Chilcotin (riv.) .... E 4
Chilko (lake) .... F 4
Chilko (riv.) .... E 4
Chilkoot (pass) .... J 1
Chuchi (lake) .... E 2
Churchill (peak) .... L 2
Clayoquot (sound) .... D 5
Clearwater (lake) .... G 4
Clearwater (riv.) .... G 4
Coast (mts.) .... D 3
Columbia (lake) .... K 5
Columbia (mt.) .... J 4
Columbia (riv.) .... H 4
Cook (cape) .... C 5
Cowichan (lake) .... J 3
Crowsnest (pass) .... K 5
Cypress Prov. Park .... K 3
Dean (chan.) .... D 4
Dean (riv.) .... D 4
Dease (lake) .... K 2
Dease (riv.) .... K 2
Devils Thumb (mt.) .... A 1
Dixon Entrance (chan.) .... A 3
Douglas (chan.) .... C 3
Dundas (isl.) .... B 3
Duncan (riv.) .... J 5
Elk (riv.) .... K 5
Elk Lakes Prov. Park .... K 5
Eutsuk (lake) .... D 3
Fairweather (mt.) .... H 1
Finlay (riv.) .... E 1
Fitzhugh (sound) .... D 4
Flathead (riv.) .... K 6
Flores (isl.) .... D 5
Fontas (riv.) .... M 2
Forbes (mt.) .... J 4
Fort Nelson (riv.) .... M 2
François (lake) .... D 3
Fraser (lake) .... E 3
Fraser (riv.) .... F 4
Fraser Reach (chan.) .... C 3
Galiano (isl.) .... K 3
Gardner (canal) .... C 3
Garibaldi Prov. Park .... F 5
Georgia (str.) .... J 3
Germansen (lake) .... E 2
Gil (isl.) .... C 3
Glacier Nat'l Park .... J 4
Golden Ears Prov. Park .... L 2
Gordon (riv.) .... H 3
Graham (isl.) .... A 3
Graham Reach (chan.) .... C 3
Grenville (chan.) .... C 3
Halfway (riv.) .... F 2
Hamber Prov. Park .... H 4
Harrison (lake) .... M 2
Hawkesbury (isl.) .... C 3
Hazelton (mts.) .... C 2
Hecate (str.) .... B 3
Hobson (lake) .... H 4
Homathko (riv.) .... E 4
Horsefly (lake) .... G 4

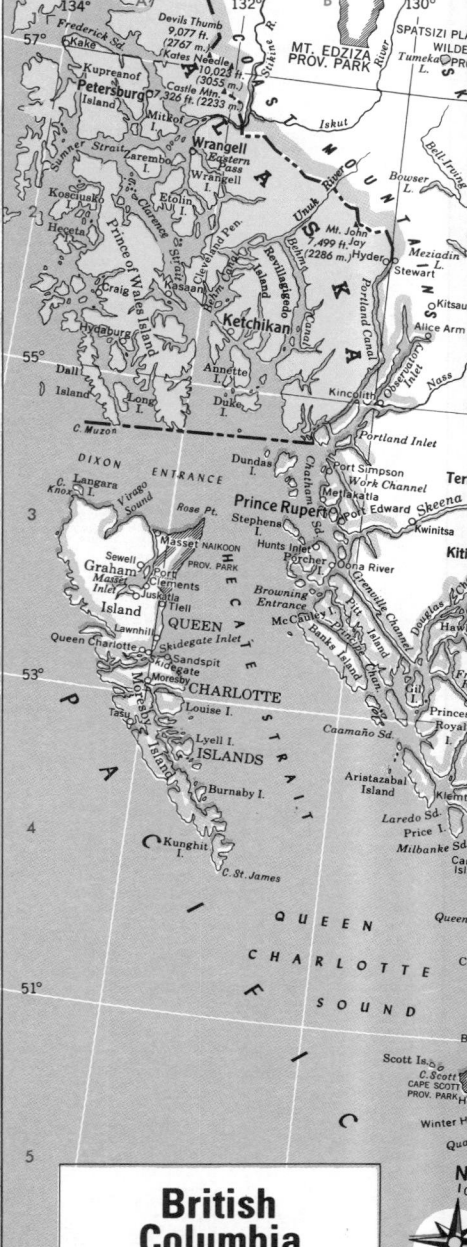

British Columbia

SCALE

0   15   30   60   90   120 MI.

0   15   30   60   90   120 KM.

Provincial Capital .... ⊛
State Capital .... ◉
International Boundaries .... ▬▬▬▬
Provincial Boundaries .... ▬ ▬ ▬

Scale 1:5,200,000

® Copyright HAMMOND INCORPORATED, Maplewood, N.J.

Howe (sound) .... K 2
Hunter (isl.) .... C 4
Inklin (riv.) .... J 2
Inzana (lake) .... E 3
Isaac (lake) .... G 3
Iskut (riv.) .... B 2
Jervis (inlet) .... E 5
John Jay (mt.) .... B 2
Johnstone (str.) .... D 5
Juan de Fuca (str.) .... J 4
Kates Needle (mt.) .... A 1
Kechika (riv.) .... L 2
Kenney (dam) .... E 3
Kettle (riv.) .... H 5
Kicking Horse (pass) .... J 4
King (isl.) .... D 4
Klinaklini (riv.) .... E 4
Kloch (lake) .... E 2
Knight (inlet) .... E 5
Knox (cape) .... A 3
Kokanee Glacier Prov. Park.... J 5
Koocanusa (lake) .... K 6
Kootenay (lake) .... J 5
Kootenay (riv.) .... K 5
Kootenay Nat'l Park .... J 4
Kotcho (lake) .... M 2
Kotcho (riv.) .... M 2
Kunghit (isl.) .... B 4
Kyuquot (sound) .... D 5
Langara (isl.) .... A 3
Laredo (sound) .... C 4
Liard (riv.) .... L 2
Lillooet (riv.) .... F 5
Louise (isl.) .... B 4
Lower Arrow (lake) .... H 5
Lyell (isl.) .... B 4
Lyell (mt.) .... J 4
Mabel (lake) .... H 5
Mahood (lake) .... G 4
Malaspina (str.) .... J 2
Manning Prov. Park .... G 5
Masset (inlet) .... A 3
McCauley (isl.) .... B 3
McGregor (riv.) .... G 3
Meziadin (lake) .... C 2
Milbanke (sound) .... C 4
Moberly (lake) .... F 2
Monashee (mts.) .... H 4
Moresby (isl.) .... B 4
Morice (lake) .... D 3
Morice (riv.) .... D 3
Mount Assiniboine Prov. Park . K 5
Mount Edziza Prov. Park and Rec. Area .... B 1
Mount Revelstoke Nat'l Park .. H 4
Mount Robson Prov. Park .... H 3
Muncho Lake Prov. Park .... L 2
Murray (riv.) .... G 3
Murtle (lake) .... H 4
Muskwa (riv.) .... M 2
Nanika (dam) .... D 3
Nass (riv.) .... C 2
Nation (riv.) .... F 2
Nechako (riv.) .... E 3
Nitinat (lake) .... H 3
Nootka (isl.) .... D 5
Nootka (sound) .... D 5
North Thompson (riv.) .... G 4
Observatory (inlet) .... C 2
Okanagan (lake) .... H 5
Okanagan Mtn. Prov. Park .... G 5
Okanogan (riv.) .... H 6
Omineca (mts.) .... E 2
Omineca (riv.) .... E 2
Ootsa (lake) .... D 3
Owikeno (lake) .... D 4
Pacific Rim Nat'l Park .... E 6
Parsnip (riv.) .... F 3
Peace (riv.) .... G 2
Pend Oreille (riv.) .... J 6
Petitot (riv.) .... M 2
Pinchi (lake) .... E 3
Pine (riv.) .... G 2
Pitt (isl.) .... C 3
Pitt (lake) .... L 2
Porcher (isl.) .... B 3
Portland (canal) .... B 2
Portland (inlet) .... C 3
Price (isl.) .... C 4
Princess Royal (isl.) .... C 3
Principe (chan.) .... C 3
Prophet (riv.) .... M 2
Purcell (mts.) .... J 5
Quatsino (sound) .... C 5
Queen Charlotte (isls.) .... B 3
Queen Charlotte (sound) .... C 4
Queen Charlotte (str.) .... D 5
Queens (sound) .... C 4
Quesnel (lake) .... G 4
Quesnel (riv.) .... F 4
Rivers (inlet) .... D 4
Robson (mt.) .... H 3
Rocky (mts.) .... F 2
Roderick (isl.) .... C 4
Rose (pt.) .... B 3
Saint James (cape) .... B 4
Salmon (riv.) .... F 3
Salmon Arm (inlet) .... J 2
San Juan (riv.) .... J 3
Schoen Lake Prov. Park .... E 5
Scott (cape) .... C 5
Scott (isls.) .... C 5
Seechelt (inlet) .... J 2
Seechelt (pen.) .... J 2
Selkirk (mts.) .... J 4
Seymour (inlet) .... D 4
Sheslay (riv.) .... J 2
Shuswap (lake) .... H 4
Sikanni Chief (riv.) .... F 1
Silver Star Prov. Park .... H 5
Sir Sandford (mt.) .... H 4
Skagit (riv.) .... G 6
Skeena (mts.) .... C 2
Skeena (riv.) .... C 3
Skidegate (inlet) .... B 3
Slocan (lake) .... J 5
Smith (sound) .... C 4
South Bentinck Arm (inlet) .... D 4
Stave (lake) .... L 3
Stephens (isl.) .... B 3
Stikine (riv.) .... B 1
Stone Mountain Prov. Park .... L 2
Strathcona Prov. Park .... E 5
Stuart (lake) .... E 3
Sustut (riv.) .... D 2
Tagish (lake) .... J 1
Tahtsa (lake) .... D 3
Takla (lake) .... D 2
Taku (riv.) .... J 2
Tatlatui (lake) .... D 2
Tatlayoko (lake) .... E 4
Tchentlo (lake) .... E 2
Teslin (lake) .... K 1
Tetachuck (lake) .... E 3
Texada (isl.) .... J 2
Tezzeron (lake) .... E 3
Thompson (riv.) .... G 5
Three Guardsmen (mt.) .... H 1
Thutade (lake) .... D 2
Tiedemann (mt.) .... E 4
Toad (riv.) .... L 2
Toba (inlet) .... E 5
Tochcha (lake) .... E 3
Top Of The World Prov. Park .. K 5
Trembleur (lake) .... E 3
Troitsa (lake) .... D 3
Tumeka (lake) .... C 1
Turnagain (riv.) .... K 2
Tuya (riv.) .... K 2
Tweedsmuir Prov. Park .... D 3
Upper Arrow (lake) .... H 5
Valdes (isl.) .... K 3
Vancouver (isl.) .... D 5
Virago (sound) .... A 3
Waddington (mt.) .... E 4
Wapiti (riv.) .... H 3
Wells Gray Prov. Park .... H 4
West Road (riv.) .... E 3
Whitesail (lake) .... D 3
Williston (lake) .... F 2
Work (chan.) .... C 3
Yellowhead (pass) .... H 4
Yoho Nat'l Park .... J 4

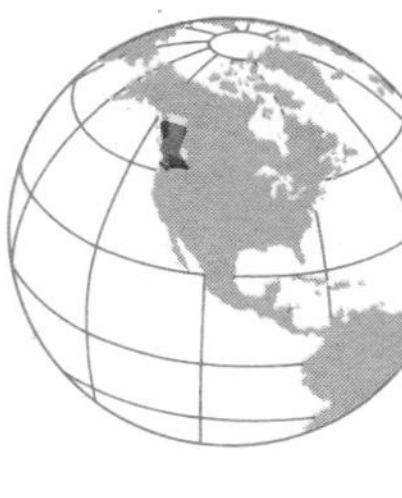

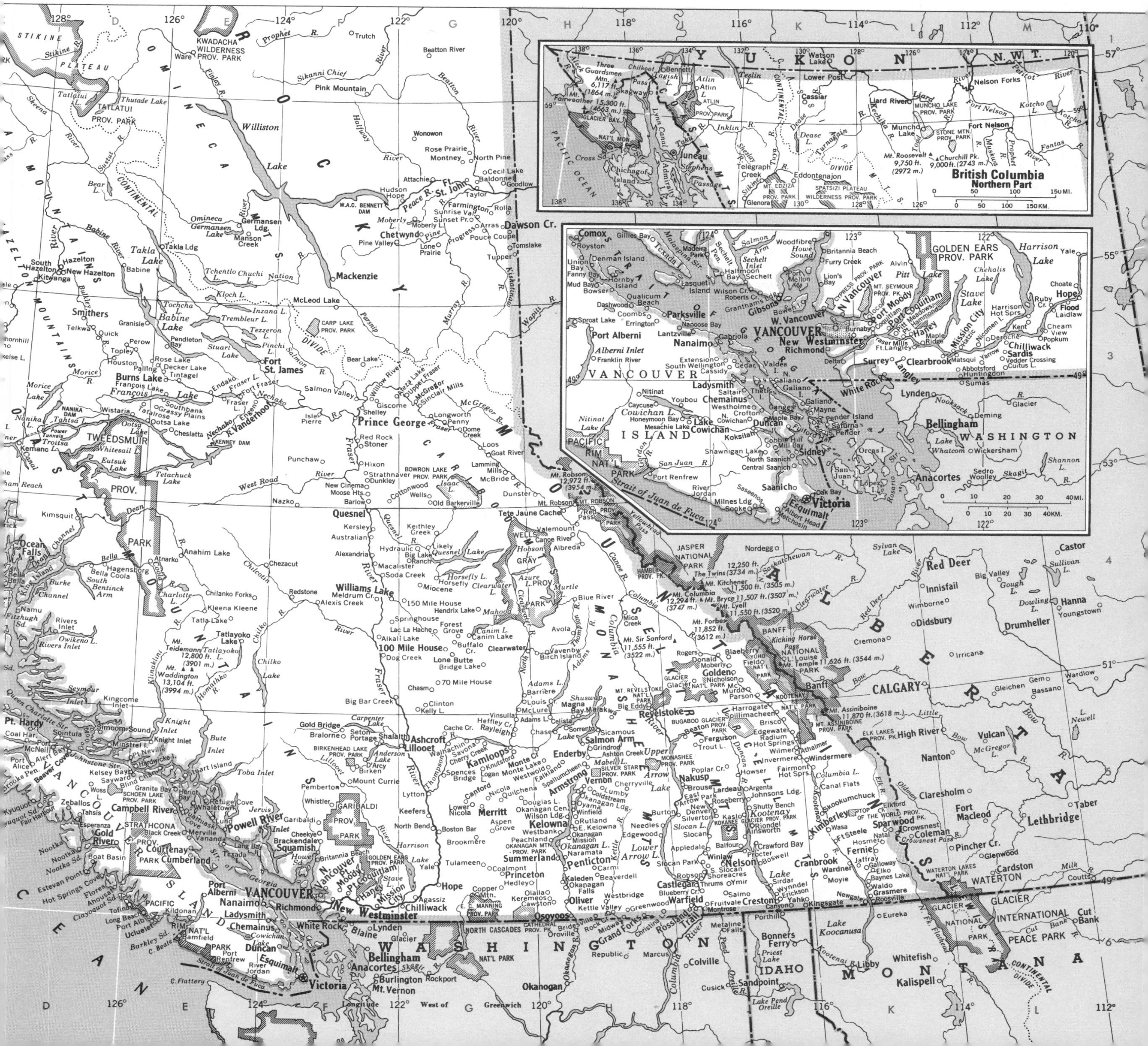

*Population of metropolitan area.
○Population of municipality.

AREA 366,253 sq. mi. (948,596 sq. km.)
POPULATION 2,744,467
CAPITAL Victoria
LARGEST CITY Vancouver
HIGHEST POINT Mt. Fairweather 15,300 ft. (4,663 m.)
SETTLED IN 1806
ADMITTED TO CONFEDERATION 1871
PROVINCIAL FLOWER Dogwood

NORTHWEST TERRITORIES

DISTRICTS

CITIES and TOWNS

OTHER FEATURES

Topography

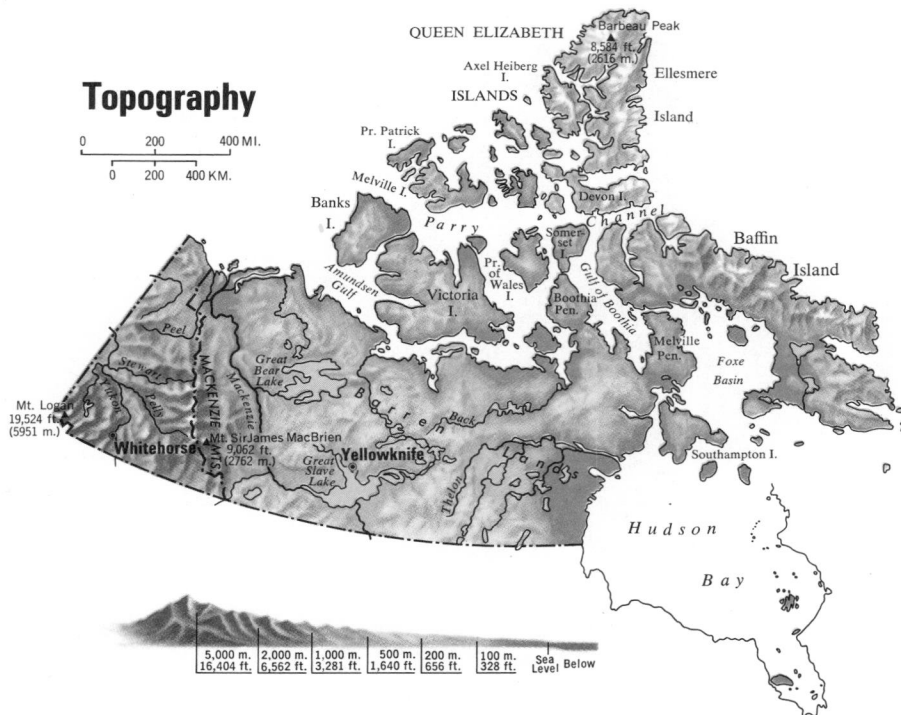

Scale: 0 200 400 MI. / 0 200 400 KM.

| 5,000 m. 16,404 ft. | 2,000 m. 6,562 ft. | 1,000 m. 3,281 ft. | 500 m. 1,640 ft. | 200 m. 656 ft. | 100 m. 328 ft. | Sea Level | Below |

Agriculture, Industry and Resources

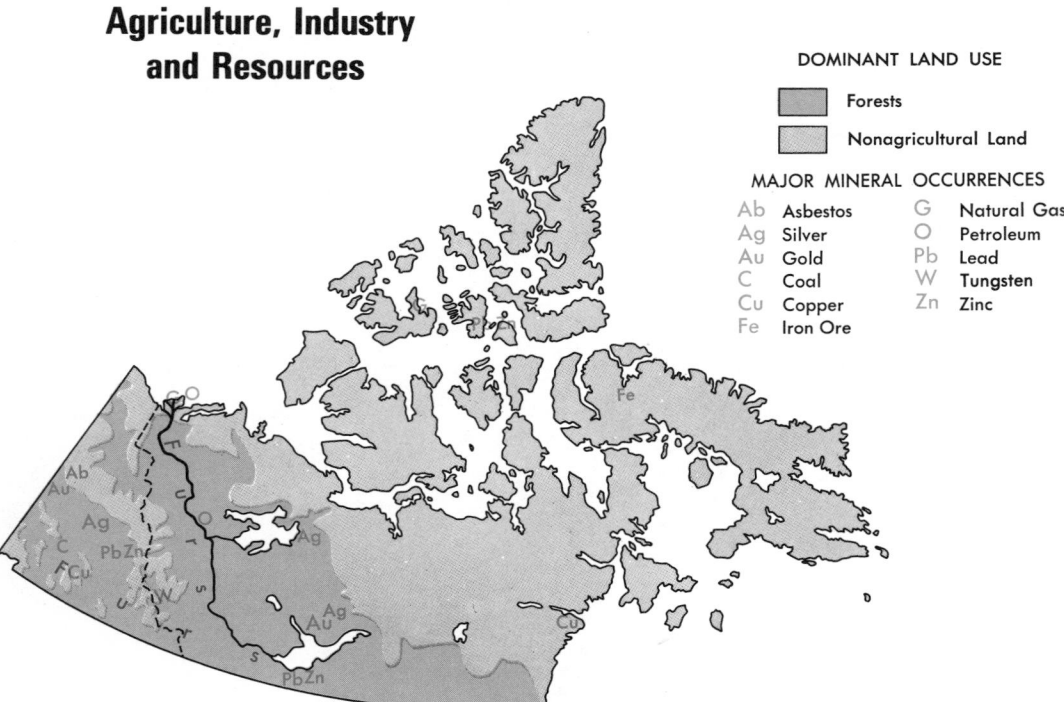

DOMINANT LAND USE

■ Forests

▨ Nonagricultural Land

MAJOR MINERAL OCCURRENCES

Ab Asbestos
Ag Silver
Au Gold
C   Coal
Cu Copper
Fe Iron Ore
G   Natural Gas
O   Petroleum
Pb Lead
W   Tungsten
Zn Zinc

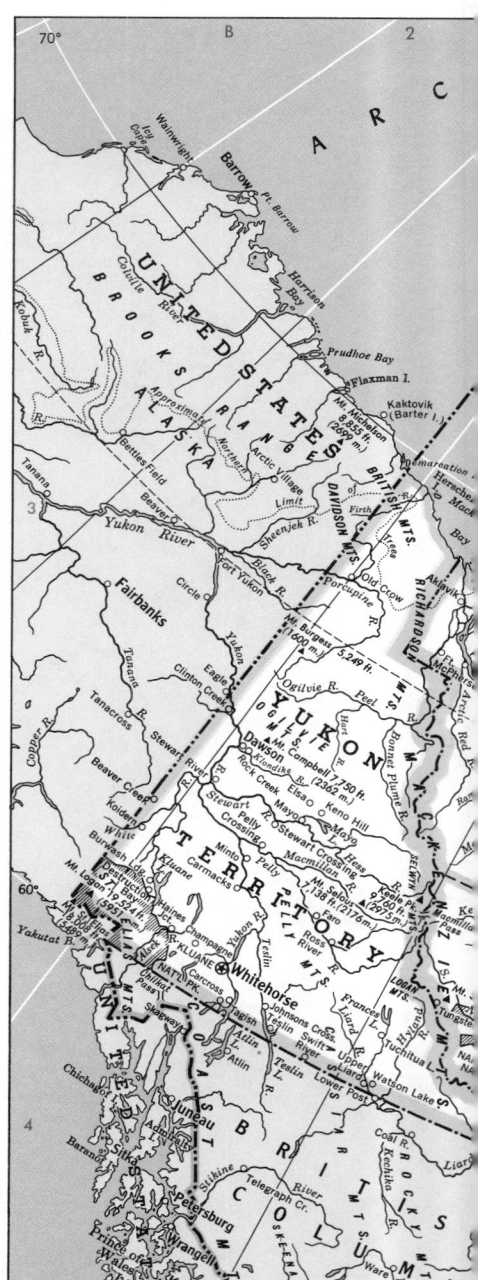

YUKON TERRITORY

AREA 207,075 sq. mi.
  (536,324 sq. km.)
POPULATION 23,153
CAPITAL Whitehorse
LARGEST CITY Whitehorse
HIGHEST POINT Mt. Logan 19,524 ft.
  (5,951 m.)
SETTLED IN 1897
ADMITTED TO CONFEDERATION 1898
PROVINCIAL FLOWER Fireweed

NORTHWEST TERRITORIES

AREA 1,304,896 sq. mi. (3,379,683 sq. km.)
POPULATION 45,741
CAPITAL Yellowknife
LARGEST CITY Yellowknife
HIGHEST POINT Mt. Sir James MacBrien
  9,062 ft. (2,762 m.)
SETTLED IN 1800
ADMITTED TO CONFEDERATION 1870
PROVINCIAL FLOWER Mountain Avens

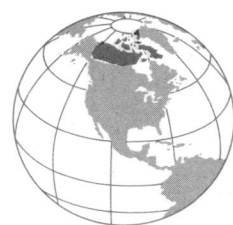

Yukon and Northwest Territories

SCALE
0   50   100   200   300 MI.
0   50 100   200   300 KM.

Territorial Capitals . . . . ⊛
Regional Capitals . . . . ⊙
International Boundaries . . . .
Provincial & Territorial Boundaries . . . .
Regional Boundaries . . . .

Scale 1:14,000,000

All islands in Hudson and James Bay lie within the Northwest Territories

© Copyright HAMMOND INCORPORATED, Maplewood, N.J.

United States

POLYCONIC PROJECTION

SCALE OF MILES

SCALE OF KILOMETERS

Capitals of Countries .... ☆
State Capitals .... △
International Boundaries .... ———

Scale 1:17,400,000

© Copyright HAMMOND INCORPORATED, Maplewood, N.J.

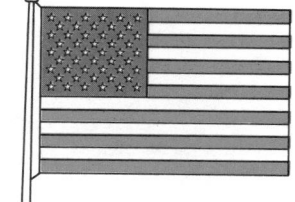

AREA 3,623,420 sq. mi.
(9,384,658 sq. km.)
POPULATION 226,504,825
CAPITAL Washington
LARGEST CITY New York
HIGHEST POINT Mt. McKinley 20,320 ft.
(6,194 m.)
MONETARY UNIT U.S. dollar
MAJOR LANGUAGE English
MAJOR RELIGIONS Protestantism,
Roman Catholicism, Judaism

Population Distribution

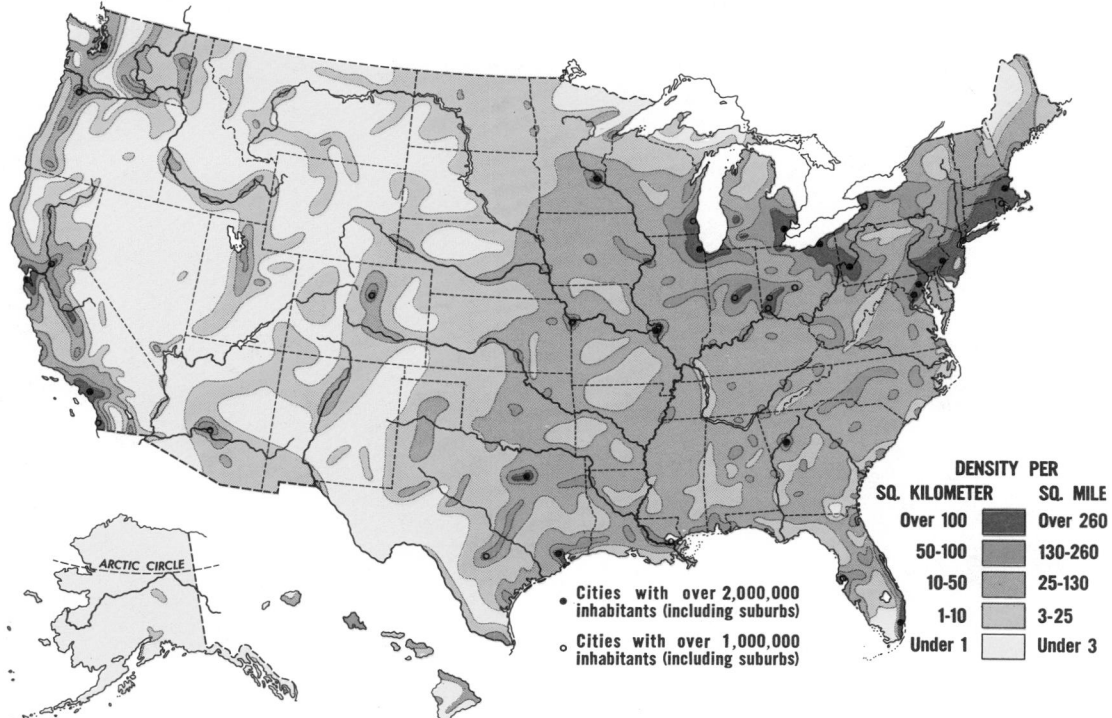

DENSITY PER

SQ. KILOMETER	SQ. MILE
Over 100	Over 260
50-100	130-260
10-50	25-130
1-10	3-25
Under 1	Under 3

• Cities with over 2,000,000 inhabitants (including suburbs)
○ Cities with over 1,000,000 inhabitants (including suburbs)

Vegetation

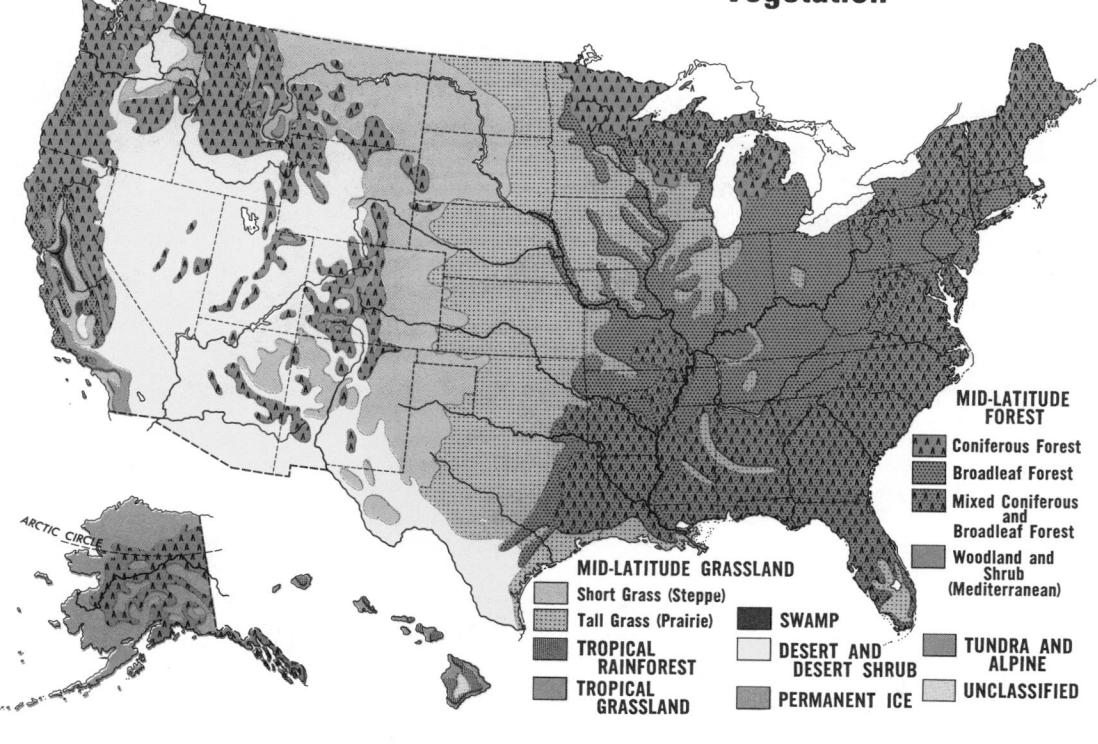

MID-LATITUDE FOREST
- Coniferous Forest
- Broadleaf Forest
- Mixed Coniferous and Broadleaf Forest
- Woodland and Shrub (Mediterranean)

MID-LATITUDE GRASSLAND
- Short Grass (Steppe)
- Tall Grass (Prairie)

- TROPICAL RAINFOREST
- TROPICAL GRASSLAND

- SWAMP
- DESERT AND DESERT SHRUB
- PERMANENT ICE

- TUNDRA AND ALPINE
- UNCLASSIFIED

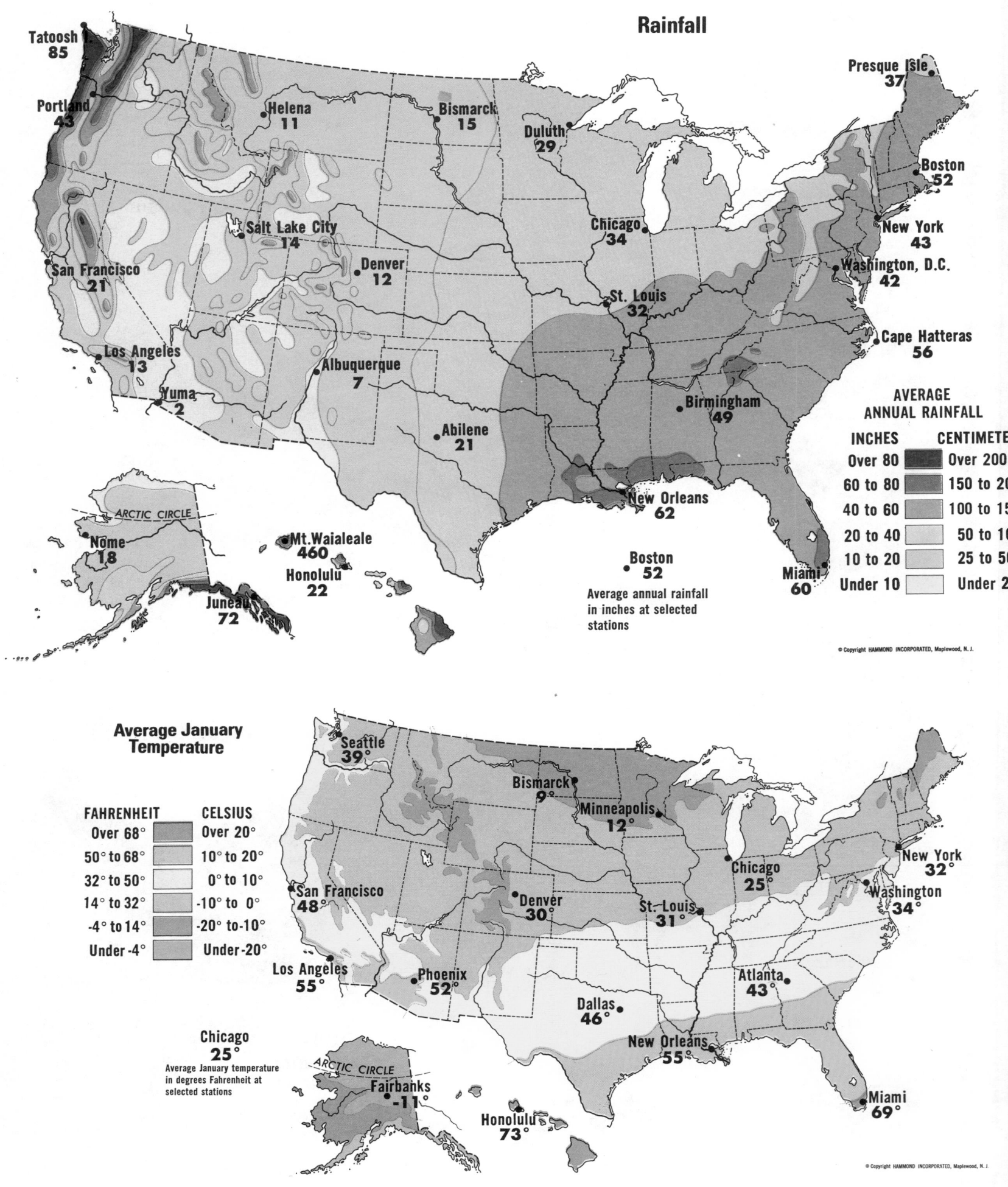

Rainfall

Tatoosh I. 85

Portland 43

Helena 11

Bismarck 15

Duluth 29

Presque Isle 37

Boston 52

Chicago 34

New York 43

Salt Lake City 14

Washington, D.C. 42

San Francisco 21

Denver 12

St. Louis 32

Los Angeles 13

Albuquerque 7

Cape Hatteras 56

Yuma 2

Birmingham 49

Abilene 21

New Orleans 62

Nome 18

Mt. Waialeale 460

Honolulu 22

Boston 52

Miami 60

ARCTIC CIRCLE

Juneau 72

Average annual rainfall in inches at selected stations

AVERAGE ANNUAL RAINFALL

INCHES	CENTIMETER
Over 80	Over 200
60 to 80	150 to 200
40 to 60	100 to 150
20 to 40	50 to 100
10 to 20	25 to 50
Under 10	Under 25

© Copyright HAMMOND INCORPORATED, Maplewood, N.J.

Average January Temperature

FAHRENHEIT	CELSIUS
Over 68°	Over 20°
50° to 68°	10° to 20°
32° to 50°	0° to 10°
14° to 32°	-10° to 0°
-4° to 14°	-20° to -10°
Under -4°	Under -20°

Seattle 39°

Bismarck 9°

Minneapolis 12°

New York 32°

San Francisco 48°

Denver 30°

Chicago 25°

St. Louis 31°

Washington 34°

Los Angeles 55°

Phoenix 52°

Atlanta 43°

Dallas 46°

New Orleans 55°

Chicago 25°

Average January temperature in degrees Fahrenheit at selected stations

ARCTIC CIRCLE

Fairbanks -11°

Honolulu 73°

Miami 69°

© Copyright HAMMOND INCORPORATED, Maplewood, N.J.

Topography

0   200   400 MI.

0   200   400 KM.

C. Flattery
Seattle
CASCADE RANGE
Mt. Rainier 14,410 ft. (4392 m.)
Mt. St. Helens 8,364 ft. (2549 m.)
COLUMBIA PLATEAU
BITTERROOT RANGE
Snake
Columbia
PACIFIC OCEAN
Great Basin
Missouri
Fort Peck Lake
Yellowstone
R O C K Y   M O U N T A I N S
Rainy
Lake Superior
Keweenaw Pen.
Minneapolis
Milwaukee
Chicago
Lake Michigan
Lake Huron
Detroit
Cleveland
Lake Erie
Lake Ontario
Niagara Falls
St. Lawrence
Lake Champlain
Gulf of Maine
Boston
C. Cod
New York
Philadelphia
Long Island
ATLANTIC
SIERRA NEVADA
Central Valley
Sacramento
San Francisco
Mt. Whitney 14,491 ft. (4418 m.)
Great Salt Lake
Lake Powell
COLORADO MOUNTAINS
Colorado
Denver
Mt. Elbert 14,431 ft. (4399 m.)
Arkansas
G R E A T   P L A I N S
N. Platte
Platte
Des Moines
Wisconsin
Illinois
Mississippi
Missouri
Kansas City
St. Louis
Ohio
Indianapolis
Washington
APPALACHIAN MTS.
ALLEGHENY MTS.
Chesapeake Bay
Pt. Conception
Mojave Desert
Mead
Grand Canyon
PLATEAU
Los Angeles
Phoenix
San Diego
Colorado
Gila
Red
LLANO ESTACADO
OZARK PLATEAU
Wheeler
Tennessee
Mt. Mitchell 6,684 ft. (2037 m.)
C. Hatteras
OCEAN
SANTA BARBARA IS.
Dallas
Memphis
Chattahoochee
Atlanta
Savannah
C. Fear
Pecos
EDWARDS PLATEAU
Brazos
Colorado
Canadian
Arkansas
Red
Houston
New Orleans
G U L F   C O A S T A L   P L A I N
Mississippi Delta
Jacksonville
ATLANTIC COASTAL PLAIN
C. Canaveral
Rio Grande
Gulf of Mexico
Okeechobee
The Everglades
Miami
FLORIDA KEYS

ARCTIC OCEAN
0   200   400 MI.
0   200   400 KM.
BROOKS RANGE
Tanana
St. Lawrence I.
Bering Str.
Yukon
Mt. McKinley 20,320 ft. (6194 m.)
Anchorage
BERING SEA
Alaska Pen.
Alaska Range
Gulf of Alaska
Kodiak I.
ALEXANDER ARCHIPELAGO
Aleutian Islands

Kauai
Oahu
Molokai
Honolulu
Maui
HAWAIIAN ISLANDS
PACIFIC OCEAN
Mauna Kea 13,796 ft. (4205 m.)
Hawaii
0   50   100 MI.
0   50   100 KM.

5,000 m. 16,404 ft. | 2,000 m. 6,562 ft. | 1,000 m. 3,281 ft. | 500 m. 1,640 ft. | 200 m. 656 ft. | 100 m. 328 ft. | Sea Level | Below

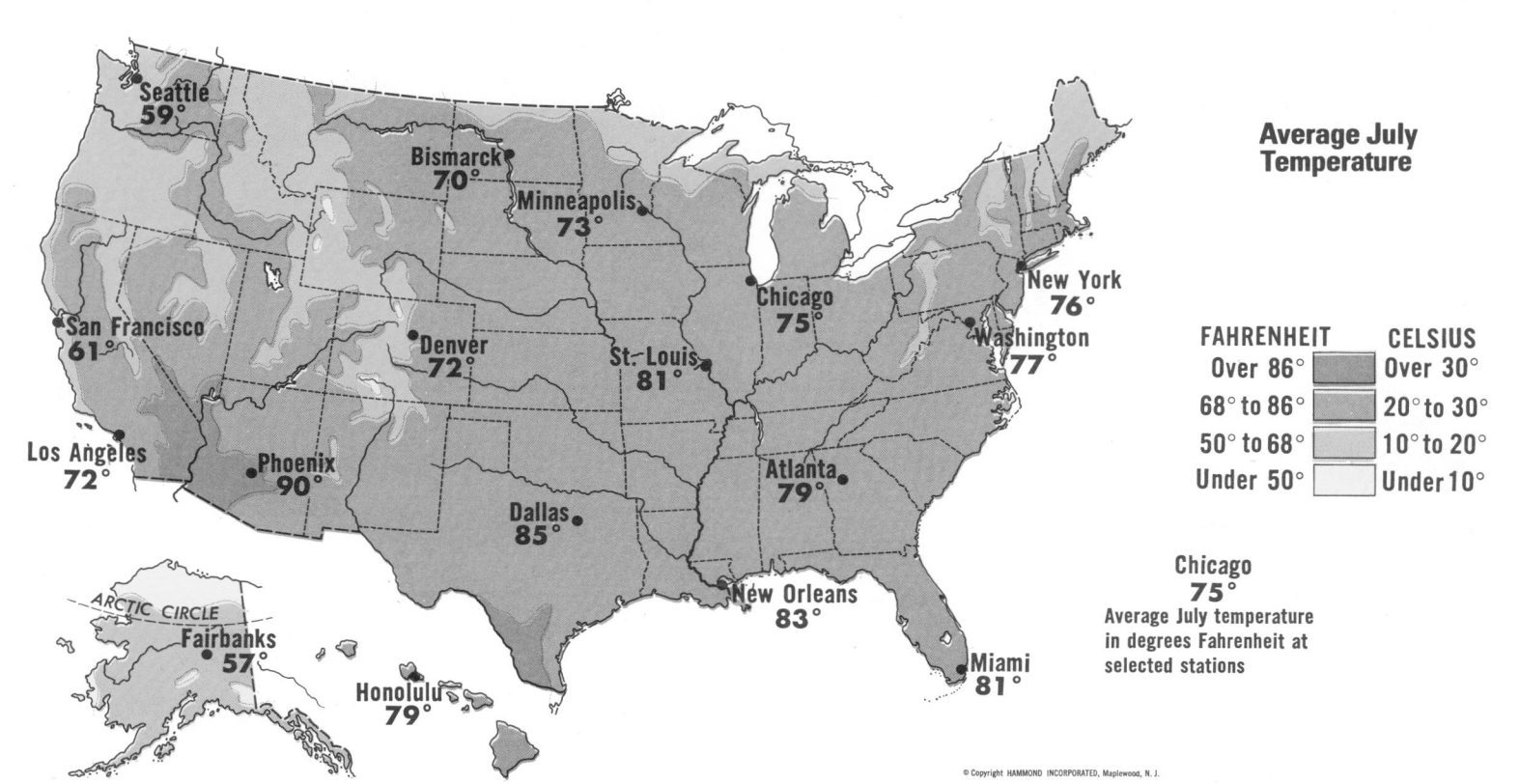

Average July Temperature

Seattle 59°
Bismarck 70°
Minneapolis 73°
Chicago 75°
New York 76°
Washington 77°
San Francisco 61°
Denver 72°
St. Louis 81°
Los Angeles 72°
Phoenix 90°
Dallas 85°
Atlanta 79°
New Orleans 83°
ARCTIC CIRCLE
Fairbanks 57°
Honolulu 79°
Miami 81°

FAHRENHEIT	CELSIUS
Over 86°	Over 30°
68° to 86°	20° to 30°
50° to 68°	10° to 20°
Under 50°	Under 10°

Chicago
75°
Average July temperature in degrees Fahrenheit at selected stations

© Copyright HAMMOND INCORPORATED, Maplewood, N. J.

United States Standard Time Zones

Established by the Uniform Time Act

Agriculture, Industry and Resources

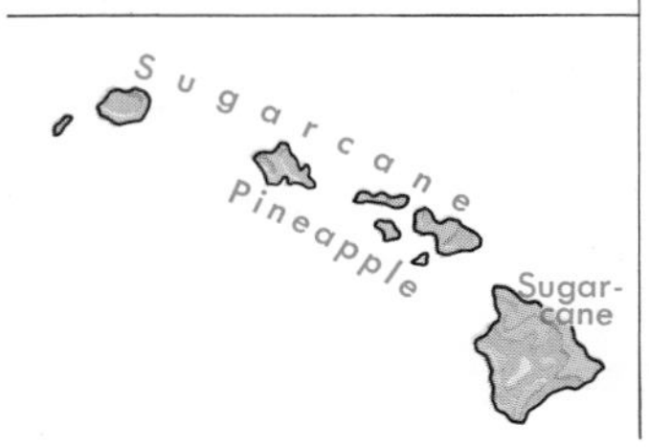

DOMINANT LAND USE

- Wheat and Small Grains
- Feed Grains and Livestock
- Dairy
- General Farming
- Cotton
- Fruit, Truck and Mixed Farming
- Tobacco and General Farming
- Special Crops and General Farming
- Range Livestock
- Forests
- Swampland
- Nonagricultural Land

MAJOR MINERAL OCCURRENCES

Ab	Asbestos	Gp	Gypsum	Sb	Antimony
Ag	Silver	Hg	Mercury	Tc	Talc
Al	Bauxite	K	Potash	Ti	Titanium
Au	Gold	Mi	Mica	U	Uranium
Bx	Borax	Mo	Molybdenum	V	Vanadium
C	Coal	Na	Salt	W	Tungsten
Cl	Clay	O	Petroleum	Zn	Zinc
Cu	Copper	P	Phosphates		
F	Fluorspar	Pb	Lead	⚡	Water Power
Fe	Iron Ore	Pt	Platinum	▨	Major Industrial Areas
G	Natural Gas	S	Sulfur		

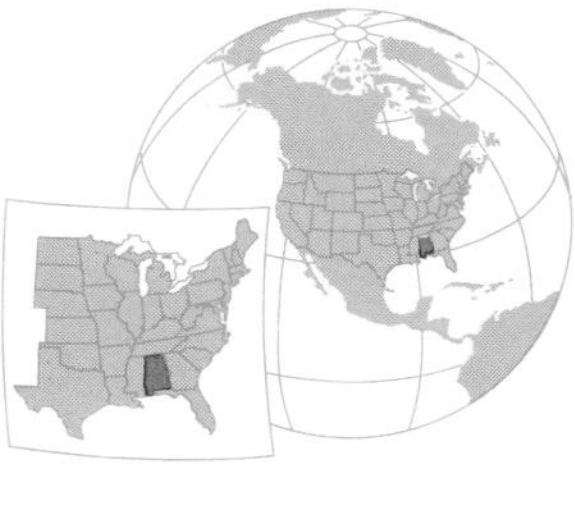

AREA 51,705 sq. mi. (133,916 sq. km.)
POPULATION 3,893,888
CAPITAL Montgomery
LARGEST CITY Birmingham
HIGHEST POINT Cheaha Mtn. 2,407 ft. (734 m.)
SETTLED IN 1702
ADMITTED TO UNION December 14, 1819
POPULAR NAME Heart of Dixie; Cotton State; Yellowhammer State
STATE FLOWER Camellia
STATE BIRD Yellowhammer

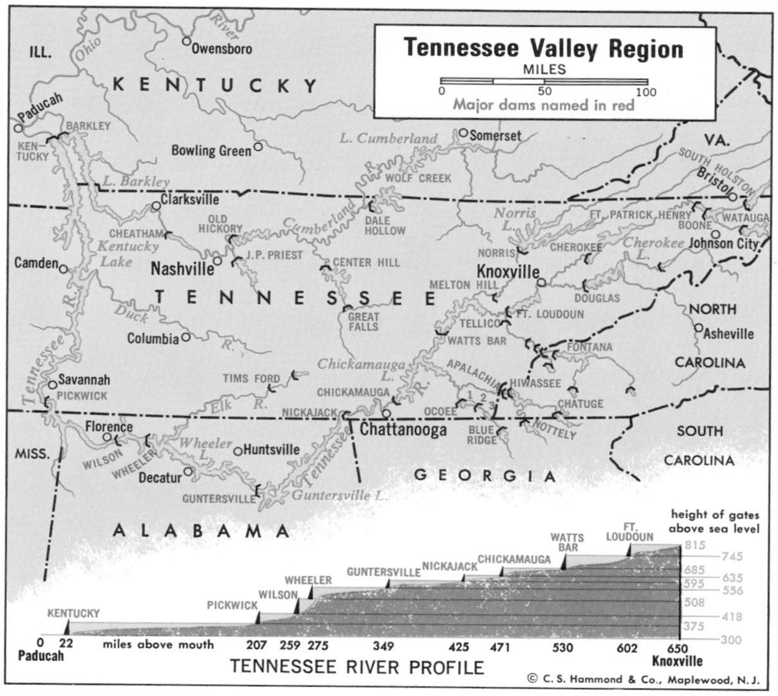
Tennessee Valley Region
MILES
0 50 100
Major dams named in red
ILL.
Owensboro
KENTUCKY
Paducah
BARKLEY
KENTUCKY
Bowling Green
L. Cumberland
Somerset
WOLF CREEK
VA.
SOUTH HOLSTON
Bristol
L. Barkley
Clarksville
OLD HICKORY
DALE HOLLOW
Norris L.
FT. PATRICK HENRY
WATAUGA
BOONE
CHEATHAM
Kentucky Lake
Nashville
J. P. PRIEST
CENTER HILL
NORRIS
CHEROKEE
Cherokee L.
Johnson City
Camden
Knoxville
MELTON HILL
TENNESSEE
DOUGLAS
NORTH
TELLICO
FT. LOUDOUN
Asheville
GREAT FALLS
WATTS BAR
FONTANA
CAROLINA
Columbia
Chickamauga L.
APALACHIA
Savannah
PICKWICK
TIMS FORD
CHICKAMAUGA
HIWASSEE
CHATUGE
Elk R.
NICKAJACK
OCOEE
Florence
Chattanooga
BLUE RIDGE
NOTTELY
SOUTH
MISS.
WILSON
Wheeler L.
Huntsville
WHEELER
GEORGIA
CAROLINA
Decatur
GUNTERSVILLE
Guntersville L.
ALABAMA
height of gates above sea level
WATTS BAR
FT. LOUDOUN
CHICKAMAUGA
NICKAJACK
GUNTERSVILLE
WHEELER
WILSON
PICKWICK
KENTUCKY
815
745
685
635
595
556
508
418
375
300
0 22 miles above mouth 207 259 275 349 425 471 530 602 650
Paducah
Knoxville
TENNESSEE RIVER PROFILE
© C. S. Hammond & Co., Maplewood, N. J.

COUNTIES

Autauga 32,259 E5
Baldwin 78,556 C9
Barbour 24,756 H7
Bibb 15,723 D5
Blount 36,459 E2
Bullock 10,596 G6
Butler 21,680 E7
Calhoun 119,761 G3
Chambers 39,191 H5
Cherokee 18,760 G2
Chilton 30,612 E5
Choctaw 16,839 B6
Clarke 27,702 C7
Clay 13,703 G4
Cleburne 12,595 G3
Coffee 38,533 G8
Colbert 54,519 C1
Conecuh 15,884 E8
Coosa 11,377 F5
Covington 36,850 F8
Crenshaw 14,110 F7
Cullman 61,642 E2
Dale 47,821 G8
Dallas 53,981 D6
De Kalb 53,658 G2
Elmore 43,390 F5
Escambia 38,440 D8
Etowah 103,057 F2
Fayette 18,809 C3
Franklin 28,350 C2
Geneva 24,253 G8
Greene 11,021 C5
Hale 15,604 C5
Henry 15,302 H7
Houston 74,632 H8
Jackson 51,407 F1
Jefferson 671,324 E3
Lamar 16,453 B3
Lauderdale 80,546 C1
Lawrence 30,170 D1
Lee 76,283 H5
Limestone 46,005 E1
Lowndes 13,253 E6
Macon 26,829 G6
Madison 196,966 E1
Marengo 25,047 C6
Marion 30,041 C2
Marshall 65,622 F2
Mobile 364,980 B9
Monroe 22,651 D7
Montgomery 197,038 F6
Morgan 90,231 E2
Perry 15,012 D5
Pickens 21,481 B4
Pike 28,050 G7
Randolph 20,075 H4
Russell 47,356 H6
Saint Clair 41,205 F3
Shelby 66,298 E4
Sumter 16,908 B5
Talladega 73,826 F4
Tallapoosa 38,676 G5
Tuscaloosa 137,541 C4
Walker 68,660 D3
Washington 16,821 B8
Wilcox 14,755 D7
Winston 21,953 D2

CITIES and TOWNS

Zip Name/Pop. Key

36310 Abbeville⊙ 3,155 H7
35440 Abernant 405 D4
35005 Adamsville 2,498 D3
35540 Addison 746 D2
35006 Adger 400 D4
35441 Akron 604 C5
35007 Alabaster 7,079 E4
35950 Albertville 12,039 F2
†35115 Aldrich 500 E4
35010 Alexander City 13,807 G5
36250 Alexandria 600 G3
35442 Aliceville 3,207 B4
35013 Allgood 387 F3
36501 Alma 500 C8
35952 Altoona 928 F2
36420 Andalusia⊙ 10,415 E8
35610 Anderson 405 D1
36201 Anniston⊙ 29,523 G3
Anniston‡ 116,936 G3
35016 Arab 5,967 E2
35805 Ardmore 1,096 E1
†35173 Argo 600 E3
36311 Ariton 844 G7
35033 Arkadelphia 150 E3
35541 Arley 276 D2
†35035 Ashby 500 E4
36312 Ashford 2,165 H8
36251 Ashland⊙ 2,052 G4
35953 Ashville⊙ 1,489 F3
35611 Athens⊙ 14,558 E1
36503 Atmore 8,789 C8
35954 Attalla 7,737 F2
36830 Auburn 28,471 H5
36003 Autaugaville 843 E6
†36312 Avon 433 H8
36505 Axis 500 B9
†36420 Babbie 553 F8
35019 Baileyton 396 E2
36005 Banks 160 G7
†36532 Barnwell 700 C10
36507 Bay Minette⊙ 7,455 C9
36509 Bayou La Batre 2,005 B10
35543 Bear Creek 353 C2
36425 Beatrice 558 D7
35544 Beaverton 360 B3
†35653 Belgreen 500 C2
35545 Belk 308 C3
36901 Bellamy 700 B6
35615 Belle Mina 675 E1
36313 Bellwood 400 G8
36785 Benton 74 E6
35546 Berry 916 C3
35020 Bessemer 31,729 D4
†36872 Beulah 500 H5
36006 Billingsley 106 E5
*35201 Birmingham⊙ 284,413 D3
Birmingham‡ 847,360 D3
36314 Black 156 G8
35031 Blountsville 1,509 E2
36201 Blue Mountain 284 G3
†36017 Blue Springs 112 G7
35957 Boaz 7,151 F2
35443 Boligee 164 C5
35032 Bon Air 118 F4
36511 Bon Secour 850 C10
†35120 Branchville 365 F3
36009 Brantley 1,151 F7
35034 Brent 2,862 D5
36426 Brewton⊙ 6,680 D8
35740 Bridgeport 2,974 G1
35020 Brighton 5,308 D4
35548 Brilliant 871 C2
35036 Brookside 1,409 E3
35444 Brookwood 492 D4
36010 Brundidge 3,213 G7
36725 Burkville 250 E6
36431 Burnt Corn 60 D7
36904 Butler⊙ 1,882 B6
†36767 Cahaba 75 D6
35040 Calera 2,035 E4
†36047 Calhoun 950 F6
36513 Calvert 600 B8
36726 Camden⊙ 2,406 D7
36850 Camp Hill 1,628 G5
†36502 Canoe 560 D8
†36726 Canton Bend 300 D6
35549 Carbon Hill 2,452 D3
35041 Cardiff 140 E3
†36420 Carolina 203 E8
35447 Carrollton⊙ 1,104 B4
†36023 Carrville 820 G5
†36548 Carson 400 C8
36432 Castleberry 847 D8
35959 Cedar Bluff 1,129 G2
35960 Centre⊙ 2,351 G2
35042 Centreville⊙ 2,504 D5
36518 Chatom⊙ 1,122 B8
35043 Chelsea 600 E4
35616 Cherokee 1,589 C1
36611 Chickasaw 7,402 B9
35044 Childersburg 5,084 F4
36254 Choccolocco 500 G3
36905 Choctaw 600 B6
†36550 Chrysler 400 C8
36521 Chunchula 700 B9
36522 Citronelle 2,841 B8
35045 Clanton⊙ 5,832 E5
†36322 Clayhatchee 560 G8
36015 Clayton⊙ 1,589 G7
35049 Cleveland 487 E3
36017 Clio 1,224 G7
35449 Coaling 400 D4
36523 Coden 600 B10
36318 Coffee Springs 339 G8
36524 Coffeeville 448 B7
35452 Coker 800 C4
35961 Collinsville 1,383 G2
36319 Columbia 881 H8
35051 Columbiana⊙ 2,655 E4
36020 Coosada 980 F5
35550 Cordova 3,123 D3
35453 Cottondale 500 D4
36320 Cottonwood 1,352 H8
†35172 County Line 199 E3
†36467 County Line 124 F8
35618 Courtland 456 D1
36321 Cowarts 418 H8
36435 Coy 950 D7
36525 Creola 1,652 B9
36906 Cromwell 650 B6
35962 Crossville 1,222 G2
36907 Cuba 486 B6
35055 Cullman⊙ 13,084 E2
36852 Cusseta 650 H5
36853 Dadeville⊙ 3,263 G5
36322 Daleville 4,250 G8
36526 Daphne 3,406 C9
36528 Dauphin Island 950 B10
36256 Daviston 334 G4
36731 Dayton 113 C6
*35601 Decatur⊙ 42,002 D1
36257 De Armanville 350 G3
36732 Demopolis 7,678 C6
35552 Detroit 326 B2
35062 Dora 2,327 D3
*36303 Dothan⊙ 48,750 H8
35553 Double Springs⊙ 1,057 D2
35964 Douglas 116 F2
36028 Dozier 494 F7
35744 Dutton 276 G1
36426 East Brewton 3,012 E8
36024 Eclectic 1,124 F5
36261 Edwardsville 207 H3
36323 Elba⊙ 4,355 F8
36530 Elberta 491 C10
35554 Eldridge 230 C3
35620 Elkmont 429 E1
36025 Elmore 600 F5
35458 Elrod 746 C4
35063 Empire 600 D3
36330 Enterprise 18,033 G8
35460 Epes 399 B5
35461 Ethelsville 95 B4
36027 Eufaula 12,097 H7
†36340 Eunola 169 G8
35462 Eutaw⊙ 2,444 C5
35621 Eva 185 E2
36401 Evergreen⊙ 4,171 E8
36439 Excel 385 D8
35746 Fackler 250 G1
36854 Fairfax 3,776 H5
35064 Fairfield 13,242 E4
36532 Fairhope 7,286 C10
35208 Fairview 450 E2
35622 Falkville 1,310 E2
36738 Faunsdale 174 C6
35555 Fayette⊙ 5,287 C3
36855 Five Points 197 H4
35966 Flat Rock 750 G1
†35601 Flint City 673 D1
36441 Flomaton 1,882 D8
36442 Florala 2,165 F8
*35630 Florence⊙ 37,029 C1
Florence‡ 135,023 C1
36535 Foley 4,003 C10
35214 Forestdale 10,814 E3
36740 Forkland 429 C5
36031 Fort Davis 500 G6
36032 Fort Deposit 1,519 E7
36856 Fort Mitchell 900 H6
35967 Fort Payne⊙ 11,485 G2
35463 Fosters 400 C4
36444 Franklin 133 G6
36445 Frisco City 1,424 D8
36539 Fruitdale 500 B8
36262 Fruithurst 239 G3
36446 Fulton 606 C7
35068 Fultondale 6,217 E3
35971 Fyffe 1,305 G2
*35901 Gadsden⊙ 47,565 G2
Gadsden‡ 103,057 G2
35464 Gainesville 207 B5
35972 Gallant 475 F2
36038 Gantt 314 E8
35070 Garden City 655 E2
35071 Gardendale 7,928 E3
35973 Gaylesville 192 G2
†35459 Geiger 200 B5
36340 Geneva⊙ 4,866 G8
36033 Georgiana 1,993 E7
35974 Geraldine 911 G2
36908 Gilbertown 218 B7
35559 Glen Allen 312 C3
35905 Glencoe 4,648 G3
36034 Glenwood 341 F7
†35010 Goldville 89 G4
†36024 Good Hope 1,442 E2
35072 Goodwater 1,895 F4
35466 Gordo 2,112 C4
36343 Gordon 362 H8
†35580 Gorgas 500 D3
36035 Goshen 365 F7
†36482 Gosport 500 C7
36541 Grand Bay 3,185 B10
35747 Grant 632 F1
35073 Graysville 2,642 D3
35074 Green Pond 750 D4
36744 Greensboro⊙ 3,248 C5
36037 Greenville⊙ 7,807 E7
†36350 Grimes 298 H8
36451 Grove Hill⊙ 1,912 C7
35563 Guin 2,418 C3
36542 Gulf Shores 1,349 C10
35976 Guntersville⊙ 7,041 F2
35748 Gurley 735 F1
†35563 Gu-Win 266 C3
35564 Hackleburg 883 C2
†36319 Haleburg 106 H8
35565 Haleyville 5,306 C2
35570 Hamilton⊙ 5,093 C2
†35989 Hammondville 369 G1
35077 Hanceville 2,220 E2
36039 Hardaway 600 G6
35078 Harpersville 934 F4
36344 Hartford 2,647 G8
35640 Hartselle 8,858 E2
36858 Hatchechubbee 840 H6
†35672 Hatton 950 D1
35079 Hayden 268 E3
36040 Hayneville⊙ 592 E6
35750 Hazel Green 1,503 E1
36345 Headland 3,327 H8
†36558 Healing Springs 100 B7
†36420 Heath 354 F8
36264 Heflin⊙ 3,014 G3
35080 Helena 2,130 E4
35978 Henagar 1,188 G1
35979 Higdon 925 G1
†35013 Highland Lake 210 F3
35643 Hillsboro 278 D1
†36201 Hobson City 1,268 G3
35571 Hodges 250 C2
35903 Hokes Bluff 3,216 G3
35082 Hollins 500 F4
35083 Holly Pond 493 E2
35752 Hollywood 1,110 G1
35209 Homewood 21,412 E4
†35216 Hoover 19,792 E4
36043 Hope Hull 975 F6
†36467 Horn Hill 186 F8
35020 Hueytown 13,478 D4
*35801 Huntsville⊙ 142,513 E1
Huntsville‡ 308,593 E1
36860 Hurtsboro 752 H6
35981 Ider 698 G1
35210 Irondale 6,510 E3
36545 Jackson 6,073 C8
36861 Jacksons Gap 800 G5
36265 Jacksonville 9,735 G3
35501 Jasper⊙ 11,894 D3
35085 Jemison 1,828 E5
35573 Kansas 267 C3
35574 Kennedy 604 B3
35645 Killen 747 D1
35091 Kimberly 1,043 E3
†36301 Kinsey 1,239 H8
36453 Kinston 604 F8
36862 Lafayette⊙ 3,647 H5
†35986 Lakeview 441 G2
36863 Lanett 6,897 H5
36864 Langdale 2,034 H5
†35768 Larkinsville 425 F1
36911 Lavaca 500 B6
35094 Leeds 8,638 E3
35983 Leesburg 116 G2
35646 Leighton 1,218 D1
36548 Leroy 699 B8
35647 Lester 117 D1
†36322 Level Plains 867 G8
35648 Lexington 884 D1
†36420 Libertyville 141 F8
35096 Lincoln 2,081 F3
36748 Linden⊙ 2,773 C6
36266 Lineville 2,257 G4
35020 Lipscomb 3,741 E4
36912 Lisman 638 B6
†36876 Little Shawmut 2,793 H5
†35653 Littleville 1,262 C1
35470 Livingston⊙ 3,187 B5
36865 Loachapoka 335 G5
36455 Lockhart 547 F8
35097 Locust Fork 488 E3
†35137 Longview 475 E4
36048 Louisville 791 G7
36751 Lower Peach Tree 926 C7
36752 Lowndesboro 207 E6
36551 Loxley 804 C9
36049 Luverne⊙ 2,639 F7
35575 Lynn 554 C2
35758 Madison 4,057 E1
36348 Madrid 172 H8
36555 Magnolia Springs 800 C10
36349 Malvern 558 G8
36750 Maplesville 754 E5
35112 Margaret 757 F3
36756 Marion⊙ 4,467 D5
35114 Maylene 500 E4
35111 McCalla 657 E4
36552 McCullough 500 D8
36553 McIntosh 319 B8
36456 McKenzie 605 E7
†35442 Memphis 95 B4
35984 Mentone 476 G1
35759 Meridianville 1,403 F1
35228 Midfield 6,203 E4
36350 Midland City 1,903 H8
36053 Midway 593 H6
†35150 Mignon 2,054 F4
36054 Millbrook 3,101 F6
35576 Millport 1,287 B3
36558 Millry 956 B7
36761 Minter 450 D6
*36601 Mobile⊙ 200,452 B9
Mobile‡ 442,819 B9
36460 Monroeville⊙ 5,674 D7
†35804 Monrovia 500 E1
35115 Montevallo 3,965 E4
*36101 Montgomery (cap.)⊙ 178,857 F6
Montgomery‡ 272,687 F3
36559 Montrose 750 C9
†35125 Moody 1,840 F3
35649 Mooresville 58 E1
35116 Morris 623 E3
35650 Moulton⊙ 3,197 D2
35474 Moundville 1,310 C5
†35957 Mountainboro 266 F2
35223 Mountain Brook 19,718 E4
36560 Mount Vernon 1,038 B8
36268 Munford 700 F3
35660 Muscle Shoals 8,911 C1
36763 Myrtlewood 252 C6
36764 Nanafalia 500 B6
36303 Napier Field 493 H8
35578 Nauvoo 259 D3
†35049 Nectar 367 E3
36765 Newbern 307 C5
36351 New Brockton 1,392 G8
35760 New Hope 1,546 F1
35761 New Market 680 F1
†35010 New Site 340 G4
36352 Newton 1,540 G8
36353 Newville 814 H8
35086 North Johns 243 D4
35476 Northport 14,291 C4
36866 Notasulga 876 G5
35006 Oak Grove 638 F4
36766 Oak Hill 63 D7
35579 Oakman 770 D3
35120 Odenville 724 F3
36271 Ohatchee 860 G3
35121 Oneonta⊙ 4,824 E3
†36467 Onycha 147 F8
36801 Opelika⊙ 21,896 H5
36467 Opp 7,204 F8
36561 Orange Beach 600 C10
36767 Orrville 349 D6
35763 Owens Cross Roads 804 E1
36203 Oxford 8,939 G3
36360 Ozark⊙ 13,188 G8
35764 Paint Rock 221 F1
35580 Parrish 1,583 D3
35124 Pelham 6,759 E4
35125 Pell City⊙ 6,616 F3
36916 Pennington 355 B6
36562 Perdido 500 C8
36471 Peterman 600 D7
36062 Petrey 93 F7
36867 Phenix City⊙ 26,928 H6
35581 Phil Campbell 1,549 C2
†35447 Pickensville 132 B4
36272 Piedmont 5,544 G3
36371 Pinckard 771 G8
36768 Pine Apple 298 E7
36769 Pine Hill 510 C7
35765 Pisgah 699 G1
36758 Plantersville 650 E5
35127 Pleasant Grove 7,102 D4
36564 Point Clear 1,812 C10
†36441 Pollard 144 D8

(continued on following page)

Agriculture, Industry and Resources

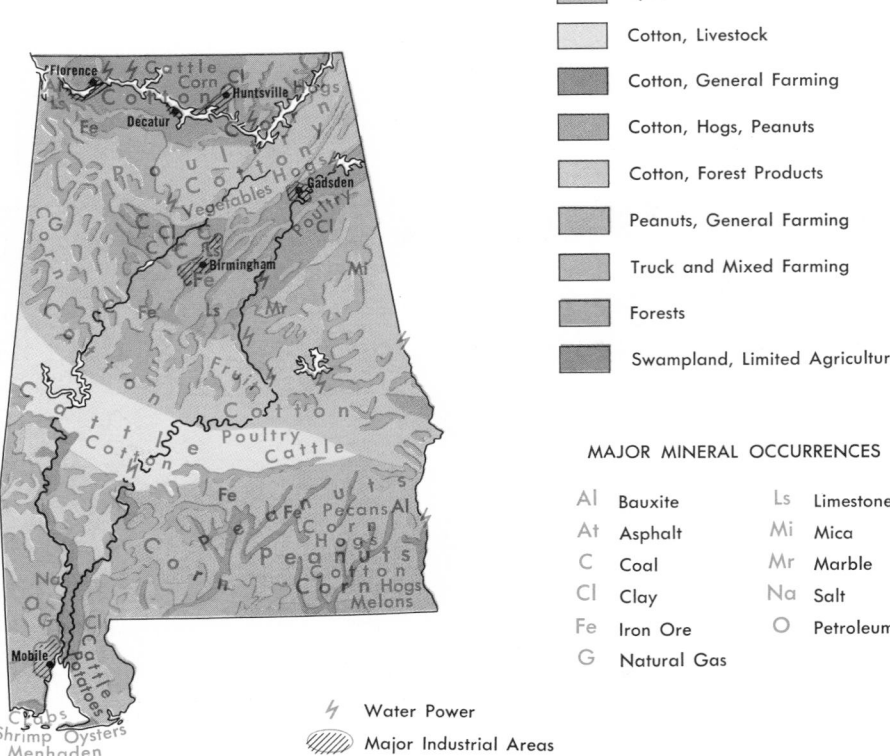

DOMINANT LAND USE

- Specialized Cotton
- Cotton, Livestock
- Cotton, General Farming
- Cotton, Hogs, Peanuts
- Cotton, Forest Products
- Peanuts, General Farming
- Truck and Mixed Farming
- Forests
- Swampland, Limited Agriculture

MAJOR MINERAL OCCURRENCES

Al	Bauxite	Ls	Limestone
At	Asphalt	Mi	Mica
C	Coal	Mr	Marble
Cl	Clay	Na	Salt
Fe	Iron Ore	O	Petroleum
G	Natural Gas		

Water Power

Major Industrial Areas

Topography

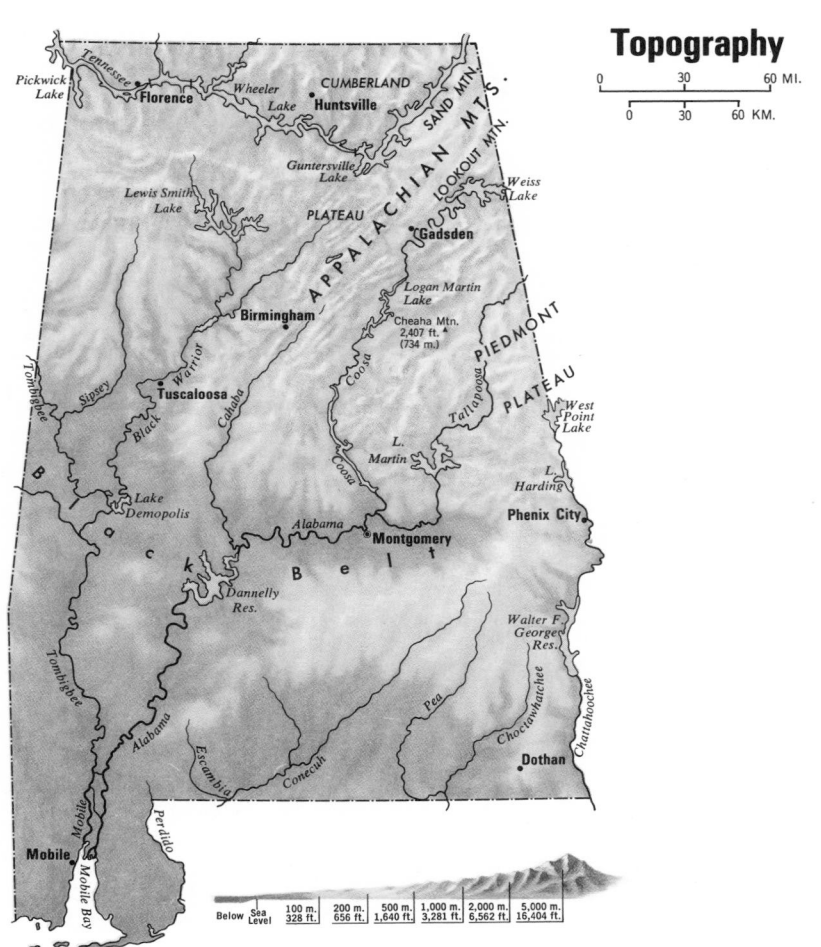

0   30   60 MI.

0   30   60 KM.

Below Sea Level | 100 m. 328 ft. | 200 m. 656 ft. | 500 m. 1,640 ft. | 1,000 m. 3,281 ft. | 2,000 m. 6,562 ft. | 5,000 m. 16,404 ft.

Alabama

SCALE

0 5 10   20   30   40 MI.

0 5 10   20   30   40 KM.

State Capitals..............⊛

County Seats...............◉

Major Limited Access Hwys._____

Scale 1:1,930,000

Copyright HAMMOND INCORPORATED, Maplewood, N. J.

Agriculture, Industry and Resources

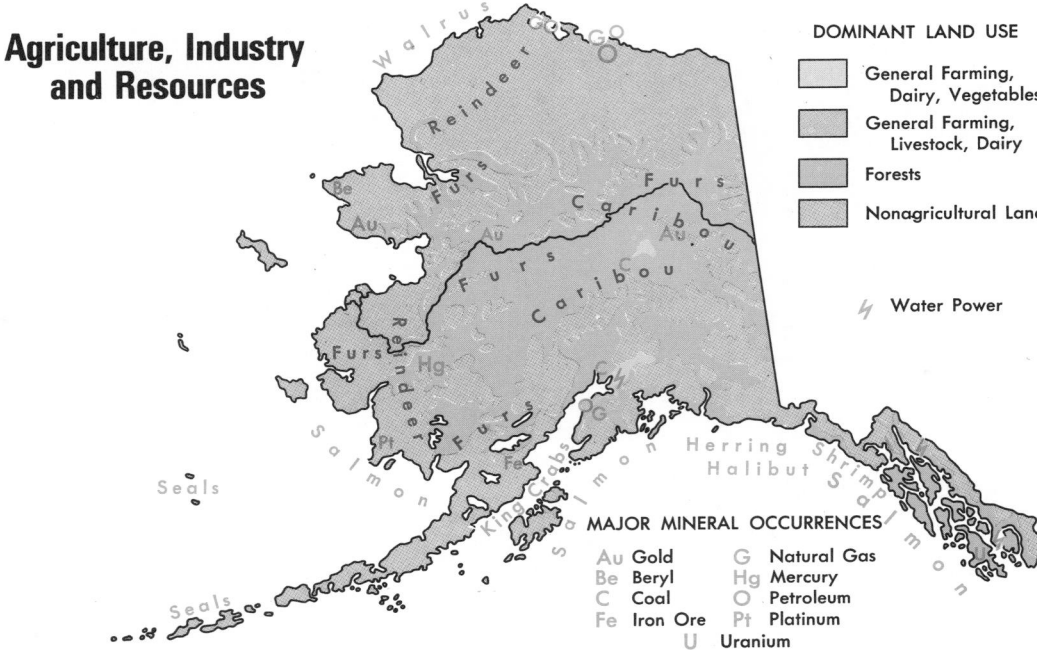

DOMINANT LAND USE

- General Farming, Dairy, Vegetables
- General Farming, Livestock, Dairy
- Forests
- Nonagricultural Land

⚡ Water Power

MAJOR MINERAL OCCURRENCES

Au	Gold	G	Natural Gas
Be	Beryl	Hg	Mercury
C	Coal	O	Petroleum
Fe	Iron Ore	Pt	Platinum
		U	Uranium

Topography

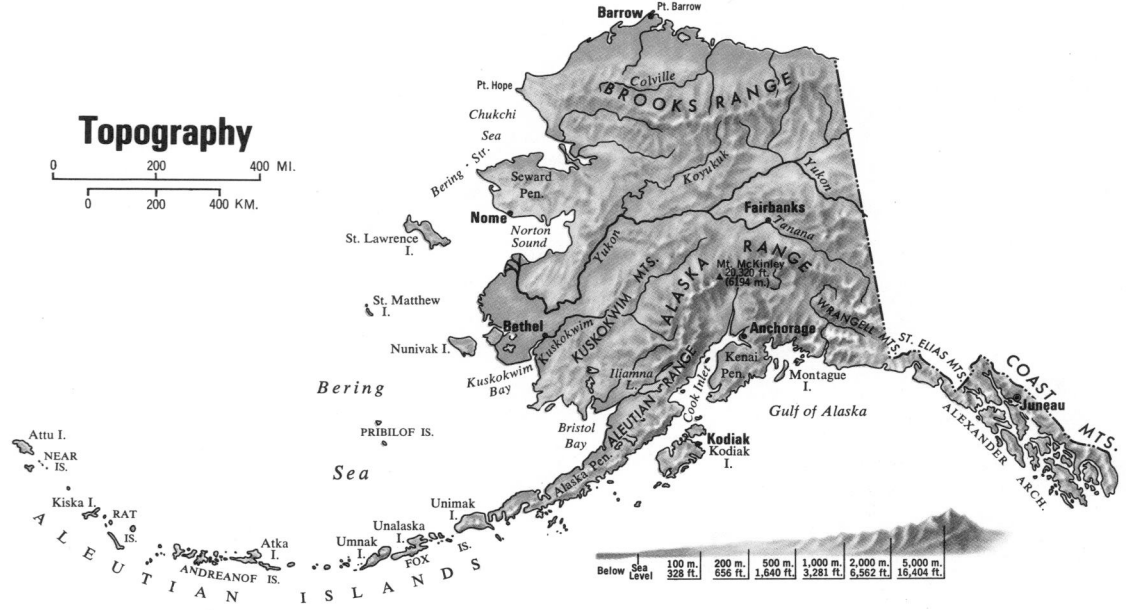

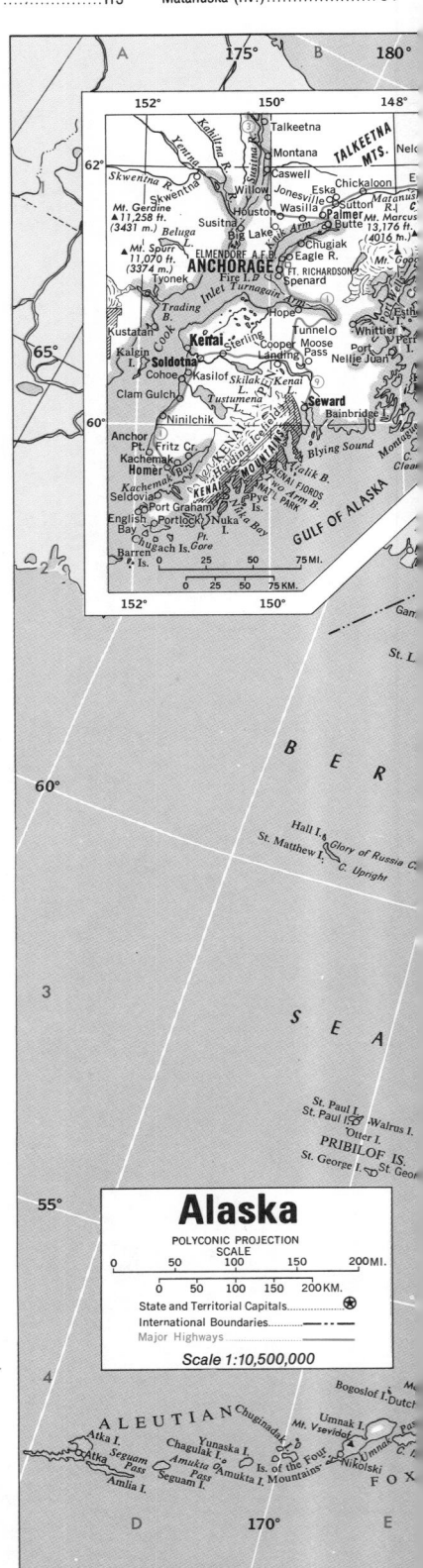

Alaska

POLYCONIC PROJECTION
SCALE

State and Territorial Capitals
International Boundaries
Major Highways

Scale 1:10,500,000

McKinley (mt.) H2
Meade (riv.) G1
Mendenhall (cape) E3
Mentasta (pass) K2
Merrill (pass) H2
Michelson (mt.) K1
Middleton (isl.) J3
Misty Fjords Nat'l Mon. ... N2
Mitkof (isl.) N2
Montague (isl.) D1
Muir (glac.) M1
Mulchatna (riv.) G2
Muzon (cape) M2
Naknek (lake) G3
Near (isls.) H3
Nelson (isl.) E2
Newenham (cape) F3
Noatak (riv.) F1
Norton (bay) F2
Norton (sound) E2
Nowitna (riv.) H2
Nuka (bay) C2
Nunivak (isl.) E3
Nushagak (riv.) G2
Nuyakuk (lake) F3
Ommaney (cape) M2
Otter (isl.) D3
Pastol (bay) F2
Pavlof (bay) F3
Pavlof (vol.) F3
Philip Smith (mts.) J1
Porcupine (riv.) K1
Port Clarence (inlet) ... E1
Port Heiden (inlet) G3

Portland Canal (inlet) ... N2
Port Moller (inlet) F3
Port Wells (inlet) C1
Pribilof (isls.) D3
Prince of Wales (cape) . E1
Prince of Wales (isl.) .. N2
Prince William (sound) . D1
Prudhoe (bay) J1
Rat (isls.) K4
Redoubt (vol.) H2
Revillagigedo (chan.) .. N2
Revillagigedo (isl.) N2
Romanzof (cape) E2
Sagavanirktok (riv.) ... J1
Saint Elias (cape) K3
Saint Elias (mts.) L2
Saint George (isl.) D3
Saint Lawrence (isl.) .. D2
Saint Matthew (isl.) ... D2
Saint Paul (isl.) D3
Salisbury (sound) M1
Sanak (isl.) F4
Sanford (mt.) K2
Schwatka (mts.) G1
Seguam (isl.) D4
Selawik (lake) F1
Semichi (isls.) J3
Semidi (isls.) G3
Semisopochnoi (isl.) ... K4
Seward (pen.) E1
Seymour (canal) N1
Sheenjek (riv.) K1
Shelikof (str.) H3
Shemya (isl.) J3

Shishaldin (vol.) E4
Shumagin (isls.) G4
Shuyak (isl.) H3
Sitka (sound) M1
Sitka Nat'l Hist. Park . M1
Sitkinak (str.) H3
Skilak (lake) C1
Skwentna (riv.) A1
Smith (bay) H1
Spencer (cape) L1
Stephens (passage) ... N1
Stevenson Entrance (str.) . H3
Stikine (riv.) N2
Stikine (str.) N2
Stony (riv.) G2
Stuart (isl.) F2
Suemez (isl.) M2
Sumner (str.) M2
Susitna (riv.) B1
Sutwik (isl.) G3
Taku (glac.) N1
Taku (riv.) N1
Talkeetna (mts.) J2
Tanaga (isl.) K4
Tanaga (vol.) K4
Tanana (riv.) J2
Taylor (mts.) G2
Tazlina (lake) D1
Tazlina (riv.) D1
Teshekpuk (lake) H1
Tigalda (isl.) F4
Tikchik (lkes.) G2
Togiak (bay) F3
Tugidak (isl.) G3

Turnagain Arm (inlet) ... B1
Tustumena (lake) C1
Two Arm (bay) C2
Ugashik (lkes.) G3
Umnak (isl.) E4
Umnak (passage) E4
Unalaska (isl.) E4
Unga (isl.) F3
Unimak (isl.) E4
Unimak (passage) F4
Utukok (riv.) F1
Valley of Ten Thousand Smokes . G3
Vancouver (mt.) L2
Veniaminof (vol.) F3
Vsevidof (mt.) E4
Walrus (isl.) E3
Walrus (isls.) F3
Waring (mts.) G1
West Point (mt.) K2
White (pass) N1
White (riv.) K2
White Mountains Nat'l Rec. Area . J1
Witherspoon (mt.) ... C1
Wrangell (cape) H3
Wrangell (isl.) N2
Wrangell (mts.) K2
Wrangell-St. Elias Nat'l Park . K2
Yakobi (isl.) M1
Yakutat (bay) K3
Yentna (riv.) A1
Yukon (riv.) F2

⊙Court House
‡Population of metropolitan area.
†Zip of nearest p.o.
* Multiple zips.

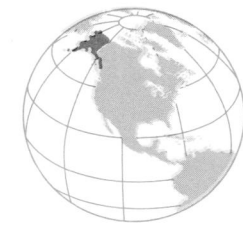

AREA 591,004 sq. mi. (1,530,700 sq. km.)
POPULATION 401,851
CAPITAL Juneau
LARGEST CITY Anchorage
HIGHEST POINT Mt. McKinley 20,320 ft.
  (6194 m.)
SETTLED IN 1801
ADMITTED TO UNION January 3, 1959
POPULAR NAME Great Land; Last Frontier
STATE FLOWER Forget-me-not
STATE BIRD Willow Ptarmigan

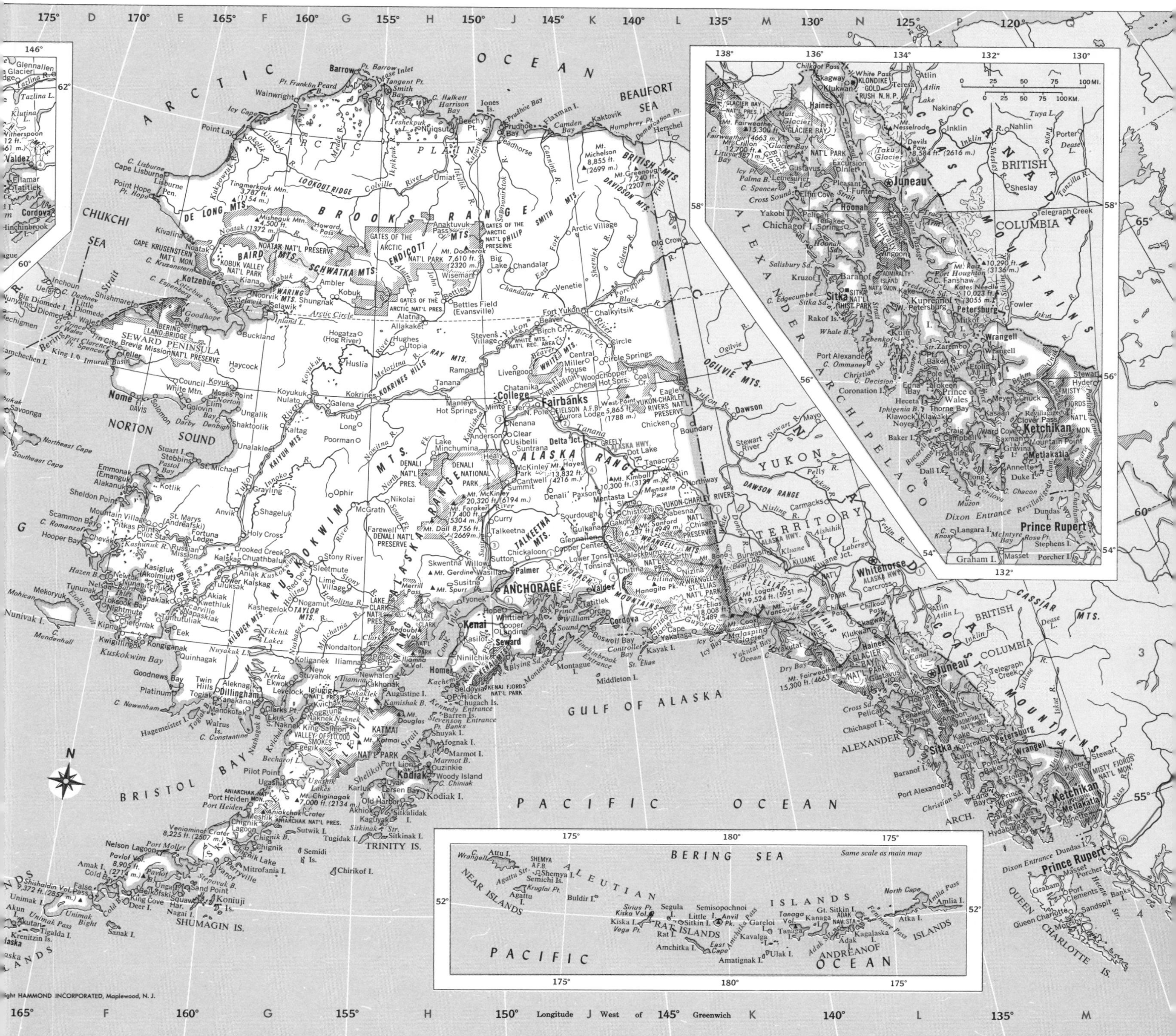

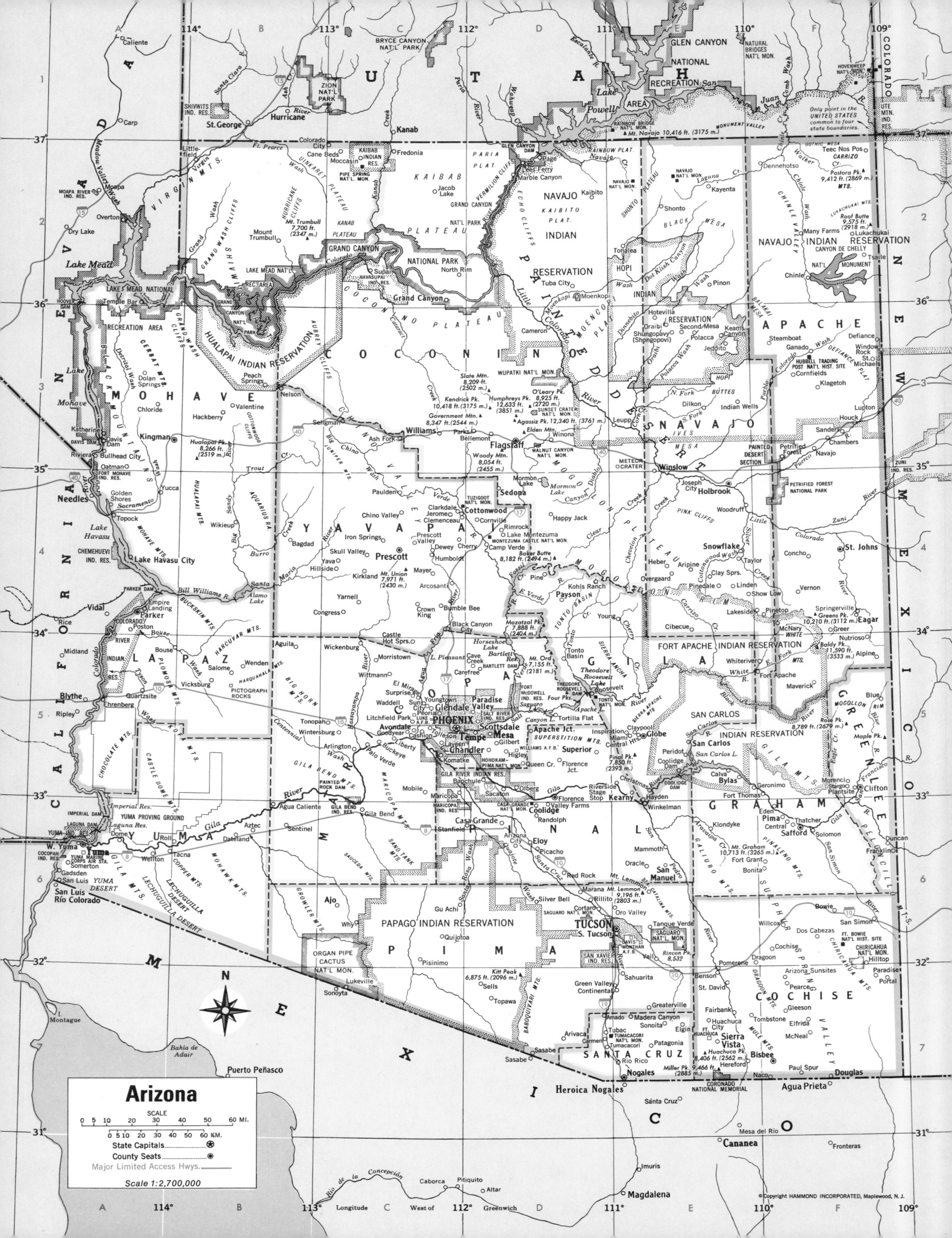

Arizona

SCALE

0 5 10 20 30 40 50 60 MI.

0 5 10 20 30 40 50 60 KM.

State Capitals .... ⊛

County Seats .... ◉

Major Limited Access Hwys. ‾‾‾‾‾‾

Scale 1:2,700,000

© Copyright HAMMOND INCORPORATED, Maplewood, N.J.

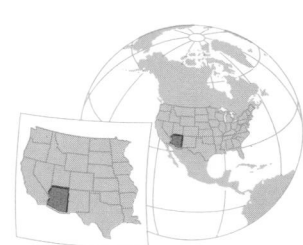

AREA 114,000 sq. mi. (295,260 sq. km.)
POPULATION 2,718,425
CAPITAL Phoenix
LARGEST CITY Phoenix
HIGHEST POINT Humphreys Pk. 12,633 ft.
(3851 m.)
SETTLED IN 1752
ADMITTED TO UNION February 14, 1912
POPULAR NAME Grand Canyon State
STATE FLOWER Saguaro Cactus Blossom
STATE BIRD Cactus Wren

Agriculture, Industry and Resources

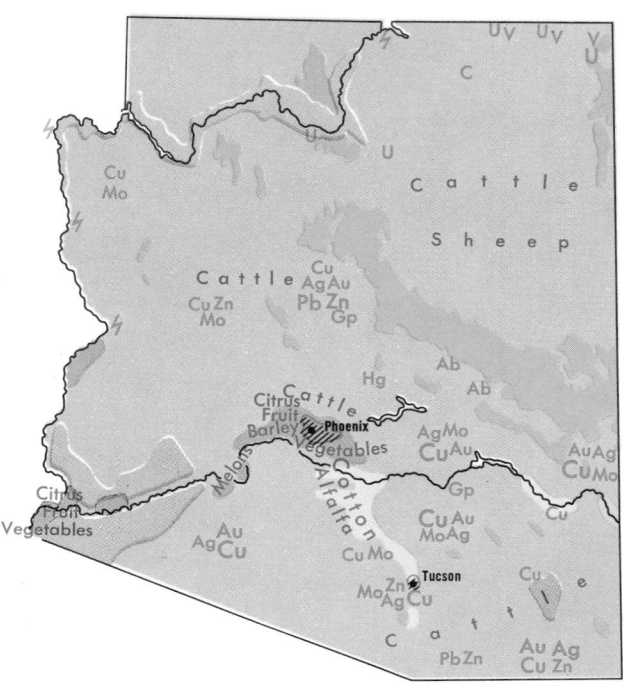

COUNTIES

Apache 52,108	F3
Cochise 85,686	F7
Coconino 75,008	C3
Gila 37,080	E5
Graham 22,862	E6
Greenlee 11,406	F5
La Paz• 13,100	A5
Maricopa 1,509,052	C5
Mohave 55,865	A3
Navajo 67,629	E3
Pima 531,443	D6
Pinal 90,918	D6
Santa Cruz 20,459	E7
Yavapai 68,145	C4
Yuma• 81,800	A6

•1982 official estimate.

CITIES and TOWNS

Zip	Name/Pop.	Key
†85333	Agua Caliente 60	B6
85320	Aguila 900	B5
85321	Ajo 5,189	C6
85920	Alpine 450	F5
85640	Amado 75	D7
85220	Apache Junction 9,935	D5
†85901	Aripine 25	E4
85601	Arivaca 400	D7
85223	Arizona City 825	D6
85625	Arizona Sunsites 825	F7
85322	Arlington 950	C5
86320	Ash Fork 800	C3

85323	Avondale 8,168	C5
†85333	Aztec 20	B6
86321	Bagdad 2,331	B4
85221	Bapchule 400	D5
86015	Bellemont 210	D3
85602	Benson 4,190	E7
85603	Bisbee⊙ 7,154	F7
85324	Black Canyon City 600	C4
85922	Blue 50	F5
†85643	Bonita 20	E6
85325	Bouse 500	A5
85605	Bowie 600	F6
85326	Buckeye 3,434	C5
86430	Bullhead City-Riviera 10,364	A3
†86301	Bumble Bee 15	C4
85530	Bylas 1,175	E5
†85530	Calva 10	E5
86020	Cameron 600	D3
86322	Camp Verde 1,125	D4
†86022	Cane Beds 30	B2
85331	Carefree 986	C5
†85640	Carmen 200	D7
85222	Casa Grande 14,971	D6
85329	Cashion 3,014	C5
†85342	Castle Hot Springs 50	C5
85331	Cave Creek 1,589	D5
85531	Central 300	F6
†85501	Central Heights-Midland City 2,791	E5
86502	Chambers 500	F3
85224	Chandler 29,673	D5
†86327	Cherry 20	C4
86503	Chinle 2,815	F2

86323	Chino Valley 2,858	C4
86431	Chloride 225	A3
†85292	Christmas 201	E5
85911	Cibecue 100	E4
86324	Clarkdale 1,512	C4
85532	Claypool 2,362	E5
†85934	Clay Springs 500	E4
†86326	Clemenceau 300	C4
85533	Clifton⊙ 4,245	F5
85606	Cochise 150	F6
86021	Colorado City 350	B2
85924	Concho 100	F4
85332	Congress 800	C4
†85640	Continental 250	D7
85228	Coolidge 6,851	D6
†85542	Coolidge Dam 42	E5
†86505	Cornfields 200	F3
86325	Cornville 425	D4
85230	Cortaro 375	D6
86326	Cottonwood 4,550	D4
86333	Crown King 100	C4
85333	Dateland 100	B6
†86430	Davis Dam 125	A3
86327	Dewey 100	C4
†86047	Dilkon 90	E3
86441	Dolan Springs 870	A3
†85364	Dome 48	A6
85607	Douglas 13,058	F7
85609	Dragoon 150	F6
85534	Duncan 603	F6
85925	Eagar 2,791	F4
85535	Eden 89	F6
85334	Ehrenburg 93	A5

(continued on following page)

MAJOR MINERAL OCCURRENCES

Ab	Asbestos	Cu	Copper	Pb	Lead
Ag	Silver	Gp	Gypsum	U	Uranium
Au	Gold	Hg	Mercury	V	Vanadium
C	Coal	Mo	Molybdenum	Zn	Zinc

DOMINANT LAND USE

▦ Fruit, Truck and Mixed Farming

□ Cotton and Alfalfa

▢ General Farming, Livestock, Special Crops

▨ Range Livestock

▨ Forests

▨ Nonagricultural Land

⚡ Water Power

▨ Major Industrial Areas

Topography

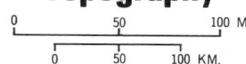

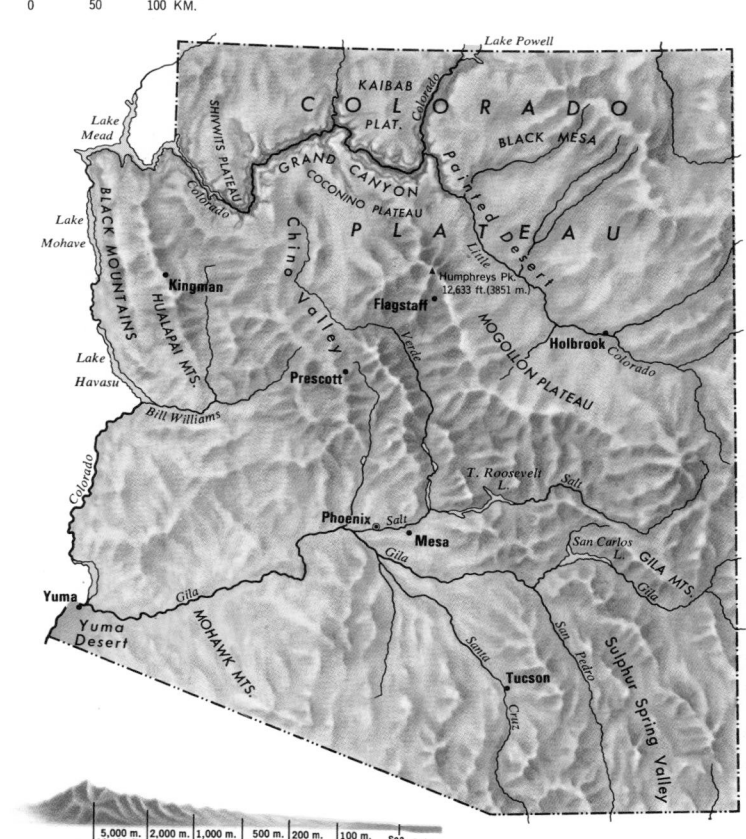

200 Arizona
(continued)

†85617 Elfrida 700 .... F7
†85637 Elgin 525 .... E7
85335 El Mirage 4,307 .... C5
85231 Eloy 6,240 .... D6
85612 Fairbank 100 .... E7
86001 Flagstaff⊙ 34,743 .... D3
85232 Florence⊙ 3,391 .... D5
†85220 Florence Junction 35 .... D5
85926 Fort Apache 500 .... F5
86504 Fort Defiance 3,431 .... F3
85643 Fort Grant 240 .... E6
85536 Fort Thomas 450 .... E5
85534 Franklin 300 .... F6
86022 Fredonia 1,040 .... C2
85336 Gadsden 250 .... A6
86505 Ganado 816 .... F3
†85536 Geronimo 25 .... F5
85337 Gila Bend 1,585 .... C6
85234 Gilbert 5,717 .... D5
†85617 Gleeson 15 .... F7
*85301 Glendale 97,172 .... C5
85501 Globe⊙ 6,886 .... E5
85323 Goodyear 2,747 .... C5
86023 Grand Canyon 1,348 .... C2
†85637 Greaterville 15 .... E7
85614 Green Valley 7,999 .... D7
85927 Greer 385 .... F4
†85634 Gu Achi 339 .... C6
86411 Hackberry 250 .... B3
86024 Happy Jack 50 .... D4
85235 Hayden 1,205 .... E5
85928 Heber 750 .... E4
85615 Hereford 10 .... E7
85236 Higley 500 .... D5
†86301 Hillside 100 .... B4
†85632 Hilltop 9 .... F6
86025 Holbrook⊙ 5,785 .... E4
86030 Hotevilla 3,009 .... E3
86506 Houck 900 .... F3
85616 Huachuca City 1,661 .... E7
86329 Humboldt 787 .... C4
86031 Indian Wells 150 .... E3
85537 Inspiration 500 .... D5
86330 Iron Springs 175 .... C4
86051 Jacob Lake 16 .... C2
†86025 Jeddito 20 .... E3
86331 Jerome 420 .... C4
86032 Joseph City 650 .... E4
86053 Kaibito 275 .... D2
†86430 Katherine 102 .... A3
86033 Kayenta 3,343 .... E2
86034 Keams Canyon 400 .... E3
85237 Kearny 2,646 .... E5
86401 Kingman⊙ 9,257 .... A3
86332 Kirkland 100 .... C4
†86505 Klagetoh 200 .... F3
85643 Klondyke 86 .... E6
85538 Kohls Ranch 100 .... D4
†85339 Komatke 300 .... C5
86403 Lake Havasu City 15,909 ... A4
86342 Lake Montezuma 900 .... D4
85929 Lakeside 1,333 .... E4
85339 Laveen 800 .... C5
†86036 Lees Ferry 10 .... D2
86035 Leupp 150 .... E3
†85326 Liberty 150 .... C5
†85901 Linden 50 .... E4
85340 Litchfield Park 3,657 .... C5
86432 Littlefield 40 .... B2
86507 Lukachukai 1,049 .... F2
85341 Lukeville 50 .... C7
86508 Lupton 250 .... F3
†85637 Madera Canyon 75 .... E7
85618 Mammoth 1,906 .... E6
86538 Many Farms 1,364 .... F2
85238 Marana 1,674 .... D6
86036 Marble Canyon 6 .... D2
85239 Maricopa 750 .... C5
†85920 Maverick 50 .... F5
86333 Mayer 810 .... C4
85930 McNary 1,320 .... F4
85617 McNeal 100 .... F7
*85201 Mesa 152,453 .... D5
85539 Miami 2,716 .... E5
†85239 Mobile 100 .... C5
†86022 Moccasin 150 .... C2
†86045 Moenkopi D2
85540 Morenci 2,736 .... F5
86038 Mormon Lake 20 .... D4
85342 Morristown 400 .... C5
85619 Mount Lemmon 400 .... E6
†84770 Mount Trumbull 14 .... B2
85620 Naco 750 .... E7
86509 Navajo 100 .... F3
†86434 Nelson 39 .... B3
85621 Nogales⊙ 15,683 .... E7
86052 North Rim 50 .... C2
85932 Nutrioso 500 .... F5
86433 Oatman 175 .... A3
†85247 Olberg 65 .... D5
85623 Oracle 2,484 .... E6
86039 Oraibi 600 .... E3
†85704 Oro Valley 1,489 .... E6
85933 Overgaard 750 .... E4
86040 Page 4,907 .... D2
85343 Palo Verde 500 .... C5
†85632 Paradise 15 .... F7
85253 Paradise Valley 11,085 .... D5
85344 Parker⊙ 2,542 .... A4
86018 Parks 175 .... C3
85624 Patagonia 980 .... E7
86334 Paulden 350 .... C4
†85607 Paul Spur 34 .... F7
85541 Payson 5,068 .... D4
86434 Peach Springs 900 .... B3
85625 Pearce 700 .... F7
85345 Peoria 12,307 .... C5
85542 Peridot 950 .... E5
86028 Petrified Forest 80 .... F3
*85001 Phoenix (cap.)⊙ 789,704 .. C5
Phoenix‡ 1,508,030 .... C5
85241 Picacho 850 .... D6
85543 Pima 1,599 .... F6
85544 Pine 800 .... D4
85934 Pinedale 400 .... E4
85935 Pinetop 1,527 .... F4
86510 Pinon 100 .... E2
85634 Pisinimo 187 .... C6
†85540 Plantsite F5
86042 Polacca 500 .... E3
85627 Pomerene 365 .... E6
85632 Portal 72 .... F7
85371 Poston 500 .... A4
86301 Prescott⊙ 20,055 .... C4
†86301 Prescott Valley 2,284 .... C4
85346 Quartzsite 255 .... A5
85242 Queen Creek 600 .... D5
†85634 Quijotoa 200 .... C6
85243 Randolph 350 .... D6
85245 Red Rock 250 .... D6
85246 Rillito 400 .... D6
86335 Rimrock 217 .... D4
85237 Riverside Stage Stop 418 .. D5
86440 Riviera-Bullhead City 10,364 .... A3
85347 Roll 700 .... A6
85545 Roosevelt 125 .... D5
85247 Sacaton 1,951 .... D5
85546 Safford⊙ 7,010 .... F6
85629 Sahuarita 200 .... E7
85630 Saint David 800 .... E7
85936 Saint Johns⊙ 3,368 .... F4
86511 Saint Michaels 250 .... F3
85348 Salome 800 .... B5
85550 San Carlos 2,668 .... E5
86512 Sanders 900 .... F3
85349 San Luis 1,946 .... A6
85631 San Manuel 5,443 .... E6
85632 San Simon 400 .... F6
85633 Sasabe 50 .... D7
*85251 Scottsdale 88,622 .... D5
86043 Second Mesa 450 .... E3
86336 Sedona 5,368 .... D4
86337 Seligman 510 .... B3
85634 Sells 1,864 .... D7
†85333 Sentinel 40 .... B6
86054 Shonto 700 .... E2
85901 Show Low 4,298 .... F4
†86043 Shungopavy (Shongopovi) 570 .... E3
85635 Sierra Vista 24,937 .... E7
85270 Silver Bell 900 .... D6
86338 Skull Valley 250 .... C4
85937 Snowflake 3,510 .... E4
85551 Solomon 700 .... F6
85350 Somerton 5,761 .... A6
85637 Sonoita 220 .... E7
85713 South Tucson 6,554 .... D6
85938 Springerville 1,452 .... F4
85272 Stanfield 150 .... C6
†85540 Stargo 1,038 .... F5
†86505 Steamboat 100 .... F3
*85351 Sun City 40,505 .... C5
86435 Supai 350 .... C2
85273 Superior 4,600 .... D5
85345 Surprise 3,723 .... C5
85352 Tacna 950 .... B6
†85701 Tanque Verde 850 .... E6
85939 Taylor 1,915 .... E4
86514 Teec Nos Pos 550 .... F2
*85282 Tempe 106,743 .... D5
86443 Temple Bar 84 .... A2
85552 Thatcher 3,374 .... F6
85353 Tolleson 4,433 .... C5
85638 Tombstone 1,632 .... F7
86044 Tonalea 125 .... E2
85354 Tonopah 54 .... B5
85553 Tonto Basin 250 .... D5
85639 Topawa 500 .... D7
86436 Topock 325 .... A4
85290 Tortilla Flat 37 .... D5
85640 Tubac 140 .... E7
86045 Tuba City 5,045 .... D2
*85701 Tucson⊙ 330,537 .... D6
Tucson‡ 531,263 .... D6
85640 Tumacacori 100 .... D7
85641 Vail 175 .... E6
86437 Valentine 120 .... B3
85291 Valley Farms 240 .... D6
85940 Vernon 75 .... F4
†85348 Vicksburg 16 .... B5
85355 Waddell 100 .... C5
85356 Wellton 911 .... A6
85357 Wenden 400 .... B5
85941 Whiteriver 2,256 .... E5
85321 Why 65 .... C6
85358 Wickenburg 3,535 .... C5
85360 Wikieup 150 .... B4
85643 Willcox 3,243 .... F6
86046 Williams 2,266 .... C3
86515 Window Rock 2,230 .... F3
85292 Winkelman 1,060 .... E6
†86001 Winona 25 .... D3
86047 Winslow 7,921 .... E3
†85322 Wintersburg 400 .... B5
85361 Wittmann 600 .... C5
85942 Woodruff 280 .... E4
85362 Yarnell 800 .... C4
†86301 Yava 40 .... C4
85554 Young 500 .... D4
85363 Youngtown 2,254 .... C5
86438 Yucca 250 .... A4
85364 Yuma⊙ 42,481 .... A6

OTHER FEATURES

Agassiz (peak) D3
Agua Fria (riv.) C5
Alamo (lake) B4
Apache (lake) D5
Aquarius (range) B4
Aravaipa (creek) E6
Aubrey (cliffs) B3
Baboquivari (mts.) D7
Baker Butte (mt.) D4
Balakai (mesa) F3
Baldy (peak) F5
Bartlett (dam) D5
Bartlett (res.) D5
Big Chino Wash (dry riv.) C3
Big Horn (mts.) B5
Big Sandy (riv.) B4
Bill Williams (riv.) B4
Black (mesa) E2
Black (mts.) A3
Black (riv.) E5
Blue (riv.) F5
Bouse Wash (dry riv.) A4
Buckskin (mts.) B4
Burro (creek) B4
Canyon (lake) D5
Canyon de Chelly Nat'l Mon. F2
Carrizo (creek) E4
Carrizo (mts.) G2
Casa Grande Ruins Nat'l Mon. D6
Castle Dome (mts.) A5
Cataract (creek) C3
Centennial Wash (dry riv.) B5
Cerbat (mts.) A3
Cherry (creek) E4
Chevelon (creek) E4
Chinle (creek) F2
Chinle (valley) F2
Chinle Wash (dry riv.) F2
Chino (valley) C3
Chiricahua (mts.) F6
Chiricahua Nat'l Mon. F6
Chocolate (mts.) A5
Clear (creek) D4
Coconino (plat.) C3
Cocopah Ind. Res. 355 .... A6
Colorado (riv.) A5
Colorado River Ind. Res. 6,640 .... A5
Coolidge (dam) E5
Copper (mts.) B6
Corn (creek) E3
Coronado Nat'l Memorial E7
Cottonwood (cliffs) B3
Cottonwood Wash (dry riv.) E4
Davis (dam) A3
Davis-Monthan A.F.B. 6,279 .... E6
Defiance (plat.) F3
Detrital Wash (dry riv.) A3
Diablo (canyon) D4
Dinnebito Wash (dry riv.) E3
Dot Klish (canyon) E2
Dragoon (mts.) F7
Eagle (creek) F5
East Verde (riv.) D4
Echo (cliffs) D2
Elden (mt.) D3
Fort Apache Ind. Res. 7,774 .... E5
Fort Bowie Nat'l Hist. Site F6
Fort Huachuca E7
Fort McDowell Ind. Res. 349 .... D5
Fort Mohave Ind. Res. 183 .... A4
Fort Pearce Wash (dry riv.) B2
Fossil (creek) D4
Four Peaks (mt.) D5
Galiuro (mts.) E6
Gila (mts.) A6
Gila (mts.) F5
Gila (riv.) B6
Gila Bend (mts.) B5
Gila Bend Ind. Res. 353 .... C6
Gila River Ind. Res. 7,445 .... C5
Glen Canyon (dam) D2
Glen Canyon Nat'l Rec. Area D1
Gothic (mesa) F2
Government (mt.) C3
Graham (mt.) F6
Grand Canyon Nat'l Park C2
Grand Wash (butte) B2
Grand Wash (riv.) B2
Greens (peak) F4
Growler (mts.) B6
Harcuvar (mts.) B5
Harquahala (mts.) B5
Hassayampa (riv.) C5
Havasu (lake) A4
Havasupai Ind. Res. 282 .... C2
Hohokam Pima Nat'l Mon. D5
Hoover (dam) A2
Hopi (buttes) E3
Hopi Ind. Res. 6,896 .... E2
Horseshoe (lake) D5
Huachuca (peak) E7
Hualapai (mts.) B4
Hualapai (peak) B3
Hualapai Ind. Res. 849 .... B3
Hubbell Trading Post Nat'l Hist. Site F3
Humphreys (peak) D3
Hurricane (cliffs) B2
Imperial (res.) A6
Ives (mesa) E3
Juniper (mts.) C3
Kaibab (plat.) C2
Kaibab Ind. Res. 173 .... C2
Kaibito (plat.) D2
Kanab (creek) C2
Kanab (plat.) C2
Kellogg (mt.) E6
Kendrick (peak) D3
Kitt (peak) D7
Kofa (mts.) B5
Laguna (creek) E2
Laguna (res.) A6
Lake Mead Nat'l Rec. Area A2
Lechuguilla (des.) A6
Lemmon (mt.) E6
Little Colorado (riv.) D3
Lukachukai (mts.) F2
Luke A.F.B. 3,515 .... C5
Maple (peak) F5
Marble Canyon Nat'l Mon. D2
Maricopa (mts.) C5
Maricopa Ind. Res. 397 .... C6
Mazatzal (peak) D4
Mead (lake) A2
Meteor (crater) E3
Miller (peak) E7
Moencopi (plat.) D3
Moenkopi Wash (dry riv.) D2
Mogollon (plat.) D4
Mogollon Rim (cliffs) D4
Mohave (lake) A3
Mohave (mts.) A4
Mohawk (mts.) B6
Montezuma Castle Nat'l Mon. D4
Mormon (lake) D4
Mule (mts.) E7
Navajo (creek) D2
Navajo Ind. Res. 76,173 .... D2
Navajo Nat'l Mon. E2
Navajo Ord. Depot D3
O'Leary (peak) D3
Oraibi Wash (dry riv.) E3
Ord (mt.) D5
Organ Pipe Cactus Nat'l Mon. C6
Painted (des.) D2
Painted Desert Section (Petrified Forest F3
Painted Rock (dam) C5
Papago Ind. Res. 7,171 .... C6
Paria (plat.) D2
Paria (riv.) D1
Parker (dam) A4
Pastora (peak) F2
Peloncillo (mts.) F6
Petrified Forest Nat'l Park F4
Pictograph (rocks) B5
Pinal (peak) E5
Pinaleno (mts.) F6
Pink (cliffs) E4
Pipe Spring Nat'l Mon. C2
Pleasant (lake) C5
Plomosa (mts.) A5
Polacca Wash (dry riv.) E3
Powell (lake) E1
Pueblo Colorado Wash (dry riv.) F3
Puerco (riv.) F3
Quajote Wash (dry riv.) D6
Rainbow (plat.) D2
Rincon (peak) E6
Roof Butte (mt.) F2
Rose (peak) F5
Sacramento Wash (dry riv.) A4
Saguaro (lake) D5
Saguaro Nat'l Mon. E6
Salt (riv.) D5
Salt River Ind. Res. 4,089 .... D5
San Carlos (lake) E5
San Carlos (riv.) E5
San Carlos Ind. Res. 6,104 .... E5
Sand Tank (mt.) C6
San Francisco (riv.) F5
San Pedro (riv.) E6
San Simon (riv.) F6
Santa Catalina (mts.) E6
Santa Cruz (riv.) D6
Santa Maria (riv.) B4
Santa Rosa Wash (dry riv.) D6
San Xavier Ind. Res. 875 .... D6
Sauceda (mts.) C6
Shivwits (plat.) B2
Shonto (plat.) E2
Sierra Ancha (mts.) D5
Sierra Apache (mts.) E5
Silver (creek) E4
Slate (mt.) D3
Sulphur Spring (valley) F6
Sunset Crater Nat'l Mon. D3
Superstition (mts.) D5
Theodore Roosevelt (lake) D5
Tonto (creek) D4
Tonto Nat'l Mon. D5
Trout (creek) B3
Trumbull (mt.) B2
Tumacacori Nat'l Mon. E7
Tuzigoot Nat'l Mon. D4
Tyson Wash (dry riv.) A5
Uinkaret (plat.) B2
Union (mt.) C4
Verde (riv.) D5
Vermilion (cliffs) D2
Virgin (mts.) B2
Walker (creek) F2
Walnut Canyon Nat'l Mon. D3
White (riv.) E5
Williams A.F.B. 3,435 .... D5
Woody (mt.) D3
Wupatki Nat'l Mon. D3
Yuma (des.) A6
Yuma Proving Ground 1,098 .... A6
Zuni (riv.) F4

⊙County seat.
‡Population of metropolitan area.
† Zip of nearest p.o. * Multiple zips.

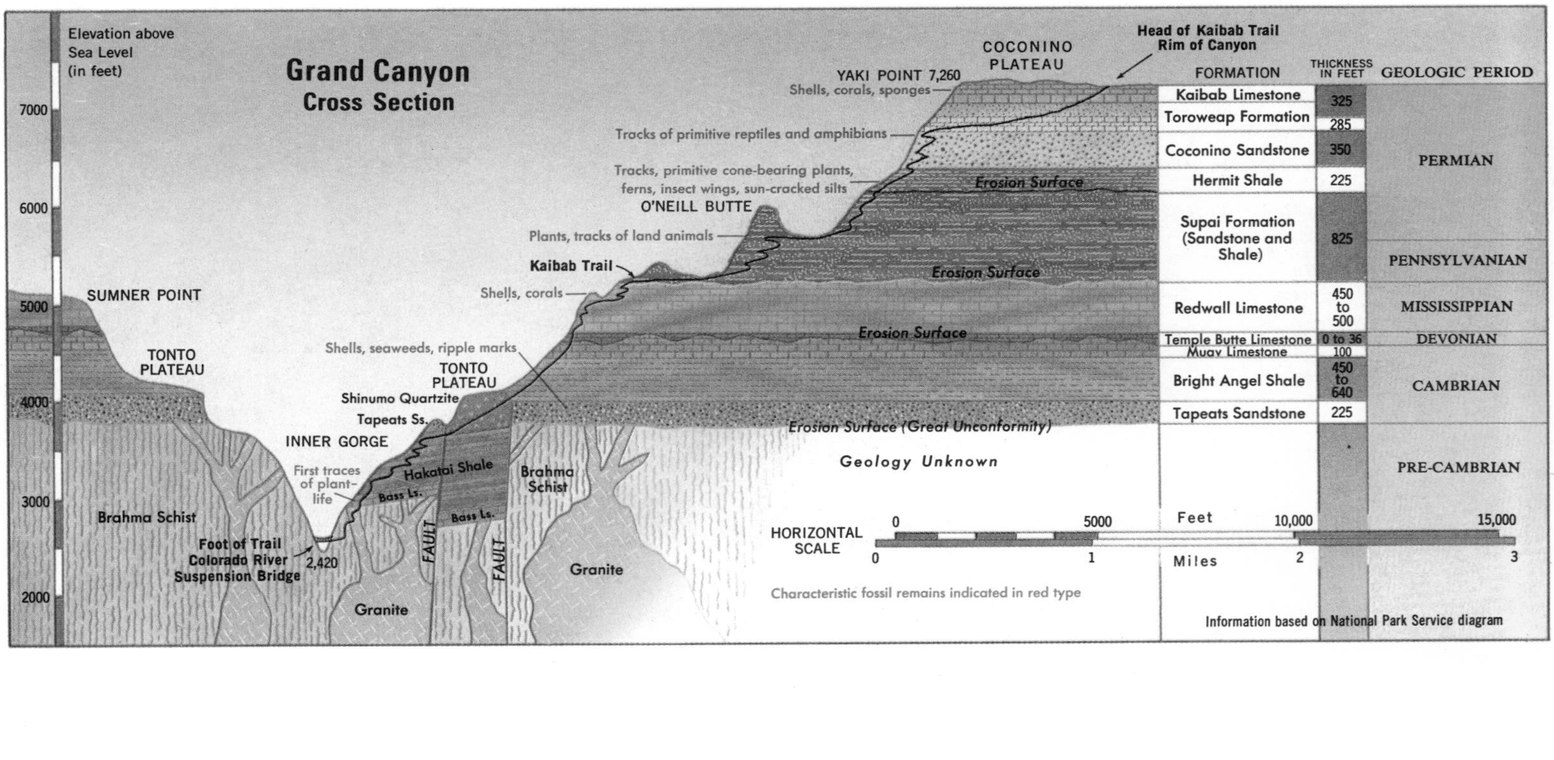

Elevation above Sea Level (in feet)
Grand Canyon Cross Section
7000
6000
5000
4000
3000
2000
YAKI POINT 7,260
COCONINO PLATEAU
Head of Kaibab Trail Rim of Canyon
Shells, corals, sponges
Tracks of primitive reptiles and amphibians
Tracks, primitive cone-bearing plants, ferns, insect wings, sun-cracked silts
O'NEILL BUTTE
Plants, tracks of land animals
Kaibab Trail
Shells, corals
SUMNER POINT
TONTO PLATEAU
Shells, seaweeds, ripple marks
TONTO PLATEAU
Shinumo Quartzite
Tapeats Ss.
INNER GORGE
First traces of plant-life
Hakatai Shale
Bass Ls.
Brahma Schist
Foot of Trail Colorado River Suspension Bridge
2,420
FAULT
Granite
Erosion Surface
Erosion Surface (Great Unconformity)
Geology Unknown
HORIZONTAL SCALE
0
5000
Feet
10,000
15,000
1
2
3
Miles
Characteristic fossil remains indicated in red type
FORMATION
THICKNESS IN FEET
GEOLOGIC PERIOD
Kaibab Limestone 325
Toroweap Formation 285
Coconino Sandstone 350
Hermit Shale 225
PERMIAN
Supai Formation (Sandstone and Shale) 825
PENNSYLVANIAN
Redwall Limestone 450 to 500
MISSISSIPPIAN
Temple Butte Limestone 0 to 36
DEVONIAN
Muav Limestone 100
Bright Angel Shale 450 to 640
Tapeats Sandstone 225
CAMBRIAN
PRE-CAMBRIAN
Information based on National Park Service diagram

AREA 53,187 sq. mi. (137,754 sq. km.)
POPULATION 2,286,435
CAPITAL Little Rock
LARGEST CITY Little Rock
HIGHEST POINT Magazine Mtn. 2,753 ft. (839 m.)
SETTLED IN 1685
ADMITTED TO UNION June 15, 1836
POPULAR NAME Land of Opportunity
STATE FLOWER Apple Blossom
STATE BIRD Mockingbird

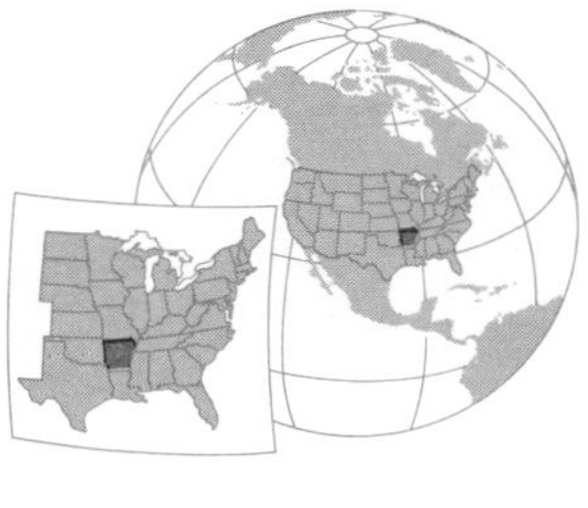

COUNTIES

Arkansas 24,175 .... H5
Ashley 26,538 .... G7
Baxter 27,409 .... F1
Benton 78,115 .... B1
Boone 26,067 .... D1
Bradley 13,803 .... F7
Calhoun 6,079 .... E6
Carroll 16,203 .... C1
Chicot 17,793 .... H7
Clark 23,326 .... D5
Clay 20,616 .... K1
Cleburne 16,909 .... F2
Cleveland 7,868 .... F6
Columbia 26,644 .... D7
Conway 19,505 .... E3
Craighead 63,239 .... J2
Crawford 36,892 .... B2
Crittenden 49,499 .... K3
Cross 20,434 .... J3
Dallas 10,515 .... E6
Desha 19,760 .... H6
Drew 17,910 .... G6
Faulkner 46,192 .... F3
Franklin 14,705 .... C2
Fulton 9,975 .... G1
Garland 70,531 .... D4
Grant 13,008 .... F5
Greene 30,744 .... J1
Hempstead 23,635 .... C6
Hot Spring 26,819 .... E5
Howard 13,459 .... C5
Independence 30,147 .... G2
Izard 10,768 .... G1
Jackson 21,646 .... H2
Jefferson 90,718 .... G5
Johnson 17,423 .... C2
Lafayette 10,213 .... C7
Lawrence 18,447 .... H1
Lee 15,539 .... J4
Lincoln 13,369 .... G6
Little River 13,952 .... B6
Logan 20,144 .... C3
Lonoke 34,518 .... G4
Madison 11,373 .... C1
Marion 11,334 .... E1
Miller 37,766 .... C7
Mississippi 59,517 .... K2
Monroe 14,052 .... H4
Montgomery 7,771 .... C4
Nevada 11,097 .... D6
Newton 7,756 .... D2
Ouachita 30,541 .... E6
Perry 7,266 .... E4
Phillips 34,772 .... J5
Pike 10,373 .... C5
Poinsett 27,032 .... J2
Polk 17,007 .... B5
Pope 39,021 .... D3
Prairie 10,140 .... G4
Pulaski 340,613 .... F4
Randolph 16,834 .... H1
Saint Francis 30,858 .... J3
Saline 53,161 .... E4
Scott 9,685 .... B4
Searcy 8,847 .... E2
Sebastian 95,172 .... B3
Sevier 14,060 .... B6
Sharp 14,607 .... G1
Stone 9,022 .... F2
Union 48,573 .... E7
Van Buren 13,357 .... E2
Washington 100,494 .... B2
White 50,835 .... G3
Woodruff 11,222 .... H3
Yell 17,026 .... D3

CITIES and TOWNS

Zip *Name/Pop.* *Key*

72001 Adona 230 .... E3
72002 Alexander 223 .... F4
72410 Alicia 246 .... H2
72820 Alix 225 .... C3
†72046 Allport 295 .... G4
72921 Alma 2,755 .... B3
72003 Almyra 294 .... H5
72611 Alpena 344 .... D1
72004 Altheimer 1,231 .... G5
72821 Altus 441 .... C3
72005 Amagon 126 .... H2
71921 Amity 859 .... D5
71922 Antoine 194 .... D5
71923 Arkadelphia⊙ 10,005 .... D5
71630 Arkansas City⊙ 668 .... H6
72310 Armorel 500 .... L2
71822 Ashdown⊙ 4,218 .... B6
72513 Ash Flat⊙ 524 .... G1
72823 Atkins 3,002 .... E3
72311 Aubrey 267 .... J4
72006 Augusta⊙ 3,496 .... H3
72007 Austin 269 .... G4
72711 Avoca 256 .... B1
72010 Bald Knob 2,756 .... G3
71631 Banks 216 .... F6
72922 Barber 35 .... B3
72923 Barling 3,761 .... B3
72313 Bassett 243 .... K2
72924 Bates B4
72501 Batesville⊙ 8,263 .... G2
72411 Bay 1,605 .... J2
71720 Bearden 1,191 .... E6
72613 Beaver C1
72012 Beebe 3,599 .... G3
72014 Beedeville 183 .... H3
†72712 Bella Vista 2,589 .... B1
†72601 Bellefonte 393 .... D1
72824 Belleville 571 .... D3
71823 Ben Lomond 155 .... B6
72015 Benton⊙ 17,717 .... E4
72712 Bentonville⊙ 8,756 .... B1
72615 Bergman 320 .... E1
72616 Berryville⊙ 2,966 .... C1
†72764 Bethel Heights 296 .... B1
72016 Bigelow 373 .... E3
72617 Big Flat 150 .... F1
72413 Biggers 363 .... J1
72017 Biscoe 486 .... H4
72414 Black Oak 309 .... K2
72415 Black Rock 848 .... H1
†71960 Black Springs 92 .... C5
71825 Blevins 314 .... C6
65611 Blue Eye 43 .... D1
72826 Blue Mountain 112 .... C3
71722 Bluff City 292 .... D6
72315 Blytheville⊙ 23,844 .... L2
†71858 Bodcaw 197 .... D6
†72901 Bonanza 553 .... B3
72416 Bono 967 .... J2
72927 Booneville⊙ 3,718 .... C3
72020 Bradford 950 .... G3
71826 Bradley 790 .... C7
72928 Branch 353 .... C3
72021 Brinkley 4,909 .... H4
72417 Brookland 840 .... J2
72022 Bryant 2,682 .... F4
71827 Buckner 436 .... D7
72619 Bull Shoals 1,312 .... E1
72321 Burdette 328 .... L2
72023 Cabot 4,806 .... F4
72322 Caldwell 283 .... J3
71828 Cale 110 .... D6
72519 Calico Rock 1,046 .... F1
71724 Calion 638 .... E7
71701 Camden⊙ 15,356 .... E6
†72201 Cammack Village 920 .... E4
†72473 Campbell Station 297 .... H2
72419 Caraway 1,165 .... K2
72024 Carlisle 2,567 .... G4
71725 Carthage 568 .... E5
72025 Casa 179 .... D3
72421 Cash 285 .... J2
72026 Casscoe 297 .... H4
†72951 Caulksville 234 .... C3
72521 Cave City 1,634 .... G2
72718 Cave Springs 429 .... B1
72932 Cedarville 375 .... B2
72719 Centerton 425 .... B1
72829 Centerville 300 .... D3
†72923 Central City 339 .... B3
72933 Charleston⊙ 1,748 .... B3
†72525 Cherokee Village-Hidden Valley 4,058 .... G1
72324 Cherry Valley 729 .... J3
72934 Chester 139 .... B2
71726 Chidester 342 .... D6
72029 Clarendon⊙ 2,361 .... H4
72325 Clarkedale 300 .... K3
72830 Clarksville⊙ 5,237 .... D3
72031 Clinton⊙ 1,284 .... F2
72832 Coal Hill 859 .... C3
72476 College City 432 .... J1
72326 Colt 378 .... J3
71831 Columbus 265 .... C6
72523 Concord 234 .... G2
72032 Conway⊙ 20,375 .... F3
72524 Cord 250 .... H2
72422 Corning⊙ 3,650 .... J1
72626 Cotter 920 .... E1
72036 Cotton Plant 1,323 .... H3
71937 Cove 391 .... B5
72037 Coy 183 .... G4
72327 Crawfordsville 685 .... K3
71635 Crossett 6,706 .... G7
71728 Curtis 300 .... D6
72526 Cushman 556 .... G2
†71950 Daisy 177 .... C5
72039 Damascus 307 .... F3
72833 Danville⊙ 1,698 .... D3
72834 Dardanelle⊙ 3,621 .... D3
72424 Datto 112 .... J1
72722 Decatur 1,013 .... A1
72425 Delaplaine 161 .... J1
71940 Delight 431 .... C5
72426 Dell 310 .... K2
†72821 Denning 238 .... C3
71832 De Queen⊙ 4,594 .... B5
71638 Dermott 4,731 .... H7
72040 Des Arc⊙ 2,001 .... G4
72041 De Valls Bluff⊙ 738 .... H4
72042 De Witt⊙ 3,928 .... H5
72644 Diamond City 650 .... E1
72043 Diaz 1,192 .... H2
71833 Dierks 1,249 .... B5
71941 Donaldson 300 .... E5
72837 Dover 948 .... D3
71639 Dumas 6,091 .... H6
72935 Dyer 608 .... B3
72330 Dyess 446 .... K2
72331 Earle 3,517 .... K3
71701 East Camden 632 .... E6
72332 Edmondson 344 .... K3
72333 Elaine 991 .... J5
71730 El Dorado⊙ 25,270 .... E7
72727 Elkins 579 .... C1
72728 Elm Springs 781 .... B1
71740 Emerson 444 .... D7
71835 Emmet 475 .... D6
72046 England 3,081 .... G4
72047 Enola 186 .... F3
71640 Eudora 3,840 .... H7
72632 Eureka Springs⊙ 1,989 .... C1
72532 Evening Shade 397 .... G1
72633 Everton 134 .... E1
72730 Farmington 1,283 .... B1
72701 Fayetteville⊙ 36,608 .... B1
Fayetteville-Springdale 07 .... B1
†71747 Felsenthal 220 .... F7
72429 Fisher 302 .... J2
72634 Flippin 1,072 .... E1
71742 Fordyce⊙ 5,175 .... F6
71836 Foreman 1,377 .... B6
72335 Forrest City⊙ 13,803 .... J3
*72901 Fort Smith⊙ 71,626 .... B3
Fort Smith‡ 203,269 .... B3
71837 Fouke 614 .... C7
71642 Fountain Hill 352 .... G7
†72016 Fourche 51 .... E4
72536 Franklin 253 .... G1
72017 Fredonia (Biscoe) 486 .... H4
71942 Friendship 163 .... E5
71838 Fulton 326 .... C6
72732 Garfield 187 .... C1
71839 Garland 660 .... C7
72052 Garner 216 .... G3
72635 Gassville 859 .... F1
72733 Gateway 75 .... B1
71840 Genoa 350 .... C7
72734 Gentry 1,468 .... A1
72636 Gilbert 43 .... E2
72055 Gillett 927 .... H5
71841 Gillham 252 .... B5
72339 Gilmore 503 .... K3
71943 Glenwood 1,402 .... C5
72340 Goodwin 225 .... J4
†72315 Gosnell 3,215 .... K2
71643 Gould 1,671 .... G6
71644 Grady 488 .... G5
71944 Grannis 349 .... B5
72838 Gravelly 300 .... C4
72736 Gravette 1,218 .... B1
72058 Greenbrier 1,423 .... F3
72638 Green Forest 1,609 .... D1
72737 Greenland 622 .... B1
72430 Greenway 317 .... K1
72936 Greenwood⊙ 3,317 .... B3
†72067 Greers Ferry 558 .... F2
72060 Griffithville 254 .... G3
72431 Grubbs 546 .... H2
72540 Guion 177 .... G2
†71923 Gum Springs 255 .... D5
71743 Gurdon 2,707 .... D6
72061 Guy 209 .... F3
72937 Hackett 505 .... B3
†71638 Halley H6
71646 Hamburg⊙ 3,394 .... G7
71744 Hampton⊙ 1,627 .... F6
72542 Hardy 643 .... H1
71745 Harrell 302 .... F7
72432 Harrisburg⊙ 1,921 .... J2
72601 Harrison⊙ 9,567 .... D1
72938 Hartford 613 .... B3
72840 Hartman 517 .... C3
†72015 Haskell 1,074 .... E4
71945 Hatfield 410 .... B5
72842 Havana 352 .... D3
72341 Haynes 359 .... J4
72064 Hazen 1,636 .... G4
72543 Heber Springs⊙ 4,589 .... G2
72843 Hector 449 .... E3
72342 Helena⊙ 9,598 .... J4
72065 Hensley 500 .... F4
71647 Hermitage 378 .... F7
72347 Hickory Ridge 478 .... J3
72067 Higden 45 .... F2
72068 Higginson 333 .... G3
†72734 Highfill 92 .... B1
72738 Hindsville C1
72069 Holly Grove 754 .... H4
†72958 Hon 250 .... B4
71801 Hope⊙ 10,290 .... C6
71842 Horatio 989 .... B3
72512 Horseshoe Bend 1,909 .... G1
71901 Hot Springs National Park⊙ 35,781 .... D4
72070 Houston 183 .... E3

(continued on following page)

Agriculture, Industry and Resources

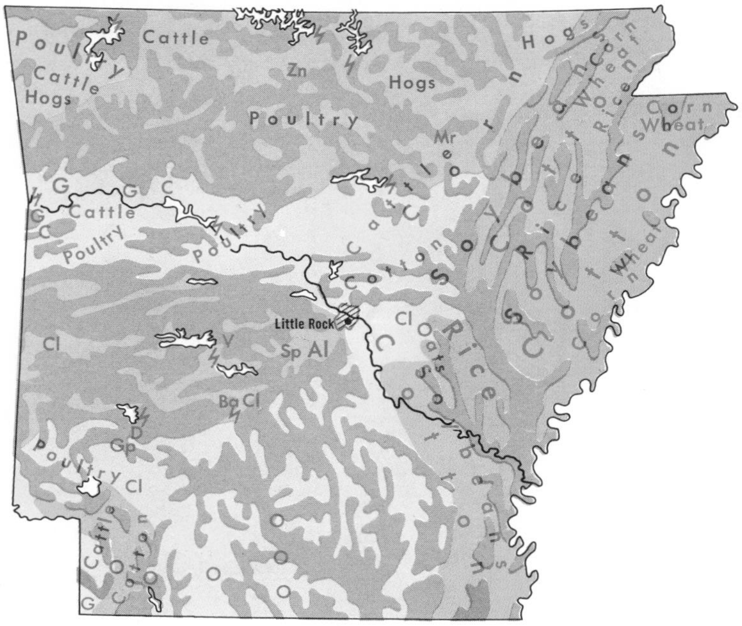

DOMINANT LAND USE

- Fruit and Mixed Farming
- Specialized Cotton
- Cotton, General Farming
- Rice, General Farming
- General Farming, Livestock, Truck Farming, Cotton
- Forests
- Swampland, Limited Agriculture

MAJOR MINERAL OCCURRENCES

Al	Bauxite	Gp	Gypsum
Ba	Barite	Mr	Marble
C	Coal	O	Petroleum
Cl	Clay	Sp	Soapstone
D	Diamonds	V	Vanadium
G	Natural Gas	Zn	Zinc

Water Power

Major Industrial Areas

Topography

Bull Shoals Lake
Norfork Lake
Beaver Lake
OZARK PLATEAU
Fayetteville
BOSTON MOUNTAINS
White
Buffalo
Greers Ferry L.
White
Black
St. Francis
Jonesboro
CROWLEY'S RIDGE
Arkansas
Fort Smith
Lake Dardanelle
Magazine Mtn. 2,753 ft. (839 m.)
Little Red
Mississippi
Fourche La Fave
OUACHITA MOUNTAINS
L. Ouachita
Little Rock
Hot Springs
De Gray Lake
Saline
White
Arkansas
L. Greeson
Ouachita
Pine Bluff
Bayou Bartholomew
Little
Millwood Lake
Red
Texarkana
El Dorado
Mississippi

Topography

| 0 | 30 | 60 MI. |
| 0 | 30 | 60 KM. |

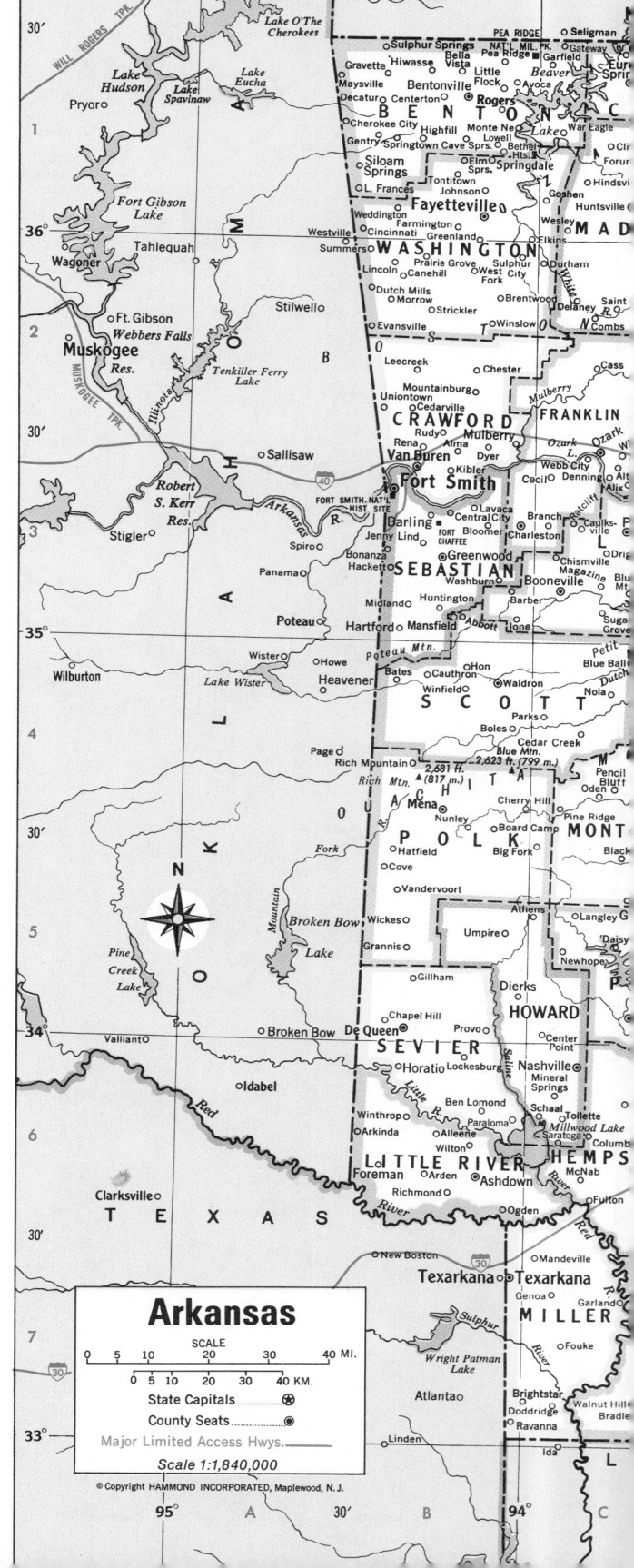

| Below Sea Level | 100 m. 328 ft. | 200 m. 656 ft. | 500 m. 1,640 ft. | 1,000 m. 3,281 ft. | 2,000 m. 6,562 ft. | 5,000 m. 16,404 ft. |

72433 Hoxie 2,961 ....H1
72348 Hughes 1,919 ....J4
72072 Humnoke 442 ....G4
72073 Humphrey 872 ....G5
72074 Hunter 170 ....H3
72940 Huntington 662 ....B3
72740 Huntsville⊙ 1,394 ......C1
71747 Huttig 976 ....F7
72434 Imboden 661 ....H1
72075 Jacksonport 288 ....H2
72076 Jacksonville 27,589 ....F4
†72501 Jamestown H2
†72641 Jasper⊙ 519 ....D1
72079 Jefferson 250 ....F5
71650 Jerome 54 ....G7
72080 Jerusalem 300 ....E3
71949 Jessieville 350 ....D4
72741 Johnson 519 ....B1
72350 Joiner 725 ....K3
72401 Jonesboro⊙ 31,530 ....J2
72081 Judsonia 2,025 ....G3
71749 Junction City 813 ....E7
72351 Keiser 962 ....K2
72082 Kensett 1,751 ....G3
72083 Keo 208 ....G4
†72956 Kibler 798 ....B3
71652 Kingsland 320 ....F6
71950 Kirby 800 ....C5
72435 Knobel 503 ....J1
72845 Knoxville 264 ....D3
72436 Lafe 215 ....H1
72437 Lake City⊙ 1,842 ......K2
72642 Lakeview 512 ....E1
†72389 Lake View 609 ....J5
71653 Lake Village⊙ 3,088 ...H7
72846 Lamar 708 ....D3
72941 Lavaca 1,092 ....B3
71750 Lawson 250 ....F7
72438 Leachville 1,882 ....K2
72644 Lead Hill 247 ....D1
72084 Leola 481 ....E5
72354 Lepanto 1,964 ....K2
72645 Leslie 501 ....E2
72085 Letona 231 ....G3
71845 Lewisville⊙ 1,476 .....C7
72355 Lexa 500 ....J4
72744 Lincoln 1,422 ....B2
†72712 Little Flock 663 ....B1
†72201 Little Rock
    (cap.)⊙ 158,461 ......F4
    Little Rock-North Little
    Rock‡ 393,494 ....F4
71846 Lockesburg 616 ....B6
72847 London 859 ....D3
72086 Lonoke⊙ 4,128 ....G4
72087 Lonsdale 117 ....E4
71751 Louann 282 ....E7
72745 Lowell 1,078 ....B1
†72856 Lurton 38 ....D2
72358 Luxora 1,739 ....K2
72440 Lynn 345 ....H2
72359 Madison 1,238 ....J4
72943 Magazine 799 ....C3
72553 Magness 196 ....H2
71753 Magnolia⊙ 11,909 .....D7
72104 Malvern⊙ 10,163 ......E5
72554 Mammoth Spring 1,158 ..G1
72442 Manila 2,553 ....K2
72944 Mansfield 1,000 ....B3
72360 Marianna⊙ 6,220 ......J4
†72395 Marie 287 ....K2
72364 Marion⊙ 2,996 ....K3

72365 Marked Tree 3,201 .....K2
72443 Marmaduke 1,168 ......K1
72650 Marshall⊙ 1,595 ......E2
72366 Marvell 1,724 ....J4
72106 Mayflower 1,381 ....F4
72444 Maynard 381 ....J1
71847 McCaskill 87 ....C6
72101 McCrory 1,942 ....H3
72441 McDougal 239 ....K1
71654 McGehee 5,671 ....H6
71752 McNeil 725 ....D7
72102 McRae 641 ....G3
72556 Melbourne⊙ 1,619 ....G1
72367 Mellwood 250 ....H5
71953 Mena⊙ 5,154 ....B4
72107 Menifee 368 ....E3
72945 Midland 286 ....B3
72445 Minturn 169 ....H2
†71639 Mitchellville 618 ......H6
72447 Monette 1,165 ....K2
72108 Monroe 250 ....H4
71655 Monticello⊙ 8,259 .....G6
71658 Montrose 641 ....H7
*72501 Moorefield 129 ....G2
72368 Moro 327 ....H4
72110 Morrilton⊙ 7,355 ......E3
71659 Moscow 325 ....G5
72946 Mountainburg 595 .....B2
72653 Mountain Home⊙ 8,066 ..F1
71956 Mountain Pine 1,068 ....D4
72560 Mountain View⊙ 2,147 ..F2
71758 Mount Holly 250 ....E7
71957 Mount Ida⊙ 1,023 .....C4
72561 Mount Pleasant 438 ....G2
72111 Mount Vernon 157 .....F3
72947 Mulberry 1,444 ....B2
71958 Murfreesboro⊙ 1,883 ...C5
71852 Nashville⊙ 4,554 .....C6
72562 Newark 1,128 ....H2
72851 New Blaine 200 ....D3
71959 Newhope 300 ....C5
72112 Newport⊙ 8,339 ......H2
72461 Nimmons 112 ....K1
*71601 Noble Lake 250 ....G5
72568 Norfork 399 ....F1
71960 Norman 539 ....C5
71759 Norphlet 756 ....E7
†72801 Norristown 625 ....D3
71635 North Crossett 3,513 ...G7
*72114 North Little Rock 64,288 ..F4
72660 Oak Grove 265 ....C1
†71801 Oakhaven 72 ....C6
71961 Oden 186 ....C4
71853 Ogden 334 ....B6
72564 Oil Trough 280 ....G2
72103 O'Kean 291 ....J1
71962 Okolona 200 ....D5
72853 Ola 1,121 ....D3
72662 Omaha 191 ....D1
72110 Oppelo 486 ....E3
72370 Osceola⊙ 8,881 ....K2
72565 Oxford 520 ....G1
71855 Ozan 111 ....C6
72949 Ozark⊙ 3,597 ....C3
72372 Palestine 976 ....J4
72121 Pangburn 673 ....G3
72450 Paragould⊙ 15,248 ....J1
72855 Paris⊙ 3,991 ....C3
71661 Parkdale 471 ....H7
72373 Parkin 2,035 ....J3
72950 Parks 600 ....B4

†71801 Patmos 88 ....C7
72123 Patterson 567 ....H3
72453 Peach Orchard 243 ....J1
71964 Pearcy 400 ....D5
72751 Pea Ridge 1,488 ....B1
†72104 Perla 149 ....E5
72125 Perry 254 ....E3
71801 Perrytown 282 ....C7
72126 Perryville⊙ 1,058 ......E3
72451 Piggott⊙ 3,762 ....K1
*71601 Pine Bluff⊙ 56,636 ....F5
    Pine Bluff‡ 90,718 .....F5
†72847 Piney 2,283 ....D3
72857 Plainview 752 ....D4
72568 Pleasant Plains 267 ....G2
72127 Plumerville 785 ....E3
72455 Pocahontas⊙ 5,995 ...H1
72456 Pollard 298 ....K1
72374 Poplar Grove 300 ......J4
72457 Portia 480 ....H1
72128 Poyen 329 ....E5
72753 Prairie Grove 1,708 ....B2
72129 Prattsville 317 ....F5
71857 Prescott⊙ 4,103 ....D6
72672 Pyatt 217 ....E1
72131 Quitman 556 ....F3
72951 Ratcliff 197 ....C3
†72333 Ratio 250 ....J5
72459 Ravenden 338 ....H1
72460 Ravenden Springs 230 ..H1
71726 Reader 127 ....D6
72461 Rector 2,336 ....K1
72132 Redfield 745 ....F5
71670 Reed 395 ....H6
72462 Reyno 521 ....J1
71665 Rison⊙ 1,325 ....F6
†72104 Rockport 231 ....E5
72134 Roe 136 ....H4
72756 Rogers 17,429 ....B1
†72355 Rondo 330 ....J4
72137 Rose Bud 202 ....F3
71858 Rosston 274 ....D6
72952 Rudy 79 ....B2
72139 Russell 232 ....G3
72801 Russellville⊙ 14,031 ...D3
72140 Saint Charles 199 .....H5
72760 Saint Paul 198 ....C2
72576 Salem⊙ 1,424 ....G1
†72658 Salesville 406 ....F1
72863 Scranton 244 ....C3
72143 Searcy⊙ 13,612 ......G3
72465 Sedgwick 205 ....J2
†72103 Shannon Hills 1,656 ...F4
72150 Sheridan⊙ 3,042 ......F5
72152 Sherrill 161 ....F5
72116 Sherwood 10,406 ......F4
72153 Shirley 354 ....F2
72577 Sidney 270 ....G1
72761 Siloam Springs 7,940 ..B1
72162 Smackover 2,453 ......E7
72466 Smithville 113 ....H1
71658 Snyder 700 ....G7
71763 Sparkman 622 ....E6
72764 Springdale 23,458 .....B1
    Springdale-Fayetteville‡
    177,850 ....B1
71860 Stamps 2,859 ....D7
71667 Star City⊙ 2,066 ......G6

71764 Stephens 1,366 ....E7
72159 Steprock 600 ....G3
72469 Strawberry 280 ....H2
71765 Strong 785 ....F7
72160 Stuttgart⊙ 10,941 .....H4
72865 Subiaco 744 ....C3
72470 Success 223 ....J1
72579 Sulphur Rock 316 ......H2
72768 Sulphur Springs 496 ...B1
72677 Summit 506 ....E1
72471 Swifton 859 ....H2
71861 Taylor 657 ....D7
55502 Texarkana⊙ 21,459 ....C7
    Texarkana‡ 127,019 ...C7
71766 Thornton 711 ....F6
71766 Tichnor 350 ....H5
71670 Tillar 280 ....H6
71767 Tinsman 112 ....F6
71851 Tollette 407 ....C6

72770 Tontitown 615 ....B1
72167 Traskwood 459 ....E5
72472 Trumann 6,405 ....J2
72168 Tucker 375 ....G5
72473 Tuckerman 2,078 ......H2
†72015 Tull 281 ....E5
72169 Tupelo 248 ....H3
72384 Turrell 1,041 ....K3
72386 Tyronza 777 ....K3
72170 Ulm 201 ....H4
71768 Urbana 500 ....E7
72682 Valley Springs 190 ....D1
72956 Van Buren⊙ 12,020 ...B3
71972 Vandervoort 98 ....B5
72370 Victoria 175 ....K2
72173 Vilonia 736 ....F3
†72002 Vimy Ridge 600 ....F4
72583 Viola 362 ....G1

Arkansas

SCALE

| 0 | 5 | 10 | 20 | 30 | 40 MI. |
| 0 | 5 | 10 | 20 | 30 | 40 KM. |

State Capitals ....⊛
County Seats ....⊙
Major Limited Access Hwys. ━━━

Scale 1:1,840,000

© Copyright HAMMOND INCORPORATED, Maplewood, N.J.

California

SCALE

State Capitals ⊛
County Seats ◉
Canals
Major Limited Access Hwys
Scale 1:4,400,000

San Francisco
and Vicinity

Sacramento
and Vicinity

Los Angeles
and Vicinity

© Copyright HAMMOND INCORPORATED, Maplewood, N.J.

AREA 158,706 sq. mi. (411,049 sq. km.)
POPULATION 23,667,565
CAPITAL Sacramento
LARGEST CITY Los Angeles
HIGHEST POINT Mt. Whitney 14,494 ft. (4418 m.)
SETTLED IN 1769
ADMITTED TO UNION September 9, 1850
POPULAR NAME Golden State
STATE FLOWER Golden Poppy
STATE BIRD California Valley Quail

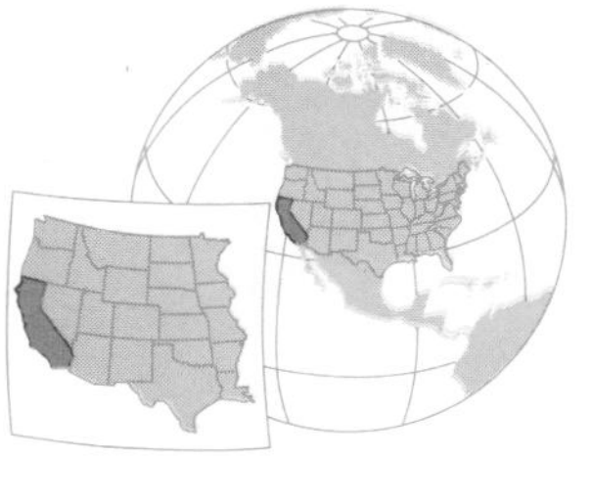

COUNTIES

Alameda 1,105,379 .... D6
Alpine 1,097 .... F5
Amador 19,314 .... E5
Butte 143,851 .... D4
Calaveras 20,710 .... E5
Colusa 12,791 .... C4
Contra Costa 656,380 .... D6
Del Norte 18,217 .... B2
El Dorado 85,812 .... E5
Fresno 514,229 .... E7
Glenn 21,350 .... C4
Humboldt 108,514 .... B3
Imperial 92,110 .... K10
Inyo 17,895 .... H7
Kern 403,089 .... G8
Kings 73,738 .... G8
Lake 36,366 .... C4
Lassen 21,661 .... E3
Los Angeles 7,477,503 .... G9
Madera 63,116 .... F6
Marin 222,592 .... C5
Mariposa 11,108 .... E6
Mendocino 66,738 .... B4
Merced 134,558 .... E6
Modoc 8,610 .... E2
Mono 8,577 .... F5
Monterey 290,444 .... D7
Napa 99,199 .... C5
Nevada 51,645 .... E4
Orange 1,932,709 .... H10
Placer 117,247 .... E4
Plumas 17,340 .... E4
Riverside 663,199 .... J10
Sacramento 783,381 .... D5
San Benito 25,005 .... D7
San Bernardino 895,016 .... J9
San Diego 1,861,846 .... J10
San Francisco (city county) 678,974 .... J2
San Joaquin 347,342 .... D6
San Luis Obispo 155,435 .... E8
San Mateo 587,329 .... J3
Santa Barbara 298,694 .... E9
Santa Clara 1,295,071 .... D6
Santa Cruz 188,141 .... C6
Shasta 115,715 .... C3
Sierra 3,073 .... E4
Siskiyou 39,732 .... C2
Solano 235,203 .... D5
Sonoma 299,681 .... C5
Stanislaus 265,900 .... D6
Sutter 52,246 .... D4
Tehama 38,888 .... C3
Trinity 11,858 .... B3
Tulare 245,738 .... G7
Tuolumne 33,928 .... F5
Ventura 529,174 .... F9
Yolo 113,374 .... D5
Yuba 49,733 .... D4

CITIES and TOWNS

Zip *Name/Pop.* *Key*

94501 Alameda 63,852 .... J2
94507 Alamo 8,505 .... K2
94706 Albany 15,130 .... J2
*91801 Alhambra 64,615 .... C10
92001 Alpine 5,368 .... J11
91001 Altadena 40,983 .... C10
96101 Alturas⊙ 3,025 .... E2
†95116 Alum Rock 16,890 .... L3
*92801 Anaheim 219,494 .... D11
Anaheim-Santa Ana-Garden Grove‡ 1,931,570 .... D11
96007 Anderson 7,381 .... C3
95222 Angels Camp 2,302 .... E5
94508 Angwin 3,526 .... C5
94509 Antioch 42,683 .... L1
92307 Apple Valley 14,305 .... H9
95003 Aptos 7,039 .... K4
91006 Arcadia 45,994 .... C10
95521 Arcata 12,850 .... A3
95825 Arden-Arcade 87,570 .... B8
93420 Arroyo Grande 11,290 .... E8
90701 Artesia 14,301 .... C11
93203 Arvin 6,863 .... G8
†94577 Ashland 13,983 .... K2
95413 Asti 75 .... C5
93422 Atascadero 16,232 .... E8
94025 Atherton 7,797 .... K3
95301 Atwater 17,530 .... E6
95603 Auburn⊙ 7,540 .... C8
90704 Avalon 2,022 .... G10
93204 Avenal 4,137 .... E8
91702 Azusa 29,380 .... D10
*93301 Bakersfield⊙ 105,735 .... G8
Bakersfield‡ 403,089 .... G8
91706 Baldwin Park 50,554 .... D10
92220 Banning 14,020 .... J10
92311 Barstow 17,690 .... H9
†93402 Baywood Park-Los Osos 10,933 .... E8
92223 Beaumont 6,818 .... J10
90201 Bell 25,450 .... C11
90706 Bellflower 53,441 .... C11
90201 Bell Gardens 34,117 .... C11
94002 Belmont 24,505 .... J3
94510 Benicia 15,376 .... K1
95005 Ben Lomond 7,238 .... K4
*94701 Berkeley 103,328 .... J2
*90210 Beverly Hills 32,367 .... B10
92315 Big Bear Lake J9
93920 Big Sur 500 .... D7
93514 Bishop 3,333 .... G6
92316 Bloomington 18,888 .... E10
92225 Blythe 6,805 .... L10
94923 Bodega Bay 800 .... B5
93516 Boron 2,040 .... H8
92004 Borrego Springs 1,405 .... J10
95006 Boulder Creek 5,662 .... J4
92227 Brawley 14,946 .... K11
92621 Brea 27,913 .... D11
94513 Brentwood 4,434 .... L2
93517 Bridgeport⊙ 525 .... F5
94005 Brisbane 2,969 .... J2
95605 Broderick-Bryte 10,194 .... B8
*90622 Buena Park 64,165 .... D11
*91501 Burbank 84,625 .... C10
94010 Burlingame 26,173 .... J2
96013 Burney 3,187 .... D3
92231 Calexico 14,412 .... K11
93505 California City 2,743 .... H8
94515 Calistoga 3,879 .... C5
93745 Calwa 6,640 .... F7
93010 Camarillo 37,797 .... F9
95008 Campbell 26,910 .... K3
*91303 Canoga Park B10
92624 Capistrano Beach 6,168 .... H10
95010 Capitola 9,095 .... K4
92007 Cardiff-by-the-Sea 10,054 .... H10
92008 Carlsbad 35,490 .... H10
93923 Carmel 4,707 .... D7
93924 Carmel Valley 4,013 .... D7
95608 Carmichael 43,108 .... C8
93013 Carpinteria 10,835 .... F9
90745 Carson 81,221 .... C11
94546 Castro Valley 44,011 .... K2
95012 Castroville 4,396 .... D7
92234 Cathedral City 4,130 .... J10
96019 Central Valley 3,424 .... C3
95307 Ceres 13,281 .... D6
†90701 Cerritos 53,020 .... C11
†94541 Cherryland 9,425 .... K2
95926 Chico 26,603 .... D4
Chico‡ 143,851 .... D4
†93555 China Lake 4,275 .... H8
95309 Chinese Camp 150 .... E6
91710 Chino 40,165 .... D10
93610 Chowchilla 5,122 .... E6
*92010 Chula Vista 83,927 .... J11
95610 Citrus Heights 85,911 .... C8
91711 Claremont 30,950 .... D10
95425 Cloverdale 3,989 .... B5
93612 Clovis 33,021 .... F7
92236 Coachella 9,129 .... J10
93210 Coalinga 6,593 .... E7
95713 Colfax 981 .... E4
92324 Colton 15,201 .... E10
95932 Colusa⊙ 4,075 .... C4
90040 Commerce 10,509 .... C10
*90220 Compton 81,286 .... C11
*94520 Concord 103,255 .... K1
93212 Corcoran 6,454 .... F7
96021 Corning 4,745 .... C4
91720 Corona 37,791 .... E11
92118 Coronado 18,790 .... H11
94925 Corte Madera 8,074 .... J2
*92626 Costa Mesa 82,562 .... D11
94928 Cotati 3,346 .... C5
*91722 Covina 33,751 .... D10
95531 Crescent City⊙ 3,075 .... A2
92325 Crestline 6,715 .... H9
90201 Cudahy 17,984 .... C11
90230 Culver City 38,139 .... B10
95014 Cupertino 34,265 .... K3
93615 Cutler 3,149 .... F7
90630 Cypress 40,391 .... D11
*94014 Daly City 78,519 .... H2
92629 Dana Point 10,602 .... H10
94526 Danville 26,446 .... K2
95616 Davis 36,640 .... B8
93215 Delano 16,491 .... F8
95315 Delhi 2,832 .... E6
92014 Del Mar 5,017 .... H11
92240 Desert Hot Springs 5,941 .... J9
93618 Dinuba 9,907 .... F7
95620 Dixon 7,541 .... B9
93620 Dos Palos 3,121 .... E6
*90240 Downey 82,602 .... C11
95936 Downieville⊙ 500 .... E4
91010 Duarte 16,766 .... D10
94566 Dublin 13,496 .... K2
93219 Earlimart 4,578 .... F8
90022 East Los Angeles 100,017 .... C10
*92020 El Cajon 73,892 .... J11
92243 El Centro⊙ 23,996 .... K11
94530 El Cerrito 22,731 .... J2
95630 El Dorado Hills 3,453 .... C8
94018 El Granada 3,582 .... H3
95624 Elk Grove 10,959 .... B9
*91731 El Monte 79,494 .... D10
†93030 El Rio 5,674 .... F9
90245 El Segundo 13,752 .... B11
92630 El Toro 38,153 .... E11
94608 Emeryville 3,714 .... J2
92024 Encinitas 10,796 .... H10
91316 Encino B10
95320 Escalon 3,127 .... E6
*92025 Escondido 64,355 .... J10
95501 Eureka⊙ 24,153 .... A3
93221 Exeter 5,606 .... F7
94930 Fairfax 7,391 .... H1
94533 Fairfield⊙ 58,099 .... K1
95628 Fair Oaks 22,602 .... C8
92028 Fallbrook 14,041 .... H10
93223 Farmersville 5,544 .... F7
95018 Felton 4,564 .... K4
93015 Fillmore 9,602 .... G9
93622 Firebaugh 3,740 .... E7
95828 Florin 16,523 .... B8
95630 Folsom 11,003 .... C8
92335 Fontana 37,107 .... E10
†93268 Ford City 3,392 .... F8
95437 Fort Bragg 5,019 .... B4
†95421 Fort Ross 30 .... B5
95540 Fortuna 7,591 .... A3
94404 Foster City 23,287 .... J2
92708 Fountain Valley 55,080 .... D11
95019 Freedom 6,416 .... L4
*94536 Fremont 131,945 .... K3
*93706 Fresno⊙ 217,289 .... F7
Fresno‡ 515,013 .... F7
*92631 Fullerton 102,034 .... D11
95632 Galt 5,514 .... C9
*90747 Gardena 45,165 .... C11
*92640 Garden Grove 123,307 .... D11
95020 Gilroy 21,641 .... D6
92509 Glen Avon Heights 8,444 .... E10
*91201 Glendale 139,060 .... C10
91740 Glendora 38,500 .... D10
93926 Gonzales 2,891 .... D7
91344 Granada Hills B10
92324 Grand Terrace 8,498 .... E10
95945 Grass Valley 6,697 .... D4
93308 Greenacres 5,381 .... F8
93927 Greenfield 4,181 .... D7
95948 Gridley 3,982 .... D4
93433 Grover City 8,827 .... E8
93434 Guadalupe 3,629 .... E9
95322 Gustine 3,142 .... D6
94019 Half Moon Bay 7,282 .... H3
93230 Hanford⊙ 20,958 .... F7
90250 Hawthorne 56,447 .... C11
*94541 Hayward 94,342 .... K2
95448 Healdsburg 7,217 .... B5
92343 Hemet 22,454 .... H10
94547 Hercules 5,963 .... J1
90254 Hermosa Beach 18,070 .... B11
92345 Hesperia 13,540 .... H9
92346 Highland 10,908 .... H9
94010 Hillsborough 10,372 .... J2
95023 Hollister⊙ 11,488 .... D7
90028 Hollywood C10
92250 Holtville 4,399 .... K11
†91720 Home Gardens 5,783 .... E11
95326 Hughson 2,943 .... E6
*92646 Huntington Beach 170,505 .... C11
90255 Huntington Park 46,223 .... C11
92251 Imperial 3,451 .... K11
92032 Imperial Beach 22,689 .... H11
93526 Independence⊙ 748 .... H7
92201 Indio 21,611 .... J10
*90301 Inglewood 94,245 .... B11
92713 Irvine 62,134 .... D11
95642 Jackson⊙ 2,331 .... C9
†94701 Kensington 5,342 .... J2
93600 Kerman 4,002 .... E7
93930 King City 5,495 .... D7
93631 Kingsburg 5,115 .... F7
91011 La Canada 20,153 .... C10
91214 La Crescenta-Montrose 16,531 .... C10
94549 Lafayette 20,879 .... K2
*92651 Laguna Beach 17,901 .... G10
92653 Laguna Hills 33,600 .... D11
92677 Laguna Niguel 12,237 .... H10
90631 La Habra 45,232 .... D11
92037 La Jolla H11
92352 Lake Arrowhead 6,272 .... H9
92330 Lake Elsinore 5,982 .... F11
93240 Lake Isabella 3,428 .... G8
95453 Lakeport⊙ 3,675 .... C4
*90712 Lakewood 74,654 .... C11
92041 La Mesa 50,308 .... H11
90638 La Mirada 40,986 .... D11
93241 Lamont 9,616 .... G8
93534 Lancaster 48,027 .... G9
*91744 La Puente 30,882 .... D10
94939 Larkspur 11,064 .... H1
95330 Lathrop 3,717 .... D6
91750 La Verne 23,508 .... D10
90260 Lawndale 23,460 .... B11
92045 Lemon Grove 20,780 .... J11
93245 Lemoore 8,832 .... F7
†92311 Lenwood 2,974 .... H9
92024 Leucadia 9,478 .... H10
95648 Lincoln 4,132 .... B8
†95901 Linda 10,225 .... D4
93247 Lindsay 6,924 .... F7
95953 Live Oak 3,103 .... D4
†95073 Live Oak 11,482 .... K4
94550 Livermore 48,349 .... L2
95334 Livingston 5,326 .... E6
95240 Lodi 35,221 .... C9
92354 Loma Linda 10,694 .... F10
90717 Lomita 18,807 .... C11
93436 Lompoc 26,267 .... E9
*90801 Long Beach 361,334 .... C11
90720 Los Alamitos 11,529 .... D11
94022 Los Altos 25,769 .... K3
94022 Los Altos Hills 7,421 .... J3
*90001 Los Angeles⊙ 2,966,850 .... C10
Los Angeles-Long Beach‡ 7,477,657 .... C10
93635 Los Banos 10,341 .... E6
95030 Los Gatos 26,906 .... K4
†93402 Los Osos-Baywood Park 10,933 .... E8
90262 Lynwood 48,548 .... C11
93637 Madera⊙ 21,732 .... E7
90265 Malibu B10
93546 Mammoth Lakes 3,929 .... G6
90266 Manhattan Beach 31,542 .... B11
95336 Manteca 24,925 .... D6
93933 Marina 20,647 .... D7
95338 Mariposa⊙ 1,150 .... F6
94553 Martinez⊙ 22,582 .... K1
95901 Marysville⊙ 9,898 .... D4
90201 Maywood 21,810 .... C10
93250 McFarland 5,151 .... F8
93023 Meiners Oaks-Mira Monte 9,512 .... F9
93640 Mendota 5,038 .... E7
94025 Menlo Park 26,369 .... J3
95340 Merced⊙ 36,499 .... E6
94030 Millbrae 20,058 .... J2
94941 Mill Valley 12,967 .... H2
95035 Milpitas 37,820 .... L3
91752 Mira Loma 8,707 .... E10
92691 Mission Viejo 50,666 .... D11
*95350 Modesto⊙ 106,602 .... D6
Modesto‡ 265,902 .... D6
93501 Mojave 2,886 .... G8
91016 Monrovia 30,531 .... D10
91763 Montclair 22,628 .... D10
90640 Montebello 52,929 .... C10
93940 Monterey 27,558 .... D7
91754 Monterey Park 54,338 .... C10
95030 Monte Sereno 3,434 .... K4
91214 Montrose-La Crescenta 16,531 .... C10
93021 Moorpark 4,030 .... G9
94556 Moraga 15,014 .... K2
95037 Morgan Hill 17,060 .... L4
93442 Morro Bay 9,064 .... D8
*94042 Mountain View 58,655 .... K3
96067 Mount Shasta 2,837 .... C5
92405 Muscoy 6,188 .... E10
94558 Napa⊙ 50,879 .... C5
92050 National City 48,772 .... J11
92363 Needles 4,120 .... L9
95959 Nevada City⊙ 2,431 .... D4
94560 Newark 32,126 .... K3
91321 Newhall 12,029 .... G9
95360 Newman 2,785 .... D6
*92660 Newport Beach 62,556 .... D11
93444 Nipomo 5,247 .... E8
91760 Norco 21,126 .... E11
95660 North Highlands 37,825 .... B8
*91601 North Hollywood B10
90650 Norwalk 85,286 .... C11
94947 Novato 43,916 .... H1
95361 Oakdale 8,474 .... E6
*94601 Oakland⊙ 339,337 .... J2
93022 Oak View 4,671 .... F9
93445 Oceano 4,478 .... E8
92054 Oceanside 76,698 .... H10
93308 Oildale 23,382 .... F8
93023 Ojai 6,816 .... F9
*91761 Ontario 88,820 .... D10
†95060 Opal Cliffs 5,041 .... K4
*92666 Orange 91,450 .... D11
93646 Orange Cove 4,026 .... F7
94563 Orinda 16,825 .... J2
95963 Orland 4,031 .... C4
93647 Orosi 4,076 .... F7
95965 Oroville⊙ 8,683 .... D4
93030 Oxnard 108,195 .... F9
Oxnard-Simi Valley-Ventura‡ 529,899 .... F9
94553 Pacheco-Vine Hill 6,129 .... K1
94044 Pacifica 36,866 .... H2
93950 Pacific Grove 15,755 .... C7
93550 Palmdale 12,277 .... G9
92260 Palm Desert 11,801 .... J10
92262 Palm Springs 32,366 .... J10
*94301 Palo Alto 55,225 .... K3
90274 Palos Verdes Estates 14,376 .... B11
95969 Paradise 22,571 .... D4
90723 Paramount 36,407 .... C11
93648 Parlier 2,902 .... F7
*91101 Pasadena 118,072 .... C10
93446 Paso Robles 9,163 .... E8
95363 Patterson 3,908 .... D6
93953 Pebble Beach C7
92370 Perris 6,827 .... F11
94952 Petaluma 33,834 .... H1
90660 Pico Rivera 53,387 .... C10
94611 Piedmont 10,498 .... J2
94564 Pinole 14,253 .... J1
93449 Pismo Beach 5,364 .... E8
94565 Pittsburg 33,034 .... L1
92670 Placentia 35,041 .... D11
95667 Placerville⊙ 6,739 .... C8
94523 Pleasant Hill 25,124 .... K2
94566 Pleasanton 35,160 .... L2
*91766 Pomona 92,742 .... D10
93257 Porterville 19,707 .... G7
93041 Port Hueneme 17,803 .... F9
94025 Portola Valley 3,939 .... J3
92064 Poway 32,263 .... J11
93534 Quartz Hill 7,421 .... G9
95971 Quincy⊙ 4,451 .... E4
92065 Ramona 8,173 .... J10
95670 Rancho Cordova 42,881 .... C8
91730 Rancho Cucamonga 55,250 .... E10
92270 Rancho Mirage 6,281 .... J10
90274 Rancho Palos Verdes 36,577 .... B11
92067 Rancho Santa Fe 4,014 .... H10
96080 Red Bluff⊙ 9,490 .... C3
96001 Redding⊙ 41,995 .... C3
Redding○ 80
92373 Redlands 43,619 .... H9
*90277 Redondo Beach 57,102 .... B11
*94061 Redwood City⊙ 54,951 .... J3
93654 Reedley 11,071 .... F7
92376 Rialto 37,474 .... E10
*94801 Richmond 74,676 .... J1
93555 Ridgecrest 15,929 .... H8
95562 Rio Dell 2,687 .... A3
95673 Rio Linda 7,359 .... B8
94571 Rio Vista 3,142 .... L1
95366 Ripon 3,509 .... D6
95367 Riverbank 5,695 .... E6
*92501 Riverside⊙ 170,591 .... E11
Riverside-San Bernardino-Ontario‡ 1,557,080 .... E11
95677 Rocklin 7,344 .... B8
94572 Rodeo 8,286 .... J1
94928 Rohnert Park 22,965 .... C5
90274 Rolling Hills 2,049 .... B11
90274 Rolling Hills Estates 7,701 .... B11
91770 Rosemead 42,604 .... C10
95678 Roseville 24,347 .... B8
94957 Ross 2,801 .... H1
92509 Rubidoux 17,048 .... E10

(continued on following page)

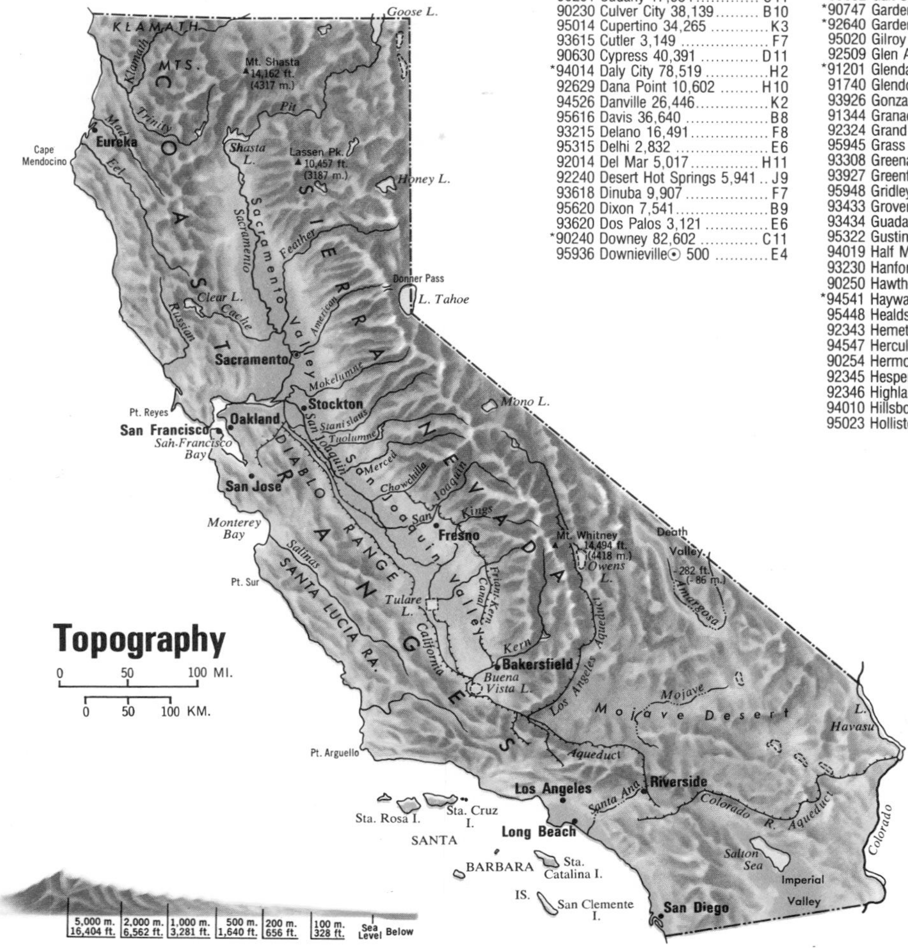
Goose L.
KLAMATH
MTS.
Mt. Shasta 14,162 ft. (4317 m.)
Pit
Trinity
Eureka
Cape Mendocino
Shasta L.
Lassen Pk.
Honey L.
Sacramento
Feather
Clear L.
Donner Pass
L. Tahoe
Sacramento
Pt. Reyes
Oakland
Stockton
San Francisco
San Francisco Bay
Mono L.
San Jose
Monterey Bay
Fresno
Mt. Whitney 14,494 ft. (4418 m.)
Death Valley
Pt. Sur
Tulare L.
Kern
Bakersfield
Buena Vista L.
Mojave Desert
Pt. Arguello
L. Havasu
Aqueduct
Los Angeles
Riverside
Sta. Rosa I.
Sta. Cruz I.
Long Beach
SANTA BARBARA
Sta. Catalina I.
IS.
San Clemente I.
Salton Sea
Imperial Valley
San Diego
Colorado
Topography
0 50 100 MI.
0 50 100 KM.
5,000 m. 16,404 ft.
2,000 m. 6,562 ft.
1,000 m. 3,281 ft.
500 m. 1,640 ft.
200 m. 656 ft.
100 m. 328 ft.
Sea Level
Below

(continued)

*95801 Sacramento (cap.)⊙ 275,741 .... B8
Sacramento‡ 1,014,002 .... B8
94574 Saint Helena 4,898 .... C5
93901 Salinas⊙ 80,479 .... D7
Salinas-Seaside-Monterey‡ 290,444 .... D7
95249 San Andreas⊙ 1,912 .... E5
94960 San Anselmo 12,067 .... H1
*92401 San Bernardino⊙ 118,794 .... E10
94066 San Bruno 35,417 .... J2
94070 San Carlos 24,710 .... J3
92672 San Clemente 27,325 .... H10
*92101 San Diego⊙ 875,538 .... H11
San Diego‡ 1,861,846 .... H11
91773 San Dimas 24,014 .... D10
*91340 San Fernando 17,731 .... C10
*94101 San Francisco⊙ 678,974 .... H2
San Francisco-Oakland‡ 3,252,721 .... H2
*91775 San Gabriel 30,072 .... C10
93657 Sanger 12,542 .... F7
92383 San Jacinto 7,098 .... H10
*95101 San Jose⊙ 629,546 .... L3
San Jose‡ 1,295,071 .... L3
†92691 San Juan Capistrano 18,959 .... H10
*94577 San Leandro 63,952 .... J2
94580 San Lorenzo 20,545 .... K2
93401 San Luis Obispo⊙ 34,252 .... E8
92069 San Marcos 17,479 .... H10
91108 San Marino 13,307 .... D10
*94401 San Mateo 77,640 .... J3
94806 San Pablo 19,750 .... J1
94964 San Quentin 450 .... H1
*94901 San Rafael⊙ 44,700 .... J1
94583 San Ramon 22,356 .... K2
93452 San Simeon 350 .... D8
*92701 Santa Ana⊙ 204,023 .... D11
*93101 Santa Barbara⊙ 74,414 .... F9
Santa Barbara-Santa Maria-Lompoc‡ 298,660 .... F9
*95050 Santa Clara 87,700 .... K3
*95060 Santa Cruz⊙ 41,483 .... K4
Santa Cruz‡ 188,141 .... K4
90670 Santa Fe Springs 14,520 .... C11
93454 Santa Maria 39,685 .... E9
*90401 Santa Monica 88,314 .... B10
93060 Santa Paula 20,552 .... F9
*95401 Santa Rosa⊙ 83,320 .... C5
Santa Rosa‡ 299,827 .... C5
92071 Santee 47,080 .... J11
95070 Saratoga 29,261 .... K4
94965 Sausalito 7,338 .... H2
95060 Scotts Valley 6,891 .... K4
90740 Seal Beach 25,975 .... C11
93955 Seaside 36,567 .... D7
95472 Sebastopol 5,595 .... C5
93662 Selma 10,942 .... F7
93263 Shafter 7,010 .... F8
96125 Sierra City 500 .... E4
91024 Sierra Madre 10,837 .... D10
†90806 Signal Hill 5,734 .... C11
*93065 Simi Valley 77,500 .... G9
92075 Solana Beach 13,047 .... H11
93960 Soledad 5,928 .... D7
93463 Solvang 3,091 .... E9
95476 Sonoma 6,054 .... C5
95370 Sonora⊙ 3,247 .... E6
95073 Soquel 6,212 .... K4
91733 South El Monte 16,623 .... C10
90280 South Gate 66,784 .... C11
95705 South Lake Tahoe 20,681 .... F5
†95965 South Oroville 7,246 .... D4
91030 South Pasadena 22,681 .... C10
94080 South San Francisco 49,393 .... J2
94305 Stanford 11,045 .... J3
90680 Stanton 23,723 .... D11
*95201 Stockton⊙ 149,779 .... D6
Stocton‡ 347,342 .... D6
94585 Suisun City 11,087 .... K1
92381 Sun City 8,460 .... F11
92388 Sunnymead 11,554 .... F11
*94086 Sunnyvale 106,618 .... K3
96130 Susanville⊙ 6,520 .... E3
95685 Sutter Creek 1,705 .... C9
93268 Taft 5,316 .... F8
95730 Tahoe City E4
93561 Tehachapi 4,126 .... G8
91780 Temple City 28,972 .... D10
†95965 Thermalito 4,961 .... D4
*91360 Thousand Oaks 77,072 .... G9
92276 Thousand Palms 1,718 .... J10
94920 Tiburon 6,685 .... J2
90290 Topanga B10
*90501 Torrance 129,881 .... C11
95376 Tracy 18,428 .... D6
93274 Tulare 22,526 .... F7
95380 Turlock 26,287 .... E6
92680 Tustin 32,317 .... D11
92277 Twentynine Palms 7,465 .... K9
†95060 Twin Lakes 4,502 .... K4
95482 Ukiah⊙ 12,035 .... B4
94587 Union City 39,406 .... K2
91786 Upland 47,647 .... E10
95688 Vacaville 43,367 .... D5
91355 Valencia 12,163 .... G9
94590 Vallejo 80,303 .... J1
Vallejo-Fairfield-Napa‡ 334,402 .... J1
*91401 Van Nuys B10
90291 Venice B11
*93001 Ventura⊙ 74,393 .... F9
92392 Victorville 14,220 .... H9
92667 Villa Park 7,137 .... D11
93277 Visalia⊙ 49,729 .... F7
Visalia-Tulare-Porterville‡ 245,738 .... F7
92083 Vista 35,834 .... H10
91789 Walnut 12,478 .... D10
*94595 Walnut Creek 53,643 .... K2
93280 Wasco 9,613 .... F8
95386 Waterford 2,683 .... E6
95076 Watsonville 23,663 .... D7
96093 Weaverville⊙ 2,787 .... B3
96094 Weed 2,879 .... C2
*91790 West Covina 80,291 .... D10
†90069 West Hollywood 35,703 .... B10
90025 West Los Angeles B10
92683 Westminster 71,133 .... D11
†90047 Westmont 27,916 .... C11
†94565 West Pittsburg 8,773 .... K1
95691 West Sacramento 10,875 .... B8
*90601 Whittier 69,717 .... D11
95490 Willits 4,008 .... B4
95988 Willows⊙ 4,777 .... C4
*90744 Wilmington C11
95388 Winton 4,995 .... E6
93286 Woodlake 4,343 .... G7
95695 Woodland⊙ 30,235 .... B8
*91364 Woodland Hills B10
94062 Woodside 5,291 .... J3
95697 Yolo 600 .... B8
92686 Yorba Linda 28,254 .... D11
94599 Yountville 2,893 .... C5
96097 Yreka⊙ 5,916 .... C2
95991 Yuba City⊙ 18,736 .... D4
Yuba City‡ 101,979 .... D4
92399 Yucaipa 23,345 .... J9
92284 Yucca Valley 8,294 .... J9

OTHER FEATURES

Agua Caliente Ind. Res. J10
Alameda (creek) K3
Alamo (riv.) K10
Alcatraz (isl.) J2
Alkali (lkes) E2
All American (canal) K11
Almanor (lake) D3
Amargosa (range) J7
Amargosa (riv.) J7
American (riv.) C8
Anacapa (isl.) F10
Angel (isl.) J2
Ano Nuevo (pt.) J4
Arena (pt.) B5
Arguello (pt.) E9
Argus (range) H7
Arroyo del Valle (dry riv.) L3
Arroyo Hondo (dry riv.) L3
Arroyo Mocho (dry riv.) L2
Arroyo Seco (dry riv.) K10
Beale A.F.B. D4
Berryessa (lake) D5
Bethany (res.) L2
Big Sage (res.) E2
Black Butte (lake) C4
Bodega (bay) B5
Bonita (pt.) H2
Bristol (lake) K9
Buchon (pt.) D8
Buena Vista (lake) F8
Cabrillo Nat'l Mon. H11
Cachuma (lake) F9
Cadiz (lake) K9
Cahuilla Ind. Res. J10
Calaveras (res.) L3
California Aqueduct E7
Camanche (res.) C9
Camp Pendleton 10,017 .... H10
Campo Ind. Res. J11
Capitan Grande Ind. Res. J11
Cascade (range) D1
Castle A.F.B. E6
Channel Islands Nat'l Park E11
China Lake Naval Weapons Center H8
Chemehuevi Valley Ind. Res. L9
Chocolate (mts.) K10
Clair Engle (lake) C3
Clear (lake) C4
Clear Lake (res.) D2
Coachella (canal) K10
Coast (ranges) D7
Colorado (riv.) L8
Colorado River Aqueduct K10
Colorado River Ind. Res. L10
Conception (pt.) E9
Cooper (pt.) D7
Copco (lake) C2
Cosumnes (riv.) C9
Cottonwood (creek) C3
Coyote (res.) L4
Crowley (lake) G6
Crystal Springs (res.) J3
Cuyama (riv.) E8
Cuyapaipe Ind. Res. J11
Danby (lake) K9
Death (valley) H7
Death Valley Nat'l Mon. H7
Delgada (pt.) A3
Del Valle (lake) L3
Devils Postpile Nat'l Mon. F6
Donner (pass) E4
Dume (pt.) G10
Duxbury (pt.) H2
Eagle (lake) E3
Eagle (peak) E2
Eagle Crags (mt.) J8
Edison (lake) F6
Edwards A.F.B. 8,554 .... H9
Eel (riv.) B4
Elsinore (lake) E11
El Toro Marine Air Sta. 7,632 .... D11
Estero (bay) D8
Estero (pt.) D8
Estrella (riv.) E8
Eugene O'Neill Nat'l Hist. Site K2
Farallon (isls.) B6
Farallons, The (gulf) H2
Feather (riv.) D4
Florence (lake) G6
Folsom (lake) C8
Fort Bidwell Ind. Res. E2
Fort Hunter Liggett D8
Fort Independence Ind. Res. G7
Fort MacArthur C11
Fort Mohave Ind. Res. L9
Fort Ord D7
Fort Point Nat'l Hist. Site J2
Freel (peak) F5

Agriculture, Industry and Resources

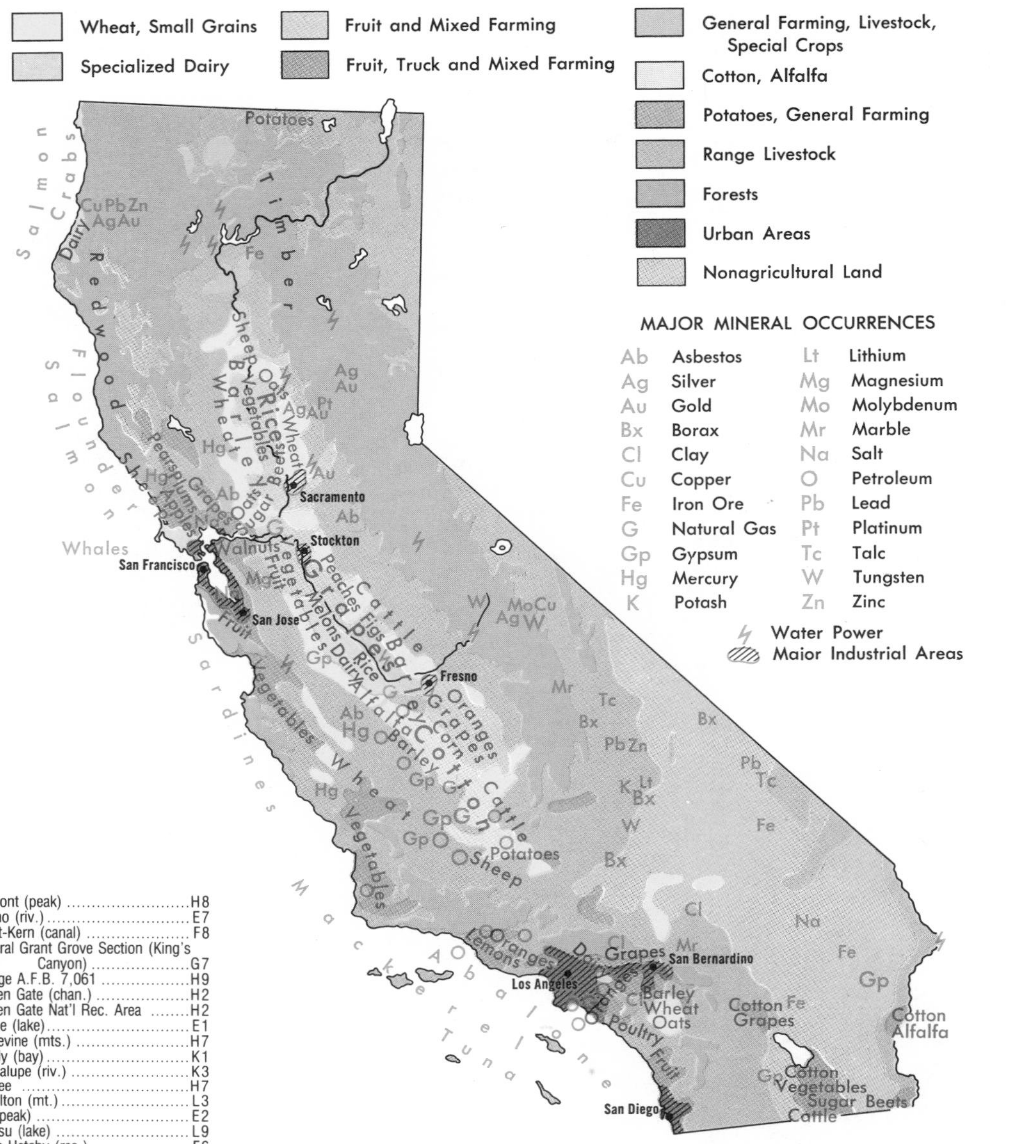
DOMINANT LAND USE
Wheat, Small Grains
Fruit and Mixed Farming
General Farming, Livestock, Special Crops
Specialized Dairy
Fruit, Truck and Mixed Farming
Cotton, Alfalfa
Potatoes, General Farming
Range Livestock
Forests
Urban Areas
Nonagricultural Land
MAJOR MINERAL OCCURRENCES
Ab Asbestos
Ag Silver
Au Gold
Bx Borax
Cl Clay
Cu Copper
Fe Iron Ore
G Natural Gas
Gp Gypsum
Hg Mercury
K Potash
Lt Lithium
Mg Magnesium
Mo Molybdenum
Mr Marble
Na Salt
O Petroleum
Pb Lead
Pt Platinum
Tc Talc
W Tungsten
Zn Zinc
Water Power
Major Industrial Areas
Sacramento
Stockton
San Francisco
San Jose
Fresno
Los Angeles
San Bernardino
San Diego
Whales
Salmon
Crabs
Flounder
Sardines
Mackerel
Albacore
Tuna
Potatoes
Timber
Redwood
Dairy
Sheep
Rice
Barley
Wheat
Oats
Vegetables
Pears
Plums
Apples
Grapes
Walnuts
Fruit
Peaches
Figs
Melons
Dairy
Alfalfa
Cattle
Cotton
Oranges
Lemons
Poultry
Sugar Beets

Fremont (peak) H8
Fresno (riv.) E7
Friant-Kern (canal) F8
General Grant Grove Section (King's Canyon) G7
George A.F.B. 7,061 .... H9
Golden Gate (chan.) H2
Golden Gate Nat'l Rec. Area H2
Goose (lake) E1
Grapevine (mts.) H7
Grizzly (bay) K1
Guadalupe (riv.) K3
Haiwee H7
Hamilton (mt.) L3
Hat (peak) E2
Havasu (lake) L9
Hetch Hetchy (res.) F6
Hoffman (mt.) D2
Honey (lake) E3
Hoopa Valley Ind. Res. A2
Humboldt (bay) A3
Imperial (res.) L10
Imperial (valley) K10
Ingalls (mt.) E3
Inyo (mts.) G6
Iron Gate (res.) C2
Isabella (lake) G8
John Muir Nat'l Hist. Site K1
Joshua Tree Nat'l Mon. J10
Kern (riv.) G8
Kings (riv.) F7
Kings Canyon Nat'l Park G7
Klamath (riv.) B2
Laguna (res.) L11
La Jolla Ind. Res. J10
Lassen (peak) D3
Lassen Volcanic Nat'l Park D3
Lava Beds Nat'l Mon. D2
Lemoore N.A.S. 5,888 .... F7
Leroy Anderson (res.) L4
Lopez (pt.) D7
Los Angeles Aqueduct G8
Los Coyotes Ind. Res. J10
Lost (riv.) D1
Lower Alkali (lake) E2
Lower Klamath (lake) D2
Mad (riv.) B3
Manzanita Ind. Res. J11
March A.F.B. 3,607 .... E11
Mare Island Navy Yard J1
Mather A.F.B. 5,245 .... C8
Mathews (lake) E11
McClellan A.F.B. B8
McClure (lake) E6
Mendocino (cape) A3
Merced (riv.) E6
Middle Alkali (lake) E2
Mill (creek) D3
Millerton (lake) F6
Moffett Nav. Air Sta. K3
Mojave (des.) H9
Mojave (riv.) J9
Mokelumne (riv.) C9
Mono (lake) G5
Monterey (bay) K4
Moon (lake) E2
Morongo Ind. Res. J10
Mountain Meadows (res.) E3
Muir Woods Nat'l Mon. H2
Nacimiento (riv.) D8
Navarro (riv.) B4
Nevada, Sierra (mts.) E4
New (riv.) K11
Norton A.F.B. F10
Noyo (riv.) B4
Oakland Army Base J2
Old (riv.) L1
Oroville (lake) D4
Owens (lake) H7
Owens (peak) H8
Owens (riv.) G6
Oxnard A.F.B. F9
Paiute Ind. Res. G6
Pala Ind. Res. H10
Palomar (mt.) J10
Panamint (range) H7
Panamint (valley) H7
Pescadero (pt.) J3
Piedras Blancas (pt.) D8
Pillar (pt.) H3
Pillsbury (lake) C4
Pine (creek) D3
Pine Flat (lake) F7
Pinnacles Nat'l Mon. D7
Pit (riv.) D2
Point Mugu Pacific Missile Test Center F9
Point Reyes Nat'l Seashore H1
Presidio J2
Providence (mts.) K8
Punta Gorda (pt.) A3
Quartz (peak) L11
Railroad Canyon (res.) E11
Redwood Nat'l Park A2
Reyes (pt.) B6
Rogers (lake) H9
Rosamond (lake) G9
Round Valley Ind. Res. B4
Russian (riv.) B4
Sacramento (riv.) D5
Sacramento Army Depot B8
Saint George (pt.) A2
Salinas (riv.) D7
Salmon (riv.) B2
Salton Sea (lake) K10
San Andreas (lake) H2
San Antonio (lake) E8
San Benito (riv.) D7
San Bernardino (mts.) J10
San Clemente (isl.) G11
San Diego (bay) H11
San Francisco (bay) J2
San Gabriel (res.) D10
San Joaquin (riv.) E6
San Joaquin (valley) D6
San Lorenzo (riv.) K4
San Luis (res.) E7
San Martin (cape) D8
San Miguel (isl.) E9
San Nicolas (isl.) F10
San Pablo (bay) J1
San Pedro (bay) C11
Santa Ana (riv.) E11
Santa Barbara (chan.) E9
Santa Barbara (isl.) G10
Santa Barbara (isls.) F10
Santa Catalina (gulf) G11
Santa Catalina (isl.) G10
Santa Cruz (chan.) F10
Santa Cruz (isl.) F10
Santa Maria (riv.) E9
Santa Monica (bay) B11
Santa Rosa (isl.) E10
Santa Rosa Ind. Res. J10
Santa Ynez (riv.) E9
Santa Ysabel Ind. Res. J10
Searles (lake) H8
Sequoia Nat'l Park G7
Sharpe Army Depot D6
Shasta (lake) C3
Shasta (mt.) C2
Shasta (riv.) C2
Sierra Army Depot E3
Sierra Nevada (mts.) E4
Siskiyou (mts.) C2
Smith (riv.) A2
Soda (lake) K8
South Bay Aqueduct L2
South Cow (creek) C3
Stony Gorge (res.) C4
Suisun (bay) K1
Sur (pt.) D7
Tahoe (lake) F4
Tamalpais (mt.) H1
Tehachapi (mts.) G9
Telescope (peak) H7
Tomales (pt.) B5
Torres Martinez Ind. Res. J10
Travis A.F.B. L1
Trinidad (head) A2
Trinity (riv.) B3
Truckee (riv.) F4
Tulare (lake) F7
Tule (lake) D2
Tule River Ind. Res. G7
Twentynine Palms Marine Base 7,079 .... J9
Twitchell (res.) E9
Upper Alkali (lake) E2
Vandenberg A.F.B. 8,136 .... E9
Vizcaino (cape) B4
Walnut (creek) K1
Wheeler (peak) F5
Whipple (mts.) L9
Whiskeytown-Shasta-Trinity Nat'l Rec. Area C3
Whitney (mt.) G7
Willow (creek) E3
Wilson (mt.) D10
Yosemite Nat'l Park F6
Yuba (riv.) D4
Yuma Ind. Res. L11

⊙County seat.
‡Population of metropolitan area.
† Zip of nearest p.o. * Multiple zips.

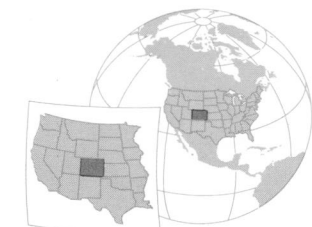

AREA 104,091 sq. mi. (269,596 sq. km.)
POPULATION 2,889,735
CAPITAL Denver
LARGEST CITY Denver
HIGHEST POINT Mt. Elbert 14,433 ft. (4399 m.)
SETTLED IN 1858
ADMITTED TO UNION August 1, 1876
POPULAR NAME Centennial State
STATE FLOWER Rocky Mountain Columbine
STATE BIRD Lark Bunting

COUNTIES

Adams 245,944	L3
Alamosa 11,799	H7
Arapahoe 293,621	L3
Archuleta 3,664	E8
Baca 5,419	O8
Bent 5,945	N7
Boulder 189,625	J2
Chaffee 13,227	G5
Cheyenne 2,153	O5
Clear Creek 7,308	H3
Conejos 7,794	G8
Costilla 3,071	J8
Crowley 2,988	M6
Custer 1,528	J6
Delta 21,225	D5
Denver 492,365	K3
Dolores 1,658	C7
Douglas 25,153	K4
Eagle 13,320	F3
Elbert 6,850	L4
El Paso 309,424	K5
Fremont 28,676	J5
Garfield 22,514	C3
Gilpin 2,441	H3
Grand 7,475	G2
Gunnison 10,689	E5
Hinsdale 408	E7
Huerfano 6,440	K7
Jackson 1,863	G1
Jefferson 371,741	J3
Kiowa 1,936	O6
Kit Carson 7,599	O4
Lake 8,830	G4
La Plata 27,195	D8
Larimer 149,184	H1
Las Animas 14,897	L8
Lincoln 4,663	M5
Logan 19,800	N1
Mesa 81,530	B5
Mineral 804	F7
Moffat 13,133	C1
Montezuma 16,510	B8
Montrose 24,352	C6
Morgan 22,513	M2
Otero 22,567	M7
Ouray 1,925	D6
Park 5,333	H4
Phillips 4,542	P1
Pitkin 10,338	F4
Prowers 13,070	P7
Pueblo 125,972	K6
Rio Blanco 6,255	C3
Rio Grande 10,511	G7
Routt 13,404	E1
Saguache 3,935	G6
San Juan 833	D7
San Miguel 3,192	C6
Sedgwick 3,266	P1
Summit 8,848	G3
Teller 8,034	J5
Washington 5,304	N3
Weld 123,438	L1

Washington 5,304	N3
Weld 123,438	L1
Yuma 9,682	P2

CITIES and TOWNS

Zip Name/Pop.	Key
80101 Agate 90	M4
81020 Aguilar 624	K8
80720 Akron⊙ 1,716	N2
81101 Alamosa⊙ 6,830	H8
80510 Allenspark 200	J2
80420 Alma 132	G4
81210 Almont 135	F5
80721 Amherst 85	P1
80801 Anton 55	N3
81120 Antonito 1,103	H8
80802 Arapahoe 300	P5
81021 Arlington 37	N6
80804 Arriba 236	N4
†81323 Arriola 56	B8
*80001 Arvada 84,576	J3
81611 Aspen⊙ 3,678	F4
80722 Atwood 100	N1
80610 Ault 1,056	K1
*80010 Aurora 158,588	K3
81410 Austin	D5
81620 Avon 640	F3
81022 Avondale 750	L6
80421 Bailey 150	H4
81621 Basalt 529	E4
81122 Bayfield 724	D8
81411 Bedrock 45	B6
†80758 Beecher Island 5	P3
80512 Bellvue 250	J1
80102 Bennett 942	L3
80513 Berthoud 2,362	J2
†80438 Berthoud Pass 40	H3
80805 Bethune 149	P4
81023 Beulah 650	K6
80908 Black Forest 3,372	K4
80422 Black Hawk 232	J3
81123 Blanca 252	H8
80421 Blue River 230	G4
†80424 Blue River 230	G4
81024 Boncarbo 200	K8
80423 Bond 65	F3
81025 Boone 431	L6
80906 Boulder⊙	J2
*80301 Boulder⊙ 76,685	J2
†81428 Bowie 18	D5
80821 Boyero 12	N5
81026 Brandon 30	P6
81027 Branson 73	M8
80424 Breckenridge⊙ 818	G4
80611 Briggsdale 85	L1
80601 Brighton⊙ 12,773	K3
81028 Bristol 200	P6
†81212 Brookside 178	J6
80020 Broomfield 20,730	J3
80723 Brush 4,082	M2
80723 Buckingham 5	L1
81211 Buena Vista 2,075	G5
80425 Buffalo Creek 150	J4

80807 Burlington⊙ 3,107	P4
80426 Burns 100	F3
80103 Byers 490	L3
81320 Cahone 200	B7
80808 Calhan 541	L4
81029 Campo 185	O8
81212 Canon City⊙ 13,037	J6
81124 Capulin 600	G8
81623 Carbondale 2,084	E4
80612 Carr 49	K1
80909 Cascade 950	K5
80104 Castle Rock⊙ 3,921	K4
81413 Cedaredge 1,184	D5
81125 Center 1,630	G7
80427 Central City⊙ 329	J3
81126 Chama 239	J8
80810 Cheyenne Wells⊙ 950	P5
81127 Chimney Rock 76	E8
81031 Chivington 20	O6
81128 Chromo 115	F8
81220 Cimarron 50	D6
80828 Clark 20	F1
81520 Clifton 5,223	C4
80429 Climax 975	G4
81221 Coal Creek 190	J6
81222 Coaldale 153	H6
80430 Coalmont 50	F1
81032 Cokedale 90	K8
81624 Collbran 344	C4
*81401 Colona 54	D6
81019 Colorado City 411	K6
*80901 Colorado Springs⊙ 214,821	K5
Colorado Springs‡ 317,458	K5
†80428 Columbine 12	E1
80022 Commerce City 16,234	K3
80432 Como 30	H4
81129 Conejos⊙ 200	G8
80812 Cope 110	O3
†80611 Cornish 15	L2
81321 Cortez⊙ 7,095	B8
81223 Cotopaxi 250	H6
80434 Cowdrey 80	G1
81625 Craig⊙ 8,133	D2
81415 Crawford 268	D5
81130 Creede⊙ 610	E7
81224 Crested Butte 959	E5
81131 Crestone 54	H7
80813 Cripple Creek⊙ 655	J5
80726 Crook 177	O1
81033 Crowley 192	M6
81055 Cuchara 45	J8
80514 Dacono 2,321	K2
†80728 Dailey 21	O1
81630 De Beque 279	C4
80135 Deckers 4	J4
80105 Deer Trail 463	M3
81059 Delhi 10	M7
81132 Del Norte⊙ 1,709	G7
81416 Delta⊙ 3,931	D5
*80201 Denver (cap.)⊙ 492,365	K3
Denver‡ 1,619,921	K3
†81054 Deora 2	O7

80435 Dillon 337	H3
81610 Dinosaur 313	B2
80814 Divide 700	J5
81323 Dolores 802	C8
81324 Dove Creek⊙ 826	A7
†81239 Doyleville 75	F6
80515 Drake 300	J2
81301 Durango⊙ 11,649	D8
81036 Eads⊙ 878	O6
81631 Eagle⊙ 950	F3
80615 Eaton 1,932	K1
80727 Eckley 262	P2
80214 Edgewater 4,766	J3
81632 Edwards 250	F3
81325 Egnar 50	B7
80106 Elbert 200	L4
†80466 Eldora 100	H3
80107 Elizabeth 789	K4
81633 Elk Springs 18	C2
80438 Empire 423	H3
†80110 Englewood 30,021	K3
80516 Erie 1,254	K2
80517 Estes Park 2,703	J2
†81433 Eureka 25	D7
80620 Evans 5,063	K2
80439 Evergreen 6,376	J3
80440 Fairplay⊙ 421	H4
81037 Farisita 116	J7
†80221 Federal Heights 7,846	J3
80520 Firestone 1,204	K2
†80810 Firstview 6	O5
80815 Flagler 550	N4
80728 Fleming 388	O1
81226 Florence 2,987	J6
80816 Florissant 130	J5
80521 Fort Collins⊙ 65,092	J1
Fort Collins‡ 149,184	J1
81133 Fort Garland 700	J8
80621 Fort Lupton 4,251	K2
81038 Fort Lyon 500	N6
80701 Fort Morgan⊙ 8,768	M2
80817 Fountain 8,324	K5
81039 Fowler 1,227	L6
80441 Foxton 12	J4
80116 Franktown 200	K4
80442 Fraser 470	H3
80530 Frederick 855	K2
80820 Freshwater (Guffey) 24	H5
80443 Frisco 1,221	G3
81521 Fruita 2,810	B4
80622 Galeton 200	K1
81134 Garcia 75	J8
81040 Gardner 100	J7
81227 Garfield 30	G5
81522 Gateway 350	B5
80818 Genoa 165	N4
80444 Georgetown⊙ 830	H3
80623 Gilcrest 1,025	K2
80624 Gill 250	L2
81634 Gilman 160	G3
80117 Kiowa⊙ 206	L4
80824 Kirk 30	P3
†80485 Glendevey 50	H1
80532 Glen Haven 110	H2
81601 Glenwood Springs⊙ 4,637	E4

80401 Golden⊙ 12,237	J3
80653 Goodrich 85	M2
†80480 Gould 12	G2
81041 Granada 557	P6
80446 Granby 963	G2
81501 Grand Junction⊙ 27,956	B4
80447 Grand Lake 382	H2
81228 Granite 47	G4
80448 Grant 50	H4
80631 Greeley⊙ 53,006	K2
Greeley‡ 123,438	K2
†80118 Greenland 21	K4
80819 Green Mountain Falls 607	K5
†81640 Greystone 2	B1
80729 Grover 158	L1
80820 Guffey 24	H5
81042 Gulnare 6	K8
81230 Gunnison⊙ 5,785	E5
81637 Gypsum 743	F3
80730 Hale 4	P3
80638 Hamilton 100	D2
81043 Hartman 122	P6
80449 Hartsel 69	H4
81044 Hasty 150	O6
81045 Haswell 126	N6
80731 Haxtun 1,014	O1
81639 Hayden 1,720	E2
80732 Hereford 50	L1
81326 Hesperus 250	C8
80733 Hillrose 213	N2
81232 Hillside 79	H6
81046 Hoehne 400	L8
81047 Holly 969	P6
80734 Holyoke⊙ 2,092	P1
81136 Hooper 71	H7
80451 Hot Sulphur Springs⊙ 405	H2
81233 Howard 200	H6
80641 Hoyt 60	L2
80642 Hudson 698	K2
80821 Hugo⊙ 776	N4
80533 Hygiene 450	J2
80452 Idaho Springs 2,077	H3
80735 Idalia 125	P3
81137 Ignacio 667	D8
80736 Iliff 218	N1
80455 Jamestown 223	J2
†80182 Jansen 267	K8
81138 Jaroso 50	H8
80456 Jefferson 50	H4
80822 Joes 100	O3
80534 Johnstown 1,535	K2
80737 Julesburg⊙ 1,528	P1
80823 Karval 51	N5
80643 Keenesburg 541	L2
†80729 Keota 4	L1
80644 Kersey 913	L2
81049 Kim 100	N8
80117 Kiowa⊙ 206	L4
80824 Kirk 30	P3
80825 Kit Carson 278	O5
80459 Kremmling 1,296	G2
†80832 Kutch 2	M5

80026 Lafayette 8,935	K3
†81132 La Garita 10	G7
80739 Laird 105	P2
81140 La Jara 858	H8
81050 La Junta⊙ 8,388	M7
81235 Lake City⊙ 206	E6
80827 Lake George 500	J5
80215 Lakewood 113,808	J3
81052 Lamar⊙ 7,713	O6
80535 Laporte 950	J1
80118 Larkspur 141	K4
80645 La Salle 1,929	K2
81054 Las Animas⊙ 2,818	N6
†81151 Lasauces 150	H8
†81153 Lavalley 237	J8
81055 La Veta 611	J8
†80452 Lawson 108	H3
†81625 Lay 40	D2
81420 Lazear 60	D5
80461 Leadville⊙ 3,879	G4
†81323 Lebanon 50	B8
81327 Lewis 150	B8
80828 Limon 1,805	M4
†81212 Lincoln Park 2,984	J6
80740 Lindon 60	N3
*80120 Littleton⊙ 28,631	K3
80536 Livermore 150	J1
†80601 Lochbuie 895	K2
†80701 Log Lane Village 709	M2
81524 Loma 265	B4
80501 Longmont 42,942	J2
†80135 Longview 10	J4
80027 Louisville 5,593	J3
80131 Louviers 300	K4
80537 Loveland 30,244	J2
80646 Lucerne 135	K2
†81054 Lycan 4	P7
80540 Lyons 1,137	J2
81525 Mack 380	B4
81421 Maher 75	D5
†80461 Malta 200	G4
81141 Manassa 945	H8
81328 Mancos 870	C8
80829 Manitou Springs 4,475	J5
81058 Manzanola 459	M6
81623 Marble 30	E4
81329 Marvel 176	C8
80541 Masonville 200	J2
†80649 Masters 50	L2
80830 Matheson 120	M4
81640 Maybell 130	C2
81057 McClave 125	O6
80463 McCoy 62	F3
80542 Mead 356	K2
81641 Meeker⊙ 2,356	D2
81642 Meredith 47	F4
80741 Merino 255	N2
80005 Mesa 120	C4
81330 Mesa Verde National Park 45	C8
81142 Mesita 70	H8
80543 Milliken 1,506	K2
80477 Milner 196	F2
81645 Minturn 1,060	G3

(continued on following page)

Agriculture, Industry and Resources

DOMINANT LAND USE

- Specialized Wheat
- Wheat, Range Livestock
- Wheat, Grain Sorghums, Range Livestock
- Dry Beans, General Farming
- Sugar Beets, Dry Beans, Livestock, General Farming
- Fruit, Mixed Farming
- General Farming, Livestock, Special Crops
- Range Livestock
- Forests
- Urban Areas
- Nonagricultural Land

MAJOR MINERAL OCCURRENCES

Ag	Silver		Mi	Mica
Au	Gold		Mo	Molybdenum
Be	Beryl		Mr	Marble
C	Coal		O	Petroleum
Cl	Clay		Pb	Lead
Cu	Copper		U	Uranium
F	Fluorspar		V	Vanadium
Fe	Iron Ore		W	Tungsten
G	Natural Gas		Zn	Zinc

⚡ Water Power

▨ Major Industrial Areas

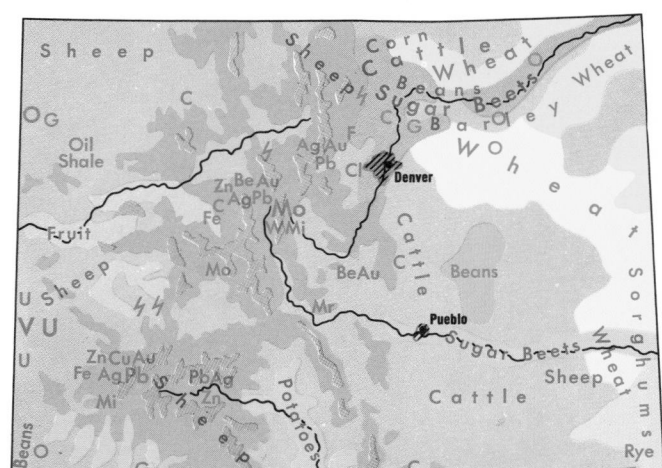

Topography

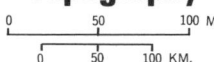

0   50   100 MI.

0   50   100 KM.

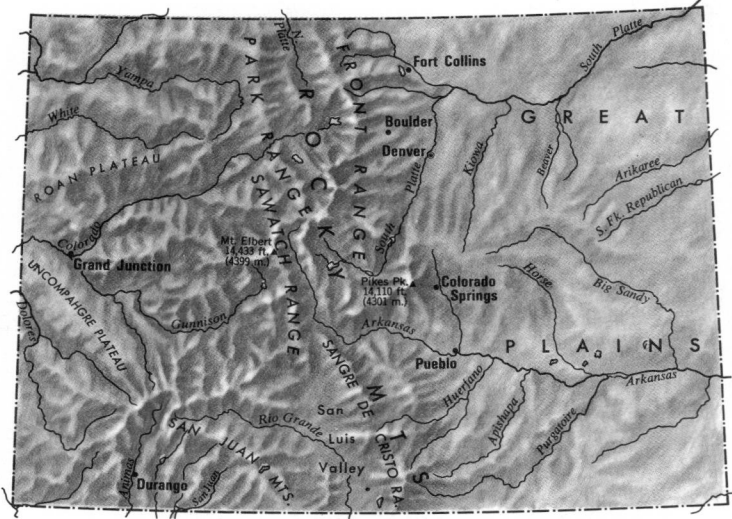

| Below Sea Level | 100 m. 328 ft. | 200 m. 656 ft. | 500 m. 1,640 ft. | 1,000 m. 3,281 ft. | 2,000 m. 6,562 ft. | 5,000 m. 16,404 ft. |

81646 Molina 200 .... D4
81144 Monte Vista 3,902 ...... G7
†80435 Montezuma 6 .... H3
81401 Montrose⊙ 8,722 .... D6
80132 Monument 690 .... K4
80465 Morrison 478 .... J3
81146 Mosca 100 .... H7
81236 Nathrop 150 .... H5
81422 Naturita 819 .... B6
80466 Nederland 1,212 .... H3
81647 New Castle 563 .... E3
80742 New Raymer 80 .... M1
†81054 Ninaview 2 .... N7
80544 Niwot 500 .... J2
†81022 North Avondale 110 ... L6
80233 Northglenn 29,847 .... K3
†81050 North La Junta 1,076 . N7
81423 Norwood 478 .... C6
81424 Nucla 1,027 .... B6
80648 Nunn 295 .... K1
80467 Oak Creek 929 .... F2
81237 Ohio 100 .... F5
81425 Olathe 1,262 .... D5
81062 Olney Springs 253 .... M6
81426 Ophir 38 .... D7
80649 Orchard 79 .... L2
†81063 Ordway⊙ 1,135 ...... M6
†81120 Ortiz 163 .... H8
80743 Otis 534 .... O2
81427 Ouray⊙ 684 .... D6
80744 Ovid 439 .... P1
80745 Padroni 100 .... N1
†81147 Pagosa Junction 15 ... E8
81147 Pagosa Springs⊙ 1,331 . E8
81526 Palisade 1,551 .... C4
80133 Palmer Lake 1,130 .... J4
80746 Paoli 81 .... P1
81428 Paonia 1,425 .... D5
81635 Parachute 338 .... C4
81429 Paradox 250 .... B6
†81212 Parkdale 21 .... H6
80134 Parker 200 .... K4
81429 Parlin 100 .... F6
80468 Parshall 80 .... G2
80747 Peetz 220 .... N1
81240 Penrose 500 .... K6
80831 Peyton 250 .... K4
80469 Phippsburg 300 .... F2
80650 Pierce 878 .... K1
80470 Pine 100 .... J4
80471 Pinecliffe 375 .... J3
†81001 Pinon 50 .... K6
81241 Pitkin 59 .... F5
81430 Placerville 375 ...... D6
†81624 Plateau City 35 ...... D4
†80743 Platner 30 .... N2
80651 Platteville 1,662 .... K2
81331 Pleasant View 300 .... B7
81242 Poncha Springs 321 ... G6
†81226 Portland 17 .... K6
†81427 Portland D6
81243 Powderhorn 100 ...... E6
81064 Pritchett 250 .... O8
†80736 Proctor 25 .... N1
81065 Pryor 50 .... K8
*81001 Pueblo⊙ 101,686 .... K6
      Pueblo‡ 125,972 ...... K6
80472 Radium 22 .... G3
80832 Ramah 119 .... L4
80473 Rand 50 .... G2
81648 Rangely 2,113 .... B2

80473 Rand 50 .... G2
81648 Rangely 2,113 .... B2
80742 Raymer (New Raymer) 80 .M1
81649 Red Cliff 409 .... G4
80545 Red Feather Lakes 150 .H1
†81326 Red Mesa 100 .... C8
†81623 Redstone 115 .... E4
81431 Redvale 300 .... B6
81066 Red Wing 200 .... J7
81332 Rico 76 .... C7
81432 Ridgway 369 .... D6
81650 Rifle 3,215 .... D3
81650 Rio Blanco 100 ...... C3
81244 Rockvale 338 .... J6
81067 Rocky Ford 4,804 .... M6
80652 Roggen 100 .... L2
81148 Romeo 308 .... G8
80833 Rush 40 .... L5
81069 Rye 232 .... K7
81149 Saguache⊙ 656 ...... G6
†81236 Saint Elmo 75 ...... G5
81201 Salida⊙ 44,870 ...... H6
81150 San Acacio 50 ...... J8
81151 Sanford 687 .... H8
†81069 San Isabel 8 .... K7
81152 San Luis⊙ 842 ..... J8
81153 San Pablo 150 ...... J8
81248 Sargents 31 .... F6
81430 Sawpit 41 .... D7
80911 Security-Widefield 18,768 . K5
80135 Sedalia 200 .... K4
80749 Sedgwick 258 .... O1
81070 Segundo 200 .... K8
80834 Seibert 180 .... O4
80546 Severance 102 ...... K1
80475 Shawnee 100 .... H4
†80110 Sheridan 5,377 ..... J3
81071 Sheridan Lake 87 ... P6
81652 Silt 923 .... D4
81249 Silver Cliff 280 ... J6
80476 Silver Plume 140 ... H3
80498 Silverthorne 989 ... G3
81433 Silverton⊙ 794 .... D7
80835 Simla 494 .... M4
81653 Slater 10 .... E1
81654 Snowmass 999 ...... E4
80750 Snyder 200 .... M2
81434 Somerset 200 .... E5
81154 South Fork 500 ..... F7
81073 Springfield⊙ 1,657 . O8
81074 Starkville 127 ..... K8
80477 Steamboat Springs⊙ 5,098 F2
80751 Sterling⊙ 11,385 ... N1
80754 Stoneham 35 .... M1
81075 Stonington 27 ...... P8
80136 Strasburg 1,005 .... L3
80836 Stratton 705 .... O4
81076 Sugar City 306 ..... M6
†81640 Sunbeam 19 .... C1
†80027 Superior 208 .... J3
81077 Swink 668 .... M7
80478 Tabernash 250 ..... H3
81435 Telluride⊙ 1,047 ... D7
†80461 Tennessee Pass 5 ... G4
81250 Texas Creek 80 ..... H6
†81082 Thatcher 50 .... L7
80229 Thornton 40,343 ... K3
†81137 Tiffany 24 .... D8
80547 Timnath 185 ...... J2
†81034 Timpas 250 .... M7
81210 Tincup 8 .... F5
80479 Toponas 55 .... F2

81334 Towaoc 300 .... B8
81080 Towner 61 .... P6
81081 Trinchera 30 .... M8
81082 Trinidad⊙ 9,663 .... L8
†80864 Truckton 10 .... L5
81251 Twin Lakes 40 ..... G4
81084 Two Buttes 84 ...... P7
†81059 Tyrone 9 .... L8
81436 Uravan 100 .... B6
†81064 Utleyville 2 .... O8
81657 Vail 2,261 .... G3
80755 Vernon 50 .... P3
80860 Victor 265 .... J5
81087 Vilas 118 .... P8
81155 Villa Grove 37 .... G6
81088 Villegreen 6 ...... M8
†81001 Vineland 100 ..... K6
80548 Virginia Dale 2 ... J1
80861 Vona 94 .... O4
†81130 Wagon Wheel Gap 20 . F7
80480 Walden⊙ 947 ...... G1
81089 Walsenburg⊙ 3,945 . K7
81090 Walsh 884 .... P8
80481 Ward 129 .... H2
80653 Weldona 200 ...... M2
80549 Wellington 1,215 .. K1
†81252 Westcliffe⊙ 324 ... H6
†80135 Westcreek 2 .... J4
80030 Westminster 50,211 . J3
81091 Weston 150 .... K8
81253 Wetmore 150 ...... J6
80033 Wheat Ridge 30,293 . J3
81527 Whitewater 300 ... C5
80654 Wiggins 531 ...... L2
80862 Wild Horse 13 .... N5
81092 Wiley 425 .... O6
†81226 Williamsburg 72 ... J6
80550 Windsor 4,277 .... J2
80482 Winter Park 480 ... H3
81655 Wolcott 30 .... F3
80863 Woodland Park 2,634 . J4
80757 Woodrow 24 ...... M3
81656 Woody Creek 400 .. F4
80758 Wray⊙ 2,131 ..... P2
80483 Yampa 472 .... F2
81335 Yellow Jacket 115 . B7
80864 Yoder 25 .... L5
80759 Yuma 2,824 ...... O2

OTHER FEATURES

Adams (mt.) H6
Adobe Creek (res.) N6
Air Force Academy 8,655 . K5
Alamosa (creek) G8
Alva B. Adams (tunnel) .. H2
Animas (riv.) D8
Antero (mt.) G5
Antero (res.) H5
Antora (peak) G6
Apishapa (riv.) K8
Arapaho Nat'l Rec. Area . G2
Arapahoe (peak) H2
Arikaree (riv.) O2
Arkansas (riv.) P6
Arkansas Divide (mts.) . L4
Baker (mt.) H2
Bald (mt.) H4
Bear (riv.) P8
Beaver (creek) M3
Bennett (peak) G7

Bent's Old Fort Nat'l Hist.
   Site M6
Big Grizzly (creek) G1
Big Sandy (creek) N4
Big Thompson (riv.) H2
Bijou (creek) L3
Black Canyon of the Gunnison Nat'l
   Mon. D5
Black Squirrel (creek) .. L5
Blanca (peak) H7
Blue (mt.) B2
Blue (riv.) G3
Blue Mesa (res.) E5
Bonny (res.) P3
Box Elder (creek) K4
Cache la Poudre (riv.) . H1
Cameron (peak) H1
Camp Hale G4
Carbon (peak) E5
Castle (peak) F5
Cebolla (creek) E6
Chacuaco (creek) .. M8
Cheesman (lake) ... J4
Clay (creek) O7

Cochetopa (creek) F6
Colorado (riv.) A5
Colorado Nat'l Mon. B4
Conejos (peak) G8
Conejos (riv.) G8
Crestone (peak) H7
Crow (creek) L1
Culebra (riv.) H8
Culebra (peak) J8
Curecanti Nat'l Rec. Area . F6
Del Norte (peak) F7
De Weese (plat.) H2
Dinosaur Nat'l Mon. .. B2
Disappointment (creek) . B7
Dolores (riv.) B5
Douglas (creek) C3
Eagle (riv.) E3
Elbert (mt.) G4
El Diente (peak) ... C7
Eleven Mile Canyon (res.) . H5
Elk (riv.) F1
Empire (res.) L2
Ent A.F.B. K6
Ethel (mt.) F1

Evans (mt.) H3
Florissant Fossil Beds Nat'l
   Mon. J5
Fort Carson 19,399 ..... K5
Fountain (creek) K5
Frenchman (creek) P1
Frenchman, North Fork (creek) . O1
Frenchman, South Fork (creek) . O1
Front (range) H1
Gore (range) G3
Graham (peak) E8
Granby (lake) G2
Great Sand Dunes Nat'l Mon. . H7
Green (riv.) A2
Green Mountain (res.) . G3
Gunnison (riv.) C5
Gunnison (tunnel) .. D6
Gunnison, North Fork (riv.) . D5
Hale, Camp G4
Handies (peak) E7
Harvard (mt.) G5
Hermosa (peak) ... D7
Hesperus (mt.) ... C8
Holy Cross (mt.) . F4

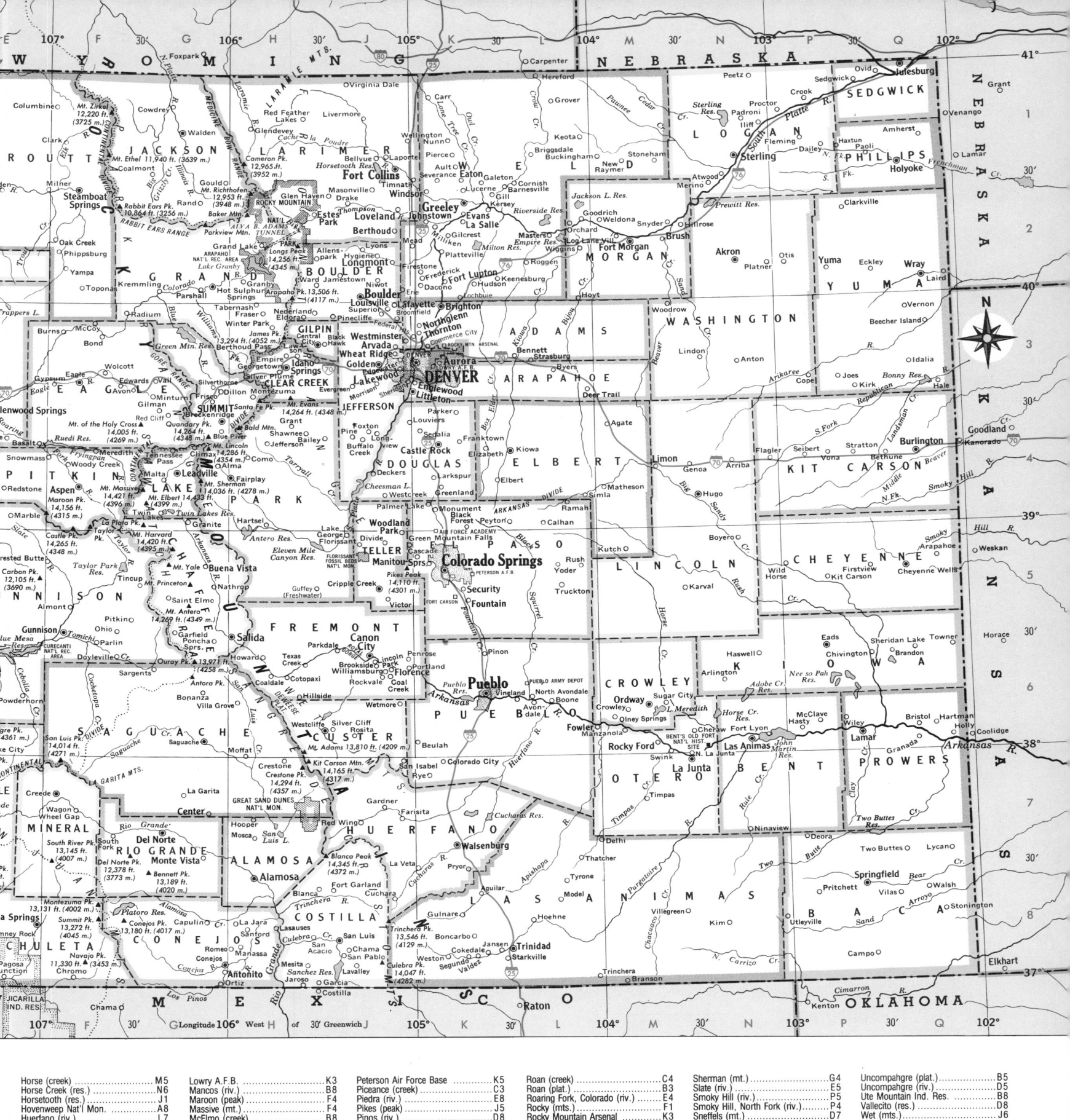

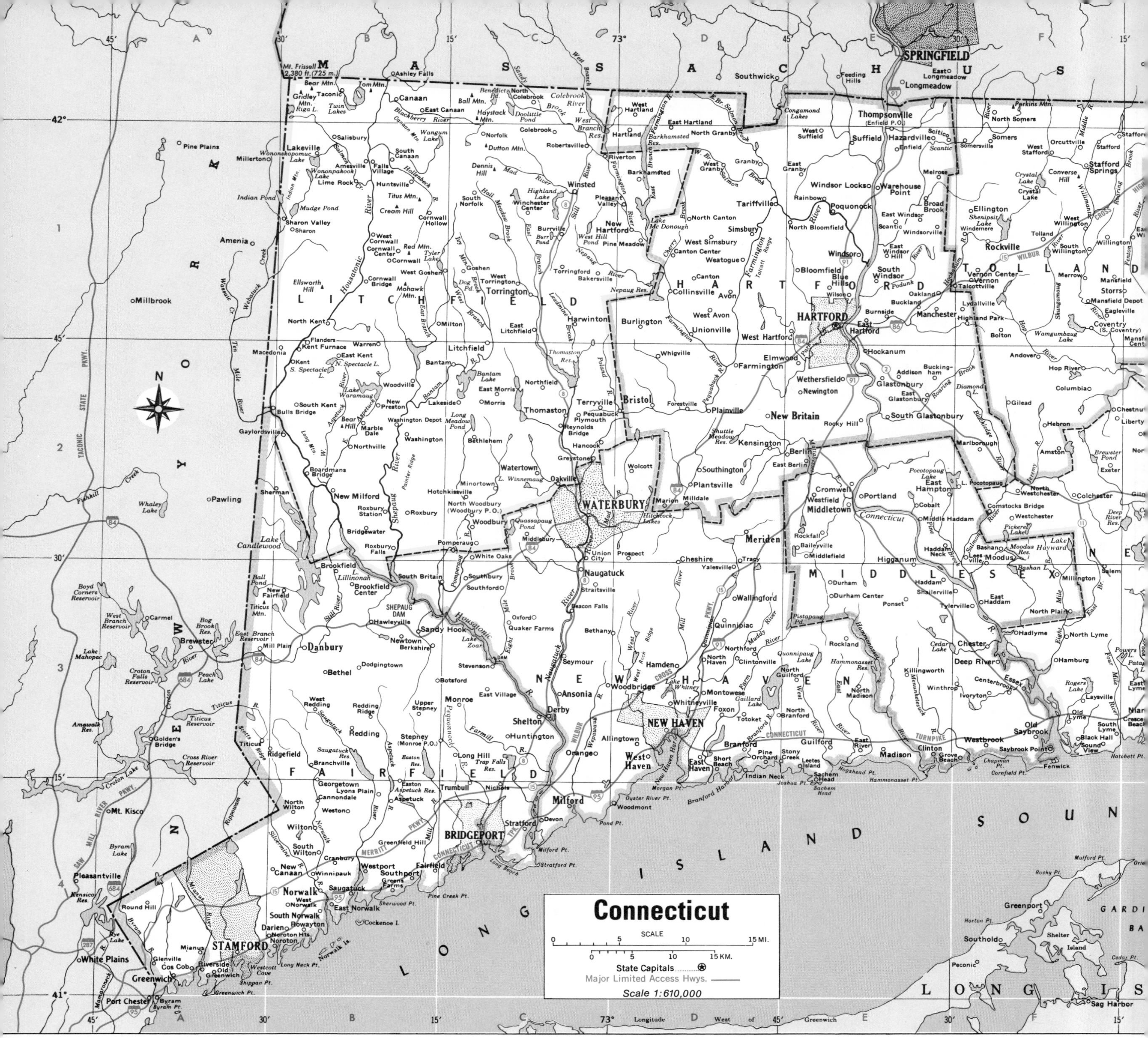

Connecticut

SCALE

0   5   10   15 MI.

0   5   10   15 KM.

State Capitals.................⊛
Major Limited Access Hwys. ————

Scale 1:610,000

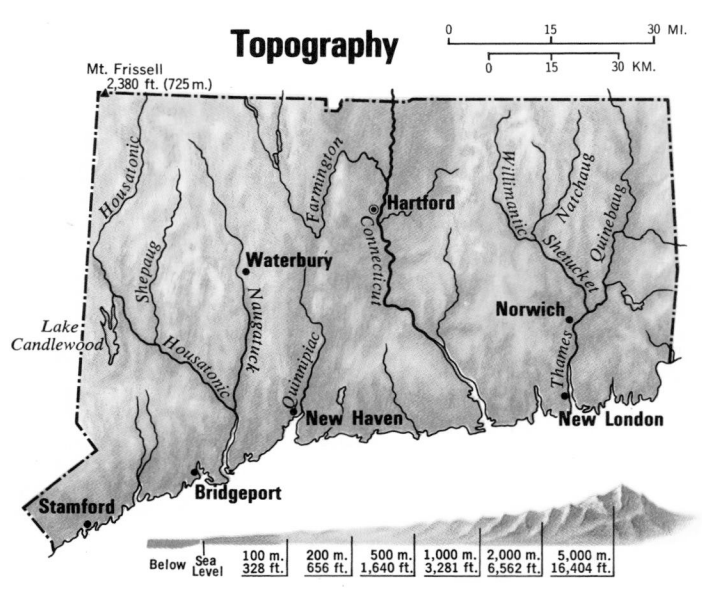

Topography

Mt. Frissell
2,380 ft. (725 m.)

0   15   30 MI.

0   15   30 KM.

Below Sea Level | 100 m. 328 ft. | 200 m. 656 ft. | 500 m. 1,640 ft. | 1,000 m. 3,281 ft. | 2,000 m. 6,562 ft. | 5,000 m. 16,404 ft.

COUNTIES

Fairfield 807,143 .... B3
Hartford 807,766 .... D1
Litchfield 156,769 .... B1
Middlesex 129,017 .... E3
New Haven 761,337 .... D3
New London 238,409 .... G2
Tolland 114,823 .... F1
Windham 92,312 .... H1

CITIES and TOWNS

Zip	Name/Pop.	Key
06230	Abington 600	G1
06231	Amston 900	F2
06232	Andover 2,144	F2
06401	Ansonia 19,039	C3
06278	Ashford 3,221	G1
06278	Ashford P.O.	
	(Warrenville) 500	G1
†06241	Attawaugan 400	H1
06001	Avon 11,201	D1
06001	Avon 1,434	D1
06233	Ballouville 800	H1
06330	Baltic	G2
06750	Bantam 860	B2
†06063	Barkhamsted 2,935	D1
†06423	Bashan 90	F2
06403	Beacon Falls 3,995	C3
06037	Berlin 15,121	E2
†06501	Bethany 4,330	C3
06801	Bethel 16,004	B3
06801	Bethel 8,755	B3
06751	Bethlehem 2,573	C2
06751	Bethlehem 1,762	C2
06002	Bloomfield 18,608	E1
06112	Blue Hills	E1
06040	Bolton 3,951	F1
06404	Botsford 400	C3
†06829	Branchville 600	B3
06405	Branford 23,363	D3
06405	Branford 5,438	D3
*06601	Bridgeport 142,546	C4
	Bridgeport‡ 395,455	C4
06752	Bridgewater 1,563	B2
06010	Bristol 57,370	D2
	Bristol‡ 73,762	D2
06016	Broad Brook	E1
06804	Brookfield 12,872	B3
06234	Brooklyn 5,691	H1
06013	Burlington 5,660	D1
06830	Byram	A4
06018	Canaan 1,002	B1
06018	Canaan 1,160	B1
†06897	Cannondale 400	B4
06331	Canterbury 3,426	H2
06019	Canton 7,635	D1
06019	Canton 1,680	D1
06409	Centerbrook 800	F3
06332	Central Village 950	H2
06235	Chaplin 1,793	G1
06410	Cheshire 21,788	D2
06410	Cheshire 5,722	D2
06412	Chester 3,068	F3
06412	Chester 1,388	F3
06413	Clinton 11,195	E3
06413	Clinton 3,168	E3
06414	Cobalt 700	E2
06415	Colchester 7,761	F2
06415	Colchester 3,190	F2
06021	Colebrook 1,221	C1
06022	Collinsville 2,555	D1
06237	Columbia 3,386	F2
06753	Cornwall 1,288	C1
06807	Cos Cob	A4
06238	Coventry 8,895	F1
06416	Cromwell 10,265	E2
06810	Danbury 60,470	B3
	Danbury‡ 146,405	B3
06239	Danielson 4,553	H1
06820	Darien 18,892	B4
06241	Dayville	H1
06417	Deep River 3,994	F3
06417	Deep River 2,495	F3
06418	Derby 12,346	C3
06422	Durham 5,143	E2
06422	Durham 2,641	E3
06023	East Berlin 950	E2
06239	East Brooklyn 1,251	H1
06024	East Canaan 800	B1
06242	Eastford 1,028	G1
06025	East Glastonbury 300	E2
06026	East Granby 4,102	E1
06423	East Haddam 5,621	F2
06424	East Hampton 8,572	E2

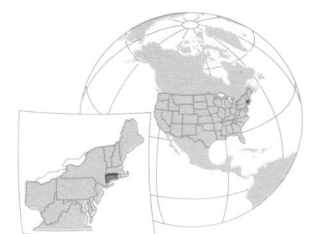

AREA 5,018 sq. mi. (12,997 sq. km.)
POPULATION 3,107,576
CAPITAL Hartford
LARGEST CITY Bridgeport
HIGHEST POINT Mt. Frissell (S. Slope) 2,380 ft. (725 m.)
SETTLED IN 1635
ADMITTED TO UNION January 9, 1788
POPULAR NAME Constitution State; Nutmeg State
STATE FLOWER Mountain Laurel
STATE BIRD Robin

06351 Lisbon○ 3,279	G2	
06759 Litchfield 7,605	C2	
06759 Litchfield 1,489	C2	
†06378 Lords Point 500	H3	
06443 Madison 14,031	E3	
06443 Madison 2,069	E3	
06040 Manchester 49,761	E1	
06040 Manchester 31,058	E1	
†06250 Mansfield 20,634	F1	
06250 Mansfield Center 1,043	G1	
06777 Marble Dale 300	B2	
06444 Marion 900	D2	
06447 Marlborough○ 4,746	F2	
06447 Marlborough 1,039	F2	
†06382 Massapeag 350	G3	
06252 Mechanicsville 425	H1	
06450 Meriden 57,118	D2	
Meriden‡ 57,118	D2	
06762 Middlebury○ 5,995	C2	
06455 Middlefield 3,796	E2	
06456 Middle Haddam 325	E2	
06457 Middletown 39,040	E2	
06460 Milford 49,101	C4	
06647 Milldale 975	D2	
†06759 Milton 600	C1	
06468 Monroe○ 14,010	C3	
06468 Monroe P.O. (Stepney)	B3	
06353 Montville○ 16,455	G3	
06353 Montville 1,711	G3	
06469 Moodus 1,179	F2	
06354 Moosup 3,308	H2	
06763 Morris 1,899	C2	
06355 Mystic 2,333	H3	
06770 Naugatuck 26,456	C3	
*06050 New Britain 73,840	E2	
New Britain‡ 142,241	E2	
06840 New Canaan○ 17,931	B4	
06810 New Fairfield 11,260	B3	
06057 New Hartford○ 4,884	C1	
06057 New Hartford 1,310	C1	
*06501 New Haven 126,109	D3	
New Haven-West Haven‡ 417,592	D3	
06111 Newington○ 28,841	E2	
06320 New London 28,842	G3	
New London-Norwich‡ 248,554	G3	
06776 New Milford○ 19,420	B2	
06776 New Milford 5,186	B2	
06777 New Preston 1,209	B2	
06470 Newtown○ 19,107	B3	
06470 Newtown 2,022	B3	
06357 Niantic 3,151	G3	
06340 Noank 1,406	G3	
06058 Norfolk○ 2,156	C1	
06471 North Branford○ 11,554	E3	
06778 Northfield 600	C2	
06254 North Franklin 500	G2	
06060 North Granby 450	D1	
06255 North Grosvenor Dale 1,856	H1	
†06437 North Guilford 500	E3	
06473 North Haven○ 22,080	D3	
06359 North Stonington 4,219	H3	
06256 North Windham 200	G1	
*06850 Norwalk 77,767	B4	
06360 Norwich 38,074	G2	
06370 Oakdale 608	G2	
06779 Oakville 8,737	C2	
06371 Old Lyme○ 6,159	F3	

06372 Old Mystic 600	H3	
06475 Old Saybrook○ 9,287	F3	
06475 Old Saybrook 1,857	F3	
06373 Oneco 550	H2	
06477 Orange○ 13,237	C3	
06483 Oxford○ 6,634	C3	
06379 Pawcatuck 5,216	H3	
06781 Pequabuck 642	C2	
06061 Pine Meadow 400	D1	
†06405 Pine Orchard 300	D3	
06374 Plainfield○ 12,774	H2	
06374 Plainfield 2,799	H2	
06062 Plainville○ 16,401	D2	
06063 Pleasant Valley 300	C1	
†06385 Pleasure Beach 1,356	G3	
06782 Plymouth○ 10,732	C2	
06258 Pomfret○ 2,775	H1	
†06340 Poquonock Bridge 2,549	G3	
06480 Portland○ 8,383	E2	
06480 Portland 5,914	E2	
06712 Prospect○ 6,807	D2	
06260 Putnam○ 8,580	H1	
06260 Putnam 6,855	H1	
06375 Quaker Hill 2,052	G3	
06262 Quinebaug 1,088	H1	
06875 Redding○ 7,272	B3	
06876 Redding Ridge 550	B3	
06877 Ridgefield○ 20,120	B3	
06877 Ridgefield 6,066	B3	
06065 Riverton 250	D1	
06481 Rockfall 900	E2	
†06066 Rockville	F1	
06067 Rocky Hill○ 14,559	E2	
06263 Rogers 650	H1	
06783 Roxbury○ 1,468	B2	
06068 Salisbury○ 3,896	B1	
06264 Scotland○ 1,072	G2	
06483 Seymour○ 13,434	C3	
06069 Sharon○ 2,623	B1	
06484 Shelton 31,314	C3	
06784 Sherman○ 2,281	B2	
06070 Simsbury○ 21,161	D1	
06070 Simsbury 5,488	D1	
06071 Somers○ 8,473	F1	
06071 Somers 1,643	F1	
06072 Somersville 750	F1	
06487 South Britain 390	B3	
06488 Southbury○ 14,156	C3	
†06238 South Coventry (Coventry) 3,769	F1	
06073 South Glastonbury	E2	
06489 Southington○ 36,879	D2	
06785 South Kent 450	B2	
06265 South Willington 450	F1	
06266 South Windham 1,399	G2	
06074 South Windsor○ 17,198	E1	
06267 South Woodstock 1,319	G1	
06075 Stafford○ 9,268	F1	
06076 Stafford Springs 3,392	F1	
06077 Staffordville 500	G1	
*06901 Stamford○ 102,453	A4	
Stamford‡ 198,854	A4	
†06468 Stepney	B3	
06377 Sterling○ 1,791	H2	
06491 Stevenson 300	C3	
06378 Stonington○ 16,220	H3	
06378 Stonington 1,228	H3	
06268 Storrs 11,394	F1	
06497 Stratford○ 50,541	C4	

06078 Suffield○ 9,294	E1	
06078 Suffield 1,122	E1	
06079 Taconic 400	B1	
06380 Taftville	G2	
06081 Tariffville 1,324	D1	
06786 Terryville 5,234	C2	
06787 Thomaston○ 6,276	C2	
06277 Thompson○ 8,141	H1	
†06082 Thompsonville	E1	
06084 Tolland○ 9,694	F1	
06790 Torrington 30,987	C1	
06611 Trumbull○ 32,989	C4	
06382 Uncasville 1,597	G3	
†06076 Union○ 546	G1	
06066 Vernon○ 27,974	F1	
06383 Versailles 540	G2	
06384 Voluntown○ 1,637	H2	
06492 Wallingford○ 37,274	D3	
06492 Wallingford 17,821	D3	
06754 Warren○ 1,027	B2	
†06278 Warrenville 500	G1	
06793 Washington○ 3,657	B2	
06794 Washington Depot 900	B2	
*06701 Waterbury 103,266	C2	
Waterbury‡ 228,178	C2	
06385 Waterford○ 17,843	G3	
06385 Waterford 2,736	G3	
06795 Watertown○ 19,489	C2	
06089 Weatogue 2,249	D1	
06498 Westbrook○ 5,216	F3	
06498 Westbrook 2,035	F3	
06796 West Cornwall 425	B1	
06090 West Granby 567	D1	
06107 West Hartford○ 61,301	D1	
06516 West Haven 53,184	D3	
06388 West Mystic 3,364	H3	
06883 Weston○ 8,284	B4	
06880 Westport○ 25,290	B4	
06896 West Redding 500	B3	
06092 West Simsbury 2,140	D1	
06109 Wethersfield○ 26,013	E2	
06517 Whitneyville	D3	
06226 Willimantic 14,652	G2	
†06279 Willington○ 4,694	F1	
06897 Wilton○ 15,351	B4	
06094 Winchester○ 10,841	C1	
06094 Winchester Center 350	C1	
06280 Windham○ 21,062	G2	
06095 Windsor○ 25,204	E1	
06095 Windsor 17,517	E1	
06096 Windsor Locks 12,190	E1	
06097 Windsorville 450	E1	
06098 Winsted 8,092	C1	
†06417 Winthrop 750	E3	
06716 Wolcott○ 13,008	D2	
†06515 Woodbridge○ 7,761	D3	
06798 Woodbury○ 6,942	C2	
06798 Woodbury 1,290	C2	
†06460 Woodmont 1,797	D4	
06281 Woodstock○ 5,117	H1	

OTHER FEATURES

Aspetuck (res.)	B4
Bantam (lake)	C2
Barkhamsted (res.)	D1
Bear (mt.)	B1
Byram (riv.)	A4
Candlewood (lake)	A2
Coast Guard Academy	G3

Colebrook River (lake)	C1
Congamond (lkes)	E1
Connecticut (riv.)	E2
Dennis (hill)	C1
Easton (res.)	B3
Eight Mile (riv.)	F3
Farmington (riv.)	D1
French (riv.)	H1
Frissell (mt.)	B1
Gaillard (lake)	D3
Gardner (lake)	G2
Hammonasset (pt.)	E3
Hammonasset (res.)	E3
Haystack (mt.)	C1
Highland (lake)	C1
Hockanum (riv.)	E1
Hop (riv.)	F1
Housatonic (riv.)	C3
Lillinonah (lake)	B3
Little (riv.)	G2
Long Island (sound)	C4
Mad (riv.)	C1
Mashapaug (lake)	G1
Mason (isl.)	H3
Mattabesset (riv.)	E2
Mianus (riv.)	A4
Mohawk (mt.)	B1
Moosup (riv.)	H2
Mount Hope (riv.)	G1
Mudge (pond)	B1
Mystic (riv.)	H3
Natchaug (riv.)	G1
Naugatuck (riv.)	C3
Nepaug (res.)	D1
Niantic (riv.)	G3
Norwalk (riv.)	B4
Pachaug (pond)	H2
Pawcatuck (riv.)	H3
Pequabuck (riv.)	D2
Pequonnock (riv.)	C3
Pocotopaug (lake)	E2
Quaddick (res.)	H1
Quinebaug (riv.)	H2
Quinnipiac (riv.)	D3
Rippowam (riv.)	A4
Sachem (head)	E4
Salmon (brook)	D1
Salmon (riv.)	F2
Saugatuck (res.)	B3
Scantic (riv.)	E1
Shenipsit (lake)	F1
Shepaug (riv.)	B2
Shetucket (riv.)	G2
Silvermine (riv.)	B4
Spectacle (lkes)	B2
Still (riv.)	B3
Still (riv.)	C1
Talcott (range)	D1
Thames (riv.)	G3
Thomaston (res.)	C2
Titicus (riv.)	A3
Trap Falls (res.)	C3
Twin (lkes)	B1
Wamgumbaug (lake)	F1
Waramaug (lake)	B2
West Rock Ridge (hills)	D3
Willimantic (riv.)	F1
Wononskopomuc (lake)	B1
Yantic (riv.)	G2

‡Population of metropolitan area.
○Population of town or township.
† Zip of nearest p.o.   * Multiple zips.

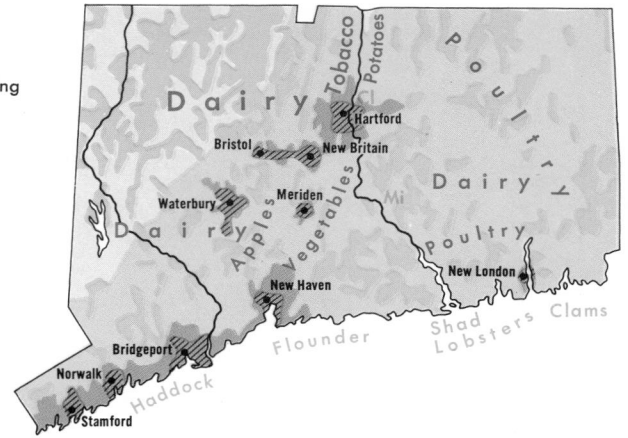

Agriculture, Industry and Resources

DOMINANT LAND USE

- Specialized Dairy
- Dairy, Poultry, Mixed Farming
- Forests
- Urban Areas

MAJOR MINERAL OCCURRENCES

Cl Clay   Mi Mica

⫽⫽ Major Industrial Areas

06424 East Hampton 2,152	E2	
06108 East Hartford○ 52,563	E1	
06027 East Hartland 900	D1	
06512 East Haven○ 25,028	D3	
06243 East Killingly 900	H1	
06333 East Lyme○ 13,870	G3	
†06763 East Morris 800	C2	
06612 Easton○ 5,962	B4	
†06088 East Windsor○ 8,925	E1	
06028 East Windsor Hill 500	E1	
06244 East Woodstock 400	H1	
06029 Ellington○ 9,711	F1	
06082 Enfield○ 42,695	E1	
06082 Enfield 8,151	E1	
06426 Essex○ 5,078	F3	
06426 Essex 2,501	F3	
06245 Fabyan 600	H1	
06430 Fairfield○ 54,849	B4	
06031 Falls Village 600	B1	
06032 Farmington○ 16,407	D2	
06334 Fitchville 400	G2	
†06254 Franklin○ 1,592	G2	
06335 Gales Ferry 1,191	G3	
06755 Gaylordsville 960	A2	
06829 Georgetown 1,834	B4	
06336 Gilman 350	G2	
06337 Glasgo 450	H2	
06033 Glastonbury○ 24,327	E2	
06033 Glastonbury 7,049	E2	
06756 Goshen○ 1,706	C1	
06035 Granby○ 7,956	D1	
06035 Granby 1,912	D1	

06830 Greenwich○ 59,578	A4	
06246 Grosvenor Dale 700	H1	
06027 Groton○ 41,062	G3	
06340 Groton 10,086	G3	
06437 Guilford○ 17,375	E3	
06437 Guilford 2,555	E3	
06438 Haddam○ 6,383	E3	
06439 Hadlyme 450	F3	
06514 Hamden○ 51,071	D3	
06247 Hampton○ 1,322	G1	
06350 Hanover 500	G2	
*06101 Hartford (cap.) 136,392	E1	
Hartford‡ 726,114	E1	
†06091 Hartland○ 1,416	D1	
06791 Harwinton○ 4,889	C1	
06791 Harwinton 3,293	C1	
06440 Hawleyville 600	B3	
06082 Hazardville 5,436	E1	
06248 Hebron○ 5,453	F2	
06441 Higganum 1,660	E2	
†06040 Highland Park 500	F1	
06351 Jewett City 3,294	H2	
06037 Kensington 7,502	D2	
06757 Kent○ 2,505	B2	
†06241 Killingly 14,519	H1	
†06413 Killingworth○ 3,976	E3	
†06424 Lake Pocotopaug 2,137	E2	
06758 Lakeside 350	B2	
06249 Lebanon○ 4,762	G2	
06339 Ledyard○ 13,735	G3	
†06437 Leetes Island 500	E3	
†06039 Lime Rock 350	B1	

© Copyright HAMMOND INCORPORATED, Maplewood, N.J.

Florida

SCALE

State Capitals........⊕
County Seats.........◎
Canals................
Major Limited Access Hwys.
Scale 1:2,550,000

Western Part of Florida

Same scale as main map

© Copyright HAMMOND INCORPORATED, Maplewood, N.J.

AREA 58,664 sq. mi. (151,940 sq. km.)
POPULATION 9,746,342
CAPITAL Tallahassee
LARGEST CITY Jacksonville
HIGHEST POINT (Walton County) 345 ft. (105 m.)
SETTLED IN 1565
ADMITTED TO UNION March 3, 1845
POPULAR NAME Sunshine State; Peninsula State
STATE FLOWER Orange Blossom
STATE BIRD Mockingbird

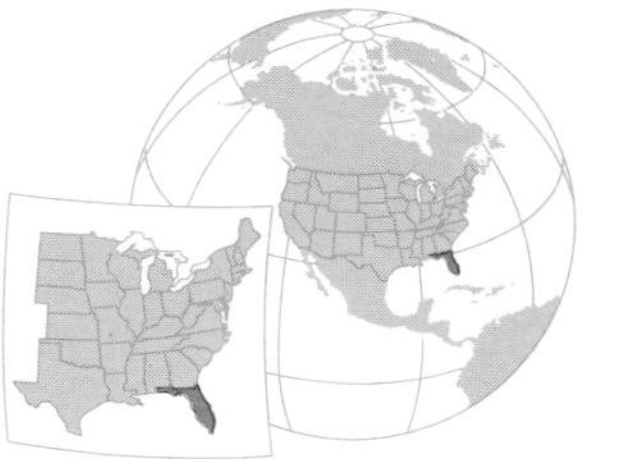

Topography

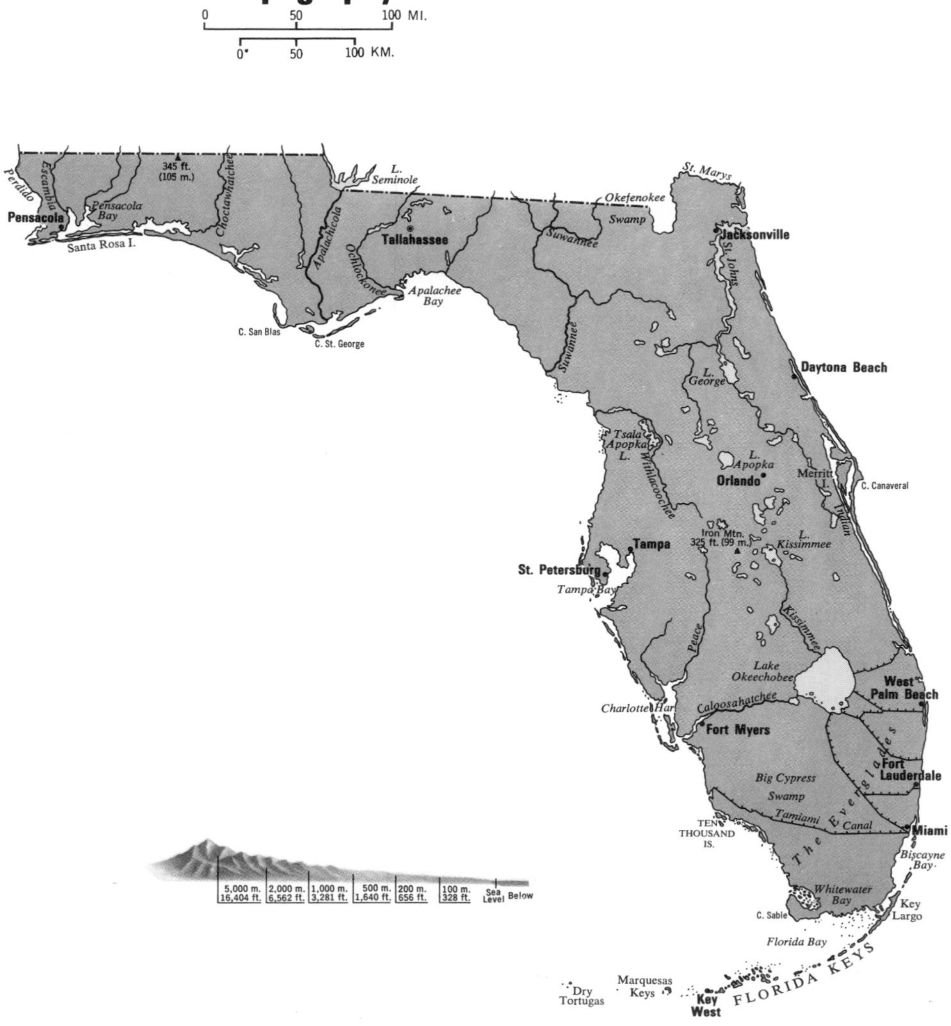

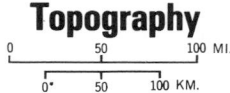

COUNTIES

Alachua 151,348 D2
Baker 15,289 D1
Bay 97,740 C6
Bradford 20,023 D2
Brevard 272,959 F3
Broward 101,820 F5
Calhoun 9,294 D6
Charlotte 58,460 E5
Citrus 54,703 D3
Clay 67,052 E2
Collier 85,791 E5
Columbia 35,399 D1
Dade 1,625,781 F6
De Soto 19,039 E4
Dixie 7,751 C2
Duval 571,003 E1
Escambia 233,794 B6
Flagler 10,913 E2
Franklin 7,661 B2
Gadsden 41,565 B1
Gilchrist 5,767 D2
Glades 5,992 E5
Gulf 10,658 D7
Hamilton 8,761 D1
Hardee 19,379 E4
Hendry 18,599 E5
Hernando 44,4693
Highlands 47,526 E4
Hillsborough 646,960 D4
Holmes 14,723 C5
Indian River 59,896 F4
Jackson 39,154 D5
Jefferson 10,703 C1
Lafayette 4,035 C2
Lake 104,870 E3
Lee 205,266 E5
Leon 148,655 B1
Levy 19,870 D2
Liberty 4,260 B1
Madison 14,894 C1
Manatee 148,442 D4
Marion 122,488 D2
Martin 64,014 F4
Monroe 63,188 E7
Nassau 32,894 E1
Okaloosa 109,920 C6
Okeechobee 20,264 F4
Orange 471,016 E3
Osceola 49,287 E3
Palm Beach 576,863 F5
Pasco 193,643 D3
Pinellas 728,531 D4
Polk 321,652 E4
Putnam 50,549 E2
Saint Johns 51,303 E2
Saint Lucie 87,182 F4
Santa Rosa 55,988 B6
Sarasota 202,251 D4
Seminole 179,752 E3
Sumter 24,272 D3
Suwannee 22,287 C1
Taylor 16,532 C1
Union 10,166 D1
Volusia 258,762 E2
Wakulla 10,887 B1
Walton 21,300 C6
Washington 14,509 C6

CITIES and TOWNS

Zip *Name/Pop.* *Key*

32615 Alachua 3,561 D2
32420 Alford 548 D6
32701 Altamonte Springs 22,028 E3
32421 Altha 478 A1
33820 Alturas 900 E4
33501 Anna Maria 1,537 D4
32320 Apalachicola⊙ 2,565 A2
33570 Apollo Beach 4,014 C3
32703 Apopka 6,019 E3
33821 Arcadia⊙ 6,002 E4
32618 Archer 1,230 D2
33502 Aripeka 450 D3
32705 Astatula 755 E3
32233 Atlantic Beach 7,847 E1
33823 Auburndale 6,501 E3
33825 Avon Park 8,026 E4
32807 Azalea Park 8,301 E3
32530 Bagdad 1,479 B6
32234 Baldwin 1,526 E1
†33101 Bal Harbour 2,973 C4
33830 Bartow⊙ 14,780 E4
32423 Bascom 134 A1
†33101 Bay Harbor Islands 4,869 B4
†32786 Bay Lake 74 E3
33504 Bay Pines 5,757 B3
33507 Bayshore Gardens 14,945 D4
†33578 Bee Ridge 3,313 D4
32619 Bell 227 D2
33540 Belleair 3,673 B2
†33540 Belleair Beach 1,643 B2
33540 Belleair Bluffs 2,522 B3
†33540 Belleair Shores 80 B3
33430 Belle Glade 16,535 F5
†33430 Belle Glade Camp 1,645 F5
†32801 Belle Isle 2,848 E3
32620 Belleview 1,913 D2
†32036 Beverly Beach 217 E2
33152 Biscayne Park 3,088 B4
†32801 Bithlo 3,143 E3
32424 Blountstown⊙ 2,632 A1
33921 Boca Grande 900 D5
*33432 Boca Raton 49,505 F5
32425 Bonifay⊙ 2,534 C5
33923 Bonita Springs 5,435 E5
33834 Bowling Green 2,310 E4
*33435 Boynton Beach 35,624 F5
*33506 Bradenton⊙ 30,170 D4
Bradenton‡ 148,442 D4
33510 Bradenton Beach 1,595 D4
33835 Bradley 1,108 D4
33511 Brandon 41,826 D4
32008 Branford 622 D2
†33435 Briny Breezes 387 G5
32321 Bristol⊙ 1,044 B1
†33314 Broadview Park 6,022 B4
32621 Bronson⊙ 853 D2
32622 Brooker 429 D2
33512 Brooksville⊙ 5,582 D3
†33311 Browardale 7,409 B4
32010 Bunnell⊙ 1,816 E2
33513 Bushnell⊙ 983 D3
32011 Callahan 869 E1
32401 Calloway 7,154 D6
32426 Campbellton 336 D5
32624 Candler 275 E2
32920 Cape Canaveral 5,733 F3
33904 Cape Coral 32,103 E5
33055 Carol City 47,349 B4
Carrabelle 1,304 B2
32427 Caryville 633 C6
32707 Casselberry 15,247 E3
†32401 Cedar Grove 1,104 D6
32625 Cedar Key 700 C2
33514 Center Hill 751 D3
32535 Century 495 B5
†33950 Charlotte Harbor 2,084 E5
32324 Chattahoochee 5,332 B1
32626 Chiefland 1,986 D2
32428 Chipley⊙ 3,330 D6
†32548 Cinco Bayou 202 B6
*33515 Clearwater⊙ 85,528 B2
32711 Clermont 5,461 E3
†33950 Cleveland 2,417 E5
33440 Clewiston 5,219 E5
32922 Cocoa 16,096 F3
32931 Cocoa Beach 10,926 F3
†33060 Coconut Creek 6,288 F5
33521 Coleman 1,022 D3
33328 Cooper City 10,140 B4
†33559 Coral Cove 2,042 D4
33134 Coral Gables 43,241 B5
33060 Coral Springs 37,349 F5
33522 Cortez 3,821 D4
32431 Cottondale 1,056 D6
32327 Crawfordville⊙ 1,110 B1
32012 Crescent City 1,722 E2
32536 Crestview⊙ 7,617 C6
32628 Cross City⊙ 2,154 C2
32629 Crystal River 2,778 D3
33157 Cutler Ridge 20,886 F6
33880 Cypress Gardens 8,043 E3
†33472 Cypress Quarters 1,479 F4
33525 Dade City⊙ 4,923 D3
33004 Dania 11,811.B4
33837 Davenport 1,509 E3
33314 Davie 20,877 B4
*32014 Daytona Beach 54,176 F2
Daytona Beach‡ 258,762 F2
32016 Daytona Beach Shores 1,324 F2
32713 De Bary 4,980 E3
33441 Deerfield Beach 39,193 F5
32433 De Funiak Springs⊙ 5,563 C6
32720 De Land⊙ 15,354 E2
32028 De Leon Springs 1,669 E2
*33444 Delray Beach 34,325 F5
32725 Deltona 15,710 E3
32541 Destin 3,672 C6
33527 Dover 2,354 D4
33838 Dundee 2,227 E3
33528 Dunedin 30,203 B2
32630 Dunnellon 1,427 D2
33839 Eagle Lake 1,678 E4
†33601 East Lake-Orient Park 5,612 C2
†33940 East Naples 12,127 E5
32031 East Palatka 1,613 E2
32328 Eastpoint 1,246 B2
32751 Eatonville 2,185 E3
32437 Ebro 233 C6
32032 Edgewater 6,726 F3
†32801 Edgewood 1,034 E3
†33614 Egypt Lake 11,932 C2
33531 Elfers 11,396 D3
†33101 El Portal 1,819 B4
33533 Englewood 9,633 D5
32504 Ensley 14,422 B6
32425 Esto 304 C5
32726 Eustis 9,453 E3
33929 Everglades City 524 E6
32634 Fairfield 450 D2
†32693 Fanning Springs (Suwannee Riv.) 314 D2
32948 Fellsmere 1,161 F4
32034 Fernandina Beach⊙ 7,224 E1
32922 Five Points 1,691 D1
32036 Flagler Beach 2,208 E2
32636 Floral City 1,181 D3
33034 Florida City 6,174 F6
†32960 Florida Ridge 4,988 F4
†33472 Fort Drum 70 F4
*33301 Fort Lauderdale⊙ 153,279 C4
Fort Lauderdale-Hollywood‡ 1,014,043 C4
33841 Fort Meade 5,546 E4
*33901 Fort Myers⊙ 36,638 E5
Fort Myers-Cape Coral‡ 205,266 E5
33931 Fort Myers Beach 5,753 E5
33842 Fort Ogden 900 E4
*33450 Fort Pierce⊙ 33,802 F4
32548 Fort Walton Beach 20,829 C6
Fort Walton Beach‡ 109,920 C6
32038 Fort White 386 D2
32438 Fountain 900 D6
32439 Freeport 669 C6
33843 Frostproof 2,995 E4
32731 Fruitland Park 2,259 D3
33578 Fruitville 3,070 D4
*32601 Gainesville⊙ 81,371 D2
Gainesville‡ 151,348 D2
32732 Geneva 1,120 E3
33534 Gibsonton 7,219 C3
32960 Gifford 6,240 F4
32040 Glen Saint Mary 462 D1
†33160 Golden Beach 612 C4
33999 Golden Gate 4,327 E5
†33444 Golf 110 F5
32560 Gonzalez 6,084 B6
33933 Goodland 600 E6
†32502 Goulding 5,352 B6
33170 Goulds 7,078 F6
32440 Graceville 2,918 D5
32442 Grand Ridge 591 A1
33463 Greenacres City 8,843 F5
32043 Green Cove Springs⊙ 4,154 E2
32330 Greensboro 562 B1
32331 Greenville 1,096 C1
32443 Greenwood 577 A1
32332 Gretna 1,448 B1
33533 Grove City 1,932 D5
32736 Groveland 1,992 E3
32561 Gulf Breeze 5,478 B6
33737 Gulfport 11,180 B3
†33444 Gulf Stream 475 F5
†33301 Hacienda Village 126 B4
33844 Haines City 10,799 E3
33009 Hallandale 36,517 B4
32044 Hampton 466 D2
33440 Harlem 2,669 F5
32045 Hastings 636 E2
32333 Havana 2,782 B1
32640 Hawthorne 1,303 D2
32642 Hernando 1,653 D3
*33010 Hialeah 145,254 B4
†33010 Hialeah Gardens 2,700 B4
33431 Highland Beach 2,030 F5
33846 Highland City 1,555 E4
32401 Highland Park 184 E4
32643 High Springs 2,491 D2
32405 Hiland Park 4,763 C6
†33827 Hillcrest Heights 177 E4
32046 Hilliard 1,869 E1
†33060 Hillsboro Beach 1,554 F5
33455 Hobe Sound 6,822 F4
32047 Hollister 980 E2
32017 Holly Hill 9,953 E2
*33020 Hollywood 121,323 B4
33509 Holmes Beach 4,023 D4
*33030 Homestead 20,668 F6
32646 Homosassa 1,426 D3
32648 Horseshoe Beach 304 C2
32334 Hosford 750 B1
32737 Howey In The Hills 626 E3
33568 Hudson 5,799 D3
†33460 Hypoluxo 573 F5
33934 Immokalee 11,038 E5
32903 Indialantic 2,883 F3
†33139 Indian Creek 103 B4
†32901 Indian Harbour Beach 5,967 F3
32960 Indian River Shores 1,254 F4
33535 Indian Rocks Beach 3,717 B3
†33535 Indian Shores 984 B3
33456 Indiantown 3,383 F4
32649 Inglis 1,173 D2
32048 Interlachen 848 E2
32650 Inverness⊙ 4,095 D3
33036 Islamorada 1,441 F7
†33101 Islandia 12 F6
*32201 Jacksonville⊙ 540,920 E1
Jacksonville‡ 737,519 E1
32250 Jacksonville Beach 15,462 E1
†33568 Jasmine Estates 11,995 D3
32052 Jasper⊙ 2,093 D1
32565 Jay 633 B5
32053 Jennings 749 C1
33457 Jensen Beach 6,639 F4
†32901 June Park 4,051 F3
†33404 Juno Beach 1,142 F5
33458 Jupiter 9,868 F5
†33455 Jupiter Island 364 F4
33849 Kathleen 1,866 D3
33156 Kendall 73,758 B5
33709 Kenneth City 4,344 B3
33149 Key Biscayne 6,313 B5
33051 Key Colony Beach 977 F7
33037 Key Largo 7,447 F6
32656 Keystone Heights 1,056 E2
33040 Key West⊙ 24,382 E7
32741 Kissimmee⊙ 15,487 E3
33935 La Belle⊙ 2,287 E5
33537 Lacoochee 1,720 D3
32658 La Crosse 170 D2
32659 Lady Lake 1,193 E3
33850 Lake Alfred 3,134 E3
†32830 Lake Buena Vista 98 E3
32054 Lake Butler⊙ 1,830 D1
†33601 Lake Carroll 13,012 C2
32055 Lake City⊙ 9,257 D1
32744 Lake Helen 2,047 E3
*33801 Lakeland 47,406 D3
Lakeland-Winter Haven‡ 321,652 D3
†33612 Lake Magdalene 13,331 D3
32746 Lake Mary 2,853 E3
33403 Lake Park 6,909 F5
33852 Lake Placid 963 E4
33853 Lake Wales 8,466 E4
*33460 Lake Worth 27,048 G5
33539 Land O'Lakes 4,515 D3
33462 Lantana 8,048 F5
*33540 Largo 58,977 B3
33308 Lauderdale-by-the-Sea 2,639 C3
†33313 Lauderdale Lakes 25,426 B3
33313 Lauderhill 37,271 B3
33545 Laurel 6,368 D4
32567 Laurel Hill 610 C5
32058 Lawtey 692 D1
†33050 Layton 88 F7
†33301 Lazy Lake 31 B3
32059 Lee 297 C1
32748 Leesburg 13,191 E3
33936 Lehigh Acres 9,604 E5
33033 Leisure City 17,905 F6
†33614 Leto 9,003 C2
33064 Lighthouse Point 11,488 F5
32060 Live Oak⊙ 6,732 D1
32662 Lochloosa 450 E2
33548 Longboat Key 4,843 D4
32750 Longwood 10,029 E3
33549 Lutz 5,555 D3
32444 Lynn Haven 6,239 C6
32063 Macclenny⊙ 3,851 D1

(continued on following page)

33738 Madeira Beach 4,520 ... B3
32340 Madison⊙ 3,487 ... C1
32751 Maitland 8,763 ... E3
32950 Malabar 1,118 ... F3
32445 Malone 897 ... A1
33550 Mango 6,493 ... D4
33050 Marathon 7,568 ... E7
33937 Marco (Marco Island) 4,679 ... E6
33063 Margate 35,900 ... F5
32446 Marianna⊙ 7,006 ... A1
†32084 Marineland 31 ... E2
32569 Mary Esther 3,530 ... B6
32753 Mascotte 1,112 ... E3
32066 Mayo⊙ 891 ... C1
32664 McIntosh 404 ... D2
†33101 Medley 537 ... B4
*32901 Melbourne 46,536 ... F3
Melbourne-Titusville-Cocoa‡ 272,959 ... F3
32951 Melbourne Beach 2,713 ... F3
†33301 Melrose Park 5,672 ... B4
†33561 Memphis 5,501 ... D4
32952 Merritt Island 30,708 ... F3
32410 Mexico Beach 632 ... D6
*33101 Miami⊙ 346,931 ... B5
Miami‡ 1,625,979 ... B5
33139 Miami Beach 96,298 ... C5
†33101 Miami Lakes 9,809 ... B4
33153 Miami Shores 9,244 ... B4
33166 Miami Springs 12,350 ... B5
32667 Micanopy 737 ... D2
†32960 Micco 3,585 ... F4
32343 Midway 950 ... B1
32570 Milton⊙ 7,206 ... B6
32754 Mims 7,583 ... F3
32755 Minneola 851 ... E3
33023 Miramar 32,813 ... B4
32577 Molino 1,456 ... B6
32344 Monticello⊙ 2,994 ... C1
32756 Montverde 397 ... E3
33471 Moore Haven⊙ 1,250 ... E5
32757 Mount Dora 5,883 ... E3
33860 Mulberry 2,932 ... E4
33938 Murdock 272 ... D4
32506 Myrtle Grove 14,238 ... B6
*33940 Naples⊙ 17,581 ... E5
†33940 Naples Park 5,438 ... E5
33032 Naranja 10,381 ... F6
32233 Neptune Beach 5,248 ... E1
32669 Newberry 1,826 ... D2
*33552 New Port Richey 11,196 ... D3
32069 New Smyrna Beach 13,557 F2
32578 Niceville 8,543 ... C6
33555 Nokomis 3,108 ... D4
32452 Noma 113 ... C5
†33169 Norland 19,471 ... B4
33141 North Bay Village 4,920 ... B4
33903 North Fort Myers 22,808 ... E5
†33063 North Lauderdale 18,653 ... B3
33161 North Miami 42,566 ... B4
33161 North Miami Beach 36,481 C4
33940 North Naples 7,950 ... E5
33403 North Palm Beach 11,344 .. F5
33595 North Port 6,205 ... D4
†33708 North Redington Beach 1,156 ... B3
32759 Oak Hill 938 ... F3
32760 Oakland 658 ... E3
33334 Oakland Park 23,035 ... B3
*32670 Ocala⊙ 37,170 ... D2
Ocala‡ 122,488 ... D2
†33457 Ocean Breeze Park 469 ... F4
33444 Ocean Ridge 1,355 ... F5
32761 Ocoee 7,803 ... E3
33163 Ojus 17,344 ... B4
32762 Okahumpka 900 ... D3
33472 Okeechobee⊙ 4,225 ... F4
33557 Oldsmar 2,608 ... B2
33558 Oneco 6,417 ... D4
33054 Opa Locka 14,460 ... B4
32763 Orange City 2,795 ... E3
32073 Orange Park 8,766 ... E1
†32970 Orchid 42 ... F4
*32801 Orlando⊙ 128,291 ... E3
Orlando‡ 700,699 ... E3
32074 Ormond Beach 21,378 ... E2
32074 Ormond-by-the-Sea 7,665 . E2
33559 Osprey 1,660 ... D4
32683 Otter Creek 167 ... D2
32765 Oviedo 3,074 ... E3
32570 Pace 5,006 ... B6
33476 Pahokee 6,346 ... F5
†32036 Painters Hill 40 ... E2
32077 Palatka⊙ 10,175 ... E2
32905 Palm Bay 18,560 ... F3
33480 Palm Beach 9,729 ... G4
†33403 Palm Beach Gardens 14,407 ... F5
†33404 Palm Beach Shores 1,232 . G5
33490 Palm City 2,177 ... F4
32037 Palm Coast 2,837 ... E2
32355 Palm Harbor 5,215 ... D3
33561 Palmetto 8,637 ... D4
33563 Palm River-Clair Mel 14,447 ... C3
†32901 Palm Shores 77 ... F3
33460 Palm Springs 8,166 ... F5
*32401 Panama City⊙ 33,346 ... C6
Panama City‡ 97,740 ... C6
32407 Panama City Beach 2,148 . C6
32401 Parker 4,298 ... C6
†33441 Parkland 545 ... F5
32538 Paxton 659 ... C5
†33023 Pembroke Park 4,783 ... B4
33024 Pembroke Pines 35,776 ... B4
32079 Penney Farms 630 ... E2
†33010 Pennsuco 15 ... B4
*32501 Pensacola⊙ 57,619 ... B6
Pensacola‡ 289,782 ... B6
33157 Perrine 16,129 ... F6
32347 Perry⊙ 8,254 ... C1
32080 Pierson 1,085 ... E2
32808 Pine Hills 35,771 ... E3
33565 Pinellas Park 32,811 ... B3
33317 Plantation 48,653 ... B4
33566 Plant City 17,064 ... D3
33868 Polk City 576 ... E3
32081 Pomona Park 791 ... E2
*33060 Pompano Beach 52,618 ... F5
32455 Ponce de Leon 454 ... C6
†32019 Ponce Inlet 1,003 ... F2
33952 Port Charlotte 25,770 ... D5
32019 Port Orange 18,756 ... F2
33568 Port Richey 2,165 ... D3
32456 Port Saint Joe 4,027 ... D6
33452 Port Saint Lucie 14,690 ... F4
33492 Port Salerno 4,511 ... F4
33032 Princeton 10,381 ... F6
*33950 Punta Gorda⊙ 6,797 ... E5
32351 Quincy⊙ 8,591 ... B1
32083 Raiford 259 ... D1
32686 Reddick 657 ... D2
33708 Redington Beach 1,708 ... B3
†33708 Redington Shores 2,142 ... B3
†33158 Richmond Heights 8,577 ... F6
†33301 Riverland 5,919 ... B4
33404 Riviera Beach 26,489 ... G5
32955 Rockledge 11,877 ... F3
32957 Roseland 1,607 ... F4
33570 Ruskin 5,117 ... C3
33572 Safety Harbor 6,461 ... B2
32084 Saint Augustine⊙ 11,985 .. E2
32084 Saint Augustine Beach 1,289 ... E2
32769 Saint Cloud 7,840 ... E3
33956 Saint James City 1,298 ... D5
33574 Saint Leo 917 ... D3
33452 Saint Lucie 593 ... F4
32355 Saint Marks 286 ... B1
*33701 Saint Petersburg 238,647 .. B3
33736 Saint Petersburg Beach 9,354 ... B3
†33508 Samoset 5,747 ... D4
†32069 Samsula 1,971 ... E2
33576 San Antonio 529 ... D3
32771 Sanford⊙ 23,176 ... E3
33957 Sanibel 3,363 ... D5
*33577 Sarasota⊙ 48,868 ... D4
Sarasota‡ 202,251 ... D4
†33577 Sarasota Springs 13,860 ... D4
32935 Satellite Beach 9,163 ... F3
32775 Scottsmoor 900 ... F3
†33301 Sea Ranch Lakes 584 ... C3
32958 Sebastian 2,831 ... F4
33870 Sebring⊙ 8,736 ... E4
33584 Seffner 6,493 ... D4
33542 Seminole 4,586 ... B3
†33457 Sewalls Point 1,187 ... F4
32579 Shalimar 390 ... C6
32959 Sharpes 4,149 ... F3
32688 Silver Springs 1,082 ... D2
32460 Sneads 1,690 ... B1
32358 Sopchoppy 444 ... B1
33493 South Bay 3,886 ... F5
32021 South Daytona 11,252 ... F2
33143 South Miami 10,944 ... B5
†33157 South Miami Heights 23,559 ... F6
33707 South Pasadena 4,188 ... B3
†32901 South Patrick Shores 9,816 ... F3
†32401 Southport 1,992 ... C6
33452 South Port Saint Lucie (Port Saint Lucie 14,690 ... F4
33595 South Venice 8,075 ... D4
32690 Sparr 902 ... D2
32401 Springfield 7,220 ... D6
32091 Starke⊙ 5,306 ... D2
33494 Stuart⊙ 9,467 ... F4
33586 Sun City ... D4
†33570 Sun City Center 5,605 ... C3
†33450 Sunland Gardens ... F4
33160 Sunny Isles 12,564 ... C4
33313 Sunrise 39,681 ... B4
33154 Surfside 3,763 ... B4
32692 Suwannee (Fanning Sprs.) 314 ... C2
†33144 Sweetwater 8,251 ... B5
†32043 Switzerland 3,906 ... E1
32809 Taft 900 ... E3
*32301 Tallahassee (cap.)⊙ 81,548 ... B1
Tallahassee‡ 159,542 ... B1
†33321 Tamarac 29,376 ... B3
*33601 Tampa⊙ 271,523 ... C2
Tampa-Saint Petersburg‡ 1,569,492 .. C2
*33589 Tarpon Springs 13,251 ... D3
32778 Tavares⊙ 4,103 ... E3
33070 Tavernier 1,834 ... F6
33617 Temple Terrace 11,097 ... C2
33458 Tequesta 3,685 ... F5
33905 Tice 6,645 ... E5
32780 Titusville⊙ 31,910 ... F3
33740 Treasure Island 6,316 ... B3
32693 Trenton⊙ 1,131 ... D2
32784 Umatilla 1,872 ... E3
33620 University 24,514 ... C2
32580 Valparaiso 6,142 ... C6
*33595 Venice 12,153 ... D4
32462 Vernon 885 ... C6
32960 Vero Beach⊙ 16,176 ... F4
†33166 Virginia Gardens 2,098 ... B5
32970 Wabasso 2,157 ... F4
†32327 Wakulla 225 ... B1
32694 Waldo 993 ... D2
†32456 Ward Ridge 104 ... D6
32507 Warrington 15,792 ... B6
†32055 Watertown 3,804 ... D1
33873 Wauchula⊙ 2,986 ... E4
32463 Wausau 347 ... D6
33877 Waverly 1,208 ... E4
33597 Webster 856 ... D3
†33512 Weeki Wachee 8 ... D3
32093 Welaka 492 ... E2
32935 West Eau Gallie 2,591 ... F3
†32901 West Melbourne 5,078 ... F3
†33101 West Miami 6,076 ... B5
*33401 West Palm Beach⊙ 63,305 F5
West Palm Beach-Boca Raton‡ 573,125 ... F5
†32502 West Pensacola 24,371 ... B6
32464 Westville 343 ... C6
†33165 Westwood Lakes 11,478 ... B5
32465 Wewahitchka⊙ 1,742 ... D6
†32465 White City 4,110 ... F4
32096 White Springs 781 ... D1
32785 Wildwood 2,665 ... D3
32696 Williston 2,240 ... D2
33334 Wilton Manors 12,742 ... B3
33598 Wimauma 1,477 ... D4
32786 Windermere 1,302 ... E3
33880 Winter Haven 21,119 ... E3
*32789 Winter Park 22,339 ... E3
†32801 Winter Springs 10,475 ... E3
32362 Woodville 1,768 ... B1
32697 Worthington Springs 220 .. D2
32698 Yankeetown 600 ... D2
32097 Yulee 3,168 ... E1
32798 Zellwood 1,760 ... E3
33599 Zephyrhills 5,742 ... D4
33890 Zolfo Springs 1,495 ... E4

OTHER FEATURES

Alapaha (riv.) ... C1
Alligator (lake) ... E3
Amelia (isl.) ... E1
Anastasia (isl.) ... E2
Anclote (keys) ... D3
Apalachee (bay) ... B2
Apalachicola (bay) ... B2
Apalachicola (riv.) ... A1
Apopka (lake) ... E3
Arbuckle (lake) ... E4
Aucilla (riv.) ... C1
Banana (riv.) ... F3
Beresford (lake) ... E2
Big Cypress (swamp) ... E5
Big Cypress Nat'l Preserve ... E5
Biscayne (bay) ... F6
Biscayne (key) ... B5
Biscayne Nat'l Park ... F6
Blackwater (riv.) ... B6
Blue Cypress (lake) ... F4
Boca Chica (key) ... E7
Boca Ciega (bay) ... B3
Boca Grande (key) ... D7
Bryant (lake) ... E2
Caloosahatchee (riv.) ... E5
Captiva (isl.) ... D5
Casey (key) ... D4
Castillo de San Marcos Nat'l Mon. ... E2
Cecil Field Naval Air Sta. ... E1
Charlotte (harb.) ... D5
Chattahoochee (riv.) ... B1
Chipola (riv.) ... D6
Choctawhatchee (riv.) ... C6
Crescent (lake) ... E2
Cumberland Island Nat'l Seashore ... E1
Cypress (lake) ... E3
De Soto Nat'l Mem. ... D4
Dead (lake) ... D6
Dexter (lake) ... E2
Dog (isl.) ... B2
Dorr (lake) ... E2
Dry Tortugas (keys) ... D7
Dumfoundling (bay) ... C4
East (pt.) ... E6
Eglin A.F.B. 7,574 ... C6
Egmont (key) ... D4
Elliott (key) ... F6
Escambia (riv.) ... B6
Estero (isl.) ... E5
Eureka (res.) ... E2
Everglades, The (swamp) ... F6
Everglades Nat'l Park ... F6
Fenholloway (riv.) ... C1
Florida (bay) ... F6
Florida (cape) ... F6
Florida (keys) ... E7
Florida (strs) ... F7
Fort Caroline Nat'l Mem. ... E1
Fort Jefferson Nat'l Mon. ... C7
Fort Matanzas Nat'l Mon. ... E2
Gasparilla (isl.) ... D5
George (lake) ... E2
Grassy (key) ... F7
Gulf Island Nat'l Seashore ... B6
Harney (lake) ... F3
Hart (lake) ... E3
Hillsborough (bay) ... C3
Hillsborough (canal) ... F5
Hillsborough (riv.) ... C2
Homosassa (isls.) ... D3
Homestead A.F.B. 7,594 ... F6
Iamonia (lake) ... B1
Indian (riv.) ... F3
Iron (mt.) ... E4
Istokpoga (lake) ... E4
Jackson (lake) ... B1
Jackson (lake) ... E4
Jacksonville Naval Air Sta. ... E1
John F. Kennedy Space Center ... F3
June in Winter (lake) ... E4
Kennedy (Canaveral) (cape) ... F3
Kerr (lake) ... E2
Key Largo (key) ... F6
Key Vaca (key) ... E7
Key West Naval Air Sta. ... E7
Kissimmee (lake) ... E4
Kissimmee (riv.) ... E4
Largo (key) ... F6
Levy (lake) ... D2
Lochloosa (lake) ... D2
Long (key) ... B3
Long (key) ... F7
Longboat (key) ... D4
Lower Matecumbe (key) ... F7
Lowery (lake) ... E3
MacDill A.F.B. ... C3
Manatee (riv.) ... D4
Marco (isl.) ... E6
Marian (lake) ... E4
Marquesas (keys) ... D7
Matanzas (inlet) ... E2
Mayport Naval Air Sta. ... E1
McCoy A.F.B. ... E3
Merritt (isl.) ... F3
Mexico (gulf) ... C4
Miami (canal) ... F5
Miami (riv.) ... B5
Miccosukee (lake) ... B1
Monroe (lake) ... E3
Mosquito (lag.) ... F3
Mullet (key) ... D4
Myakka (riv.) ... D4
Nassau (riv.) ... E1
Nassau (sound) ... E1
New (riv.) ... B1
New (riv.) ... D1
Newnans (lake) ... D2
North Merritt (isl.) ... F3
North New River (canal) ... F5
Ochlockonee (riv.) ... B1
Okaloacoochee Slough (swamp) ... E5
Okeechobee (lake) ... F5
Okefenokee (swamp) ... D1
Oklawaha (riv.) ... E2
Old Rhodes (key) ... F6
Old Tampa (bay) ... B3
Olustee (riv.) ... D1
Orange (lake) ... D2
Patrick A.F.B. 2,843 ... F3
Peace (riv.) ... E4
Pensacola (bay) ... B6
Pensacola Naval Air Sta. ... B6
Perdido (riv.) ... B6
Pine (isl.) ... D5
Pine Island (sound) ... D5
Pine Log (creek) ... C6
Pinellas (pt.) ... C3
Piney (isl.) ... B1
Piney (pt.) ... C2
Placid (lake) ... E4
Plantation (key) ... F7
Poinsett (lake) ... F3
Ponce de Leon (bay) ... E6
Port Everglades (harb.) ... C4
Port Tampa (harb.) ... B3
Reedy (lake) ... E4
Romano (cape) ... E6
Sable (cape) ... E6
Saint Andrew (pt.) ... D6
Saint George (cape) ... A2
Saint George (isl.) ... B2
Saint George (sound) ... B2
Saint Johns (riv.) ... E2
Saint Joseph (bay) ... D6
Saint Joseph (pt.) ... D6
Saint Lucie (canal) ... F4
Saint Lucie (inlet) ... F4
Saint Marys (riv.) ... D1
Saint Marys Entrance (inlet) ... E1
Saint Vincent (isl.) ... D7
San Blas (cape) ... D7
Sand (key) ... B3
Sands (key) ... F6
Sanibel (isl.) ... D5
Santa Fe (lake) ... D2
Santa Fe (riv.) ... D2
Santa Rosa (isl.) ... B6
Santa Rosa (sound) ... B6
Sarasota (pt.) ... D4
Seminole (lake) ... B1
Seminole Ind. Res. ... E4
Seminole Ind. Res. ... F5
Shark (pt.) ... E6
Shoal (riv.) ... C6
Snake Creek (canal) ... B4
South New River (canal) ... F5
Stafford (lake) ... D2
Sugarloaf (key) ... E7
Suwannee (riv.) ... C2
Suwannee (sound) ... C2
Talbot (isl.) ... E1
Talquin (lake) ... B1
Tamiami (canal) ... E6
Tampa (bay) ... D4
Ten Thousand (isls.) ... E6
Torch (key) ... E7
Treasure (isl.) ... B3
Tsala Apopka (lake) ... D3
Tyndall A.F.B. 4,542 ... C6
Upper Matecumbe (key) ... F7
Vaca (key) ... E7
Virginia (key) ... B5
Waccasassa (bay) ... D2
Waccasassa (riv.) ... D2
Washington (lake) ... F3
Weir (lake) ... E2
Weohyakapka (lake) ... E4
West Palm Beach (canal) ... F5
Whitewater (bay) ... F6
Whiting Field Naval Air Sta. ... B6
Wimico (lake) ... A2
Winder (lake) ... F3
Withlacoochee (riv.) ... C1
Withlacoochee (riv.) ... D2
Yale (lake) ... E3
Yellow (riv.) ... B6

⊙County seat.
‡Population of metropolitan area.
† Zip of nearest p.o. * Multiple zips.

Agriculture, Industry and Resources

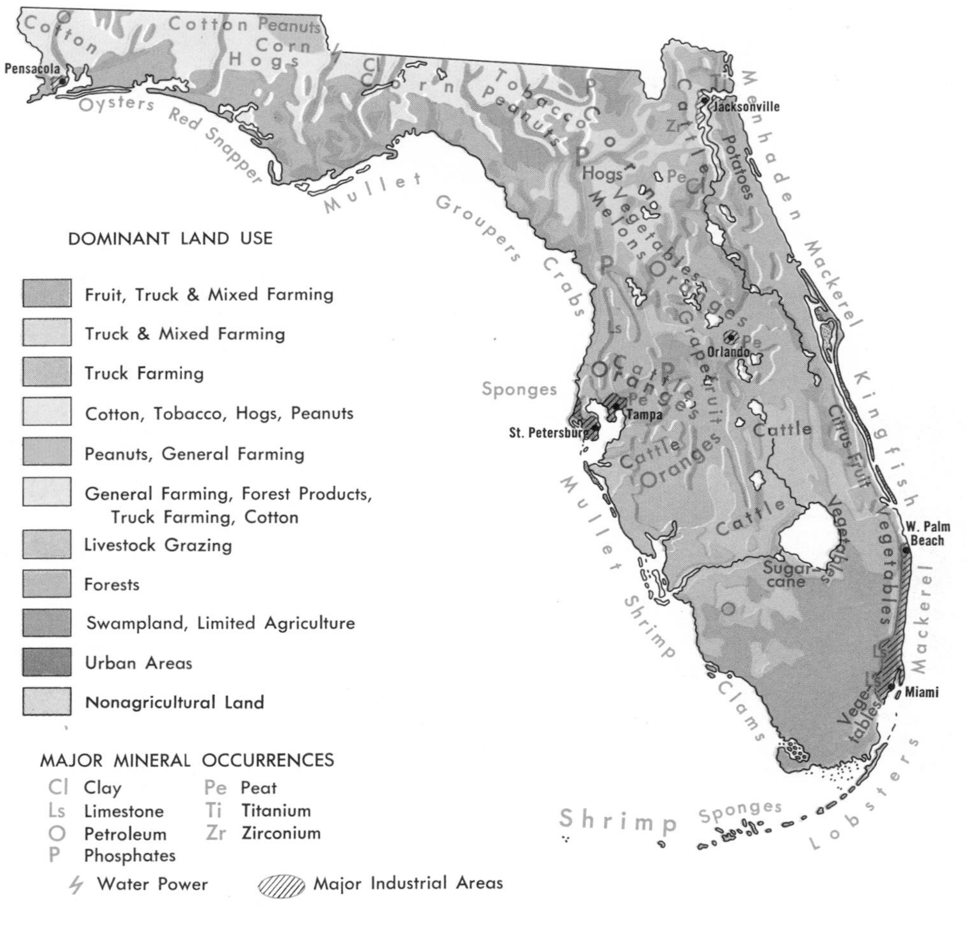

DOMINANT LAND USE
Fruit, Truck & Mixed Farming
Truck & Mixed Farming
Truck Farming
Cotton, Tobacco, Hogs, Peanuts
Peanuts, General Farming
General Farming, Forest Products, Truck Farming, Cotton
Livestock Grazing
Forests
Swampland, Limited Agriculture
Urban Areas
Nonagricultural Land
MAJOR MINERAL OCCURRENCES
Cl Clay
Ls Limestone
O Petroleum
P Phosphates
Pe Peat
Ti Titanium
Zr Zirconium
Water Power
Major Industrial Areas
Pensacola
Jacksonville
Orlando
Tampa
St. Petersburg
W. Palm Beach
Miami
Oysters
Red Snapper
Mullet
Groupers
Crabs
Sponges
Shrimp
Clams
Lobsters
Menhaden
Mackerel
Kingfish
Cattle
Oranges
Sugar-cane
Potatoes

AREA 58,910 sq. mi. (152,577 sq. km.)
POPULATION 5,463,105
CAPITAL Atlanta
LARGEST CITY Atlanta
HIGHEST POINT Brasstown Bald 4,784 ft. (1458 m.)
SETTLED IN 1733
ADMITTED TO UNION January 2, 1788
POPULAR NAME Empire State of the South; Peach State
STATE FLOWER Cherokee Rose
STATE BIRD Brown Thrasher

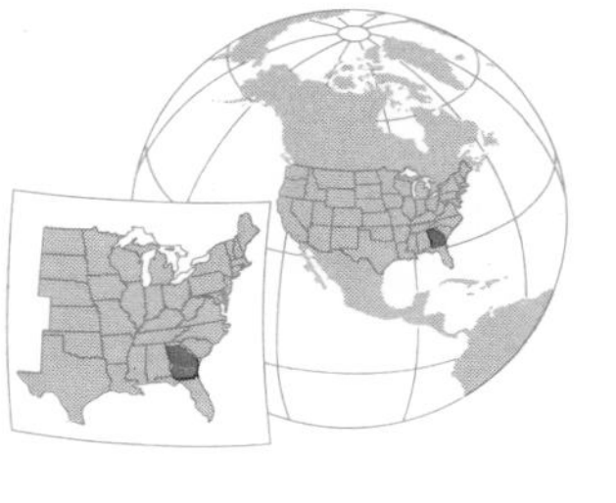

COUNTIES

Appling 15,565 H7
Atkinson 6,141 G8
Bacon 9,379 G7
Baker 3,808 D8
Baldwin 34,686 F4
Banks 8,702 E2
Barrow 21,293 E2
Bartow 40,760 C2
Ben Hill 16,000 F7
Berrien 13,525 F8
Bibb 151,085 E5
Bleckley 10,767 F6
Brantley 8,701 J8
Brooks 15,255 E9
Bryan 10,175 K6
Bulloch 35,785 J6
Burke 19,349 J4
Butts 13,665 E4
Calhoun 5,717 C7
Camden 13,371 J9
Candler 7,518 H6
Carroll 56,346 B3
Catoosa 36,991 B1
Charlton 7,343 H9
Chatham 202,226 K6
Chattahoochee 21,732 C6
Chattooga 21,856 B1
Cherokee 51,699 D2
Clarke 74,498 F3
Clay 3,553 B7
Clayton 150,357 D3
Clinch 6,660 G9
Cobb 297,694 C3
Coffee 26,894 G8
Colquitt 35,376 E8
Columbia 40,118 H3
Cook 13,490 F8
Coweta 39,268 C4
Crawford 7,684 E5
Crisp 19,489 E7
Dade 12,318 A1
Dawson 4,774 D2
Decatur 25,495 C9
De Kalb 483,024 D3
Dodge 16,955 F6
Dooly 10,826 E6
Dougherty 100,978 D7
Douglas 54,573 C3
Early 13,158 C8
Echols 2,297 G9
Effingham 18,327 K6
Elbert 18,758 G2
Emanuel 20,795 H5
Evans 8,428 J6
Fannin 14,748 D1
Fayette 29,043 C4
Floyd 79,800 B2
Forsyth 27,958 D2
Franklin 15,185 F2
Fulton 589,904 D3
Gilmer 11,110 D1
Glascock 2,382 G4
Glynn 54,981 J8
Gordon 30,070 C2
Grady 19,845 D9
Greene 11,391 F3
Gwinnett 166,903 D2
Habersham 25,020 E1
Hall 75,649 E2
Hancock 9,466 G4
Haralson 18,422 B3
Harris 15,464 C5
Hart 18,585 G2
Heard 6,520 B4
Henry 36,309 D4
Houston 77,605 E6
Irwin 8,988 F7
Jackson 25,343 E2
Jasper 7,553 E4
Jeff Davis 11,473 G7
Jefferson 18,403 H4
Jenkins 8,841 J5
Johnson 8,660 G5
Jones 16,579 E5
Lamar 12,215 D4
Lanier 5,654 F8
Laurens 36,990 G6
Lee 11,684 D7
Liberty 37,583 J7
Lincoln 6,949 H3
Long 4,524 J7
Lowndes 67,972 F9
Lumpkin 10,762 D1
Macon 14,003 D6
Madison 17,747 F2
Marion 5,297 C6
McDuffie 18,546 H4
McIntosh 8,046 K7
Meriwether 21,229 C4
Miller 7,038 C8
Mitchell 21,114 D8
Monroe 14,610 E4
Montgomery 7,011 G6
Morgan 11,572 F3
Murray 19,685 C1
Muscogee 170,108 C6
Newton 34,489 E3
Oconee 12,427 F3
Oglethorpe 8,929 F3
Paulding 26,042 C3
Peach 19,151 E5
Pickens 11,652 D2
Pierce 11,897 H8
Pike 8,937 D4
Polk 32,386 B3
Pulaski 8,950 E6
Putnam 10,295 F4
Quitman 2,357 B7
Rabun 10,466 F1
Randolph 9,599 C7
Richmond 181,629 H4
Rockdale 36,747 D3
Schley 3,433 D6
Screven 14,043 J5
Seminole 9,057 C9
Spalding 47,899 D4
Stephens 21,763 F1
Stewart 5,896 C6
Sumter 29,360 D6
Talbot 6,536 C5
Taliaferro 2,032 G3
Tattnall 18,134 J6
Taylor 7,902 D5
Telfair 11,445 G7
Terrell 12,017 D7
Thomas 38,098 E9
Tift 32,862 E7
Toombs 22,592 H6
Towns 5,638 E1
Treutlen 6,087 G6
Troup 50,003 B4
Turner 9,510 E7
Twiggs 9,354 F5
Union 9,390 E1
Upson 25,998 D5
Walker 56,470 B1
Walton 31,211 E3
Ware 37,180 H8
Warren 6,583 G4
Washington 18,842 G4
Wayne 20,750 J7
Webster 2,341 C6
Wheeler 5,155 G6
White 10,120 E1
Whitfield 65,780 B1
Wilcox 7,682 F7
Wilkes 10,951 G3
Wilkinson 10,368 F5
Worth 18,064 E8

CITIES and TOWNS

Zip *Name/Pop.* *Key*

31001 Abbeville⊙ 985 F7
30101 Acworth 3,648 C2
30103 Adairsville 1,739 C2
31620 Adel⊙ 5,592 F8
31002 Adrian 756 G5
30410 Ailey 579 G6
30411 Alamo⊙ 993 G6
31622 Alapaha 771 F8
*31701 Albany⊙ 74,550 D7
Albany‡ 112,456 D7
†30204 Aldora 139 D4
31301 Allenhurst 606 J7
31003 Allentown 321 F5
31510 Alma⊙ 3,819 G7
30201 Alpharetta 3,128 D2
30412 Alston 111 H6
30510 Alto 618 E2
†30161 Alto Park B2
31512 Ambrose 360 G7
31709 Americus⊙ 16,120 D6
31711 Andersonville 267 D6
30802 Appling⊙ 150 H3
31712 Arabi 376 E7
30104 Aragon 855 B2
†30549 Arcade 223 E2
†31520 Arco J8
31623 Argyle 206 G8
31713 Arlington 1,572 C8
30619 Arnoldsville 187 F3
31714 Ashburn⊙ 4,766 E7
*30601 Athens⊙ 42,549 F3
Athens‡ 130,015 F3
*30301 Atlanta (cap.)⊙ 425,022 K1
Atlanta‡ 2,029,618 K1
31715 Attapulgus 623 D9
30203 Auburn 692 E2
*30901 Augusta⊙ 47,532 J4
Augusta‡ 327,372 J4
30001 Austell 3,939 J1
†30557 Avalon 200 F1
30803 Avera 248 G4
30002 Avondale Estates 1,313 L1
31716 Baconton 763 D8
31717 Bainbridge⊙ 10,553 C9
30511 Baldwin 1,080 E2
30107 Ball Ground 640 D2
30204 Barnesville⊙ 4,887 D4
31625 Barney 146 E8
30413 Bartow 357 G5
31720 Barwick 413 E9
31513 Baxley⊙ 3,586 H7
†31554 Beach G8
30414 Bellville 173 H6
31721 Benevolence 138 C7
†30136 Berkeley Lake 503 D3
31722 Berlin 538 E8
30620 Bethlehem 281 E3
†31901 Bibb City 667 B5
30621 Bishop 172 F3
31516 Blackshear⊙ 3,222 H8
30512 Blairsville⊙ 530 E1
31723 Blakely⊙ 5,880 C8
31302 Bloomingdale 1,855 K6
30513 Blue Ridge⊙ 1,376 D1
31724 Bluffton 132 C7
30805 Blythe 367 H4
30622 Bogart 819 E3
31626 Boston 1,424 E9
30623 Bostwick 357 E3
30108 Bowdon 1,743 B3
30516 Bowersville 318 G2
30624 Bowman 890 G2
30517 Braselton 308 E2
†30153 Braswell 282 C3
30110 Bremen 3,966 B3
31725 Brinson 274 C9
31726 Bronwood 524 D7
30415 Brooklet 1,035 J6
30205 Brooks 199 D4
31519 Broxton 1,117 G7
31520 Brunswick⊙ 17,605 K8
30113 Buchanan⊙ 1,019 B3
30625 Buckhead 219 F3
31803 Buena Vista⊙ 1,544 C6
30518 Buford 6,578 D2
31006 Butler⊙ 1,959 D5
31007 Byromville 567 E6
31008 Byron 1,661 E5
31009 Cadwell 353 G6
31728 Cairo⊙ 8,777 D9
30701 Calhoun⊙ 5,335 C1
30807 Camak 283 G4
31730 Camilla⊙ 5,414 D8
30520 Canon 704 F2
30114 Canton⊙ 3,601 C2
30203 Carl 239 E3
30627 Carlton 291 F2
30521 Carnesville⊙ 465 F2
30117 Carrollton⊙ 14,078 C3
30120 Cartersville⊙ 9,247 C2
30124 Cave Spring 883 B2
31627 Cecil 280 F8
30125 Cedartown⊙ 8,619 B2
†30601 Center 330 F2
31028 Centerville 2,622 E5
†30217 Centralhatchee 240 B4
†31816 Chalybeate Springs 265 C5
30341 Chamblee 7,137 K1
30705 Chatsworth⊙ 2,493 C1
31011 Chauncey 350 F6
31012 Chester 409 F6
30707 Chickamauga 2,232 B1
30523 Clarkesville⊙ 1,348 F1
30021 Clarkston 4,539 L1
30417 Claxton⊙ 2,694 J6
30525 Clayton⊙ 1,838 F1
30527 Clermont 300 E2
30528 Cleveland⊙ 1,578 E1
31734 Climax 407 D9
31735 Cobb E7
30420 Cobbtown 494 H6
31014 Cochran⊙ 5,121 F6
30710 Cohutta 407 C1
30628 Colbert 498 F2
31736 Coleman 164 C7
30337 College Park 24,632 K2
30421 Collins 639 H6
31737 Colquitt⊙ 2,065 C8
*31901 Columbus⊙ 169,441 C6
Columbus‡ 239,196 C6
30629 Comer 930 F2
30529 Commerce 4,092 E2
30206 Concord 317 D4
*30207 Conyers⊙ 6,567 D3
31738 Coolidge 736 E8
31015 Cordele⊙ 11,184 E7
30531 Cornelia 3,203 E1
31739 Cotton 122 D8
30209 Covington⊙ 10,586 E3
30711 Crandall C1
30630 Crawford 498 F3
30631 Crawfordville⊙ 594 G3
†31771 Crosland E8
31016 Culloden 281 D5
30130 Cumming⊙ 2,094 D2
31805 Cusseta⊙ 1,218 C6
31740 Cuthbert⊙ 4,340 C7
30211 Dacula 1,577 E3
30533 Dahlonega⊙ 2,844 D1
30423 Daisy 174 J6
30132 Dallas⊙ 2,440 C3
30720 Dalton⊙ 20,743 C1
31741 Damascus 403 C8
30633 Danielsville⊙ 354 F2
31017 Danville 529 F5
31305 Darien⊙ 1,731 K8
31601 Dasher 659 F9
31018 Davisboro 433 G5
31742 Dawson⊙ 5,699 D7
30534 Dawsonville⊙ 342 D2
30808 Dearing 539 H4
*30030 Decatur⊙ 18,404 K1
†31501 Deenwood H8
31082 Deepstep 120 G4
30535 Demorest 1,130 F1
31532 Denton 286 G7
31743 De Soto 248 D7
31019 Dexter 527 G6
30537 Dillard 238 F1
31629 Dixie 259 E9
†31520 Dock Junction (Arco) J8
31744 Doerun 1,062 E8
31745 Donalsonville⊙ 3,320 C8
30340 Doraville 7,414 K1
31533 Douglas⊙ 10,980 G7
*30133 Douglasville⊙ 7,641 C3
31021 Dublin⊙ 16,083 G5
31022 Dudley 425 F5
30136 Duluth 2,956 D2
31630 Du Pont 267 G9
†31830 Durand 206 C5
31021 East Dublin 2,916 G5
30539 East Ellijay 469 C1

(continued on following page)

Agriculture, Industry and Resources

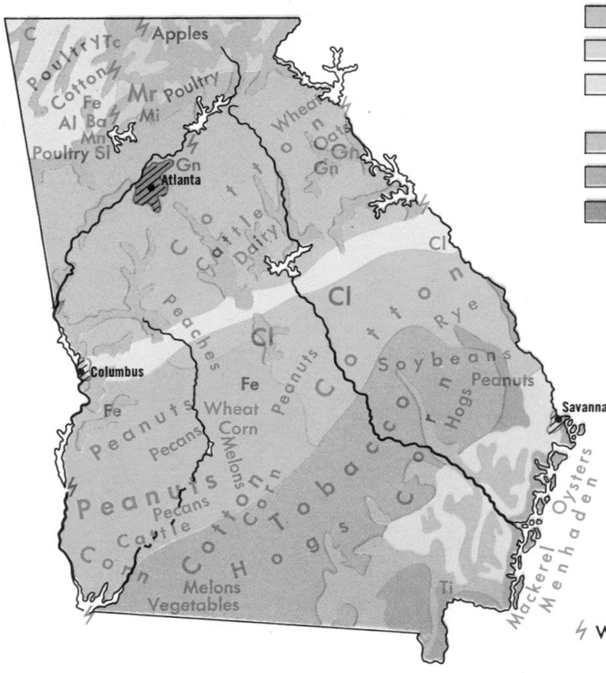

DOMINANT LAND USE

Specialized Cotton
Cotton, General Farming
Cotton, Tobacco, Hogs, Peanuts
Peanuts, General Farming
General Farming, Livestock, Fruit, Tobacco
General Farming, Forest Products, Cotton, Truck Farming
Forests
Swampland, Limited Agriculture
Urban Areas

MAJOR MINERAL OCCURRENCES

Al Bauxite
Ba Barite
C Coal
Cl Clay
Fe Iron Ore
Gn Granite
Mi Mica
Mn Manganese
Mr Marble
Sl Slate
Tc Talc
Ti Titanium

Water Power
Major Industrial Areas

†31046 East Juliette E4
31023 Eastman⊙ 5,330 F6
†30263 East Newnan C4
30344 East Point 37,486 K2
†30677 Eastville E3
31024 Eatonton⊙ 4,833 F4
31307 Eden 990 K6
31746 Edison 1,128 C7
30635 Elberton⊙ 5,686 G2
31806 Ellaville⊙ 1,684 D6
31747 Ellenton 277 E8
31807 Ellerslie 700 C5
30540 Ellijay⊙ 1,507 C1
30137 Emerson 1,110 C2
31749 Enigma 574 F8
†30217 Ephesus 184 B4
30724 Eton 301 C1
†30120 Euharlee 477 C2
30809 Evans H3
30212 Experiment D4
30213 Fairburn 3,466 J2
30139 Fairmount 842 C2
30214 Fayetteville⊙ 2,715 C4
†31071 Finleyson 101 F6
31750 Fitzgerald⊙ 10,187 F7
†31313 Flemington 440 K7
30216 Flovilla 458 E4
30542 Flowery Branch 755 E2
31537 Folkston⊙ 2,243 H9
30050 Forest Park 18,782 K2
31029 Forsyth⊙ 4,624 E4
31751 Fort Gaines⊙ 1,260 C7
30742 Fort Oglethorpe 5,443 B1
31030 Fort Valley⊙ 9,000 E5
30217 Franklin⊙ 711 B4
30639 Franklin Springs 797 F2
31753 Funston 337 E8
30501 Gainesville⊙ 15,280 E2
31408 Garden City 6,895 K6
30425 Garfield 222 H5
30218 Gay 175 C4
31810 Geneva 232 C5
31754 Georgetown⊙ 935 B7
30810 Gibson⊙ 730 G4
30426 Girard 225 J4
30427 Glennville 4,144 J7
30428 Glenwood 824 L1
30641 Good Hope 200 E3
31031 Gordon 2,768 F5
30220 Grantville 1,110 C4
31032 Gray⊙ 2,145 F4
30221 Grayson 464 E3
30726 Graysville 193 B1
30642 Greensboro⊙ 2,985 F3
30222 Greenville⊙ 1,213 C4
30223 Griffin⊙ 20,728 D4
30813 Grovetown 3,491 H4
31312 Guyton 749 K6
31033 Haddock 800 F4
30429 Hagan 880 J6
31632 Hahira 1,534 F9
31811 Hamilton⊙ 506 C5
30228 Hampton 2,059 D4
30354 Hapeville 6,166 K2
30229 Haralson 123 C4
31034 Hardwick F4
30814 Harlem 1,485 H4
31035 Harrison 456 G5
30643 Hartwell⊙ 4,855 G2
31036 Hawkinsville⊙ 4,372 E6
31539 Hazlehurst⊙ 4,249 G7
30545 Helen 265 E1
31037 Helena 1,390 G6
30815 Hephzibah 1,452 H4
30546 Hiawassee⊙ 491 E1
†30410 Higgston 152 G6
30467 Hilltonia 515 J5
31313 Hinesville⊙ 11,309 J7
30141 Hiram 711 C3
31542 Hoboken 514 H8
30230 Hogansville 3,362 C4
30142 Holly Springs 687 D2
†31537 Homeland 683 H9
30547 Homer⊙ 734 F2
31634 Homerville⊙ 3,112 G8
30548 Hoschton 490 E2
30646 Hull 188 F2
31041 Ideal 619 D6
30647 Ila 287 F2
†30705 Industrial City 1,054 C1
31759 Iron City 367 C8
31042 Irwinton⊙ 841 F5
†31031 Ivey 455 F5
30233 Jackson⊙ 4,133 E4
31544 Jacksonville 206 G7
31761 Jakin 194 C8
30143 Jasper⊙ 1,556 D2
30549 Jefferson⊙ 1,820 F2
31044 Jeffersonville⊙ 1,473 F5
30234 Jenkinsburg 360 E4
30235 Jersey 201 E3
31545 Jesup⊙ 9,418 J7
30236 Jonesboro⊙ 4,132 D4
31812 Junction City 254 C5
30144 Kennesaw 5,095 C2
31548 Kingsland 2,008 J9
30145 Kingston 733 C2
31049 Kite 328 G5
31050 Knoxville⊙ 75 E5
30728 La Fayette⊙ 6,517 B1
30240 La Grange⊙ 24,204 B4
30252 Lake 2,963 D3
31635 Lakeland⊙ 2,647 F8
31636 Lake Park 448 F9
30553 Lavonia 2,024 F2
30245 Lawrenceville⊙ 8,928 D3
31762 Leary 783 C8
30146 Lebanon 800 D2
31763 Leesburg⊙ 1,301 D7
31637 Lenox 965 F8
31764 Leslie 470 D7
30648 Lexington⊙ 278 F3
30247 Lilburn 3,765 D3
31051 Lilly 202 E6
†30286 Lincoln Park D5
30817 Lincolnton⊙ 1,406 G3
30147 Lindale B2
†30728 Linwood 417 B1
30058 Lithonia 2,637 D3
30248 Locust Grove 1,479 D4
30249 Loganville 1,841 E3
30433 Lollie G6
†30230 Lone Oak 119 C4
†30741 Lookout Mountain 1,505 B1
30434 Louisville⊙ 2,823 H4
30250 Lovejoy 205 D4
31316 Ludowici⊙ 1,286 J7
30554 Lula 857 E2
31549 Lumber City 1,426 G7
31815 Lumpkin⊙ 1,335 C6
30251 Luthersville 597 C4
30730 Lyerly 482 B2
30436 Lyons⊙ 4,203 H6
30059 Mableton J1
*31201 Macon⊙ 116,860 E5
Macon‡ 254,623 E5
30650 Madison⊙ 2,954 F3
30438 Manassas 116 H6
31816 Manchester 4,796 C5
30255 Mansfield 435 E4
*30060 Marietta⊙ 30,805 J1
31057 Marshallville 1,540 D6
30557 Martin 305 F2
30671 Maxeys 205 F3
30558 Maysville 619 E2
30555 McCaysville 1,219 D1
30253 McDonough⊙ 2,778 D4
31054 McIntyre 386 F5
31055 McRae⊙ 3,409 G6
30256 Meansville 303 D4
30040 Mechanicsville L1
31765 Meigs 1,231 D8
30731 Menlo 611 B2
†31792 Metcalf E9
30439 Metter⊙ 3,531 H6
30441 Midville 670 H5
31320 Midway 457 K7
31060 Milan 1,115 G6
31061 Milledgeville⊙ 12,176 F4
30442 Millen⊙ 3,988 J5
30257 Milner 320 D4
30207 Milstead D3
30559 Mineral Bluff 130 D1
30820 Mitchell 214 G4
30258 Molena 379 D4
30655 Monroe⊙ 8,854 E3
31063 Montezuma 4,830 E6
31064 Monticello⊙ 2,382 E4
31065 Montrose 170 F5
30259 Moreland 358 C4
31766 Morgan⊙ 364 C7
30560 Morganton 263 D1
30260 Morrow 3,791 K2
31638 Morven 471 E9
31768 Moultrie⊙ 15,708 E8
30562 Mountain City 701 F1
†30075 Mountain Park 378 D2
30563 Mount Airy 670 F1
30149 Mount Berry B2
30445 Mount Vernon⊙ 1,737 G6
30261 Mountville 168 C4
30150 Mount Zion 445 B3
31553 Nahunta⊙ 951 H8
31639 Nashville⊙ 4,831 F8
31641 Naylor 228 F9
30151 Nelson 562 D2
30262 Newborn 391 E3
30446 Newington 402 J5
30263 Newnan⊙ 11,449 C4
31770 Newton⊙ 711 D8
31554 Nicholls 1,114 G7
30565 Nicholson 491 F2
*30071 Norcross 3,317 D3
31771 Norman Park 757 E8
†30645 North High Shoals 256 F3
30821 Norwood 306 G4
30448 Nunez 168 H5
31772 Oakfield 113 E7
30732 Oakman 150 C1
31903 Oak Park 256 H6
30566 Oakwood 723 E2
31773 Ochlocknee 627 E9
31774 Ocilla⊙ 3,436 F7
31067 Oconee 306 G5
†30222 Odessadale 142 C5
31555 Odum 401 H7
31406 Oglethorpe⊙ 1,305 D6
30449 Oliver 239 J5
31821 Omaha 169 C6
31775 Omega 996 E8
30266 Orchard Hill 162 D4
30267 Oxford 1,750 E3
30268 Palmetto 2,086 C3
31777 Parrott 222 D7
31557 Patterson 763 H8
31778 Pavo 830 E9
†31201 Payne 196 E5
30269 Peachtree City 6,429 C4
31642 Pearson⊙ 1,827 G8
31779 Pelham 4,306 D8
31321 Pembroke⊙ 1,400 J6
30567 Pendergrass 302 E2
31069 Perry⊙ 9,453 E6
†31794 Phillipsburg E8
31070 Pinehurst 431 E6
30072 Pine Lake 901 D3
31822 Pine Mountain 984 C5
†31312 Pineora 387 K6
†31728 Pine Park D9
31071 Pineview 564 F6
31072 Pitts 384 E7
31073 Plainfield 128 F6
31780 Plains 651 D6
30733 Plainville 281 C2
31322 Pooler 2,543 K6
30450 Portal 694 J5
30270 Porterdale 1,451 E3
31407 Port Wentworth 3,947 K6
31781 Poulan 818 E8
30073 Powder Springs 3,381 C3
31824 Preston⊙ 429 C6
30451 Pulaski 257 J6
31643 Quitman⊙ 5,188 E9
30734 Ranger 171 C2
31645 Ray City 658 F8
30660 Rayle 177 G3
31783 Rebecca 272 E7
30453 Reidsville⊙ 2,296 H6
31601 Remerton 443 F9
31075 Rentz 337 G6
†30518 Rest Haven 231 E2
31076 Reynolds 1,298 D5
31077 Rhine 590 F7
31323 Riceboro 216 K7
31825 Richland 1,802 C6
31324 Richmond Hill 1,177 K7
†31018 Riddleville 154 G5
31326 Rincon 1,988 K6
30736 Ringgold⊙ 1,821 B1
*30274 Riverdale 7,121 K2
†31768 Riverside 99 E8
†30759 Riverside B2
31078 Roberta 859 D5
31079 Rochelle 1,626 F7
30153 Rockmart 3,645 B2
30455 Rocky Ford 223 J5
30161 Rome⊙ 29,654 B2
30170 Roopville 229 B4
30741 Rossville 3,851 B1
*30075 Roswell 23,337 D2
30662 Royston 2,404 F2
†30680 Russell 378 E3
30663 Rutledge 694 E3
31558 Saint Marys 3,596 J9
31522 Saint Simons Island K8
31784 Sale City 336 D8
31082 Sandersville⊙ 6,137 G5
†20436 Santa Claus 167 H6
30456 Sardis 1,180 J5
30275 Sargent 800 C4
31785 Sasser 407 D7
*31401 Savannah⊙ 141,634 L6
Savannah‡ 230,728 L6
31083 Scotland 222 G6
31095 Scott 139 G5
31560 Screven 872 H7
30276 Senoia 900 C4
31084 Seville 209 E7
31085 Shady Dale 155 E4
30172 Shannon B2
30664 Sharon 140 G3
30277 Sharpsburg 194 C4
31786 Shellman 1,254 C7
31826 Shiloh 392 C5
30665 Siloam 446 F3
31787 Smithville 867 D7
30080 Smyrna 20,312 K1
30278 Snellville 8,514 D3
30279 Social Circle 2,591 E3
30457 Soperton⊙ 2,981 G6
31647 Sparks 1,353 F8
31087 Sparta⊙ 1,754 F4
31329 Springfield⊙ 1,075 K6
†30705 Spring Place 246 C1
30823 Stapleton 388 H4
31648 Statenville⊙ 700 G9
30458 Statesboro⊙ 14,866 J6
30666 Statham 1,101 E3
30464 Stillmore 527 H6
30281 Stockbridge 2,103 D3
*30083 Stone Mountain 4,867 D3
†30518 Sugar Hill 2,473 E2
30746 Sugar Valley C1
30466 Summertown 215 H5
30747 Summerville⊙ 4,878 B2
31789 Sumner 213 E7
30284 Sunny Side 338 D4
31563 Surrency 368 H7
30174 Suwanee 1,026 D2
30401 Swainsboro⊙ 7,602 H5
31790 Sycamore 474 E7
30467 Sylvania⊙ 3,352 J5
31791 Sylvester⊙ 5,860 E7
31827 Talbotton⊙ 1,140 C5
30176 Tallapoosa 2,647 B3
30573 Tallulah Falls 162 F1
30575 Talmo E2
30470 Tarrytown 145 H6
30178 Taylorsville 266 C2
30179 Temple 1,520 B3
31089 Tennille 1,709 G5
30285 The Rock 78 D5
30286 Thomaston⊙ 9,682 D5
31792 Thomasville⊙ 18,463 E9
30824 Thomson⊙ 7,001 H4
†31404 Thunderbolt 2,165 K6
31794 Tifton⊙ 13,749 F8
30576 Tiger 299 F1
30668 Tignall 733 G3
30577 Toccoa⊙ 9,104 F1
31090 Toomsboro 673 F5
30752 Trenton⊙ 1,636 A1
30753 Trion 1,732 B1
30755 Tunnel Hill 867 C1
30289 Turin 260 C4
30471 Twin City 1,402 H5
31328 Tybee Island 2,240 L6
30290 Tyrone 1,038 C4
31795 Ty Ty 618 E8
31091 Unadilla 1,566 E6
30291 Union City 4,780 J2
30669 Union Point 1,750 F3
†31794 Unionville F8
30473 Uvalda 646 H6
31601 Valdosta⊙ 37,596 F9
30672 Vanna F2
†30153 Van Wert 303 B3
30756 Varnell 288 C1
†31401 Vernonburg 178 K7
30474 Vidalia 10,393 H6
†30830 Vidette H4
31092 Vienna⊙ 2,886 E6
30180 Villa Rica 3,420 C3
30182 Waco 471 B3
30477 Wadley 2,438 H5
30183 Waleska 450 D2
†30209 Walnut Grove 387 E3
31333 Walthourville 905 J7
31830 Warm Springs 425 C5
31093 Warner Robins 39,893 E5
30828 Warrenton⊙ 2,172 G4
31796 Warwick 488 E7
30673 Washington⊙ 4,662 G3
30677 Watkinsville⊙ 1,240 E3
31831 Waverly Hall 913 C5
31501 Waycross⊙ 19,371 H8
30830 Waynesboro⊙ 5,760 J4
31832 Weston 109 C7
31833 West Point 4,294 B5
31797 Whigham 507 D9
30184 White 501 C2
31568 White Oak 450 J8
30678 White Plains 231 F4
30185 Whitesburg 775 B4
31650 Willacoochee 1,166 G8
30292 Williamson 250 D4
31410 Wilmington Island L7
30680 Winder⊙ 6,705 E3
31406 Windsor Forest K7
30683 Winterville 621 F3
31569 Woodbine⊙ 910 J9
30293 Woodbury 1,738 C5
31836 Woodland 664 D5
30188 Woodstock 2,699 D2
30670 Woodville 455 F3
30833 Wrens 2,415 H4
31096 Wrightsville⊙ 2,526 G5
31097 Yatesville 390 D5
30582 Young Harris 687 E1
30295 Zebulon⊙ 995 D4

OTHER FEATURES

Alapaha (riv.) F7
Allatoona (lake) C2
Altamaha (riv.) H7
Andersonville Nat'l Hist. Site D6
Atlanta Nav. Air Sta. J1
Banks (lake) F9
Bartletts Ferry (dam) B5
Blackshear (lake) E7
Blue Ridge (mts.) D1
Brasstown Bald (mt.) E1
Burton (lake) E1
Carters (lake) C1
Chattahoochee (riv.) B8
Chattahoochee River Nat'l Rec. Area K1
Chattooga (riv.) A2
Chattooga (riv.) F1
Chatuge (lake) E1
Chickamauga and Chattanooga Nat'l Mil. Park B1
Clark Hill (lake) H3
Coosa (riv.) A2
Coosawattee (riv.) C1
Cumberland (isl.) K9
Cumberland Island Nat'l Seashore K9
Dobbins A.F.B. J1
Doboy (sound) K8
Etowah (riv.) C2
Eufaula (Walter F. George Res.) (lake) B7
Flint (riv.) D8
Fort Benning B6
Fort Frederica Nat'l Mon. K8
Fort Gordon H4
Fort McPherson K1
Fort Pulaski Nat'l Mon. L6
Fort Stewart J7
Goat Rock (lake) B5
Harding (lake) B5
Hartwell (lake) G2
Jekyll (isl.) K8
Kennesaw Mtn. Nat'l Battlefield Park J1
Lawson A.A.F. B6
Martin Luther King, Jr., Nat'l Hist. Site K1
Moody A.F.B. F9
Nottely (lake) D1
Ochlockonee (riv.) C10
Ocmulgee (riv.) E5
Ocmulgee Nat'l Mon. F5
Oconee (riv.) F5
Ogeechee (riv.) J5
Okefenokee (swamp) H9
Oliver (lake) B5
Oostanaula (riv.) B2
Ossabaw (sound) K7
Rabun (lake) E1
Robins A.F.B. F5
Saint Andrew (sound) K9
Saint Catherines (isl.) K7
Saint Marys (riv.) J9
Saint Simons K8
Sapelo (isl.) K8
Satilla (riv.) G8
Savannah (riv.) K5
Sea (isls.) K9
Seminole (lake) B9
Sidney Lanier (lake) D2
Sinclair (lake) F4
Skidaway (isl.) L7
Springer (mt.) D1
Suwannee (riv.) G10
Tugaloo (riv.) F1
Walter F. George (res.) B7
Wassaw (sound) L7
Weiss (lake) A2
West Point (lake) B4

⊙County seat.
‡Population of metropolitan area.
† Zip of nearest p.o. * Multiple zips.

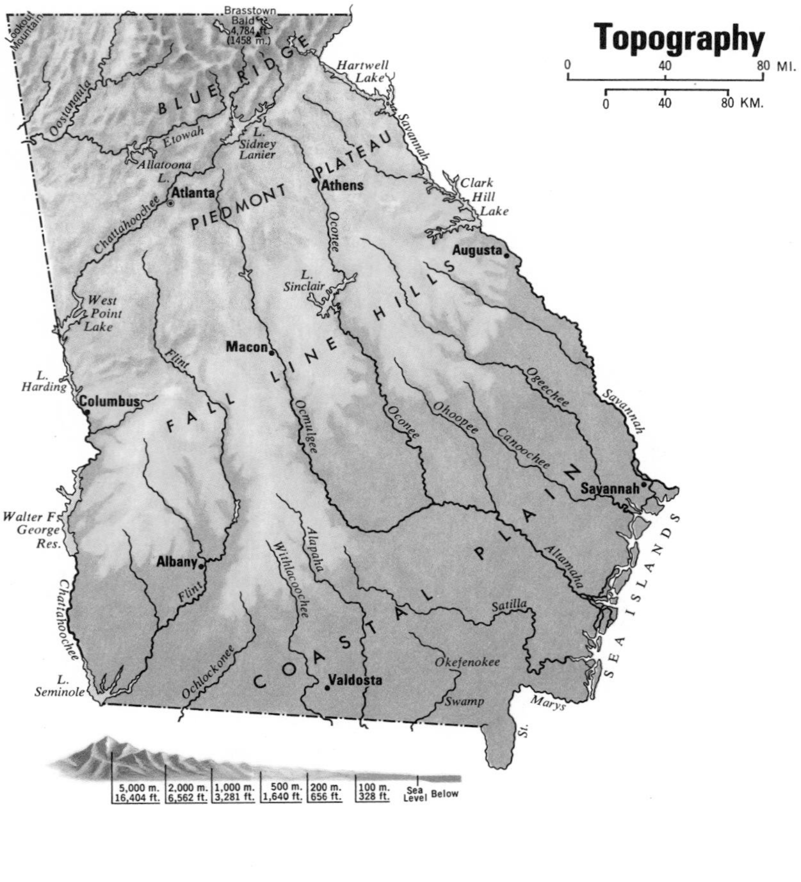

COUNTIES

Hawaii 92,053 ....K7
Honolulu 762,565 ....D3
Kalawao 144 ....G1
Kauai 39,082 ....A1
Maui 70,847 ....J1

CITIES and TOWNS

Zip   Name/Pop.   Key

96701 Aiea 32,879 ....B3
96821 Aina Haina F2
　Ala Moana 96,820 ....C4
96703 Anahola 915 ....C1
†96706 Barbers Point 1,373 ...E2
96704 Captain Cook 2,008 ....G5
96705 Eleele 580 ....C2
96706 Ewa 2,637 ....A4
96706 Ewa Beach 14,369 ......A4
96701 Foster Village B3
†96714 Haena 200 ....C1
96708 Haiku 619 ....J2
96710 Hakalau J4
†96711 Halawa, Hawaii 50 ....G3
†96748 Halawa, Molokai 15 ...H1
†96701 Halawa Heights B3
96712 Haleiwa 2,412 ....E1
†96718 Halfway House 150 ....H6
96787 Haliimaile 741 ....J2

†96713 Hamoa 35 ....K2
96713 Hana 643 ....K2
96714 Hanalei 483 ....C1
96715 Hanamaulu 3,227 ....C1
96716 Hanapepe 1,417 ....C2
96717 Hauula 2,997 ....E1
96825 Hawaii Kai F2
96718 Hawaii Nat'l Park 250 ...J6
96824 Hickam Housing 4,425 ..B4
96720 Hilo⊙ 35,269 ....J5
96725 Holualoa 1,243 ....G5
96726 Honaunau 950 ....G6
96727 Honokaa 1,936 ....H4
†96761 Honokahua 309 ....H1
*96801 Honolulu (cap.)⊙ 365,048 ...C4
　Honolulu‡ 762,874 ....C4
96728 Honomu 559 ....J4
96729 Hoolehua G1
†96706 Iroquois Point 3,915 ...A4
96730 Kaaawa 959 ....F1
†96761 Kaanapali 541 ....H2
96793 Kahakuloa 75 ....J1
†96801 Kahala D5
†96744 Kahaluu 2,925 ....E2
96731 Kahuku 935 ....E1
96732 Kahului 12,978 ....J2
96740 Kohala (Kapaau) 612 ...G3
96734 Kailua (Oahu) 35,812 ...F2

96740 Kailua Kona 4,751 ....F5
†96750 Kainaliu 512 ....G5
96741 Kalaheo 2,500 ....C2
96742 Kalaupapa⊙ 170 ....G1
96754 Kalihiwai 40 ....C1
96748 Kaluaaha 20 ....H1
96743 Kamuela 1,179 ....G3
96744 Kaneohe 29,919 ....F2
96746 Kapaa 4,467 ....C1
96755 Kapaau 612 ....G3
96817 Kapalama C4
96747 Kaumakani 888 ....C2
96748 Kaunakakai 2,231 ....G1
96708 Kaupakulua 600 ....K2
†96713 Kaupo 65 ....K2
96743 Kawaihae 50 ....G4
†96712 Kawailoa 200 ....E1
96749 Keaau 775 ....J5
†96750 Kealakekua 1,033 .....G5
96751 Kealia, Kauai 300 ....D1
96708 Keanae 280 ....K2
96752 Kekaha 3,260 ....C2
96754 Kilauea 895 ....C1
†96713 Kipahulu 75 ....K2
†96713 Koali 60 ....K2
†96755 Kokee (Kapaau) 612 ...G3
96708 Kokomo 500 ....K2
96756 Koloa 1,457 ....C2

96756 Koloa Landing C2
96757 Kukaiau 75 ....H4
†96775 Kukaiau 75 ....H4
96727 Kukuihaele 332 ....H3
96790 Kula 800 ....J2
96759 Kunia 550 ....E2
96760 Kurtistown 900 ....J5
96761 Lahaina 6,095 ....H1
96762 Laie 4,643 ....E1
96763 Lanai City 2,092 ....H2
96764 Laupahoehoe 500 ....J4
96765 Lawai 950 ....C2
96766 Lihue⊙ 4,000 ....C2
†96779 Lower Paia 1,500 ....J1
96719 Mahukona 2 ....G3
96792 Maili 5,026 ....D2
96732 Makaha 6,582 ....D2
96706 Makakilo 7,691 ....E2
96768 Makawao 2,900 ....K2
96769 Makaweli 500 ....B2
†96790 Makena 100 ....J2
96822 Makiki C4
96770 Maunaloa 633 ....G1
96744 Maunawili 5,239 ....F2
96789 Mililani Town 21,365 ...E2
96828 Moiliili C4
96734 Mokapu 11,615 ....F2
96771 Mountainview 540 ....J5
96772 Naalehu 1,168 ....H7
†96713 Nahiku 50 ....K2

96792 Nanakuli 8,185 ....D2
96761 Napili-Honokowai 2,446 ...H1
96773 Ninole 75 ....J4
†96781 Onomea 10 ....J4
96774 Ookala 401 ....J4
96775 Paauhau 450 ....H4
96776 Paauilo 755 ....H4
96777 Pahala 1,619 ....H6
96778 Pahoa 923 ....J5
96779 Paia J2
96780 Papaaloa J4
96781 Papaikou 1,567 ....J5
†96781 Paukaa 544 ....J5
96708 Pauwela 468 ....K2
96708 Peahi 308 ....K2
96782 Pearl City 42,575 ....B3
96783 Pepeekeo J4
†96756 Poipu 685 ....C2
96714 Princeville 500 ....C1
96766 Puhi 991 ....C2
96788 Pukalani 3,950 ....J2
96748 Pukoo 50 ....H1
†96713 Puuiki 75 ....K2
96784 Puunene 572 ....J2
†96801 Puunui C4
96786 Schofield Barracks 18,851 .E2
96779 Spreckelsville 350 ....J1
†96708 Ulumalu 25 ....K2
†96776 Umikoa 25 ....H4
96785 Volcano 400 ....J6

96786 Wahiawa 16,911 ....E2
†96788 Waiakoa J2
96816 Waialae D4
†96731 Waialee 50 ....E1
96748 Waialua, Molokai 30 ....H1
96791 Waialua, Oahu 4,051 ...E2
96792 Waianae 7,941 ....D2
96793 Waihee 413 ....J2
96793 Waikapu 698 ....J2
96815 Waikiki C4
†96748 Wailau 20 ....H1
†96710 Wailea, Hawaii 150 .....J4
96790 Wailea, Maui 1,124 ......J2
96746 Wailua 1,587 ....D2
96793 Wailuku⊙ 10,260 ....J2
96708 Waimanalo 3,562 ....F2
†96795 Waimanalo Bch. 4,161 .F2
96743 Waimea (Kamuela),
　Hawaii 1,179 ....G3
96796 Waimea, Kauai 1,569 ...B2
†96720 Wainaku 1,045 ....J5
96714 Wainiha 175 ....C1
96797 Waipahu 29,139 ....A3
†96786 Waipio Acres 4,091 .....E2
†96786 Whitmore Village 2,318 .E1

OTHER FEATURES

Alalakeiki (chan.) J3
Alenuihaha (chan.) E7

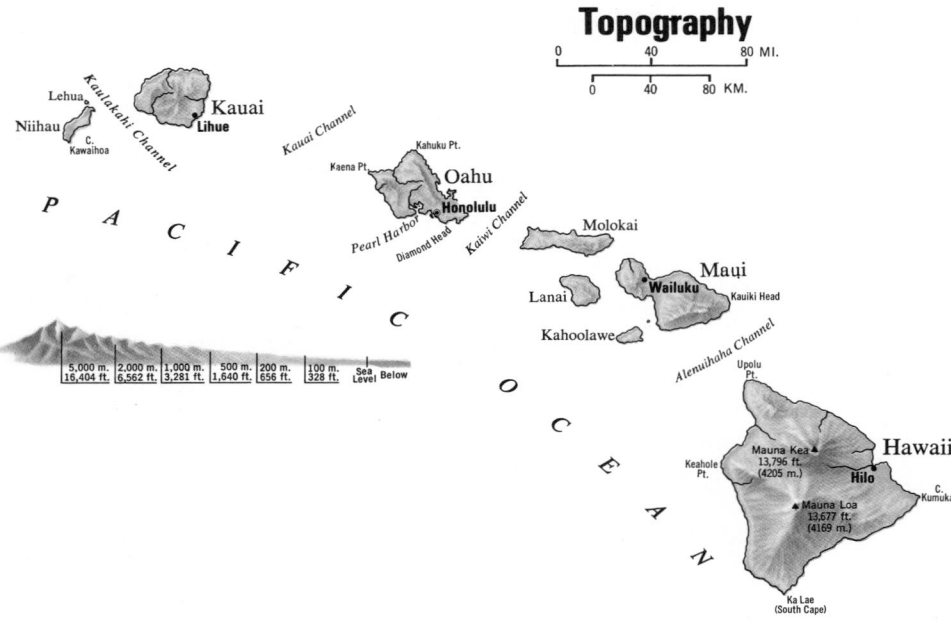

Topography

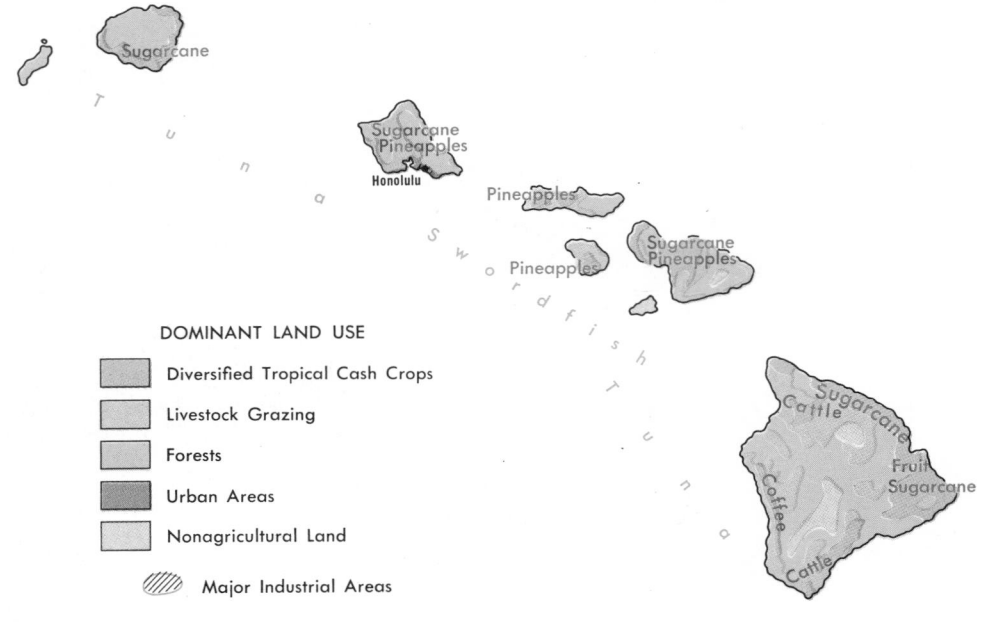

Agriculture, Industry and Resources

DOMINANT LAND USE

Diversified Tropical Cash Crops
Livestock Grazing
Forests
Urban Areas
Nonagricultural Land

Major Industrial Areas

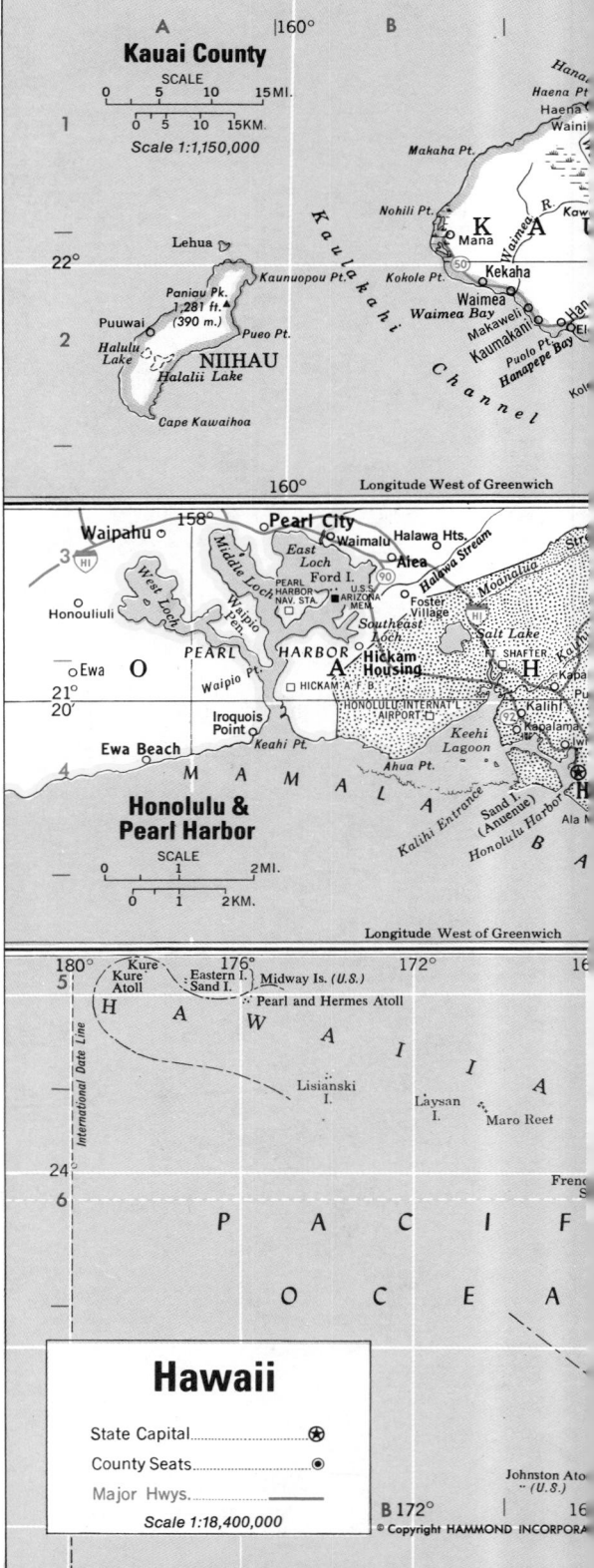

Kauai County

SCALE
0　5　10　15 MI.
0　5　10　15KM.
Scale 1:1,150,000

Honolulu & Pearl Harbor

SCALE
0　1　2 MI.
0　1　2KM.

Hawaii

State Capital ....⊛
County Seats ....⊙
Major Hwys. _____

Scale 1:18,400,000

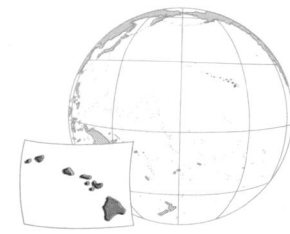

AREA 6,471 sq. mi. (16,760 sq. km.)
POPULATION 964,691
CAPITAL Honolulu
LARGEST CITY Honolulu
HIGHEST POINT Mauna Kea 13,796 ft. (4205 m.)
SETTLED IN —
ADMITTED TO UNION August 21, 1959
POPULAR NAME Aloha State
STATE FLOWER Hibiscus
STATE BIRD Nene (Hawaiian Goose)

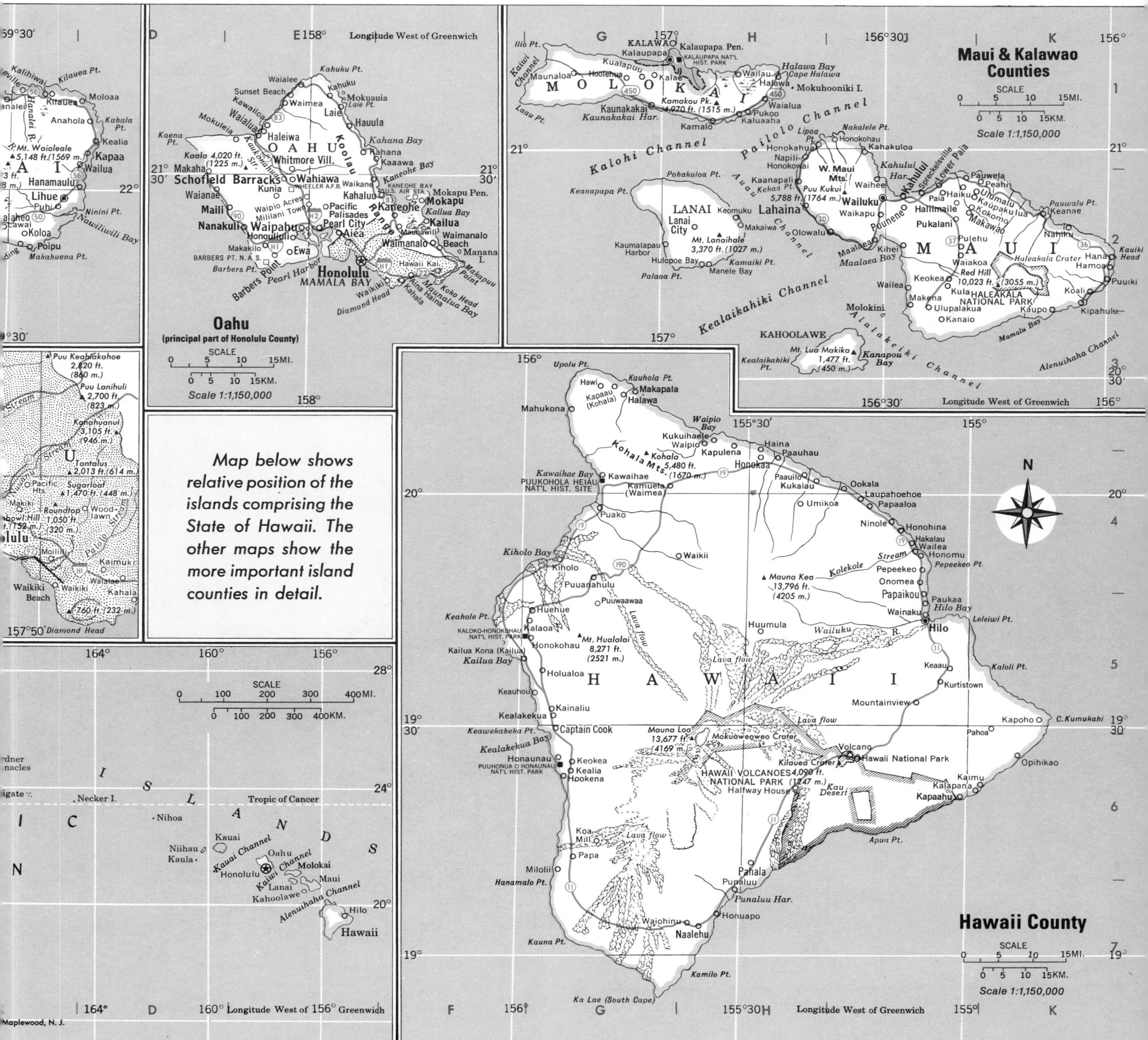

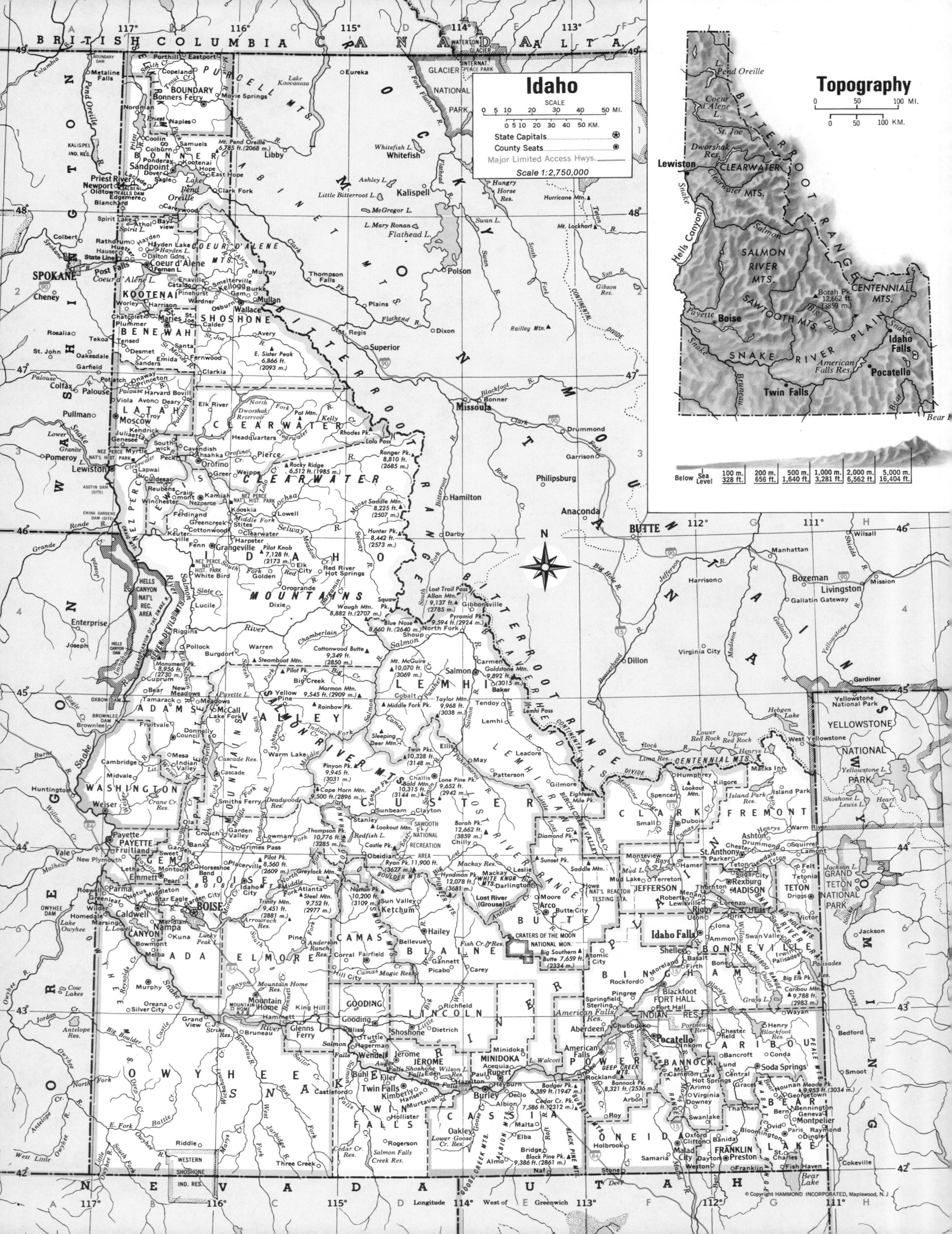

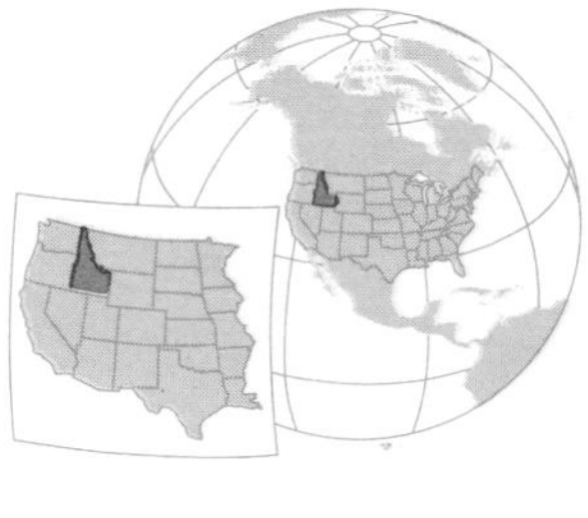

AREA 83,564 sq. mi. (216,431 sq. km.)
POPULATION 944,038
CAPITAL Boise
LARGEST CITY Boise
HIGHEST POINT Borah Pk. 12,662 ft. (3859 m.)
SETTLED IN 1842
ADMITTED TO UNION July 3, 1890
POPULAR NAME Gem State
STATE FLOWER Syringa
STATE BIRD Mountain Bluebird

COUNTIES

Ada 173,036 ..... B6
Adams 3,347 ..... B5
Bannock 65,421 ..... F7
Bear Lake 6,931 ..... G7
Benewah 8,292 ..... B2
Bingham 36,489 ..... F6
Blaine 9,841 ..... D6
Boise 2,999 ..... C6
Bonner 24,163 ..... B1
Bonneville 65,980 ..... G6
Boundary 7,289 ..... B1
Butte 3,342 ..... E6
Camas 818 ..... D6
Canyon 83,756 ..... B6
Caribou 8,695 ..... G7
Cassia 19,427 ..... E7
Clark 798 ..... F5
Clearwater 10,390 ..... C3
Custer 3,385 ..... D5
Elmore 21,565 ..... C6
Franklin 8,895 ..... G7
Fremont 10,813 ..... G5
Gem 11,972 ..... B6
Gooding 11,874 ..... D6
Idaho 14,769 ..... C4
Jefferson 15,304 ..... F6
Jerome 14,840 ..... D7
Kootenai 59,770 ..... B2
Latah 28,749 ..... B3
Lemhi 7,460 ..... D4
Lewis 4,118 ..... B3
Lincoln 3,436 ..... D6
Madison 19,480 ..... G6
Minidoka 19,718 ..... E7
Nez Perce 33,220 ..... B3
Oneida 3,258 ..... F7
Owyhee 8,272 ..... B7
Payette 15,825 ..... B5
Power 6,844 ..... F7
Shoshone 19,226 ..... B2
Teton 2,897 ..... G6
Twin Falls 52,927 ..... D7
Valley 5,604 ..... C5
Washington 8,803 ..... B5

CITIES and TOWNS

Zip *Name/Pop.* *Key*

83210 Aberdeen 1,528 ..... F7
83350 Acequia 100 ..... E7
83311 Albion 286 ..... E7
83211 American Falls⊙ 3,626 ..... E7
†83401 Ammon 4,669 ..... G6
83213 Arco⊙ 1,241 ..... E6
83214 Arimo 338 ..... F7
83420 Ashton 1,219 ..... G5
83801 Athol 312 ..... B2
83217 Bancroft 505 ..... G7
83218 Basalt 414 ..... F6
83313 Bellevue 1,016 ..... D6
83221 Blackfoot⊙ 10,065 ..... F6
83314 Bliss 208 ..... D7
83223 Bloomington 212 ..... G7
*83701 Boise (cap.)⊙ 102,160 ..... B6
Boise‡ 173,036 ..... B6
83805 Bonners Ferry⊙ 1,906 ..... B1
83806 Bovill 289 ..... B3
83316 Buhl 3,629 ..... D7
83318 Burley⊙ 8,761 ..... E7
83213 Butte City 93 ..... E6
83605 Caldwell⊙ 17,699 ..... B6
83610 Cambridge 428 ..... B5
83611 Cascade⊙ 945 ..... C5
83321 Castleford 191 ..... C7
83226 Challis⊙ 758 ..... D5
†83851 Chatcolet 181 ..... B2
83202 Chubbuck 7,052 ..... F7
83811 Clark Fork 449 ..... B1
83227 Clayton 43 ..... D5
83228 Clifton 208 ..... F7
83814 Coeur d'Alene⊙ 20,054 ..... B2
83522 Cottonwood 941 ..... B3
83612 Council⊙ 917 ..... B5
83523 Craigmont 617 ..... B3
†83622 Crouch 69 ..... B5
83524 Culdesac 261 ..... B3
†83814 Dalton Gardens 1,795 ..... B2
83232 Dayton 368 ..... F7
83823 Deary 539 ..... B3
83323 Declo 276 ..... E7
83324 Dietrich 101 ..... D7
83615 Donnelly 139 ..... B5
83234 Downey 645 ..... F7
83422 Driggs⊙ 727 ..... G6
83423 Dubois⊙ 413 ..... F5
83616 Eagle 2,620 ..... B6
†83836 East Hope 258 ..... B1
83325 Eden 355 ..... D7
83827 Elk River 265 ..... B3
83617 Emmett⊙ 4,605 ..... B6
83327 Fairfield⊙ 404 ..... D6
83526 Ferdinand 144 ..... B3
†83814 Fernan Lake 178 ..... B2
83328 Filer 1,645 ..... D7
83236 Firth 460 ..... F6
83203 Fort Hall 750 ..... F6
83237 Franklin 423 ..... G7
83619 Fruitland 2,456 ..... B6
†83704 Garden City 4,571 ..... B6
83832 Genesee 791 ..... B3
83239 Georgetown 544 ..... G7
83623 Glenns Ferry 1,374 ..... C7
83330 Gooding⊙ 2,949 ..... D7
83241 Grace 1,216 ..... G7
83624 Grand View 366 ..... B7
83530 Grangeville⊙ 3,666 ..... B4
83626 Greenleaf 663 ..... B6
83332 Hagerman 602 ..... D7
83333 Hailey⊙ 2,109 ..... D6
83425 Hamer 93 ..... F6
83334 Hansen 1,078 ..... D7
83833 Harrison 260 ..... B2
†83854 Hauser 305 ..... A2
†83835 Hayden 2,586 ..... B2
83835 Hayden Lake 273 ..... B2
83335 Hazelton 496 ..... E7
83336 Heyburn 2,889 ..... E7
†83301 Hollister 167 ..... D7
83628 Homedale 2,078 ..... A6
83836 Hope 106 ..... B1
83629 Horseshoe Bend 700 ..... B6
†83854 Huetter 65 ..... B2
83631 Idaho City⊙ 300 ..... C6
*83401 Idaho Falls⊙ 39,590 ..... F6
83245 Inkom 830 ..... F7
83427 Iona 1,072 ..... G6
83428 Irwin 113 ..... G6
83429 Island Park 154 ..... G5
83338 Jerome⊙ 6,891 ..... D7
83535 Juliaetta 522 ..... B3
83536 Kamiah 1,478 ..... B3
83837 Kellogg 3,417 ..... B2
83537 Kendrick 395 ..... B3
83340 Ketchum 2,200 ..... D6
83341 Kimberly 2,307 ..... D7
83539 Kooskia 784 ..... C3
83840 Kootenai 280 ..... B1
83634 Kuna 1,767 ..... B6
83540 Lapwai 1,043 ..... B3
83246 Lava Hot Springs 467 ..... F7
83464 Leadore 114 ..... E5
83501 Lewiston⊙ 27,986 ..... A3
83431 Lewisville 502 ..... F6
83251 Mackay 541 ..... E6
83252 Malad City⊙ 1,915 ..... F7
83342 Malta 196 ..... E7
83639 Marsing 786 ..... B6
83638 McCall 2,188 ..... C5
83250 McCammon 770 ..... F7
83641 Melba 276 ..... B6
83434 Menan 605 ..... F6
83642 Meridian 6,658 ..... B6
83644 Middleton 1,901 ..... B6
83645 Midvale 205 ..... B5
83343 Minidoka 101 ..... E7
83254 Montpelier 3,107 ..... G7
83255 Moore 210 ..... E6
83843 Moscow⊙ 16,513 ..... B3
83647 Mountain Home⊙ 7,540 ..... C6
83845 Moyie Springs 386 ..... B1
†83450 Mud Lake 243 ..... F6
83846 Mullan 1,269 ..... C2
83650 Murphy⊙ 200 ..... B6
83344 Murtaugh 114 ..... D7
83651 Nampa 25,112 ..... B6
83436 Newdale 329 ..... G6
83654 New Meadows 576 ..... B4
83655 New Plymouth 1,186 ..... B6
83543 Nezperce⊙ 517 ..... B3
83656 Notus 437 ..... B6
83346 Oakley 663 ..... D7
†99156 Oldtown 257 ..... A1
†83855 Onaway 254 ..... B3
83544 Orofino⊙ 3,711 ..... B3
83849 Osburn 2,220 ..... B2
†83263 Oxford 66 ..... F7
83261 Paris⊙ 707 ..... G7
83438 Parker 262 ..... G6
83660 Parma 1,820 ..... B6
83347 Paul 940 ..... E7
83661 Payette⊙ 5,448 ..... B5
83545 Peck 209 ..... B3
83546 Pierce 1,060 ..... C3
83850 Pinehurst 2,183 ..... B2
83851 Plummer 634 ..... B2
*83201 Pocatello⊙ 46,340 ..... F7
83852 Ponderay 399 ..... B1
83854 Post Falls 5,736 ..... A2
83855 Potlatch 819 ..... A3
83263 Preston⊙ 3,759 ..... G7
83856 Priest River 1,639 ..... A1
83858 Rathdrum 1,369 ..... A2
83548 Reubens 87 ..... B3
83440 Rexburg⊙ 11,559 ..... G6
83349 Richfield 357 ..... D6
83442 Rigby⊙ 2,624 ..... F6
83549 Riggins 527 ..... B4
83443 Ririe 555 ..... G6
83444 Roberts 466 ..... F6
83271 Rockland 283 ..... F7
83350 Rupert⊙ 5,476 ..... E7
83445 Saint Anthony⊙ 3,212 ..... G6
83272 Saint Charles 211 ..... G7
83861 Saint Maries⊙ 2,794 ..... B2
83467 Salmon⊙ 3,308 ..... D4
83864 Sandpoint⊙ 4,460 ..... B1
83274 Shelley 3,300 ..... F6
83352 Shoshone⊙ 1,242 ..... D7
†83650 Silver City 1 ..... B6
83868 Smelterville 776 ..... B2
83276 Soda Springs⊙ 4,051 ..... G7
83869 Spirit Lake 834 ..... A2
83278 Stanley 99 ..... D5
83552 Stites 253 ..... C3
83448 Sugar City 1,022 ..... G6
83353 Sun Valley 545 ..... D6
83449 Swan Valley 135 ..... G6
83870 Tensed 113 ..... B2
83451 Teton 559 ..... G6
83452 Tetonia 191 ..... G6
83871 Troy 820 ..... B3
83301 Twin Falls⊙ 26,209 ..... D7
83454 Ucon 833 ..... F6
83455 Victor 323 ..... G6
83873 Wallace⊙ 1,736 ..... C2
†83837 Wardner 423 ..... B2
83553 Weippe 828 ..... C3
83672 Weiser⊙ 4,771 ..... B5
83355 Wendell 1,974 ..... D7
83286 Weston 310 ..... F7
83554 White Bird 154 ..... B4
83676 Wilder 1,260 ..... A6
83555 Winchester 343 ..... B3
83876 Worley 206 ..... B2

OTHER FEATURES

Albeni Falls (dam) B1
Albion (mts.) E7
Allan (mt.) D4
American Falls (res.) F6
Anderson Ranch (res.) C6
Antelope (creek) E6
Arrowrock (res.) C6
Auger (falls) D7
Badger (peak) E7
Bald (mt.) D5
Bannock (creek) F7
Bannock (peak) F7
Bannock (range) F7
Bargamin (creek) C4
Battle (creek) B7
Bear (lake) G7
Bear (riv.) G7
Beaver (creek) F5
Beaverhead (mts.) E4
Big (creek) C4
Big Boulder (creek) B7
Big Elk (peak) G6
Big Hole (mts.) G6
Big Lost (riv.) E6
Big Southern (butte) E6
Big Wood (riv.) D6
Birch (creek) F5
Birch Creek (valley) E5
Bitterroot (range) D3
Blackfoot (res.) G7
Black Pine (mts.) E7
Blue Nose (mt.) D4
Boise (mts.) B6
Boise (riv.) B6
Borah (peak) E5
Boulder (mts.) D6
Brownlee (dam) B5
Bruneau (riv.) C7
Camas (creek) D5
Camas (creek) D6
Camas (creek) F5
Canyon (creek) C6
Cape Horn (mt.) C5
Caribou (mt.) G6
Caribou (range) G6
Cascade (res.) C5
Castle (creek) B7
Castle (peak) D5
Cedar Creek (peak) E7
Cedar Creek (res.) D7
Centennial (mts.) F5
Clearwater (mts.) C3
Clearwater (riv.) B3
Coeur d'Alene (lake) B2
Coeur d'Alene (mts.) C2
Coeur d'Alene (riv.) B2
Cottonwood (butte) C4
Craig (mts.) B4
Crane Creek (res.) B5
Craters of the Moon Nat'l Mon. E6
Deadwood (res.) C5
Deep (creek) B7
Deep (creek) F7
Deep Creek (mts.) F7
Diamond (peak) E5
Dworshak (res.) C3
East Sister (peak) C2
Eighteen Mile (peak) E5
Fish Creek (res.) E6
Fort Hall Ind. Res. F6
Goldstone (mt.) E4
Goose (creek) E7
Goose Creek (mts.) E7
Grand Canyon of the Snake River (canyon) B4
Grays (lake) G6
Grays Lake Outlet (creek) G6
Greylock (mt.) C6
Hayden (lake) B2
Hells (canyon) B4
Hells Canyon Nat'l Rec. Area B4
Henrys (lake) G5
Henrys Fork, Snake (riv.) G5
Hunter (peak) D3
Hyndman (peak) D6
Indian (creek) C5
Island Park (res.) G5
Jarbidge (riv.) C7
Johnson (creek) C5
Jordan (creek) A7
Kootenai (riv.) C1
Lemhi (pass) E5
Lemhi (range) E5
Lemhi (riv.) E5
Little Lost (riv.) E5
Little Owyhee (riv.) B7
Little Salmon (riv.) B4
Little Weiser (riv.) B5
Little Wood (riv.) D6
Lochsa (riv.) C3
Lolo (creek) C3
Lolo (pass) D3
Lone Pine (peak) D5
Lookout (mt.) D5
Lookout (mt.) F5
Lost River (range) E5
Lost Trail (pass) E4
Lowell (lake) B6
Lower Goose Creek (res.) D7
Lower Granite (lake) A3
Lucky Peak (lake) B6
Mackay (res.) E6
Magic (res.) D6
Malad (riv.) F7
Marsh (creek) F7
McGuire (mt.) D4
Meade (peak) G7
Meadow (creek) C4
Medicine Lodge (creek) F5
Middle Fork (peak) D5
Monument (peak) B4
Moose (creek) D3
Mores (creek) C6
Mormon (mt.) D4
Mountain Home (res.) C6
Mountain Home A.F.B. 6,403 ..... C6
Moyie (riv.) B1
Mud (lake) F6
National Reactor Testing Sta. F6
Nez Perce Nat'l Hist. Park B-C3
North Fork (riv.) B7
Norton (peak) D6
Orofino (creek) C3
Owyhee (mts.) B6
Owyhee, East Fork (riv.) B7
Oxbow (dam) B5
Pack (riv.) B1
Pahsimeroi (riv.) E5
Palisades (res.) G6
Palouse (riv.) B3
Panther (creek) D4
Payette (lake) C4
Payette (mts.) B5
Payette (riv.) B6
Peale (mts.) G7
Pend Oreille (lake) B1
Pend Oreille (mt.) B1
Pend Oreille (riv.) A1
Pilot (peak) C4
Pilot (peak) C6
Pilot Knob (mt.) C4
Pinyon (peak) C5
Pioneer (mts.) D6
Portneuf (res.) F7
Pot (mt.) C3
Potlatch (riv.) B3
Priest (lake) B1
Priest (riv.) B1
Purcell (mts.) B1
Pyramid (peak) E4
Raft (riv.) E7
Rainbow (mt.) C4
Ranger (peak) D3
Rays (lake) F6
Red (riv.) C4
Redfish (lake) D5
Reynolds (creek) B6
Rhodes (peak) D3
Rocky (mts.) D1
Rocky Ridge (mt.) C3
Ryan (peak) D6
Saddle (mt.) D3
Saddle (mt.) F6
Sailor (creek) C7
Saint Joe (riv.) B2
Saint Maries (riv.) B2
Salmon (falls) C7
Salmon (riv.) B4
Salmon Falls (creek) D7
Salmon Falls Creek (res.) D7
Salmon River (mts.) C5
Sawtooth (range) C6
Sawtooth Nat'l Rec. Area D5
Secesh (riv.) C4
Selkirk (mts.) B1
Selway (riv.) C3
Seven Devils (mts.) B4
Shoshone (falls) D7
Sleeping Deer (mt.) D5
Smith (creek) B1
Smoky (mts.) D6
Snake (riv.) A3
Snake River (plain) D7
Snake River (range) G6
Spirit (lake) B2
Squaw (creek) B5
Squaw (peak) D4
Steamboat (mt.) C4
Steel (mt.) C6
Strike, C.J. (res.) C7
Sublett (mts.) E7
Sunset (peak) E6
Taylor (mt.) D5
Teton (riv.) G6
Thompson (peak) C5
Trinity (mt.) C6
Trout (creek) B1
Twin (falls) D7
Twin Peaks (mt.) D5
Walcott (lake) E7
Wasatch (range) G7
Waugh (mt.) D4
Weiser (riv.) B5
Western Shoshone Ind. Res. B7
White Knob (mts.) E6
Wickahoney (creek) C7
Willow (creek) G6
Wilson Lake (res.) D7
Yankee Fork, Salmon (riv.) D5
Yellowstone Nat'l Park G5

⊙County seat.
‡Population of metropolitan area.
† Zip of nearest p.o.
* Multiple zips.

Agriculture, Industry and Resources

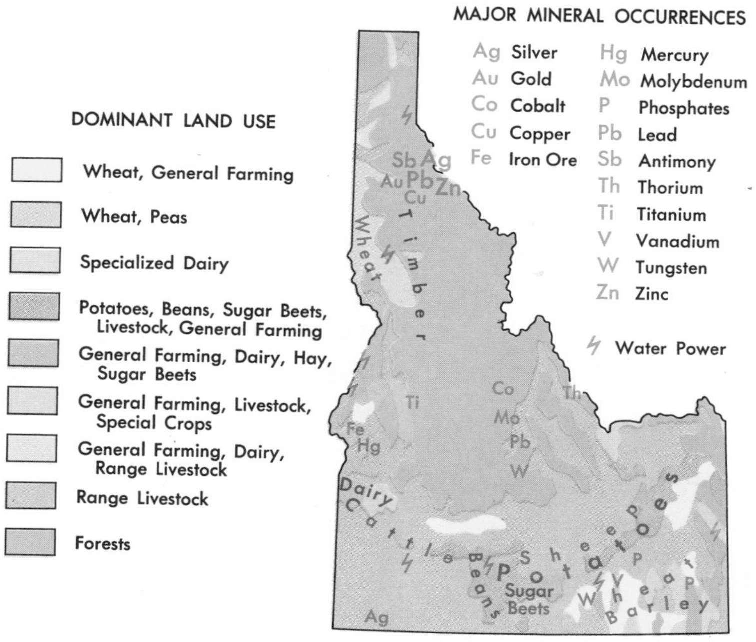
MAJOR MINERAL OCCURRENCES
Ag Silver
Au Gold
Co Cobalt
Cu Copper
Fe Iron Ore
Hg Mercury
Mo Molybdenum
P Phosphates
Pb Lead
Sb Antimony
Th Thorium
Ti Titanium
V Vanadium
W Tungsten
Zn Zinc
Water Power
DOMINANT LAND USE
Wheat, General Farming
Wheat, Peas
Specialized Dairy
Potatoes, Beans, Sugar Beets, Livestock, General Farming
General Farming, Dairy, Hay, Sugar Beets
General Farming, Livestock, Special Crops
General Farming, Dairy, Range Livestock
Range Livestock
Forests
Timber
Wheat
Dairy
Cattle
Sheep
Potatoes
Beans
Sugar Beets
Wheat
Barley

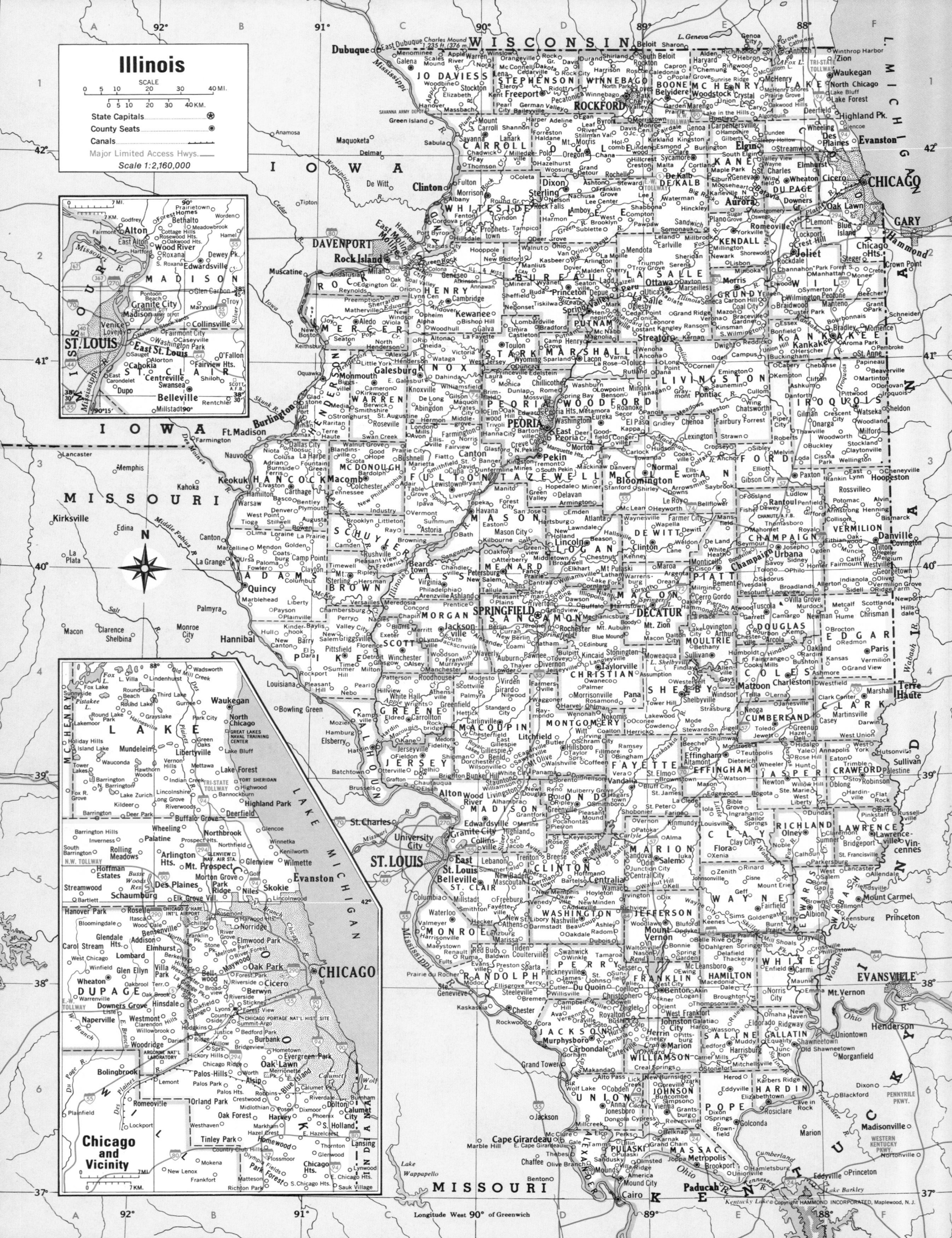

Illinois

SCALE

0 5 10   20   30   40 MI.

0 5 10 20   30   40 KM.

State Capitals .... ⊛
County Seats .... ◉
Canals
Major Limited Access Hwys. ....

Scale 1:2,160,000

Chicago and Vicinity

0   7MI.

0   7 KM.

AREA 56,345 sq. mi. (145,934 sq. km.)
POPULATION 11,426,596
CAPITAL Springfield
LARGEST CITY Chicago
HIGHEST POINT Charles Mound 1,235 ft. (376 m.)
SETTLED IN 1720
ADMITTED TO UNION December 3, 1818
POPULAR NAME Prairie State; Land of Lincoln
STATE FLOWER Native Violet
STATE BIRD Cardinal

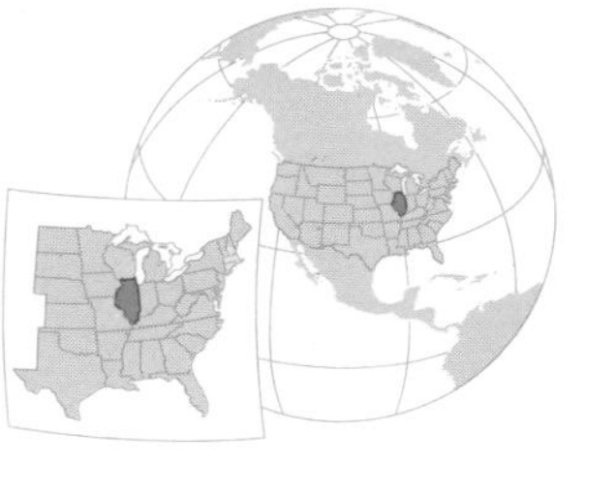

COUNTIES

Adams 71,622 ... B4
Alexander 12,264 ... D6
Bond 16,224 ... D5
Boone 28,630 ... E1
Brown 5,411 ... C4
Bureau 39,114 ... D2
Calhoun 5,867 ... C4
Carroll 18,779 ... D1
Cass 15,084 ... C4
Champaign 168,392 ... E3
Christian 36,446 ... D4
Clark 16,913 ... F4
Clay 15,283 ... E5
Clinton 32,617 ... D5
Coles 52,260 ... E4
Cook 5,253,655 ... F2
Crawford 20,818 ... F4
Cumberland 11,062 ... E4
De Kalb 74,624 ... E2
De Witt 18,108 ... E3
Douglas 19,774 ... E4
Du Page 658,835 ... E2
Edgar 21,725 ... F4
Edwards 7,961 ... E5
Effingham 30,944 ... E4
Fayette 22,167 ... D4
Ford 15,265 ... E3
Franklin 43,201 ... E5
Fulton 43,687 ... C3
Gallatin 7,590 ... E6
Greene 16,661 ... C4
Grundy 30,582 ... E2
Hamilton 9,172 ... E5
Hancock 23,877 ... B3
Hardin 5,383 ... E6
Henderson 9,114 ... C3
Henry 57,968 ... C2
Iroquois 32,976 ... F3
Jackson 61,522 ... D6
Jasper 11,318 ... E4
Jefferson 36,354 ... E5
Jersey 20,538 ... C4
Jo Daviess 23,520 ... C1
Johnson 9,624 ... E6
Kane 278,405 ... E2
Kankakee 102,926 ... F2
Kendall 37,202 ... E2
Knox 61,607 ... C3
Lake 440,372 ... E1
La Salle 112,033 ... E2
Lawrence 17,807 ... F5
Lee 36,328 ... D2
Livingston 41,381 ... E3
Logan 31,802 ... D3
Macon 131,375 ... E4
Macoupin 49,384 ... D4
Madison 247,691 ... D5
Marion 43,523 ... E5
Marshall 14,479 ... D2
Mason 19,492 ... D3
Massac 14,990 ... E6
McDonough 37,467 ... C3
McHenry 147,897 ... E1
McLean 119,149 ... E3
Menard 11,700 ... D3
Mercer 19,286 ... C2
Monroe 20,117 ... C5
Montgomery 31,686 ... D4
Morgan 37,502 ... C4
Moultrie 14,546 ... E4
Ogle 46,338 ... D1
Peoria 200,466 ... D3
Perry 21,714 ... D5
Piatt 16,581 ... E4
Pike 18,896 ... C4
Pope 4,404 ... E6
Pulaski 8,840 ... D6
Putnam 6,085 ... D2
Randolph 35,652 ... D5
Richland 17,587 ... E5
Rock Island 165,968 ... C2
Saint Clair 267,531 ... D5
Saline 28,448 ... E6
Sangamon 176,089 ... D4
Schuyler 8,365 ... C3
Scott 6,142 ... C4
Shelby 23,923 ... E4
Stark 7,389 ... D2
Stephenson 49,536 ... D1
Tazewell 132,078 ... D3
Union 17,765 ... D6
Vermilion 95,222 ... F3
Wabash 13,713 ... F5
Warren 21,943 ... C3
Washington 15,472 ... D5
Wayne 18,059 ... E5
White 17,864 ... E5
Whiteside 65,970 ... D2
Will 324,460 ... F2
Williamson 56,538 ... E6
Winnebago 250,884 ... D1
Woodford 33,320 ... D3

CITIES and TOWNS

Zip *Name/Pop.* *Key*

61410 Abingdon 4,210 ... C3
60101 Addison 29,826 ... B5
61230 Albany 1,014 ... C2
62806 Albion⊙ 2,285 ... E5
61231 Aledo⊙ 3,881 ... C2
61412 Alexis 1,076 ... C2
60102 Algonquin 5,834 ... E1
62207 Alorton 2,237 ... B2
61413 Alpha 815 ... C2
†60658 Alsip 17,134 ... B6
62411 Altamont 2,389 ... E4
62002 Alton 34,171 ... A2
61310 Amboy 2,377 ... D2
61232 Andalusia 1,238 ... C2
62906 Anna 5,408 ... D6
61234 Annawan 908 ... C2
60002 Antioch 4,419 ... E1
61910 Arcola 2,714 ... E4
62501 Argenta 994 ... E4
*60004 Arlington Heights 66,116 ... B5
61911 Arthur 2,122 ... E4
60911 Ashkum 735 ... E3
62612 Ashland 1,351 ... C4
62808 Ashley 658 ... D5
61912 Ashmore 883 ... F4
61006 Ashton 1,140 ... D2
62510 Assumption 1,283 ... E4
61501 Astoria 1,370 ... C3
62613 Athens 1,371 ... D4
61235 Atkinson 1,138 ... C2
61723 Atlanta 1,807 ... D3
61913 Atwood 1,464 ... E4
62615 Auburn 3,616 ... D4
62311 Augusta 764 ... C3
*60504 Aurora 81,293 ... E2
62907 Ava 811 ... D6
62216 Aviston 846 ... D5
61415 Avon 1,019 ... C3
†60015 Bannockburn 1,316 ... B5
60010 Barrington 9,029 ... A5
†60010 Barrington Hills 3,631 ... A5
62312 Barry 1,487 ... B4
60103 Bartlett 13,254 ... A5
61607 Bartonville 6,137 ... D3
60510 Batavia 12,574 ... E2
62618 Beardstown 6,338 ... C3
62219 Beckemeyer 1,119 ... D5
60401 Beecher 2,024 ... F2
*62220 Belleville⊙ 41,580 ... B3
60104 Bellwood 19,811 ... B5
61008 Belvidere⊙ 15,176 ... E1
61813 Bement 1,770 ... E4
62009 Benld 1,638 ... D4
60106 Bensenville 16,124 ... B5
62812 Benton⊙ 7,778 ... E6
60162 Berkeley 5,467 ... B5
60402 Berwyn 46,849 ... B6
62010 Bethalto 8,630 ... B2
61914 Bethany 1,550 ... E4
61420 Blandinsville 886 ... C3
60108 Bloomingdale 12,659 ... A5
61701 Bloomington⊙ 44,189 ... D3
Bloomington-Normal‡ 119,149 ... D3
60406 Blue Island 21,855 ... B6
62513 Blue Mound 1,338 ... D4
62621 Bluffs 821 ... C4
60439 Bolingbrook 37,261 ... A6
60914 Bourbonnais 13,280 ... F2
60407 Braceville 721 ... E2
61421 Bradford 924 ... D2
60915 Bradley 11,008 ... F2
60408 Braidwood 3,429 ... E2
62230 Breese 3,516 ... D5
62417 Bridgeport 2,281 ... F5
60455 Bridgeview 14,155 ... B6
62012 Brighton 2,364 ... C4
61517 Brimfield 890 ... D3
60153 Broadview 8,618 ... B6
60513 Brookfield 19,395 ... B6
†62059 Brooklyn (Lovejoy) 1,233 ... A2
62910 Brookport 1,128 ... E6
61314 Buda 668 ... D2
†60090 Buffalo Grove 22,230 ... B5
62014 Bunker Hill 1,700 ... D4
60459 Burbank 28,462 ... B6
†60601 Burnham 4,030 ... C6
†60558 Burr Ridge 3,833 ... B6
61422 Bushnell 3,811 ... C3
61010 Byron 2,035 ... D1
62206 Cahokia 18,904 ... A3
62914 Cairo⊙ 5,931 ... D6
60409 Calumet City 39,697 ... C6
†60643 Calumet Park 8,788 ... C6
62915 Cambria 1,090 ... D6
61238 Cambridge⊙ 2,217 ... C2
62320 Camp Point 1,285 ... B3
61520 Canton 14,626 ... C3
61239 Carbon Cliff 1,578 ... C2
62901 Carbondale 26,414 ... D6
62626 Carlinville⊙ 5,439 ... D4
62231 Carlyle⊙ 3,388 ... D5
62821 Carmi⊙ 6,264 ... E5
†60187 Carol Stream 15,472 ... A5
60110 Carpentersville 23,272 ... E1
62917 Carrier Mills 2,268 ... E6
62016 Carrollton⊙ 2,816 ... C4
62918 Carterville 3,445 ... D6
62321 Carthage⊙ 2,978 ... B3
60013 Cary 6,640 ... E1
62420 Casey 3,026 ... F4
62232 Caseyville 4,308 ... B2
61817 Catlin 2,226 ... F3
61013 Cedarville 766 ... D1
†62801 Central City 1,505 ... D5
62801 Centralia 15,126 ... D5
62206 Centreville 9,747 ... B3
61818 Cerro Gordo 1,553 ... E4
61820 Champaign 58,133 ... E3
Champaign-Urbana-Rantoul‡ 168,392 ... E3
62627 Chandlerville 842 ... C3
60410 Channahon 3,734 ... E2
61920 Charleston⊙ 19,355 ... E4
62629 Chatham 5,597 ... D4
60921 Chatsworth 1,187 ... E3
60922 Chebanse 1,191 ... F3
61726 Chenoa 1,847 ... E3
61016 Cherry Valley 946 ... D1
62233 Chester⊙ 8,401 ... D6
*60601 Chicago⊙ 3,005,072 ... C5
Chicago‡ 7,102,328 ... C5
60411 Chicago Heights 37,026 ... C6
60415 Chicago Ridge 13,473 ... B6
61523 Chillicothe 6,176 ... D3
61924 Chrisman 1,413 ... F4
62822 Christopher 3,086 ... D6
60650 Cicero 61,232 ... B5
60924 Cissna Park 825 ... F3
60514 Clarendon Hills 6,870 ... B6
62824 Clay City 1,038 ... E5
62324 Clayton 889 ... B3
60927 Clifton 1,390 ... F3
61727 Clinton⊙ 8,014 ... E3
60416 Coal City 3,028 ... E2
61240 Coal Valley 3,800 ... C2
62920 Cobden 1,210 ... D6
62017 Coffeen 842 ... D4
62326 Colchester 1,729 ... C3
61728 Colfax 920 ... E3
62234 Collinsville 19,613 ... B2
61241 Colona 2,172 ... C2
62236 Columbia 4,269 ... C5
60112 Cortland 1,019 ... E2
62018 Cottage Hills ... B2
62237 Coulterville 1,118 ... D5
†60525 Countryside 6,538 ... B6
62922 Creal Springs 845 ... E6
60431 Crest Hill 9,252 ... E2
†60445 Crestwood 10,852 ... B6
60417 Crete 5,417 ... F2
61611 Creve Coeur 6,851 ... D3
62827 Crossville 944 ... F5
60014 Crystal Lake 18,590 ... E1
61427 Cuba 1,648 ... C3
62330 Dallas City 1,408 ... B3
61320 Dalzell 824 ... D2
61732 Danvers 921 ... D3
61832 Danville⊙ 38,985 ... F3
†60559 Darien 14,536 ... B6
*62521 Decatur⊙ 94,081 ... E4
Decatur‡ 131,375 ... E4
60015 Deerfield 17,430 ... B5
†60010 Deer Park 1,368 ... A5
60115 De Kalb 33,099 ... E2
61734 Delavan 1,973 ... D3
61322 Depue 1,873 ... D2
62924 De Soto 1,589 ... D6
*60016 Des Plaines 53,568 ... B5
62530 Divernon 1,081 ... D4
†60469 Dixmoor 4,175 ... C6
61021 Dixon⊙ 15,701 ... D2
60419 Dolton 24,766 ... C6
62926 Dongola 886 ... D6
60515 Downers Grove 42,572 ... A6
60118 Dundee (East and West Dundee) 6,169 ... E1
61525 Dunlap 824 ... D3
62239 Dupo 3,039 ... A3
62832 Du Quoin 6,594 ... D5
61024 Durand 1,073 ... D1
60420 Dwight 4,146 ... E2
60518 Earlville 1,382 ... E2
62024 East Alton 7,096 ... A2
†60411 East Chicago Heights 5,347 ... C6
61025 East Dubuque 2,194 ... C1
†60118 East Dundee (Dundee) 2,618 ... E1
61430 East Galesburg 928 ... C3
†60429 East Hazelcrest 1,362 ... C6
61244 East Moline 20,907 ... C2
61611 East Peoria 22,385 ... D3
*62201 East Saint Louis 55,200 ... A2
62531 Edinburg 1,231 ... D4
62025 Edwardsville⊙ 12,480 ... B2
62401 Effingham⊙ 11,270 ... E4
60119 Elburn 1,224 ... E2
62930 Eldorado 5,198 ... E6
60120 Elgin 63,981 ... E1
61028 Elizabeth 772 ... C1
62931 Elizabethtown⊙ 478 ... E6
60007 Elk Grove Village 28,907 ... B5
62932 Elkville 973 ... D6
60126 Elmhurst 44,276 ... B5
61529 Elmwood 2,117 ... D3
60635 Elmwood Park 24,016 ... B5
61738 El Paso 2,676 ... D3
62028 Elsah 990 ... C5
60421 Elwood 814 ... E2
62933 Energy 1,138 ... E6
62835 Enfield 890 ... E5
62934 Equality 831 ... E6
61250 Erie 1,725 ... C2
61530 Eureka⊙ 4,306 ... D3
*60201 Evanston 73,706 ... B5
62242 Evansville 863 ... D5
60642 Evergreen Park 22,260 ... B6
61739 Fairbury 3,544 ... E3
62837 Fairfield⊙ 5,954 ... E5
†62201 Fairmont City 2,313 ... B2
61841 Fairmount 851 ... F3
62208 Fairview Heights 12,414 ... B3
61842 Farmer City 2,252 ... E3
61531 Farmington 3,118 ... C3
62534 Findlay 868 ... E4
61843 Fisher 1,572 ... E3
61740 Flanagan 978 ... E3
62839 Flora 5,379 ... E5
60422 Flossmoor 8,423 ... B6
60130 Forest Park 15,177 ... B5
†60402 Forest View 764 ... B6
61741 Forrest 1,246 ... E3
61030 Forreston 1,384 ... D1
60020 Fox Lake 6,831 ... A4
60021 Fox River Grove 2,515 ... A5
60423 Frankfort 4,357 ... B6
61031 Franklin Grove 965 ... D2
60131 Franklin Park 17,507 ... B5
62243 Freeburg 2,989 ... D5
61032 Freeport⊙ 26,266 ... D1
61252 Fulton 3,936 ... C2
62935 Galatia 1,042 ... E6
61036 Galena⊙ 3,876 ... C1
61401 Galesburg⊙ 35,305 ... C3
61434 Galva 3,185 ... D2
60424 Gardner 1,322 ... E2
61254 Geneseo 6,373 ... C2
60134 Geneva⊙ 9,881 ... E2
60135 Genoa 3,276 ... E1
61846 Georgetown 4,220 ... F4
62245 Germantown 1,191 ... D5
60936 Gibson City 3,498 ... E3
61847 Gifford 848 ... E3
62033 Gillespie 3,740 ... D4
60938 Gilman 1,913 ... E3
62640 Girard 2,246 ... D4
61533 Glasford 1,201 ... D3
62034 Glen Carbon 5,197 ... B2
60022 Glencoe 9,200 ... B5
†60108 Glendale Heights 23,163 ... A5
60137 Glen Ellyn 23,717 ... A5
60025 Glenview 32,060 ... B5
60425 Glenwood 10,538 ... C6
62035 Godfrey ... A2
62938 Golconda⊙ 960 ... E6
62939 Goreville 978 ... E6
62037 Grafton 1,024 ... C5
62942 Grand Tower 748 ... D6
†62701 Grandview 1,794 ... D4
62040 Granite City 36,815 ... A2
60940 Grant Park 1,038 ... F2
61326 Granville 1,537 ... D2
60030 Grayslake 5,260 ... B4
62844 Grayville 2,313 ... B4
62044 Greenfield 1,090 ... C4
†60048 Green Oaks 1,415 ... B4
†61241 Green Rock 3,324 ... C2
62428 Greenup 1,655 ... E4
61534 Green Valley 768 ... D3
62642 Greenview 830 ... D3
62246 Greenville⊙ 5,271 ... D5
61744 Gridley 1,246 ... E3
62340 Griggsville 1,301 ... C4
60031 Gurnee 7,179 ... B4
62341 Hamilton 3,509 ... B3
60140 Hampshire 1,735 ... E1
61256 Hampton 1,873 ... C2
61536 Hanna City 1,361 ... D3
61041 Hanover 1,069 ... C1
60103 Hanover Park 28,719 ... A5
62047 Hardin⊙ 1,107 ... C4
62946 Harrisburg⊙ 10,410 ... E6
62537 Harristown 1,456 ... D4
62048 Hartford 1,887 ... A2
60033 Harvard 5,126 ... E1
60426 Harvey 35,810 ... B6
60656 Harwood Heights 8,228 ... B5
62644 Havana⊙ 4,277 ... D3
†60047 Hawthorn Woods 1,658 ... B5
60429 Hazel Crest 13,973 ... B6
60034 Hebron 786 ... E1
†61832 Hegeler 1,853 ... F3
61327 Hennepin⊙ 716 ... D2
61537 Henry 2,740 ... D2
62948 Herrin 10,708 ... E6
60941 Herscher 1,214 ... E2
61745 Heyworth 1,598 ... E3
60457 Hickory Hills 13,778 ... B6
62249 Highland 7,122 ... D5
60035 Highland Park 30,611 ... B5
60040 Highwood 5,452 ... B5
62049 Hillsboro⊙ 4,408 ... D4
60162 Hillside 8,279 ... B5
60520 Hinckley 1,447 ... E2
60521 Hinsdale 16,726 ... B6
60525 Hodgkins 2,005 ... B6
60195 Hoffman Estates 37,272 ... A5
61849 Homer 1,279 ... F3
60456 Hometown 5,324 ... B6
60430 Homewood 19,724 ... B6
60942 Hoopeston 6,411 ... F3
61747 Hohedale 913 ... D3
61748 Hudson 929 ... E3

(continued on following page)

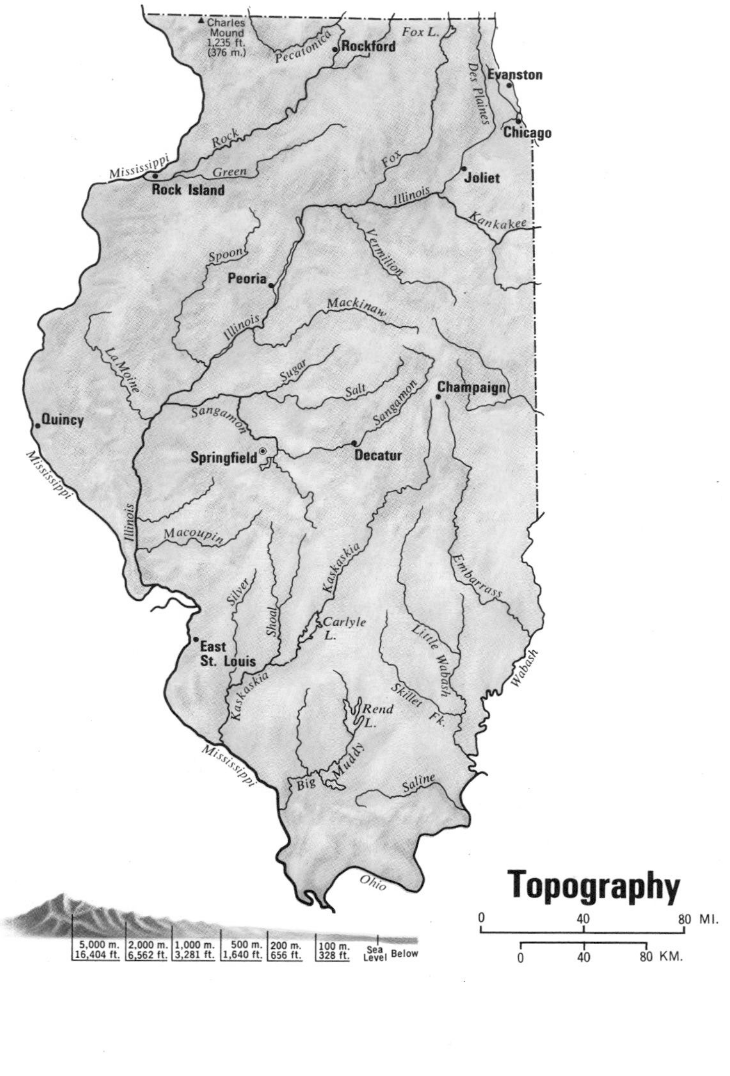
Charles Mound 1,235 ft. (376 m.)
Rockford
Pecatonica
Fox L.
Evanston
Des Plaines
Chicago
Rock
Mississippi
Green
Rock Island
Fox
Joliet
Illinois
Kankakee
Spoon
Vermilion
Peoria
Mackinaw
Illinois
La Moine
Sugar
Salt
Sangamon
Champaign
Quincy
Sangamon
Springfield
Decatur
Mississippi
Illinois
Macoupin
Embarrass
Kaskaskia
Silver
Shoal
Carlyle L.
East St. Louis
Little Wabash
Wabash
Kaskaskia
Skillet Fk.
Rend L.
Mississippi
Big Muddy
Saline
Ohio
5,000 m. 16,404 ft.
2,000 m. 6,562 ft.
1,000 m. 3,281 ft.
500 m. 1,640 ft.
200 m. 656 ft.
100 m. 328 ft.
Sea Level
Below
0 40 80 MI.
0 40 80 KM.

Topography

Agriculture, Industry and Resources

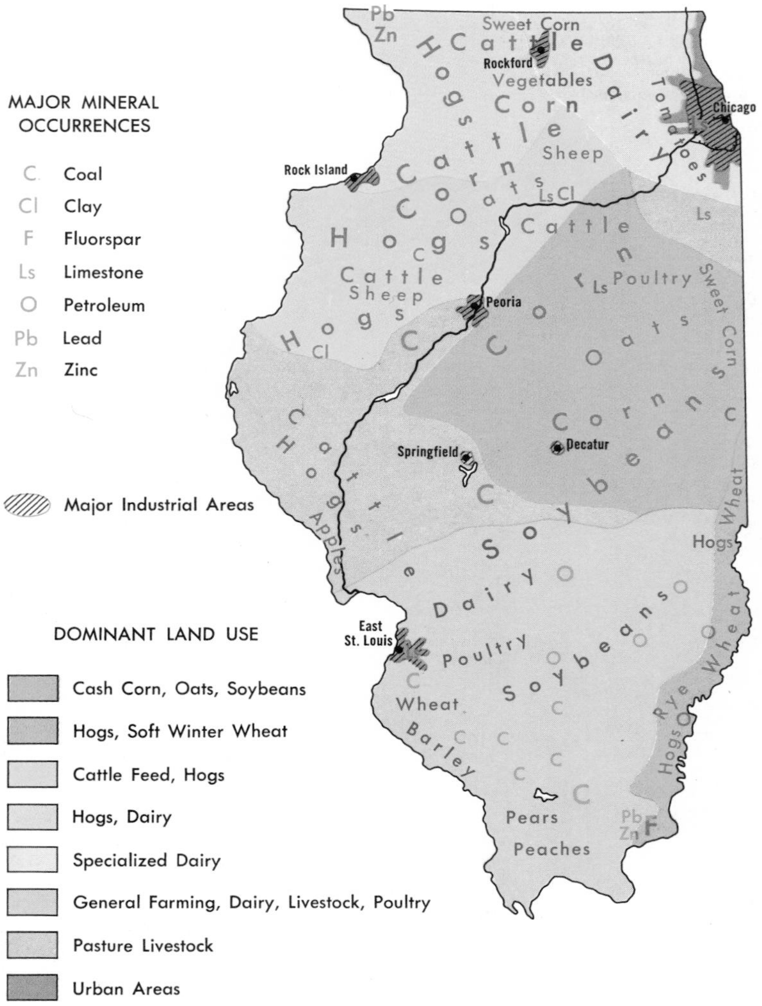
MAJOR MINERAL OCCURRENCES
C Coal
Cl Clay
F Fluorspar
Ls Limestone
O Petroleum
Pb Lead
Zn Zinc
Major Industrial Areas
DOMINANT LAND USE
Cash Corn, Oats, Soybeans
Hogs, Soft Winter Wheat
Cattle Feed, Hogs
Hogs, Dairy
Specialized Dairy
General Farming, Dairy, Livestock, Poultry
Pasture Livestock
Urban Areas
Sweet Corn
Cattle
Rockford
Vegetables
Corn
Dairy
Tomatoes
Chicago
Rock Island
Sheep
Hogs
Oats
Poultry
Peoria
Springfield
Decatur
Soybeans
Wheat
Apples
East St. Louis
Barley
Rye
Pears
Peaches

60142 Huntley 1,646 E1
62949 Hurst 938 D6
62539 Illiopolis 1,118 D4
†60067 Inverness 4,046 A5
62848 Irvington 789 D5
60042 Island Lake 2,293 A4
60143 Itasca 7,129 B5
62650 Jacksonville⊙ 20,284 C4
†62701 Jerome 1,374 D4
62052 Jerseyville⊙ 7,506 C4
62436 Jewett 230 E4
62951 Johnston City 3,873 E6
*60431 Joliet⊙ 77,956 E2
62952 Jonesboro⊙ 1,842 D6
†60458 Justice 10,552 B6
60901 Kankakee⊙ 30,141 F2
Kankakee‡ 102,926 F2
61933 Kansas 791 F4
†63673 Kaskaskia 33 C6
61442 Keithsburg 936 B2
60043 Kenilworth 2,708 B5
61443 Kewanee 14,508 C2
†60069 Kildeer 1,609 A5
62540 Kincaid 1,591 D4
62854 Kinmundy 945 E5
60146 Kirkland 1,155 E1
61447 Kirkwood 1,008 C3
61448 Knoxville 3,432 C3
61540 Lacon⊙ 2,135 D2
61329 Ladd 1,337 D2
60525 La Grange 15,445 B6
60525 La Grange Park 13,359 B5
61450 La Harpe 1,471 C3
†60010 Lake Barrington 2,320 A5
60044 Lake Bluff 4,434 B4
†60002 Lake Catherine 1,335 E1
60045 Lake Forest 15,245 B4
†60102 Lake in the Hills 5,651 E1
60046 Lake Villa 1,462 A4
62438 Lakewood 1,254 E4
60047 Lake Zurich 8,225 A5
61330 La Moille 734 D2
61046 Lanark 1,483 D1
60438 Lansing 29,039 C6
61301 La Salle 10,347 E2
62439 Lawrenceville⊙ 5,652 F5
62254 Lebanon 3,245 D5
60531 Leland 775 E2
60439 Lemont 5,640 B6
61048 Lena 2,295 D1
61752 Le Roy 2,870 E3
61542 Lewistown⊙ 2,758 C3
61753 Lexington 1,806 E3
60048 Libertyville 16,520 B4
62656 Lincoln⊙ 16,327 D3
†60015 Lincolnshire 4,151 B5
†60645 Lincolnwood 11,921 B5
†60046 Lindenhurst 6,220 B4
60532 Lisle 13,625 A6
62056 Litchfield 7,204 D4
62058 Livingston 949 D5
62661 Loami 770 D4
60441 Lockport 9,170 B6
60148 Lombard 36,897 B5
60047 Long Grove 2,013 B5
62858 Louisville⊙ 1,166 E5
62059 Lovejoy 1,233 A2
61111 Loves Park 13,192 E1
61937 Lovington 1,313 E4
61261 Lyndon 777 D2
†60411 Lynwood 4,195 C6
60534 Lyons 9,925 B6
61755 Mackinaw 1,354 D3
61455 Macomb⊙ 19,863 C3
62544 Macon 1,300 E4
62060 Madison 5,915 A2
61853 Mahomet 1,986 E3
60150 Malta 995 E2
60442 Manhattan 1,944 F2
61546 Manito 1,869 D3
61854 Mansfield 921 E3
60950 Manteno 3,155 F2
60152 Marengo 4,361 E1
62061 Marine 957 D5
62959 Marion⊙ 14,031 E6
62257 Marissa 2,568 D5
60426 Markham 15,172 B6
61756 Maroa 1,760 E3
†61554 Marquette Heights 3,386 D3
61341 Marseilles 4,766 E2
62441 Marshall⊙ 3,655 F4
62442 Martinsville 1,298 F4
62062 Maryville 1,937 B2
62258 Mascoutah 4,962 D5
62664 Mason City 2,719 D3
61263 Matherville 793 C2
60443 Matteson 10,223 B6
61938 Mattoon 19,055 E4
60153 Maywood 27,998 B5
60444 Mazon 828 E2
60050 McHenry 10,908 E1
†60050 McHenry Shores 1,041 E1
61754 McLean 836 D3
62859 McLeansboro⊙ 2,960 E5
†62010 Meadowbrook 1,082 B2
*60160 Melrose Park 20,735 B5
62351 Mendon 979 B3
61342 Mendota 7,134 D2
62665 Meredosia 1,272 C4
†60601 Merrionette Park 2,054 B6
61548 Metamora 2,482 D3
62960 Metropolis⊙ 7,171 E6
60445 Midlothian 14,274 B6
61264 Milan 6,264 C2
60953 Milford 1,716 F3
61051 Milledgeville 1,209 D1
62260 Millstadt 2,736 B3
61759 Minier 1,261 D3
61760 Minonk 2,039 D3
60447 Minooka 1,565 E2
60448 Mokena 4,578 B6
61265 Moline 46,278 C2
60954 Momence 3,297 F2
60449 Monee 993 F2
61462 Monmouth⊙ 10,706 C3
60538 Montgomery 3,369 E2
61856 Monticello⊙ 4,753 E3
60450 Morris⊙ 8,833 E2
61270 Morrison⊙ 4,605 C2
62546 Morrisonville 1,208 D4
61550 Morton 14,178 D3
60053 Morton Grove 23,747 B5
62963 Mound City⊙ 1,102 D6
62964 Mounds 1,669 D6
62863 Mount Carmel⊙ 8,908 F5
61053 Mount Carroll⊙ 1,936 D1
61054 Mount Morris 2,989 D1
62069 Mount Olive 2,357 D4
60056 Mount Prospect 52,634 B5
62548 Mount Pulaski 1,783 D3
62353 Mount Sterling⊙ 2,186 C4
62864 Mount Vernon⊙ 17,193 E5
62549 Mount Zion 4,563 E4
62550 Moweaqua 1,922 E4
60060 Mundelein 17,053 A4
62966 Murphysboro⊙ 9,866 D6
60540 Naperville 42,601 A6
62263 Nashville⊙ 3,186 D5
62354 Nauvoo 1,133 B3
62447 Neoga 1,736 E4
60541 Newark 798 E2
62264 New Athens 1,937 D5
62265 New Baden 2,476 D5
62670 New Berlin 834 D4
61272 New Boston 731 B2
60451 New Lenox 5,792 B6
61942 Newman 1,079 B6
62448 Newton⊙ 3,186 E5
61465 New Windsor 863 C2
62551 Niantic 761 D4
60648 Niles 30,363 B5
62868 Noble 832 E5
62075 Nokomis 2,656 D4
61761 Normal 35,672 E3
†60656 Norridge 16,483 B5
62869 Norris City 1,515 E6
60542 North Aurora 5,205 E2
†60010 North Barrington 1,475 A5
60062 Northbrook 30,778 B5
60064 North Chicago 38,774 B4
60093 Northfield 5,807 B5
60164 Northlake 12,166 B5
†61111 North Park 15,806 D1
†61554 North Pekin 1,824 D3
60546 North Riverside 6,764 B5
†61373 North Utica (Utica) 1,067 E2
60521 Oak Brook 6,641 B6
†60181 Oakbrook Terrace 2,285 B5
60452 Oak Forest 26,096 B6
61943 Oakland 1,035 F4
*60453 Oak Lawn 60,590 B6
*60303 Oak Park 54,887 B5
61858 Oakwood 1,627 F3
62449 Oblong 1,840 F5
60460 Odell 1,083 E2
62870 Odin 1,285 D5
62269 O'Fallon 12,241 B2
61859 Ogden 818 F3
61348 Oglesby 3,979 D2
62271 Okawville 1,337 D5
62450 Olney⊙ 9,026 E5
60461 Olympia Fields 4,146 B6
60955 Onarga 1,269 F3
61467 Oneida 765 C2
61469 Oquawka⊙ 1,533 C3
62554 Oreana 999 E4
61061 Oregon⊙ 3,559 D1
61273 Orion 2,013 C2
60462 Orland Park 23,045 B6
60543 Oswego 3,021 E2
61350 Ottawa⊙ 18,166 E2
60067 Palatine 32,166 B5
62451 Palestine 1,718 F4
62674 Palmyra 864 C4
60463 Palos Heights 11,096 B6
60465 Palos Hills 16,654 B6
60464 Palos Park 3,150 B6
62557 Pana 6,040 D4
61944 Paris⊙ 9,885 F4
†60085 Park City 3,673 B4
60466 Park Forest 26,222 B6
60466 Park Forest South 6,245 F2
60068 Park Ridge 38,704 B5
62558 Pawnee 2,577 D4
61353 Pawpaw 839 E2
60957 Paxton⊙ 4,258 E3
62360 Payson 1,065 B4
61063 Pecatonica 1,732 D1
61554 Pekin⊙ 33,967 D3
*61601 Peoria⊙ 124,160 D3
Peoria‡ 365,864 D3
61614 Peoria Heights 7,453 D3
60468 Peotone 2,832 F2
62272 Percy 1,053 D5
61354 Peru 10,886 D2
62675 Petersburg⊙ 2,419 D4
61864 Philo 973 E3
†60426 Phoenix 2,850 C6
62274 Pinckneyville⊙ 3,319 D5
60959 Piper City 905 E3
62363 Pittsfield⊙ 4,170 C4
60544 Plainfield 3,767 A6
60545 Plano 4,875 E2
62366 Pleasant Hill 1,112 C4
62275 Pocahontas 866 D5
61074 Polo 2,643 D1
61764 Pontiac⊙ 11,227 E3
†62040 Pontoon Beach 3,336 A2
61065 Poplar Grove 818 E1
61275 Port Byron 1,289 C2
60469 Posen 4,642 B6
61865 Potomac 874 F3
61470 Prairie City 580 C3
61356 Princeton⊙ 7,342 D2
61559 Princeville 1,712 D3
61277 Prophetstown 2,141 D2
60070 Prospect Heights 11,808 B5
62301 Quincy⊙ 42,554 B4
62080 Ramsey 1,058 D4
60960 Rankin 727 F3
61866 Rantoul 20,161 E3
61278 Rapids City 1,058 C2
62560 Raymond 957 D4
62278 Red Bud 2,850 D5
60071 Richmond 1,068 E1
60471 Richton Park 9,403 B6
61870 Ridge Farm 1,096 F4
62979 Ridgway 1,245 E6
60627 Riverdale 13,233 C6
60305 River Forest 12,392 B5
60171 River Grove 10,368 B5
60546 Riverside 9,236 B6
62561 Riverton 2,783 D4
†60015 Riverwoods 2,804 B5
61561 Roanoke 2,001 D3
60472 Robbins 8,853 B6
62454 Robinson⊙ 7,285 F5
61068 Rochelle 8,982 D2
62563 Rochester 2,488 D4
60436 Rockdale 1,913 E2
61071 Rock Falls 10,633 D2
*61101 Rockford⊙ 139,712 D1
Rockford‡ 279,514 D1
61201 Rock Island⊙ 46,928 C2
Rock Island-Moline-Davenport‡ 383,958 C2
61072 Rockton 2,313 E1
60008 Rolling Meadows 20,167 A5
61562 Rome 2,744 D3
60441 Romeoville 15,519 B6
62082 Roodhouse 2,364 C4
61073 Roscoe 1,388 D1
60172 Roselle 16,948 A5
60018 Rosemont 4,137 B5
61473 Roseville 1,254 C3
†62024 Rosewood Heights 5,085 B2
62982 Rosiclare 1,441 E6
60963 Rossville 1,363 F3
60673 Round Lake 2,644 A4
†60673 Round Lake Beach 12,921 A4
†60673 Round Lake Heights 1,192 E1
†60673 Round Lake Park 4,032 A4
62084 Roxana 1,587 B2
62983 Royalton 1,320 D6
62681 Rushville⊙ 3,348 C3
60964 Saint Anne 1,421 F2
60174 Saint Charles 17,492 E2
61563 Saint David 786 C3
62458 Saint Elmo 1,611 E4
62460 Saint Francisville 1,040 F5
62281 Saint Jacob 792 D5
61873 Saint Joseph 1,900 E3
62881 Salem⊙ 7,813 E5
62882 Sandoval 1,734 D5
60548 Sandwich 5,244 E2
62682 San Jose 784 D3
60411 Sauk Village 10,906 C6
61074 Savanna 4,529 C1
61874 Savoy 2,126 E3
61770 Saybrook 882 E3
60194 Schaumburg 53,305 A5
60176 Schiller Park 11,458 B5
61360 Seneca 2,098 E2
62884 Sesser 2,238 D5
60550 Shabbona 851 E2
61078 Shannon 938 D1
62984 Shawneetown⊙ 1,841 E6
61361 Sheffield 1,130 D2
62565 Shelbyville⊙ 5,259 E4
60966 Sheldon 1,215 F3
62684 Sherman 1,501 D4
61281 Sherrard 811 C2
†62220 Shiloh 1,045 B3
60435 Shorewood 4,714 E2
61877 Sidney 886 E3
61282 Silvis 7,130 C2
*60076 Skokie 60,278 B5
†60118 Sleepy Hollow 2,000 E1
62285 Smithton 1,447 C5
60552 Somonauk 1,344 E2
†60010 South Barrington 1,168 A5
61080 South Beloit 4,088 E1
60411 South Chicago Heights 3,932 C6
60177 South Elgin 5,970 E2
60473 South Holland 24,977 C6
†62650 South Jacksonville 3,382 C4
61564 South Pekin 1,243 D3
62087 South Roxana 2,286 B2
60474 South Wilmington 747 E2
62286 Sparta 4,957 D5
*62701 Springfield (cap.)⊙ 100,054 D4
Springfield‡ 187,789 D4
61362 Spring Valley 5,822 D2
61774 Stanford 720 D3
62088 Staunton 4,744 D5
62288 Steeleville 2,240 D6
60475 Steger 9,269 F2
61081 Sterling 16,281 D2
62463 Stewardson 745 E4
60402 Stickney 5,893 B6
61084 Stillman Valley 961 D1
61085 Stockton 1,872 C1
†60160 Stone Park 4,273 B5
62567 Stonington 1,184 D4
60103 Streamwood 23,456 A5
61364 Streator 14,795 E2
61480 Stronghurst 865 C3
60554 Sugar Grove 1,366 E2
61951 Sullivan⊙ 4,526 E4
60501 Summit-Argo 10,110 B6
62466 Sumner 1,238 F5
†60050 Sunnyside 1,432 A4
62221 Swansea 5,347 B3
60178 Sycamore⊙ 9,219 E2
62888 Tamaroa 885 D5
62988 Tamms 826 D6
61283 Tampico 966 D2
62568 Taylorville⊙ 11,386 D4
62467 Teutopolis 1,414 E4
62689 Thayer 759 D4
61878 Thomasboro 1,242 E3
61285 Thomson 911 C2
60476 Thornton 3,024 C6
62292 Tilden 1,025 D5
†61832 Tilton 2,405 F3
60477 Tinley Park 26,171 B6
61368 Tiskilwa 990 D2
62468 Toledo⊙ 1,284 E4
61880 Tolono 2,434 E3
61369 Toluca 1,471 D2
61483 Toulon⊙ 1,390 D2
†60010 Tower Lakes 1,177 A4
61568 Tremont 2,096 D3
62293 Trenton 2,504 D5
62294 Troy 3,772 B2
61953 Tuscola⊙ 3,839 E4
61801 Urbana⊙ 35,978 E3
61373 Utica 1,067 E2
62891 Valier 729 D5
†60120 Valley View 2,112 E2
62295 Valmeyer 898 C5
62471 Vandalia⊙ 5,338 D5
62090 Venice 3,480 A2
61484 Vermont 885 C3
60061 Vernon Hills 9,827 B4
62995 Vienna⊙ 1,420 E6
61956 Villa Grove 2,707 E4
60181 Villa Park 23,185 B5
61486 Viola 1,144 C2
62690 Virden 3,899 D4
62691 Virginia⊙ 1,825 C4
60083 Wadsworth 1,104 B4
61376 Walnut 1,513 D2
†62801 Wamac 1,665 D5
61777 Wapella 768 E3
61087 Warren 1,595 C1
62573 Warrensburg 1,372 D4
60555 Warrenville 7,519 A6
62379 Warsaw 1,842 B3
61570 Washburn 1,206 D3
61571 Washington 10,364 D3
62204 Washington Park 8,223 B2
61488 Wataga 996 C2
62298 Waterloo⊙ 4,646 C5
60556 Waterman 943 E2
60970 Watseka⊙ 5,543 F3
60084 Wauconda 5,688 A4
60085 Waukegan⊙ 67,653 B4
62692 Waverly 1,537 D4
60184 Wayne 940 E2
62895 Wayne City 1,132 E5
61377 Wenona 1,025 E2
60153 Westchester 17,730 B5
60185 West Chicago 12,550 A5
†60118 West Dundee (Dundee) 3,551 E1
60558 Western Springs 12,876 B6
62474 Westfield 733 F4
62896 West Frankfort 9,437 E6
†60462 Westhaven 2,784 B6
60559 Westmont 16,718 B6
62476 West Salem 1,145 F5
61883 Westville 3,573 F3
60187 Wheaton⊙ 43,043 A5
60090 Wheeling 23,266 B5
62092 White Hall 2,935 C4
62693 Williamsville 996 D4
†60521 Willowbrook 4,953 B6
60480 Willow Springs 4,147 B6
60091 Wilmette 28,229 B5
60481 Wilmington 4,424 E2
62694 Winchester⊙ 1,716 C4
61957 Windsor 1,228 E4
†61465 Windsor (New Windsor) 863 C2
60190 Winfield 4,422 A5
61088 Winnebago 1,644 D1
60093 Winnetka 12,772 B5
60096 Winthrop Harbor 5,431 F1
62094 Witt 1,205 D4
60191 Wood Dale 11,251 B5
61490 Woodhull 901 C2
†60517 Woodridge 22,561 B6
62095 Wood River 12,446 B2
60098 Woodstock⊙ 11,725 E1
62097 Worden 953 B2
60482 Worth 11,592 B6
61379 Wyanet 1,069 D2
61491 Wyoming 1,614 D2
61572 Yates City 860 C3
60560 Yorkville⊙ 3,422 E2
62999 Zeigler 1,858 D6
60099 Zion 17,861 F1

OTHER FEATURES

Apple (creek) C4
Apple (riv.) C1
Argonne Nat'l Laboratory B6
Big Bureau (riv.) D2
Big Muddy (riv.) D6
Bonpas (creek) F5
Cache (riv.) D6
Calumet (lake) C6
Carlyle (lake) D5
Chanute A.F.B. E3
Charles Mound (hill) C1
Chicago Portage Nat'l Hist. Site B6
Crab Orchard (lake) E6
Des Plaines (riv.) A6
Du Page (riv.) E2
Edwards (riv.) C2
Embarras (riv.) E4
Fort Sheridan B5
Fox (lake) A4
Fox (riv.) E2
Fox (riv.) E5
Glenview Nav. Air. Sta. B5
Granite City Army Depot A2
Great Lakes Nav. Trng. Ctr. B4
Green (riv.) D2
Henderson (riv.) C2
Illinois (riv.) C4
Illinois - Mississippi (canal) C2
Iroquois (riv.) F3
Kankakee (riv.) F2
Kaskaskia (riv.) E4
La Moine (riv.) C3
Little Wabash (riv.) E5
Mackinaw (riv.) E3
Macoupin (riv.) C4
Michigan (lake) F1
Mississippi (riv.) C5
O'Hare Field-Chicago International Airport B5
Ohio (riv.) E6
Plum (riv.) C1
Pope (creek) C2
Rend (lake) E5
Rock (creek) D2
Rock (riv.) C2
Rock Island Arsenal C2
Saline (riv.) E6
Salt (creek) D3
Sangamon (riv.) C3
Savanna Army Depot C1
Scott A.F.B. 8,648 B3
Shelbyville (lake) E4
Spoon (riv.) C3
Wabash (riv.) F5

⊙County seat.
‡Population of metropolitan area.
† Zip of nearest p.o. * Multiple zips.

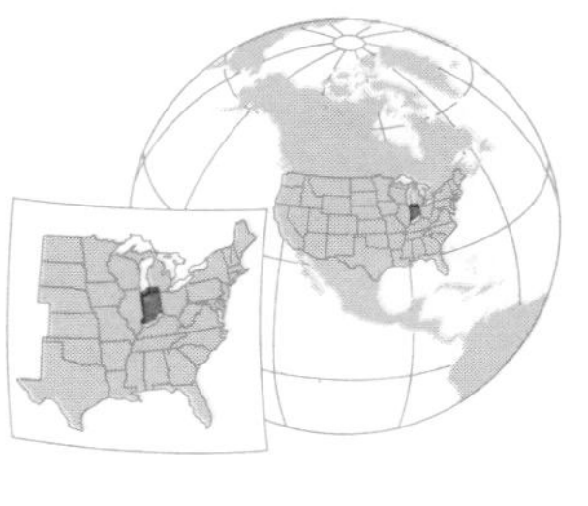

AREA 36,185 sq. mi. (93,719 sq. km.)
POPULATION 5,490,260
CAPITAL Indianapolis
LARGEST CITY Indianapolis
HIGHEST POINT 1,257 ft. (383 m.) (Wayne County)
SETTLED IN 1730
ADMITTED TO UNION December 11, 1816
POPULAR NAME Hoosier State
STATE FLOWER Peony
STATE BIRD Cardinal

COUNTIES

Adams 29,619 ..... H3
Allen 294,335 ..... G2
Bartholomew 65,088 ..... F6
Benton 10,218 ..... C3
Blackford 15,570 ..... G4
Boone 36,446 ..... E4
Brown 12,377 ..... E6
Carroll 19,722 ..... D3
Cass 40,936 ..... E3
Clark 88,838 ..... F8
Clay 24,862 ..... C6
Clinton 31,545 ..... E4
Crawford 9,820 ..... E8
Daviess 27,836 ..... C7
Dearborn 34,291 ..... H6
Decatur 23,841 ..... G6
De Kalb 33,606 ..... H2
Delaware 128,587 ..... G4
Dubois 34,238 ..... D8
Elkhart 137,330 ..... F1
Fayette 28,272 ..... G5
Floyd 61,169 ..... F8
Fountain 19,033 ..... C4
Franklin 19,612 ..... G6
Fulton 19,335 ..... E2
Gibson 33,156 ..... B8
Grant 80,934 ..... F3
Greene 30,416 ..... D6
Hamilton 82,027 ..... E4
Hancock 43,939 ..... F5
Harrison 27,276 ..... E8
Hendricks 69,804 ..... D5
Henry 53,336 ..... G5
Howard 86,896 ..... E4
Huntington 35,596 ..... G3
Jackson 36,523 ..... E7
Jasper 26,138 ..... C2
Jay 23,239 ..... G4
Jefferson 30,419 ..... G7
Jennings 22,854 ..... F7
Johnson 77,240 ..... E6
Knox 41,838 ..... C7
Kosciusko 59,555 ..... F2
Lagrange 25,550 ..... G1
Lake 522,965 ..... C2
LaPorte 108,632 ..... D1
Lawrence 4,272 ..... E7
Madison 139,336 ..... F4
Marion 765,233 ..... E5
Marshall 39,155 ..... E2
Martin 11,001 ..... D7
Miami 39,820 ..... E3
Monroe 98,785 ..... D6
Montgomery 35,501 ..... D4
Morgan 51,999 ..... E6
Newton 14,844 ..... C3
Noble 35,443 ..... G2
Ohio 5,114 ..... H7
Orange 18,677 ..... E7
Owen 15,841 ..... D6
Parke 16,372 ..... C5
Perry 19,346 ..... D8
Pike 13,465 ..... C8
Porter 119,816 ..... C2
Posey 26,414 ..... B8
Pulaski 13,258 ..... D2
Putnam 29,163 ..... D5
Randolph 29,997 ..... G4
Ripley 24,398 ..... G6
Rush 19,604 ..... G5
Saint Joseph 241,617 ..... E1
Scott 20,422 ..... F7
Shelby 39,887 ..... F5
Spencer 19,361 ..... C9
Starke 21,997 ..... D2
Steuben 24,694 ..... G1
Sullivan 21,107 ..... C6
Switzerland 7,153 ..... G7
Tippecanoe 121,702 ..... D4
Tipton 16,819 ..... E4
Union 6,860 ..... H5
Vanderburgh 167,515 ..... B8
Vermillion 18,229 ..... C5
Vigo 112,385 ..... C6
Wabash 36,640 ..... F3
Warren 8,976 ..... C4
Warrick 41,474 ..... C8
Washington 21,932 ..... E7
Wayne 76,058 ..... G5
Wells 25,401 ..... G3
White 23,867 ..... D3
Whitley 26,215 ..... F2

CITIES and TOWNS

Zip *Name/Pop.* *Key*

47240 Adams 250 ..... F6
†46947 Adamsboro 325 ..... E3
46102 Advance 559 ..... D5
46910 Akron 1,045 ..... E2
47320 Albany 2,625 ..... G4
46701 Albion⊙ 1,637 ..... G2
†47283 Alert 102 ..... F6
46001 Alexandria 6,028 ..... F4
†46738 Altona 263 ..... G2
47917 Ambia 274 ..... C4
46911 Amboy 450 ..... F3
†46131 Amity 200 ..... E6
46103 Amo 444 ..... D5
*46011 Anderson⊙ 64,695 ..... F4
Anderson‡ 139,336 ..... F4
†47024 Andersonville 225 ..... G5
46702 Andrews 1,243 ..... F3
46703 Angola⊙ 5,486 ..... G1
46030 Arcadia 1,801 ..... E4
46704 Arcola 300 ..... G2
†46624 Ardmore 800 ..... E1
46501 Argos 1,547 ..... E2
46104 Arlington 500 ..... F5
46705 Ashley 841 ..... G1
46031 Atlanta 657 ..... E4
47918 Attica 3,841 ..... C4
46502 Atwood 300 ..... F2
46706 Auburn⊙ 8,122 ..... G2
47001 Aurora 3,816 ..... H6
47102 Austin 4,857 ..... F7
46710 Avilla 1,272 ..... G2
47420 Avoca 400 ..... D7
46105 Bainbridge 644 ..... D5
46106 Bargersville 1,647 ..... E5
47006 Batesville 4,152 ..... G6
47920 Battle Ground 812 ..... D3
47421 Bedford⊙ 14,410 ..... E7
46107 Beech Grove 13,196 ..... E5
†46526 Benton 220 ..... F2
46711 Berne 3,300 ..... H3
†46111 Bethany 127 ..... E5
46301 Beverly Shores 864 ..... C1
47512 Bicknell 4,713 ..... C7
46713 Bippus 300 ..... F3
47513 Birdseye 533 ..... D8
†46406 Black Oak C1
47831 Blanford 500 ..... B5
47138 Blocher 400 ..... F7
47424 Bloomfield⊙ 2,705 ..... D6
47832 Bloomingdale 409 ..... C5
47401 Bloomington⊙ 52,044 ..... D6
Bloomington‡ 98,387 ..... D6
†47360 Blountsville 213 ..... G4
†46176 Blue Ridge 219 ..... F5
46714 Bluffton⊙ 8,705 ..... G3
46110 Boggstown 200 ..... F5
46302 Boone Grove 220 ..... C2
47601 Boonville⊙ 6,300 ..... C8
47106 Borden 384 ..... F8
47324 Boston 189 ..... H5
47921 Boswell 810 ..... C3
46504 Bourbon 1,522 ..... E2
47833 Bowling Green 200 ..... D6
47107 Bradford 350 ..... E8
47834 Brazil⊙ 7,852 ..... C5
46506 Bremen 3,565 ..... E2
47836 Bridgeton 250 ..... C5
†45030 Bright 450 ..... H6
46720 Brimfield 292 ..... G2
46913 Bringhurst 275 ..... E3
46507 Bristol 1,203 ..... F1
47922 Brook 926 ..... C3
46111 Brooklyn 889 ..... E5
†47250 Brooksburg 132 ..... G7
47923 Brookston 1,701 ..... D3
47012 Brookville⊙ 2,874 ..... G6
46112 Brownsburg 6,242 ..... E5
47220 Brownstown⊙ 2,704 ..... F7
47325 Brownsville 250 ..... H5
47516 Bruceville 646 ..... C7
47326 Bryant 277 ..... G3
47924 Buck Creek 225 ..... D4
47647 Buckskin 200 ..... C8
47925 Buffalo 500 ..... D3
46914 Bunker Hill 984 ..... E3
46508 Burket 260 ..... F2
46915 Burlington 680 ..... E4
47926 Burnettsville 496 ..... D3
47222 Burney 300 ..... F6
†46401 Burns Harbor 920 ..... C1
46916 Burrows 250 ..... E3
46721 Butler 2,509 ..... H2
47223 Butlerville 300 ..... F6
†46371 Byron 200 ..... C5
†47362 Cadiz 180 ..... G5
47327 Cambridge City 2,407 ..... G5
46917 Camden 618 ..... D3
47108 Campbellsburg 695 ..... E7
47224 Canaan 90 ..... G7
47519 Cannelburg 152 ..... C7
47520 Cannelton⊙ 2,373 ..... D9
47837 Carbon 307 ..... C5
47838 Carlisle 717 ..... C7
46032 Carmel 18,272 ..... E5
46114 Cartersburg 300 ..... E5
46115 Carthage 886 ..... F5
47927 Cates 125 ..... C4
47928 Cayuga 1,258 ..... C5
47016 Cedar Grove 217 ..... H6
46303 Cedar Lake 8,754 ..... C2
47521 Celestine 150 ..... D8
†47842 Centenary 150 ..... B5
†46901 Center 310 ..... E4
47840 Centerpoint 242 ..... C6
46116 Centerton 250 ..... E5
47330 Centerville 2,284 ..... H5
47929 Chalmers 554 ..... D3
47610 Chandler 3,043 ..... C8
47111 Charlestown 5,596 ..... F8
46117 Charlottesville 300 ..... F5
†47138 Chelsea 200 ..... F7
46017 Chesterfield 2,701 ..... F4
46304 Chesterton 8,531 ..... D1
47611 Chrisney 537 ..... C8
46723 Churubusco 1,638 ..... G2
46034 Cicero 2,557 ..... E4
47225 Clarksburg 300 ..... G6
47930 Clarks Hill 653 ..... D4
47130 Clarksville 15,164 ..... F8
47841 Clay City 883 ..... C6
46510 Claypool 464 ..... F2
46118 Clayton 703 ..... D5
47426 Clear Creek 200 ..... E6
†46737 Clear Lake 301 ..... H1
47226 Clifford 310 ..... F6
47842 Clinton 5,267 ..... C5
46120 Cloverdale 1,357 ..... D5
†47834 Cloverland 175 ..... C6
47427 Coal City 225 ..... D6
47845 Coalmont 450 ..... C6
46121 Coatesville 474 ..... D5
47931 Colburn 300 ..... D3
46035 Colfax 823 ..... D4
47978 Collegeville 1,059 ..... C3
46725 Columbia City⊙ 5,091 ..... G2
47201 Columbus⊙ 30,614 ..... E6
47331 Connersville⊙ 17,023 ..... G5
46919 Converse 1,279 ..... F3
47228 Cortland 175 ..... F7
46730 Corunna 304 ..... G2
47112 Corydon⊙ 2,724 ..... E8
47932 Covington⊙ 2,883 ..... C4
†47302 Cowan 428 ..... G4
47114 Crandall 176 ..... E8
47522 Crane D7
47933 Crawfordsville⊙ 13,325 ..... D4
46732 Cromwell 458 ..... F2
47229 Crothersville 1,747 ..... F7
46307 Crown Point⊙ 16,455 ..... C2
46511 Culver 1,601 ..... E2
46229 Cumberland 3,375 ..... E5
47612 Cynthiana 874 ..... B8
47523 Dale 1,693 ..... D8
47334 Daleville F4
47847 Dana 803 ..... C5
46122 Danville⊙ 4,220 ..... D5
47940 Darlington 811 ..... D4
47618 Darmstadt 1,280 ..... B8
47941 Dayton 781 ..... D4
46733 Decatur⊙ 8,649 ..... H3
47524 Decker 256 ..... B7
†46917 Deer Creek 250 ..... E3
46923 Delphi⊙ 3,042 ..... D3
46310 Demotte 2,559 ..... C2
46926 Denver 589 ..... E3
47230 Deputy 200 ..... F7
47302 Desoto 385 ..... G4
47018 Dillsboro 1,038 ..... G6
46513 Donaldson 320 ..... E2
†47118 Doolittle Mills 200 ..... D8
47335 Dublin 979 ..... G5
47525 Dubois 550 ..... D8
47848 Dugger 1,118 ..... C6
†46304 Dune Acres 291 ..... C1
47336 Dunkirk 3,180 ..... G4
†46514 Dunlap 5,397 ..... F1
47337 Dunreith 184 ..... F5
47231 Dupont 392 ..... G7
46311 Dyer 9,555 ..... C1
†46074 Eagletown 306 ..... E4
47942 Earl Park 469 ..... C3
46312 East Chicago 39,786 ..... C1
47019 East Enterprise 250 ..... H7
†47370 East Germantown (Pershing) 438 ..... G5
47338 Eaton 1,804 ..... G4
47116 Eckerty 108 ..... D8
47339 Economy 237 ..... G5
†46011 Edgewood 2,215 ..... F4
46124 Edinburgh 4,856 ..... E6
47528 Edwardsport 459 ..... C7
†47150 Edwardsville 700 ..... F8
47613 Elberfeld 640 ..... C8
47117 Elizabeth 178 ..... F8
47232 Elizabethtown 603 ..... F6
46514 Elkhart 41,305 ..... F1
Elkhart‡ 137,330 ..... F1
47429 Ellettsville 3,328 ..... D6
47529 Elnora 756 ..... C7
†47018 Elrod 200 ..... G6
†47901 Elston 500 ..... D4
46036 Elwood 10,867 ..... F4
46125 Eminence 200 ..... D5
47118 English⊙ 633 ..... E8
46524 Etna Green 522 ..... E2
†47928 Eugene 400 ..... B5
*47701 Evansville⊙ 130,496 ..... C9
Evansville‡ 309,408 ..... C9
†47331 Everton 500 ..... G5
46126 Fairland 950 ..... F5
46928 Fairmount 3,286 ..... F4
†47842 Fairview Park 1,545 ..... C5
47850 Farmersburg 1,240 ..... C6
47340 Farmland 1,560 ..... G4
†47421 Fayetteville 180 ..... D7
47532 Ferdinand 2,192 ..... D8
46128 Fillmore 550 ..... D5
46129 Finly 400 ..... F5
46038 Fishers 2,008 ..... E5
47234 Flat Rock 323 ..... F6
46929 Flora 2,303 ..... E3
47119 Floyds Knobs 500 ..... F8
47851 Fontanet 325 ..... C5
46039 Forest 400 ..... E4
47648 Fort Branch 2,504 ..... B8
46040 Fortville 2,787 ..... F5
*46801 Fort Wayne⊙ 172,028 ..... G2
Fort Wayne‡ 382,961 ..... G2
47341 Fountain City 839 ..... H5
46130 Fountaintown 225 ..... F5
47944 Fowler⊙ 2,319 ..... C3
46930 Fowlerton 300 ..... F4
47946 Francesville 944 ..... D3
47649 Francisco 612 ..... B8
46041 Frankfort⊙ 15,168 ..... E4
46131 Franklin⊙ 11,563 ..... E6
46044 Frankton 2,080 ..... F4
47120 Fredericksburg 233 ..... E8
47431 Freedom 100 ..... D6
47535 Freelandville 600 ..... C7
47235 Freetown 600 ..... E7
46737 Fremont 1,180 ..... H1
47432 French Lick 2,265 ..... D7
46931 Fulton 393 ..... E3
†47119 Galena 1,186 ..... F8
46932 Galveston 1,822 ..... E3
46738 Garrett 4,751 ..... G2
*46401 Gary 151,953 ..... C1
Gary-Hammond-East Chicago‡ 642,781 ..... C1
46933 Gas City 6,370 ..... F4
47342 Gaston 1,150 ..... G4
46740 Geneva 1,430 ..... H3
47537 Gentryville 299 ..... C8
47122 Georgetown 1,494 ..... F8
46133 Glenwood 370 ..... G5
†47567 Glezen 300 ..... C8
46045 Goldsmith 235 ..... E4

(continued on following page)

Agriculture, Industry and Resources

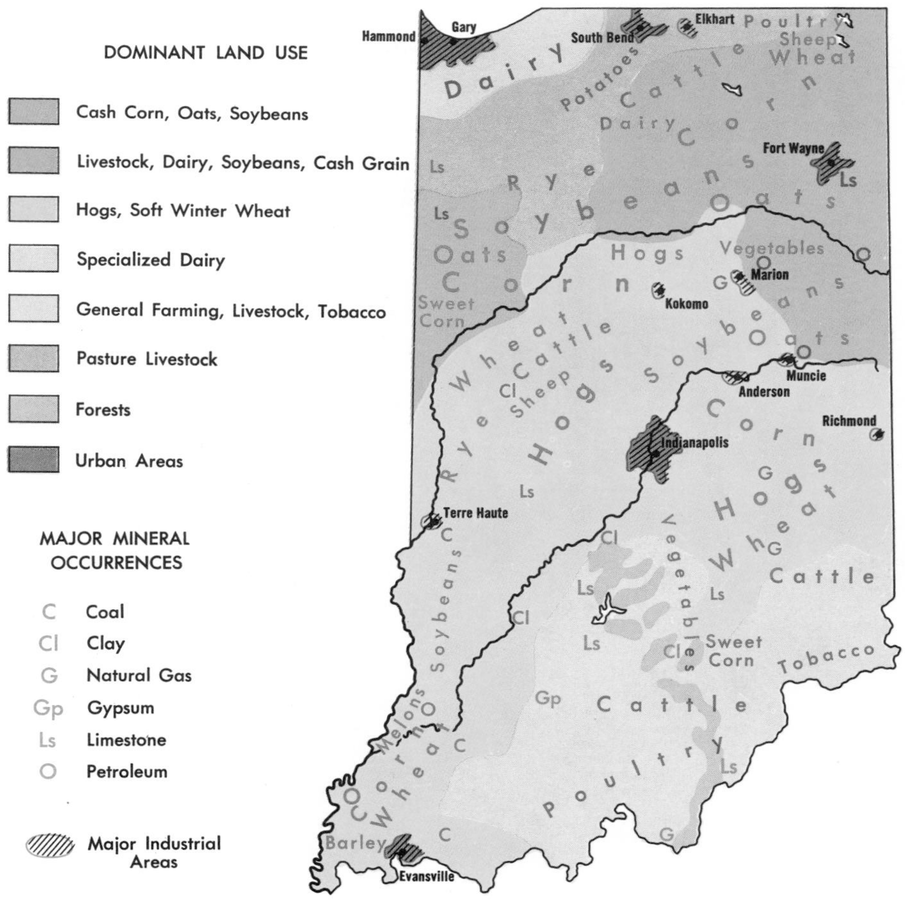
DOMINANT LAND USE
Cash Corn, Oats, Soybeans
Livestock, Dairy, Soybeans, Cash Grain
Hogs, Soft Winter Wheat
Specialized Dairy
General Farming, Livestock, Tobacco
Pasture Livestock
Forests
Urban Areas
MAJOR MINERAL OCCURRENCES
C Coal
Cl Clay
G Natural Gas
Gp Gypsum
Ls Limestone
O Petroleum
Major Industrial Areas
Hammond
Gary
South Bend
Elkhart
Fort Wayne
Marion
Kokomo
Muncie
Anderson
Richmond
Indianapolis
Terre Haute
Evansville
Dairy
Potatoes
Cattle
Poultry
Sheep
Wheat
Corn
Rye
Soybeans
Oats
Hogs
Vegetables
Sweet Corn
Tobacco
Melons
Barley

47948 Goodland 1,200 ....C3
46526 Goshen⊙ 19,665 ....F1
47433 Gosport 729 ....D6
46741 Grabill 658 ....H2
47615 Grandview 670 ....C9
46530 Granger 350 ....E1
46135 Greencastle⊙ 8,403 ......D5
†47025 Greendale 3,795 ....H6
46140 Greenfield⊙ 11,299 ......F5
47344 Greensboro 175 ....G5
47240 Greensburg⊙ 9,254 ....G6
47345 Greens Fork 426 ....H5
46936 Greentown 2,265 ....E4
47124 Greenville 537 ....F8
46142 Greenwood 19,327 ....F5
47616 Griffin 192 ....B8
46319 Griffith 17,026 ....C1
46144 Gwynneville 250 ....F5
47346 Hagerstown 1,950 ....G5
46742 Hamilton 587 ....H1
46532 Hamlet 738 ....D2
*46320 Hammond 93,714 ....B1
46340 Hanna 550 ....D2
47243 Hanover 4,054 ....F7
47125 Hardinsburg 298 ....E8
46743 Harlan 840 ....H2
47853 Harmony 613 ....C5
47434 Harrodsburg 400 ....D6
47348 Hartford City⊙ 7,622 ....G4
47244 Hartsville 379 ....F6
47617 Hatfield 800 ....C9
47639 Haubstadt 1,389 ....B8
†47546 Haysville 600 ....D8
47640 Hazleton 368 ....B8
46341 Hebron 2,696 ....C2
47436 Heltonville 400 ....E7
46937 Hemlock 300 ....F4
47126 Henryville 1,132 ....F7
46322 Highland 25,935 ....B1
47949 Hillsboro 561 ....C4
47854 Hillsdale 500 ....C5
46745 Hoagland 600 ....H3
46342 Hobart 22,987 ....C1
46047 Hobbs 200 ....E4
47541 Holland 683 ....D8
47023 Holton 487 ....G6
46146 Homer 250 ....F5
47246 Hope 2,185 ....F6
†46069 Hortonville 240 ....E4
46746 Howe 800 ....G1
46747 Hudson 447 ....G1
46552 Hudson Lake 1,347 .....D1
46748 Huntertown 1,265 ......G2
47542 Huntingburg 5,376 .....D8
46750 Huntington⊙ 16,202 ...G3
†46064 Huntsville 120 ....G4
47437 Huron 250 ....D7
47855 Hymera 1,054 ....C6
47950 Idaville 655 ....D3
*46201 Indianapolis (cap.)⊙
         700,807 ....E5
     Indianapolis‡ 1,166,929 ...E5
†46601 Indian Village 151 .....E1
46048 Ingalls 909 ....F5
47545 Ireland 600 ....C8
46147 Jamestown 924 ....D5
47438 Jasonville 2,497 ......C6
47546 Jasper⊙ 9,097 ....D8
47130 Jeffersonville⊙ 21,220 .F8
†47565 Johnson 100 ....B8
46074 Jolietville 300 ....E4
46938 Jonesboro 2,279 ......F4
47247 Jonesville 213 ....F6
46049 Kempton 410 ....E4
46755 Kendallville 7,299 .....G2
47351 Kennard 441 ....G5
47951 Kentland⊙ 1,936 ......C3
46939 Kewanna 711 ....E2
46759 Keystone 204 ....G3
46760 Kimmell 250 ....F2
47952 Kingman 566 ....C5
46345 Kingsbury 329 ....D1
46346 Kingsford Heights 1,618 .D2
46050 Kirklin 662 ....E4
46148 Knightstown 2,325 ....F5
47857 Knightsville 763 ......C5
46534 Knox⊙ 3,674 ....D2
46901 Kokomo⊙ 47,808 ......E4
     Kokomo‡ 103,715 ......E4
†46574 Koontz Lake 1,436 ....D2
46347 Kouts 1,619 ....C2
46348 La Crosse 713 ....D2
47954 Ladoga 1,151 ....D5
*47901 Lafayette⊙ 43,011 ....D4
     Lafayette-West Lafayette‡
           121,702 ....D4
46940 La Fontaine 946 ....F3
47761 Lagrange⊙ 2,164 .....F1
46941 Lagro 549 ....F3
46157 Lake Hart 231 ....H1
†46703 Lake James 400 ....H1
46943 Laketon 500 ....F3
46349 Lake Village 900 ......C2
46536 Lakeville 629 ....E1
46944 Landess 150 ....F3
47136 Lanesville 570 ....E8
46763 Laotto 361 ....G2
46537 Lapaz 651 ....E2
46051 Lapel 1,881 ....E4
46350 LaPorte⊙ 21,796 .....D1
46764 Larwill 286 ....F2
47024 Laurel 819 ....G6
46226 Lawrence 25,591 ......E5
47025 Lawrenceburg⊙ 4,403 .H6
47137 Leavenworth 356 ......E8
46052 Lebanon⊙ 11,456 .....D4
46538 Leesburg 629 ....F2
46945 Leiters Ford 280 ......E2
46765 Leo 500 ....G2
47551 Leopold 175 ....D8
46355 Leroy 400 ....C2
†47240 Letts 247 ....G6
47352 Lewisville 577 ....G5
47138 Lexington 100 ....F7
47353 Liberty⊙ 1,844 ......H5
46766 Liberty Center 275 ....G3
46946 Liberty Mills 200 .....F2

46767 Ligonier 3,134 ....F2
47955 Linden 700 ....D4
46769 Linn Grove 175 ....H3
47441 Linton 6,315 ....C6
†46755 Lisbon 200 ....G2
47139 Little York 150 ....F7
46149 Lizton 456 ....D5
46947 Logansport⊙ 17,731 ..E3
†46360 Long Beach 2,262 .....D1
47553 Loogootee 3,100 ......D7
47354 Losantville 306 ......G4
46356 Lowell 5,827 ....C2
47354 Lucerne 135 ....E3
†46601 Lydick E1
†47874 Lyford 400 ....C5
47355 Lynn 1,250 ....H4
47619 Lynnville 566 ....C8
47443 Lyons 782 ....C7
46951 Macy 282 ....E3
47250 Madison⊙ 12,472 ....G7
47865 Magnet 75 ....D8
†47001 Manchester 250 ......H6
46150 Manilla 350 ....F5
†47872 Mansfield 200 ....C5
47443 Marco 150 ....C7
47140 Marengo 892 ....E8
47556 Mariah Hill 300 ......D8
†46176 Marietta 234 ....F6
46952 Marion⊙ 35,874 .....F3
46770 Markle 975 ....G3
46056 Markleville 427 ......F5
47453 Marshall 413 ....C5
46151 Martinsville⊙ 11,311 .D6
46957 Matthews 745 ....F4
46154 Maxwell 300 ....F5
46055 McCordsville 600 .....F5
47860 Mecca 482 ....C5
47957 Medaryville 731 ......D2
47260 Medora 853 ....E7
47958 Mellott 294 ....C4
47143 Memphis 300 ....F8
46539 Mentone 973 ....E2
47861 Merom 360 ....B6
46410 Merrillville 27,677 ...C2
47030 Metamora 350 ....G6
†46703 Metz 200 ....H1
46057 Miami 350 ....E3
†49117 Michiana Shores 464 ..D1
46360 Michigan City 36,850 ..C1
46057 Michigantown 453 ....E4
46540 Middlebury 1,665 ....F1
47356 Middletown 2,978 ....F4
47445 Midland 250 ....C6
47031 Milan 1,566 ....G6
46542 Milford 1,153 ....F2
†47240 Milford 177 ....F6
47261 Millhousen 214 ......G6
47145 Milltown 1,006 ......E8
†47362 Millville 275 ....G5
46156 Milroy 750 ....G6
47357 Milton 729 ....G5
46544 Mishawaka 40,201 ...E1
47446 Mitchell 4,641 ......E7
47358 Modoc 243 ....G4
46771 Mongo 225 ....G1
47359 Monon 1,540 ....D3
46772 Monroe 739 ....H3
47557 Monroe City 569 .....C7
46773 Monroeville 1,372 ....H3
46157 Monrovia 800 ....E5
46960 Monterey 236 ....D2
47862 Montezuma 1,352 ....C5
47558 Montgomery 390 .....C7
†47960 Monticello⊙ 5,162 ...D3
47962 Montmorenci 300 ....D4
47359 Montpelier 1,995 .....G3
47360 Mooreland 479 ....G5
47032 Moores Hill 566 .....G6
46158 Mooresville 5,349 ....E5
46160 Morgantown 897 .....E6
47963 Morocco 1,348 ......C3
47033 Morris 350 ....G6
46161 Morristown 989 ......F5
†47327 Mount Auburn 192 ...G5
47964 Mount Ayr 207 ......C3
47361 Mount Summit 357 ...G4
†47620 Mount Vernon⊙ 7,656 .B9
46058 Mulberry 1,225 ......D4
46321 Munster 20,671 ......B1
47147 Nabb 150 ....F7
47034 Napoleon 246 ....G6
46550 Nappanee 4,694 .....F2
47448 Nashville⊙ 705 ......E6
†47421 Needmore 200 ....E7
47150 New Albany⊙ 37,103 .F8
47449 Newberry 246 ....C7
47630 Newburgh 2,906 .....C9
46552 New Carlisle 1,439 ...E1
47362 New Castle⊙ 20,056 .G5
†46342 New Chicago 3,284 ...C1
47863 New Goshen 500 .....B5
47631 New Harmony 945 ....B8
46774 New Haven 6,714 ....H2
47366 New Lisbon 300 .....G5
†46979 New London 200 .....E4
47965 New Market 608 .....D5
46163 New Palestine 749 ...F5
46553 New Paris 1,062 .....F2
†47165 New Pekin 1,125 .....F7
47263 New Point 296 ......G6
46967 Newport⊙ 704 ....C5
†47106 New Providence
         (Borden) 384 ......F8
47967 New Richmond 403 ...D4
47968 New Ross 306 ....D5
†46173 New Salem 200 ......G5
47161 New Salisbury 350 ...E8
47632 Newtonville 136 .....D8
47969 Newtown 277 ....C4
47170 New Trenton 200 ....H6
47162 New Washington 800 .F7
46961 New Waverly 162 ....E3
46184 New Whiteland 4,502 .E5

†46122 New Winchester 180 ...D5
46060 Noblesville⊙ 12,056 ...F4
46366 North Judson 1,653 ...D2
46554 North Liberty 1,211 ...E1
46962 North Manchester 5,998 .F3
46165 North Salem 581 .....D5
47805 North Terre Haute C5
47265 North Vernon 5,768 ...F6
46555 North Webster 709 ...F2
46556 Notre Dame E1
†47331 Nulltown 235 ....G5
46965 Oakford 325 ....E4
47660 Oakland City 3,301 ...C8
47561 Oaktown 776 ....C7
47367 Oakville 220 ....G4
47562 Odon 1,463 ....C7
†46401 Ogden Dunes 1,489 ...C1
47036 Oldenburg 770 ....G6
47451 Oolitic 1,495 ....E7
47343 Orange 200 ....G5
46063 Orestes 539 ....F4
46776 Orland 424 ....G1
47452 Orleans 2,161 ....D7
46561 Osceola 1,990 ....E1
47037 Osgood 1,554 ....G6
46777 Ossian 1,945 ....G3
46367 Otis 250 ....D1
47163 Otisco 425 ....F7
47970 Otterbein 1,118 ......C4
47564 Otwell 600 ....C8
47453 Owensburg 785 ......D7
47665 Owensville 1,261 ....B8
47971 Oxford 1,327 ....C3
†46508 Palestine 800 ....F2
47164 Palmyra 692 ....E8
47454 Paoli⊙ 3,637 ....E7
46166 Paragon 538 ....D6
47368 Parker City 1,414 ....G4
47666 Patoka 832 ....B8
47455 Patricksburg 250 ....D6
47038 Patriot 265 ....H7
47865 Paxton 200 ....C6
47165 Pekin 950 ....E7
46064 Pendleton 2,130 .....F5
47369 Pennville 805 ....G4
†46011 Perkinsville 175 .....F4
47974 Perrysville 532 ......C4
47370 Pershing 438 ....G5
†46975 Pershing 425 ....E2
46970 Peru⊙ 13,764 ....E3
47567 Petersburg⊙ 2,987 ...C7
46778 Petroleum 210 ......G3
46562 Pierceton 1,086 .....F2
47866 Pimento 150 ....C6
†46350 Pine Lake 1,676 .....D1
47975 Pine Village 257 ....C4
46167 Pittsboro 891 ....D5
†46923 Pittsburg 175 ....D3
46168 Plainfield 9,191 .....E5
47568 Plainville 556 ....C7
46779 Pleasant Lake 800 ...H1
46563 Plymouth⊙ 7,693 ....E2
†47068 Poland 200 ....D6
46781 Poneto 250 ....G3
46368 Portage 27,409 .....C1
46304 Porter 2,988 ....C1
47371 Portland⊙ 7,074 ....H4
47633 Poseyville 1,247 ....B8
†46360 Pottawattamie Park 284 .C1
47870 Prairie Creek 275 ....C6
47870 Prairieton 200 ......B6
46782 Preble 150 ....H3
†46164 Princes Lakes 937 ...E6
†46670 Princeton⊙ 8,976 ....B8
46170 Putnamville 250 ....D5
47456 Quincy 250 ....D6
47573 Ragsdale 135 ....C7
46737 Ray 200 ....H1
†47224 Reddington 400 ......F6
46171 Reelsville 210 ....D5
47977 Remington 1,268 ....C3
47978 Rensselaer⊙ 4,944 ...C3
47980 Reynolds 632 ....D3
47634 Richland 500 ....C9
47374 Richmond⊙ 41,349 ...H5
47380 Ridgeville 933 ......G4
47871 Riley 269 ....C6
47040 Rising Sun⊙ 2,478 ...H7
46172 Roachdale 958 ......D5
46974 Roann 548 ....F3
46783 Roanoke 891 ....G3
46975 Rochester⊙ 5,050 ...E2
46977 Rockfield 300 ....D3
47635 Rockport⊙ 2,590 ....C9
47872 Rockville⊙ 2,785 ....C5
46371 Rolling Prairie 550 ...D1
47574 Rome 500 ....D8
46784 Rome City 1,319 ....G1
47981 Romney 353 ....D4
47874 Rosedale 744 ....C5
†46601 Roseland 800 ....E1
46310 Roselawn 200 ....C2
46065 Rossville 1,148 ......D4
46978 Royal Center 908 ....E3
†47302 Royerton 300 ....G4
†46173 Russellville 376 ......D5
46975 Russiaville 973 ......E4
47575 Saint Anthony 470 ...D8
47875 Saint Bernice 500 ...C5
46785 Saint Joe 546 ....H2
46383 Saint John 3,974 ....C1
46373 Saint Leon 515 ......H6
47876 Saint Mary-of-
         the-Woods 920 ....B6
†46556 Saint Marys E1
47577 Saint Meinrad 910 ...D8
47272 Saint Paul 976 ......F6
†47012 Saint Peter 175 .....H6
†47620 Saint Philip 400 .....B9
47638 Saint Wendel 250 ...B8
47167 Salem⊙ 5,290 ......E7
47578 Sandborn 576 ......C7
†47401 Sanders 65 ....E6
46374 San Pierre 325 .....D2
47579 Santa Claus 514 ....D8

47382 Saratoga 338 ....H4
†47283 Sardinia 133 ....F6
46375 Schererville 13,209 ...C2
46376 Schneider 364 ....C2
47580 Schnellville 250 .....D8
47273 Scipio 200 ....F6
46066 Scircleville 125 ......E4
47170 Scottsburg⊙ 5,068 ...F7
47878 Seelyville 1,374 .....C5
47172 Sellersburg 3,211 ....F8
47383 Selma 1,056 ....G4
46068 Sharpsville 617 ......E4
47879 Shelburn 1,259 ......C6
46377 Shelby 700 ....C2
46176 Shelbyville⊙ 14,989 ..F6
47880 Shepardsville 325 ...B5
46069 Sheridan 2,200 ......E4
†47338 Shideler 275 ....G4
46565 Shipshewana 466 ....F1
†46797 Shirley City (Woodburn)
         1,002 ....H2
47581 Shoals⊙ 967 ....D7
46566 Sidney 194 ....F2
46982 Silver Lake 576 .....F2
46983 Sims 250 ....F3
†46142 Smith Valley E5
47458 Smithville 500 ......D6
46984 Somerset 350 ....F3
47683 Somerville 340 ......C8
*46601 South Bend⊙ 109,727 .E1
       South Bend‡ 280,772 ..E1
46786 South Milford 270 ...G1
†46201 Southport 2,266 .....E5
46787 South Whitley 1,575 ..F2
†47355 Spartanburg 201 .....H4
47112 Speed 800 ....F8
46224 Speedway 12,641 ....E5
†47808 Spelterville 200 .....C5
47460 Spencer⊙ 2,732 ....D6
46788 Spencerville 400 ....G2
47385 Spiceland 940 ......F5
†47374 Spring Grove 469 ...H5
†46140 Spring Lake 236 ....F5
47386 Springport 221 .....G4
47462 Spurgeon 279 ......D7
47584 Spurgeon 250 ......C8
47463 Stanford 300 ....D6
46985 Star City 351 ....D3
47982 State Line 233 ......C4
47881 Staunton 607 ....C6
47585 Stendal 175 ....C8
47636 Stewartsville 225 ...B8
46180 Stilesville 350 ......D5
46351 Stilesville 300 ......D5
47464 Stinesville 227 .....D6
47983 Stockwell 310 ......D4
47387 Straughn 331 ......G5
46789 Stroh 350 ....G1
47882 Sullivan⊙ 4,774 ....C6
47388 Sulphur Springs 345 .G4
46379 Sumava Resorts 300 .C2
46070 Summitville 1,085 ...F4
47041 Sunman 924 ....G6
46987 Sweetser 944 ......F3
47465 Switz City 300 .....C6
47567 Syracuse 2,579 ....F2
47280 Taylorsville 1,247 ..F6
47586 Tell City 8,704 .....D9
47637 Tennyson 331 ......C8
*47801 Terre Haute⊙ 61,125 .C6
       Terre Haute‡ 176,583 .C6
46381 Thayer 350 ....C2
46071 Thorntown 1,468 ...D4
†46975 Tiosa 100 ....E2
46570 Tippecanoe 320 ....E2
46072 Tipton⊙ 5,004 .....E4
46571 Topeka 876 ....F1
†46360 Town of Pines 962 ..D1
46181 Trafalgar 466 ......E6
†46360 Trail Creek 2,581 ..D1
46725 Tri Lakes 1,356 ...G2
47588 Troy 550 ....D9
46988 Twelve Mile 240 ...E3
46572 Tyner 245 ....E2
47177 Underwood 550 ....F7
47390 Union City 3,908 ...H4
46791 Uniondale 303 .....G3
46382 Union Mills 650 ...D2
47468 Unionville 225 .....E6
47884 Universal 428 .....C5
46989 Upland 3,335 .....F4
46990 Urbana 400 ....F3
†47130 Utica 501 ....F8
47281 Vallonia 345 ......E7
46383 Valparaiso⊙ 22,247 .C2
46991 Van Buren 935 ....F3
47987 Veedersburg 2,261 .C4
47590 Velpen 375 ....C8
47282 Vernon⊙ 329 .....F7
47042 Versailles⊙ 1,560 .G6
47043 Vevay⊙ 1,343 ....G7
†47441 Vicksburg 175 ....C6
47170 Vienna 175 ....F7
†47302 Vincennes⊙ 20,857 .C7
47591 Vincennes⊙ 20,857 .C7
46992 Wabash⊙ 12,985 ..F3
47638 Wadesville 450 ...B8
46573 Wakarusa 1,281 ..F1
46182 Waldron 850 .....F6
47201 Walkerton 214 ....F6
46574 Walkerton 2,051 ..E2
46802 Wallen 945 ......G2
46994 Walton 1,202 ....E3
46390 Wanatah 879 .....C2
46792 Warren 1,254 ....G3
46580 Warsaw⊙ 10,647 .F2
47501 Washington⊙ 11,325 .C7
46173 Waterloo 1,951 ...G2
†47130 Watson 200 ......F8
47989 Waveland 559 ...D5
46794 Wawaka 320 .....F2
47990 Waynetown 915 ..C4
47392 Webster 350 ....H5
47469 West Baden Springs 796 .D7
†47353 West College Corner 614 .H5
46074 Westfield 2,783 ....E4

†45030 West Harrison 328 ......H6
47906 West Lafayette 21,247 ...D4
47991 West Lebanon 946 ......C4
46995 West Middleton 327 ....E4
47596 West Middlebury 300 ...C7
47992 Westpoint 375 ....C4
47283 Westport 1,450 ....F6
47885 West Terre Haute 2,806 .B6
46391 Westville 2,887 ....D1
46392 Wheatfield 755 ....C2
47597 Wheatland 532 ....C7
46393 Wheeler 540 ....C1
†47342 Wheeling 180 ....G4
46184 Whiteland 1,956 ......E5
46075 Whitestown 497 ......E5
46394 Whiting 5,630 ....C1
46186 Wilkinson 493 ....F5
47470 Williams 350 ....D7
47993 Williamsport⊙ 1,747 ..C4
46996 Winamac⊙ 2,370 ....D2
47394 Winchester⊙ 5,659 ..G4
46076 Windfall 911 ....F4
47994 Wingate 373 ....C4
46590 Winona Lake 2,827 ..F2
47598 Winslow 1,017 ......C8
47995 Wolcott 923 ....C3
46795 Wolcottville 890 .....G1
46796 Wolflake 230 ....F2
46797 Woodburn 1,002 ....H2
†46624 Woodland 400 ......E1
47471 Worthington 1,574 ..C6
46595 Wyatt 250 ....E1
†47030 Yankeetown 250 ....C9
46798 Yoder 250 ....G3
47396 Yorktown 3,945 ....G4
46998 Young America 259 ..E3
†47808 Youngstown 350 ....C6
46799 Zanesville 575 ......G3
46077 Zionsville 3,948 ....E5

OTHER FEATURES

Anderson (riv.) D8
Bass (lake) D2
Beanblossom (creek) D6
Big (creek) D6
Big (creek) C8
Big Blue (riv.) F5
Big Pine (creek) C4
Big Raccoon (creek) C5
Big Walnut (creek) D5
Blue (riv.) E8
Brookville (lake) G6
Buck (creek) E8
Busseron (creek) C7
Camp (creek) E6
Cedar (creek) G2
Clifty (creek) F6
Coal (creek) C4
Crooked (creek) D2
Cypress (pond) B8
Deer (creek) E3
Deer (creek) D5
Eagle (creek) C6
Eel (riv.) C6
Eel (riv.) F3
Elkhart (riv.) F1

Fawn (riv.) G1
Flatrock (creek) F5
Fort Benjamin Harrison .E5
Freeman (lake) D3
Geist (res.) F5
George Rogers Clark Nat'l Hist.
    Park B7
Graham (creek) F5
Grissom A.F.B. 4,676 ..E3
Huntington (lake) F3
Indian (creek) E8
Indian (creek) D6
Indiana Dunes Nat'l Lakeshore .C1
Iroquois (riv.) C2
Jefferson Proving Ground .G7
Kankakee (riv.) C2
Lemon (lake) F5
Lincoln Boyhood Nat'l Mem. .C8
Little (riv.) G3
Little Elkhart (riv.) ...F1
Little Pigeon (creek) ..C8
Little Vermilion (riv.) .B5
Lost (riv.) D7
Maria (creek) C7
Maumee (riv.) H2
Maxinkuckee (lake) ..E2
Michigan (lake) C1
Mill (creek) D5
Mississinewa (lake) ..F3
Mississinewa (riv.) ..F3
Monroe (lake) E6
Morse (res.) E4
Muscatatuck (riv.) ...E4
Ohio (riv.) B9
Patoka (riv.) C8
Pigeon (creek) C8
Pigeon (riv.) F1
Pipe (creek) F4
Prairie (creek) C6
Richland (creek) D7
Saint Joseph (riv.) ...E1
Saint Joseph (riv.) ...H3
Saint Marys (riv.) ...H3
Saint Marys (riv.) ...H3
Salamonie (lake) F3
Salamonie (riv.) G4
Salt (creek) E6
Sand (creek) F6
Shafer (lake) D3
Silver (creek) F8
Sugar (creek) B5
Sugar (creek) F3
Sugar (creek) C5
Tippecanoe (riv.) ...E2
Vermilion (riv.) B5
Vernon Fork (creek) .F7
Wabash (riv.) B8
Wawasee (lake) F2
White (riv.) B8
White, East Fork (riv.) .C7
White, West Fork (riv.) .C7
Whitewater (riv.) H6
Wildcat (creek) E4

⊙County seat.
‡Population of metropolitan area.
† Zip of nearest p.o.   * Multiple zips.

Topography

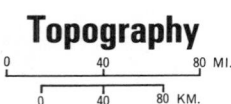

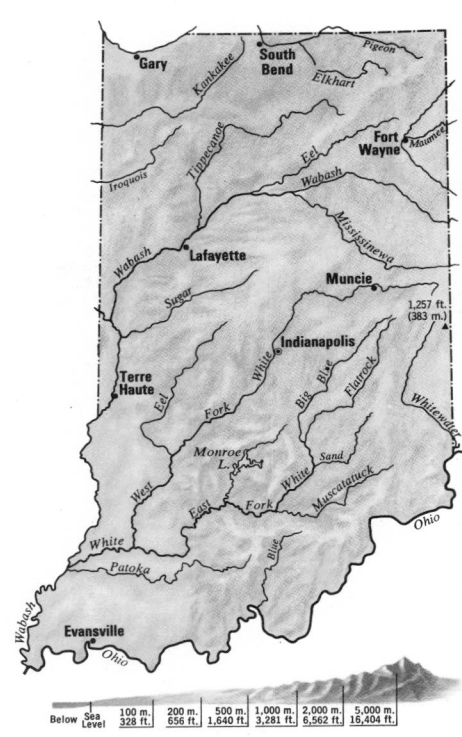

0   40   80 MI.

0   40   80 KM.

| | Below Sea Level | 100 m. 328 ft. | 200 m. 656 ft. | 500 m. 1,640 ft. | 1,000 m. 3,281 ft. | 2,000 m. 6,562 ft. | 5,000 m. 16,404 ft. |

1,257 ft. (383 m.)

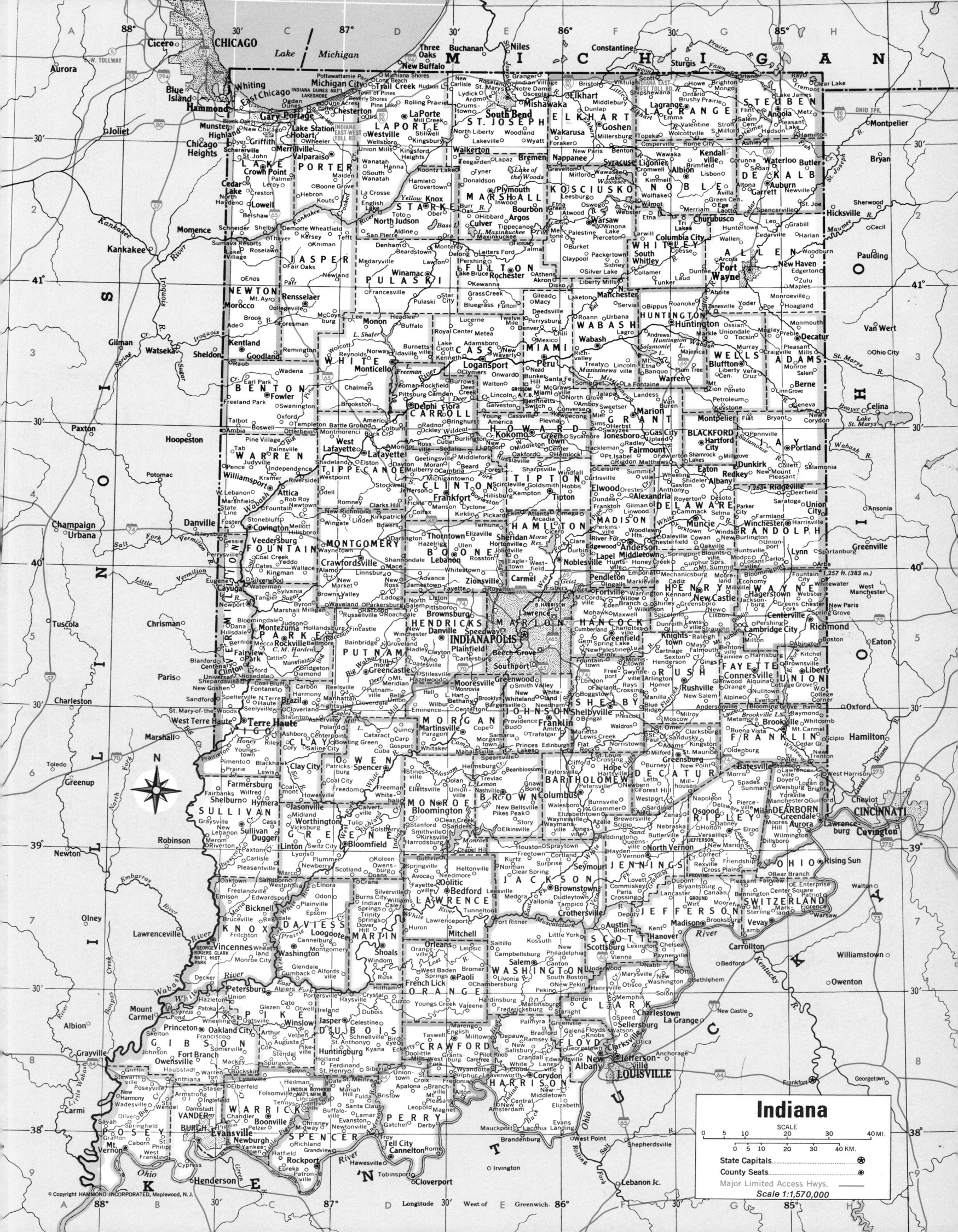

COUNTIES

Name	Pop.	Key
Adair	9,509	E6
Adams	5,731	D6
Allamakee	15,108	L2
Appanoose	15,511	H7
Audubon	8,559	D5
Benton	23,649	J4
Black Hawk	137,961	J4
Boone	26,184	F5
Bremer	24,820	J3
Buchanan	22,900	K4
Buena Vista	20,774	C3
Butler	17,668	H3
Calhoun	13,542	D4
Carroll	22,951	D4
Cass	16,932	D6
Cedar	18,635	L5
Cerro Gordo	48,458	G2
Cherokee	16,238	B3
Chickasaw	15,437	J2
Clarke	8,612	F6
Clay	19,576	C2
Clayton	21,098	L3
Clinton	57,122	M5
Crawford	18,935	C4
Dallas	29,513	E5
Davis	9,104	J7
Decatur	9,794	F7
Delaware	18,933	L4
Des Moines	46,203	L7
Dickinson	15,629	C2
Dubuque	93,745	M4
Emmet	13,336	D2
Fayette	25,488	K3
Floyd	19,597	H2
Franklin	13,036	G3
Fremont	9,401	B7
Greene	12,119	E5
Grundy	14,366	H4
Guthrie	11,983	D5
Hamilton	17,862	F4
Hancock	13,833	F2
Hardin	21,776	G4
Harrison	16,348	B5
Henry	18,890	K6
Howard	11,114	J2
Humboldt	12,246	E3
Ida	8,908	C4
Iowa	15,429	J5
Jackson	22,503	M4
Jasper	36,425	G5
Jefferson	16,316	K6
Johnson	81,717	K5
Jones	20,401	L4
Keokuk	12,921	J6
Kossuth	21,891	E2
Lee	43,106	L7
Linn	169,775	K4
Louisa	12,055	L6
Lucas	10,313	G6
Lyon	12,896	A2
Madison	12,597	E6
Mahaska	22,867	H6
Marion	29,669	G6
Marshall	41,652	G4
Mills	13,406	B6
Mitchell	12,329	H2
Monona	12,197	B4
Monroe	9,209	H7
Montgomery	13,413	C6
Muscatine	40,436	L5
O'Brien	16,972	B2
Osceola	8,371	B2
Page	19,063	C7
Palo Alto	12,721	D2
Plymouth	24,743	A3
Pocahontas	11,369	D3
Polk	303,170	F5
Pottawattamie	86,561	B6
Poweshiek	19,306	H5
Ringgold	6,112	E7
Sac	14,118	C4
Scott	160,022	M5
Shelby	15,043	C5
Sioux	30,813	A2
Story	72,326	G4
Tama	19,533	H4
Taylor	8,353	D7
Union	13,858	E7
Van Buren	8,626	K7
Wapello	40,241	J6
Warren	34,878	F6
Washington	20,141	K6
Wayne	8,199	G7
Webster	45,953	E4
Winnebago	13,010	F2
Winneshiek	21,876	K2
Woodbury	100,884	B4
Worth	9,075	G2
Wright	16,319	F3

CITIES and TOWNS

Zip	Name/Pop.	Key
50601	Ackley 1,900	G3
50002	Adair 883	D6
50003	Adel⊙ 2,846	E5
50830	Afton 985	E6
52530	Agency 657	J7
52201	Ainsworth 547	K6
51001	Akron 1,517	A3
50510	Albert City 818	C3
52531	Albia⊙ 4,184	H6
52202	Alburnett 411	K4
50006	Alden 953	G4
50511	Algona⊙ 6,289	E2
50007	Alleman 307	F5
50008	Allerton 670	G7
50602	Allison⊙ 1,132	H3
51002	Alta 1,720	C3
50603	Alta Vista 314	J2
51003	Alton 986	A3
50009	Altoona 5,764	G5
51230	Alvord 246	A2
52203	Amana 300	K5
50010	Ames 45,775	F4
52205	Anamosa⊙ 4,958	L4
50020	Andrew 349	M4
50021	Ankeny 15,429	F5
51004	Anthon 687	B4
50604	Aplington 1,027	H3
51430	Arcadia 454	C4
50606	Arlington 498	K3
51231	Armstrong 1,153	D2
52310	Arnolds Park 1,051	C2
51431	Arthur 288	C4
†52001	Asbury 2,017	M4
51232	Ashton 441	B2
52720	Atalissa 360	L5
52206	Atkins 678	K4
50022	Atlantic⊙ 7,789	D6

51433 Auburn 320 .... D4
50025 Audubon⊙ 2,841 .... D5
51005 Aurelia 1,143 .... C3
50607 Aurora 248 .... K3
51521 Avoca 1,650 .... C6
50515 Ayrshire 243 .... D2
50516 Badger 653 .... E3
50026 Bagley 370 .... E5
50517 Bancroft 1,082 .... E2
50027 Barnes City 266 .... H6
51006 Battle Creek 919 .... B4
50028 Baxter 951 .... G5
50029 Bayard 637 .... D5
52534 Beacon 530 .... H6
50833 Bedford⊙ 1,692 .... D7
52208 Belle Plaine 2,903 .... J5
52031 Bellevue 2,450 .... M4
50421 Belmond 2,505 .... F3
52721 Bennett 458 .... L5
50032 Berwick 600 .... G5
52722 Bettendorf 27,381 .... N5
52535 Birmingham 410 .... K7
50034 Blairsburg 288 .... F4

52209 Blairstown 695 .... J5
52536 Blakesburg 404 .... H7
51523 Blencoe 247 .... A5
50836 Blockton 280 .... D7
52537 Bloomfield⊙ 2,849 .... J7
52726 Blue Grass 1,377 .... M5
50519 Bode 406 .... E3
52620 Bonaparte 489 .... K7
50035 Bondurant 1,283 .... G5
50036 Boone⊙ 12,602 .... F4
50040 Boxholm 267 .... E4
51234 Boyden 708 .... B2
52210 Brandon 337 .... K4
51436 Breda 502 .... C4
50837 Bridgewater 233 .... D6
52540 Brighton 804 .... K6
50611 Bristow 252 .... H3
50423 Britt 2,185 .... F2
51007 Bronson 289 .... A4
52211 Brooklyn 1,509 .... J5
52728 Buffalo 1,569 .... M6
50424 Buffalo Center 1,233 ... F2
52601 Burlington⊙ 29,529 .... L7
50522 Burt 689 .... E2

AREA 56,275 sq. mi. (145,752 sq. km.)
POPULATION 2,913,808
CAPITAL Des Moines
LARGEST CITY Des Moines
HIGHEST POINT (Osceola Co.) 1670 ft.
  (509 m.)
SETTLED IN 1788
ADMITTED TO UNION December 28, 1846
POPULAR NAME Hawkeye State
STATE FLOWER Wild Rose
STATE BIRD Eastern Goldfinch

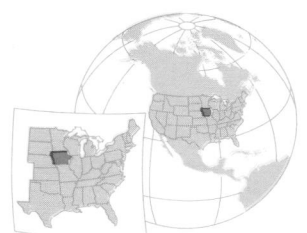

Iowa

SCALE
0 5 10   20   30   40 MI.
0 5 10   20   30   40 KM.

State Capitals .... ⊛
County Seats .... ⊙
Major Limited Access Hwys. ___
Scale 1:1,700,000

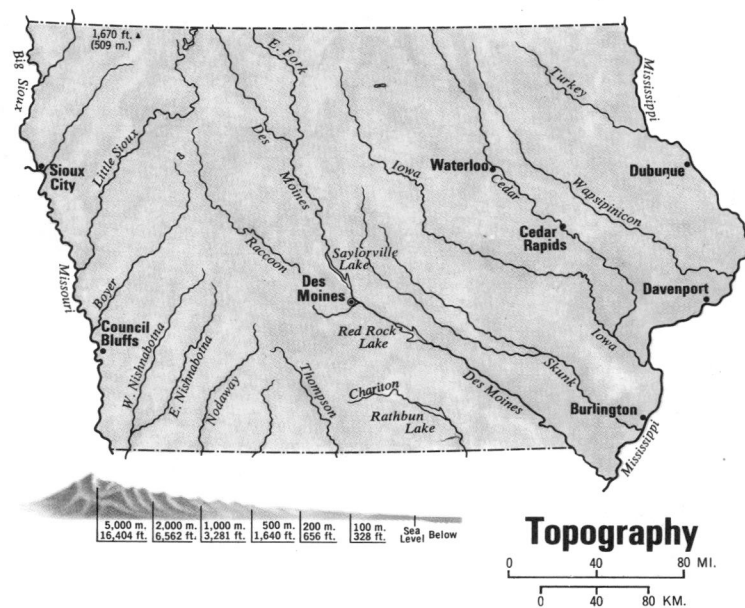

Topography

| 5,000 m. 16,404 ft. | 2,000 m. 6,562 ft. | 1,000 m. 3,281 ft. | 500 m. 1,640 ft. | 200 m. 656 ft. | 100 m. 328 ft. | Sea Level | Below |

0   40   80 MI.
0   40   80 KM.

50044 Bussey 579 .... H6
52729 Calamus 452 .... M5
50523 Callender 446 .... E4
52132 Calmar 1,053 .... K2
52730 Camanche 4,725 .... N5
50046 Cambridge 732 .... G5
52542 Cantril 299 .... J7
50047 Carlisle 3,073 .... G6
51441 Carroll⊙ 9,705 .... D4
51525 Carson 716 .... C6
†68101 Carter Lake 3,438 ...... B6
52033 Cascade 1,912 .... L4
50048 Casey 473 .... D5
50613 Cedar Falls 36,322 .... H3
*52401 Cedar Rapids⊙ 110,243 . K5
  Cedar Rapids‡ 169,775 .. K5
52213 Center Point 1,591 .... K4
52544 Centerville⊙ 6,558 .... H7
52214 Central City 1,067 .... K4
50049 Chariton⊙ 4,987 .... G6
50616 Charles City⊙ 8,778 ...... H2
51442 Charlotte 442 .... M5
51439 Charter Oak 615 .... C4
52215 Chelsea 357 .... J5
51012 Cherokee⊙ 7,004 .... B3
50050 Churdan 540 .... D4
52549 Cincinnati 598 .... G7
52216 Clarence 1,001 .... M5
51632 Clarinda⊙ 5,458 .... C7
50525 Clarion⊙ 3,060 .... F3
50619 Clarksville 1,424 .... H3
50840 Clearfield 410 .... D7
50428 Clear Lake 7,458 .... G2
51014 Cleghorn 275 .... B3
52135 Clermont 602 .... K3
52732 Clinton⊙ 32,828 .... N5
50318 Clive 6,064 .... F5
52217 Clutier 249 .... J4
52218 Coggon 639 .... L4
51636 Coin 316 .... C7
52035 Colesburg 463 .... L3
50054 Colfax 2,234 .... G5
51637 College Springs 307 .... C7
50055 Collins 451 .... G4
50056 Colo 808 .... G4
52737 Columbus City 367 .... L6
52738 Columbus Junction 1,429 . L6
52739 Conesville 301 .... L6
50631 Conrad 1,133 .... H4
52220 Conroy 250 .... J5
50058 Coon Rapids 1,448 .... D5
52241 Coralville 7,687 .... K5
50841 Corning⊙ 1,939 .... D7
51016 Correctionville 935 ... B4
50430 Corwith 480 .... F3
50060 Corydon⊙ 1,818 .... G7
50431 Coulter 264 .... G3
51501 Council Bluffs⊙ 56,449 . B6
52621 Crawfordsville 290 .... K6
51526 Crescent 647 .... B6
52136 Cresco⊙ 3,860 .... J2
50801 Creston⊙ 8,429 .... D6
50432 Crystal Lake 314 ...... F2
50843 Cumberland 351 ...... D6

51018 Cushing 270 .... B4
50529 Dakota City⊙ 1,072 .... E3
50063 Dallas 451 .... G6
50062 Dallas Center 1,360 .... E5
51019 Danbury 492 .... B4
52623 Danville 994 .... L7
*52801 Davenport⊙ 103,264 .. M5
  Davenport-Rock
  Island-Moline‡ 383,958 M5
50065 Davis City 327 .... F7
50530 Dayton 941 .... E4
52101 Decorah⊙ 7,991 .... K2
51440 Dedham 321 .... D5
52222 Deep River 323 .... J5
51527 Defiance 383 .... C5
52223 Delhi 511 .... L4
52037 Delmar 633 .... M4
51441 Deloit 345 .... C4
52550 Delta 482 .... J6
51442 Denison⊙ 6,675 ..... C4
52624 Denmark 480 .... L7
50622 Denver 1,647 .... J3
*50301 Des Moines
  (cap.)⊙ 191,003 ... G5
  Des Moines‡ 338,048 .. G5
50069 De Soto 1,035 ...... E5
50623 Dewar 230 .... J3
52742 De Witt 4,512 ..... N5
50070 Dexter 678 .... E5
50845 Diagonal 362 ...... E7
51333 Dickens 289 .... C2
50624 Dike 987 .... H4
52745 Dixon 312 .... M5
52746 Donahue 289 ..... M5
52625 Donnellson 972 ... K7
51235 Doon 537 .... A2
52551 Dorards 425 ...... J7
51528 Dow City 616 .... B5
50071 Dows 771 .... F3
52001 Dubuque⊙ 62,321 . M3
  Dubuque‡ 93,745 .. M3
50625 Dumont 815 ..... H3
50532 Duncombe 504 ... E4
50626 Dunkerton 718 .. J3
51529 Dunlap 1,374 .... B5
52747 Durant 1,583 .... M5
52040 Dyersville 3,825 . L3
52224 Dysart 1,355 .... J4
50533 Eagle Grove 4,324 . F3
50072 Earlham 1,140 ... E6
51530 Earling 520 ..... C5
50534 Earlville 844 .... L4
50535 Early 670 .... C4
52042 Edgewood 900 ... K3
52554 Eldon 1,255 .... J7
50627 Eldora⊙ 3,063 .. G4
51528 Eldridge 3,279 . M5
52141 Elgin 702 .... K3
52043 Elkader⊙ 1,688 . L3
50073 Elkhart 256 .... F5
51531 Elk Horn 746 ... C5
†50700 Elk Run Heights 1,186 . J4
51532 Elliott 493 ..... C6

50075 Ellsworth 480 .... F4
50628 Elma 714 .... J2
52227 Ely 425 .... K5
51533 Emerson 502 .... C6
50536 Emmetsburg⊙ 4,621 . D2
52045 Epworth 1,380 ...... M4
51638 Essex 1,001 .... C7
51334 Estherville⊙ 7,518 . D2
50707 Evansdale 4,798 ... J4
51338 Everly 796 .... C2
50076 Exira 978 .... D5
50629 Fairbank 980 ..... K3
52228 Fairfax 683 .... K5
52556 Fairfield⊙ 9,428 . J6
52046 Farley 1,287 ..... L4
52047 Farmersburg 276 . L3
52626 Farmington 869 . K7
50538 Farnhamville 461 . E4
51639 Farragut 603 .... C7
52142 Fayette 1,515 ... K3
50539 Fenton 394 ..... E2
50434 Fertile 372 ..... G2
50435 Floyd 408 ...... H2
50540 Fonda 863 ...... D3
50846 Fontanelle 805 . E6
50436 Forest City⊙ 4,270 . F2
52144 Fort Atkinson 374 . K3
50501 Fort Dodge⊙ 29,423 . E3
52627 Fort Madison⊙ 13,520 . L7
51340 Fostoria 261 ..... C2
50630 Fredericksburg 1,075 . J3
50631 Frederika 223 ... J3
52561 Fremont 730 .... H6
52749 Fruitland 461 ... L6
51020 Galva 420 ...... C3
50103 Garden Grove 297 . F7
52049 Garnavillo 723 . L3
50438 Garner⊙ 2,908 . F2
52229 Garrison 411 ... J4
50632 Garwin 626 .... H4
51237 George 1,241 .. B2
50105 Gilbert 805 .... F4
50634 Gilbertville 740 . J4
50106 Gilman 642 .... H5
50541 Gilmore City 626 . D3
50635 Gladbrook 970 . H4
51534 Glenwood⊙ 5,280 . B6
51443 Glidden 1,076 . D4
50542 Goldfield 789 .. F3
52750 Goose Lake 274 . N5
50543 Gowrie 1,089 .. E4
51342 Graettinger 923 . D2
50440 Grafton 255 ... G2
50107 Grand Junction 970 . E4
52751 Grand Mound 674 . M5
52752 Grandview 473 . L6
50109 Granger 619 ... F5
51022 Granville 336 .. B3
50848 Gravity 245 .... D7
52050 Gray 313 ...... L3
50636 Greene 1,332 .. H3
50849 Greenfield⊙ 2,243 . D6
50111 Grimes 1,973 .. F5
50112 Grinnell 8,868 . H5

(continued on following page)

Agriculture, Industry and Resources

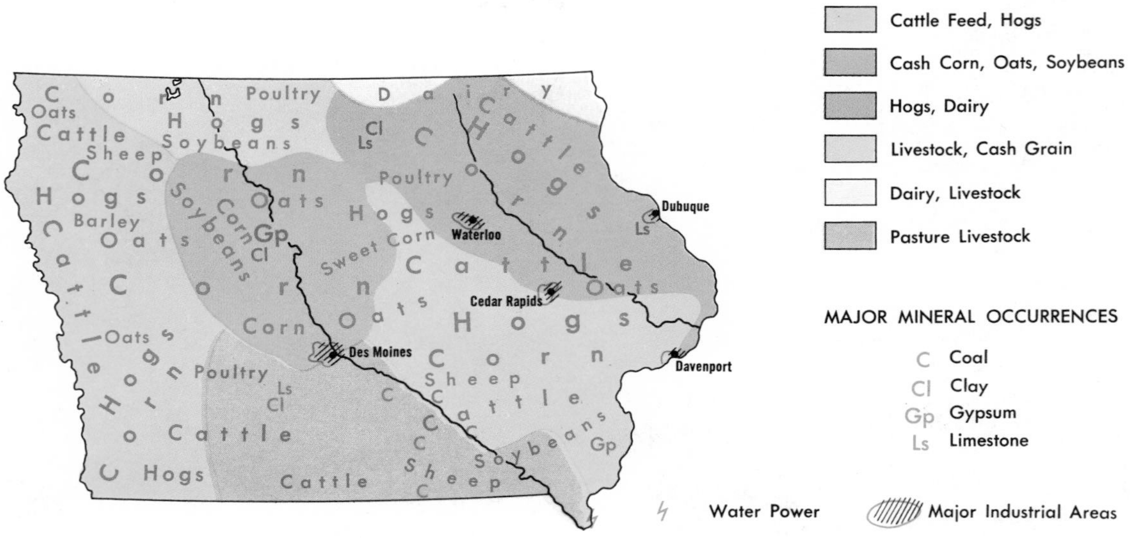
DOMINANT LAND USE
Cattle Feed, Hogs
Cash Corn, Oats, Soybeans
Hogs, Dairy
Livestock, Cash Grain
Dairy, Livestock
Pasture Livestock
MAJOR MINERAL OCCURRENCES
C Coal
Cl Clay
Gp Gypsum
Ls Limestone
Water Power
Major Industrial Areas
Dubuque
Waterloo
Cedar Rapids
Des Moines
Davenport

51535 Griswold 1,176 ..... C6
50638 Grundy Center⊙ 2,880 ..... H4
50115 Guthrie Center⊙ 1,713 ..... D5
52052 Guttenberg 2,428 ..... L3
51640 Hamburg 1,597 ..... B7
50441 Hampton⊙ 4,630 ..... G3
51536 Hancock 254 ..... C6
50544 Harcourt 347 ..... E4
51537 Harlan⊙ 5,357 ..... C5
52146 Harpers Ferry 258 ..... L2
50118 Hartford 761 ..... G6
51346 Hartley 1,700 ..... C2
50119 Harvey 275 ..... H6
50546 Havelock 279 ..... D3
51023 Hawarden 2,722 ..... A2
52147 Hawkeye 512 ..... J3
50641 Hazleton 877 ..... K3
52563 Hedrick 847 ..... J6
51541 Henderson 236 ..... B6
52233 Hiawatha 4,825 ..... K4
52235 Hills 547 ..... K5
52630 Hillsboro 208 ..... K7
51024 Hinton 659 ..... A3
50642 Holland 278 ..... H4
51025 Holstein 1,477 ..... B4
52053 Holy Cross 310 ..... L3
52237 Hopkinton 774 ..... L4
51026 Hornick 239 ..... A4
51238 Hospers 655 ..... B2
50122 Hubbard 852 ..... G4
50643 Hudson 2,267 ..... H4
51239 Hull 1,714 ..... A2
50548 Humboldt 4,794 ..... E3
50123 Humeston 671 ..... G7
50124 Huxley 1,884 ..... F5
51445 Ida Grove⊙ 2,285 ..... B4
50644 Independence⊙ 6,392 ..... K4
50125 Indianola⊙ 10,843 ..... F6
51240 Inwood 755 ..... A2
50645 Ionia 350 ..... J2
52240 Iowa City⊙ 50,508 ..... L5
Iowa City○‡ 81,717 ..... L5
50126 Iowa Falls 6,174 ..... G3
51027 Ireton 588 ..... A3
51446 Irwin 427 ..... C5
50128 Jamaica 275 ..... E5
50647 Janesville 840 ..... J3
50129 Jefferson⊙ 4,854 ..... E4
50648 Jesup 2,343 ..... J4
50130 Jewell 1,145 ..... F4
50131 Johnston 2,617 ..... F5
52247 Kalona 1,862 ..... K6
50447 Kanawha 756 ..... F3
50133 Kellerton 278 ..... E7
50134 Kelley 237 ..... F5
50135 Kellogg 654 ..... H5
50448 Kensett 360 ..... G2
52632 Keokuk⊙ 13,536 ..... L8
52565 Keosauqua⊙ 1,003 ..... J7
52248 Keota 1,034 ..... K6
50136 Keswick 300 ..... J6
52249 Keystone 618 ..... J5
51543 Kimballton 362 ..... D5
51028 Kingsley 1,209 ..... A3
51448 Kiron 317 ..... C4
50449 Klemme 620 ..... F3
50138 Knoxville⊙ 8,143 ..... G6
50139 Lacona 376 ..... G6
52251 Ladora 289 ..... J5
51449 Lake City 2,006 ..... D4
50450 Lake Mills 2,281 ..... F2
51347 Lake Park 1,123 ..... C2
50588 Lakeside 589 ..... C3
51450 Lake View 1,291 ..... C4
50451 Lakota 330 ..... E2
50140 Lamoni 2,705 ..... E7
50650 Lamont 554 ..... K3
52054 La Motte 322 ..... M4
52151 Lansing 1,181 ..... L2
50651 La Porte City 2,324 ..... J4
51241 Larchwood 701 ..... A2
50452 Latimer 441 ..... G3
50141 Laurel 278 ..... H5
50554 Laurens 1,606 ..... D3
52154 Lawler 534 ..... J2
51030 Lawton 447 ..... A4
52753 Le Claire 2,899 ..... N5
50142 Le Grand 921 ..... H5
50557 Lehigh 654 ..... E4
50453 Leland 274 ..... F2
51031 Le Mars⊙ 8,276 ..... A3
50851 Lenox 1,338 ..... D7
50144 Leon⊙ 2,094 ..... F7
51242 Lester 274 ..... A2
52754 Letts 473 ..... L6
51544 Lewis 497 ..... C6
52567 Libertyville 281 ..... K7
52155 Lime Springs 476 ..... J2
50146 Linden 264 ..... E5
50147 Lineville 319 ..... G7
52253 Lisbon 1,458 ..... L5
50148 Liscomb 296 ..... H4
51243 Little Rock 490 ..... B2
51545 Little Sioux 251 ..... B5
50558 Livermore 490 ..... E3
52635 Lockridge 271 ..... K7
51546 Logan⊙ 1,540 ..... B5
51453 Lohrville 521 ..... D4
52755 Lone Tree 1,014 ..... L6
52756 Long Grove 596 ..... M5
50149 Lorimor 405 ..... E6
52254 Lost Nation 524 ..... M5
50150 Lovilia 637 ..... H6
52255 Lowden 717 ..... L5
52757 Low Moor 346 ..... N5
52156 Luana 246 ..... K2
50151 Lucas 292 ..... G6
50560 Lu Verne 418 ..... E3
52056 Luxemburg 271 ..... L3
50153 Lynnville 406 ..... H5
50561 Lytton 377 ..... D4
51549 Macedonia 279 ..... C6
50156 Madrid 2,281 ..... F5
50157 Malcom 418 ..... H5
50562 Mallard 407 ..... D3
51551 Malvern 1,244 ..... B7
52057 Manchester⊙ 4,942 ..... L3
51454 Manilla 1,020 ..... C5
50456 Manly 1,496 ..... G2
51455 Manning 1,609 ..... C5
50563 Manson 1,924 ..... D3
51034 Mapleton 1,495 ..... B4
52060 Maquoketa⊙ 6,313 ..... M4
50565 Marathon 442 ..... C3
50653 Marble Rock 419 ..... H3
51035 Marcus 1,206 ..... B3
52301 Marengo⊙ 2,308 ..... J5
52302 Marion 19,474 ..... K4
52158 Marquette 528 ..... L2
50158 Marshalltown⊙ 26,938 ..... G4
52305 Martelle 316 ..... L4
50160 Martensdale 438 ..... F6
50401 Mason City⊙ 30,144 ..... G2
50853 Massena 518 ..... D6
51036 Maurice 288 ..... A3
50161 Maxwell 783 ..... G5
50655 Maynard 561 ..... K3
50154 McCallsburg 304 ..... G4
52758 McCausland 381 ..... M5
52157 McGregor 945 ..... L2
52306 Mechanicsville 1,166 ..... L5
52637 Mediapolis 1,685 ..... L6
50162 Melbourne 732 ..... G5
50163 Melcher 953 ..... G6
51350 Melvin 277 ..... B2
50164 Menlo 410 ..... E5
51037 Meriden 233 ..... B3
51038 Merrill 737 ..... A3
50457 Meservey 324 ..... G3
52307 Middle 335 ..... K5
52638 Middletown 487 ..... L7
52064 Miles 398 ..... N4
51351 Milford 2,076 ..... C2
50166 Milo 778 ..... G6
52570 Milton 567 ..... J7
50167 Minburn 390 ..... E5
51553 Minden 419 ..... C6
50168 Mingo 303 ..... G5
51555 Missouri Valley 3,107 ..... B5
50169 Mitchellville 1,530 ..... G5
51556 Modale 373 ..... B5
51557 Mondamin 423 ..... B5
52159 Monona 1,530 ..... L2
50170 Monroe 1,875 ..... G5
50171 Montezuma⊙ 1,485 ..... H5
52310 Monticello 3,641 ..... L4
50173 Montour 387 ..... H5
52759 Montpelier 250 ..... M6
52639 Montrose 1,038 ..... L7
51558 Moorhead 264 ..... B5
50566 Moorland 257 ..... E4
52571 Moravia 706 ..... H7
52640 Morning Sun 959 ..... L6
52760 Moscow 350 ..... L5
52572 Moulton 762 ..... H7
50854 Mount Ayr⊙ 1,938 ..... E7
52641 Mount Pleasant⊙ 7,322 ..... L7
52314 Mount Vernon 3,325 ..... K5
51039 Moville 1,273 ..... A4
50174 Murray 703 ..... F6
52761 Muscatine⊙ 23,467 ..... L6
52574 Mystic 665 ..... H7
50658 Nashua 1,846 ..... J3
51559 Neola 839 ..... B6
50201 Nevada⊙ 5,912 ..... G5
52160 New Albin 609 ..... L2
50568 Newell 913 ..... D3
52315 Newhall 899 ..... K5
50660 New Hartford 764 ..... H3
52645 New London 2,043 ..... L7
51646 New Market 554 ..... D7
50206 New Providence 249 ..... G4
50207 New Sharon 1,225 ..... H6
50208 Newton⊙ 15,292 ..... H5
52065 New Vienna 430 ..... L3
50210 New Virginia 512 ..... F6
52766 Nichols 375 ..... L6
50458 Nora Springs 1,572 ..... H2
52316 North English 990 ..... J5
52317 North Liberty 2,046 ..... K5
50459 Northwood⊙ 2,193 ..... G2
50211 Norwalk 2,676 ..... F6
52318 Norway 633 ..... K5
52319 Oakdale 300 ..... K5
51560 Oakland 1,552 ..... C6
52646 Oakville 470 ..... L6
51354 Ocheyedan 599 ..... B2
51458 Odebolt 1,299 ..... C4
50662 Oelwein 7,564 ..... K3
50212 Ogden 1,953 ..... E4
51355 Okoboji 559 ..... C2
52320 Olin 735 ..... L5
52576 Ollie 232 ..... J6
51040 Onawa⊙ 3,283 ..... A4
51041 Orange City⊙ 4,588 ..... A2
50858 Orient 416 ..... E6
†51360 Orleans 546 ..... C2
50461 Osage⊙ 3,718 ..... H2
50213 Osceola⊙ 3,750 ..... F6
52577 Oskaloosa⊙ 10,984 ..... H6
52161 Ossian 829 ..... K2
50569 Otho 692 ..... E4
52501 Ottumwa⊙ 27,381 ..... J6
52322 Oxford 676 ..... K5
52323 Oxford Junction 600 ..... M4
51561 Pacific Junction 511 ..... B6
50571 Palmer 288 ..... D3
52324 Palo 529 ..... K4
51562 Panama 229 ..... B5
50216 Panora 1,211 ..... E5
50665 Parkersburg 1,968 ..... H3
52325 Parnell 234 ..... J5
50217 Paton 291 ..... E4
51046 Paullina 1,224 ..... B3
50219 Pella 8,349 ..... H6
50220 Perry 7,053 ..... E5
50221 Pershing 325 ..... G6
51563 Persia 355 ..... B5
51047 Peterson 470 ..... C3
51048 Pierson 408 ..... B3
51564 Pisgah 307 ..... B5
50666 Plainfield 469 ..... J3
50225 Pleasantville 1,531 ..... G6
50464 Plymouth 463 ..... G2
50574 Pocahontas⊙ 2,352 ..... D3
50226 Polk City 1,658 ..... F5
50575 Pomeroy 895 ..... D3
51565 Portsmouth 240 ..... C5
52162 Postville 1,475 ..... K2
50228 Prairie City 1,278 ..... G5
50859 Prescott 349 ..... D6
52069 Preston 1,120 ..... N4
Primghar⊙ 1,050 ..... B2
52768 Princeton 965 ..... N5
52163 Protivin 368 ..... J2
52584 Pulaski 267 ..... J7
52326 Quasqueton 599 ..... K4
51049 Quimby 424 ..... B3
50230 Radcliffe 593 ..... G4
50465 Rake 283 ..... F2
50667 Raymond 655 ..... J4
50668 Readlyn 858 ..... J3
50232 Reasnor 277 ..... G5
50233 Redfield 959 ..... E5
51566 Red Oak⊙ 6,810 ..... C6
50669 Reinbeck 1,808 ..... H4
50576 Rembrandt 291 ..... C3
51050 Remsen 1,592 ..... B3
50577 Renwick 410 ..... E3
50234 Rhodes 367 ..... G5
50466 Riceville 919 ..... H2
52585 Richland 600 ..... K6
52165 Ridgeway 308 ..... K2
50578 Ringsted 557 ..... D2
50235 Rippey 304 ..... E5
†52722 Riverdale 462 ..... N5
52327 Riverside 826 ..... K6
51650 Riverton 342 ..... B7
52328 Robins 726 ..... K4
50468 Rockford 1,012 ..... H2
51246 Rock Rapids⊙ 2,693 ..... A2
51247 Rock Valley 2,706 ..... A2
50469 Rockwell 1,039 ..... G3
50579 Rockwell City⊙ 2,276 ..... D4
50236 Roland 1,005 ..... F4
50581 Rolfe 796 ..... D3
50470 Rowan 259 ..... F3
52329 Rowley 275 ..... K4
51357 Royal 522 ..... C2
50471 Rudd 460 ..... H2
50237 Runnells 377 ..... G5
50238 Russell 593 ..... G7
51358 Ruthven 769 ..... D2
52330 Ryan 390 ..... K4
52070 Sabula 824 ..... N4
50583 Sac City⊙ 3,000 ..... C4
†52001 Sageville 291 ..... M3
50472 Saint Ansgar 1,100 ..... H2
50240 Saint Charles 507 ..... F6
52649 Salem 463 ..... K7
51052 Salix 429 ..... A4
51248 Sanborn 1,398 ..... B2
51053 Schaller 832 ..... C4
51461 Schleswig 868 ..... B4
51462 Scranton 748 ..... D4
51054 Sergeant Bluff 2,416 ..... A4
52590 Seymour 1,036 ..... G7
50475 Sheffield 1,224 ..... G3
51570 Shelby 665 ..... C5
50243 Sheldahl 315 ..... F5
51201 Sheldon 5,003 ..... B2
50670 Shell Rock 1,478 ..... H3
52332 Shellsburg 771 ..... K4
51601 Shenandoah 6,274 ..... C7
†52401 Shueyville 287 ..... K5
51249 Sibley⊙ 3,051 ..... B2
51652 Sidney⊙ 1,308 ..... B7
52591 Sigourney⊙ 2,330 ..... J6
51571 Silver City 291 ..... B6
51250 Sioux Center 4,588 ..... A2
*51101 Sioux City⊙ 82,003 ..... A3
Sioux City‡ 117,457 ..... A3
50585 Sioux Rapids 897 ..... C3
50244 Slater 1,312 ..... F5
51055 Sloan 978 ..... A4
51056 Smithland 282 ..... B4
51572 Soldier 257 ..... B5
52333 Solon 969 ..... L5
51301 Spencer⊙ 11,726 ..... C2
52168 Spillville 415 ..... J2
51360 Spirit Lake⊙ 3,976 ..... C2
52336 Springville 1,165 ..... L4
50476 Stacyville 538 ..... H2
50246 Stanhope 492 ..... F4
51573 Stanton 747 ..... C7
52337 Stanwood 705 ..... L5
50247 State Center 1,292 ..... G5
50672 Steamboat Rock 387 ..... G4
52651 Stockport 272 ..... K7
52769 Stockton 240 ..... M5
50588 Storm Lake⊙ 8,814 ..... C3
50248 Story City 2,762 ..... F4
50249 Stratford 806 ..... F4
52076 Strawberry Point 1,463 ..... K3
50250 Stuart 1,650 ..... E6
50251 Sully 828 ..... H5
50674 Sumner 2,335 ..... J3
51058 Sutherland 897 ..... B3
50590 Swea City 813 ..... E2
52338 Swisher 654 ..... K5
51653 Tabor 1,088 ..... B7
52339 Tama 2,968 ..... H5
51463 Templeton 319 ..... D5
51364 Terril 420 ..... C2
50478 Thompson 668 ..... F2
50479 Thornton 442 ..... G3
52340 Tiffin 413 ..... K5
52772 Tipton⊙ 3,055 ..... L5
50480 Titonka 607 ..... E2
52342 Toledo⊙ 2,445 ..... H4
50675 Traer 1,703 ..... J4
51575 Treynor 981 ..... B6
50676 Tripoli 1,280 ..... J3
50257 Truro 407 ..... F6
51576 Underwood 448 ..... B6
50258 Union 515 ..... G4
†52240 University Heights 1,069 ..... K5
52595 University Park 645 ..... H6
52345 Urbana 574 ..... K4
50322 Urbandale 17,869 ..... F5
51060 Ute 479 ..... B4
51465 Vail 490 ..... C4
52346 Van Horne 682 ..... J4
50261 Van Meter 747 ..... E5
50262 Van Wert 245 ..... F7
50482 Ventura 614 ..... F2
52347 Victor 1,046 ..... J5
50864 Villisca 1,434 ..... C7
52349 Vinton⊙ 5,040 ..... J4
52077 Volga 310 ..... L3
52169 Wadena 230 ..... K3
†51360 Wahpeton 372 ..... C2
52773 Walcott 1,425 ..... M5
52351 Walford 285 ..... K5
52352 Walker 733 ..... K4
51365 Wallingford 256 ..... D2
51466 Wall Lake 892 ..... C4
51577 Walnut 897 ..... C6
52653 Wapello⊙ 2,011 ..... L6
52353 Washington⊙ 6,584 ..... K6
51061 Washta 320 ..... B3
*50701 Waterloo⊙ 75,985 ..... J4
Waterloo-Cedar Falls‡ 137,961 ..... J4
52171 Waucoma 308 ..... J2
50263 Waukee 2,227 ..... F5
52172 Waukon⊙ 3,983 ..... L2
50677 Waverly⊙ 8,444 ..... J3
52654 Wayland 720 ..... K6
52356 Wellman 1,125 ..... K6
50680 Wellsburg 761 ..... H4
50483 Wesley 598 ..... E2
50597 West Bend 941 ..... D3
52358 West Branch 1,867 ..... L5
52655 West Burlington 3,371 ..... L7
50318 West Des Moines 21,894 ..... F5
50681 Westgate 263 ..... K3
52776 West Liberty 2,723 ..... L5
†51351 West Okoboji 435 ..... C2
52656 West Point 1,133 ..... K7
51467 Westside 387 ..... C4
52175 West Union⊙ 2,783 ..... K3
50268 What Cheer 803 ..... J6
52777 Wheatland 840 ..... M5
51063 Whiting 734 ..... A4
50598 Whittemore 647 ..... E2
50271 Williams 410 ..... F3
52361 Williamsburg 2,033 ..... J5
52778 Wilton 2,502 ..... M5
50311 Windsor Heights 5,474 ..... F5
52659 Winfield 1,042 ..... L6
50273 Winterset⊙ 4,021 ..... E6
50682 Winthrop 767 ..... K4
50484 Woden 287 ..... F2
51579 Woodbine 1,463 ..... B5
50276 Woodward 1,212 ..... E5
50599 Woolstock 235 ..... F3
52078 Worthington 432 ..... L4
52362 Wyoming 702 ..... L4
50277 Yale 299 ..... E5
50278 Zearing 630 ..... G4

OTHER FEATURES

Big Sioux (riv.) A3
Boyer (riv.) B5
Cedar (riv.) K4
Chariton (riv.) G7
Clear (lake) G2
Eagle (lake) F2
East Nishnabotna (riv.) C6
Effigy Mounds Nat'l Mon. L2
Five Island (lake) D2
Floyd (riv.) A3
Herbert Hoover Nat'l Hist. Site L5
Iowa (riv.) H4
Little Sioux (riv.) B3
Lost Island (lake) D2
Mississippi (riv.) L7
Missouri (riv.) A4
Nodaway (riv.) D7
Palo Alto (lake) D2
Platte (riv.) D8
Raccoon (riv.) D4
Rathbun (lake) G7
Red Rock (lake) G6
Rock (riv.) A2
Sac and Fox Ind. Res. H5
Saylorville (lake) F5
Skunk (riv.) K6
Spirit (lake) C2
Storm (lake) C3
Thompson (riv.) E7
Trumbull (lake) C2
Turkey (riv.) K2
Upper Iowa (riv.) K2
Wapsipinicon (riv.) J3
West Nishnabotna (riv.) C6

⊙County seat.
‡Population of metropolitan area.
† Zip of nearest p.o. * Multiple zips.

AREA 82,277 sq. mi. (213,097 sq. km.)
POPULATION 2,364,236
CAPITAL Topeka
LARGEST CITY Wichita
HIGHEST POINT Mt. Sunflower 4,039 ft. (1231 m.)
SETTLED IN 1831
ADMITTED TO UNION January 29, 1861
POPULAR NAME Sunflower State
STATE FLOWER Sunflower
STATE BIRD Western Meadowlark

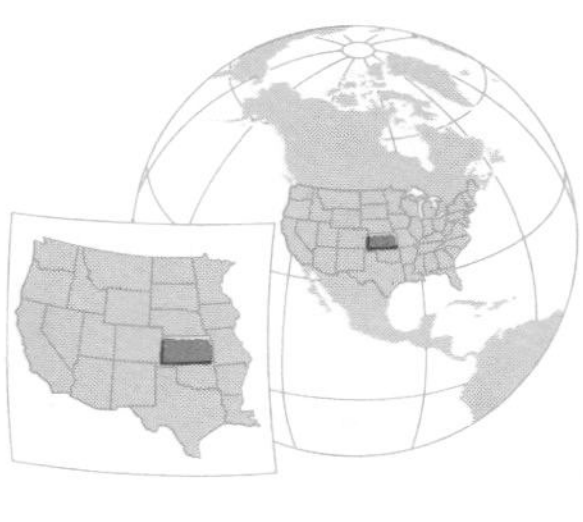

Agriculture, Industry and Resources

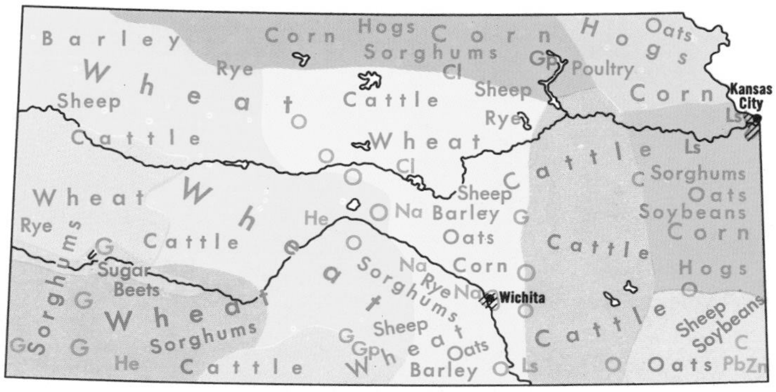

DOMINANT LAND USE

- Specialized Wheat
- Wheat, General Farming
- Wheat, Range Livestock
- Wheat, Grain Sorghums, Range Livestock
- Cattle Feed, Hogs
- Livestock, Cash Grain
- Livestock, Cash Grain, Dairy
- General Farming, Livestock, Cash Grain
- General Farming, Livestock, Special Crops
- Range Livestock

MAJOR MINERAL OCCURRENCES

C	Coal	Ls	Limestone
Cl	Clay	Na	Salt
G	Natural Gas	O	Petroleum
Gp	Gypsum	Pb	Lead
He	Helium	Zn	Zinc

Major Industrial Areas

COUNTIES

Allen 15,654 ... G4
Anderson 8,749 ... G3
Atchison 18,397 ... G2
Barber 6,548 ... D4
Barton 31,343 ... D3
Bourbon 15,969 ... H4
Brown 11,955 ... G2
Butler 44,782 ... F4
Chase 3,309 ... F3
Chautauqua 5,016 ... F4
Cherokee 22,304 ... H4
Cheyenne 3,678 ... A2
Clark 2,599 ... C4
Clay 9,802 ... E2
Cloud 12,494 ... E2
Coffey 9,370 ... G3
Comanche 2,554 ... C4
Cowley 36,824 ... F4
Crawford 37,916 ... H4
Decatur 4,509 ... B2
Dickinson 20,175 ... E3
Doniphan 9,268 ... G2
Douglas 67,640 ... G3
Edwards 4,271 ... C4
Elk 3,918 ... F4
Ellis 26,098 ... C3
Ellsworth 6,640 ... D3
Finney 23,825 ... B3
Ford 24,315 ... C4
Franklin 22,062 ... G3
Geary 29,852 ... F3
Gove 3,726 ... B3
Graham 3,995 ... C2
Grant 6,977 ... A4
Gray 5,138 ... B4
Greeley 1,845 ... A3
Greenwood 8,764 ... F4
Hamilton 2,514 ... A3
Harper 7,778 ... D4
Harvey 30,531 ... E3
Haskell 3,814 ... B4
Hodgeman 2,269 ... C3
Jackson 11,644 ... G2
Jefferson 15,207 ... G2
Jewell 5,241 ... D2
Johnson 270,269 ... H3
Kearny 3,435 ... A3
Kingman 8,960 ... D4
Kiowa 4,046 ... C4
Labette 25,682 ... G4
Lane 2,472 ... B3
Leavenworth 54,809 ... G2
Lincoln 4,145 ... D2
Linn 8,234 ... H3
Logan 3,478 ... A3
Lyon 35,108 ... F3
Marion 13,522 ... E3
Marshall 12,787 ... F2
McPherson 26,855 ... E3
Meade 4,788 ... B4
Miami 21,618 ... H3
Mitchell 8,117 ... D2
Montgomery 42,281 ... G4
Morris 6,419 ... F3
Morton 3,454 ... A4
Nemaha 11,211 ... F2
Neosho 18,967 ... G4
Ness 4,498 ... C3
Norton 6,689 ... C2
Osage 15,319 ... G3
Osborne 5,959 ... D2
Ottawa 5,971 ... E2
Pawnee 8,065 ... C3
Phillips 7,406 ... C2
Pottawatomie 14,782 ... F2
Pratt 10,275 ... D4
Rawlins 4,105 ... A2
Reno 64,983 ... D4
Republic 7,569 ... E2
Rice 11,900 ... D3
Riley 63,505 ... F2
Rooks 7,006 ... C2
Rush 4,516 ... C3
Russell 8,868 ... D3
Saline 48,905 ... E3
Scott 5,782 ... B3
Sedgwick 367,088 ... E4
Seward 17,071 ... B4
Shawnee 154,916 ... G2
Sheridan 3,544 ... B2
Sherman 7,759 ... A2
Smith 5,947 ... D2
Stafford 5,694 ... D3
Stanton 2,339 ... A4
Stevens 4,736 ... A4
Sumner 24,928 ... E4
Thomas 8,451 ... A2
Trego 4,165 ... C3
Wabaunsee 6,867 ... F3
Wallace 2,045 ... A3
Washington 8,543 ... E2
Wichita 3,041 ... A3
Wilson 12,128 ... G4
Woodson 4,600 ... G4
Wyandotte 172,335 ... H2

CITIES and TOWNS

Zip *Name/Pop.* *Key*

67510 Abbyville 123 ... D4
67410 Abilene⊙ 6,572 ... E3
66830 Admire 158 ... F3
66930 Agenda 106 ... E2
67621 Agra 321 ... C2
67511 Albert 236 ... C3
67512 Alden 214 ... D3
67513 Alexander 116 ... C3
66833 Allen 205 ... F3
66401 Alma⊙ 925 ... F2
67622 Almena 517 ... C2
67330 Altamont 1,054 ... G4
66834 Alta Vista 430 ... F3
67623 Alton 135 ... D2
66710 Altoona 564 ... G4
66835 Americus 915 ... F3
67001 Andale 538 ... E4
67002 Andover 2,801 ... E4
67003 Anthony⊙ 2,661 ... D4
66711 Arcadia 460 ... H4
67004 Argonia 587 ... E4
67005 Arkansas City 13,201 ... E4
67514 Arlington 631 ... D4
66712 Arma 1,676 ... H4
67831 Ashland⊙ 1,096 ... C4
67416 Assaria 414 ... E3
66002 Atchison⊙ 11,407 ... G2
66932 Athol 90 ... D2
67008 Atlanta 256 ... F4
67009 Attica 730 ... D4
67730 Atwood⊙ 1,665 ... B2
66402 Auburn 890 ... G3
67010 Augusta 6,968 ... F4
67417 Aurora 130 ... E2
66403 Axtell 470 ... F2
66404 Baileyville 130 ... F2
66006 Baldwin City 2,829 ... G3
67418 Barnard 163 ... D2
66933 Barnes 257 ... F2
67332 Bartlett 163 ... G4
66007 Basehor 1,483 ... G2
†66749 Bassett 31 ... G4
66713 Baxter Springs 4,730 ... H4
67516 Bazine 385 ... C3
66406 Beattie 316 ... F2
67013 Belle Plaine 1,706 ... E4
66935 Belleville⊙ 2,805 ... E2
67420 Beloit⊙ 4,367 ... D2
67519 Belpre 154 ... C4
66407 Belvue 212 ... F2
66714 Benedict 111 ... G4
67422 Bennington 579 ... E2
67016 Bentley 311 ... E4
67017 Benton 609 ... E4
66408 Bern 220 ... F2
67423 Beverly 171 ... E2
67731 Bird City 546 ... A2
67520 Bison 279 ... C3
66010 Blue Mound 319 ... H3
66411 Blue Rapids 1,280 ... F2
67018 Bluff City 95 ... E4
67625 Bogue 197 ... C2
66012 Bonnėr Springs 6,266 ... H2
67732 Brewster 327 ... A2
66716 Bronson 414 ... H4
67425 Brookville 259 ... E3
67521 Brownell 92 ... C3
67834 Bucklin 786 ... C4
66717 Buffalo 386 ... G4
67522 Buhler 1,188 ... E3
67626 Bunker Hill 124 ... D3
67019 Burden 518 ... F4
67523 Burdett 275 ... C3
66413 Burlingame 1,239 ... G3
66839 Burlington⊙ 2,901 ... G3
66840 Burns 224 ... F3
66936 Burr Oak 366 ... D2
67020 Burrton 976 ... E3
66841 Bushong 62 ... F3
67427 Bushton 388 ... D3
67021 Byers 47 ... D4
67022 Caldwell 1,401 ... E4
67023 Cambridge 113 ... F4
67333 Caney 2,284 ... G4
67428 Canton 926 ... E3
66414 Carbondale 1,518 ... G3
67429 Carlton 49 ... E3
66842 Cassoday 122 ... F3
67430 Cawker City 640 ... D2
67628 Cedar 53 ... D2
66843 Cedar Point 66 ... F3
67024 Cedar Vale 848 ... F4
66415 Centralia 486 ... F2
66720 Chanute 10,506 ... G4
67431 Chapman 1,255 ... E3
67524 Chase 753 ... D3
67334 Chautauqua 156 ... F4
67025 Cheney 1,404 ... E4
66724 Cherokee 775 ... H4
67335 Cherryvale 2,769 ... G4
67336 Chetopa 1,751 ... G4
67835 Cimarron⊙ 1,491 ... B4
66416 Circleville 164 ... G2
67525 Claflin 764 ... D3
67432 Clay Center⊙ 4,948 ... E2
67629 Clayton 102 ... B2
67026 Clearwater 1,684 ... E4
66937 Clifton 695 ... E2
67027 Climax 81 ... F4
66938 Clyde 909 ... E2
67028 Coats 153 ... D4
67337 Coffeyville 15,185 ... G4
67701 Colby⊙ 5,544 ... A2
67029 Coldwater⊙ 989 ... C4
67631 Collyer 151 ... B2
66015 Colony 474 ... G3
66725 Columbus⊙ 3,426 ... H4
67030 Colwich 935 ... E4
66901 Concordia⊙ 6,847 ... E2
67031 Conway Springs 1,313 ... E4
67836 Coolidge 82 ... A3
67837 Copeland 323 ... B4
66417 Corning 158 ... F2
66845 Cottonwood Falls⊙ 954 ... F3
66846 Council Grove⊙ 2,381 ... F3
66939 Courtland 377 ... E2
66727 Coyville 98 ... G4
66940 Cuba 286 ... E2
†67124 Cullison 154 ... D4
67435 Culver 167 ... E3
67035 Cunningham 540 ... D4
67632 Damar 204 ... C2
67036 Danville 71 ... E4
67340 Dearing 475 ... G4
67838 Deerfield 538 ... A4
66418 Delia 181 ... G2
67436 Delphos 570 ... E2
66419 Denison 231 ... G2
66017 Denton 156 ... G2
67037 Derby 9,786 ... E4
66018 De Soto 2,061 ... H3
67038 Dexter 366 ... F4
67839 Dighton⊙ 1,390 ... B3
67801 Dodge City⊙ 18,001 ... B4
67634 Dorrance 220 ... D3
67039 Douglass 1,450 ... F4
67437 Downs 1,324 ... D2
67635 Dresden 84 ... B2
66848 Dunlap 82 ... F3
67438 Durham 130 ... E3
66849 Dwight 320 ... F3
†66720 Earlton 79 ... G4
†67201 Eastborough 854 ... E4
66020 Easton 460 ... G2
66021 Edgerton 1,214 ... H3
67636 Edmond 56 ... C2
67342 Edna 537 ... G4
66113 Edwardsville 3,364 ... H2
66023 Effingham 634 ... G2
67041 Elbing 175 ... E3
67042 El Dorado⊙ 10,510 ... F4
†67361 Elgin 139 ... F4
67344 Elk City 404 ... G4
67345 Elk Falls 151 ... F4
67950 Elkhart⊙ 2,243 ... A4
67526 Ellinwood 2,508 ... D3
67637 Ellis 2,062 ... C3
67439 Ellsworth⊙ 2,465 ... D3
66850 Elmdale 109 ... F3
66732 Elsmore 104 ... G4
66024 Elwood 1,275 ... H2
66422 Emmett 223 ... F2
66801 Emporia⊙ 25,287 ... F3
67840 Englewood 111 ... C4
67841 Ensign 209 ... B4
67441 Enterprise 839 ... E3
66733 Erie⊙ 1,415 ... G4
66941 Esbon 234 ... D2
66423 Eskridge 603 ... F3
66025 Eudora 2,934 ... G3
67045 Eureka⊙ 3,425 ... F4
66424 Everest 331 ... G2
66425 Fairview 258 ... G2
†66101 Fairway 4,619 ... H2
67047 Fall River 173 ... G4
66851 Florence 729 ... E3
66026 Fontana 173 ... H3
67842 Ford 272 ... C4
66942 Formoso 166 ... D2
67843 Fort Dodge 400 ... C4
66027 Fort Leavenworth ... H2
66701 Fort Scott⊙ 8,893 ... H4
67844 Fowler 592 ... B4
66427 Frankfort 1,038 ... F2
66735 Franklin 400 ... H4
66736 Fredonia⊙ 3,047 ... G4
67049 Freeport 12 ... E4
66762 Frontenac 2,586 ... H4
66738 Fulton 194 ... H4
66739 Galena 3,587 ... H4
66740 Galesburg 181 ... G4
67443 Galva 651 ... E3
67846 Garden City⊙ 18,256 ... B4
67050 Garden Plain 775 ... E4
66030 Gardner 2,392 ... H3
67529 Garfield 277 ... C3
66032 Garnett⊙ 3,310 ... G3
66742 Gas 543 ... G4
67638 Gaylord 203 ... D2
67734 Gem 101 ... B2
67444 Geneseo 496 ... D3
67051 Geuda Springs 217 ... E4
66743 Girard⊙ 2,888 ... H4
67639 Glade 131 ... C2
67445 Glasco 710 ... E2
67446 Glen Elder 491 ... D2
67052 Goddard 1,427 ... E4
67053 Goessel 421 ... E3
66428 Goff 196 ... G2
67735 Goodland⊙ 5,708 ... A2
67640 Gorham 355 ... D3
67736 Gove⊙ 148 ... B3
67737 Grainfield 417 ... B2
†66441 Grandview Plaza 1,189 ... F2
66429 Grantville 220 ... G2
67530 Great Bend⊙ 16,608 ... D3
66033 Greeley 405 ... G3
67447 Green 155 ... E2
66943 Greenleaf 462 ... E2
67054 Greensburg⊙ 1,885 ... C4
67346 Grenola 335 ... F4
66852 Gridley 404 ... G3
67738 Grinnell 410 ... B2
67448 Gypsum 423 ... E3
66944 Haddam 239 ... E2
67056 Halstead 1,994 ... E4
66853 Hamilton 363 ... F4
66945 Hanover 802 ... F2
67849 Hanston 257 ... C3
67057 Hardtner 336 ... D4
67058 Harper 1,823 ... D4
66854 Hartford 551 ... F3
66431 Harveyville 280 ... F3
67347 Havana 169 ... G4
67543 Haven 1,125 ... E4
66432 Havensville 183 ... F2
67059 Haviland 770 ... C4

(continued on following page)

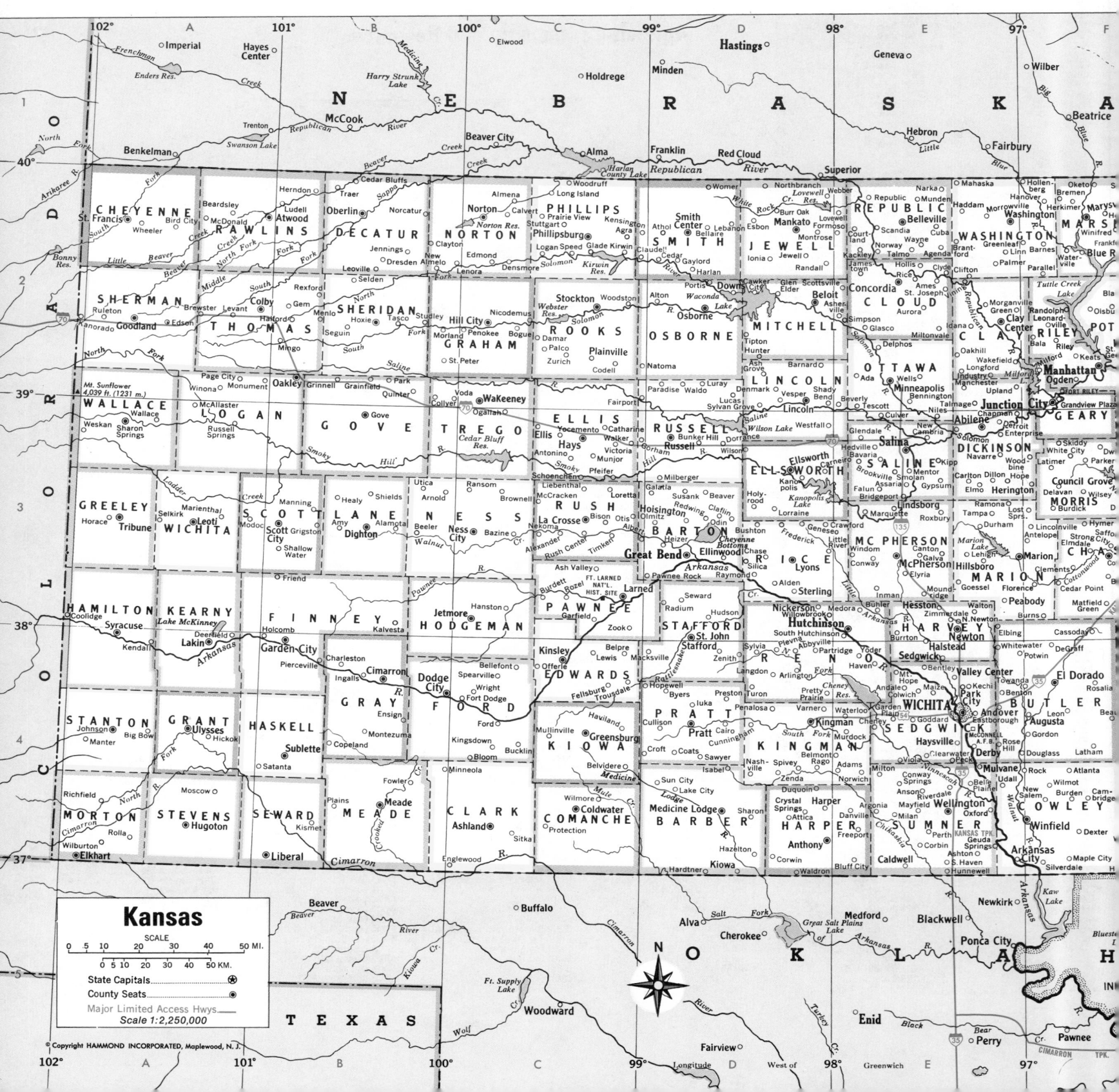

Kansas

SCALE
0 5 10   20   30   40   50 MI.
0 5 10 20 30 40 50 KM.

State Capitals .... ⊛
County Seats .... ⊙
Major Limited Access Hwys. ____
Scale 1:2,250,000

© Copyright HAMMOND INCORPORATED, Maplewood, N.J.

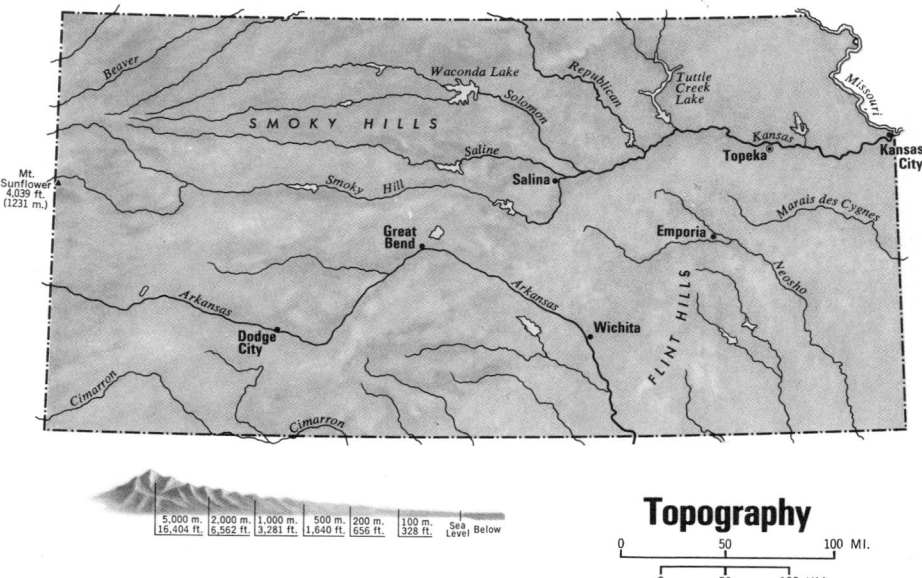

Topography

KENTUCKY

COUNTIES

Adair 15,233 ....L6
Allen 14,128 ....J7
Anderson 12,567 ....M5
Ballard 8,798 ....C6
Barren 34,009 ....K7
Bath 10,025 ....O4
Bell 34,330 ....O7
Boone 45,842 ....M3
Bourbon 19,405 ....N4
Boyd 55,513 ....R4
Boyle 25,066 ....M5
Bracken 7,738 ....N3
Breathitt 17,004 ....P5
Breckinridge 16,861 ....H5
Bullitt 43,346 ....K5
Butler 11,064 ....H6
Caldwell 13,473 ....F6
Calloway 30,031 ....E7
Campbell 83,317 ....N3
Carlisle 5,487 ....C7
Carroll 9,270 ....L3
Carter 25,060 ....P4
Casey 14,818 ....M6
Christian 66,878 ....F7
Clark 28,322 ....N4
Clay 22,752 ....O6
Clinton 9,321 ....L7
Crittenden 9,207 ....E6
Cumberland 7,289 ....L7
Daviess 85,949 ....G5
Edmonson 9,962 ....J6
Elliott 6,908 ....P4
Estill 14,495 ....O5
Fayette 204,165 ....N4
Fleming 12,323 ....O4
Floyd 48,764 ....R5
Franklin 41,830 ....M4
Fulton 8,971 ....C7
Gallatin 4,842 ....M3
Garrard 10,853 ....N5
Grant 13,308 ....M3
Graves 34,049 ....D7
Grayson 20,854 ....J5
Green 11,043 ....K6
Greenup 39,132 ....R3
Hancock 7,742 ....H5
Hardin 88,917 ....K5
Harlan 41,889 ....P7
Harrison 15,166 ....N4
Hart 15,402 ....K6
Henderson 40,849 ....F5
Henry 12,740 ....L4
Hickman 6,065 ....C7
Hopkins 46,174 ....F6
Jackson 11,996 ....O6
Jefferson 684,565 ....K4
Jessamine 26,065 ....M5
Johnson 24,432 ....R5
Kenton 137,058 ....M3
Knott 17,940 ....Q6
Knox 30,239 ....O7
Larue 11,922 ....K5
Laurel 38,982 ....N6
Lawrence 14,121 ....R4
Lee 7,754 ....O5
Leslie 14,882 ....P6
Letcher 30,687 ....R6
Lewis 14,545 ....P3
Lincoln 19,053 ....M6
Livingston 9,219 ....E6
Logan 24,138 ....H7

Lyon 6,490 ....E6
Madison 53,352 ....N5
Magoffin 13,515 ....P5
Marion 17,910 ....L5
Marshall 25,637 ....E7
Martin 13,925 ....R5
Mason 17,765 ....O3
McCracken 61,310 ....D6
McCreary 15,634 ....N7
McLean 10,090 ....G5
Meade 22,854 ....J5
Menifee 5,117 ....O5
Mercer 19,011 ....M5
Metcalfe 9,484 ....K7
Monroe 12,353 ....K7
Montgomery 20,046 ....O4
Morgan 12,103 ....P5
Muhlenberg 32,238 ....G6
Nelson 27,584 ....K5
Nicholas 7,157 ....N4
Ohio 21,765 ....H6
Oldham 27,795 ....L4
Owen 8,924 ....M3
Owsley 5,709 ....O6
Pendleton 10,989 ....N3
Perry 33,763 ....P6
Pike 81,123 ....S6
Powell 11,101 ....O5
Pulaski 45,803 ....M6
Robertson 2,265 ....N3
Rockcastle 13,973 ....N6
Rowan 19,049 ....P4
Russell 13,708 ....L7
Scott 21,813 ....M4
Shelby 23,328 ....L4
Simpson 14,673 ....H7
Spencer 5,929 ....L4
Taylor 21,178 ....L6
Todd 11,874 ....G7
Trigg 9,384 ....F7
Trimble 6,253 ....L3
Union 17,821 ....F5
Warren 71,828 ....H6
Washington 10,764 ....L5
Wayne 17,022 ....M7
Webster 14,832 ....F5
Whitley 33,396 ....N7
Wolfe 6,698 ....O5
Woodford 17,778 ....M4

CITIES and TOWNS

Zip Name/Pop. Key

42202 Adairville 1,105 ....H7
42602 Albany 2,083 ....L7
41001 Alexandria 4,735 ....N3
41601 Allen 338 ....R5
42204 Allensville 170 ....G7
40023 Anchorage 1,726 ....L2
41101 Ashland 27,064 ....R4
  Ashland-Huntington‡
    311,350 ....R4
42206 Auburn 1,467 ....H7
†40201 Audubon Park 1,571 ....J2
41002 Augusta 1,455 ....N3
41602 Auxier 900 ....R5
†40222 Bancroft 725 ....K1
41603 Banner 950 ....R5
†40201 Barbourmeade 1,038 ....K1
40906 Barbourville 3,333 ....O7
40004 Bardstown 6,155 ....L5
42023 Bardwell 988 ....D7
42024 Barlow 746 ....D6
41311 Beattyville 1,068 ....O5
42320 Beaver Dam 3,185 ....H6

40006 Bedford 835 ....L3
40359 Beechwood Village 1,462 ....K2
†40201 Bellemeade 918 ....L2
41073 Bellevue 7,678 ....S1
40807 Benham 936 ....R7
42025 Benton 3,700 ....E7
40403 Berea 8,226 ....N5
41003 Berry 287 ....N3
41124 Blaine 358 ....R4
40008 Bloomfield 954 ....L5
†40201 Blue Ridge Manor 465 ....L2
42713 Bonnieville 372 ....K6
40403 Boone 300 ....N5
41314 Booneville 191 ....O6
42101 Bowling Green 40,450 ....H7
40009 Bradfordsville 331 ....L6
40108 Brandenburg 1,831 ....J4
†42025 Briensburg E7
40409 Brodhead 686 ....N6
†41016 Bromley 844 ....S2
40109 Brooks 1,344 ....K4
41004 Brooksville 680 ....N3
†40201 Brownsboro Farm 790 ....L1
42210 Brownsville 674 ....J6
40218 Buechel 6,709 ....K2
40310 Burgin 1,008 ....M5
42717 Burkesville 2,051 ....L7
41005 Burlington 500 ....R2
42519 Burnside 775 ....M6
41006 Butler 663 ....N3
42211 Cadiz 1,661 ....F7
42327 Calhoun 1,080 ....G5
42029 Calvert City 2,388 ....E7
40011 Campbellsburg 714 ....L3
42718 Campbellsville 8,715 ....L6
41301 Campton 486 ....O5
42721 Caneyville 642 ....J6
40311 Carlisle 1,757 ....N4
41008 Carrollton 3,967 ....L3
42030 Carrsville 99 ....E6
†42459 Caseyville 43 ....E5
41129 Catlettsburg 3,005 ....R4
42127 Cave City 2,098 ....K6
†41522 Cedarville 81 ....S6
42328 Centertown 462 ....H6
42330 Central City 5,214 ....G6
42726 Clarkson 666 ....J6
42404 Clay 1,356 ....F6
40312 Clay City 1,279 ....O5
40313 Clearfield 1,250 ....P4
42031 Clinton 1,720 ....D7
40111 Cloverport 1,585 ....H5
†41501 Coal Run 348 ....R5
41076 Cold Spring 2,117 ....T2
42728 Columbia 3,710 ....L6
42032 Columbus 296 ....C7
41729 Combs 900 ....P6
41131 Concord 67 ....P3
40701 Corbin 8,075 ....N7
41010 Corinth 258 ....M3
42406 Corydon 874 ....F5
†41011 Covington 49,563 ....S2
40419 Crab Orchard 843 ....M6
†41016 Crescent Springs 1,951 ....S2
41076 Crestview 528 ....S2
†41017 Crestview Hills 1,408 ....R2
40014 Crestwood 531 ....L4
41030 Crittenden 597 ....M3
42217 Crofton 823 ....G6
40823 Cumberland 3,712 ....R6
41031 Cynthiana 5,881 ....N4

40422 Danville 12,942 ....M5
42408 Dawson Springs 3,275 ....F6
41074 Dayton 6,979 ....T1
†40201 Devondale 1,164 ....K2
42036 Dexter E7
42409 Dixon 533 ....F5
41034 Dover 305 ....O3
41035 Dry Ridge 1,250 ....M3
42037 Dycusburg 64 ....E6
42038 Eddyville 1,949 ....E6
†41017 Edgewood 7,230 ....S2
42129 Edmonton 1,401 ....K7
41018 Elizabethtown 15,380 ....K5
42220 Elkton 1,815 ....G7
†41018 Elsmere 7,203 ....R2
40826 Eolia 875 ....R6
41018 Erlanger 14,433 ....R2
40827 Essie 650 ....P6
42567 Eubank 207 ....M6
40828 Evarts 1,234 ....P7
41039 Ewing 144 ....O4
40118 Fairdale 7,315 ....K4
42020 Fairfield 169 ....L5
41101 Fairview 198 ....S2
41040 Falmouth 2,482 ....N3
41524 Fedscreek 950 ....S6
42533 Ferguson 1,009 ....M6
†40222 Fincastle 804 ....L1
42139 Flatwoods 8,354 ....R4
41816 Fleming-Neon 1,195 ....R6
41041 Flemingsburg 2,835 ....O4
41042 Florence 15,586 ....R2
42343 Fordsville 561 ....H5
40121 Fort Knox 31,055 ....K5
41017 Fort Mitchell 7,297 ....S2
41075 Fort Thomas 16,012 ....S2
†41011 Fort Wright 4,481 ....S2
41043 Foster 80 ....N3
42133 Fountain Run 340 ....K7
40601 Frankfort (cap.) 25,973 ....M4
42134 Franklin 7,738 ....J7
42411 Fredonia 535 ....E6
40322 Frenchburg 550 ....O5
†41175 Fullerton 950 ....P3
42041 Fulton 3,137 ....D7
42140 Gamaliel 456 ....K7
40324 Georgetown 10,972 ....M4
41044 Germantown 347 ....O3
41045 Ghent 439 ....L3
42044 Gilbertsville E7
42141 Glasgow 12,958 ....J7
40046 Glencoe 354 ....M3
†40222 Glenview 212 ....K1
†40222 Goose Creek 394 ....L1
42045 Grand Rivers 428 ....E7
†41005 Grant 150 ....M3
40327 Gratz 124 ....M4
†40201 Graymoor 1,167 ....K1
41143 Grayson 3,423 ....R4
42743 Greensburg 2,377 ....K6
41144 Greenup 1,386 ....R3
42345 Greenville 4,631 ....G6
42234 Guthrie 1,361 ....G7
42413 Hanson 485 ....G6
42048 Hardin 545 ....E7
40143 Hardinsburg 2,211 ....H5
41531 Hardy 900 ....S5
40831 Harlan 3,024 ....P7

40330 Harrodsburg 7,265 ....M5
42347 Hartford 2,512 ....H6
42348 Hawesville 1,036 ....H5
41701 Hazard 5,371 ....P6
42049 Hazel 465 ....E7
40949 Heidrick 400 ....O7
42420 Henderson 24,834 ....F5
42050 Hickman 2,894 ....C7
42051 Hickory D7
41076 Highland Heights 4,435 ....T2
41822 Hindman 876 ....R6
42152 Hiseville 349 ....K7
42748 Hodgenville 2,531 ....K5
†40228 Hollow Creek 1,023 ....K4
42240 Hopkinsville 27,318 ....F7
42749 Horse Cave 2,045 ....K6
40437 Houston Acres 608 ....K2
40437 Hustonville 339 ....M6
†41018 Hyden 488 ....P6
40051 Independence 7,998 ....M3
†40201 Indian Hills 787 ....K1
41224 Inez 413 ....S5
40336 Irvine 2,889 ....O5
40146 Irvington 1,409 ....J5
42350 Island 532 ....G6
41642 Ivel 850 ....R5
41339 Jackson 2,651 ....P5
42629 Jamestown 1,441 ....L7
40299 Jeffersontown 15,795 ....L2
40337 Jeffersonville 1,528 ....O5
41537 Jenkins 3,271 ....R6
40440 Junction City 2,045 ....M5
40737 Keavy 900 ....N6
†41011 Kenton Vale 145 ....S2
42053 Kevil 382 ....D6
†40201 Kingsley 464 ....K2
42055 Kuttawa 560 ....E6
42056 La Center 1,044 ....C6
41643 Lackey R6
42254 La Fayette 160 ....F7
40031 La Grange 2,971 ....L4
†41017 Lakeside Park 3,038 ....R2
40444 Lancaster 3,365 ....M5
40342 Lawrenceburg 5,167 ....M4
40033 Lebanon 6,590 ....L5
40150 Lebanon Junction 1,581 ....K5
42754 Leitchfield 4,533 ....J6
42256 Lewisburg 972 ....G6
42351 Lewisport 1,832 ....H5
42539 Liberty 2,206 ....M6
42352 Livermore 1,672 ....G5
40445 Livingston 334 ....N6
40036 Lockport 84 ....M4
40741 London 4,002 ....N6
42001 Lone Oak 443 ....D6
40037 Loretto 954 ....L5
41230 Louisa 1,832 ....R4
*40201 Louisville 298,840 ....J2
  Louisville‡ 906,240 ....J2
40854 Loyall 1,210 ....P7
40016 Ludlow 4,959 ....S2
40855 Lynch 1,614 ....R7
†40201 Lynnview 1,157 ....K4
40040 Mackville 229 ....L5
42431 Madisonville 16,979 ....F6
40962 Manchester 1,838 ....O6
42064 Marion 3,392 ....E6
41649 Martin 827 ....R5
42066 Mayfield 10,705 ....D7
41056 Maysville 7,983 ....O3
41543 McAndrews 975 ....S5
42354 McHenry 582 ....H6

40447 McKee 759 ....O6
41835 McRoberts 1,106 ....R6
†40201 Meadow Vale 1,008 ....L1
41059 Melbourne 628 ....T2
†41060 Mentor 169 ....N3
40965 Middlesboro 12,251 ....O7
40243 Middletown 414 ....L2
40347 Midway 1,445 ....M4
40045 Milton 718 ....L3
40348 Millersburg 987 ....N4
†40201 Minor Lane Heights 1,882 ....K4
†40359 Monterey 186 ....M4
42633 Monticello 5,677 ....M7
†40223 Moorland 513 ....L2
40351 Morehead 7,789 ....P4
42437 Morganfield 3,781 ....E5
42261 Morgantown 2,000 ....H6
42440 Mortons Gap 1,201 ....F6
41064 Mount Olivet 346 ....N3
†40437 Mount Salem 50 ....M6
40353 Mount Sterling 5,820 ....N4
40456 Mount Vernon 2,334 ....N6
40047 Mount Washington 3,997 ....K4
41548 Mouthcard 900 ....S6
40155 Muldraugh 1,752 ....J5
42765 Munfordville 1,783 ....J6
42071 Murray 14,248 ....E7
42441 Nebo 269 ....F6
41840 Neon-Fleming 1,195 ....R6
40050 New Castle 832 ....L4
40051 New Haven 926 ....K5
*41071 Newport 21,587 ....S2
40356 Nicholasville 10,319 ....N5
†40201 Northfield 906 ....K1
40357 North Middletown 637 ....N4
42442 Nortonville 1,336 ....G6
42262 Oak Grove 2,088 ....G7
42159 Oakland 264 ....J6
41238 Oil Springs 900 ....P5
40219 Okolona 20,039 ....K4
41164 Olive Hill 2,539 ....P4
42301 Owensboro 54,450 ....G5
  Owensboro‡ 85,949 ....G5
40359 Owenton 1,341 ....M3
40360 Owingsville 1,419 ....O4
42001 Paducah 29,315 ....D6
41240 Paintsville 3,815 ....R5
40361 Paris 7,935 ....N4
42160 Park City 614 ....J6
†41011 Park Hills 3,500 ....S2
†40201 Parkway Village 754 ....J2
42266 Pembroke 636 ....G7
40468 Pewee Valley 982 ....L4
41553 Phelps 1,126 ....S6
41501 Pikeville 4,756 ....S6
42635 Pine Knot 1,389 ....M7
40977 Pineville 2,599 ....O7
†40201 Plantation 969 ....K1
40258 Pleasure Ridge
  Park 27,332 ....J4
40057 Pleasureville 837 ....L4
†42101 Plum Springs 393 ....J7
42367 Powderly 848 ....G6
41653 Prestonsburg 4,011 ....R5
†41008 Prestonville 205 ....L3
42445 Princeton 7,073 ....F6
40059 Prospect 1,981 ....K4
42450 Providence 4,434 ....F5
41169 Raceland 2,179 ....R3
40160 Radcliff 14,519 ....K5
40472 Ravenna 793 ....O5
40475 Richmond 21,705 ....N5
†40222 Riverwood 435 ....K1
42273 Rochester 289 ....H6

Agriculture, Industry and Resources

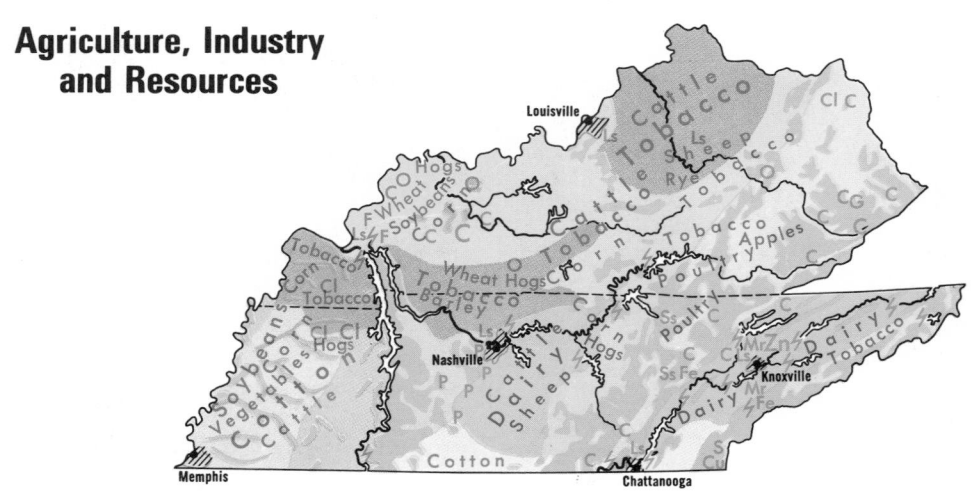

DOMINANT LAND USE

Hogs, Soft Winter Wheat
Tobacco, General Farming
General Farming, Livestock, Tobacco
General Farming, Livestock, Dairy
General Farming, Livestock, Fruit, Tobacco
Specialized Cotton
Cotton, General Farming
Cotton, Livestock
Forests
Swampland, Limited Agriculture

MAJOR MINERAL OCCURRENCES

C Coal
Cl Clay
Cu Copper
F Fluorspar
Fe Iron Ore
G Natural Gas
Ls Limestone
Mr Marble
O Petroleum
P Phosphates
S Pyrites
Ss Sandstone
Zn Zinc

⚡ Water Power   ▨ Major Industrial Areas

KENTUCKY

AREA 40,409 sq. mi. (104,659 sq. km.)
POPULATION 3,660,257
CAPITAL Frankfort
LARGEST CITY Louisville
HIGHEST POINT Black Mtn. 4,145 ft. (1263 m.)
SETTLED IN 1774
ADMITTED TO UNION June 1, 1792
POPULAR NAME Bluegrass State
STATE FLOWER Goldenrod
STATE BIRD Cardinal

TENNESSEE

AREA 42,144 sq. mi. (109,153 sq. km.)
POPULATION 4,591,120
CAPITAL Nashville
LARGEST CITY Memphis
HIGHEST POINT Clingmans Dome 6,643 ft. (2025 m.)
SETTLED IN 1757
ADMITTED TO UNION June 1, 1796
POPULAR NAME Volunteer State
STATE FLOWER Iris
STATE BIRD Mockingbird

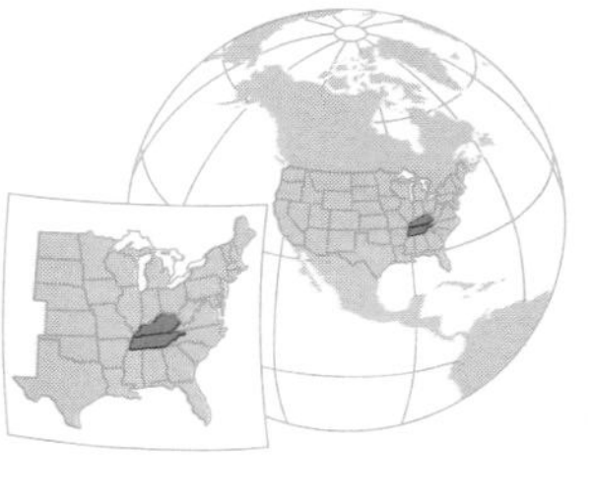

42369 Rockport 511 H6
†40201 Rolling Fields 731 K2
†40201 Rolling Hills 1,122 L1
41169 Russell 3,824 R3
42642 Russell Springs 1,831 L6
42276 Russellville⊙ 7,520 H7
†41015 Ryland Heights 252 M3
42372 Sacramento 538 G6
40370 Sadieville 253 M4
42453 Saint Charles 405 F6
40207 Saint Matthews 13,519 K2
†40201 Saint Regis Park 1,735 K2
42078 Salem 833 E6
40371 Salt Lick 347 O4
41465 Salyersville⊙ 1,352 P5
41083 Sanders 332 M3
41171 Sandy Hook⊙ 627 P4
41056 Sardis 198 O3
42553 Science Hill 655 M6
42164 Scottsville⊙ 4,278 J7
42455 Sebree 1,516 F5
†40201 Seneca Gardens 748 K2
40983 Sextons Creek 975 O6
40374 Sharpsburg 339 O4
40065 Shelbyville⊙ 5,329 L4
40165 Shepherdsville⊙ 4,454 K4
40216 Shively 16,819 K4
41085 Silver Grove 1,260 T2
40067 Simpsonville 642 L4
42456 Slaughters 269 F6
41764 Smilax 987 P6
40068 Smithfield 137 L4
42081 Smithland⊙ 512 E6
42171 Smiths Grove 767 J6
42501 Somerset⊙ 10,649 M6
42776 Sonora 416 K5
42374 South Carrollton 262 G6
41071 Southgate 2,833 T2
41174 South Portsmouth 900 P3
41175 South Shore 1,525 R3
25661 South Williamson 1,016 S5
41086 Sparta 192 M3
42458 Spottsville 914 G5
40069 Springfield⊙ 3,179 L5
†40201 Springlee 498 K2
40379 Stamping Ground 562 M4
40484 Stanford⊙ 2,764 M5
40380 Stanton⊙ 2,691 O5
42647 Stearns 1,557 N7
41567 Stone 900 S5
†40201 Strathmoor Village 466 J2
42459 Sturgis 2,293 F5
†41011 Taylor Mill 4,509 S2
40071 Taylorsville⊙ 801 L4
†40222 Thornhill 233 K1
41189 Tollesboro 808 O3
42167 Tompkinsville⊙ 4,366 K7
42286 Trenton 465 G7
41091 Union 601 M3
42461 Uniontown 1,169 F5
42784 Upton 731 K6
40272 Valley Station 24,474 K4
41179 Vanceburg⊙ 1,939 P3
41265 Van Lear 2,035 R5
†40828 Verda 1,133 P7
40383 Versailles⊙ 6,427 M4
41773 Vicco 456 P6
†41017 Villa Hills 4,402 R2
40175 Vine Grove 3,583 K5
†41063 Visalia 198 N3
40873 Wallins Creek 459 O7
41094 Walton 1,651 M3
41095 Warsaw⊙ 1,328 M3
41096 Washington 624 O3
42085 Water Valley 395 D7
42462 Waverly 434 F5
41666 Wayland 601 R6
41667 Weeksbury 850 R6
†40201 Wellington 653 K2
†40218 West Buechel 1,205 K2
41472 West Liberty⊙ 1,381 P5
40177 West Point 1,339 J4
†42501 West Somerset 850 M6
41101 Westwood 5,973 R4
†40207 Westwood 826 L1
42463 Wheatcroft 325 F5
41669 Wheelwright 865 R6
41390 Whick 280 P6
42464 White Plains 859 G6
41858 Whitesburg⊙ 1,525 R6
42378 Whitesville 788 H5
42653 Whitley City⊙ 1,683 N7
42087 Wickliffe⊙ 1,034 C7
†41071 Wilders 633 S2
40769 Williamsburg⊙ 5,560 N7
41097 Williamstown⊙ 2,502 M3
40078 Willisburg 235 L5
40390 Wilmore 3,787 M5
40391 Winchester⊙ 15,216 N5
†40201 Windy Hills 2,214 K1
42088 Wingo 606 D7
40771 Woodbine 900 N7
42170 Woodburn 330 J7
†40201 Woodland Hills 839 L2
†42001 Woodlawn-Oakdale 4,722 D6
†41071 Woodlawn 331 T2
†40201 Woodlawn Park 1,052 K2
41183 Worthington 1,948 R3
41098 Worthville 272 L3
41144 Wurtland 1,301 R3

OTHER FEATURES

Abraham Lincoln Birthplace Nat'l Hist. Site K5
Barkley (dam) E6
Barkley (lake) F7
Barren (riv.) H6
Barren River (lake) J7
Beech Fork (riv.) L5
Big Sandy (riv.) R4
Black (mt.) R7
Buckhorn (lake) O6
Chaplin (riv.) L5
Clarks, East Fork (riv.) E7
Cove Run (lake) O4
Cumberland (lake) M7
Cumberland (mt.) P7
Cumberland (riv.) K8
Cumberland Gap Nat'l Hist. Park P7
Dale Hollow (lake) L7
Dewey (lake) R5
Dix (riv.) M5
Drakes (creek) J7
Dry (creek) R3
Eagle (creek) M3
Fishtrap (lake) S6
Fort Campbell G7
Grayson (lake) P4
Green (riv.) G6
Green River (lake) L6
Herrington (lake) M5
Hinkston (creek) N4
Kentucky (dam) E7
Kentucky (lake) E8
Kentucky (riv.) M3
Land Between The Lakes Rec. Area E7
Laurel River (lake) N6
Lexington Blue Grass Army Depot N5
Licking (riv.) N3
Mammoth Cave Nat'l Park J6
Mayfield (creek) C7
Mississippi (riv.) A10
Mud (riv.) H7
Nolin (lake) K6
Nolin (riv.) J6
Obion (creek) C7
Ohio (riv.) F5
Paint Lick (riv.) M5
Panther (creek) G5
Pine (mt.) O7
Pond (riv.) G6
Red (riv.) O5
Red (riv.) G7
Rockcastle (riv.) N6
Rolling Fork (riv.) L5
Rough (riv.) H5
Rough River (lake) J5
Salt (riv.) K5
Tennessee (riv.) D6
Tradewater (riv.) F6
Tug Fork (riv.) S5

TENNESSEE

COUNTIES

Anderson 67,346 N8
Bedford 27,916 J9
Benton 14,901 E8
Bledsoe 9,478 L9
Blount 77,770 O9
Bradley 67,547 M10
Campbell 34,923 N8
Cannon 10,234 J9
Carroll 28,285 E9
Carter 50,205 S8
Cheatham 21,616 G8
Chester 12,727 D10
Claiborne 24,595 O8
Clay 7,676 K7
Cocke 28,792 P9
Coffee 38,311 J9
Crockett 14,941 C9
Cumberland 28,676 L9
Davidson 477,811 H8
Decatur 10,857 E9
De Kalb 13,589 K9
Dickson 30,037 G8
Dyer 34,663 C8
Fayette 25,305 C10
Fentress 14,826 M8
Franklin 31,983 J10
Gibson 49,467 D9
Giles 24,625 G10
Grainger 16,751 O8
Greene 54,422 R8
Grundy 13,787 K10
Hamblen 49,300 P8
Hamilton 287,740 L10
Hancock 6,887 P7
Hardeman 23,873 C10
Hardin 22,280 E10
Hawkins 43,751 P8
Haywood 20,318 C9
Henderson 21,390 E9
Henry 28,656 E8
Hickman 15,151 G9
Houston 6,871 F8
Humphreys 15,957 F8
Jackson 9,398 K8
Jefferson 31,284 P8
Johnson 13,745 T7
Knox 319,694 O9
Lake 7,455 B8
Lauderdale 24,555 B9
Lawrence 34,110 G10
Lewis 9,700 F9
Lincoln 26,483 H10
Loudon 28,553 N9
Macon 15,700 J7
Madison 74,546 D9
Marion 24,416 K10
Marshall 19,698 H10
Maury 51,095 G9
McMinn 41,878 M10
McNairy 22,525 D10
Meigs 7,431 M9
Monroe 28,700 N10
Montgomery 83,342 G8
Moore 4,510 J10
Morgan 16,604 M8
Obion 32,781 C8
Overton 17,575 L8
Perry 6,111 F9
Pickett 4,358 M7
Polk 13,602 N10
Putnam 47,690 K8
Rhea 24,235 M9
Roane 48,425 M9
Robertson 37,021 H7
Rutherford 84,058 J9
Scott 19,259 M8
Sequatchie 8,605 L10
Sevier 41,418 O9
Shelby 777,113 B10
Smith 14,935 J8
Stewart 8,665 F7
Sullivan 143,968 S7
Sumner 85,790 J8
Tipton 32,930 B9
Trousdale 6,137 J8
Unicoi 16,362 S8
Union 11,707 O8
Van Buren 4,728 L9
Warren 32,653 K9
Washington 88,755 R8
Wayne 13,946 F10
Weakley 32,896 D8
White 19,567 L9
Williamson 58,108 H9
Wilson 56,064 J8

CITIES and TOWNS

Zip Name/Pop. Key

†38301 Adair 70 D9
37010 Adams 600 G7
38310 Adamsville 1,453 E10
38001 Alamo⊙ 2,615 C9
37701 Alcoa 6,870 N9
37012 Alexandria 689 J8
38501 Algood 2,406 K8
38504 Allardt 654 M8
37301 Altamont⊙ 679 K10
38449 Ardmore 835 H10
38002 Arlington 1,778 B10
37015 Ashland City⊙ 2,329 G8
37303 Athens⊙ 12,080 M10
38004 Atoka 691 B10
38220 Atwood 1,143 D9
37016 Auburntown 204 J9
37743 Baileyton 333 R8
†37650 Banner Hill 2,913 R8
38134 Bartlett 17,170 B10
38544 Baxter 1,411 K8
37305 Beersheba Springs 643 K10
37020 Bell Buckle 450 J9
37205 Belle Meade 3,182 H8
38006 Bells 1,571 C9
37307 Benton⊙ 1,115 M10
†37201 Berry Hill 1,113 H8
†37027 Berry's Chapel 2,703 H9
38315 Bethel Springs 873 D10
38221 Big Sandy 650 E8
37709 Blaine 1,147 O8
37660 Bloomingdale 12,088 R7
37617 Blountville⊙ 2,554 S7
37618 Bluff City 1,121 S8
38008 Bolivar⊙ 6,597 C10
38010 Braden 293 B10
38316 Bradford 1,146 D8
37027 Brentwood 9,431 H8
37710 Briceville 850 N8
38011 Brighton 976 B10
37620 Bristol 23,986 S7
38012 Brownsville⊙ 9,307 C9
38317 Bruceton 1,579 E8
37711 Bulls Gap 821 P8
38015 Burlison 386 B9
37029 Burns 777 G8
38549 Byrdstown⊙ 884 L7
37309 Calhoun 590 M10
38320 Camden⊙ 3,279 E8
37030 Carthage⊙ 2,672 K8
37714 Caryville 2,039 N8
37032 Cedar Hill 420 H7
38551 Celina⊙ 1,580 K7
†37110 Centertown 300 K9
37033 Centerville⊙ 2,824 G9
37034 Chapel Hill 861 H9
37310 Charleston 756 M10
37036 Charlotte⊙ 788 G8
*37401 Chattanooga⊙ 169,558 K10
Chattanooga‡ 426,540 K10
37642 Church Hill 4,110 R7
38324 Clarksburg 400 E9
37040 Clarksville⊙ 54,777 G7
Clarksville‡ 150,220 G7
37311 Cleveland⊙ 26,415 M10
38425 Clifton 773 F10
37716 Clinton⊙ 5,245 N8
37313 Coalmont 625 K10
37315 Collegedale 4,607 M10
38017 Collierville 7,839 B10
38450 Collinwood 1,064 F10
37663 Colonial Heights 6,744 R8
38401 Columbia⊙ 26,571 G9
37720 Concord 8,569 N9
38501 Cookeville⊙ 20,535 L8
37317 Copperhill 418 N10
37047 Cornersville 722 H10
38224 Cottage Grove 117 E8
38326 Counce 975 E10
38019 Covington⊙ 6,065 B9
37318 Cowan 1,790 K10
37723 Crab Orchard 1,065 M9
37049 Cross Plains 655 H7
38555 Crossville⊙ 6,394 L9
37050 Cumberland City 276 F8
37724 Cumberland Gap 263 O8
37725 Dandridge⊙ 1,383 O8
37321 Dayton⊙ 5,913 L9
37322 Decatur⊙ 1,069 M9
38329 Decaturville⊙ 1,004 E9
37324 Decherd 2,233 J10
38391 Denmark 51 D9
37055 Dickson 7,040 G8
37058 Dover⊙ 1,197 F8
37059 Dowelltown 341 K8
38559 Doyle 344 K9
38225 Dresden⊙ 2,256 D8
37326 Ducktown 583 N10
37327 Dunlap⊙ 3,681 L10
38330 Dyer 2,419 D8
38024 Dyersburg⊙ 15,856 C8
†37801 Eagleton Village 5,331 O9
37060 Eagleville 444 H9
37412 East Ridge 21,236 L11
†38367 Eastview 552 D10
37643 Elizabethton⊙ 12,431 S8
38455 Elkton 540 H10
38029 Ellendale 850 B10
37329 Englewood 1,840 M10
38332 Enville 287 E10
37061 Erin⊙ 1,614 F8
37650 Erwin⊙ 4,739 S8
37330 Estill Springs 1,324 J10
38456 Ethridge 548 G10
37331 Etowah 3,758 M10
37062 Fairview 3,648 G9
37656 Fall Branch 1,340 R8
37334 Fayetteville⊙ 7,559 H10
38334 Finger 245 D10
38030 Finley 1,014 B8
†37201 Forest Hills 4,516 H8
37064 Franklin⊙ 12,407 H9
38034 Friendship 763 C9
37737 Friendsville 694 N9
38337 Gadsden 683 D9
38562 Gainesboro⊙ 1,119 K8
37066 Gallatin⊙ 17,191 H8
38036 Gallaway 804 B10
†38019 Garland 301 B9
38037 Gates 729 C9
37738 Gatlinburg 3,210 O9
38138 Germantown 21,482 B10
38338 Gibson 458 D9
†38015 Gilt Edge 142 B9
38229 Gleason 1,335 D8
37072 Goodlettsville 8,327 H8
38563 Gordonsville 893 K8
38039 Grand Junction 360 C10
37338 Graysville 1,380 L10
37742 Greenback 546 N9
37073 Greenbrier 3,180 H8
37743 Greeneville⊙ 14,097 R8
38230 Greenfield 2,109 D8
37339 Gruetli 910 K10
38040 Halls 2,444 C9
37658 Hampton 2,236 S8
37748 Harriman 8,303 M9
37341 Harrison 6,206 L10
37752 Harrogate-Shawanee 2,530 O8
37074 Hartsville⊙ 2,674 J8
38340 Henderson⊙ 4,449 D10
37075 Hendersonville 26,561 H8
38041 Henning 638 B9
38231 Henry 295 E8
38042 Hickory Valley 252 C10
38462 Hohenwald⊙ 3,922 F9
38342 Hollow Rock 955 E8
38232 Hornbeak 452 C8
38044 Hornsby 401 D10
38343 Humboldt 10,209 D9
38344 Huntingdon⊙ 3,962 E8
37345 Huntland 983 J10
37756 Huntsville⊙ 519 N8
37078 Hurricane Mills 850 F9
38463 Iron City 482 F10
37757 Jacksboro⊙ 1,722 N8
38301 Jackson⊙ 49,131 D9
38556 Jamestown⊙ 2,364 M8
37347 Jasper⊙ 2,633 K10
37760 Jefferson City 5,612 P8
37762 Jellico 2,798 N7
37601 Johnson City 39,753 S8
Johnson City-Kingspoint-Bristol‡ 433,638 S8
37659 Jonesboro⊙ 2,829 R8
37921 Karns 1,173 N9
38233 Kenton 1,551 C8
†37347 Kimball 1,220 K10
*37660 Kingsport 32,027 R7
37763 Kingston⊙ 4,441 N9
37082 Kingston Springs 1,017 G8
*37901 Knoxville⊙ 175,045 O9
Knoxville‡ 476,517 O9
37083 Lafayette⊙ 3,808 J7
37766 La Follette 8,198 N8
38046 La Grange 185 C10
37769 Lake City 2,335 N8
†38134 Lakeland 612 B10
†37379 Lakesite 651 L10
†37138 Lakewood 2,325 H8
37086 La Vergne 5,495 H9
38464 Lawrenceburg⊙ 10,184 G10
37087 Lebanon⊙ 11,872 J8
37771 Lenoir City 5,446 N9
37091 Lewisburg⊙ 8,760 H10
38351 Lexington⊙ 5,934 E9
37095 Liberty 365 K8
37096 Linden⊙ 1,087 F9
38570 Livingston⊙ 3,372 L8
37097 Lobelville 993 F9
37350 Lookout Mountain 1,886 L11
38469 Loretto 1,612 G10
37774 Loudon⊙ 3,943 N9
37779 Luttrell 962 O8
37352 Lynchburg⊙ 668 J10
38472 Lynnville 383 G10
37354 Madisonville⊙ 2,884 N9
37355 Manchester⊙ 7,250 J10
38237 Martin 8,898 D8
37801 Maryville⊙ 17,480 O9
37806 Mascot 2,203 O8
38049 Mason 471 B10
38050 Maury City 989 C9
37807 Maynardville⊙ 924 O8
37101 McEwen 1,352 F8
38201 McKenzie 5,405 E8
38235 McLemoresville 311 D9
37110 McMinnville⊙ 10,683 K9
38355 Medina 687 D9
38356 Medon 169 D10
*38101 Memphis⊙ 646,174 B10
Memphis‡ 912,887 B10
38357 Michie 530 E10
38052 Middleton 596 D10
38358 Milan 8,083 D9
38359 Milledgeville 392 E10
38053 Millington 20,236 B10
38473 Minor Hill 564 G10
37119 Mitchellville 209 J7
37356 Monteagle 1,126 K10
38574 Monterey 2,610 L8
37357 Morrison 587 K9
†37660 Morrison City 2,032 R7
37814 Morristown⊙ 19,683 P8
38057 Moscow 499 C10
37818 Mosheim 1,539 R8
37683 Mountain City⊙ 2,125 T8
37642 Mount Carmel 3,764 R8
37122 Mount Juliet 2,879 H8
38474 Mount Pleasant 3,375 G9
38058 Munford 2,336 B10
37130 Murfreesboro⊙ 32,845 J9
*37201 Nashville (cap.)⊙ 455,651 H8
Nashville-Davidson‡ 850,505 H8
38059 Newbern 2,794 C8
†37380 New Hope 681 K11
37134 New Johnsonville 1,824 E8
37820 New Market 1,216 O8
37821 Newport⊙ 7,580 P9
37825 New Tazewell 1,677 O8
37826 Niota 765 M9
37360 Normandy 118 J10
37828 Norris 1,374 N8
37829 Oakdale 323 M9
†37201 Oak Hill 4,609 H8
38060 Oakland 472 B10
37830 Oak Ridge 27,662 N8
38240 Obion 1,282 C8
37840 Oliver Springs 3,659 N8
37841 Oneida 3,717 N7
37363 Ooltewah 950 M10
†37660 Orebank 1,284 R7
37141 Orlinda 382 H7
35740 Orme 181 K10
37365 Palmer 1,027 K10
38242 Paris⊙ 10,728 E8
37843 Parrottsville 118 P8
38363 Parsons 2,422 E9
37143 Pegram 1,081 H8
37144 Petersburg 681 H10
37845 Petros 1,286 M8
37846 Philadelphia 507 M9
37863 Pigeon Forge 1,822 O9
37367 Pikeville⊙ 2,085 L9
†38017 Piperton 746 B10
†37738 Pittman Center 488 P9
38578 Pleasant Hill 371 L9
37148 Portland 4,030 H7
37849 Powell 7,220 N8
†37397 Powells Crossroads 918 L10
38478 Pulaski⊙ 7,184 G10
38251 Puryear 624 E8
38367 Ramer 429 D10
37415 Red Bank 13,299 L10
37150 Red Boiling Springs 1,173 K7
†37641 Rheatown R8
†37380 Richard City 87 K11
38080 Ridgely 1,932 B8
†37401 Ridgeside 417 L10
37152 Ridgetop 1,225 H8
38063 Ripley⊙ 6,366 B9
38253 Rives 386 C8
37687 Roan Mountain 1,108 S8
37853 Rockford 567 O9
37854 Rockwood 5,767 M9
37857 Rogersville⊙ 4,368 P8
38053 Rosemark 950 B10
38066 Rossville 379 B10
37860 Russellville 1,069 P8
38369 Rutherford 1,378 C8
37861 Rutledge⊙ 1,058 P8
38481 Saint Joseph 897 G10
37373 Sale Creek 900 L10
38370 Saltillo 434 E10
38254 Samburg 465 C8
38371 Sardis 301 E10
38067 Saulsbury 156 C10
38372 Savannah⊙ 6,992 E10
38374 Scotts Hill 668 E10
38375 Selmer⊙ 3,979 D10
37862 Sevierville⊙ 4,556 P9
37375 Sewanee 2,298 K10
38255 Sharon 1,134 D8
37160 Shelbyville⊙ 13,530 H10
37376 Sherwood 900 K10
37377 Signal Mountain 5,818 L10
38377 Silerton 100 D10
37165 Slayden 69 G8
37166 Smithville⊙ 3,839 K9
37167 Smyrna 8,839 H9
37869 Sneedville⊙ 1,110 P7
37319 Soddy-Daisy 8,388 L10
38068 Somerville⊙ 2,264 C10
†37030 South Carthage 1,004 K8
†37311 South Cleveland 4,360 M10
†37716 South Clinton 1,671 N8
†42041 South Fulton 2,735 D8
37380 South Pittsburg 3,636 K10
37171 Southside 800 G8
38583 Sparta⊙ 4,864 K9
38585 Spencer⊙ 1,126 L9
37381 Spring City 1,951 M9
37172 Springfield⊙ 10,814 H8
37174 Spring Hill 989 H9
38069 Stanton 540 C10
38379 Stantonville 271 E10
†37660 Sullivan Gardens 2,513 R8
38483 Summertown 850 G10
37873 Surgoinsville 1,536 R8
37874 Sweetwater 4,725 N9
37877 Talbott 975 P8
37879 Tazewell⊙ 2,090 O8
37385 Tellico Plains 698 N10
37178 Tennessee Ridge 1,325 F8
38079 Tiptonville⊙ 2,438 B8
38381 Toone 355 D10
37882 Townsend 351 O9
37387 Tracy City 1,356 K10
38382 Trenton⊙ 4,601 D9
38258 Trezevant 921 D8
38259 Trimble 722 C8
38260 Troy 1,093 C8
37388 Tullahoma 15,800 J10
37743 Tusculum 1,242 R8
38261 Union City⊙ 10,436 C8
37181 Vanleer 401 G8
†37397 Victoria 800 K10
37394 Viola 149 K9

(continued on following page)

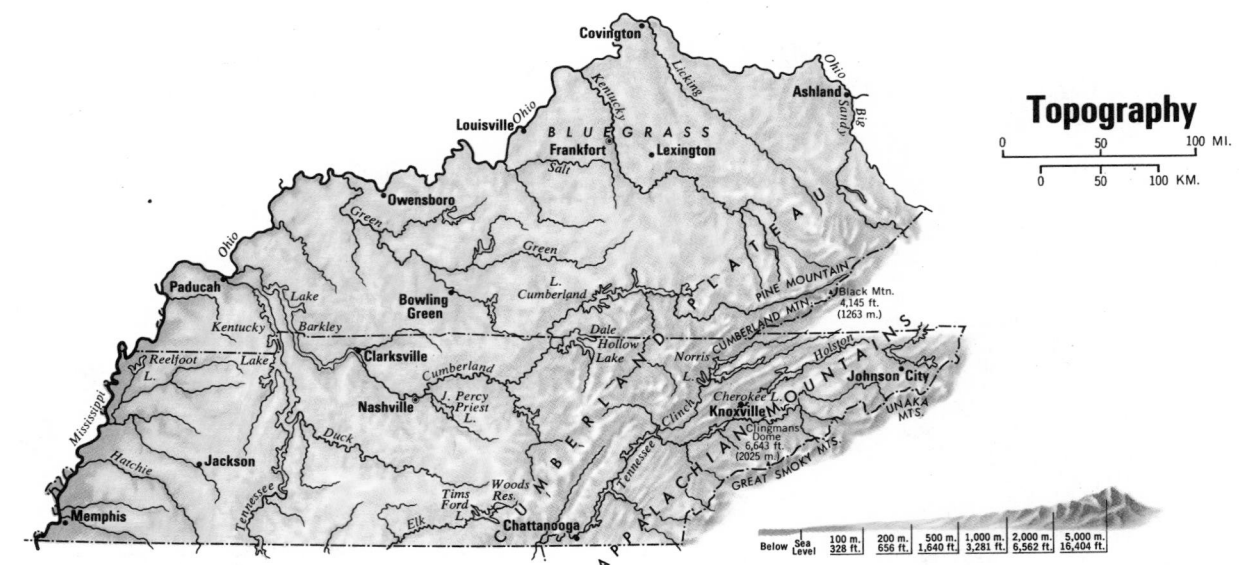

Topography

Below Sea Level | 100 m. 328 ft. | 200 m. 656 ft. | 500 m. 1,640 ft. | 1,000 m. 3,281 ft. | 2,000 m. 6,562 ft. | 5,000 m. 16,404 ft.

Kentucky and Tennessee

SCALE
0 5 10 20 30 40 MI.
0 5 10 20 30 40 KM.

State Capitals ⊛
County Seats ⊙
Major Limited Access Hwys.

Scale 1:1,970,000

© Copyright HAMMOND INCORPORATED, Maplewood, N.J.

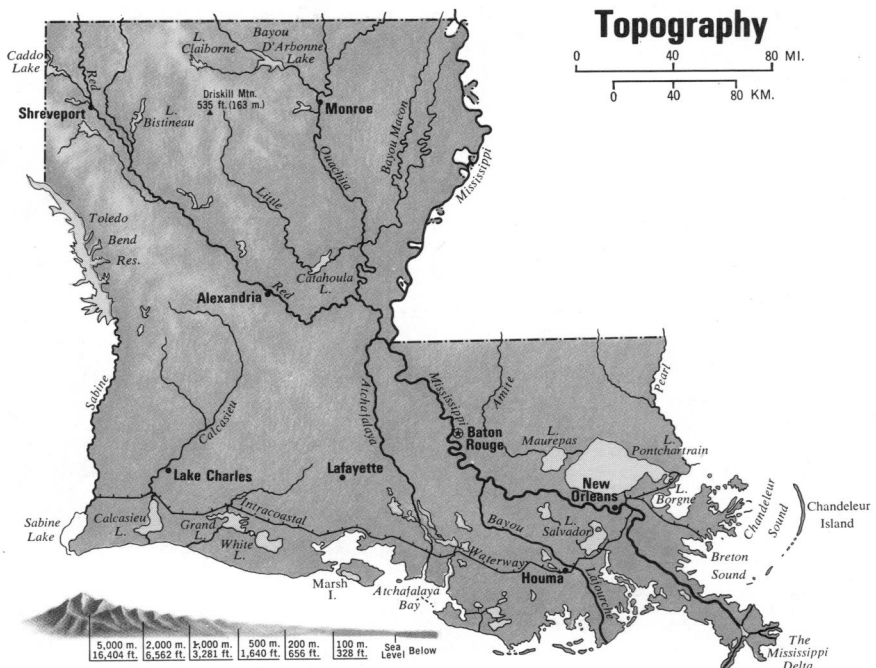

Topography

5,000 m. | 2,000 m. | 1,000 m. | 500 m. | 200 m. | 100 m. | Sea Level | Below
16,404 ft. | 6,562 ft. | 3,281 ft. | 1,640 ft. | 656 ft. | 328 ft.

The Mississippi Delta

PARISHES

Parish	Key
Acadia 56,427	F6
Allen 21,390	E5
Ascension 50,068	J6
Assumption 22,084	H7
Avoyelles 41,393	G4
Beauregard 29,692	D5
Bienville 16,387	D2
Bossier 80,721	C1
Caddo 252,358	C1
Calcasieu 167,223	D6
Caldwell 10,761	F2
Cameron 9,336	D7
Catahoula 12,287	G3
Claiborne 17,095	D1
Concordia 22,981	G4
De Soto 25,727	C2
East Baton Rouge 366,191	K1
East Carroll 11,772	H1
East Feliciana 19,015	H5
Evangeline 33,343	F5
Franklin 24,141	G2
Grant 16,703	E3
Iberia 63,752	G7
Iberville 32,159	H6
Jackson 17,321	E2
Jefferson 454,592	K7
Jefferson Davis 32,168	E6
Lafayette 150,017	F6
Lafourche 82,483	K7
La Salle 17,004	F3
Lincoln 39,763	E1
Livingston 58,806	L2
Madison 15,975	H2
Morehouse 34,803	G1
Natchitoches 39,863	D3
Orleans 557,515	L6
Ouachita 139,241	F2
Plaquemines 26,049	L8
Pointe Coupee 24,045	G5
Rapides 135,282	E4
Red River 10,433	D2
Richland 22,187	G2
Sabine 25,280	C3
Saint Bernard 64,097	L7
Saint Charles 37,259	K7
Saint Helena 9,827	J5
Saint James 21,495	L3
Saint John the Baptist 31,924	M3
Saint Landry 84,128	F5
Saint Martin 40,214	G6
Saint Mary 64,253	H7
Saint Tammany 110,869	L6
Tangipahoa 80,698	K5
Tensas 8,525	H2
Terrebonne 94,393	J8
Union 21,167	F1
Vermilion 48,458	F7
Vernon 53,475	D4
Washington 44,207	K5
Webster 43,631	D1
West Baton Rouge 19,086	H6
West Carroll 12,922	H1
West Feliciana 12,186	H5
Winn 17,253	E3

CITIES and TOWNS

Zip	Name/Pop.	Key
70510	Abbeville⊙ 12,391	F7
70420	Abita Springs 1,072	L6
71316	Acme 235	G4
70710	Addis 1,320	J2
71401	Aimwell 55	G3
70421	Akers 150	N2

70711	Albany 857	M1
71301	Alexandria⊙ 51,565	E4
	Alexandria‡ 151,985	E4
†70458	Alton 500	L6
70422	Amite⊙ 4,301	K5
70340	Amelia 3,617	H7
71403	Anacoco 820	D4
70426	Angie 311	L5
70712	Angola 600	G5
70032	Arabi 10,248	P4
71001	Arcadia⊙ 3,403	E1
71218	Archibald 425	G2
70512	Arnaudville 1,679	G6
71002	Ashland 307	D2
71003	Athens 419	E1
70513	Avery Island 500	G7
70714	Baker 12,865	K1
70514	Baldwin 2,644	H7
71405	Ball 3,405	F4
†70401	Baptist 150	M1
70036	Barataria 1,123	K7
70515	Basile 2,635	E5
71219	Baskin 286	G2
71220	Bastrop⊙ 15,527	G1
70715	Batchelor 500	G5
*70801	Baton Rouge	
	(cap.)⊙ 219,419	K2
	Baton Rouge‡ 493,973	K2
†70360	Bayou Cane 15,723	J7
†70380	Bayou Vista 5,805	H7
71004	Belcher 436	C1
70630	Bell City 400	D6
70037	Belle Chasse 5,412	O4
71407	Bentley 28	E3
71006	Benton⊙ 1,864	C1
†70558	Bermuda 50	D3
71222	Bernice 1,956	E1
70342	Berwick 4,466	H7
71007	Bethany 300	B2
71008	Bienville 300	D2
71009	Blanchard 1,128	C1
70427	Bogalusa 16,976	L5
†71064	Bolinger 200	C1
71223	Bonita 503	G1
71320	Bordelonville 350	G4
*71111	Bossier City 50,817	C1
70343	Bourg 2,073	J7
71409	Boyce 1,198	E4
70040	Braithwaite 350	P4
70516	Branch 200	F6
70517	Breaux Bridge 5,922	G6
70718	Brittany 475	L3
70518	Broussard 2,923	F6
70719	Brusly 1,762	J2
71014	Bryceland 94	E2
71321	Buckeye 280	E4
71322	Bunkie 5,364	F5
70041	Buras-Triumph 4,137	L8
70519	Cade 175	G6
71225	Calhoun 350	F2
71410	Calvin 263	E3
70631	Cameron⊙ 1,736	D7
71411	Campti 1,069	D3
†70584	Cankton 303	F6
70520	Carencro 3,712	G6
70042	Carlisle 975	L7
70721	Carville 1,037	K3
71015	Caspiana 50	C2
71016	Castor 195	D2
70522	Centerville 600	H7
70043	Chalmette 33,847	P4
†70767	Chamberlin 20	J1
71324	Chase 200	G2
70524	Chataignier 431	F5

71226	Chatham 714	F2
70344	Chauvin 3,338	J8
71325	Cheneyville 865	F4
71412	Chopin 175	E4
71227	Choudrant 809	F1
70525	Church Point 4,599	F6
71414	Clarence 612	E3
71415	Clarks 931	F2
71326	Clayton 1,204	H3
70722	Clinton⊙ 1,919	J5
71416	Cloutierville 100	E3
71417	Colfax⊙ 1,680	E3
71229	Collinston 439	G1
71418	Columbia⊙ 687	F2
70723	Convent⊙ 400	L3
71419	Converse 449	C3
†71107	Cooper Road	C1
71327	Cottonport 1,911	F5
71018	Cotton Valley 1,445	D1
71019	Coushatta⊙ 2,084	D2
70433	Covington⊙ 7,892	K5
†70510	Cow Island 200	F7
†70656	Cravens 200	E5
71020	Creston 135	E3
70526	Crowley⊙ 16,036	F6
71230	Crowville 400	G2
71021	Cullen 1,869	D1
70345	Cut Off 5,049	K7
71420	Cypress 55	D3
70046	Davant 600	L7
70528	Delcambre 2,216	G7
71232	Delhi 3,290	H2
71233	Delta 295	J2
70726	Denham Springs 8,563	L2
70633	De Quincy 3,966	D6
70634	De Ridder⊙ 11,057	D5
71421	Derry 75	E3
70030	Des Allemands 2,920	N4
70047	Destrehan 2,382	N4
†71055	Dixie Inn 453	D1
71422	Dodson 469	E2
70346	Donaldsonville⊙ 7,901	K3
70352	Donner 500	J7
71234	Downsville 213	F1
71023	Doyline 801	D1
70637	Dry Creek 300	D5
71423	Dry Prong 526	E3
71235	Dubach 1,161	E1
71024	Dubberly 421	D1
70353	Dulac 675	J8
71236	Dunn 225	G2
70728	Duplessis 500	K2
70529	Duson 1,253	F6
†71247	East Hodge 439	E2
71025	East Point 100	D2
71330	Echo 525	F4
70049	Edgard⊙ 400	M3
†71019	Edgefield 312	D2
71331	Effie 300	F4
70638	Elizabeth 454	E5
71424	Elmer 200	E4
71051	Elm Grove 100	C2
70532	Elton 1,450	E6
71425	Enterprise 375	G3
71332	Eola 47	F5
71237	Epps 672	G1
70533	Erath 2,133	F7
71238	Eros 158	F2
70534	Estherwood 691	F6
70730	Ethel 250	H5
70535	Eunice 12,479	F6
70639	Evans 1,253	D5
71333	Evergreen 272	F5
71240	Fairbanks 300	F1
71241	Farmerville⊙ 3,768	F1
70640	Fenton 491	E6

(continued)

Louisiana

SCALE
0 5 10 20 30 40 MI.
0 5 10 20 30 40 KM.

State Capitals .... ⊛
Parish Seats .... ⊙
Canals ....
Major Limited Access Hwys. ....

Scale 1:2,000,000

AREA 47,752 sq. mi. (123,678 sq. km.)
POPULATION 4,206,312
CAPITAL Baton Rouge
LARGEST CITY New Orleans
HIGHEST POINT Driskill Mtn. 535 ft. (163 m.)
SETTLED IN 1699
ADMITTED TO UNION April 30, 1812
POPULAR NAME Pelican State
STATE FLOWER Magnolia
STATE BIRD Eastern Brown Pelican

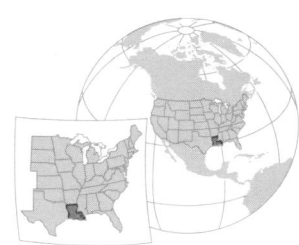

New Orleans, Baton Rouge and Vicinity

© Copyright HAMMOND INCORPORATED, Maplewood, N.J.

(continued)

71334 Ferriday 4,472 ... G3
71426 Fisher 325 ... D4
71427 Flatwoods 360 ... E4
71428 Flora 300 ... D3
71429 Florien 964 ... D4
70436 Fluker 400 ... K5
70437 Folsom 319 ... K5
70732 Fordoche 676 ... G5
71242 Forest 299 ... H1
71430 Forest Hill 494 ... E4
70538 Franklin⊙ 9,584 ... G7
70438 Franklinton⊙ 4,119 ... K5
70733 French Settlement 761 ... L2
†71447 Galbraith 30 ... E4
70354 Galliano 5,159 ... K8
70540 Garden City 225 ... H7
70051 Garyville 2,856 ... M3
71432 Georgetown 381 ... F3
70355 Gheens 350 ... K7
71028 Gibsland 1,354 ... E1
71336 Gilbert 800 ... G2
71029 Gilliam 244 ... C1
71244 Girard 150 ... G2
71433 Glenmora 1,479 ... E5
71030 Gloster 780 ... C2
70736 Glynn 700 ... H5
70357 Golden Meadow 2,282 ... K8
71031 Goldonna 526 ... D2
70737 Gonzales 7,287 ... L2
†70079 Good Hope 500 ... N3
†71342 Good Pine-Trout 1,033 ... F3
71434 Gorum 150 ... E4
71338 Goudeau 25 ... G5
71245 Grambling 4,226 ... E1
70052 Gramercy 3,211 ... M3
71032 Grand Cane 252 ... C2
70541 Grand Coteau 1,165 ... G6
70358 Grand Isle 1,982 ... L8
70644 Grant 225 ... E5
71435 Grayson 564 ... F2
70441 Greensburg⊙ 662 ... J5
70739 Greenwell Springs 350 ... K1
71033 Greenwood 1,043 ... B2
70053 Gretna⊙ 20,615 ... O4
70740 Grosse Tete 749 ... G6
70542 Gueydan 1,695 ... E6
70057 Hahnville⊙ 2,947 ... N4
71034 Hall Summit 276 ... D2
70401 Hammond 15,043 ... N1
71035 Hanna 138 ... D3
70123 Harahan 11,384 ... O4
71340 Harrisonburg⊙ 610 ... G3
70058 Harvey 22,709 ... O4
71037 Haughton 1,510 ... C1
†71446 Hawthorn 400 ... D4
70646 Hayes 600 ... E6
71038 Haynesville 3,454 ... D1
71039 Heflin 279 ... D2
†70517 Henderson 1,560 ... G6
71341 Hessmer 743 ... F4
70743 Hester 250 ... L3
71437 Hicks 379 ... E4
71438 Hineston 400 ... E4
71247 Hodge 708 ... E2
70744 Holden 600 ... M1
71248 Holly Ridge 100 ... G2
71040 Homer⊙ 4,307 ... D1
71439 Hornbeck 470 ... D4
71043 Hosston 480 ... C1
70360 Houma⊙ 32,602 ... J7
70746 Iberville 367 ... K2
71044 Ida 306 ... C1
70443 Independence 1,684 ... M1
70747 Innis 200 ... G5
70543 Iota 1,326 ... E6
70647 Iowa 2,437 ... D6
†70427 Isabel 550 ... K5
70748 Jackson 3,133 ... H5
71045 Jamestown 131 ... D2
70544 Jeanerette 6,511 ... G7
†70067 Jean Lafitte 936 ... K7
70121 Jefferson 15,550 ... O4
71342 Jena⊙ 4,375 ... F3
70546 Jennings⊙ 12,401 ... E6
71249 Jigger 300 ... G2
71250 Jones 350 ... G1
71251 Jonesboro⊙ 5,061 ... E2
71343 Jonesville 2,828 ... G3
71749 Junction City 727 ... E1
70548 Kaplan 5,016 ... F6
71046 Keatchie 342 ... C2
71441 Kelly 325 ... F3
70062 Kenner 66,382 ... N4
70444 Kentwood 2,667 ... J5
71253 Kilbourne 286 ... H1
†70462 Killian 611 ... M2
70066 Killona 950 ... M3
70648 Kinder 2,603 ... E6
70371 Kraemer 350 ... M4
70750 Krotz Springs 1,374 ... G5
71443 Kurthwood 65 ... D4
70372 Labadieville 2,138 ... K4
71444 Lacamp 150 ... E4
70650 Lacassine 400 ... E6
70445 Lacombe 5,146 ... L6
*70501 Lafayette⊙ 81,961 ... F6
Lafayette‡ 150,017 ... F6
70067 Lafitte 1,312 ... K7
70549 Lake Arthur 3,615 ... E6
*70601 Lake Charles⊙ 75,226 ... D6
Lake Charles‡ 167,048 ... D6
70752 Lakeland 800 ... H5
71254 Lake Providence⊙ 6,361 ... H1
70068 La Place 16,112 ... N3
70373 Larose 5,234 ... K7
71344 Larto 500 ... G4
70550 Lawtell 1,014 ... F5
71445 Leander 145 ... E4
71345 Lebeau 200 ... F5
70651 Le Blanc 400 ... E5
71346 Lecompte 1,661 ... F4
71446 Leesville⊙ 9,054 ... D4
71447 Lena 300 ... E4
70551 Leonville 1,143 ... G6
†71008 Liberty Hill 50 ... E2
71348 Libuse 500 ... F4
71256 Lillie 172 ... E1

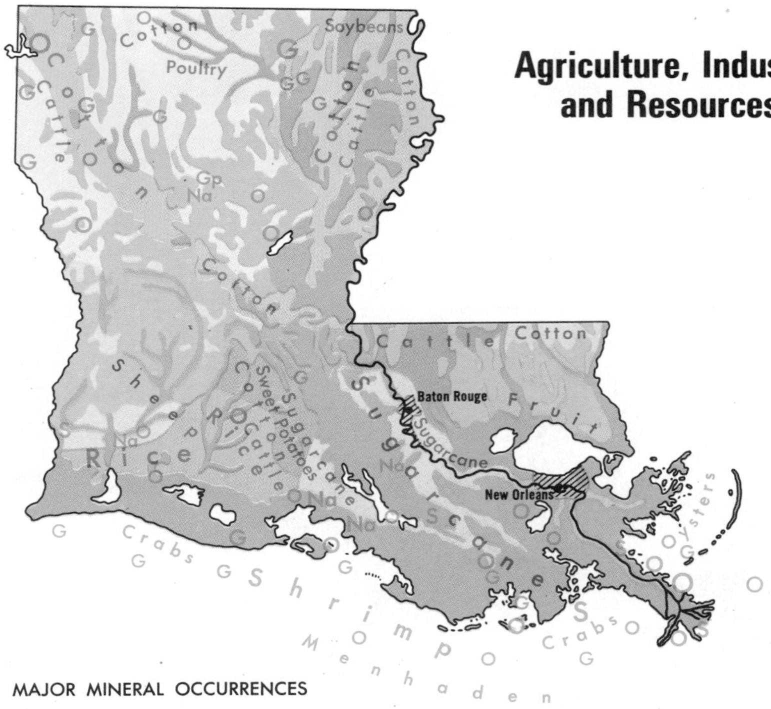

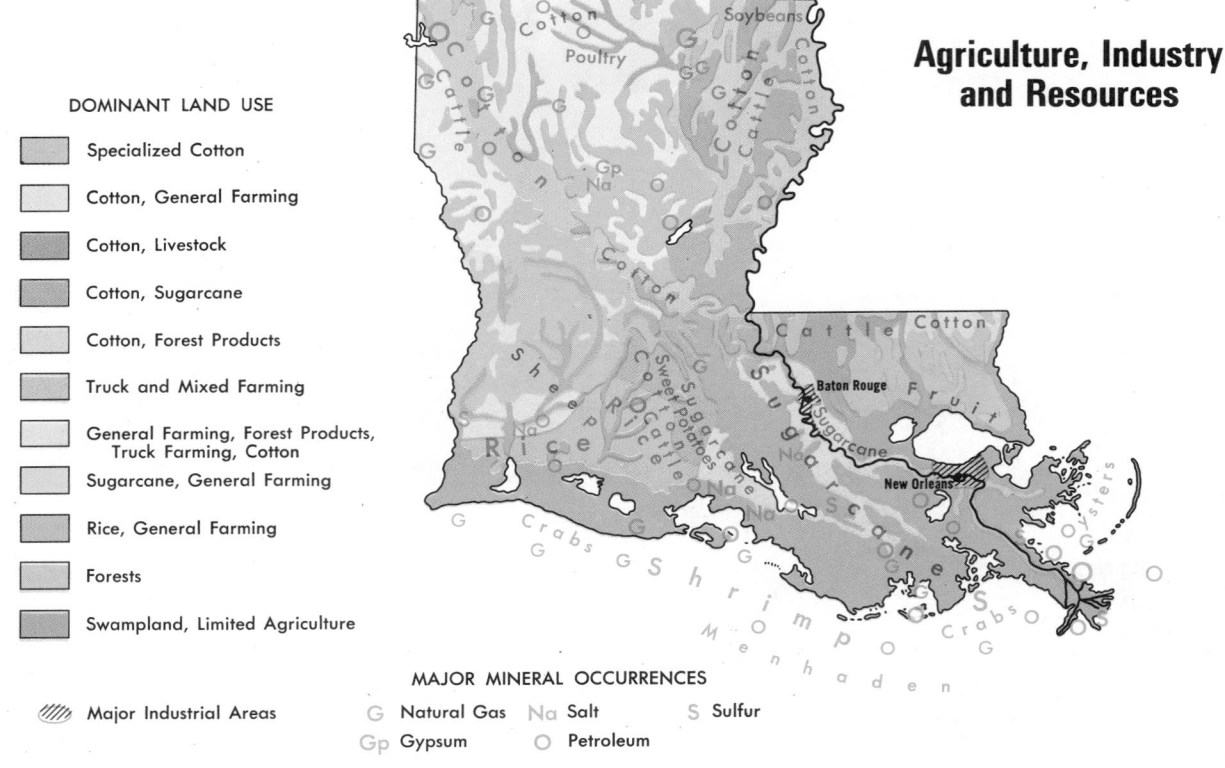

Agriculture, Industry and Resources

DOMINANT LAND USE

- Specialized Cotton
- Cotton, General Farming
- Cotton, Livestock
- Cotton, Sugarcane
- Cotton, Forest Products
- Truck and Mixed Farming
- General Farming, Forest Products, Truck Farming, Cotton
- Sugarcane, General Farming
- Rice, General Farming
- Forests
- Swampland, Limited Agriculture

Major Industrial Areas

MAJOR MINERAL OCCURRENCES

G Natural Gas Na Salt S Sulfur
Gp Gypsum O Petroleum

71257 Linville 150 ... F1
71048 Lisbon 138 ... E1
70754 Livingston⊙ 1,260 ... L1
70755 Livonia 980 ... G5
†70767 Lobdell 200 ... J1
70374 Lockport 2,424 ... K7
71049 Logansport 1,565 ... C3
71448 Longleaf 80 ... E4
71050 Longstreet 281 ... B2
70652 Longville 300 ... D5
70446 Loranger 250 ... N1
70552 Loreauville 860 ... G6
70756 Lottie 400 ... G5
†71008 Lucky 370 ... E2
70070 Luling 4,006 ... N4
70071 Lutcher 4,730 ... L3
70447 Madisonville 799 ... K6
70554 Mamou 3,194 ... F5
70448 Mandeville 6,076 ... L6
71259 Mangham 867 ... G2
71052 Mansfield⊙ 6,485 ... C2
71350 Mansura 2,074 ... G4
71449 Many⊙ 3,988 ... C3
70757 Maringouin 1,291 ... G6
71260 Marion 989 ... F1
71351 Marksville⊙ 5,113 ... G4
70072 Marrero 36,548 ... O4
†71019 Martin 584 ... D2
70555 Maurice 478 ... F6
†71433 McNary 240 ... E5
71346 Meeker 50 ... F4
71451 Melder 150 ... E4
71452 Melrose 500 ... E3
71353 Melville 1,764 ... G5
70556 Mermentau 771 ... E6
71261 Mer Rouge 802 ... G1
70653 Merryville 1,286 ... D5
*70001 Metairie 164,160 ... O4
70557 Midland 560 ... F6
70558 Milton 450 ... F6
†70070 Mimosa Park 3,737 ... N4
71055 Minden⊙ 15,074 ... D1
71059 Mira 354 ... C1
71453 Mitchell 155 ... C3
70376 Modeste 225 ... K3
*71201 Monroe⊙ 57,597 ... F1
Monroe‡ 139,241 ... F1
71454 Montgomery 843 ... E3
†70422 Montpelier 219 ... M1
71060 Mooringsport 911 ... B1
71455 Mora 427 ... E4
71355 Moreauville 853 ... G4
70380 Morgan City 16,114 ... H7
70759 Morganza 846 ... G5
71356 Morrow 600 ... F5
70559 Morse 835 ... F6
71262 Mound 40 ... H2
70450 Mount Hermon 170 ... K5
†71028 Mount Lebanon 105 ... D2
70390 Napoleonville⊙ 829 ... K4
70451 Natalbany 900 ... N1
71456 Natchez 527 ... D3
71457 Natchitoches⊙ 16,664 ... D3
71460 Negreet 400 ... C4
71357 Newellton 1,726 ... H2
70560 New Iberia⊙ 32,766 ... G6
71461 Newllano 2,213 ... D4
*70101 New Orleans⊙ 557,927 ... O4
New Orleans‡ 1,186,725 ... O4
70760 New Roads⊙ 3,924 ... G5

70078 New Sarpy 2,249 ... N4
71462 Noble 194 ... C3
70079 Norco 4,416 ... N3
†71247 North Hodge 573 ... E2
70761 Norwood 421 ... H5
71463 Oakdale 7,155 ... E5
71263 Oak Grove⊙ 2,214 ... H1
71264 Oak Ridge 257 ... G1
70655 Oberlin⊙ 1,764 ... E5
71061 Oil City 1,323 ... C1
71465 Olla 1,603 ... F3
70570 Opelousas⊙ 18,903 ... G5
70762 Oscar 650 ... H5
71466 Otis 400 ... E4
70391 Paincourtville 2,004 ... K3
71358 Palmetto 327 ... G5
70582 Parks 545 ... G6
70392 Patterson 4,693 ... H7
70452 Pearl River 1,693 ... L6
71063 Pelican 250 ... C3
70575 Perry 230 ... F7
70081 Pilottown 175 ... M8
70453 Pine Grove 570 ... J5
70576 Pine Prairie 734 ... E5
71360 Pineville 12,034 ... F4
71266 Pioneer 221 ... H1
70656 Pitkin 600 ... E5
71064 Plain Dealing 1,213 ... C1
70764 Plaquemine⊙ 7,521 ... J2
70393 Plattenville 205 ... K4
71362 Plaucheville 196 ... G5
71065 Pleasant Hill 776 ... C3
70082 Pointe a la Hache⊙ 750 ... L7
71467 Pollock 399 ... F3
70454 Ponchatoula 5,469 ... N2
70767 Port Allen⊙ 6,114 ... J2
70577 Port Barre 2,625 ... G5
70083 Port Sulphur 3,318 ... L8
†70726 Port Vincent 450 ... L2
71066 Powhatan 279 ... D3
71468 Provencal 695 ... D3
71268 Quitman 231 ... E2
70394 Raceland 6,302 ... J7
70578 Rayne 9,066 ... F6
71269 Rayville⊙ 4,610 ... G2
70580 Reddell 500 ... F5
70658 Reeves 199 ... D5
70084 Reserve 7,288 ... M3
†71282 Richmond 505 ... H2
†71201 Richwood 1,223 ... F2
†71334 Ridgecrest 895 ... G3
71068 Ringgold 1,655 ... D2
†70427 Rio 400 ... L5
70581 Roanoke 800 ... E6
71469 Robeline 238 ... D3
71069 Rodessa 337 ... B1
71364 Rosa 300 ... G5
70772 Rosedale 658 ... G6
70456 Roseland 1,346 ... J5
70659 Rosepine 953 ... D5
71365 Ruby 400 ... F4
71270 Ruston⊙ 20,585 ... E1
70457 Saint Benedict 190 ... K5
70775 Saint Francisville⊙ 1,471 ... H5
71366 Saint Joseph⊙ 1,687 ... H3
71367 Saint Landry 550 ... F5
70582 Saint Martinville⊙ 7,965 ... G6
71471 Saint Maurice 560 ... E3
71070 Saline 293 ... E2

71071 Sarepta 831 ... D1
70807 Scotlandville 15,113 ... J1
70583 Scott 2,239 ... F6
†70764 Seymourville 2,891 ... J2
71072 Shongaloo 163 ... D1
*71101 Shreveport⊙ 205,820 ... C2
Shreveport‡ 376,646 ... C2
71073 Sibley 1,211 ... D1
71368 Sicily Island 691 ... G3
71472 Sieper 226 ... E4
71473 Sikes 226 ... F2
71369 Simmesport 2,293 ... G5
71474 Simpson 534 ... D4
71275 Simsboro 553 ... E1
70660 Singer 250 ... D5
71475 Slagle 650 ... D4
70777 Slaughter 729 ... H5
70458 Slidell 26,718 ... L6
71276 Sondheimer 225 ... H1
70778 Sorrento 1,197 ... L3
†71052 South Mansfield 1,463 ... C3
71277 Spearsville 181 ... E1
71278 Spencer 50 ... F1
70462 Springfield 424 ... M2
71075 Springhill 6,516 ... D1
†71049 Stanley 151 ... C3
71280 Sterlington 1,400 ... F1
71078 Stonewall 1,175 ... C2
70662 Sugartown 375 ... D5
70663 Sulphur 19,709 ... D6
70463 Sun 404 ... L5
70584 Sunset 2,300 ... F6
70464 Talisheek 315 ... L5
71282 Tallulah⊙ 11,634 ... H2
70465 Tangipahoa 493 ... J5
71080 Taylor 500 ... D1
71476 Temple 250 ... E4
71285 Terry 50 ... H1
†70053 Terry Town 23,548 ... O4
70397 Theriot 450 ... J8
70301 Thibodaux⊙ 15,810 ... J7
70466 Tickfaw 571 ... M1
71286 Transylvania 400 ... H1
71081 Trees 327 ... B1
†70041 Triumph-Buras 4,137 ... L8
71371 Trout-Good Pine 1,033 ... F3
71479 Tullos 776 ... F3
70782 Tunica 500 ... G5
70585 Turkey Creek 366 ... F5
71480 Urania 849 ... F3
70090 Vacherie 2,169 ... L3
70467 Varnado 249 ... L5
71481 Verda 100 ... E3
71373 Vidalia⊙ 5,936 ... G3
†71270 Vienna 519 ... E1
70586 Ville Platte⊙ 9,201 ... F5
70668 Vinton 3,631 ... C6
70092 Violet 11,678 ... P4
71082 Vivian 4,146 ... B1
†71418 Vixen 40 ... F2
70784 Wakefield 400 ... H5
†70433 Waldheim 25 ... L5
70785 Walker 2,957 ... L1
71289 Warden 130 ... H1
70589 Washington 1,266 ... G5
71375 Waterproof 1,339 ... H3
70786 Watson 800 ... L1
70591 Welsh 3,515 ... E6
70669 Westlake 5,246 ... D6
71291 West Monroe 14,993 ... F1

70094 Westwego 12,663 ... O4
70787 Weyanoke 500 ... H5
70788 White Castle 2,160 ... J3
†71371 White Sulphur Springs 50 ... F3
71376 Whiteville 150 ... F5
71377 Wildsville 800 ... G3
†70040 Wills Point 150 ... L7
70789 Wilson 656 ... H5
71483 Winnfield⊙ 7,311 ... E3
71295 Winnsboro⊙ 5,921 ... G2
71378 Wisner 1,424 ... G3
71485 Woodworth 412 ... E4
70592 Youngsville 1,053 ... G6
70791 Zachary 7,297 ... K1
†71371 Zenoria 76 ... F3
†71409 Zimmerman 20 ... E4
71486 Zwolle 2,602 ... C3

OTHER FEATURES

Allemands (lake) ... M4
Alligator (pt.) ... L6
Amite (riv.) ... L2
Anacoco (lake) ... D4
Atchafalaya (bay) ... H8
Atchafalaya (riv.) ... G6
Barataria (bay) ... L8
Barataria (passage) ... L8
Barksdale A.F.B. ... C2
Bayou D'Arbonne (lake) ... F1
Bird (isl.) ... M8
Bistineau (lake) ... D2
Black (lake) ... D3
Black Lake (bayou) ... D1
Boeuf (lake) ... J7
Boeuf (riv.) ... G1
Bonnet Carré Spillway and Floodway ... N3
Borgne (lake) ... L7
Boudreau (bay) ... M7
Boudreaux (lake) ... J8
Breton (isls.) ... M8
Breton (sound) ... M7
Bundick (lake) ... D5
Caddo (lake) ... B1
Caillou (bay) ... J8
Calcasieu (lake) ... D7
Calcasieu (passage) ... D7
Calcasieu (riv.) ... E5
Catahoula (lake) ... F4
Cataouatche (lake) ... N4
Cat Island (chan.) ... M6
Cat Island (passage) ... J8
Chandeleur (isls.) ... N7
Chandeleur (sound) ... M7
Chenier (lake) ... F2
Chicot (pt.) ... M7
Claiborne (lake) ... E1
Clear (lake) ... D3
Cocodrie (lake) ... E5
Cotile (lake) ... E4
Cross (lake) ... C2
Curlew (isls.) ... M7
Dernieres (isls.) ... J8
Door (pt.) ... M6
Driskill (mt.) ... E2
Drum (bay) ... M7
East (bay) ... M8
East Cote Blanche (bay) ... G7
Edwards (lake) ... C2
Eloi (bay) ... M7
England A.F.B. ... E4
Fields (lake) ... J7
Fort Polk 14,142 ... D4
Free Mason (isls.) ... M7
Garden Island (bay) ... M8
Grand (lake) ... E7
Grand (lake) ... H8
Grand Terre (isls.) ... L8
Iatt (lake) ... E3
Jean Lafitte Nat'l Hist. Park ... P4
Lafourche (bayou) ... K8
Little (riv.) ... F3
Louisiana (pt.) ... C7
Macon (bayou) ... H1
Main (passage) ... M8
Manchac (passage) ... N2
Marsh (isl.) ... G7
Maurepas (lake) ... M2
Mermentau (riv.) ... E7
Mexico (gulf) ... F8
Mississippi (delta) ... M8
Mississippi (riv.) ... H3
Mississippi (sound) ... M6
Mississippi River Gulf Outlet (canal) ... L7
Mozambique (pt.) ... M7
Mud (lake) ... D7
Naval Air Sta. ... O4
North (isls.) ... M7
North (pass) ... N8
North (pt.) ... M7
Northeast (pass) ... M8
Ouachita (riv.) ... F1
Palourde (lake) ... H7
Pearl (riv.) ... L5
Point au Fer (isl.) ... H8
Point au Fer (pt.) ... H8
Pontchartrain (lake) ... O3
Pontchartrain Causeway ... O3
Raccoon (pt.) ... H8
Red (riv.) ... G4
Sabine (lake) ... C7
Sabine (passage) ... C7
Sabine (riv.) ... C5
Saline (lake) ... E3
Salvador (lake) ... K7
Smithport (lake) ... C2
South (pass) ... M8
South (pt.) ... G8
Southeast (pass) ... M8
Southwest (pass) ... L8
Tangipahoa (riv.) ... N1
Tensas (riv.) ... G3
Terrebonne (bay) ... J8
Tickfaw (riv.) ... M1
Timbalier (bay) ... K8
Timbalier (isl.) ... K8
Toledo Bend (res.) ... C3
Turkey Creek (lake) ... G3
Vermilion (bay) ... F7
Vernon (lake) ... D4
Verret (lake) ... H7
Wallace (lake) ... C2
West (bay) ... M8
West Cote Blanche (bay) ... G7
White (lake) ... E7

⊙Parish seat.
‡Population of metropolitan area.
† Zip of nearest p.o. * Multiple zips.

AREA 33,265 sq. mi. (86,156 sq. km.)
POPULATION 1,125,027
CAPITAL Augusta
LARGEST CITY Portland
HIGHEST POINT Katahdin 5,268 ft. (1606 m.)
SETTLED IN 1624
ADMITTED TO UNION March 15, 1820
POPULAR NAME Pine Tree State
STATE FLOWER White Pine Cone & Tassel
STATE BIRD Chickadee

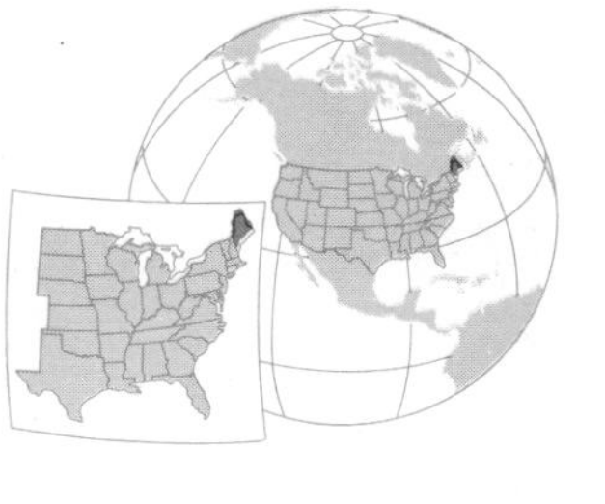

COUNTIES

Androscoggin 99,657 .... C7
Aroostook 91,331 .... F2
Cumberland 215,789 .... C8
Franklin 27,098 .... B5
Hancock 41,781 .... G6
Kennebec 109,889 .... D7
Knox 32,941 .... E7
Lincoln 25,691 .... D7
Oxford 48,968 .... B7
Penobscot 137,015 .... F5
Piscataquis 17,634 .... E4
Sagadahoc 28,795 .... D7
Somerset 45,028 .... C4
Waldo 28,414 .... E6
Washington 34,963 .... H6
York 139,666 .... B9

CITIES and TOWNS

Zip *Name/Pop.* *Key*

04406 Abbot Village○ 576 .... D5
04001 Acton○ 1,228 .... B8
04606 Addison○ 1,061 .... H6
04910 Albion○ 1,551 .... E6
†04610 Alexander○ 385 .... H5
04002 Alfred○ 1,890 .... B9
†04774 Allagash○ 448 .... F1
†04938 Allens Mills 100 .... C6
04535 Alna○ 425 .... D7
†04468 Alton○ 468 .... F5
†04408 Amherst○ 203 .... G6
04216 Andover○ 850 .... B6
04911 Anson○ 2,226 .... D6
†04862 Appleton○ 818 .... E7
†04468 Argyle 225 .... F5
04732 Ashland○ 1,865 .... G2
04607 Ashville 36 .... G7
04912 Athens○ 802 .... D6
†04426 Atkinson○ 306 .... E5
04608 Atlantic 120 .... G7
04210 Auburn⊙ 23,128 .... C7
04330 Augusta (cap.)⊙ 21,819 .... D7
04408 Aurora○ 110 .... G6
04003 Bailey Island 500 .... D8
†04497 Bancroft○ 61 .... H4
04401 Bangor⊙ 31,643 .... F6
Bangor‡ 83,919 .... F6
04609 Bar Harbor○ 4,124 .... G7
04609 Bar Harbor 2,685 .... G7
†04619 Baring○ 308 .... J5
04004 Bar Mills 800 .... C8
04653 Bass Harbor 450 .... G7
04530 Bath⊙ 10,246 .... D8
†04915 Bayside F7
04611 Beals○ 695 .... H7
†04622 Beddington○ 36 .... H6
04915 Belfast⊙ 6,243 .... F7
04917 Belgrade○ 2,043 .... D7
†04915 Belmont○ 520 .... E7
04733 Benedicta○ 225 .... G4
†04937 Benton○ 2,188 .... D6
03901 Berwick○ 4,149 .... B9
03901 Berwick 2,378 .... B9
04217 Bethel○ 2,340 .... B7
04005 Biddeford 19,638 .... B9
04920 Bingham○ 1,184 .... D5
04920 Bingham 1,074 .... D5
04613 Birch Harbor 300 .... H7
04734 Blaine○ 922 .... H2
04734 Blaine-Mars Hill 1,921 .... H2
04614 Blue Hill○ 1,644 .... F7
04615 Blue Hill Falls 135 .... F7
04537 Boothbay○ 2,308 .... D8
04538 Boothbay Harbor 2,207 .... D8
04008 Bowdoinham○ 1,828 .... D7
†04481 Bowerbank○ 27 .... E5
04410 Bradford○ 888 .... F5
†04410 Bradford Center 105 .... F5
04411 Bradley○ 1,149 .... F6
04412 Brewer 9,017 .... F6
04735 Bridgewater○ 742 .... H3
04009 Bridgton○ 3,528 .... B7
04009 Bridgton 1,639 .... B7
†04990 Brighton○ 74 .... D5
04539 Bristol○ 2,095 .... D8
04616 Brooklin○ 619 .... F7
04921 Brooks○ 804 .... E6
04617 Brooksville○ 753 .... F7
04413 Brookton 175 .... H4
04010 Brownfield○ 767 .... B8
04414 Brownville○ 1,545 .... E5
04011 Brunswick○ 17,366 .... C8
04011 Brunswick 10,990 .... C8
04219 Bryant Pond 600 .... B7
†04232 Buckfield○ 1,333 .... C7
04618 Bucks Harbor 300 .... J6
04416 Bucksport○ 4,345 .... F6
04416 Bucksport 2,853 .... F6
04540 Burkettville 120 .... E7
04417 Burlington○ 322 .... G5
04922 Burnham○ 951 .... E6
†04093 Buxton○ 5,775 .... C8
†04275 Byron○ 114 .... B6
04619 Calais 4,262 .... J5
04923 Cambridge○ 445 .... E5
04843 Camden○ 4,584 .... F7
04843 Camden 3,743 .... F7
04924 Canaan○ 1,189 .... D6
04221 Canton○ 831 .... C7
03902 Cape Neddick 850 .... B9
04014 Cape Porpoise 500 .... C9
04736 Caribou 9,916 .... G2
04419 Carmel○ 1,695 .... E6
†04947 Carrabassett Valley○ 107 .... C5
†04487 Carroll○ 175 .... G5
†04224 Carthage○ 438 .... C6
†04465 Cary○ 229 .... H4
04015 Casco○ 2,243 .... B7
04421 Castine○ 1,304 .... F7
†04941 Center Montville 16 .... E7
†04623 Centerville○ 28 .... H6
†04757 Chapman○ 406 .... G2
04422 Charleston○ 1,037 .... F5
†04666 Charlotte○ 300 .... J5
04017 Chebeague Island 900 .... C8
†04345 Chelsea○ 2,522 .... D7
04622 Cherryfield○ 983 .... H6
†04458 Chester○ 434 .... F5
†04938 Chesterville○ 869 .... C6
†04478 Chesuncook 6 .... D3
04926 China○ 2,918 .... E7
†04239 Chisholm 1,796 .... C7
†04428 Clifton○ 462 .... G6
04927 Clinton○ 2,696 .... D6
04927 Clinton 1,305 .... D6
†04623 Columbia○ 275 .... H6
04623 Columbia Falls○ 517 .... H6
†04638 Cooper○ 105 .... H6
04624 Corea 375 .... H7
04928 Corinna○ 1,887 .... E6
04020 Cornish○ 1,047 .... B8
†04976 Cornville○ 838 .... D6
04625 Cranberry Isles○ 198 .... G7
†04610 Crawford○ 86 .... H5
†04015 Crescent Lake 325 .... C7
†04851 Criehaven 5 .... F8
04738 Crouseville 450 .... G2
†04747 Crystal○ 349 .... G4
04021 Cumberland Center○ 5,284 .... C8
04021 Cumberland Center 2,015 .... C8
04563 Cushing○ 795 .... E7
04626 Cutler○ 726 .... J6
04543 Damariscotta○ 1,493 .... E7
04543 Damariscotta-Newcastle
1,411 .... E7
04424 Danforth○ 826 .... H4
†04622 Deblois○ 44 .... H6
†04429 Dedham○ 841 .... F6
04627 Deer Isle○ 1,492 .... F7
04022 Denmark○ 672 .... B8
04628 Dennysville○ 296 .... J6
04929 Detroit○ 744 .... E6
04930 Dexter○ 4,286 .... E5
04930 Dexter 3,118 .... E5
04224 Dixfield○ 2,389 .... C6
04224 Dixfield 1,725 .... C6
04932 Dixmont○ 812 .... E6
04426 Dover-Foxcroft○ 4,323 .... E5
04426 Dover-Foxcroft⊙ 2,974 .... E5
†04426 Dover South Mills 54 .... E5
04342 Dresden○ 998 .... D7
†04747 Dyer Brook○ 275 .... G3
04739 Eagle Lake○ 1,019 .... F1
04226 East Andover 250 .... B6
04544 East Boothbay 800 .... D8
04427 East Corinth 525 .... F5
04227 East Dixfield 250 .... C6
04429 East Holden 600 .... F6
04027 East Lebanon 950 .... B9
04228 East Livermore 500 .... C7
04630 East Machias○ 1,233 .... J6
04430 East Millinocket○ 2,372 .... F4
04430 East Millinocket 2,361 .... F4
04740 Easton○ 1,305 .... H2
04028 East Parsonfield 400 .... B8
04229 East Peru 200 .... C7
†04210 East Poland 200 .... C7
04631 Eastport 1,982 .... K6
04231 East Stoneham 300 .... B7
†04607 East Sullivan 496 .... G6
†04220 East Sumner 120 .... C7
†04862 East Union 75 .... E7
†04428 Eddington○ 1,769 .... F6
†04556 Edgecomb○ 841 .... D8
03903 Eliot○ 4,948 .... B9
04605 Ellsworth⊙ 5,179 .... F6
04031 Emery Mills 100 .... B8
04433 Enfield○ 1,397 .... F5
04434 Etna○ 758 .... E6
04936 Eustis○ 582 .... B5
04435 Exeter○ 823 .... E6
†04938 Fairbanks 400 .... C6
04937 Fairfield○ 6,113 .... D6
04937 Fairfield 3,169 .... D6
04105 Falmouth○ 6,853 .... C8
04105 Falmouth 1,655 .... C8
†04345 Farmingdale○ 2,535 .... D7
†04345 Farmingdale 2,014 .... D7
04938 Farmington○ 6,730 .... C6
04938 Farmington⊙ 3,583 .... C6
04940 Farmington Falls 500 .... C6
†04349 Fayette○ 812 .... C7
04546 Five Islands 225 .... D8
04742 Fort Fairfield○ 4,376 .... H2
04742 Fort Fairfield 2,282 .... H2
04743 Fort Kent○ 4,826 .... F1
04743 Fort Kent 2,375 .... F1
04744 Fort Kent Mills 200 .... F1
04438 Frankfort○ 783 .... F6
04634 Franklin○ 979 .... G6
04941 Freedom○ 458 .... E7
04032 Freeport○ 5,863 .... C8
04032 Freeport 1,906 .... C8
04635 Frenchboro○ 43 .... G7
04745 Frenchville○ 1,450 .... G1
04547 Friendship○ 1,000 .... E7
04037 Fryeburg○ 2,715 .... A7
04037 Fryeburg 1,644 .... A7
04345 Gardiner 6,485 .... D7
04939 Garland○ 718 .... E5
04548 Georgetown○ 735 .... D8
†04217 Gilead○ 191 .... B7
†04401 Glenburn○ 2,319 .... F6
04846 Glen Cove 250 .... E7
04038 Gorham○ 10,101 .... C8
04038 Gorham 4,052 .... C8
†04607 Gouldsboro○ 1,574 .... H7
04746 Grand Isle○ 719 .... G1
04637 Grand Lake Stream○ 198 .... H5
04039 Gray○ 4,344 .... C8
†04408 Great Pond○ 45 .... G6
04236 Greene○ 3,037 .... C7
04441 Greenville○ 1,839 .... D5
04441 Greenville 1,640 .... D5
04442 Greenville Junction 650 .... D5
04443 Guilford○ 1,793 .... E5
04443 Guilford 1,235 .... E5
04347 Hallowell 2,502 .... D7
†04785 Hamlin○ 340 .... H1
04444 Hampden○ 5,250 .... F6
04444 Hampden 3,538 .... F6
04445 Hampden Highlands 950 .... F6
04640 Hancock○ 1,409 .... G6
04237 Hanover○ 256 .... B7
04942 Harmony○ 755 .... D6
†04011 Harpswell○ 3,796 .... D8
04643 Harrington○ 859 .... H6
04040 Harrison○ 1,667 .... B7
†04221 Hartford○ 480 .... C7
04943 Hartland○ 1,669 .... D6
04943 Hartland 1,041 .... D6
04446 Haynesville○ 169 .... G4
04238 Hebron○ 665 .... C7
†04401 Hermon○ 3,170 .... F6
04944 Hinckley 140 .... D6
04041 Hiram○ 1,067 .... B8
†04730 Hodgdon○ 1,084 .... H3
04042 Hollis Center○ 2,892 .... B8
04847 Hope○ 730 .... E7
04730 Houlton○ 6,766 .... H3
04730 Houlton⊙ 5,730 .... H3
04448 Howland○ 1,602 .... F5
04448 Howland 1,502 .... F5
04449 Hudson○ 797 .... F5
04644 Hulls Cove 200 .... G7
04747 Island Falls○ 981 .... G3
04645 Isle Au Haut○ 57 .... F7
04848 Islesboro○ 521 .... F7
04945 Jackman○ 1,003 .... C4
†04630 Jacksonville 200 .... J6
04239 Jay○ 5,080 .... C7
04348 Jefferson○ 1,616 .... D7
04648 Jonesboro○ 553 .... J6
04649 Jonesport○ 1,512 .... H6
04649 Jonesport 1,050 .... H6
04450 Kenduskeag○ 1,210 .... E6
04043 Kennebunk○ 6,621 .... B9
04043 Kennebunk 3,294 .... B9
†04043 Kennebunk Beach 200 .... C9
04046 Kennebunkport○ 2,952 .... C9
04046 Kennebunkport 1,685 .... C9
04349 Kents Hill 300 .... D7
04947 Kingfield○ 1,083 .... C6
04451 Kingman 281 .... G4
†04990 Kingsbury○ 4 .... D5
03904 Kittery○ 9,314 .... B9
03904 Kittery 5,465 .... B9
03905 Kittery Point 1,260 .... B9
†04986 Knox○ 558 .... E6
04453 La Grange○ 509 .... F5
†04463 Lake View○ 20 .... F5
†04605 Lamoine○ 953 .... G7
04455 Lee○ 688 .... G5
†04263 Leeds○ 1,463 .... C7
04456 Levant○ 1,117 .... F6
04240 Lewiston 40,481 .... C7
Lewiston-Auburn‡ 72,378 .... C7
04949 Liberty○ 694 .... E7
04749 Lille 300 .... G1
04048 Limerick○ 1,356 .... B8
04750 Limestone○ 8,719 .... H2
04750 Limestone 1,334 .... H2
04049 Limington○ 2,203 .... B8
04457 Lincoln○ 5,066 .... G5
04457 Lincoln 3,524 .... G5
04849 Lincolnville○ 1,414 .... E7
04850 Lincolnville Center 200 .... E7
†04730 Linneus○ 752 .... H3
04250 Lisbon○ 8,769 .... C7
04250 Lisbon-Lisbon
Center 1,865 .... C7
04252 Lisbon Falls 4,370 .... D7
04350 Litchfield○ 1,954 .... D7
†04627 Little Deer Isle 475 .... F7
04082 Little Falls-South
Windham 1,366 .... C8
†04760 Littleton○ 1,009 .... H3
04253 Livermore○ 1,826 .... C7
04254 Livermore Falls○ 3,572 .... C7
04254 Livermore Falls 2,441 .... C7
04255 Locke Mills 600 .... B7
04051 Lovell○ 767 .... B7
†04433 Lowell○ 194 .... F5
04652 Lubec○ 2,045 .... K6
†04730 Ludlow○ 403 .... G3
04654 Machias○ 2,458 .... J6
04654 Machias⊙ 1,277 .... J6
04655 Machiasport○ 1,108 .... H6
†04451 Macwahoc○ 126 .... G4
04756 Madawaska○ 5,282 .... G1
04756 Madawaska 4,165 .... G1
04950 Madison○ 4,367 .... D6
04950 Madison 2,788 .... D6
†04966 Madrid○ 178 .... B6
†04942 Mainstream 100 .... D6
04351 Manchester○ 1,949 .... D7
04757 Mapleton○ 1,895 .... G2
04758 Mars Hill○ 1,892 .... H2
04758 Mars Hill-Blaine 1,921 .... H2
04759 Masardis○ 328 .... G3
04851 Matinicus 66 .... F8
04459 Mattawamkeag○ 1,000 .... G5
04256 Mechanic Falls○ 2,616 .... C7
04256 Mechanic Falls 2,198 .... C7
04657 Meddybemps○ 110 .... J5
†04453 Medford○ 163 .... F5
†04453 Medford Center 100 .... F5
04460 Medway○ 1,871 .... G4
04957 Mercer○ 448 .... D6
04257 Mexico○ 3,698 .... B6
04257 Mexico 3,207 .... B6
†04216 Middledam 10 .... B6
04658 Milbridge○ 1,306 .... H6
04461 Milford○ 2,160 .... F6
04461 Milford 1,688 .... F6
04462 Millinocket○ 7,567 .... F4

(continued on following page)

Agriculture, Industry and Resources

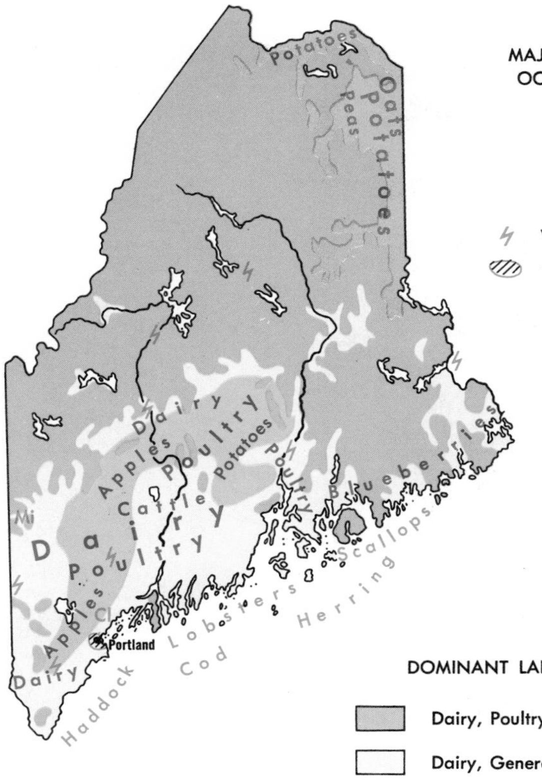

MAJOR MINERAL OCCURRENCES

Cl Clay
Mi Mica

Water Power
Major Industrial Areas

DOMINANT LAND USE

Dairy, Poultry, Mixed Farming
Dairy, General Farming
Potatoes, General Farming
Forests

(continued)

04463 Milo○ 2,624 F5
04463 Milo 2,255 F5
04258 Minot○ 1,631 C7
04659 Minturn 150 G7
†04776 Monarda 100 G4
04852 Monhegan○ 109 E8
04259 Monmouth○ 2,888 D7
04951 Monroe○ 657 E6
04464 Monson○ 804 E5
04760 Monticello○ 950 H3
†04941 Montville○ 631 E7
04054 Moody 500 B9
†04478 Moosehead 6 D4
†04945 Moose River○ 252 C4
04952 Morrill○ 506 E7
04660 Mount Desert○ 2,063 G7
04352 Mount Vernon○ 1,021 D7
04055 Naples○ 1,833 B8
04552 Newagen 100 D8
†04445 Newburgh○ 1,228 F6
04553 Newcastle○ 1,227 D7
04553 Newcastle-Damariscotta 1,411 E7
04056 Newfield○ 644 B8
04260 New Gloucester○ 3,180 C8
04554 New Harbor 850 E8
04761 New Limerick○ 513 G3
04953 Newport○ 2,755 E6
04953 Newport 1,748 E6
04954 New Portland○ 651 C6
04261 Newry○ 235 B6
04955 New Sharon○ 969 C6
04762 New Sweden○ 737 G2
04956 New Vineyard○ 607 C6
04555 Nobleboro○ 1,154 D7
†04462 Norcross 13 F4
04957 Norridgewock○ 2,552 D6
04957 Norridgewock 1,318 D6
04958 North Anson 950 D6
03906 North Berwick○ 2,878 B9
03906 North Berwick 1,436 B9
04057 North Bridgton 300 B7
†04938 North Chesterville 50 C6
†04441 North East Carry 2 D4
04662 Northeast Harbor 800 G7
†04654 Northfield○ 88 H6
04853 North Haven○ 373 F7
04262 North Jay 800 C6
†04254 North Livermore 250 C7
04961 North New Portland 500 C6
†04476 North Penobscot 246 F7
†04849 Northport○ 958 E7
†04274 North Raymond 225 C8
04266 North Turner 350 C7
04962 North Vassalboro 950 D7
04267 North Waterford 390 B7
04062 North Windham 5,492 C8
†04219 North Woodstock 75 B7
†04096 North Yarmouth○ 1,919 C8
04268 Norway○ 4,042 B7
04268 Norway 2,653 B7
†04268 Norway Lake 75 B7
04763 Oakfield○ 847 G3
04963 Oakland○ 5,162 D6
04963 Oakland 3,387 D6
04063 Ocean Park 200 C9
03907 Ogunquit 1,492 B9
04064 Old Orchard Beach○ 6,291 C9
04064 Old Orchard Beach 6,023 C9
04468 Old Town 8,422 F6
04964 Oquossoc 150 B6
04471 Orient○ 97 H4
04472 Orland○ 1,645 F6
04473 Orono○ 10,578 F6
04473 Orono 9,891 F6
04474 Orrington○ 3,244 F6
04066 Orrs Island 600 D8
†04270 Otisfield○ 897 B7
04665 Otter Creek 260 G7
04854 Owls Head○ 1,633 F7
04764 Oxbow○ 84 G3
04270 Oxford○ 3,143 B7
04354 Palermo○ 760 E7
04965 Palmyra○ 1,485 E6
04271 Paris○ 4,168 B7
†04443 Parkman○ 621 D5
04475 Passadumkeag○ 430 F5
04765 Patten○ 1,368 F4
04765 Patten 1,057 F4
04558 Pemaquid 200 E8
04666 Pembroke○ 920 J6
04476 Penobscot○ 1,104 F7
04766 Perham○ 437 G2
04667 Perry○ 737 J6
04272 Peru○ 1,564 C6
04966 Phillips○ 1,092 C6
04562 Phippsburg○ 1,527 D8
04967 Pittsfield○ 4,125 E6
04967 Pittsfield 3,117 E6
†04345 Pittston○ 2,267 D7
†04767 Plaisted 125 F1
†04925 Pleasant Pond 18 D5
04969 Plymouth○ 811 E6
04273 Poland○ 3,578 C7
04562 Popham Beach 40 D8
04768 Portage○ 562 G2
04855 Port Clyde 400 E8
04068 Porter○ 1,222 B8
*04101 Portland⊙ 61,572 C8
Portland‡ 183,625 C8
04069 Pownal○ 1,189 C8
†04487 Prentiss○ 205 G5
04769 Presque Isle 11,172 H2
04668 Princeton○ 994 H5
†04981 Prospect○ 511 F6
04669 Prospect Harbor 445 H7
04770 Quimby 50 F2
†04345 Randolph○ 1,834 D7
04970 Rangeley○ 1,023 B6
04071 Raymond○ 2,251 B8
04355 Readfield○ 1,943 D7
04357 Richmond○ 2,627 D7
04357 Richmond 1,578 D7
†04262 Riley 50 C6
†04930 Ripley○ 439 E5
04671 Robbinston○ 492 J5
†04734 Robinsons 160 H3
04841 Rockland⊙ 7,919 E7
04856 Rockport○ 2,749 F7
04478 Rockwood 265 D4
†04957 Rome○ 627 D6
†04654 Roque Bluffs○ 244 H6
04564 Round Pond 400 E8
04275 Roxbury○ 373 B6
04276 Rumford○ 8,240 B6
04276 Rumford 6,256 B6
04279 Rumford Point 320 B6
04280 Sabattus○ 3,081 C7
04280 Sabattus 1,234 C7
04072 Saco 12,921 C8
04772 Saint Agatha○ 1,035 G1
04971 Saint Albans○ 1,400 E6
04773 Saint David 915 G1
04774 Saint Francis○ 839 E1
04857 Saint George○ 1,948 E7
†04743 Saint John○ 322 F1
†04983 Salem 125 C6
†04009 Sandy Creek 132 B7
04972 Sandy Point 350 F7
04073 Sanford○ 18,020 B9
04073 Sanford 10,268 B9
04479 Sangerville○ 1,219 E5
†04417 Saponac 8 G5
04074 Scarborough○ 11,347 C8
04074 Scarborough 2,280 C8
04674 Seal Cove 215 G7
04675 Seal Harbor 500 G7
04973 Searsmont○ 782 E7
04974 Searsport○ 2,309 F7
04974 Searsport 1,348 F7
04075 Sebago Lake 800 B8
04481 Sebec○ 469 E5
04484 Seboeis○ 53 F5
†04478 Seboomook 3 D4
04676 Sedgwick○ 795 F7
04076 Shapleigh○ 1,370 B8
04975 Shawmut 500 D6
04775 Sheridan 300 F2
†04777 Sherman○ 1,021 G4
04777 Sherman Station 650 F4
04485 Shirley Mills○ 242 D5
†04330 Sidney○ 2,052 D7
04779 Sinclair 264 G1
04976 Skowhegan○ 8,098 D6
04976 Skowhegan⊙ 6,517 D6
04567 Small Point 22 D8
04978 Smithfield○ 748 D6
04780 Smyrna Mills○ 354 G3
04979 Solon○ 827 D6
†04341 Somerville○ 377 D7
†04660 Somesville (Mount Desert) 150 G7
04677 Sorrento○ 276 G7
03908 South Berwick○ 4,046 B9
†04009 South Bridgton 373 B8
04568 South Bristol○ 800 D8
04077 South Casco 750 B8
†03903 South Eliot 1,681 B9
†04928 South Exeter 100 E6
04080 South Hiram 350 B8
†04862 South Hope 200 E7
†04453 South La Grange 150 F5
†04259 South Monmouth 400 C7
04281 South Paris⊙ 2,128 C7
†04538 Southport○ 598 D8
04106 South Portland 22,712 C8
04858 South Thomaston○ 1,064 E7
†04864 South Union 50 E7
04081 South Waterford 300 B7
04679 Southwest Harbor○ 1,855 G7
04679 Southwest Harbor 1,052 G7
04082 South Windham (Little Falls-South Windham) 1,366 C8
04487 Springfield○ 443 G5
04083 Springvale 2,940 B9
04782 Stacyville○ 554 F4
04084 Standish○ 5,946 B8
†04980 Starks○ 440 D6
04488 Stetson○ 618 E6
04680 Steuben○ 970 H6
04489 Stillwater 700 F6
04783 Stockholm○ 319 G1
04981 Stockton Springs○ 1,230 F7
04681 Stonington○ 1,273 F7
†04058 Stow○ 186 A7
04982 Stratton 600 B5
04983 Strong○ 1,506 C6
†04689 Sullivan○ 967 G6
†04292 Sumner○ 613 C7
04232 Sumner-East Sumner C7
04683 Sunset 165 F7
†04627 Sunshine 100 G7
04684 Surry○ 894 F7
04685 Swans Island○ 337 G7
†04915 Swanville○ 873 E6
†04040 Sweden○ 163 B7
04984 Temple○ 518 C6
04860 Tenants Harbor 900 E8
04861 Thomaston○ 2,900 E7
04861 Thomaston 2,348 E7
04986 Thorndike○ 603 E6
04490 Topsfield○ 240 H5
04086 Topsham○ 6,431 D8
04086 Topsham 4,657 D8
†04653 Tremont○ 1,222 G7
†04605 Trenton○ 718 G7
04571 Trevett 400 D8
04987 Troy○ 701 E6
04282 Turner○ 3,539 C7
04862 Union○ 1,569 E7
04988 Unity○ 1,431 E6
†04293 Upper Dam 2 B6
04784 Upper Frenchville 405 G1
04261 Upton○ 65 B6
04785 Van Buren○ 3,557 G1
04785 Van Buren 3,282 G1
04491 Vanceboro○ 256 J4
04989 Vassalboro○ 3,410 D7
04401 Veazie○ 1,610 F6
04360 Vienna○ 454 D6
04863 Vinalhaven○ 1,211 F7
04492 Waite○ 130 H5
†04915 Waldo○ 495 E7
04572 Waldoboro○ 3,985 E7
04572 Waldoboro 1,195 E7
†04605 Waltham○ 186 G6
04864 Warren○ 2,566 E7
04786 Washburn○ 2,028 G2
04786 Washburn 1,221 G2
04574 Washington○ 954 E7
04087 Waterboro○ 2,943 B8
04088 Waterford○ 951 B7
04901 Waterville 17,779 D6
04284 Wayne○ 680 D7
04285 Weld○ 435 C6
04990 Wellington○ 287 D5
04090 Wells○ 8,211 B9
04686 Wesley○ 140 H6
†04530 West Bath○ 1,309 D8
04092 Westbrook 14,976 C8
04493 West Enfield 609 F5
04787 Westfield○ 647 G2
04985 West Forks○ 72 D5
†04649 West Jonesport 400 H6
04094 West Kennebunk 750 B9
†04938 West Mills 75 C6
04288 West Minot 400 C7
04095 West Newfield 300 B8
04424 Weston○ 155 H4
04289 West Paris○ 1,390 B7
04290 West Peru 700 C7
04291 West Poland 250 C7
04074 West Scarborough 500 C8
04690 West Tremont 250 G7
04362 Whitefield○ 1,606 D7
04691 Whiting○ 335 J6
04692 Whitneyville○ 264 H6
†04443 Willimantic○ 164 E5
04293 Wilsons Mills 50 B6
04294 Wilton○ 4,382 C6
04294 Wilton 2,262 C6
04363 Windsor○ 1,702 D7
04495 Winn○ 503 G5
†04901 Winslow○ 8,057 D6
†04901 Winslow 5,903 D6
04693 Winter Harbor○ 1,120 G7
04496 Winterport○ 2,675 F6
04496 Winterport 1,126 F6
04788 Winterville○ 235 F2
04364 Winthrop○ 5,889 C7
04364 Winthrop 3,264 C7
04578 Wiscasset○ 2,832 D7
04694 Woodland○ 1,363 H5
04579 Woolwich○ 2,156 D8
04497 Wytopitlock 130 G4
04096 Yarmouth○ 6,585 C8
04096 Yarmouth 2,981 C8
03909 York○ 8,465 B9
03909 York 4,530 B9
03910 York Beach 900 B9
03911 York Harbor 950 B9

OTHER FEATURES

Abraham (mt.) C5
Acadia Nat'l Park G7
Allagash (lake) D3
Allagash (riv.) E2
Androscoggin (riv.) C7
Aroostook (riv.) G2
Attean (pond) C4
Baker (lake) D3
Baskahegan (lake) H5
Bear (riv.) B6
Big (brook) E2
Big (lake) H5
Big Black (riv.) D2
Bigelow (bight) C9
Big Spencer (mt.) E4
Black (pond) D3
Blue (mt.) C6
Blue Hill (bay) G7
Bog (lake) H6
Brassua (lake) D4
Casco (bay) C8
Cathance (lake) J6
Caucomgomoc (lake) D3
Center (pond) E5
Chamberlain (lake) E3
Chemquasabamticook (lake) D3
Chesuncook (lake) E3
Chiputneticook (lakes) H4
Clayton (lake) D2
Clifford (lake) H5
Cold Stream (pond) G5
Crawford (lake) H5
Cross (isl.) J6
Cross (lake) G1
Cupsuptic (riv.) B5
Dead (riv.) C5
Deer (isl.) F7
Duck (isls.) G7
Eagle (lake) E3
Eagle (lake) F1
East Machias (riv.) H6
East Musquash (lake) H5
Elizabeth (cape) C8
Ellis (pond) B6
Ellis (riv.) B6
Embden (pond) D6
Endless (lake) F5
Englishman (bay) J6
Eskutassis (pond) G5
Fifth (lake) H5
Fish (riv.) F2
Fish River (lake) F2
Flagstaff (lake) C5
Fourth (lake) H5
Frenchman (bay) G7
Gardner (lake) J6
Georges (isls.) E8
Graham (lake) G6
Grand (lake) H4
Grand Falls (lake) H5
Grand Lake Seboeis (lake) F3
Grand Manan (chan.) K6
Great Moose (lake) D6
Great Wass (isl.) J7
Green (isl.) F8
Harrington (lake) E4
Haut (isl.) G7
Indian Pond (lake) D4
Islesboro (isl.) F7
Jo-Mary (lakes) E4
Katahdin (mt.) F4
Kennebec (riv.) D7
Kezar (lake) B7
Kezar (pond) B7
Kingsbury (pond) D5
Little Black (riv.) E1
Little Madawaska (riv.) G2
Lobster (lake) E4
Long (lake) B7
Long (lake) E2
Long (lake) G1
Long (pond) C4
Long (pond) D6
Long (pond) E5
Long Falls (dam) C5
Longfellow (mts.) B6
Loon (lake) E3
Loring A.F.B. 6,572 H2
Lower Roach (pond) E4
Lower Sysladobsis (lake) G5
Machias (bay) J6
Machias (riv.) F2
Machias (riv.) H6
Machias Seal (isl.) J7
Madagascal (pond) G5
Marshall (isl.) G7
Matinicus Rock (isl.) F8
Mattamiscontis (lake) F4
Mattawamkeag (lake) G4
Mattawamkeag (riv.) G4
Meddybemps (lake) J5
Metinic (isl.) E8
Millinocket (lake) F4
Millinocket (lake) F3
Molunkus (lake) G4
Monhegan (isl.) E8
Moose (pond) B7
Moose (riv.) D4
Moosehead (lake) D4
Mooseleuk (stream) F2
Mooselookmeguntic (lake) B6
Mopang (lake) H6
Mount Desert (isl.) G7
Mount Desert Rock (isl.) G8
Moxie (lake) D5
Munsungan (lake) E3
Muscongus (bay) E8
Musquacook (lakes) E2
Nahmakanta (lake) E4
Nicatous (lake) G5
Nollesemic (lake) F4
Old (stream) H6
Onawa (lake) E5
Parlin (pond) C4
Parmachenee (lake) B5
Passamaquoddy (bay) J5
Passamaquoddy Ind. Res. J6
Pemadumcook (lake) E4
Penobscot (bay) F7
Penobscot (lake) C4
Penobscot (riv.) F5
Penobscot Ind. Res. F6
Pierce (pond) C5
Piscataqua (riv.) B9
Piscataquis (riv.) E5
Pleasant (lake) E3
Pleasant (lake) G3
Pleasant (lake) H5
Pleasant (riv.) H6
Pocomoonshine (lake) H5
Portage (lake) F2
Presque Isle A.F.B. G2
Priestly (lake) E2
Pushaw (lake) F6
Ragged (isl.) F8
Ragged (lake) E4
Rainbow (lake) E4
Rangeley (lake) B6
Richardson (lakes) B6
Rocky (lake) J6
Round (pond) E2
Rowe (lake) F2
Saco (riv.) B8
Saint Croix (riv.) J5
Saint Croix Isl. Nat'l Mon. J5
Saint Francis (riv.) E1
Saint Froid (lake) F2
Saint John (pond) D3
Saint John (riv.) G1
Salmon Falls (riv.) B9
Sandy (riv.) C6
Schoodic (lake) F5
Scraggly (lake) F3
Scraggly (lake) H5
Seal (isl.) F8
Sebago (lake) B8
Sebasticook (lake) E6
Seboeis (lake) F5
Seboeis (riv.) F3
Seboomook (lake) D4
Shallow (lake) E3
Small (cape) D8
Sourdnahunk (lake) F3
Spencer (pond) D4
Spencer (stream) C5
Spider (lake) E3
Squa Pan (lake) G2
Square (lake) G1
Sunday (riv.) B6
Swift (riv.) B6
Sysladobsis, Lower (lake) G5
Third (lake) H5
Twin (lakes) F4
Umbagog (lake) A6
Umcalcus (lake) G3
Umsaskis (lake) E2
Union, West Branch (riv.) G6
Vinalhaven (isl.) F7
Wassataquoik (stream) F4
Webb (lake) C6
Webster (brook) E3
West Grand (lake) H5
West Musquash (lake) H5
West Quoddy (head) K6
Wilson E5
Winnecook (lake) E6
Wooden Ball (isl.) F8
Wyman (lake) C5
Wytopitlock (lake) G4

⊙County seat.
‡Population of metropolitan area.
○Population of town or township.
† Zip of nearest p.o.
* Multiple zips.

Topography

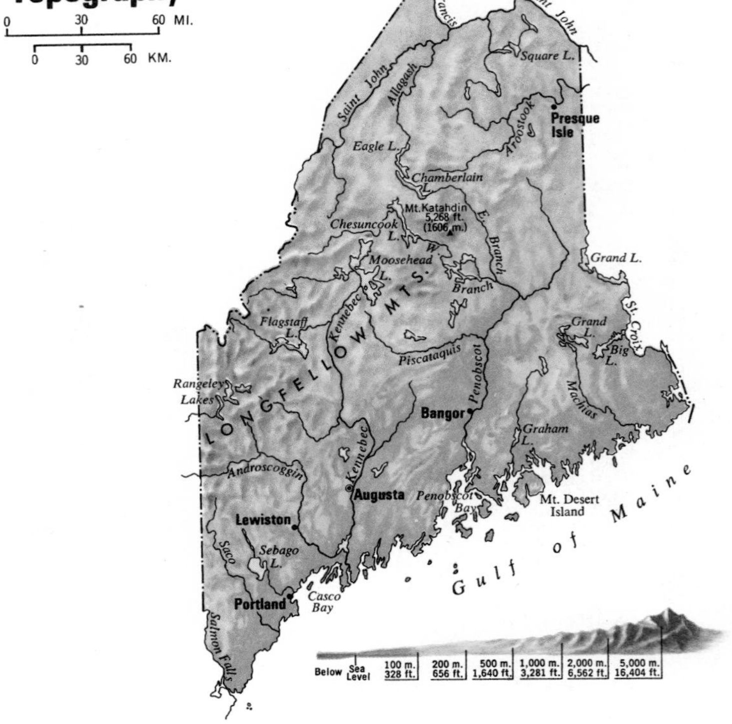
0 30 60 MI.
0 30 60 KM.
St. Francis
Saint John
Square L.
Saint John
Allagash
Presque Isle
Aroostook
Eagle L.
Chamberlain
Mt. Katahdin 5,268 ft. (1606 m.)
Chesuncook L.
E. Branch
W. Branch
Moosehead L.
Grand L.
St. Croix
Flagstaff L.
Kennebec
LONGFELLOW MTS.
Grand L.
Big L.
Piscataquis
Penobscot
Rangeley Lakes
Machias
Bangor
Graham L.
Androscoggin
Kennebec
Augusta
Penobscot Bay
Mt. Desert Island
Lewiston
Saco
Sebago L.
Portland
Casco Bay
Gulf of Maine
Salmon Falls
Below Sea Level
100 m. 328 ft.
200 m. 656 ft.
500 m. 1,640 ft.
1,000 m. 3,281 ft.
2,000 m. 6,562 ft.
5,000 m. 16,404 ft.

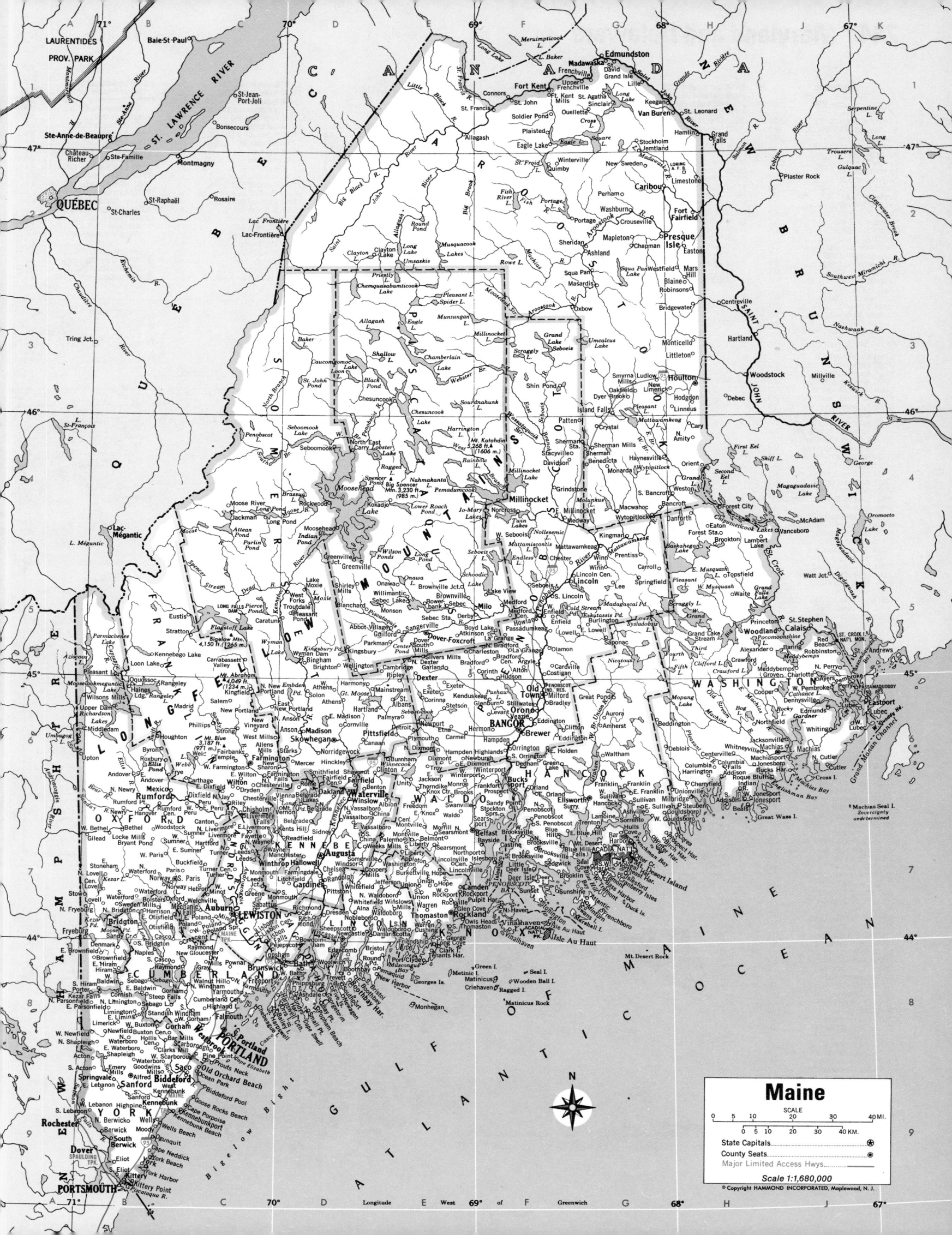

Maine

SCALE
0 5 10   20   30   40 MI.
0 5 10   20   30   40 KM.

State Capitals........................⊛
County Seats..........................◉
Major Limited Access Hwys...........

Scale 1:1,680,000

© Copyright HAMMOND INCORPORATED, Maplewood, N.J.

MARYLAND

COUNTIES

CITIES and TOWNS

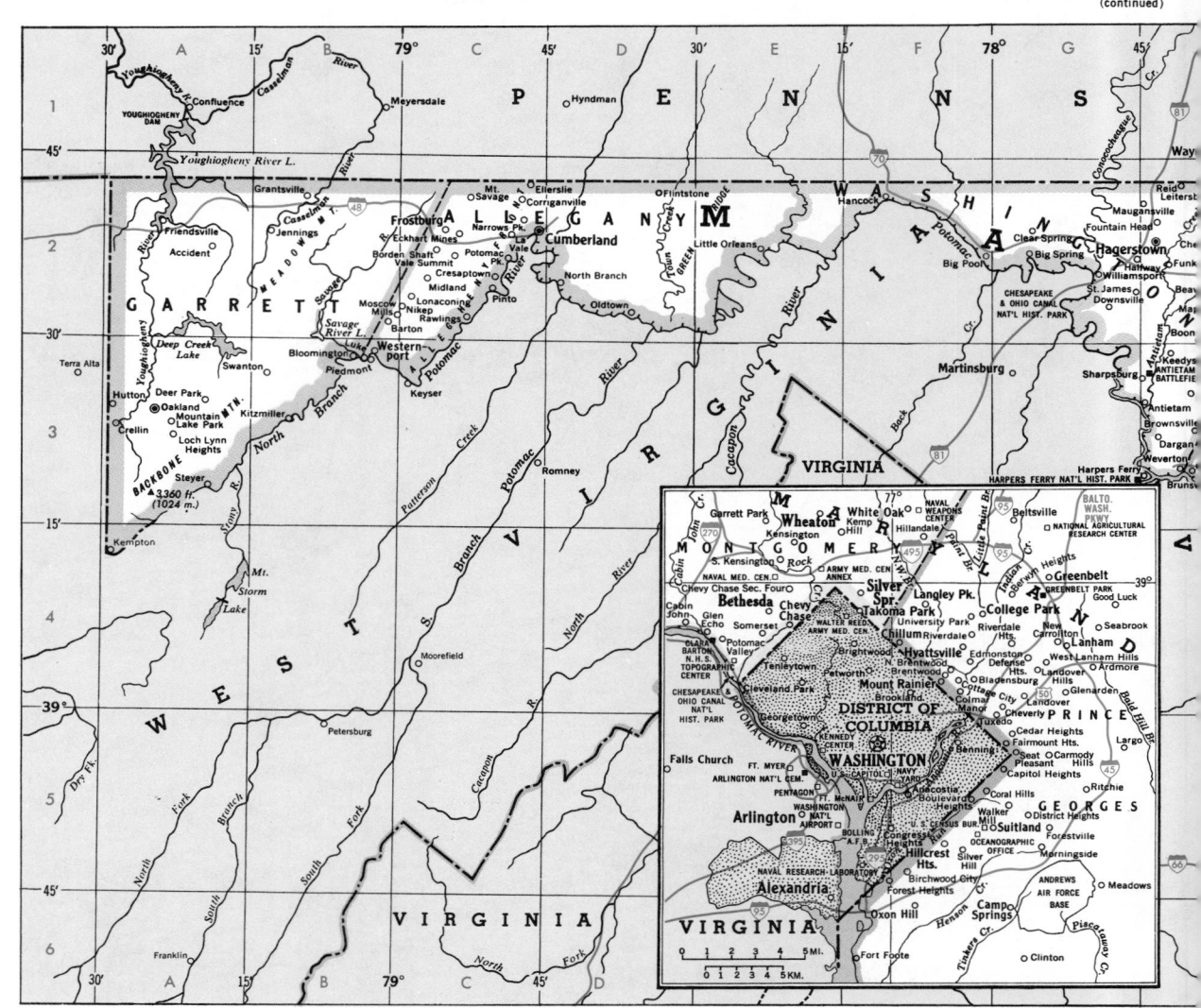

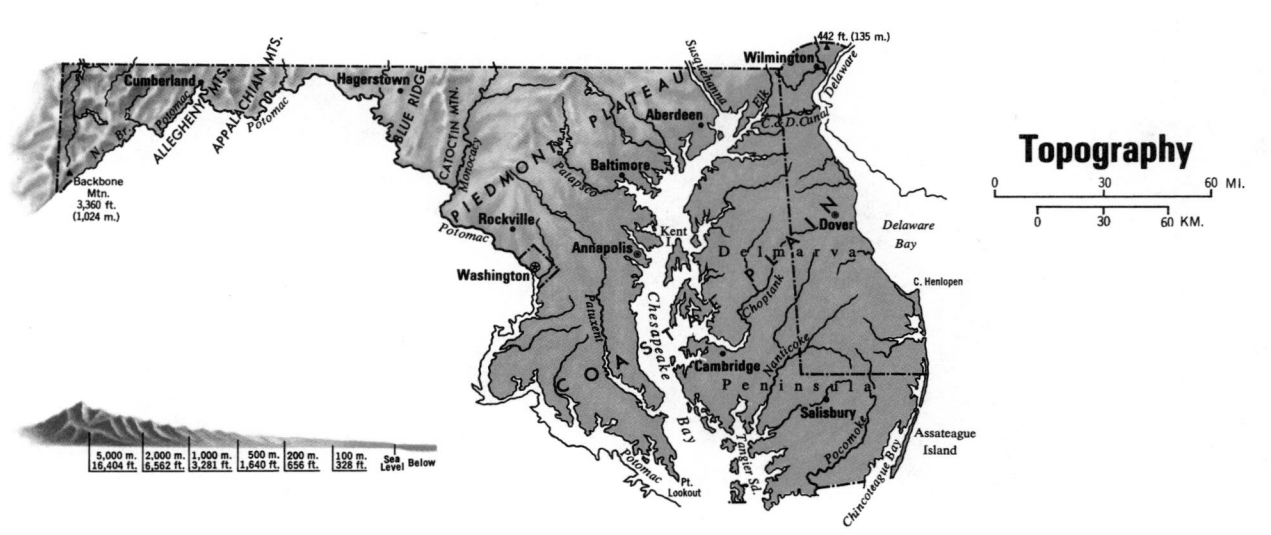

Topography

0   30   60 MI.

0   30   60 KM.

5,000 m. 2,000 m. 1,000 m. 500 m. 200 m. 100 m. Sea
16,404 ft. 6,562 ft. 3,281 ft. 1,640 ft. 656 ft. 328 ft. Level Below

MARYLAND

AREA 10,460 sq. mi. (27,091 sq. km.)
POPULATION 4,216,975
CAPITAL Annapolis
LARGEST CITY Baltimore
HIGHEST POINT Backbone Mtn. 3,360 ft. (1024 m.)
SETTLED IN 1634
ADMITTED TO UNION April 28, 1788
POPULAR NAME Old Line State; Free State
STATE FLOWER Black-eyed Susan
STATE BIRD Baltimore Oriole

DELAWARE

AREA 2,044 sq. mi. (5,294 sq. km.)
POPULATION 594,317
CAPITAL Dover
LARGEST CITY Wilmington
HIGHEST POINT Ebright Road 442 ft. (135 m.)
SETTLED IN 1627
ADMITTED TO UNION December 7, 1787
POPULAR NAME First State; Diamond State
STATE FLOWER Peach Blossom
STATE BIRD Blue Hen Chicken

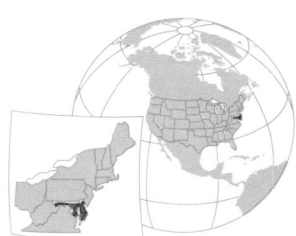

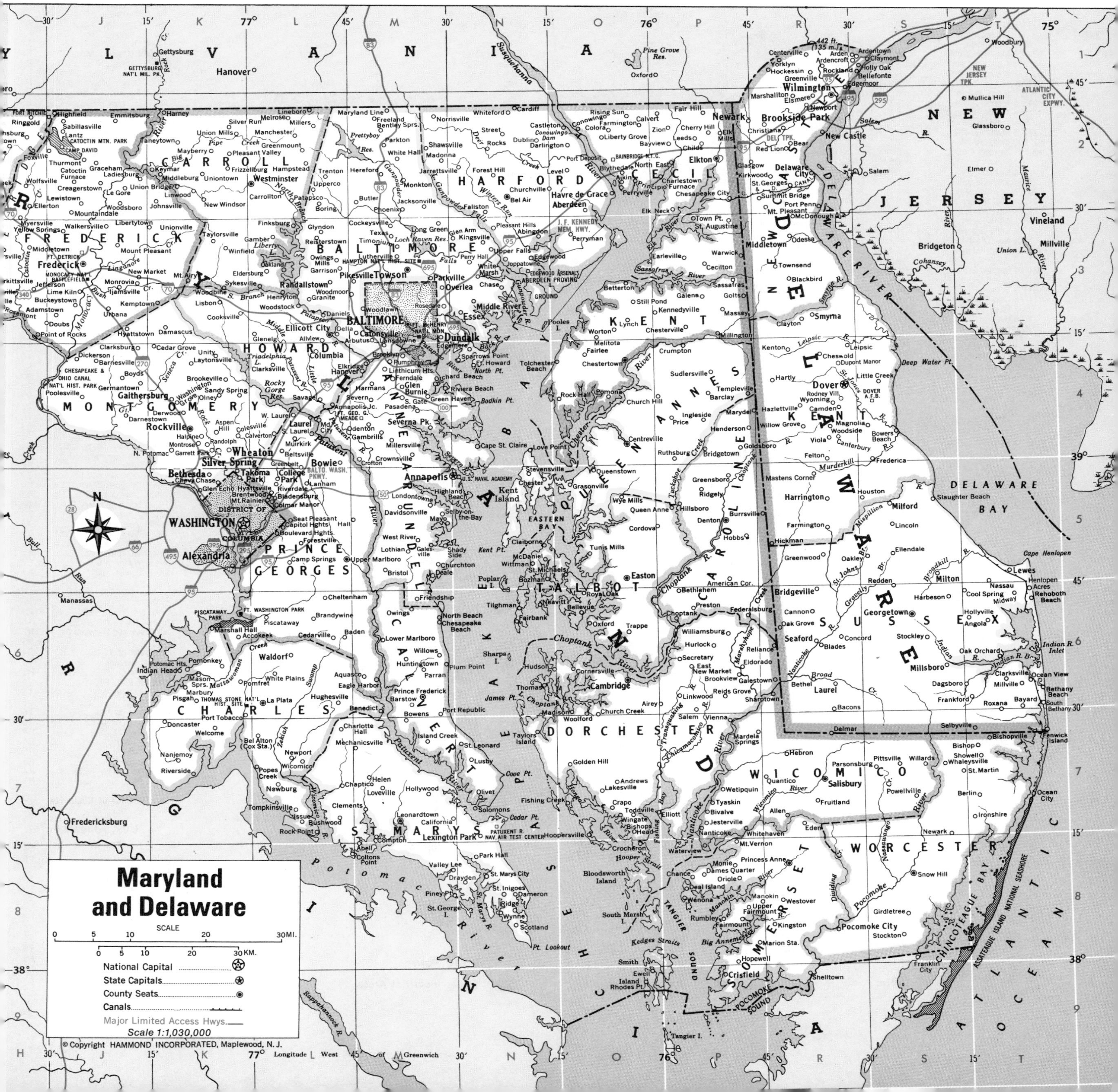

Maryland and Delaware

SCALE

0 5 10 20 30 MI.
0 5 10 20 30 KM.

National Capital .... ★
State Capitals .... ⊛
County Seats .... ⊙
Canals ....
Major Limited Access Hwys. ......
Scale 1:1,030,000

© Copyright HAMMOND INCORPORATED, Maplewood, N.J.

(continued)

21701 Lewistown 600 .... J2
20653 Lexington Park 10,361 ..... M7
21762 Libertytown 400 .... J3
21090 Linthicum Heights 7,457 .. M4
21766 Little Orleans 600 .... E2
†21550 Loch Lynn Heights 503 ..... A3
21539 Lonaconing 1,420 .... C2
†21035 Londontowne 6,052 .... M4
21092 Long Green 1,626 .... M3
20656 Loveville 600 .... M7
21540 Luke 329 .... B3
21093 Lutherville-Timonium
16,871 .... M3
21648 Madison 350 .... O6
21102 Manchester 1,830 .... L2
20658 Marbury 1,189 .... K6
21837 Mardela Springs 320 .... P7
21838 Marion Station 400 .... R8
†20616 Marshall Hall 325 .... K6
21649 Marydel 152 .... P4
†21113 Maryland City 6,949 .... L4
21767 Maugansville 1,707 .... H2
21106 Mayo 2,795 .... M5
20659 Mechanicsville 784 .... M7
21220 Middle River 26,756 .... N3
21769 Middletown 1,748 .... J3
21542 Midland 601 .... C2
21108 Millersville 380 .... M4
21651 Millington 546 .... P3
†20028 Morningside 1,395 .... G5
†21701 Mountaindale 400 .... J2
21550 Mountain Lake Park 1,597 . A3
21771 Mount Airy 2,450 .... K3
†21701 Mount Pleasant 400 .... J3
20822 Mount Rainier 7,361 .... F4
21545 Mount Savage 1,640 .... C2
†21853 Mount Vernon 900 .... P8
†20705 Muirkirk 950 .... L4
21773 Myersville 432 .... H3
21840 Nanticoke 450 .... P7
†21502 Narrows Park-La
Vale 5,523 .... C2
21841 Newark 900 .... S7
20664 Newburg 550 .... L7
20784 New Carrollton 12,632 ...... G4
21774 New Market 306 .... J3
21776 New Windsor 799 .... K2
20831 North Beach 1,504 .... N6
†20722 North Brentwood 580 .... F4
21901 North East 1,469 .... P2
†20854 North Potomac K4
21550 Oakland⊙ 1,994 .... A3
†21784 Oakland 2,242 .... L3
21842 Ocean City 4,946 .... T7
21113 Odenton 13,270 .... M4
†21228 Oella 600 .... L3
20832 Olney 13,026 .... K4
21206 Overlea 12,965 .... N3
20836 Owings 700 .... M6
21117 Owings Mills 9,526 .... L3
21654 Oxford 754 .... O6
20745 Oxon Hill 36,267 .... F6
20667 Park Hall 775 .... N8
21234 Parkville 35,159 .... M3
21122 Pasadena 7,439 .... M4
21128 Perry Hall 13,455 .... N3
21130 Perryman 1,819 .... O3
21903 Perryville 2,018 .... O2
21208 Pikesville 22,555 .... M3
20674 Piney Point 950 .... M8
†20735 Piscataway 500 .... L6
20640 Pisgah 650 .... K6
21850 Pittsville 519 .... S7
†21087 Pleasant Hills 2,790 .... N3
21851 Pocomoke City 3,558 .... R8
20675 Pomfret 600 .... L6
†20640 Pomonkey 410 .... K6
20837 Poolesville 3,428 .... J4
21904 Port Deposit 664 .... O2
20677 Port Tobacco 40 .... K6
20640 Potomac Heights 2,456 .... K6
†21502 Potomac Park-Bowling
Green 2,275 .... C2
21852 Powellville 400 .... S7
21655 Preston 498 .... P6
20678 Prince Frederick⊙ 1,805 .. M6
21853 Princess Anne⊙ 1,499 ..... P8
†21090 Pumphrey 5,666 .... M4
21657 Queen Anne 259 .... O5
21658 Queenstown 491 .... O5
21133 Randallstown 25,927 .... L3
21557 Rawlings 500 .... C2
21136 Reisterstown 19,385 .... L3
20680 Ridge 550 .... N8
21660 Ridgely 933 .... P5
21911 Rising Sun 1,160 .... O2
†20027 Ritchie 950 .... G5
†20840 Riverdale Heights G4
†21061 Riviera Beach 8,812 .... N4
21661 Rock Hall 1,511 .... O4
†21084 Rocks 450 .... N2
*20850 Rockville⊙ 43,811 .... K4
21779 Rohrersville 525 .... H3
21237 Rosedale 19,956 .... M3
†21758 Rosemont 305 .... H3
21662 Royal Oak 600 .... O6
21780 Sabillasville 450 .... J2
20684 Saint Inigoes 750 .... N8
21663 Saint Michaels 1,301 .... N5
21801 Salisbury⊙ 16,429 .... R7
20860 Sandy Spring-Ashton 2,659 K4
20863 Savage-Guilford 2,928 ...... L4
20687 Scotland 475 .... N8
20801 Seabrook-Lanham 15,814 .. G4
20027 Seat Pleasant 5,217 .... G5
21664 Secretary 487 .... P6
†21037 Selby-on-the-Bay 3,125 ..... N5
21144 Severn 20,147 .... M4
21146 Severna Park 21,253 .... M4
20867 Shady Side 2,877 .... M5
21782 Sharpsburg 721 .... G3
21861 Sharptown 654 .... R6
20023 Silver
Hill-Suitland 32,164 ...... F5
†21157 Silver Run 350 .... K2
*20901 Silver Spring 72,893 .... F4
21783 Smithsburg 833 .... H2
21863 Snow Hill⊙ 2,192 .... S8
†20015 Somerset 1,101 .... E4
†21113 South Gate 24,185 .... M4
†20795 South Kensington 9,344 .... E4
†20810 South Laurel 18,034 .... L4
21219 Sparrows Point N4
21666 Stevensville 500 .... N5
21667 Still Pond 350 .... O3
21864 Stockton 400 .... S8
21668 Sudlersville 443 .... P4
†20746 Suitland-Silver
Hill 32,164 .... F5
21784 Sykesville 1,712 .... K3
20912 Takoma Park 16,231 .... F4
21787 Taneytown 2,618 .... K2
21669 Taylors Island 400 .... N7
21670 Templeville 96 .... P4
21788 Thurmont 2,934 .... J2
21671 Tilghman 979 .... N6
21093 Timonium-Lutherville
16,871 .... M3
21672 Toddville 500 .... O7
21204 Towson⊙ 51,083 .... M3
21673 Trappe 739 .... O6
†20780 Tuxedo 500 .... G5
21791 Union Bridge 927 .... K2
†20740 University Park 2,536 .... F4
21155 Upperco 500 .... L2
21867 Upper Fairmount 500 .... P8
21156 Upper Falls 550 .... N3
20870 Upper Marlboro⊙ 828 ..... M5
20692 Valley Lee 600 .... M8
21869 Vienna 300 .... P7
20601 Waldorf 9,782 .... L6
†20023 Walker Mill 10,651 .... F5
21793 Walkersville 2,212 .... J3
21912 Warwick 550 .... P3
20880 Washington Grove 527 ..... K4
20693 Welcome 438 .... K7
21562 Westernport 2,706 .... B3
†20784 West Lanham Hills 350 ..... G4
21157 Westminster⊙ 8,808 .... L2
21871 Westover 450 .... R8
20902 Wheaton-Glenmont 48,598 E3
21160 Whiteford 500 .... N2
21161 White Hall 360 .... M2
21162 White Marsh 500 .... N3
†20901 White Oak 13,700 .... F3
20695 White Plains 5,167 .... L6
21874 Willards 540 .... S7
21795 Williamsport 2,153 .... G2
21676 Wittman 544 .... N5
21797 Woodbine 872 .... K3
21798 Woodsboro 506 .... J2
21163 Woodstock 700 .... L3
21677 Woolford 330 .... O7
21679 Wye Mills 315 .... O5
†20680 Wynne 450 .... N8
†21701 Yellow Springs 940 .... H3

OTHER FEATURES

Aberdeen Proving Ground 5,722 .... N3
Allegheny Front (mts.) C2
Andrews A.F.B. 10,064 .... G5
Antietam (creek) H2
Antietam Nat'l Battlefield H3
Army Chemical Center O3
Back (riv.) N4
Backbone (mt.) A3
Bainbridge N.T.C. O2
Bald Hill Branch (riv.) G4
Big Annemessex (riv.) P8
Big Pipe (creek) K2
Bloodsworth (isl.) O8
Blue Ridge (mts.) H3
Bodkin (pt.) N4
Bush (creek) J3
Cabin John (creek) E4
Camp David J2
Casselman (riv.) B2
Catoctin (creek) H3
Catoctin Mt. Park J2
Cedar (pt.) N7
Census Bureau F5
Chesapeake (bay) N7
Chesapeake and Delaware
(canal) R2
Chesapeake and Ohio Canal Nat'l Hist.
Park J4
Chester (riv.) O4
Chicamacomico (riv.) P7
Chincoteague (bay) S8
Choptank (riv.) O6
Clara Barton Nat'l Hist. Site E4
Conococheague (creek) G1
Conowingo (dam) O2
Cove (pt.) N7
Deep Creek (lake) A3
Deer (creek) N2
Dividing (creek) R8
Eastern (bay) N5
Elk (riv.) P3
Fishing (bay) O7
Fort Detrick J3
Fort George G. Meade 14,083 .... L4
Fort McHenry Nat'l Mon. M3
Fort Ritchie 1,754 .... H2
Fort Washington Park L6
Great Seneca (creek) J4
Greenbelt Park G4
Green Ridge (mts.) E2
Gunpowder (riv.) N3
Gunpowder Falls (creek) M2
Hampton Nat'l Hist. Site M3
Harpers Ferry Nat'l Hist. Park G3
Henson (creek) F6
Honga (riv.) O7
Hooper (str.) O8
Indian (creek) G4
James (pt.) N6
Kedges (strs) O8
Kent (isl.) N5
Kent (pt.) N5
Liberty (lake) L3
Linganore (creek) J3
Little Choptank (riv.) N6
Little Gunpowder Falls
(creek) M2
Little Paint Branch (riv.) F4
Little Patuxent (riv.) L4
Loch Raven (res.) M3
Lookout (pt.) N8
Manokin (riv.) P8
Marshyhope (creek) P6
Mattawoman (creek) K6
Meadow (mt.) B2
Middle Patuxent (riv.) L3
Monocacy (riv.) J3
Monocacy Nat'l Battlefield J3
Nanticoke (riv.) P7
Nassawango (creek) S8
National Agricultural Research
Center G3
Naval Academy, U.S. 5,367 .... N5
Naval Medical Center E4
Naval Weapons Center F3
North (pt.) N4
Oceanographic Office F5
Oxon Run (riv.) F5
Paint Branch (riv.) F4
Patapsco (riv.) M4
Patuxent (riv.) M7
Patuxent River Nav. Air Test
Ctr. N7
Piscataway (creek) G6
Piscataway Park K6
Pocomoke (riv.) S8
Pocomoke (sound) P9
Pooles (isl.) O3
Poplar (isl.) N5
Potomac (riv.) M8
Prettyboy (res.) M2
Rock (creek) K4
Rocky Gorge (res.) L4
Saint George (isl.) M8
Saint Marys (riv.) N8
Sassafras (riv.) P3
Savage (riv.) B2
Savage River (lake) B2
Severn (riv.) N4
Sharps (isl.) N6
Smith (isl.) O8
South Marsh (isl.) O8
Susquehanna (riv.) N1
Tangier (sound) P8
Thomas Stone Nat'l Hist.
Site K6
Tinkers (creek) F6
Topographic Center E4
Town (creek) E2
Transquaking (riv.) P7
Triadelphia (lake) L4
Tuckahoe (creek) P5
Walter Reed Army Med. Ctr.
Annex E4
Wicomico (riv.) L7
Wicomico (riv.) R7
Winters Run (creek) N2
Youghiogheny (riv.) A3
Youghiogheny River
(lake) A2
Zekiah Swamp (riv.) L7

DELAWARE

COUNTIES

Kent 98,219 .... R4
New Castle 398,115 .... R2
Sussex 97,983 .... S6

CITIES and TOWNS

Zip *Name/Pop.* *Key*

†19801 Arden 516 .... R1
†19810 Ardencroft 267 .... R1
†19810 Ardentown 307 .... S1
19809 Bellefonte 1,279 .... S1
19930 Bethany Beach 330 .... T6
19931 Bethel 197 .... R6
†19973 Blades 664 .... R6
†19962 Bowers Beach 198 .... S4
19993 Bridgeville 1,238 .... R6
19711 Brookside 15,255 .... R2
19934 Camden 1,757 .... R4
†19801 Centerville 800 .... R1
19936 Cheswold 269 .... R4
†19711 Christiana 500 .... R2
19937 Clarksville 350 .... T6
19703 Claymont 10,022 .... S1
19938 Clayton 1,216 .... R3
19930 Dagsboro 344 .... S6
19706 Delaware City 1,858 .... R2
19940 Delmar 948 .... R7
19901 Dover (cap.)⊙ 23,507 ...... R4
†19901 Dupont Manor 1,059 .... R4
†19801 Edgemoor 7,397 .... S1
19941 Ellendale 361 .... S5
†19801 Elsmere 6,493 .... R2
19942 Farmington 141 .... R5
19943 Felton 547 .... R4
19944 Fenwick Island 114 .... T7
19945 Frankford 828 .... S6
19946 Frederica 864 .... S4
19947 Georgetown⊙ 1,710 .... S6
†19711 Glasgow 350 .... R2
19950 Greenwood 578 .... R5
19952 Harrington 2,405 .... R5
†19971 Henlopen Acres 176 .... T6
19707 Hockessin 950 .... R1
†19801 Holly Oak S1
19954 Houston 357 .... S5
19955 Kenton 243 .... R4
19708 Kirkwood 350 .... R2
19956 Laurel 3,052 .... R6
†19901 Leipsic 228 .... S4
19958 Lewes 2,197 .... T5
19960 Lincoln 757 .... S5
19961 Little Creek 230 .... S4
19962 Magnolia 197 .... R4
19709 Middletown 2,946 .... R3
19963 Milford 5,366 .... S5
19966 Millsboro 1,233 .... S6
19967 Millville 178 .... T6
19968 Milton 1,359 .... S5
19711 Newark 25,247 .... P2
19720 New Castle 4,907 .... R2
19804 Newport 1,167 .... R2
†19966 Oak Orchard 350 .... T6
19970 Ocean View 495 .... T6
19730 Odessa 384 .... R3
19971 Rehoboth Beach 1,730 ..... T6
19901 Rodney Village 1,753 .... R4
19733 Saint Georges 450 .... R2
19973 Seaford 5,256 .... R6
19975 Selbyville 1,251 .... S7
†19963 Slaughter Beach 121 .... S5
19977 Smyrna 4,750 .... R3
†19930 South Bethany 115 .... T6
19734 Townsend 386 .... R3
19979 Viola 167 .... R4
*19801 Wilmington⊙ 70,195 .... R2
Wilmington‡ 524,108 .... R2
19980 Woodside 248 .... R4
19934 Wyoming 960 .... R4
19736 Yorklyn 600 .... R1

OTHER FEATURES

Broad (creek) R6
Broadkill (riv.) S5
Chesapeake and Delaware (canal) ... R2
Choptank (riv.) P5
Deep Water (pt.) S4
Delaware (bay) T5
Delaware (riv.) R3
Dover A.F.B. 4,391 .... S4
Henlopen (cape) T5
Indian (riv.) S6
Indian River (bay) T6
Indian River (inlet) T6
Leipsic (riv.) R4
Mispillion (riv.) S5
Murderkill (riv.) R5
Nanticoke (riv.) R6
Saint Jones (riv.) R4
Smyrna (res.) R3

DISTRICT OF COLUMBIA

CITIES and TOWNS

Zip *Name/Pop.* *Key*

20007 Georgetown E5
*20001 Washington, D.C. (cap.),
U.S. 638,432 .... F5
Washington‡ 3,060,240 .... F5

OTHER FEATURES

Anacostia (riv.) F5
Bolling A.F.B. E5
Fort Lesley J. McNair E5
Kennedy Center A5
Naval Yard F5
U.S. Capitol F5
Walter Reed Army Med. Ctr. E4

⊙County seat.
‡Population of metropolitan area.
† Zip of nearest p.o.
* Multiple zips.

Agriculture, Industry and Resources

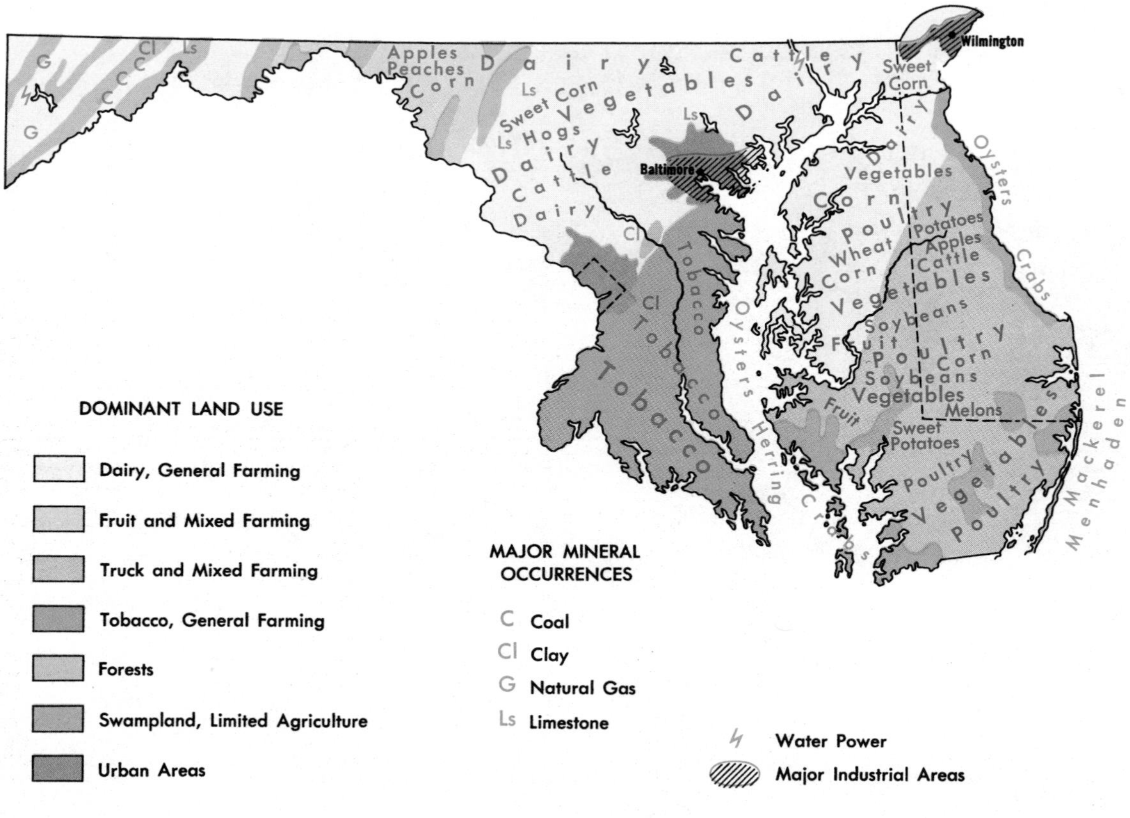
Apples
Peaches
Corn
Dairy
Cattle
Sweet Corn
Vegetables
Hogs
Wilmington
Baltimore
Poultry
Wheat
Potatoes
Apples
Soybeans
Fruit
Tobacco
Oysters
Crabs
Herring
Melons
Sweet Potatoes
Mackerel
Menhaden
DOMINANT LAND USE
Dairy, General Farming
Fruit and Mixed Farming
Truck and Mixed Farming
Tobacco, General Farming
Forests
Swampland, Limited Agriculture
Urban Areas
MAJOR MINERAL OCCURRENCES
C Coal
Cl Clay
G Natural Gas
Ls Limestone
Water Power
Major Industrial Areas

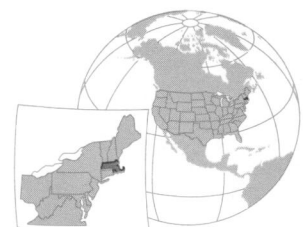

MASSACHUSETTS

AREA 8,284 sq. mi. (21,456 sq. km.)
POPULATION 5,737,037
CAPITAL Boston
LARGEST CITY Boston
HIGHEST POINT Mt. Greylock 3,491 ft. (1064 m.)
SETTLED IN 1620
ADMITTED TO UNION February 6, 1788
POPULAR NAME Bay State; Old Colony
STATE FLOWER Mayflower
STATE BIRD Chickadee

RHODE ISLAND

AREA 1,212 sq. mi. (3,139 sq. km.)
POPULATION 947,154
CAPITAL Providence
LARGEST CITY Providence
HIGHEST POINT Jerimoth Hill 812 ft. (247 m.)
SETTLED IN 1636
ADMITTED TO UNION May 29, 1790
POPULAR NAME Little Rhody; Ocean State
STATE FLOWER Violet
STATE BIRD Rhode Island Red

Agriculture, Industry and Resources

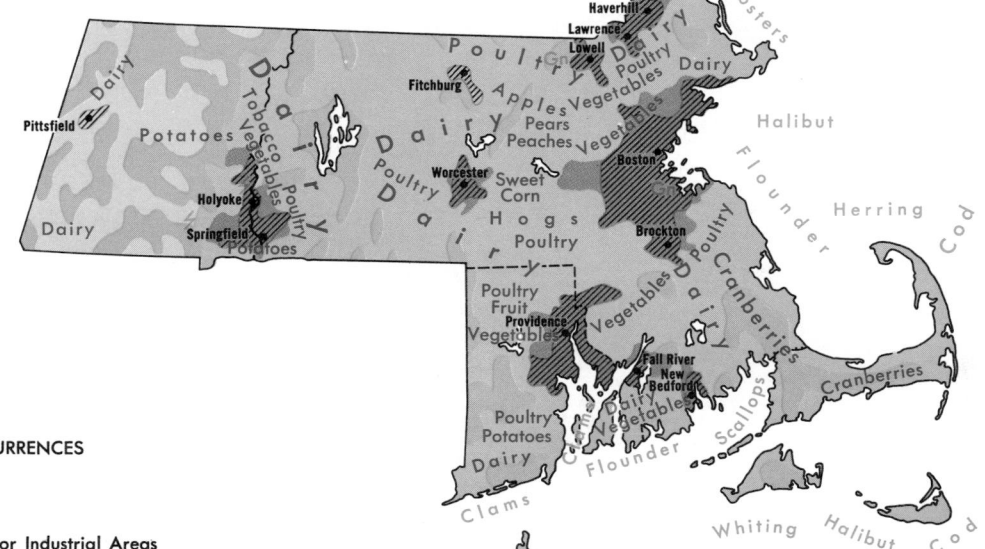

DOMINANT LAND USE

- Specialized Dairy
- Dairy, Poultry, Mixed Farming
- Forests
- Urban Areas

MAJOR MINERAL OCCURRENCES

Gn Granite

⚡ Water Power ▨ Major Industrial Areas

(continued on following page)

01266 West Stockbridge○ 1,280 ...A3
02575 West Tisbury○ 1,010 ......M7
01587 West Upton-Upton 2,184 ...H4
02576 West Wareham 1,837 ......L5
02090 Westwood 13,212 ....B8
02673 West Yarmouth 3,852 ....N6
02188 Weymouth 55,601 ....D8
01093 Whately○ 1,341 ....D3
01588 Whitinsville 5,379 ......H4
02382 Whitman 13,534 ....L4
01095 Wilbraham 12,053 ....E4
01095 Wilbraham 3,379 ....E4
01096 Williamsburg 2,237 ......C3
01267 Williamstown○ 8,741 ....B2
01267 Williamstown 4,798 ......B2
01887 Wilmington 17,471 ......C5
01475 Winchendon 7,019 ....F2
01475 Winchendon 4,030 ....F2
01890 Winchester 20,701 ......C6
01270 Windsor○ 598 ....B2

02152 Winthrop○ 19,294 ....D6
01801 Woburn 36,626 ....C6
02543 Woods Hole 1,080 ....M6
*01601 Worcester⊙ 161,799 ....H3
Worcester‡ 372,940 ...H3
01098 Worthington○ 932 ....C3
02093 Wrenthem 7,580 ....J4
Yarmouth 18,449 .....O6
02675 Yarmouth Port 2,490 ....N6

OTHER FEATURES

Adams Nat'l Hist. Site D7
Agawam (riv.) M5
Allerton (pt.) E7
Ann (cape) M2
Ashmere (lake) B3
Assabet (riv.) H3
Assawompset (pond) L5
Bachelor (brook) D3

Berkshire (hills) B4
Big (pond) B4
Bigelow (bight) M1
Blackstone (riv.) G3
Blue (hills) C8
Boston (bay) E6
Boston (harb.) D7
Boston Nat'l Hist. Park D6
Brewster (isls.) E7
Buel (lake) A4
Buzzards (bay) L7
Cambridge (res.) B6
Cape Cod (bay) N5
Cape Cod (canal) N5
Cape Cod Nat'l Seashore P5
Chappaquiddick (isl.) N7
Charles (riv.) C7
Chicopee (riv.) D4
Cobble Mountain (res.) C4
Cochituate (lake) A7

Cod (cape) O4
Concord (riv.) J2
Congamond (lkes.) D4
Connecticut (riv.) D2
Cuttyhunk (isl.) L7
Deer (isl.) E7
Deerfield (riv.) C2
East (pt.) E6
East Chop (pt.) M7
Eastern (pt.) M2
Elizabeth (isls.) L7
Everett (mt.) A4
Falls (riv.) A4
Fort Devens H2
Fort Rodman L6
Fresh (pond) C6
Gammon (pt.) N6
Gay Head (prom.) L7
Grace (mt.) B2
Great (pt.) O7
Green (riv.) B2
Greylock (mt.) B2
Gurnet (pt.) M4
Hingham (bay) E7
Holyoke (range) D3
Hoosac (mts.) B2
Hoosic (riv.) A1
Housatonic (riv.) A4
Ipswich (riv.) L2
John F. Kennedy Nat'l Hist.
Site C7
Knightville (res.) C3
Laurence G. Hanscom Field ..B6
Little (riv.) C4
Logan Internat'l Airport ...D7
Long (isl.) E7
Long (pt.) O4
Long (pond) L5
Lowell Nat'l Hist. Park J2
Maine (gulf) M2
Manhan (riv.) D4
Manomet (pt.) N5
Marblehead (neck) F6
Martha's Vineyard (isl.) ...M7
Massachusetts (bay) M4
Merrimack (riv.) K1
Mill (riv.) C3
Mill (riv.) D3
Millers (riv.) E2
Minute Man Nat'l Hist. Park .B6
Mishaum (pt.) L6
Monomonac (lake) G2
Monomoy (isl.) O6
Monomoy (pt.) O6
Mount Hope (bay) K6
Muskeget (chan.) N7
Muskeget (isl.) N7
Mystic (lake) C6
Mystic (riv.) C6
Nahant (bay) E6
Nantucket (isl.) O8
Nantucket (sound) N6
Nashawena (isl.) L7
Nashua (riv.) H3
Naushon (isl.) L7
Neponset (riv.) C8
Nomans Land (isl.) L7
Nonamesset (isl.) M6
North (riv.) D2
North (riv.) L4
Onota (lake) A3
Otis (res.) B4

Otis A.F.B. M6
Pasque (isl.) L7
Plum (isl.) L2
Plymouth (bay) M5
Poge (cape) N7
Pontoosuc (lake) A3
Quabbin (res.) E3
Quaboag (riv.) F4
Quincy (bay) D7
Quinebaug (riv.) F4
Race (pt.) N4
Salem Maritime Nat'l Hist.
Site E5
Saugus Iron Works Nat'l Hist.
Site D6
Shawshine (riv.) K2
Silver (lake) L4
South (riv.) D2
Springfield Armory Nat'l Hist.
Site D4
Squibnocket (pt.) M7
Stillwater (riv.) G3
Sudbury (res.) H3
Sudbury (riv.) A6
Swift (riv.) E4
Taconic (mts.) A2
Taunton (riv.) K5
Thompson (isl.) D7
Toby (mt.) E3
Tom (mt.) D4
Tuckernuck (isl.) N7
Vineyard (sound) L7
Wachusett (res.) G3
Wachusett (mt.) G3
Walden (pond) A6
Ware (riv.) F3
Watuppa (pond) K6
Webster (lake) G4
Wellfleet (harb.) O5
West (riv.) H4
West Branch, Farmington
(riv.) B4
West Chop (pt.) M7
Westfield (riv.) C3
Westover A.F.B. D4
Weweantic (riv.) L5
Whitman (riv.) G2
Winter I. Coast Guard Air Sta. .E5

RHODE ISLAND

COUNTIES

Bristol 46,942 ....J6
Kent 154,163 ....H6
Newport 81,383 ....J7
Providence 571,349 ....H5
Washington 93,317 ....H7

CITIES and TOWNS

Zip	Name/Pop.	Key
02804	Ashaway 1,747	G7
02806	Barrington 16,174	J6
02807	Block Island 620	H8
02808	Bradford 1,354	H7
02809	Bristol⊙ 20,128	J6
02863	Central Falls 16,995	J5
02816	Coventry 27,065	H6
02910	Cranston 71,992	J5
02818	East Greenwich⊙ 10,211	H6
02914	East Providence 50,980	J5

02822 Exeter○ 4,453 ....H6
02825 Foster○ 3,370 ....H5
02828 Greenville 7,516 .....H5
02830 Harrisville 1,224 ....H5
02832 Hope Valley 1,414 ....H6
02833 Hopkinton○ 6,406 .....H7
02835 Jamestown○ 4,040 .....J6
02835 Jamestown 2,156 ......J6
02881 Kingston 5,479 ....J7
02837 Little Compton○ 3,085 .K6
02840 Middletown 17,216 ....J6
02882 Narragansett 12,088 ..J7
02882 Narragansett 3,342 ...J7
02840 Newport⊙ 29,259 ......J7
†02807 New Shoreham (Block
Island)○ 620 ....H8
02852 North Kingstown○
21,938 ....J6
02908 North Providence○
29,188 ....J5
02859 Pascoag 3,807 ....H5
*02860 Pawtucket 71,204 ....J5
02883 Peace
Dale-Wakefield 6,474 .J7
02871 Portsmouth○ 14,257 ...J6
*02901 Providence
(cap.)⊙ 156,804 ......H5
Providence-Warwick-
Pawtucket‡ 919,216 ...H5
02878 Tiverton 13,526 .....K6
02878 Tiverton 7,653 ......K6
†02864 Valley Falls 10,892 ..J5
*02879 Wakefield-Peace
Dale 6,474 ....J7
02885 Warren○ 10,640 ......J6
*02886 Warwick 87,123 ......J6
02891 Westerly○ 18,580 ....G7
02891 Westerly⊙ 14,093 ....G7
02893 West Warwick 27,026 ..H6
02895 Woonsocket⊙ 45,914 ...J4

OTHER FEATURES

Black Rock (pt.) H8
Block (isl.) H8
Block Island (sound) H8
Brenton (pt.) J7
Conanicut (isl.) J6
Dickens (pt.) H8
Durfee (hill) G5
Grace (pt.) H8
Jerimoth (hill) G5
Judith (pt.) J7
Mount Hope (bay) K6
Narragansett (bay) J6
Noyes (pt.) H7
Pawcatuck (riv.) G7
Prudence (isl.) J6
Rhode Island (isl.) J6
Rhode Island (sound) J7
Roger Williams Nat'l Mem. ..J5
Sakonnet (pt.) K7
Sakonnet (riv.) K7
Sandy (pt.) H8
Scituate (res.) H5
Stillwater (res.) C2
Touro Synagogue Nat'l Hist.
Site J7
Watch Hill (pt.) G7

○County seat (Shire town).
⊙County seat (Shire town).
‡Population of metropolitan area.
○Population of town or township.
† Zip of nearest p.o.   * Multiple zips.

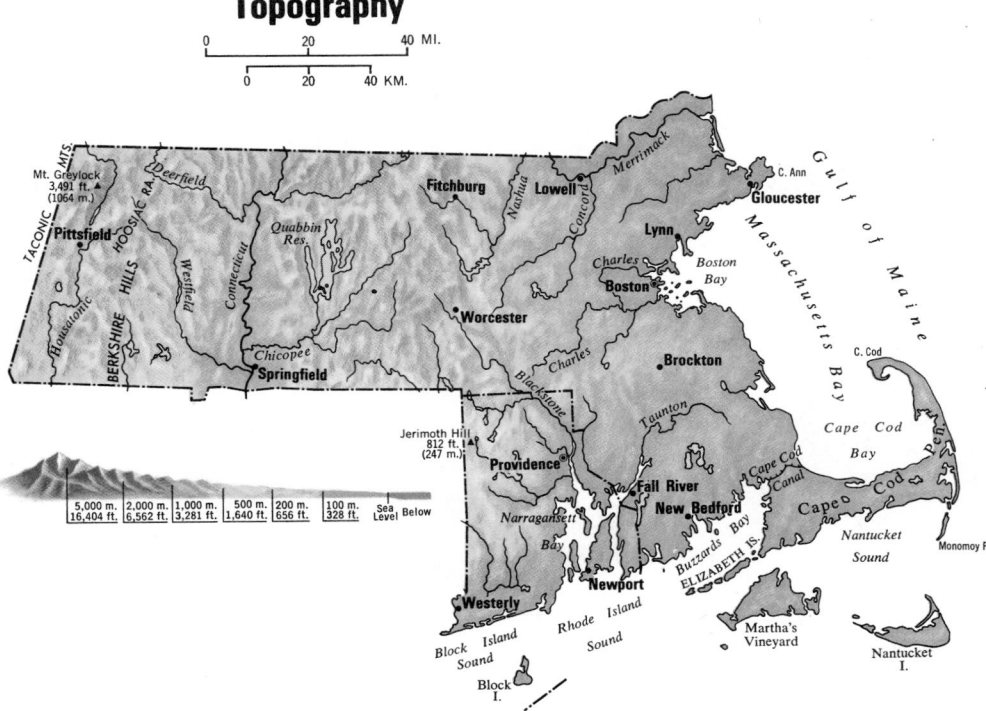

Topography

Michigan

SCALE
0 5 10 20 30 40 50 MI.
0 5 10 20 30 40 50 KM.

State Capitals ⊛
County Seats ⊙
Canals ⊐

Major Limited Access Hwys. ━━━

Scale 1:2,360,000

© Copyright HAMMOND INCORPORATED, Maplewood, N.J.

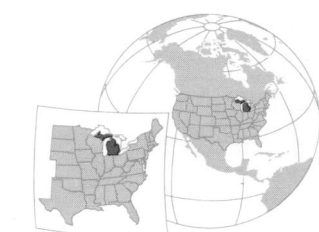

AREA 58,527 sq. mi. (151,585 sq. km.)
POPULATION 9,262,078
CAPITAL Lansing
LARGEST CITY Detroit
HIGHEST POINT Mt. Curwood 1,980 ft. (604 m.)
SETTLED IN 1650
ADMITTED TO UNION January 26, 1837
POPULAR NAME Wolverine State
STATE FLOWER Apple Blossom
STATE BIRD Robin

Topography

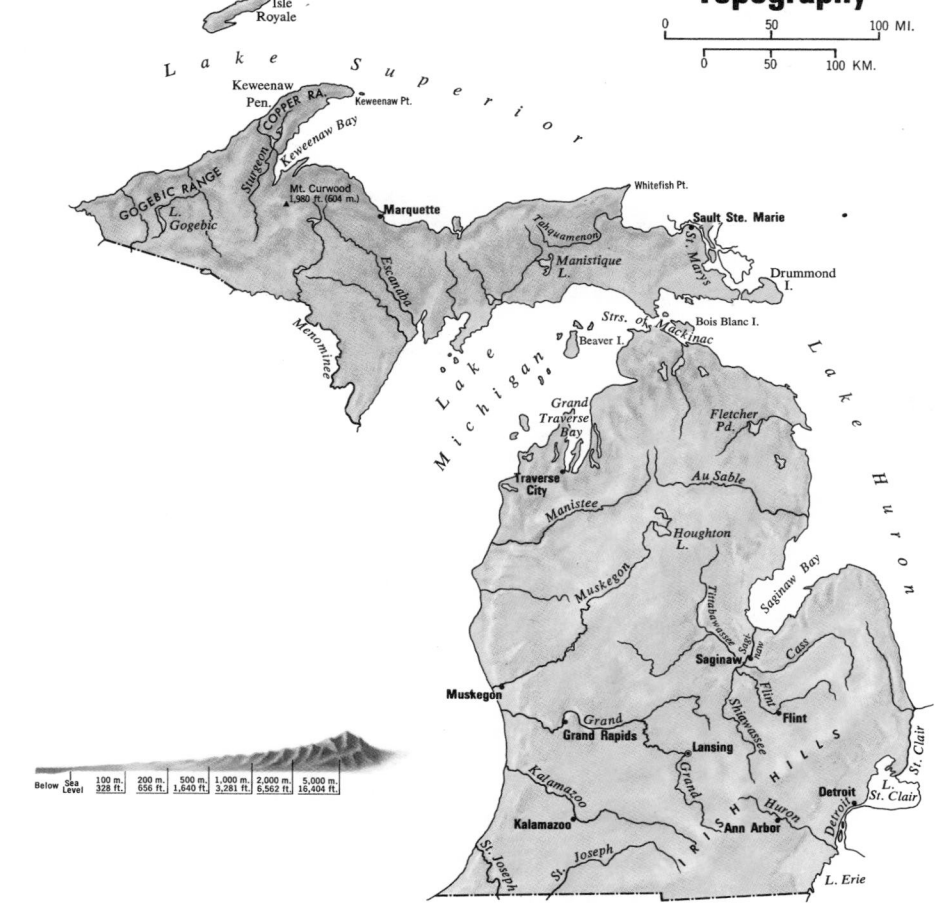

COUNTIES

Alcona 9,740	F4
Alger 9,225	C2
Allegan 81,555	D6
Alpena 32,315	F4
Antrim 16,194	D3
Arenac 14,706	F4
Baraga 8,484	A2
Barry 45,781	D6
Bay 119,881	E5
Benzie 11,205	C4
Berrien 171,276	C7
Branch 40,188	D7
Calhoun 141,557	D6
Cass 49,499	C7
Charlevoix 19,907	D3
Cheboygan 20,649	E3
Chippewa 29,029	E2
Clare 23,822	E5
Clinton 55,893	E6
Crawford 9,465	E4
Delta 38,947	C2
Dickinson 25,341	B2
Eaton 88,337	E6
Emmet 22,992	E3
Genesee 450,449	F5
Gladwin 19,957	E4
Gogebic 19,686	F2
Grand Traverse 54,899	D4
Gratiot 40,448	E5
Hillsdale 42,071	E7
Houghton 37,872	G1
Huron 36,459	F5
Ingham 275,520	E6
Ionia 51,815	D6
Iosco 28,349	F4
Iron 13,635	G2
Isabella 54,110	E5
Jackson 151,495	E6
Kalamazoo 212,378	D6
Kalkaska 10,952	D4
Kent 444,506	D5
Keweenaw 1,963	A1
Lake 7,711	D5
Lapeer 70,038	F5
Leelanau 14,007	D4
Lenawee 89,948	E7
Livingston 100,289	F6
Luce 6,659	D2
Mackinac 10,178	D2
Macomb 694,600	G6
Manistee 23,019	C4
Marquette 74,101	B2
Mason 26,365	C4
Mecosta 36,961	D5
Menominee 26,201	B3
Midland 73,578	E5
Missaukee 10,009	D4
Monroe 134,659	F7
Montcalm 47,555	D5
Montmorency 7,492	E3
Muskegon 157,589	C5
Newaygo 34,917	D5
Oakland 1,011,793	F6
Oceana 22,002	C5
Ogemaw 16,436	E4
Ontonagon 9,861	F1
Osceola 18,928	D5
Oscoda 6,858	E4
Otsego 14,993	E3
Ottawa 157,174	C6
Presque Isle 14,267	F3
Roscommon 16,374	E4
Saginaw 228,059	E5
Saint Clair 138,802	G6
Saint Joseph 56,083	D7
Sanilac 40,789	G5
Schoolcraft 8,575	C2
Shiawassee 71,140	E6
Tuscola 56,961	F5
Van Buren 66,814	C6
Washtenaw 264,748	F6
Wayne 2,337,891	F6
Wexford 25,102	D4

CITIES and TOWNS

Zip	Name/Pop.	Key
49220	Addison 655	E7
49221	Adrian⊙ 21,186	F7
48701	Akron 538	F5
†48763	Alabaster 46	F4
49224	Albion 11,059	E6
48001	Algonac 4,412	G6
49010	Allegan⊙ 4,576	D6
48101	Allen Park 34,196	B7
48801	Alma 9,652	E5
48003	Almont 1,857	F6
49707	Alpena⊙ 12,214	F3
*48103	Ann Arbor⊙ 107,966	F6
	Ann Arbor‡ 264,748	F6
48005	Armada 1,392	G6
48806	Ashley 570	E5
49011	Athens 960	D6
49709	Atlanta⊙ 475	E3
48611	Auburn 1,921	F5
48703	Au Gres 768	F4
49012	Augusta 913	D6
†48750	Au Sable 1,240	F4
48413	Bad Axe⊙ 3,184	G5
49304	Baldwin⊙ 674	D5
48414	Bancroft 618	E6
49013	Bangor 2,001	C6
49908	Baraga 1,055	G1
49101	Baroda 627	C7
*49014	Battle Creek 35,724	D6
	Battle Creek‡ 187,338	D6
48706	Bay City⊙ 41,593	F5
	Bay City‡ 119,881	F5
48612	Beaverton 1,025	E5
†49423	Beechwood 2,333	C6
48809	Belding 5,634	D5
49615	Bellaire⊙ 1,063	D4
48111	Belleville 3,366	F6
49021	Bellevue 1,289	E6
49022	Benton Harbor 14,707	C6
	Benton Harbor‡ 171,276	C6
†49022	Benton Heights 6,787	C6
48072	Berkley 18,637	B6
49103	Berrien Springs 2,042	C7
49911	Bessemer⊙ 2,553	F2
49617	Beulah⊙ 454	C4
†48010	Beverly Hills 11,598	B6
49307	Big Rapids⊙ 14,361	D5
48415	Birch Run 1,196	F5
*48008	Birmingham 21,689	B6
49228	Blissfield 3,107	F7
48013	Bloomfield Hills 3,985	B6
49026	Bloomingdale 537	C6
49712	Boyne City 3,348	E3
48615	Breckenridge 1,495	E5
49106	Bridgman 2,235	C7
48116	Brighton 4,268	F6
49229	Britton 693	F6
49028	Bronson 2,271	D7
49230	Brooklyn 1,110	E6
48416	Brown City 1,163	G5
49107	Buchanan 5,142	C7
49030	Burr Oak 853	D7
48507	Burton 29,976	F6
48418	Byron 689	E6
49601	Cadillac⊙ 10,199	D4
49316	Caledonia 722	D6
49913	Calumet 1,013	A1
48014	Capac 1,377	G5
48117	Carleton 2,786	F6
48723	Caro⊙ 4,317	F5
48724	Carrollton 7,482	E5
48811	Carson City 1,229	E5
48419	Carsonville 622	G5
48725	Caseville 851	F5
49915	Caspian 1,038	G2
48726	Cass City 2,258	F5
49031	Cassopolis⊙ 1,933	C7
49319	Cedar Springs 2,615	D5
49233	Cement City 539	E6
48015	Center Line 9,293	B6
49622	Central Lake 895	D3
49032	Centreville⊙ 1,202	D7
49720	Charlevoix⊙ 3,296	D3
48813	Charlotte⊙ 8,251	E6
49721	Cheboygan⊙ 5,106	E3
48118	Chelsea 3,816	E6
48616	Chesaning 2,656	E5
48617	Clare 3,300	E5
48016	Clarkston 968	F6
48017	Clawson 15,103	B6
49034	Climax 619	D6
49236	Clinton 2,342	F6
48420	Clio 2,669	F5
49036	Coldwater⊙ 9,461	D7
48618	Coleman 1,429	E5
49038	Coloma 1,833	C6
49040	Colon 1,190	D7
48421	Columbiaville 953	F5
49041	Comstock⊙ 11,162	D6
49237	Concord 900	E6
49042	Constantine 1,680	D7
48817	Coopersville 2,889	C5
48822	Corunna⊙ 3,206	E6
48422	Croswell 2,073	G5
49920	Crystal Falls⊙ 1,965	A2
49508	Cutlerville 8,256	D6
48423	Davison 6,087	F5
*48120	Dearborn 90,660	B7
48127	Dearborn Heights 67,706	B7
49045	Decatur 1,915	C6
48427	Deckerville 887	G5
49238	Deerfield 957	F7
49408	Fennville 934	C6
48430	Fenton 8,098	F6
48220	Ferndale 26,227	B6
49409	Ferrysburg 2,440	C5
48134	Flat Rock 6,853	F6
*48501	Flint⊙ 159,611	F5
	Flint‡ 521,589	F5
48433	Flushing 8,624	F5
48835	Fowler 1,021	E5
48836	Fowlerville 2,289	F6
48428	Dryden 650	F6
48131	Dundee 2,575	F7
48429	Durand 4,241	E6
49924	Eagle River⊙ 20	A1
48021	East Detroit 38,280	B6
48023	East Detroit 38,280	B6
†49506	East Grand Rapids 10,914	D6
49412	East Jordan 2,185	D3
†49801	East Kingsford	A3
48823	East Lansing 51,392	E6
48730	East Tawas 2,584	F4
†49001	Eastwood 7,186	D6
48827	Eaton Rapids 4,510	E6
49111	Eau Claire 573	C6
48229	Ecorse 14,447	B7
48829	Edmore 1,176	E5
49112	Edwardsburg 1,135	C7
49628	Elberta 556	C4
49629	Elk Rapids 1,504	D4
48731	Elkton 953	F5
48831	Elsie 1,022	E5
49837	Gladstone 4,533	C3
48624	Gladwin⊙ 2,479	E5
49055	Gobles 816	D6
48438	Goodrich 795	F6
48439	Grand Blanc 6,848	F6
49417	Grand Haven⊙ 11,763	C5
49337	Grand Ledge 6,920	E6
*49501	Grand Rapids⊙ 181,843	D5
	Grand Rapids‡ 601,680	D5
49418	Grandville 12,412	D6
49327	Grant 683	D5
49240	Grass Lake 962	E6
49738	Grayling⊙ 1,792	E4
48838	Greenville 8,019	D5
48138	Grosse Ile 9,320	B7
48236	Grosse Pointe 5,901	B7
†48236	Grosse Pointe Farms 10,551	B6
48734	Frankenmuth 3,753	F5
49635	Frankfort 1,603	C4
48025	Franklin 2,864	B6
48026	Fraser 14,560	B6
48623	Freeland 1,364	E5
49412	Fremont 3,672	D5
49415	Fruitport 1,143	C5
49053	Galesburg 1,822	D6
49113	Galien 692	C7
48135	Garden City 35,640	F6
49735	Gaylord⊙ 3,011	E3
48173	Gibraltar 4,458	F6
†48236	Grosse Pointe Park 13,639	B7
†48236	Grosse Pointe Shores 3,122	B6
†48236	Grosse Pointe Woods 18,886	B6
49841	Gwinn 1,408	B2
48212	Hamtramck 21,300	B6
49930	Hancock 5,122	G1
48441	Harbor Beach 2,000	G5
49740	Harbor Springs 1,567	D3
48225	Harper Woods 16,361	B6
48625	Harrison⊙ 1,700	E4
48740	Harrisville⊙ 559	F4
49420	Hart⊙ 1,888	C5
49057	Hartford 2,493	C6
48840	Haslett 7,025	E6
49058	Hastings⊙ 6,418	D6
48030	Hazel Park 20,914	B6
48626	Hemlock 1,362	E5
49421	Hesperia 876	D5
48203	Highland Park 27,909	B6
49242	Hillsdale⊙ 7,432	E7
49423	Holland 26,281	C6
48842	Holt 10,097	E6
49245	Homer 1,791	E6
49931	Houghton⊙ 7,512	G1
48629	Houghton Lake 2,449	E4
48630	Houghton Lake Heights	E4
49329	Howard City 1,118	D5
48843	Howell⊙ 6,976	F6
49934	Hubbell 1,278	A1
49247	Hudson 2,545	E7
49426	Hudsonville 4,844	D6
48444	Imlay City 2,495	F5
48141	Inkster 35,190	B7
49643	Interlochen 600	D4
48846	Ionia⊙ 5,920	D6
49801	Iron Mountain⊙ 8,341	B3
49935	Iron River 2,426	A2
49938	Ironwood 7,741	F2
49849	Ishpeming 7,538	B2
48847	Ithaca⊙ 2,950	E5
*49201	Jackson⊙ 39,739	E6
	Jackson‡ 151,495	E6
49428	Jenison 16,330	D6
49250	Jonesville 2,172	E6
*49001	Kalamazoo⊙ 79,722	D6
	Kalamazoo-Portage‡ 279,192	D6
49646	Kalkaska⊙ 1,654	D4
48030	Keego Harbor 3,083	F6
49330	Kent City 860	D5
49508	Kentwood 30,438	D6
48445	Kinde 600	G5
49801	Kingsford 5,290	A3
49649	Kingsley 664	D4
48848	Laingsburg 1,145	E6
49651	Lake City⊙ 843	D4
49945	Lake Linden 1,181	A1
†49039	Lake Michigan Beach 2,001	C6
48849	Lake Odessa 2,171	D6
48035	Lake Orion 2,907	F6
48850	Lakeview 1,139	D5
†49440	Lakewood Club 695	C5
48144	Lambertville 6,341	F7
49946	L'Anse⊙ 2,500	G1
*48901	Lansing (cap.) 130,414	E6
	Lansing-East Lansing‡ 468,482	E6
48446	Lapeer⊙ 6,198	F5
49913	Laurium 2,678	A1
49064	Lawrence 903	C6
49065	Lawton 1,558	D6
49654	Leland⊙ 776	D3
48449	Lennon 600	E5
49251	Leslie 2,110	E6
48450	Lexington 765	G5
48742	Lincoln 361	F4
48146	Lincoln Park 45,105	B7
48451	Linden 2,174	F6
49252	Litchfield 1,353	E6
*48150	Livonia 104,814	F6
49331	Lowell 3,707	D6
49431	Ludington⊙ 8,937	C5

(continued on following page)

48157 Luna Pier 1,443 F7
48851 Lyons 708 E6
49757 Mackinac Island 479 E3
49701 Mackinaw City 820 E3
48071 Madison Heights 35,375 B6
49659 Mancelona 1,432 E4
48158 Manchester 1,686 E6
49660 Manistee⊙ 7,566 C4
49854 Manistique⊙ 3,962 C3
49663 Manton 1,212 D4
48853 Maple Rapids 683 E5
49067 Marcellus 1,134 D6
48039 Marine City 4,414 G6
49665 Marion 816 D4
48453 Marlette 1,761 G5
49855 Marquette⊙ 23,288 B2
49068 Marshall⊙ 7,201 E6
49070 Martin 447 D6
48040 Marysville 7,345 G6
48854 Mason⊙ 6,019 E6
49071 Mattawan 2,143 D6
48744 Mayville 958 F5
49657 McBain 519 D4
48122 Melvindale 12,322 B7
48041 Memphis 1,171 G6
49072 Mendon 951 D7
49858 Menominee⊙ 10,099 B3
48637 Merrill 851 E5
48455 Metamora 552 F6
49254 Michigan Center 5,244 E6
49333 Middleville 1,797 D6
48640 Midland⊙ 37,250 E5
48160 Milan 4,182 F6
48042 Milford 5,041 F6
48746 Millington 1,237 F5
48647 Mio⊙ 975 E4
48161 Monroe⊙ 23,531 F7
49437 Montague 2,332 C5
48457 Montrose 1,706 F5
49256 Morenci 2,110 E7
49336 Morley 507 D5
48857 Morrice 733 E6
48043 Mount Clemens⊙ 18,806 G6
48458 Mount Morris 3,246 F5
48858 Mount Pleasant⊙ 23,746 E5
48860 Muir 698 D5
48861 Mulliken 550 E6
49862 Munising⊙ 3,083 C2
*49440 Muskegon⊙ 40,823 C5
Muskegon-Norton Shores-Muskegon Heights‡ 179,591 C5
49444 Muskegon Heights 14,611 C5
49261 Napoleon 1,400 E6
49073 Nashville 1,628 D6
49866 Negaunee 5,189 B2
49337 Newaygo 1,271 D5
48047 New Baltimore 5,439 G6
49868 Newberry⊙ 2,120 D2
48164 New Boston 1,200 F6
49117 New Buffalo 2,821 C7
48048 New Haven 1,871 G6
48460 New Lothrop 646 F5
49120 Niles 13,115 C7
49262 North Adams 565 E7
48461 North Branch 896 F5
49445 North Muskegon 4,024 C5
49670 Northport 611 D3
48167 Northville 5,698 F6
†49441 Norton Shores 22,025 C5
49870 Norway 2,919 B3
48050 Novi 22,525 F6
48237 Oak Park 31,537 B6
48864 Okemos 8,882 E6
49076 Olivet 1,604 E6
49765 Onaway 1,084 E3
49675 Onekama 582 C4
49265 Onsted 670 E6
49953 Ontonagon⊙ 2,182 F1
48033 Orchard Lake 1,798 F6
48462 Ortonville 1,190 F6
48750 Oscoda 2,431 F4
48463 Otisville 682 F5
49078 Otsego 3,802 D6
48866 Ovid 1,712 E5
48867 Owosso 16,455 E5
48051 Oxford 2,746 F6
49004 Parchment 1,817 D6
49269 Parma 873 E6
49079 Paw Paw⊙ 3,211 D6
†49038 Paw Paw Lake 4,193 C6
48052 Pearl Beach 3,430 G6
48466 Peck 606 G5
49769 Pellston 565 E3
49449 Pentwater 1,165 C5
48872 Perry 2,051 E6
49270 Petersburg 1,222 F7
49770 Petoskey⊙ 6,097 E3
48755 Pigeon 1,247 F5
48169 Pinckney 1,390 F6
48650 Pinconning 1,430 F5
49080 Plainwell 3,751 D6
48069 Pleasant Ridge 3,217 B6
*48170 Plymouth 9,986 F6
*48053 Pontiac⊙ 76,715 F6
49081 Portage 38,157 D6
48467 Port Austin 839 F4
48060 Port Huron⊙ 33,981 G6
48875 Portland 3,963 E6
48469 Port Sanilac 598 G5
49776 Posen 270 F3
48876 Potterville 1,502 E6
49082 Quincy 1,569 E7
49959 Ramsay F2
49451 Ravenna 951 D5
49274 Reading 1,203 E7
49677 Reed City⊙ 2,221 D5
48757 Reese 1,645 F5
48062 Richmond 3,536 G6
48218 River Rouge 12,912 B7
48192 Riverview 14,569 B7
48063 Rochester 7,203 F6
49341 Rockford 3,324 D5
48173 Rockwood 3,346 F6
49779 Rogers City⊙ 3,923 F3
48065 Romeo 3,509 F6
48174 Romulus 24,857 F6
49444 Roosevelt Park 4,015 C5
48653 Roscommon⊙ 834 E4
48654 Rose City 661 E4
48066 Roseville 54,311 B6
49452 Rothbury 522 C5
*48067 Royal Oak 70,893 B6
*48601 Saginaw⊙ 77,508 F5
Saginaw‡ 228,059 F5
48655 Saint Charles 2,276 E5
48079 Saint Clair 4,780 G6
*48080 Saint Clair Shores 76,210 B6
49781 Saint Ignace⊙ 2,632 E3
48879 Saint Johns⊙ 7,376 E6
49085 Saint Joseph⊙ 9,622 C6
48880 Saint Louis 4,107 E5
48176 Saline 6,483 F6
48471 Sandusky⊙ 2,216 G5
48657 Sanford 864 E5
48881 Saranac 1,421 D6
49453 Saugatuck 1,079 C6
49783 Sault Sainte Marie⊙ 14,448 E2
49087 Schoolcraft 1,359 D6
49454 Scottville 1,241 C5
48759 Sebewaing 2,046 F5
49455 Shelby 1,624 C5
48883 Shepherd 1,534 E5
48884 Sheridan 664 D5
†49085 Shoreham 742 C6
†49125 Shorewood 1,735 C7
*48034 Southfield 75,568 F6
48195 Southgate 32,058 F6
49090 South Haven 5,943 C6
48178 South Lyon 5,214 F6
†48161 South Monroe 4,232 F7
49963 South Range 861 G1
48179 South Rockwood 1,353 F7
†48060 Sparlingville 1,718 G6
49345 Sparta 3,373 D5
49283 Spring Arbor 2,101 E6
49015 Springfield 5,917 D6
49456 Spring Lake 2,731 C5
49284 Springport 675 E6
49964 Stambaugh 1,442 G2
48658 Standish⊙ 1,264 F5
48888 Stanton⊙ 1,315 D5
49887 Stephenson 967 B3
48659 Sterling 457 E4
48077 Sterling Heights 108,999 B6
49127 Stevensville 1,268 C6
49285 Stockbridge 1,213 E6
49091 Sturgis 9,468 D7
48890 Sunfield 591 D6
49682 Suttons Bay 504 D3
48473 Swartz Creek 5,013 F6
†48053 Sylvan Lake 1,949 F6
48763 Tawas City⊙ 1,967 F4
48180 Taylor 77,568 B7
49286 Tecumseh 7,320 E7
49092 Tekonsha 755 E6
49128 Three Oaks 1,774 C7
49093 Three Rivers 7,015 D7
49684 Traverse City⊙ 15,516 D4
48183 Trenton 22,762 B7
*48084 Troy 67,102 B6
48475 Ubly 862 G5
49094 Union City 1,667 D6
49129 Union Pier 1,039 C7
48767 Unionville 578 F5
*48087 Utica 5,282 F6
49095 Vandalia 447 D7
49795 Vanderbilt 525 E3
48768 Vassar 2,727 F5
49096 Vermontville 832 E6
48476 Vernon 1,008 F6
49097 Vicksburg 2,224 D6
49968 Wakefield 2,591 F2
49288 Waldron 570 E7
49504 Walker 15,088 D6
48088 Walled Lake 4,748 F6
*48089 Warren 161,134 B6
49098 Watervliet 1,867 C6
49348 Wayland 2,023 D6
48184 Wayne 21,159 F6
48892 Webberville 1,535 E6
49894 Wells B3
48661 West Branch⊙ 1,785 E4
48185 Westland 84,603 F6
48894 Westphalia 896 E6
49349 White Cloud⊙ 1,101 D5
49461 Whitehall 2,856 C5
49099 White Pigeon 1,478 D7
49971 White Pine 1,142 F1
48189 Whitmore Lake 2,920 F6
48770 Whittemore 438 F4
48895 Williamston 2,981 E6
48096 Wixom 6,705 F6
†49440 Wolf Lake 3,876 D5
49799 Wolverine 364 E3
†48183 Woodhaven 10,902 F6
48897 Woodland 431 D6
48192 Wyandotte 34,006 B7
49509 Wyoming 59,616 D6
48097 Yale 1,814 G5
48197 Ypsilanti 24,031 F6
49464 Zeeland 4,764 D6
†48601 Zilwaukee 2,201 F5

OTHER FEATURES

Abbaye (pt.) B2
Au Sable (pt.) C2
Au Sable (pt.) F4
Au Sable (riv.) E4
Au Train (bay) C2
Bad (riv.) E5
Barques (pt.) C3
Beaver (isl.) D3
Beaver (lake) F4
Belle (riv.) G6
Bete Grise (bay) B1
Betsy (riv.) D2
Big Bay (pt.) B2
Big Bay de Noc (bay) C3
Big Iron (riv.) F1
Big Sable (pt.) C4
Big Sable (riv.) C4
Big Star (lake) C5
Black (lake) E3
Black (riv.) E3
Black (riv.) G5
Blake (pt.) E1
Boardman (riv.) D4
Bois Blanc (isl.) E3
Bond Falls (res.) G2
Brevoort (lake) D3
Brule (riv.) A3
Burt (lake) E3
Cass (riv.) F5
Cedar (lake) F4
Charlevoix (lake) D3
Chippewa (riv.) E5
Crisp (pt.) D2
Crystal (lake) C4
Curwood (mt.) A2
Dead (riv.) B2
Deer (riv.) A2
De Tour (passage) E3
Detour (pt.) C3
Detroit (riv.) B7
Drummond (isl.) F2
Duck (lake) F4
Elk (lake) D4
Erie (lake) G7
Escanaba (riv.) B2
False Detour (chan.) F3
Fawn (riv.) D7
Fence (riv.) A2
Firesteel (riv.) G1
Fletcher (pond) F4
Flint (riv.) F5
Ford (riv.) B2
Forty Mile (pt.) F3
Fourteen Mile (pt.) F1
Garden (isl.) D3
Garden (pen.) C3
Glen (lake) C4
Gogebic (lake) F2
Good Harbor (bay) D3
Government (peak) F1
Grand (isl.) C2
Grand (lake) F3
Grand (riv.) D6
Grand Traverse (bay) D3
Granite (pt.) B2
Green (bay) B4
Gun (lake) D6
Hamlin (lake) C4
Higgins (lake) E4
High (isl.) D3
Hog (isl.) D3
Houghton (lake) E4
Hubbard (lake) F4
Huron (bay) A2
Huron (lake) G4
Huron (riv.) F6
Huron River (pt.) B2
Independence (lake) B2
Indian (lake) C2
Isle Royale Nat'l Park E1
Kalamazoo (riv.) C6
Keweenaw (bay) A1
Keweenaw (pt.) B1
K.I. Sawyer A.F.B. 7,345 B2
L'Anse Ind. Res. A2
Laughing Fish (pt.) B2
Leelanau (lake) D4
Light House (pt.) D3
Little Bay de Noc (bay) B3
Little Girl (pt.) E1
Little Sable (pt.) C5
Little Summer (isl.) C3
Little Traverse (bay) D3
Long (lake) F3
Lookingglass (riv.) E6
Mackinac (isl.) E3
Mackinac (str.) E3
Manistee (riv.) C4
Manistique (lake) D2
Manistique (riv.) C2
Manitou (isl.) B1
Maple (riv.) E5
Margrethe (lake) E4
Marquette (isl.) E3
Maumee (bay) F7
Menominee (riv.) B3
Michigamme (lake) A2
Michigamme (res.) B2
Michigamme (riv.) A2
Michigan (lake) B5
Mill (creek) G5
Millecoquins (lake) D2
Misery (bay) G1
Misery (riv.) G1
Montreal (riv.) F1
Mullett (lake) E3
Munuscong (lake) E2
Muskegon (riv.) C5
Neebish (isl.) E2
Net (riv.) G2
Ninemile (pt.) E3
North (chan.) F2
North (pt.) F3
North Fox (isl.) D3
North Manitou (isl.) C3
Oak (pt.) F5
Ontonagon (riv.) G1
Ontonagon Ind. Res. F1
Otsego (lake) E4
Paint (riv.) A2
Paradise (lake) E3
Passage (isl.) E1
Patterson (pt.) D3
Paw Paw (riv.) C6
Peninsula (pt.) C3
Perch (lake) G2
Perch (riv.) G2
Pere Marquette (riv.) D5
Pictured Rocks (cliff) C2
Pictured Rocks Nat'l Lakeshore C2
Pigeon (riv.) D7
Pigeon (riv.) E3
Pine (lake) F4
Pine (riv.) D4
Pine (riv.) E5
Platte (lake) C4
Porcupine (mts.) F1
Potagannissing (bay) F2
Poverty (isl.) C3
Prairie (riv.) D7
Presque Isle (riv.) F1
Rabbit (riv.) D6
Raisin (riv.) F7
Rapid (riv.) B2
Reedsburg (res.) E4
Rifle (riv.) E4
Royale (isl.) E1
Saginaw (bay) F5
Saginaw (riv.) F5
Saint Clair (lake) G6
Saint Clair (riv.) G6
Saint Joseph (riv.) C7
Saint Martin (bay) E3
Saint Martin (isl.) C3
Saint Marys (riv.) E2
Salt (pt.) E2
Sand (pt.) F5
Seul Choix (pt.) D3
Shiawassee (riv.) E5
Siskiwit (bay) E1
Sleeping Bear Dunes Nat'l Lakeshore C4
South (bay) C2
South (chan.) E3
South (pt.) F4
South Fox (isl.) D3
South Manitou (isl.) C3
Sturgeon (riv.) C2
Sugar (isl.) E2
Summer (isl.) C3
Superior (lake) C2
Tahquamenon (falls) D2
Tahquamenon (riv.) D2
Tawas (lake) F4
Tawas (pt.) F4
Thunder (bay) F4
Thunder Bay (riv.) F3
Tittabawassee (riv.) E5
Torch (lake) D3
Traverse (isl.) A1
Traverse (pt.) A1
Turtle (lake) F4
Two Hearted (riv.) D2
Vieux Desert (lake) G2
Walloon (lake) E3
White (riv.) C5
Whitefish (bay) E2
Whitefish (pt.) E2
Whitefish (riv.) C2
Wood (isl.) C2
Wurtsmith A.F.B. 5,166 F4
Yellow Dog (riv.) B2

⊙County seat.
‡Population of metropolitan area.
○Population of township.
† Zip of nearest p.o. * Multiple zips.

Agriculture, Industry and Resources

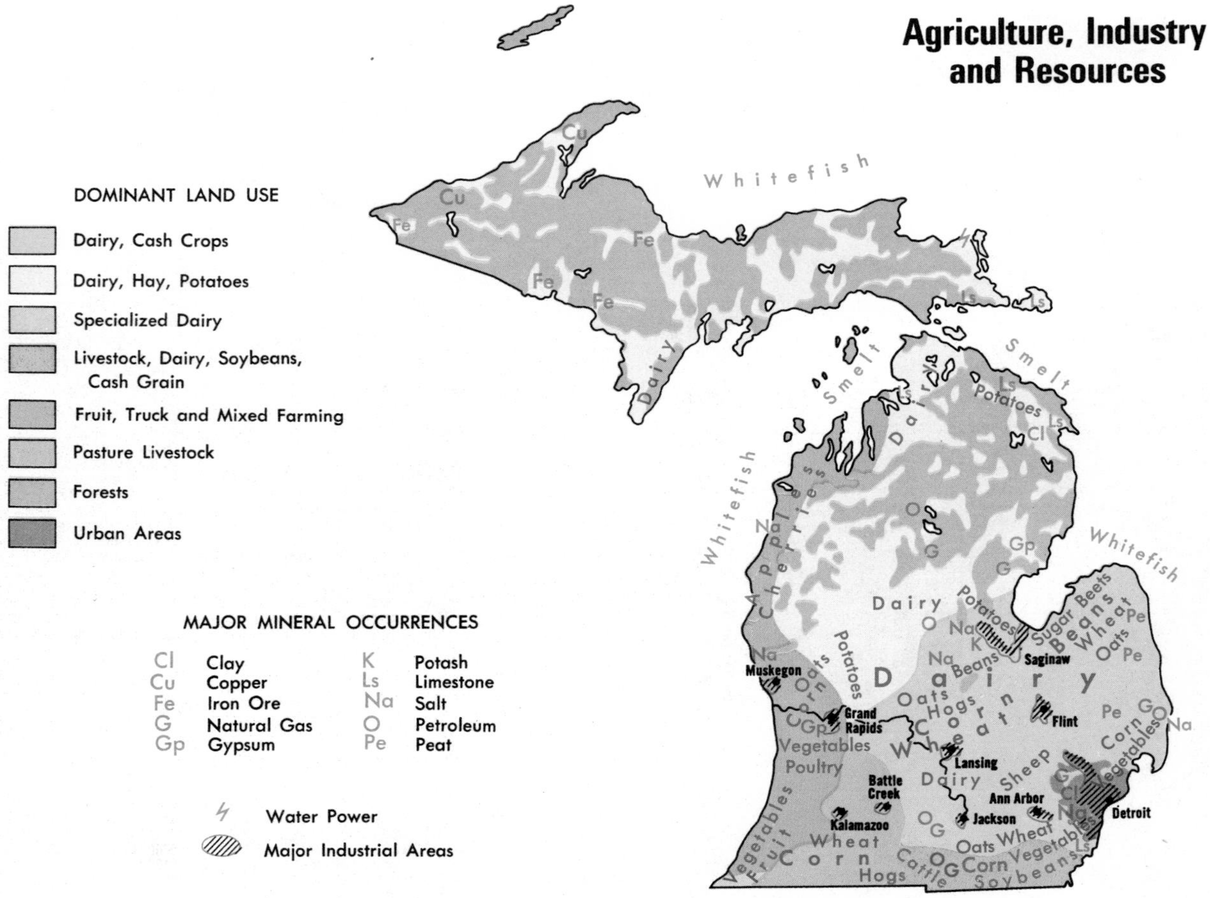
DOMINANT LAND USE
Dairy, Cash Crops
Dairy, Hay, Potatoes
Specialized Dairy
Livestock, Dairy, Soybeans, Cash Grain
Fruit, Truck and Mixed Farming
Pasture Livestock
Forests
Urban Areas
MAJOR MINERAL OCCURRENCES
Cl Clay
Cu Copper
Fe Iron Ore
G Natural Gas
Gp Gypsum
K Potash
Ls Limestone
Na Salt
O Petroleum
Pe Peat
Water Power
Major Industrial Areas
Whitefish
Smelt
Dairy
Potatoes
Cherries
Oats
Beans
Sugar Beets
Wheat
Hogs
Corn
Vegetables
Poultry
Sheep
Fruit
Cattle
Soybeans
Muskegon
Grand Rapids
Saginaw
Flint
Lansing
Battle Creek
Kalamazoo
Jackson
Ann Arbor
Detroit

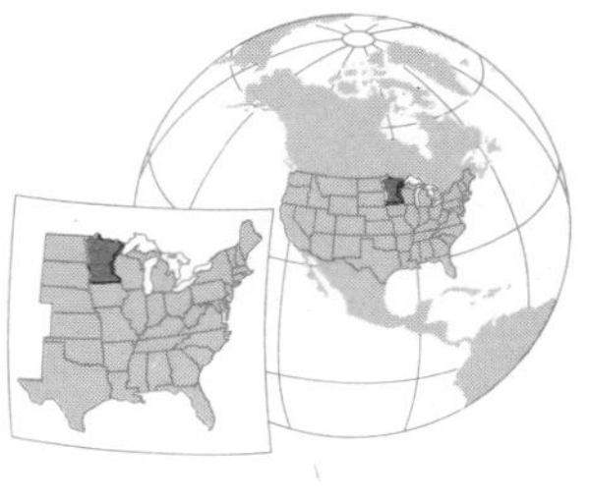

AREA 84,402 sq. mi. (218,601 sq. km.)
POPULATION 4,075,970
CAPITAL St. Paul
LARGEST CITY Minneapolis
HIGHEST POINT Eagle Mtn. 2,301 ft. (701 m.)
SETTLED IN 1805
ADMITTED TO UNION May 11, 1858
POPULAR NAME North Star State; Gopher State
STATE FLOWER Pink & White Lady's-Slipper
STATE BIRD Common Loon

COUNTIES

Aitkin 13,404 .... E4
Anoka 195,998 .... E5
Becker 29,336 .... C4
Beltrami 30,982 .... C2
Benton 25,187 .... D5
Big Stone 7,716 .... B5
Blue Earth 52,314 .... D6
Brown 28,645 .... D6
Carlton 29,936 .... F4
Carver 37,046 .... E6
Cass 21,050 .... D4
Chippewa 14,941 .... C5
Chisago 25,717 .... F5
Clay 49,327 .... B4
Clearwater 8,761 .... C3
Cook 4,092 .... H3
Cottonwood 14,854 .... C6
Crow Wing 41,722 .... D4
Dakota 194,279 .... E6
Dodge 14,773 .... F7
Douglas 27,839 .... C5
Faribault 19,714 .... D7
Fillmore 21,930 .... F7
Freeborn 36,329 .... E7
Goodhue 38,749 .... F6
Grant 7,171 .... B5
Hennepin 941,411 .... E5
Houston 18,382 .... G7
Hubbard 14,098 .... D3
Isanti 23,600 .... E5
Itasca 43,069 .... E3
Jackson 13,690 .... C7
Kanabec 12,161 .... E5
Kandiyohi 36,763 .... C5
Kittson 6,672 .... B2
Koochiching 17,571 .... E2
Lac qui Parle 10,592 .... B6
Lake 13,043 .... G3
Lake of the Woods 3,764 .... D2
Le Sueur 23,434 .... E6
Lincoln 8,207 .... B6
Lyon 25,207 .... C6
Mahnomen 5,535 .... C3
Marshall 13,027 .... B2
Martin 24,687 .... D7
McLeod 29,657 .... D6
Meeker 20,594 .... D5
Mille Lacs 18,430 .... E5
Morrison 29,311 .... D4
Mower 40,390 .... F7
Murray 11,507 .... C6
Nicollet 26,929 .... D6
Nobles 21,840 .... C7
Norman 9,379 .... B3
Olmsted 92,006 .... F7
Otter Tail 51,937 .... C4
Pennington 15,258 .... B2
Pine 19,871 .... F4
Pipestone 11,690 .... B6
Polk 34,844 .... B3
Pope 11,657 .... C5
Ramsey 459,784 .... E5
Red Lake 5,471 .... B3
Redwood 19,341 .... C6
Renville 20,401 .... C6
Rice 46,087 .... E6
Rock 10,703 .... B7
Roseau 12,574 .... C2
Saint Louis 222,229 .... F3
Scott 43,784 .... E6
Sherburne 29,908 .... E5
Sibley 15,448 .... D6
Stearns 108,161 .... D5
Steele 30,328 .... E7
Stevens 11,322 .... B5
Swift 12,920 .... C5
Todd 24,991 .... D4
Traverse 5,542 .... B5
Wabasha 19,335 .... F6
Wadena 14,192 .... D4
Waseca 18,448 .... E6
Washington 113,571 .... F5
Watonwan 12,361 .... D7
Wilkin 8,454 .... B4
Winona 46,256 .... G6
Wright 58,681 .... D5
Yellow Medicine 13,653 .... B6

CITIES and TOWNS

Zip *Name/Pop.* *Key*

56510 Ada⊙ 1,971 .... B3
55909 Adams 797 .... F7
56110 Adrian 1,336 .... C7
55001 Afton 2,550 .... F6
56430 Ah-Gwah-Ching 400 .... D3
56431 Aitkin⊙ 1,770 .... E4
56433 Akeley 486 .... D3
56307 Albany 1,569 .... D5
56207 Alberta 145 .... B5
56007 Albert Lea⊙ 19,200 .... E7
55301 Albertville 564 .... E5
56009 Alden 687 .... E7
56308 Alexandria⊙ 7,608 .... C5
56111 Alpha 180 .... D7
55910 Altura 354 .... G6
56710 Alvarado 385 .... B2
56010 Amboy 606 .... D7
†55303 Andover 9,387 .... E5
55302 Annandale 1,568 .... D5
55303 Anoka⊙ 15,634 .... E5
56208 Appleton 1,842 .... C5
†55124 Apple Valley 21,818 .... G6
56713 Argyle 741 .... B2
55307 Arlington 1,779 .... D6
56309 Ashby 486 .... C4
55704 Askov 350 .... F4
56209 Atwater 1,128 .... D5
56511 Audubon 383 .... C4
55705 Aurora 2,670 .... F3
55912 Austin⊙ 23,020 .... E7
56114 Avoca 201 .... C7
56310 Avon 804 .... D5
55706 Babbitt 2,435 .... G3
56435 Backus 255 .... D4
56714 Badger 320 .... B2
56621 Bagley⊙ 1,321 .... C3
56115 Balaton 752 .... C6
56514 Barnesville 2,207 .... B4
55707 Barnum 464 .... F4
56311 Barrett 388 .... B5
56515 Battle Lake 708 .... C4
56623 Baudette⊙ 1,170 .... D2
†56401 Baxter 2,625 .... D4
55003 Bayport 2,932 .... F5
56211 Beardsley 344 .... B5
55601 Beaver Bay 283 .... G3
56116 Beaver Creek 260 .... B7
55308 Becker 601 .... E5
56312 Belgrade 805 .... C5
†55027 Bellechester 220 .... F6
56011 Belle Plaine 2,754 .... E6
56212 Bellingham 290 .... B5
56214 Belview 438 .... C6
56601 Bemidji⊙ 10,949 .... D3
56626 Bena 153 .... D3
56215 Benson⊙ 3,656 .... C5
56437 Bertha 510 .... C4
55005 Bethel 272 .... E5
56117 Bigelow 249 .... C7
56627 Big Falls 490 .... E2
56628 Bigfork 457 .... E3
55309 Big Lake 2,210 .... E5
56118 Bingham Lake 222 .... C7
55310 Bird Island 1,372 .... D6
55708 Biwabik 1,428 .... F3
56630 Blackduck 653 .... D3
†55433 Blaine 28,558 .... G5
56216 Blomkest 200 .... D6
55917 Blooming Prairie 1,969 .... E7
55420 Bloomington 81,831 .... G6
56013 Blue Earth⊙ 4,132 .... D7
56518 Bluffton 206 .... C4
56519 Borup 160 .... B3
55709 Bovey 813 .... E3
56314 Bowlus 276 .... D5
56218 Boyd 329 .... C6
55006 Braham 1,015 .... E5
56401 Brainerd⊙ 11,489 .... D4
†55056 Branch 1,866 .... F5
56315 Brandon 473 .... C5
56520 Breckenridge⊙ 3,909 .... B4
†56472 Breezy Point 384 .... D4
56119 Brewster 559 .... C7
56014 Bricelyn 487 .... E7
55429 Brooklyn Center 31,230 .... G5
†55444 Brooklyn Park 43,332 .... G5
56715 Brooks 173 .... B3
56316 Brooten 647 .... C5
56438 Browerville 693 .... D4
55918 Brownsdale 691 .... F7
56219 Browns Valley 887 .... B5
55919 Brownsville 418 .... G7
55312 Brownton 697 .... D6
56317 Buckman 171 .... D5
55313 Buffalo⊙ 4,560 .... E5
55314 Buffalo Lake 782 .... D6
55713 Buhl 1,284 .... F3
55337 Burnsville 35,674 .... E6
56318 Burtrum 177 .... D5
56120 Butterfield 634 .... D7
55920 Byron 1,715 .... F6
55921 Caledonia⊙ 2,691 .... G7
56521 Callaway 238 .... C3
55716 Calumet 469 .... E3
55008 Cambridge⊙ 3,287 .... E5
56522 Campbell 286 .... B4
56220 Canby 2,143 .... B6
55009 Cannon Falls 2,653 .... F6
55922 Canton 386 .... F7
56319 Carlos 364 .... C5
55718 Carlton⊙ 862 .... F4
55315 Carver 642 .... E6
56633 Cass Lake 1,001 .... D3
55012 Center City⊙ 458 .... F5
†55038 Centerville 734 .... E5
56121 Ceylon 543 .... D7
55316 Champlin 9,006 .... G5
56122 Chandler 344 .... C7
55317 Chanhassen 6,359 .... F6
55318 Chaska⊙ 8,346 .... F6
55923 Chatfield 2,055 .... F7
55013 Chisago City 1,634 .... E5
55719 Chisholm 5,930 .... E3
56221 Chokio 559 .... B5
55014 Circle Pines 3,321 .... G5
56222 Clara City 1,574 .... C6
55924 Claremont 591 .... E6
56440 Clarissa 663 .... C4
56223 Clarkfield 1,171 .... C6
56016 Clarks Grove 620 .... E7
56634 Clearbrook 579 .... C3
55319 Clear Lake 266 .... E5
55320 Clearwater 379 .... D5
56224 Clements 227 .... D6
56017 Cleveland 699 .... E6
56523 Climax 273 .... B3
56225 Clinton 622 .... B5
56226 Clontarf 196 .... C5
55720 Cloquet 11,142 .... F4
†55068 Coates 207 .... E6
55321 Cokato 2,056 .... D5
56320 Cold Spring 2,294 .... D5
55722 Coleraine 1,116 .... E3
55322 Cologne 545 .... E6
55421 Columbia Heights 20,029 .... G5
56019 Comfrey 548 .... D6
56020 Conger 183 .... E7
55723 Cook 800 .... F3
55433 Coon Rapids 35,826 .... G5
†55340 Corcoran 4,252 .... F5
56228 Cosmos 571 .... D6
55016 Cottage Grove 18,994 .... F6
56229 Cottonwood 924 .... C6
56021 Courtland 399 .... D6
55726 Cromwell 229 .... F4
56716 Crookston⊙ 8,628 .... B3
56441 Crosby 2,218 .... D4
56442 Crosslake 1,064 .... E4
†55428 Crystal 25,543 .... G5
55323 Crystal Bay (Orono) 6,845 .... F5
56123 Currie 359 .... C6
56323 Cyrus 334 .... C5
55925 Dakota 350 .... G7
56324 Dalton 248 .... C4
56230 Danube 590 .... C6
56231 Danvers 152 .... C5
56022 Darfur 139 .... D6
55324 Darwin 282 .... D5
55325 Dassel 1,066 .... D5
56232 Dawson 1,901 .... B6
55327 Dayton 4,070 .... E5
55391 Deephaven 3,716 .... G5
56527 Deer Creek 392 .... C4
56636 Deer River 907 .... E3
56444 Deerwood 580 .... E4
56233 De Graff 179 .... C5
55328 Delano 2,480 .... E5
56023 Delavan 262 .... D7
†55110 Dellwood 751 .... F5
56528 Dent 167 .... C4
56501 Detroit Lakes⊙ 7,106 .... C4
55926 Dexter 279 .... F7
56529 Dilworth 2,585 .... B4
55927 Dodge Center 1,816 .... F6
56235 Donnelly 317 .... B5
55929 Dover 312 .... F7
*55801 Duluth⊙ 92,811 .... F4
Duluth-Superior‡ 266,650 .... F4
56236 Dumont 173 .... B5
55019 Dundas 422 .... E6
56127 Dunnell 216 .... D7
55111 Eagan 20,700 .... G6
56446 Eagle Bend 593 .... D4
56024 Eagle Lake 1,470 .... E6
†55005 East Bethel 6,626 .... E5
56721 East Grand Forks 8,537 .... B3
†56401 East Gull Lake 586 .... D4
56025 Easton 283 .... E7
56237 Echo 334 .... C6
55344 Eden Prairie 16,263 .... G6
55329 Eden Valley 763 .... D5
56128 Edgerton 1,123 .... B7
55424 Edina 46,073 .... G5
55931 Eitzen 226 .... G7
†55910 Elba 198 .... F6
56531 Elbow Lake⊙ 1,358 .... B5
55932 Elgin 667 .... F6
56533 Elizabeth 195 .... B4
55020 Elko 274 .... E6
55330 Elk River⊙ 6,785 .... E5
56026 Ellendale 555 .... E7
56129 Ellsworth 629 .... C7
56027 Elmore 882 .... D7
56325 Elrosa 214 .... C5
55731 Ely 4,820 .... G3
56028 Elysian 454 .... E6
56447 Emily 588 .... E4
56029 Emmons 465 .... E7
56534 Erhard 194 .... B4
56535 Erskine 585 .... B3
56326 Evansville 571 .... C4
55734 Eveleth 5,042 .... F3
55331 Excelsior 2,523 .... E6
55934 Eyota 1,244 .... F7
55332 Fairfax 1,405 .... D6
56031 Fairmont⊙ 11,506 .... D7
55113 Falcon Heights 5,291 .... G5
55021 Faribault⊙ 16,241 .... E6
55024 Farmington 4,370 .... E6
56641 Federal Dam 192 .... D3
56536 Felton 264 .... B3
56537 Fergus Falls⊙ 12,519 .... B4
56540 Fertile 869 .... B3
56448 Fifty Lakes 263 .... D4
55735 Finlayson 202 .... F4
56723 Fisher 453 .... B3
56328 Flensburg 256 .... D5
55736 Floodwood 648 .... E4
56329 Foley⊙ 1,606 .... D5
†56308 Forada 191 .... C5
55025 Forest Lake 4,596 .... F5
56330 Foreston 283 .... E5
56542 Fosston 1,599 .... C3
55935 Fountain 327 .... F7
56543 Foxhome 161 .... B4
55333 Franklin 512 .... D6
56544 Frazee 1,284 .... C4
56032 Freeborn 323 .... E7
56331 Freeport 563 .... D5
55432 Fridley 30,228 .... G5
56033 Frost 293 .... D7
56131 Fulda 1,308 .... C7
56332 Garfield 284 .... C5
56450 Garrison 174 .... E4
56132 Garvin 172 .... C6
56545 Gary 241 .... B3
55334 Gaylord⊙ 1,933 .... D6
56035 Geneva 417 .... E7
56239 Ghent 356 .... C6
55335 Gibbon 787 .... D6
55741 Gilbert 2,721 .... F3
56333 Gilman 156 .... E5
55336 Glencoe⊙ 4,396 .... D6
56036 Glenville 851 .... E7
56334 Glenwood⊙ 2,523 .... C5
56547 Glyndon 882 .... B4
55427 Golden Valley 22,775 .... G5
56644 Gonvick 362 .... C3
55027 Goodhue 657 .... F6
56725 Goodridge 191 .... C2
56037 Good Thunder 560 .... D6
55027 Goodview 2,567 .... G6
56240 Graceville 780 .... B5
56039 Granada 377 .... D7
55604 Grand Marais⊙ 1,289 .... G2
55936 Grand Meadow 965 .... F7
55744 Grand Rapids⊙ 7,934 .... E3
56241 Granite Falls⊙ 3,451 .... C6
55030 Grasston 123 .... E5
56726 Greenbush 817 .... B2
†55373 Greenfield 1,391 .... F5
55338 Green Isle 357 .... E6
56335 Greenwald 259 .... D5
56336 Grey Eagle 338 .... D5
56243 Grove City 596 .... D5
56727 Grygla 216 .... C2
56452 Hackensack 285 .... D4
56728 Hallock⊙ 1,405 .... A2
56548 Halstad 690 .... B3
55339 Hamburg 475 .... D6
55340 Hamel 2,623 .... F5
55304 Ham Lake 7,832 .... E5
55938 Hammond 178 .... F6
55031 Hampton 299 .... E6
56244 Hancock 877 .... C5
56245 Hanley Falls 265 .... C6
55341 Hanover 647 .... E5
56041 Hanska 429 .... D6
56134 Hardwick 279 .... B7
55939 Harmony 1,133 .... F7
55032 Harris 678 .... F5
56042 Hartland 322 .... E7
55033 Hastings⊙ 12,827 .... F6
56549 Hawley 1,634 .... B4
55940 Hayfield 1,243 .... F7
56043 Hayward 294 .... E7
55342 Hector 1,252 .... D6
56044 Henderson 739 .... E6
56136 Hendricks 737 .... B6
56550 Hendrum 336 .... B3
56551 Henning 832 .... C4
56248 Herman 600 .... B5
†55811 Hermantown 6,759 .... F4
56137 Heron Lake 783 .... C7
56453 Hewitt 299 .... C4
55746 Hibbing 21,193 .... F3
55748 Hill City 533 .... E4
56138 Hills 598 .... B7
55037 Hinckley 963 .... E4
56552 Hitterdal 253 .... B4

(continued on following page)

Agriculture, Industry and Resources

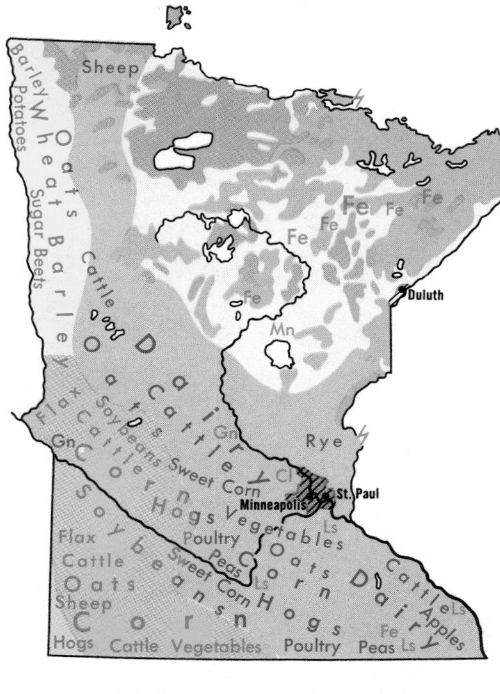

DOMINANT LAND USE

- Wheat, General Farming
- Dairy, Livestock
- Dairy, Hay, Potatoes
- Cattle Feed, Hogs
- Livestock, Cash Grain
- Forests
- Swampland, Limited Agriculture
- Urban Areas

MAJOR MINERAL OCCURRENCES

Cl Clay
Fe Iron Ore
Gn Granite
Ls Limestone
Mn Manganese

Water Power
Major Industrial Areas

56339 Hoffman 631 C5
55941 Hokah 686 G7
56340 Holdingford 635 D5
56139 Holland 234 B6
56045 Hollandale 290 E7
56249 Holloway 142 C5
55343 Hopkins 15,336 G5
55943 Houston 1,057 G7
55349 Howard Lake 1,240 D5
55750 Hoyt Lakes 3,186 F3
55038 Hugo 3,771 E5
55350 Hutchinson 9,244 D6
†55359 Independence 2,640 F5
56649 International Falls⊙ 5,611 E2
55075 Inver Grove Heights 17,171 E6
56141 Iona 248 C7
56455 Ironton 537 D4
55040 Isanti 858 E5
56342 Isle 573 E4
56142 Ivanhoe⊙ 761 B6
56143 Jackson⊙ 3,797 C7
56048 Janesville 1,897 E6
56144 Jasper 731 B7
56145 Jeffers 437 C6
56456 Jenkins 219 D4
55352 Jordan 2,663 E6
56251 Kandiyohi 447 D5
56732 Karlstad 934 B2
56050 Kasota 739 D6
55944 Kasson 2,827 F6
55753 Keewatin 1,443 E3
56650 Kelliher 324 D3
55945 Kellogg 440 G6
55754 Kelly Lake 900 F3
56733 Kennedy 405 B2
56343 Kensington 331 C5
55946 Kenyon 1,529 E6
56252 Kerkhoven 761 C5
56051 Kiester 670 E7
56052 Kilkenny 177 E6
55353 Kimball 651 D5
55758 Kinney 447 F3
55947 La Crescent 3,674 G7
56054 Lafayette 507 D6
56149 Lake Benton 869 B6
56734 Lake Bronson 298 B2
55041 Lake City 4,505 F6
56055 Lake Crystal 2,078 D6
55042 Lake Elmo 5,296 F6
56150 Lakefield 1,845 C7
†55398 Lake Fremont (Zimmerman) 1,074 E5
55043 Lakeland 1,812 F6
56253 Lake Lillian 329 C6
56554 Lake Park 716 B4
†55043 Lake Saint Croix Beach 1,176 F6
†56401 Lake Shore 583 D4
55044 Lakeville 14,790 E6
56151 Lake Wilson 380 B7
56152 Lamberton 1,032 C6
56735 Lancaster 368 B2
55949 Lanesboro 923 G7
56461 Laporte 160 D3
†55744 La Prairie 536 E3
56344 Lastrup 150 D4
†55101 Lauderdale 1,985 G5
56057 Le Center⊙ 1,967 E6
55951 Le Roy 930 F7
55354 Lester Prairie 1,229 D6
56058 Le Sueur 3,763 E6
55952 Lewiston 1,226 G7
56060 Lewisville 273 D7
†55014 Lexington 2,150 G5
†55050 Lilydale 417 G5
55045 Lindstrom 1,972 F5
†55038 Lino Lakes 4,966 G5
56155 Lismore 276 B7
55355 Litchfield⊙ 5,904 D5
56345 Little Falls⊙ 7,250 D5
56653 Littlefork 918 E2
†56334 Long Beach 263 C5
55356 Long Lake 1,747 F5
56347 Long Prairie⊙ 2,859 D5
56655 Longville 191 D4
55046 Lonsdale 1,160 E6
55357 Loretto 297 F5
56349 Lowry 283 C5
56255 Lucan 262 C6
56156 Luverne⊙ 4,568 B7
55953 Lyle 576 F7
56157 Lynd 304 C6
55954 Mabel 861 G7
56062 Madelia 2,130 D6
56256 Madison⊙ 2,212 B5
56063 Madison Lake 592 E6
56158 Magnolia 234 B7
56557 Mahnomen⊙ 1,283 C3
55115 Mahtomedi 3,851 F5
56001 Mankato⊙ 28,651 E6
55955 Mantorville⊙ 705 F6
†55369 Maple Grove 20,525 G5
55358 Maple Lake 1,132 D5
55359 Maple Plain 1,421 F5
56065 Mapleton 1,516 E7
†55912 Mapleview 253 E7
55109 Maplewood 26,990 G5
55764 Marble 757 E3
56257 Marietta 279 B5
55047 Marine on Saint Croix 543 F5
56258 Marshall⊙ 11,161 C6
55360 Mayer 388 E6
56260 Maynard 428 C6
55956 Mazeppa 680 F6
55760 McGregor 447 E4
56556 McIntosh 681 C3
55761 McKinley 230 F3
55049 Medford 775 E6
55441 Medicine Lake 419 G5
†55340 Medina (Hamel) 2,623 F5
†56352 Meire Grove 174 C5
56252 Melrose 2,409 D5
56464 Menahga 980 C4
55050 Mendota 219 G5
†55050 Mendota Heights 7,288 G6
56736 Mentor 219 B3
56737 Middle River 349 B2
†55033 Miesville 179 F6
56262 Milan 417 C5
55957 Millville 186 F6
56263 Milroy 242 C6
56354 Miltona 187 C4
*55401 Minneapolis⊙ 370,951 G5
Minneapolis-Saint Paul‡ 2,114,256 G5
56264 Minneota 1,470 C6
55959 Minnesota City 265 G6
56068 Minnesota Lake 744 E7
55343 Minnetonka 38,683 G5
†55364 Minnetrista 3,236 F5
56265 Montevideo⊙ 5,845 C6
56069 Montgomery 2,349 E6
55362 Monticello 2,830 E5
55363 Montrose 762 E5
56560 Moorhead⊙ 29,998 B4
Moorhead-Fargo‡ 137,574 B4
55767 Moose Lake 1,408 F4
55051 Mora⊙ 2,890 E5
56266 Morgan 975 D6
56267 Morris⊙ 5,367 C5
55052 Morristown 639 E6
56270 Morton 549 C6
56466 Motley 444 D4
56364 Mound 9,280 E6
†55112 Mounds View 12,593 G5
55768 Mountain Iron 4,134 F3
56159 Mountain Lake 2,277 D7
56271 Murdock 343 C5
55769 Nashwauk 1,419 E3
56355 Nelson 209 C5
55053 Nerstrand 255 E6
56467 Nevis 332 D4
55366 New Auburn 331 D6
55112 New Brighton 23,269 G5
56738 Newfolden 384 B2
55367 New Germany 347 E6
†55428 New Hope 23,087 G5
56273 New London 812 C5
55054 New Market 286 E6
56356 New Munich 302 D5
55055 Newport 3,323 F6
56071 New Prague 2,952 E6
56072 New Richland 1,263 E7
56073 New Ulm⊙ 13,755 D6
56567 New York Mills 972 C4
56074 Nicollet 709 D6
56568 Nielsville 145 B3
56468 Nisswa 1,407 D4
55056 North Branch 1,597 F5
55057 Northfield 12,562 E6
56001 North Mankato 9,145 D6
†55101 North Oaks 2,846 G5
56661 Northome 312 D3
56275 North Redwood 206 D6
56075 Northrop 269 D7
55109 North Saint Paul 11,921 G5
55368 Norwood 1,219 E6
†55109 Oakdale 12,123 E5
56276 Odessa 177 B5
56160 Odin 134 D7
56569 Ogema 215 C3
56358 Ogilvie 423 E5
56161 Okabena 263 C7
56742 Oklee 536 C3
56277 Olivia⊙ 2,802 C6
56359 Onamia 691 E4
56162 Ormsby 181 D7
†55323 Orono 6,845 F5
55960 Oronoco 574 F6
55771 Orr 294 F2
56278 Ortonville⊙ 2,550 B5
56360 Osakis 1,355 C5
56744 Oslo 379 A2
55369 Osseo 2,974 G5
55961 Ostrander 293 F7
56571 Ottertail 239 C4
55060 Owatonna⊙ 18,632 E6
56469 Palisade 155 E4
56361 Parkers Prairie 917 C4
56470 Park Rapids⊙ 2,976 D4
56362 Paynesville 2,140 D5
56363 Pease 174 E5
†56472 Pelican Lakes (Breezy Point) 384 D4
56572 Pelican Rapids 1,867 B4
56078 Pemberton 208 E7
56279 Pennock 410 C5
56472 Pequot Lakes 681 D4
56573 Perham 2,086 C4
55962 Peterson 291 G7
†56364 Pierz 1,018 D5
56473 Pillager 341 D4
55063 Pine City⊙ 2,489 F5
55963 Pine Island 1,986 F6
56474 Pine River 881 D4
56164 Pipestone⊙ 4,887 B7
55964 Plainview 2,416 F6
55370 Plato 390 D6
56748 Plummer 353 B3
†55441 Plymouth 31,615 G5
56280 Porter 211 B6
55965 Preston⊙ 1,478 F7
55371 Princeton 3,146 E5
56281 Prinsburg 557 C6
55372 Prior Lake 7,284 E6
55810 Proctor 3,180 F4
55967 Racine 285 F7
56475 Randall 527 D4
55065 Randolph 351 E6
56668 Ranier 237 E2
56282 Raymond 723 C5
56750 Red Lake Falls⊙ 1,732 B3
55066 Red Wing⊙ 13,736 F6
56283 Redwood Falls⊙ 5,210 C6
56672 Remer 396 E3
56284 Renville 1,493 C6
56166 Revere 158 C6
56367 Rice 499 D5
55423 Richfield 37,851 G6
56368 Richmond 867 D5
55422 Robbinsdale 14,422 G5
55901 Rochester⊙ 57,890 F6
Rochester‡ 91,971 F6
55067 Rock Creek 890 F5
55373 Rockford 2,408 F5
56369 Rockville 597 D5
55374 Rogers 652 E5
55969 Rollingstone 528 G6
56371 Roscoe 154 D5
56751 Roseau⊙ 2,272 C2
55970 Rose Creek 371 F7
55068 Rosemount 5,083 E6
55113 Roseville 35,820 G5
56579 Rothsay 476 B4
56167 Round Lake 480 C7
56373 Royalton 660 D5
55069 Rush City 1,198 F5
55971 Rushford 1,478 G7
56168 Rushmore 387 C7
56169 Russell 412 C6
56170 Ruthton 328 B6
55778 Rutledge 185 F4
56580 Sabin 446 B4
56285 Sacred Heart 666 C6
55414 Saint Anthony 7,981 G5
55375 Saint Bonifacius 857 F5
55972 Saint Charles 2,184 F7
56080 Saint Clair 655 E6
56301 Saint Cloud⊙ 42,566 D5
Saint Cloud‡ 163,256 D5
55070 Saint Francis 1,184 E5
56754 Saint Hilaire 388 B3
56081 Saint James⊙ 4,346 D7
56374 Saint Joseph 2,994 D5
55426 Saint Louis Park 42,931 G5
56376 Saint Martin 220 D5
55376 Saint Michael 1,519 E5
*55101 Saint Paul (cap.)⊙ 270,230 G6
Saint Paul-Minneapolis‡ 2,114,256 G5
55071 Saint Paul Park 4,864 G6
56082 Saint Peter⊙ 9,056 E6
56375 Saint Stephen 453 D5
56755 Saint Vincent 141 A2
56083 Sanborn 518 C6
55072 Sandstone 1,594 F4
56377 Sartell 3,427 D5
56378 Sauk Centre 3,709 D5
56379 Sauk Rapids 5,793 D5
55337 Savage 3,954 G6
†55720 Scanlon 1,050 F4
56477 Sebeka 774 C4
55074 Shafer 180 F5
55379 Shakopee⊙ 9,941 F6
56581 Shelly 276 B3
56171 Sherburn 1,275 D7
56676 Shevlin 193 C3
†55112 Shoreview 17,300 G5
†55331 Shorewood 4,646 F5
55614 Silver Bay 2,917 G3
55381 Silver Lake 698 D6
†56001 Skyline 399 D6
56172 Slayton⊙ 2,420 C7
56085 Sleepy Eye 3,581 D6
†56345 Sobieski 219 D5
55382 South Haven 205 D5
56679 South International Falls 2,806 E2
55075 South Saint Paul 21,235 G6
56288 Spicer 909 C5
56087 Springfield 2,303 C6
55974 Spring Grove 1,275 G7
†55432 Spring Lake Park 6,477 E5
55384 Spring Park 1,465 F5
55975 Spring Valley 2,616 F7
56681 Squaw Lake 162 D3
55079 Stacy 996 E5
56479 Staples 2,887 D4
56381 Starbuck 1,224 C5
56173 Steen 153 B7
56757 Stephen 898 A2
55385 Stewart 616 D6
55976 Stewartville 3,925 F7
55082 Stillwater⊙ 12,290 F5
55988 Stockton 517 G6
56174 Storden 341 C6
56758 Strandquist 136 B2
55783 Sturgeon Lake 222 F4
†55075 Sunfish Lake 344 E6
56382 Swanville 295 D5
55786 Taconite 331 E3
56291 Taunton 177 B6
55084 Taylors Falls 623 F5
56683 Tenstrike 159 D3
56701 Thief River Falls⊙ 9,105 B2
†56319 Thomson 152 F4
†55331 Tonka Bay 1,354 F5
55790 Tower 640 F3
56175 Tracy 2,478 C6
56176 Trimont 805 D7
56088 Truman 1,392 D7
56089 Twin Lakes 210 E7
56584 Twin Valley 907 B3
55616 Two Harbors⊙ 4,039 G3
56178 Tyler 1,353 B6
56585 Ulen 514 B3
56586 Underwood 332 C4
56384 Upsala 400 D5
55979 Utica 249 G7
†55101 Vadnais Heights 5,111 G5
56587 Vergas 287 C4
55085 Vermillion 438 F6
56481 Verndale 504 C4
56090 Vernon Center 365 D7
56292 Vesta 360 C6
55386 Victoria 1,425 F6
56385 Villard 275 C5
55792 Virginia 11,056 F3
55981 Wabasha⊙ 2,372 G6
56293 Wabasso 745 C6
55387 Waconia 2,638 E6
56482 Wadena⊙ 4,699 C4
56386 Wahkon 271 E4
56387 Waite Park 3,496 D5
56091 Waldorf 249 E7
56484 Walker⊙ 970 D3
56180 Walnut Grove 753 C6
55982 Waltham 176 F7
55983 Wanamingo 717 F6
55743 Warba 150 E3
56762 Warren⊙ 2,105 B2
56763 Warroad 1,216 C2
56093 Waseca⊙ 8,219 E6
55388 Watertown 1,818 E6
56096 Waterville 1,717 E6
55389 Watkins 757 D5
56295 Watson 238 C5
56589 Waubun 390 C3
55390 Waverly 470 E5
55391 Wayzata 3,621 G5
56181 Welcome 855 D7
56097 Wells 2,777 E7
56590 Wendell 216 B4
56183 Westbrook 978 C6
55985 West Concord 762 F6
55118 West Saint Paul 18,527 G5
56296 Wheaton⊙ 1,969 B5
55110 White Bear Lake 22,538 G5
55090 Willernie 654 G5
56686 Williams 217 D2
56201 Willmar⊙ 15,895 C5
55795 Willow River 303 F4
56185 Wilmont 380 C7
56687 Wilton 176 C3
56101 Windom⊙ 4,666 C7
56592 Winger 200 B3
56098 Winnebago 1,869 D7
55987 Winona⊙ 25,075 G6
55395 Winsted 1,522 D6
55396 Winthrop 1,376 D6
55796 Winton 276 G3
56594 Wolverton 177 B4
†55798 Woodbury 10,297 F6
56297 Wood Lake 420 C6
56186 Woodstock 180 B7
56187 Worthington⊙ 10,243 C7
55797 Wrenshall 333 F4
55798 Wright 162 E4
55990 Wykoff 482 F7
55092 Wyoming 1,559 F5
55397 Young America 1,237 E6
55398 Zimmerman 1,074 E5
55991 Zumbro Falls 208 F6
55992 Zumbrota 2,129 F6

OTHER FEATURES

Ash (riv.) F2
Bald Eagle (lake) G3
Basswood (lake) G2
Battle (riv.) D3
Baudette (riv.) D2
Bear (riv.) E3
Bemidji (lake) D3
Benton (lake) B6
Big Fork (riv.) E2
Big Sandy (lake) E4
Big Stone (lake) B5
Birch (lake) G3
Black (riv.) D2
Blue Earth (riv.) D7
Bois de Sioux (riv.) B4
Bowstring (lake) E3
Buffalo (riv.) B4
Burntside (lake) F3
Cass (lake) D3
Cedar (riv.) F7
Chippewa (riv.) C5
Christina (lake) C4
Clearwater (riv.) C3
Cloquet (riv.) F4
Cobb (riv.) E7
Cottonwood (riv.) C6
Crooked (creek) F4
Crooked (lake) G2
Crow (riv.) F5
Crow Wing (riv.) D4
Cuyuna (range) D4
Dead (lake) C4
Deer (lake) E3
Des Moines (riv.) C7
Eagle (mt.) G2
East Swan (riv.) F3
Elbow (lake) C3
Emily (lake) C5
Fond du Lac Ind. Res. F4
Grand Portage Ind. Res. G2
Grand Portage Nat'l Mon. G2
Green (lake) D5
Greenwood (lake) G3
Gull (lake) D4
Heron (lake) C7
Hill (riv.) C3
Independence (lake) F5
Isabella (lake) G3
Itasca (lake) C3
Kabetogama (lake) E2
Kanaranzi (creek) C7
Kettle (riv.) F4
Knife (lake) G2
La Croix (lake) F2
Lac qui Parle (lake) C5
Lac qui Parle (riv.) B6
Lake of the Woods (lake) D1
Leaf (riv.) C4
Leech (lake) D3
Leech Lake Ind. Res. D3
Lida (lake) C4
Little Fork (riv.) E2
Little Rock (creek) D5
Long (lake) C7
Long (lake) F3
Long Prairie (riv.) D4
Lost (riv.) C3
Lower Red (lake) C3
Maple (lake) B3
Maple (riv.) E7
Marsh (lake) B5
Mary (lake) C5
Mesabi (range) E3
Middle (riv.) B2
Mille Lac Ind. Res. E4
Mille Lacs (lake) E4
Miltona (lake) C4
Minneapolis-Saint Paul Airport G5
Minnesota (riv.) E6
Minnetonka (lake) F5
Minnewaska (lake) C5
Misquah (hills) F2
Mississippi (riv.) D4
Moose (riv.) C2
Mud (lake) C2
Mud (riv.) C2
Muskeg (bay) C2
Mustinka (riv.) B5
Nemadji (riv.) F4
Nett (lake) E2
Nett Lake Ind. Res. E2
North (lake) F1
Otter Tail (lake) C4
Otter Tail (riv.) B4
Partridge (riv.) G3
Pelican (lake) C4
Pelican (lake) D4
Pelican (lake) F2
Pelican (riv.) B4
Pelican (riv.) F2
Pepin (lake) F6
Pigeon (riv.) G2
Pike (riv.) F3
Pipestone Nat'l Mon. B6
Pokegama (lake) E3
Pomme de Terre (riv.) C5
Poplar (riv.) C3
Prairie (riv.) E3
Rainy (lake) E2
Rainy (riv.) D2
Rapid (riv.) D2
Redeye (riv.) D4
Red Lake (riv.) B2
Red Lake Ind. Res. C2
Red River of the North (riv.) A2
Redwood (riv.) C6
Reno (lake) C5
Rice (lake) E4
Rock (riv.) B7
Root (riv.) G7
Roseau (riv.) B2
Rum (riv.) E5
Saganaga (lake) H2
Saint Croix (riv.) F5
Saint Louis (riv.) F4
Sand (creek) F5
Sand Hill (riv.) B3
Sarah (lake) F5
Schoolcraft (riv.) C3
Shakopee (creek) C5
Shell (riv.) C4
Shetek (lake) C6
Sleepy Eye (creek) C6
Snake (riv.) A2
Snake (riv.) E4
South Fowl (lake) G1
Star (lake) C4
Sturgeon (riv.) F3
Superior (lake) G3
Swan (lake) D6
Tamarac (riv.) A2
Tamarack (riv.) D2
Thief (lake) C2
Thief (riv.) B2
Traverse (lake) B5
Trout (lake) F2
Two Rivers (riv.) A1
Upper Red (lake) D2
Vermilion (lake) F3
Vermilion (range) F3
Vermilion (riv.) F2
Voyageurs Nat'l Park F2
Wabatawangang (lake) D3
West Swan (riv.) F3
White Earth Ind. Res. C3
Whiteface (riv.) F3
Whitefish (lake) D4
White Iron (lake) G3
Wild Rice (lake) F4
Wild Rice (riv.) B3
Willow (riv.) E4
Winnibigoshish (lake) D3
Woods (lake) D1
Zumbro (riv.) F6

⊙County seat.
‡Population of metropolitan area.
† Zip of nearest p.o. * Multiple zips.

Topography

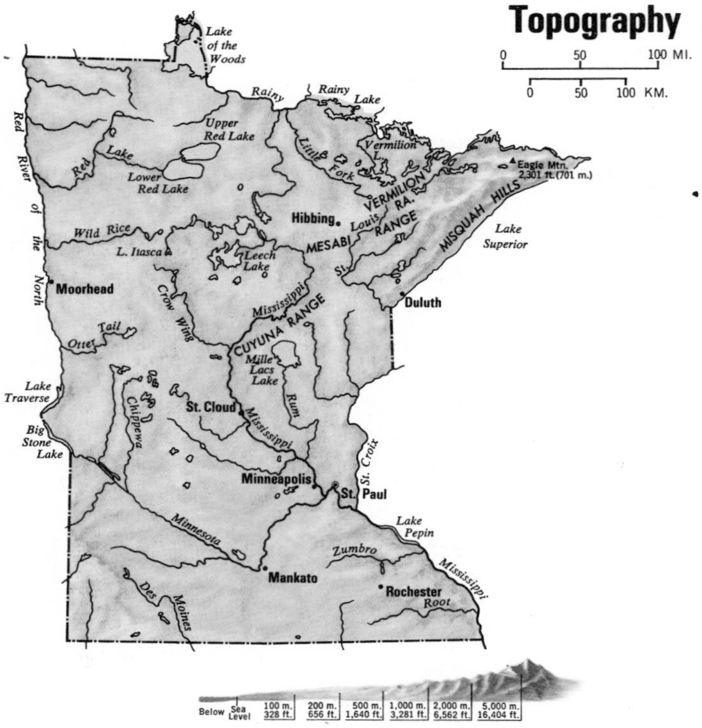
0 50 100 MI.
0 50 100 KM.
Lake of the Woods
Rainy
Rainy Lake
Upper Red Lake
Red Lake
Lower Red Lake
Red River of the North
Vermilion
Little Fork
VERMILION RA.
Eagle Mtn. 2,301 ft. (701 m.)
MISQUAH HILLS
Hibbing
Louis
MESABI RANGE
Lake Superior
Wild Rice
L. Itasca
Leech Lake
Moorhead
Crow Wing
Mississippi
CUYUNA RANGE
Duluth
Otter Tail
Mille Lacs Lake
Lake Traverse
Big Stone Lake
Chippewa
St. Cloud
Rum
St. Croix
Minneapolis
St. Paul
Lake Pepin
Minnesota
Zumbro
Mississippi
Mankato
Rochester
Root
Des Moines
Below Sea Level
100 m. 328 ft.
200 m. 656 ft.
500 m. 1,640 ft.
1,000 m. 3,281 ft.
2,000 m. 6,562 ft.
5,000 m. 16,404 ft.

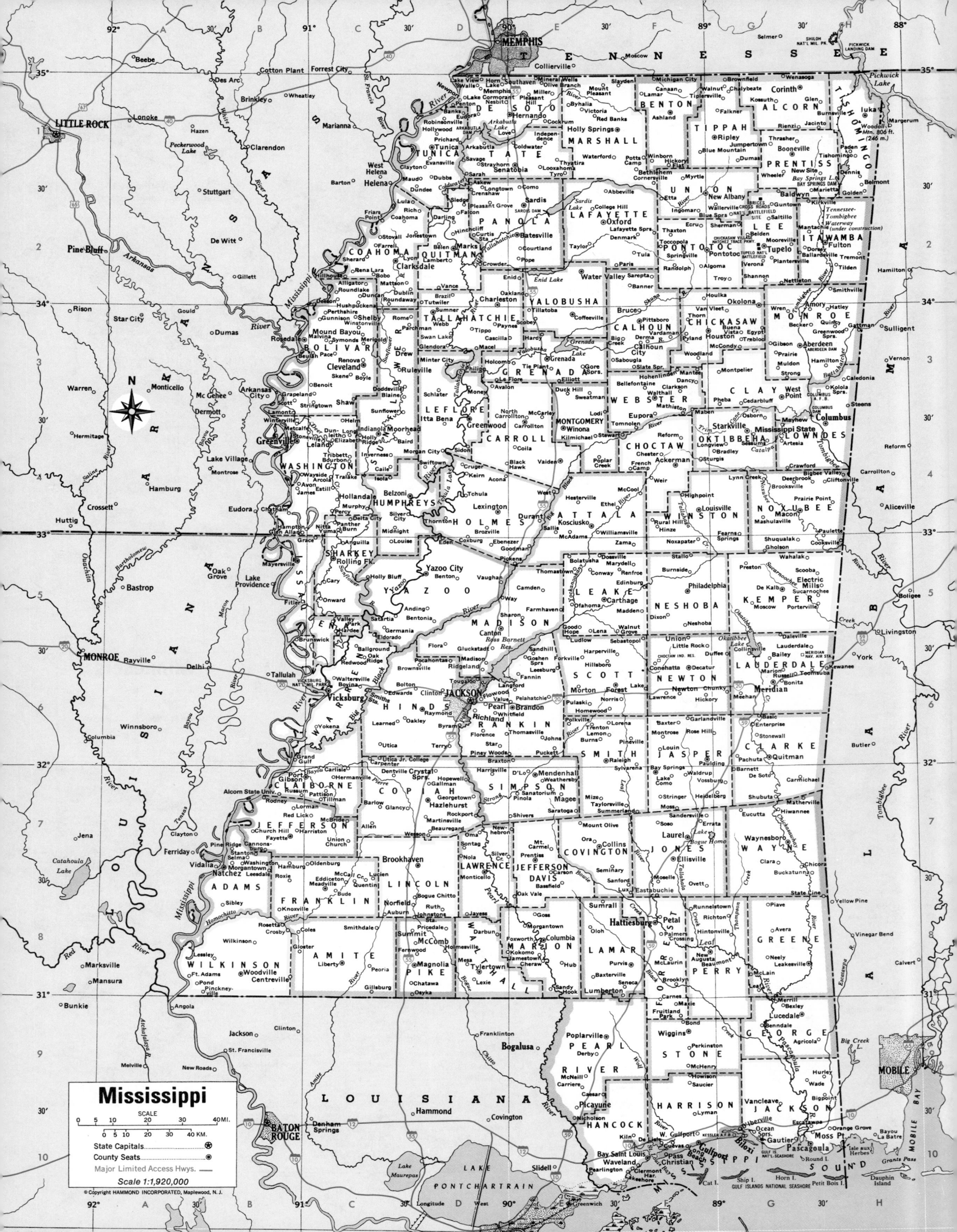

Mississippi

SCALE
0 5 10 20 30 40 MI.
0 5 10 20 30 40 KM.

State Capitals..............⊛
County Seats.............⊛
Major Limited Access Hwys.......

Scale 1:1,920,000

© Copyright HAMMOND INCORPORATED, Maplewood, N.J.

AREA 47,689 sq. mi. (123,515 sq. km.)
POPULATION 2,520,638
CAPITAL Jackson
LARGEST CITY Jackson
HIGHEST POINT Woodall Mtn. 806 ft. (246 m.)
SETTLED IN 1716
ADMITTED TO UNION December 10, 1817
POPULAR NAME Magnolia State
STATE FLOWER Magnolia
STATE BIRD Mockingbird

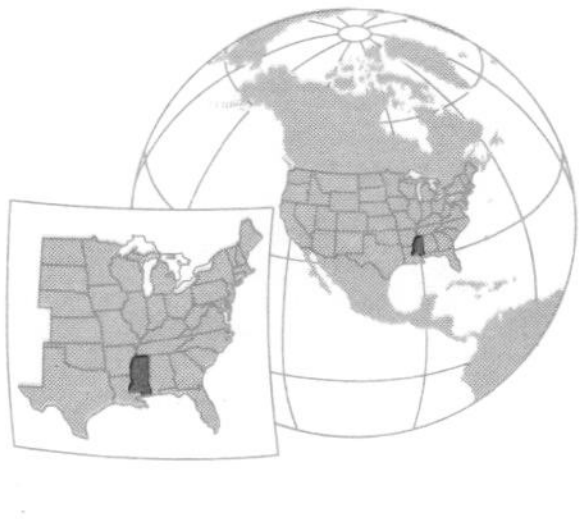

Topography

0 40 80 MI.
0 40 80 KM.

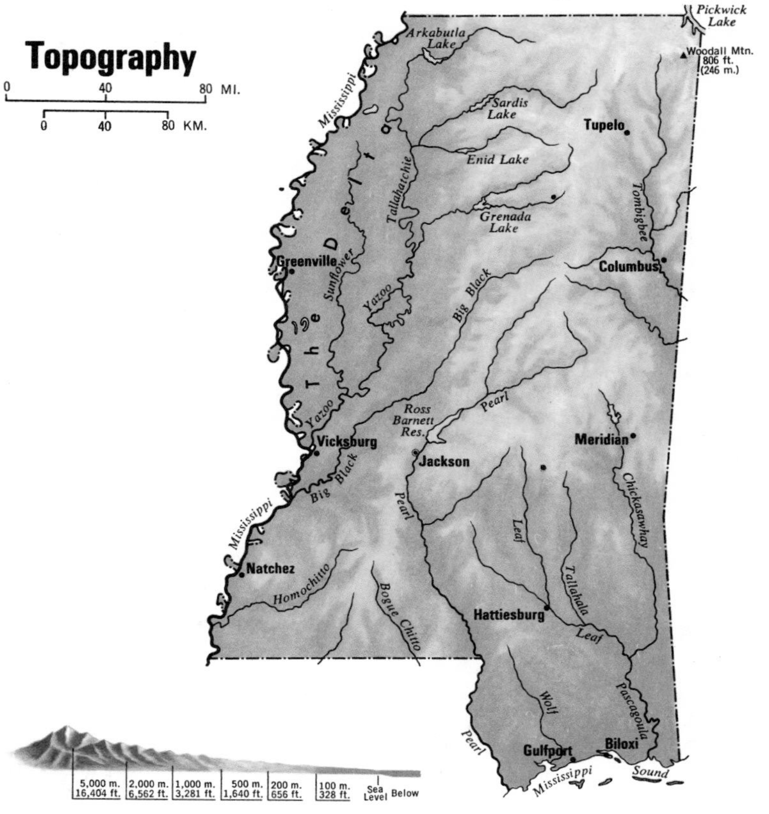

COUNTIES

Adams 38,035 B8
Alcorn 33,036 G1
Amite 13,369 C8
Attala 19,865 E4
Benton 8,153 F1
Bolivar 45,965 C3
Calhoun 15,664 F3
Carroll 9,776 E4
Chickasaw 17,853 G3
Choctaw 8,996 F4
Claiborne 12,279 C7
Clarke 16,945 G6
Clay 21,082 G3
Coahoma 36,918 C2
Copiah 26,503 D7
Covington 15,927 E7
De Soto 53,930 E1
Forrest 66,018 F8
Franklin 8,208 C8
George 15,297 G9
Greene 9,827 G8
Grenada 21,043 E3
Hancock 24,537 E10
Harrison 157,665 F10
Hinds 250,998 D6
Holmes 22,970 D4
Humphreys 13,931 C4
Issaquena 2,513 B5
Itawamba 20,518 H2
Jackson 118,015 G9
Jasper 17,265 F6
Jefferson 9,181 B7
Jefferson Davis 13,846 E7
Jones 61,912 F7
Kemper 10,148 G5
Lafayette 31,030 E2
Lamar 23,821 E8
Lauderdale 77,285 G6
Lawrence 12,518 D7
Leake 18,790 E5
Lee 57,061 G2
Leflore 41,525 D3
Lincoln 30,174 D8
Lowndes 57,304 H4
Madison 41,613 D5
Marion 25,708 E8
Marshall 29,296 E1
Monroe 36,404 H3
Montgomery 13,366 E4
Neshoba 23,789 F5
Newton 19,944 F6
Noxubee 13,212 G4
Oktibbeha 36,018 G4
Panola 28,164 E2
Pearl River 33,795 E9
Perry 9,864 G8
Pike 36,173 D8
Pontotoc 20,918 F2
Prentiss 24,025 G1
Quitman 12,636 D2
Rankin 69,427 E6
Scott 24,556 E6
Sharkey 7,964 C5
Simpson 23,441 E7
Smith 15,077 E6
Stone 9,716 F9
Sunflower 34,844 C3
Tallahatchie 17,157 D3
Tate 20,119 E1
Tippah 18,739 G1
Tishomingo 18,434 H1
Tunica 9,652 D1
Union 21,741 F2
Walthall 13,761 D8
Warren 51,627 C6
Washington 72,344 C4
Wayne 19,135 G7
Webster 10,300 F3
Wilkinson 10,021 B8
Winston 19,474 F4
Yalobusha 13,139 E2
Yazoo 27,349 D5

CITIES and TOWNS

Zip Name/Pop. Key

38601 Abbeville 448 F2
39730 Aberdeen⊙ 7,184 H3
39735 Ackerman⊙ 1,567 F4
39096 Alcorn State University B7
38820 Algoma 175 G2
†39083 Allen 15 C7
38720 Alligator 256 C2
38821 Amory 7,307 H3
38721 Anguilla 950 C5
38722 Arcola 588 C4
38602 Arkabutla 400 D1
39736 Artesia 526 G4
38603 Ashland⊙ 532 F1
38604 Askew 300 D1
†39664 Auburn 500 C8
38912 Avalon 100 D3
38723 Avon 400 B4
39320 Bailey 320 G6
38724 Baird 150 C4
38824 Baldwyn 3,427 G2
†39156 Ballground 30 C5
38913 Banner 120 E2
†39083 Barlow 20 C7
†39330 Basic 60 G6
39421 Bassfield 325 E8
38606 Batesville⊙ 4,692 E2
†39343 Baxter 75 F6
†39455 Baxterville 100 E8
39520 Bay Saint Louis⊙ 7,891 F10
39422 Bay Springs⊙ 1,884 F7
39423 Beaumont 1,112 G8
†39191 Beauregard 185 D7
38825 Becker 350 G3
38826 Belden 241 G2
38609 Belen 400 D2
39737 Bellefontaine 400 F3
38827 Belmont 1,420 H1
39038 Belzoni⊙ 2,982 C4
†39450 Benndale 500 G9
38725 Benoit 499 C3
39039 Benton 350 D5
39040 Bentonia 518 D5
†38659 Bethlehem 210 F1
38726 Beulah 431 B3
39738 Bigbee Valley 370 H4
38914 Big Creek 146 F3
†39567 Bigpoint 350 H9
*39530 Biloxi 49,311 G10
Biloxi-Gulfport‡ 191,918 G10
†38917 Black Hawk 41 E4
38727 Blaine 75 C3
38610 Blue Mountain 867 G1
38828 Blue Springs 131 G2
†38614 Bobo 200 C2
39629 Bogue Chitto 575 D8
39041 Bolton 664 D6
39550 Bond 350 F9
†39301 Bonita 300 G6
38829 Booneville⊙ 6,199 G1
†38756 Bourbon 200 C4
†39180 Bovina 50 C6
38730 Boyle 888 C3
39042 Brandon⊙ 9,626 E6
39044 Braxton 172 D6
38963 Brazil 229 D2
39601 Brookhaven⊙ 10,800 C7
39425 Brooklyn 450 F8
39739 Brooksville 1,038 G4
†38683 Brownfield 125 G1
38915 Bruce 2,208 F3
39322 Buckatunna 500 G7
39630 Bude 1,092 C8
38833 Burnsville 889 H1
38611 Byhalia 757 E1
†39205 Byram 250 D6
†38754 Caile 30 C4
39740 Caledonia 497 H3
38916 Calhoun City 2,033 F3
39045 Camden 150 E5
38612 Canaan 200 F1
39046 Canton⊙ 11,116 D5
39049 Carlisle 425 C7
†39360 Carmichael 75 G7
39050 Carpenter 200 C6
39426 Carriere 900 E9
38917 Carrollton⊙ 338 E4
39427 Carson 400 E7
39051 Carthage⊙ 3,453 E5
39054 Cary 470 C5
38920 Cascilla 230 D3
39741 Cedarbluff 175 G3
39631 Centreville 1,844 B8
38684 Chalybeate 350 G1
38921 Charleston⊙ 2,878 D2
39632 Chatawa 300 D8
38731 Chatham 150 B4
39323 Chunky 277 G6
39055 Church Hill 350 B7
39324 Clara 275 G7
38614 Clarksdale⊙ 21,137 D2
39551 Clermont Harbor 550 F10
38732 Cleveland⊙ 14,524 C3
39056 Clinton 14,660 D6
38617 Coahoma 350 C2
†38632 Cockrum 150 E1
38922 Coffeeville⊙ 1,129 E3
38923 Coila 75 E4
38618 Coldwater 1,505 E1
†39638 Coles 150 C8
†38655 College Hill 150 E2
39428 Collins⊙ 2,131 E7
39325 Collinsville 700 G6
39429 Columbia⊙ 7,733 E8
39701 Columbus⊙ 27,383 H3
38619 Como 1,378 E1
39057 Conehatta 200 F6
†39051 Conway 25 E5
38834 Corinth⊙ 13,839 G1
†38659 Cornersville 65 F1
38620 Courtland 381 E2
†39095 Coxburg 300 D5
39743 Crawford 495 G4
38621 Crenshaw 1,019 D2
39633 Crosby 349 B8
38622 Crowder 789 D2
38924 Cruger 540 D4
39059 Crystal Springs 4,902 D7
†38606 Curtis Station 350 D2
39326 Daleville 210 G5
†39643 Darbun 100 D8
38623 Darling 275 D2
39327 Decatur⊙ 1,148 F6
†39739 Deerbrook 30 G4
39328 De Kalb⊙ 1,159 G5
†39571 De Lisle 450 F10
39061 Delta City 310 C4
†38655 Denmark 40 F2
38838 Dennis 150 H1
†39059 Dentville 175 C7
†39470 Derby 298 E9
38839 Derma 793 F3
†39532 D'Iberville 13,369 G10
39062 D'Lo 463 E7
38736 Doddsville 232 C3
38737 Drew 2,528 C3
38739 Dublin 100 C2
38925 Duck Hill 706 E3
†39337 Duffee 175 G6
39326 Dumas 312 G1
38740 Duncan 501 C2
38626 Dundee 600 D1
39063 Durant 2,889 E4
39436 Eastabuchie 200 F8
39064 Ebenezer 200 D5
38841 Ecru 687 F2
39634 Eddiceton 65 C8
39065 Eden 150 D5
39066 Edwards 1,515 C6
†39156 Eldorado 20 C5
39329 Electric Mills 100 G5
38742 Elizabeth 500 C4
38926 Elliott 200 E3
39437 Ellisville⊙ 4,652 F7
38927 Enid E2
39330 Enterprise 607 G6
†39440 Errata 85 F7
39552 Escatawpa 5,367 G10
39067 Ethel 486 F4
38627 Etta 75 F2
39744 Eupora 2,048 F3
†38676 Evansville 60 D1
38628 Falcon 260 D2
38629 Falkner 251 G1
38630 Farrell 300 C2
39069 Fayette⊙ 2,033 B7
39635 Fernwood 500 D8
39070 Fitler 175 B5
39071 Flora 1,507 D5
39073 Florence 1,111 D6
†39201 Flowood 943 D6
39074 Forest⊙ 5,229 F6
39076 Forkville 185 E6
39636 Fort Adams 75 B8
39483 Foxworth 800 E8
39745 French Camp 306 F4
38631 Friars Point 1,400 C2
39577 Fruitland Park 75 F9
38843 Fulton⊙ 3,238 H2
39077 Gallman D7
38844 Gattman 151 H3
39553 Gautier 8,917 G10
39078 Georgetown 343 D7
†39354 Gholson 50 G5
†39083 Glancy 25 C7
38846 Glen 100 H1
38744 Glen Allan 650 B4
38928 Glendora 220 D3
39638 Gloster 1,726 B8
†39110 Gluckstadt 150 D5
38847 Golden 292 H2
39079 Goodman 1,285 E5
38929 Gore Springs 125 E3
38745 Grace 325 C5
†38725 Grapeland 200 B3
38701 Greenville⊙ 40,613 B4
38930 Greenwood⊙ 20,115 D4
38848 Greenwood Springs 170 H3
38901 Grenada⊙ 12,641 E3
*39501 Gulfport⊙ 39,676 F10
38746 Gunnison 708 C3
38849 Guntown 359 G2
†39661 Hamburg 150 B7
39746 Hamilton 500 H3
†38901 Hardy 45 E3
39080 Harperville 200 E6
39081 Harriston 500 C7
39082 Harrisville 500 D7
†38821 Hatley 497 H3
39401 Hattiesburg⊙ 40,829 F8
39083 Hazlehurst⊙ 4,437 D7
39439 Heidelberg 1,098 F7
39086 Hermanville 750 C7
38632 Hernando⊙ 2,969 E1
†39192 Hesterville 25 E4
39332 Hickory 670 F6
38633 Hickory Flat 458 F1
39087 Hillsboro 800 E6
†38646 Hinchcliff 60 D2
†39462 Hintonville 300 F8
†39108 Hinze 30 F4
†39751 Hohenlinden 96 F3
38940 Holcomb 50 D3
38748 Hollandale 4,336 C4
39088 Holly Bluff 700 C5
38749 Holly Ridge 350 C4
38635 Holly Springs⊙ 7,285 E1
†38676 Hollywood 80 D1
†39648 Holmesville 50 D8
38637 Horn Lake 4,326 D1
38850 Houlka 710 G2
38851 Houston⊙ 3,747 G3
†39574 Howison 300 F9
†39429 Hub 80 E8
39555 Hurley 500 H9
†38774 Hushpuckena 60 C2
38638 Independence 150 E1
38751 Indianola⊙ 8,221 C4
†38652 Ingomar 150 F2
38753 Inverness 1,034 C4
38754 Isola 834 C4
38941 Itta Bena 2,904 D4
38852 Iuka⊙ 2,846 H1
†38865 Jacinto 65 H1
*39201 Jackson (cap.)⊙ 202,895 D6
Jackson‡ 320,425 D6
39641 Jayess 200 D8
38639 Jonestown 1,231 D2
†38829 Jumpertown 472 G1
†38924 Keirn 3 D4
†39364 Kewanee 250 H6
39747 Kilmichael 906 E4
39556 Kiln 800 F10
†39661 Knoxville 65 B8
39643 Kokomo 250 E8
†39740 Kolola Springs 100 H3
39090 Kosciusko⊙ 7,415 E4
38834 Kossuth 190 G1
38640 Lafayette Springs 80 F2
39092 Lake 524 F6
38641 Lake Cormorant 300 D1
39558 Lakeshore 550 F10
38642 Lamar 200 F1
38643 Lambert 1,624 D2
38755 Lamont 400 B3
39335 Lauderdale 600 G5
39440 Laurel⊙ 21,897 F7
39336 Lawrence 250 F6
39450 Leaf 250 G8
39451 Leakesville⊙ 1,120 G8
39093 Learned 113 C6
38756 Leland 6,667 C4
39094 Lena 231 E5
†39667 Lexie 40 D8
39095 Lexington⊙ 2,628 D4
39645 Liberty⊙ 669 C8
39337 Little Rock 70 F5
39560 Long Beach 7,967 F10
†39759 Longview 800 G4
39096 Lorman 350 B7
39338 Louin 338 F6
39097 Louise 400 C5
39339 Louisville⊙ 7,323 G4
†38632 Love 50 D1
39452 Lucedale⊙ 2,429 G9
39646 Lucien 75 C7
39098 Ludlow 350 E5
38644 Lula 394 C2
39455 Lumberton 2,217 E8
†39501 Lyman 500 F10
†39739 Lynn Creek 20 G4
38645 Lyon 531 D2
39750 Maben 855 F3
39341 Macon⊙ 2,396 G4
39109 Madden 450 F5
39110 Madison 2,241 D6
39111 Magee 3,497 E7
39652 Magnolia⊙ 2,461 D8
†38769 Malvina 100 C3
38855 Mantachie 732 H2
39751 Mantee 158 F3
38856 Marietta 298 H2
39342 Marion 771 G6
38646 Marks⊙ 2,260 D2
†39083 Martinsville 30 D7
†39051 Marydell 99 F5
39752 Mathiston 632 F3
38758 Mattson 200 C2
†39458 Maxie 233 F9
39113 Mayersville⊙ 378 B5
39753 Mayhew 150 G4
39107 McAdams 350 E4
†39144 McBride 2 C7
39647 McCall Creek 250 C7
38943 McCarley 250 E3
39648 McComb 12,331 D8
38854 McCondy 150 G3
39108 McCool 203 F4
39561 McHenry 660 F9
39456 McLain 688 G8
39457 McNeill 800 E9
39653 Meadville⊙ 575 C8
39114 Mendenhall⊙ 2,533 E7
39301 Meridian⊙ 46,577 G6
38759 Merigold 574 C3
†39667 Mesa 30 D8
38760 Metcalfe 952 B4
38647 Michigan City 350 F1
39115 Midnight 500 C4
38648 Mineral Wells 250 E1
38944 Minter City 150 D3
39762 Mississippi State G4
39116 Mize 363 E7
38945 Money 350 D3
39654 Monticello⊙ 1,834 D7
39754 Montpelier 175 G3
†39338 Montrose 120 F6
38857 Mooreville 200 G2
38761 Moorhead 2,358 C4
38946 Morgan City 319 D4
39484 Morgantown 325 E8
†39120 Morgantown 3,445 B7
39117 Morton 3,303 E6
†39328 Moscow 30 G5
39459 Moselle 525 F8
39460 Moss 65 F7
39563 Moss Point 18,998 G10
38762 Mound Bayou 2,917 C3
†39474 Mount Carmel 30 E7
39119 Mount Olive 993 E7
38649 Mount Pleasant 250 E1
38650 Myrtle 402 F1
39120 Natchez⊙ 22,015 B7
39461 Neely 270 G8
38651 Nesbit 366 D1
39365 Neshoba 250 F5
38858 Nettleton 1,911 G2
38652 New Albany⊙ 7,072 G2
39462 New Augusta⊙ 589 F8
39140 Newhebron 470 D7
38850 New Houlka (Houlka) 710 G2
38859 New Site 100 H1
39345 Newton 3,708 F6
39463 Nicholson 400 E10
38763 Nitta Yuma 150 C4
†39629 Norfield 75 C8
38947 North Carrollton 859 E3
39346 Noxapater 516 F5
38948 Oakland 540 E2
†39154 Oakley 133 D6
39656 Oak Vale E8
39564 Ocean Springs 14,504 G10
39141 Ofahoma 350 E5
38860 Okolona⊙ 3,409 G2
38654 Olive Branch 2,067 E1
†39482 Oloh 93 E8
†39654 Oma 200 D7
†39501 Orange Grove 13,476 H10
39657 Osyka 581 D8
39464 Ovett 600 F8
38655 Oxford⊙ 9,882 F2
38764 Pace 519 C3
39347 Pachuta 256 G6
38861 Paden 119 H1
†39401 Palmers Crossing 2,765 F8
38765 Panther Burn 300 C4
38738 Parchman 200 D3
38949 Paris 253 F2
39567 Pascagoula⊙ 29,318 G10
Pascagoula-Moss Point‡ 118,015 G10
39571 Pass Christian 5,014 F10
39144 Pattison 540 C7
39348 Paulding⊙ 630 F6
39349 Paulette 230 H4
†38920 Paynes 100 D3
39028 Pearl 18,580 D6
39572 Pearlington 500 E10
39145 Pelahatchie 1,445 E6
39573 Perkinston 950 F9
†38746 Perthshire 25 C3
39465 Petal 8,476 F8
39755 Pheba 280 G3
39350 Philadelphia⊙ 6,434 F5
38950 Philipp 975 D3
†39476 Piave 150 G8
39466 Picayune 10,361 E9
39146 Pickens 1,386 E5
39148 Piney Woods 450 D6
39149 Pinola E7

(continued on following page)

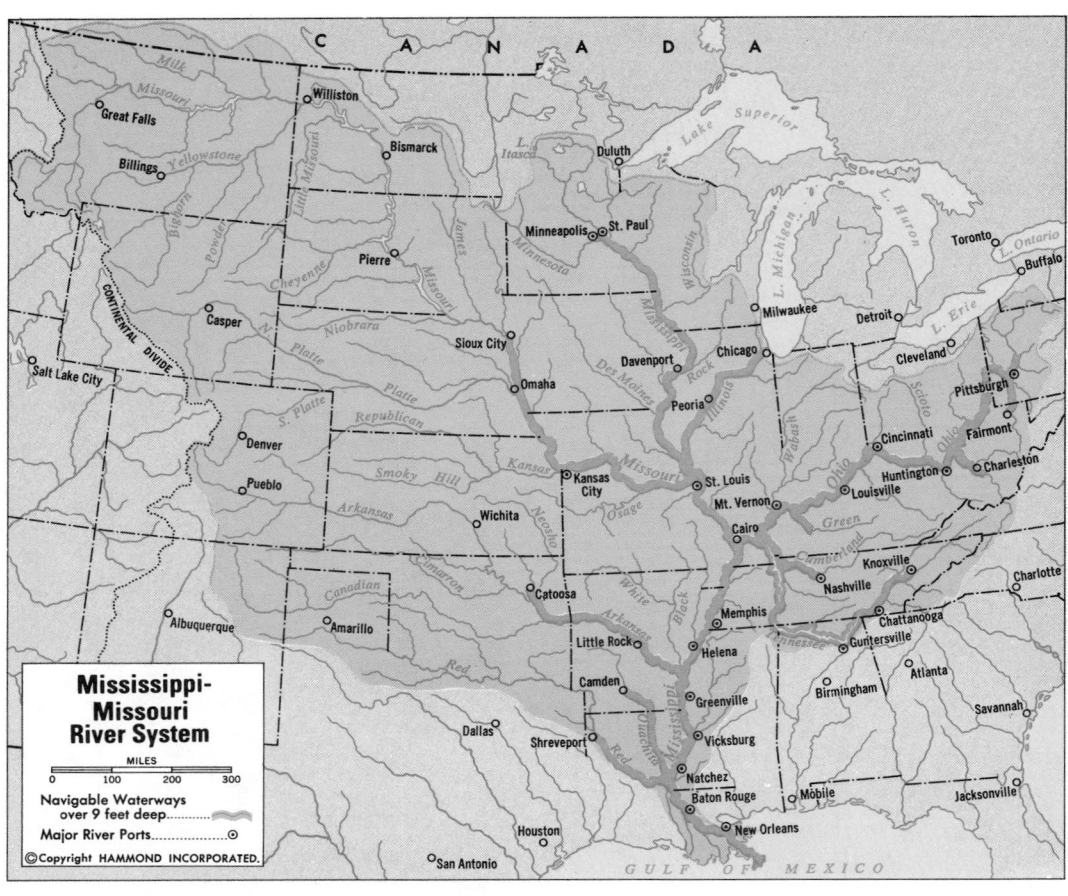

Mississippi-Missouri River System

MILES
0   100   200   300

Navigable Waterways over 9 feet deep
Major River Ports...............⊙

© Copyright HAMMOND INCORPORATED.

Agriculture, Industry and Resources

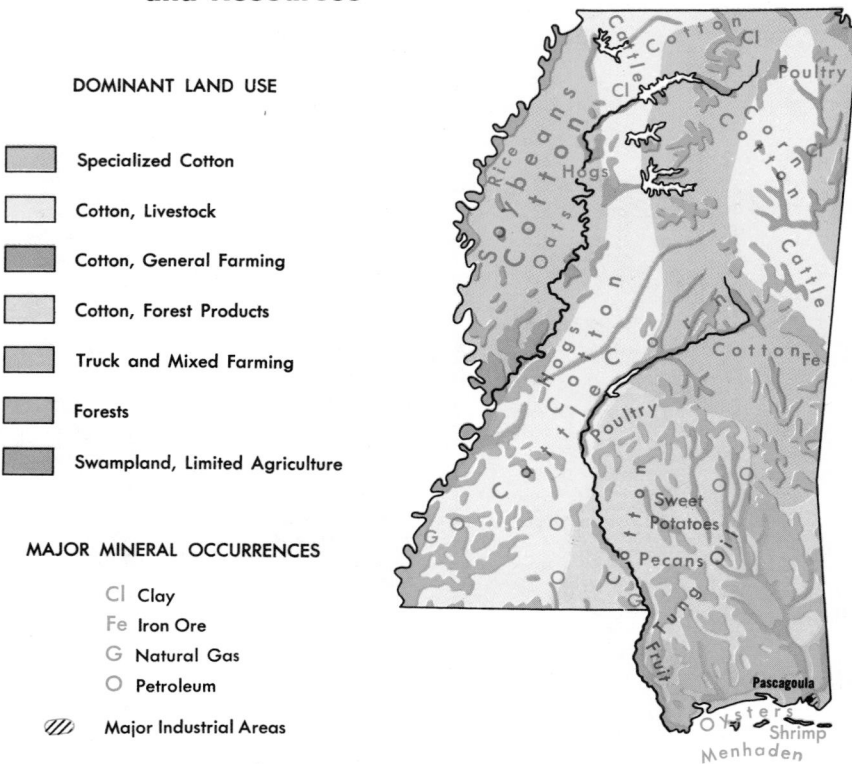

DOMINANT LAND USE

Specialized Cotton

Cotton, Livestock

Cotton, General Farming

Cotton, Forest Products

Truck and Mixed Farming

Forests

Swampland, Limited Agriculture

MAJOR MINERAL OCCURRENCES

Cl   Clay
Fe   Iron Ore
G   Natural Gas
O   Petroleum

⧄   Major Industrial Areas

AREA 69,697 sq. mi. (180,515 sq. km.)
POPULATION 4,916,759
CAPITAL Jefferson City
LARGEST CITY St. Louis
HIGHEST POINT Taum Sauk Mtn. 1,772 ft. (540 m.)
SETTLED IN 1764
ADMITTED TO UNION August 10, 1821
POPULAR NAME Show Me State
STATE FLOWER Hawthorn
STATE BIRD Bluebird

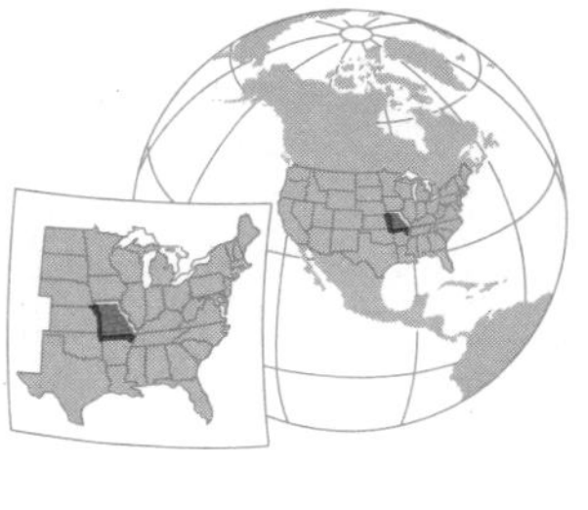

COUNTIES

Adair 24,870 G2
Andrew 13,980 C3
Atchison 8,605 B2
Audrain 26,458 J4
Barry 24,408 E9
Barton 11,292 D7
Bates 15,873 D6
Benton 12,183 F6
Bollinger 10,301 M8
Boone 100,376 H4
Buchanan 87,888 C3
Butler 37,693 M9
Caldwell 8,660 E3
Callaway 32,252 J5
Camden 20,017 G6
Cape Girardeau 58,837 N8
Carroll 12,131 F4
Carter 5,428 L9
Cass 51,029 D5
Cedar 11,894 E7
Chariton 10,489 F3
Christian 22,402 F9
Clark 8,493 J2
Clay 136,488 D4
Clinton 15,916 D3
Cole 56,663 H6
Cooper 14,643 G5
Crawford 18,300 K7
Dade 7,383 E8
Dallas 12,096 F7
Daviess 8,905 E3
De Kalb 8,222 D3
Dent 14,517 J7
Douglas 11,594 G9
Dunklin 36,324 M10
Franklin 71,233 K6
Gasconade 13,181 J6
Gentry 7,887 D2
Greene 185,302 F8
Grundy 11,959 E2
Harrison 9,890 E2
Henry 19,672 E6
Hickory 6,367 F7
Holt 6,882 B2
Howard 10,008 G4
Howell 28,807 J9
Iron 11,084 L7
Jackson 629,266 R5
Jasper 86,958 D8
Jefferson 146,183 L6
Johnson 39,059 E5
Knox 5,508 H2
Laclede 24,323 G7
Lafayette 29,925 E4
Lawrence 28,973 E8
Lewis 10,901 J2
Lincoln 22,193 L4
Linn 15,495 F3
Livingston 15,739 E3
Macon 16,313 G3
Madison 10,725 M8
Maries 7,551 J6
Marion 28,638 J3
McDonald 14,917 D9
Mercer 4,685 E2
Miller 18,532 H6
Mississippi 15,726 O9
Moniteau 12,068 G5
Monroe 9,716 H3
Montgomery 11,537 K5
Morgan 13,807 G6
New Madrid 22,945 N9
Newton 40,555 D9
Nodaway 21,996 C2
Oregon 10,238 K9
Osage 12,014 J6
Ozark 7,961 H9
Pemiscot 24,987 N10
Perry 16,784 N7
Pettis 36,378 F5
Phelps 33,633 J7
Pike 17,568 K4
Platte 46,341 C4
Polk 18,822 F7
Pulaski 42,011 H7
Putnam 6,092 F2
Ralls 8,984 J3
Randolph 25,460 G3
Ray 21,378 E4
Reynolds 7,230 L8
Ripley 12,458 L9
Saint Charles 144,107 M2
Saint Clair 8,622 E6
Sainte Genevieve 15,180 M7
Saint Francois 42,600 M7
Saint Louis 973,896 O3
Saint Louis (city county) 453,085 P3
Saline 24,919 F4
Schuyler 4,979 G2
Scotland 5,415 H2
Scott 39,647 N8
Shannon 7,885 K8
Shelby 7,826 H3
Stoddard 29,009 N9
Stone 15,587 F9
Sullivan 7,434 F2
Taney 20,467 F9
Texas 21,070 J8
Vernon 19,806 D7
Warren 14,900 K5
Washington 17,983 L7
Wayne 11,277 L8
Webster 20,414 G8
Worth 3,008 D2
Wright 16,188 H8

CITIES and TOWNS

Zip Name/Pop. Key

64720 Adrian 1,484 D6
63730 Advance 1,054 N8
63123 Affton 23,181 P4
64401 Agency 419 C3
64830 Alba 474 D8
64402 Albany⊙ 2,152 D2
63430 Alexandria 417 K2
64001 Alma 445 E4
65606 Alton⊙ 721 K9
64421 Amazonia 314 C3
64723 Amsterdam 231 D6
64831 Anderson 1,237 D9
63620 Annapolis 370 L8
63820 Anniston 320 O9
64724 Appleton City 1,257 D6
63821 Arbyrd 704 M10
63621 Arcadia 683 L7
64725 Archie 753 D5
65230 Armstrong 360 G4
63010 Arnold 19,141 M6
65604 Ash Grove 1,157 E8
65010 Ashland 1,021 H5
63530 Atlanta 441 H3
63332 Augusta 308 L5
65605 Aurora 6,437 E9
65231 Auxvasse 858 J4
65608 Ava⊙ 2,761 G9
64010 Avondale 612 P5
63011 Ballwin 12,656 N3
64011 Bates City 199 E5
†65619 Battlefield 1,227 F8
†63101 Bella Villa 758 R4
63735 Bell City 539 N8
65013 Belle 1,233 J6
†63137 Bellefontaine Neighbors 12,082 R2
63333 Bellflower 403 K4
†63101 Bel-Nor 2,047 P2
†63101 Bel-Ridge 3,682 P2
64012 Belton 12,708 C5
63736 Benton⊙ 674 O8
63134 Berkeley 15,922 P2
63822 Bernie 1,975 M9
63823 Bertrand 688 O9
64424 Bethany⊙ 3,095 E2
63532 Bevier 733 G3
65610 Billings 911 F8
65438 Birch Tree 622 K9
63624 Bismarck 1,625 L7
65321 Blackburn 314 F4
†63031 Black Jack 5,293 R1
65014 Bland 662 J6
63825 Bloomfield⊙ 1,795 M9
63627 Bloomsdale 397 M6
64015 Blue Springs 25,927 R6
†64101 Blue Summit R5
65613 Bolivar⊙ 5,919 F7
63628 Bonne Terre 3,797 L7
65233 Boonville⊙ 6,959 G5
64723 Bosworth 394 F4
65441 Bourbon 1,259 K6
63334 Bowling Green⊙ 3,022 K4
65616 Branson 2,550 F9
63533 Brashear 332 H2
64624 Braymer 986 E3
64625 Breckenridge 523 E3
†63114 Breckenridge Hills 5,666 O2
63144 Brentwood 8,209 P3
63044 Bridgeton 18,445 O2
†63044 Bridgeton Terrace 334 O2
64628 Brookfield 5,555 F3
64630 Browning 368 F2
65236 Brunswick 1,272 F4
64631 Bucklin 713 G3
64016 Buckner 2,848 R5
65622 Buffalo⊙ 2,217 F7
65237 Bunceton 419 G5
63629 Bunker 673 K8
64428 Burlington Junction 657 B2
64730 Butler⊙ 4,107 D6
65689 Cabool 2,090 H8
64632 Cainsville 496 E2
65239 Cairo 315 H4
65323 Calhoun 427 E6
65018 California⊙ 3,381 H5
63534 Callao 326 G3
†63101 Calverton Park 1,717 P2
65020 Camdenton⊙ 2,303 G6
64429 Cameron 4,519 D3
63933 Campbell 2,134 M9
63828 Canalou 369 N9
63435 Canton 2,435 J2
63701 Cape Girardeau 34,361 O8
63829 Cardwell 831 M10
64834 Carl Junction 3,937 C8
64633 Carrollton⊙ 4,700 E4
64835 Carterville 1,973 D8
64836 Carthage⊙ 11,104 D8
63830 Caruthersville⊙ 7,958 N10
65625 Cassville⊙ 2,091 E9
65022 Cedar City 427 H5
63436 Center 669 J3
65023 Centertown 304 H5
63633 Centerville⊙ 241 L8
65240 Centralia 3,537 H4
63740 Chaffee 3,241 N8
65024 Chamois 546 J5
†63101 Charlack 1,537 P2
63834 Charleston⊙ 5,230 O9
64733 Chilhowee 349 E5
64601 Chillicothe⊙ 9,089 E3
63437 Clarence 1,147 H3
65243 Clark 304 H4
65025 Clarksburg 352 G5
64430 Clarksdale 278 D3
†63017 Clarkson Valley 1,435 N3
63336 Clarksville 585 K4
63837 Clarkton 1,228 M10
†64119 Claycomo 1,671 P5
63105 Clayton⊙ 14,273 P3
64734 Cleveland 485 C5
65631 Clever 551 F8
64735 Clinton⊙ 8,366 E6
65325 Cole Camp 1,022 F6
65201 Columbia⊙ 62,061 H5
Columbia‡ 100,376 H5
†63128 Concord 20,896 P4
64020 Concordia 2,129 E5
65632 Conway 601 G7
†63101 Cool Valley 2,084 P2
63839 Cooter 479 N10
64021 Corder 483 E4
†64501 Country Club Village 1,234 C3
64437 Craig 379 B2
65633 Crane 1,185 E9
64739 Creighton 301 D6
†63126 Crestwood 12,815 O3
63141 Creve Coeur 11,757 O2
65452 Crocker 979 H7
63019 Crystal City 3,618 M6
†63101 Crystal Lake Park 496 O3
65453 Cuba 2,120 K6
63339 Curryville 323 K4
64439 Dearborn 547 C3
64740 Deepwater 475 E6
64440 De Kalb 245 C3
†63135 Dellwood 6,200 R2
63744 Delta 524 N8
63636 Des Arc 237 L8
63601 Desloge 3,481 M7
63020 De Soto 5,993 L6
63131 Des Peres 8,254 O3
63841 Dexter 7,043 N9
64840 Diamond 766 D9
65459 Dixon 1,402 H6
63935 Doniphan⊙ 1,921 L9
†65550 Doolittle 701 J7
63536 Downing 462 H2
64742 Drexel 908 C6
64841 Duenweg 703 D8
†64801 Duquesne 1,252 D8
64442 Eagleville 364 D2
64443 Easton 313 C3
63845 East Prairie 3,713 O9
64444 Edgerton 584 C3
63537 Edina⊙ 1,520 H2
†63101 Edmundson 1,374 O2
65026 Eldon 4,342 G6
64744 El Dorado Springs 3,868 E7
63638 Ellington 1,215 L8
†63011 Ellisville 6,233 M3
63937 Ellsinore 362 L9
63343 Elsberry 1,272 L4
63639 Elvins 1,548 L7
65466 Eminence⊙ 614 K8
63344 Eolia 401 L4
63846 Essex 545 N9
†63601 Esther 1,038 M7
63025 Eureka 3,862 M4
65646 Everton 317 E8
63440 Ewing 400 J2
64024 Excelsior Springs 10,424 R4
65647 Exeter 588 D9
64446 Fairfax 835 B2
65648 Fair Grove 863 F8
65649 Fair Play 384 E7
63345 Farber 503 J4
63640 Farmington⊙ 8,270 M7
65248 Fayette⊙ 2,983 G4
63026 Fenton 2,417 O4
63135 Ferguson 24,740 P2
64163 Ferrelview 447 O4
63028 Festus 7,574 M6
64449 Fillmore 265 C2
63940 Fisk 450 M9
63601 Flat River 4,443 M7
*63031 Florissant 55,372 P1
65652 Fordland 569 G8
64451 Forest City 387 B3
65653 Forsyth⊙ 1,010 F9
63441 Frankford 443 K4
63645 Fredericktown⊙ 4,036 M7
65035 Freeburg 554 J6
64746 Freeman 485 C5
†63101 Frontenac 3,654 O3
65251 Fulton⊙ 11,046 J5
65655 Gainesville⊙ 707 G9
65656 Galena⊙ 423 F9
64640 Gallatin⊙ 2,063 E3
64641 Galt 323 F2
64747 Garden City 1,021 D5
63037 Gerald 921 K6
63848 Gideon 1,240 N10
64642 Gilman City 414 D2
64118 Gladstone 24,990 P5
65254 Glasgow 1,336 G4
†64068 Glenaire 541 R5
63122 Glendale 6,035 P3
64748 Golden City 900 D8
63843 Goodman 1,030 C9
63543 Gorin H2
64454 Gower 1,276 C3
64029 Grain Valley 1,327 S6
64844 Granby 1,908 D9
64030 Grandview 24,502 P6
64456 Grant City⊙ 1,068 D2
†63155 Grantwood Village 1,002 O4
65037 Gravois Mills G6
63545 Green City 719 F2
65661 Greenfield⊙ 1,394 E8
65332 Green Ridge 488 F5
63546 Greentop 538 H2
63944 Greenville⊙ 393 M8
64034 Greenwood 1,315 R6
64643 Hale 529 F3
65255 Hallsville 624 H4
64644 Hamilton 1,582 E3
†63101 Hanley Hills 2,439 P2
63401 Hannibal 18,811 K3
64035 Hardin 688 E4
64701 Harrisonville⊙ 6,372 D5
65667 Hartville⊙ 576 G8
63945 Harviell M9
63349 Hawk Point 386 K5
63851 Hayti 3,964 N10
†63851 Hayti Heights 1,023 N10
†63736 Haywood City 425 N9
*63042 Hazelwood 12,935 P2
64036 Henrietta 424 E4
63048 Herculaneum 2,293 M6
65041 Hermann⊙ 2,695 K5
65668 Hermitage⊙ 384 F7
65257 Higbee 817 H4
64037 Higginsville 4,595 E4
63350 High Hill 254 K5
63050 Hillsboro⊙ 1,508 L6
†63101 Hillsdale 2,247 R2
63852 Holcomb 632 N10
64040 Holden 2,195 E5
63853 Holland 295 N10
65672 Hollister 1,439 F9
64048 Holt 276 D4
65043 Holts Summit 2,540 H5
†63879 Homestown 306 N10
64461 Hopkins 634 C1
63855 Hornersville 704 M10
65483 Houston⊙ 2,157 J8
65333 Houstonia 327 F5
†64152 Houston Lake 280 O5
†63869 Howardville 536 N9
65674 Humansville 907 E7
64752 Hume 315 C6
63443 Hunnewell 235 J3
†63101 Huntleigh 428 O3
65259 Huntsville⊙ 1,657 H4
63547 Hurdland 227 H2
65486 Iberia 852 H6
63754 Illmo 1.368 O8

(continued on following page)

Agriculture, Industry and Resources

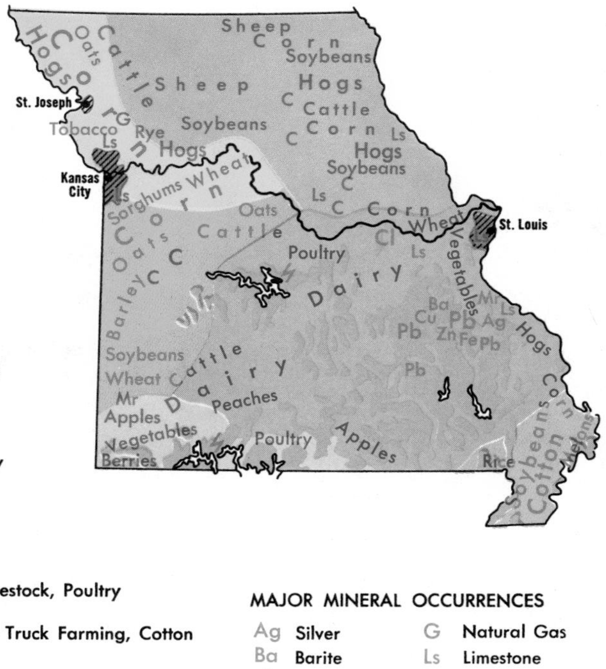

DOMINANT LAND USE

Cattle Feed, Hogs
Livestock, Cash Grain, Dairy
Pasture Livestock
Specialized Cotton
General Farming, Dairy, Livestock, Poultry
General Farming, Livestock, Truck Farming, Cotton
Fruit and Mixed Farming
Forests
Urban Areas

MAJOR MINERAL OCCURRENCES

Ag Silver
Ba Barite
C Coal
Cl Clay
Cu Copper
Fe Iron Ore
G Natural Gas
Ls Limestone
Mr Marble
Pb Lead
Zn Zinc

Water Power
Major Industrial Areas

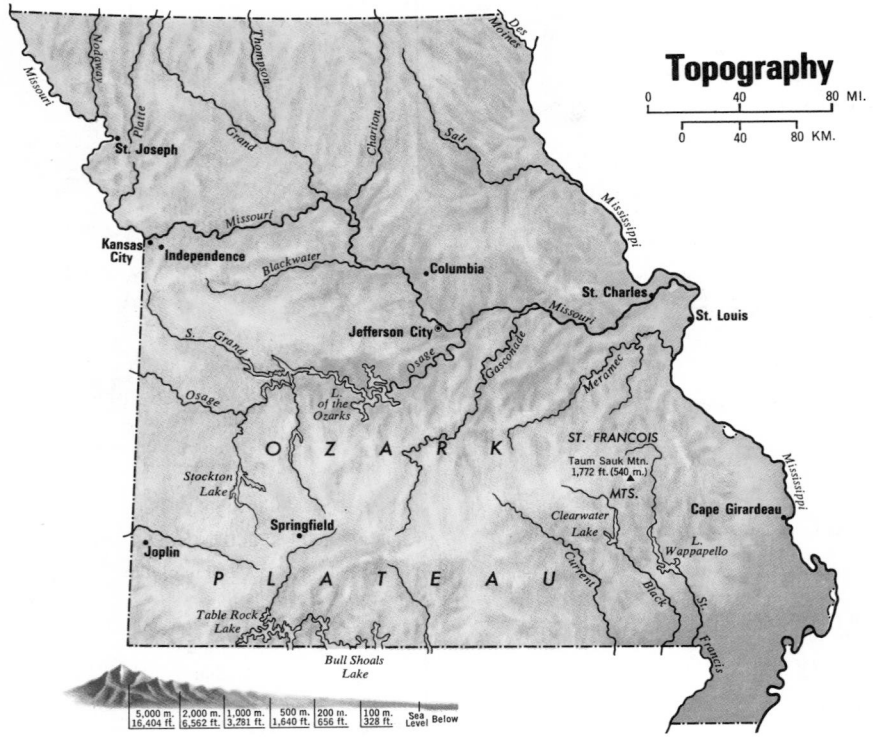

Topography

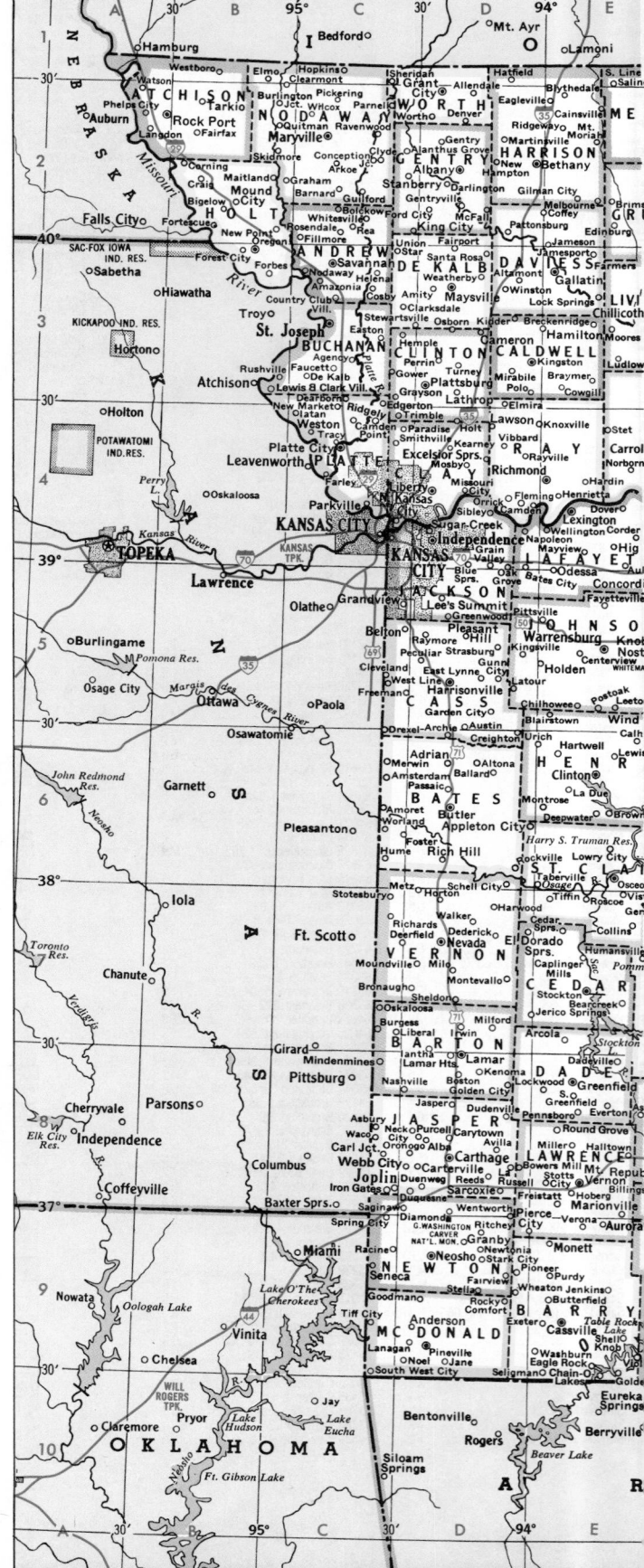

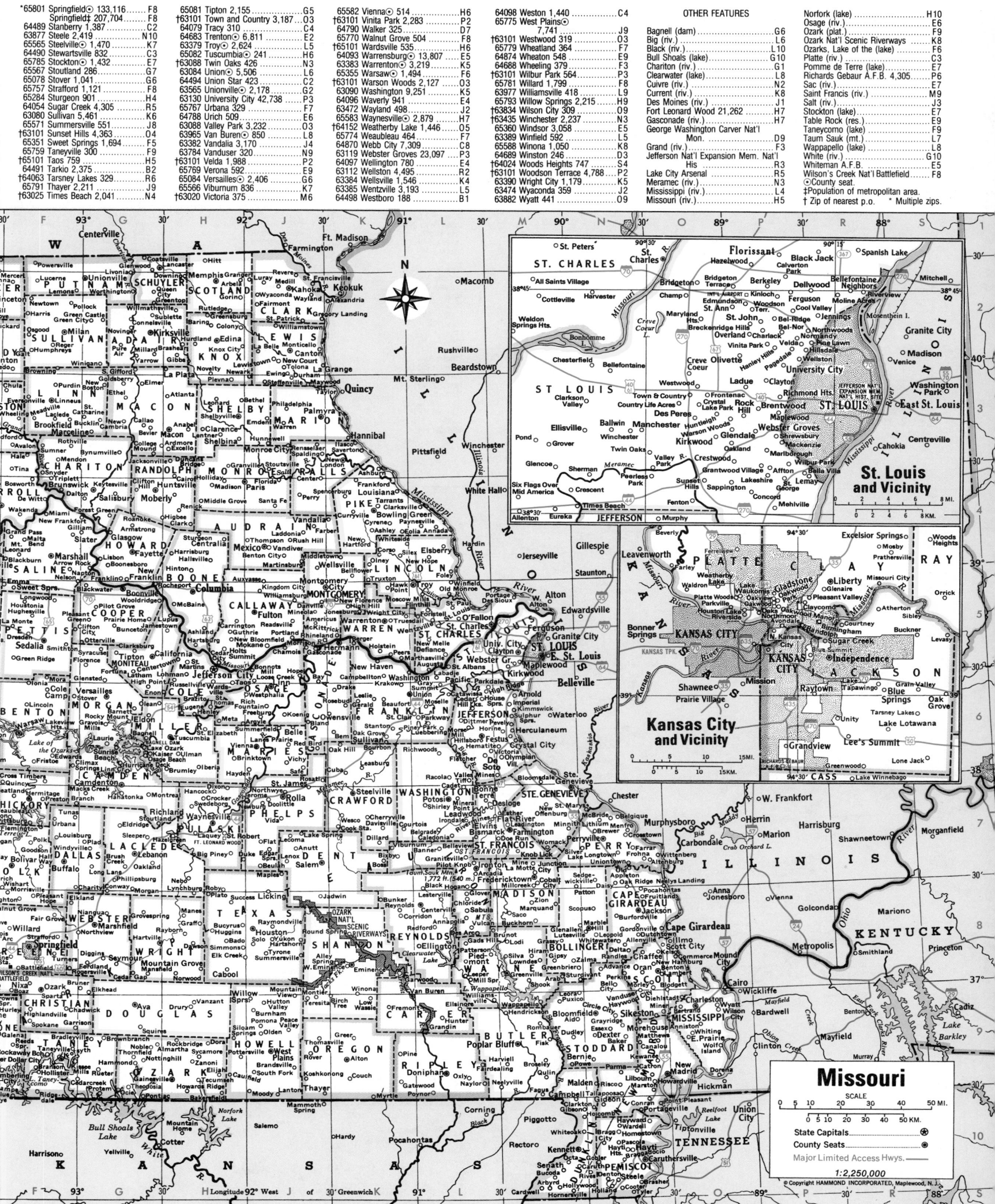

Agriculture, Industry and Resources

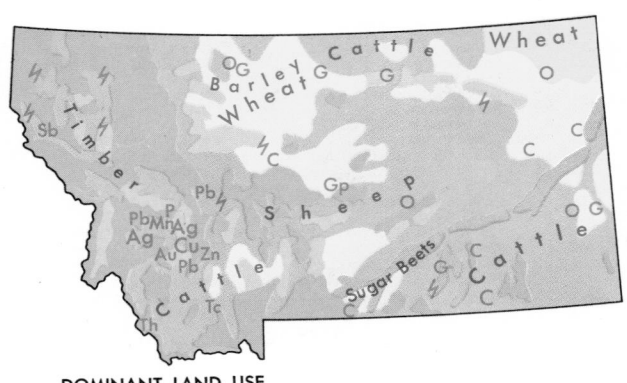

DOMINANT LAND USE

- Specialized Wheat
- Wheat, Range Livestock
- General Farming, Dairy, Range Livestock
- General Farming, Livestock, Special Crops
- Range Livestock
- Sugar Beets, Beans, Livestock, General Farming
- Forests

MAJOR MINERAL OCCURRENCES

Ag	Silver	O	Petroleum
Au	Gold	P	Phosphates
C	Coal	Pb	Lead
Cu	Copper	Sb	Antimony
G	Natural Gas	Tc	Talc
Gp	Gypsum	Th	Thorium
Mn	Manganese	Zn	Zinc

⚡ Water Power

COUNTIES

Beaverhead 8,186 .... C5
Big Horn 11,096 .... J5
Blaine 6,999 .... G2
Broadwater 3,267 .... E4
Carbon 8,099 .... G5
Carter 1,799 .... M5
Cascade 80,696 .... E3
Chouteau 6,092 .... F3
Custer 13,109 .... L4
Daniels 2,835 .... L2
Dawson 11,805 .... M3
Deer Lodge 12,518 .... C5
Fallon 3,763 .... M4
Fergus 13,076 .... G3
Flathead 51,966 .... B2
Gallatin 42,865 .... E5
Garfield 1,656 .... J3
Glacier 10,628 .... C2
Golden Valley 1,026 .... G4
Granite 2,700 .... C4
Hill 17,985 .... F2
Jefferson 7,029 .... D4
Judith Basin 2,646 .... F4
Lake 19,056 .... B3
Lewis and Clark 43,039 .... D3
Liberty 2,329 .... E2
Lincoln 17,752 .... B2
Madison 5,448 .... D5
McCone 2,702 .... L3
Meagher 2,154 .... F4
Mineral 3,675 .... B3
Missoula 76,016 .... C3
Musselshell 4,428 .... H4
Park 12,869 .... F5
Petroleum 655 .... H3
Phillips 5,367 .... J2
Pondera 6,731 .... D2
Powder River 2,520 .... L5
Powell 6,958 .... D4
Prairie 1,836 .... L4
Ravalli 22,493 .... B4
Richland 12,243 .... M3
Roosevelt 10,467 .... L2
Rosebud 9,899 .... K4
Sanders 8,675 .... A3
Sheridan 5,414 .... M2
Silver Bow 38,092 .... D5
Stillwater 5,598 .... G5
Sweet Grass 3,216 .... G5
Teton 6,491 .... D3
Toole 5,559 .... E2
Treasure 981 .... J4
Valley 10,250 .... K2
Wheatland 2,359 .... G4
Wibaux 1,476 .... M4
Yellowstone 108,035 .... H4
Yellowstone Nat'l Park 275 .... F6

CITIES and TOWNS

Zip	Name/Pop.	Key
59001	Absarokee 830	G5
59820	Alberton 368	B3
59710	Alder 120	D5
†59741	Amsterdam 130	E5
59711	Anaconda-Deer Lodge County⊙ 12,518	C4
59312	Angela 50	K4
59211	Antelope 83	M2
59821	Arlee 200	B3
59003	Ashland 600	K5
59410	Augusta 497	D3
59713	Avon 125	D4
59411	Babb 150	C2
59313	Baker⊙ 2,354	M4
†59725	Bannack 2	C5
59613	Basin 350	D4
59006	Ballantine 380	J5
59007	Bearcreek 61	G5
59008	Belfry 300	H5
59714	Belgrade 2,336	E5
59412	Belt 825	E3
59314	Biddle 28	L5
59910	Big Arm 250	B3
59520	Big Sandy 835	G2
59911	Big Timber 1,690	G5
*59101	Billings⊙ 66,842	H5
	Billings‡ 108,035	H5
59012	Birney 100	K5
59414	Black Eagle 1,500	E3

Zip	Name/Pop.	Key
59415	Blackfoot 100	D2
59823	Bonner-West Riverside 1,742	C4
59632	Boulder⊙ 1,441	E4
59521	Box Elder 300	F2
59715	Bozeman⊙ 21,645	E5
59416	Brady 450	E2
59014	Bridger 724	H5
59317	Broadus⊙ 712	L5
59015	Broadview 120	H4
59213	Brockton 374	M2
59417	Browning 1,226	C2
59016	Busby 700	J5
59701	Butte-Silver Bow County⊙ 37,205	D5
59720	Cameron 150	E5
59633	Canyon Creek 100	D4
†59347	Cartersville 115	K4
59421	Cascade 773	E3
59824	Charlo 250	B3
59522	Chester⊙ 963	E2
59523	Chinook⊙ 1,660	G2
59422	Choteau⊙ 1,798	D3
59215	Circle⊙ 931	L3
59634	Clancy 550	E4
59018	Clyde Park 283	F5
†59351	Coalwood 2	L5
59322	Cohagen 12	K3
59323	Colstrip 1,476	K5
59912	Columbia Falls 3,112	B2
59019	Columbus⊙ 1,439	G5
59826	Condon 300	C3
59827	Conner 420	B5
59425	Conrad⊙ 3,074	D2
59020	Cooke City 120	G5
59913	Coram 450	C2
59828	Corvallis 500	C4
59217	Crane 163	M3
59022	Crow Agency 975	J5
59218	Culbertson 887	M2
59024	Custer 300	J4
59427	Cut Bank⊙ 3,688	D2
59829	Darby 581	B4
59914	Dayton 140	B3
59830	De Borgia 300	A3
59025	Decker 150	K5
59722	Deer Lodge⊙ 4,023	D4
59430	Denton 356	G3

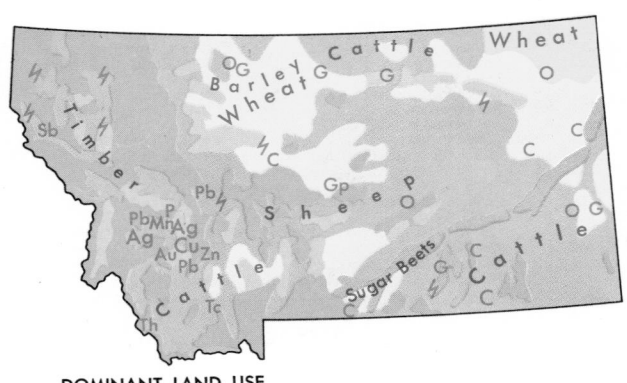

Montana

SCALE

0 5 10 20 40 60 MI.

0 5 10 20 40 60KM.

⊛ State Capitals

⊙ County Seats

Major Limited Access Hwys.

Scale 1:3,450,000

© Copyright HAMMOND INCORPORATED, Maplewood, N.J.

Topography

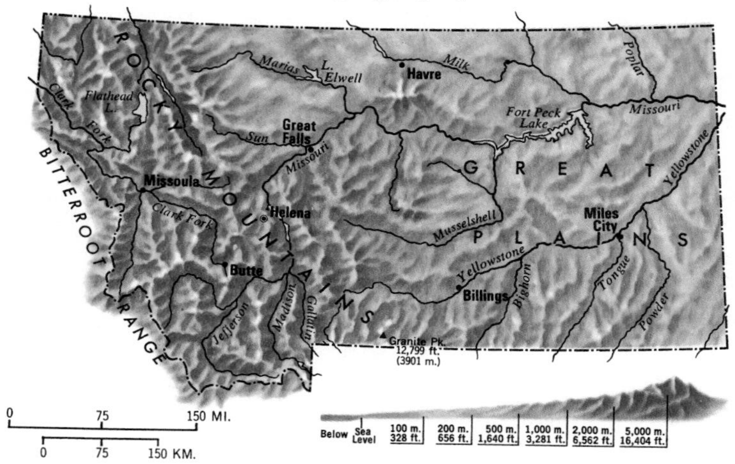

AREA 147,046 sq. mi. (380,849 sq. km.)
POPULATION 786,690
CAPITAL Helena
LARGEST CITY Billings
HIGHEST POINT Granite Pk. 12,799 ft. (3901 m.)
SETTLED IN 1809
ADMITTED TO UNION November 8, 1889
POPULAR NAME Treasure State; Big Sky Country
STATE FLOWER Bitterroot
STATE BIRD Western Meadowlark

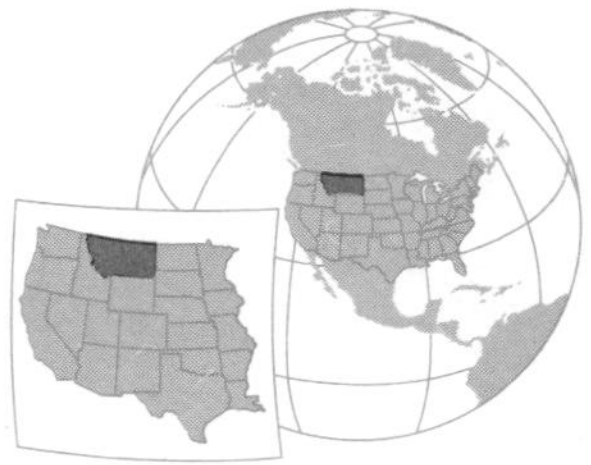

59725 Dillon⊙ 3,976 .... D5
59727 Divide 275 .... D5
59831 Dixon 550 .... B3
59524 Dodson 158 .... H2
59832 Drummond 414 .... D4
59432 Dupuyer 105 .... D2
59433 Dutton 359 .... E3
59434 East Glacier Park 475 .... C2
59635 East Helena 1,647 .... E4
59026 Edgar 220 .... H5
59324 Ekalaka⊙ 620 .... M5
59728 Elliston 250 .... D4
59915 Elmo 250 .... B3
59729 Ennis 660 .... E5
59917 Eureka 1,119 .... B2
59436 Fairfield 650 .... D3
59221 Fairview 1,366 .... M3
59326 Fallon 225 .... L4
59222 Flaxville 142 .... L2
59833 Florence 700 .... B4
59441 Forestgrove 100 .... H3
59327 Forsyth⊙ 2,553 .... K4
†59526 Fort Belknap 185 .... H2
59442 Fort Benton⊙ 1,693 .... F3
59918 Fortine 250 .... A2
59223 Fort Peck 456 .... K2
59443 Fort Shaw 200 .... E3
†59075 Fort Smith 300 .... J5
59225 Frazer 200 .... K2
59834 Frenchtown 300 .... B3
59226 Froid 323 .... M2
59029 Fromberg 469 .... H5
59444 Galata 100 .... E2
59730 Gallatin Gateway 600 .... E5
59030 Gardiner 600 .... F5
59731 Garrison 300 .... D4
59031 Garryowen 200 .... J5
59446 Geraldine 305 .... F3
59447 Geyser 125 .... F3
59525 Gildford 250 .... F2
59230 Glasgow⊙ 4,455 .... K2
59330 Glendive⊙ 5,978 .... M3
59733 Goldcreek 100 .... D4
59835 Grantsdale 500 .... B4
59032 Grass Range 139 .... H3
59401 Great Falls⊙ 56,725 .... E3
Great Falls‡ 80,696 .... E3
59836 Greenough 120 .... C4
59837 Hall 130 .... C4
59840 Hamilton⊙ 2,661 .... B4
59034 Hardin⊙ 3,300 .... J5
59526 Harlem 1,023 .... H2
59036 Harlowton⊙ 1,181 .... F4
59735 Harrison 94 .... E5
59842 Haugan 90 .... A3
59501 Havre⊙ 10,891 .... G2
59527 Hays 400 .... H2
59448 Heart Butte 300 .... C2
59601 Helena (cap.)⊙ 23,938 .... E4
59843 Helmville 250 .... C4
59450 Highwood 150 .... F3
59528 Hingham 186 .... F2
59241 Hinsdale 260 .... K2
59452 Hobson 261 .... G4
59845 Hot Springs 601 .... B3
59919 Hungry Horse 700 .... C2
59037 Huntley 250 .... H5
59846 Huson 97 .... B3
59038 Hysham⊙ 449 .... J4
59530 Inverness 150 .... F2
59336 Ismay 31 .... M4
59736 Jackson 210 .... C5
59638 Jefferson City 162 .... E4
59041 Joliet 580 .... G5
59531 Joplin 300 .... F2
59337 Jordan⊙ 485 .... J3
59453 Judith Gap 213 .... G4
59901 Kalispell⊙ 10,648 .... B2
59454 Kevin 208 .... D2
59920 Kila 350 .... B2
59338 Kinsey 100 .... L4
†59072 Klein 250 .... H4
59532 Kremlin 304 .... F2
59922 Lakeside 663 .... B2
59243 Lambert 203 .... M3
59043 Lame Deer 460 .... K5
59044 Laurel 5,481 .... H5
59046 Lavina 164 .... H4
59457 Lewistown⊙ 7,104 .... G3
59923 Libby⊙ 2,748 .... A2
59739 Lima 272 .... D6
59639 Lincoln 473 .... D4
59047 Livingston⊙ 6,994 .... F5
59050 Lodge Grass 771 .... J5
†59524 Lodge Pole 292 .... H2
59847 Lolo 2,418 .... B4
†59847 Lolo Hot Springs 25 .... B4
59460 Loma 200 .... F3
59225 Lustre 25 .... K2
59538 Malta⊙ 2,367 .... J2
59741 Manhattan 988 .... E5
59925 Marion 450 .... B2
59052 McLeod 150 .... G5
59247 Medicine Lake 408 .... M2
59743 Melrose 350 .... D5
59054 Melstone 238 .... H4
59055 Melville 100 .... F4
59301 Miles City⊙ 9,602 .... L4
59851 Milltown 300 .... C4
*59801 Missoula⊙ 33,388 .... C4
59463 Monarch 120 .... F3
59464 Moore 229 .... G4
59059 Musselshell 117 .... H4
59248 Nashua 495 .... K2
59465 Neihart 91 .... F4
†59501 North Havre 1,230 .... G2
59853 Noxon 800 .... A3
59927 Olney 200 .... B2
59250 Opheim 210 .... K2
59252 Outlook 122 .... M2
59854 Ovando 300 .... C3
59855 Pablo 500 .... B3
59856 Paradise 400 .... B3
59063 Park City 800 .... H5
59253 Peerless 110 .... L2
59467 Pendroy 100 .... D2
59858 Philipsburg⊙ 1,138 .... C4
59859 Plains 1,116 .... B3
59254 Plentywood⊙ 2,476 .... M2
59344 Plevna 191 .... M4
59860 Polson⊙ 2,798 .... B3
59064 Pompeys Pillar 300 .... J5
59747 Pony 130 .... E5
59255 Poplar 995 .... L2
59468 Power 159 .... E3
59929 Proctor 150 .... B3
59066 Pryor 146 .... H5
59641 Radersburg 104 .... E4
59863 Ravalli 150 .... B3
59068 Red Lodge⊙ 1,896 .... G5
59069 Reedpoint 160 .... G5
59258 Reserve 80 .... M2
59930 Rexford 130 .... A2
59259 Richey 417 .... L3
59642 Ringling 102 .... F4
59070 Roberts 312 .... G5
59931 Rollins 200 .... B3
59864 Ronan 1,530 .... C3
59347 Rosebud 259 .... K4
59072 Roundup⊙ 2,119 .... H4
59471 Roy 200 .... H3
59540 Rudyard 450 .... F2
59074 Ryegate⊙ 273 .... G4
59261 Saco 252 .... J2
59865 Saint Ignatius 877 .... C3
59866 Saint Regis 500 .... A3
59075 Saint Xavier 200 .... J5
59867 Saltese 90 .... A3
59472 Sand Coulee 600 .... E3
59473 Santa Rita 120 .... D2
59262 Savage 300 .... M3
59263 Scobey⊙ 1,382 .... L2
59868 Seeley Lake 900 .... C3
59474 Shelby⊙ 3,142 .... E2
59079 Shepherd 200 .... H5
59749 Sheridan 646 .... D5
59270 Sidney⊙ 5,726 .... M3
59751 Silver Star 125 .... D5
59477 Simms 200 .... E3
59932 Somers 700 .... B2
59479 Stanford⊙ 595 .... F3
59870 Stevensville 1,207 .... C4
59480 Stockett 500 .... E3
59933 Stryker 96 .... B2
59871 Sula 200 .... B5
59482 Sunburst 476 .... E2
59483 Sun River 300 .... E3
59872 Superior⊙ 1,054 .... B3
59911 Swan Lake 100 .... C3
59484 Sweetgrass 250 .... E2
59349 Terry⊙ 929 .... L4
59873 Thompson Falls⊙ 1,478 .... A3
59752 Three Forks 1,247 .... E5
59644 Townsend⊙ 1,587 .... E4
59874 Trout Creek 300 .... A3
59935 Troy 1,088 .... A2
59542 Turner 150 .... H2
59754 Twin Bridges 437 .... D5
59085 Twodot 285 .... F4
59485 Ulm 450 .... E3
59486 Valier 640 .... D2
59487 Vaughn 2,270 .... E3
59875 Victor 700 .... B4
59755 Virginia City⊙ 192 .... E5
59351 Volborg 125 .... L5
59701 Walkerville 887 .... D4
59756 Warmsprings 500 .... D4
59275 Westby 291 .... M2
59936 West Glacier 150 .... C2
59758 West Yellowstone 735 .... E6
59937 Whitefish 3,703 .... B2
59759 Whitehall 1,030 .... D5
59645 White Sulphur Springs⊙ 1,302 .... E4
59276 Whitetail 150 .... L2
59544 Whitewater 100 .... J2
59353 Wibaux⊙ 782 .... M3
59760 Willow Creek 150 .... E5
59086 Wilsall 250 .... F5
59489 Winifred 155 .... G3
59087 Winnett⊙ 207 .... H4
59647 Winston 120 .... E4
59761 Wisdom 140 .... C5
59762 Wise River 150 .... C5
59648 Wolf Creek 500 .... D3
59201 Wolf Point⊙ 3,074 .... L2
59088 Worden 600 .... H5
59089 Wyola 350 .... J5

OTHER FEATURES

Absaroka (range) F5
Allen (mt.) C2
Arrow (creek) F3
Ashley (lake) B2
Battle (creek) G1
Bearhat (mt.) C2
Bearpaw (mts.) G2
Beartooth (mts.) G5
Beaver (creek) J2
Beaverhead (riv.) D5
Benton (lake) E3
Big (lake) G5
Big Belt (mts.) E4
Big Dry (creek) K3
Big Hole (riv.) C5
Big Hole Nat'l Battlefield C5
Bighorn (lake) H5
Bighorn (riv.) J5
Bighorn Canyon Nat'l Rec. Area H5
Big Muddy (riv.) M2
Big Porcupine (creek) J4
Birch (creek) D2
Birch Creek (res.) D2
Bitterroot (range) B4
Bitterroot (riv.) B4
Blackfeet Ind. Res. D2
Blackfoot (riv.) C4
Blackmore (mt.) F5
Bowdoin (lake) J2
Boxelder (creek) H3
Boxelder (creek) M5
Bynum (res.) D2
Cabinet (mts.) A2
Canyon Ferry (lake) E4
Clark Canyon (res.) D6
Clark Fork (riv.) A3
Clarks Fork, Yellowstone (riv.) G6
Cottonwood (creek) E2
Cow (creek) G2
Crazy (peak) F4
Crow Ind. Res. H5
Custer Battlefield Nat'l Mon. J5
Cut Bank (creek) D2
Douglas (mt.) F5
Earthquake (lake) E6
Electric (peak) F6
Elwell (lake) E2
Emigrant (peak) F5
Ennis (lake) E5
Flathead (lake) C3
Flathead (riv.) B2
Flathead, North Fork (riv.) B2
Flathead, South Fork (riv.) C3
Flathead Ind. Res. B3
Flatwillow (creek) H4
Fort Belknap Ind. Res. H2
Fort Peck (lake) K3
Fort Union Trading Post Nat'l Hist. Site N2
Frances (lake) D2
Freezeout (lake) D3
Frenchman (riv.) J1
Fresno (res.) F2
Gallatin (peak) E5
Gallatin (riv.) E5
Georgetown (lake) C4
Gibson (res.) D3
Glacier Nat'l Park C2
Granite (peak) F5
Grant-Kohrs Ranch Nat'l Hist. Site D4
Hauser (lake) E4
Haystack (peak) A3
Hebgen (lake) E6
Helena (lake) E4
Holter (lake) D4
Hungry Horse (res.) C2
Hurricane (mt.) D2
Hyalite (peak) E5
Jackson (mt.) C2
Jefferson (riv.) D5
Judith (riv.) G3
Koocanusa (lake) A2
Kootenai (riv.) A2
Lemhi (pass) C6
Lewis (range) C2
Lima (res.) D6
Little Bighorn (riv.) J5
Little Bitterroot (lake) B2
Little Dry (creek) K3
Little Missouri (riv.) M5
Lockhart (mt.) D3
Lodge (creek) G1
Lolo (pass) B4
Lone (mt.) E5
Lost Trail (pass) B5
Lower Red Rock (lake) E6
Lower Saint Mary (lake) C2
Madison (riv.) E5
Malmstrom A.F.B. 6,675 .... E3
Marias (riv.) D2
Martinsdale (res.) F4
Mary Ronan (lake) B3
McDonald (lake) B2
McGloughlin (peak) C4
McGregor (lake) B3
Medicine (lake) M2
Milk (riv.) J2
Mission (range) C3
Missouri (riv.) L3
Musselshell (riv.) J3
Nelson (res.) J2
Ninepipe (res.) C3
Northern Cheyenne Indian Reservation K5
O'Fallon (creek) L4
Pishkun (res.) D3
Poplar (riv.) L2
Porcupine (creek) K2
Powder (riv.) L4
Purcell (mts.) A2
Railley (mt.) C3
Red Rock (lkes) E6
Red Rock (riv.) D6
Redwater (riv.) L3
Rock (creek) C4
Rocky (mts.) D4
Rocky Boy's Ind. Res. G2
Rosebud (creek) K4
Ruby (riv.) D5
Ruby River (res.) D5
Sage (creek) F2
Saint Mary (lake) C2
Saint Mary (riv.) C1
Sandy (creek) F2
Sheep (mt.) C2
Shields (riv.) F4
Siyeh (mt.) C2
Smith (riv.) E3
Sphinx (mt.) E5
Stillwater (riv.) G5
Stimson (mt.) C2
Sun (riv.) D3
Swan (lake) C3
Teton (riv.) E3
Tongue (riv.) K5
Upper Red Rock (lake) E6
Ward (peak) A3
Waterton-Glacier Int'l Peace Park C2
Whitefish (lake) B2
Willow (creek) E2
Willow Creek (res.) D3
Yellowstone (riv.) M3
Yellowstone National Park F6

⊙County seat.
‡Population of metropolitan area.
† Zip of nearest p.o. * Multiple zips.

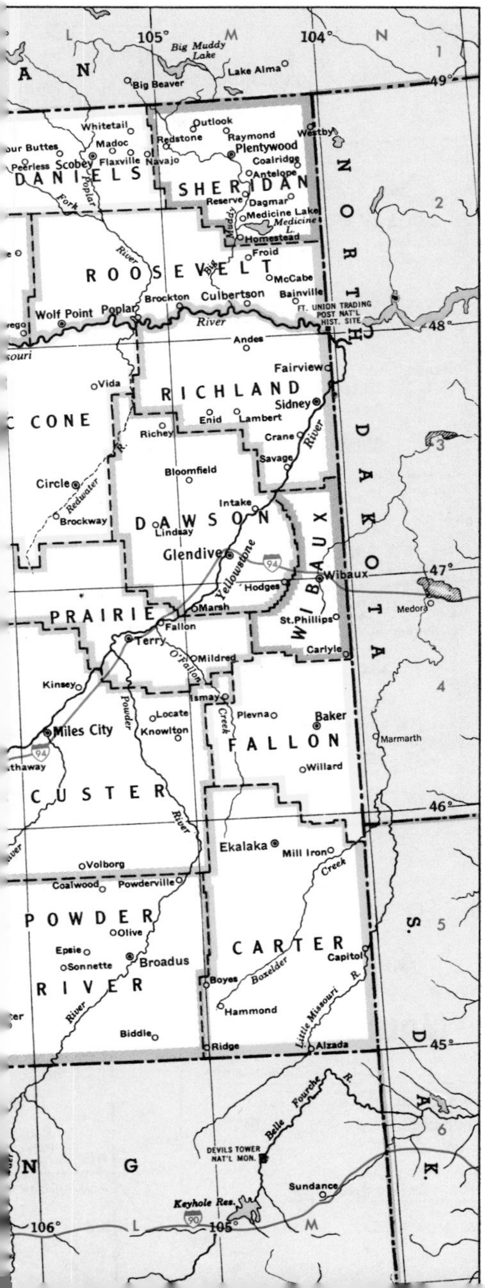

COUNTIES

Adams 30,656 ... F4
Antelope 8,675 ... F2
Arthur 513 ... C3
Banner 918 ... A3
Blaine 867 ... E3
Boone 7,391 ... F3
Box Butte 13,696 ... A2
Boyd 3,331 ... F2
Brown 4,377 ... E2
Buffalo 34,797 ... E4
Burt 8,813 ... H3
Butler 9,330 ... G3
Cass 20,297 ... H4
Cedar 11,375 ... G2
Chase 4,758 ... C4
Cherry 6,758 ... C2
Cheyenne 10,057 ... A3
Clay 8,106 ... F4
Colfax 9,890 ... G3
Cuming 11,664 ... H3
Custer 13,877 ... E3
Dakota 16,573 ... H2
Dawes 9,609 ... A2
Dawson 22,304 ... E4
Deuel 2,462 ... B3
Dixon 7,137 ... H2
Dodge 35,847 ... H3
Douglas 397,038 ... H3
Dundy 2,861 ... C4
Fillmore 7,920 ... G4
Franklin 4,377 ... F4
Frontier 3,647 ... D4
Furnas 6,486 ... E4
Gage 24,456 ... H4
Garden 2,802 ... B3
Garfield 2,363 ... F3
Gosper 2,140 ... E4
Grant 877 ... C3
Greeley 3,462 ... F3
Hall 47,690 ... F4
Hamilton 9,301 ... F4
Harlan 4,292 ... E4
Hayes 1,356 ... C4
Hitchcock 4,079 ... C4
Holt 13,552 ... F2
Hooker 990 ... C3
Howard 6,773 ... F3
Jefferson 9,817 ... G4
Johnson 5,285 ... H4
Kearney 7,053 ... F4
Keith 9,364 ... C3
Keya Paha 1,301 ... E2
Kimball 4,882 ... A3
Knox 11,457 ... G2
Lancaster 192,884 ... H4
Lincoln 36,455 ... D4
Logan 983 ... D3
Loup 859 ... E3
Madison 31,382 ... G3
McPherson 593 ... C3
Merrick 8,945 ... F3
Morrill 6,085 ... A3
Nance 4,740 ... F3
Nemaha 8,367 ... J4
Nuckolls 6,726 ... F4
Otoe 15,183 ... H4
Pawnee 3,937 ... H4
Perkins 3,637 ... C4
Phelps 9,769 ... E4
Pierce 8,481 ... G2
Platte 28,852 ... G3
Polk 6,320 ... G3
Red Willow 12,615 ... D4
Richardson 11,315 ... J4
Rock 2,383 ... E2
Saline 13,131 ... G4
Sarpy 86,015 ... H3
Saunders 18,716 ... H3
Scotts Bluff 38,344 ... A3
Seward 15,789 ... G4
Sheridan 7,544 ... B2
Sherman 4,226 ... F3
Sioux 1,845 ... A2
Stanton 6,549 ... G3
Thayer 7,582 ... G4
Thomas 973 ... D3
Thurston 7,186 ... H2
Valley 5,633 ... E3
Washington 15,508 ... H3
Wayne 9,858 ... G2
Webster 4,858 ... F4
Wheeler 1,060 ... F3
York 14,798 ... G4

CITIES and TOWNS

Zip Name/Pop. Key

68301 Adams 395 ... H4
69210 Ainsworth⊙ 2,256 ... D2
68620 Albion⊙ 1,997 ... F3
68810 Alda 601 ... F4
68710 Allen 390 ... H2
69301 Alliance⊙ 9,920 ... A2
68920 Alma⊙ 1,369 ... E4
68304 Alvo 144 ... H4
68812 Amherst 269 ... E4
68814 Ansley 644 ... E3
68922 Arapahoe 1,107 ... E4
68815 Arcadia 412 ... F3
68002 Arlington 1,117 ... H3
69120 Arnold 813 ... D3
69121 Arthur⊙ 124 ... C3
68003 Ashland 2,274 ... H3
68713 Atkinson 1,521 ... E2
68305 Auburn⊙ 3,482 ... J4
68818 Aurora⊙ 3,717 ... F4
68924 Axtell 602 ... E4
68004 Bancroft 552 ... H2
68622 Bartlett⊙ 144 ... F3
69020 Bartley 342 ... D4
68714 Bassett⊙ 1,009 ... E2
68715 Battle Creek 948 ... G3
69334 Bayard 1,435 ... A3
68310 Beatrice⊙ 12,891 ... H4
68926 Beaver City⊙ 775 ... E4
68313 Beaver Crossing 458 ... G4
68716 Beemer 853 ... H3
68005 Bellevue 21,813 ... J3
68624 Bellwood 407 ... G3
69021 Benkelman⊙ 1,235 ... C4
68317 Bennet 523 ... H4
68007 Bennington 631 ... H3
68927 Bertrand 775 ... E4
69122 Big Springs 505 ... B3
68928 Bladen 298 ... F4
68008 Blair⊙ 6,418 ... H3
68718 Bloomfield 1,393 ... G2
68930 Blue Hill 883 ... F4
68318 Blue Springs 521 ... H4
68010 Boys Town 622 ... H3
68319 Bradshaw 373 ... G4
69123 Brady 377 ... D3
68821 Brewster⊙ 46 ... D3
69336 Bridgeport⊙ 1,668 ... A3
68822 Broken Bow⊙ 3,979 ... E3
69127 Brule 438 ... C3
68322 Bruning 330 ... G4
68823 Burwell⊙ 1,383 ... E3
68722 Butte⊙ 529 ... F2
68824 Cairo 737 ... F3
68825 Callaway 579 ... D3
69022 Cambridge 1,206 ... D4
68932 Campbell 441 ... F4
68015 Cedar Bluffs 632 ... H3
68016 Cedar Creek 311 ... H3
68627 Cedar Rapids 447 ... F3
68724 Center⊙ 123 ... G2
68826 Central City⊙ 3,083 ... F3
68017 Ceresco 836 ... H3
69337 Chadron⊙ 5,933 ... B2
68725 Chambers 390 ... F2
68827 Chapman 349 ... F3
69129 Chappell⊙ 1,095 ... B3
68327 Chester 435 ... G4
68628 Clarks 445 ... G3
68629 Clarkson 817 ... G3
68328 Clatonia 273 ... H4
68933 Clay Center⊙ 962 ... F4
68726 Clearwater 409 ... F2
†69343 Clinton 80 ... B2
68727 Coleridge 673 ... G2
68601 Columbus⊙ 17,328 ... G3
68329 Cook 341 ... H4
68331 Cortland 403 ... H4
69130 Cozad 4,453 ... E4
69339 Crawford 1,315 ... A2
68729 Creighton 1,341 ... G2
68333 Crete 4,872 ... G4
68730 Crofton 948 ... G2
69024 Culbertson 767 ... C4
69025 Curtis 1,014 ... D4
68731 Dakota City⊙ 1,440 ... H2
69131 Dalton 345 ... B3
68831 Dannebrog 356 ... F3
68335 Davenport 445 ... G4
68632 David City⊙ 2,514 ... G3
68020 Decatur 723 ... H2
68340 Deshler 997 ... G4
68341 De Witt 642 ... G4
68342 Diller 311 ... H4
69133 Dix 275 ... A3
68633 Dodge 815 ... H3
68832 Doniphan 696 ... F4
68343 Dorchester 611 ... G4
68634 Duncan 410 ... G3
68347 Eagle 832 ... H4
68935 Edgar 705 ... F4
68636 Elgin 807 ... F3
68022 Elkhorn 1,344 ... H3
68836 Elm Creek 862 ... E4
68349 Elmwood 598 ... H4
68937 Elwood⊙ 716 ... E4
68733 Emerson 874 ... H2
68350 Endicott 198 ... G4
69028 Eustis 460 ... D4
68735 Ewing 520 ... F2
68351 Exeter 807 ... G4
68352 Fairbury⊙ 4,885 ... G4
68938 Fairfield 543 ... G4
68354 Fairmont 767 ... G4
68355 Falls City⊙ 5,374 ... J4
69029 Farnam 268 ... D4
68358 Firth 384 ... H4
68023 Fort Calhoun 641 ... J3
68939 Franklin⊙ 1,167 ... E4
68025 Fremont⊙ 23,979 ... H3
68359 Friend 1,079 ... G4
68638 Fullerton⊙ 1,506 ... F3
68361 Geneva⊙ 2,400 ... G4
68640 Genoa 1,090 ... G3
69341 Gering⊙ 7,760 ... A3
68840 Gibbon 1,531 ... F4
68841 Giltner 400 ... F4
68941 Glenvil 363 ... F4
69343 Gordon 2,167 ... B2
69138 Gothenburg 3,479 ... D4
68801 Grand Island⊙ 33,180 ... F4
69140 Grant⊙ 1,270 ... C4
68842 Greeley⊙ 597 ... F3
68366 Greenwood 587 ... H3
68367 Gresham 320 ... G3
68028 Gretna 1,609 ... H3
68942 Guide Rock 344 ... F4
68738 Hadar 286 ... G2
68368 Hallam 290 ... H4
68843 Hampton 419 ... G4
69346 Harrison⊙ 361 ... A2
68739 Hartington⊙ 1,730 ... G2
68944 Harvard 1,217 ... F4
68901 Hastings⊙ 23,045 ... F4
69032 Hayes Center⊙ 231 ... C4
69347 Hay Springs 794 ... B2
68370 Hebron⊙ 1,906 ... G4
69348 Hemingford 1,023 ... A2
68371 Henderson 1,072 ... G4
68029 Herman 340 ... H3
69143 Hershey 633 ... D3
68372 Hickman 687 ... H4
68947 Hildreth 394 ... E4
68948 Holbrook 297 ... D4
68949 Holdrege⊙ 5,624 ... E4
68030 Homer 564 ... H2
68031 Hooper 932 ... H3
68740 Hoskins 306 ... G2
68641 Howells 677 ... H3
68376 Humboldt 1,176 ... J4
68642 Humphrey 799 ... G3
69350 Hyannis⊙ 336 ... C3
69033 Imperial⊙ 1,941 ... C4
69034 Indianola 856 ... D4
68743 Jackson 287 ... H2
68378 Johnson 341 ... J4
68955 Juniata 703 ... F4
68847 Kearney⊙ 21,158 ... E4
68956 Kenesaw 854 ... F4
68034 Kennard 372 ... H3
69145 Kimball⊙ 3,120 ... A3
69035 Lamar 60 ... C4
68745 Laurel 1,031 ... G2
†68046 La Vista 9,588 ... J3
68957 Lawrence 350 ... F4
68643 Leigh 509 ... G3
69147 Lewellen 368 ... B3
68850 Lexington⊙ 7,040 ... E4
*68501 Lincoln (cap.)⊙ 171,932 ... H4
Lincoln‡ 192,884 ... H4
68644 Lindsay 383 ... G3
69149 Lodgepole 413 ... B3
69217 Long Pine 521 ... E2
68958 Loomis 447 ... E4
68037 Louisville 1,022 ... H3
68853 Loup City⊙ 1,368 ... E3
69352 Lyman 551 ... A3
68746 Lynch 357 ... F2
68038 Lyons 1,214 ... H3
68748 Madison⊙ 1,950 ... G3
69150 Madrid 284 ... C4
68402 Malcolm 355 ... H4
68854 Marquette 303 ... G4
69151 Maxwell 410 ... D3
69038 Maywood 332 ... D4
69001 McCook⊙ 8,404 ... D4
68401 McCool Junction 404 ... G4
68041 Mead 506 ... H3
68752 Meadow Grove 400 ... G2
68856 Merna 389 ... E3
68405 Milford 2,108 ... H4
68406 Milligan 332 ... G4
69356 Minatare 969 ... A3
68959 Minden⊙ 2,939 ... F4
69357 Mitchell 1,956 ... A3
68647 Monroe 294 ... G3
69358 Morrill 1,097 ... A3
69152 Mullen⊙ 720 ... C2
68409 Murray 465 ... J4
68410 Nebraska City⊙ 7,127 ... J4
68413 Nehawka 270 ... H4
68756 Neligh⊙ 1,893 ... G2
68961 Nelson⊙ 733 ... F4
68757 Newcastle 348 ... H2
68758 Newman Grove 930 ... G3
68760 Niobrara 419 ... G2
68962 Nora 24 ... G4
68701 Norfolk 19,449 ... G2
68649 North Bend 1,368 ... H3
68859 North Loup 405 ... F3
69101 North Platte⊙ 24,509 ... D3
68761 Oakdale 410 ... F2
68045 Oakland 1,393 ... H3
68415 Odell 322 ... H4
69153 Ogallala⊙ 5,638 ... C3
*68101 Omaha⊙ 313,911 ... J3
Omaha‡ 570,399 ... J3
68763 O'Neill⊙ 4,049 ... F2
68764 Orchard 482 ... F2
68862 Ord⊙ 2,658 ... F3
68966 Orleans 527 ... E4
68651 Osceola⊙ 975 ... G3
69154 Oshkosh⊙ 1,057 ... B3
68765 Osmond 871 ... G2
68863 Overton 633 ... E4
68967 Oxford 1,109 ... E4
69040 Palisade 401 ... C4
68864 Palmer 487 ... F3
68418 Palmyra 512 ... H4
68046 Papillion⊙ 6,399 ... J3
68420 Pawnee City⊙ 1,156 ... H4
69155 Paxton 568 ... C3
68047 Pender⊙ 1,318 ... H2
68421 Peru 998 ... J4
68652 Petersburg 381 ... G3
68865 Phillips 405 ... F4
68767 Pierce⊙ 1,535 ... G2
68768 Pilger 400 ... G2
68769 Plainview 1,483 ... G2
68653 Platte Center 367 ... G3
68048 Plattsmouth⊙ 6,295 ... J3
68866 Pleasanton 349 ... E4
68424 Plymouth 506 ... G4
68654 Polk 440 ... G3
68770 Ponca⊙ 1,057 ... H2
68867 Poole ... F4
69156 Potter 369 ... A3
68050 Prague 285 ... H3
68127 Ralston 5,143 ... J3
68771 Randolph 1,106 ... G2
68869 Ravenna 1,296 ... F4
68970 Red Cloud⊙ 1,300 ... F4
68658 Rising City 392 ... G3
69360 Rushville⊙ 1,217 ... B2
68660 Saint Edward 891 ... G3
68873 Saint Paul⊙ 2,094 ... F3
†68760 Santee 388 ... G2
68874 Sargent 828 ... E3
68661 Schuyler⊙ 4,151 ... G3
68875 Scotia 349 ... F3
69361 Scottsbluff 14,156 ... A3
68057 Scribner 1,011 ... H3
68434 Seward⊙ 5,713 ... H4
68662 Shelby 724 ... G3
68876 Shelton 1,046 ... F4
68436 Shickley 413 ... G4
69162 Sidney⊙ 6,010 ... B3
68663 Silver Creek 496 ... G3
68664 Snyder 387 ... H3
68776 South Sioux City 9,339 ... H2
68665 Spalding 645 ... F3
68777 Spencer 596 ... F2
68059 Springfield 782 ... H3
68778 Springview⊙ 326 ... E2
68779 Stanton⊙ 1,603 ... G3
68439 Staplehurst 306 ... G4
69163 Stapleton⊙ 340 ... D3
68442 Stella 289 ... J4
68443 Sterling 526 ... H4
69042 Stockville⊙ 45 ... D4
69043 Stratton 499 ... C4
68666 Stromsburg 1,290 ... G3
68780 Stuart 641 ... E2
68978 Superior 2,502 ... F4
69165 Sutherland 1,238 ... C3
68979 Sutton 1,416 ... G4
68446 Syracuse 1,638 ... H4
68447 Table Rock 393 ... H4

Agriculture, Industry and Resources

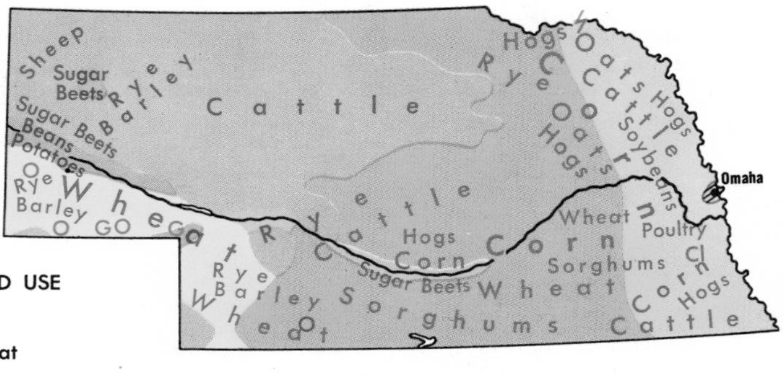
Sheep
Sugar Beets
Rye
Barley
Cattle
Hogs
Oats
Corn
Soybeans
Potatoes
Wheat
Poultry
Sorghums
Omaha

DOMINANT LAND USE

Specialized Wheat
Cattle Feed, Hogs
Livestock, Cash Grain
General Farming, Livestock, Special Crops
Sugar Beets, Dry Beans, Livestock, General Farming
Range Livestock

MAJOR MINERAL OCCURRENCES

Cl Clay
G Natural Gas
O Petroleum
Water Power
Major Industrial Areas

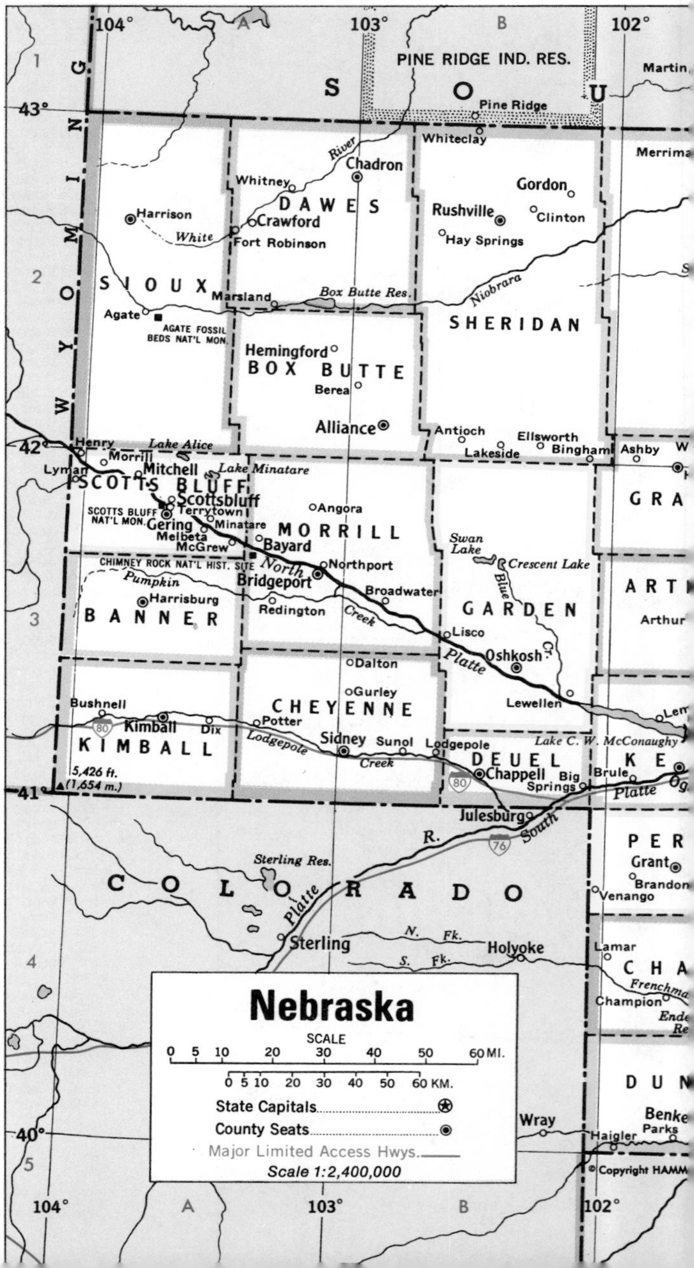
PINE RIDGE IND. RES.
SOUTH DAKOTA
WYOMING
COLORADO
DAWES
SIOUX
SHERIDAN
BOX BUTTE
SCOTTS BLUFF
MORRILL
BANNER
GARDEN
KIMBALL
CHEYENNE
DEUEL
Chadron
Whitney
Crawford
Fort Robinson
Harrison
Agate
AGATE FOSSIL BEDS NAT'L MON.
Marsland
Box Butte Res.
Hemingford
Berea
Alliance
Rushville
Gordon
Clinton
Hay Springs
Whiteclay
Pine Ridge
Antioch
Lakeside
Ellsworth
Bingham
Ashby
Henry
Morrill
Lyman
Mitchell
Lake Alice
Lake Minatare
Scottsbluff
Terrytown
Gering
Minatare
Melbeta
McGrew
Bayard
Angora
SCOTTS BLUFF NAT'L MON.
CHIMNEY ROCK NAT'L HIST. SITE
Northport
Bridgeport
Broadwater
Harrisburg
Redington
Swan Lake
Crescent Lake
Lisco
Oshkosh
Lewellen
Dalton
Gurley
Bushnell
Kimball
Dix
Potter
Sidney
Sunol
Lodgepole
Chappell
Big Springs
Brule
Lake C. W. McConaughy
Julesburg
Sterling Res.
Sterling
Holyoke
Lamar
Grant
Brandon
Venango
Champion
Wray
Haigler
Benkelman
Parks
Martin
Merriman
Arthur
5,426 ft. (1,654 m.)
Nebraska
SCALE
0 5 10 20 30 40 50 60 MI.
0 5 10 20 30 40 50 60 KM.
State Capitals
County Seats
Major Limited Access Hwys.
Scale 1:2,400,000
© Copyright HAMMOND

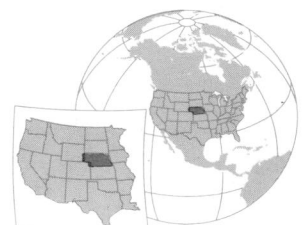

AREA 77,355 sq. mi. (200,349 sq. km.)
POPULATION 1,569,825
CAPITAL Lincoln
LARGEST CITY Omaha
HIGHEST POINT (Kimball Co.) 5,246 ft. (1654 m.)
SETTLED IN 1847
ADMITTED TO UNION March 1, 1867
POPULAR NAME Cornhusker State
STATE FLOWER Goldenrod
STATE BIRD Western Meadowlark

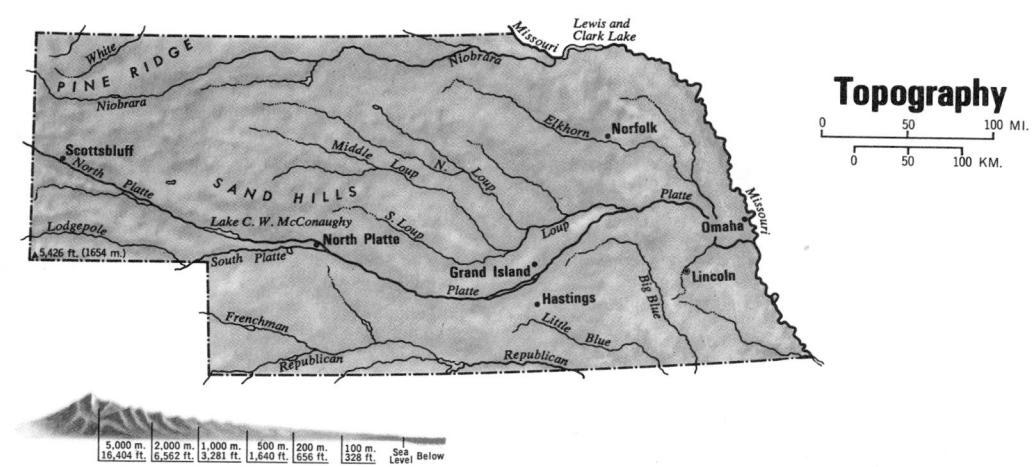

Topography

5,000 m. / 16,404 ft. | 2,000 m. / 6,562 ft. | 1,000 m. / 3,281 ft. | 500 m. / 1,640 ft. | 200 m. / 656 ft. | 100 m. / 328 ft. | Sea Level | Below

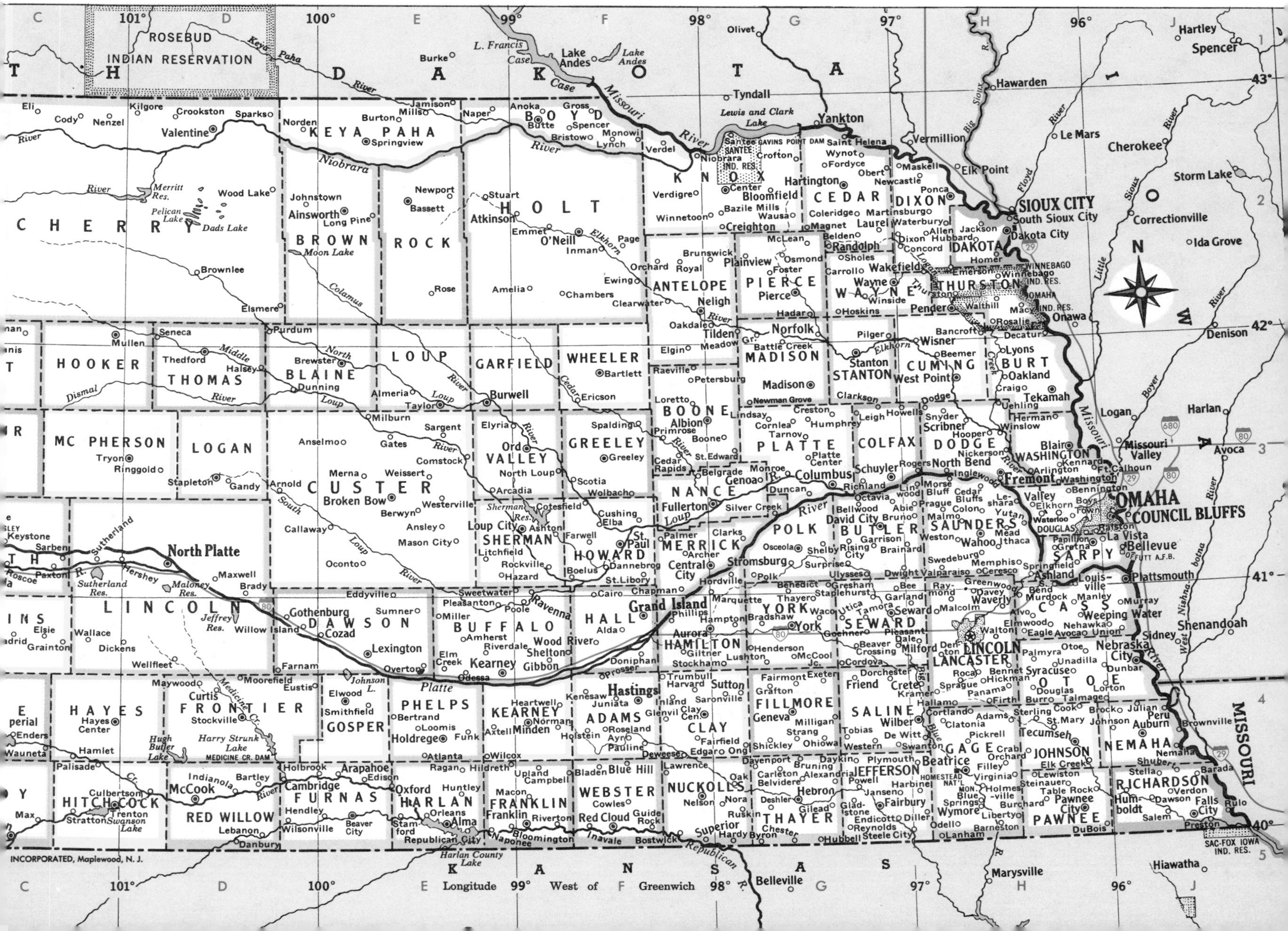

INCORPORATED, Maplewood, N.J.

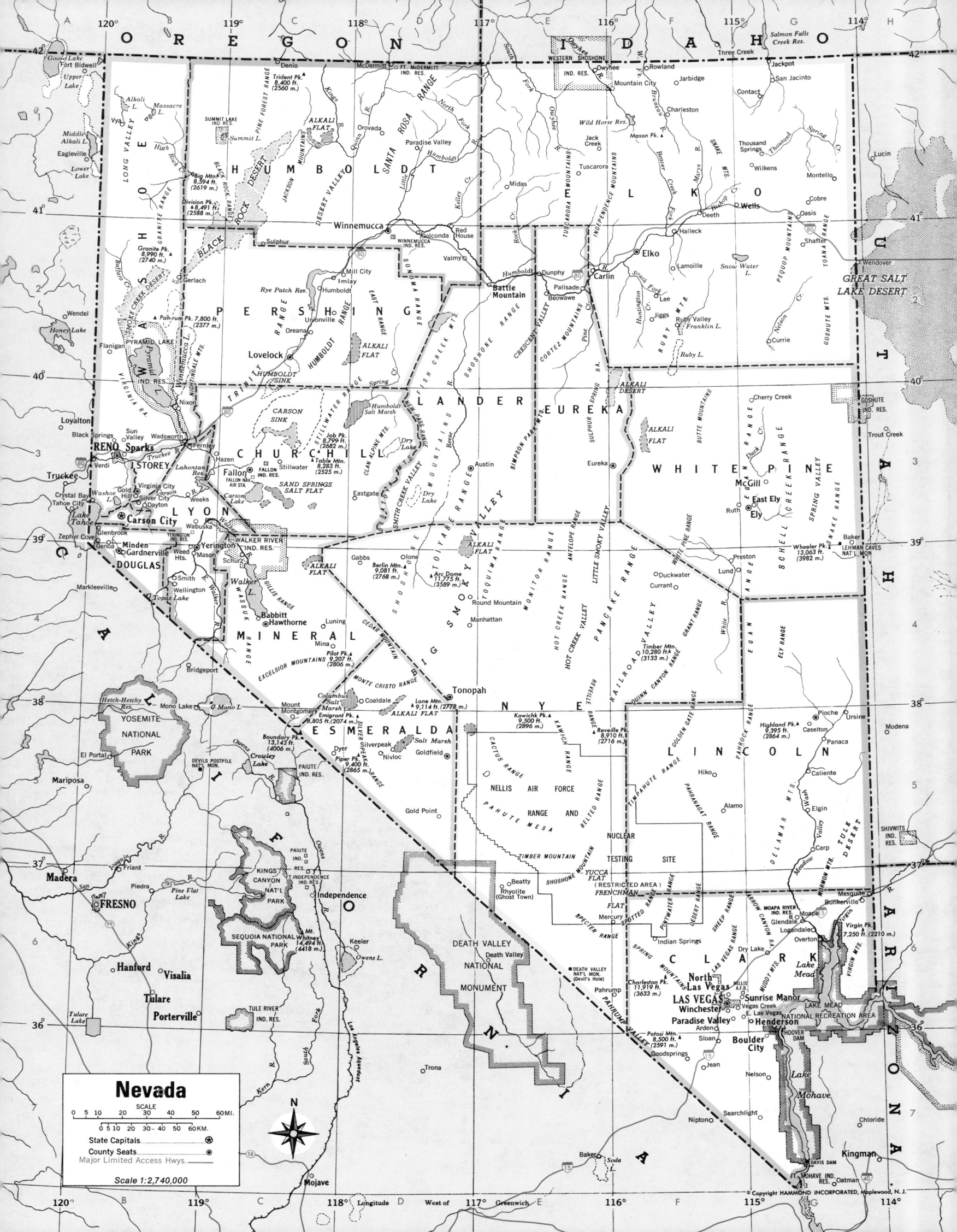

AREA 110,561 sq. mi. (286,353 sq. km.)
POPULATION 800,493
CAPITAL Carson City
LARGEST CITY Las Vegas
HIGHEST POINT Boundary Pk. 13,143 ft. (4006 m.)
SETTLED IN 1850
ADMITTED TO UNION October 31, 1864
POPULAR NAME Silver State; Sagebrush State
STATE FLOWER Sagebrush
STATE BIRD Mountain Bluebird

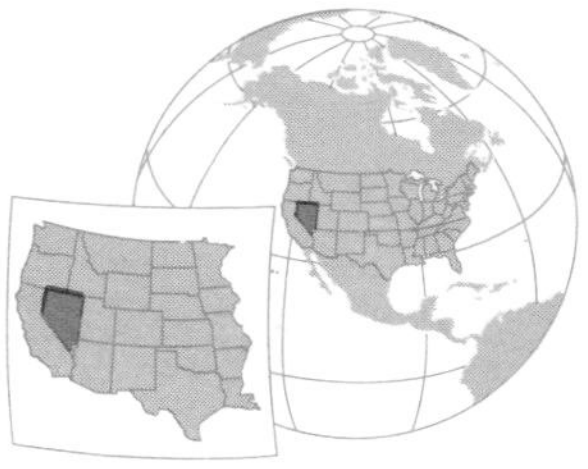

Agriculture, Industry and Resources

MAJOR MINERAL OCCURRENCES

- Ag Silver
- Au Gold
- Ba Barite
- Cu Copper
- Gp Gypsum
- Hg Mercury
- Lt Lithium
- Mg Magnesium
- Mo Molybdenum
- Na Salt
- O Petroleum
- Pb Lead
- S Sulfur
- W Tungsten
- Zn Zinc
- Water Power

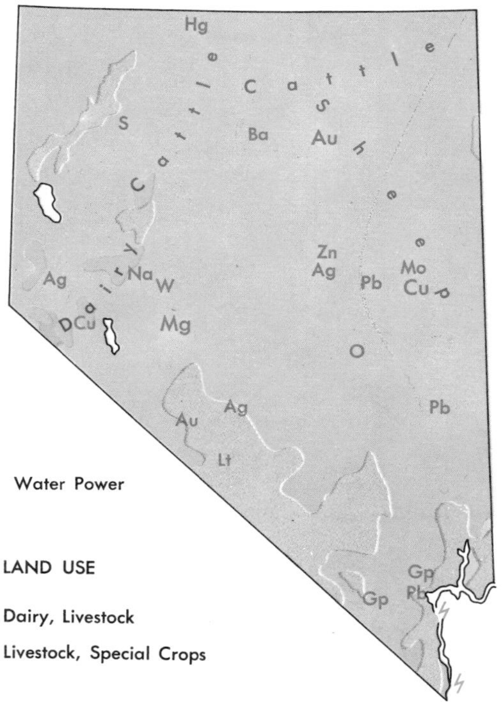
Hg
Cattle
Sheep
S
Ba
Au
Zn
Ag
Mo
Cu
Pb
Na
W
Mg
O
Lt
Gp

DOMINANT LAND USE

- General Farming, Dairy, Livestock
- General Farming, Livestock, Special Crops
- Range Livestock
- Forests
- Nonagricultural Land

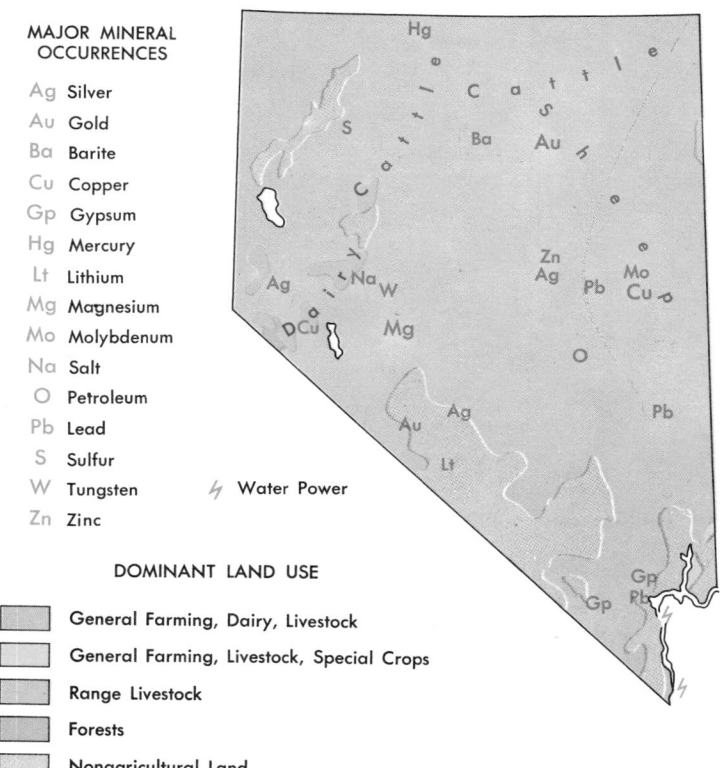

Topography

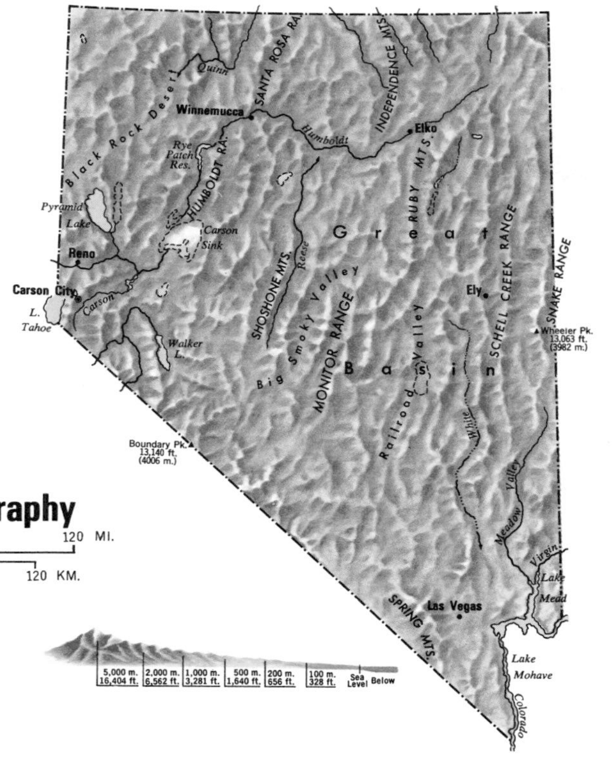
Quinn
Winnemucca
SANTA ROSA RA.
INDEPENDENCE MTS.
Humboldt
Elko
Black Rock Desert
Rye Patch Res.
HUMBOLDT RA.
RUBY MTS.
Pyramid Lake
Reno
Carson Sink
Carson City
Carson
L. Tahoe
Walker L.
SHOSHONE MTS.
Big Smoky Valley
MONITOR RANGE
Great Basin
Railroad Valley
Ely
SCHELL CREEK RANGE
SNAKE RANGE
Wheeler Pk. 13,063 ft. (3982 m.)
White
Boundary Pk. 13,140 ft. (4006 m.)
Meadow Valley
Virgin
Lake Mead
Las Vegas
SPRING MTS.
Lake Mohave
Colorado
0 60 120 MI.
0 60 120 KM.
5,000 m. 16,404 ft.
2,000 m. 6,562 ft.
1,000 m. 3,281 ft.
500 m. 1,640 ft.
200 m. 656 ft.
100 m. 328 ft.
Sea Level
Below

COUNTIES

Carson City (city) 32,022 ..... B3
Churchill 13,917 ..... C3
Clark 463,087 ..... F6
Douglas 19,421 ..... B4
Elko 17,269 ..... F1
Esmeralda 777 ..... D5
Eureka 1,198 ..... E3
Humboldt 9,434 ..... C1
Lander 4,076 ..... D3
Lincoln 3,732 ..... F5
Lyon 13,594 ..... B3
Mineral 6,217 ..... C4
Nye 9,048 ..... E4
Pershing 3,408 ..... C2
Storey 1,503 ..... B3
Washoe 193,623 ..... B2
White Pine 8,167 ..... F3

CITIES and TOWNS

Zip *Name/Pop.* *Key*

89001 Alamo 300 ..... F5
89310 Austin⊙ 300 ..... E3
89416 Babbitt C4
89311 Baker 140 ..... G3
89820 Battle Mountain 2,749 ..... E2
89003 Beatty 600 ..... E6
89821 Beowawe 77 ..... E2
†89508 Black Springs 180 ..... B3
89005 Boulder City 9,590 ..... G7
89007 Bunkerville 300 ..... G6
89008 Caliente 982 ..... G5
89822 Carlin 1,232 ..... E2
†89008 Carp 30 ..... G5
89701 Carson City (cap.) 32,022 ..... B3
†89043 Caselton G5
†89301 Cherry Creek 80 ..... G3
89402 Crystal Bay 6,225 ..... A3
89403 Dayton 350 ..... B3
89823 Deeth 125 ..... F1
89404 Denio 35 ..... C1
89314 Duckwater 80 ..... F4
89010 Dyer 56 ..... C5
89315 East Ely G3
89112 East Las Vegas 6,449 ..... F6
89801 Elko⊙ 8,758 ..... F2
89301 Ely⊙ 4,882 ..... G3
89316 Eureka⊙ 300 ..... E3
89406 Fallon⊙ 4,262 ..... C3
89408 Fernley 750 ..... B3
89409 Gabbs 811 ..... D4
89410 Gardnerville 1,610 ..... B4
89411 Genoa 254 ..... B4
89412 Gerlach 400 ..... B2
89413 Glenbrook 800 ..... B3
89414 Golconda 275 ..... D2
89013 Goldfield⊙ 500 ..... D5
89019 Goodsprings 80 ..... F7
89824 Halleck 68 ..... F2
89415 Hawthorne⊙ 3,741 ..... C4
89417 Hazen 76 ..... C3
89015 Henderson 24,363 ..... G6
89017 Hiko 210 ..... F5
†89418 Humboldt 14 ..... C2
89418 Imlay 250 ..... C2
89018 Indian Springs 500 ..... F6
†89310 Ione 20 ..... D4
†89834 Jack Creek E1
89825 Jackpot 400 ..... G1
89826 Jarbidge 11 ..... F1
89019 Jean 125 ..... F7
89828 Lamoille 100 ..... F2
*89101 Las Vegas⊙ 164,674 ..... F6
Las Vegas‡ 461,816 ..... F6
89829 Lee 125 ..... F2
89021 Logandale 410 ..... G6
89419 Lovelock⊙ 1,680 ..... C2
89317 Lund 380 ..... F4
89420 Luning 90 ..... C4
89022 Manhattan 93 ..... E4
†89447 Mason 200 ..... B4
89421 McDermitt 240 ..... D1
89318 McGill 1,419 ..... G3
89023 Mercury 900 ..... E6
89024 Mesquite 500 ..... G6
89422 Mina 450 ..... C4
89423 Minden⊙ 1,029 ..... B4
89025 Moapa 275 ..... G6
89830 Montello 100 ..... G1
89831 Mountain City 100 ..... F1
‡89046 Nelson 75 ..... G7
89424 Nixon 400 ..... B3
89030 North Las Vegas 42,739 ..... F6
89425 Orovada 200 ..... D1
89040 Overton 1,111 ..... G6
89041 Pahrump 400 ..... E6
89042 Panaca 650 ..... G5
89119 Paradise Valley 84,818 ..... F6
89426 Paradise Valley 115 ..... D1
89043 Pioche⊙ 850 ..... G5
*89501 Reno⊙ 100,756 ..... B3
Reno‡ 193,623 ..... B3
†89003 Rhyolite (Ghost Town) 8 ..... E6
89045 Round Mountain 400 ..... E4
89833 Ruby Valley 150 ..... F2
89319 Ruth 455 ..... F3
89427 Schurz 800 ..... C4
89046 Searchlight 500 ..... F7
89428 Silver City 150 ..... B3
89047 Silverpeak 100 ..... D5
89430 Smith 200 ..... B4
89431 Sparks 40,780 ..... B3
†89406 Stillwater 150 ..... C3
†89445 Sulphur C2
†89110 Sunrise Manor 44,155 ..... F6
†89431 Sun Valley 8,822 ..... B3
†89835 Thousand Springs G1
89049 Tonopah⊙ 1,952 ..... D4
89834 Tuscarora 24 ..... E1
89438 Valmy 200 ..... D2
89121 Vegas Creek G6
89440 Virginia City⊙ 750 ..... B3
89442 Wadsworth 400 ..... B3
89443 Weed Heights 8 ..... B4
89444 Wellington 505 ..... B4
89835 Wells 1,218 ..... G1
†89109 Winchester 19,728 ..... F6
89445 Winnemucca⊙ 4,140 ..... D2
89447 Yerington⊙ 2,021 ..... B4
89448 Zephyr Cove 1,316 ..... A3

OTHER FEATURES

Alkali (lake) B1
Antelope (range) E3
Arc Dome (mt.) D4
Arrow Canyon (range) G6
Beaver Creek Fork, Humboldt (riv.) F1
Belted (range) E5
Berlin (mt.) D4
Big (mt.) B1
Big Smoky (valley) D4
Bishop (creek) F1
Black Rock (des.) B2
Black Rock (range) B1
Boundary (peak) C5
Buffalo (creek) B2
Butte (mts.) F3
Cactus (range) E5
Carson (lake) C3
Carson (riv.) B3
Carson (sink) C3
Cedar (mt.) D4
Charleston (peak) F6
Clan Alpine (mts.) D3
Columbus Salt (marsh) C4
Cortez (mts.) E2
Crescent (valley) E2
Davis (dam) G7
Death Valley Nat'l Mon. E6
Delamar (mts.) G5
Desatoya (mts.) D3
Desert (range) F6
Desert (valley) C1
Devil's Hole (Death Valley Nat'l Mon.) E6
Division (peak) B1
Duck (creek) G3
East (range) D2
East Walker (riv.) B4
Egan (range) G4
Ely (range) G4
Emigrant (peak) C5
Excelsior (mts.) C4
Fallon Ind. Res. C3
Fallon Nav. Air Sta. C3
Fish Creek (mts.) D2
Fort McDermitt Ind. Res. D1
Fort Mohave Ind. Res. G7
Franklin (lake) F2
Frenchman Flat (basin) F6
Gillis (range) C4
Golden Gate (range) F5
Goshute (mts.) G2
Goshute Ind. Res. G3
Granite (peak) B2
Granite (range) B2
Grant (range) F4
Great Salt Lake (des.) H2
High Rock (creek) B1
Highland (peak) G5
Hoover (dam) G7
Hot Creek (range) E4
Hot Creek (valley) E4
Humboldt (range) C2
Humboldt (riv.) E2
Humboldt (sink) C2
Humboldt Salt (marsh) D3
Huntington (creek) F2
Independence (mts.) E1
Jackson (mts.) C1
Job (peak) C3
Kawich (peak) E5
Kawich (range) E5
Kelley (creek) D1
Kings (riv.) C1
Lahontan (res.) B3
Lake Mead Nat'l Rec. Area G6
Las Vegas (range) F6
Lehman Caves Nat'l Mon. G4
Little Humboldt (riv.) D1
Little Smoky (valley) E4
Lone (mt.) D4
Long (valley) B1
Marys (riv.) F1
Mason (peak) F1
Massacre (lake) B1
Mead (lake) G6
Meadow Valley Wash (riv.) G5
Moapa River Ind. Res. G6
Mohave (lake) G7
Monitor (range) E4
Monte Cristo (range) D4
Mormon (mts.) G5
Muddy (mts.) G6
Nellis A.F.B. 7,476 ..... F6
Nellis Air Force Range and Nuclear Testing Site E5
Nelson (creek) G2
New Pass (range) D3
Nightingale (mts.) B2
Owyhee (riv.) E1
Pahranagat (range) F5
Pahrock (range) F5
Pah-rum (peak) B2
Pahrump (valley) F6
Pahute (mesa) E5
Pancake (range) F4
Pequop (mts.) G2
Pilot (peak) C4
Pine (creek) E2
Pine Forest (range) C1
Pintwater (range) F6
Piper (peak) D5
Potosi (mt.) F7
Pyramid (lake) B2
Pyramid Lake Ind. Res. B2
Quinn (riv.) D1
Quinn Canyon (range) F4
Railroad (valley) F4
Reese (riv.) D3
Reveille (peak) E5
Reveille (range) E4
Ruby (lake) F2
Ruby (mts.) F2
Rye Patch (res.) C2
Sand Springs (salt flat) C3
Santa Rosa (range) D1
Schell Creek (range) G3
Sheep (range) F6
Shoshone (mt.) E6
Shoshone (mts.) D3
Shoshone (range) E2
Silver Peak (range) D5
Simpson Park (mts.) E3
Smith Creek (valley) D3
Smoke Creek (des.) B2
Snake (mts.) F1
Snake (range) G3
Snow Water (lake) G2
Sonoma (range) D2
Specter (range) E6
Spotted (range) F6
Spring (creek) D2
Spring (mts.) F6
Spring (valley) G3
Stillwater (range) C3
Sulphur Spring (range) E3
Summit (lake) C1
Summit Lake Ind. Res. B1
Table (mt.) C3
Tahoe (lake) B3
Thousand Spring (creek) G1
Timber (mt.) F4
Timber (mt.) E5
Timpahute (range) F5
Toana (range) G2
Toiyabe (range) D3
Topaz (lake) B4
Toquima (range) E4
Trident (peak) C1
Trinity (range) C2
Truckee (riv.) B3
Tule (des.) G5
Tuscarora (mts.) E1
Virgin (mts.) G6
Virgin (peak) G6
Virgin (riv.) G6
Virginia (range) B3
Walker (lake) C4
Walker (riv.) C3
Walker River Ind. Res. C3
Washoe (lake) B3
Wassuk (range) C4
Western Shoshone Ind. Res. E1
Wheeler (peak) G4
White (riv.) F4
White Pine (range) F3
Wild Horse (res.) E1
Winnemucca (lake) B2
Winnemucca Ind. Res. D2
Yerington Ind. Res. B3
Yucca Flat (basin) E6

⊙County seat.
‡Population of metropolitan area.
† Zip of nearest p.o.
* Multiple zips.

NEW HAMPSHIRE
AREA 9,279 sq. mi. (24,033 sq. km.)
POPULATION 920,610
CAPITAL Concord
LARGEST CITY Manchester
HIGHEST POINT Mt. Washington 6,288 ft. (1917 m.)
SETTLED IN 1623
ADMITTED TO UNION June 21, 1788
POPULAR NAME Granite State
STATE FLOWER Purple Lilac
STATE BIRD Purple Finch

VERMONT
AREA 9,614 sq. mi. (24,900 sq. km.)
POPULATION 511,456
CAPITAL Montpelier
LARGEST CITY Burlington
HIGHEST POINT Mt. Mansfield 4,393 ft. (1339 m.)
SETTLED IN 1764
ADMITTED TO UNION March 4, 1791
POPULAR NAME Green Mountain State
STATE FLOWER Red Clover
STATE BIRD Hermit Thrush

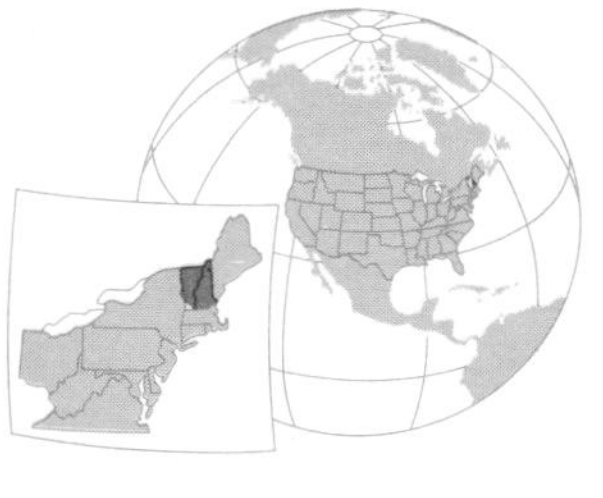

Topography

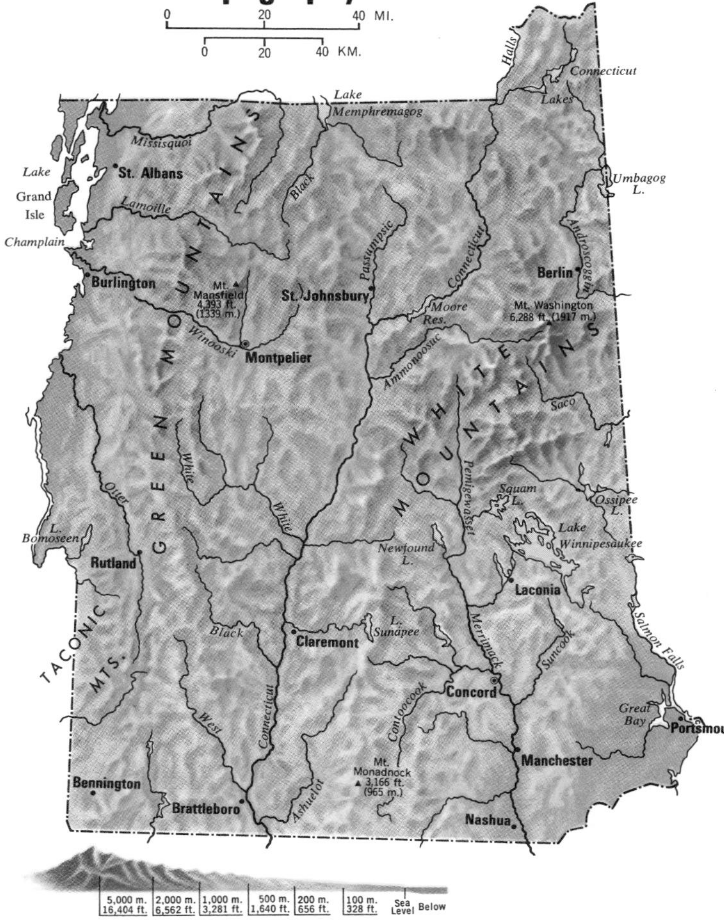

0 20 40 MI.
0 20 40 KM.
Lake Memphremagog
Missisquoi
St. Albans
Lake
Grand
Isle
Champlain
Lamoille
Black
Umbagog L.
Connecticut Lakes
Halls
Androscoggin
Passumpsic
Connecticut
Burlington
Mt. Mansfield 4,393 ft. (1339 m.)
St. Johnsbury
Moore Res.
Berlin
Mt. Washington 6,288 ft. (1917 m.)
Winooski
Montpelier
Ammonoosuc
Saco
White
Otter
Pemigewasset
Squam L.
Ossipee L.
Lake Winnipesaukee
L. Bomoseen
Rutland
Newfound L.
Laconia
L. Sunapee
Claremont
Black
Merrimack
Suncook
Salmon Falls
TACONIC MTS.
Contoocook
Concord
Great Bay
Portsmouth
West
Connecticut
Mt. Monadnock 3,166 ft. (965 m.)
Manchester
Bennington
Ashuelot
Brattleboro
Nashua
5,000 m. 16,404 ft.
2,000 m. 6,562 ft.
1,000 m. 3,281 ft.
500 m. 1,640 ft.
200 m. 656 ft.
100 m. 328 ft.
Sea Level
Below

NEW HAMPSHIRE

COUNTIES

Belknap 42,884 D4
Carroll 27,931 E4
Cheshire 62,116 C6
Coos 35,147 E2
Grafton 65,806 D4
Hillsborough 276,608 D6
Merrimack 98,302 D5
Rockingham 190,345 E5
Strafford 85,408 E5
Sullivan 36,063 C5

CITIES and TOWNS

Zip *Name/Pop.* *Key*

03601 Acworth○ 590 C5
†03864 Albany○ 383 E4
†03222 Alexandria○ 706 D4
†03275 Allenstown○ 4,398 E5
03602 Alstead○ 1,461 C5
03809 Alton○ 2,440 E5
03810 Alton Bay 500 E5
03031 Amherst○ 8,243 D6
03216 Andover○ 1,587 D5
03440 Antrim○ 2,208 D5
03440 Antrim 1,142 D5
03217 Ashland○ 1,807 D4
03217 Ashland 1,479 D4
03441 Ashuelot 810 C6
03811 Atkinson○ 4,397 E6
03032 Auburn○ 2,883 E5
03218 Barnstead○ 2,292 E5
†03825 Barrington○ 4,404 F5
03812 Bartlett○ 1,566 E3
03740 Bath○ 761 D3
03102 Bedford○ 9,481 D6
03220 Belmont○ 4,026 E5
03442 Bennington○ 890 D5
†03785 Benton○ 333 D3
03570 Berlin 13,084 E3
03574 Bethlehem○ 1,784 D3
03301 Boscawen○ 3,435 D5
03221 Bradford○ 1,115 D5
†03833 Brentwood○ 2,004 E6
†03222 Bridgewater○ 606 D4
03222 Bristol○ 2,198 D4
03222 Bristol 1,258 D4
†03872 Brookfield○ 385 E4
03033 Brookline○ 1,766 D6
03223 Campton○ 1,694 D4
03741 Canaan○ 2,456 C4
03034 Candia○ 2,989 E5
03224 Canterbury○ 1,410 D5
†03595 Carroll○ 647 D3
03813 Center Conway 558 E4
03226 Center Harbor○ 808 E4
03814 Center Ossipee 800 E4
03603 Charlestown○ 4,417 C5
03603 Charlestown 1,294 C5
†04037 Chatham○ 189 E3
03036 Chester○ 2,006 E6
03443 Chesterfield○ 2,561 C6
†03258 Chichester○ 1,492 E5
03817 Chocorua 575 E4
03743 Claremont 14,557 C5
†05902 Clarksville○ 262 E1
03576 Colebrook○ 2,459 E2
03576 Colebrook 1,131 E2
03301 Concord (cap.)⊙ 30,400 D5
03229 Contoocook 1,499 D5
03818 Conway○ 7,158 E4
03818 Conway 1,781 E4
03746 Cornish Flat 450 C4
†03753 Croydon○ 457 C5
†03598 Dalton○ 672 D3
03230 Danbury○ 680 D4
03819 Danville○ 1,318 E6
03037 Deerfield○ 1,979 E5
†03244 Deering○ 1,041 D5
03038 Derry○ 18,875 E6
03038 Derry 12,248 E6
†03266 Dorchester○ 244 D4
03820 Dover⊙ 22,377 F5
03444 Dublin○ 1,303 C6
†03588 Dummer○ 390 E2
†03301 Dunbarton○ 1,174 D5
03824 Durham○ 10,652 F5
03824 Durham 8,448 F5
03231 East Andover 500 D5
03826 East Hampstead 900 E6
03827 East Kingston○ 1,135 F6
†03580 Easton○ 124 D3
03446 East Swanzey 500 C6
03832 Eaton (Eaton Center)○ 256 E4
†03264 Ellsworth○ 53 D4
03748 Enfield○ 3,175 C4
03748 Enfield 1,581 C4
03042 Epping○ 3,460 E5
03042 Epping 1,384 E5
03234 Epsom○ 2,743 E5
03579 Errol○ 313 E2
03750 Etna 550 C4
03833 Exeter○ 11,024 F6
03833 Exeter⊙ 8,947 F6
03835 Farmington○ 4,630 E5
03835 Farmington 3,284 E5
03447 Fitzwilliam○ 1,795 C6
03043 Francestown○ 830 D6
03580 Franconia○ 743 D3
03235 Franklin 7,901 D5
03836 Freedom○ 720 E4
03044 Fremont○ 1,333 E6
†03246 Gilford○ 4,841 E4
03237 Gilmanton○ 1,941 E5
03448 Gilsum○ 652 C5
03838 Glen 600 E3
03045 Goffstown○ 11,315 D5
03581 Gorham○ 3,322 E3
03581 Gorham 2,180 E3
03752 Goshen○ 549 C5
03240 Grafton○ 739 D4
03753 Grantham○ 704 C5
03047 Greenfield○ 972 D6
03840 Greenland○ 2,129 F5
03048 Greenville○ 1,988 D6
03048 Greenville 1,447 D6
†03241 Groton○ 255 D4
03582 Groveton 1,389 D2
03754 Guild 500 C5
03841 Hampstead○ 3,785 E6
03842 Hampton○ 10,493 F6
03842 Hampton 6,779 F6
03844 Hampton Falls○ 1,372 F6
03449 Hancock○ 1,193 C6
03755 Hanover○ 9,119 C4
03755 Hanover 6,861 C4
03450 Harrisville○ 860 C6
03765 Haverhill○ 3,445 C3
03241 Hebron○ 349 D4
03242 Henniker○ 3,246 D5
03242 Henniker 1,538 D5
03243 Hill○ 736 D4
03244 Hillsboro○ 3,437 D5
03244 Hillsboro 1,797 D5
03451 Hinsdale○ 3,631 C6
03451 Hinsdale 1,546 C6
03245 Holderness○ 1,586 D4
03049 Hollis○ 4,679 D6
03106 Hooksett○ 7,303 E5
03106 Hooksett 1,868 E5
03301 Hopkinton○ 3,861 D5
03051 Hudson○ 14,022 E6
03051 Hudson 6,248 E6
03845 Intervale 725 E3
03846 Jackson○ 642 E3
03452 Jaffrey○ 4,349 C6
03452 Jaffrey 2,684 C6
03583 Jefferson○ 803 D3
03431 Keene⊙ 21,449 C6
03848 Kingston○ 4,111 E6
03246 Laconia⊙ 15,575 E4
03584 Lancaster○ 3,401 D3
03584 Lancaster⊙ 2,134 D3
†03585 Landaff○ 266 D3
†03602 Langdon○ 437 C5
03766 Lebanon 11,134 C4
†03857 Lee○ 2,111 F5
03606 Lempster○ 637 C5
03251 Lincoln○ 1,313 D3
03585 Lisbon○ 1,517 D3
03585 Lisbon 1,151 D3
†03051 Litchfield○ 4,150 E6
03561 Littleton○ 5,558 D3
03561 Littleton 4,480 D3
03053 Londonderry○ 13,598 E6
03301 Loudon○ 2,454 E5
†03585 Lyman○ 281 D3
03768 Lyme○ 1,289 C4
†03082 Lyndeborough○ 1,070 D6
†03820 Madbury○ 987 F5
03849 Madison○ 1,051 E4
*03101 Manchester 90,936 E6
Manchester‡ 160,767 E6
03455 Marlborough○ 1,846 C6
03455 Marlborough 1,184 C6
03456 Marlow○ 542 C5
03850 Melvin Village 450 E4
03253 Meredith○ 4,646 D4
03253 Meredith 1,202 D4
03770 Meriden 800 C4
03054 Merrimack○ 15,406 D6
†03887 Middleton○ 734 E5
03588 Milan○ 1,013 E2
03055 Milford○ 8,685 D6
03055 Milford 6,269 D6
03851 Milton○ 2,438 F5
03852 Milton Mills 450 F4
03771 Monroe○ 619 C3
03057 Mont Vernon○ 1,444 D6
03254 Moultonboro○ 2,206 E4
03060 Nashua⊙ 67,865 D6
Nashua‡ 114,221 D6
†03457 Nelson○ 442 C5
03070 New Boston○ 1,928 D6
03255 Newbury○ 961 C5
03854 New Castle○ 936 F5
03855 New Durham○ 1,183 E5
03856 Newfields○ 817 F5
03256 New Hampton○ 1,249 D4
†03801 Newington○ 716 F5
03071 New Ipswich○ 2,433 D6
03257 New London○ 2,935 D5
03257 New London 1,335 D5
03857 Newmarket○ 4,290 F5
03857 Newmarket 3,749 F5
03773 Newport○ 6,229 C5
03773 Newport⊙ 4,388 C5
03858 Newton○ 3,068 E6
03859 Newton Junction 450 E6
03860 North Conway 2,104 E3
†03276 Northfield○ 3,051 D5
†03276 Northfield-Tilton 2,574 D5
03862 North Hampton○ 3,425 F6
03590 North Stratford 600 D2
†03582 Northumberland○ 2,520 D2
03261 Northwood○ 2,175 E5
03262 North Woodstock 750 D3
03290 Nottingham○ 1,952 E5
†03741 Orange○ 197 D4
03777 Orford○ 928 C4
03864 Ossipee 2,465 E4
03076 Pelham○ 8,090 E6
†03275 Pembroke○ 4,861 E5
03458 Peterborough○ 4,895 D6
03458 Peterborough 2,568 D6
03779 Piermont○ 507 C4
03592 Pittsburg○ 780 E1
03263 Pittsfield○ 2,889 E5
03263 Pittsfield 1,584 E5
03781 Plainfield○ 1,749 C4
03865 Plaistow○ 5,609 E6
03264 Plymouth○ 5,094 D4
03264 Plymouth 3,628 D4
03801 Portsmouth 26,254 F5
Portsmouth-Dover-Rochester‡ 163,880 F5
03593 Randolph○ 274 E3
03077 Raymond○ 5,453 E5
03077 Raymond 1,192 E5
†03470 Richmond○ 518 C6
03461 Rindge○ 3,375 C6
03867 Rochester 21,560 E5
†03431 Roxbury○ 190 C6
03266 Rumney○ 1,212 D4
03870 Rye○ 4,508 F5
03871 Rye Beach 600 F6
03079 Salem○ 24,124 E6
03268 Salisbury○ 781 D5
03269 Sanbornton○ 1,679 D5
03872 Sanbornville 750 F4
03873 Sandown○ 2,057 E6
03270 Sandwich○ 905 E4
03874 Seabrook○ 5,917 F6
†03458 Sharon○ 184 D6
†03581 Shelburne○ 318 E3
03878 Somersworth 10,350 F5
†01913 South Hampton○ 660 F6
03462 Spofford 750 C6
†03284 Springfield○ 532 C4
†03582 Stark○ 470 E2
†03576 Stewartstown○ 943 E2
03464 Stoddard○ 482 C5
03884 Strafford○ 1,663 E5
†03590 Stratford○ 989 D2
03885 Stratham○ 2,507 F5
03585 Sugar Hill○ 397 D3
†03445 Sullivan○ 585 C5
03782 Sunapee○ 2,312 C5
03275 Suncook 4,698 D5
03431 Surry○ 656 C5
†03260 Sutton○ 1,091 D5
†03431 Swanzey○ 5,183 C6
03886 Tamworth○ 1,672 E4
03084 Temple○ 692 D6
†03285 Thornton○ 952 D4
03276 Tilton○ 3,387 D5
03276 Tilton-Northfield 2,574 D5
03465 Troy○ 2,131 C6
03465 Troy 1,318 C6
†03816 Tuftonboro○ 1,500 E4
03595 Twin Mountain 500 D3
†03743 Unity○ 1,092 C5
†03872 Wakefield○ 2,237 F4
03608 Walpole○ 3,188 C5
03278 Warner○ 1,963 D5
03279 Warren○ 650 D4
03280 Washington○ 411 C5
03223 Waterville Valley○ 180 D4
03281 Weare○ 3,232 D5
†03301 Webster○ 1,095 D5
03282 Wentworth○ 527 D4
†03579 Wentworths Location○ 49 E2
†03242 West Henniker 500 D5
03784 West Lebanon C4
03467 Westmoreland○ 1,452 C6
03597 West Stewartstown 700 E2
03469 West Swanzey 1,022 C6
03865 Westville 750 E6
03598 Whitefield○ 1,681 D3
03598 Whitefield 1,005 D3
†03287 Wilmot○ 725 D5
03287 Wilmot Flat 450 D5
03086 Wilton○ 2,669 D6
03086 Wilton 1,310 D6
03470 Winchester○ 3,465 C6
03470 Winchester 1,732 C6
03087 Windham○ 5,664 E6
03289 Winnisquam 500 E5
03894 Wolfeboro○ 3,968 E4
03894 Wolfeboro 2,271 E4
03896 Wolfeboro Falls 600 E4
03293 Woodstock○ 1,008 D4
03785 Woodsville⊙ 1,195 C3

OTHER FEATURES

Adams (mt.) E3
Ammonoosuc (riv.) D3
Androscoggin (riv.) E2
Ashuelot (riv.) C6
Back (lake) E1
Baker (riv.) D4
Bearcamp (riv.) E4
Beaver (brook) E6
Belknap (mt.) E5
Blackwater (res.) D5
Blue (mt.) E2
Bond (mt.) E3
Bow (lake) E5
Cabot (mt.) E2
Cannon (mt.) D3
Cardigan (mt.) D4
Carrigain (mt.) E3
Carter Dome (mt.) E3
Chocorua (mt.) E4
Cocheco (riv.) E5
Cold (riv.) C5
Comerford (dam) D3
Connecticut (riv.) B6
Contoocook (riv.) D6
Conway (lake) E4
Crawford Notch (pass) E3
Croydon (peak) C5
Croydon Branch, Sugar (riv.) C5
Crystal (lake) E5
Cube (mt.) D4
Dixville (peak) E2
Dixville Notch (pass) E2
Edward MacDowell (res.) D6
Ellis (riv.) E3
Everett (dam) D5
Exeter (riv.) E6
First Connecticut (lake) E1
Francis (lake) E1
Franconia Notch (pass) D3
Franklin Falls (res.) D4
Gale (riv.) D3
Great (bay) F5
Halls (stream) E1
Hancock (mt.) D3
Highland (lake) C5
Hutchins (mt.) E2
Indian (stream) E1
Jefferson (mt.) E3
Kearsarge (mt.) D5
Kinsman (mt.) D3
Kinsman Notch (pass) D3
Lafayette (mt.) D3
Lamprey (riv.) E5
Liberty (mt.) D3
Lincoln (mt.) D3
Long (mt.) E2
Mad (riv.) D4
Madison (mt.) E3
Mascoma (lake) C4
Massabesic (lake) E6
Merrimack (riv.) D5
Merrymeeting (lake) E5
Mohawk (riv.) E2
Monadnock (mt.) C6
Monroe (mt.) E3
Moore (dam) D3
Moore (res.) D3
Moosilauke (mt.) D3
Nash (stream) E2
Newfound (lake) D4
North Carter (mt.) E3
North Twin (mt.) D3
Nubanusit (lake) C5
Osceola (mt.) E3
Ossipee (lake) E4
Ossipee (mts.) E4
Ossipee (riv.) F4
Passaconaway (mt.) E4
Pawtuckaway (pond) E5
Pease A.F.B. F5
Pemigewasset (riv.) D4
Perry (stream) E1
Pine (riv.) E4
Pinkham Notch (pass) E3
Piscataqua (riv.) F5
Piscataquog (riv.) D5
Presidential (range) E3
Rice (mt.) E2
Saco (riv.) E3
Saint-Gaudens Nat'l Hist. Site B4
Salmon Falls (riv.) F5

(continued on following page)

Agriculture, Industry and Resources

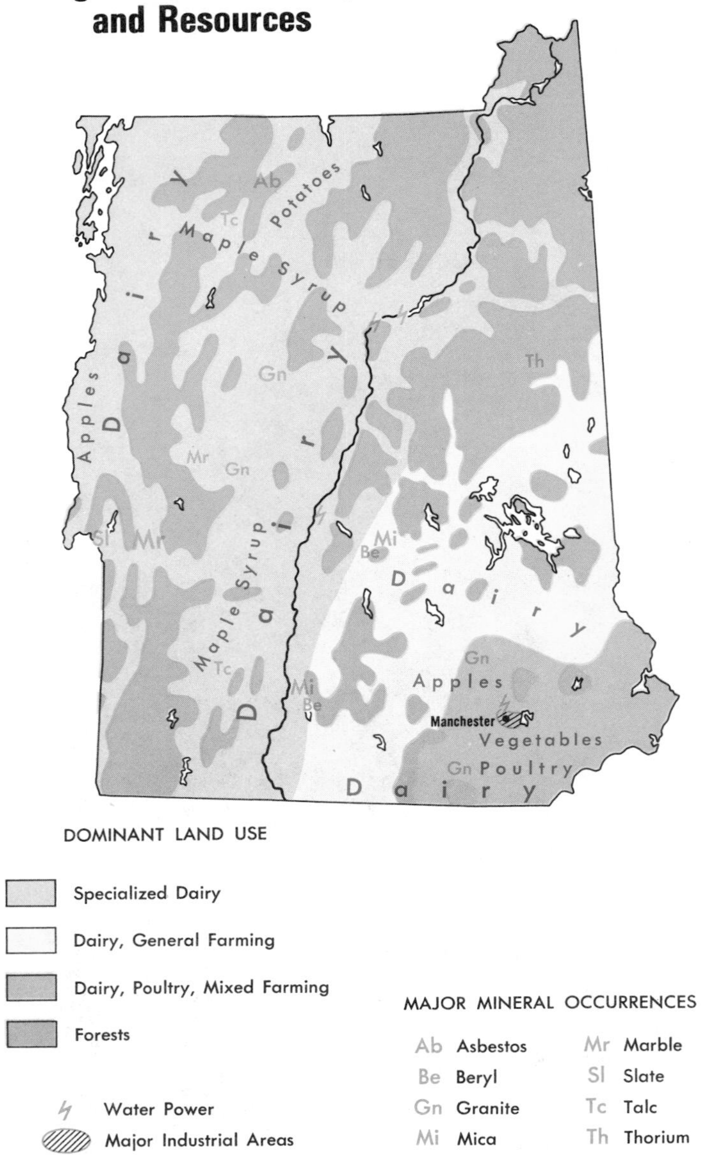
Dairy
Maple Syrup
Potatoes
Apples
Vegetables
Poultry
Manchester
Ab
Tc
Gn
Mr
Sl
Mi
Be
Th
DOMINANT LAND USE
Specialized Dairy
Dairy, General Farming
Dairy, Poultry, Mixed Farming
Forests
Water Power
Major Industrial Areas
MAJOR MINERAL OCCURRENCES
Ab Asbestos
Be Beryl
Gn Granite
Mi Mica
Mr Marble
Sl Slate
Tc Talc
Th Thorium

Sandwich (mt.) ... E4
Sandwich (range) ... E4
Second (lake) ... E1
Shaw (mt.) ... E4
Shoals (isls.) ... F6
Smarts (mt.) ... C4
Souhegan (riv.) ... D6
South Twin (mt.) ... D3
Squam (lake) ... E4
Starr King (mt.) ... E3
Stub Hill (mt.) ... E1
Sugar (riv.) ... C5
Sunapee (lake) ... C5
Suncook (lkes) ... E5
Suncook (riv.) ... E5
Surry Mountain (lake) ... C5
Tarleton (lake) ... D4
Tecumseh (mt.) ... D4
Third (lake) ... E1
Tom (mt.) ... E3
Umbagog (lake) ... E2
Upper Ammonoosuc (riv.) ... E2
Warner (riv.) ... D5
Washington (mt.) ... E3
Waumbek (mt.) ... E3
Wentworth (lake) ... E4
White (isl.) ... F6
White (mts.) ... E3
Whiteface (mt.) ... E4
Wild Ammonoosuc (riv.) ... D3
Wilder (dam) ... C4
Winnipesaukee (lake) ... E4
Winnipesaukee (riv.) ... D5
Winnisquam (lake) ... D4

VERMONT

COUNTIES

Addison 29,406 ... A3
Bennington 33,345 ... A6
Caledonia 25,808 ... C2
Chittenden 115,534 ... A3
Essex 6,313 ... D2
Franklin 34,788 ... B2
Grand Isle 4,613 ... A2
Lamoille 16,767 ... B2
Orange 22,739 ... C3
Orleans 23,440 ... C2
Rutland 58,347 ... A4
Washington 52,393 ... B3
Windham 36,933 ... B5
Windsor 51,030 ... B4

CITIES and TOWNS

Zip *Name/Pop.* *Key*

05820 Albany○ 705 ... C2
05440 Alburg○ 1,352 ... A2
05440 Alburg 496 ... A2
†05143 Andover○ 350 ... B5
05250 Arlington○ 2,184 ... A5
05250 Arlington 1,309 ... A5
05441 Bakersfield○ 852 ... B2
05031 Barnard○ 790 ... B4
05821 Barnet○ 1,338 ... C3
05641 Barre 9,824 ... C3
05641 Barre○ 7,090 ... C3
05822 Barton○ 2,990 ... C2
05822 Barton 1,062 ... C2
05823 Beebe Plain 500 ... C2
05902 Beecher Falls 950 ... D2
05101 Bellows Falls 3,456 ... C5
05442 Belvidere○ 218 ... B2
05201 Bennington○ 15,815 ... A6
05201 Bennington⊙ 9,349 ... A6
05731 Benson○ 739 ... A4
†05476 Berkshire○ 1,116 ... B2
05032 Bethel○ 1,715 ... B4
05032 Bethel 1,016 ... B4
†03590 Bloomfield○ 188 ... D2
†05466 Bolton○ 715 ... B3
05732 Bomoseen 700 ... A4
05340 Bondville 500 ... B5
05033 Bradford○ 2,191 ... C3
05033 Bradford 831 ... C3
†05669 Braintree○ 1,065 ... B4
05733 Brandon○ 4,194 ... A4
05733 Brandon 1,925 ... A4
05301 Brattleboro○ 11,886 ... B6
05301 Brattleboro 8,596 ... B6
05034 Bridgewater○ 867 ... B4
05734 Bridport○ 997 ... A4
05443 Bristol○ 3,293 ... A3
05443 Bristol 1,793 ... A3
05036 Brookfield○ 959 ... B3
†05345 Brookline○ 310 ... B5
†05860 Brownington○ 708 ... C2
†05871 Burke○ 1,385 ... D2
05401 Burlington⊙ 37,712 ... A3
Burlington‡ 114,070 ... A3
05647 Cabot○ 958 ... C3
05647 Cabot 259 ... C3
05648 Calais○ 1,207 ... B3
05444 Cambridge○ 2,019 ... B2
05444 Cambridge 217 ... B2
05903 Canaan○ 1,196 ... D2
05735 Castleton○ 3,637 ... A4
05142 Cavendish○ 1,355 ... B5
05736 Center Rutland 465 ... A4
05445 Charlotte○ 2,561 ... A3
05038 Chelsea 1,091 ... C4
05143 Chester○ 2,791 ... B5
05143 Chester-Chester Depot 1,267 ... B5
05737 Chittenden○ 927 ... B4
†05759 Clarendon○ 2,372 ... A4
05446 Colchester○ 12,629 ... A2
05824 Concord○ 1,125 ... D3
05039 Corinth○ 904 ... C3
†05753 Cornwall○ 993 ... A4
05825 Coventry○ 674 ... C2
05826 Craftsbury○ 844 ... C2
05739 Danby○ 992 ... A5
05828 Danville○ 1,705 ... C3
05829 Derby○ 4,222 ... C2
05829 Derby (Derby Center) 598 ... C2
05830 Derby Line 874 ... C2
05251 Dorset○ 1,648 ... A5
†05676 Duxbury○ 877 ... B3
05252 East Arlington 600 ... A5
05649 East Barre-Graniteville 2,172 ... C3
05253 East Dorset 550 ... A5
05837 East Haven○ 280 ... D2
05740 East Middlebury 550 ... A4
05651 East Montpelier○ 2,205 ... B3
05741 East Poultney 450 ... A4
05742 East Wallingford 500 ... B5
05652 Eden○ 612 ... B2
05450 Enosburg Falls 1,207 ... B2
05451 Essex○ 14,392 ... A2
05452 Essex Junction 7,033 ... A3
05454 Fairfax○ 1,805 ... B2
05455 Fairfield○ 1,493 ... B2
05743 Fair Haven○ 2,819 ... A4
05743 Fair Haven 2,363 ... A4
05045 Fairlee○ 770 ... C4
05456 Ferrisburg○ 2,117 ... A3
†05444 Fletcher○ 626 ... B2
05745 Forest Dale 500 ... A4
05457 Franklin○ 1,006 ... B2
†05478 Georgia○ 2,818 ... A2
05904 Gilman 600 ... D3
05839 Glover○ 843 ... C2
05146 Grafton○ 604 ... B5
05840 Granby○ 70 ... D2
05458 Grand Isle○ 1,238 ... A2
05654 Graniteville-East Barre 2,172 ... C3
05747 Granville○ 288 ... B4
05841 Greensboro○ 677 ... C2
05046 Groton○ 667 ... C3
05905 Guildhall 202 ... D2
†05301 Guilford○ 1,532 ... B6
†05358 Halifax○ 488 ... B6
05748 Hancock○ 334 ... B4
05843 Hardwick○ 2,613 ... C2
05843 Hardwick 1,476 ... C2
05047 Hartford○ 7,963 ... C4
05048 Hartland○ 2,396 ... C4
†05459 Highgate○ 2,493 ... B2
05461 Hinesburg○ 2,690 ... A3
†05830 Holland○ 473 ... D2
05749 Hubbardton○ 490 ... A4
05462 Huntington○ 1,161 ... B3
05655 Hyde Park○ 2,021 ... B2
05655 Hyde Park⊙ 475 ... B2
05750 Hydeville 500 ... A4
†05777 Ira○ 354 ... A4
05845 Irasburg○ 870 ... C2
05846 Island Pond 1,216 ... D2
05463 Isle La Motte○ 393 ... A2
05342 Jacksonville 252 ... B6
05343 Jamaica○ 681 ... B5
†05859 Jay○ 302 ... C2
05464 Jeffersonville 491 ... B2
05465 Jericho○ 3,575 ... A2
05465 Jericho 1,340 ... A2
05656 Johnson○ 2,581 ... B2
05656 Johnson 1,393 ... B2
05751 Killington 700 ... B4
†05752 Leicester○ 803 ... A4
†03576 Lemington○ 108 ... D2
†05443 Lincoln○ 870 ... B3
05148 Londonderry○ 1,510 ... B5
05847 Lowell○ 573 ... C2
05149 Ludlow○ 2,414 ... B5
05149 Ludlow 1,352 ... B5
05906 Lunenburg○ 1,138 ... D3
05849 Lyndon○ 4,924 ... C2
05850 Lyndon Center ... C2
05851 Lyndonville 1,401 ... D2
†05905 Maidstone○ 100 ... D2
05254 Manchester○ 3,261 ... A5
05254 Manchester⊙ 563 ... A5
05255 Manchester Center 1,719 ... A5
05344 Marlboro○ 695 ... B6
05658 Marshfield○ 1,267 ... C3
05658 Marshfield 301 ... C3
†05701 Mendon○ 1,056 ... B4
05753 Middlebury○ 7,574 ... A3
05753 Middlebury⊙ 5,591 ... A3
†05602 Middlesex○ 1,235 ... B3
05757 Middletown Springs○ 603 ... A5
05468 Milton○ 6,829 ... A2
05468 Milton 1,411 ... A2
05469 Monkton○ 1,201 ... A3
05470 Montgomery○ 681 ... B2
05471 Montgomery Center 400 ... B2
05602 Montpelier (cap.)⊙ 8,241 ... B3
05660 Moretown○ 1,221 ... B3
05853 Morgan○ 460 ... D2
†05661 Morristown○ 4,448 ... B2
05661 Morrisville 2,074 ... B2
05758 Mount Holly○ 938 ... B5
†05739 Mount Tabor○ 211 ... B5
†05871 Newark○ 280 ... D2
05051 Newbury○ 1,699 ... C3
05051 Newbury 425 ... C3
05345 Newfane○ 1,129 ... B6
05345 Newfane⊙ 119 ... B6
05472 New Haven○ 1,217 ... A3
05855 Newport○ 1,319 ... C2
05855 Newport⊙ 4,756 ... C2
05257 North Bennington 1,685 ... A6
05663 Northfield○ 5,435 ... B3
05663 Northfield 2,033 ... B3
05664 Northfield Falls 600 ... B3
05052 North Hartland 500 ... C4
05474 North Hero 442 ... A2
05665 North Hyde Park 450 ... B2
05053 North Pomfret 400 ... B4
05260 North Pownal 700 ... A6
05150 North Springfield ... B5
05859 North Troy 717 ... C2
†05101 North Westminster 310 ... B5
05907 Norton○ 184 ... D2
05055 Norwich○ 2,398 ... C4
†05201 Old Bennington 353 ... A6
†05649 Orange○ 752 ... C3
05860 Orleans 983 ... C2
05760 Orwell○ 901 ... A4
†05491 Panton○ 537 ... A3
05761 Pawlet○ 1,244 ... A5
05862 Peacham○ 531 ... C3
05151 Perkinsville 187 ... B5
05152 Peru○ 312 ... B5
05762 Pittsfield○ 396 ... B4
05763 Pittsford○ 2,590 ... A4
05763 Pittsford 666 ... A4
05667 Plainfield○ 1,249 ... C3
05667 Plainfield 599 ... C3
05056 Plymouth○ 405 ... B4
†05067 Pomfret○ 856 ... B4
05058 Post Mills 500 ... C4
05764 Poultney○ 3,196 ... A4
05764 Poultney 1,554 ... A4
05261 Pownal○ 3,269 ... A6
05765 Proctor○ 1,998 ... A4
05153 Proctorsville 481 ... B5
05346 Putney○ 1,850 ... B6
05059 Quechee 900 ... C4
05060 Randolph○ 4,689 ... B4
05060 Randolph 2,217 ... B4
05062 Reading○ 647 ... B5
05350 Readsboro○ 638 ... B6
05350 Readsboro 402 ... B6
05476 Richford○ 2,206 ... B2
05476 Richford 1,471 ... B2
05477 Richmond○ 3,159 ... A3
05477 Richmond 865 ... A3
05766 Ripton○ 327 ... A4
05767 Rochester○ 1,054 ... B4
†05101 Rockingham○ 5,538 ... B5
05669 Roxbury○ 452 ... B3
†05068 Royalton○ 2,100 ... B4
05768 Rupert○ 605 ... A5
05701 Rutland○ 3,300 ... B4
05701 Rutland⊙ 18,436 ... B4
05042 Ryegate○ 1,000 ... C3
05478 Saint Albans○ 3,555 ... A2
05478 Saint Albans⊙ 7,308 ... A2
†05401 Saint George○ 677 ... A2
05819 Saint Johnsbury○ 7,938 ... D3
05819 Saint Johnsbury⊙ 7,150 ... D3
05863 Saint Johnsbury Center 400 ... D3
05769 Salisbury○ 881 ... A4
†05250 Sandgate○ 234 ... A5
05154 Saxtons River 593 ... B5
†05363 Searsburg○ 72 ... A6
05262 Shaftsbury○ 3,001 ... A6
05065 Sharon○ 828 ... C4
05866 Sheffield○ 435 ... C2
05482 Shelburne○ 5,000 ... A3
05483 Sheldon○ 1,618 ... B2
05770 Shoreham○ 972 ... A4
†05738 Shrewsbury○ 866 ... B4
05670 South Barre 1,301 ... B3
05401 South Burlington 10,679 ... A3
05486 South Hero○ 1,188 ... A2
05155 South Londonderry 500 ... B5
05068 South Royalton 700 ... C4
05069 South Ryegate 400 ... C3
05156 Springfield○ 10,190 ... B5
05156 Springfield 5,603 ... B5
05352 Stamford○ 773 ... A6
05487 Starksboro○ 1,336 ... A3
05772 Stockbridge○ 508 ... B4
05672 Stowe○ 2,991 ... B3
05672 Stowe 531 ... B3
05072 Strafford○ 731 ... C4
†05360 Stratton○ 122 ... B5
†05733 Sudbury○ 380 ... A4
†05250 Sunderland○ 768 ... A5
05867 Sutton○ 667 ... C2
05488 Swanton○ 5,141 ... A2
05488 Swanton 2,520 ... A2
05074 Thetford○ 2,188 ... C4
†05773 Tinmouth○ 406 ... A5
05076 Topsham○ 767 ... C3
05353 Townshend○ 849 ... B5
05868 Troy○ 1,498 ... C2
05077 Tunbridge○ 925 ... C4
05489 Underhill○ 2,172 ... B2
05490 Underhill Center 575 ... B2
05491 Vergennes 2,273 ... A3
05354 Vernon○ 1,175 ... B6
05079 Vershire○ 442 ... C4
05673 Waitsfield○ 1,300 ... B3
†05873 Walden○ 575 ... C3
05773 Wallingford○ 1,893 ... B5
05773 Wallingford 1,141 ... B5
†05491 Waltham○ 394 ... A3
05355 Wardsboro○ 505 ... B5
05674 Warren○ 956 ... B3
05675 Washington○ 855 ... C3
05676 Waterbury○ 4,465 ... B3
05676 Waterbury 1,892 ... B3
05492 Waterville○ 470 ... B2
05678 Websterville 700 ... B3
05774 Wells○ 815 ... A5
05081 Wells River 396 ... C3
05301 West Brattleboro 2,795 ... B6
05871 West Burke 338 ... C2
05356 West Dover 550 ... B6
05083 West Fairlee○ 427 ... C4
05874 Westfield○ 418 ... C2
05494 Westford○ 1,413 ... A2
05875 West Glover ... C2
†05743 West Haven○ 253 ... A4
05158 Westminster○ 2,493 ... C5
05158 Westminster 319 ... C5
†05860 Westmore○ 257 ... C2
05161 Weston○ 627 ... B5
05777 West Rutland○ 2,351 ... A4
05777 West Rutland 2,169 ... A4
05359 West Townshend 500 ... B5
†05753 Weybridge○ 667 ... A3
†05851 Wheelock○ 444 ... C2
05001 White River Junction 2,582 ... C4
05778 Whiting○ 379 ... A4
05361 Whitingham○ 1,043 ... B6
05088 Wilder 1,461 ... C4
05679 Williamstown○ 2,284 ... B3
05495 Williston○ 3,843 ... A3
05363 Wilmington○ 1,808 ... B6
†05359 Windham○ 223 ... B5
05089 Windsor○ 4,084 ... C5
05089 Windsor 3,478 ... C5
05404 Winooski 6,318 ... A2
05680 Wolcott○ 986 ... C2
05681 Woodbury○ 573 ... C3
†05201 Woodford○ 314 ... A6
05091 Woodstock○ 3,214 ... B4
05091 Woodstock⊙ 1,178 ... B4
05682 Worcester○ 727 ... B3

OTHER FEATURES

Abraham (mt.) ... B3
Arrowhead Mountain (lake) ... A2
Ascutney (mt.) ... C5
Bald (mt.) ... D2
Barton (riv.) ... C2
Batten Kill (riv.) ... A5
Belvidere (mt.) ... B2
Black (riv.) ... B5
Black (riv.) ... C2
Bloodroot (mt.) ... B4
Bolton (mt.) ... B3
Bomoseen (lake) ... A4
Brandon Gap (pass) ... B4
Bread Loaf (mt.) ... A3
Bromley (mt.) ... B5
Brown's (riv.) ... A2
Burke (mt.) ... D2
Camels Hump (mt.) ... B3
Carmi (lake) ... B2
Caspian (lake) ... C2
Champlain (lake) ... A2
Chittenden (res.) ... B4
Clyde (riv.) ... C2
Comerford (dam) ... D3
Connecticut (riv.) ... C4
Crystal (lake) ... C2
Dorset (peak) ... A5
Dunmore (lake) ... A4
Echo (lake) ... D2
Ellen (mt.) ... B3
Equinox (mt.) ... A5
Fairfield (pond) ... A2
Glastenbury (mt.) ... A6
Gore (mt.) ... D2
Green (mts.) ... B4
Green River (res.) ... B2
Groton (lake) ... C3
Hardwick (lake) ... C2
Harriman (res.) ... B6
Harveys (lake) ... C3
Haystack (mt.) ... B6
Hoosic (riv.) ... A6
Hortonia (lake) ... A4
Hunger (mt.) ... B3
Iroquois (lake) ... A3
Island (pond) ... D2
Jay (peak) ... B2
Joes (brook) ... C3
Killington (peak) ... B4
Lamoille (riv.) ... A2
Lewis (creek) ... A3
Lincoln Gap (pass) ... B3
Little (riv.) ... B3
Mad (riv.) ... B3
Maidstone (lake) ... D2
Mansfield (mt.) ... B2
Memphremagog (lake) ... C1
Mettawee (riv.) ... A5
Middlebury Gap (pass) ... B4
Mill (riv.) ... B4
Missisquoi (riv.) ... B2
Mollys Falls (pond) ... C3
Moore (dam) ... D3
Moore (res.) ... D3
Moose (riv.) ... D2
Norton (pond) ... D2
Nulhegan (riv.) ... D2
Ottauquechee (riv.) ... B4
Otter (creek) ... A3
Passumpsic (riv.) ... D2
Pico (peak) ... B4
Poultney (riv.) ... A4
Saint Catherine (lake) ... A5
Salem (lake) ... C2
Seymour (lake) ... D2
Shelburne (pond) ... A3
Smugglers Notch (pass) ... B2
Snow (mt.) ... B6
Somerset (res.) ... A5
Spruce (mt.) ... C3
Stratton (mt.) ... B5
Tabor (mt.) ... B5
Trout (riv.) ... B2
Waits (riv.) ... C3
Waterbury (res.) ... B3
Wells (riv.) ... C3
West (riv.) ... B5
White (riv.) ... C4
White Face (mt.) ... B2
Wilder (dam) ... C4
Willoughby (lake) ... D2
Winooski (riv.) ... B3

⊙County seat.
‡Population of metropolitan area.
○Population of town or township.
† Zip of nearest p.o. * Multiple zips.

AREA 7,787 sq. mi. (20,168 sq. km.)
POPULATION 7,364,823
CAPITAL Trenton
LARGEST CITY Newark
HIGHEST POINT High Point 1,803 ft. (550 m.)
SETTLED IN 1617
ADMITTED TO UNION December 18, 1787
POPULAR NAME Garden State
STATE FLOWER Purple Violet
STATE BIRD Eastern Goldfinch

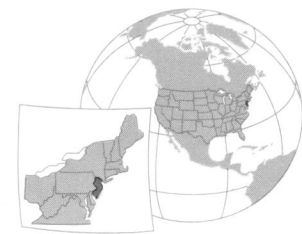

Agriculture, Industry and Resources

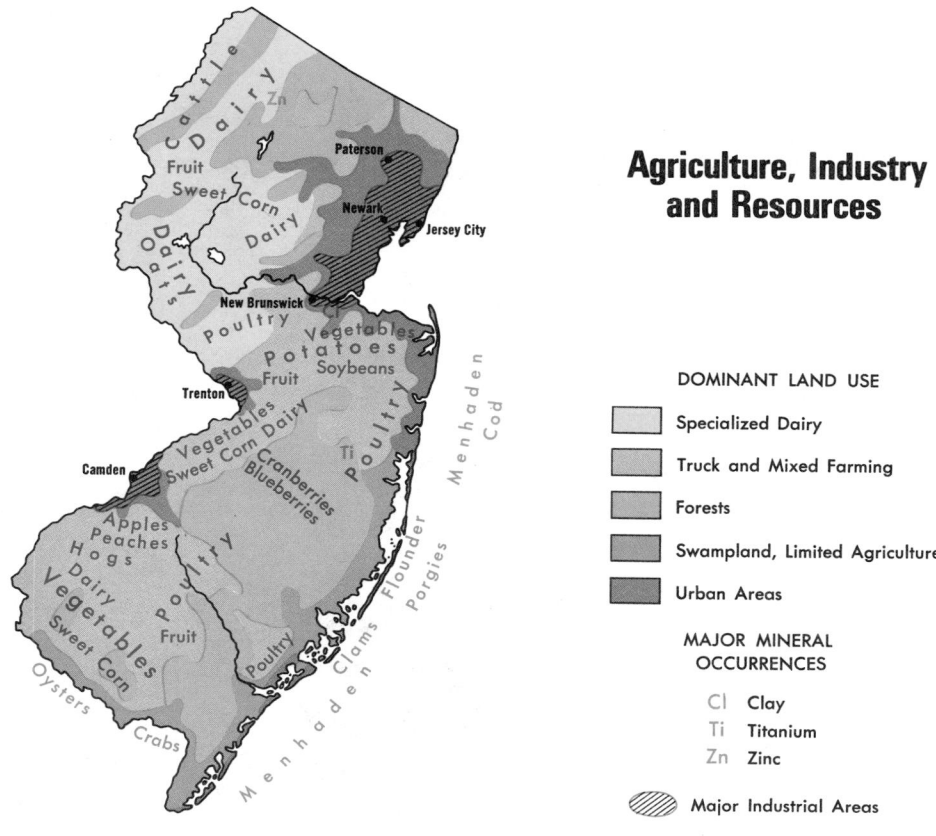

DOMINANT LAND USE

- Specialized Dairy
- Truck and Mixed Farming
- Forests
- Swampland, Limited Agriculture
- Urban Areas

MAJOR MINERAL OCCURRENCES

- Cl   Clay
- Ti   Titanium
- Zn   Zinc

Major Industrial Areas

The Urban Northeast

- Urbanized Areas
- Places with more than 10,000 inhabitants
- Places with 5,000-10,000 inhabitants
- Places with 2,500-5,000 inhabitants

© Copyright HAMMOND INCORPORATED, Maplewood, N.J.

COUNTIES

Atlantic 194,119	D5
Bergen 845,385	E2
Burlington 362,542	D4
Camden 471,650	D4
Cape May 82,266	D5
Cumberland 132,866	C5
Essex 851,116	E2
Gloucester 199,917	C4
Hudson 556,972	E2
Hunterdon 87,361	D2
Mercer 307,863	D3
Middlesex 595,893	E3
Monmouth 503,173	E3
Morris 407,630	D2
Ocean 346,038	E4
Passaic 447,585	E1
Salem 64,676	C4
Somerset 203,129	D2
Sussex 116,119	D1
Union 504,094	E2
Warren 84,429	C2

CITIES and TOWNS

Zip	Name/Pop.	Key
08201	Absecon 6,859	D5
07820	Allamuchy 600	D2
07401	Allendale 5,901	B1
07711	Allenhurst 912	F3
08501	Allentown 1,962	D3
08720	Allenwood	E3
08001	Alloway 1,370	C4
08865	Alpha 2,644	C2
07620	Alpine 1,549	C1
07821	Andover 892	D2
08801	Annandale 1,040	D2
07712	Asbury Park 17,015	F3
	Asbury Park-Long Branch‡ 503,173	F3
†08033	Ashland	B3
08004	Atco	D4
*08401	Atlantic City 40,199	E5
	Atlantic City‡ 194,119	E5
07716	Atlantic Highlands 4,950	F3
08106	Audubon 9,533	B3
†08106	Audubon Park 1,274	B3
08202	Avalon 2,162	D5
07001	Avenel	E2
07717	Avon By The Sea 2,337	E3
08005	Barnegat 1,012	E4
08006	Barnegat Light 619	E4
08007	Barrington 7,418	B3
07920	Basking Ridge	D2
08742	Bay Head 1,340	E3
07002	Bayonne 65,047	B2
08008	Beach Haven 1,714	E4
08722	Beachwood 7,687	E4
07921	Bedminster○ 2,469	D2
08502	Belle Mead	D3
07109	Belleville 35,367	B2
08031	Bellmawr 13,721	B3
07719	Belmar 6,771	F3
07823	Belvidere○ 2,475	C2
07621	Bergenfield 25,568	C1
07922	Berkeley Heights○ 12,549	E2
08009	Berlin 5,786	D4
07924	Bernardsville 6,715	D2
08010	Beverly 2,919	D3
08012	Blackwood 5,219	C4
07825	Blairstown○ 4,360	C2
07003	Bloomfield 47,792	B2
07403	Bloomingdale 7,867	E1
08804	Bloomsbury 864	C2
07603	Bogota 8,344	B2
07005	Boonton 8,620	E2
08505	Bordentown 4,441	D3
08805	Bound Brook 9,710	D2
07720	Bradley Beach 4,772	F3
07826	Branchville 870	D1
08723	Breton Woods	E3
08723	Brick○ 53,629	E3
08014	Bridgeport 750	C4
08302	Bridgeton○ 18,795	C5
08807	Bridgewater○ 29,175	D2
08730	Brielle 4,068	E3
08203	Brigantine 8,318	E5
08030	Brooklawn 2,133	B3
08015	Browns Mills 10,568	D4
07828	Budd Lake 6,523	D2
08310	Buena 3,642	D4
08016	Burlington 10,246	D3
07405	Butler 7,616	E2
07006	Caldwell 7,624	B2
07830	Califon 1,023	D2
*08101	Camden○ 84,910	B3
†08701	Candlewood 6,750	E3
08204	Cape May 4,853	D6
08210	Cape May Court House○ 3,597	D5
07072	Carlstadt 6,166	B2
08069	Carneys Point 7,574	C4
07008	Carteret 20,598	E2
07009	Cedar Grove○ 12,600	B2
†08723	Cedarwood Park	E3
07928	Chatham 8,537	E2
08019	Chatsworth 700	D4
08879	Cheesequake	E3
*08034	Cherry Hill○ 68,785	B3
†08089	Chesilhurst 1,590	D4
07930	Chester 1,433	D2
†08505	Chesterfield○ 3,867	D3
08077	Cinnaminson○ 16,072	B3
07066	Clark○ 16,699	A3
08020	Clarksboro	C4
08510	Clarksburg 800	E3
08312	Clayton 6,013	C4
08021	Clementon 5,764	D4
07010	Cliffside Park 21,464	C2
07721	Cliffwood	E3
*07011	Clifton 74,388	B2
08809	Clinton 1,910	D2
08108	Collingswood 15,838	B3
08213	Cologne 800	D4
07722	Colts Neck 950	E3
07832	Columbia 600	C2
08022	Columbus 800	D3
07961	Convent Station	E2
†08270	Corbin City 254	D5
†07821	Cranberry Lake 500	D2
08512	Cranbury 1,255	E3
07016	Cranford○ 24,573	E2
07626	Cresskill 7,609	C1
08515	Crosswicks 265	D3
07723	Deal 1,952	F3
08023	Deepwater 800	C4
08110	Delair	B3
08075	Delanco○ 3,730	D3
08075	Delran○ 14,811	B3
07627	Demarest 4,963	C1
08214	Dennisville 890	D5
08096	Deptford○ 23,473	B4
08317	Dorothy 900	D5
07801	Dover 14,681	D2
07628	Dumont 18,334	C1
08812	Dunellen 6,593	D2
08816	East Brunswick 37,711	E3
07936	East Hanover○ 9,319	E2
07734	East Keansburg	E3
08873	East Millstone 950	D3
†07100	East Newark 1,923	B2
*07017	East Orange 77,690	B2
07073	East Rutherford 7,849	B2
07724	Eatontown 12,703	E3
07020	Edgewater 4,628	C2
†08010	Edgewater Park○ 9,273	D3
*08817	Edison○ 70,193	E2
08215	Egg Harbor City 4,618	D4
07740	Elberon	F3
*07201	Elizabeth○ 106,201	B2
08318	Elmer 1,569	C4
†07407	Elmwood Park 18,377	B2
08217	Elwood 1,538	D4
07630	Emerson 7,793	B1
*07631	Englewood 23,701	C2
07632	Englewood Cliffs 5,698	C2
07726	Englishtown 976	E3
07021	Essex Fells 2,363	B2
08319	Estell Manor 848	D5
08025	Ewan 610	C4
07006	Fairfield○ 7,987	A2
07701	Fair Haven 5,679	E3
07410	Fair Lawn 32,229	B1
08320	Fairton 1,107	C5
07022	Fairview 10,519	C2
07023	Fanwood 7,767	E2
07931	Far Hills 677	D2
07727	Farmingdale 1,348	E3
†08505	Fieldsboro 597	D3
07836	Flanders	D2
08822	Flemington○ 4,132	D2
08518	Florence-Roebling 7,677	D3
07932	Florham Park 9,359	E2
†08037	Folsom 1,892	D4
08863	Fords	E2
08731	Forked River 900	E4
07024	Fort Lee 32,449	C2
07416	Franklin 4,486	D1
07417	Franklin Lakes 8,769	B1
†08823	Franklin Park○ 31,358	D3
08322	Franklinville	C4
07728	Freehold○ 10,020	E3
08825	Frenchtown 1,573	C2
07026	Garfield 26,803	B2
07027	Garwood 4,752	E2
08026	Gibbsboro 2,510	B4
08027	Gibbstown	C4
†08753	Gilford Park 6,528	E4
07933	Gillette	E2
08028	Glassboro 14,574	C4
08029	Glendora 5,632	B4
08826	Glen Gardner 834	D2
07028	Glen Ridge 7,855	B2
07452	Glen Rock 11,497	B1
08030	Gloucester City 13,121	B3
07435	Green Pond 800	E1
07935	Green Village 800	D2
08323	Greenwich○ 973	C5
08032	Grenloch 700	C4

(continued on following page)

07093 Guttenberg 7,340 C2
*07601 Hackensack⊙ 36,039 B2
07840 Hackettstown 8,850 D2
08033 Haddonfield 12,337 B3
08035 Haddon Heights 8,361 B3
08036 Hainesport○ 3,236 D4
07508 Haledon 6,607 B1
07419 Hamburg 1,832 D1
08690 Hamilton Square-Mercerville 25,446 D3
08037 Hammonton 12,298 D4
08827 Hampton 1,614 D2
07640 Harrington Park 4,532 C1
07029 Harrison 12,242 B2
†08057 Hartford 650 D4
08008 Harvey Cedars 363 E4
07604 Hasbrouck Heights 12,166 B2
07641 Haworth 3,509 C1
07507 Hawthorne 18,200 B2
07730 Hazlet 23,013 E3
08828 Helmetta 955 E3
07421 Hewitt 950 E1
08829 High Bridge 3,435 D2
07422 Highland Lakes 2,888 E1
08904 Highland Park 13,396 D2
07732 Highlands 5,187 F3
08520 Hightstown 4,581 D3
07642 Hillsdale 10,495 B1
07205 Hillside○ 21,440 B2
†08083 Hi-Nella 1,250 B4
07030 Hoboken 42,460 C2
07423 Ho Ho Kus 4,129 B1
07733 Holmdel○ 8,447 E3
07843 Hopatcong 15,531 D2
07844 Hope 310 D2
08525 Hopewell 2,001 D3
07731 Howell○ 25,065 E3
†07712 Interlaken 1,037 E3
07845 Ironia D2
07111 Irvington 61,493 B2
08830 Iselin E2
08732 Island Heights 1,575 E4
08527 Jackson○ 25,644 E3
08831 Jamesburg 4,114 E3
*07301 Jersey City⊙ 223,532 B2
Jersey City‡ 556,972 B2
07734 Keansburg 10,613 E3
07032 Kearny 35,735 B2
08824 Kendall Park 7,419 D3
07033 Kenilworth 8,221 E2
07735 Keyport 7,413 E3
08528 Kingston D3
07405 Kinnelon 7,770 E2
07848 Lafayette 900 D1
07034 Lake Hiawatha E2
07849 Lake Hopatcong D2
08733 Lakehurst 2,908 E3
†07871 Lake Mohawk 8,498 D1
08701 Lakewood 22,863 E3
08530 Lambertville 4,044 D3
07850 Landing D2
08734 Lanoka Harbor E4
08021 Laurel Springs 2,249 B4
08879 Laurence Harbor 6,737 E3
08735 Lavallette 2,072 E4
08045 Lawnside 3,042 B3
08648 Lawrenceville 19,724 D3
08833 Lebanon 820 D2
07852 Ledgewood D2
08327 Leesburg 700 D5
07737 Leonardo E3
07605 Leonia 8,027 C2
07938 Liberty Corner D2
07035 Lincoln Park 8,806 A1
07738 Lincroft E3
07036 Linden 37,836 A3
08021 Lindenwold 18,196 B4
08221 Linwood 6,144 D5
07424 Little Falls○ 11,496 B2
07643 Little Ferry 9,399 B2
07739 Little Silver 5,548 F3
07039 Livingston○ 28,040 E2
07644 Lodi 23,956 B2
07740 Long Branch 29,819 F3
Long Branch-Asbury Park‡ 503,173 F3
08403 Longport 1,249 D5
07853 Long Valley 1,682 D2
08048 Lumberton 600 D4
07071 Lyndhurst○ 20,326 B2
07939 Lyons D2
07940 Madison 15,357 E2
08049 Magnolia 4,881 B3
07430 Mahwah○ 12,127 E1
08328 Malaga 950 C4
08050 Manahawkin 1,469 E4
08736 Manasquan 5,354 E3
08738 Mantoloking 433 E3
08051 Mantua○ 9,193 C4
08835 Manville 11,278 D2
08052 Maple Shade○ 20,525 B3
07040 Maplewood○ 22,950 E2
08402 Margate City 9,179 E5
07746 Marlboro○ 17,560 E3
08053 Marlton 9,411 D4
08223 Marmora 650 D5
08836 Martinsville D2
07747 Matawan 8,837 E3
08330 Mays Landing⊙ 2,054 D5
07607 Maywood 9,895 B2
07428 McAfee 800 D1
†08232 McKee City 950 D5
08055 Medford D4
08055 Medford Lakes 4,958 D4
07945 Mendham 4,899 D2
08837 Menlo Park E2
08619 Mercerville-Hamilton Square 25,446 D3
08109 Merchantville 3,972 B3
08840 Metuchen 13,762 E2
08846 Middlesex 13,480 E2
07748 Middletown○ 62,574 E3
07432 Midland Park 7,381 B1
08848 Milford 1,368 C2
07041 Millburn○ 19,543 E2
07946 Millington 975 D2
†08876 Millstone 530 D2
08850 Milltown 7,136 E3
08332 Millville 24,815 C5
†07801 Mine Hill○ 3,325 D2
08342 Mizpah 900 D5
07750 Monmouth Beach 3,318 F3
08852 Monmouth Junction 2,579 D3
07434 Monroe○ 15,858 E3
*07042 Montclair 38,321 B2
07645 Montvale 7,318 B1
07045 Montville○ 14,290 E2
†07070 Moonachie 2,706 B2
08057 Moorestown 13,695 B3
07950 Morris Plains 5,305 D2
07960 Morristown⊙ 16,614 D2
07046 Mountain Lakes 4,153 E2
07092 Mountainside 7,118 E2
07856 Mount Arlington 4,251 D2
08059 Mount Ephraim 4,863 B3
07970 Mount Freedom D2
08060 Mount Holly 10,818 D4
†08054 Mount Laurel○ 17,614 D4
†07828 Mount Olive○ 18,748 D2
08061 Mount Royal 900 C4
08062 Mullica Hill 1,050 C4
08087 Mystic Islands 4,929 E4
08063 National Park 3,552 B3
07752 Navesink E3
07753 Neptune○ 28,366 E3
07753 Neptune City 5,276 E3
07857 Netcong 3,557 D2
*07101 Newark⊙ 329,248 B2
Newark‡ 1,965,304 B2
*08901 New Brunswick⊙ 41,442 E3
New Brunswick-Perth Amboy-Sayreville‡ 595,893 E3
08533 New Egypt 2,111 E3
08344 Newfield 1,563 D4
07435 Newfoundland 900 D1
08224 New Gretna 800 E4
07646 New Milford 16,876 B1
07974 New Providence 12,426 E2
07860 Newton⊙ 7,748 D1
08346 Newtonville 950 D4
07976 New Vernon D2
07032 North Arlington 16,587 B2
07047 North Bergen○ 47,019 B2
08876 North Branch 610 D2
08902 North Brunswick○ 22,220 D3
†07006 North Caldwell 5,832 B2
08204 North Cape May 4,029 C6
08225 Northfield 7,795 D5
07508 North Haledon 8,177 B1
07060 North Plainfield 19,108 E2
07647 Northvale 5,046 F1
08260 North Wildwood 4,714 D6
07648 Norwood 4,413 C1
07110 Nutley 28,998 B2
07755 Oakhurst E3
07436 Oakland 13,443 B1
08107 Oaklyn 4,223 B3
08226 Ocean City 13,949 D5
08740 Ocean Gate 1,385 E4
07756 Ocean Grove F3
07757 Oceanport 5,888 F3
07439 Ogdensburg 2,737 D1
08857 Old Bridge 21,815 E3
07675 Old Tappan 4,168 C1
07649 Oradell 8,658 B1
*07050 Orange 31,136 B2
08723 Osbornsville E3
07863 Oxford 1,587 C2
07470 Packanack Lake B1
07650 Palisades Park 13,732 C2
08065 Palmyra 7,085 B3
07652 Paramus 26,474 B1
07656 Park Ridge 8,515 B1
07054 Parsippany-Troy Hills○ 49,868 E2
07055 Passaic 52,463 E2
*07501 Paterson⊙ 137,970 B2
Paterson-Clifton-Passaic‡ 447,585 B2
08066 Paulsboro 6,944 C4
07977 Peapack-Gladstone 2,038 D2
08067 Pedricktown C4
08068 Pemberton 1,198 D4
08534 Pennington 2,109 D3
08110 Pennsauken○ 33,775 B3
08069 Penns Grove 5,760 C4
08070 Pennsville 12,467 C4
07440 Pequannock○ 13,776 B1
*08861 Perth Amboy 38,951 E2
08865 Phillipsburg 16,647 C2
08741 Pine Beach 1,796 E4
07058 Pine Brook E2
08021 Pine Hill 8,684 D4
08854 Piscataway○ 42,223 D2
08071 Pitman 9,744 C4
*07060 Plainfield 45,555 E2
08536 Plainsboro D3
08232 Pleasantville 13,435 D5
08742 Point Pleasant 17,747 E3
08742 Point Pleasant Beach 5,415 E3
08240 Pomona 2,358 D5
07442 Pompton Lakes 10,660 A1
07444 Pompton Plains B1
07758 Port Monmouth E3
†07850 Port Morris 616 D2
07865 Port Murray 250 C2
08349 Port Norris 1,730 C5
08241 Port Republic 837 D4
08540 Princeton 12,035 D3
08550 Princeton Junction 2,419 D3
†07885 Prospect Park 5,142 B1
08867 Quinton 750 C4
*07065 Rahway 26,723 E2
†08054 Ramblewood 6,475 D4
07446 Ramsey 12,899 B1
†07801 Randolph○ 17,828 D2
08869 Raritan 6,128 D2
07701 Red Bank 12,031 E3
07657 Ridgefield 10,294 B2
07660 Ridgefield Park 12,738 B2
*07450 Ridgewood 25,208 B1
08551 Ringoes 682 D2
07456 Ringwood 12,625 E1
08242 Rio Grande 2,016 D5
07457 Riverdale 2,530 A1
07661 River Edge 11,111 B1
08075 Riverside○ 7,941 B3
08077 Riverton 3,068 B3
07675 River Vale○ 9,489 B1
07662 Rochelle Park○ 5,603 B2
07866 Rockaway 6,852 D2
07647 Rockleigh 192 C1
08553 Rocky Hill 717 D3
08554 Roebling-Florence 7,677 D3
08555 Roosevelt 835 E3
07068 Roseland 5,330 A2
07203 Roselle 20,641 B2
07204 Roselle Park 13,377 A2
08352 Rosenhayn 950 C5
†07876 Roxbury○ 18,878 D2
07760 Rumson 7,623 F3
08078 Runnemede 9,461 B3
*07070 Rutherford 19,068 B2
07662 Saddle Brook○ 14,084 B1
07458 Saddle River 2,763 B1
08079 Salem⊙ 6,959 C4
08872 Sayreville 29,969 E3
07076 Scotch Plains○ 20,774 E2
07760 Sea Bright 1,812 F3
08302 Seabrook 1,411 C5
08750 Sea Girt 2,650 E3
08243 Sea Isle City 2,644 D5
08751 Seaside Heights 1,802 E4
08752 Seaside Park 1,795 E4
07094 Secaucus 13,719 B2
07077 Sewaren E2
08080 Sewell C4
08353 Shiloh 604 C5
08008 Ship Bottom 1,427 E4
07078 Short Hills E2
07701 Shrewsbury 2,962 E3
08081 Sicklerville D4
08558 Skillman D3
08201 Smithville 70 E5
08083 Somerdale 5,900 B4
08244 Somers Point 10,330 D5
08876 Somerville⊙ 11,973 D2
08879 South Amboy 8,322 E3
†07719 South Belmar 1,566 E3
08880 South Bound Brook 4,331 E2
†08852 South Brunswick○ 17,127 E3
07079 South Orange○ 15,864 A2
07080 South Plainfield 20,521 E2
08882 South River 14,361 E3
08753 South Toms River 3,954 E4
07871 Sparta○ 13,333 D1
08884 Spotswood 7,840 E3
07081 Springfield○ 13,955 E2
07762 Spring Lake 4,215 F3
†07762 Spring Lake Heights 5,424 E3
07874 Stanhope 3,638 D2
08886 Stewartsville 950 C2
07980 Stirling E2
07460 Stockholm D1
08559 Stockton 643 D3
08247 Stone Harbor 1,187 D5
08084 Stratford 8,005 B4
†07747 Strathmore E3
07876 Succasunna 10,931 D2
07901 Summit 21,071 E2
08008 Surf City 1,571 E4
07461 Sussex 2,418 D1
08085 Swedesboro 2,031 C4
07878 Tabor E2
07666 Teaneck○ 39,007 B2
07670 Tenafly 13,552 C1
07608 Teterboro 19 B2
08086 Thorofare B4
08887 Three Bridges 750 D2
07724 Tinton Falls 7,740 E3
08753 Toms River⊙ 7,465 E4
07512 Totowa 11,448 B1
07082 Towaco E2
*08601 Trenton (cap.)⊙ 92,124 D3
Trenton‡ 307,863 D3
08087 Tuckerton 2,472 E4
07083 Union○ 50,184 A2
07735 Union Beach 6,354 E3
07087 Union City 55,593 C2
†07421 Upper Greenwood Lake 2,734 E1
†07458 Upper Saddle River 7,958 B1
08406 Ventnor City 11,704 E5
07462 Vernon 800 E1
07044 Verona 14,166 B2
08251 Villas 5,909 D5
08088 Vincentown 900 D4
08360 Vineland 53,753 C5
Vineland-Millville-Bridgeton‡ 132,866 C5
†08043 Voorhees○ 12,919 B3
07463 Waldwick 10,802 B1
07719 Wall○ 18,952 E3
07057 Wallington 10,741 B2
†07712 Wanamassa E3
07465 Wanaque 10,025 B1
08758 Waretown 1,175 E4
†07060 Warren○ 9,805 D2
07882 Washington 6,429 D2
07060 Watchung 5,290 E2
07470 Wayne○ 46,474 A1
07087 Weehawken○ 13,168 C2
08090 Wenonah 2,303 C4
07006 West Caldwell 11,407 A2
†08204 West Cape May 1,091 D6
08092 West Creek 827 E4
†08086 West Deptford○ 18,002 B3
*07090 Westfield 30,447 E2
07764 West Long Branch 7,380 F3
07480 West Milford 950 E1
08108 Westmont 15,875 B3
07093 West New York 39,194 C2
07052 West Orange 39,510 A2
07424 West Paterson 11,293 B2
08628 West Trenton D3
08093 Westville 4,786 B3
†08260 West Wildwood 360 D6
07675 Westwood 10,714 B1
07885 Wharton 5,485 D2

Topography

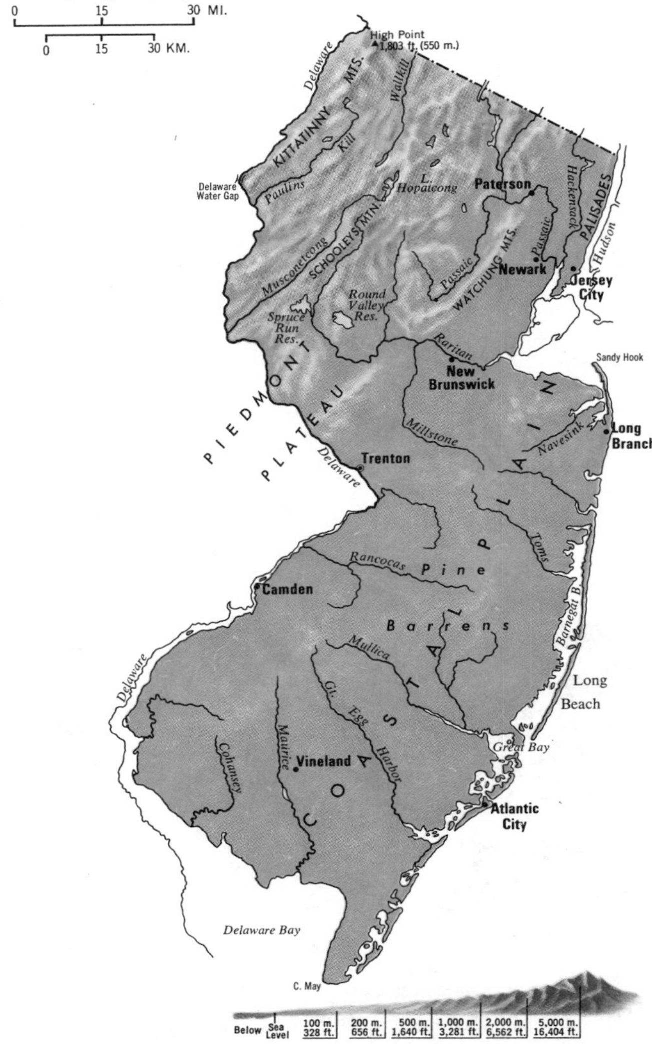

0 15 30 MI.
0 15 30 KM.
High Point 1,803 ft. (550 m.)
Delaware
Kittatinny Mts.
Wallkill
Delaware Water Gap
Paulins Kill
L. Hopatcong
Paterson
Hackensack
Palisades
Hudson
Passaic
Schooleys Mtn.
Musconetcong
Watchung Mts.
Newark
Jersey City
Round Valley Res.
Spruce Run Res.
Raritan
Sandy Hook
New Brunswick
Piedmont Plateau
Millstone
Navesink
Long Branch
Trenton
Delaware
Toms
Rancocas
Pine Barrens
Camden
Mullica
Coastal Plain
Barnegat B.
Long Beach
Great Bay
Gt. Egg Harbor
Maurice
Cohansey
Vineland
Atlantic City
Delaware Bay
C. May
Below Sea Level
100 m. 328 ft.
200 m. 656 ft.
500 m. 1,640 ft.
1,000 m. 3,281 ft.
2,000 m. 6,562 ft.
5,000 m. 16,404 ft.

07981 Whippany E2
08889 White House Station D2
†07866 White Meadow Lake 8,429 D2
08252 Whitesboro 1,583 D5
07765 Wickatunk 950 E3
08260 Wildwood 4,913 D6
08260 Wildwood Crest 4,149 D6
08094 Williamstown 5,768 D4
08046 Willingboro○ 39,912 D3
†07036 Winfield○ 1,785 B2
08270 Woodbine 2,809 D5
07095 Woodbridge○ 90,074 E2
08096 Woodbury⊙ 10,353 B4
08097 Woodbury Heights 3,460 B4
07675 Woodcliff Lake 5,644 B1
†08107 Wood-Lynne 2,578 B3
†07885 Woodport D2
07075 Wood-Ridge 7,929 B2
08098 Woodstown 3,250 C4
08562 Wrightstown 3,031 D3
07481 Wyckoff○ 15,500 B1
08620 Yardville 9,414 D3

OTHER FEATURES

Absecon (inlet) E5
Alloways (creek) C4
Arthur Kill (str.) E2
Atlantic Highlands (ridge) E3
Barnegat (bay) E4
Batsto (riv.) D4
Bayonne Military Ocean Terminal B2
Beach Haven (inlet) E4
Beaver (brook) C2
Ben Davis (pt.) C5
Big Flat (brook) D1
Big Timber (creek) C4
Boonton (res.) E2
Brigantine (inlet) E5
Budd (lake) D2
Canistear (res.) E1
Cedar (creek) E4
Clinton (res.) E1
Cohansey (riv.) C5
Cold Spring (inlet) D6
Cooper (riv.) B3
Corson (inlet) D5
Crosswicks (creek) D3
Culvers (lake) D1
Delaware (bay) C5
Delaware (riv.) D3
Delaware Water Gap Nat'l Rec. Area C1
Earle Naval Weapons Sta. E3
Echo (lake) E1
Edison Nat'l Hist. Site A2
Egg Island (pt.) C5
Fort Dix 14,297 D3
Fort Hancock F3
Fort Monmouth E3
Gateway Nat'l Rec. Area E2
Great (bay) E4
Great Egg Harbor (inlet) E5
Greenwood (lake) E1
Hackensack (riv.) C1
Hereford (inlet) D5
High Point (mt.) D1
Hopatcong (lake) D2
Hudson (riv.) C1
Island (beach) E4
Kill Van Kull (str.) B2
Kittatinny (mts.) D1
Lakehurst Naval Air Engineering Center E3
Lamington (riv.) D2
Landing (creek) D4
Little Egg (harb.) E4
Lockatong (creek) C3
Long (beach) E4
Long Beach (isl.) E4
Lower New York (bay) E2
Manasquan (riv.) E3
Manumuskin (riv.) D5
Maurice (riv.) C4
May (cape) C6
McGuire A.F.B. 7,853 D3
Metedeconk (riv.) E3
Mill (creek) E4
Millstone (riv.) D3
Mohawk (lake) D1
Morristown Nat'l Hist. Park D2
Mullica (riv.) D4
Musconetcong (riv.) C2
Navesink (riv.) E3
Newark (bay) B2
Oak Ridge (res.) D1
Oldmans (creek) C4
Oradell (res.) B1
Oswego (riv.) E4
Owassa (lake) D1
Palisades C1
Passaic (riv.) E2
Paulins Kill (riv.) D1
Pennsauken (creek) B3
Pequest (riv.) D2
Picatinny Arsenal D2
Pohatcong (creek) C2
Pompton (lake) B1
Raccoon (creek) C4
Ramapo (riv.) E1
Rancocas (creek) D3
Raritan (bay) E3
Raritan (riv.) D2
Ridgeway Branch, Toms (riv.) E3
Round Valley (res.) D2
Saddle (riv.) B1
Salem (riv.) C4
Sandy Hook (spit) F3
Shoal Branch, Wading (riv.) D4
Spruce Run (res.) D2
Statue of Liberty Nat'l Mon. B2
Stony (brook) D3
Stow (creek) C5
Swartswood (lake) D1
Tappan (lake) C1
The Narrows (str.) E2
Toms (riv.) E3
Townsend (inlet) D5
Tuckahoe (riv.) D5
Union (lake) C5
Upper New York (bay) B2
Wading (riv.) D4
Wallkill (riv.) D1
Wanaque (res.) E1
Wawayanda (lake) E1

⊙County seat.
‡Population of metropolitan area.
○Population of town or township.
† Zip of nearest p.o. * Multiple zips.

COUNTIES

Bernalillo 419,700 .... C4
Catron 2,720 .... A4
Chaves 51,103 .... E5
Cibola B3
Colfax 13,667 .... E2
Curry 42,019 .... F4
De Baca 2,454 .... E4
Dona Ana 96,340 .... C6
Eddy 47,855 .... E6
Grant 26,204 .... A5
Guadalupe 4,496 .... E4
Harding 1,090 .... F3
Hidalgo 6,049 .... A7
Lea 55,993 .... F6
Lincoln 10,997 .... D5

Los Alamos 17,599 .... C3
Luna 15,585 .... B6
McKinley 56,449 .... A3
Mora 4,205 .... D6
Otero 44,665 .... D6
Quay 10,577 .... F3
Rio Arriba 29,282 .... B2
Roosevelt 15,695 .... F4
Sandoval 34,799 .... C3
San Juan 81,433 .... A2
San Miguel
   22,751 .... D3
Santa Fe 75,360 .... C3
Sierra 8,454 .... B5
Socorro 12,566 .... C5
Taos 19,456 .... D2
Torrance 7,491 .... D4
Union 4,725 .... F2
Valencia 61,115 .... C4

CITIES and TOWNS

Zip   Name/Pop.   Key

87510 Abiquiu 500 .... C2
†87034 Acoma 150 .... B4
†87034 Acomita (Pueblo of
        Acoma) 975 .... B3
88310 Alamogordo⊙ 24,024 .... C6
*87101 Albuquerque⊙ 331,767 .. C3
       Albuquerque† 454,499 ... C3
87511 Alcalde 975 .... C2
87001 Algodones 195 .... C3
88312 Alto 285 .... D5
87512 Amalia 200 .... D2
88021 Anthony 3,285 .... C6
87711 Anton Chico 400 .... D3
87930 Arrey 367 .... B6
87513 Arroyo Hondo 400 ...... D2

87514 Arroyo Seco 500 .... D2
88210 Artesia 10,385 .... E6
87410 Aztec⊙ 5,512 .... B2
88023 Bayard 3,036 .... A6
87002 Belen 5,617 .... C4
88314 Bent 294 .... D5
88026 Berino 600 .... C6
87004 Bernalillo⊙ 3,012 ...... C3
87412 Blanco 200 .... B2
87413 Bloomfield 4,881 .... A2
87005 Bluewater 300 .... A3
87006 Bosque (Bosque
        Farms) 3,353 .... C4
87712 Buena Vista 178 .... D3
87515 Canjilon 380 .... C2
87516 Canones 300 .... C2
88316 Capitan 762 .... D5
88414 Capulin 100 .... F2
88220 Carlsbad⊙ 25,496 ...... E6

87514 Carrizozo⊙ 1,222 .... D5
87007 Casa Blanca 560 .... B4
88113 Causey 81 .... F5
87518 Cebolla 100 .... C2
87008 Cedar Crest 600 .... C3
†87410 Cedar Hill 145 .... B2
88026 Central 1,968 .... A6
87010 Cerrillos 500 .... D3
87519 Cerro 400 .... D2
87713 Chacon 310 .... D2
87520 Chama 1,090 .... C2
88027 Chamberino 700 .... C6
87521 Chamisal 642 .... D2
87522 Chimayo 1,993 .... D3
87714 Cimarron 888 .... E2
88415 Clayton⊙ 2,968 .... F2
87715 Cleveland 450 .... D2
88028 Cliff 600 .... A6
88317 Cloudcroft 521 .... D6

88101 Clovis⊙ 31,194 .... F4
†87041 Cochiti 983 .... C3
88029 Columbus 414 .... B7
88416 Conchas Dam 240 ...... E3
87523 Cordova 750 .... D2
88318 Corona 236 .... D4
87048 Corrales 2,791 .... C3
87524 Costilla 400 .... D2
87313 Crownpoint 1,134 ...... A3
†86504 Crystal 200 .... A2
87013 Cuba 609 .... C3
87014 Cubero 300 .... B3
87821 Datil 150 .... B4
88030 Deming⊙ 9,964 .... B6
87933 Derry 175 .... B6
88418 Des Moines 178 .... F2
88230 Dexter 882 .... E5
87527 Dixon 800 .... D2
88032 Dona Ana 800 .... C6

New Mexico map with counties, cities, towns, highways, and geographic features.

New Mexico

SCALE
0 5 10   20   30   40   50   60 MI.
0 5 10   20   30   40   50 60 KM.

State Capitals .... ⊛
County Seats .... ⊙
Major Limited Access Hwys.

Scale 1 : 2,910,000

© Copyright HAMMOND INCORPORATED, Maplewood, N.J.

88115 Dora 168 .... F5
87528 Dulce 1,648 .... B2
87718 Eagle Nest 202 .... D2
88116 Elida 202 .... F5
87529 El Prado 200 .... D2
87530 El Rito 475 .... C2
87531 Embudo 400 .... C2
88321 Encino 155 .... D4
87532 Espanola 6,803 .... C3
87016 Estancia⊙ 830 .... D4
88231 Eunice 2,970 .... F6
88033 Fairacres 700 .... C6
87401 Farmington 31,222 .... A2
†88041 Fierro 200 .... A6
87415 Flora Vista 500 .... A2
88118 Floyd 146 .... F4
88419 Folsom 73 .... F2
88036 Fort Bayard 400 .... A6
88323 Fort Stanton 80 .... D5
88119 Fort Sumner⊙ 1,421 .... E4
87316 Fort Wingate 800 .... A3
87416 Fruitland 800 .... A2
†87540 Galisteo 125 .... D3
87017 Gallina 420 .... C2
87301 Gallup⊙ 18,167 .... A3
87317 Gamerco 800 .... A3
87936 Garfield 600 .... B6
88038 Gila 350 .... A6
88324 Glencoe 125 .... D5
88039 Glenwood 220 .... A5
87535 Glorieta 300 .... D3
88120 Grady 122 .... F4
87020 Grants 11,439 .... B3
88424 Grenville 39 .... F2
87722 Guadalupita 300 .... D2
88232 Hagerman 936 .... E5
88041 Hanover 300 .... A6
87937 Hatch 1,028 .... B6
87537 Hernandez 500 .... C2
88325 High Rolls-Mountain Park 555 .... D5
88042 Hillsboro 175 .... B6
88240 Hobbs 29,153 .... F6
87723 Holman 400 .... D2
88336 Hondo 425 .... D5
88250 Hope 111 .... E6
87901 Hot Springs (Truth or Consequences)⊙ 5,219 . B5
88121 House 117 .... F4
88043 Hurley 1,616 .... A6
87022 Isleta 1,246 .... C4
88252 Jal 2,675 .... F6
87023 Jarales 700 .... C4
87024 Jemez Pueblo 1,503 .... C3
87025 Jemez Springs 316 .... C3
87417 Kirtland 2,358 .... A2
87026 Laguna 900 .... B3
87027 La Jara 210 .... B2
88253 Lake Arthur 327 .... E5
88337 La Luz 1,194 .... C6
87539 La Madera 200 .... C2
88044 La Mesa 900 .... C6
87418 La Plata 150 .... A2
88001 Las Cruces⊙ 45,086 .... C6
Las Cruces‡ 96,340 .... C6
87701 Las Vegas⊙ 14,322 .... D3
87725 Ledoux 300 .... D3
87823 Lemitar 800 .... B4
88338 Lincoln 100 .... D5
87543 Llano 325 .... D2
88255 Loco Hills 375 .... F6
88426 Logan 735 .... F3
88045 Lordsburg⊙ 3,195 .... A6
87544 Los Alamos⊙ 11,039 .... C3
87031 Los Lunas⊙ 3,525 .... C4
†87101 Los Ranchos De Albuquerque 2,702 .... C3
88256 Loving 1,355 .... E6
88260 Lovington⊙ 9,727 .... F6
87547 Lumberton 175 .... C2
87824 Luna 200 .... A5
87825 Magdalena 1,022 .... B4
88263 Malaga 300 .... E6
87728 Maxwell 316 .... E2
88339 Mayhill 300 .... D6
†79901 Meadow Vista 3,377 .... C7
88124 Melrose 649 .... F4
87319 Mentmore 315 .... A3
88340 Mescalero 1,259 .... D5
88046 Mesilla 2,029 .... C6
88047 Mesilla Park C6
88048 Mesquite 500 .... C6
87320 Mexican Springs 150 .... A3
87729 Miami 112 .... E2
87021 Milan 3,747 .... B3
88049 Mimbres 300 .... B6
87731 Montezuma 250 .... D3
87939 Monticello 125 .... B5
88265 Monument 300 .... F6
87732 Mora⊙ D3
87035 Moriarty 1,276 .... D4
87733 Mosquero⊙ 197 .... F3
87036 Mountainair 1,170 .... C4
†87501 Nambe 1,017 .... D3
88430 Nara Visa 250 .... F3
87328 Navajo 920 .... A3
†87325 Newcomb 500 .... A2
87038 New Laguna 250 .... B4
88266 Oil Center 236 .... F6
87549 Ojo Caliente 600 .... D2
87735 Ojo Feliz 133 .... E2
87550 Ojo Sarco 380 .... D2
88052 Organ 300 .... C6
87040 Paguate 500 .... B3
87552 Pecos 885 .... D3
87041 Pena Blanca 700 .... C3
87553 Penasco 860 .... D2
87042 Peralta 400 .... C4
88343 Picacho 100 .... D5
88053 Pinos Altos 250 .... A6
87044 Ponderosa 300 .... C3
88130 Portales⊙ 9,940 .... F4
87045 Prewitt 300 .... B3
88432 Puerto de Luna 175 .... E4
87829 Quemado 450 .... A4
87556 Questa 1,202 .... D2
88054 Radium Springs 150 .... B6
87736 Rainsville 350 .... D2
87321 Ramah 574 .... A3
87557 Ranches of Taos 1,411 .... D2
87740 Raton⊙ 8,225 .... E2
87558 Red River 332 .... D2
87322 Rehoboth 200 .... A3
87830 Reserve⊙ 439 .... A5
87560 Ribera 84 .... D3
87940 Rincon 300 .... C6
87124 Rio Rancho 9,985 .... C3
87561 Rodarte 650 .... D2
88201 Roswell⊙ 39,676 .... E5
87562 Rowe 290 .... D3
87743 Roy 381 .... E3
88345 Ruidoso 4,260 .... D5
88346 Ruidoso Downs 949 .... D5
87941 Salem 400 .... B6
87831 San Acacia 286 .... B4
87832 San Antonio 359 .... B5
87564 San Cristobal 350 .... D2
87047 Sandia Park 450 .... C3
†87001 San Felipe Pueblo 1,465 .... C3
†87501 San Ildefonso 232 .... C3
88434 San Jon 341 .... F3
87565 San Jose 150 .... D3
87566 San Juan Pueblo 870 .... C2
88041 San Lorenzo 200 .... B6
87050 San Mateo 200 .... B3
88058 San Miguel 400 .... C6
88348 San Patricio 300 .... D5
87051 San Rafael 300 .... A3
87567 Santa Cruz 754 .... D2
87501 Santa Fe (cap.)⊙ 48,953 .... C3
†88041 Santa Rita 600 .... B6
88435 Santa Rosa⊙ 2,469 .... E4
87052 Santo Domingo Pueblo 2,082 .... C3
87053 San Ysidro 199 .... C3
87745 Sapello 600 .... D3
87055 Seboyeta 125 .... B3
87568 Sena 150 .... D3
87569 Serafina 225 .... D3
87420 Shiprock 7,237 .... A2
88061 Silver City⊙ 9,887 .... A6
87801 Socorro⊙ 7,173 .... C4
†87565 Soham 104 .... D3
87747 Springer 1,657 .... E2
87057 Tajique 145 .... C4
87571 Taos⊙ 3,369 .... D2
†87571 Taos Pueblo 900 .... D2
88267 Tatum 896 .... F5
87574 Tesuque 1,014 .... C3
88135 Texico 958 .... F4
87323 Thoreau 1,099 .... A3
87575 Tierra Amarilla⊙ 850 .... C2
87059 Tijeras 311 .... C3
87324 Toadlena 200 .... A2
87325 Tohatchi 1,011 .... A3
87060 Tome 500 .... C4
87577 Tres Piedras 200 .... D2
87578 Truchas 275 .... D2
†87701 Trujillo 148 .... E3
87901 Truth or Consequences⊙ 5,219 .... B5
88401 Tucumcari⊙ 6,765 .... F3
88352 Tularosa 2,536 .... C5
88003 University Park 4,353 .... C6
87579 Vadito 400 .... D2
88072 Vado 325 .... C6
87580 Valdez 300 .... D2
†87031 Valencia 500 .... C4
87581 Vallecitos 450 .... C2
88073 Vanadium 150 .... A6
88353 Vaughn 737 .... D4
87582 Velarde 950 .... C2
87583 Villanueva 500 .... D3
†88055 Virden 246 .... A6
87752 Wagon Mound 416 .... E2
87421 Waterflow 475 .... A2
87753 Watrous 175 .... D3
87544 White Rock 6,560 .... C3
88002 White Sands Missile Range 3,120 .... C6
87063 Willard 166 .... D4
87942 Williamsburg 433 .... B5
88136 Yeso 200 .... E4
87064 Youngsville 125 .... C2
†87053 Zia Pueblo 500 .... C3
87327 Zuni 5,551 .... A3

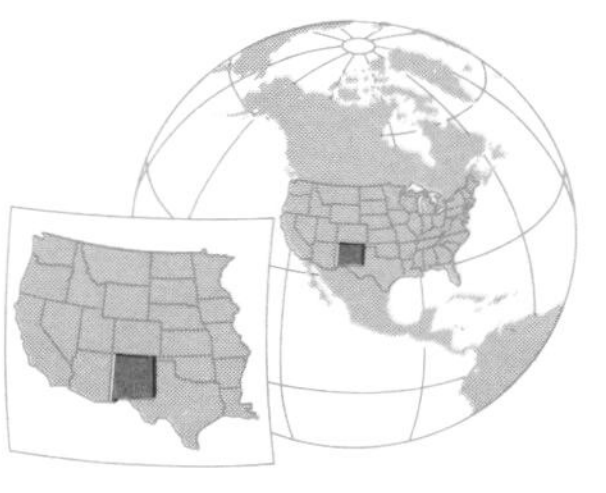

AREA 121,593 sq. mi. (314,926 sq. km.)
POPULATION 1,302,981
CAPITAL Santa Fe
LARGEST CITY Albuquerque
HIGHEST POINT Wheeler Pk. 13,161 ft. (4011 m.)
SETTLED IN 1605
ADMITTED TO UNION January 6, 1912
POPULAR NAME Land of Enchantment
STATE FLOWER Yucca
STATE BIRD Road Runner

OTHER FEATURES

Abiquiu (res.) C2
Alamosa (riv.) B5
Animas (riv.) B1
Avalon (res.) E6
Aztec Ruins Nat'l Mon. A2
Baldy (peak) D3
Bandelier Nat'l Mon. C3
Big Burro (mts.) A6
Black (mt.) A6
Black (range) B5
Blanco (creek) F4
Bluewater (creek) B4
Bluewater (creek) D6
Bluewater (lake) A3
Boulder (lake) C2
Brazos (peak) C2
Burford (lake) C2
Caballo (res.) B6
Canadian (riv.) F3
Cannon A.F.B. 3,798 .... F4
Canyon Blanco (creek) B2
Capitan (mts.) D5
Capitan (peak) D5
Capulin Mountain Nat'l Mon. E2
Carlsbad Caverns Nat'l Park E6
Carrizo (creek) F2
Chaco (mesa) B3
Chaco (riv.) A2
Chaco Culture Nat'l Hist. Park B2
Chico Arroyo (creek) B3
Chivato (mesa) B3
Chupadera (mesa) C5
Chuska (mts.) A2
Cimarron (riv.) E2
Colorado, Arroyo (riv.) B4
Compañero, Arroyo (creek) B2
Conchas (lake) E3
Conchas (riv.) E3
Cookes (range) B6
Corrumpa (creek) F2
Costilla (peak) D2
Cuchillo Negro (creek) B5
Cuervo (creek) E3
Dark Canyon (creek) E6
Datil (mts.) B4
Dry Cimarron (riv.) F2
Eagle Nest (lake) D2
Elephant Butte (res.) B5
El Morro Nat'l Mon. A3
El Rito (riv.) C2
Fifteenmile Arroyo (creek) D4
Florida (mts.) B7
Fort Bliss Mil. Res. C6
Fort Union Nat'l Mon. E3
Gallinas (mts.) B4
Gallinas (riv.) E3
Gila (riv.) A6
Gila Cliff Dwellings Nat'l Mon. A5
Grouse (mt.) A5
Guadalupe (mts.) D6
Hatchet (mts.) A7
Holloman A.F.B. 7,245 .... C6
Hueco (mts.) D6
Jemez (riv.) C3
Jemez Canyon (res.) C3
Jicarilla Ind. Res. B2
Jornada del Muerto (valley) C5
Kirtland A.F.B. C3
Ladron (mts.) B4
La Plata (riv.) A1
Largo, Cañon (creek) B2
Las Animas (creek) B5
Llano Estacado (Staked) (plain) F5
Lucero (lake) C6
Macho, Arroyo del (creek) D5
Magdalena (mts.) B4
Manzano (mts.) C4
Manzano (peak) C4
McMillan (lake) E6
Mescalero (ridge) F6
Mescalero (valley) F5
Mescalero Apache Ind. Res. D5
Mimbres (mts.) B6
Mimbres (riv.) B6
Mogollon (mts.) A5
Mogollon Baldy (peak) A5
Montosa (mesa) E3
Mora (riv.) E3
Nacimiento (mts.) C3
Nacimiento (peak) C2
Navajo (res.) B2
Navajo Ind. Res. A2
North Truchas (peak) D3
Ocate (creek) E2
O'Keeffe Nat'l Hist. Site C2
Oscura (mts.) C5
Osha (peak) C4
Padilla (creek) D5
Pajarito (creek) A2
Pecos (riv.) E5
Pecos Nat'l Mon. D3
Peloncillo (mts.) A6
Perro (mts.) D4
Pinos, Rio de los (riv.) B2
Pintada Arroyo (creek) E4
Playas (lake) A7
Potrillo (mts.) B7
Pueblo Ind. Res. B4
Pueblo Ind. Res. D3
Pueblo Ind. Res. C4
Pueblo Ind. Res. D2
Puerco (riv.) A3
Red Bluff (lake) E7
Revuelto (creek) F3
Rio Brazos (riv.) C2
Rio Chama (riv.) C2
Rio Felix (riv.) E5
Rio Grande (riv.) C5
Rio Hondo (riv.) E5
Rio Penasco (riv.) E6
Rio Puerco (riv.) C4
Rio Salado (riv.) B4
Rocky (mts.) C1
Sacramento (mts.) D6
Salinas Nat'l Mon. C4
Salt (creek) E5
Salt (lake) F4
San Agustin (plains) B5
San Andres (mts.) C6
San Antonio (peak) C2
Sandia (peak) C3
San Francisco (riv.) A5
Sangre de Cristo (mts.) D3
San Jose (riv.) B3
San Juan (riv.) B2
San Mateo (mts.) B5
Seven Rivers (riv.) E6
Ship Rock (peak) A2
Sierra Blanca (peak) C5
Staked (Llano Estacado) (plain) F5
Sumner (lake) E4
Taylor (mt.) B3
Tecolote (creek) D3
Tequesquite (creek) E2
Thompson (peak) D3
Tierra Blanca (creek) B6
Tramperos (creek) F2
Tularosa (valley) C6
Ute (creek) F3
Ute (peak) D2
Ute (res.) F3
Ute Mountain Ind. Res. A1
Vermejo (riv.) E2
Wheeler (peak) D2
White Sands (des.) C5
White Sands Missile Range C5
White Sands Nat'l Mon. C6
Whitewater Baldy (mt.) A5
Wingate Army Depot A3
Yeso (creek) E4
Zuni (mts.) A3
Zuni (riv.) A3
Zuni Ind. Res. A3

⊙County seat.
‡Population of metropolitan area.
† Zip of nearest p.o. * Multiple zips.

Topography

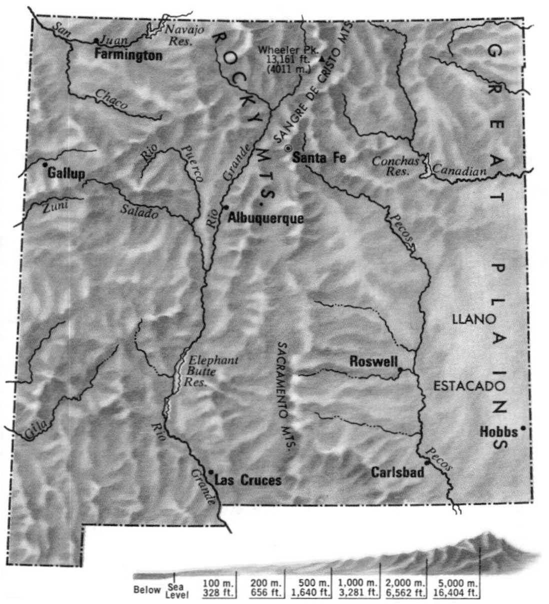
0 50 100 MI.
0 50 100 KM.
San Juan
Navajo Res.
Farmington
Wheeler Pk. 13,161 ft. (4011 m.)
ROCKY MTS.
SANGRE DE CRISTO MTS.
Chaco
Gallup
Rio Puerco
Santa Fe
Conchas Res.
Canadian
Zuni
Salado
Rio Grande
Albuquerque
Pecos
GREAT PLAINS
LLANO
ESTACADO
Elephant Butte Res.
SACRAMENTO MTS.
Roswell
Hobbs
Gila
Rio Grande
Las Cruces
Carlsbad
Pecos
Below Sea Level
100 m. 328 ft.
200 m. 656 ft.
500 m. 1,640 ft.
1,000 m. 3,281 ft.
2,000 m. 6,562 ft.
5,000 m. 16,404 ft.

Agriculture, Industry and Resources

DOMINANT LAND USE

- Wheat, Grain Sorghums, Range Livestock
- General Farming, Livestock, Special Crops
- General Farming, Livestock, Cash Grain
- Dry Beans, General Farming
- Cotton, Forest Products
- Range Livestock
- Forests
- Nonagricultural Land

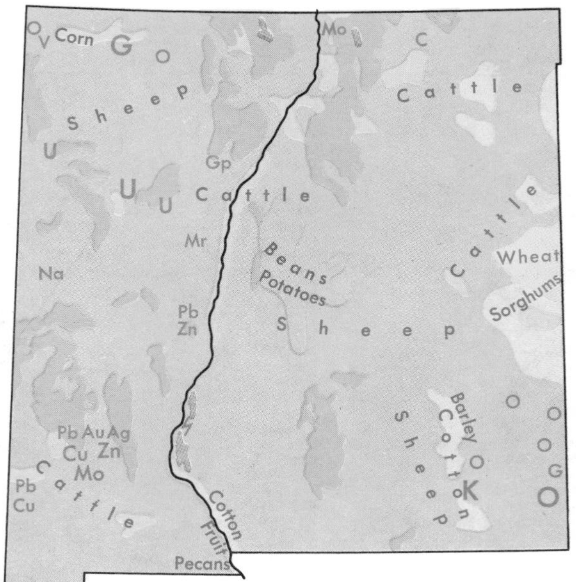
Corn
Sheep
Cattle
Gp
Cattle
Mr
Beans
Potatoes
Wheat
Na
Sorghums
Pb Zn
Sheep
Barley
Cotton
Pb Au Ag
Cu Zn
Mo
Pb
Cu
Cattle
Sheep
Cotton
Fruit
Pecans

MAJOR MINERAL OCCURRENCES

Ag	Silver	Gp	Gypsum			U	Uranium		
Au	Gold	K	Potash						
C	Coal	Mo	Molybdenum						
Cu	Copper	Mr	Marble	O	Petroleum	V	Vanadium	ϟ	Water Power
G	Natural Gas	Na	Salt	Pb	Lead	Zn	Zinc		

New York
SCALE
0 5 10 20 30 40 MI.
0 5 10 20 30 40 KM.
State Capitals............⊛
County Seats.............⊙
Canals...................
Major Limited Access Hwys.____
Scale 1:1,920,000

COUNTIES

Albany 285,909 ...... M5
Allegany 51,742 ...... D6
Bronx 1,168,972 ...... N9
Broome 213,648 ...... J6
Cattaraugus 85,697 ...... C6
Cayuga 79,894 ...... G4
Chautauqua 146,925 ...... B6
Chemung 97,656 ...... G6
Chenango 49,344 ...... J6
Clinton 80,750 ...... N1
Columbia 59,487 ...... N6
Cortland 48,820 ...... H5
Delaware 46,824 ...... K6
Dutchess 245,055 ...... N7
Erie 1,015,472 ...... C5
Essex 36,176 ...... N2
Franklin 44,929 ...... M1
Fulton 55,153 ...... M4
Genesee 59,400 ...... D4
Greene 40,861 ...... M6
Hamilton 5,034 ...... L3
Herkimer 66,714 ...... L4
Jefferson 88,151 ...... J2
Kings 2,230,936 ...... N9
Lewis 25,035 ...... K3
Livingston 57,006 ...... E5
Madison 65,150 ...... J5
Monroe 702,238 ...... E4
Montgomery 53,439 ...... M5
Nassau 1,321,582 ...... N9
New York 1,428,285 ...... M9
Niagara 227,354 ...... C4
Oneida 253,466 ...... J4
Onondaga 463,920 ...... H5
Ontario 88,909 ...... F5
Orange 259,603 ...... M8
Orleans 38,496 ...... D4
Oswego 113,901 ...... H4
Otsego 59,075 ...... K5
Putnam 77,193 ...... N8
Queens 1,891,325 ...... N9
Rensselaer 151,966 ...... O5
Richmond 352,121 ...... M9
Rockland 259,530 ...... M8
Saint Lawrence 114,254 ...... K2
Saratoga 153,759 ...... N4
Schenectady 149,946 ...... M5
Schoharie 29,710 ...... M5
Schuyler 17,686 ...... G6
Seneca 33,733 ...... G5
Steuben 99,217 ...... F6
Suffolk 1,284,231 ...... P9
Sullivan 65,155 ...... L7
Tioga 49,812 ...... H6
Tompkins 87,085 ...... H6
Ulster 158,158 ...... M7
Warren 54,854 ...... N3
Washington 54,795 ...... O4
Wayne 84,581 ...... F4
Westchester 866,599 ...... N8
Wyoming 39,895 ...... D5
Yates 21,459 ...... F5

CITIES and TOWNS
Zip Name/Pop. Key

13605 Adams 1,701 ...... J3
14801 Addison 2,028 ...... F6
14001 Akron 2,971 ...... C4
*12201 Albany (cap.)⊛⊙ 101,727 ...... N5
Albany-Schenectady-Troy‡ 795,019 ...... N5
14411 Albion⊙ 4,897 ...... D4
14004 Alden 2,488 ...... C5
13607 Alexandria Bay 1,265 ...... J2
14802 Alfred 4,967 ...... E6
14706 Allegany 2,078 ...... C6
12009 Altamont 1,292 ...... M5
11930 Amagansett 2,188 ...... R9
11701 Amityville 9,076 ...... O9
12010 Amsterdam 21,872 ...... M5
14006 Angola 2,292 ...... C5
14009 Arcade 2,052 ...... D5
10502 Ardsley 4,183 ...... O6
12603 Arlington 11,305 ...... N7
12015 Athens 1,738 ...... N6
11509 Atlantic Beach 1,775 ...... P7
14011 Attica 2,659 ...... D5
13021 Auburn⊙ 32,548 ...... G5
13026 Aurora 926 ...... G5
12018 Averill Park 1,337 ...... O5
14414 Avon 3,006 ...... E5
*11702 Babylon 12,388 ...... O9
13733 Bainbridge 1,603 ...... J6
11510 Baldwin 31,630 ...... R7
13027 Baldwinsville 6,446 ...... H4
12020 Ballston Spa⊙ 4,711 ...... N5
†12550 Ballville 2,919 ...... M7
14020 Batavia⊙ 16,703 ...... D5
14810 Bath⊙ 6,042 ...... F6
11705 Bayport 9,282 ...... O9
11706 Bay Shore 10,784 ...... O9
11709 Bayville 7,034 ...... N7
12508 Beacon 12,937 ...... N7
11710 Bellmore 18,106 ...... R7
11713 Bellport 2,809 ...... P9
14813 Belmont⊙ 1,024 ...... E6
11714 Bethpage 16,840 ...... R7
14814 Big Flats 2,892 ...... G6
*13901 Binghamton⊙ 55,860 ...... J6
Binghamton‡ 301,336 ...... J6

13612 Black River 1,384 ...... J3
14219 Blasdell 3,288 ...... C5
14715 Bolivar 1,345 ...... D6
13309 Boonville 2,344 ...... K4
13613 Brasher
Falls-Winthrop 1,454 ...... L1
11717 Brentwood 44,321 ...... O9
13029 Brewerton 2,472 ...... H4
10509 Brewster 1,650 ...... N8
11932 Bridgehampton 1,941 ...... R9
†12524 Brinckerhoff 3,030 ...... N7
12025 Broadalbin 1,415 ...... M4
14420 Brockport 9,776 ...... D4
14716 Brocton 1,416 ...... B6
*10401 Bronx
(borough)⊙ 1,168,972 ...... N9
10708 Bronxville 6,267 ...... O7
*11201 Brooklyn
(borough)⊙ 2,230,936 ...... N9
†11545 Brookville 3,290 ...... R6
10511 Buchanan 2,041 ...... N8
*14201 Buffalo⊙ 357,870 ...... B5
Buffalo‡ 1,242,573 ...... B5
12413 Cairo 1,281 ...... M6
14423 Caledonia 2,188 ...... E5
12816 Cambridge 1,820 ...... O4
13316 Camden 2,667 ...... J4
13031 Camillus 1,298 ...... H4
13317 Canajoharie 2,412 ...... L5
14424 Canandaigua⊙ 10,419 ...... F5
14823 Canaseraga 926 ...... E6
14823 Canisteo 2,679 ...... E6
13032 Canastota 4,773 ...... J4
13617 Canton⊙ 7,055 ...... K1
10512 Carmel⊙ 27,948 ...... N8
13619 Carthage 3,643 ...... J3
12033 Castleton-on-Hudson 1,627 ...... N5
12414 Catskill⊙ 4,718 ...... N6
†14850 Cayuga Heights 3,170 ...... H6

13035 Cazenovia 2,599 ...... J5
11516 Cedarhurst 6,162 ...... P7
14720 Celoron 1,405 ...... B6
11720 Centereach 30,136 ...... O9
11934 Center Moriches 5,703 ...... P9
11722 Central Islip 19,734 ...... O9
10917 Central Valley 1,705 ...... M8
13036 Central Square 1,418 ...... H4
12919 Champlain 1,410 ...... N1
12037 Chatham 2,001 ...... N6
14225 Cheektowaga 92,145 ...... C5
10918 Chester 1,910 ...... M8
13037 Chittenango 4,290 ...... J4
14428 Churchville 1,399 ...... E4
14031 Clarence 18,146 ...... C5
13624 Clayton 1,816 ...... H2
†12118 Clifton Park 23,989 ...... N5
14432 Clifton Springs 2,039 ...... F4
13323 Clinton 2,107 ...... K4
14433 Clyde 2,491 ...... G4
12043 Cobleskill 5,272 ...... L5
12047 Cohoes 18,144 ...... N5
10516 Cold Spring 2,161 ...... N8
11724 Cold Spring Harbor 5,336 ...... R6
†12201 Colonie 8,869 ...... N5
11725 Commack 34,719 ...... O9
13326 Cooperstown⊙ 2,342 ...... L5
11726 Copiague 20,132 ...... O9
12822 Corinth 2,702 ...... N4
14830 Corning 12,953 ...... F6
12518 Cornwall On Hudson 3,164 ...... M8
13045 Cortland⊙ 20,138 ...... H5
12051 Coxsackie 2,786 ...... N6
10520 Croton-on-Hudson 6,889 ...... N8
14727 Cuba 1,739 ...... D6
11935 Cutchogue-New
Suffolk 2,788 ...... P8
12929 Dannemora 3,770 ...... N1

AREA 49,108 sq. mi. (127,190 sq. km.)
POPULATION 17,558,072
CAPITAL Albany
LARGEST CITY New York
HIGHEST POINT Mt. Marcy 5,344 ft. (1629 m.)
SETTLED IN 1614
ADMITTED TO UNION July 26, 1788
POPULAR NAME Empire State
STATE FLOWER Rose
STATE BIRD Bluebird

Topography

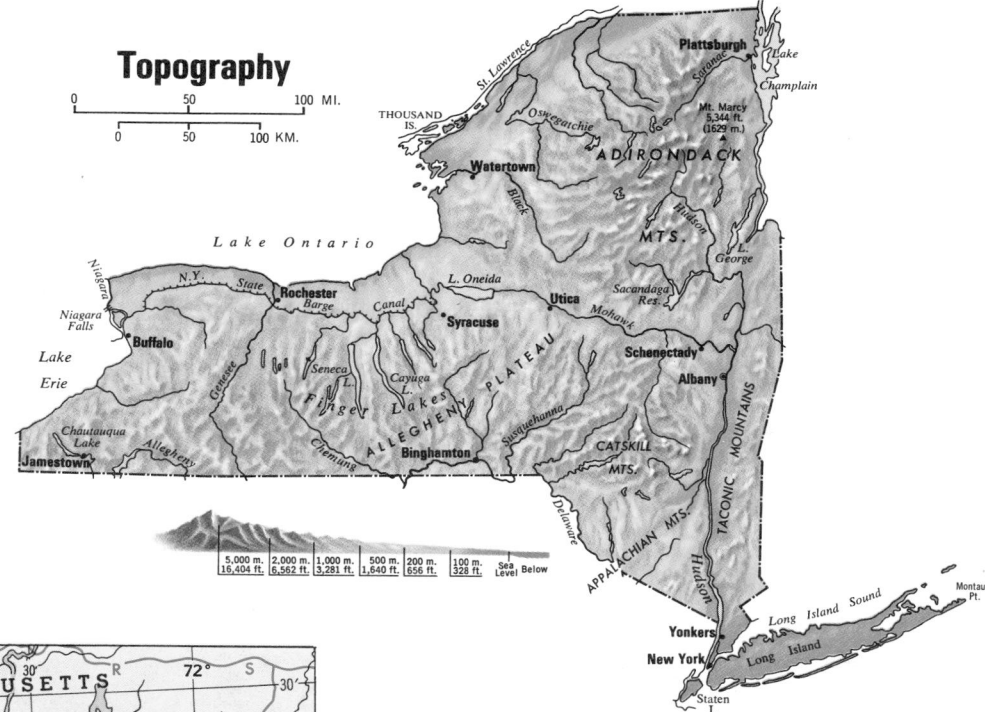

5,000 m.	2,000 m.	1,000 m.	500 m.	200 m.	100 m.	Sea
16,404 ft.	6,562 ft.	3,281 ft.	1,640 ft.	656 ft.	328 ft.	Level Below

(continued on following page)

© Copyright HAMMOND INCORPORATED, Maplewood, N.J.

(continued)

11751 Islip 13,438 ... O9
14850 Ithaca⊙ 28,732 ... G6
*11401 Jamaica⊙ ... N9
14701 Jamestown 35,775 ... B6
11753 Jericho 12,739 ... R6
13790 Johnson City 17,126 ... J6
12095 Johnstown⊙ 9,360 ... M4
13080 Jordan 1,371 ... H4
12944 Keeseville 2,025 ... O2
14271 Kenmore 18,474 ... C5
12446 Kerhonkson 1,646 ... M7
12106 Kinderhook 1,377 ... N6
11754 Kings Park 16,131 ... O9
11024 Kings Point 5,234 ... P6
12401 Kingston⊙ 24,481 ... M7
14218 Lackawanna 22,701 ... B5
10512 Lake Carmel 7,295 ... N8
†14006 Lake Erie Beach 4,625 ... B5
12845 Lake George⊙ 1,047 ... N4
12449 Lake Katrine 2,011 ... M7
12846 Lake Luzerne-Hadley 1,988 N4
12946 Lake Placid 2,490 ... N2
12108 Lake Pleasant⊙ 700 ... M4
11040 Lake Success 2,396 ... P7
14750 Lakewood 3,941 ... B6
14086 Lancaster 13,056 ... C5
14882 Lansing 3,039 ... H5
10538 Larchmont 6,308 ... P7
12110 Latham 11,182 ... N5
†11560 Lattingtown 1,749 ... R6
11559 Lawrence 6,175 ... P7
14482 Le Roy 4,900 ... E5
11756 Levittown 57,045 ... R7
14092 Lewiston 3,326 ... B4
12754 Liberty 4,293 ... L7
14485 Lima 2,025 ... E5
11757 Lindenhurst 26,919 ... O9
13365 Little Falls 6,156 ... L4
14755 Little Valley⊙ 1,203 ... C6
13088 Liverpool 2,849 ... H4
12758 Livingston Manor 1,436 ... L7
†11743 Lloyd Harbor 3,405 ... R6
14094 Lockport⊙ 24,844 ... C4
†11791 Locust Grove 9,670 ... R6
11561 Long Beach 34,073 ... R7
13367 Lowville⊙ 3,364 ... J3
11563 Lynbrook 20,424 ... P7
14489 Lyons⊙ 4,160 ... F4
14502 Macedon 1,400 ... F4
10541 Mahopac 7,681 ... N8
12953 Malone⊙ 7,668 ... M1
11565 Malverne 9,262 ... R7
10543 Mamaroneck 17,616 ... P7
14504 Manchester 1,698 ... F5
11030 Manhasset 8,485 ... P7
*10001 Manhattan (borough) 1,428,285 ... M9
13104 Manlius 5,241 ... J5
13108 Marcellus 1,870 ... H5
12542 Marlboro 2,275 ... M7
11758 Massapequa 24,454 ... R7
11762 Massapequa Park 19,779 .. R7
13662 Massena 12,851 ... L1
11950 Mastic Beach 8,318 ... P9
11952 Mattituck 3,923 ... P9
12543 Maybrook 2,007 ... M8
14757 Mayville⊙ 1,626 ... A6
12118 Mechanicville 5,500 ... N5
14103 Medina 6,392 ... D4
†13021 Melrose Park 2,171 ... G5
11746 Melville 8,139 ... O9
†12201 Menands 4,012 ... N5
11566 Merrick 24,478 ... R7
13114 Mexico 1,621 ... H4
12122 Middleburgh 1,358 ... M5
12550 Middle Hope 3,229 ... M7
14105 Middleport 1,995 ... C4
10940 Middletown 21,454 ... L8
†12020 Milton 2,063 ... N4
11501 Mineola⊙ 20,757 ... R7
13115 Minetto 1,629 ... H4
12956 Mineville-Witherbee 1,925 .. O2
11516 Minoa 3,640 ... H4
13407 Mohawk 2,956 ... L4
10950 Monroe 5,996 ... M8
10952 Monsey 12,380 ... J8
12549 Montgomery 2,316 ... M7
12701 Monticello⊙ 6,306 ... L7
14865 Montour Falls 1,791 ... G6
13118 Moravia 1,582 ... H5
12962 Morrisonville 1,721 ... N1
13408 Morrisville 2,707 ... J5
10549 Mount Kisco 8,025 ... N8
14510 Mount Morris 3,039 ... E5
*10550 Mount Vernon 66,713 ... O7
10954 Nanuet 12,578 ... K8
12123 Nassau 1,285 ... N5
Nassau-Suffolk‡ 2,605,813 R7
14513 Newark 10,017 ... G4
13411 New Berlin 1,392 ... K5
12550 Newburgh 23,438 ... M7
Newburgh-Middletown‡ 259,603 ... M7
10956 New City⊙ 35,859 ... K8
14108 Newfane 3,120 ... C4
13413 New Hartford 2,313 ... K4
11040 New Hyde Park 9,801 ... P7
12561 New Paltz 4,938 ... M7
*10801 New Rochelle 70,794 ... P7
†10901 New Square 1,750 ... K8
12550 New Windsor 7,812 ... N8
*10001 New York⊙ 7,071,639 ... M9
New York‡ 9,119,737 ... M9
13417 New York Mills 3,549 ... K4
*14301 Niagara Falls 71,384 ... C4
†12301 Niskayuna 5,223 ... N5
13667 Norfolk 1,599 ... K1
14110 North Boston 2,743 ... C5
14111 North Collins 1,496 ... C5
11768 Northport 7,651 ... O9
13212 North Syracuse 7,970 ... H4
10591 North Tarrytown 7,994 ... O6
14120 North Tonawanda 35,760 .. C4
12134 Northville 1,304 ... M4
13815 Norwich⊙ 8,082 ... J5
13368 Norwood 1,902 ... L1
10960 Nyack 6,428 ... K8
14125 Oakfield 1,791 ... D4
11572 Oceanside 33,639 ... R7
13669 Ogdensburg 12,375 ... K1
14126 Olcott 1,571 ... C4
14760 Olean 18,207 ... D6
13421 Oneida 10,810 ... J4
13820 Oneonta 14,933 ... K6
14127 Orchard Park 3,671 ... C5
13424 Oriskany 1,680 ... K4
10562 Ossining 20,196 ... N8
13126 Oswego⊙ 19,793 ... G4
14521 Ovid⊙ 666 ... G5
13827 Owego⊙ 4,364 ... H6
13830 Oxford 1,765 ... J6
11771 Oyster Bay 6,497 ... R6
14870 Painted Post 2,196 ... F6
14522 Palmyra 3,729 ... F4
11772 Patchogue 11,291 ... P9
12564 Pawling 1,996 ... N7
10965 Pearl River 15,893 ... K8
10566 Peekskill 18,236 ... N8
10803 Pelham 6,848 ... O7
†10803 Pelham Manor 6,130 ... O7
14527 Penn Yan⊙ 5,242 ... F5
14530 Perry 4,198 ... D5
12972 Peru 1,716 ... N1
14532 Phelps 2,004 ... F5
12565 Philmont 1,539 ... N6
13135 Phoenix 2,357 ... H4
10968 Piermont 2,269 ... K8
12567 Pine Plains 1,303 ... N7
14534 Pittsford 1,568 ... E4
11803 Plainview 28,037 ... R7
12901 Plattsburgh⊙ 21,057 ... O1
10570 Pleasantville 6,749 ... N8
13140 Port Byron 1,400 ... G4
10573 Port Chester 23,565 ... P7
†13901 Port Dickinson 1,974 ... J6
12466 Port Ewen 2,813 ... N7
12974 Port Henry 1,450 ... O2
11777 Port Jefferson 6,731 ... P9
12771 Port Jervis 8,699 ... L8
11050 Port Washington 14,521 ... R6
13676 Potsdam 10,635 ... K1
*12601 Poughkeepsie⊙ 29,757 ... N7
Poughkeepsie‡ 245,055 ... N7
14873 Prattsburg○ 1,657 ... F5
13142 Pulaski 2,415 ... H3
10579 Putnam Valley○ 8,994 ... N8
*11101 Queens (borough) 1,891,325 ... N9
14772 Randolph 1,398 ... C6
14131 Ransomville 1,401 ... C4
12143 Ravena 3,091 ... N6
12571 Red Hook 1,692 ... N7
†12601 Red Oaks Mill 5,236 ... N7
12144 Rensselaer 9,047 ... N5
12572 Rhinebeck 2,542 ... N7
13439 Richfield Springs 1,561 ... K5
*10301 Richmond (Staten Island) (borough) 352,121 ... M9
11901 Riverhead⊙ 6,339 ... P9
*14601 Rochester⊙ 241,741 ... E4
Rochester‡ 971,879 ... E4
*11570 Rockville Centre 25,412 ... R7
13440 Rome 43,826 ... J4
11575 Roosevelt 14,109 ... R7
11576 Roslyn 2,134 ... R6
12979 Rouses Point 2,266 ... O1
10580 Rye 15,083 ... P6
11963 Sag Harbor 2,581 ... R8
11780 Saint James 12,122 ... O9
13452 Saint Johnsville 1,974 ... L5
14779 Salamanca 6,890 ... C6
†13132 Sand Ridge 1,293 ... H4
†11050 Sands Point 2,742 ... P6
12983 Saranac Lake 5,578 ... M2
12866 Saratoga Springs 23,906 ... N4
12477 Saugerties 3,882 ... M6
13146 Savannah○ 1,905 ... G4
11782 Sayville 12,013 ... O9
10583 Scarsdale 17,650 ... P6
*12301 Schenectady⊙ 67,972 ... M5
12157 Schoharie⊙ 1,016 ... M5
12871 Schuylerville 1,256 ... N4
12302 Scotia 7,280 ... N5
14546 Scottsville 1,789 ... E4
11579 Sea Cliff 5,364 ... R6
11783 Seaford 16,117 ... R7
13148 Seneca Falls 7,466 ... G5
13460 Sherburne 1,561 ... K5
13461 Sherrill 2,830 ... J4
14548 Shortsville 1,669 ... F5
13838 Sidney 4,861 ... K6
14136 Silver Creek 3,088 ... B5
13152 Skaneateles 2,789 ... H5
†14201 Sloan 4,529 ... C5
10974 Sloatsburg 3,154 ... M8
11787 Smithtown 30,906 ... O9
14551 Sodus 1,790 ... G4
14555 Sodus Point 1,334 ... G4
13209 Solvay 7,140 ... H4
11968 Southampton 4,000 ... R9
12779 South Fallsburg 2,196 ... L7
†12801 South Glens Falls 3,714 ... N4
†10960 South Nyack 3,602 ... K8
11971 Southold 4,770 ... P8
†14901 Southport 8,329 ... G6
14559 Spencerport 3,424 ... E4
10977 Spring Valley 20,537 ... K8
14141 Springville 4,285 ... C5
*10301 Staten Island (borough) 352,121 ... M9
12170 Stillwater 1,572 ... N5
11790 Stony Brook 16,155 ... O9
10980 Stony Point 8,686 ... M8
12172 Stottville 1,387 ... N6
10901 Suffern 10,794 ... J8
11791 Syosset 9,818 ... R6
*13201 Syracuse⊙ 170,105 ... H4
Syracuse‡ 642,375 ... H4
10983 Tappan 8,267 ... K8
10591 Tarrytown 10,648 ... O6
†11020 Thomaston 2,684 ... P7
12883 Ticonderoga 2,938 ... N3
12486 Tillson 1,529 ... M7
14150 Tonawanda 18,693 ... B4
*12180 Troy⊙ 56,638 ... N5
14886 Trumansburg 1,722 ... G5
10707 Tuckahoe 6,076 ... O7
12986 Tupper Lake 4,478 ... M2
13849 Unadilla 1,367 ... K6
11553 Uniondale 20,016 ... R7
*13501 Utica⊙ 75,632 ... K4
Utica-Rome‡ 320,180 ... K4
12184 Valatie 1,492 ... N6
10989 Valley Cottage 8,214 ... K8
*11580 Valley Stream 35,769 ... P7
13850 Vestal○ 27,238 ... H6
14564 Victor 2,370 ... F5
†10901 Viola 5,340 ... J8
12186 Voorheesville 3,320 ... M5
12586 Walden 5,659 ... M7
12589 Wallkill 2,064 ... M7
13856 Walton 3,329 ... K6
13163 Wampsville⊙ 569 ... J4
11793 Wantagh 19,817 ... R7
12590 Wappingers Falls 5,110 ... N7
12885 Warrensburg 2,834 ... N3
14569 Warsaw⊙ 3,619 ... D5
10990 Warwick 4,320 ... M8
10992 Washingtonville 2,380 ... M8
12188 Waterford 2,405 ... N5
13165 Waterloo⊙ 5,303 ... G5
13601 Watertown⊙ 27,861 ... J3
13480 Waterville 1,672 ... K5
12189 Watervliet 11,354 ... N5
14891 Watkins Glen⊙ 2,440 ... G6
14892 Waverly 4,738 ... G7
14572 Wayland 1,846 ... E5
14580 Webster 5,499 ... F4
13166 Weedsport 1,952 ... G4
14895 Wellsville 5,769 ... E6
11590 Westbury 13,871 ... R7
†13619 West Carthage 1,824 ... J3
†14901 West Elmira 5,485 ... G6
14787 Westfield 3,446 ... A6
†12801 West Glens Falls 5,331 ... N4
11977 Westhampton 2,774 ... P9
11978 Westhampton Beach 1,629 P9
12491 West Hurley 2,382 ... M6
10994 West Nyack 8,553 ... K8
14788 Westons Mills 1,837 ... D6
10996 West Point 8,105 ... M8
11796 West Sayville 8,185 ... O9
14224 West Seneca 51,210 ... C5
12887 Whitehall 3,241 ... O3
*10601 White Plains⊙ 46,999 ... P6
13492 Whitesboro 4,460 ... K4
14588 Willard 1,339 ... G5
14589 Williamson 1,768 ... F4
14221 Williamsville 6,017 ... C5
11596 Williston Park 8,216 ... R7
13865 Windsor 1,155 ... J6
13697 Winthrop-Brasher Falls 1,454 ... L1
12998 Witherbee-Mineville 1,925 .. N2
14590 Wolcott 1,496 ... G4
11598 Woodmere 17,205 ... P7
12498 Woodstock 2,280 ... M6
12790 Wurtsboro 1,128 ... L7
11798 Wyandanch 13,215 ... N9
*10701 Yonkers 195,351 ... O6
10598 Yorktown Heights 7,696 ... N8
13495 Yorkville 3,115 ... K4
14174 Youngstown 2,191 ... C4

OTHER FEATURES

Adirondack (mts.) ... M3
Algonquin (peak) ... M2
Allegany Ind. Res. 1,243 ... C6
Allegheny (res.) ... C7
Allegheny (riv.) ... C6
Ashokan (res.) ... M7
Ausable (riv.) ... N2
Batten Kill (riv.) ... O4
Beaver (riv.) ... K3
Big Moose (lake) ... L3
Black (lake) ... J1
Black (riv.) ... K3
Block Island (sound) ... S8
Blue Mountain (lake) ... M3
Bonaparte (lake) ... K2
Brandreth (lake) ... L3
Brant (lake) ... N3
Brookhaven Nat'l Lab. ... P9
Butterfield (lake) ... J2
Canandaigua (lake) ... F5
Canisteo (riv.) ... F6
Cannonsville (res.) ... K6
Catskill (mts.) ... L6
Cattaraugus (creek) ... C6
Cattaraugus Ind. Res. 1,994 ... C5
Cayuga (lake) ... G5
Champlain (lake) ... O1
Chateaugay, Upper (lake) ... M1
Chautauqua (lake) ... A6
Chazy (lake) ... N1
Chenango (riv.) ... J6
Cohocton (riv.) ... F6
Conesus (lake) ... E5
Conewango (creek) ... B6
Cranberry (lake) ... L2
Deer (riv.) ... J3
Deer (riv.) ... L1
Delaware (riv.) ... K7
East (riv.) ... N9
Erie (lake) ... A5
Fire Island Nat'l Seashore ... P9
Fishers (isl.) ... S8
Forked (lake) ... L3
Fort Drum ... J2
Fort Niagara ... C4
Fort Stanwix Nat'l Mon. ... J4
Fulton Chain (lkes) ... K3
Galloo (isl.) ... H3
Gardiners (bay) ... R8
Gardiners (isl.) ... R8
Gateway Nat'l Rec. Area ... M9
Genesee (riv.) ... E5
George (lake) ... N4
Grand (isl.) ... B5
Grass (riv.) ... K1
Great Sacandaga (lake) ... M4
Great South (bay) ... O9
Great South (beach) ... O9
Greenwood (lake) ... M8
Grenadier (isl.) ... H2
Griffiss A.F.B. ... K4
Haystack (mt.) ... N2
Hemlock (lake) ... E5
Hinckley (res.) ... K4
Honeoye (lake) ... F5
Honnedaga (lake) ... L3
Hudson (riv.) ... N7
Hunter (mt.) ... M6
Indian (lake) ... M3
Jones (beach) ... R7
Keuka (lake) ... F5
Lila (lake) ... L2
Little Tupper (lake) ... L2
Long (isl.) ... P9
Long (lake) ... M2
Long Island (sound) ... P9
Manhattan (isl.) ... M9
Marcy (mt.) ... N2
Martin Van Buren Nat'l Hist. Site ... N6
Meacham (lake) ... M1
Mohawk (riv.) ... L5
Montauk (pt.) ... S8
Moose (riv.) ... K3
Neversink (res.) ... L7
New York State Barge (canal) ... C4
Niagara (riv.) ... B4
Oil Spring Ind. Res. 6 ... D6
Oneida (lake) ... J4
Onondaga Ind. Res. 596 ... H5
Ontario (lake) ... F3
Orient (pt.) ... R8
Oswegatchie (riv.) ... K2
Oswego (riv.) ... H4
Otisco (lake) ... H5
Otsego (lake) ... L5
Otselic (riv.) ... J5
Owasco (lake) ... G5
Peconic (bay) ... R9
Peninsula (pt.) ... H3
Pepacton (res.) ... L6
Piseco (lake) ... M4
Placid (lake) ... N2
Plattsburgh A.F.B. 5,905 ... N1
Pleasant (lake) ... M4
Plum (isl.) ... R8
Poosepatuck Ind. Res. 203 ... P9
Raquette (lake) ... L3
Rondout (res.) ... M7
Round (lake) ... L2
Sacandaga (lake) ... L3
Sackets (harb.) ... H3
Sagamore Hill Nat'l Hist. Site ... R6
Saint Lawrence (lake) ... K1
Saint Lawrence (riv.) ... J2
Saint Regis (riv.) ... L1
Saint Regis Ind. Res. 1,802 ... M1
Salmon (res.) ... J3
Salmon (riv.) ... H3
Salmon (riv.) ... M1
Saranac (lkes) ... M2
Saranac (riv.) ... N1
Saratoga (lake) ... N4
Saratoga Nat'l Hist. Park ... N4
Schoharie (res.) ... M6
Schroon (lake) ... N3
Seneca (lake) ... G5
Seneca (riv.) ... G5
Shelter (isl.) ... R8
Shinnecock Ind. Res. 297 ... R9
Silver (lake) ... N1
Skaneateles (lake) ... H5
Skylight (mt.) ... M2
Slide (mt.) ... L6
Staten (isl.) ... M9
Statue of Liberty Nat'l Mon. ... M9
Stony (isl.) ... H3
Stony (pt.) ... H3
Susquehanna (riv.) ... H6
Thousand (isls.) ... H2
Tioughnioga (riv.) ... H6
Titus (lake) ... M1
Tomhannock (res.) ... O5
Tonawanda Ind. Res. 467 ... D4
Toronto (res.) ... L7
Tupper (lake) ... M2
Tuscarora Ind. Res. 921 ... B4
Unadilla (riv.) ... K5
Upper Chateaugay (lake) ... M1
Valcour (isl.) ... N1
Wallkill (riv.) ... L8
Whiteface (mt.) ... N2
Whitney Point (lake) ... J6
Woodhull (lake) ... L3

⊙County seat.
‡Population of metropolitan area.
○Population of town or township.
† Zip of nearest p.o. * Multiple zips.

Agriculture, Industry and Resources

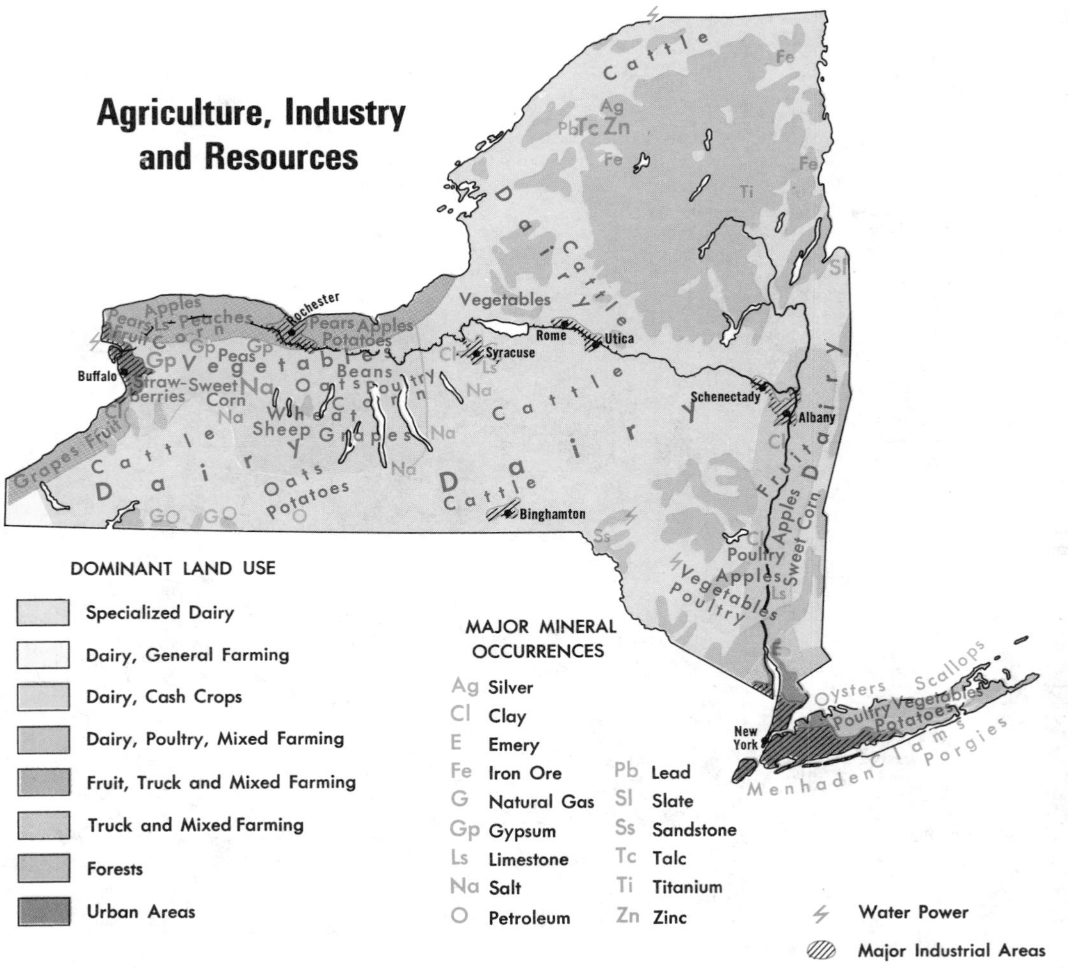

Cattle
Dairy
Vegetables
Apples
Peaches
Pears
Corn
Potatoes
Beans
Oats
Poultry
Wheat
Sheep
Grapes
Fruit
Straw-berries
Sweet Corn
Sweet Corn
Oysters
Scallops
Clams
Porgies
Menhaden
Rochester
Buffalo
Syracuse
Rome
Utica
Schenectady
Albany
Binghamton
New York
DOMINANT LAND USE
Specialized Dairy
Dairy, General Farming
Dairy, Cash Crops
Dairy, Poultry, Mixed Farming
Fruit, Truck and Mixed Farming
Truck and Mixed Farming
Forests
Urban Areas
MAJOR MINERAL OCCURRENCES
Ag Silver
Cl Clay
E Emery
Fe Iron Ore
G Natural Gas
Gp Gypsum
Ls Limestone
Na Salt
O Petroleum
Pb Lead
Sl Slate
Ss Sandstone
Tc Talc
Ti Titanium
Zn Zinc
Water Power
Major Industrial Areas

AREA 52,669 sq. mi. (136,413 sq. km.)
POPULATION 5,881,813
CAPITAL Raleigh
LARGEST CITY Charlotte
HIGHEST POINT Mt. Mitchell 6,684 ft. (2037 m.)
SETTLED IN 1650
ADMITTED TO UNION November 21, 1789
POPULAR NAME Tarheel State
STATE FLOWER Flowering Dogwood
STATE BIRD Cardinal

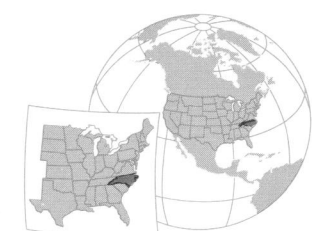

COUNTIES

Alamance 99,319 ....L3
Alexander 24,999 ....G3
Alleghany 9,587 ....G1
Anson 25,649 ....J4
Ashe 22,325 ....F2
Avery 14,409 ....F2
Beaufort 40,355 ....R4
Bertie 21,024 ....P2
Bladen 30,491 ....M5
Brunswick 35,777 ....N6
Buncombe 160,934 ....D3
Burke 72,504 ....F3
Cabarrus 85,895 ....H4
Caldwell 67,746 ....F3
Camden 5,829 ....S2
Carteret 41,092 ....R5
Caswell 20,705 ....L2
Catawba 105,208 ....G3
Chatham 33,415 ....L3
Cherokee 18,933 ....A4
Chowan 12,558 ....R2
Clay 6,619 ....B4
Cleveland 83,435 ....F4
Columbus 51,037 ....M6
Craven 71,043 ....P4
Cumberland 247,160 ....M4
Currituck 11,089 ....S2
Dare 13,377 ....T3
Davidson 113,162 ....J3
Davie 24,599 ....H3
Duplin 40,952 ....O5
Durham 152,785 ....M3
Edgecombe 55,988 ....O3
Forsyth 243,683 ....J2
Franklin 30,055 ....N2
Gaston 162,568 ....G4
Gates 8,875 ....R2
Graham 7,217 ....B4
Granville 34,043 ....M2
Greene 16,117 ....O3
Guilford 317,154 ....K3
Halifax 55,286 ....O2
Harnett 59,570 ....M4
Haywood 46,495 ....C3
Henderson 58,580 ....D4
Hertford 23,368 ....P2
Hoke 20,383 ....L4
Hyde 5,873 ....S3
Iredell 82,538 ....H3
Jackson 25,811 ....C4
Johnston 70,599 ....N4
Jones 9,705 ....P4

Lee 36,718 ....L4
Lenoir 59,819 ....O4
Lincoln 42,372 ....G3
Macon 20,178 ....B4
Madison 16,827 ....D3
Martin 25,948 ....P3
McDowell 35,135 ....E3
Mecklenburg 404,270 ....H4
Mitchell 14,428 ....E2
Montgomery 22,469 ....K4
Moore 50,505 ....L4
Nash 67,153 ....O2
New Hanover 103,471 ....O6
Northampton 22,584 ....P2
Onslow 112,784 ....P5
Orange 77,055 ....L2
Pamlico 10,398 ....R4
Pasquotank 28,462 ....S2
Pender 22,215 ....O5
Perquimans 9,486 ....S2
Person 29,164 ....M2
Pitt 90,146 ....P3
Polk 12,984 ....E4
Randolph 91,728 ....K3
Richmond 45,481 ....K4
Robeson 101,610 ....L5
Rockingham 83,426 ....K2
Rowan 99,186 ....H3
Rutherford 53,787 ....E4
Sampson 49,687 ....N4
Scotland 32,273 ....L5
Stanly 48,517 ....J4
Stokes 33,086 ....J2
Surry 59,449 ....H2
Swain 10,283 ....B3
Transylvania 23,417 ....D4
Tyrrell 3,975 ....S3
Union 70,380 ....H4
Vance 36,748 ....N2
Wake 301,327 ....M3
Warren 16,232 ....N2
Washington 14,801 ....R3
Watauga 31,666 ....F2
Wayne 97,054 ....N4
Wilkes 58,657 ....G2
Wilson 63,132 ....O3
Yadkin 28,439 ....H2
Yancey 14,934 ....E3

CITIES and TOWNS

Zip	Name/Pop.	Key

28315 Aberdeen 1,945 ....L4
27910 Ahoskie 4,887 ....P2
27201 Alamance 320 ....K2
28001 Albemarle⊙ 15,110 ....J4
†28043 Alexander Mills 643 ....F4
28509 Alliance 616 ....R4
28702 Almond 140 ....B4
28901 Andrews 1,621 ....B4
27501 Angier 1,709 ....M4
28007 Ansonville 794 ....J4
27502 Apex 2,847 ....M3
28510 Arapahoe 467 ....R4
27263 Archdale 5,326 ....K3
†28642 Arlington 872 ....H2
28420 Ash 150 ....N6
27203 Asheboro⊙ 15,252 ....K3
*28801 Asheville⊙ 53,583 ....D3
    Asheville‡ 177,761 ....D3
†27983 Askewville 227 ....R2
28421 Atkinson 298 ....N5
28512 Atlantic Beach 941 ....R5
27805 Aulander 1,214 ....P2
27806 Aurora 698 ....R4
28318 Autryville 228 ....M4

27915 Avon 500 ....U4
28513 Ayden 4,361 ....P4
27916 Aydlett 205 ....T2
28009 Badin 1,514 ....J4
27807 Bailey 685 ....N3
28705 Bakersville⊙ 373 ....E2
28706 Balfour 1,772 ....E4
28707 Balsam 200 ....C4
28604 Banner Elk 1,087 ....F2
†27030 Bannertown 1,028 ......H1
27008 Barber 155 ....H3
†28739 Barker Heights 1,267 ...D4
28710 Bat Cave 450 ....E4
27808 Bath 207 ....R4
27809 Battleboro 632 ....O2
28515 Bayboro⊙ 759 ....R4
†27892 Beargrass 82 ....P3
28516 Beaufort⊙ 3,826 ....R5
27810 Belhaven 2,430 ....R3
27811 Bellarthur 350 ....O3
28012 Belmont 4,607 ....H4
†28451 Belville 102 ....N6

†28090 Belwood 613 ....F4
†27208 Bennett 254 ....K3
27504 Benson 2,792 ....N4
28016 Bessemer City 4,787 ....G4
27812 Bethel 1,825 ....P3
28518 Beulaville⊙ 1,060 ....O5
†28803 Biltmore Forest 1,499 ...E3
27209 Biscoe 1,334 ....K4
27813 Black Creek 523 ....O3
28711 Black Mountain 4,083 ...E3
28320 Bladenboro 1,428 ....M5
27212 Blanch 200 ....L2
28605 Blowing Rock 1,337 .....F2
28092 Boger City 2,252 ....G4
28461 Boiling Spring Lakes 998 ..N7
28017 Boiling Springs 2,381 ...F4
28422 Bolivia 252 ....N6
28423 Bolton 563 ....N6
27213 Bonlee 300 ....L3
28606 Boomer 250 ....G2
28607 Boone⊙ 10,191 ....F2
27011 Boonville 1,028 ....H2
28322 Bowdens 200 ....N4
28712 Brevard⊙ 5,323 ....D4
28519 Bridgeton 461 ....R4
27505 Broadway 908 ....L4
†28601 Brookford 467 ....G3
28424 Brunswick 223 ....M6
28713 Bryson City⊙ 1,556 ....C4
27506 Buies Creek 1,939 ......M4
27507 Bullock 525 ....M2
27508 Bunn 505 ....N3
28425 Burgaw⊙ 1,738 ....N5
27215 Burlington 37,266 ......K2
    Burlington‡ 99,136 ....F2
28714 Burnsville⊙ 1,452 ......E3
27509 Butner 4,240 ....M2
27312 Bynum 350 ....L3
†29566 Calabash 128 ....M7
28325 Calypso 689 ....N4
28326 Cameron 225 ....L4
27229 Candor 868 ....K4
28716 Canton 4,631 ....D3
†28584 Cape Carteret 944 .....P5
28428 Carolina Beach 2,000 ..O6
27510 Carrboro 7,336 ....L3
28327 Carthage⊙ 925 ....K4
27511 Cary 21,763 ....M3
28020 Casar 346 ....F3
28717 Cashiers 553 ....C4
27816 Castalia 358 ....O2
28429 Castle Hayne 1,087 ....O6
†28461 Caswell Beach 110 .....N7
28609 Catawba 509 ....G3
27230 Cedar Falls 400 ....K3
27231 Cedar Grove 250 ....L2
28520 Cedar Island 310 ....S5
†27549 Centerville 135 ....N2
28430 Cerro Gordo 295 ....M6
28431 Chadbourn 1,975 ....M6
†28445 Chadwick Acres 15 .....P6
27514 Chapel Hill 32,421 .....L3
*28201 Charlotte⊙ 314,447 ....H4
    Charlotte-Gastonia‡
        637,218 ....H4
28021 Cherryville 4,844 ....G4
28023 China Grove 2,081 .....H3
28521 Chinquapin 280 ....O5
27817 Chocowinity 644 ....P4
28610 Claremont 880 ....G3
28433 Clarkton 664 ....M6
27520 Clayton 4,091 ....N3
27012 Clemmons 7,401 ....J2

28328 Clinton⊙ 7,552 ....N5
28721 Clyde 1,008 ....D3
27521 Coats 1,385 ....M4
27922 Cofield 465 ....R2
27924 Colerain 284 ....R2
27925 Columbia⊙ 758 ....S3
28722 Columbus⊙ 727 ....E4
28522 Comfort 325 ....O5
27818 Como 89 ....P1
28025 Concord⊙ 16,942 ......H4
27819 Conetoe 215 ....O3
28613 Conover 4,245 ....G3
27820 Conway 678 ....P2
27014 Cooleemee 1,448 ......H3
28031 Cornelius 1,460 ....H4
27927 Corolla 158 ....T2
28523 Cove City 500 ....P4
28032 Cramerton 1,869 ....G4
27522 Creedmoor 1,641 ......M2
27928 Creswell 426 ....S3
27852 Crisp 435 ....O3
28616 Crossnore 297 ....F2
28331 Cumberland 400 ....M5
27237 Cumnock 200 ....L3
27929 Currituck⊙ 700 ....T2
28034 Dallas 3,340 ....G4
27016 Danbury⊙ 140 ....J2
28036 Davidson 3,241 ....H4
28524 Davis 612 ....R5
27239 Denton 949 ....J3
28725 Dillsboro 179 ....C4
27017 Dobson⊙ 1,222 ....H2
†27801 Dortches 885 ....O2
28526 Dover 600 ....P4
28619 Drexel 1,392 ....F3
28332 Dublin 477 ....M5
28334 Dunn 8,962 ....M4
*27701 Durham⊙ 100,538 .....M2
    Durham-Raleigh‡ 530,673 ..M2
27242 Eagle Springs 280 .....K4
28038 Earl 206 ....F4
†28434 East Arcadia 461 ....N6
27018 East Bend 602 ....H2
28726 East Flat Rock 3,365 ..E4
†28723 East Laport 150 ....C4
28352 East Laurinburg 536 ...L5
†28752 East Marion 1,851 .....F3
28039 East Spencer 2,150 ...J3
27288 Eden 15,672 ....K1
27932 Edenton⊙ 5,357 ....R2
27909 Elizabeth City⊙ 14,004 ..S2
28337 Elizabethtown⊙ 3,551 ..M5
28621 Elkin 2,858 ....H2
28622 Elk Park 535 ....E2
28040 Ellenboro 560 ....F4
28338 Ellerbe 1,415 ....K4
27822 Elm City 1,561 ....O3
27244 Elon College 2,873 ....L2
†28557 Emerald Isle 865 ....P5
27823 Enfield 2,995 ....O2
28728 Enka 5,567 ....D3
28339 Erwin 2,828 ....M4
27247 Ether 425 ....K4
27935 Eure 300 ....R2
27830 Eureka 303 ....O3
27825 Everetts 213 ....P3
28438 Evergreen 310 ....M6
28439 Fair Bluff 1,095 ....M6
27826 Fairfield 900 ....S3
28340 Fairmont 2,658 ....L6
28730 Fairview 1,122 ....D3
28341 Faison 636 ....N4
28041 Faith 552 ....J3
(continued on following page)

Agriculture, Industry and Resources

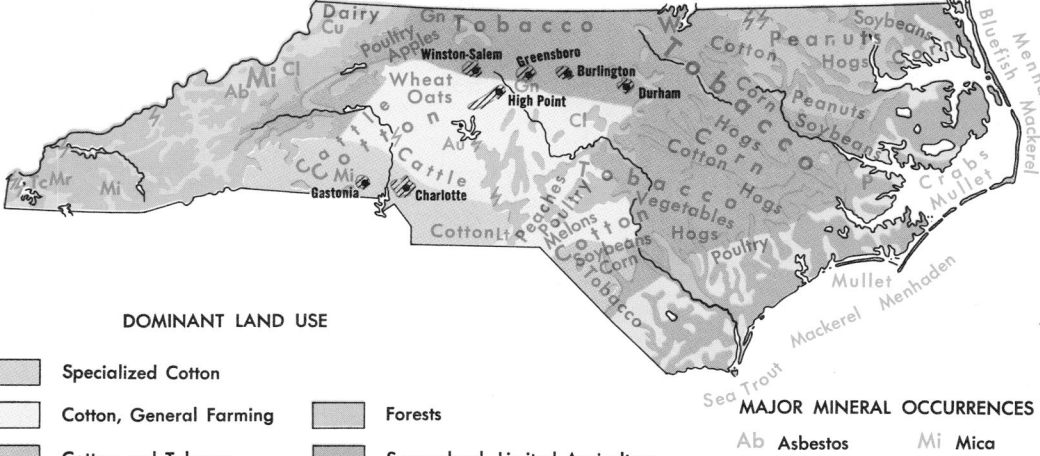

DOMINANT LAND USE

Specialized Cotton

Cotton, General Farming

Cotton and Tobacco

Tobacco, General Farming

Peanuts, General Farming

General Farming, Livestock, Fruit, Tobacco

General Farming, Truck Farming, Tobacco, Livestock

Forests

Swampland, Limited Agriculture

Nonagricultural Land

⚡ Water Power

▨ Major Industrial Areas

MAJOR MINERAL OCCURRENCES

Ab Asbestos
Au Gold
Cl Clay
Cu Copper
Gn Granite
Lt Lithium

Mi Mica
Mr Marble
P Phosphates
Tc Talc
W Tungsten

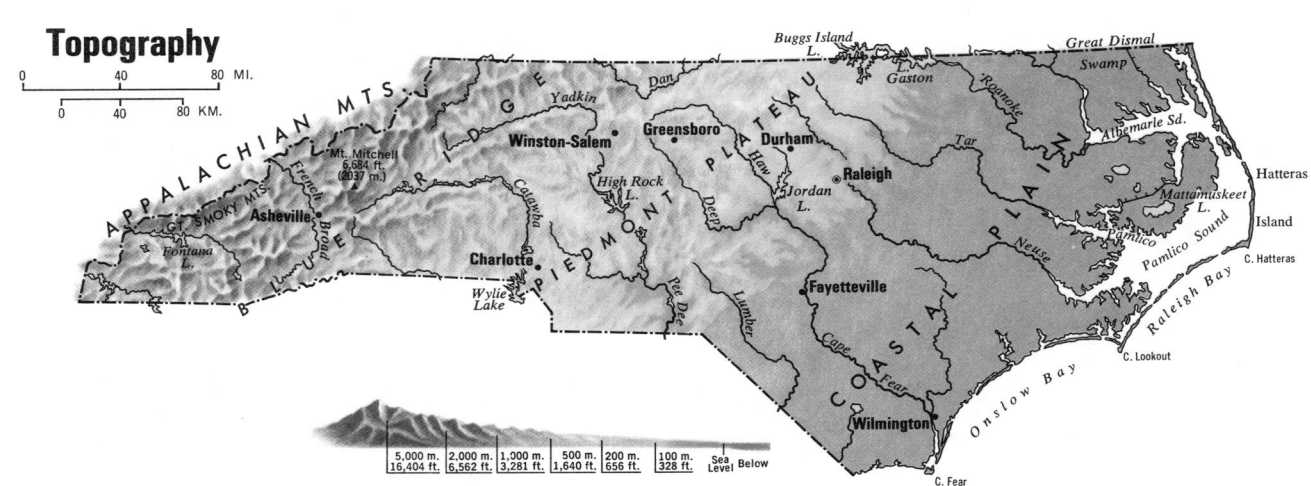

Topography

Topography scale: 0 40 80 MI. / 0 40 80 KM.

5,000 m. 16,404 ft.   2,000 m. 6,562 ft.   1,000 m. 3,281 ft.   500 m. 1,640 ft.   200 m. 656 ft.   100 m. 328 ft.   Sea Level   Below

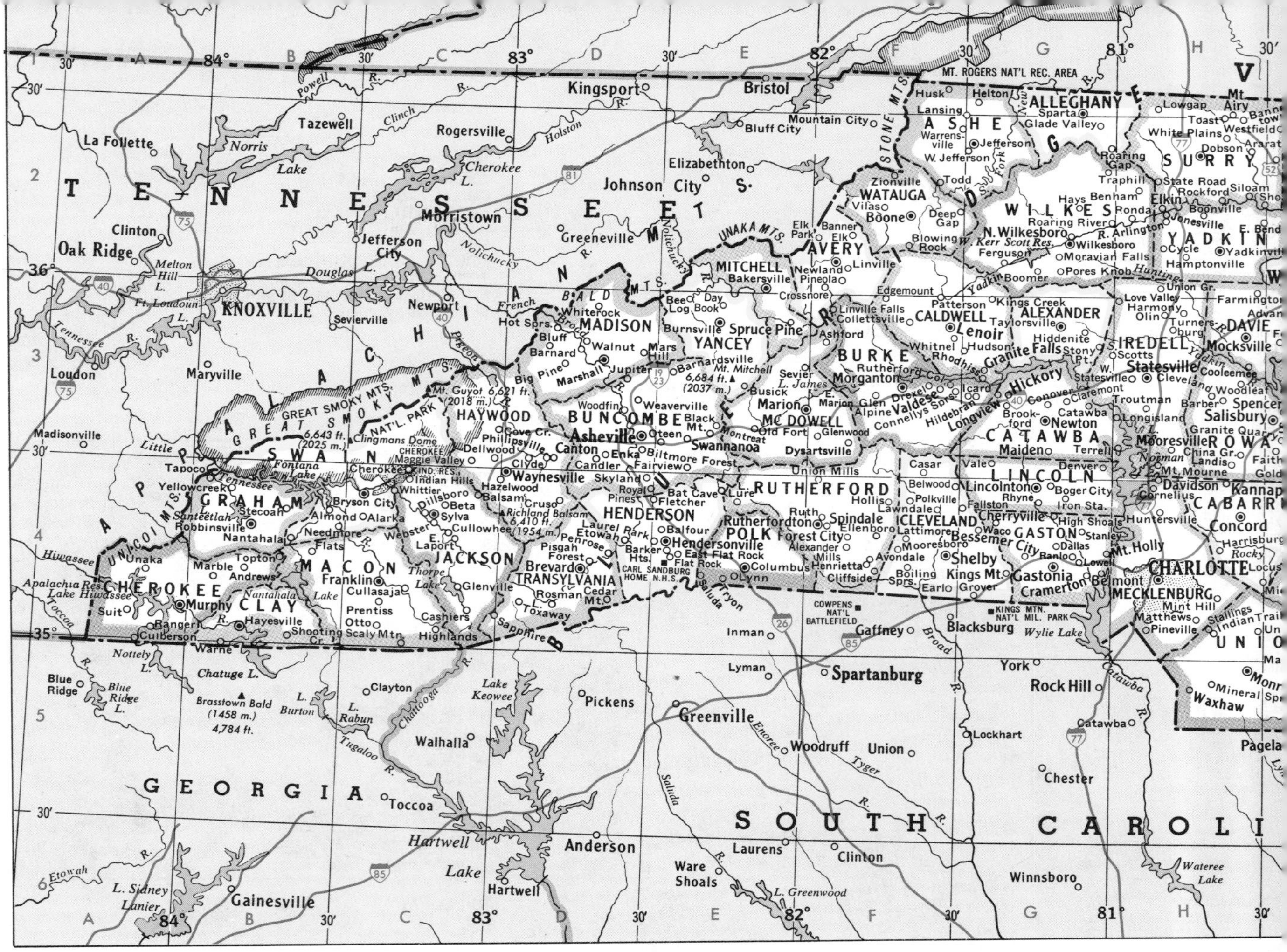

North Carolina

SCALE
0 5 10   20   30   40   50 MI.
0 5 10   20   30   40   50 KM.

State Capitals..............⊛
County Seats................⊙
Canals......................

Major Limited Access Hwys. ___

Scale 1:2,070,000

© Copyright HAMMOND INCORPORATED, Maplewood, N.J.

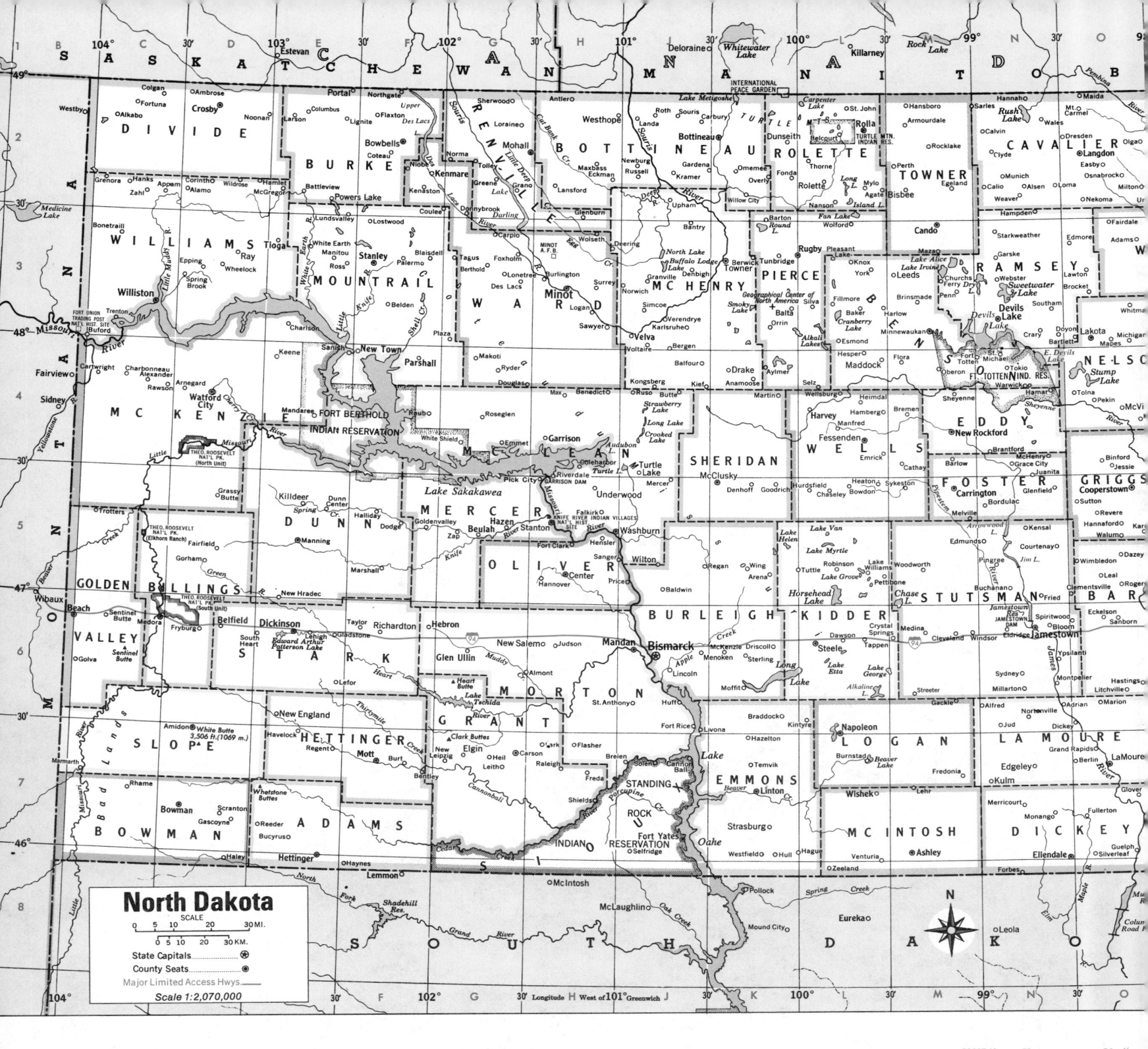

North Dakota

SCALE

0 5 10   20   30 MI.

0 5 10   20   30 KM.

State Capitals..⊛

County Seats..⊛

Major Limited Access Hwys...................

Scale 1:2,070,000

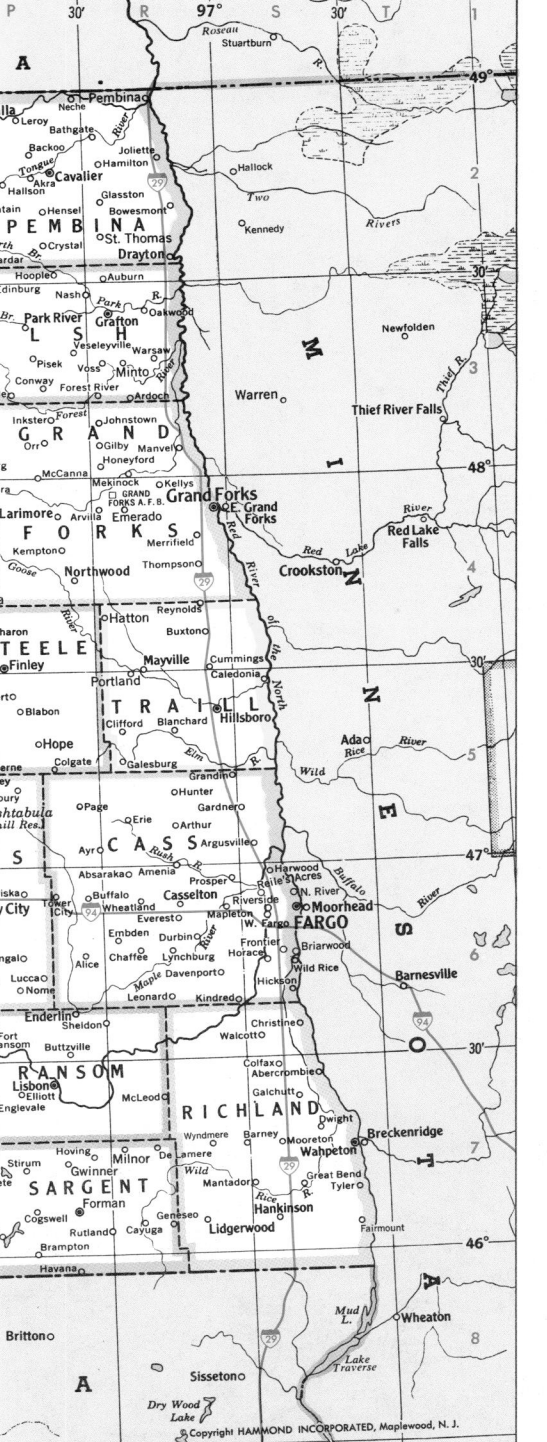

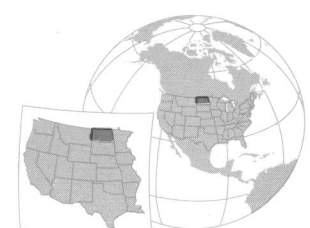

AREA 70,702 sq. mi. (183,118 sq. km.)
POPULATION 652,717
CAPITAL Bismarck
LARGEST CITY Fargo
HIGHEST POINT White Butte 3,506 ft. (1069 m.)
SETTLED IN 1780
ADMITTED TO UNION November 2, 1889
POPULAR NAME Flickertail State; Sioux State
STATE FLOWER Wild Prairie Rose
STATE BIRD Western Meadowlark

58276 Saint Thomas 528 ....R2
58780 Sanish E4
58781 Sawyer 417 ....H3
58653 Scranton 415 ....D7
58568 Selfridge 273 ....J7
58654 Sentinel Butte 86 ....C6
58068 Sheldon 173 ....P6
58782 Sherwood 294 ....G2
58374 Sheyenne 307 ....M4
58655 South Heart 294 ....D6
58850 Spring Brook 52 ....D3
58784 Stanley⊙ 1,631 ....F3
58571 Stanton⊙ 623 ....H5
58482 Steele⊙ 796 ....L6
58573 Strasburg 623 ....K7
58483 Streeter 264 ....M6
58785 Surrey 999 ....H3
58487 Tappen 271 ....L6
58656 Taylor 239 ....F6
58278 Thompson 785 ....R4
58852 Tioga 1,597 ....E3
58380 Tolna 241 ....O4
58071 Tower City 293 ....P6
58788 Towner⊙ 867 ....K3
58575 Turtle Lake 802 ....J4
58576 Underwood 1,329 ....H5
58072 Valley City⊙ 7,774 ....P6
58790 Velva 1,101 ....J3
58792 Voltaire 65 ....J3
58075 Wahpeton⊙ 9,064 ....S7
58281 Wales 74 ....N2
58282 Walhalla 1,429 ....P2
58577 Washburn⊙ 1,767 ....J5
58854 Watford City⊙ 2,119 .....D4
58078 West Fargo 10,099 ....S6
58793 Westhope 741 ....H2
58794 White Earth 98 ....E3
58795 Wildrose 214 ....D2
58801 Williston⊙ 13,336 ....C3
58384 Willow City 329 ....K2
58579 Wilton 950 ....J5
58492 Wimbledon 330 ....O5
58495 Wishek 1,345 ....L7
58385 Wolford 76 ....L3
58801 Wyndmere 550 ....R7
58386 York 69 ....L3
58580 Zap 511 ....G5
58581 Zeeland 253 ....L8

OTHER FEATURES

Alkali (lke)s L3
Alkaline (lke) L6
Apple (creek) J6
Arrowwood (lake) N5
Ashtabula (lake) P5
Audubon (lake) H4
Bad Lands (reg.) C7
Baldhill (Ashtabula) (res.) P5
Bear (creek) O7
Beaver (creek) B5
Beaver (creek) K7
Beaver (lake) L7
Buffalo Lodge (lake) J3
Cannonball (riv.) G7
Carpenter (lake) L2
Cedar (creek) G7
Chase (lake) M5
Cherry (creek) D4
Clark (butte) G7
Coteau du Missouri (plain) G3
Cranberry (lake) L3
Crooked (lake) J4
Cut Bank (creek) H2
Darling (lake) G2
Deep (riv.) J1
Des Lacs (riv.) G3
Devils (lake) N3
Dry (lake) M3
East Devils (lake) N4
Egg (lake) H3
Elm (riv.) N8
Elm (riv.) R5
Etta (lake) L6

Fan (lake) L2
Forest (riv.) P3
Fort Berthold Ind. Res. E4
Fort Totten Ind. Res. N4
Fort Union Trading Post Nat'l Hist.
 Site B3
Garrison (dam) H5
George (lake) L6
Goose (riv.) P4
Grand, North Fork (riv.) E8
Grand Forks A.F.B. 9,390 ......R4
Green (riv.) D5
Grove (lake) L5
Heart (butte) G6
Heart (riv.) F6
Helen (lake) K5
Horsehead (lake) L5
International Peace Garden K1
Irvine (lake) M3
Island (lake) L2
James (riv.) N6
Jamestown (res.) N6
Jim (lake) N5
Knife (riv.) G5
Knife R. Indian Villages Nat'l Hist.
 Site H5
Little Deep (creek) G2
Little Knife (riv.) F3

Little Missouri (riv.) D4
Little Muddy (riv.) C3
Long (lake) J4
Long (lake) K6
Long (lake) L2
Maple (riv.) O8
Maple (riv.) R6
Metigoshe (lake) K2
Minot A.F.B. 9,880 ....H3
Missouri (riv.) H5
Muddy (creek) G6
Myrtle (lake) L5
North (lake) J3
Oahe (lake) J7
Oak (creek) J8
Park (riv.) R3
Patterson, Edward A. (lake) ...E6
Pembina (riv.) O1
Pipestem (creek) M5
Porcupine (creek) J7
Red River of the North (riv.) .S4
Round (lake) K3
Rush (lake) N2
Rush (riv.) R5
Sakakawea (lake) G5
Sentinel (butte) C6
Shell (creek) F3
Sheyenne (riv.) O6

Smoky (lake) K3
Souris (riv.) J2
Spring (creek) E5
Standing Rock Ind. Res. J7
Strawberry (lake) J4
Stump (lake) O4
Sweetwater (lake) N3
Theodore Roosevelt Nat'l Mem. Park
 ....C5, D4, D6
Thirty Mile (creek) F6
Tongue (riv.) P2
Tschida (lake) G6
Turtle (lake) H4
Turtle (mts.) K2
Turtle Mountain Ind. Res. L2
Upper Des Lacs (lake) F2
Van (lake) L5
Whetstone (buttes) E7
White (butte) D7
White Butte (mt.) D7
White Earth (riv.) E3
Wild Rice (riv.) R7
Yellowstone (riv.) B4

⊙ County seat.
‡ Population of metropolitan area.
† Zip of nearest p.o.
* Multiple zips.

Topography

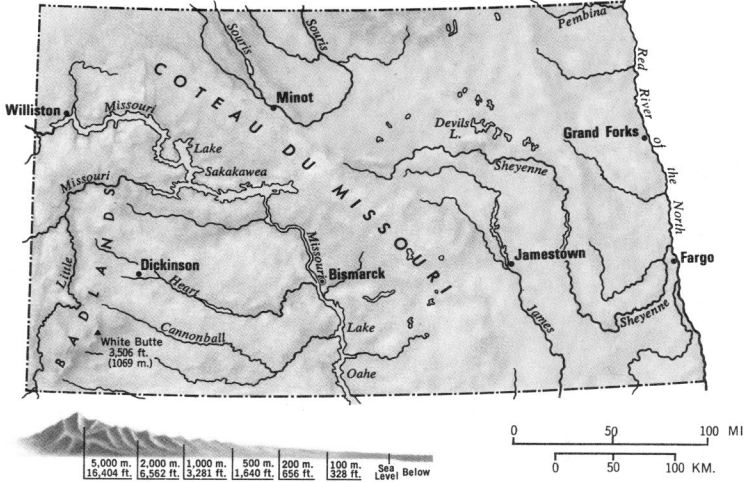

5,000 m. 16,404 ft.	2,000 m. 6,562 ft.	1,000 m. 3,281 ft.	500 m. 1,640 ft.	200 m. 656 ft.	100 m. 328 ft.	Sea Level / Below

0   50   100 MI.
0   50   100 KM.

†58501 Lincoln 656 ....J6
58552 Linton⊙ 1,561 ....K7
58054 Lisbon⊙ 2,283 ....P7
58461 Litchville 251 ....O6
58056 Luverne 65 ....P5
58348 Maddock 677 ....L4
58554 Mandan⊙ 15,513 ....J6
58642 Manning⊙ 75 ....E5
58058 Mantador 76 ....R7
58256 Manvel 308 ....R3
58059 Mapleton 306 ....R6
58643 Marmarth 190 ....B7
58759 Max 317 ....H4
58257 Mayville 2,255 ....R4
58463 McClusky⊙ 658 ....K4
58254 McVille 626 ....O4
58467 Medina 521 ....M6
58645 Medora⊙ 94 ....C6
58260 Michigan 502 ....O3
58060 Milnor 716 ....R7
58351 Minnewaukan⊙ 461 ....M3
58701 Minot⊙ 32,843 ....H3
58261 Minto 592 ....R3
58761 Mohall⊙ 1,049 ....G2
58471 Monango 59 ....N7
58472 Montpelier 96 ....N6
58646 Mott⊙ 1,315 ....F7
58352 Munich 300 ....N2
58561 Napoleon⊙ 1,103 ......L6
58265 Neche 471 ....P2
58467 New England 825 ....E6
58562 New Leipzig 352 ....G7
58356 New Rockford 1,791 ....N4

58563 New Salem 1,081 ....G6
58763 New Town 1,335 ....F4
58266 Niagara 76 ....P4
58062 Nome 67 ....P6
58765 Noonan 283 ....D2
†58102 North River 65 ....S6
58267 Northwood 1,240 ....P4
58474 Oakes 2,112 ....O7
58063 Oriska 125 ....P6
58064 Page 329 ....P5
58769 Palermo 97 ....F3
58270 Park River 1,844 ......P3
58770 Parshall 1,059 ....F4
58271 Pembina 673 ....R2
58476 Pingree 88 ....N5
58772 Portal 238 ....E2
58274 Portland 627 ....R5
58773 Powers Lake 466 ....E2
58849 Ray 766 ....D3
58649 Reeder 355 ....E7
58477 Regan 71 ....K5
58650 Regent 297 ....E7
58275 Reynolds 309 ....R4
58651 Rhame 222 ....C7
58652 Richardton 699 ....F6
†58078 Riverside 465 ....S6
58365 Rocklake 287 ....M2
58479 Rogers 68 ....O5
58366 Rolette 667 ....L2
58367 Rolla⊙ 1,538 ....L2
58368 Rugby⊙ 3,335 ....L3
58067 Rutland 250 ....P7
58369 Saint John 401 ....L2

Agriculture, Industry and Resources

DOMINANT LAND USE

- Specialized Wheat
- Wheat, General Farming
- Wheat, Range Livestock
- Livestock, Cash Grain
- Sugar Beets, Dry Beans, Livestock, General Farming
- Range Livestock
- ⚡ Water Power

MAJOR MINERAL OCCURRENCES

- Cl Clay
- G   Natural Gas
- Lg Lignite
- Na Salt
- O   Petroleum
- U   Uranium

Ohio

SCALE

0 5 10   20   30   40 MI.

0 5 10   20   30   40 KM.

State Capitals............⊛
County Seats.............◉
Major Limited Access Hwys.

Scale 1:1,800,000

© Copyright HAMMOND INCORPORATED, Maplewood, N.J.

AREA 41,330 sq. mi. (107,045 sq. km.)
POPULATION 10,797,624
CAPITAL Columbus
LARGEST CITY Cleveland
HIGHEST POINT Campbell Hill 1,550 ft. (472 m.)
SETTLED IN 1788
ADMITTED TO UNION March 1, 1803
POPULAR NAME Buckeye State
STATE FLOWER Scarlet Carnation
STATE BIRD Cardinal

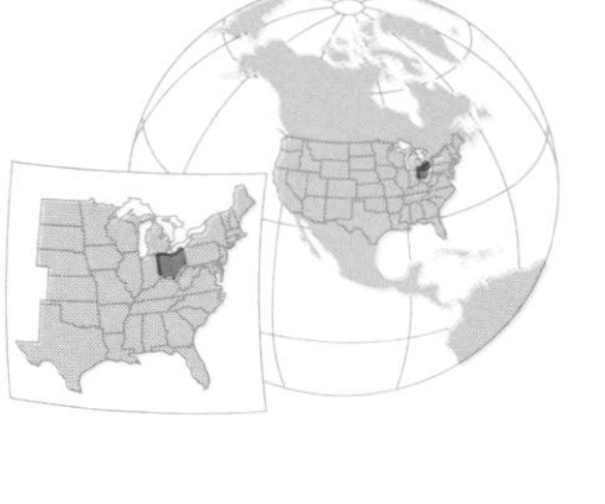

Topography

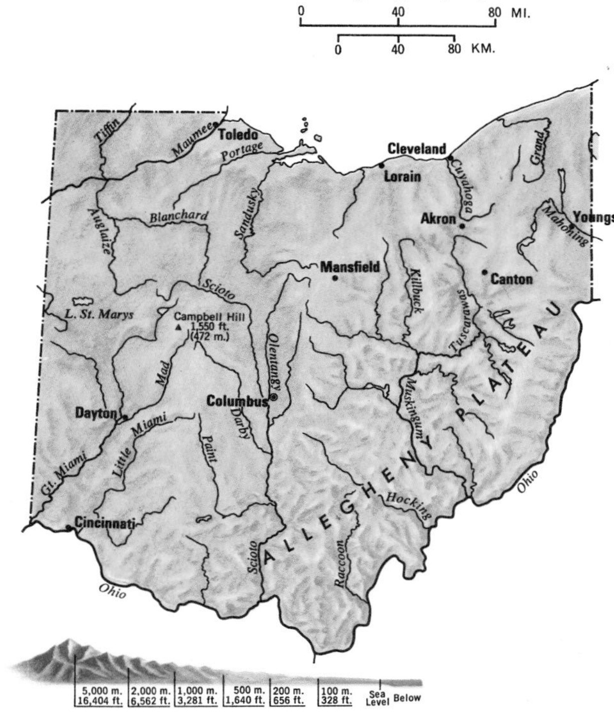

COUNTIES

County	Key
Adams 24,328	D8
Allen 112,241	B4
Ashland 46,178	F4
Ashtabula 104,215	J2
Athens 56,399	F7
Auglaize 42,554	B4
Belmont 82,569	J5
Brown 31,920	C8
Butler 258,787	A7
Carroll 25,598	H4
Champaign 33,649	C5
Clark 150,236	C6
Clermont 128,483	B7
Clinton 34,603	C7
Columbiana 113,572	J4
Coshocton 36,024	G5
Crawford 50,075	E4
Cuyahoga 1,498,400	G3
Darke 55,096	A5
Defiance 39,987	A3
Delaware 53,840	D5
Erie 79,655	E3
Fairfield 93,678	E6
Fayette 27,467	D6
Franklin 869,126	E5
Fulton 37,751	B2
Gallia 30,098	F8
Geauga 74,474	H3
Greene 129,769	C6
Guernsey 42,024	H5
Hamilton 873,224	A7
Hancock 64,581	C3
Hardin 32,719	C4
Harrison 18,152	H5
Henry 28,383	B3
Highland 33,477	C7
Hocking 24,304	F6
Holmes 29,416	G4
Huron 54,608	E3
Jackson 30,592	E7
Jefferson 91,564	J5
Knox 46,304	F5
Lake 212,801	H2
Lawrence 63,849	E8
Licking 120,981	F5
Logan 39,155	C5
Lorain 274,909	F3
Lucas 471,741	C2
Madison 33,004	D6
Mahoning 289,487	J4
Marion 67,974	D4
Medina 113,150	G3
Meigs 23,641	F7
Mercer 38,334	A4
Miami 90,381	B5
Monroe 17,382	H6
Montgomery 571,697	B6
Morgan 14,241	G6
Morrow 26,480	E4
Muskingum 83,340	G5
Noble 11,310	G6
Ottawa 40,076	D2
Paulding 21,302	A3
Perry 31,032	F6
Pickaway 43,662	D6
Pike 22,802	D7
Portage 135,856	H3
Preble 38,223	A6
Putnam 32,991	B3
Richland 131,205	E4
Ross 65,004	D7
Sandusky 63,267	D3
Scioto 84,545	D8
Seneca 61,901	D3
Shelby 43,089	B5
Stark 378,823	H4
Summit 524,472	G3
Trumbull 241,863	J3
Tuscarawas 84,614	H5
Union 29,536	D5
Van Wert 30,458	A4
Vinton 11,584	E7
Warren 99,276	B7
Washington 64,266	H7
Wayne 97,408	G4
Williams 36,369	A2
Wood 107,372	C3
Wyandot 22,651	D4

CITIES and TOWNS

Zip	Name/Pop.	Key
45101	Aberdeen 1,566	C8
45810	Ada 5,669	C4
45001	Addyston 1,195	B9
43101	Adelphi 472	E7
43901	Adena 1,062	J5
*44301	Akron⊙ 237,177	G3
	Akron‡ 660,328	G3
45710	Albany 905	F7
43001	Alexandria 489	E5
45812	Alger 992	C4
44601	Alliance 24,315	H4
43102	Amanda 720	E6
†45201	Amberley 3,442	C9
45102	Amelia 1,108	D10
44001	Amherst 10,638	F3
43903	Amsterdam 783	J5
44003	Andover 1,205	J2
45302	Anna 1,038	B5
45303	Ansonia 1,267	A5
45813	Antwerp 1,765	A3
44606	Apple Creek 741	G4
44804	Arcadia 580	D3
45304	Arcanum 2,002	A6
43502	Archbold 3,318	B2
45814	Arlington 1,187	C4
†45201	Arlington Heights 1,082	C9
44805	Ashland⊙ 20,326	F4
43003	Ashley 1,057	E5
44004	Ashtabula 23,449	J2
43103	Ashville 2,046	E6
45701	Athens⊙ 19,743	F7
44807	Attica 865	E3
44201	Atwater 975	H3
44202	Aurora 8,177	H3
44010	Austinburg 900	J2
44515	Austintown 33,636	J3
44011	Avon 7,241	F3
44012	Avon Lake 13,222	F2
†43512	Ayersville 950	B3
†44805	Bailey Lakes 397	F4
45612	Bainbridge 1,042	D7
43804	Baltic 563	G5
43105	Baltimore 2,689	E6
44203	Barberton 29,751	G4
43713	Barnesville 4,633	H6
43905	Barton 1,039	J5
45103	Batavia⊙ 1,896	B7
†44870	Bay View 804	E3
44140	Bay Village 17,846	G9
44608	Beach City 1,083	G4
44122	Beachwood 9,983	J9
43716	Beallsville 601	J6
45808	Beaverdam 492	C4
44146	Bedford 15,056	H9
†44146	Bedford Heights 13,214	J9
43906	Bellaire 8,241	J5
45305	Bellbrook 5,174	C6
43310	Belle Center 930	C4
43311	Bellefontaine⊙ 11,888	C5
44811	Bellevue 8,187	E3
44813	Bellville 1,714	E4
43718	Belmont 714	J5
44609	Beloit 1,093	J4
45714	Belpre 7,193	G7
44017	Berea 19,567	G10
43908	Bergholz 914	J4
44814	Berlin Heights 756	F3
45106	Bethel 2,231	B8
43719	Bethesda 1,429	H5
44815	Bettsville 752	D3
45715	Beverly 1,471	G6
43209	Bexley 13,405	E6
45107	Blanchester 3,202	B7
44817	Bloomdale 744	D3
43106	Bloomingburg 869	D6
44818	Bloomville 1,019	D3
†45242	Blue Ash 9,506	C9
45817	Bluffton 3,310	C4
44512	Boardman 39,161	J3
44612	Bolivar 989	G4
†44264	Boston Heights 781	J10
45306	Botkins 1,372	B5
44695	Bowerston 487	H5
43402	Bowling Green⊙ 25,728	C3
45308	Bradford 2,166	B5
43406	Bradner 1,175	C3
44211	Brady Lake 470	H3
†44101	Bratenahl 1,485	H9
44141	Brecksville 10,132	H10
43107	Bremen 1,432	F6
44613	Brewster 2,321	G4
43912	Bridgeport 2,642	J5
†45211	Bridgetown 11,460	B9
43913	Brilliant 1,751	J5
†44240	Brimfield 3,161	H3
44402	Bristolville 900	J3
†44141	Broadview Heights 10,920	H10
44403	Brookfield 1,527	J3
44144	Brooklyn 12,342	H9
†44131	Brooklyn Heights 1,653	H9
44142	Brook Park 26,195	G9
†43912	Brookside 887	J5
45309	Brookville 4,322	B6
44212	Brunswick 28,104	G3
43506	Bryan⊙ 7,879	A3
45716	Buchtel 585	F7
43008	Buckeye Lake	F6
44820	Bucyrus⊙ 13,433	E4
†45680	Burlington 900	F9
44021	Burton 1,401	H3
44822	Butler 991	F4
43723	Byesville 2,572	G6
43907	Cadiz⊙ 4,058	J5
45820	Cairo 596	B4
43920	Calcutta 1,121	J4
43724	Caldwell⊙ 1,935	G6
43314	Caledonia 759	D4
43725	Cambridge⊙ 13,573	G5
45311	Camden 1,971	A6
44405	Campbell 11,619	J3
45111	Camp Dennison 625	D9
44614	Canal Fulton 3,481	H4
43110	Canal Winchester 2,749	E6
44406	Canfield 5,535	J3
*44701	Canton⊙ 93,077	H4
	Canton‡ 404,421	H4
43315	Cardington 1,665	E5
43316	Carey 3,674	D4
45005	Carlisle 4,276	B6
43112	Carroll 641	E6
44615	Carrollton⊙ 3,065	J4
44824	Castalia 973	E3
45314	Cedarville 2,799	C6
45822	Celina⊙ 9,137	A4
43011	Centerburg 1,275	E5
45459	Centerville 18,886	B6
44022	Chagrin Falls 4,335	J9
†45631	Chambersburg	F8
44024	Chardon⊙ 4,434	H2
45719	Chauncey 1,050	F7
†45202	Cherry Grove 850	C10
45619	Chesapeake 1,370	E9
44026	Chesterland 2,301	H2
†45211	Cheviot 9,888	B9
45601	Chillicothe⊙ 23,420	E7
45389	Christiansburg 593	C5
*45201	Cincinnati⊙ 385,457	B9
	Cincinnati‡ 1,401,403	B9
43113	Circleville⊙ 11,700	D6
43915	Clarington 558	J6
43115	Clarksburg 483	D7
45113	Clarksville 525	C7
45315	Clayton 752	B6
*44101	Cleveland⊙ 573,822	H9
	Cleveland‡ 1,898,720	H9
44118	Cleveland Heights 56,438	H9
45002	Cleves 2,094	B9
44216	Clinton 1,277	G4
43410	Clyde 5,489	E3
†45638	Coal Grove 2,602	E9
45621	Coalton 639	E7
45828	Coldwater 4,220	A5
†44034	Colebrook 700	J2
44028	Columbia Station 518	G10
44408	Columbiana 4,987	J4
*43201	Columbus (cap.)⊙ 565,032	E6
	Columbus‡ 1,093,293	E6
45830	Columbus Grove 2,313	B4
43811	Conesville 451	G5
44030	Conneaut 13,835	J2
45831	Continental 1,179	B3
45832	Convoy 1,140	A4
45723	Coolville 649	G7
43730	Corning 789	F6
44410	Cortland 5,011	J3
43812	Coshocton⊙ 13,405	G5
†45238	Covedale 5,830	B10
45318	Covington 2,610	B5
†44429	Craig Beach 1,657	H3
44827	Crestline 5,406	E4
44217	Creston 1,828	G3
45806	Cridersville 1,843	B4
43731	Crooksville 2,766	F6
45623	Crown City 513	F8
†45341	Crystal Lakes 1,463	C6
*44221	Cuyahoga Falls 43,890	G3
†44101	Cuyahoga Heights 739	H9
43413	Cygnet 646	C3
44618	Dalton 1,357	G4
43014	Danville 1,127	F5
†43123	Darbydale 825	D6
*45401	Dayton⊙ 193,444	B6
	Dayton‡ 830,070	B6
44411	Deerfield 800	H3
45236	Deer Park 6,745	C9
43512	Defiance⊙ 16,810	B3
43318	Degraff 1,358	C5
43015	Delaware⊙ 18,780	E5
45833	Delphos 7,314	B4
43515	Delta 2,831	B2
44621	Dennison 3,398	H5
†45202	Dent 800	B9
43516	Deshler 1,870	C3
45750	Devola 2,708	H7
43917	Dillonvale 912	J5
44622	Dover 11,782	G4
44230	Doylestown 2,493	G4
43821	Dresden 1,646	G5
43017	Dublin 3,855	D5
43734	Duncan Falls 900	G6
45836	Dunkirk 954	C4
44730	East Canton 1,721	H4
44112	East Cleveland 36,957	H9
†44094	Eastlake 22,104	J8
43920	East Liverpool 16,687	J4
44413	East Palestine 5,306	J4
44626	East Sparta 868	H4
45320	Eaton⊙ 6,839	A6
†44035	Eaton Estates 1,806	G3
43517	Edgerton 1,813	A3
†44004	Edgewood 3,099	J2
43320	Edison 504	E4
43518	Edon 947	A2
45321	Eldorado 509	A6
45807	Elida 1,349	B4
43416	Elmore 1,271	D3
45216	Elmwood Place 2,840	B9
*44035	Elyria⊙ 57,538	F3
45322	Englewood 11,329	B6
45323	Enon 2,597	C6
44117	Euclid 59,999	J9
†45201	Evendale 1,954	C9
45042	Excello 900	B7
45324	Fairborn 29,702	B6
†45201	Fairfax 2,222	C9
45014	Fairfield 30,777	A7
44313	Fairlawn 6,100	G3
44077	Fairport Harbor 3,357	H2
44126	Fairview Park 19,311	G9
45325	Farmersville 950	A6
43521	Fayette 1,222	B2
45120	Felicity 929	B8
45840	Findlay⊙ 35,594	C3
45326	Fletcher 498	B5
43977	Flushing 1,266	J5
45843	Forest 1,633	C4
45405	Forest Park 18,675	B9
45230	Forestville 950	C10
45844	Fort Jennings 538	B4
45845	Fort Loramie 977	B5
†45426	Fort McKinley	B6
45846	Fort Recovery 1,370	A5
†45801	Fort Shawnee 4,541	B4
44830	Fostoria 15,743	D3
45628	Frankfort 1,008	D7
45005	Franklin 10,711	B6
45629	Franklin Furnace 1,093	E8
43822	Frazeysburg 1,025	F5
44627	Fredericksburg 511	G4
43019	Fredericktown 2,299	F5
43973	Freeport 525	H5
43420	Fremont⊙ 17,834	D3
45630	Friendship 900	D8
43230	Gahanna 18,001	E5
44833	Galion 12,391	E4
45631	Gallipolis⊙ 5,576	F8
43022	Gambier 2,056	F5
44125	Garfield Heights 34,938	J9
44231	Garrettsville 1,769	H3
44040	Gates Mills 2,236	J9
44041	Geneva 6,655	J2
44043	Geneva-on-the-Lake 1,634	H2
43430	Genoa 2,213	D2
45121	Georgetown⊙ 3,467	C8
45327	Germantown 5,015	B6
45328	Gettysburg 545	A5
43431	Gibsonburg 2,479	D3
44420	Girard 12,517	J3
45848	Glandorf 746	B3
45246	Glendale 2,368	C9
†44139	Glenwillow 492	J10
45732	Glouster 2,211	F6
44629	Gnadenhutten 1,320	G5
†45201	Golf Manor 4,317	C9
45122	Goshen	B7
44044	Grafton 2,231	F3
43522	Grand Rapids 962	C3
44045	Grand River 412	H2
†43212	Grandview Heights 7,420	D6
43023	Granville 3,851	E5
45330	Gratis 809	A6
43322	Green Camp 475	D4
45123	Greenfield 5,150	D7
45218	Greenhills 4,927	B9
44232	Greensburg 950	G4
44836	Green Springs 1,568	E3
44630	Greentown 300	H4
45331	Greenville⊙ 12,999	A5
44837	Greenwich 1,458	E3
43123	Grove City 16,816	D6
43125	Groveport 3,286	E6
45849	Grover Hill 486	B3
45634	Hamden 1,010	F7
45130	Hamersville 688	C8
*45011	Hamilton⊙ 63,189	A7
	Hamilton-Middletown‡ 258,787	A7
43524	Hamler 625	B3
43931	Hannibal 550	J6
†43055	Hanover 926	F5
43126	Harrisburg 363	D6
45030	Harrison 5,855	A9
45850	Harrod 506	C4
†44085	Hartsgrove 200	J2
44632	Hartville 1,772	H4
43525	Haskins 568	C3
43127	Haydenville 395	F7
44838	Hayesville 518	F4
43055	Heath 6,969	F5
43025	Hebron 2,035	E6
43526	Hicksville 3,929	A3
†44143	Highland Heights 5,739	J9
43026	Hilliard 8,008	D5
45133	Hillsboro⊙ 6,356	C7
44234	Hiram 1,360	H3
43527	Holgate 1,315	B3
43528	Holland 1,048	C2
45033	Hooven 550	A9
43976	Hopedale 857	J5
44425	Hubbard 9,245	J3
45424	Huber Heights 35,480	B6
44236	Hudson 4,615	H3
†44022	Hunting Valley 786	J9
44839	Huron 7,123	E3
44131	Independence 6,607	H9
†45201	Indian Hill 5,521	C9
43932	Irondale 535	J4
45638	Ironton⊙ 14,290	E8
45640	Jackson⊙ 6,675	E7
45334	Jackson Center 1,310	B5
45740	Jacksonville 651	F7
45335	Jamestown 1,702	C6
44047	Jefferson⊙ 2,952	J2
†43162	Jefferson (West Jefferson) 4,448	D6
43128	Jeffersonville 1,252	C6
44840	Jeromesville 582	F4
43437	Jerry City 512	C3
43986	Jewett 972	H5
43031	Johnstown 3,158	E5
43748	Junction City 754	F6
45853	Kalida 1,019	B4
44240	Kent 26,164	H3
43326	Kenton⊙ 8,605	C4
45429	Kettering 61,186	B6
44637	Killbuck 937	G5
45034	Kings Mills 500	B7
45644	Kingston 1,208	E7
44048	Kingsville	J2
44428	Kinsman 900	J3
43033	Kirkersville 626	E6
†44094	Kirtland 5,969	H2
43951	Lafferty 855	H5
44050	Lagrange 1,258	F3
44250	Lakemore 2,744	H3
43440	Lakeside 850	E2
43331	Lakeview 1,089	C4
44107	Lakewood 61,963	G9
43130	Lancaster⊙ 34,953	E6
43934	Lansing 950	J5
43332	La Rue 861	D4
43135	Laurelville 591	E7
†45501	Lawrenceville 307	C6
45036	Lebanon⊙ 9,636	B7
45135	Leesburg 1,019	D7
44431	Leetonia 2,121	J4
45856	Leipsic 2,171	C3
45338	Lewisburg 1,450	A6
44904	Lexington 3,823	E4
43532	Liberty Center 1,111	B3
*45801	Lima⊙ 47,381	B4
	Lima‡ 218,244	B4
†45201	Lincoln Heights 5,259	C9
43442	Lindsey 571	D3
44432	Lisbon⊙ 3,159	J4
44253	Litchfield 650	F3
43136	Lithopolis 652	E6
45742	Little Hocking 800	G7
45215	Lockland 4,292	C9
44254	Lodi 2,942	F3
43138	Logan⊙ 6,557	F6
43140	London⊙ 6,958	C6
*44052	Lorain 75,416	F3
	Lorain-Elyria‡ 274,909	F3
†44481	Lordstown 3,280	J3
44842	Loudonville 2,945	F4
44641	Louisville 7,996	H4
45140	Loveland 9,106	D9
45744	Lowell 729	H6
44436	Lowellville 1,558	J3
44843	Lucas 753	F4
45648	Lucasville 3,349	E8
43443	Luckey 895	D3
45142	Lynchburg 1,205	C7
44124	Lyndhurst 18,092	J9
43533	Lyons 596	B2
44056	Macedonia 6,571	J10
†45202	Mack	B9
45243	Madeira 9,341	C9
44057	Madison 2,291	H2
44643	Magnolia 986	H4
43758	Malta 956	G6
44644	Malvern 1,032	H4
45144	Manchester 2,313	C8
*44901	Mansfield⊙ 53,927	F4
	Mansfield‡ 131,205	F4
44255	Mantua 1,041	H3
44137	Maple Heights 29,735	H9
†43440	Marblehead 679	E2
45860	Maria Stein 950	A5

(continued on following page)

Agriculture, Industry and Resources

DOMINANT LAND USE

- Hogs, Soft Winter Wheat
- Livestock, Dairy, Soybeans, Cash Grain
- Dairy, General Farming
- General Farming, Livestock, Tobacco
- Fruit, Truck and Mixed Farming
- Forests
- Urban Areas

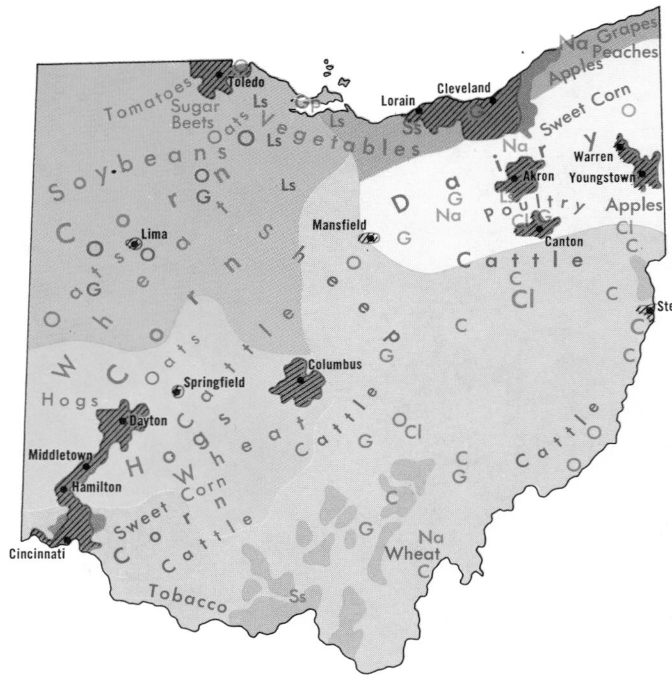
Toledo
Lorain
Cleveland
Warren
Youngstown
Akron
Mansfield
Lima
Canton
Steubenville
Columbus
Springfield
Dayton
Middletown
Hamilton
Cincinnati
Grapes
Peaches
Apples
Tomatoes
Sugar Beets
Oats
Vegetables
Sweet Corn
Soybeans
Dairy
Poultry
Apples
Cattle
Hogs
Wheat
Sweet Corn
Cattle
Tobacco

MAJOR MINERAL OCCURRENCES

- C Coal
- Cl Clay
- G Natural Gas
- Gp Gypsum
- Ls Limestone
- Na Salt
- O Petroleum
- Ss Sandstone
- Major Industrial Areas

45227 Mariemont 3,295 ....C9
45750 Marietta⊙ 16,467 ....G7
43302 Marion⊙ 37,040.............D4
44645 Marshallville 788 ....G4
43935 Martins Ferry 9,331 .... J5
45146 Martinsville 539 ....C7
43040 Marysville⊙ 7,414 ....D5
45040 Mason 8,692 ....B7
44646 Massillon 30,557 ....H4
44438 Masury 1,836 .... J3
†45069 Maud 800 ....B7
43537 Maumee 15,747 ....C2
44124 Mayfield 3,577 .... J9
44124 Mayfield Heights 21,550.... J9
45651 McArthur⊙ 1,912 .... F7
43534 McClure 694 ....C3
45858 McComb 1,608 ....C3
43756 McConnelsville⊙ 2,018.....G6
44437 McDonald 3,744 .... J3
45859 McGuffey 646 ....C4
43044 Mechanicsburg 1,792.......D5
44256 Medina⊙ 15,268 ....G3
45862 Mendon 749 ....A4
44060 Mentor 42,065 ....H2
44060 Mentor-on-the-Lake 7,919 .G2
43540 Metamora 556................C2
45342 Miamisburg 15,304 ....B6
45041 Miamitown 800...............A9
44652 Middlebranch 300............H4
†44017 Middleburg Heights 16,218G10
44062 Middlefield 1,997 ....H3
45863 Middle Point 709.............B4
45760 Middleport 2,971 .... F7
45042 Middletown 43,719...........A6
44653 Midvale 654...................H5
44846 Milan 1,569................... E3
45150 Milford 5,232.................D9
43045 Milford Center 764...........D5
43447 Millbury 955 ....D2
44654 Millersburg⊙ 3,247 .... F4
43046 Millersport 844 .... E6
†45011 Millville 809 ....A7
44656 Mineral City 884 ....H4
44657 Minerva 4,549.................H4
†43201 Minerva Park 1,618 .... E5
43938 Mingo Junction 4,834 ...... J5
45865 Minster 2,557 ....B5
44260 Mogadore 4,190 ....H3
45050 Monroe 4,256 ....B7
44847 Monroeville 1,329 .... E3
45242 Montgomery 10,088 ....C9
43543 Montpelier 4,431..............A2
†45439 Moraine 5,325.................B6
†44022 Moreland Hills 3,083 .... J9
45152 Morrow 1,254 ....B7
43338 Mount Gilead⊙ 2,911 ...... E4
45231 Mount Healthy 7,562.........B9
45154 Mount Orab 1,573............C7
43939 Mount Pleasant 616 .... J5
43143 Mount Sterling 1,623 ....D6
43050 Mount Vernon⊙ 14,323 ... E5
43340 Mount Victory 667...........D4
44262 Munroe Falls 4,731..........H3
43144 Murray City 579.............. F6
43545 Napoleon⊙ 8,614 ....B3
44662 Navarre 1,343 ....H4
43940 Neffs 1,106 .... J5
44441 Negley 917 .... J4
45764 Nelsonville 4,567............. F7
44849 Nevada 945 ....D4
43055 Newark⊙ 41,200 .... F5
Newark‡ 120,981............ F5
45662 New Boston 3,188............E8
45869 New Bremen 2,393...........B5
†44101 Newburgh Heights 2,678...H9
†45201 New Burlington 900 ....B9
45344 New Carlisle 6,498 ....C6
43832 Newcomerstown 3,986 .....G5
43762 New Concord 1,860..........G6
43145 New Holland 783 ....D6
45871 New Knoxville 760............B5
45345 New Lebanon 4,501..........B6
43764 New Lexington⊙ 5,179 .... F6
44851 New London 2,449.......... F3
45346 New Madison 1,008.........A6
45767 New Matamoras.............. J6
45011 New Miami 2,980.............A7
44442 New Middletown 2,195 ..... J4
45347 New Paris 1,709 ....A6
44663 New Philadelphia⊙ 16,883 G5
45768 Newport 975...................H7
45157 New Richmond 2,769.......B8
43766 New Straitsville 937 .... F6
44444 Newton Falls 4,960........... J3
45244 Newtown 1,817 .... C10
45159 New Vienna 1,133 ....C7
44854 New Washington 1,213..... E4
44445 New Waterford 1,314 .... J4
44446 Niles 23,088 .... J3
45872 North Baltimore 3,127 ......C3
45052 North Bend 546 ....B9
44450 North Bloomfield 650 .... J3
44720 North Canton 14,228........H4
45239 North College Hill 11,114 ..B9
44855 North Fairfield 525...........E3
44067 Northfield 3,913.............J10
44707 North Industry H4
44068 North Kingsville 2,939 ...... J2
43060 North Lewisburg 1,072 .....C5
44452 North Lima 800 .... J4
†44057 North Madison 8,741 ....H2
44070 North Olmsted 36,486 ......G9
†44081 North Perry 897..............H2
†44101 North Randall 1,054.........H9
45414 Northridge 9,720.............B6
44039 North Ridgeville 21,522 .... F3
44133 North Royalton 17,671 ... H10
†43619 Northwood 5,495 ....D2
†43701 North Zanesville 2,166......G6
44203 Norton 12,242.................G3
44857 Norwalk⊙ 14,358 .... E3
45212 Norwood 26,342.............C9
43449 Oak Harbor 2,678 ....D2
45656 Oak Hill 1,713 .... E8
†45419 Oakwood 9,372 ....B6
†44146 Oakwood 3,786 ....H9
45873 Oakwood 886..................B3
44074 Oberlin 8,660 .... F3
†43201 Obetz 3,095.................... E6
45874 Ohio City 881 ....A4
44138 Olmsted Falls 5,868 ....G9
44862 Ontario 4,123.................. E4
†44101 Orange 2,376.................. J9
43616 Oregon 18,675 ....D2
44667 Orrville 7,511 ....G4
44076 Orwell 1,067................... J2
45875 Ottawa⊙ 3,874 ....B3
†43601 Ottawa Hills 4,065...........C2
45876 Ottoville 833 ....B4
45160 Owensville 858 ....B7
45056 Oxford 17,655.................A6
44077 Painesville⊙ 16,391 ....H2
45877 Pandora 977 ....C4
44080 Parkman 600 ....H3
44129 Parma 92,548 ....H9
†44130 Parma Heights 23,112......G9
43062 Pataskala 2,284 .... E5
45879 Paulding⊙ 2,754 ....A3
45880 Payne 1,399 ....A3
45660 Peebles 1,790 ....D8
43450 Pemberville 1,321 ....C3
44264 Peninsula 604 ....G3
†44124 Pepper Pike 6,177 .... J9
44081 Perry 961.......................H2
43551 Perrysburg 10,215............C2
44864 Perrysville 836................ F4
45354 Phillipsburg 705..............B6
43771 Philo 799.......................G6
43147 Pickerington 3,917 .... E6
45661 Piketon 1,726.................. E7
43554 Pioneer 1,133 ....A2
45356 Piqua 20,480 ....B5
43064 Plain City 2,102..............D5
43772 Pleasant City 481 ....G6
45359 Pleasant Hill 1,051 ....B5
43148 Pleasantville 780 .... F6
44865 Plymouth 1,939............... E4
44514 Poland 3,084 .... J3
45769 Pomeroy⊙ 2,728............G7
43452 Port Clinton⊙ 7,223 ....E2
45770 Portland 150...................G7
45662 Portsmouth⊙ 25,943.......D8
43837 Port Washington 622 ....G5
43942 Powhatan Point 2,181 ...... J6
45669 Proctorville 975 .... F9
43342 Prospect 1,159...............D5
43456 Put-in-Bay 146 ....E2
43773 Quaker City 698 ....H6
43343 Quincy 633.....................C5
45771 Racine 908.....................G8
44265 Randolph 900 ....H3
44266 Ravenna⊙ 11,987...........H3
43943 Rayland 566 .... J5
45215 Reading 12,843 ....C9
†44202 Reminderville 1,960 ....J10
†45202 Remington 600................C9
45773 Reno 576.......................H7
†43412 Reno Beach D2
44867 Republic 656..................D3
43068 Reynoldsburg 20,661 .... E6
44286 Richfield 3,437 ....G3
43944 Richmond 624................ J5
†44045 Richmond (Grand
River) 412 ....H2
45673 Richmond Dale 950 .... E7
44143 Richmond Heights 10,095 .H9
43344 Richwood 2,181 ....D5
45674 Rio Grande 864 .... F8
45167 Ripley 2,174 ....C8
43457 Risingsun 698 ....C3
44270 Rittman 6,063 ....G4
†43085 Riverlea 528 ....D5
44670 Robertsville 600 ....H4
44084 Rock Creek 652 .... J2
45882 Rockford 1,245 ....A4
44116 Rocky River 21,084 ....G9
44085 Rome 210...................... J2
44272 Rootstown 900 ....H3
†45662 Rosemount 1,747............D8
43777 Roseville 1,915............... F6
45061 Ross 2,767 ....B9
43460 Rossford 5,978 ....C2
45236 Rossmoyne C9
†43943 Rush Run 560................. J5
43347 Rushsylvania 610 ....C5
43348 Russells Point 1,156 ....C5
45775 Rutland 635................... F7
45169 Sabina 2,799 ....C7
†44067 Sagamore Hills J10
45217 Saint Bernard 5,396.........B9
43950 Saint Clairsville⊙ 5,452 .... J5
45883 Saint Henry 1,596 ....A5
45885 Saint Marys 8,414...........B4
43072 Saint Paris 1,742 ....C5
44460 Salem 12,869 .... J4
43945 Salineville 1,629.............. J4
44870 Sandusky⊙ 31,360 .... E3
44671 Sandyville 500 ....H4
45171 Sardinia 826 ....C7
43946 Sardis 865 .... J6
43988 Scio 1,003 ....H5
†45662 Sciotodale 1,191 .... E8
45679 Seaman 1,039.................C8
44672 Sebring 5,078 ....H4
†44131 Seven Hills 13,650 ....H9
45062 Seven Mile 841...............A7
44273 Seville 1,568...................G3
43947 Shadyside 4,315 .... J6
44120 Shaker Heights 32,487 .....H9
45241 Sharonville 10,108...........C9
43782 Shawnee 924 .... F6
†44052 Sheffield 1,886 .... F3
44054 Sheffield Lake 10,484....... F3
44875 Shelby 9,646 .... E4
43556 Sherwood 915.................A3
44878 Shiloh 857 .... E4
44676 Shreve 1,608 .... F4
45365 Sidney⊙ 17,657..............B5
†44221 Silver Lake 2,915 ....G3
†45201 Silverton 6,172...............C9
43948 Smithfield 1,308 .... J5
44677 Smithville 1,467..............G4
44139 Solon 14,341 .... J9
43783 Somerset 1,432.............. F6
†44001 South Amherst 1,848 .... F3
†43103 South Bloomfield 934 ....D6
45368 South Charleston 1,682 ....C6
44121 South Euclid 25,713 ....H9
45065 South Lebanon 2,700.......B7
45680 South Point 3,918 .... E9
†44022 South Russell 2,784.........H3
45369 South Vienna 464.............C6
45682 South Webster 886.......... E8
43701 South Zanesville 1,739 ..... F6
44275 Spencer 764 .... F3
45887 Spencerville 2,184 ....B4
45066 Springboro 4,962.............B6
45246 Springdale 10,111 ....B9
*45501 Springfield⊙ 72,563 ....C6
Springfield‡ 183,885........C6
45370 Spring Valley 541 ....C6
44276 Sterling 600....................G4
43952 Steubenville⊙ 26,400....... J5
Steubenville-Weirton‡
163,099 .... J5
43787 Stockport 558 ....G6
43154 Stoutsville 537................ E6
44224 Stow 25,303....................H3
44680 Strasburg 2,091...............G4
44240 Streetsboro 9,055 ....H3
44136 Strongsville 28,577 .... G10
44471 Struthers 13,624 .... J3
43557 Stryker 1,423 ....B3
†44260 Suffield 650 ....H3
44681 Sugarcreek 1,966 ....G5
43074 Sunbury 2,101 .... E5
43558 Swanton 3,424 ....C2
44882 Sycamore 1,059 ....D4
43560 Sylvania 15,527 ....C2
45779 Syracuse 946 ....G7
44278 Tallmadge 15,269............H3
†43771 Taylorsville (Philo) 799......G6
45174 Terrace Park 2,044 ....D9
45780 The Plains 2,044............. F7
43076 Thornville 838 .... F6
44883 Tiffin⊙ 19,549 ....D3
43963 Tiltonsville 1,750............. J5
†44094 Timberlake 885............... J8
45371 Tipp City 5,595...............B6
†45245 Tobasco 950 .... C10
*43601 Toledo⊙ 354,635 ....D2
Toledo‡ 791,599 ....D2
43964 Toronto 6,934 .... J5
45067 Trenton 6,401 ....B7
45782 Trimble 579 .... F7
45426 Trotwood 7,802...............B6
45373 Troy⊙ 19,086.................B5
44682 Tuscarawas 917..............H5
44087 Twinsburg 7,632............J10
44683 Uhrichsville 6,130............H5
45322 Union 5,219 ....B6
†47390 Union City 1,716.............A5
44685 Uniontown 875 ....H4
44118 University Heights 15,401..H9
43221 Upper Arlington 35,648.....D6
43351 Upper Sandusky⊙ 5,967 ..D4
43078 Urbana⊙ 10,762 ....C5
†43123 Urbancrest 880...............D6
43080 Utica 2,238 .... F5
†43201 Valley View 730 ....D6
†44101 Valleyview 1,576 ....H9
45377 Vandalia 13,161 ....B6
45890 Vanlue 390.....................C4
45891 Van Wert⊙ 11,035.........A4
44089 Vermilion 11,012 .... F3
45378 Verona 571.....................A6
45380 Versailles 2,384 ....A5
44473 Vienna 900.................... J3
44281 Wadsworth 15,166 ....G3
†44094 Waite Hill 529 ....H2
45687 Wakefield 300 .... E8
44889 Wakeman 906 .... F3
43465 Walbridge 2,900 ....C2
44687 Walnut Creek 550............G4
†44146 Walton Hills 2,199..........J10
45895 Wapakoneta⊙ 8,402........B4
45785 Warner 250 ....H6
*44481 Warren⊙ 56,629 .... J3
44128 Warrensville
Heights 16,565 ....H9
43844 Warsaw 765 ....G5
43160 Washington Court
House⊙ 12,682...........D6
44490 Washingtonville 865......... J4
45786 Waterford 600.................G6
43566 Waterville 3,884..............C3
43567 Wauseon⊙ 6,173 ....B2
45690 Waverly⊙ 4,603 ....D7
43466 Wayne 894.....................C3
44688 Waynesburg 1,160 ....H4
45896 Waynesfield 826 ....C4
45068 Waynesville 1,796 ....B6
44090 Wellington 4,146............. F3
45692 Wellston 6,016 .... F7
43968 Wellsville 5,095 .... J4
45381 West Alexandria 1,313......A6
45449 West Carrollton 13,148 .....B6
43081 Westerville 23,414............D5
44491 West Farmington 563 .... J3
44251 Westfield Center 791 ....G3
43162 West Jefferson 4,448 ....D6
43845 West Lafayette 2,225 ....G5
44145 Westlake 19,483..............G9
43357 West Liberty 1,653............C5
43358 West Mansfield 716 ....C5
45383 West Milton 4,119............B6
43569 Weston 1,708 ....C3
†45662 West Portsmouth 4,095 ....D8
44287 West Salem 1,357............ F4
45693 West Union⊙ 2,791 ....C8
43570 West Unity 1,639.............B2
45694 Wheelersburg 4,796......... E8
43213 Whitehall 21,299............. E6
43571 Whitehouse 2,137 ....C2
44092 Wickliffe 16,790.............. J9
44890 Willard 5,720 .... E3
45176 Williamsburg 1,952..........B7
44093 Williamsfield 950............. J2
43164 Williamsport 792.............D6
44094 Willoughby 19,329 .... J8
†44094 Willoughby Hills 8,612...... J9
44094 Willowick 17,834 .... J8
45898 Willshire 564...................A4
45177 Wilmington⊙ 10,431 ....C7
45697 Winchester 1,080............C8
44288 Windham 3,721...............H3
43952 Wintersville 4,724............ J5
45245 Withamsville 975........... C10
†45201 Woodlawn 2,715..............C9
†44101 Woodmere 877................ J9
43793 Woodsfield⊙ 3,145 ....H6
43469 Woodville 2,050...............D3
44691 Wooster⊙ 19,289............G4
43085 Worthington 15,016......... E5
45215 Wyoming 8,282...............C9
45385 Xenia⊙ 24,653 ....C6
45387 Yellow Springs 4,077 ....C6
43971 Yorkville 1,447 .... J5
*44501 Youngstown⊙ 115,436 .... J3
Youngstown-Warren‡
531,350...................... J3
43701 Zanesville⊙ 28,655 ....G6
44697 Zoar 264........................H4
44698 Zoarville 125 ....H4

OTHER FEATURES

Atwood (lake) H4
Auglaize (riv.) B4
Berlin (lake) H4
Big Walnut (creek) E5
Black (riv.)............................. F3
Black Fork, Mohican (riv.)........... F4
Blanchard (riv.) C4
Blennerhassett (isl.)...................G7
Buckeye (lake) F6
Campbell (hill) C5
Captina (creek).........................J6
Cedar (pt.)..............................D2
Chagrin (riv.)........................... J8
Clear Fork (res.)....................... E4
Clear Fork, Mohican (riv.) F4
Clendening (lake) H5
Cleveland-Hopkins Mun. Airport G9
Cuyahoga (riv.) H10
Darby (creek) D5
Deer (creek)............................D6
Delaware (lake) E5
Dillon (lake) F5
Dover (lake) H4
Duck (creek) H6
Erie (lake)..............................H1
Eufaula (res.)..........................L4
Grand (riv.)............................H2
Great Miami (riv.) A7
Hocking (riv.) F7
Hoover (res.)........................... E5
Huron (riv.)............................ E3
Indian (lake)...........................C5
James A. Garfield Nat'l Hist.
Site G2
Kelleys (isl.)........................... E2
Keystone (res.) K2
Killbuck (creek) G4
Kokosing (riv.)......................... E5
Leesville (lake) H5
Licking (riv.) F5
Little Beaver (creek).................. J4
Little Miami (riv.).....................B6
Little Miami, East Fork (riv.) C7
Little Muskingum (riv.)...............H6
Loramie (lake) B5
Mad (riv.)...............................C6
Maumee (bay) D2
Maumee (riv.)..........................A3
Middle Bass (isl.) E2
Mohican (riv.)......................... F4
Mosquito Creek (lake) J3
Mound City Group Nat'l Mon. E7
Muskingum (riv.).......................G6
North Bass (isl.)....................... E2
Ohio (riv.) B8
Ohio Brush (creek)....................D8
Olentangy (riv.) D4
Paint (creek)...........................D7
Perry's Victory and Int'l Peace
Mem. E2
Piedmont (lake)........................H5
Portage (riv.)...........................D3
Pymatuning (res.)..................... J2
Raccoon (creek) F8
Rattlesnake (creek)...................C7
Rickenbacker Air Force Base 1,763. E6
Rocky (riv.).............................G9
Rocky, West Branch (riv.).......... G10
Rocky Fork (lake) D7
Saint Joseph (riv.) A3
Saint Marys (lake).....................A4
Saint Marys (riv.) A4
Salt Fork (creek).......................H5
Sandusky (bay) E3
Sandusky (riv.) D3
Scioto (riv.) D8
Senecaville (lake) H6
Sevenmile (creek) A6
South Bass (isl.) E2
Stillwater (riv.) B5
Symmes (creek) F8
Tappan (lake) H5
Tiffin (riv.) B3
Tuscarawas (riv.).....................H5
Vermilion (riv.)........................ F3
Wabash (riv.) A5
West Sister (isl.) D2
Whiteoak (creek) C7
William H. Taft Nat'l Hist. Site ... C10
Wills (creek)...........................G5
Wills Creek (lake).....................G5
Wright-Patterson Air Force Base
9,155 ....B6
Yellow (creek).......................... J4

⊙County seat.
‡Population of metropolitan area.
† Zip of nearest p.o. * Multiple zips.

AREA 69,956 sq. mi. (181,186 sq. km.)
POPULATION 3,025,290
CAPITAL Oklahoma City
LARGEST CITY Oklahoma City
HIGHEST POINT Black Mesa 4,973 ft. (1516 m.)
SETTLED IN 1889
ADMITTED TO UNION November 16, 1907
POPULAR NAME Sooner State
STATE FLOWER Mistletoe
STATE BIRD Scissor-tailed Flycatcher

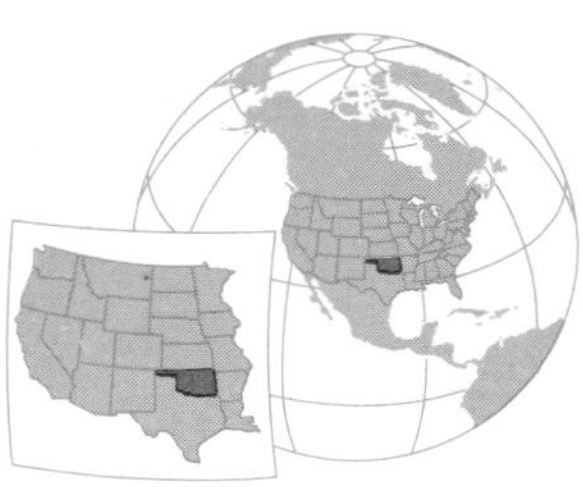

COUNTIES

Adair 18,575 ..... S3
Alfalfa 7,077 ..... K1
Atoka 12,748 ..... O6
Beaver 6,806 ..... E1
Beckham 19,243 ..... G4
Blaine 13,443 ..... K3
Bryan 30,535 ..... O7
Caddo 30,905 ..... K4
Canadian 56,452 ..... K3
Carter 43,610 ..... M6
Cherokee 30,684 ..... R3
Choctaw 17,203 ..... P6
Cimarron 3,648 ..... A1
Cleveland 133,173 ..... M4
Coal 6,041 ..... O5
Comanche 112,456 ..... K5
Cotton 7,338 ..... K6
Craig 15,014 ..... R1
Creek 59,016 ..... O3
Custer 25,995 ..... H3
Delaware 23,946 ..... S2
Dewey 5,922 ..... H2
Ellis 5,596 ..... G2
Garfield 62,820 ..... L2
Garvin 27,856 ..... M5
Grady 39,490 ..... L5
Grant 6,518 ..... L1
Greer 7,028 ..... G5
Harmon 4,519 ..... G5
Harper 4,715 ..... G1
Haskell 11,010 ..... R4
Hughes 14,338 ..... O4
Jackson 30,356 ..... H5
Jefferson 8,183 ..... L6
Johnston 10,356 ..... N6
Kay 49,852 ..... M1
Kingfisher 14,187 ..... L3
Kiowa 12,711 ..... J5
Latimer 9,840 ..... R5
Le Flore 40,698 ..... S5
Lincoln 26,601 ..... N3
Logan 26,881 ..... M3
Love 7,469 ..... M7
Major 8,772 ..... K2
Marshall 10,550 ..... N6
Mayes 32,261 ..... R2
McClain 20,291 ..... L5
McCurtain 36,151 ..... S6
McIntosh 15,562 ..... P4
Murray 12,147 ..... M6
Muskogee 66,939 ..... R3
Noble 11,573 ..... M2
Nowata 11,486 ..... P1
Okfuskee 11,125 ..... O3
Oklahoma 568,933 ..... M3
Okmulgee 39,169 ..... P3
Osage 39,327 ..... O1
Ottawa 32,870 ..... S1
Pawnee 15,310 ..... N2
Payne 62,435 ..... N2
Pittsburg 40,524 ..... P5
Pontotoc 32,598 ..... N5
Pottawatomie 55,239 ..... N4
Pushmataha 11,773 ..... R6
Roger Mills 4,799 ..... G3
Rogers 46,436 ..... P2
Seminole 27,473 ..... N4
Sequoyah 30,749 ..... S3
Stephens 43,419 ..... L6
Texas 17,727 ..... C1
Tillman 12,398 ..... J6
Tulsa 470,593 ..... P2
Wagoner 41,801 ..... P3
Washington 48,113 ..... P1
Washita 13,798 ..... J4
Woods 10,923 ..... J1
Woodward 21,172 ..... H2

CITIES and TOWNS

Zip *Name/Pop.* *Key*

74720 Achille 480 ..... O7
74820 Ada⊙ 15,902 ..... N5
74330 Adair 508 ..... R2
73901 Adams 150 ..... D1
73520 Addington 141 ..... L6
74331 Afton 1,174 ..... S1
74824 Agra 354 ..... N3
74721 Albany 65 ..... O7
73001 Albert 100 ..... K4
74521 Albion 165 ..... R5
74522 Alderson 366 ..... P5
73002 Alex 769 ..... L5
73716 Aline 313 ..... K1
74825 Allen 998 ..... O5
73521 Altus⊙ 23,101 ..... H5
73717 Alva⊙ 6,416 ..... J1
73004 Amber 416 ..... L4
73718 Ames 314 ..... K2
73719 Amorita 66 ..... K1
73005 Anadarko⊙ 6,378 ..... K4
74523 Antlers⊙ 2,989 ..... P6
73006 Apache 1,560 ..... K5
73620 Arapaho⊙ 851 ..... H3
73401 Ardmore⊙ 23,689 ..... M6
74901 Arkoma 2,175 ..... T4
73832 Arnett⊙ 714 ..... G2
74826 Asher 659 ..... N5
74524 Ashland 72 ..... O5
74525 Atoka⊙ 3,409 ..... O6
74827 Atwood 225 ..... O5
74001 Avant 461 ..... O2
†73860 Avard 51 ..... J1
73930 Baker 70 ..... D1
74002 Barnsdall 1,501 ..... O1
†74965 Baron 300 ..... S3
74003 Bartlesville⊙ 34,568 ..... O1
74722 Battiest 250 ..... S6
73932 Beaver⊙ 1,939 ..... F1
74421 Beggs 1,428 ..... P3
†74966 Bengal 300 ..... R5
74723 Bennington 302 ..... P7
74331 Bernice 318 ..... S1
73622 Bessie 245 ..... H4
73008 Bethany 22,130 ..... L3
74724 Bethel 350 ..... S6
†74801 Bethel Acres 2,314 ..... M4
74332 Big Cabin 252 ..... R1
74630 Billings 632 ..... M1
73009 Binger 791 ..... K4
73720 Bison 103 ..... L2
74008 Bixby 6,969 ..... P3
74058 Blackburn 114 ..... N2
74631 Blackwell 8,400 ..... M1
73526 Blair 1,092 ..... H5
73010 Blanchard 1,688 ..... L4
74528 Blanco 215 ..... P5
74529 Blocker 135 ..... P4
†74701 Blue 150 ..... O7
74333 Bluejacket 247 ..... R1
73933 Boise City⊙ 1,761 ..... B1
74726 Bokchito 628 ..... O6
74930 Bokoshe 556 ..... S4
74829 Boley 423 ..... O4
74727 Boswell 702 ..... P6
74830 Bowlegs 522 ..... N4
74009 Bowring 115 ..... O1
74422 Boynton 518 ..... P3
73011 Bradley 284 ..... L5
74423 Braggs 351 ..... R3
74632 Braman 355 ..... M1
73012 Bray 591 ..... L5
73721 Breckinridge 261 ..... L2
†73047 Bridgeport 115 ..... K3
74010 Bristow 4,702 ..... O3
74012 Broken Arrow 35,761 ..... P2
74728 Broken Bow 3,965 ..... S7
74530 Bromide 180 ..... N6
†74873 Brooksville 46 ..... M4
†74437 Bryant 74 ..... P4
73834 Buffalo⊙ 1,381 ..... G1
74931 Bunch 64 ..... S3
74633 Burbank 161 ..... N1
73722 Burlington 206 ..... K1
73430 Burneyville 150 ..... M7
73624 Burns Flat 2,431 ..... H4
73625 Butler 388 ..... H3
74831 Byars 353 ..... N5
†74820 Byng 833 ..... N5
73723 Byron 67 ..... K1
73527 Cache 1,661 ..... J5
74729 Caddo 923 ..... O6
74730 Calera 1,390 ..... O7
73014 Calumet 469 ..... K3
74531 Calvin 315 ..... O5
73835 Camargo 264 ..... H2
74932 Cameron 365 ..... T4
74425 Canadian 279 ..... P4
74533 Caney 147 ..... O6
73724 Canton 854 ..... J2
73626 Canute 676 ..... H4
73725 Capron 54 ..... J1
74335 Cardin 500 ..... S1
73726 Carmen 516 ..... J1
73015 Carnegie 2,016 ..... J4
74832 Carney 622 ..... N3
73727 Carrier 259 ..... K2
73627 Carter 367 ..... H4
74934 Cartersville 79 ..... S4
73016 Cashion 547 ..... L3
74833 Castle 130 ..... O4
74015 Catoosa 1,561 ..... P2
73017 Cement 884 ..... K5
74534 Centrahoma 166 ..... O5
74834 Chandler⊙ 2,926 ..... N3
73528 Chattanooga 403 ..... J6
74426 Checotah 3,454 ..... R4
74016 Chelsea 1,754 ..... P1
73728 Cherokee⊙ 2,105 ..... K1
73838 Chester 104 ..... J2
73628 Cheyenne⊙ 1,207 ..... G3
73018 Chickasha⊙ 15,828 ..... L4
74635 Chilocco 400 ..... M1
73020 Choctaw 7,520 ..... M3
74337 Chouteau 1,559 ..... R2
†74965 Christie 375 ..... S3
73111 Cimarron L3
74017 Claremore⊙ 12,085 ..... R2
74535 Clarita 72 ..... O6
74536 Clayton 833 ..... R5
74835 Clearview 250 ..... O4
73729 Cleo Springs 514 ..... K2
74020 Cleveland 2,972 ..... O2
73601 Clinton 8,796 ..... H3
74538 Coalgate⊙ 2,001 ..... O5
74733 Colbert 1,122 ..... O7
74338 Colcord 530 ..... S2
†73010 Cole 309 ..... L5
73432 Coleman 200 ..... O6
74021 Collinsville 3,556 ..... P2
73021 Colony 185 ..... J4
73529 Comanche 1,937 ..... L6
74339 Commerce 2,556 ..... R1
73022 Concho 300 ..... L3
†73041 Cooperton 31 ..... J5
74022 Copan 960 ..... P1
73632 Cordell⊙ 3,301 ..... H4
73024 Corn 542 ..... J4
†73456 Cornish 115 ..... L6
74428 Council Hill 141 ..... P3
73025 Countyline 550 ..... L6
73730 Covington 715 ..... L2
74429 Coweta 4,554 ..... P3
†74934 Cowlington 546 ..... S4
73027 Coyle 345 ..... M3
73638 Crawford 53 ..... G3
73028 Crescent 1,651 ..... L3
74837 Cromwell 337 ..... N4
74430 Crowder 431 ..... P4
†73446 Cumberland 100 ..... N6
74023 Cushing 7,720 ..... N3
73639 Custer City 530 ..... J3
73029 Cyril 1,220 ..... K5
73731 Dacoma 226 ..... J1
74838 Dale 160 ..... M4
74026 Davenport 974 ..... N3
73530 Davidson 501 ..... J6
73030 Davis 2,782 ..... M5
74636 Deer Creek 174 ..... L1
74027 Delaware 544 ..... P1
73115 Del City 28,523 ..... L4
74028 Depew 682 ..... O3
73531 Devol 186 ..... J6
74431 Dewar 1,048 ..... P4
74029 Dewey 3,545 ..... P1
73031 Dibble 348 ..... L4
†73401 Dickson 996 ..... M6
73641 Dill City 649 ..... H4
74340 Disney 464 ..... S2
73032 Dougherty 210 ..... M6
73733 Douglas 89 ..... L2
74341 Douthat 30 ..... S1
73734 Dover 570 ..... L3
73735 Drummond 482 ..... L2
74030 Drumright 3,162 ..... N3
73533 Duncan⊙ 22,517 ..... L5
74701 Durant⊙ 11,972 ..... O6
73642 Durham 30 ..... G3
74839 Dustin 498 ..... O4
74734 Eagletown 650 ..... S6
73033 Eakly 452 ..... K4
74840 Earlsboro 266 ..... N4
†73532 East Duke 484 ..... H5
73034 Edmond 34,637 ..... M3
73537 Eldorado 688 ..... G6
73538 Elgin 1,003 ..... K5
73644 Elk City 9,579 ..... G4
73539 Elmer 131 ..... H6
73035 Elmore City 582 ..... M5
73935 Elmwood 300 ..... F1
73036 El Reno⊙ 15,486 ..... K3
†73529 Empire City 13 ..... L6
73701 Enid⊙ 50,363 ..... L2
73645 Erick 1,375 ..... G4
74342 Eucha 210 ..... S2
74432 Eufaula⊙ 3,159 ..... P4
74637 Fairfax 1,949 ..... N1
74343 Fairland 1,073 ..... S1
73736 Fairmont 419 ..... L2
†74080 Fair Oaks 346 ..... P2
73737 Fairview⊙ 3,370 ..... J2
†74881 Fallis 22 ..... M3
74935 Fanshawe 416 ..... S5
73840 Fargo 409 ..... G2
73540 Faxon 140 ..... J6
73646 Fay 140 ..... J3
73937 Felt 120 ..... A1
74543 Finley 350 ..... R6
74842 Fittstown 500 ..... N5
74843 Fitzhugh 150 ..... N5
†73569 Fleetwood 12 ..... L7
73541 Fletcher 1,074 ..... K5
74652 Foraker 34 ..... Q1
†73101 Forest Park 1,148 ..... M3
73938 Forgan 611 ..... E1
73038 Fort Cobb 760 ..... K4
74434 Fort Gibson 2,477 ..... R3
73841 Fort Supply 559 ..... G1
74735 Fort Towson 789 ..... R7
73647 Foss 188 ..... H4
73039 Foster 100 ..... M5
73435 Fox 400 ..... M6
74031 Foyil 191 ..... R2
74844 Francis 365 ..... N5
73542 Frederick⊙ 6,153 ..... H6
73842 Freedom 339 ..... H1
73843 Gage 667 ..... G2
74936 Gans 346 ..... S4
73738 Garber 1,215 ..... M2
74736 Garvin 162 ..... S7
73844 Gate 146 ..... F1
73040 Geary 1,700 ..... K3
73436 Gene Autry 178 ..... N6
73543 Geronimo 726 ..... K6
†74531 Gerty 149 ..... O5
74032 Glencoe 490 ..... M2
74033 Glenpool 2,706 ..... P3
74737 Golden 300 ..... S6
†73093 Goldsby 603 ..... L4
73739 Goltry 305 ..... K1
†74740 Goodwater 240 ..... S7
73939 Goodwell 1,186 ..... C1
74435 Gore 445 ..... R3
73041 Gotebo 457 ..... J4
73544 Gould 318 ..... G5
74545 Gowen 75 ..... R5
73042 Gracemont 503 ..... K4
73545 Grady 85 ..... L6
73437 Graham 200 ..... M6
†74652 Grainola 67 ..... N1
73546 Grandfield 1,445 ..... J6
†74349 Grand Lake Towne 36 ..... S1
73547 Granite 1,617 ..... H5
†74437 Grayson 150 ..... P3
73043 Greenfield 233 ..... K3
74344 Grove 3,378 ..... S1
73044 Guthrie⊙ 10,312 ..... M3
73942 Guymon⊙ 8,492 ..... D1
74546 Haileyville 832 ..... P5
74034 Hallett 186 ..... N2
†73069 Hall Park 577 ..... M4
73650 Hammon 866 ..... H3
74845 Hanna 157 ..... P4
74846 Harden City 250 ..... N5
73944 Hardesty 243 ..... D1
73832 Harmon 27 ..... G2
73045 Harrah 2,897 ..... M4
†74740 Harris 192 ..... S7
74547 Hartshorne 2,380 ..... R5
74436 Haskell 1,953 ..... P3
73548 Hastings 246 ..... K6
74740 Haworth 341 ..... S7
73549 Headrick 223 ..... H5
73438 Healdton 3,769 ..... M6
74937 Heavener 2,776 ..... S5
73741 Helena 710 ..... K1
74741 Hendrix 106 ..... O7
73046 Hennepin 300 ..... M5
73742 Hennessey 2,287 ..... L2
74437 Henryetta 6,432 ..... O4
†73086 Hickory 95 ..... N5
73743 Hillsdale 110 ..... K1
73047 Hinton 1,432 ..... K4
73744 Hitchcock 172 ..... K3
74438 Hitchita 126 ..... P3
73651 Hobart⊙ 4,735 ..... J5
74439 Hoffman 407 ..... P4
74848 Holdenville⊙ 5,469 ..... O4
73550 Hollis⊙ 2,958 ..... G5
73551 Hollister 82 ..... J6
74035 Hominy 3,130 ..... O2
74549 Honobia 80 ..... R5
73945 Hooker 1,788 ..... D1
†74366 Hoot Owl 3 ..... R2
73746 Hopeton 42 ..... J1
74940 Howe 562 ..... S5
74440 Hoyt 160 ..... R4
74743 Hugo⊙ 7,172 ..... P7
74441 Hulbert 633 ..... R3
74640 Hunter 276 ..... L1
73048 Hydro 938 ..... J3
74745 Idabel⊙ 7,622 ..... S7
73552 Indiahoma 364 ..... J5
74442 Indianola 254 ..... P4
74036 Inola 1,550 ..... P2
73747 Isabella 113 ..... K2
74346 Jay⊙ 2,100 ..... S2
†73759 Jefferson 92 ..... L1
74037 Jenks 5,876 ..... P2
74038 Jennings 395 ..... N2
73749 Jet 352 ..... K1
73049 Jones 2,270 ..... M3
74347 Kansas 491 ..... S2
74641 Kaw City 283 ..... N1
74039 Kellyville 960 ..... O3

(continued on following page)

Agriculture, Industry and Resources

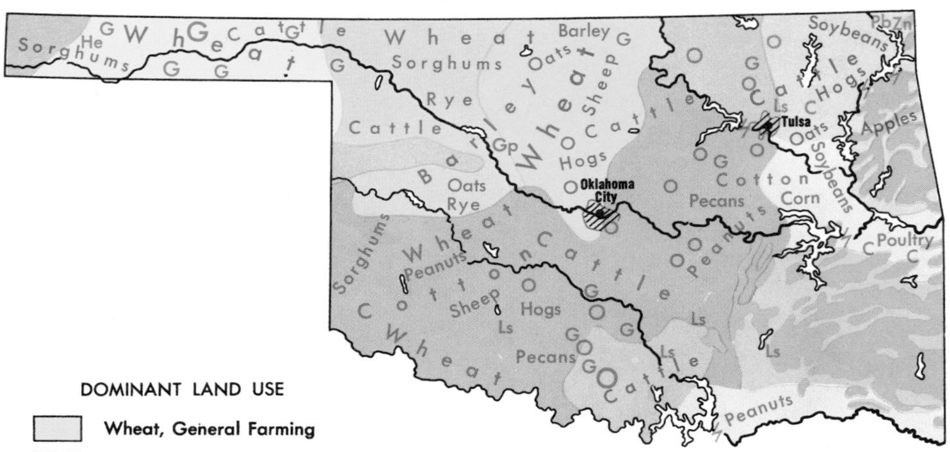

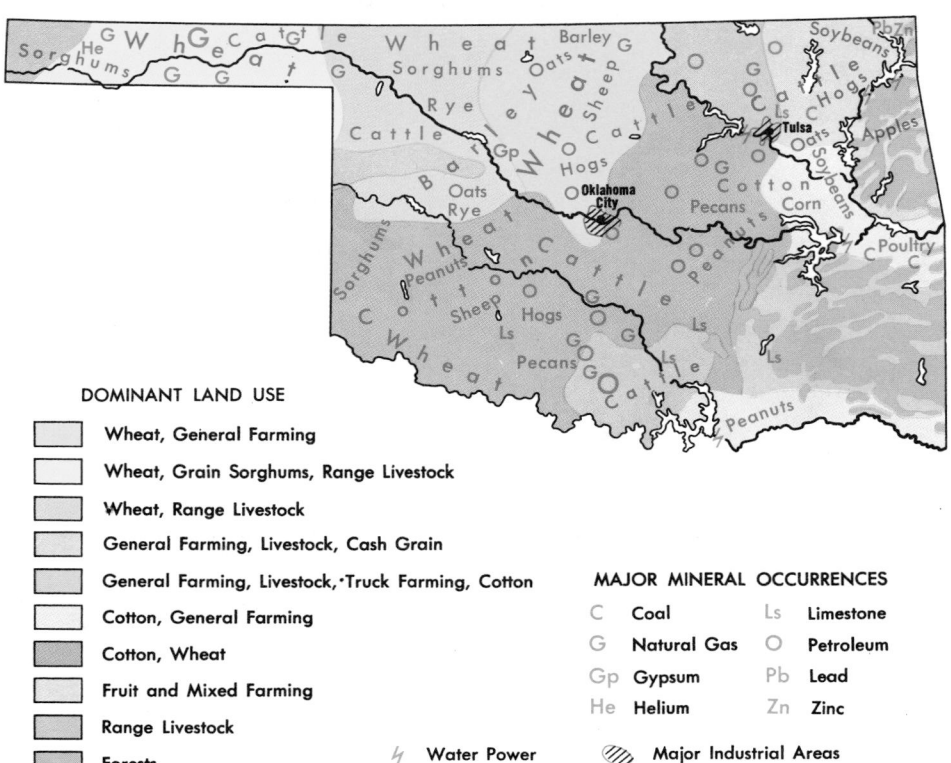

DOMINANT LAND USE

- Wheat, General Farming
- Wheat, Grain Sorghums, Range Livestock
- Wheat, Range Livestock
- General Farming, Livestock, Cash Grain
- General Farming, Livestock, Truck Farming, Cotton
- Cotton, General Farming
- Cotton, Wheat
- Fruit and Mixed Farming
- Range Livestock
- Forests

Water Power

MAJOR MINERAL OCCURRENCES

C Coal
G Natural Gas
Gp Gypsum
He Helium
Ls Limestone
O Petroleum
Pb Lead
Zn Zinc

Major Industrial Areas

74747 Kemp 178.....O7
†74741 Kemp City (Hendrix) 106.....O7
74040 Kendrick 132.....N3
74748 Kenefic 140.....O6
†74365 Kenwood 400.....S2
74941 Keota 661.....S4
74349 Ketchum 326.....R1
73947 Keyes 557.....B1
74041 Kiefer 912.....O3
74601 Kildare 112.....M1
73750 Kingfisher⊙ 4,245.....L3
73439 Kingston 1,171.....N7
74552 Kinta 303.....R4
74553 Kiowa 866.....P5
73847 Knowles 44.....F1
74849 Konawa 1,711.....N5
74554 Krebs 1,754.....P5
73753 Kremlin 301.....L1
73754 Lahoma 537.....K2
74850 Lamar 121.....O4
†73728 Lambert 20.....J1
74643 Lamont 571.....L1
74350 Langley 582.....R2
73050 Langston 443.....M3
73848 Laverne 1,563.....G1
73501 Lawton⊙ 80,054.....K5
   Lawton‡ 112,456.....K5
74351 Leach 350.....S2
73440 Lebanon 382.....N7
73654 Leedey 499.....H3
74942 Leflore 322.....S5
74556 Lehigh 284.....O6
74042 Lenapah 350.....P1
73441 Leon 120.....M7
74043 Leonard 400.....P3
74943 Lequire 250.....R4
73051 Lexington 1,731.....M4
74858 Lima (New Lima) 256.....D4
73052 Lindsay 3,454.....L5
73442 Loco 215.....L6
74352 Locust Grove 1,179.....R2
73849 Logan 18.....F1
73443 Lone Grove 3,369.....M6
73655 Lone Wolf 613.....H5
73755 Longdale 405.....K2
73053 Lookeba 221.....K4
†73842 Lookout 3.....H1
†74063 Lotsee 7.....O2
73553 Loval 21.....J6
73756 Loyal 112.....K3
73757 Lucien 350.....M2
73054 Luther 1,159.....M3
74578 Lutie 100.....R5
74852 Macomb 58.....M4
73446 Madill⊙ 3,173.....N6
73758 Manchester 146.....L1
73554 Mangum⊙ 3,833.....G5
73555 Manitou 322.....J5
74044 Mannford 1,610.....O2
73447 Mannsville 568.....N6
74045 Maramec 101.....N2
74945 Marble City 294.....S3
73448 Marietta⊙ 2,494.....M7
74644 Marland 340.....M1
73055 Marlow 5,017.....K5
73056 Marshall 372.....L2
73556 Martha 219.....H5
74854 Maud 1,444.....N4
73851 May 89.....G1
73656 Mayfield 17.....G4
73057 Maysville 1,396.....M5
74353 Mazie 118.....R2
74501 McAlester⊙ 17,255.....P5
†74441 McBride 91.....N7
74944 McCurtain 549.....R4
74851 McLoud 4,061.....M4
73445 McMillan 50.....M6
73449 Mead 143.....O7
73759 Medford⊙ 1,419.....L1
73557 Medicine Park 437.....J5
74855 Meeker 1,032.....N4
73760 Meno 171.....K2
73058 Meridian 78.....M3
74354 Miami⊙ 14,237.....S1
73110 Midwest City 49,559.....M4
73450 Milburn 376.....O6
74046 Milfay 200.....N3
74856 Mill Creek 431.....N6
74750 Millerton 262.....S7
73451 Milo 25.....M6
73059 Minco 1,489.....L4
74946 Moffett 269.....S4

74947 Monroe 150.....S4
74444 Moodys 250.....S2
73160 Moore 35,063.....M4
73852 Mooreland 1,383.....H2
74445 Morris 1,288.....P3
73061 Morrison 671.....M2
74047 Mounds 1,086.....O3
73559 Mountain Park 557.....J5
73062 Mountain View 1,189.....J4
74557 Moyers 312.....P6
73063 Mulhall 301.....M2
74949 Muldrow 2,538.....S4
74949 Muse 350.....S5
74401 Muskogee⊙ 40,011.....R3
73064 Mustang 7,496.....L4
73853 Mutual 135.....H2
†74354 Narcissa 100.....S1
74646 Nardin 98.....M1
73761 Nash 301.....K1
74558 Nashoba 50.....R6
74049 New Alluwe 129.....R1
73065 Newcastle 3,076.....L4
†73632 New Cordell
   (Cordell)⊙ 3,301.....H4
74647 Newkirk⊙ 2,413.....N1
74884 New Lima 256.....O4
†74060 New Prue (Prue) 554.....O2
74751 New Tulsa 252.....P2
†73116 Nichols Hills 4,171.....L3
74866 Nicoma Park 2,588.....M4
73068 Noble 3,497.....M4
73018 Norge 87.....K4
*73069 Norman⊙ 68,020.....M4
†73701 North Enid 992.....L2

74358 North Miami 544.....R1
74048 Nowata⊙ 4,270.....P1
74452 Oakland 485.....N6
74359 Oaks 591.....S2
73658 Oakwood 140.....J3
74051 Ochelata 480.....P1
74958 Octavia 30.....S5
74052 Oilton 1,244.....N2
73762 Okarche 1,064.....L3
74446 Okay 554.....R3
73763 Okeene 1,601.....K2
74859 Okemah⊙ 3,381.....O4
*73101 Oklahoma City
   (cap.)⊙ 403,136.....L4
   Oklahoma City‡ 834,088.....L4
74447 Okmulgee⊙ 16,263.....O3
74450 Oktaha 376.....R3
74538 Olney 125.....O6
73560 Olustee 721.....H5
73764 Omega 50.....K3
74053 Oologah 798.....P2
73765 Orienta 25.....J2
73073 Orlando 218.....M2
74054 Osage 243.....O2
73561 Oscar 60.....L7
73453 Overbrook 443.....M6
74055 Owasso 6,149.....P2
73659 Putnam 74.....J3
74860 Paden 448.....N3
74951 Panama 1,425.....S4
74559 Panola 75.....R5
73074 Paoli 573.....M5
74435 Paradise Hill 154.....R3
74451 Park Hill 200.....R3

73075 Pauls Valley⊙ 5,664.....M5
74056 Pawhuska⊙ 4,771.....O1
74058 Pawnee⊙ 1,688.....N2
74301 Pensacola 82.....R2
74059 Perkins 1,762.....M3
73076 Pernell 110.....M5
73077 Perry⊙ 5,796.....M2
74862 Pharoah 100.....O4
†74538 Phillips 178.....O6
74360 Picher 2,180.....S1
74752 Pickens 525.....S6
73078 Piedmont 2,016.....L3
74873 Pink 911.....M4
74560 Pittsburg 305.....P5
73079 Pocasset 220.....L4
74902 Pocola 3,268.....T4
74601 Ponca City 26,238.....M1
73766 Pond Creek 949.....L1
74454 Porter 642.....R3
74455 Porum 668.....R4
74953 Poteau⊙ 7,089.....S4
74864 Prague 2,208.....N4
74456 Preston 350.....P3
74060 Prue 554.....O2
74361 Pryor⊙ 8,483.....R2
73080 Purcell⊙ 4,638.....M4
73659 Putnam 74.....J3
74363 Quapaw 1,097.....S1
74085 Quay 50.....N2
†73852 Quinlan 64.....J2
74561 Quinton 1,228.....R4
74650 Ralston 495.....N2
74061 Ramona 567.....P1

†73160 Ranchwood Manor 296.....L4
73562 Randlett 461.....K6
73081 Ratliff City 350.....M6
74562 Rattan 332.....R6
73455 Ravia 487.....N6
74458 Redbird 199.....P3
74563 Red Oak 676.....R5
74651 Red Rock 376.....M2
73563 Reed 48.....G5
†74801 Remus.....N4
†73759 Renfrow 27.....L1
74459 Rentiesville 78.....R4
73660 Reydon 252.....G3
73456 Ringling 1,561.....L6
74754 Ringold 200.....R6
73768 Ringwood 389.....K2
74932 Ripley 451.....N2
73661 Rocky 242.....J4
74865 Roff 729.....N5
74954 Roland 1,472.....S4
73564 Roosevelt 396.....J5
74364 Rose 100.....R2
74831 Rosedale 97.....M5
73855 Rosston 66.....G1
73457 Rubottom 35.....M7
74755 Rufe 150.....R6
73082 Rush Springs 1,451.....L5
73565 Ryan 1,083.....L6
74866 Saint Louis 109.....N4
74365 Salina 1,115.....R2
74955 Sallisaw⊙ 6,403.....S4
73449 Sand Point 179.....N7
74063 Sand Springs 13,121.....O2

74066 Sapulpa⊙ 15,853.....O3
74867 Sasakwa 335.....N5
74565 Savanna 828.....P5
74756 Sawyer 200.....R7
73662 Sayre⊙ 3,177.....G4
74460 Schulter 600.....P3
73663 Seiling 1,103.....J2
73856 Selman 25.....H1
74868 Seminole 8,590.....N4
73664 Sentinel 1,016.....H4
74956 Shady Point 235.....S4
74068 Shamrock 218.....N3
73857 Sharon 171.....H2
73858 Shattuck 1,759.....G2
74801 Shawnee⊙ 26,506.....N4
74652 Shidler 708.....N1
†74701 Silo 43.....N6
74069 Skedee 117.....N2
74070 Skiatook 3,596.....O2
†73051 Slaughterville 1,953.....M4
74071 Slick 187.....O3
74957 Smithville 133.....S5
74567 Snow 200.....R6
73566 Snyder 1,848.....J5
74759 Soper 465.....P6
74072 South Coffeyville 873.....P1
74869 Sparks 772.....N3
73084 Spencer 4,064.....M3
74760 Spencerville 275.....R6
74073 Sperry 1,276.....P2
74959 Spiro 2,221.....S4
73458 Springer 679.....M6
73567 Sterling 702.....K5

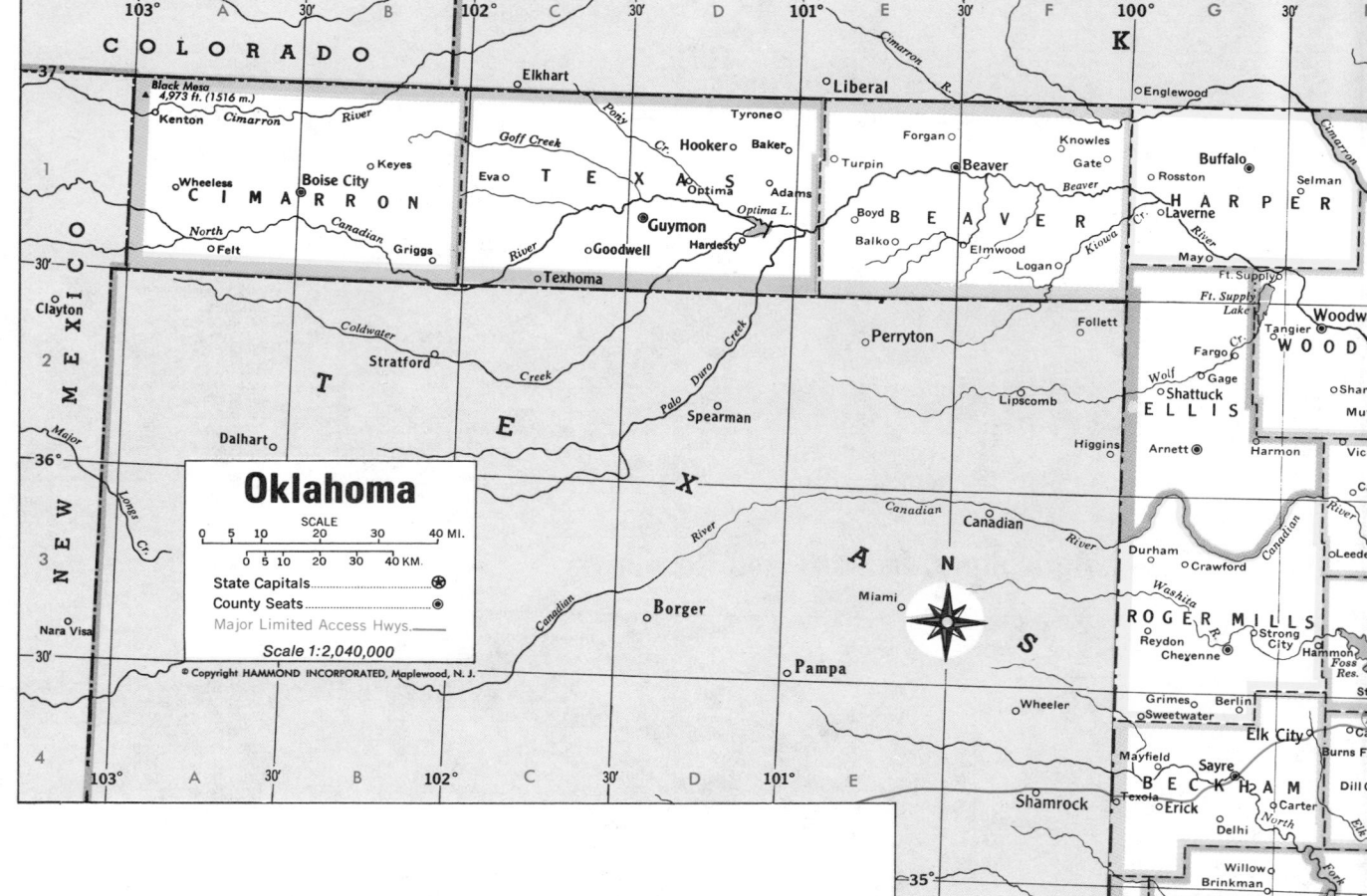

Oklahoma

SCALE
0 5 10 20 30 40 MI.
0 5 10 20 30 40 KM.

State Capitals ⊛
County Seats ⊙
Major Limited Access Hwys.

Scale 1:2,040,000

© Copyright HAMMOND INCORPORATED, Maplewood, N.J.

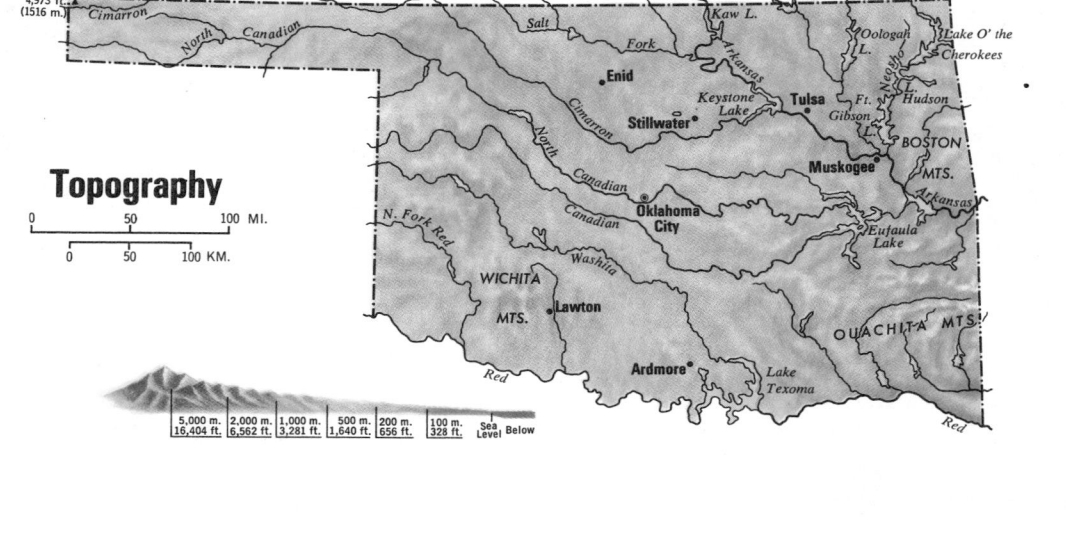

Topography

0 50 100 MI.
0 50 100 KM.

Black Mesa 4,973 ft. (1516 m.)

| 5,000 m. 16,404 ft. | 2,000 m. 6,562 ft. | 1,000 m. 3,281 ft. | 500 m. 1,640 ft. | 200 m. 656 ft. | 100 m. 328 ft. | Sea Level | Below |

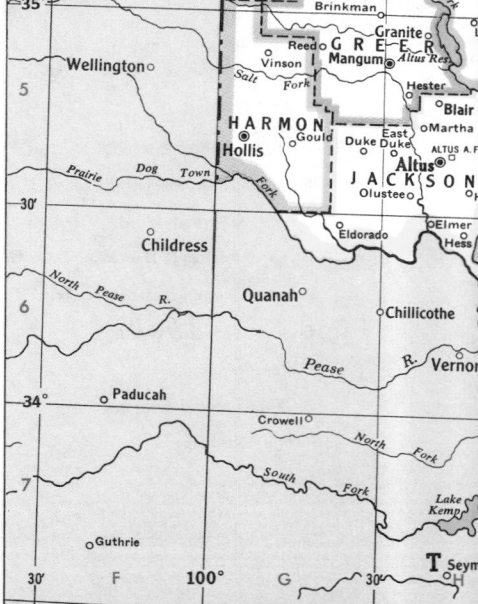

OTHER FEATURES

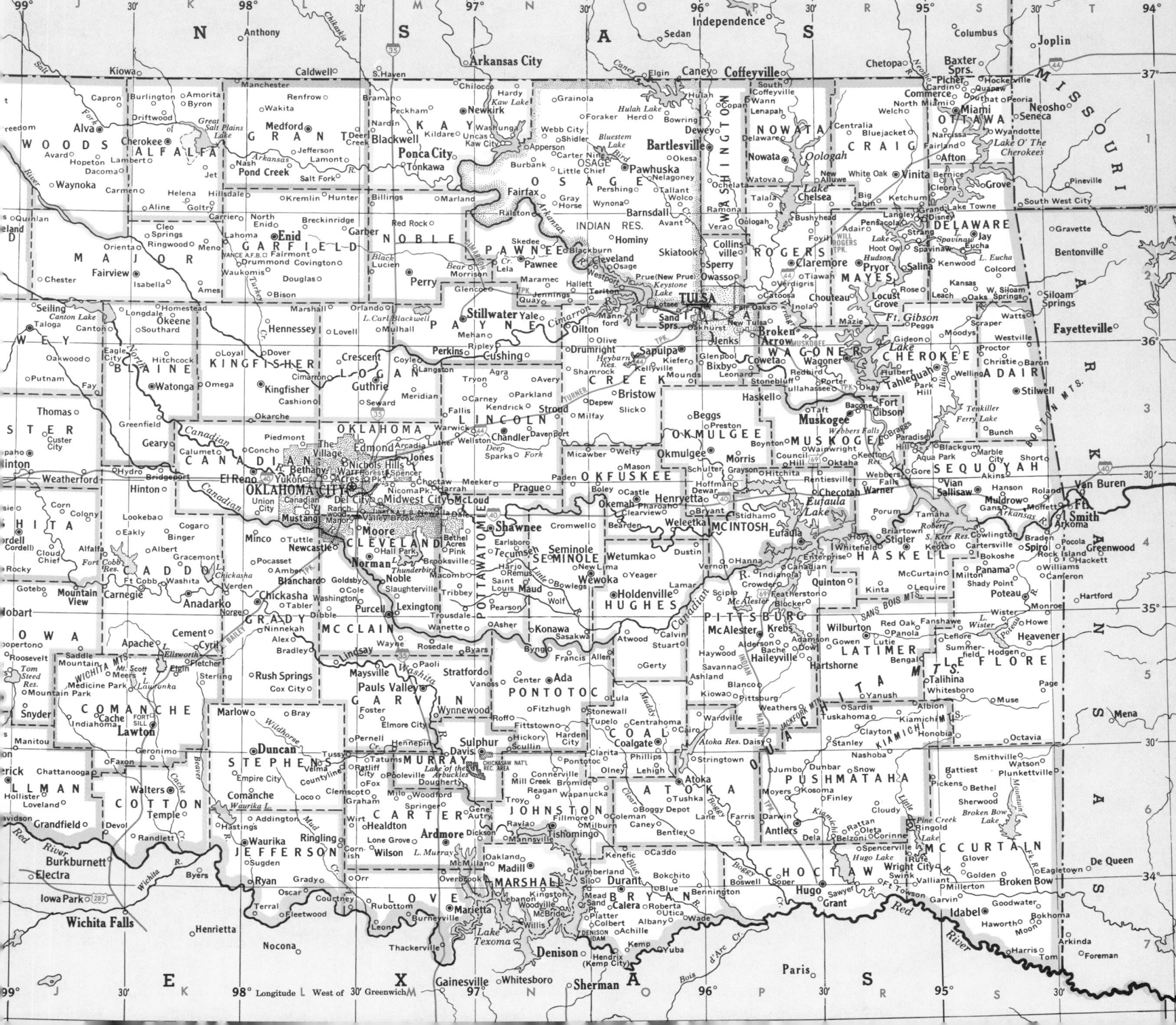

290 Oregon

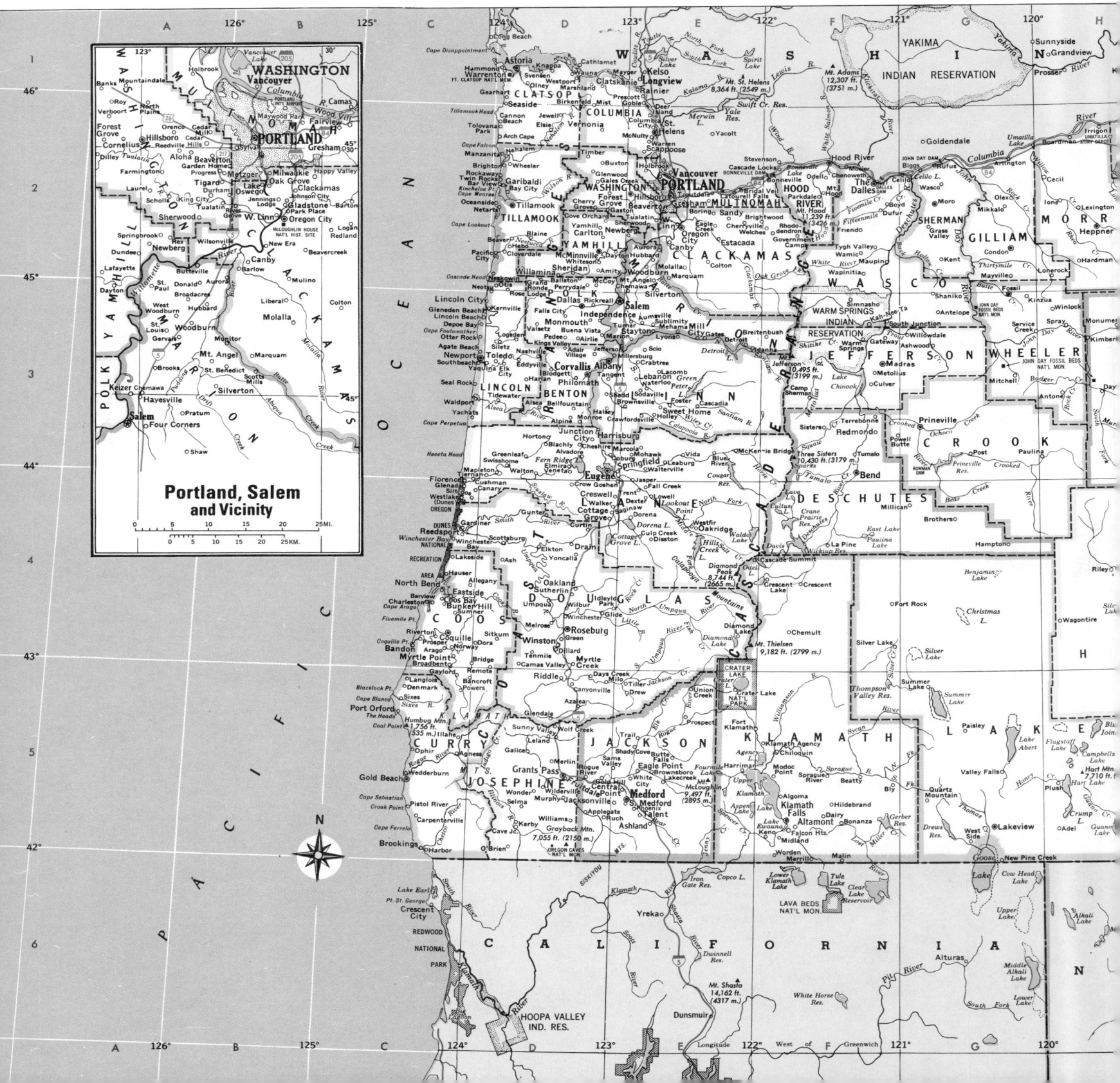

AREA 97,073 sq. mi. (251,419 sq. km.)
POPULATION 2,633,149
CAPITAL Salem
LARGEST CITY Portland
HIGHEST POINT Mt. Hood 11,239 ft.
  (3426 m.)
SETTLED IN 1810
ADMITTED TO UNION February 14, 1859
POPULAR NAME Beaver State
STATE FLOWER Oregon Grape
STATE BIRD Western Meadowlark

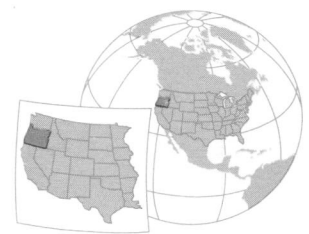

Topography

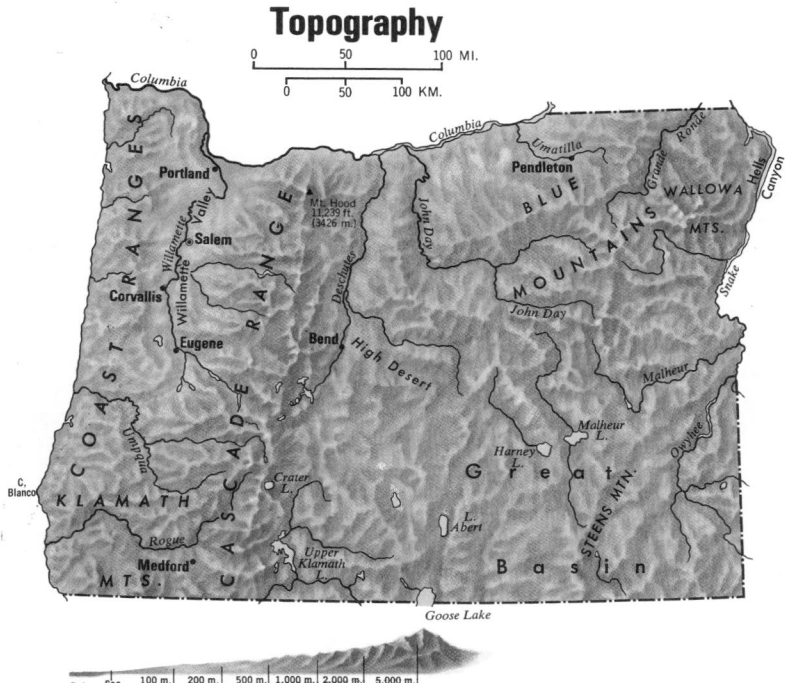

Goose Lake

	Below Sea Level	100 m. 328 ft.	200 m. 656 ft.	500 m. 1,640 ft.	1,000 m. 3,281 ft.	2,000 m. 6,562 ft.	5,000 m. 16,404 ft.

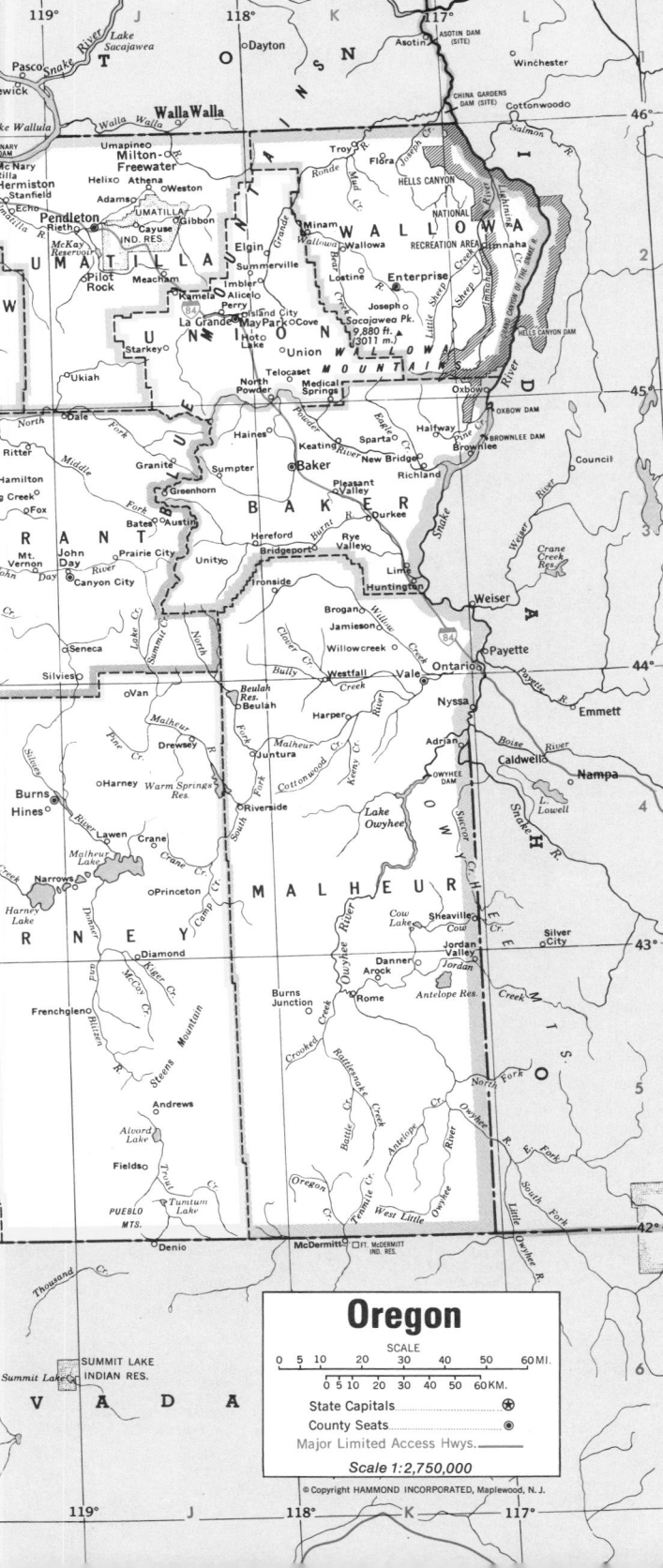

Oregon

SCALE

0 5 10 20 30 40 50 60 MI.

0 5 10 20 30 40 50 60 KM.

State Capitals .... ✳
County Seats .... ⊙
Major Limited Access Hwys. _____

Scale 1:2,750,000

© Copyright HAMMOND INCORPORATED, Maplewood, N.J.

(continued on following page)

Agriculture, Industry and Resources

DOMINANT LAND USE

- Specialized Wheat
- Wheat, Peas
- Specialized Dairy
- Dairy, Poultry, Mixed Farming
- Fruit and Mixed Farming
- Potatoes, General Farming
- General Farming, Dairy, Hay, Sugar Beets
- General Farming, Livestock, Special Crops
- Range Livestock
- Forests
- Nonagricultural Land

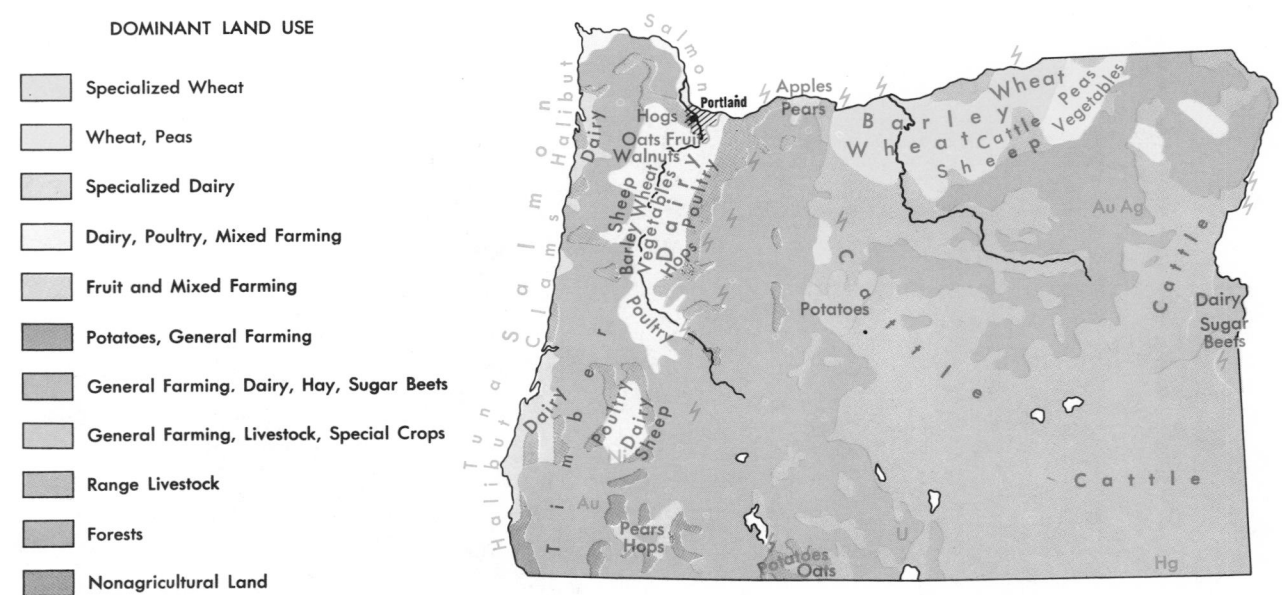

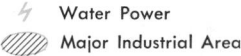

MAJOR MINERAL OCCURRENCES

- Ag Silver
- Au Gold
- Hg Mercury
- Ni Nickel
- U Uranium
- Water Power
- Major Industrial Areas

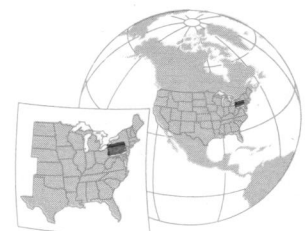

DOMINANT LAND USE

- Specialized Dairy
- Dairy, General Farming
- Fruit and Mixed Farming
- Fruit, Truck and Mixed Farming
- General Farming, Livestock, Tobacco
- General Farming, Livestock, Fruit, Tobacco
- Forests
- Urban Areas

AREA 45,308 sq. mi. (117,348 sq. km.)
POPULATION 11,863,895
CAPITAL Harrisburg
LARGEST CITY Philadelphia
HIGHEST POINT Mt. Davis 3,213 ft. (979 m.)
SETTLED IN 1682
ADMITTED TO UNION December 12, 1787
POPULAR NAME Keystone State
STATE FLOWER Mountain Laurel
STATE BIRD Ruffed Grouse

MAJOR MINERAL OCCURRENCES

C	Coal	G	Natural Gas	Sl	Slate
Cl	Clay	Ls	Limestone	Ss	Sandstone
Co	Cobalt	O	Petroleum	Zn	Zinc
Fe	Iron Ore				

Water Power
Major Industrial Areas

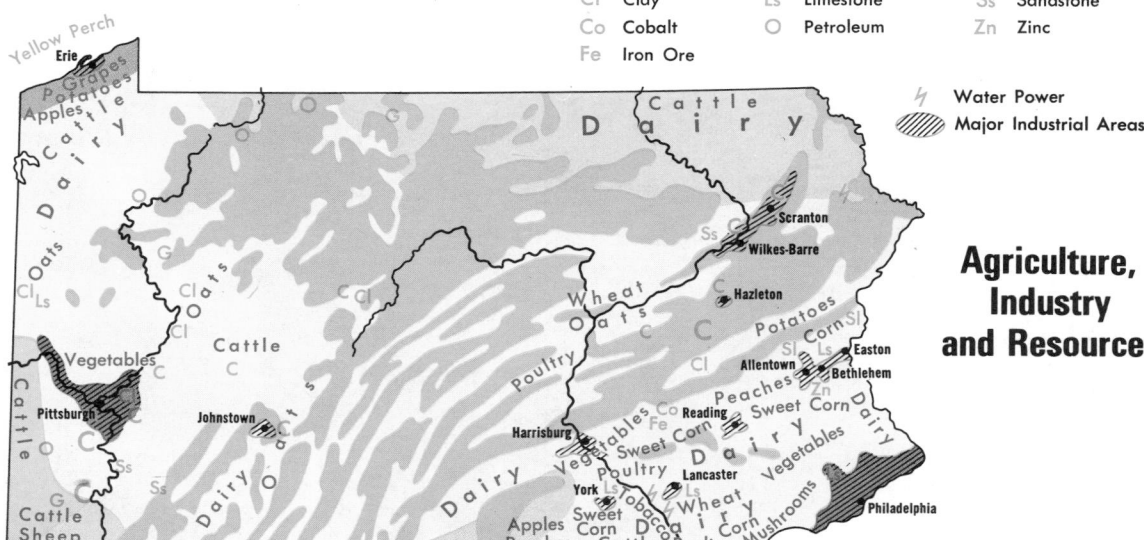

Agriculture, Industry and Resources

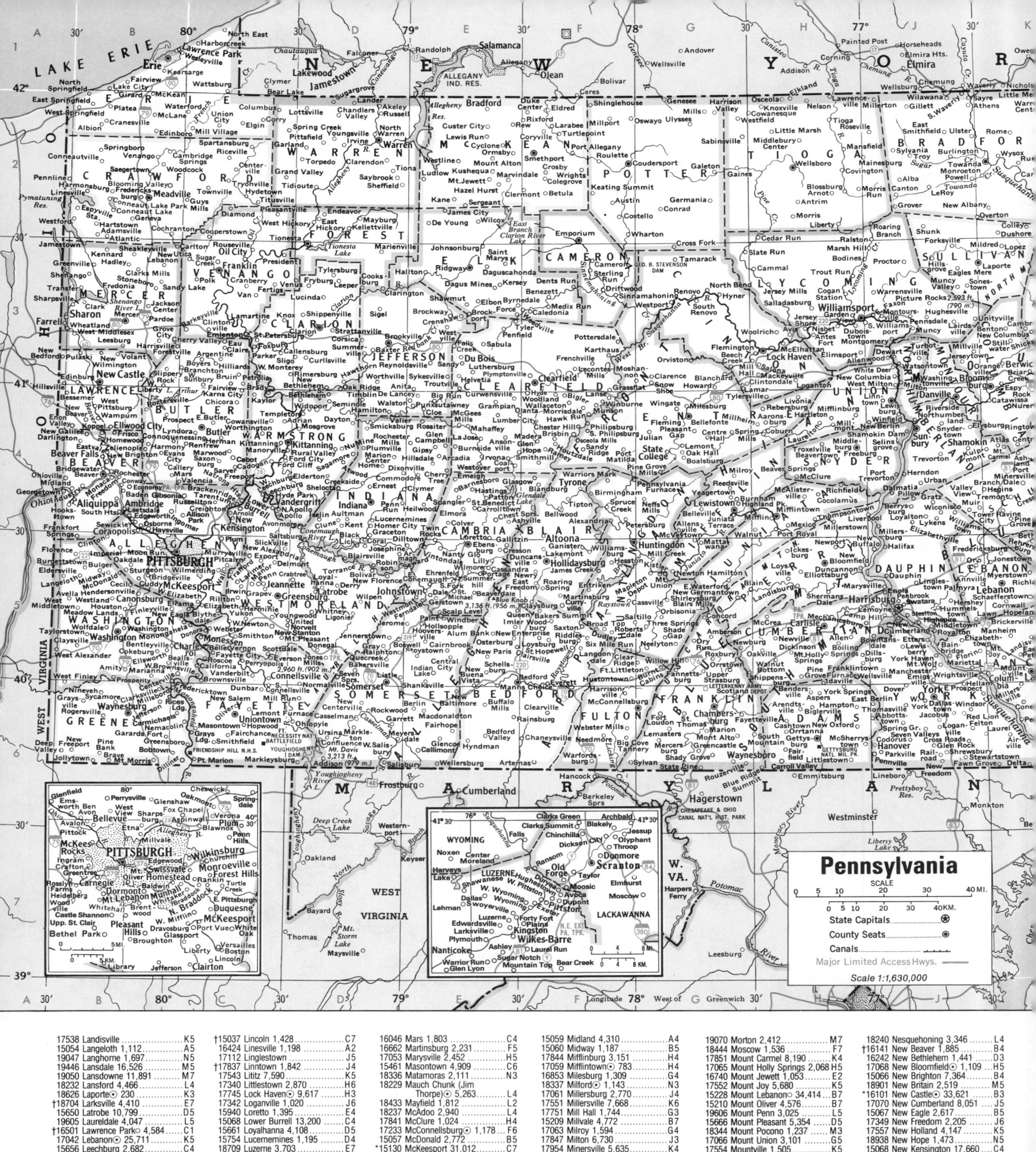

Pennsylvania

SCALE

State Capitals ⊛
County Seats ⊙
Canals

Major Limited Access Hwys. ———

Scale 1:1,630,000

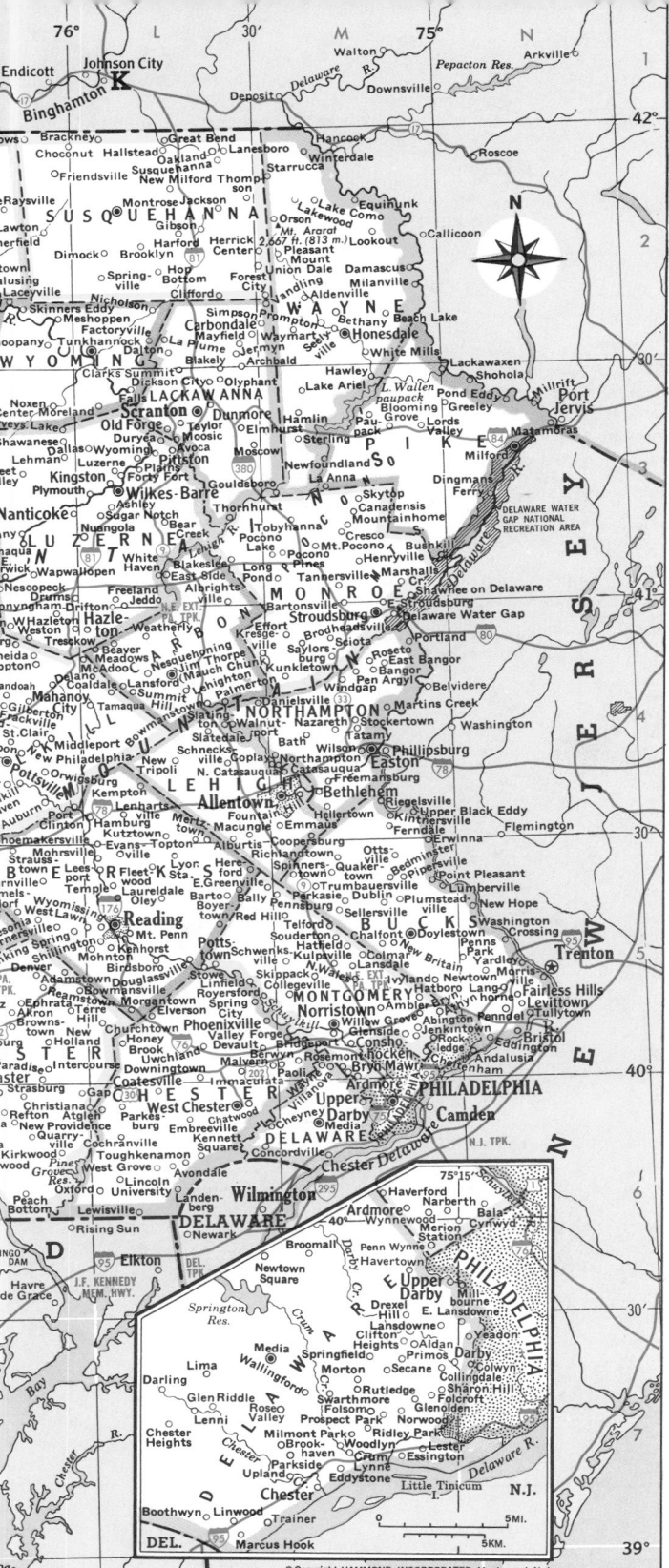

16823 Pleasant Gap 1,859 ....G4
15236 Pleasant Hills 9,676 ....B7
16341 Pleasantville 1,099 ....C2
15239 Plum 25,390...............C5
18651 Plymouth 7,605 ....E7
15474 Point Marion 1,642 ....C6
16342 Polk 1,884 ....C3
15946 Portage 3,510 ....E5
16743 Port Allegany 2,593 ....F2
17965 Port Carbon 2,576.........K4
†15133 Port Vue 5,316 ....C7
19464 Pottstown 22,729 ....L5
17901 Pottsville⊙ 18,195 ....K4
19076 Prospect Park 6,593 ....M7
15767 Punxsutawney 7,479 ....E4
18951 Quakertown 8,867 ....M5
17566 Quarryville 1,558 ....K6
†15104 Rankin 2,892 ....C7
*19601 Reading⊙ 78,686 ....L5
          Reading‡ 312,509.........L5
17567 Reamstown 1,308 ....K5
18076 Red Hill 1,727 ....L5
17356 Red Lion 5,824 ....J6
17084 Reedsville 1,023 ....G4
17764 Renovo 1,812 ....G3
17087 Richland 1,470 ....K5
18955 Richlandtown 1,180 ....M5
15853 Ridgway⊙ 5,604 ....E3
19078 Ridley Park 7,889 ....M7
18077 Riegelsville 993 ....M4
16248 Rimersburg 1,096 ....D3
17868 Riverside 2,266 ....J4
16673 Roaring Spring 2,962 ....F5
19551 Robesonia 1,748 ....K5
15074 Rochester 4,759 ....B4
†19101 Rockledge 2,538 ....M5
15557 Rockwood 1,058 ....D6
15477 Roscoe 1,123 ....C5
18013 Roseto 1,484 ....M4
†19065 Rose Valley 1,038 ....L7
17250 Rouzerville 1,371 ....G6
19468 Royersford 4,243 ....L5
16249 Rural Valley 1,033 ....D4
15076 Russellton 1,878 ....C4
17970 Saint Clair 4,037 ....K4
15857 Saint Marys 6,417 ....E3
15951 Saint Michael 1,445 ....E5
15681 Saltsburg 964 ....C4
†15801 Sandy 1,835 ....E3
16056 Saxonburg 1,336 ....C4
18840 Sayre 6,951 ....K2
†15963 Scalp Level 1,186 ....E5
15963 Schuylkill Haven 5,977 ....K4
19473 Schwenksville 1,041 ....L5
15683 Scottdale 5,833 ....C5
*18501 Scranton⊙ 88,117 ....F7
          Scranton (Northeast
          Pa.)‡ 640,396 ....F7
17870 Selinsgrove 5,227 ....J4
18960 Sellersville 3,143 ....M5
15143 Sewickley 4,778 ....B4
17872 Shamokin 10,357 ....J4
17876 Shamokin Dam 1,622 ....J4
16146 Sharon 19,057 ....B3
          Sharon‡ 128,299 ....B3
19079 Sharon Hill 6,221 ....N7
15215 Sharpsburg 4,351 ....B6
16150 Sharpsville 5,375 ....A3
16347 Sheffield 1,471 ....D2
17976 Shenandoah 7,589 ....K4
18655 Shickshinny 1,192 ....K3
19607 Shillington 5,601 ....K5
16748 Shinglehouse 1,310 ....F2
17257 Shippensburg 5,261 ....H5
19555 Shoemakersville 1,391 ....K4
17361 Shrewsbury 2,688 ....J6
19608 Sinking Spring 2,617 ....K5
18080 Slatington 4,277 ....L4
15684 Slickville 1,178 ....C5
16057 Slippery Rock 3,047 ....B3
16749 Smethport⊙ 1,797 ....F2
15478 Smithfield 1,084 ....C6
18964 Souderton 6,657 ....M5
15425 South Connellsville 2,296 ....C6
15956 South Fork 1,401 ....E5
†18840 South Waverly 1,176 ....J2

17701 South Williamsport 6,581 ..J3
15775 Spangler 2,399 ....E4
19475 Spring City 3,389 ....L5
15144 Springdale 4,418 ....C6
19064 Springfield 25,326 ....M7
17362 Spring Grove 1,832 ....J6
16801 State College 36,130 ....G4
          State College‡ 112,760......G4
17263 State Line 1,253 ....G6
17113 Steelton 6,484 ....J5
17363 Stewartstown 1,072 ....K6
16153 Stoneboro 1,177 ....B3
19464 Stowe 3,860 ....L5
17579 Strasburg 1,999 ....K6
18360 Stroudsburg⊙ 5,148 ....M4
15082 Sturgeon 1,312 ....B5
†16323 Sugar Creek 5,954 ....C3
18706 Sugar Notch 1,191 ....E7
18250 Summit Hill 3,418 ....L4
17801 Sunbury⊙ 12,292 ....J4
18847 Susquehanna 1,994 ....L2
19081 Swarthmore 5,950 ....M7
15218 Swissvale 11,345 ....C7
18704 Swoyersville 5,795 ....E7
15865 Sykesville 1,537 ....E3
18252 Tamaqua 8,843 ....L4
15084 Tarentum 6,419 ....C4
18517 Taylor 7,246 ....F7
18969 Telford 3,507 ....M5
19560 Temple 1,486 ....L5
17581 Terre Hill 1,217 ....L5
18512 Throop 4,166 ....F7
16351 Tidioute 844 ....D2
16353 Tionesta⊙ 659 ....C2
16684 Tipton 1,348 ....F4
16354 Titusville 6,884 ....C2
15962 Topton 1,818 ....L5
19374 Toughkenamon 1,111 ....L6
18848 Towanda⊙ 3,526 ....J2
17980 Tower City 1,667 ....J4
15085 Trafford 3,662 ....C5
†19013 Trainer 2,056 ....L7
17981 Tremont 1,796 ....K4
18254 Tresckow 1,128 ....K4
17881 Trevorton 2,192 ....J4
16947 Troy 1,381 ....J2
19007 Tullytown 2,277 ....N5
18657 Tunkhannock⊙ 2,144 ....L2
15145 Turtle Creek 6,959 ....C7
16686 Tyrone 6,346 ....F4
16438 Union City 3,623 ....C2
15401 Uniontown⊙ 14,510 ....C6
†19013 Upland 3,458 ....L7
*19082 Upper Darby⊙ 84,054 ....M6
15241 Upper Saint Claire 19,023 B7
19481 Valley Forge 400 ....L5
17983 Valley View 1,722 ....J4
15690 Vandergrift 6,823 ....D4
15147 Verona 3,179 ....C6
15132 Versailles 2,150 ....C7
19085 Villanova M6
18088 Walnutport 2,007 ....L4
16365 Warren⊙ 12,146 ....D2
15301 Washington⊙ 18,363 ....B5
16441 Waterford 1,568 ....B2
17777 Watsontown 2,366 ....J3
19087 Wayne M6
17268 Waynesboro 9,726 ....G6
15370 Waynesburg⊙ 4,482 ....B6
18255 Weatherly 2,891 ....L4
16901 Wellsboro⊙ 3,805 ....H2
19565 Wernersville 1,811 ....K5
16510 Wesleyville 3,998 ....C1
15417 West Brownsville 1,433 ....C5
19380 West Chester⊙ 17,435 ....L6
16950 Westfield 1,268 ....H2
19390 West Grove 1,820 ....L6
18201 West Hazleton 4,871 ....K4
†16201 West Kittanning 1,591 ....C4
†15656 West Leechburg 1,395 ....C4
16159 West Middlesex 1,064 ....B3
15122 West Mifflin 26,279 ....C7
†15905 Westmont 6,113 ....D5
15089 West Newton 3,387 ....C5
16160 West Pittsburg 1,133 ....B4
18643 West Pittston 5,980 ....F7
15229 West View 7,648 ....C7

18644 West Wyoming 3,288.........E7
†17401 West York 4,526 ....J6
15120 Whitaker 1,615 ....C7
†15234 Whitehall 15,206 ....B7
18661 White Haven 1,921 ....L3
15131 White Oak 9,480 ....C7
17097 Wiconisco 1,321 ....J4
*18701 Wilkes-Barre⊙ 51,551 ....F7
15221 Wilkinsburg 23,669 ....C7
16693 Williamsburg 1,400 ....F5
17701 Williamsport⊙ 33,401 ....H3
          Williamsport‡ 118,416 .....H3
17098 Willow Grove M5
19090 Willow Grove M5
15148 Wilmerding 2,421 ....C5
15025 Wilson 7,564 ....M4
15963 Windber 5,585 ....E5
18091 Windgap 2,651 ....M4
19567 Womelsdorf 1,827 ....K5
19094 Woodlyn M7
17368 Wrightsville 2,365 ....J5
18644 Wyoming 3,655 ....E7
19610 Wyomissing 6,551 ....K5
19067 Yardley 2,533 ....N5
19050 Yeadon 11,727 ....N7
17099 Yeagertown 1,305 ....G4
*17401 York⊙ 44,619 ....J6
          York‡ 381,255 ....J6
16371 Youngsville 2,006 ....D2
15697 Youngwood 3,749 ....D5
16063 Zelienople 3,502 ....B4

OTHER FEATURES

Allegheny (res.) E2
Allegheny (riv.) D2
Allegheny Front (mts.) E5
Appalachian (mts.) H4
Ararat (mt.) M2
Arthur (lake) C4
Beaver (riv.) B4
Blue (mt.) G5
Blue Knob (mt.) E5
Casselman (riv.) D6
Clarion (riv.) D3
Conemaugh (riv.) D5
Conemaugh River (lake) D5
Conewango (creek) D1
Davis (mt.) D6
Delaware (riv.) N3
Delaware Water Gap Nat'l Rec.
          Area N3
Erie (lake) B1
Fort Necessity Nat'l
          Battlefield C6
George B. Stevenson (dam) G3
Gettysburg Nat'l Mil. Park H6
Glendale (lake) F4
Juniata (riv.) G5
Laurel Hill (mt.) D5
Lehigh (riv.) L3
Letterkenny Army Depot G6
Licking (creek) F6
Little Tinicum (isl.) M7
Lycoming (creek) H3
Monongahela (riv.) C6
North (mt.) K3
Ohio (riv.) A4
Oil (creek) C2
Pine (creek) H2
Pine Grove (res.) K6
Pocono (mts.) M3
Pymatuning (res.) A2
Redbank (creek) D3
Schuylkill (riv.) M5
Shenango River (lake) A3
Sinnemahoning (creek) F3
South (mt.) H6
Susquehanna (riv.) H1
Tioga (riv.) H1
Tionesta Creek (lake) D3
Towanda (creek) J2
Tuscarora (riv.) G5
Wallenpaupack (lake) M3
Youghiogheny River (lake) D6

⊙County seat.
‡Population of metropolitan area.
○Population of town or township.
† Zip of nearest p.o.   * Multiple zips.

Topography

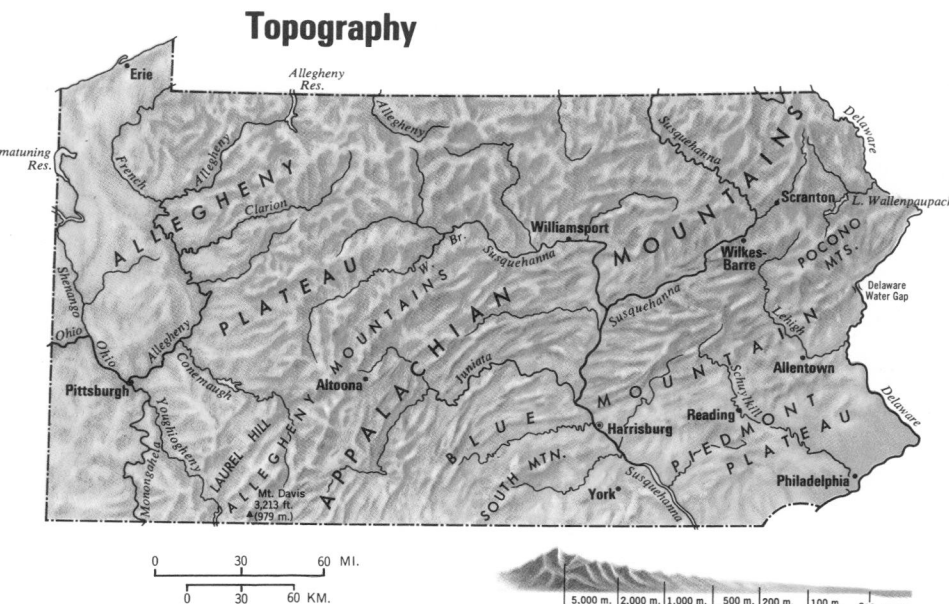

18067 Northampton 8,240 ....M4
15673 North Apollo 1,487 ....D4
15104 North Braddock 8,711 ....C7
†18032 North Catasauqua 2,554 ....L4
16428 North East 4,568 ....C1
17857 Northumberland 3,636 ....J4
19454 North Wales 3,391 ....M5
†16365 North Warren 1,232 ....D2
15674 Norvelt 2,541 ....D5
19074 Norwood 6,647 ....M7
15071 Oakdale 1,955 ....B5
15139 Oakmont 7,039 ....C6
†15059 Ohioville 4,217 ....B4
16301 Oil City 13,881 ....C3
15472 Oliver 3,777 ....C6
18447 Olyphant 5,204 ....F7
17961 Orwigsburg 2,700 ....K4
16666 Osceola Mills 1,466 ....F4
19363 Oxford 3,633 ....K6
†15963 Paint 1,177 ....E5
18071 Palmerton 5,455 ....L4
17078 Palmyra 7,228 ....J5
19301 Paoli 5,277 ....M5

17562 Paradise 1,107 ....K5
19365 Parkesburg 2,578 ....L6
†19013 Parkside 2,464 ....M7
†17331 Parkville 5,009 ....J6
16668 Patton 2,441 ....E4
18072 Pen Argyl 3,388 ....M4
17103 Penbrook 3,006 ....J5
19047 Penndel 2,703 ....N5
18073 Pennsburg 2,339 ....M5
†17331 Pennville 1,398 ....J6
†19151 Penn Wynne M6
18944 Perkasie 5,241 ....M5
15473 Perryopolis 2,139 ....C5
*19101 Philadelphia⊙ 1,688,210...N6
          Philadelphia‡ 4,716,818...N6
16866 Philipsburg 3,533 ....F4
19460 Phoenixville 14,165 ....L5
17963 Pine Grove 2,244 ....K4
16868 Pine Grove Mills 1,030 ....G4
15140 Pitcairn 4,175 ....C5
*15201 Pittsburgh⊙ 423,938 ....B7
          Pittsburgh‡ 2,263,894 ....B7
*18640 Pittston 9,930 ....F7
†18701 Plains 5,455 ....F7

© Copyright HAMMOND INCORPORATED, Maplewood, N.J.

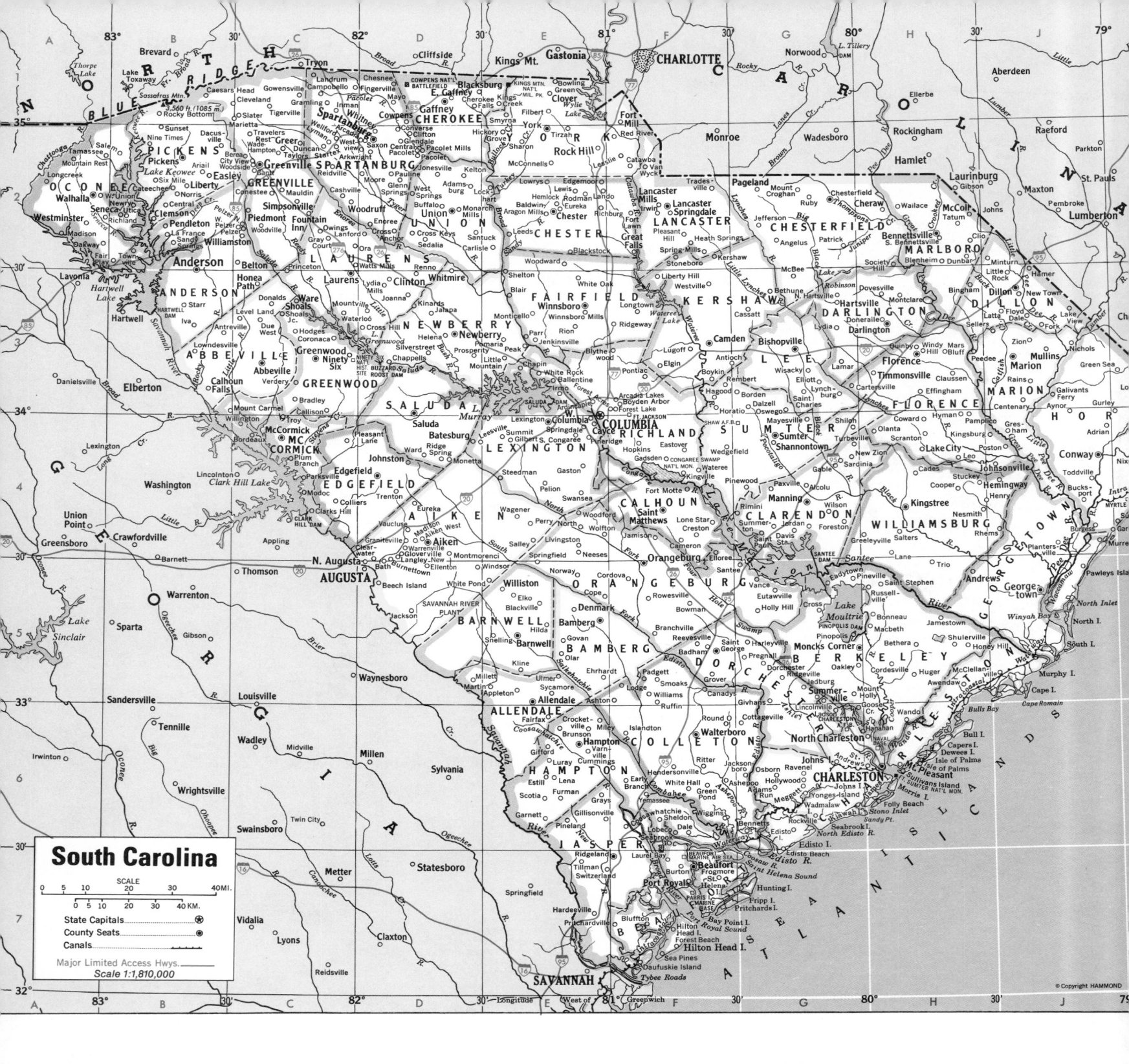

South Carolina

SCALE
0 5 10 20 30 40 MI.
0 5 10 20 30 40 KM.

State Capitals............⊛
County Seats.............⊙
Canals

Major Limited Access Hwys.
Scale 1:1,810,000

© Copyright HAMMOND

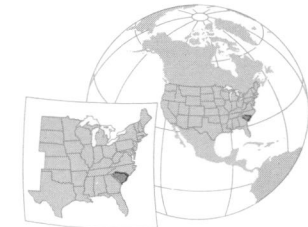

Agriculture, Industry and Resources

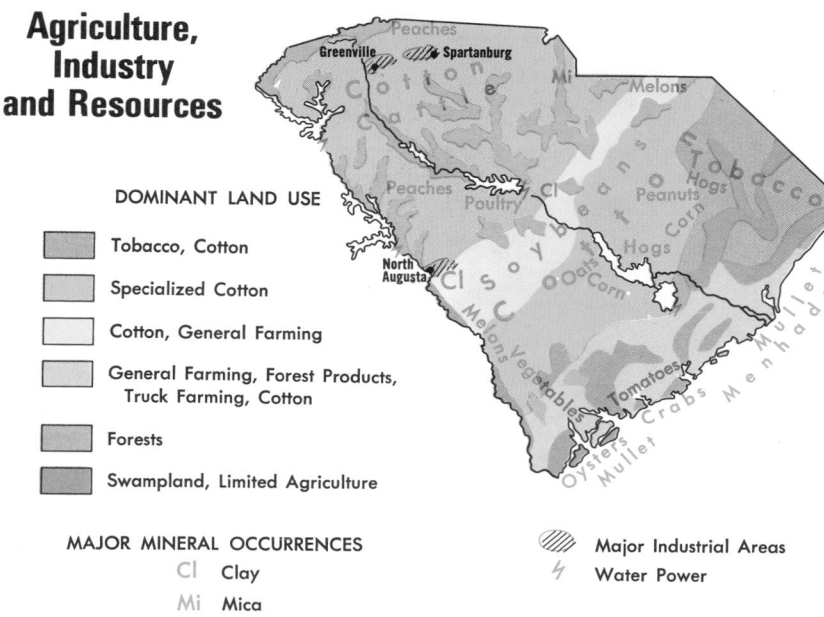

DOMINANT LAND USE

- Tobacco, Cotton
- Specialized Cotton
- Cotton, General Farming
- General Farming, Forest Products, Truck Farming, Cotton
- Forests
- Swampland, Limited Agriculture

MAJOR MINERAL OCCURRENCES

Cl Clay
Mi Mica

◢ Major Industrial Areas
⚡ Water Power

AREA 31,113 sq. mi. (80,583 sq. km.)
POPULATION 3,121,833
CAPITAL Columbia
LARGEST CITY Columbia
HIGHEST POINT Sassafras Mtn. 3,560 ft. (1085 m.)
SETTLED IN 1670
ADMITTED TO UNION May 23, 1788
POPULAR NAME Palmetto State
STATE FLOWER Carolina (Yellow) Jessamine
STATE BIRD Carolina Wren

†29720 Lancaster Mills 2,096 .... F2
29356 Landrum 2,141 .... C1
29564 Lane 554 .... H5
29834 Langley 1,714 .... D4
29565 Latta 1,804 .... J3
29902 Laurel Bay 5,238 .... F7
29360 Laurens⊙ 10,587 .... C3
29070 Leesville 2,296 .... E4
†29730 Lesslie 1,102 .... E2
29072 Lexington⊙ 2,131 .... E4
29657 Liberty 3,167 .... B2
†29483 Lincolnville G6
29075 Little Mountain 282 .... E3
29076 Livingston 166 .... E4
29364 Lockhart 85 .... E2
29082 Lodge 145 .... F5
29569 Loris 2,193 .... K3
29659 Lowndesville 197 .... B3
†29706 Lowrys 225 .... E2
29078 Lugoff 2,939 .... F3
29932 Luray 149 .... E6
29325 Lydia Mills 925 .... D3
29365 Lyman 1,067 .... C2
29080 Lynchburg 534 .... G3
†29829 Madison 1,150 .... D4
29102 Manning⊙ 4,746 .... G4
29661 Marietta-Slater 1,834 .... C1
29571 Marion⊙ 7,700 .... J3
29662 Mauldin 8,143 .... C2
29104 Mayesville 663 .... G4
29101 McBee 774 .... G3
29458 McClellanville 436 .... H5
29570 McColl 2,677 .... H2
29726 McConnells 171 .... E2
29835 McCormick⊙ 1,725 .... C4
29460 Meggett 249 .... G6
†29379 Monarch Mills 2,353 .... D2
29461 Moncks Corner⊙ 3,699 .... G5
29105 Monetta 167 .... D4
29840 Mount Carmel 182 .... C3
29727 Mount Croghan 146 .... G2
29464 Mount Pleasant 14,209 .... H6
29574 Mullins 6,068 .... J3
29576 Murrells Inlet 2,410 .... K4
29577 Myrtle Beach 18,446 .... K4
29107 Neeses 557 .... E4
29108 Newberry⊙ 9,866 .... D3
29809 New Ellenton 2,628 .... D5
†29536 New Town 950 .... J3
29581 Nichols 606 .... J3
29666 Ninety Six 2,249 .... C3
29667 Norris 903 .... B2
29112 North 1,304 .... E4
29841 North Augusta 13,593 .... C5
29406 North Charleston 62,534 .... G6
†29550 North Hartsville 2,650 .... G3
29582 North Myrtle Beach 3,960 .... K4
29113 Norway 518 .... E5
29114 Olanta 699 .... H4
29843 Olar 381 .... E5
29115 Orangeburg⊙ 14,933 .... F4
29372 Pacolet 1,556 .... D2
29373 Pacolet Mills 1,051 .... D2
29728 Pageland 2,720 .... G2
29583 Pamplico 1,213 .... H4
29844 Parksville 157 .... C4
29584 Patrick 375 .... G2
29102 Paxville 244 .... G4
29122 Peak 82 .... E3
29123 Pelion 213 .... E4
29669 Pelzer 130 .... B2
29670 Pendleton 3,154 .... B2
29124 Perry 273 .... E4
29671 Pickens⊙ 3,199 .... B2
29673 Piedmont 2,992 .... C2
29934 Pineland 800 .... E6
†29169 Pineridge 1,287 .... E4
29468 Pineville 900 .... H5
29125 Pinewood 689 .... G4
29469 Pinopolis 788 .... G5
29845 Plum Branch 73 .... C4
29126 Pomaria 271 .... E3
29935 Port Royal 2,977 .... F7
29127 Prosperity 803 .... D3
†29501 Quinby 952 .... H3
29470 Ravenel 1,655 .... G6

29471 Reevesville 241 .... F5
29729 Richburg 269 .... E2
29936 Ridgeland⊙ 1,143 .... E7
29129 Ridge Spring 969 .... D4
29472 Ridgeville 603 .... G5
29130 Ridgeway 343 .... F3
29730 Rock Hill 35,344 .... E2
Rock Hill‡ 106,720 .... E2
29133 Rowesville 388 .... F5
29741 Ruby 256 .... G2
29407 Saint Andrews 9,908 .... G6
29477 Saint George⊙ 2,134 .... F5
29135 Saint Matthews⊙ 2,496 .... F4
29479 Saint Stephen 1,850 .... H5
29676 Salem 194 .... A2
29137 Salley 584 .... E4
29138 Saluda⊙ 2,752 .... D4
29142 Santee 612 .... F5
29301 Saxon 4,383 .... D2
29939 Scotia 72 .... E6
29591 Scranton 861 .... H4
29592 Sellers 388 .... H3
29678 Seneca 7,436 .... A2
29742 Sharon 323 .... E2
29145 Silverstreet 200 .... D3
29681 Simpsonville 9,037 .... C2
29682 Six Mile 470 .... B2
29683 Slater-Marietta 1,834 .... C1
29481 Smoaks 165 .... F5
29743 Smyrna 47 .... E1
29301 Spartanburg⊙ 43,826 .... C1
29169 Springdale 2,985 .... E4
†29720 Springdale 2,570 .... F2
29146 Springfield 604 .... E4
†29067 Spring Mills 1,419 .... F2
29684 Starr 241 .... B3
29377 Startex 1,006 .... C2
29554 Stuckey 222 .... H4
29482 Sullivans Island 1,867 .... H6
29148 Summerton 1,173 .... G4
29483 Summerville 6,706 .... G5
29054 Summit 172 .... E4
29150 Sumter⊙ 24,890 .... G4
29577 Surfside Beach 2,522 .... K4
29160 Swansea 888 .... E4
29846 Sycamore 261 .... E5
29594 Tatum 101 .... H2
29687 Taylors 15,801 .... C2
29688 Tigerville 975 .... C1
29161 Timmonsville 2,112 .... H3
29690 Travelers Rest 3,017 .... C2
29847 Trenton 404 .... D4
29848 Troy 705 .... C4
29162 Turbeville 549 .... G4
29849 Ulmer 91 .... E5
29379 Union⊙ 10,523 .... D2
†29678 Utica 1,501 .... B2
29163 Vance 89 .... G5
29944 Varnville 1,999 .... E5
†29607 Wade-Hampton 20,180 .... C2
29164 Wagener 903 .... E4
29691 Walhalla⊙ 3,977 .... A2
29488 Walterboro⊙ 6,209 .... F6
29166 Ward 98 .... D4
29692 Ware Shoals 2,370 .... C3
29851 Warrenville 1,029 .... D4
29384 Waterloo 200 .... C3
29360 Watts Mills 1,324 .... D2
29385 Wellford 2,143 .... C2
29169 West Columbia 10,409 .... E4
29693 Westminster 3,114 .... A2
29669 West Pelzer 944 .... B2
29696 West Union 300 .... B2
†29301 Westview 1,999 .... C2
29178 Whitmire 2,038 .... D3
29303 Whitney 4,052 .... D1
29493 Williams 205 .... F5
29697 Williamston 4,310 .... B2
29853 Williston 3,173 .... E5
29856 Windsor 55 .... E5
†29501 Windy Hill 1,622 .... H3
29180 Winnsboro⊙ 2,919 .... E3

†29180 Winnsboro Mills 1,890 .... E3
†29112 Woodford 206 .... E4
29388 Woodruff 5,171 .... D2
29945 Yemassee 789 .... F6
29745 York⊙ 6,412 .... E1

OTHER FEATURES

Ashepoo (riv.) F6
Ashley (riv.) G6
Bay Point (isl.) F7
Beaufort Marine Air Sta. F7
Big Black (creek) G2
Black (riv.) H4
Blue Ridge (mts.) B1
Broad (riv.) D2
Broad (riv.) F7
Buck (creek) J3
Bull (isl.) H6
Bullock (creek) E2
Bulls (bay) H6
Bush (riv.) D3
Buzzard Roost (dam) D3
Cape (isl.) J5
Capers (isl.) H6
Catawba (riv.) F2
Catfish (creek) J3
Charleston A.F.B. G6
Chattooga (riv.) A2
Clark Hill (dam) C4
Clark Hill (lake) C4
†29812 Snelling 111 .... E5
Combahee (riv.) F6
Congaree (riv.) F4
†29512 South Bennettsville 1,065 .... H2
Congaree Nat'l Mon. F4
†29169 South Congaree 2,113 .... E4
Cooper (riv.) H6
Coosaw (riv.) G7
Coosawhatchie (riv.) E6
Cowpens Nat'l Battlefield D1
Crooked (riv.) H2
Deep (creek) B2
Dewees (isl.) H6
Donaldson A.F.B. C2

Edisto (isl.) G6
Edisto (riv.) G7
Enoree (riv.) C2
Fort Jackson F4
Fort Sumter Nat'l Mon. H6
Four Hole Swamp (creek) F5
Fripp (isl.) G7
Great Pee Dee (riv.) J4
Greenwood (lake) D3
Hartwell (dam) B3
Hartwell (lake) A3
Hilton Head (isl.) F7
Hunting (isl.) G7
Intracoastal Waterway H5
James (isl.) H6
Johns (isl.) G6
Juniper (creek) H2
Keowee (lake) B2
Keowee (riv.) B2
Kiawah (isl.) G6
Kings Mountain Nat'l Mil. Park E1
Little (riv.) C3
Little (riv.) D3
Little Lynches (riv.) G3
Little Pee Dee (riv.) J4
Little River (inlet) L4
Lumber (riv.) J3
Lynches (riv.) H3
Marion (lake) G5
Morris (isl.) H6
Moultrie (lake) G5
Murphy (isl.) J5
Murray (lake) D4
Myrtle Beach A.F.B. K4
Naval Base H6
New (riv.) E6
Ninety Six Nat'l Hist. Site C3
North (inlet) J5
North (isl.) J5
North Edisto (riv.) G6
Pacolet (riv.) D1
Palms, Isle of (isl.) H6

Parris Island Marine Base F7
Pee Dee (riv.) H2
Pinopolis (dam) G5
Pocotaligo (riv.) G4
Port Royal (sound) F7
Pritchards (isl.) G7
Reedy (riv.) C2
Robinson (lake) G3
Romain (cape) J6
Saint Helena (isl.) F7
Saint Helena (sound) G7
Salkehatchie (riv.) E5
Saluda (riv.) D3
Sandy (pt.) H6
Sandy (riv.) E2
Santee (dam) G4
Santee (riv.) H5
Sassafras (mt.) B1
Savannah (riv.) E6
Savannah River Plant D5
Sea (isls.) G7
Seabrook (isl.) G6
Seneca (riv.) B2
Shaw A.F.B. 6,939 .... F4
South (isl.) J5
Stevens (creek) C4
Stono (inlet) H6
Thompsons (creek) G2
Tugaloo (riv.) A2
Turkey (creek) E2
Tybee Roads (chan.) F7
Tyger (riv.) D2
Waccamaw (riv.) J5
Wadmalaw (isl.) G6
Wando (riv.) H6
Wateree (lake) F3
Wateree (riv.) F3
Winyah (bay) J5
Wylie (lake) E1

⊙County seat.
‡Population of metropolitan area.
† Zip of nearest p.o.   * Multiple zips.

29554 Hemingway 853 .... J4
†29706 Hemlock (Eureka) 1,627 .... E2
29717 Hickory Grove 344 .... E2
29813 Hilda 355 .... E5
29928 Hilton Head Island 11,344 .... F7
29653 Hodges 154 .... C3
29059 Holly Hill 1,785 .... G5
29449 Hollywood 729 .... G6
29654 Honea Path 4,114 .... C3
29349 Inman 1,554 .... C1
29063 Irmo 3,957 .... E3
†29720 Irwin 1,373 .... F2
29451 Isle of Palms 3,421 .... H6
29655 Iva 1,369 .... B3
29831 Jackson 1,771 .... D5
29453 Jamestown 193 .... H5
†29483 Jedburg 900 .... G5
29718 Jefferson 651 .... G2
29351 Joanna 1,839 .... D3
29555 Johnsonville 1,421 .... J4
29832 Johnston 2,624 .... D4
29353 Jonesville 1,201 .... D2
29067 Kershaw 1,993 .... F2
29556 Kingstree⊙ 4,147 .... H4
29814 Kline 315 .... E5
29456 Ladson 13,246 .... G6
29560 Lake City 6,731 .... H4
29563 Lake View 939 .... J3
29069 Lamar 1,333 .... G3
29720 Lancaster⊙ 9,703 .... F2

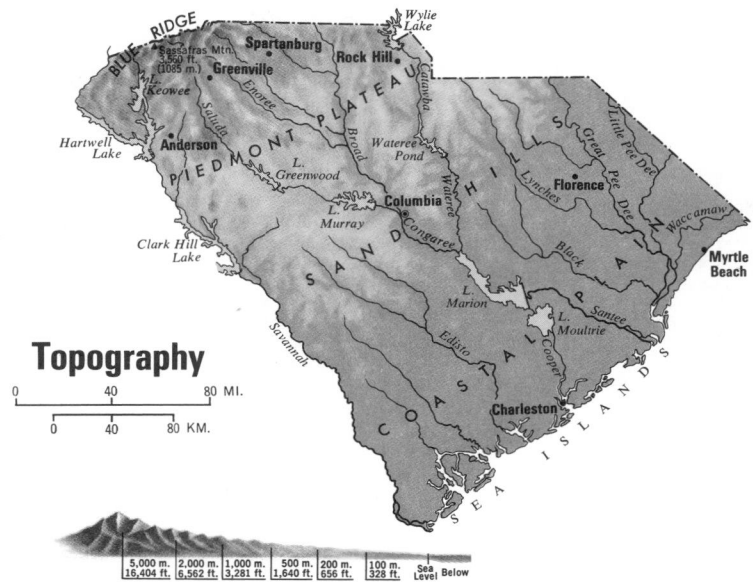

Topography

0   40   80 MI.
0   40   80 KM.

	5,000 m.	2,000 m.	1,000 m.	500 m.	200 m.	100 m.	Sea
	16,404 ft.	6,562 ft.	3,281 ft.	1,640 ft.	656 ft.	328 ft.	Level Below

COUNTIES

County	Pop.	Key
Aurora	3,628	M6
Beadle	19,195	N5
Bennett	3,044	F7
Bon Homme	8,059	O7
Brookings	24,332	R5
Brown	36,962	N2
Brule	5,245	L6
Buffalo	1,795	L5
Butte	8,372	B4
Campbell	2,243	J2
Charles Mix	9,680	M7
Clark	4,894	O4
Clay	13,689	P8
Codington	20,885	P4
Corson	5,196	G2
Custer	6,000	B6
Davison	17,820	N6
Day	8,133	O3
Deuel	5,289	R4
Dewey	5,366	G3
Douglas	4,181	N7
Edmunds	5,159	L3
Fall River	8,439	B7
Faulk	3,327	L3
Grant	9,013	R3
Gregory	6,015	L7
Haakon	2,794	F5
Hamlin	5,261	P4
Hand	4,948	L4
Hanson	3,415	O6
Harding	1,700	B2
Hughes	14,220	J5
Hutchinson	9,350	O7
Hyde	2,069	K4
Jackson	3,437	F6
Jerauld	2,929	M5
Jones	1,463	H6
Kingsbury	6,679	O5
Lake	10,724	P5
Lawrence	18,339	B5
Lincoln	13,942	R7

County	Pop.	Key
Lyman	3,864	J6
Marshall	5,404	O2
McCook	6,444	P6
McPherson	4,027	L2
Meade	20,717	D5
Mellette	2,249	H6
Miner	3,739	O5
Minnehaha	109,435	R6
Moody	6,692	R5
Pennington	70,361	C6
Perkins	4,700	D3
Potter	3,674	J3
Roberts	10,911	P2
Sanborn	3,213	N5
Shannon	11,323	D7
Spink	9,201	N4
Stanley	2,533	H5
Sully	1,990	J4
Todd	7,328	H7
Tripp	7,268	K7
Turner	9,255	P7
Union	10,938	R8
Walworth	7,011	J3

CITIES and TOWNS

Zip	Name/Pop.	Key
	Yankton 18,952	P7
	Ziebach 2,308	F4
57424	Ashton 154	N3
57213	Astoria 154	S4
57425	Athol 38	M3
57002	Aurora 507	R5
57315	Avon 576	N8
57214	Badger 99	P5
57401	Aberdeen⊙ 25,851	M3
57310	Academy 10	M7
57520	Agar 139	J4
57420	Akaska 49	J3
57210	Albee 23	S3
57001	Alcester 885	R7
57311	Alexandria⊙ 588	O6
57714	Allen 300	F7
57312	Alpena 288	N5
57211	Altamont 58	R4
57421	Amherst 75	O2
57422	Andover 139	O3
57715	Ardmore 16	B7
57313	Armour⊙ 819	N7
57423	Artas 43	K2
57314	Artesian 227	O6
57316	Bancroft 41	O4
57426	Barnard 65	N2
57716	Batesland 163	E7
57427	Bath 175	N3
57717	Belle Fourche⊙ 4,692	B4
57521	Belvidere 80	G6
57215	Bemis 37	R4
57004	Beresford 1,865	R7
57216	Big Stone City 672	S3
†57310	Bijou Hills 12	L6
57620	Bison⊙ 457	E2
57718	Black Hawk 1,608	C5
57522	Blunt 424	J4
57428	Bowdle 644	K3
57317	Bonesteel 358	M7
57719	Box Elder 3,186	D5

Zip	Name/Pop.	Key
57217	Bradley 135	O3
57005	Brandon 2,589	R6
57218	Brandt 129	R4
57429	Brentford 91	N3
57319	Bridgewater 653	P6
57219	Bristol 445	O3
57430	Britton⊙ 1,590	O2
†57350	Broadland 49	N4
57006	Brookings⊙ 14,951	R5
57220	Bruce 254	R5
57221	Bryant 388	P4
57720	Buffalo⊙ 453	B2
57722	Buffalo Gap 186	C6
57621	Bullhead 400	G2
57010	Burbank 92	R8
57523	Burke⊙ 859	L7
†57276	Bushnell 76	R5
57222	Butler 22	O3
57724	Camp Crook 100	B2
57012	Canistota 626	P6
57321	Canova 194	O6
57013	Canton⊙ 2,886	R7
57725	Caputa 50	D5

South Dakota

SCALE

0 5 10 20 40 60 MI.

0 5 10 20 40 60 KM.

State Capitals ⊛

County Seats ⊙

Major Limited Access Hwys.

Scale 1:2,220,000

© Copyright HAMMOND INCORPORATED, Maplewood, N.J.

(continued on following page)

AREA 77,116 sq. mi. (199,730 sq. km.)
POPULATION 690,768
CAPITAL Pierre
LARGEST CITY Sioux Falls
HIGHEST POINT Harney Pk. 7,242 ft. (2207 m.)
SETTLED IN 1856
ADMITTED TO UNION November 2, 1889
POPULAR NAME Coyote State; Sunshine State
STATE FLOWER Pasqueflower
STATE BIRD Ring-necked Pheasant

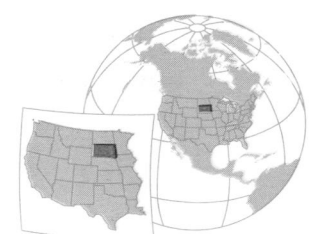

Topography

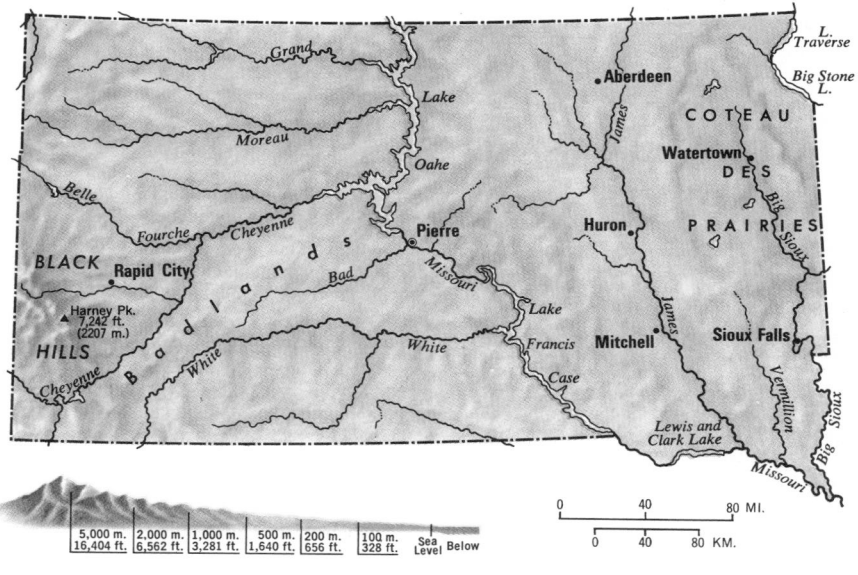

5,000 m.	2,000 m.	1,000 m.	500 m.	200 m.	100 m.	Sea
16,404 ft.	6,562 ft.	3,281 ft.	1,640 ft.	656 ft.	328 ft.	Level Below

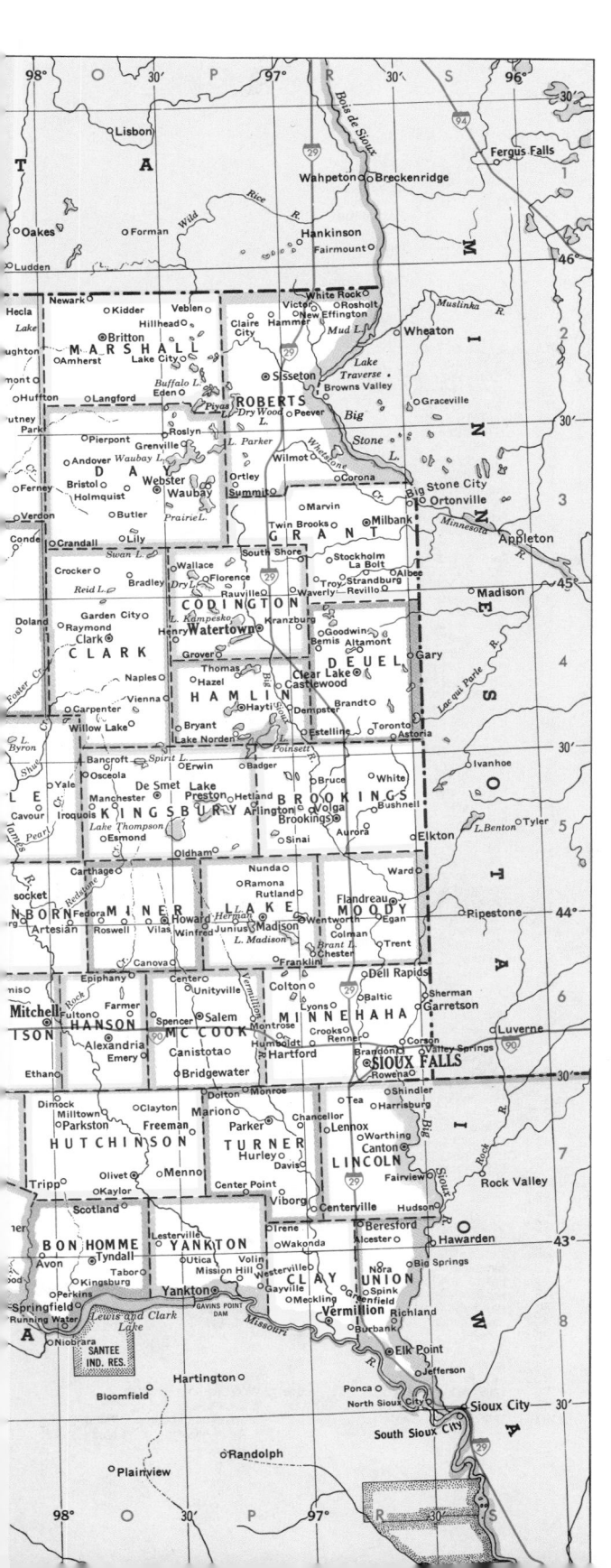

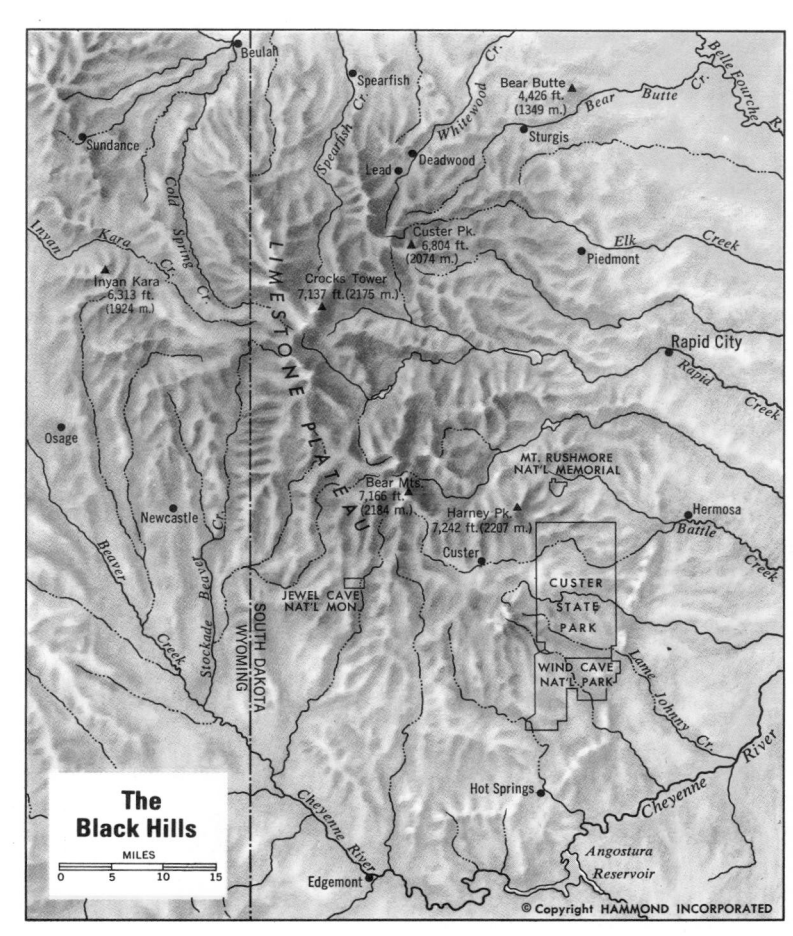

The Black Hills

MILES
0   5   10   15

Agriculture, Industry and Resources

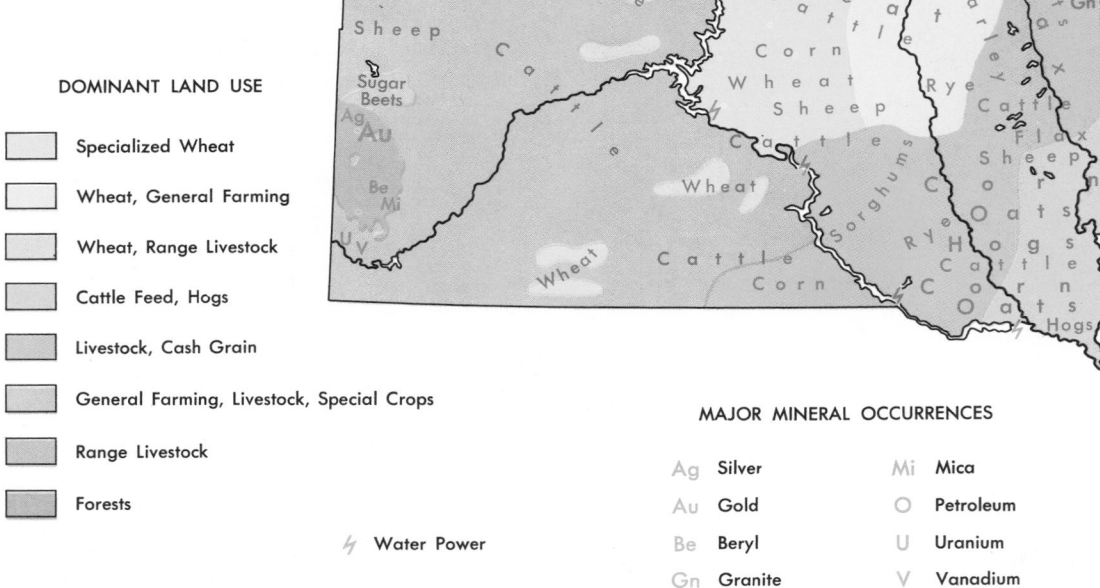

DOMINANT LAND USE

- Specialized Wheat
- Wheat, General Farming
- Wheat, Range Livestock
- Cattle Feed, Hogs
- Livestock, Cash Grain
- General Farming, Livestock, Special Crops
- Range Livestock
- Forests

⚡ Water Power

MAJOR MINERAL OCCURRENCES

Ag	Silver	Mi	Mica
Au	Gold	O	Petroleum
Be	Beryl	U	Uranium
Gn	Granite	V	Vanadium

COUNTIES

Anderson 38,381 .... J6
Andrews 13,323 .... B5
Angelina 64,172 .... K6
Aransas 14,260 .... H10
Archer 7,266 .... F4
Armstrong 1,994 .... C3
Atascosa 25,055 .... F9
Austin 17,726 .... H8
Bailey 8,168 .... B3
Bandera 7,084 .... E8
Bastrop 24,726 .... G7
Baylor 4,919 .... E4
Bee 26,030 .... G9
Bell 157,820 .... G6
Bexar 988,798 .... F8
Blanco 4,681 .... F8
Borden 859 .... C5
Bosque 13,401 .... G6
Bowie 75,301 .... K4
Brazoria 169,587 .... J8
Brazos 93,588 .... H7
Brewster 7,573 .... A8
Briscoe 2,579 .... C3
Brooks 8,428 .... F11
Brown 33,057 .... F6
Burleson 12,313 .... H7
Burnet 17,803 .... F7
Caldwell 23,637 .... G8
Calhoun 19,574 .... H9
Callahan 10,992 .... E5
Cameron 209,727 .... G11
Camp 9,275 .... K5
Carson 6,672 .... C2
Cass 29,430 .... K4
Castro 10,556 .... B3
Chambers 18,538 .... K8
Cherokee 38,127 .... J6
Childress 6,950 .... D3
Clay 9,582 .... F4
Cochran 4,825 .... B4
Coke 3,196 .... D6
Coleman 10,439 .... E6
Collin 144,576 .... H4
Collingsworth 4,648 .... D3
Colorado 18,823 .... H8
Comal 36,446 .... F8
Comanche 12,617 .... F5
Concho 2,915 .... E6
Cooke 27,656 .... G4
Coryell 56,767 .... G6
Cottle 2,947 .... D3
Crane 4,600 .... B6
Crockett 4,608 .... C7
Crosby 8,859 .... C4
Culberson 3,315 .... C11
Dallam 6,531 .... B1
Dallas 1,556,390 .... H5
Dawson 16,184 .... C5
Deaf Smith 21,165 .... B3
Delta 4,839 .... J4
Denton 143,126 .... G4
De Witt 18,903 .... G9
Dickens 3,539 .... D4
Dimmit 11,367 .... E9
Donley 4,075 .... D2
Duval 12,517 .... F10
Eastland 19,480 .... F5
Ector 115,374 .... B6
Edwards 2,033 .... D7
Ellis 59,743 .... H5
El Paso 479,899 .... A10
Erath 22,560 .... F5
Falls 17,946 .... H6
Fannin 24,285 .... H4
Fayette 18,832 .... H8
Fisher 5,891 .... D5
Floyd 9,834 .... C3
Foard 2,158 .... E3
Fort Bend 130,846 .... J8
Franklin 6,893 .... J4
Freestone 14,830 .... H6
Frio 13,785 .... E9
Gaines 13,150 .... B5
Galveston 195,940 .... K8
Garza 5,336 .... C4
Gillespie 13,532 .... F7
Glasscock 1,304 .... C6
Goliad 5,193 .... G9
Gonzales 15,949 .... G8
Gray 26,386 .... D2
Grayson 89,796 .... H4
Gregg 99,495 .... K5
Grimes 13,580 .... J7
Guadalupe 46,708 .... G8
Hale 37,592 .... C3
Hall 5,594 .... D3
Hamilton 8,297 .... F6
Hansford 6,209 .... C1
Hardeman 6,368 .... E3
Hardin 40,721 .... K7
Harris 2,409,547 .... J8
Harrison 52,265 .... K5
Hartley 3,987 .... B2
Haskell 7,725 .... E4
Hays 40,594 .... F7
Hemphill 5,304 .... D2
Henderson 42,606 .... J5
Hidalgo 283,323 .... F11
Hill 25,024 .... G5
Hockley 23,230 .... B4
Hood 17,714 .... G5
Hopkins 25,247 .... J4
Houston 22,299 .... J6
Howard 33,142 .... C5
Hudspeth 2,728 .... B10
Hunt 55,248 .... H4
Hutchinson 26,304 .... C2
Irion 1,386 .... C6
Jack 7,408 .... F4
Jackson 13,352 .... H9
Jasper 30,781 .... K7
Jeff Davis 1,647 .... C11
Jefferson 250,938 .... K8
Jim Hogg 5,168 .... F11
Jim Wells 36,498 .... F10
Johnson 67,649 .... G5
Jones 17,268 .... E5
Karnes 13,593 .... G9
Kaufman 39,029 .... H5
Kendall 10,635 .... F8
Kenedy 543 .... G11
Kent 1,145 .... D4
Kerr 28,780 .... E7
Kimble 4,063 .... E7
King 425 .... D4
Kinney 2,279 .... D8
Kleberg 33,358 .... G10
Knox 5,329 .... E4
Lamar 42,156 .... J4
Lamb 18,669 .... B3
Lampasas 12,005 .... F6
La Salle 5,514 .... E9
Lavaca 19,004 .... H8
Lee 10,952 .... H7
Leon 9,594 .... J6
Liberty 47,088 .... K7
Limestone 20,224 .... H6
Lipscomb 3,766 .... D1
Live Oak 9,606 .... F9
Llano 10,144 .... F7
Loving 91 .... A6
Lubbock 211,651 .... C4
Lynn 8,605 .... C4
Madison 10,649 .... J6
Marion 10,360 .... K5
Martin 4,684 .... C5
Mason 3,683 .... E7
Matagorda 37,828 .... H9
Maverick 31,398 .... D9
McCulloch 8,735 .... E6
McLennan 170,755 .... G6
McMullen 789 .... F9
Medina 23,164 .... E8
Menard 2,346 .... E7
Midland 82,636 .... B6
Milam 22,732 .... H7
Mills 4,477 .... F6
Mitchell 9,088 .... D5
Montague 17,410 .... G4
Montgomery 128,487 .... J7
Moore 16,575 .... C2
Morris 14,629 .... K4
Motley 1,950 .... D3
Nacogdoches 46,786 .... K6
Navarro 35,323 .... H5
Newton 13,254 .... L7
Nolan 17,359 .... D5
Nueces 268,215 .... G10
Ochiltree 9,588 .... D1
Oldham 2,283 .... B2
Orange 83,838 .... L7
Palo Pinto 24,062 .... F5
Panola 20,724 .... K5
Parker 44,609 .... G5
Parmer 11,038 .... B3
Pecos 14,618 .... B7
Polk 24,407 .... K7
Potter 98,637 .... C2
Presidio 5,188 .... C12
Rains 4,839 .... J5
Randall 75,062 .... C2
Reagan 4,135 .... C6
Real 2,469 .... E8
Red River 16,101 .... J4
Reeves 15,801 .... D11
Refugio 9,289 .... G9
Roberts 1,187 .... D2
Robertson 14,653 .... H6
Rockwall 14,528 .... H5
Runnels 11,872 .... E6
Rusk 41,382 .... K5
Sabine 8,702 .... L6
San Augustine 8,785 .... K6
San Jacinto 11,434 .... J7
San Patricio 58,013 .... G10
San Saba 6,204 .... F6
Schleicher 2,820 .... D7
Scurry 18,192 .... D5
Shackelford 3,915 .... E5
Shelby 23,084 .... K6
Sherman 3,174 .... C1
Smith 128,366 .... J5
Somervell 4,154 .... G5
Starr 27,266 .... F11
Stephens 9,926 .... F5
Sterling 1,206 .... C6
Stonewall 2,406 .... D4
Sutton 5,130 .... D7
Swisher 9,723 .... C3
Tarrant 860,880 .... G5
Taylor 110,932 .... E5
Terrell 1,595 .... B7
Terry 14,581 .... B4
Throckmorton 2,053 .... E4
Titus 21,442 .... K4
Tom Green 84,784 .... D6
Travis 419,573 .... G7
Trinity 9,450 .... J6
Tyler 16,223 .... K7
Upshur 28,595 .... K5
Upton 4,619 .... B6
Uvalde 22,441 .... E8
Val Verde 35,910 .... C8
Van Zandt 31,426 .... J5
Victoria 68,807 .... H9
Walker 41,789 .... J7
Waller 19,798 .... J8
Ward 13,976 .... A6
Washington 21,998 .... H7
Webb 99,258 .... E10
Wharton 40,242 .... H8
Wheeler 7,137 .... D2
Wichita 121,082 .... F3
Wilbarger 15,931 .... E3
Willacy 17,495 .... G11
Williamson 76,507 .... G7
Wilson 16,756 .... F8
Winkler 9,944 .... A6
Wise 26,575 .... G4
Wood 24,697 .... J5
Yoakum 8,299 .... B4
Young 19,083 .... F4
Zapata 6,628 .... E11
Zavala 11,666 .... E9

AREA 266,807 sq. mi. (691,030 sq. km.)
POPULATION 14,229,288
CAPITAL Austin
LARGEST CITY Houston
HIGHEST POINT Guadalupe Pk. 8,749 ft. (2667 m.)
SETTLED IN 1686
ADMITTED TO UNION December 29, 1845
POPULAR NAME Lone Star State
STATE FLOWER Bluebonnet
STATE BIRD Mockingbird

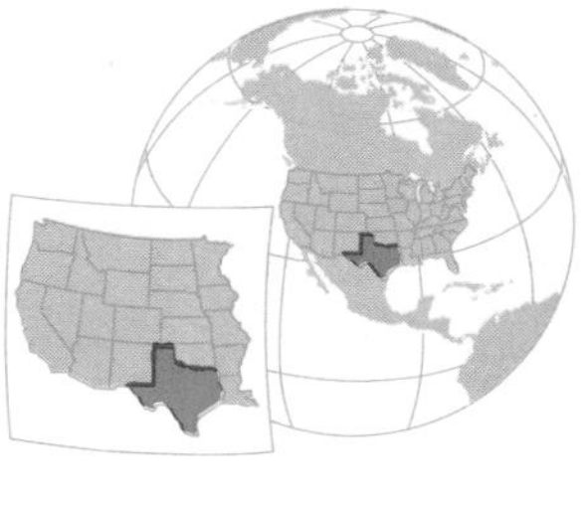

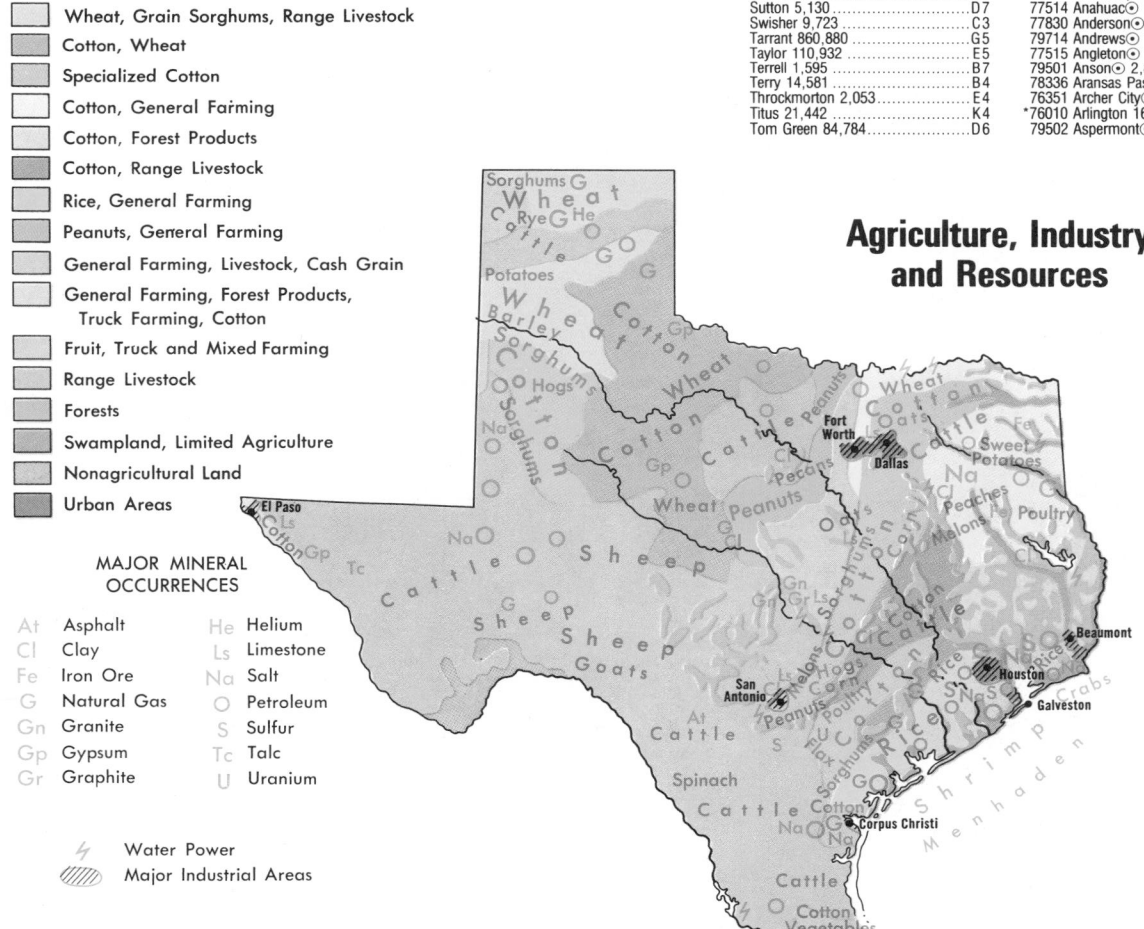

CITIES and TOWNS

Zip *Name/Pop.* *Key*

*79601 Abilene⊙ 98,315 .... E5
Abilene‡ 139,192 .... E5
78516 Alamo 5,831 .... F11
78209 Alamo Heights 6,252 .... K10
76430 Albany⊙ 2,450 .... E5
78332 Alice⊙ 20,961 .... F10
75002 Allen 8,314 .... H1
79830 Alpine⊙ 5,465 .... D12
77511 Alvin 16,515 .... J3
*79101 Amarillo⊙ 149,230 .... C2
Amarillo‡ 173,699 .... C2
77514 Anahuac⊙ 1,840 .... K8
77830 Anderson⊙ 500 .... J7
79714 Andrews⊙ 11,061 .... B5
77515 Angleton⊙ 13,929 .... J8
79501 Anson⊙ 2,831 .... E5
78336 Aransas Pass 7,173 .... G10
76351 Archer City⊙ 1,862 .... F4
*76010 Arlington 160,123 .... F2
79502 Aspermont⊙ 1,357 .... D4
75751 Athens⊙ 10,197 .... J5
75551 Atlanta 6,272 .... K4
*78701 Austin (cap.)⊙ 345,496 .... G7
Austin‡ 536,450 .... G7
76020 Azle 5,822 .... E2
77518 Bacliff 4,851 .... K2
79504 Baird⊙ 1,696 .... E5
75180 Balch Springs 13,746 .... H2
†78201 Balcones Heights 2,511 .... J10
76821 Ballinger⊙ 4,207 .... E6
78003 Bandera⊙ 947 .... F8
77532 Barrett 3,183 .... K1
78602 Bastrop⊙ 3,789 .... G7
77414 Bay City⊙ 17,837 .... H9
77520 Baytown 56,923 .... L2
*77701 Beaumont⊙ 118,102 .... K7
Beaumont-Port Arthur-Orange‡ 375,497 K7
76021 Bedford 20,821 .... F2
78102 Beeville⊙ 14,574 .... G9
77401 Bellaire 14,950 .... J2
76704 Bellmead 7,569 .... H6
77418 Bellville⊙ 2,860 .... H8
76513 Belton⊙ 10,660 .... G7
76126 Benbrook 13,579 .... E2
79505 Benjamin⊙ 257 .... E4
76932 Big Lake⊙ 3,404 .... C6
79720 Big Spring⊙ 24,804 .... C5
78006 Boerne⊙ 3,229 .... J10
75418 Bonham⊙ 7,338 .... H4
79007 Borger 15,837 .... C2
75557 Boston⊙ 400 .... K4
76230 Bowie 5,610 .... G4
78832 Brackettville⊙ 1,676 .... D8
76825 Brady⊙ 5,969 .... E6
77422 Brazoria 3,025 .... J9
76024 Breckenridge⊙ 6,921 .... F5
77833 Brenham⊙ 10,966 .... H7
77611 Bridge City 7,667 .... L7
79316 Brownfield⊙ 10,387 .... B4
*78520 Brownsville⊙ 84,997 .... G12
Brownsville-Harlingen-San Benito‡ 209,680 .... G12
76801 Brownwood⊙ 19,396 .... F6
77801 Bryan⊙ 44,337 .... H7
Bryan-College Station‡ 93,588 .... H7
76354 Burkburnett 10,668 .... F3
76028 Burleson 11,734 .... F3
78611 Burnet⊙ 3,410 .... F7
77836 Caldwell⊙ 2,953 .... H7
76520 Cameron⊙ 5,721 .... H7
79014 Canadian⊙ 3,491 .... D2
75103 Canton⊙ 2,845 .... J5
79015 Canyon⊙ 10,724 .... C3
78834 Carrizo Springs⊙ 6,886 .... E9
*75006 Carrollton 40,595 .... G2
75633 Carthage⊙ 6,447 .... K5
†78213 Castle Hills 4,773 .... J10
75104 Cedar Hill 6,849 .... G3
75935 Center⊙ 5,827 .... K6
75833 Centerville⊙ 799 .... H6
77530 Channelview 17,471 .... K1
79018 Channing⊙ 304 .... B2
79201 Childress⊙ 5,817 .... D3
76437 Cisco 4,517 .... E5
79226 Clarendon⊙ 2,220 .... C3
75426 Clarksville⊙ 4,917 .... K4
79019 Claude⊙ 1,112 .... C2
†77565 Clear Lake Shores 755 .... K2
76031 Cleburne⊙ 19,218 .... G5
77327 Cleveland 5,977 .... K7
77531 Clute 9,577 .... J9
77331 Coldspring⊙ 569 .... J7
76834 Coleman⊙ 5,960 .... E6
77840 College Station 37,272 .... H7
76034 Colleyville 6,700 .... F2
79512 Colorado City⊙ 5,405 .... C5
78934 Columbus⊙ 3,923 .... H8
76442 Comanche⊙ 4,075 .... F6
75428 Commerce 8,136 .... J4
*77301 Conroe⊙ 18,034 .... J7
78109 Converse 5,150 .... K11
75432 Cooper⊙ 2,338 .... J4
76522 Copperas Cove 19,469 .... G6
*78401 Corpus Christi⊙ 231,999 .... G10
Corpus Christi‡ 326,228 .... G10
75110 Corsicana⊙ 21,712 .... H5
78014 Cotulla⊙ 3,912 .... E9
79731 Crane⊙ 3,622 .... B6
75835 Crockett⊙ 7,405 .... J6
79322 Crosbyton⊙ 2,289 .... C4
79227 Crowell⊙ 1,509 .... E4
76036 Crowley 5,852 .... E3
78839 Crystal City⊙ 8,334 .... E9
77954 Cuero⊙ 7,124 .... G8
75638 Daingerfield⊙ 3,030 .... K4
79022 Dalhart⊙ 6,854 .... B1
*75201 Dallas⊙ 904,078 .... G2
Dallas-Ft. Worth‡ 2,974,878 .... G2
77535 Dayton 4,908 .... J7
76234 Decatur⊙ 4,104 .... G4
77536 Deer Park 22,648 .... K2
76444 De Leon 2,478 .... F5
78840 Del Rio⊙ 30,034 .... D8
75020 Denison 23,884 .... H4
76201 Denton⊙ 48,063 .... G4

(continued on following page)

Agriculture, Industry and Resources

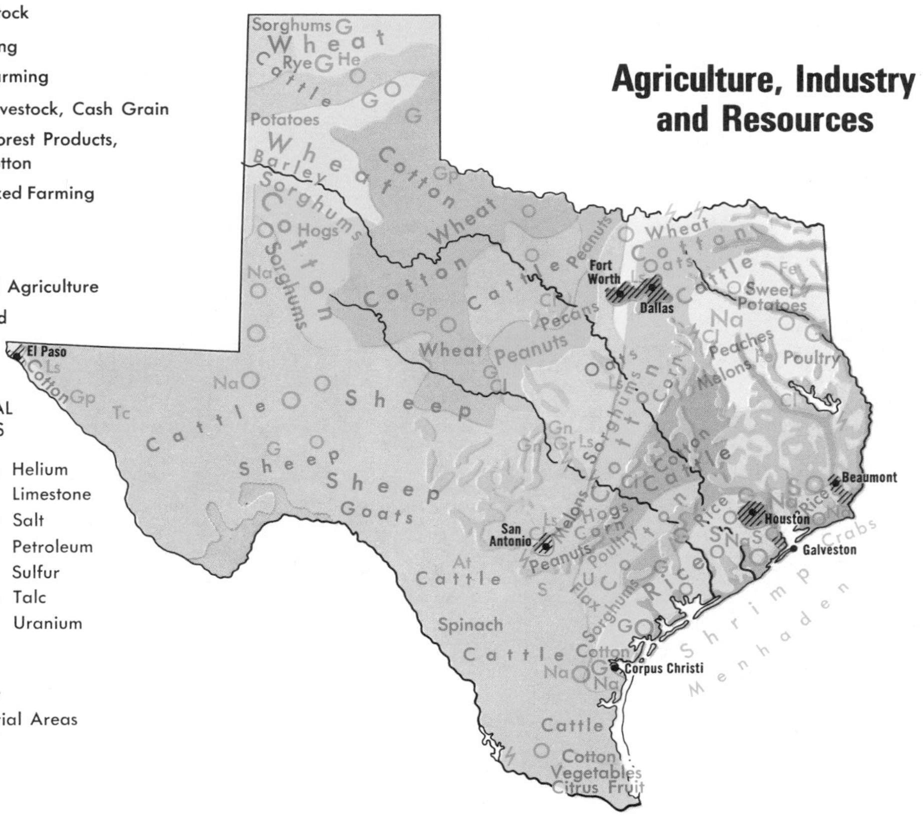

DOMINANT LAND USE

- Wheat, Grain Sorghums, Range Livestock
- Cotton, Wheat
- Specialized Cotton
- Cotton, General Farming
- Cotton, Forest Products
- Cotton, Range Livestock
- Rice, General Farming
- Peanuts, General Farming
- General Farming, Livestock, Cash Grain
- General Farming, Forest Products, Truck Farming, Cotton
- Fruit, Truck and Mixed Farming
- Range Livestock
- Forests
- Swampland, Limited Agriculture
- Nonagricultural Land
- Urban Areas

MAJOR MINERAL OCCURRENCES

At	Asphalt	He	Helium
Cl	Clay	Ls	Limestone
Fe	Iron Ore	Na	Salt
G	Natural Gas	O	Petroleum
Gn	Granite	S	Sulfur
Gp	Gypsum	Tc	Talc
Gr	Graphite	U	Uranium

Water Power
Major Industrial Areas

79323 Denver City 4,704 .... B4
75115 De Soto 15,538 .... G3
78016 Devine 3,756 .... E8
75941 Diboll 5,227 .... K6
79229 Dickens⊙ 409 .... D4
77539 Dickinson 7,505 .... K3
79027 Dimmitt⊙ 5,019 .... B3
78537 Donna 9,952 .... F11
79029 Dumas⊙ 12,194 .... C2
75116 Duncanville 27,781 .... G3
78852 Eagle Pass⊙ 21,407 .... D9
76448 Eastland⊙ 3,747 .... F5
78539 Edinburg⊙ 24,075 .... F11
77957 Edna⊙ 5,650 .... H9
77437 El Campo 10,462 .... H8
76936 Eldorado⊙ 2,061 .... D7
78621 Elgin 4,535 .... G7
*79901 El Paso⊙ 425,259 .... A10
El Paso‡ 479,899 .... A10
78543 Elsa 5,061 .... G11
75440 Emory⊙ 813 .... J5
75119 Ennis 12,110 .... H5
76039 Euless 24,002 .... F2
76140 Everman 5,387 .... F3
79838 Fabens 4,285 .... B10
75840 Fairfield⊙ 3,505 .... H6
78355 Falfurrias⊙ 6,103 .... F10
75234 Farmers Branch 24,863 .... G2
79325 Farwell⊙ 1,354 .... A3
78114 Floresville⊙ 4,381 .... K11
†75067 Flower Mound 4,402 .... F1
79235 Floydada⊙ 4,193 .... C3
†76119 Forest Hill 11,684 .... F2
79734 Fort Davis⊙ 900 .... D11
79735 Fort Stockton⊙ 8,688 .... A7
*76101 Fort Worth⊙ 385,164 .... F2
77856 Franklin⊙ 1,349 .... H7
78624 Fredericksburg⊙ 6,412 .... E7
76842 Fredonia 50 .... E7
77541 Freeport 13,444 .... J9
77546 Friendswood 10,719 .... J2
79035 Friona 3,809 .... B3
75034 Frisco 3,499 .... H4
79738 Gail⊙ 171 .... C5
76240 Gainesville⊙ 14,081 .... G4
77547 Galena Park 9,879 .... J1
*77550 Galveston⊙ 61,902 .... L3
Galveston-Texas
City‡ 195,940 .... L3
79739 Garden City⊙ 350 .... C6
*75040 Garland 138,857 .... H2
76528 Gatesville⊙ 6,260 .... G6
78626 Georgetown⊙ 9,468 .... G7
78022 George West⊙ 2,627 .... F9
78942 Giddings⊙ 3,950 .... H7
75644 Gilmer⊙ 5,167 .... J5
75647 Gladewater 6,548 .... K5
76043 Glen Rose⊙ 2,075 .... G5
76844 Goldthwaite⊙ 1,783 .... F6
77963 Goliad⊙ 1,990 .... G9
78629 Gonzales⊙ 7,152 .... G8
76046 Graham⊙ 9,170 .... F4
76048 Granbury⊙ 3,332 .... G5
*75050 Grand Prairie 71,462 .... G2
76051 Grapevine 11,801 .... F2
75401 Greenville⊙ 22,161 .... H4
76642 Groesbeck⊙ 3,373 .... H6
77619 Groves 17,090 .... L8
75845 Groveton⊙ 1,262 .... J7
79236 Guthrie⊙ 170 .... D4
77964 Hallettsville⊙ 2,865 .... G8
76117 Haltom City 29,014 .... F2
76531 Hamilton⊙ 3,189 .... G6
78550 Harlingen 43,543 .... G11
79521 Haskell⊙ 3,782 .... E4
77859 Hearne 5,418 .... H7
78361 Hebbronville⊙ 4,684 .... F10
75948 Hemphill⊙ 1,353 .... L6
77445 Hempstead⊙ 3,456 .... J7
75652 Henderson⊙ 11,473 .... K5
76365 Henrietta⊙ 3,149 .... F4
79045 Hereford⊙ 15,853 .... B3
†75201 Highland Park 8,909 .... G2
77562 Highlands 6,467 .... K1
76645 Hillsboro⊙ 7,397 .... G5
77563 Hitchcock 6,655 .... K3
78861 Hondo⊙ 6,057 .... E8
*77001 Houston⊙ 1,595,138 .... J2
Houston‡ 2,905,350 .... J2
*77338 Humble 6,729 .... J7
†77001 Hunters Creek
Village 4,215 .... J1
77340 Huntsville⊙ 23,936 .... J7
76053 Hurst 31,420 .... F2
76367 Iowa Park 6,184 .... F4
*75061 Irving 109,943 .... G2
77029 Jacinto City 8,953 .... J1
76056 Jacksboro⊙ 4,000 .... F4
75766 Jacksonville 12,264 .... J5
75951 Jasper⊙ 6,959 .... L7
79528 Jayton⊙ 638 .... D4
75657 Jefferson⊙ 2,643 .... K5
†77001 Jersey Village 4,084 .... J1
78636 Johnson City⊙ 872 .... F7
78026 Jourdanton⊙ 2,743 .... F9
76849 Junction⊙ 2,593 .... E7
78118 Karnes City⊙ 3,296 .... G9
77450 Katy 5,660 .... J8
75142 Kaufman⊙ 4,658 .... H5
76248 Keller 4,156 .... F2
78119 Kenedy 4,356 .... G9
79745 Kermit⊙ 8,015 .... B6
78028 Kerrville⊙ 15,276 .... E7
75662 Kilgore 11,006 .... K5
76541 Killeen 46,296 .... G6
Killeen-Temple‡ 214,656 .... G6
78363 Kingsville⊙ 28,808 .... G10
†78109 Kirby 6,435 .... K11
77625 Kountze⊙ 2,716 .... K7
78945 La Grange⊙ 3,768 .... G8
77566 Lake Jackson 19,102 .... J8
76135 Lake Worth 4,394 .... E2
77568 La Marque 15,372 .... K3
79331 Lamesa⊙ 11,790 .... C5
76550 Lampasas⊙ 6,165 .... F6
*75146 Lancaster 14,807 .... G3
77571 La Porte 14,062 .... K2

*78040 Laredo⊙ 91,449 .... E10
Laredo‡ 99,258 .... E10
77573 League City 16,578 .... K2
78873 Leakey⊙ 468 .... E8
†78201 Leon Valley 9,088 .... J10
79336 Levelland⊙ 13,809 .... B4
*75067 Lewisville 24,273 .... G1
77575 Liberty⊙ 7,945 .... K7
75563 Linden⊙ 2,443 .... K4
79056 Lipscomb⊙ 52 .... D1
79339 Littlefield⊙ 7,409 .... B4
†78201 Live Oak 8,183 .... K10
77351 Livingston⊙ 4,928 .... K7
78643 Llano⊙ 3,071 .... F7
78644 Lockhart⊙ 7,953 .... G8
79241 Lockney 2,334 .... C3
*75601 Longview⊙ 62,762 .... K5
Longview-Marshall‡
151,752 .... K5
*79401 Lubbock⊙ 173,979 .... C4
Lubbock‡ 211,651 .... C4
75901 Lufkin⊙ 28,562 .... K6
78648 Luling 5,039 .... G8
77864 Madisonville⊙ 3,660 .... J7
76063 Mansfield 8,092 .... F3
77578 Manvel 3,549 .... J3
79843 Marfa⊙ 2,466 .... C12
76661 Marlin⊙ 7,099 .... H6
75670 Marshall⊙ 24,921 .... K5
76856 Mason⊙ 2,153 .... E7
79244 Matador⊙ 1,052 .... D3
78368 Mathis 5,667 .... G9
78501 McAllen 66,281 .... F11
McAllen-Pharr-Edinburg‡
283,229 .... F11
76657 McGregor 4,513 .... G6
75069 McKinney⊙ 16,256 .... H4
†77520 McNair K1
79245 Memphis⊙ 3,352 .... D3
76859 Menard⊙ 1,697 .... E7
79754 Mentone⊙ 50 .... D10
78570 Mercedes 11,851 .... F12
76665 Meridian⊙ 1,330 .... G6
76941 Mertzon⊙ 687 .... C6
*75149 Mesquite 67,053 .... H2
76667 Mexia 7,094 .... H6
79059 Miami⊙ 813 .... D2
*79701 Midland⊙ 70,525 .... C6
Midland‡ 82,636 .... C6
76065 Midlothian 3,219 .... G5
75773 Mineola 4,346 .... J5
76067 Mineral Wells 14,468 .... F5
78572 Mission 22,653 .... F11
77459 Missouri City 24,533 .... J2
79756 Monahans⊙ 8,397 .... B6
76251 Montague⊙ 1,253 .... G4
79346 Morton⊙ 2,674 .... B4
75455 Mount Pleasant⊙ 11,003 .... K4
75457 Mount Vernon⊙ 2,025 .... J4
79347 Muleshoe⊙ 4,842 .... B3
75961 Nacogdoches⊙ 27,149 .... J6
†77598 Nassau Bay 4,526 .... K2
77868 Navasota 5,971 .... J7
77627 Nederland 16,855 .... K8
75570 New Boston 4,628 .... K4
78130 New Braunfels⊙ 22,402 .... K10
75966 Newton⊙ 1,620 .... L7
76118 North Richland
Hills 30,592 .... F2
79760 Odessa⊙ 90,027 .... B6
Odessa‡ 115,374 .... B6
76374 Olney 4,060 .... F4
77630 Orange⊙ 23,628 .... L7
76943 Ozona⊙ 3,766 .... C7
79248 Paducah⊙ 2,216 .... D4
76866 Paint Rock⊙ 256 .... E6
77465 Palacios 4,667 .... H9
75801 Palestine⊙ 15,948 .... J6
76072 Palo Pinto⊙ 350 .... F5
79065 Pampa⊙ 21,396 .... D2
79068 Panhandle⊙ 2,226 .... C2
75460 Paris⊙ 25,498 .... J4
*77501 Pasadena 112,560 .... J2
77581 Pearland 13,248 .... J2
78061 Pearsall⊙ 7,383 .... E9
79772 Pecos⊙ 12,855 .... D10
79070 Perryton⊙ 7,991 .... D1
78577 Pharr 21,381 .... F11
75686 Pittsburg⊙ 4,245 .... J4
79355 Plains⊙ 1,457 .... B4
79072 Plainview⊙ 22,187 .... C3
75074 Plano 72,331 .... G1
78064 Pleasanton 6,346 .... F9
77640 Port Arthur 61,251 .... K8
78578 Port Isabel 3,769 .... G11
78374 Portland 12,023 .... G10
77979 Port Lavaca⊙ 10,911 .... H9
77651 Port Neches 13,944 .... K7
79356 Post⊙ 3,961 .... C4
78065 Poteet 3,086 .... F8
77445 Prairie View 3,993 .... J7
79845 Presidio 1,723 .... C12
79252 Quanah⊙ 3,890 .... E3
76470 Ranger 3,142 .... F5
79778 Rankin⊙ 1,216 .... B6
78580 Raymondville⊙ 9,493 .... G11
78377 Refugio⊙ 3,898 .... G9
75080 Richardson 72,496 .... G2
76118 Richland Hills 7,977 .... F2
77469 Richmond⊙ 9,692 .... J8
78582 Rio Grande City⊙ 8,930 .... F11
77019 River Oaks 6,890 .... E2
76945 Robert Lee⊙ 1,202 .... D6
78380 Robstown 12,100 .... G10
79543 Roby⊙ 814 .... D5
76567 Rockdale 5,611 .... G7
78382 Rockport⊙ 3,686 .... H9
78880 Rocksprings⊙ 1,317 .... D8
75087 Rockwall⊙ 5,939 .... H5
78584 Roma-Los Saenz 3,384 .... E11
77471 Rosenberg 17,995 .... J8
78664 Round Rock 12,740 .... G7
75088 Rowlett 7,522 .... H2
75785 Rusk⊙ 4,681 .... J6
76179 Saginaw 5,736 .... E2
*76901 San Angelo⊙ 73,240 .... D6
San Angelo‡ 84,784 .... D6

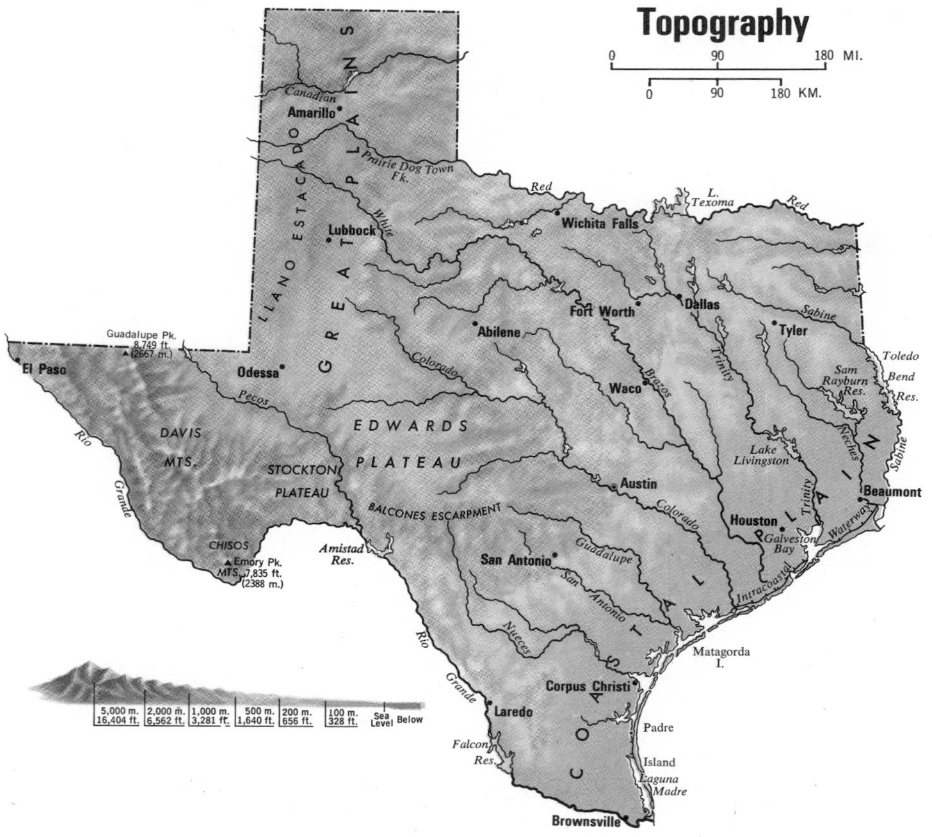

*78201 San Antonio⊙ 786,023 .... J11
San Antonio‡ 1,071,954 .... J11
75972 San Augustine⊙ 2,930 .... K6
78586 San Benito 17,988 .... G12
79848 Sanderson⊙ 1,241 .... B7
78384 San Diego⊙ 5,225 .... F10
76266 Sanger 2,574 .... G4
78589 San Juan 7,608 .... F11
78666 San Marcos⊙ 23,420 .... F8
76877 San Saba⊙ 2,847 .... F6
†76101 Sansom Park Village 3,921 E2
†77510 Santa Fe 6,172 .... K3
78385 Sarita⊙ 200 .... G10
78154 Schertz 7,262 .... K10
77586 Seabrook 4,670 .... K2
75159 Seagoville 7,304 .... H3
77474 Sealy 3,875 .... H8
78155 Seguin⊙ 17,854 .... G8
79360 Seminole⊙ 6,080 .... B5
†78357 Seven Sisters 2 .... F9
76380 Seymour⊙ 3,657 .... E4
75090 Sherman⊙ 30,413 .... H4
Sherman-Denison‡ 89,796 H4
79851 Sierra Blanca⊙ 800 .... B11
77656 Silsbee 7,684 .... K7
79257 Silverton⊙ 918 .... C3
78387 Sinton⊙ 6,044 .... G9
79364 Slaton 6,804 .... C4
78957 Smithville 3,470 .... G7
79549 Snyder⊙ 12,705 .... D5
76950 Sonora⊙ 3,856 .... D7
77587 South Houston 13,293 .... J2
79081 Spearman⊙ 3,413 .... C1
*77373 Spring J7
†77001 Spring Valley 3,353 .... J1
77477 Stafford 4,755 .... J2
79553 Stamford 4,542 .... E5
79782 Stanton⊙ 2,314 .... C5
76401 Stephenville⊙ 11,881 .... F5
76951 Sterling City⊙ 915 .... D6
79083 Stinnett⊙ 2,222 .... C2
79084 Stratford⊙ 1,917 .... C1
77478 Sugar Land 8,826 .... J8
75482 Sulphur Springs⊙ 12,804 .... J4
77480 Sweeny 3,538 .... J8
79556 Sweetwater⊙ 12,242 .... D5
78390 Taft 3,686 .... G9
79373 Tahoka⊙ 3,262 .... C4
76574 Taylor 10,619 .... G7
†77586 Taylor Lake Village 3,669 .... K2
75860 Teague 3,390 .... H6
76501 Temple 42,354 .... G6
79852 Terlingua 100 .... D12
75160 Terrell 13,269 .... H5
†78201 Terrell Hills 4,644 .... K11
*75501 Texarkana 31,271 .... L4
Texarkana, Tex.-Texarkana,
Ark.‡ 27,019 .... L4
77590 Texas City 41,403 .... K3
73949 Texhoma 358 .... C1
The Colony 11,586 .... G1
76083 Throckmorton⊙ 1,174 .... F4
78072 Tilden⊙ 450 .... F9
77375 Tomball 3,996 .... J7
75862 Trinity 2,620 .... J7
79088 Tulia⊙ 5,033 .... C3
*75701 Tyler⊙ 70,508 .... J5
Tyler‡ 128,366 .... J5
78148 Universal City 10,720 .... K10
†75205 University Park 22,254 .... G2
78801 Uvalde⊙ 14,178 .... E8
75095 Van Alstyne 1,860 .... H4

79855 Van Horn⊙ 2,772 .... C11
79092 Vega⊙ 900 .... B2
76384 Vernon⊙ 12,695 .... E3
77901 Victoria⊙ 50,695 .... H9
Victoria‡ 68,807 .... H9
77662 Vidor 11,834 .... L7
*76701 Waco⊙ 101,261 .... G6
Waco‡ 170,755 .... G6
75501 Wake Village 3,865 .... K4
75165 Waxahachie⊙ 14,624 .... H5
76086 Weatherford⊙ 12,049 .... G5
79095 Wellington⊙ 3,043 .... D3
78596 Weslaco 19,331 .... F11
77486 West Columbia 4,109 .... J8
77630 West Orange 4,610 .... L7
†77005 West University
Place 12,010 .... J2
†76101 Westworth 3,651 .... E2
77488 Wharton⊙ 9,033 .... J8
79096 Wheeler⊙ 1,584 .... D2
75693 White Oak 4,415 .... K5
76273 Whitesboro 3,197 .... H4
76108 White Settlement 13,508 .... E2
*76301 Wichita Falls⊙ 94,201 .... F4
Wichita Falls‡ 130,664 .... F4
†78201 Windcrest 5,332 .... K11
75494 Winnsboro 3,458 .... J5
79567 Winters 3,061 .... E6
75979 Woodville⊙ 2,821 .... K7
75098 Wylie 3,152 .... H1
78076 Zapata⊙ 3,831 .... E11

OTHER FEATURES

Amistad (res.) C8
Amistad Nat'l Rec. Area D8
Angelina (riv.) K6
Apache (mts.) C11
Aransas (passage) H10
Arlington (lake) F2
Baffin (bay) G10
Balcones Escarpment (plat.) E8
Beals (creek) C5
Benbrook (lake) E3
Bergstrom A.F.B. G7
Big Bend Nat'l Park A8
Bolivar (pen.) K8
Brazos (riv.) H7
Brownwood (lake) E6
Buchanan (lake) F7
Buck (creek) D3
Caddo (lake) L5
Canadian (riv.) D1
Carrizo (creek) A1
Carswell A.F.B. E2
Cathedral (mt.) D12
Cavallo (passage) H9
Cedar (lake) B5
Cerro Alto (mt.) B10
Chamizal Nat'l Mem. A10
Chase N.A.S. G9
Chinati (mts.) C12
Chinati (peak) C12
Chisos (mts.) A8
Cibolo (creek) K11
Clear Fork, Brazos (riv.) D5
Coldwater (creek) B1
Colorado (riv.) F7
Copano (bay) G9
Corpus Christi (lake) F9

Corpus Christi N.A.S. G10
Cottonwood Draw (dry riv.) C10
Davis (mts.) C11
Deep (creek) C5
Delaware (creek) C10
Delaware (mts.) C10
Denison (dam) H4
Devils (riv.) D7
Diablo, Sierra (mts.) C10
Double Mountain Fork, Brazos
(riv.) C4
Dyess A.F.B. D5
Eagle (peak) C11
Eagle Mountain (lake) E2
Edwards (plat.) C7
Elephant (mt.) D12
Ellington A.F.B. K2
Elm Fork, Trinity (riv.) G2
Emory (peak) A8
Falcon (res.) E11
Finlay (mts.) B10
Fort Bliss 12,687 .... A10
Fort Davis Nat'l Hist. Site D11
Fort Hood 31,250 .... G6
Frio (riv.) E8
Galveston (bay) L2
Galveston (isl.) K8
Glass (mts.) A7
Goodfellow A.F.B. D6
Grapevine (lake) F2
Guadalupe (mts.) C10
Guadalupe (peak) B10
Guadalupe (riv.) G8
Guadalupe Mts. Nat'l Park C10
Houston (lake) J8
Houston Ship (chan.) K2
Howard (creek) C7
Hubbard Creek (lake) F5
Hueco (mts.) B10
Intracoastal Waterway J9
Johnson Draw (dry riv.) C7
Kelly A.F.B. J11
Kemp (lake) E4
Kingsville N.A.S. G10
Kiowa (creek) D1
Lackland A.F.B. 14,459 .... J11
Lake Meredith Nat'l Rec. Area C2
Lampasas (riv.) G6
Laughlin A.F.B. 2,994 .... D8
Lavon (lake) H1
Leon (riv.) F6
Livermore (mt.) C11
Livingston (lake) K7
Llano (riv.) D7
Llano Estacado (plain) B4
Locke (mt.) D11
Los Olmos (creek) F10
Los Olmos (creek) F11
Lyndon B. Johnson Nat'l Hist.
Site F7
Lyndon B. Johnson Space Ctr. K2
Madre (lag.) G11
Maravillas (creek) A7
Matagorda (bay) H9
Matagorda (isl.) H9
Matagorda (pen.) J9
Matagorda Isl. Bombing and Gunnery
Range H9
Medina (lake) E8
Medina (riv.) J11
Mexico (gulf) K9
Middle Concho (riv.) C6

Mountain Creek (lake) G2
Mustang (creek) A1
Mustang (isl.) G10
Mustang Draw (dry riv.) B5
Navasota (riv.) H7
Navidad (riv.) H8
Neches (riv.) K6
North Concho (riv.) C6
North Pease (riv.) D3
Nueces (riv.) F9
Padre (isl.) G10
Padre Island Nat'l Seashore G11
Palo Duro (creek) B2
Palo Duro (creek) C1
Pease (riv.) D3
Pecos (riv.) C7
Pedernales (riv.) F7
Possum Kingdom (lake) F5
Prairie Dog Town Fork, Red (riv.) C3
Quitman (mts.) B11
Red (riv.) F3
Red Bluff (lake) A6
Reese A.F.B. 1,934 .... B4
Rio Grande (riv.) D9
Rita Blanca (creek) B2
Sabine (riv.) L7
Salt Fork, Red (riv.) D3
Sam Rayburn (res.) K6
San Antonio (bay) H9
San Antonio (mt.) B10
San Antonio Missions Nat'l Hist.
Park J11
San Francisco (creek) B8
San Luis (passage) K8
San Martine Draw (dry riv.) C11
San Saba (riv.) D7
Santa Isabel (creek) E10
Santiago (mts.) A8
Santiago (peak) D12
Sheppard A.F.B. F3
Sierra Diablo (mts.) C10
Sierra Vieja (mts.) C11
Staked (Llano Estacado) (plain) B4
Stamford (lake) E4
Stockton (plat.) B7
Sulphur (riv.) J4
Sulphur Draw (dry riv.) B4
Sulphur Springs (creek) B4
Tenmile (creek) G3
Terlingua (creek) D12
Texoma (lake) H3
Tierra Blanca (creek) B3
Toledo Bend (res.) L6
Toyah (creek) D11
Toyah (lake) A6
Travis (lake) G7
Trinity (bay) L2
Trinity (riv.) H5
Trinity, West Fork (riv.) G2
Trujillo (creek) A2
Vieja, Sierra (mts.) C11
Walnut (creek) F3
Washita (riv.) D2
West (bay) K3
White (riv.) C3
White River (lake) C4
White Rock (creek) G2
Wichita (riv.) F4
Wolf (creek) D1
Worth (lake) E2

⊙County seat.
‡Population of metropolitan area.
† Zip of nearest p.o. * Multiple zips.

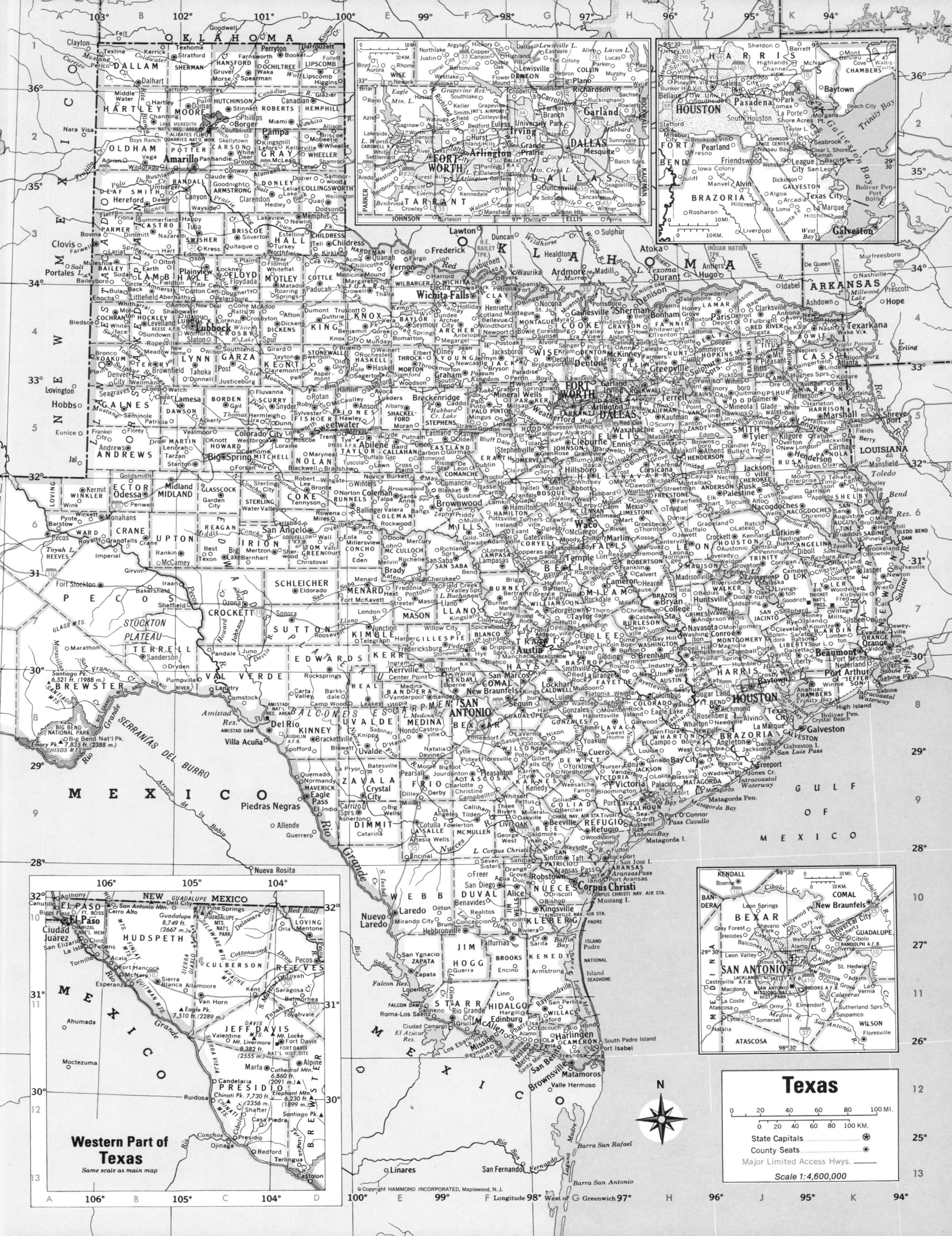

Texas

State Capitals .... ⊛
County Seats .... ⊙
Major Limited Access Hwys. ——————

Scale 1:4,600,000

Western Part of Texas
Same scale as main map

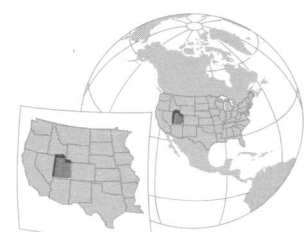

AREA 84,899 sq. mi. (219,888 sq. km.)
POPULATION 1,461,037
CAPITAL Salt Lake City
LARGEST CITY Salt Lake City
HIGHEST POINT Kings Pk. 13,528 ft. (4123 m.)
SETTLED IN 1847
ADMITTED TO UNION January 4, 1896
POPULAR NAME Beehive State
STATE FLOWER Sego Lily
STATE BIRD Sea Gull

COUNTIES

Beaver 4,378 ....A5
Box Elder 33,222 ....A2
Cache 57,176 ....C2
Carbon 22,179 ....D4
Daggett 769 ....E3
Davis 146,540 ....B3
Duchesne 12,565 ....D3
Emery 11,451 ....D4
Garfield 3,673 ....C6
Grand 8,241 ....E5
Iron 17,349 ....A6
Juab 5,530 ....A4
Kane 4,024 ....B6
Millard 8,970 ....A4
Morgan 4,917 ....C2
Piute 1,329 ....B5
Rich 2,100 ....C2
Salt Lake 619,066 ....B3
San Juan 12,253 ....E6
Sanpete 14,620 ....C4
Sevier 14,727 ....C5
Summit 10,198 ....D3
Tooele 26,033 ....A3
Uintah 20,506 ....E3
Utah 218,106 ....C3
Wasatch 8,523 ....C3
Washington 26,065 ....A6
Wayne 1,911 ....C5
Weber 144,616 ....B2

CITIES and TOWNS

Zip Name/Pop. Key
†84003 Alpine 2,649 ....C3
 84003 American Fork 12,693 ...C3
 84713 Beaver⊙ 1,792 ....B5
 84511 Blanding 3,118 ....E6
†84065 Bluffdale 1,300 ....B3
 84010 Bountiful 32,877 ....C3
 84302 Brigham City⊙ 15,596 ..C2
†84101 Brighton 150 ....C3
 84513 Castle Dale⊙ 1,910 ....D4
 84720 Cedar City 10,972 ......A6
 84014 Centerville 8,069 ......C3
 84015 Clearfield 17,982 ......B2
 84017 Coalville⊙ 1,031 ......C2
 84624 Delta 1,930 ....B4
 84020 Draper 5,521 ....C3
 84021 Duchesne⊙ 1,677 ......D3
 84022 Dugway 1,646 ....B3
 84520 East Carbon 1,942 .....D4
 84109 East Millcreek 24,150 ..C3
 84627 Ephraim 2,810 ....C4
 84025 Farmington⊙ 4,691 ....C3
 84523 Ferron 1,718 ....C4
 84631 Fillmore⊙ 2,083 ......B5
†84037 Fruit Heights 2,728 ...C2
 84312 Garland 1,405 ....B2
 84029 Grantsville 4,419 ......B3
 84525 Green River 1,048 .....D4
 84634 Gunnison 1,255 ....C4
†84401 Harrisville 1,371 ......C2
 84032 Heber City⊙ 4,362 ....C3
 84526 Helper 2,724 ....D4
†84043 Highland 2,435 ....C3
†84767 Hilldale 1,009 ....A6
 84117 Holladay 22,189 ....C3
 84528 Huntington 2,316 .....C4
 84737 Hurricane 2,361 ....A6
 84318 Hyde Park 1,495 ....C2
 84319 Hyrum 3,952 ....C2
 84740 Junction⊙ 151 ....B5
 84036 Kamas 1,064 ....C3
 84741 Kanab⊙ 2,148 ....B6
 84037 Kaysville 9,811 ....B2
 84118 Kearns 21,353 ....B3
 84745 La Verkin 1,174 ....A6
 84041 Layton 22,862 ....C2
 84043 Lehi 6,848 ....C3
 84320 Lewiston 1,438 ....C2
†84062 Lindon 2,796 ....C3
 84747 Loa⊙ 364 ....C5
 84321 Logan⊙ 26,844 ......C2
†84078 Maeser 2,216 ....E3
 84044 Magna 13,138 ....B3
 84046 Manila⊙ 272 ....E3
 84642 Manti⊙ 2,080 ....C4
†84663 Mapleton 2,726 ....C3
 84531 Mexican Hat 250 ......E6
 84047 Midvale 10,146 ....B3
 84049 Midway 1,194 ....C3
 84751 Milford 1,293 ....A5
 84532 Moab⊙ 5,333 ....E5
 84754 Monroe 1,476 ....B5
 84535 Monticello⊙ 1,929 ...E6
 84050 Morgan⊙ 1,896 ......C2
 84646 Moroni 1,086 ....C4
 84647 Mount Pleasant 2,049 .C4
 84107 Murray 25,750 ....C3
 84648 Nephi⊙ 3,285 ....C4
†84321 Nibley 1,036 ....C2
†84404 North Ogden 9,309 ...C2
†84010 North Salt Lake 5,548 .C3
*84401 Ogden⊙ 64,407 ......C2
  Ogden-Salt Lake City‡
  936,255 ....C3
 84537 Orangeville 1,309 .....C4
 84057 Orem 52,399 ....C3
  Orem-Provo‡ 218,106 ..C3
 84759 Panguitch⊙ 1,343 ....B6
 84060 Park City 2,823 ....C3
 84761 Parowan⊙ 1,836 .....C6
 84651 Payson 8,246 ....C3
†84302 Perry 1,084 ....C2
†84401 Plain City 2,379 ......B2
 84062 Pleasant Grove 10,833 .C3
†84401 Pleasant View 3,983 ..B2
 84501 Price⊙ 9,086 ....D4
 84332 Providence 2,675 .....C2
 84601 Provo⊙ 74,108 ....C3
  Provo-Orem‡ 218,106 ..C3
 84064 Randolph⊙ 659 ......C2
 84701 Richfield⊙ 5,482 ....B5
 84333 Richmond 1,705 ......C2
†84321 River Heights 1,211 ..C2
 84065 Riverton 7,293 ....B3
 84066 Roosevelt 3,842 ......D3
 84067 Roy 19,694 ....C2
  Saint George⊙ 11,350 .A6
 84653 Salem 2,233 ....C3
 84654 Salina 1,992 ....C5
*84101 Salt Lake City (cap)⊙
  163,697 ....C3
  Salt Lake City-Ogden‡
  936,255 ....C3
*84070 Sandy 52,210 ....C3
 84765 Santa Clara 1,091 ....A6
 84655 Santaquin 2,175 ......C3
 84335 Smithfield 4,993 .....C2
†84065 South Jordan 7,492 ..B3
†84403 South Ogden 11,366 .C2
 84115 South Salt Lake 9,884 .C3
 84660 Spanish Fork 9,825 ...C3
 84663 Springville 12,101 ....C3
*84015 Sunset 5,733 ....B2
†84041 Syracuse 3,702 ......C2
†84101 Taylorsville 17,448 ...B3
 84074 Tooele⊙ 14,335 .....B3
 84337 Tremonton 3,464 .....B2
 84078 Vernal⊙ 6,600 ......E3
 84780 Washington 3,092 ....A6
†84403 Washington Terrace 8,212 .B2
 84542 Wellington 1,406 .....D4
 84339 Wellsville 1,952 .....C2
 84083 Wendover 1,099 ......A3
†84087 West Bountiful 3,556 .B3
 84084 West Jordan 27,192 ..B3
 84340 Willard 1,241 ....C2
 84087 Woods Cross 4,263 ...B3

OTHER FEATURES

Abajo (mts.) E6
Agassiz (mt.) D3
Antelope (isl.) B3
Aquarius (plat.) C5
Arches Nat'l Park E5
Assay (creek) B6
Bad Land (cliffs) D4
Baldy (peak) B5
Bear (lake) C2
Bear (mts.) B2
Bear (riv.) B2
Beaver (mts.) A5
Beaver (riv.) A5
Beaver Dam Wash (creek) A6
Birch (creek) B5
Blue (creek) B2
Bonneville (salt flats) A3
Book (cliffs) E4
Brown (Roan) (cliffs) E4
Bryce Canyon Nat'l Park B6
Canyonlands Nat'l Park D5
Capitol Reef Nat'l Park C5
Castle (valley) D4
Cedar (mts.) B3
Chalk (creek) C3
Chinle (creek) E6
Clear (lake) B4
Cliff (creek) E3
Coal (cliffs) C5
Colorado (riv.) E5
Confusion (range) A4
Cottonwood (creek) C4
Cub (creek) C1
Deep (creek) B1
Deep Creek (range) A4
Delano (peak) B5
Desolation (canyon) E4
Dinosaur Nat'l Mon. E3
Dirty Devil (riv.) D5
Dolores (riv.) E5
Dry Coal (creek) A6
Duchesne (riv.) D3
Dugway (range) A3
Dugway Proving Grounds B3
Dutton (mt.) B5
East Canyon (res.) C3
Echo (res.) C3
Elk (ridge) E6
Ellen (mt.) D5
Emmons (mt.) D3
Escalante (des.) A6
Escalante (riv.) C6
Fish (lake) C5
Fish (riv.) C5
Fish Springs (range) A4
Flaming Gorge (res.) E3
Flaming Gorge Nat'l Rec. Area .E2
Fool Creek (res.) B4
Fremont (isl.) B2
Fremont (riv.) C5
Glen Canyon Nat'l Rec. Area ...D6
Golden Spike Nat'l Hist. Site ..B2
Goshute Ind. Res. A4
Government (creek) B3
Gray (canyon) D4
Great Salt (lake) B2
Great Salt Lake (des.) A3
Greeley (creek) B3
Green (riv.) D4
Grouse (creek) A2
Grouse Creek (mts.) A2
Gunnison (res.) C4
Henry (mts.) D6
Hilgard (mt.) D3
Hill (creek) E4
Hill A.F.B. C2
Hill Creek Ext., Uintah and Ouray Ind.
  Res. E4
Hillers (mt.) D6
House (range) A4
Hovenweep Nat'l Mon. E6
Huntington (creek) C4
Indian (creek) B5
Jordan (riv.) C3
Kaiparowits (plat.) C6
Kanab (creek) B7
Kanosh Ind. Res. B5
Kings (peak) D3
Koosharem Ind. Res. C5
Little Creek (peak) B6
Little Salt (lake) A6
Malad (riv.) B1
Marsh (creek) E3
Marvine (mt.) C5
Mineral (mts.) B5
Mona (res.) C4
Monroe (peak) B5
Montezuma (creek) E6
Monument (valley) D6
Muddy (creek) C4
Natural Bridges Nat'l Mon. ...E6
Navajo (mt.) D6
Navajo Ind. Res. D7
Nebo (mt.) C4
Newfoundland (mts.) A2
Nine Mile (creek) D4
North (lake) B2
Orange (cliffs) D5
Otter (creek) D5
Otter Creek (res.) C5
Paria (riv.) B6
Paunsaugunt (plat.) B6
Pavant (mts.) B5
Peale (mt.) E5
Pennell (mt.) D6
Piute (res.) B5
Plumber (creek) C2
Powell (lake) D6
Price (riv.) D4
Provo (peak) C3
Provo (riv.) C3
Raft River (mts.) A2
Rainbow Bridge Nat'l Mon. ...C6
Roan (cliffs) E4
Rockport (lake) C3
Salvation (creek) C5
San Juan (riv.) D6
San Pitch (riv.) C4
San Rafael (riv.) D4
San Rafael Swell (mts.) D5
Santa Clara (riv.) A6
Sevier (des.) B4
Sevier (lake) A5
Sevier (riv.) B4
Sevier Bridge (res.) C4
Shivwits Ind. Res. A6
Silver Island (mts.) A3
Skull Valley Ind. Res. B3
Spanish Fork (riv.) C3
Strait (cliffs) C6
Strawberry (res.) C3
Strawberry (riv.) D3
Swan (lake) B4
Tavaputs (plat.) D4
Thomas (range) A4
Thousand Lake (mt.) C5
Timpanogos Cave
  Nat'l Mon. C3
Tokewanna (peak) D3
Tooele Army Depot B3
Two Water (creek) E4
Uinta (mts.) D3
Uinta (riv.) D3
Uintah and Ouray Ind. Res. .D3
Utah (lake) C3
Virgin (riv.) A6
Waas (mt.) E5
Wah Wah (mts.) A5
Wahweap (creek) C6
Wasatch (range) C3
Washakie Ind. Res. B2
Waterpocket Fold (cliffs) .D6
Weber (riv.) C3
White (riv.) E3
Willow (creek) E4
Zion Nat'l Park A6
⊙County seat.
‡Population of metropolitan area.
† Zip of nearest p.o.
* Multiple zips.

Agriculture, Industry and Resources

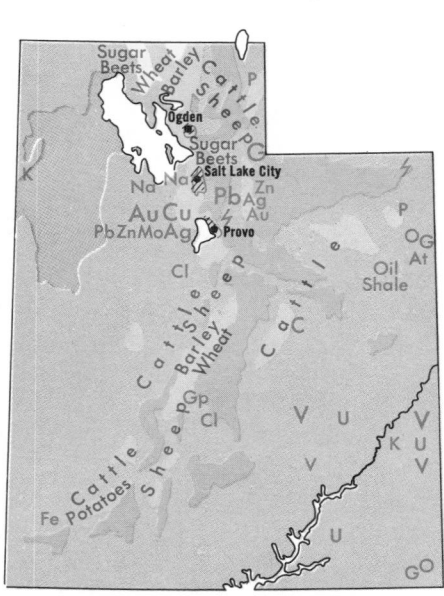

DOMINANT LAND USE

Wheat, General Farming

General Farming, Livestock, Special Crops

Range Livestock

Forests

Nonagricultural Land

MAJOR MINERAL OCCURRENCES

Ag Silver
At Asphalt
Au Gold
C Coal
Cl Clay
Cu Copper

Fe Iron Ore
G Natural Gas
Gp Gypsum
K Potash
Mo Molybdenum
Na Salt

O Petroleum
P Phosphates
Pb Lead
U Uranium
V Vanadium
Zn Zinc

⚡ Water Power
▨ Major Industrial Areas

Topography

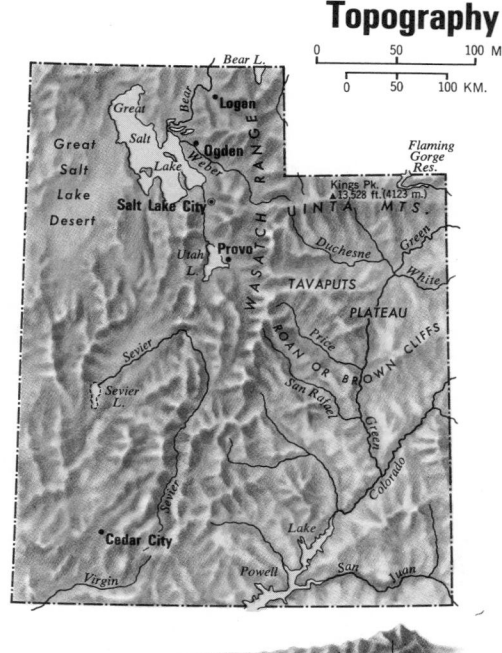

Topography

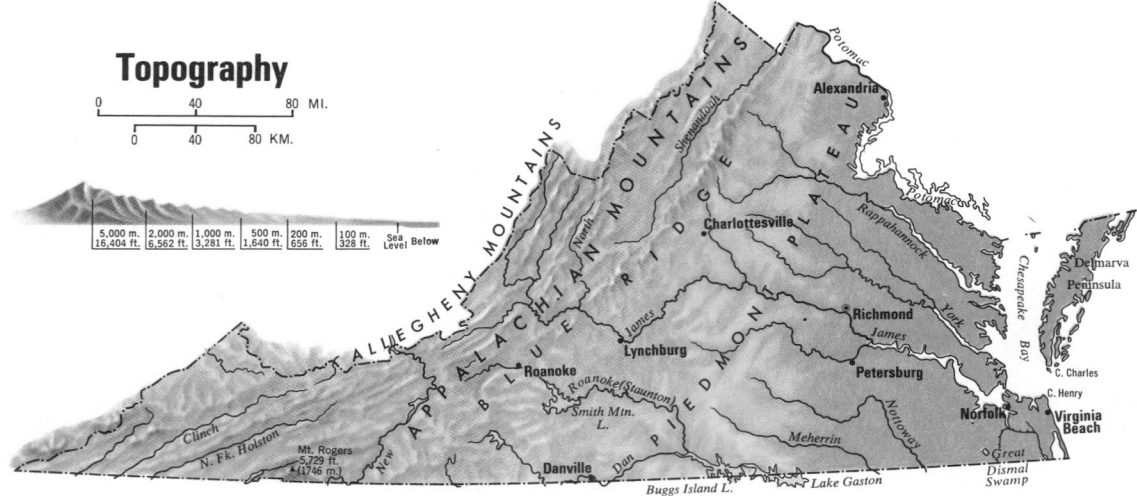

0   40   80 MI.

0   40   80 KM.

5,000 m. | 2,000 m. | 1,000 m. | 500 m. | 200 m. | 100 m. | Sea
16,404 ft. | 6,562 ft. | 3,281 ft. | 1,640 ft. | 656 ft. | 328 ft. | Level Below

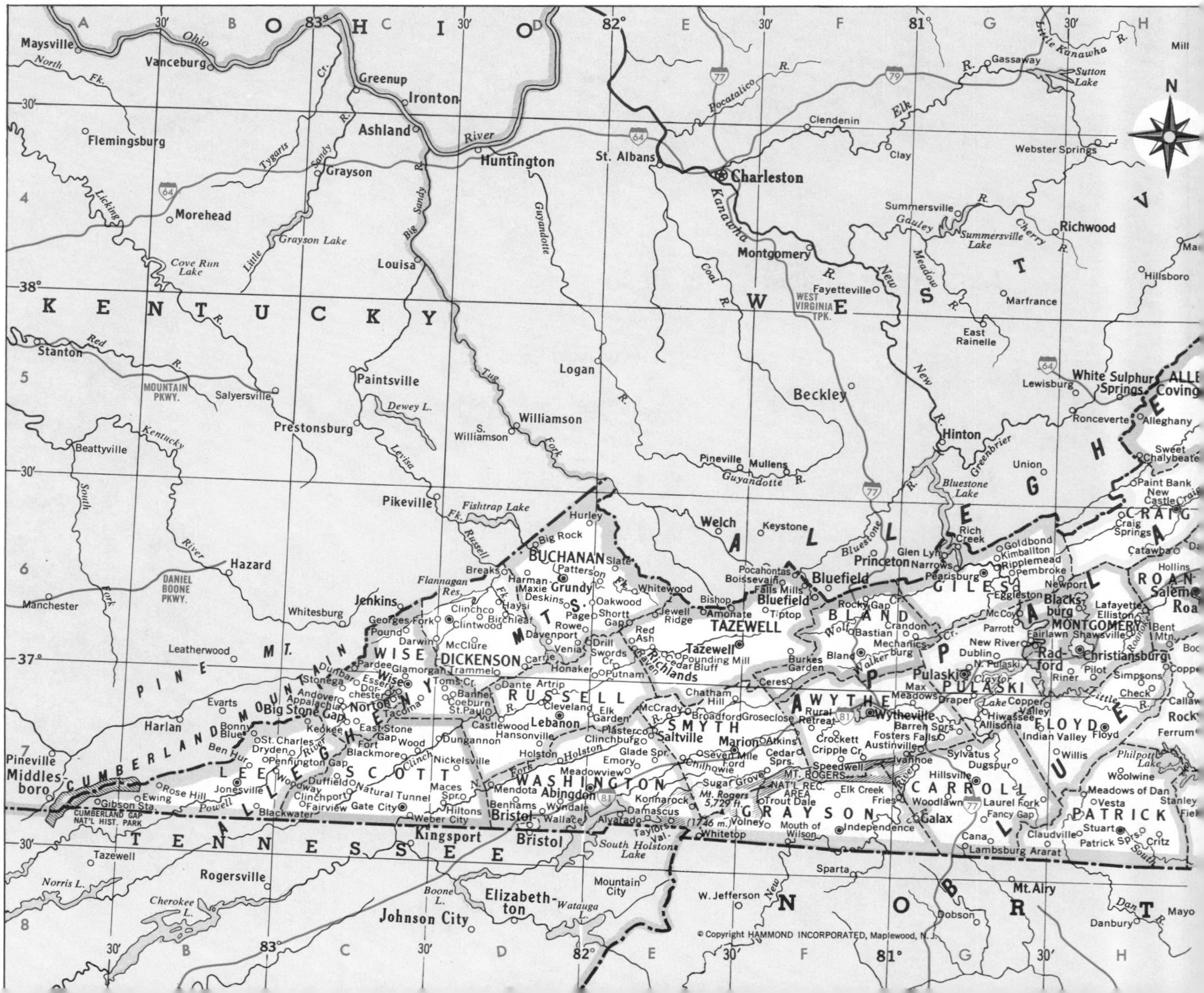

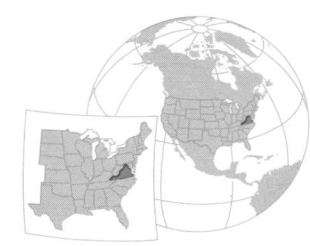

AREA 40,767 sq. mi. (105,587 sq. km.)
POPULATION 5,346,818
CAPITAL Richmond
LARGEST CITY Norfolk
HIGHEST POINT Mt. Rogers 5,729 ft. (1746 m.)
SETTLED IN 1607
ADMITTED TO UNION June 26, 1788
POPULAR NAME Old Dominion
STATE FLOWER Dogwood
STATE BIRD Cardinal

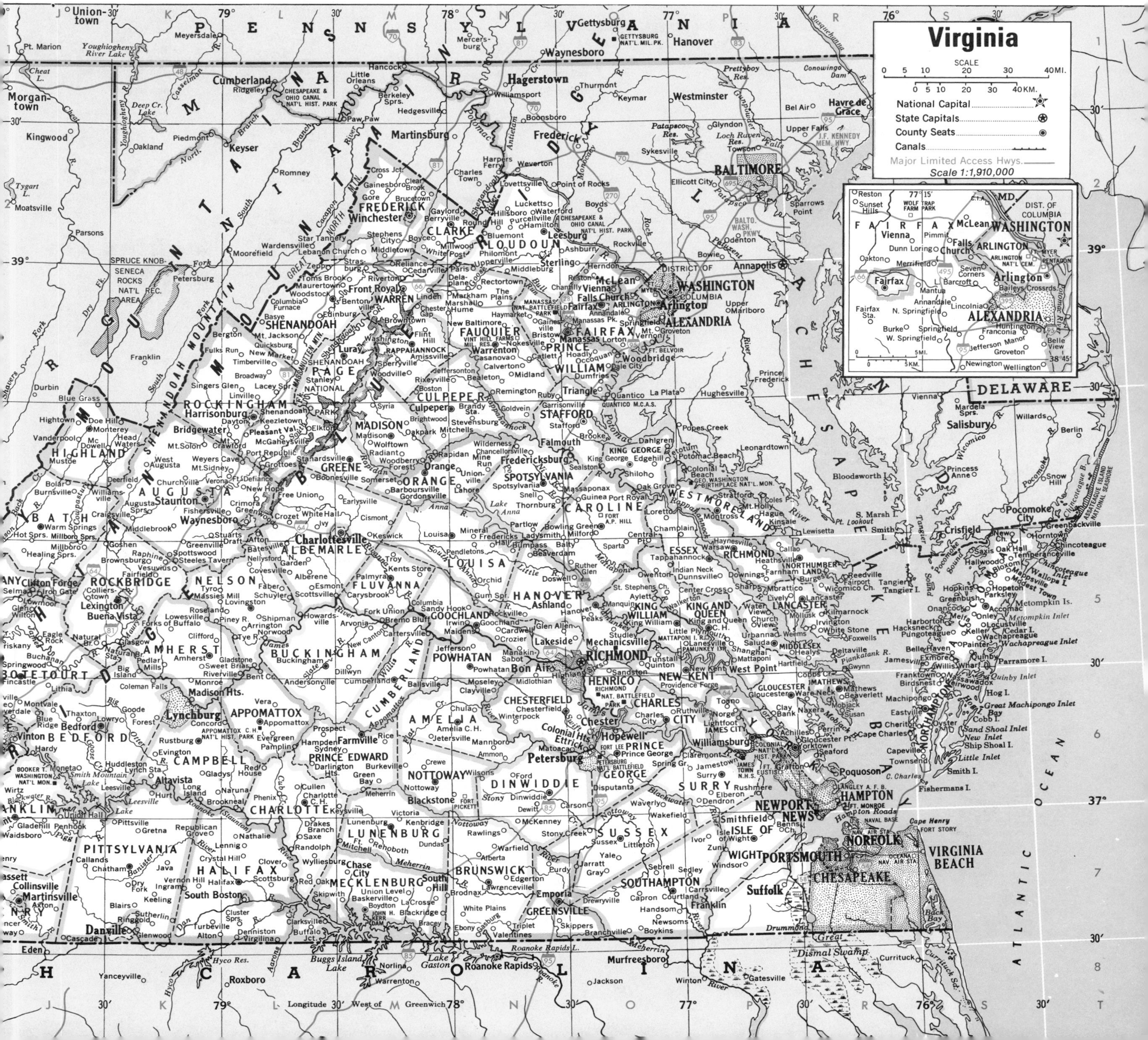

(continued on following page)

Agriculture, Industry and Resources

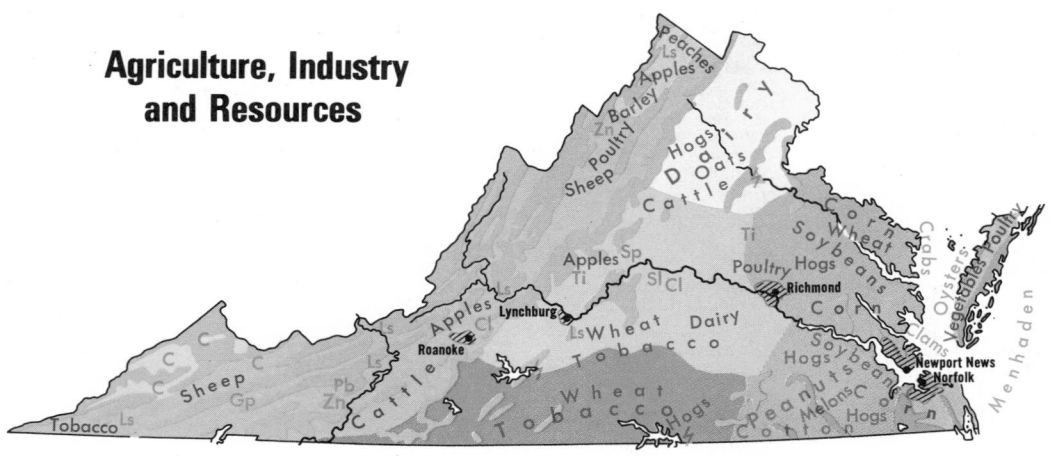

DOMINANT LAND USE

- Dairy, General Farming
- General Farming, Livestock, Dairy
- General Farming, Livestock, Tobacco
- General Farming, Livestock, Fruit, Tobacco
- General Farming, Truck Farming, Tobacco, Livestock
- Tobacco, General Farming
- Peanuts, General Farming
- Fruit and Mixed Farming
- Truck and Mixed Farming
- Forests
- Swampland, Limited Agriculture

MAJOR MINERAL OCCURRENCES

C	Coal	Sl	Slate
Cl	Clay	Sp	Soapstone
Gp	Gypsum	Ti	Titanium
Ls	Limestone	Zn	Zinc
Pb	Lead		

⚡ Water Power

▨ Major Industrial Areas

AREA 68,139 sq. mi. (176,480 sq. km.)
POPULATION 4,132,180
CAPITAL Olympia
LARGEST CITY Seattle
HIGHEST POINT Mt. Rainier 14,410 ft. (4392 m.)
SETTLED IN 1811
ADMITTED TO UNION November 11, 1889
POPULAR NAME Evergreen State
STATE FLOWER Western Rhododendron
STATE BIRD Willow Goldfinch

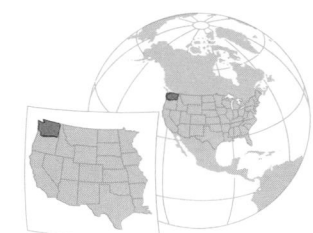

COUNTIES

Adams 13,267 ...... G3
Asotin 16,823 ...... H4
Benton 109,444 ...... F4
Chelan 45,061 ...... E3
Clallam 51,648 ...... B2
Clark 192,227 ...... C5
Columbia 4,057 ...... H4
Cowlitz 79,548 ...... C4
Douglas 22,144 ...... F3
Ferry 5,811 ...... G2
Franklin 35,025 ...... G4
Garfield 2,468 ...... H4
Grant 48,522 ...... F3
Grays Harbor 66,314 ...... B3
Island 44,048 ...... C2
Jefferson 15,965 ...... B3
King 1,269,749 ...... D3
Kitsap 147,152 ...... C3
Kittitas 24,877 ...... E3
Klickitat 15,822 ...... E5
Lewis 56,028 ...... C4
Lincoln 9,604 ...... G3
Mason 31,184 ...... B3
Okanogan 30,639 ...... F2
Pacific 17,237 ...... B4
Pend Oreille 8,580 ...... H2
Pierce 485,667 ...... C3
San Juan 7,838 ...... C2
Skagit 64,138 ...... D2
Skamania 7,919 ...... D5
Snohomish 337,720 ...... D2
Spokane 341,835 ...... H3
Stevens 28,979 ...... H2
Thurston 124,264 ...... C4
Wahkiakum 3,832 ...... B4
Walla Walla 47,435 ...... G4
Whatcom 106,701 ...... D2
Whitman 40,103 ...... H4
Yakima 172,508 ...... E4

CITIES and TOWNS

Zip — Name/Pop. — Key

98520 Aberdeen 18,739 ...... B3
98220 Acme 500 ...... C2
99001 Airway Heights 1,730 ...... H3
99102 Albion 631 ...... H4
†98328 Alder 300 ...... C4
98002 Algona 1,467 ...... C3
98524 Allyn 850 ...... C3
99103 Almira 330 ...... G3
98526 Amanda Park 495 ...... A3
98601 Amboy 480 ...... C5
98221 Anacortes 9,013 ...... C2
98603 Ariel 386 ...... C5
98223 Arlington 3,282 ...... C2
98304 Ashford 300 ...... C4
99402 Asotin⊙ 943 ...... H4
98002 Auburn 26,417 ...... C3
98110 Bainbridge Island-Winslow (Winslow) 2,196 ...... A2
98604 Battle Ground 2,774 ...... C5
†98004 Beaux Arts Village 328 ...... B2
98305 Beaver 450 ...... A2
98528 Belfair 500 ...... C3
*98004 Bellevue 73,903 ...... B2
98225 Bellingham⊙ 45,794 ...... C2
   Bellingham‡ 106,701 ...... C2
99320 Benton City 1,980 ...... F4
98605 Bingen 644 ...... D5
98010 Black Diamond 1,170 ...... D3
98230 Blaine 2,363 ...... C2
†98390 Bonney Lake 5,328 ...... C3
98011 Bothell 7,943 ...... B1
98310 Bremerton 36,208 ...... A2
   Bremerton‡ 146,609 ...... A2
98812 Brewster 1,337 ...... F2
98813 Bridgeport 1,174 ...... F3
†98036 Brier 2,915 ...... C3
98320 Brinnon 500 ...... B3
†98101 Bryn Mawr-Skyway 11,754 ...... B2
98321 Buckley 3,143 ...... C3
98530 Bucoda 519 ...... C4
98921 Buena 590 ...... E4
98166 Burien 23,189 ...... A2
98233 Burlington 3,894 ...... C2
98013 Burton 650 ...... C3
98607 Camas 5,681 ...... C5
98323 Carbonado 456 ...... C3
98324 Carlsborg 500 ...... B2
98814 Carlton 410 ...... F2
98014 Carnation 913 ...... D3
98610 Carson 500 ...... D5
98815 Cashmere 2,240 ...... E3
98611 Castle Rock 2,162 ...... B4
98612 Cathlamet⊙ 635 ...... B4
98531 Centralia 11,555 ...... C4
98520 Central Park 2,709 ...... B3
98532 Chehalis⊙ 6,100 ...... C4
98816 Chelan 2,802 ...... E3
99004 Cheney 7,630 ...... H3
99109 Chewelah 1,888 ...... H2
98614 Chinook 928 ...... B4
98326 Clallam Bay 600 ...... A2
99403 Clarkston 6,903 ...... H4
98235 Clearlake 750 ...... C2
98922 Cle Elum 1,773 ...... E3
98236 Clinton 900 ...... C3
†98004 Clyde Hill 3,229 ...... B2
†98055 Coalfield 500 ...... B2
99111 Colfax⊙ 2,780 ...... H4
99304 College Place 5,771 ...... G4
99113 Colton 307 ...... H4
†98632 Columbia Heights 2,515 ...... C4
99114 Colville⊙ 4,510 ...... H2
98819 Conconully 157 ...... F2
98237 Concrete 592 ...... D2
99326 Connell 1,981 ...... G4
98535 Copalis Beach 600 ...... A3
98536 Copalis Crossing 500 ...... B3
98537 Cosmopolis 1,575 ...... B4
99115 Coulee City 510 ...... F3
98116 Coulee Dam 1,412 ...... G3
98239 Coupeville⊙ 1,006 ...... C2
99012 Fairfield 582 ...... H4
99117 Creston 309 ...... G3
99119 Cusick 246 ...... H2
98240 Custer 300 ...... C2
98617 Dallesport 600 ...... D5
98241 Darrington 1,064 ...... D2
99122 Davenport⊙ 1,559 ...... G3
98328 Dayton⊙ 2,565 ...... H4
98243 Deer Harbor 400 ...... B2
99006 Deer Park 2,140 ...... H3
98188 Des Moines 7,378 ...... B2
99213 Dishman 10,169 ...... H3
99329 Dixie 210 ...... G4
98821 Dryden 500 ...... E3
†98382 Dungeness 675 ...... B2
98327 Du Pont 559 ...... C3
98019 Duvall 729 ...... D3
98245 Eastsound 800 ...... B2
98801 East Wenatchee 1,640 ...... E3
98328 Eatonville 998 ...... C4
98020 Edmonds 27,679 ...... C3
99123 Electric City 927 ...... F3
98926 Ellensburg⊙ 11,752 ...... E3
98541 Elma 2,720 ...... B4
99124 Elmer City 312 ...... G2
99125 Endicott 290 ...... H4
†98901 Fairview-Sumach 2,788 ...... E4
98024 Fall City 1,528 ...... D3
99128 Farmington 176 ...... H3
98248 Ferndale 3,855 ...... C2
98424 Fife 1,823 ...... C3
98466 Fircrest 5,477 ...... C3
†98531 Fords Prairie 2,582 ...... B4
98331 Forks 3,060 ...... A3
99014 Four Lakes 500 ...... H3
98250 Friday Harbor⊙ 1,200 ...... B2
†98901 Fruitvale 3,967 ...... E4
99130 Garfield 599 ...... H3
†99362 Garrett 1,134 ...... G4
98824 George 261 ...... F3
98335 Gig Harbor 2,429 ...... C3
98336 Glenoma 500 ...... C4
98619 Glenwood 626 ...... D4
98251 Gold Bar 794 ...... D3
98620 Goldendale⊙ 3,575 ...... E5
98337 Gorst 750 ...... C3
99133 Grand Coulee 1,180 ...... G3
99930 Grandview 5,615 ...... F4
98932 Granger 1,812 ...... E4
98252 Granite Falls 911 ...... D2
98547 Grayland 750 ...... A4
98621 Grays River 350 ...... B4
98253 Greenbank 600 ...... C2
98339 Hadlock-Irondale 1,752 ...... C2
98255 Hamilton 268 ...... D2
†98366 Harper 300 ...... A2
98933 Harrah 343 ...... E4
99134 Harrington 507 ...... G3
99135 Hartline 165 ...... F3
99332 Hatton 81 ...... G4
98025 Hobart 500 ...... D3
98548 Hoodsport 500 ...... B3
98550 Hoquiam 9,719 ...... A3
†98004 Hunts Point 480 ...... B2
98624 Ilwaco 604 ...... A4
98256 Index 147 ...... D3
98342 Indianola 800 ...... A1
99139 Ione 594 ...... H2
98027 Issaquah 5,536 ...... C3
98343 Joyce 375 ...... B2
98033 Juanita 17,232 ...... B1
99335 Kahlotus 203 ...... G4
98625 Kalama 1,216 ...... C4
98344 Kapowsin 500 ...... C4
98626 Kelso⊙ 11,129 ...... C4
98028 Kenmore 7,281 ...... B1
99336 Kennewick 34,397 ...... F4
98031 Kent 23,152 ...... C3
99141 Kettle Falls 1,087 ...... H2
98345 Keyport 900 ...... A2
98346 Kingston 950 ...... C3
98033 Kirkland 18,779 ...... B2
98934 Kittitas 782 ...... E4
98628 Klickitat 750 ...... D5
†98832 Krupp (Marlin) 83 ...... F3
98629 La Center 439 ...... C5
98503 Lacey 13,940 ...... C3
98257 La Conner 633 ...... C2
99143 Lacrosse 373 ...... H4
†98101 Lake Forest Park 2,485 ...... B1
98258 Lake Stevens 1,660 ...... D3
99017 Lamont 101 ...... H4
98260 Langley 650 ...... C2
98350 La Push 500 ...... A3
99018 Latah 155 ...... H3
98826 Leavenworth 1,522 ...... E3
99019 Liberty Lake 1,599 ...... J3
98555 Lilliwaup 75 ...... B3
99341 Lind 567 ...... G4
98556 Littlerock 850 ...... B4
98631 Long Beach 1,199 ...... A4
98351 Longbranch 640 ...... C3
98632 Longview 31,052 ...... B4
99148 Loon Lake 500 ...... H2
98262 Lummi Island 675 ...... C2
98635 Lyle 580 ...... D5
98263 Lyman 285 ...... D2
98264 Lynden 4,022 ...... C2
98036 Lynnwood 22,641 ...... C3
98935 Mabton 1,248 ...... E4
98149 Malden 200 ...... H3
98829 Malott 350 ...... F2
98353 Manchester 400 ...... A2
98830 Mansfield 315 ...... F3
98266 Maple Falls 300 ...... D2
98038 Maple Valley 900 ...... C3
98151 Marcus 174 ...... H2
98268 Marietta-Alderwood 2,324 ...... C2
98832 Marlin 83 ...... F3
98270 Marysville 5,080 ...... C2
99344 Mattawa 299 ...... F4
98557 McCleary 1,419 ...... B3
99022 Medical Lake 3,600 ...... H3
98039 Medina 3,220 ...... B2
98040 Mercer Island (city) 21,522 ...... B2
99343 Mesa 278 ...... G4
99152 Metaline 190 ...... H2
99153 Metaline Falls 296 ...... H2
†99210 Millwood 1,717 ...... H3
98354 Milton 3,162 ...... C3
98355 Mineral 550 ...... C4
98562 Moclips 500 ...... A3
98836 Monitor 650 ...... E3
98272 Monroe 2,869 ...... D3
98563 Montesano⊙ 3,247 ...... B4
98356 Morton 1,264 ...... C4
98837 Moses Lake 10,629 ...... F3
98564 Mossyrock 463 ...... C4
98043 Mountlake Terrace 16,534 ...... B1
98273 Mount Vernon⊙ 13,009 ...... C2
98936 Moxee City 687 ...... E4
98275 Mukilteo 1,426 ...... C3
98937 Naches 644 ...... E4
98565 Napavine 611 ...... C4
98638 Naselle 500 ...... B4
†98310 Navy Yard City 2,594 ...... A2
98357 Neah Bay 800 ...... A2
99155 Nespelem 284 ...... G2
†98283 Newhalem 350 ...... D2
99156 Newport⊙ 1,665 ...... H2
†98501 Nisqually 500 ...... C3
98276 Nooksack 429 ...... C2
98358 Nordland 706 ...... C2
†98100 Normandy Park 4,268 ...... A2
98045 North Bend 1,701 ...... D3
98639 North Bonneville 394 ...... C5
98157 Northport 368 ...... H2
99158 Oakesdale 444 ...... H3
98277 Oak Harbor 12,271 ...... C2
98568 Oakville 537 ...... B4
98569 Ocean City 350 ...... A3
98640 Ocean Park 918 ...... A4
98551 Ocean Shores 1,692 ...... A3
†98520 Ocosta 369 ...... B4
99159 Odessa 1,009 ...... G3
98840 Okanogan⊙ 2,302 ...... F2
98359 Olalla 500 ...... A2
*98501 Olympia (cap.)⊙ 27,447 ...... C3
   Olympia‡ 124,264 ...... C3
98841 Omak 4,007 ...... F2
98570 Onalaska 600 ...... C4
99214 Opportunity 21,241 ...... H3
98662 Orchards 8,828 ...... C5
98844 Oroville 1,483 ...... F2
98360 Orting 1,787 ...... C3
99344 Othello 4,454 ...... F4
99027 Otis Orchards-East Farms 4,597 ...... H3
98938 Outlook 300 ...... E4
98047 Pacific 2,261 ...... C3
98571 Pacific Beach 900 ...... A3
98361 Packwood 800 ...... D4
99161 Palouse 1,005 ...... H4
98939 Parker 500 ...... E4
98444 Parkland 23,355 ...... C3
99301 Pasco⊙ 18,425 ...... F4
98846 Pateros 555 ...... E2
98572 Pe Ell 617 ...... B4
98847 Peshastin 500 ...... E3
98281 Point Roberts 500 ...... B2
98101 Pomeroy⊙ 1,716 ...... H4
98362 Port Angeles⊙ 17,311 ...... B2
†98601 Port Blakely 600 ...... A2
98366 Port Orchard⊙ 4,787 ...... A2
98368 Port Townsend⊙ 6,067 ...... C2
†98584 Potlach 100 ...... B3
98370 Poulsbo 3,453 ...... A1
98348 Prescott 341 ...... G4
98050 Preston 500 ...... D3
99350 Prosser⊙ 3,896 ...... F4
99163 Pullman 23,579 ...... H4
98371 Puyallup 18,251 ...... C3
98376 Quilcene 900 ...... B3
98575 Quinault 450 ...... B3
98848 Quincy 3,525 ...... F3
98576 Rainier 891 ...... C4

(continued on following page)

Agriculture, Industry and Resources

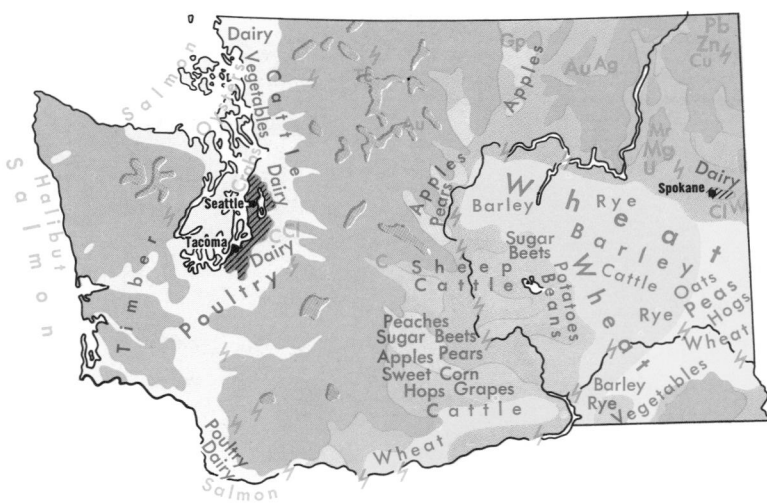

DOMINANT LAND USE

- Specialized Wheat
- Wheat, Peas
- Dairy, Poultry, Mixed Farming
- Fruit and Mixed Farming
- General Farming, Dairy, Range Livestock
- General Farming, Livestock, Special Crops
- Range Livestock
- Forests
- Urban Areas
- Nonagricultural Land

MAJOR MINERAL OCCURRENCES

Ag Silver
Au Gold
C Coal
Cl Clay
Cu Copper
Gp Gypsum
Mg Magnesium

Mr Marble
Pb Lead
Tc Talc
U Uranium
W Tungsten
Zn Zinc

⚡ Water Power
▨ Major Industrial Areas

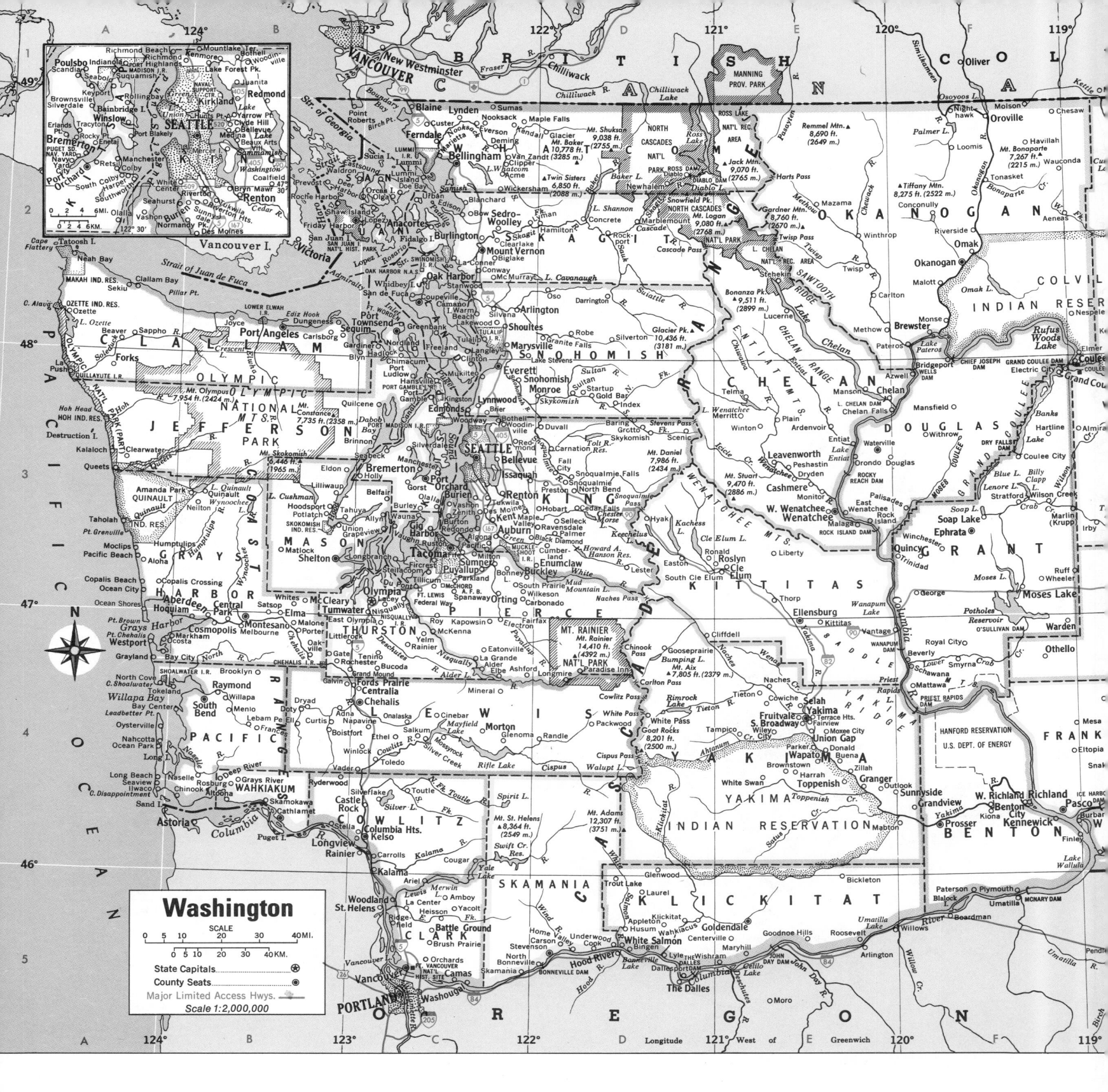

Washington

SCALE
0   5   10   20   30   40 MI.
0   5 10   20   30   40 KM.

State Capitals .... ⊛
County Seats .... ◉
Major Limited Access Hwys.
Scale 1:2,000,000

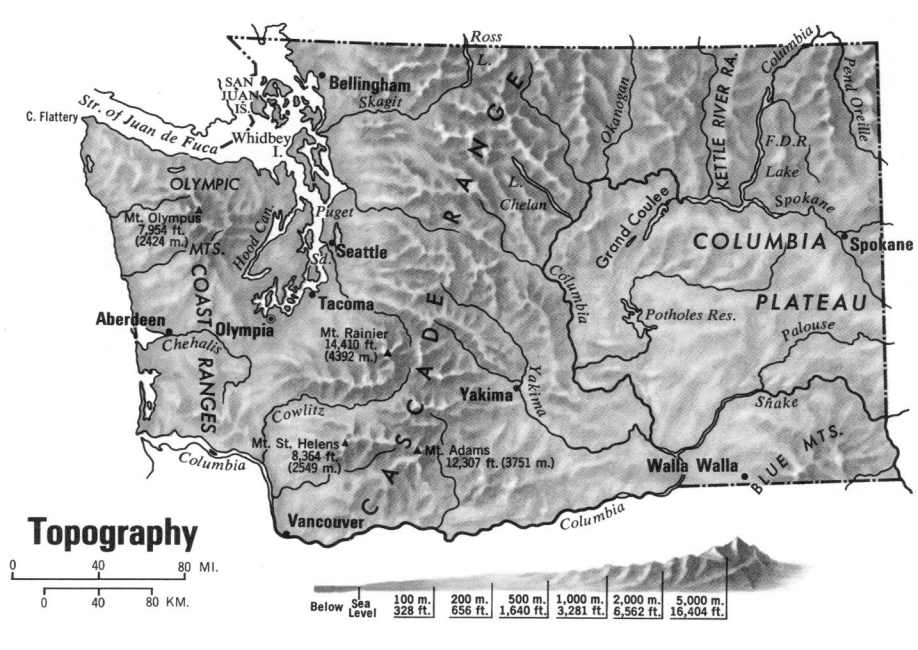

Topography

Below Sea Level	100 m. 328 ft.	200 m. 656 ft.	500 m. 1,640 ft.	1,000 m. 3,281 ft.	2,000 m. 6,562 ft.	5,000 m. 16,404 ft.

Scale: 0 — 40 — 80 MI.
0 — 40 — 80 KM.

Map labels (topography): Ross L., Bellingham, Skagit, C. Flattery, Str. of Juan de Fuca, Whidbey I., SAN JUAN IS., Okanogan, Chelan, KETTLE RIVER RA., Columbia, Pend Oreille, F.D.R. Lake, Spokane, COLUMBIA PLATEAU, Grand Coulee, OLYMPIC MTS., Mt. Olympus 7,954 ft. (2424 m.), Hood Canal, Puget Sound, Seattle, CASCADE RANGE, Potholes Res., COAST RANGES, Aberdeen, Olympia, Tacoma, Chehalis, Mt. Rainier 14,410 ft. (4392 m.), Yakima, Yakima, Palouse, Snake, Cowlitz, Mt. St. Helens 8,364 ft. (2549 m.), Mt. Adams 12,307 ft. (3751 m.), Walla Walla, BLUE MTS., Vancouver, Columbia, Columbia

Index (first list)

Name	Grid
Deer (lake)	H2
Deschutes (riv.)	C4
Destruction (isl.)	A3
Diablo (lake)	D2
Diamond (lake)	H2
Disappointment (cape)	A4
Dry Falls (dam)	F3
Ediz Hook (pen.)	B2
Elwha (riv.)	B3
Entiat (lake)	E3
Entiat (mts.)	E2
Entiat (riv.)	E3
Fairchild A.F.B. 5,353	H3
Fidalgo (isl.)	C2
Flattery (cape)	A2
Fort Lewis 23,761	C3
Fort Vancouver Nat'l Hist. Site	C5
Fort Worden	C2
Franklin D. Roosevelt (lake)	G2
Gardner (mt.)	E2
Georgia (str.)	B2
Glacier (peak)	D2
Goat Rocks (mt.)	D4
Grand Coulee (canyon)	F3
Grand Coulee (dam)	F3
Grande Ronde (riv.)	H5
Grays (harb.)	A4
Green (lake)	A2
Green (riv.)	C3
Grenville (pt.)	A3
Hanford Reservation-U.S. Dept. of Energy	F4
Haro (str.)	B2
Harts (pass)	E2
Hells Canyon Nat'l Rec. Area	H5
Hoh (head)	A3
Hoh (riv.)	A3
Hoh Ind. Res.	A3
Hood (canal)	B3
Howard A. Hanson (res.)	D3
Humptulips (riv.)	B3
Ice Harbor (dam)	G4
Icicle (creek)	E3
Jack (riv.)	E2
John Day (dam)	E5
Juan de Fuca (str.)	A2
Kachess (lake)	D3
Kalama (riv.)	C4
Kalispel Ind. Res.	H2
Keechelus (lake)	D3
Kettle (riv.)	G2
Kettle River (range)	G2
Klickitat (riv.)	D4
Lake (creek)	G3
Lake Chelan Nat'l Rec. Area	E2
Latah (creek)	H3
Leadbetter (pt.)	A4
Lenore (lake)	F3
Lewis (riv.)	C5
Little Goose (dam)	G4
Little Spokane (riv.)	H3
Logan (mt.)	E2
Long (isl.)	A4
Long (lake)	H3
Loon (lake)	H2
Lopez (isl.)	B2
Lower Crab (creek)	F4
Lower Elwha Ind. Res.	B2
Lower Granite (dam)	H4
Lower Monumental (lake)	G4
Lummi (isl.)	C2
Lummi Ind. Res.	C2
Makah Ind. Res.	A2
Mayfield (lake)	C4
McChord A.F.B. 5,746	C3
McNary (dam)	F5
Merwin (lake)	C4
Methow (riv.)	E2

Index (second list)

Name	Grid
Moses (lake)	F3
Moses Coulee (canyon)	F3
Mount Rainier Nat'l Park	D4
Muckleshoot Ind. Res.	C3
Mud Mountain (lake)	D3
Naches (pass)	D3
Naches (riv.)	E4
Naselle (riv.)	B4
Naval Support Ctr.	B1
Newman (lake)	H3
Nisqually (riv.)	C4
Nisqually Ind. Res.	C4
Nooksack (riv.)	C2
North (riv.)	B4
North Cascades Nat'l Park	D2
Oak Harbor Naval Air Sta.	C2
Okanogan (riv.)	F2
Olympic (mts.)	B3
Olympic Nat'l Park	B3
Olympus (mt.)	B3
Omak (lake)	F2
Orcas (isl.)	C2
Osoyoos (lake)	F1
O'Sullivan (dam)	F4
Ozette (lake)	A2
Ozette Ind. Res.	A2
Padilla (bay)	C2
Palmer (lake)	F2
Palouse (riv.)	G4
Pasayten (riv.)	E2
Pataha (creek)	H4
Pateros (lake)	F2
Pend Oreille (riv.)	H2
Pillar (pt.)	A2
Pine (creek)	H3
Port Angeles Ind. Res.	B2
Port Gamble Ind. Res.	C3
Port Madison Ind. Res.	A1
Potholes (res.)	F3
Priest Rapids (lake)	E4
Puget (isl.)	B4
Puget (sound)	C2
Puget Sound Navy Yard	A2
Puyallup (riv.)	C4
Queets (riv.)	A3
Quillayute Ind. Res.	A3
Quinault (lake)	B3
Quinault (riv.)	A3
Quinault Ind. Res.	A3
Rainier (mt.)	D4
Remmel (mt.)	E2
Rifle (lake)	C4
Rimrock (lake)	D4
Rock (creek)	H3
Rock (lake)	H3
Rock Island (dam)	E3
Rocky (mts.)	H2
Rocky Reach (dam)	E3
Rosario (str.)	C2
Ross (dam)	D2
Ross (lake)	D2
Ross Lake Nat'l Rec. Area	E2
Rufus Woods (lake)	F2
Sacajawea (lake)	G4
Sacheen (lake)	H2
Saddle (mts.)	E4
Saint Helens (mt.)	C4
Samish (lake)	C2
Sammamish (lake)	C3
Sand (isl.)	A4
San Juan (isl.)	B2
San Juan Island Nat'l Hist. Park	B2
Sanpoil (riv.)	F2
Satus (creek)	E4
Sauk (riv.)	D2
Sawtooth (ridge)	E2
Shannon (lake)	D2

Index (third list)

Name	Grid
Shoalwater (cape)	A4
Shoalwater Ind. Res.	B4
Shuksan (mt.)	D2
Silver (lake)	C4
Similkameen (riv.)	F1
Skagit (riv.)	C2
Skokomish (mt.)	B3
Skokomish Ind. Res.	B3
Skykomish (riv.)	D3
Snake (riv.)	G4
Snohomish (riv.)	C3
Snoqualmie (pass)	D3
Snoqualmie (riv.)	D3
Snow (peak)	G2
Snowfield (peak)	D2
Soap (lake)	F3
Soleduck (riv.)	A3
Spirit (lake)	C4
Spokane (mt.)	H3
Spokane (riv.)	H3
Spokane Ind. Res.	G3
Sprague (lake)	G3
Stevens (pass)	D3
Stuart (mt.)	E3
Sucia (isl.)	C2
Suiattle (riv.)	D2
Sullivan (lake)	H2
Sultan (riv.)	D3
Swift Creek (res.)	C4
Swinomish Ind. Res.	C2
Sylvan (lake)	G3
Tatoosh (isl.)	A2
The Dalles (dam)	D5
Tieton (riv.)	D4
Tiffany (mt.)	F2
Tolt River (res.)	D3
Toppenish (creek)	E4
Touchet (riv.)	G4
Toutle, North Fork (riv.)	C4
Toutle, South Fork (riv.)	C4
Tucannon (riv.)	G4
Tulalip Ind. Res.	C2
Tule (lake)	G3
Twin (lkes.)	G2
Twin Sisters (mt.)	D2
Twisp (pass)	E2
Twisp (riv.)	E2
Umatilla (lake)	E5
Union (lake)	B2
Vancouver (lake)	C5
Walla Walla (riv.)	G4
Wallula (lake)	F4
Walupt (lake)	D4
Wanapum (lake)	E3
Washington (lake)	B2
Wells (dam)	F3
Wenas (lake)	E4
Wenatchee (lake)	E3
Wenatchee (mts.)	E3
Wenatchee (riv.)	E3
Whatcom (lake)	C2
Whidbey (isl.)	C2
White (pass)	D4
White (riv.)	D3
White Salmon (riv.)	D4
Whitman Mission Nat'l Hist. Site	G4
Willapa (bay)	A4
Wilson (creek)	F3
Wind (riv.)	D5
Wynoochee (lake)	B3
Wynoochee (riv.)	B3
Yakima (ridge)	E4
Yakima (riv.)	F4
Yakima Ind. Res.	E4

⊙County seat.
‡Population of metropolitan area.
† Zip of nearest p.o. * Multiple zips.

Index (bottom-left list)

Name	Grid
Adams (mt.)	D4
Admiralty (inlet)	B2
Ahtanum (creek)	D4
Aix (mt.)	D4
Alava (cape)	A2
Alder (lake)	C4
Asotin (creek)	H4
Asotin (dam)	J4
Bainbridge (isl.)	A2
Baker (lake)	D2
Baker (mt.)	D2
Baker (riv.)	D2
Banks (lake)	F3
Birch (pt.)	C2
Blalock (isl.)	F5
Blue (lake)	F3
Blue (mts.)	H4
Bonanza (peak)	E2
Bonaparte (creek)	F2
Bonaparte (mt.)	F2
Bonneville (dam)	D5
Bonneville (lake)	D5
Boundary (bay)	C1

Name	Grid
Boundary (dam)	H2
Boundary (lake)	H2
Box Canyon (dam)	H2
Brown (pt.)	A4
Bumping (lake)	D4
Camano (isl.)	C2
Carlton (pass)	D4
Cascade (pass)	D2
Cascade (range)	D2
Cascade (riv.)	D2
Cavanaugh (lake)	C2
Cedar (riv.)	B2
Celilo (lake)	D5
Chehalis (pt.)	A4
Chehalis (riv.)	C4
Chehalis Ind. Res.	B4
Chelan (lake)	E2
Chelan (range)	E2
Chester Morse (lake)	D3
Chewack (riv.)	E2
Chief Joseph (dam)	F3
China Gardens (dam)	J4
Chinook (pass)	D4

Name	Grid
Chiwawa (riv.)	E2
Cispus (pass)	D4
Cispus (riv.)	D4
Cle Elum (lake)	E3
Coal (creek)	G3
Coast (ranges)	B3
Columbia (riv.)	B4
Colville (riv.)	H2
Colville Ind. Res.	G2
Constance (mt.)	B3
Coulee Dam Nat'l Rec. Area	G2
Cow (creek)	G3
Cowlitz (pass)	D4
Cowlitz (riv.)	C4
Crab (creek)	F3
Crescent (lake)	B2
Curlew (lake)	G2
Cushman (lake)	B3
Dabob (bay)	C3
Dalles, The (dam)	D5
Daniel (mt.)	D3
Deadman (creek)	H4

Main map labels (left): COLUMBIA, Grand Forks, Rossland, Trail, Fruitvale, Christina L., Danville, Laurier, Northport, Mt. Abercrombie 7,308 ft. (2227 m.), Boundary Dam, Metaline Falls, Metaline, Box Canyon Dam, Ione, Tiger, Sullivan L., Priest L., Curlew, Orient, Leadpoint, Snow Pk. 7,109 ft. (2167 m.), Bossburg, Evans, Marcus, Kettle Falls, Lost Creek, Ruby, Pend Oreille, PEND OREILLE, KETTLE RIVER RANGE, FERRY, STEVENS, Malo, Colville, Orin, Park Rapids, Cusick, Usk, KALISPEL IND. RES., Kettle Falls, Rice, Arden, Addy, Bluecreek, Chewelah, Dalkena, Newport, Priest River, ALBENI FALLS DAM, Inchelium, Gifford, Daisy, Impach, Springdale, Valley, Deer L., Sacheen, Diamond, Kewa, Cedonia, Hunters, Fruitland, Loon Lake, Elk, PRIEST R., Roosevelt, Lincoln, Creston, Davenport, Reardan, Deepcreek, Espanola, Medical Lake, FAIRCHILD A.F.B. HTS., Four Lakes, Geiger HTS., Cheney, Tyler, Edwall, Waukon, Spokane, Spokane, Town & Country, Dishman, Opportunity, Veradale, Greenacres, Liberty Lake, Coeur d'Alene L., Coeur d'Alene, Mica, Rockford, Mohler, Harrington, Sprague, Amber, Plaza, Spangle, Fairfield, Waverly, Latah, Plummer, Rosalia, Tekoa, LINCOLN, ADAMS, SPOKANE, Ritzville, Lind, Ralston, Benge, Washtucna, Cunningham, Hooper, Kahlotus, Marengo, Lamont, Pine City, Oakesdale, Thornton, Belmont, Farmington, Garfield, Steptoe, Elberton, Palouse, Colfax, Moscow, WHITMAN, Dusty, Lacrosse, Winona, Endicott, Diamond, Albion, Pullman, Deadman Cr., Hay, L. Bryan, Almota, Colton, Uniontown, Clarkston, Lewiston, GARFIELD, COLUMBIA, ASOTIN, Pomeroy, Pataha, Turner, Anatone, Cloverland, Starbuck, Ayer, Clyde, Riparia, Dayton, Huntsville, Waitsburg, Prescott, Eureka, Dixie, Garrett, Walla Walla, College Place, Milton-Freewater, WALLA WALLA, BLUE MTS., HELLS CANYON NAT'L REC. AREA, Wallowa, Elgin, Enterprise, IDAHO, LEWIS

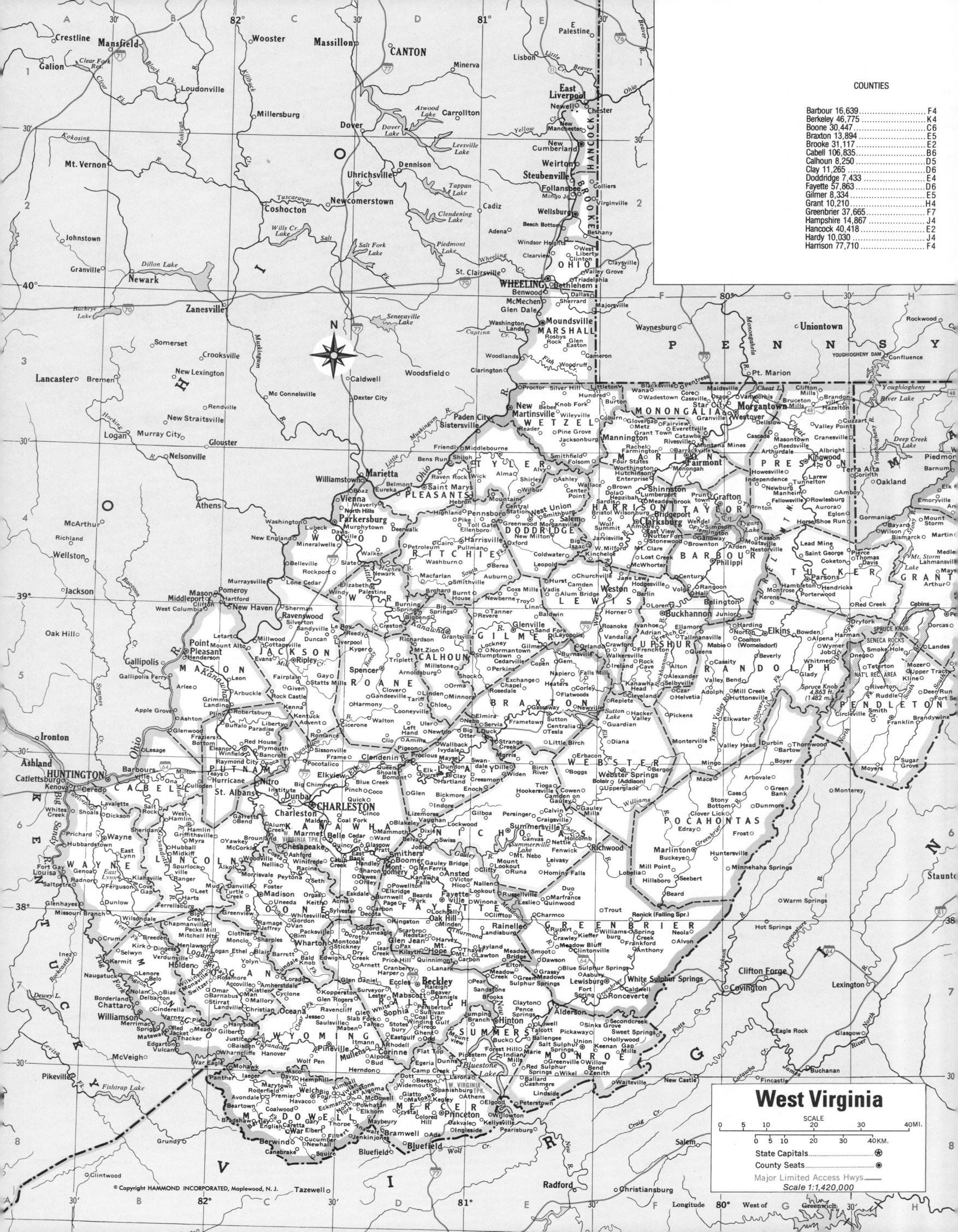

West Virginia

SCALE

0   5   10   20   30   40 MI.

0   5 10   20   30   40 KM.

State Capitals .... ⊛

County Seats .... ◎

Major Limited Access Hwys. ——————

Scale 1:1,420,000

COUNTIES

County	Pop.	Grid
Barbour	16,639	F4
Berkeley	46,775	K4
Boone	30,447	C6
Braxton	13,894	E5
Brooke	31,117	E2
Cabell	106,835	B6
Calhoun	8,250	D5
Clay	11,265	D6
Doddridge	7,433	E4
Fayette	57,863	D6
Gilmer	8,334	E5
Grant	10,210	H4
Greenbrier	37,665	F7
Hampshire	14,867	J4
Hancock	40,418	E2
Hardy	10,030	J4
Harrison	77,710	F4

Jackson 25,794 ....C5
Jefferson 30,302 ....L4
Kanawha 231,414 ....C6
Lewis 18,813 ....E4
Lincoln 23,675 ....B6
Logan 50,679 ....C7
Marion 65,789 ....F4
Marshall 41,608 ....E3
Mason 27,045 ....B5
McDowell 49,899 ....C8
Mercer 73,942 ....D8
Mineral 27,234 ....J4
Mingo 37,336 ....B7
Monongalia 75,024 ....F3
Monroe 12,873 ....E7
Morgan 10,711 ....K3
Nicholas 28,126 ....E6
Ohio 61,389 ....E2
Pendleton 7,910 ....H5
Pleasants 8,236 ....D4

Pocahontas 9,919 ....F6
Preston 30,460 ....G4
Putnam 38,181 ....C6
Raleigh 86,821 ....D7
Randolph 28,734 ....G5
Ritchie 11,442 ....D4
Roane 15,952 ....D5
Summers 15,875 ....E7
Taylor 16,584 ....F4
Tucker 8,675 ....G4
Tyler 11,320 ....E4
Upshur 23,427 ....F5
Wayne 46,021 ....B6
Webster 12,245 ....E6
Wetzel 21,874 ....E3
Wirt 4,922 ....D4
Wood 93,648 ....D4
Wyoming 35,993 ....C7

CITIES and TOWNS

Zip / Name/Pop. / Key

25606 Accoville 975 ....C7
†26288 Addison (Webster Springs)⊙ 939 ....F6
26210 Adrian 510 ....F5
26519 Albright 357 ....G3
24910 Alderson 1,375 ....E7
25044 Algoma 200 ....D8
25501 Alkol 500 ....C6
26320 Alma 197 ....E4
24710 Alpoca 200 ....D7
26321 Alum Bridge 150 ....E4
25003 Alum Creek 900 ....C6
26322 Alvy 150 ....E4
25004 Ameagle 230 ....D7
25607 Amherstdale 1,075 ....C7
25005 Amma 200 ....D5
24808 Anawalt 652 ....D8

AREA 24,231 sq. mi. (62,758 sq. km.)
POPULATION 1,950,279
CAPITAL Charleston
LARGEST CITY Charleston
HIGHEST POINT Spruce Knob 4,863 ft. (1482 m.)
SETTLED IN 1774
ADMITTED TO UNION June 20, 1863
POPULAR NAME Mountain State
STATE FLOWER Big Rhododendron
STATE BIRD Cardinal

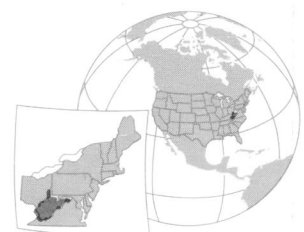

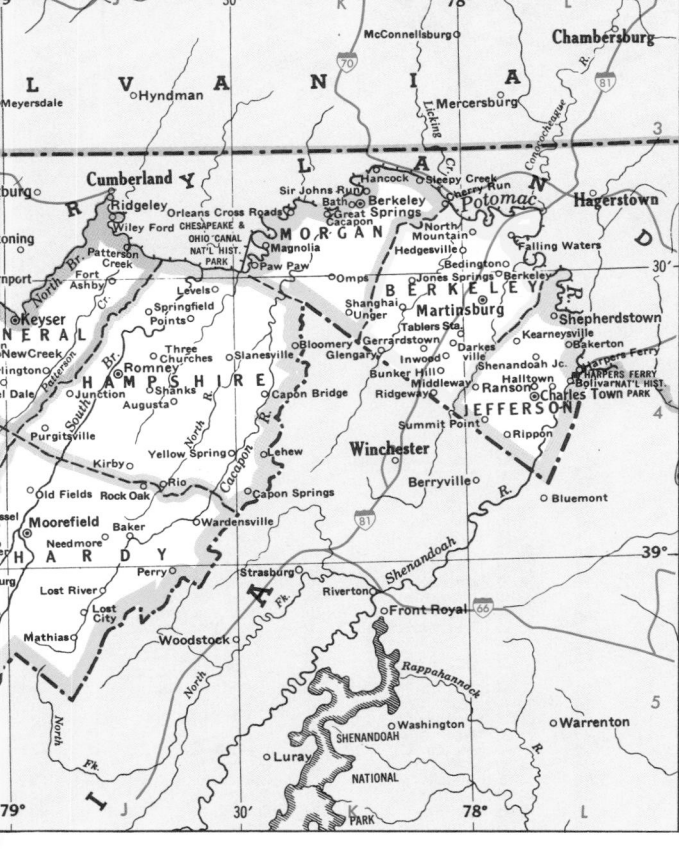

Topography

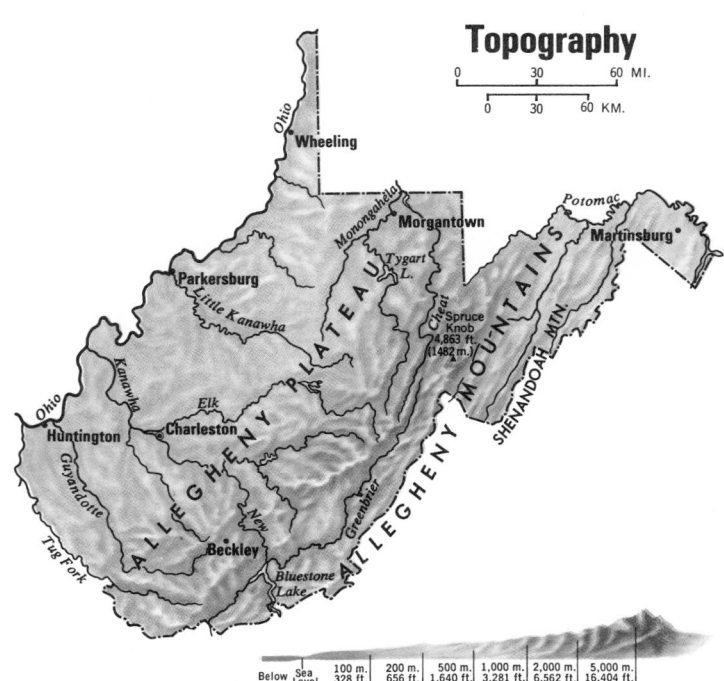

| | Below Sea Level | Sea Level | 100 m. 328 ft. | 200 m. 656 ft. | 500 m. 1,640 ft. | 1,000 m. 3,281 ft. | 2,000 m. 6,562 ft. | 5,000 m. 16,404 ft. |

26323 Anmoore 865 ....F4
25812 Ansted 1,952 ....D6
25502 Apple Grove 900 ....B5
24915 Arbovale 610 ....G6
26816 Arthur 350 ....H4
26520 Arthurdale 1,063 ....G3
24916 Asbury 280 ....E7
24809 Asco 175 ....C8
25009 Ashford 400 ....C6
25503 Ashton 259 ....B5
26325 Auburn 614 ....E4
26704 Augusta 750 ....J4
26705 Aurora 250 ....G4
24811 Avondale 250 ....C8
25608 Baisden 500 ....C7
26801 Baker 200 ....J4
25410 Bakerton 125 ....L4
25010 Bald Knob 356 ....C7
26326 Baldwin 92 ....E5
25011 Bancroft 528 ....C5
25504 Barboursville 2,871 ....B6
25609 Barnabus 750 ....C7
26559 Barrackville 1,815 ....F3
25013 Barrett 950 ....C7
24813 Bartley 900 ....C8
24920 Bartow 500 ....G5
†25411 Bath (Berkeley Springs) 789 ....K3
26707 Bayard 540 ....H4
25014 Beards Fork 400 ....D6
25813 Beaver (Glen Hedrick) 1,122 ....D7
25801 Beckley⊙ 20,492 ....D7
26030 Beech Bottom 507 ....E2
24714 Beeson 300 ....D8
26250 Belington 2,038 ....F4
25015 Belle 1,621 ....C6
26133 Belleville 105 ....C4
26134 Belmont 887 ....D4
26656 Belva 275 ....D6
26135 Bens Run 85 ....D4
26031 Benwood 1,994 ....E2
26298 Bergoo 220 ....F6
25411 Berkeley Springs (Bath)⊙ 789 ....K3
24815 Berwind 615 ....C8
26032 Bethany 1,336 ....E2
†26003 Bethlehem 3,045 ....E2
26253 Beverly 475 ....G5
25019 Bickmore 300 ....D6
26136 Bigbend 120 ....D5
25302 Big Chimney 450 ....C6
25505 Big Creek 500 ....B7
26137 Big Springs 485 ....D5
25021 Bim 500 ....C7
26610 Birch River 650 ....E6
26521 Blacksville 248 ....F3
25022 Blair 800 ....C7
26817 Bloomery 200 ....K4
25026 Blue Creek 650 ....D6
26288 Bolair 450 ....F6
†25425 Bolivar 672 ....L4
25030 Bomont 170 ....D6
25031 Boomer 1,051 ....D6
24817 Bradshaw 1,002 ....C8
24715 Bramwell 989 ....D8
26523 Brandonville 92 ....G3
26802 Brandywine 300 ....H5
25666 Breeden 600 ....B7
26330 Bridgeport 6,604 ....F4
25957 Brooks 196 ....E7
26334 Brownton 400 ....F4
26525 Bruceton Mills 296 ....G3
24924 Buckeye 125 ....F6
26201 Buckhannon⊙ 6,820 ....F5
24716 Bud 400 ....D7
25033 Buffalo 1,034 ....C5
25413 Bunker Hill 600 ....K4
26710 Burlington 300 ....J4
26335 Burnsville 531 ....E5
26336 Burnt House 175 ....D4
26562 Burton 200 ....F3
25035 Cabin Creek 900 ....C6
26337 Cairo 428 ....D4
24925 Caldwell 795 ....F7
26660 Calvin 400 ....E6
26208 Camden on Gauley 236 ....E6
26033 Cameron 1,474 ....E3
24819 Canebrake 300 ....C8
26662 Canvas 300 ....E6
26711 Capon Bridge 191 ....K4
26823 Capon Springs 580 ....K4
25037 Carbon 300 ....D6
24821 Caretta 650 ....C8
24927 Cass 148 ....G6
26527 Cassville 800 ....F3
25039 Cedar Grove 1,479 ....C6
26339 Center Point 250 ....E4
26612 Centralia 100 ....E6
26340 Central Station 200 ....E4
26214 Century 250 ....F4
25507 Ceredo 2,255 ....B6
25508 Chapmanville 1,164 ....B7

*25301 Charleston (cap.)⊙ 63,968 ....C6
Charleston‡ 269,595 ....C6
25414 Charles Town⊙ 2,857 ....L4
25958 Charmco 800 ....E6
25667 Chattaroy 1,383 ....B7
25418 Cherry Run 120 ....L3
†25301 Chesapeake 2,364 ....C6
26034 Chester 3,297 ....E1
26301 Clarksburg⊙ 22,371 ....F4
25043 Clay⊙ 940 ....D6
25044 Clear Creek 300 ....D7
†26003 Clearview 740 ....E2
25045 Clendenin 1,373 ....D5
26215 Cleveland 74 ....F5
25822 Clifftop 100 ....E6
25237 Clifton 325 ....B5
24928 Clintonville 250 ....E7
25046 Clio 300 ....D5
25047 Clothier 900 ....C7
25823 Coal City 2,300 ....D7
25306 Coal Fork 2,775 ....D6
26257 Coalton 306 ....G5
24824 Coalwood 650 ....C8
25048 Colcord 600 ....D7
26035 Colliers 864 ....E2
26615 Copen 50 ....E5
25826 Corinne 900 ....D7
25051 Costa 200 ....C6
25239 Cottageville 300 ....C5
25509 Cove Gap 650 ....B6
26206 Cowen 723 ....E6
26342 Coxs Mills 275 ....E4
26205 Craigsville 1,562 ....E6
25828 Cranberry 315 ....D7
24931 Crawley 395 ....E7
25669 Crum 500 ....B7
24826 Cucumber 274 ....C8
25510 Culloden 2,931 ....B6
24827 Cyclone 500 ....C7
26036 Dallas 450 ....E2
25832 Daniels 1,959 ....D7
25053 Danville 727 ....C6
†25428 Darkesville 150 ....L4
26260 Davis 979 ....H4
24828 Davy 882 ....C8
25054 Dawes 800 ....D6
24932 Dawson 300 ....E7
25670 Delbarton 981 ....B7
26531 Dellslow 300 ....G3
26217 Diana 500 ....F5
26617 Dille 300 ....E6
25671 Dingess 600 ....B7
25059 Dixie 985 ....D6
25060 Dorothy 400 ....D7
24721 Dott 100 ....D8
25062 Dry Creek 441 ....D7
26263 Dryfork 425 ....H5
25063 Duck 500 ....E5
25064 Dunbar 9,285 ....C6
24934 Dunmore 280 ....G6
26264 Durbin 379 ....G5
25067 East Bank 1,155 ....D6
25835 Eastgulf 300 ....D7
25512 East Lynn 150 ....B6
†26301 East View 1,222 ....F4
25836 Eccles 1,162 ....D7
24829 Eckman 750 ....C8
25672 Edgarton 415 ....B7
26716 Eglon 70 ....G4
24830 Elbert 400 ....C8
26143 Elizabeth⊙ 856 ....D4
26717 Elk Garden 291 ....H4
26241 Elkins⊙ 8,536 ....G5
25071 Elkview 1,161 ....C6
26267 Ellamore 250 ....F5
25965 Ellenboro 357 ....D4
25965 Elton 200 ....E7
24832 English 500 ....C8
26568 Enterprise 1,110 ....F4
25075 Eskdale 400 ....D6
25076 Ethel 450 ....C7
26144 Eureka 125 ....D4
25241 Evans 400 ....C5
26533 Everettville 175 ....F3
26554 Fairmont 23,863 ....F4
26570 Fairview 759 ....F3
†24966 Falling Spring (Renick) 240 ....F6
26571 Farmington 583 ....F3
25840 Fayetteville⊙ 2,366 ....D6
26202 Fenwick 500 ....E6
24835 Filbert 130 ....D8
25841 Flat Top 550 ....D7
26621 Flatwoods 405 ....E5
26347 Flemington 452 ....F4
26037 Follansbee 3,994 ....E2
26348 Folsom 360 ....E4
24935 Forest Hill 314 ....E7
25514 Fort Ashby 1,205 ....J4
24836 Fort Gay 886 ....A6
24937 Fort Seybert 200 ....H5
24936 Fort Spring 250 ....E7
25081 Foster 500 ....C6

26572 Four States 500 ....F4
25071 Frame 76 ....C5
26623 Frametown 150 ....E5
26807 Franklin⊙ 780 ....H5
25082 Fraziers Bottom 250 ....B5
26219 Frenchton 102 ....F5
26146 Friendly 242 ....D3
25515 Gallipolis Ferry 325 ....B5
25243 Gandeeville 150 ....D5
24941 Gap Mills 300 ....F7
24836 Gary 2,233 ....C8
26624 Gassaway 1,225 ....E5
25085 Gauley Bridge 1,177 ....D6
26240 Gauley Mills 165 ....E6
25244 Gay 300 ....C5
25420 Gerrardstown 240 ....K4
25843 Ghent 500 ....D7
25621 Gilbert 757 ....C7
26671 Gilboa 500 ....E6
26350 Gilmer 110 ....E5
26268 Glady 175 ....G5
25086 Glasgow 1,031 ....D6
25088 Glen 175 ....D6
26038 Glen Dale 1,875 ....E3
26039 Glen Easton 100 ....E3
25090 Glen Ferris 200 ....D6
25421 Glengary 250 ....K4
†25813 Glen Hedrick (Beaver) 1,122 ....D7
25846 Glen Jean D7
25848 Glen Rogers 500 ....D7
26351 Glenville⊙ 2,155 ....E5
25849 Glen White 300 ....D7
25520 Glenwood 400 ....B5
†26585 Glovergap 100 ....F3
25093 Gordon 300 ....C7
26720 Gormania 100 ....H4
26354 Grafton⊙ 6,845 ....G4
26147 Grantsville⊙ 788 ....D5
26574 Grant Town 987 ....F3
26534 Granville 992 ....F3
24943 Grassy Meadows 100 ....E7
25422 Great Cacapon 750 ....K3
24944 Green Bank 115 ....G6
25966 Green Sulphur Springs 225 ....E7
24945 Greenville 125 ....E7
26360 Greenwood 750 ....E4
25095 Grimms Landing 350 ....B5
26221 Guardian 175 ....D7
26222 Hacker Valley 440 ....F5
25423 Halltown 375 ....L4
26269 Hambleton 403 ....G4
25523 Hamlin⊙ 1,219 ....B6
25623 Hampden 300 ....C7
25424 Hancock 175 ....K3
25102 Handley 633 ....D6
†26250 Harding 100 ....G5
26270 Harman 181 ....G5
25246 Harmony 600 ....D5
25851 Harper 400 ....D7
25425 Harpers Ferry 361 ....L4
26362 Harrisville⊙ 1,673 ....E4
25247 Hartford 556 ....C4
25524 Harts 400 ....B6
25852 Harvey 300 ....D7
24841 Havaco 350 ....C8
26627 Heaters 440 ....E5
25427 Hedgesville 217 ....K3
26224 Helvetia 130 ....F5
24842 Hemphill 700 ....C8
25106 Henderson 604 ....B5
26271 Hendricks 390 ....G4
25624 Henlawson 900 ....B7
26369 Hepzibah 600 ....F4
24726 Herndon 500 ....D7
25854 Hico 750 ....D6
24946 Hillsboro 276 ....F6
25951 Hinton⊙ 4,622 ....E7
25625 Holden 2,036 ....B7
26372 Homer 125 ....C7
26769 Horse Shoe Run 500 ....G4
†25506 Hubball 145 ....B6
26273 Huttonsville 242 ....G5
*25701 Huntington⊙ 63,684‡ A6
Huntington-Ashland‡ 311,350 ....A6
25526 Hurricane 3,751 ....C6
26273 Huttonsville 242 ....G5
24844 Iaeger 833 ....C8
26374 Independence 200 ....G4
24949 Indian Mills 150 ....E7
25111 Indore 300 ....D6
25112 Institute C6
25428 Inwood 1,159 ....K4
24847 Itmann 600 ....D7
25113 Ivydale 800 ....D5
26377 Jacksonburg 400 ....E3
25114 Jeffrey 900 ....C7
26378 Jane Lew 406 ....F4
24848 Jenkinjones 750 ....D8
24849 Jesse 400 ....C7
26674 Jodie 440 ....D6
25969 Jumping Branch 700 ....E7
26824 Junction 75 ....J4

(continued on following page)

Agriculture, Industry and Resources

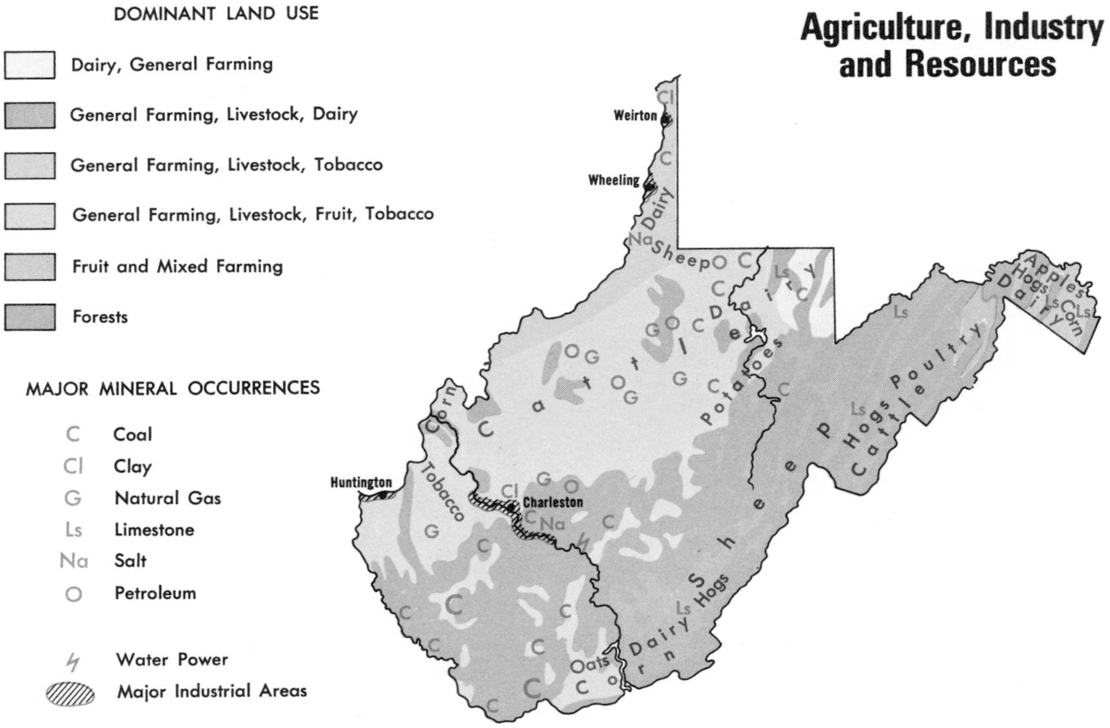
DOMINANT LAND USE
Dairy, General Farming
General Farming, Livestock, Dairy
General Farming, Livestock, Tobacco
General Farming, Livestock, Fruit, Tobacco
Fruit and Mixed Farming
Forests
MAJOR MINERAL OCCURRENCES
C Coal
Cl Clay
G Natural Gas
Ls Limestone
Na Salt
O Petroleum
Water Power
Major Industrial Areas
Weirton
Wheeling
Huntington
Charleston
Dairy
Sheep
Cattle
Potatoes
Corn
Tobacco
Poultry
Hogs
Apples
Oats

26275 Junior 591 G5
24851 Justice 600 C7
25115 Kanawha Falls 105 D6
25430 Kearneysville 250 L4
24731 Kegley 900 D8
24732 Kellysville 165 E8
25248 Kenna 150 C5
25530 Kenova 4,454 A6
25249 Kentuck 200 C5
25674 Kermit 705 B7
26726 Keyser⊙ 6,569 J4
24852 Keystone 902 D8
24950 Kieffer 135 E7
25859 Kilsyth 200 D7
24853 Kimball 871 C8
25120 Kingston 189 D7
26537 Kingwood⊙ 2,877 G4
26729 Kirby 110 J4
25628 Kistler 200 C7
26579 Knob Fork 106 E3
24854 Kopperston 700 C7
26731 Lahmansville 200 H4
25860 Lanark 559 D7
25629 Landville 400 C7
25535 Lavalette 600 B6
25863 Lawton 100 E7
25864 Layland 500 E7
†26430 Layopolis (Sand Fork) 280 E5
25251 Left Hand 700 D5
26676 Leivasy 200 E6
25676 Lenore 800 B7
25123 Leon 228 C5
25971 Lerona 550 D8
25537 Lesage 600 B5
25972 Leslie 350 E6
25865 Lester 626 D7
25253 Letart 350 C5
25431 Levels 180 J4
24901 Lewisburg⊙ 3,065 E7
26384 Linn 165 E4
26629 Little Birch 400 E5
26581 Littleton 335 F3
25125 Lizemores 400 D6
25866 Lochgelly 250 D6
25258 Lockney 190 E5
25601 Logan⊙ 3,029 B7
25630 Lorado 400 C7
†26201 Lorentz 200 F4
26810 Lost City 130 J5
26385 Lost Creek 604 F4
26811 Lost River 500 J5
†26101 Lubeck 1,356 C4
26386 Lumberport 939 F4
25631 Lundale 525 C7
25870 Maben 450 D7
26278 Mabie 550 F5
25871 Mabscott 1,668 D7
26148 Macfarlan 436 D4
25130 Madison⊙ 3,228 C6
26541 Maidsville 500 F3
25306 Malden 900 C6
25634 Mallory 1,330 C7
25132 Mammoth 563 D6
25635 Man 1,333 C7
26582 Mannington 3,036 F3
25975 Marfrance 225 E6
24954 Marlinton⊙ 1,352 F6
25315 Marmet 2,196 C6
25401 Martinsburg⊙ 13,063 K4
25260 Mason 1,432 B4
26542 Masontown 1,052 G3
25678 Matewan 822 B7
24736 Matoaka 613 D8
24861 Maybeury 300 D8
26833 Maysville 150 H4
24858 McDowell 500 D8
26040 McMechen 2,402 E3
26401 McWhorter 150 F4
24958 Meadow Bluff 250 E7
25976 Meadow Bridge 530 E7
26404 Meadowbrook 500 F4
25977 Meadow Creek 300 E7
26585 Metz 150 F3
26149 Middlebourne⊙ 941 E3
25540 Midkiff 650 B6
26280 Mill Creek 801 G5
24959 Mill Point 148 F6
25261 Millstone 850 D5
25262 Millwood 800 C5
25541 Milton 2,178 B6
25879 Minden 800 D7
26150 Mineralwells 325 C4
26281 Mingo 350 F5
25263 Minnora 500 D5
26405 Moatsville 150 G4
25636 Monaville 950 B7
26554 Monongah 1,132 F4
26586 Montana Mines 200 F3
25135 Montcoal 150 D7
26282 Monterville 250 F5
25136 Montgomery 3,104 D6
26283 Montrose 129 G4
26836 Moorefield⊙ 2,257 J4
26505 Morgantown⊙ 27,605 G3
25542 Morrisvale 450 C6
26041 Moundsville⊙ 12,419 E3
26407 Mountain 200 E4
25264 Mount Alto 200 C5
25139 Mount Carbon 450 D7
26408 Mount Clare 950 F4
25637 Mount Gay 4,366 C7
25880 Mount Hope 1,849 D7
26678 Mount Lookout 500 E6
26679 Mount Nebo 535 E6
26739 Mount Storm 500 H4
25882 Mullens 2,919 D7
26680 Nallen 250 E6
26631 Napier 158 E5
25685 Naugatuck 500 B7
25141 Nebo 200 D5
25142 Nellis 600 C6
24961 Neola 300 F7
26681 Nettie 500 E6
26410 Newburg 418 G4
26047 New Cumberland⊙ 1,752 E2
26050 Newell 2,032 E1
26154 New England 335 C4
24866 Newhall 400 C8
25265 New Haven 1,723 C5
26056 New Manchester 800 E1
26155 New Martinsville⊙ 7,109 E3
25266 Newton 390 D5
26632 Newville 160 E5
25143 Nitro 8,074 C6
25687 Nolan 250 B7
25267 Normantown 112 E5
24868 Northfork 1,105 D8
†26101 North Hills 940 D4
26285 Norton 400 G5
26301 Nutter Fort 2,078 F4
25901 Oak Hill 7,120 D6
24739 Oakvale 208 D8
24870 Oceana 2,143 C7
25902 Odd 500 D7
25147 Ohley 450 D6
25638 Omar 900 C7
26886 Onego 400 H5
25148 Orgas 500 C6
26412 Orlando 700 E5
25268 Orma D5
26543 Osage 285 F3
25151 Packsville 225 C7
26159 Paden City 3,671 D3
25152 Page 600 D6
26160 Palestine 110 D4
24872 Panther 450 C8
26101 Parkersburg⊙ 39,967 D4
Parkersburg-Marietta‡ 162,836 D4
26287 Parsons⊙ 1,937 G4
26746 Patterson Creek 157 J3
25434 Paw Paw 644 K3
25904 Pax 274 D7
†25955 Pear 100 E7
25547 Pecks Mill 350 B7
25905 Pemberton 300 D7
24962 Pence Springs 300 E7
26415 Pennsboro 1,652 E4
26544 Pentress 250 F3
26847 Petersburg⊙ 2,084 H5
24963 Peterstown 648 E8
25154 Peytona 175 C6
26416 Philippi⊙ 3,194 G4
24964 Pickaway 225 E7
26230 Pickens 240 F5
25689 Pie 250 B7
26750 Piedmont 1,491 H4
25156 Pinch 800 D6
26419 Pine Grove 767 E3
24874 Pineville⊙ 1,140 C7
25158 Pliny 900 B5
25159 Poca 1,142 C6
†25301 Pocotalico 2,420 C6
25550 Point Pleasant⊙ 5,682 B5
25437 Points 250 J4
25161 Powellton 1,339 D6
24877 Powhatan 400 D8
25162 Pratt 821 D6
24878 Premier 400 C8
†25880 Price Hill 175 D7
25555 Prichard 500 A6
24740 Princeton⊙ 7,493 D8
25164 Procious 600 D5
26055 Proctor 350 E3
26421 Pullman 196 E4
26852 Purgitsville 450 J4
25045 Quick 400 D6
†25015 Quincy 150 C6
25981 Quinwood 460 E6
26587 Rachel 550 F3
25165 Racine 725 C6
25556 Radnor 300 A6
25962 Rainelle 1,983 E7
25911 Raleigh 900 D7
25166 Ramage 350 C7
25557 Ranger 300 B6
25438 Ranson 2,471 L4
25913 Ravencliff 350 C7
26164 Ravenswood 4,126 C5
26167 Reader 950 E3
26289 Red Creek 125 H4
25168 Red House 600 C5
25692 Red Jacket 850 B7
26547 Reedsville 564 G3
25270 Reedy 338 D5
24966 Renick 240 F6
25915 Rhodell 472 D7
26261 Richwood 3,568 F6
26753 Ridgeley 994 J3
25440 Ridgeway 200 K4
26755 Rio 140 J4
25271 Ripley⊙ 3,464 C5
25441 Rippon 500 L4
26588 Rivesville 1,327 F3
26234 Rock Cave 400 F5
24881 Roderfield 900 C8
26757 Romney⊙ 2,094 J4
24970 Ronceverte 2,312 F7
26636 Rosedale 400 E5
25643 Rossmore 200 C7
26425 Rowlesburg 966 G4
26688 Runa 150 E6
25984 Rupert 1,276 E7
26689 Russellville 280 E6
25177 Saint Albans 12,402 C6
26290 Saint George 150 G4
26170 Saint Marys⊙ 2,219 D4
26426 Salem 2,706 E4
25559 Salt Rock 350 B6
26430 Sand Fork 280 E5
25985 Sandstone 300 E7
25275 Sandyville 500 C5
25876 Saulsville 250 C7
25917 Scarbro 800 D7
24975 Seebert 100 F6
25181 Seth 950 C6
26761 Shanks 500 J4
25182 Sharon 450 D6
25183 Sharples 250 C7
25443 Shepherdstown 1,791 L4
26173 Sherman 104 C5
26431 Shinnston 3,059 F4
26434 Shirley 275 E4
25562 Shoals 150 B6
26638 Shock 200 D5
†26164 Silverton 250 C5
26435 Simpson 250 F4
24976 Sinks Grove 156 F7
25320 Sissonville 450 C5
26175 Sistersville 2,367 D3
25920 Slab Fork 210 D7
25444 Slanesville 250 K4
26436 Smithburg 130 E4
25186 Smithers 1,482 D6
26437 Smithfield 278 E4
26178 Smithville 200 D4
24977 Smoot 300 E7
25921 Sophia 1,216 D7
25303 South Charleston 15,968 C6
25922 Spanishburg 550 D8
25276 Spencer⊙ 2,799 D5
25693 Sprigg 225 B7
26763 Springfield 250 J4
25565 Spurlockville 250 B6
24884 Squire 900 C8
26505 Star City 1,464 F3
25279 Statts Mills 400 C5
25188 Stickney 150 D7
25645 Stirrat 250 C7
26301 Stonewood 2,058 F4
24979 Stony Bottom 50 F6
25280 Stumptown 125 E5
26651 Summersville⊙ 2,972 E6
25446 Summit Point 455 K4
25932 Surveyor 300 D7
26601 Sutton⊙ 1,192 E5
26690 Swiss 500 D6
25647 Switzer 1,034 B7
25193 Sylvester 256 C6
24981 Talcott 800 E7
26237 Tallmansville 140 F5
26179 Tanner 375 E5
26764 Terra Alta 1,946 H4
26640 Tesla 300 E5
25694 Thacker 525 B7
26292 Thomas 747 H4
26440 Thornton 200 G4
24888 Thorpe 600 D8
26765 Three Churches 350 J4
25936 Thurmond 67 D7
26691 Tioga 825 E6
26059 Triadelphia 1,461 E2
26443 Troy 110 E4
26444 Tunnelton 510 G4
25203 Turtle Creek 566 C6
25205 Uneeda 700 C6
25447 Unger 300 K4
24983 Union⊙ 743 E7
26266 Upperglade 750 F6
26866 Upper Tract 155 H5
26445 Vadis 130 E4
26293 Valley Bend 950 F5
26060 Valley Grove 597 E2
26294 Valley Head 900 G5
25206 Van 800 C7
25696 Varney 750 B7
25649 Verdunville 950 B7
25938 Victor 500 D6
26105 Vienna 11,618 D4
24891 Vivian 500 D8
26238 Volga 125 F4
25697 Vulcan 130 B7
26589 Wadestown 300 F3
24984 Waiteville 230 F8
26180 Walker 100 D4
26448 Wallace 325 E4
25286 Walton 550 D5
26590 Wana 150 F3
24892 War 2,158 C8
26851 Wardensville 241 J4
26181 Washington 450 C4
26184 Waverly 500 D4
25570 Wayne⊙ 1,495 B6
26288 Webster Springs⊙ 939 F6
26062 Weirton 25,371 E2
Weirton-Steubenville‡ 163,099 E2
24801 Welch⊙ 3,885 C8
26070 Wellsburg⊙ 3,963 E2
25287 West Columbia 245 B5
25571 West Hamlin 643 B6
26074 West Liberty 744 E2
25601 West Logan 630 C7
26451 West Milford 510 F4
26452 Weston⊙ 6,250 F4
26505 Westover 4,884 G3
26456 West Union⊙ 1,090 E4
25651 Wharncliffe 900 C7
25208 Wharton 450 C7
26003 Wheeling⊙ 43,070 E2
Wheeling‡ 185,566 E2
24986 White Sulphur Springs 3,371 F7
25209 Whitesville 689 C6
26296 Whitmer 400 G5
25211 Widen 230 E6
26767 Wiley Ford 1,224 J3
26186 Wileyville 175 E3
25653 Wilkinson 975 B7
24991 Williamsburg 350 F7
25661 Williamson⊙ 5,219 B7
26187 Williamstown 3,095 C4
26461 Wilsonburg 350 F4
25699 Wilsondale 250 B7
26075 Windsor Heights 800 E2
25213 Winfield⊙ 329 C5
25214 Winifrede 750 C6
25942 Winona 250 E6
26462 Wolf Summit 750 F4
†26257 Womelsdorf (Coalton) 306 G5
25572 Woodville 300 C6
26591 Worthington 329 F4
25573 Yawkey 985 C6
26865 Yellow Spring 280 J4
25654 Yolyn 400 C7

OTHER FEATURES

Big Sandy (riv.) A6
Bluestone (lake) E7
Buckhannon (riv.) F5
Cacapon (riv.) J4
Cheat (riv.) G3
Cherry (riv.) E6
Chesapeake and Ohio Canal Nat'l Hist. Pa J3
Clear Fork, Guyandotte (riv.) C7
Coal (riv.) C6
Dry Fork (riv.) C8
Dry Fork (riv.) G5
East Lynn (lake) B6
Elk (riv.) D6
Fish (creek) E3
Gauley (riv.) D6
Greenbrier (riv.) F6
Guyandotte (riv.) B6
Harpers Ferry Nat'l Hist. Park L4
Hughes (riv.) D4
Kanawha (riv.) C5
Little Kanawha (riv.) D5
Meadow (riv.) E6
Mill (creek) C5
Monongahela (riv.) G3
Mount Storm (lake) H4
Mud (riv.) B6
New (riv.) E7
North (riv.) J4
Ohio (riv.) B5
Patterson (creek) J4
Pigeon (creek) B7
Pocatalico (riv.) C5
Pond Fork (riv.) C6
Potomac (riv.) L3
Potts (creek) F7
Reedy (creek) D5
Shavers Fork (riv.) G5
Shenandoah (riv.) K4
Spruce Knob (mt.) G5
Spruce Knob-Seneca Rocks Nat'l Rec. Area H5
Stony (riv.) H4
Summersville (lake) E6
Sutton (lake) F5
Tug Fork (riv.) B7
Twelvepole (creek) A6
Tygart (lake) G4
Tygart Valley (riv.) F5
West Fork (riv.) E5
Williams (riv.) F6

⊙County seat.
‡Population of metropolitan area.
† Zip of nearest p.o. * Multiple zips.

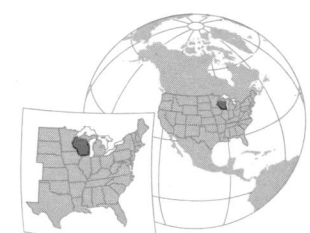

AREA 56,153 sq. mi. (145,436 sq. km.)
POPULATION 4,705,521
CAPITAL Madison
LARGEST CITY Milwaukee
HIGHEST POINT Timms Hill 1,951 ft. (595 m.)
SETTLED IN 1670
ADMITTED TO UNION May 29, 1848
POPULAR NAME Badger State
STATE FLOWER Wood Violet
STATE BIRD Robin

COUNTIES

Adams 13,457 G7
Ashland 16,783 E3
Barron 38,730 C5
Bayfield 13,822 D3
Brown 175,280 L7
Buffalo 14,309 C7
Burnett 12,340 B4
Calumet 30,867 K7
Chippewa 52,127 D5
Clark 32,910 E6
Columbia 43,222 H9
Crawford 16,556 E9
Dane 323,545 H9
Dodge 75,064 J9
Door 25,029 M6
Douglas 44,421 C3
Dunn 34,314 C6
Eau Claire 78,805 D6
Florence 4,172 K4
Fond du Lac 88,964 K8
Forest 9,044 J4
Grant 51,736 E10
Green 30,012 G10
Green Lake 18,370 H8
Iowa 19,802 F9
Iron 6,730 F3
Jackson 16,831 E7
Jefferson 66,152 J9
Juneau 21,039 F8
Kenosha 123,137 K10
Kewaunee 19,539 L6
La Crosse 91,056 D8
Lafayette 17,412 F10
Langlade 19,978 H5
Lincoln 26,555 G5
Manitowoc 82,918 L7
Marathon 111,270 G6
Marinette 39,314 K5
Marquette 11,672 H8
Menominee 3,373 J5
Milwaukee 964,988 L9
Monroe 35,074 E8
Oconto 28,947 K6
Oneida 31,216 G4
Outagamie 128,799 K7
Ozaukee 66,981 L9
Pepin 7,477 C6
Pierce 31,149 B6
Polk 32,351 B5
Portage 57,420 G6
Price 15,788 F4
Racine 173,132 K10
Richland 17,476 F9
Rock 139,420 H10
Rusk 15,589 D5
Saint Croix 43,262 B5
Sauk 43,469 G9
Sawyer 12,843 D4
Shawano 35,928 J6
Sheboygan 100,935 L8
Taylor 18,817 E5
Trempealeau 26,158 D7
Vernon 25,642 E8
Vilas 16,535 G3
Walworth 71,507 J10
Washburn 13,174 C4
Washington 84,848 K9
Waukesha 280,080 K9
Waupaca 42,831 J6
Waushara 18,526 H7
Winnebago 131,722 J8
Wood 72,799 F7

CITIES and TOWNS

Zip Name/Pop. Key

54405 Abbotsford 1,901 F6
53910 Adams 1,744 G8
53001 Adell 545 L8
53501 Afton 225 H10
53502 Albany 1,051 G10
†53534 Albion 300 H10
54201 Algoma 3,656 M6
53002 Allenton 915 K9
†54301 Allouez 14,882 L7
54610 Alma⊙ 876 C7
54611 Alma Center 454 E7
54805 Almena 526 B5
54909 Almond 477 G7
54720 Altoona 4,393 C6
54102 Amberg 875 K5
54001 Amery 2,404 B5
54406 Amherst 701 H7
54407 Amherst Junction 225 H7
54408 Aniwa 273 H6
54409 Antigo⊙ 8,653 H5
54911 Appleton⊙ 58,913 J7
Appleton-Oshkosh‡ 291,325 J7
†54568 Arbor Vitae 900 G4
54612 Arcadia 2,109 D7
53503 Arena 451 G9
54511 Argonne 600 J4
53504 Argyle 720 G10
54721 Arkansaw 400 B6
53911 Arlington 440 H9
54103 Armstrong Creek 615 K4
54410 Arpin 361 G6
53003 Ashippun 750 H1
54806 Ashland⊙ 9,115 E2
54304 Ashwaubenon 14,486 K7
54411 Athens 988 G5
54412 Auburndale 641 F6
54722 Augusta 1,560 D6
53506 Avoca 505 F9
†53520 Avon 120 H10
54413 Babcock 250 F7
53801 Bagley 317 D10
54202 Baileys Harbor 250 M5
54002 Baldwin 1,620 B6
54810 Balsam Lake⊙ 749 B5
54921 Bancroft 355 G7
54614 Bangor 1,012 E8
53913 Baraboo⊙ 8,081 G9
†54873 Barnes 225 D3
53507 Barneveld 579 F10
54812 Barron⊙ 2,595 C5
†53001 Batavia 125 K8
54723 Bay City 543 B6
54814 Bayfield 778 E2
†53201 Bayside 4,724 M1
54922 Bear Creek 454 J6
53916 Beaver Dam 14,149 J9
53802 Beetown 150 E10
53004 Belgium 892 L8
†54631 Bell Center 124 E9
53508 Belleville 1,302 G10
53510 Belmont 826 F10
53511 Beloit 35,207 H10
53803 Benton 983 F10
54923 Berlin 5,478 H8
†54410 Bethel 210 F6
†54440 Bevent 200 H6
53103 Big Bend 1,345 K2
54926 Big Falls 107 H6
54817 Birchwood 437 C4
54414 Birnamwood 688 H6
†54494 Biron 698 G7
54106 Black Creek 1,097 K7
53515 Black Earth 1,145 G9
54615 Black River Falls⊙ 3,434 E7
†54541 Blackwell 550 J4
54616 Blair 1,142 D7
53516 Blanchardville 803 G10
54617 Bloom City 167 E8
54724 Bloomer 3,342 D5
53804 Bloomington 743 E10
53517 Blue Mounds 387 G9
53518 Blue River 412 E9
†53581 Boaz 161 E9
†53105 Bohners Lake 1,507 K10
54107 Bonduel 1,160 K6
53805 Boscobel 2,662 E9
54512 Boulder Junction 780 G3
54416 Bowler 339 J6
54725 Boyceville 862 C5
54726 Boyd 660 E6
54203 Branch 300 L7
53919 Brandon 862 J8
54513 Brantwood 500 F4
53920 Briggsville 250 H8
54110 Brillion 2,907 L7
53520 Brodhead 3,153 G10
54417 Brokaw 298 G5
53005 Brookfield 34,035 K1
53521 Brooklyn 627 H10
53209 Brown Deer 12,921 L1
†53105 Brown's Lake 1,648 K3
53006 Brownsville 433 J8
53522 Browntown 284 G10
54819 Bruce 905 D5
54820 Brule 335 C2
54204 Brussels 500 L6
†54622 Buffalo 894 C7
53105 Burlington 8,385 K10
53922 Burnett 260 J9
53007 Butler 2,059 K1
54514 Butternut 438 E3
53009 Byron 40 K8
54821 Cable 227 D3
54727 Cadott 1,247 D6
53923 Cambria 680 H8
53523 Cambridge 844 H9
54822 Cameron 1,115 C5
†53019 Campbellsport 1,740 K8
54618 Camp Douglas 589 F8
53109 Camp Lake 2,060 K10
54823 Canton 100 C5
54928 Caroline 450 J6
53011 Cascade 615 K8
54205 Casco 484 L6
54619 Cashton 827 E8
53806 Cassville 1,270 E10
54620 Cataract 200 E7
54515 Catawba 205 E4
54206 Cato 85 L7
53924 Cazenovia 259 F8
54111 Cecil 445 K6
53012 Cedarburg 9,005 L9
53013 Cedar Grove 1,420 L8
54824 Centuria 711 A5
54621 Chaseburg 279 D8
54419 Chelsea 120 F5
†53029 Chenequa 532 J1
54728 Chetek 1,931 C5
54420 Chili 185 F6
53014 Chilton⊙ 2,965 K7
54729 Chippewa Falls⊙ 12,270 D6
54004 Clayton 425 B5
54005 Clear Lake 899 B5
53015 Cleveland 1,270 L8
53525 Clinton 1,751 J10
54929 Clintonville 4,567 J6
53016 Clyman 317 J9
53526 Cobb 409 F10
54622 Cochrane 512 C7
54421 Colby 1,496 F6
54112 Coleman 852 L5
54730 Colfax 1,149 C6
54930 Coloma 367 H7
53925 Columbus 4,049 H9
54113 Combined Locks 2,573 K7
†53147 Como 1,376 K10
54519 Conover 480 H3
54731 Conrath 86 E5
54623 Coon Valley 758 E8
54732 Cornell 1,583 D5
54827 Cornucopia 250 D2
54520 Crandon⊙ 1,969 H4
54114 Crivitz 1,041 L5
53528 Cross Plains 2,156 G9
53807 Cuba City 2,129 F10
53110 Cudahy 19,547 M2
54829 Cumberland 1,983 C4
54422 Curtiss 127 F6
54006 Cushing 150 A4
54931 Dale 410 J7
54733 Dallas 477 C5
53926 Dalton 300 H8
53529 Dane 518 G9
53114 Darien 1,152 J10
53530 Darlington⊙ 2,300 F10
53531 Deerfield 1,466 H9
54007 Deer Park 232 B5
53532 De Forest 3,367 H9
53018 Delafield 4,083 J1
53115 Delavan 5,684 J10
†53115 Delavan Lake 2,082 J10
†54856 Delta 35 D3
54208 Denmark 1,475 L7
54115 De Pere 14,892 K7
†54663 De Soto 318 D9
†54014 Diamond Bluff 100 A6
53808 Dickeyville 1,156 E10
54625 Dodge 185 D7
53533 Dodgeville⊙ 3,458 F10
54425 Dorchester 613 F5
53118 Dousman 1,153 J1
54734 Downing 242 B5
54735 Downsville 200 C6
53928 Doylestown 294 H9
54009 Dresser 670 A5
54832 Drummond 200 D3
54736 Durand⊙ 2,047 C6
53119 Eagle 1,008 H2
54521 Eagle River⊙ 1,326 H4
54626 Eastman 371 D9
53120 East Troy 2,385 J2
54701 Eau Claire⊙ 51,509 D6
Eau Claire‡ 130,507 D6
53019 Eden 534 K8
54426 Edgar 1,194 G6
53534 Edgerton 4,335 H10
54209 Egg Harbor 238 M5
54427 Eland 230 H6
54428 Elcho 500 H5
54429 Elderon 191 H6
54932 Eldorado 200 J8
54738 Eleva 593 D6
53020 Elkhart Lake 1,054 L8
53121 Elkhorn⊙ 4,605 J10
54739 Elk Mound 773 C6
54210 Ellison Bay 112 M5
54011 Ellsworth⊙ 2,143 A6
53122 Elm Grove 6,735 K1
54740 Elmwood 885 B6
†53401 Elmwood Park 483 M3
53929 Elroy 1,504 F8
54430 Elton 150 J5
54933 Embarrass 496 J6
53930 Endeavor 335 G8
54211 Ephraim 319 M5
54627 Ettrick 462 D7
53536 Evansville 2,835 H10
54835 Exeland 219 D4
54741 Fairchild 577 D6
53931 Fair Water 310 J8
54742 Fall Creek 1,148 D6
53932 Fall River 850 H9
†54840 Falun 95 A4
54120 Fence 200 K4
53809 Fennimore 2,212 E9
54431 Fenwood 165 F6
54628 Ferryville 227 D9
54524 Fifield 310 F4
54212 Fish Creek 119 M5
54121 Florence⊙ 780 K4
54935 Fond du Lac⊙ 35,863 K8
53125 Fontana 1,764 J10
53537 Footville 794 H10
54123 Forest Junction 140 K7
54213 Forestville 455 L6
53538 Fort Atkinson 9,785 J10
54629 Fountain City 963 C7
54836 Foxboro 360 B2
53933 Fox Lake 1,373 J8
†53117 Fox Point 7,649 M1
54214 Francis Creek 589 L7
53132 Franklin 16,871 L2
54837 Frederic 1,039 B4
53021 Fredonia 1,437 L8
54940 Fremont 510 J7
53934 Friendship⊙ 744 G8
53935 Friesland 267 H8
54630 Galesville 1,239 D7
54631 Gays Mills 627 E9
53127 Genesee Depot 350 J2
54632 Genoa 283 D8
53128 Genoa City 1,202 K11
53022 Germantown 10,729 K1
54124 Gillett 1,356 K6
54433 Gilman 436 E5
54743 Gilmanton 300 C7
54435 Gleason 200 G5
53023 Glenbeulah 423 L8
†53209 Glendale 13,882 M1
54526 Glen Flora 83 E4
53810 Glen Haven 160 E10
54013 Glenwood City 950 B5
54527 Glidden 940 E3
54125 Goodman 875 K4
54838 Gordon 600 C3
53540 Gotham 250 F9
53024 Grafton 8,381 L9
53936 Grand Marsh 725 G8
54839 Grand View 447 D3
54436 Granton 399 E6
54840 Grantsburg⊙ 1,153 A4
53541 Gratiot 280 F10
*54301 Green Bay⊙ 87,899 K6
Green Bay‡ 175,280 K6
53129 Greendale 16,928 L2
53220 Greenfield 31,467 L2
54941 Green Lake⊙ 1,208 H8
54126 Greenleaf 300 L7
54942 Greenville 900 J7
54437 Greenwood 1,124 E6
54128 Gresham 534 J6
54014 Hager City 110 A6
53130 Hales Corners 7,110 K2
54015 Hammond 991 A6
54943 Hancock 419 G7
54529 Harshaw 87 G4
53027 Hartford 7,046 K9
53029 Hartland 5,559 J1
54440 Hatley 300 H6
54841 Haugen 251 C4
54530 Hawkins 407 E4
54842 Hawthorne 200 C3
54843 Hayward⊙ 1,698 D3
53811 Hazel Green 1,282 F11
54531 Hazelhurst 630 G4
†53538 Hebron 450 J10
53137 Helenville 300 J10
54844 Herbster 100 D2
54441 Hewitt 470 F6
53543 Highland 860 F9
54129 Hilbert 1,176 K7
†54511 Hiles 350 J4

(continued on following page)

Agriculture, Industry and Resources

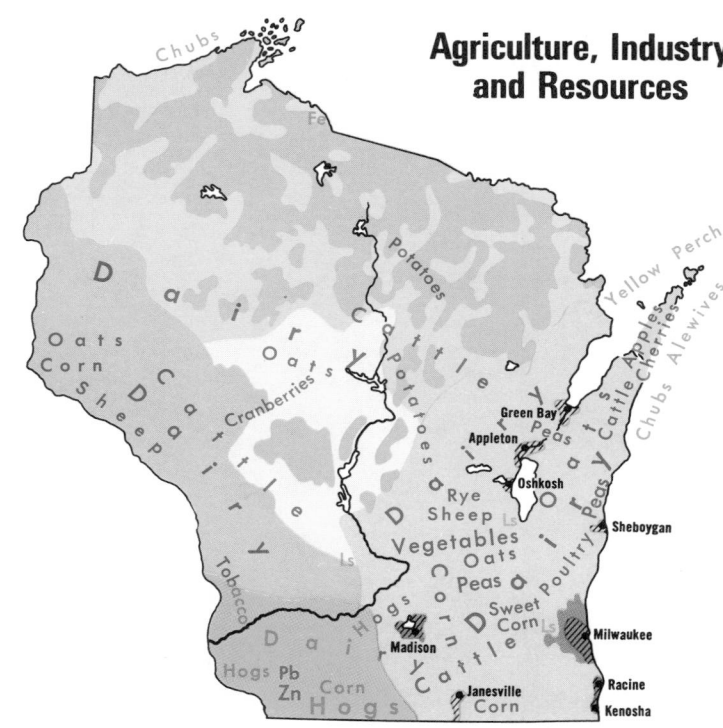

DOMINANT LAND USE

Specialized Dairy
Dairy, Hay, Potatoes
Dairy, General Farming
Hogs, Dairy
Dairy, Livestock
Forests
Urban Areas

MAJOR MINERAL OCCURRENCES

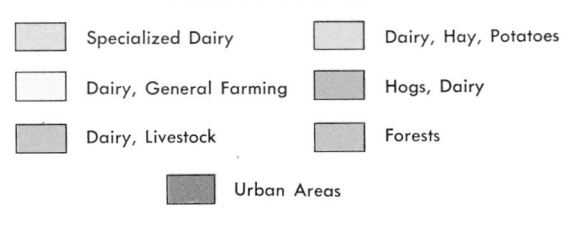

Fe Iron Ore
Pb Lead
Ls Limestone
Zn Zinc

Major Industrial Areas

54634 Hillsboro 1,263 F8
53061 Hingham 250 K8
54635 Hixton 364 E7
54745 Holcombe 200 D5
53544 Hollandale 271 G10
54636 Holmen 2,411 D8
53138 Honey Creek 300 J3
53032 Horicon 3,584 J9
54944 Hortonville 2,016 J7
†55082 Houlton 915 A5
54303 Howard 8,240 K6
53081 Howards Grove-Millersville 1,838 L8
53033 Hubertus 600 K1
54016 Hudson⊙ 5,434 A6
54746 Humbird 190 E6
54534 Hurley⊙ 2,015 F3
53034 Hustisford 874 J9
54637 Hustler 170 F8
54747 Independence 1,180 D7
54945 Iola 957 H6
54536 Iron Belt 300 F3
53035 Iron Ridge 766 K9
54847 Iron River 878 D2
†53941 Ironton 206 F8
53036 Ixonia 525 H1
53037 Jackson 1,817 K9
†54235 Jacksonport 150 M6
53545 Janesville⊙ 51,071 H10
Janesville-Beloit‡ 139,420 H10
53549 Jefferson⊙ 5,647 J10
54748 Jim Falls 100 D5
53038 Johnson Creek 1,136 J9
53550 Juda 500 H10
54443 Junction City 523 G6
53039 Juneau⊙ 2,045 J9
53139 Kansasville 150 L3
54130 Kaukauna 11,310 K7
†53050 Kekoskee 224 J8
54215 Kellnersville 369 L7
54638 Kendall 486 F8
54537 Kennan 194 F5
*53140 Kenosha⊙ 77,685 M3
Kenosha‡ 123,137 M3
54135 Keshena⊙ 980 J6
53040 Kewaskum 2,381 K8
54216 Kewaunee⊙ 2,801 M7
53042 Kiel 3,083 L8
53812 Kieler 800 E10
54136 Kimberly 5,881 K7
53939 Kingston 328 H8
54749 Knapp 419 B6
†54455 Knowlton 127 G6
53044 Kohler 1,651 L8
53147 Krakow 345 K6
54538 Lac du Flambeau 500 G4
†53066 Lac La Belle 289 H1
54601 La Crosse⊙ 48,347 D8
La Crosse‡ 91,056 D8
54848 Ladysmith⊙ 3,826 D5
54639 La Farge 746 E8
53940 Lake Delton 1,158 G8
53147 Lake Geneva 5,612 K10
53551 Lake Mills 3,670 H9
54849 Lake Nebagamon 780 C3
54538 Lake Tomahawk 600 H4
†54494 Lake Wazeecha 2,176 G7
†54729 Lake Wissota 1,788 D6
54138 Lakewood 425 K5
53813 Lancaster⊙ 4,076 E10
54540 Land O'Lakes 786 H3
53046 Lannon 987 K1
53941 La Valle 412 F8
53047 Lebanon 250 H1
54139 Lena 585 K6
†54656 Leon 100 E8
54948 Leopolis 200 J6
54851 Lewis 200 B4
53942 Limeridge 191 F9
53553 Linden 395 F10
54140 Little Chute 7,907 K7
53554 Livingston 642 E10
53555 Lodi 1,959 G9
53943 Loganville 239 F9
†54970 Lohrville 336 H7
53048 Lomira 1,446 J8
53556 Lone Rock 577 F9
54542 Long Lake 150 J4
53557 Lowell 326 J9
54446 Loyal 1,252 E6
54447 Lublin 142 E5
54853 Luck 997 B4
54217 Luxemburg 1,040 L6
53944 Lyndon Station 375 F8
54640 Lynxville 174 D9
53148 Lyons 550 K10
*53701 Madison (cap.)⊙ 170,616 H9
Madison‡ 323,545 H9
54750 Maiden Rock 172 B6
54949 Manawa 1,205 J7
54220 Manitowoc⊙ 32,547 L7
54226 Maplewood 200 M6
54448 Marathon 1,552 G6
54855 Marengo 130 E3
54227 Maribel 363 L7
54143 Marinette⊙ 11,965 L5
54950 Marion 1,348 J6
53946 Markesan 1,446 J8
53947 Marquette 204 H8
53559 Marshall 2,363 H9
54449 Marshfield 18,290 F6
54856 Mason 102 D3
54450 Mattoon 382 J5
53948 Mauston⊙ 3,284 F8
53050 Mayville 4,333 K9
53560 Mazomanie 1,248 G9
53558 McFarland 3,783 H10
54543 McNaughton 450 H4
54451 Medford⊙ 4,035 F5
54546 Mellen 1,046 E3
54642 Melrose 507 E7
54619 Melvina 117 E8
54952 Menasha 14,728 J7
53051 Menomonee Falls 27,845 K1
54751 Menomonie⊙ 12,769 C6
53092 Mequon 16,193 L1
54452 Merrill⊙ 9,578 G5
54754 Merrillan 587 E7
53561 Merrimac 365 G9
53056 Merton 1,045 K1
53562 Middleton 11,848 G9
54857 Mikana 200 C4
54453 Milan 153 F6
†53038 Milford 35 J9
54454 Milladore 250 G6
54643 Millston 110 E7
54858 Milltown 732 B4
53563 Milton 4,092 J10
*53201 Milwaukee⊙ 636,236 M1
Milwaukee‡ 1,397,143 M1
54644 Mindoro 200 D7
53565 Mineral Point 2,259 F10
54548 Minocqua 950 G4
54859 Minong 557 C3
54228 Mishicot 1,503 L7
54755 Mondovi 2,545 C6
54549 Monico 250 H4
53716 Monona 8,809 H9
53566 Monroe⊙ 10,027 G10
53949 Montello⊙ 1,273 H8
53569 Montfort 616 E10
53570 Monticello 1,021 G10
54550 Montreal 887 F3
53571 Morrisonville 375 G9
54455 Mosinee 3,015 G6
54149 Mountain 250 K5
53057 Mount Calvary 585 K8
53816 Mount Hope 197 D10
53572 Mount Horeb 3,251 G10
54645 Mount Sterling 223 D9
†53572 Mount Vernon 138 G10
53149 Mukwonago 4,014 J2
53573 Muscoda 1,331 F9
53150 Muskego 15,277 K2
53058 Nashotah 513 J1
54646 Necedah 773 F7
54956 Neenah 22,432 J7
54456 Neillsville⊙ 2,780 E6
54457 Nekoosa 2,519 G7
54756 Nelson 389 C7
54458 Nelsonville 199 H7
54150 Neopit 1,065 J6
53059 Neosho 575 J9
54960 Neshkoro 386 H8
54551 Newald 375 J4
54757 New Auburn 466 D5
53151 New Berlin 30,529 K2
53060 Newburg 783 K9
†61075 New Diggings 65 F10
54229 New Franken 150 L6
53574 New Glarus 1,763 G10
53061 New Holstein 3,412 K8
53950 New Lisbon 1,390 F8
54961 New London 6,210 J7
54017 New Richmond 4,306 A5
54151 Niagara 2,079 K4
54152 Nichols 267 K6
†53401 North Bay 219 M3
†54935 North Fond du Lac 3,844 J8
53951 North Freedom 616 G9
†54016 North Hudson 2,218 A5
53064 North Lake 400 J1
53217 North Shore 14,930 M1
54648 Norwalk 517 E8
53154 Oak Creek 16,932 M2
54649 Oakdale 150 F8
53065 Oakfield 990 J8
53066 Oconomowoc 9,909 H1
†53066 Oconomowoc Lake 524 H1
54153 Oconto⊙ 4,505 L6
54154 Oconto Falls 2,500 K6
54962 Ogdensburg 214 J7
54459 Ogema 238 F5
53069 Okauchee 3,958 J1
†53555 Okee 250 H9
†54880 Oliver 253 B2
54963 Omro 2,763 J7
54650 Onalaska 9,249 D8
54155 Oneida 900 K7
54651 Ontario 398 E8
53070 Oostburg 1,647 L8
53575 Oregon 3,876 H10
53576 Orfordville 1,143 H10
54020 Osceola 1,581 A5
54901 Oshkosh⊙ 49,620 J8
54758 Osseo 1,474 D6
54460 Owen 998 F6
53952 Oxford 432 H8
53953 Packwaukee 271 G8
†53168 Paddock Lake 2,207 K10
53156 Palmyra 1,515 H2
53954 Pardeeville 1,594 H8
54552 Park Falls 3,192 F4
†54481 Park Ridge 643 H6
53817 Patch Grove 259 D10
53157 Pell Lake 1,826 K10
54553 Pence 234 F3
54759 Pepin 890 B7
54157 Peshtigo 2,807 L5
53072 Pewaukee 4,637 K1
54554 Phelps 950 H3
54555 Phillips⊙ 1,522 E4
54464 Phlox 150 J5
54465 Pickerel 107 J5
54760 Pigeon Falls 338 D7
54466 Pittsville 810 F7
53577 Plain 676 F9
54966 Plainfield 813 G7
†53017 Plat 120 K1
53818 Platteville 9,580 F10
53158 Pleasant Prairie 950 L10
54467 Plover 5,310 G7
54761 Plum City 505 B6
53073 Plymouth 6,027 L8
†54423 Polonia 200 H6
54864 Poplar 569 C2
53901 Portage⊙ 7,896 G8
54469 Port Edwards 2,077 G7
53074 Port Washington⊙ 8,612 L9
54865 Port Wing 290 D2
53820 Potosi 736 E10
54160 Potter 330 K7
54161 Pound 407 L5
53955 Poynette 1,447 G9
54967 Poy Sippi 425 J7
53821 Prairie du Chien⊙ 5,859 D9
53578 Prairie du Sac 2,145 G9
54762 Prairie Farm 387 C5
54556 Prentice 605 F4
54021 Prescott 2,654 A6
54968 Princeton 1,479 H8
54162 Pulaski 1,875 K6
54164 Pulcifer 35 K6
*53401 Racine⊙ 85,725 M3
Racine‡ 173,132 M3
54867 Radisson 280 D4
53956 Randolph 1,691 H8
53075 Random Lake 1,287 K8
†53126 Raymond 300 L2
54652 Readstown 396 E9
54970 Redgranite 976 J7
53959 Reedsburg 5,038 G8
54230 Reedsville 1,134 L7
53579 Reeseville 649 J9
53580 Rewey 233 F10
54501 Rhinelander⊙ 7,873 H4
54470 Rib Lake 945 F5
54868 Rice Lake 7,691 C5
53581 Richland Center⊙ 4,997 F9
54763 Ridgeland 300 B5
53582 Ridgeway 503 F10
53960 Rio 785 H9
54971 Ripon 7,111 J8
54022 River Falls 9,019 A6
†53201 River Hills 1,642 M1
54023 Roberts 833 A6
53167 Rochester 746 K3
†53523 Rockdale 200 J10
53077 Rockfield 200 L1
54653 Rockland 383 D8
53961 Rock Springs 426 F8
†53178 Rome 200 H1
54974 Rosendale 725 J8
54473 Rosholt 520 H6
54474 Rothschild 3,338 G6
†53583 Roxbury 260 G9
54475 Rudolph 392 G7
†54751 Rusk 40 C6
53079 Saint Cloud 560 K8
54024 Saint Croix Falls 1,497 A5
†53207 Saint Francis 10,042 M2
†54601 Saint Joseph Ridge 450 D8
54232 Saint Nazianz 738 L7
54765 Sand Creek 225 C5
53583 Sauk City 2,703 G9
53080 Saukville 3,494 L9
54559 Saxon 375 F3
54977 Scandinavia 292 H7
54476 Schofield 2,226 H6
†54843 Seeley 68 D3
54654 Seneca 235 E9
53584 Sextonville 225 F9
54165 Seymour 2,530 K6
53585 Sharon 1,280 J11
54166 Shawano⊙ 7,013 J6
53081 Sheboygan⊙ 48,085 L8
Sheboygan‡ 100,935 L8
53085 Sheboygan Falls 5,253 L8
54766 Sheldon 292 D5
54871 Shell Lake⊙ 1,135 C4
54169 Sherwood 372 K7
54170 Shiocton 805 K7
53211 Shorewood 14,327 M1
†53701 Shorewood Hills 1,837 G9
53586 Shullsburg 1,484 F10
53170 Silver Lake 1,598 K10
54872 Siren 896 B4
54234 Sister Bay 564 M5
53086 Slinger 1,612 K9
54655 Soldiers Grove 622 E9
54873 Solon Springs 590 C3
54025 Somerset 860 A5
53172 South Milwaukee 21,069 M2
53587 South Wayne 495 G10
54656 Sparta⊙ 6,934 E8
54479 Spencer 1,754 F6
54801 Spooner 2,365 B4
53588 Spring Green 1,265 G9
54767 Spring Valley 982 B6
54768 Stanley 2,095 E6
54026 Star Prairie 420 A5
54480 Stetsonville 487 F5
54657 Steuben 175 E9
54481 Stevens Point⊙ 22,970 G7
54172 Stiles 300 L6
53825 Stitzer 190 E10
53088 Stockbridge 567 K7
54769 Stockholm 104 B7
54658 Stoddard 762 D8
54876 Stone Lake 210 C4
53589 Stoughton 7,589 H10
54484 Stratford 1,385 F6
54770 Strum 944 D6
54235 Sturgeon Bay⊙ 8,847 M6
53177 Sturtevant 4,130 M3
54173 Suamico 900 K6
53178 Sullivan 434 H1
54485 Summit Lake 250 H5
53590 Sun Prairie 12,931 H9
54880 Superior⊙ 29,571 C2
Superior-Duluth‡ 266,650 C2
†54880 Superior Village 580 B2
54174 Suring 581 K5
53089 Sussex 3,482 K1
53090 Taycheedah 350 K8
54659 Taylor 411 E7
†53820 Tennyson 476 E10
53091 Theresa 766 K8
53092 Thiensville 3,341 L1
54771 Thorp 1,635 E6
54562 Three Lakes 950 H4
54486 Tigerton 865 H6
54240 Tisch Mills 315 L7
54660 Tomah 7,204 F8
54487 Tomahawk 3,527 G5
54563 Tony 146 E5
54888 Trego 280 C4
54661 Trempealeau 956 C8
54662 Tunnel City 200 E7
54889 Turtle Lake 762 B5
53181 Twin Lakes 3,474 K11

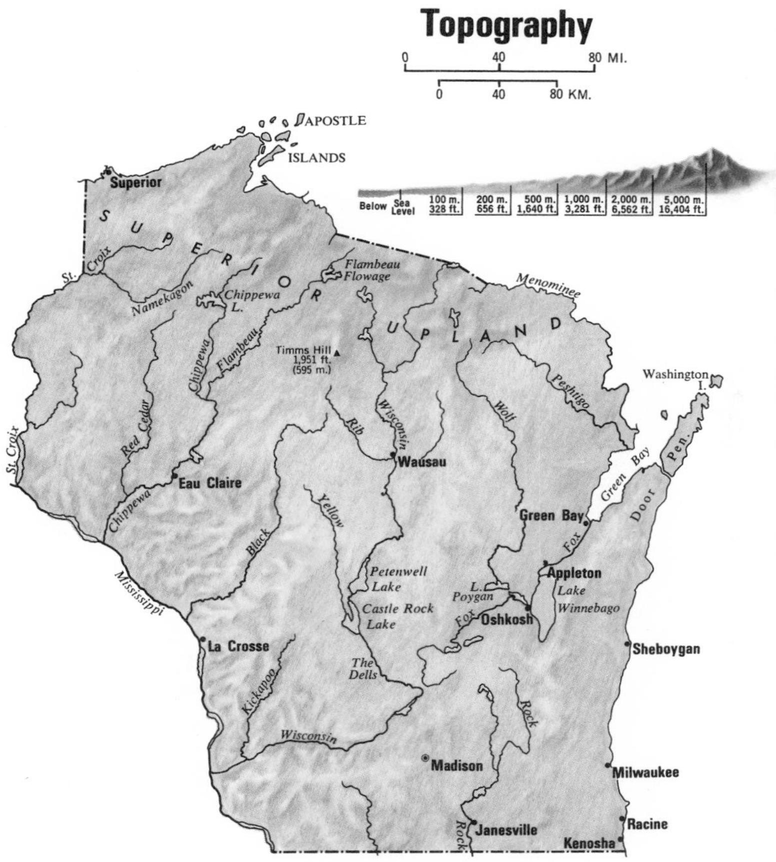
Topography
0 40 80 MI.
0 40 80 KM.
APOSTLE ISLANDS
Superior
Below Sea Level
100 m. 328 ft.
200 m. 656 ft.
500 m. 1,640 ft.
1,000 m. 3,281 ft.
2,000 m. 6,562 ft.
5,000 m. 16,404 ft.
SUPERIOR UPLAND
St. Croix
Namekagon
Chippewa L.
Flambeau Flowage
Menominee
Timms Hill 1,951 ft. (595 m.)
Washington I.
Red Cedar
Chippewa
Flambeau
Rib
Wisconsin
Wolf
Peshtigo
Wausau
Green Bay
Door Pen.
Eau Claire
Mississippi
Black
Yellow
Petenwell Lake
Castle Rock Lake
L. Poygan
Oshkosh
Appleton
Lake Winnebago
Fox
La Crosse
Sheboygan
The Dells
Kickapoo
Rock
Madison
Milwaukee
Racine
Janesville
Kenosha

54241 Two Rivers 13,354 M7
53962 Union Center 216 F8
53182 Union Grove 3,517 L3
54488 Unity 418 F6
54245 Valders 984 L7
53593 Verona 3,336 G9
54489 Vesper 554 F7
54664 Viola 696 E8
54665 Viroqua⊙ 3,716 D8
54566 Wabeno 800 J5
53093 Waldo 416 L8
53183 Wales 1,992 J1
53184 Walworth 1,607 J10
54666 Warrens 300 E7
54890 Wascott 70 C3
54891 Washburn⊙ 2,080 D2
54246 Washington Island 550 M5
53185 Waterford 2,051 K3
53594 Waterloo 2,393 J9
53094 Watertown 18,113 J9
53021 Waubeka 450 L9
53186 Waukesha⊙ 50,365 K1
53597 Waunakee 3,866 G9
54981 Waupaca⊙ 4,472 H7
53963 Waupun 8,132 J8
54401 Wausau⊙ 32,426 G6
Wausau‡ 111,270 G6
54177 Wausaukee 648 K5
54982 Wautoma⊙ 1,629 H7
53226 Wauwatosa 51,308 L1
53826 Wauzeka 580 E9
†54126 Wayside 140 L7
54893 Webster 610 B4
53214 West Allis 63,982 L1
†53913 West Baraboo 846 G9
53095 West Bend⊙ 21,484 K9
54490 Westboro 750 F5
54667 Westby 1,797 E8
53964 Westfield 1,033 H8
†53201 West Milwaukee 3,535 L1
†54476 Weston 8,775 G6
54669 West Salem 3,276 D8
54983 Weyauwega 1,549 H7
54895 Weyerhaeuser 313 D5
54772 Wheeler 231 C5
54773 Whitehall⊙ 1,530 D7
54491 White Lake 309 J5
54247 Whitelaw 649 L7
53190 Whitewater 11,520 J10
†54481 Whiting 2,050 H7
54984 Wild Rose 741 H7
53191 Williams Bay 1,763 J10
54027 Wilson 155 B6
54670 Wilton 465 F8
54567 Winchester 300 G3
53185 Wind Lake 900 K2
†53401 Wind Point 1,695 M2
53598 Windsor 827 H9
54985 Winnebago 1,433 J8
54986 Winneconne 1,935 J7
54896 Winter 376 E4
53965 Wisconsin Dells 2,521 G8
54494 Wisconsin Rapids⊙ 17,995 G7
54498 Withee 509 E6
54499 Wittenberg 997 H6
53968 Wonewoc 842 F8
53827 Woodman 116 E9
54568 Woodruff 850 G4
54028 Woodville 725 B6
54180 Wrightstown 1,169 K7
54671 Wyeville 163 F7
53969 Wyocena 548 H9
54182 Zachow 135 K6

OTHER FEATURES

Apostle (isls.) F2
Apostle Islands Nat'l Lakeshore E1
Apple (riv.) A5
Bad River Ind. Res. E2
Bardon (lake) C3
Bear (isl.) E1
Beaver Dam (lake) J9
Beulah (lake) J2
Big Eau Pleine (res.) G6
Big Muskego (lake) L2
Big Rib (riv.) G5
Black (riv.) E7
Butternut (lake) J4
Castle Rock (lake) G8
Cat (isl.) E1
Chambers (isl.) M5
Chequamegon (bay) E2
Chetac (lake) D4
Chippewa (lake) D4
Chippewa (riv.) B7
Clam (lake) B4
Clam (riv.) A4
Dells, The (valley) G8
Denoon (lake) K2
Du Bay (lake) G6
Eagle (lake) H2
Eagle (lake) K3
Eau Claire (riv.) D6
Flambeau (riv.) E4
Flambeau Flowage (res.) F3
Fox (riv.) K2
Fox (riv.) K7
General Mitchell Field M2
Geneva (lake) K10
Golden (lake) H1
Green (bay) L6
Grindstone (lake) C4
Holcombe Flowage (res.) D5
Jump (riv.) E5
Kegonsa (lake) H10
Kickapoo (riv.) E9
Koshkonong (lake) H10
La Belle (lake) H1
Lac Court Oreilles Ind. Res. D4
Lac du Flambeau Ind. Res. G3
Long (lake) C4
Madeline (isl.) E2
Mendota (lake) H9
Menominee (riv.) L5
Metonga (lake) J4
Michigan (isl.) F2
Michigan (lake) M9
Mississippi (riv.) D10
Montreal (riv.) F2
Moose (lake) E3
Moose (lake) F3
Nagawicka (lake) J1
Namekagon (lake) D3
Namekagon (riv.) C3
North (lake) J1
Oak (isl.) E2
Oconomowoc (lake) H1
Oconto (riv.) K5
Okauchee (lake) J1
Outer (isl.) F1
Owen (lake) D3
Pecatonica (riv.) H11
Pelican (lake) H4
Pepin (lake) B7
Peshtigo (riv.) K5
Petenwell (lake) G7
Pewaukee (lake) K1
Phantom (lake) J2
Pine (lake) J1
Porte des Morts (str.) N5
Poygan (lake) J7
Puckaway (lake) H8
Red Cedar (riv.) C5
Red Cliff Ind. Res. E2
Rib (mt.) G6
Rock (riv.) J9
Round (lake) F4
Round (lake) D3
Saint Croix (lake) A6
Saint Croix (riv.) A4
Saint Croix Flowage (res.) C3
Saint Louis (riv.) A2
Sand (isl.) D2
Shawano (lake) K6
Shell (lake) C4
Spider (lake) D3
Stockbridge Ind. Res. J6
Stockton (isl.) F2
Sugar (riv.) H10
Sugarbush Hill (mt.) J4
Superior (lake) F1
Thunder (lake) H4
Tichigan (lake) K2
Timms Hill (mt.) F5
Trempealeau (riv.) C7
Trout (lake) G3
Vieux Desert (lake) J3
Washington (isl.) M5
Willow (res.) F4
Wind (lake) K2
Winnebago (lake) K7
Wisconsin (riv.) E9
Wolf (riv.) J5
Yellow (lake) B4
Yellow (riv.) F7

⊙County seat.
‡Population of metropolitan area.
† Zip of nearest p.o. * Multiple zips.

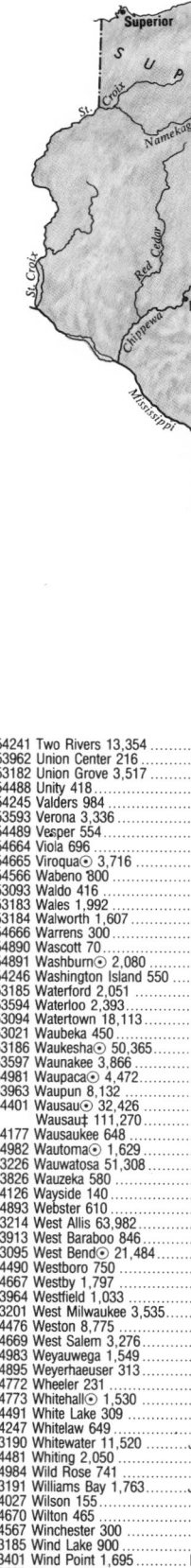

Wisconsin

SCALE
0 5 10 20 30 40 MI.
0 5 10 20 30 40 KM.
State Capitals .... ⊛
County Seats .... ⊚
Canals ....
Major Limited Access Hwys. ━━━
Scale 1:2,270,000

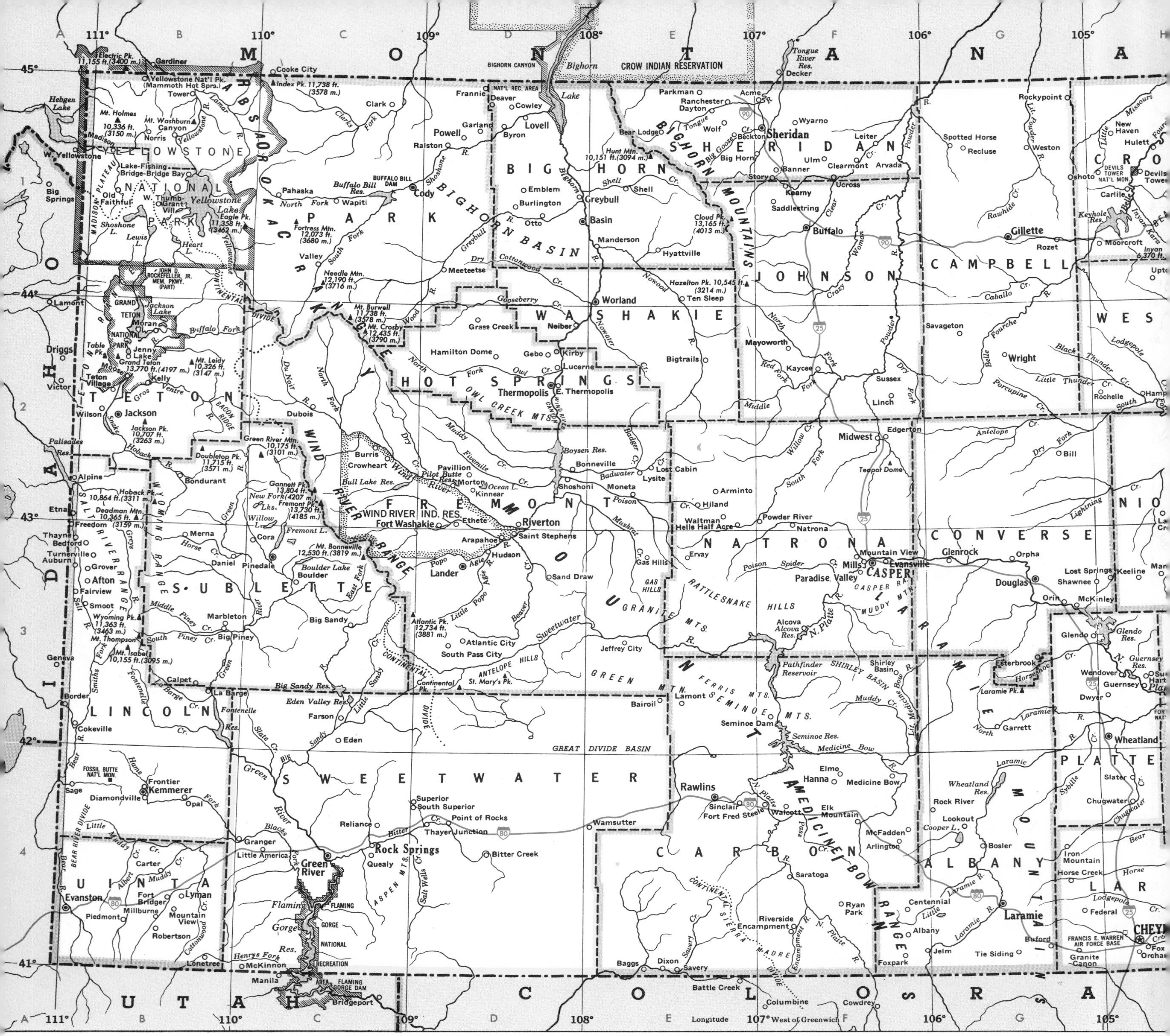

Agriculture, Industry and Resources

DOMINANT LAND USE

- Specialized Wheat
- Specialized Dairy
- General Farming, Livestock, Special Crops
- Sugar Beets, Dry Beans, Livestock, General Farming
- Range Livestock
- Forests
- Nonagricultural Land

MAJOR MINERAL OCCURRENCES

- C Coal
- Cl Clay
- Fe Iron Ore
- G Natural Gas
- O Petroleum
- P Phosphates
- So Soda Ash
- U Uranium
- V Vanadium
- ⚡ Water Power

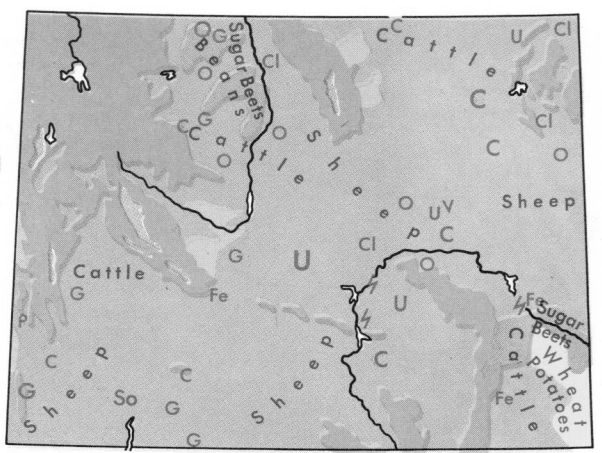

COUNTIES

County	Pop.	Key
Albany	29,062	G4
Big Horn	11,896	E1
Campbell	24,367	G1
Carbon	21,896	F4
Converse	14,069	G3
Crook	5,308	H1
Fremont	38,992	D2
Goshen	12,040	H4
Hot Springs	5,710	D2
Johnson	6,700	F1
Laramie	68,649	H4
Lincoln	12,177	B3
Natrona	71,856	F3
Niobrara	2,924	H2
Park	21,639	C1
Platte	11,975	H4
Sheridan	25,048	F1
Sublette	4,548	C3
Sweetwater	41,723	D4
Teton	9,355	B2
Uinta	13,021	B4
Washakie	9,496	E2
Weston	7,106	H2

CITIES and TOWNS

Zip	Name/Pop.	Key
83110	Afton 1,481	B3
82050	Albin 128	H4
82620	Alcova 275	F3

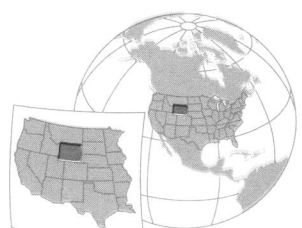

Wyoming

SCALE
0 5 10 20 30 40 MI.
0 5 10 20 30 40 KM.

State Capitals .... ⊛
County Seats .... ⊛
Major Limited Access Hwys. ____

Scale 1:2,410,000

AREA 97,809 sq. mi. (253,325 sq. km.)
POPULATION 469,557
CAPITAL Cheyenne
LARGEST CITY Casper
HIGHEST POINT Gannett Pk. 13,804 ft. (4207 m.)
SETTLED IN 1834
ADMITTED TO UNION July 10, 1890
POPULAR NAME Equality State
STATE FLOWER Indian Paintbrush
STATE BIRD Meadowlark

Topography

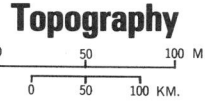

0   50   100 MI.
0   50   100 KM.

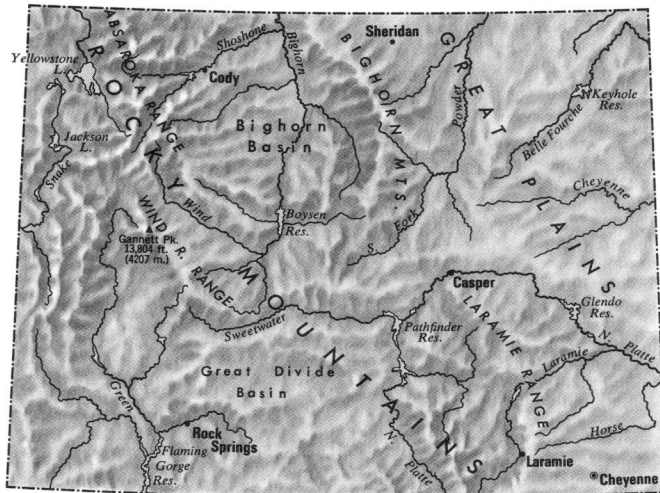

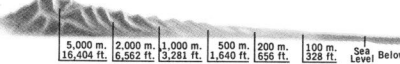

5,000 m.	2,000 m.	1,000 m.	500 m.	200 m.	100 m.	Sea
16,404 ft.	6,562 ft.	3,281 ft.	1,640 ft.	656 ft.	328 ft.	Level Below

83001 Jackson⊙ 4,511	B2
82310 Jeffrey City 1,882	E3
82639 Kaycee 271	F2
83011 Kelly 100	B2
83101 Kemmerer⊙ 3,273	B4
82516 Kinnear 145	D2
82430 Kirby 129	D2
83123 La Barge 302	B3
82221 Lagrange 232	H4
82520 Lander⊙ 7,867	D3
82070 Laramie⊙ 24,410	G4
82640 Linch 187	F2
82223 Lingle 475	H3
82929 Little America 175	C4
†82642 Lost Cabin 25	E2
82224 Lost Springs 9	G3
82431 Lovell 2,447	D1
†82443 Lucerne 240	D2
82225 Lusk⊙ 1,650	H3
82937 Lyman 2,284	B4
82642 Lysite 175	E2
†82190 Mammoth Hot Springs (Yellowstone Nat'l Park 350	B1
82432 Manderson 174	E1
82227 Manville 94	H3
†83113 Marbleton 537	B3
82938 McKinnon 135	C4
82329 Medicine Bow 953	F4
82433 Meeteetse 512	D1
82643 Midwest 638	F2
82644 Mills 2,139	F3
82721 Moorcroft 1,014	H1
83012 Moose 150	B2
83013 Moran 200	B2
†82601 Mountain View	F3
82939 Mountain View 628	B4
82701 Newcastle⊙ 3,596	H2
82190 Old Faithful 75	B1
†82001 Orchard Valley 3,327	H4
82723 Osage 500	H2
†82601 Paradise Valley	F3
82523 Pavillion 287	D2
82082 Pine Bluffs 1,077	H4
82941 Pinedale⊙ 1,066	C3
82942 Point of Rocks 425	D4
82435 Powell 5,310	D1
82839 Ranchester 655	E1
82301 Rawlins⊙ 11,547	E4
82725 Recluse 285	G1
82943 Reliance 325	C4
†82325 Riverside 55	F4
82501 Riverton 9,247	D2
82944 Robertson 142	B4
82083 Rock River 415	G4
82901 Rock Springs 19,458	C4
82331 Saratoga 2,410	F4
82801 Sheridan⊙ 15,146	F1
82615 Shirley Basin 400	F3
82649 Shoshoni 879	D2
82334 Sinclair 586	E4
83126 Smoot 310	B3
†82945 South Superior 586	D4

82842 Story 637	F1
82729 Sundance⊙ 1,087	H1
82945 Superior 500	D4
82442 Ten Sleep 407	E1
83127 Thayne 256	A3
82443 Thermopolis⊙ 3,852	D2
82240 Torrington⊙ 5,441	H3
82730 Upton 1,193	H1
82242 Van Tassell 10	H3
82335 Walcott 200	F4
82336 Wamsutter 681	E4
82201 Wheatland⊙ 5,816	H3
82401 Worland⊙ 6,391	E1
82732 Wright 1,117	G2
82190 Yellowstone Nat'l Pk. 350	B1
82244 Yoder 110	H4

OTHER FEATURES

Absaroka (range)	C1
Antelope (creek)	G2
Antelope (hills)	D3
Aspen (mts.)	C4
Atlantic (peak)	D3
Badwater (creek)	E2
Bear (creek)	H4
Bear (riv.)	B4
Bear Lodge (mts.)	H1
Bear River Divide (mts.)	B4
Beaver (creek)	D3
Beaver (creek)	H2
Belle Fourche (riv.)	H1
Big Goose (creek)	E1
Bighorn (basin)	D1
Bighorn (lake)	D1
Bighorn (mts.)	E1
Bighorn (riv.)	D1
Bighorn Canyon Nat'l Rec. Area	D1
Big Sandy (riv.)	C3
Bitter (creek)	C4
Blacks Fork, Green (riv.)	C4
Black Thunder (creek)	G2
Bonneville (mt.)	C3
Boysen (res.)	D2
Buffalo Bill (dam)	C1
Buffalo Bill (res.)	C1
Buffalo Fork, Snake (riv.)	B2
Burwell (mt.)	C2
Caballo (creek)	G1
Casper (range)	F3
Cheyenne (riv.)	H2
Chugwater (creek)	H4
Clarks Fork (riv.)	C1
Clear (creek)	F1
Cloud (peak)	E1
Cottonwood (creek)	B4
Crazy Woman (creek)	F1
Crosby (mt.)	C2
Crow (creek)	H4
Deadman (mt.)	B2
Devils Tower Nat'l Mon.	H1

Doubletop (peak)	B2
Dry (creek)	C2
Dry Cottonwood (creek)	D1
Eagle (peak)	B1
Fivemile (creek)	D2
Flaming Gorge (res.)	C4
Flaming Gorge Nat'l Rec. Area	C4
Fontenelle (creek)	B3
Fontenelle (res.)	B3
Fort Laramie Nat'l Hist. Site	H3
Fortress (mt.)	C1
Fossil Butte Nat'l Mon.	B4
Francis E. Warren A.F.B. 3,627	G4
Fremont (lake)	C2
Fremont (peak)	C2
Gannett (peak)	C2
Gas (hills)	E3
Glendo (res.)	H3
Gooseberry (creek)	D1
Grand Teton (mt.)	B2
Grand Teton Nat'l Park	B2
Granite (mts.)	E3
Great Divide (basin)	E3
Green (mt.)	E3
Green (riv.)	C4
Green, East Fork (riv.)	C3
Green River (mt.)	C2
Greybull (riv.)	D1
Greys (riv.)	B3
Gros Ventre (riv.)	B2
Guernsey (res.)	H3
Hams Fork (riv.)	B4
Hazelton (peak)	E1
Henrys Fork, Green (riv.)	C4
Hoback (peak)	B2
Hoback (riv.)	B2
Holmes (mt.)	B1
Horse (creek)	H4
Horseshoe (creek)	G3
Hunt (mt.)	C1
Index (peak)	C1
Inyan Kara (creek)	H1
Inyan Kara (mt.)	H1
Isabel (mt.)	C2
Jackson (lake)	B2
Jackson (mt.)	B2
John D. Rockefeller, Jr., Mem. Pkwy.	B1
Keyhole (res.)	H1
Lamar (riv.)	B1
Lance (creek)	H2
Laramie (mts.)	G3
Laramie (peak)	G3
Laramie (riv.)	G4
Leidy (mt.)	B2
Lewis (lake)	B1
Lightning (creek)	H2
Little Missouri (riv.)	H1
Little Muddy (creek)	B3
Little Powder (riv.)	G1
Little Sandy (creek)	C3
Little Thunder (creek)	G2

Lodgepole (creek)	H2
Lodgepole (creek)	H4
Madison (plat.)	B1
Medicine Bow (range)	F4
Medicine Bow (riv.)	F3
Middle Piney (creek)	B3
Muddy (creek)	D2
Muskrat (creek)	E2
Needle (mt.)	C1
Niobrara (riv.)	J3
North Laramie (riv.)	G3
North Platte (riv.)	H3
Nowater (creek)	E2
Nowood (riv.)	E1
Owl, North Fork (creek)	D2
Owl Creek (mts.)	D2
Palisades (res.)	A2
Pass (creek)	F4
Pathfinder (res.)	F3
Poison (creek)	E2
Poison Spider (creek)	F3
Popo Agie (riv.)	D3
Powder (riv.)	F2
Rattlesnake (range)	E3
Rawhide (creek)	G1
Rawhide (creek)	H3
Rocky (mts.)	C1
Salt (riv.)	B3
Salt River (range)	B3
Salt Wells (creek)	D4
Seminoe (mts.)	E3
Seminoe (res.)	F3
Shell (creek)	E1
Shirley (basin)	F3
Shoshone (lake)	B1
Shoshone (riv.)	D1
Sierra Madre (mts.)	E4
Slate (creek)	C3
Smiths Fork (riv.)	B3
Snake (riv.)	B2
South Cheyenne (riv.)	H2
South Piney (creek)	B3
Sweetwater (riv.)	D3
Sybille (creek)	G4
Teapot Dome (mt.)	F2
Teton (range)	B2
Tongue (riv.)	E1
Washburn (mt.)	B1
Wheatland (res.)	G4
Willow (creek)	F2
Wind (riv.)	D2
Wind River (canyon)	D2
Wind River (mts.)	C2
Wind River Ind. Res.	C2
Wood (riv.)	C2
Wyoming (peak)	B3
Wyoming (range)	B2
Yellowstone (lake)	B1
Yellowstone (riv.)	B1
Yellowstone Nat'l Park	B1
⊙County seat.	

† Zip of nearest p.o.   * Multiple zips.

© Copyright HAMMOND INCORPORATED, Maplewood, N.J.

82510 Arapahoe 682	D3
83111 Auburn 360	A3
82321 Baggs 433	E4
82322 Bairoil 300	E3
82410 Basin⊙ 1,349	E1
†82801 Beckton 110	E1
83112 Bedford 350	A3
•82712 Beulah 184	H1
82833 Big Horn 350	E1
83113 Big Piney 530	B3
82051 Bosler 195	G4
82834 Buffalo⊙ 3,799	F1
82411 Burlington 300	D1
82053 Burns 268	H4
82412 Byron 633	D1
82601 Casper⊙ 51,016	F3
82055 Centennial 140	F4
82001 Cheyenne (cap.)⊙ 47,283	H4
82210 Chugwater 282	H4
82835 Clearmont 191	F1
82414 Cody⊙ 6,790	D1
82420 Cowley 455	D1
82512 Cokeville 515	B3
83114 Cokeville 515	B3
83115 Daniel 130	B3
82421 Deaver 178	D1
83116 Diamondville 1,000	B4
82323 Dixon 82	E4
82633 Douglas⊙ 6,030	G3
82513 Dubois 1,067	C2
†82443 East Thermopolis 359	D2

82926 Eden 198	C3
82635 Edgerton 510	F2
82324 Elk Mountain 338	F4
82325 Encampment 611	F4
83118 Etna 200	A2
82930 Evanston⊙ 6,421	B4
82636 Evansville 2,335	F3
83119 Fairview 150	B3
82932 Farson 350	C3
82933 Fort Bridger 300	B4
82212 Fort Laramie 356	H3
82514 Fort Washakie 400	C2
†82001 Fox Farm 2,850	H4
82423 Frannie 138	D1
83120 Freedom 400	B3
83121 Frontier 150	B4
82501 Gas Hills 150	D2
82716 Gillette⊙ 12,134	G1
82213 Glendo 367	G3
82637 Glenrock 2,736	G3
82934 Granger 177	C4
82425 Grass Creek 152	D2
82935 Green River⊙ 12,807	C4
82426 Greybull 2,277	E1
83122 Grover 425	B3
82214 Guernsey 1,512	H3
82327 Hanna 2,288	F4
82215 Hartville 149	H3
82060 Hillsdale 160	H4
82061 Horse Creek 225	G4
82515 Hudson 514	D3
82720 Hulett 291	H1

Acquisitions of Territory

WASHINGTON
OREGON COUNTRY
OREGON 1846
Treaty with Great Britain
IDAHO
MONTANA
NORTH DAKOTA
RED RIVER
Title Established 1818
MINNESOTA
MICHIGAN
WISCONSIN
NEW YORK
MAINE
VT. N.H.
MASS.
CONN.
R.I.
NEVADA
UTAH
WYOMING
SOUTH DAKOTA
NEBRASKA
IOWA
ILLINOIS
INDIANA
OHIO
PENNSYLVANIA
NEW JERSEY
CALIFORNIA
MEXICAN CESSION 1848
COLORADO
KANSAS
MISSOURI
WEST VIRGINIA
VIRGINIA
MD.
DEL.
UNITED STATES
KENTUCKY
ARIZONA
NEW MEXICO
OKLAHOMA
ARKANSAS
TENNESSEE 1783
NORTH CAROLINA
SOUTH CAROLINA
GADSDEN PURCHASE 1853
TEXAS
Annexed in 1845
MISSISSIPPI
ALABAMA
GEORGIA
LOUISIANA
FLORIDA 1819
Treaty with Spain
LOUISIANA
Purchased from France
1803

ALASKA
1867
Purchased from Russia

HAWAII
Annexed in 1898

The United States in 1783 comprised the thirteen original states and included lands acquired by conquest during the Revolution and by the Treaty of 1783.

Rank by Area

Rank by Population

YEAR OF ADMISSION TO THE UNION

State	Year
DELAWARE ☆	1787
PENNSYLVANIA ☆	
NEW JERSEY ☆	
GEORGIA ☆	1788
CONNECTICUT ☆	
MASSACHUSETTS ☆	
MARYLAND ☆	
SOUTH CAROLINA ☆	
NEW HAMPSHIRE ☆	
VIRGINIA ☆	
NEW YORK ☆	
NORTH CAROLINA ☆	1789
RHODE ISLAND ☆	1790
VERMONT ☆	1791
KENTUCKY ☆	1792
TENNESSEE ☆	1796
OHIO ☆	1803
LOUISIANA ☆	1812
INDIANA ☆	1816
MISSISSIPPI ☆	1817
ILLINOIS ☆	1818
ALABAMA ☆	1819
MAINE ☆	1820
MISSOURI ☆	1821

1959 ☆ HAWAII
☆ ALASKA

1912 ☆ ARIZONA
☆ NEW MEXICO

1907 ☆ OKLAHOMA

☆ NORTH DAKOTA
☆ SOUTH DAKOTA
WEST VIRGINIA ☆
MINNESOTA ☆
CALIFORNIA ☆
WISCONSIN ☆
IOWA ☆
ARKANSAS ☆
MICHIGAN ☆
UTAH ☆
IDAHO ☆
MONTANA ☆
NEVADA ☆
KANSAS ☆
OREGON ☆
FLORIDA ☆
WYOMING ☆
WASHINGTON ☆
COLORADO ☆
NEBRASKA ☆
TEXAS ☆

| 1896 | 1889 | 1876 | 1867 | 1864 | 1861 | 1858 | 1848 | 1845 | 1836 |
| 1890 | | | | 1863 | 1859 | | 1850 | 1846 | 1837 |

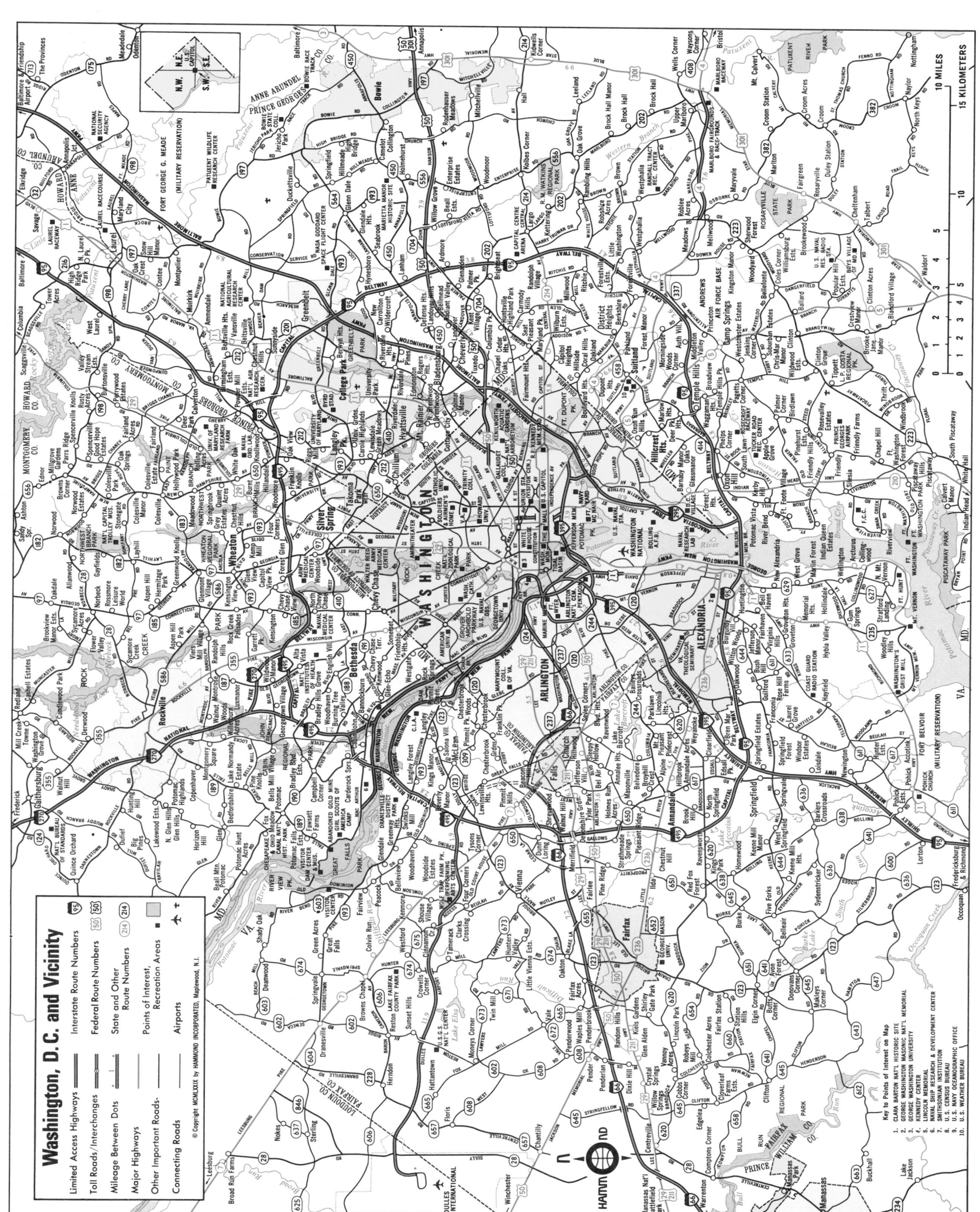

Washington, D.C. and Vicinity

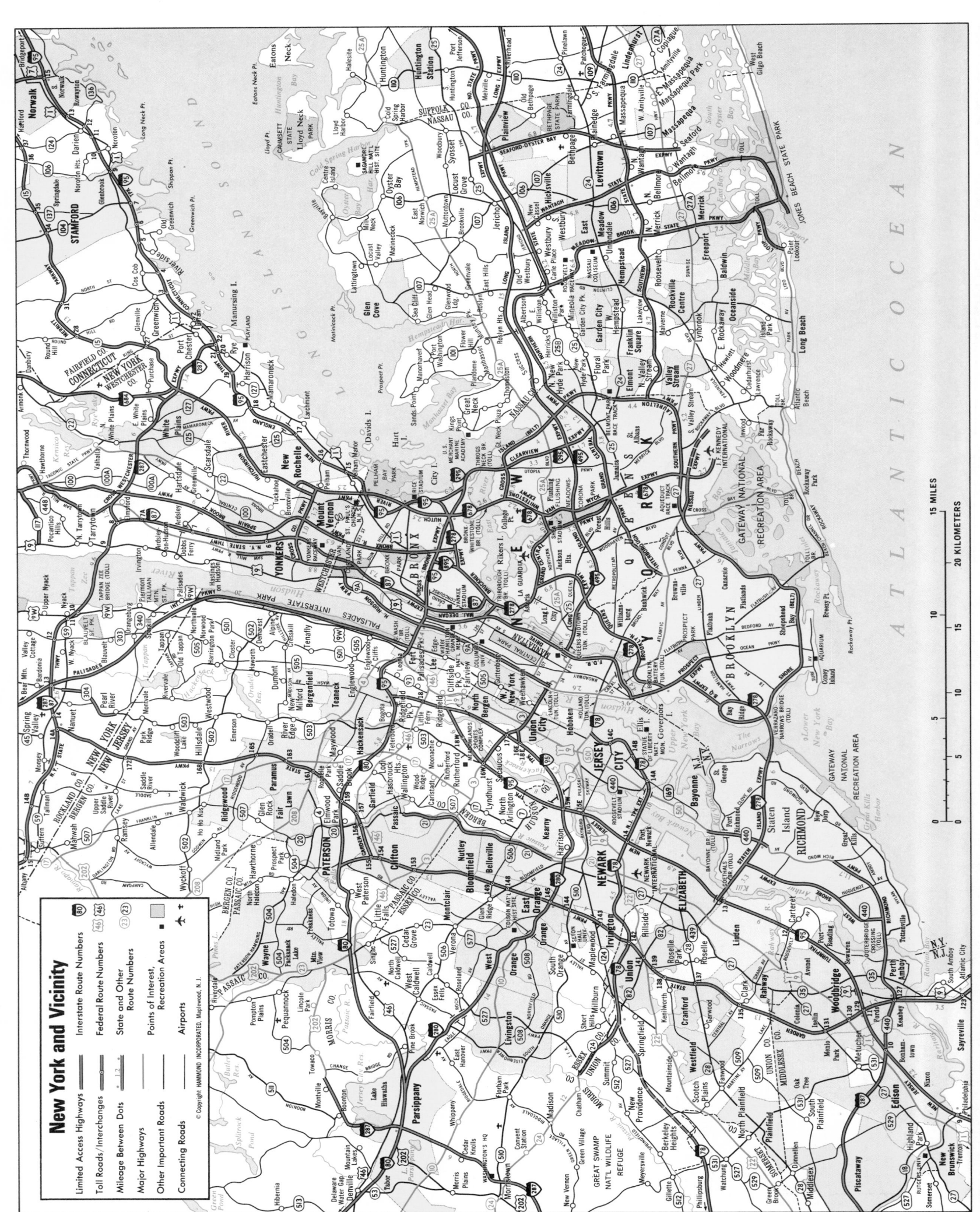

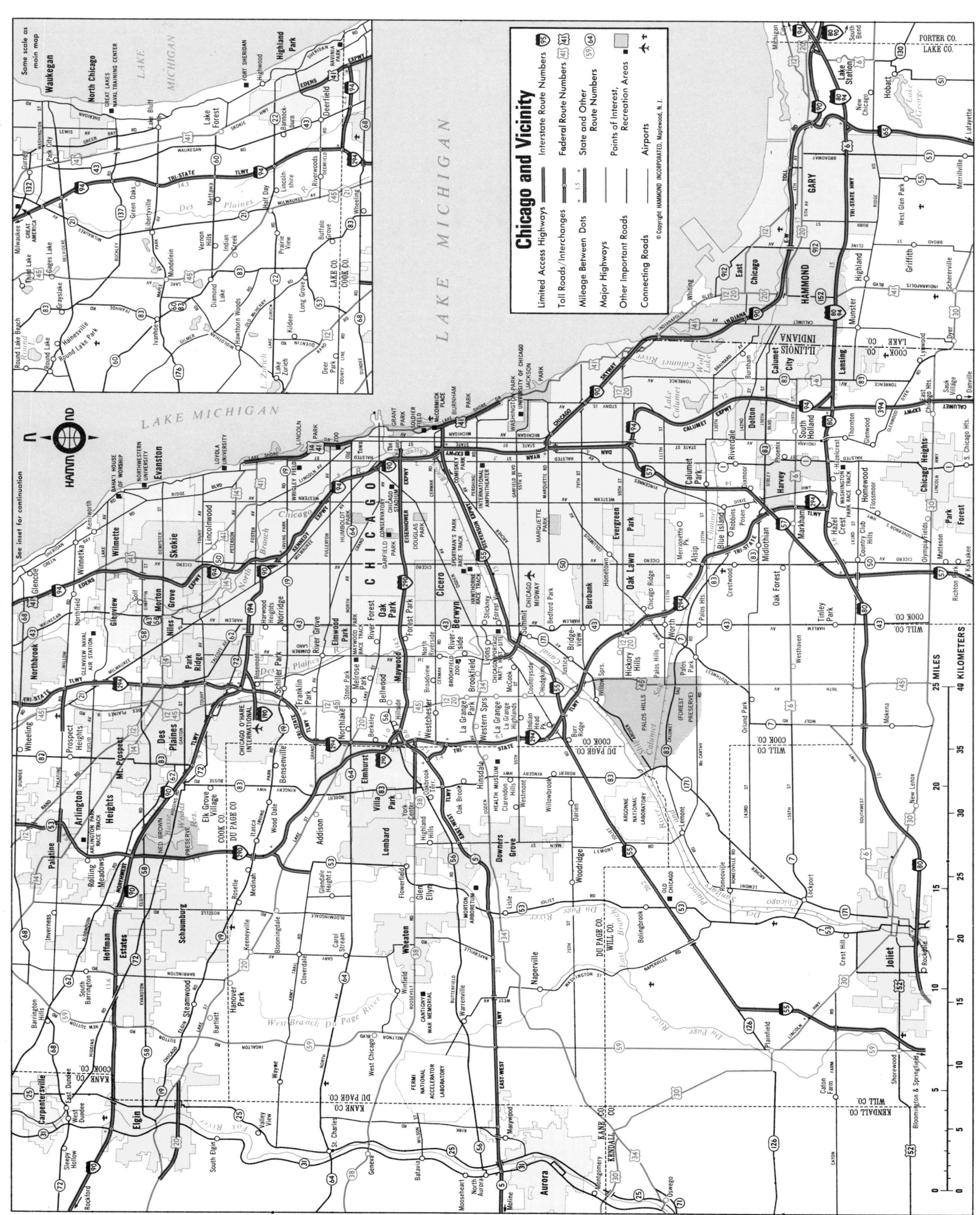

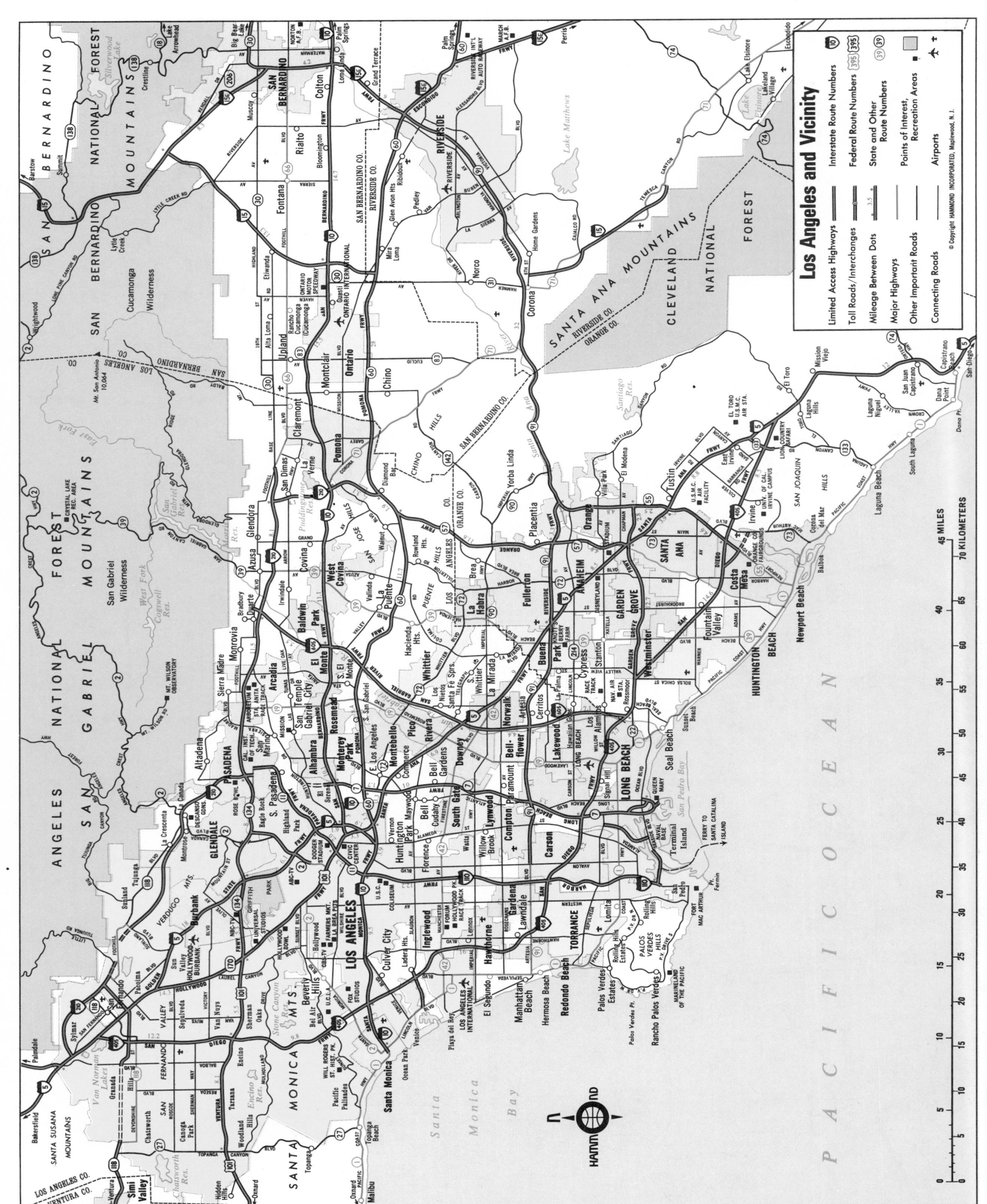

Los Angeles and Vicinity

INDEX OF THE WORLD

Introduction

This index contains a complete alphabetical listing of more than one hundred thousand names shown on all the maps included in this atlas. Names not found in the individual indexes accompanying the maps appear here. The user who is unfamiliar with the location of a country, town, or physical feature, or who is in doubt as to which country, state or province a place belongs will find the answers to his questions in this index. Entries are indexed to all maps or insets showing the place.

The name of the feature sought will be found in its proper alphabetical sequence, followed by the name of the political division in which it is located, the page number of the map on which it will be found, and the key reference necessary for finding its location on the map. After noting the key reference letter-number combination for the place name, turn to the page number indicated. The place name will be found within the square formed by the two lines of latitude and the two lines of longitude which enclose the coordinates—i.e., the marginal letters and numbers. An open circle (○) after the name signifies a township — better known as a town — in the northeastern U.S.

All index entries for cities and towns in the United States are followed by a five-digit postal ZIP code number applying to the community. This useful feature permits the reader to address his mail so that it will be routed and delivered more efficiently and quickly by the U.S. Postal Service. A dagger (†) designates those places that do not possess a post office. The ZIP code number listed in such cases refers to that of the nearest post office. An asterisk (*) marks those larger cities which are divided into multiple ZIP code areas. Using the single ZIP code number listed in such cases will direct your letter to the proper city with dispatch. However, if the precise ZIP code number of the address within the city is needed, it is suggested that the reader refer to the latest National ZIP Code Directory at his local post office. This detailed guide lists every street in a multiple ZIP code city with the proper ZIP code for the street.

Because of limitations of space on the map, place names do not always appear in their complete form on the map. The complete forms are, however, given in the index. Variant spellings of names and alternate names are also given in this index. The alternate form or spelling of the name appears first, followed in parentheses by the name as it appears on the map. Physical features are usually listed under their proper names and not according to their generic terms; that is to say, Rio Negro will be found under Negro and not under Rio Negro. Exceptions are familiar names such as Rio Grande.

The abbreviations for the political division names and geographical features are explained on page XVI of the atlas. In addition, reference can be made to the Gazetteer-Index appearing on pages IX through XIII in which area, population, capital, map reference and population source data may be found for all major political and physical divisions of the world. Population figures for most entries are also included in the comprehensive individual indexes accompanying each map.

A

Aa (riv.), Switzerland 39/F3
Aachen, W. Germany 22/B3
Aadorf, Switzerland 39/G2
Aalen, W. Germany 22/D4
Aalsmeer, Netherlands 27/F4
Aalst, Belgium 27/D7
Aalten, Netherlands 27/K5
Aalter, Belgium 27/C6
Äänekoski, Finland 18/O5
Aarau, Switzerland 39/F2
Aarberg, Switzerland 39/D2
Aarburg, Switzerland 39/E2
Aardenburg, Netherlands 27/C6
Aare (riv.), Switzerland 39/E3
Aargau (canton), Switzerland 39/F2
Aarlen (Arlon), Belgium 27/H9
Aarons (creek), Va. 307/L7
Aaronsburg, Pa. (16820) 294/H4
Aarschot, Belgium 27/F7
Aat (Ath), Belgium 27/D7
Aba, China 77/F5
Aba, Hungary 41/E3
Aba, Nigeria 106/F7
Aba, Nigeria 102/C4
Aba, Zaire 115/F3
Aba as Sa'ud, Saudi Arabia 59/D6
Abacaxis (riv.), Brazil 132/B4
Abadan, Iran 54/F6
Abadan, Iran 66/F5
Abadan, Iran 59/E3
Abadeh, Iran 66/H5
Abadeh, Iran 59/F3
Abadla, Algeria 106/D2
Abádszalók, Hungary 41/F3
Abaeté, Brazil 132/E7
Abaetetuba, Brazil 132/D3
Abaetetuba, Brazil 120/E3
Abagnar (Silinhot), China 77/J3
Abaí, Paraguay 144/E4
Abaiang (atoll), Kiribati 87/H5
'Abaila, Saudi Arabia 59/F5
Abajo (mts.), Utah 304/E6
Abakan, U.S.S.R. 54/L4
Abakan, U.S.S.R. 48/K4
Abala, Congo 115/C4
Abalos (pt.), Cuba 158/A2
Abana, Turkey 63/F2
Abancay, Peru 120/B4
Abancay, Peru 128/F9
Abapó, Bolivia 136/D6
Abaq, China 77/J3
Abarqu, Iran 59/F3
Abarqu, Iran 66/H5
'Abasan, Gaza Strip 65/A5
Abashiri, Japan 81/M1
Abashiri (riv.), Japan 81/M1
Abau, Papua N.G. 85/C7
Abaújszántó, Hungary 41/F2
Abay (riv.), Ethiopia 111/G5
Abay, U.S.S.R. 48/H5
Abaya (lake), Ethiopia 111/G6
Abaza, U.S.S.R. 48/J4
Abbaye (pt.), Mich. 250/B2
Abbe (lake), Djibouti 111/H5
Abbeville, Ala. (36310) 195/H7
Abbeville, France 28/D2
Abbeville, Georgia (31001) 217/F7
Abbeville, La. (70510) 238/F7
Abbeville, Miss. (38601) 256/F2
Abbeville (co.), S.C. 296/B3
Abbeville, S.C. (29620) 296/C3
Abbey, Sask. 181/C5
Abbey (head), Scotland 15/E6
Abbeydorney, Ireland 17/B7
Abbeyfeale, Ireland 10/B4
Abbeyfeale, Ireland 17/C7
Abbeylara, Ireland 17/F4
Abbeyleix, Ireland 17/G6
Abbotsford, Br. Col. 184/L3
Abbotsford, Wis. (54405) 317/F6
Abbott, Ark. (†72944) 202/B3
Abbott, N. Mex. (†87747) 274/E2
Abbott, Texas (76621) 303/G6
Abbottabad, Pakistan 68/C2
Abbottabad, Pakistan 59/K3
Abbottsburg, N.C. (28321) 281/M5
Abbottsford, Georgia (†30240) 217/B4
Abbottstown, Pa. (17301) 294/J6
Abbot Village○, Maine (04406) 243/D5
Abbyville, Kansas (67510) 232/D4
'Abdul 'Aziz, Jebel (mts.), Syria 63/J4
Abdulino, U.S.S.R. 52/H4
Abéché, Chad 102/D3
Abéché, Chad 111/D5
Abee, Alberta 182/D2
Abell, Md. (20606) 245/M8
Abemama (atoll), Kiribati 87/H5
Abengourou, Ivory Coast 106/D7
Abengourou, Ivory Coast 102/B4
Åbenrå, Denmark 18/F9
Åbenrå, Denmark 21/C7
Abeokuta, Niger 106/E7
Abeokuta, Nigeria 102/C4
Aberaeron, Wales 13/C5
Aberaeron, Wales 10/D4
Abercarn, Wales 13/B6
Aberchirder, Scotland 15/F3
Abercorn, Québec 172/E4
Abercorn (Mbala), Zambia 115/F5
Abercrombie, N. Dak. (58001) 282/S7
Abercrombie, Nova Scotia 168/F3
Abercrombie (mt.), Wash. 310/H2
Aberdare, Wales 13/A6
Aberdare, Wales 10/E5
Aberdaron, Wales 13/C5
Aberdeen, Idaho (83210) 220/F7
Aberdeen, Ky. (42201) 237/H6
Aberdeen, Md. (21001) 245/O2
Aberdeen, Miss. (39730) 256/H3
Aberdeen (dam), Miss. 256/H3
Aberdeen○, N.J. (†07747) 273/E3
Aberdeen, N.S. Wales 97/F3
Aberdeen, N.C. (28315) 281/L4
Aberdeen (lake), N.W. Terrs. 187/J3
Aberdeen, Ohio (45101) 284/C8
Aberdeen, Sask. 181/E3
Aberdeen, Scotland 7/D3
Aberdeen, Scotland 15/F3
Aberdeen, Scotland 10/F2
Aberdeen (trad. co.), Scotland 15/B5
Aberdeen, S. Africa 118/C6
Aberdeen, S. Dak. 146/J5
Aberdeen, S. Dak. 188/G1
Aberdeen, S. Dak. (57401) 298/M3
Aberdeen, Wash. 188/B1
Aberdeen, Wash. (98520) 310/B3
Aberdeen Proving Ground, Md. 245/N3
Aberdour, Scotland 15/D1
Aberfeldy, Sask. 181/B2
Aberfeldy, Scotland 10/D2
Aberfeldy, Scotland 15/E4
Aberfoyle, Scotland 15/D4
Abergavenny, Wales 13/B6
Abergavenny, Wales 10/E5
Abergele, Wales 13/D4
Aberlady, Scotland 15/F4
Aberlour, Scotland 15/E3
Abernant, Ala. (35440) 195/D4
Abernathy, Texas (79311) 303/B4
Abernethy, Sask. 181/H5
Abernethy, Scotland 15/E4
Aberporth, Wales 13/C5
Abert (lake), Oreg. 188/C2
Abert (lake), Oreg. 291/G5
Abertillery, Wales 13/B6
Abertillery, Wales 10/E5
Aberystwyth, Wales 13/C5
Aberystwyth, Wales 10/D4
Abez', U.S.S.R. 52/K1
Abha, Saudi Arabia 59/D6
Abha, Saudi Arabia 54/F8
Abhar, Iran 66/F2
Abiad, Ras el (Blanc) (cape), Tunisia 106/G1
Abibe, Serranía de (mts.), Colombia 126/B3
'Abidiya, Sudan 59/B6
Abidjan (cap.), Ivory Coast 2/J5
Abidjan (cap.), Ivory Coast 102/B4
Abidjan (cap.), Ivory Coast 106/D7
Abie, Nebr. (68001) 264/H3
Abilene, Kansas (67410) 232/E3
Abilene, Texas 146/J6
Abilene, Texas (*79601) 303/E5
Abilene, Texas 188/G4
Abingdon, England 10/F5
Abingdon, England 13/F6
Abingdon, Ill. (61410) 222/C3
Abingdon, Iowa (†52533) 229/J6
Abingdon, Md. (21009) 245/N3
Abingdon, Va. (24210) 307/D7
Abingdon Downs, Queensland 95/B3
Abington, Conn. (06230) 210/G1
Abington, Ind. (†47330) 227/H5
Abington○, Mass. (02351) 249/L4
Abington, Pa. (19001) 294/M5
Abington, Scotland 15/E5
Abiqua (creek), Oreg. 291/B3
Abiquiu, N. Mex. (87510) 274/C2
Abiquiu (res.), N. Mex. 274/C2
Abita Springs, La. (70420) 238/L6
Abitibi (riv.), Ont. 162/H5
Abitibi (lake), Ont. 162/H6
Abitibi (lake), Ontario 175/E3
Abitibi (riv.), Ontario 175/D2
Abitibi (riv.), Ontario 177/J5
Abitibi (terr.), Québec 174/B3
Abitibi (county), Québec 174/B2
Abkhaz A.S.S.R., U.S.S.R. 48/E5
Abkhaz A.S.S.R., U.S.S.R. 52/F6
Abminga, S. Australia 94/D2
Abner, N.C. (†27371) 281/K4
Abnûb, Egypt 111/J4
Åbo (Turku), Finland 18/N6
Aboisso, Ivory Coast 106/D7
Aboite, Ind. (†46783) 227/G3
Abomey, Benin 106/E7
Abong-Mbang, Cameroon 115/B3
Abony, Hungary 41/E3
Abor (hills), India 68/G3
Aborlan, Philippines 82/B6
Abou Deïa, Chad 111/C5
Aboyne, Scotland 15/F3
Abqaiq, Saudi Arabia 59/E4
Abra (prov.), Philippines 82/C2
Abra (riv.), Philippines 82/C2
Abraham (lake), Alberta 182/B3
Abraham (mt.), Maine 243/C5
Abraham, Utah (†84635) 304/B4
Abraham (mt.), Vt. 268/B3
Abraham Lincoln Birthplace Nat'l Hist. Site, Ky. 237/K5
Abrams, Wis. (54101) 317/L6
Abrantes, Portugal 33/B3
Abra Pampa, Argentina 143/C1
Abreus, Cuba 158/D2
'Abri, Sudan 111/F3
Abricots, Haiti 158/A6
Abruzzi (reg.), Italy 34/D3
Absaraka, N. Dak. (58002) 282/P6
Absaroka (range), Mont. 262/F5
Absaroka (range), Wyo. 319/C1
Absarokee, Mont. (59001) 262/G5
Absecon, N.J. (08201) 273/D5
Absecon (inlet), N.J. 273/E5
Abu, India 68/C4
Abu 'Arish, Saudi Arabia 59/D6
Abu Dara, Ras (cape), Sudan 59/C5
Abu Dara, Ras (cape), Sudan 111/G3
Abu Deleiq, Sudan 59/B6
Abu Dhabi (cap.), U.A.E. 54/G7
Abu Dhabi (cap.), U.A.E. 59/F5
Abu ed Duhur, Syria 63/G5
Abu Habl, Wadi (dry riv.), Sudan 111/F5
Abu Hadriya, Saudi Arabia 59/E4
Abu Hamed, Sudan 111/F4
Abu Hamed, Sudan 59/B6
Abuja, Niger 106/F7
Abu Kemal, Syria 59/D3
Abu Kemal, Syria 63/J5
Abukuma (riv.), Japan 81/K4
Abu-Mad, Ras (cape), Saudi Arabia 59/C5
Abu Matariq, Sudan 111/E5
Abumombazi, Zaire 115/D3
Abuná (riv.), Bolivia 136/B2
Abunã, Brazil 132/H10
Abunã (riv.), Brazil 132/G10
Abu Qir (bay), Egypt 111/J2
Abu Qurqâs, Egypt 111/J4
Abu Road, India 68/C4
Abu Rujmein, Jebel (mts.), Syria 63/H5
Abu Shagara, Ras (cape), Sudan 111/G3
Abu Shagara, Ras (cape), Sudan 59/C5
Abut (head), N. Zealand 100/B5
Abu Tabari (well), Sudan 111/E4
Abuyog, Philippines 82/E5
Abu Zabad, Sudan 59/A7
Abu Zabad, Sudan 111/E5
Abwong, Sudan 111/F6
Aby (lag.), Ivory Coast 106/D8
Åbybro, Denmark 21/C3
Abydos (ruins), Egypt 111/F2
Abydos (ruins), Turkey 63/B6
Abyei, Sudan 111/E6
Acacías, Colombia 126/D6
Acaciaville, Nova Scotia 168/C4
Academy, S. Dak. (57310) 298/M7
Acadia (par.), La. 238/F6
Acadia Nat'l Park, Maine 243/G7
Acadia Valley, Alberta 182/E4
Acadie Siding, New Bruns. 170/E2
Acadieville, New Bruns. 170/E2
Acahay, Paraguay 144/B5
Acajutla, El Salvador 154/B4
Acala, Mexico 150/N8
Acala, Texas (†79839) 303/B10
Acámbaro, Mexico 150/J7
Acampo, Calif. (95220) 204/C9
Acandí, Colombia 126/B3
Acaponeta, Mexico 150/G5
Acapulco de Juárez, Mexico 146/H8
Acapulco de Juárez, Mexico 150/K8
Acaraí, Serra do (range), Brazil 132/B2
Acarai (mts.), Guyana 131/B5
Acaraú, Brazil 132/F3
Acaray (riv.), Paraguay 144/E4
Acarí, Peru 128/E10
Acarí (riv.), Peru 128/E10
Acarigua, Venezuela 124/D3
Acatlán de Osorio, Mexico 150/K7
Acatzingo de Hidalgo, Mexico 150/N2
Acayucan, Mexico 150/M8
Acchilla, Bolivia 136/C7
Accident, Md. (21520) 245/A2
Accokeek, Md. (20607) 245/L6
Accomac, Va. (23301) 307/S5
Accomack (co.), Va. 307/S5
Accord, Mass. (02018) 249/E8
Accord, N.Y. (12404) 276/M7
Accoville, W. Va. (25606) 312/C7
Accra (cap.), Ghana 102/B4
Accra (cap.), Ghana 106/D7
Accra (cap.), Ghana 2/J5
Accrington, England 10/G1
Accrington, England 13/H1
Aceguá, Uruguay 145/E2
Acequia, Idaho (83350) 220/E7
Acevedo, Argentina 143/F6
Achacachi, Bolivia 136/A5
Achaguas, Venezuela 124/D4
Achalpur, India 68/D4
Achao, Chile 138/D4
Achar, Uruguay 145/C3
Acharacle, Scotland 15/C4
Achégour (well), Niger 106/G5
Achenkirch, Austria 41/A3
Achill (head), Ireland 10/A4
Achill (head), Ireland 17/A4
Achill (isl.), Ireland 10/A4
Achill (isl.), Ireland 17/A4
Achille, Okla. (74720) 288/O7
Achilles, Va. (23001) 307/R6
Achill Sound, Ireland 17/B4
Achiltibuie, Scotland 15/C3
Achinsk, U.S.S.R. 48/K4
Achnasheen, Scotland 10/D2
Achnasheen, Scotland 15/C3
Achourat (well), Mali 106/D4
A'Chralaig (mt.), Scotland 15/C3
Acı (lake), Turkey 63/C4
Acıgöl, Turkey 63/F3
Acıpayam, Turkey 63/C4
Acireale, Italy 34/E6
Ackerly, Texas (79713) 303/C5
Ackerman, Miss. (39735) 256/F4
Ackerville, Ala. (†36778) 195/D6
Ackley, Iowa (50601) 229/G3
Acklins (isl.), Bahamas 146/L7
Acklins (isl.), Bahamas 156/C2
Ackworth, Iowa (50001) 229/G6
Aclare, Ireland 17/D3
Acle, England 13/J5
Acme, Alberta 182/D4
Acme, La. (71316) 238/G4
Acme, Mich. (49610) 250/D4
Acme, N.C. (†28456) 281/N6
Acme, Texas (†79252) 303/E3
Acme, Wash. (98220) 310/C2
Acme, W. Va. (†25122) 312/D6
Acme, Wyo. (82839) 319/E1
Acoaxet, Mass. (†02837) 249/K7
Acobamba, Peru 128/E9
Acolla, Peru 128/E8
Acoma, N. Mex. (†87034) 274/B4
Acomayo, Cusco, Peru 128/G9
Acomayo, Huánuco, Peru 128/E7
Acomita (Pueblo of Acoma), N. Mex. (†87034) 274/B3
Acona, Miss. (†39095) 256/D4
Aconcagua (mt.) 120/C6
Aconcagua, Cerro (mt.), Argentina 143/C3
Aconcagua, Chile 138/A9
Aconcagua (riv.), Chile 138/F2
Aconchi, Mexico 150/D2
Acopiara, Brazil 132/G4
Acora, Peru 128/H11
Acorizal, Brazil 132/C6
Acoyapa, Nicaragua 154/E5
Acqui Terme, Italy 34/B2
Acraman (lake), S. Australia 94/D5
Acre (state), Brazil 132/G10
Acre (riv.), Brazil 132/G10
Acre, Israel 65/C2

Allgäu 327

Alabat (isl.), Philippines 82/D3
Alaca, Turkey 63/F2
Alacahan, Turkey 63/G3
Alaçam, Turkey 63/F2
Alachua (co.), Fla. 212/D2
Alachua, Fla. (32615) 212/D2
Alacrán (reef), Mexico 150/P5
Alacranes, Cuba 158/D1
Aladağ (mt.), Turkey 63/F4
Aladagh, Kuh-i- (mt.), Iran 59/G2
'Aladagh, Kuh-e (mts.), Iran 66/K2
Aladdin, Wyo. (82710) 319/H1
Alaejos, Spain 33/D2
Alagir, U.S.S.R. 52/F6
Alagoa Grande, Brazil 132/H4
Alagoas (state), Brazil 132/G5
Alagoinhas, Brazil 120/F4
Alagoinhas, Brazil 132/G6
Alagón, Spain 33/F2
Alagón (riv.), Spain 33/C2
Alah (riv.), Philippines 82/E7
Al Ahqaf (Bahr es Safi) (des.), Saudi Arabia 59/E6
Al 'Ain, Saudi Arabia 59/C4
Alajuela, C. Rica 154/E6
Alakanuk, Alaska (99554) 196/E2
Alakol' (lake), U.S.S.R. 48/J5
Al 'Ala, Saudi Arabia 59/C4
Alalakeiki (chan.), Hawaii 218/J3
Alalapadu, Suriname 131/C4
Alamagan (isl.), No. Marianas 87/E4
Alamance (co.), N.C. 281/L3
Alamance, N.C. (27201) 281/K2
Alameda (co.), Calif. 204/D6
Alameda, Calif. (94501) 204/J2
Alameda (creek), Calif. 204/K3
Alameda, N. Mex. (87114) 274/C3
Alameda, Sask. 181/J6
Alamikamba, Nicaragua 154/E4
Alamo (lake), Ariz. 198/B4
Alamo (riv.), Calif. 204/K10
Alamo, Georgia (30411) 217/G6
Alamo, Ind. (47916) 227/C5
Alamo, Mexico 150/L6
Alamo, Nev. (89001) 266/F5
Alamo, N. Dak. (58830) 282/D2
Alamo, Tenn. (38001) 237/C9
Alamo, Texas (78516) 303/F11
Ala Moana, Hawaii 218/C4
Alamo-Danville, Calif. (94507) 204/K2
Alamogordo, N. Mex. 188/E4
Alamogordo, N. Mex. (88310) 274/C6
Alamo Heights, Texas (78209) 303/K10
Álamos, Mexico 150/E3
Alamosa (co.), Colo. 208/H7
Alamosa, Colo. (81101) 208/H8
Alamosa (creek), Colo. 208/G8
Alamosa (riv.), N. Mex. 274/B5
Alamota, Kansas (67830) 232/B3
Åland (Ahvenanmaa) (prov.), Finland 18/L6
Åland (isls.), Finland 7/F2
Åland (isls.), Finland 18/L6
Alanje, Panama 154/F6
Alanreed, Texas (79002) 303/D2
Alanson, Mich. (49706) 250/E3
Alanthus Grove, Mo. (†64489) 261/D2
Alanya, Turkey 59/B2
Alanya, Turkey 63/D4
Alaotra (lake), Madagascar 118/H3
Alapaha (riv.), Fla. 212/C1
Alapaha, Georgia (31622) 217/F8
Alapaha (riv.), Georgia 217/F7
Alaqua (creek), Fla. 212/C6
Alarcón (res.), Spain 33/E3
Alarka, N.C. (†28713) 281/C4
Alas (str.), Indonesia 85/F7
Alaşehir, Turkey 63/C3
Alashtar, Iran 66/E4
Alaska (reg.) 4/C17
Alaska 188/C5
Alaska (gulf) 146/D4
ALASKA 196
Alaska (gulf), Alaska 188/D6
Alaska (pen.), Alaska 188/C6
Alaska (range), Alaska 188/C6
Alaska (range), Alaska 146/C3
Alaska (pen.), Alaska 146/C4
Alaska (gulf), Alaska 196/K3
Alaska (pen.), Alaska 196/G3
Alaska (range), Alaska 196/H2
Alaska, Mich. (†49316) 250/D6
Alaska (state), U.S. 2/B2
Alaska (state), U.S. 146/C3
Alaska (range), U.S. 4/C17
Alaska (pen.), U.S. 4/D18
Alaska (gulf), U.S. 4/D17
Alaska Highway, Yukon 187/E3
Alassio, Italy 34/A2
Alatna, Alaska (†99720) 196/H1
Alatna (riv.), Alaska 196/H1
Alatri, Italy 34/D4
Alatyr', U.S.S.R. 52/G4
Al 'Auda, Saudi Arabia 59/E4
Alausí, Ecuador 128/C4
Álava (prov.), Spain 33/E1
Alava (cape), Wash. 188/A1
Alava (cape), Wash. 310/A2
Alaverdi, U.S.S.R. 52/F6
Alavus, Finland 18/N5
Alayor, Spain 33/J3
Al 'Azair, Iraq 66/E5
Alazeya (riv.), U.S.S.R. 48/Q3
Al'Aziziya, Iraq 59/E3
Al 'Aziziya, Iraq 66/D4
Alba, Italy 34/B2
Alba, Mich. (49611) 250/E4
Alba, Mo. (64830) 261/D8
Alba, Pa. (16910) 294/J2
Alba, Texas (75410) 303/J5
Albacete (prov.), Spain 33/E3
Albacete, Spain 7/D5
Albacete, Spain 33/F3
Alba de Tormes, Spain 33/D2
Albaida, Spain 33/F3
Alba Iulia, Romania 45/F2
Albalate del Arzobispo, Spain 33/F2
Alban, Ontario 177/D1
Albanel, Québec 172/E1
Albanel (lake), Québec 174/C2
Albania 2/K3
Albania 7/G4
ALBANIA 45/E5
Albano (lake), Italy 34/F7
Albano Laziale, Italy 34/F7
Albany, Australia 87/B9
Albany, Calif. (94706) 204/J2
Albany, Ga. 146/K6
Albany, Georgia (*31701) 217/D7
Albany, Ill. (61230) 222/C2
Albany, Ind. (47320) 227/G4
Albany, Jamaica 158/J6
Albany, Ky. (42602) 237/L7
Albany, La. (70711) 238/M1
Albany, Minn. (56307) 255/D5
Albany, Mo. (64402) 261/D2
Albany○, N.H. (†03864) 268/E4
Albany (cap.), N.Y. 188/M2
Albany (cap.), N.Y. 146/L5
Albany (co.), N.Y. 276/M5
Albany (cap.), N.Y. (*12201) 276/N5
Albany, N. Zealand 100/B1
Albany, Nova Scotia 168/C4
Albany, Ohio (45710) 284/F7
Albany, Okla. (74721) 288/O7
Albany (riv.), Ont. 146/K4
Albany (riv.), Ont. 162/H5
Albany (riv.), Ontario 175/C2
Albany, Oreg. 188/B2
Albany, Oreg. (97321) 291/D3
Albany, Pr. Edward I. 168/E2
Albany, Texas (76430) 303/E5
Albany, Vt. (05820) 268/C2
Albany○, Vt. (05820) 268/C2
Albany, W. Australia 88/B6
Albany, W. Australia 92/B6
Albany, Wis. (53502) 317/G10
Albany (co.), Wyo. 319/G4
Albany, Wyo. (†82055) 319/F4
Albany Creek, Queensland 88/J2
Albardon, Argentina 143/C3
Albarracín, Spain 33/F2
Albatross (pt.), N. Zealand 100/E3
Albatross (bay), Queensland 88/G2
Albatross (bay), Queensland 95/B2
Albay (prov.), Philippines 82/D4
Albay (gulf), Philippines 82/D4
Albee, S. Dak. (57210) 298/S3
Albemarle (pt.), Ecuador 128/B9
Albemarle (sound), N.C. 188/L3
Albemarle, N.C. (28001) 281/J4
Albemarle (sound), N.C. 281/S2
Albemarle (co.), Va. 307/L5
Albenga, Italy 34/B3
Albeni Falls (dam), Idaho 220/B1
Alberdi, Paraguay 144/D5
Alberene, Va. (†22959) 307/L5
Alberga, S. Australia 94/D2
Alberga, The (riv.), S. Australia 94/D2
Alberga, The (riv.), S. Australia 88/E5
Alberhill, Calif. (†92330) 204/E11
Alberni (inlet), Br. Col. 184/H3
Albers, Ill. (62215) 222/D5
Albert (canal), Belgium 27/F6
Albert, France 28/E2
Albert, Kansas (67511) 232/C3
Albert (co.), New Bruns. 170/F3
Albert, N. Mex. (87733) 274/F3
Albert, N.S. Wales 97/D3
Albert, Okla. (73001) 288/K4
Albert (lake), Québec 172/C1
Albert (Mobuto Sese Seko) (lake), Uganda 115/F3
Albert (creek), Wyo. 319/B4
Albert (Mobuto Sese Seko) (lake), Zaire 115/F3
Alberta (prov.) 162/E5
Alberta (prov.) Canada 146/G4
Alberta, Ala. (36720) 195/D6
ALBERTA 182
Alberta (mt.), Alberta 182/B3
Alberta (mt.), Alta. 162/E5
Alberta, La. (†71016) 238/D2
Alberta, Minn. (56207) 255/B5
Alberta, Va. (23821) 307/N7
Alberta Beach, Alberta 182/C3
Albert City, Iowa (50510) 229/C3
Albert Edward (bay), N.W. Terrs. 187/H3
Albert Head, Br. Col. 184/J4
Alberti, Argentina 143/G7
Albertirsa, Hungary 41/E3
Albert Lea, Minn. (56007) 255/E7
Albert Mines, New Bruns. 170/F3
Alberton, Mont. (59820) 262/B3
Alberton, Pr. Edward I. 168/E2
Alberton, S. Africa 118/H6
Albert Town, Jamaica 158/H6
Albertville, Ala. (35950) 195/F2
Albertville, France 28/G5
Albertville, Minn. (55301) 255/E5
Albertville, Sask. 181/F2
Albeuve, Switzerland 39/D3
Albi, France 28/E6
Albia, Iowa (52531) 229/H6
Albin, Wyo. (82050) 319/H4
Albina, Suriname 131/D3
Albino, Italy 34/B2
Albion, Calif. (95410) 204/B4
Albion, Idaho (83311) 220/E7
Albion (mts.), Idaho 220/E7
Albion, Ill. (62806) 222/E5
Albion, Ind. (46701) 227/G2
Albion, Iowa (50005) 229/H4
Albion○, Maine (04910) 243/E6
Albion, Mich. (49224) 250/E6
Albion, Nebr. (68620) 264/F3
Albion, N.Y. (14411) 276/D4
Albion, Okla. (74521) 288/R5
Albion, Pa. (16401) 294/B2
Albion, R.I. (02802) 249/H5
Albion, Wash. (99102) 310/H4
Albion, Wis. (†53534) 317/H10
Al Birk, Saudi Arabia 59/D6
Albocácer, Spain 33/F2
Alborán (isl.), Spain 7/D5
Alborán (isl.), Spain 33/E5
Ålborg, Denmark 7/F3
Ålborg, Denmark 18/G8
Ålborg (bay), Denmark 21/D4
Alborn, Minn. (55702) 255/F4
Albox, Spain 33/E4
Albreda, Br. Col. 184/H4
Albright, W. Va. (26519) 312/G3
Albrightsville, Pa. (18210) 294/L3
Albristhorn (mt.), Switzerland 39/D4
Albufeira, Portugal 33/B4
Albuñol, Spain 33/E4
Albuquerque (cays), Colombia 126/A10
Albuquerque, N. Mex. 146/H6
Albuquerque, N. Mex. 188/E3
Albuquerque, N. Mex. (*87101) 274/C3
Alburg, Vt. (05440) 268/A2
Alburg○, Vt. (05440) 268/A2
Alburnett, Iowa (52202) 229/K4
Alburquerque, Spain 33/C3
Alburtis, Pa. (18011) 294/L5
Albury, Australia 87/E9
Albury, N. S. Wales 88/H7
Albury, N.S. Wales 97/D5
Albury, N. Zealand 100/C6
Alca, Peru 128/F10
Alcácer do Sal, Portugal 33/B3
Alcalá, Bolivia 136/C6
Alcalá de Chivert, Spain 33/G2
Alcalá de Guadaira, Spain 33/D4
Alcalá de Henares, Spain 33/G4
Alcalá de los Gazules, Spain 33/D4
Alcalá la Real, Spain 33/E4
Alcalde, N. Mex. (87511) 274/C2
Alcamo, Italy 34/D6
Alcanar, Spain 33/G2
Alcañices, Spain 33/C2
Alcañiz, Spain 33/F2
Alcàntara, Portugal 33/A1
Alcántara, Spain 33/C3
Alcántara (res.), Spain 33/C3
Alcántaratara (res.), Portugal 33/C3
Alcantarilla, Spain 33/F4
Alcaraz, Argentina 143/G5
Alcaraz, Spain 33/E3
Alcaraz, Sierra de (range), Spain 33/E3
Alcatraz (isl.), Calif. 204/J2
Alcaudete, Spain 33/E4
Alcázar de San Juan, Spain 33/E3
Alcester, S. Dak. (57001) 298/R7
Alcida, New Bruns. 170/E1
Alcira, Spain 33/F3
Alco, Ark. (72610) 202/F2
Alco, La. (71402) 238/D4
Alcoa, Tenn. (37701) 237/N9
Alcobaça, Brazil 132/G7
Alcobaça, Portugal 33/B3
Alcolu, S.C. (29001) 296/G4
Alcomdale, Alberta 182/C3
Alcona (co.), Mich. 250/F4
Alcona Beach, Ontario 177/E3
Alcones, Chile 138/F5
Alcony, Ohio (†45373) 284/B5
Alcora, Spain 33/F2
Alcorisa, Spain 33/F2
Alcorn, Ky. (†40447) 237/O5
Alcorn (co.), Miss. 256/G1
Alcorn State University, Miss. (39096) 256/B7
Alcorta, Argentina 143/F6
Alcoutim, Portugal 33/C4
Alcova, Wyo. (82620) 319/F3
Alcova (res.), Wyo. 319/F3
Alcoy, Spain 33/F3
Alcudia (bay), Spain 33/H3
Alda, Nebr. (68810) 264/F4
Aldabra (isls.), Seychelles 102/G5
Aldabra (isls.), Seychelles 118/H1
Aldama, Chihuahua, Mexico 150/G2
Aldama, Tamaulipas, Mexico 150/L5
Aldan, Pa. (†19018) 294/M7
Aldan, U.S.S.R. 54/O4
Aldan (riv.), U.S.S.R. 54/P3
Aldan, U.S.S.R. 48/N4
Aldan (plat.), U.S.S.R. 48/N4
Aldan (riv.), U.S.S.R. 48/O3
Aldeburgh, England 13/J5
Aldeburgh, England 10/G4
Aldeia Carajá, Brazil 132/D6
Aldeia Nova de São Bento, Portugal 33/C4
Alden, Ill. (60001) 222/E1
Alden, Iowa (50006) 229/G4
Alden, Kansas (67512) 232/D3
Alden, Mich. (49612) 250/D4
Alden, Minn. (56009) 255/E7
Alden, N.Y. (14004) 276/C5
Alden Bridge, La. (†71006) 238/C1
Aldenville, Pa. (18401) 294/M2
Alder, Mont. (59710) 262/D5
Alder, Wash. (†98328) 310/C4
Alder (lake), Wash. 310/C4
Alder Creek, N.Y. (13301) 276/K4
Alder Flats, Alberta 182/C3
Alderley, Wis. (†53066) 317/J1
Alderney (isl.), Chan. Is. 10/E6
Alderney (isl.), Chan. Is. 13/E8
Alderpoint, Calif. (95411) 204/B3
Alder Point, Nova Scotia 168/H2
Aldershot, England 10/F5
Aldershot, England 13/G8
Aldershot, Nova Scotia 168/D3
Alderson, Okla. (74522) 288/P5
Alderson, W. Va. (24910) 312/E7
Aldersyde, Alberta 182/C4
Aldine, Ind. (†46366) 227/D2
Aldora, Georgia (†30204) 217/D4
Aldouane, New Bruns. 170/E2
Aldrich, Ala. (†35115) 195/E4
Aldrich, Minn. (56434) 255/C4
Aldrich, Mo. (65601) 261/F7
Aldridge Brownhills, England 10/G3
Aldridge Brownhills, England 13/E5
Aledo, Ill. (61231) 222/C2
Aledo, Texas (76008) 303/E2
Aleg, Mauritania 106/B5
Alegre, Brazil 135/F2
Alegre, Brazil 132/F8
Alegrete, Brazil 132/B10
Alegrete, Brazil 120/D5
'Aleih, Lebanon 63/F6
Alejandra, Argentina 143/F5
Alejandría, Bolivia 136/C3
Alejandro Selkirk (isl.), Chile 120/A6
Aleknagik, Alaska (99555) 196/G3
Aleksandriya, U.S.S.R. 52/D5
Aleksandrov Gay, U.S.S.R. 52/G4
Aleksandrovsk, U.S.S.R. 52/J3
Aleksandrovsk-Sakhalinsky, U.S.S.R. 54/R4
Aleksandrovsk-Sakhalinskiy, U.S.S.R. 48/P5
Aleksandrów Kujawski, Poland 47/D2
Aleksandrów Łódzki, Poland 47/D3
Alekseyevka, U.S.S.R. 48/H4
Alekseyevka, U.S.S.R. 52/E4
Aleksin, U.S.S.R. 52/E4
Aleksinac, Yugoslavia 45/E4
Além Paraíba, Brazil 135/E2
Alençon, France 28/D3
Alenquer, Brazil 132/C3
Alenquer, Brazil 120/D3
Alenuihaha (chan.), Hawaii 218/E7
Aleppo (prov.), Syria 63/G4
Aleppo, Syria 54/E6
Aleppo, Syria 59/C2
Aleppo, Syria 63/G4
Aléria, France 28/B6
Alert, Canada 4/A12
Alert, Ind. (†47283) 227/F6
Alert, N.C. (†27589) 281/N2
Alert, N.W.T. 162/N3
Alert, N.W. Terrs. 187/M1
Alert (pt.), N.W. Terrs. 187/K1
Alert Bay, Br. Col. 184/D5
Alès, France 28/E5
Alessandria (prov.), Italy 34/B2
Alessandria, Italy 34/B2
Ålestrup, Denmark 21/C4
Ålesund, Norway 7/E2
Ålesund, Norway 18/D5
Aletschhorn (mt.), Switzerland 39/F4
Aleutian (isls.), Alaska 188/D6
Aleutian (isls.), Alaska 196/J4
Aleutian (range), Alaska 196/G3
Aleutian (isls.), U.S. 4/D18
Aleutian (isls.), U.S. 2/A3
Alex, Okla. (73002) 288/L5
Alexander (arch.), Alaska 146/E4
Alexander (arch.), Alaska 196/L1
Alexander (isl.) 5/B15
Alexander, Ark. (72002) 202/F4
Alexander (lake), Conn. 210/H1
Alexander, Georgia (30801) 217/J4
Alexander (co.), Ill. 222/D6
Alexander, Ill. (62601) 222/D4
Alexander, Iowa (50420) 229/G3
Alexander, Kansas (67513) 232/C3
Alexander○, Maine (†04610) 243/H5
Alexander, Manitoba 179/B5
Alexander, N.Y. (14005) 276/D5
Alexander (co.), N.C. 281/G3
Alexander, N. Dak. (58831) 282/C4
Alexander (cape), Solomon Is. 86/D2
Alexander (arch.), U.S. 4/D16
Alexander, W. Va. (26218) 312/F5
Alexander Bay, S. Africa 102/D7
Alexander Bay, S. Africa 118/B5
Alexander City, Ala. (35010) 195/G5
Alexander Mills, N.C. (†28043) 281/F4
Alexandra, N. Zealand 100/B6
Alexandra, S. Africa 118/H6
Alexandra, Victoria 97/C5
Alexandra Land (isl.), U.S.S.R. 4/A8
Alexandra Land (isl.), U.S.S.R. 48/E1
Alexandretta (Iskenderun), Turkey 63/G4
Alexandretta (gulf), Turkey 63/F4
Alexandria, Ala. (36250) 195/G3
Alexandria, Br. Col. 184/F4
Alexandria, Egypt 2/L4
Alexandria, Egypt 102/E1
Alexandria, Egypt 59/A3
Alexandria, Egypt 111/J2
Alexandria, Ind. (46001) 227/F4
Alexandria, Jamaica 158/J6
Alexandria, Ky. (41001) 237/N3
Alexandria, La. 146/J6
Alexandria, La. 188/H4
Alexandria, La. (71301) 238/E4
Alexandria, Minn. (56308) 255/C5
Alexandria, Mo. (63430) 261/K2
Alexandria, Nebr. (68303) 264/G4
Alexandria○, N.H. (†03222) 268/D4
Alexandria, North. Terr. 93/E5
Alexandria, Ohio (43001) 284/E5
Alexandria, Ontario 177/K2
Alexandria, Pa. (16611) 294/F4
Alexandria, Romania 45/G3
Alexandria, Scotland 15/A1
Alexandria, Scotland 10/A1
Alexandria, S. Dak. (57311) 298/O6
Alexandria, Tenn. (37012) 237/J8
Alexandria, Va. 188/L3
Alexandria (I.C.), Va. (*22301) 307/S3
Alexandria Bay, N.Y. (13607) 276/J2
Alexandrina (lake), S. Australia 94/F6
Alexandroúpolis, Greece 45/H5
Alexis, Ill. (61412) 222/C2
Alexis (riv.), Newf. 166/C3
Alexis Creek, Br. Col. 184/F4
Aleysk, U.S.S.R. 48/J4
Aleza Lake, Br. Col. 184/G3
Alfalfa (co.), Okla. 288/K1
Alfalfa, Okla. (†73015) 288/J4
Al Falluja, Iraq 59/D3
Al Falluja, Iraq 66/C4
Alfaro, Spain 33/F1
Alfatar, Bulgaria 45/H4
Al Fatha, Iraq 59/D3
Al Fatha, Iraq 66/C3
Alfeld, W. Germany 22/C2
Alfenas, Brazil 135/D2
Alférez (riv.), Uruguay 145/E5
Alford, England 13/H4
Alford, Fla. (32420) 212/D6
Alford○, Mass. (†01261) 249/A4
Alford, Scotland 15/F3
Alford, Scotland 10/E2
Alfordsville, Ind. (†47553) 227/C7
Alfred, Maine (04002) 243/B9
Alfred○, Maine (04002) 243/B9
Alfred, N.Y. (14802) 276/E6
Alfred, N. Dak. (58411) 282/N6
Alfred, Ontario 177/K2
Alfredton, N. Zealand 100/F4
Alfreton, England 13/F4
Alga, U.S.S.R. 48/F5
Ålgård, Norway 18/D7
Algarrobo, Chile 138/F3
Algarrobo (pt.), P. Rico 161/A2
Algarrobo del Águila, Argentina 143/C4
Algeciras, Colombia 126/C6
Algeciras, Spain 33/D4
Algemesí, Spain 33/F3
Alger (co.), Mich. 250/C2
Alger, Mich. (48610) 250/E4
Alger, Ohio (45812) 284/C4
Algeria 2/J4
Algeria 102/C2
ALGERIA 106/D3
Algés, Portugal 33/A1
Algete, Spain 33/G4
Alghero, Italy 34/B4
Algiers (cap.), Algeria 102/C1
Algiers (cap.), Algeria 106/E1
Algiers (cap.), Algeria 2/K4
Algiers, Ind. (†47567) 227/C7
Algoa, Ark. (†72112) 202/H3
Algoa (bay), S. Africa 118/D6
Algoa, Texas (†77511) 303/K3
Algodones, N. Mex. (87001) 274/C3
Algoma, Miss. (38820) 256/G2
Algoma (terr. dist.), Ontario 177/J5
Algoma (terr. dist.), Ontario 175/D3
Algoma, Oreg. (†97601) 291/F5
Algoma, W. Va. (24807) 312/D8
Algoma, Wis. (54201) 317/M6
Algoma Mills, Ontario 177/B1
Algona, Iowa (50511) 229/E2
Algona, Wash. (98002) 310/C3
Algonac, Mich. (48001) 250/G6
Algonquin, Ill. (60102) 222/E1
Algonquin (peak), N.Y. 276/M2
Algonquin Park, Ontario 177/F2
Algonquin Prov. Park, Ontario 177/F2
Algonquin Prov. Park, Ontario 175/E3
Algood, Tenn. (38501) 237/K8
Algorta, Uruguay 145/B3
Algrove, Sask. 181/H3
Alhama de Granada, Spain 33/E4
Alhama de Murcia, Spain 33/F4
Alhambra, Alberta 182/C3
Alhambra, Calif. (*91801) 204/C10
Alhambra, Ill. (62001) 222/D5
Al Hawtah, P.D.R. Yemen 59/E6
Al Hilla, Saudi Arabia 59/E5
Al Hoceima, Morocco 106/D1
Alhos Vedros, Portugal 33/B3
Alhué, Estero de (riv.), Chile 138/F4
Alía, Spain 33/D3
'Aliabad, Kuh-e (mt.), Iran 59/F3
'Aliabad, Kuh-e (mt.), Iran 66/G3
Aliağa, Turkey 63/B3
Alibag, India 68/C5
Alibates Flint Quarries Nat'l Mon., Texas 303/C2
Ali-Bayramly, U.S.S.R. 52/G7
Alibeyköyü, Turkey 63/D6
Alicante (prov.), Spain 33/F3
Alicante, Spain 33/F3
Alicante, Spain 7/D5
Alice (lake), Nebr. 264/A2
Alice, N. Dak. (58003) 282/P6
Alice (lake), N. Dak. 282/M3
Alice, Ontario 177/G2
Alice (chan.), Philippines 82/B8
Alice (riv.), Queensland 95/C4
Alice, Texas (78332) 303/F10
Alice Arm, Br. Col. 184/C2
Alicel, Oreg. (†97824) 291/J2
Alice Springs, Australia 87/D8
Alice Springs, North. Terr. 88/E4
Alice Springs, North. Terr. 93/D7
Aliceville, Ala. (35442) 195/B4
Aliceville (dam), Ala. 195/B4
Aliceville, Kansas (66832) 232/G3
Alicia, Ark. (72410) 202/H2
Alicia (bank), Colombia 126/B8
Alicudi (isl.), Italy 34/E5
Alida, Minn. (†56676) 255/C3
Alida, Sask. 181/K6
Aligarh, India 68/D3
'Ali Gharbi, Iraq 66/E4
Alijó, Portugal 33/C2
Alima (riv.), Congo 115/B4
Alimodian, Philippines 82/D5
Alindao, Cent. Afr. Rep. 115/D2
Aline, Georgia (†30420) 217/H6
Aline, Okla. (73716) 288/K1
Alingly, Sask. 181/E2
Alingsås, Sweden 18/H7
Alipore, India 68/F2
Aliquippa, Pa. (15001) 294/B4
Ali Sabieh, Djibouti 111/H5
'Ali Sharqi, Iraq 66/E4
Aliskerovo, U.S.S.R. 48/R3
Alivérion, Greece 45/G6
Aliwal North, S. Africa 118/D6
Alix, Alberta 182/D3
Alix, Ark. (72820) 202/C3
Aljezur, Portugal 33/B4
Aljojuca, Mexico 150/O1
Aljustrel, Portugal 33/B4
Alkabo, N. Dak. (58832) 282/C2
Alkali (lakes), Calif. 204/E2
Alkali (lake), Nev. 266/B1
Alkali (lakes), N. Dak. 282/L3
Alkali Lake, Br. Col. 184/F4
Alkaline (lake), N. Dak. 282/L6
Alken, Belgium 27/G7
Alkmaar, Netherlands 27/F3
Alkmaardermeer (lake), Netherlands 27/F3
Alkol, W. Va. (25501) 312/C6
Al Kufa, Iraq 66/D4
Al Kumait, Iraq 66/E4
Al Kuwait (cap.), Kuwait 59/E4
Al Kuwait (cap.), Kuwait 54/F7
Allagash○, Maine (†04774) 243/F1
Allagash (lake), Maine 243/D3
Allagash (riv.), Maine 243/E2
Allahabad, India 68/E3
Allahabad, India 54/K7
Allaine (riv.), Switzerland 39/D2
Allaire, N.J. (†07727) 273/E3
Allakaket, Alaska (99720) 196/H1
Allakh-Yun', U.S.S.R. 48/O3
Allamakee (co.), Iowa 229/L2
Allaman, Switzerland 39/B4
All American (canal), Calif. 204/K11
Allamoore, Texas (†79855) 303/C11
Allamuchy, N.J. (07820) 273/D2
Allan (mt.), Idaho 220/D4
Allan, Sask. 181/E4
Allan (hills), Sask. 181/E4
Allanmyo, Burma 72/B3
Allanwater, Ontario 175/C2
Allanwater, Ontario 177/G4
'Allaqi, Wadi (dry riv.), Egypt 111/F3
Allard (lake), Québec 174/E2
Allardt, Tenn. (38504) 237/M8
Allardville, New Bruns. 170/E1
Allariz, Spain 33/C1
Allatoona (lake), Georgia 217/C2
Alle, Switzerland 39/D2
Alleene, Ark. (71820) 202/B6
Allegan (co.), Mich. 250/D6
Allegan, Mich. (49010) 250/D6
Allegany (co.), Md. 245/C2
Allegany (co.), N.Y. 276/D6
Allegany, N.Y. (14706) 276/C6
Allegany, Oreg. (97407) 291/D4
Allegany Ind. Res., N.Y. 276/C6
Alleghany, Calif. (95910) 204/E4
Alleghany (co.), N.C. 281/G1
Alleghany (co.), Va. 307/H5
Alleghany, Va. (†24426) 307/H5
Allegheny (res.), N.Y. 276/C7
Allegheny (riv.), N.Y. 276/C6
Allegheny (co.), Pa. 294/B5
Allegheny (res.), Pa. 294/E2
Allegheny (riv.), Pa. 294/D2
Allegheny (mts.), Va. 307/H5
Allegheny Front (mts.), Md. 245/C2
Allegheny Front (mts.), Pa. 294/E5
Allègre (pt.), Guadeloupe 161/A6
Allegre, Ky. (42203) 237/G7
Alleman, Iowa (50007) 229/F5
Allemands (lake), La. 238/M4
Allen, Ala. (36419) 195/C7
Allen, Argentina 143/C4
Allen (co.), Ind. 227/G2
Allen, Lough (lake), Ireland 10/C3
Allen (lake), Ireland 17/E3
Allen, Bog of (marsh), Ireland 17/H5
Allen (co.), Kansas 232/G4
Allen, Kansas (66833) 232/F3
Allen (co.), Ky. 237/J7
Allen, Ky. (41601) 237/R5
Allen (par.), La. 238/E5
Allen, La. (†71469) 238/D3
Allen, Md. (21810) 245/R7
Allen, Mich. (49227) 250/E7
Allen, Miss. (†39083) 256/C7
Allen (mt.), Mont. 262/C2
Allen, Nebr. (68710) 264/H2
Allen (co.), Ohio 284/B4
Allen, Okla. (74825) 288/O5
Allen, Pa. (†17007) 294/H5
Allen, S. Dak. (57714) 298/F7
Allen, Texas (75002) 303/H1
Allendale, England 13/E3
Allendale, Ill. (62410) 222/F5
Allendale, Mo. (†64456) 261/D2
Allendale, N.J. (07401) 273/B1
Allendale (co.), S.C. 296/E6
Allendale, S.C. (29810) 296/E5
Allende, Coahuila, Mexico 150/J2
Allende, Nuevo León, Mexico 150/J4
Allendorf, Iowa (51330) 229/B2
Allenford, Ontario 177/C3
Allenhurst, Georgia (31301) 217/J7
Allenhurst, N.J. (07711) 273/F3
Allen Park, Mich. (48101) 250/B7
Allens Mills, Maine (†04938) 243/C6
Allenspark, Colo. (80510) 208/J2
Allen Springs, Ky. (†42122) 237/J7
Allenstein (Olsztyn), Poland 47/E2
Allenstown○, N.H. (†03275) 268/E5
Allensville, Ky. (42204) 237/G7
Allensville, Ohio (45611) 284/E7
Allensville, Pa. (17002) 294/G4
Allenton, Mo. (63001) 261/M4
Allenton, R.I. (†02852) 249/H6
Allenton, Wis. (53002) 317/K9
Allentown, Georgia (31003) 217/F5
Allentown, N.J. (08501) 273/D3
Allentown, N.Y. (14707) 276/E6
Allentown, Ohio (†45801) 284/B4
Allentown, Pa. 188/L2
Allentown, Pa. (*18101) 294/L4
Allentsteig, Austria 41/C2
Allenville, Ill. (†61951) 222/E4
Allenville, Mo. (†63740) 261/N8
Allenwood, N.J. (08720) 273/E3
Allenwood, Pa. (17810) 294/H3
Alleppey-Cochin, India 68/D7
Aller (riv.), W. Germany 22/C2
Allerton, Ill. (61810) 222/F4
Allerton, Iowa (50008) 229/G7
Allerton, Mass. (02045) 249/E7
Allerton (pt.), Mass. 249/E7
Alley, Jamaica 158/J7
Alley Spring, Mo. (†65466) 261/J8
Allgäu (reg.), W. Germany 22/D5

Antsiranana 329

Amritsar, India 68/C2
Amrum (isl.), W. Germany 22/C1
Amsden, Ohio (44803) 284/D3
Amstelveen, Netherlands 27/B5
Amsterdam (isl.) 2/N7
Amsterdam, Georgia (31734) 217/D9
Amsterdam, Mo. (64723) 261/D6
Amsterdam, Mont. (†59741) 262/E5
Amsterdam (cap.), Netherlands 27/B4
Amsterdam (cap.), Netherlands 7/E3
Amsterdam, N.Y. (12010) 276/M5
Amsterdam, Ohio (43903) 284/J5
Amsterdam, Sask. 181/J4
Amstetten, Austria 41/C2
Amston, Conn. (06231) 210/F2
Am-Timan, Chad 111/D5
Amuay, Venezuela 124/C2
Amudar'ya (riv.) 2/N3
Amudar'ya (riv.), U.S.S.R. 54/H5
Amudar'ya (riv.), U.S.S.R. 48/G5
Amukta (isl.), Alaska 196/D4
Amukta (passage), Alaska 196/D4
Amuku (mts.), Guyana 131/B4
Amulet, Sask. 181/G6
Amund Ringnes (isl.), N.W.T. 162/M3
Amund Ringnes (isl.), N.W. Terrs. 187/J2
Amundsen (sea) 2/D10
Amundsen (bay) 5/C3
Amundsen (sea) 5/B13
Amundsen (gulf), Canada 4/B16
Amundsen (gulf), N.W.T. 162/D1
Amundsen (gulf), N.W.T. 146/F2
Amundsen (gulf), N.W. Terrs. 187/F2
Amundsen-Scott Station 5/A14
Amuntai, Indonesia 85/F6
Amur (riv.) 2/R3
Amur (riv.) 54/P5
Amur (Heilong Jiang) (riv.), China 77/L2
'Amur, Wadi (dry riv.), Sudan 111/G4
Amur (riv.), U.S.S.R. 48/O4
Amurang, Indonesia 85/G5
Amursk, U.S.S.R. 48/O4
Amy, Kansas (†67850) 232/B3
Amya (pass), Burma 72/C4
Amya (pass), Thailand 72/C4
Amyun, Lebanon 63/F5
An, Burma 72/B3
'Ana, Iraq 66/B3
'Ana, Iraq 59/D3
Anaa (atoll), Fr. Poly. 87/M7
Anabar (riv.), U.S.S.R. 48/M2
Anabel, Mo. (63431) 261/H3
Ana Branch, Darling (riv.), N.S. Wales 97/A3
'Anabta, West Bank 65/C3
Anacapa (isl.), Calif. 204/F10
Anaco, Venezuela 124/F3
Anacoco, La. (71403) 238/D4
Anacoco (lake), La. 238/D4
Anaconda, Mont. 188/D1
Anaconda-Deer Lodge County, Mont. (59711) 262/C4
Anacortes, Wash. (98221) 310/C2
Anacostia, D.C. (20020) 245/F5
Anacostia (riv.), D.C. 245/F5
Anadarko, Okla. (73005) 288/K4
Anadia, Portugal 33/B2
Anadolufeneri, Turkey 63/D5
Anadoluhisarı, Turkey 63/D6
Anadyr', U.S.S.R 2/T2
Anadyr', U.S.S.R. 4/C1
Anadyr' (gulf), U.S.S.R. 4/C18
Anadyr' (gulf), U.S.S.R. 54/V3
Anadyr' (riv.), U.S.S.R. 54/U3
Anadyr' (riv.), U.S.S.R. 4/C1
Anadyr', U.S.S.R. 48/S3
Anadyr' (gulf), U.S.S.R. 48/T3
Anadyr' (range), U.S.S.R. 48/S3
Anadyr' (riv.), U.S.S.R. 48/S3
Anadyr' U.S.S.R. 54/U3
Anáfi (isl.), Greece 45/G7
Anagance, New Bruns. 170/E3
Anaheim, Calif. 188/C4
Anaheim, Calif. (*92801) 204/D11
Anahim Lake, Br. Col. 184/E4
Anahola, Hawaii (96703) 218/C1
Anáhuac, Chihuahua, Mexico 150/F2
Anáhuac, Nuevo León, Mexico 150/J3
Anahuac, Texas (77514) 303/K8
Anaï (well), Algeria 106/G4
Anai Mudi (mt.), India 68/D6
'Anaiza, Saudi Arabia 59/D4
'Anaiza, Saudi Arabia 54/F7
Anak, N. Korea 81/B4
Anakapalle, India 68/E5
Anaktalik Brook (riv.), Newf. 166/B2
Anaktuvuk Pass, Alaska (99721) 196/H1
Analalava, Madagascar 118/H2
Ana María (gulf), Cuba 158/F3
Anambas (isls.), Indonesia 85/D5
Anambra (state), Nigeria 106/F7
Anamoose, N. Dak. (58710) 282/K4
Anamosa, Iowa (52205) 229/L4
Anamur, Turkey 63/E4
Anamur (cape), Turkey 59/B2
Anamur (cape), Turkey 63/E5
Anan, Japan 81/G7
Anandale, La. (†71301) 238/F4
Ananea, Bolivia 136/A4
Anantapur, India 68/D6
Anantnag, India 68/D2
Anapa, U.S.S.R. 52/E6
Anápolis, Brazil 132/D7
Anápolis, Brazil 120/E4
Anar, Iran 66/J5
Anar, Iran 59/G3
Anarak, Iran 66/H4
Anarak, Iran 59/F3
Anar Darreh, Afghanistan 59/H3
Anar Darreh, Afghanistan 68/A2
Añasco, P. Rico 161/A1
Añasco, P. Rico 156/F1
Añasco (bay), P. Rico 161/A1
Anastasia (isl.), Fla. 212/E2
Anatahan (isl.), No. Marianas 87/E4
Anatolia (reg.), Turkey 63/D3
Anatone, Wash. (99401) 310/H4
Añatuya, Argentina 143/D2
Anauá (riv.), Brazil 132/B2
Anawalt, W. Va. (24808) 312/D8
Anaye (well), Niger 106/G5
Anbar (gov.), Iraq 66/B4
Ancash (dept.), Peru 128/D7
Ancaster, Ontario 177/D4
Anceney, Mont. (†59741) 262/E5
Ancenis, France 28/C4
Anchieta, Brazil 132/F8
Ancho, N. Mex. (†88301) 274/D5
Anchor, Ill. (61720) 222/E3
Anchorage, Alaska 188/D6
Anchorage, Alaska 146/D3
Anchorage, Alaska (*99501) 196/B1
Anchorage, Ky. (40223) 237/L2
Anchorage, U.S. 2/B2
Anchorage, U.S. 4/D17
Anchorena, Argentina 143/C4
Anchor Point, Alaska (99556) 196/B2
Anchor Point, Newf. 166/C3
Anchorville, Mich. (48004) 250/G6
Anchovy, Jamaica 158/H5
Ancienne-Lorette, Québec 172/H3
Anclitas (cay), Cuba 158/F3
Anclote (keys), Fla. 212/D3
Anco, Ky. (41711) 237/P6
Ancohuma (mt.), Bolivia 120/C4
Ancohuma, Nevada (mt.), Bolivia 136/A4
Ancón, Peru 128/D8
Ancona, Ill. (61311) 222/E2
Ancona (prov.), Italy 34/D3
Ancona, Italy 34/D3
Ancona, Italy 7/F4
Ancón de Sardinas (bay), Colombia 126/A7
Ancón de Sardinas (bay), Ecuador 128/C2
Ancoraimes, Bolivia 136/A4
Ancram, N.Y. (12502) 276/N6
Ancroft, England 13/F2
Ancrum, Scotland 15/F5
Ancud, Chile 120/B7
Ancud, Chile 138/D4
Ancud (gulf), Chile 138/D4
Anda (Anta), China 77/L2
Andacollo, Argentina 143/B4
Andacollo, Chile 138/A8
Andado, North. Terr. 93/D8
Andahuaylas, Peru 128/F9
Andale, Kansas (67001) 232/E4
Andalgalá, Argentina 143/C2
Åndalsnes, Norway 18/F5
Andalusia, Ala. (36420) 195/E8
Andalusia, Ill. (61232) 222/C2
Andalusia, Pa. (†19020) 294/N5
Andalusia (reg.), Spain 33/C4
Andaman (sea) 54/L8
Andaman (sea), Burma 72/B4
Andaman (isls.), India 2/P5
Andaman (isls.), India 54/L8
Andaman (isls.), India 68/G6
Andaman (sea), India 68/G6
Andaman and Nicobar Isls. (terr.), India 68/G6
Andamarca, Bolivia 136/B6
Andamarca, Peru 128/E8
Andamooka, S. Australia 94/E4
Andapa, Madagascar 118/H2
Andaraí, Brazil 132/F6
Andau, Austria 41/D3
Andeer, Switzerland 39/H3
Andelfingen, Switzerland 39/G1
Andenne, Belgium 27/G8
Anderlecht, Belgium 27/B9
Anderlues, Belgium 27/E8
Andermatt, Switzerland 39/G3
Andernach, W. Germany 22/B3
Anderson, Ala. (35610) 195/D1
Anderson, Alaska (†99760) 196/H2
Anderson, Argentina 143/F7
Anderson, Calif. (96007) 204/C3
Anderson, Ind. 188/J2
Anderson, Ind. (*46011) 227/F4
Anderson (riv.), Ind. 227/D8
Anderson, Iowa (†51652) 229/B7
Anderson (co.), Kansas 232/G3
Anderson (co.), Ky. 237/M5
Anderson (lake), Manitoba 179/D2
Anderson (pt.), Manitoba 179/F3
Anderson, Mo. (64831) 261/D9
Anderson (riv.), N.W.T. 162/D2
Anderson (riv.), N.W. Terrs. 187/F3
Anderson, S.C. 188/K4
Anderson (co.), S.C. 296/B2
Anderson, S.C. (*29621) 296/B2
Anderson (bay), Tasmania 99/D2
Anderson (co.), Tenn. 237/N8
Anderson, Tenn. (†37376) 237/K10
Anderson (co.), Texas 303/J6
Anderson, Texas (77830) 303/J7
Anderson Ranch (res.), Idaho 220/C6
Andersonville, Georgia (31711) 217/D6
Andersonville, Ind. (†47024) 227/G5
Andersonville, Tenn. (37705) 237/O8
Andersonville, Va. (23911) 307/L6
Andersonville Nat'l Hist. Site, Georgia 217/D6
Andes (range), 120/B2-6
Andes, Cordillera de los (mts.), Argentina 143/C2
Andes, Cordillera de los (mts.), Chile 138/C5,E
Andes, Colombia 126/C5
Andes, Mont. (†59218) 262/M3
Andes, N.Y. (13731) 276/L6
Andes, Cordillera de los (mts.), Peru 128/F10
Andes (lake), S. Dak. 298/N7
Andheri, India 68/B7
Andhra Pradesh (state), India 68/D5
Andijk, Netherlands 27/G3
Andikithira (isl.), Greece 45/F8
Andilamena, Madagascar 118/H3
Andimeshk, Iran 66/F4
Anding, Miss. (†39040) 256/D5
Andırın, Turkey 63/G4
Ándissa, Greece 45/H6
Andizhan, U.S.S.R. 54/J5
Andizhan, U.S.S.R. 48/H5
Andkhvoy, Afghanistan 68/A1
Andkhvoy, Afghanistan 59/H2
Andoas Nuevo, Ecuador 128/D4
Andoma, Zaire 115/E3
Andong, S. Korea 81/D5
Andorra 7/E4
ANDORRA 33/G1
Andorra, Spain 33/F2
Andorra la Vella (cap.), Andorra 33/G1
Andover○, Conn. (06232) 210/F2
Andover, England 10/F5
Andover, England 13/F6
Andover, Ill. (61233) 222/C2
Andover, Iowa (52701) 229/N5
Andover, Kansas (67002) 232/E4
Andover, Maine (04216) 243/B6
Andover○, Maine (04216) 243/B6
Andover, Mass. (01810) 249/K2
Andover○, Mass. (01810) 249/K2
Andover, Minn. (†55303) 255/E5
Andover○, N.H. (03216) 268/D5
Andover, N.J. (07821) 273/D2
Andover, N.Y. (14806) 276/E6
Andover, Ohio (44003) 284/J2
Andover, S. Dak. (57422) 298/O3
Andover○, Vt. (†05143) 268/B5
Andover, Va. (24215) 307/C7
Andøya (isl.), Norway 18/J2
Andradas, Brazil 135/C3
Andradina, Brazil 132/D8
Andraitx, Spain 33/H3
Andravídha, Greece 45/E6
Andre (lake), Newf. 166/A3
Andreafski (Saint Marys), Alaska (†99658) 196/F2
Andreanof (isls.), Alaska 196/L4
Andreas (cape), Cyprus 63/F5
Andrelândia, Brazil 135/D2
Andrés, Nicaragua 154/F3
Andrespol, Poland 47/D3
Andrew, Alberta 182/D3
Andrew, Iowa (52030) 229/M4
Andrew, La. (†70548) 238/F6
Andrew (co.), Mo. 261/C3
Andrew (isl.), Nova Scotia 168/H3
Andrew Johnson Nat'l Hist. Site, Tenn. 237/R8
Andrews, (†21626) 245/O7
Andrews, Ind. (46702) 227/F3
Andrews, N.C. (28901) 281/B4
Andrews, Oreg. (†97732) 291/J5
Andrews, S.C. (29510) 296/H5
Andrews (co.), Texas 303/B5
Andrews, Texas (79714) 303/B5
Andrews A.F.B., Md. 245/G5
Andreyevka, U.S.S.R. 52/H4
Andria, Italy 34/F4
Androka, Madagascar 118/G5
Andros (isl.), Bahamas 146/L7
Andros (isl.), Bahamas 156/B1
Ándros, Greece 45/G7
Ándros (isl.), Greece 45/G7
Androscoggin (co.), Maine 243/C7
Androscoggin (riv.), Maine 243/C7
Androscoggin (riv.), N.H. 268/E2
Androth (isl.), India 68/C6
Andrychów, Poland 47/D4
Andsfjorden (fjord), Norway 18/K2
Andújar, Spain 33/D3
Andul, India 68/F2
Andulo, Angola 102/D6
Andulo, Angola 115/C6
Anéfis, Mali 106/E5
Anegada (isl.), Virgin Is. (Br.) 156/H1
Anegada (passage), Virgin Is. (Br.) 156/F3
Aného (Anécho), Togo 106/E7
Aneityum (Anatom) (isl.), Vanuatu 87/H8
'Aneiza, Jebel (mt.), Iraq 66/A4
'Aneiza, Jebel (mt.), Iraq 59/C3
'Aneiza, Jebel (mt.), Jordan 59/C3
'Aneiza, Jebel (mt.), Saudi Arabia 59/C3
Añelo, Argentina 143/C4
Anerley, Sask. 181/D4
Aneroid, Sask. 181/D6
Aneta, N. Dak. (58212) 282/P4
Aneth, Utah (84510) 304/E6
Aneto (peak), Spain 33/G1
Angaki (Quirino), Philippines 82/C2
Angamos (isl.), Chile 138/D8
Angamos (pt.), Chile 138/A4
Angara (riv.), U.S.S.R. 54/L4
Angara (riv.), U.S.S.R. 48/K4
Angarsk, U.S.S.R. 54/M4
Angarsk, U.S.S.R. 48/L4
Angas Downs, North. Terr. 93/C8
Angaston, S. Australia 94/F6
Angaur (isl.), Belau 87/D5
Ånge, Sweden 18/J5
Ange-Gardien, Québec 172/E4
Angel (isl.), Calif. 204/J2
Angel (falls), Venezuela 120/C2
Angel (fall), Venezuela 124/G5
Angela, Mont. (59312) 262/K4
Ángel de la Guarda (isl.), Mexico 150/C2
Angeles, Philippines 82/C3
Ángeles, P. Rico 161/B2
Ängelholm, Sweden 18/H8
Angélica, Argentina 143/E5
Angelica, N.Y. (14709) 276/E6
Angelica, Wis. (†54162) 317/K6
Angelina (co.), Texas 303/K6
Angelina (riv.), Texas 303/K6
Angelo, Wis. (†54656) 317/E8
Angels Camp, Calif. (95222) 204/E5
Angelus, S.C. (†29718) 296/G2
Angerman (riv.), Sweden 7/F2
Ångermanälven (riv.), Sweden 18/K5
Angermünde, E. Germany 22/E2
Angers, France 7/D4
Angers, France 28/C4
Angers, Québec 172/B4
Angicos, Brazil 132/G4
Angie, La. (70426) 238/L5
Angier, N.C. (27501) 281/M4
Angijak (isl.), N.W. Terrs. 187/M3
Angikuni (lake), N.W. Terrs. 187/J3
Angkor Wat (ruins), Cambodia 72/E4
Angle, Utah (†84712) 304/C5
Angle Inlet, Minn. (56711) 255/C1
Anglem (mt.), N. Zealand 100/A7
Anglesey (isl.), Wales 13/C4
Anglesey (isl.), Wales 10/D4
Angleton, Texas (77515) 303/J8
Anglia, Sask. 181/C4
Angliers, Québec 174/B3
Angmagssalik, Greenl. 4/C11
Angmagssalik, Greenland 146/Q3
Ango, Zaire 115/E3
Angoche, Mozambique 118/G3
Angoche, Mozambique 102/G6
Angoche (isl.), Mozambique 118/G3
Angol, Chile 138/D1
Angola 2/K6
Angola 102/D6
ANGOLA 115/C6
Angola, Del. (†19966) 245/T6
Angola, Ind. (46703) 227/G1
Angola, Kansas (67331) 232/G4
Angola, La. (70712) 238/G5
Angola, N.Y. (14006) 276/C5
Angola (swamp), N.C. 281/O5
Angola on the Lake, N.Y. (†14006) 276/B5
Angoon, Alaska (99820) 196/M1
Angora, Minn. (55703) 255/F3
Angora, Nebr. (69331) 264/A3
Angoram, Papua N.G. 85/B6
Angostura (falls), Colombia 120/B2
Angostura (falls), Colombia 126/E6
Angostura, Mexico 150/E4
Angostura (res.), S. Dak. 298/B7
Angoulême, France 28/D5
Angoumois (trad. prov.), France, 29
Angra do Heroísmo (dist.), Portugal 33/C1
Angra do Heroísmo, Portugal 33/C1
Angra dos Reis, Brazil 135/D3
Angren, U.S.S.R. 48/H5
Ang Thong, Thailand 72/C4
Anguil, Argentina 143/D4
Anguilla (isl.) 146/M8
ANGUILLA 156
Anguilla, Anguilla 156/F3
Anguilla, Miss. (38721) 256/C5
Anguillara Sabazia, Italy 34/F6
Anguille (cape), Newf. 166/C4
Angurugu, North. Terr. 93/E3
Angus, Iowa (†50220) 229/E5
Angus, Minn. (56712) 255/B2
Angus, Ontario 177/E3
Angus (trad. prov.), Scotland, 15/B5
Angusville, Manitoba 179/A4
Angwin, Calif. (94508) 204/C5
Anhée, Belgium 27/F8
Anholt, Denmark 21/E4
Anholt (isl.), Denmark 21/E4
Anholt (isl.), Denmark 18/G8
Anhua, China 77/H6
Anhui (Anhwei), China 77/J5
Aniak, Alaska (99557) 196/G2
Aniakchak (vol.), Alaska 196/G3
Aniakchak Nat'l Mon., Alaska 196/G3
Aniakchak Nat'l Preserve, Alaska 196/G3
Anicuns, Brazil 132/D7
Aniene (riv.), Italy 34/F6
Animas (riv.), Colo. 208/D8
Animas, N. Mex. (88020) 274/A7
Animas (riv.), N. Mex. 274/B1
Añimbo, Bolivia 136/C7
Anin, Burma 72/C4
Anin, West Bank 65/C2
Anina, Romania 45/E3
Anita, Iowa (50020) 229/D6
Anita, Pa. (15711) 294/D3
Aniva (cape), U.S.S.R. 48/P5
Aniwa, Wis. (54408) 317/H6
'Anjara, Jordan 65/D3
Anjidiv (Angedeva) (isl.), India 68/C6
Anjou (trad. prov.), France, 29
Anjou, Québec 172/H4
Anjouan (isl.), Comoros 102/G6
Anjouan (isl.), Comoros 118/G2
Anju, N. Korea 81/B4
Anjum, Netherlands 27/J2
Ankang, China 77/G5
Ankara (prov.), Turkey 63/E3
Ankara (cap.), Turkey 63/E3
Ankara (cap.), Turkey 2/L4
Ankara (cap.), Turkey 54/E5
Ankara (cap.), Turkey 59/B2
Ankara (riv.), Turkey 63/D3
Ankazoabo, Madagascar 118/G4
Ankeny, Iowa (50021) 229/F5
Anker (riv.), England 10/G3
Ankerton, Alberta 182/D3
Ankhor, Somalia 115/J1
Anking (Anqing), China 77/J5
Anklam, E. Germany 22/E2
Ankober, Ethiopia 111/H6
Ankona, Fla. (†33450) 212/F4
Ankoro, Zaire 115/E5
An Loc (Binh Long), Vietnam 72/E5
Anlu, China 77/H5
Anmoore, W. Va. (26323) 312/F4
Ann (cape), Mass. 249/M2
Anna, Ill. (62906) 222/D6
Anna, Ky. (†42270) 237/J6
Anna, Ohio (45302) 284/B5
Anna, Texas (75003) 303/H4
Anna (lke), Va. 307/N4
Annaba, Algeria 102/C1
Annaba, Algeria 106/F1
Annabella, Utah (84711) 304/B5
Annaberg-Buchholz, E. Germany 22/E3
Anna Creek, S. Australia 94/D3
Annada, Mo. (63330) 261/L4
Annadel, Tenn. (†37770) 237/M8
Annagry, Ireland 17/E1
Annaheim, Sask. 181/G3
Annai, Guyana 131/B4
An Najaf (gov.), Iraq 66/C5
An Najaf, Iraq 59/D3
An Najaf, Iraq 66/D5
An Najaf, Iraq 54/F6
Annalee (riv.), Ireland 17/G3
Annalong, N. Ireland 17/K3
Annaly (bay), Virgin Is. (U.S.) 161/E3
Anna Maria, Fla. (33501) 212/D4
Annan, Scotland 15/E6
Annan, Scotland 10/E3
Annan (riv.), Scotland 15/E5
Annandale, Minn. (55302) 255/D5
Annandale, N.J. (08801) 273/D2
Annandale, Va. (22003) 307/S3
Annandale-on-Hudson, N.Y. (12504) 276/N6
Anna Plains, W. Australia 92/C2
Annapolis, Calif. (95412) 204/B5
Annapolis, Ill. (62413) 222/F4
Annapolis (cap.), Md. (*21401) 245/M5
Annapolis (cap.), Md. 188/L3
Annapolis, Mo. (63620) 261/L8
Annapolis (co.), Nova Scotia 168/C4
Annapolis (basin), Nova Scotia 168/C4
Annapolis (riv.), Nova Scotia 168/C4
Annapolis Junction, Md. (20701) 245/M4
Annapolis Royal, Nova Scotia 168/C4
Annapurna (mt.), Nepal 68/E3
Ann Arbor, Mich. 188/K2
Ann Arbor, Mich. (*48103) 250/F6
Anna Regina, Guyana 131/B2
Annascaul, Ireland 17/B7
An Nasiriya, Iraq 59/E3
An Nasiriya, Iraq 66/D5
Annat, Scotland 15/C3
Annaville, Québec 172/E3
Annawan, Ill. (61234) 222/C2
Annbank Station, Scotland 15/D5
Anne (mt.), Tasmania 99/C4
Anne Arundel (co.), Md. 245/M4
Annecy, France 28/G5
Annemanie, Ala. (36721) 195/D6
Anner (riv.), Ireland 17/F7
Anneta, Ky. (†42754) 237/J6
Annette, Alaska (99920) 196/N2
An Nhon, Vietnam 72/F4
Annieopscotch (mts.), Newf. 166/C4
Anniston, Ala. 188/J4
Anniston, Ala. (36201) 195/G3
Anniston, Mo. (63820) 261/O9
Anniston Army Depot, Ala. 195/F3
Annobon (isl.), Equat. Guinea 102/C5
Annona, Texas (75550) 303/K4
Annonay, France 28/F5
Annotto Bay, Jamaica 156/C3
Annotto Bay, Jamaica 158/K6
Annville, Ky. (40402) 237/O6
Annville, Pa. (17003) 294/J5
Annweiler am Trifels, W. Germany 22/B4
Anoka (co.), Minn. 255/E5
Anoka, Minn. (55303) 255/E5
Anoka, Nebr. (†68722) 264/F2
Anola, Manitoba 179/F5
Ano Nuevo (pt.), Calif. 204/J4
Áno Viánnos, Greece 45/G8
Anóyia, Greece 45/G8
Anqing (Anking), China 77/J5
Ans, Belgium 27/H7
Ansager, Denmark 21/B6
Ansai, China 77/G4
Ansbach, W. Germany 22/D4
Anse à Galets, Haiti 158/B6
Anse-à-Pitre, Haiti 158/C6
Anse-au-Griffon, Québec 172/D1
Anse-aux-Gascons, Québec 172/D2
Anse-à-Veau, Haiti 158/B6
Anse-Bertrand, Guadeloupe 161/A5
Anse-Bleue, New Bruns. 170/E1
Anse Boileau, Seychelles 118/H5
Anse-d'Hainault, Haiti 158/A6
Anse la Raye, St. Lucia 161/F6
Anselmo, Nebr. (68813) 264/E3
Anser Group (isls.), Tasmania 99/C1
Anserma, Colombia 126/B5
Anse Rouge, Haiti 158/B5
Anse Royale, Seychelles 118/H5
Anshan, China 77/K3
Anshan, China 54/O5
Anshun, China 77/G6
Ansley, Ala. (36001) 195/F7
Ansley, La. (†71228) 238/E2
Ansley, Nebr. (68814) 264/E3
Anson, Kansas (†67103) 232/E4
Anson, Maine (04911) 243/D6
Anson○, Maine (04911) 243/D6
Anson (pt.), Norfolk I. 88/K5
Anson (bay), Norfolk I. 88/K5
Anson (co.), N.C. 281/J4
Anson (bay), North. Terr. 88/D2
Anson, Texas (79501) 303/E5
Ansŏng, S. Korea 81/C5
Ansongo, Mali 106/E5
Ansonia, Conn. (06401) 210/C3
Ansonia, Ohio (45303) 284/A5
Ansonville, N.C. (28007) 281/J4
Ansonville, Pa. (†16656) 294/E4
Ansted, W. Va. (25812) 312/D6
Anta, Peru 128/F9
Antabamba, Peru 128/F10
Antakya, Turkey 59/C2
Antakya, Turkey 63/G4
Antalaha, Madagascar 118/J2
Antalaha, Madagascar 102/H6
Antalya (prov.), Turkey 63/D4
Antalya, Turkey 54/D6
Antalya, Turkey 63/D4
Antalya, Turkey 59/B2
Antalya (gulf), Turkey 63/D4
Antalya (gulf), Turkey 59/B2
Antananarivo (prov.), Madagascar 118/H3
Antananarivo (cap.), Madagascar 2/M6
Antananarivo (cap.), Madagascar 102/G6
Antananarivo (cap.), Madagascar 118/H3
Antarctic (pen.), Ant. 2/G9
Antarctic (pen.) 5/C15
Antarctica 2/E11
ANTARCTICA 5
Antarctic Circle 2/A9
An Teallach (mt.), Scotland 15/C3
Antelope (creek), Idaho 220/E6
Antelope, Kansas (66836) 232/F3
Antelope, Mont. (59211) 262/M2
Antelope (co.), Nebr. 264/F2
Antelope (range), Nev. 266/E3
Antelope, Oreg. (97001) 291/G3
Antelope (creek), Oreg. 291/K5
Antelope (res.), Oreg. 291/K5
Antelope, Sask. 181/C5
Antelope (lake), Sask. 181/C5
Antelope (creek), S. Dak. 298/D3
Antelope, Texas (76350) 303/F4
Antelope (isl.), Utah 304/B3
Antelope (creek), Wyo. 319/G2
Antelope (hills), Wyo. 319/D3
Antequera, Paraguay 144/D4
Antequera, Spain 33/D4
Antero (mt.), Colo. 208/G5
Antero (res.), Colo. 208/H5
Antes Fort, Pa. (17720) 294/H3
Anthon, Iowa (51004) 229/B4
Anthony, Fla. (32617) 212/D2
Anthony, Ind. (†47302) 227/G4
Anthony, Kansas (67003) 232/D4
Anthony, N. Mex. (88021) 274/C6
Anthony, R.I. (†02816) 249/H6
Anthony, Texas (88021) 303/A10
Anthony, W. Va. (24914) 312/F7
Anthony Lagoon, North. Terr. 88/E3
Anthony Lagoon, North. Terr. 93/D4
Anthracite, Alberta 182/C4
Anti-Atlas (ranges), Morocco 106/C3
Antibes, France 28/G6
Anticosti (isl.), Que. 146/M5
Anticosti (isl.), Que. 162/K6
Anticosti (isl.), Québec 174/E3
Antietam, Md. (†21782) 245/H3
Antietam (creek), Md. 245/H2
Antietam Nat'l Battlefield, Md. 245/H3
Antigo, Wis. (54409) 317/H5
Antigonish (co.), Nova Scotia 168/F3
Antigonish, Nova Scotia 168/F3
Antigonish (harb.), Nova Scotia 168/G3
Antigua (isl.) 146/M8
ANTIGUA & BARBUDA 156
ANTIGUA & BARBUDA 161
Antigua (isl.), Ant. & Bar. 161/E11
Antigua (isl.), Ant. & Bar. 156/G3
Antigua, Guatemala 154/B3
Antigua (riv.), Mexico 150/Q1
Antigua, Spain 33/B4
Antigues (pt.), Guadeloupe 161/A5
Antiguo Morelos, Mexico 150/K5
Antilla, Cuba 156/C2
Antilla, Cuba 158/J3
Antilles, Greater (isls.), W. Indies 156/B2
Antilles, Lesser (isls.), W. Indies 156/E4
Antimony, Utah (84712) 304/C5
Antioch, Calif. (94509) 204/L1
Antioch, Georgia (†30240) 217/B4
Antioch, Ill. (60002) 222/E1
Antioch, Nebr. (69340) 264/B2
Antioch, Ohio (43710) 284/H6
Antioch, S.C. (†29020) 296/F3
Antioch (Antakya), Turkey 63/G4
Antioch, W. Va. (†26743) 312/H4
Antioquia (dept.), Colombia 126/B4
Antioquia, Colombia 126/B4
Antique (prov.), Philippines 82/D5
Antiquity, Ohio (†45771) 284/G8
Antisana (mt.), Ecuador 128/D3
Anti-Taurus (mts.), Turkey 63/G3
Antler, N. Dak. (58711) 282/H2
Antler, Sask. 181/K6
Antler (riv.), Sask. 181/K6
Antler Lake, Alberta 182/D3
Antlers, Okla. (74523) 288/P6
Antofagasta (reg.), Chile 138/B4
Antofagasta, Chile 120/B5
Antofagasta, Chile 2/F7
Antofagasta, Chile 138/A4
Antofagasta de la Sierra, Argentina 143/C2
Antoine, Ark. (71922) 202/D5
Antoing, Belgium 27/C7
Anton, Colo. (80801) 208/N3
Antón, Panama 154/G6
Anton, Texas (79313) 303/B4
Anton Chico, N. Mex. (87711) 274/D3
Antone, Oreg. (†97750) 291/H3
Antongil (bay), Madagascar 118/J3
Antonina, Brazil 135/B4
Antonino, Kansas (67624) 232/C3
Antonito, Colo. (81120) 208/H8
Antony, France 28/B2
Antora (peak), Colo. 208/G6
Antreville, S.C. (†29620) 296/B3
Antrim (co.), Mich. 250/D3
Antrim, Mich. (†49659) 250/D4
Antrim, N.H. (03440) 268/D5
Antrim○, N.H. (03440) 268/D5
Antrim (dist.), N. Ireland 17/J2
Antrim, N. Ireland 10/C3
Antrim, N. Ireland 17/J2
Antrim, Ohio (†43973) 284/H5
Antrim, Pa. (†16901) 294/H2
Antsalova, Madagascar 118/G3
Antsirabe, Madagascar 102/G7
Antsirabe, Madagascar 118/H3
Antsiranana (prov.), Madagascar 118/H2
Antsiranana, Madagascar 118/H2
Antsiranana, Madagascar 102/G6

330 Antsia

Antsia, U.S.S.R. 53/D2
Antsohihy, Madagascar 118/H2
Antu, China 77/L3
An Tuc (An Khe), Vietnam 72/F4
Antwerp (prov.), Belgium 27/F6
Antwerp, Belgium 7/E3
Antwerp, Belgium 27/E6
Antwerp, N.Y. (13608) 276/J2
Antwerp, Ohio (45813) 284/A3
Antwerpen (Antwerp), Belgium 27/E6
An Uaimh, Ireland 10/C4
An Uaimh, Ireland 17/H4
Anuenue (Sand) (isl.), Hawaii 218/C4
Anuradhapura, Sri Lanka 68/E7
Anutt, Mo. (†65401) 261/J7
Anvik, Alaska (99558) 196/F2
Anvil (peak), Alaska 196/K4
Anxi, China 77/E3
Anxious (bay), S. Australia 94/D5
Anyang, China 77/H4
A'nyêmaqên Shan (mts.), China 77/E5
Anykščiai, U.S.S.R. 53/C3
Anzá, Colombia 126/C4
'Anza, West Bank 65/C3
Anzac, Alberta 182/E1
Anzaldo, Bolivia 136/C5
Anzhero-Sudzhensk, U.S.S.R. 54/K4
Anzhero-Sudzhensk, U.S.S.R. 48/J4
Anzio, Italy 34/D4
Anzoátegui (state), Venezuela 124/F3
Aoiz, Spain 33/F1
Aoji-ri, N. Korea 81/E2
Aomori (pref.), Japan 81/K3
Aomori, Japan 54/R5
Aomori, Japan 81/K3
Ao Paray (riv.), Paraguay 144/A5
Aosta (reg.), Italy 34/A2
Aosta (prov.), Italy 34/A2
Aosta, Italy 34/A2
Aouara, Fr. Guiana 131/E3
Aouinet Bel Egrâ (well), Algeria 106/C3
Aoulef, Algeria 106/E3
Aozou, Chad 111/C3
Apa (riv.), Paraguay 144/D3
Apache (co.), Ariz. 198/F3
Apache (lake), Ariz. 198/D5
Apache, Okla. (73006) 288/K5
Apache (mts.), Texas 303/C11
Apache Creek, N. Mex. (†87830) 274/A5
Apache Junction, Ariz. (85220) 198/D5
Apalachee (bay), Fla. 188/K5
Apalachee (bay), Fla. 212/B2
Apalachee, Georgia (†30650) 217/E3
Apalachia (res.), N.C. 281/A4
Apalachicola, Fla. (32320) 212/A2
Apalachicola (bay), Fla. 212/B2
Apalachicola (riv.), Fla. 212/A1
Apalachin, N.Y. (13732) 276/H6
Apalona, Ind. (†47576) 227/D8
Apan, Mexico 150/M1
Apaporis (riv.), Colombia 126/F8
Aparecida, Brazil 135/D3
Aparri, Philippines 82/C1
Aparri, Philippines 85/G2
Aparurén, Venezuela 124/G5
Apataki (atoll), Fr. Poly. 87/M7
Apatin, Yugoslavia 45/D3
Apatity, U.S.S.R. 52/D1
Apatzingán de la Constitución, Mexico 150/H7
Ape, U.S.S.R. 53/D2
Apeldoorn, Netherlands 27/H4
Apennines (mts.), Italy 7/F4
Apennines, Central (range), Italy 34/D3
Apennines, Northern (range), Italy 34/B2
Apennines, Southern (range), Italy 34/E4
Apere (riv.), Bolivia 136/C4
Apex, N.C. (27502) 281/M3
Apgar, Mont. (†59936) 262/B2
Apia (cap.), W. Samoa 2/A6
Apia (cap.), W. Samoa 87/J7
Apia (cap.), W. Samoa 86/M8
Apiaí, Brazil 135/B4
Apishapa (riv.), Colo. 208/L8
Apison, Tenn. (37302) 237/L10
Ap Iwan, Cerro (mt.), Chile 138/E6
Apizaco, Mexico 150/N1
Aplao, Peru 128/F11
Aplin, Ark. (†72126) 202/E4
Aplington, Iowa (50604) 229/H3
Ap Long Ha, Vietnam 72/F5
Apo (vol.), Philippines 82/E7
Apohaqui, New Bruns. 170/E3
Apolda, E. Germany 22/D3
Apolima (str.), W. Samoa 86/L8
Apollo, Georgia (†31024) 217/F4
Apollo, Pa. (15613) 294/C4
Apollo Bay, Victoria 97/B6
Apollo Beach, Fla. (33570) 212/C3
Apolo, Bolivia 136/A4
Aponguao (riv.), Venezuela 124/H5
Apopka, Fla. (32703) 212/E3
Apopka (lake), Fla. 212/E3
Aporé (riv.), Brazil 132/D7
Apostle (isls.), Wis. 317/F2
Apostle Islands Nat'l Lakeshore, Wis. 317/E1
Apóstoles, Argentina 143/E2
Apoteri, Guyana 131/B3
Appalachia, Va. (24216) 307/C7
Appalachian (mts.) 188/K3
Appalachian (mts.), N.C. 281/D2
Appalachian (mts.), Pa. 294/H4
Appalachian (mts.), Tenn. 237/M10
Appalachian (mts.), U.S. 146/K6
Appalachian (mts.), Va. 307/J5
Appam, N. Dak. (†58830) 282/C2
Appanoose (co.), Iowa 229/H7
Appelscha, Netherlands 27/J3
Appenzell, Ausser Rhoden (canton), 39/H2
Appenzell, Inner Rhoden (canton), Switzerland 39/H2
Appenzell, Switzerland 39/H2
Apperson, Okla. (†74633) 288/N1
Appin, Ontario 177/C5
Appin (dist.), Scotland 15/C4
Appingedam, Netherlands 27/K2
Apple (creek), Ill. 222/C4
Apple (riv.), Ill. 222/C1
Apple (creek), N. Dak. 282/J6
Apple (riv.), Wis. 317/A5
Appleby, England 13/E3
Appleby, England 10/E3
Appleby, Texas (75961) 303/K6
Apple Creek, Ohio (44606) 284/G4
Applecross, Scotland 15/C3
Appledale, Br. Col. 184/J5
Applegate, Calif. (95703) 204/E5
Applegate, Mich. (48401) 250/G5
Applegate, Oreg. (97530) 291/D5
Apple Grove, W. Va. (25502) 312/B5
Apple Hill, Ontario 177/K2
Apple River, Ill. (61001) 222/C1
Apple River, Nova Scotia 168/D3
Apples, Switzerland 39/B3
Appleton, Ark. (72822) 202/E3
Appleton, Maine (†04540) 243/E7
Appleton○, Maine (†04862) 243/E7
Appleton, Minn. (56208) 255/C5
Appleton (Old Appleton), Mo. (†63770) 261/N7
Appleton, N.Y. (14008) 276/C4
Appleton, Ontario 177/H2
Appleton, S.C. (†29836) 296/E5
Appleton, Wash. (98602) 310/D5
Appleton, Wis. 188/J2
Appleton, Wis. (54911) 317/J7
Appleton City, Mo. (64724) 261/D6
Apple Valley, Calif. (92307) 204/H9
Apple Valley, Minn. (†55124) 255/G6
Appling (co.), Georgia 217/H7
Appling, Georgia (30802) 217/H3
Appomattox (co.), Va. 307/L6
Appomattox, Va. (24522) 307/L6
Appomattox (riv.), Va. 307/M6
Appomattox Court House Nat'l Hist. Park, Va. 307/K6
Apponaug, R.I. (†02887) 249/J6
Approuague (riv.), Fr. Guiana 131/E4
Apra (harb.), Guam 86/K7
Aprilia, Italy 34/D4
Apsheron (pen.), U.S.S.R. 52/H6
Apsheronsk, U.S.S.R. 52/F6
Apsley, Ontario 177/F3
Apsley, Victoria 97/A5
Apt, France 28/F6
Aptos, Calif. (95003) 204/K4
Apua (pt.), Hawaii 218/J6
Apulia (Puglia) (reg.), Italy 34/F4
Apulia Station, N.Y. (13020) 276/H5
Apure (state), Venezuela 124/D4
Apure (riv.), Venezuela 124/E4
Apurímac (dept.), Peru 128/F10
Apurímac (riv.), Peru 120/B4
Apurímac (riv.), Peru 128/F9
Apurito, Venezuela 124/D4
Ap Vinh Hao, Vietnam 72/F5
Aqaba (gulf) 54/E7
'Aqaba (gulf), Egypt 111/G2
'Aqaba (gulf), Egypt 59/C4
'Aqaba (gulf), Israel 65/D6
'Aqaba, Jordan 65/D6
'Aqaba, Jordan 59/C4
Aqaba (gulf), Jordan 65/D6
'Aqaba (gulf), Saudi Arabia 59/C4
Aqcheh, Afghanistan 68/B1
Aqcheh, Afghanistan 59/J2
Aq Darband, Iran 66/M2
'Aqiq, Sudan 111/G4
'Aqqaba, West Bank 65/C3
Aqqikkol Hu (lake), China 77/C4
'Aqra, Iraq 66/D2
'Aqraba, West Bank 65/C3
Aqsu (Aksu), China 77/B3
Aquades Beach, Sask. 181/C2
Aquaforte, Newf. 166/D2
Aqua Park, Okla. (†74435) 288/R3
Aquarius (range), Ariz. 198/B4
Aquarius (plat.), Utah 304/C5
Aquasco, Md. (20608) 245/L6
Aquia, Peru 128/D8
Aquidabán (riv.), Paraguay 144/D3
Aquidauana, Brazil 120/D5
Aquidauana, Brazil 132/C8
Aquila, Mexico 150/H7
Aquila, Switzerland 39/G3
Aquiles Serdán, Mexico 150/G2
Aquilla, Ohio (†44024) 284/H2
Aquin, Haiti 158/B6
Ara (riv.), Japan 81/O2
Arab, Ala. (35016) 195/E2
'Arab, Shatt-al- (riv.), Iran 59/E4
'Arab, Shatt-al- (riv.), Iran 66/F5
'Arab, Shatt-al- (riv.), Iraq 59/E4
'Arab, Shatt-al- (riv.), Iraq 66/F5
Arab, Mo. (63733) 261/M8
'Araba, Wadi (valley), Israel 65/D5
'Araba, Wadi (valley), Jordan 65/D5
Arabela, N. Mex. (†88351) 274/D5
Arabella, Sask. 181/K3
Arabi, Georgia (31712) 217/E7
'Arabi (isl.), Iran 66/G7
Arabi, La. (70032) 238/P4
Arabia, Ky. (†40437) 237/M6
Arabia, Ohio (†45659) 284/F8
Arabian (sea) 54/H8
Arabian (sea) 2/N5
Arabian (des.), Egypt 111/F2
Arabian (des.), Egypt 59/B4
Arabian (sea), India 68/B5
Arabian (sea), Pakistan 68/B5
Arabian (sea), P.D.R. Yemen 59/H5
Arabopó, Venezuela 124/H5
Araç, Turkey 63/E2
Araca, Bolivia 136/B5
Aracaju, Brazil 120/F4
Aracaju, Brazil 132/G5
Aracataca, Colombia 126/D2
Aracati, Brazil 132/G4
Araçatuba, Brazil 132/D8
Araçatuba, Brazil 135/A2
Araceli, Philippines 82/C5
Aracena, Spain 33/C4
Araçuaí, Brazil 132/F7
Arad, Israel 65/C5
Arad, Romania 7/G4
Arad, Romania 45/E2
Arada, Chad 111/D4
'Aradah, U.A.E. 59/F5
Aradan, Iran 66/H3
Arafat, Jebel (mt.), Saudi Arabia 59/D5
Arafura (sea) 87/D6
Arafura (sea) 2/R6
Arafura (sea) 88/E2
Arafura (sea), Indonesia 85/J8
Arafura (sea), North. Terr. 93/D1
Arago, Minn. (†56470) 255/C3
Arago, Oreg. (97458) 291/C4
Arago (cape), Oreg. 291/C4
Aragon, Georgia (30104) 217/B2
Aragon, N. Mex. (87820) 274/A5
Aragón (reg.), Spain 33/F2
Aragón (riv.), Spain 33/F1
Aragona, Italy 34/D6
Aragua (state), Venezuela 124/E3
Araguacema, Brazil 132/D5
Aragua de Barcelona, Venezuela 124/F3
Aragua de Maturín, Venezuela 124/G3
Araguaia (riv.), Brazil 120/E3
Araguaia (riv.), Brazil 132/D4
Araguaiana, Brazil 132/C6
Araguaína, Brazil 120/E3
Araguari, Brazil 120/E4
Araguari, Brazil 132/D7
Araguari (riv.), Brazil 132/D2
Araioses, Brazil 132/F3
Arak, Algeria 106/E3
Arak, Iran 54/G6
Arak, Iran 59/E3
Arak, Iran 66/F3
Arakan (state), Burma 72/B3
Arakan Yoma (mts.), Burma 72/B3
Araks (riv.) 54/F6
Araks (riv.), Iran 59/E2
Araks (Aras) (riv.), Iran 66/E1
Araks (riv.), Turkey 63/K2
Araks (riv.), U.S.S.R. 7/J5
Araks (riv.), U.S.S.R. 52/G7
Aral (sea), U.S.S.R. 54/G5
Aral (sea), U.S.S.R. 48/F5
Aralık, Turkey 63/L3
Aral Sea (lake), U.S.S.R. 2/M3
Aral'sk, U.S.S.R. 54/H5
Aral'sk, U.S.S.R. 48/G5
Aramac, Queensland 95/C4
Aramberri, Mexico 150/J5
Arampampa, Bolivia 136/B5
Aran (isl.), Ireland 10/B3
Aran (isl.), Ireland 17/D2
Aran (isls.), Ireland 17/B5
Aran (isls.), Ireland 10/B4
Aranda de Duero, Spain 33/E2
Arandas, Mexico 150/H6
Aran Fawddwy (mt.), Wales 13/C5
Arani, Bolivia 136/C5
Aranjuez, Spain 33/E2
Aransas (co.), Texas 303/H10
Aransas (passage), Texas 303/H10
Aransas Pass, Texas (78336) 303/G10
Araoua (mts.), Fr. Guiana 131/E4
Araouane, Mali 106/D5
Araouane, Mali 102/B3
Arapaho, Okla. (73620) 288/H3
Arapahoe (co.), Colo. 208/L3
Arapahoe, Colo. (80802) 208/P5
Arapahoe (peak), Colo. 208/H2
Arapahoe, Nebr. (68922) 264/E4
Arapahoe, N.C. (28510) 281/R4
Arapahoe, Wyo. (82510) 319/D3
Arapaho Nat'l Rec. Area, Colo. 208/G2
Arapey, Uruguay 145/B1
Arapey Chico (riv.), Uruguay 145/B1
Arapey Grande (riv.), Uruguay 145/B2
Arapicos, Ecuador 128/D3
Arapiraca, Brazil 120/F3
Arapkir, Turkey 63/H3
Arapkir, Turkey 59/C2
'Ar'ar, Wadi (dry riv.), Iraq 66/B5
'Ar'ar, Wadi (dry riv.), Iraq 59/D3
'Ar'ar, Wadi (dry riv.), Saudi Arabia 59/D3
Araracuara, Colombia 126/E8
Araracuara, Cerros de (mts.), Colombia 126/E7
Araranguá, Brazil 132/D10
Araraquara, Brazil 132/E8
Araraquara, Brazil 135/B2
Araras, Brazil 135/C3
Ararat, Ala. (†36921) 195/B7
Ararat, N.C. (27007) 281/H2
Ararat (mt.), Pa. 294/M2
Ararat (mt.), Turkey 54/F6
Ararat (mt.), Turkey 63/L3
Ararat (mt.), Turkey 59/D2
Ararat, Victoria 88/G7
Ararat, Victoria 97/B5
Ararat, Va. (24053) 307/G7
Arari, Brazil 132/E3
Araruama (lake), Brazil 135/E3
Aras (Araks) (riv.), Iran 66/E1
Aras (Araks) (riv.), Iran 59/E2
Aratürük (Yiwu), China 77/D3
Arauca (riv.) 120/C2
Arauca (inten.), Colombia 126/E4
Arauca, Colombia 120/B2
Arauca, Colombia 126/E4
Arauca (riv.), Colombia 126/E4
Arauca (riv.), Venezuela 124/E4
Arauco, Chile 138/D1
Arauco (gulf), Chile 138/D1
Arauquita, Colombia 126/E4
Araure, Venezuela 124/D3
Aravaca, Spain 33/F4
Aravaipa (creek), Ariz. 198/E6
Arawa, Papua N.G. 86/C2
Arawe, Papua N.G. 86/B2
Arax (Araks)(riv.), Asia 59/E2
Araxá, Brazil 132/E7
Araya, Venezuela 124/F2
Arba, Ind. (†47355) 227/H4
Arba Mench, Ethiopia 111/G6
Arba Mench, Ethiopia 102/F4
Arbeca, Spain 33/G2
Arbedo-Castione, Switzerland 39/G4
Arbela (Erbil), Iraq 59/D2
Arbela (Erbil), Iraq 66/D2
Arbela, Mo. (63432) 261/H2
Arboga, Sweden 18/J7
Arbois, France 28/F4
Arbon, Idaho (83212) 220/F7
Arbon, Switzerland 39/H1
Arborea, Italy 34/B5
Arborfield, Sask. 181/H2
Arborg, Manitoba 179/E4
Arbor Vitae, Wis. (†54568) 317/G4
Arbovale, W. Va. (24915) 312/G6
Arbrå, Sweden 18/K6
Arbroath, Scotland 15/F4
Arbroath, Scotland 10/E2
Arbroth, La. (†70736) 238/H5
Arbucias, Spain 33/H2
Arbuckle, Calif. (95912) 204/C4
Arbuckle (lake), Fla. 212/E4
Arbuckle, W. Va. (25006) 312/C5
Arbuckles, Lake of the (lake), Okla. 288/M6
Arbuthnot, Sask. 181/E6
Arbutus, Md. (†21227) 245/M4
Arbyrd, Mo. (63821) 261/M10
Arcachon, France 28/C5
Arcachon (bay), France 28/C5
Arcade, Georgia (†30549) 217/E2
Arcade, N.Y. (14009) 276/D5
Arcadia, Calif. (91006) 204/C10
Arcadia, Fla. (33821) 212/E4
Arcadia, Ind. (46030) 227/E4
Arcadia, Iowa (51430) 229/C4
Arcadia, Kansas (66711) 232/H4
Arcadia, La. (71001) 238/E1
Arcadia, Mich. (49613) 250/C4
Arcadia, Mo. (63621) 261/L7
Arcadia, Nebr. (68815) 264/F3
Arcadia, Nova Scotia 168/B5
Arcadia, Ohio (44804) 284/D3
Arcadia, Okla. (73007) 288/M3
Arcadia, Pa. (15712) 294/E4
Arcadia, R.I. (†02832) 249/H6
Arcadia, S.C. (29320) 296/C2
Arcadia, Texas (77517) 303/K3
Arcadia, Utah (†84012) 304/D3
Arcadia, Wis. (54612) 317/D7
Arcadia Lakes, S.C. (†29201) 296/F3
Arcahaie, Haiti 158/C6
Arcanum, Ohio (45304) 284/A6
Arcas (cay), Mexico 150/N6
Arcata, Calif. (95521) 204/A3
Arc Dome (mt.), Nev. 266/D4
Arcelia, Mexico 150/J7
Arch, N. Mex. (†88130) 274/F4
Archambault (lake), Québec 172/C3
Archangel, U.S.S.R. 4/C7
Archangel, U.S.S.R. 2/M2
Archangel, U.S.S.R. 7/J2
Archangel (Arkhangel'sk), U.S.S.R. 48/E3
Archangel (Arkhangel'sk), U.S.S.R. 52/F2
Archbald, Pa. (18403) 294/F6
Archbold, Ohio (43502) 284/B2
Arch Cape, Oreg. (97102) 291/D2
Archdale, N.C. (27263) 281/K3
Archena, Spain 33/F3
Archer, Fla. (32618) 212/D2
Archer, Iowa (51231) 229/B2
Archer, Nebr. (68816) 264/F3
Archer (fiord), N.W. Terrs. 187/M1
Archer (riv.), Queensland 95/B2
Archer (co.), Texas 303/F4
Archer City, Texas (76351) 303/F4
Archerfield, Queensland 88/K3
Archerfield, Queensland 95/D3
Archerwill, Sask. 181/H3
Arches Nat'l Park, Utah 304/E5
Archibald, La. (71218) 238/G2
Archidona, Ecuador 128/D3
Archidona, Spain 33/D4
Archie, La. (†71343) 238/G3
Archie, Mo. (64725) 261/D5
Archiestown, Scotland 15/E3
Archuleta (co.), Colo. 208/E8
Archydal, Sask. 181/F5
Arcis-sur-Aube, France 28/F3
Arckaringa (creek), S. Australia 94/D2
Arco, Georgia (†31520) 217/J8
Arco, Idaho (83213) 220/E6
Arco, Idaho 188/D2
Arco, Minn. (56113) 255/B6
Arcola, Ill. (61910) 222/E4
Arcola, Ind. (46704) 227/G2
Arcola, La. (†70456) 238/K5
Arcola, Miss. (38722) 256/C4
Arcola, Mo. (65603) 261/E7
Arcola, N.C. (27589) 281/N2
Arcola, Sask. 181/J6
Arcopongo, Bolivia 136/B5
Arcosanti, Ariz. (†86333) 198/C4
Arcos de Jalón, Spain 33/E2
Arcos de la Frontera, Spain 33/D4
Arcos de Valdevez, Portugal 33/B2
Arcot, India 68/D6
Arcoverde, Brazil 132/G5
Arctic (ocean) 54/C1
Arctic (ocean) 146/B2
Arctic (plain), Alaska 196/G1
Arctic, R.I. (†02893) 249/J6
Arctic Bay, Canada 4/B14
Arctic Bay, N.W.T. 162/H1
Arctic Bay, N.W. Terrs. 187/K2
Arctic Circle 2/J2
Arctic Ocean 2/B2
Arctic Ocean 4/B14
Arctic Ocean, U.S.S.R. 48/K1
Arctic Red (riv.), N.W. Terrs. 187/E3
Arctic Red River, N.W.T. 162/C2
Arctic Red River, N.W. Terrs. 187/E3
Arctic Village, Alaska (99722) 196/K1
Arda (riv.), Greece 45/G5
Ardabil, Iran 54/F6
Ardabil, Iran 59/E2
Ardabil, Iran 66/F1
Ardagh, Limerick, Ireland 17/C7
Ardagh, Longford, Ireland 17/F4
Ardahan, Turkey 59/D1
Ardahan, Turkey 63/K2
Ardal, Iran 66/G4
Årdal, Norway 18/E7
Årdalstangen, Norway 18/F6
Ardanuç, Turkey 63/K2
Ardara, Ireland 17/E2
Ardath, Sask. 181/D4
Ardavasar, Scotland 15/B3
Ardbeg, Ontario 177/D2
Ardèche (dept.), France 28/F5
Ardee, Ireland 17/H4
Ardee, Ireland 10/C4
Arden, Ark. (†71822) 202/B6
Arden, Del. (†19801) 245/R1
Arden, Denmark 21/C4
Arden, Manitoba 179/C4
Arden, Ontario 177/G3
Arden, Wash. (†99114) 310/H2
Arden, W. Va. (†26405) 312/G4
Arden-Arcade, Calif. (95825) 204/B8
Ardencroft, Del. (†19810) 245/R1
Ardennes (for.), Belgium 27/F9
Ardennes (dept.), France 28/F3
Ardenode, Alberta 182/D4
Ardentown, Del. (†19810) 245/S1
Ardenvoir, Wash. (98811) 310/E3
Ardersier, Scotland 15/E3
Ardeşen, Turkey 63/J2
Ardestan, Iran 59/F3
Ardestan, Iran 66/H4
Ardez, Switzerland 39/K3
Ardfert, Ireland 17/B7
Ardfinnan, Ireland 17/F7
Ardgay, Scotland 15/D3
Ardglass, N. Ireland 17/K3
Ardgour (dist.), Scotland 15/C4
Ardhéa, Greece 45/F5
Ardila (riv.), Spain 33/C3
Ardill, Sask. 181/F6
Ardino, Bulgaria 45/G5
Ardivachar (pt.), Scotland 15/A3
Ardle (riv.), Scotland 15/E4
Ardlethan, N.S. Wales 97/D4
Ardmore, Ala. (35805) 195/E1
Ardmore, Alberta 182/E2
Ardmore, Ind. (†46624) 227/E1
Ardmore, Ireland 17/F8
Ardmore, Md. (†20785) 245/G4
Ardmore, Mo. (†65247) 261/H3
Ardmore, Okla. 188/G4
Ardmore, Okla. (73401) 288/M6
Ardmore, Pa. (19003) 294/M6
Ardmore, S. Dak. (57715) 298/B7
Ardmore, Tenn. (38449) 237/H10
Ardnamurchan (pen.), Scotland 15/B4
Ardnamurchan (pt.), Scotland 15/B4
Ardoch, N. Dak. (58213) 282/R3
Ardon, Switzerland 39/D4
Ardooie, Belgium 27/C7
Ardrahan, Ireland 17/D5
Ardrishaig, Scotland 15/C4
Ardrossan, Alberta 182/D3
Ardrossan, Scotland 10/D3
Ardrossan, Scotland 15/D5
Ards (dist.), N. Ireland 17/K2
Ardsley, N.Y. (10502) 276/O6
Åre, Sweden 18/H5
Arecibo (dist.), P. Rico 161/C1
Arecibo, P. Rico 156/G1
Arecibo, P. Rico 161/B1
Aredale, Iowa (50605) 229/H3
Areguá, Paraguay 144/B4
Areia Branca, Brazil 132/G4
Arelee, Sask. 181/D3
Arena (pt.), Calif. 188/B3
Arena (pt.), Calif. 204/B5
Arena (pt.), Mexico 150/E5
Arena, N. Dak. (58412) 282/K5
Arena (isl.), Philippines 82/C6
Arena, Wis. (53503) 317/G9
Arenac (co.), Mich. 250/F4
Arenales, Cerro (mt.), Chile 138/D7
Arenas (pt.), Argentina 143/C7
Arenas (cay), Mexico 150/O5
Arenas (pt.), P. Rico 161/F2
Arenas de San Pedro, Spain 33/D2
Arendal, Norway 18/F7
Arendjelovac, Yugoslavia 45/E3
Arendonk, Belgium 27/G6
Arendtsville, Pa. (17303) 294/H6
Arenillas, Ecuador 128/B4
Arenys de Mar, Spain 33/H2
Arenzville, Ill. (62611) 222/C4
Areópolis, Greece 45/F7
Arequipa (dept.), Peru 128/F10
Arequipa, Peru 128/G11
Arequipa, Peru 120/B4
Arequipa, Peru 2/F6
Arequipa, Peru 128/72
Aresji, Neth. Ant. 161/D9
Areuse (riv.), Switzerland 39/C3
Arévalo, Spain 33/D2
Areyonga, North. Terr. 88/E4
Areyonga, North. Terr. 93/C8
Arezzo (prov.), Italy 34/C3
Arezzo, Italy 34/C3
Arfa Deh, Iran 66/H3
Arga (riv.), Spain 33/F1
Argadargada, North. Terr. 93/E6
Argalant, Mongolia 77/G3
Argalastí, Greece 45/F6
Argamasilla de Alba, Spain 33/E3
Arganda, Spain 33/G4
Argao, Philippines 82/D6
Argenta, Br. Col. 184/J5
Argenta, Ill. (62501) 222/E4
Argenta, Italy 34/D2
Argentan, France 28/D3
Argentat, France 28/D5
Argenteuil, France 28/A1
Argenteuil (co.), Québec 172/C4
Argentia, Newf. 166/C2
Argentina 2/F7
Argentina 120/C6
ARGENTINA 143
Argentine, Pa. (†16040) 294/C3
Argentino (lake), Argentina 143/B7
Argenton-sur-Creuse, France 28/D4
Argeş (riv.), Romania 45/G3
Argo, Ala. (†35173) 195/E3
Argo, Sudan 111/F4
Argo, Sudan 59/B6
Argolis (gulf), Greece 45/F7
Argonia, Kansas (67004) 232/E4
Argonne, Wis. (54511) 317/J4
Argonne Nat'l Laboratory, Ill. 222/B6
Árgos, Greece 45/F7
Argos, Ind. (46501) 227/E2
Argos (cape), Nova Scotia 168/G3
Argostólion, Greece 45/E6
Arguello (pt.), Calif. 204/E9
Arguin (bay), Mauritania 106/A4
Argun (riv.) 54/N4
Argun' (Ergun He) (riv.), China 77/K1
Argun' (riv.), U.S.S.R. 48/M4
Argungu, Nigeria 106/E6
Argus (range), Calif. 204/H7
Argusville, N. Dak. (58005) 282/R5
Arguvan, Turkey 63/H3
Argyle, Fla. (32422) 212/C6
Argyle, Georgia (31623) 217/G8
Argyle, Iowa (52619) 229/K7
Argyle, Maine (†04468) 243/F5
Argyle, Manitoba 179/E4
Argyle, Mich. (48410) 250/G5
Argyle, Minn. (56713) 255/B2
Argyle, Mo. (65001) 261/J6
Argyle, New Bruns. 170/C2
Argyle, N.Y. (12809) 276/O4
Argyle, Texas (76226) 303/F1
Argyle (lake), W. Australia 88/D3
Argyle (lake), W. Australia 92/E2
Argyle, Wis. (53504) 317/G10
Argyle Downs, W. Australia 92/E2
Argyll (dist.), Scotland 15/C4
Argyll (trad. co.), Scotland 15/B5
Arhangay, Mongolia 77/F2
Arhavi, Turkey 63/J2
Arhli (Arlit), Niger 106/F4
Ar Horqin, China 77/K3
Århus (co.), Denmark 21/D5
Århus, Denmark 7/E3
Århus, Denmark 21/D5
Århus, Denmark 18/F8
Aria, N. Zealand 100/E3
Ariah Park, N.S. Wales 97/D4
Ariail, S.C. (†29640) 296/B2
Ariano Irpino, Italy 34/E4
Ariari (riv.), Colombia 126/D6
Aribinda, Upper Volta 106/D6
Arica, Chile 120/B4
Arica, Chile 138/A1
Arica, Colombia 126/E9
Aricagua, Venezuela 124/C3
Ariccia, Italy 34/F7
Arichat, Nova Scotia 168/H3
Arichuna, Venezuela 124/E4
Arichuna (riv.), Venezuela 124/D4
Arid (cape), W. Australia 88/C6
Arid (cape), W. Australia 92/C6
Ariège (dept.), France 28/D6
Ariel, Wash. (98603) 310/C5
Ariguaní (riv.), Colombia 126/D3
Ariha (Jericho), West Bank 65/C4
Arikaree (riv.), Colo. 208/O3
Arima, Trin. & Tob. 156/G5
Arima, Trin. & Tob. 161/B10
Arimo, Idaho (83214) 220/F7
Arinagour, Scotland 15/B4
Aringa, Uganda 115/F3
Arinos (riv.), Brazil 132/B5
Ario de Rosales, Mexico 150/J7
Arion, Iowa (51520) 229/B5
Aripao, Venezuela 124/F4
Aripeka, Fla. (33502) 212/D3
Aripine, Ariz. (†85901) 198/E4
Aripo, El Cerro del (mt.), Trin. & Tob. 161/B10
Ariporo (riv.), Colombia 126/E4
Aripuanã, Brazil 120/C3
Aripuanã, Brazil 132/A5
Aripuanã (riv.), Brazil 120/D3
Aripuanã (riv.), Brazil 132/A4
Arisaig, Scotland 15/C4
Arisaig (sound), Scotland 15/C4
Arismendi, Venezuela 124/D3
Arispe, Iowa (50831) 229/E7
Aristazabal (isl.), Br. Col. 184/C4
Aritao, Philippines 82/C2
Ariton, Ala. (36311) 195/G7
Arivaca, Ariz. (85601) 198/D7
Arivonimamo, Madagascar 118/H3
Arixang (Wenquan), China 77/B3
Ariza, Spain 33/E2
Arizaro, Salar de (salt dep.), Argentina 143/C2
Arizona 188/D4
ARIZONA 198
Arizona (state), U.S. 146/G6
Arizona City, Ariz. (85223) 198/D6
Arizona Sunsites, Ariz. (85625) 198/F7
Arizpe, Mexico 150/D1
Årjäng, Sweden 18/H7
Arjay, Ky. (40902) 237/O7
Arjeplog, Sweden 18/L3
Arjona, Colombia 126/C2
Arkabutla, Miss. (38602) 256/D1
Arkabutla (dam), Miss. 256/D1
Arkabutla (lake), Miss. 256/D1
Arkadelphia, Ala. (35033) 195/E3
Arkadelphia, Ark. (71923) 202/D5
Arkaig, Loch (lake), Scotland 15/C4
Arkaig, Loch (lake), Scotland 10/D2
Arkalyk, U.S.S.R. 48/G4
Arkansas 188/H3
Arkansas (riv.) 188/H3
ARKANSAS 202
Arkansas (co.), Ark. 202/H5

Atchison 331

Arkansas (riv.), Ark. 202/G5
Arkansas (riv.), Colo. 208/P6
Arkansas (riv.), Kansas 232/D3
Arkansas (riv.), Okla. 288/S4
Arkansas (state), U.S. 146/J6
Arkansas (riv.), U.S. 2/E4
Arkansas (riv.), U.S. 146/J6
Arkansas City, Ark. (71630) 202/H6
Arkansas City, Kans. 188/G3
Arkansas City, Kansas (67005) 232/E4
Arkansas Divide (mts.), Colo. 208/L4
Arkansas Post Nat'l Mem., Ark. 202/H5
Arkansaw, Wis. (54721) 317/B6
Arkdale, Wis. (54613) 317/G7
Arkhángelos, Greece 45/J7
Arkhipo-Osipovka, U.S.S.R. 52/E6
Arkinda, Ark. (71821) 202/B6
Arklow, Ireland 10/C4
Arklow, Ireland 17/J6
Arklow (bank), Ireland 17/K6
Arkoe, Mo. (†64468) 261/C2
Arkoma, Okla. (74901) 288/T4
Arkona (cape), E. Germany 22/E1
Arkona, Ontario 177/C4
Arkport, N.Y. (14807) 276/E6
Arkticheskiy Institut (isls.), U.S.S.R. 48/H2
Arkville, N.Y. (12406) 276/L6
Arkwright, S.C. (†29301) 296/C2
Arlee, Mont. (59821) 262/B3
Arlee, W. Va. (†25106) 312/B5
Arles, France 28/F6
Arley, Ala. (35541) 195/D2
Arlington, Ala. (36722) 195/C6
Arlington, Ariz. (85322) 198/C5
Arlington, Colo. (81021) 208/N6
Arlington, Georgia (31713) 217/C8
Arlington, Ill. (61312) 222/D2
Arlington, Ind. (46104) 227/F5
Arlington, Iowa (50606) 229/K3
Arlington, Kansas (67514) 232/D4
Arlington, Ky. (42021) 237/D7
Arlington○, Mass. (02174) 249/C6
Arlington, Minn. (55307) 255/D6
Arlington, Nebr. (68002) 264/H3
Arlington, N.Y. (12603) 276/N7
Arlington, N.C. (†28642) 281/H2
Arlington, Ohio (45814) 284/C4
Arlington, Oreg. (97812) 291/G2
Arlington, S. Dak. (57212) 298/P5
Arlington, Tenn. (38002) 237/B10
Arlington, Tex. 188/G4
Arlington, Texas (*76010) 303/F2
Arlington (lake), Texas 303/F2
Arlington, Vt. (05250) 268/A5
Arlington○, Vt. (05250) 268/A5
Arlington (co.), Va. 307/S2
Arlington, Va. (*22201) 307/T3
Arlington, Wash. (98223) 310/C2
Arlington, Wis. (53911) 317/H9
Arlington, Wyo. (†82080) 319/F4
Arlington Beach, Sask. 181/F4
Arlington Heights, Ill. (*60004) 222/B5
Arlington Heights, Ohio (†45201) 284/C9
Arlington Nat'l Cemetery, Va. 307/T3
Arlit (Arhli), Niger 106/F4
Arló, Hungary 41/F2
Arlon, Belgium 27/H9
Arltunga, North. Terr. 93/D7
Arm (riv.), Sask. 181/F5
Arma, Kansas (66712) 232/H4
Arma (plat.), Saudi Arabia 59/E4
Armada, Alberta 182/D4
Armada, Mich. (48005) 250/G6
Armadale, Scotland 15/C2
Armadale, Scotland 10/B1
Armagh (dist.), N. Ireland 17/H3
Armagh, N. Ireland 10/C3
Armagh, N. Ireland 17/H3
Armagh, Pa. (15920) 294/E5
Armagh, Québec 172/G3
Armathwaite, Tenn. (38506) 237/M8
Armavir, U.S.S.R. 7/J4
Armavir, U.S.S.R. 48/E5
Armavir, U.S.S.R. 52/F5
Armena, Alberta 182/D3
Armenia, Colombia 120/B2
Armenia, Colombia 126/B5
Armenian S.S.R., U.S.S.R. 7/J4
Armenian S.S.R., U.S.S.R. 52/F6
Armenian S.S.R., U.S.S.R. 48/E6
Armentières, France 28/E2
Armería, Mexico 150/G7
Armero, Colombia 126/C5
Armidale, Australia 87/F9
Armidale, N.S. Wales 88/J6
Armidale, N.S. Wales 97/F2
Armington, Ill. (61721) 222/D3
Armington, Mont. (†59412) 262/F3
Arminto, Wyo. (82630) 319/E2
Armistead, La. (†71019) 238/D3
Armit (lake), Manitoba 179/A2
Armley, Sask. 181/G2
Armona, Calif. (93202) 204/F7
Armorel, Ark. (72310) 202/L2
Armour, S. Dak. (57313) 298/N7
Armourdale, N. Dak. (†58365) 282/M2
Armoy, N. Ireland 17/J1
Armstrong, Br. Col. 184/H5
Armstrong, Ill. (61812) 222/F3
Armstrong, Ind. (†47708) 227/B8
Armstrong, Iowa (50514) 229/D2
Armstrong, Mo. (65230) 261/G4
Armstrong, Ont. 162/H5
Armstrong, Ontario 175/C2
Armstrong, Ontario 177/H4
Armstrong (co.), Pa. 294/D4
Armstrong (co.), Texas 303/C3
Armstrong, Texas (78338) 303/G11
Armstrong Brook, New Bruns. 170/E1
Armstrong Creek, Wis. (54103) 317/K4
Armstrong Mills, Ohio (43904) 284/J6
Armuchee, Georgia (30105) 217/B2
Army Chemical Center, Md. 245/O3
Army Med. Ctr. Annex (Walter Reed), Md. 245/E4
Arnaía, Greece 45/F5
Arnaud, Manitoba 179/E5
Arnaud (riv.), Québec 174/F1
Arnaudville, La. (70512) 238/G6
Arnauti (cape), Cyprus 59/B2
Arnauti (cape), Cyprus 63/E5
Arnavutköy, Turkey 63/D6
Arnedo, Spain 33/E1
Arnegard, N. Dak. (58835) 282/D4
Årnes, Norway 18/G6
Arnett, Okla. (73832) 288/G2
Arnett, W. Va. (25007) 312/D7
Arney (riv.), N. Ireland 17/F3
Arnheim, Mich. (†49958) 250/G1
Arnhem (cape), Australia 87/D7
Arnhem, Netherlands 27/H4
Arnhem (cape), North. Terr. 88/F2
Arnhem (cape), North. Terr. 93/E2
Arnhem Land (reg.), Australia 87/D7
Arnhem Land (reg.), North. Terr. 88/E2
Arnhem Land (reg.), North. Terr. 93/D2
Arnhem Land Aboriginal Reserve, North. Terr. 88/E2
Arnhem Land Aboriginal Res., North. Terr. 93/C2
Arno (riv.), Italy 34/C3
Arno (atoll), Marshall Is. 87/H5
Arnold, Calif. (95223) 204/E5
Arnold, England 13/F4
Arnold, Kansas (67515) 232/B3
Arnold, Mich. (49819) 250/B2
Arnold, Minn. (†55801) 255/F4
Arnold, Mo. (63010) 261/M6
Arnold, Nebr. (69120) 264/D3
Arnold (riv.), North. Terr. 93/D3
Arnold, Pa. (15068) 294/C4
Arnold Mills, R.I. (†02864) 249/J5
Arnoldsburg, W. Va. (25234) 312/D5
Arnold's Cove, Newf. 166/C2
Arnolds Park, Iowa (51331) 229/C2
Arnoldstein, Austria 41/B3
Arnoldsville, Georgia (30619) 217/F3
Arnot, Pa. (16911) 294/H2
Arnøya (isl.), Norway 18/M1
Arnprior, Ontario 177/H2
Arnsberg, W. Germany 22/C3
Arnstadt, E. Germany 22/D3
Årø (isl.), Denmark 21/C7
Aro (riv.), Venezuela 124/F4
Aroa, Venezuela 124/D2
Aroab, Namibia 118/B5
Aroche, Spain 33/C4
Arock, Oreg. (97902) 291/K5
Aroland, Ontario 177/H4
Aroland, Ontario 175/C2
Arolla, Switzerland 39/E4
Arolsen, W. Germany 22/C3
Aroma, Bolivia 136/B6
Aroma, Sudan 111/G4
Aroma Park, Ill. (60910) 222/F2
Aromas, Calif. (95004) 204/D7
Aroostook (co.), Maine 243/F2
Aroostook (riv.), Maine 243/G2
Aroostook, New Bruns. 170/C2
Arorae (atoll), Kiribati 87/H6
Aroroy, Philippines 82/D4
Arosa, Ría de (est.), Spain 33/B1
Arosa, Switzerland 39/J3
Aroser Rothorn (mt.), Switzerland 39/J3
Årøsund, Denmark 21/C7
Arouca, Trin. & Tob. 161/B10
Arp, Georgia (†31783) 217/F7
Arp, Texas (75750) 303/J5
Arpa (riv.), Turkey 63/K2
Arpaçay, Turkey 63/K2
Arpin, Wis. (54410) 317/G6
Arque, Bolivia 136/B5
'Arraba, West Bank 65/C3
'Arrabe, Israel 65/C2
Arrah, India 68/E3
Ar Rahhaliya, Iraq 66/C4
Ar Rahhaliya, Iraq 59/D3
Arraias, Brazil 132/E6
Arran, Fla. (†32327) 212/B1
Arran, Sask. 181/K4
Arran (isl.), Scotland 15/C5
Arran (isl.), Scotland 10/D3
Arras, Br. Col. 184/G2
Arras, France 28/E2
Arrecifal, Colombia 126/F6
Arrecife, Spain 106/B3
Arrecife, Spain 33/C4
Arrecife de la Media Luna (reefs), Honduras 154/F3
Arrecifes, Argentina 143/F7
Arrecifes (riv.), Argentina 143/G6
Arrey, N. Mex. (87930) 274/B6
Arriaga, Mexico 150/N8
Arriba, Colo. (80804) 208/N4
Arribeños, Argentina 143/F7
Arrington, Kansas (†66436) 232/G2
Arrington, Tenn. (37014) 237/H9
Arrington, Va. (22922) 307/L5
Arriola, Colo. (†81323) 208/B8
Arrochar, Scotland 15/D4
Arronches, Portugal 33/C3
Arrow (lake), Ireland 17/E3
Arrow (creek), Mont. 262/F3
Arrow Canyon (range), Nev. 266/G6
Arrow Creek, Mont. (†59424) 262/F3
Arrowhead Mountain (lake), Vt. 268/A2
Arrow River, Manitoba 179/B4
Arrowrock (res.), Idaho 220/C6
Arrow Rock, Mo. (65320) 261/F4
Arrowsmith, Ill. (61722) 222/E3
Arrowtown, N. Zealand 100/B6
Arrowwood, Alberta 182/D4
Arrowwood (lake), N. Dak. 282/N5
Arroyas, Los (lake), Bolivia 136/C3
Arroyo, P. Rico 161/E3
Arroyo, P. Rico 156/G1
Arroyo Blanco, Cuba 158/F2
Arroyo de la Luz, Spain 33/C3
Arroyo del Valle (dry riv.), Calif. 204/L3
Arroyo Grande, Bolivia 136/A2
Arroyo Grande, Calif. (93420) 204/E8
Arroyo Hondo (dry riv.), Calif. 204/L3
Arroyo Hondo, N. Mex. (87513) 274/D2
Arroyo Mocho (dry riv.), Calif. 204/L2
Arroyo Seco, Argentina 143/F6
Arroyo Seco (dry riv.), Calif. 204/K10
Arroyo Seco, N. Mex. (87514) 274/D2
Arroyos y Esteros, Paraguay 144/B4
Ar Rumaila, Iraq 66/E5
Års, Denmark 21/C4
Ars-en-Ré, France 28/C4
Arsen'yev, U.S.S.R. 48/O5
Arsin, Turkey 63/H2
Arslanköy, Turkey 63/F4
Árta, Greece 45/E6
Artá, Spain 33/H3
Artas, S. Dak. (57423) 298/K2
Artawiya, Saudi Arabia 59/E4
Arteaga, Mexico 150/H7
Artem, U.S.S.R. 48/O5
Artemas, Pa. (17211) 294/E6
Artemisa, Cuba 158/B1
Artemisa, Cuba 156/A2
Artemovskiy, U.S.S.R. 48/M4
Artemus, Ky. (40903) 237/O7
Artena, Italy 34/F7
Artesia, Calif. (90701) 204/C11
Artesia, Miss. (39736) 256/G4
Artesia, N. Mex. 188/F4
Artesia, N. Mex. (88210) 274/E6
Artesian, S. Dak. (57314) 298/O6
Artesia Wells, Texas (78001) 303/E9
Arth, Switzerland 39/F2
Arthabaska (co.), Québec 172/E4
Arthabaska, Québec 172/F3
Arthur, Ill. (61911) 222/E4
Arthur, Ind. (†47598) 227/C8
Arthur, Iowa (51431) 229/C4
Arthur (co.), Nebr. 264/C3
Arthur, Nebr. (69121) 264/C3
Arthur (range), N. Zealand 100/D4
Arthur, N. Dak. (58006) 282/R5
Arthur, Ontario 177/D4
Arthur (lake), Pa. 294/C4
Arthur (lake), Tasmania 99/D4
Arthur (range), Tasmania 99/C5
Arthur (riv.), Tasmania 99/B3
Arthur, Tenn. (37707) 237/O7
Arthur (riv.), W. Australia 92/B2
Arthur, W. Va. (26816) 312/H4
Arthurdale, W. Va. (26520) 312/G3
Arthuret, England 13/E2
Arthurette, New Bruns. 170/C2
Arthur Kill (str.), N.J. 273/B3
Arthur's (pass), N. Zealand 100/C5
Arthurstown, Ireland 17/H7
Artibonite (dept.), Haiti 158/C5
Artibonite (riv.), Haiti 158/C5
Artigas (dept.), Uruguay 145/B1
Artigas, Uruguay 145/C1
Artillery (lake), N.W. Terrs. 187/H3
Artland, Sask. 181/B3
Artois, Calif. (95913) 204/C4
Artois (trad. prov.), France 29
Artova, Turkey 63/G2
Artux (Atushi), China 77/A4
Artvin (prov.), Turkey 63/J2
Artvin, Turkey 59/D1
Artvin, Turkey 63/J2
Aru (isls.), Indonesia 85/K7
Aru, Zaire 115/F3
Arua, Uganda 115/F3
Aruba (isl.), Neth. Ant. 161/E9
Aruba (isl.), Neth. Ant. 156/E4
Arucas, Spain 33/B5
Arunachal Pradesh (terr.), India 68/G3
Arundel, England 13/G7
Arundel, England 10/F5
Arundel, Québec 172/C4
Årup, Denmark 21/D7
Aruppukkottai, India 68/D7
'Arura, West Bank 65/C3
Arus, P. Rico 161/C3
Arusha (reg.), Tanzania 115/G4
Arusha, Tanzania 102/F5
Arusha, Tanzania 115/G4
Arusi (prov.), Ethiopia 111/G6
Aruwimi (riv.), Zaire 115/E3
Arva, Ireland 17/F4
Arva, Ontario 177/C4
Arvada, Colo. (*80001) 208/J3
Arvada, Wyo. (82831) 319/F1
Arvayheer, Mongolia 77/F2
Arvel, Ky. (†40447) 237/O5
Arvi, India 68/D4
Arvida, Québec 172/F1
Arvidsjaur, Sweden 18/L4
Arvika, Sweden 18/H7
Arvilla, N. Dak. (58214) 282/P4
Arvin, Calif. (93203) 204/G8
Arvonia, Va. (23004) 307/M5
Arwad (Ruad) (isl.), Syria 63/F5
Arxan, China 77/K2
Arys', U.S.S.R. 48/G5
Arzamas, U.S.S.R. 48/E4
Arzamas, U.S.S.R. 52/F3
Arzúa, Spain 33/B1
Aš, Belgium 27/H6
Aš, Czech. 41/B1
Aså, Denmark 21/D3
Asaba, Nigeria 106/F7
Asadabad, Iran 66/F3
Asahan (riv.), Indonesia 85/B5
Asahi, Japan 81/K6
Asahi (mt.), Japan 81/J4
Asahikawa, Japan 81/L2
Asahikawa, Japan 54/P5
Asama (mt.), Japan 81/J5
Asansol, India 68/F4
Åsarna, Sweden 18/J5
Asau, W. Samoa 86/L8
Asbest, U.S.S.R. 48/G4
Asbestos, Québec 172/F4
Asbury, Iowa (†52001) 229/M4
Asbury, Mo. (64832) 261/C8
Asbury, N.J. (08802) 273/C2
Asbury, W. Va. (24916) 312/E7
Asbury Park, N.J. (07712) 273/F3
As Busaiya, Iraq 66/E5
Ascención (Añez), Bolivia 136/D4
Ascensión, Argentina 143/F7
Ascension (par.), La. 238/J6
Ascensión, Mexico 150/E1
Ascension, Neth. Ant. 161/F8
Ascension (isl.), St. Helena 102/A5
Ascension (isl.), St. Helena 2/J6
Aschaffenburg, W. Germany 22/C4
Aschendorf, W. Germany 22/B2
Aschersleben, E. Germany 22/D3
Asco, W. Va. (24809) 312/C8
Ascog, Scotland 15/A2
Ascoli Piceno (prov.), Italy 34/D3
Ascoli Piceno, Italy 34/D3
Ascona, Switzerland 39/G4
Ascope, Peru 128/C6
Ascot, Queensland 88/K2
Ascot, Queensland 95/E2
Ascotán, Chile 138/B3
Ascotán, Salar de (salt dep.), Chile 138/B3
Ascot Corner, Québec 172/F4
Ascrib (isls.), Scotland 15/B3
Ascutney, Vt. (05030) 268/C5
Ascutney (mt.), Vt. 268/C5
Åseda, Sweden 18/J8
Åsele, Sweden 18/K4
Asenovgrad, Bulgaria 45/G5
Asèr, Ras (cape), Somalia 2/M5
Asèr, Ras (cape), Somalia 115/K1
Ash (riv.), Minn. 255/F2
Ash, N.C. (28420) 281/N6
Ash, Oreg. (†97473) 291/D4
Ash (creek), Utah 304/A6
'Ashaira, Saudi Arabia 59/D5
Ashanti (reg.), Ghana 102/B4
Ashanti (reg.), Ghana 106/D7
Ashaway, R.I. (02804) 249/G7
Ashboro, Ind. (†47840) 227/C6
Ashburn, Georgia (31714) 217/E7
Ashburn, Mo. (63433) 261/K3
Ashburn, Va. (22011) 307/O2
Ashburnham, Mass. (01430) 249/G2
Ashburnham○, Mass. (01430) 249/G2
Ashburton (riv.), Australia 87/B8
Ashburton, England 13/D7
Ashburton, N. Zealand 100/C5
Ashburton (riv.), W. Australia 88/B4
Ashburton (riv.), W. Australia 92/A3
Ashburton Downs, W. Australia 88/B4
Ashby, Ala. (†35035) 195/E4
Ashby○, Mass. (01431) 249/G2
Ashby, Minn. (56309) 255/C4
Ashby, Nebr. (69333) 264/C2
Ashbyburg, Ky. (†42456) 237/G5
Ash Creek, Minn. (†56173) 255/B7
Ashcroft, Br. Col. 184/G5
Ashdale, Maine (†04565) 243/D8
Ashdod, Israel 65/B4
Ashdot Ya'aqov, Israel 65/D2
Ashdown, Ark. (71822) 202/B6
Ashe (co.), N.C. 281/F2
Ashe (isl.), N.C. 281/P6
Asheboro, N.C. (27203) 281/K3
Ashepoo, S.C. (†29446) 296/G6
Ashepoo (riv.), S.C. 296/F6
Asher, Okla. (74826) 288/N5
Ashern, Manitoba 179/D3
Asherton, Texas (78827) 303/E9
Asherville, Ind. (†47834) 227/C6
Asherville, Kansas (67420) 232/D2
Asheville, N.C. 188/K3
Asheville, N.C. (*28801) 281/D3
Asheweig (riv.), Ontario 175/C2
Ashfield○, Mass. (01330) 249/C2
Ashfield, N.S. Wales 88/K4
Ashfield, N.S. Wales 97/J3
Ash Flat, Ark. (72513) 202/G1
Ashford, Ala. (36312) 195/H8
Ashford○, Conn. (06278) 210/G1
Ashford, England 10/G5
Ashford, England 13/H6
Ashford, Ireland 17/J5
Ashford, N.S. Wales 97/F1
Ashford, N.C. (†28752) 281/F3
Ashford, Wash. (98304) 310/C4
Ashford, W. Va. (25009) 312/C6
Ashford P.O. (Warrenville), Conn. (06278) 210/G1
Ash Fork, Ariz. (86320) 198/C3
Ash Grove, Kansas (†67455) 232/D2
Ash Grove, Mo. (65604) 261/E8
Ashgrove, Queensland 88/K2
Ashhurst, N. Zealand 100/E4
Ashibetsu, Japan 81/L2
Ashikaga, Japan 81/J5
Ashington, England 13/F2
Ashington, England 10/F3
Ashippun, Wis. (53003) 317/H1
Ashiya, Japan 81/H8
Ashizuri (cape), Japan 81/F7
Ashkhabad, U.S.S.R. 54/G6
Ashkhabad, U.S.S.R. 48/F6
Ashkum, Ill. (60911) 222/E3
Ash Lake, Minn. (†55771) 255/F2
Ashland, Ala. (36251) 195/G4
Ashland, Calif. (†94577) 204/K2
Ashland, Georgia (†30521) 217/F2
Ashland, Ill. (62612) 222/C4
Ashland, Kansas (67831) 232/C4
Ashland, Ky. (41101) 237/R4
Ashland, Ky. 188/K3
Ashland, La. (71002) 238/D2
Ashland, Maine (04732) 243/G2
Ashland○, Maine (04732) 243/G2
Ashland○, Mass. (01721) 249/J3
Ashland, Miss. (38603) 256/F1
Ashland, Mo. (65010) 261/H5
Ashland, Mont. (59003) 262/K5
Ashland, Nebr. (68003) 264/H3
Ashland, N.H. (03217) 268/D4
Ashland○, N.H. (03217) 268/D4
Ashland, N.J. (†08033) 273/B3
Ashland, N.Y. (12407) 276/M6
Ashland (co.), Ohio 284/F4
Ashland, Ohio (44805) 284/F4
Ashland, Okla. (74524) 288/O5
Ashland, Oreg. (97520) 291/E5
Ashland, Pa. (17921) 294/K4
Ashland, Va. (23005) 307/N5
Ashland (co.), Wis. 317/E3
Ashland, Wis. (54806) 317/E2
Ashland City, Tenn. (37015) 237/G8
Ashley (co.), Ark. 202/G7
Ashley, Ill. (62808) 222/D5
Ashley, Ind. (46705) 227/G1
Ashley, Mich. (48806) 250/E5
Ashley, Mo. (†63334) 261/K4
Ashley (lake), Mont. 262/B2
Ashley, N.S. Wales 97/E1
Ashley, N. Dak. (58413) 282/M7
Ashley, Ohio (43003) 284/E5
Ashley, Pa. (18706) 294/E7
Ashley (riv.), S.C. 296/G6
Ashley, W. Va. (†26339) 312/E4
Ashley Falls, Mass. (01222) 249/A4
Ashmere (lake), Mass. 249/B3
Ashmont, Alberta 182/E2
Ashmore, Ill. (61912) 222/F4
Ashmore, Nova Scotia 168/C4
Ashmore (isls.), Terr. of Ashmore and Cartier Is. 88/C2
Ashmore and Cartier Is., Terr. of, 88/C2
Ashokan, N.Y. (†12491) 276/M7
Ashokan (res.), N.Y. 276/M7
Ashport, Tenn. (†38063) 237/B9
Ashqelon, Israel 65/A4
Ash Shabicha, Iraq 66/C5
Ashtabula (lake), N. Dak. 282/P5
Ashtabula (co.), Ohio 284/J2
Ashtabula, Ohio (44004) 284/J2
Ashton, Idaho (83420) 220/G5
Ashton, Ill. (61006) 222/D2
Ashton, Iowa (51232) 229/B2
Ashton, Kansas (†67051) 232/E4
Ashton, Mich. (†49677) 250/D5
Ashton, Nebr. (68817) 264/F3
Ashton, R.I. (02864) 249/J5
Ashton, S.C. (†29082) 296/E5
Ashton, S. Dak. (57424) 298/N3
Ashton, W. Va. (25503) 312/B5
Ashton Creek, Br. Col. 184/H5
Ashton-under-Lyne, England 13/H2
Ashton-under-Lyne, England 10/G2
Ashuanipi (lake), Newf. 166/A3
Ashuanipi (riv.), Newf. 166/A3
Ashuapi, Newf. 166/A3
Ashuelot, N.H. (03441) 268/C6
Ashuelot (riv.), N.H. 268/C6
Ash Valley, Kansas (†67550) 232/C3
Ashville, Ala. (35953) 195/F3
Ashville, Maine (04607) 243/G7
Ashville, Manitoba 179/B3
Ashville, Ohio (43103) 284/E6
Ashville, Pa. (16613) 294/F4
Ashwaubenon, Wis. (54304) 317/K7
Ashwood, Oreg. (97711) 291/G3
'Asi (Orontes) (riv.), Syria 63/G5
Asia 2/P3
Asia (isls.), Indonesia 85/J5
Asid (gulf), Philippines 82/D4
Asidonhoppo, Suriname 131/D4
Asilah, Morocco 106/C1
Asinara (gulf), Italy 34/B4
Asinara (isl.), Italy 34/B4
Asino, U.S.S.R. 48/J4
'Asir (reg.), Saudi Arabia 59/D6
Aşkale, Turkey 63/J3
Askeaton, Ireland 17/D6
Askew, Miss. (38604) 256/D1
Askewville, N.C. (†27983) 281/R2
Askim, Norway 18/E4
Askim, Sweden 18/G8
Aski Mosul, Iraq 66/C2
Askival (mt.), Scotland 15/B4
Askov, Denmark 21/C7
Askov, Minn. (55704) 255/F4
Askvoll, Norway 18/D6
Asmara, Ethiopia 111/G4
Asmara, Ethiopia 59/C6
Asmara, Ethiopia 102/F3
Asnaes, Denmark 21/E6
Åsnen (lake), Sweden 18/J8
Asnières-sur-Seine, France 28/A1
Aso (mt.), Japan 81/E7
Aso National Park, Japan 81/E7
Asosa, Ethiopia 111/F5
Asoteriba, Jebel (mt.), Sudan 111/G3
Asotin (co.), Wash. 310/H4
Asotin, Wash. (99402) 310/H4
Asotin (creek), Wash. 310/H4
Asotin (dam), Wash. 310/J4
Aspang Markt, Austria 41/D3
Aspatria, England 13/D3
Aspe, Spain 33/F3
Aspelund, Minn. (†55946) 255/F6
Aspen, Colo. (81611) 208/F4
Aspen, Nova Scotia 168/F3
Aspen (lake), Oreg. 291/E5
Aspen (mts.), Wyo. 319/C4
Aspen Grove, Br. Col. 184/G5
Aspen Hill, Md. 245/K4
Aspermont, Texas (79502) 303/D4
Aspers, Pa. (17304) 294/H6
Aspetuck, Conn. (†06880) 210/B4
Aspetuck (res.), Conn. 210/B4
Aspetuck (riv.), Conn. 210/B3
Aspinwall, Iowa (51432) 229/C5
Aspinwall, Pa. (15215) 294/C6
Aspiring (mt.), N. Zealand 100/B6
Aspley, Queensland 88/K2
Aspy (bay), Nova Scotia 168/H2
Asquith, Sask. 181/D3
Assab, Ethiopia 59/D7
Assab, Ethiopia 111/H5
Assaba (reg.), Mauritania 106/B5
Assabet (riv.), Mass. 249/H3
Assad, Bahrat (lake), Syria 63/H4
Assakarai (dry riv.), Niger 106/F5
Assale (lake), Ethiopia 111/H5
As Salman, Iraq 59/E3
As Salman, Iraq 66/D5
Assam (state), India 68/G3
Assapan (riv.), Manitoba 179/G2
Assaria, Kansas (67416) 232/E3
Assateague Island Nat'l Seashore, Va. 307/T4
Assawompset (pond), Mass. 249/L5
Assay (creek), Utah 304/B6
Asse, Belgium 27/E7
Asselar (well), Mali 106/D5
Asselle, Ethiopia 102/F4
Asselle, Ethiopia 111/G6
Assen, Netherlands 27/K3
Assenede, Belgium 27/D6
Assens, Århus, Denmark 21/D4
Assens, Fyn, Denmark 21/D7
Assesse, Belgium 27/G8
Assigny (lake), Newf. 166/A3
Assiniboia, Sask. 181/E6
Assiniboine (mt.), Alberta 182/C4
Assiniboine (mt.), Br. Col. 184/K5
Assiniboine (riv.), Manitoba 179/C5
Assiniboine (riv.), Sask. 181/J3
Assinica (lake), Québec 174/C3
Assinika (lake), Manitoba 179/G2
Assinika (riv.), Manitoba 179/G2
Assinippi, Mass. (02339) 249/E8
Assis, Brazil 132/D8
Assis, Brazil 135/A3
Assisi, Italy 34/D3
Assonet, Mass. (02702) 249/K5
Assumption, Ill. (62510) 222/E4
Assumption (par.), La. 238/H7
Assumption, Ohio (†43540) 284/B2
Assumption (isl.), Seychelles 118/H1
Assynt (dist.), Scotland 15/C2
Assynt, Loch (lake), Scotland 15/D2
Assyria, Mich. (†49021) 250/D6
Astara, U.S.S.R. 52/G7
Astatula, Fla. (32705) 212/E3
Asten, Netherlands 27/H6
Asterabad (Gorgan), Iran 59/F2
Asterabad (Gorgan), Iran 66/J2
Asti, Calif. (95413) 204/C5
Asti (prov.), Italy 34/B2
Asti, Italy 34/B2
Astillero, Peru 128/H9
Astipálaia, Greece 45/H7
Astipálaia (isl.), Greece 45/H7
Astle, New Bruns. 170/D2
Aston (bay), N.W. Terrs. 187/J2
Aston-Jonction, Québec 172/E3
Astor, Fla. (32002) 212/E2
Astorga, Spain 33/C1
Astoria, Ill. (61501) 222/C3
Astoria, Oreg. 188/B1
Astoria, Oreg. (97103) 291/D1
Astoria, S. Dak. (57213) 298/S4
Astorville, Ontario 177/E1
Astove (isl.), Seychelles 102/G6
Astove (isl.), Seychelles 118/H2
Astra, Argentina 143/C6
Astrakhan', U.S.S.R. 7/J4
Astrakhan', U.S.S.R. 52/G5
Astrakhan', U.S.S.R. 48/E5
Astray (lake), Newf. 166/A3
Astudillo, Spain 33/D1
Asturias (reg.), Spain 33/C1
Asunción, Bolivia 136/B2
Asuncion (isl.), No. Marianas 87/E4
Asunción, Paraguay 144/A4
Asunción (cap.), Paraguay 2/F7
Asunción (dept.), Paraguay 144/A4
Asunción (cap.), Paraguay 120/D5
Asuncion (passage), Philippines 82/D5
Asunción Mita, Guatemala 154/C3
Asunción Nochixtlán, Mexico 150/L8
Asunta, Bolivia 136/B5
Aswad, Ras al (cape), Saudi Arabia 59/C5
Aswân, Egypt 111/F3
Aswân, Egypt 59/B5
Aswân, Egypt 102/F2
Aswân (dam), Egypt 59/B5
Aswân (dam), Egypt 111/F3
Aswân High (dam), Egypt 102/F2
Aswân High (dam), Egypt 111/F3
Asyût, Egypt 111/J4
Asyût, Egypt 102/F2
Asyût, Egypt 59/B4
Aszód, Hungary 41/E3
Atabapo (riv.), Colombia 126/G6
Atabapo (riv.), Venezuela 124/E6
Atacama, Puna de (reg.), Argentina 143/C2
Atacama (reg.), Chile 138/B6
Atacama (des.), Chile 120/C5
Atacama (des.), Chile 138/B4
Atacama, Salar de (salt dep.), Chile 138/C4
Atafu (atoll), Tokelau Is. 87/J6
Atahona, Uruguay 145/B4
Atakora (mts.), Benin 106/E6
Atakpamé, Togo 106/E7
Atalándi, Greece 45/F6
Atalaya, Peru 128/E8
Atalissa, Iowa (52720) 229/L5
Atambua, Indonesia 85/G7
Atami, Japan 81/J6
Atapirire, Venezuela 124/F3
Atar, Mauritania 106/B4
Atar, Mauritania 102/A2
Ataran (riv.), Burma 72/C4
Atascadero, Calif. (93422) 204/E8
Atascosa (co.), Texas 303/F9
Atascosa, Texas (78002) 303/J11
Atbara (riv.), Ethiopia 111/G4
Atbara, Sudan 111/F4
Atbara, Sudan 59/B6
Atbara, Sudan 102/F3
Atbara (riv.), Sudan 59/C6
Atbara (riv.), Sudan 111/G4
Atbasar, U.S.S.R. 48/G4
Atchafalaya (bay), La. 238/H8
Atchafalaya (riv.), La. 238/G6
Atchison, Kans. 188/G3

Aytos, Bulgaria 45/H4
Ayu (isls.), Indonesia 85/J5
Ayun, Saudi Arabia 59/D4
Ayutla de los Libres, Mexico 150/K8
Ayutthaya (Phra Nakhon Si Ayutthaya), Thailand 72/D4
Ayvacık, Turkey 63/B3
Ayvalık, Turkey 59/A2
Ayvalık, Turkey 63/B3
Aywaille, Belgium 27/H8
Azalea, Oreg. (97410) 291/D5
Azalea Park, Fla. (32807) 212/E3
Azalia, Ind. (†47232) 227/F6
Azalia, Mich. (48110) 250/F6
Azamgarh, India 68/E3
Azángaro, Peru 128/H10
Azángaro (riv.), Peru 128/G10
Azaoua (reg.), Niger 106/E5
Azaouad (reg.), Mali 106/D5
Azaouak (dry riv.), Mali 106/E5
Azapa, Chile 138/A1
Azapa, Quebrada (riv.), Chile 138/B1
Azare, Nigeria 106/G6
Azaz, Syria 63/G4
Azbine (Aïr) (mts.), Niger 106/F5
Azcapotzalco, Mexico 150/L1
Azdavay, Turkey 63/E2
Azemmour, Morocco 106/C2
Azerbaidzhan S.S.R., U.S.S.R. 7/J4
Azerbaidzhan S.S.R., U.S.S.R. 48/E5
Azerbaidzhan S.S.R., U.S.S.R. 52/G6
Azerbaijan, East (prov.), Iran 66/E1
Azerbaijan, West (prov.), Iran 66/D1
Azerbaijan (reg.), Iran 66/D1
Aziscoos (lake), Maine 243/A5
Azle, Texas (76020) 303/E2
Azogues, Ecuador 128/C4
AZORES 33
Azores (isls.), Portugal 2/H4
Azores (isls.), Portugal 33/A2
Azoum, Bahr, Chad 111/D5
Azov (sea), U.S.S.R. 7/H4
Azov, U.S.S.R. 52/E5
Azov (sea), U.S.S.R. 52/E5
Azov (sea), U.S.S.R. 48/D5
Azoyú, Mexico 150/K8
Azpeitia, Spain 33/E1
Azrou, Morocco 106/C2
Aztec, Ariz. (†85333) 198/B6
Aztec, N. Mex. (87410) 274/B2
Aztec Ruins Nat'l Mon., N. Mex. 274/A2
Azua (prov.), Dom. Rep. 158/D6
Azua, Dom. Rep. 156/D3
Azua, Dom. Rep. 158/D6
Azuaga, Spain 33/D3
Azuara, Spain 33/F2
Azuay (prov.), Ecuador 128/C4
Azuero (pen.), Panama 154/G7
Azul, Argentina 143/E4
Azul, Argentina 120/D6
Azul (riv.), Guatemala 154/C2
Azul, Cordillera (mts.), Peru 128/E7
Azurduy, Bolivia 136/C6
Azure (lake), Br. Col. 184/G4
Azusa, Calif. (91702) 204/D10
Azwell, Wash. (†98846) 310/F3
Azzel Mati, Sebkha (lake), Algeria 106/E3
Az Zubair, Iraq 66/E5

B

Ba, Fiji 86/P10
Baa, Indonesia 85/G8
Baaba (isl.), New Caled. 86/G4
Ba'albek, Lebanon 63/G5
Baan Baa, N.S. Wales 97/E2
Baar, Switzerland 39/F2
Baarle-Nassau, Netherlands 27/F6
Baarn, Netherlands 27/G4
Baatsagaan, Mongolia 77/E2
Baba, Ecuador 128/C3
Baba (cape), Turkey 63/D2
Baba (cape), Turkey 63/A3
Babadag, Romania 45/J3
Babadağ, Turkey 63/C4
Babaeski, Turkey 63/B2
Babahoyo, Ecuador 128/C3
Babanusa, Sudan 111/E5
Babar (isl.), Indonesia 85/H7
Babar (isls.), Indonesia 85/H7
Babati, Tanzania 115/G4
Babayevo, U.S.S.R. 52/E3
Babb, Mont. (59411) 262/C2
Babbie, Ala. (†36420) 195/F8
Babbitt, Minn. (55706) 255/G3
Babbitt, Nev. (89416) 266/C4
Babcock, Wis. (54413) 317/F7
Babel (isls.), Tasmania 99/E1
Bab el Mandeb (str.) 102/G3
Bab el Mandeb (str.), Djibouti 111/H5
Babelthuap (isl.), Belau 87/D5
Babia (riv.), Mexico 150/J2
Babil (heads), Iraq 66/D4
Babine (lake), Br. Col. 162/D5
Babine, Br. Col. 184/D2
Babine (lake), Br. Col. 184/E3
Babine (riv.), Br. Col. 184/D2
Babo, Indonesia 85/K7
Babol, Iran 54/G6
Babol, Iran 59/F2
Babol, Iran 66/H2
Babol Sar, Iran 66/H2
Baboquivari (mts.), Ariz. 198/D7
Baboua, Cent. Afr. Rep. 115/C2
Babson Park, Fla. (33827) 212/E4
Babuyan (isls.), Philippines 54/O8
Babuyan (chan.), Philippines 82/A3
Babuyan (isl.), Philippines 82/B2
Babuyan (isls.), Philippines 85/G2
Babuyan (isls.), Philippines 82/A2
Babylon (ruins), Iraq 66/D4
Babylon, N.Y. (*11702) 276/O9
Baca (co.), Colo. 208/O8
Bacabal, Brazil 120/E3
Bacabal, Maranhão, Brazil 132/E4
Bacabal, Pará, Brazil 132/B4
Bacadéhuachi, Mexico 150/E2
Bacalar, Mexico 150/P7
Bacalar (lake), Mexico 150/P7
Bacan (isls.), Indonesia 85/H6
Bacanora, Mexico 150/E2
Bacarra, Philippines 82/C1
Bacău, Romania 7/G4
Bacău, Romania 45/H2
Baccalieu (isl.), Newf. 166/D2
Bac Can, Vietnam 72/E2
Baccaro (pt.), Nova Scotia 168/C5
Bacchus Marsh, Victoria 97/C5
Bacerac, Mexico 150/E1
Bac Giang, Vietnam 72/E2
Bach, Mich. (†48759) 250/F5
Bachaquero, Venezuela 124/C3
Bache (pen.), N.W. Terrs. 187/L2
Bache, Okla. (74526) 288/P5
Bachelor (brook), Mass. 249/D3
Bachiniva, Mexico 150/F2
Bach Long Vi, Dao (isl.), Vietnam 72/F2
Bachu (Maralwexi), China 77/A4
Back (bay), India 68/B7
Back (riv.), Md. 245/N4
Back (lake), N.H. 268/E1
Back (riv.), N.W.T. 146/H3
Back (riv.), N.W.T. 162/G2
Back (riv.), N.W. Terrs. 187/J3
Back (bay), Va. 307/S7
Back (creek), Va. 307/J4
Bačka Topola, Yugoslavia 45/D3
Back Bay, New Bruns. 170/D3
Backbone (mt.), Md. 245/A3
Backnang, W. Germany 22/C4
Backoo, N. Dak. (58215) 282/P2
Backus, Minn. (56435) 255/D4
Backway, The (inlet), Newf. 166/C3
Bac Lieu, Vietnam 72/E5
Bacliff, Texas (77518) 303/K2
Bac Ninh, Vietnam 72/E2
Baco (mt.), Philippines 82/C4
Bacolod, Philippines 85/G3
Bacolod, Philippines 54/O8
Bacolod, Philippines 82/D5
Bacon (co.), Georgia 217/G7
Bacone, Okla. (†74401) 288/R3
Bacon Ridge (mts.), Wyo. 319/B2
Bacons, Del. (†19940) 245/R6
Baconton, Georgia (31716) 217/D8
Bácsalmás, Hungary 41/E3
Bács-Kiskun (co.), Hungary 41/E3
Bacum, Mexico 150/D3
Bacuna, Neth. Ant. 161/E8
Bacup, England 13/H1
Bacup, England 10/G1
Bad (riv.), Mich. 250/E5
Bad (hills), Sask. 181/C4
Bad (lake), Sask. 181/C4
Bad (riv.), S. Dak. 298/G5
Badacsonytomaj, Hungary 41/D3
Badagara, India 68/D6
Bad Aibling, W. Germany 22/D5
Badajoz (prov.), Spain 33/C3
Badajoz, Spain 33/C3
Badalona, Spain 33/H2
Bad Aussee, Austria 41/B3
Bad Axe, Mich. (48413) 250/G5
Bad Berleburg, W. Germany 22/C3
Bad Berneck, W. Germany 22/D3
Bad Bramstedt, W. Germany 22/C2
Bad Brückenau, W. Germany 22/C3
Baddeck, Nova Scotia 168/H2
Baddeck (riv.), Nova Scotia 168/H2
Bad Doberan, E. Germany 22/D1
Bad Driburg, W. Germany 22/C3
Bad Dürkheim, W. Germany 22/C4
Bad Dürrenberg, E. Germany 22/D3
Bad Ems, W. Germany 22/B3
Baden, Austria 41/D2
Baden, Manitoba 179/A2
Baden, Md. (†20613) 245/M6
Baden, Ontario 177/D4
Baden, Pa. (15005) 294/B4
Baden, Switzerland 39/F2
Ba Den, Nui (mt.), Vietnam 72/E5
Baden-Baden, W. Germany 22/C4
Badenoch (dist.), Scotland 15/D4
Badenweiler, W. Germany 22/B5
Baden-Württemberg (state), W. Germany 22/C4
Bad Freienwalde, E. Germany 22/F2
Bad Gandersheim, W. Germany 22/D3
Badgastein, Austria 41/B3
Badger (peak), Idaho 220/E7
Badger, Iowa (50516) 229/E3
Badger, Minn. (56714) 255/B2
Badger, Newf. 166/C4
Badger (creek), Oreg. 291/H3
Badger, S. Dak. (57214) 298/P5
Badger (creek), Wyo. 319/E2
Badger's Quay, Newf. 166/D4
Bad Goisern, Austria 41/B3
Badham, S.C. (†29471) 296/F5
Bad Harzburg, W. Germany 22/D3
Bad Hersfeld, W. Germany 22/C3
Badhoevedorp, Netherlands 27/B5
Bad Hofgastein, Austria 41/B3
Bad Homburg vor der Höhe, W. Germany 22/C3
Bad Honnef, W. Germany 22/B3
Badian, Philippines 82/D6
Badin, N.C. (28009) 281/J4
Badin, Pakistan 68/B4
Badiraguato, Mexico 150/F4
Bad Ischl, Austria 41/B3
Bad Kissingen, W. Germany 22/D3
Bad Kreuznach, W. Germany 22/B4
Bad Land (butte), Utah 304/D4
Bad Lands (reg.), N. Dak. 282/C7
Badlands Nat'l Park, S. Dak. 298/E6
Bad Langensalza, E. Germany 22/D3
Bad Lauterberg im Harz, W. Germany 22/D3
Bad Leonfelden, Austria 41/C2
Bad Liebenwerda, E. Germany 22/E3
Bad Lippspringe, W. Germany 22/C3
Bad Mergentheim, W. Germany 22/C4
Bad Münster-Ebernburg, W. Germany 22/B4
Bad Münstereifel, W. Germany 22/B3
Bad Muskau, E. Germany 22/F3
Bad Nauheim, W. Germany 22/C3
Bad Neuenahr-Ahrweiler, W. Germany 22/B3
Bad Neustadt an der Saale, W. Germany 22/D3
Bado, Mo. (†65447) 261/H8
Bad Oldesloe, W. Germany 22/D2
Ba Don, Vietnam 72/E3
Bad Orb, W. Germany 22/C3
Bad Pyrmont, W. Germany 22/C3
Badr, Saudi Arabia 59/C5
Badra, Iraq 66/D4
Bad Ragaz, Switzerland 39/H2
Bad Reichenhall, W. Germany 22/E5
Bad River Ind. Res., Wis. 317/E2
Bad Sachsa, W. Germany 22/D3
Bad Salzschlirf, W. Germany 22/C3
Bad Salzuflen, W. Germany 22/C2
Bad Salzungen, E. Germany 22/C3
Bad Sankt-Leonhard im Lavanttal, Austria 41/C3
Bad Schwartau, W. Germany 22/D2
Bad Segeberg, W. Germany 22/D2
Bad Tölz, W. Germany 22/D5
Baduen, Somalia 115/J2
Badulla, Sri Lanka 68/E7
Bad Vilbel, W. Germany 22/C3
Bad Waldsee, W. Germany 22/C5
Badwater (creek), Wyo. 319/E2
Bad Wildungen, W. Germany 22/C3
Bad Wimpfen, W. Germany 22/C4
Baelum, Denmark 21/D4
Baena, Spain 33/D4
Baerle-Hertog, Belgium 27/F6
Báez, Cuba 158/E2
Baeza, Ecuador 128/D3
Baeza, Spain 33/E4
Bafa (lake), Turkey 63/B4
Baffin (bay) 4/B13
Baffin (bay) 146/M2
Baffin (isl.), Canada 2/F2
Baffin (isl.), Canada 4/C13
Baffin (bay), Canada 2/F2
Baffin (isl.), N.W.T. 146/L2
Baffin (isl.), N.W.T. 162/J1
Baffin (bay), N.W.T. 162/J1
Baffin (dist.), N.W. Terrs. 187/K2
Baffin (bay), N.W. Terrs. 187/M2
Baffin (isl.), N.W. Terrs. 187/L2
Baffin (bay), Texas 303/G10
Bafia, Cameroon 115/B3
Bafing (riv.), Guinea 106/B6
Bafing (riv.), Mali 106/B6
Bafoulabé, Mali 106/B6
Bafoussam, Cameroon 115/B2
Bafq, Iran 59/G3
Bafq, Iran 66/J5
Bafra, Turkey 59/C1
Bafra, Turkey 63/F2
Bafra (cape), Turkey 59/C1
Bafra (cape), Turkey 63/G2
Baft, Iran 66/K6
Baft, Iran 59/G4
Baga, Nigeria 106/G6
Bagabag, Philippines 82/C2
Bagac, Philippines 82/C3
Bagaces, C. Rica 154/E5
Bagadó, Colombia 126/B5
Bagalkot, India 68/D5
Bagam (well), Niger 106/F5
Bagamoyo, Tanzania 115/G5
Baganga, Philippines 82/F7
Baganian (pen.), Philippines 82/D7
Bagansiapiapi, Indonesia 85/C5
Bagata, Zaire 115/C4
Bagdad, Ariz. (86321) 198/B4
Bagdad, Fla. (32530) 212/B6
Bagdad, Ky. (40003) 237/L4
Bagdad, Tasmania 99/D4
Bagdarin, U.S.S.R. 48/M4
Bagé, Brazil 120/D6
Bagé, Brazil 132/C10
Bagenalstown, Ireland 10/C4
Bagenalstown (Muinebeag), Ireland 17/H6
Bagenkop, Denmark 21/D8
Baggs, Wyo. (82321) 319/E4
Baghbaghu, Iran 66/M3
Baghdad (heads), Iraq 66/D4
Baghdad (cap.), Iraq 59/E3
Baghdad (cap.), Iraq 54/F6
Baghdad (cap.), Iraq 2/M4
Baghdad (cap.), Iraq 66/D4
Bagheria, Italy 34/D5
Baghlan, Afghanistan 54/H6
Baghlan, Afghanistan 59/J2
Baghlan, Afghanistan 68/B1
Baghu, Iran 66/K7
Bağırpaşa Daği (mt.), Turkey 59/D2
Bağırpaşa Dağı (mt.), Turkey 63/J3
Bagley, Iowa (50026) 229/E5
Bagley, Minn. (56621) 255/C3
Bagley, N.C. (†27542) 281/N3
Bagley, Wis. (53801) 317/D10
Bagnell, Mo. (†65026) 261/G6
Bagnell (dam), Mo. 261/G6
Bagnères-de-Bigorre, France 28/D6
Bagnères-de-Luchon, France 28/D6
Bagnolet, France 28/B2
Bagnols-sur-Cèze, France 28/F5
Bågø (isl.), Denmark 21/C7
Bago, Philippines 82/D5
Bagoé (riv.), Ivory Coast 106/C6
Bagoé (riv.), Mali 106/C6
Bagot, Manitoba 179/D5
Bagot (co.), Québec 172/E4
Bagrax (Bosten Hu) (lake), China 77/C3
Bagua, Peru 128/C5
Báguanos, Cuba 158/J3
Baguio, Philippines 54/N8
Baguio, Philippines 85/G2
Baguio, Philippines 82/C2
Baguirmi (reg.), Chad 111/C5
Bagwell, Texas (75412) 303/J4
Bahama, N.C. (27503) 281/M2
Bahamas 2/F4
Bahamas 146/L7
BAHAMAS 156/C1
Bahariya (oasis), Egypt 111/E2
Bahariya (oasis), Egypt 59/A4
Bahawalnagar, Pakistan 68/C2
Bahawalpur, Pakistan 54/J7
Bahawalpur, Pakistan 68/C3
Bahawalpur, Pakistan 59/K4
Bahçe, Turkey 63/G4
Bahçesaray, Turkey 63/K3
Bahia (state), Brazil 132/F6
Bahia (Salvador), Brazil 132/G6
Bahía (isls.), Honduras 154/D2
Bahía Blanca, Argentina 2/F7
Bahía Blanca, Argentina 143/D4
Bahía Blanca, Argentina 120/C6
Bahía Bustamante, Argentina 143/C6
Bahía de Caráquez, Ecuador 128/B3
Bahía Honda, Cuba 158/B1
Bahía Kino, Mexico 150/C2
Bahía San Blas, Argentina 143/D5
Bahía Thetis, Argentina 143/C7
Bahía Tortugas, Mexico 150/B3
Bahir Dar, Ethiopia 111/G5
Bahomamey, P. Rico 161/A1
Bahoruco (prov.), Dom. Rep. 158/D6
Bahoruco, Sierra de (mts.), Dom. Rep. 158/D6
Bahraich, India 68/E3
Bahrain 54/G7
BAHRAIN 59/F4
Bahramabad (Rafsanjan), Iran 66/K5
Bahr Azoum (riv.), Sudan 111/D5
Bahr el 'Arab (riv.), Sudan 111/E6
Bahr el Ghazal (dry riv.), Chad 111/C5
Bahr El Ghazal (prov.), Sudan 111/E6
Bahr es Safi (des.), Saudi Arabia 59/E6
Bahr ez Zeraf (riv.), Sudan 111/F6
Bahr Yusef (stream), Egypt 111/J4
Baia de Aramă, Romania 45/F3
Baía dos Tigres, Angola 115/B7
Baia Farta, Angola 115/B6
Baia Mare, Romania 45/F2
Baião, Brazil 132/D3
Baibiene, Argentina 143/G4
Baibokoum, Chad 111/C6
Bai Bung, Mui (Ca Mau) (pt.), Vietnam 72/E5
Baicheng (Bay), Xinjiang Uygur, China 77/B3
Baicheng, Jilin, China 77/K2
Baida, Libya 102/E1
Baida, Libya 111/D1
Baidyabati, India 68/F1
Baie-Comeau, Québec 172/A1
Baie-Comeau, Québec 174/D3
Baie de Henne, Haiti 158/B5
Baie-des-Bacons, Québec 172/H1
Baie-des-Moutons, Québec 174/F2
Baie-des-Rochers, Québec 172/H2
Baie-des-Sables, Québec 172/A1
Baie-du-Poste, Québec 174/C2
Baie-d'Urfé, Québec 172/G4
Baie-du-Vieux-Fort, Québec 174/F2
Baie-Johan-Beetz, Québec 174/E2
Baie-Mahault, Guadeloupe 161/A6
Baiersbronn, W. Germany 22/C4
Baie-Sainte-Anne, New Bruns. 170/F1
Baie-Sainte-Catherine, Québec 172/H1
Baie-Saint-Paul, Que. 162/J6
Baie-Saint-Paul, Québec 174/C3
Baie-Saint-Paul, Québec 172/G2
Baie-Trinité, Québec 172/B1
Baie-Verte, New Bruns. 170/F2
Baie Verte, Newf. 166/C4
Baieville, Québec 172/E3
Baigorrita, Argentina 143/F7
Baiji, Iraq 66/C3
Baildon, Sask. 181/F5
Baile Átha Cliath (Dublin) (cap.), Ireland 17/K5
Baile Átha Cliath (Dublin) (cap.), Ireland 10/C4
Băile Herculane, Romania 45/F3
Bailén, Spain 33/E3
Băileşti, Romania 45/F3
Bailey, Colo. (80421) 208/H4
Bailey, Iowa (†50455) 229/H2
Bailey, Mich. (49303) 250/D5
Bailey, Miss. (39320) 256/G6
Bailey, N.C. (27807) 281/N3
Bailey (co.), Texas 303/B3
Baileyboro, Texas (†79371) 303/B3
Bailey Island, Maine (04003) 243/D8
Bailey Lakes, Ohio (†44805) 284/F4
Bailey's Crossroads, Va. (22041) 307/S3
Baileys Harbor, Wis. (54202) 317/M5
Baileyton, Ala. (35019) 195/E2
Baileyton, Tenn. (37743) 237/R8
Baileyville, Conn. (†06455) 210/E2
Baileyville, Ill. (61007) 222/D1
Baileyville, Kansas (66404) 232/F2
Bailieborough, Ireland 17/G4
Bailique (isl.), Brazil 132/D2
Bailivanish, Scotland 15/A3
Baillie (isls.), N.W. Terrs. 187/F2
Baillieston, Scotland 15/B2
Baillif, Guadeloupe 161/A7
Bailundo, Angola 115/C6
Baima, China 77/E5
Bainbridge (isl.), Alaska 196/C1
Bainbridge, Georgia (31717) 217/C9
Bainbridge, Ind. (46105) 227/D5
Bainbridge, N.Y. (13733) 276/J6
Bainbridge (dist.), N. Ireland 17/J3
Bainbridge, Ohio (45612) 284/D7
Bainbridge, Pa. (17502) 294/J5
Bainbridge (isl.), Wash. 310/A2
Bainbridge Island-Winslow (Winslow), Wash. (98110) 310/A2
Bainbridge N.T.C., Md. 245/O2
Bainet, Haiti 158/B6
Baingoin, China 77/D5
Bains, La. (70713) 238/H5
Bainville, Mont. (59212) 262/M2
Baird (inlet), Alaska 196/F2
Baird (mts.), Alaska 196/F1
Baird, Miss. (38724) 256/C4
Baird (pen.), N.W. Terrs. 187/L3
Baird, Texas (79504) 303/E5
Bairdstown, Ohio (†45872) 284/C3
Bairdsville, New Bruns. 170/C2
Baire, Cuba 158/H4
Bairiki (cap.), Kiribati 87/H5
Bairin Zuoqi, China 77/J3
Bairnsdale, Victoria 88/H7
Bairnsdale, Victoria 97/D5
Bairoil, Wyo. (82322) 319/E3
Bais, Philippines 82/D6
Baisden, W. Va. (25608) 312/C7
Baïse (riv.), France 28/D6
Baisha, China 77/G8
Baitadi, Nepal 68/E3
Bait al Faqih, Yemen Arab Rep. 59/D7
Bai Thuong, Vietnam 72/E3
Baixa da Banheira, Portugal 33/B3
Baixoaixo (isl.), Portugal 33/B2
Baixo Guandu, Brazil 132/F7
Baja, Hungary 41/E3
Baja California (state), Mexico 150/B1
Baja California Sur (state), Mexico 150/C3
Bajadero, P. Rico 161/C1
Bajgiran, Iran 66/L2
Bajo Boquete, Panama 154/F6
Bajo Nuevo (shoal), Colombia 126/C8
Bajos de Haina, Dom. Rep. 158/E6
Bajram Curri, Albania 45/D4
Bakala, Cent. Afr. Rep. 115/D2
Bakar, Yugoslavia 45/B3
Bakel, Senegal 106/B6
Baker (isl.), Alaska 196/M2
Baker, Calif. (92309) 204/J8
Baker (riv.), Chile 138/D7
Baker (mt.), Colo. 208/H2
Baker (co.), Fla. 212/D1
Baker, Fla. (32531) 212/C5
Baker (co.), Georgia 217/D8
Baker, Idaho (†83467) 220/E4
Baker, La. (70714) 238/K1
Baker (lake), Maine 243/C4
Baker, Minn. (56513) 255/B4
Baker, Mo. (†63846) 261/N9
Baker, Mont. (59313) 262/M4
Baker, Nev. (89311) 266/G3
Baker (riv.), N.H. 268/D4
Baker, N. Dak. (†58386) 282/L3
Baker (lake), N.W. Terrs. 187/J3
Baker, Okla. (73930) 288/D1
Baker, Oreg. 188/C2
Baker (co.), Oreg. 291/K3
Baker, Oreg. (97814) 291/K3
Baker (isl.), Pacific 87/J5
Baker (creek), Utah 304/A4
Baker (lake), Wash. 310/D2
Baker (mt.), Wash. 310/D2
Baker (riv.), Wash. 310/D2
Baker, W. Va. (26801) 312/J4
Baker Brook, New Bruns. 170/B1
Baker Butte (mt.), Ariz. 198/D4
Baker Hill, Ala. (36004) 195/H7
Baker Lake, N.W.T. 162/G3
Baker Lake, N.W. Terrs. 187/J3
Bakers (isl.), Mass. 249/F5
Bakersfield, Calif. 146/G6
Bakersfield, Calif. 188/C3
Bakersfield, Calif. (*93301) 204/G8
Bakersfield, Mo. (65609) 261/H9
Bakersfield, Texas (†79752) 303/B7
Bakersfield○, Vt. (05441) 268/B2
Bakers Summit, Pa. (16614) 294/F5
Bakersville, Conn. (†06057) 210/C1
Bakersville, N.C. (28705) 281/E2
Bakersville, Ohio (43803) 284/G5
Bakersville, Pa. (†15501) 294/D5
Bakerton, Ky. (42711) 237/L7
Bakerton, W. Va. (25410) 312/L4
Bakerville, Tenn. (†37185) 237/F9
Bakewell, England 10/G2
Bakewell, England 13/J2
Bakewell, Tenn. (37304) 237/L10
Bakharz, Kuhha-ye (mt.), Iran 66/M3
Bakhchisaray, U.S.S.R. 52/D6
Bakhmach, U.S.S.R. 52/D4
Bakhtegan (lake), Iran 66/J6
Bakhtiari (gov.), Iran 66/F4
Bakhun, Kuh-e (mt.), Iran 66/K6
Bakhuys (mts.), Suriname 131/C3
Bakia, Cent. Afr. Rep. 115/E2
Bakırköy, Turkey 63/D6
Baklan, Turkey 63/C4
Bako, Ethiopia 111/G6
Bakony (mts.), Hungary 41/D3
Bakool (prov.), Somalia 115/H3
Bakouma, Cent. Afr. Rep. 115/D2
Bakoy (riv.), Guinea 106/B6
Bakoy (riv.), Mali 106/B6
Bakraband, Kuh-e (mts.), Iran 66/M7
Baktalórántháza, Hungary 41/G2
Baktu (Paektu) (mt.), N. Korea 81/C3
Baku, U.S.S.R. 2/M3
Baku, U.S.S.R. 7/J4
Baku, U.S.S.R. 48/F5
Baku, U.S.S.R. 52/H6
Bala, Kansas (†66531) 232/F2
Bala, Ontario 177/E2
Bala, Turkey 63/E3
Bala, Wales 13/D5
Bala, Wales 10/E4
Balabac, Philippines 82/A7
Balabac (isl.), Philippines 85/F4
Balabac (isl.), Philippines 82/A7
Balabac (str.), Philippines 85/F4
Balabac (str.), Philippines 82/A7
Balabalagan (isls.), Indonesia 85/F6
Balabio (isl.), New Caled. 86/G4
Balaclava, Jamaica 158/H6
Bala-Cynwyd, Pa. (19004) 294/N6
Balad, Somalia 115/J3
Balaghat, India 68/E4
Balaguer, Spain 33/G2
Balaïtous (mt.), Spain 33/F1
Balakai (mesa), Ariz. 198/F3
Balakhna, U.S.S.R. 52/F3
Balaklava, S. Australia 94/F6
Balaklava, U.S.S.R. 52/D6
Balakovo, U.S.S.R. 7/J3
Balakovo, U.S.S.R. 48/E4
Balakovo, U.S.S.R. 52/G4
Balallan, Scotland 15/B2
Bal'ama, Jordan 65/E3
Balambangan (isl.), Malaysia 85/F4
Balancán de Domínguez, Mexico 150/O8
Balandra (pt.), Dom. Rep. 158/F5
Balanga, Philippines 82/C3
Balangala, Zaire 115/D3
Ba Lang An, Mui (cape), Vietnam 72/F4
Balangiga, Philippines 82/E5
Balao, Ecuador 128/C4
Balashi, Neth. Ant. 161/E10
Balashov, U.S.S.R. 7/J3
Balashov, U.S.S.R. 52/F4
Balashov, U.S.S.R. 48/E4
Balasore, India 68/F4
Balassagyarmat, Hungary 41/E2
Balaton (lake), Hungary 7/F4
Balaton (lake), Hungary 41/D3
Balaton, Minn. (56115) 255/C6
Balatonfüred, Hungary 41/D3
Balatonszentgyörgy, Hungary 41/D3
Balayan (bay), Philippines 82/C4
Balbi (mt.), Papua N.G. 86/C2
Balboa, Panama 154/H6
Balbriggan, Ireland 17/J4
Balbriggan, Ireland 10/C4
Balcarce, Argentina 143/E4
Balcarres, Sask. 181/H5
Balchik, Bulgaria 45/H4
Balch Springs, Texas (75180) 303/H2
Balclutha, N. Zealand 100/B7
Balcones Escarpment (plat.), Texas 303/E8
Balcones Heights, Texas (†78201) 303/J10
Bald (mt.), Colo. 208/H4
Bald (hill), Conn. 210/G1
Bald (mt.), Idaho 220/D5
Bald (mt.), New Bruns. 170/C1
Bald (mts.), N.C. 281/D3
Bald (mts.), Tenn. 237/R9
Bald (mt.), Utah 304/C3
Bald (mt.), Vt. 268/D2
Bald (head), W. Australia 88/B7
Bald (head), W. Australia 92/B6
Bald Eagle (lake), Minn. 255/G3
Baldeggersee (lake), Switzerland 39/F2
Baldhill (Ashtabula) (res.), N. Dak. 282/P5
Bald Hill Branch (riv.), Md. 245/G4
Bald Hills, Queensland 88/K2
Bald Knob, Ark. (72010) 202/G3
Bald Knob, W. Va. (25010) 312/C7
Baldonnel, Br. Col. 184/G2
Baldur, Manitoba 179/C5
Baldwin (co.), Ala. 195/C9
Baldwin, Fla. (32234) 212/E1
Baldwin (co.), Georgia 217/F4
Baldwin, Georgia (30511) 217/E2
Baldwin, Ill. (62217) 222/D5
Baldwin, Iowa (52207) 229/M4
Baldwin, La. (70514) 238/H7
Baldwin, Mich. (49304) 250/D5
Baldwin, N.Y. (11510) 276/R7
Baldwin, N. Dak. (58521) 282/J5
Baldwin, Pa. (†15208) 294/B7
Baldwin, W. Va. (26326) 312/E5
Baldwin, Wis. (54002) 317/B6
Baldwin-Aragon Mills, S.C. (†29706) 296/E2
Baldwin City, Kansas (66006) 232/G3
Baldwin Park, Calif. (91706) 204/D10
Baldwinsville, N.Y. (13027) 276/H4
Baldwinton, Sask. 181/B3
Baldwinville, Mass. (01436) 249/F2
Baldwyn, Miss. (38824) 256/G2
Baldy (peak), Ariz. 198/F5
Baldy (mt.), Manitoba 179/B3
Baldy (peak), N. Mex. 274/D3
Baldy (peak), Utah 304/B5
Bale (prov.), Ethiopia 111/H6
Bale (mt.), Ethiopia 111/G6
Baleares (prov.), Spain 33/H3
Balearic (isls.), Spain 7/E5
Balearic (Baleares) (isls.), Spain 33/H3
Baleine, Grande R. de la (riv.), Que. 162/J4
Baleine, Grand Rivière de la (riv.), Québec 174/B1
Baleine, Petite Rivière de la (riv.), Québec 174/B1
Baleine (riv.), Québec 174/D1
Baleine, R. à la (riv.), Que. 162/K4
Balen, Belgium 27/G6
Baler, Philippines 82/C3
Baler (bay), Philippines 82/C3
Balerna, Switzerland 39/G5
Balerno, Scotland 15/D2
Baleshare (isl.), Scotland 15/A3
Balestrand, Norway 18/E6
Baley, U.S.S.R. 48/M4
Balfate, Honduras 154/D3
Balfour, Br. Col. 184/J5
Balfour, N.C. (28706) 281/E4
Balfour, N. Dak. (58712) 282/J4
Balfron, Scotland 15/B1
Balgonie, Sask. 181/G5
Balhaf, P.D.R. Yemen 59/E7
Bal Harbour, Fla. (†33101) 212/C4
Bali, Cameroon 115/A2
Bali (isl.), Indonesia 54/N10
Bali (isl.), Indonesia 85/F7
Bali (sea), Indonesia 85/F7
Bali (str.), Indonesia 85/E7

Baxterville 335

Barham, N.S. Wales 97/C4
Bar Harbor, Maine (04609) 243/G7
Bar Harbor○, Maine (04609) 243/G7
Bari (prov.), Italy 34/F4
Bari, Italy 34/F4
Bari, Italy 7/F4
Bari (prov.), Somalia 115/J1
Baria (riv.), Venezuela 124/E7
Barich, Alberta 182/D2
Barichara, Colombia 126/D4
Barida, Ras (cape), Saudi Arabia 59/C5
Barima (riv.), Guyana 131/B2
Barinas (state), Venezuela 124/D3
Barinas, Venezuela 124/C3
Barinas, Venzuela 120/C2
Baring, Maine (†04619) 243/J5
Baring○, Maine (†04619) 243/J5
Baring, Mo. (63531) 261/H2
Baring (head), N. Zealand 100/B3
Baring (cape), N.W. Terrs. 187/G3
Baring, Sask. 181/J5
Baring, Wash. (98224) 310/D3
Barinitas, Venezuela 124/C3
Baripada, India 68/F4
Bariri, Brazil 135/B3
Bariri (res.), Brazil 135/B3
Bâris, Egypt 111/F3
Barisal, Bangladesh 68/G4
Barisan (mts.), Indonesia 85/C6
Baritbog (riv.), New Bruns. 170/E1
Barito (riv.), Indonesia 85/E6
Bark (lake), Ontario 177/G2
Barkam, China 77/F5
Barker, N.Y. (14012) 276/C4
Barker Heights, N.C. (†28739) 281/D4
Barkeyville, Pa. (†16038) 294/C3
Barkhamsted○, Conn. (†06063) 210/D1
Barkhamsted (res.), Conn. 210/D1
Barkhan, Pakistan 68/B3
Barkhan, Pakistan 59/J4
Barking, England 10/C5
Barking, England 13/H8
Barkley (sound), Br. Col. 184/E6
Barkley (dam), Ky. 237/E6
Barkley (lake), Ky. 237/F7
Barkley (lake), Tenn. 237/F7
Barkly Downs, Queensland 95/A4
Barkly East, S. Africa 118/D6
Barkly Tableland (plat.), Australia 87/D7
Barkly Tableland, North. Terr. 88/F3
Barkly Tableland, North. Terr. 93/D4
Barkly Tableland, Queensland 95/A4
Barkmere, Québec 172/C3
Barkol, China 77/D3
Bark River, Mich. (49807) 250/B3
Barksdale, Texas (78828) 303/D8
Barksdale A.F.B., La. 238/C2
Barlby, England 13/G4
Bar-le-Duc, France 28/F3
Barlee (lake), Australia 87/B8
Barlee (lake), W. Australia 88/B5
Barlee (lake), W. Australia 92/B5
Barletta, Italy 34/F4
Barlinek, Poland 47/B2
Barling, Ark. (72923) 202/B3
Barlow, Br. Col. 184/F3
Barlow, Ky. (42024) 237/D6
Barlow, Miss. (†39083) 256/C7
Barlow, N. Dak. (†58421) 282/M4
Barlow, Ohio (45612) 284/G7
Barlow, Oreg. (†97013) 291/B2
Barlow Bend, Ala. (†36545) 195/C8
Barmedman, N.S. Wales 97/D4
Barmer, India 68/C3
Barmera, S. Australia 94/G6
Bar Mills, Maine (04004) 243/C8
Barmouth, Wales 10/D4
Barmouth, Wales 13/C5
Barna, Ireland 17/C5
Barnabus, W. Va. (25609) 312/C7
Barnaby (riv.), New Bruns. 170/E2
Barnaby River, New Bruns. 170/E2
Barnard, Kansas (67418) 232/D2
Barnard, Mo. (64423) 261/C2
Barnard, N.C. (†28753) 281/D3
Barnard, S. Dak. (57426) 298/N2
Barnard○, Vt. (05031) 268/B4
Barnard Castle, England 13/E3
Barnardsville, N.C. (28709) 281/E3
Barnaul, U.S.S.R. 54/K4
Barnaul, U.S.S.R. 48/J4
Barn Bluff (mt.), Tasmania 99/B3
Barnegat, Alberta 182/E2
Barnegat, N.J. (08005) 273/E4
Barnegat (bay), N.J. 273/E4
Barnegat (inlet), N.J. 273/E4
Barnegat Light, N.J. (08006) 273/E4
Barnes (sound), Fla. 212/F6
Barnes, Kansas (66933) 232/F2
Barnes (co.), N. Dak. 282/O5
Barnes, Wis. (†54873) 317/D3
Barnesboro, Pa. (15714) 294/E4
Barnes City, Iowa (50027) 229/H6
Barnes Corners, N.Y. (13610) 276/J3
Barneston, Nebr. (68309) 264/H4
Barnesville, Colo. (†80624) 208/L2
Barnesville, Georgia (30204) 217/D4
Barnesville, Md. (20703) 245/J4
Barnesville, Minn. (56514) 255/B4
Barnesville, N.C. (28319) 281/L6
Barnesville, Ohio (43713) 284/H6
Barnet, England 13/H7
Barnet, England 10/B5
Barnet○, Vt. (05821) 268/C3
Barnett, Georgia (†30821) 217/G3
Barnett, Miss. (†39347) 256/G7
Barnett, Mo. (65011) 261/G6
Barnettville, New Bruns. 170/E2
Barneveld, Netherlands 27/H4
Barneveld, N.Y. (13304) 276/K4
Barneveld, Wis. (53507) 317/F10
Barneville-Carteret, France 28/C3
Barney, Georgia (31625) 217/E8
Barney, N. Dak. (58008) 282/S7
Barnhart, Texas (76930) 303/C6
Barnhill, Ohio (†44663) 284/H5
Barnoldswick, England 13/H1
Barnrock, Ky. (†41219) 237/R5
Barnsdall, Okla. (74002) 288/O1
Barnsley, England 13/J2
Barnsley, England 10/F4
Barnstable (co.), Mass. 249/N6
Barnstable, Mass. (02630) 249/N6
Barnstable○, Mass. (02630) 249/N6
Barnstaple, England 10/E5
Barnstaple, England 13/D6
Barnstaple (bay), England 10/D5
Barnstaple (bay), England 13/C6
Barnstead○, N.H. (03218) 268/E5
Barnum, Iowa (50518) 229/E3
Barnum, Minn. (55707) 255/F4
Barnum, W. Va. (†26726) 312/H4
Barnum, Wis. (†54631) 317/E9
Barnwell, Ala. (†36532) 195/C10
Barnwell, Alberta 182/D5
Barnwell (co.), S.C. 296/E5
Barnwell, S.C. (29812) 296/E5
Baro (riv.), Ethiopia 111/G6
Baro, Nigeria 106/F7
Baroda (Vadodara), India 68/C4
Baroda, India 54/J7
Baroda, Mich. (49101) 250/C7
Baroghil (pass), Afghanistan 68/C1
Baroghil (pass), Pakistan 68/C1
Baron, Okla. (†74965) 288/S3
Baron Bluff (prom.), Virgin Is. (U.S.) 161/E3
Barons, Alberta 182/D4
Barooga, N.S. Wales 97/C4
Barossa (res.), S. Australia 94/C6
Barotseland (reg.), Zambia 115/D7
Barpeta, India 68/G3
Barqa (Cyrenaica) (reg.), Libya 111/D1
Barques (pt.), Mich. 250/C3
Barquisimeto, Venezuela 124/D2
Barquisimeto, Venezuela 120/C2
Barr, Scotland 15/D5
Barr, Tenn. (†38040) 237/B9
Barra, Brazil 132/F5
Barra (head), Scotland 10/C2
Barra (head), Scotland 15/A4
Barra (isl.), Scotland 15/A4
Barra (isl.), Scotland 10/C2
Barra (isls.), Scotland 10/C2
Barra (sound), Scotland 15/A3
Barraba, N.S. Wales 97/F2
Barra Bonita (res.), Brazil 135/B3
Barrackpore, India 68/F1
Barrackville, W. Va. (26559) 312/F3
Barra de Río Grande, Nicaragua 154/F4
Barra do Bugres, Brazil 132/B6
Barra do Corda, Brazil 132/E4
Barra do Piraí, Brazil 132/E8
Barra do Piraí, Brazil 135/E3
Barra Isles (isls.), Scotland 15/A4
Barra Mansa, Brazil 135/D3
Barranca, Lima, Peru 128/C8
Barranca, Loreto, Peru 128/D5
Barrancabermeja, Colombia 126/C4
Barranca de Upía, Colombia 126/D5
Barrancas, Argentina 143/F6
Barrancas (riv.), Argentina 143/G5
Barrancas, Chile 138/G3
Barrancas, Colombia 126/D2
Barrancas, Barinas, Venezuela 124/C3
Barrancas, Monagas, Venezuela 124/G3
Barranco de Loba, Colombia 126/C3
Barrancos, Cerro (mt.), Chile 138/D7
Barrancos, Portugal 33/C3
Barranqueras, Argentina 143/E2
Barranquilla, Colombia 120/B1
Barranquilla, Colombia 126/C2
Barranquitas, P. Rico 161/D2
Barras (riv.), Bolivia 136/B6
Barras, Brazil 132/F4
Barras, Colombia 126/D8
Barraute, Québec 174/B3
Barre, Mass. (01005) 249/F3
Barre○, Mass. (01005) 249/F3
Barre, Québec 172/G3
Barre, Vt. (05641) 268/C3
Barre○, Vt. (05641) 268/C3
Barreal, Argentina 143/C3
Barreau (pt.), New Bruns. 170/F1
Barre Center, N.Y. (†14411) 276/D4
Barreiras, Brazil 120/E4
Barreiras, Brazil 132/E6
Barreirinha, Brazil 132/B3
Barreirinhas, Brazil 132/F3
Barreiro, Portugal 33/B1
Barreiros, Brazil 132/H5
Barren (isls.), Alaska 196/B2
Barren (isl.), India 68/G6
Barren (co.), Ky. 237/K7
Barren (riv.), Ky. 237/H6
Barren (isls.), Madagascar 118/G3
Barren (isl.), Nova Scotia 168/G4
Barren (cape), Tasmania 99/E2
Barren Plains, Tenn. (†37172) 237/H7
Barren River (lake), Ky. 237/J7
Barren Springs, Va. (24313) 307/G7
Barre Plains, Mass. (†01005) 249/F3
Barrera, Bolivia 136/B3
Barretos, Brazil 132/D8
Barretos, Brazil 135/B2
Barrett, Minn. (56311) 255/B5
Barrett, Texas (77532) 303/K1
Barrett, W. Va. (25013) 312/C7
Barretts, Georgia (†31601) 217/F8
Barrhead, Alberta 182/C2
Barrhead, Scotland 10/A1
Barrhead, Scotland 15/B2
Barrhill, Scotland 15/D5
Barrie, Ontario 177/E3
Barrie (isl.), Ontario 177/B1
Barrière, Br. Col. 184/H4
Barrineau Park, Fla. (†32533) 212/B6
Barrington, Ill. (60010) 222/A5
Barrington○, N.H. (†03825) 268/F5
Barrington, N.J. (08007) 273/B3
Barrington, Nova Scotia 168/C5
Barrington (bay), Nova Scotia 168/C5
Barrington○, R.I. (02806) 249/J6
Barrington, Tasmania 99/C3
Barrington Hills, Ill. (†60010) 222/A5
Barrington P.O. (East Barrington), N.H. (03825) 268/F5
Barrington Passage, Nova Scotia 168/C5
Barrington Tops (mt.), N.S. Wales 97/F2
Barringun, N.S. Wales 97/C1
Barron (co.), Wis. 317/C5
Barron, Wis. (54812) 317/C5
Barronett, Wis. (54813) 317/B4
Barrouallie, St. Vin. & Grens. 161/A9
Barroui, Dominica 161/E6
Barrow, Alaska (99723) 196/G1
Barrow, Alaska 188/C5
Barrow, Alaska 146/C2
Barrow (pt.), Alaska 146/C2
Barrow (pt.), Alaska 196/G1
Barrow (isl.), Australia 87/B8
Barrow (co.), Georgia 217/E2
Barrow (riv.), Ireland 17/H7
Barrow (riv.), Ireland 10/C4
Barrow (str.), N.W.T. 162/G1
Barrow (str.), N.W. Terrs. 187/J2
Barrow (bay), Ontario 177/C2
Barrow, U.S. 4/B17
Barrow (pt.), U.S. 2/B2
Barrow (pt.), U.S. 4/B18
Barrow (isl.), W. Australia 88/A4
Barrow (isl.), W. Australia 92/A3
Barrow Creek, North. Terr. 93/D6
Barrow-in-Furness, England 10/E3
Barrow-in-Furness, England 13/D3
Barrows, Manitoba 179/A2
Barrowsville, Mass. (†02766) 249/K5
Barr Smith (mt.) 5/C5
Barruelo de Santullán, Spain 33/D1
Barry, Ill. (62312) 222/B4
Barry (co.), Mich. 250/D6
Barry, Minn. (56210) 255/B5
Barry (co.), Mo. 261/E9
Barry (mts.), Victoria 97/D5
Barry, Wales 13/B7
Barry, Wales 10/E5
Barry's Bay, Ontario 177/G2
Barryton, Mich. (49305) 250/D5
Barryville, N.Y. (12719) 276/L8
Barsi, India 68/D5
Barsinghausen, W. Germany 22/C2
Barss Corners, Nova Scotia 168/D4
Barstow, Calif. (92311) 204/H9
Barstow, Md. (20610) 245/M6
Barstow, Texas (79719) 303/A6
Bar-sur-Aube, France 28/F3
Bar-sur-Seine, France 28/F3
Bartelso, Ill. (62218) 222/D5
Barterville, Ky. (†40311) 237/N4
Barth, E. Germany 22/E1
Barth, Fla. (†32533) 212/B6
Barthel, Sask. 181/B2
Bartholomew (bayou), Ark. 202/G6
Bartholomew (co.), Ind. 227/F6
Bartibog Bridge, New Bruns. 170/E1
Bartica, Guyana 120/D2
Bartica, Guyana 131/B2
Bartın, Turkey 63/E2
Bartle, Cuba 158/H3
Bartle Frere (mt.), Queensland 88/H3
Bartle Frere (mt.), Queensland 95/C3
Bartlesville, Okla. (74003) 288/O1
Bartlett (dam), Ariz. 198/D5
Bartlett (res.), Ariz. 198/D5
Bartlett, Ill. (60103) 222/A5
Bartlett, Iowa (51655) 229/B7
Bartlett, Kansas (67332) 232/G4
Bartlett, Nebr. (68622) 264/F3
Bartlett○, N.H. (03812) 268/E3
Bartlett, N. Dak. (†58344) 282/N3
Bartlett, Ohio (45713) 284/G7
Bartlett, Tenn. (38134) 237/B10
Bartlett, Texas (76511) 303/G7
Bartlett Deep, Cayman Is. 156/B3
Bartletts Ferry (dam), Ala. 195/H5
Bartletts Ferry (dam), Georgia 217/B5
Bartley, Nebr. (69020) 264/D4
Bartley, W. Va. (24813) 312/C8
Barto, Pa. (19504) 294/L5
Bartolomeu Dias, Mozambique 118/F4
Barton, Ala. (†35616) 195/C1
Barton, Ark. (72312) 202/J4
Barton (co.), Kansas 232/D3
Barton, Md. (21521) 245/B2
Barton (co.), Mo. 261/D7
Barton, N. Dak. (58315) 282/K2
Barton, Ohio (43905) 284/J5
Barton, Oreg. (†97009) 291/B2
Barton, Vt. (05822) 268/C2
Barton○, Vt. (05822) 268/C2
Barton (riv.), Vt. 268/C2
Barton City, Mich. (48705) 250/F4
Barton Hills, Mich. (48105) 250/F6
Bartonsville, Pa. (18321) 294/M4
Bartonsville, Vt. (†05143) 268/B5
Barton-upon-Humber, England 13/G4
Barton-upon-Humber, England 10/F4
Bartonville, Ill. (61607) 222/D3
Bartonville, Texas (†76226) 303/F1
Bartoszyce, Poland 47/E1
Bartow, Fla. (33830) 212/E4
Bartow (co.), Georgia 217/C2
Bartow, Georgia (30413) 217/G5
Bartow, W. Va. (24920) 312/G5
Bartra Antiguo, Peru 128/E4
Bartra Nuevo, Peru 128/E4
Barú (isl.), Colombia 126/C2
Barú (vol.), Panama 154/F6
Baruipur, India 68/F2
Barus, Indonesia 85/B5
Barut, Tanjong (cape), Malaysia 85/E5
Baruun-Urt, Mongolia 77/H2
Barvas, Scotland 10/C1
Barvas, Scotland 15/B2
Barview, Oreg. (†97420) 291/C4
Bar View, Oreg. (†97136) 291/C2
Barville, Québec 174/B3
Barwani, India 68/D4
Barwick, Georgia (31720) 217/E9
Barwick, Ontario 175/B3
Barwick, Ontario 177/F5
Barwon (riv.) 88/H5
Barwon (riv.), N.S. Wales 97/D2
Barysh, U.S.S.R. 52/G4
Baryulgil, N.S. Wales 97/G1
Basalt, Colo. (81621) 208/E4
Basalt, Idaho (83218) 220/F6
Basankusu, Zaire 115/C3
Basavilbaso, Argentina 143/G6
Bas-Caraquet, New Bruns. 170/F1
Bascharage, Luxembourg 27/H9
Basco, Ill. (62313) 222/B3
Basco, Philippines 82/A2
Bascom, Fla. (32423) 212/A1
Bascom, Ohio (44809) 284/D3
Bascuñán (cape), Chile 138/A7
Basehor, Kansas (66007) 232/G2
Basel, Switzerland 39/E1
Basel, Switzerland 7/E4
Baselland (canton), Switzerland 39/E2
Baselstadt (canton), Switzerland 39/E1
Basey, Philippines 82/E5
Bashan, Conn. (†06423) 210/F2
Bashan (lake), Conn. 210/F3
Bashaw, Alberta 182/D3
Bashi, Ala. (†36784) 195/C7
Bashi (chan.), China 77/K7
Bashi (chan.), Philippines 82/A1
Bashkir A.S.S.R., U.S.S.R. 48/F4
Bashkir A.S.S.R., U.S.S.R. 52/J4
Basht, Iran 66/G5
Basic, Miss. (†39330) 256/G6
Basilan (prov.), Philippines 82/D7
Basilan, Philippines 82/C7
Basilan (isl.), Philippines 85/G4
Basilan (isl.), Philippines 82/D7
Basilan (str.), Philippines 82/C7
Basildon, England 13/J8
Basildon, England 10/G5
Basile, La. (70515) 238/E5
Basilicata (reg.), Italy 34/F4
Basim, India 68/D4
Basin, Mont. (59613) 262/D4
Basin (lake), Sask. 181/F3
Basin, Wyo. (82410) 319/E1
Basinger, Fla. (†33472) 212/F4
Basingstoke, England 10/F5
Basingstoke, England 13/F6
Basirhat, India 68/F4
Basit (cape), Syria 63/F5
Baskahegan (lake), Maine 243/H5
Başkale, Turkey 63/K3
Baskatong (res.), Que. 162/J6
Baskatong (res.), Québec 172/B3
Baskerville, Va. (23915) 307/M7
Basket (lake), Manitoba 179/C3
Baskett, Ky. (42402) 237/F5
Baskil, Turkey 63/H3
Baskin, La. (71219) 238/G2
Basking Ridge, N.J. (07920) 273/D2
Başmakçı, Turkey 63/C4
Basodino (peak), Switzerland 39/G4
Basoko, Zaire 115/D3
Basom, N.Y. (14013) 276/D4
Basongo, Zaire 115/D4
Basora (pt.), Neth. Ant. 161/E10
Basra (gov.), Iraq 66/E5
Basra, Iraq 2/M4
Basra, Iraq 66/E5
Basra, Iraq 59/E3
Basra, Iraq 54/F6
Bas-Rhin (dept.), France 28/G3
Bass (str.) 88/H7
Bass (str.), Australia 87/E9
Bass (isls.), Fr. Poly. 87/M8
Bass (lake), Ind. 227/D2
Bass (str.), Tasmania 99/C1
Bassano, Alberta 182/D4
Bassano del Grappa, Italy 34/C2
Bassas da India (isl.), Réunion 102/F7
Bassas da India (isl.), Réunion 118/F4
Bassecourt, Switzerland 39/D2
Bassein, Burma 54/L8
Bassein, Burma 72/B3
Bassein, India 68/C5
Basse-Pointe, Martinique 161/C5
Basse-Sambre, Belgium 27/F8
Basse Santa Su, Gambia 106/B6
Basse-Terre (cap.), Guadeloupe 161/A7
Basse-Terre (cap.), Guadeloupe 156/F3
Basse-Terre (isl.), Guadeloupe 161/A6
Basseterre (cap.), St. Chris.-Nevis 161/C10
Basseterre (cap.), St. Chris.-Nevis 156/F3
Basse Terre, Trin. & Tob. 161/B11
Bassett, Ark. (72313) 202/K2
Bassett, Iowa (†50645) 229/J2
Bassett, Kansas (†66749) 232/G4
Bassett, Nebr. (68714) 264/E2
Bassett, Va. (24055) 307/J7
Bassfield, Miss. (39421) 256/E8
Bass Harbor, Maine (04653) 243/G7
Bassikounou, Mauritania 106/C5
Bassin Bleu, Haiti 158/B5
Bass River, New Bruns. 170/E2
Bass River, Nova Scotia 168/E3
Bassum, W. Germany 22/C2
Basswood, Manitoba 179/B4
Basswood (lake), Minn. 255/G2
Basswood (lake), Ontario 175/B3
Båstad, Sweden 18/H8
Bastak, Iran 66/J7
Bastam, Iran 66/J2
Bastar, India 68/E5
Bastelica, France 28/B6
Bastenaken (Bastogne), Belgium 27/H9
Bastia, France 7/E4
Bastia, France 28/B6
Bastian, Va. (24314) 307/F6
Bastimentos (isl.), Panama 154/G6
Bastogne, Belgium 27/H9
Bastrop, La. (71220) 238/G1
Bastrop (co.), Texas 303/G7
Bastrop, Texas (78602) 303/G7
Bastuträsk, Sweden 18/L4
Basye, Va. (22810) 307/L3
Bas-Zaïre (prov.), Zaire 115/B4
Bata, Equat. Guinea 102/C4
Bata, Equat. Guinea 115/B3
Bataan (prov.), Philippines 82/C3
Batabanó (gulf), Cuba 158/C2
Batabanó (gulf), Cuba 156/A2
Batag (isl.), Philippines 82/E4
Batagay, U.S.S.R. 48/O3
Batala, India 68/D2
Batalha, Brazil 132/F3
Batalha, Portugal 33/B3
Batan (isls.), Philippines 54/O7
Batan, Albay (isl.), Philippines 82/E4
Batan, Batanes (isl.), Philippines 82/B2
Batan (isls.), Philippines 85/G1
Batan (isls.), Philippines 82/A2
Batanes (prov.), Philippines 82/A2
Batang, China 77/E5
Batang, China 54/L6
Batang, Indonesia 85/J2
Batangafo, Cent. Afr. Rep. 115/C2
Batangas (prov.), Philippines 82/C4
Batangas, Philippines 82/C4
Batangas, Philippines 85/G3
Batas (isl.), Philippines 82/B5
Bátaszék, Hungary 41/E3
Batatais, Brazil 135/C2
Batavia, Ill. (60510) 222/E2
Batavia (Jakarta) (cap.), Indonesia 85/H1
Batavia, Iowa (52533) 229/J7
Batavia, Mich. (†49036) 250/D7
Batavia, N.Y. (14020) 276/D5
Batavia, Ohio (45103) 284/B7
Batavia, Wis. (†53001) 317/K8
Batawa, Ontario 177/G3
Bataysk, U.S.S.R. 52/E5
Bat Cave, N.C. (28710) 281/E4
Batchelor, La. (70715) 238/G5
Batchelor, North. Terr. 93/B2
Batchtown, Ill. (62006) 222/C4
Batchwana Bay, Ontario 177/J5
Batdambang, Cambodia 54/M8
Batdambang (Battambang), Cambodia 72/D4
Bateman, Sask. 181/E5
Batemans Bay, N.S. Wales 97/F4
Bates, Ark. (72924) 202/B4
Bates, Mich. (†49690) 250/D4
Bates (co.), Mo. 261/D6
Bates (mt.), Norfolk I. 88/L5
Bates, Oreg. (97817) 291/J3
Batesburg, S.C. (29006) 296/D4
Bates City, Mo. (64011) 261/E5
Batesland, S. Dak. (57716) 298/E7
Batesville, Ala. (†36018) 195/H6
Batesville, Ark. (72501) 202/G2
Batesville, Ind. (47006) 227/G6
Batesville, Miss. (38606) 256/E2
Batesville, Ohio (43715) 284/H6
Batesville, Texas (78829) 303/E9
Batesville, Va. (22924) 307/L5
Bath, England 13/E6
Bath, England 10/E5
Bath, Ill. (62617) 222/C3
Bath, Ind. (47010) 227/H5
Bath, Jamaica 158/K6
Bath (co.), Ky. 237/O4
Bath, Maine (04530) 243/D8
Bath, Mich. (48808) 250/E6
Bath, Netherlands 27/E6
Bath, New Bruns. 170/C2
Bath○, N.H. (03740) 268/D3
Bath, N.Y. (14810) 276/F6
Bath, N.C. (27808) 281/R4
Bath, Ontario 177/H3
Bath, Pa. (18014) 294/M4
Bath, S.C. (29816) 296/D5
Bath, S. Dak. (57427) 298/N3
Bath (co.), Va. 307/J4
Bath (Berkeley Springs), W. Va. (†25411) 312/K3
Batha (riv.), Chad 111/C5
Bathgate, N. Dak. (58216) 282/P2
Bathgate, Scotland 15/C2
Bathgate, Scotland 10/C1
Bathsheba, Barbados 161/B8
Bath Springs, Tenn. (38311) 237/E10
Bathurst (isl.), Australia 87/C7
Bathurst (isl.), Canada 4/B14
Bathurst (Banjul)(cap.), Gambia 106/A6
Bathurst, N. Br. 162/K6
Bathurst, New Bruns. 170/E1
Bathurst, N. S. Wales 88/H6
Bathurst, N.S. Wales 97/E3
Bathurst (isl.), North Terr. 88/D2
Bathurst (isl.), North Terr. 93/A1
Bathurst (isl.), N.W.T. 162/F1
Bathurst (isl.), N.W.T. 146/H2
Bathurst (cape), N.W.T. 162/D1
Bathurst (cape), N.W.Terrs. 187/F2
Bathurst (inlet), N.W. Terrs. 187/H3
Bathurst (isl.), N.W. Terrs. 187/H2
Bathurst (harb.), Tasmania 99/C5
Bathurst Inlet, N.W. Terrs. 187/H3
Bathurst Island, North. Terr. 93/B1
Bathurst Island Mission, North. Terr. 88/E2
Bathurst Mines, New Bruns. 170/E1
Batié, Upper Volta 106/D7
Batı Fırat (riv.), Turkey 63/H3
Batin, Wadi al (dry riv.), Iraq 59/E4
Batin, Wadi al (dry riv.), Iraq 66/E6
Batin, Wadi al (dry riv.), Saudi Arabia 59/E4
Batina (reg.), Oman 59/G5
Batini (mt.), Fiji 86/Q10
Batiscan, Québec 172/E3
Batiscan (lake), Québec 172/E2
Batiscan (riv.), Québec 172/E2
Batley, England 13/J1
Batlow, N.S. Wales 97/E4
Batman, Turkey 63/J4
Batna, Algeria 102/C1
Batna, Algeria 106/F1
Bato, Catanduanes, Philippines 82/E4
Bato, Leyte, Philippines 82/E5
Bato-Bato, Philippines 82/C8
Batobato, Philippines 82/E7
Batoche, Sask. 181/E3
Batoche Nat'l Hist. Site, Sask. 181/E3
Baton Rouge (cap.), La. 146/J6
Baton Rouge (cap.), La. 188/H4
Baton Rouge (cap.), La. (*70801) 238/K2
Batopilas, Mexico 150/F3
Batouri, Cameroon 115/B3
Batovi, Uruguay 145/D2
Batrun, Lebanon 63/F5
Bat Shelomo, Israel 65/B2
Batson, Texas (77519) 303/K7
Batsto, N.J. (08037) 273/D4
Batsto (riv.), N.J. 273/D4
Batten Kill (riv.), N.Y. 276/O4
Batten Kill (riv.), Vt. 268/A5
Batterbee (cape), Ant. 2/N9
Batterbee (cape) 5/C3
Bätterkinden, Switzerland 39/E2
Battersea, Ontario 177/H3
Batticaloa, Sri Lanka 68/E7
Battiest, Okla. (74722) 288/S6
Batti Malv (isl.), India 68/G7
Battle (riv.) 162/E5
Battle (riv.), Alberta 182/D3
Battle, England 13/H7
Battle, England 10/G5
Battle (creek), Idaho 220/B7
Battle (riv.), Minn. 255/D3
Battle (creek), Mont. 262/G1
Battle (creek), Oreg. 291/K5
Battle (creek), Sask. 181/B6
Battle (riv.), Sask. 181/B3
Battle (creek), S. Dak. 298/C6
Battleboro, N.C. (27809) 281/O2
Battle Creek, Iowa (51006) 229/B4
Battle Creek, Mich. 188/J2
Battle Creek, Mich. (*49014) 250/D6
Battle Creek, Nebr. (68715) 264/G3
Battlefield, Mo. (†65619) 261/F8
Battleford, Sask. 162/E5
Battleford, Sask. 181/C3
Battle Ground, Ind. (47920) 227/D3
Battle Ground, Wash. (98604) 310/C5
Battle Harbour, Newf. 166/C3
Battle Harbour, Newf. 162/L5
Battle Lake, Alberta 182/C3
Battle Lake, Minn. (56515) 255/C4
Battle Mountain, Nev. (89820) 266/E2
Battles Wharf, Ala. (†36532) 195/C10
Battletown, Ky. (40104) 237/J4
Battleview, N. Dak. (58714) 282/E2
Battock (mt.), Scotland 15/F4
Battonya, Hungary 41/F3
Battrum, Sask. 181/C5
Batu (isls.), Indonesia 85/B6
Batuco, Chile 138/G3
Batu Gajah, Malaysia 72/D6
Batulaki, Philippines 82/E8
Batumi, U.S.S.R. 48/E5
Batumi, U.S.S.R. 52/F6
Batu Pahat, Malaysia 72/D7
Baturaja, Indonesia 85/C6
Baturité, Brazil 132/G4
Batusangkar, Indonesia 85/C6
Bat Yam, Israel 65/B3
Bauang, Philippines 82/C2
Baubau, Indonesia 85/G7
Bauchi (state), Nigeria 106/F6
Bauchi, Nigeria 106/F6
Baudette, Minn. (56623) 255/D2
Baudette (riv.), Minn. 255/D2
Baudh, India 68/E4
Baudó, Serranía de (mts.), Colombia 126/B5
Baudó (riv.), Colombia 126/B5
Baugé, France 28/D4
Bauld (cape), Newf. 166/C3
Bauld (cape), Newf. 162/L5
Bauline, Newf. 166/D2
Baulkham Hills, N. S. Wales 88/K4
Baulkham Hills, N.S. Wales 97/H3
Baulmes, Switzerland 39/C3
Bauma, Switzerland 39/G2
Baumann (fjord), N.W. Terrs. 187/K2
Baume-les-Dames, France 28/G4
Baures, Bolivia 136/D3
Baures (riv.), Bolivia 136/D3
Bauria, India 68/E2
Baurtregaum (mt.), Ireland 17/A7
Bauru, Brazil 120/E5
Bauru, Brazil 135/B3
Bauru, Brazil 132/D8
Bauska, U.S.S.R. 53/B2
Bauta, Cuba 158/C1
Bauta (riv.), P. Rico 161/C2
Bautzen, E. Germany 22/F3
Bauxite, Ark. (72011) 202/F4
Bavaria, Kansas (67419) 232/E3
Bavaria (state), W. Germany 22/D4
Bavarian (for.), W. Germany 22/E4
Bavarian Alps (mts.), Austria 41/A3
Bavarian Alps (range), W. Germany 22/D5
Baviácora, Mexico 150/E2
Bavispe, Mexico 150/E1
Bavispe, Río de (riv.), Mexico 150/E1
Bawean (isl.), Indonesia 85/K1
Bawku, Ghana 106/D6
Bawlf, Alberta 182/D3
Ba Xian, China 77/J4
Baxley, Georgia (31513) 217/H7
Baxoi, China 77/E5
Baxter (co.), Ark. 202/F1
Baxter, Iowa (50028) 229/G5
Baxter, Minn. (†56401) 255/D4
Baxter, Miss. (†39343) 256/F6
Baxter, Pa. (†15829) 294/D3
Baxter, Tenn. (38544) 237/K8
Baxter Springs, Kansas (66713) 232/H4
Baxterville, Miss. (†39455) 256/E8

Blandburg 339

Big Spencer (mt.), Maine 243/E4
Big Spring, Georgia (†30240) 217/C5
Big Spring, Ky. (40106) 237/J5
Big Spring, Md. (21722) 245/G2
Big Spring, Tenn. (37323) 237/M10
Big Spring, Texas 188/F4
Big Spring, Texas (79720) 303/C5
Big Springs, Nebr. (69122) 264/B3
Big Springs, S. Dak. (†57001) 298/S8
Big Springs, W. Va. (26137) 312/D5
Big Star (lake), Mich. 250/C5
Bigstick (lake), Sask. 181/B5
Big Stone, Alberta 182/E4
Bigstone (lake), Manitoba 179/J3
Bigstone (pt.), Manitoba 179/E2
Bigstone (riv.), Manitoba 179/J3
Big Stone (co.), Minn. 255/B5
Big Stone (lake), Minn. 255/B5
Big Stone (lake), S. Dak. 298/R3
Big Stone City, S. Dak. (57216) 298/S3
Big Stone Gap, Va. (24219) 307/C7
Big Sur, Calif. (93920) 204/D7
Big Thicket Nat'l Preserve, Texas 303/K7
Big Thompson (riv.), Colo. 208/H2
Big Timber, Mont. (59011) 262/G5
Big Timber (creek), N.J. 273/C4
Big Tracadie (riv.), New Bruns. 170/E1
Bigtrails, Wyo. (†82442) 319/E2
Big Trout (lake), Ontario 177/F2
Big Trout (lake), Ontario 175/B2
Big Trout Lake, Ontario 175/C2
Big Valley, Alberta 182/D3
Big Walnut (creek), Ind. 227/D5
Big Walnut (creek), Ohio 284/E5
Big Wells, Texas (78830) 303/E9
Big Whiteshell Lake, Manitoba 179/G4
Big Wood (riv.), Idaho 220/D6
Bihać, Yugoslavia 45/B3
Bihar (state), India 68/F4
Bihar, India 68/F3
Biharamulo, Tanzania 115/F4
Biharkeresztes, Hungary 41/F3
Biharnagybajom, Hungary 41/F3
Bijagós (isls.), Guinea-Biss. 106/A6
Bijagós (isls.), Guinea-Biss. 102/A3
Bijapur, Karnataka, India 68/D5
Bijapur, Madhya Pradesh, India 68/E5
Bijar, Iran 66/E3
Bijeljina, Yugoslavia 45/D3
Bijelo Polje, Yugoslavia 45/D4
Bijiang, China 77/E6
Bijie, China 77/G6
Bijnor, India 68/D3
Bijou (creek), Colo. 208/L3
Bijou Hills, S. Dak. (†57310) 298/L6
Bikaner, India 54/J7
Bikaner, India 68/C3
Bikar (atoll), Marshall Is. 87/H4
Bikin, U.S.S.R. 48/O5
Bikini (atoll), Marshall Is. 87/G4
Bikoro, Zaire 115/C4
Bikoro, Zaire 102/D5
Bilaspur, India 68/E4
Bilauktaung (range), Burma 72/C4
Bilauktaung (range), Thailand 72/C4
Bilbao, Spain 33/E1
Bilbao, Spain 7/D4
Bileća, Yugoslavia 45/D4
Bilecik (prov.), Turkey 63/D2
Bilecik, Turkey 59/A1
Bilecik, Turkey 63/D2
Biłgoraj, Poland 47/F3
Bilibino, U.S.S.R. 4/C1
Bilibino, U.S.S.R. 48/R3
Bilin, Burma 72/C3
Bílina, Czech. 41/B1
Biliran (isl.), Philippines 82/E5
Bill, Wyo. (82631) 319/G2
Billate (riv.), Ethiopia 111/G6
Billerica○, Mass. (01821) 249/J2
Billings (lake), Conn. 210/H2
Billings, Mo. (65610) 261/F8
Billings, Mont. 146/H5
Billings, Mont. 188/E1
Billings, Mont. (*59101) 262/H5
Billings (co.), N. Dak. 282/D5
Billings, Okla. (74630) 288/M1
Billingsgate (isl.), Mass. 249/O5
Billingshurst, England 13/G6
Billingsley, Ala. (36006) 195/E5
Billiton (isl.), Indonesia 54/M10
Billiton (isl.), Indonesia 85/D6
Bill Williams (riv.), Ariz. 198/B4
Billy Clapp (lake), Wash. 310/F3
Bilma, Niger 102/D3
Bilma, Niger 106/G5
Biloela, Queensland 88/J4
Biloela, Queensland 95/D5
Biloku, Guyana 131/B5
Biloxi, Miss. 146/K6
Biloxi, Miss. 188/J4
Biloxi, Miss. (*39530) 256/G10
Biltine, Chad 111/D5
Biltine, Chad 102/D3
Biltmore Forest, N.C. (†28803) 281/E3
Bilwaskarma, Nicaragua 154/F3
Bilzen, Belgium 27/G7
Bim, W. Va. (25021) 312/C7
Biminis, The (isls.), Bahamas 156/B1
Bina-Itawa, India 68/D4
Binalbagan, Philippines 82/D5
Binalong, N.S. Wales 97/E4
Binboğa (mts.), Turkey 63/G3
Binbrook, Ontario 177/E4
Binche, Belgium 27/E8
Binda, N.S. Wales 97/E4
Bindloss, Alberta 182/E4
Bindoon, W. Australia 92/B1
Bindura, Zimbabwe 118/E3
Binéfar, Spain 33/G2
Binevenagh (mt.), N. Ireland 17/H1
Binford, N. Dak. (58416) 282/O4
Binga (mt.), Mozambique 118/E3
Bingara, N.S. Wales 97/F1
Bingen, Wash. (98605) 310/D5
Bingen, W. Germany 22/B4
Binger, Okla. (73009) 288/K4
Bingerville, Ivory Coast 106/D7
Bingham (co.), Idaho 220/F6
Bingham, Ill. (62011) 222/D4
Bingham, Maine (04920) 243/D5
Bingham○, Maine (04920) 243/D5
Bingham, Nebr. (69335) 264/B2
Bingham, N. Mex. (87815) 274/C5
Bingham, S.C. (†29565) 296/H3
Bingham Lake, Minn. (56118) 255/C7
Binghamton, N.Y. 188/L2
Binghamton, N.Y. (*13901) 276/J6
Bingöl (prov.), Turkey 63/J3
Bingöl (Çapakçur), Turkey 63/J3
Bingöl Dağları (mts.), Turkey 63/J3
Binhai, China 77/K5
Binh Long (An Loc), Vietnam 72/E5
Binh Son, Vietnam 72/F4
Binjai, Indonesia 85/B5
Binn, Switzerland 39/F4
Binnaway, N.S. Wales 97/E2
Binningen, Switzerland 39/D1
Binongko (isl.), Indonesia 85/G7
Binscarth, Manitoba 179/A4
Bintan (isl.), Indonesia 85/C5
Bintuhan, Indonesia 85/C6
Bintulu, Malaysia 85/E5
Binyamina, Israel 65/B2
Binyang, China 77/G7
Biobío (reg.), Chile 138/E1
Bío-Bío (riv.), Chile 138/E2
Biograd, Yugoslavia 45/B4
Bioko (isl.), Equat. Guinea 102/C4
Bioko (terr.), Equat. Guinea 115/A3
Bioko (isl.), Equat. Guinea 115/A3
Biola, Calif. (93606) 204/E7
Bippus, Ind. (46713) 227/F3
Bir, India 68/D5
Bira, U.S.S.R. 48/O5
Birag, Kuh-e (mts.), Iran 66/M7
Bir 'Ali, P.D.R. Yemen 59/E7
Birama (pt.), Cuba 158/G4
Birao, Cent. Afr. Rep. 115/D1
Biratnagar, Nepal 68/F3
Biratori, Japan 81/L2
Bir Bala, Iran 66/L8
Bir Bala, Iran 59/G4
Bircao, Somalia 115/H4
Birch (creek), Alaska 196/J1
Birch (hills), Alberta 182/A2
Birch (lake), Alberta 182/E3
Birch (mts.), Alberta 182/B5
Birch (riv.), Alberta 182/B5
Birch (creek), Idaho 220/F5
Birch (isl.), Manitoba 179/C2
Birch (lake), Minn. 255/G3
Birch (creek), Mont. 262/D2
Birch (lake), Sask. 181/C2
Birch (creek), Utah 304/B5
Birch (pt.), Wash. 310/C2
Birch Creek, Alaska (†99740) 196/J1
Birch Creek (valley), Idaho 220/E5
Birch Creek (res.), Mont. 262/D2
Birchdale, Minn. (56629) 255/D2
Birch Harbor, Maine (04613) 243/H7
Birch Hills, Sask. 181/F3
Birchip, Victoria 97/B4
Birch Island, Br. Col. 184/H4
Birchleaf, Va. (24220) 307/D6
Birch River, Manitoba 179/A2
Birch River, W. Va. (26610) 312/E6
Birch Run, Mich. (48415) 250/F5
Birchtown, Nova Scotia 168/C5
Birch Tree, Mo. (65438) 261/K9
Birchwood, Md. (†20021) 245/F5
Birchwood, Tenn. (37308) 237/M10
Birchwood, Wis. (54817) 317/C4
Birchy Bay, Newf. 166/D4
Bird (isl.), La. 238/M8
Bird (creek), Okla. 288/O1
Bird City, Kansas (67731) 232/A2
Bird Cove, Newf. 166/C3
Bird Island, Minn. (55310) 255/D6
Birds, Ill. (62415) 222/F5
Birdsboro, Pa. (19508) 294/L5
Birdseye, Ind. (47513) 227/D8
Birds Hill, Manitoba 179/F4
Birdsnest, Va. (23307) 307/S6
Birdsong, Ark. (†72386) 202/K3
Birdsville, Ky. (†42081) 237/D6
Birdsville, Queensland 88/F5
Birdsville, Queensland 95/A5
Birdtail, Manitoba 179/B4
Birdum, North. Terr. 93/C3
Birdwood, S. Australia 94/C7
Birecik, Turkey 63/H4
Bir el Khzaim (well), Mauritania 106/C4
Bireuen, Indonesia 85/B4
Bir Ganduz (well), Western Sahara 106/A4
Birganj, Nepal 68/F3
Bir Hakeim (ruins), Libya 111/D1
Birigui, Brazil 135/A2
Birjand, Iran 66/L4
Birjand, Iran 59/G3
Birjand, Iran 54/G6
Birken, Br. Col. 184/F5
Birkenfeld, Oreg. (97016) 291/D1
Birkenfeld, W. Germany 22/B4
Birkenhead, England 13/G2
Birkenhead, England 10/F2
Birkenhead, N. Zealand 100/B1
Birkenhead Lake Prov. Park, Br. Col. 184/F5
Birkerød, Denmark 21/F6
Birket Qârûn (lake), Egypt 111/J3
Bir Ksaib Ounane (well), Mali 106/C4
Birksgate (range), S. Australia 94/A2
Bîrlad, Romania 45/H2
Bîrlad (riv.), Romania 45/H2
Birmingham, Ala. 146/K6
Birmingham, Ala. 188/J4
Birmingham, Ala. 195/D3
Birmingham, England 7/D3
Birmingham, England 10/G3
Birmingham, England 13/F5
Birmingham, Iowa (52535) 229/K7
Birmingham, Mich. (*48008) 250/B6
Birmingham, Mo. (†64068) 261/R5
Birmingham, N.J. (08011) 273/D4
Birmingham, Ohio (44816) 284/F3
Birmingham, Pa. (†16686) 294/F4
Birmingham, Sask. 181/H5
Birmitrapur, India 68/E4
Bir Mogreïn, Mauritania 106/B3
Birnam, Scotland 15/E4
Birnamwood, Wis. (54414) 317/H6
Birney, Mont. (59012) 262/K5
Birnie, Manitoba 179/C4
Birnin Kebbi, Nigeria 106/E6
Birni-N'Konni, Niger 106/E6
Birni-N'Konni, Niger 102/C3
Bir Nzaran (well), Western Sahara 106/B4
Birobidzhan, U.S.S.R. 54/O5
Birobidzhan, U.S.S.R. 48/O5
Biron, Wis. (†54494) 317/G7
Bir Ounane (well), Mali 106/D4
Birqin, West Bank 65/C3
Birr, Ireland 17/F5
Birr, Ireland 10/B4
Birregurra, Victoria 97/B6
Birrie (riv.), N. S. Wales 88/H5
Birrie (riv.), N.S. Wales 97/D1
Birrimbah, North. Terr. 93/C3
Birrindudu, North. Terr. 93/A5
Birriwa, N.S. Wales 97/E3
Birs (riv.), Switzerland 39/D2
Birsay, Sask. 181/D4
Birsk, U.S.S.R. 52/J3
Birta, Ark. (†72853) 202/D3
Bir Taba, Egypt 59/B4
Bir Taba (well), Egypt 111/F2
Birtle, Manitoba 179/B4
Biru, China 77/D5
Biruaca, Venezuela 124/E4
Biruni, U.S.S.R. 48/G5
Biržai, U.S.S.R. 53/C2
Bir Zeit, West Bank 65/C4
Bisbee, Ariz. 188/E4
Bisbee, Ariz. (85603) 198/F7
Bisbee, N. Dak. (58317) 282/M2
Biscarrosse (lake), France 28/C5
Biscay (bay) 2/J3
Biscay (bay) 7/D4
Biscay (bay), France 28/B5
Biscay, Minn. (†55336) 255/D6
Biscay (bay), Spain 33/E1
Biscay Bay (riv.), Newf. 166/D2
Biscayne (bay), Fla. 212/F6
Biscayne (key), Fla. 212/B5
Biscayne Nat'l Park, Fla. 212/F6
Biscayne Park, Fla. (33152) 212/B4
Bisceglie, Italy 34/F4
Bischofshofen, Austria 41/B3
Bischofswerda, E. Germany 22/F3
Bischofszell, Switzerland 39/H1
Biscoe (isls.) 5/C15
Biscoe, Ark. (72017) 202/H4
Biscoe, N.C. (27209) 281/K4
Biscotasing, Ontario 177/J5
Biscotasing, Ontario 175/D3
Biscucuy, Venezuela 124/D3
Bisha, Saudi Arabia 59/D5
Bisha, Wadi (dry riv.), Saudi Arabia 59/D5
Bishiara (well), Libya 111/D3
Bisho (cap.), Ciskei, S. Africa 102/E8
Bishop, Calif. (93514) 204/G6
Bishop, Georgia (30621) 217/F3
Bishop, Md. (†21813) 245/S7
Bishop (creek), Nev. 266/F1
Bishop, Texas (78343) 303/G10
Bishop (creek), Utah 304/A3
Bishop, Va. (24604) 307/E6
Bishop Auckland, England 10/E3
Bishop Auckland, England 13/E3
Bishopbriggs, Scotland 15/B2
Bishop Hill, Ill. (61419) 222/C2
Bishopric, Sask. 181/F5
Bishop's Falls, Newf. 166/C4
Bishops Head, Md. (21611) 245/O7
Bishops Mitre (mt.), Newf. 166/B2
Bishop's Stortford, England 10/G5
Bishop's Stortford, England 13/H6
Bishopton, Québec 172/F4
Bishopton, Scotland 15/B2
Bishopville, Md. (21813) 245/T7
Bishopville, S.C. (29010) 296/G3
Bishri, Jebel el (mts.), Syria 63/H5
Biskra, Algeria 106/F2
Biskra, Algeria 102/C1
Biskupiec, Poland 47/E2
Bislig, Philippines 85/H4
Bislig, Philippines 82/F6
Bismarck, Ark. (71929) 202/D5
Bismarck, Ill. (61814) 222/F3
Bismarck, Mo. (63624) 261/L7
Bismarck (cap.), N. Dak. 146/H5
Bismarck (cap.), N. Dak. 188/G1
Bismarck (cap.), N. Dak. (58501) 282/J6
Bismarck (arch.), Papua N.G. 87/E6
Bismarck (arch.), Papua N.G. 86/B1
Bismarck (sea), Papua N.G. 86/B1
Bismarck (arch.), Papua N.G. 2/S6
Bismarck, W. Va. (†26739) 312/H4
Bismil, Turkey 63/J4
Bison (lake), Alberta 182/B1
Bison, Kansas (67520) 232/C3
Bison, Okla. (73720) 288/L2
Bison, S. Dak. (57620) 298/E2
Bispgården, Sweden 18/K5
Bissau (cap.), Guinea-Biss. 106/A6
Bissau (cap.), Guinea-Biss. 102/A3
Bissett, Manitoba 179/G4
Bistineau (lake), La. 238/D2
Bistriţa, Romania 45/G2
Bita (riv.), Colombia 126/F5
Bitagron, Suriname 131/C3
Bitam, Gabon 115/B3
Bitburg, W. Germany 22/B4
Bitely, Mich. (49309) 250/D5
Bithlo, Fla. (†32801) 212/E3
Bitkine, Chad 111/C5
Bitlis (prov.), Turkey 63/J3
Bitlis, Turkey 63/J3
Bitlis, Turkey 59/D2
Bitola, Yugoslavia 45/E5
Bitola, Yugoslavia 7/G4
Bitonto, Italy 34/F4
Bitter (lakes), Egypt 111/K3
Bitter (lake), Sask. 181/B6
Bitter (creek), Wyo. 319/C4
Bitter Creek, Wyo. (†82901) 319/D4
Bitterfeld, E. Germany 22/E3
Bitterfontein, S. Africa 118/B6
Bittern (lake), Alberta 182/D3
Bittern Lake, Alberta 182/D3
Bitterroot (range) 188/D1
Bitterroot (range), Idaho 220/D3
Bitterroot (range), Mont. 262/B4
Bitterroot (riv.), Mont. 262/B4
Bitterroot (range), U.S. 146/G5
Bitti, Italy 34/B4
Bitumount, Alberta 182/E1
Bitung, Indonesia 85/H5
Biu, Nigeria 106/G6
Biu (plat.), Nigeria 106/G6
Bivalve, Md. (21814) 245/P7
Bivalve, N.J. (08301) 273/C5
Bivolari, Romania 45/H2
Biwa (lake), Japan 81/H6
Biwabik, Minn. (55708) 255/F3
Bixby, Minn. (55916) 255/E7
Bixby, Mo. (65439) 261/K7
Bixby, Okla. (74008) 288/P3
Biyang, China 77/H5
Biysk, U.S.S.R. 54/K4
Biysk, U.S.S.R. 48/J4
Bizcocho, Uruguay 145/B4
Bizerte, Tunisia 106/F1
Bizerte, Tunisia 102/C1
Bjargtangar (pt.), Iceland 21/A1
Bjelovar, Yugoslavia 45/C3
Bjerringbro, Denmark 21/C5
Bjorkdale, Sask. 181/H3
Bjørnafjorden (fjord), Norway 18/D6
Bjorne (pen.), N.W. Terrs. 187/K2
Bjørnøya (isl.), Norway 18/D3
Blabon, N. Dak. (†58046) 282/P5
Blachly, Oreg. (97412) 291/D3
Black (sea) 2/L3
Black (sea) 54/E5
Black (sea) 7/H4
Black, Ala. (36314) 195/G8
Black (riv.), Alaska 196/K1
Black (mesa), Ariz. 198/E2
Black (mts.), Ariz. 198/A3
Black (riv.), Ariz. 198/E5
Black (riv.), Ark. 202/H2
Black (sea), Bulgaria 45/J4
Black (pond), Conn. 210/G1
Black (pt.), Conn. 210/G3
Black (mts.), England 13/D6
Black (creek), Fla. 212/E1
Black (head), Ireland 17/C5
Black (riv.), Jamaica 158/H6
Black (mt.), Ky. 237/R7
Black (lake), La. 238/D3
Black (pond), Maine 243/D3
Black (isl.), Manitoba 179/F3
Black (riv.), Manitoba 179/F4
Black (lake), Mich. 250/E3
Black (riv.), Mich. 250/E3
Black (riv.), Mich. 250/G5
Black (riv.), Minn. 255/D2
Black (creek), Miss. 256/F8
Black, Mo. (63625) 261/L7
Black (riv.), Mo. 261/L10
Black (mt.), N. Mex. 274/A6
Black (range), N. Mex. 274/B5
Black (lake), N.Y. 276/J1
Black (riv.), N.Y. 276/K3
Black (riv.), N.C. 281/N5
Black (riv.), Ohio 284/F3
Black (riv.), Ontario 177/E3
Black (sea), Romania 45/J4
Black (lake), Sask. 181/M2
Black (riv.), S.C. 296/H4
Black (sea), Turkey 63/E1
Black (sea), U.S.S.R. 48/D5
Black (sea), U.S.S.R. 52/D6
Black (creek), Vt. 268/B2
Black (riv.), Vt. 268/C2
Black (riv.), Vt. 268/B5
Black (riv.), Vietnam 72/D2
Black (mts.), Wales 13/D6
Black (for.), W. Germany 22/C4
Black (riv.), Wis. 317/E7
Black (riv.), Yukon 187/D3
Blackall, Australia 87/E8
Blackall, Queensland 88/H4
Blackall, Queensland 95/C5
Black Bear (creek), Okla. 288/M2
Blackberry (riv.), Conn. 210/B1
Blackbird, Del. (†19734) 245/R3
Blackbourne (pt.), Norfolk I. 88/L6
Black Branch, Nulhegan (riv.), Vt. 268/D2
Blackburn (mt.), Alaska 196/K2
Blackburn, England 13/H1
Blackburn, England 10/G1
Blackburn, La. (†71038) 238/D1
Blackburn, Mo. (65321) 261/F4
Blackburn, Okla. (74058) 288/N2
Blackburn, Ontario 177/J2
Blackburn, Scotland 15/C2
Black Butte (lake), Calif. 204/C4
Black Canyon City, Ariz. (85324) 198/C4
Black Canyon of the Gunnison Nat'l Mon., Colo. 208/D5
Black Creek, Br. Col. 184/E5
Black Creek, N.C. (27813) 281/O3
Black Creek, Wis. (54106) 317/K7
Black Diamond, Alberta 182/C4
Black Diamond, Wash. (98010) 310/D3
Blackduck, Minn. (56630) 255/D3
Black Duck (riv.), Ontario 175/C1
Black Eagle, Mont. (59414) 262/E3
Black Earth, Wis. (53515) 317/G9
Black Elster (riv.), E. Germany 22/E3
Blackey, Ky. (41804) 237/R6
Blackfalds, Alberta 182/D3
Blackfeet Ind. Res., Mont. 262/D2
Blackfoot, Alberta 182/E3
Blackfoot, Idaho (83221) 220/F6
Blackfoot (res.), Idaho 220/G7
Blackfoot (riv.), Idaho 220/G6
Blackfoot, Mont. (59415) 262/D2
Blackfoot (riv.), Mont. 262/C4
Blackford (co.), Ind. 227/G4
Blackford, Ky. (42403) 237/F6
Blackford, Scotland 15/E4
Black Forest, Colo. (80908) 208/K4
Blackfork, Ohio (45615) 284/E8
Black Fork, Mohican (riv.), Ohio 284/F4
Blackgum, Okla. (†74962) 288/S3
Black Hall, Conn. (†06371) 210/F3
Black Hawk, Colo. (80422) 208/J3
Blackhawk, Ind. (†47866) 227/C6
Black Hawk (co.), Iowa 229/J4
Black Hawk, Miss. (†38917) 256/E4
Black Hawk, S. Dak. (57718) 298/C5
Blackhead (bay), Newf. 166/D2
Blackhead Road, Newf. 166/D2
Black Hills (mts.) 188/F2
Black Hills (mts.), S. Dak. 298/B5
Blackie, Alberta 182/D4
Black Isle (pen.), Scotland 15/D3
Black Jack, Mo. (†63031) 261/R1
Black Lake (bayou), La. 238/D1
Black Lake, Québec 172/F3
Black Lake, Sask. 181/M2
Blackledge (riv.), Conn. 210/F2
Black Lick, Pa. (15716) 294/D4
Blacklock (pt.), Oreg. 291/C5
Black Mesa (mt.), Okla. 288/A1
Blackmore (mt.), Mont. 262/F5
Black Mountain, N.C. (28711) 281/E3
Black Oak, Ark. (72414) 202/K2
Black Oak, Ind. (†46406) 227/C1
Black Pine (mts.), Idaho 220/E7
Black Pine (peak), Idaho 220/E7
Black Pine (creek), S. Dak. 298/G6
Black Point, Calif. (†94947) 204/J1
Black Point, Conn. (†06357) 210/G3
Black Point, New Bruns. 170/D1
Blackpool, England 13/G1
Blackpool, England 10/F1
Blackridge, Va. (23916) 307/M7
Black River, Jamaica 158/H6
Black River, Jamaica 156/B3
Black River (bay), Jamaica 158/G6
Black River, Mich. (48721) 250/F4
Black River, New Bruns. 170/E3
Black River (pond), Newf. 166/C2
Black River, N.Y. (13612) 276/J3
Black River Bridge, New Bruns. 170/E2
Black River Falls, Wis. (54615) 317/E7
Black Rock, Ark. (72415) 202/H1
Black Rock (des.), Nev. 266/B2
Black Rock (range), Nev. 266/B1
Black Rock (pt.), R.I. 249/H8
Black Rock, Utah (†84751) 304/B5
Blacksburg, S.C. (29702) 296/D1
Blacksburg, Va. (24060) 307/H6
Blacks Fork, Green (riv.), Wyo. 319/C4
Blacks Harbour, New Bruns. 170/D3
Blackshear, Georgia (31516) 217/H8
Blackshear (lake), Georgia 217/E7
Blacksher, Ala. (†36507) 195/C8
Blacksod (bay), Ireland 17/A3
Black Springs, Ark. (†71960) 202/C5
Black Springs, Nev. (†89508) 266/B3
Black Squirrel (creek), Colo. 208/L5
Blackstairs (mt.), Ireland 17/H6
Blackstock, Ontario 177/F3
Blackstock, S.C. (29014) 296/E2
Blackstone○, Mass. (01504) 249/H4
Blackstone (riv.), Mass. 249/G3
Blackstone, Va. (23824) 307/N6
Blacksville, W. Va. (26521) 312/F3
Black Thunder (creek), Wyo. 319/G2
Black Tickle, Newf. 166/C3
Blackton, Ark. (†72069) 202/H4
Blacktown, N. S. Wales 88/K4
Blacktown, N.S. Wales 97/H3
Blackville, New Bruns. 170/E2
Blackville, S.C. (29817) 296/E5
Black Volta (riv.) 102/B3
Black Volta (riv.), Ghana 106/D6
Black Volta (riv.), Ivory Coast 106/D6
Black Volta (riv.), Upper Volta 106/D6
Black Warrior (riv.), Ala. 195/C5
Blackwater (riv.), England 13/H6
Blackwater (riv.), Fla. 212/B6
Blackwater, Ireland 17/J7
Blackwater (riv.), Ireland 10/B4
Blackwater (riv.), Ireland 17/D7
Blackwater (riv.), Ireland 17/H4
Blackwater, Mo. (65322) 261/G5
Blackwater (res.), N.H. 268/D5
Blackwater (riv.), N. Ireland 17/H3
Blackwater, Queensland 95/D4
Blackwater, Queensland 88/H4
Blackwater (res.), Scotland 15/D4
Blackwater, Va. (24221) 307/B7
Blackwater (riv.), Va. 307/J6
Blackwater (riv.), Va. 307/O6
Blackwell, Ark. (72019) 202/E3
Blackwell (brook), Conn. 210/H1
Blackwell, Okla. (74631) 288/M1
Blackwell, Texas (79506) 303/D5
Blackwell, Wis. (†54541) 317/J4
Blackwood (Ngunju) (cape), Indonesia 85/F8
Blackwood, N.J. (08012) 273/C4
Blackwood Terrace, N.J. (†08096) 273/C4
Bladen, Nebr. (68928) 264/F4
Bladen (co.), N.C. 281/M5
Bladenboro, N.C. (28320) 281/M5
Bladensburg, Md. (20710) 245/G4
Bladensburg, Ohio (43005) 284/F5
Blades, Del. (†19973) 245/R6
Bladon Springs, Ala. (36902) 195/B7
Bladworth, Sask. 181/E4
Blaeberry, Br. Col. 184/J4
Blaenavon, Wales 13/B6
Blagodarnoye, U.S.S.R. 52/F5
Blagoevgrad, Bulgaria 45/F5
Blagoveshchensk, U.S.S.R. 54/O4
Blagoveshchensk, U.S.S.R. 48/N4
Blagoveshchensk, U.S.S.R. 52/J4
Blain, France 28/C4
Blain, Pa. (17006) 294/H5
Blaine, Georgia (†30175) 217/C1
Blaine (co.), Idaho 220/D6
Blaine, Kansas (66410) 232/F2
Blaine, Ky. (41124) 237/R4
Blaine○, Maine (04734) 243/H2
Blaine, Mich. (†48032) 250/G5
Blaine, Minn. (†55433) 255/G5
Blaine, Miss. (38727) 256/C3
Blaine (co.), Mont. 262/G2
Blaine (co.), Nebr. 264/E3
Blaine, Ohio (43909) 284/J5
Blaine (co.), Okla. 288/K3
Blaine, Oreg. (†97108) 291/D2
Blaine, Tenn. (37709) 237/O8
Blaine, Wash. (98230) 310/C2
Blaine Lake, Sask. 181/D3
Blaine-Mars Hill, Maine (04734) 243/H2
Blainville, Québec 172/H4
Blair, Kansas (†66090) 232/H2
Blair, Nebr. (68008) 264/H3
Blair, Okla. (73526) 288/H5
Blair (co.), Pa. 294/F4
Blair, S.C. (29015) 296/E3
Blair, W. Va. (25022) 312/C7
Blair, Wis. (54616) 317/D7
Blair Athol, Queensland 95/C4
Blair Atholl, Scotland 10/E2
Blair Atholl, Scotland 15/E4
Blairgowrie and Rattray, Scotland 15/E4
Blairgowrie and Rattray, Scotland 10/E2
Blairmore, Alberta 182/C5
Blairs, Va. (24527) 307/K7
Blairsburg, Iowa (50034) 229/F4
Blairsden, Calif. (96103) 204/E4
Blairs Mills, Ky. (41402) 237/P4
Blairs Mills, Pa. (17213) 294/G5
Blairstown, Iowa (52209) 229/J5
Blairstown, Mo. (64726) 261/E5
Blairstown○, N.J. (07825) 273/C2
Blairsville, Georgia (30512) 217/E1
Blairsville, Pa. (15717) 294/D5
Blaisdell, N. Dak. (58720) 282/F3
Blaj, Romania 45/F2
Blake (pt.), Mich. 250/E1
Blakeley, Minn. (†56011) 255/E6
Blakeley, W. Va. (†25160) 312/D6
Blakely, Georgia (31723) 217/C8
Blakely, Pa. (18447) 294/F6
Blakesburg, Iowa (52536) 229/H7
Blakeslee, Ohio (43505) 284/A2
Blakeslee, Pa. (18610) 294/L3
Blaketown, Newf. 166/D2
Blalock, Ala. (†36773) 195/D6
Blalock, Georgia (†30525) 217/E1
Blalock (isl.), Wash. 310/F5
Blanc (cape) 2/J4
Blanc (mt.), France 7/E4
Blanc (mt.), France 28/G5
Blanc (mt.), Italy 34/A2
Blanc (cape), Mauritania 102/A2
Blanc (cape), Mauritania 106/A4
Blanc (cape), Tunisia 106/G1
Blanc (cape), Western Sahara 106/A4
Blanca (bay), Argentina 120/C6
Blanca (bay), Argentina 143/D4
Blanca (lag.), Chile 138/E10
Blanca (peak), Colo. 188/F3
Blanca, Colo. (81123) 208/H8
Blanca (peak), Colo. 208/H7
Blanca (pt.), C. Rica 154/F5
Blanca, Cordillera (mts.), Peru 128/D7
Blanch, N.C. (27212) 281/L2
Blanchard, Idaho (83804) 220/A1
Blanchard, Iowa (51630) 229/C7
Blanchard, La. (71009) 238/C1
Blanchard○, Maine (†04406) 243/D5
Blanchard, Mich. (49310) 250/D5
Blanchard, N. Dak. (58009) 282/R5
Blanchard (riv.), Ohio 284/C4
Blanchard, Okla. (73010) 288/L4
Blanchard, Pa. (16826) 294/G3
Blanchard, Wash. (†98232) 310/C2
Blanchardstown, Ireland 17/H5
Blanchardville, Wis. (53516) 317/G10
Blanche, Ky. (†40902) 237/O7
Blanche (riv.), Québec 172/E2
Blanche (lake), S. Australia 88/F5
Blanche (lake), S. Australia 94/F3
Blanche, Tenn. (†38488) 237/H10
Blanche (lake), W. Australia 88/C4
Blanche Marie (fall), Suriname 131/C3
Blanchester, Ohio (45107) 284/B7
Blanchisseuse, Trin. & Tob. 161/B10
Blanco (riv.), Argentina 143/C2
Blanco (riv.), Bolivia 136/D4
Blanco (lake), Chile 138/F10
Blanco (cape), C. Rica 154/E6
Blanco (peak), C. Rica 154/F6
Blanco (riv.), Mexico 150/Q2
Blanco, N. Mex. (87412) 274/B2
Blanco (creek), N. Mex. 274/F4
Blanco, Okla. (74528) 288/P5
Blanco (cape), Oreg. 188/A2
Blanco (cape), Oreg. 291/C5
Blanco (cape), Peru 128/B5
Blanco (riv.), Peru 128/F6
Blanco (co.), Texas 303/F8
Blanco, Texas (78606) 303/F7
Blanc-Sablon, Québec 174/F2
Bland, Mo. (65014) 261/J6
Bland (co.), Va. 307/F6
Bland, Va. (24315) 307/F6
Blandburg, Pa. (16619) 294/F4

340 Blandford

Blandford○, Mass. (01008) 249/C4
Blandford, Nova Scotia 168/D4
Blandford Forum, England 13/E7
Blandford Forum, England 10/E5
Blanding, Utah (84511) 304/E6
Blandinsville, Ill. (61420) 222/C3
Blandville, Ky. (42026) 237/D7
Blanefield, Scotland 15/B1
Blanes, Spain 33/H2
Blaney Park, Mich. (†49836) 250/D2
Blanford, Ind. (47831) 227/B5
Blankenberge, Belgium 27/C6
Blankenburg am Harz, E. Germany 22/D3
Blanket, Texas (76432) 303/F6
Blanquillo, Uruguay 145/D3
Blansko, Czech. 41/D2
Blanton, Ala. (†36872) 195/H5
Blanton, Fla. (†33525) 212/D3
Blantyre, Malawi 115/F7
Blantyre, Malawi 102/F6
Blantyre, Scotland 15/B2
Blarney, Ireland 10/B5
Blarney, Ireland 17/D8
Blas (peak), Switzerland 39/G3
Blasdell, N.Y. (14219) 276/C5
Blasket (isls.), Ireland 10/A4
Blasket (isls.), Ireland 17/A7
Blatná, Czech. 41/B2
Blato, Yugoslavia 45/C4
Blatten, Switzerland 39/E4
Blaubeuren, W. Germany 22/C4
Blauvelt, N.Y. (10913) 276/K8
Blåvands Huk (pt.), Denmark 21/A6
Blawenburg, N.J. (08504) 273/D3
Blawnox, Pa. (15238) 294/C6
Blaydon, England 10/F3
Blaydon, England 13/H3
Blaye, France 28/C5
Blayney, N.S. Wales 97/E3
Blaze (pt.), North. Terr. 88/D2
Blaze (pt.), North. Terr. 93/A2
Bleckley (co.), Georgia 217/F6
Bled, Yugoslavia 45/A2
Bledsoe (co.), Tenn. 237/L9
Bledsoe, Texas (79314) 303/A4
Bleecker, Ala. (†36874) 195/H5
Blekinge (co.), Sweden 18/J8
Blencoe, Iowa (51523) 229/A5
Blenheim, N. Zealand 100/D4
Blenheim, Ontario 177/C5
Blenheim, S.C. (29516) 296/H2
Blenker, Wis. (54415) 317/F6
Blennerhassett (isl.), Ohio 284/G7
Blerick, Netherlands 27/J6
Blesbok (riv.), S. Africa 118/J7
Blessing, Texas (77419) 303/H9
Blessington, Ireland 17/J5
Blevins, Ark. (71825) 202/C6
Blewett, Texas (†78801) 303/D8
Blida, Algeria 106/E1
Blida, Algeria 102/C1
Bligh (sound), N. Zealand 100/A6
Bligh Water (bay), Fiji 86/P10
Blind Channel, Br. Col. 184/E5
Blind River, Ont. 162/H6
Blind River, Ontario 177/J5
Blind River, Ontario 175/D3
Blinman, S. Australia 88/F6
Blinman, S. Australia 94/F4
Blinnenhorn (mt.), Switzerland 39/F4
Bliss, Idaho (83314) 220/D7
Bliss, N.Y. (14024) 276/D5
Blissfield, Mich. (49228) 250/F7
Blissfield, New Bruns. 170/D2
Blissfield, Ohio (43805) 284/G5
Blitar, Indonesia 85/K2
Blitchton, Georgia (†31308) 217/J6
Blocher, Ind. (47138) 227/F7
Block (isl.), R.I. 249/H8
Blocker, Okla. (74529) 288/P4
Block House, Nova Scotia 168/D4
Block Island (sound), N.Y. 276/S8
Block Island, R.I. (02807) 249/H8
Block Island (sound), R.I. 249/H8
Blockton, Iowa (50836) 229/D7
Blodgett, Mo. (63824) 261/O8
Blodgett, Oreg. (97326) 291/D3
Blodgett Landing, N.H. (†03255) 268/D5
Bloemendaal, Netherlands 27/E4
Bloemfontein, S. Africa 102/E7
Bloemfontein, S. Africa 118/C5
Blois, France 28/D4
Blokzijl, Netherlands 27/H3
Blomkest, Minn. (56216) 255/D6
Blonie, Poland 47/E2
Bloodroot (mt.), Vt. 268/B4
Bloodsworth (isl.), Md. 245/O8
Bloodvein (riv.), Manitoba 179/F3
Bloodvein (riv.), Ontario 175/A2
Bloodvein River, Manitoba 179/F3
Bloody Foreland (prom.), Ireland 17/E1
Bloody Foreland (prom.), Ireland 10/B3
Bloom, Kansas (67833) 232/C4
Bloom, N. Dak. (†58401) 282/N6
Bloomburg, Texas (75556) 303/L4
Bloom City, Wis. (54617) 317/E8
Bloomdale, Ohio (44817) 284/D3
Bloomer, Ark. (†72933) 202/B3
Bloomer, Wis. (54724) 317/D5
Bloomery, W. Va. (26817) 312/K4
Bloomfield, Sierra (mts.), Bolivia 136/D4
Bloomfield○, Conn. (06002) 210/E1
Bloomfield, Ind. (47424) 227/D6
Bloomfield, Iowa (52537) 229/J7
Bloomfield, Ky. (40008) 237/L5
Bloomfield, Mo. (63825) 261/M9
Bloomfield, Mont. (59315) 262/M3
Bloomfield, Nebr. (68718) 264/G2
Bloomfield, Newf. 166/D2
Bloomfield, N.J. (07003) 273/B2
Bloomfield, N. Mex. (87413) 274/A2
Bloomfield, Ontario 177/G4
Bloomfield (New Bloomfield), Pa. (17068) 294/H5
Bloomfield○, Vt. (†03590) 268/D2
Bloomfield Hills, Mich. (48013) 250/B6
Bloomfield Ridge, New Bruns. 170/D2
Bloomfield Station, New Bruns. 170/E3
Bloomingburg, N.Y. (12721) 276/L7
Bloomingburg, Ohio (43106) 284/D6
Bloomingdale, Georgia (31302) 217/K6
Bloomingdale, Ill. (60108) 222/A5
Bloomingdale, Ind. (47832) 227/C5
Bloomingdale, Mich. (49026) 250/C6
Bloomingdale, N.J. (07403) 273/E1
Bloomingdale, N.Y. (12913) 276/M2
Bloomingdale, Ohio (43910) 284/J5
Bloomingdale, Tenn. (37660) 237/R7
Bloomingdale, Wis. (†54667) 317/E8
Blooming Grove, Ind. (†47012) 227/G5
Blooming Grove, Pa. (†18428) 294/M3
Blooming Grove, Texas (76626) 303/H5
Bloomingport, Ind. (†47355) 227/G5
Blooming Prairie, Minn. (55917) 255/E7
Bloomington, Calif. (92316) 204/E10
Bloomington, Idaho (83223) 220/G7
Bloomington, Ill. 188/J2
Bloomington, Ill. (61701) 222/D3
Bloomington, Ind. (47401) 227/D6
Bloomington, Md. (21523) 245/B3
Bloomington, Minn. (55420) 255/G6
Bloomington, Nebr. (68929) 264/F4
Bloomington, Texas (77951) 303/H9
Bloomington, Wis. (53804) 317/E10
Bloomington Springs, Tenn. (38545) 237/K8
Blooming Valley, Pa. (†16335) 294/B2
Bloomsburg, Pa. (17815) 294/J3
Bloomsbury, Alberta 182/C2
Bloomsbury, N.J. (08804) 273/C2
Bloomsdale, Mo. (63627) 261/M6
Bloomville, N.Y. (13739) 276/L6
Bloomville, Ohio (44818) 284/D3
Blora, Indonesia 85/K2
Blossburg, Pa. (16912) 294/H2
Blossom, Texas (75416) 303/J4
Bloubergstrand, S. Africa 118/E6
Blount (co.), Ala. 195/E2
Blount (co.), Tenn. 237/O9
Blounts Creek, N.C. (27814) 281/P4
Blount Springs, Ala. (†35079) 195/E3
Blountstown, Fla. (32424) 212/A1
Blountsville, Ala. (35031) 195/E2
Blountsville, Ind. (†47360) 227/G4
Blountville, Tenn. (37617) 237/S7
Blowering (res.), N.S. Wales 97/E4
Blowing Rock, N.C. (28605) 281/F2
Bloxom, Va. (23308) 307/S5
Bludenz, Austria 41/A3
Blue, Ariz. (85922) 198/F5
Blue (riv.), Ariz. 198/F5
Blue (mt.), Colo. 208/B2
Blue (riv.), Colo. 208/G3
Blue (riv.), Ind. 227/E8
Blue (mts.), Jamaica 158/J6
Blue (mt.), Maine 243/C6
Blue (hills), Mass. 249/C8
Blue (creek), Nebr. 264/B3
Blue (mt.), New Bruns. 170/D1
Blue (mt.), N.H. 268/E2
Blue (mts.), N. S. Wales 88/H6
Blue (mts.), N.S. Wales 97/F3
Blue, Okla. (†74701) 288/O7
Blue (riv.), Okla. 288/O6
Blue (mts.), Oreg. 291/J3
Blue (mt.), Pa. 294/G5
Blue (creek), Utah 304/B2
Blue (lake), Utah 304/B4
Blue (lake), Wash. 310/F3
Blue (mts.), Wash. 310/H4
Blue Ash, Ohio (†45242) 284/C9
Blue Ball, Ark. (†72866) 202/C4
Blue Bell, S. Dak. (†57773) 298/C6
Bluebell, Utah (84007) 304/D3
Blueberry Creek, Br. Col. 184/J5
Blueberry Mountain, Alberta 182/A2
Blue Creek, Ohio (45616) 284/D8
Blue Creek, Utah (†84337) 304/B2
Bluecreek, Wash. (†99109) 310/H2
Blue Creek, W. Va. (25026) 312/D6
Blue Cypress (lake), Fla. 212/F4
Blue Diamond, Ky. (41718) 237/P6
Blue Earth (co.), Minn. 255/D6
Blue Earth, Minn. (56013) 255/D7
Blue Earth (riv.), Minn. 255/D7
Blue Eye, Ark. (65611) 202/D1
Blue Eye, Mo. (65611) 261/F9
Bluefield, Va. (24605) 307/F6
Bluefield, W. Va. 188/K3
Bluefield, W. Va. (24701) 312/D8
Bluefields, Jamaica 158/G6
Bluefields, Nicaragua 154/F4
Bluegrass, Ind. (†46939) 227/E3
Blue Grass, Iowa (52726) 229/M5
Blue Grass, Minn. (†56477) 255/C4
Blue Grass, Va. (24413) 307/J3
Blue Heron, Sask. 181/E2
Blue Hill, Maine (04614) 243/F7
Blue Hill○, Maine (04614) 243/F7
Blue Hill (bay), Maine 243/G7
Blue Hill, Nebr. (68930) 264/F4
Blue Hill Falls, Maine (04615) 243/F7
Blue Hills, Conn. (06112) 210/E1
Blue Island, Ill. (60406) 222/B6
Bluejacket, Okla. (74333) 288/R1
Blue Jay, Calif. (92317) 204/H9
Blue Joint (lake), Oreg. 291/H5
Blue Knob (mt.), Pa. 294/E5
Blue Lake, Calif. (95525) 204/A3
Blue Mesa (res.), Colo. 208/E5
Bluemont, Va. (22012) 307/N2
Blue Mound, Ill. (62513) 222/D4
Blue Mound, Kansas (66010) 232/H3
Blue Mound, Texas (†76101) 303/E2
Blue Mounds, Wis. (53517) 317/G9
Blue Mountain, Ala. (36201) 195/G3
Blue Mountain, Ark. (72826) 202/C3
Blue Mountain (lake), Ark. 202/C3
Blue Mountain (peak), Jamaica 158/K6
Blue Mountain (peak), Jamaica 156/C3
Blue Mountain, Miss. (38610) 256/G1
Blue Mountain (lake), N.Y. 276/M3
Blue Mountain Lake, N.Y. (12812) 276/M3
Blue Mountains, Australia 87/E9
Blue Mountains, N. S. Wales 88/J6
Blue Mountains, N.S. Wales 97/F3
Blue Nile (riv.) 102/F3
Blue Nile (Abay) (riv.), Ethiopia 111/G5
Blue Nile (prov.), Sudan 111/F5
Blue Nile (riv.), Sudan 59/B6
Blue Nile (riv.), Sudan 111/F5
Blue Nose (mt.), Idaho 220/D4
Bluenose (lake), N.W. Terrs. 187/G3
Blue Rapids, Kansas (66411) 232/F2
Blue Ridge, Alberta 182/C2
Blue Ridge, Georgia (30513) 217/D1
Blue Ridge (lake), Georgia 217/D1
Blue Ridge (mts.), Georgia 217/D1
Blue Ridge, Ind. (†46176) 227/F5
Blue Ridge (mts.), Md. 245/H3
Blue Ridge (mts.), N.C. 281/E3
Blue Ridge (mts.), S.C. 296/B1
Blue Ridge, Va. (24064) 307/J6
Blue Ridge (mts.), Va. 307/J6
Blue Ridge Manor, Ky. (†40201) 237/L2
Blue Ridge Summit, Pa. (17214) 294/G6
Blue River, Br. Col. 184/H4
Blue River, Colo. (†80424) 208/G4
Blue River, Oreg. (97413) 291/E3
Blue River, Wis. (53518) 317/E9
Blue Rock, Nova Scotia 168/D4
Blue Rock (Gaysport), Ohio (43720) 284/G6
Blue Sea Lake, Québec 172/A3
Bluesky, Alberta 182/A1
Blue Spring (hills), Utah 304/B1
Blue Springs, Ala. (†36017) 195/G7
Blue Springs, Miss. (38828) 256/G2
Blue Springs, Mo. (64015) 261/R6
Blue Springs, Nebr. (68318) 264/H4
Blue Stack (mts.), Ireland 17/E2
Bluestem (lake), Okla. 288/O1
Bluestone (lake), Va. 307/G5
Bluestone (lake), W. Va. 312/E7
Blue Sulphur Springs, W. Va. (†25545) 312/E7
Blue Summit, Mo. (†64101) 261/R5
Bluevale, Ontario 177/C4
Bluewater, N. Mex. (87005) 274/A3
Bluewater (creek), N. Mex. 274/B4
Bluewater (creek), N. Mex. 274/D6
Bluewater (lake), N. Mex. 274/A3
Bluff (cape), Newf. 166/C3
Bluff, N. Zealand 100/B7
Bluff, N.C. (†28743) 281/D3
Bluff, Utah (84512) 304/E6
Bluff City, Ark. (71722) 202/D6
Bluff City, Ill. (†62624) 222/E5
Bluff City, Kansas (67018) 232/E4
Bluff City, Tenn. (37618) 237/S8
Bluff Dale, Texas (76433) 303/F5
Bluffdale, Utah (†84065) 304/B3
Bluff Knoll (mt.), W. Australia 92/B6
Bluff Park, Ala. (35226) 195/E4
Bluffs, Ill. (62621) 222/C4
Bluffsprings, Fla. (†32535) 212/B5
Bluffton, Alberta 182/C3
Bluffton, Ark. (72827) 202/C4
Bluffton, Georgia (31724) 217/C7
Bluffton, Ind. (46714) 227/G3
Bluffton, Minn. (56518) 255/C4
Bluffton, Ohio (45817) 284/C4
Bluffton, S.C. (29910) 296/F7
Bluford, Ill. (62814) 222/E5
Blum, Texas (76627) 303/G5
Blumenau, Brazil 132/D9
Blumenau, Brazil 120/E5
Blumenfeld, Manitoba 179/D5
Blumenheim, Sask. 181/E3
Blumenhof, Sask. 181/D5
Blumenort, Manitoba 179/E5
Blumenort, Manitoba 179/F5
Blumenort, Sask. 181/D6
Blumenstein, Switzerland 39/E3
Blumenthal, Sask. 181/E3
Blümlisalp (mt.), Switzerland 39/E3
Blunt, S. Dak. (57522) 298/J4
Bly, Oreg. (97622) 291/F5
Blying (sound), Alaska 196/C1
Blyn, Wash. (†98382) 310/B3
Blyth, England 13/F2
Blyth, England 10/F3
Blyth, Ontario 177/C4
Blyth Bridge, Scotland 15/E5
Blythe, Calif. (92225) 204/L10
Blythe, Georgia (30805) 217/H4
Blythedale, Md. (†21904) 245/O2
Blythedale, Mo. (64426) 261/E2
Blythedale, Pa. (†15018) 294/C5
Blytheswood, Ontario 177/B5
Blytheville, Ark. 188/H3
Blytheville, Ark. (72315) 202/L2
Blytheville A.F.B., Ark. 202/K2
Blythewood, S.C. (29016) 296/E3
Bo, S. Leone 102/A4
Bo, S. Leone 106/B7
Boac, Philippines 82/C4
Boaco, Nicaragua 154/E4
Boa Esperança, Brazil 135/D2
Boalsburg, Pa. (16827) 294/G4
Boano (isl.), Indonesia 85/H6
Boa Nova, Brazil 132/B5
Board Camp, Ark. (71932) 202/B4
Boardman (riv.), Mich. 250/D4
Boardman, N.C. (†28438) 281/M6
Boardman, Ohio (44512) 284/J3
Boardman, Oreg. (97818) 291/H2
Boardman, Wis. (†54016) 317/A5
Boardmans Bridge, Conn. (†06776) 210/B2
Boas (riv.), N.W. Terrs. 187/K3
Boat Basin, Br. Col. 184/D5
Boat Harbour, Tasmania 99/B2
Boat of Garten, Scotland 15/E3
Boa Vista, Brazil 120/C2
Boa Vista, Brazil 132/H8
Boa Vista (isl.), C. Verde 106/B8
Boayan (isl.), Philippines 82/B5
Boaz, Ala. (35957) 195/F2
Boaz, Ky. (42027) 237/D7
Boaz, Mo. (†65631) 261/F8
Boaz, W. Va. (†26187) 312/D4
Boaz, Wis. (†53581) 317/E9
Bobadah, N.S. Wales 97/D3
Bobai, China 77/H7
Bobaomby (cape), Madagascar 102/G6
Bobaomby (Amber) (cape), Madagascar 118/H2
Bobare, Venezuela 124/D2
Bobbili, India 68/E5
Bobbitt, N.C. (†27544) 281/N2
Bobcaygeon, Ontario 177/F3
Bobigny, France 28/B1
Böblingen, W. Germany 22/C4
Bobo, Miss. (†38614) 256/C2
Bobo Dioulasso, Upper Volta 106/D6
Bobo Dioulasso, Upper Volta 102/B3
Bobon, Philippines 82/F7
Bobonaza (riv.), Ecuador 128/D3
Bobonong, Botswana 118/D4
Bobotov Kuk (mt.), Yugoslavia 45/D4
Bobr (riv.), Poland 47/B3
Bobrov, U.S.S.R. 52/F4
Bobruysk, U.S.S.R. 7/G3
Bobruysk, U.S.S.R. 52/C4
Bobruysk, U.S.S.R. 48/C4
Bobs (lake), Ontario 177/H3
Bobtown, Pa. (15315) 294/B6
Bobures, Venezuela 124/C3
Boby, Pic (mt.), Madagascar 118/H4
Bocabec, New Bruns. 170/C3
Boca Chica, Dom. Rep. 158/E6
Boca Chica (key), Fla. 212/E7
Boca Ciega (bay), Fla. 212/B3
Boca de Aroa, Venezuela 124/D2
Boca del Mangle, Venezuela 124/D2
Boca del Pao, Venezuela 124/F3
Boca del Pepé, Colombia 126/B5
Boca del Río, Mexico 150/Q2
Boca del Soco, Dom. Rep. 158/F6
Boca do Acre, Brazil 132/G10
Boca Grande, Fla. (33921) 212/D5
Boca Grande (key), Fla. 212/D7
Boca Grande (passage), Trin. & Tob. 161/A10
Boca Grande (gulf), Venezuela 124/H3
Bocaiúva, Brazil 132/E7
Bocaranga, Cent. Afr. Rep. 115/C2
Boca Raton, Fla. (*33432) 212/F5
Bocas del Toro, Panama 154/F6
Bocay, Nicaragua 154/E3
Bochnia, Poland 47/E4
Bocholt, Belgium 27/H6
Bocholt, W. Germany 22/B3
Bochov, Czech. 41/B1
Bochum, W. Germany 22/B3
Bock, Minn. (56313) 255/E5
Boco, Chile 138/F2
Boconó, Venezuela 124/C3
Boda, Cent. Afr. Rep. 115/C3
Bodalla, N.S. Wales 97/F5
Bodaybo, U.S.S.R. 54/N4
Bodaybo, U.S.S.R. 48/M4
Bodcaw, Ark. (†71858) 202/D6
Boddam, Scotland 15/G3
Boddington, W. Australia 92/B2
Bode, Iowa (50519) 229/E3
Bodega (bay), Calif. 204/B5
Bodega (head), Calif. 204/B5
Bodega Bay, Calif. (94923) 204/B5
Bodegraven, Netherlands 27/F4
Bodélé (depr.), Chad 102/D3
Bodélé (depr.), Chad 111/C4
Boden, Sweden 18/M4
Bodensee (Constance) (lake), Austria 41/A3
Bodensee (Constance) (lake), Switzerland 39/H1
Bodensee (Constance) (lake), W. Germany 22/C5
Boderg (lake), Ireland 17/E4
Bodfish, Calif. (93205) 204/G8
Bodhan, India 68/D5
Bodie (isl.), N.C. 281/T2
Bodinayakkanur, India 68/D6
Bodines, Pa. (17722) 294/H3
Bodio, Switzerland 39/G4
Bodkin (pt.), Md. 245/N4
Bodmin, England 13/C7
Bodmin, England 10/D5
Bodmin, Sask. 181/D2
Bodo, Alberta 182/E3
Bodø, Norway 18/J3
Bodø, Norway 7/F2
Bodrum, Turkey 63/B4
Bodrum, Turkey 59/A2
Bo Duc, Vietnam 72/E4
Bódvaszilas, Hungary 41/F2
Boelus, Nebr. (68820) 264/F3
Boende, Zaire 115/D4
Boerne, Texas (78006) 303/J10
Boeuf (lake), La. 238/J7
Boeuf (riv.), La. 238/G1
Boffa, Guinea 106/B6
Bog (lake), Maine 243/H6
Bogalusa, La. 188/H4
Bogalusa, La. (70427) 238/L5
Bogan (riv.), N.S. Wales 97/D2
Bogandé, Upper Volta 106/E6
Bogan Gate, N.S. Wales 97/D3
Bogantungan, Queensland 95/C4
Bogard, Mo. (64622) 261/E4
Bogart, Georgia (30622) 217/E3
Bogata, Texas (75417) 303/J4
Bogatynia, Poland 47/B3
Boğazlıyan, Turkey 63/F3
Bogen, W. Germany 22/E4
Bogenfels, Namibia 118/B5
Bogense, Denmark 21/D6
Boger City, N.C. (28092) 281/G4
Boggabilla, N.S. Wales 97/F1
Boggabri, N.S. Wales 97/F2
Boggeragh (mts.), Ireland 17/D7
Boggstown, Ind. (46110) 227/F5
Boggy (peak), Ant. & Bar. 161/D11
Boggy Creek, Manitoba 179/A3
Boggy Depot, Okla. (†74525) 288/O6
Bogia, Papua N.G. 85/B6
Bogie (riv.), Scotland 15/F3
Bognor Regis, England 13/G7
Bognor Regis, England 10/F5
Bogny-sur-Meuse, France 28/F3
Bogo, Philippines 82/E5
Bogon (riv.), N. S. Wales 88/H6
Bogong (mt.), Victoria 97/D5
Bogor, Indonesia 54/M10
Bogor, Indonesia 85/H2
Bogoslof (isl.), Alaska 196/E4
Bogotá (cap.), Colombia 126/D5
Bogotá (cap.), Colombia 120/B2
Bogotá (cap.), Colombia 2/F5
Bogota, Ill. (†62448) 222/E5
Bogota, N.J. (07603) 273/B2
Bogota, Tenn. (38007) 237/C8
Bogra, Bangladesh 68/F4
Boguchar, U.S.S.R. 52/F5
Bogue, Kansas (67625) 232/C2
Bogué, Mauritania 106/B5
Bogue Chitto, Miss. (39629) 256/D8
Bogue Chitto (riv.), Miss. 256/D8
Bogue Homo (lake), Miss. 256/F7
Boguszów-Gorce, Poland 47/B3
Bog Walk, Jamaica 158/J6
Bo Hai (gulf), China 77/J4
Boharm, Sask. 181/F5
Bohemian (for.), Czech. 41/B2
Bohemian (for.), W. Germany 22/E4
Bohemian-Moravian Heights (hills), Czech. 41/C2
Boherbue, Ireland 17/C7
Bohners Lake, Wis. (†53105) 317/K10
Bohodleh, Somalia 115/J2
Bohol (prov.), Philippines 82/E6
Bohol (isl.), Philippines 85/G4
Bohol (isl.), Philippines 82/E6
Bohol (sea), Philippines 82/E6
Bohol (str.), Philippines 82/D6
Böhönye, Hungary 41/D3
Bohu (Bagrax), China 77/C3
Boicourt, Kansas (†66075) 232/H3
Boiestown, New Bruns. 170/D2
Boiling Spring Lakes, N.C. (28461) 281/N7
Boiling Springs, N.C. (28017) 281/F4
Boiling Springs, Pa. (17007) 294/H5
Bois Blanc (isl.), Mich. 250/E3
Boischatel, Québec /J3
Boisdale, Nova Scotia 168/H2
Boisdale, Loch (inlet), Scotland 15/A3
Bois D'Arc, Mo. (65612) 261/F8
Bois-des-Filion, Québec 172/H4
Bois de Sioux (riv.), Minn. 255/B4
Bois de Sioux (riv.), S. Dak. 298/R1
Boise (co.), Idaho 220/C6
Boise (cap.), Idaho 146/G5
Boise (cap.), Idaho (*83701) 220/B6
Boise (cap.), Idaho 188/C2
Boise (mts.), Idaho 220/B6
Boise (riv.), Idaho 220/B6
Boise City, Okla. (73933) 288/B1
Boissevain, Man. 162/G6
Boissevain, Manitoba 179/C5
Boissevain, Va. (24606) 307/F6
Boistfort, Wash. (†98532) 310/B4
Boisvert (pt.), Québec 172/J1
Boizenburg an der Elbe, E. Germany 22/D2
Bojador (cape), W. Sahara 102/A2
Bojador (cape), Western Sahara 106/B3
Bojeador (cape), Philippines 82/C1
Bojnurd, Iran 66/K2
Bojnurd, Iran 59/G2
Bojonegoro, Indonesia 85/J2
Bokchito, Okla. (74726) 288/O6
Boké, Guinea 106/B6
Bokeelia, Fla. (33922) 212/D5
Bokel (cay), Belize 154/D2
Bokhara (riv.), N.S. Wales 97/D1
Bokhoma, Okla. (†71821) 288/S7
Boknafjord (fjord), Norway 18/D7
Boko, Congo 115/B4
Bokoro, Chad 111/C5
Bokoshe, Okla. (74930) 288/S4
Bokote, Zaire 115/D4
Bokpyin, Burma 72/C5
Boksburg, S. Africa 118/J6
Bokungu, Zaire 115/D4
Bol, Chad 111/B5
Bol, Chad 102/D3
Bolair, W. Va. (26288) 312/F6
Bolama, Guinea-Biss. 106/A6
Bolan (pass), Pakistan 68/B3
Bolangir, India 68/E4
Bolar, Va. (24414) 307/J4
Bolatusha, Miss. (†39160) 256/E5
Bolayır, Turkey 63/C5
Bolbec, France 28/D3
Bolckow, Mo. (64427) 261/C2
Bolderslev, Denmark 21/C8
Bolding, Ark. (†71747) 202/F7
Boldman, Ky. (†41501) 237/R5
Boldon, England 13/J3
Bolduc, Québec 172/G4
Bole, China 77/B3
Bole, Ghana 106/D7
Boles, Ark. (72926) 202/B4
Bolesławiec, Poland 47/B3
Boley, Okla. (74829) 288/O4
Bolgatanga, Ghana 106/D6
Boli, China 77/M2
Boligee, Ala. (35443) 195/C5
Bolinao, Philippines 82/B2
Bolinao (cape), Philippines 82/B2
Bolinas, Calif. (94924) 204/H1
Boling, Texas (77420) 303/H8
Bolingbroke, Georgia (31004) 217/E5
Bolingbrook, Ill. (60439) 222/A6
Bolinger, Ala. (36903) 195/B7
Bolinger, La. (†71064) 238/C1
Bolívar, Argentina 143/D4
Bolívar, Bolivia 136/B3
Bolívar (dept.), Colombia 126/C3
Bolívar, Antioquia, Colombia 126/C5
Bolívar, Cauca, Colombia 126/B7
Bolívar (prov.), Ecuador 128/C3
Bolívar, Ecuador 128/C2
Bolivar (co.), Miss. 256/C3
Bolivar, Mo. (65613) 261/F7
Bolivar, N.Y. (14715) 276/D6
Bolivar, Ohio (44612) 284/G4
Bolivar, Pa. (15923) 294/D5
Bolívar, Peru 128/D6
Bolivar, Tenn. (38008) 237/C10
Bolivar (pen.), Texas 303/K8
Bolívar (state), Venezuela 124/F7
Bolívar, Cerro (mt.), Venezuela 124/G4
Bolívar, Pico (peak), Venezuela 124/C3
Bolivar, W. Va. (†25425) 312/L4
Bolivia 2/F6
Bolivia 120/C4
BOLIVIA 136
Bolivia, N.C. (28422) 281/N6
Bolkar (mts.), Turkey 63/F4
Bolkhov, U.S.S.R. 52/E4
Bolligen, Switzerland 39/E3
Bolling, Ala. (36007) 195/E7
Bolling A.F.B., D.C. 245/E5
Bollinger (co.), Mo. 261/M8
Bollington, England 10/G2
Bollington, England 13/H2
Bollnäs, Sweden 18/K6
Bollon, Queensland 95/C6
Bollon, Queensland 88/H5
Bollstabruk, Sweden 18/L5
Bolmen (lake), Sweden 18/H8
Bolobo, Zaire 115/C4
Bologna (prov.), Italy 34/C2
Bologna, Italy 34/C2
Bologna, Italy 7/F4
Bolognesi, Peru 128/F8
Bolognesi, Peru 128/F6
Bologoye, U.S.S.R. 52/D3
Bolomba, Zaire 115/C3
Bolonchén de Rejón, Mexico 150/O7
Bolondrón, Cuba 156/B2
Bolondrón, Cuba 158/D1
Bolovens (plat.), Laos 72/E4
Bolpebra, Bolivia 136/A2
Bolsena (lake), Italy 34/C3
Bol'shevik (isl.) U.S.S.R. 54/N2
Bol'shevik (isl.), U.S.S.R. 4/A4
Bol'shevik (isl.), U.S.S.R. 48/K2
Bol'shoy Lyakhov (isl.), U.S.S.R. 54/R2
Bol'shoy Lyakhovskiy (isl.), U.S.S.R. 48/P2
Bolsover, England 13/J2
Bolsters Mills, Maine (†04040) 243/B7
Bolsward, Netherlands 27/H2
Boltaña, Spain 33/F1
Boltigen, Switzerland 39/D3
Bolton○, Conn. (06040) 210/F1
Bolton, England 10/G2
Bolton, England 13/H2
Bolton○, Mass. (01740) 249/H3
Bolton, Miss. (39041) 256/D6
Bolton, N.C. (28423) 281/N6
Bolton○, Vt. (†05466) 268/B3
Bolton (mt.), Vt. 268/B3
Bolton Landing, N.Y. (12814) 276/N3
Bolu (prov.), Turkey 63/D2
Bolu, Turkey 59/B1
Bolu, Turkey 63/D2
Bolus (head), Ireland 17/A8
Bolvadin, Turkey 63/D3
Bolvanskiy Nos (cape), U.S.S.R. 52/K1
Bolvanskiy Nos (cape), U.S.S.R. 48/G2
Bolzano (Bolzen), Italy 34/C1
Bolzano, Italy 7/F4
Bolzano-Bozen (prov.), Italy 34/C1
Bolzen (Bolzano), Italy 34/C1
Boma, Zaire 102/D5
Boma, Zaire 115/B5
Bomaderry-Nowra, N.S. Wales 97/F4
Bomarton, Texas (†76380) 303/E4
Bomba (gulf), Libya 111/D1
Bombala, N.S. Wales 97/E5
Bombardopolis, Haiti 158/B5
Bombay, India 54/J8
Bombay, India 2/N5
Bombay (harb.), India 68/B7
Bombay, Minn. (†55946) 255/F6
Bombay, N.Y. (12914) 276/M1
Bomboma, Zaire 115/C3
Bom Conselho, Brazil 132/G5
Bom Despacho, Brazil 135/D1
Bom Despacho, Brazil 132/E7
Bomdila, India 68/G3
Bom Futuro, Brazil 120/C4
Bom Futuro, Brazil 132/A5
Bomi, China 77/E6
Bom Jesus, Brazil 132/E5
Bom Jesus da Lapa, Brazil 120/E4
Bom Jesus da Lapa, Brazil 132/F6
Bom Jesus do Itabapoana, Brazil 135/F2
Bomongo, Zaire 115/C3
Bomont, W. Va. (25030) 312/D6
Bomoseen, Vt. (05732) 268/A4
Bomoseen (lake), Vt. 268/A4
Bom Retiro, Brazil 132/D10
Bom Sucesso, Brazil 135/D2
Bomu (riv.), Cent. Afr. Rep. 102/E4
Bomu (riv.), Cent. Afr. Rep. 115/D3
Bomu (riv.), Zaire 115/D3
Bon (cape), Tunisia 102/D1
Bon (cape), Tunisia 106/G1
Bona (mt.), Alaska 196/K2
Bonabéri, Cameroon 115/A3
Bonacca (Guanaja) (isl.), Honduras 154/E2
Bon Accord, Alberta 182/D3
Bonaduz, Switzerland 39/H3
Bon Air, Ala. (35032) 195/F4
Bonair, Iowa (†52155) 229/J2
Bon Air, Tenn. (†38583) 237/L9
Bon Air, Va. (23235) 307/N5
Bonaire (isl.), Neth. Ant. 156/E4
Bonaire (isl.), Neth. Ant. 161/E9
Bonalbo, N.S. Wales 97/G1

Boyne City 341

Bonanza, Alberta 182/A2
Bonanza, Ark. (†72901) 202/B3
Bonanza, Colo. (†81155) 208/G6
Bonanza, Nicaragua 154/E4
Bonanza, Oreg. (97623) 291/F5
Bonanza, Utah (84008) 304/E3
Bonanza (peak), Wash. 310/E2
Bonao, Dom. Rep. 158/E6
Bonaparte, Iowa (52620) 229/K7
Bonaparte (lake), N.Y. 276/K2
Bonaparte (creek), Wash. 310/F2
Bonaparte (mt.), Wash. 310/F2
Bonaparte (arch.), W. Australia 88/C2
Bonaparte (arch.), W. Australia 92/D1
Bon Aqua, Tenn. (37025) 237/G9
Bonar Bridge, Scotland 15/D3
Bonaventure (cape), Newf. 166/D2
Bonaventure (co.), Québec 172/C2
Bonaventure (county), Québec 174/D3
Bonaventure, Québec 172/C2
Bonaventure (isl.), Québec 172/D1
Bonaventure (riv.), Québec 172/C1
Bonavista, Newf. 166/D2
Bonavista (bay), Newf. 166/D1
Bonavista (cape), Newf. 166/D1
Bonavista, Newf. 162/L6
Boncarbo, Colo. (81024) 208/K8
Bonchester Bridge, Scotland 15/F5
Boncourt, Switzerland 39/C2
Bond, Colo. (80423) 208/F3
Bond (co.), Ill. 222/D5
Bond, Ky. (40407) 237/N6
Bond, Miss. (39550) 256/F9
Bond (mt.), N.H. 268/E3
Bondeno, Italy 34/C2
Bond Falls (res.), Mich. 250/G2
Bondi (beach), N.S. Wales 97/K3
Bondiss, Alberta 182/D2
Bondo, Zaire 115/D3
Bondoukou, Ivory Coast 106/D7
Bondowoso, Indonesia 85/L2
Bondsville, Mass. (01009) 249/E4
Bonduel, Wis. (54107) 317/K6
Bondurant, Iowa (50035) 229/G5
Bondurant, Wyo. (82922) 319/B2
Bondville, Ill. (61815) 222/E3
Bondville, Ky. (40308) 237/M5
Bondville, Vt. (05340) 268/B5
Bondy, France 28/B1
Bône (Annaba), Algeria 106/F1
Bone, Idaho (†83401) 220/G6
Bone (gulf), Indonesia 54/O10
Bone (gulf), Indonesia 85/G7
Bone Cave, Tenn. (†38581) 237/L9
Bone Gap, Ill. (62815) 222/F5
Bo'ness, Scotland 10/C1
Bo'ness, Scotland 15/C1
Bonesteel, S. Dak. (57317) 298/M7
Bonet (riv.), Ireland 17/E3
Boneta, Utah (†84051) 304/D3
Bonete (dam), Uruguay 145/C3
Bonetraill, N. Dak. (†58801) 282/C3
Boneville, Georgia (30806) 217/G4
Bonfield, Ill. (60913) 222/E2
Bonfield, Ontario 177/E1
Bonfol, Switzerland 39/D2
Bong (range), Liberia 106/B7
Bongabong, Philippines 82/C4
Bongandanga, Zaire 115/D3
Bonggaw, Philippines 82/B8
Bongo (isl.), Philippines 82/D7
Bongor, Chad 111/C5
Bongor, Chad 102/D3
Bong Son (Hoai Nhon), Vietnam 72/F4
Bonham, Texas (75418) 303/H4
Bonhill, Scotland 15/B1
Bonhomme (isl.), Mo. 261/N2
Bon Homme (co.), S. Dak. 298/O7
Bonifacio, France 28/B7
Bonifacio (str.), France 28/B7
Bonifacio (str.), Italy 34/B4
Bonifay, Fla. (32425) 212/C5
Bönigen, Switzerland 39/E3
Bonilla, S. Dak. (†57348) 298/N4
Bonin (isls.), Japan 2/S4
Bonin (isls.), Japan 54/R7
Bonin (isls.), Japan 87/E3
Bonin (isls.), Japan 81/M3
Bonita, Ariz. (†85643) 198/E6
Bonita (pt.), Calif. 204/H2
Bonita, La. (71223) 238/G1
Bonita, Miss. (†39301) 256/G6
Bonita Springs, Fla. (33923) 212/E5
Bonlee, N.C. (27213) 281/L3
Bonn (cap.), W. Germany 7/E3
Bonn (cap.), W. Germany 22/B3
Bonne (bay), Newf. 166/C4
Bonneau, S.C. (29431) 296/H5
Bonner (co.), Idaho 220/B1
Bonners Ferry, Idaho (83805) 220/B1
Bonner Springs, Kansas (66012) 232/H2
Bonner-West Riverside, Mont. (59823) 262/C4
Bonnet (lake), Manitoba 179/G4
Bonnétable, France 28/D3
Bonnet Carré Spillway and Floodway, La. 238/N3
Bonne Terre, Mo. (63628) 261/L7
Bonnet Plume (riv.), Yukon 187/E3
Bonneville, France 28/G4
Bonneville (co.), Idaho 220/G6
Bonneville, Oreg. (97008) 291/F2
Bonneville (dam), Oreg. 291/E2
Bonneville (salt flats), Utah 304/A3
Bonneville (dam), Wash. 310/D5
Bonneville (lake), Wash. 310/D5
Bonneville, Wyo. (†82649) 319/E2
Bonneville (mt.), Wyo. 319/C3
Bonney Lake, Wash. (†98390) 310/C3
Bonnie, Ill. (62816) 222/E5
Bonnieville, Ky. (42713) 237/K6
Bonnots Mill, Mo. (65016) 261/J5
Bonny (res.), Colo. 208/P3
Bonny, Nigeria 106/F8
Bonny (bight), Nigeria 106/F8
Bonnybridge, Scotland 15/C1
Bonnyman, Ky. (41719) 237/P6
Bonnyrigg, N. S. Wales 88/K4
Bonnyrigg, N.S. Wales 97/H3
Bonnyrigg and Lasswade, Scotland 10/C1
Bonnyrigg and Lasswade, Scotland 15/D2
Bonny River, New Bruns. 170/D3
Bonnyville, Alberta 182/E2
Bono, Ark. (72416) 202/J2
Bono, Ohio (†43445) 284/D2
Bonorva, Italy 34/B4
Bonpas (creek), Ill. 222/F5
Bonpland (mt.), N. Zealand 100/A6
Bon Secour, Ala. (36511) 195/C10
Bon Secour (bay), Ala. 195/C10
Bonsecours, Québec 172/E4
Bonshaw, Pr. Edward I. 168/E2
Bonthain, Indonesia 85/F7
Bonthe, S. Leone 106/B7
Bontoc, Philippines 85/G2
Bontoc, Philippines 82/C2
Bon Wier, Texas (75928) 303/L7
Bonyhád, Hungary 41/E3
Boody, Ill. (62514) 222/D4
Book (cliffs), Utah 304/E4
Booker, Texas (79005) 303/D1
Booker T. Washington Nat'l Mon., Va. 307/J6
Boolaloo, W. Australia 92/B3
Booligal, N.S. Wales 97/C3
Boom, Belgium 27/E6
Boom, Tenn. (†38573) 237/L7
Boomer, N.C. (28606) 281/G2
Boomer, W. Va. (25031) 312/D6
Boomi, N. S. Wales 88/H5
Boomi, N.S. Wales 97/E1
Boon (pt.), Ant. & Bar. 161/E11
Boon, Mich. (49618) 250/D4
Boondall, Queensland 88/K2
Boone (co.), Ark. 202/D1
Boone, Colo. (81025) 208/L6
Boone (co.), Ill. 222/E1
Boone (co.), Ind. 227/E4
Boone (co.), Iowa 229/F5
Boone, Iowa (50036) 229/F4
Boone (co.), Ky. 237/M3
Boone, Ky. (†40403) 237/N5
Boone (co.), Mo. 261/H4
Boone (co.), Nebr. 264/F3
Boone, Nebr. (68625) 264/F3
Boone, N.C. (28607) 281/F2
Boone (lake), Tenn. 237/S8
Boone (co.), W. Va. 312/C6
Boone Grove, Ind. (46302) 227/C2
Boonesboro, Mo. (†65250) 261/G4
Boones Mill, Va. (24065) 307/J6
Boonesville, Va. (†22935) 307/L4
Booneville, Ark. (72927) 202/C3
Booneville, Ky. (41314) 237/O6
Booneville, Miss. (38829) 256/G1
Boonsboro, Md. (21713) 245/H2
Boonton, N.J. (07005) 273/E2
Boonton (res.), N.J. 273/E2
Boonville, Calif. (95415) 204/B5
Boonville, Ind. (47601) 227/C8
Boonville, Mo. (65233) 261/G5
Boonville, N.Y. (13309) 276/K4
Boonville, N.C. (27011) 281/H2
Boopi (riv.), Bolivia 136/B4
Boorooban, N.S. Wales 97/C4
Boorowa, N.S. Wales 97/E4
Boort, Victoria 97/B5
Booth, Ala. (36008) 195/E6
Boothbay, Maine (04537) 243/D8
Boothbay○, Maine (04537) 243/D8
Boothbay Harbor, Maine (04538) 243/D8
Boothia (pen.), Canada 4/B14
Boothia (gulf), Canada 4/B14
Boothia (pen.), N.W.T. 146/J2
Boothia (gulf), N.W.T. 146/J2
Boothia (isthmus), N.W.T. 162/G2
Boothia (pen.), N.W.T. 162/G1
Boothia (gulf), N.W.T. 162/G1
Boothia (gulf), N.W. Terrs. 187/K3
Boothia (pen.), N.W. Terrs. 187/J2
Boothville, La. (70038) 238/M8
Boothwyn, Pa. (19061) 294/L7
Bootle, England 10/F2
Bootle, England 13/G2
Booué, Gabon 115/B3
Bophuthatswana (bantustan), S. Africa 102/E7
Bophuthatswana (rep.), S. Africa 118/D5
Boppard, W. Germany 22/B3
Boquerón, Cuba 158/K4
Boquerón, Cuba 156/C3
Boquerón, (dept.), Paraguay 144/B3
Boquerón, El (pass), Peru 128/E7
Boquerón, P. Rico 156/F1
Boquerón, P. Rico 161/A3
Boquerón (bay), P. Rico 161/A3
Boquilla del Carmen, Mexico 150/H2
Bor, Czech. 41/B2
Bor, Sudan 111/F6
Bor, Turkey 63/F4
Bor, U.S.S.R. 52/F3
Bor, Yugoslavia 45/E3
Bora-Bora (isl.), Fr. Poly. 87/L7
Borah (peak), Idaho 188/D2
Borah (peak), Idaho 220/E5
Borama, Somalia 115/H1
Borås, Sweden 7/F3
Borås, Sweden 18/H8
Borazjan, Iran 66/G6
Borazjan, Iran 59/F4
Borba, Brazil 120/D3
Borba, Brazil 132/H9
Borba, Portugal 33/C3
Borbón, Venezuela 124/F4
Borçka, Turkey 63/J2
Borculo, Netherlands 27/J4
Bordeaux, France 28/C5
Bordeaux, France 7/D4
Bordeaux, S.C. (†29835) 296/C4
Bordeaux (mt.), Virgin Is. (U.S.) 161/C4
Bordelonville, La. (71320) 238/G4
Borden (isl.), Canada 4/B15
Borden, Ind. (47106) 227/F8
Borden (isl.), N.W. Terrs. 187/G2
Borden (pen.), N.W. Terrs. 187/K2
Borden, Pr. Edward I. 168/E2
Borden, Sask. 181/D3
Borden, S.C. (29017) 296/G3
Borden (co.), Texas 303/C5
Borden, W. Australia 92/B6
Borden Shaft, Md. (†21532) 245/B2
Borden Springs, Ala. (†36262) 195/H3
Bordentown, N.J. (08505) 273/D3
Border, Minn. (†56623) 255/D2
Border, Wyo. (†83114) 319/B3
Borderland, W. Va. (25665) 312/B7
Borders (reg.), Scotland 15/E5
Bordertown, S. Australia 88/F7
Bordertown, S. Australia 94/G7
Bordighera, Italy 34/A3
Bordj Bou Arreridj, Algeria 106/E1
Bordj Fly Sainte Marie, Algeria 106/D3
Bordj Omar Driss, Algeria 106/F3
Bordj Omar Driss, Algeria 102/C2
Bordulac, N. Dak. (58417) 282/N5
Boreing, Ky. (†40740) 237/N6
Boreray (isl.), Scotland 15/A2
Boreray (isl.), Scotland 15/A3
Borgå, Finland 18/O6
Borge, Norway 18/H2
Borger, Netherlands 27/K3
Borger, Texas (79007) 303/C2
Borger, Texas 188/F3
Borgerhout, Belgium 27/E6
Borgholm, Sweden 18/K8
Borghorst, W. Germany 22/B2
Borgloon, Belgium 27/G7
Borgne (lake), La. 238/L7
Borgne (riv.), Switzerland 39/D4
Borgo, Italy 34/C1
Borgomanero, Italy 34/B2
Borgo San Lorenzo, Italy 34/C2
Borgworm (Waremme), Belgium 27/G7
Borikan, Laos 72/D3
Boring, Md. (21020) 245/L2
Boring, Oreg. (97009) 291/E2
Borinquen (pt.), P. Rico 156/F1
Borinquen (pt.), P. Rico 161/A1
Borislav, U.S.S.R. 52/B5
Borisoglebsk, U.S.S.R. 48/E4
Borisoglebsk, U.S.S.R. 52/F4
Borisov, U.S.S.R. 52/C4
Borisovka, U.S.S.R. 52/E4
Bo River Post, Sudan 111/E6
Borja, Peru 128/D5
Borja, Spain 33/F2
Borjas Blancas, Spain 33/G2
Borken, W. Germany 22/B3
Børkop, Denmark 21/C6
Borku, Chad 111/C4
Borkum, W. Germany 22/B2
Borkum (isl.), W. Germany 22/B2
Borlänge, Sweden 18/J6
Borna, E. Germany 22/E3
Borndiep (chan.), Netherlands 27/H2
Borne, Netherlands 27/K4
Borneo (isl.) 2/Q6
Borneo (isl.) 54/N9
Borneo (isl.), Indonesia 85/E5
Borneo (isl.), Malaysia 85/E5
Bornheim, W. Germany 22/B3
Bornholm (co.), Denmark 21/F9
Bornholm (isl.), Denmark 7/F3
Bornholm (isl.), Denmark 18/J9
Bornholm (isl.), Denmark 21/F9
Borno (state), Nigeria 106/G6
Bornova, Turkey 63/B3
Borocay (isl.), Philippines 82/D5
Borojó, Venezuela 124/C2
Boron, Calif. (93516) 204/H8
Borongan, Philippines 82/E5
Borot Kidod (well), Israel 65/C5
Borovichi, U.S.S.R. 52/D3
Borradaile, Alberta 182/E3
Borre, Norway 18/D4
Borrego Springs, Calif. (92004) 204/J10
Borris, Ireland 17/H6
Borris-in-Ossory, Ireland 17/F6
Borrisokane, Ireland 17/E6
Borrisoleigh, Ireland 17/E6
Borroloola, North. Terr. 88/F3
Borroloola, North. Terr. 93/E4
Borşa, Romania 45/G2
Borsod-Abaúj-Zemplén (co.), Hungary 41/F2
Bortala (Bole), China 77/B3
Borth, Wales 13/C5
Bort-les-Orgues, France 28/E5
Boruca, C. Rica 154/F6
Borujerd, Iran 59/E3
Borujerd, Iran 66/F4
Borup, Denmark 21/E7
Borup, Minn. (56519) 255/B3
Börzsöny (mts.), Hungary 41/E3
Borzya, U.S.S.R. 48/M4
Bosa, Italy 34/B4
Bosanska Dubica, Yugoslavia 45/C3
Bosanska Gradiška, Yugoslavia 45/C3
Bosanska Kostajnica, Yugoslavia 45/B3
Bosanska Krupa, Yugoslavia 45/C3
Bosanski Brod, Yugoslavia 45/D3
Bosanski Novi, Yugoslavia 45/C3
Bosanski Petrovac, Yugoslavia 45/C3
Bosanski Šamac, Yugoslavia 45/D3
Bosaso, Somalia 115/J1
Bosaso, Somalia 102/G3
Boscawen○, N.H. (03301) 268/D5
Bosch, van den (cape), Indonesia 85/J6
Bosco, La. (†71201) 238/F2
Boscobel, Wis. (53805) 317/E9
Bose, China 77/G7
Boshan, China 77/J4
Boskoop, Netherlands 27/F4
Boskovice, Czech. 41/D2
Bosler, Wyo. (82051) 319/G4
Bosna (riv.), Yugoslavia 45/D3
Bosnia and Hercegovina (rep.), Yugoslavia 45/C3
Boso (pen.), Japan 81/K6
Bosobolo, Zaire 115/D3
Bosporus (str.), Turkey 7/G4
Bosporus (str.), Turkey 59/A1
Bosporus (str.), Turkey 63/C2
Bosque (Bosque Farms), N. Mex. (87006) 274/C4
Bosque (co.), Texas 303/G6
Boss, Mo. (65440) 261/K7
Bossangoa, Cent. Afr. Rep. 102/D4
Bossangoa, Cent. Afr. Rep. 115/C2
Bossburg, Wash. (†99126) 310/H2
Bossé, New Bruns. 170/B1
Bossembele, Cent. Afr. Rep. 115/C2
Bossier (par.), La. 238/C1
Bossier City, La. (*71111) 238/C1
Bosso, Niger 106/G6
Bostan, Iran 66/F5
Bostan, Pakistan 68/B2
Bostanabad-e-Bala, Iran 66/E2
Bosten (Bagrax) Hu (lake), China 77/C3
Boston (mts.), Ark. 202/B2
Boston, England 13/G5
Boston, England 10/F4
Boston, Georgia (31626) 217/E9
Boston, Ind. (47324) 227/H5
Boston, Ky. (40107) 237/K5
Boston (cap.), Mass. 146/L5
Boston (cap.), Mass. 188/M2
Boston (cap.), Mass. (*02101) 249/D7
Boston (bay), Mass. 249/E6
Boston (harb.), Mass. 249/D7
Boston, Mo. (†64759) 261/D8
Boston, N.Y. (14025) 276/C5
Boston (mts.), Okla. 288/S3
Boston, Pa. (15135) 294/C7
Boston, Tenn. (†37064) 237/G9
Boston, Texas (75557) 303/K4
Boston, U.S. 2/F3
Boston, Va. (22713) 307/M3
Boston Bar, Br. Col. 184/G5
Boston Heights, Ohio (†44264) 284/J10
Bostonnais (isl.), Québec 172/E2
Bostonnais, Grand Lac (lake), Québec 172/E2
Bostonnais (riv.), Québec 172/E2
Boston Nat'l Hist. Park, Mass. 249/D6
Bostwick, Fla. (32007) 212/E2
Bostwick, Georgia (30623) 217/E3
Bostwick, Nebr. (†68978) 264/F4
Boswell, Ark. (72516) 202/F1
Boswell, Br. Col. 184/J5
Boswell, Ind. (47921) 227/C3
Boswell, Okla. (74727) 288/P6
Boswell, Pa. (15531) 294/E5
Boswell Bay, Alaska (†99574) 196/J2
Boswil, Switzerland 39/F2
Bosworth, Mo. (64723) 261/F4
Bot (riv.), S. Africa 118/G7
Botany, N. S. Wales 88/L4
Botany (bay), N. S. Wales 88/L4
Botany, N.S. Wales 97/J4
Botany (bay), N.S. Wales 97/J4
Botene, Laos 72/D3
Botetourt (co.), Va. 307/J5
Botevgrad, Bulgaria 45/F4
Botha, Alberta 182/D3
Botha (riv.), Alberta 182/B1
Bothell, Wash. (98011) 310/B1
Bothnia (gulf) 7/G2
Bothnia (gulf), Finland 18/M5
Bothnia (gulf), Sweden 18/N4
Bothwell, Ontario 177/C5
Bothwell, Tasmania 99/C4
Bothwell, Utah (†84337) 304/B2
Botkins, Ohio (45306) 284/B5
Botna, Iowa (†51454) 229/C5
Botoşani, Romania 45/H2
Botrange (mt.), Belgium 27/J8
Botrivier, S. Africa 118/F7
Botsford, Conn. (06404) 210/C3
Botswana 2/L7
Botswana 102/E7
BOTSWANA 118/C4
Bottesford, England 13/G4
Bottineau (co.), N. Dak. 282/J2
Bottineau, N. Dak. (58318) 282/J2
Bottrel, Alberta 182/C4
Bottrop, W. Germany 22/B3
Botucatu, Brazil 135/B3
Botucatu, Brazil 132/D8
Botwood, Newf. 166/C4
Bouaflé, Ivory Coast 106/C7
Bouaké, Ivory Coast 102/B4
Bouaké, Ivory Coast 106/D7
Bouali, Cent. Afr. Rep. 115/C3
Bouar, Cent. Afr. Rep. 102/D4
Bouar, Cent. Afr. Rep. 115/C2
Bou Arfa, Morocco 106/D2
Bouca, Cent. Afr. Rep. 115/C2
Boucaut (bay), North. Terr. 93/D1
Boucherville, Québec 172/J4
Boucherville (isl.), Québec 172/J4
Bouches-du-Rhône (dept.), France 28/F6
Bouchette, Québec 172/A3
Buckville, N.Y. (13310) 276/J5
Bou Djebeha, Mali 106/D5
Boudreau (bay), La. 238/M7
Boudreaux, La. (†70353) 238/J8
Boudreaux (lake), La. 238/J8
Boudry, Switzerland 39/C3
Boufarik, Algeria 106/E1
Bougainville (reef), 95/C2
Bougainville (reef), Coral Sea Is. Terr. 88/H3
Bougainville (isl.), Papua N.G. 87/F6
Bougainville (isl.), Papua N.G. 86/C2
Bougainville (str.), Papua N.G. 86/D2
Bougainville (str.), Solomon Is. 86/D2
Bougainville (cape), W. Australia 88/D2
Bougainville (cape), W. Australia 92/D1
Bougaroun (cape), Algeria 106/F1
Boughton (isl.), Pr. Edward I. 168/F2
Bougie (Béjaïa), Algeria 106/F1
Bougouni, Mali 106/C6
Bouillante, Guadeloupe 161/A6
Bouillon, Belgium 27/G9
Bou Izakarn, Morocco 106/C3
Boujad, Morocco 106/C2
Boula, Cent. Afr. Rep. 115/C3
Boulanger, Québec 172/E1
Boularderie (isl.), Nova Scotia 168/H2
Boulder, Australia 87/C9
Boulder, Colo. 188/E2
Boulder, Colo. 146/H6
Boulder (co.), Colo. 208/J2
Boulder, Colo. (*80301) 208/J2
Boulder (mts.), Idaho 220/D6
Boulder, Mont. (59632) 262/E4
Boulder (lake), N. Mex. 274/C2
Boulder, Utah (84716) 304/C6
Boulder (creek), Utah 304/C6
Boulder, W. Australia 88/C6
Boulder, Wyo. (82923) 319/C3
Boulder (lake), Wyo. 319/C3
Boulder City, Nev. (89005) 266/G7
Boulder Creek, Calif. (95006) 204/J4
Boulder Junction, Wis. (54512) 317/G3
Boulder-Kalgoorlie, W. Australia 92/C5
Boulevard, Calif. (92005) 204/J11
Boulevard Heights, Md. (†20027) 245/F5
Boulia, Queensland 95/A4
Boulia, Queensland 88/F4
Boulogne, Fla. (†32046) 212/E1
Boulogne-Billancourt, France 28/A2
Boulogne-sur-Mer, France 28/D2
Bouna, Ivory Coast 106/D7
Boundary, Alaska (†99732) 196/K2
Boundary (co.), Idaho 220/B1
Boundary (peak), Nev. 266/C5
Boundary (plat.), Sask. 181/B6
Boundary (bay), Wash. 310/C1
Boundary (dam), Wash. 310/H2
Boundary (lake), Wash. 310/H2
Boundary Bend, Victoria 97/B4
Bound Brook, N.J. (08805) 273/D2
Boundiali, Ivory Coast 106/C7
Boundji, Congo 115/C4
Boun Nua, Laos 72/D2
Bountiful, Utah (84010) 304/C3
Bounty (isls.), N. Zealand 87/H10
Bounty, Sask. 181/D4
Bourail, New Caled. 87/G8
Bourail, New Caled. 86/G4
Bourbon, Ill. (†61953) 222/E4
Bourbon, Ind. (46504) 227/E2
Bourbon (co.), Kansas 232/H4
Bourbon (co.), Ky. 237/N4
Bourbon, Miss. (†38756) 256/C4
Bourbon, Mo. (65441) 261/K6
Bourbonnais (trad. prov.), France 29
Bourbonnais, Ill. (60914) 222/F2
Bourem, Mali 106/E5
Bourg, La. (70343) 238/J7
Bourganeuf, France 28/D5
Bourg-des-Saintes, Guadeloupe 161/A7
Bourg-en-Bresse, France 28/F4
Bourgeois, New Bruns. 170/F2
Bourges, France 28/E4
Bourget, Ontario 177/J2
Bourg-Léopold (Leopoldsburg), Belgium 27/G6
Bourgoin-Jallieu, France 28/F5
Bourg Saint-Pierre, Switzerland 39/D5
Bourke, N. S. Wales 88/H6
Bourke, N.S. Wales 97/D2
Bourne, England 13/G5
Bourne, Mass. (02532) 249/M6
Bourne○, Mass. (02532) 249/M6
Bournedale, Mass. (†02532) 249/M5
Bournemouth, England 13/F7
Bournemouth, England 10/F5
Bourneville, Ohio (45617) 284/D7
Bou Saâda, Algeria 106/E1
Bouse, Ariz. (85325) 198/A5
Bouse Wash (dry riv.), Ariz. 198/A4
Boussac, France 28/D4
Bousso, Chad 111/C5
Boussu, Belgium 27/D8
Boutilimit, Mauritania 106/B5
Boutilimit, Mauritania 102/A3
Bouton, Iowa (50039) 229/E5
Boutte, La. (70039) 238/N4
Bouvard (cape), W. Australia 92/A2
Bouvet (isl.) 5/D1
Bouvetøya (Bouvet) (isl.) 5/D1
Boven Bolivia, Neth. Ant. 161/E8
Boves, Italy 34/A2
Bovey, Minn. (55709) 255/E3
Bovey Tracey, England 13/D7
Bovill, Idaho (83806) 220/B3
Bovina, Miss. (†39180) 256/C6
Bovina, Texas (79009) 303/A3
Bovril, Argentina 143/G5
Bow (riv.), Alberta 182/D4
Bow (riv.), Alta. 162/E5
Bow (lake), N.H. 268/E5
Bow, Wash. (98232) 310/C2
Bowbells, N. Dak. (58721) 282/F2
Bow City, Alberta 182/D4
Bowden, Alberta 182/C4
Bowden, Jamaica 158/K6
Bowden, W. Va. (26254) 312/G5
Bowdens, N.C. (28322) 281/N4
Bowdle, S. Dak. (57428) 298/K3
Bowdoin (lake), Mont. 262/J2
Bowdoinham○, Maine (04008) 243/D7
Bowdon, Georgia (30108) 217/B3
Bowdon, N. Dak. (58418) 282/L5
Bowdon Junction, Georgia (30109) 217/B3
Bowell, Alberta 182/E4
Bowen, Australia 87/E7
Bowen, Ill. (62316) 222/B3
Bowen, Ky. (40309) 237/O5
Bowen, Queensland 95/D3
Bowen, Queensland 88/H3
Bowen Island, Br. Col. 184/K3
Bowens, Md. (†20678) 245/M6
Bowerbank○, Maine (†04481) 243/E5
Bowers, Ind. (†47940) 227/D4
Bowers Beach, Del. (†19962) 245/S4
Bowers Mill, Mo. (†64848) 261/E8
Bowerston, Ohio (44695) 284/H5
Bowersville, Georgia (30516) 217/G2
Bowersville, Ohio (44695) 284/C6
Bowes, England 13/F3
Bowesmont, N. Dak. (58217) 282/R2
Bowie, Ariz. (85605) 198/F6
Bowie, Colo. (†81428) 208/D5
Bowie, Md. (20715) 245/L4
Bowie (creek), Miss. 256/E7
Bowie (co.), Texas 303/K4
Bowie, Texas (76230) 303/G4
Bow Island, Alberta 182/E5
Bowkan, Iran 66/E2
Bowlegs, Okla. (74830) 288/N4
Bowler, Wis. (54416) 317/J6
Bowling Green, Fla. (33834) 212/E4
Bowling Green, Ind. (47833) 227/D6
Bowling Green, Ky. (42101) 237/H7
Bowling Green, Ky. 188/J3
Bowling Green, Mo. (63334) 261/K4
Bowling Green, Ohio (43402) 284/C3
Bowling Green (cape), Queensland 88/H3
Bowling Green (cape), Queensland 95/C3
Bowling Green, S.C. (29703) 296/E1
Bowling Green, Va. (22427) 307/O4
Bowlus, Minn. (56314) 255/D5
Bowman, Calif. (95604) 204/C8
Bowman, Georgia (30624) 217/G2
Bowman (co.), N. Dak. 282/C7
Bowman, N. Dak. (58623) 282/D7
Bowman (bay), N.W.T. 162/J2
Bowman (bay), N.W. Terrs. 187/L3
Bowman (dam), Oreg. 291/G3
Bowman, S.C. (29018) 296/F5
Bowmansdale, Pa. (17008) 294/J5
Bowmanstown, Pa. (18030) 294/L4
Bowmansville, Pa. (17507) 294/L5
Bow Mills, N.H. (†03301) 268/D5
Bowmont, Idaho (†83651) 220/B6
Bowmore, Scotland 15/B5
Bowmore, Scotland 10/C3
Bowral, N.S. Wales 97/F4
Bowraville, N.S. Wales 97/G2
Bowring, Okla. (74009) 288/O1
Bowron Lake Prov. Park, Br. Col. 184/G3
Bowser, Br. Col. 184/H2
Bowser (lake), Br. Col. 184/C2
Bowsman, Manitoba 179/A2
Bowstring, Minn. (56631) 255/E3
Bowstring (lake), Minn. 255/E3
Boxborough○, Mass. (01719) 249/H3
Box Butte (co.), Nebr. 264/A2
Box Butte (res.), Nebr. 264/A2
Box Canyon (dam), Wash. 310/H2
Box Elder (creek), Colo. 208/K4
Box Elder, Mont. (59521) 262/F2
Boxelder (creek), Mont. 262/M5
Boxelder (creek), Mont. 262/H3
Box Elder, S. Dak. (57719) 298/D5
Boxelder (creek), S. Dak. 298/D5
Box Elder (co.), Utah 304/A2
Boxford, Mass. (01921) 249/L2
Boxford○, Mass. (01921) 249/L2
Box Hill, Victoria 97/J5
Box Hill, Victoria 88/L7
Boxholm, Iowa (50040) 229/E4
Bo Xian (Pohsien), China 77/J5
Boxley, Ark. (†72742) 202/D2
Boxmeer, Netherlands 27/H5
Box Springs, Georgia (31801) 217/C5
Boxtel, Netherlands 27/G5
Boyabat, Turkey 63/F2
Boyacá (dept.), Colombia 126/D5
Boyama (Stanley) (falls), Zaire 102/E5
Boyama (Stanley) (falls), Zaire 115/D3
Boyanup, W. Australia 92/A2
Boyce, La. (71409) 238/E4
Boyce, Va. (22620) 307/M2
Boyceville, Wis. (54725) 317/C5
Boyd, Ala. (†35470) 195/B5
Boyd, Fla. (†32347) 212/C1
Boyd (co.), Ky. 237/R4
Boyd, Minn. (56218) 255/C6
Boyd, Mont. (59013) 262/G5
Boyd (co.), Nebr. 264/F2
Boyd, Okla. (†73931) 288/E1
Boyd, Oreg. (†97021) 291/F2
Boyd, Texas (76023) 303/E1
Boyd, Wis. (54726) 317/E6
Boydell, Ark. (†71658) 202/H7
Boyden, Iowa (51234) 229/B2
Boyden Arbor, S.C. (†29128) 296/F3
Boyd Lake, Maine (†04463) 243/F5
Boyds, Md. (20720) 245/J4
Boyds, Wash. (99107) 310/G2
Boydton, Va. (23917) 307/M7
Boyer (riv.), Alberta 182/A5
Boyer, Iowa (†51448) 229/C4
Boyer (riv.), Iowa 229/B5
Boyer, W. Va. (†24915) 312/G5
Boyer Ahmediyeh and Kohkiluyeh (gov.), Iran 66/G5
Boyero, Colo. (80821) 208/N5
Boyers, Pa. (16020) 294/C3
Boyertown, Pa. (19512) 294/L5
Boyes, Mont. (59316) 262/M5
Boykin, Georgia (†31737) 217/C8
Boykin, S.C. (†29128) 296/F3
Boykins, Va. (23827) 307/O7
Boyle, Alberta 182/D2
Boyle, Ireland 17/E4
Boyle, Ireland 10/B3
Boyle (co.), Ky. 237/M5
Boyle, Miss. (38730) 256/C3
Boyleston, Ind. (†46057) 227/E4
Boylston○, Mass. (01505) 249/H3
Boylston, Nova Scotia 168/G3
Boyne (riv.), Ireland 17/J4
Boyne City, Mich. (49712) 250/E3

342 Boyne Falls

Boyne Falls, Mich. (49713) 250/E3
Boyne Lake, Alberta 182/E5
Boynton, Okla. (74422) 288/P3
Boynton Beach, Fla. (*33435) 212/F5
Boy River, Minn. (56632) 255/D3
Boysen (res.), Wyo. 319/D2
Boysen Bay, N.Y. (†13212) 276/H4
Boys Ranch, Texas (79010) 303/B2
Boys Town, Nebr. (68010) 264/H3
Boyuibe, Bolivia 136/D7
Bozcaada (isl.), Turkey 63/A3
Bozdoğan, Turkey 63/C4
Bozeman, Mont. 188/D1
Bozeman, Mont. (59715) 262/E5
Bozkır, Turkey 63/E4
Bozkurt, Turkey 63/F2
Bozman, Md. (21612) 245/N5
Bozoum, Cent. Afr. Rep. 115/C2
Bozova, Turkey 63/H4
Bozqush, Kuh-e (mts.), Iran 66/E2
Bozüyük, Turkey 59/B2
Bozüyük, Turkey 63/C3
Bra, Italy 34/A2
Brabant (prov.), Belgium 27/F7
Brabant Lake, Sask. 181/M3
Brač (isl.), Yugoslavia 45/C4
Bracadale, Loch (inlet), Scotland 15/B3
Bracciano, Italy 34/C3
Bracciano (lake), Italy 34/D3
Bracebridge, Ontario 177/E2
Braceville, Ill. (60407) 222/E2
Bracey, Va. (23919) 307/M7
Bräcke, Sweden 18/J5
Bracken (co.), Ky. 237/N3
Bracken, Sask. 181/C6
Brackendale, Br. Col. 184/F5
Brackenridge, Pa. (15014) 294/C4
Brackett, Wis. (†54742) 317/D6
Brackettville (canton), Texas 303/D8
Brackley, England 10/F4
Brackley, England 13/F5
Bracknell, England 13/G8
Bracknell, Tasmania 99/C3
Brackney, Pa. (18812) 294/K2
Brackwede, W. Germany 22/C3
Braço Maior do Araguaia (riv.), Brazil 132/D5
Braço Menor do Araguaia (riv.), Brazil 132/D6
Brad, Romania 45/F2
Bradbury, Calif. (91010) 204/D10
Braddock, N. Dak. (58524) 282/K6
Braddock, Pa. (15104) 294/C7
Braddock, Sask. 181/D5
Braddyville, Iowa (51631) 229/D7
Braden, Okla. (†74959) 288/S4
Braden, Tenn. (38010) 237/B10
Bradenton, Fla. (*33506) 212/D4
Bradenton Beach, Fla. (33510) 212/D4
Bradford, Ark. (72020) 202/G3
Bradford, England 13/J1
Bradford, England 10/H1
Bradford (co.), Fla. 212/D2
Bradford, Ill. (61421) 222/D2
Bradford, Ind. (47107) 227/E8
Bradford, Iowa (50041) 229/G3
Bradford, Ky. (†41043) 237/N3
Bradford, Maine (04410) 243/F5
Bradford○, Maine (04410) 243/F5
Bradford○, N.H. (03221) 268/D5
Bradford, Ohio (45308) 284/B5
Bradford, Ontario 177/E3
Bradford (co.), Pa. 294/J2
Bradford, Pa. (16701) 294/E2
Bradford, R.I. (02808) 249/H7
Bradford, Tenn. (38316) 237/D8
Bradford, Vt. (05033) 268/C3
Bradford○, Vt. (05033) 268/C3
Bradford Center, Maine (†04410) 243/F5
Bradford-on-Avon, England 13/E6
Bradfordsville, Ky. (40009) 237/L6
Bradgate, Iowa (50520) 229/E3
Bradley (co.), Ark. 202/F7
Bradley, Ark. (71826) 202/C7
Bradley, Calif. (93426) 204/E8
Bradley, Fla. (33835) 212/D4
Bradley, Georgia (†31032) 217/E4
Bradley, Ill. (60915) 222/F2
Bradley○, Maine (04411) 243/F6
Bradley, Miss. (†39759) 256/G4
Bradley, Ohio (†43917) 284/J5
Bradley, Okla. (73011) 288/L5
Bradley, S.C. (29819) 296/C3
Bradley, S. Dak. (57217) 298/O3
Bradley (co.), Tenn. 237/M10
Bradley, Wis. (†54487) 317/G4
Bradley Beach, N.J. (07720) 273/F3
Bradleyton, Ala. (†36041) 195/F7
Bradleyville, Mo. (65614) 261/F9
Bradner, Ohio (43406) 284/C3
Bradshaw, Nebr. (68371) 264/G4
Bradshaw, Texas (†79567) 303/D5
Bradshaw, W. Va. (24817) 312/C8
Bradwardine, Manitoba 179/B5
Bradwell, Sask. 181/E4
Brady (glac.), Alaska 196/M1
Brady, Mont. (59416) 262/E2
Brady, Nebr. (69123) 264/D3
Brady (mt.), S. Australia 94/D3
Brady, Texas (76825) 303/E6
Brady Lake, Ohio (44211) 284/H3
Bradyville, Tenn. (37026) 237/J9
Brae, Scotland 15/G2
Braedstrup, Denmark 21/C6
Braemar, Scotland 15/E3
Braemar, Scotland 10/E2
Braemar (dist.), Scotland 15/E3
Braemar, Tenn. (37658) 237/S8
Braeside, Ontario 177/H2
Braeside, W. Australia 92/C3
Braga (dist.), Portugal 33/B2
Braga, Portugal 7/D4
Braga, Portugal 33/B2
Bragado, Argentina 143/F7
Bragança, Brazil 120/E3
Bragança, Brazil 132/E3
Bragança (dist.), Portugal 33/C2
Bragança, Portugal 33/C2
Bragança Paulista, Brazil 135/C3
Bragança Paulista, Brazil 132/E8
Braggadocio, Mo. (63826) 261/N10
Bragg City, Mo. (63827) 261/N10
Bragg Creek, Alberta 182/C4
Braggs, Ala. (†36761) 195/E6
Braggs, Okla. (74423) 288/R3
Bragman's Bluff (Puerto Cabezas), Nicaragua 154/F3
Braham, Minn. (55006) 255/E5
Brahmaputra (riv.) 54/L7
Brahmaputra (riv.), Bangladesh 68/G3
Brahmaputra (riv.), India 68/G3
Braich-y-Pwll (prom.), Wales 10/D4
Braich-y-Pwll (prom.), Wales 13/C5
Braidwood, Ill. (60408) 222/E2
Braidwood, N.S. Wales 97/E4
Brăila, Romania 7/G4
Brăila, Romania 45/H3
Brăila (marshes), Romania 45/H3
Brainard, Nebr. (68626) 264/G3
Brainards, N.J. (08865) 273/C2
Braine-l'Alleud, Belgium 27/E7
Braine-le-Comte, Belgium 27/D7
Brainerd, Minn. 188/H1
Brainerd, Minn. (56401) 255/D4
Braintree○, Mass. (02184) 249/D8
Braintree (West Braintree), Vt. 268/B4
Braintree○, Vt. (†05669) 268/B4
Braintree and Bocking, England 13/H6
Braintree and Bocking, England 10/G5
Braithwaite, La. (70040) 238/P4
Brak, Libya 102/D2
Brak, Libya 111/B2
Brake, W. Germany 22/C2
Brakna (reg.), Mauritania 106/B5
Brakpan, S. Africa 118/J6
Bralorne, Br. Col. 184/F5
Braman, Okla. (74632) 288/M1
Bramber, Nova Scotia 168/D3
Bramberg am Wildkogel, Austria 41/B3
Bramble (bay), Queensland 95/E2
Bramming, Denmark 21/B7
Bramon, Venezuela 124/B4
Brampton, England 13/E3
Brampton, Mich. (49810) 250/B3
Brampton, N. Dak. (58010) 282/P7
Brampton, Ontario 177/J4
Bramsche, W. Germany 22/B2
Bramwell, W. Va. (24715) 312/B8
Bran (riv.), Scotland 15/D3
Brancepeth, Sask. 181/F2
Branch, Ark. (72928) 202/C3
Branch, La. (70516) 238/F6
Branch (co.), Mich. 250/D7
Branch, Mich. (49402) 250/D5
Branch, Minn. (†55056) 255/F5
Branch, Mo. (†65786) 261/G7
Branch, Newf. 166/D2
Branch (riv.), Newf. 166/C2
Branch, Wis. (54203) 317/L7
Branch Dale, Pa. (17923) 294/K4
Branchport, N.Y. (14418) 276/F5
Branchton, Pa. (16021) 294/C3
Branchville, Ala. (†35120) 195/F3
Branchville, Conn. (†06829) 210/B3
Branchville, Ind. (47514) 227/D8
Branchville, N.J. (07826) 273/D1
Branchville, S.C. (29432) 296/F5
Branchville, Va. (23828) 307/O7
Branco (riv.), Brazil 120/C2
Branco (riv.), Brazil 132/H8
Brandberg (mt.), Namibia 118/A4
Brande, Denmark 21/B6
Brandenburg, E. Germany 22/E2
Brandenburg (reg.), E. Germany 22/E2
Brandenburg, Ky. (40108) 237/J4
Brandon, Colo. (81026) 208/P6
Brandon, England 13/H5
Brandon, Fla. (33511) 212/D4
Brandon, Iowa (52210) 229/K4
Brandon (bay), Ireland 17/A7
Brandon (head), Ireland 17/A7
Brandon (mt.), Ireland 17/A7
Brandon, Man. 146/H4
Brandon, Man. 162/F6
Brandon, Manitoba 179/C5
Brandon, Minn. (56315) 255/C5
Brandon, Miss. (39042) 256/E6
Brandon, Nebr. (69102) 264/C4
Brandon, Ohio (†43050) 284/F5
Brandon, S. Dak. (57005) 298/R6
Brandon, Vt. (05733) 268/A4
Brandon○, Vt. (05733) 268/A4
Brandon, Wis. (53919) 317/J8
Brandon Gap (pass), Vt. 268/B4
Brandonville, W. Va. (26523) 312/G3
Brandreth (lake), N.Y. 276/L3
Brandsville, Mo. (65688) 261/J9
Brandt, Ohio (†45371) 284/B6
Brandt, S. Dak. (57218) 298/R4
Brandvlei, S. Africa 118/B6
Brandýs nad Labem-Stará Boleslavv, Czech. 41/C1
Brandy Station, Va. (22714) 307/N4
Brandywine, Md. (20613) 245/L6
Brandywine, W. Va. (26802) 312/H5
Branford, Conn. (06405) 210/D3
Branford○, Conn. (06405) 210/D3
Branford (harb.), Conn. 210/D4
Branford (riv.), Conn. 210/D3
Branford, Fla. (32008) 212/D2
Braniewo, Poland 47/D1
Brannock (isls.), Ireland 17/A5
Bransfield (str.) 5/C16
Branson, Colo. (81027) 208/M8
Branson, Mo. (65616) 261/F9
Brant, Alberta 182/D4
Brant, Mich. (48614) 250/E5
Brant, N.Y. (14027) 276/B5
Brant (lake), N.Y. 276/N3
Brant (county), Ontario 177/D4
Brant (lake), S. Dak. 298/R6
Brant Beach, N.J. (†08008) 273/E4
Brantford, Kansas (†66938) 232/E2
Brantford, N. Dak. (†58356) 282/N4
Brantford, Ontario 177/D4
Brant Lake, N.Y. (12815) 276/N3
Brantley, Ala. (36009) 195/F7
Brantley (co.), Georgia 217/J8
Brant Rock-Ocean Bluff, Mass. (02020) 249/M4
Brantville, New Bruns. 170/E1
Brantwood, Wis. (54513) 317/F4
Branxholm, Tasmania 99/D3
Branxholme, Victoria 97/A5
Branxton-Greta, N.S. Wales 97/F3
Bras d'Or, Nova Scotia 168/H2
Bras d'Or (lake), Nova Scotia 168/H3
Braselton, Georgia (30517) 217/E2
Brasfield, Ark. (†72017) 202/H4
Brashear, Mo. (63533) 261/H2
Brasher, Mo. (†63830) 261/N10
Brasher Falls-Winthrop, N.Y. (13613) 276/L1
Brasiléia, Brazil 132/G10
Brasília (cap.), Brazil 2/G6
Brasília (cap.), Brazil 120/E4
Brasília (cap.), Brazil 132/E6
Brasília de Minas, Brazil 132/F7
Brașov, Romania 45/G3
Brașov, Romania 7/G4
Brass, Nigeria 106/F8
Brass (isls.), Virgin Is. (U.S.) 161/A4
Brassey (range), W. Australia 92/C4
Brasstown Bald (mt.), Georgia 217/E1
Brassua (lake), Maine 243/D4
Braswell, Georgia (†30153) 217/C3
Brate, Norway 18/G7
Bratenahl, Ohio (†44101) 284/H9
Bratislava, Czech. 7/F4
Bratislava (city), Czech. 41/D2
Bratislava, Czech. 41/D2
Bratsk, U.S.S.R. 54/M4
Bratsk, U.S.S.R. 48/L4
Bratsk (res.), U.S.S.R. 48/L4
Brattleboro, Vt. (05301) 268/B6
Brattleboro○, Vt. (05301) 268/B6
Bratton, Sask. 181/D4
Braunau am Inn, Austria 41/B2
Braunlage, W. Germany 22/D3
Braunschweig (Brunswick), W. Germany 22/D2
Braunton, England 13/C6
Brava (isl.), C. Verde 106/B8
Brava, Somalia 115/H3
Brava, Somalia 102/G4
Brava (pt.), Uruguay 145/B7
Brave, Pa. (15316) 294/B6
Bravo (riv.), Chile 138/D7
Bravo (Grande) (riv.), Mexico 150/G2
Brawley, Calif. 188/C4
Brawley, Calif. (92227) 204/K11
Braxton, Miss. (39044) 256/D6
Braxton (co.), W. Va. 312/E5
Bray, Ireland 17/K5
Bray, Ireland 10/C4
Bray (head), Ireland 17/A8
Bray (isl.), N.W. Terrs. 187/L3
Bray, Okla. (73012) 288/L5
Braymer, Mo. (64624) 261/E3
Brayton, Iowa (50042) 229/D5
Brazeau (dam), Alberta 182/C3
Brazeau (mt.), Alberta 182/B3
Brazeau (riv.), Alberta 182/B3
Brazil 2/F6
Brazil 120/D4
BRAZIL 132, 135
Brazil, Ind. (47834) 227/C5
Brazil, Miss. (38963) 256/D2
Brazil, Tenn. (†38382) 237/C9
Brazilian Highlands (plat.), Brazil 120/E4
Brazilton, Kansas (†66743) 232/H4
Brazito, Mo. (†65101) 261/H6
Brazoria (co.), Texas 303/J8
Brazoria, Texas (77422) 303/J9
Brazos (peak), N. Mex. 274/C2
Brazos (co.), Texas 303/H7
Brazos (riv.), Texas 188/G4
Brazos (riv.), Texas 146/J6
Brazos (riv.), Texas 303/H7
Brazo Sur, Pilcomayo (riv.), Argentina 143/E1
Brazzaville (cap.), Congo 115/C4
Brazzaville (cap.), Congo 2/K6
Brazzaville (cap.), Congo 102/D5
Brčko, Yugoslavia 45/D3
Brda (riv.), Poland 47/C2
Brea, Calif. (92621) 204/D11
Breadalbane (dist.), Scotland 15/D4
Bread Loaf, Vt. (05753) 268/B4
Bread Loaf (mt.), Vt. 268/A3
Breakabeen, N.Y. (†12122) 276/M5
Breakeyville, Québec 172/J3
Breaks, Va. (24607) 307/D6
Breaksea (sound), N. Zealand 100/A6
Bream (bay), N. Zealand 100/E1
Breasclete, Scotland 15/B2
Breathitt (co.), Ky. 237/P5
Breau-Village, New Bruns. 170/F2
Breaux Bridge, La. (70517) 238/G6
Brebes, Indonesia 85/H2
Brébeuf, Québec 172/C3
Brébeuf (lake), Québec 172/G1
Brechin, Ontario 177/E3
Brechin, Scotland 10/E2
Brechin, Scotland 15/F4
Brecht, Belgium 27/F6
Breckenridge, Colo. (80424) 208/G4
Breckenridge, Mich. (48615) 250/E5
Breckenridge, Minn. (56520) 255/B4
Breckenridge, Mo. (64625) 261/E3
Breckenridge, Texas (76024) 303/F5
Breckenridge Hills, Mo. (†63114) 261/O2
Breckinridge (co.), Ky. 237/H5
Breckinridge, Okla. (73721) 288/L2
Brecknock (Brecon), Wales 13/D6
Brecksville, Ohio (44141) 284/H10
Břeclav, Czech. 41/D2
Brecon, Wales 13/D6
Brecon, Wales 10/E5
Brecon Beacons (mt.), Wales 13/D6
Brecon Beacons National Park, Wales 13/D6
Breda, Iowa (51436) 229/C4
Breda, Netherlands 27/F5
Bredasdorp, S. Africa 118/B6
Bredasdorp Nat'l Park, S. Africa 118/C6
Bredbo, N.S. Wales 97/E4
Bredbyn, Sweden 18/L5
Bredebro, Denmark 21/B7
Bredenbury, Sask. 181/K5
Bredene, Belgium 27/B6
Bredstedt, W. Germany 22/C1
Bree, Belgium 27/H6
Breed, Wis. (†54174) 317/K5
Breeden, W. Va. (25666) 312/B7
Breeding, Ky. (42715) 237/L7
Breedsville, Mich. (49027) 250/C6
Breese, Ill. (62230) 222/D5
Breesport, N.Y. (14816) 276/G6
Breezand, Netherlands 27/F3
Breezy Point, Minn. (†56472) 255/D4
Bregenz, Austria 41/A3
Bregovo, Bulgaria 45/F3
Breidhafjördhur (fjord), Iceland 7/B2
Breidhafjördhur (fjord), Iceland 21/B1
Breien, N. Dak. (58525) 282/H7
Breil-Brigels, Switzerland 39/H3
Breil-sur-Roya, France 28/G6
Breisach am Rhein, W. Germany 22/B4
Breisgau (reg.), W. Germany 22/B5
Breitenbach, Switzerland 39/E2
Breitenbush, Oreg. (†97342) 291/F3
Breithorn (mt.), Switzerland 39/E5
Breithorn (mt.), Switzerland 39/E4
Brejo, Brazil 132/F3
Bremanger (isl.), Norway 18/D6
Bremen, Ala. (35033) 195/E3
Bremen, Georgia (30110) 217/B3
Bremen, Ill. (†62233) 222/D6
Bremen, Ind. (46506) 227/E2
Bremen, Kansas (66412) 232/F2
Bremen, Ky. (42325) 237/G6
Bremen, N. Dak. (58319) 282/M4
Bremen, Ohio (43107) 284/F6
Bremen, Sask. 181/F3
Bremen, W. Germany 7/E3
Bremen (state), W. Germany 22/C2
Bremen, W. Germany 22/C2
Bremer (co.), Iowa 229/J3
Bremer, Iowa (†50677) 229/J3
Bremerhaven, W. Germany 22/C2
Bremerton, Wash. 188/B1
Bremerton, Wash. (98310) 310/A2
Bremervörde, W. Germany 22/C2
Bremgarten, Switzerland 39/F2
Bremo Bluff, Va. (23022) 307/M5
Bremond, Texas (76629) 303/H6
Brenham, Texas (77833) 303/H7
Brenner (pass), Austria 41/A3
Brenner (pass), Italy 34/C1
Brent, Ala. (35034) 195/D5
Brent, England 13/H8
Brent, England 10/B5
Brent, Ontario 177/F1
Brentford, S. Dak. (57429) 298/N3
Brenton (pt.), R.I. 249/J7
Brentwood, Ark. (†72959) 202/B2
Brentwood, Calif. (94513) 204/L2
Brentwood, England 10/C5
Brentwood, England 13/J8
Brentwood, Md. (20722) 245/F4
Brentwood, Mo. (63144) 261/P3
Brentwood○, N.H. (†03833) 268/E6
Brentwood, N.Y. (11717) 276/O9
Brentwood, Pa. (15227) 294/B7
Brentwood, Tenn. (37027) 237/H8
Brentwood Park, S. Africa 118/J6
Brereton Lake, Manitoba 179/G5
Bresaylor, Sask. 181/C3
Brescia (prov.), Italy 34/C2
Brescia, Italy 7/E4
Brescia, Italy 34/C2
Breskens, Netherlands 27/C6
Breslau (Wrocław), Poland 47/C3
Bressanone, Italy 34/C1
Bressay (isl.), Scotland 15/G2
Bressay (isl.), Scotland 10/G1
Bressuire, France 28/C4
Brest, France 7/D4
Brest, France 28/A3
Brest, Georgia (†31716) 217/D8
Brest, New Bruns. 170/E2
Brest, U.S.S.R. 7/G3
Brest, U.S.S.R. 48/C4
Brest, U.S.S.R. 52/B4
Bretaña, Peru 128/E5
Brethren, Mich. (49619) 250/D4
Breton, Alberta 182/C3
Breton (isls.), La. 238/M8
Breton (sound), La. 238/M7
Breton (cape), Nova Scotia 168/J3
Breton Cove, Nova Scotia 168/H2
Breton Woods, N.J. (08723) 273/E3
Brett (cape), N. Zealand 100/E1
Bretten, W. Germany 22/C4
Bretton Woods, N.H. (03575) 268/E3
Brevard (co.), Fla. 212/F3
Brevard, N.C. (28712) 281/D4
Breves, Brazil 132/D3
Brevig Mission, Alaska (99785) 196/E1
Brevik, Minn. (†56655) 255/D3
Brevoort (lake), Mich. 250/D3
Brevoort (isl.), N.W. Terrs. 187/M3
Brevort, Mich. (†49760) 250/E2
Brewarrina, N. S. Wales 88/H5
Brewarrina, N.S. Wales 97/D1
Brewer, Maine (04412) 243/F6
Brewer, Mo. (†63775) 261/N7
Brewers, Ky. (†42025) 237/E7
Brewers Mills, New Bruns. 170/C2
Brewersville, Ind. (†47265) 227/F6
Brewerton, N.Y. (13029) 276/H4
Brewster (pond), Conn. 210/F2
Brewster, Kansas (67732) 232/A2
Brewster, Mass. (02631) 249/O5
Brewster○, Mass. (02631) 249/O5
Brewster (isls.), Mass. 249/E7
Brewster, Minn. (56119) 255/C7
Brewster, Nebr. (68821) 264/D3
Brewster (lake), N.S. Wales 97/D3
Brewster, N.Y. (10509) 276/N8
Brewster, Ohio (44613) 284/G4
Brewster, Cerro (mt.), Panama 154/H6
Brewster (co.), Texas 303/A8
Brewster, Wash. (98812) 310/F2
Brewton, Ala. (36426) 195/D8
Breynat, Alberta 182/D2
Brežice, Yugoslavia 45/B3
Brezina, Algeria 106/E2
Březnice, Czech. 41/B2
Breznik, Bulgaria 45/F4
Brezno, Czech. 41/E2
Bria, Cent. Afr. Rep. 102/E4
Bria, Cent. Afr. Rep. 115/D2
Briançon, France 28/G5
Brian Head, Utah (84719) 304/B6
Briar, Texas (†76023) 303/E1
Briar Creek, Pa. (†18603) 294/K3
Briare, France 28/E4
Briartown, Okla. (†74455) 288/R4
Briarwood, (†58102) 282/S6
Bribbaree, N.S. Wales 97/D3
Brice, Ohio (43109) 284/E6
Bricelyn, Minn. (56014) 255/E7
Brices Cross Roads Nat'l Battlefield Site, Miss.256/G2
Briceville, Tenn. (37710) 237/N8
Brí Chualann (Bray), Ireland 17/K5
Brick○, N.J. (08723) 273/E3
Brickaville (Vohibinany), Madagascar 118/H3
Brickerville, Pa. (†17543) 294/K5
Brickeys, Ark. (72320) 202/J4
Bricks, N.C. (†27891) 281/O2
Brickton, Nova Scotia 168/C4
Bridal Veil, Oreg. (97010) 291/E2
Bride (riv.), Ireland 17/E7
Bridesville, Br. Col. 184/H6
Bridge, Idaho (†83342) 220/E7
Bridge, Oreg. (†97458) 291/D4
Bridgeboro, Georgia (31705) 217/E8
Bridge City, Texas (77611) 303/L7
Bridgedale, New Bruns. 170/F3
Bridgeford, Sask. 181/E5
Bridgehampton, N.Y. (11932) 276/R9
Bridge Lake, Br. Col. 184/G4
Bridgeland, Utah (84012) 304/D3
Bridgend, Wales 13/A7
Bridgenorth, Ontario 177/F3
Bridge of Allan, Scotland 10/B1
Bridge of Allan, Scotland 15/C1
Bridge of Don, Scotland 15/F3
Bridge of Weir, Scotland 15/A2
Bridgeport, Ala. (35740) 195/G1
Bridgeport, Calif. (93517) 204/F5
Bridgeport, Conn. 188/M2
Bridgeport, Conn. (*06601) 210/C4
Bridgeport, Ill. (62417) 222/F5
Bridgeport, Kansas (67416) 232/E3
Bridgeport, Mich. (48722) 250/F5
Bridgeport, Nebr. (69336) 264/A3
Bridgeport, N.J. (08014) 273/C4
Bridgeport, N.Y. (13030) 276/J4
Bridgeport, Ohio (43912) 284/J5
Bridgeport, Okla. (†73047) 288/K3
Bridgeport, Oreg. (97819) 291/K3
Bridgeport, Pa. (19405) 294/M5
Bridgeport, Texas (76026) 303/G4
Bridgeport, Wash. (98813) 310/F3
Bridgeport, W. Va. (26330) 312/F4
Bridgeport, Wis. (†53821) 317/D9
Bridger, Mont. (59014) 262/H5
Bridgeton, Ind. (47836) 227/C5
Bridgeton, Mich. (†49327) 250/D5
Bridgeton, Mo. (63044) 261/O2
Bridgeton, N.J. (08302) 273/C5
Bridgeton, N.C. (28519) 281/R4
Bridgeton Terrace, Mo. (†63044) 261/O2
Bridgetown (cap.), Barbados 156/G4
Bridgetown (cap.), Barbados 161/B9
Bridgetown, Md. (†21640) 245/P4
Bridgetown, Nova Scotia 168/C4
Bridgetown, Ohio (†45211) 284/B9
Bridgetown, W. Australia 88/B6
Bridgetown, W. Australia 92/B6
Bridgeview, Ill. (60455) 222/B6
Bridgeville, Calif. (95526) 204/B3
Bridgeville, Del. (19993) 245/R6
Bridgeville, Nova Scotia 168/F3
Bridgeville, Pa. (15017) 294/B5
Bridgeville, Québec 172/D1
Bridgewater○, Conn. (06752) 210/B2
Bridgewater, Iowa (50837) 229/D6
Bridgewater○, Maine (04735) 243/H3
Bridgewater, Mass. (02324) 249/K5
Bridgewater○, Mass. (02324) 249/K5
Bridgewater○, N.H. (†03222) 268/D4
Bridgewater○, N.J. (08807) 273/D2
Bridgewater, N.Y. (13313) 276/K5
Bridgewater, N.S. 162/K7
Bridgewater, Nova Scotia 168/D4
Bridgewater, Pa. (15009) 294/B4
Bridgewater, S. Dak. (57319) 298/P6
Bridgewater, Tasmania 99/D4
Bridgewater○, Vt. (05034) 268/B4
Bridgewater (cape), Victoria 97/A6
Bridgewater, Va. (22812) 307/K4
Bridgewater Center, Vt. (†05034) 268/B4
Bridgewater Corners, Vt. (05035) 268/B4
Bridgman, Mich. (49106) 250/C7
Bridgnorth, England 13/E5
Bridgnorth, England 10/E4
Bridgton, Maine (04009) 243/B7
Bridgton○, Maine (04009) 243/B7
Bridgwater, England 10/E5
Bridgwater, England 13/E6
Bridlington, England 13/G3
Bridlington, England 10/F3
Bridlington (bay), England 13/G3
Bridport, England 13/E7
Bridport, England 10/E5
Bridport, Tasmania 99/D3
Bridport○, Vt. (05734) 268/A4
Brieg (Brzeg), Poland 47/C3
Brielle, Netherlands 27/E5
Brielle, N.J. (08730) 273/E3
Briensburg, Ky. (†42025) 237/E7
Brienz, Switzerland 39/F3
Brienzer Rothorn (mt.), Switzerland 39/F3
Brienzersee (lake), Switzerland 39/F3
Brier (isl.), Nova Scotia 168/B4
Brier, Wash. (†98036) 310/C3
Briercrest, Sask. 181/F5
Brierfield, Ala. (35035) 195/E4
Brier Hill, N.Y. (13614) 276/J1
Brig, Switzerland 39/F4
Brigantine, N.J. (08203) 273/E5
Brigantine (inlet), N.J. 273/E5
Brigden, Ontario 177/B5
Brigg, England 13/G4
Briggs, Texas (78608) 303/F7
Briggs Corner, New Bruns. 170/E2
Briggsdale, Colo. (80611) 208/L1
Briggsville, Ark. (72828) 202/C4
Briggsville, Wis. (53920) 317/H8
Brigham City, Utah 188/D2
Brigham City, Utah (84302) 304/C2
Brighowe, England 13/J1
Bright, Ind. (†45030) 227/H6
Bright, Victoria 97/D5
Brightlingsea, England 13/J6
Brightlingsea, England 10/G5
Brighton, Ala. (35020) 195/D4
Brighton, Colo. (80601) 208/K3
Brighton, England 10/F5
Brighton, England 13/H7
Brighton, Fla. (†33472) 212/E4
Brighton, Ill. (62012) 222/C4
Brighton, Ind. (†46746) 227/G1
Brighton, Iowa (52540) 229/K6
Brighton○, Maine (†04990) 243/D5
Brighton, Mich. (48116) 250/F6
Brighton, Mo. (65617) 261/F8
Brighton, Nova Scotia 168/C4
Brighton, Ohio (†44090) 284/F3
Brighton, Ontario 177/G3
Brighton, Oreg. (†97136) 291/C2
Brighton, S. Australia 88/D8
Brighton, S. Australia 94/A8
Brighton, Tasmania 99/D4
Brighton, Tenn. (38011) 237/B10
Brighton, Utah (†84101) 304/C3
Brighton, Victoria 97/J5
Brighton, Victoria 88/L7
Brighton, Wis. (†53139) 317/K3
Brightons, Scotland 15/C1
Brightsand (lake), Sask. 181/B2
Brights Grove, Ontario 177/B4
Brightshade, Ky. (40962) 237/O7
Brightstar, Ark. (†75556) 202/C7
Brightwood, D.C. (20011) 245/F4
Brightwood, Oreg. (97001) 291/E2
Brightwood, Va. (22715) 307/M4
Brignoles, France 28/G6
Brigus, Newf. 166/D2
Brihuega, Spain 33/E2
Brikama, Gambia 106/A6
Brill, Wis. (54818) 317/C4
Brilliant, Ala. (35548) 195/C2
Brilliant, Ohio (43913) 284/J5
Brillion, Wis. (54110) 317/L7
Brilon, W. Germany 22/C3
Brimfield, Ill. (61517) 222/D3
Brimfield, Ind. (46720) 227/G2
Brimfield○, Mass. (01010) 249/F4
Brimfield, Ohio (†44240) 284/H3
Brimley, Mich. (49715) 250/E2
Brimson, Minn. (55602) 255/F3
Brimson, Mo. (64642) 261/E2
Brimstone (hill), St. Chris.-Nevis 161/C10
Brinckerhoff, N.Y. (†12524) 276/N7
Brindakit, U.S.S.R. 48/O4
Brindisi (prov.), Italy 34/G4
Brindisi, Italy 7/F4
Brindisi, Italy 34/G4
Bringhurst, Ind. (46913) 227/E3
Brinkhaven, Ohio (43006) 284/F5
Brinkley, Ark. (72021) 202/H4
Brinkman, Okla. (†73673) 288/G4
Brinktown, Mo. (65443) 261/J6
Brinnon, Wash. (98320) 310/B3
Brinsmade, N. Dak. (58320) 282/M3
Brinson, Georgia (31725) 217/C9
Briny Breezes, Fla. (†33435) 212/G5
Brione, Switzerland 39/G4
Brioude, France 28/E5
Brisbane, Australia 2/S7
Brisbane, Calif. (94005) 204/J2
Brisbane (cap.), Queensland 95/D2
Brisbane (cap.), Queensland 88/K3
Brisbane (riv.), Queensland 88/J3
Brisbane (riv.), Queensland 95/D2
Brisbane Airport, Queensland 95/E2
Brisbane International Airport, Queensland 88/K2
Brisbane Water, N. S. Wales 88/J6
Brisbane Water, N.S. Wales 97/F3
Brisbin, Pa. (16620) 294/F4
Brisco, Br. Col. 184/J5
Briscoe (co.), Texas 303/C3
Briscoe, Texas (79011) 303/D2
Brisighella, Italy 34/C2
Brissago, Switzerland 39/G4
Bristol (bay), Alaska 188/C6
Bristol (bay), Alaska 146/B4
Bristol (bay), Alaska 196/F3
Bristol (lake), Calif. 204/K9
Bristol, Colo. (81028) 208/P6
Bristol, Conn. (06010) 210/D2
Bristol, England 13/E6
Bristol, England 7/D3
Bristol, England 10/E5
Bristol (chan.), England 13/C6
Bristol (chan.), England 10/E5
Bristol, Fla. (32321) 212/B1
Bristol, Georgia (31518) 217/H8
Bristol, Ind. (46507) 227/F1

Caltagirone 345

Butler (co.), Ala. 195/E7
Butler, Ala. (36904) 195/B6
Butler, Georgia (31006) 217/D5
Butler, Ill. (62015) 222/D4
Butler, Ind. (46721) 227/H2
Butler (co.), Iowa 229/H3
Butler (co.), Kansas 232/F4
Butler (co.), Ky. 237/H6
Butler, Ky. (41006) 237/N3
Butler, Md. (21023) 245/M2
Butler, Minn. (†56567) 255/C4
Butler (co.), Mo. 261/M9
Butler, Mo. (64730) 261/D6
Butler (co.), Nebr. 264/G3
Butler, N.J. (07405) 273/E2
Butler (co.), Ohio 284/A7
Butler, Ohio (44822) 284/F4
Butler, Okla. (73625) 288/H3
Butler (co.), Pa. 294/C4
Butler, Pa. (16001) 294/C4
Butler, S. Dak. (57222) 298/O3
Butler, Tenn. (37640) 237/T8
Butler (bay), Virgin Is. (U.S.) 161/E4
Butler, Wis. (53007) 317/K1
Butler Springs, Ala. (†36030) 195/E7
Butlerville, Ark. (†72176) 202/G4
Butlerville, Ind. (47223) 227/F6
Butlerville, Ohio (†45162) 284/B7
Butner, N.C. (27509) 281/M2
Bütschelegg (mt.), Switzerland 39/D3
Bütschwil, Switzerland 39/H2
Buttahatchee (riv.), Ala. 195/B3
Buttahatchee (riv.), Miss. 256/H3
Butte (co.), Calif. 204/D4
Butte (co.), Idaho 220/E6
Butte, Mont. 146/G5
Butte, Mont. 188/D1
Butte, Nebr. (68722) 264/F2
Butte (mts.), Nev. 266/F3
Butte, N. Dak. (58723) 282/J4
Butte (creek), Oreg. 291/G2
Butte (creek), Oreg. 291/B3
Butte (co.), S. Dak. 298/B4
Butte City, Calif. (95920) 204/C4
Butte City, Idaho (83213) 220/E6
Butte Des Morts, Wis. (†54901) 317/J7
Butte Falls, Oreg. (97522) 291/E5
Butter (creek), Oreg. 291/H2
Butterfield, Ark. (†72104) 202/E5
Butterfield, Minn. (56120) 255/D7
Butterfield, Mo. (65623) 261/E9
Butterfield (lake), N.Y. 276/J2
Butternut, Mich. (†48811) 250/E5
Butternut, Wis. (54514) 317/E3
Butternut (lake), Wis. 317/J4
Butter Pot Prov. Park, Newf. 166/D2
Butters, N.C. (28324) 281/M5
Butterworth, Malaysia 72/D6
Butterworth (Gcuwa), S. Africa 118/D6
Buttes, Switzerland 39/C3
Butte-Silver Bow County, Mont. (59701) 262/D5
Buttevant, Ireland 17/D7
Butteville, Oreg. (†97002) 291/A2
Butt of Lewis (prom.), Scotland 15/B2
Button (isls.), N.W. Terrs. 187/M3
Buttonwillow, Calif. (93206) 204/F8
Butts (co.), Georgia 217/E4
Buttzville, N.J. (07829) 273/D2
Buttzville, N. Dak. (†58054) 282/P6
Butuan, Philippines 82/E6
Butuan, Philippines 85/H4
Butuan, Philippines 54/O9
Butuan (bay), Philippines 82/E6
Butumi, U.S.S.R. 7/J4
Butung (isl.), Indonesia 54/O10
Butung (isl.), Indonesia 85/G6
Buturlinovka, U.S.S.R. 52/F4
Butzbach, W. Germany 22/C3
Bützow, E. Germany 22/E2
Buxtehude, W. Germany 22/C2
Buxton, England 10/G2
Buxton, England 13/J2
Buxton○, Maine (†04093) 243/C8
Buxton, N.C. (27920) 281/U4
Buxton, N. Dak. (58218) 282/R4
Buxton, Oreg. (97109) 291/D2
Buxton Center, Maine (†04093) 243/B8
Buy, U.S.S.R. 52/F3
Buyck, Minn. (55771) 255/F2
Buynaksk, U.S.S.R. 52/G6
Büyükada, Turkey 63/D6
Büyük Ağrı (Ararat) (mt.), Turkey 63/L3
Büyük Ağrı (Ararat) (mt.), Turkey 59/D2
Büyükanafarta, Turkey 63/B6
Büyükdere, Turkey 63/D5
Büyük Hasan Dağı, Turkey 63/E3
Büyük Menderes (riv.), Turkey 59/A2
Buzău, Romania 45/H3
Buzău (riv.), Romania 45/H3
Buzeima (well), Libya 111/D3
Buziaş, Romania 45/E3
Buzios (cape), Brazil 135/F3
Buzuluk, U.S.S.R. 52/H4
Buzuluk, U.S.S.R. 48/F4
Buzzard Roost (dam), S.C. 296/D3
Buzzards (bay), Mass. 249/L7
Buzzards Bay, Mass. (02532) 249/M5
Byala, Bulgaria 45/G4
Byala Slatina, Bulgaria 45/F4
Byam Martin (chan.), N.W. Terrs. 187/H2
Byam Martin (isl.), N.W. Terrs. 187/H2
Byars, Okla. (74831) 288/N5
Bybee, Tenn. (37713) 237/P8
Bydgoszcz (prov.), Poland 47/C2
Bydgoszcz, Poland 47/C2
Bydgoszcz, Poland 7/F3
Byemoor, Alberta 182/D4
Byers, Colo. (80103) 208/L3
Byers, Kansas (67021) 232/D4
Byers, Texas (76357) 303/F3
Byesville, Ohio (43723) 284/G6
Byfield, Mass. (01922) 249/L1
Byford, W. Australia 88/B2
Bygland, Minn. (†56723) 255/B3
Bygland, Norway 18/F7
Byhalia, Miss. (38611) 256/E1
Bykhov, U.S.S.R. 52/C4
Bylas, Ariz. (85530) 198/E5
Bylot (isl.), N.W.T. 146/L2
Bylot (isl.), N.W.T. 162/J1
Bylot (isl.), N.W. Terrs. 187/L2
Byng, Okla. (†74820) 288/N5
Byng Inlet, Ontario 177/D2
Byng Inlet, Ontario 175/D3
Bynum, Mont. (59419) 262/D3
Bynum (res.), Mont. 262/D2
Bynum, N.C. (27312) 281/L3
Bynumville, Mo. (†65281) 261/G3
Byram, Conn. (06830) 210/A4
Byram (pt.), Conn. 210/A4
Byram (riv.), Conn. 210/A4
Byram, Miss. (†39205) 256/D6
Byrd Station 5/A12
Byrdstown, Tenn. (38549) 237/L7
Byrnedale, Pa. (15827) 294/E3
Byrock, N.S. Wales 97/D2
Byromville, Georgia (31007) 217/E6
Byron, Calif. (94514) 204/L2
Byron (isl.), Chile 138/D7
Byron, Georgia (31008) 217/E5
Byron, Ill. (61010) 222/D1
Byron, Ind. (†46371) 227/C5
Byron, Maine (†04275) 243/B6
Byron○, Maine (†04275) 243/B6
Byron, Mich. (48418) 250/E6
Byron, Minn. (55920) 255/F6
Byron, Nebr. (68325) 264/G4
Byron (bay), Newf. 166/C3
Byron (cape), N. S. Wales 88/J5
Byron (cape), N. S. Wales 97/G1
Byron, N.Y. (14422) 276/D4
Byron, Okla. (73723) 288/K1
Byron (lake), S. Dak. 298/N4
Byron, Wis. (53009) 317/K8
Byron, Wyo. (82412) 319/D1
Byron Bay, N.S. Wales 97/G1
Byron Center, Mich. (49315) 250/D6
Byrum, Denmark 21/E3
Byskeälv (riv.), Sweden 18/L4
Bystřice nad Pernštejnem, Czech. 41/D2
Bystřice pod Hostýnem, Czech. 41/D2
Bystrzyca Kłodzka, Poland 47/C3
Bytča, Czech. 41/E2
Bytom, Poland 47/A3
Bytów, Poland 47/C1

C

Caacupé, Paraguay 144/B5
Caaguazú (dept.), Paraguay 144/D-E4
Caaguazú, Paraguay 144/D4
Caála, Angola 115/C6
Caamaño (sound), Br. Col. 184/C4
Caapucú, Paraguay 144/D5
Caatingas (for.), Brazil 120/E3
Caazapá (dept.), Paraguay 144/D-E5
Caazapá, Paraguay 144/D5
Caba, Philippines 82/C2
Cabadbaran, Philippines 82/E6
Cabaiguán, Cuba 158/E2
Cabalasan (mt.), Philippines 82/E5
Caballero, Paraguay 144/B5
Caballo, N. Mex. (87931) 274/B6
Caballo (res.), N. Mex. 274/B6
Caballo (creek), Wyo. 319/G1
Caballococha, Peru 128/G4
Caballones (chan.), Cuba 158/F3
Cabana, Peru 128/C7
Cabañaquinta, Spain 33/D1
Cabañas, Cuba 158/B1
Cabanatuan, Philippines 54/O8
Cabanatuan, Philippines 82/C3
Cabanatuan, Philippines 85/G2
Cabanes, Spain 33/F2
Cabano, Québec 172/J2
Cabarroquis, Philippines 82/C2
Cabarrus (co.), N.C. 281/H4
Cabazon, Calif. (92230) 204/J10
Cabbage Tree (creek), Queensland 95/D2
Cabedelo, Brazil 132/H4
Cabell (co.), W. Va. 312/B6
Cabery, Ill. (60919) 222/E3
Cabet, Pitons du (mt.), Martinique 161/C6
Cabeza del Buey, Spain 33/D3
Cabezas, Bolivia 136/D6
Cabezas, Cuba 158/D1
Cabildo, Chile 138/A9
Cabimas, Venezuela 120/B1
Cabimas, Venezuela 124/C2
Cabin Creek, W. Va. (25035) 312/C6
Cabinda (dist.), Angola 115/B5
Cabinda, Angola 115/B5
Cabinda, Angola 102/D5
Cabinet (mts.), Mont. 262/A2
Cabin John (creek), Md. 245/E4
Cabin John-Brookmont, Md. (20731) 245/E4
Cabins, W. Va. (26855) 312/H4
Cable, Minn. (†56301) 255/D5
Cable, Ohio (43009) 284/C5
Cable, Wis. (54821) 317/D3
Cabo Blanco, Peru 128/B5
Cabo Delgado (prov.), Mozambique 118/F2
Cabo Frio, Brazil 132/F8
Cabo Frio, Brazil 135/F3
Cabo Gracias a Dios, Nicaragua 154/F3
Cabonga (res.), Québec 174/B3
Cabool, Mo. (65689) 261/H8
Cabora Bassa (dam), Mozambique 118/E3
Caborn, Ind. (†47620) 227/B9
Cabo Rojo, P. Rico 161/A2
Cabo San Lucas, Mexico 150/E5
Cabot (str.) 162/K6
Cabot, Ark. (72023) 202/F4
Cabot (str.), Canada 146/N5
Cabot (lake), Newf. 166/B2
Cabot (str.), Newf. 166/B4
Cabot (mt.), N.H. 268/E2
Cabot (head), Ontario 177/C2
Cabot, Pa. (16023) 294/C4
Cabot, Vt. (05647) 268/C3
Cabot○, Vt. (05647) 268/C3
Cabo Vírgenes, Argentina 143/C7
Cabra, Spain 33/D4
Cabra de Santo Cristo, Spain 33/E4
Cabral, Dom. Rep. 158/D6
Cabral (lag.), Paraguay 144/A5
Cabrera, Dom. Rep. 158/E5
Cabrera (isl.), Spain 33/H3
Cabri, Sask. 181/C5
Cabri (lake), Sask. 181/B4
Cabrillo Nat'l Mon., Calif. 204/H11
Cabrits (isl.), Martinique 161/D7
Cabrón (cape), Dom. Rep. 158/F5
Cabruta, Venezuela 124/E4
Cabudare, Venezuela 124/D3
Cabugao, Philippines 82/C2
Cabulauan (isls.), Philippines 82/C5
Cabullones (pt.), P. Rico 161/C3
Caburai (mt.), Guyana 131/A3
Cabure, Venezuela 124/D2
Caçador, Brazil 132/D9
Cacahoatán, Mexico 150/N9
Čačak, Yugoslavia 45/E4
Caçapava, Brazil 135/D3
Caçapava do Sul, Brazil 132/C10
Cacapon (riv.), W. Va. 312/J4
Cáceres (lag.), Bolivia 136/G6
Cáceres, Brazil 132/B7
Cáceres, Brazil 120/D4
Cáceres, Colombia 126/C4
Cáceres (prov.), Spain 33/C3
Cáceres, Spain 33/C3
Cáceres, Spain 7/D5
Cachapoal (riv.), Chile 138/G5
Cache (riv.), Ark. 202/H3
Cache (riv.), Ill. 222/D6
Cache, Okla. (73527) 288/J5
Cache (creek), Okla. 288/K6
Cache (co.), Utah 304/C2
Cache Bay, Ontario 177/D1
Cache Creek, Br. Col. 184/G5
Cache Junction, Utah (84304) 304/C2
Cache la Poudre (riv.), Colo. 208/H1
Cacheu, Guinea-Biss. 106/A6
Cachi, Argentina 143/C2
Cachina, Quebrada (riv.), Chile 138/A5
Cachipo, Venezuela 124/G3
Cachoeira, Brazil 132/G6
Cachoeira de Itapemirim, Brazil 120/E5
Cachoeira do Arari, Brazil 132/D3
Cachoeira do Sul, Brazil 132/C10
Cachoeira do Sul, Brazil 120/D6
Cachoeiro de Itapemirim, Brazil 132/G8
Cachorras, Colombia 126/D8
Cachos (pt.), Chile 138/A6
Cachuela Esperanza, Bolivia 136/C2
Cachuma (lake), Calif. 204/F9
Cacocum, Cuba 158/H3
Cacocum, Cuba 156/C2
Cacolo, Angola 115/C6
Caconda, Angola 115/B6
Cacouna, Québec 172/H2
Cactus (range), Nev. 266/E5
Cactus (hills), Sask. 181/F5
Cactus, Texas (79013) 303/B1
Cactus Lake, Sask. 181/B3
Cacuri, Venezuela 124/F5
Cacuso, Angola 115/C5
Čadca, Czech. 41/E2
Caddo (riv.), Ark. 202/D5
Caddo (par.), La. 238/C1
Caddo (lake), La. 238/B1
Caddo (co.), Okla. 288/K4
Caddo, Okla. (74729) 288/O6
Caddo, Texas (76029) 303/F5
Caddo (lake), Texas 303/L5
Caddo Gap, Ark. (71935) 202/C5
Caddo Valley, Ark. (†71923) 202/D5
Caddy Lake, Manitoba 179/G5
Cade, La. (70519) 238/G6
Cadereyta Jiménez, Mexico 150/K4
Cades, S.C. (29518) 296/H4
Cades, Tenn. (†38358) 237/D9
Cades Cove, Tenn. (†37882) 237/O9
Cadet, Mo. (63630) 261/L6
Cadibarrawirracanna (lake), S. Australia 94/D3
Cadillac, Mich. (49601) 250/D4
Cadillac, Québec 174/B3
Cadillac, Sask. 181/D6
Cadiz, Calif. (92319) 204/K9
Cadiz (lake), Calif. 204/K9
Cadiz, Ind. (†47362) 227/G5
Cadiz, Ky. (42211) 237/F7
Cadiz, Ohio (43907) 284/J5
Cadiz, Philippines 82/D5
Cádiz (prov.), Spain 33/D4
Cádiz, Spain 33/C4
Cádiz, Spain 7/D5
Cádiz (gulf), Spain 33/C4
Cádizadiz (gulf), Portugal 33/C4
Cadogan, Alberta 182/E3
Cadogan○, Pa. (16212) 294/C4
Cadomin, Alberta 182/B3
Cadott, Wis. (54727) 317/D6
Cadotte (lake), Alberta 182/B1
Cadotte (riv.), Alberta 182/B1
Cadotte Lake, Alberta 182/B1
Cadron (creek), Ark. 202/F3
Caduruan (pt.), Philippines 82/D5
Cadwell, Georgia (31009) 217/G6
Cadyville, N.Y. (12918) 276/N1
Caen, France 28/C3
Caen, France 7/E4
Caerleon, Wales 13/B6
Caernarfon, Wales 13/C4
Caernarfon, Wales 10/D4
Caernarfon (bay), Wales 13/C4
Caernarfon (bay), Wales 10/D4
Caerphilly, Wales 13/B6
Caerphilly, Wales 10/E5
Caesar, Miss. (†39466) 256/E9
Caesarea, Ontario 177/F3
Caesars Head, S.C. (†29635) 296/B1
Caeté, Brazil 135/E1
Caetité, Brazil 132/F6
Cafayate, Argentina 143/C2
Cafelândia, Brazil 135/B2
Cagayan (prov.), Philippines 82/C1
Cagayan (isls.), Philippines 82/C6
Cagayan (isls.), Philippines 85/F4
Cagayan (riv.), Philippines 82/C2
Cagayancillo, Philippines 82/C6
Cagayan de Oro, Philippines 82/E6
Cagayan de Oro, Philippines 85/G4
Cagayan Sulu (isl.), Philippines 85/F4
Cagayan Sulu (isl.), Philippines 82/B7
Cagle, Tenn. (†37327) 237/L10
Cagles Mill (lake), Ind. 227/D6
Cagli, Italy 34/D3
Cagliari (prov.), Italy 34/B5
Cagliari, Italy 7/E5
Cagliari, Italy 34/B5
Cagliari (gulf), Italy 34/B5
Cagua (vol.), Philippines 82/D1
Cagua, Venezuela 124/E2
Caguán (riv.), Colombia 126/C7
Caguas, P. Rico 161/E2
Caguas, P. Rico 156/G1
Caha (mts.), Ireland 17/B8
Cahaba, Ala. (†36767) 195/D6
Cahaba (riv.), Ala. 195/D5
Cahabón, Guatemala 154/C3
Cahir, Ireland 10/B4
Cahir, Ireland 17/F7
Cahirciveen, Ireland 17/A8
Cahirciveen, Ireland 10/A5
Cahokia, Ill. (62206) 222/A3
Cahone, Colo. (81320) 208/B7
Cahore (pt.), Ireland 17/J6
Cahors, France 28/D5
Cahuapanas, Peru 128/D5
Cahuilla Ind. Res., Calif. 204/J10
Cahuinari (riv.), Colombia 126/E8
Cahuita (pt.), C. Rica 154/F6
Caiapônia, Brazil 132/C7
Caibarién, Cuba 158/F2
Caibarién, Cuba 156/B2
Caibiran, Philippines 82/E5
Caicara, Venezuela 124/G3
Caicara de Orinoco, Venezuela 124/E4
Caicedonia, Colombia 126/C5
Caicó, Brazil 120/F3
Caicó, Brazil 132/G4
Caicos (passage), Bahamas 156/D2
Caicos (bank), Turks & Caicos 156/D2
Caicos (isls.), Turks & Caicos 156/D2
Caicos (passage), Turks & Caicos 156/D2
Caile, Miss. (†38754) 256/C4
Cailloma, Peru 128/G10
Caillou (bay), La. 238/J8
Caimanera, Cuba 158/J4
Caimanera, Cuba 156/C3
Cain (creek), S. Dak. 298/N5
Cainde, Angola 115/B7
Cains (riv.), New Bruns. 170/D2
Cains Store, Ky. (42520) 237/M6
Cainsville, Mo. (64632) 261/E2
Cainsville, Tenn. (†37085) 237/J9
Caird Coast (reg.) 5/B17
Cairnbaan, Scotland 15/C4
Cairnbrook, Pa. (15924) 294/E5
Cairndow, Scotland 15/D4
Cairn Gorm (mt.), Scotland 15/E3
Cairngorm (mts.), Scotland 15/E3
Cairnryan, Scotland 15/D6
Cairns, Australia 87/E7
Cairns, Queensland 95/C3
Cairns, Queensland 88/H3
Cairnsmore (mt.), Scotland 15/D5
Cairn Toul (mt.), Scotland 15/E3
Cairo (cap.), Egypt 102/F2
Cairo (cap.), Egypt 111/J3
Cairo (cap.), Egypt 2/L4
Cairo, Egypt 59/B4
Cairo, Georgia (31728) 217/D9
Cairo, Ill. 188/J3
Cairo, Ill. (62914) 222/D6
Cairo, Kansas (†67035) 232/D4
Cairo, Mo. (65239) 261/H4
Cairo, Nebr. (68824) 264/F3
Cairo, N.Y. (12413) 276/M6
Cairo, Ohio (45820) 284/B4
Cairo, Okla. (†74538) 288/O5
Cairo, W. Va. (26337) 312/D4
Caissie (pt.), New Bruns. 170/F2
Caister-on-Sea, England 13/J5
Caistor, England 13/G4
Caithness (trad. co.), Scotland 15/B4
Caiundo, Angola 102/D6
Caiundo, Angola 115/C7
Caiza, Bolivia 136/C7
Cajabamba, Ecuador 128/C3
Cajabamba, Peru 128/C6
Cajacay, Peru 128/D8
Caja de Muertos (isl.), P. Rico 161/C3
Cajamarca (dept.), Peru 128/C6
Cajamarca, Peru 128/C6
Cajamarca, Peru 120/B3
Cajatambo, Peru 128/D8
Cajazeiras, Brazil 132/G4
Cajidiocan, Philippines 82/D4
Cajuata, Bolivia 136/B5
Cajuru, Brazil 135/C2
Čakovec, Yugoslavia 45/C2
Çal, Turkey 63/C3
Çala, Turkey 63/K2
Calabar, Nigeria 102/D4
Calabar, Nigeria 106/F7
Calabash, N.C. (†29566) 281/M7
Calabazar de Sagua, Cuba 158/E1
Calabogie, Ontario 177/H2
Calabozo, Venezuela 124/E3
Calabria (reg.), Italy 34/F5
Cala Burras (pt.), Spain 33/D4
Calaceite, Spain 33/G2
Calacoto, Bolivia 136/A5
Caladesi (isl.), Fla. 212/B2
Calafat, Romania 45/F3
Calafate, Argentina 143/B7
Calafquén (lake), Chile 138/E3
Calagnaan (isl.), Philippines 82/D5
Calagua (isls.), Philippines 82/D3
Calahoo, Alberta 182/D3
Calahorra, Spain 33/E1
Calais, Alberta 182/B2
Calais, France 28/D2
Calais, France 7/E3
Calais (Dover) (str.), France 28/D2
Calais, Maine 188/N1
Calais, Maine (04619) 243/J5
Calais○, Vt. (05648) 268/B3
Calama, Brazil 132/H10
Calama, Chile 120/C5
Calama, Chile 138/B3
Calamar, Bolívar, Colombia 126/C2
Calamar, Vaupés, Colombia 126/D7
Calamarca, Bolivia 136/A5
Calamba, Laguna, Philippines 82/C3
Calamba, Misamis Occ., Philippines 82/D6
Calamian Group (isls.), Philippines 85/F3
Calamian Group (isls.), Philippines 82/B4
Calamine, Ark. (72418) 202/H1
Calamocha, Spain 33/F2
Calamus, Iowa (52729) 229/M5
Calanasan, Philippines 82/C1
Calancasca (riv.), Switzerland 39/H4
Calanda, Spain 33/F2
Calang, Indonesia 85/B5
Calansho, Serir (des.), Libya 111/D2
Calansho Sand Sea (des.), Libya 111/D2
Calapan, Philippines 82/C4
Calapan, Philippines 85/G3
Calapooia (riv.), Oreg. 291/E3
Calapooya (mts.), Oreg. 291/E4
Călăraşi, Romania 45/H3
Calarcá, Colombia 126/C5
Calasparra, Spain 33/F3
Calatayud, Spain 33/F2
Calatorao, Spain 33/F2
Calauag, Philippines 82/D4
Calaveras (co.), Calif. 204/E5
Calaveras (res.), Calif. 204/L3
Calaveras (lake), Texas 303/K11
Calavite (cape), Philippines 82/C4
Calayan, Philippines 82/A2
Calayan (isl.), Philippines 82/A2
Calbayog, Philippines 82/E4
Calbe, E. Germany 22/D3
Calbuco, Chile 138/D4
Calca, Peru 128/G9
Calcasieu (par.), La. 238/D6
Calcasieu, La. (71433) 238/E4
Calcasieu (lake), La. 238/D7
Calcasieu (passage), La. 238/D7
Calcasieu (riv.), La. 238/E5
Calceta, Ecuador 128/C3
Calchaquí, Argentina 143/F5
Calcis, Ala. (†35178) 195/F4
Calcutta, India 68/F2
Calcutta, India 54/K7
Calcutta, India 2/P4
Calcutta, Ohio (43920) 284/J4
Calcutta, Suriname 131/C3
Caldas (dept.), Colombia 126/C5
Caldas da Rainha, Portugal 33/B3
Caldas Novas, Brazil 132/D7
Calder, Idaho (83808) 220/B2
Calder, Sask. 181/K4
Calder, Loch (lake), Scotland 15/E2
Caldera, Chile 120/B5
Caldera, Chile 138/A6
Calderas (bay), Dom. Rep. 158/D6
Calderas, Venezuela 124/C3
Calderwood, Tenn. (†37801) 237/N9
Caldicot, Wales 13/E6
Çaldıran, Turkey 63/K3
Caldwell, Ark. (72322) 202/J3
Caldwell, Idaho (83605) 220/B6
Caldwell, Idaho 188/C2
Caldwell, Kansas (67022) 232/E4
Caldwell (co.), Ky. 237/F6
Caldwell (par.), La. 238/F2
Caldwell (co.), Mo. 261/E3
Caldwell, N.J. (07006) 273/B2
Caldwell (co.), N.C. 281/F3
Caldwell, Ohio (43724) 284/G6
Caldwell (co.), Texas 303/G8
Caldwell, Texas (77836) 303/H7
Caldwell, W. Va. (24925) 312/F7
Caldwell, Wis. (†53149) 317/J2
Caldy (isl.), Wales 13/C6
Cale, Ark. (71828) 202/D6
Cale, Ind. (†47544) 227/D7
Caledon, N. Ireland 17/H3
Caledon, Ontario 177/E4
Caledon, S. Africa 118/G7
Caledonia, Ill. (61011) 222/E1
Caledonia, Mich. (49316) 250/D6
Caledonia, Minn. (55921) 255/G7
Caledonia, Miss. (39740) 256/H3
Caledonia, Mo. (63631) 261/L7
Caledonia, N.Y. (14423) 276/E5
Caledonia, N. Dak. (58219) 282/S5
Caledonia, Guysborough, Nova Scotia 168/F3
Caledonia, Queens, Nova Scotia 168/C4
Caledonia, Ohio (43314) 284/D4
Caledonia, Pa. (†15868) 294/F3
Caledonia (co.), Vt. 268/C2
Caledonia, Wis. (53108) 317/L2
Caledonian (canal), Scotland 15/D3
Calella, Spain 33/H2
Calenzana, France 28/B6
Calera, Ala. (35040) 195/E4
Calera, Okla. (74730) 288/O7
Calera de Tango, Chile 138/G4
Caleta Barquito, Chile 138/A6
Caleta Clarencia, Chile 138/E10
Caleta Olivia, Argentina 143/C6
Caleta Olivia, Argentina 120/C7
Caleta Pan de Azúcar, Chile 138/A5
Caleu, Chile 138/G2
Caleufú, Argentina 143/C4
Calexico, Calif. (92231) 204/K11
Calf of Man (isl.), I. of Man 13/C3
Calfsound, Scotland 15/F1
Calgary, Alberta 182/C4
Calgary, Alta. 162/E5
Calgary (cap.), Alta.. 146/G4
Calgary, Canada 2/D3
Calhan, Colo. (80808) 208/L4
Calheta, Portugal 33/A2
Calhoun (co.), Ala. 195/G3
Calhoun, Ala. (†36047) 195/F6
Calhoun (co.), Ark. 202/E6
Calhoun (co.), Fla. 212/D6
Calhoun (co.), Georgia 217/C7
Calhoun, Georgia (30701) 217/C1
Calhoun (co.), Ill. 222/C4
Calhoun, Ill. (62419) 222/E5
Calhoun (co.), Iowa 229/D4
Calhoun, Ky. (42327) 237/G5
Calhoun, La. (71225) 238/F2
Calhoun (co.), Mich. 250/D6
Calhoun (co.), Miss. 256/F3
Calhoun, Mo. (65323) 261/E6
Calhoun (co.), S.C. 296/F4
Calhoun, Tenn. (37309) 237/M10
Calhoun (co.), Texas 303/H9
Calhoun (co.), W. Va. 312/D5
Calhoun City, Miss. (38916) 256/F3
Calhoun Falls, S.C. (29628) 296/B3
Cali, Colombia 126/B6
Cali, Colombia 120/B2
Calicito, Cuba 158/H4
Calicoan (isl.), Philippines 82/E5
Calico Rock, Ark. (72519) 202/F1
Calicut (Kozhikode), India 68/D6
Caliente, Nev. (89008) 266/G5
Califon, N.J. (07830) 273/D2
California 188/B3
CALIFORNIA 204
California, Ky. (41007) 237/N3
California, Md. (20619) 245/M7
California (gulf), Mexico 146/G7
California (gulf), Mexico 150/D3
California, Mo. (65018) 261/H5
California, Pa. (15419) 294/C5
California, Trin. & Tob. 161/A11
California (state), U.S. 146/G6
California Aqueduct, Calif. 204/E7
California City, Calif. (93505) 204/H8
California Hot Springs, Calif. (93207) 204/G8
California Junction, Iowa (†51555) 229/B5
Calimete, Cuba 158/D1
Calio, N. Dak. (58322) 282/N2
Calion, Ark. (71724) 202/E7
Calipatria, Calif. (92233) 204/K10
Calistoga, Calif. (94515) 204/C5
Calixa-Lavallée, Québec 172/J4
Calkiní, Mexico 150/O6
Çalköy, Turkey 63/C3
Call, Texas (75933) 303/L7
Callabonna (lake), S. Australia 88/G5
Callabonna (lake), S. Australia 94/F3
Callafo, Ethiopia 111/H6
Callahan, Calif. (96014) 204/C2
Callahan, Fla. (32011) 212/E1
Callahan (co.), Texas 303/E5
Callalli, Peru 128/G10
Callan, Ireland 17/G7
Callan, Ireland 10/C4
Callander, Ont. 162/H6
Callander, Ontario 177/E1
Callander, Scotland 10/D2
Callander, Scotland 15/D4
Callands, Va. (24530) 307/J7
Callantsoog, Netherlands 27/F3
Callao, Mo. (63534) 261/G3
Callao (prov.), Peru 128/D9
Callao, Peru 128/D9
Callao, Peru 2/F6
Callao, Peru 120/B4
Callao, Utah (†84034) 304/A4
Callao, Va. (22435) 307/P5
Callapa, Bolivia 136/A5
Callaway, Minn. (56521) 255/C3
Callaway (co.), Mo. 261/J5
Callaway, Nebr. (68825) 264/D3
Callaway, Va. (24067) 307/H7
Calle Larga, Chile 138/G2
Callender, Iowa (50523) 229/E4
Callensburg, Pa. (16213) 294/D3
Callery, Pa. (16024) 294/C4
Calleuque, Chile 138/F5
Calliaqua, St. Vin. & Grens. 161/A9
Callicoon, N.Y. (12723) 276/K7
Callicoon Center, N.Y. (12724) 276/L7
Callihan, Texas (78007) 303/F9
Callimont, Pa. (†15552) 294/E6
Calling (lake), Alberta 182/D2
Callis, Somalia 115/J2
Callison, S.C. (29819) 296/C3
Callosa de Ensarriá, Spain 33/G3
Calloway, Fla. (32401) 212/D6
Calloway (co.), Ky. 237/E7
Calmar, Alberta 182/D3
Calmar, Iowa (52132) 229/K2
Calmer, Ark. (†71665) 202/F6
Calnali, Mexico 150/K6
Calne, England 13/F6
Calobre, Panama 154/G6
Caloosahatchee (riv.), Fla. 212/E5
Caloundra, Queensland 88/J5
Caloundra, Queensland 95/E5
Čalovo, Czech. 41/D3
Calpella, Calif. (95418) 204/B4
Calpet, Wyo. (†83123) 319/B3
Calpulálpan, Mexico 150/M1
Calstock, England 13/C7
Caltagirone, Italy 34/E6

346 Caltanissetta

Caltanissetta (prov.), Italy 34/D6
Caltanissetta, Italy 34/D6
Caluire-et-Cuire, France 28/F5
Calulo, Angola 115/C6
Calumet (lake), Ill. 222/C6
Calumet, Iowa (51009) 229/B3
Calumet, La. (†70538) 238/H7
Calumet, Mich. 188/J1
Calumet, Mich. (49913) 250/A1
Calumet, Minn. (55716) 255/E3
Calumet, Okla. (73014) 288/K3
Calumet, Québec 172/C4
Calumet (co.), Wis. 317/K7
Calumet City, Ill. (60409) 222/C6
Calumet Park, Ill. (†60643) 222/C6
Calumetville, Wis. (†53049) 317/K8
Caluquembe, Angola 102/D6
Caluquembe, Angola 115/B6
Calva, Ariz. (†85530) 198/E5
Calvados (dept.), France 28/C3
Calvary, Georgia (31729) 217/D9
Calvary, Ky. (†40033) 237/L6
Calvert, Ala. (36513) 195/B8
Calvert (isl.), Br. Col. 184/C4
Calvert, Kansas (†67622) 232/C2
Calvert (co.), Md. 245/M6
Calvert, Md. (†21911) 245/O2
Calvert, Newf. 166/D2
Calvert, Texas (77837) 303/H7
Calvert City, Ky. (42029) 237/E6
Calvert Hills, North. Terr. 93/E4
Calverton, Md. (†20705) 245/L4
Calverton, Va. (22016) 307/N3
Calverton Park, Mo. (†63101) 261/P2
Calvertville, Ind. (†47424) 227/D6
Calvi, France 28/B6
Calvillo, Mexico 150/H6
Calvin, Ky. (40813) 237/O7
Calvin, La. (71410) 238/E3
Calvin, N. Dak. (58323) 282/N2
Calvin, Okla. (74531) 288/O5
Calvin, W. Va. (26660) 312/E6
Calvinia, S. Africa 102/E8
Calvinia, S. Africa 118/B6
Calwa, Calif. (93745) 204/F7
Calypso, N.C. (28325) 281/N4
Calzada de Calatrava, Spain 33/E3
Camabatela, Angola 115/C5
Camacho, Bolivia 136/C7
Camacupa, Angola 115/C6
Camaguán, Venezuela 124/E3
Camagüey (prov.), Cuba 158/G2
Camagüey, Cuba 158/G3
Camagüey, Cuba 146/L7
Camagüey, Cuba 156/B2
Camagüey (arch.), Cuba 158/G2
Camaiore, Italy 34/C3
Camajuaní, Cuba 158/E2
Camak, Georgia (30807) 217/G4
Camaná, Peru 128/F11
Camanche (res.), Calif. 204/C9
Camanche, Iowa (52730) 229/N5
Camano (isl.), Wash. 310/C2
Camanongue, Angola 115/D6
Camanongue, Angola 102/E6
Camaquã, Brazil 132/C10
Câmara de Lobos, Portugal 33/A2
Çamardı, Turkey 63/F4
Camargo, Bolivia 136/C7
Camargo, Ill. (61919) 222/E4
Camargo, Ky. (†40337) 237/K4
Camargo, Okla. (73835) 288/H2
Camarillo, Calif. (93010) 204/F9
Camarines Norte (prov.), Philippines 82/D3
Camarines Sur (prov.), Philippines 82/D4
Camarón (cape), Honduras 154/E2
Camarones, Argentina 143/C5
Camarones, Chile 138/B2
Camarones (riv.), Chile 138/A2
Camas (co.), Idaho 220/D6
Camas (creek), Idaho 220/D6
Camas (creek), Idaho 220/F5
Camas (creek), Idaho 220/D5
Camas, Wash. (98607) 310/C5
Camas Prairie, Mont. (†59857) 262/B3
Camas Valley, Oreg. (97416) 291/D4
Camatagua, Venezuela 124/E3
Camatindi, Bolivia 136/D7
Ca Mau (Mui Bai Bung) (pt.), Vietnam 72/E5
Cambará, Brazil 135/A3
Cambará, Brazil 132/D8
Cambay, India 68/C4
Cambay (gulf), India 54/J7
Cambay (gulf), India 68/C4
Camberwell, Victoria 88/L7
Camberwell, Victoria 97/J5
Cambodia 2/Q5
Cambodia 54/M8
CAMBODIA (KAMPUCHEA) 72
Camborne-Redruth, England 10/D5
Camborne-Redruth, England 13/B7
Cambra, Pa. (18611) 294/K3
Cambrai, France 28/E2
Cambria, Alberta 182/D4
Cambria, Calif. (93428) 204/D8
Cambria, Ill. (62915) 222/D6
Cambria, Ind. (†46041) 227/D4
Cambria, Iowa (†50060) 229/G7
Cambria, Mich. (†49242) 250/E7
Cambria, Minn. (†56073) 255/D6
Cambria (co.), Pa. 294/E4
Cambria, Wis. (53923) 317/H8
Cambrian (mts.), Wales 13/D5
Cambridge, England 13/G5
Cambridge, England 10/G4
Cambridge, Idaho (83610) 220/B5
Cambridge, Ill. (61238) 222/C2
Cambridge, Iowa (50046) 229/G5
Cambridge, Jamaica 158/H6
Cambridge, Kansas (67023) 232/F4
Cambridge○, Maine (04923) 243/E5
Cambridge, Md. (21613) 245/O6
Cambridge, Mass. (02138) 249/C7
Cambridge (res.), Mass. 249/B6
Cambridge, Minn. (55008) 255/E5
Cambridge, Nebr. (69022) 264/D4
Cambridge, N.Y. (12816) 276/O4
Cambridge, N. Zealand 100/E2
Cambridge, Ohio (43725) 284/G5
Cambridge, Ontario 177/D4
Cambridge, Tasmania 99/D4
Cambridge, Vt. (05444) 268/B2
Cambridge○, Vt. (05444) 268/B2
Cambridge, Wis. (53523) 317/H9
Cambridge Bay, Canada 4/B15
Cambridge Bay, N.W.T. 162/F2
Cambridge Bay, N.W. Terrs. 187/H3
Cambridge City, Ind. (47327) 227/G5
Cambridge-Narrows, New Bruns. 170/E3
Cambridgeport, Vt. (05141) 268/B5
Cambridgeshire (co.), England 13/G5
Cambridge Springs, Pa. (16403) 294/C2
Cambridge Station, Nova Scotia 168/D3
Cambuí, Brazil 135/C3
Cambulo, Angola 115/D5
Cambulo, Angola 102/E5
Cambuslang, Scotland 15/B2
Camden, Ala. (36726) 195/D7
Camden (bay), Alaska 196/K1
Camden, Ark. (71701) 202/E6
Camden, Del. (19934) 245/R4
Camden, England 13/H8
Camden, England 10/B5
Camden (co.), Georgia 217/J9
Camden, Ill. (62319) 222/C3
Camden, Ind. (46917) 227/D3
Camden, Maine (04843) 243/F7
Camden○, Maine (04843) 243/F7
Camden, Mich. (49232) 250/E7
Camden, Miss. (39045) 256/E5
Camden (co.), Mo. 261/G6
Camden, Mo. (64017) 261/D4
Camden, N.J. 188/M3
Camden (co.), N.J. 273/D4
Camden, N.J. (*08101) 273/B3
Camden, N.S. Wales 97/F4
Camden, N.Y. (13316) 276/J4
Camden (co.), N.C. 281/S2
Camden, N.C. (27921) 281/S2
Camden, Ohio (45311) 284/A6
Camden, S.C. (29020) 296/F3
Camden, Tenn. (38320) 237/E8
Camden, Texas (75934) 303/K7
Camden, W. Va. (26338) 312/E4
Camden Haven, N.S. Wales 97/G2
Camden on Gauley, W. Va. (26208) 312/E6
Camden Park, St. Vin. & Grens. 161/A9
Camden Point, Mo. (64018) 261/C4
Camdenton, Mo. (65020) 261/G6
Cameia, Angola 115/D6
Camelford, England 13/C7
Çameli, Turkey 63/C4
Camels Hump (mt.), Vt. 268/B3
Camerino, Italy 34/D3
Cameron, Ariz. (86020) 198/D3
Cameron (peak), Colo. 208/H1
Cameron (par.), La. 238/D7
Cameron, La. (70631) 238/D7
Cameron, Mo. (64429) 261/D3
Cameron, Mont. (59720) 262/E5
Cameron, N.Y. (14819) 276/F6
Cameron (mts.), N. Zealand 100/A7
Cameron, N.C. (28326) 281/L4
Cameron (isl.), N.W. Terrs. 187/H2
Cameron, Ohio (43914) 284/J6
Cameron, Okla. (74932) 288/T4
Cameron (co.), Pa. 294/F3
Cameron, Pa. (†15834) 294/F3
Cameron, S.C. (29030) 296/F4
Cameron (co.), Texas 303/G11
Cameron, Texas (76520) 303/H7
Cameron, W. Va. (26033) 312/E3
Cameron, Wis. (54822) 317/C5
Cameron Falls, Ontario 177/H5
Cameron Highlands, Malaysia 72/D6
Cameroon 2/K5
Cameroon 102/D4
CAMEROON 115/B2
Cameroon (mt.), Cameroon 102/C4
Cameroon (mt.), Cameroon 115/A3
Camerota, Italy 34/E4
Cametá, Brazil 132/D3
Camiguin (prov.), Philippines 82/E6
Camiguin, Cagayan (isl.), Philippines 82/B3
Camiguin, Camiguin (isl.), Philippines 82/E6
Camiling, Philippines 82/C3
Camilla, Georgia (31730) 217/D8
Camillus, N.Y. (13031) 276/H4
Camiña, Chile 138/B2
Camiña, Quebrada (riv.), Chile 138/B2
Caminha, Portugal 33/B2
Camino, Calif. (95709) 204/E5
Camiri, Bolivia 120/C5
Camiri, Bolivia 136/D7
Camlachie, Ontario 177/B4
Çamlıdere, Turkey 63/E2
Cammack, Ind. (†47302) 227/G4
Cammack Village, Ark. (†72201) 202/E4
Cammal, Pa. (17723) 294/H3
Camoapa, Nicaragua 154/E4
Camocim, Brazil 132/F3
Camolin, Ireland 17/J6
Camooweal, Queensland 88/F3
Camooweal, Queensland 95/A3
Camopi, Fr. Guiana 131/E4
Camopi (riv.), Fr. Guiana 131/E4
Camorta (isl.), India 68/G7
Camoruco, Colombia 126/E4
Camotes (isls.), Philippines 82/E5
Camotes (sea), Philippines 82/E5
Camp (creek), Georgia 217/J2
Camp (creek), Ind. 227/E6
Camp (creek), Oreg. 291/J4
Camp (co.), Texas 303/K5
Campaign, Tenn. (38550) 237/K9
Campamento, Uruguay 145/C1
Campana, Argentina 143/G6
Campana (isl.), Chile 120/B7
Campana (isl.), Chile 138/D7
Campanario, Cerro (mt.), Argentina 143/C4
Campanario, Cerro (mt.), Chile 138/A10
Campanario, Spain 33/D3
Campanha, Brazil 135/D2
Campania, Georgia (†30814) 217/H4
Campania (reg.), Italy 34/E4
Campaspe (riv.), Victoria 97/C5
Campbell, Ala. (36727) 195/C7
Campbell, Alaska (†99901) 196/M2
Campbell, Calif. (95008) 204/K3
Campbell (co.), Ky. 237/N3
Campbell, Minn. (56522) 255/B4
Campbell, Mo. (63933) 261/M9
Campbell, Nebr. (68932) 264/F4
Campbell, N.Y. (14821) 276/F6
Campbell (cape), N. Zealand 100/E4
Campbell, Ohio (44405) 284/J3
Campbell (hill), Ohio 284/C5
Campbell (co.), S. Dak. 298/J2
Campbell (co.), Tenn. 237/N8
Campbell (co.), Va. 307/K6
Campbell (co.), Wyo. 319/G1
Campbell (mt.), Yukon 187/E3
Campbellford, Ontario 177/G3
Campbell Hall, N.Y. (10916) 276/M8
Campbell Hill, Ill. (62916) 222/D6
Campbell Island, Br. Col. 184/C4
Campbellpore, Pakistan 68/C2
Campbell River, Br. Col. 184/E5
Campbells (lake), Oreg. 291/H5
Campbellsburg, Ind. (47108) 227/E7
Campbellsburg, Ky. (40011) 237/L3
Campbellsport, Wis. (†53019) 317/K8
Campbell Station, Ark. (†72473) 202/H2
Campbellsville, Ky. (42718) 237/L6
Campbellton, Fla. (32426) 212/D5
Campbellton, Mo. (†63068) 261/K5
Campbellton, N. Br. 162/K6
Campbellton, N. Br. 146/M5
Campbellton, New Bruns. 170/D1
Campbellton, Newf. 166/D4
Campbellton, Pr. Edward I. 168/D2
Campbellton, Texas (78008) 303/F9
Campbelltown, N.S. Wales 97/F4
Campbelltown, S. Australia 88/E8
Campbelltown, S. Australia 94/B7
Campbell Town, Tasmania 99/D3
Campbeltown, Scotland 15/C5
Campbeltown, Scotland 10/C3
Camp Creek, Alberta 182/C2
Camp Creek, W. Va. (25820) 312/D7
Camp Crook, S. Dak. (57724) 298/B2
Camp David, Md. 245/J2
Camp Dennison, Ohio (45111) 284/D9
Camp Dix, Ky. (41127) 237/P3
Camp Douglas, Wis. (54618) 317/F8
Campeche (state), Mexico 150/O7
Campeche, Mexico 146/J8
Campeche, Mexico 150/O7
Campeche (bay), Mexico 146/J7
Campeche (bank), Mexico 150/O6
Campeche (bay), Mexico 150/N7
Campechuela, Cuba 158/G4
Camper, Manitoba 179/D3
Camperdown, Victoria 97/C6
Camperville, Manitoba 179/B2
Camp Grove, Ill. (61424) 222/D2
Camp Hale, Colo. 208/G4
Camp Hill, Ala. (36850) 195/G5
Camp Hill, Pa. (17011) 294/H5
Camp Hill, Queensland 88/K3
Camp Hill, Queensland 95/E3
Campiglia Marittima, Italy 34/C3
Campile, Ireland 17/H7
Campillo de Altobuey, Spain 33/F3
Campillos, Spain 33/D4
Campina Grande, Brazil 120/F3
Campina Grande, Brazil 132/G4
Campinas, Brazil 120/E5
Campinas, Brazil 135/C3
Campinas, Brazil 132/E8
Campina Verde, Brazil 135/B1
Campina Verde, Brazil 132/D7
Camp Lake, Wis. (53109) 317/K10
Camp Lejeune Marine Corps Base, N.C. 281/P5
Campli, Italy 34/D3
Camp Morton, Manitoba 179/E4
Camp Nelson, Calif. (93208) 204/G7
Campo, Calif. (92006) 204/J11
Campo, Cameroon 115/B3
Campo, Colo. (81029) 208/O8
Campoalegre, Colombia 126/C6
Campobasso (prov.), Italy 34/E4
Campobasso, Italy 34/E4
Campobello (isl.), New Bruns. 170/D4
Campobello, S.C. (29322) 296/C1
Campo Belo, Brazil 132/E8
Campo Belo, Brazil 135/D2
Campo Claro, Venezuela 124/G2
Campo de Criptana, Spain 33/E3
Campo de la Cruz, Colombia 126/C2
Campo Florido, Brazil 135/B1
Campo Formoso, Brazil 132/F5
Campo Grande, Brazil 120/D5
Campo Grande, Brazil 132/8
Campo Ind. Res., Calif. 204/J11
Campo Largo, Brazil 135/B4
Campo Maior, Brazil 132/F4
Campo Maior, Portugal 33/C3
Campos, Brazil 132/F8
Campos, Brazil 135/F2
Campos, Brazil 120/E5
Campos (reg.), Brazil 120/E4
Campos Altos, Brazil 135/C1
Campo Seco, Calif. (95226) 204/D9
Campo Tencia (peak), Switzerland 39/G4
Campo Tures, Italy 34/C1
Camp Pendleton, Calif. 204/H10
Camp Perrin, Haiti 158/A6
Camp Point, Ill. (62320) 222/B3
Camp Robinson, Ontario 177/G4
Camp Robinson, Ontario 175/B2
Camp Sherman, Oreg. (97730) 291/F3
Camp Springs, Md. (20748) 245/G6
Campti, La. (71411) 238/D3
Campton, Georgia (†30655) 217/E3
Campton, Ky. (41301) 237/O5
Campton○, N.H. (03223) 268/D4
Camptown, Pa. (18815) 294/K2
Campus, Ill. (60920) 222/E2
Camp Verde, Ariz. (86322) 198/D4
Campville, Fla. (†32640) 212/D2
Camp Wood, Texas (78833) 303/D8
Cam Ranh, Vietnam 72/F5
Cam Ranh, Vinh (bay), Vietnam 72/F5
Camrose, Alberta 182/D3
Camrose, Alta. 162/E5
Camsell (riv.), N.W. Terrs. 187/G3
Camsell Portage, Sask. 181/L2
Camuy, P. Rico 161/B1
Camuy, P. Rico 156/F1
Camuy (riv.), P. Rico 161/B1
Çan, Turkey 63/B2
Čaňa, Czech. 41/F2
Cana (pt.), Dom. Rep. 158/F6
Cana, Sask. 181/J5
Cana, Va. (24317) 307/G7
Canaan, Conn. (06018) 210/B1
Canaan○, Conn. (06018) 210/B1
Canaan (mt.), Conn. 210/B1
Canaan, Ind. (47224) 227/G7
Canaan○, Maine (04924) 243/D6
Canaan, Miss. (38612) 256/F1
Canaan, New Bruns. 170/E2
Canaan (riv.), New Bruns. 170/E2
Canaan○, N.H. (03741) 268/C4
Canaan, N.Y. (12029) 276/O6
Canaan○, Vt. (05903) 268/D2
Canaan Center, N.H. (†03741) 268/C4
Canaan Forks, 170/E2
Canaan Road, New Bruns. 170/E2
Canada 2/D3
Canada 4/C13
Canada 146/G4
CANADA, 163
Cañada, La (mt.), Cuba 158/B2
Canada, Ky. (41519) 237/S5
Canada (bay), Newf. 166/C3
Cañada de Gómez, Argentina 143/F6
Cañada Nieto, Uruguay 145/B4
Canadensis, Pa. (18325) 294/M3
Canadian (riv.) 188/F3
Canadian (riv.), N. Mex. 274/F3
Canadian (co.), Okla. 288/K3
Canadian, Okla. (74425) 288/P4
Canadian (riv.), Okla. 288/O4
Canadian, Texas (79014) 303/D2
Canadian (riv.), Texas 303/D1
Canadian (riv.), U.S. 146/H6
Canadian City, Okla. (†73064) 288/L4
Canadice (lake), N.Y. 276/F5
Canadys, S.C. (29433) 296/F5
Canagua (riv.), Venezuela 124/C3
Canajoharie, N.Y. (13317) 276/L5
Çanakkale (prov.), Turkey 63/B2
Çanakkale, Turkey 63/B6
Çanakkale, Turkey 59/A2
Çanakkale Boğazı (Dardanelles) (str.), Turkey 63/B6
Çanakkale Boğazı (str.), Turkey 59/A2
Canal (creek), Alberta 182/E5
Canala, New Caled. 86/G4
Canala (bay), New Caled. 86/H4
Canal Flats, Br. Col. 184/K5
Canal Fulton, Ohio (44614) 284/H4
Canalou, Mo. (63828) 261/N9
Canal Point, Fla. (33438) 212/F5
Canals, Argentina 143/D3
Canal Winchester, Ohio (43110) 284/E6
Canandaigua, N.Y. (14424) 276/F5
Canandaigua (lake), N.Y. 276/F5
Cananea, Mexico 150/D1
Cananéia, Brazil 132/E9
Cananéia, Brazil 135/C4
Canonova, Cuba 158/K3
Cañar (prov.), Ecuador 128/C4
Cañar, Ecuador 128/C4
Canaries, St. Lucia 161/G6
Canaries, Piton (mt.), St. Lucia 161/G6
Canarreos, Los (arch.), Cuba 158/C2
Canary, Oreg. (†97493) 291/D4
Canary (isls.), Spain 102/A2
Canary (isls.), Spain 2/H4
Canary (isls.), Spain 33/B4
Canary (isls.), Spain 106/A3
Cañas, C. Rica 154/E5
Cañas, Cuba 158/B1
Cañas (range), Uruguay 145/C2
Canaseraga, N.Y. (14822) 276/E6
Cañasgordas, Colombia 126/B4
Canasí, Cuba 158/C1
Canastota, N.Y. (13032) 276/J4
Canatlán, Mexico 150/G4
Canaveral (cape), Fla. 146/L7
Canaveral (Kennedy) (cape), Fla. 188/L5
Canaveral (cape), U.S. 2/F4
Canavieiras, Brazil 132/G6
Cañazas, Panama 154/G6
Canbelego, N.S. Wales 97/D2
Canberra (cap.), Australia 87/F9
Canberra (cap.), Australia 2/S7
Canberra (cap.), Australia, Aust. Cap. Terr. 97/E4
Canby, Calif. (96015) 204/E2
Canby, Minn. (56220) 255/B6
Canby, Oreg. (97013) 291/B2
Cancún, Mexico 150/Q6
Candala, Somalia 115/J1
Candarave, Peru 128/G11
Çandarlı (gulf), Turkey 63/B3
Candás, Spain 33/D1
Candéias, Brazil 120/F4
Candela, Mexico 150/J3
Candelaria, Bolivia 136/F5
Candelaria (riv.), Bolivia 136/F5
Candelaria, Cuba 158/B1
Candelaria, Mexico 150/O7
Candelaria (riv.), Mexico 150/O8
Candelaria, Philippines 82/B3
Candelaria, Texas (†79843) 303/C12
Candelaria, Venezuela 124/F4
Candeleda, Spain 33/D2
Candelero (pt.), P. Rico 161/F2
Candelo, N.S. Wales 97/E5
Candia (Iráklion), Greece 45/G8
Candia○, N.H. (03034) 268/E5
Candiac, Québec 172/J4
Candiac, Sask. 181/H5
Cândido Mendes, Brazil 132/E3
Çandır, Turkey 63/F3
Candle (lake), Sask. 181/F2
Candle Lake, Sask. 181/F2
Candler, Fla. (32624) 212/E2
Candler (co.), Georgia 217/H6
Candler, N.C. (28715) 281/D3
Candlewood (lake), Conn. 210/A2
Candlewood, N.J. (†08701) 273/E3
Cando, N. Dak. (58324) 282/M3
Cando, Sask. 181/C3
Candon, Philippines 82/C2
Candor, N.Y. (13743) 276/H6
Candor, N.C. (27229) 281/K4
Cane (creek), Utah 304/E5
Canea (Khaniá), Greece 45/G8
Caneadea, N.Y. (14717) 276/D6
Canebay, Virgin Is. (U.S.) 161/E3
Cane Beds, Ariz. (†86022) 198/B2
Canebrake, W. Va. (24819) 312/C8
Caneel (bay), Virgin Is. (U.S.) 161/B4
Canehill, Ark. (72717) 202/B2
Canelones (dept.), Uruguay 145/D5
Canelones, Uruguay 120/D6
Canelones, Uruguay 145/B6
Canelos, Ecuador 128/D3
Canendiyu (dept.), Paraguay 144/E4
Cañete (riv.), 128/D9
Cañete, Chile 138/D2
Cañete, Spain 33/F2
Cane Valley, Ky. (42720) 237/L6
Caney, Kansas (67333) 232/G4
Caney, Ky. (41407) 237/P5
Caney, Okla. (74533) 288/O6
Caney (riv.), Okla. 288/O1
Caney Fork (riv.), Tenn. 237/L9
Caneyville, Ky. (42721) 237/J6
Canfield, Ark. (71829) 202/C7
Canfield, Ohio (44406) 284/J3
Canford, Br. Col. 184/G5
Cangallo, Peru 128/E9
Cangamba, Angola 115/C6
Cangas, Spain 33/B1
Cangas de Narcea, Spain 33/C1
Cangas de Onís, Spain 33/D1
Canguaretama, Brazil 132/H4
Cangyuan, China 77/E7
Cangzhou (Tsangchow), China 77/J4
Caniapiscau (riv.), Que. 162/K4
Caniapiscau, Québec 174/D1
Caniapiscau (res.), Québec 174/D2
Caniapiscau (riv.), Québec 174/D1
Canicattì, Italy 34/E6
Canigao (chan.), Philippines 82/E5
Canik (mts.), Turkey 63/G2
Caniles, Spain 33/E4
Canim (lake), Br. Col. 184/G4
Canim Lake, Br. Col. 184/G4
Canindé, Brazil 132/G4
Canistear (res.), N.J. 273/E1
Canisteo, N.Y. (14823) 276/E6
Canisteo (riv.), N.Y. 276/F6
Canistota, S. Dak. (57012) 298/P6
Cañitas de Felipe Pescador, Mexico 150/H5
Canjáyar, Spain 33/E4
Canje (riv.), Guyana 131/C2
Canjilon, N. Mex. (87515) 274/C2
Çankaya, Turkey 63/E3
Çankırı (prov.), Turkey 63/E2
Çankırı, Turkey 63/E2
Çankırı, Turkey 59/B1
Cankton, La. (†70584) 238/F6
Canlaon, Philippines 82/D5
Canlaon (peak), Philippines 82/D5
Canmer, Ky. (42722) 237/K6
Canmore, Alberta 182/C4
Canna (isl.), Scotland 10/C2
Canna (isl.), Scotland 15/B3
Canna (sound), Scotland 15/B3
Cannalville, Ohio (†43777) 284/F6
Cannanore, India 68/D6
Cannelburg, Ind. (47519) 227/C7
Cannel City, Ky. (41408) 237/P5
Cannelles (pt.), St. Lucia 161/G7
Cannelles (riv.), St. Lucia 161/G6
Cannelton, Ind. (47520) 227/D9
Cannes, France 28/G6
Cannich, Scotland 15/D3
Canning (riv.), Alaska 196/J1
Canning, Nova Scotia 168/D3
Canning, S. Dak. (†57501) 298/K5
Canning (riv.), W. Australia 88/B3
Canning (res.), W. Australia 88/B2
Canning, W. Australia 92/A1
Cannington, Ontario 177/E3
Cannington Manon Hist. Park, Sask. 181/J6
Cannock, England 10/G2
Cannock, England 13/E5
Cannon, Del. (19935) 245/R6
Cannon (mt.), N.H. 268/D3
Cannon (co.), Tenn. 237/J9
Cannon A.F.B., N. Mex. 274/F4
Cannon Ball, N. Dak. (58528) 282/J7
Cannonball (riv.), N. Dak. 282/G7
Cannon Beach, Oreg. (97110) 291/D2
Cannondale, Conn. (†06897) 210/B4
Cannon Falls, Minn. (55009) 255/F6
Cannonsburg, Miss. (†39120) 256/B7
Cannonsville (res.), N.Y. 276/K6
Cannonville, Utah (84718) 304/B6
Cann River, Victoria 97/E5
Caño (isl.), C. Rica 154/F6
Canoas, Brazil 132/D10
Canoas, Brazil 120/D5
Canobie Lake, N.H. (†03079) 268/E6
Caño Capure (riv.), Venezuela 124/H3
Canoe, Ala. (†36502) 195/D8
Canoe (riv.), Br. Col. 184/H4
Canoe (lake), Sask. 181/L3
Canoe Lake, Sask. 181/L3
Canoe River, Br. Col. 184/H4
Canoga Park, Calif. (*91303) 204/B10
Canoinhas, Brazil 132/D9
Caño Macareo (riv.), Venezuela 124/H3
Caño Mánamo (riv.), Venezuela 124/G3
Canon, Georgia (30520) 217/F2
Canonbie, Scotland 15/F5
Canonchet, R.I. (†02833) 249/H7
Canon City, Colo. (81212) 208/J6
Canones, N. Mex. (87516) 274/C2
Canonsburg, Pa. (15317) 294/B5
Canoochee, Georgia (30416) 217/H5
Canoose Flowage (lake), New Bruns. 170/C3
Canora, Sask. 181/J4
Canosa di Puglia, Italy 34/E4
Canouan (isl.), St. Vin. & Grens. 156/G4
Canova, S. Dak. (57321) 298/O6
Canovanas (riv.), P. Rico 161/E1
Canowindra, N.S. Wales 97/E3
Canquella, Bolivia 136/A7
Cansado, Mauritania 106/A4
Canso, Nova Scotia 168/H3
Canso (cape), Nova Scotia 168/H3
Canso (str.), Nova Scotia 168/G3
Canta, Peru 128/D8
Cantabrian (range), Spain 33/C1
Cantagalo, Brazil 135/E3
Cantal (dept.), France 28/E5
Cantal, Sask. 181/K6
Cantalejo, Spain 33/D2
Cantanhede, Portugal 33/B2
Cantaura, Venezuela 124/F3
Canterbury○, Conn. (06331) 210/H2
Canterbury, Del. (†19943) 245/R4
Canterbury, England 10/G5
Canterbury, England 13/H6
Canterbury, New Bruns. 170/C3
Canterbury○, N.H. (03224) 268/D5
Canterbury, N.S. Wales 88/K4
Canterbury, N.S. Wales 97/J3
Canterbury (bight), N. Zealand 100/D6
Can Tho, Vietnam 72/E5
Can Tho, Vietnam 54/M9
Cantil, Calif. (93519) 204/H8
Cantiles (cay), Cuba 158/C3
Cantillana, Alto de (mt.), Chile 138/G4
Cantley, Québec 172/B4
Canto del Agua, Chile 138/A7
Canto do Buriti, Brazil 132/F5
Canton (Guangzhou), China 77/H7
Canton, China 54/N7
Canton, China 2/Q4
Canton, Conn. (06019) 210/D1
Canton○, Conn. (06019) 210/D1
Canton, Georgia (30114) 217/C2
Canton, Ill. (61520) 222/C3
Canton, Ind. (†47167) 227/E7
Canton, Kansas (67428) 232/E3
Canton, Ky. (42212) 237/F7
Canton (isl.), Kiribati 87/J6
Canton○, Maine (04221) 243/C7
Canton○, Mass. (02021) 249/C8
Canton, Minn. (55922) 255/F7
Canton, Miss. (39046) 256/D5
Canton, Mo. (63435) 261/J2
Canton, N.J. (†08079) 273/C5
Canton, N.Y. (13617) 276/K1
Canton, N.C. (28716) 281/D3
Canton (Hensel), N. Dak. (†58241) 282/P2
Canton, Ohio 188/K2
Canton, Ohio (*44701) 284/H4
Canton, Okla. (73724) 288/J2
Canton (lake), Okla. 288/J2
Canton, Pa. (17724) 294/J2
Canton, S. Dak. (57013) 298/R7
Canton, Texas (75103) 303/J5
Canton, Wis. (54823) 317/C5
Canton-Bégin, Québec 172/F1
Canton Bend, Ala. (†36726) 195/D6
Canton Center, Conn. (06020) 210/D1
Cantonment, Fla. (32533) 212/B6
Canton-Patapédia, Québec 172/B2
Cantoria, Spain 33/E4
Cantrall, Ill. (62625) 222/D4
Cantril, Iowa (52542) 229/J7
Cantù, Italy 34/B2
Cantuar, Sask. 181/C5
Cantwell, Alaska (99729) 196/J2
Canuck, Sask. 181/C6
Cañuelas, Argentina 143/G7
Canumã (riv.), Brazil 132/B4
Canutama, Brazil 132/G9
Canute, Okla. (73626) 288/H4
Canutillo, Texas (79835) 303/A10
Canvas, W. Va. (26662) 312/E6
Canvey Island, England 13/J8
Canvey Island, England 10/G5
Canwood, Sask. 181/E2
Canyon (lake), Ariz. 198/D5
Canyon, Br. Col. 184/J5
Canyon, Calif. (94516) 204/K2
Canyon (co.), Idaho 220/B6
Canyon (creek), Idaho 220/C6
Canyon, Minn. (55717) 255/F3
Canyon, Texas (79015) 303/C3
Canyon, Wyo. (82190) 319/B1
Canyon Blanco (creek), N. Mex. 274/B2
Canyon City, Oreg. (97820) 291/J3
Canyon Creek, Alberta 182/C2
Canyon Creek, Mont. (59633) 262/D4
Canyon de Chelly Nat'l Mon., Ariz. 198/F2
Canyon Ferry, Mont. (†59601) 262/E4
Canyon Ferry (lake), Mont. 262/E4
Canyonlands Nat'l Park, Utah 304/D5
Canyonville, Oreg. (97417) 291/D5
Cao Bang, Vietnam 72/E2
Caol, Scotland 15/C4
Cao Lanh, Vietnam 72/E5
Caonao, Cuba 158/E2
Caonillas (lake), P. Rico 161/C2

Changyŏn 349

Ceclavín, Spain 33/C3
Cedar (pt.), Ala. 195/B10
Cedar, Br. Col. 184/J3
Cedar (creek), Colo. 208/M1
Cedar (lake), Conn. 210/E3
Cedar (creek), Ind. 227/G2
Cedar (co.), Iowa 229/L5
Cedar, Iowa (52543) 229/H6
Cedar (riv.), Iowa 188/H2
Cedar (riv.), Iowa 229/K4
Cedar, Kansas (67628) 232/D2
Cedar (lake), Manitoba 179/B1
Cedar (pt.), Md. 245/N7
Cedar, Mich. (49621) 250/D4
Cedar (lake), Mich. 250/F4
Cedar (riv.), Minn. 255/F7
Cedar (co.), Mo. 261/E7
Cedar (co.), Nebr. 264/G2
Cedar (riv.), Nebr. 264/F3
Cedar (mt.), Nev. 266/D4
Cedar (creek), N.J. 273/E4
Cedar (creek), N. Dak. 282/G7
Cedar (pt.), Ohio 284/D2
Cedar (lake), Ontario 177/F1
Cedar (lake), Texas 303/B5
Cedar (mts.), Utah 304/B3
Cedar (isl.), Va. 307/S5
Cedar (riv.), Wash. 310/B2
Cedar Bluff, Ala. (35959) 195/G2
Cedar Bluff, Iowa (†52772) 229/L5
Cedar Bluff (res.), Kansas 232/C3
Cedarbluff, Miss. (39741) 256/G3
Cedar Bluff, Va. (24609) 307/E6
Cedar Bluffs, Kansas (†67749) 232/B2
Cedar Bluffs, Nebr. (68015) 264/H3
Cedar Breaks Nat'l Mon., Utah 304/B6
Cedar Brook, N.J. (08018) 273/D4
Cedarburg, Wis. (53012) 317/L9
Cedarbutte, S. Dak. (57527) 298/H6
Cedar City, Mo. (65022) 261/H5
Cedar City, Utah 188/D3
Cedar City, Utah (84720) 304/A6
Cedar Cove, Ala. (†35453) 195/D4
Cedar Creek, Ark. (†72950) 202/C4
Cedar Creek (peak), Idaho 220/E7
Cedar Creek (res.), Idaho 220/D7
Cedarcreek, Mo. (†65680) 261/G9
Cedar Creek, Nebr. (68016) 264/H3
Cedar Crest, N. Mex. (87008) 274/C3
Cedaredge, Colo. (81413) 208/D5
Cedar Falls, Iowa (50613) 229/H3
Cedar Falls, N.C. (27230) 281/K3
Cedar Falls, Wash. (†98045) 310/D3
Cedar Falls, Wis. (†54751) 317/C6
Cedar Fort, Utah (†84013) 304/B3
Cedar Gap, Mo. (†65746) 261/G8
Cedar Grove, Ant. & Bar. 161/E11
Cedar Grove, Fla. (†32401) 212/D6
Cedar Grove, Georgia (†30727) 217/L2
Cedar Grove, Ind. (47016) 227/H6
Cedar Grove, Md. (†20767) 245/K4
Cedar Grove○, N.J. (07009) 273/B2
Cedar Grove, N.C. (27231) 281/L2
Cedar Grove, Tenn. (38321) 237/D9
Cedar Grove, W. Va. (25039) 312/D6
Cedar Grove, Wis. (53013) 317/L8
Cedar Heights, Md. (†20027) 245/G5
Cedar Hill, N. Mex. (†87410) 274/B2
Cedar Hill, Tenn. (37032) 237/H7
Cedar Hill, Texas (75104) 303/G3
Cedar Hill Lakes, Mo. (63016) 261/L6
Cedar Hills, Oreg. (97225) 291/A2
Cedarhurst, N.Y. (11516) 276/P7
Cedar Island, N.C. (28520) 281/S5
Cedar Key, Fla. (32625) 212/C2
Cedar Knolls, N.J. (07927) 273/E2
Cedar Lake, Ind. (46303) 227/C2
Cedar Lake, Minn. (†56431) 255/E4
Cedar Mill, Oreg. (†97005) 291/A2
Cedar Mills, Minn. (55351) 255/D6
Cedar Mountain, N.C. (28718) 281/D4
Cedar Park, Texas (78613) 303/G7
Cedar Point, Ill. (61316) 222/D2
Cedar Point, Kansas (66843) 232/F3
Cedar Rapids, Iowa 188/H2
Cedar Rapids, Iowa (*52401) 229/K5
Cedar Rapids, Iowa 146/J5
Cedar Rapids, Nebr. (68627) 264/F3
Cedar River, Mich. (49813) 250/B3
Cedar Run, N.J. (†08092) 273/E4
Cedar Run, Pa. (17727) 294/H2
Cedar Springs, Georgia (31732) 217/C8
Cedar Springs, Mich. (49319) 250/D5
Cedar Springs, Mo. (†64744) 261/E7
Cedar Springs, Ontario 177/B5
Cedar Springs, Va. (†24368) 307/F7
Cedar Swamp (pond), Conn. 210/G2
Cedartown, Georgia (30125) 217/B2
Cedarvale, Br. Col. 184/C2
Cedar Vale, Kansas (67024) 232/F4
Cedarvale, N. Mex. (87009) 274/D4
Cedar Valley, Utah (84013) 304/B3
Cedarville, Ark. (72932) 202/B2
Cedarville, Calif. (96104) 204/E2
Cedarville, Ill. (61013) 222/D1
Cedarville, Ind. (†46741) 227/G2
Cedarville, Ky. (†41522) 237/S6
Cedarville, Md. (†20613) 245/L6
Cedarville, Mich. (49719) 250/E2
Cedarville, N.J. (08311) 273/C5
Cedarville, N.Y. (†13357) 276/K5
Cedarville, Ohio (45314) 284/C6
Cedarville, Va. (†22630) 307/M3
Cedarville, W. Va. (26611) 312/E5
Cedarwood Park, N.J. (†08723) 273/E3
Cedonia, Wash. (99137) 310/G2
Cedoux, Sask. 181/H6
Cedral, Mexico 150/J5
Cedros, Honduras 154/D3
Cedros (isl.), Mexico 146/G7
Cedros (isl.), Mexico 150/B2
Cedros, Trin. & Tob. 161/A11
Ceduna, S. Australia 88/E6
Ceduna, S. Australia 94/D5
Cee Vee, Texas (79223) 303/D3
Cefalù, Italy 34/E5
Cegléd, Hungary 41/E3
Ceglie Messapico, Italy 34/F4
Cehegín, Spain 33/F3
Ceiba, P. Rico 161/F2
Çekerek, Turkey 63/F2
Çekerek (riv.), Turkey 63/F3
Cela, Angola 115/C6
Celada Cué, Paraguay 144/D3
Celano, Italy 34/D3
Celanova, Spain 33/B1
Celaya, Mexico 150/J6
Celbridge, Ireland 17/H5
Celebes (sea) 54/O9
Celebes (isl.), Indonesia 54/N10
Celebes (isl.), Indonesia 2/R6
Celebes (Sulawesi) (isl.), Indonesia 85/G5
Celebes (sea), Indonesia 85/G5
Celebes (sea), Philippines 82/D8
Celendín, Peru 128/D6
Celerigna-Schlarigna, Switzerland 39/J3
Celeste, Texas (75423) 303/H4
Celestine, Ind. (47521) 227/D8
Celestún, Mexico 150/O6
Celica, Ecuador 128/B4
Céligny, Switzerland 39/B4
Çelikhan, Turkey 63/H3
Celilo, Oreg. (†97058) 291/G2
Celilo (lake), Oreg. 291/G2
Celilo (lake), Wash. 310/E5
Celina, Minn. (†55788) 255/E3
Celina, Ohio (45822) 284/A4
Celina, Tenn. (38551) 237/K7
Celina, Texas (75009) 303/H4
Celista, Br. Col. 184/H5
Celje, Yugoslavia 45/B2
Cella, Spain 33/F2
Cellar (head), Scotland 15/B2
Celldömölk, Hungary 41/D3
Celle, W. Germany 22/D2
Celorico da Beira, Portugal 33/C2
Celoron, N.Y. (14720) 276/B6
Cement, Okla. (73017) 288/K5
Cement City, Mich. (49233) 250/E6
Çemişkezek, Turkey 63/H3
Cemmaes (head), Wales 13/C5
Cenderawasih (bay), Indonesia 85/K6
Ceneri (mt.), Switzerland 39/G4
Cenia, Spain 33/G2
Census Bureau, Md. 245/F5
Centenary, Ind. (†47842) 227/B5
Centenary, S.C. (29519) 296/J3
Centennial (mts.), Idaho 220/F5
Centennial, Wyo. (82055) 319/F4
Centennial Wash (dry riv.), Ariz. 198/B5
Center, Colo. (81125) 208/G7
Center, Georgia (†30601) 217/F2
Center, Ind. (†46901) 227/E4
Center, Ky. (42214) 237/K6
Center (pond), Maine 243/E5
Center, Mo. (63436) 261/J3
Center, Nebr. (68724) 264/G2
Center, N. Dak. (58530) 282/H5
Center, Okla. (†74820) 288/N5
Center, S. Dak. (†57058) 298/P6
Center, Texas (75935) 303/K6
Center Barnstead, N.H. (03225) 268/E5
Center Belpre, Ohio (†45714) 284/G7
Centerbrook, Conn. (06409) 210/F3
Centerburg, Ohio (43011) 284/E5
Center City, Minn. (55012) 255/F5
Center Conway, N.H. (03813) 268/E4
Center Cross, Va. (22437) 307/P5
Centerdale, R.I. (02911) 249/H5
Centereach, N.Y. (11720) 276/O9
Centerfield, Utah (84622) 304/C4
Center Groton, Conn. (†06340) 210/G3
Center Harbor○, N.H. (03226) 268/E4
Center Hill, Ark. (72143) 202/G3
Center Hill, Fla. (33514) 212/D3
Center Hill (lake), Tenn. 237/K9
Center Junction, Iowa (52212) 229/L4
Center Line, Mich. (48015) 250/B6
Center Lovell, Maine (04016) 243/B7
Center Montville, Maine (†04941) 243/E7
Center Moreland, Pa. (18657) 294/E7
Center Moriches, N.Y. (11934) 276/P9
Center Ossipee, N.H. (03814) 268/E4
Center Point, Ark. (71830) 202/C5
Centerpoint, Ind. (47840) 227/C6
Center Point, Iowa (52213) 229/K4
Center Point, La. (71323) 238/F4
Center Point, S. Dak. (†57070) 298/P7
Center Point, Texas (78010) 303/E8
Center Point, W. Va. (26339) 312/E4
Center Ridge, Ark. (72027) 202/E3
Center Rutland, Vt. (05736) 268/A4
Center Sandwich, N.H. (03227) 268/D4
Center Square, Ind. (†47043) 227/H7
Center Strafford, N.H. (03815) 268/E5
Centerton, Ark. (72719) 202/B1
Centerton, Ind. (46116) 227/E5
Centerton, N.J. (†08318) 273/C4
Centertown, Ky. (42328) 237/G6
Centertown, Mo. (65023) 261/H5
Centertown, Tenn. (†37110) 237/K9
Center Tuftonboro, N.H. (03816) 268/E4
Centerview, Mo. (64019) 261/E5
Center Village, Ohio (†43021) 284/E5
Centerville, Ark. (72829) 202/D3
Centerville, Del. (†19801) 245/R1
Centerville, Georgia (31028) 217/E5
Centerville, Ind. (47330) 227/H5
Centerville, Iowa (52544) 229/H7
Centerville, Kansas (66014) 232/H3
Centerville, Ky. (†41522) 237/S6
Centerville, La. (70522) 238/H7
Centerville○, Maine (†04623) 243/H6
Centerville, Mass. (02632) 249/N6
Centerville, Minn. (†55038) 255/E5
Centerville, Mo. (63633) 261/L8
Centerville, N.C. (†27549) 281/N2
Centerville, Ohio (45459) 284/B6
Centerville, Pa. (15417) 294/B6
Centerville, Pa. (16404) 294/C2
Centerville, S. Dak. (57014) 298/R7
Centerville, Tenn. (37033) 237/G9
Centerville, Texas (75833) 303/H6
Centerville, Utah (84014) 304/C3
Centerville, Wash. (98613) 310/D5
Centrahoma, Okla. (74534) 288/O5
Central, Ala. (36014) 195/F5
Central (sen. dist.), Alaska 196/H2
Central, Alaska (99730) 196/J1
Central, Ariz. (85531) 198/F6
Central, Cordillera (range), Bolivia 136/C6
Central, Cordillera (range), Colombia 126/C5
Central, Cordillera (range), Dom. Rep. 158/D5
Central, Idaho (†83241) 220/G7
Central, Ind. (47110) 227/E8
Central (Markazi) (prov.), Iran 66/G3
Central (dist.), Israel 65/B3
Central (prov.), Kenya 115/G4
Central, La. (†70723) 238/L3
Central, N. Mex. (88026) 274/A6
Central (dept.), Paraguay 144/D4
Central (Baganga), Philippines 82/F7
Central, Cordillera (range), P. Rico 161/C2
Central (reg.), Scotland 15/D4
Central, S.C. (29630) 296/B2
Central, Utah (†84701) 304/A6
Central, Utah (84722) 304/B5
Central Aboriginal Reserve, W. Australia 88/D4
Central Aboriginal Res., W. Australia 92/E3
Central African Republic 2/K5
Central African Republic 102/D4
CENTRAL AFRICAN REPUBLIC 115/C2
Central Aguirre, P. Rico 161/D3
Central Amancio Rodríguez, Cuba 158/G3
Central America 2/E5
Central América, Cuba 158/J4
Central Bedeque, Pr. Edward I. 168/E2
Central Blissville, New Bruns. 170/D3
Central Bolivia, Cuba 158/G2
Central Brasil, Cuba 158/G2
Central Bridge, N.Y. (12035) 276/M5
Central Butte, Sask. 181/E5
Central Cándido González, Cuba 158/G3
Central City, Ark. (†72923) 202/B3
Central City, Colo. (80427) 208/J3
Central City, Ill. (†62801) 222/D5
Central City, Iowa (52214) 229/K4
Central City, Ky. (42330) 237/G6
Central City, Nebr. (68826) 264/F3
Central City, Pa. (15926) 294/E5
Central City, S. Dak. (†57754) 298/B5
Central Colombia, Cuba 158/G3
Central Falls, R.I. (02863) 249/J5
Central Frank País, Cuba 158/K3
Central Greece and Euboea (reg.), Greece 45/F6
Central Guatemala, Cuba 158/J3
Central Haití, Cuba 158/G3
Centralhatchee, Georgia (†30217) 217/B4
Central Heights-Midland City, Ariz. (†85501)198/E5
Centralia, Ill. (62801) 222/D5
Centralia, Iowa (†52068) 229/M4
Centralia, Kansas (66415) 232/F2
Centralia, Mo. (65240) 261/H4
Centralia, Okla. (74336) 288/R1
Centralia, Pa. (17927) 294/K4
Centralia, Texas (75834) 303/K6
Centralia, Wash. 188/B1
Centralia, Wash. (98531) 310/C4
Centralia, W. Va. (26612) 312/E5
Central Intelligence Agency (C.I.A.), Va. 307/S2
Central Islip, N.Y. (11722) 276/O9
Central Lake, Mich. (49622) 250/D3
Central Los Reynaldos, Cuba 158/J4
Central Loynaz Echevarría, Cuba 158/J3
Central Manuel Tames, Cuba 158/K4
Central Niágara, Cuba 158/B1
Central Pacolet, S.C. (†29372) 296/D2
Central Park, Wash. (98520) 310/B3
Central Patricia, Ontario 175/B2
Central Point, Oreg. (97502) 291/D5
Central Point, Va. (†22427) 307/O4
Central Saanich, Br. Col. 184/K3
Central Square, N.Y. (13036) 276/H4
Central Station, W. Va. (26340) 312/E4
Central Ural (mts.), U.S.S.R. 52/J2
Central Valley, Calif. (96019) 204/C3
Central Valley, N.Y. (10917) 276/M8
Central Village, Conn. (06332) 210/H2
Central Village, Mass. (02790) 249/K6
Central Wedge (mt.), North. Terr. 93/C7
Centre, Ala. (35960) 195/G2
Centre (co.), Pa. 294/G4
Centre Hall, Pa. (16828) 294/G4
Centre Island, N.Y. (†11771) 276/R6
Centre-Saint-Simon, New Bruns. 170/E1
Centreville, Ala. (35042) 195/D5
Centreville, Ill. (62206) 222/B3
Centreville, Md. (21617) 245/O4
Centreville, Mich. (49032) 250/D7
Centreville, Miss. (39631) 256/B8
Centreville, New Bruns. 170/C2
Centreville, Digby, Nova Scotia 168/B4
Centreville, Kings, Nova Scotia 168/D3
Centreville (Thurman), Ohio (†45685) 284/F8
Centuria, Wis. (54824) 317/A5
Centurión, Uruguay 145/F3
Century, Fla. (32535) 212/B5
Century, W. Va. (26214) 312/F4
Cephalonia (Kefallinía) (isl.), Greece 45/E6
Ceram (isl.), Indonesia 54/P10
Ceram (isl.), Indonesia 85/H6
Cerbat (mts.), Ariz. 198/A3
Cercal, Portugal 33/B4
Cerca la Source, Haiti 158/C5
Cereal, Alberta 182/E4
Ceredo, W. Va. (25507) 312/B6
Ceres, Argentina 143/D2
Ceres, Brazil 132/D6
Ceres, Brazil 120/E4
Ceres, Calif. (95307) 204/D6
Ceres, N.Y. (14721) 276/D6
Ceres, S. Africa 118/B6
Ceres, Va. (24318) 307/F6
Ceresco, Nebr. (68017) 264/H3
Céret, France 28/E6
Cereté, Colombia 126/C3
Cerf (lake), Québec 172/B3
Cerf (isl.), Seychelles 118/H5
Cerfontaine, Belgium 27/E8
Cerignola, Italy 34/E4
Çerkeş, Turkey 63/E2
Çerkezköy, Turkey 63/C2
Çermik, Turkey 63/H3
Cernavodă, Romania 45/J3
Cernier, Switzerland 39/C2
Cernobbio, Italy 34/B2
Cerralvo (isl.), Mexico 150/E4
Cerrillos, N. Mex. (87010) 274/D3
Cerrillos, Uruguay 145/A6
Cerrito, Paraguay 144/D5
Cerritos, Calif. (†90701) 204/C11
Cerritos, Mexico 150/J5
Cerro, N. Mex. (87519) 274/D2
Cerro Aconcagua (mt.) 120/C6
Cerro Alto (mt.), Texas 303/B10
Cêrro Azul, Brazil 135/B4
Cerro Azul, Mexico 150/L6
Cerro Azul, Peru 128/D9
Cerro Castillo, Chile 138/E9
Cerro Chato, Cerro Largo, Uruguay 145/F3
Cerro Chato, Rivera, Uruguay 145/D2
Cerro Chato, Treinta y Tres, Uruguay 145/D4
Cerro Colorado, Uruguay 145/D4
Cerro Corá, Paraguay 144/E3
Cerro de las Armas, Uruguay 145/B5
Cerro de las Cuentas, Uruguay 145/E3
Cerro de Pasco, Peru 120/B4
Cerro de Pasco, Peru 128/D8
Cerro de San Antonio, Colombia 126/C
Cerro Gordo, Ill. (61818) 222/E4
Cerro Gordo (co.), Iowa 229/G2
Cerro Gordo, N.C. (28430) 281/M6
Cerro Gordo (pt.), P. Rico 161/D1
Cerro Gordo, Tenn. (38322) 237/E10
Cerro Largo (dept.), Uruguay 145/E3
Cerro Manantiales, Chile 138/F10
Cerulean, Ky. (42215) 237/F7
Cervera, Spain 33/G2
Cervera del Río Alhama, Spain 33/E1
Cervera de Pisuerga, Spain 33/D1
Cerveteri, Italy 34/E6
Cervione, France 28/B6
Cesano, Italy 34/F6
César (dept.), Colombia 126/D3
César (riv.), Colombia 126/D2
Cesena, Italy 34/D2
Cesenatico, Italy 34/D2
Cēsis, U.S.S.R. 53/C2
Cēsis, U.S.S.R. 52/C3
Česká Kamenice, Czech. 41/C1
Česká Lípa, Czech. 41/C1
Česká Třebová, Czech. 41/D2
České Budějovice, Czech. 41/C2
Český Brod, Czech. 41/C1
Český Krumlov, Czech. 41/C2
Český Těšín, Czech. 41/E2
Çeşme, Turkey 63/B3
Céspedes, Cuba 158/G2
Cessford, Alberta 182/E4
Cessnock-Bellbird, N.S. Wales 88/J6
Cessnock-Bellbird, N.S. Wales 97/F3
Cestos (riv.), Liberia 106/C7
Cetinje, Yugoslavia 45/D4
Çetinkaya, Turkey 63/G3
Ceuta, Spain 106/C1
Ceuta, Spain 7/D5
Ceuta, Spain 102/B1
Ceuta, Spain 33/D5
Cévennes (mts.), France 28/E5
Cevio, Switzerland 39/G4
Cevizli, Turkey 63/D4
Ceyhan, Turkey 63/F4
Ceyhan (riv.), Turkey 63/F4
Ceyhan (riv.), Turkey 59/C2
Ceylânpınar, Turkey 63/H4
Ceylon (Sri Lanka) 54/K9
Ceylon, Minn. (56121) 255/D7
Ceylon, Sask. 181/G6
Chabás, Argentina 143/F6
Chaca, Chile 138/B1
Chacabuco, Argentina 143/F7
Chacabuco, Chile 138/G2
Chacachacare (isl.), Trin. & Tob. 161/A10
Chacahoula, La. (†70395) 238/J7
Chacalluta, Chile 138/A1
Chachacomani, Bolivia 136/A6
Chachapoyas, Peru 128/D6
Chachapoyas, Peru 120/B3
Chachoengsao, Thailand 72/D4
Chachro, Pakistan 68/C3
Chaco (prov.), Argentina 143/D2
Chaco (mesa), N. Mex. 274/B3
Chaco (riv.), N. Mex. 274/A2
Chaco (dept.), Paraguay 144/B-C2
Chaco Austral (reg.), Argentina 143/D2
Chaco Boreal (reg.), Paraguay 144/B2-3
Chaco Central (reg.), Argentina 143/D1
Chaco Culture Nat'l Hist. Park, N. Mex. 274/B2
Chacoma, Bolivia 136/A6
Chacon (cape), Alaska 196/N2
Chacon, N. Mex. (87713) 274/D2
Chacuaco (creek), Colo. 208/M8
Chad 2/K5
Chad 102/D3
Chad (lake) 102/D3
CHAD 111/C4
Chad (lake), Chad 111/C5
Chad (lake), Niger 106/G6
Chad (lake), Nigeria 106/G6
Chadan, U.S.S.R. 48/K4
Chadbourn, N.C. (28431) 281/M6
Chadron, Nebr. (69337) 264/B2
Chadwick, Ill. (61014) 222/D1
Chadwick, Mo. (65629) 261/G9
Chadwick Acres, N.C. (†28445) 281/P6
Chadwicks, N.Y. (13319) 276/K4
Chadyr-Lunga, U.S.S.R. 52/C5
Chaffee (co.), Colo. 208/G5
Chaffee, Mo. (63740) 261/N8
Chaffee, N.Y. (14030) 276/C5
Chaffee, N. Dak. (58014) 282/R6
Chaffers (isl.), Chile 138/D5
Chafurray, Colombia 126/D6
Chagai (hills), Afghanistan 68/A3
Chagai, Pakistan 59/H4
Chagai, Pakistan 68/A3
Chagai (hills), Pakistan 68/A3
Chagai (hills), Pakistan 59/H4
Chagda, U.S.S.R. 48/O4
Chaghcharan, Afghanistan 68/B2
Chagoda, U.S.S.R. 52/D3
Chagoness, Sask. 181/G3
Chagos (arch.), Br. Ind. Ocean Terr. 2/N6
Chagos (arch.), Br. Ind. Ocean Terr. 54/J10
Chagrin (riv.), Ohio 284/J8
Chagrin Falls, Ohio (44022) 284/J9
Chaguanas, Trin. & Tob. 161/B10
Chaguaramas, Trin. & Tob. 161/A10
Chaguaramas, Venezuela 124/E3
Chaguaya, Bolivia 136/C7
Chagulak (isl.), Alaska 196/D4
Chahal, Guatemala 154/C3
Chahar Borjak, Afghanistan 59/H3
Chahar Borjak, Afghanistan 68/A2
Chah Bahar, Afghanistan 59/H4
Chah Bahar, Iran 66/M8
Chahuites, Mexico 150/M8
Chai Badan, Thailand 72/D4
Chaibasa, India 68/F4
Chai Buri, Thailand 72/D3
Chainat, Thailand 72/D4
Chain-O-Lakes, Mo. (†65641) 261/E9
Chaira, Laguna (lake), Colombia 126/C7
Chaires, Fla. (†32302) 212/B1
Chaitén, Chile 138/E4
Chaiya, Thailand 72/C5
Chaiyaphum, Thailand 72/D4
Chajarí, Argentina 143/G5
Chajul, Guatemala 154/B3
Chake Chake, Tanzania 115/H5
Chala, Peru 128/E10
Chalais, Switzerland 39/E4
Chalatenango, El Salvador 154/C3
Chalchihuites, Mexico 150/G5
Chalco de Díaz Covarrubias, Mexico 150/M1
Chaleur (bay), New Bruns. 170/E1
Chaleur (bay), Québec 172/C2
Chaleur (bay), Québec 174/D3
Chalfont, Pa. (18914) 294/M5
Chalhuanca, Peru 128/F10
Chaling, China 77/H6
Chalk (creek), Utah 304/C3
Chalk River, Ontario 175/E3
Chalk River, Ontario 177/G1
Chalkyitsik, Alaska (99788) 196/K1
Challacollo, Bolivia 136/B6
Challana, Bolivia 136/A4
Challapata, Bolivia 136/B6
Challenger (mts.), N.W. Terrs. 187/L1
Challis, Idaho (83226) 220/D5
Challviri (salt dep.), Bolivia 136/B8
Chalmers, Ind. (47929) 227/D3
Chalmette, La. (70043) 238/P4
Chalna Port, Bangladesh 68/F4
Chalonnes-sur-Loire, France 28/C4
Châlons-sur-Marne, France 28/F3
Chalon-sur-Saône, France 28/F4
Chaltel, Cerro (mt.), Chile 138/E8
Chalus, Iran 59/F2
Chalus, Iran 66/G2
Chalybeate, Miss. (38684) 256/G1
Chalybeate Springs, Georgia (†31816) 217/C5
Chalybeate Springs, N.C. (†27526) 281/M3
Cham, Switzerland 39/F2
Cham, W. Germany 22/E4
Chama, Colo. (81126) 208/J8
Chama, N. Mex. (87520) 274/C2
Chaman, Pakistan 68/B2
Chaman, Pakistan 59/J3
Chamba, India 68/D2
Chambal (riv.), India 68/D3
Chambas, Cuba 158/F2
Chamberino, N. Mex. (88027) 274/C6
Chamberlain (creek), Idaho 220/C4
Chamberlain (lake), Maine 243/E3
Chamberlain, Sask. 181/F5
Chamberlain, S. Dak. (57325) 298/L6
Chamberlain, Uruguay 145/C3
Chamberlin, La. (†70767) 238/J1
Chambers (co.), Ala. 195/H5
Chambers, Ariz. (86502) 198/F3
Chambers, Nebr. (68725) 264/F2
Chambers (co.), Texas 303/K8
Chambers (isl.), Wis. 317/M5
Chambersburg, Ill. (62323) 222/C4
Chambersburg, Ind. (†47454) 227/E7
Chambersburg, Ohio (†45631) 284/F8
Chambersburg, Pa. (17201) 294/G6
Chambéry, France 28/F5
Chambeshi (riv.), Zambia 115/F6
Chambeyron (mt.), France 28/G5
Chambeyron (mt.), Italy 34/A2
Chambi, Jebel (mt.), Tunisia 106/F2
Chamblee, Georgia (30341) 217/K1
Chambly (co.), Québec 172/J4
Chambly, Québec 172/J4
Chambord, France 28/D4
Chambord, Québec 172/E1
Chamdo (Qamdo), China 77/E5
Chame (pt.), Panama 154/H6
Chamela (bay), Mexico 150/G7
Chamical, Argentina 143/C3
Chamisal, N. Mex. (87521) 274/D2
Chamizal Nat'l Mem., Texas 303/A10
Chamizo, Uruguay 145/D5
Chamo (lake), Ethiopia 111/G6
Chamois, Mo. (65024) 261/J5
Chamonix-Mont-Blanc, France 28/G5
Chamoson, Switzerland 39/D4
Champ, Mo. (†63042) 261/O2
Champagne (trad. prov.), France 29
Champagne, Yukon 187/E3
Champaign, Ill. 188/J2
Champaign (co.), Ill. 222/E3
Champaign, Ill. (61820) 222/E3
Champaign (co.), Ohio 284/C5
Champasak, Laos 72/E4
Champdani, India 68/F1
Champerico, Guatemala 154/A3
Champéry, Switzerland 39/C4
Champex, Switzerland 39/D4
Champigny-sur-Marne, France 28/C2
Champion, Alberta 182/D4
Champion, Mich. (49814) 250/B2
Champion, Nebr. (69023) 264/C4
Champlain (lake) 188/M2
Champlain, N.Y. (12919) 276/N1
Champlain (lake), N.Y. 276/O1
Champlain (county), Québec 174/C3
Champlain (co.), Québec 172/E2
Champlain, Québec 172/E3
Champlain (lake), Québec 172/D4
Champlain (lake), Vt. 268/A2
Champlain, Va. (22438) 307/O4
Champlain Park, N.Y. (†12901) 276/O1
Champlin, Minn. (55316) 255/G5
Champney's West, Newf. 166/D2
Champotón, Mexico 150/O7
Chamusa, Sierra (mts.), Colombia 126/C6
Chamusca, Portugal 33/B3
Chan, Ko (isl.), Thailand 72/C5
Chana, Ill. (61015) 222/D2
Chañaral, Chile 120/B5
Chañaral, Chile 138/A6
Chañaral (isl.), Chile 138/A7
Chancay, Peru 128/D8
Chance, Ala. (36729) 195/C7
Chance, Ky. (†42728) 237/L7
Chance, Md. (21816) 245/P8
Chance Cove, Newf. 166/D2
Chance Cove (cape), Newf. 166/D2
Chance Harbour, New Bruns. 170/D3
Chancellor, Ala. (36316) 195/G8
Chancellor, Alberta 182/D4
Chancellor, S. Dak. (57015) 298/R7
Chancellorsville, Va. (†22401) 307/N4
Chanco, Chile 138/A11
Chancy, Switzerland 39/A4
Chandalar, Alaska (†99726) 196/J1
Chandalar (riv.), Alaska 196/J1
Chandalar, East Fork (riv.), Alaska 196/J1
Chandeleur (isls.), La. 238/N7
Chandeleur (sound), La. 238/M7
Chanderi, India 68/D4
Chandernagore, India 68/F1
Chandigarh (terr.), India 68/D2
Chandigarh, India 68/D2
Chandler, Ariz. (85224) 198/D5
Chandler, Ind. (47610) 227/C8
Chandler, Minn. (56122) 255/C7
Chandler, Okla. (74834) 288/N3
Chandler, Que. 162/K6
Chandler, Québec 174/E3
Chandler, Québec 172/D2
Chandler, Texas (75758) 303/J5
Chandler Springs, Ala. (†35160) 195/F4
Chandlers Valley, Pa. (16312) 294/D2
Chandlersville, Ohio (43727) 284/G6
Chandlerville, Ill. (62627) 222/C3
Chandmanĭ, Mongolia 77/E2
Chandolin, Switzerland 39/E4
Chandos (lake), Ontario 177/G3
Chandrapur, India 68/D5
Chaneysville, Pa. (†21530) 294/F6
Chang, Ko (isl.), Thailand 72/D4
Changane (riv.), Mozambique 118/E4
Changbaek-sanmaek (mts.), N. Korea 81/D2
Changchih (Changzhi), China 77/H4
Changchow (Zhangzhou), China 77/J7
Changchow (Changzhou), China 77/J5
Changchun, China 77/K3
Changchun, China 54/O5
Changchun, China 2/R3
Changde (Changteh), China 77/H6
Changde, China 54/N7
Change Islands, Newf. 166/D4
Changewater, N.J. (07831) 273/D2
Changhua, China 77/K7
Changhŭng, S. Korea 81/C6
Changji, China 77/C3
Changjiang, China 77/G8
Chang Jiang (Yangtze) (riv.), China 2/Q4
Chang Jiang (Yangtze) (riv.), China 54/N6
Chang Jiang (Yangtze) (riv.), China 77/K5
Changjin (res.), N. Korea 81/C3
Chang Khoeng, Thailand 72/C3
Changling, China 77/K3
Changsha, China 77/H6
Changsha, China 2/Q4
Changsha, China 54/N7
Changshun, China 77/G6
Changsŏng, S. Korea 81/C6
Changteh (Changde), China 77/H6
Changuinola, Panama 154/F6
Changwu, China 77/G4
Changyang, China 77/H5
Changyeh (Zhangye), China 77/F4
Changyŏn, N. Korea 81/B4

350 **Changzhi**

Changzhi (Changchih), China 77/H4
Changzhi, China 54/N6
Changzhou (Changchow), China 77/K5
Chanhassen, Minn. (55317) 255/F6
Chankiang (Zhanjiang), China 77/H7
Channahon, Ill. (60410) 222/E2
Channel (isls.) 7/D4
Channel (isl.), Manitoba 179/B2
CHANNEL ISLANDS 10/E6
CHANNEL ISLANDS 13/E8
Channel Islands Nat'l Park, Calif. 204/E11
Channel-Port aux Basques, Newf. 166/C4
Channel-Port aux Basques, Newf. 162/L6
Channelview, Texas (77530) 303/K1
Channing, Mich. (49815) 250/B2
Channing, Texas (79018) 303/B2
Chantada, Spain 33/C1
Chanthaburi, Thailand 72/D4
Chantilly, France 28/E3
Chantilly, Va. (22021) 307/O3
Chantonnay, France 28/C4
Chantrey (inlet), N.W. Terrs. 187/J3
Chanute, Kansas (66720) 232/G4
Chanute A.F.B., Ill. 222/E3
Chao, Peru 128/C7
Chao'an (Chaochow), China 77/J7
ChaoChao (isl.), Portugal 33/B2
Chao Phraya, Mae Nam (riv.), Thailand 72/D4
Chaotung (Zhaotung), China 77/F6
Chaoyang, Guangdong, China 77/J7
Chaoyang, Liaoning, China 77/J3
Chapa, Vietnam 72/E2
Chapacura, Bolivia 136/A2
Chapais, Québec 174/B3
Chapala (lake), Mexico 150/H6
Chapanoke, N.C. (†27944) 281/S2
Chaparé (riv.), Bolivia 136/C5
Chaparra, Cuba 158/H3
Chaparral, Colombia 126/C6
Chapayevsk, U.S.S.R. 48/F4
Chapayevsk, U.S.S.R. 52/G4
Chapecó, Brazil 132/C9
Chapel, W. Va. (†26624) 312/E5
Chapel Arm, Newf. 166/D2
Chapel en le Frith, England 13/J2
Chapel Hill, Ark. (†71832) 202/B5
Chapel Hill, Ind. (†47436) 227/E6
Chapel Hill, N.C. (27514) 281/L3
Chapel Hill, Tenn. (37034) 237/H9
Chapelton, Jamaica 158/J6
Chapicuy, Uruguay 145/B2
Chapin, Ill. (62628) 222/C4
Chapin, Iowa (50427) 229/G3
Chapin, S.C. (29036) 296/E3
Chapleau, Ont. 162/H6
Chapleau, Ontario 175/D3
Chapleau, Ontario 177/J5
Chaplin○, Conn. (06235) 210/G1
Chaplin, Ky. (40012) 237/L5
Chaplin (riv.), Ky. 237/L5
Chaplin, Sask. 181/E5
Chaplin (lake), Sask. 181/E5
Chapman, Ala. (36015) 195/E7
Chapman (pt.), Conn. 210/F3
Chapman, Kansas (67431) 232/E3
Chapman○, Maine (†04757) 243/G2
Chapman, Nebr. (68827) 264/F3
Chapmansboro, Tenn. (37035) 237/G8
Chapmanville, W. Va. (25508) 312/B7
Chappaquiddick (isl.), Mass. 249/N7
Chappell, Ky. (40816) 237/P7
Chappell, Nebr. (69129) 264/B3
Chappell (isls.), Tasmania 99/D2
Chappell Hill, Texas (77426) 303/H7
Chappells, S.C. (29037) 296/D3
Chapra, India 68/F3
Chaptico, Md. (20621) 245/M7
Chapultepec, Mexico 150/A1
Chaquí, Bolivia 136/C6
Chara, U.S.S.R. 48/M4
Charadai, Argentina 143/D2
Charagua, Bolivia 136/D6
Charagua, Sierra de (mts.), Bolivia 136/D6
Charagua, Paraguay 144/D3
Charak, Iran 66/J7
Charambirá (pt.), Colombia 126/B5
Charaña, Bolivia 136/A5
Charata, Argentina 143/D2
Charbon, N.S. Wales 97/F3
Charbonneau, N. Dak. (†58831) 282/C4
Charcas, Mexico 150/J5
Charcot (isl.) 5/C15
Chard, Alberta 182/E2
Chard, England 13/E7
Chard, England 10/E5
Chardon, Ohio (44024) 284/H2
Chardonnière, Haiti 158/A6
Chardzhou, U.S.S.R. 54/H6
Chardzhou, U.S.S.R. 48/G6
Charente (dept.), France 28/D5
Charente (riv.), France 28/C5
Charente-Maritime (dept.), France 28/C5
Charenton, La. (70523) 238/H7
Charenton-le-Pont, France 28/B2
Charette, Québec 172/D3
Charikar, Afghanistan 68/B1
Charikar, Afghanistan 59/J2
Charing, Georgia (†31058) 217/D6
Charing Cross, Ontario 177/B5
Chariton, Iowa (50049) 229/G6
Chariton (riv.), Iowa 229/G7
Chariton (co.), Mo. 261/F3
Chariton (riv.), Mo. 261/G1
Charity, Guyana 131/B2
Charity, Mo. (†65644) 261/G7
Charkhlig (Ruoqiang), China 77/C4
Charlack, Mo. (†63101) 261/P2
Charlemagne, Québec 172/H4
Charlemont○, Mass. (01339) 249/C2
Charleroi, Belgium 27/E8
Charleroi, Pa. (15022) 294/C5
Charles, Georgia (†30474) 217/H6
Charles (co.), Md. 245/K6
Charles (riv.), Mass. 249/C7
Charles (isl.), N.W. Terrs. 187/L3
Charles (cape), Va. 188/L3
Charles (cape), Va. 307/R6
Charlesbourg, Québec 172/J3
Charles City, Iowa (50616) 229/H2
Charles City (co.), Va. 307/O6
Charles City, Va. (23030) 307/O6
Charles Mix (co.), S. Dak. 298/M7
Charles Mound (hill), Ill. 222/C1
Charleston, Ark. (72933) 202/B3
Charleston, Ill. (61920) 222/E4
Charleston, Kansas (†67853) 232/B4
Charleston○, Maine (04422) 243/F5
Charleston, Miss. (38921) 256/D2
Charleston, Mo. (63834) 261/O9
Charleston, Nev. (†89801) 266/F1
Charleston (peak), Nev. 266/F6
Charleston (lake), Ontario 177/J3
Charleston, Oreg. (97420) 291/C4
Charleston, S.C. 146/L6
Charleston, S.C. 188/L4
Charleston (co.), S.C. 296/H6
Charleston, S.C. (*29401) 296/G6
Charleston, Tenn. (37310) 237/M10
Charleston, Utah (†84032) 304/C3
Charleston (cap.), W. Va. 188/K3
Charleston (cap.), W. Va. 146/K6
Charleston (cap.), W. Va. (*25301) 312/C6
Charleston A.F.B., S.C. 296/G6
Charlestown, Ind. (47111) 227/F8
Charlestown, Md. (21914) 245/P2
Charlestown, N.H. (03603) 268/C5
Charlestown○, N.H. (03603) 268/C5
Charlestown, R.I. (02813) 249/H7
Charlestown, St. Chris.-Nevis 161/C11
Charlestown (cap.), Nevis, St. Chris.-Nevis 156/F3
Charles Town, W. Va. (25414) 312/L4
Charlestown-Bellahy, Ireland 17/D4
Charleville, Australia 87/E8
Charleville (Rathluirc), Ireland 17/D7
Charleville, Queensland 95/C5
Charleville, Queensland 88/H5
Charleville-Mézières, France 28/F3
Charlevoix (co.), Mich. 250/D3
Charlevoix, Mich. (49720) 250/D3
Charlevoix (lake), Mich. 250/D3
Charlevoix-Est (co.), Québec 172/G2
Charlevoix-Est (county), Québec 174/C3
Charlevoix-Ouest (co.), Québec 172/G2
Charlevoix-Ouest (county), Québec 174/C3
Charley, Ky. (†41230) 237/R5
Charlie Lake, Br. Col. 184/G2
Charlo, Mont. (59824) 262/B3
Charlo, New Bruns. 170/D1
Charlo (riv.), New Bruns. 170/D1
Charlotte, Ark. (72522) 202/H2
Charlotte (lake), Br. Col. 184/E4
Charlotte (harb.), Fla. 188/K5
Charlotte (co.), Fla. 212/E5
Charlotte (harb.), Fla. 212/D5
Charlotte, Iowa (52731) 229/M5
Charlotte○, Maine (†04666) 243/J5
Charlotte, Mich. (48813) 250/E6
Charlotte (co.), New Bruns. 170/C3
Charlotte, N.C. (*28201) 281/H4
Charlotte, N.C. 188/L3
Charlotte, N.C. 146/K6
Charlotte (lake), Nova Scotia 168/F4
Charlotte, Tenn. (37036) 237/G8
Charlotte, Texas (78011) 303/F9
Charlotte○, Vt. (05445) 268/A3
Charlotte (co.), Va. 307/L6
Charlotte Amalie (cap.), Virgin Is. (U.S.) 156/H1
Charlotte Amalie (cap.), Virgin Is. (U.S.) 161/B4
Charlotte Court House, Va. (23923) 307/L6
Charlotte Hall, Md. (20622) 245/M7
Charlotte Harbor, Fla. (†33950) 212/E5
Charlottenberg, Sweden 18/H6
Charlottenburg, W. Germany 22/E4
Charlottesville, Ind. (46117) 227/F5
Charlottesville, Va. 188/L3
Charlottesville (I.C.), Va. (*22901) 307/M4
Charlottetown, Newf. 166/D2
Charlottetown, Newf. 166/C3
Charlottetown (cap.), P.E.I. 146/M5
Charlottetown (cap.), P.E.I. 162/K6
Charlottetown (cap.), Pr. Edward I. 168/E2
Charlotteville, N.Y. (12036) 276/L5
Charlotte Waters, North. Terr. 93/D8
Charlson, N. Dak. (58726) 282/E3
Charlton (co.), Georgia 217/H9
Charlton○, Mass. (01507) 249/F4
Charlton (isl.), N.W.T. 162/H5
Charlton, Ontario 177/K5
Charlton, Ontario 175/D3
Charlton, Victoria 97/B5
Charlton City, Mass. (01508) 249/F4
Charlton Depot, Mass. (01509) 249/F4
Charlton Kings, England 13/F6
Charmco, W. Va. (25958) 312/E6
Charmey, Switzerland 39/D3
Charny, Québec 172/J3
Charolles, France 28/F4
Charouine, Algeria 106/D3
Charqueada Aguas de São Pedro, Brazil 135/B3
Charron (lake), Manitoba 179/G2
Charsk, U.S.S.R. 48/J5
Charter Oak, Iowa (51439) 229/C4
Charters, Ky. (†41179) 237/P3
Charters Towers, Australia 87/E7
Charters Towers, Queensland 95/C4
Charters Towers, Queensland 88/H4
Chartierville, Québec 172/F4
Chartley, Mass. (02712) 249/K5
Chartres, France 28/D3
Chascomús, Argentina 143/H7
Chase, Ala. (†35811) 195/E1
Chase, Br. Col. 184/H5
Chase (co.), Kansas 232/F3
Chase, Kansas (67524) 232/D3
Chase, La. (71324) 238/G2
Chase, Md. (21027) 245/N3
Chase, Mich. (49623) 250/D5
Chase (co.), Nebr. 264/C4
Chase (lake), N. Dak. 282/M5
Chaseburg, Wis. (54621) 317/D8
Chase City, Va. (23924) 307/M7
Chaseley, N. Dak. (58423) 282/L5
Chase Mills, N.Y. (13621) 276/K1
Chase N.A.S., Texas 303/G9
Chaska, Minn. (55318) 255/F6
Chaska, Tenn. (†37729) 237/N7
Chasm, Br. Col. 184/G4
Chasŏng, N. Korea 81/C3
Chasseron (mt.), Switzerland 39/C3
Chastang, Ala. (36517) 195/B8
Chastre, Belgium 27/F7
Chaswood, Nova Scotia 168/E3
Chataignier, La. (70524) 238/F5
Chatanika, Alaska (99731) 196/J1
Chatawa, Miss. (39632) 256/D8
Chatcolet, Idaho (†83851) 220/B2
Chateaubelair, St. Vin. & Grens. 161/A8
Châteaubriant, France 28/C4
Château-Chinon, France 28/E4
Château-d'Oex, Switzerland 39/D4
Château-du-Loir, France 28/D4
Châteaudun, France 28/D3
Chateaugay, N.Y. (12920) 276/N1
Chateaugay, Upper (lake), N.Y. 276/M1
Château-Gontier, France 28/C4
Châteauguay (co.), Québec 172/D4
Châteauguay, Québec 172/H4
Châteauguay-Centre, Québec 172/H4
Châteauneuf-sur-Loire, France 28/E4
Château-Renault, France 28/D4
Château-Richer, Québec 172/F3
Châteauroux, France 28/D4
Château-Salins, France 28/G3
Château-Thierry, France 28/E3
Châteaux (pt.), Guadeloupe 161/B6
Chateh, Alberta 182/A5
Châtelet, Belgium 27/F8
Châtellerault, France 28/D4
Châtel-Saint-Denis, Switzerland 39/C3
Chater, Manitoba 179/C5
Chatfield, Ark. (†72348) 202/K3
Chatfield, Manitoba 179/E4
Chatfield, Minn. (55923) 255/F7
Chatfield, Ohio (44825) 284/E4
Chatham (str.), Alaska 196/M1
Chatham (sound), Br. Col. 184/B3
Chatham (isl.), Chile 138/D9
Chatham, England 13/J8
Chatham, England 10/G5
Chatham (co.), Georgia 217/K6
Chatham, Ill. (62629) 222/D4
Chatham, La. (71226) 238/F2
Chatham, Mass. (02633) 249/P6
Chatham○, Mass. (02633) 249/P6
Chatham, Mich. (49816) 250/B2
Chatham, Miss. (38731) 256/B4
Chatham, N. Br. 162/K6
Chatham, New Bruns. 170/E1
Chatham○, N.H. (†04037) 268/E3
Chatham○, N.J. (07928) 273/E2
Chatham, N.Y. (12037) 276/N6
Chatham (isls.), N. Zealand 87/J10
Chatham (isl.), N. Zealand 100/D7
Chatham (isls.), N. Zealand 100/D7
Chatham (co.), N.C. 281/L3
Chatham, Ontario 177/B5
Chatham, Va. (24531) 307/K7
Chatham Center, N.Y. (†12037) 276/N6
Chatham Head, New Bruns. 170/E2
Chatham Port, Mass. (†02650) 249/P6
Châtillon, France 28/B2
Châtillon-sur-Indre, France 28/D4
Châtillon-sur-Seine, France 28/F4
Chato, Cerro (mt.), Argentina 143/B5
Chato, Cerro (mt.), Chile 138/E4
Chatom, Ala. (36518) 195/B8
Chatou, France 28/A1
Chatrapur, India 68/F5
Chatsworth, Calif. (91311) 204/B10
Chatsworth, Georgia (30705) 217/C1
Chatsworth, Ill. (60921) 222/E3
Chatsworth, Iowa (51011) 229/A3
Chatsworth, N.J. (08019) 273/D4
Chatsworth, Ontario 177/D3
Chattahoochee (riv.) 188/K4
Chattahoochee (riv.), Ala. 195/H8
Chattahoochee, Fla. (32324) 212/B1
Chattahoochee (riv.), Fla. 212/B1
Chattahoochee (co.), Georgia 217/C6
Chattahoochee (riv.), Georgia 217/B8
Chattahoochee River Nat'l Rec. Area, Georgia 217/K1
Chattanooga, Ohio (†45882) 284/A4
Chattanooga, Okla. (73528) 288/J6
Chattanooga, Tenn. 188/J3
Chattanooga, Tenn. 146/K6
Chattanooga, Tenn. (*37401) 237/K10
Chattaroy, Wash. (99003) 310/H3
Chattaroy, W. Va. (25667) 312/B7
Chatteris, England 13/H5
Chattooga (riv.), Ala. 195/H2
Chattooga (co.), Georgia 217/B1
Chattooga (riv.), Georgia 217/A2
Chattooga (riv.), Georgia 217/F1
Chattooga (riv.), S.C. 296/A2
Chatuge (lake), Georgia 217/E1
Chatuge (lake), N.C. 281/B5
Chatwood, Pa. (†19380) 294/L6
Chaud (lake), Québec 172/C3
Chaudière (riv.), Québec 172/G4
Chauk, Burma 72/B2
Chauk, Burma 54/L7
Chaukan (pass), Burma 72/C1
Chaumont, France 28/F3
Chaumont, N.Y. (13622) 276/H2
Chauncey, Georgia (31011) 217/F6
Chauncey, Ohio (45719) 284/F7
Chauny, France 28/E3
Chau Phu, Vietnam 72/E5
Chauques (isls.), Chile 138/D4
Chautauqua, Ill. (†62028) 222/C5
Chautauqua (co.), Kansas 232/F4
Chautauqua, Kansas (67334) 232/F4
Chautauqua (co.), N.Y. 276/B6
Chautauqua, N.Y. (14722) 276/A6
Chautauqua (lake), N.Y. 276/A6
Chauvin, Alberta 182/E3
Chauvin, La. (70344) 238/J8
Chavantes, Serra dos (range), Brazil 132/D5
Chaves, Brazil 132/D3
Chaves (Santa Cruz) (isl.), Ecuador 128/C9
Chaves (co.), N. Mex. 274/E5
Chaves, Portugal 33/C2
Chavies, Ky. (41727) 237/P6
Chavornay, Switzerland 39/C3
Chayanta, Bolivia 136/B6
Chaykovskiy, U.S.S.R. 52/H3
Chazelles-sur-Lyon, France 28/F5
Chazy, N.Y. (12921) 276/N1
Chazy (lake), N.Y. 276/N1
Cheadle, Alberta 182/D4
Cheadle, England 13/E5
Cheadle and Gatley, England 13/H2
Cheadle and Gatley, England 10/G2
Cheaha (mt.), Ala. 195/G4
Cheam View, Br. Col. 184/M3
Cheap (chan.), Chile 138/D7
Cheat (lake), W. Va. 312/G3
Cheat (riv.), W. Va. 312/G3
Cheatham (co.), Tenn. 237/G8
Cheatham (dam), Tenn. 237/G8
Cheatham (lake), Tenn. 237/H8
Cheb, Czech. 41/B1
Chebanse, Ill. (60922) 222/F3
Chebeague Island, Maine (04017) 243/C8
Chebogue (harb.), Nova Scotia 168/B5
Cheboksary, U.S.S.R. 7/J3
Cheboksary, U.S.S.R. 52/G3
Cheboksary, U.S.S.R. 48/E4
Cheboygan, Mich. 188/K1
Cheboygan (co.), Mich. 250/E3
Cheboygan, Mich. (49721) 250/E3
Chech, Erg (des.), Algeria 106/D3
Chech, Erg (des.) 102/B2
Chech, Erg (des.), Mali 106/D4
Chechaouene, Morocco 106/D1
Chechen-Ingush A.S.S.R., U.S.S.R. 48/E5
Chechen-Ingush A.S.S.R., U.S.S.R. 52/G6
Chech'ŏn, S. Korea 81/D5
Check, Va. (24072) 307/H6
Checker Hall, Barbados 161/B8
Checotah, Okla. (74426) 288/R4
Chedabucto (bay), Nova Scotia 168/G3
Cheduba (isl.), Burma 72/B3
Cheektowaga, N.Y. (14225) 276/C5
Cheekye, Br. Col. 184/F5
Cheesequake, N.J. (08879) 273/E3
Cheesman (lake), Colo. 208/J4
Chefoo (Yantai), China 77/K4
Chefornak, Alaska (99561) 196/F2
Chegdomyn, U.S.S.R. 48/O4
Chegga (well), Mauritania 106/C3
Chehalis (lake), Br. Col. 184/L3
Chehalis, Wash. (98532) 310/C4
Chehalis (pt.), Wash. 310/A4
Chehalis (riv.), Wash. 310/B4
Chehalis Ind. Res., Wash. 310/B4
Chehar Deh, Iran 66/K4
Cheju (isl.), S. Korea 54/O6
Cheju, S. Korea 81/C7
Cheju (isl.), S. Korea 81/C7
Cheju (str.), S. Korea 81/C7
Chekiang (Zhejiang), China 77/K6
Chelan, Sask. 181/H3
Chelan (lake), Wash. 188/B1
Chelan (co.), Wash. 310/E3
Chelan, Wash. (98816) 310/E3
Chelan (dam), Wash. 310/E3
Chelan (lake), Wash. 310/E2
Chelan (range), Wash. 310/E2
Chelan Falls, Wash. (98817) 310/E3
Cheleken, U.S.S.R. 48/F6
Chelia (mt.), Algeria 106/F1
Chelif (riv.), Algeria 106/E1
Chelkar, U.S.S.R. 48/F5
Chelles, France 28/C1
Chelm (prov.), Poland 47/F3
Chełm, Poland 47/F3
Chełmno, Poland 47/D2
Chelmsford, England 13/J7
Chelmsford, England 10/G5
Chelmsford○, Mass. (01824) 249/J2
Chełmża, Poland 47/D2
Chelsea, Ala. (35043) 195/E4
Chelsea, Ind. (†47138) 227/F7
Chelsea, Iowa (52215) 229/J5
Chelsea○, Maine (†04345) 243/D7
Chelsea, Mass. (02150) 249/D6
Chelsea, Mich. (48118) 250/E6
Chelsea, Okla. (74016) 288/P1
Chelsea, S. Dak. (57431) 298/M3
Chelsea, Vt. (05038) 268/C4
Chelsea, Victoria 88/L8
Chelsea, Victoria 97/J6
Chelsea, Wis. (54419) 317/F5
Cheltenham, England 13/E6
Cheltenham, England 10/F5
Cheltenham, Md. (20623) 245/L6
Cheltenham○, Pa. (19012) 294/M5
Chelva, Spain 33/F3
Chelyabinsk, U.S.S.R. 2/N3
Chelyabinsk, U.S.S.R. 54/H4
Chelyabinsk, U.S.S.R. 48/G4
Chelyuskin (cape), U.S.S.R. 54/N2
Chelyuskin (cape), U.S.S.R. 4/B4
Chelyuskin (cape), U.S.S.R. 48/M2
Chemainus, Br. Col. 184/J3
Chemawa, Oreg. (97306) 291/A3
Chemba, Mozambique 118/E3
Chembur, India 68/B7
Chemehuevi Valley Ind. Res., Calif. 204/L9
Chemeketa Park-Redwood Estates, Calif. (95044) 204/K4
Chemnitz (Karl-Marx-Stadt), E. Germany 22/E3
Chemquasabamticook (lake), Maine 243/D3
Chemult, Oreg. (97731) 291/F4
Chemung, Ill. (†60033) 222/E1
Chemung (co.), N.Y. 276/G6
Chemung, N.Y. (14825) 276/G6
Chenab (riv.), India 68/C2
Chenab (riv.), Pakistan 68/C2
Chenab (riv.), Pakistan 59/K4
Chenachane, Algeria 106/D3
Chena Hot Springs, Alaska (†99701) 196/J1
Chenango (co.), N.Y. 276/J6
Chenango (riv.), N.Y. 276/J6
Chenango Bridge, N.Y. (13745) 276/J6
Chenango Forks, N.Y. (13746) 276/J6
Chen Barag, China 77/J2
Chêne-Bougeries, Switzerland 39/B4
Chenequa, Wis. (†53029) 317/J1
Chénéville, Québec 172/B4
Cheney, Kansas (67025) 232/E4
Cheney (res.), Kansas 232/E4
Cheney, Wash. (99004) 310/H3
Cheneyville, Ill. (†60942) 222/F3
Cheneyville, La. (71325) 238/F4
Chengchow (Zhengzhou), China 77/H5
Chengde (Chengteh), China 77/J3
Chengdu (Chengtu), China 77/F5
Chengdu, China 54/M6
Chengdu, China 2/P4
Chengkou, China 77/G5
Chengteh (Chengde), China 77/J3
Chengtu (Chengdu), China 77/F5
Chenier (lake), La. 238/F2
Chenoa, Ill. (61726) 222/E3
Chenoa, Ky. (40925) 237/O7
Chenoweth, Oreg. (†97058) 291/F2
Chen Xian, China 77/H6
Chepachet, R.I. (02814) 249/H5
Chepén, Peru 128/C6
Chépénéhé, New Caled. 86/H4
Chepes, Argentina 143/C3
Chépica, Chile 138/A10
Chepo, Panama 154/H6
Chepo (riv.), Panama 154/H6
Chepstow, Ontario 177/C3
Chepstow, Wales 10/E5
Chepstow, Wales 13/E6
Chequamegon (bay), Wis. 317/E2
Cher (dept.), France 28/E4
Cher (riv.), France 28/D4
Cheraw, Colo. (81030) 208/N6
Cheraw, Miss. (†39483) 256/E8
Cheraw, S.C. (29520) 296/H2
Cherbourg, France 28/C3
Cherbourg, France 7/D4
Cherbourg, Queensland 95/D5
Cherchell, Algeria 106/E1
Cherchen (Qiemo), China 77/C4
Cherdyn', U.S.S.R. 52/J2
Cheremkhovo, U.S.S.R. 54/L4
Cheremkhovo, U.S.S.R. 48/L4
Cherepovets, U.S.S.R. 7/H3
Cherepovets, U.S.S.R. 52/E3
Cherepovets, U.S.S.R. 48/D4
Chergui, Chott Ech (salt lake), Algeria 106/E2
Cherhill, Alberta 182/C3
Cherial (riv.), India 68/F2
Cheriton, Va. (23316) 307/R6
Cherkassy, U.S.S.R. 7/H4
Cherkassy, U.S.S.R. 52/D5
Cherkessk, U.S.S.R. 48/E5
Cherkessk, U.S.S.R. 52/F6
Chermside, Queensland 88/K2
Chermside, Queensland 95/D2
Chernigov, U.S.S.R. 7/H3
Chernigov, U.S.S.R. 48/D4
Chernigov, U.S.S.R. 52/D4
Chernogorsk, U.S.S.R. 48/K4
Chernorechenskiy, U.S.S.R. 52/H2
Chernovtsy, U.S.S.R. 7/G4
Chernovtsy, U.S.S.R. 52/C5
Chernovtsy, U.S.S.R. 48/C5
Chernushka, U.S.S.R. 52/J3
Chernyshevsk, U.S.S.R. 48/M4
Chernyshevskiy, U.S.S.R. 48/M3
Cherokee (co.), Ala. 195/G2
Cherokee, Ala. (35616) 195/C1
Cherokee (co.), Georgia 217/D2
Cherokee (co.), Iowa 229/B3
Cherokee, Iowa (51012) 229/B3
Cherokee (co.), Kansas 232/H4
Cherokee, Kansas (66724) 232/H4
Cherokee, Ky. (†41180) 237/R4
Cherokee (co.), N.C. 281/A4
Cherokee, N.C. (28719) 281/C4
Cherokee (co.), Okla. 288/R3
Cherokee, Okla. (73728) 288/K1
Cherokee (co.), S.C. 296/D1
Cherokee (dam), Tenn. 237/P8
Cherokee (lake), Tenn. 237/P8
Cherokee (co.), Texas 303/J6
Cherokee, Texas (76832) 303/F7
Cherokee City, Ark. (†72734) 202/A1
Cherokee Falls, S.C. (29705) 296/D1
Cherokee Ind. Res., N.C. 281/C3
Cherokees, Lake O'The (lake), Okla. 288/S1
Cherokee Village, Ark. (†72525) 202/G1
Cherrapunji, India 68/G3
Cherry, Ariz. (†86327) 198/C4
Cherry (creek), Ariz. 198/E4
Cherry (brook), Conn. 210/D1
Cherry, Ill. (61317) 222/D2
Cherry (co.), Nebr. 264/C2
Cherry, N.C. (†27928) 281/R3
Cherry (creek), N. Dak. 282/D4
Cherry (creek), S. Dak. 298/F5
Cherry (creek), S. Dak. 298/F4
Cherry, Tenn. (†38041) 237/B9
Cherry (creek), Utah 304/B4
Cherry (riv.), W. Va. 312/E6
Cherry Creek, Br. Col. 184/G5
Cherry Creek, Nev. (†89301) 266/G3
Cherry Creek, N.Y. (14723) 276/B6
Cherry Creek, S. Dak. (57622) 298/F4
Cherryfield○, Maine (04622) 243/H6
Cherry Fork, Ohio (45618) 284/C8
Cherry Grove, Alberta 182/E2
Cherry Grove, Minn. (†55975) 255/F7
Cherry Grove, Ohio (†45202) 284/C10
Cherry Grove, Oreg. (†97119) 291/D2
Cherry Hill, Ark. (†71953) 202/B4
Cherry Hill, Md. (†21921) 245/P2
Cherry Hill○, N.J. (*08034) 273/B3
Cherry Lake Farms, Fla. (†32350) 212/C1
Cherryland, Calif. (†94541) 204/K2
Cherrylog, Georgia (30522) 217/D1
Cherry Point, Alberta 182/A1
Cherry Point Marine Air Sta., N.C. 281/R5
Cherry Run, W. Va. (25418) 312/L3
Cherry Tree, Pa. (15724) 294/E4
Cherryvale, Kansas (67335) 232/G4
Cherry Valley, Ark. (72324) 202/J3
Cherry Valley, Ill. (61016) 222/D1
Cherry Valley, Mass. (01611) 249/G3
Cherry Valley, N.Y. (13320) 276/L5
Cherry Valley, Ontario 177/G4
Cherry Valley, Pa. (†16030) 294/C3
Cherryville, Br. Col. 184/H5
Cherryville, Mo. (65446) 261/K7
Cherryville, N.C. (28021) 281/G4
Cherryville, Oreg. (†97055) 291/E2
Cherskiy, U.S.S.R. 54/T3
Cherskiy, U.S.S.R. 4/C1
Cherskiy (range), U.S.S.R. 54/R3
Cherskiy, U.S.S.R. 48/Q3
Cherskiy (range), U.S.S.R. 48/P3
Cherta, Spain 33/G2
Chertsey, England 13/G8
Chertsey, England 10/B6
Chervonograd, U.S.S.R. 52/B4
Chesaning, Mich. (48616) 250/E5
Chesapeake (bay) 188/L3
Chesapeake (bay), Md. 245/N7
Chesapeake, Ohio (45619) 284/E9
Chesapeake (bay), U.S. 146/L6
Chesapeake (I.C.), Va. (*23320) 307/R7
Chesapeake (bay), Va. 307/R5
Chesapeake, W. Va. (†25301) 312/C6
Chesapeake and Delaware (canal), Del. 245/R2
Chesapeake and Delaware (canal), Md. 245/R2
Chesapeake and Ohio Canal Nat'l Hist. Park, Md. 245/J4
Chesapeake and Ohio Canal Nat'l Mon., Va. 307/O2
Chesapeake and Ohio Canal Nat'l Hist. Park, W. Va. 312/J3
Chesapeake Beach, Md. (20732) 245/N6
Chesapeake City, Md. (21915) 245/P2
Chesaw, Wash. (98818) 310/G2
Chésery, Pointe de (mt.), Switzerland 39/C4
Chesham, England 10/F5
Chesham, England 13/G7
Chesham, N.H. (†03455) 268/C6
Cheshire, Conn. (06410) 210/D2
Cheshire○, Conn. (06410) 210/D2
Cheshire (co.), England 13/E4
Cheshire○, Mass. (01225) 249/B2
Cheshire (res.), Mass. 249/A2
Cheshire (co.), N.H. 268/C6
Cheshire, Ohio (45620) 284/F8
Cheshire, Oreg. (97419) 291/D3
Cheshskaya (bay), U.S.S.R. 7/J2
Cheshskaya (bay), U.S.S.R. 52/G1
Cheshunt, England 13/H7
Cheshunt, England 10/B5
Chesilhurst, N.J. (†08089) 273/D4
Cheslatta, Br. Col. 184/E3
Chesley, Ontario 177/C3
Chesnaye, Manitoba 179/K2
Chesnee, S.C. (29323) 296/D1
Chester, Ark. (72934) 202/B2
Chester, Calif. (96020) 204/D3
Chester, Conn. (06412) 210/F3
Chester○, Conn. (06412) 210/F3
Chester, England 10/F2
Chester, England 13/G2
Chester, Georgia (31012) 217/F6
Chester, Idaho (83421) 220/G5
Chester, Ill. (62233) 222/D6
Chester, Ind. (†47374) 227/H5
Chester, Iowa (52134) 229/J2
Chester○, Maine (†04458) 243/F5
Chester, Md. (21619) 245/N5
Chester (riv.), Md. 245/O4
Chester○, Mass. (01011) 249/C3
Chester, Minn. (55904) 255/F6
Chester, Miss. (†39735) 256/F4
Chester, Mont. (59522) 262/E2
Chester, Nebr. (68327) 264/G4
Chester○, N.H. (03036) 268/E6
Chester, N.J. (07930) 273/D2
Chester, N.Y. (10918) 276/M8
Chester, Nova Scotia 168/D4
Chester, Ohio (45720) 284/G7
Chester, Okla. (73838) 288/J2
Chester (co.), Pa. 294/L6
Chester, Pa. (*19013) 294/L7
Chester (creek), Pa. 294/L7
Chester (co.), S.C. 296/E2
Chester, S.C. (29706) 296/E2
Chester, S. Dak. (57016) 298/R6
Chester (co.), Tenn. 237/D10
Chester, Texas (75936) 303/K7
Chester, Utah (84023) 304/C4
Chester○, Vt. (05143) 268/B5
Chester, Va. (23831) 307/O6
Chester, W. Va. (26034) 312/E1
Chester Basin, Nova Scotia 168/D4
Chester-Chester Depot, Vt. (05143) 268/B5
Chesterfield, Conn. (†06370) 210/G3
Chesterfield, England 13/J2

Dent d'Hérens 359

Davis (co.), Iowa 229/J7
Davis (dam), Nev. 266/G7
Davis, N.C. (28524) 281/R5
Davis (str.), N.W.T. 162/K1
Davis (str.), N.W. Terrs. 187/M3
Davis, Okla. (73030) 288/M5
Davis (lake), Oreg. 291/F4
Davis (mt.), Pa. 294/D6
Davis, Sask. 181/F2
Davis, S. Dak. (57021) 298/P7
Davis (mts.), Texas 303/C11
Davis (co.), Utah 304/B3
Davis, W. Va. (26260) 312/H4
Davisboro, Georgia (31018) 217/G5
Davis City, Iowa (50065) 229/F7
Davis Cove, Newf. 166/D4
Davis Creek, Calif. (96108) 204/E2
Davis Dam, Ariz. (†86430) 198/A3
Davis Inlet, Newf. 166/B2
Davis Junction, Ill. (61020) 222/D1
Davis-Monthan A.F.B., Ariz. 198/E6
Davison, Mich. (48423) 250/F5
Davison (co.), S. Dak. 298/N6
Davis Station 5/C4
Davis Station, S.C. (29041) 296/G4
Daviston, Ala. (36256) 195/G4
Davisville, Mo. (65456) 261/K7
Davisville, R.I. (02854) 249/H6
Davisville, W. Va. (26142) 312/C4
Davlekanovo, U.S.S.R. 52/H4
Davos, Switzerland 39/J3
Davos (valley), Switzerland 39/J3
Davy, W. Va. (24828) 312/C8
Dawa (riv.), Ethiopia 111/G7
Dawasir, Hadhb (range), Saudi Arabia 59/D5
Dawasir, Wadi (dry riv.), Saudi Arabia 59/E5
Dawes (co.), Nebr. 264/A2
Dawes, W. Va. (25054) 312/D6
Dawlish, England 13/D7
Dawn, Mo. (64638) 261/E3
Dawn, Texas (79025) 303/B3
Dawna (range), Burma 72/C3
Dawson, Ala. (35963) 195/G2
Dawson, Canada 4/C16
Dawson (isl.), Chile 138/E10
Dawson (co.), Georgia 217/D2
Dawson, Georgia (31742) 217/D7
Dawson, Ill. (62520) 222/D4
Dawson, Iowa (50066) 229/E5
Dawson (bay), Manitoba 179/B2
Dawson, Minn. (56232) 255/B6
Dawson, Mo. (†65548) 261/H8
Dawson (co.), Mont. 262/M3
Dawson (co.), Nebr. 264/E4
Dawson, Nebr. (68337) 264/J4
Dawson, N. Dak. (58428) 282/L6
Dawson (inlet), N.W. Terrs. 187/J3
Dawson (riv.), Queensland 88/H4
Dawson (riv.), Queensland 95/D5
Dawson (co.), Texas 303/C5
Dawson, Texas (76639) 303/H6
Dawson, W. Va. (24932) 312/E7
Dawson, Yukon 146/E3
Dawson, Yukon 162/C3
Dawson, Yukon 187/E3
Dawson Bay, Manitoba 179/B2
Dawson Creek, Br. Col. 146/F4
Dawson Creek, Br. Col. 162/D4
Dawson Creek, Br. Col. 184/G2
Dawson Springs, Ky. (42408) 237/F6
Dawsonville, Georgia (30534) 217/D2
Dawsonville, New Bruns. 170/C1
Dawu, China 77/H5
Dawu, China 77/F5
Dax, France 28/C6
Da Xian, China 77/G5
Day, Fla. (32013) 212/C1
Day, Minn. (†55006) 255/E5
Day (co.), S. Dak. 298/O3
Day Book, N.C. (†28714) 281/E3
Daykin, Nebr. (68338) 264/G4
Daylesford, Victoria 97/C5
Daylight, Tenn. (†37110) 237/K9
Daymán, Uruguay 145/B2
Daymán (range), Uruguay 145/B2
Daymán (riv.), Uruguay 145/B2
Dayong, China 77/H6
Days Creek, Oreg. (97429) 291/D5
Daysland, Alberta 182/D3
Daysville, Ky. (†42276) 237/G7
Dayton, Ala. (36731) 195/C6
Dayton, Idaho (83232) 220/F7
Dayton, Ill. (†61350) 222/E2
Dayton, Ind. (47941) 227/D4
Dayton, Iowa (50530) 229/E4
Dayton, Ky. (41074) 237/T1
Dayton, Mich. (†49113) 250/C7
Dayton, Minn. (55327) 255/E5
Dayton, Mont. (59914) 262/B3
Dayton, Nev. (89403) 266/B3
Dayton, N.J. (08810) 273/D3
Dayton, N.Y. (4041) 276/C6
Dayton, Ohio (*45401) 284/B6
Dayton, Ohio 146/K6
Dayton, Ohio 188/K3
Dayton, Oreg. (97114) 291/A3
Dayton, Pa. (16222) 294/D4
Dayton, Tenn. (37321) 237/L9
Dayton, Texas (77535) 303/J7
Dayton, Va. (22821) 307/L4
Dayton, Wash. (99328) 310/H4
Dayton, Wis. (†53508) 317/H10
Dayton, Wyo. (82836) 319/E1
Daytona Beach, Fla. 188/K5
Daytona Beach, Fla. 146/K7
Daytona Beach, Fla. (*32014) 212/F2
Daytona Beach Shores, Fla. (32016) 212/F2
Dayu, China 77/H6
Dayville, Conn. (06241) 210/H1
Dayville, Oreg. (97825) 291/H3
Dazey, N. Dak. (58429) 282/O5
Dazhai, China 77/H4
Dazkırı, Turkey 63/D4
De Aar, S. Africa 118/C6
Dead (lake), Fla. 212/D6
Dead (sea), Israel 65/C4
Dead (sea), Israel 59/C3
Dead (sea), Jordan 59/C3
Dead (sea), Jordan 65/C4
Dead (riv.), Maine 243/C5
Dead (riv.), Mich. 250/B2
Dead (lake), Minn. 255/C4
Dead (sea), West Bank 59/C3
Deadhorse, Alaska (†99723) 196/J1
Deadman (creek), Wash. 310/H4
Deadman (mt.), Wyo. 319/B2
Deadwood, Alberta 182/B1
Deadwood (res.), Idaho 220/C5
Deadwood (riv.), Idaho 220/C5
Deadwood, S. Dak. (57732) 298/B5
Deaf Smith (co.), Texas 303/B3
Deal, England 13/J6
Deal, England 10/G5
Deal, N.J. (07723) 273/F3
Deal (isl.), Tasmania 99/D1
Deale, Md. (20751) 245/M5
Deal Island, Md. (21821) 245/P8
Dean (chan.), Br. Col. 184/D4
Dean (riv.), Br. Col. 184/D4
Dean, Nova Scotia 168/F3
Deán Funes, Argentina 143/D3
Deanville, Texas (77852) 303/H7
Dearborn (co.), Ind. 227/H6
Dearborn, Mich. (*48120) 250/B7
Dearborn, Mo. (64439) 261/C3
Dearborn Heights, Mich. (48127) 250/B7
Dearing, Georgia (30808) 217/H4
Dearing, Kansas (67340) 232/G4
De Armanville, Ala. (36257) 195/G3
Dearne, England 13/K2
Deary, Idaho (83823) 220/B3
Dease (inlet), Alaska 196/H1
Dease (lake), Br. Col. 184/K2
Dease (riv.), Br. Col. 184/K2
Dease (str.), N.W.T. 146/G3
Dease (str.), N.W.T. 162/F2
Dease (str.), N.W. Terrs. 187/H3
Dease Arm (inlet), N.W. Terrs. 187/F3
Death (valley), Calif. 204/H7
Death Valley (depr.), Calif. 188/C3
Death Valley, Calif. (92328) 204/J7
Death Valley Junction, Calif. (92328) 204/J7
Death Valley Nat'l Mon., Calif. 204/H7
Death Valley Nat'l Mon., Nev. 266/E6
Deatsville, Ala. (36022) 195/F5
Deauville, France 28/C3
Deauville, Québec 172/E4
Deaver, Wyo. (82421) 319/D1
Deavertown, Ohio (†43731) 284/G6
De Baca (co.), N. Mex. 274/E4
Deba Habe, Nigeria 106/G6
Debar, Yugoslavia 45/E5
De Bary, Fla. (32713) 212/E3
Debden, Sask. 181/E2
Débé, Trin. & Tob. 161/B11
Debec, New Bruns. 170/C2
De Beque, Colo. (81630) 208/C4
De Berry, Texas (75639) 303/L5
Debert, Nova Scotia 168/E3
Dębica, Poland 47/E3
De Bilt, Netherlands 27/G4
Dęblin, Poland 47/E3
Deblois○, Maine (†04622) 243/H6
Dębno, Poland 47/B2
Debo (lake), Mali 106/D5
Debolt, Alberta 182/B2
De Borgia, Mont. (59830) 262/A3
Debra Birhan, Ethiopia 111/G6
Debra Markos, Ethiopia 111/G5
Debra Markos, Ethiopia 102/F3
Debra Tabor, Ethiopia 111/G5
Debrecen, Hungary 41/F3
Debrecen, Hungary 7/G4
Decatur, Ala. (*35601) 195/D1
Decatur, Ark. (72722) 202/A1
Decatur (co.), Georgia 217/C9
Decatur, Georgia (*30030) 217/K1
Decatur, Ill. 188/J3
Decatur, Ill. 146/K6
Decatur, Ill. (*62521) 222/E4
Decatur (co.), Ind. 227/G6
Decatur, Ind. (46733) 227/H3
Decatur (co.), Iowa 229/F7
Decatur, Iowa (50067) 229/F7
Decatur (co.), Kansas 232/B2
Decatur, Mich. (49045) 250/C6
Decatur, Miss. (39327) 256/F6
Decatur, Nebr. (68020) 264/H2
Decatur, Ohio (45115) 284/C8
Decatur (co.), Tenn. 237/E9
Decatur, Tenn. (37322) 237/M9
Decatur, Texas (76234) 303/G4
Decaturville, Tenn. (38329) 237/E9
Decazeville, France 28/E5
Deccan (plat.), India 68/D6
Decherd, Tenn. (37324) 237/J10
Děčín, Czech. 41/C1
Decision (cape), Alaska 196/M2
Decize, France 28/E4
Decker, Ind. (47524) 227/B7
Decker, Manitoba 179/B4
Decker, Mich. (48426) 250/F5
Decker, Mont. (59025) 262/K5
Decker Lake, Br. Col. 184/E3
Deckers, Colo. (†80135) 208/J4
Deckerville, Ark. (†72386) 202/K3
Deckerville, Mich. (48427) 250/G5
Declo, Idaho (83323) 220/E7
Decorah, Iowa (52101) 229/K2
Decota, W. Va. (†25122) 312/D6
Decoy, Ky. (41321) 237/P5
Dededo, Guam 86/K6
Dedegül Dağı (mt.), Turkey 63/D4
Dedemsvaart, Netherlands 27/J3
Dederick, Mo. (†64744) 261/D7
Dedham, Iowa (51440) 229/D5
Dedham, Maine (†04429) 243/F6
Dedham○, Maine (†04429) 243/F6
Dedham, Mass. (02026) 249/C7
Dédougou, Upper Volta 106/D6
Dedza, Malawi 115/F6
Dee (riv.), England 13/D4
Dee (riv.), England 10/E4
Dee (riv.), Ireland 17/H4
Dee (riv.), Scotland 15/D5
Dee (riv.), Scotland 15/F3
Dee (riv.), Scotland 10/E2
Dee (riv.), Tasmania 99/C4
Dee (riv.), Wales 10/E4
Dee (riv.), Wales 13/D4
Deedsville, Ind. (46921) 227/E3
Deel (riv.), Ireland 17/C3
Deel (riv.), Ireland 17/G4
Deel (riv.), Ireland 17/D7
Deele (riv.), Ireland 17/F2
Deenwood, Georgia (†31501) 217/H8
Deep (creek), Idaho 220/F7
Deep (creek), Idaho 220/B7
Deep (inlet), Newf. 166/B2
Deep (riv.), N.C. 281/K3
Deep (riv.), N. Dak. 282/J1
Deep (creek), S.C. 296/B2
Deep (creek), Texas 303/C5
Deep (creek), Utah 304/B1
Deep (creek), Utah 304/A3
Deep Bight, Newf. 166/C2
Deep Brook, Nova Scotia 168/C4
Deep Creek (mts.), Idaho 220/F7
Deep Creek (lake), Md. 245/A3
Deep Creek (range), Utah 304/A4
Deepcreek, Wash. (†99010) 310/H3
Deepdale, Manitoba 179/A3
Deep Fork, North Canadian (riv.), Okla. 288/N3
Deep Gap, N.C. (28618) 281/F2
Deephaven, Minn. (55391) 255/G5
Deeping Saint James, England 13/G5
Deep River, Conn. (06417) 210/F3
Deep River○, Conn. (06417) 210/F3
Deep River (res.), Conn. 210/F2
Deep River, Iowa (52222) 229/J5
Deep River, Ontario 177/G1
Deep River, Ontario 175/E3
Deep River, Wash. (†98638) 310/B4
Deep Run, N.C. (28525) 281/O4
Deep Springs, Calif. (†93513) 204/H6
Deepstep, Georgia (31082) 217/G4
Deep Valley, Pa. (†15352) 294/A6
Deep Water (pt.), Del. 245/S4
Deepwater, Mo. (64740) 261/E6
Deepwater, N.J. (08023) 273/C4
Deepwater, N.S. Wales 97/F1
Deer (isl.), Alaska 196/F4
Deer, Ariz. (72628) 202/D2
Deer (creek), Ind. 227/D5
Deer (creek), Ind. 227/E3
Deer (isl.), Maine 243/F7
Deer (creek), Md. 245/N2
Deer (isl.), Mass. 249/E7
Deer (riv.), Mich. 250/A2
Deer (lake), Minn. 255/E3
Deer (creek), Miss. 256/C4
Deer (isl.), New Bruns. 170/D4
Deer (harb.), Newf. 166/D2
Deer (riv.), N.Y. 276/L1
Deer (riv.), N.Y. 276/J3
Deer (creek), Ohio 284/D6
Deer (lake), Wash. 310/H2
Deerbrook, Miss. (†39739) 256/G4
Deerbrook, Wis. (54424) 317/H5
Deer Creek, Ill. (61733) 222/D3
Deer Creek, Ind. (†46917) 227/E3
Deer Creek, Minn. (56527) 255/C4
Deer Creek (lake), Ohio 284/D6
Deer Creek, Okla. (74636) 288/L1
Deerfield, Ill. (60015) 222/B5
Deerfield, Ind. (†47380) 227/H4
Deerfield, Kansas (67838) 232/A4
Deerfield○, Mass. (01342) 249/D2
Deerfield (riv.), Mass. 249/C2
Deerfield, Mich. (49238) 250/F7
Deerfield, Mo. (64741) 261/D7
Deerfield○, N.H. (03037) 268/E5
Deerfield, Ohio (44411) 284/H3
Deerfield (riv.), Vt. 268/B6
Deerfield, Va. (24432) 307/K4
Deerfield, Wis. (53531) 317/H9
Deerfield Beach, Fla. (33441) 212/F5
Deerfield Street, N.J. (08313) 273/C4
Deerford, La. (†70791) 238/K1
Deer Grove, Ill. (61243) 222/D2
Deer Harbor, Wash. (98243) 310/B2
Deerhorn, Manitoba 179/E4
Deering, Alaska (99736) 196/F1
Deering○, N.H. (†03244) 268/D5
Deering, N. Dak. (58731) 282/J3
Deer Island, Oreg. (97054) 291/E2
Deer Isle, Maine (04627) 243/F7
Deer Isle○, Maine (04627) 243/F7
Deer Lake, Newf. 166/C4
Deer Lake, Ontario 175/B2
Deer Lodge (co.), Mont. 262/C5
Deer Lodge, Mont. (59722) 262/D4
Deer Lodge, Tenn. (37726) 237/M8
Deer Park, Ala. (36529) 195/B8
Deer Park, Calif. (94576) 204/C5
Deer Park, Fla. (†32901) 212/F3
Deer Park, Ill. (†60010) 222/A5
Deer Park, Md. (21550) 245/A3
Deer Park, N.Y. (11729) 276/O9
Deer Park, Ohio (45236) 284/C9
Deer Park, Texas (77536) 303/K2
Deer Park, Wash. (99006) 310/H3
Deer Park, Wis. (54007) 317/B5
Deer River, Minn. (56636) 255/E3
Deer River, N.Y. (13627) 276/J3
Deer Run, W. Va. (†26807) 312/H5
Deersville, Ohio (44693) 284/H5
Deerton, Mich. (49822) 250/B2
Deer Trail, Colo. (80105) 208/M3
Deerwalk, W. Va. (†26180) 312/D4
Deerwood, Minn. (56444) 255/E4
Deesa, India 68/C4
Deeson, Miss. (†38740) 256/C2
Deeth, Nev. (89823) 266/F1
Dee Why, N.S. Wales 88/L4
Dee Why, N.S. Wales 97/K3
Defense Heights, Md. (†20784) 245/G4
Deferiet, N.Y. (13628) 276/J2
Defiance (plat.), Ariz. 198/F3
Defiance, Iowa (51527) 229/C5
Defiance, Mo. (63341) 261/L5
Defiance (co.), Ohio 284/A3
Defiance, Ohio (43512) 284/B3
De Fluessen (lake), Netherlands 27/G3
Defoe, Ky. (40017) 237/L4
Deford, Mich. (48729) 250/F5
De Forest, Wis. (53532) 317/H9
Defoy, Québec 172/E3
De Funiak Springs, Fla. (32433) 212/C6
Dégelis, Québec 172/J2
Degema, Nigeria 106/F8
Degersheim, Switzerland 39/H2
Deggendorf, W. Germany 22/E4
De Graff, Kansas (†66840) 232/F4
De Graff, Minn. (56233) 255/C5
Degraff, Ohio (43318) 284/C5
Degrasse, N.Y. (13629) 276/L2
De Gray (lake), Ark. 202/D5
De Grey, W. Australia 88/B4
De Grey, W. Australia 92/B3
De Grey (riv.), W. Australia 88/C4
De Grey (riv.), W. Australia 92/B3
De Haan, Belgium 27/C6
Deh Bid, Iran 66/H5
Dehdez, Iran 66/G5
Deheq, Iran 66/G4
Dehiwala-Mt. Lavinia, Sri Lanka 68/D7
Dehkhvareqan, Iran 66/D2
Dehlco, La. (†71269) 238/G2
De Honte (bay), Netherlands 27/D6
Dehra Dun, India 68/D2
Dehua, China 77/J6
Deim Zubeir, Sudan 111/E6
Deinze, Belgium 27/C7
Deir Abu Sa'id, Jordan 65/D3
Deir Ballut, West Bank 65/C3
Deir el Balah, Gaza Strip 65/A5
Deir ez Zor (prov.), Syria 63/H5
Deir ez Zor, Syria 63/H5
Deir ez Zor, Syria 59/C2
Deir Sharaf, West Bank 65/C3
Dej, Romania 45/F2
De Kalb (co.), Ala. 195/G2
De Kalb (co.), Georgia 217/D3
De Kalb (co.), Ill. 222/E2
De Kalb, Ill. (60115) 222/E2
De Kalb (co.), Ind. 227/H2
De Kalb, Miss. (39328) 256/G5
De Kalb (co.), Mo. 261/D3
De Kalb, Mo. (64440) 261/C3
De Kalb (co.), Tenn. 237/K9
De Kalb, Texas (75559) 303/K4
De Kalb Junction, N.Y. (13630) 276/K2
Dekese, Zaire 115/D4
Dekoa, Cent. Afr. Rep. 115/C2
De Koog, Netherlands 27/F2
De Koven, Ky. (†42459) 237/E5
Dela, Okla. (†74523) 288/P6
Delacour, Alberta 182/D4
Delacroix, La. (†70085) 238/L7
Delafield, Ill. (†62859) 222/E5
Delafield, Wis. (53018) 317/J1
Delagoa (bay), Mozambique 118/E5
Delair, N.J. (08110) 273/B3
Delamar (mts.), Nev. 266/G5
De Lamere, N. Dak. (58022) 282/R7
DeLancey, Pa. (15733) 294/D4
Delanco○, N.J. (08075) 273/D3
De Land, Fla. (32720) 212/E2
De Land, Ill. (61839) 222/E3
Delaney, Ark. (†72727) 202/C2
Delano, Calif. (93215) 204/F8
Delano, Minn. (55328) 255/E5
Delano, Pa. (18220) 294/K4
Delano, Tenn. (37325) 237/M10
Delano (peak), Utah 304/B5
Delanson, N.Y. (12053) 276/M5
Delaplaine, Ark. (72425) 202/J1
Delaplane, Va. (22025) 307/N3
Delaram, Afghanistan 59/H3
Delaram, Afghanistan 68/A2
Delaronde (lake), Sask. 181/E1
Delavan, Ill. (61734) 222/D3
Delavan, Kansas (66847) 232/F3
Delavan, Minn. (56023) 255/D7
Delavan, Wis. (53115) 317/J10
Delavan Lake, Wis. (†53115) 317/J10
Delaware 188/L3
Delaware (bay) 188/M3
Delaware, Ark. (72835) 202/D3
DELAWARE 245
Delaware (bay), Del. 245/T5
Delaware (riv.), Del. 245/R3
Delaware (co.), Ind. 227/G4
Delaware, Ind. (†47037) 227/G6
Delaware (co.), Iowa 229/L4
Delaware, Iowa (52036) 229/L4
Delaware, N.J. (07833) 273/C2
Delaware (bay), N.J. 273/C5
Delaware (riv.), N.J. 273/D3
Delaware (co.), N.Y. 276/K6
Delaware (riv.), N.Y. 276/K7
Delaware (co.), Ohio 284/D5
Delaware, Ohio (43015) 284/E5
Delaware (lake), Ohio 284/E5
Delaware (co.), Okla. 288/S2
Delaware, Okla. (74027) 288/P1
Delaware, Ontario 177/C5
Delaware (co.), Pa. 294/M6
Delaware (riv.), Pa. 294/N3
Delaware (creek), Texas 303/C10
Delaware (mts.), Texas 303/C10
Delaware (state), U.S. 146/L6
Delaware City, Del. (19706) 245/R2
Delaware Water Gap Nat'l Rec. Area, N.J. 273/C1
Delaware Water Gap, Pa. (18327) 294/M4
Delaware Water Gap Nat'l Rec. Area, Pa. 294/N3
Delbarton, W. Va. (25670) 312/B7
Del Bonita, Alberta 182/D5
Delburne, Alberta 182/D3
Delcambre, La. (70528) 238/G7
Del City, Okla. (73115) 288/L4
Delco, N.C. (28436) 281/N6
Deldoul, Algeria 106/E3
Deleau, Manitoba 179/B5
Delegate, N.S. Wales 97/E5
Delémont, Switzerland 39/D2
De Leon, Texas (76444) 303/F5
De Leon Springs, Fla. (32028) 212/E2
Delevan, N.Y. (14042) 276/D6
Delfi, Greece 45/F6
Delft, Minn. (56124) 255/C7
Delft, Netherlands 27/E4
Delfzijl, Netherlands 27/K2
Delgada (pt.), Argentina 143/D5
Delgada (pt.), Calif. 204/A3
Delgada (pt.), Mexico 150/L7
Delgado (cape), Mozambique 102/G6
Delgado (cape), Mozambique 118/G2
Delgado Chalbaud, Cerro (mt.), Venezuela 124/G6
Delgertsogt, Mongolia 77/G2
Delgo, Sudan 111/F3
Delhi, Calif. (95315) 204/E6
Delhi, Colo. (†81059) 208/M7
Delhi, Ill. (†62052) 222/C4
Delhi (terr.), India 68/D3
Delhi, India 68/D3
Delhi, India 54/J7
Delhi, India 2/N4
Delhi, Iowa (52223) 229/L4
Delhi, La. (71232) 238/H2
Delhi, Minn. (56234) 255/C6
Delhi, N.Y. (13753) 276/L6
Delhi, Okla. (†73662) 288/G4
Delhi, Ontario 177/D5
Delia, Alberta 182/D4
Delia, Kansas (66418) 232/G2
Delice, Dominica 161/F7
Delice, Turkey 63/E3
Delice (riv.), Turkey 63/F3
Délices, Fr. Guiana 131/E3
Delicias, Cuba 158/H3
Delicias, Venezuela 124/B4
Delight, Ark. (71940) 202/C5
Delijan, Iran 66/G4
Delingha, China 77/E4
De Lisle, Miss. (†39571) 256/F10
Delisle, Québec 172/F1
Delisle, Sask. 181/D4
Delitzsch, E. Germany 22/E3
Dell, Ark. (72426) 202/K2
Dell, Mont. (59724) 262/D6
Dell City, Texas (79837) 303/C10
Dell Rapids, S. Dak. (57022) 298/R6
Dellrose, Tenn. (38453) 237/H10
Dellroy, Ohio (44620) 284/H4
Dells, The (valley), Wis. 317/G8
Dellslow, W. Va. (26531) 312/G3
Dellwood, Minn. (†55110) 255/F5
Dellwood, Mo. (†63135) 261/R2
Dellwood, N.C. (†28786) 281/C3
Dellwood, Wis. (53927) 317/G7
Dellys, Algeria 106/E1
Delmar, Ala. (35551) 195/C2
Del Mar, Calif. (92014) 204/H11
Delmar, Del. (19940) 245/R7
Delmar, Iowa (52037) 229/M4
Delmar, Md. (21875) 245/R7
Delmar, N.Y. (12054) 276/N5
Delmas, Sask. 181/C3
Delmas, S. Africa 118/J6
Delmenhorst, W. Germany 22/C2
Delmont, N.J. (08314) 273/C5
Delmont, Pa. (15626) 294/D5
Delmont, S. Dak. (57330) 298/N7
Del Norte (co.), Calif. 204/B2
Del Norte, Colo. (81132) 208/G7
Del Norte (peak), Colo. 208/F7
Deloit, Iowa (51441) 229/C4
DeLong (mts.), Alaska 196/F1
De Long, Ill. (†61436) 222/C3
Delong, Ind. (46922) 227/E2
Deloraine, Man. 162/G6
Deloraine, Manitoba 179/B5
Deloraine, Tasmania 99/C3
Delorme (lake), Québec 174/C2
Deloro, Ontario 177/G3
Delphi, Ind. (46923) 227/D3
Delphia, Ky. (41735) 237/P6
Delphos, Iowa (50844) 229/E7
Delphos, Kansas (67436) 232/E2
Delphos, Ohio (45833) 284/B4
Delpine, Mont. (†59053) 262/F4
Delran○, N.J. (08075) 273/B3
Delray Beach, Fla. (*33444) 212/F5
Del Rey Oaks, Calif. (93940) 204/D7
Del Rio, Tenn. (37727) 237/P9
Del Rio, Texas 188/F5
Del Rio, Texas 146/H7
Del Rio, Texas (78840) 303/D8
Del Rosa, Calif. (92404) 204/E10
Delson, Québec 172/H4
Delta, Ala. (36258) 195/G4
Delta, Br. Col. 184/K3
Delta (co.), Colo. 208/D5
Delta, Colo. (81416) 208/D5
Delta, Iowa (52550) 229/J6
Delta, La. (71233) 238/J2
Delta, Manitoba 179/D4
Delta (co.), Mich. 250/C2
Delta, Mo. (63744) 261/N8
Delta, Ohio (43515) 284/B2
Delta, Ontario 177/H3
Delta, Pa. (17314) 294/K6
Delta (co.), Texas 303/J4
Delta, Utah (84624) 304/B4
Delta, Wis. (†54856) 317/D3
Delta Amacuro (terr.), Venezuela 124/H3
Delta City, Miss. (39061) 256/C4
Delta Junction, Alaska (99737) 196/J2
Deltaville, Va. (23043) 307/R5
Delton, Mich. (49046) 250/D6
Deltona, Fla. (32725) 212/E3
Delungra, N.S. Wales 97/F1
Del Valle, Argentina 143/F7
Del Valle (lake), Calif. 204/L3
Delvin, Ireland 17/G4
Delvinákion, Greece 45/E6
Delvinë, Albania 45/D6
Delwin, Mich. (†48858) 250/E5
Demaine, Sask. 181/D5
Demak, Indonesia 85/J2
Demanda, Sierra de la (range), Spain 33/E1
Demarcation (pt.), Alaska 196/K1
Demarest, N.J. (07627) 273/C1
Demavend (Damavend) (mt.), Iran 66/G3
Demba, Zaire 115/D5
Dembidollo, Ethiopia 111/F6
Demchok, India 68/D2
Demerara (riv.), Guyana 131/B3
Demidov, U.S.S.R. 52/D3
Deming, N. Mex. (88030) 274/B6
Deming, Wash. (98244) 310/C2
Demini (riv.), Brazil 132/H8
Demirci, Turkey 63/C3
Demirkent, Turkey 63/E4
Demirköy, Turkey 63/B2
Demir Qapu, Syria 63/J4
Demmin, E. Germany 22/E2
Democracia, Venezuela 124/E6
Demopolis, Ala. (36732) 195/C6
Demopolis (dam), Ala. 195/C5
Demopolis (lake), Ala. 195/C5
Demorest, Georgia (30535) 217/F1
De Mossville, Ky. (41033) 237/N3
Demotte, Ind. (46310) 227/C2
Dempo (mt.), Indonesia 85/C6
Dempster, S. Dak. (57230) 298/R4
Demster, N.Y. (†13126) 276/H3
Demta, Indonesia 85/L6
Denain, France 28/E2
Denali, Alaska (†99729) 196/J2
Denali Nat'l Park, Alaska 196/H2
Denali Nat'l Preserve, Alaska 196/H2
Denare Beach, Sask. 181/M4
Denau, U.S.S.R. 48/G6
Denbigh (cape), Alaska 196/F2
Denbigh, N. Dak. (58732) 282/J3
Denbigh, Ontario 177/G2
Denbigh, Wales 13/D4
Denbigh, Wales 10/E4
Den Burg, Netherlands 27/F2
Denby, S. Dak. (57733) 298/E7
Denby Dale, England 13/J2
Den Chai, Thailand 72/C3
Dender (riv.), Belgium 27/D7
Denderleeuw, Belgium 27/E7
Dendermonde, Belgium 27/E6
Dendron, Va. (23839) 307/P6
Denekamp, Netherlands 27/L4
Denezhkin Kamen' (mt.), U.S.S.R. 52/J2
Dengkou, China 77/G3
Dêngqên, China 77/E5
Denham, Ind. (46925) 227/D2
Denham, Minn. (55728) 255/F4
Denham, W. Australia 92/A4
Denham Springs, La. (70726) 238/L2
Den Helder, Netherlands 27/F3
Denhoff, N. Dak. (58430) 282/K5
Denholm, Sask. 181/C3
Denholm, Scotland 15/F5
Denia, Spain 33/G3
Deniliquin, N. S. Wales 88/G7
Deniliquin, N.S. Wales 97/C4
Denio, Nev. (89404) 266/C1
Denison, Iowa (51442) 229/C4
Denison, Kansas (66419) 232/G2
Denison (dam), Okla. 288/O7
Denison (range), Tasmania 99/C4
Denison, Texas 188/G4
Denison, Texas (75020) 303/H4
Denison (dam), Texas 303/H4
Denison, Wash. (†99006) 310/H3
Denizli (prov.), Turkey 63/C4
Denizli, Turkey 63/C4
Denizli, Turkey 59/A2
Denman, N.S. Wales 97/F3
Denman Island, Br. Col. 184/H2
Denmark 2/K3
Denmark 7/E3
Denmark (strait) 4/C11
Denmark (str.) 146/S3
Denmark (str.) 7/B2
DENMARK 18/D9
DENMARK 21/E6
Denmark, Iowa (52624) 229/L7
Denmark, Kansas (†67455) 232/D2
Denmark○, Maine (04022) 243/B8
Denmark, Miss. (†38655) 256/F2
Denmark (bay), N.W. Terrs. 187/H2
Denmark, Oreg. (†97450) 291/C5
Denmark, S.C. (29042) 296/E5
Denmark, Tenn. (38391) 237/D9
Denmark, W. Australia 88/B7
Denmark, W. Australia 92/B6
Denmark, Wis. (54208) 317/L7
Dennard, Ark. (72629) 202/E2
Dennehotso, Ariz. (86535) 198/F2
Dennery, St. Lucia 161/G6
Denning, Ark. (†72821) 202/C3
Dennis (hill), Conn. 210/C1
Dennis, Kansas (67341) 232/G4
Dennis○, Mass. (02638) 249/O5
Dennis, Miss. (38838) 256/H1
Dennis (head), Scotland 15/F1
Dennison, Minn. (55018) 255/E6
Dennison, Ohio (44621) 284/H5
Dennis Port, Mass. (02639) 249/O6
Denniston, Va. (†24520) 307/L7
Dennisville, N.J. (08214) 273/D5
Dennisville, Sask. 181/K6
Denny and Dunipace, Scotland 10/B1
Denny and Dunipace, Scotland 15/C1
Dennysville○, Maine (04628) 243/J6
Den Oever, Netherlands 27/G3
Denoon (lake), Wis. 317/K2
Denpasar, Indonesia 85/E7
Densmore, Kansas (67633) 232/C2
Dent, Minn. (56528) 255/C4
Dent (co.), Mo. 261/J7
Dent, Ohio (†45202) 284/B9
Dent Blanche (mt.), Switzerland 39/E4
Dent de Lys (mt.), Switzerland 39/D4
Dent de Ruth (mt.), Switzerland 39/D3
Dent d'Hérens (mt.), Switzerland 39/E5

Dovray 361

Disko (isl.), Greenland 146/N3
Disko, Ind. (†46982) 227/E2
Disley, Sask. 181/F5
Dismal (riv.), Nebr. 264/C3
Dismal (Great) (swamp), N.C. 281/S1
Disney, Okla. (74340) 288/S2
Dison, Belgium 27/H7
Dispur, India 68/G3
Disputanta, Va. (23842) 307/O6
Disraeli (bay), N.W. Terrs. 187/L1
Disraëli, Québec 172/F4
Diss, England 13/J5
Diss, England 10/G4
Disston (lake), Fla. 212/E2
Disston, Oreg. (†97427) 291/E4
District Heights, Md. (20747) 245/G5
District of Columbia 146/L6
District of Columbia 188/L3
DISTRICT OF COLUMBIA 245
Distrito Especial, Colombia 126/C5
Distrito Federal, Argentina 143/H7
Distrito Federal, Mexico 150/L1
Distrito Federal, Venezuela 124/E2
Distrito Nacional, Dom. Rep. 158/E6
Disûq, Egypt 111/J3
Dittmer, Mo. (63023) 261/L6
Ditton (riv.), Québec 172/F4
Diu, India 68/C4
Diu (dist.), India 68/C4
Diuata (mts.), Philippines 82/E6
Divernon, Ill. (62530) 222/D4
Divide, Colo. (80814) 208/J5
Divide, Mont. (59727) 262/D5
Divide (co.), N. Dak. 282/C2
Dividing (creek), Md. 245/R8
Dividing Creek, N.J. (08315) 273/C5
Divino, Brazil 135/E2
Divinópolis, Brazil 132/E8
Divinópolis, Brazil 120/E5
Divinópolis, Brazil 135/D2
Divis (mt.), N. Ireland 17/J2
Divisa Nova, Brazil 135/C2
Division (peak), Nev. 266/B1
Divo, Ivory Coast 106/C7
Divriği, Turkey 63/H3
Divriği, Turkey 59/C2
Dix, Ill. (62830) 222/E5
Dix (riv.), Ky. 237/M5
Dix, Nebr. (69133) 264/A3
Dixfield, Maine (04224) 243/C6
Dixfield○, Maine (04224) 243/C6
Dix Hills, N.Y. (11746) 276/O9
Dixie, Ala. (†36420) 195/E8
Dixie (co.), Fla. 212/C2
Dixie, Georgia (31629) 217/E9
Dixie, Idaho (83525) 220/C4
Dixie, La. (†71107) 238/C1
Dixie, Wash. (99329) 310/G4
Dixie, W. Va. (25059) 312/D6
Dixie Inn, La. (†71055) 238/D1
Dixmont, Maine (04932) 243/E6
Dixmont○, Maine (04932) 243/E6
Dixmoor, Ill. (†60469) 222/C6
Dixmude (Diksmuide), Belgium 27/B6
Dixon, Calif. (95620) 204/B9
Dixon, Ill. (61021) 222/D2
Dixon, Iowa (52745) 229/M5
Dixon, Ky. (42409) 237/F5
Dixon, Miss. (†39350) 256/F5
Dixon, Mo. (65459) 261/H6
Dixon, Mont. (59831) 262/B3
Dixon (co.), Nebr. 264/H2
Dixon, Nebr. (68732) 264/H2
Dixon, N. Mex. (87527) 274/D2
Dixon, N.C. (†28445) 281/O5
Dixon, Ohio (†46773) 284/A4
Dixon, S. Dak. (57530) 298/L7
Dixon, Wyo. (82323) 319/E4
Dixon Entrance (chan.) 146/E4
Dixon Entrance (chan.), Alaska 196/M2
Dixon Entrance (chan.), Br. Col. 184/A3
Dixons Mills, Ala. (36736) 195/C6
Dixon Springs, Ill. (†62911) 222/E6
Dixon Springs, Tenn. (37057) 237/J8
Dixonville, Ala. (†36426) 195/E8
Dixonville, Alberta 182/B1
Dixonville, Pa. (15734) 294/D4
Dixville (peak), N.H. 268/E2
Dixville, Québec 172/F4
Dixville Notch, N.H. (†03576) 268/E2
Dixville Notch (pass), N.H. 268/E2
Diyadin, Turkey 63/K3
Diyala (heads), Iraq 66/D4
Diyala (riv.), Iraq 66/D4
Diyarbakır (prov.), Turkey 63/H4
Diyarbakır, Turkey 54/F6
Diyarbakır, Turkey 63/H4
Diyarbakır, Turkey 59/C2
Dizful (Dezful), Iran 66/F4
Dja (riv.), Cameroon 115/B3
Dja (riv.), Congo 115/B3
Djado (plat.) 102/D2
Djado, Niger 102/D2
Djado, Niger 106/G4
Djado (plat.), Niger 106/G4
Djakarta (Jakarta) (cap.), Indonesia 85/H1
Djakovica, Yugoslavia 45/E4
Djakovo, Yugoslavia 45/D3
Djambala, Congo 115/B4
Djambi (Jambi), Indonesia 85/C6
Djanet, Algeria 106/F4
Djanet, Algeria 102/C2
Djelfa, Algeria 106/E2
Djema, Cent. Afr. Rep. 115/E2
Djemaa, Algeria 106/F2
Djenné, Mali 102/B3
Djenné, Mali 106/D6
Djerba (isl.), Tunisia 106/G2
Djerid, Shott el (salt lake), Tunisia 106/F2
Djibo, Upper Volta 106/D6
Djibouti 2/L5
Djibouti 102/G3
DJIBOUTI 111/H5
Djibouti (cap.), Djibouti 111/H5
Djibouti (cap.), Djibouti 102/G3
Djokjakarta (Yogyakarta), Indonesia 85/J2
Djolu, Zaire 115/D3
Djouf, El (des.), Mauritania 106/C4
Djougou, Benin 106/E7
Djoum, Cameroon 115/B3
Djugu, Zaire 115/F3
D'Lo, Miss. (39062) 256/E7
Dmitriya Lapteva (str.), U.S.S.R. 4/B2
Dmitriya Lapteva (str.), U.S.S.R. 48/O2
Dneprodzerzhinsk, U.S.S.R. 7/H4
Dneprodzerzhinsk, U.S.S.R. 52/D5
Dnepropetrovsk, U.S.S.R. 7/H4
Dnepropetrovsk, U.S.S.R. 48/D5
Dnepropetrovsk, U.S.S.R. 52/D5
Dnieper (riv.), U.S.S.R. 7/H3
Dnieper (riv.), U.S.S.R. 48/D5
Dnieper (riv.), U.S.S.R. 52/D5
Dniester (riv.), U.S.S.R. 7/G4
Dniester (riv.), U.S.S.R. 52/C5
Dniester (riv.), U.S.S.R. 48/C5
Dno, U.S.S.R. 52/D3
Doaghbeg, Ireland 17/F1
Doaktown, New Bruns. 170/D2
Doans, Ind. (†47424) 227/D7
Doba, Chad 111/C6
Doba, Chad 102/D4
Dobbie (mt.), North. Terr. 93/E7
Dobbin (bay), N.W. Terrs. 187/L2
Dobbins A.F.B., Georgia 217/J1
Dobbs Ferry, N.Y. (10522) 276/O6
Dobbyn, Queensland 95/A3
Dobele, U.S.S.R. 53/B2
Döbeln, E. Germany 22/E3
Doberai (pen.), Indonesia 85/J6
Dobiegniew, Poland 47/B2
Dobias, Argentina 143/D4
Dobo, Indonesia 85/J7
Doboj, Yugoslavia 45/C3
Doboy (sound), Georgia 217/K8
Dobřany, Czech. 41/B2
Dobre Miasto, Poland 47/E2
Dobrich (Tolbukhin), Bulgaria 45/H4
Dobříš, Czech. 41/C2
Dobrush, U.S.S.R. 52/D4
Dobruška, Czech. 41/D1
Dobryanka, U.S.S.R. 52/J3
Dobšiná, Czech. 41/F2
Dobson, N.C. (27017) 281/H2
Doce (riv.), Brazil 135/E2
Doce (riv.), Brazil 132/F7
Doce Leguas (cays), Cuba 158/F3
Docker River, North. Terr. 93/A8
Docking, England 13/H5
Dock Junction (Arco), Georgia (†31520) 217/J8
Doctor Arroyo, Mexico 150/K5
Doctor Cecilio Báez, Paraguay 144/D4
Doctor Juan L. Mallorquín, Paraguay 144/E4
Doctor Juan Manuel Frutos, Paraguay 144/E4
Doctor M. Irala, Paraguay 144/E4
Doctor Pedro P. Peña, Paraguay 144/A3
Doctors Inlet, Fla. (32030) 212/E1
Doctortown, Georgia (†31545) 217/J7
Doddridge, Ark. (71834) 202/Ci
Doddridge (co.), W. Va. 312/E4
Dodds, Alberta 182/D3
Doddsville, Miss. (38736) 256/C3
Dodecanese (isls.), Greece 45/H8
Dodge (co.), Georgia 217/F6
Dodge, Mass. (†01507) 249/G4
Dodge (co.), Minn. 255/F7
Dodge (co.), Nebr. 264/H3
Dodge, Nebr. (68633) 264/H3
Dodge, N. Dak. (58625) 282/F5
Dodge, Texas (77334) 303/J7
Dodge (co.), Wis. 317/J9
Dodge, Wis. (54625) 317/D7
Dodge Center, Minn. (55927) 255/F6
Dodge City, Kans. 188/F3
Dodge City, Kansas (67801) 232/B4
Dodgeville, Wis. (53533) 317/F10
Dodgingtown, Conn. (†06470) 210/B3
Dodman (pt.), England 13/C7
Dodoma (reg.), Tanzania 115/G5
Dodoma, Tanzania 102/F5
Dodoma, Tanzania 115/G5
Dodsland, Sask. 181/C4
Dodson, La. (71422) 238/E2
Dodson, Mont. (59524) 262/H2
Dodson, Texas (79230) 303/D3
Doe (lake), Ontario 177/E2
Doe (bay), Wash. 310/C2
Doe Bay, Wash. (†98279) 310/C2
Doe Hill, Va. (24433) 307/K4
Doering, Wis. (†54435) 317/G5
Doerun, Georgia (31744) 217/E8
Doe Run, Mo. (63637) 261/M7
Doesburg, Netherlands 27/J4
Doetinchem, Netherlands 27/J5
Dog (pond), Conn. 210/C1
Dog (isl.), Fla. 212/B2
Dog (lake), Manitoba 179/D3
Dog (isl.), Newf. 166/B2
Dog (lake), Ontario 177/G5
Dogai Coring (lake), China 77/C5
Doğanbey, Turkey 63/D4
Doğanhisar, Turkey 63/D3
Doğanşehir, Turkey 63/G3
Dog Creek, Br. Col. 184/G4
Dog Ear (creek), S. Dak. 298/K6
Döger, Turkey 63/D3
Dogo (isl.), Japan 81/F5
Dogondoutchi, Niger 106/E6
Dogondoutchi, Niger 102/C3
Dogpatch, Ark. (72648) 202/D1
Dog Pound, Alberta 182/C4
Dogskin (lake), Manitoba 179/G3
Doğubeyazıt, Turkey 63/K3
Dogwood (pt.), St. Chris.-Nevis 161/D11
Doha (cap.), Qatar 54/G7
Doha (cap.), Qatar 59/F4
Dohad, India 68/C4
Doheny, Québec 172/E2
Dohuk (gov.), Iraq 66/C2
Dohuk, Iraq 66/C2
Doi Inthanon (mt.), Thailand 72/C3
Doilungdêqên, China 77/C6
Doi Pha Hom Pok (mt.), Thailand 72/C2
Doi Pia Fai (mt.), Thailand 72/D4
Doische, Belgium 27/F8
Dois Córregos, Brazil 135/B3
Dois Irmãos, Serra (range), Brazil 132/F5
Dokkum, Netherlands 27/H2
Doksy, Czech. 41/C1
Dokterstuin, Neth. Ant. 161/F8
Dola, Ohio (45835) 284/C4
Dola, W. Va. (†26386) 312/F4
Dolan, Ind. (†47401) 227/E6
Doland, S. Dak. (57436) 298/N4
Dolan Springs, Ariz. (86441) 198/A3
Dolavon, Argentina 143/C5
Dolbeau, Québec 174/C3
Dolbeau, Québec 172/E1
Doldenhorn (mt.), Switzerland 39/E4
Dole, France 28/F4
Dolega, Panama 154/F6
Dolent (mt.), Switzerland 39/C5
Doles, Georgia (†31791) 217/E7
Dolgellau, Wales 13/D5
Dolgellau, Wales 10/E4
Dolgeville, N.Y. (13329) 276/L4
Dolgiy (isl.), U.S.S.R. 52/J1
Dolinsk, U.S.S.R. 48/P5
Dollar, Scotland 10/B1
Dollar, Scotland 15/E4
Dollar Bay, Mich. (49922) 250/G1
Dollard (bay), Netherlands 27/L2
Dollard, Sask. 181/C6
Dollard-des-Ormeaux, Québec 172/H4
Dollart (est.), W. Germany 22/B2
Dollarville, Mich. (†49868) 250/D2
Dolliver, Iowa (50531) 229/D2
Dolný Kubín, Czech. 41/E2
Dolo, Ethiopia 111/H7
Dolomite, Ala. (35061) 195/D4
Dolomite Alps (range), Italy 34/C1
Dolores, Argentina 143/E4
Dolores, Argentina 120/D6
Dolores (co.), Colo. 208/C7
Dolores, Colo. (81323) 208/C8
Dolores (riv.), Colo. 208/B5
Dolores, Guatemala 154/C2
Dolores, Philippines 82/E4
Dolores, Spain 33/F3
Dolores, Uruguay 145/A4
Dolores (riv.), Utah 304/E5
Dolores, Venezuela 124/D3
Dolores Hidalgo de la Independencia Nacional, Mexico 150/J6
Dolphin and Union (str.), N.W. Terrs. 187/G3
Dölsach, Austria 41/B3
Dolton, Ill. (60419) 222/C6
Dolton, S. Dak. (57023) 298/P7
Dom (mt.), Switzerland 39/E4
Domain, Manitoba 179/E5
Domanic, Turkey 63/C3
Domar (dry riv.), Chad 111/C4
Domat-Ems, Switzerland 39/H3
Domažlice, Czech. 41/B2
Dombås, Norway 18/F5
Dombe Grande, Angola 115/B6
Dombóvár, Hungary 41/E3
Dombrád, Hungary 41/F2
Dombresson, Switzerland 39/C2
Domburg, Netherlands 27/C5
Domburg, Suriname 131/D3
Dome, Ariz. (†85364) 198/A6
Dome Creek, Br. Col. 184/G3
Domeiko, Chile 138/A7
Domeyko, Cordillera (mts.), Chile 138/B4
Dominguez, Argentina 143/G6
Dominica 2/F5
Dominica 146/M8
DOMINICA 156/G4
DOMINICA 161/E7
Dominica (passage), Dominica 161/E5
Dominican Republic 2/F4
Dominican Republic 146/L8
DOMINICAN REPUBLIC 156/D3
DOMINICAN REPUBLIC 158
Dominion (lake), Newf. 166/B3
Dominion (cape), N.W. Terrs. 187/L3
Dominion, Nova Scotia 168/J2
Dominion City, Manitoba 179/E5
Domino, Newf. 166/C3
Dömitz, E. Germany 22/D2
Domjor, India 68/F1
Domleschg (valley), Switzerland 39/E2
Dommel (riv.), Netherlands 27/H6
Domo, Ethiopia 111/J6
Domodossola, Italy 34/A1
Dom Pedrito, Brazil 132/C10
Dompu, Indonesia 85/F7
Domremy, Sask. 181/F3
Domrémy-la-Pucelle, France 28/F3
Dom Silvério, Brazil 135/E2
Dömsöd, Hungary 41/E3
Domuyo (vol.), Argentina 143/B4
Don (riv.), England 10/F4
Don (riv.), England 13/F4
Don (riv.), Ontario 177/J4
Don (riv.), Scotland 15/F3
Don (riv.), Scotland 10/E2
Don (riv.), U.S.S.R. 7/J4
Don (riv.), U.S.S.R. 48/E5
Don (riv.), U.S.S.R. 52/F5
Dona Ana (Mutarara), Mozambique 118/F3
Dona Ana (co.), N. Mex. 274/C6
Dona Ana, N. Mex. (88032) 274/C6
Donabate, Ireland 17/J5
Donaghadee, N. Ireland 17/K2
Donahue, Iowa (52746) 229/M5
Donald, Br. Col. 184/J4
Donald, Oreg. (97020) 291/A3
Donald, Victoria 97/B5
Donald, Wash. (†98951) 310/E4
Donald, Wis. (†54433) 317/E5
Donalda, Alberta 182/D3
Donalds, S.C. (29638) 296/C3
Donaldson, Ark. (71941) 202/E5
Donaldson, Ind. (46513) 227/E2
Donaldson, Minn. (56720) 255/B2
Donaldson A.F.B., S.C. 296/C2
Donaldsonville, La. (70346) 238/K3
Donalsonville, Georgia (31745) 217/C8
Donansburg, Ky. (†42743) 237/K6
Donath, Switzerland 39/H3
Donatville, Alberta 182/D2
Donau (Danube) (riv.), Austria 41/D2
Donau (Danube) (riv.), W. Germany 22/C4
Donaueschingen, W. Germany 22/C5
Donauwörth, W. Germany 22/D4
Donavon, Sask. 181/D4
Donbar, Queensland 95/B3
Don Benito, Spain 33/C3
Doncaster, England 13/F4
Doncaster, England 10/F4
Doncaster, Md. (†20646) 245/K7
Doncaster and Templestowe, Victoria 88/L7
Doncaster and Templestowe, Victoria 97/J5
Dondo, Angola 115/B5
Dondo, Mozambique 118/F3
Dondra (head), Sri Lanka 68/E7
Dondra Head (cape), Sri Lanka 54/K9
Donegal (co.), Ireland 17/K2
Donegal, Ireland 10/B3
Donegal, Ireland 17/F2
Donegal (bay), Ireland 17/D3
Donegal (bay), Ireland 10/B3
Donegal (harb.), Ireland 17/E2
Donegal (pt.), Ireland 17/B6
Donegal, Pa. (15628) 294/D5
Donel, Honduras 154/E3
Doneraile, Ireland 17/D7
Doneraile, S.C. (†29532) 296/H3
Donets (riv.), U.S.S.R. 7/H4
Donets (riv.), U.S.S.R. 48/D5
Donets (riv.), U.S.S.R. 52/E5
Donetsk, U.S.S.R. 7/H4
Donetsk, U.S.S.R. 48/D5
Donetsk, U.S.S.R. 52/E5
Donga (riv.), Cameroon 115/B2
Donga, Nigeria 106/G7
Donga (riv.), Nigeria 106/G7
Dongara, W. Australia 92/A5
Dongchuan, China 77/F6
Dongen, Netherlands 27/F5
Dongfang, China 77/G8
Dongfanghong, China 77/M2
Donggala, Indonesia 85/F6
Dônghén, Laos 72/E3
Dong Hoi, Vietnam 72/E3
Dongio, Switzerland 39/H4
Dongning, China 77/M3
Dongo, Zaire 115/C3
Dongola, Ill. (62926) 222/D6
Dongola, Sudan 102/E3
Dongola, Sudan 59/B6
Dongola, Sudan 111/F4
Dongou, Congo 115/C3
Dong Rak (mts.), Thailand 72/D4
Dongsha (isl.), China 77/J7
Dongsheng, China 77/H4
Dongtai, China 77/K5
Dongting (lake), China 54/N7
Dongting Hu (riv.), China 77/H6
Dong Ujimqin, China 77/J2
Dongwe (riv.), Zambia 115/D6
Donie, Texas (75838) 303/H6
Doñihue, Chile 138/G5
Doniphan (co.), Kansas 232/G2
Doniphan, Mo. (63935) 261/L9
Doniphan, Nebr. (68832) 264/F4
Donji Vakuf, Yugoslavia 45/C3
Donkin, Nova Scotia 168/J2
Donley (co.), Texas 303/D2
Dønna (isl.), Norway 18/H3
Donna, Texas (78537) 303/F11
Donnacona, Québec 172/F3
Donnan, Iowa (52139) 229/K3
Donnellson, Ill. (62019) 222/D4
Donnellson, Iowa (52625) 229/K7
Donnelly, Alberta 182/B2
Donnelly, Idaho (83615) 220/B5
Donnelly, Minn. (56235) 255/B5
Donner (pass), Calif. 204/E4
Donner, La. (70352) 238/J7
Donner and Blitzen (riv.), Oreg. 291/J4
Donnybrook, N. Dak. (58734) 282/G2
Donnybrook, Queensland 95/D5
Donnybrook, W. Australia 92/A2
Donora, Pa. (15033) 294/C5
Donovan, Georgia (†31096) 217/G5
Donovan, Ill. (60931) 222/F3
Donsol, Philippines 82/D4
Donwell, Sask. 181/J4
Donzère, France 28/F5
Dooagh-Keel, Ireland 17/A4
Doole, Texas (76836) 303/E6
Dooling, Georgia (†31063) 217/E6
Doolittle (pond), Conn. 210/C1
Doolittle, Mo. (†65550) 261/J7
Doolittle Mills, Ind. (†47118) 227/D8
Dooly (co.), Georgia 217/E6
Doon, Iowa (51235) 229/A2
Doon, Ireland 17/E6
Doon, Loch (lake), Scotland 15/D5
Doon (riv.), Scotland 15/D5
Doonerak (mt.), Alaska 196/H1
Doonside, Sask. 181/K6
Door (pt.), La. 238/M6
Door (co.), Wis. 317/M6
Door (pen.), Wis. 317/M6
Doorn, Netherlands 27/G4
Doornik (Tournai), Belgium 27/C7
Doqa, Saudi Arabia 59/D6
Dor, Israel 65/B2
Dora, Ala. (35062) 195/D3
Dora, Mo. (65637) 261/H9
Dora, N. Mex. (88115) 274/F5
Dora, Oreg. (†97458) 291/D4
Dora (lake), W. Australia 88/C4
Dora (lake), W. Australia 92/C3
Dora Baltea (riv.), Italy 34/A2
Dorado, P. Rico 161/D1
Dora Lake, Minn. (†56661) 255/D3
Doran, Minn. (56530) 255/B4
Dora Riparia (riv.), Italy 34/A2
Doraville, Georgia (30340) 217/K1
D'Orbigny, Bolivia 136/D7
Dorbiljin (Emin), China 77/B2
Dorbod, China 77/K2
Dorcas, W. Va. (26835) 312/H5
Dorchester, England 10/E5
Dorchester, England 13/E7
Dorchester, Georgia (†31317) 217/K7
Dorchester, Ill. (62020) 222/D4
Dorchester, Iowa (52140) 229/L2
Dorchester (co.), Md. 245/O7
Dorchester, Mass. (†02122) 249/D7
Dorchester, Nebr. (68343) 264/G4
Dorchester, New Bruns. 170/F3
Dorchester○, N.H. (†03266) 268/D4
Dorchester, N.J. (08316) 273/D5
Dorchester (cape), N.W. Terrs. 187/L3
Dorchester, Ontario 177/C5
Dorchester (co.), Québec 172/C3
Dorchester (co.), S.C. 296/G5
Dorchester, S.C. (29437) 296/G5
Dorchester, Wis. (54425) 317/F5
Dorchester Crossing, New Bruns. 170/F2
Dordogne (dept.), France 28/D5
Dordogne (riv.), France 7/E4
Dordogne (riv.), France 28/D5
Dordrecht, Netherlands 27/F5
Doré (lake), Ontario 177/G2
Doré (lake), Sask. 181/L3
Dore Alps (mts.), France 28/E5
Doré Lake, Sask. 181/L4
Dorena, Mo. (†63845) 261/O9
Dorena, Oreg. (97434) 291/E4
Dorena (lake), Oreg. 291/E4
Dorenlee, Alberta 182/D3
Dores, Scotland 15/D3
Dores do Indaiá, Brazil 132/E7
Dorgali, Italy 34/B4
Dörgön Nuur (lake), Mongolia 77/D2
Dori, Mali 102/B3
Dori, Upper Volta 106/D6
Doring (riv.), S. Africa 118/B6
Dorintosh, Sask. 181/L4
Dorion, Ontario 177/H5
Dorion, Québec 172/C4
Dorking, England 13/G8
Dorking, England 10/F5
Dormont, Pa. (15216) 294/B7
Dornach, Switzerland 39/E2
Dornbirn, Austria 41/A3
Dornie, Scotland 15/C3
Dornoch, Scotland 10/D2
Dornoch, Scotland 15/D3
Dornoch (firth), Scotland 15/E3
Dornoch (firth), Scotland 10/E2
Dornod, Mongolia 77/H2
Dornogovĭ, Mongolia 77/G3
Dorog, Hungary 41/E3
Dorohoi, Romania 45/H2
Dorotea, Sweden 18/K4
Dorothy, Alberta 182/D4
Dorothy, Minn. (†56750) 255/B3
Dorothy, N.J. (08317) 273/D5
Dorothy, W. Va. (25060) 312/D7
Dorr (lake), Fla. 212/E2
Dorr, Mich. (49323) 250/D6
Dorrance, Kansas (67634) 232/D3
Dorre (isl.), W. Australia 88/A5
Dorre (isl.), W. Australia 92/A4
Dorreen, Br. Col. 184/C3
Dorrigo, N.S. Wales 97/G2
Dorris, Calif. (96023) 204/D2
Dorset (co.), England 13/E7
Dorset, Minn. (†56470) 255/D4
Dorset, Ohio (44032) 284/J2
Dorset○, Vt. (05251) 268/A5
Dorset (peak), Vt. 268/A5
Dorset Heights (hills), England 13/E7
Dorsey, Miss. (†38801) 256/H2
Dorsten, W. Germany 22/B3
Dortches, N.C. (†27801) 281/O2
Dortmund, W. Germany 7/E3
Dortmund, W. Germany 22/B3
Dorton, Ky. (41520) 237/R6
Dörtyol, Turkey 63/F4
Doruma, Zaire 115/E3
Dorval, Québec 172/H4
Dory Point, N.W. Terrs. 187/G3
Dos Bahías (cape), Argentina 143/D5
Dos Cabezas, Ariz. (†85643) 198/F6
Dos Caminos, Cuba 158/J4
Dos de Mayo, Peru 128/E6
Dos Hermanas, Spain 33/D4
Dos Palos, Calif. (93620) 204/E6
Dosquet, Québec 172/F3
Dos Reyes (pt.), Chile 138/A5
Dos Rios, Cuba 158/J4
Dosso, Niger 106/E6
Dossor, U.S.S.R. 48/F5
Dossville, Miss. (†39051) 256/F5
Doswell, Va. (23047) 307/N5
Dothan, Ala. 188/J4
Dothan, Ala. (*36303) 195/H8
Doti, Nepal 68/E3
Dot Klish (canyon), Ariz. 198/E2
Dot Lake, Alaska (99737) 196/K2
Dott, W. Va. (24721) 312/D8
Döttingen, Switzerland 39/F1
Doty, Wash. (98539) 310/B4
Douai, France 28/E2
Douala, Cameroon 115/B3
Douala, Cameroon 102/D4
Douarnenez, France 28/A3
Double Branches, Georgia (†30817) 217/H3
Double Mer (lake), Newf. 166/C3
Double Mountain Fork, Brazos (riv.), Texas 303/C4
Double Oak, Texas (†76226) 303/F1
Double Springs, Ala. (35553) 195/D2
Doubletop (peak), Wyo. 319/B2
Doubs (dept.), France 28/G4
Doubs (riv.), France 28/G4
Doubs, Md. (†21710) 245/J3
Doubs (riv.), Switzerland 39/C2
Doubtful (sound), N. Zealand 100/A6
Doubtless (bay), N. Zealand 100/D1
Doucette, Texas (79542) 303/K7
Douds, Iowa (52551) 229/J7
Doué-la-Fontaine, France 28/C4
Douentza, Mali 106/D6
Douentza, Mali 102/B3
Dougherty (co.), Georgia 217/D7
Dougherty, Iowa (50433) 229/G3
Dougherty, Okla. (73032) 288/M6
Dougherty, Texas (79231) 303/C4
Douglas, Ala. (35964) 195/F2
Douglas (mt.), Alaska 196/H3
Douglas, Ariz. 146/G6
Douglas, Ariz. 188/E4
Douglas, Ariz. (85607) 198/F7
Douglas (chan.), Br. Col. 184/C3
Douglas (co.), Colo. 208/K4
Douglas (creek), Colo. 208/B3
Douglas (bay), Dominica 161/E5
Douglas (co.), Georgia 217/C3
Douglas, Georgia (31533) 217/G7
Douglas (co.), Ill. 222/E4
Douglas, Ireland 17/D8
Douglas (cap.), I. of Man 13/C3
Douglas (cap.), I. of Man 10/D3
Douglas (co.), Kansas 232/G3
Douglas, Manitoba 179/C5
Douglas○, Mass. (†01516) 249/H4
Douglas, Mich. (49406) 250/C6
Douglas (co.), Minn. 255/C5
Douglas, Minn. (†55960) 255/F6
Douglas (co.), Mo. 261/G9
Douglas (mt.), Mont. 262/F5
Douglas (co.), Nebr. 264/J3
Douglas, Nebr. (68344) 264/H4
Douglas (co.), Nev. 266/B4
Douglas, N. Dak. (58735) 282/G4
Douglas, North. Terr. 93/B2
Douglas, Okla. (73733) 288/L2
Douglas, Ontario 177/H2
Douglas (pt.), Ontario 177/C3
Douglas (co.), Oreg. 291/D4
Douglas, Scotland 15/E5
Douglas, S. Africa 118/C5
Douglas (co.), S. Dak. 298/N7
Douglas (lake), Tenn. 237/P9
Douglas (co.), Wash. 310/F3
Douglas, Wash. (†98858) 310/F3
Douglas (co.), Wis. 317/C3
Douglas, Wyo. (82633) 319/G3
Douglas Harbour, New Bruns. 170/D3
Douglas Lake, Br. Col. 184/H5
Douglas Prov. Park, Sask. 181/E4
Douglass, Kansas (67039) 232/F4
Douglass, Texas (75943) 303/K6
Douglass Hills, Ky. (†40243) 237/L2
Douglassville, Pa. (19518) 294/L5
Douglastown, New Bruns. 170/E1
Douglastown, Québec 172/D1
Douglasville, Georgia (*30133) 217/C3
Doullens, France 28/E2
Doulus (head), Ireland 17/A8
Doumé, Cameroon 115/B3
Dounby, Scotland 15/E1
Doune, Scotland 15/D4
Dour, Belgium 27/D8
Dourados, Brazil 120/D5
Dourados, Brazil 132/C8
Douro (riv.), Portugal 7/D4
Douro (riv.), Portugal 33/B2
Douro (riv.), Spain 33/C2
Dousman, Wis. (53118) 317/J1
Douthat, Okla. (74341) 288/S1
Douville, Québec 172/D4
Dove (riv.), England 13/J2
Dove (creek), Utah 304/A2
Dove Creek, Colo. (81324) 208/A7
Dover, Ark. (72837) 202/D3
Dover (cap.), Del. 146/L6
Dover (cap.), Del. 188/L3
Dover (cap.), Del. (19901) 245/R4
Dover, England 7/E3
Dover, England 10/G5
Dover, England 13/J6
Dover (str.), England 13/J7
Dover (str.), England 10/G5
Dover, Fla. (33527) 212/D4
Dover, Georgia (30424) 217/J5
Dover, Idaho (83825) 220/B1
Dover, Ill. (61323) 222/D2
Dover, Ind. (†46052) 227/H6
Dover, Kansas (66420) 232/G3
Dover, Ky. (41034) 237/O3
Dover, Mass. (02030) 249/B7
Dover○, Mass. (02030) 249/B7
Dover, Minn. (55929) 255/F7
Dover, Mo. (64022) 261/E4
Dover, N.H. (03820) 268/F5
Dover, N.J. (07801) 273/D2
Dover, N.C. (28526) 281/P4
Dover, Ohio (44622) 284/G4
Dover (lake), Ohio 284/H4
Dover, Okla. (73734) 288/L3
Dover, Pa. (17315) 294/J6
Dover, Tasmania 99/C5
Dover, Tenn. (37058) 237/F8
Dover (pt.), W. Australia 88/D6
Dover (pt.), W. Australia 92/D6
Dover A.F.B., Del. 245/S4
Doverel, Georgia (†31742) 217/D7
Dover-Foxcroft, Maine (04426) 243/E5
Dover-Foxcroft○, Maine (04426) 243/E5
Dover Hill, Ind. (†47581) 227/D7
Dover Plains, N.Y. (12522) 276/O7
Dover South Mills, Maine (†04426) 243/E5
Dovesville, S.C. (29540) 296/H3
Dovey (riv.), Wales 10/D4
Dovey (riv.), Wales 13/D5
Dovns Klint (cliff), Denmark 21/D8
Dovray, Minn. (56125) 255/C6

362 Dovre

Dovre, Norway 18/F6
Dovrefjell (hills), Norway 18/F5
Dow (Xau) (lake), Botswana 118/C4
Dow, Ill. (62022) 222/C4
Dow, Okla. (†74547) 288/P5
Dowa, Malawi 115/F6
Dowagiac, Mich. (49047) 250/D6
Dow City, Iowa (51528) 229/B5
Dowell, Ill. (62927) 222/D6
Dowelltown, Tenn. (37059) 237/K8
Dowlatabad, Afghanistan 59/H3
Dowlatabad, Afghanistan 68/A2
Dowlatabad, Kerman, Iran 66/K6
Dowlatabad, Khorasan, Iran 66/M2
Dowlat Yar, Afghanistan 59/J3
Dowlat Yar, Afghanistan 68/B2
Dowling, Alberta 182/E4
Dowling (lake), Alberta 182/D4
Dowling, Mich. (49050) 250/D6
Dowling Park, Fla. (32060) 212/C1
Down (dist.), N. Ireland 17/K3
Downe, Sask. 181/C4
Downer, Minn. (†56514) 255/B4
Downers Grove, Ill. (60515) 222/A6
Downey, Calif. (*90240) 204/C11
Downey, Idaho (83234) 220/F7
Downey, Iowa (†52358) 229/L5
Downfall (creek), Queensland 95/D2
Downham Market, England 13/H5
Downham Market, England 10/G4
Downieville, Calif. (95936) 204/E4
Downing, Mo. (63536) 261/H2
Downing, Wis. (54734) 317/B5
Downings, Va. (†22460) 307/P5
Downingtown, Pa. (19335) 294/L5
Downpatrick (head), Ireland 17/C3
Downpatrick, N. Ireland 10/C3
Downpatrick, N. Ireland 17/K3
Downs, Ill. (61736) 222/E3
Downs, Kansas (67437) 232/D2
Downsville, La. (71234) 238/F1
Downsville, Md. (†21795) 245/G2
Downsville, N.Y. (13755) 276/L6
Downsville, Wis. (54735) 317/C6
Downton, England 13/F6
Dows, Iowa (50071) 229/F3
Dowshi, Afghanistan 59/J2
Dowshi, Afghanistan 68/B1
Doyle, Calif. (96109) 204/E3
Doyle, Georgia (†31803) 217/D6
Doyle, Tenn. (38559) 237/K9
Doylestown, Ohio (44230) 284/G4
Doylestown, Pa. (18901) 294/M5
Doylestown, Wis. (53928) 317/H9
Doyleville, Colo. (†81239) 208/F6
Doyline, La. (71023) 238/D1
Doyon, N. Dak. (58328) 282/O3
Dozen (isls.), Japan 81/F5
Dozier, Ala. (36028) 195/F7
Dozier, Texas (†79079) 303/D2
Dozois (res.), Québec 174/B3
Dra, Wadi (dry riv.), Morocco 106/C3
Drachten, Netherlands 27/J2
Dracut○, Mass. (01826) 249/J2
Drăgănești Olt, Romania 45/G3
Drăgășani, Romania 45/F3
Dragonera (isl.), Spain 33/H3
Dragons Mouth (str.), Trin. & Tob. 156/F5
Dragons Mouth (str.), Trin. & Tob. 161/A10
Dragons Mouth (str.), Venezuela 124/H2
Dragoon, Ariz. (85609) 198/F6
Dragoon (mts.), Ariz. 198/F7
Draguignan, France 28/G6
Drain, Oreg. (97435) 291/D4
Drake (passage) 2/F8
Drake (passage) 5/C15
Drake (passage), Chile 138/E11
Drake, Colo. (80515) 208/J2
Drake, Mo. (†65066) 261/K6
Drake, N. Dak. (58736) 282/K4
Drake, Sask. 181/G4
Drakensberg (range), Lesotho 118/D6
Drakensberg (range), S. Africa 118/D6
Drakensberg (range), Swaziland 118/D6
Drakes (creek), Ky. 237/J7
Drakesboro, Ky. (42337) 237/H6
Drakes Branch, Va. (23937) 307/L7
Drakesville, Iowa (52552) 229/J7
Draketown, Georgia (†30179) 217/B3
Dráma, Greece 45/F5
Drammen, Norway 7/E3
Drammen, Norway 18/C4
Drance (riv.), Switzerland 39/D4
Drancy, France 28/B1
Drang, Ia (riv.), Cambodia 72/E4
Draper, S. Dak. (57531) 298/J6
Draper, Utah (84020) 304/C3
Draper, Va. (24324) 307/G7
Draper, Wis. (†54852) 317/E4
Draperstown, N. Ireland 17/H2
Draperstown, N. Ireland 10/C3
Drasco, Ark. (72530) 202/G2
Drau (riv.), Austria 41/C3
Drava (riv.) 7/F4
Dráva (riv.), Hungary 41/D3
Drava (riv.), Yugoslavia 45/C3
Dravosburg, Pa. (15034) 294/C7
Drawsko Pomorskie, Poland 47/B2
Drax Hall, Barbados 161/B8
Drayden, Md. (20630) 245/N8
Drayton, N. Dak. (58225) 282/R2
Drayton, Ontario 177/D4
Drayton Plains, Mich. (48020) 250/F6
Drayton Valley, Alberta 182/C3
Drenthe (prov.), Netherlands 27/K3
Dresbach, Minn. (55930) 255/G7
Dresden, E. Germany 7/F3
Dresden (dist.), E. Germany 22/E3
Dresden, E. Germany 22/E3
Dresden, Kansas (67635) 232/B2
Dresden○, Maine (04342) 243/D7
Dresden, Mo. (†65301) 261/F5
Dresden, N.Y. (14441) 276/F5
Dresden, N. Dak. (†58249) 282/O2
Dresden, Ohio (43821) 284/G5
Dresden, Ontario 177/B5
Dresden, Tenn. (38225) 237/D8
Dresden Station, N.Y. (†12887) 276/O3
Dresser, Wis. (54009) 317/A5
Dreux, France 28/D3
Drew (co.), Ark. 202/G6
Drew, Miss. (38737) 256/C3
Drew, Oreg. (†97484) 291/E5
Drewry, Ala. (†36460) 195/D8
Drewryville, Va. (23844) 307/O7
Drews (res.), Oreg. 291/G5
Drewsey, Oreg. (97904) 291/J4
Drewsville, N.H. (03604) 268/C5
Drexel, Mo. (64742) 261/C6
Drexel, N.C. (28619) 281/F3
Drexel Hill, Pa. (19026) 294/M6
Dreyfus, Ky. (40426) 237/N5
Drezdenko, Poland 47/B2
Driebergen, Netherlands 27/G4
Driffield, England 13/G3
Driffield, England 10/F4
Drift (creek), Oreg. 291/B3
Drifton, Pa. (18221) 294/L3
Driftwood, Okla. (†73722) 288/K1
Driftwood, Pa. (15832) 294/F3
Driggs, Ark. (†72943) 202/C3
Driggs, Idaho (83422) 220/G6
Drill, Va. (†24260) 307/E6
Drimoleague, Ireland 17/C8
Drin (riv.), Albania 45/E4
Drina (riv.), Yugoslavia 45/D3
Drinkwater, Sask. 181/F5
Dripping Springs, Texas (78620) 303/F7
Driscoll, N. Dak. (58532) 282/K6
Driscoll, Texas (78351) 303/G10
Drishane, Ireland 17/C7
Driskill (mt.), La. 238/E2
Drøbak, Norway 18/D4
Drobeta-Turnu Severin, Romania 45/F3
Drogenbos, Belgium 27/B10
Drogheda, Ireland 17/J4
Drogheda, Ireland 10/C4
Drogobych, U.S.S.R. 52/B5
Drogobych, U.S.S.R. 48/C5
Droichead Nua, Ireland 10/C4
Droichead Nua, Ireland 17/H5
Droitwich, England 13/E5
Dromahair, Ireland 17/F3
Drome (dept.), France 28/F5
Drome (riv.), France 28/F5
Dromore, Bainbridge, N. Ireland 17/J3
Dromore, Omagh, N. Ireland 17/G3
Dromore West, Ireland 17/D3
Dronfield, England 13/J2
Drongan, Scotland 15/D5
Dronne (riv.), France 28/D5
Dronninglund, Denmark 21/D3
Dronten (prov.), Netherlands 27/H4
Dronten, Netherlands 27/H3
Dropmore, Manitoba 179/A3
Drouin, Victoria 97/C6
Druid, Sask. 181/C4
Druif, Neth. Ant. 161/D10
Drum (hills), Ireland 17/F7
Drum (bay), La. 238/M7
Drum (inlet), N.C. 281/S5
Drumaness, N. Ireland 17/K3
Drumbeg, Scotland 15/C2
Drumbo, Ontario 177/D4
Drumcar, Ireland 17/J4
Drumconrath, Ireland 17/H4
Drumheller, Alberta 182/D4
Drumheller, Alta. 162/E5
Drumhill, N.C. (†27937) 281/R1
Drumkeerin, Ireland 17/E3
Drumlish, Ireland 17/F4
Drummond, Idaho (†83420) 220/G5
Drummond (isl.), Mich. 250/F2
Drummond, Mont. (59832) 262/D4
Drummond, New Bruns. 170/C1
Drummond (mt.), North. Terr. 93/E5
Drummond, Okla. (73735) 288/L2
Drummond (co.), Québec 172/E4
Drummond (range), Queensland 88/H4
Drummond (range), Queensland 95/C5
Drummond (lake), Va. 307/P7
Drummond, Wis. (54832) 317/D3
Drummond Island, Mich. (49726) 250/F3
Drummonds, Tenn. (38023) 237/A10
Drummondville, Québec 172/E4
Drummondville-Nord, Québec 172/E4
Drummondville-Sud, Québec 172/E4
Drummore, Scotland 15/D6
Drummoyne, N.S. Wales 88/K4
Drummoyne, N.S. Wales 97/J3
Drumnadrochit, Scotland 15/D3
Drumquin, N. Ireland 17/G3
Drumright, Okla. (74030) 288/N3
Drums, Pa. (18222) 294/K3
Drumshanbo, Ireland 17/E3
Drury, Mo. (65638) 261/H9
Druskininkai, U.S.S.R. 53/C3
Druten, Netherlands 27/H5
Druz, Jebel ed (mts.), Syria 63/G6
Druzhba, U.S.S.R. 48/J5
Druzhina, U.S.S.R. 48/P3
Drvar, Yugoslavia 45/C3
Dry (bay), Alaska 196/L3
Dry (creek), Ky. 237/R3
Dry (lake), N. Dak. 282/M3
Dry (riv.), North. Terr. 88/E3
Dry (riv.), North. Terr. 93/C3
Dry (creek), S. Dak. 298/G4
Dry (lake), S. Dak. 298/P3
Dry (creek), Wyo. 319/C2
Dryad, Wash. (†98532) 310/B4
Dryanovo, Bulgaria 45/G4
Dry Branch, Georgia (31020) 217/F5
Dry Cimarron (riv.), N. Mex. 274/F2
Dry Coal (creek), Utah 304/A6
Dry Cottonwood (creek), Wyo. 319/D1
Dry Creek, La. (70637) 238/D5
Dry Creek, W. Va. (25062) 312/D7
Dryden, Ark. (†72401) 202/J2
Dryden, Maine (04225) 243/C6
Dryden, Mich. (48428) 250/F6
Dryden, N.Y. (13053) 276/H6
Dryden, Ontario 177/G4
Dryden, Ontario 175/B3
Dryden, Texas (78851) 303/C7
Dryden, Va. (24243) 307/B7
Dryden, Wash. (98821) 310/E3
Dry Falls (dam), Wash. 310/F3
Dry Fork, Va. (24549) 307/K7
Dryfork, W. Va. (26263) 312/H5
Dry Fork (riv.), W. Va. 312/G5
Dry Fork (riv.), W. Va. 312/C8
Dry Fork, Cheyenne (riv.), Wyo. 319/G2
Dry Fork, Powder (riv.), Wyo. 319/F2
Dry Lake, Nev. (†89040) 266/G6
Drymen, Scotland 15/B1
Dry Mills, Maine (†04039) 243/C8
Dry Prong, La. (71423) 238/E3
Dry Ridge, Ky. (41035) 237/M3
Dry Run, Pa. (17220) 294/G5
Drysdale (riv.), W. Australia 88/D3
Drysdale (riv.), W. Australia 92/D1
Dry Tortugas (keys), Fla. 212/D7
Drytown, Calif. (95699) 204/C8
Dry Wood (lake), S. Dak. 298/P2
Dschang, Cameroon 115/A2
Duaca, Venezuela 124/D2
Duaringa, Queensland 95/D4
Duart, Ontario 177/C5
Duarte, Calif. (91010) 204/D10
Duarte (prov.), Dom. Rep. 158/E5
Duarte (peak), Dom. Rep. 158/D5
Dubach, La. (71235) 238/E1
Dubai, U.A.E. 59/F4
Dubawnt (lake), N.W.T. 162/F3
Dubawnt (lake), N.W.T. 146/H3
Dubawnt (lake), N.W. Terrs. 187/H3
Dubawnt (riv.), N.W.T. 162/F3
Dubawnt (riv.), N.W. Terrs. 187/H3
Du Bay (lake), Wis. 317/G6
Dubberly, La. (71024) 238/D1
Dubbo, N. S. Wales 88/H6
Dubbo, N.S. Wales 97/E3
Dubbs, Miss. (†38626) 256/D1
Dübendorf, Switzerland 39/G2
Dublin, Calif. (94566) 204/K2
Dublin, Georgia (31021) 217/G5
Dublin, Ind. (47335) 227/G5
Dublin (co.), Ireland 17/J5
Dublin (cap.), Ireland 7/D3
Dublin (cap.), Ireland 17/K5
Dublin (cap.), Ireland 10/C4
Dublin (bay), Ireland 10/C4
Dublin (bay), Ireland 17/J5
Dublin, Ky. (†42039) 237/D7
Dublin, Md. (†21154) 245/N2
Dublin, Mich. (†49689) 250/D4
Dublin, Miss. (38739) 256/C2
Dublin○, N.H. (03444) 268/C6
Dublin, N.C. (28332) 281/M5
Dublin, Ohio (43017) 284/D5
Dublin, Ontario 177/C4
Dublin, Pa. (18917) 294/M5
Dublin, Texas (76446) 303/F5
Dublin, Va. (24084) 307/G6
Dubna, U.S.S.R. 52/E4
Dubna, U.S.S.R. 52/E3
Dubnica nad Váhom, Czech. 41/E2
Dubno, U.S.S.R. 52/C4
Dubois, Idaho (83423) 220/F5
Dubois, Ill. (62831) 222/D5
Dubois (co.), Ind. 227/D8
Dubois, Ind. (47525) 227/D8
Du Bois, Nebr. (68345) 264/H4
DuBois, Pa. (15801) 294/E3
Dubois, Wyo. (82513) 319/C2
Duboistown, Pa. (†17701) 294/H3
Dubréka, Guinea 106/B7
Dubreuilville, Ontario 177/J5
Dubrovnik, Yugoslavia 45/C4
Dubrueilville, Ontario 175/D3
Dubuc, Sask. 181/J5
Dubuque (co.), Iowa 229/M4
Dubuque, Iowa 188/H2
Dubuque, Iowa (52001) 229/M3
Duchcov, Czech. 41/B1
Duchesne (co.), Utah 304/D3
Duchesne, Utah (84021) 304/D3
Duchesne (riv.), Utah 304/D3
Duchess, Alberta 182/E4
Duchess, Queensland 88/F4
Duchess, Queensland 95/A4
Ducie (isl.), Pitcairn Is. 87/O8
Duck (isls.), Maine 243/G7
Duck (lake), Mich. 250/F4
Duck (creek), Nev. 266/G3
Duck, N.C. (†27949) 281/T2
Duck (creek), Ohio 284/H6
Duck (isl.), Ontario 177/H4
Duck (isls.), Ontario 177/A2
Duck (riv.), Tenn. 237/F9
Duck, W. Va. (25063) 312/E5
Duck Bay, Manitoba 179/B2
Duck Hill, Miss. (38925) 256/E3
Duck Lake, Sask. 181/E3
Duck Lake Hist. Park, Sask. 181/E3
Duck Lake Post, Manitoba 179/J2
Duck Mountain Prov. Park, Manitoba 179/B3
Duck Mountain Prov. Park, Sask. 181/K4
Duck River, Tenn. (38454) 237/G9
Ducktown, Georgia (†30130) 217/D2
Ducktown, Tenn. (37326) 237/N10
Duckwater, Nev. (89314) 266/F4
Duclos, Québec 172/A4
Ducor, Calif. (93218) 204/G8
Ducos, Martinique 161/D6
Dudelange, Luxembourg 27/J10
Dudenville, Mo. (†64748) 261/D8
Duderstadt, W. Germany 22/D3
Dudhi, India 68/E4
Dudignac, Argentina 143/F7
Düdingen, Switzerland 39/D3
Dudinka, U.S.S.R. 54/K3
Dudinka, U.S.S.R. 4/B2
Dudinka, U.S.S.R. 48/J3
Dudley, England 13/E5
Dudley, England 10/G3
Dudley, Georgia (31022) 217/F5
Dudley○, Mass. (01570) 249/G4
Dudley, Mo. (63936) 261/M9
Dudley, N.C. (28333) 281/N4
Dudley, Pa. (16634) 294/F5
Dudley (lake), Québec 172/B4
Dudleytown, Ind. (†47274) 227/F7
Dudváh (riv.), Czech. 41/D2
Dudweiler, W. Germany 22/B4
Dueñas, Spain 33/D2
Duenweg, Mo. (64841) 261/D8
Duero (Douro) (riv.), Spain 33/C2
Due West, S.C. (29639) 296/C3
Duff, Sask. 181/H5
Duff, Tenn. (37729) 237/N8
Duffee, Miss. (†39337) 256/G6
Duffel, Belgium 27/F6
Dufferin (county), Ontario 177/D3
Duffield, Alberta 182/C3
Duffield, Va. (24244) 307/C7
Dufftown, Scotland 10/E2
Dufftown, Scotland 15/E3
Dufourspitze (mt.), Switzerland 39/E5
Dufresne, Manitoba 179/F5
Dufrost, Manitoba 179/E5
Dufur, Oreg. (97021) 291/F2
Dugald, Manitoba 179/F5
Dugger, Ind. (47848) 227/C6
Dugi Otok (isl.), Yugoslavia 45/B3
Dugspur, Va. (24325) 307/G7
Duguayville, New Bruns. 170/E1
Du Gué (riv.), Québec 174/C1
Dugway, Utah (84022) 304/B3
Dugway (range), Utah 304/A3
Dugway Proving Grounds, Utah 304/B3
Duhamel, Alberta 182/D3
Duhamel, Québec 172/B3
Duich, Loch (inlet), Scotland 15/C3
Duida, Cerro (mt.), Venezuela 124/F6
Duifken (pt.), Queensland 88/G2
Duifken (pt.), Queensland 95/B2
Duiker (pt.), S. Africa 118/E6
Duinain (riv.), Scotland 15/D3
Duirinish (dist.), Scotland 15/B3
Duisburg, W. Germany 22/B3
Duitama, Colombia 126/D5
Duiveland (isl.), Netherlands 27/D5
Duivendrecht, Netherlands 27/C5
Duke, Ala. (†36279) 195/G3
Duke (isl.), Alaska 196/N2
Duke, Mo. (65461) 261/H7
Duke, Okla. (73532) 288/G5
Duke Center, Pa. (16729) 294/F2
Dukedom, Tenn. (38226) 237/D8
Duke of Gloucester (isls.), Fr. Poly. 87/M8
Dukes (co.), Mass. 249/M7
Dukes, Mich. (†49885) 250/B2
Dukhan, Qatar 59/F4
Duki, Pakistan 68/B2
Dukla (pass), Czech. 41/F2
Dukla (pass), Poland 47/E4
Dukou, China 77/F6
Dulac, La. (70353) 238/J8
Dulah, N.C. (†28463) 281/M6
Dulan, China 77/E4
Dulce (riv.), Argentina 143/D2
Dulce (gulf), C. Rica 154/F6
Dulce, N. Mex. (87528) 274/B2
Duleek, Ireland 17/J4
Dulgalakh (riv.), U.S.S.R. 48/O3
Dülmen, W. Germany 22/B3
Dulunguin (pt.), Philippines 82/C7
Duluth, Georgia (30136) 217/D2
Duluth, Kansas (66421) 232/F2
Duluth, Minn. 146/J5
Duluth, Minn. 188/H1
Duluth, Minn. (*55801) 255/F4
Dulverton, England 13/D6
Duma, Syria 63/G6
Duma, West Bank 65/C3
Dumagasa (pt.), Philippines 82/C7
Dumaguete, Philippines 82/D6
Dumaguete, Philippines 85/G4
Dumanquilas (bay), Philippines 82/D7
Dumaran (isl.), Philippines 85/G3
Dumaran (isl.), Philippines 82/C5
Dumaresq (riv.), N.S. Wales 97/F1
Dumas, Ark. (71639) 202/H6
Dumas, Miss. (38625) 256/G1
Dumas, Sask. 181/J6
Dumas, Texas (79029) 303/C2
Dumbarton, New Bruns. 170/C3
Dumbarton, Scotland 10/A1
Dumbarton, Scotland 15/B1
Dum Dum, India 68/F1
Dume (pt.), Calif. 204/G10
Dumeir, Syria 63/G6
Dumfoundling (bay), Fla. 212/C4
Dumfries, New Bruns. 170/C3
Dumfries, Scotland 15/E5
Dumfries, Scotland 10/E3
Dumfries (trad. co.), Scotland, 15/B5
Dumfries, Va. (22026) 307/O3
Dumfries and Galloway (reg.), Scotland 15/E5
Dumlu, Turkey 63/J2
Dummer○, N.H. (†03588) 268/E2
Dummer, Sask. 181/G6
Dümmersee (lake), W. Germany 22/C2
Dumont, Iowa (50625) 229/H3
Dumont, Minn. (56236) 255/B5
Dumont, N.J. (07628) 273/C1
Dumont, Texas (79232) 303/D4
Dumont d'Urville Station 5/C7
Dumyât (Damietta), Egypt 111/J3
Dumyat (Damietta), Egypt 59/B3
Dun (isl.), Scotland 15/A2
Duna (Danube) (riv.), Hungary 41/E3
Dunaff (head), Ireland 17/F1
Dunaföldvár, Hungary 41/E3
Dunaharaszti, Hungary 41/E3
Dunajec (riv.), Czech. 41/F2
Dunajec (riv.), Poland 47/E4
Dunajská Streda, Czech. 41/D3
Dunakeszi, Hungary 41/E3
Dunalley, Tasmania 99/D4
Dunany (pt.), Ireland 17/J4
Dunaszekcső, Hungary 41/E3
Dunaújváros, Hungary 41/E3
Dunav (Danube) (riv.), Bulgaria 45/H4
Dunavecse, Hungary 41/E3
Dunbar, Iowa (†50158) 229/H5
Dunbar, Nebr. (68346) 264/J4
Dunbar, Okla. (†74557) 288/P6
Dunbar, Pa. (15431) 294/C6
Dunbar, Scotland 10/E2
Dunbar, Scotland 15/F4
Dunbar, S.C. (†29525) 296/H2
Dunbar, W. Va. (25064) 312/C6
Dunbar, Wis. (54119) 317/K4
Dunbarton○, N.H. (†03301) 268/D5
Dunbarton (trad. co.), Scotland 15/A5
Dunbarton Center, N.H. (†03301) 268/D5
Dunbeath, Scotland 15/E2
Dunbeg, Scotland 15/C4
Dunblane, Sask. 181/D4
Dunblane, Scotland 15/E4
Dunblane, Scotland 10/D1
Dunbridge, Ohio (43414) 284/C3
Duncan, Ariz. (85534) 198/F6
Duncan, Br. Col. 184/J3
Duncan (riv.), Br. Col. 184/J5
Duncan (isls.), China 85/E2
Duncan, Ill. (†61559) 222/D3
Duncan (passage), India 68/G6
Duncan, Miss. (38740) 256/C2
Duncan, Nebr. (68634) 264/G3
Duncan, Okla. (73533) 288/L5
Duncan (lake), Québec 174/B2
Duncan, S.C. (29334) 296/C2
Duncan, W. Va. (25240) 312/C5
Duncan Falls, Ohio (43734) 284/G6
Duncannon, Ireland 17/H7
Duncannon, Pa. (17020) 294/H5
Duncans, Jamaica 158/H5
Duncans Bridge, Mo. (†63437) 261/H3
Duncansby (head), Scotland 15/F2
Duncansby (head), Scotland 10/E1
Duncansville, Pa. (16635) 294/F5
Duncanville, Ala. (35456) 195/D4
Duncanville, Texas (75116) 303/G3
Dunchurch, Ontario 177/E2
Duncombe, Iowa (50532) 229/E4
Duncombe (bay), Norfolk I. 88/L5
Dundaga, U.S.S.R. 53/B2
Dundalk, Ireland 17/H3
Dundalk, Ireland 10/C4
Dundalk (bay), Ireland 10/C4
Dundalk (bay), Ireland 17/J4
Dundalk, Md. (21222) 245/N3
Dundalk, Ontario 177/D3
Dundarrach, N.C. (†28386) 281/L5
Dundas (isl.), Br. Col. 184/B3
Dundas, Greenl. 4/B13
Dundas, Greenland 146/M2
Dundas, Ill. (62425) 222/E5
Dundas, Minn. (55019) 255/E6
Dundas (str.), North. Terr. 88/E2
Dundas (str.), North. Terr. 93/B1
Dundas (pen.), N.W. Terrs. 187/G2
Dundas, Ohio (45625) 284/E7
Dundas (county), Ontario 177/J2
Dundas, Ontario 177/D4
Dundas, Va. (23938) 307/M7
Dundas (lake), W. Australia 88/C6
Dundas (lake), W. Australia 92/C6
Dundee, Fla. (33838) 212/E3
Dundee (East and West Dundee), Ill. (60118) 222/E1
Dundee, Ind. (†47348) 227/F4
Dundee, Iowa (52038) 229/L3
Dundee, Ky. (42338) 237/H5
Dundee, Mich. (48131) 250/F7
Dundee, Minn. (56126) 255/C7
Dundee, Miss. (38626) 256/D1
Dundee, N.Y. (14837) 276/F5
Dundee, Oreg. (97115) 291/A2
Dundee, Scotland 7/D3
Dundee, Scotland 15/F4
Dundee, Scotland 10/E2
Dundee, S. Africa 118/E5
Dundee, Texas (76358) 303/F4
Dundgovĭ, Mongolia 77/G2
Dundon, W. Va. (†25043) 312/D6
Dundonald, Scotland 15/D5
Dundrum, N. Ireland 17/K3
Dundrum (bay), N. Ireland 17/K3
Dundurn, Sask. 181/E4
Dundy (co.), Nebr. 264/C4
Dune Acres, Ind. (†46304) 227/C1
Dunedin, Fla. (33528) 212/B2
Dunedin, N. Zealand 2/T8
Dunedin, N. Zealand 100/C6
Dunedoo, N.S. Wales 97/E3
Dunellen, N.J. (08812) 273/D2
Dunes (Westlake), Oreg. (†97493) 291/C4
Dunfanaghy, Ireland 17/F1
Dunfee, Ind. (†46802) 227/G2
Dunfermline, Ill. (61524) 222/D3
Dunfermline, Sask. 181/D3
Dunfermline, Scotland 15/D1
Dunfermline, Scotland 10/C1
Dungalear Station, N.S. Wales 97/D1
Dungannon (dist.), N. Ireland 17/H3
Dungannon, N. Ireland 17/H3
Dungannon, Ontario 177/C4
Dungannon, Va. (24245) 307/D7
Dungarpur, India 68/C4
Dungarvan, Ireland 10/C4
Dungarvan, Ireland 17/F7
Dungarvan (harb.), Ireland 10/C4
Dungarvan (harb.), Ireland 17/G7
Dungarvon (riv.), New Bruns. 170/D2
Dungeness (pt.), Argentina 143/C7
Dungeness (pt.), Chile 138/F10
Dungeness (prom.), England 13/J7
Dungeness (prom.), England 10/G5
Dungeness, Wash. (†98382) 310/B2
Dungiven, N. Ireland 17/H2
Dungloe, Ireland 17/E2
Dungog, N.S. Wales 97/F3
Dungu, Zaire 115/E3
Dungunab, Sudan 59/C5
Dungunab, Sudan 111/G3
Dunham, Québec 172/E4
Dunhua (Tunhwa), China 77/L3
Dunhuang, China 77/E3
Dunkeld, Queensland 95/D5
Dunkeld, Scotland 15/E4
Dunkeld, Victoria 97/B5
Dunkellin (riv.), Ireland 17/D5
Dunkerton, Iowa (50626) 229/J3
Dunkery (hill), England 13/D6
Dunkineely, Ireland 17/E2
Dunkirk (riv.), Alberta 182/D1
Dunkirk (Dunkerque), France 28/E2
Dunkirk, France 28/E2
Dunkirk, Ind. (47336) 227/G4
Dunkirk, N.Y. (14048) 276/B5
Dunkirk, Ohio (45836) 284/C4
Dunkley, Br. Col. 184/F3
Dunklin (co.), Mo. 261/M10
Dunkwa, Ghana 106/D7
Dún Laoghaire, Ireland 10/D4
Dún Laoghaire, Ireland 17/K5
Dunlap, Ill. (61525) 222/D3
Dunlap, Ind. (†46514) 227/F1
Dunlap, Iowa (51529) 229/B5
Dunlap, Kansas (66848) 232/F3
Dunlap, Tenn. (37327) 237/L10
Dunlavin, Ireland 17/H5
Dunleath, Sask. 181/K4
Dunleer, Ireland 17/J4
Dunleith, Miss. (†38756) 256/C4
Dunlow, W. Va. (25511) 312/B6
Dunloy, N. Ireland 17/J1
Dunmanus (bay), Ireland 17/B8
Dunmanway, Ireland 17/C8
Dunmanway, Ireland 10/B5
Dunmor, Ky. (42339) 237/G6
Dunmore, Alberta 182/E5
Dunmore, Ireland 17/D4
Dunmore, Pa. (18512) 294/F7
Dunmore (lake), Vt. 268/A4
Dunmore, W. Va. (24934) 312/G6
Dunmore East, Ireland 17/G7
Dunn, La. (71236) 238/G2
Dunn, N.C. (28334) 281/M4
Dunn (co.), N. Dak. 282/E5
Dunn, Texas (79516) 303/D5
Dunn (co.), Wis. 317/C6
Dunnamanagh, N. Ireland 17/G2
Dunn Center, N. Dak. (58626) 282/E5
Dunnegan, Mo. (65640) 261/E7
Dunnell, Minn. (56127) 255/D7
Dunnellon, Fla. (32630) 212/D2
Dunnet, Scotland 15/E2
Dunnet (bay), Scotland 15/E2
Dunnet (head), Scotland 10/E1
Dunnet (head), Scotland 15/E2
Dunnigan, Calif. (95937) 204/C5
Dunning, Nebr. (68833) 264/D3
Dunning, Scotland 15/E4
Dunn Loring, Va. (22027) 307/S2
Dunnottar, Manitoba 179/E4
Dunnottar, S. Africa 118/J6
Dunns, W. Va. (†25841) 312/D7
Dunnsville, Va. (22454) 307/P5
Dunnville, Ky. (42528) 237/M6
Dunnville, Ontario 177/E5
Du Noir (riv.), Wyo. 319/C2
Dunolly, Victoria 97/B5
Dunoon, Scotland 15/A2
Dunoon, Scotland 10/A1
Dunphy, Nev. (†89821) 266/E2
Dunragit, Scotland 15/D6
Dunrea, Manitoba 179/C5
Dunreith, Ind. (47337) 227/F5
Duns, Scotland 10/E3
Duns, Scotland 15/F5
Dunscore, Scotland 15/E5
Dunseith, N. Dak. (58329) 282/K2
Dunshaughlin, Ireland 17/H5
Dunsmuir, Calif. (96025) 204/C2
Dunstable, England 10/F5
Dunstable, England 13/G6
Dunstable○, Mass. (01827) 249/J2
Dunster, Br. Col. 184/G3
Duntochter, Scotland 15/B2
Dunure, Scotland 15/D5
Dunvegan, Nova Scotia 168/F4
Dunvegan, Scotland 15/B3
Dunvegan, Loch (inlet), Scotland 15/B3
Dunville, Newf. 166/D2
Dunwoody, Georgia (†30338) 217/K1
Duo, W. Va. (†25984) 312/E6
Duolun, China 77/J3
Duong Dong, Vietnam 72/D5
Du Page (co.), Ill. 222/E2
Du Page, East Branch (riv.), Ill. 222/A6
Du Page, West Branch (riv.), Ill. 222/A6
Du Page (riv.), Ill. 222/E2
Duparquet, Québec 174/B3
Duperow, Sask. 181/C4
Duplessis, La. (70728) 238/K2
Duplin (co.), N.C. 281/O5
Dupo, Ill. (62239) 222/A3
Du Pont, Georgia (31630) 217/G9
Dupont, Ind. (47231) 227/G7
Dupont, Ohio (45837) 284/B3
Dupont, Pa. (18641) 294/F7
Du Pont, Wash. (98327) 310/C3
Dupont Manor, Del. (†19901) 245/R4
Dupree, S. Dak. (57623) 298/F3
Dupuis Corner, New Bruns. 170/F2
Dupuy, Québec 174/B3
Dupuyer, Mont. (59432) 262/D2
Duque de Bragança, Angola 115/C5
Duque de Caxias, Brazil 135/E3
Duque de York (isl.), Chile 138/C9
Duquesne, Mo. (†64801) 261/D8
Duquesne, Pa. (15110) 294/C7
Duquette, Minn. (55729) 255/F4
Du Quoin, Ill. (62832) 222/D5
Duquoin, Kansas (†67058) 232/D4
Dura, West Bank 65/C4
Durack (range), W. Australia 88/D3
Durağan, Turkey 63/F2
Duran, N. Mex. (88319) 274/D4
Durance (riv.), France 28/F6

Eastsound 363

Durand, Georgia (†31830) 217/C5
Durand, Ill. (61024) 222/D1
Durand, Mich. (48429) 250/E6
Durand, Wis. (54736) 317/C6
Durango, Colo. 188/E3
Durango, Colo. (81301) 208/D8
Durango, Iowa (52039) 229/M3
Durango (state), Mexico 150/G4
Durango, Mexico 146/H7
Durango, Mexico 150/G4
Durango, Spain 33/E1
Duranillin, W. Australia 92/B2
Durant, Iowa (52747) 229/M5
Durant, Miss. (39063) 256/E4
Durant, Okla. 188/G4
Durant, Okla. (74701) 288/O6
Duratón (riv.), Spain 33/E2
Durazno (dept.), Uruguay 145/C3
Durazno, Uruguay 145/C4
Durazno, Grande del (range), Uruguay 145/D4
Durban, Manitoba 179/A3
Durban, S. Africa 2/L7
Durban, S. Africa 102/F7
Durban, S. Africa 118/E5
Durbanville, S. Africa 118/F6
Durbe, U.S.S.R. 53/A2
Durbin, Ind. (†46060) 227/F4
Durbin, N. Dak. (58023) 282/R6
Durbin, W. Va. (26264) 312/G5
Durbuy, Belgium 27/H8
Düren, W. Germany 22/B3
Durfee (hill), R.I. 249/G5
Durg, India 68/E4
Durgapur, India 68/F4
Durgerdam, Netherlands 27/C4
Durham, Ark. (†72701) 202/C2
Durham, Calif. (95938) 204/D4
Durham, Conn. (06422) 210/E3
Durham○, Conn. (06422) 210/E3
Durham (co.), England 13/F3
Durham, England 13/J3
Durham, England 10/F3
Durham, Kansas (67438) 232/E3
Durham, Mo. (63438) 261/J3
Durham, N.H. (03824) 268/F5
Durham○, N.H. (03824) 268/F5
Durham (pt.), N. Zealand 100/D7
Durham, N.C. 188/L3
Durham (co.), N.C. 281/M3
Durham, N.C. (*27701) 281/M2
Durham, Okla. (73642) 288/G3
Durham (reg. munic.), Ontario 177/F3
Durham, Ontario 177/D3
Durham, Oreg. (†97233) 291/A2
Durham Bridge, New Bruns. 170/D2
Durham Center, Conn. (†06422) 210/E3
Durham Downs, Queensland 95/B5
Durham-Sud, Québec 172/E4
Durhamville, N.Y. (13054) 276/J4
Duri, N.S. Wales 97/F2
Durkee, Oreg. (97905) 291/K3
Durness, Scotland 15/D2
Durnford (pt.), Western Sahara 106/A4
Dürnten, Switzerland 39/G2
Duror, Scotland 15/C4
Durrell, Newf. 166/D4
Dürrenroth, Switzerland 39/E2
Durrës (Durazzo), Albania 45/D5
Durrës, Albania 7/F4
Durrington, England 13/F6
Durrow, Laoighis, Ireland 17/G6
Durrow, Offaly, Ireland 17/F5
Dursey (isl.), Ireland 17/A8
Dursunbey, Turkey 63/C3
Duruh, Iran 59/H3
Duruh, Iran 66/M4
D'Urville (isl.), N. Zealand 100/D4
Duryea, Pa. (18642) 294/F7
Dusa Marreb, Somalia 115/J2
Dûsh, Egypt 59/B5
Dûsh, Egypt 111/F3
Dushan, China 77/G6
Dushanbe, U.S.S.R. 54/H6
Dushanbe, U.S.S.R. 2/N4
Dushanbe, U.S.S.R. 48/G6
Dushore, Pa. (18614) 294/K2
Dusky (sound), N. Zealand 100/A6
Duson, La. (70529) 238/F6
Düsseldorf, W. Germany 7/E3
Düsseldorf, W. Germany 22/B3
Dustin, Okla. (74839) 288/O4
Dusty, N. Mex. (87934) 274/B5
Dusty, Wash. (†99143) 310/H4
Dutch (creek), Ark. 202/C4
Dutch Cap (cay), Virgin Is. (U.S.) 161/A4
Dutchess (co.), N.Y. 276/N7
Dutch Flat, Calif. (95714) 204/E4
Dutch Harbor, Alaska (†99685) 196/E4
Dutch John, Utah (84023) 304/E3
Dutch Mills, Ark. (†72744) 202/B2
Dutch Neck, N.J. (†08550) 273/D3
Dutchtown, Mo. (63745) 261/N8
Dutton, Ala. (35744) 195/G1
Dutton, Ark. (†72760) 202/C2
Dutton (mt.), Conn. 210/C1
Dutton, Mont. (59433) 262/E3
Dutton, Ontario 177/C5
Dutton (mt.), Utah 304/B5
Duval (co.), Fla. 212/E1
Duval, Sask. 181/G4
Duval (co.), Texas 303/F10
Duvalierville, Haiti 158/C6
Duvall, Wash. (98019) 310/D3
Duvergé, Dom. Rep. 158/D6
Duvernay, Alberta 182/E3
Duwadami, Saudi Arabia 59/D5
Duxbury (pt.), Calif. 204/H2
Duxbury, Mass. (02332) 249/M4
Duxbury○, Mass. (02332) 249/M4
Duxbury○, Vt. (†05676) 268/B3
Duyun (Tuyün), China 77/G6
Düzce, Turkey 63/D2
Duzdab (Zahedan), Iran 66/M6
Dvina, (bay), U.S.S.R. 52/E2
Dvina, Northern (riv.), U.S.S.R. 4/C7
Dvina, Northern (riv.), U.S.S.R. 7/J2
Dvina, Northern (riv.), U.S.S.R. 48/E3
Dvina, Northern (riv.), U.S.S.R. 52/F2
Dvina, Western (riv.) U.S.S.R. 53/C2
Dvina, Western (riv.), U.S.S.R. 48/C4
Dvina, Western (riv.), U.S.S.R. 52/C3
Dvina, Western (riv.), U.S.S.R. 7/G3
Dvinsk (Daugavpils), U.S.S.R. 52/C3
Dvory nad Žitavou, Czech. 41/E3
Dvůr Králové nad Labem, Austria 41/C1
Dwale, Ky. (41621) 237/R5
Dwarka, India 68/B4
Dwellingup, W. Australia 92/B2
Dwight, Ill. (60420) 222/E2
Dwight, Kansas (66849) 232/F3
Dwight, Nebr. (68635) 264/G3
Dwight, N. Dak. (58024) 282/S7
Dwight, Ontario 177/F2
Dworshak (res.), Idaho 220/C3
Dwyer, N. Mex. (†88034) 274/B6
Dwyer, Wyo. (82211) 319/G3
Dyas, Ala. (†36507) 195/C9
Dyat'kovo, U.S.S.R. 52/D4
Dybvad, Denmark 21/D3
Dyce, Scotland 15/F3
Dyckesville, Wis. (†54217) 317/L6
Dycusburg, Ky. (42037) 237/E6
Dyer, Ark. (72935) 202/B3
Dyer, Ind. (46311) 227/C1
Dyer, Ky. (†40115) 237/J5
Dyer, Nev. (89010) 266/C5
Dyer (cape), N.W.T. 162/K2
Dyer (cape), N.W. Terrs. 187/M3
Dyer (co.), Tenn. 237/C8
Dyer, Tenn. (38330) 237/D8
Dyer Brook○, Maine (†04747) 243/G3
Dyersburg, Tenn. (38024) 237/C8
Dyersville, Iowa (52040) 229/L3
Dyess, Ark. (72330) 202/K2
Dyess A.F.B., Texas 303/D5
Dyfed, Wales 13/C6
Dyje (riv.), Czech. 41/D2
Dyke (lake), Newf. 166/A3
Dykh-Tau (mt.), U.S.S.R. 52/F6
Dyle (riv.), Belgium 27/F7
Dysart, Iowa (52224) 229/J4
Dysart, Sask. 181/H5
Dysartsville, N.C. (†28761) 281/F3
Dzamïn Üüd, Mongolia 77/H3
Dzaoudzi (cap.), Comoros 118/H2
Dzavhan, Mongolia 77/E2
Dzavhan Gol (riv.), Mongolia 77/D2
Dzerzhinsk, U.S.S.R. 7/J3
Dzerzhinsk, U.S.S.R. 48/E4
Dzerzhinsk, U.S.S.R. 52/F3
Dzhalal-Abad, U.S.S.R. 48/H5
Dzhalilabad, U.S.S.R. 52/G7
Dzhalinda, U.S.S.R. 48/N4
Dzhambul, U.S.S.R. 54/J5
Dzhambul, U.S.S.R. 48/H5
Dzhankoy, U.S.S.R. 52/D5
Dzhelinda, U.S.S.R. 48/M2
Dzhetygara, U.S.S.R. 48/G4
Dzhezkazgan, U.S.S.R. 54/H5
Dzhezkazgan, U.S.S.R. 48/G5
Dzhugdzhur (range), U.S.S.R. 54/P4
Dzhugdzhur (range), U.S.S.R. 48/O4
Dzhul'fa, U.S.S.R. 52/G7
Dzhusaly, U.S.S.R. 48/G5
Działdowo, Poland 47/E2
Dzibalchén, Mexico 150/P7
Dzibichaltún (ruin), Mexico 150/P6
Dzidzantún, Mexico 150/P6
Dzierzoniów, Poland 47/C3
Dzilam de Bravo, Mexico 150/P6
Dzitbalché, Mexico 150/P6
Dzurh, Mongolia 77/E2
Dzüünharaa, Mongolia 77/G2
Dzuunmod, Mongolia 77/G2

E

Eabamet (lake), Ontario 175/C2
Eads, Colo. (81036) 208/O6
Eads, Tenn. (38028) 237/B10
Eadytown, S.C. (†29468) 296/G5
Eagan, Minn. (55111) 255/G6
Eagan, Tenn. (37730) 237/O7
Eagar, Ariz. (85925) 198/F4
Eagarville, Ill. (†62033) 222/D4
Eagle, Alaska 188/D5
Eagle, Alaska (99738) 196/K2
Eagle (creek), Ariz. 198/F5
Eagle (lake), Calif. 204/E3
Eagle (peak), Calif. 204/E2
Eagle (co.), Colo. 208/F3
Eagle, Colo. (81631) 208/F3
Eagle (riv.), Colo. 208/E3
Eagle, Idaho (83616) 220/B6
Eagle (creek), Ind. 227/E4
Eagle (lake), Iowa 229/F2
Eagle (creek), Ky. 237/M3
Eagle (lake), Maine 243/F1
Eagle (lake), Maine 243/E3
Eagle, Mich. (48822) 250/E6
Eagle (mt.), Minn. 255/G2
Eagle, Nebr. (68347) 264/H4
Eagle (riv.), Newf. 166/C3
Eagle, Ontario 177/C5
Eagle (lake), Ontario 177/F5
Eagle (lake), Ontario 177/E2
Eagle (creek), Oreg. 291/K3
Eagle (hills), Sask. 181/C3
Eagle (peak), Texas 303/C11
Eagle (mt.), Virgin Is. (U.S.) 161/E4
Eagle, Wis. (53119) 317/H2
Eagle (lake), Wis. 317/H2
Eagle (lake), Wis. 317/G3
Eagle (peak), Wyo. 319/B1
Eagle Bay, N.Y. (13331) 276/L3
Eagle Bend, Minn. (56446) 255/D4
Eagle Bridge, N.Y. (12057) 276/O5
Eagle Butte, S. Dak. (57625) 298/G4
Eagle City, Okla. (73658) 288/J3
Eagle Crags (mt.), Calif. 204/J8
Eagle Creek, Oreg. (97022) 291/E2
Eagle Grove, Iowa (50533) 229/F3
Eagle Harbor, Md. (†20608) 245/M6
Eagle Harbor, Mich. (49951) 250/A1
Eaglehawk, Victoria 97/C5
Eaglehill (creek), Sask. 181/D4
Eagle Lake, Fla. (33839) 212/E4
Eagle Lake, Maine (04739) 243/F1
Eagle Lake○, Maine (04739) 243/F1
Eagle Lake, Minn. (56024) 255/E6
Eagle Lake, Ontario 177/F2
Eagle Lake, Texas (77434) 303/H8
Eagle Mills, Ark. (71729) 202/E6
Eagle Mountain, Calif. (92241) 204/K10
Eagle Mountain (lake), Texas 303/E2
Eagle Nest, N. Mex. (87718) 274/D2
Eagle Nest (lake), N. Mex. 274/D2
Eagle Pass, Texas (78852) 303/D9
Eagle Point, Oreg. (97524) 291/E5
Eagle River, Alaska (99577) 196/C1
Eagle River, Mich. (49924) 250/A1
Eagle River, Wis. (54521) 317/H4
Eagle Rock, Mo. (65641) 261/E9
Eagle Rock, Va. (24085) 307/J5
Eaglesfield, Scotland 15/E5
Eaglesham, Alberta 182/B2
Eaglesham, Scotland 15/D5
Eagles Mere, Pa. (17731) 294/J3
Eagle Springs, N.C. (27242) 281/K4
Eagleton Village, Tenn. (†37801) 237/O9
Eagletown, Ind. (†46074) 227/E4
Eagletown, Okla. (74734) 288/S6
Eagleville, Calif. (96110) 204/E2
Eagleville, Conn. (†06268) 210/F1
Eagleville, Mo. (64442) 261/D2
Eagleville, Tenn. (37060) 237/H9
Eakly, Okla. (73033) 288/K4
Ealing, England 13/H8
Ealing, England 10/B5
Ear (lake), Sask. 181/B3
Earby, England 13/H1
Eardley (lake), Manitoba 179/F2
Ear Falls, Ontario 175/B2
Earl (lake), Calif. 204/A2
Earl, N.C. (28038) 281/F4
Earl, Wis. (54833) 317/C4
Earle, Ark. (72331) 202/K3
Earle Naval Weapons Sta., N.J. 273/E3
Earleton, Fla. (32631) 212/D2
Earleville, Md. (21919) 245/P3
Earl Grey, Sask. 181/G5
Earlham, Iowa (50072) 229/E6
Earlimart, Calif. (93219) 204/F8
Earling, Iowa (51530) 229/C5
Earlington, Ky. (42410) 237/F6
Earl Park, Ind. (47942) 227/C3
Earlsboro, Okla. (74840) 288/N4
Earlston, Scotland 15/F5
Earlton, Kansas (†66720) 232/G4
Earlton, Ontario 177/K5
Earltown, Nova Scotia 168/E3
Earlville, Ill. (60518) 222/E2
Earlville, Iowa (52041) 229/L4
Earlville, N.Y. (13332) 276/J5
Early (co.), Georgia 217/C8
Early, Iowa (50535) 229/C4
Early Branch, S.C. (29916) 296/F6
Earlysville, Va. (22936) 307/M4
Earn, Loch (lake), Scotland 15/D4
Earn (riv.), Scotland 15/E4
Earnslaw (mt.), N. Zealand 100/B6
Earp, Calif. (92242) 204/L9
Earth, Texas (79031) 303/B3
Earthquake (lake), Mont. 262/E6
Easby, N. Dak. (†58249) 282/O2
Easington, England 13/J3
Easingwold, England 13/F3
Eask (lake), Ireland 17/E2
Easky, Ireland 17/D3
Easley, S.C. (29640) 296/B2
East (cape), Alaska 196/K4
East (riv.), Conn. 210/E3
East (pt.), Fla. 212/E6
East (bay), La. 238/M8
East (pt.), Mass. 249/E6
East (range), Nev. 266/D2
East (pt.), N.S. Wales 97/J2
East (riv.), N.Y. 276/N9
East (cape), N. Zealand 87/H9
East (cape), N. Zealand 100/G2
East (bay), Nova Scotia 168/H3
East (riv.), Nova Scotia 168/F3
East (lake), Oreg. 291/F4
East (pt.), Pr. Edward I. 168/G2
East (Dezhnev) (cape), U.S.S.R. 4/C18
East (pt.), Virgin Is. (U.S.) 161/G4
Eastaboga, Ala. (36260) 195/F3
Eastabuchie, Miss. (39436) 256/F8
East Albany, Vt. (†05820) 268/C2
East Alburg, Vt. (†05440) 268/A2
East Aldfield, Québec 172/A4
East Alligator (riv.), North. Terr. 93/C2
East Alton, Ill. (62024) 222/A2
East Andover, Maine (04226) 243/B6
East Andover, N.H. (03231) 268/D5
East Angus, Québec 172/F4
Eastanollee, Georgia (30538) 217/F1
East Arcadia, N.C. (†28434) 281/N6
East Arlington, Vt. (05252) 268/A5
East Arrow Park, Br. Col. 184/J5
East Aspetuck (riv.), Conn. 210/B2
East Aurora, N.Y. (14052) 276/C5
East Baldwin, Maine (04024) 243/B8
East Bangor, Pa. (18013) 294/M4
East Bank, W. Va. (25067) 312/D6
East Barnet, Vt. (†05821) 268/C3
East Barre-Graniteville, Vt. (05649) 268/C3
East Barrington, N.H. (03825) 268/F5
East Baton Rouge (par.), La. 238/K1
East Bay, Nova Scotia 168/H3
East Bay (hills), Nova Scotia 168/H3
East Bend, N.C. (27018) 281/H2
East Berbice-Corantyne (dist.), Guyana 131/C3
East Berkshire, Vt. (05447) 268/B2
East Berlin, Conn. (06023) 210/E2
East Berlin, Pa. (17316) 294/J6
East Bernard, Texas (77435) 303/H8
East Bernstadt, Ky. (40729) 237/N6
East Berwick, Pa. (†18603) 294/K3
East Bethany, N.Y. (14054) 276/D5
East Bethel, Minn. (†55005) 255/E5
East Bethel, Vt. (†05032) 268/B4
East Bloomfield, N.Y. (14443) 276/E5
East Blue Hill, Maine (04629) 243/G7
East Blythe, Calif. (†92225) 204/L10
East Boothbay, Maine (04544) 243/D8
Eastborough, Kansas (†67201) 232/E4
Eastbourne, England 13/H7
Eastbourne, England 10/G5
Eastbourne, N. Zealand 100/B3
East Brady, Pa. (16028) 294/C3
East Braintree, Manitoba 179/G5
East Braintree, Mass. (†02184) 249/D8
East Braintree, Vt. (†05060) 268/B3
East Branch, N.Y. (13756) 276/K7
East Branch, Rocky (riv.), Ohio 284/G10
East Brewster, Mass. (†02631) 249/O5
East Brewton, Ala. (36426) 195/E8
East Bridgewater○, Mass. (02333) 249/L4
East Brisbane, Queensland 88/K3
East Brisbane, Queensland 95/E3
East Brookfield, Mass. (01515) 249/G4
East Brookfield○, Mass. (01515) 249/G4
East Brookfield, Vt. (†05036) 268/C3
East Brooklyn, Conn. (†06239) 210/H1
East Broughton, Québec 172/F3
East Broughton Station, Québec 172/F3
East Brownfield, Maine (†04010) 243/B8
East Brunswick○, N.J. (08816) 273/E3
East Burke, Vt. (05832) 268/D2
East Butler, Pa. (16029) 294/C4
East Calais, Vt. (05650) 268/C3
East Calder, Scotland 15/D2
East Camden, Ark. (71701) 202/E6
East Canaan, Conn. (06024) 210/B1
East Candia, N.H. (03040) 268/E5
East Canton, Ohio (44730) 284/H4
East Canyon (res.), Utah 304/C3
East Cape Girardeau, Ill. (†62957) 222/D6
East Carbon, Utah (84520) 304/D4
East Carondelet, Ill. (62240) 222/A3
East Carroll (par.), La. 238/H1
East Chain, Minn. (†56031) 255/D7
East Charleston, Vt. (05833) 268/D2
Eastchester, N.Y. (10709) 276/P6
East Chester, Nova Scotia 168/D4
East Chevington, England 13/F2
East Chezzetcook, Nova Scotia 168/E4
East Chicago, Ind. (46312) 227/C1
East Chicago Heights, Ill. (†60411) 222/C6
East China (sea) 54/O7
East China (sea), China 77/L6
East China (sea), Japan 81/C8
East China (sea), S. Korea 81/C8
East Chop (pt.), Mass. 249/M7
East Claridon, Ohio (44033) 284/H2
East Cleveland, Ohio (44112) 284/H9
East Coast Bays, N. Zealand 100/B1
East Concord, Vt. (†05906) 268/D3
East Conemaugh, Pa. (15909) 294/E5
East Corinth, Maine (04427) 243/F5
East Corinth, Vt. (05040) 268/C3
East Cote Blanche (bay), La. 238/G7
East Coulée, Alberta 182/D4
East Craftsbury, Vt. (†05826) 268/C2
East Dedham, Mass. (02026) 249/C8
East Demerara-West Coast Berbice (dist.), Guyana 131/C2
East Dennis, Mass. (02641) 249/O5
East Dereham, England 13/H5
East Dereham, England 10/G4
East Derry, N.H. (03041) 268/E6
East Detroit, Mich. (48021) 250/B6
East Devils (lake), N. Dak. 282/N4
East Dixfield, Maine (04227) 243/C6
East Dixmont, Maine (†04932) 243/E6
East Dorset, Vt. (05253) 268/A5
East Douglas, Mass. (01516) 249/G4
East Dover, Vt. (05341) 268/B6
East Dublin, Georgia (31021) 217/G5
East Dubuque, Ill. (61025) 222/C1
East Duke, Okla. (†73532) 288/H5
East Dundee (Dundee), Ill. (†60118) 222/E1
East Durham, N.Y. (12423) 276/M6
East Eddington, Maine (04428) 243/F6
East Ellijay, Georgia (30539) 217/C1
East Ely, Nev. 266/G3
Eastend, Sask. 181/C6
Eastend, Virgin Is. (U.S.) 161/D4
East Enterprise, Ind. (47019) 227/H7
Easter (isl.), Chile 87/Q8
Easter (isl.), Chile 2/D7
Eastern (pt.), Conn. 210/G3
Eastern (Arabian) (des.), Egypt 111/F2
Eastern (prov.), Kenya 115/G4
Eastern (bay), Md. 245/N5
Eastern (pt.), Mass. 249/M2
Eastern (creek), N.S. Wales 97/H3
Eastern Channel (str.), Japan 81/D7
Eastern Ghats (mts.), India 68/D6
Eastern Samar (prov.), Philippines 82/E5
Eastern Scheldt (est.), Netherlands 27/D5
Eastern Taurus (mts.), Turkey 63/J3
Eastern Wolf (isl.), New Bruns. 170/D4
Easterville, Manitoba 179/C1
East Fairfield, Vt. (05448) 268/B2
East Falkland (isl.), 143/E7
East Falkland (isl.), Falk. Is. 120/D8
East Falmouth (Teaticket), Mass. (02536) 249/M6
East Farnham, Québec 172/E4
East Faxon, Pa. (†17701) 294/J3
East Feliciana (par.), La. 238/H5
East Ferry, Nova Scotia 168/B4
East Flanders (prov.), Belgium 27/D7
East Flat Rock, N.C. (28726) 281/E4
Eastford○, Conn. (06242) 210/G1
East Fork, Little Miami (riv.), Ohio 284/C7
East Fork, Green (riv.), Wyo. 319/C3
East Foxboro, Mass. (†02035) 249/K4
East Franklin, Maine (†04634) 243/G6
East Franklin, Vt. (†05457) 268/B2
East Freedom, Pa. (16637) 294/E5
East Freetown, Mass. (02717) 249/L5
East Friesland (reg.), W. Germany 22/B2
East Frisian (isls.), W. Germany 22/B2
East Gaffney, S.C. (†29340) 296/D1
East Galesburg, Ill. (61430) 222/C3
Eastgate, Nev. (†89406) 266/D3
East Georgia, Vt. (†05455) 268/A2
East Germantown (Pershing), Ind. (†47370) 227/G5
East Germany 7/F3
EAST GERMANY 22
East Gillespie, Ill. (†62033) 222/D4
East Glacier Park, Mont. (59434) 262/C2
East Glastonbury, Conn. (06025) 210/E2
East Grafton, N.H. (†03240) 268/D4
East Granby○, Conn. (06026) 210/E1
East Grand Forks, Minn. (56721) 255/B3
East Grand Rapids, Mich. (†49506) 250/D6
East Granville, Vt. (†05669) 268/B3
East Greenbush, N.Y. (12061) 276/N5
East Green Harbour, Nova Scotia 168/C5
East Greenville, Ohio (†44666) 284/G4
East Greenville, Pa. (18041) 294/L5
East Greenwich, R.I. (02818) 249/H6
East Grinstead, England 10/G5
East Grinstead, England 13/G6
Eastgulf, W. Va. (25835) 312/D7
East Gull Lake, Minn. (†56401) 255/D4
East Haddam○, Conn. (06423) 210/F3
Eastham○, Mass. (02642) 249/O5
East Hampstead, N.H. (†03826) 268/E6
East Hampton, Conn. (06424) 210/E2
East Hampton○, Conn. (06424) 210/E2
Easthampton○, Mass. (01027) 249/D3
East Hampton, N.Y. (11937) 276/R9
East Hanover○, N.J. (07936) 273/E2
East Hardin, Ill. (†62031) 222/C4
East Hardwick, Vt. (05836) 268/C2
East Hartford○, Conn. (06108) 210/E1
East Hartland, Conn. (06027) 210/D1
East Harwich, Mass. (†02645) 249/O6
East Haven○, Conn. (06512) 210/D3
East Haven○, Vt. (05837) 268/D2
East Haverhill, N.H. (†03780) 268/D3
East Hazelcrest, Ill. (†60429) 222/C6
East Hebron, N.H. (03232) 268/D4
East Helena, Mont. (59635) 262/E4
East Hereford, Québec 172/F4
East Herkimer, N.Y. 276/L4
East Hickory, Pa. (16321) 294/D2
East Hills, N.Y. (†11576) 276/R7
East Hiram, Maine (†04041) 243/B8
East Hodge, La. (†71247) 238/E2
East Holden, Maine (04429) 243/F6
East Hope, Idaho (†83836) 220/B1
East Jackson, Maine (†04986) 243/E6
East Jamaica, Vt. (†05343) 268/B5
East Jordan, Mich. (49727) 250/D3
East Juliette, Georgia (†31046) 217/E4
East Keansburg, N.J. (07734) 273/E3
East Kelowna, Br. Col. 184/H5
East Kent, Conn. (†06785) 210/B2
East Kilbride, Scotland 15/B2
East Killingly, Conn. (06243) 210/H1
East Kingsford, Mich. (†49801) 250/A3
East Kingston○, N.H. (03827) 268/F6
East Knox, Maine (†04921) 243/E7
East Korea (bay), N. Korea 81/D4
East Lake, Mich. (49626) 250/C4
East Lake, Minn. (†55760) 255/E4
East Lake, N.C. (27931) 281/S3
Eastlake, Ohio (†44094) 284/J8
East Lake-Orient Park, Fla. (†33601) 212/C2
Eastland, Tenn. (†38583) 237/L9
Eastland (co.), Texas 303/F5
Eastland, Texas (76448) 303/F5
East Lansdowne, Pa. (†19050) 294/M7
East Lansing, Mich. (48823) 250/E6
East Laport, N.C. (†28723) 281/C4
East Las Vegas, Nev. (89112) 266/F6
East Laurinburg, N.C. (28352) 281/L5
East Lebanon, Maine (04027) 243/B9
East Lee, Mass. (†01238) 249/B3
Eastleigh, England 13/F7
Eastleigh, England 10/F5
East Lempster, N.H. (03605) 268/C5
East Limington, Maine (†04049) 243/B8
East Linton, Scotland 15/F5
East Litchfield, Conn. (†06759) 210/C1
East Livermore, Maine (04228) 243/C7
East Liverpool, Ohio (43920) 284/J4
East Loch (inlet), Hawaii 218/B3
East Loch Tarbert (inlet), Scotland 15/B3
East London, S. Africa 102/E8
East London, S. Africa 118/D6
East Longmeadow○, Mass. (01028) 249/E4
East Los Angeles, Calif. (90022) 204/C10
East Lowell, Maine (†04433) 243/G5
East Lyme○, Conn. (06333) 210/G3
East Lynn, Ill. (60932) 222/F3
East Lynn, W. Va. (25512) 312/B6
East Lynn (lake), W. Va. 312/B6
East Lynne, Mo. (64743) 261/D5
East Machias, Maine (04630) 243/J6
East Machias○, Maine (04630) 243/J6
East Machias (riv.), Maine 243/H6
East Madison, Maine (†04950) 243/D6
East Madison, N.H. (†03849) 268/E4
Eastmain, Que. 162/J5
Eastmain (riv.), Que. 146/L4
Eastmain (riv.), Que. 162/J5
Eastmain, Québec 174/B2
Eastmain (riv.), Québec 174/B2
Eastman, Georgia (31023) 217/F6
Eastman, Québec 172/E4
Eastman, Wis. (54626) 317/D9
East Marion, N.C. (†28752) 281/F3
East Meadow, N.Y. (11554) 276/R7
East Meredith, N.Y. (13757) 276/L6
East Middlebury, Vt. (05740) 268/A4
East Millcreek, Utah (84109) 304/C3
East Millinocket, Maine (04430) 243/F4
East Millinocket○, Maine (04430) 243/F4
East Millstone, N.J. (08873) 273/D3
East Milton, Mass. (†02186) 249/D7
East Mines, Nova Scotia 168/E3
East Moline, Ill. (61244) 222/C2
East Montpelier○, Vt. (05651) 268/B3
East Moriches, N.Y. (11940) 276/P9
East Morris, Conn. (†06763) 210/C2
East Murton, England 13/J3
East Musquash (lake), Maine 243/H5
East Naples, Fla. (†33940) 212/E5
East Newark, N.J. (†07100) 273/B2
East New Market, Md. (21631) 245/P6
East Newnan, Georgia (†30263) 217/C4
East New Portland, Maine (†04954) 243/D6
East Nishnabotna (riv.), Iowa 229/C6
East Northfield, Mass. (†01360) 249/E2
East Northport, N.Y. (11731) 276/O9
East Norton, Mass. (†02766) 249/K5
East Norwalk, Conn. (†06856) 210/B4
East Olympia, Wash. (98540) 310/B4
Easton, Calif. (93706) 204/F7
Easton○, Conn. (06612) 210/B4
Easton (res.), Conn. 210/B3
Easton, Ill. (62633) 222/D3
Easton, Kansas (66020) 232/G2
Easton, La. (†70586) 238/F5
Easton○, Maine (04740) 243/H2
Easton, Md. (21601) 245/O5
Easton○, Mass. (02334) 249/K4
Easton, Minn. (56025) 255/E7
Easton, Mo. (64443) 261/C3
Easton○, N.H. (03580) 268/D3
Easton, Pa. (18042) 294/M4
Easton, Wash. (98925) 310/D3
Easton, Wis. (†53936) 317/G8
Eastondale, Mass. (†02375) 249/K4
East Orange, N.J. (*07017) 273/B2
East Orland, Maine (04431) 243/F6
East Orleans, Mass. (02643) 249/P5
East Otis, Mass. (01029) 249/B4
East Otisfield, Maine (†04270) 243/B7
East Otto, N.Y. (14729) 276/C6
Eastover, S.C. (29044) 296/F4
East Palatka, Fla. (32031) 212/E2
East Palestine, Ohio (44413) 284/J4
East Park (res.), Calif. 204/C4
East Parsonfield, Maine (04028) 243/B8
East Peacham, Vt. (†05821) 268/C3
East Pembroke, Mass. (†02359) 249/M4
East Pembroke, N.Y. (14056) 276/D5
East Peoria, Ill. (61611) 222/D3
East Pepperell, Mass. (01437) 249/H2
East Peru (Peru), Iowa (†50222) 229/F6
East Peru, Maine (04229) 243/C7
East Petersburg, Pa. (17520) 294/K5
East Pleasant Plain, Iowa (†52540) 229/K6
Eastpoint, Fla. (32328) 212/B2
East Point, Georgia (30344) 217/K2
East Point, Ky. (41216) 237/R5
East Point, La. (71025) 238/D2
East Poland, Maine (†04210) 243/C7
East Poplar, Sask. 181/F6
Eastport, Idaho (83826) 220/B1
Eastport, Maine 188/N2
Eastport, Maine (04631) 243/K6
Eastport, Mich. (49627) 250/D3
Eastport, Newf. 166/D1
Eastport, N.Y. (11941) 276/P9
East Poultney, Vt. (05741) 268/A4
East Prairie, Mo. (63845) 261/O9
East Preston, England 13/G7
East Prospect, Pa. (17317) 294/J6
East Providence, R.I. (02914) 249/J5
East Putnam, Conn. (†06260) 210/H1
East Randolph, N.Y. (14730) 276/C6
East Randolph, Vt. (05041) 268/B4
East Retford, England 13/G4
East Retford, England 10/F4
East Richford, Vt. (†05476) 268/B2
East Ridge, Tenn. (37412) 237/L11
Eastriggs, Scotland 15/E5
East Rindge, N.H. (†03461) 268/D6
East River, Conn. (†06443) 210/E3
East River Saint Marys, Nova Scotia 168/F3
East Riverside-Kingshurst, New Bruns. 170/E3
East Rochester, N.Y. (14445) 276/F4
East Rochester, Ohio (44625) 284/H4
East Rockaway, N.Y. (11518) 276/R7
East Rutherford, N.J. (07073) 273/B2
Eastry, England 13/J6
East Ryegate, Vt. (05042) 268/C3
East Saint Louis, Ill. 188/J3
East Saint Louis, Ill. (*62201) 222/A2
East Sandwich, Mass. (02537) 249/N6
East Saugus, Mass. (†01906) 249/D6
East Sebago, Maine (04029) 243/B8
East Selkirk, Manitoba 179/F4
East Shoal (lake), Manitoba 179/E4
East Siberian (sea), U.S.S.R. 4/B1
East Siberian (sea), U.S.S.R. 54/T2
East Siberian (sea), U.S.S.R. 48/S2
Eastside, Oreg. (97420) 291/C4
East Side, Pa. (18634) 294/L3
East Sister (peak), Idaho 220/C2
East Sister (isl.), Tasmania 99/E1
East Smithfield, Pa. (18817) 294/J2
Eastsound, Wash. (98245) 310/B2

364 East Sparta

East Sparta, Ohio (44626) 284/H4
East Spencer, N.C. (28039) 281/J3
East Springfield, N.Y. (13333) 276/L5
East Springfield, Pa. (16411) 294/A2
East Stone Gap, Va. (24246) 307/C7
East Stoneham, Maine (04231) 243/B7
East Stroudsburg, Pa. (18301) 294/M4
East Sullivan, Maine (†04607) 243/G6
East Sullivan, N.H. (03445) 268/C6
East Sumner, Maine (†04220) 243/C7
East Sussex (co.), England 13/H7
East Swan (riv.), Minn. 255/F3
East Swanzey, N.H. (03446) 268/C6
East Syracuse, N.Y. (13057) 276/H4
East Tawas, Mich. (48730) 250/F4
East Templeton, Mass. (01438) 249/G2
East Thermopolis, Wyo. (†82443) 319/D2
East Thetford, Vt. (05043) 268/C4
East Thompson, Conn. (†06255) 210/H1
East Tintic (creek), Utah 304/B4
East Tohopekaliga (lake), Fla. 212/E3
East Troy, Wis. (53120) 317/J2
East Union, Maine (†04862) 243/E7
Eastvale, Pa. (†15010) 294/B4
Eastvale, Texas (†75067) 303/G1
East Vassalboro, Maine (04935) 243/D7
East Verde (riv.), Ariz. 198/D4
Eastview, Tenn. (†38367) 237/D10
East View, W. Va. (†26301) 312/F4
East Village, Conn. (†06468) 210/C3
Eastville, Georgia (†30677) 217/E3
Eastville, Va. (23347) 307/R6
East Wakefield, N.H. (03830) 268/E4
East Walker (riv.), Nev. 266/B4
East Wallingford, Vt. (05742) 268/B5
East Walpole, Mass. (02032) 249/C8
East Wareham, Mass. (02538) 249/M5
East Washington, Pa. (†15301) 294/B5
East Waterboro, Maine (04030) 243/B8
East Waterford, Pa. (17021) 294/G5
East Wenatchee, Wash. (98801) 310/E3
East Weymouth, Mass. (†02189) 249/E8
East Whately, Mass. (†01373) 249/D3
East Williamson, N.Y. (14449) 276/F4
East Willington, Conn. (†06279) 210/G1
East Wilton, Maine (04234) 243/C6
East Windsor○, Conn. (†06088) 210/E1
East Windsor Hill, Conn. (06028) 210/E1
East Winn, Maine (†04495) 243/G5
East Wolfeboro, N.H. (†03894) 268/E4
Eastwood, Mich. (†49001) 250/D6
Eastwood, N.S. Wales 88/K4
Eastwood, N.S. Wales 97/J3
Eastwood, Ontario 177/D4
East Woodstock, Conn. (06244) 210/H1
East Worcester, N.Y. (12064) 276/L5
East York, Ontario 177/J4
Eaton, Colo. (80615) 208/K1
Eaton, Ill. (†62454) 222/F4
Eaton, Ind. (47338) 227/G4
Eaton, Maine (†04424) 243/H4
Eaton (co.), Mich. 250/E6
Eaton (Eaton Center)○, N.H. (03832) 268/E4
Eaton, N.Y. (13334) 276/J5
Eaton, Ohio (45320) 284/A6
Eaton, Tenn. (38331) 237/C9
Eaton Center, N.H. (03832) 268/E4
Eaton Estates, Ohio (†44035) 284/G3
Eatonia, Sask. 181/B4
Eaton Rapids, Mich. (48827) 250/E6
Eatonton, Georgia (31024) 217/F4
Eatontown, N.J. (07724) 273/E3
Eatonville, Fla. (32751) 212/E3
Eatonville, Wash. (98328) 310/C4
Eau Claire, Mich. (49111) 250/C6
Eau Claire, Pa. (16030) 294/C3
Eau Claire, Lac à l' (lake), Que. 162/J4
Eau Claire (lake), Québec 174/C1
Eau Claire, Wis. 188/H2
Eau Claire (co.), Wis. 317/D6
Eau Claire, Wis. (54701) 317/D6
Eau Claire (riv.), Wis. 317/D6
Eau Galle, Wis. (54737) 317/B6
Eauripik (atoll), Micronesia 87/E5
Ebal (mt.), Jordan 65/C3
Ebano, Mexico 150/K5
Ebb, Fla. (†32331) 212/C1
Ebb and Flow (lake), Manitoba 179/C3
Ebbw Vale, Wales 13/B6
Ebbw Vale, Wales 10/E5
Ebeltoft, Denmark 21/D5
Ebeltoft, Denmark 18/G8
Ebenezer, Miss. (39064) 256/D5
Ebenezer, Sask. 181/J4
Ebenfurth, Austria 41/D3
Eben Junction, Mich. (49825) 250/B2
Ebensburg, Pa. (15931) 294/E5
Ebensee, Austria 41/B3
Eberbach, W. Germany 22/C4
Ebersbach, E. Germany 22/F3
Eberswalde-Finow, E. Germany 22/E2
Ebetsu, Japan 81/K2
Ebingen, W. Germany 22/C4
Ebinur Hu (lake), China 77/B2
Ebnat-Kappel, Switzerland 39/H2
Eboli, Italy 34/E4
Ebolowa, Cameroon 102/D4
Ebolowa, Cameroon 115/B3
Ebon (atoll), Marshall Is. 87/G5
Ebony, Va. (23845) 307/N7
Ebor, Manitoba 179/A5
Ebrach, W. Germany 22/D4
Ebrié (lag.), Ivory Coast 106/D8
Ebro, Fla. (32437) 212/C6
Ebro, Minn. (†56621) 255/C3
Ebro (riv.), Spain 7/D4
Ebro (riv.), Spain 33/G2
Ecatepec de Morelos, Mexico 150/L1
Ecaussinnes, Belgium 27/E7
Ecclefechan, Scotland 15/E5
Eccles, W. Va. (25836) 312/D7
Ecclesville, Trin. & Tob. 161/B11
Eceabat, Turkey 63/B6
Echallens, Switzerland 39/C3
Echarate, Peru 128/F9
Echeconnee, Georgia (†31008) 217/E5
Echmiadzin, U.S.S.R. 52/F6
Echo, Ala. (†36360) 195/G8
Echo (cliffs), Ariz. 198/D2
Echo, La. (71330) 238/F4
Echo, Minn. (56237) 255/C6
Echo (lake), N.J. 273/E1
Echo, Oreg. (97826) 291/H2
Echo (lake), Tasmania 99/C4
Echo, Utah (84024) 304/C3
Echo (res.), Utah 304/C3
Echo (lake), Vt. 268/D2
Echo Bay, Ontario 177/J5
Echo Bay, Ontario 175/D3
Echola, Ala. (35457) 195/C4
Echo Lake, N.J. (†07435) 273/E1
Echo Lake, Nova Scotia 168/E4
Echols (co.), Georgia 217/G9
Echols, Ky. (42340) 237/H6
Echo Valley Prov. Park, Sask. 181/G5
Echt, Netherlands 27/H6
Echternach, Luxembourg 27/J9
Echuca, Victoria 97/C5
Echuca, Victoria 88/G7
Écija, Spain 33/D4
Eck, Loch (lake), Scotland 15/A1
Eckelson, N. Dak. (58432) 282/O6
Eckerman, Mich. (49728) 250/E2
Eckernförde, W. Germany 22/D1
Eckerty, Ind. (47116) 227/D8
Eckhart Mines, Md. (21528) 245/C2
Eckley, Colo. (80727) 208/P2
Eckman, N. Dak. (†58760) 282/H2
Eckman, W. Va. (24829) 312/C8
Eckville, Alberta 182/C3
Eclectic, Ala. (36024) 195/F5
Eclipse (harb.), Newf. 166/B2
Eclipse (sound), N.W. Terrs. 187/L2
Economy, Ind. (47339) 227/G5
Economy, Nova Scotia 168/D3
Economy, Pa. (†15005) 294/B4
Écorce (lake), Québec 172/A2
Écorces (riv.), Québec 172/F1
Ecorse, Mich. (48229) 250/B7
Écrins, Les (mt.), France 28/G5
Ecru, Miss. (38841) 256/F2
Ector (co.), Texas 303/B6
Ecuador 2/D6
Ecuador 120/B3
ECUADOR 128
Écublens, Switzerland 39/B3
Ecum Secum, Nova Scotia 168/F3
Ecum Secum Bridge, Nova Scotia 168/F4
Edam, Sask. 181/C2
Edam-Volendam, Netherlands 27/G4
Eday (isl.), Scotland 10/E1
Eday (isl.), Scotland 15/F1
Edberg, Alberta 182/D3
Edcouch, Texas (78538) 303/G11
Edd, Ethiopia 111/H5
Edd, Ethiopia 59/D7
Ed Da'ein, Sudan 111/E5
Ed Damazin, Sudan 111/F5
Ed Damer, Sudan 111/F4
Ed Damer, Sudan 59/B6
Ed Damer, Sudan 102/F3
Ed Debba, Sudan 111/F4
Ed Debba, Sudan 59/B6
Edderton, Scotland 15/D3
Eddiceton, Miss. (39634) 256/C8
Eddington, Maine (†04428) 243/F6
Eddington○, Maine (†04428) 243/F6
Eddington, Pa. (19020) 294/N5
Eddleston, Scotland 15/E5
Eddontenajon, Br. Col. 184/K2
Eddrachillis (bay), Scotland 15/C2
Ed Dueim, Sudan 59/B7
Ed Dueim, Sudan 111/F5
Ed Dueim, Sudan 102/F3
Eddy (co.), N. Mex. 274/E6
Eddy (co.), N. Dak. 282/N4
Eddy, Texas (76524) 303/G6
Eddystone (rocks), England 13/C7
Eddystone (rocks), England 10/D5
Eddystone, Manitoba 179/C3
Eddystone, Pa. (†19013) 294/M7
Eddystone (pt.), Tasmania 88/H8
Eddystone (pt.), Tasmania 99/E2
Eddyville, Ill. (62928) 222/E6
Eddyville, Iowa (52553) 229/H6
Eddyville, Ky. (42038) 237/E6
Eddyville, Nebr. (68834) 264/E3
Eddyville, Oreg. (97343) 291/D3
Ede, Netherlands 27/H4
Ede, Nigeria 106/E7
Edéa, Cameroon 115/B3
Edelény, Hungary 41/F2
Edelstein, Ill. (61526) 222/D3
Eden, Ariz. (85535) 198/F6
Edén, Ecuador 128/E3
Eden (riv.), England 13/E3
Eden (riv.), England 10/E3
Eden, Georgia (31307) 217/K6
Eden, Idaho (83325) 220/D7
Eden, Ind. (†46140) 227/F5
Eden, Manitoba 179/C4
Eden, Md. (21822) 245/R7
Eden, Miss. (39065) 256/D5
Eden, Mont. (†59401) 262/E3
Eden, N.S. Wales 97/E5
Eden, N.Y. (14057) 276/C5
Eden, N.C. (27288) 281/K1
Eden (riv.), Scotland 15/F4
Eden, S. Dak. (57232) 298/P2
Eden, Texas (76837) 303/E6
Eden, Utah (84310) 304/C2
Eden○, Vt. (05652) 268/B2
Eden, Wis. (53019) 317/K8
Eden, Wyo. (82926) 319/C3
Edenburg, Sask. 181/E3
Edenburg, S. Africa 118/D5
Edendale, S. Africa 118/D5
Edenderry, Ireland 10/C4
Edenderry, Ireland 17/G5
Edenhope, Victoria 97/A5
Eden Mills, Ontario 177/D4
Eden Mills, Vt. (05653) 268/C2
Eden Prairie, Minn. (55344) 255/G6
Edenton, N.C. (27932) 281/R2
Edenton, Ohio (†45122) 284/C7
Edenvale, S. Africa 118/H6
Eden Valley, Minn. (55329) 255/D5
Eden Valley (res.), Wyo. 319/C3
Edenville, Mich. (48620) 250/E5
Edenwold, Sask. 181/G5
Eder (res.), W. Germany 22/C3
Eder (riv.), W. Germany 22/C3
Ederney and Kesh, N. Ireland 17/F2
Edgar (co.), Ill. 222/F4
Edgar, Mont. (59026) 262/H5
Edgar, Nebr. (68935) 264/F4
Edgar, Wis. (54426) 317/G6
Edgard, La. (70049) 238/M3
Edgar Springs, Mo. (65462) 261/J7
Edgarton, W. Va. (25672) 312/B7
Edgartown, Mass. (02539) 249/M7
Edgartown○, Mass. (02539) 249/M7
Edge (isl.), Norway 4/B8
Edgecliff, Texas (†76101) 303/E2
Edgecomb○, Maine (†04556) 243/D8
Edgecombe (co.), N.C. 281/O3
Edgecumbe (cape), Alaska 196/L1
Edgecumbe, N. Zealand 100/F2
Edgefield, La. (†71019) 238/D2
Edgefield (co.), S.C. 296/D4
Edgefield, S.C. (29824) 296/C4
Edge Hill, Georgia (†30810) 217/G4
Edgehill, Va. (†22485) 307/O4
Edgeley, N. Dak. (58433) 282/N7
Edgeley, Sask. 181/H5
Edgell (isl.), N.W. Terrs. 187/M3
Edgemere, Idaho (†83856) 220/B1
Edgemere, Md. (†21219) 245/N4
Edgemont, Ark. (72044) 202/F2
Edgemont, S. Dak. (57735) 298/B7
Edgemoor, Del. (†19801) 245/S1
Edgemoor, S.C. (29712) 296/E2
Edgemount, N.C. (28645) 281/F2
Edgeøya (isl.), Norway 18/E2
Edgerly, La. (†70668) 238/C6
Edgerton, Alberta 182/E3
Edgerton, Ind. (†46797) 227/H2
Edgerton, Kansas (66021) 232/H3
Edgerton, Minn. (56128) 255/B7
Edgerton, Mo. (64444) 261/C3
Edgerton, Ohio (43517) 284/A3
Edgerton, Va. (†23868) 307/N7
Edgerton, Wis. (53534) 317/H10
Edgerton, Wyo. (82635) 319/F2
Edgewater, Br. Col. 184/J5
Edgewater, Colo. (80214) 208/J3
Edgewater, Fla. (32032) 212/F3
Edgewater, N.J. (07020) 273/C2
Edgewater, Wis. (54834) 317/D4
Edgewater Park○, N.J. (†08010) 273/D3
Edgewood, Br. Col. 184/H5
Edgewood, Calif. (96094) 204/C2
Edgewood, Fla. (†32801) 212/E3
Edgewood, Ill. (62426) 222/E5
Edgewood, Ind. (†46011) 227/F4
Edgewood, Iowa (52042) 229/K3
Edgewood, Ky. (†41017) 237/S2
Edgewood, Md. (21040) 245/N3
Edgewood, N. Mex. (87015) 274/C3
Edgewood, Ohio (†44004) 284/J2
Edgewood, Pa. (†15218) 294/B7
Edgeworth, Pa. (†15143) 294/B4
Edgington, Ill. (†61284) 222/C2
Édhessa, Greece 45/F5
Edievale, N. Zealand 100/B6
Edina, Minn. (55424) 255/G5
Edina, Mo. (63537) 261/H2
Edinboro, Pa. (16412) 294/B2
Edinburg, Ill. (62531) 222/D4
Edinburg, Miss. (†39051) 256/F5
Edinburg, Mo. (†64683) 261/E2
Edinburg, N. Dak. (58227) 282/P3
Edinburg, Pa. (16116) 294/B3
Edinburg, Texas (78539) 303/F11
Edinburg, Va. (22824) 307/M3
Edinburgh, Ind. (46124) 227/E6
Edinburgh (cap.), Scotland 7/D3
Edinburgh (cap.), Scotland 15/D1
Edinburgh (cap.), Scotland 10/C1
Edingen (Enghien), Belgium 27/D7
Edirne (prov.), Turkey 63/B2
Edirne, Turkey 7/G4
Edirne, Turkey 63/B2
Edirne, Turkey 59/A1
Edison, Calif. (93220) 204/G8
Edison (lake), Calif. 204/F6
Edison, Georgia (31746) 217/C7
Edison, Nebr. (68936) 264/E4
Edison○, N.J. (*08817) 273/E2
Edison, Ohio (43320) 284/E4
Edison, Wash. (98246) 310/C2
Edison Nat'l Hist. Site, N.J. 273/A2
Edisto (isl.), S.C. 296/G6
Edisto (riv.), S.C. 296/G7
Edisto Beach, S.C. (†29438) 296/G7
Edisto Island, S.C. (29438) 296/G6
Edith, Georgia (†31631) 217/G9
Edithburgh, S. Australia 94/E6
Ediz Hook (pen.), Wash. 310/B2
Edjeleh, Algeria 106/F3
Edmeston, N.Y. (13335) 276/K5
Edmond, Kansas (67636) 232/C2
Edmond, Okla. (73034) 288/M3
Edmonds, Wash. (98020) 310/C3
Edmondson, Ark. (72332) 202/K3
Edmondt, Fr. Guiana 131/E3
Edmonson (co.), Ky. 237/J6
Edmonson, Texas (79032) 303/C3
Edmonston, Md. (†20781) 245/F4
Edmonton (cap.), Alberta 182/D3
Edmonton, Alta. 146/G4
Edmonton (cap.), Alta. 162/E5
Edmonton, Canada 2/D3
Edmonton, Ky. (42129) 237/K7
Edmonton Beach, Alberta 182/C3
Edmore, Mich. (48829) 250/E5
Edmore, N. Dak. (58330) 282/O3
Edmore, Sask. 181/H4
Edmund, Wis. (†53533) 317/F9
Edmunds, Maine (†04628) 243/J6
Edmunds, N. Dak. (†58746) 282/M5
Edmunds (co.), S. Dak. 298/L3
Edmundson, Mo. (†63101) 261/O2
Edmundston, N. Br. 162/K6
Edmundston, New Bruns. 170/B1
Edna, Ala. (†36922) 195/B6
Edna, Iowa (†51246) 229/A2
Edna, Kansas (67342) 232/G4
Edna, Texas (77957) 303/H9
Edna Bay, Alaska (†99901) 196/M2
Edo (riv.), Japan 81/P2
Edolo, Italy 34/C1
Edom, Texas (†75656) 303/J5
Edon, Ohio (43518) 284/A2
Édouard (lake), Québec 172/E2
Edrans, Manitoba 179/C4
Edray, W. Va. (†24954) 312/F6
Edremit, Turkey 63/B3
Edremit, Turkey 59/A2
Edremit (gulf), Turkey 63/B3
Edri, Libya 111/B2
Edsbyn, Sweden 18/J6
Edson, Alberta 182/B3
Edson, Alta. 162/E5
Edson, Kansas (67733) 232/A2
Eduardo Castex, Argentina 143/D4
Edwall, Wash. (99008) 310/H3
Edwand, Alberta 182/D2
Edward (lake) 102/E5
Edward, N.C. (27821) 281/R4
Edward (lake), Uganda 115/E4
Edward (lake), Zaire 115/E4
Edward MacDowell (res.), N.H. 268/D6
Edwards, Colo. (81632) 208/F3
Edwards (co.), Ill. 222/E5
Edwards, Ill. (61528) 222/D3
Edwards (riv.), Ill. 222/C2
Edwards (co.), Kansas 232/C4
Edwards (lake), La. 238/C2
Edwards, Miss. (39066) 256/C6
Edwards, Mo. (65326) 261/F6
Edwards, N.Y. (13635) 276/K2
Edwards (co.), Texas 303/D7
Edwards (plat.), Texas 303/C7
Edwards A.F.B., Calif. 204/H9
Edwardsburg, Mich. (49112) 250/C7
Edwardsport, Ind. (47528) 227/C7
Edwardsville, Ala. (36261) 195/H3
Edwardsville, Ill. (62025) 222/B2
Edwardsville, Ind. (†47150) 227/F8
Edwardsville, Kansas (66113) 232/H2
Edwardsville, Pa. (18704) 294/E7
Edward VII (pen.) 5/B11
Edward VIII (bay) 5/C4
Edwight, W. Va. (†25189) 312/C7
Edwin, Ala. (†36317) 195/H7
Edwin, Manitoba 179/D5
Edzell, Scotland 15/F4
Eefde, Netherlands 27/J4
Eek, Alaska (99578) 196/F2
Eeklo, Belgium 27/D6
Eel (riv.), Calif. 204/B4
Eel (riv.), Ind. 227/C6
Eel (riv.), Ind. 227/F3
Eel River Bridge, New Bruns. 170/F1
Eel River Crossing, New Bruns. 170/D1
Eems (riv.), Netherlands 27/K2
Eersterivier, S. Africa 118/F6
Efate (isl.), Vanuatu 87/G7
Eferding, Austria 41/B2
Effie, La. (71331) 238/F4
Effie, Minn. (56639) 255/E3
Effigy Mounds Nat'l Mon., Iowa 229/L2
Effingham (co.), Georgia 217/K6
Effingham (co.), Ill. 222/E4
Effingham, Ill. (62401) 222/E4
Effingham, Kansas (66023) 232/G2
Effingham, S.C. (29541) 296/H3
Effingham Falls, N.H. (†03814) 268/E4
Effort, Pa. (18330) 294/M4
Efland, N.C. (27243) 281/L2
Eflâni, Turkey 63/E2
Egadi (isls.), Italy 34/C6
Egan, Ill. (61026) 222/D1
Egan (range), Nev. 266/G4
Egan, S. Dak. (57024) 298/R6
Egaña, Uruguay 145/B4
Eganville, Ontario 177/G2
Egbert, Wyo. (†82053) 319/H4
Ege, Ind. (†46763) 227/G2
Egegik, Alaska (99579) 196/G3
Egeland, N. Dak. (58331) 282/M2
Eger, Hungary 41/F3
Egeria, W. Va. (†25902) 312/D7
Egernsund, Denmark 21/C8
Egerton (mt.), W. Australia 92/B4
Egg (isl.), Manitoba 179/E3
Egg (creek), N. Dak. 282/H3
Egg, Switzerland 39/G2
Eggenburg, Austria 41/C2
Eggertsville, N.Y. (†14226) 276/C5
Egg Harbor, Wis. (54209) 317/M5
Egg Harbor City, N.J. (08215) 273/D4
Egg Island (pt.), N.J. 273/C5
Eggiwil, Switzerland 39/E3
Egg Lagoon, Tasmania 99/A1
Eggleston, Va. (24086) 307/G6
Egham, England 13/G8
Egham, England 10/B5
Éghezée, Belgium 27/F7
Egilsay (isl.), Scotland 15/F1
Eglin A.F.B., Fla. 212/C6
Eglington (isl.), N.W.T. 162/L3
Eglinton (cape), N.W. Terrs. 187/M2
Eglinton (isl.), N.W. Terrs. 187/F2
Eglisau, Switzerland 39/G1
Eglon, W. Va. (26716) 312/G4
Egmond aan Zee, Netherlands 27/E3
Egmondville, Ontario 177/C4
Egmont (key), Fla. 212/D4
Egmont (cape), N. Zealand 100/D3
Egmont (mt.), N. Zealand 100/D3
Egmont (cape), Nova Scotia 168/H2
Egmont (bay), Pr. Edward I. 168/D2
Egmont (cape), Pr. Edward I. 168/D2
Egnach, Switzerland 39/H1
Egnar, Colo. (81325) 208/B7
Egremont, Alberta 182/D2
Egremont, England 13/D3
Eğridir, Turkey 63/D4
Eğridir (lake), Turkey 59/B2
Eğridir (lake), Turkey 63/D4
Egtved, Denmark 21/C6
Egvekinot, U.S.S.R. 48/S3
Egyek, Hungary 41/F3
Egypt 2/L4
Egypt 102/E2
EGYPT 111/E2
EGYPT 59/A4
Egypt, Georgia (†31329) 217/K6
Egypt, Miss. (†38860) 256/G3
Egypt Lake, Fla. (†33614) 212/C2
Eha Amufu, Nigeria 106/F7
Ehime (pref.), Japan 81/F7
Ehingen, W. Germany 22/C4
Ehrenberg (range), North. Terr. 93/B7
Ehrenburg, Ariz. (85334) 198/A5
Ehrenfeld, Pa. (†15956) 294/E5
Ehrhardt, S.C. (29081) 296/E5
Ehrwald, Austria 41/A3
Eiao (isl.), Fr. Poly. 87/M6
Eibar, Spain 33/E1
Eichstätt, W. Germany 22/D4
Eider (riv.), W. Germany 22/C1
Eidfjord, Norway 18/E6
Eidsfoss, Norway 18/C4
Eidson, Tenn. (37731) 237/P7
Eidsvold, Queensland 95/D5
Eidsvoll, Norway 18/G6
Eielson A.F.B., Alaska 196/J2
Eigenbrakel (Braine-l'Alleud), Belgium 27/E7
Eigersund, Norway 18/D7
Eigg (mt.), Nova Scotia 168/F3
Eigg (isl.), Scotland 15/B4
Eigg (isl.), Scotland 10/C2
Eigg (sound), Scotland 15/B4
Eight Degree (chan.), India 68/C7
Eighteen Mile (peak), Idaho 220/E5
Eight Mile (brook), Conn. 210/C3
Eight Mile (riv.), Conn. 210/F3
Eights Coast (reg.) 5/B14
Eighty Eight, Ky. (42130) 237/K7
Eighty Mile (beach), W. Australia 88/C3
Eighty Mile (beach), W. Australia 92/C2
Eijerlandsche Gat (str.), Netherlands 27/F2
Eil, Loch (lake), Scotland 15/C4
Eil, Somalia 115/J2
Eildon, Victoria 97/C5
Eildon (lake), Victoria 97/C5
Eileen, Ill. (†60416) 222/E2
Eileen (lake), N.W.T. 162/F3
Eilenburg, E. Germany 22/E3
Eilerts de Haan (mts.), Suriname 131/C4
Eina, Norway 18/G6
Einbeck, W. Germany 22/C3
Eindhoven, Netherlands 27/G6
'Ein Gedi, Israel 65/C5
'Ein Harod, Israel 65/C2
'Ein Netafim (well), Israel 65/D5
Einsiedeln, Switzerland 39/G2
Eirunepé, Brazil 132/G10
Eirunepé, Brazil 120/B3
Eisenach, E. Germany 22/D3
Eisenberg, E. Germany 22/D3
Eisenerz, Austria 41/C3
Eisenhower (mt.), Alberta 182/C4
Eisenhüttenstadt, E. Germany 22/F2
Eisenkappel-Vellach, Austria 41/C3
Eisenstadt, Austria 41/D3
Eiserfeld, W. Germany 22/C3
Eishort, Loch (inlet), Scotland 15/B3
Eisleben, E. Germany 22/D3
Eisling (mts.), Luxembourg 27/H9
Eitzen, Minn. (55931) 255/G7
Ejby, Denmark 21/C7
Ejea de los Caballeros, Spain 33/F1
Ejido, Venezuela 124/C3
Ejin, China 77/F3
Ejin Horo, China 77/G4
Ejutla de Crespo, Mexico 150/L8
Ekalaka, Mont. (59324) 262/M5
Ekenäs, Finland 18/N6
Ekeren, Belgium 27/E6
Eketahuna, N. Zealand 100/E4
Ekibastuz, U.S.S.R. 48/H4
Ekibin, Queensland 88/K3
Ekimchan, U.S.S.R. 48/O4
Ekin, Ind. (†46072) 227/E4
Ekonk, Conn. (†06384) 210/H2
Ekron, Ky. (40117) 237/J5
Eksjö, Sweden 18/J8
Ekuk, Alaska (†99569) 196/G3
Ekwan (riv.), Ont. 162/H5
Ekwan (riv.), Ontario 175/C2
Ekwok, Alaska (99580) 196/G3
El Aaiún (Laayoune), Morocco 102/A2
El Aaiún (Laayoune), Western Sahara 106/B3
El Abbasiya, Sudan 111/F5
El Abiar, Libya 111/D1
El Abiod Sidi Cheikh, Algeria 106/E2
El Agheila, Libya 111/C1
Elaine, Ark. (72333) 202/J5
El 'Al, Jordan 65/D4
El 'Alamein, Egypt 111/E1
El 'Alamein, Egypt 59/A3
El Almacén, Venezuela 124/G4
El Amparo de Apure, Venezuela 124/C4
Elams, N.C. (†23919) 281/O1
Elamton, Ky. (41420) 237/P5
Elamville, Ala. (†36311) 195/G7
Eland, Wis. (54427) 317/H6
El Ángel, Ecuador 128/C2
El Arahal, Spain 33/D4
El 'Arish, Egypt 59/B3
El 'Arish, Egypt 111/F1
El Asiento, Bolivia 136/B6
El Asnam, Algeria 106/E1
El Asnam, Algeria 102/C1
Elassón, Greece 45/F6
Elat, Israel 65/D6
Elath (Elat), Israel 65/D6
Elath, Israel 59/B4
El Athale (lake), Somalia 115/J3
Elato (atoll), Micronesia 87/E5
El 'Atrun (oasis), Sudan 111/E4
El 'Auja, Israel 65/D5
Elâzığ (prov.), Turkey 63/H3
Elâzığ, Turkey 59/C2
Elâzığ, Turkey 63/H3
El Azizia, Libya 111/B1
El Azúcar (res.), Mexico 150/K3
Elba, Idaho (83326) 220/E7
Elba, Ala. (36323) 195/F8
Elba (isl.), Italy 7/E4
Elba (isl.), Italy 34/C3
Elba, Minn. (†55910) 255/F6
Elba, Nebr. (68835) 264/F3
Elba, N.Y. (14058) 276/D4
Elba, Ohio (45786) 284/H6
El Bab, Syria 63/G4
El Balqa (dist.), Jordan 65/D4
El Banco, Colombia 126/D3
El Barco, Spain 33/C1
El Barco de Ávila, Spain 33/D2
El Bardi, Libya 111/D1
El Barkat, Libya 111/B3
Elbasan, Albania 45/E5
El Baúl, Venezuela 124/D3
El Bawiti, Egypt 111/E2
El Bawiti, Egypt 102/E2
El Bawiti, Egypt 59/A4
El Bayadh, Algeria 106/E2
El Bayadh, Algeria 102/C1
Elbe (riv.) 7/F3
Elbe (riv.), E. Germany 22/D2
Elbe, Wash. (98330) 310/C4
Elbe (riv.), W. Germany 22/C2
El Beida, Yemen Arab Rep. 59/E7
El Beni (dept.), Bolivia 136/C3
Elberfeld, Ind. (47613) 227/C8
Elberon, Iowa (52225) 229/J4
Elberon, N.J. (07740) 273/F3
Elberon, Va. (23846) 307/P6
Elbert (mt.), Colo. 188/E3
Elbert (co.), Colo. 208/L4
Elbert, Colo. (80106) 208/L4
Elbert (mt.), Colo. 208/G4
Elbert (co.), Georgia †17/G2
Elbert, Texas (76359) 303/E4
Elbert, W. Va. (24830) 312/C8
Elberta, Ala. (36530) 195/C10
Elberta, Georgia (†31093) 217/E5
Elberta, Mich. (49628) 250/C4
Elberta, Utah (84626) 304/B4
Elberton, Georgia (30635) 217/G2
Elberton, Wash. (†99130) 310/H4
Elbeuf, France 28/D3
Elbing, Kansas (67041) 232/E3
Elbing (Elblag), Poland 47/D1
El Bira, West Bank 65/C4
Elbistan, Turkey 63/G3
Elblag (prov.), Poland 47/D1
Elblag, Poland 47/D1
Elblag, Poland 7/F3
El Bolsón, Argentina 143/B5
Elbon, Pa. (†15823) 294/E3
El Bonillo, Spain 33/E3
El Boquerón (pass), Peru 128/E7
El Borma, Tunisia 106/F2
Elbow (riv.), Alberta 182/C4
Elbow (lake), Manitoba 179/G4
Elbow (lake), Minn. 255/C3
Elbow, Sask. 181/E4
Elbow Lake, Minn. (56531) 255/B5
Elbridge, N.Y. (13060) 276/G5
Elbridge, Tenn. (38227) 237/C8
El'brus (mt.), U.S.S.R. 7/J4
El'brus (mt.), U.S.S.R. 52/F6
El Buheyrat (prov.), Sudan 111/E6
El Bur, Somalia 115/J3
Elburg, Netherlands 27/H4
El Burgo de Osma, Spain 33/E2
Elburn, Ill. (60119) 222/E2
Elburz (mts.), Iran 59/F2
Elburz (mts.), Iran 66/G2
El Cajon, Calif. (*92020) 204/J11
El Callao, Venezuela 124/G4
El Calvario, Venezuela 124/E3
El Campo, Texas (77437) 303/H8
El Caney, Cuba 158/J4
El Carmen, El Beni, Bolivia 136/D3
El Carmen, Santa Cruz, Bolivia 136/F6
El Carmen, Ñuble, Chile 138/A11
El Carmen, O'Higgins, Chile 138/F5
El Carmen, Chocó, Colombia 126/B5
El Carmen, Nariño, Colombia 126/A6
El Carmen, Norte de Santander, Colombia 126/D3
El Carmen de Bolívar, Colombia 126/C3
El Carre, Ethiopia 111/H6
El Centro, Calif. 188/C4
El Centro, Calif. (92243) 204/K11
El Centro, Colombia 126/D4
El Cercado, Dom. Rep. 158/D6
El Cerrito, Calif. (94530) 204/J2
El Cerrito, Colombia 126/B6
El Cerro, Bolivia 136/E5
El Chaparro, Venezuela 124/F3
Elche, Spain 33/F3
Elche de la Sierra, Spain 33/E3
Elcho (isl.), North. Terr. 93/D1
Elcho, Wis. (54428) 317/H5
El Chocón (res.), Argentina 143/C4
Elcho Island Mission, North. Terr. 93/D1
El Choro, Bolivia 136/B6
El Chorro, Argentina 143/D1
Elco, Ill. (62929) 222/D6
El Cobre, Chile 138/A4
El Cobre, Cuba 158/J4
El Cocuy, Colombia 126/D4
El Convento, Chile 138/F4
El Corazón, Ecuador 128/C3
El Cristo, Venezuela 124/G4
El Cuey, Dom. Rep. 158/F6
El Cuy, Argentina 143/C4
Elda, Spain 33/F3
El Dara, Ill. (†62312) 222/B4

Fairhaven 367

Espada (pt.), Colombia 126/E1
Espada (pt.), Dom. Rep. 158/F6
Espagnol (pt.), St. Vin. & Grens. 161/A8
Espaillat (prov.), Dom. Rep. 158/E5
Espalion, France 28/E5
Española (isl.), Ecuador 128/C10
Espanola, Fla. (†32010) 212/E2
Espanola, N. Mex. (87532) 274/C3
Espanola, Ontario 177/J5
Espanola, Ontario 175/D3
Espanola, Wash. (†99022) 310/H3
Esparta, C. Rica 154/E5
Esparto, Calif. (95627) 204/C5
Espejo, Chile 138/G3
Espejo, Spain 33/D4
Espelkamp, W. Germany 22/C2
Espenberg (cape), Alaska 196/F1
Esperança, Brazil 132/G4
Esperance, Australia 87/C9
Esperance, N.Y. (12066) 276/M5
Esperance, W. Australia 88/C6
Esperance, W. Australia 92/C6
Esperance (bay), W. Australia 92/C6
Esperanza, Argentina 143/F5
Esperanza, Br. Col. 184/D5
Esperanza, Cuba 158/E2
Esperanza, Dom. Rep. 158/D5
Esperanza (mts.), Honduras 154/E3
Esperanza, Puebla, Mexico 150/O2
Esperanza, Sonora, Mexico 150/E3
Esperanza, Peru 128/G7
Esperanza, P. Rico 161/G2
Esperanza, Texas (†79841) 303/B11
Esperanza, Venezuela 124/E6
Espichel (cape), Portugal 33/B3
Espigão Mestre (Geral de Goiás) (range), Brazil 132/E6
Espinal, Colombia 126/C5
Espinhaço (mts.), Brazil 120/E4
Espinhaço, Serra do (range), Brazil 132/F7
Espinho, Portugal 33/B2
Espinillo, Argentina 143/E2
Espinillo (pt.), Uruguay 145/A7
Espino, Venezuela 124/F3
Espírito Santo (state), Brazil 132/F7
Espírito Santo (state), Brazil 135/F2
Espíritu Santo (isl.), Mexico 150/D4
Espiritu Santo (cape), Philippines 85/H3
Espiritu Santo (cape), Philippines 82/E4
Espiritu Santo (isl.), Vanuatu 87/G7
Espita, Mexico 150/Q6
Espiye, Turkey 63/H2
Esplanada, Brazil 132/G5
Espluga de Francolí, Spain 33/G2
Espoir (bay), Newf. 166/C4
Espoo, Finland 18/O6
Esposende, Portugal 33/B2
Esprit-Saint, Québec 172/J1
Espungabera, Mozambique 118/E4
Espy, Pa. (17815) 294/K4
Espyville Station, Pa. (16414) 294/B2
Esqueda, Mexico 150/E1
Esquel, Argentina 143/B5
Esquel, Argentina 120/B7
Esquimalt, Br. Col. 184/K4
Esquina, Argentina 143/G5
Esquipulas, Nicaragua 154/E4
Es Sahab, Jordan 65/E4
Es Salt, Jordan 65/D3
Es Salt, Jordan 59/C3
Essaouira, Morocco 106/B2
Essaouira, Morocco 102/A1
Essé, Cameroon 115/B3
Essen, Belgium 27/F6
Essen, W. Germany 7/E3
Essen, W. Germany 22/B3
Essendon, Victoria 88/K7
Essendon, Victoria 97/H5
Essequibo (riv.), Guyana 120/D2
Essequibo (riv.), Guyana 131/B3
Esserville, Va. (24274) 307/G2
Essex, Calif. (92332) 204/K9
Essex, Conn. (06426) 210/F3
Essex○, Conn. (06426) 210/F3
Essex (co.), England 13/H6
Essex, Ill. (60935) 222/E2
Essex, Iowa (51638) 229/C7
Essex, Md. (21221) 245/N3
Essex (co.), Mass. 249/L2
Essex, Mass. (01929) 249/L2
Essex○, Mass. (01929) 249/L2
Essex, Mo. (63846) 261/N9
Essex, Mont. (59916) 262/C2
Essex (co.), N.J. 273/E2
Essex (co.), N.Y. 276/N2
Essex, N.Y. (12936) 276/O2
Essex (county), Ontario 177/B5
Essex, Ontario 177/B5
Essex (co.), Vt. 268/D2
Essex○, Vt. (05451) 268/A2
Essex (co.), Va. 307/P5
Essex Fells, N.J. (07021) 273/B2
Essex Junction, Vt. (05452) 268/A3
Essexville, Mich. (48732) 250/F5
Es Sidr, Libya 111/C1
Essie, Ky. (40827) 237/P6
Essig, Minn. (56030) 255/D6
Essington, Pa. (19029) 294/M7
Esslingen am Neckar, W. Germany 22/C4
Essonne (dept.), France 28/E3
Es Sukhna, Jordan 65/E3
Es Sukhne, Syria 59/C3
Es Sukhne, Syria 63/H5
Es Suki, Sudan 59/B7
Es Suweida (prov.), Syria 63/G6
Es Suweida, Syria 59/C3
Es Suweida, Syria 63/G6
Est (pt.), Haiti 158/C4
Est (lake), Québec 172/H2
Estacada, Oreg. (97023) 291/E2
Estaca de Vares (pt.), Spain 33/C1
Estación Atlántida, Uruguay 145/B6
Estación Cuaró, Uruguay 145/C1
Estación J. J. Castro, Uruguay 145/C4
Estación José Ignacio, Uruguay 145/E5
Estación La Floresta, Uruguay 145/C7
Estación Lasala, Uruguay 145/C7
Estación Laureles, Uruguay 145/C2
Estación Margat, Uruguay 145/B6
Estación Migues, Uruguay 145/C6
Estación Pampa, Uruguay 145/C3
Estación Puma, Uruguay 145/D5
Estación Rincón, Uruguay 145/F3
Estación Sosa Díaz, Uruguay 145/C6
Estación Tapia, Uruguay 145/C6
Estación Villasboas, Uruguay 145/C4
Estación Yí, Uruguay 145/C4
Estados (isl.), Argentina 120/C8
Estados, Los (isl.), Argentina 143/D7
Estahbanat, Iran 59/F4
Estahbanat, Iran 66/J6
Estaire, Ontario 177/D1
Estampuis, Belgium 27/C7
Estância, Brazil 132/G5
Estância, Brazil 120/F4
Estancia, N. Mex. (87016) 274/D4
Estancia Caleta Josefina, Chile 138/F10
Estancia Laguna Blanca, Chile 138/E9
Estancia Morro Chico, Chile 138/E9
Estancia Punta Delgada, Chile 138/E9
Estancia San Gregorio, Chile 138/E9
Estancia Springhill (Cerro Manantiales), Chile 138/F10
Estanzuela, Uruguay 145/B5
Estanzuelas, El Salvador 154/C4
Estarca, Bolivia 136/C7
Estats (peak), Spain 33/G1
Estavayer-le-Lac, Switzerland 39/C3
Estcourt, S. Africa 118/D5
Este (pt.), Cuba 158/C3
Este, Italy 34/C2
Este (pt.), P. Rico 161/G2
Este (pt.), Uruguay 120/D6
Este (pt.), Uruguay 145/D6
Esteban Rams, Argentina 143/F5
Estelí, Nicaragua 154/D4
Estella, Spain 33/E1
Estelline, S. Dak. (57234) 298/R4
Estelline, Texas (79233) 303/D3
Estell Manor, N.J. (08319) 273/D5
Estepa, Spain 33/D4
Estepona, Spain 33/D4
Ester, Alaska (99725) 196/J2
Esterbrook, Wyo. (†82633) 319/G3
Estérel, Québec 172/C3
Esterhazy, Sask. 181/K5
Estero (bay), Calif. 204/D8
Estero (pt.), Calif. 204/D8
Estero, Fla. (33928) 212/E5
Estero (isl.), Fla. 212/E5
Estes Park, Colo. (80517) 208/J2
Este Sudeste (cays), Colombia 126/A10
Estevan, Sak. 162/F6
Estevan, Sask. 181/J6
Estevan Point, Br. Col. 184/D5
Estey, Mich. (†48652) 250/E5
Esther (isl.), Alaska 196/C1
Esther, Alberta 182/E4
Esther, La. (†70510) 238/F7
Esther, Mo. (†63601) 261/M7
Estherville, Iowa (51334) 229/D2
Estherwood, La. (70534) 238/F6
Estill (co.), Ky. 237/O5
Estill, Miss. (†38748) 256/C4
Estill, S.C. (29918) 296/E6
Estillfork, Ala. (35745) 195/F1
Estill Springs, Tenn. (37330) 237/J10
Estlin, Sask. 181/G5
Esto, Fla. (32425) 212/C5
Eston, England 13/F3
Eston, Sask. 162/F5
Eston, Sask. 181/C4
ESTONIA 53
Estonian S.S.R., U.S.S.R. 7/G3
Estonian S.S.R., U.S.S.R. 48/C4
Estonian S.S.R, U.S.S.R. 52/C3
Estoril, Portugal 33/B3
Estral Beach, Mich. (†48166) 250/F7
Estreito (res.), Brazil 135/C2
Estrela, Serra da (mts.), Portugal 33/C2
Estrella (riv.), Calif. 204/E8
Estremadura (reg.), Spain 33/C3
Estremoz, Portugal 33/C3
Estrondo, Serra do (range), Brazil 132/D4
Estuary, Sask. 181/B5
Esztergom, Hungary 41/E3
Etadunna, S. Australia 94/F3
Etalle, Belgium 27/H9
Étampes, France 28/E3
Étaples, France 28/D2
Etawah, India 68/D3
Etawney (lake), Manitoba 179/J2
Etchojoa, Mexico 150/E3
Ethan, S. Dak. (57334) 298/N6
Ethel, Ark. (72048) 202/H5
Ethel (mt.), Colo. 208/F1
Ethel, La. (70730) 238/H5
Ethel, Miss. (39067) 256/F4
Ethel, Mo. (63539) 261/G3
Ethel, Ontario 177/C4
Ethel, Wash. (98542) 310/C4
Ethel, W. Va. (25076) 312/C7
Ethelbert, Manitoba 179/B3
Ethel Creek, W. Australia 92/C3
Ethelsville, Ala. (35461) 195/B4
Ethelton, Sask. 181/G3
Ether, N.C. (27247) 281/K4
Ethete, Wyo. (82520) 319/D2
Ethiopia 2/L5
Ethiopia 102/F4
ETHIOPIA 59/C7
ETHIOPIA 111/G5
Ethridge, Mont. (59435) 262/D2
Ethridge, Tenn. (38456) 237/G10
Etive, Loch (inlet), Scotland 15/C4
Etiwanda, Calif. (91739) 204/E10
Etna, Calif. (96027) 204/C2
Etna, Ind. (†46725) 227/F2
Etna (vol.), Italy 7/F5
Etna (vol.), Italy 34/E6
Etna○, Maine (04434) 243/E6
Etna, N.H. (03750) 268/C4
Etna, Ohio (43018) 284/E6
Etna, Pa. (15223) 294/B6
Etna, Utah (†84313) 304/A2
Etna, Wyo. (83118) 319/A2
Etna Green, Ind. (46524) 227/E2
Etobicoke, Ontario 177/J4
Etoile, Ky. (42131) 237/K7
Etoile, Zaire 115/E6
Etolin (isl.), Alaska 196/N2
Etolin (str.), Alaska 196/E2
Etomami (riv.), Manitoba 179/F2
Etomami (riv.), Sask. 181/J3
Eton, England 10/F5
Eton, England 13/G8
Eton, Georgia (30724) 217/C1
Etosha Pan (salt pan), Namibia 118/B3
Etosha Salt Pan, Namibia 102/D6
Etoumbi, Congo 115/B3
Etowah (co.), Ala. 195/F2
Etowah, Ark. (72428) 202/K2
Etowah (riv.), Georgia 217/C2
Etowah, N.C. (28729) 281/D4
Etowah, Tenn. (37331) 237/M10
Étretat, France 28/D3
Etta, Miss. (38627) 256/F2
Etta (lake), N. Dak. 282/L6
Et Tafila, Jordan 65/E5
Et Taiyiba, Jordan 65/D2
Ettelbruck, Luxembourg 27/J9
Et Tell el Abyad, Syria 63/H4
Etten-Leur, Netherlands 27/F5
Etter, Minn. (†55033) 255/F6
Etterbeek, Belgium 27/B9
Etters, Pa. (17319) 294/J5
Etters Beach, Sask. 181/F4
Ettington, Sask. 181/F6
Ettlingen, W. Germany 22/C4
Ettrick, Scotland 15/E5
Ettrick, Va. (23803) 307/O6
Ettrick, Wis. (54627) 317/D7
Ettrick Pen (mt.), Scotland 15/E5
Etty, Ky. (41523) 237/R6
Etzatlán, Mexico 150/G6
Etzikom, Alberta 182/E5
Etzikom Coulee (riv.), Alberta 182/E5
Eu, France 28/D3
Euabalong, N.S. Wales 97/D3
Eubank, Ky. (42567) 237/M6
Euboea (Évvoia) (isl.), Greece 45/G6
Eucha, Okla. (74342) 288/S2
Eucha (lake), Okla. 288/S2
Eucla, W. Australia 92/E5
Euclid, Minn. (56722) 255/B3
Euclid, Ohio (44117) 284/J9
Eucumbene (lake), N.S. Wales 97/E5
Eucutta, Miss. (†39360) 256/G7
Eudora, Ark. (71640) 202/H7
Eudora, Kansas (66025) 232/G3
Eudora, Miss. (†38632) 256/D1
Eudora, Mo. (65645) 261/E7
Eufaula, Ala. (36027) 195/H7
Eufaula (Walter F. George Res.) (lake), Ala 195/H7
Eufaula (Walter F. George Res.) (lake), Georgia 217/B7
Eufaula (res.), Ohio 284/L4
Eufaula, Okla. (74432) 288/P4
Eufaula (lake), Okla. 288/P4
Eugene, Ind. (†47928) 227/B5
Eugene, Mo. (65032) 261/H6
Eugene, Oreg. 188/B2
Eugene, Oreg. 146/F5
Eugene, Oreg. (*97401) 291/D3
Eugene O'Neill Nat'l Hist. Site, Calif. 204/K2
Eugowra, N.S. Wales 97/E3
Euharlee, Georgia (†30120) 217/C2
Euless, Texas (76039) 303/F2
Eulo, Queensland 95/C6
Eulonia, Georgia (†31331) 217/K7
Eumungerie, N.S. Wales 97/E2
Eunice, La. (70535) 238/F6
Eunice, N. Mex. (88231) 274/F6
Eunola, Ala. (†36340) 195/G8
Eupen, Belgium 27/J7
Euphrates (riv.) 54/F6
Euphrates (riv.), Iran 59/E3
Euphrates (riv.), Iraq 59/E3
Euphrates (riv.), Iraq 66/D4
Euphrates (riv.), Syria 59/E3
Euphrates (El Furat) (riv.), Syria 63/H4
Euphrates (Fırat) (riv.), Turkey 63/G4
Eupora, Miss. (39744) 256/F3
Eure (dept.), France 28/D3
Eure (riv.), France 28/D3
Eure, N.C. (27935) 281/R2
Eure-et-Loir (dept.), France 28/D3
Eureka, Calif. 188/B2
Eureka, Calif. 146/F5
Eureka, Calif. (95501) 204/A3
Eureka, Canada 4/A14
Eureka, Colo. (†81433) 208/D7
Eureka (res.), Fla. 212/E2
Eureka, Ill. (61530) 222/D3
Eureka, Ind. (†47635) 227/C9
Eureka, Kansas (67045) 232/F4
Eureka, Mo. (63025) 261/M4
Eureka, Mont. (59917) 262/B2
Eureka (co.), Nev. 266/E3
Eureka, Nev. (89316) 266/E3
Eureka, N.C. (27830) 281/O3
Eureka, N.W.T. 146/K2
Eureka, N.W.T. 162/N3
Eureka, N.W. Terrs. 187/K2
Eureka (sound), N.W. Terrs. 187/K2
Eureka, Nova Scotia 168/F3
Eureka, S.C. (†29706) 296/E2
Eureka, S.C. (†29847) 296/D4
Eureka, S. Dak. (57437) 298/K2
Eureka, Utah (84628) 304/B4
Eureka, Wash. (†99348) 310/G4
Eureka, W. Va. (26144) 312/D4
Eureka Lodge, Alaska (†99588) 196/C1
Eureka Springs, Ark. (72632) 202/C1
Euroa, Victoria 97/C5
Europa (pt.), Gibraltar 33/D4
Europa (isl.), Réunion 102/G7
Europa (isl.), Réunion 118/G4
Europe 2/K3
Europoort, Netherlands 27/E5
Eusebio Ayala, Paraguay 144/B4
Euskirchen, W. Germany 22/B3
Eustace, Texas (75124) 303/H5
Eustis, Fla. (32726) 212/E3
Eustis, Maine (04936) 243/B5
Eustis○, Maine (04936) 243/B5
Eustis, Nebr. (69028) 264/D4
Euston, N.S. Wales 97/B4
Eutaw, Ala. (35462) 195/C5
Eutawville, S.C. (29048) 296/G5
Eutin, W. Germany 22/D1
Eutsuk (lake), Br. Col. 184/D3
Eva, Ala. (35621) 195/E2
Eva (lake), Alberta 182/B5
Eva, La. (†71354) 238/G4
Eva, Okla. (†73949) 288/C1
Eva, Tenn. (38333) 237/E8
Evadale, Texas (77615) 303/L7
Eva Downs, North. Terr. 93/D5
Évain, Québec 174/B3
Evan, Minn. (56238) 255/D6
Evan (lake), Québec 174/B2
Evandale, New Bruns. 170/D3
Evandale, Tasmania 99/D3
Evangeline (par.), La. 238/F5
Evangeline, La. (70537) 238/F6
Evangeline, New Bruns. 170/F1
Evans, Colo. (80620) 208/K2
Evans (mt.), Colo. 208/H3
Evans (co.), Georgia 217/J6
Evans, Georgia (30809) 217/H3
Evans, La. (70639) 238/D5
Evans (head), N.S. Wales 97/G1
Evans (str.), N.W.T. 162/H3
Evans (str.), N.W. Terrs. 187/K3
Evans, Wash. (99126) 310/H2
Evans, W. Va. (25241) 312/C5
Evansburg, Alberta 182/C3
Evans Center, N.Y. (†14006) 276/B5
Evans City, Pa. (16033) 294/B4
Evansdale, Iowa (50707) 229/J4
Evans Head, N.S. Wales 97/G1
Evans Mills, N.Y. (13637) 276/J2
Evansport, Ohio (43519) 284/B3
Evanston, Ill. (*60201) 222/B5
Evanston, Ind. (47531) 227/D8
Evanston, Wyo. 188/D2
Evanston, Wyo. (82930) 319/B4
Evansville (Bettles Field), Alaska (†99726) 196/H1
Evansville, Ark. (72729) 202/B2
Evansville, Ill. (62242) 222/D5
Evansville, Ind. 188/J3
Evansville, Ind. 146/K6
Evansville, Ind. (*47701) 227/C9
Evansville, Minn. (56326) 255/C4
Evansville, Miss. (†38676) 256/D1
Evansville, Pa. (19521) 294/L5
Evansville, Wis. (53536) 317/H10
Evansville, Wyo. (82636) 319/F3
Evant, Texas (76525) 303/G6
Evanton, Scotland 15/D3
Evart, Mich. (49631) 250/D5
Evarts, Ky. (40828) 237/P7
Evaton, S. Africa 118/H7
Evaz, Iran 66/J7
Eveleth, Minn. (55734) 255/F3
Evelyn, La. (†71052) 238/D3
Evendale, Ohio (†45201) 284/C9
Evening Shade, Ark. (72532) 202/G1
Evenki Aut. Okr., U.S.S.R. 48/K3
Evensk, U.S.S.R. 4/C1
Evensk, U.S.S.R. 48/Q3
Evensville, Tenn. (37332) 237/M9
Even Yehuda, Israel 65/B3
Everard (lake), S. Australia 88/E6
Everard (lake), S. Australia 94/D4
Everard (ranges), S. Australia 94/C2
Evere, Belgium 27/C9
Everest (mt.) 54/K7
Everest (mt.), China 77/C6
Everest, Kansas (66424) 232/G2
Everest (mt.), Nepal 68/F3
Everest, N. Dak. (†58023) 282/R6
Everett, Georgia (31536) 217/J8
Everett, Mass. (02149) 249/D6
Everett (mt.), Mass. 249/A4
Everett, New Bruns. 170/C1
Everett (dam), N.H. 268/D5
Everett (mts.), N.W. Terrs. 187/M3
Everett, Ontario 177/E3
Everett, Pa. (15537) 294/F5
Everett, Wash. 188/B1
Everett, Wash. (*98201) 310/C3
Everetts, N.C. (27825) 281/P3
Everettville, W. Va. (26533) 312/F3
Evergem, Belgium 27/D6
Everglades, The (swamp), Fla. 212/F6
Everglades, The (swamp), Fla. 188/K5
Everglades City, Fla. (33929) 212/E6
Everglades Nat'l Park, Fla. 212/F6
Evergreen, Ala. (36401) 195/E8
Evergreen, Colo. (80439) 208/J3
Evergreen, La. (71333) 238/F5
Evergreen, N.C. (28438) 281/M6
Evergreen, Va. (23939) 307/L6
Evergreen Park, Ill. (60642) 222/B6
Everly, Iowa (51338) 229/C2
Everman, Texas (76140) 303/F3
Everson, Pa. (15631) 294/C5
Everson, Wash. (98247) 310/C2
Eversonville, Mo. (†64688) 261/F3
Everton, Ark. (72633) 202/E1
Everton, Ind. (†47331) 227/G5
Everton, Mo. (65646) 261/E8
Evesham, England 10/E4
Evesham, England 13/F5
Evesham, Sask. 181/B3
Evington, Va. (24550) 307/K6
Evolène, Switzerland 39/D4
Évora (dist.), Portugal 33/C3
Évora, Portugal 7/D5
Évora, Portugal 33/C3
Évreux, France 28/D3
Évros (riv.), Greece 45/H5
Évry, France 28/E3
Évvoia (isl.), Greece 7/G5
Évvoia (isl.), Greece 45/G6
Ewa, Hawaii (96706) 218/A4
Ewab (Kai) (isls.), Indonesia 85/J7
Ewa Beach, Hawaii (96706) 218/A4
Ewan, N.J. (08025) 273/C4
Ewan, Wash. (99127) 310/H3
Ewaninga, North. Terr. 93/D7
Ewart, Iowa (†50171) 229/H5
Ewarton, Jamaica 156/C3
Ewarton, Jamaica 158/J6
Ewauna (lake), Oreg. 291/F5
Ewe, Loch (inlet), Scotland 15/C3
Ewell, Md. (21824) 245/O9
Ewen, Mich. (49925) 250/F2
Ewing, Ill. (62836) 222/E5
Ewing, Ky. (41039) 237/O4
Ewing, Mo. (63440) 261/J2
Ewing, Nebr. (68735) 264/F2
Ewing (mt.), North. Terr. 93/E7
Ewing, Va. (24248) 307/B7
Ewington, Ohio (45627) 284/F8
Ewo, Congo 115/B4
Exaltación, Bolivia 136/C3
Excel, Ala. (36439) 195/D8
Excel, Alberta 182/E4
Excello, Mo. (65247) 261/H3
Excello, Ohio (45042) 284/B7
Excelsior, Minn. (55331) 255/E6
Excelsior (mts.), Nev. 266/C4
Excelsior, Wis. (†53518) 317/E9
Excelsior Springs, Mo. (64024) 261/R4
Exchange, W. Va. (26619) 312/E5
Excursion Inlet, Alaska (†99826) 196/M1
Exe (riv.), England 13/D7
Exe (riv.), England 10/E5
Executive Committee (range) 5/B12
Exeland, Wis. (54835) 317/D4
Exeter, Calif. (93221) 204/F7
Exeter, Conn. (†06249) 210/F2
Exeter, England 13/D7
Exeter, England 10/E5
Exeter, Ill. (†62694) 222/C4
Exeter, Maine (04435) 243/E6
Exeter○, Maine (04435) 243/E6
Exeter, Mo. (65647) 261/D9
Exeter, Nebr. (68351) 264/G4
Exeter, N.H. (03833) 268/F6
Exeter○, N.H. (03833) 268/F6
Exeter (riv.), N.H. 268/E6
Exeter (sound), N.W. Terrs. 187/M3
Exeter, Ontario 177/C4
Exeter○, R.I. (02822) 249/H6
Exeter, Tasmania 99/C3
Exira, Iowa (50076) 229/D5
Exline, Iowa (52555) 229/H7
Exminster, England 13/D7
Exmoor National Park, England 13/D6
Exmore, Va. (23350) 307/S5
Exmouth, England 13/D7
Exmouth, England 10/E5
Exmouth, W. Australia 88/A4
Exmouth (gulf), W. Australia 88/A4
Exmouth, W. Australia 92/A3
Exmouth (gulf), W. Australia 92/A3
Expanse, Sask. 181/E6
Experiment, Georgia (30212) 217/D4
Exploits (riv.), Newf. 166/C4
Export, Pa. (15632) 294/C5
Exshaw, Alberta 182/C4
Extension, Br. Col. 184/J3
Extension, La. (71239) 238/G3
Exu, Brazil 132/G4
Exuma (cays), Bahamas 156/C1
Exuma (sound), Bahamas 156/C1
Eyasi (lake), Tanzania 115/F4
Eye, England 10/G4
Eye, England 13/J5
Eye (pen.), Scotland 15/B2
Eyebrow, Sask. 181/E5
Eyebrow (lake), Sask. 181/E5
Eyehill (creek), Sask. 181/B3
Eyemouth, Scotland 15/F5
Eyemouth, Scotland 10/F3
Eynesil, Turkey 63/H2
Eynhallow (sound), Scotland 15/E1
Eynort, Loch (inlet), Scotland 15/A3
Eyota, Minn. (55934) 255/F7
Eyre (lake), Australia 87/D8
Eyre (bay), Chile 138/D8
Eyre (mts.), N. Zealand 100/B6
Eyre (riv.), Queensland 88/F5
Eyre (lake), S. Australia 88/F5
Eyre (pen.), S. Australia 88/F6
Eyre (pen.), S. Australia 94/D5
Eyre, W. Australia 92/D6
Eyrecourt, Ireland 17/E5
Eyre North (lake), S. Australia 94/E3
Eyre South (lake), S. Australia 94/E3
Eysturoy (isl.), Denmark 21/B3
Eyüp, Turkey 63/D6
Ezel, Ky. (41425) 237/P5
Ezequiel Montes, Mexico 150/K6
Ezibider, Turkey 63/H2
Ezine, Turkey 63/B3
Ezna, Iran 66/F4
Ez Zababida, West Bank 65/C3
Ez Zarqa', Jordan 65/E3
Ez Zuetina, Libya 111/D1

F

Faaa, Fr. Poly. 86/S13
Fabens, Texas (79838) 303/B10
Faber (lake), N.W. Terrs. 187/G3
Faber, Va. (22938) 307/L5
Fabius, Ala. (35965) 195/G1
Fabius, N.Y. (13063) 276/J5
Fåborg, Denmark 21/D7
Fåborg, Denmark 18/G9
Fabriano, Italy 34/D3
Fabyan, Alberta 182/E3
Fabyan, Conn. (06245) 210/H1
Fabyan House, N.H. (†03595) 268/E3
Facatativá, Colombia 126/C5
Faceville, Georgia (†31717) 217/C9
Fachi, Niger 106/G5
Fackler, Ala. (35746) 195/G1
Factoryville, Pa. (18419) 294/L2
Facundo, Argentina 143/C6
Fada, Chad 111/D4
Fada-N'Gourma, Upper Volta 106/E6
Fadd, Hungary 41/E3
Faddeyevskiy (isl.), U.S.S.R. 4/B2
Faddeyevskiy (isl.), U.S.S.R. 48/P2
Faden, Newf. 166/A3
Faenza, Italy 34/D2
Faerøe (isls.), Den. 4/C10
Faerøe (isls.), Denmark 7/D2
Faerøe (isls.), Denmark 21/B2
FAERØE ISLANDS, Denmark 21/B2
Faerøe Islands, Denmark 21/B2
Fafan (riv.), Ethiopia 111/H6
Fafe, Portugal 33/B2
Fagan, Ky. (†40322) 237/O5
Făgăraş, Romania 45/G3
Fagernes, Norway 18/F6
Fagersta, Sweden 18/J6
Fagnano (lake), Argentina 143/C7
Fagnano (lake), Chile 138/F11
Faguibine (lake), Mali 106/D5
Fagundes, Brazil 132/C4
Fagus, Mo. (63938) 261/M9
Fahan, Ireland 17/G1
Fahrej (Iranshahr), Iran 66/M7
Fahrej (Iranshahr), Iran 59/H4
Faial (isl.), Portugal 33/B1
Faid, Saudi Arabia 59/D4
Faido, Switzerland 39/G4
Fainaven (mt.), Scotland 15/D2
Fair (head), N. Ireland 17/J1
Fair (isl.), Scotland 10/F1
Faircres, N. Mex. (88033) 274/C6
Fairbank, Ariz. (85612) 198/E7
Fairbank, Iowa (50629) 229/K3
Fairbank, Md. (†21671) 245/N6
Fairbanks, Alaska 146/D3
Fairbanks, Alaska (99701) 196/J2
Fairbanks, Alaska 188/D5
Fairbanks, Fla. (†32601) 212/D2
Fairbanks, Ind. (47849) 227/B6
Fairbanks, La. (71240) 238/F1
Fairbanks, Maine (†04938) 243/C6
Fairbanks, Minn. (†55602) 255/G3
Fairbanks, U.S. 4/C17
Fairbanks, U.S. 2/C2
Fair Bluff, N.C. (28439) 281/M6
Fairborn, Ohio (45324) 284/B6
Fairburn, Georgia (30213) 217/J2
Fairburn, S. Dak. (57738) 298/C6
Fairbury, Ill. (61739) 222/E3
Fairbury, Nebr. (68352) 264/G4
Fairchance, Pa. (15436) 294/C6
Fairchild, Wis. (54741) 317/D6
Fairchild A.F.B., Wash. 310/H3
Fairdale, Ill. (†60146) 222/E1
Fairdale, Ky. (40118) 237/K4
Fairdale, N. Dak. (58229) 282/O3
Fairdealing, Mo. (63939) 261/L9
Fairfax, Ala. (36854) 195/H5
Fairfax, Calif. (94930) 204/H1
Fairfax, Iowa (52228) 229/K5
Fairfax, Manitoba 179/B5
Fairfax, Minn. (55332) 255/D6
Fairfax, Mo. (64446) 261/B2
Fairfax, Ohio (†45201) 284/C9
Fairfax, Okla. (74637) 288/N1
Fairfax, S.C. (29827) 296/E6
Fairfax, S. Dak. (57335) 298/M7
Fairfax○, Vt. (05454) 268/B2
Fairfax (co.), Va. 307/O3
Fairfax (I.C.), Va. (22030) 307/R3
Fairfax, Wash. (†98323) 310/C4
Fairfax Station, Va. (22039) 307/R3
Fairfield, Ala. (35064) 195/E4
Fairfield, Calif. (94533) 204/K1
Fairfield (co.), Conn. 210/B3
Fairfield○, Conn. (06430) 210/B4
Fairfield, Fla. (32634) 212/D2
Fairfield, Idaho (83327) 220/D6
Fairfield, Ill. (62837) 222/E5
Fairfield, Iowa (52556) 229/J6
Fairfield, Ky. (40020) 237/L5
Fairfield, Maine (04937) 243/D6
Fairfield○, Maine (04937) 243/D6
Fairfield, Mont. (59436) 262/D3
Fairfield, Nebr. (68938) 264/G4
Fairfield, New Bruns. 170/E3
Fairfield○, N.J. (07006) 273/A2
Fairfield, N.S. Wales 88/K4
Fairfield, N.S. Wales 97/H3
Fairfield, N. Zealand 100/C6
Fairfield, N.C. (27826) 281/S3
Fairfield, N. Dak. (58627) 282/D5
Fairfield (co.), Ohio 284/E6
Fairfield, Ohio (45014) 284/A7
Fairfield, Pa. (17320) 294/H6
Fairfield (co.), S.C. 296/E3
Fairfield, Tenn. (†37183) 237/J9
Fairfield, Texas (75840) 303/H6
Fairfield, Utah (†84013) 304/B3
Fairfield○, Vt. (05455) 268/B2
Fairfield (pond), Vt. 268/A2
Fairfield, Va. (24435) 307/K5
Fairfield, Wash. (99012) 310/H3
Fairfield Center, Maine (†04937) 243/D6
Fairford, Ala. (†36553) 195/B8
Fairford, Manitoba 179/D3
Fairgrange, Ill. (†61920) 222/E4
Fairgrove, Mich. (48733) 250/F5
Fair Grove, Mo. (65648) 261/F8W
Fair Harbour, Br. Col. 184/D5
Fairhaven○, Mass. (02719) 249/L6
Fair Haven, Mich. (48023) 250/G6
Fairhaven, Minn. (†55382) 255/D5
Fairhaven, New Bruns. 170/C4

Fontaine 369

Feshi, Zaire 115/C5
Fessenden, N. Dak. (58438) 282/L4
Fesserton, Ontario 177/E3
Festina, Iowa (52143) 229/K2
Festus, Mo. (63028) 261/M6
Feteşti, Romania 45/H3
Fethard, Tipperary, Ireland 17/F7
Fethard, Wexford, Ireland 17/H7
Fethiye, Turkey 63/C4
Fethiye, Turkey 59/A2
Fetlar (isl.), Scotland 15/G2
Fetlar (isl.), Scotland 10/H1
Feudal, Sask. 181/D4
Feuerkogel (mt.), Austria 41/B3
Feuerthalen, Switzerland 39/G1
Feuilles (riv.), Que. 162/J4
Feuilles (riv.), Que. 146/L4
Feuilles (riv.), Québec 174/C1
Feversham, Ontario 177/D3
Fevzipaşa, Turkey 63/G4
Feyzabad, Afghanistan 54/H6
Feyzabad, Afghanistan 59/K2
Feyzabad, Afghanistan 68/C1
Fezzan (reg.), Libya 102/D2
Fezzan (reg.), Libya 111/B2
Ffestiniog, Wales 10/E4
Ffestiniog, Wales 13/D5
Fiambalá, Argentina 143/C2
Fianarantsoa (prov.), Madagascar 118/H4
Fianarantsoa, Madagascar 102/G7
Fianarantsoa, Madagascar 118/H4
Fianga, Chad 111/C6
Fiat, Ind. (†47326) 227/G3
Fiatt, Ill. (61433) 222/C3
Fichtelberg (mt.), E. Germany 22/E3
Fichtelgebirge (range), W. Germany 22/D3
Fickle, Ind. (†46035) 227/D4
Ficklin, Georgia (†30673) 217/G3
Ficksburg, S. Africa 118/D5
Fidalgo (isl.), Wash. 310/C2
Fidelity, Ill. (62030) 222/C4
Fidenza, Italy 34/B2
Fieberbrunn, Austria 41/B3
Field, Br. Col. 184/J4
Field, Ky. (40934) 237/O7
Field, Ontario 177/E1
Fieldale, Va. (24089) 307/H7
Field Creek, Texas (†76869) 303/F7
Fielding, New Bruns. 170/C2
Fielding, Sask. 181/D3
Fielding, Utah (84311) 304/B2
Fieldon, Ill. (62031) 222/C4
Fields, La. (70641) 238/C5
Fields (lake), La. 238/J7
Fields, Oreg. (97710) 291/J5
Fieldsboro, N.J. (†08505) 273/D3
Fieldton, Texas (79326) 303/B3
Fier, Albania 45/D5
Fierro, N. Mex. (†88041) 274/A6
Fiesch, Switzerland 39/F4
Fiesole, Italy 34/C3
Fife (lake), Sask. 181/E6
Fife (reg.), Scotland 15/E4
Fife (trad. co.), Scotland 15/B5
Fife, Wash. (98424) 310/C3
Fife Lake, Mich. (49633) 250/D4
Fife Lake, Sask. 181/F6
Fife Ness (prom.), Scotland 15/F4
Fifield, N.S. Wales 97/D3
Fifield, Wis. (54524) 317/F4
Fifteenmile (creek), Oreg. 291/F2
Fifteenmile Arroyo (creek), N. Mex. 274/D4
Fifth (lake), Maine 243/H5
Fifth Cataract, Sudan 111/F4
Fifth Cataract, Sudan 59/B6
Fifth Cataract (dam), Sudan 102/F3
Fifty Lakes, Minn. (56448) 255/D4
Fiftysix, Ark. (72533) 202/F2
Fig (riv.), Newf. 166/B3
Figeac, France 28/D5
Figueira da Foz, Portugal 33/B2
Figueras, Spain 33/H1
Figuig, Morocco 102/B1
Figuig, Morocco 106/D2
Figuras (pt.), P. Rico 161/E3
Fiji 2/A6
Fiji 87/H8
FIJI 86/P11
Filadelfia, Bolivia 136/A2
Filadelfia, C. Rica 154/E5
Filadelfia, Paraguay 144/B3
Fil'akovo, Czech. 41/E2
Filbert, S.C. (†29745) 296/E1
Filbert, W. Va. (24835) 312/D8
Filchner Ice Shelf, Ant. 2/H10
Filchner Ice Shelf, Ant. 5/B16
Fil di Remia (peak), Switzerland 39/H4
File (hills), Sask. 181/H5
Filer, Idaho (83328) 220/D7
Filer City, Mich. (49634) 250/C4
Filey, England 13/G3
Filey, England 10/F3
Filiátes, Greece 45/E6
Filiatrá, Greece 45/E7
Filicudi (isl.), Italy 34/E5
Filingué, Niger 106/E6
Filion, Mich. (48432) 250/G5
Filippiás, Greece 45/E6
Filipstad, Sweden 18/H7
Filisur, Switzerland 39/J3
Filley, Nebr. (68357) 264/H4
Fillmore, Calif. (93015) 204/G9
Fillmore, Ill. (62032) 222/D4
Fillmore, Ind. (46128) 227/D5
Fillmore (co.), Minn. 255/F7
Fillmore, Minn. (†55990) 255/F7
Fillmore, Mo. (64449) 261/C2
Fillmore (co.), Nebr. 264/G4
Fillmore, N.Y. (14735) 276/D6
Fillmore, N. Dak. (58333) 282/L3
Fillmore, Okla. (†73450) 288/N6
Fillmore, Sask. 181/H6
Fillmore, Utah (84631) 304/B5
Filtu, Ethiopia 111/H6
Filyos (riv.), Turkey 63/D2
Fimi (riv.), Zaire 115/C4
Finale Emilia, Italy 34/C2
Finale Ligure, Italy 34/B2
Fiñana, Spain 33/E4
Fincastle, Ind. (†46172) 227/D5
Fincastle, Ky. (†40222) 237/L1
Fincastle, Va. (24090) 307/J6
Finch, Mont. (†59076) 262/K4
Finch, Ontario 177/J2
Finchburg, Ala. (†36444) 195/D7
Finchville, Ky. (40022) 237/L4
Findhorn, Scotland 15/E3
Findhorn (riv.), Scotland 15/E3
Fındıklı, Turkey 63/J2
Findlater, Sask. 181/F5
Findlay, Ill. (62534) 222/E4
Findlay, Ohio (45840) 284/C3
Findley Lake, N.Y. (14736) 276/A6
Findochty, Scotland 15/E3
Findon, Mont. (†59053) 262/F4
Fine, N.Y. (13639) 276/K2
Finesville, N.J. (†08865) 273/C2
Fingal, N. Dak. (58031) 282/P6
Fingal, Ontario 177/C5
Fingal, Tasmania 99/E3
Finger (lake), Ontario 175/B2
Finger, Tenn. (38334) 237/D10
Fingerville, S.C. (29338) 296/D1
Fingoè, Mozambique 118/E2
Finhaut, Switzerland 39/C4
Finike, Turkey 63/D4
Finistère (dept.), France 28/A3
Finisterre (cape), Spain 7/C4
Finisterre (cape), Spain 33/B1
Finke (riv.), North. Terr. 88/E5
Finke (riv.), North. Terr. 93/C8
Finke (riv.), S. Australia 94/C1
Finksburg, Md. (21048) 245/L3
Finland 2/L2
Finland 4/C8
Finland 7/G2
Finland (gulf) 7/G3
FINLAND 18
Finland (gulf), Finland 18/P7
Finland, Minn. (55603) 255/G3
Finland (gulf), U.S.S.R. 52/C3
Finland (gulf), U.S.S.R. 48/C4
Finland (gulf), U.S.S.R. 53/D1
Finlay (riv.), Br. Col. 162/D4
Finlay (riv.), Br. Col. 184/E1
Finlay (mts.), Texas 303/B10
Finlayson, Minn. (55735) 255/F4
Finley, Ky. (42736) 237/L6
Finley, N. S. Wales 88/H7
Finley, N.S. Wales 97/C4
Finley, N. Dak. (58230) 282/P4
Finley, Okla. (74543) 288/R6
Finley, Tenn. (38030) 237/B8
Finley, Wash. (†99336) 310/F4
Finleyson, Georgia (†31071) 217/F6
Finleyville, Pa. (15332) 294/B5
Finly, Ind. (46129) 227/F5
Finn (riv.), Ireland 17/F2
Finn (riv.), Ireland 17/G3
Finnegan, Alberta 182/E4
Finney (co.), Kansas 232/B3
Finnmark (co.), Norway 18/O2
Finschhafen, Papua N.G. 86/B2
Finschhafen, Papua N.G. 85/C7
Finspång, Sweden 18/J7
Finsteraarhorn (mt.), Switzerland 39/F3
Finstermünz (pass), Switzerland 39/K3
Finsterwalde, E. Germany 22/E3
Finstown, Scotland 15/E1
Fintona, N. Ireland 17/G3
Fintry, Scotland 15/B1
Fionn Loch (lake), Scotland 15/C3
Fir (riv.), Sask. 181/J2
Fırat (riv.), Turkey 63/G4
Fircrest, Wash. (98466) 310/C3
Fire (isl.), Alaska 196/B1
Firebag (riv.), Alberta 182/E1
Firebaugh, Calif. (93622) 204/E7
Firebrick, Ky. (41137) 237/P3
Fireco, W. Va. (†25856) 312/D7
Fire Island National Seashore, N.Y. 276/P9
Firenze (Florence), Italy 34/C3
Fires (bay), Tasmania 99/E3
Firesteel (riv.), Mich. 250/G1
Firesteel, S. Dak. (57628) 298/G3
Firesteel (creek), S. Dak. 298/N6
Firestone, Colo. (80520) 208/K2
Firgrove, S. Africa 118/F6
Firmat, Argentina 143/F6
Firminy, France 28/F5
Fir Mountain, Sask. 181/E6
Firozabad, India 68/D3
Firozpur, India 68/C2
First (lake), New Bruns. 170/B1
First Cataract, Egypt 59/B5
First Connecticut (lake), N.H. 268/E1
First Eel (lake), New Bruns. 170/C3
Firstview, Colo. (†80810) 208/O5
Firth (riv.), Alaska 196/K1
Firth, Idaho (83236) 220/F6
Firth, Nebr. (68358) 264/H4
Firth (riv.), Yukon 187/D3
Firuzabad, Iran 66/H6
Firuzkuh, Iran 66/H3
Fischot Islands, Newf. 166/C3
Fish (creek), Ind. 227/H2
Fish (riv.), Maine 243/F2
Fish (riv.), Namibia 118/B5
Fish (creek), Oreg. 291/E4
Fish (lake), Utah 304/C5
Fish (creek), W. Va. 312/E3
Fish Camp, Calif. (93623) 204/F6
Fish Creek (res.), Idaho 220/E6
Fish Creek (mts.), Nev. 266/D2
Fish Creek, Wis. (54212) 317/M5
Fisher, Ark. (72429) 202/J2
Fisher (isl.), Fla. 212/B5
Fisher, Ill. (61843) 222/E3
Fisher, La. (71426) 238/D4
Fisher (bay), Manitoba 179/E3
Fisher (riv.), Manitoba 179/E3
Fisher, Minn. (56723) 255/B3
Fisher (str.), N.W.T. 162/H3
Fisher (str.), N.W. Terrs. 187/K3
Fisher (lake), Nova Scotia 168/C4
Fisher, S. Australia 94/B4
Fisher (co.), Texas 303/D5
Fisher, W. Va. (26818) 312/H4
Fisher Bay, Manitoba 179/E3
Fisher Branch, Manitoba 179/E3
Fishermans (isl.), Va. 307/S6
Fishers, Ind. (46038) 227/E5
Fishers (isl.), N.Y. 276/S8
Fishers Island, N.Y. (06390) 276/R8
Fishersville, Va. (22939) 307/K4
Fisherville (South Grafton), Mass. (01560) 249/H4
Fishguard and Goodwick, Wales 13/B5
Fishguard and Goodwick, Wales 10/D4
Fish Haven, Idaho (83261) 220/G7
Fishing (lake), Manitoba 179/G2
Fishing (bay), Md. 245/O7
Fishing (creek), N.C. 281/O2
Fishing Creek, Md. (21634) 245/N7
Fishing Lake, Alberta 182/E3
Fishing Ships Harbour, Newf. 166/C3
Fishkill, N.Y. (12524) 276/N7
Fish River (lake), Maine 243/F2
Fishs Eddy, N.Y. (13774) 276/K8
Fish Springs (range), Utah 304/A4
Fishtail, Mont. (59028) 262/G5
Fishtoft, England 13/H5
Fishtrap, Ky. (41525) 237/S6
Fishtrap (lake), Ky. 237/S6
Fisk, Mo. (63940) 261/M9
Fiskdale, Mass. (01518) 249/F4
Fiske, Sask. 181/C4
Fiskeville, R.I. (02823) 249/H6
Fitch Bay, Québec 172/E4
Fitchburg, Mass. (01420) 249/G2
Fitchville, Conn. (06334) 210/G2
Fitchville, Ohio (†44851) 284/E3
Fithian, Ill. (61844) 222/F3
Fitler, Miss. (39070) 256/B5
Fitri (lake), Chad 111/C5
Fittstown, Okla. (74842) 288/N5
Fitzcarrald, Peru 128/G8
Fitzgerald, Alberta 182/C4
Fitzgerald, Georgia (31750) 217/F7
Fitzgerald, N.W.T. 162/E4
Fitzhugh (sound), Br. Col. 184/D4
Fitzhugh, Okla. (74843) 288/N5
Fitzmaurice (riv.), North. Terr. 93/B3
Fitzpatrick, Ala. (36029) 195/G6
Fitzpatrick, Georgia (†31044) 217/F5
Fitzroy (riv.), Australia 87/C7
Fitz Roy (Chaltel) (mt.), Chile 138/E8
Fitzroy, North. Terr. 93/B4
Fitzroy (riv.), Queensland 88/J4
Fitzroy (riv.), Queensland 95/D4
Fitzroy, Victoria 97/H5
Fitzroy, Victoria 88/L7
Fitzroy (riv.), W. Australia 88/C3
Fitzroy (riv.), W. Australia 92/D2
Fitzroy Crossing, W. Australia 88/D3
Fitzroy Crossing, W. Australia 92/D2
Fitzroy Harbour, Ontario 177/H2
Fitzwilliam○, N.H. (03447) 268/C6
Fitzwilliam (isl.), Ontario 177/C2
Fitzwilliam Depot, N.H. (03447) 268/C6
Fiume (Rijeka), Yugoslavia 45/B3
Fiumicino, Italy 34/F7
Five (isls.), Nova Scotia 168/D3
Five Fingers, New Bruns. 170/C1
Five Island (lake), Iowa 229/D2
Five Islands, Maine (04546) 243/D8
Five Islands, Nova Scotia 168/D3
Five Mile (riv.), Conn. 210/H1
Fivemile (creek), Oreg. 291/F2
Fivemile (pt.), Oreg. 291/C4
Fivemile (creek), Wyo. 319/D2
Fivemiletown, N. Ireland 17/G3
Five Points, Ala. (36855) 195/H4
Five Points, Fla. (32922) 212/D1
Five Points, Tenn. (38457) 237/G10
Five Stars, Guyana 131/A2
Fivizzano, Italy 34/B2
Fizi, Zaire 115/E4
Fjerritslev, Denmark 21/C3
Flagler, Colo. (80815) 208/N4
Flagler (co.), Fla. 212/E2
Flagler Beach, Fla. (32036) 212/E2
Flag Pond, Tenn. (37657) 237/R8
Flagstaff, Ariz. 146/G6
Flagstaff, Ariz. 188/D3
Flagstaff, Ariz. (86001) 198/D3
Flagstaff (lake), Maine 243/C5
Flagstaff (lake), Oreg. 291/H5
Flagtown, N.J. (08821) 273/D2
Flambeau (riv.), Wis. 317/E4
Flambeau Flowage (res.), Wis. 317/F3
Flamborough (head), England 13/G3
Flamborough (head), England 10/G3
Flamenco de San Pedro, Cuba 158/F3
Flaming Gorge (dam), Utah 304/E3
Flaming Gorge (res.), Utah 304/E3
Flaming Gorge (res.), Wyo. 319/C4
Flaming Gorge Nat'l Rec. Area, Utah 304/E2
Flaming Gorge Nat'l Rec. Area, Wyo. 319/C4
Flamingo (cay), Bahamas 156/C2
Flanagan, Ill. (61740) 222/E3
Flanagan (passage), Virgin Is. (Br.) 161/D4
Flanagan (passage), Virgin Is. (U.S.) 161/D4
Flanagin Town, Trin. & Tob. 161/B10
Flanders, Conn. (†06757) 210/B1
Flanders (trad. prov.) France 29
Flanders, N.J. (07836) 273/D2
Flanders, Ontario 175/B3
Flanders-Riverside, N.Y. (†11901) 276/P9
Flandreau, S. Dak. (57028) 298/R5
Flanigan, Nev. (†89501) 266/B2
Flannagan (res.), Va. 307/C6
Flannan (isls.), Scotland 15/A2
Flannan (isls.), Scotland 10/C1
Flasher, N. Dak. (58535) 282/H7
Flat, Ky. (41325) 237/O5
Flat, Mo. (†65550) 261/J7
Flat (isl.), Philippines 85/F3
Flat, Texas (76526) 303/G6
Flat (creek), Va. 307/M6
Flat (cays), Virgin Is. (U.S.) 161/A4
Flat Bay, Newf. 166/C4
Flatbrookville, N.J. (†07832) 273/D1
Flatbush, Alberta 182/C2
Flat Creek, Tenn. (†37160) 237/H10
Flat Creek-Wegra, Ala. (†35129) 195/D3
Flat Fork, Ky. (41427) 237/P5
Flatgap, Ky. (41219) 237/R5
Flathead (riv.), Br. Col. 184/K6
Flathead (co.), Mont. 262/B2
Flathead (lake), Mont. 188/D1
Flathead (lake), Mont. 262/C3
Flathead (riv.), Mont. 262/B2
Flatheand, North Fork (riv.), Mont. 262/B2
Flathead, South Fork (riv.), Mont. 262/C3
Flathead Ind. Res., Mont. 262/B3
Flatlands, New Bruns. 170/D1
Flat Lick, Ky. (40935) 237/O7
Flatonia, Texas (78941) 303/G8
Flat River, Mo. (63601) 261/M7
Flat Rock, Ala. (35966) 195/G1
Flat Rock, Ill. (62427) 222/F5
Flat Rock, Ind. (47234) 227/F6
Flatrock (creek), Ind. 227/F5
Flat Rock, Ky. (†42634) 237/M7
Flat Rock, Mich. (48134) 250/F6
Flat Rock, Newf. 166/D2
Flat Rock, N.C. (†27043) 281/E4
Flat Rock, Ohio (44828) 284/E3
Flats, N.C. (†28781) 281/B4
Flattery (cape), Br. Col. 162/D6
Flattery (cape), Queensland 88/H2
Flattery (cape), Queensland 95/C2
Flattery (cape), Wash. 146/F5
Flattery (cape), Wash. 188/A1
Flattery (cape), Wash. 310/A2
Flat Top, W. Va. (25841) 312/D7
Flatwillow (creek), Mont. 262/H4
Flatwood, Ala. (†36739) 195/C6
Flatwoods, Ky. (41139) 237/R4
Flatwoods, La. (71427) 238/E4
Flatwoods, Tenn. (38458) 237/F9
Flatwoods, W. Va. (26621) 312/E5
Flawil, Switzerland 39/H2
Flaxcombe, Sask. 181/B4
Flaxman (isl.), Alaska 196/J1
Flaxton, N. Dak. (58737) 282/F2
Flaxville, Mont. (59222) 262/L2
Fleet, Alberta 182/E3
Fleet, England 13/G8
Fleet, Loch (inlet), Scotland 15/D3
Fleetwood, England 10/E4
Fleetwood, England 13/D4
Fleetwood, Okla. (†73569) 288/L7
Fleetwood, Pa. (19522) 294/L5
Fleischmanns, N.Y. (12430) 276/L6
Flekkefjord, Norway 18/E7
Flémalle, Belgium 27/G7
Fleming, Colo. (80728) 208/O1
Fleming, Georgia (31309) 217/K7
Fleming (co.), Ky. 237/O4
Fleming, Mo. (†64077) 261/D4
Fleming, Pa. (19375) 294/G4
Fleming, Sask. 181/K5
Fleming-Neon, Ky. (41816) 237/R6
Flemingsburg, Ky. (41041) 237/O4
Flemington, Georgia (†31313) 217/K7
Flemington, Mo. (65650) 261/F7
Flemington, N.J. (08822) 273/D2
Flemington, Pa. (†17745) 294/G3
Flemington, W. Va. (26347) 312/F4
Flen, Sweden 18/K7
Flensburg, Minn. (56328) 255/D5
Flensburg, W. Germany 22/C1
Flers, France 28/C3
Flesherton, Ontario 177/D3
Flesk (riv.), Ireland 17/C7
Fleta, Ala. (†36043) 195/F6
Fletcher (pond), Mich. 250/F4
Fletcher, Mo. (63030) 261/L6
Fletcher, N.C. (28732) 281/E4
Fletcher, Ohio (45326) 284/B5
Fletcher, Okla. (73541) 288/K5
Fletcher○, Vt. (†05444) 268/B2
Fletschhorn (mt.), Switzerland 39/F4
Fleurance, France 28/D6
Fleur de Lys, Newf. 166/C3
Fleur-de-May (lake), Newf. 166/B3
Fleurier, Switzerland 39/C3
Fleurus, Belgium 27/E8
Flevoland Polders, Netherlands 27/G4
Flims, Switzerland 39/H3
Flinders (reefs), 95/D3
Flinders (riv.), Australia 87/E7
Flinders (reef), Coral Sea Is. Terr. 88/H3
Flinders (riv.), Queensland 88/G3
Flinders (riv.), Queensland 95/B3
Flinders (range), S. Australia 88/F6
Flinders (range), S. Australia 94/F4
Flinders (isl.), Tasmania 88/H7
Flinders (isl.), Tasmania 99/D1
Flinders (bay), W. Australia 88/A6
Flinders (bay), W. Australia 92/A6
Flin Flon, Man. 146/H4
Flin Flon, Manitoba 179/H3
Flin Flon, Man.-Sask. 162/F4
Flin Flon, Sask. 181/N4
Flint (riv.), Ga. 188/K4
Flint, Georgia (†31716) 217/D8
Flint (riv.), Georgia 217/D8
Flint, Ind. (†46703) 227/G1
Flint (isl.), Kiribati 87/L7
Flint, Mich. 146/K5
Flint, Mich. 188/K2
Flint, Mich. (*48501) 250/F5
Flint (riv.), Mich. 250/F5
Flint (lake), N.W. Terrs. 187/L3
Flint, Wales 13/G2
Flint City, Ala. (†35601) 195/D1
Flinthill, Mo. (63346) 261/L5
Flint Hill, Va. (22627) 307/M3
Flinton, Ontario 177/G3
Flint Rock (creek), S. Dak. 298/E3
Flintstone, Georgia (30725) 217/B1
Flintstone (lake), Manitoba 179/G4
Flintstone, Md. (21530) 245/D2
Flintville, Tenn. (37335) 237/H10
Flippen, Georgia (30215) 217/D3
Flippin, Ark. (72634) 202/E1
Flippin, Ky. (42132) 237/K7
Flix, Spain 33/G2
Flom, Minn. (56541) 255/B3
Flomaton, Ala. (36441) 195/D8
Flomot, Texas (79234) 303/D3
Flood, Br. Col. 184/M3
Floodwood, Minn. (55736) 255/E4
Flora, Ill. (62839) 222/E5
Flora, Ind. (46929) 227/E3
Flora, La. (71428) 238/D3
Flora, Miss. (39071) 256/D5
Flora, N. Dak. (†58348) 282/M4
Flora (riv.), North. Terr. 93/B3
Flora, Norway 18/D6
Flora, Oreg. (†97828) 291/K2
Florac, France 28/E5
Florahome, Fla. (32635) 212/E2
Floral, Ark. (72534) 202/G2
Florala, Ala. (36442) 195/F8
Floral City, Fla. (32636) 212/D3
Floral Park, N.Y. (*11001) 276/P7
Floraville, Queensland 95/B3
Flora Vista, N. Mex. (87415) 274/A2
Floreana (Sta. Maria), Ecuador 128/B10
Floreana (Santa Maria) (isl.), Ecuador 128/B10
Florence, Ala. 188/J4
Florence, Ala. (*35630) 195/C1
Florence, Ariz. (85232) 198/D5
Florence, Ark. (†71655) 202/G6
Florence (lake), Calif. 204/G6
Florence, Colo. (81226) 208/J6
Florence, Ill. (†62363) 222/C4
Florence, Ind. (47020) 227/H7
Florence (prov.), Italy 34/C3
Florence, Italy 7/F4
Florence, Italy 34/C3
Florence, Kansas (66851) 232/E3
Florence, Ky. (41042) 237/R2
Florence, Minn. (56130) 255/B6
Florence, Miss. (39073) 256/D6
Florence, Mo. (65329) 261/G5
Florence, Mont. (59833) 262/B4
Florence, N.Y. (†13316) 276/J4
Florence, N.C. (†28556) 281/R4
Florence, Nova Scotia 168/H2
Florence, Ontario 177/B5
Florence, Oreg. (97439) 291/C4
Florence, Pa. (†15021) 294/A5
Florence, S.C. 188/L4
Florence (co.), S.C. 296/H3
Florence, S.C. (29501) 296/H3
Florence, S. Dak. (57235) 298/P3
Florence (riv.), Tasmania 99/C4
Florence, Tenn. (†37130) 237/H9
Florence, Texas (76527) 303/G7
Florence, Vt. (05744) 268/A4
Florence (co.), Wis. 317/K4
Florence, Wis. (54121) 317/K4
Florence Junction, Ariz. (†85220) 198/D5
Florence-Roebling, N.J. (08518) 273/D3
Florenceville, New Bruns. 170/C2
Florencia, Colombia 126/C7
Florencia, Colombia 120/B2
Florencia, Cuba 158/F2
Florennes, Belgium 27/F8
Florenton, Minn. (†55792) 255/F3
Florenville, Belgium 27/G9
Flores, Las (riv.), Argentina 143/G7
Flores, Brazil 132/G4
Flores (isl.), Br. Col. 184/D5
Flores, Guatemala 154/C2
Flores (isl.), Indonesia 54/O10
Flores (isl.), Indonesia 85/G7
Flores (sea), Indonesia 2/Q6
Flores (sea), Indonesia 54/N10
Flores (sea), Indonesia 85/F7
Flores (isl.), Portugal 33/A1
Flores (dept.), Uruguay 145/C4
Flores (isl.), Uruguay 145/D5
Floresville, Texas (78114) 303/K11
Florey, Texas (†79714) 303/B5
Florham Park, N.J. (07932) 273/E2
Floriano, Brazil 132/F4
Floriano, Brazil 120/E3
Florianópolis, Brazil 132/E9
Florianópolis, Brazil 120/E5
Florida 188/K5
FLORIDA 212
Florida (strs.) 146/K7
Florida, Bolivia 136/D6
Florida, Cuba 158/G3
Florida (str.), Cuba 156/B1
Florida (bay), Fla. 188/K6
Florida (bay), Fla. 212/F6
Florida (cape), Fla. 212/F6
Florida (keys), Fla. 188/K6
Florida (keys), Fla. 212/E7
Florida (strs.), Fla. 188/K6
Florida (strs.), Fla. 212/F7
Florida○, Mass. (†01247) 249/B2
Florida, Mo. (†65283) 261/J4
Florida (mts.), N. Mex. 274/B7
Florida, N.Y. (10921) 276/M8
Florida, Ohio (†43545) 284/B3
Florida, P. Rico 161/C1
Florida (isls.), Solomon Is. 86/E3
Florida (state), U.S. 146/K7
Florida (dept.), Uruguay 145/D4
Florida, Uruguay 145/C5
Florida City, Fla. (33034) 212/F6
Florida Ridge, Fla. (†32960) 212/F4
Floridia, Italy 34/E6
Florien, La. (71429) 238/D4
Florin, Calif. (95828) 204/B8
Florin, Pa. (†17552) 294/J5
Flórina, Greece 45/E5
Floris, Iowa (52560) 229/J7
Florissant, Colo. (80816) 208/J5
Florissant, Mo. (*63031) 261/P1
Florissant Fossil Beds Nat'l Mon., Colo. 208/J5
Flossmoor, Ill. (60422) 222/B6
Flovilla, Georgia (30216) 217/E4
Flowerdale, Tasmania 99/B2
Floweree, Mont. (59440) 262/E3
Flower Mound, Texas (†75067) 303/F1
Flowerpot (isl.), Ontario 177/C2
Flowers (bay), Newf. 166/B2
Flowers Cove, Newf. 166/C3
Flowery Branch, Georgia (30542) 217/E2
Flowood, Miss. (†39201) 256/D6
Floyd (co.), Georgia 217/B2
Floyd, Georgia (30059) 217/J1
Floyd (co.), Ind. 227/F8
Floyd (co.), Iowa 229/H2
Floyd, Iowa (50435) 229/H2
Floyd (riv.), Iowa 229/A3
Floyd (co.), Ky. 237/R5
Floyd, La. (†71266) 238/H1
Floyd, N. Mex. (88118) 274/F4
Floyd (co.), Texas 303/C3
Floyd (co.), Va. 307/H7
Floyd, Va. (24091) 307/H7
Floydada, Texas (79235) 303/C3
Floyd Dale, S.C. (29542) 296/J3
Floyds Knobs, Ind. (47119) 227/F8
Fluchthorn (mt.), Switzerland 39/K3
Flüela (pass), Switzerland 39/J3
Flüelen, Switzerland 39/G3
Fluhberg (mt.), Switzerland 39/G2
Fluker, La. (70436) 238/K5
Flums, Switzerland 39/H2
Flushing, Mich. (48433) 250/F5
Flushing, Netherlands 27/C6
Flushing, Ohio (43977) 284/J5
Fluvanna, Texas (79517) 303/D5
Fluvanna (co.), Va. 307/M5
Fly, Ohio (45730) 284/H6
Fly (riv.), Papua N.G. 87/E6
Fly (riv.), Papua N.G. 85/A7
Fly Creek, N.Y. (13337) 276/K5
Flying H, N. Mex. (88322) 274/E5
Flying Shot, Alberta 182/A2
Flynns Lick, Tenn. (†38562) 237/K8
Foam Lake, Sask. 181/H4
Foard (co.), Texas 303/E3
Foça, Turkey 63/B3
Foča, Yugoslavia 45/D4
Fochabers, Scotland 15/E3
Focşani, Romania 45/H3
Foge (isl.), Nigeria 106/E6
Foggia (prov.), Italy 34/E4
Foggia, Italy 7/F4
Foggia, Italy 34/E4
Fogo (isl.), C. Verde 106/B8
Fogo, Newf. 166/D4
Fogo (isl.), Newf. 166/D4
Fogo (isl.), Newf. 162/L6
Fohnsdorf, Austria 41/C3
Föhr (isl.), W. Germany 22/C1
Foisy, Alberta 182/E3
Foix, France 28/D6
Foix (trad. prov.) France 29
Folcroft, Pa. (19032) 294/M7
Folda (fjord), Norway 18/J3
Folda (fjord), Norway 18/G4
Földeák, Hungary 41/F3
Földes, Hungary 41/F2
Foley, Ala. (36535) 195/C10
Foley, Fla. (†32347) 212/C1
Foley, Minn. (56329) 255/D5
Foley, Mo. (63347) 261/L4
Foley (isl.), N.W. Terrs. 187/L3
Foleyet, Ontario 177/J5
Foleyet, Ontario 175/D3
Folgares, Angola 115/C6
Foligno, Italy 34/D3
Folkestone, England 13/J6
Folkestone, England 10/G5
Folkston, Georgia (31537) 217/H9
Folkstone, N.C. (†28445) 281/O5
Follansbee, W. Va. (26037) 312/E2
Follett, Texas (79034) 303/D1
Föllinge, Sweden 18/J5
Folly Beach, S.C. (29439) 296/H6
Folsom, Calif. (95630) 204/C8
Folsom (lake), Calif. 204/C8
Folsom, La. (70437) 238/K5
Folsom, N.J. (†08037) 273/D4
Folsom, N. Mex. (88419) 274/F2
Folsom, Pa. (19033) 294/M7
Folsom, W. Va. (26348) 312/E4
Folsomville, Ind. (47614) 227/C8
Folteşti, Romania 45/H3
Fomboni, Comoros 118/G2
Fomento, Cuba 158/E2
Fonda, Iowa (50540) 229/D3
Fonda, N.Y. (12068) 276/M5
Fonda, N. Dak. (†58366) 282/K2
Fond d'Or (bay), St. Lucia 161/G6
Fond-du-Lac (riv.), Sask. 162/F4
Fond du Lac, Sask. 181/L2
Fond du Lac (riv.), Sask. 181/M2
Fond du Lac, Wis. 188/J2
Fond du Lac (co.), Wis. 317/K8
Fond du Lac, Wis. (54935) 317/K8
Fond du Lac Ind. Res., Minn. 255/F4
Fonde, Ky. (40937) 237/O7
Fondi, Italy 34/D4
Fond-Lahaye, Martinique 161/C6
Fond-Saint-Denis, Martinique 161/C6
Fond Verrettes, Haiti 158/C6
Fonehill, Sask. 181/J4
Fongafale (cap.), Tuvalu 87/H6
Fonsagrada, Spain 33/C1
Fonseca, Colombia 126/D2
Fonseca (gulf), El Salvador 154/D4
Fonseca (gulf), Honduras 154/D4
Fonseca (gulf), Nicaragua 154/D4
Fontaine, New Bruns. 170/F2

370 Fontainebleau

Fontainebleau, France 28/E3
Fontainebleau, Québec 172/F4
Fontana, Calif. (92335) 204/E10
Fontana, Kansas (66026) 232/H3
Fontana (lake), N.C. 281/B4
Fontana, Wis. (53125) 317/J10
Fontanelle, Iowa (50846) 229/E6
Fontanet, Ind. (47851) 227/C5
Fontas (riv.), Br. Col. 184/M2
Fonte Boa, Brazil 132/G9
Fontein, Neth. Ant. 161/E8
Fontenay-le-Comte, France 28/C4
Fontenay-sous-Bois, France 28/C2
Fonteneau (lake), Newf. 166/B3
Fontenelle, Québec 172/D1
Fontenelle (creek), Wyo. 319/B3
Fontenelle (res.), Wyo. 319/B3
Fontibón, Colombia 126/C5
Fontur (prom.), Iceland 7/C2
Fontur (pt.), Iceland 21/D1
Fonyód, Hungary 41/D3
Foochow (Fuzhou), China 77/J6
Fool Creek (res.), Utah 304/B4
Foosland, Ill. (61845) 222/E3
Foothills, Alberta 182/B3
Footscray, Victoria 97/H5
Footscray, Victoria 88/K7
Footville, Ohio (†44084) 284/J2
Footville, Wis. (53537) 317/H10
Foping, China 77/G5
Forada, Minn. (†56308) 255/C5
Foraker (mt.), Alaska 196/H2
Foraker, Ind. (46525) 227/F1
Foraker, Ohio (†45812) 284/C4
Foraker, Okla. (74652) 288/O1
Forbach, France 28/G3
Forbes (mt.), Alberta 182/B4
Forbes (mt.), Br. Col. 184/J4
Forbes (isl.), Fla. 212/D6
Forbes, Minn. (55738) 255/F3
Forbes, Mo. (†64473) 261/B3
Forbes, N. S. Wales 88/H6
Forbes, N.S. Wales 97/E3
Forbes, N. Dak. (58439) 282/N8
Forbes (lake), Québec 172/C3
Forbing, La. (71106) 238/C2
Forbus, Tenn. (38561) 237/M7
Forcados, Nigeria 106/E7
Forcalquier, France 28/F6
Force, Pa. (15841) 294/E3
Forchheim, W. Germany 22/D4
Forchu (bay), Nova Scotia 168/H3
Forchu (cape), Nova Scotia 168/B5
Ford, England 13/F2
Ford (isl.), Hawaii 218/B3
Ford (co.), Ill. 222/E3
Ford (co.), Kansas 232/C4
Ford, Kansas (67842) 232/C4
Ford, Ky. (40320) 237/N5
Ford (riv.), Mich. 250/B2
Ford (cape), North. Terr. 88/D2
Ford (cape), North. Terr. 93/A2
Ford, Va. (23850) 307/N6
Ford, Wash. (99013) 310/H3
Ford City, Calif. (†93268) 204/F8
Ford City, Mo. (†64463) 261/C2
Ford City, Pa. (16226) 294/D4
Ford Cliff, Pa. (16228) 294/D4
Fordland, Mo. (65652) 261/G8
Fordoche, La. (70732) 238/G5
Ford Ranges (mts.) 5/B11
Fords, N.J. (08863) 273/E2
Ford's Bridge, N.S. Wales 97/C1
Fords Prairie, Wash. (†98531) 310/B4
Fordsville, Ky. (42343) 237/H5
Fordville, N. Dak. (58231) 282/P3
Fordwich, Ontario 177/C4
Fordyce, Ark. (71742) 202/F6
Fordyce, Nebr. (68736) 264/G2
Forécariah, Guinea 106/B7
Foreman, Ark. (71836) 202/B6
Foremost, Alberta 182/E5
Foresman, Ind. (†47922) 227/C3
Forest, Belgium 27/B9
Forest, Ind. (46039) 227/E4
Forest, La. (71242) 238/H1
Forest, Miss. (39074) 256/F6
Forest (riv.), N. Dak. 282/P3
Forest, Ohio (45843) 284/C4
Forest, Ontario 177/C4
Forest (co.), Pa. 294/D2
Forest, Va. (24551) 307/K6
Forest (co.), Wis. 317/J4
Forest Acres, S.C. (29206) 296/E3
Forest Beach, S.C. (†29928) 296/F7
Forestburg, Alberta 182/E3
Forestburg, S. Dak. (57338) 298/N5
Forestburg, Texas (76239) 303/G4
Forest City, Ill. (61532) 222/D3
Forest City, Iowa (50436) 229/F2
Forest City, Maine (04413) 243/H4
Forest City, Mo. (64451) 261/B3
Forest City, New Bruns. 170/C3
Forest City, N.C. (28043) 281/E4
Forest City, Pa. (18421) 294/L2
Forestdale, Ala. (35214) 195/E3
Forestdale, R.I. (02824) 249/H5
Forest Dale, Vt. (05745) 268/A4
Forester, Mich. (†48419) 250/G5
Foresters Falls, Ontario 177/H2
Forest Glen, Georgia (†31001) 217/F7
Forest Green, Mo. (†65281) 261/G4
Forest Grove, Br. Col. 184/G4
Forestgrove, Mont. (59441) 262/H3
Forest Grove, Oreg. (97116) 291/A2
Forest Heights, Md. (†20001) 245/F5
Foresthill, Calif. (†95703) 204/E4
Forest Hill, Ind. (†47240) 227/F6
Forest Hill, La. (71430) 238/E4
Forest Hill, Md. (21050) 245/N2
Forest Hill, N.S. Wales 97/D4
Forest Hill, Texas (†76119) 303/F2
Forest Hill, W. Va. (24935) 312/E7
Forest Hills, Ky. (41527) 237/L2
Forest Hills, Pa. (†15221) 294/C7
Forest Hills, Tenn. (†37201) 237/H8
Forest Home, Ala. (36030) 195/E7
Forest Homes, Ill. (†62018) 222/B2
Forestier (cape), Tasmania 99/E4
Forestier (pen.), Tasmania 99/E4
Forest Junction, Wis. (54123) 317/K7
Forest Knolls-Lagunitas, Calif. (94933) 204/H1
Forest Lake, Mich. (49832) 250/C2
Forest Lake, Minn. (55025) 255/F5
Foreston, Minn. (56330) 255/E5
Foreston, S.C. (†29102) 296/G4
Forest Park, Georgia (30050) 217/K2
Forest Park, Ill. (60130) 222/B5
Forest Park, Ohio (45405) 284/B9
Forest Park, Okla. (†73101) 288/M3
Forestport, N.Y. (13338) 276/K4
Forest River, N. Dak. (58233) 282/P3
Forest Station, Maine (†04413) 243/H4
Forest View, Ill. (†60402) 222/B6
Forestville, Conn. (†06010) 210/D2
Forestville, Md. (†20028) 245/G5
Forestville, Mich. (48434) 250/G5
Forestville, N.Y. (14062) 276/B6
Forestville, Ohio (45230) 284/C10
Forestville, Pa. (16035) 294/B3
Forestville, Québec 172/H1
Forestville, Québec 174/D3
Forestville, Wis. (54213) 317/L6
Forez (mts.), France 28/E5
Forfar, Scotland 10/E2
Forfar, Scotland 15/F4
Forgan, Okla. (73938) 288/E1
Forgan, Sask. 181/D4
Forget, Sask. 181/J6
Forge Village, Mass. (01828) 249/H2
Forillon Nat'l Park, Que. 162/K6
Forillon Nat'l Park, Québec 172/D1
Foristell, Mo. (63348) 261/L5
Fork, N.C. (†27028) 281/J3
Fork, S.C. (29543) 296/J3
Forked (lake), N.Y. 276/L3
Forked Deer (riv.), Tenn. 237/C9
Forked Deer, Middle Fork (riv.), Tenn. 237/C9
Forked Deer, North Fork (riv.), Tenn. 237/C8
Forked Deer, South Fork (riv.), Tenn. 237/C9
Forked River, N.J. (08731) 273/E4
Fork Lake, Alberta 182/E2
Forkland, Ala. (36740) 195/C5
Fork Mountain, Tenn. (†37728) 237/N8
Fork River, Manitoba 179/B3
Forks, Wash. (98331) 310/A3
Forks of Buffalo, Va. (†24521) 307/K5
Forks of Elkhorn, Ky. (†40601) 237/M4
Forks of Salmon, Calif. (96031) 204/B2
Forksville, Pa. (18616) 294/J3
Fork Union, Va. (23055) 307/M5
Forkville, Miss. (39076) 256/E6
Forlì (prov.), Italy 34/D2
Forlì, Italy 34/D2
Forman, N. Dak. (58032) 282/P7
Formartine (dist.), Scotland 15/F3
Formby, England 13/G2
Formby, England 10/F2
Formby (head), England 13/G2
Formentera (isl.), Spain 33/G3
Formentor (cape), Spain 33/H2
Formia, Italy 34/D4
Formiga, Brazil 135/D2
Formiga, Brazil 132/E8
Formosa (prov.), Argentina 143/D1
Formosa, Argentina 143/E2
Formosa, Argentina 120/D5
Formosa, Ark. (†72031) 202/E3
Formosa, Brazil 132/E6
Formosa, Serra (range), Brazil 132/C5
Formosa (Taiwan) (isl.), China 2/R4
Formosa (Taiwan) (isl.), China 77/K7
Formosa (Taiwan) (str.), China 77/J7
Formosa (bay), Kenya 115/H4
Formosa, Ontario 177/C3
Formosa, Paraguay 144/C5
Formoso, Kansas (66942) 232/D2
Forney, Ala. (†30124) 195/H2
Forney, Texas (75126) 303/H5
Forres, Scotland 10/E2
Forres, Scotland 15/E3
Forrest, Ill. (61741) 222/E3
Forrest (co.), Miss. 256/F8
Forrest, N. Mex. (†88401) 274/F4
Forrest (lake), Sask. 181/L3
Forrest, W. Australia 88/D6
Forrest (lakes), W. Australia 88/D5
Forrest, W. Australia 92/D5
Forrest City, Ark. (72335) 202/J3
Forreston, Ill. (61030) 222/D1
Forrest River Aboriginal Res., W. Australia 92/D1
Forrest River Mission, W. Australia 92/D1
Forrest Station, Manitoba 179/C5
Forsan, Texas (79733) 303/C5
Forsayth, Queensland 95/B3
Forsayth, Queensland 88/G3
Forshaga, Sweden 18/H7
Forssa, Finland 18/N6
Forst, E. Germany 22/F3
Forster-Tuncurry, N.S. Wales 97/G3
Forsyth (co.), Georgia 217/D2
Forsyth, Georgia (31029) 217/E4
Forsyth, Ill. (62535) 222/D4
Forsyth, Mo. (65653) 261/F9
Forsyth, Mont. (59327) 262/K4
Forsyth (co.), N.C. 281/J2
Fort (pt.), St. Chris.-Nevis 161/C11
Fort (mt.), Switzerland 39/D4
Fort A.P. Hill, Va. 307/O4
Fort Adams, Miss. (39636) 256/B8
Fort à la Corne, Sask. 181/G2
Fort Albany, Ont. 146/K4
Fort Albany, Ont. 162/H5
Fort Albany, Ontario 175/D2
Fort Alexander, Manitoba 179/F4
Fortaleza, Bolivia 136/C1
Fortaleza, Bolivia 136/B3
Fortaleza, Brazil 132/G3
Fortaleza, Brazil 120/F3
Fortaleza, Brazil 2/H6
Fortaleza de Santa Teresa, Uruguay 145/F5
Fort Ann, N.Y. (12827) 276/N4
Fort Apache, Ariz. (85926) 198/F5
Fort Apache Ind. Res., Ariz. 198/E5
Fort Ashby, W. Va. (26719) 312/J4
Fort Assiniboine, Alberta 182/C2
Fort Atkinson, Iowa (52144) 229/J2
Fort Atkinson, Wis. (53538) 317/J10
Fort Augustus, Scotland 10/D2
Fort Augustus, Scotland 15/D3
Fort Battleford Nat'l Hist. Park, Sask. 181/C3
Fort Bayard, N. Mex. (88036) 274/A6
Fort Beaufort, S. Africa 118/D6
Fort Beauséjour Nat'l Hist. Park, New Bruns 170/F3
Fort Belknap, Mont. (†59526) 262/H2
Fort Belknap Ind. Res., Mont. 262/H2
Fort Belvoir, Va. 307/O3
Fort Bend (co.), Texas 303/J8
Fort Benjamin Harrison, Ind. 227/E5
Fort Benning, Georgia 217/B6
Fort Benton, Mont. (59442) 262/F3
Fort Berthold Ind. Res., N. Dak. 282/E4
Fort Bidwell, Calif. (96112) 204/E2
Fort Bidwell Ind. Res., Calif. 204/E2
Fort Blackmore, Va. (24250) 307/C7
Fort Bliss, Texas 303/A10
Fort Bliss Mil. Res., N. Mex. 274/C6
Fort Bowie Nat'l Hist. Site, Ariz. 198/F6
Fort Bragg, Calif. (95437) 204/B4
Fort Bragg, N.C. 281/M4
Fort Branch, Ind. (47648) 227/B8
Fort Bridger, Wyo. (82933) 319/B4
Fort Calhoun, Nebr. (68023) 264/J3
Fort Campbell, Ky. 237/G7
Fort Campbell, Tenn. 237/G7
Fort Carlton Hist. Park, Sask. 181/E3
Fort Caroline Nat'l Mem., Fla. 212/E1
Fort Carson, Colo. 208/K5
Fort Chaffee, Ark. 202/B3
Fort Chambly Nat'l Hist. Park, Québec 172/J4
Fort-Chimo, Que. 162/K4
Fort-Chimo, Québec 174/F2
Fort Chipewyan, Alberta 182/C5
Fort Chipewyan, Alta 162/E4
Fort Chipewyan, Alta. 146/G4
Fort Churchill, Manitoba 179/K2
Fort Clark, N. Dak. (†58571) 282/H5
Fort Clatsop Nat'l Mem., Oreg. 291/C1
Fort Cobb, Okla. (73038) 288/K4
Fort Cobb (res.), Okla. 288/J4
Fort Collins, Colo. 146/H6
Fort Collins, Colo. 188/E2
Fort Collins, Colo. (80521) 208/J1
Fort Covington○, N.Y. (12937) 276/M1
Fort-Dauphin (Faradofay), Madagascar 118/H5
Fort Davis, Ala. (36031) 195/G6
Fort Davis, Alaska 196/E2
Fort Davis, Texas (79734) 303/D11
Fort Davis Nat'l Hist. Site, Texas 303/D11
Fort Defiance, Ariz. (86504) 198/F3
Fort Defiance, Va. (24437) 307/L4
Fort-de-France (cap.), Martinique 161/C6
Fort-de-France (cap.), Martinique 156/G4
Fort-de-France (bay), Martinique 161/C6
Fort Denaud, Fla. (†33935) 212/E5
Fort Deposit, Ala. (36032) 195/E7
Fort-Desaix, Martinique 161/D6
Fort Detrick, Md. 245/J3
Fort Devens, Mass. 249/H2
Fort Dick, Calif. (95531) 204/A2
Fort Dix, N.J. 273/D3
Fort Dodge, Iowa (50501) 229/E3
Fort Dodge, Iowa 188/H2
Fort Dodge, Kansas (67843) 232/C4
Fort Donelson Nat'l Mil. Park, Tenn. 237/F8
Fort Drum, Fla. (†33472) 212/F4
Fort Drum, N.Y. 276/J2
Fort Duchesne, Utah (84026) 304/E3
Forteau, Newf. 166/C3
Fort Edward, N.Y. (12828) 276/O4
Forte República, Angola 115/C5
Forte República, Angola 102/D5
Fort Erie, Ontario 177/E5
Fortescue, Mo. (64452) 261/B2
Fortescue, N.J. (08321) 273/C5
Fortescue (riv.), W. Australia 88/B4
Fortescue (riv.), W. Australia 92/B3
Fort Eustis, Va. 307/P6
Fort Fairfield, Maine (04742) 243/H2
Fort Fairfield○, Maine (04742) 243/H2
Fort Foote, Md. (†20022) 245/F6
Fort-Foureau (Kousseri), Cameroon 115/B1
Fort Frances, Ont. 162/G6
Fort Frances, Ontario 177/F5
Fort Frances, Ontario 175/B3
Fort Franklin, N.W.T. 162/D3
Fort Franklin, N.W. Terrs. 187/F3
Fort Fraser, Br. Col. 184/E3
Fort Frederica Nat'l Mon., Georgia 217/K8
Fort Fred Steele, Wyo. (†82301) 319/E4
Fort Gaines, Ala. 195/B10
Fort Gaines, Georgia (31751) 217/C7
Fort Garland, Colo. (81133) 208/J8
Fort Gay, W. Va. (25514) 312/A6
Fort-George, Que. 146/K4
Fort-George, Que. 162/J5
Fort-George, Québec 174/B2
Fort George G. Meade, Md. 245/L4
Fort Gibson, Okla. (74434) 288/R3
Fort Gibson (lake), Okla. 288/R2
Fort Good Hope, N.W.T. 162/D2
Fort Good Hope, N.W. Terrs. 187/F3
Fort Gordon, Georgia 217/H4
Fort-Gouraud (Fdérik), Mauritania 106/B4
Fort Grant, Ariz. (85643) 198/E6
Fort Greely, Alaska 196/J2
Fort Green, Fla. (33834) 212/E4
Forth, Scotland 15/C2
Forth (firth), Scotland 10/E2
Forth (firth), Scotland 15/F4
Forth (riv.), Scotland 15/B1
Forth (riv.), Scotland 10/C1
Forth, Tasmania 99/C3
Forth (riv.), Tasmania 99/C3
Fort Hall, Idaho (83203) 220/F6
Fort Hall, Kenya 115/G4
Fort Hall Ind. Res., Idaho 220/F6
Fort Hancock, N.J. 273/F3
Fort Hancock, Texas (79839) 303/B11
Forth and Clyde (canal), Scotland 10/B1
Forth and Clyde (canal), Scotland 15/B2
Fort Hertz (Putao), Burma 72/C1
Fort Hood, Texas 303/G6
Fort Howard, Md. (21052) 245/N4
Fort Huachuca, Ariz. 198/E7
Fort Hunter Liggett, Calif. 204/D8
Fortierville, Québec 172/F3
Fortín 10 de Octubre, Paraguay 144/A2
Fortín Ávalos Sánchez, Paraguay 144/C3
Fortín Boquerón, Paraguay 144/C3
Fortín Buenos Aires, Paraguay 144/B3
Fortín Campero, Bolivia 136/C8
Fortín Capitán Escobar, Paraguay 144/B3
Fortín Carlos Antonio López (Pitiantuta), Paraguay 144/C2
Fortín Casanillo, Paraguay 144/C3
Fortín Coronel Bogado, Paraguay 144/C2
Fortín Coronel Sánchez, Paraguay 144/C1
Fortín de las Flores, Mexico 150/P2
Fort Independence Ind. Res., Calif. 204/G7
Fortine, Mont. (59918) 262/A2
Fortín Falcon, Paraguay 144/C3
Fortín Florida, Paraguay 144/C2
Fortín Galpón, Paraguay 144/C1
Fortín General Bruguez, Paraguay 144/C4
Fortín General Caballero, Paraguay 144/C4
Fortín General Delgado, Paraguay 144/B4
Fortín General Díaz, Paraguay 144/B3
Fortín Guaraní, Paraguay 144/C3
Fortín Hernandarias, Paraguay 144/A2
Fortín Infante Rivarola, Paraguay 144/A2
Fortín Isla Poi, Paraguay 144/C3
Fortín Lagerenza i, Paraguay 144/B2
Fortín Madrejón, Paraguay 144/B2
Fortín Max Paredes, Bolivia 136/F6
Fortín Mayor Alberto Gardel, Paraguay 144/A3
Fortín Mayor Rodríguez, Paraguay 144/B3
Fortín Mutum, Bolivia 136/F6
Fortín Nueva Asunción (Picuiba), Paraguay 144/B2
Fortín Olmos, Argentina 143/F4
Fortín Palmar de las Islas, Paraguay 144/B1
Fortín Pilcomayo, Paraguay 144/B3
Fortín Presidente Ayala, Paraguay 144/C3
Fortín Presidente Cardozo, Paraguay 144/B5
Fortín Ravelo, Bolivia 136/E6
Fortín Santiago Rodríguez, Paraguay 144/A2
Fortín Suárez Arana, Bolivia 136/F6
Fortín Teniente Américo Picco, Paraguay 144/C1
Fortín Teniente E. Ochoa, Paraguay 144/B2
Fortín Teniente Esteban Martínez, Paraguay 144/C3
Fortín Teniente Gabino Mendoza, Paraguay 144/B2
Fortín Teniente Juan E. López, Paraguay 144/B2
Fortín Teniente Martínez, Paraguay 144/C2
Fortín Teniente Montenía, Paraguay 144/B3
Fortín Teniente Primero Anselmo Escobar, Paraguay 144/A3
Fortín Teniente Primero M. Cabello, Paraguay 144/B3
Fortín Teniente Primero Ramiro Espínola, Paraguay 144/B2
Fortín Toledo, Paraguay 144/B3
Fortín Torres, Paraguay 144/C2
Fortín Vanguardia, Bolivia 136/F6
Fortín Zalazar, Paraguay 144/C3
Fort Jackson, N.Y. (12938) 276/L1
Fort Jackson, S.C. 296/F4
Fort Jefferson Nat'l Mon., Fla. 212/C7
Fort Jennings, Ohio (45844) 284/B4
Fort Jesup, La. (†71449) 238/C3
Fort Johnson, N.Y. (12070) 276/M5
Fort Jones, Calif. (96032) 204/C2
Fort Kent, Alberta 182/E2
Fort Kent, Maine (04743) 243/F1
Fort Kent○, Maine (04743) 243/F1
Fort Kent Mills, Maine (04744) 243/F1
Fort Klamath, Oreg. (97626) 291/E5
Fort Knox, Ky. (40121) 237/K5
Fort Lallemand, Algeria 106/F2
Fort Lamar, Georgia (†30633) 217/F2
Fort Langley, Br. Col. 184/L3
Fort Laramie, Wyo. (82212) 319/H3
Fort Laramie Nat'l Hist. Site, Wyo. 319/H3
Fort Larned Nat'l Hist. Site, Kansas 232/C3
Fort Lauderdale, Fla. 188/K5
Fort Lauderdale, Fla. (*33301) 212/C4
Fort Lawn, S.C. (29714) 296/F2
Fort Lawrence, Nova Scotia 168/D3
Fort Leavenworth, Kansas (66027) 232/H2
Fort Lee, N.J. (07024) 273/C2
Fort Lee, Va. 307/O6
Fort Leonard Wood, Mo. 261/H7
Fort Lesley J. McNair, D.C. 245/E5
Fort Lewis, Wash. 310/C3
Fort Liard, N.W.T. 146/F3
Fort Liard, N.W.T. 162/D3
Fort Liard, N.W. Terrs. 187/F3
Fort Liberté, Haiti 156/D3
Fort Liberté, Haiti 158/C5
Fort Littleton, Pa. (17223) 294/F5
Fort Loramie, Ohio (45845) 284/B5
Fort Loudon, Pa. (17224) 294/G6
Fort Loudoun (lake), Tenn. 237/N9
Fort Lupton, Colo. (80621) 208/K2
Fort Lyon, Colo. (81038) 208/N6
Fort MacArthur, Calif. 204/C11
Fort Mackay, Alta. 162/E4
Fort Macleod, Alberta 182/D5
Fort Macleod, Alta. 162/E6
Fort MacMahon, Algeria 106/E3
Fort Madison, Iowa 188/H2
Fort Madison, Iowa (52627) 229/L7
Fort Matanzas Nat'l Mon., Fla. 212/E2
Fort McClellan Mil. Res., Ala. 195/G3
Fort McCoy, Fla. (32637) 212/E2
Fort McCoy, Wis. 317/E7
Fort McDermitt Ind. Res., Nev. 266/D1
Fort McDowell Ind. Res., Ariz. 198/D5
Fort McHenry Nat'l Mon., Md. 245/M3
Fort McKavett, Texas (76841) 303/E7
Fort McKay, Alberta 182/E1
Fort McKinley, Ohio (†45426) 284/B6
Fort McMurray, Alberta 182/E1
Fort McMurray, Alta. 146/G4
Fort McMurray, Alta. 162/E4
Fort McPherson, Georgia 217/K1
Fort McPherson, N.W.T. 146/E3
Fort McPherson, N.W.T. 162/C2
Fort McPherson, N.W. Terrs. 187/E3
Fort Meade, Fla. (33841) 212/E4
Fort Meade, Uruguay (57741) 298/C5
Fort Mill, S.C. (29715) 296/F1
Fort Miribel, Algeria 106/E3
Fort Mitchell, Ala. (36856) 195/H6
Fort Mitchell, Ky. (41017) 237/S2
Fort Mitchell, Va. (23941) 307/M7
Fort Mohave Ind. Res., Ariz. 198/A4
Fort Mohave Ind. Res., Calif. 204/L9
Fort Mohave Ind. Res., Nev. 266/G7
Fort Monmouth, N.J. 273/E3
Fort Monroe, Va. 307/R6
Fort Morgan, Ala. 195/C10
Fort Morgan, Colo. (80701) 208/M2
Fort Motte, S.C. (29050) 296/F4
Fort Myer, Va. 307/T2
Fort Myers, Fla. 188/K5
Fort Myers, Fla. (*33901) 212/E5
Fort Myers Beach, Fla. (33931) 212/E5
Fort Necessity, La. (71243) 238/G2
Fort Necessity Nat'l Battlefield, Pa. 294/C6
Fort Nelson, Br. Col. 146/F4
Fort Nelson, Br. Col. 162/D4
Fort Nelson, Br. Col. 184/M2
Fort Nelson (riv.), Br. Col. 184/M2
Fort Niagara, N.Y. 276/C4
Fort Norman, N.W.T. 162/D3
Fort Norman, N.W.T. 146/F3
Fort Norman, N.W. Terrs. 187/F3
Fort Ogden, Fla. (33842) 212/E4
Fort Oglethorpe, Georgia (30742) 217/B1
Fort Ord, Calif. 204/D7
Fort Payne, Ala. (35967) 195/G2
Fort Pearce Wash (dry riv.), Ariz. 198/B2
Fort Pearce Wash (creek), Utah 304/A6
Fort Peck, Mont. (59223) 262/K2
Fort Peck (dam), Mont. 262/K3
Fort Peck (lake), Mont. 262/K3
Fort Peck (lake), Mont. 146/H5
Fort Peck (lake), Mont. 188/E1
Fort Pickett, Va. 307/N6
Fort Pierce, Fla. 188/K5
Fort Pierce, Fla. (*33450) 212/F4
Fort Pierre, S. Dak. (57532) 298/H5
Fort Pillow, Tenn. (38032) 237/B9
Fort Pitt Hist. Park, Sask. 181/B2
Fort Plain, N.Y. (13339) 276/L5
Fort Point Nat'l Hist. Site, Calif. 204/J2
Fort Polk, La. 238/D4
Fort Portal, Uganda 115/F3
Fort Providence, N.W.T. 162/E3
Fort Providence, N.W. Terrs. 187/G3
Fort Pulaski Nat'l Mon., Georgia 217/L6
Fort Qu'Appelle, Sask. 181/H5
Fort Raleigh Nat'l Hist. Site, N.C. 281/T3
Fort Randall (dam), S. Dak. 298/N7
Fort Ransom, N. Dak. (58033) 282/P6
Fort Recovery, Ohio (45846) 284/A5
Fort Resolution, N.W.T. 146/G3
Fort Resolution, N.W.T. 162/E3
Fort Resolution, N.W. Terrs. 187/G3
Fortress (mt.), Wyo. 319/C1
Fort Rice, N. Dak. (58537) 282/J6
Fort Richardson, Alaska 196/C1
Fort Riley-Camp Whiteside, Kansas 232/F2
Fort Ripley, Minn. (56449) 255/D4
Fort Ritchie, Md. 245/H2
Fort Ritner, Ind. (47430) 227/E7
Fort Robinson, Nebr. (†69339) 264/A2
Fort Rock, Oreg. (97735) 291/G4
Fort Rodman, Mass. 249/L6
Fortrose, Scotland 10/D2
Fortrose, Scotland 15/D3
Fort Rosebery (Mansa), Zambia 115/E6
Fort Ross, Calif. (†95421) 204/B5
Fort Rucker, Ala. 195/G8
Fort-Rupert, Que. 146/L4
Fort Rupert (Rupert House), Québec 174/B2
Fort Saint James, Br. Col. 162/D5
Fort Saint James, Br. Col. 184/E3
Fort Saint John, Br. Col. 162/D4
Fort Saint John, Br. Col. 184/G2
Fort Sam Houston, Texas 303/K11
Fort San, Sask. 181/H5
Fort Sandeman, Pakistan 68/B2
Fort Sandeman, Pakistan 59/J3
Fort Saskatchewan, Alberta 182/D3
Fort Saskatchewan, Alta. 162/E5
Fort Scott, Kans. 188/H3
Fort Scott, Kansas (66701) 232/H4
Fort Seneca, Ohio (44829) 284/D3
Fort Severn, Ontario 175/C1
Fort Seward, Calif. (†95440) 204/B3
Fort Seybert, W. Va. (26806) 312/H5
Fort Shafter, Hawaii 218/C3
Fort Shaw, Mont. (59443) 262/E3
Fort Shawnee, Ohio (†45801) 284/B4
Fort Sheridan, Ill. 222/B5
Fort-Shevchenko, U.S.S.R. 48/F5
Fort Sill, Okla. 288/K5
Fort Simpson, Canada 4/C15
Fort Simpson, N.W.T. 146/F3
Fort Simpson, N.W.T. 162/D3
Fort Simpson, N.W. Terrs. 187/F3
Fort Smith, Ark. 188/H3
Fort Smith, Ark. 146/J6
Fort Smith, Ark. (*72901) 202/B3
Fort Smith, Mont. (†59075) 262/J5
Fort Smith, N.W.T. 146/G3
Fort Smith, N.W.T. 162/E3
Fort Smith (dist.), N.W. Terrs. 187/G3
Fort Smith, N.W. Terrs. 187/G4
Fort Smith Nat'l Hist. Site, Ark. 202/B3
Fort Spring, W. Va. (24936) 312/E7
Fort Stanton, N. Mex. (88323) 274/D5
Fort Stanwix Nat'l Mon., N.Y. 276/J4
Fort Steele, Br. Col. 184/K5
Fort Stewart, Georgia 217/J7
Fort Stewart, Ontario 177/G2
Fort Stockton, Texas (79735) 303/A7
Fort Story, Va. 307/S7
Fort Sumner, N. Mex. (88119) 274/E4
Fort Sumter Nat'l Mon., S.C. 296/H6
Fort Supply, Okla. (73841) 288/G1
Fort Supply (lake), Okla. 288/G1
Fort Tarat, Algeria 106/F3
Fort Thomas, Ariz. (85536) 198/E5
Fort Thomas, Ky. (41075) 237/S2
Fort Thompson, S. Dak. (57339) 298/L5
Fort Ticonderoga, N.Y. (†12883) 276/O3
Fort Totten, N. Dak. (58335) 282/M4
Fort Totten Ind. Res., N. Dak. 282/N4
Fort Towson, Okla. (74735) 288/R7
Fortuna, Calif. (95540) 204/A3
Fortuna, Mo. (65034) 261/G5
Fortuna, N. Dak. (58844) 282/C2
Fortuna, Spain 33/F3
Fortuna Ledge, Alaska (99585) 196/F2
Fortune, Newf. 166/C4
Fortune (bay), Newf. 166/C4
Fort Union Nat'l Mon., N. Mex. 274/E3
Fort Union Trading Post Nat'l Hist. Site, Mont. 262/N2
Fort Union Trading Post Nat'l Hist. Site, N. Dak. 282/B3
Fort Valley, Georgia (31030) 217/E5
Fort Vancouver Nat'l Hist. Site, Wash. 310/C5
Fort Vermilion, Alberta 182/B5
Fort Vermilion, Alta. 162/E4
Fort Vermilion, Alta. 146/G4
Fort Victoria, Zimbabwe 102/F7
Fort Victoria, Zimbabwe 118/E4
Fortville, Ind. (46040) 227/F5
Fort Wainwright, Alaska 196/J1
Fort Walsh Nat'l Hist. Park, Sask. 181/A6
Fort Walton Beach, Fla. (32548) 212/C6
Fort Washakie, Wyo. (82514) 319/C2
Fort Washington, Md. (†20744) 245/L6
Fort Washington Park, Md. 245/L6
Fort Wayne, Ind. 188/J2
Fort Wayne, Ind. (*46801) 227/G2
Fort Wellington, Guyana 131/C2
Fort White, Fla. (32038) 212/D2
Fort William, Scotland 10/D2
Fort William, Scotland 15/C4
Fort Wingate, N. Mex. (87316) 274/A3
Fort Worden, Wash. 310/C2
Fort Worth, Texas 146/J6
Fort Worth, Texas (*76101) 303/F2
Fort Worth, Texas 188/G4
Fort Wright, Ky. (†41011) 237/S2
Fort Yates, N. Dak. (58538) 282/J7
Forty Fort, Pa. (18704) 294/F7
Forty Mile (pt.), Mich. 250/F3
Fort Yukon, Alaska 146/D3
Fort Yukon, Alaska (99740) 196/J1
Fort Yukon, Alaska 188/D5
Fort Yukon, U.S. 4/C17
Forum, Ark. (†72740) 202/C1
Fosforescente (bay), P. Rico 161/A3
Foshan (Fatshan), China 77/H7
Fosheim (pen.), N.W. Terrs. 187/K1
Foss, Okla. (73647) 288/H4
Foss (res.), Okla. 288/H3
Fossano, Italy 34/A2
Fosses-La-Ville, Belgium 27/F8
Fossil (creek), Ariz. 198/D4
Fossil, Oreg. (97830) 291/G2
Fossil Butte Nat'l Mon., Wyo. 319/B4
Fossombrone, Italy 34/D3
Fosston, Minn. (56542) 255/C3
Fosston, Sask. 181/H3
Foster, Ind. (†47932) 227/C4
Foster, Ky. (41043) 237/N3
Foster, Mo. (64745) 261/D6
Foster, Nebr. (68737) 264/G2
Foster (co.), N. Dak. 282/N5
Foster, Okla. (73039) 288/M5
Foster, Oreg. (97345) 291/E3
Foster○, R.I. (02825) 249/H5

Front 371

Foster (riv.), Sask. 181/M3
Foster (creek), S. Dak. 298/N4
Foster, W. Va. (25081) 312/C6
Foster, Wis. (†54758) 317/D6
Foster Center (Foster P.O.), R.I. (†02825) 249/H5
Foster City, Calif. (94404) 204/J2
Foster City, Mich. (49834) 250/B3
Fosters, Ala. (35463) 195/C4
Fosters, Mich. (†48415) 250/F5
Fosters Falls, Va. (24329) 307/G7
Fosterton, Sask. 181/C5
Foster Village, Hawaii (†96701) 218/B3
Fosterville, New Bruns. 170/C3
Fosterville, Tenn. (37063) 237/J9
Fostoria, Ala. (†36737) 195/E6
Fostoria, Iowa (51340) 229/C2
Fostoria, Kansas (66426) 232/F2
Fostoria, Mich. (48435) 250/F5
Fostoria, Ohio (44830) 284/D3
Fougamou, Gabon 115/A4
Fougères, France 28/C3
Fouke, Ark. (71837) 202/C7
Foul (bay), Egypt 111/G3
Foul (sound), Ireland 17/B5
Foula (isl.), Scotland 15/F2
Foula (isl.), Scotland 10/G1
Foules, La. (†71326) 238/G3
Foulness Island (pen.), England 13/J6
Foulpointe, Madagascar 118/H3
Foulweather (cape), Oreg. 291/C3
Foulwind (cape), N. Zealand 100/C4
Foumban, Cameroon 115/B2
Foumban, Cameroon 102/D4
Fountain, Ala. (36460) 195/D7
Fountain, Colo. (80817) 208/K5
Fountain (creek), Colo. 208/K5
Fountain, Fla. (32438) 212/D6
Fountain (co.), Ind. 227/C4
Fountain, Ind. (†47918) 227/C4
Fountain, Mich. (49410) 250/C4
Fountain, Minn. (55935) 255/F7
Fountain, N.C. (27829) 281/O3
Fountain City, Ind. (47341) 227/H5
Fountain City, Wis. (54629) 317/C7
Fountain Green, Ill. (†62321) 222/C3
Fountain Green, Utah (84632) 304/C4
Fountain Head, Md. (†21740) 245/G2
Fountain Head, Tenn. (†37148) 237/J7
Fountain Hill, Ark. (71642) 202/G7
Fountain Hill, Pa. (†18015) 294/L4
Fountain Inn, S.C. (29644) 296/C2
Fountain Run, Ky. (42133) 237/K7
Fountaintown, Ind. (46130) 227/F5
Fountain Valley, Calif. (92708) 204/D11
Four (peaks), Newf. 166/B2
Four Buttes, Mont. (59224) 262/L2
Fourche, Ariz. (†72016) 202/E4
Fourche LaFave (riv.), Ark. 202/D4
Four Corners, Oreg. (97301) 291/A3
Four Corners, Wyo. (82715) 319/H1
Four Falls, New Bruns. 170/C2
Four Hole Swamp (creek), S.C. 296/F5
Four Lakes, Wash. (99014) 310/H3
Fourmies, France 28/F2
Four Mile (riv.), Conn. 210/F3
Fourmile (lake), Oreg. 291/E5
Four Mountains (isls.), Alaska 196/E4
Fournier (cape), N. Zealand 100/E7
Fournier, Ontario 177/K2
Four Oaks, N.C. (27524) 281/M4
Four Paths, Jamaica 158/J6
Four Peaks (mt.), Ariz. 198/D5
Four States, W. Va. (26572) 312/F4
Fourteen Mile (pt.), Mich. 250/F1
Fourth (lake), Maine 243/H5
Fourth Cataract, Sudan 111/F4
Fourth Cataract, Sudan 59/B6
Fourth Cataract (dam), Sudan 102/F3
Foveaux (str.), N. Zealand 87/G10
Foveaux (str.), N. Zealand 100/A7
Fowler, Calif. (93625) 204/F7
Fowler, Colo. (81039) 208/L6
Fowler, Ill. (62338) 222/B3
Fowler, Ind. (47944) 227/C3
Fowler, Kansas (67844) 232/B4
Fowler, Mich. (48835) 250/E5
Fowlerton, Ind. (46930) 227/F4
Fowlerton, Texas (78021) 303/F9
Fowlerville, Mich. (48836) 250/F6
Fowlkes, Tenn. (38033) 237/C9
Fowlstown, Georgia (31752) 217/D9
Fowman, Iran 66/F2
Fowyang (Fuyang), China 77/J5
Fox (isls.), Alaska 196/E4
Fox, Ark. (72051) 202/F2
Fox (lake), Ill. 222/A4
Fox (riv.), Ill. 222/E5
Fox (riv.), Ill. 222/E2
Fox (riv.), Manitoba 179/K2
Fox, Mich. (†49813) 250/B3
Fox (isl.), New Bruns. 170/F1
Fox, Okla. (73435) 288/M6
Fox, Oreg. (97831) 291/H3
Fox (riv.), Wis. 317/K7
Fox (riv.), Wis. 317/K2
Foxboro, Mass. (02035) 249/J4
Foxboro○, Mass. (02035) 249/J4
Foxboro, Ontario 177/G3
Foxboro, Wis. (54836) 317/B2
Foxburg, Pa. (16036) 294/C3
Fox Chapel, Pa. (†15238) 294/C6
Fox Creek, Alberta 182/B2
Foxe (basin), Canada 4/C13
Foxe (basin), N.W.T. 146/L3
Foxe (basin), N.W.T. 162/J2
Foxe (basin), N.W. Terrs. 187/L3
Foxe (chan.), N.W.T. 162/H2
Foxe (chan.), N.W.T. 146/K3
Foxe (chan.), N.W. Terrs. 187/K3
Foxe (pen.), N.W.T. 146/L3
Foxe (pen.), N.W.T. 162/J3
Foxe (pen.), N.W. Terrs. 187/L3
Fox Farm, Wyo. (†82001) 319/H4
Foxfire, N.C. (†28373) 281/K4
Foxford, Ireland 17/C4
Foxford, Sask. 181/F2
Fox Glacier, N. Zealand 100/B5
Fox Harbour, Newf. 166/D2
Fox Harbour, Newf. 166/C3
Foxholm, N. Dak. (58738) 282/G3
Foxhome, Minn. (56543) 255/B4
Fox Lake, Alberta 182/B5
Fox Lake, Ill. (60020) 222/A4
Fox Lake, Wis. (53933) 317/J8
Foxon, Conn. (†06512) 210/D3
Foxpark, Wyo. (82057) 319/F4
Fox Point, Wis. (†53117) 317/M1
Fox River, Nova Scotia 168/D3
Fox River Grove, Ill. (60021) 222/A5
Foxton, Colo. (80441) 208/J4
Foxton, N. Zealand 100/E4
Fox Valley, Sask. 181/B5
Foxville, Md. (†21760) 245/H2
Foxwarren, Manitoba 179/A4
Foxwells, Va. (22578) 307/R5
Foxworth, Miss. (39483) 256/E8
Foyers, Scotland 15/D3
Foyil, Okla. (74031) 288/R2
Foyle (inlet), Ireland 17/G1
Foyle, Lough (inlet), Ireland 10/C3
Foyle (riv.), Ireland 17/G2
Foyle, Lough (inlet), N. Ireland 10/C3
Foyle (inlet), N. Ireland 17/G1
Foyle (riv.), N. Ireland 17/G2
Foynes, Ireland 10/B4
Foynes, Ireland 17/C6
Foz do Breu, Brazil 132/F10
Foz do Cunene, Angola 115/B7
Foz do Iguaçu, Brazil 132/C9
Frackville, Pa. (17931) 294/K4
Fraga, Spain 33/G2
Fragoso (cay), Cuba 158/F1
Fraile Muerto, Uruguay 145/E3
Frailes, Los (isl.), Dom. Rep. 158/C7
Fram, Paraguay 144/E5
Framboise, Nova Scotia 168/H3
Framboise Cove (bay), Nova Scotia 168/H3
Frame, W. Va. (25071) 312/C5
Frameries, Belgium 27/D8
Frametown, W. Va. (26623) 312/E5
Framingham○, Mass. (01701) 249/A7
Framingham Center, Mass. (01701) 249/J3
Framlingham, England 13/J5
Frampton, Québec 172/G3
Franca, Brazil 135/C2
Franca, Brazil 132/E8
Francavilla Fontana, Italy 34/F4
France 2/J3
France 7/E4
FRANCE 28
Francés (cape), Cuba 158/B2
Francés (cape), Cuba 158/A2
Frances (lake), Mont. 262/D2
Frances, Wash. (†98577) 310/B4
Frances (lake), Yukon 187/E3
Francestown○, N.H. (03043) 268/D6
Francés Viejo (cape), Dom. Rep. 158/E5
Francesville, Ind. (47946) 227/D3
Franceville, Gabon 115/B4
Franche Comté (trad. prov.), France 29
Francia, Uruguay 145/C3
Francis (lake), N.H. 268/E1
Francis, Okla. (74844) 288/N5
Francis, Sask. 181/H5
Francis, Utah (†84036) 304/C3
Francis Case (lake), S. Dak. 188/F2
Francis Case (lake), S. Dak. 146/J5
Francis Case (lake), S. Dak. 298/L7
Francisco, Ala. (†37345) 195/F1
Francisco, Ind. (47649) 227/B8
Francisco, N.C. (†27053) 281/J2
Francisco de Orellana, Peru 128/F4
Francisco I. Madero, Mexico 150/H4
Francis Creek, Wis. (54214) 317/L7
Francis E. Warren A.F.B., Wyo. 319/G4
Francistown, Botswana 118/D4
Francoeur, Québec 172/F3
Francois (lake), Br. Col. 162/D5
François (lake), Br. Col. 184/D3
François, Newf. 166/C4
François Lake, Br. Col. 184/D3
Franconia○, N.H. (03580) 268/D3
Franconia, Va. (22310) 307/S3
Franconian Jura (range), W. Germany 22/D4
Franconia Notch (pass), N.H. 268/D3
Franeker, Netherlands 27/H2
Frank, Alberta 182/C5
Frankel City, Texas (79737) 303/B5
Frankenberg-Eder, W. Germany 22/C3
Frankenmarkt, Austria 41/B3
Frankenmuth, Mich. (48734) 250/F5
Frankenthal, W. Germany 22/C4
Frankenwald (for.), W. Germany 22/D3
Frankewing, Tenn. (38459) 237/H10
Frankfield, Jamaica 158/H6
Frankford, Del. (19945) 245/S6
Frankford (Kilcormac), Ireland 17/F5
Frankford, Mo. (63441) 261/K4
Frankford, Ontario 177/G3
Frankford, W. Va. (24938) 312/F7
Frankfort, Ala. (†35653) 195/C1
Frankfort, Ill. (60423) 222/B6
Frankfort, Ind. (46041) 227/E4
Frankfort, Kansas (66427) 232/F2
Frankfort (cap.), Ky. (40601) 237/M4
Frankfort (cap.), Ky. 188/K3
Frankfort (cap.), Ky. 146/K6
Frankfort○, Maine (04438) 243/F6
Frankfort, Mich. (49635) 250/C4
Frankfort, N.Y. (13340) 276/K4
Frankfort, Ohio (45628) 284/D7
Frankfort, S. Dak. (57440) 298/N4
Frankfort Springs, Pa. (†15050) 294/A4
Frankfurt (dist.), E. Germany 22/F2
Frankfurt, W. Germany 7/E3
Frankfurt am Main, W. Germany 22/C3
Frankfurt an der Oder, E. Germany 22/F2
Frankland (cape), Tasmania 99/D1
Frankland (range), Tasmania 99/B4
Franklin (co.), Ala. 195/C2
Franklin, Ala. (36444) 195/G6
Franklin (pt.), Alaska 196/G1
Franklin, Ariz. (85534) 198/F6
Franklin (co.), Ark. 202/C2
Franklin, Ark. (72536) 202/G1
Franklin○, Conn. (†06254) 210/G2
Franklin (co.), Fla. 212/B2
Franklin (co.), Georgia 217/F2
Franklin, Georgia (30217) 217/B4
Franklin (co.), Idaho 220/G7
Franklin, Idaho (83237) 220/G7
Franklin (co.), Ill. 222/E5
Franklin, Ill. (62638) 222/C4
Franklin (co.), Ind. 227/G6
Franklin, Ind. (46131) 227/E6
Franklin (co.), Iowa 229/G3
Franklin, Iowa (†52625) 229/L7
Franklin (co.), Kansas 232/G3
Franklin, Kansas (66735) 232/H4
Franklin (co.), Ky. 237/M4
Franklin, Ky. (42134) 237/J7
Franklin (par.), La. 238/G2
Franklin, La. (70538) 238/G7
Franklin (co.), Maine 243/B5
Franklin, Maine (04634) 243/G6
Franklin○, Maine (04634) 243/G6
Franklin, Manitoba 179/C4
Franklin (co.), Mass. 249/D2
Franklin, Mass. (02038) 249/J4
Franklin○, Mass. (02038) 249/J4
Franklin, Mich. (48025) 250/B6
Franklin, Minn. (†55792) 255/F3
Franklin, Minn. (55333) 255/D6
Franklin (co.), Miss. 256/C8
Franklin (co.), Mo. 261/K6
Franklin, Mo. (65250) 261/G4
Franklin, Mont. (†59074) 262/G4
Franklin (co.), Nebr. 264/F4
Franklin, Nebr. (68939) 264/E4
Franklin (lake), Nev. 266/F2
Franklin, N.H. (03235) 268/D5
Franklin, N.J. (07416) 273/D1
Franklin (co.), N.Y. 276/M1
Franklin, N.Y. (13775) 276/K6
Franklin (co.), N.C. 281/N2
Franklin, N.C. (28734) 281/C4
Franklin (dist.), N.W.T. 162/H1
Franklin (bay), N.W.Terrs. 187/F2
Franklin (lake), N.W. Terrs. 187/J3
Franklin (mts.), N.W. Terrs. 187/F3
Franklin (str.), N.W. T. 162/G1
Franklin (str.), N.W. Terrs. 187/J2
Franklin (co.), Ohio 284/E5
Franklin, Ohio (45005) 284/B6
Franklin (co.), Pa. 294/G6
Franklin, Pa. (16323) 294/C3
Franklin, S. Dak. (†57042) 298/P6
Franklin, Tasmania 99/C5
Franklin (riv.), Tasmania 99/B4
Franklin (co.), Tenn. 237/J10
Franklin, Tenn. (37064) 237/H9
Franklin (co.), Texas 303/J4
Franklin, Texas (77856) 303/H7
Franklin (co.), Vt. 268/B2
Franklin○, Vt. (05457) 268/B2
Franklin (co.), Va. 307/J6
Franklin (I.C.), Va. (23851) 307/P7
Franklin (co.), Wash. 310/G4
Franklin, W. Va. (26807) 312/H5
Franklin, Wis. (53132) 317/L2
Franklin D. Roosevelt (lake), Wash. 310/G2
Franklin Falls (res.), N.H. 268/D4
Franklin Furnace, Ohio (45629) 284/E8
Franklin Grove, Ill. (61031) 222/D2
Franklin Lakes, N.J. (07417) 273/B1
Franklin Park, Ill. (60131) 222/B5
Franklin Park○, N.J. (†08823) 273/D3
Franklin River, Br. Col. 184/H3
Franklin Springs, Georgia (30639) 217/F2
Franklin Square, N.Y. (11010) 276/R7
Franklinton, La. (70438) 238/K5
Franklinton, N.C. (27525) 281/N2
Franklintown, Pa. (17323) 294/H5
Franklinville, N.J. (08322) 273/C4
Franklinville, N.Y. (14737) 276/D6
Franklinville, N.C. (27248) 281/K3
Franks (pond), Newf. 166/D2
Frankslake, Sask. 181/G5
Frankston, Texas (75763) 303/J5
Franksville, Wis. (53126) 317/M3
Frankton, Ind. (46044) 227/F4
Franktown, Colo. (80116) 208/K4
Franktown, Ontario 177/H2
Franktown, Va. (23354) 307/S6
Frankville, Ala. (36538) 195/B7
Frankville, Iowa (†52162) 229/K2
Frankville, Nova Scotia 168/G3
Frankville, Ontario 177/J2
Frannie, Wyo. (82423) 319/D1
Franquelin, Québec 172/B1
Franquia, Uruguay 145/B1
Franschhoek, S. Africa 118/F6
Fransfontein, Namibia 118/A4
Františkovy Lázně, Czech. 41/B1
Franz, Ontario 177/J5
Franz, Ontario 175/D3
Franz Josef Land (isls.), U.S.S.R. 2/L1
Franz Josef Land (isls.), U.S.S.R. 4/A7
Franz Josef Land (isls.), U.S.S.R. 48/F1
Frascati, Italy 34/F7
Fraser (isl.), Australia 87/F8
Fraser (riv.), Br. Col. 146/F4
Fraser (riv.), Br. Col. 162/D5
Fraser (lake), Br. Col. 184/E3
Fraser (riv.), Br. Col. 184/F4
Fraser, Colo. (80442) 208/H3
Fraser, Iowa (†50036) 229/E4
Fraser, Mich. (48026) 250/B6
Fraser, Minn. (†55719) 255/F3
Fraser (riv.), Newf. 166/B2
Fraser (isl.), Queensland 88/J4
Fraser (isl.), Queensland 95/E5
Fraserburgh, Scotland 15/G3
Fraserburgh, Scotland 10/E2
Fraserdale, Ontario 175/D3
Fraserdale, Ontario 177/J5
Fraser Lake, Br. Col. 184/E3
Fraser Mills, Br. Col. 184/K3
Fraser Reach (chan.), Br. Col. 184/C3
Frasertown, N. Zealand 100/F3
Fraserwood, Manitoba 179/E4
Frasnes-lez Anvaing, Belgium 27/D7
Frauenfeld, Switzerland 39/G1
Frauenkirchen, Austria 41/D3
Fray Benito, Cuba 158/J3
Fray Bentos, Uruguay 145/A4
Fray Marcos, Uruguay 145/D5
Frazee, Minn. (56544) 255/C4
Frazer, Mont. (59225) 262/K2
Frazeysburg, Ohio (43822) 284/F5
Frazier Park, Calif. (93225) 204/F9
Fraziers Bottom, W. Va. (25082) 312/B5
Frechen, W. Germany 22/B3
Fred, Texas (77616) 303/K7
Freda, N. Dak. (†58569) 282/H7
Fredensborg, Denmark 21/F6
Fredensdal, Virgin Is. (U.S.) 161/F4
Frederic, Mich. (49733) 250/E4
Frederic, Wis. (54837) 317/B4
Frederica, Del. (19946) 245/S4
Fredericia, Denmark 21/C6
Fredericia, Denmark 18/F9
Frederick (sound), Alaska 196/N1
Frederick, Colo. (80530) 208/K2
Frederick, Ill. (62639) 222/C3
Frederick, Kansas (†67444) 232/D3
Frederick (co.), Md. 245/J3
Frederick, Md. (21701) 245/J3
Frederick, Okla. (73542) 288/H6
Frederick, S. Dak. (57441) 298/N2
Frederick (co.), Va. 307/M2
Fredericksburg, Ind. (47120) 227/E8
Fredericksburg, Iowa (50630) 229/J3
Fredericksburg, Ohio (44627) 284/G4
Fredericksburg, Pa. (17026) 294/J5
Fredericksburg, Pa. (†16335) 294/B2
Fredericksburg, Texas (78624) 303/E7
Fredericksburg (I.C.), Va. (*22401) 307/N4
Fredericks Hall, Va. (†23117) 307/N4
Frederickton, N.S. Wales 97/G2
Fredericktown, Mo. (63645) 261/M7
Fredericktown, Ohio (43019) 284/F5
Fredericktown, Pa. (15333) 294/C6
Fredericton, N. Br. 146/M5
Fredericton, N. Br. 162/K6
Fredericton (cap.), New Bruns. 170/D3
Fredericton Junction, New Bruns. 170/D3
Frederika, Iowa (50631) 229/J3
Frederik Hendrik (Kolepom) (isl.), Indonesia 85/K7
Frederiksberg (commune), Denmark 21/F6
Frederiksberg, Denmark 21/F6
Frederiksborg (co.), Denmark 21/E5
Frederikshåb, Greenl. 4/C12
Frederikshåb, Greenland 146/N3
Frederikshavn, Denmark 18/G8
Frederikshavn, Denmark 21/D3
Frederikssund, Denmark 21/E6
Frederiksted, Virgin Is. (U.S.) 161/E4
Frederiksted, Virgin Is. (U.S.) 156/G2
Frederiksvaerk, Denmark 21/E6
Frederiksvaerk, Denmark 18/G8
Frederik Willem IV (falls), Suriname 131/C4
Fredonia, Ala. (†31833) 195/H5
Fredonia, Ariz. (86022) 198/C2
Fredonia (Biscoe), Ark. (72017) 202/H4
Fredonia, Ind. (†47137) 227/E8
Fredonia, Iowa (†52738) 229/L6
Fredonia, Kansas (66736) 232/G4
Fredonia, Ky. (42411) 237/E6
Fredonia, N.Y. (14063) 276/B6
Fredonia, N. Dak. (58440) 282/M7
Fredonia, Pa. (16124) 294/B3
Fredonia, Texas (76842) 303/E7
Fredonia, Wis. (53021) 317/L8
Fredric, Iowa (†52531) 229/H6
Fredrika, Sweden 18/L4
Fredrikstad, Norway 18/D4
Freeborn (co.), Minn. 255/E7
Freeborn, Minn. (56032) 255/E7
Freeburg, Ill. (62243) 222/D5
Freeburg, Minn. (†55921) 255/G7
Freeburg, Mo. (65035) 261/J6
Freeburg, Pa. (17827) 294/H4
Freeburn, Ky. (41528) 237/S5
Freedhem, Minn. (†56345) 255/D4
Freedom, Calif. (95019) 204/L4
Freedom, Ind. (47431) 227/D6
Freedom, Ky. (†42157) 237/K7
Freedom○, Maine (04941) 243/E7
Freedom○, N.H. (03836) 268/E4
Freedom, Okla. (73842) 288/H1
Freedom, Pa. (15042) 294/B4
Freedom, Wyo. (83120) 319/B3
Freehold, N.J. (07728) 273/E3
Freehold, N.Y. (12431) 276/N6
Freel (peak), Calif. 204/F5
Freeland, Md. (21053) 245/M2
Freeland, Mich. (48623) 250/E5
Freeland, N.C. (28440) 281/N6
Freeland, Pa. (18224) 294/L3
Freeland, Wash. (98249) 310/C2
Freeland Park, Ind. (†47944) 227/C3
Freelandville, Ind. (47535) 227/C7
Freels (cape), Newf. 166/D3
Freelton, Ontario 177/D4
Freeman (riv.), Alberta 182/C2
Freeman, Ind. (†47460) 227/D6
Freeman (lake), Ind. 227/D3
Freeman, Mo. (64746) 261/C5
Freeman, S. Dak. (57029) 298/O7
Freeman, Wash. (99015) 310/H3
Freemansburg, Pa. (†18017) 294/M4
Freemanville, Ala. (†36502) 195/D8
Free Mason (isls.), La. 238/M7
Freemont, Calif. 188/B3
Freemont, Sask. 181/B3
Freeport, Bahamas 156/B1
Freeport, Fla. (32439) 212/C6
Freeport, Ill. 188/J2
Freeport, Ill. (61032) 222/D1
Freeport, Ind. (†46161) 227/F5
Freeport, Kansas (67049) 232/E4
Freeport, Maine (04032) 243/C8
Freeport○, Maine (04032) 243/C8
Freeport, Mich. (49325) 250/D6
Freeport, Minn. (56331) 255/D5
Freeport, N.Y. (11520) 276/R7
Freeport, Nova Scotia 168/B4
Freeport, Ohio (43973) 284/H5
Freeport, Pa. (16229) 294/C4
Freeport, Texas (77541) 303/J9
Freer, Texas (78357) 303/F10
Free Soil, Mich. (49411) 250/C4
Freestone (co.), Texas 303/H6
Freetown, Ant. & Bar. 161/E11
Freetown, Ind. (47235) 227/E7
Freetown, N.Y. (†11937) 276/R9
Freetown (cap.), S. Leone 102/A4
Freetown (cap.), S. Leone 106/B7
Free Union, Va. (22940) 307/L4
Freeville, N.Y. (13068) 276/H5
Freezeout (lake), Mont. 262/D3
Fregenal de la Sierra, Spain 33/C3
Fregene, Italy 34/F6
Freiberg, E. Germany 22/E3
Freiburg, W. Germany 7/E4
Freiburg im Breisgau, W. Germany 22/B5
Freidberg, Austria 41/D3
Freienbach, Switzerland 39/G2
Freire, Chile 138/E2
Freirina, Chile 138/A7
Freising, W. Germany 22/D4
Freistadt, Austria 41/C2
Freistatt, Mo. (65654) 261/E8
Freital, E. Germany 22/E3
Freixo de Espada à Cinta, Portugal 33/C2
Fréjus, France 28/G6
Fréjus (pass), France 28/G5
Fréjus (pass), Italy 34/A2
Frelighsburg, Québec 172/E4
Fremantle, Australia 2/Q7
Fremantle, Australia 87/B9
Fremantle, W. Australia 88/B6
Fremantle, W. Australia 92/A1
Fremington, England 13/C6
Fremont, Calif. (*94536) 204/K3
Fremont (peak), Calif. 204/H8
Fremont (co.), Colo. 208/J5
Fremont (co.), Idaho 220/G5
Fremont, Ind. (46737) 227/H1
Fremont (co.), Iowa 229/B7
Fremont, Iowa (52561) 229/H6
Fremont, Mich. (49412) 250/D5
Fremont, Mo. (63941) 261/K9
Fremont, Nebr. 188/G2
Fremont, Nebr. (68025) 264/H3
Fremont○, N.H. (03044) 268/E6
Fremont, N.C. (27830) 281/N3
Fremont, Ohio (43420) 284/D3
Fremont, Utah (84727) 304/C5
Fremont (isl.), Utah 304/B2
Fremont (riv.), Utah 304/C5
Fremont, Wis. (54940) 317/J7
Fremont (co.), Wyo. 319/D2
Fremont (lake), Wyo. 319/C3
Fremont (peak), Wyo. 319/C2
French, Argentina 143/F7
French (riv.), Conn. 210/H1
French (riv.), Ontario 177/D1
French (creek), Pa. 294/C2
French (creek), S. Dak. 298/C6
French (isl.), Victoria 97/C6
Frenchboro○, Maine (04635) 243/G7
French Broad (riv.), N.C. 281/D3
French Broad (riv.), Tenn. 237/R9
Frenchburg, Ky. (40322) 237/O5
French Camp, Miss. (39745) 256/F4
French Creek, W. Va. (26218) 312/F5
French Frigate (shoal), Hawaii 188/F6
French Frigate (shoals), Hawaii 87/K3
French Frigate (shoals), Hawaii 218/C6
Frenchglen, Oreg. (97736) 291/H5
French Guiana 2/G5
French Guiana 120/D2
FRENCH GUIANA 131/E3
French Lick, Ind. (47432) 227/D7
Frenchman (creek), Colo. 208/P1
Frenchman (bay), Maine 243/G7
Frenchman (riv.), Mont. 188/E1
Frenchman (riv.), Mont. 262/J1
Frenchman (creek), Nebr. 264/C4
Frenchman (riv.), Sask. 181/C6
Frenchman (cay), Virgin Is. (Br.) 161/C4
Frenchman Butte, Sask. 181/B2
Frenchman Flat (basin), Nev. 266/F6
Frenchmans Cap (mt.), Tasmania 99/B4
Frenchmans Island, Newf. 166/C3
Frenchpark, Ireland 17/E4
French Polynesia 87/L8
French River, Minn. (†55801) 255/G4
French River, Ontario 177/D1
French Settlement, La. (70733) 238/L2
Frenchton, W. Va. (26219) 312/F5
Frenchtown, Mont. (59834) 262/B3
Frenchtown, N.J. (08825) 273/C2
Frenchville, Maine (04745) 243/G1
Frenchville○, Maine (04745) 243/G1
Frenchville, Pa. (16836) 294/F3
Frenštát pod Radhoštěm, Czech. 41/E2
Fresco, Ivory Coast 106/C7
Fresh (pond), Mass. 249/C6
Freshford, Ireland 17/G6
Freshwater, Calif. (†95501) 204/B3
Freshwater (Guffey), Colo. (80820) 208/H5
Freshwater, England 13/F7
Freshwater, Newf. 166/D2
Fresia, Chile 138/D3
Fresillo, Mexico 146/H7
Fresnillo de González Echeverría, Mexico 150/H5
Fresno (co.), Calif. 204/E7
Fresno, Calif. 146/G6
Fresno, Calif. 188/C3
Fresno, Calif. (*93706) 204/F7
Fresno (riv.), Calif. 204/E7
Fresno, Colombia 126/C5
Fresno, Mont. (†59532) 262/G2
Fresno (res.), Mont. 262/F2
Fresno, Texas (77545) 303/J2
Freudenstadt, W. Germany 22/C4
Frew, Ky. (41744) 237/P6
Frewena, North. Terr. 93/D5
Frewsburg, N.Y. (14738) 276/B6
Freycinet (pen.), Tasmania 99/E4
Fria, Guinea 106/B6
Fria (cape), Namibia 102/D6
Fria (cape), Namibia 118/A3
Friant, Calif. (93626) 204/F7
Friant-Kern (canal), Calif. 204/F8
Friars Point, Miss. (38631) 256/C2
Frias, Argentina 143/D2
Fribourg (canton), Switzerland 39/D3
Fribourg, Switzerland 39/D3
Frick, Switzerland 39/E1
Friday Harbor, Wash. (98250) 310/B2
Fridley, Minn. (55432) 255/G5
Fried, N. Dak. (†58401) 282/N5
Friedberg, W. Germany 22/C3
Friedland, E. Germany 22/E2
Friedrichshafen, W. Germany 22/C5
Friedrichstadt, W. Germany 22/C1
Friend, Kansas (67845) 232/B3
Friend, Nebr. (68359) 264/G4
Friend, Oreg. (97021) 291/F2
Friendly, W. Va. (26146) 312/D3
Friendship, Ark. (71942) 202/E5
Friendship, Ind. (47021) 227/G7
Friendship, Maine (04547) 243/E7
Friendship○, Maine (04547) 243/E7
Friendship, Md. (20758) 245/M6
Friendship, N.Y. (14739) 276/D6
Friendship, Ohio (45630) 284/D8
Friendship, Tenn. (38034) 237/C9
Friendship, Wis. (53934) 317/G8
Friendship Hill Nat'l Hist. Site, Pa. 294/C6
Friendsville, Ill. (†62863) 222/F5
Friendsville, Md. (21531) 245/A2
Friendsville, Pa. (18818) 294/L2
Friendsville, Tenn. (37737) 237/N9
Friendswood, Texas (77546) 303/J2
Friesenberg (mt.), Switzerland 39/D2
Frierson, La. (71027) 238/C2
Fries, Va. (24330) 307/F7
Friesach, Austria 41/C3
Friesche Gat (chan.), Netherlands 27/J2
Friesland, Minn. (†55037) 255/E4
Friesland (prov.), Netherlands 27/H2
Friesland, Wis. (53935) 317/H8
Frigate (isl.), Seychelles 118/J5
Frigate Bay, St. Chris.-Nevis 161/C10
Frimley and Camberley, England 13/G8
Frink, Fla. (†32430) 212/D6
Frinton and Walton, England 10/G5
Frinton and Walton, England 13/J6
Frio (cape), Brazil 120/E5
Frio (cape), Brazil 135/F3
Frio (co.), Texas 303/E9
Frio (riv.), Texas 303/E8
Friockheim, Scotland 15/F4
Friol, Spain 33/C1
Friona, Texas (79035) 303/B3
Fripp (isl.), S.C. 296/G7
Frisches Haff (lag.), Poland 47/D1
Frisco, Colo. (80443) 208/G3
Frisco, N.C. (27936) 281/T4
Frisco, Pa. (†16117) 294/B4
Frisco, Texas (75034) 303/H4
Frisco City, Ala. (36445) 195/D8
Frisian (isls.) 7/E3
Frisian, North (isls.), Denmark 21/B7
Frisian, West (isls.), Netherlands 27/G2
Frisian, East (isls.), W. Germany 22/B2
Frisian, North (isls.), W. Germany 22/B1
Frissell (mt.), Conn. 210/B1
Fristoe, Mo. (†65355) 261/F6
Fritch, Texas (79036) 303/C2
Fritchton, Ind. (†47591) 227/C7
Fritz Creek, Alaska (†99603) 196/B2
Fritzlar, W. Germany 22/C3
Friuli-Venezia Giulia (reg.), Italy 34/D1
Frizzellburg, Md. (†21157) 245/K2
Frobisher (bay), N.W.T. 162/K3
Frobisher (bay), N.W. Terrs. 187/M3
Frobisher, Sask. 181/J6
Frobisher (lake), Sask. 181/L3
Frobisher Bay, N.W.T. 162/K3
Frobisher Bay, N.W. Terrs. 187/M3
Froelich, Iowa (†52047) 229/L2
Frog (lake), Alberta 182/E3
Frog Lake, Alberta 182/E3
Frogmore, S.C. (29920) 296/F7
Frogue, Ky. (†42714) 237/L7
Frohavet (bay), Norway 18/F5
Frohna, Mo. (63748) 261/N7
Frohnleiten, Austria 41/C3
Froid, Mont. (59226) 262/M2
Froidchapelle, Belgium 27/E8
Frolovo, U.S.S.R. 48/E5
Frolovo, U.S.S.R. 52/F5
Fromberg, Mont. (59029) 262/H5
Frome (lake), Australia 87/E9
Frome, England 10/E5
Frome, England 13/E6
Frome, Jamaica 158/G6
Frome (lake), S. Australia 88/G6
Frome (lake), S. Australia 94/G4
Front (range), Colo. 208/H1

372 Fronteira

Fronteira, Portugal 33/C3
Fronteiras, Brazil 132/F4
Frontenac, Kansas (66762) 232/H4
Frontenac, Minn. (55026) 255/F6
Frontenac, Mo. (†63101) 261/O3
Frontenac (county), Ontario 177/H3
Frontenac (co.), Québec 172/G4
Frontera, Mexico 150/N7
Frontier, Mich. (49239) 250/E7
Frontier (co.), Nebr. 264/D4
Frontier, N. Dak. (†58102) 282/S6
Frontier, Sask. 181/C6
Frontier, Wyo. (83121) 319/B4
Front Royal, Va. (22630) 307/M3
Frosinone (prov.), Italy 34/D4
Frosinone, Italy 34/D4
Frösö, Sweden 18/J5
Frost, La. (†70753) 238/L2
Frost, Minn. (56033) 255/D7
Frost, Texas (76641) 303/H5
Frost, W. Va. (†24954) 312/G6
Frostburg, Md. (21532) 245/C2
Frostproof, Fla. (33843) 212/E4
Froude, Sask. 181/H6
Frövi, Sweden 18/J7
Frøya (isl.), Norway 18/F5
Frozen (str.), N.W.T. 162/H2
Frozen (str.), N.W. Terrs. 187/K3
Fruita, Colo. (81521) 208/B4
Fruita, Utah (†84775) 304/C5
Fruitdale, Ala. (36539) 195/B8
Fruitdale, S. Dak. (57742) 298/B4
Fruitdale-Harbeck, Oreg. (†97526) 291/D5
Fruitgrove, Queensland 88/K3
Fruit Heights, Utah (†84037) 304/C2
Fruithurst, Ala. (36262) 195/G3
Fruitland, Idaho (83619) 220/B6
Fruitland, Iowa (52749) 229/L6
Fruitland, Md. (21826) 245/R7
Fruitland, Mo. (†63755) 261/N8
Fruitland, N. Mex. (87416) 274/A2
Fruitland, Tenn. (†38343) 237/D9
Fruitland, Utah (84027) 304/D3
Fruitland, Wash. (99129) 310/G2
Fruitland Park, Fla. (32731) 212/D3
Fruitland Park, Miss. (39577) 256/F9
Fruitport, Mich. (49415) 250/C5
Fruitvale, Br. Col. 184/J5
Fruitvale, Idaho (83620) 220/B5
Fruitvale, Tenn. (38336) 237/C9
Fruitvale, Wash. (†98901) 310/E4
Fruitville, Fla. (33578) 212/D4
Frunze, U.S.S.R. 54/J5
Frunze, U.S.S.R. 48/H5
Frutal, Brazil 135/B2
Frutigen, Switzerland 39/E3
Frutillar, Chile 138/D3
Fry, Georgia (37317) 217/D1
Fryburg, N. Dak. (†58622) 282/D6
Fryburg, Ohio (†45895) 284/B4
Fryburg, Pa. (16326) 294/D3
Fry Canyon, Utah (†84511) 304/D6
Frýdek-Místek, Czech. 41/E2
Frýdlant nad Ostravicí, Czech. 41/E2
Frýdlant v. Čechách, Czech. 41/C1
Frye, Maine (04235) 243/B6
Fryeburg, La. (†71039) 238/D2
Fryeburg, Maine (04037) 243/A7
Fryeburg○, Maine (04037) 243/A7
Fu'an, China 77/K6
Fuchu, Hiroshima, Japan 81/F6
Fuchu, Tokyo, Japan 81/O2
Fuding, China 77/K6
Fuengirola, Spain 33/D4
Fuensalida, Spain 33/D2
Fuente-Álamo, Spain 33/F4
Fuente de Cantos, Spain 33/C3
Fuentelapeña, Spain 33/D2
Fuente Obejuna, Spain 33/D3
Fuenterrabía, Spain 33/E1
Fuentesaúco, Spain 33/D2
Fuentes de Andalucía, Spain 33/D4
Fuentes de Oñoro, Spain 33/C2
Fuerte (isl.), Colombia 126/B3
Fuerte (riv.), Mexico 150/E3
Fuerte Bulnes, Chile 138/E10
Fuerte Olimpo, Argentina 120/D5
Fuerte Olimpo, Paraguay 144/C2
Fuerteventura (isl.), Spain 102/A2
Fuerteventura (isl.), Spain 106/B3
Fuerteventura (isl.), Spain 33/C4
Fuga (isl.), Philippines 82/A3
Fuglebjerg, Denmark 21/E7
Fugu, China 77/H4
Fuhai (Burultokay), China 77/C2
Fuik, Neth. Ant. 161/G9
Fujairah, U.A.E. 59/G4
Fuji, Japan 81/J6
Fuji (mt.), Japan 81/J6
Fuji (riv.), Japan 81/J6
Fujian (Fukien), China 77/J6
Fujieda, Japan 81/J6
Fuji-Hakone-Izu National Park, Japan 81/H6
Fujin, China 77/M2
Fujisawa, Japan 81/O3
Fukagawa, Japan 81/L2
Fukang, China 77/C3
Fukuchiyama, Japan 81/G6
Fukue, Japan 81/D7
Fukui (pref.), Japan 81/G5
Fukui, Japan 81/G5
Fukuoka (pref.), Japan 81/D7
Fukuoka, Japan 54/O6
Fukuoka, Japan 81/D7
Fukushima (pref.), Japan 81/K5
Fukushima, Japan 81/K5
Fukuyama, Japan 81/F6
Fulbourn, England 13/H5
Fulbright, Texas (75436) 303/J4
Fulda, Ind. (47536) 227/D8
Fulda, Minn. (56131) 255/C7
Fulda, Sask. 181/F3
Fulda, W. Germany 22/C3
Fulda (riv.), W. Germany 22/C3
Fulford, England 13/F4
Fulford Harbour, Br. Col. 184/K3
Fuling, China 77/G6
Fulks Run, Va. (22830) 307/L3
Fullarton, Trin. & Tob. 161/A11
Fullerton, Calif. (*92631) 204/D11
Fullerton, Ky. (†41175) 237/P3
Fullerton, La. (70642) 238/D4
Fullerton, Nebr. (68638) 264/F3
Fullerton, N. Dak. (58441) 282/O7
Fully, Switzerland 39/D4
Fulnek, Czech. 41/D2
Fulpmes, Austria 41/A3
Fulton, Ala. (36446) 195/C7
Fulton (co.), Ark. 202/G1
Fulton, Ark. (71838) 202/C6
Fulton (co.), Georgia 217/D3
Fulton (co.), Ill. 222/C3
Fulton, Ill. (61252) 222/C2
Fulton (co.), Ind. 227/E2
Fulton, Ind. (46931) 227/E3
Fulton, Iowa (†52060) 229/M4
Fulton, Kansas (66738) 232/H4
Fulton (co.), Ky. 237/C7
Fulton, Ky. (42041) 237/D7
Fulton, Mich. (49052) 250/D6
Fulton, Miss. (38843) 256/H2
Fulton, Mo. (65251) 261/J5
Fulton (co.), N.Y. 276/M4
Fulton, N.Y. (13069) 276/H4
Fulton (co.), Ohio 284/B2
Fulton, Ohio (43321) 284/E5
Fulton (co.), Pa. 294/F6
Fulton, S. Dak. (57340) 298/O6
Fulton, Tenn. (†38041) 237/B9
Fulton, Texas (78358) 303/H9
Fulton Chain (lakes), N.Y. 276/K3
Fultondale, Ala. (35068) 195/E3
Fultonham, Ohio (43738) 284/F6
Fultonville, N.Y. (12072) 276/M5
Fults, Ill. (62244) 222/C5
Fulwood, England 10/G1
Fulwood, England 13/G1
Funabashi, Japan 81/P2
Funafuti (atoll), Tuvalu 87/H6
Funchal (cap.), Madeira, Port. 102/A1
Funchal (dist.), Portugal 33/A2
Funchal (cap.), Madeira, Portugal 106/A2
Funchal, Portugal 33/A2
Fundación, Colombia 126/C2
Fundão, Portugal 33/C2
Fundy (bay) 162/K7
Fundy (bay), New Bruns. 170/E3
Fundy (bay), Nova Scotia 168/C3
Fundy Nat'l Park, New Bruns. 170/E3
Funhalouro, Mozambique 118/E4
Funing, China 77/K5
Funk, Nebr. (68940) 264/E4
Funk (isl.), Newf. 166/D4
Funkley, Minn. (†56630) 255/D3
Funkstown, Md. (21734) 245/H2
Funston, Georgia (31753) 217/E8
Funter, Alaska (†99801) 196/M1
Funtua, Nigeria 106/F6
Fuping, China 77/H4
Fuquay-Varina, N.C. (27526) 281/M3
Furancungo, Mozambique 118/E2
Furka (pass), Switzerland 39/F3
Furman, Ala. (36741) 195/E6
Furman, S.C. (29921) 296/E6
Furmanov, U.S.S.R. 52/F3
Furnace, Ky. (†40472) 237/O5
Furnace, Mass. (†01031) 249/F3
Furnace, Scotland 15/C4
Furnas (res.), Brazil 120/E5
Furnas (dam), Brazil 135/C2
Furnas (co.), Nebr. 264/E4
Furneaux Group (isls.), Australia 87/E9
Furneaux Group (isls.), Tasmania 88/H8
Furneaux Group (isls.), Tasmania 99/E1
Furnes (Veurne), Belgium 27/B6
Furness, Sask. 181/B2
Furry Creek, Br. Col. 184/K2
Fürstenberg, E. Germany 22/E2
Fürstenfeld, Austria 41/C3
Fürstenfeldbruck, W. Germany 22/D4
Fürstenwalde, E. Germany 22/F2
Fürth, W. Germany 22/D4
Furth im Wald, W. Germany 22/E4
Furukawa, Japan 81/K4
Fury and Hecla (str.), N.W.T. 162/H2
Fury and Hecla (str.), N.W. Terrs. 187/K3
Fusagasugá, Colombia 126/C5
Fushun, China 77/K3
Fushun, China 54/O5
Fusilier, Sask. 181/B4
Fusin (Fuxin), China 77/K3
Fusingchen (Simao), China 77/F7
Fusio, Switzerland 39/G4
Fusong, China 77/L3
Füssen, W. Germany 22/D5
Futa Jallon (mts.), Guinea 106/B6
Futaleufú, Chile 138/E4
Futrono, Chile 138/E3
Futuna (Hoorn) (isls.), Wallis and Futuna 87/J7
Fu Xian, Liaoning, China 77/K4
Fu Xian, Shaanxi, China 77/G4
Fuxin (Fusin), China 77/K3
Fuxin, China 54/O5
Fuyang (Fowyang), China 77/J5
Fuyu, Heilongjiang, China 77/K2
Fuyu, Jilin, China 77/L2
Fuyuan, Heilongjiang, China 77/M2
Fuyuan, Yunnan, China 77/F6
Fuyun, China 77/C2
Füzesabony, Hungary 41/F3
Füzesgyarmat, Hungary 41/F3
Fuzhou (Foochow), Fujian, China 77/J6
Fuzhou, Jiangxi, China 77/J6
Fuzhou, China 2/R4
Fuzhou, China 54/N7
Fyffe, Ala. (35971) 195/G2
Fylingdales, England 13/G3
Fyn (co.), Denmark 21/D7
Fyn (isl.), Denmark 21/D7
Fyn (isl.), Denmark 18/G9
Fyne, Loch (inlet), Scotland 10/D2
Fyne, Loch (inlet), Scotland 15/C5
Fyns Hoved (pt.), Denmark 21/D6
Fyvie, Scotland 15/F3
Fyzabad, Trin. & Tob. 161/A11

G

Gaastra, Mich. (49927) 250/G2
Gabarus, Nova Scotia 168/H3
Gabarus (bay), Nova Scotia 168/H3
Gabarus (cape), Nova Scotia 168/J3
Gabbettville, Georgia (†30240) 217/B5
Gabbs, Nev. (89409) 266/D4
Gabela, Angola 115/B6
Gabès, Tunisia 106/F2
Gabès, Tunisia 102/D1
Gabès (gulf), Tunisia 106/G2
Gabgaba, Wadi (dry riv.), Sudan 111/F3
Gable, S.C. (29051) 296/G4
Gabon 2/K6
Gabon 102/D4
GABON 115/B4
Gaborone (cap.), Botswana 2/L7
Gaborone (cap.), Botswana 118/D4
Gaborone (cap.), Botswana 102/E7
Gabras, Sudan 111/E5
Gabredarre, Ethiopia 111/H6
Gabriel (str.), N.W. Terrs. 187/M3
Gabrik (riv.), Iran 66/L7
Gabriola, Br. Col. 184/J3
Gabrovo, Bulgaria 45/G4
Gachalá, Colombia 126/D5
Gach Saran, Iran 59/F3
Gach Saran, Iran 66/G5
Gackle, N. Dak. (58442) 282/M6
Gacko, Yugoslavia 45/D4
Gadag-Betgeri, India 68/D5
Gäddede, Sweden 18/J4
Gadê, China 77/E5
Gadebusch, E. Germany 22/D2
Gadmen, Switzerland 39/F3
Gadsby, Alberta 182/D3
Gadsden, Ala. 188/J4
Gadsden, Ala. (*35901) 195/G2
Gadsden, Ariz. (85336) 198/A6
Gadsden (co.), Fla. 212/B1
Gadsden, S.C. (29052) 296/F4
Gadsden, Tenn. (38337) 237/D9
Gads Hill, Mo. (†63957) 261/L8
Gadston (pt.), Fla. 212/C3
Gadwal, India 68/D5
Gadyach, U.S.S.R. 52/D4
Găeşti, Romania 45/G3
Gaeta, Italy 34/D4
Gaeta (gulf), Italy 34/D4
Gaferut (isl.), Micronesia 87/E5
Gaffney, S.C. (29340) 296/D1
Gafsa, Tunisia 106/F2
Gagarin, U.S.S.R. 52/D3
Gage, Alberta 182/A1
Gage (co.), Nebr. 264/H4
Gage, N. Mex. (†88030) 274/A6
Gage, Okla. (73843) 288/G2
Gagetown, Mich. (48735) 250/F5
Gagetown, New Bruns. 170/D3
Gaggenau, W. Germany 22/C4
Gagnoa, Ivory Coast 102/B4
Gagnoa, Ivory Coast 106/C7
Gagnon, Que. 162/K5
Gagnon, Québec 174/D2
Gagnon (lake), Québec 172/B3
Gagny, France 28/C1
Gagra, U.S.S.R. 52/E6
Gahanna, Ohio (43230) 284/E5
Gaiba (lag.), Bolivia 136/F5
Gail, Saudi Arabia 59/E5
Gail, Texas (79738) 303/C5
Gaillac, France 28/D6
Gaillard (lake), Conn. 210/D3
Gaillard, Georgia (†31078) 217/D5
Gaima, Papua N.G. 85/B7
Gaiman, Argentina 143/C5
Gaines, Mich. (48436) 250/F6
Gaines, Pa. (16921) 294/G2
Gaines (co.), Texas 303/B5
Gainesboro, Tenn. (38562) 237/K8
Gainesboro, Va. (†22601) 307/M2
Gainestown, Ala. (36540) 195/C8
Gainesville, Ala. (35464) 195/B5
Gainesville (dam), Ala. 195/B5
Gainesville, Fla. 188/K5
Gainesville, Fla. (*32601) 212/D2
Gainesville, Georgia (30501) 217/E2
Gainesville, Mo. (65655) 261/G9
Gainesville, N.Y. (14066) 276/D5
Gainesville, Texas (76240) 303/G4
Gainesville, Va. (22065) 307/N3
Gainsborough, England 10/F4
Gainsborough, England 13/G4
Gainsborough, Sask. 181/K6
Gairdner (lake), Australia 87/D9
Gairdner (lake), S. Australia 88/F6
Gairdner (lake), S. Australia 94/D4
Gairloch, Scotland 15/C3
Gairloch, Loch (inlet), Scotland 15/C3
Gais, Switzerland 39/H2
Gaithersburg, Md. (20760) 245/K4
Gajdel, Czech. 41/E2
Gakona, Alaska (99586) 196/K2
Galadi, Ethiopia 111/J6
Galahad, Alberta 182/E3
Galana (riv.), Kenya 115/G4
Galand, Iran 66/J2
Galanta, Czech. 41/D2
Galápagos (isls.), Ecuador 2/E6
Galápagos (isls.), Ecuador 128/C8
Galashiels, Scotland 10/E3
Galashiels, Scotland 15/F5
Galata, Mont. (59444) 262/E2
Galata, Turkey 63/C6
Galaţi, Romania 7/G4
Galaţi, Romania 45/H3
Galatia, Ill. (62935) 222/E6
Galatia, Kansas (†67567) 232/D3
Galatina, Italy 34/G4
Galatone, Italy 34/F4
Galax (I.C.), Va. (24333) 307/G7
Galbally, Ireland 17/E7
Galbraith, La. (†71447) 238/E4
Galcaio, Somalia 102/G4
Galcaio, Somalia 115/J2
Galchutt, N. Dak. (58034) 282/S7
Gale, Ill. (62936) 222/D6
Gale (riv.), N.H. 268/D3
Galeana, Chihuahua, Mexico 150/F1
Galeana, Nuevo León, Mexico 150/J4
Galela, Indonesia 85/H5
Galen, Mont. (†59722) 262/D4
Galena, Alaska (99741) 196/G2
Galena, Ill. (61036) 222/C1
Galena, Ind. (†47119) 227/F8
Galena, Kansas (66739) 232/H4
Galena, Md. (21635) 245/P3
Galena, Mo. (65656) 261/F9
Galena, Ohio (43021) 284/E5
Galena Park, Texas (77547) 303/J1
Galeota (pt.), Trin. & Tob. 161/B11
Galera (pt.), Chile 138/D3
Galera (pt.), Ecuador 128/B2
Galera (pt.), Trin. & Tob. 161/C10
Galera (pt.), Trin. & Tob. 156/G5
Galesburg, Ill. 188/H2
Galesburg, Ill. (61401) 222/C3
Galesburg, Kansas (66740) 232/G4
Galesburg, Mich. (49053) 250/D6
Galesburg, N. Dak. (58035) 282/R5
Gales Creek, Oreg. (97117) 291/D2
Gales Ferry, Conn. (06335) 210/G3
Galestown, Md. (†19973) 245/P6
Galesville, Md. (20765) 245/M5
Galesville, Wis. (54630) 317/D7
Galeton, Colo. (80622) 208/K1
Galeton, Pa. (16922) 294/G2
Galetta, Ontario 177/H2
Galgenberg (hill), Netherlands 27/H4
Galguduud (prov.), Somalia 115/J2
Galiano, Br. Col. 184/K3
Galiano (isl.), Br. Col. 184/K3
Galice, Oreg. (†97532) 291/D5
Galich, U.S.S.R. 52/F3
Galicia (reg.), Spain 33/B1
Galien, Mich. (49113) 250/C7
Galilee, Sea of (lake), Israel 59/C3
Galilee, Sea of (Tiberias) (lake), Israel 65/D2
Galilee (reg.), Israel 65/C2
Galilee (lake), Queensland 95/C4
Galina (pt.), Jamaica 158/J6
Galion (bay), Martinique 161/D6
Galion, Ohio (44833) 284/E4
Galisteo, N. Mex. (†87540) 274/D3
Galiuro (mts.), Ariz. 198/E6
Galivants Ferry, S.C. (29544) 296/J3
Gallabat, Sudan 111/G5
Gallan (head), Scotland 15/A2
Gallant, Ala. (35972) 195/F2
Gallarate, Italy 34/B2
Gallatin (co.), Ill. 222/E6
Gallatin (co.), Ky. 237/M3
Gallatin, Mo. (64640) 261/E3
Gallatin (co.), Mont. 262/E5
Gallatin (peak), Mont. 262/E5
Gallatin (riv.), Mont. 262/E5
Gallatin, Tenn. (37066) 237/H8
Gallatin Gateway, Mont. (59730) 262/E5
Gallaway, Tenn. (38036) 237/B10
Galle, Sri Lanka 54/J9
Galle, Sri Lanka 68/D7
Gallegos (riv.), Argentina 143/B7
Gallegos, N. Mex. (†87733) 274/F3
Galley (head), Ireland 17/D9
Gallia (co.), Ohio 284/F8
Galliano, La. (70354) 238/K8
Gallina, N. Mex. (87017) 274/C2
Gallinas (pt.), Colombia 120/B1
Gallinas (pt.), Colombia 126/E1
Gallinas (mts.), N. Mex. 274/B4
Gallinas (riv.), N. Mex. 274/E3
Gallion, Ala. (36742) 195/C6
Gallion, La. (†71223) 238/G1
Gallipoli, Italy 34/F4
Gallipoli, Turkey 59/A1
Gallipoli, Turkey 63/C5
Gallipolis, Ohio (45631) 284/F8
Gallipolis Ferry, W. Va. (25515) 312/B5
Gallitzin, Pa. (16641) 294/E4
Gällivare, Sweden 18/M3
Gallman, Miss. (39077) 256/D7
Gallo (pt.), Chile 138/G3
Gallo (mt.), Dom. Rep. 158/D5
Gällö, Sweden 18/J5
Galloo (isl.), N.Y. 276/H3
Galloway, Ark. (†72114) 202/F4
Galloway, Br. Col. 184/K5
Galloway (dist.), Scotland 15/D5
Galloway, Mull of (prom.), Scotland 15/D6
Galloway, Mull of (prom.), Scotland 10/D3
Galloway, W. Va. (26349) 312/F4
Galloway, Wis. (54432) 317/H6
Gallup, N. Mex. 188/E3
Gallup, N. Mex. (87301) 274/A3
Gallur, Spain 33/F2
Galole, Kenya 115/G4
Gal'on, Israel 65/B4
Galston, Scotland 10/D3
Galston, Scotland 15/D5
Galt, Calif. (95632) 204/C9
Galt, Iowa (50101) 229/F3
Galt, Mo. (64641) 261/F2
Galtee (mts.), Ireland 17/E7
Galtymore (mt.), Ireland 17/E7
Galva, Ill. (61434) 222/D2
Galva, Iowa (51020) 229/C3
Galva, Kansas (67443) 232/E3
Galván (mt.), Paraguay 144/C3
Galvarino, Chile 138/D2
Galveston, Ind. (46932) 227/E3
Galveston (co.), Texas 303/K8
Galveston, Texas 146/J7
Galveston, Texas 188/H5
Galveston, Texas (*77550) 303/L3
Galveston (bay), Texas 188/H5
Galveston (bay), Texas 303/L2
Galveston (isl.), Texas 303/K8
Gálvez, Argentina 143/F6
Galvez, La. (†70769) 238/L2
Gálvez, Spain 33/D3
Galvin, Wash. (98544) 310/B4
Galway (co.), Ireland 17/D5
Galway, Ireland 17/C5
Galway, Ireland 7/D3
Galway, Ireland 10/B4
Galway (bay), Ireland 17/C5
Galway (bay), Ireland 10/B4
Galway, N.Y. (12074) 276/N4
Gamaliel, Ky. (42140) 237/K7
Gamarra, Colombia 126/D3
Gamas Ab (riv.), Iran 66/E3
Gamay, Philippines 82/E4
Gamay (bay), Philippines 82/E4
Gamba, China 77/C6
Gambaga, Ghana 106/D6
Gambela, Ethiopia 111/F6
Gambell, Alaska (99742) 196/D2
Gamber, Md. (†21048) 245/L3
Gambia 2/J5
Gambia 102/A3
GAMBIA 106/A6
Gambia (riv.), Gambia 106/B6
Gambia (riv.), Senegal 106/B6
Gambier (isls.), Fr. Poly. 87/N8
Gambier, Ohio (43022) 284/F5
Gambo, Newf. 166/D4
Gamboma, Congo 115/C4
Gambos, Angola 115/B6
Gambrills, Md. (21054) 245/M4
Gamerco, N. Mex. (87317) 274/A3
Gaming, Austria 41/C3
Gamleby, Sweden 18/J8
Gammon (riv.), Manitoba 179/G3
Gammon (pt.), Mass. 249/N6
Gampel, Switzerland 39/E4
Gamu-Gofa (prov.), Ethiopia 111/G6
Gamvik, Norway 18/Q1
Ganado, Ariz. (86505) 198/F3
Ganado, Texas (77962) 303/H8
Ganale Dorya (riv.), Ethiopia 111/H6
Gananoque, Ontario 177/H3
Ganassi, Philippines 82/D7
Ganaveh, Iran 66/G6
Ganda, Angola 115/B6
Gandajika, Zaire 115/D5
Gandara, Philippines 82/E4
Gándara, Spain 33/C1
Gandava, Pakistan 68/B3
Gandava, Pakistan 59/J4
Gandeeville, W. Va. (25243) 312/D5
Gander, Newf. 166/D4
Gander (lake), Newf. 166/D4
Gander (riv.), Newf. 166/D4
Gander, Newf. 162/L6
Gandesa, Spain 33/G2
Gandhinagar, India 68/C4
Gandía, Spain 33/F3
Gandy, Nebr. (†69163) 264/D3
Gandy, Utah (†84728) 304/A4
Gandzha (Kirovabad), U.S.S.R. 52/G6
Ganga (Ganges) (riv.), India 68/F3
Gan Gan, Argentina 143/C5
Ganganagar, India 68/C3
Gangapur, India 68/D3
Gangara, Niger 106/F6
Gangaw, Burma 72/B2
Gangca, China 77/F4
Gangdisê Shan (range), China 77/B5
Ganges (riv.) 54/K7
Ganges (riv.) 2/P4
Ganges, Mouths of the (delta), Bangladesh 68/F3
Ganges (riv.), Bangladesh 68/F3
Ganges, Br. Col. 184/K3
Ganges, Mouths of the (delta), India 68/F4
Ganges (riv.), India 68/F3
Gangtok, India 68/F3
Gan He (riv.), China 77/K2
Gani, Indonesia 85/H6
Ganister, Pa. (†16693) 294/F5
Ganmain, N.S. Wales 97/E1
Gann (Brinkhaven), Ohio (†43006) 284/F5
Gannat, France 28/E4
Gannett, Idaho (†83313) 220/D6
Gannett (peak), Wyo. 188/D2
Gannett (peak), Wyo. 319/C2
Gannvalley, S. Dak. (57341) 298/L5
Ganquan, China 77/H4
Gans, Okla. (74936) 288/S4
Gänserndorf, Austria 41/D2
Gansevoort, N.Y. (12831) 276/N4
Ganshoren, Belgium 27/B9
Gansu (Kansu), China 77/E3
Gansville, La. (†71422) 238/E2
Gantt, Ala. (36038) 195/E8
Gantt, S.C. (†29609) 296/C2
Ganzhou (Kanchow), China 77/H6
Gao (mt.), Cent. Afr. Rep. 115/C2
Gao, Mali 102/C3
Gao, Mali 106/E5
Gao'an, China 77/H6
Gaolan, China 77/F4
Gaotai, China 77/F4
Gaoua, Upper Volta 106/D6
Gaoual, Guinea 106/B6
Gaoyou Hu (lake), China 77/J5
Gap, France 28/G5
Gap, Pa. (17527) 294/L6
Gap (creek), Sask. 181/B6
Gapan, Philippines 82/C3
Gapcreek, Ky. (†42603) 237/M7
Gap Mills, W. Va. (24941) 312/F7
Gar, China 77/B5
Gara (lake), Ireland 17/D4
Gara, Lough (lake), Ireland 10/B4
Garachiné, Panama 154/H6
Garad, Somalia 115/J2
Garadice (lake), Ireland 17/F3
Garah, N.S. Wales 97/E1
Garamba Nat'l Park, Zaire 115/E3
Garanhuns, Brazil 120/F3
Garanhuns, Brazil 132/G5
Garards Fort, Pa. (15334) 294/B6
Garbahaarrey, Somalia 115/H3
Garba Tula, Kenya 115/G3
Garber, Iowa (52048) 229/L3
Garber, Okla. (73738) 288/M2
Garberville, Calif. (95440) 204/B3
Garbosh, Kuh-e (mt.), Iran 66/G4
Garbsen, W. Germany 22/C2
Garça, Brazil 135/B3
Garcia, Colo. (81134) 208/J8
García de Sola (res.), Spain 33/D3
Garcitas, Venezuela 124/C3
Gard (dept.), France 28/F6
Gard (riv.), France 28/F5
Garda (lake), Italy 34/C2
Gardanne, France 28/F6
Gardar, N. Dak. (58234) 282/P2
Gardelegen, E. Germany 22/D2
Garden, Mich. (49835) 250/C3
Garden (isl.), Mich. 250/D3
Garden (pen.), Mich. 250/C3
Garden (co.), Nebr. 264/B3
Garden (isl.), W. Australia 88/A2
Garden (isl.), W. Australia 92/A1
Gardena, Calif. (*90747) 204/C11
Gardena, Idaho (†83629) 220/B5
Gardena, N. Dak. (58739) 282/J2
Garden City, Ala. (35070) 195/E2
Garden City, Georgia (31408) 217/K6
Garden City, Idaho (†83704) 220/B6
Garden City, Iowa (50102) 229/G4
Garden City, Kans. 188/F3
Garden City, Kansas (67846) 232/B4
Garden City, La. (70540) 238/H7
Garden City, Mich. (48135) 250/F6
Garden City, Minn. (56034) 255/D6
Garden City, Mo. (64747) 261/D5
Garden City, N.Y. (11530) 276/R7
Garden City, S. Dak. (57236) 298/O4
Garden City, Texas (79739) 303/C6
Garden City, Utah (84028) 304/C2
Garden City Beach, S.C. (29576) 296/K4
Gardendale, Ala. (35071) 195/E3
Garden Grove, Calif. (*92640) 204/D11
Garden Grove, Iowa (50103) 229/F7
Garden Home-Whitford, Oreg. (97223) 291/A2
Garden Island (bay), La. 238/M8
Garden Plain, Kansas (67050) 232/E4
Garden Prairie, Ill. (61038) 222/E1
Garden Reach, India 68/F2
Garden River, Alberta 182/B5
Gardenstown, Scotland 15/F3
Gardenton, Manitoba 179/F5
Garden Valley, Idaho (83622) 220/C5
Garden View, Pa. (†17701) 294/H3
Garden Village, Ontario 177/E1
Gardez, Afghanistan 59/J3
Gardez, Afghanistan 68/B2
Gardi, Georgia (†31545) 217/J7
Gardiner, Maine (04345) 243/D7
Gardiner, Mont. (59030) 262/F5
Gardiner, Oreg. (97441) 291/C4
Gardiner (dam), Sask. 181/D4
Gardiner, Wash. (98334) 310/B2
Gardiners (bay), N.Y. 276/R8
Gardiners (isl.), N.Y. 276/R8
Gardner (canal), Br. Col. 184/C3
Gardner, Colo. (81040) 208/J7
Gardner (lake), Conn. 210/G2
Gardner, Fla. (†33890) 212/E4
Gardner, Ill. (60424) 222/E2
Gardner, Kansas (66030) 232/H3
Gardner (isl.), Kiribati 87/J6
Gardner (lake), Maine 243/J6
Gardner, Mass. (01440) 249/G2
Gardner, N. Dak. (58036) 282/R5
Gardner, Tenn. (†38237) 237/D8
Gardner (mt.), Wash. 310/E2
Gardner Creek, New Bruns. 170/E3
Gardner Pinnacles (isls.), Hawaii 87/K3
Gardner Pinnacles (isls.), Hawaii 188/F6
Gardner Pinnacles (isls.), Hawaii 218/C6
Gardnerville, Nev. (89410) 266/B4
Gardo, Somalia 115/J2
Gardula, Ethiopia 111/G6
Gare Loch (inlet), Scotland 15/A1
Garelochhead, Scotland 15/A1
Garelochhead, Scotland 10/A1
Gareloi (isl.), Alaska 196/K4
Garessio, Italy 34/A2
Garfield, Ark. (72732) 202/C1
Garfield (co.), Colo. 208/C3
Garfield, Colo. (81227) 208/G5
Garfield, Georgia (30425) 217/H5
Garfield, Kansas (67529) 232/C3
Garfield, Ky. (40140) 237/J5
Garfield, Minn. (56332) 255/C5
Garfield (co.), Mont. 262/J3
Garfield (co.), Nebr. 264/F3
Garfield, N.J. (07026) 273/B2
Garfield, N. Mex. (87936) 274/B6
Garfield (co.), Okla. 288/L2
Garfield (co.), Utah 304/C6
Garfield (co.), Wash. 310/H4
Garfield, Wash. (99130) 310/H3
Garfield Heights, Ohio (44125) 284/J9
Gargaliánoi, Greece 45/E7
Gargunnock, Scotland 15/B1
Garibaldi, Br. Col. 184/F5
Garibaldi, Oreg. (97118) 291/D2
Garibaldi Prov. Park, Br. Col. 184/F5
Garies, S. Africa 118/B6
Garioch (dist.), Scotland 15/F3
Garissa, Kenya 115/G4
Garita, N. Mex. (88421) 274/E3
Garland, Ala. (†36456) 195/E7
Garland (co.), Ark. 202/D4

Ghemines 373

Garland, Ark. (71839) 202/C7
Garland, Kansas (66741) 232/H4
Garland, Maine (04939) 243/E5
Garland○, Maine (04939) 243/E5
Garland, Manitoba 179/B3
Garland, Nebr. (68360) 264/G4
Garland, N.C. (28441) 281/N5
Garland, Pa. (16416) 294/C2
Garland, Tenn. (†38019) 237/B9
Garland, Tex. 188/G4
Garland, Texas (*75040) 303/H2
Garland, Utah (84312) 304/B2
Garland, Wyo. (†82435) 319/D1
Garlandville, Miss. (†39345) 256/F6
Garlieston, Scotland 15/D6
Garlin, Ky. (†42728) 237/L6
Garmisch-Partenkirchen, W. Germany 22/D5
Garmouth, Scotland 15/E3
Garmsar, Iran 59/F2
Garmsar, Iran 66/H3
Garnavillo, Iowa (52049) 229/L3
Garneill, Mont. (59445) 262/G4
Garner, Ark. (72052) 202/G3
Garner, Iowa (50438) 229/F2
Garner (lake), Manitoba 179/G4
Garner, N.C. (27529) 281/M3
Garnet, Mich. (†49762) 250/D2
Garnet, Mont. (†59832) 262/C4
Garnet (bay), N.W. Terrs. 187/L3
Garnett, Kansas (66032) 232/G3
Garnett, S.C. (29922) 296/E6
Garnish, Newf. 166/C4
Garoe, Somalia 115/J2
Garonne (riv.), France 7/D4
Garonne (riv.), France 28/C5
Garoua, Cameroon 102/D4
Garoua, Cameroon 115/B2
Garrabost, Scotland 15/B2
Garrard (co.), Ky. 237/M5
Garretson, S. Dak. (57030) 298/S6
Garrett, Ill. (†61913) 222/E4
Garrett, Ind. (46738) 227/G2
Garrett, Ky. (41630) 237/R6
Garrett (co.), Md. 245/A2
Garrett, Pa. (15542) 294/D6
Garrett, Wash. (†99362) 310/G4
Garrett, Wyo. (82058) 319/G3
Garrett Park, Md. (20766) 245/E3
Garretts Bend, W. Va. (†25523) 312/C6
Garrettsville, Ohio (44231) 284/H3
Garrick, Sask. 181/G2
Garrison, Iowa (52229) 229/J4
Garrison, Ky. (41141) 237/P3
Garrison, Md. (21055) 245/L3
Garrison, Minn. (56450) 255/E4
Garrison, Mo. (65657) 261/F9
Garrison, Mont. (59731) 262/D4
Garrison, Nebr. (68632) 264/G3
Garrison, N.Y. (10524) 276/N8
Garrison, N. Dak. (58540) 282/H4
Garrison (dam), N. Dak. 282/H5
Garrison, Texas (75946) 303/K6
Garrison, Utah (84728) 304/A5
Garrisonville, Va. (22463) 307/N4
Garron (pt.), N. Ireland 17/K1
Garrovillas, Spain 33/C3
Garry (lake), Canada 4/C14
Garry (lake), N.W.T. 162/G2
Garry (lake), N.W. Terrs. 187/H3
Garry, Loch (lake), Scotland 15/D3
Garry (riv.), Scotland 15/D4
Garryowen, Mont. (59031) 262/J5
Garsen, Kenya 115/G4
Garske, N. Dak. (†58382) 282/N3
Garson (lake), Alberta 182/E1
Garson, Manitoba 179/F4
Garstang, England 13/G1
Gartan (lake), Ireland 17/F2
Gartmore, Scotland 15/B1
Garulia, India 68/F1
Garut, Indonesia 85/H2
Garvagh, N. Ireland 17/H2
Garvan (isls.), Ireland 17/G1
Garvin, Minn. (56132) 255/C6
Garvin (co.), Okla. 288/M5
Garvin, Okla. (74736) 288/S7
Garwin, Iowa (50632) 229/H4
Garwolin, Poland 47/E3
Garwood, Mo. (†63965) 261/L8
Garwood, N.J. (07027) 273/E2
Garwood, Texas (77442) 303/H8
Gary, Ind. 146/K5
Gary, Ind. 188/J2
Gary, Ind. (*46401) 227/C1
Gary, Minn. (56545) 255/B3
Gary, S. Dak. (57237) 298/S4
Gary, Texas (75643) 303/K5
Gary, W. Va. (24836) 312/C8
Garyarsa (Gartok), China 77/B5
Garyarsa, China 54/K6
Garysburg, N.C. (27831) 281/O2
Garyville, La. (70051) 238/M3
Garza (co.), Texas 303/C4
Garzê, China 77/F5
Garzón, Colombia 126/C6
Garzón, Uruguay 145/E5
Garzón (lag.), Uruguay 145/E5
Gas, Kansas (66742) 232/G4
Gas (hills), Wyo. 319/E3
Gasan-Kuli, U.S.S.R. 48/F6
Gasburg, Va. (23857) 307/N7
Gas City, Ind. (46933) 227/F4
Gasconade (co.), Mo. 261/J6
Gasconade, Mo. (65036) 261/J5
Gasconade (riv.), Mo. 261/H7
Gascony (trad. prov.), France 29
Gascoyne (riv.), Australia 87/B8
Gascoyne, N. Dak. (58629) 282/D7
Gascoyne (riv.), W. Australia 88/A4
Gascoyne (riv.), W. Australia 92/B4
Gascoyne Junction, W. Australia 92/A4
Gash (Mareb) (riv.), Ethiopia 59/C7
Gash (riv.), Sudan 59/C6
Gashaka, Nigeria 106/G7
Gas Hills, Wyo. (82501) 319/E3
Gash Mareb (riv.), Ethiopia 111/G5
Gasht, Iran 66/M7
Gasker (isl.), Scotland 15/A3
Gaskiers, Newf. 166/D2
Gasmata, Papua N.G. 86/B2
Gaspar, Cuba 158/F2
Gaspar Hernández, Dom. Rep. 158/E5
Gasparilla (isl.), Fla. 212/D5
Gaspé, Que. 162/K6
Gaspé, Québec 172/D1
Gaspé, Québec 174/E3
Gaspé (bay), Québec 172/D1
Gaspé (cape), Québec 172/D1
Gaspé (pen.), Québec 172/D2
Gaspé-Est (county), Québec 174/E3
Gaspé-Est (co.), Québec 172/D1
Gaspé-Ouest (co.), Québec 172/C1
Gaspé-Ouest (county), Québec 174/D3
Gaspereau (riv.), New Bruns. 170/D2
Gaspereau (lake), Nova Scotia 168/D4
Gaspésie Prov. Park, Québec 174/D3
Gaspésie Prov. Park, Québec 172/C1
Gasport, N.Y. (14067) 276/C4
Gasque, Ala. (†36542) 195/C10
Gassan (mt.), Japan 81/J4
Gassaway, Tenn. (†37095) 237/K9
Gassaway, W. Va. (26624) 312/E5
Gassetts, Vt. (†05144) 268/B5
Gassville, Ark. (72635) 202/F1
Gaston, Ind. (47342) 227/G4
Gaston (co.), N.C. 281/G4
Gaston, N.C. (27832) 281/O1
Gaston (res.), N.C. 281/O2
Gaston, Oreg. (97119) 291/D2
Gaston, S.C. (29053) 296/E4
Gaston (lake), Va. 307/M8
Gastonburg, Ala. (†36728) 195/C6
Gastonia, N.C. 188/K3
Gastonia, N.C. (28052) 281/G4
Gastre, Argentina 143/C5
Gat, Israel 65/B4
Gata (cape), Cyprus 59/B3
Gata (cape), Cyprus 63/E5
Gata (cape), Spain 33/F4
Gata (mts.), Spain 33/C2
Gatchel, Ind. (†47586) 227/D8
Gatchina, U.S.S.R. 52/C3
Gate, Okla. (73844) 288/F1
Gate, Wash. (†98579) 310/B4
Gate City, Va. (24251) 307/C7
Gatehouse of Fleet, Scotland 10/E3
Gatehouse of Fleet, Scotland 15/D6
Gates, Nebr. (68839) 264/E3
Gates (co.), N.C. 281/R2
Gates, N.C. (27937) 281/R2
Gates, Oreg. (97346) 291/E3
Gates, Tenn. (38037) 237/C9
Gateshead, England 10/F3
Gateshead, England 13/J3
Gateshead (isl.), N.W. Terrs. 187/J2
Gates Mills, Ohio (44040) 284/J9
Gates of the Arctic Nat'l Park, Alaska 196/H1
Gates of the Arctic Nat'l Preserve, Alaska 196/H1
Gatesville, N.C. (27938) 281/R2
Gatesville, Texas (76528) 303/G6
Gateswood, Ala. (†36507) 195/C9
Gateway, Ark. (72733) 202/B1
Gateway, Colo. (81522) 208/B5
Gateway, Oreg. (†97741) 291/F3
Gateway Nat'l Rec. Area, N.J. 273/E2
Gateway Nat'l Rec. Area, N.Y. 276/M9
Gatewood, Mo. (63942) 261/K9
Gatico, Chile 138/A4
Gatineau (co.), Québec 172/B4
Gatineau (county), Québec 174/B3
Gatineau, Québec 172/B4
Gatineau (riv.), Québec 172/B3
Gatliff, Ky. (†40769) 237/O7
Gatlinburg, Tenn. (37738) 237/O9
Gatooma, Zimbabwe 118/D3
Gatooma, Zimbabwe 102/E6
Gatow, W. Germany 22/E4
Gatteville-le-Phare, France 28/C3
Gattman, Miss. (38844) 256/H3
Gatton, Queensland 88/J5
Gatton, Queensland 95/E5
Gatun (lake), Panama 154/G6
Gatzke, Minn. (56724) 255/C2
Gaucín, Spain 33/D4
Gauhati, India 68/G3
Gauhati, India 54/L7
Gauja (riv.), U.S.S.R. 53/C2
Gauley (riv.), W. Va. 312/D6
Gauley Bridge, W. Va. (25085) 312/D6
Gauley Mills, W. Va. (26240) 312/E6
Gaultois, Newf. 166/C4
Gausdale, Ky. (40906) 237/N7
Gause, Texas (77857) 303/H7
Gaussberg (mt.) 5/C5
Gautier, Miss. (39553) 256/G10
Gavater, Iran 59/H5
Gavater, Iran 66/M8
Gávdhos (isl.), Greece 45/F8
Gave de Pau (riv.), France 28/C6
Gavião, Portugal 33/C3
Gavins Point (dam), Nebr. 264/G2
Gavins Point (dam), S. Dak. 298/P8
Gaviota, Calif. (†93017) 204/E9
Gavkhuni (lake), Iran 59/F3
Gavkhuni (marsh), Iran 66/H4
Gävle, Sweden 7/F2
Gävle, Sweden 18/K6
Gävleborg (co.), Sweden 18/K6
Gawai, Burma 72/C1
Gawler, S. Australia 88/F6
Gawler (ranges), S. Australia 88/F6
Gawler, S. Australia 94/B6
Gawler (ranges), S. Australia 94/E5
Gawler (riv.), S. Australia 94/B6
Gay, Georgia (30218) 217/C4
Gay, Mich. (49928) 250/A1
Gay, U.S.S.R. 52/J4
Gay, W. Va. (25244) 312/C5
Gaya, India 68/F4
Gaya, Niger 106/E6
Gay Head○, Mass. (†02535) 249/L7
Gay Head (prom.), Mass. 249/L7
Gay Hill, Texas (†77833) 303/H7
Gayle, Jamaica 158/J6
Gaylesville, Ala. (35973) 195/G2
Gaylord, Kansas (67638) 232/D2
Gaylord, Mich. (49735) 250/E3
Gaylord, Minn. (55334) 255/D6
Gaylord, Oreg. (97458) 291/C5
Gaylord, Va. (†22611) 307/M2
Gaylordsville, Conn. (06755) 210/A2
Gayndah, Queensland 95/D5
Gayndah, Queensland 88/J5
Gayny, U.S.S.R. 52/H2
Gays, Ill. (61928) 222/E4
Gaysin, U.S.S.R. 52/C5
Gays Mills, Wis. (54631) 317/E9
Gaysport, Ohio (†43720) 284/G6
Gaysville, Vt. (05746) 268/B4
Gayville, S. Dak. (57031) 298/P8
Gaza, Cent. Afr. Rep. 115/C3
Gaza, Egypt 59/B3
Gaza, Gaza Strip 65/A5
Gaza, Iowa (†51245) 229/B2
Gaza (prov.), Mozambique 118/E4
Gaza, N.H. (†03269) 268/D4
GAZA STRIP 59/B3
Gaza Strip 65/A5
Gazelle, Calif. (96034) 204/C2
Gazelle (pen.), Papua N.G. 86/B2
Gaziantep (prov.), Turkey 63/G4
Gaziantep, Turkey 54/E6
Gaziantep, Turkey 63/G4
Gaziantep, Turkey 59/C2
Gazik, Iran 66/L4
Gazipaşa, Turkey 63/E4
Gbarnga, Liberia 106/C7
Gbarnga, Liberia 102/B4
Gbogo, Nigeria 106/F7
Gcuwa, S. Africa 118/D6
Gdańsk (prov.), Poland 47/D1
Gdańsk, Poland 7/F3
Gdańsk, Poland 47/D1
Gdov, U.S.S.R. 52/C3
Gdynia, Poland 7/F3
Gdynia, Poland 47/D1
Gearhart, Oreg. (97138) 291/C1
Geary (co.), Kansas 232/F3
Geary, New Bruns. 170/D3
Geary, Okla. (73040) 288/K3
Geashill, Ireland 17/G5
Geauga (co.), Ohio 284/H3
Gebe (isl.), Indonesia 85/H6
Gebeit Mine, Sudan 111/G3
Gebo, Wyo. (†82430) 319/D2
Gebze, Turkey 63/C2
Gedaref, Sudan 111/G5
Gedaref, Sudan 59/C7
Gedaref, Sudan 102/F3
Geddes, S. Dak. (57342) 298/M7
Gede (mt.), Indonesia 85/H2
Gedera, Israel 65/B4
Gedi (ruins), Kenya 115/G4
Gedinne, Belgium 27/F9
Gediz, Turkey 63/C3
Gediz (riv.), Turkey 63/C3
Gedo, Ethiopia 111/G6
Gedo (prov.), Somalia 115/H3
Gedser, Denmark 21/F8
Gedser Odde (pt.), Denmark 21/E8
Gedsted, Denmark 21/C4
Geebung, Queensland 88/K2
Geebung, Queensland 95/E2
Geel, Belgium 27/F6
Geelong, Victoria 88/L7
Geelong, Victoria 97/C6
Geelong West, Victoria 88/G7
Geelong West, Victoria 97/C6
Geelvink (Cenderawasih) (bay), Indonesia 85/K6
Geelvink (chan.), W. Australia 88/A5
Geelvink (chan.), W. Australia 92/A5
Geertruidenberg, Netherlands 27/F5
Geesthacht, W. Germany 22/D2
Geetingsville, Ind. (†46041) 227/D4
Geeveston, Tasmania 99/C5
Geff, Ill. (62842) 222/E5
Gê'gyai, China 77/B5
Geh, Iran 59/H4
Geh, Iran 66/L7
Gehua, Papua N.G. 85/C8
Geidam, Nigeria 106/G6
Geiger, Ala. (†35459) 195/B5
Geiger Heights, Wash. (†99219) 310/H3
Geikie (riv.), Sask. 181/M3
Geilo, Norway 18/F6
Geiranger, Norway 18/E5
Geislingen an der Steige, W. Germany 22/C4
Geismar, La. (70734) 238/K3
Geist (res.), Ind. 227/F5
Geistown, Pa. (15904) 294/E5
Geita, Tanzania 115/F4
Gejiu (Kokiu), China 77/F7
Gejiu, China 54/M7
Gela, Italy 34/E6
Gelang, Tanjong (pt.), Malaysia 72/D6
Geldenaken (Jodoigne), Belgium 27/F7
Gelderland (prov.), Netherlands 27/H4
Geldermalsen, Netherlands 27/G5
Geldern, W. Germany 22/B3
Geldrop, Netherlands 27/H6
Geleen, Netherlands 27/H7
Gelendzhik, U.S.S.R. 52/E6
Gelgia (riv.), Switzerland 39/J3
Gelibolu (Gallipoli), Turkey 63/C5
Gelidonya (cape), Turkey 59/B2
Gelidonya (cape), Turkey 63/D4
Gelligaer, Wales 13/A6
Gelnhausen, W. Germany 22/C3
Gelnica, Czech. 41/F2
Gelså (riv.), Denmark 21/C7
Gelsenkirchen, W. Germany 22/B3
Gelsted, Denmark 21/C7
Gelterkinden, Switzerland 39/E2
Gem, Alberta 182/D4
Gem (co.), Idaho 220/B6
Gem, Idaho (†83873) 220/C2
Gem, Ind. (†46140) 227/F5
Gem, Kansas (67734) 232/B2
Gem (lake), Manitoba 179/G4
Gem, W. Va. (26625) 312/E5
Gemas, Malaysia 72/D7
Gembloux-sur-Orneau, Belgium 27/F7
Gemena, Zaire 115/D3
Gemena, Zaire 102/E4
Gemerek, Turkey 63/G3
Gemert, Netherlands 27/H5
Gemlik, Turkey 63/C2
Gemmell, Minn. (†56660) 255/D3
Gemona, Italy 34/D1
Gemsa, Egypt 111/F2
Genç, Turkey 63/J3
Gendringen, Netherlands 27/J5
Gene Autry, Okla. (73436) 288/N6
Genemuiden, Netherlands 27/H3
General Acha, Argentina 143/C4
General Alvear, Buenos Aires, Argentina 143/F7
General Alvear, Mendoza, Argentina 143/C3
General Arenales, Argentina 143/F7
General Artigas, Paraguay 144/D5
General Belgrano, Argentina 143/G7
General Bravo, Mexico 150/K4
General Campos, Argentina 143/G5
General Cepeda, Mexico 150/J4
General Conesa, Argentina 143/C5
General Elizardo Aquino, Paraguay 144/D4
General Enrique Martínez, Uruguay 145/F4
General Eugenio A. Garay, Paraguay 144/A2
General Galarza, Argentina 143/C6
General Grant Grove Section (King's Canyon), Calif. 204/G7
General Güemes, Argentina 143/D1
General Guido, Argentina 143/E4
General José de San Martín, Argentina 143/E2
General Juan Madariaga, Argentina 143/E4
General Lagos, Chile 138/B1
General La Madrid, Argentina 143/D4
General Las Heras, Argentina 143/G7
General Lavalle, Argentina 143/E4
General Manuel Belgrano, Cerro (mt.), Argentina 143/C2
General Mitchell Field, Wis. 317/M2
General O'Brien, Argentina 143/F7
General Paz, Argentina 143/E2
General Paz, Argentina 143/H7
General Paz (lake), Chile 138/E5
General Pico, Argentina 143/D4
General Ramírez, Argentina 143/F6
General Roca, Argentina 143/C4
General Saavedra, Bolivia 136/D5
General San Martín, Argentina 143/D4
General San Martín, Argentina 143/G4
General Santos, Philippines 82/E7
General Terán, Mexico 150/K4
General Tinio, Philippines 82/C3
General-Toshevo, Bulgaria 45/H4
General Viamonte, Argentina 143/F7
General Villegas, Argentina 143/D4
Generoso (mt.), Switzerland 39/H5
Genesee, Idaho (83832) 220/B3
Genesee (co.), Mich. 250/F5
Genesee (co.), N.Y. 276/D4
Genesee (riv.), N.Y. 276/E5
Genesee, Pa. (16923) 294/G2
Genesee, Wis. (†53127) 317/J2
Genesee Depot, Wis. (53127) 317/J2
Geneseo, Ill. (61254) 222/C2
Geneseo, Kansas (67444) 232/D3
Geneseo, N.Y. (14454) 276/E5
Geneseo, N. Dak. (58037) 282/R7
Geneva (lake) 7/E4
Geneva (co.), Ala. 195/G8
Geneva, Ala. (36340) 195/G8
Geneva, Fla. (32732) 212/E3
Geneva (lake), France 28/G4
Geneva, Georgia (31810) 217/C5
Geneva, Idaho (83238) 220/G7
Geneva, Ill. (60134) 222/E2
Geneva, Ind. (46740) 227/H3
Geneva, Iowa (50633) 229/G3
Geneva, Ky. (†42406) 237/F5
Geneva, Minn. (56035) 255/E7
Geneva, Nebr. (68361) 264/G4
Geneva, N.Y. (14456) 276/G5
Geneva, Ohio (44041) 284/J2
Geneva, Pa. (16316) 294/B2
Geneva (Genève) (canton), Switzerland 39/B4
Geneva (Genève), Switzerland 39/B4
Geneva, Switzerland 7/E4
Geneva (lake), Switzerland 39/C4
Geneva, Texas (75947) 303/L6
Geneva (lake), Wis. 317/K10
Geneva-on-the-Lake, Ohio (44043) 284/H2
Genezin, Turkey 63/F3
Genichesk, U.S.S.R. 52/E5
Genil (riv.), Spain 33/D4
Genk, Belgium 27/H7
Gennargentu, Monti del (mt.), Italy 34/B5
Gennep, Netherlands 27/H5
Gennevilliers, France 28/B1
Genoa, Ark. (71840) 202/C7
Genoa, Colo. (80818) 208/N4
Genoa, Ill. (60135) 222/E1
Genoa (prov.), Italy 34/B2
Genoa, Italy 7/E4
Genoa, Italy 34/B2
Genoa (gulf), Italy 34/B2
Genoa, Nebr. (68640) 264/G3
Genoa, Nev. (89411) 266/B4
Genoa, N.Y. (13071) 276/G5
Genoa, Ohio (43430) 284/D2
Genoa, W. Va. (25517) 312/A6
Genoa, Wis. (54632) 317/D8
Genoa City, Wis. (53128) 317/K11
Genola, Minn. (†56364) 255/D5
Genola, Utah (†84655) 304/C4
Genova (Genoa), Italy 34/B2
Genovesa (isl.), Ecuador 128/C9
Gent (Ghent), Belgium 27/D6
Genthin, E. Germany 22/E2
Gentilly, France 28/B2
Gentilly, Minn. (†56716) 255/B3
Genting, Indonesia 85/D5
Gentofte, Denmark 21/F6
Gentry, Ark. (72734) 202/A1
Gentry (co.), Mo. 261/D2
Gentry, Mo. (64453) 261/D2
Gentryville, Ind. (47537) 227/C8
Gentryville, Mo. (†64402) 261/D2
Genzano di Roma, Italy 34/F7
Geographe (chan.), W. Australia 88/A4
Geographe (bay), W. Australia 92/A6
Geographe (chan.), W. Australia 92/A4
Geographical Center of North America, N. Dak. 282/K3
Geographical Center of U.S., S. Dak. 298/B4
George (isl.), 143/E7
George (lake), Fla. 212/E2
George, Iowa (51237) 229/B2
George (isl.), Manitoba 179/E2
George (lake), Manitoba 179/G4
George (co.), Miss. 256/G9
George (isl.), Newf. 166/C3
George (lake), N.S. Wales 97/E4
George (lake), N.Y. 276/N4
George (sound), N. Zealand 100/A6
George (lake), N. Dak. 282/L6
George (cape), Nova Scotia 168/G3
George (lake), Nova Scotia 168/B5
George (riv.), Que. 162/K4
George (riv.), Que. 146/M4
George (riv.), Québec 174/F2
George, S. Africa 118/C6
George (lake), Uganda 115/F4
George, Wash. (98824) 310/F3
George A.F.B., Calif. 204/H9
George B. Stevenson (dam), Pa. 294/G3
George Land (isl.), U.S.S.R. 4/B7
George Land (isl.), U.S.S.R. 48/E1
George Rogers Clark Nat'l Hist. Park, Ind. 227/B7
Georges (isls.), Maine 243/E8
Georges (riv.), N. S. Wales 88/K4
Georges (riv.), N. S. Wales 97/H4
Georges Brook, Newf. 166/D2
George's Cove, Newf. 166/C3
Georges Fork, Va. (†24228) 307/C6
Georges Mills, N.H. (03751) 268/C5
Georgetown, Ark. (72054) 202/G3
Georgetown, Calif. (95634) 204/E5
George Town (cap.), Cayman Is. 156/B3
Georgetown, Colo. (80444) 208/H3
Georgetown, Conn. (06829) 210/B4
Georgetown, Del. (19947) 245/S6
Georgetown, D.C. (20007) 245/E5
Georgetown, Fla. (32039) 212/E2
Georgetown, Gambia 106/A6
Georgetown, Georgia (31754) 217/B7
Georgetown (cap.), Guyana 2/G5
Georgetown (cap.), Guyana 131/C2
Georgetown (cap.), Guyana 120/D2
Georgetown, Idaho (83239) 220/G7
Georgetown, Ill. (61846) 222/F4
Georgetown, Ind. (47122) 227/F8
Georgetown, Ky. (40324) 237/M4
Georgetown, La. (71432) 238/F3
Georgetown, Maine (04548) 243/D8
Georgetown○, Maine (04548) 243/D8
George Town (Pinang), Malaysia 72/C6
George Town, Malaysia 54/M9
Georgetown, Mass. (01833) 249/L2
Georgetown○, Mass. (01833) 249/L2
Georgetown, Minn. (56546) 255/B3
Georgetown, Miss. (39078) 256/D7
Georgetown (lake), Mont. 262/C4
Georgetown, Ohio (45121) 284/C8
Georgetown, Pa. (15043) 294/A4
Georgetown, Pr. Edward I. 168/F2
Georgetown, Queensland 88/G3
Georgetown, Queensland 95/B3
Georgetown, St. Vin. & Grens. 161/A8
Georgetown, St. Vin. & Grens. 156/G4
Georgetown (co.), S.C. 296/J5
Georgetown, S.C. 188/L4
Georgetown, S.C. (29440) 296/J5
George Town, Tasmania 99/C3
George Town, Tasmania 88/H8
Georgetown, Tenn. (37336) 237/L10
Georgetown, Texas (78626) 303/G7
George V Coast (reg.) 5/C8
Georgeville, Minn. (†56312) 255/C5
Georgeville, Nova Scotia 168/F3
George Washington Carver Nat'l Mon., Mo. 261/D9
George Washington Birthplace Nat'l Mon., Va. 307/P4
George West, Texas (78022) 303/F9
Georgia 188/K4
GEORGIA 217
Georgia (str.), Br. Col. 184/J3
Georgia (state), U.S. 146/K6
Georgia○, Vt. (†05478) 268/A2
Georgia (str.), Wash. 310/B2
Georgia Center, Vt. (†05478) 268/A2
Georgian (bay), Ont. 162/H6
Georgian (bay), Ontario 177/D2
Georgian (bay), Ontario 175/D3
Georgiana, Ala. (36033) 195/E7
Georgian Bay Is. Nat'l Park, Ontario 177/C2D3
Georgian S.S.R., U.S.S.R. 7/J4
Georgian S.S.R., U.S.S.R. 52/F6
Georgian S.S.R., U.S.S.R. 48/D5
Georgiaville, R.I. (†02917) 249/H5
Georgina (riv.), North. Terr. 93/E6
Georgina (isl.), Ontario 177/E3
Georgina (riv.), Queensland 88/F4
Georgina (riv.), Queensland 95/A4
Georgiu-Dezh, U.S.S.R. 52/E4
Georgsmarienhütte, W. Germany 22/B2
Gera (dist.), E. Germany 22/D3
Gera, E. Germany 22/E3
Geraardsbergen, Belgium 27/D7
Gerald, Mo. (63037) 261/K6
Gerald, Sask. 181/K5
Geral de Goiás, Serra (range), Brazil 132/E6
Geraldine, Ala. (35974) 195/G2
Geraldine, Mont. (59446) 262/F3
Geraldine, N. Zealand 100/C6
Geraldton, Australia 87/B8
Geraldton, Ont. 162/H6
Geraldton, Ontario 177/H5
Geraldton, Ontario 175/C3
Geraldton, W. Australia 88/A5
Geraldton, W. Australia 92/A5
Gerar (dry riv.), Israel 65/B5
Gerber, Calif. (96035) 204/C3
Gerber (res.), Oreg. 291/F5
Gercüş, Turkey 63/J4
Gerdine (mt.), Alaska 196/A1
Gerede, Turkey 63/E2
Gereshk, Afghanistan 59/H3
Gereshk, Afghanistan 68/A2
Geretsried, W. Germany 22/D5
Gérgal, Spain 33/E4
Gerger, Turkey 63/H3
Gerik, Malaysia 72/D6
Gering, Nebr. (69341) 264/A3
Gerlach, Nev. (89412) 266/B2
Gerlachovka (mt.), Czech. 41/E2
Gerlogubi, Ethiopia 111/H6
Germania, Miss. (†39162) 256/C5
Germania, Pa. (16922) 294/G2
Germania, Wis. (†54968) 317/H8
Germano, Ohio (†43825) 284/J5
Germansen (lake), Br. Col. 184/E2
Germansen Landing, Br. Col. 184/E2
Germanton, N.C. (27019) 281/J2
Germantown, Ill. (62245) 222/D5
Germantown, Ky. (41044) 237/O3
Germantown, Md. (20767) 245/J4
Germantown, New Bruns. 170/F3
Germantown, N.Y. (12526) 276/N6
Germantown, Ohio (45327) 284/B6
Germantown, Tenn. (38138) 237/B10
Germantown, Wis. (53022) 317/K1
German Valley, Ill. (61039) 222/D1
Germany (East) 2/K3
Germany (West) 2/K3
GERMANY, EAST 22/E2
GERMANY, WEST 22
Germencik, Turkey 63/B4
Germersheim, W. Germany 22/C4
Germfask, Mich. (49836) 250/C2
Germiston, S. Africa 102/E7
Germiston, S. Africa 118/H6
Gerofit, Israel 65/D5
Gerolstein, W. Germany 22/B3
Gerona (prov.), Spain 33/H1
Gerona, Spain 33/H2
Geronimo, Ariz. (†85536) 198/F5
Geronimo, Okla. (73543) 288/K6
Gerpinnes, Belgium 27/F8
Gerpir (cape), Iceland 21/D1
Gerra, Switzerland 39/G4
Gerrardstown, W. Va. (25420) 312/K4
Gerringong, N.S. Wales 97/F4
Gerrish, N.H. (†03301) 268/D5
Gerry, N.Y. (14740) 276/B6
Gers (dept.), France 28/D6
Gers (riv.), France 28/D6
Gersau, Switzerland 39/G2
Gersfeld, W. Germany 22/C3
Gerster, Mo. (†64776) 261/E7
Gerty, Okla. (†74531) 288/O5
Gervais, Oreg. (97026) 291/A3
Gervasio, Uruguay 145/F4
Gêrzê, China 77/B5
Gerze, Turkey 63/F2
Geser, Indonesia 85/J6
Gesher, Israel 65/C2
Gesher Haziv, Israel 65/C1
Gessie, Ind. (†47974) 227/C4
Getafe, Spain 33/F4
Getaway, Ohio (†45675) 284/F9
Gettysburg, Ohio (45328) 284/A5
Gettysburg, Pa. (17325) 294/H6
Gettysburg, S. Dak. (57442) 298/K3
Gettysburg Nat'l Mil. Park, Pa. 294/H6
Getulio Vargas, Uruguay 145/F3
Getz Ice Shelf 5/B12
Geuda Springs, Kansas (67051) 232/E4
Geurie, N.S. Wales 97/E3
Gevar'am, Israel 65/B4
Gevaş, Turkey 63/K3
Gevgelija, Yugoslavia 45/F5
Gex, France 28/G4
Geyser, Mont. (59447) 262/F3
Geyserville, Calif. (95441) 204/B5
Geyve, Turkey 63/D2
Gezira, El (reg.), Sudan 111/F5
Ghabaghib, Syria 63/H5
Ghadames, Libya 102/D2
Ghadames, Libya 111/A2
Ghaghra (riv.), India 68/E3
Ghaida, P.D.R. Yemen 59/F6
Ghalla, Wadi el (dry riv.), Sudan 111/E5
Ghana 2/J5
Ghana 102/B4
GHANA 106/D7
Ghanzi, Botswana 118/C4
Ghard Abu Muharik (des.), Egypt 111/J4
Ghardaïa, Algeria 106/E2
Ghardaïa, Algeria 102/C1
Gharian, Libya 102/D1
Gharian, Libya 111/B1
Gharib, Jebel (mt.), Egypt 59/B4
Ghat, Libya 102/D2
Ghat, Libya 111/B3
Ghat Kopar, India 68/B7
Ghazaouet, Algeria 106/D2
Ghaziabad, India 68/D3
Ghazipur, India 68/E3
Ghazni, Afghanistan 68/B2
Ghazni, Afghanistan 59/J3
Ghea (riv.), India 68/F1
Gheen, Minn. (55740) 255/F3
Gheens, La. (70355) 238/K7
Ghemines, Libya 111/C1

Guadalupe Bravo 377

Great Torrington, England 10/D5
Great Torrington, England 13/C7
Great Valley, N.Y. (14741) 276/C6
Great Victoria (des.) 88/D5
Great Victoria (desert), Australia 87/C8
Great Victoria (des.), S. Australia 94/B3
Great Victoria (des.), W. Australia 92/D5
Great Village, Nova Scotia 168/E3
Great Wall (ruins), China 54/N5
Great Wall (ruins), China 77/G4,J
Great Wass (isl.), Maine 243/J7
Great Western Tiers (mts.), Tasmania 99/C3
Great Yarmouth, England 13/J5
Great Yarmouth, England 10/G4
Great Zab (riv.), Iraq 66/C2
Grecco, Uruguay 145/B3
Grecia, C. Rica 154/E5
Greco (cape), Cyprus 63/F5
Gredos, Sierra de (range), Spain 33/D2
Greece 2/L4
Greece 7/G5
GREECE 45/F6
Greece, N.Y. (14616) 276/E4
Greeley, Colo. 188/F2
Greeley, Colo. (80631) 208/K2
Greeley, Iowa (52050) 229/L3
Greeley (co.), Kansas 232/A3
Greeley, Kansas (66033) 232/G3
Greeley (co.), Nebr. 264/F3
Greeley, Nebr. (68842) 264/F3
Greeley, Pa. (18425) 294/N3
Greeley (creek), Utah 304/B3
Greeleyville, S.C. (29056) 296/H4
Greely (fjord), N.W. Terrs. 187/K1
Greely, Ontario 177/J2
Green (bay) 188/J1
Green (riv.) 188/D3
Green (isl.), Ant. & Bar. 161/E11
Green (riv.), Colo. 208/A2
Green (isl.), Grenada 161/D8
Green (riv.), Ill. 222/D2
Green, Kansas (67447) 232/E2
Green (co.), Ky. 237/K6
Green (riv.), Ky. 237/G6
Green (isl.), Maine 243/F8
Green (riv.), Mass. 249/B2
Green, Mich. (†49953) 250/F1
Green (bay), Mich. 250/B4
Green (lake), Minn. 255/D5
Green (riv.), New Bruns. 170/B1
Green (cape), N.S. Wales 97/F5
Green (swamp), N.C. 281/N6
Green (riv.), N. Dak. 282/D5
Green (pt.), Nova Scotia 168/C5
Green (isl.), Ontario 177/A2
Green, Oreg. (†97470) 291/D4
Green (isls.), Papua N.G. 86/C2
Green (lake), Sask. 181/D1
Green (riv.), Tenn. 237/F10
Green (riv.), U.S. 146/H6
Green (riv.), Utah 304/D4
Green (mts.), Vt. 268/B4
Green (cay), Virgin Is. (U.S.) 161/F4
Green (lake), Wash. 310/A2
Green (riv.), Wash. 310/C3
Green (co.), Wis. 317/G10
Green (bay), Wis. 317/L6
Green (mt.), Wyo. 319/E3
Green (riv.), Wyo. 319/C4
Greenacres, Calif. (93308) 204/F8
Green Acres, Sask. 181/F2
Greenacres, Wash. (99016) 310/J3
Greenacres City, Fla. (33463) 212/F5
Greenan, Sask. 181/C4
Greenback, Tenn. (37742) 237/N9
Greenbackville, Va. (23356) 307/T5
Green Bank, N.J. (†08215) 273/D4
Greenbank, Wash. (98253) 310/C2
Green Bank, W. Va. (24944) 312/G6
Green Bay, N. Zealand 100/B1
Green Bay, Va. (23942) 307/M6
Green Bay, Wis. 188/J2
Green Bay, Wis. 146/J5
Green Bay, Wis. (*54301) 317/K6
Greenbelt, Md. (20770) 245/G4
Greenbelt Park, Md. 245/G4
Greenbrier, Ala. (†35758) 195/E1
Greenbrier, Ark. (72058) 202/F3
Greenbrier, Mo. (†63730) 261/M8
Greenbrier, Tenn. (37073) 237/H8
Greenbrier (co.), W. Va. 312/F7
Greenbrier (riv.), W. Va. 312/F6
Green Brook, N.J. (08812) 273/D2
Greenbush, Mass. (02040) 249/F8
Greenbush, Mich. (48738) 250/F4
Greenbush, Minn. (56726) 255/B2
Greenbush, Va. (23357) 307/S5
Green Camp, Ohio (43322) 284/D4
Greencastle, Ind. (46135) 227/D5
Greencastle, Ireland 17/H1
Green Castle, Mo. (63544) 261/G2
Greencastle, Pa. (17225) 294/G6
Green Center, Ind. (†46701) 227/G2
Green City, Mo. (63545) 261/F2
Green Court, Alberta 182/C2
Green Cove Springs, Fla. (32043) 212/E2
Greencreek, Idaho (83533) 220/B3
Green Creek, N.J. (08219) 273/D5
Greendale, Ind. (†47025) 227/H6
Greendale, Wis. (53129) 317/L2
Greendell, N.J. (07839) 273/D2
Greene (co.), Ala. 195/C5
Greene (co.), Ark. 202/J1
Greene (co.), Georgia 217/F3
Greene (co.), Ill. 222/C4
Greene (co.), Ind. 227/D6
Greene (co.), Iowa 229/E5
Greene, Iowa (50636) 229/H3
Greene○, Maine (04236) 243/C7
Greene (co.), Miss. 256/G8
Greene (co.), Mo. 261/F8
Greene (co.), N.Y. 276/M6
Greene, N.Y. (13778) 276/J6
Greene (co.), N.C. 281/O3
Greene, N. Dak. (†58787) 282/G2
Greene (co.), Ohio 284/C6
Greene (co.), Pa. 294/B6
Greene, R.I. (02827) 249/G6
Greene (co.), Tenn. 237/R8
Greene (co.), Va. 307/M4
Greenevers, N.C. (†28521) 281/O5
Greeneville, Tenn. (37743) 237/R8
Greenfield, Calif. (93927) 204/D7
Greenfield, Ill. (62044) 222/C4
Greenfield, Ind. (46140) 227/F5
Greenfield, Iowa (50849) 229/D6
Greenfield, Mass. (01301) 249/D2
Greenfield○, Mass. (01301) 249/D2
Greenfield, Minn. (†55373) 255/F5
Greenfield, Mo. (65661) 261/E8
Greenfield○, N.H. (03047) 268/D6
Greenfield, Nova Scotia 168/D4
Greenfield, Ohio (45123) 284/D7
Greenfield, Okla. (73043) 288/K3
Greenfield, S. Dak. (†57010) 298/R8
Greenfield, Tenn. (38230) 237/D8
Greenfield, Wis. (53220) 317/L2
Greenfield Hill, Conn. (†06430) 210/B4
Greenfield Park, Québec 172/J4
Greenford, Ohio (44422) 284/J4
Green Forest, Ark. (72638) 202/D1
Green Hall, Ky. (41328) 237/O6
Green Harbor, Mass. (02041) 249/M4
Green Haven, Md. (21122) 245/M4
Greenhills, Ohio (45218) 284/B9
Greenhorn, Oreg. (†97877) 291/J3
Green Island, Iowa (52051) 229/N4
Green Island, Jamaica 158/G6
Green Island, N.Y. (12183) 276/N5
Green Island, N. Zealand 100/C7
Greenisland, N. Ireland 17/K2
Green Island (bay), Philippines 82/B5
Green Island Cove, Newf. 166/C3
Green Isle, Minn. (55338) 255/E6
Green Lake, Maine (†04429) 243/F6
Green Lake, Sask. 181/L4
Green Lake (co.), Wis. 317/H8
Green Lake, Wis. (54941) 317/H8
Greenland 2/G2
Greenland 4/B12
Greenland 146/P2
Greenland (sea) 146/T2
Greenland (sea) 4/B10
Greenland, Ark. (72737) 202/B1
Greenland, Barbados 161/B8
Greenland, Colo. (†80118) 208/K4
Greenland, Mich. (49929) 250/G1
Greenland○, N.H. (03840) 268/F5
Greenlaw, Scotland 15/F5
Greenleaf, Idaho (83626) 220/B6
Greenleaf, Kansas (66943) 232/E2
Greenleaf, Minn. (†55355) 255/D6
Greenleaf, Oreg. (97445) 291/D3
Greenleaf, Wis. (54126) 317/L7
Greenleafton, Minn. (†55965) 255/F7
Greenlee (co.), Ariz. 198/F5
Green Lowther (mt.), Scotland 15/E5
Greenmount, Ky. (†40741) 237/N6
Greenmount, Md. (†21074) 245/L2
Green Mountain (res.), Colo. 208/G3
Green Mountain, Iowa (50637) 229/H4
Green Mountain, N.C. (28740) 281/E3
Green Mountain Falls, Colo. (80819) 208/K5
Green Oaks, Ill. (†60048) 222/B4
Greenock, Scotland 10/A1
Greenock, Scotland 15/A2
Greenore, Ireland 17/J4
Greenore (pt.), Ireland 17/J7
Greenough (mt.), Alaska 196/K1
Greenough, Georgia (†31716) 217/D8
Greenough, Mont. (59836) 262/C4
Green Peter (lake), Oreg. 291/E3
Green Pond, Ala. (35074) 195/D4
Green Pond, N.J. (07435) 273/E1
Green Pond, S.C. (29446) 296/F6
Greenport, N.Y. (11944) 276/P8
Green Ridge (mts.), 245/E2
Green Ridge, Mo. (65332) 261/F5
Green River (lake), Ky. 237/L6
Green River, Utah (84525) 304/D4
Green River (res.), Vt. 268/B2
Green River, Wyo. 188/E2
Green River, Wyo. (82935) 319/C4
Green River (mt.), Wyo. 319/C2
Green Rock, Ill. (†61241) 222/C2
Greens (peak), Ariz. 198/F4
Greensboro, Ala. (36744) 195/C5
Greensboro, Fla. (32330) 212/B1
Greensboro, Georgia (30642) 217/F3
Greensboro, Ind. (47344) 227/G5
Greensboro, Md. (21639) 245/P5
Greensboro, N.C. 146/L6
Greensboro, N.C. 188/K3
Greensboro, N.C. (*27401) 281/K2
Greensboro, Pa. (15338) 294/B6
Greensboro○, Vt. (05841) 268/C2
Greensburg, Ind. (47240) 227/G6
Greensburg, Kansas (67054) 232/C4
Greensburg, Ky. (42743) 237/K6
Greensburg, La. (70441) 238/J5
Greensburg, Mo. (†63531) 261/H2
Greensburg, Ohio (44232) 284/G4
Greensburg, Pa. (15601) 294/D5
Green Sea, S.C. (29545) 296/J3
Greens Farms, Conn. (06436) 210/B4
Greens Fork, Ind. (47345) 227/H5
Green's Harbour, Newf. 166/D2
Greenshields, Alberta 182/E3
Greenslopes, Queensland 88/K3
Greenslopes, Queensland 95/E3
Greenspond, Newf. 166/D4
Green Springs, Ohio (44836) 284/E3
Greenstone (pt.), Scotland 15/C3
Greenstreet, Sask. 181/A2
Green Sulphur Springs, W. Va. (25966) 312/E7
Greensville (co.), Va. 307/N7
Greentop, Mo. (63546) 261/H2
Greentown, Ind. (46936) 227/E4
Greentown, Ohio (44630) 284/H4
Greentree, Pa. (15242) 294/B7
Greenup, Ill. (62428) 222/E4
Greenup (co.), Ky. 237/R3
Greenup, Ky. (41144) 237/R3
Greenvale, Queensland 95/C3
Green Valley, Ariz. (85614) 198/D7
Green Valley, Ill. (61534) 222/D3
Green Valley, Minn. (†56258) 255/C6
Green Valley, Ontario 177/K2
Green Valley, Wis. (54127) 317/K6
Greenview, Calif. (96037) 204/B2
Greenview, Ill. (62642) 222/D3
Greenview, W. Va. (†25166) 312/C6
Green Village, N.J. (07935) 273/D2
Greenville, Ala. (36037) 195/E7
Greenville, Calif. (95947) 204/E3
Greenville, Del. (19807) 245/R1
Greenville, Fla. (32331) 212/C1
Greenville, Georgia (30222) 217/C4
Greenville, Ill. (62246) 222/D5
Greenville, Ind. (47124) 227/F8
Greenville, Iowa (51343) 229/C3
Greenville, Ky. (42345) 237/G6
Greenville, Liberia 106/C8
Greenville, Maine (04441) 243/D5
Greenville○, Maine (04441) 243/D5
Greenville, Mich. (48838) 250/D5
Greenville, Miss. 146/J6
Greenville, Miss. 188/H4
Greenville, Miss. (38701) 256/B4
Greenville, Mo. (63944) 261/M8
Greenville, N.H. (03048) 268/D6
Greenville○, N.H. (03048) 268/D6
Greenville, N.C. (27834) 281/P3
Greenville, Ohio (45331) 284/A5
Greenville, Pa. (16125) 294/B3
Greenville, R.I. (02828) 249/H5
Greenville, S.C. 146/K6
Greenville, S.C. 188/K4
Greenville (co.), S.C. 296/C2
Greenville, S.C. (*29601) 296/C2
Greenville, Texas 188/G4
Greenville, Texas (75401) 303/H4
Greenville, Utah (84731) 304/B5
Greenville, Va. (24440) 307/K5
Greenville, W. Va. (24945) 312/E7
Greenville, Wis. (54942) 317/J7
Greenville Junction, Maine (04442) 243/D5
Greenwald, Minn. (56335) 255/D5
Greenwater Lake, Sask. 181/H3
Greenwater Lake Prov. Park, Sask. 181/H3
Greenway, Ark. (72430) 202/K1
Greenway, Manitoba 179/C5
Greenway, S. Dak. (†57437) 298/K2
Greenwell Springs, La. (70739) 238/K1
Greenwich○, Conn. (06830) 210/A4
Greenwich (pt.), Conn. 210/A4
Greenwich, England 13/H8
Greenwich, England 10/B5
Greenwich (Kapingamarangi) (atoll), Micronesia 87/F5
Greenwich○, N.J. (08323) 273/C5
Greenwich, N.Y. (12834) 276/O4
Greenwich, Ohio (44837) 284/E3
Greenwich, Utah (84732) 304/B5
Greenwood, Ark. (72936) 202/B3
Greenwood, Br. Col. 184/H5
Greenwood, Calif. (95635) 204/E5
Greenwood, Del. (19950) 245/R5
Greenwood, Fla. (32443) 212/A1
Greenwood, Ind. (46142) 227/E5
Greenwood (co.), Kansas 232/F4
Greenwood, Ky. (†42634) 237/N7
Greenwood, La. (71033) 238/B2
Greenwood, Mass. (01880) 249/D6
Greenwood (lake), Minn. 255/G3
Greenwood, Miss. (38930) 256/D4
Greenwood, Mo. (64034) 261/R6
Greenwood, Nebr. (68366) 264/H3
Greenwood (lake), N.J. 273/E1
Greenwood, N.Y. (14839) 276/E6
Greenwood (lake), N.Y. 276/M8
Greenwood, S.C. 188/K4
Greenwood (co.), S.C. 296/C3
Greenwood, S.C. (29646) 296/C3
Greenwood (lake), S.C. 296/D3
Greenwood, S. Dak. (†57380) 298/N8
Greenwood, Va. (22943) 307/L4
Greenwood, W. Va. (26360) 312/E4
Greenwood, Wis. (54437) 317/E6
Greenwood Lake, N.Y. (10925) 276/M8
Greenwood Springs, Miss. (38848) 256/H3
Greer, Ariz. (85927) 198/F4
Greer, Idaho (†83544) 220/B3
Greer, Mo. (†65606) 261/K9
Greer, Ohio (†44628) 284/F4
Greer (co.), Okla. 288/G5
Greer, S.C. (29651) 296/C2
Greers Ferry, Ark. (†72067) 202/F2
Greers Ferry (lake), Ark. 202/G2
Greeson (lake), Ark. 202/C5
Gregg (co.), Texas 303/K5
Greggs, Georgia (†31620) 217/F8
Gregory, Ark. (72059) 202/H3
Gregory, Mich. (48137) 250/E6
Gregory (range), Queensland 95/B3
Gregory (riv.), Queensland 88/F3
Gregory (riv.), Queensland 95/A3
Gregory (lake), S. Australia 88/F5
Gregory (lake), S. Australia 94/F3
Gregory (co.), S. Dak. 298/L7
Gregory, S. Dak. (57533) 298/L7
Gregory (lake), W. Australia 92/C4
Gregory Landing, Mo. (†63435) 261/K2
Gregory's (sound), Ireland 17/B5
Greian (head), Scotland 15/A3
Greifensee (lake), Switzerland 39/G2
Greifswald, E. Germany 22/E1
Grein, Austria 41/C2
Greina (pass), Switzerland 39/G3
Greiz, E. Germany 22/E3
Grelton, Ohio (43523) 284/C3
Gremikha, U.S.S.R. 52/E1
Gremyachinsk, U.S.S.R. 52/J3
Grenå, Denmark 21/D5
Grenå, Denmark 18/G8
Grenada 2/F5
Grenada 146/M8
Grenada, Calif. (96038) 204/C2
GRENADA 161/D9
GRENADA 156/G4
Grenada (isl.), Grenada 156/G4
Grenada (co.), Miss. 256/E3
Grenada, Miss. (38901) 256/E3
Grenada (lake), Miss. 256/E3
Grenadier (isl.), N.Y. 276/H2
Grenadines (isls.), Grenada 156/G4
Grenadines (isls.), St. Vin. & Grens. 156/G4
Grenchen, Switzerland 39/D2
Grenfell, N.S. Wales 97/E3
Grenfell, Sask. 181/J5
Grenloch, N.J. (08032) 273/C4
Grenoble, France 7/E4
Grenoble, France 28/F5
Grenola, Kansas (67346) 232/F4
Grenora, N. Dak. (58845) 282/C2
Grenville (chan.), Br. Col. 184/C3
Grenville, Grenada 161/D8
Grenville (bay), Grenada 161/D8
Grenville, N. Mex. (88424) 274/F2
Grenville (county), Ontario 177/J3
Grenville, Québec 172/C4
Grenville (cape), Queensland 88/G2
Grenville (cape), Queensland 95/B1
Grenville, S. Dak. (57239) 298/O3
Grenville (pt.), Wash. 310/A3
Gresham, Nebr. (68367) 264/G3
Gresham, Oreg. (97030) 291/B2
Gresham, S.C. (29546) 296/J4
Gresham, Wis. (54128) 317/J6
Greshamville, Georgia (†30650) 217/F3
Gresik, Indonesia 85/K2
Gresston, Georgia (†31023) 217/F6
Greta-Branxton, N.S. Wales 97/F3
Greta East, N.S. Wales 97/F3
Gretna, Fla. (32332) 212/B1
Gretna, La. (70053) 238/O4
Gretna, Manitoba 179/E5
Gretna, Nebr. (68028) 264/H3
Gretna, Scotland 10/E3
Gretna, Scotland 15/E5
Gretna, Tasmania 99/D4
Gretna, Va. (24557) 307/K7
Grevelingen (str.), Netherlands 27/E5
Greven, W. Germany 22/B2
Grevená, Greece 45/E5
Grevenbroich, W. Germany 22/B3,
Grevenmacher, Luxembourg 27/J9
Grevesmühlen, E. Germany 22/D2
Greville (bay), Nova Scotia 168/D3
Grey (isls.), Newf. 166/C3
Grey (riv.), N. Zealand 100/C5
Grey (cape), North. Terr. 88/F2
Grey (cape), North. Terr. 93/E2
Grey (county), Ontario 177/D3
Grey (range), Queensland 88/G5
Grey (range), Queensland 95/B5
Grey Abbey, N. Ireland 17/K2
Greybull, Wyo. (82426) 319/E1
Greybull (riv.), Wyo. 319/D1
Greycliff, Mont. (59033) 262/G5
Grey Eagle, Minn. (56336) 255/D5
Grey Forest, Texas (†78201) 303/J10
Grey Islands, Newf. 166/C3
Greylock (mt.), Idaho 220/C6
Greylock (mt.), Mass. 249/B2
Greymouth, N. Zealand 100/C5
Greymouth, N. Zealand 87/G10
Grey River, Newf. 166/C4
Greys (riv.), Wyo. 319/B3
Greystone, Colo. (†81640) 208/B1
Greystone, Conn. (†06786) 210/C2
Greystone Park, N.J. (07950) 273/D2
Greystones-Delgany, Ireland 10/D4
Greystones-Delgany, Ireland 17/K5
Greytown, N. Zealand 100/E4
Greytown (San Juan del Norte), Nicaragua 154/F5
Greytown, S. Africa 118/E5
Grez-Doiceau, Belgium 27/F7
Gribbles Settlement, North. Terr. 93/B1
Gridley, Calif. (95948) 204/D4
Gridley (mt.), Conn. 210/B1
Gridley, Ill. (61744) 222/E3
Gridley, Kansas (66852) 232/G3
Gridone (mt.), Switzerland 39/G4
Griend (isl.), Netherlands 27/G2
Grier, N. Mex. (†88101) 274/F4
Gries am Brenner, Austria 41/A3
Griesheim, W. Germany 22/C4
Grieskirchen, Austria 41/B2
Griffin, Georgia (30223) 217/D4
Griffin, Ind. (47616) 227/B8
Griffin, Sask. 181/H6
Griffiss A.F.B., N.Y. 276/K4
Griffith, Ind. (46319) 227/C1
Griffith, N. S. 88/H6
Griffith, N.S. Wales 97/C4
Griffith (isl.), Ontario 177/D3
Griffithsville, W. Va. (25521) 312/B6
Griffithville, Ark. (72060) 202/G3
Grifton, N.C. (28530) 281/P4
Griggs (co.), N. Dak. 282/O5
Griggs, Okla. (†73949) 288/B1
Griggsville, Ill. (62340) 222/C4
Grigston, Kansas (†67871) 232/B3
Grijalva (riv.), Mexico 150/N7
Grim (cape), Tasmania 99/A2
Grimari, Cent. Afr. Rep. 115/C2
Grimbergen, Belgium 27/E7
Grimes, Ala. (†36350) 195/H8
Grimes, Calif. (95950) 204/C4
Grimes, Iowa (50111) 229/F5
Grimes, Okla. (†73628) 288/G4
Grimes (co.), Texas 303/J7
Grimesland, N.C. (27837) 281/P3
Griminish, Scotland 15/A3
Grimma, E. Germany 22/E3
Grimmen, E. Germany 22/E1
Grimms Landing, W. Va. (25095) 312/B5
Grimsby, England 13/G4
Grimsby, England 10/F4
Grimsby, Ontario 177/E4
Grimsel (pass), Switzerland 39/F3
Grimsey (isl.), Iceland 21/C1
Grimshaw, Alberta 182/B1
Grimsley, Tenn. (38565) 237/L2
Grimstad, Norway 18/F7
Grindelwald, Switzerland 39/E3
Grindrod, Br. Col. 184/H5
Grindsted, Denmark 21/B6
Grindstone, Maine (†04460) 243/F4
Grindstone (isl.), New Bruns. 170/F3
Grindstone (lake), Wis. 317/C4
Grind Stone City, Mich. (48467) 250/G4
Grindstone Prov. Rec. Park, Manitoba 179/F3
Grinnell, Iowa (50112) 229/H5
Grinnell, Kansas (67738) 232/B2
Grinnell (pen.), N.W. Terrs. 187/J2
Grippon, Guadeloupe 161/B6
Griqualand West (reg.), S. Africa 118/C5
Griquatown, S. Africa 118/C5
Grise Fiord, Canada 4/B13
Grise Fiord, N.W.T. 162/H1
Grise Fiord, N.W. Terrs. 187/K2
Gris-Nez (cape), France 28/D2
Grisons (Graubünden) (elec. div.), Switzerland 39/H3
Grissom A.F.B., Ind. 227/E3
Griswold, Iowa (51535) 229/C6
Griswold, Manitoba 179/B5
Griswoldville, Mass. (01345) 249/D2
Griva, U.S.S.R. 53/D3
Grizzly (bay), Calif. 204/K1
Grizzly Flats, Calif. (95636) 204/E5
Groais (isl.), Newf. 166/C3
Grobiņa, U.S.S.R. 53/A2
Grodno, U.S.S.R. 7/G3
Grodno, U.S.S.R. 48/C4
Grodno, U.S.S.R. 52/B4
Grodzisk Mazowiecki, Poland 47/E2
Grodzisk Wielkopolski, Poland 47/C2
Groenlo, Netherlands 27/K4
Groesbeck, Ohio (45239) 284/B9
Groesbeck, Texas (76642) 303/H6
Groesbeek, Netherlands 27/H5
Groix (isl.), France 28/B4
Grójec, Poland 47/E3
Grömitz, W. Germany 22/D1
Gronau, W. Germany 22/B2
Grondines, Québec 172/E3
Grong, Norway 18/H4
Grong Grong, N.S. Wales 97/D4
Groningen, Minn. (†55072) 255/E4
Groningen (prov.), Netherlands 27/K2
Groningen, Netherlands 27/K2
Groningen, Suriname 131/D2
Groninger Wad (sound), Netherlands 27/J2
Gronlid, Sask. 181/G2
Grønnedal, Greenl. 4/C12
Grono, Switzerland 39/H4
Groom, Texas (79039) 303/C2
Groomsport, N. Ireland 17/K2
Groot-Drakenstein, S. Africa 118/F6
Groote (isl.), North. Terr. 88/F2
Groote (riv.), S. Africa 118/C6
Groote Eylandt (isl.), Australia 87/D7
Groote Eylandt (isl.), North. Terr. 93/E3
Groote IJ Polder, Netherlands 27/B4
Grootfontein, Namibia 118/B3
Groot Sint Joris, Neth. Ant. 161/G9
Gros (pt.), Grenada 161/C8
Gros Islet, St. Lucia 161/G5
Gros Islet (bay), St. Lucia 161/G5
Grosmont (Island Lake), Alberta 182/D2
Gros Morne, Haiti 158/B5
Gros-Morne, Martinique 161/D6
Gros Morne (mt.), Newf. 166/C4
Gros-Morne, Québec 172/C1
Gros Morne Nat'l Park, Newf. 166/C4
Gros Piton (mt.), St. Lucia 161/G6
Gross, Nebr. (†68719) 264/F2
Grosse Ile, Mich. (48138) 250/B7
Grosse Isle, Manitoba 179/E4
Grosse Emme (riv.), Switzerland 39/E2
Grossenbrode, W. Germany 22/D1
Grossenhain, E. Germany 22/E3
Grosse Pointe, Mich. (48236) 250/B7
Grosse Pointe Farms, Mich. (†48236) 250/B6
Grosse Pointe Park, Mich. (†48236) 250/B7
Grosse Pointe Shores, Mich. (†48236) 250/B6
Grosse Pointe Woods, Mich. (†48236) 250/B6
Grosser Arber (mt.), W. Germany 22/E4
Grosser Peilstein (mt.), Austria 41/C2
Grosses Coques, Nova Scotia 168/B4
Grosses-Roches, Québec 172/B1
Grosse Tete, La. (70740) 238/G6
Grosseto (prov.), Italy 34/C3
Grosseto, Italy 34/C3
Grossglockner (mt.), Austria 41/B3
Gross Litzner (mt.), Switzerland 39/K3
Grossräschen, E. Germany 22/E3
Grosssiegharts, Austria 41/C2
Grosswangen, Switzerland 39/F2
Grosvenor Dale, Conn. (06246) 210/H1
Gros Ventre (riv.), Wyo. 319/B2
Groswater (bay), Newf. 166/C3
Groton, Conn. (06340) 210/G3
Groton○, Conn. (06340) 210/G3
Groton, Mass. (01450) 249/H2
Groton○, Mass. (01450) 249/H2
Groton○, N.H. (†03241) 268/D4
Groton, N.Y. (13073) 276/H5
Groton, S. Dak. (57445) 298/N3
Groton○, Vt. (05046) 268/C3
Groton (lake), Vt. 268/C3
Groton Long (pt.), Conn. 210/H3
Groton Long Point, Conn. (†06340) 210/G3
Grottaferrata, Italy 34/F7
Grottaglie, Italy 34/F4
Grotto, Wash. (98288) 310/D3
Grottoes, Va. (24441) 307/L4
Grouard, Alberta 182/B2
Grouard Mission, Alberta 182/C2
Grouard Mission, Alta. 162/E4
Groundhog (riv.), Ontario 175/D3
Grouse (Lost River), Idaho (†83255) 220/E6
Grouse (mt.), N. Mex. 274/A5
Grouse (creek), Utah 304/A2
Grouse Creek, Utah (84313) 304/A2
Grouse Creek (mts.), Utah 304/A2
Grouw, Netherlands 27/H2
Grovania, Georgia (†31036) 217/E6
Grove, Maine (04638) 243/J5
Grove (lake), N. Dak. 282/L5
Grove, Okla. (74344) 288/S1
Grove Beach, Conn. (†06413) 210/E3
Grove Center, Ky. (†42437) 237/F5
Grove City, Fla. (33533) 212/D5
Grove City, Minn. (56243) 255/D5
Grove City, Ohio (43123) 284/D6
Grove City, Pa. (16127) 294/B3
Grovedale, Alberta 182/A2
Grove Hill, Ala. (36451) 195/C7
Groveland, Calif. (95321) 204/E6
Groveland, Fla. (32736) 212/E3
Groveland, Georgia (†31321) 217/J6
Groveland, Ind. (†46121) 227/D5
Groveland○, Mass. (01830) 249/L1
Groveland, N.Y. (14462) 276/E5
Groveoak, Ala. (35975) 195/F2
Grove Place, Virgin Is. (U.S.) 161/E4
Groveport, Ohio (43125) 284/E6
Grover, Colo. (80729) 208/L1
Grover, Mo. (63040) 261/M3
Grover, N.C. (28073) 281/G4
Grover, Pa. (17735) 294/J2
Grover, S.C. (29447) 296/F5
Grover, S. Dak. (†57201) 298/P4
Grover, Utah (†84773) 304/C5
Grover, Wyo. (83122) 319/B3
Grover City, Calif. (93433) 204/E8
Grover Hill, Ohio (45849) 284/B3
Grovertown, Ind. (46531) 227/D2
Groves, Texas (77619) 303/L8
Grovespring, Mo. (65662) 261/G8
Groveton, N.H. (03582) 268/D2
Groveton, Texas (75845) 303/J7
Groveton, Va. (†22306) 307/T3
Grovetown, Georgia (30813) 217/H4
Groveville, N.J. (†08601) 273/D3
Growler (mts.), Ariz. 198/B6
Groznyy, U.S.S.R. 7/J4
Groznyy, U.S.S.R. 48/E5
Groznyy, U.S.S.R. 52/G6
Grubbs, Ark. (72431) 202/H2
Grubišno Polje, Yugoslavia 45/C3
Grudovo, Bulgaria 45/H4
Grudziądz, Poland 47/D2
Gruenthal, Sask. 181/E3
Gruetli, Tenn. (37339) 237/K10
Gruinard (bay), Scotland 15/C3
Grulla, Texas (78548) 303/F11
Grünberg (Zielona Góra), Poland 47/B3
Grünburg, Austria 41/C3
Grundy (co.), Ill. 222/E2
Grundy (co.), Iowa 229/H4
Grundy (co.), Mo. 261/E2
Grundy (co.), Tenn. 237/K10
Grundy, Va. (24614) 307/D6
Grundy Center, Iowa (50638) 229/H4
Grunthal, Manitoba 179/F5
Gruver, Iowa (51344) 229/D2
Gruver, Texas (79040) 303/C1
Gruyères, Switzerland 39/D3
Gryazi, U.S.S.R. 52/F4
Gryazovets, U.S.S.R. 52/F3
Gryfice, Poland 47/B2
Gryfino, Poland 47/B2
Grygla, Minn. (56727) 255/C2
Gryon, Switzerland 39/D4
Grytviken 5/D17
Gstaad, Switzerland 39/D4
Gsteig, Switzerland 39/D4
Guacamaya, Colombia 126/C6
Guacamayo, Colombia 126/F6
Guacanayabo (gulf), Cuba 156/C2
Guacanayabo (gulf), Cuba 158/G4
Guacara, Venezuela 124/D2
Guachara, Venezuela 124/D4
Gu Achi, Ariz. (†85634) 198/C6
Guácimo, C. Rica 154/F5
Guacui, Brazil 135/F2
Guadalajara, Mexico 2/D5
Guadalajara, Mexico 150/H6
Guadalajara, Mexico 146/H7
Guadalajara (prov.), Spain 33/E2
Guadalajara, Spain 33/E2
Guadalcanal (isl.), Solomon Is. 87/F7
Guadalcanal (isl.), Solomon Is. 86/D3
Guadalcanal, Spain 33/D3
Guadalimar (riv.), Spain 33/E3
Guadaloupe (isl.), Mexico 146/G7
Guadalquivir (riv.), Spain 7/D5
Guadalquivir (riv.), Spain 33/C4
Guadalupe, Potosí, Bolivia 136/B7
Guadalupe, Santa Cruz, Bolivia 136/C6
Guadalupe, Calif. (93434) 204/E9
Guadalupe (riv.), Calif. 204/K3
Guadalupe, Nuevo León, Mexico 150/K4
Guadalupe, Zacatecas, Mexico 150/H5
Guadalupe (co.), N. Mex. 274/E4
Guadalupe (mts.), N. Mex. 274/D6
Guadalupe, Peru 128/E9
Guadalupe, Spain 33/D3
Guadalupe, Sierra de (range), Spain 33/D3
Guadalupe (co.), Texas 303/G8
Guadalupe (mts.), Texas 303/C10
Guadalupe (peak), Texas 303/B10
Guadalupe (riv.), Texas 303/G8
Guadalupe Bravo, Mexico 150/F1

Hardesty 379

Ha! Ha! (riv.) Qué. 172/G1
Hahatonka, Mo. (†65020) 261/G7
Hahira, Georgia (31632) 217/F9
Hahndorf, S. Australia 94/C8
Hahnville, La. (70057) 238/N4
Hai, Iraq 59/E3
Hai, Iraq 66/E4
Haifa (dist.), Israel 65/C2
Haifa, Israel 65/B2
Haifa, Israel 59/B3
Haifa (bay), Israel 65/C2
Haifeng, China 77/J7
Haig (lake), Alberta 182/B1
Haight, Alberta 182/D3
Haigler, Nebr. (69030) 264/C4
Haikang, China 77/G7
Haikou (Hoihow), China 77/H7
Haikou, China 54/N8
Haiku, Hawaii (96708) 218/J2
Hail, Saudi Arabia 54/F7
Hail, Saudi Arabia 59/D4
Hailar, China 77/J2
Hailar He (riv.), China 77/K2
Haile, La. (†71260) 238/F1
Hailesboro, N.Y. (13645) 276/K2
Hailey, Idaho (83333) 220/D6
Haileybury, Ontario 177/K5
Haileybury, Ontario 175/D3
Haileyville, Okla. (74546) 288/P5
Hailong, China 77/L3
Hailsham, England 13/H7
Hailun, China 77/L2
Hailuoto, Finland 18/O4
Hailuoto (isl.), Finland 18/O4
Haina, Hawaii (96727) 218/H3
Hainan (isl.), China 2/Q5
Hainan (isl.), China 54/N8
Hainan (isl.), China 77/H8
Hainaut (prov.), Belgium 27/D7
Hainburg an der Donau, Austria 41/D2
Haines, Alaska (99827) 196/M1
Haines, Oreg. (97833) 291/J3
Hainesburg, N.J. (†07832) 273/C2
Haines City, Fla. (33844) 212/E3
Haines Junction, Yukon 187/E3
Haines Landing, Maine (†04964) 243/B6
Hainesport○, N.J. (08036) 273/D4
Hainesville, Ill. (†60030) 222/A4
Hainesville, N.J. (†07826) 273/D1
Hainfeld, Austria 41/C2
Haiphong, Vietnam 54/M7
Hairy Hill, Alberta 182/D3
Haiti 2/F5
Haiti 146/L8
HAITI 158
HAITI 156/D3
Haiwee, Calif. 204/H7
Haiya Junction, Sudan 59/C6
Haiya Junction, Sudan 111/G4
Haiyan, China 77/F4
Haiyang, China 77/K4
Haiyuan, China 77/G4
Hajara, Al (plain), Iraq 66/D5
Hajarain, P.D.R. Yemen 59/E6
Hajdú-Bihar (co.), Hungary 41/F3
Hajdúböszörmény, Hungary 41/F3
Hajdúdorog, Hungary 41/F3
Hajdúhadház, Hungary 41/F3
Hajdúnánás, Hungary 41/F3
Hajdúsámson, Hungary 41/F3
Hajdúszoboszló, Hungary 41/F3
Haji Ibraham (mt.), Iraq 66/D2
Hajja, Yemen Arab Rep. 59/D6
Hajnowka, Poland 47/F2
Hajós, Hungary 41/E3
Haka, Burma 72/B2
Hakalau, Hawaii (96710) 218/J4
Hakkâri (prov.), Turkey 63/K4
Hakkâri (Çölemerik), Turkey 63/K4
Hakkâri (mts.), Turkey 63/K4
Hakken (mt.), Japan 81/H6
Hakodate, Japan 81/K3
Hakodate, Japan 54/R5
Haku (mt.), Japan 81/H5
Hakui, Japan 81/H5
Hakusan National Park, Japan 81/H5
Hal (Halle), Belgium 27/E7
Halabja, Iraq 66/D3
Halachó, Mexico 150/O6
Halaib, Sudan 59/C5
Halaib, Sudan 111/G3
Halalii (lake), Hawaii 218/A2
Halaula, Hawaii 188/G5
Halawa, Hawaii, Hawaii (†96711) 218/G3
Halawa, Molokai, Hawaii (†96748) 218/H1
Halawa (bay), Hawaii 218/H1
Halawa (cape), Hawaii 218/H1
Halawa (stream), Hawaii 218/B3
Halawa Heights, Hawaii (†96701) 218/B3
Halberstadt, E. Germany 22/D3
Halbrite, Sask. 181/H6
Halbur, Iowa (51444) 229/D4
Halcon (mt.), Philippines 82/C4
Halcyon Dale, Georgia (†30467) 217/J5
Haldane, Ill. (†61030) 222/D1
Haldeman, Ky. (40329) 237/P4
Halden, Norway 18/G7
Haldensleben, E. Germany 22/D2
Haldimand, Ontario 177/E5
Haldimand-Norfolk (reg. munic.), Ontario 177/E5
Hale (co.), Ala. 195/C5
Hale, Argentina 143/F7
Hale, Colo. (80730) 208/P3
Hale, Camp, Colo. 208/G4
Hale, England 13/H2
Hale, Iowa (52230) 229/L4
Hale, Mich. (48739) 250/F4
Hale, Mo. (64643) 261/F3
Hale (riv.), North. Terr. 93/D8
Hale (co.), Texas 303/C3
Hale (mt.), W. Australia 92/B4
Haleakala (crater), Hawaii 218/K2
Haleakala Nat'l Park, Hawaii 218/K2
Haleb (Aleppo), Syria 59/C2
Haleb (Aleppo), Syria 63/G4
Haleburg, Ala. (†36319) 195/H8
Hale Center, Texas (79041) 303/C3
Haledon, N.J. (07508) 273/B1
Haleiwa, Hawaii (96712) 218/E1
Halen, Belgium 27/G7
Hales Corners, Wis. (53130) 317/K2
Halesowen, England 13/E5
Halesowen, England 10/G3
Hales Point, Tenn. (†38040) 237/B9
Halesworth, England 13/J5
Haley, N. Dak. (†58629) 282/D8
Haley Station, Ontario 177/H2
Haleyville, Ala. (35565) 195/C2
Haleyville, N.J. (†08349) 273/C5
Half Assini, Ghana 106/D8
Halfeti, Turkey 63/H4
Half Island Cove, Nova Scotia 168/G3
Half Moon (cay), Belize 154/D2
Halfmoon Bay, Alberta 182/C3
Halfmoon Bay, Br. Col. 184/J2
Half Moon Bay, Calif. (94019) 204/H3
Half Moon Bay (Oban), N. Zealand 100/B7
Half Moon Lake, Alberta 182/D2
Halford, Kansas (†67701) 232/B2
Halfway (riv.), Br. Col. 184/F2
Halfway, Ky. (42150) 237/J7
Halfway, Md. (†21740) 245/G2
Half Way, Mo. (65663) 261/F7
Halfway, Oreg. (97834) 291/K3
Halfway House, Hawaii (†96718) 218/H6
Halfway House, S. Africa 118/H6
Halfweg, Netherlands 27/B4
Halhul, West Bank 65/C4
Haliburton (county), Ontario 177/F2
Haliburton, Ontario 177/F2
Haliburton (lake), Ontario 177/F2
Halieli, Turkey 63/B6
Halifax, Canada 2/F3
Halifax, England 13/J1
Halifax, England 10/G1
Halifax (harb.), Grenada 161/C8
Halifax○, Mass. (02338) 249/L5
Halifax (co.), N.C. 281/O2
Halifax, N.C. (27839) 281/O2
Halifax (co.), Nova Scotia 168/E4
Halifax (cap.), N.S. 162/K7
Halifax (cap.), N.S. 146/M5
Halifax (cap.), Nova Scotia 168/E4
Halifax (harb.), Nova Scotia 168/E4
Halifax, Pa. (17032) 294/J5
Halifax (bay), Queensland 88/H3
Halifax (bay), Queensland 95/C3
Halifax○, Vt. (†05358) 268/B6
Halifax (co.), Va. 307/L7
Halifax, Va. (24558) 307/L7
Halifax Center, Vt. (†05358) 268/B6
Haliimaile, Hawaii (96787) 218/J2
Halil (riv.), Iran 59/G4
Halin, Somalia 115/J2
Halkett (cape), Alaska 196/H1
Halkirk, Alberta 182/D3
Halkirk, Scotland 10/E1
Halkirk, Scotland 15/E2
Hall (isl.), Alaska 196/D2
Hall (co.), Georgia 217/E2
Hall, Ind. (†46157) 227/D5
Hall, Ky. (†41840) 237/R6
Hall, Md. (†20716) 245/L5
Hall (isls.), Micronesia 87/F5
Hall, Mont. (59837) 262/C4
Hall (co.), Nebr. 264/F4
Hall (basin), N.W. Terrs. 187/M1
Hall (lake), N.W. Terrs. 187/K3
Hall (pen.), N.W.T. 162/K3
Hall (pen.), N.W. Terrs. 187/M3
Hall (riv.), Québec 172/C2
Hall (co.), Texas 303/D3
Hall, W. Va. (†26201) 312/F4
Halla (mt.), S. Korea 81/C7
Hallam, Nebr. (68368) 264/H4
Hallam, Victoria 97/K5
Halland (co.), Sweden 18/H8
Hallandale, Fla. (33009) 212/B4
Hallandale (riv.), Scotland 15/E2
Hallaniya (isl.), P.D.R. Yemen 59/G6
Hallau, Switzerland 39/F1
Hall Beach, N.W. Terrs. 187/K3
Hallboro, Manitoba 179/C4
Halle, Belgium 27/E7
Halle, E. Germany 7/F3
Halle (dist.), E. Germany 22/D3
Halle, E. Germany 22/D3
Halleck, Nev. (89824) 266/F2
Hällefors, Sweden 18/J7
Hallein, Austria 41/B3
Halle-Neustadt, E. Germany 22/D3
Hallett, Okla. (74034) 288/N2
Hallettsville, Texas (77964) 303/G8
Halley, Ark. (†71638) 202/H6
Halliday, N. Dak. (58636) 282/F5
Hallie, Wis. (†54729) 317/D6
Halligen (isls.), W. Germany 22/C1
Hall Meadow (brook), Conn. 210/C1
Hallock, Minn. (56728) 255/A2
Hallonquist, Sask. 181/D5
Hallowell, Kansas (66744) 232/H4
Hallowell, Maine (04347) 243/D7
Hall Park, Okla. (†73069) 288/M4
Halls (stream), N.H. 268/E1
Halls, Tenn. (38040) 237/C9
Halls (creek), Utah 304/D6
Hallsberg, Sweden 18/J7
Hallsboro, N.C. (28442) 281/M6
Halls Creek, Australia 87/C7
Halls Creek, W. Australia 88/D3
Halls Creek, W. Australia 92/D2
Halls Crossroads, Tenn. (37918) 237/O8
Hallson, N. Dak. (†58220) 282/P2
Halls Summit, Kansas (†66871) 232/G3
Hallstahammar, Sweden 18/K7
Hallstatt, Austria 41/B3
Hallstavik, Sweden 18/L6
Hallstead, Pa. (18822) 294/L2
Hall Summit, La. (71034) 238/D2
Hallsville, Ill. (†61727) 222/D3
Hallsville, Mo. (65255) 261/H4
Hallsville, Ohio (45633) 284/E7
Hallsville, Texas (75650) 303/K5
Hallton, Pa. (†15860) 294/E3
Halltown, Mo. (65664) 261/E8
Halltown, W. Va. (25423) 312/L4
Hallum, Netherlands 27/H2
Hallwilersee (lake), Switzerland 39/F2
Hallwood, Va. (23359) 307/S5
Halma, Minn. (56729) 255/B2
Halmahera (isl.), Indonesia 54/O9
Halmahera (isl.), Indonesia 85/H5
Halmahera (sea), Indonesia 85/H5
Halmstad, Sweden 18/H8
Halpine, Md. (†20852) 245/K4
Halq el Oued, Tunisia 106/G1
Hals, Denmark 21/D3
Halsell, Ala. (†36912) 195/B6
Halsey, Nebr. (69142) 264/D3
Halsey, Oreg. (97348) 291/D3
Halstad, Minn. (56548) 255/B3
Halstead, England 13/H6
Halstead, England 10/G5
Halstead, Kansas (67056) 232/E4
Haltdalen, Norway 18/G5
Haltemprice, England 13/G4
Haltemprice, England 10/F4
Haltern, W. Germany 22/B3
Haltiatunturi (mt.), Finland 18/M2
Haltom City, Texas (76117) 303/F2
Halton (reg. munic.), Ontario 177/E4
Halton Hills, Ontario 177/E4
Haltwhistle, England 13/E2
Halulu (lake), Hawaii 218/A2
Ham, Chad 111/C5
Ham, France 28/E3
Hama (prov.), Syria 63/G5
Hama, Syria 63/G5
Hama, Syria 59/C2
Hamada, Jebel (mt.), Egypt 59/B5
Hamada, Japan 81/E6
Hamadan (gov.), Iran 66/F3
Hamadan, Iran 66/F3
Hamadan, Iran 59/E3
Hamadan, Iran 54/F6
Hamamatsu, Japan 54/P6
Hamamatsu, Japan 81/H6
Hamar, N. Dak. (58336) 282/N4
Hamar, Norway 18/G6
Hamar, Saudi Arabia 59/E5
Hambantota, Sri Lanka 68/E7
Hamberg, N. Dak. (58337) 282/L4
Hamber Prov. Park, Br. Col. 184/H4
Hamblen (co.), Tenn. 237/P8
Hambleton, W. Va. (26269) 312/G4
Hamburg, Ark. (71646) 202/G7
Hamburg, Conn. (†06371) 210/F3
Hamburg, Ill. (62045) 222/C4
Hamburg, Iowa (51640) 229/B7
Hamburg, Mich. (48139) 250/F6
Hamburg, Minn. (55339) 255/D6
Hamburg, Miss. (†39661) 256/B7
Hamburg, N.J. (07419) 273/D1
Hamburg, N.Y. (14075) 276/C5
Hamburg, Pa. (19526) 294/L4
Hamburg, W. Germany 7/F3
Hamburg (state), W. Germany 22/D2
Hamburg, W. Germany 22/D2
Hamburg, Wis. (54438) 317/G5
Hamda, Saudi Arabia 59/D6
Hamden○, Conn. (06514) 210/D3
Hamden, N.Y. (13782) 276/K6
Hamden, Ohio (45634) 284/F7
Häme (prov.), Finland 18/O6
Hämeenlinna, Finland 18/O6
Hamel, Ill. (62046) 222/B2
Hamel, Minn. (55340) 255/F5
Hamel, Québec 172/G3
Hamelin Pool, W. Australia 88/A5
Hamelin Pool, W. Australia 92/A4
Hameln, W. Germany 22/C2
Hamer, Idaho (83425) 220/F6
Hamer, S.C. (29547) 296/J3
Hamersley (range), W. Australia 88/B4
Hamersley (range), W. Australia 92/B3
Hamersville, Ohio (45130) 284/C8
Hamhung, N. Korea 81/C4
Hami (Kumul), China 77/D3
Hami, China 54/L5
Hamill, S. Dak. (57534) 298/K6
Hamilton, Ala. (35570) 195/C2
Hamilton (lake), Ark. 202/D5
Hamilton (cap.), Bermuda 156/G3
Hamilton (mt.), Calif. 204/L3
Hamilton, Colo. (81638) 208/D2
Hamilton (co.), Fla. 212/D1
Hamilton, Georgia (31811) 217/C5
Hamilton (co.), Ill. 222/E5
Hamilton, Ill. (62341) 222/B3
Hamilton (co.), Ind. 227/E4
Hamilton, Ind. (46742) 227/H1
Hamilton (co.), Iowa 229/F4
Hamilton, Iowa (50116) 229/H6
Hamilton (co.), Kansas 232/A3
Hamilton, Kansas (66853) 232/F4
Hamilton○, Mass. (01936) 249/L2
Hamilton, Mich. (49419) 250/C6
Hamilton, Miss. (39746) 256/H3
Hamilton, Mo. (64644) 261/E3
Hamilton, Mont. (59840) 262/B4
Hamilton (co.), Nebr. 264/F4
Hamilton (inlet), Newf. 166/C3
Hamilton (inlet), Newf. 146/N4
Hamilton (inlet), Newf. 162/L5
Hamilton (sound), Newf. 166/D4
Hamilton (co.), N.Y. 276/L3
Hamilton, N.Y. (13346) 276/J5
Hamilton, N. Zealand 100/E2
Hamilton, N.C. (27840) 281/P3
Hamilton, N. Dak. (58238) 282/R2
Hamilton (co.), Ohio 284/A7
Hamilton, Ohio 188/K3
Hamilton, Ohio (*45011) 284/A7
Hamilton, Ont. 146/K5
Hamilton, Ont. 162/H7
Hamilton, Ontario 177/E4
Hamilton, Oreg. (†97856) 291/H3
Hamilton, Pa. (15744) 294/D4
Hamilton (riv.), Queensland 95/B4
Hamilton, R.I. (†02852) 249/J6
Hamilton, Scotland 15/C2
Hamilton, Scotland 10/B1
Hamilton, The (riv.), S. Australia 94/D2
Hamilton, The (riv.), S. Australia 88/E5
Hamilton, Tasmania 99/C4
Hamilton (co.), Tenn. 237/L10
Hamilton (co.), Texas 303/F6
Hamilton, Texas (76531) 303/G6
Hamilton, Victoria 88/G7
Hamilton, Victoria 97/B5
Hamilton, Va. (22068) 307/N2
Hamilton, Wash. (98255) 310/D2
Hamilton City, Calif. (95951) 204/C4
Hamilton Dome, Wyo. (82427) 319/D2
Hamilton Square-Mercerville, N.J. (08690) 273/D3
Hamilton-Wentworth (reg. munic.), Ontario 177/D4
Hamina, Finland 18/P6
Hamiota, Manitoba 179/B4
Ham Lake, Minn. (55304) 255/E5
Hamler, Ohio (43524) 284/B3
Hamlet, Ind. (46532) 227/D2
Hamlet, Nebr. (69031) 264/C4
Hamlet, N.Y. (†14138) 276/B6
Hamlet, N.C. (28345) 281/K5
Hamlet, N. Dak. (†58795) 282/E2
Hamlet, Ohio (†45102) 284/B8
Hamletsburg, Ill. (62944) 222/E6
Hamlin, Alberta 182/D2
Hamlin, Iowa (50117) 229/D5
Hamlin, Kansas (†66434) 232/G2
Hamlin, Ky. (42046) 237/E7
Hamlin○, Maine (†04785) 243/H1
Hamlin (lake), Mich. 250/C4
Hamlin, N.Y. (14464) 276/E4
Hamlin, Pa. (18427) 294/M3
Hamlin, Sask. 181/C3
Hamlin (co.), S. Dak. 298/P4
Hamlin, Texas (79520) 303/E5
Hamlin, W. Va. (25523) 312/B6
Hamm, W. Germany 22/B3
Hammamet (gulf), Tunisia 106/G1
Hammar, Hor al (lake), Iraq 66/E5
Hammarstrand, Sweden 18/J5
Hamme, Belgium 27/E6
Hammel, Denmark 21/C5
Hammelburg, W. Germany 22/C3
Hammer, S. Dak. (†57255) 298/R2
Hammerdal, Sweden 18/J5
Hammerfest, Norway 4/B9
Hammerfest, Norway 18/N1
Hammerfest, Norway 7/G1
Hammersmith, England 10/B5
Hammersmith, England 13/H8
Hammerum, Denmark 21/C5
Hammett, Idaho (83627) 220/C7
Hammon, Okla. (73650) 288/H3
Hammonasset (pt.), Conn. 210/E3
Hammonasset (res.), Conn. 210/E3
Hammonasset (riv.), Conn. 210/E3
Hammond, Ill. (61929) 222/E4
Hammond, Ind. (*46320) 227/B1
Hammond, Ky. (†40935) 237/O7
Hammond, La. (70401) 238/N1
Hammond, Minn. (55938) 255/F6
Hammond, Mo. (†65762) 261/G9
Hammond, Mont. (59332) 262/M5
Hammond (riv.), New Bruns. 170/E3
Hammond, N.Y. (13646) 276/J2
Hammond, Oreg. (97121) 291/C1
Hammond, Wis. (54015) 317/A6
Hammondsport, N.Y. (14840) 276/F6
Hammondsville, Ohio (43930) 284/J4
Hammondvale, New Bruns. 170/E3
Hammondville, Ala. (†35989) 195/G1
Hammonton, N.J. (08037) 273/D4
Hamnavoe, Scotland 15/G2
Ham-Nord, Québec 172/F4
Hamoa, Hawaii (†96713) 218/K2
Hamois, Belgium 27/G8
Hamont-Achel, Belgium 27/H6
Hampden, Maine (04444) 243/F6
Hampden○, Maine (04444) 243/F6
Hampden (co.), Mass. 249/D4
Hampden○, Mass. (01036) 249/E4
Hampden, Newf. 166/C4
Hampden, N. Zealand 100/C6
Hampden, N. Dak. (58338) 282/N2
Hampden, W. Va. (25623) 312/C7
Hampden Highlands, Maine (04445) 243/F6
Hampden-Sydney, Va. (23943) 307/L6
Hampshire (co.), England 13/F6
Hampshire, Ill. (60140) 222/E1
Hampshire (co.), Mass. 249/D3
Hampshire, Tenn. (38461) 237/G9
Hampshire (co.), W. Va. 312/J4
Hampshire, Wyo. (†82701) 319/H2
Hampstead, Dominica 161/E5
Hampstead, Md. (21074) 245/L2
Hampstead, New Bruns. 170/D3
Hampstead○, N.H. (03841) 268/E6
Hampstead, N.C. (28443) 281/O6
Hampstead, Québec 172/H4
Hampton, Ark. (71744) 202/F6
Hampton○, Conn. (06247) 210/G1
Hampton, Fla. (32044) 212/D2
Hampton, Georgia (30228) 217/D4
Hampton, Ill. (61256) 222/C2
Hampton, Iowa (50441) 229/G3
Hampton, Ky. (42047) 237/E6
Hampton, Minn. (55031) 255/E6
Hampton, Miss. (†38744) 256/B4
Hampton, Nebr. (68843) 264/G4
Hampton, New Bruns. 170/E3
Hampton, N.H. (03842) 268/F6
Hampton○, N.H. (03842) 268/F6
Hampton, N.J. (08827) 273/D2
Hampton, N.Y. (12837) 276/O3
Hampton, Nova Scotia 168/C4
Hampton, Oreg. (†97712) 291/G4
Hampton, Pa. (†17350) 294/H6
Hampton (co.), S.C. 296/E6
Hampton, S.C. (29924) 296/E6
Hampton, Tenn. (37658) 237/S8
Hampton (I.C.), Va. (*23601) 307/R6
Hampton Bays, N.Y. (11946) 276/R9
Hampton Beach, N.H. (03842) 268/F6
Hampton Falls○, N.H. (03844) 268/F6
Hampton Nat'l Hist. Site, Md. 245/M3
Hampton Park, Victoria 97/K6
Hampton Park, Victoria 88/M8
Hampton Roads (est.), Va. 307/R7
Hampton Springs, Fla. (†32347) 212/C1
Hamptonville, N.C. (27020) 281/H2
Hamrat esh Sheikh, Sudan 111/E5
Hamrin, Jabal (mts.), Iraq 66/D3
Hams Bluff (prom.), Virgin Is. (U.S.) 161/E3
Hams Fork (riv.), Wyo. 319/B4
Ham-Sud, Québec 172/F4
Hamton, Sask. 181/J4
Hamtramck, Mich. (48212) 250/B6
Hamur, Turkey 63/K3
Han (riv.), China 54/N6
Han (riv.), S. Korea 81/C5
Hana, Hawaii 188/F5
Hana, Hawaii (96713) 218/K2
Hanac, Turkey 63/K2
Hanaford (Logan), Ill. (†62856) 222/E6
Hanagita (peak), Alaska 196/K2
Hanahan, S.C. (29410) 296/H6
Hanakiya, Saudi Arabia 59/D5
Hanalei, Hawaii (96714) 218/C1
Hanalei (bay), Hawaii 218/C1
Hanalei (riv.), Hawaii 218/C1
Hanamaki, Japan 81/K4
Hanamalo (pt.), Hawaii 218/F7
Hanamaulu, Hawaii (96715) 218/C1
Hanapepe, Hawaii (96716) 218/C2
Hanapepe (bay), Hawaii 218/C2
Hanau, W. Germany 22/C3
Hanbogd, Mongolia 77/G3
Hanceville, Ala. (35077) 195/E2
Hancheng, China 77/H4
Hanchung (Hanzhong), China 77/G5
Hancock, Conn. (†06786) 210/C2
Hancock (co.), Georgia 217/G4
Hancock (co.), Ill. 222/B3
Hancock (co.), Ind. 227/F5
Hancock (co.), Iowa 229/F2
Hancock, Iowa (51536) 229/C6
Hancock (co.), Ky. 237/H5
Hancock (co.), Maine 243/G6
Hancock○, Maine (04640) 243/G6
Hancock, Md. (21750) 245/F2
Hancock○, Mass. (01237) 249/A2
Hancock, Mich. (49930) 250/G1
Hancock, Minn. (56244) 255/C5
Hancock (co.), Miss. 256/E10
Hancock, Mo. (†65452) 261/H7
Hancock○, N.H. (03449) 268/C6
Hancock (mt.), N.H. 268/D3
Hancock, N.Y. (13783) 276/K7
Hancock (co.), Ohio 284/C3
Hancock (co.), Tenn. 237/P7
Hancock○, Vt. (05748) 268/B4
Hancock (co.), W. Va. 312/E2
Hancock, W. Va. (25424) 312/K3
Hancock, Wis. (54943) 317/G7
Hancocks Bridge, N.J. (08038) 273/C4
Hand (co.), S. Dak. 298/L4
Handa (isl.), Scotland 15/C2
Handan (Hantan), China 77/H4
Handan, China 54/N6
Handel, Sask. 181/C3
Handeni, Tanzania 115/G5
Handies (peak), Colo. 208/E7
Handley, W. Va. (25102) 312/D6
Handlová, Czech. 41/E2
Handsom, Va. (23859) 307/O7
Handsworth, Sask. 181/J6
Haney, Br. Col. 184/L3
Hanford, Calif. (93230) 204/F7
Hanford Reservation, Wash. 310/F4
Hangayn Nuruu (mts.), Mongolia 77/E2
Hangchow (Hangzhou), China 77/J5
Hanggin, China 77/G4
Hanging Rock, Ohio (45635) 284/E8
Hangklip (cape), S. Africa 118/F7
Hangö, Finland 18/N7
Hangöudd (prom.), Finland 18/N7
Hangzhou (Hangchow), China 77/J5
Hangzhou, China 54/N6
Hangzhou Wan (bay), China 77/K5
Hanh, Mongolia 77/F1
Hani, Turkey 63/J3
Haniqra, Rosh (cape), Israel 65/C1
Hanish (isls.), Yemen Arab Rep. 59/D7
Hankinson, N. Dak. (58041) 282/S7
Hanko (Hangö), Finland 18/N7
Hanks, N. Dak. (†58856) 282/C2
Hanksville, Utah (84734) 304/D5
Hanle, India 68/D2
Hanley, Sask. 181/E4
Hanley Falls, Minn. (56245) 255/C6
Hanley Hills, Mo. (†63101) 261/P2
Hanlontown, Iowa (50444) 229/G2
Hanmer, N. Zealand 100/D5
Hann (mt.), W. Australia 92/D1
Hanna, Alberta 182/E4
Hanna, Alta. 162/E5
Hanna, Ind. (46340) 227/D2
Hanna, La. (71035) 238/D3
Hanna, Okla. (74845) 288/P4
Hanna, Utah (84031) 304/D3
Hanna, Wyo. (82327) 319/F4
Hanna City, Ill. (61536) 222/D3
Hannaford, N. Dak. (58448) 282/O5
Hannah, N. Dak. (58239) 282/N2
Hannah (bay), Ontario 175/D2
Hannawa Falls, N.Y. (13647) 276/L1
Hannibal, Mo. (63401) 261/K3
Hannibal, Mo. 188/H3
Hannibal, N.Y. (13074) 276/G4
Hannibal, Ohio (43931) 284/J6
Hannibal, Wis. (54439) 317/E5
Hanno, Japan 81/O2
Hannover, N. Dak. (58543) 282/H5
Hannover, W. Germany 7/E3
Hannover, W. Germany 22/C2
Hannuit (Hannut), Belgium 27/G7
Hannut, Belgium 27/G7
Hanöbukten (bay), Sweden 18/J9
Hanoi (cap.), Vietnam 2/Q4
Hanoi (cap.), Vietnam 54/M7
Hanover (isl.), Chile 120/B8
Hanover (isl.), Chile 138/D9
Hanover, Conn. (06350) 210/G2
Hanover, Ill. (61041) 222/C1
Hanover, Ind. (47243) 227/F7
Hanover, Kansas (66945) 232/F2
Hanover○, Maine (04237) 243/B7
Hanover, Md. (21201) 245/M4
Hanover○, Mass. (02339) 249/L4
Hanover, Mich. (49241) 250/E6
Hanover, Minn. (55341) 255/E5
Hanover, N.H. (03755) 268/C4
Hanover○, N.H. (03755) 268/C4
Hanover, N. Mex. (88041) 274/A6
Hanover, Ohio (†43055) 284/F5
Hanover, Ontario 177/C3
Hanover, Pa. (17331) 294/J6
Hanover (co.), Va. 307/N5
Hanover, Va. (23069) 307/O5
Hanover, W. Va. (24839) 312/C7
Hanover Park, Ill. (60103) 222/A5
Hanoverton, Ohio (44423) 284/J4
Hansboro, N. Dak. (58339) 282/M2
Hansell, Iowa (50640) 229/G3
Hansen, Idaho (83334) 220/D7
Hansford (co.), Texas 303/C1
Han Shui (riv.), China 77/H5
Hanska, Minn. (56041) 255/D6
Hans Lollik (isls.), Virgin Is. (U.S.) 161/B4
Hanson, Ky. (42413) 237/G6
Hanson, Mass. (02341) 249/L4
Hanson○, Mass. (02341) 249/L4
Hanson (bay), N. Zealand 100/E7
Hanson (riv.), North. Terr. 93/C6
Hanson, Okla. (†74955) 288/S4
Hanson (co.), S. Dak. 298/O6
Hansonville, Va. (†24266) 307/D7
Hanstholm, Denmark 21/B3
Hanston, Kansas (67849) 232/C3
Hansville, Wash. (98340) 310/C3
Hantan (Handan), China 77/H4
Hants (co.), Nova Scotia 168/D4
Hant's Harbour, Newf. 166/D2
Hantsport, Nova Scotia 168/D3
Hantzsch (riv.), N.W. Terrs. 187/L3
Hanumangarh, India 68/C3
Hanwood, N.S. Wales 97/C4
Hanyuan, China 77/F6
Hanzhong (Hanchung), China 77/G5
Hao (atoll), Fr. Poly. 87/N7
Haouach, Wadi (dry riv.), Chad 111/C4
Haparanda, Sweden 18/N4
Hapeville, Georgia (30354) 217/K2
Happy, Ky. (41746) 237/P6
Happy, Texas (79042) 303/C3
Happy Adventure, Newf. 166/D2
Happy Camp, Calif. (96039) 204/B2
Happy Jack, Ariz. (86024) 198/D4
Happy Jack, La. (†70083) 238/L7
Happy Valley, Oreg. (†97222) 291/B2
Happy Valley-Goose Bay, Newf. 166/B3
Haqi, Saudi Arabia 59/C4
Harad, Saudi Arabia 59/E5
Harads, Sweden 18/M3
Harahan, La. (70123) 238/O4
Haraja, Saudi Arabia 59/D6
Haralson (co.), Georgia 217/B3
Haralson, Georgia (30229) 217/C4
Haramachi, Japan 81/K5
Harar (prov.), Ethiopia 111/H6
Harar, Ethiopia 111/H6
Harar, Ethiopia 102/G4
Harardera, Somalia 115/J3
Harare (Salisbury) (cap.), Zimbabwe 102/E6
Haraz, Chad 111/C5
Harbel, Liberia 106/B7
Harbeson, Del. (19951) 245/S6
Harbin, China 77/L2
Harbin, China 2/R3
Harbin, China 54/O5
Harbine, Nebr. (†68377) 264/G4
Harbinger, N.C. (27941) 281/T2
Harboør, Denmark 21/B4
Harbor, Oreg. (97415) 291/C5
Harbor Beach, Mich. (48441) 250/G5
Harbor City, Calif. (90710) 204/C11
Harborcreek, Pa. (16421) 294/C1
Harbor Springs, Mich. (49740) 250/D3
Harborton, Va. (23389) 307/S5
Harbor View, Ohio (43434) 284/C2
Harbour (isl.), Bahamas 156/C1
Harbour Breton, Newf. 166/C4
Harbour Deep, Newf. 166/C3
Harbour Grace, Newf. 166/D2
Harbour Grace, Newf. 162/L6
Harbour Main, Newf. 166/D2
Harbourton, N.J. (†08530) 273/D3
Harbourville, Nova Scotia 168/D3
Harburg-Wilhelmsburg, W. Germany 22/C2
Hårby, Denmark 21/D7
Harco, Ill. (†62935) 222/E6
Harcourt, Iowa (50544) 229/E4
Harcourt, New Bruns. 170/E2
Harcourt, Ontario 177/F2
Harcuvar (mts.), Ariz. 198/B5
Harda, India 68/D4
Hardangerfjord (fjord), Norway 18/D7
Hardangerfjorden (fjord), Norway 7/E3
Hardangervidda (plat.), Norway 18/E6
Hardaway, Ala. (36039) 195/G6
Hardburly, Ky. (41747) 237/P6
Hardee (co.), Fla. 212/E4
Hardee, Miss. (†39177) 256/C5
Hardeeville, S.C. (29927) 296/E7
Hardeman (co.), Tenn. 237/C10
Hardeman (co.), Texas 303/E3
Hardenberg, Netherlands 27/J3
Harden City, Okla. (74846) 288/N5
Harderwijk, Netherlands 27/H4
Hardesty, Okla. (73944) 288/D1

Hérouxville 381

Hay, Wales 10/E4
Hay, Wales 13/D5
Hay, Wash. (99136) 310/H4
Hayama, Japan 81/O3
Hayange, France 28/F3
Haycock, Alaska (†99762) 196/F1
Hayden, Ala. (35079) 195/E3
Hayden, Ariz. (85235) 198/E5
Hayden, Colo. (81639) 208/E2
Hayden, Idaho (†83835) 220/B2
Hayden (lake), Idaho 220/B2
Hayden, Ind. (47245) 227/F7
Hayden, Mo. (†65459) 261/H6
Hayden, N. Mex. (†88410) 274/F3
Hayden (peak), Utah 304/C3
Haydenburg, Tenn. (†38588) 237/K8
Hayden Lake, Idaho (83835) 220/B2
Haydenville, Mass. (01039) 249/C3
Haydenville, Ohio (43127) 284/F7
Hayes (mt.), Alaska 196/J2
Hayes (pen.), Greenl. 4/B13
Hayes, Jamaica 158/J6
Hayes, La. (70646) 238/E6
Hayes (riv.), Man. 162/G4
Hayes (riv.), Manitoba 179/K3
Hayes (co.), Nebr. 264/C4
Hayes (riv.), N.W. Terrs. 187/J3
Hayes, S. Dak. (57537) 298/H5
Hayes, Wis. (†54174) 317/J5
Hayes Center, Nebr. (69032) 264/C4
Hayesville, Iowa (52562) 229/J6
Hayesville, New Bruns. 170/D2
Hayesville, N.C. (28904) 281/B4
Hayesville, Ohio (44838) 284/F4
Hayesville, Oreg. (†97301) 291/A3
Hayfield, Iowa (50445) 229/F2
Hayfield, Minn. (55940) 255/F7
Hayfork, Calif. (96041) 204/B3
Hay Fork, Trinity (riv.), Calif. 204/B3
Hay Lakes, Alberta 182/D3
Hayle, England 13/B7
Haylow, Georgia (†31648) 217/G9
Haymana, Turkey 63/E3
Haymarket, Va. (22069) 307/N3
Hayne, N.C. (†28318) 281/M5
Haynes, Alberta 182/D3
Haynes, Ark. (72341) 202/J4
Haynes, N. Dak. (58637) 282/F8
Haynesville, La. (71038) 238/D1
Haynesville○, Maine (04446) 243/G4
Haynesville, Va. (22472) 307/P5
Hayneville, Ala. (36040) 195/E6
Hayrabolu, Turkey 63/B2
Hay River, N.W.T. 162/E3
Hay River, N.W.T. 146/G3
Hay River, N.W. Terrs. 187/G3
Hays, Alberta 182/E4
Hays, Kansas (67601) 232/C3
Hays, Mont. (59527) 262/H2
Hays, N.C. (28635) 281/G2
Hays (co.), Texas 303/F7
Haysi, Va. (24256) 307/D6
Hay Springs, Nebr. (69347) 264/B2
Haystack (mt.), Conn. 210/C1
Haystack (peak), Mont. 262/A3
Haystack (mt.), N.Y. 276/N2
Haystack (mt.), Vt. 268/B6
Haysville, Ind. (†47546) 227/D8
Haysville, Kansas (67060) 232/E4
Haysville, Pa. (†15143) 294/B4
Hayter, Alberta 182/E3
Hayti, Mo. (63851) 261/N10
Hayti, S. Dak. (57241) 298/P4
Hayti Heights, Mo. (†63851) 261/N10
Hayton, Wis. (†53014) 317/K7
Hayward, Calif. (*94541) 204/K2
Hayward (lake), Conn. 210/F2
Hayward, Minn. (56043) 255/E7
Hayward, Mo. (†63873) 261/N10
Hayward, Wis. (54843) 317/D3
Haywards-Manor Park, N. Zealand 100/B2
Haywood, Manitoba 179/D5
Haywood (co.), N.C. 281/C3
Haywood, N.C. (†27559) 281/L3
Haywood, Okla. (74548) 288/P5
Haywood (co.), Tenn. 237/C9
Haywood City, Mo. (†63736) 261/N9
Hazar (lake), Turkey 63/H3
Hazaran, Kuh-e (mt.), Iran 66/K6
Hazard, Ky. (41701) 237/P6
Hazard, Nebr. (68844) 264/F3
Hazardville, Conn. (06082) 210/E1
Hazaribagh, India 68/F4
Hazar Qadam, Afghanistan 59/J3
Hazar Qadam, Afghanistan 68/B2
Hazebrouck, France 28/E2
Hazel, Ky. (42049) 237/E7
Hazel, S. Dak. (57242) 298/P4
Hazel Cliffe, Sask. 181/J5
Hazel Crest, Ill. (60429) 222/B6
Hazeldean, New Bruns. 170/C2
Hazel Dell, Ill. (62430) 222/E4
Hazel Dell, Sask. 181/H4
Hazeldine, Alberta 182/E3
Hazel Green, Ala. (35750) 195/E1
Hazel Green, Ky. (41332) 237/O5
Hazelgreen, Mo. (†65556) 261/H7
Hazel Green, Wis. (53811) 317/F11
Hazel Grove and Bramhall, England 13/H2
Hazel Hill, Nova Scotia 168/G3
Hazelhurst, Ill. (†61064) 222/D2
Hazel Hurst, Pa. (16733) 294/E2
Hazelhurst, Wis. (54531) 317/G4
Hazel Park, Mich. (48030) 250/B6
Hazel Patch, Ky. (†40729) 237/N6
Hazelridge, Manitoba 179/F5
Hazelrigg, Ind. (†46052) 227/D4
Hazel Run, Minn. (56247) 255/C6
Hazelton, Br. Col. 162/D5
Hazelton, Br. Col. 184/D2
Hazelton (mts.), Br. Col. 184/C2
Hazelton, Idaho (83335) 220/E7
Hazelton, Kansas (67061) 232/D4
Hazelton, N. Dak. (58544) 282/K7
Hazelton, W. Va. (26535) 312*G3
Hazelton (peak), Wyo. 319/E1
Hazelwood, Ind. (†46118) 227/D5
Hazelwood, Mo. (*63042) 261/P2
Hazelwood, N.C. (28738) 281/C4
Hazen (bay), Alaska 196/E2
Hazen, Ark. (72064) 202/G4
Hazen, Nev. (89417) 266/C3
Hazen, N. Dak. (58545) 282/G5
Hazen (lake), N.W. Terrs. 187/L1
Hazen (str.), N.W. Terrs. 187/G2
Hazenmore, Sask. 181/D6
Hazerim, Israel 65/B5
Hazlehurst, Georgia (31539) 217/G7
Hazlehurst, Miss. (39083) 256/D7
Hazlet, N.J. (07730) 273/E3
Hazlet, Sask. 181/C5
Hazleton, Ind. (47640) 227/B8
Hazleton, Iowa (50641) 229/K3
Hazleton, Pa. (18201) 294/L4
Hazlett (lake), W. Australia 88/D4
Hazlettville, Del. (†19953) 245/R4
Hazor Hagelilit, Israel 65/D2
Hazro, Turkey 63/J3
Heacham, England 13/H5
Headford, Ireland 17/C5
Headland, Ala. (36345) 195/H8
Headlee, Ind. (†47960) 227/D3
Head of Amherst, Nova Scotia 168/E3
Head of Bay d'Espoir, Newf. 166/C4
Head of Bight (bay), S. Australia 94/B4
Head of Grassy, Ky. (41145) 237/P4
Head of Island, La. (†70462) 238/L2
Head of Jeddore, Nova Scotia 168/E4
Head of Millstream, New Bruns. 170/E3
Head of Saint Margarets Bay, Nova Scotia 168/E4
Headquarters, Idaho (83534) 220/C3
Headrick, Okla. (73549) 288/H5
Heads, The (prom.), Oreg. 291/C5
Heads of Ayr (cape), Scotland 15/D5
Head Waters, Va. (24442) 307/K4
Heafford Junction, Wis. (54532) 317/G4
Healdsburg, Calif. (95448) 204/B5
Healdton, Okla. (73438) 288/M6
Healdville, Vt. (05147) 268/B5
Healesville, Victoria 97/C5
Healing Springs, Ala. (†36558) 195/B7
Healing Springs, Va. (†24445) 307/J5
Healy, Alaska (99743) 196/H2
Healy, Kansas (67850) 232/B3
Healys, Va. (†23071) 307/R5
Heanor, England 13/F4
Heard (isl.), Australia 2/N8
Heard (co.), Georgia 217/B4
Hearne, Sask. 181/F5
Hearne, Texas (77859) 303/H7
Hearst (isl.) 5/B16
Hearst, Ont. 162/H6
Hearst, Ontario 177/J5
Hearst, Ontario 175/D3
Heart (lake), Alberta 182/E2
Heart (butte), N. Dak. 282/G6
Heart (riv.), N. Dak. 282/F6
Heart (lake), Wyo. 319/B1
Heart Butte, Mont. (59448) 262/C2
Heart River Settlement, Alberta 182/B2
Heart's Content, Newf. 166/D2
Heart's Delight, Newf. 166/D2
Heart's Desire, Newf. 166/D2
Hearts Hill, Sask. 181/B3
Heartwell, Nebr. (68945) 264/F4
Heartwellville, Vt. (†05350) 268/A6
Heaters, W. Va. (26627) 312/E5
Heath, Ala. (†36420) 195/F8
Heath, Alberta 182/E3
Heath (riv.), Bolivia 136/A3
Heath○, Mass. (01346) 249/C2
Heath, Mont. (†59457) 262/G3
Heath, Ohio (43055) 284/F5
Heath (riv.), Peru 128/H9
Heath (pt.), Québec 174/E3
Heathcote, Victoria 97/C5
Heatherton, Newf. 166/C4
Heatherton, Nova Scotia 168/G3
Heathhall, Scotland 15/E5
Heath Springs, S.C. (29058) 296/F2
Heath Steele, New Bruns. 170/D1
Heathsville, Va. (22473) 307/P5
Heaton, N. Dak. (58450) 282/L5
Heavener, Okla. (74937) 288/S5
Hebbardsville, Ky. (†42420) 237/G5
Hebbronville, Texas (78361) 303/F10
Hebbs Cross, Nova Scotia 168/D4
Hebburn, England 13/J3
Hebei (Hopei) (prov.), China 77/J4
Hebel, Queensland 95/C6
Heber, Ariz. (85928) 198/E4
Heber, Calif. (92249) 204/K11
Heber City, Utah (84032) 304/C3
Heber Springs, Ark. (72543) 202/G2
Hebert, La. (71436) 238/G2
Hébert (riv.), Nova Scotia 168/D3
Hébertville, Québec 172/F1
Hébertville-Station, Québec 172/F1
Hebgen (dam), Mont. 262/E6
Hebgen (lake), Mont. 262/E6
Hebi, China 77/H4
Hebo, Oreg. (97122) 291/D2
Hebrides, Inner (isls.), Scotland 10/C2
Hebrides, Inner (isls.), Scotland 15/B4
Hebrides, Outer (isls.), Scotland 10/C2
Hebrides, Outer (isls.), Scotland 15/A3
Hebrides (sea), Scotland 15/B3
Hebrides (sea), Scotland 10/C2
Hebron○, Conn. (06248) 210/F2
Hebron, Ill. (60034) 222/E1
Hebron, Ind. (46341) 227/C2
Hebron, Ky. (41048) 237/R2
Hebron○, Maine (04238) 243/C7
Hebron, Md. (21830) 245/R7
Hebron, Nebr. (68370) 264/G4
Hebron, Newf. 146/M4
Hebron, Newf. 162/K4
Hebron (fjord), Newf. 166/B2
Hebron○, N.H. (03241) 268/D4
Hebron, N. Dak. (58638) 282/G6
Hebron, Nova Scotia 168/B5
Hebron, Ohio (43025) 284/E6
Hebron, Texas (†75067) 303/G1
Hebron, West Bank 65/C4
Hebron, West Bank 59/C3
Hebron, W. Va. (26368) 312/D4
Hebron, Wis. (†53538) 317/J10
Hecate (str.), Br. Col. 162/C5
Hecate (str.), Br. Col. 146/E4
Hecate (str.), Br. Col. 184/B3
Hecelchakán, Mexico 150/O6
Heceta (isl.), Alaska 196/M2
Heceta (head), Oreg. 291/C3
Hechi, China 77/G7
Hechingen, W. Germany 22/C4
Hechuan (Hochwan), China 77/G5
Hecker, Ill. (62248) 222/D5
Hecla, Manitoba 179/F3
Hecla (isl.), Manitoba 179/F3
Hecla, S. Dak. (57446) 298/N2
Hecla Prov. Park, Manitoba 179/F3
Hector, Ark. (72843) 202/E3
Hector, Minn. (55342) 255/D6
Hector, N.Y. (14841) 276/G5
Hede, Sweden 18/H5
Hedemora, Sweden 18/K6
Hedenäset, Sweden 18/N3
Hedensted, Denmark 21/C6
Hedgesville, Mont. (†59078) 262/G4
Hedgesville, W. Va. (25427) 312/K3
Hedley, Br. Col. 184/G5
Hedley, Texas (79237) 303/D3
Hedmark (co.), Norway 18/G6
Hedon, England 13/G4
Hedrick, Iowa (52563) 229/J6
Hedville, Kansas (†67401) 232/E3
Hedwig Village, Texas (†77001) 303/H1
Heemskerk, Netherlands 27/F3
Heemstede, Netherlands 27/F4
Heer, Netherlands 27/H7
Heerde, Netherlands 27/H4
Heerenveen, Netherlands 27/H3
Heerhugowaard, Netherlands 27/F3
Heerlen, Netherlands 27/J7
Heesch, Netherlands 27/G5
Hefei (Hofei), China 77/J5
Hefei, China 54/N6
Heffley Creek, Br. Col. 184/G5
Heflin, Ala. (36264) 195/G3
Heflin, La. (71039) 238/D2
Hegang (Hokang), China 77/L2
Hegang, China 54/O5
Hegau (reg.), W. Germany 22/C5
Hegeler, Ill. (†61832) 222/F3
Hegins, Pa. (17938) 294/K4
Heiban, Sudan 111/F5
Heiberger, Ala. (†36756) 195/D5
Heide, W. Germany 22/C1
Heidelberg, Ky. (41333) 237/O5
Heidelberg, Minn. (†56071) 255/E6
Heidelberg, Miss. (39439) 256/F7
Heidelberg, Pa. (15106) 294/B7
Heidelberg, S. Africa 118/J7
Heidelberg, Victoria 97/J5
Heidelberg, Victoria 88/L7
Heidelberg, W. Germany 22/C4
Heiden, Switzerland 39/H2
Heidenau, E. Germany 22/E3
Heidenheim an der Brenz, W. Germany 22/D4
Heidenreichstein, Austria 41/C2
Heidrick, Ky. (40949) 237/O7
Heihe (Aihui) (Aigun), China 77/L1
Heijo (P'yŏngyang) (cap.), N. Korea 81/C4
Heil, N. Dak. (58546) 282/G7
Heilbron, S. Africa 118/D5
Heilbronn, W. Germany 22/C4
Heiligenblut, Austria 41/B3
Heiligenhafen, W. Germany 22/D1
Heiligenstadt, E. Germany 22/D3
Heilman, Ind. (†47523) 227/C8
Heilongjiang (Heilungkiang) (prov.), China 77/K2
Heilong Jiang (Amur) (riv.), China 77/L2
Heiloo, Netherlands 27/F3
Heilwood, Pa. (15745) 294/E4
Heimberg, Switzerland 39/E3
Heimdal, N. Dak. (58342) 282/L4
Heinola, Finland 18/P6
Heinola, Minn. (†56567) 255/C4
Heinsburg, Alberta 182/E3
Heinze Chaung (bay), Burma 72/C4
Heise, Idaho (†83443) 220/G6
Heiskell, Tenn. (37754) 237/O8
Heisler, Alberta 182/D3
Heislerville, N.J. (08324) 273/D5
Heisson, Wash. (98622) 310/C5
Heist-Knokke, Belgium 27/C6
Heist-op-den-Berg, Belgium 27/F6
Heizer, Kansas (†67530) 232/D3
Hejaz (reg.), Saudi Arabia 59/C4
Hejian, China 77/J4
Hejing, China 77/C3
Hekimhan, Turkey 63/G3
Hekla (mt.), Iceland 4/C11
Hekla (mt.), Iceland 7/C2
Hekla (vol.), Iceland 21/B1
Hekou, China 77/F7
Hel, Poland 47/D1
Hel (pen.), Poland 47/D1
Helan, China 77/G4
Heldens (pt.), St. Chris.-Nevis 161/C10
Helechawa, Ky. (41334) 237/P5
Helen, Georgia (30545) 217/E1
Helen, Md. (20635) 245/M7
Helen (lake), N. Dak. 282/K5
Helena, Ala. (35080) 195/E4
Helena, Ark. (72342) 202/J4
Helena, Calif. (96042) 204/B3
Helena, Georgia (31037) 217/G6
Helena, Mo. (64459) 261/C3
Helena (cap.), Mont. 146/G5
Helena (cap.), Mont. 188/D1
Helena (cap.), Mont. (59601) 262/E4
Helena (lake), Mont. 262/E4
Helena, N.Y. (13649) 276/L1
Helena, Ohio (43435) 284/D3
Helena, Okla. (73741) 288/K1
Helena, S.C. (†29108) 296/D3
Helensburgh, N.S. Wales 97/F4
Helensburgh, Scotland 10/A1
Helensburgh, Scotland 15/A1
Helen Springs, North. Terr. 93/C5
Helensville, N. Zealand 100/B1
Helenville, Wis. (53137) 317/J10
Helenwood, Tenn. (37755) 237/M8
Helez, Israel 65/B4
Helgoland (bay), W. Germany 22/C1
Helgoland (isl.), W. Germany 22/B1
Heliopolis, Egypt 111/J3
Helix, Oreg. (97835) 291/J2
Hellam, Pa. (17406) 294/J6
Hell Canyon (creek), S. Dak. 298/B6
Hellebaek, Denmark 21/F5
Hellendoorn, Netherlands 27/J4
Hellertown, Pa. (18055) 294/M4
Helles (cape), Turkey 63/B6
Hellevoetsluis, Netherlands 27/E5
Hellier, Ky. (41534) 237/S6
Hellín, Spain 33/F3
Hells (canyon), Idaho 220/B4
Hells Canyon (dam), Idaho 220/B4
Hells Canyon (dam), Oreg. 291/L2
Hells Canyon Nat'l Rec. Area, Idaho 220/B4
Hells Canyon Nat'l Rec. Area, Oreg. 291/K2
Hells Canyon Nat'l Rec. Area, Wash. 310/H5
Hells Half Acre, Wyo. (82601) 319/E2
Hell-Ville, Madagascar 102/G6
Hell-Ville, Madagascar 118/H2
Helm, Miss. (†38756) 256/C4
Helmand (riv.), Afghanistan 54/H6
Helmand (riv.), Afghanistan 59/J3
Helmand (riv.), Afghanistan 68/B2
Helmand (Sistan, Daryacheh-ye) (lake), Iran 66/M5
Helmer, Ind. (46744) 227/G1
Helmetta, N.J. (08828) 273/E3
Helmond, Netherlands 27/H6
Helmsburg, Ind. (47435) 227/E6
Helmsdale, Scotland 10/E1
Helmsdale, Scotland 15/E2
Helmsdale (riv.), Scotland 15/E2
Helmsley, England 13/G3
Helmstedt, W. Germany 22/D2
Helmville, Mont. (59843) 262/C4
Helotes, Texas (78023) 303/J10
Helper, Utah (84526) 304/D4
Helsenhorn (mt.), Switzerland 39/F4
Helsingborg, Sweden 18/H8
Helsingborg, Sweden 7/F3
Helsinge, Denmark 21/F6
Helsingør, Denmark 21/F6
Helsingør, Denmark 18/H8
Helsinki (cap.), Finland 18/O6
Helsinki (cap.), Finland 7/G2
Helsinki (cap.), Finland 2/L2
Helston, England 13/B7
Helston, England 10/D5
Helston, Manitoba 179/C4
Helton, Ky. (40840) 237/P7
Helton, N.C. (†28631) 281/G1
Heltonville, Ind. (47436) 227/E7
Helvecia, Argentina 143/F5
Helvetia, Pa. (†15848) 294/E3
Helvetia, W. Va. (26224) 312/F5
Helvick (head), Ireland 17/G7
Helwân, Egypt 59/B4
Helwân, Egypt 111/J3
Hemar (dry riv.), Israel 65/C5
Hemaruka, Alberta 182/E4
Hematite, Mo. (63047) 261/L6
Hemel Hempstead, England 10/F5
Hemel Hempstead, England 13/G7
Hemet, Calif. (92343) 204/H10
Hemford, Nova Scotia 168/D4
Hemingford, Nebr. (69348) 264/A2
Hemingway, S.C. (29554) 296/J4
Hemlock, Ind. (46937) 227/F4
Hemlock, Mich. (48626) 250/E5
Hemlock, N.Y. (14466) 276/E5
Hemlock (lake), N.Y. 276/E5
Hemlock, Ohio (43743) 284/F6
Hemlock (Eureka), S.C. (†29706) 296/E2
Hemlock Grove, Ohio (45738) 284/F7
Hemmingford, Québec 172/D4
Hemnes, Norway 18/J3
Hemphill (co.), Texas 303/D2
Hemphill, Texas (75948) 303/L6
Hemphill, W. Va. (24842) 312/C8
Hemple, Mo. (†64490) 261/D3
Hempstead (co.), Ark. 202/C6
Hempstead, N.Y. (*11550) 276/R7
Hempstead, Texas (77445) 303/J7
Hemse, Sweden 18/L8
Henagar, Ala. (35978) 195/G1
Henan (Honan) (prov.), China 77/H5
Henan, China 77/F5
Hen and Chickens (isls.), N. Zealand 100/E1
Henares (riv.), Spain 33/G4
Henbury, North. Terr. 93/C8
Hendaye, France 28/C6
Hendek, Turkey 63/D2
Henderson, Ala. (†36035) 195/F7
Henderson (co.), Ill. 222/C3
Henderson, Ill. (61439) 222/C2
Henderson (riv.), Ill. 222/C2
Henderson, Ind. (†46173) 227/F5
Henderson, Iowa (51541) 229/B6
Henderson (co.), Ky. 237/F5
Henderson, Ky. (42420) 237/F5
Henderson, La. (†70517) 238/G6
Henderson, Md. (21640) 245/P4
Henderson, Minn. (56044) 255/E6
Henderson, Nebr. (68371) 264/G4
Henderson, Nev. (89015) 266/G6
Henderson, N.Y. (13650) 276/H3
Henderson, N. Zealand 100/B1
Henderson (co.), N.C. 281/D4
Henderson, N.C. (27536) 281/N2
Henderson (isl.), Pitcairn Is. 87/O8
Henderson (co.), Tenn. 237/E9
Henderson, Tenn. (38340) 237/D10
Henderson (co.), Texas 303/J5
Henderson, Texas (75652) 303/K5
Henderson, W. Va. (25106) 312/B5
Hendersonville, N.C. (28739) 281/E4
Hendersonville, Pa. (15339) 294/B5
Hendersonville, S.C. (†29945) 296/F6
Hendersonville, Tenn. (37075) 237/H8
Hendley, Nebr. (68946) 264/D4
Hendon, Sask. 181/H3
Hendorabi (isl.), Iran 66/H7
Hendra, Queensland 88/K2
Hendricks (co.), Ind. 227/D5
Hendricks, Ky. (41441) 237/P5
Hendricks, Minn. (56136) 255/B6
Hendricks, W. Va. (26271) 312/G4
Hendrickson, Mo. (†63967) 261/M9
Hendrix, Okla. (74741) 288/O7
Hendrix Lake, Br. Col. 184/G4
Hendrum, Minn. (56550) 255/B3
Hendry (co.), Fla. 212/E5
Hendrysburg, Ohio (43744) 284/H5
Henefer, Utah (84033) 304/C2
Hengchun, China 77/K7
Hengduan Shan (mts.), China 77/E6
Hengelo, Gelderland, Netherlands 27/J4
Hengelo, Overijssel, Netherlands 27/K4
Hengshan, China 77/G4
Hengshui, China 77/J4
Heng Xian, China 77/G7
Hengyang, China 77/H6
Hengyang, China 54/N7
Henik (lakes), N.W. Terrs. 187/J3
Hénin-Beaumont, France 28/E2
Henjam (isl.), Iran 66/J7
Henlawson, W. Va. (25624) 312/B7
Henley, Mo. (65040) 261/H6
Henley and Grange, S. Australia 88/D8
Henley Harbour, Newf. 166/C3
Henley on Klip, S. Africa 118/H7
Henley-on-Thames, England 13/G8
Henlopen (cape), Del. 245/T5
Henlopen Acres, Del. (†19971) 245/T6
Henne, Denmark 21/B6
Hennebont, France 28/B4
Hennef, W. Germany 22/B3
Hennepin, Ill. (61327) 222/D2
Hennepin (co.), Minn. 255/E5
Hennepin, Okla. (73046) 288/M5
Hennessey, Okla. (73742) 288/L2
Hennigsdorf bei Berlin, E. Germany 22/E3
Henniker, N.H. (03242) 268/D5
Henniker○, N.H. (03242) 268/D5
Henning, Ill. (61848) 222/F3
Henning, Minn. (56551) 255/C4
Henning, Tenn. (38041) 237/B9
Henribourg, Sask. 181/F2
Henrico (co.), Va. 307/O6
Henrietta, Mo. (64036) 261/E4
Henrietta, N.Y. (14467) 276/E4
Henrietta, N.C. (28076) 281/F4
Henrietta, Texas (76365) 303/F4
Henrietta Maria (cape), Ont. 162/H4
Henrietta Maria (cape), Ontario 175/D1
Henriette, Minn. (55036) 255/E5
Henrieville, Utah (84736) 304/C6
Henry (co.), Ala. 195/H7
Henry (co.), Georgia 217/D4
Henry, Idaho (†83230) 220/G7
Henry (co.), Ill. 222/C2
Henry, Ill. (61537) 222/D2
Henry (co.), Ind. 227/G5
Henry (co.), Iowa 229/K6
Henry (co.), Ky. 237/L4
Henry (co.), Mo. 261/E6
Henry, Nebr. (69349) 264/A2
Henry (isl.), Nova Scotia 168/G3
Henry (co.), Ohio 284/B3
Henry, S.C. (†29554) 296/J4
Henry, S. Dak. (57243) 298/P4
Henry (co.), Tenn. 237/E8
Henry, Tenn. (38231) 237/E8
Henry (mts.), Utah 304/D6
Henry (co.), Va. 307/J7
Henry, Va. (24102) 307/J7
Henry (cape), Va. 307/R7
Henryetta, Okla. (74437) 288/O4
Henry House, Alberta 182/B3
Henry Kater (cape), N.W. Terrs. 187/M3
Henrys (lake), Idaho 220/G5
Henrys Fork, Snake (riv.), Idaho 220/G5
Henrys Fork, Green (riv.), Wyo. 319/C4
Henryton, Md. (21080) 245/L3
Henryville, Ind. (47126) 227/F7
Henryville, Pa. (18332) 294/M3
Henryville, Québec 172/D4
Henryville, Tenn. (†38483) 237/G10
Hensall, Ontario 177/C4
Hensel, N. Dak. (58241) 282/P2
Henshaw, Ky. (†42459) 237/F5
Hensies, Belgium 27/D8
Hensler, N. Dak. (58547) 282/H5
Hensley, Ark. (72065) 202/F4
Henson (creek), Md. 245/F6
Hentiy, Mongolia 77/H2
Henty, N.S. Wales 97/D4
Henzada, Burma 72/B3
Henzada, Burma 54/L8
Hepburn, Iowa (†51632) 229/C7
Hepburn, Ohio (†43326) 284/D4
Hepburn, Sask. 181/E3
Hephzibah, Georgia (30815) 217/H4
Hepler, Kansas (66746) 232/H4
Heppner, Oreg. (97836) 291/H2
Hepu (Hoppo), China 77/G7
Hepworth, Ontario 177/C3
Hepzibah, W. Va. (26369) 312/F4
Hequ, China 77/H4
Herald, Calif. (95638) 204/C9
Heralds (cays), 95/D3
Herat, Afghanistan 54/H6
Herat, Afghanistan 59/H3
Herat, Afghanistan 68/A2
Hérault (dept.), France 28/E6
Hérault (riv.), France 28/E6
Herbert, Ala. (†36401) 195/E8
Herbert (riv.), Queensland 88/H3
Herbert, Sask. 181/D5
Herbert Hoover Nat'l Hist. Site, Iowa 229/L5
Herbes (isl.), Ala. 195/B10
Herbeumont, Belgium 27/G9
Herb Lake, Manitoba 179/H3
Herborn, W. Germany 22/C3
Herbst, Ind. (†46952) 227/F3
Herbster, Wis. (54844) 317/D2
Herceg Novi, Yugoslavia 45/D4
Herchmer, Man. 162/G4
Herchmer, Manitoba 179/K2
Herculaneum, Mo. (63048) 261/M6
Hercules, Calif. (94547) 204/J1
Herd, Okla. (†74056) 288/O1
Heredia, C. Rica 154/E5
Hereford, Ariz. (85615) 198/E7
Hereford, Colo. (80732) 208/L1
Hereford, England 13/E5
Hereford, England 10/E4
Hereford, Md. (†21111) 245/M2
Hereford (inlet), N.J. 273/D5
Hereford, Oreg. (97837) 291/K3
Hereford, Pa. (18056) 294/L5
Hereford, S. Dak. (57743) 298/D5
Hereford, Texas (79045) 303/B3
Hereford and Worcester (co.), England 13/E5
Hérémence, Switzerland 39/D4
Herencia, Spain 33/E3
Herentals, Belgium 27/F6
Heretaunga-Pinehaven, N. Zealand 100/C2
Herford, W. Germany 22/C2
Hergiswil, Switzerland 39/F3
Héricourt, France 28/G4
Heringsdorf, E. Germany 22/F1
Herington, Kansas (67449) 232/E3
Heriot Bay, Br. Col. 184/E5
Herisau, Switzerland 39/H2
Herkimer, Kansas (66433) 232/F2
Herkimer (co.), N.Y. 276/L4
Herkimer, N.Y. (13350) 276/L4
Herlen Gol (Kerulen) (riv.), Mongolia 77/H2
Herlong, Calif. (96113) 204/E3
Herm (isl.), Chan. Is. 13/E8
Hermagor-Preseggersee, Austria 41/B3
Herman, Mich. (†49946) 250/A2
Herman, Minn. (56248) 255/B5
Herman, Nebr. (68029) 264/H3
Herman, Pa. (16039) 294/C4
Herman (lake), S. Dak. 298/P5
Herma Ness (prom.), Scotland 15/G2
Hermann, Mo. (65041) 261/K5
Hermannsburg, North. Terr. 88/E4
Hermannsburg, North. Terr. 93/C7
Hermansverk, Norway 18/E6
Hermansville, Mich. (49847) 250/B3
Hermantown, Minn. (†55811) 255/F4
Hermanus, S. Africa 118/G7
Hermanville, Miss. (39086) 256/C7
Hermidale, N.S. Wales 97/D2
Hermil, Lebanon 63/G5
Herminie, Pa. (15637) 294/C5
Hermiston, Oreg. (97838) 291/H2
Hermitage, Ark. (71647) 202/F7
Hermitage, Grenada 161/D8
Hermitage, Mo. (65668) 261/F7
Hermitage, Newf. 166/C4
Hermitage (bay), Newf. 166/C4
Hermitage Springs, Tenn. (†37150) 237/K7
Hermite (isls.), Chile 138/F11
Hermleigh, Texas (79526) 303/D5
Hermon, Ill. (†61458) 222/C3
Hermon○, Maine (†04401) 243/F6
Hermon, N.Y. (13652) 276/K2
Hermon (mt.), Syria 63/F6
Hermosa (peak), Colo. 208/D7
Hermosa, S. Dak. (57744) 298/C6
Hermosa Beach, Calif. (90254) 204/B11
Hermosillo, Mexico 146/G7
Hermosillo, Mexico 150/D2
Hermsdorf, W. Germany 22/E3
Hernád (riv.), Hungary 41/F2
Hernandarias, Argentina 143/F5
Hernandarias, Paraguay 144/E4
Hernández, Argentina 143/F6
Hernandez, N. Mex. (87537) 274/C2
Hernando, Argentina 143/D3
Hernando (co.), Fla. 212/D3
Hernando, Fla. (32642) 212/D3
Hernando, Miss. (38632) 256/E1
Herndon, Georgia (†30442) 217/H5
Herndon, Iowa (†50128) 229/E5
Herndon, Kansas (67739) 232/B2
Herndon, Ky. (42236) 237/G7
Herndon, Pa. (17830) 294/J4
Herndon, Va. (*22070) 307/O3
Herndon, W. Va. (24726) 312/D7
Herne, Belgium 27/E7
Herne, W. Germany 22/B3
Herning, Denmark 18/F8
Herning, Denmark 21/B5
Herod, Georgia (†31742) 217/D7
Herod, Ill. (62947) 222/E6
Heroica Caborca, Mexico 150/C1
Heroica Nogales, Mexico 150/D1
Heron (lake), Minn. 255/C7
Heron, Mont. (59844) 262/A2
Heron (isl.), New Bruns. 170/D1
Heron Bay, Ontario 177/H5
Heron Bay, Ontario 175/C3
Heron Lake, Minn. (56137) 255/C7
Hérouxville, Québec 172/E3

Isle of Palms, S.C. (29451) 296/H6
Isle of Whithorn, Scotland 15/D6
Isle of Wight (co.), England 13/F7
Isle of Wight (co.), Va. 307/P7
Isle of Wight, Va. (23397) 307/P7
Isle Pierre, Br. Col. 184/F3
Isle Royale (isl.), Mich. 250/D1
Isle Royale National Park, Mich. (†55605) 250/E1
Isle Royale Nat'l Park, Mich. 250/E1
Islesboro, Maine (04848) 243/F7
Islesboro○, Maine (04848) 243/F7
Islesboro (isl.), Maine 243/F7
Islesford, Maine (04646) 243/G7
Isles of Scilly, England 13/A7
Isleta, N. Mex. (87022) 274/C4
Isleton, Calif. (95641) 204/L1
Islington, England 10/B5
Islington, England 13/H8
Islington, Mass. (02090) 249/C8
Islip, N.Y. (11751) 276/O9
Ismailia, Egypt 111/K3
Ismailia, Egypt 59/B3
Ismay, Mont. (59336) 262/M4
Isna, Egypt 111/F2
Isna, Egypt 59/B4
Isney, Ala. (†36919) 195/B7
Isny im Allgäu, W. Germany 22/D5
Isojoki, Finland 18/M5
Isoka, Zambia 115/F6
Isola, Miss. (38754) 256/C4
Isonville, Ky. (41149) 237/P4
Isparta (prov.), Turkey 63/D4
Isparta, Turkey 63/D4
Isparta, Turkey 59/B2
Isperikh, Bulgaria 45/H4
Ispir, Turkey 63/J2
Israel 2/L4
Israel 54/E6
ISRAEL 59/B3
ISRAEL 65
Issano, Guyana 131/B3
Issaouane Erg (des.), Algeria 106/F3
Issaquah, Wash. (98027) 310/C3
Issaquena (co.), Miss. 256/B5
Issia, Ivory Coast 106/C7
Issineru, Guyana 131/A2
Issoire, France 28/E5
Issoudun, France 28/D4
Issue, Md. (20645) 245/L7
Issyk-Kul' (lake), U.S.S.R. 54/J5
Issyk-Kul' (lake), U.S.S.R. 48/H5
Issy-les-Moulineaux, France 28/A2
Istanbul (prov.), Turkey 63/C2
Istanbul, Turkey 2/L3
Istanbul, Turkey 7/G4
Istanbul, Turkey 63/D6
Istanbul, Turkey 59/A1
Isthmus (bay), Ontario 177/C2
Istiaía, Greece 45/F6
Istmina, Colombia 126/B5
Istokpoga (lake), Fla. 212/E4
Istranca (mts.), Turkey 63/B2
Istres, France 28/F6
Istria (pen.), Yugoslavia 45/A3
Isulan, Philippines 82/E7
Itá, Paraguay 144/B5
Itabaiana, Paraíba, Brazil 132/H4
Itabaiana, Sergipe, Brazil 132/G5
Itaberaba, Brazil 132/F6
Itabira, Brazil 120/E4
Itabira, Brazil 132/F7
Itabirito, Brazil 135/E2
Itabuna, Brazil 132/G6
Itabuna, Brazil 120/F4
Itacoatiara, Brazil 132/B3
Itacoatiara, Brazil 120/D3
Itacurubí, Paraguay 144/B5
Itacurubí del Rosario, Paraguay 144/D4
Itaguara, Brazil 135/D2
Itaguatins, Brazil 132/D4
Itagüí, Colombia 126/C4
Itaí, Brazil 135/B3
Itaipu (dam) 120/D5
Itaipu (dam), Brazil 132/C9
Itaipu (dam), Paraguay 144/E4
Itaituba, Brazil 132/C4
Itajaí, Brazil 120/E5
Itajaí, Brazil 132/D9
Itajubá, Brazil 135/D3
Itajubá, Brazil 132/E8
Itala, Somalia 115/J3
Italy 2/K3
Italy 7/F4
ITALY 34
Italy, Texas (76651) 303/H5
Itamarandiba, Brazil 132/F7
Itami, Japan 81/H7
Itanagar, India 68/G3
Itanhaem, Brazil 135/C4
Itapagipe, Brazil 135/B1
Itapé, Paraguay 144/C5
Itapeby, Uruguay 145/B2
Itapecerica, Brazil 135/D2
Itapecuru (riv.), Brazil 132/F4
Itapecuru-Mirim, Brazil 132/F3
Itapemirim, Brazil 132/F8
Itaperuna, Brazil 135/F2
Itapetinga, Brazil 120/F4
Itapetinga, Brazil 132/G6
Itapetininga, Brazil 135/B3
Itapetininga, Brazil 132/D8
Itapeva, Brazil 132/D8
Itapeva, Brazil 135/B3
Itapi (riv.), Brazil 132/B3
Itapicuru, Brazil 132/G5
Itapicuru (riv.), Brazil 132/G5
Itapipoca, Brazil 132/G3
Itapira, Brazil 135/C3
Itapiranga, Brazil 132/B3
Itápolis, Brazil 132/D8
Itápolis, Brazil 135/B2
Itaporanga, Brazil 132/G4
Itapúa (dept.), Paraguay 144/E5
Itaqui, Brazil 132/B10
Itaquyry, Paraguay 144/E4
Itararé, Brazil 132/D9
Itararé, Brazil 135/B4
Itararé (riv.), Brazil 135/B3
Itariri, Brazil 135/C4
Itarsi, India 68/D4
Itasca, Ill. (60143) 222/B5
Itasca (co.), Minn. 255/E3
Itasca (lake), Minn. 255/C3
Itasca, Texas (76055) 303/G5
Itasy (lake), Madagascar 118/H3
Itata (riv.), Chile 138/A11
Itatí, Argentina 143/E2
Itatiba, Brazil 135/C3
Itaú, Bolivia 136/D7
Itauguá, Paraguay 144/B5
Itaúna, Brazil 135/D2
Itawamba (co.), Miss. 256/H2
Itbayat (isl.), Philippines 82/A2
Itchen (lake), N.W. Terrs. 187/G3
Iténez (Guaporé) (riv.), Bolivia 136/C3
Ithaca, Mich. (48847) 250/E5
Ithaca, Nebr. (68033) 264/H3
Ithaca, N.Y. (14850) 276/G6
Ithaca, Ohio (†45329) 284/A6
Ithaca, Queensland 88/K2
Ithaca, Wis. (†53581) 317/F9
Itháki, Greece 45/E6
Itháki (Ithaca) (isl.), Greece 45/E6
Itigi, Tanzania 115/F5
Itimbiri (riv.), Zaire 115/D3
Itkillik (riv.), Alaska 196/H1
Itmann, W. Va. (24847) 312/D7
Itnay (riv.), Fr. Guiana 120/D2
Ito, Japan 81/J6
Itoigawa, Japan 81/H5
Itoman, Japan 81/N6
Itonamas (riv.), Bolivia 136/C3
Itta Bena, Miss. (38941) 256/D4
Ittre, Belgium 27/E7
Itu, Brazil 135/C3
Ituaçu, Brazil 132/F6
Ituango, Colombia 126/C4
Ituberá, Brazil 132/G6
Ituiutaba, Brazil 132/D7
Itumbiara, Brazil 120/E4
Itumbiara, Brazil 132/D7
Ituna, Sask. 181/H4
Ituni, Guyana 131/B3
Itupiranga, Brazil 132/D4
Iturama, Brazil 135/A1
Iturbe, Paraguay 144/C5
Ituri (for.), Zaire 115/E3
Iturup (isl.), U.S.S.R. 54/R5
Iturup (isl.), U.S.S.R. 48/P5
Ituverava, Brazil 135/C2
Ituzaingó, Argentina 143/E2
Ituzaingó, Uruguay 145/A6
Itzehoe, W. Germany 22/C2
Iuka, Ill. (62849) 222/E5
Iuka, Kansas (67066) 232/D4
Iuka, Ky. (42052) 237/E6
Iuka, Miss. (38852) 256/H1
Iul'tin, U.S.S.R. 48/T3
Iva, S.C. (29655) 296/B3
Ivaí (riv.), Brazil 132/C8
Ivalo, Finland 18/P2
Ivalojoki (riv.), Finland 18/P2
Ivan, Ark. (71748) 202/F6
Ivan, La. (†71006) 238/C1
Ivančice, Czech. 41/D2
Ivangrad, Yugoslavia 45/E4
Ivanhoe, Calif. (93235) 204/F7
Ivanhoe, Minn. (56142) 255/B6
Ivanhoe, N. S. Wales 88/G6
Ivanhoe, N.S. Wales 97/C3
Ivanhoe, N.C. (28447) 281/N5
Ivanhoe, Va. (24350) 307/G7
Ivanhoe, W. Australia 92/E1
Ivanhoe, W. Va. (†26201) 312/F5
Ivanjica, Yugoslavia 45/E4
Ivanof, Alaska (†99502) 196/G3
Ivano-Frankovsk, U.S.S.R. 7/G4
Ivano-Frankovsk, U.S.S.R. 48/C5
Ivano-Frankovsk, U.S.S.R. 52/B5
Ivanovo, U.S.S.R. 7/J3
Ivanovo, U.S.S.R. 48/E4
Ivanovo, U.S.S.R. 52/E3
Ivarib, Namibia 118/B4
Ivaylovgrad, Bulgaria 45/H5
Ivdel, U.S.S.R. 48/G3
Ivel, Ky. (41642) 237/R5
Ives (mesa), Ariz. 198/E3
Ivesdale, Ill. (61851) 222/E4
Ivey, Georgia (†31031) 217/F5
Ivigtut, Greenl. 4/D12
Ivindo (riv.), Cameroon 115/B3
Ivindo (riv.), Congo 115/B3
Ivindo (riv.), Gabon 115/B3
Ivins, Utah (84738) 304/A6
Ivohibe, Madagascar 118/H4
Ivón, Bolivia 136/C2
Ivor, Va. (23866) 307/P7
Ivory Coast 2/J5
Ivory Coast 102/B4
IVORY COAST 106/C7
Ivory Coast (reg.), Ivory Coast 106/C8
Ivoryton, Conn. (06442) 210/F3
Ivrea, Italy 34/B2
Ivrindi, Turkey /B3
Ivry-sur-Seine, France 28/B2
Ivujivik, Que. 162/J3
Ivujivik, Québec 174/E1
Ivy, Va. (22945) 307/L4
Ivybridge, England 13/D7
Ivydale, W. Va. (25113) 312/D5
Ivyland, Pa. (†18974) 294/M5
Ivy Mountain (brook), Conn. 210/C1
Ivyton, Ky. (41444) 237/P5
Ivyton, Tenn. (†38543) 237/L8
Iwaizumi, Japan 81/K4
Iwaki, Japan 54/R6
Iwaki, Japan 81/K5
Iwaki (mt.), Japan 81/K3
Iwakuni, Japan 81/E6
Iwami, Japan 81/G6
Iwamizawa, Japan 81/L2
Iwanai, Japan 81/K2
Iwasaki, Japan 81/J3
Iwata, Japan 81/H6
Iwate (pref.), Japan 81/K4
Iwate (mt.), Japan 81/K4
Iwatsuki, Japan 81/O2
Iwilei, Hawaii (†96801) 218/C4
Iwo (isl.), Japan 87/E3
Iwo (isl.), Japan 81/M4
Iwo, Nigeria 106/E7
Iwŏn, N. Korea 81/D3
Ixelles, Belgium 27/C9
Ixiamas, Bolivia 136/A3
Ixmiquilpan, Mexico 150/K6
Ixonia, Wis. (53036) 317/H1
Ixtapa, Mexico 150/J8
Ixtapalapa, Mexico 150/L1
Ixtenco, Mexico 150/N1
Ixtepec, Mexico 150/M8
Ixtlán del Río, Mexico 150/G6
Iyo, Japan 81/F7
Iyo (sea), Japan 81/E7
Izabal (lake), Guatemala 154/C3
Izamal, Mexico 150/P6
Izard (co.), Ark. 202/G1
Izberbash, U.S.S.R. 52/G6
Izegem, Belgium 27/C7
Izeh, Iran 66/F5
Izhevsk, U.S.S.R. 7/K3
Izhevsk, U.S.S.R. 48/F4
Izhevsk, U.S.S.R. 52/H3
Izhma (riv.), U.S.S.R. 52/H2
Izigan (cape), Alaska 196/E4
Izmail, U.S.S.R. 48/C5
Izmail, U.S.S.R. 52/C5
İzmir (prov.), Turkey 63/B3
İzmir, Turkey 54/D6
İzmir, Turkey 63/B3
İzmir, Turkey 59/A2
İzmir (gulf), Turkey 63/B3
İzmit, Turkey 59/A1
İzmit, Turkey 63/D2
Iznájar, Spain 33/D4
Iznalloz, Spain 33/E4
İznik, Turkey 63/C2
İznik (lake), Turkey 63/C2
Izozog, Bolivia 136/D6
Izozog (swamp), Bolivia 136/E6
Izra, Syria 63/G6
Izsák, Hungary 41/E3
Izsófalva, Hungary 41/F2
Iztapa, Guatemala 154/B4
Izu (isls.), Japan 81/J6
Izu (pen.), Japan 81/J6
Izúcar de Matamoros, Mexico 150/M2
Izuhara, Japan 81/D6
Izumi, Japan 81/J8
Izumiotsu, Japan 81/J8
Izumisano, Japan 81/G6
Izumo, Japan 81/F6
Izyum, U.S.S.R. 52/E5

J

Jaba, West Bank 65/C3
Jabaliya, Gaza Strip 65/A4
Jabalpur, India 54/K7
Jabalpur, India 68/D4
Jaba Rud (riv.), Iran 66/L2
Jabbeke, Belgium 27/C6
Jabir, Jordan 65/E2
Jablonec nad Nisou, Czech. 41/C1
Jablonica, Czech. 41/D2
Jablunka (pass), Czech. 41/E2
Jablunkov, Czech. 41/E2
Jaboatão, Brazil 120/F3
Jaboatão, Brazil 132/H5
Jaboticabal, Brazil 135/B2
Jaboticabal, Brazil 132/D8
Jabrin, Saudi Arabia 59/E5
Jaca, Spain 33/F1
Jacaguas (riv.), P. Rico 161/C2
Jacaleapa, Honduras 154/D3
Jacaltenango, Guatemala 154/B3
Jacaréacanga, Brazil 132/B4
Jacareí, Brazil 132/E8
Jacareí, Brazil 135/D3
Jacarezinho, Brazil 135/A3
Jacarezinho, Brazil 132/D8
Jáchal, Argentina 143/C3
Jachin, Ala. (36910) 195/B6
Jáchymov, Czech. 41/B1
Jacinto, Miss. (†38865) 256/H1
Jacinto City, Texas (77029) 303/J1
Jack, Ala. (36346) 195/F7
Jack (creek), Minn. 255/C7
Jack (lake), Ontario 177/F3
Jack (co.), Texas 303/F4
Jack (mt.), Wash. 310/E2
Jack Creek, Nev. (†89834) 266/E1
Jackfish (riv.), Alberta 182/B5
Jackfish (lake), Sask. 181/C2
Jackfish Lake, Sask. 181/C2
Jackfork (mt.), Okla. 288/P5
Jackman, Maine (04945) 243/C4
Jackman○, Maine (04945) 243/C4
Jackpot, Nev. (89825) 266/G1
Jacksboro, Tenn. (37757) 237/N8
Jacksboro, Texas (76056) 303/F4
Jacks Creek, Tenn. (38347) 237/D10
Jacks Fork (riv.), Mo. 261/J8
Jackson (co.), Ala. 195/F1
Jackson, Ala. (36545) 195/C8
Jackson (co.), Ark. 202/H2
Jackson, Calif. (95642) 204/C9
Jackson (co.), Colo. 208/G1
Jackson (co.), Fla. 212/D5
Jackson (lake), Fla. 212/B1
Jackson (lake), Fla. 212/E4
Jackson (co.), Georgia 217/E2
Jackson, Georgia (30233) 217/E4
Jackson (lake), Georgia 217/E4
Jackson (co.), Ill. 222/D6
Jackson (co.), Ind. 227/E7
Jackson (co.), Iowa 229/M4
Jackson (co.), Kansas 232/G2
Jackson (co.), Ky. 237/N6
Jackson, Ky. (41339) 237/P5
Jackson (par.), La. 238/E2
Jackson, La. (70748) 238/H5
Jackson (co.), Mich. 250/E6
Jackson, Mich. 188/J2
Jackson, Mich. (*49201) 250/E6
Jackson (co.), Minn. 255/C7
Jackson, Minn. (56143) 255/C7
Jackson (co.), Miss. 256/G9
Jackson (cap.), Miss. 146/K6
Jackson (cap.), Miss. 188/J4
Jackson (cap.), Miss. (*39201) 256/D6
Jackson (co.), Mo. 261/R5
Jackson, Mo. (63755) 261/N8
Jackson, Mont. (59736) 262/C5
Jackson (mt.), Mont. 262/C2
Jackson, Nebr. (68743) 264/H2
Jackson (mts.), Nev. 266/C1
Jackson○, N.H. (03846) 268/E3
Jackson○, N.J. (08527) 273/E3
Jackson (bay), N. Zealand 100/B5
Jackson (co.), N.C. 281/C4
Jackson, N.C. (27845) 281/P2
Jackson (co.), Ohio 284/E7
Jackson, Ohio (45640) 284/E7
Jackson (co.), Okla. 288/H5
Jackson (co.), Oreg. 291/E5
Jackson (creek), Oreg. 291/E5
Jackson, Pa. (18825) 294/L2
Jackson, S.C. (29831) 296/D5
Jackson (co.), S. Dak. 298/F6
Jackson (co.), Tenn. 237/K8
Jackson, Tenn. 188/J3
Jackson, Tenn. (38301) 237/D9
Jackson (co.), Texas 303/H9
Jackson (riv.), Va. 307/J4
Jackson (co.), W. Va. 312/C5
Jackson (co.), Wis. 317/E7
Jackson, Wis. (53037) 317/K9
Jackson (lake), Wyo. 188/E2
Jackson, Wyo. (83001) 319/B2
Jackson (lake), Wyo. 319/B2
Jackson (peak), Wyo. 319/B2
Jacksonboro, S.C. (29452) 296/G6
Jacksonburg, Ind. (†47327) 227/G5
Jacksonburg, Ohio (†45067) 284/B6
Jacksonburg, W. Va. (26377) 312/E3
Jackson Center, Ohio (45334) 284/B5
Jackson Center, Pa. (16133) 294/B3
Jackson Junction, Iowa (52150) 229/K2
Jackson Lake (res.), Colo. 208/L2
Jacksonport, Ark. (72075) 202/H2
Jacksonport, Wis. (†54235) 317/M6
Jackson's Arm, Newf. 166/C4
Jacksons Gap, Ala. (36861) 195/G5
Jackson Springs, N.C. (27281) 281/K4
Jacksontown, Ohio (43030) 284/F6
Jacksonville, Ala. (36265) 195/G3
Jacksonville, Ark. (72076) 202/F4
Jacksonville, Fla. 146/K6
Jacksonville, Fla. 188/K4
Jacksonville, Fla. (*32201) 212/E1
Jacksonville, Georgia (31544) 217/G7
Jacksonville, Ill. (62650) 222/C4
Jacksonville, Maine (†04630) 243/J6
Jacksonville, Md. (†21131) 245/M2
Jacksonville, Mo. (65260) 261/G3
Jacksonville, New Bruns. 170/C2
Jacksonville, N.C. (28540) 281/O5
Jacksonville, Ohio (45740) 284/F7
Jacksonville, Oreg. (97530) 291/D5
Jacksonville (Kent), Pa. (15752) 294/D4
Jacksonville, Texas (75766) 303/J5
Jacksonville, Vt. (05342) 268/B6
Jacksonville Beach, Fla. (32250) 212/E1
Jacksonville Naval Air Sta., Fla. 212/E1
Jacmel, Haiti 158/C6
Jacmel, Haiti 156/D3
Jacobabad, Pakistan 59/J4
Jacobabad, Pakistan 68/B3
Jacobina, Brazil 120/E4
Jacobina, Brazil 132/F5
Jacob Lake, Ariz. (86051) 198/C2
Jacobson, Minn. (55752) 255/E4
Jacobstown, N.J. (†08562) 273/D3
Jacobsville, Mich. (†49945) 250/A1
Jacobus, Pa. (17407) 294/J6
Jacques-Cartier (lake), Québec 172/F2
Jacques-Cartier (mt.), Québec 172/C1
Jacques-Cartier (passage), Québec 174/E3
Jacques-Cartier (riv.), Québec 172/F2
Jacquet (riv.), New Bruns. 170/D1
Jacquet River, New Bruns. 170/E1
Jacquinot (bay), Papua N.G. 86/B2
Jacuípe (riv.), Brazil 132/F5
Jacumba, Calif. (92034) 204/J11
Jacupiranga, Brazil 135/B4
Jaddi, Ras (cape), Pakistan 59/H4
Jaddi, Ras (pt.), Pakistan 68/A4
Jade (bay), W. Germany 22/C2
Jadwin, Mo. (65501) 261/K8
Jaén, Peru 128/C5
Jaén (prov.), Spain 33/E4
Jaén, Spain 7/D5
Jaén, Spain 33/E4
Jaffa (cape), S. Australia 94/F7
Jaffna, Sri Lanka 68/E7
Jaffna, Sri Lanka 54/K9
Jaffray, Br. Col. 184/K5
Jaffrey, N.H. (03452) 268/C6
Jaffrey○, N.H. (03452) 268/C6
Jaffrey Center, N.H. (03454) 268/C6
Jafura (des.), Saudi Arabia 59/F5
Jagdalpur, India 68/E5
Jagdaqi, China 77/K1
Jagersfontein, S. Africa 118/D5
Jagfontein, S. Africa 118/G7
Jaghbub (Jarabub), Libya 111/D2
Jagin (riv.), Iran 66/L8
Jagna, Philippines 82/E6
Jagtial, India 68/D5
Jagua, Cuba 158/D2
Jaguaquara, Brazil 132/F6
Jaguara (res.), Brazil 135/C2
Jaguarão, Brazil 132/C11
Jaguariaíva, Brazil 132/D9
Jaguariaíva, Brazil 135/B4
Jaguaribe (riv.), Brazil 132/G4
Jagüey Grande, Cuba 158/D2
Jagüey Grande, Cuba 156/B2
Jahrom, Iran 59/F4
Jahrom, Iran 66/H6
Jaicoa, Cordillera (mts.), P. Rico 161/B1
Jaicós, Brazil 132/F4
Jailolo, Indonesia 85/H5
Jainca, China 77/F4
Jaipur, India 54/J7
Jaipur, India 68/D3
Jaisalmer, India 68/C3
Jajarm, Iran 66/K2
Jajce, Yugoslavia 45/C3
Jajpur, India 68/F4
Jakarta (cap.), Indonesia 2/Q6
Jakarta (cap.), Indonesia 54/M10
Jakarta (cap.), Indonesia 85/H1
Jakin, Georgia (31761) 217/C8
Jakobstad, Finland 18/N5
Jakubany, Czech. 41/F2
Jal, N. Mex. (88252) 274/F6
Jala, Mexico 150/G6
Jalacingo, Mexico 150/P1
Jalaid, China 77/K2
Jalalabad, Afghanistan 68/B2
Jalalabad, Afghanistan 59/K3
Jalama, West Bank 65/C3
Jalapa, Guatemala 154/B3
Jalapa, Ind. (†46952) 227/F3
Jalapa, Nicaragua 154/E4
Jalapa, S.C. (†29108) 296/D3
Jalapa Enríquez, Mexico 146/J8
Jalapa Enríquez, Mexico 150/P1
Jalbun, West Bank 65/C3
Jaleswar, Nepal 68/F3
Jalgaon, India 68/D4
Jalingo, Nigeria 106/G7
Jalisco (state), Mexico 150/H6
Jalkot, Pakistan 59/K2
Jalna, India 68/D4
Jalo, Libya 111/D2
Jalo (oasis), Libya 111/D2
Jalón (riv.), Spain 33/E2
Jalor, India 68/C3
Jalpa, Mexico 150/H6
Jalpa de Méndez, Mexico 150/N7
Jalpaiguri, India 68/F3
Jalpan, Mexico 150/K6
Jalq, Iran 66/N7
Jáltipan de Morelos, Mexico 150/M8
Jalud, West Bank 65/C3
Jaluit (atoll), Marshall Is. 87/G5
Jam, Iran 66/H7
Jama, Ecuador 128/B3
Jamaica 2/F5
Jamaica 146/L8
Jamaica, Cuba 158/K4
Jamaica (chan.), Haiti 156/C3
Jamaica, Iowa (50128) 229/E5
JAMAICA 158
JAMAICA 156/C3
Jamaica (chan.), Jamaica 156/C3
Jamaica, N.Y. (*11401) 276/N9
Jamaica○, Vt. (05343) 268/B5
Jamaica Plain, Mass. (02130) 249/C7
Jamaiké, Suriname 131/D4
Jamalpur, Bangladesh 68/F4
Jamalpur, India 68/F3
Jamama, Somalia 115/H3
Jamanota (mt.), Neth. Ant. 161/E10
Jamanxim (riv.), Brazil 132/C4
Jambi, Indonesia 85/C6
Jambi, Indonesia 54/M10
Jambuair (cape), Indonesia 85/B4
James (bay) 162/H5
James (riv.) 188/G2
James (bay), Canada 146/K4
James (isl.), Chile 138/D5
James (peak), Colo. 208/H3
James, Georgia (†31032) 217/E5
James, Iowa (†51101) 229/A3
James (pt.), Md. 245/N6
James, Miss. (†38748) 256/B4
James (lake), N.C. 281/E3
James (riv.), N. Dak. 282/N6
James (bay), Ontario 175/D2
James (bay), Québec 174/A2
James (isl.), S.C. 296/H6
James (riv.), S. Dak. 298/N5
James (riv.), Va. 307/O6
James A. Garfield Nat'l Hist. Site, Ohio 284/G2
James Bay, Ontario 177/E2
Jamesburg, N.J. (08831) 273/E3
James City, N.C. (28550) 281/R4
James City, Pa. (16734) 294/E2
James City (co.), Va. 307/P6
James Creek, Pa. (16657) 294/F5
Jameson, Mo. (64647) 261/E2
Jameson Park, S. Africa 118/J7
Jamesport, Mo. (64648) 261/E3
James Ross (isl.) 5/C16
James Ross (str.), N.W.T. 162/G1
James Ross (str.), N.W. Terrs. 187/J3
Jamestown, Ala. (†35973) 195/G2
Jamestown, Ark. (†72501) 202/G2
Jamestown, Calif. (95327) 204/E6
Jamestown, Colo. (80455) 208/J2
Jamestown, Ill. (†62238) 222/D5
Jamestown, Ind. (46147) 227/D5
Jamestown, Kansas (66948) 232/E2
Jamestown, Ky. (42629) 237/L7
Jamestown, La. (71045) 238/D2
Jamestown, Miss. (†39483) 256/E8
Jamestown, Mo. (65046) 261/G5
Jamestown, N.Y. 188/F2
Jamestown, N.Y. (14701) 276/B6
Jamestown, N.C. (27282) 281/K3
Jamestown, N.Dak. 188/G1
Jamestown, N. Dak. (58401) 282/N6
Jamestown (dam), N. Dak. 282/N6
Jamestown (res.), N. Dak. 282/N6
Jamestown, Ohio (45335) 284/C6
Jamestown, Pa. (16134) 294/A3
Jamestown, R.I. (02835) 249/J6
Jamestown○, R.I. (02835) 249/J6
Jamestown, S. Australia 88/F6
Jamestown, S. Australia 94/F5
Jamestown, S.C. (29453) 296/H5
Jamestown, Tenn. (38556) 237/M8
Jamestown, Va. (23081) 307/P6
Jamestown Nat'l Hist. Site, Va. 307/P6
Jamesville, N.Y. (13078) 276/H5
Jamesville, N.C. (27846) 281/R3
Jamesville, Va. (23398) 307/S5
Jamieson, Fla. (†32333) 212/B1
Jamieson, Oreg. (97909) 291/K3
Jamison, Nebr. (†68759) 264/E2
Jamison, S.C. (†29115) 296/F4
Jamma, Somalia 102/G4
Jammerbugt (bay), Denmark 21/C3
Jammu, India 54/J6
Jammu, India 68/D2
Jammu and Kashmir (state), India 68/D2
Jamnagar, India 68/B4
Jamnagar, India 54/H7
Jampur, Pakistan 59/K4
Jämsä, Finland 18/O6
Jamshedpur, India 54/K7
Jamshedpur, India 68/F4
Jämtland (co.), Sweden 18/J5
Jamursba (cape), Indonesia 85/J5
Janakpur, Nepal 68/F3
Jandaq, Iran 66/J3
Jandowae, Queensland 95/D5
Jane, Mo. (64846) 261/D9
Jane Lew, W. Va. (26378) 312/F4
Janesville, Calif. (96114) 204/E3
Janesville, Ill. (62435) 222/E4
Janesville, Iowa (50647) 229/J3
Janesville, Minn. (56048) 255/E6
Janesville (Smithmill), Pa. (16680) 294/F4
Janesville, Wis. 188/J2
Janesville, Wis. (53545) 317/H10
Janesville-Beloit, Wis. 317/80
Janetstown, Scotland 15/E2
Janeville, New Bruns. 170/E1
Jánico, Dom. Rep. 158/D5
Janikowo, Poland 47/C2
Janiuay, Philippines 82/D5
Jan Mayen (isl.), Norway 4/B10
Jan Mayen (isl.), Norway 7/D1
Janos, Mexico 150/F1
Jánoshalma, Hungary 41/E3
Jánosháza, Hungary 41/D3
Janów Lubelski, Poland 47/F3
Jansen, Colo. (†81082) 208/K8
Jansen, Nebr. (68377) 264/G4
Jansen, Sask. 181/G4
Jantetelco, Mexico 150/L2
Januária, Brazil 120/E4
Januária, Brazil 132/E6
Janvrin (isl.), Nova Scotia 168/G3
Jaora, India 68/D4
Japan 2/S4
Japan 54/R6
Japan (sea) 2/R4
Japan (sea) 54/P6
JAPAN 81
Japan (sea), Japan 81/G4
Japan (sea), N. Korea 81/G4
Japan (sea), S. Korea 81/G4
Japan (sea), U.S.S.R. 48/O6
Japurá, Brazil 132/G9
Japurá (riv.), Brazil 120/C3
Japurá (riv.), Brazil 132/G9
Jaquet (pt.), Dominica 161/E5
Jara, Cerrito (mt.), Bolivia 136/F6
Jara (hill), Paraguay 144/C1
Jarabacoa, Dom. Rep. 158/E5
Jarabub, Libya 102/E2
Jarabub, Libya 111/D2
Jaragua, Dom. Rep. 158/D6
Jaraíz de la Vera, Spain 33/D2
Jarales, N. Mex. (87023) 274/C4
Jarama (riv.), Spain 33/E2
Jaramillo, Argentina 143/C6
Jarandilla de la Vera, Spain 33/D2
Jarash, Jordan 65/D3
Jarbalo, Kansas (†66048) 232/G2
Jarbidge (riv.), Idaho 220/C7
Jarbidge, Nev. (89826) 266/F1
Jardim, Brazil 132/G4
Jardine, Mont. (†59030) 262/F5
Jardines de la Reina (arch.), Cuba 158/F3
Jardines de la Reina (arch.), Cuba 156/B2
Jargalant, Mongolia 77/J2
Jari (riv.), Brazil 120/D2
Jari (riv.), Brazil 132/C3
Järna, Sweden 18/G2
Jarnac, France 28/C5
Jaro, Philippines 82/E5
Jarocin, Poland 47/C3
Jaroměř, Czech. 41/C1
Jarosław, Poland 47/F4
Jaroso, Colo. (81138) 208/H8
Järpen, Sweden 18/H5
Jarrahdale, W. Australia 88/B3
Jarrahdale, W. Australia 92/B2
Jarratt, Va. (23867) 307/O7
Jarrettsville, Md. (21084) 245/M2
Jarrow, Alberta 182/E3
Jarrow, England 13/J3
Jarrow, England 10/F3
Jars (plain), Laos 72/D3
Jartai, China 77/G4
Jaruco, Cuba 158/C1
Jarud, China 77/K3
Järvenpää, Finland 18/O6
Jarvie, Alberta 182/D2
Jarvis (isl.), Pacific 87/K6
Jarvisburg, N.C. (27947) 281/T2
Jarvisville, W. Va. (†26462) 312/F4
Järvsö, Sweden 18/K6
Jask, Iran 59/G4

Kamienna Góra 389

Jones Creek, Texas (†77541) 303/J9
Jonesdale, Wis. (†53565) 317/F10
Jones Mills, Ark. (72105) 202/E5
Jones Mills, Pa. (15646) 294/D5
Jonesport, Maine (04649) 243/H6
Jonesport○, Maine (04649) 243/H6
Jones Springs, W. Va. (25427) 312/K4
Jonestown, Miss. (38639) 256/D2
Jonestown, Pa. (17038) 294/K5
Jonesville, Alaska (†99674) 196/B1
Jonesville, Ind. (47247) 227/F6
Jonesville, Ky. (41052) 237/M3
Jonesville, La. (71343) 238/G3
Jonesville, Mich. (49250) 250/E6
Jonesville, N.C. (28642) 281/H2
Jonesville, S.C. (29353) 296/D2
Jonesville, Vt. (05466) 268/B3
Jonesville, Va. (24263) 307/B7
Jonglei, Sudan 111/F6
Joniškis, U.S.S.R. 53/B2
Jönköping (co.), Sweden 18/H8
Jönköping, Sweden 18/H8
Jönköping, Sweden 7/F3
Jonquière, Que. 162/J6
Jonquière, Québec 172/F1
Jonquière, Québec 174/C3
Jonuta, Mexico 150/N7
Jonzac, France 28/C5
Joplin, Mo. (64801) 261/C8
Joplin, Mo. 146/J6
Joplin, Mo. 188/H3
Joplin, Mont. (59531) 262/F2
Joppa, Ala. (35087) 195/E2
Joppa, Ill. (62953) 222/E6
Joppa, Tenn. (†37861) 237/O8
Joppatowne, Md. (†21085) 245/N3
Jorat (mt.), Switzerland 39/C3
Jordan 2/L4
Jordan 54/E6
JORDAN 59/C3
Jordan (dam), Ala. 195/F5
Jordan (lake), Ala. 195/F5
Jordan, (creek) Idaho 220/A7
Jordan, Iowa (†50036) 229/F4
Jordan (riv.), Israel 65/D3
Jordan (riv.), Jordan 65/D3
Jordan, Minn. (55352) 255/E6
Jordan, Mont. (59337) 262/J3
Jordan, N.Y. (13080) 276/H4
Jordan, B. Everett (lake), N.C. 281/M3
Jordan (bay), Nova Scotia 168/C5
Jordan (lake), Nova Scotia 168/C4
Jordan (riv.), Nova Scotia 168/C5
Jordan (creek), Oreg. 291/K5
Jordan, S.C. (†29102) 296/G4
Jordan (riv.), Utah 304/C3
Jordan Falls, Nova Scotia 168/C5
Jordan River, Sask. 181/H2
Jordan Valley, Oreg. (97910) 291/K5
Jorge Montt (isl.), Chile 138/D9
Jorhat, India 68/G3
Jorm, Afghanistan 68/C1
Jorm, Afghanistan 59/K2
Jörn, Sweden 18/M4
Jornada del Muerto (valley), N. Mex. 274/C5
Jorquera (riv.), Chile 138/B6
Jõrva-Jaani, U.S.S.R. 53/D1
Jos, Nigeria 106/F7
Jos, Nigeria 102/C4
Jos (plat.), Nigeria 106/F7
Jose Abad Santos, Philippines 82/E8
José Agustín Palacios, Bolivia 136/B3
José Batlle y Ordóñez, Uruguay 145/D4
José Cardel, Mexico 150/Q1
José de San Martín, Argentina 143/B5
José Enrique Rodó, Uruguay 145/B4
José Ignacio (lag.), Uruguay 145/E5
José M. Micheo, Argentina 143/G7
Jose Panganiban, Philippines 82/D3
José Pedro Varela, Uruguay 145/E4
Joseph (lake), Newf. 166/B3
Joseph (lake), Ontario 177/E2
Joseph, Oreg. (97846) 291/K2
Joseph (creek), Oreg. 291/K2
Joseph, Utah (84739) 304/B5
Joseph Bonaparte (gulf) 88/D2
Joseph Bonaparte (gulf), Australia 87/C7
Joseph Bonaparte (gulf), North. Terr. 93/A3
Joseph Bonaparte (gulf), W. Australia 92/E1
Joseph City, Ariz. (86032) 198/E4
Josephine, Ala. (†36530) 195/C10
Josephine (co.), Oreg. 291/D5
Josephine, Pa. (15750) 294/D5
Joshinetsu-Kogen National Park, Japan 81/J5
Joshua (pt.), Conn. 210/E4
Joshua Tree, Calif. (92252) 204/J9
Joshua Tree Nat'l Mon., Calif. 204/J10
Jostedal, Norway 18/E6
Jostedalsbreen (glac.), Norway 18/E6
Jost Van Dyke (isl.), Virgin Is. (Br.) 161/C3
Jost Van Dyke (isl.), Virgin Is. (Br.) 156/G1
Joubert, S. Dak. (†57344) 298/M7
Jourdanton, Texas (78026) 303/F9
Joure, Netherlands 27/H3
Joussard, Alberta 182/B2
Joux (lake), Switzerland 39/B3
Jovellanos, Cuba 156/B2
Jovellanos, Cuba 158/D1
Joveyn (riv.), Iran 66/K2
Joy, Ill. (61260) 222/C2
Joy, Ky. (†42047) 237/E6
Joyce, La. (71440) 238/E3
Joyce, Wash. (98343) 310/B2
Joyce's Country (dist.), Ireland 17/B4
Joyo, Japan 81/J7
Juab (co.), Utah 304/A4
Juana Díaz, P. Rico 161/C2
Juan Aldama, Mexico 150/H4
Juan D. Jackson, Uruguay 145/C4
Juan de Fuca (str.) 146/F5
Juan de Fuca (str.), Br. Col. 162/D6
Juan de Fuca (str.), Br. Col. 184/J4
Juan de Fuca (str.), Wash. 188/A1
Juan de Fuca (str.), Wash. 310/A2
Juan de Mena, Paraguay 144/D4
Juan de Nova (isl.), Réunion 102/G6
Juan de Nova (isl.), Réunion 118/G3
Juan Fernández (isls.), Chile 2/E7
Juan Fernández (isls.), Chile 120/B6
Juangriego, Venezuela 124/G2
Juani (isl.), Tanzania 115/G5
Juanita, N. Dak. (58453) 282/N4
Juanita, Wash. (98033) 310/B1
Juanjuí, Peru 128/D6
Juan L. Lacaze, Uruguay 145/B5
Juan Stuven (isl.), Chile 138/D7
Juárez, Argentina 143/D4
Juárez, Mexico 150/J3
Juazeiro, Brazil 132/G5
Juàzeiro, Brazil 120/E3
Juazeiro do Norte, Brazil 132/F4
Juàzeiro do Norte, Brazil 120/F3
Juba, Sudan 111/F7
Juba, Sudan 102/F4
Jubail, Saudi Arabia 59/F4
Jubba, Saudi Arabia 59/D4
Jubbada Hoose (prov.), Somalia 115/H3
Jubbulpore (Jabalpur), India 68/D4
Jubilee (lake), W. Australia 88/D5
Juby (cape), Morocco 106/B3
Júcar (riv.), Spain 7/D5
Júcar (riv.), Spain 33/F3
Júcaro, Cuba 158/F2
Juchipila, Mexico 150/H6
Juchique de Ferrer, Mexico 150/Q1
Juchitán de Zaragoza, Mexico 150/M8
Jucuarán, El Salvador 154/C4
Jud, N. Dak. (58454) 282/N6
Juda, Wis. (53550) 317/H10
Judaea (reg.), Israel 65/B5
Judaea (reg.), Jordan 65/C4
Judas (pt.), C. Rica 154/E6
Judenburg, Austria 41/C3
Judibana, Venezuela 124/C2
Judique, Nova Scotia 168/G3
Judith (riv.), Mont. 262/G3
Judith (pt.), R.I. 249/J7
Judith Basin (co.), Mont. 262/F4
Judith Gap, Mont. (59453) 262/G4
Judson, Ind. (47856) 227/C5
Judson, Minn. (†56055) 255/D6
Judson, N. Dak. (†58563) 282/H6
Judsonia, Ark. (72081) 202/G3
Judyville, Ind. (†47993) 227/C4
Juelsminde, Denmark 21/D6
Juhu, India 68/B7
Juichin (Ruijin), China 77/J6
Juigalpa, Nicaragua 154/E4
Juist (isl.), W. Germany 22/B2
Juiz de Fora, Brazil 120/E5
Juiz de Fora, Brazil 135/E2
Juiz de Fora, Brazil 132/F8
Jujuy (prov.), Argentina 143/C1
Jujuy, Argentina 143/C1
Jujuy, Argentina 120/C5
Jukskei (riv.), S. Africa 118/H6
Julesburg, Colo. (80737) 208/P1
Juli, Peru 128/H11
Juliaca, Peru 120/B4
Juliaca, Peru 128/G10
Julia Creek, Queensland 88/G4
Julia Creek, Queensland 95/B4
Juliaetta, Idaho (83535) 220/B3
Julian, Calif. (92036) 204/J10
Julian, Nebr. (68379) 264/J4
Julian, N.C. (27283) 281/K3
Julian, Pa. (16844) 294/G4
Julian Alps (range), Italy 34/D1
Julianatop (mt.), Suriname 131/C4
Julianehåb, Greenl. 4/D12
Julianehåb, Greenland 2/G2
Julianehåb, Greenland 146/P3
Jülich, W. Germany 22/B3
Juliette, Georgia (31046) 217/E4
Juliff, Texas (†77583) 303/J3
Julio María Sanz, Uruguay 145/E4
Juliustown, N.J. (08042) 273/D3
Jullundur, India 68/D2
Jumbilla, Peru 128/C5
Jumbo, Okla. (†74523) 288/P6
Jumilla, Spain 33/F3
Jumla, Nepal 68/E3
Jumna (riv.), India 68/E3
Jump (riv.), Wis. 317/E5
Jumpertown, Miss. (†38829) 256/G1
Jumping Branch, W. Va. (25969) 312/E7
Jump River, Wis. (54434) 317/E5
Junagadh, India 68/B4
Junaina, Saudi Arabia 59/D5
Juncal, Argentina 143/F6
Juncos, P. Rico 161/E2
Juncos, P. Rico 156/G1
Junction, Ill. (62954) 222/E6
Junction, Texas (76849) 303/E7
Junction, Utah (84740) 304/B5
Junction, W. Va. (26824) 312/J4
Junction City, Ark. (71749) 202/E7
Junction City, Georgia (31812) 217/C5
Junction City, Ill. (†61601) 222/D5
Junction City, Kansas (66441) 232/E2
Junction City, Ky. (40440) 237/M5
Junction City, La. (71749) 238/E1
Junction City, Mo. (†63645) 261/M7
Junction City, Ohio (43748) 284/F6
Junction City, Oreg. (97448) 291/D3
Junction City, Wis. (54443) 317/G6
Jundah, Queensland 95/B5
Jundah, Queensland 88/G4
Jundiaí, Brazil 135/C3
Jundiaí, Brazil 132/E8
Juneau, Alaska 146/E4
Juneau (cap.), Alaska 188/E6
Juneau (cap.), Alaska (99801) 196/N1
Juneau, U.S. 4/D16
Juneau, U.S. 2/C3
Juneau (co.), Wis. 317/F8
Juneau, Wis. (53039) 317/J9
Juneda, Spain 33/G2
Junee, N.S. Wales 97/D4
June in Winter (lake), Fla. 212/E4
June Lake, Calif. (93529) 204/G6
June Park, Fla. (†32901) 212/F3
Jungar, China 77/H4
Jungfrau (mt.), Switzerland 39/E3
Jungfraujoch, Switzerland 39/E3
Junggar Pendi (desert basin), China 77/C2
Junglei (prov.), Sudan 111/F6
Juniata, Nebr. (68955) 264/F4
Juniata (co.), Pa. 294/H4
Juniata (riv.), Pa. 294/G5
Juniata Terrace, Pa. (†17044) 294/G4
Junín, Argentina 143/F7
Junín, Argentina 120/C6
Junín (dept.), Peru 128/E8
Junín, Peru 128/E8
Junín (lake), Peru 128/E8
Junín de los Andes, Argentina 143/B4
Junior, W. Va. (26275) 312/G5
Juniper (mts.), Ariz. 198/C3
Juniper (mt.), Colo. 208/C1
Juniper, Georgia (31801) 217/C6
Juniper, New Bruns. 170/C2
Juniper (creek), S.C. 296/H2
Junius, S. Dak. (†57042) 298/P6
Juniye, Lebanon 63/F5
Junlian, China 77/F6
Juno, Georgia (30534) 217/D2
Juno, North. Terr. 93/C5
Juno, Tenn. (†38351) 237/E9
Juno, Texas (76943) 303/C7
Juno Beach, Fla. (†33404) 212/F5
Junosuando, Sweden 18/N3
Juntura, Oreg. (97911) 291/K4
Jun Xian, China 77/H5
Juojärvi (lake), Finland 18/Q5
Jupiter, Fla. (33458) 212/F5
Jupiter, N.C. (28787) 281/D3
Jupiter Island, Fla. (†33455) 212/F4
Juquiá, Brazil 135/C4
Jur (riv.), Sudan 111/E6
Jura (dept.), France 28/F4
Jura (mts.), France 28/F4
Jura (isl.), Scotland 10/D3
Jura (isl.), Scotland 15/C5
Jura (sound), Scotland 15/C5
Jura (sound), Scotland 10/D3
Jura (canton), Switzerland /D2
Jura (mts.), Switzerland 39/B3
Juradó, Colombia 126/B4
Jurbarkas, U.S.S.R. 53/B3
Jurmala, U.S.S.R. 53/B2
Jurmala, U.S.S.R. 52/B3
Jurong, Singapore 72/E6
Juruá (riv.), Brazil 120/C3
Juruá (riv.), Brazil 132/G10
Juruá (riv.), Peru 128/F7
Juruena, Brazil 132/B6
Juruena (riv.), Brazil 120/D4
Juruena (riv.), Brazil 132/B5
Juruti, Brazil 132/B3
Jusepín, Venezuela 124/G3
Juskatla, Br. Col. 184/A3
Jussy, Switzerland 39/B4
Justice, Ill. (†60458) 222/B6
Justice, Manitoba 179/C4
Justice, W. Va. (24851) 312/C7
Justiceburg, Texas (79330) 303/C5
Justin, Texas (76247) 303/F1
Justus, Ohio (†44662) 284/G4
Jutaí (riv.), Brazil 132/G9
Jüterbog, E. Germany 22/E3
Jutiapa, Guatemala 154/B3
Jutiapa, Honduras 154/D3
Juticalpa, Honduras 154/D3
Jutland (pen.), Denmark 21/C5
Jutland (pen.), Denmark 18/F9
Jutland, N.J. (08809) 273/D2
Juuka, Finland 18/Q5
Juventud (municipio especial), Cuba 158/C2
Juventud (isl.), Cuba 146/K7
Juventud, Isla de la (Pines), Cuba 158/B3
Juventud (Pines) (isl.), Cuba 156/A2
Juwara, Oman 59/G6
Ju Xian, China 77/J4
Juye, China 77/J4
Jyderup, Denmark 21/E6
Jylland (Jutland) (pen.), Denmark 21/C5
Jyske Ås (hills), Denmark 21/D3
Jyväskylä, Finland 7/G2
Jyväskylä, Finland 18/O5

K

K2 (mt.) 54/J6
K2 (mt.), Pakistan 68/D1
Kaawa, Hawaii (96730) 218/F1
Kaabong, Uganda 115/F3
Kaala (mt.), Hawaii 218/D1
Kaanapali, Hawaii (†96761) 218/H2
Kaba (Habahe), China 77/C2
Kaba, Hungary 41/F2
Kabacan, Philippines 82/E7
Kabaena (isl.), Indonesia 85/G7
Kabala, S. Leone 106/B7
Kabale, Uganda 115/E4
Kabalo, Zaire 115/E5
Kabambare, Zaire 115/E4
Kabardin-Balkar A.S.S.R., U.S.S.R. 48/E5
Kabardin-Balkar A.S.S.R., U.S.S.R. 52/F6
Kabare, Zaire 115/E4
Kabarega Nat'l Park, Uganda 115/F3
Kabasalan, Philippines 82/D7
Kabba, Nigeria 106/F7
Kabetogama, Minn. (†56669) 255/F2
Kabetogama (lake), Minn. 255/E2
Kabinakagami (riv.), Ontario 177/J5
Kabin Buri, Thailand 72/D4
Kabinda, Zaire 115/D5
Kabir Kuh (mts.), Iran 66/E4
Kabompo, Zambia 115/D6
Kabompo (riv.), Zambia 115/D6
Kabong, Malaysia 85/E5
Kabongo, Zaire 115/E5
Kabud Gonbad, Iran 66/L2
Kabul (cap.), Afghanistan 68/B2
Kabul (cap.), Afghanistan 59/J3
Kabul (cap.), Afghanistan 54/H6
Kabul (cap.), Afghanistan 2/N4
Kabul (riv.), Afghanistan 68/C2
Kabul (riv.), Afghanistan 59/K3
Kabul (riv.), Pakistan 68/C2
Kabunda, Zaire 115/E6
Kabwe, Zambia 102/E6
Kabwe, Zambia 115/E6
Kabylia (reg.), Algeria 106/E1
Kachemak, Alaska (†99663) 196/B2
Kachemak (bay), Alaska 196/B2
Kachess (lake), Wash. 310/D3
Kachin (state), Burma 72/C1
Kachug, U.S.S.R. 48/L4
Kaçkar Dağı (mt.), Turkey 63/J2
Kackley, Kansas (†66948) 232/E2
Kadaň, Czech. 41/B1
Kadan Kyun (isl.), Burma 72/C4
Kadavu (Kandavu) (isl.), Fiji 87/H7
Kadayanallur, India 68/D7
Kadei (riv.), Cameroon 115/C3
Kadei (riv.), Cent. Afr. Rep. 115/C3
Kadei (riv.), Congo 115/C3
Kadıköy, Turkey 63/D6
Kadina, S. Australia 88/F6
Kadina, S. Australia 94/F5
Kadınhanı, Turkey 63/E3
Kadiolo, Mali 106/C6
Kadiri, India 68/D6
Kadirli, Turkey 63/F4
Kadiyevka (Stakhanov), U.S.S.R. 52/E5
Kadmat (isl.), India 68/C6
Kadoka, S. Dak. (57543) 298/F6
Kadoma, Japan 81/J7
Kadoma (Gatooma), Zimbabwe 118/D3
Kadugli, Sudan 111/E5
Kadugli, Sudan 102/E3
Kaduna (state), Nigeria 106/F6
Kaduna, Nigeria 102/C3
Kaduna, Nigeria 106/F6
Kaduna (riv.), Nigeria 106/F7
Kadzherom, U.S.S.R. 52/J2
Kaech'ŏn, N. Korea 81/B4
Kaédi, Mauritania 106/B5
Kaédi, Mauritania 102/A3
Kaélé, Cameroon 115/B1
Kaena (pt.), Hawaii 218/D1
Kaeo, N. Zealand 100/D1
Kaesŏng, N. Korea 81/C4
Kaf, Saudi Arabia 59/C3
Kafan, U.S.S.R. 52/G7
Kafar Kanna, Israel 65/C2
Kaffa (prov.), Ethiopia 111/G6
Kaffrine, Senegal 106/A6
Kafia Kingi, Sudan 111/D6
Kafirévs (cape), Greece 45/G6
Kafr Yasif, Israel 65/C2
Kafue, Zambia 115/E7
Kafue (riv.), Zambia 115/E7
Kafue Nat'l Park, Zambia 115/E6
Kaga, Japan 81/H5
Kaga Bandoro, Cent. Afr. Rep. 115/C2
Kagalaska (isl.), Alaska 196/L4
Kagan, U.S.S.R. 48/G6
Kagawa (pref.), Japan 81/G6
Kagawong, Ontario 177/B2
Kagawong (lake), Ontario 177/B2
Kagera Nat'l Park, Rwanda 115/F4
Kağıthane, Turkey 63/D6
Kağızman, Turkey 63/K2
Kagoshima (pref.), Japan 81/E8
Kagoshima, Japan 81/E8
Kagoshima, Japan 54/O6
Kagoshima (bay), Japan 81/E8
Kagul, U.S.S.R. 52/C5
Kaguyak, Alaska (†99608) 196/H3
Kahakuloa, Hawaii (†96793) 218/J1
Kahala, Hawaii (†96801) 218/D5
Kahala (pt.), Hawaii 218/D1
Kahaluu, Hawaii (†96744) 218/E2
Kahama, Tanzania 115/F4
Kahana, Hawaii (†96717) 218/F1
Kahana (bay), Hawaii 218/F1
Kahayan (riv.), Indonesia 85/E6
Kahemba, Zaire 115/C5
Kahiltna (riv.), Alaska 196/B1
Kahlotus, Wash. (99335) 310/G4
Kah-Nee-Ta, Oreg. (†97761) 291/F3
Kahoka, Mo. (63445) 261/J2
Kahoolawe (isl.), Hawaii 188/F5
Kahoolawe (isl.), Hawaii 87/L6
Kahoolawe (isl.), Hawaii 218/H3
Kahouanne (isl.), Guadeloupe 161/A6
Kahramanmaraş (prov.), Turkey 63/G4
Kâhta, Turkey 63/H4
Kahuku, Hawaii (96731) 218/E1
Kahuku, Hawaii 188/F5
Kahuku (pt.), Hawaii 218/E1
Kahului, Hawaii (96732) 218/J2
Kahului, Hawaii 188/F5
Kahului (harb.), Hawaii 218/J1
Kai (isls.), Indonesia 85/J7
Kaiama, Nigeria 106/E7
Kaiapit, Papua N.G. 85/B7
Kaiapoi, N. Zealand 100/D5
Kaibab (plat.), Ariz. 198/C2
Kaibab Ind. Res., Ariz. 198/C2
Kaibito, Ariz. (86053) 198/D2
Kaibito (plat.), Ariz. 198/D2
Kaieteur (fall), Guyana 131/B3
Kaifeng, China 77/H5
Kaifeng, China 54/N6
Kaikohe, N. Zealand 100/D1
Kaikoura, N. Zealand 100/D5
Kaikoura (pen.), N. Zealand 100/E5
Kaikoura (range), N. Zealand 100/D5
Kaili, China 77/G6
Kailu, China 77/K3
Kailua (Kailua Kona), Hawaii, Hawaii (96740) 218/F5
Kailua, Oahu, Hawaii (96734) 218/F2
Kailua (bay), Hawaii 218/F2
Kailua (bay), Hawaii 218/F5
Kailua Kona, Hawaii (96740) 218/F5
Kaimana, Indonesia 85/J6
Kaimanawa (range), N. Zealand 100/E3
Kaimu, Hawaii (†96778) 218/J6
Kaimuki, Hawaii (96816) 218/D4
Kainaliu, Hawaii (†96750) 218/G5
Kainaliu, Hawaii 188/F6
Kainan (bay) 5/B10
Kaingaroa, N. Zealand 100/E7
Kainji (res.), Nigeria 106/E6
Kaipara (harb.), N. Zealand 100/D2
Kaipara (riv.), N. Zealand 100/A1
Kaiparowits (plat.), Utah 304/C6
Kaipokok (bay), Newf. 166/B2
Kaipokok (riv.), Newf. 166/B3
Kairouan, Tunisia 106/F1
Kairuku, Papua N.G. 85/B7
Kaiser, Mo. (65047) 261/G6
Kaiseregg (mt.), Switzerland 39/D3
Kaiserslautern, W. Germany 22/B4
Kaiserstuhl (mt.), W. Germany 22/B4
Kaitaia, N. Zealand 100/D1
Kaitangata, N. Zealand 100/C7
Kaitumälv (riv.), Sweden 18/M3
Kaiwi (chan.), Hawaii 218/E6
Kaiyuan, Liaoning, China 77/K3
Kaiyuan, Yunnan, China 77/F7
Kaiyuh (mts.), Alaska 196/G2
Kaizuka, Japan 81/H8
Kajaani, Finland 7/G2
Kajaani, Finland 18/P4
Kajabbi, Queensland 88/G3
Kajabbi, Queensland 95/A4
Kajiado, Kenya 115/G4
Kajok, Sudan 111/E6
Kaka, Cent. Afr. Rep. 115/E2
Kaka, Sudan 111/F5
Kakabeka Falls, Ontario 177/G5
Kakabeka Falls, Ontario 175/B3
Kakamega, Kenya 115/F3
Kake, Alaska (99830) 196/M1
Kakhk, Iran 66/L3
Kakhonak, Alaska (†99647) 196/H3
Kakhovka, U.S.S.R. 52/D5
Kakhovka (res.), U.S.S.R. 48/D5
Kakhovka (res.), U.S.S.R. 52/D5
Kakinada, India 54/K8
Kakinada, India 68/E5
Kakisa, N.W. Terrs. 187/G3
Kakkiviak (cape), Newf. 166/B1
Kakogawa, Japan 81/G6
Kaktovik, Alaska (99747) 196/K1
Kakwa (riv.), Alberta 182/A2
Kalaa-Kebira, Tunisia 106/F1
Kalabahi, Indonesia 85/G7
Kalabo, Zambia 115/D6
Kalach, U.S.S.R. 52/F4
Kalachinsk, U.S.S.R. 48/H4
Kalach-na-Donu, U.S.S.R. 52/F5
Kaladan (riv.), Burma 72/B2
Kaladar, Ontario 177/H3
Kalae, Hawaii (†96757) 218/G1
Ka Lae (cape), Hawaii 218/G7
Kalahari (des.) 102/E7
Kalahari (des.), Botswana 118/C4
Kalahari (des.), Namibia 118/C4
Kalahari Gemsbok Nat'l Park, S. Africa 118/C5
Kalaheo, Hawaii (96741) 218/C2
Kalajoki, Finland 18/N4
Kalajoki (riv.), Finland 18/O4
Kalakan, U.S.S.R. 48/M4
Kalaloch, Wash. (†98331) 310/A3
Kalam, Pakistan 68/C1
Kalama, Wash. (98625) 310/C4
Kalama (riv.), Wash. 310/C4
Kalámai, Greece 7/G5
Kalámai, Greece 45/F7
Kalamazoo, Mich. 188/J2
Kalamazoo (co.), Mich. 250/D6
Kalamazoo, Mich. (*49001) 250/D6
Kalamazoo (riv.), Mich. 250/C6
Kalambo (falls), Tanzania 115/F5
Kalambo (falls), Zambia 115/F5
Kalamo, Mich. (†49096) 250/D6
Kalampáka, Greece 45/E6
Kalamunda, W. Australia 88/B2
Kalan, Turkey 63/H3
Kalao (isl.), Indonesia 85/G7
Kalaoa, Hawaii (†96740) 218/G5
Kalaotoa (isl.), Indonesia 85/G5
Kalapana, Hawaii (†96778) 218/J6
Kalasin, Thailand 72/D3
Kalat (Qalat), Afghanistan 68/B2
Kalat (Qalat), Afghanistan 59/J3
Kalat, Pakistan 54/H7
Kalat, Pakistan 59/J4
Kalat, Pakistan 68/B3
Kalâtdlit-Nunât (Greenland) 4/B12
Kalâtdlit-Nunât (Greenland) 146/P2
Kalaupapa, Hawaii (96742) 218/G1
Kalaupapa (pen.), Hawaii 218/H1
Kalaupapa Nat'l Hist. Park, Hawaii 218/H1
Kalávrita, Greece 45/F6
Kalawao (co.), Hawaii 218/G1
Kalbarri, W. Australia 92/A4
Kale, Turkey 63/C4
Kalecik, Turkey 63/E2
Kaleden, Br. Col. 184/H5
Kalegauk (isl.), Burma 72/C4
Kalehe, Zaire 115/E4
Kaleida, Manitoba 179/D5
Kalemie, Zaire 115/E5
Kalemie, Zaire 102/E5
Kalemyo, Burma 72/B2
Kaleva, Mich. (49645) 250/C4
Kalevala, U.S.S.R. 52/D1
Kalewa, Burma 72/B2
Kalgan (Zhangjiakou), China 77/J3
Kalgin (isl.), Alaska 196/B1
Kalgoorlie, Australia 2/R7
Kalgoorlie, W. Australia 88/C6
Kalgoorlie, W. Australia 92/C5
Kalgoorlie-Boulder, W. Australia 92/C5
Kaliakra (cape), Bulgaria 45/J4
Kalianda, Indonesia 85/D7
Kalibo, Philippines 82/D5
Kalida, Ohio (45853) 284/B4
Kalihi, Hawaii (†96801) 218/C4
Kalihi (stream), Hawaii 218/C3
Kalihi Entrance (str.), Hawaii 218/B4
Kalihiwai, Hawaii (†96754) 218/C1
Kalima, Zaire 115/E4
Kalimantan (reg.), Indonesia 85/E5
Kálimnos, Greece 45/H7
Kálimnos (isl.), Greece 45/H7
Kalinga, Queensland 88/K2
Kalinga-Apayao (prov.), Philippines 82/C1
Kalinin, U.S.S.R. 7/H3
Kalinin, U.S.S.R. 48/D4
Kalinin, U.S.S.R. 52/E3
Kaliningrad, U.S.S.R. 7/G3
Kaliningrad, U.S.S.R. 48/B4
Kaliningrad, Kaliningrad, U.S.S.R. 52/B4
Kaliningrad, Moscow Oblast, U.S.S.R. 52/E3
Kalininsk, U.S.S.R. 52/F4
Kalinkovichi, U.S.S.R. 52/C4
Kalispel Ind. Res., Wash. 310/H2
Kalispell, Mont. 188/C1
Kalispell, Mont. (59901) 262/B2
Kalisz (prov.), Poland 47/D3
Kalisz, Poland 7/F3
Kalisz, Poland 47/D3
Kaliua, Tanzania 115/F5
Kalix, Sweden 18/N4
Kalixälv (riv.), Sweden 18/N3
Kalkaska (co.), Mich. 250/D4
Kalkaska, Mich. (49646) 250/D4
Kalkfeld, Namibia 118/B4
Kalkfontein, Botswana 118/C4
Kallaste, U.S.S.R. 53/D1
Kallavesi (lake), Finland 18/P5
Kallsjö (lake), Sweden 18/H5
Kalmalo, Nigeria 106/F6
Kalmar (co.), Sweden 18/K8
Kalmar, Sweden 7/F3
Kalmar, Sweden 18/K8
Kalmarsund (sound), Sweden 18/K8
Kalmthout, Belgium 27/F6
Kalmuck A.S.S.R., U.S.S.R. 52/F5
Kalmuck A.S.S.R., U.S.S.R. 48/E5
Kalmunai, Sri Lanka 68/E7
Kalmykovo, U.S.S.R. 48/F5
Kalo, Iowa (†50569) 229/E4
Kalocsa, Hungary 41/E3
Kalohi (chan.), Hawaii 218/G1
Kaloko-Honokohau Nat'l Hist. Park, Hawaii 218/F6
Kaloli (pt.), Hawaii 218/K5
Kalomo, Zambia 115/E7
Kalona, Iowa (52247) 229/K6
Kalpeni (isl.), India 68/C7
Kalpin, China 77/A3
Kalskag, Alaska (99607) 196/F2
Kaltag, Alaska (99748) 196/G2
Kaltbrunn, Switzerland 39/H2
Kaluaaha, Hawaii (†96748) 218/H1
Kaluga, U.S.S.R. 7/H3
Kaluga, U.S.S.R. 48/D4
Kaluga, U.S.S.R. 52/E4
Kalumburu Mission, W. Australia 88/D2
Kalumburu Mission, W. Australia 92/D1
Kalundborg, Denmark 21/D6
Kalundborg, Denmark 18/G9
Kalush, U.S.S.R. 52/B5
Kalutara, Sri Lanka 68/D7
Kalvarija, U.S.S.R. 53/B3
Kalvesta, Kansas (67856) 232/B3
Kalyan, India 68/C5
Kama, Burma 72/B3
Kama (res.), U.S.S.R. 52/J3
Kama (riv.), U.S.S.R. 7/K3
Kama (riv.), U.S.S.R. 52/H2
Kama, Zaire 115/E4
Kamaiki (pt.), Hawaii 218/H2
Kamaing, Burma 72/C1
Kamaishi, Japan 81/L4
Kamakou (peak), Hawaii 218/H1
Kamakura, Japan 81/O3
Kamakusa, Guyana 131/A3
Kamalino, Hawaii (†96769) 218/A2
Kamalo, Hawaii (†96748) 218/H1
Kaman, Turkey 63/E3
Kamaniskeg (lake), Ontario 177/G2
Kamanjab, Namibia 118/A3
Kamaran (isl.), P.D.R. Yemen 59/D6
Kamarang, Guyana 131/A3
Kamarhati, India 68/F1
Kamaria (falls), Guyana 131/B2
Kamas, Utah (84036) 304/C3
Kamay, Texas (76369) 303/F4
Kambalda, W. Australia 88/C6
Kambalda, W. Australia 92/C5
Kambia, S. Leone 106/B7
Kambove, Zaire 115/E6
Kambove, Zaire 102/E6
Kamchatka (pen.), U.S.S.R. 54/S4
Kamchatka (pen.), U.S.S.R. 2/T3
Kamchatka (pen.), U.S.S.R. 48/Q4
Kamela, Oreg. (†97859) 291/J2
Kamenets-Podol'skiy, U.S.S.R. 52/C5
Kamenice, Czech. 41/C2
Kamenjak (cape), Yugoslavia 45/A3
Kamenka, Archangel, U.S.S.R. 52/F1
Kamenka, Penza, U.S.S.R. 52/F4
Kamen'-na-Obi, U.S.S.R. 48/H4
Kamenskoye, U.S.S.R. 48/R3
Kamensk-Shakhtinskiy, U.S.S.R. 52/F5
Kamensk-Ural'skiy, U.S.S.R. 48/G4
Kamenz, E. Germany 22/F3
Kameoka, Japan 81/J7
Kames, Scotland 15/C5
Kamet (mt.), India 68/D2
Kamiah, Idaho (83536) 220/B3
Kamienna Góra, Poland 47/B3

Kazan-retto (Volcano) (isls.), Japan 81/M4
Kazatin, U.S.S.R. 52/C5
Kazbek (mt.), U.S.S.R. 52/F6
Kazerun, Iran 66/G6
Kazerun, Iran 59/F4
Kazhim, U.S.S.R. 52/H2
Kazimierza Wielka, Poland 47/E3
Kazımkarabekir, Turkey 63/E4
Kazincbarcika, Hungary 41/F2
Kazlu-Rūda, U.S.S.R. 53/B3
Kazumba, Zaire 115/D5
Kazvin (Qazvin), Iran 66/F2
Kbenhaven (co.), Denmark 21/F6
Kbenhavn (Copenhagen) (commune), Denmark 21/F6
Kdyně, Czech. 41/B2
Kéa, Greece 45/G7
Kéa (isl.), Greece 45/G7
Keaau, Hawaii 188/G6
Keaau, Hawaii (96749) 218/J5
Keady, N. Ireland 17/H3
Keahi (pt.), Hawaii 218/A4
Keahole (pt.), Hawaii 218/F5
Kealaikahiki (chan.), Hawaii 218/H3
Kealaikahiki (pt.), Hawaii 218/H3
Kealakekua, Hawaii (96750) 218/G5
Kealakekua (bay), Hawaii 218/F6
Kealia, Hawaii (†96704) 218/G6
Kealia, Kauai, Hawaii (96751) 218/D1
Keams Canyon, Ariz. (86034) 198/E3
Keanae, Hawaii (†96708) 218/K2
Keanapapa (pt.), Hawaii 218/G2
Keansburg, N.J. (07734) 273/E3
Kearney, Mo. (64060) 261/D4
Kearney, Nebr. 188/G2
Kearney (co.), Nebr. 264/F4
Kearney, Nebr. (68847) 264/E4
Kearney, Ontario 177/E2
Kearneysville, W. Va. (25430) 312/L4
Kearns, Utah (84118) 304/B3
Kearny, Ariz. (85237) 198/E5
Kearny (co.), Kansas 232/A3
Kearny, N.J. (07032) 273/B2
Kearny, Wyo. (†82832) 319/F1
Kearsarge, N.H. (03847) 268/E3
Kearsarge (mt.), N.H. 268/D5
Kearsarge, Pa. (†16501) 294/B1
Keasbey, N.J. (08832) 273/E2
Keatchie, La. (71046) 238/C2
Keating, Oreg. (†97814) 291/K3
Keating Summit, Pa. (16737) 294/F2
Keatley, Sask. 181/D3
Keaton, Ky. (41226) 237/P5
Keats, Kansas (†66502) 232/F2
Keats (mt.), W. Australia 92/A2
Keauhou, Hawaii (†96725) 218/F5
Keavy, Ky. (40737) 237/N6
Keawekaheka (pt.), Hawaii 218/F5
Keban, Turkey 63/H3
Kebang (mt.), S. Korea 81/D5
Ke Bao, Vietnam 72/E2
Kebbi (riv.), Nigeria 106/E6
Kebnekaise (mt.), Sweden 7/F2
Kebnekaise (mt.), Sweden 18/L3
Kebock (head), Scotland 15/B2
Kebumen, Indonesia 85/J2
Kecel, Hungary 41/E3
Kechi, Kansas (67067) 232/E4
Kechika (riv.), Br. Col. 184/L2
Keçiborlu, Turkey 63/D4
Kecskemét, Hungary 7/F4
Kecskemét, Hungary 41/E3
Kedah (state), Malaysia 72/D6
Kedainiai, U.S.S.R. 53/C3
Keddie, Calif. (95952) 204/E3
Kedges (strs), Md. 245/O8
Kedgwick, New Bruns. 170/C1
Kedgwick (riv.), New Bruns. 170/C1
Kedgwick Ouest, New Bruns. 170/C1
Kedgwick River, New Bruns. 170/C1
Kediri, Indonesia 85/K2
Kédougou, Senegal 106/B6
Kedron (brook), Queensland 95/D2
Kedzierzyn-Koźle, Poland 47/C3
Keechelus (lake), Wash. 310/D3
Keedysville, Md. (21756) 245/H3
Keefers, Br. Col. 184/G5
Keefton, Okla. (†74401) 288/R3
Keegan, Maine (†04785) 243/G1
Keego Harbor, Mich. (48030) 250/F6
Keehi (lag.), Hawaii 218/B4
Keel-Dooagh, Ireland 17/A4
Keele (riv.), N.W. Terrs. 187/F3
Keele (peak), Yukon 187/E3
Keeler, Calif. (93530) 204/H7
Keeler, Sask. 181/F5
Keeline, Wyo. (82220) 319/H3
Keeling (Cocos) (isls.), Australia 2/P6
Keeling, Va. (24566) 307/K7
Keels, Newf. 166/D1
Keelung, China 77/K6
Keenan, W. Va. (†24983) 312/F7
Keenan Siding, New Bruns. 170/E2
Keene, Calif. (93531) 204/G8
Keene, Ky. (40339) 237/M5
Keene, N.H. (03431) 268/C6
Keene, N.Y. (12942) 276/N2
Keene, N. Dak. (58847) 282/E4
Keene, Ohio (43828) 284/G5
Keene, Ontario 177/F3
Keene, Texas (76059) 303/G5
Keener, Ala. (†35954) 195/G2
Keenes, Ill. (62851) 222/E5
Keenesburg, Colo. (80643) 208/L2
Keene Valley, N.Y. (12943) 276/N2
Keensburg, Ill. (62852) 222/F5
Keeny (creek), Oreg. 291/K4
Keeper (hill), Ireland 17/E6
Keerweer (cape), Queensland 88/G2
Keerweer (cape), Queensland 95/B2
Keeseville, N.Y. (12944) 276/O2
Keesler A.F.B., Miss. 256/G10
Keetley, Utah (†84060) 304/C3
Keetmanshoop, Namibia 118/B5
Keetmanshoop, Namibia 102/D7
Keewatin, Minn. (55753) 255/E3
Keewatin (dist.), N.W.T. 162/G3
Keewatin (dist.), N.W. Terrs. 187/J3
Keewatin, Ontario 177/F5
Keewatin, Ontario 175/A3
Keewong, N.S. Wales 97/C3
Keezletown, Va. (22832) 307/L4
Kefallinía (isl.), Greece 45/E6
Kefar Blum, Israel 65/D1
Kefar Gil'adi, Israel 65/C1
Kefar Ruppin, Israel 65/D3
Kefar Sava, Israel 65/B3
Kefar Vitkin, Israel 65/B3
Kefar Zekhariya, Israel 65/B4
Keffi, Nigeria 106/F7
Keflavík, Iceland 21/B1
Kégashka, Québec 174/E2
Kegley, W. Va. (24731) 312/D8
Kegonsa (lake), Wis. 317/H10
Keg River, Alberta 182/A5
Kehl, W. Germany 22/B4
Kehoe, Ky. (†41144) 237/P4
Kehra, U.S.S.R. 53/C1
Keila, U.S.S.R. 53/C1
Keilor, Victoria 88/K7
Keilor, Victoria 97/H5
Keimoes, S. Africa 118/C5
Keirn, Miss. (†38924) 256/D4
Keiser, Ark. (72351) 202/K2
Keiss, Scotland 15/E2
Keitele (lake), Finland 18/O5
Keith (co.), Nebr. 264/C3
Keith, Scotland 10/E2
Keith, Scotland 15/F3
Keith, S. Australia 94/G7
Keith, W. Va. (†25148) 312/C6
Keith Arm (inlet), N.W. Terrs. 187/F3
Keithley Creek, Br. Col. 184/G4
Keithsburg, Ill. (61442) 222/B2
Keithville, La. (71047) 238/C2
Keizer, Oreg. (97303) 291/A3
Kejimkujik (lake), Nova Scotia 168/C4
Kejimkujik Nat'l Park, Nova Scotia 168/C4
Kekaa (pt.), Hawaii 218/H2
Kekaha, Hawaii (96752) 218/C2
Kekaha, Hawaii 188/E5
Kekertaluk (isl.), N.W. Terrs. 187/M3
Kékes (mt.), Hungary 41/E3
Kekoskee, Wis. (†53050) 317/J8
Kelang, Malaysia 72/D7
Kelantan (state), Malaysia 72/D6
Kelantan, Sungai (riv.), Malaysia 72/D6
Kelasa (str.), Indonesia 85/D6
Keldron, S. Dak. (57634) 298/F2
Keles, Turkey 63/C3
Kelfield, Sask. 181/C4
Kelford, N.C. (27847) 281/P2
Kelheim, W. Germany 22/D4
Kelkit, Turkey 63/H2
Kelkit (riv.), Turkey 59/C1
Kelkit (riv.), Turkey 63/G2
Kell, Ill. (62853) 222/E5
Kellé, Congo 115/B4
Keller (lake), N.W. Terrs. 187/F3
Keller, Texas (76248) 303/F2
Keller, Va. (23401) 307/S5
Keller, Wash. (99140) 310/G2
Kellerberrin, W. Australia 88/B6
Kellerberrin, W. Australia 92/B5
Kellerman, Ala. (35468) 195/D4
Kellerton, Iowa (50133) 229/E7
Kellerville, Texas (79057) 303/D2
Kellett (cape), N.W.T. 162/D1
Kellett (cape), N.W. Terrs. 187/F2
Kellett (str.), N.W. Terrs. 187/G2
Kellettville, Pa. (†16353) 294/D2
Kelley, Iowa (50134) 229/F5
Kelley (creek), Nev. 266/D1
Kelleys (isl.), Ohio 284/E2
Kelleys Island, Ohio (43438) 284/E2
Kelligrews, Newf. 166/D2
Kelliher, Minn. (56650) 255/D3
Kelliher, Sask. 181/H4
Kellnersville, Wis. (54215) 317/L7
Kellogg (mt.), Ariz. 198/E6
Kellogg, Idaho (83837) 220/B2
Kellogg, Iowa (50135) 229/H5
Kellogg, Minn. (55945) 255/G6
Kelloggsville, Ohio (†44048) 284/J2
Kelloselkä, Finland 18/Q3
Kells (Ceanannus Mór), Ireland 17/G4
Kells, Ireland 17/G6
Kells, N. Ireland 17/J2
Kelly, Georgia (31048) 217/E4
Kelly (creek), Idaho 220/C3
Kelly, Kansas (66446) 232/G2
Kelly, Ky. (†42240) 237/G7
Kelly, La. (71441) 238/F3
Kelly, N.C. (28448) 281/N6
Kelly, Wyo. (83011) 319/B2
Kelly A.F.B., Texas 303/J11
Kelly Lake, Br. Col. 184/G4
Kelly Lake, Minn. (55754) 255/F3
Kellys, N. Dak. (†58201) 282/R4
Kellysville, W. Va. (24732) 312/E8
Kellyton, Ala. (35089) 195/F5
Kellyville, Okla. (74039) 288/O3
Kelme, U.S.S.R. 53/B3
Kélo, Chad 111/C6
Kélo, Chad 102/D4
Kelowna, Br. Col. 146/G4
Kelowna, Br. Col. 162/E6
Kelowna, Br. Col. 184/H5
Kelsey, Alberta 182/D3
Kelsey, Minn. (55755) 255/F3
Kelsey Bay, Br. Col. 184/D5
Kelseyville, Calif. (95451) 204/C5
Kelso, Ark. (†71674) 202/H6
Kelso, Calif. (92351) 204/K8
Kelso, Mo. (63758) 261/O8
Kelso, Sask. 181/K6
Kelso, Scotland 10/E3
Kelso, Scotland 15/F5
Kelso, Tenn. (37348) 237/J10
Kelso, Wash. (98626) 310/C4
Kelstern, Sask. 181/E5
Kelston West, N. Zealand 100/B1
Keltie (cape) 5/C7
Keltner, Ky. (†42761) 237/K6
Kelton, S.C. (†29353) 296/D2
Kelty, Scotland 10/C1
Kelty, Scotland 15/D1
Keluang, Malaysia 72/D7
Kelvington, Sask. 181/H3
Kelwood, Manitoba 179/C4
Kem', U.S.S.R. 7/H2
Kem', U.S.S.R. 4/C8
Kem', U.S.S.R. 52/D2
Kem', U.S.S.R. 48/D3
Ké-Macina, Mali 106/C6
Kemah, Texas (77565) 303/K2
Kemah, Turkey 63/H3
Kemaliye, Turkey 63/H3
Kemalpaşa, Turkey 63/J2
Kemano, Br. Col. 184/D3
Kemasik, Malaysia 72/D6
Kembe, Cent. Afr. Rep. 115/D3
Kemble, Ontario 177/D3
Kemboma, Gabon 115/B3
Kemecse, Hungary 41/F2
Kemer, Turkey 63/D4
Kemerburgaz, Turkey 63/D5
Kemerovo, U.S.S.R. 54/K4
Kemerovo, U.S.S.R. 48/J4
Kemi, Finland 7/G2
Kemi, Finland 18/O4
Kemi (riv.), Finland 7/G2
Kemijärvi, Finland 18/P3
Kemijärvi (lake), Finland 18/Q3
Kemijoki (riv.), Finland 18/O3
Kemikli, Büyük (cape), Turkey 63/B6
Kemirhisar, Turkey 63/F4
Kemmerer, Wyo. (83101) 319/B4
Kemnay, Manitoba 179/B5
Kemnay, Scotland 15/F3
Kemp, Ill. (†61910) 222/E4
Kemp, Okla. (74747) 288/O7
Kemp, Texas (75143) 303/H5
Kemp (lake), Texas 303/E4
Kemp City (Hendrix), Okla. (†74741) 288/O7
Kemp Coast (reg.) 5/C3
Kemper (co.), Miss. 256/G5
Kemp Mill, Md. (†20901) 245/F3
Kempsey, N.S. Wales 88/J6
Kempsey, N.S. Wales 97/G2
Kempster, Wis. (54444) 317/H5
Kempston, England 13/G5
Kempt, Nova Scotia 168/C4
Kempt (lake), Québec 172/C2
Kempten, W. Germany 22/D5
Kempton, Ill. (60946) 222/E3
Kempton, Ind. (46049) 227/E4
Kempton, Md. (†26292) 245/A4
Kempton, N. Dak. (†58267) 282/P4
Kempton, Pa. (19529) 294/L4
Kempton, Tasmania 99/D4
Kempton Park, S. Africa 118/J6
Kemptown, Md. (†21770) 245/J3
Kemptown, Nova Scotia 168/E3
Kemptville, Nova Scotia 168/C4
Kemptville, Ontario 177/J2
Ken, Afghanistan 68/A2
Ken, Afghanistan 59/H3
Kenadsa, Algeria 106/D2
Kenai, Alaska (99611) 196/B1
Kenai (lake), Alaska 196/C1
Kenai (mt.), Alaska 196/C2
Kenai (pen.), Alaska 196/C2
Kenai Fjords Nat'l Park, Alaska 196/C3
Kenamu (riv.), Newf. 166/B3
Kenansville, Fla. (32739) 212/F4
Kenansville, N.C. (28349) 281/O5
Kenaston, N. Dak. (†58746) 282/F2
Kenaston, Sask. 181/E4
Kenbridge, Va. (23944) 307/M7
Kendal, Barbados 161/B8
Kendal, England 13/E3
Kendal, England 10/E3
Kendal, Indonesia 85/J2
Kendal, Sask. 181/H5
Kendall, Fla. (33156) 212/B5
Kendall (co.), Ill. 222/E2
Kendall, Kansas (67857) 232/A4
Kendall, N.S. Wales 97/G2
Kendall, N.Y. (14476) 276/E4
Kendall (cape), N.W. Terrs. 187/K3
Kendall (co.), Texas 303/F8
Kendall, Wash. (†98244) 310/C2
Kendall, Wis. (54638) 317/F8
Kendall Park, N.J. (08824) 273/D3
Kendallville, Ind. (46755) 227/G2
Kendallville, Iowa (†52136) 229/K2
Kendari, Indonesia 85/G6
Kendawangan, Indonesia 85/D6
Kendrapara, India 68/F4
Kendrick (peak), Ariz. 198/D3
Kendrick, Fla. (†32670) 212/D2
Kendrick, Idaho (83537) 220/B3
Kendrick, Okla. (74040) 288/N3
Kenduskeag○, Maine (04450) 243/E6
Kenedy (co.), Texas 303/G11
Kenedy, Texas (78119) 303/G9
Kenefic, Okla. (74748) 288/O6
Kenel, S. Dak. (†57642) 298/H2
Kenema, S. Leone 102/A4
Kenema, S. Leone 106/B7
Kenesaw, Nebr. (68956) 264/F4
Kengah (isls.); Indonesia 85/F7
Kenge, Zaire 115/C4
Keng Hkam, Burma 72/C2
Keng Tung, Burma 72/C2
Kenhardt, S. Africa 118/C5
Kenhorst, Pa. (†19607) 294/L5
Kéniéba, Mali 106/B6
Kenilworth, England 13/F5
Kenilworth, Ill. (60043) 222/B5
Kenilworth, N.J. (07033) 273/E2
Kenilworth, Ontario 177/D4
Kenilworth, Utah (84529) 304/D4
Keningau, Malaysia 85/F4
Kenitra, Morocco 102/B1
Kenitra, Morocco 106/C2
Kenli, China 77/J4
Kenly, N.C. (27542) 281/N3
Kenmare, Ireland 10/B5
Kenmare, Ireland 17/B8
Kenmare (riv.), Ireland 17/A8
Kenmare, N. Dak. (58746) 282/G2
Kenmore, N.Y. (14271) 276/C5
Kenmore, Queensland 88/J3
Kenmore, Scotland 15/E4
Kenmore, Wash. (98028) 310/B1
Kenna, N. Mex. (88122) 274/F5
Kenna, W. Va. (25248) 312/C5
Kennan, Wis. (54537) 317/F5
Kennard, Ind. (47351) 227/G5
Kennard, Nebr. (68034) 264/H3
Kennard, Pa. (†16125) 294/B3
Kennard, Texas (75847) 303/J6
Kennebago Lake, Maine (†04970) 243/B5
Kennebec (co.), Maine 243/D7
Kennebec (riv.), Maine 243/D7
Kennebec, S. Dak. (57544) 298/K6
Kennebecasis (bay), New Bruns. 170/E3
Kennebecasis (riv.), New Bruns. 170/E3
Kennebunk, Maine (04043) 243/B9
Kennebunk○, Maine (04043) 243/B9
Kennebunk Beach, Maine (†04043) 243/C9
Kennebunkport, Maine (04046) 243/C9
Kennebunkport○, Maine (04046) 243/C9
Kennedale, Texas (76060) 303/F3
Kennedy, Ala. (35574) 195/B3
Kennedy (Canaveral) (cape), Fla. 212/F3
Kennedy, Minn. (56733) 255/B2
Kennedy, N.Y. (14747) 276/B6
Kennedy (chan.), N.W.T. 162/N3
Kennedy (chan.), N.W. Terrs. 187/M1
Kennedy, Sask. 181/J5
Kennedy Center, D.C. 245/A5
Kennedy Entrance (str.), Alaska 196/H3
Kennedyville, Md. (21645) 245/P3
Kenner, La. (70062) 238/N4
Kennesaw, Georgia (30144) 217/C2
Kennesaw Mtn. Nat'l Battlefield Park, Georgia 217/J1
Kennet (riv.), England 13/F6
Kennetcook, Nova Scotia 168/E3
Kennetcook (riv.), Nova Scotia 168/E3
Kenneth, Ind. (†46947) 227/E3
Kenneth, Minn. (56147) 255/B7
Kenneth City, Fla. (33709) 212/B3
Kennett, Mo. (63857) 261/M10
Kennett Square, Pa. (19348) 294/L6
Kennewick, Wash. (99336) 310/F4
Kenney (dam), Br. Col. 184/E3
Kenney, Ill. (61749) 222/D3
Kennisis (lake), Ontario 177/F2
Keno, Oreg. (97627) 291/F5
Kenogami (riv.), Ont. 162/H5
Kenogami (riv.), Ontario 177/H4
Kenogami (riv.), Ontario 175/C2
Kénogami (lake), Québec 172/F1
Keno Hill, Yukon 187/E3
Kenoma, Mo. (†64759) 261/D8
Kenora (terr. dist.), Ont. 177/G5
Kenora (terr. dist.), Ont. 175/C2
Kenora, Ont. 146/J4
Kenora, Ont. 162/G5
Kenora, Ontario 175/B3
Kenora, Ontario 177/F4
Kenosee Park, Sask. 181/J6
Kenosha (co.), Wis. 317/K10
Kenosha, Wis. (*53140) 317/M3
Kenova, W. Va. (25530) 312/A6
Kensal, N. Dak. (58455) 282/N5
Kenscoff, Haiti 158/C6
Kensett, Ark. (72082) 202/G3
Kensett, Iowa (50448) 229/G2
Kensington, Calif. (†94701) 204/J2
Kensington, Conn. (06037) 210/D2
Kensington, Kansas (66951) 232/C2
Kensington, Md. (20795) 245/E4
Kensington, Minn. (56343) 255/C5
Kensington, N.S. Wales 97/J4
Kensington, Ohio (44427) 284/J4
Kensington, Pr. Edward I. 168/E2
Kensington and Chelsea, England 13/G8
Kensington and Chelsea, England 10/B5
Kensington and Norwood, S. Australia 88/E8
Kensington and Norwood, S. Australia 94/B8
Kent, Ala. (36045) 195/G5
Kent, Br. Col. 184/M3
Kent○, Conn. (06757) 210/B2
Kent (co.), Del. 245/R4
Kent (co.), England 13/H6
Kent, Ill. (61044) 222/D1
Kent, Ind. (†47250) 227/F7
Kent, Iowa (50850) 229/E7
Kent (co.), Md. 245/O3
Kent (isl.), Md. 245/N5
Kent (pt.), Md. 245/N5
Kent (co.), Mich. 250/D5
Kent, Minn. (56553) 255/B4
Kent (co.), New Bruns. 170/E2
Kent (pen.), N.W. Terrs. 187/H3
Kent, Ohio (44240) 284/H3
Kent (county), Ontario 177/B5
Kent, Oreg. (97033) 291/G2
Kent, Pa. (15752) 294/D4
Kent (co.), R.I. 249/H6
Kent (co.), Texas 303/D4
Kent, Texas (79855) 303/C11
Kent, Wash. (98031) 310/C3
Kentau, U.S.S.R. 48/G5
Kent Bridge, Ontario 177/B5
Kent City, Mich. (49330) 250/D5
Kent Furnace, Conn. (†06757) 210/B2
Kent Group (isls.), Tasmania 99/D1
Kent Junction, New Bruns. 170/E2
Kent Lake, New Bruns. 170/E2
Kentland, Ind. (47951) 227/C3
Kenton, Del. (19955) 245/R4
Kenton (co.), Ky. 237/M3
Kenton, Ky. (41053) 237/N3
Kenton, Manitoba 179/B5
Kenton, Mich. (49943) 250/G2
Kenton, Ohio (43326) 284/C4
Kenton, Okla. (73946) 288/A1
Kenton, Tenn. (38233) 237/C8
Kenton Vale, Ky. (†41011) 237/S2
Kents Hill, Maine (04349) 243/D7
Kents Store, Va. (23084) 307/M5
Kentuck, W. Va. (25249) 312/C5
Kentucky 188/J3
Kentucky (lake) 188/J3
KENTUCKY 237
Kentucky (dam), Ky. 237/E7
Kentucky (lake), Ky. 237/E8
Kentucky (riv.), Ky. 237/M3
Kentucky (lake), Tenn. 237/E8
Kentucky (state), U.S. 146/K6
Kentville, Nova Scotia 168/D3
Kentwood, La. (70444) 238/J5
Kentwood, Mich. (49508) 250/D6
Kenville, Manitoba 179/A3
Kenvir, Ky. (40847) 237/P7
Kenwood, Georgia (†30214) 217/D3
Kenwood, Okla. (†74365) 288/S2
Kenya 2/L5
Kenya 102/F4
KENYA 115/G3
Kenya (mt.), Kenya 102/F4
Kenya (mt.), Kenya 115/G4
Kenyon, Minn. (55946) 255/E6
Kenyon, R.I. (02836) 249/H7
Kenyonville, Conn. (†06281) 210/G1
Keo, Ark. (72083) 202/G4
Keokea, Hawaii, Hawaii (†96704) 218/G6
Keokea, Maui, Hawaii (†96790) 218/J2
Keokee, Va. (24265) 307/C7
Keokuk (co.), Iowa 229/J6
Keokuk, Iowa 188/H2
Keokuk, Iowa (52632) 229/L8
Keoma, Alberta 182/D4
Keomah, Iowa (†52577) 229/J6
Keomuku, Hawaii (†96763) 218/H2
Keonjhar, India 68/F4
Keosauqua, Iowa (52565) 229/J7
Keota, Colo. (†80729) 208/L1
Keota, Iowa (52248) 229/K6
Keota, Okla. (74941) 288/S4
Keowee (lake), S.C. 296/B2
Keowee (riv.), S.C. 296/B2
Kepez, Turkey 63/B6
Kepi, Indonesia 85/K7
Kępno, Poland 47/C3
Keppel (harb.), Singapore 72/F6
Kepsut, Turkey 63/C3
Kerala (state), India 68/D6
Kerama (isls.), Japan 81/M6
Kerang, Victoria 97/B4
Kerava, Finland 18/O6
Kerby, Oreg. (97531) 291/D5
Kerch', U.S.S.R. 7/H4
Kerch', U.S.S.R. 52/E5
Kerchoual, Mali 106/E5
Kerema, Papua N.G. 85/B7
Keremeos, Br. Col. 184/G5
Kerempe (cape), Turkey 63/E1
Keren, Ethiopia 59/C6
Keren, Ethiopia 111/G4
Kerens, Texas (75144) 303/H5
Kerens, W. Va. (26276) 312/G4
Keret', U.S.S.R. 52/D1
Kerguélen (isl.), 2/N8
Kerhonkson, N.Y. (12446) 276/M7
Kericho, Kenya 115/F4
Kerinci (mt.), Indonesia 85/C6
Keriya (Yutian), China 77/B4
Keriya He (riv.), China 77/B4
Keriya Shankou (pass), China 77/B4
Kerkdriel, Netherlands 27/G5
Kerkennah (isls.), Tunisia 106/G2
Kerkhoven, Minn. (56252) 255/C5
Kerki, U.S.S.R. 48/G6
Kérkira, Greece 45/D6
Kérkira (isl.), Greece 7/F5
Kérkira (isl.), Greece 45/D6
Kerkrade, Netherlands 27/J7
Kerlin, Ark. (†71753) 202/D7
Kerma, Sudan 111/F4
Kerma, Sudan 59/B6
Kermadec (isls.), N. Zealand 2/T7
Kermadec (isls.), N. Zealand 87/J9
Kerman, Calif. (93600) 204/E7
Kerman (prov.), Iran 66/K6
Kerman, Iran 54/G6
Kerman, Iran 59/G3
Kerman, Iran 66/K5
Kermanshah, Iran 54/F6
Kermanshah, Iran 59/E3
Kermanshah, Iran 66/E3
Kermanshahan (prov.), Iran 66/E3
Kerme (gulf), Turkey 63/B4
Kermit, Texas (79745) 303/B6
Kermit, W. Va. (25674) 312/B7
Kern (co.), Calif. 204/G8
Kern (riv.), Calif. 204/G8
Kernan, Ill. (†61364) 222/E2
Kernersville, N.C. (27284) 281/J2
Kerns, Switzerland 39/F3
Kernville, Calif. (93238) 204/G8
Kernville, Oreg. (†97367) 291/D3
Kérouané, Guinea 106/C7
Kerr (lake), Fla. 212/E2
Kerr, N.C. (†28444) 281/N5
Kerr, W. Scott (res.), N.C. 281/G2
Kerr, Robert S. (res.), Okla. 288/S4
Kerr (co.), Texas 303/E7
Kerrera (isl.), Scotland 15/C4
Kerrick, Minn. (55756) 255/F4
Kerrick, Texas (79051) 303/B1
Kerrobert, Sask. 181/C4
Kerrville, Tenn. (†38053) 237/B10
Kerrville, Texas (78028) 303/E7
Kerry (co.), Ireland 17/B7
Kerry (head), Ireland 17/A7
Kerry, Wales 13/D5
Kersey, Colo. (80644) 208/L2
Kersey, Ind. (†46310) 227/C2
Kersey, Pa. (15846) 294/E3
Kershaw (co.), S.C. 296/F3
Kershaw, S.C. (29067) 296/G2
Kersley, Br. Col. 184/F4
Kerteminde, Denmark 21/D7
Kerulen (riv.) 54/N5
Kerulen (riv.), Mongolia 77/H2
Kerwood, Ontario 177/C5
Kerzaz, Algeria 106/D3
Kerzers, Switzerland 39/D3
Kesagami (lake), Ontario 175/E2
Keşan, Turkey 63/B2
Keşap, Turkey 63/H2
Kesch (peak), Switzerland 39/J3
Kesennuma, Japan 81/K4
Kesgrave, England 13/J5
Kesh, N. Ireland 17/F3
Keshena, Wis. (54135) 317/J6
Keşiş Tepesi (mt.), Turkey 63/H3
Keskin, Turkey 63/E3
Keski-Suomi (prov.), Finland 18/O5
Kesley, Iowa (50649) 229/H3
Kessel, W. Va. (†26818) 312/H4
Kesten'ga, U.S.S.R. 52/D1
Kesteren, Netherlands 27/G5
Keswick, England 13/D3
Keswick, England 10/E3
Keswick, Iowa (50136) 229/J6
Keswick, New Bruns. 170/D3
Keswick (riv.), New Bruns. 170/C2
Keswick, Ontario 177/E3
Keswick, Va. (22947) 307/M4
Keswick Grove, N.J. (†08759) 273/E4
Keszthely, Hungary 41/D3
Keta, Ghana 106/E7
Ketapang, Indonesia 85/E6
Ketchen, Sask. 181/J3
Ketch Harbour, Nova Scotia 168/E4
Ketchikan, Alaska 146/E4
Ketchikan, Alaska 188/E6
Ketchikan, Alaska (99901) 196/N2
Ketchum, Idaho (83340) 220/D6
Ketchum, Okla. (74349) 288/R1
Kétegyháza, Hungary 41/F3
Kete Krachi, Ghana 106/E7
Kętrzyn, Poland 47/E1
Kettering, England 13/G5
Kettering, England 10/F4
Kettering, Ohio (45429) 284/B6
Kettering, Tasmania 99/D5
Kettle (riv.), Br. Col. 184/H5
Kettle (riv.), Minn. 255/F4
Kettle (pt.), Ontario 177/B4
Kettle (riv.), Wash. 310/G2
Kettle Falls, Wash. (99141) 310/H2
Kettleman City, Calif. (93239) 204/E7
Kettle River, Minn. (55757) 255/E4
Kettle River (range), Wash. 310/G2
Kettlersville, Ohio (45336) 284/B5
Kettle Valley, Br. Col. 184/H5
Keuka (lake), N.Y. 276/F5
Keuka Park, N.Y. (14478) 276/F5
Keuterville, Idaho (83538) 220/B3
Kevelaer, W. Germany 22/B3
Kevil, Ky. (42053) 237/D6
Kevin, Mont. (59454) 262/D2
Kevisville, Alberta 182/C4
Kew, Victoria 88/L7
Kew, Victoria 97/J5
Kewa, Wash. (†99138) 310/G2
Kewanee, Ill. (61443) 222/C2
Kewanee, Miss. (†39364) 256/H6
Kewanee, Mo. (63860) 261/N9
Kewanna, Ind. (46939) 227/E2
Kewaskum, Wis. (53040) 317/K8
Kewaunee (co.), Wis. 317/L6
Kewaunee, Wis. (54216) 317/M7
Keweenaw (co.), Mich. 250/A1
Keweenaw (bay), Mich. 250/A1
Keweenaw (pt.), Mich. 250/B1
Keweenaw Bay, Mich. (49944) 250/G1
Key, Ala. (†35960) 195/G2
Key (lake), Ireland 17/E3
Keya Paha (co.), Nebr. 264/E2
Keya Paha (riv.), Nebr. 264/D1
Keyapaha, S. Dak. (57545) 298/J7
Keya Paha (riv.), S. Dak. 298/K7
Key Biscayne, Fla. (33149) 212/B5
Key Colony Beach, Fla. (33051) 212/F7
Keyes, Calif. (95328) 204/E6
Keyes, Manitoba 179/C4
Keyes, Okla. (73947) 288/B1
Keyesport, Ill. (62253) 222/D5
Keyhole (res.), Wyo. 319/H1
Key Largo, Fla. (33037) 212/F6
Key Largo (key), Fla. 212/F6
Keymar, Md. (21757) 245/K2
Keynsham, England 13/E6
Keyport, N.J. (07735) 273/E3
Keyport, Wash. (98345) 310/A2
Keysbrook, W. Australia 88/B3
Keyser, W. Va. (26726) 312/J4
Keystone, Ind. (46759) 227/G3
Keystone, Iowa (52249) 229/J5
Keystone, Nebr. (69144) 264/C3
Keystone (res.), Ohio 284/K2
Keystone (lake), Okla. 288/O2
Keystone, S. Dak. (57751) 298/C6
Keystone, W. Va. (24852) 312/D8
Keystone Heights, Fla. (32656) 212/E2
Keystown, Sask. 181/F5
Keysville, Georgia (30816) 217/H4
Keysville, Va. (23947) 307/M6
Keytesville, Mo. (65261) 261/G4
Key Vaca (key), Fla. 212/E7
Key West, Fla. 146/K7
Key West, Fla. 188/K6
Key West, Fla. (33040) 212/E7
Key West Naval Air Sta., Fla. 212/E7
Kezar (lake), Maine 243/B7
Kezar (pond), Maine 243/B7
Kezar Falls, Maine (04047) 243/B8
Kežmarok, Czech. 41/F2
Khabake (Habahe), China 77/C2
Khabarovsk, U.S.S.R. 54/P5
Khabarovsk, U.S.S.R. 2/R3
Khabarovsk, U.S.S.R. 48/O5
Khabur (riv.), Syria 63/J5
Khabur (riv.), Syria 59/D2
Khachmas, U.S.S.R. 52/G6

Kongsberg 393

Kintampo, Ghana 106/D7
Kintnersville, Pa. (18930) 294/M4
Kintore, Scotland 15/F3
Kintyre, N. Dak. (58549) 282/L6
Kintyre (pen.), Scotland 15/C5
Kintyre, Mull of (prom.), Scotland 15/C5
Kinuso, Alberta 182/C2
Kinvara, Ireland 17/D5
Kinwow (bay), Manitoba 179/E2
Kinyangiri, Tanzania 115/G4
Kinyeti (mt.), Sudan 111/F7
Kinzel Springs, Tenn. (†37882) 237/O9
Kinzua, Oreg. (97849) 291/H3
Kioa (isl.), Fiji 86/R10
Kioga (lake), Uganda 102/F4
Kioga (lake), Uganda 115/F3
Kiona, Wash. (†99320) 310/F4
Kiosk, Ontario 177/F1
Kiowa (co.), Colo. 208/O6
Kiowa, Colo. (80117) 208/L4
Kiowa (creek), Colo. 208/L3
Kiowa (co.), Kansas 232/C4
Kiowa, Kansas (67070) 232/D4
Kiowa (co.), Okla. 288/J5
Kiowa, Okla. (74553) 288/P5
Kiowa (creek), Okla. 288/F1
Kiowa (creek), Texas 303/D1
Kipabiskau, Sask. 181/G3
Kipahulu, Hawaii (†96713) 218/K2
Kiparissia, Greece 45/E7
Kiparissia (gulf), Greece 45/E7
Kipawa, Québec 174/B3
Kipili, Tanzania 115/F5
Kipini, Kenya 115/H4
Kipisa, N.W. Terrs. 187/M3
Kipling, N.C. (27543) 281/M4
Kipling, Sask. 181/J5
Kipnuk, Alaska (99614) 196/F2
Kipp, Alberta 182/D5
Kipp, Kansas (†67401) 232/E3
Kippel, Switzerland 39/E4
Kippen, Scotland 15/B1
Kippens, Newf. 166/C4
Kippure (mt.), Ireland 17/J5
Kipton, Ohio (44049) 284/F3
Kipushi, Zaire 115/E6
Kipushi, Zaire 102/E6
Kiput, Philippines 82/C8
Kira Kira, Solomon Is. 86/E3
Kiraz, Turkey 63/C3
Kirazlı, Turkey 63/C6
Kirby, Ark. (71950) 202/C5
Kirby, Mont. (†59016) 262/J5
Kirby, Ohio (43330) 284/D4
Kirby, Texas (†78109) 303/K11
Kirby, W. Va. (26729) 312/J4
Kirby, Wyo. (82430) 319/D2
Kirbyville, Texas (75956) 303/K7
Kirchberg, Bern, Switzerland 39/E2
Kirchberg, St. Gallen, Switzerland 39/G2
Kirchdorf an der Krems, Austria 41/C3
Kirchheim unter Teck, W. Germany 22/C4
Kircubbin, N. Ireland 17/K3
Kirensk, U.S.S.R. 48/L4
Kirgiz S.S.R., U.S.S.R. 54/J5
Kirgiz S.S.R., U.S.S.R. 48/H5
Kiri, Zaire 115/C4
Kiribati 2/A6
Kiribati 87/J6
Kiribati 2/T6
Kirigalpota (mt.), Sri Lanka 68/E7
Kırıkhan, Turkey 63/G4
Kırıkkale, Turkey 63/E3
Kirillov, U.S.S.R. 52/E2
Kirin (Jilin) (prov.), China 77/L3
Kirin (Jilin), China 77/L3
Kirishi, U.S.S.R. 52/D3
Kirishima-Yaku National Park, Japan 81/E7
Kiriwina (isl.), Papua N.G. 85/C7
Kirk, Colo. (80824) 208/P3
Kirk, Ky. (†40143) 237/H5
Kirk, W. Va. (†25671) 312/B7
Kırkağaç, Turkey 63/B3
Kirkburton, England 13/J2
Kirkby, England 13/G2
Kirkby, England 10/F2
Kirkby Lonsdale, England 13/E3
Kirkbymoorside, England 13/F3
Kirkby Stephen, England 13/E3
Kirkcaldy, Alberta 182/D4
Kirkcaldy, Scotland 15/D1
Kirkcaldy, Scotland 10/C1
Kirkcolm, Scotland 15/C6
Kirkconnel, Scotland 15/E5
Kirkcowan, Scotland 15/D6
Kirkcudbright, Scotland 15/E6
Kirkcudbright, Scotland 10/E3
Kirkcudbright (trad. co.), Scotland 15/A5
Kirkee, India 68/C5
Kirkella, Manitoba 179/A4
Kirkenes, Norway 18/Q2
Kirkersville, Ohio (43033) 284/E6
Kirkfield, Ontario 177/E3
Kirkham, England 13/G1B
Kirkham, England 10/F1
Kirkhill, Scotland 15/D3
Kirkinner, Scotland 15/D6
Kirkintilloch, Scotland 10/B1
Kirkintilloch, Scotland 15/B2
Kirkland, Ariz. (86332) 198/C4
Kirkland, Georgia (†31642) 217/G8
Kirkland, Ill. (60146) 222/E1
Kirkland, New Bruns. 170/C3
Kirkland, Québec 172/H4
Kirkland, Tenn. (†37046) 237/H9
Kirkland, Texas (79238) 303/D3
Kirkland, Wash. (98033) 310/B2
Kirkland Lake, Ont. 162/H6
Kirkland Lake, Ont. 146/K5
Kirkland Lake, Ontario 177/K5
Kirkland Lake, Ontario 175/D3
Kırklareli (prov.), Turkey 63/B2
Kırklareli, Turkey 63/B2
Kirklin, Ind. (46050) 227/E4
Kirkman, Iowa (51447) 229/C5
Kirkmansville, Ky. (†42216) 237/G6
Kirkmuirhill, Scotland 15/E5
Kirkpatrick (lake), Alberta 182/E4
Kirkpatrick (mt.) 5/A8
Kirkpatrick, Ind. (†47955) 227/D4
Kirkpatrick, Ohio (†43302) 284/D4
Kirksey, Ky. (42054) 237/E7
Kirksville, Ind. (†47401) 227/D6
Kirksville, Ky. (†40475) 237/N5
Kirksville, Mo. (63501) 261/H2
Kirkton of Glenisla, Scotland 15/E4
Kirkuk, Iraq 54/F6
Kirkuk, Iraq 59/D2
Kirkuk, Iraq 66/D3
Kirkville, Iowa (52566) 229/H6
Kirkville, Miss. (†38856) 256/H2
Kirkwall, Scotland 10/E1
Kirkwall, Scotland 15/E2
Kirkwood, Del. (19708) 245/R2
Kirkwood, Ill. (61447) 222/C3
Kirkwood, Mo. (63122) 261/O3
Kirkwood, N.J. (08043) 273/B4
Kirkwood, N.Y. (13795) 276/J6
Kirkwood, Pa. (17536) 294/K6
Kirkwood, S. Africa 118/D6
Kirmastı (riv.), Turkey 63/C3
Kirn, W. Germany 22/B4
Kiron, Iowa (51448) 229/C4
Kirov, U.S.S.R. 7/J3
Kirov, U.S.S.R. 48/E4
Kirov, Kirov, U.S.S.R. 52/G3
Kirov, Kaluga, U.S.S.R. 52/D4
Kirovabad, U.S.S.R. 7/J4
Kirovabad, U.S.S.R. 52/G6
Kirovabad, U.S.S.R. 48/E5
Kirovakan, U.S.S.R. 52/G6
Kirovo-Chepetsk, U.S.S.R. 52/H3
Kirovograd, U.S.S.R. 7/H4
Kirovograd, U.S.S.R. 48/D5
Kirovograd, U.S.S.R. 52/D5
Kirovsk, U.S.S.R. 52/D1
Kirovskiy, U.S.S.R. 48/H5
Kirriemuir, Alberta 182/E4
Kirriemuir, Scotland 10/E2
Kirriemuir, Scotland 15/E4
Kirs, U.S.S.R. 52/H3
Kirsanov, U.S.S.R. 52/F4
Kırşehir (prov.), Turkey 63/F3
Kırşehir, Turkey 63/F3
Kırşehir, Turkey 59/B2
Kirte, Turkey 63/B6
Kirtland, N. Mex. (87417) 274/A2
Kirtland, Ohio (†44094) 284/H2
Kirtland A.F.B., N. Mex. 274/C3
Kirtland Hills, Ohio (†44094) 284/H2
Kirton, England 13/H5
Kiruna, Sweden 4/C8
Kiruna, Sweden 7/G2
Kiruna, Sweden 18/L3
Kirundu, Zaire 115/E4
Kirwin, Kansas (67644) 232/C2
Kirwin (res.), Kansas 232/C2
Kiryu, Japan 81/J5
Kisa, Sweden 18/J7
Kisangani, Zaire 115/E3
Kisangani, Zaire 102/E4
Kisar (isl.), Indonesia 85/H7
Kisarazu, Japan 81/P3
Kisatchie, La. (†71468) 238/D4
K.I. Sawyer A.F.B., Mich. 250/B2
Kisbér, Hungary 41/D3
Kisbey, Sask. 181/J6
Kiselevsk, U.S.S.R. 48/J4
Kishangarh, India 68/D3
Kishinev, U.S.S.R. 7/G4
Kishinev, U.S.S.R. 48/C5
Kishinev, U.S.S.R. 52/C5
Kishiwada, Japan 81/J8
Kishorganj, Bangladesh 68/G4
Kishtwar, India 68/D2
Kisi (Jixi), China 77/M2
Kisii, Kenya 115/F4
Kisiju, Tanzania 115/G5
Kiska (isl.), Alaska 188/D6
Kiska (isl.), Alaska 196/J4
Kiska (vol.), Alaska 196/J4
Kiskatinaw (riv.), Br. Col. 184/G2
Kiskissink, Québec 172/E2
Kiskissink (lake), Québec 172/E2
Kiskőrös, Hungary 41/E3
Kiskunfélegyháza, Hungary 41/E3
Kiskunhalas, Hungary 41/E3
Kiskunmajsa, Hungary 41/E3
Kislovodsk, U.S.S.R. 7/J4
Kislovodsk, U.S.S.R. 52/F6
Kismayu (Chisimayu), Somalia 115/H4
Kismet, Kansas (67859) 232/B4
Kispest, Hungary 41/E3
Kissamos, Greece 45/G8
Kissee Mills, Mo. (65680) 261/G9
Kissidougou, Guinea 106/B7
Kissimmee, Fla. (32741) 212/E3
Kissimmee (lake), Fla. 212/E4
Kissimmee (riv.), Fla. 212/E4
Kississing (lake), Manitoba 179/H2
Kistelek, Hungary 41/E3
Kisten (pass), Switzerland 39/H3
Kisterenye, Hungary 41/E2
Kistler, Pa. (†17066) 294/G5
Kistler, W. Va. (25628) 312/C7
Kistna (riv.), India 54/J8
Kistna (Krishna) (riv.), India 68/D5
Kistrand, Norway 18/O1
Kisújszállás, Hungary 41/F3
Kisumu, Kenya 115/F3
Kisumu, Kenya 102/F5
Kisvárda, Hungary 41/G2
Kita, Mali 102/B3
Kita, Mali 106/C6
Kitaibaraki, Japan 81/K5
Kita Iwo (isl.), Japan 87/D3
Kita Iwo (isl.), Japan 81/M4
Kitakami, Japan 81/K4
Kitakami (riv.), Japan 81/K4
Kitakata, Japan 81/J5
Kitakyushu, Japan 81/E6
Kitakyushu, Japan 54/P6
Kitakyushu, Japan 2/R4
Kitale, Kenya 102/F4
Kitale, Kenya 115/G3
Kitami, Japan 81/L2
Kit Carson (co.), Colo. 208/O4
Kit Carson, Colo. (80825) 208/O5
Kit Carson (mt.), Colo. 208/H7
Kitchel, Ind. (†47353) 227/H5
Kitchener (mt.), Alberta 182/B3
Kitchener, Ontario 177/D4
Kite, Georgia (31049) 217/G5
Kite, Ky. (41828) 237/R6
Kitgum, Uganda 115/F3
Kíthira, Greece 45/F7
Kíthira (isl.), Greece 45/F7
Kíthnos (isl.), Greece 45/G7
Kitim, Jordan 65/D3
Kitimat, Br. Col. 162/D5
Kitimat, Br. Col. 146/F4
Kitimat, Br. Col. 184/C3
Kitinen (riv.), Finland 18/P3
Kitsap (co.), Wash. 310/C3
Kitsault, Br. Col. 184/C2
Kitscoty, Alberta 182/E3
Kitt (peak), Ariz. 198/D7
Kittanning, Pa. (16201) 294/D4
Kittatinny (mts.), N.J. 273/D1
Kittery, Maine (03904) 243/B9
Kittery○, Maine (03904) 243/B9
Kittery Point, Maine (03905) 243/B9
Kittilä, Finland 18/O3
Kittitas (co.), Wash. 310/E3
Kittitas, Wash. (98934) 310/E4
Kittrell, N.C. (27544) 281/M2
Kitts, Ky. (40848) 237/P7
Kitts Hill, Ohio (45645) 284/E8
Kittson (co.), Minn. 255/B2
Kitty Hawk, N.C. (27949) 281/T2
Kitui, Kenya 115/G4
Kitunda, Tanzania 115/F5
Kitwanga, Br. Col. 184/D2
Kitwe, Zambia 115/E6
Kitwe, Zambia 102/E6
Kitzbühel, Austria 41/B3
Kitzingen, W. Germany 22/C4
Kitzmiller, Md. (21538) 245/B3
Kiuchüan (Jiuquan), China 77/E4
Kiukiang (Jiujiang), China 77/J6
Kiunga, Papua N.G. 85/B7
Kivalina, Alaska (99750) 196/E1
Kivijärvi (lake), Finland 18/O5
Kiviõli, U.S.S.R. 53/D1
Kivu (lake) 102/E5
Kivu (lake), Rwanda 115/E4
Kivu (prov.), Zaire 115/E4
Kivu (lake), Zaire 115/E4
Kiyiu (lake), Sask. 181/C4
Kizel', U.S.S.R. 7/K3
Kizel, U.S.S.R. 48/F4
Kizel, U.S.S.R. 52/J3
Kızılcahamam, Turkey 63/E2
Kızılhisar, Turkey 63/C4
Kızılırmak (riv.), Turkey 63/F2
Kızılırmak (riv.), Turkey 59/B1
Kızıltepe, Turkey 63/J4
Kızıltoprak, Turkey 63/D6
Kızılviran, Turkey 63/E4
Kizimkazi, Tanzania 115/G5
Kizlyar, U.S.S.R. 52/G6
Kizu, Japan 81/J7
Kizyl-Arvat, U.S.S.R. 48/F6
Kjeller, Norway 18/E3
Kjellerup, Denmark 21/C5
Kjölen (mts.) 7/F2
Kjölen (mts.), Norway 18/K3
Kladanj, Yugoslavia 45/D3
Kladno, Czech. 41/B1
Kladovo, Yugoslavia 45/F3
Klagenfurt, Austria 41/C3
Klagetoh, Ariz. (†86505) 198/F3
Klaipeda, U.S.S.R. 7/F3
Klaipeda, U.S.S.R. 53/A3
Klaipeda, U.S.S.R. 52/B3
Klaipeda, U.S.S.R. 48/B4
Klaksvík, Denmark 21/B2
Klamath, Calif. (95548) 204/B2
Klamath (riv.), Calif. 188/B2
Klamath (riv.), Calif. 204/B2
Klamath (co.), Oreg. 291/F5
Klamath (mts.), Oreg. 291/C5
Klamath (riv.), Oreg. 291/E6
Klamath Agency, Oreg. (97624) 291/F5
Klamath Falls, Oreg. 146/F5
Klamath Falls, Oreg. 188/B2
Klamath Falls, Oreg. (97601) 291/F5
Klapmuts, S. Africa 118/F6
Klar (riv.), Sweden 7/F2
Klarälv (riv.), Sweden 18/H6
Klaten, Indonesia 85/J2
Klatovy, Czech. 41/B2
Klausen (pass), Switzerland 39/G3
Klawock, Alaska (99925) 196/M2
Klazienaveen, Netherlands 27/L3
Kleberg (co.), Texas 303/G10
Kleefeld, Manitoba 179/F5
Kleena Kleene, Br. Col. 184/E4
Klein, Mont. (†59072) 262/H4
Klein Bonaire (isl.), Neth. Ant. 161/E8
Kleine Emme (riv.), Switzerland 39/F3
Klein Karas, Namibia 118/B5
Kleinlützel, Switzerland 39/D2
Kleinmachnow, E. Germany 22/E4
Kleinmond, S. Africa 118/F7
Klemme, Iowa (50449) 229/F3
Klemtu, Br. Col. 184/C4
Klerksdorp, S. Africa 118/D5
Kleve, W. Germany 22/B3
Klickitat (co.), Wash. 310/E5
Klickitat, Wash. (98628) 310/D5
Klickitat (riv.), Wash. 310/D4
Klides (isls.), Cyprus 63/F5
Klinaklini (riv.), Br. Col. 184/E4
Kline, S.C. (29814) 296/E5
Kline, W. Va. (†26866) 312/H5
Kling, Philippines 82/E8
Klingenthal, E. Germany 22/E3
Klingnau, Switzerland 39/F1
Klintehamn, Sweden 18/K8
Klintsy, U.S.S.R. 52/D4
Klip (riv.), S. Africa 118/H6
Kliprivier, S. Africa 118/H7
Klitmøller, Denmark 21/B3
Ključ, Yugoslavia 45/C3
Kłobuck, Poland 47/D3
Kloch (lake), Br. Col. 184/E2
Kłodawa, Poland 47/D2
Kłodnica (riv.), Poland 47/A4
Kłodzko, Poland 47/C3
Klondike (riv.), Yukon 187/E3
Klondike Gold Rush Nat'l Hist. Park, Alaska 196/N1
Klondyke, Ariz. (85643) 198/E6
Klossner, Minn. (56053) 255/D6
Klosterneuburg, Austria 41/D2
Klosters Dorf, Switzerland 39/J3
Kloten, N. Dak. (58248) 282/O4
Kloten, Switzerland 39/G2
Klotzville, La. (†70341) 238/K3
Kluane (lake), Yukon 162/C3
Kluane (lake), Yukon 187/E3
Kluane Nat'l Park, Yukon 187/E3
Kluane Nat'l Park, Yukon 162/C3
Kluczbork, Poland 47/D3
Klukwan, Alaska (†99827) 196/M1
Klutina (lake), Alaska 196/D1
Klyuchevskaya Sopka (vol.), U.S.S.R. 48/Q4
Knapdale (dist.), Scotland 15/C5
Knapp, Minn. (†55321) 255/D5
Knapp, Wis. (54749) 317/B6
Knappa, Oreg. (†97103) 291/D1
Knapp Creek, N.Y. (14749) 276/C6
Knaresborough, England 13/F4
Knaresborough, England 10/F3
Knee (lake), Manitoba 179/J3
Knierim, Iowa (50552) 229/D4
Knife (lake), Minn. 255/G2
Knife (riv.), N. Dak. 282/G5
Knife R. Indian Villages Nat'l Hist. Site, N. Dak. 282/H5
Knife River, Minn. (55609) 255/G4
Knifley, Ky. (42753) 237/L6
Knight (isl.), Alaska 196/D1
Knight (inlet), Br. Col. 184/E5
Knightdale, N.C. (27545) 281/N3
Knight Inlet, Br. Col. 184/E5
Knighton, Wales 10/E4
Knighton, Wales 13/D5
Knightsen, Calif. (94548) 204/L1
Knights Landing, Calif. (95645) 204/B8
Knightstown, Ind. (46148) 227/F5
Knightstown, Ireland 17/A8
Knightsville, Ind. (47857) 227/C5
Knightville (res.), Mass. 249/C3
Knik Arm (inlet), Alaska 196/B1
Kniman, Ind. (†46392) 227/C2
Knin, Yugoslavia 45/C3
Knippa, Texas (78870) 303/E8
Knittelfeld, Austria 41/C3
Knjaževac, Yugoslavia 45/F4
Knobel, Ark. (72435) 202/J1
Knob Fork, W. Va. (26579) 312/E3
Knob Lick, Ky. (42154) 237/K6
Knob Lick, Mo. (63651) 261/M7
Knob Noster, Mo. (65336) 261/E5
Knock, Ireland 17/D4
Knockadoon (head), Ireland 17/F8
Knockanefune (mt.), Ireland 17/C7
Knockboy (mt.), Ireland 17/B8
Knocklayd (mt.), N. Ireland 17/J1
Knocklong, Ireland 17/D7
Knockmealdown (mts.), Ireland 17/F7
Knocknagashel, Ireland 17/C7
Knoke, Iowa (50553) 229/D3
Knokke-Heist, Belgium 27/C6
Knøsen (mt.), Denmark 21/D3
Knott (co.), Ky. 237/R6
Knott, Texas (79748) 303/C5
Knotts Island, N.C. (27950) 281/T2
Knottsville, Ky. (†42366) 237/H5
Knowles, Okla. (73847) 288/F1
Knowlesville, New Bruns. 170/C2
Knowlesville, N.Y. (14479) 276/D4
Knowlton, Mont. (†59336) 262/L4
Knowlton, Québec 172/E4
Knowlton, Wis. (†54455) 317/G6
Knox (cape), Br. Col. 162/C5
Knox (cape), Br. Col. 184/A3
Knox (co.), Ill. 222/C3
Knox (co.), Ind. 227/C7
Knox, Ind. (46534) 227/D2
Knox (co.), Ky. 237/O7
Knox (co.), Maine 243/E7
Knox○, Maine (†04986) 243/E6
Knox (co.), Mo. 261/H2
Knox (co.), Nebr. 264/G2
Knox (lake), Newf. 166/A3
Knox, N. Dak. (58343) 282/L3
Knox (co.), Ohio 284/F5
Knox, Pa. (16232) 294/C3
Knox (co.), Tenn. 237/O9
Knox (co.), Texas 303/E4
Knox, Victoria 97/K5
Knox, Victoria 88/M7
Knoxboro, N.Y. (13362) 276/J5
Knox Center, Maine (†04986) 243/E6
Knox City, Mo. (63446) 261/H2
Knox City, Texas (79529) 303/E4
Knox Coast (reg.) 5/C6
Knoxville, Ala. (35469) 195/C4
Knoxville, Ark. (72845) 202/D3
Knoxville, Georgia (31050) 217/E5
Knoxville, Ill. (61448) 222/C3
Knoxville, Iowa (50138) 229/G6
Knoxville, Md. (21758) 245/H3
Knoxville, Miss. (†39661) 256/B8
Knoxville, Mo. (†64084) 261/E4
Knoxville, Pa. (16928) 294/H2
Knoxville, Tenn. 146/K6
Knoxville, Tenn. 188/K3
Knoxville, Tenn. (*37901) 237/O9
Knud Rasmussen Land (reg.), Greenl. 4/B12
Knudshoved (pt.), Denmark 21/D7
Knurów, Poland 47/A4
Knutsford, Br. Col. 184/G5
Knutsford, England 13/H2
Knutsford, England 10/G2
Knutsford, Pr. Edward I. 168/D2
Knysna, S. Africa 118/C6
Koah Kong (isl.), Cambodia 72/D5
Koah Nhek, Cambodia 72/E4
Koah Rung (isl.), Cambodia 72/D5
Koah Tang (isl.), Cambodia 72/D5
Koali, Hawaii (†96713) 218/K2
Koa Mill, Hawaii (†96704) 218/G6
Koani, Tanzania 115/G5
Koartac, Québec 174/F1
Kobayashi, Japan 81/E8
Kobbfjorden (fjord), Norway 18/O1
Kobdo (Hovd), Mongolia 77/D2
Kobe, Japan 81/H7
Kobe, Japan 54/P6
København (Copenhagen) (cap.), Denmark 21/F6
Koblenz, Switzerland 39/F1
Koblenz, W. Germany 22/B3
Kobrin, U.S.S.R. 52/B4
Kobroor (isl.), Indonesia 85/K7
Kobuk, Alaska (99751) 196/G1
Kobuk (riv.), Alaska 188/C5
Kobuk (riv.), Alaska 196/G1
Kobuk Valley Nat'l Park, Alaska 196/F1
Kobuleti, U.S.S.R. 52/F6
Koca (riv.), Turkey 63/C3
Koca (riv.), Turkey 63/C6
Koca (riv.), Turkey 63/E2
Kocaeli (prov.), Turkey 63/C2
Kocaeli (İzmit), Turkey 63/D2
Kočani, Yugoslavia 45/F5
Koçarlı, Turkey 63/B4
Kočevje, Yugoslavia 45/B3
Koch (isl.), N.W. Terrs. 187/L3
Koch'ang, S. Korea 81/C6
Kochevo, U.S.S.R. 52/J3
Kochi (pref.), Japan 81/F7
Kochi, Japan 81/F7
Kodaira, Japan 81/O2
Kodak, Tenn. (37764) 237/O9
Kodiak, Alaska 188/D6
Kodiak, Alaska (99615) 196/H3
Kodiak (isl.), Alaska 146/C4
Kodiak (isl.), Alaska 196/H3
Kodiak, U.S. 4/D17
Kodiak (isl.), U.S. 4/D17
Kodok, Sudan 111/F6
Kodok, Sudan 102/F4
Koekelare, Belgium 27/B6
Koekelberg, Belgium 27/B9
Koenig, Mo. (†65013) 261/J6
Koenton, Ala. (†36558) 195/B7
Koes, Namibia 118/B5
Kofa (mts.), Ariz. 198/B5
Kofçaz, Turkey 63/B2
Koffiefontein, S. Africa 118/D5
Köflach, Austria 41/C3
Koforidua, Ghana 106/D7
Kofu, Japan 81/J6
Koga, Japan 81/J5
Kogaluc (riv.), Québec 174/E1
Kogaluk (riv.), Newf. 166/B2
Koganei, Japan 81/O2
Kogarah, N. S. Wales 88/K4
Kogarah, N. S. Wales 97/J4
Køge, Denmark 21/F7
Køge (bay), Denmark 21/F7
Koggiung, Alaska (†99633) 196/G3
Kohala (Kapaau), Hawaii (†96755) 218/G3
Kohala (mts.), Hawaii 218/G4
Kohala (peak), Hawaii 218/G4
Kohat, Pakistan 59/K3
Kohat, Pakistan 68/C2
Kohila, U.S.S.R. 53/C1
Kohima, India 68/G3
Kohler, Wis. (53044) 317/L8
Kohls Ranch, Ariz. (85538) 198/D4
Kohtla-Järve, U.S.S.R. 52/C3
Kohtla-Järve, U.S.S.R. 53/D1
Kohŭng, S. Korea 81/C6
Koidern, Yukon 187/D3
Koitere (lake), Finland 18/R5
Kŏje (isl.), S. Korea 81/D6
Kojetín, Czech. 41/D2
Kojonup, W. Australia 88/B6
Kojonup, W. Australia 92/B6
Kokadjo, Maine (†04441) 243/E4
Kokand, U.S.S.R. 48/H5
Kokanee Glacier Prov. Park, Br. Col. 184/J5
Kokava nad Rimavicou, Czech. 41/E2
Kokchetav, U.S.S.R. 54/J4
Kokchetav, U.S.S.R. 48/H4
Kokemäki, Finland 18/N6
Kokish, Br. Col. 184/D5
Kokiu (Gejiu), China 77/F7
Kokkola, Finland 18/N5
Koko (head), Hawaii 218/F2
Koko, Nigeria 106/F7
Kokoda, Papua N.G. 85/C7
Kokole (pt.), Hawaii 218/B2
Kokolik (riv.), Alaska 196/F1
Kokomo, Hawaii (†96708) 218/K2
Kokomo, Ind. 188/J2
Kokomo, Ind. (46901) 227/E4
Kokomo, Miss. (39643) 256/E8
Kokonau, Indonesia 85/K6
Kokopo, Papua N.G. 86/B2
Kokosing (riv.), Ohio 284/E5
Kokrines, Alaska (†99768) 196/G1
Kokrines (hills), Alaska 196/H1
Koksan, N. Korea 81/C4
Koksijde, Belgium 27/B6
Koksilah, Br. Col. 184/J3
Koksoak (riv.), Que. 162/K4
Koksoak (riv.), Québec 174/D1
Kokstad, S. Africa 118/D6
Kokubu, Japan 81/E8
Kola, Manitoba 179/A5
Kola (pen.), U.S.S.R. 7/H2
Kola (pen.), U.S.S.R. 4/C8
Kola (pen.), U.S.S.R. 52/E1
Kola (pen.), U.S.S.R. 48/D3
Kolahun, Liberia 106/C7
Kolaka, Indonesia 85/G6
Kolar, India 68/D6
Kolar Gold Fields, India 68/D6
Kolari, Finland 18/O3
Kolárovo, Czech. 41/D3
Kolašin, Yugoslavia 45/D4
Kolberg (Kołobrzeg), Poland 47/B1
Kolbio, Kenya 115/H4
Kolbuszowa, Poland 47/E3
Kolda, Senegal 106/B6
Kolding, Denmark 18/F9
Kolding, Denmark 21/C7
Kole, Haut-Zaïre, Zaire 115/E3
Kole, Kasai-Oriental, Zaire 115/D4
Koleen, Ind. (47439) 227/D7
Kolekole (stream), Hawaii 218/J4
Kölen (mts.), Sweden 18/K3
Kolepom (isl.), Indonesia 85/K7
Kolguyev (isl.), U.S.S.R. 7/J2
Kolguyev (isl.), U.S.S.R. 4/B7
Kolguyev (isl.), U.S.S.R. 52/G1
Kolguyev (isl.), U.S.S.R. 48/E3
Kolhapur, India 68/C5
Kolhapur, India 54/J8
Koliganek, Alaska (99576) 196/G3
Kolín, Czech. 41/C1
Kolin, Mont. (†59462) 262/G3
Kolind, Denmark 21/D5
Kölliken, Switzerland 39/F2
Kollum, Netherlands 27/J2
Kolmanskop, Namibia 118/B5
Köln (Cologne), W. Germany 22/B3
Kolno, Poland 47/F2
Koło, Poland 47/D2
Koloa, Hawaii 188/E5
Koloa, Hawaii (96756) 218/C2
Koloa Landing, Hawaii (†96756) 218/C2
Kołobrzeg, Poland 47/B1
Kologriv, U.S.S.R. 52/F3
Kolokani, Mali 106/C6
Kolola Springs, Miss. (†39740) 256/H3
Kolombangara (isl.), Solomon Is. 86/D2
Kolomiya, U.S.S.R. 52/B5
Kolomna, U.S.S.R. 7/H3
Kolomna, U.S.S.R. 48/D4
Kolomna, U.S.S.R. 52/E4
Kolondiéba, Mali 106/C6
Kolonia (cap.), Micronesia 87/F5
Kolonodale, Indonesia 85/G6
Kolovrat (mt.), Solomon Is. 86/E3
Kolpashevo, U.S.S.R. 54/K4
Kolpashevo, U.S.S.R. 48/J4
Kolpino, U.S.S.R. 52/D3
Kolva (riv.), U.S.S.R. 52/J1
Kolwezi, Zaire 102/E6
Kolwezi, Zaire 115/E6
Kolyma (range), U.S.S.R. 54/S3
Kolyma (range), U.S.S.R. 48/Q3
Kolyma (range), U.S.S.R. 4/C1
Kolyma (riv.), U.S.S.R. 48/Q3
Kolyma (riv.), U.S.S.R. 54/S3
Kolyma (riv.), U.S.S.R. 4/C2
Koma, Burma 72/C4
Komádi, Hungary 41/F3
Komadugu Yobe (riv.), Niger 106/G6
Komadugu Yobe (riv.), Nigeria 106/G6
Komaga (mt.), Japan 81/K2
Komagane, Japan 81/H6
Komandorskiye (isls.), U.S.S.R. 54/T4
Komandorskiye (isls.), U.S.S.R. 2/T3
Komandorskiye (isls.), U.S.S.R. 48/R4
Komárno, Czech. 41/D3
Komarno, Manitoba 179/E4
Komárom (co.), Hungary 41/E3
Komárom, Hungary 41/E3
Komatke, Ariz. (†85339) 198/C5
Komatsu, Japan 81/H5
Komba, Zaire 115/D3
Kŏmdŏk (mt.), N. Korea 81/D3
Komi A.S.S.R., U.S.S.R. 48/F3
Komi A.S.S.R., U.S.S.R. 52/H2
Komi-Permyak Aut. Okr., U.S.S.R. 52/H3
Komi-Permyak Aut. Okr., U.S.S.R. 48/F4
Komló, Hungary 41/E3
Kommetjie, S. Africa 118/E7
Kommunarsk, U.S.S.R. 52/E5
Komodo (isl.), Indonesia 85/F7
Komoka, Ontario 177/C5
Kôm Ombo, Egypt 111/F3
Kôm Ombo, Egypt 59/B5
Komono, Congo 115/B4
Komoran (isl.), Indonesia 85/K7
Komotini, Greece 45/G5
Komrat, U.S.S.R. 52/C5
Komsomolets (isl.), U.S.S.R. 4/A5
Komsomolets (isl.), U.S.S.R. 54/M1
Komsomolets (isl.), U.S.S.R. 48/L1
Komsomol'sk, U.S.S.R. 54/P4
Komsomol'sk, U.S.S.R. 48/G4
Komsomol'skiy, U.S.S.R. 52/K1
Komsomol'sk-na-Amure, U.S.S.R. 48/O4
Kona, Ky. (41829) 237/R6
Konahuanui (peaks), Hawaii 218/C3
Konar (riv.), Afghanistan 68/C1
Konar (riv.), Afghanistan 59/K2
Konar (riv.), Pakistan 68/C1
Konawa, Okla. (74849) 288/N5
Kondoa, Tanzania 115/G4
Kondopoga, U.S.S.R. 52/D2
Kondopoga, U.S.S.R. 48/D3
Kondoros, Hungary 41/F3
Koné, New Caled. 86/G4
Kong, Koh (isl.), Cambodia 72/D5
Kong, Ivory Coast 106/D7
Kongiganak, Alaska (99559) 196/F3
Kongju, S. Korea 81/C5
Kong Karls Land (isl.), Norway 18/E1
Kongmoon (Jiangmen), China 77/H7
Kongolo, Zaire 115/E5
Kongolo, Zaire 102/E5
Kongor, Sudan 111/F6
Kongsberg, N. Dak. (†58792) 282/J4

394 Kongsberg

Kongsberg, Norway 18/F7
Kongsfjorden (fjord), Norway 18/B2
Kongsvinger, Norway 18/H6
Kongur Shan (mt.), China 77/A4
Kongwa, Tanzania 115/G5
Koni (pen.), U.S.S.R. 48/Q4
Koniecpol, Poland 47/D3
Königsberg (Kaliningrad), U.S.S.R. 52/B4
Königssee (lake), W. Germany 22/E5
Königswiesen, Austria 41/C2
Königswinter, W. Germany 22/B3
Königs Wusterhausen, E. Germany 22/E2
Konin (prov.), Poland 47/D2
Konin, Poland 47/D2
Kónitsa, Greece 45/E5
Koniuji (isls.), Alaska 196/G3
Köniz, Switzerland 39/D3
Konjic, Yugoslavia 45/D4
Konkiep, Namibia 118/B5
Konnagar, India 68/F1
Konolfingen, Switzerland 39/E3
Konomoc (lake), Conn. 210/G3
Konosha, U.S.S.R. 52/F2
Konotop, U.S.S.R. 52/D4
Konqi He (riv.), China 77/C3
Końskie, Poland 47/E3
Konstantinovka, U.S.S.R. 52/E5
Konstantynów Łódzki, Poland 47/D3
Konstanz, W. Germany 22/C5
Kontagora, Nigeria 106/F6
Kontcha, Cameroon 115/B2
Kontich, Belgium 27/E6
Kontiomäki, Finland 18/Q4
Kontum, Vietnam 72/E4
Kontum (plat.), Vietnam 72/E4
Konya (prov.), Turkey 63/E4
Konya, Turkey 63/E4
Konya, Turkey 59/B2
Konya, Turkey 54/E6
Konza, Kenya 115/G4
Koocanusa (lake), Br. Col. 184/K6
Koocanusa (lake), Mont. 262/A2
Koochiching (co.), Minn. 255/E2
Koog aan de Zaan, Netherlands 27/A4
Koolan (isl.), W. Australia 88/C3
Koolan (isl.), W. Australia 92/C1
Koolau (range), Hawaii 218/E2
Kooline Station, W. Australia 92/B3
Koolpinyah, North. Terr. 93/B2
Koolyanobbing, W. Australia 88/B6
Koolyanobbing, W. Australia 92/B5
Koondrook, Victoria 97/B4
Koonibba, S. Australia 88/E6
Koonibba, S. Australia 94/C4
Koontz Lake, Ind. (†46574) 227/D2
Koorawatha, N.S. Wales 97/E4
Koosharem, Utah (84744) 304/C5
Koosharem Ind. Res., Utah 304/C5
Kooskia, Idaho (83539) 220/C3
Koostatak, Manitoba 179/E3
Kootenai (co.), Idaho 220/B2
Kootenai, Idaho (83840) 220/B1
Kootenai (riv.), Idaho 220/C1
Kootenai (riv.), Mont. 262/A2
Kootenay (lake), Br. Col. 162/E5
Kootenay (lake), Br. Col. 184/J5
Kootenay (riv.), Br. Col. 184/K5
Kootenay Nat'l Park, Br. Col. 184/J4
Kootenay Nat'l Pk., Br. Col. 162/E5
Kootingal, N.S. Wales 97/F2
Kópavogur, Iceland 21/B1
Köpenick, E. Germany 22/F4
Koper, Yugoslavia 45/A3
Kopervik, Norway 18/D7
Kopeysk, U.S.S.R. 48/G4
Köping, Sweden 18/J7
Koppal, India 68/D5
Koppang, Norway 18/G6
Kopparberg (co.), Sweden 18/J6
Kopparberg, Sweden 18/J7
Koppel, Pa. (16136) 294/B4
Kopperston, W. Va. (24854) 312/C7
Koprivnica, Yugoslavia 45/C2
Köprü (riv.), Turkey 63/D4
Kor (riv.), Iran 66/H6
Korab (mt.), Albania 45/E5
Korab (mt.), Yugoslavia 45/E5
Koraka (cape), Turkey 63/B3
Koran, La. (†71037) 238/D2
Koraput, India 68/E5
Korba, India 68/E4
Korbach, W. Germany 22/C3
Korbel, Calif. (95550) 204/B3
Korçë, Albania 45/E5
Korčula (isl.), Yugoslavia 45/C4
Kordestan (Kurdistan) (prov.), Iran 66/E3
Kord Kuy, Iran 66/J2
Kordofan, Southern (prov.), Sudan 111/E5
Kordofan, Northern (prov.), Sudan 111/E5
Korea (North) 2/R4
KOREA (NORTH) 81
Korea (South) 2/R4
KOREA (SOUTH) 81
Korea (bay), N. Korea 81/B4
Korea (str.), S. Korea 81/D6
Korenovsk, U.S.S.R. 52/E5
Korf, U.S.S.R. 54/T3
Korf, U.S.S.R. 4/C1
Korf, U.S.S.R. 48/R3
Korhogo, Ivory Coast 106/C7
Korhogo, Ivory Coast 102/B4
Körishegy (mt.), Hungary 41/D3
Koriyama, Japan 81/K5
Korkuteli, Turkey 63/D4
Korla, China 77/C3
Kormakiti (cape), Cyprus 59/B2
Kormakiti (cape), Cyprus 63/E5
Körmend, Hungary 41/D3
Kornat (isl.), Yugoslavia 45/B4
Korneuburg, Austria 41/D2
Kornsjø, Norway 18/G7
Kornwestheim, W. Germany 22/C4
Koro (isl.), Fiji 86/Q10
Koro (sea), Fiji 86/Q10
Köroğlu (mts.), Turkey 63/E2
Köroğlu Dağı (mt.), Turkey 63/E2
Korogwe, Tanzania 115/G5
Koroit, Victoria 97/B6
Korona, Fla. (†32010) 212/E2
Koronadal, Philippines 82/E7
Koronowo, Poland 47/C2
Koropí, Greece 45/G7
Koror (cap.), Belau 87/D5
Kororoit (creek), Victoria 97/H5
Kororoit (creek), Victoria 88/K7
Körös (riv.), Hungary 41/F3
Körösladány, Hungary 41/F3
Korosten', U.S.S.R. 52/C4
Korostyshev, U.S.S.R. 52/C4
Koro Toro, Chad 111/C4
Korpilombolo, Sweden 18/N3
Korsakov, U.S.S.R. 48/P5
Korsnäs, Finland 18/M5
Korsør, Denmark 21/E7
Korsør, Denmark 18/G9
Kortemark, Belgium 27/C6
Korti, Sudan 111/F4
Korti, Sudan 59/B6
Kortrijk, Belgium 27/C7
Korumburra, Victoria 97/D6
Koryak (range), U.S.S.R. 54/U3
Koryak (range), U.S.S.R. 48/S3
Koryak Aut. Okr., U.S.S.R. 48/R3
Koryazhma, U.S.S.R. 52/G2
Kos, Greece 45/H7
Kos (isl.), Greece 45/H7
Kościan, Poland 47/C2
Kościerzyna, Poland 47/C1
Kosciusko (mt.), Australia 87/F9
Kosciusko (co.), Ind. 227/F2
Kosciusko, Miss. (39090) 256/E4
Kosciusko (mt.), N. S. Wales 88/H7
Kosciusko (mt.), N.S. Wales 97/E5
Koshigaya, Japan 81/P2
Koshiki (isls.), Japan 81/D8
Koshke-e Kohneh, Afghanistan 68/A2
Koshkonong, Mo. (65692) 261/J9
Koshkonong (lake), Wis. 317/H10
Košice, Czech. 7/G4
Košice, Czech. 41/F2
Koslan, U.S.S.R. 48/E3
Koslan, U.S.S.R. 52/G2
Köslin (Koszalin), Poland 47/C1
Kosoma, Okla. (†74557) 288/P6
Kosŏng, N. Korea 81/D4
Kosovo (aut. reg.), Yugoslavia 45/E4
Kosovska Mitrovica, Yugoslavia 45/E4
Kosrae (isl.), Micronesia 87/G5
Kosse, Texas (76653) 303/H6
Kössen, Austria 41/B3
Kossou, Lac de (lake), Ivory Coast 106/C7
Kossuth, Ind. (†47167) 227/E7
Kossuth (co.), Iowa 229/E2
Kossuth, Miss. (38834) 256/G1
Kostajnica, Yugoslavia 45/C3
Kostelec nad Černými Lesy, Czech. 41/C2
Kostelec nad Orlicí, Czech. 41/D1
Kosti, Sudan 59/B7
Kosti, Sudan 111/F5
Kosti, Sudan 102/F3
Kostopol', U.S.S.R. 52/C4
Kostroma, U.S.S.R. 7/J3
Kostroma, U.S.S.R. 52/F3
Kostroma, U.S.S.R. 48/E4
Kostrzyń, Poland 47/B2
Koszalin (prov.), Poland 47/C1
Koszalin, Poland 7/F3
Koszalin, Poland 47/C1
Kőszeg, Hungary 41/D3
Koszta, Iowa (†52208) 229/J5
Kota, India 68/D3
Kota, India 54/J7
Kotaagung, Indonesia 85/C7
Kotabaharu, Indonesia 85/E6
Kota Baharu, Malaysia 54/M9
Kota Baharu, Malaysia 72/D6
Kotabaru, Indonesia 85/F6
Kotabumi, Indonesia 85/C7
Kota Kinabalu, Malaysia 54/N9
Kota Kinabalu, Malaysia 85/F4
Kotamobagu, Indonesia 85/G5
Kota Tinggi, Malaysia 72/F5
Kotawaringin, Indonesia 85/E6
Kotcho (lake), Br. Col. 184/M2
Kotcho (riv.), Br. Col. 184/M2
Kotel, Bulgaria 45/H4
Kotel'nich, U.S.S.R. 52/G3
Kotel'nikovo, U.S.S.R. 52/F5
Kotel'nyy (isl.), U.S.S.R. 4/B2
Kotel'nyy (isl.), U.S.S.R. 48/O2
Köthen, E. Germany 22/E3
Kotido, Uganda 115/F3
Kotka, Finland 7/G2
Kotka, Finland 18/P6
Kotlas, U.S.S.R. 7/J2
Kotlas, U.S.S.R. 48/E3
Kotlas, U.S.S.R. 52/G2
Kotlik, Alaska (99620) 196/F2
Kotor, Yugoslavia 45/D4
Kotovo, U.S.S.R. 52/G4
Kotovsk, Odessa, U.S.S.R. 52/C5
Kotovsk, Tambov, U.S.S.R. 52/F4
Kotri, Pakistan 68/B3
Kötschach-Mauthen, Austria 41/B3
Kottaguden, India 68/E5
Kottayam, India 68/D7
Kotto (riv.), Cent. Afr. Rep. 115/D2
Kotturu, India 68/D6
Kotuy (riv.), U.S.S.R. 4/B4
Kotuy (riv.), U.S.S.R. 54/M2
Kotuy (riv.), U.S.S.R. 48/L3
Kotzebue, Alaska (99752) 196/F1
Kotzebue, Alaska 146/B3
Kotzebue, Alaska 188/C5
Kotzebue (sound), Alaska 196/F1
Kotzebue, U.S. 4/C18
Kouango, Cent. Afr. Rep. 115/D2
Kouchibouguac, New Bruns. 170/F2
Kouchibouguac (bay), New Bruns. 170/F2
Kouchibouguacis (riv.), New Bruns. 170/E2
Kouchobouguac Nat'l Park, New Bruns. 170/F2
Koudougou, Upper Volta 106/D6
Kouilou (riv.), Congo 115/B4
Koukdjuak (riv.), N.W. Terrs. 187/L3
Kouki, Cent. Afr. Rep. 115/C2
Koula-Moutou, Gabon 115/B4
Koula-Moutou, Gabon 102/D5
Koulikoro, Mali 106/C6
Koulikoro, Mali 102/B3
Koumala, Queensland 95/D4
Koumbi Saleh (ruins), Mauritania 106/C5
Koumra, Chad 102/D4
Koumra, Chad 111/C6
Koundara, Guinea 106/B6
Kounde, Cent. Afr. Rep. 115/B2
Kouno, Chad 111/C6
Kounradskiy, U.S.S.R. 48/H5
Kountze, Texas (77625) 303/K7
Koupela, Upper Volta 106/D6
Kourou, Fr. Guiana 131/E3
Kourouba, Mali 106/B6
Kouroussa, Guinea 106/C6
Kousseri, Cameroon 115/B1
Koutiala, Mali 106/C6
Koutiala, Mali 102/B3
Kouts, Ind. (46347) 227/C2
Kouvola, Finland 18/P6
Kovdor, U.S.S.R. 52/D1
Kovel', U.S.S.R. 52/C4
Kovel', U.S.S.R. 48/C4
Kovrov, U.S.S.R. 52/F3
Kovrov, U.S.S.R. 48/E4
Kovur, India 68/E6
Kovylkino, U.S.S.R. 52/F4
Kowary, Poland 47/B3
Kowloon, Hong Kong 77/H7
Kowt-e 'Ashrow, Afghanistan 68/B2
Koyama, Japan 81/E8
Köyceğiz, Turkey 63/C4
Köyceğiz (lake), Turkey 63/C4
Koyuk, Alaska (99753) 196/F1
Koyukuk, Alaska (99754) 196/G1
Koyukuk (riv.), Alaska 188/C5
Koyukuk (riv.), Alaska 196/G1
Koyulhisar, Turkey 63/G2
Kozaklı, Turkey 63/F3
Kozan, Turkey 63/F4
Kozáni, Greece 45/F5
Kozhevnikovo, U.S.S.R. 48/L2
Kozhikode, India 68/D6
Kozhikode, India 54/J8
Kozhva, U.S.S.R. 52/J1
Kozienice, Poland 47/E3
Kozlu, Turkey 63/D2
Kozluk, Turkey 63/J3
Kozmin, Poland 47/C3
Kozuchów, Poland 47/B3
Kpalimé, Togo 106/E7
Kpandu, Ghana 106/D7
Kpémé, Togo 106/E7
Kra (isth.), Thailand 72/C5
Kraaifontein, S. Africa 118/F6
Kraainem, Belgium 27/C9
Krabi, Thailand 72/C5
Kra Buri, Thailand 72/C5
Kracheh, Cambodia 72/E4
Kraemer, La. (70371) 238/M4
Kragan, Indonesia 85/K2
Kragerø, Norway 18/F7
Kragujevac, Yugoslavia 45/E3
Kragujevac, Yugoslavia 7/G4
Krakatau (Rakata) (isl.), Indonesia 85/C7
Krakow, Mo. (†63090) 261/K6
Kraków (Cracow), Poland 47/E4
Krakow, Wis. (53147) 317/K6
Kralendijk (cap.), Bonaire, Neth. Ant. 161/E8
Kralendijk, Neth. Ant. 156/E4
Králíky, Czech. 41/D1
Kraljevo, Yugoslavia 45/E4
Kralovice, Czech. 41/B2
Král'ovský Chlmec, Czech. 41/G2
Kralupy nad Vltavou, Czech. 41/C1
Kramatorsk, U.S.S.R. 52/E5
Kramer, Ind. (†47918) 227/C4
Kramer, Nebr. (†68333) 264/H4
Kramer, N. Dak. (58748) 282/J2
Kramfors, Sweden 18/L5
Kranídhion, Greece 45/F7
Kranj, Yugoslavia 45/B2
Kranzburg, S. Dak. (57245) 298/R4
Krapkowice, Poland 47/D3
Krasino, U.S.S.R. 52/H1
Krasino, U.S.S.R. 48/F2
Krāslava, U.S.S.R. 53/D3
Kraslice, Czech. 41/B1
Krásná Lípa, Czech. 41/C1
Kraśnik Fabryczny, Poland 47/F3
Krasnoarmeysk, U.S.S.R. 52/G4
Krasnoborsk, U.S.S.R. 52/G2
Krasnodar, U.S.S.R. 7/H4
Krasnodar, U.S.S.R. 48/E5
Krasnodar, U.S.S.R. 52/E6
Krasnograd, U.S.S.R. 52/E5
Krasnokamensk, U.S.S.R. 48/M4
Krasnokamsk, U.S.S.R. 52/H3
Krasnokamsk, U.S.S.R. 48/F4
Krasnoperekopsk, U.S.S.R. 52/D5
Krasnoslobodsk, U.S.S.R. 52/G5
Krasnotur'insk, U.S.S.R. 48/G3
Krasnoural'sk, U.S.S.R. 48/G4
Krasnovishersk, U.S.S.R. 52/J2
Krasnovodsk, U.S.S.R. 54/G5
Krasnovodsk, U.S.S.R. 48/F5
Krasnoyarsk, U.S.S.R. 54/L4
Krasnoyarsk, U.S.S.R. 2/P3
Krasnoyarsk, U.S.S.R. 48/K4
Krasnystaw, Poland 47/F3
Krasnyy Kut, U.S.S.R. 52/G4
Krasnyy Luch, U.S.S.R. 52/E5
Krasnyy Sulin, U.S.S.R. 52/F5
Krasnyy Yar, U.S.S.R. 52/G5
Kraulshavn, Greenl. 4/B13
Krause Lagoon (chan.), Virgin Is. (U.S.) 161/F4
Krawang, Indonesia 85/H2
Krebs, Okla. (74554) 288/P5
Krefeld, W. Germany 22/B3
Kremenchug, U.S.S.R. 7/H4
Kremenchug, U.S.S.R. 48/D5
Kremenchug, U.S.S.R. 52/D5
Kremlin, Mont. (59532) 262/F2
Kremlin, Okla. (73753) 288/L1
Kremmling, Colo. (80459) 208/G2
Kremnica, Czech. 41/E2
Krems an der Donau, Austria 41/C2
Krenitzin (isls.), Alaska 196/E4
Kresgeville, Pa. (18333) 294/L4
Kress, Texas (79052) 303/C3
Kretinga, U.S.S.R. 53/A3
Kreutztal, W. Germany 22/C3
Kreuzlingen, Switzerland 39/H1
Kribi, Cameroon 115/B3
Krichev, U.S.S.R. 52/D4
Kriens, Switzerland 39/F2
Krimml, Austria 41/B3
Krimpen aan den IJssel, Netherlands 27/F5
Kriós (cape), Greece 45/F8
Krishna (Kistna) (riv.), India 68/D5
Krishnanagar, India 68/F4
Kristiansand, Norway 18/F8
Kristiansand, Norway 7/E3
Kristianstad (co.), Sweden 18/J8
Kristianstad, Sweden 18/J9
Kristiansund, Norway 7/E2
Kristiansund, Norway 18/E5
Kristiinankaupunki (Kristinestad), Finland 18/N5
Kristinehamn, Sweden 18/H7
Kristinestad, Finland 18/N5
Kríti (Crete) (isl.), Greece 45/G8
Krivoy Rog, U.S.S.R. 7/H4
Krivoy Rog, U.S.S.R. 48/D5
Krivoy Rog, U.S.S.R. 52/D5
Križevci, Yugoslavia 45/C2
Krk, Yugoslavia 45/B3
Krk (isl.), Yugoslavia 45/B3
Krnov, Czech. 41/D1
Krolevets, U.S.S.R. 52/D4
Kroměříž, Czech. 41/D2
Krompachy, Czech. 41/F2
Kronach, W. Germany 22/D3
Kronau, Sask. 181/G5
Krong Kaoh Kong, Cambodia 72/D4
Krong Keb, Cambodia 72/E5
Kronoberg (co.), Sweden 18/J8
Kronshtadt, U.S.S.R. 52/C3
Kroonstad, S. Africa 118/D5
Kropotkin, U.S.S.R. 52/F5
Kroschel, Minn. (†55037) 255/E4
Krosno (prov.), Poland 47/E4
Krosno, Poland 47/E4
Krosno Odrzanskie, Poland 47/B2
Krotoszyn, Poland 47/C3
Krotz Springs, La. (70750) 238/G5
Krško, Yugoslavia 45/B3
Kru Coast (reg.), Liberia 106/C8
Kruger Nat'l Park, S. Africa 118/E4
Krugersdorp, S. Africa 118/H6
Krugloi (pt.), Alaska 196/J3
Kruis (riv.), S. Africa 118/F6
Krujë, Albania 45/D5
Krum, Texas (76249) 303/G4
Krumbach, W. Germany 22/D4
Krummenau, Switzerland 39/H2
Krumovgrad, Bulgaria 45/G5
Krung Thep (Bangkok) (cap.), Thailand 72/D4
Krupina, Czech. 41/E2
Krupka, Czech. 41/B1
Krupp (Marlin), Wash. (†98832) 310/F3
Krusenstern (cape), Alaska 196/F1
Krusenstern (cape), N.W. Terrs. 187/G3
Kruševac, Yugoslavia 45/E4
Krušné Hory (Erzgebirge) (mts.), Czech. 41/B1
Kruszwica, Poland 47/D2
Kruzof (isl.), Alaska 196/M1
Krydor, Sask. 181/D3
Krymsk, U.S.S.R. 52/E5
Krynica, Poland 47/E4
Krypton, Ky. (41754) 237/P6
Krzyz, Poland 47/C2
Ksar el Boukhari, Algeria 106/E1
Ksar el Kebir, Morocco 106/C2
Ksar es Souk, Morocco 106/D2
Ktima, Cyprus 63/E5
Kuala Dungun, Malaysia 72/D6
Kualakapuas, Indonesia 85/E6
Kuala Kerai, Malaysia 72/D6
Kualakurun, Indonesia 85/E6
Kuala Lipis, Malaysia 72/D6
Kuala Lumpur (cap.), Malaysia 72/D7
Kuala Lumpur (cap.), Malaysia 54/M9
Kuala Lumpur (cap.), Malaysia 2/P5
Kuala Pilah, Malaysia 72/D7
Kualapuu, Hawaii (96757) 218/G1
Kuala Rompin, Malaysia 72/D7
Kuala Selangor, Malaysia 72/D7
Kuala Terengganu, Malaysia 72/D6
Kuancheng, China 77/J3
Kuantan, Malaysia 72/D7
Kuba, U.S.S.R. 52/G6
Kubachi, U.S.S.R. 52/G6
Kubaisa, Iraq 66/C4
Kuban' (riv.), U.S.S.R. 7/J4
Kuban' (riv.), U.S.S.R. 52/E5
Kubbum, Sudan 111/D5
Kubeno (lake), U.S.S.R. 52/E3
Kūblis, Switzerland 39/J3
Kubohama, Japan 81/F7
Kubrat, Bulgaria 45/H4
Kuching, Malaysia 54/N9
Kuching, Malaysia 85/E5
Kuchino (isl.), Japan 81/O4
Kuçovë (Stalin), Albania 45/D5
Küçükköy, Turkey 63/C3
Kudarebe (pt.), Neth. Ant. 161/D9
Kudat, Malaysia 85/F4
Kudowa Zdroj, Poland 47/B3
Kudus, Indonesia 85/J2
Kudymkar, U.S.S.R. 48/F4
Kudymkar, U.S.S.R. 52/H3
Kufra (oasis), Libya 102/E2
Kufra (oasis), Libya 111/D3
Kufrinja, Jordan 65/D3
Kufstein, Austria 41/A3
Kuh (cape), Iran 66/K8
Kuhak, Iran 66/N7
Kuhestan, Afghanistan 59/H3
Kuhestan, Afghanistan 68/A2
Kühlungsborn, E. Germany 22/D1
Kuhmo, Finland 18/Q4
Kuhpayeh, Iran 66/H4
Kuilsrivier, S. Africa 118/F6
Kuiseb (riv.), Namibia 118/B4
Kuiu (isl.), Alaska 196/M2
Kuivaniemi, Finland 18/O4
Kuji, Japan 81/K3
Kuju (mt.), Japan 81/E7
Kuk (riv.), Alaska 196/G1
Kukaiau, Hawaii (†96775) 218/H4
Kukaklek (lake), Alaska 196/G3
Kukalar, Kuh-e (mt.), Iran 59/F3
Kukalar, Kuh-e (mt.), Iran 66/G5
Kukalaya (riv.), Nicaragua 154/F4
Kukawa, Nigeria 106/G6
Kukës, Albania 45/E4
Kuki, Japan 81/O2
Kukpowruk (riv.), Alaska 196/F1
Kukui (riv.), Guyana 131/A3
Kukuihaele, Hawaii (96727) 218/H3
Kula, Bulgaria 45/F4
Kula, Hawaii (96790) 218/J2
Kula, Turkey 63/C3
Kulai, Malaysia 72/F5
Kula Kangri (mt.), Bhutan 68/G3
Kuldīga, U.S.S.R. 53/A2
Kuldja (Yining), China 77/B3
Kulebaki, U.S.S.R. 52/F3
Kulen, Cambodia 72/E4
Kulen Vakuf, Yugoslavia 45/B3
Kulgera, North. Terr. 88/E5
Kulgera, North. Terr. 93/C8
Kulkyne (creek), N.S. Wales 97/C1
Kulm, N. Dak. (58456) 282/N7
Kulmbach, W. Germany 22/D3
Kuloy, U.S.S.R. 52/F2
Kulp, Turkey 63/J3
Kulpmont, Pa. (17834) 294/J4
Kulpsville, Pa. (19443) 294/M5
Kul'sary, U.S.S.R. 48/F5
Kulu, India 68/D2
Kulu, Turkey 63/E3
Kulunda, U.S.S.R. 48/H4
Kulyab, U.S.S.R. 48/H6
Kŭm (riv.), S. Korea 81/C5
Kuma (riv.), U.S.S.R. 7/J4
Kuma (riv.), U.S.S.R. 48/E5
Kuma (riv.), U.S.S.R. 52/G5
Kumagaya, Japan 81/J5
Kumai, Indonesia 85/E6
Kumaka, Guyana 131/B4
Kumamoto (pref.), Japan 81/E7
Kumamoto, Japan 54/P6
Kumamoto, Japan 81/E7
Kumano, Japan 81/H7
Kumanovo, Yugoslavia 45/E4
Kumara, N. Zealand 100/C5
Kumasi, Ghana 106/D7
Kumasi, Ghana 102/B4
Kumba, Cameroon 115/A3
Kumbakonam, India 68/D6
Kumbo, Cameroon 115/B2
Kum-Dag, U.S.S.R. 48/F6
Kume (isl.), Japan 81/M6
Kumertau, U.S.S.R. 52/J4
Kumeu, N. Zealand 100/B1
Kŭmgang (mt.), N. Korea 81/D4
Kumiyama, Japan 81/J7
Kumkale, Turkey 63/B6
Kumköy, Turkey 63/B6
Kumla, Sweden 18/J7
Kumluca, Turkey 63/D4
Kummerowersee (lake), E. Germany 22/E2
Kumo (riv.), Finland 7/G2
Kumo, Nigeria 106/G7
Kumphawapi, Thailand 72/D3
Kumta, India 68/C6
Kumukahi (cape), Hawaii 218/K5
Kumul (Hami), China 77/D3
Kuna, Idaho (83634) 220/B6
Kunágota, Hungary 41/F3
Kunashir (isl.), U.S.S.R. 54/R5
Kunda, U.S.S.R. 52/C3
Kunda, U.S.S.R. 53/D1
Kundiawa, Papua N.G. 85/B7
Kundl, Austria 41/A3
Künes (Xinyuan), China 77/B3
Künes He (riv.), China 77/B3
Kungälv, Sweden 18/G8
Kunghit (isl.), Br. Col. 184/B4
Kungsbacka, Sweden 18/G8
Kungu, Zaire 102/D4
Kungu, Zaire 115/C3
Kungur, U.S.S.R. 7/K3
Kungur, U.S.S.R. 48/F4
Kungur, U.S.S.R. 52/J3
Kunhegyes, Hungary 41/F3
Kunia, Hawaii (96759) 218/E2
Kuningan, Indonesia 85/H2
Kunkle, Ohio (43531) 284/A2
Kunkletown, Pa. (18058) 294/M4
Kunlong, Burma 72/C2
Kunlun (range), China 54/K6
Kunlun (range), India 68/D1
Kunlun Shan (range), China 77/B4
Kunmadaras, Hungary 41/F3
Kunming, China 77/F6
Kunming, China 2/Q4
Kunming, China 54/M7
Kunsan, S. Korea 81/C6
Kunszentmárton, Hungary 41/F3
Kunszentmiklós, Hungary 41/E3
Kununurra, W. Australia 88/D3
Kununurra, W. Australia 92/E2
Kuolayarvi, U.S.S.R. 52/D1
Kuopio (prov.), Finland 18/P5
Kuopio, Finland 7/G2
Kuopio, Finland 18/Q5
Kupa (riv.), Yugoslavia 45/B3
Kupang, Indonesia 54/O11
Kupang, Indonesia 85/G8
Kuparuk (riv.), Alaska 196/H1
Kupino, U.S.S.R. 48/H4
Kupiškis, U.S.S.R. 53/C3
Kupreanof (isl.), Alaska 196/N1
Kupyansk, U.S.S.R. 52/E5
Kuqa, China 77/B3
Kur (isl.), Indonesia 85/J7
Kura (riv.), U.S.S.R. 48/E6
Kura (riv.), U.S.S.R. 52/G6
Kuraiyima, Jordan 65/D3
Kurang (riv.), Iran 66/G4
Kurashiki, Japan 81/F6
Kurayoshi, Japan 81/F6
Kurdistan (Kordestan) (prov.), Iran 66/E3
Kurdistan (reg.), Iran 59/D2
Kurdistan (reg.), Iran 66/D2
Kurdistan (reg.), Iraq 59/D2
Kurdistan (reg.), Iraq 66/C2
Kurdistan (reg.), Turkey 59/D2
Kŭrdzhali, Bulgaria 45/G5
Kure (atoll), Hawaii 87/J3
Kure (atoll), Hawaii 218/A5
Kure (isl.), Hawaii 218/A5
Kure, Japan 81/F6
Küre, Turkey 63/E2
Küre (mts.), Turkey 63/E2
Kure Beach, N.C. (28449) 281/O7
Kuressaare, U.S.S.R. 53/B1
Kuressaare, U.S.S.R. 52/B3
Kurgan, U.S.S.R. 54/H4
Kurgan, U.S.S.R. 48/G4
Kurgan-Tyube, U.S.S.R. 48/G6
Kuria Muria (isls.), Oman 54/G8
Kuria Muria (isls.), Oman 59/G6
Kurikka, Finland 18/M5
Kuril (isls.), U.S.S.R. 2/S3
Kuril (isls.), U.S.S.R. 54/R5
Kuril (isls.), U.S.S.R. 48/P5
Kuril'sk, U.S.S.R. 48/P5
Ku-ring-gai, N. S. Wales 88/K4
Kuring Kuru, Namibia 118/B3
Kurla, India 68/B7
Kurmuk, Sudan 111/F5
Kurnell (pen.), N.S. Wales 97/J4
Kurnool, India 54/J8
Kurnool, India 68/D5
Kuroiso, Japan 81/K5
Kuroki, Sask. 181/H4
Kurow, N. Zealand 100/C6
Kurri Kurri-Weston, N.S. Wales 97/F3
Kuršenai, U.S.S.R. 53/B2
Kursk, U.S.S.R. 7/H3
Kursk, U.S.S.R. 48/D4
Kursk, U.S.S.R. 52/E4
Kurşunlu, Turkey 63/E2
Kurtalan, Turkey 63/J3
Kurthwood, La. (71443) 238/D4
Kurtistown, Hawaii (96760) 218/J5
Kurtz, Ind. (47249) 227/E7
Kurucaşile, Turkey 63/E2
Kuruçay (riv.), Turkey 63/K2
Kuruktag Shan (range), China 77/C3
Kuruman, S. Africa 118/C5
Kurume, Japan 81/E7
Kurundi, North. Terr. 93/D6
Kurunegala, Sri Lanka 68/E7
Kurungiku (mts.), Guyana 131/B3
Kurupukari, Guyana 131/B3
Kuş (lake), Turkey 63/B2
Kuşada (gulf), Turkey 63/B4
Kuşadası, Turkey 63/B4
Kushchevskaya, U.S.S.R. 52/E5
Kushequa, Pa. (†16735) 294/E2
Kushikino, Japan 81/E8
Kushima, Japan 81/E8
Kushimoto, Japan 81/G7
Kushiro, Japan 54/R5
Kushiro, Japan 81/M2
Kushka, U.S.S.R. 48/G6
Kushog (lake), Ontario 177/F2
Kuskokwim (bay), Alaska 196/F3
Kuskokwim (mts.), Alaska 196/G2
Kuskokwim (riv.), Alaska 188/C6
Kuskokwim (riv.), Alaska 196/G2
Kuskokwim (riv.), Alaska 146/C3
Kuskokwim, North Fork (riv.), Alaska 196/H2
Kuskokwim, South Fork (riv.), Alaska 196/H2
Kuskokwim (riv.), U.S. 4/C17
Küsnacht, Switzerland 39/G2
Kusŏng, N. Korea 81/B4
Küssnacht am Rigi, Switzerland 39/F2
Kustanay, U.S.S.R. 54/H4
Kustanay, U.S.S.R. 48/G4
Kustatan, Alaska (†99682) 196/B1
Küstrin, Poland 47/B2
Kut, Iraq 59/E3
Kut, Iraq 66/D4
Kut, Ko (isl.), Thailand 72/D5
Kuta, Nigeria 106/F7
Kütahya (prov.), Turkey 63/C3
Kütahya, Turkey 59/B2
Kütahya, Turkey 63/C3
Kutaisi, U.S.S.R. 7/J4
Kutaisi, U.S.S.R. 48/E5
Kutaisi, U.S.S.R. 52/F6
Kutaraja (Banda Aceh), Indonesia 85/A4
Kutari (riv.), Guyana 131/C4
Kutari (riv.), Suriname 131/C4
Kutch, Colo. (†80832) 208/M5
Kutch (gulf), India 68/B4
Kutch (reg.), India 68/B4
Kutch, Rann of (salt marsh), 54/H7
Kutch, Rann of (salt marsh), India 68/B4
Kutch, Rann of (salt marsh), Pakistan 68/B4
Kutch, Rann of (salt lake), Pakistan 59/K5
Kutcharo (lake), Japan 81/M2

Lake Chelan 395

Kutina, Yugoslavia 45/C3
Kutná Hora, Czech. 41/C2
Kutno, Poland 47/D2
Kutoarjo, Indonesia 85/J2
Kuttawa, Ky. (42055) 237/E6
Küttigen, Switzerland 39/F2
Kutu, Zaire 115/C4
Kutum, Sudan 111/D5
Kúty, Czech. 41/D2
Kutztown, Pa. (19530) 294/L4
Kuusamo, Finland 18/Q4
Kuusamojärvi (lake), Finland 18/Q4
Kuusankoski, Finland 18/P6
Kuvandyk, U.S.S.R. 52/J4
Kuwait 2/M4
Kuwait 54/F7
KUWAIT 59/E4
Kuybyshev, U.S.S.R. 2/M3
Kuybyshev, U.S.S.R. 7/K3
Kuybyshev, U.S.S.R. 48/F4
Kuybyshev, U.S.S.R. 52/H4
Kuybyshev, U.S.S.R. 48/H4
Kuybyshev (res.), U.S.S.R. 7/K3
Kuybyshev (res.), U.S.S.R. 48/F4
Kuybyshev (res.), U.S.S.R. 52/G4
Kuyto (lake), U.S.S.R. 52/D2
Kuytun, China 77/C3
Kuyucak, Turkey 63/C4
Kuyuwini (riv.), Guyana 131/B4
Kuznetsk, U.S.S.R. 52/G4
Kuzomen', U.S.S.R. 52/E1
Kvaenangen (fjord), Norway 18/N2
Kvaerndrup, Denmark 21/D7
Kvaløy (isl.), Norway 18/K2
Kvaløya (isl.), Norway 18/01
Kvarner (gulf), Yugoslavia 45/B3
Kvichak, Alaska (†99625) 196/G3
Kvichak (bay), Alaska 196/G3
Kvikkjokk, Sweden 18/K3
Kvinnherad, Norway 18/E6
Kvissleby, Sweden 18/K5
Kviteseid, Norway 18/F7
Kwa (riv.), Zaire 115/C4
Kwai (Mae Nam Khwae Noi) (riv.), Thailand 72/C4
Kwajalein (atoll), Marshall Is. 87/G5
Kwakoegron, Suriname 131/D3
Kwakwani, Guyana 131/C3
Kwale, Kenya 102/F5
Kwale, Kenya 115/G4
Kwamouth, Zaire 115/C4
Kwangchow (Canton), China 77/H7
Kwangju, S. Korea 54/06
Kwangju, S. Korea 81/C6
Kwango (riv.), Zaire 115/C5
Kwangsi Chuang Aut. Reg. (Guangxi Zhuangzu), China 77/G7
Kwangtung (Guangdong) (prov.), China 77/H7
Kwanmo (mt.), N. Korea 81/D3
Kwara (state), Nigeria 106/E7
Kweichow (Guizhou)(prov.),China 77/G6
Kweilin (Guilin), China 77/G6
Kweisui (Hohhot), China 77/H3
Kweiyang (Guiyang), China 77/G6
Kwekwe (Que Que), Zimbabwe 118/D3
Kwethluk, Alaska (99621) 196/F2
Kwidzin, Poland 47/D2
Kwigillingok, Alaska (99622) 196/F3
Kwilu (riv.), Angola 115/C5
Kwilu (riv.), Zaire 115/C5
Kwinana New Town, W. Australia 88/B2
Kwinana New Town, W. Australia 92/A1
Kwinitsa, Br. Col. 184/C3
Kwitaro (riv.), Guyana 131/B4
Kyabé, Chad 111/C6
Kyabram, Victoria 97/C5
Kyaikto, Burma 72/C3
Kya-in Seikkyi, Burma 72/C3
Kyakhta, U.S.S.R. 54/M4
Kyakhta, U.S.S.R. 48/L4
Kyalite, N.S. Wales 97/B4
Kyana, Ind. (47549) 227/D8
Kyancutta, S. Australia 94/D5
Kyangin, Burma 72/B3
Kyaukme, Burma 72/C2
Kyaukpadaung, Burma 72/B2
Kyaukpyu, Burma 72/B3
Kyaukse, Burma 72/C2
Kybartai, U.S.S.R. 53/B3
Kyeburn, N. Zealand 100/C6
Kyger, Ohio (†45620) 284/F8
Kyger, W. Va. (†25270) 312/D5
Kyjov, Czech. 41/D2
Kyle, Sask. 181/C5
Kyle, S. Dak. (57752) 298/E7
Kyle, Texas (78640) 303/G8
Kyleakin, Scotland 15/C3
Kylemore, Sask. 181/H4
Kyle of Lochalsh, Scotland 15/C3
Kyle of Tongue (inlet), Scotland 15/D2
Kyles Ford, Tenn. (37765) 237/R7
Kylestrome, Scotland 15/D2
Kymi (prov.), Finland 18/Q6
Kyneton, Victoria 97/C5
Kynšperk, Czech. 41/B1
Kynuna, Queensland 95/B4
Kyogle, N.S. Wales 97/G1
Kyonan, Japan 81/O3
Kyŏnghŭng, N. Korea 81/E2
Kyŏngju, S. Korea 81/D6
Kyoto (pref.), Japan 81/J7
Kyoto, Japan 54/P6
Kyoto, Japan 81/J7
Kyrenia, Cyprus 63/E5
Kyritz, E. Germany 22/E2
Kysucké Nové Mesto, Czech. 41/E2
Kythrea, Cyprus 63/E5
Kyuquot, Br. Col. 184/D5
Kyuquot (sound), Br. Col. 184/D5
Kyushu (isl.), Japan 2/R4
Kyushu (isl.), Japan 54/P6
Kyushu (isl.), Japan 81/E7
Kyustendil, Bulgaria 45/F4
Kyusyur, U.S.S.R. 48/N2
Kywebwe, Burma 72/C3
Kyzyl, U.S.S.R. 48/K4
Kyzyl (riv.), U.S.S.R. 54/L4
Kyzyl-Kum (des.), U.S.S.R. 48/G5
Kzyl-Orda, U.S.S.R. 54/H5
Kzyl-Orda, U.S.S.R. 48/G5

L

Laa an der Thaya, Austria 41/D2
La Aduana, Venezuela 124/D3
Laager, Tenn. (37349) 237/K10
La Aguja (cape), Colombia 126/C2
Laakirchen, Austria 41/B3
La Almunia de Doña Godina, Spain 33/F2
La Altagracia (prov.), Dom. Rep. 158/F6
La Anna, Pa. (†18326) 294/M3
La Antigua Veracruz, Mexico 150/Q1
La Araucanía (reg.), Chile 138/E2
La Asunción, Venezuela 124/G2
Laau (pt.), Hawaii 218/G1
Laax, Switzerland 39/H3
Laayoune, W. Sahara 102/A2
Laayoune, Western Sahara 106/B3
Labadie, Mo. (63055) 261/L5
Labadieville, La. (70372) 238/K4
La Baie, Québec 172/G1
La Baie-de-Shawinigan, Québec 172/E3
La Banda, Argentina 143/D2
La Bandera (pt.), P. Rico 161/F1
La Bañeza, Spain 33/C1
La Barca, Mexico 150/H6
La Barge, Wyo. (83123) 319/B3
La Barge (creek), Wyo. 319/B3
La Barra de Navidad, Mexico 150/G7
Labasheeda, Ireland 17/C6
La Baule-Escoublac, France 28/B4
L'Abbaye, Switzerland 39/B3
Labe (riv.), Czech. 41/C1
Labé, Guinea 106/B6
La Bella (lag.), Paraguay 144/B4
La Belle, Fla. (33935) 212/E5
La Belle, Mo. (63447) 261/J2
Labelle (co.), Québec 172/B3
Labelle, Québec 172/C3
Labelle (lake), Québec 172/C3
La Belle (lake), Wis. 317/H1
Laberge (lake), Yukon 162/C3
Laberinto de las Doce Leguas (cays), Cuba 158/F3
La Berra (mt.), Switzerland 39/D3
Labette (co.), Kansas 232/G4
Labette, Kansas (67350) 232/G4
Labinsk, U.S.S.R. 52/F6
La Bisbal, Spain 33/H1
La Blanquilla (isl.), Venezuela 124/F2
Labo, Philippines 82/D3
Labo (mt.), Philippines 82/D3
La Bolsa, Uruguay 145/C1
La Bolt, S. Dak. (57246) 298/R3
La Bonita, Ecuador 128/D2
La Boquilla (res.), Mexico 150/G3
Laborec (riv.), Czech. 41/F2
Laborie, St. Lucia 161/G7
La Bostonnais, Québec 172/E2
Labougle, Argentina 143/G5
Laboulaye, Argentina 143/D3
Labrador (sea) 146/N4
Labrador (sea) 162/L4
Labrador (reg.), Canada 2/G3
Labrador (sea), Newf. 166/C2
Labrador (reg.), Newf. 166/B2
Labrador (reg.), Newf. 146/M4
Labrador (reg.), Newf. 162/K4
Labrador City, Newf. 166/A3
La Branche, Mich. (†49873) 250/B3
Lábrea, Brazil 132/G10
La Brea, Trin. & Tob. 161/A11
Labrieville, Québec 174/C3
La Broquerie, Manitoba 179/F5
Labuan, Malaysia 85/E4
Labuan (isl.), Malaysia 85/E4
Labuha, Indonesia 85/H6
Labuhan, Indonesia 85/G2
Labuk (bay), Malaysia 85/F4
Labutta, Burma 72/B3
Labyrinth (canyon), Utah 304/D5
Labytnangi, U.S.S.R. 48/G3
Lac (bay), Neth. Ant. 161/D9
Lac-à-Beauce, Québec 172/E2
Lacadena, Sask. 181/C5
Lacadie, Québec 172/J4
La Cahouane, Haiti 158/A6
Lac-à-la-Croix, Québec 172/F1
La Calera, Chile 138/F2
Lac-Alouette, Québec 172/D4
Lacamp, La. (71444) 238/E4
La Canada, Calif. (91011) 204/C10
Lacanau (lake), France 28/C5
La Canoa, Venezuela 124/G3
Lacantum (riv.), Mexico 150/O8
La Capilla, 136/C8
La Carlota, Argentina 143/D3
La Carlota, Philippines 82/D5
La Carlota, Spain 33/D4
La Carolina, Spain 33/E3
Lacassine, La. (70650) 238/E6
Lac-au-Saumon, Québec 172/B2
Lac-aux-Sables, Québec 172/E3
Lac Baker, New Bruns. 170/B1
Lac-Beauport, Québec 172/F3
Lac-Bouchette, Québec 172/E1
Laccadive (isls.), India 54/H8
Laccadive (isls.), India 68/C6
Lac-Carré, Québec 172/C3
Lac-Cayamant, Québec 172/A3
Lac-Chat, Québec 172/E2
Lac Court Oreilles Ind. Res., Wis. 317/D4
Lac de Gras (lake), N.W. Terrs. 187/G3
Lac-Delage, Québec 172/H3
Lac-des-Aigles, Québec 172/J2
Lac des Arcs, Alberta 182/C4
Lac-des-Écorces, Québec 172/B3
Lac-des-Îles, Québec 172/B3
Lac-Drolet, Québec 172/G4
Lac du Bonnet, Manitoba 179/G4
Lac-du-Cerf, Québec 172/B3
Lac du Flambeau, Wis. (54538) 317/G4
Lac du Flambeau Ind. Res., Wis. 317/G3
Lac-Édouard, Québec 172/E2
La Ceiba, Hond. 146/K8
La Ceiba, Honduras 154/D3
La Ceiba, Apure, Venezuela 124/C4
La Ceiba, Trujillo, Venezuela 124/C3
La Center, Ky. (42056) 237/C6
La Center, Wash. (98629) 310/C5
Lacepede (bay), S. Australia 88/F7
Lacepede (bay), S. Australia 94/F7
Lacepede (isls.), W. Australia 92/C2
Lacepede (range), W. Australia 88/D3
La Cerbatana, Serranía de (mts.), Venezuela 124/E4
Lac-Etchemin, Québec 172/G3
Lacey, Ark. (†71655) 202/G7
Lacey, Wash. (98503) 310/C3
Lacey Spring, Va. (22833) 307/L3
Laceys Spring, Ala. (35754) 195/E1
Laceyville, Pa. (18623) 294/K2
Lac-Frontière, Québec 172/H3
Lac Giao (Ban Me Thuot), Vietnam 72/E4
Lacha (lake), U.S.S.R. 52/E2
La Chapelle, Haiti 158/C5
La Charité-sur-Loire, France 28/E4
La Châtre, France 28/D4
La Chaux-de-Fonds, Switzerland 39/C2
Lachay (pt.), Peru 128/D8
Lachen, Switzerland 39/G2
Lachenaie, Québec 172/D4
Lachine, Mich. (49753) 250/F3
Lachine, Québec 172/H2
Lachlan (range), N.S. Wales 97/C3
Lachlan (riv.), N. W. Wales 88/G6
Lachlan (riv.), N.S. Wales 97/C3
La Chorrera, Colombia 126/D8
La Chorrera, Panama 154/H6
Lac-Humqui, Québec 172/B2
Lachute, Québec 172/C4
La Ciénaga, Dom. Rep. 158/D6
La Ciotat, France 28/F6
Lackawanna, N.Y. (14218) 276/B5
Lackawanna (co.), Pa. 294/L3
Lackawaxen, Pa. (18435) 294/N3
Lackey, Ky. (41643) 237/R6
Lackland A.F.B., Texas 303/J11
Lac La Belle, Wis. (†53066) 317/H1
Lac La Biche, Alberta 182/E2
Lac La Biche, Alta. 162/E5
Lac La Hache, Br. Col. 184/G4
Lac la Martre, N.W. Terrs. 187/G3
La Clarita, Argentina 143/G5
Lac La Ronge Prov. Park, Sask. 181/M3
Laclede, Idaho (83841) 220/B1
La Clede, Ill. (62437) 222/E5
Laclede (co.), Mo. 261/G7
Laclede, Mo. (64651) 261/F3
Lac-Mégantic, Québec 172/G4
Lacolle, Québec 172/D4
La Colmena, Paraguay 144/B5
La Coloma, Cuba 158/B2
La Colonia, Chile 138/D7
Lacomb, Oreg. (†97355) 291/E3
Lacombe, Alberta 182/D3
Lacombe, Alta. 162/E5
Lacombe, La. (70445) 238/L6
Lacon, Ill. (61540) 222/D2
Lacona, Iowa (50139) 229/G6
Lacona, N.Y. (13083) 276/J3
La Concepción, Honduras 154/E3
La Concepción, Panama 154/F6
La Concepción, Venezuela 124/C2
La Concepción, Venezuela 124/B2
La Conception, Québec 172/C3
La Concordia, Mexico 150/N9
Laconia, Ind. (47135) 227/E8
Laconia, N.H. (03246) 268/E4
Laconia, Tenn. (38045) 237/C10
La Conner, Wash. (98257) 310/C2
La Conquista, Nicaragua 154/D5
Lacoochee, Fla. (33537) 212/D3
La Corey, Alberta 182/E2
La Coronilla, Uruguay 145/F4
La Coruña (prov.), Spain 33/B1
La Coruña, Spain 33/B1
La Coruña, Spain 7/D4
La Coste, Texas (78039) 303/J11
La Courneuve, France 28/B1
Lacovia, Jamaica 158/H6
Lac Pelletier, Sask. 181/C6
Lac-Poulin, Québec 172/G3
Lac qui Parle (co.), Minn. 255/B6
Lac qui Parle, Minn. (†56265) 255/B5
Lac qui Parle (lake), Minn. 255/C5
Lac qui Parle (riv.), Minn. 255/B6
Lacre (pt.), Neth. Ant. 161/E9
La Crescent, Minn. (55947) 255/G7
La Crescenta-Montrose, Calif. (91214) 204/C10
La Crete, Alberta 182/B5
La Croche, Québec 172/E2
La Croix (lake), Minn. 255/F2
La Crosse, Fla. (32658) 212/D2
La Crosse, Georgia (†31806) 217/D6
La Crosse, Ind. (46348) 227/D2
La Crosse, Kansas (67548) 232/C3
La Crosse, Va. (23950) 307/M7
Lacrosse, Wash. (99143) 310/H4
La Crosse (co.), Wis. 317/D8
La Crosse, Wis. 146/J5
La Crosse, Wis. 188/H2
La Crosse, Wis. (54601) 317/D8
La Cruz, Argentina 143/E2
La Cruz, Chile 138/F2
La Cruz, Colombia 126/B7
La Cruz, Chihuahua, Mexico 150/G3
La Cruz, Sinaloa, Mexico 150/F5
La Cruz, Nicaragua 154/E4
La Cruz, Uruguay 145/C4
Lac-Saguay, Québec 172/B3
Lac-Saint-Charles, Québec 172/H3
Lac-Sainte-Marie, Québec 172/A4
Lac-Saint-Jean-Est (co.), Québec 172/F1
Lac-Saint-Jean-Est (county), Québec 174/C3
Lac-Saint-Jean-Ouest (co.), Québec 172/E1
Lac-Saint-Jean-Ouest (county), Québec 174/C2
Lac-Saint-Joseph, Québec 172/F3
Lac-Saint-Paul, Québec 172/B3
Lac-Sergent, Québec 172/F3
Lac Seul, Ontario 175/B2
La Cuchilla, Uruguay 145/F3
La Cueva, N. Mex. (†87712) 274/D3
La Cumbre, Argentina 143/C3
La Cure, Switzerland 39/B4
Lacuy (pen.), Chile 138/D4
Lac Vert, Sask. 181/G3
La Cygne, Kansas (66040) 232/H3
Ladakh (reg.), India 68/D2
Ladd, Ill. (61329) 222/D2
Ladder (creek), Kansas 232/A3
Ladder (hills), Scotland 15/E3
Laddonia, Mo. (63352) 261/J4
La Decharge, Québec 172/F1
Ladelle, Ark. (†71655) 202/G7
Ladgasht (Qila Ladgasht), Pakistan 68/A3
Ladhar Bheinn (mt.), Scotland 15/C3
Ladiesburg, Md. (21759) 245/J2
La Digue (isl.), Seychelles 118/J5
Lâdik, Turkey 63/G2
Ladispoli, Italy 34/E6
Ladiz, Iran 66/M6
Ladner, S. Dak. (†57720) 298/B2
Lado, Sudan 111/F6
Ladoga, Ind. (47954) 227/D5
Ladoga (lake), U.S.S.R. 7/H2
Ladoga (lake), U.S.S.R. 48/D3
Ladoga (lake), U.S.S.R. 52/D2
La Dôle (mt.), Switzerland 39/B4
Ladonia, Texas (75449) 303/J4
Ladora, Iowa (52251) 229/J5
La Dorada, Colombia 126/C5
Ladrillero (gulf), Chile 138/C8
Ladrillero (mt.), Chile 138/E10
Ladrillo (pt.), Cuba 158/E3
Ladron (mts.), N. Mex. 274/B4
Ladrones (isls.), Panama 154/F7
Ladson, S.C. (29456) 296/G6
La Due, Mo. (†64735) 261/E6
Ladue, Mo. (†63124) 261/P3
La Durantaye, Québec 172/G3
Lady (pond), Newf. 166/D2
Lady Ann (str.), N.W. Terrs. 187/K2
Ladybank, Scotland 15/E4
Lady Barron, Tasmania 99/E2
Ladybrand, S. Africa 118/D5
Lady Franklin (bay), N.W. Terrs. 187/M1
Lady Franklin (isl.), N.W. Terrs. 187/M3
Lady Lake, Fla. (32659) 212/E3
Lady Lake, Sask. 181/J3
Lady's Island Lake (inlet), Ireland 17/J7
Ladysmith, Br. Col. 184/J3
Ladysmith, S. Africa 102/F7
Ladysmith, S. Africa 118/D5
Ladysmith, Va. (22501) 307/N4
Ladysmith, Wis. (54848) 317/D5
Ladywood, Manitoba 179/F4
Lae, Papua N.G. 85/B7
Lae, Papua N.G. 86/A2
Lae, Papua N.G. 87/E6
Lae, Thailand 72/D3
Laem Chong Phra (cape), Thailand 72/C5
Laem Pho (cape), Thailand 72/D6
Laem Talumphuk (cape), Thailand 72/D5
Laerdal, Norway 18/E6
La Esmeralda, Argentina 143/G5
La Esmeralda, Bolivia 136/D8
La Esmeralda, Venezuela 124/F6
Laesø (isl.), Denmark 18/G8
Laesø (isl.), Denmark 21/D3
La Esperanza, Argentina 143/B7
La Esperanza, Bolivia 136/D4
La Esperanza, Honduras 154/C3
La Esperanza, Venezuela 124/H3
La Estrada, Spain 33/B1
La Estrella, Chile 138/F5
La Estrelleta (prov.), Dom. Rep. 158/C5
La Falda, Argentina 143/D3
La Farge, Wis. (54639) 317/E8
La Fargeville, N.Y. (13656) 276/J2
Lafayette, Ala. (36862) 195/H5
Lafayette (co.), Ark. 202/C7
Lafayette, Calif. (94549) 204/K2
Lafayette, Colo. (80026) 208/K3
Lafayette (co.), Fla. 212/C2
La Fayette, Georgia (30728) 217/B1
La Fayette, Ill. (61449) 222/C2
Lafayette, Ind. 188/J2
Lafayette, Ind. (*47901) 227/D4
La Fayette, Ky. (42254) 237/F7
Lafayette (par.), La. 238/F6
Lafayette, La. (*70501) 238/F6
Lafayette, Minn. (56054) 255/D6
Lafayette (co.), Miss. 256/E2
Lafayette (co.), Mo. 261/E4
Lafayette (mt.), N.H. 268/D3
Lafayette, N.J. (07848) 273/D1
La Fayette, N.Y. (13084) 276/H5
Lafayette, Ohio (45854) 284/C4
Lafayette, Oreg. (97127) 291/A2
La Fayette, R.I. (†02852) 249/H6
Lafayette, Tenn. (37083) 237/J7
Lafayette (co.), Wis. 317/F10
Lafayette-Elliston, Va. (24108) 307/H6
Lafayette Springs, Miss. (38640) 256/F2
Lafe, Ark. (72436) 202/J1
La Fe, Cuba 158/A2
La Feria, Texas (78559) 303/G11
La Ferté-Macé, France 28/C3
Lafferty, Ohio (43951) 284/H5
Lafia, Nigeria 106/F7
Lafiagi, Nigeria 106/F7
Lafitte, La. (70067) 238/K7
La Flèche, France 28/C4
Lafleche, Sask. 181/E6
La Floresta, Uruguay 145/C7
Lafnitz (riv.), Austria 41/D3
La Follette, Tenn. (37766) 237/N8
La Fontaine, Ind. (46940) 227/F3
Lafontaine, Kansas (66750) 232/G4
Lafontaine, Québec 172/C4
Lafourche (par.), La. 238/K7
Lafourche, La. (†70301) 238/J7
Lafourche (bayou), La. 238/K8
La France, S.C. (29656) 296/B2
La Fría, Venezuela 124/B3
Laful, India 68/G7
Lagacéville, New Bruns. 170/E1
La Gallareta, Argentina 143/F5
Lagan (riv.), N. Ireland 17/K2
Lagarfljót (stream), Iceland 21/C1
La Garita, Colo. (†81132) 208/G7
La Garita (mts.), Colo. 208/F7
Lagawe, Philippines 82/C2
Lagayan, Philippines 82/C2
Lage, W. Germany 22/C3
Lågen (riv.), Norway 18/G6
Lages, Brazil 132/D9
Lages, Brazil 120/D5
Laggan, Scotland 15/D3
Laggan, Scotland 10/D2
Laggan (bay), Scotland 15/B5
Laggan, Loch (lake), Scotland 15/D4
Laghouat, Algeria 106/E2
Laghouat, Algeria 102/C1
Laghy, Ireland 17/E2
La Gineta, Spain 33/E3
Lagkadia, Greece 45/E7
La Glace, Alberta 182/A2
La Gloria, Colombia 126/D3
La Gloria, Cuba 158/G2
Lago, Neth. Ant. 161/E10
Lagoa, Portugal 33/B4
Lagoa da Prata, Brazil 135/D2
Lagoa Dourada, Brazil 135/D2
Lago Blanco, Argentina 143/B6
Lagoen, Neth. Ant. 161/F8
La Goleta, Colombia 126/B3
La Gomera, Guatemala 154/B3
Lagonegro, Italy 34/E4
Lagonoy (gulf), Philippines 82/E4
Lagoon (lake), S. Australia 88/F6
Lago Ranco, Chile 138/E3
Lagos (state), Nigeria 106/E7
Lagos (cap.), Nigeria 2/K5
Lagos (cap.), Nigeria 102/C4
Lagos (cap.), Nigeria 106/E7
Lagos, Portugal 33/B4
Lagos de Moreno, Mexico 150/J6
Lagosta (Lastovo) (isl.), Yugoslavia 45/C4
La Goulette (Halq el Oued), Tunisia 106/G1
Lago Verde, Chile 138/E5
La Grand-Combe, France 28/E5
La Grande, Oreg. 188/C1
La Grande, Oreg. (97850) 291/J2
La Grande, Wash. (98348) 310/C4
La Grand Rivière (riv.), Que. 162/J5
La Grange, Ark. (72352) 202/J4
La Grange, Australia 87/C7
La Grange, Calif. (95329) 204/E6
La Grange, Ga. 188/K4
La Grange, Georgia (30240) 217/B4
La Grange, Ill. (60525) 222/B6
Lagrange (co.), Ind. 227/G1
Lagrange, Ind. (46761) 227/F1
La Grange, Ky. (40031) 237/L4
La Grange, Maine (04453) 243/F5
La Grange○, Maine (04453) 243/F5
La Grange, Mo. (63448) 261/K2
La Grange, N.C. (28551) 281/O4
Lagrange, Ohio (44050) 284/F3
La Grange, Tenn. (38046) 237/C10
La Grange, Texas (78945) 303/G8
La Grange, W. Australia 92/C2
Lagrange, Wyo. (82221) 319/H4
La Grange Park, Ill. (60525) 222/B5
La Granja (San Ildefonso), Spain 33/E2
La Gran Sabana (plain), Venezuela 124/G5
La Grita, Venezuela 124/C3
Lagro, Ind. (46941) 227/F3
La Grue (bayou), Ark. 202/H5
La Guadeloupe, Québec 172/F4
La Guaira, Venezuela 124/E2
La Guaira, Venezuela 120/C1
La Guajira (dept.), Colombia 126/D2
La Guardia, Bolivia 136/D5
La Guardia, Spain 33/B2
Laguardia, Spain 33/E1
La Guata, Honduras 154/D3
Laguna (creek), Ariz. 198/E2
Laguna (dam), Ariz. 198/A6
Laguna (res.), Ariz. 198/A6
Laguna, Brazil 132/D10
Laguna (res.), Calif. 204/L11
Laguna, N. Mex. (87026) 274/B3
Laguna (prov.), Philippines 82/C3
Laguna Beach, Calif. (*92651) 204/G10
Laguna de Perlas, Nicaragua 154/F4
Laguna Hills, Calif. (92653) 204/D11
Laguna Niguel, Calif. (92677) 204/H10
Laguna Paiva, Argentina 143/F5
Lagunas, Chile 138/B3
Lagunas, Peru 128/E5
Laguna Yema, Argentina 143/D1
Lagunetas, Venezuela 124/C3
Lagunillas, Bolivia 136/D6
Lagunillas, Chile 138/F3
Lagunillas, Venezuela 124/C2
Lagunitas-Forest Knolls, Calif. (94938) 204/H1
La Habra, Calif. (90631) 204/D11
Lahad Datu, Malaysia 85/F5
Lahaina, Hawaii (96761) 218/H2
Lahaina, Hawaii 188/F5
Laham, Indonesia 85/F5
Lahan, Nong (lake), Thailand 72/D3
La Harpe, Ill. (61450) 222/C3
La Harpe, Kansas (66751) 232/G4
Lahat, Indonesia 85/C6
La Have, Nova Scotia 168/D4
La Have (isl.), Nova Scotia 168/D4
La Have (riv.), Nova Scotia 168/D4
Lahej, P.D.R. Yemen 59/E7
La Higuera, Chile 138/A7
Lahijan, Iran 66/G2
Lahinch, Ireland 17/C6
Lahmansville, W. Va. (26731) 312/H4
Lahn, W. Germany 22/C3
Lahn (riv.), W. Germany 22/C3
Lahnstein, W. Germany 22/B3
Laholm, Sweden 18/H8
Lahoma, Okla. (73754) 288/K2
La Honda, Calif. (94020) 204/J3
Lahontan (res.), Nev. 266/B3
Lahore, Pakistan 59/K3
Lahore, Pakistan 68/C2
Lahore, Pakistan 54/J6
Lahore, Va. (22502) 307/N4
La Horqueta, Venezuela 124/G3
Lahr, W. Germany 22/B4
Lahri, Pakistan 68/B3
Lahti, Finland 7/G2
Lahti, Finland 18/O6
La Huaca, Peru 128/B5
La Huerta, Mexico 150/G7
Laï, Chad 111/C6
Laï, Chad 102/D4
Lai Chau, Vietnam 72/D2
Laidlaw, Br. Col. 184/M3
Laidon, Loch (lake), Scotland 15/D4
Laie, Hawaii (96762) 218/E1
Laie (pt.), Hawaii 218/E1
L'Aigle, France 28/D3
Lai-hka, Burma 72/C2
Laila, Saudi Arabia 59/E5
Lailan, Iraq 66/D3
La Inglesa, Venezuela 124/G3
Laings, Ohio (43752) 284/J6
Laingsburg, Mich. (48848) 250/E6
Lainioälv (riv.), Sweden 18/N3
Lair, Ky. (†41031) 237/N4
Laird, Colo. (80739) 208/P2
Laird, Sask. 181/E3
Lairdsville, Pa. (17742) 294/J3
Lairg, Scotland 10/D1
Lairg, Scotland 15/D2
Lais, Philippines 82/E7
Laisamis, Kenya 115/G3
La Isla, Texas (†79838) 303/A10
Laiwui, Indonesia 85/H6
Laiyang, China 77/K4
Laja (riv.), Chile 138/E1
La Jalca, Peru 128/D6
La Jara, Colo. (81140) 208/H8
La Jara, N. Mex. (87027) 274/B2
Lajas, P. Rico 161/A2
Lajes do Pico, Portugal 33/B1
Lajinha, Brazil 135/F2
La Jolla, Calif. (92037) 204/H11
La Jolla Ind. Res., Calif. 204/J10
Lajord, Sask. 181/G5
La Jose, Pa. (15753) 294/E4
Lajosmizse, Hungary 41/E3
La Joya, Bolivia 136/B5
Lajoya, N. Mex. (87028) 274/C4
La Joya, Peru 128/G11
La Joya, Texas (78560) 303/F11
La Junta, Colo. 188/F3
La Junta, Colo. (81050) 208/M7
Lak Dera (dry riv.), Kenya 115/H3
Lak Dera (dry riv.), Somalia 115/H3
Lake (co.), Calif. 204/C4
Lake (co.), Colo. 208/G4
Lake (co.), Fla. 212/E3
Lake (co.), Ill. 222/E1
Lake (co.), Ind. 227/C2
Lake, Ky. (†40741) 237/O6
Lake (co.), Mich. 250/D5
Lake, Mich. (48632) 250/E5
Lake (co.), Minn. 255/G3
Lake, Miss. (39092) 256/F6
Lake (co.), Mont. 262/B3
Lake (co.), Ohio 284/H2
Lake (co.), Oreg. 291/G5
Lake (creek), Oreg. 291/J3
Lake (co.), S. Dak. 298/P5
Lake (riv.), Tasmania 99/D3
Lake (co.), Tenn. 237/B8
Lake (creek), Utah 304/A5
Lake (creek), Wash. 310/G3
Lake Alfred, Fla. (33850) 212/E3
Lake Alma, Sask. 181/G6
Lake Alpine, Calif. (†95223) 204/F5
Lake Andes, S. Dak. (57356) 298/M7
Lake Ann, Mich. (49650) 250/D4
Lake Ariel, Pa. (18436) 294/M3
Lake Arrowhead, Calif. (92352) 204/H9
Lake Arthur, La. (70549) 238/E6
Lake Arthur, N. Mex. (88253) 274/E5
Lake Arthur, N.S. Wales 97/D4
Lake Barcroft, Va. (†22041) 307/S3
Lake Barrington, Ill. (†60010) 222/A5
Lake Benton, Minn. (56149) 255/B6
Lake Beulah, Wis. (†53120) 317/J2
Lake Bluff, Ill. (60044) 222/B4
Lake Boga, Victoria 97/B4
Lake Bolac, Victoria 97/B5
Lake Bronson, Minn. (56734) 255/B2
Lake Bruce, Ind. (†46939) 227/E2
Lake Buena Vista, Fla. (†32830) 212/E3
Lake Butler, Fla. (32054) 212/D1
Lake Butte Des Morts (Butte Des Morts), Wis. (†54901) 317/J7
Lake Cargelligo, N.S. Wales 97/D3
Lake Carmel, N.Y. (10512) 276/N8
Lake Carroll, Fla. (†33601) 212/C2
Lake Catherine, Ill. (†60002) 222/E1
Lake Charles, La. 188/H4
Lake Charles, La. (*70601) 238/D6
Lake Chelan Nat'l Rec. Area, Wash. 310/E2

Lingshan 399

Leti (isls.), Indonesia 85/H7
Leticia, Colombia 126/F10
Leticia, Colombia 120/B3
L'Etivaz, Switzerland 39/D4
Letka, U.S.S.R. 52/H3
Leto, Fla. (†33614) 212/C2
Letohatchee, Ala. (36047) 195/E6
Leton, La. (†71072) 238/D1
Letona, Ark. (72085) 202/G3
Letong, Indonesia 85/D5
Le Touquet-Paris-Plage, France 28/D2
Letpadan, Burma 72/C3
Le Tréport, France 28/D2
Letsôk-aw Kyun (isl.), Burma 72/C5
Lette, N.S. Wales 97/B4
Letterkenny, Ireland 10/B3
Letterkenny, Ireland 17/F2
Letterkenny Army Depot, Pa. 294/G6
Lettermullan (isl.), Ireland 17/B5
Letts, Ind. (†47240) 227/F6
Letts, Iowa (52754) 229/L6
Lettsworth, La. (70753) 238/G5
Leucadia, Calif. (92024) 204/H10
Leucate (mts.), France 28/E6
Leuchars, Scotland 15/F4
Leuk, Switzerland 39/E4
Leukerbad, Switzerland 39/E4
Leupp, Ariz. (86035) 198/E3
Leurbost, Scotland 15/B2
Leuser (mt.), Indonesia 85/B5
Leuven, Belgium 27/F7
Leuze-en-Hainaut, Belgium 27/D7
Levádhia, Greece 45/F6
Levallois-Perret, France 28/A1
Levan, Utah (84639) 304/C4
Levanger, Norway 18/G5
Levant, Kansas (67743) 232/A2
Levant○, Maine (04456) 243/F6
Levanzo (isl.), Italy 34/D5
Levasy, Mo. (64066) 261/S5
Le Vauclin, Martinique 161/D6
Levee, Ky. (†40337) 237/O5
Level, Md. (†21078) 245/O2
Level Green, Ky. (†40456) 237/N6
Level Land, S.C. (†29655) 296/C3
Levelland, Texas (79336) 303/B4
Levelock, Alaska (99625) 196/G3
Level Plains, Ala. (†36322) 195/G8
Levels, W. Va. (25431) 312/J4
Leven, Scotland 10/E2
Leven, Scotland 15/F4
Leven, Loch (inlet), Scotland 15/D4
Leven (lake), Scotland 15/E4
Leven (riv.), Tasmania 99/B3
Leveque (cape), Australia 87/C7
L'Eveque (cape), N. Zealand 100/D7
Lévêque (cape), W. Australia 88/C3
Lévêque (cape), W. Australia 92/C2
Leverburgh, Scotland 15/B3
Le Verdon-sur-Mer, France 28/C5
Leverett○, Mass. (01054) 249/E3
Levering, Mich. (49755) 250/E3
Leverkusen, W. Germany 22/B3
Levesque, New Bruns. 170/C1
Levice, Czech. 41/E2
Levick (mt.) 5/B8
Levie, France 28/B7
Le Vigan, France 28/E5
Levin, N. Zealand 100/E4
Lévis (co.), Québec 172/J3
Lévis, Québec 172/J3
Lévis, Québec 174/C3
Levisa Fork (riv.), Va. 307/C5
Levítha (isl.), Greece 45/H7
Levittown, N.Y. (11756) 276/R7
Levittown, Pa. (*19053) 294/N5
Levittown, P. Rico 161/D1
Levkás, Greece 45/E6
Levkás (isl.), Greece 45/E6
Levoča, Czech. 41/F2
Lévrier (bay), Mauritania 106/A4
Levuka, Fiji 87/H7
Levukaa, Fiji 86/Q10
Levy (co.), Fla. 212/D2
Levy (lake), Fla. 212/D2
Levy, N. Mex. (†87752) 274/E2
Lewe, Burma 72/B3
Lewellen, Nebr. (69147) 264/B3
Lewes, Del. (19958) 245/T5
Lewes, England 13/H7
Lewes, England 10/G5
Lewis, Colo. (81327) 208/B8
Lewis (isl.), Fla. 212/B3
Lewis (co.), Idaho 220/B3
Lewis, Ind. (47858) 227/C6
Lewis, Iowa (51544) 229/C6
Lewis, Kansas (67552) 232/C4
Lewis (co.), Ky. 237/P3
Lewis, Manitoba 179/F5
Lewis (lake), Manitoba 179/G2
Lewis (co.), Mo. 261/J2
Lewis, Mo. (†64735) 261/E6
Lewis (range), Mont. 262/C2
Lewis (co.), N.Y. 276/K3
Lewis, N.Y. (12950) 276/N2
Lewis (dist.), Scotland 15/B2
Lewis (dist.), Scotland 10/C1
Lewis, Butt of (prom.), Scotland 15/B2
Lewis, Butt of (prom.), Scotland 10/C1
Lewis, S.C. (†29706) 296/E2
Lewis (co.), Tenn. 237/F9
Lewis (creek), Vt. 268/A3
Lewis (co.), Wash. 310/C4
Lewis (riv.), Wash. 310/C5
Lewis (co.), W. Va. 312/E4
Lewis, Wis. (54851) 317/B4
Lewis (lake), Wyo. 319/B1
Lewis and Clark (co.), Mont. 262/D3
Lewis and Clark (lake), Nebr. 264/G2
Lewis and Clark (lake), S. Dak. 298/O8
Lewis and Clark Village, Mo. (†64484) 261/C3
Lewisberry, Pa. (17339) 294/J5
Lewisburg, Ky. (42256) 237/G6
Lewisburg, La. (†70525) 238/F6
Lewisburg, Ohio (45338) 284/A6
Lewisburg, Pa. (17837) 294/J4
Lewisburg, Tenn. (37091) 237/H10
Lewisburg, W. Va. (24901) 312/E7
Lewis Center, Ohio (43035) 284/D5
Lewis Creek, Ind. (†47234) 227/F6
Lewisetta, Va. (22505) 307/R4
Lewisham, England 10/B5
Lewisham, England 13/H8
Lewis Hill (mt.), Newf. 166/C4
Lewisport, Ky. (42351) 237/H5
Lewisporte, Newf. 166/C4
Lewis Run, Pa. (16738) 294/E2
Lewis Smith (dam), Ala. 195/D3
Lewis Smith (lake), Ala. 195/D2
Lewiston, Calif. (96052) 204/C3
Lewiston, Idaho 188/C1
Lewiston, Idaho (83501) 220/A3
Lewiston, Maine 188/N2
Lewiston, Maine (04240) 243/C7
Lewiston, Mich. (49756) 250/E4
Lewiston, Minn. (55952) 255/G7
Lewiston, Nebr. (68380) 264/H4
Lewiston, N.Y. (14092) 276/B4
Lewiston, N.C. (27849) 281/P2
Lewiston, Utah (84320) 304/C2
Lewiston, Vt. (†05055) 268/C4
Lewistown, Ill. (61542) 222/C3
Lewistown, Md. (21701) 245/J2
Lewistown, Mo. (63452) 261/J2
Lewistown, Mont. (59457) 262/G3
Lewistown, Ohio (43333) 284/C5
Lewistown, Pa. (17044) 294/G4
Lewisville, Ark. (71845) 202/C7
Lewisville, Idaho (83431) 220/F6
Lewisville, Ind. (47352) 227/G5
Lewisville, Minn. (56060) 255/D7
Lewisville, Ohio (43754) 284/H6
Lewisville (Ulysses), Pa. (16948) 294/G2
Lewisville, Pa. (19351) 294/L6
Lewisville, Texas (*75067) 303/G1
Lewisville (lake), Texas 303/G1
Lewvan, Sask. 181/H5
Lexa, Ark. (72355) 202/J4
Lexie, Miss. (†39667) 256/D8
Lexington, Ala. (35648) 195/D1
Lexington, Ark. (†72153) 202/F2
Lexington, Georgia (30648) 217/F3
Lexington, Ill. (61753) 222/E3
Lexington, Ind. (47138) 227/F7
Lexington, Ky. (*40501) 237/N4
Lexington, Ky. 146/K6
Lexington, Ky. 188/K3
Lexington○, Mass. (02173) 249/B6
Lexington, Mich. (48450) 250/G5
Lexington, Minn. (†55014) 255/G5
Lexington, Miss. (39095) 256/D4
Lexington, Mo. (64067) 261/E4
Lexington, Nebr. (68850) 264/E4
Lexington, N.Y. (12452) 276/M6
Lexington, N.C. (27292) 281/J3
Lexington, Ohio (44904) 284/E4
Lexington, Okla. (73051) 288/M4
Lexington, Oreg. (97839) 291/H2
Lexington (co.), S.C. 296/E4
Lexington, S.C. (29072) 296/E4
Lexington, Tenn. (38351) 237/E9
Lexington, Texas (78947) 303/G7
Lexington (I.C.), Va. (24450) 307/J5
Lexington Blue Grass Army Depot, Ky. 237/N5
Lexington Park, Md. (20653) 245/M7
Lexsy, Georgia (†30401) 217/H6
Leyba, N. Mex. (87542) 274/D3
Leyburn, England 13/F3
Leyden○, Mass. (†01301) 249/D2
Leye, China 77/G7
Leyland, England 13/G1
Leyland, England 10/F1
Leyond (riv.), Manitoba 179/F3
Leysin, Switzerland 39/C4
Leyte (prov.), Philippines 82/E5
Leyte (isl.), Philippines 54/O8
Leyte (gulf), Philippines 82/E5
Leyte (isl.), Philippines 85/H3
Leyte (isl.), Philippines 82/E5
Lezajsk, Poland 47/F3
Lezama, Argentina 143/H7
Lézarde (riv.), Martinique 161/D6
Lezhë, Albania 45/D5
Lézignan-Corbières, France 28/E6
Lezuza, Spain 33/E3
L'gov, U.S.S.R. 52/E4
Lhanbryde, Scotland 15/E3
Lhari, China 77/D5
Lhasa, China 77/D6
Lhasa, China 2/P4
Lhasa, China 54/L7
Lhazê (Lhatse), China 77/C6
Lhazhong, China 77/C5
Lhokseumawe, Indonesia 85/B4
Lhorong, China 77/E5
Lhozhag, China 77/D6
Lhünzê, China 77/D6
Lhünzhub, China 77/D5
Liancheng, China 77/J6
Lianga, Philippines 82/E6
Lianga (bay), Philippines 82/F6
Lianping, China 77/H7
Lian Xian, China 77/H7
Lianyungang (Lienyünkang), China 77/J5
Lianyunggang, China 54/N6
Liao (riv.), China 54/O5
Liaodong Bandao (pen.), China 77/K3
Liao He (riv.), China 77/K3
Liaoning (prov.), China 77/K3
Liaoyang, China 77/K3
Liaoyuan, China 77/K3
Liard (riv.) 162/D3
Liard (riv.), Br. Col. 184/L2
Liard (riv.), Canada 146/F3
Liard (riv.), N.W. Terrs. 187/F4
Liard (riv.), Yukon 187/E3
Liard River, Br. Col. 184/L2
Libáň, Czech. 41/C1
Libano, Colombia 126/C5
Libau, Manitoba 179/F4
Libby, Minn. (†55760) 255/E4
Libby, Mont. (59923) 262/A2
Libenge, Zaire 115/C3
Liberal, Kansas (67901) 232/B4
Liberal, Mo. (64762) 261/D7
Liberal, Oreg. (†97042) 291/B3
Liberdade, Brazil 135/D3
Liberec, Czech. 41/C1
Liberia 2/J5
Liberia 102/B4
LIBERIA 106/C7
Liberia, C. Rica 154/E5
Liberta, Ant. & Bar. 161/E11
Libertad, Belize 154/C1
Libertad, Uruguay 145/C5
Libertad, Barinas, Venezuela 124/D3
Libertad, Cojedes, Venezuela 124/D3
Liberty, Ariz. (†85326) 198/C5
Liberty (co.), Fla. 212/B1
Liberty (co.), Georgia 217/J7
Liberty, Ill. (62347) 222/B4
Liberty, Ind. (47353) 227/H5
Liberty, Kansas (67351) 232/G4
Liberty, Ky. (42539) 237/M6
Liberty, Maine (04949) 243/E7
Liberty○, Maine (04949) 243/E7
Liberty (lake), Md. 245/L3
Liberty, Miss. (39645) 256/C8
Liberty, Mo. (64068) 261/R5
Liberty (co.), Mont. 262/E2
Liberty, Nebr. (68381) 264/H4
Liberty (mt.), N.H. 268/D3
Liberty, N.Y. (12754) 276/L7
Liberty, N.C. (27298) 281/K3
Liberty, Pa. (16930) 294/H2
Liberty, Pa. (†15100) 294/C7
Liberty, Sask. 181/F4
Liberty, S.C. (29657) 296/B2
Liberty, Tenn. (37095) 237/K8
Liberty (co.), Texas 303/K7
Liberty, Texas (77575) 303/K7
Liberty, Wash. (†98922) 310/E3
Liberty, W. Va. (25124) 312/C5
Liberty Center, Ind. (46766) 227/G3
Liberty Center, Iowa (50145) 229/F6
Liberty Center, Ohio (43532) 284/B3
Liberty Corner, N.J. (07938) 273/D2
Liberty Grove, Md. (†21918) 245/O2
Liberty Hill, Conn. (†06249) 210/G2
Liberty Hill, La. (†71008) 238/E2
Liberty Hill, S.C. (29074) 296/F3
Liberty Lake, Wash. (99019) 310/J3
Liberty Mills, Ind. (46946) 227/F2
Liberty Pole, Wis. (†54665) 317/D8
Libertytown, Md. (21762) 245/J3
Libertyville, Ala. (†36420) 195/F8
Libertyville, Ill. (60048) 222/B4
Libertyville, Iowa (52567) 229/K7
Libiaz, Poland 47/D3
Libin, Belgium 27/G9
Libochovice, Czech. 41/B1
Libon, Philippines 82/D4
Libong, Ko (isl.), Thailand 72/C6
Libourne, France 28/C5
Libramont-Chevigny, Belgium 27/G9
Library, Pa. (15129) 294/B7
Libres, Mexico 150/O1
Libreville (cap.), Gabon 2/K6
Libreville (cap.), Gabon 115/A3
Libreville (cap.), Gabon 102/C4
Libuse, La. (71348) 238/F4
Libya 2/K4
Libya 102/D2
LIBYA 111/B2
Libyan (des.) 102/E2
Libyan (des.), Egypt 111/E2
Libyan (plat.), Egypt 111/E1
Libyan (des.), Libya 111/D2
Libyan (plat.), Libya 111/D1
Libyan (des.), Sudan 111/E3
Licancábur, Cerro (mt.), Chile 138/B4
Licantén, Chile 138/A10
Licata, Italy 34/D6
Lice, Turkey 63/J3
Lichfield, England 13/F5
Lichfield, England 10/G2
Lichinga, Mozambique 102/F6
Lichinga, Mozambique 118/F2
Lichtenberg, E. Germany 22/F4
Lichtenfels, W. Germany 22/D3
Lichtenrade, W. Germany 22/F4
Lichterfelde, W. Germany 22/E4
Lichtervelde, Belgium 27/C6
Lick (creek), Tenn. 237/R8
Lick Creek, Ill. (†62912) 222/D6
Licking, North Fork (riv.), Ky. 237/O3
Licking, South Fork (riv.), Ky. 237/N3
Licking (riv.), Ky. 237/N3
Licking, Mo. (65542) 261/J8
Licking (co.), Ohio 284/F5
Licking (riv.), Ohio 284/F5
Licking (creek), Pa. 294/F6
Licosa (cape), Italy 34/E4
Lida, Ky. (†40741) 237/O6
Lida (lake), Minn. 255/C4
Lida, U.S.S.R. 52/C4
Lidcombe, N.S. Wales 97/J3
Liddel Water (riv.), Scotland 15/F5
Lidderdale, Iowa (51452) 229/D4
Liddes, Switzerland 39/D5
Liddon (gulf), N.W. Terrs. 187/G4
Lidgerwood, N. Dak. (58053) 282/R7
Lidice, Czech. 41/C1
Lidingö, Sweden 18/H1
Lidköping, Sweden 18/H7
Lido di Ostia, Italy 34/F7
Lido di Venezia, Italy 34/D2
Lidzbark, Poland 47/D2
Lidzbark Warmiński, Poland 47/E1
Liebenthal, Kansas (67553) 232/C3
Liebenthal, Sask. 181/B5
Liechtensteig, Switzerland 39/H2
Liechtenstein 7/F4
LIECHTENSTEIN 39/J2
Liedekerke, Belgium 27/D7
Liége (riv.), Alberta 182/D1
Liège (prov.), Belgium 27/H7
Liège, Belgium 7/E3
Liège, Belgium 27/H7
Liegnitz (Legnica), Poland 47/C3
Lieksa, Finland 18/R5
Lienyünkang (Lianyungang), China 77/J5
Lienz, Austria 41/B3
Liepāja, U.S.S.R. 7/F3
Liepāja, U.S.S.R. 53/A2
Liepāja, U.S.S.R. 48/B4
Liepāja, U.S.S.R. 52/B3
Lier, Belgium 27/F6
Lierneux, Belgium 27/H8
Lierre (Lier), Belgium 27/F6
Liestal, Switzerland 39/E2
Liévin, France 28/E2
Lièvre (riv.), Québec 172/B4
Lièvres (isl.), Québec 172/H2
Liezen, Austria 41/C3
Liffey (riv.), Ireland 17/H5
Liffey (riv.), Ireland 10/C4
Lifford, Ireland 10/C3
Lifford, Ireland 17/F2
Lifu (isl.), New Caled. 87/G8
Lifu (isl.), New Caled. 86/H4
Ligao, Philippines 82/D4
Ligatne, U.S.S.R. 53/C2
Liggett, Ky. (†40831) 237/P7
Lightfoot, Va. (23090) 307/P6
Lighthouse (pt.), Fla. 212/B2
Light House (pt.), Mich. 250/D3
Lighthouse Point, Fla. (33064) 212/F5
Lightning (creek), Oreg. 291/L2
Lightning (creek), Wyo. 319/G2
Lightning Ridge, N.S. Wales 97/E1
Lightsville, Ohio (†45362) 284/A5
Lignite, N. Dak. (58752) 282/F2
Ligon, Ky. (41646) 237/R6
Ligonha (riv.), Mozambique 118/F3
Ligonier, Ind. (46767) 227/F2
Ligonier, Pa. (15658) 294/D5
Liguria (reg.), Italy 34/B2
Ligurian (sea), Italy 34/B3
Lihir Group (isls.), Papua N.G. 86/C1
Lihou (cays), Coral Sea Is. Terr. 88/J3
Lihue, Hawaii (96766) 218/C2
Lihue, Hawaii 188/E5
Lihula, U.S.S.R. 53/C1
Lijiang, China 77/F6
Likasi, Panda-, Zaire 115/E6
Likati, Zaire 115/D3
Likely, Br. Col. 184/G4
Likely, Calif. (96116) 204/E2
Likhoslavl', U.S.S.R. 52/E3
Likouala (riv.), Congo 115/C3
Lila (lake), N.Y. 276/L2
Lilac, Sask. 181/D3
Lilbourn, Mo. (63862) 261/N9
Lilburn, Georgia (30247) 217/D3
Lileah, Tasmania 99/B2
L'Île-Rousse, France 28/B6
Liles (pt.), Chile 138/F2
Lilesville, N.C. (28091) 281/K5
Lilienfeld, Austria 41/C3
Lille, France 7/E3
Lille, France 28/E2
Lille, Maine (04749) 243/G1
Lilleå (riv.), Denmark 21/B5
Lille Baelt (chan.), Denmark 21/C7
Lillehammer, Norway 18/F6
Lillesand, Norway 18/F7
Lillestrøm, Norway 18/E3
Lillian, Ala. (36549) 195/D10
Lillie, La. (71256) 238/E1
Lilliesleaf, Scotland 15/F5
Lillington, N.C. (27546) 281/M4
Lillinonah (lake), Conn. 210/B3
Lilliwaup, Wash. (98555) 310/B3
Lillo, Spain 33/E3
Lillooet, Br. Col. 162/D5
Lillooet, Br. Col. 184/G5
Lillooet (riv.), Br. Col. 184/F5
Lilly, Georgia (31051) 217/E6
Lilly, Ill. (†61755) 222/D3
Lilly, Pa. (15938) 294/E5
Lilly Chapel, Ohio (†43162) 284/D6
Lillydale, Victoria 97/J4
Lilongwe (cap.), Malawi 2/L6
Lilongwe (cap.), Malawi 102/F6
Lilongwe (cap.), Malawi 115/F6
Liloy, Philippines 82/D6
Lily, Ky. (40740) 237/N6
Lily, S. Dak. (57250) 298/O3
Lily, Wis. (54445) 317/J5
Lilydale, Minn. (†55050) 255/G5
Lily Dale, N.Y. (14752) 276/B6
Lilydale, Tasmania 99/D3
Lily Plain, Sask. 181/E2
Lim (fjord), Denmark 18/E8
Lim (riv.), Yugoslavia 45/D4
Lima, Ill. (62348) 222/B3
Lima (isls.), Indonesia 85/F7
Lima, Pulau (isl.), Malaysia 72/F6
Lima, Mont. (59739) 262/D6
Lima (res.), Mont. 262/D6
Lima, N.Y. (14485) 276/E5
Lima, Ohio (*45801) 284/B4
Lima, Ohio 188/K2
Lima (New Lima), Okla. (†74858) 288/D4
Lima, Paraguay 144/D3
Lima, Pa. (†19037) 294/L7
Lima (dept.), Peru 128/D8
Lima (cap.), Peru 2/F6
Lima (cap.), Peru 120/B4
Lima (cap.), Peru 128/D8
Lima (riv.), Portugal 33/B2
Lima (pt.), P. Rico 161/F2
Lima Center, Wis. (†53190) 317/J10
Limache, Chile 138/F2
Lima Duarte, Brazil 135/E2
Limal, Bolivia 136/C8
Limanowa, Poland 47/E4
Limarí (riv.), Chile 138/A8
Limasawa (isl.), Philippines 82/E6
Limassol, Cyprus 59/B3
Limassol, Cyprus 63/E5
Limavady (dist.), N. Ireland 17/H1
Limavady, N. Ireland 10/C3
Limavady, N. Ireland 17/H1
Limaville, Ohio (44640) 284/H4
Limay (riv.), Argentina 120/C6
Limay (riv.), Argentina 143/C4
Limbach-Oberfrohna, E. Germany 22/E3
Limbani, Peru 128/H10
Limbaži, U.S.S.R. 53/C2
Limbé, Haiti 158/C5
Limbourg, Belgium 27/J7
Limbunya, North. Terr. 93/B4
Limburg (prov.), Belgium 27/G7
Limburg (Limbourg), Belgium 27/J7
Limburg (prov.), Netherlands 27/H6
Limburg an der Lahn, W. Germany 22/C3
Lime, Oreg. (†97907) 291/K3
Limedsforsen, Sweden 18/H6
Limeira, Brazil 132/E8
Limeira, Brazil 135/C3
Lime Kiln, Md. (†21701) 245/J3
Limekilns, Scotland 15/D1
Limenária, Greece 45/G5
Limerick (co.), Ireland 17/D7
Limerick, Ireland 17/D6
Limerick, Ireland 10/B4
Limerick, Ireland 7/D3
Limerick○, Maine (04048) 243/B8
Limerick, Sask. 181/E6
Limeridge, Wis. (53942) 317/F9
Lime Rock, Conn. (†06039) 210/B1
Lime Springs, Iowa (52155) 229/J2
Limestone (co.), Ala. 195/E1
Limestone, Ark. (72628) 202/D2
Limestone, Fla. (†33865) 212/E4
Limestone, Maine (04750) 243/H2
Limestone○, Maine (04750) 243/H2
Limestone, Mont. (†59028) 262/F5
Limestone, N.Y. (14753) 276/C6
Limestone, Tenn. (37681) 237/R8
Limestone (co.), Texas 303/H6
Lime Village, Alaska (†99673) 196/G2
Limfjorden (fjord), Denmark 21/D4
Limfjorden (fjord), Denmark 21/A4
Limington, Maine (04049) 243/B8
Limington○, Maine (04049) 243/B8
Limmat (riv.), Switzerland 39/F2
Limmen (bight), North. Terr. 88/F2
Limmen (bight), North. Terr. 93/D3
Limmen Bight (riv.), North. Terr. 88/F3
Limmen Bight (riv.), North. Terr. 93/D4
Límni, Greece 45/F6
Límnos (isl.), Greece 45/G6
Limoeiro, Brazil 132/H4
Limoeiro do Norte, Brazil 132/G4
Limoges, France 7/E4
Limoges, France 28/D5
Limoges, Ontario 177/J2
Limon, Colo. (80828) 208/M4
Limón, C. Rica 146/K8
Limón, C. Rica 154/F6
Limón, Honduras 154/E3
Limonade, Haiti 158/C5
Limonar, Cuba 158/D1
Limoquije, Bolivia 136/C4
Limousin (trad. prov.), France, 29
Limousin (reg.), France 28/D5
Limoux, France 28/E6
Limpio, Paraguay 144/B4
Limpopo (riv.) 102/E7
Limpopo (riv.), Botswana 118/D4
Limpopo (riv.), Mozambique 118/E4
Limpopo (riv.), S. Africa 118/D4
Lim Rock, Ala. (†35776) 195/F1
Linapacan (isl.), Philippines 82/B5
Linapacan (str.), Philippines 82/B5
Linard (peak), Switzerland 39/K3
Linares, Chile 138/A11
Linares, Chile 120/B6
Linares, Mexico 150/K4
Linares, Spain 33/E3
Linares, Spain 7/D5
Linaria, Alberta 182/C2
Lincang, China 77/E7
Linch, Wyo. (82640) 319/F2
Linckiaen, N.Y. (†13052) 276/J5
Lincoln (sea) 146/M1
Lincoln (sea) 4/A12
Lincoln, Ala. (35096) 195/F3
Lincoln, Argentina 143/F7
Lincoln (co.), Ark. 202/G6
Lincoln, Ark. (72744) 202/B2
Lincoln, Calif. (95648) 204/B8
Lincoln (isl.), China 85/E2
Lincoln (co.), Colo. 208/M5
Lincoln (mt.), Colo. 208/G4
Lincoln, Del. (19960) 245/S5
Lincoln, England 13/G4
Lincoln, England 10/F4
Lincoln (co.), Georgia 217/H3
Lincoln (co.), Idaho 220/D6
Lincoln, Ill. (62656) 222/D3
Lincoln, Ind. (†46994) 227/E3
Lincoln, Iowa (50652) 229/H4
Lincoln (co.), Kansas 232/D2
Lincoln, Kansas (67455) 232/D2
Lincoln (co.), Ky. 237/M6
Lincoln (par.), La. 238/E1
Lincoln (co.), Maine 243/D7
Lincoln, Maine (04457) 243/G5
Lincoln○, Maine (04457) 243/G5
Lincoln○, Mass. (01773) 249/B6
Lincoln, Mich. (48742) 250/F4
Lincoln (co.), Minn. 255/B6
Lincoln (co.), Miss. 256/D8
Lincoln (co.), Mo. 261/L4
Lincoln, Mo. (65338) 261/E6
Lincoln (co.), Mont. 262/A2
Lincoln, Mont. (59639) 262/D4
Lincoln (co.), Nebr. 264/D4
Lincoln (cap.), Nebr. 146/J5
Lincoln (cap.), Nebr. 188/G2
Lincoln (cap.), Nebr. (*68501) 264/H4
Lincoln (co.), Nev. 266/F5
Lincoln○, N.H. (03251) 268/D3
Lincoln (mt.), N.H. 268/D3
Lincoln (co.), N. Mex. 274/D5
Lincoln, N. Mex. (88338) 274/D5
Lincoln (co.), N.C. 281/G3
Lincoln, N. Dak. (†58501) 282/J6
Lincoln (sea), N.W. Terrs. 187/M1
Lincoln (co.), Okla. 288/N3
Lincoln, Ontario 177/E4
Lincoln (co.), Oreg. 291/D3
Lincoln, Pa. (†15037) 294/C7
Lincoln (co.), S. Dak. 298/R7
Lincoln (co.), Tenn. 237/H10
Lincoln, Texas (78948) 303/H7
Lincoln (creek), Utah 30r/C2
Lincoln○, Vt. (†05443) 268/B3
Lincoln (co.), Wash. 310/G3
Lincoln, Wash. (99147) 310/G3
Lincoln (co.), W. Va. 312/B6
Lincoln (co.), Wis. 317/G5
Lincoln (co.), Wyo. 319/B3
Lincoln Beach, Oreg. (†97341) 291/C3
Lincoln Boyhood Nat'l Mem., Ind. 227/C8
Lincoln Center, Maine (04458) 243/G5
Lincoln Center, Mass. (01773) 249/B6
Lincoln City, Ind. (47552) 227/C8
Lincoln City, Oreg. (97367) 291/C3
Lincoln Gap (pass), Vt. 268/B3
Lincoln Heights, Ohio (†45201) 284/C9
Lincolnia, Va. (†22313) 307/S3
Lincoln Park, Colo. (†81212) 208/J6
Lincoln Park, Georgia (†30286) 217/D5
Lincoln Park, Mich. (48146) 250/B7
Lincoln Park, N.J. (07035) 273/A1
Lincolnshire (co.), England 13/G4
Lincolnshire, Ill. (†60015) 222/B5
Lincolnton, Georgia (30817) 217/G3
Lincolnton, N.C. (28092) 281/G4
Lincoln University, Pa. (19352) 294/L6
Lincolnville, Ind. (†46992) 227/F3
Lincolnville, Kansas (66858) 232/F3
Lincolnville, Maine (04849) 243/E7
Lincolnville○, Maine (04849) 243/E7
Lincolnville, Nova Scotia 168/G3
Lincolnville, S.C. (†29483) 296/G6
Lincolnville Center, Maine (04850) 243/E7
Lincoln Wolds (hills), England 13/G4
Lincolnwood, Ill. (†60645) 222/B5
Lincroft, N.J. (07738) 273/E3
L'Incudine (mt.), France 28/B7
Lind, Wash. (99341) 310/G4
Linda, Calif. (†95901) 204/D4
Lindale, Alberta 182/C3
Lindale, Georgia (30147) 217/B2
Lindale, Texas (75771) 303/J5
Lindau, W. Germany 22/C5
Lindberg, Alberta 182/E3
Linden, Ala. (36748) 195/C6
Linden, Alberta 182/D4
Linden, Ariz. (†85901) 198/E4
Linden, Calif. (95236) 204/D5
Linden, Guyana 131/L2
Linden, Ind. (47955) 227/D4
Linden, Iowa (50146) 229/E5
Linden, Mich. (48451) 250/F6
Linden, N.J. (07036) 273/A3
Linden, N.C. (28356) 281/M4
Linden (mts.), Switzerland 39/F2
Linden, Tenn. (37096) 237/F9
Linden, Texas (75563) 303/K4
Linden, Va. (22642) 307/M3
Linden, W. Va. (25256) 312/D5
Linden, Wis. (53553) 317/F10
Linden Beach, Ontario 177/B6
Lindenhurst, Ill. (†60046) 222/B4
Lindenhurst, N.Y. (11757) 276/O9
Lindenwold, N.J. (08021) 273/B4
Lindenwood, Ill. (61049) 222/D1
Lindesberg, Sweden 18/J7
Lindesnes (cape), Norway 7/E3
Lindesnes (cape), Norway 18/E8
Lindi (reg.), Tanzania 115/G5
Lindi, Tanzania 102/F5
Lindi, Tanzania 115/G5
Lindi (riv.), Zaire 115/E3
Lindisfarne (Holy) (dist.), England 13/F2
Lindisfarne (Holy) (isl.), England 10/F3
Lindley, N.Y. (14858) 276/F6
Lindon, Colo. (80740) 208/N3
Lindon, Utah (†84062) 304/C3
Líndos, Greece 45/J7
Lindrith, N. Mex. (87029) 274/C2
Lindsay, Calif. (93247) 204/F7
Lindsay, La. (†70748) 238/H5
Lindsay, Mont. (59339) 262/L3
Lindsay, Nebr. (68644) 264/G3
Lindsay, Okla. (73052) 288/L5
Lindsay, Ontario 177/F3
Lindsborg, Kansas (67456) 232/E3
Lindsey, Ohio (43442) 284/D3
Lindsey, Wis. (†54449) 317/F6
Lindside, W. Va. (24951) 312/E8
Lindstrom, Minn. (55045) 255/F5
Line (isls.) 2/B6
Line (isls.), Pacific 87/K5
Lineboro, Md. (21088) 245/L2
Linesville, Pa. (16424) 294/A2
Lineville, Ala. (36266) 195/G4
Lineville, Iowa (50147) 229/G7
Linfen, China 77/H4
Linfield, Pa. (19468) 294/L5
Linganore (creek), Md. 245/J3
Lingao, China 77/G8
Lingayen, Philippines 85/F2
Lingayen, Philippines 82/C2
Lingayen (gulf), Philippines 82/C2
Lingen, W. Germany 22/B2
Lingga (arch.), Indonesia 85/D5
Lingga (isl.), Indonesia 85/D6
Lingle, Wyo. (82223) 319/H3
Linglestown, Pa. (17112) 294/J5
Lingling, China 77/H6
Lingo, N. Mex. (88123) 274/F5
Lingqui, China 77/H6
Lingshan, China 77/G7

402 Lost

Lost (riv.), Ind. 227/D7
Lost (riv.), Minn. 255/C3
Lost (riv.), Oreg. 291/F5
Lost (creek), Utah 304/C5
Lostallo, Switzerland 39/H4
Lostant, Ill. (61334) 222/D2
Los Taques, Venezuela 124/C2
Lost Cabin, Wyo. (†82642) 319/E2
Lost City, W. Va. (26810) 312/J5
Lost Creek, Ky. (41348) 237/P6
Lost Creek, Wash. (†99180) 310/H2
Lost Creek, W. Va. (26385) 312/F4
Los Teques, Venezuela 120/C2
Los Teques, Venezuela 124/E2
Los Testigos (isls.), Venezuela 124/G2
Lost Hills, Calif. (93249) 204/F8
Lostine, Oreg. (97857) 291/K2
Lost Island (lake), Iowa 229/D2
Lost Nation, Iowa (52254) 229/M5
Lost River, Idaho (†83255) 220/E6
Lost River (range), Idaho 220/E5
Lost River, W. Va. (26811) 312/J5
Lost Springs, Kansas (66859) 232/E3
Lost Springs, Wyo. (82224) 319/G3
Lost Trail (pass), Idaho 220/E4
Lost Trail (pass), Mont. 262/B5
Lostwood, N. Dak. (†58784) 282/F3
Los Vilos, Chile 138/A9
Los Yébenes, Spain 33/E3
Lot (dept.), France 28/D5
Lot (riv.), France 28/D5
Lota, Chile 138/D1
Lotagipi Swamp (plain), Sudan 111/F6
Lotbinière (co.), Québec 172/F3
Lotbinière, Québec 172/F3
Lot-et-Garonne (dept.), France 28/D5
Lothair, Ky. (†41701) 237/P6
Lothair, Mont. (59461) 262/E2
Lothian, Md. (20820) 245/M5
Lothian (reg.), Scotland 15/E5
Lothain (trad. co.), Scotland 15/A5
Loto, Zaire 115/D4
Lötschberg (tunnel), Switzerland 39/E4
Lotsee, Okla. (†74063) 288/O2
Lott, Texas (76656) 303/H6
Lottie, Ala. (†36552) 195/C8
Lottie, La. (70756) 238/G5
Lottsville, Pa. (†16402) 294/D2
Lotus, Calif. (95651) 204/C8
Lotzwil, Switzerland 39/E2
Louang Namtha, Laos 72/D2
Louangphrabang, Laos 72/D3
Louangphrabang, Laos 54/M7
Louann, Ark. (71751) 202/E7
Loubomo, Congo 115/B4
Loubomo, Congo 102/D5
Loudéac, France 28/B3
Loudima, Congo 115/B4
Loudon○, N.H. (03301) 268/E5
Loudon (co.), Tenn. 237/N9
Loudon, Tenn. (37774) 237/N9
Loudonville, Ohio (44842) 284/F4
Loudoun (co.), Va. 307/N2
Loudun, France 28/D4
Louellen, Ky. (40853) 237/P7
Louga, Senegal 106/A5
Loughborough, England 13/F5
Loughborough, England 10/F4
Loughbrickland, N. Ireland 17/J3
Lougheed, Alberta 182/E3
Lougheed (isl.), N.W. Terrs. 187/H2
Loughman, Fla. (33858) 212/E3
Loughrea, Ireland 17/E5
Loughrea, Ireland 10/B4
Loughros More (bay), Ireland 17/D2
Louin, Miss. (39338) 256/F6
Louisa (co.), Iowa 229/L6
Louisa, Ky. (41230) 237/R4
Louisa, La. (†70538) 238/G7
Louisa (lake), Ontario 177/F2
Louisa (co.), Va. 307/N5
Louisa, Va. (23093) 307/M4
Louisbourg, Nova Scotia 168/J3
Louisbourg Nat'l Hist. Park, Nova Scotia 168/J3
Louisburg, Kansas (66053) 232/H3
Louisburg, Minn. (56254) 255/B5
Louisburg, Mo. (65685) 261/F7
Louisburg, N.C. (27549) 281/N2
Louisburgh, Ireland 17/B4
Louis Creek, Br. Col. 184/H4
Louisdale, Nova Scotia 168/G3
Louise (isl.), Alaska 196/C1
Louise (isl.), Br. Col. 184/B4
Louise, Miss. (39097) 256/C5
Louise (lake), Québec 172/C4
Louise, Texas (77455) 303/H8
Louiseville, Québec 172/E3
Louisiade (arch.), Papua N.G. 87/F7
Louisiade (arch.), Papua N.G. 85/D8
Louisiana 188/H4
LOUISIANA 238
Louisiana (pt.), La. 238/C7
Louisiana, Mo. (63353) 261/K4
Louisiana (state), U.S. 146/J6
Louis Trichardt, S. Africa 118/E4
Louisville, Ala. (36048) 195/G7
Louisville, Colo. (80027) 208/J3
Louisville, Georgia (30434) 217/H4
Louisville, Ill. (62858) 222/E5
Louisville, Kansas (66450) 232/F2
Louisville, Ky. (*40201) 237/J2
Louisville, Ky. 146/K6
Louisville, Miss. (39339) 256/G4
Louisville, Nebr. (68037) 264/H3
Louisville, Ohio (44641) 284/H4
Louisville, Tenn. (37777) 237/N9
Louisville, Ky. 188/J3
Louis XIV (pt.), Que. 162/H5
Louis XIV (pt.), Québec 174/B2
Loukhi, U.S.S.R. 52/D1
Loulé, Portugal 33/B4
Louny, Czech. 41/B1
Loup (co.), Nebr. 264/E3
Loup (riv.), Nebr. 264/F3
Loup (riv.), Québec 172/H2
Loup City, Nebr. (68853) 264/E3
Lourdes, France 28/C6
Lourdes, Newf. 166/C4
Lourdes, N. Mex. (†87701) 274/D3
Lourdes, Québec 172/F3
Louriçal, Portugal 33/B3
Lourinhã, Portugal 33/B3
Lousã, Portugal 33/B2
Lousana, Alberta 182/D3
Louth, England 13/H4
Louth, England 10/F4
Louth (co.), Ireland 17/J4
Louth, Ireland 17/J4
Louth, N.S. Wales 97/C2
Loutrá Aidhipsoú, Greece 45/F6
Louvain (Leuven), Belgium 27/F7
Louvale, Georgia (31814) 217/C6
Louviers, Colo. (80131) 208/K4
Louviers, France 28/D3
Lövånger, Sweden 18/M4
Lovango (cay), Virgin Is. (U.S.) 161/C4
Lovat' (riv.), U.S.S.R. 52/D3
Love, Miss. (†38632) 256/D1
Love (co.), Okla. 288/M7
Love, Sask. 181/G2
Lovech, Bulgaria 45/G4
Lovejoy, Georgia (30250) 217/D4
Lovejoy, Ill. (62059) 222/A2
Loveladeville, Ky. (42060) 237/D7
Lovelady, Texas (75851) 303/J6
Loveland, Colo. 188/E2
Loveland, Colo. (80537) 208/J2
Loveland, Iowa (†51555) 229/B6
Loveland, Ohio (45140) 284/D9
Loveland, Okla. (73553) 288/J6
Lovell, Maine (04051) 243/B7
Lovell○, Maine (04051) 243/B7
Lovell, Okla. (†73028) 288/L2
Lovell, Wyo. (82431) 319/D1
Lovells, Mich. (†49738) 250/E4
Lovelock, Nev. (89419) 266/C2
Lovely, Ky. (41231) 237/S5
Lovenia (mt.), Utah 304/D3
Love Point, Md. (†21617) 245/N4
Loverna, Sask. 181/B4
Loves Park, Ill. (61111) 222/E1
Lovett, Georgia (†31021) 217/G5
Lovett, Ind. (†47265) 227/F7
Lovettsville, Va. (22080) 307/N2
Love Valley, N.C. (28677) 281/H3
Loveville, Md. (20656) 245/M7
Lovewell, Kansas (†66942) 232/D2
Lovewell (res.), Kansas 232/D2
Lovilia, Iowa (50150) 229/H6
Loving, N. Mex. (88256) 274/E6
Loving (co.), Texas 303/A6
Lovingston, Va. (22949) 307/L5
Lovington, Ill. (61937) 222/E4
Lovington, N. Mex. (88260) 274/F6
Lovisa, Finland 18/P6
Lövö, Hungary 41/D3
Lovosice, Czech. 41/C1
Lóvua, Angola 115/D5
Low (cape), N.W.T. 162/H3
Low (cape), N.W. Terrs. 187/K3
Low, Québec 172/B4
Lowa (riv.), Zaire 115/E4
Low Bush River, Ontario 177/K5
Low Bush River, Ontario 175/E3
Lowden, Iowa (52255) 229/L5
Lowder, Ill. (62662) 222/D4
Lowe Farm, Manitoba 179/E5
Lowell, Ark. (72745) 202/B1
Lowell, Fla. (32663) 212/D2
Lowell, Idaho (†83539) 220/C3
Lowell (lake), Idaho 220/B6
Lowell, Ind. (46356) 227/C2
Lowell, Iowa (†52645) 229/L7
Lowell, Maine (†04433) 243/F5
Lowell○, Maine (†04433) 243/F5
Lowell, Mass. 188/M2
Lowell, Mass. (*01850) 249/J2
Lowell, Mich. (49331) 250/D6
Lowell, N.C. (28098) 281/G4
Lowell, Ohio (45744) 284/H6
Lowell, Oreg. (97452) 291/E4
Lowell○, Vt. (05847) 268/C2
Lowell, W. Va. (†24910) 312/E7
Lowell, Wis. (53557) 317/J9
Lowell Nat'l Hist. Park, Mass. 249/J2
Lowellville, Ohio (44436) 284/J3
Lower Alkali (lake), Calif. 204/E2
Lower Argyle, Nova Scotia 168/C5
Lower Arrow (lake), Br. Col. 184/H5
Lower Austria (prov.), Austria 41/C2
Lower Bank, N.J. (†08215) 273/E4
Lower Barneys River, Nova Scotia 168/F3
Lower Brule, S. Dak. (57548) 298/K5
Lower Brule Ind. Res., S. Dak. 298/K5
Lower Burrell, Pa. (15068) 294/C4
Lower Cabot, Vt. (†05658) 268/C3
Lower California (pen.), Mexico 2/D4
Lower California (pen.), Mexico 146/G7
Lower California (pen.), Mexico 150/C3
Lower Cloverdale, New Bruns. 170/F2
Lower Crab (creek), Wash. 310/F4
Lower Derby, New Bruns. 170/E2
Lower Durham, New Bruns. 170/D2
Lower East Pubnico, Nova Scotia 168/C5
Lower Elwah Ind. Res., Wash. 310/B2
Lower Engadine (valley), Switzerland 39/K3
Lower Goose Creek (res.), Idaho 220/D7
Lower Granite (lake), Idaho 220/A3
Lower Granite (dam), Wash. 310/H4
Lower Granite (lake), Wash. 310/H4
Lower Hainesville, New Bruns. 170/C2
Lower Hutt, N. Zealand 100/B2
Lower Island Cove, Newf. 166/D2
Lower Kalskag, Alaska (99626) 196/F2
Lower Kars, New Bruns. 170/E3
Lower Klamath (lake), Calif. 204/D2
Lower Lake, Calif. (95457) 204/C5
Lower L'Ardoise, Nova Scotia 168/H3
Lower Marlboro, Md. (†20836) 245/M6
Lower Matecumbe (key), Fla. 212/F7
Lower Millstream, New Bruns. 170/E3
Lower Montague, Pr. Edward I. 168/F2
Lower Monumental (dam), Wash. 310/G4
Lower Monumental (lake), Wash. 310/G4
Lower New York (bay), N.J. 273/E2
Lower Nicola, Br. Col. 184/G5
Lower Ohio, Nova Scotia 168/C5
Lower Paia, Hawaii (†96779) 218/J1
Lower Peach Tree, Ala. (36751) 195/C7
Lower Post, Br. Col. 184/K1
Lower Red (lake), Minn. 255/C3
Lower Red Rock (lake), Mont. 262/E6
Lower Rhine (riv.), Netherlands 27/H5
Lower Roach (pond), Maine 243/E4
Lower Saint Mary (lake), Mont. 262/C2
Lower Salem, Ohio (45745) 284/H6
Lower Sapin, New Bruns. 170/F2
Lower Saranac (lake), N.Y. 276/M2
Lower Saxony (state), W. Germany 22/C2
Lower Southampton, New Bruns. 170/C2
Lower South River, Nova Scotia 168/F3
Lower Sysladobsis (lake), Maine 243/G5
Lower Tonsina, Alaska (†99566) 196/J2
Lower Tunguska (riv.), U.S.S.R. 54/L3
Lower Tunguska (riv.), U.S.S.R. 48/K3
Lower Waterford, Vt. (05848) 268/D3
Lower Wedgeport, Nova Scotia 168/C5
Lower West Pubnico, Nova Scotia 168/C5
Lower Woods Harbour, Nova Scotia 168/C5
Lowery, Ala. (†36453) 195/F8
Lowery (lake), Fla. 212/E3
Lowes, Ky. (42061) 237/D7
Lowestoft, England 13/J5
Lowestoft, England 10/G4
Lowesville, Va. (22951) 307/K5
Lowgap, N.C. (27024) 281/H1
Łowicz, Poland 47/D2
Lowland, N.C. (28552) 281/S4
Lowman, Idaho (83637) 220/C5
Lowmansville, Ky. (41232) 237/R5
Low Moor, Iowa (52757) 229/N5
Lowmoor, Va. (24457) 307/J5
Lowndes (co.), Ala. 195/E6
Lowndes (co.), Georgia 217/F9
Lowndes (co.), Miss. 256/H4
Lowndes, Mo. (63951) 261/M8
Lowndesboro, Ala. (36752) 195/E6
Lowndesville, S.C. (29659) 296/B3
Lowpoint, Ill. (61545) 222/D3
Low Rocky (pt.), Tasmania 99/B4
Lowry, Minn. (56349) 255/C5
Lowry, S. Dak. (†57472) 298/K3
Lowry, Va. (24570) 307/K6
Lowry A.F.B., Colo. 208/K3
Lowry City, Mo. (64763) 261/E6
Lowrys, S.C. (†29706) 296/E2
Lowther (isl.), N.W. Terrs. 187/J2
Lowville, N.Y. (13367) 276/J3
Low Wassie, Mo. (†65588) 261/K9
Loxahatchee, Fla. (33470) 212/F5
Loxley, Ala. (36551) 195/C9
Loxton, S. Australia 94/G6
Loxton North, S. Australia 94/G6
Loyal, Okla. (73756) 288/K3
Loyal, Loch (lake), Scotland 15/D2
Loyal, Wis. (54446) 317/E6
Loyalhanna, Pa. (15661) 294/D5
Loyalist, Alberta 182/E4
Loyall, Ky. (40854) 237/P7
Loyalton, Calif. (96118) 204/E4
Loyalton, Pa. (†17048) 294/J4
Loyalton, S. Dak. (†57471) 298/L3
Loyalty (isls.), New Caled. 87/G8
Loyalty (isls.), New Caled. 86/H4
Loyang (Luoyang), China 77/H5
Loyd, Wis. (†53924) 317/F9
Loyne, Loch (lake), Scotland 15/C3
Loysburg, Pa. (16659) 294/F5
Loysville, Pa. (17047) 294/H5
Lozeau (lake), Newf. 166/B3
Lozère (dept.), France 28/E5
Loznica, Yugoslavia 45/D3
Lozovaya, U.S.S.R. 52/E5
Lua (riv.), Zaire 115/C3
Luacano, Angola 115/D6
Luachimo, Angola 115/D5
Lualaba (riv.), Zaire 102/E5
Lualaba (riv.), Zaire 115/E4
Lua Makika (mt.), Hawaii 218/J3
Lu'an, China 77/J5
Luana, Iowa (52156) 229/K2
Luana (pt.), Jamaica 158/G6
Luanchuan, China 77/H5
Luanda (dist.), Angola 115/B5
Luanda (cap.), Angola 2/K6
Luanda (cap.), Angola 115/B5
Luanda (cap.), Angola 102/D5
Luang, Thale (lag.), Thailand 72/D6
Luang (mt.), Thailand 72/C5
Luang Prabang (Loungphrabang), Laos 72/D3
Luangwa (Feira), Zambia 115/E7
Luangwa (riv.), Zambia 115/F6
Luanshya, Zambia 115/E6
Luanshya, Zambia 102/E6
Luao, Angola 115/D6
Luapula (riv.), Zaire 115/E6
Luapula (riv.), Zambia 115/E6
Luarca, Spain 33/C1
Luashi, Zaire 115/D6
Luba, Equat. Guinea 115/A3
Lubaczów, Poland 47/F3
Lubań, Poland 47/B3
Lubāna (lake), U.S.S.R. 53/D2
Lubang, Philippines 82/C4
Lubang (isls.), Philippines 85/F3
Lubang (isls.), Philippines 82/B4
Lubango, Angola 115/B6
Lubango, Angola 102/D6
Lubartów, Poland 47/F3
Lubawa, Poland 47/D2
Lübben, E. Germany 22/E3
Lübbenau, E. Germany 22/F3
Lubbock (co.), Texas 303/C4
Lubbock, Texas 146/H6
Lubbock, Texas (*79401) 303/C4
Lubbock, Texas 188/F4
Lubec, Maine (04652) 243/K6
Lubec○, Maine (04652) 243/K6
Lübeck, W. Germany 7/E3
Lübeck, W. Germany 22/D2
Lubeck, W. Va. (†26101) 312/C4
Lubefu, Zaire 115/D4
Lubero, Zaire 115/E4
L'ubica, Czech. 41/F2
Lubicon (lake), Alberta 182/C1
Lubien Kujawski, Poland 47/D2
Lubilash (riv.), Zaire 115/D5
Lublin, Poland 47/C3
Lublin (prov.), Poland 47/F3
Lublin, Poland 47/F3
Lublin, Poland 7/G3
Lublin, Wis. (54447) 317/E5
Lubliniec, Poland 47/D3
Lubny, U.S.S.R. 52/D4
Luboń, Poland 47/C2
Lubrín, Spain 33/F4
Lubsko, Poland 47/B3
Lubuagan, Philippines 82/C2
Lubudi, Zaire 115/E5
Lubuklinggau, Indonesia 85/C6
Lubuksikaping, Indonesia 85/B5
Lubumbashi, Zaire 2/L6
Lubumbashi, Zaire 115/E6
Lubumbashi, Zaire 102/E6
Lubutu, Zaire 115/E4
Lübz, E. Germany 22/D2
Lucama, N.C. (27851) 281/N3
Lucan, Minn. (56255) 255/C6
Lucan, Ontario 177/C4
Luc An Chau, Vietnam 72/E2
Lucan-Doddsborough, Ireland 17/J5
Lucas (co.), Iowa 229/G6
Lucas, Iowa (50151) 229/G6
Lucas, Kansas (67648) 232/D2
Lucas, Ky. (42156) 237/K7
Lucas, Mich. (†49657) 250/D4
Lucas (co.), Ohio 284/C2
Lucas, Ohio (44843) 284/F4
Lucas, S. Dak. (57549) 298/L7
Lucas, Texas (†75069) 303/H1
Lucas E. de Peña, Dom. Rep. 158/D5
Lucas González, Argentina 143/G6
Lucasville, Ohio (45648) 284/E8
Lucban, Philippines 82/C3
Lucca (prov.), Italy 34/C3
Lucca, Italy 34/C3
Lucca, N. Dak. (†58027) 282/P6
Luce (co.), Mich. 250/D2
Luce, Minn. (†56573) 255/C4
Luce (bay), Scotland 10/D3
Luce (bay), Scotland 15/D6
Lucea, Jamaica 158/G5
Lucedale, Miss. (39452) 256/G9
Lucena, Philippines 85/G3
Lucena, Philippines 82/C4
Lucena, Spain 33/D4
Lucena del Cid, Spain 33/F2
Lučenec, Czech. 41/E2
Lucens, Switzerland 39/C3
Lucera, Italy 34/E4
Lucerna, Peru 128/H9
Lucerne, Calif. (95458) 204/C4
Lucerne, Colo. (80646) 208/K2
Lucerne, Ind. (46950) 227/E3
Lucerne, Mo. (64655) 261/F2
Lucerne, Québec 172/B4
Lucerne (Luzern) (canton), Switzerland 39/F2
Lucerne, Switzerland 39/F2
Lucerne (lake), Switzerland 39/F3
Lucerne, Wash. (†98816) 310/E2
Lucerne, Wyo. (†82443) 319/D2
Lucernemines, Pa. (15754) 294/D4
Lucerne Valley, Calif. (92356) 204/J9
Lucero (lake), N. Mex. 274/C6
Luceville, Québec 172/J1
Luchow (Luzhou), China 77/G6
Lüchow, W. Germany 22/D2
Lucia, Calif. (†93920) 204/D7
Lucie (riv.), Suriname 131/C4
Lucien, Miss. (39646) 256/C7
Lucien, Okla. (73757) 288/M2
Lucile, Georgia (†31723) 217/C8
Lucile, Idaho (83542) 220/B4
Lucile, Ky. (†41171) 237/P4
Lucinda, Pa. (16235) 294/D3
Lucira, Angola 115/B6
Luck, Wis. (54853) 317/B4
Luckau, E. Germany 22/E3
Luckenwalde, E. Germany 22/E2
Lucketts, Va. (†22075) 307/N2
Luckey, Ohio (43443) 284/D3
Lucknow, India 68/E3
Lucknow, India 54/K7
Lucknow, Ontario 177/C4
Lucky, La. (†71008) 238/E2
Lucky Lake, Sask. 181/D5
Lucky Peak (lake), Idaho 220/B6
Luçon, France 28/C4
Lucrecia (cape), Cuba 158/J3
Lucy, La. (†70049) 238/M3
Lucy, Tenn. (†38053) 237/B10
Lucy Creek, North. Terr. 93/E7
Lüda (Lüta), China 77/K4
Lüda, China 2/R4
Lüda, China 54/O6
Ludden, N. Dak. (58462) 282/O7
Ludell, Kansas (67744) 232/B2
Lüdenscheid, W. Germany 22/B3
Lüderitz, Namibia 118/A5
Lüderitz, Namibia 102/D7
Lüderitz (bay), Namibia 118/A5
Ludhiana, India 54/J6
Ludhiana, India 68/D2
Ludington, Mich. (49431) 250/C5
Ludlow, Calif. (†92365) 204/J9
Ludlow, England 10/E4
Ludlow, England 13/E5
Ludlow, Ill. (60949) 222/E3
Ludlow, Ky. (41016) 237/S2
Ludlow○, Maine (†04730) 243/G3
Ludlow○, Mass. (01056) 249/E4
Ludlow, Miss. (39098) 256/E5
Ludlow, Mo. (64656) 261/E3
Ludlow, New Bruns. 170/D2
Ludlow, Pa. (16333) 294/E2
Ludlow, S. Dak. (57755) 298/C2
Ludlow, Vt. (05149) 268/B5
Ludlow○, Vt. (05149) 268/B5
Ludlow (mt.), Vt. 268/B5
Ludlow Center, Mass. (†01056) 249/E4
Ludlow Falls, Ohio (45339) 284/B6
Ludowici, Georgia (31316) 217/J7
Luduş, Romania 45/G2
Ludvika, Sweden 18/J6
Ludville, Georgia (†30175) 217/C2
Ludwigsburg, W. Germany 22/C4
Ludwigshafen am Rhein, W. Germany 22/C4
Ludwigslust, E. Germany 22/D2
Ludza, U.S.S.R. 53/D2
Lue, N.S. Wales 97/E3
Luebbering, Mo. (63061) 261/L6
Luebo, Zaire 115/D5
Lueders, Texas (79533) 303/E5
Luella, Georgia (†30248) 217/D4
Luena, Angola 115/C6
Luepa, Venezuela 124/H5
Lüeyang, China 77/G5
Lufeng, China 77/J7
Lufira (riv.), Zaire 115/E5
Lufkin, Texas (75901) 303/K6
Luga, U.S.S.R. 52/C3
Luga, U.S.S.R. 48/D4
Lugano, Switzerland 39/G4
Lugano (lake), Switzerland 39/H5
Luganville, Vanuatu 87/G7
Lugareño, Cuba 158/G3
Lugenda (riv.), Mozambique 118/F2
Lugerville, Wis. (†54555) 317/E4
Lugnaquillia (mt.), Ireland 17/J5
Lugo, Italy 34/D2
Lugo (prov.), Spain 33/C1
Lugo, Spain 33/C1
Lugoff, S.C. (29078) 296/F3
Lugoj, Romania 45/F3
Luhaiya, Yemen Arab Rep. 59/D6
Luiana, Angola 115/D7
Luiana, Angola 102/E6
Luik (Liège), Belgium 27/H7
Luilaka (riv.), Zaire 115/C4
Luimneach (Limerick), Ireland 10/B4
Luimneach (Limerick), Ireland 17/D6
Luina, Tasmania 99/B3
Luing (isl.), Scotland 15/C4
Luís Correia, Brazil 132/F3
Luis de Saboya, Cerro (mt.), Chile 138/F11
Luishia, Zaire 115/E6
Luitpold Coast (reg.) 5/B17
Luiza, Zaire 115/D5
Luján, Argentina 143/G7
Lujiang, China 77/J5
Lukachukai, Ariz. (86507) 198/F2
Lukachukai (mts.), Ariz. 198/F2
Lukapa, Angola 115/D5
Luke, Md. (21540) 245/B3
Luke A.F.B., Ariz. 198/C5
Lukenie (riv.), Zaire 115/D4
Lukeville, Ariz. (85341) 198/C7
Lukolela, Equateur, Zaire 115/C4
Lukolela, Kasai-Oriental, Zaire 115/D5
Lukovit, Bulgaria 45/G4
Łuków, Poland 47/F3
Lukuga (riv.), Zaire 115/E5
Lukula, Zaire 115/B5
Lukulu, Zambia 115/D6
Lula, Georgia (30554) 217/E2
Lula, Miss. (38644) 256/C2
Lula, Okla. (†74825) 288/O5
Luleå (riv.), Sweden 7/G2
Luleå, Sweden 7/G2
Luleå, Sweden 18/N4
Luleälv (riv.), Sweden 18/M4
Lüleburgaz, Turkey 63/B2
Lules, Argentina 143/C2
Luling, La. (70070) 238/N4
Luling, Texas (78648) 303/G8
Lulu, Fla. (32061) 212/D1
Lulua (riv.), Zaire 115/D5
Lum, Mich. (48452) 250/F5
Lumajang, Indonesia 85/K2
Lumajangdong Co (lake), China 77/B5
Lumbala, Angola 115/D6
Lumber (riv.), N.C. 281/L6
Lumber (riv.), S.C. 296/J3
Lumber Bridge, N.C. (28357) 281/L5
Lumber City, Georgia (31549) 217/G7
Lumber City, Pa. (†16833) 294/E4
Lumberport, W. Va. (26386) 312/F4
Lumberton, Miss. (39455) 256/E8
Lumberton, N.J. (08048) 273/D4
Lumberton, N. Mex. (87547) 274/C2
Lumberton, N.C. (28358) 281/L5
Lumberton, Texas (†77656) 303/K7
Lumberville, Pa. (18933) 294/N5
Lumbo, Mozambique 118/G3
Lumbrales, Spain 33/C2
Lumbrein, Switzerland 39/H3
Lumby, Br. Col. 184/H5
Lumding, India 68/G3
Lummen, Belgium 27/G7
Lummi (isl.), Wash. 310/C2
Lummi Ind. Res., Wash. 310/C2
Lummi Island, Wash. (98262) 310/C2
Lumphat, Cambodia 72/E4
Lumpkin (co.), Georgia 217/D1
Lumpkin, Georgia (31815) 217/C6
Lumsden, Newf. 166/D4
Lumsden, N. Zealand 100/B6
Lumsden, Sask. 181/G5
Lumsden, Scotland 15/F3
Lumsden Beach, Sask. 181/F5
Lumut, Malaysia 72/D6
Luna, Ark. (†71653) 202/H7
Luna (co.), N. Mex. 274/B6
Luna, N. Mex. (87824) 274/A5
Luna Pier, Mich. (48157) 250/F7
Luncarty, Scotland 15/E4
Lund, Br. Col. 184/E5
Lund, Idaho (†83241) 220/G7
Lund, Nev. (89317) 266/F4
Lund, Sweden 18/H9
Lund, Utah (†84720) 304/A5
Lundale, W. Va. (25631) 312/C7
Lunda Norte (dist.), Angola 115/C5
Lundar, Manitoba 179/D4
Lunda Sul (dist.), Angola 115/D5
Lundazi, Zambia 115/F6
Lundbreck, Alberta 182/C5
Lundby, Denmark 21/E7
Lundell, Ark. (†72367) 202/H5
Lunderskov, Denmark 21/C7
Lundi (riv.), Zimbabwe 118/E4
Lunds Corner, Mass. (02745) 249/L6
Lundsvalley, N. Dak. (†58724) 282/E3
Lundy (isl.), England 13/C6
Lundy (isl.), England 10/D5
Lune (riv.), England 13/E3
Lüneburg, W. Germany 22/D2
Lüneburger Heide (dist.), W. Germany 22/C2
Lunel, France 28/E6
Lünen, W. Germany 22/B3
Lunenburg, Mass. (01462) 249/H2
Lunenburg○, Mass. (01462) 249/H2
Lunenburg, N.S. 162/K7
Lunenburg (co.), Nova Scotia 168/D4
Lunenburg, Nova Scotia 168/D4
Lunenburg (bay), Nova Scotia 168/D4
Lunenburg○, Vt. (05906) 268/D3
Lunenburg (co.), Va. 307/M7
Lunenburg, Va. (23952) 307/M7
Lunéville, France 28/G3
Lung (riv.), Ireland 17/D4
Lungchen (Longzhen), China 77/L2
Lungdo, China 77/B5
Lungern, Switzerland 39/F3
Lungi, S. Leone 106/B7
Lungleh, India 68/G4
Lungwebungu (riv.), Angola 115/D6
Lungwebungu (riv.), Zambia 115/D6
Luni (riv.), India 68/C3
Luninets, U.S.S.R. 52/C4
Luning, Nev. (89420) 266/C4
Lunita, La. (†70661) 238/C6
Lunsford, Ark. (†72437) 202/K2
Luocheng, China 77/G7
Luodian, China 77/G6
Luoding, China 77/H7
Luohe, China 77/H5
Luoyang (Loyang), China 77/H5
Luoyang, China 54/N6
Luozi, Zaire 115/B5
Lupeni, Romania 45/F3
Luperón, Dom. Rep. 158/D5
Lupon, Philippines 82/E7
Lupton, Ariz. (86508) 198/F3
Lupton, Mich. (48635) 250/F4
Lupus, Mo. (†65046) 261/H5
Luputa, Zaire 115/D5
Luqu, China 77/F5
Luque, Paraguay 144/B4
Luquillo, P. Rico 161/F1
Luquillo, Sierra de (mts.), P. Rico 161/E2
Lurah (riv.), Afghanistan 68/B2
Lurah (riv.), Afghanistan 59/J3
Luray, Kansas (67649) 232/D2
Luray, Mo. (63453) 261/J2
Luray, S.C. (29932) 296/E6
Luray, Tenn. (38352) 237/D9
Luray, Va. (22835) 307/M3
Lure, France 28/G4
Lurgan, N. Ireland 17/J3
Luribay, Bolivia 136/B5
Lurín, Peru 128/D9
Lúrio, Mozambique 118/G2
Lúrio (riv.), Mozambique 118/F2
Luristan (Lorestan) (gov.), Iran 66/F4
Lurton, Ark. (†72856) 202/D2
Lusaka (cap.), Zambia 115/E7
Lusaka (cap.), Zambia 102/E6
Lusaka (cap.), Zambia 2/L6
Lusambo, Zaire 102/E5
Lusambo, Zaire 115/D4
Lusatia (reg.), E. Germany 22/F3
Lusby, Md. (20657) 245/N7
Luseland, Sask. 181/B3
Lushi, China 77/H5
Lushnje, Albania 45/D5
Lushoto, Tanzania 115/G4
Lushton, Nebr. (†68371) 264/G4
Lushui, China 77/E6
Lüshun, China 77/K4
Lusk, Ireland 17/J4
Lusk, Wyo. (82225) 319/H3
Luso, Angola 102/E6
Luss, Scotland 15/A1
Lustenau, Austria 41/A3
Lustre, Mont. (59225) 262/K2
Lut, Dasht-e (des.), Iran 59/G3
Lut, Dasht-e (des.), Iran 66/L5
Lüta (Lüda), China 77/K4
Lutcher, La. (70071) 238/L3
Lutesville, Mo. (63762) 261/M8
Luther, Iowa (50152) 229/F5
Luther, Mich. (49656) 250/D4
Luther, Mont. (59051) 262/G5
Luther, Okla. (73054) 288/M3
Luther, Tenn. (†37869) 237/P8
Luthern, Switzerland 39/E2
Luthersburg, Pa. (15848) 294/E3
Luthersville, Georgia (30251) 217/C4
Lutherville-Timonium, Md. (21093) 245/M3
Lutie, Okla. (†74578) 288/R5
Luton, England 13/G6
Luton, England 10/F5
Luton, Iowa (†51052) 229/A4
Lutry, Switzerland 39/C3

404 Magalia

Magalia, Calif. (95954) 204/D4
Magaliesburg, S. Africa 118/G6
Magallanes (reg.), Chile 138/E10
Magallanes (Magellan) (str.), Chile 138/D10
Magallanes, Philippines 82/D4
Magallenes (Magellan) (str.), Argentina 143/C7
Magangué, Colombia 126/C3
Maganoy, Philippines 82/E7
Mağara, Turkey 63/G3
Magarabomba, Cuba 158/G2
Magaria, Niger 106/F6
Magazine, Ark. (72943) 202/C3
Magazine (mt.), Ark. 202/C3
Magdagachi, U.S.S.R. 48/N4
Magdala, Ethiopia 111/G5
Magdalen (isls.), Que. 162/K6
Magdalena, Argentina 143/H7
Magdalena, Bolivia 136/C3
Magdalena (isl.), Chile 138/D5
Magdalena (dept.), Colombia 126/C3
Magdalena (riv.), Colombia 120/B2
Magdalena (riv.), Colombia 126/C3
Magdalena (bay), Mexico 150/C4
Magdalena, N. Mex. (87825) 274/B4
Magdalena (mts.), N. Mex. 274/B4
Magdalena de Kino, Mexico 150/D1
Magdeburg, E. Germany 7/F3
Magdeburg (dist.), E. Germany 22/D2
Magdeburg, E. Germany 22/D2
Magdelaine (cays), Coral Sea Is. Terr. 88/H3
Magé, Brazil 135/E3
Magee, Miss. (39111) 256/E7
Magee, Island (pen.), N. Ireland 17/K2
Magelang, Indonesia 85/J2
Magellan (str.) 120/C8
Magellan (str.) 2/F8
Magellan (str.), Argentina 143/C7
Magellan (str.), Chile 138/D10
Magen, Israel 65/A5
Magens (bay), Virgin Is. (U.S.) 161/B4
Magerøya (isl.), Norway 18/P1
Magerrain (mt.), Switzerland 39/H2
Magetan, Indonesia 85/K2
Maggia, Switzerland 39/G4
Maggia (riv.), Switzerland 39/G4
Maggie Valley, N.C. (28751) 281/C3
Maggiore (lake), Fla. 212/B3
Maggiore (lake), Italy 34/B1
Maggiore (lake), Switzerland 39/G5
Maggotty, Jamaica 158/H6
Maghâgha, Egypt 59/B4
Maghâgha, Egypt 111/J4
Maghama, Mauritania 102/A3
Maghama, Mauritania 106/B5
Maghera, N. Ireland 17/H2
Magherafelt (dist.), N. Ireland 17/H2
Magherafelt, N. Ireland 10/C3
Magherafelt, N. Ireland 17/H2
Magic (res.), Idaho 220/D6
Magilligan (pt.), N. Ireland 17/H1
Maglaj, Yugoslavia 45/D3
Magley, Ind. (†46733) 227/G3
Maglie, Italy 34/G4
Magna, Utah (84044) 304/B3
Magna Bay, Br. Col. 184/H4
Magness, Ark. (72553) 202/H2
Magnet, Ark. (†72104) 202/E5
Magnet, Ind. (47555) 227/D8
Magnet, Manitoba 179/C3
Magnet, Nebr. (68749) 264/G2
Magnetawan, Ontario 177/E2
Magnetawan (riv.), Ontario 177/D2
Magnetic Springs, Ohio (43036) 284/D5
Magnitogorsk, U.S.S.R. 54/H4
Magnitogorsk, U.S.S.R. 48/G4
Magnolia, Ala. (36754) 195/C6
Magnolia, Ark. (71753) 202/D7
Magnolia, Del. (19962) 245/R4
Magnolia, Ill. (61336) 222/D2
Magnolia, Iowa (51550) 229/B5
Magnolia, Minn. (56158) 255/B7
Magnolia, Miss. (39652) 256/D8
Magnolia, N.J. (08049) 273/B3
Magnolia, N.C. (28453) 281/O5
Magnolia, Ohio (44643) 284/H4
Magnolia, Texas (77355) 303/J7
Magnolia, W. Va. (†25422) 312/K3
Magnolia Springs, Ala. (36555) 195/C10
Màgoé, Mozambique 118/E3
Magoffin (co.), Ky. 237/P5
Magog, Québec 172/E4
Magpie, Québec 174/E2
Magpie (lake), Québec 174/E2
Magrath, Alberta 182/D5
Magude, Mozambique 118/E5
Maguindanao (prov.), Philippines 82/E7
Maguse (lake), N.W. Terrs. 187/J3
Magwe (div.), Burma 72/B2
Magwe, Burma 72/B2
Mahabad, Iran 59/E2
Mahabad, Iran 66/D2
Mahabaleshwar, India 68/C5
Mahabo, Madagascar 118/G4
Mahaena, Fr. Poly. 86/T13
Mahaffey, Pa. (15757) 294/E4
Mahagi, Zaire 115/F3
Mahaica, Guyana 131/C2
Mahaicony Village, Guyana 131/C2
Mahajamba (bay), Madagascar 118/H2
Mahajanga (prov.), Madagascar 118/H3
Mahajanga, Madagascar 102/G6
Mahakam (riv.), Indonesia 85/F6
Mahalapye, Botswana 118/D4
Mahalapye, Botswana 102/E7
Mahalasville, Ind. (†46151) 227/E6
Mahallat, Iran 66/G4
Mahan, Iran 66/K5
Mahanadi (riv.), India 68/E4
Mahanoro, Madagascar 118/H3
Mahanoy City, Pa. (17948) 294/K4
Maharashtra (state), India 68/C5
Maha Sarakham, Thailand 72/D3
Mahaska (co.), Iowa 229/H6
Mahaska, Kansas (66955) 232/E2
Mahaxai, Laos 72/E3
Mahbubnagar, India 68/D5
Mahdia, Guyana 131/B3
Mahdia, Tunisia 106/G1
Mahe, India 68/D6
Mahé (isl.), Seychelles 118/H5
Mahébourg, Mauritius 118/G5
Mahenge, Tanzania 115/G5
Maheno, N. Zealand 100/C6
Maher, Colo. (81421) 208/D5
Maheshkhali, Bangladesh 68/G4
Mahia (pen.), N. Zealand 100/G3
Mahim, India 68/C5
Mahim (bay), India 68/B7
Mahkonce, Minn. (†56557) 255/C3
Mahlaing, Burma 72/B2
Mahmudiye, Turkey 63/D3
Mahnomen (co.), Minn. 255/C3
Mahnomen, Minn. (56557) 255/C3
Maho (bay), Virgin Is. (U.S.) 161/C4
Mahoba, India 68/D3
Mahomet, Ill. (61853) 222/E3
Mahón, Spain 33/J3
Mahone (bay), Nova Scotia 168/D4
Mahone Bay, Nova Scotia 168/D4
Mahoning (co.), Ohio 284/J4
Mahood (lake), Br. Col. 184/G4
Mahopac, N.Y. (10541) 276/N8
Mahout, Dominica 161/E6
Mahto, S. Dak. (57643) 298/H2
Mahtomedi, Minn. (55115) 255/F5
Mahtowa, Minn. (55762) 255/F4
Mahukona, Hawaii (†96719) 218/G3
Mahuva, India 68/C4
Mahwah○, N.J. (07430) 273/E1
Maia, Portugal 33/B2
Maicao, Colombia 126/D2
Maicuru (riv.), Brazil 132/C2
Maida, N. Dak. (58255) 282/O2
Maida, Yemen Arab Rep. 59/D6
Maidan, Iraq 66/D3
Maidan, Iraq 59/E3
Maidani, Ras (cape), Iran 59/G4
Maiden, N.C. (28650) 281/G3
Maidenhead, England 10/F5
Maidenhead, England 13/G8
Maiden Rock, Wis. (54750) 317/B6
Maidens, The (isls.), N. Ireland 17/K2
Maidens, Scotland 15/D5
Maidens, Va. (23102) 307/N5
Maidstone, England 13/J8
Maidstone, England 10/G5
Maidstone, Ontario 177/B5
Maidstone, Sask. 181/B2
Maidstone○, Vt. (†05905) 268/D2
Maidstone (lake), Vt. 268/D2
Maidsville, W. Va. (26541) 312/F3
Maiduguri, Nigeria 106/G6
Maiduguri, Nigeria 102/D3
Maienfeld, Switzerland 39/J2
Maigatari, Nigeria 106/F6
Maigualida, Sierra (range), Venezuela 124/F4
Maigue (riv.), Ireland 17/D6
Maihara, Japan 81/G6
Maili, Hawaii (†96792) 218/D2
Maillard, Québec 172/G2
Ma'in, Jordan 65/D4
Main (passage), La. 238/M8
Main (riv.), N. Ireland 17/J2
Main (chan.), Ontario 177/C2
Main (str.), Singapore 72/F6
Main (riv.), W. Germany 22/C4
Main-à-Dieu, Nova Scotia 168/J2
Main Barrier (range), N. S. Wales 88/G6
Main Barrier (range), N.S. Wales 97/A2
Main Brook, Newf. 166/C3
Main Centre, Sask. 181/D5
Mai-Ndombe (lake), Zaire 115/C4
Maine 188/N1
MAINE 243
Maine (gulf) 188/N2
Maine (gulf) 162/K7
Maine (trad. prov.), France, 29
Maine (riv.), Ireland 17/C7
Maine (gulf), Mass. 249/M2
Maine, N.Y. (13802) 276/H6
Maine (state), U.S. 146/M5
Maine-et-Loire (dept.), France 28/C4
Mainesburg, Pa. (16932) 294/J2
Mainé-Soroa, Niger 106/G6
Maineville, Ohio (45039) 284/C9
Maingard (lake), Québec 172/G1
Maingkwan, Burma 72/C1
Mainit, Philippines 82/E6
Mainit (lake), Philippines 82/E6
Mainland, Orkney Is. (isl.), Scotland 10/E1
Mainland, Shetland Is. (isl.), Scotland 10/G1
Mainland (isl.), Scotland 15/G2
Mainland (isl.), Scotland 15/E1
Mainling, China 77/D6
Mainoru, North. Terr. 93/C3
Mainstream, Maine (†04942) 243/D6
Maintirano, Madagascar 118/G3
Main Topsail (mt.), Newf. 166/C4
Mainz, W. Germany 22/C4
Maio (isl.), C. Verde 106/B8
Maipo (vol.), Argentina 143/C3
Maipo (riv.), Chile 138/F4
Maipú, Argentina 143/E4
Maipú, Chile 138/G3
Maipú (vol.), Chile 138/B10
Maipures, Colombia 126/F5
Maiquetía, Venezuela 120/C1
Maiquetía, Venezuela 124/E2
Mairana, Bolivia 136/D6
Maisí, Cuba 158/K4
Maisí (cape), Cuba 158/K4
Maisí (cape), Cuba 156/D2
Maison de Pierre (lake), Québec 172/C3
Maisonnette, New Bruns. 170/E1
Maisons-Alfort, France 28/B2
Maisons-Laffitte, France 28/A1
Maïssade, Haiti 158/C5
Maitencillo, Chile 138/A8
Maitland, Australia 87/F9
Maitland, Fla. (32751) 212/E3
Maitland, Mo. (64466) 261/B2
Maitland, N. S. Wales 88/J6
Maitland, N.S. Wales 97/F3
Maitland, Annapolis, Nova Scotia 168/C4
Maitland, Hants, Nova Scotia 168/E3
Maitland, Ontario 177/J3
Maitland, S. Australia 94/E6
Maitum, Philippines 82/E7
Maize, Kansas (67101) 232/E4
Maiz Grande (Great Corn) (isl.), Nicaragua 154/F4
Maizhokunggar, China 77/D6
Maiz Pequeña (Little Corn) (isl.), Nicaragua 154/F4
Maizuru, Japan 81/G6
Majagua, Cuba 158/F2
Majagual, Colombia 126/C3
Majalengka, Indonesia 85/H2
Majene, Indonesia 85/F6
Majenica, Ind. (†46750) 227/F3
Majes (riv.), Peru 128/F11
Majestic, Ky. (41547) 237/S5
Maji, Ethiopia 111/G6
Majma'a, Saudi Arabia 59/D4
Majoli, Suriname 131/D4
Major (co.), Okla. 288/K2
Major, Sask. 181/B4
Majorca (isl.), Spain 7/E5
Majorca (isl.), Spain 33/H3
Majorsville, W. Va. (†26036) 312/F3
Majunga, Madagascar 118/H3
Majuro (atoll) (cap.), Marshall Is. 87/H5
Makaha, Hawaii (†96792) 218/D2
Makaha (pt.), Hawaii 218/B1
Makah Ind. Res., Wash. 310/A2
Makahuena (pt.), Hawaii 218/C2
Makaiwa, Hawaii (†96763) 218/H2
Makakilo, Hawaii (96706) 218/E2
Makale, Ethiopia 102/F3
Makale, Ethiopia 111/G5
Makallé, Argentina 143/E2
Makanda, Ill. (62958) 222/D6
Makanza, Zaire 115/C3
Makapala, Hawaii (†96711) 218/G3
Makapuu (pt.), Hawaii 218/F2
Makara Beach, N. Zealand 100/A2
Makara-Ohariu, N. Zealand 100/A3
Makari, Cameroon 115/B1
Makaroff, Manitoba 179/A3
Makarov, U.S.S.R. 48/P5
Makarska, Yugoslavia 45/C4
Makar'yev, U.S.S.R. 52/F3
Makassar (Ujung Pandang), Indonesia 85/F7
Makassar (str.), Indonesia 54/N10
Makassar (str.), Indonesia 85/F6
Makatea (isl.), Fr. Poly. 87/L7
Makawao, Hawaii (96768) 218/K2
Makaweli, Hawaii (96769) 218/B2
Makena, Hawaii (†96790) 218/J2
Makeni, S. Leone 102/A4
Makeni, S. Leone 106/B7
Makepeace, Alberta 182/D4
Makeyevka, U.S.S.R. 7/H4
Makeyevka, U.S.S.R. 52/E5
Makgadikgadi (salt pan), Botswana 102/E7
Makgadikgadi (salt pan), Botswana 118/D3
Makhachkala, U.S.S.R. 7/J4
Makhachkala, U.S.S.R. 48/E5
Makhachkala, U.S.S.R. 52/G6
Makharadze, U.S.S.R. 52/F6
Makhmur, Iraq 66/C3
Makiki, Hawaii (96822) 218/C4
Makin (Butaritari) (atoll), Kiribati 87/H5
Makinak, Manitoba 179/C4
Makinen, Minn. (55763) 255/F3
Makinsk, U.S.S.R. 48/H4
Makinson (inlet), N.W. Terrs. 187/L2
Makkovik, Newf. 166/C2
Makkovik (cape), Newf. 166/C2
Makkum, Netherlands 27/G2
Makó, Hungary 41/F3
Makokou, Gabon 115/B3
Makoti, N. Dak. (58756) 282/G4
Makoua, Congo 115/C3
Maków Mazowiecki, Poland 47/E2
Makran (reg.), Iran 66/M8
Makteïr (des.), Mauritania 106/B4
Maku, Iran 66/D1
Makubetsu, Japan 81/L2
Makumbako, Tanzania 115/G5
Makurazaki, Japan 81/O3
Makurdi, Nigeria 102/C4
Makurdi, Nigeria 106/F7
Makushin (vol.), Alaska 196/E4
Makwa, Sask. 181/C2
Makwa (lake), Sask. 181/B1
Makwa (riv.), Sask. 181/B1
Mal, Mauritania 106/B5
Mala, Punta (cape), Panama 154/H7
Malå, Sweden 18/L4
Malabang, Philippines 82/D7
Malabar, Fla. (32950) 212/F3
Malabar (hill), India 68/B7
Malabar (pt.), India 68/B7
Malabar Coast (reg.), India 68/C6
Malabo (cap.), Equat. Guinea 102/C4
Malabo (cap.), Equat. Guinea 115/A3
Malabrigo, Argentina 143/F4
Mal Abrigo, Uruguay 145/C5
Malabungan, Philippines 82/A6
Malacca (str.) 54/M9
Malacca (str.), Indonesia 85/C5
Malacca (Melaka), Malaysia 72/D7
Malacca (str.), Malaysia 72/D7
Malacky, Czech. 41/D2
Malad (riv.), Idaho 220/F7
Malad, India 68/B6
Malad (creek), India 68/B7
Malad (riv.), Utah 304/B1
Malad City, Idaho (83252) 220/F7
Maladers, Switzerland 39/J3
Málaga, Colombia 126/D4
Malaga, N.J. (08328) 273/C4
Malaga, N. Mex. (88263) 274/E6
Malaga, Ohio (43757) 284/H6
Málaga (prov.), Spain 33/D4
Málaga, Spain 7/D5
Málaga, Spain 33/D4
Malaga, Wash. (98828) 310/E3
Malagash, Nova Scotia 168/E3
Malagash (pt.), Nova Scotia 168/E3
Malagón, Spain 33/E3
Malagueta (bay), Cuba 158/H3
Malahide, Ireland 17/J5
Malaita (isl.), 86/E3
Malaita (isl.), Solomon Is. 87/G6
Malakal, Sudan 111/F6
Malakal, Sudan 102/F4
Malakanagiri, India 68/E5
Malakand, Pakistan 68/C2
Malakand, Pakistan 59/K3
Malakoff, France 28/A2
Malakoff, Texas (75148) 303/H5
Malakwa, Br. Col. 184/H5
Malalag, Philippines 82/E7
Malamir (Izeh), Iran 66/F5
Malang, Indonesia 54/N10
Malang, Indonesia 85/K2
Malange (dist.), Angola 115/C6
Malange, Angola 102/D5
Malange, Angola 115/C5
Malangka (cape), Indonesia 85/G5
Malans, Switzerland 39/J3
Malanville, Benin 106/E6
Mälaren (lake), Sweden 18/G1
Malargüe, Argentina 120/C6
Malargüe, Argentina 143/C4
Malartic, Québec 174/B3
Malaspina (glac.), Alaska 196/K3
Malaspina (str.), Br. Col. 184/J2
Malatya (prov.), Turkey 63/H3
Malatya, Turkey 59/C2
Malatya, Turkey 54/E6
Malatya, Turkey 63/H3
Malawi 2/L6
Malawi 102/F6
MALAWI 115/F6
Malawi (Nyasa) (lake), Malawi 115/F6
Malay (pen.), Malaysia 72/D6
Malay (pen.), Malaysia 85/B4
Malay (pen.), Thailand 72/D6
MALAYA, MALAYSIA 72
Malaya (reg.), Malaysia 54/M9
Malaya (reg.), Malaysia 72/E6
Malaya Vishera, U.S.S.R. 52/D3
Malaybalay, Philippines 82/E6
Malayer, Iran 66/F3
Malaysia 2/Q5
Malaysia 54/M9
MALAYSIA 85/D4
Malazgirt, Turkey 63/K3
Malbaie (riv.), Québec 172/G2
Malbon, Queensland 95/B4
Malbork (Marienburg), Poland 47/D1
Malchinersee (lake), E. Germany 22/E2
Malchow, E. Germany 22/E2
Malcolm, Ala. (36556) 195/B8
Malcolm, Nebr. (68402) 264/H4
Malcom, Iowa (50157) 229/H5
Maldegem, Belgium 27/C6
Malden, Ill. (61337) 222/D2
Malden, Ind. (†46383) 227/C2
Malden (isl.), Kiribati 87/L6
Malden, Mass. (02148) 249/D6
Malden, Mo. (63863) 261/M9
Malden, New Bruns. 170/G2
Malden, Wash. (99149) 310/H3
Malden, W. Va. (25306) 312/C6
Maldives 2/N5
MALDIVES 68
Maldives 54/J9
Maldives (isls.) 68/C7
Maldon, England 10/G5
Maldon, England 13/H6
Maldon, Victoria 97/C5
Maldonado (pt.), Mexico 150/K8
Maldonado (dept.), Uruguay 145/E5
Maldonado, Uruguay 145/D6
Male (cap.), Maldives 54/J9
Male (cap.), Maldives 2/N5
Maléa (cape), Greece 45/F7
Malebo (Stanley Pool) (lake), Zaire 115/C4
Malegaon, India 54/J7
Malegaon, India 68/C4
Malekula (isl.), Vanuatu 87/G7
Malema, Mozambique 118/F2
Malemba-Nkulu, Zaire 115/E5
Malente, W. Germany 22/D1
Maler Kotla, India 68/D2
Malesus, Tenn. (†38301) 237/D9
Malgobek, U.S.S.R. 52/F6
Malhão da Estrela (mt.), Portugal 33/C2
Malheur (lake), Oreg. 188/C2
Malheur (co.), Oreg. 291/K4
Malheur (lake), Oreg. 291/J4
Malheur (riv.), Oreg. 291/J4
Mali 2/J5
Mali 102/B2
Mali (riv.), Burma 72/C1
Mali, Guinea 106/B6
MALI 106/D5
Malibu, Calif. (90265) 204/B10
Malignant Cove, Nova Scotia 168/F3
Maligne (lake), Alberta 182/B3
Mali Kyun (isl.), Burma 72/C4
Malili, Indonesia 85/G6
Malin, Ireland 17/G1
Malin (head), Ireland 17/F1
Malin (head), Ireland 10/C3
Malin, Oreg. (97632) 291/F5
Malin, U.S.S.R. 52/C4
Malinau, Indonesia 85/F5
Malindang (mt.), Philippines 82/D6
Malindi, Kenya 102/B2
Malindi, Kenya 115/H4
Malines (Mechelen), Belgium 27/F6
Malinta, Ohio (43535) 284/B3
Malita, Philippines 82/E7
Maliwun, Burma 72/C5
Malkapur, India 68/D4
Malkara, Turkey 63/B2
Malkiya, Israel 65/D1
Malko Tŭrnovo, Bulgaria 45/H4
Mallacoota, Victoria 97/E5
Mallaig, Alberta 182/E2
Mallaig, Scotland 10/D2
Mallaig, Scotland 15/C4
Mallanganee, N.S. Wales 97/G1
Mallard, Iowa (50562) 229/D3
Mallawi, Egypt 111/J4
Mallawi, Egypt 59/B4
Mallén, Spain 33/F2
Malleray, Switzerland 39/D2
Mallet Creek, Ohio (†44256) 284/G3
Malling, Denmark 21/D5
Mallnitz, Austria 41/B3
Malloa, Chile 138/G5
Malloch (cape), N.W. Terrs. 187/H2
Mallorca (Majorca) (isl.), Spain 33/H3
Mallory, N.Y. (13103) 276/H4
Mallory, W. Va. (25634) 312/C7
Mallorytown, Ontario 177/J3
Mallow, Ireland 17/D7
Mallow, Ireland 10/B4
Malmanoury, Fr. Guiana 131/E3
Malmberget, Sweden 18/M3
Malmédy, Belgium 27/J8
Malmesbury, England 13/E6
Malmesbury, S. Africa 118/B6
Malmköping, Sweden 18/F1
Malmo, Minn. (†56431) 255/E4
Malmo, Nebr. (68040) 264/H3
Malmö, Sweden 7/F3
Malmö, Sweden 18/H9
Malmöhus (co.), Sweden 18/H9
Malmok (mt.), Neth. Ant. 161/E8
Malmstrom A.F.B., Mont. 262/E3
Malo, Wash. (99150) 310/G2
Maloca, Brazil 132/C4
Maloca, Brazil 120/D3
Maloelap (atoll), Marshall Is. 87/H5
Malolos, Philippines 82/C3
Malone, Fla. (32445) 212/A1
Malone, Ky. (41451) 237/P5
Malone, N.Y. (12953) 276/M1
Malone, Texas (76660) 303/H6
Malone, Wash. (98559) 310/B4
Maloneton, Ky. (41158) 237/R3
Maloney (res.), Nebr. 264/D3
Malonton, Manitoba 179/E4
Malott, Wash. (98829) 310/F2
Maloy, Iowa (50852) 229/E7
Malpartida de Cáceres, Spain 33/C3
Malpartida de Plasencia, Spain 33/C2
Malpelo (isl.), Colombia 120/A2
Malpeque (bay), Pr. Edward I. 168/E2
Malta 2/K4
Malta 7/F5
Malta, Colo. (†80461) 208/G4
Malta, Idaho (83342) 220/E7
Malta, Ill. (60150) 222/E2
Malta (chan.), Italy 34/E6
MALTA 34
Malta (isl.), Malta 34/E7
Malta, Mont. (59538) 262/J2
Malta, Ohio (43758) 284/G6
Malta Bend, Mo. (65339) 261/F4
Maltahöhe, Namibia 118/B4
Maltepe, Turkey 63/D6
Malters, Switzerland 39/F2
Malton, England 13/G3
Malton, England 10/F3
Maltrata, Mexico 150/O2
Malung, Sweden 18/H6
Malvaglia, Switzerland 39/H4
Malvan, India 68/C5
Malvern, Ala. (36349) 195/G8
Malvern, Ark. (72104) 202/E5
Malvern, England 13/E5
Malvern, England 10/E4
Malvern, Iowa (51551) 229/B7
Malvern, Jamaica 158/H6
Malvern, Ohio (44644) 284/H4
Malvern, Pa. (19355) 294/L5
Malvern, Victoria 88/L7
Malvern, Victoria 97/J5
Malverne, N.Y. (11565) 276/R7
Malvina, Miss. (†38769) 256/C3
Malvinas (Falkland) (isls.), 143/D7
Malhye Karmakuly, U.S.S.R. 52/H1
Mama, U.S.S.R. 48/M4
Mamala (bay), Hawaii 218/B4
Mamalu (bay), Hawaii 218/K3
Mamanguape, Brazil 132/H4
Mamaroneck, N.Y. (10543) 276/P7
Mambahenauhan (isl.), Philippines 82/B7
Mambajao, Philippines 82/E6
Mambasa, Zaire 115/E3
Mamberamo (riv.), Indonesia 85/K6
Mambrui, Kenya 115/H4
Mamburao, Philippines 82/C4
Ma-Me-O Beach, Alberta 182/D3
Mamer, Luxembourg 27/H9
Mamers, France 28/D3
Mamers, N.C. (27552) 281/L4
Mamfé, Cameroon 115/A2
Mamie, N.C. (27952) 281/T2
Mamiña, Chile 138/B2
Mammoth, Ariz. (85618) 198/E6
Mammoth, Utah (†84628) 304/B4
Mammoth (creek), Utah 304/B6
Mammoth, W. Va. (25132) 312/D6
Mammoth Cave Nat'l Park, Ky. 237/J6
Mammoth Hot Springs (Yellowstone Nat'l Park), Wyo. (†82190) 319/B1
Mammoth Lakes, Calif. (93546) 204/G6
Mammoth Spring, Ark. (72554) 202/G1
Mamoré (riv.), Bolivia 120/C4
Mamoré (riv.), Bolivia 136/C2
Mamou, Guinea 106/B6
Mamou, La. (70554) 238/F5
Mampong, Ghana 106/D7
Mamry, Jezioro (lake), Poland 47/E1
Mamuju, Indonesia 85/F6
Man (isl.), I. of Man 13/C3
Man, Ivory Coast 106/C7
Man, Ivory Coast 102/B4
Man, W. Va. (25635) 312/C7
Mana, Fr. Guiana 131/E3
Mana (riv.), Fr. Guiana 131/E3
Mana (isl.), N. Zealand 100/B2
Manabí (prov.), Ecuador 128/B3
Manacacías (riv.), Colombia 126/D6
Manacapuru, Brazil 120/C3
Manacapuru, Brazil 132/H9
Manacas, Cuba 158/E1
Manacle (pt.), England 13/C7
Manacor, Spain 33/H3
Manado, Indonesia 54/O9
Manado, Indonesia 85/G5
Manage, Belgium 27/E7
Managua (cap.), Nic. 146/K8
Managua (cap.), Nicaragua 154/D4
Managua (lake), Nicaragua 154/E4
Manah, Oman 59/G5
Manahawkin, N.J. (08050) 273/E4
Manaia, N. Zealand 100/E3
Manakara, Madagascar 118/H4
Manakara, Madagascar 102/G7
Manakha, Yemen Arab Rep. 59/D6
Manakin-Sabot, Va. (23103) 307/N5
Manalapan, N.J. (†07746) 273/E3
Manama (cap.), Bahrain 59/F4
Manana (isl.), Hawaii 218/F2
Mananara, Madagascar 118/J3
Mananara (riv.), Madagascar 118/H4
Mananbao (riv.), Madagascar 118/G3
Mananjary, Madagascar 118/H4
Mananjary, Madagascar 102/G7
Manannah, Minn. (†56243) 255/D5
Manapire (riv.), Venezuela 124/E3
Manapouri (lake), N. Zealand 100/A6
Manaqil, Sudan 59/B7
Manar, Jebel (mt.), Yemen Arab Rep. 59/D7
Manare, Colombia 126/E4
Manas, China 77/C3
Manas He (riv.), China 77/C3
Manas Hu (lake), China 77/C2
Manasquan, N.J. (08736) 273/E3
Manasquan (riv.), N.J. 273/E3
Manassa, Colo. (81141) 208/H8
Manassas, Georgia (30438) 217/H6
Manassas (I.C.), Va. (22110) 307/O3
Manassas Nat'l Battlefield Park, Va. 307/K3
Manassas Park (I.C.), Va. (22110) 307/O3
Manatee (co.), Fla. 212/D4
Manatee (riv.), Fla. 212/D4
Manatí, Cuba 158/H3
Manatí, P. Rico 156/G1
Manatí, P. Rico 161/C1
Manaus, Brazil 2/F6
Manaus, Brazil 120/D3
Manaus, Brazil 132/H9
Manavgat, Turkey 63/D4
Manawa, Wis. (54949) 317/J7
Manay, Philippines 82/F7
Mancelona, Mich. (49659) 250/E4
Mancha, La (reg.), Spain 33/E3
Manchac (passage), La. 238/N2
Manchaca, Texas (78652) 303/G7
Mancha Real, Spain 33/E4
Manchaug, Mass. (01526) 249/G4
Manche (dept.), France 28/C3
Manche, La (English) (chan.), France 28/B3
Manchester, Ala. (†35501) 195/D3
Manchester, Calif. (95459) 204/B5
Manchester, Conn. (06040) 210/E1
Manchester○, Conn. (06040) 210/E1
Manchester, Greater (co.), England 13/H2
Manchester, England 7/D3
Manchester, England 10/G2
Manchester, England 13/H2
Manchester, Georgia (31816) 217/C5
Manchester, Ill. (62663) 222/C4
Manchester, Ind. (†47001) 227/H6
Manchester, Iowa (52057) 229/L3
Manchester, Kansas (67463) 232/E2
Manchester, Ky. (40962) 237/O6
Manchester○, Maine (04351) 243/D7
Manchester, Md. (21102) 245/L2
Manchester○, Mass. (01944) 249/F5
Manchester, Mich. (48158) 250/E6
Manchester, Minn. (56064) 255/E7
Manchester, Mo. (63011) 261/O3
Manchester, N.H. 188/M2
Manchester, N.H. (*03101) 268/E6
Manchester, N.Y. (14504) 276/F5
Manchester, Ohio (45144) 284/C8
Manchester, Okla. (73758) 288/L1
Manchester, Pa. (17345) 294/J5
Manchester, S. Dak. (†57353) 298/O5
Manchester, Tenn. (37355) 237/J10
Manchester, Vt. (05254) 268/A5
Manchester○, Vt. (05254) 268/A5
Manchester, Wash. (98353) 310/A2
Manchester, Wis. (†53946) 317/J8
Manchester Center, Vt. (05255) 268/A5
Manchester Depot, Vt. (†05254) 268/B5
Manchioneal, Jamaica 158/K6
Manchouli (Manzhouli), China 77/J2
Máncora, Peru 128/B5
Mancos, Colo. (81328) 208/C8
Mancos (riv.), Colo. 208/B8
Manda, Tanzania 115/F6
Mandabe, Madagascar 118/G4
Mandah, Mongolia 77/G3
Mandal, Norway 18/E7
Mandalay (div.), Burma 72/B2
Mandalay, Burma 54/L7
Mandalay, Burma 72/C2

Mariano Roque Alonso 405

Mandalgovĭ, Mongolia 77/G2
Mandali, Iraq 66/D4
Mandal-Ovoo, Mongolia 77/F3
Mandalya (gulf), Turkey 63/B4
Mandan, N. Dak. 188/F1
Mandan, N. Dak. (58554) 282/J6
Mandaon, Philippines 82/D4
Mandar (cape), Indonesia 85/F6
Mandaree, N. Dak. (58757) 282/E4
Mandaue, Philippines 82/E5
Mandeb, Bab el (str.), Saudi Arabia 59/D7
Mandeb, Bab el (str.), Yemen Arab Rep. 59/D7
Mandera, Kenya 115/H3
Manderson, S. Dak. (57756) 298/D7
Manderson, Wyo. (82432) 319/E1
Mandeville, Ark. (†75501) 202/C7
Mandeville, Jamaica 158/H6
Mandeville, La. (70448) 238/L6
Mandi, India 68/D2
Mandié, Mozambique 118/E3
Mandimba, Mozambique 118/F2
Mandinga, Panama 154/H6
Mandioré (lag.), Bolivia 136/F6
Mandla, India 68/E4
Mándok, Hungary 41/G2
Mandritsara, Madagascar 118/H3
Mand Rud (riv.), Iran 59/F4
Mand Rud (riv.), Iran 66/G6
Mandsaur, India 68/C4
Mandurah, W. Australia 88/B3
Mandurah, W. Australia 92/A2
Manduria, Italy 34/F4
Mandvi, India 68/B4
Manele (bay), Hawaii 218/H2
Manele Bay, Hawaii (†96763) 218/H2
Manendragarh, India 68/E4
Manes, Mo. (†65711) 261/H8
Manfalût, Egypt 111/J4
Manfalût, Egypt 59/B4
Manfred, N. Dak. (58465) 282/L4
Manfredonia, Italy 34/F4
Manfredonia (gulf), Italy 34/F4
Manga, Brazil 132/E6
Manga, Uruguay 145/B7
Mangai, Zaire 115/C4
Mangaia (isl.), Cook Is. 87/L8
Mangakino, N. Zealand 100/E3
Mangalia, Romania 45/J4
Mangalore, India 54/J8
Mangalore, India 68/C6
Mangareva (isl.), Fr. Poly. 87/N8
Mangaweka, N. Zealand 100/E3
Mangere (isl.), N. Zealand 100/E7
Mangerton (mt.), Ireland 17/C8
Mangham, La. (71259) 238/G2
Mangkalihat (cape), Indonesia 85/F5
Manglaralto, Ecuador 128/B3
Mangle (pt.), Cuba 158/J3
Manglillo (pt.), P. Rico 161/B3
Mangnai, China 77/D4
Mango, Fla. (33550) 212/D4
Mango, Togo 106/E6
Mangochi, Malawi 115/G6
Mangoky (riv.), Madagascar 102/G7
Mangoky (riv.), Madagascar 118/G4
Mangole (isl.), Indonesia 85/H6
Mangonui, N. Zealand 100/D1
Mangoro (riv.), Madagascar 118/H3
Mangotsfield, England 10/E5
Mangotsfield, England 13/E6
Mangrol, India 68/B4
Mangsee (isls.), Philippines 82/A7
Mangualde, Portugal 33/C2
Mangueigne, Chad 111/D5
Mangueira (lag.), Brazil 132/D11
Manguera Azul, Uruguay 145/D4
Mangui, China 77/K1
Manguito, Cuba 158/D1
Mangum, Okla. (73554) 288/G5
Mangyshlak (pen.), U.S.S.R. 48/F5
Manhan (riv.), Mass. 249/D4
Manhasset, N.Y. (11030) 276/P7
Manhattan, Ill. (60442) 222/F2
Manhattan, Ind. (†46171) 227/D5
Manhattan, Kansas (66502) 232/F2
Manhattan, Mont. (59741) 262/E5
Manhattan, Nev. (89022) 266/E4
Manhattan (borough), N.Y. (*10001) 276/M9
Manhattan (isl.), N.Y. 276/M9
Manhattan Beach, Calif. (90266) 204/B11
Manhattan Beach, Minn. (56463) 255/E4
Manhay, Belgium 27/H8
Manheim, Pa. (17545) 294/K5
Manheim, W. Va. (26403) 312/G4
Manhiça, Mozambique 118/E5
Man Hpang, Burma 72/C2
Manhuaçu, Brazil 132/F8
Manhuaçu, Brazil 135/E2
Manhumirim, Brazil 135/E2
Maní, Colombia 126/D5
Maniamba, Mozambique 102/F6
Maniamba, Mozambique 118/F2
Manibridge, Manitoba 179/J2
Manica (prov.), Mozambique 118/E4
Manica, Mozambique 118/E3
Manicani (isl.), Philippines 82/E5
Manicaragua, Cuba 158/E2
Manicoré, Brazil 120/C3
Manicoré, Brazil 132/H9
Manicouagan, Québec 174/D2
Manicouagan (pt.), Québec 172/B1
Manicouagan (res.), Québec 174/D2
Manicouagan (riv.), Que. 162/K5
Manicouagan (riv.), Québec 174/D2
Manifest, La. (†71340) 238/G3
Manifold (cape), Queensland 88/J4
Manifold (cape), Queensland 95/D4
Manigotagan, Manitoba 179/F3
Manigotagan (lake), Manitoba 179/G4
Manigotagan (riv.), Manitoba 179/G3
Manigouche, Québec 174/C3
Manihiki (atoll), Cook Is. 87/K7
Manila, Ala. (†36586) 195/C7
Manila, Ark. (72442) 202/K2
Manila (prov.), Philippines 82/C3
Manila (cap.), Philippines 2/R5
Manila (cap.), Philippines 85/G3
Manila (cap.), Philippines 82/C3
Manila (cap.), Philippines 54/N8
Manila (bay), Philippines 82/C3
Manila, Utah (84046) 304/E3
Manildra, N.S. Wales 97/E3
Manilla, Ind. (46150) 227/F5
Manilla, Iowa (51454) 229/C5
Manilla, N.S. Wales 97/F2
Maningrida, North. Terr. 93/C2
Manipa (str.), Indonesia 85/H6
Manipur (riv.), Burma 72/B2
Manipur (state), India 68/G4
Manisa (prov.), Turkey 63/B3
Manisa, Turkey 63/B3
Manisa, Turkey 59/A2
Manistee, Mich. 188/J2
Manistee (co.), Mich. 250/C4
Manistee, Mich. (49660) 250/C4
Manistee (riv.), Mich. 250/C4
Manistique, Mich. (49854) 250/C3
Manistique (lake), Mich. 250/D2
Manistique (riv.), Mich. 250/C2
Manito, Ill. (61546) 222/D3
Manito (lake), Sask. 181/B3
Manitoba (prov.) 162/G5
Manitoba (prov.), Canada 146/J4
MANITOBA 179
Manitoba (lake), Man. 146/H4
Manitoba (lake), Man. 162/G5
Manitoba (lake), Manitoba 179/D4
Manitou, Ky. (42436) 237/F6
Manitou, Manitoba 179/D5
Manitou (isl.), Mich. 250/B1
Manitou, N. Dak. (†58776) 282/E3
Manitou, Okla. (73555) 288/J5
Manitou (lake), Ontario 177/C2
Manitou (lake), Québec 172/C3
Manitou Beach, Sask. 181/F4
Manitoulin (terr. dist.), Ontario 175/D3
Manitoulin (terr. dist.), Ontario 177/B2
Manitoulin (isl.), Ont. 162/H6
Manitoulin (isl.), Ontario 175/D3
Manitoulin (isl.), Ontario 177/B2
Manitou Springs, Colo. (80829) 208/J5
Manitouwadge, Ontario 177/H5
Manitouwadge, Ontario 175/C3
Manitowaning, Ontario 177/C2
Manitowish, Wis. (†54547) 317/F3
Manitowoc (co.), Wis. 317/L7
Manitowoc, Wis. (54220) 317/L7
Maniwaki, Québec 174/B3
Maniwaki, Québec 172/B3
Manizales, Colombia 126/C5
Manizales, Colombia 120/B2
Manja, Jordan 65/D4
Manja, Madagascar 118/G4
Manjacaze, Mozambique 118/E5
Manjimup, W. Australia 88/B6
Manjimup, W. Australia 92/B6
Mankato, Kansas (66956) 232/D2
Mankato, Minn. 188/H2
Mankato, Minn. (56001) 255/E6
Mankono, Ivory Coast 106/C7
Mankota, Sask. 181/D6
Manley, Nebr. (68403) 264/H4
Manley Hot Springs, Alaska (99756) 196/H2
Manlius, Ill. (61338) 222/D2
Manlius, N.Y. (13104) 276/J5
Manlleu, Spain 33/H1
Manly, Iowa (50456) 229/G2
Manly, N. S. Wales 88/L4
Manly, N.S. Wales 97/K3
Manly, N.C. (†28387) 281/L4
Manly, Queensland 88/L2
Manmad, India 68/C4
Manmanoc (mt.), Philippines 82/C2
Mann (riv.), North. Terr. 93/D2
Manna, Indonesia 85/C6
Mannahill, S. Australia 94/F5
Mannar (gulf) 54/J9
Mannar (gulf), India 68/D7
Mannar, Sri Lanka 68/E7
Mannar (gulf), Sri Lanka 68/D7
Mannargudi, India 68/E6
Mannboro, Va. (23105) 307/N6
Männedorf, Switzerland 39/G2
Mannersdorf am Leithagebirge, Austria 41/D3
Manners Sutton, New Bruns. 170/D3
Mannford, Okla. (74044) 288/O2
Mannheim, W. Germany 7/E4
Mannheim, W. Germany 22/C4
Manning, Alberta 182/B1
Manning, Ark. (71757) 202/E5
Manning, Iowa (51455) 229/C5
Manning, Kansas (†67871) 232/B3
Manning (riv.), N.S. Wales 97/F2
Manning, N. Dak. (58642) 282/E5
Manning (cape), N.W. Terrs. 187/F2
Manning (str.), Solomon Is. 86/D2
Manning, S.C. (29102) 296/G4
Manning Prov. Park, Br. Col. 184/G5
Mannington, Ky. (†42217) 237/G6
Mannington, W. Va. (26582) 312/F3
Männlifluh (mt.), Switzerland 39/E3
Manns Choice, Pa. (15550) 294/E6
Manns Harbor, N.C. (27953) 281/T3
Mannsville, Ky. (42758) 237/L6
Mannsville, N.Y. (13661) 276/H3
Mannsville, Okla. (73447) 288/N6
Mannu (riv.), Italy 34/B5
Mannum, S. Australia 94/F6
Mannville, Alberta 182/E3
Mano (riv.), Liberia 106/B7
Mano (riv.), S. Leone 106/B7
Manoa, Bolivia 136/C1
Manokin, Md. (21836) 245/P8
Manokin (riv.), Md. 245/P8
Manokotak, Alaska (99628) 196/G3
Manokwari, Indonesia 85/J6
Manola, Alberta 182/C2
Manombo, Madagascar 118/G4
Manomet, Mass. (02345) 249/M5
Manomet (pt.), Mass. 249/N5
Manono, Zaire 115/E5
Manono, Zaire 102/E5
Manor, Georgia (31550) 217/G8
Manor, Pa. (15665) 294/C5
Manor, Sask. 181/K6
Manor, Texas (78653) 303/G7
Manorhamilton, Ireland 17/E3
Manori, India 68/B6
Manori (creek), India 68/B7
Manorville, N.Y. (11949) 276/P9
Manorville, Pa. (16238) 294/C4
Manosque, France 28/G6
Manotick, Ontario 177/J2
Manouane, Québec 172/C2
Manouane (lake), Québec 174/C2
Manp'o, N. Korea 81/B3
Manquin, Va. (23106) 307/O5
Manra (Sydney) (isl.), Kiribati 87/K6
Manresa, Spain 33/G2
Mansa, Zambia 115/E6
Mansa, Zambia 102/E6
Mansalay, Philippines 82/C4
Mansavillagra, Uruguay 145/D4
Manseau, Québec 172/E3
Mansel (isl.), N.W.T. 162/H3
Mansel (isl.), N.W.T. 146/K3
Mansel (isl.), N.W. Terrs. 187/K3
Mansel'ka (mts.), U.S.S.R. 52/C1
Mansfield, Ark. (72944) 202/B3
Mansfield○, Conn. (†06250) 210/F1
Mansfield, England 13/K2
Mansfield, England 10/F4
Mansfield, Georgia (30255) 217/E4
Mansfield, Ill. (61854) 222/E3
Mansfield, Ind. (†47872) 227/C5
Mansfield, La. (71052) 238/C2
Mansfield, Mass. (02048) 249/J4
Mansfield○, Mass. (02048) 249/J4
Mansfield, Minn. (†56009) 255/E7
Mansfield, Mo. (65704) 261/G8
Mansfield, Ohio 188/K2
Mansfield, Ohio (*44901) 284/F4
Mansfield, Pa. (16933) 294/H2
Mansfield, S. Dak. (57460) 298/N3
Mansfield, Tenn. (38236) 237/E8
Mansfield, Texas (76063) 303/F3
Mansfield (mt.), Vt. 268/B2
Mansfield, Victoria 97/D5
Mansfield, Wash. (98830) 310/F3
Mansfield Center, Conn. (06250) 210/G1
Mansfield Depot, Conn. (06251) 210/F1
Mansfield Woodhouse, England 13/F4
Mansilla de las Mulas, Spain 33/D1
Manso (riv.), Brazil 132/C6
Manso (riv.), Chile 138/E4
Manson, Ind. (†46041) 227/D4
Manson, Iowa (50563) 229/D3
Manson, Manitoba 179/A4
Manson, N.C. (27553) 281/N2
Manson, Wash. (98831) 310/E3
Manson Creek, Br. Col. 184/E2
Mansonville, Québec 172/E4
Mansura, La. (71350) 238/G4
Manta, Ecuador 128/B3
Manta, Ecuador 120/A3
Manta (bay), Ecuador 128/B3
Mantachie, Miss. (38855) 256/H2
Mantador, N. Dak. (58058) 282/R7
Mantagao (lake), Manitoba 179/E3
Mantagao (riv.), Manitoba 179/E3
Mantalingajan (mt.), Philippines 82/A6
Mantario, Sask. 181/B4
Mantaro (riv.), Peru 128/E8
Mantas (well), Niger 106/E5
Manteca, Calif. (95336) 204/D6
Mantecal, Apure, Venezuela 124/D4
Mantecal, Bolívar, Venezuela 124/F4
Mantee, Miss. (39751) 256/F3
Manteigas, Portugal 33/C2
Manteno, Ill. (60950) 222/F2
Manteo, N.C. (27954) 281/T3
Manter, Kansas (67862) 232/A4
Mantes-la-Jolie, France 28/D3
Manti, Utah (84642) 304/C4
Mantiqueira (range), Brazil 135/D3
Manto, Honduras 154/D3
Mantoloking, N.J. (08738) 273/E3
Manton, Calif. (96059) 204/D3
Manton, Mich. (49663) 250/D4
Manton, R.I. (†02904) 249/J5
Mantorville, Minn. (55955) 255/F6
Mänttä, Finland 18/O6
Mantua, Ala. (35472) 195/C4
Mantua, Cuba 158/A2
Mantua (prov.), Italy 34/C2
Mantua, Italy 34/C2
Mantua○, N.J. (08051) 273/C4
Mantua, Ohio (44255) 284/H3
Mantua, Utah (†84302) 304/C2
Mantua, Va. (†22030) 307/S3
Manturovo, U.S.S.R. 52/F3
Manú, Peru 128/G9
Manú (riv.), Peru 128/G8
Manua (isls.), Amer. Samoa 87/K7
Manuae (atoll), Cook Is. 87/K7
Manuel Benavides, Mexico 150/H2
Manuelito, N. Mex. (†86506) 274/A3
Manuel Rodríguez (isl.), Chile 138/D10
Manuels, New Bruns. 170/F1
Manuels, Newf. 166/D2
Manui (isl.), Indonesia 85/G6
Manukan, Philippines 82/D6
Manukau, N. Zealand 100/C1
Manukau (harb.), N. Zealand 100/B1
Manulla, Ireland 17/C4
Manumuskin (riv.), N.J. 273/D5
Manunui, N. Zealand 100/E3
Manuripi (riv.), Bolivia 136/B2
Manus (isl.), Papua N.G. 87/E6
Manus (isl.), Papua N.G. 86/A1
Manutuke, N. Zealand 100/F3
Manvel, N. Dak. (58256) 282/R3
Manvel, Texas (77578) 303/J3
Manville, N.J. (08835) 273/D2
Manville, R.I. (02838) 249/H5
Manville, Wyo. (82227) 319/H3
Many, La. (71449) 238/C3
Manyara (lake), Tanzania 115/G4
Manyas, Turkey 63/B3
Manyberries, Alberta 182/E5
Manych-Gudilo (lake), U.S.S.R. 52/F5
Many Farms, Ariz. (86538) 198/F2
Manyoni, Tanzania 115/G5
Manzai, Pakistan 59/K3
Manzanar, Chile 138/F2
Manzanares, Spain 33/E3
Manzanares (riv.), Spain 33/F4
Manzanillo, Cuba 158/H4
Manzanillo, Cuba 156/C2
Manzanillo (bay), Dom. Rep. 158/C5
Manzanillo (bay), Haiti 158/C5
Manzanillo, Mexico 150/G7
Manzanillo, Mexico 146/H8
Manzanillo (pt.), Panama 154/H6
Manzanita, Oreg. (97130) 291/C2
Manzanita Ind. Res., Calif. 204/J11
Manzano, N. Mex. (†87016) 274/C4
Manzano (mts.), N. Mex. 274/C4
Manzano (peak), N. Mex. 274/C4
Manzanola, Colo. (81058) 208/M6
Manzhouli (Manchouli), China 77/J2
Manzini, Swaziland 118/E5
Mao, Chad 111/C5
Mao, Dom. Rep. 158/D5
Maoke (mts.), Indonesia 85/K6
Maoming (Mowming), China 77/H7
Mapai, Mozambique 118/E4
Mapararí, Venezuela 124/D2
Mapastepec, Mexico 150/N9
Mapes, N. Dak. (58349) 282/O3
Mapia (isls.), Indonesia 85/J5
Mapimí, Mexico 150/G4
Mapimí (depr.), Mexico 150/G3
Mapire, Venezuela 124/F4
Mapiri, Bolivia 136/B4
Mapiripán, Laguna (lake), Colombia 126/E6
Maple (peak), Ariz. 198/F5
Maple (riv.), Mich. 250/E5
Maple (lake), Minn. 255/B3
Maple (riv.), Minn. 255/E7
Maple (riv.), N. Dak. 282/O8
Maple (riv.), N. Dak. 282/R6
Maple (creek), Sask. 181/B5
Maple (riv.), S. Dak. 298/M1
Maple, Wis. (54854) 317/C2
Maple Bay, Br. Col. 184/K3
Maple Bay, Minn. (†56736) 255/B3
Maple City, Kansas (67102) 232/F4
Maple City, Mich. 250/D4
Maple Creek, Sask. 162/F6
Maple Creek, Sask. 181/B6
Maple Falls, Wash. (98266) 310/D2
Maple Grove, Minn. (†55369) 255/G5
Maple Grove, Ontario 177/F4
Maple Grove, Québec 172/H4
Maple Heights, Ohio (44137) 284/H9
Maple Hill, Iowa (50564) 229/D2
Maple Hill, Kansas (66507) 232/F2
Maple Hill, N.C. (28454) 281/O5
Maple Island, Minn. (†55082) 255/E7
Maple Lake, Minn. (55358) 255/D5
Maple Park, Ill. (60151) 222/E2
Maple Plain, Minn. (55359) 255/F5
Maple Rapids, Mich. (48853) 250/E5
Maple Ridge, Br. Col. 184/L3
Maple River, Iowa (†51401) 229/D4
Maples, Ind. (†46802) 227/H2
Maples, Mo. (†65542) 261/J7
Maple Shade○, N.J. (08052) 273/B3
Maplesville, Ala. (36750) 195/E5
Mapleton, Iowa (51034) 229/B4
Mapleton, Kansas (66754) 232/H3
Mapleton○, Maine (04757) 243/G2
Mapleton, Mich. (†49684) 250/D4
Mapleton, Minn. (56065) 255/E7
Mapleton, N.C. (†27855) 281/P2
Mapleton, N. Dak. (58059) 282/R6
Mapleton, Oreg. (97453) 291/C3
Mapleton (Mapleton Depot), Pa. (17052) 294/F5
Mapleton, Utah (†84663) 304/C3
Mapleton, Wis. (†53066) 317/J1
Mapleton Depot, Pa. (17052) 294/F5
Maple Valley, Wash. (98038) 310/C3
Mapleview, Minn. (†55912) 255/E7
Mapleview, New Bruns. 170/C2
Mapleville, Md. (†21713) 245/H2
Mapleville, R.I. (02839) 249/H5
Maplewood, La. (†70663) 238/D6
Maplewood, Minn. (55109) 255/G5
Maplewood, Mo. (63143) 261/P3
Maplewood, N.H. (†03574) 268/D3
Maplewood○, N.J. (07040) 273/E2
Maplewood, Ohio (45340) 284/B5
Maplewood, Wis. (54226) 317/M6
Mapocho (riv.), Chile 138/G3
Mapoon Mission Station, Queensland 88/G2
Mapoon Mission Station, Queensland 95/B1
Maporal, Venezuela 124/C4
Mapos (Amazones), Cuba 158/F2
Mappsville, Va. (23407) 307/T5
Mapuera (riv.), Brazil 132/B3
Maputo (city) (prov.), Mozambique 118/E5
Maputo (prov.), Mozambique 118/E5
Maputo (cap.), Mozambique 2/L7
Maputo (cap.), Mozambique 118/E5
Maputo (cap.), Mozambique 102/F7
Maqatin (ruins), P.D.R. Yemen 59/E7
Maqên, China 77/F5
Maqna, Saudi Arabia 59/C4
Ma Qu (Huang He) (riv.), China 77/F5
Maquapit (lake), New Bruns. 170/D3
Maqueda (chan.), Philippines 82/D3
Maquela do Zombo, Angola 102/D5
Maquela do Zombo, Angola 115/C5
Maquereau (pt.), Québec 172/D2
Maquinchao, Argentina 143/C5
Maquoketa, Iowa (52060) 229/M4
Maquon, Ill. (61458) 222/C3
Mar (mts.), Brazil 120/E5
Mar (range), Brazil 135/C4
Mar, Serra do (range), Brazil 132/E9
Mar (dist.), Scotland 15/F3
Mara, Guyana 131/C3
Mara (reg.), Tanzania 115/F4
Marabá, Brazil 132/D4
Marabá, Brazil 120/E3
Marabahan, Indonesia 85/E6
Marabella, Trin. & Tob. 161/A11
Maracá (isl.), Brazil 120/E2
Maracá (isl.), Brazil 132/D2
Maracaibo, Venezuela 124/C2
Maracaibo, Venezuela 120/B1
Maracaibo (lake), Venezuela 120/B2
Maracaibo (lake), Venezuela 124/C3
Maracaju, Brazil 132/C8
Maracas (bay), Trin. & Tob. 161/C10
Maracay, Venezuela 124/E2
Maracay, Venezuela 120/C2
Marada, Libya 111/C2
Maradi, Niger 106/F6
Maradi, Niger 102/C3
Maragheh, Iran 59/E2
Maragheh, Iran 66/E2
Maragogipe, Brazil 132/G6
Maraira (pt.), Philippines 82/C1
Marajó (est.), Brazil 120/E2
Marajó (isl.), Brazil 120/E3
Marajó (bay), Brazil 132/E2
Marajó (isl.), Brazil 132/D3
Maralal, Kenya 115/G3
Maralinga, S. Australia 88/E6
Maralwexi (Bachu), China 77/A4
Maramag, Philippines 82/E7
Maramec, Okla. (74045) 288/N2
Marampa, S. Leone 106/B7
Marana, Ariz. (85238) 198/D6
Marand, Iran 59/E2
Marand, Iran 66/D1
Marandellas, Zimbabwe 118/E3
Marang, Malaysia 72/D6
Maranguape, Brazil 132/G3
Maranhão (state), Brazil 132/E4
Maranoa (riv.), Queensland 95/C5
Marañón (riv.), Peru 120/B3
Marañón (riv.), Peru 128/E5
Marapanim, Brazil 132/E3
Maras (mt.), Indonesia 85/D6
Maraş, Turkey 59/C2
Maraş (Kahramanmaraş), Turkey 63/G4
Marathon, Fla. (33050) 212/E7
Marathón, Greece 45/G6
Marathon, Iowa (50565) 229/C3
Marathon, N.Y. (13803) 276/J6
Marathon, Ohio (45145) 284/C7
Marathon, Ont. 162/H6
Marathon, Ontario 177/H5
Marathon, Ontario 175/C3
Marathon, Texas (79842) 303/A7
Marathon (co.), Wis. 317/G6
Marathon, Wis. (54448) 317/G6
Maratua (isl.), Indonesia 85/F5
Maravillas, Bolivia 136/B2
Maravillas (creek), Texas 303/A7
Marawi, Philippines 85/G4
Marawi, Philippines 82/E6
Marbach, Switzerland 39/E3
Marbach am Neckar, W. Germany 22/C4
Marbella, Spain 33/D4
Marble, Ark. (72746) 202/C1
Marble, Colo. (†81623) 208/E4
Marble, Minn. (55764) 255/E3
Marble, N.C. (28905) 281/B4
Marble (isl.), N.W.T. 162/G3
Marble (isl.), N.W. Terrs. 187/J3
Marble Bar, Australia 87/C8
Marble Bar, W. Australia 88/B4
Marble Bar, W. Australia 92/C3
Marble Canyon, Ariz. (86036) 198/D2
Marble Canyon Nat'l Mon., Ariz. 198/D2
Marble City, Okla. (74945) 288/S3
Marble Dale, Conn. (06777) 210/B2
Marble Falls, Texas (78654) 303/F7
Marblehead, Ill. (†62301) 222/B4
Marblehead○, Mass. (01945) 249/E7
Marblehead (neck), Mass. 249/F6
Marblehead, Ohio (†43440) 284/E2
Marble Hill, Georgia (30148) 217/D2
Marble Hill, Mo. (63764) 261/N8
Marblemount, Wash. (98267) 310/D2
Marble Rock, Iowa (50653) 229/H3
Marbleton, Québec 172/F4
Marbleton, Wyo. (†83113) 319/B3
Marble Valley, Ala. (†35150) 195/F4
Marburg an der Lahn, W. Germany 22/C3
Marbury, Ala. (36051) 195/E5
Marbury, Md. (20658) 245/K6
Marcala, Honduras 154/C3
Marcali, Hungary 41/D3
Marcapata, Peru 128/G9
Marcelin, Sask. 181/E3
Marceline, Mo. (64658) 261/F3
Marcell, Minn. (56657) 255/E3
Marcella, Ark. (72555) 202/G2
Marcella, N.J. (†07866) 273/E2
Marcelline, Ill. (†62376) 222/B3
Marcellus, Mich. (49067) 250/D6
Marcellus, N.Y. (13108) 276/H5
Marcelville, New Bruns. 170/E2
March (riv.), Austria 41/D2
March, England 10/G4
March, England 13/H5
March A.F.B., Calif. 204/E11
Marchand, Manitoba 179/F5
Marche, Ark. (†72114) 202/F4
Marche (trad. prov.) France 29
Marche (reg.), Italy 34/D3
Marche-en-Famenne, Belgium 27/G8
Marchegg, Austria 41/D2
Marchena (isl.), Ecuador 128/B9
Marchena, Spain 33/D4
Marchfield, Barbados 161/B9
Marchigüe, Chile 138/F5
Marchin, Belgium 27/G8
Mar Chiquita (lake), Argentina 143/D3
Marchwell, Sask. 181/K5
Marco (Marco Island), Fla. (33937) 212/E6
Marco (isl.), Fla. 212/E6
Marco, Ind. (†47443) 227/C7
Marco, La. (†71447) 238/E3
Marcola, Oreg. (97454) 291/E3
Marcona, Peru 128/E10
Marcos Juárez, Argentina 143/D3
Marcus, Iowa (51035) 229/B3
Marcus (isl.), Japan 87/F3
Marcus, S. Dak. (57757) 298/E4
Marcus, Wash. (99151) 310/H2
Marcus Baker (mt.), Alaska 196/C1
Marcus Hook, Pa. (19061) 294/L7
Marcy, N.Y. (13403) 276/K4
Marcy (mt.), N.Y. 276/N2
Mardan, Pakistan 68/C2
Mardan, Pakistan 59/K3
Mardela Springs, Md. (21837) 245/P7
Mar del Plata, Argentina 143/E4
Mar del Plata, Argentina 120/D6
Mardin (prov.), Turkey 63/J4
Mardin, Turkey 63/J4
Mardin, Turkey 59/D2
Maré (isl.), New Caled. 87/G8
Mare (isl.), New Caled. 86/J4
Mareb (riv.), Ethiopia 59/C7
Marechal Deodoro, Brazil 132/H5
Maree, Loch (lake), Scotland 10/D2
Mare, Loch (lake), Scotland 15/C3
Mareeba, Queensland 95/C3
Mareeba, Queensland 88/G3
Mare Island Navy Yard, Calif. 204/J1
Marengo (co.), Ala. 195/C6
Marengo, Ala. (†36736) 195/C6
Marengo, Ill. (60152) 222/E1
Marengo, Ind. (47140) 227/E8
Marengo, Iowa (52301) 229/J5
Marengo, Ohio (43334) 284/E5
Marengo, Sask. 181/B4
Marengo, Wash. (†99004) 310/G3
Marengo, Wis. (54855) 317/E3
Marenisco, Mich. (49947) 250/F2
Marennes, France 28/C5
Mareth, Tunisia 106/F2
Marettimo (isl.), Italy 34/C6
Marfa, Texas (79843) 303/C12
Marfield, N.S. Wales 97/C3
Marfrance, W. Va. (25975) 312/E6
Margai Caka (lake), China 77/C4
Marganets, U.S.S.R. 52/E5
Margao, India 68/C5
Margaree, Nova Scotia 168/G2
Margaree (isl.), Nova Scotia 168/F4
Margaree Centre, Nova Scotia 168/H2
Margaree Forks, Nova Scotia 168/G2
Margaree Harbour, Nova Scotia 168/G2
Margaree Valley, Nova Scotia 168/H2
Margaret, Ala. (35112) 195/F3
Margaret (lake), Alberta 182/B5
Margaret, Manitoba 179/C5
Margaret, Texas (†79227) 303/E3
Margaret (riv.), W. Australia 88/D3
Margaret River, W. Australia 88/A6
Margaret River, W. Australia 92/A6
Margaret River Station, W. Australia 92/D2
Margaretsville, Nova Scotia 168/C3
Margaretville, N.Y. (12455) 276/L6
Margarita, Argentina 143/F5
Margarita (isl.), Venezuela 120/C1
Margarita (isl.), Venezuela 124/F2
Margate, England 13/J6
Margate, England 10/G5
Margate, Fla. (33063) 212/F5
Margate, S. Africa 118/E6
Margate, Tasmania 99/D4
Margate City, N.J. (08402) 273/E5
Margento, Colombia 126/C4
Margerum, Ala. (†35616) 195/B1
Margherita (Jamama), Somalia 115/H3
Margherita (mt.), Uganda 115/E3
Margherita (mt.), Zaire 102/E4
Margherita (mt.), Zaire 115/E3
Margie, Minn. (56658) 255/E2
Margo, Sask. 181/H4
Margos, Peru 128/D8
Margosatubig, Philippines 82/D7
Margow, Dasht-e (des.), Afghanistan 59/H3
Margow, Dasht-e (des.), Afghanistan 68/A2
Margraten, Netherlands 27/H7
Margret, Georgia (†30536) 217/D1
Margrethe (lake), Mich. 250/E4
Marguerite (bay) 5/C15
María (isl.), Fr. Poly. 87/L8
Maria (creek), Ind. 227/C7
Maria, Québec 172/C2
Maria (isls.), St. Lucia 161/G7
Maria (isl.), Tasmania 99/E4
Mari A.S.S.R., U.S.S.R. 52/G3
Mari A.S.S.R., U.S.S.R. 48/E4
María Albina, Uruguay 145/E4
María Cleófas (isl.), Mexico 150/F6
María Elena, Chile 138/B3
Mariager, Denmark 21/D4
Mariager, Denmark 18/G8
Mariager (fjord), Denmark 21/D4
Mariah Hill, Ind. (47556) 227/D8
María Madre (isl.), Mexico 150/F6
María Magdalena (isl.), Mexico 150/F6
Marian (lake), Fla. 212/E4
Marian (lake), N.W. Terrs. 187/G3
Marian, Queensland 88/H4
Marian, Queensland 95/D4
Mariana, Brazil 135/E2
Mariana Lake, Alberta 182/D2
Marianao, Cuba 158/C1
Marianao, Cuba 156/A2
Marianas, Northern 87/E4
Mariana Trench 87/E4
Marianna, Ark. (72360) 202/J4
Marianna, Fla. (32446) 212/A1
Marianna, Pa. (15345) 294/B5
Mariano I. Loza, Argentina 143/G4
Mariano Roque Alonso, Paraguay 144/A4

406 Mariánské Lázně

Mariánské Lázně, Czech. 41/B2
Maria Pinto, Chile 138/G3
Mariapolis, Manitoba 179/C5
Marías, Islas (isls.), Mexico 150/F6
Marias (riv.), Mont. 188/D1
Marias (riv.), Mont. 262/D2
Maria Stein, Ohio (45860) 284/A5
Mariato, Punta (cape), Panama 154/G7
María Trinidad Sánchez (prov.), Dom. Rep. 158/E5
Maria van Diemen (cape), N. Zealand 100/D1
Mariazell, Austria 41/C3
Marib, Saudi Arabia 59/E6
Marib, Yemen Arab Rep. 59/D6
Mariba, Ky. (40345) 237/O5
Maribel, Wis. (54227) 317/L7
Maribo, Denmark 21/E8
Maribor, Yugoslavia 7/F4
Maribor, Yugoslavia 45/B2
Maribyrnong (riv.), Victoria 97/H5
Maribyrnong (riv.), Victoria 88/K7
Maricao, P. Rico 161/B2
Maricopa (co.), Ariz. 198/C5
Maricopa, Ariz. (85239) 198/C5
Maricopa (mts.), Ariz. 198/C5
Maricopa, Calif. (93252) 204/F8
Maricopa Ind. Res., Ariz. 198/C6
Maricourt, Que. 162/J3
Maricourt, Québec 174/F1
Maricunga, Salar de (salt dep.), Chile 138/B6
Maridi, Sudan 111/E7
Marie (lake), Alberta 182/E2
Marie, Ark. (†72395) 202/K2
Marie, W. Va. (†24910) 312/E7
Marie Byrd Land (reg.), Ant. 2/D10
Marie Byrd Land (reg.) 5/B13
Mariefred, Sweden 18/F1
Marie-Galante (isl.), Guadeloupe 161/B7
Marie-Galante (isl.), Guadeloupe 156/G4
Mariehamn, Finland 18/M7
Mariel, Cuba 158/B1
Mariemont, Ohio (45227) 284/C9
Marienberg, Papua N.G. 85/B6
Marienburg (Malbork), Poland 47/D1
Mariënburg, Suriname 131/D2
Mariental, Namibia 118/B4
Mariental, Namibia 102/D7
Marienthal, Kansas (67863) 232/A3
Marienville, Pa. (16239) 294/D3
Marie-Reine, Alberta 182/B1
Maries (co.), Mo. 261/J6
Mariestad, Sweden 18/H7
Marietta, Georgia (*30060) 217/J1
Marietta, Ill. (61459) 222/C3
Marietta, Ind. (†46176) 227/F6
Marietta, Minn. (56257) 255/B5
Marietta, Miss. (38856) 256/H2
Marietta, N.C. (28362) 281/L6
Marietta, Ohio (45750) 284/G7
Marietta, Okla. (73448) 288/M7
Marietta, Pa. (17547) 294/J5
Marietta-Alderwood, Wash. (98268) 310/C2
Marietta-Slater, S.C. (29661) 296/C1
Marieval, Sask. 181/J5
Marieville, Québec 172/D4
Marigot, Dominica 161/F6
Marigot, Haiti 158/C6
Marigot, Martinique 161/D5
Marigot, St. Lucia 161/G6
Marigüitar, Venezuela 124/G2
Marihatag, Philippines 82/F6
Marília, Brazil 120/D5
Marília, Brazil 135/A3
Marília, Brazil 132/D8
Marilla, N.Y. (14102) 276/C5
Marin (co.), Calif. 204/C5
Marin, Spain 33/B1
Marin, Calif. (93933) 204/D7
Marinduque (prov.), Philippines 82/C4
Marinduque (isl.), Philippines 82/C4
Marine, Ill. (62061) 222/D5
Marine City, Mich. (48039) 250/G6
Marineland, Fla. (†32084) 212/E2
Marine on Saint Croix, Minn. (55047) 255/F5
Marinette (co.), Wis. 317/K5
Marinette, Wis. (54143) 317/L5
Maringá, Brazil 120/D5
Maringá, Brazil 132/D8
Maringouin, La. (70757) 238/G6
Marinha Grande, Portugal 33/B3
Marinhas, Portugal 33/B2
Marino, Italy 34/F7
Marion (reef), 95/E3
Marion (co.), Ala. 195/C2
Marion, Ala. (36756) 195/D5
Marion (lake), Alberta 182/D3
Marion (co.), Ark. 202/E1
Marion, Ark. (72364) 202/K3
Marion, Conn. (06444) 210/D2
Marion (co.), Fla. 212/D2
Marion (co.), Georgia 217/C6
Marion (co.), Ill. 222/E5
Marion, Ill. (62959) 222/E6
Marion (co.), Ind. 227/E5
Marion, Ind. 188/J2
Marion, Ind. (46952) 227/F3
Marion (co.), Iowa 229/G6
Marion, Iowa (52302) 229/K4
Marion (co.), Kansas 232/E3
Marion, Kansas (66861) 232/F3
Marion (lake), Kansas 232/E3
Marion (co.), Ky. 237/L5
Marion, Ky. (42064) 237/E6
Marion, La. (71260) 238/F1
Marion, Mass. (02738) 249/L6
Marion○, Mass. (02738) 249/L6
Marion, Mich. (49665) 250/D4
Marion (co.), Miss. 256/E8
Marion, Miss. (39342) 256/G6
Marion (co.), Mo. 261/J3
Marion, Mont. (59925) 262/B2
Marion, N.Y. (14505) 276/F4
Marion, N.C. (28752) 281/E3
Marion, N. Dak. (58466) 282/O6
Marion (co.), Ohio 284/D4
Marion, Ohio 188/K2
Marion, Ohio (43302) 284/D4
Marion (co.), Oreg. 291/E3
Marion, Oreg. (97359) 291/D3
Marion, Pa. (17235) 294/G6
Marion (res.), Queensland 88/J3
Marion, S. Australia 88/D8
Marion, S. Australia 94/A8
Marion (lake), S.C. 188/K4
Marion (co.), S.C. 296/J3
Marion, S.C. (29571) 296/J3
Marion (lake), S.C. 296/G5
Marion, S. Dak. (57043) 298/P7
Marion (bay), Tasmania 99/E4
Marion (co.), Tenn. 237/K10
Marion (co.), Texas 303/K5
Marion, Va. (24354) 307/E7
Marion (co.), W. Va. 312/F4
Marion, Wis. (54950) 317/J6
Marion Bridge, Nova Scotia 168/H3
Marion Center, Pa. (15759) 294/D4
Marion Junction, Ala. (36759) 195/D6
Marion Station, Md. (21838) 245/R8
Marionville, Mo. (65705) 261/E8
Maripa, Fr. Guiana 131/E4
Maripa, Venezuela 124/F4
Maripasoula, Fr. Guiana 131/D4
Mariposa (co.), Calif. 204/E6
Mariposa, Calif. (95338) 204/F6
Mariscala, Uruguay 145/E5
Mariscal Estigarribia, Paraguay 120/C5
Mariscal Estigarribia, Paraguay 144/B3
Marismas, Las (marsh), Spain 33/C4
Marissa, Ill. (62257) 222/D5
Maritime Alps (range), France 28/G5
Maritime Alps (range), Italy 34/A2
Maritsa, Bulgaria 45/H4
Maritsa (riv.), Bulgaria 45/G4
Mariupol' (Zhdanov), U.S.S.R. 52/E5
Marivan (Dezh Shahpur), Iran 66/E3
Mariveles, Philippines 82/C3
Märjamaa, U.S.S.R. 53/C1
Mark (riv.), Belgium 27/F6
Mark, Ill. (61340) 222/D2
Mark (riv.), Netherlands 27/F6
Marka (Merka), Somalia 115/H3
Marka, Somalia 102/G4
Markam, China 77/E6
Markaryd, Sweden 18/H8
Mark Center, Ohio (43536) 284/A3
Markdale, Ontario 177/D3
Marked Tree, Ark. (72365) 202/K2
Marken (isl.), Netherlands 27/G4
Markerwaard Polder, Netherlands 27/G3
Markesan, Wis. (53946) 317/J8
Market Drayton, England 10/E4
Market Drayton, England 13/E5
Market Harborough, England 13/G5
Markethill, N. Ireland 17/H3
Market Rasen, England 13/G4
Market Weighton, England 13/G4
Markha (riv.), U.S.S.R. 48/M3
Markham (mt.) 5/A8
Markham, Ill. (60426) 222/B6
Markham (bay), N.W. Terrs. 187/L3
Markham (inlet), N.W. Terrs. 187/L1
Markham, Ontario 177/K4
Markham, Va. (22643) 307/N3
Markham, Wash. (†98520) 310/B4
Markinch, Sask. 181/G5
Markinch, Scotland 15/E4
Markit, China 77/A4
Markkleeberg, E. Germany 22/E3
Markland, Ind. (†47020) 227/G7
Markland, Newf. 166/D2
Markle, Ind. (46770) 227/G3
Markleeville, Calif. (96120) 204/F5
Marklesburg (James Creek), Pa. (16657) 294/F5
Markleton, Pa. (15551) 294/D6
Markleville, Ind. (46056) 227/F5
Markleysburg, Pa. (15459) 294/C6
Markounda, Cent. Afr. Rep. 115/C2
Markovo, U.S.S.R. 4/C1
Markovo, U.S.S.R. 48/S3
Marks, Miss. (38646) 256/D2
Marks, U.S.S.R. 52/G4
Markstay, Ontario 177/D1
Marksville, La. (71351) 238/G4
Marktredwitz, W. Germany 22/E4
Markville, Minn. (55048) 255/F4
Marl, W. Germany 22/B3
Marland, Okla. (74644) 288/M1
Marlbank, Ontario 177/G3
Marlboro, Alberta 182/B3
Marlboro○, N.J. (07746) 273/E3
Marlboro, N.Y. (12542) 276/M7
Marlboro (co.), S.C. 296/H2
Marlboro○, Vt. (05344) 268/B6
Marlborough, Conn. (06447) 210/F2
Marlborough○, Conn. (06447) 210/F2
Marlborough, England 13/F6
Marlborough, England 10/F5
Marlborough, Mass. (01752) 249/H3
Marlborough, Mo. (†63101) 261/P3
Marlborough, N.H. (03455) 268/C6
Marlborough○, N.H. (03455) 268/C6
Marlborough, Queensland 95/D4
Marlette, Mich. (48453) 250/G5
Marlin, Texas (76661) 303/H6
Marlin, Wash. (98832) 310/F3
Marlinton, W. Va. (24954) 312/F6
Marlow, Ala. (†36580) 195/C10
Marlow, England 13/G8
Marlow, Georgia (†31312) 217/K6
Marlow○, N.H. (03456) 268/C5
Marlow, Okla. (73055) 288/K5
Marlton, N.J. (08053) 273/D4
Marmaduke, Ark. (72443) 202/K1
Marmagao, India 68/C5
Marmande, France 28/C5
Marmara (sea), Turkey 7/G4
Marmara (isl.), Turkey 63/B2
Marmara (sea), Turkey 63/C2
Marmara (sea), Turkey 59/A1
Marmaris, Turkey 63/C4
Marmarth, N. Dak. (58643) 282/B7
Mar Menor (lag.), Spain 33/F4
Marmet, W. Va. (25315) 312/C6
Marmolada (mt.), Italy 34/C1
Marmontana (mt.), Switzerland 39/H4
Marmora, N.J. (08223) 273/D5
Marmora, Ontario 177/G3
Marmot (bay), Alaska 196/H3
Marmot (isl.), Alaska 196/H3
Mar Muerto (lag.), Mexico 150/N9
Marne (dept.), France 28/F3
Marne (riv.), France 28/C2
Marne, Iowa (51552) 229/C6
Marne, Mich. (49435) 250/D5
Marne, W. Germany 22/C2
Maro (dry riv.), Chad 111/C4
Maro (reef), Hawaii 188/F6
Maro (reef), Hawaii 218/C6
Maroa, Ill. (61756) 222/E3
Maroa, Venezuela 124/E6
Maroantsetra, Madagascar 118/J3
Marolambo, Madagascar 118/H4
Maromokotro (mt.), Madagascar 102/G6
Maromokotro (mt.), Madagascar 118/H2
Maroni (riv.) 120/D2
Maroni (riv.), Fr. Guiana 131/D3
Maroochydore-Mooloolaba, Queensland 88/J5
Maroochydore-Mooloolaba, Queensland 95/E5
Maroon (peak), Colo. 208/F4
Maroon Town, Jamaica 158/H6
Maros (riv.), Hungary 41/F3
Maros, Indonesia 85/F6
Maroua, Cameroon 102/D3
Maroua, Cameroon 115/B1
Maroubra, N.S. Wales 97/K3
Marouini (riv.), Fr. Guiana 131/D4
Marovoay, Madagascar 102/G6
Marovoay, Madagascar 118/H3
Marowijne (dist.), Suriname 131/D4
Marowijne (riv.), Suriname 131/D3
Marquam, Oreg. (97362) 291/B3
Marquand, Mo. (63655) 261/M8
Marquesas (keys), Fla. 212/D7
Marquesas (isls.), Fr. Polynesia 2/B6
Marquesas (isls.), Fr. Poly. 87/N6
Marquette, Iowa (52158) 229/L2
Marquette, Kansas (67464) 232/E3
Marquette, Manitoba 179/E4
Marquette, Mich. 146/K5
Marquette, Mich. 188/J1
Marquette (co.), Mich. 250/B2
Marquette, Mich. (49855) 250/B2
Marquette (isl.), Mich. 250/E3
Marquette, Nebr. (68854) 264/G4
Marquette (co.), Wis. 317/H8
Marquette, Wis. (53947) 317/H8
Marquette Heights, Ill. (†61554) 222/D3
Marquez, Texas (77865) 303/H6
Marquis, Grenada 161/D8
Marquis, St. Lucia 161/G6
Marquis, Sask. 181/F5
Marra, Jebel (mt.), Sudan 102/E3
Marra (creek), N.S. Wales 97/D2
Marra, Jebel (mt.), Sudan 111/D5
Marracuene, Mozambique 118/E5
Marrakech, Morocco 102/B1
Marrakech, Morocco 106/C2
Marrawah, Tasmania 99/A2
Marree, S. Australia 88/F5
Marree, S. Australia 94/E3
Marrero, La. (70072) 238/O4
Marrickville, N.S. Wales 88/L4
Marrickville, N.S. Wales 97/J3
Marriott, Sask. 181/D4
Marromeu, Mozambique 118/F3
Marrowbone, Ky. (42759) 237/K7
Marrowie (creek), N.S. Wales 97/C3
Marrupa, Mozambique 118/F2
Mars, Pa. (16046) 294/C4
Mars (riv.), Québec 172/G1
Marsabit, Kenya 115/G3
Marsabit, Kenya 102/F4
Marsa el Brega, Libya 111/D1
Marsa el Hariga, Libya 111/D1
Marsala, Italy 34/D6
Marsa Oseif, Sudan 111/G3
Mars Bluff, S.C. (†29501) 296/H3
Marsciano, Italy 34/D3
Marsden, N.S. Wales 97/D3
Marsden, Sask. 181/B3
Marsden Park, N.S. Wales 97/H3
Marsdiep (chan.), Netherlands 27/F3
Marseille, France 7/E4
Marseille, France 28/F6
Marseilles, Ill. (61341) 222/E2
Marseilles, Ohio (†43351) 284/D4
Marsh (creek), Idaho 220/F7
Marsh (isl.), La. 238/G7
Marsh (lake), Minn. 255/B5
Marsh, Mont. (†59326) 262/M4
Marsh (peak), Utah 304/E3
Marshall (co.), Ala. 195/F2
Marshall, Ark. (72650) 202/E2
Marshall (co.), Ill. 222/D2
Marshall, Ill. (62441) 222/F4
Marshall (co.), Ind. 227/E2
Marshall, Ind. (47859) 227/C5
Marshall (co.), Iowa 229/G4
Marshall (co.), Kansas 232/F2
Marshall (co.), Ky. 237/E7
Marshall, Liberia 106/B7
Marshall (isl.), Maine 243/G7
Marshall, Mich. (49068) 250/E6
Marshall (co.), Minn. 255/B2
Marshall, Minn. (56258) 255/C6
Marshall (co.), Miss. 256/E1
Marshall, Mo. (65340) 261/F4
Marshall, N.C. (28753) 281/D3
Marshall, N. Dak. (58644) 282/F5
Marshall (riv.), North. Terr. 88/F4
Marshall (riv.), North. Terr. 93/D7
Marshall, Ohio (†45133) 284/C7
Marshall (co.), Okla. 288/N6
Marshall, Okla. (73056) 288/L2
Marshall (isls.), Pacific Is. Terr. 2/T5
Marshall, Sask. 181/B2
Marshall (co.), S. Dak. 298/O2
Marshall (co.), Tenn. 237/H10
Marshall, Texas 188/H4
Marshall, Texas (75670) 303/K5
Marshall, Va. (22115) 307/N3
Marshall (co.), W. Va. 312/E3
Marshall, Wis. (53559) 317/H9
Marshallberg, N.C. (28553) 281/S5
Marshall Hall, Md. (†20616) 245/K6
Marshall Islands 87/G4
Marshalls Creek, Pa. (18335) 294/M3
Marshallton, Del. (19808) 245/R2
Marshalltown, Iowa (50158) 229/G4
Marshalltown, Iowa 188/H2
Marshallville, Georgia (31057) 217/D6
Marshallville, Ohio (44645) 284/G4
Marshes Siding, Ky. (42631) 237/M7
Marshfield, Ind. (47956) 227/C4
Marshfield, Mass. (02050) 249/M4
Marshfield○, Mass. (02050) 249/M4
Marshfield, Mo. (65706) 261/G8
Marshfield, Vt. (05658) 268/C3
Marshfield○, Vt. (05658) 268/C3
Marshfield, Wis. (54449) 317/F6
Marshfield Hills, Mass. (02051) 249/M4
Marsh Hill, Pa. (†17722) 294/H3
Mars Hill○, Maine (04758) 243/H2
Mars Hill, N.C. (28754) 281/D3
Mars Hill-Blaine, Maine (04758) 243/H2
Marshland, Oreg. (†97016) 291/D1
Marshville, N.C. (28103) 281/J4
Marshy (lake), Manitoba 179/B5
Marshyhope (creek), Md. 245/P6
Marsing, Idaho (83639) 220/B6
Marsland, Nebr. (69354) 264/A2
Marsoui, Québec 172/C1
Märsta, Sweden 18/K7
Marstal, Denmark 21/D8
Marston, Mo. (63866) 261/N9
Marston, N.C. (28363) 281/K5
Marstons Mills, Mass. (02648) 249/N6
Marstrand, Sweden 18/G8
Mart, Texas (76664) 303/H6
Martaban, Burma 72/C3
Martaban (gulf), Burma 54/L8
Martaban (gulf), Burma 72/C4
Martapura, Indonesia 85/F6
Martel, Ohio (43335) 284/E4
Martel, Tenn. (†37771) 237/N9
Martelange, Belgium 27/H9
Martell, Calif. (95654) 204/C9
Martell, Wis. (†54767) 317/B6
Martelle, Iowa (52305) 229/L4
Marten (mt.), Alberta 182/C2
Martensdale, Iowa (50160) 229/F6
Martensville, Sask. 181/E3
Martha, Ky. (41159) 237/R4
Martha, Okla. (73556) 288/H5
Martha, Tenn. (†37087) 237/J8
Marthaguy (creek), N.S. Wales 97/D2
Marthasville, Mo. (63357) 261/L5
Martha's Vineyard (isl.), Mass. 188/N2
Martha's Vineyard (isl.), Mass. 249/M7
Marthaville, La. (71450) 238/D3
Martí, Camagüey, Cuba 158/G3
Martí, Matanzas, Cuba 158/D1
Martí, Cuba 156/C2
Martigny, Switzerland 39/C4
Martigues, France 28/F6
Martin (dam), Ala. 195/G5
Martin (lake), Ala. 195/G5
Martin, Czech. 41/E2
Martin (co.), Fla. 212/F4
Martin, Georgia (30557) 217/F2
Martin (co.), Ind. 227/D7
Martin (co.), Ky. 237/R5
Martin, Ky. (41649) 237/R5
Martin, La. (†71019) 238/D2
Martin, Mich. (49070) 250/D6
Martin (co.), Minn. 255/D7
Martin, New Bruns. 170/C1
Martin (head), New Bruns. 170/E3
Martin (co.), N.C. 281/P3
Martin, N. Dak. (58758) 282/K4
Martin, Ohio (43445) 284/D2
Martin, S.C. (29836) 296/D5
Martin, S. Dak. (57551) 298/F7
Martin, Tenn. (38237) 237/D8
Martin (co.), Texas 303/C5
Martin, W. Va. (†26702) 312/H4
Martina Franca, Italy 34/F4
Martinborough, N. Zealand 100/E4
Martín Chico, Uruguay 145/A5
Martinez, Calif. (94553) 204/K1
Martinez, Georgia (30907) 217/H3
Martínez de la Torre, Mexico 150/L6
Martín García (isl.), Argentina 143/H6
Martinique (isl.) 146/M8
Martinique (passage), Dominica 161/E7
MARTINIQUE 161/D5
MARTINIQUE 156/G4
Martinique (passage), Martinique 161/C5
Martin Luther King, Jr., Nat'l Hist. Site, Georgia 217/K1
Martinsburg, Ind. (†47165) 227/E8
Martinsburg, Iowa (52568) 229/J6
Martinsburg, Mo. (65264) 261/J4
Martinsburg, Nebr. (†68770) 264/H2
Martinsburg, N.Y. (13404) 276/J3
Martinsburg, Ohio (43037) 284/F5
Martinsburg, Pa. (16662) 294/F5
Martinsburg, W. Va. (25401) 312/K4
Martins Creek, Pa. (18063) 294/M4
Martinsdale, Mont. (59053) 262/F4
Martinsdale (res.), Mont. 262/F4
Martins Ferry, Ohio (43935) 284/J5
Martins Mills, Tenn. (†38471) 237/F10
Martins River, Nova Scotia 168/D4
Martinsville, Ill. (62442) 222/F4
Martinsville, Ind. (46151) 227/D6
Martinsville, Miss. (†39083) 256/D7
Martinsville, Mo. (64467) 261/D2
Martinsville, N.J. (08836) 273/D2
Martinsville, Ohio (45146) 284/C7
Martinsville (I.C.), Va. (24112) 307/J7
Martinton, Ill. (60951) 222/F3
Martintown, Ontario 177/K2
Martin Van Buren Nat'l Hist. Site, N.Y. 276/N6
Martinville, Ark. (†72039) 202/F3
Martinville, Québec 172/F4
Martock, England 13/E7
Martofte, Denmark 21/D6
Marton, N. Zealand 100/E4
Martos, Spain 33/E4
Martre, Lac la (LAKE(, N.W.T. 162/E3
Martwick, Ky. (†42330) 237/H6
Marty, S. Dak. (57361) 298/N8
Marudi (mts.), Guyana 131/B5
Marudi, Malaysia 85/E5
Ma'ruf, Afghanistan 68/B2
Ma'ruf, Afghanistan 59/J3
Maruim, Brazil 132/G5
Marulan, N.S. Wales 97/E4
Marungu (mts.), Zaire 115/E5
Marutea (atoll), Fr. Poly. 87/N8
Marv Dasht, Iran 66/H6
Marvejols, France 28/E5
Marvel, Ala. (†35115) 195/D4
Marvel, Colo. (81329) 208/C8
Marvell, Ark. (72366) 202/J4
Marvin, S. Dak. (57251) 298/R3
Marvindale, Pa. (†16749) 294/E2
Marvine (mt.), Utah 304/C5
Marvyn, Ala. (†36801) 195/H6
Marwayne, Alberta 182/E3
Marwood, Pa. (16047) 294/C4
Mary, Ky. (41350) 237/O5
Mary (lake), Minn. 255/C5
Mary (riv.), Queensland 95/E5
Mary, U.S.S.R. 54/H6
Mary (Merv), U.S.S.R. 48/G6
Maryborough, Australia 87/F8
Maryborough (Portlaoighise), Ireland 17/G5
Maryborough (Portlaoighise), Ireland 10/C4
Maryborough, Queensland 95/E5
Maryborough, Queensland 88/J5
Maryborough, Victoria 97/B5
Maryborough, Victoria 88/G7
Marydel, Md. (21649) 245/P4
Marydell, Miss. (†39051) 256/F5
Mary Esther, Fla. (32569) 212/B6
Maryfield, Sask. 181/K6
Maryhill, Wash. (†98620) 310/E5
Mary Kathleen, Queensland 88/G4
Mary Kathleen, Queensland 95/A4
Marykirk, Scotland 15/F4
Maryland 188/L3
MARYLAND 245
Maryland, N.Y. (12116) 276/L5
Maryland (state), U.S. 146/L6
Maryland City, Md. (†21113) 245/L4
Maryland Heights, Mo. (63043) 261/O2
Maryland Line, Md. (21105) 245/M2
Maryneal, Texas (79535) 303/D5
Maryport, England 10/E3
Maryport, England 13/D3
Mary Ronan (lake), Mont. 262/B3
Marys (creek), Idaho 220/C7
Marys (riv.), Nev. 266/F1
Mary's Harbour, Newf. 166/C3
Marystown, Newf. 166/D4
Marysvale, Utah (84750) 304/B5
Marysvale (peak), Utah 304/B5
Marysville, Calif. 188/B3
Marysville, Calif. (95901) 204/D4
Marysville, Ind. (47141) 227/F7
Marysville, Iowa (†50116) 229/G6
Marysville, Kansas (66508) 232/F2
Marysville, Mich. (48040) 250/G6
Marysville, Mont. (59640) 262/D4
Marysville, Ohio (43040) 284/D5
Marysville, Pa. (17053) 294/H5
Marysville, Wash. (98270) 310/C2
Marytown, W. Va. (†24889) 312/C8
Maryvale, Queensland 95/C3
Maryvale, Queensland 88/H3
Maryville, Ill. (62062) 222/B2
Maryville, Mo. (64468) 261/C2
Maryville, Tenn. (37801) 237/O9
Marzo (pt.), Colombia 126/B4
Masagua, Guatemala 154/B3
Masahim, Kuh-e (mt.), Iran 66/J5
Masai (steppe), Tanzania 115/G4
Masaka, Uganda 115/F4
Masamba, Indonesia 85/G6
Masan, S. Korea 81/D6
Masardis○, Maine (04759) 243/G3
Masaryktown, Fla. (33512) 212/D3
Masasi, Tanzania 115/G6
Masatepe, Nicaragua 154/D5
Masaya, Nicaragua 154/D5
Masbate (prov.), Philippines 82/D4
Masbate, Philippines 82/D4
Masbate (isl.), Philippines 82/D4
Masbate (isl.), Philippines 85/G3
Mascara, Algeria 106/D1
Mascarene (isls.), Mauritius 118/F5
Mascarene (isls.), Réunion 118/F5
Mascoma, N.H. (†03748) 268/C4
Mascoma (lake), N.H. 268/C4
Mascot, Tenn. (37806) 237/O8
Mascota, Mexico 150/G6
Mascotte, Fla. (32753) 212/E3
Mascouche, Québec 172/H4
Mascoutah, Ill. (62258) 222/D5
Masefield, Sask. 181/D6
Masela (isl.), Indonesia 85/H7
Maseru (cap.), Lesotho 102/E8
Maseru (cap.), Lesotho 118/D5
Mash 'Abbe Sade, Israel 65/B6
Mashabi (isl.), Saudi Arabia 59/C4
Masham, England 13/F3
Mashapaug, Conn. (†06076) 210/G1
Mashapaug (lake), Conn. 210/G1
Mashash, Wadi (dry riv.), Jordan 65/C4
Mashhad (Meshed), Iran 66/L2
Mashike, Japan 81/K2
Mashkel, Hamun-i- (swamp), Pakistan 68/A3
Mashkel, Hamun-i- (swamp), Pakistan 59/H4
Mashkid (riv.), Iran 66/N7
Mashkid (riv.), Iran 59/H4
Mashkid (riv.), Pakistan 59/H4
Mashkid (riv.), Pakistan 68/A3
Mashonaland (reg.), Zimbabwe 118/E3
Mashpee○, Mass. (02649) 249/M6
Mashulaville, Miss. (†39341) 256/G4
Masi-Manimba, Zaire 115/C4
Masindi, Uganda 115/F3
Masinloc, Philippines 82/B3
Masio (cay), Cuba 158/C2
Masira (isl.), Oman 54/G7
Masira (gulf), Oman 59/G6
Masira (isl.), Oman 59/G5
Masisea, Peru 128/E7
Masisi, Zaire 115/E4
Masjed Soleyman, Iran 66/F5
Mask (lake), Ireland 17/C4
Mask, Lough (lake), Ireland 10/B4
Maskell, Nebr. (68751) 264/H2
Maskinongé (co.), Québec 172/D3
Maskinongé (county), Québec 174/C3
Maskinongé, Québec 172/E3
Maskinongé (riv.), Québec 172/D3
Masoala (pen.), Madagascar 118/J3
Masoller, Uruguay 145/C2
Mason (isl.), Conn. 210/H3
Mason (co.), Ill. 222/D3
Mason, Ill. (62443) 222/E5
Mason (co.), Ky. 237/O3
Mason, Ky. (†41097) 237/M3
Mason (co.), Mich. 250/C4
Mason, Mich. (48854) 250/E6
Mason, Nev. (†89447) 266/B4
Mason (peak), Nev. 266/F1
Mason (bay), N. Zealand 100/A7
Mason, Ohio (45040) 284/B7
Mason, Okla. (74859) 288/O3
Mason, Tenn. (38049) 237/B10
Mason (co.), Texas 303/E7
Mason, Texas (76856) 303/E7
Mason (co.), Wash. 310/B3
Mason (co.), W. Va. 312/B5
Mason, W. Va. (25260) 312/B4
Mason, Wis. (54856) 317/D3
Mason City, Ill. (62664) 222/D3
Mason City, Iowa (50401) 229/G2
Mason City, Iowa 188/H2
Mason City, Nebr. (68855) 264/E3
Mason Hall, Tenn. (†38233) 237/C8
Mason Springs, Md. (†20640) 245/K6
Masontown, Pa. (15461) 294/C6
Masontown, W. Va. (26542) 312/G3
Masonville, Colo. (80541) 208/J2
Masonville, Iowa (50654) 229/K4
Masonville, N.Y. (13804) 276/K6
Masqat (Muscat) (cap.), Oman 59/G5
Massa, Italy 34/C2
Massabesic (lake), N.H. 268/E6
Massac (co.), Ill. 222/E6
Massa-Carrara (prov.), Italy 34/C2
Massachusetts 188/M2
MASSACHUSETTS 249
Massachusetts (bay), Mass. 249/M4
Massachusetts (state), U.S. 146/L5
Massacre (bay), Amer. Samoa 86/N9
Massacre (lake), Nev. 266/B1
Massafra, Italy 34/F4
Massakory, Chad 111/C5
Massa Marittima, Italy 34/C3
Massangena, Mozambique 118/E4
Massango (Forte República), Angola 115/C5
Massanutten (mt.), Va. 307/L3
Massapê, Brazil 132/G3
Massapeag, Conn. (†06382) 210/G3
Massapequa, N.Y. (11758) 276/R7
Massapequa Park, N.Y. (11762) 276/R7
Massaponax, Va. (†22553) 307/O4
Massawa, Ethiopia 111/G4
Massawa, Ethiopia 59/C6
Massawa, Ethiopia 102/F3
Massbach, Ill. (†61028) 222/C1
Mass City, Mich. (49948) 250/G1
Massena, Iowa (50853) 229/D6
Massena, N.Y. (13662) 276/L1
Massénya, Chad 111/C5
Masset, Br. Col. 184/B3
Masset (inlet), Br. Col. 184/A3
Massey, Md. (21650) 245/P3
Massey, N. Zealand 100/B1
Massey, Ontario 177/C1
Massies Mill, Va. (22954) 307/K5
Massillon, Ala. (†36759) 195/D6
Massillon, Iowa (†52255) 229/L5
Massillon, Ohio (44646) 284/H4
Massinga, Mozambique 118/F4
Massingir, Mozambique 118/E4
Massive (mt.), Colo. 208/F4
Masson, Québec 172/B4
Massueville, Québec 172/E4
Mastaba, Saudi Arabia 59/C5
Mastens Corner, Del. (†19943) 245/R5
Masters, Colo. (†80649) 208/L2
Masterton, N. Zealand 100/E4
Mastic Beach, N.Y. (11950) 276/P9
Mastuj, Pakistan 59/K2
Mastung, Pakistan 59/J4
Mastung, Pakistan 68/B3
Mastura, Saudi Arabia 59/C5
Masuda, Japan 81/E6
Masurian (lakes), Poland 47/E2
Masury, Ohio (44438) 284/J3
Masyaf, Syria 63/G5
Matabeleland (reg.), Zimbabwe 118/D3
Matachewan, Ontario 177/J5
Matachewan, Ontario 175/D3
Mata de São João, Brazil 132/G6
Matadi, Zaire 115/B5

McKinley 407

Matadi, Zaire 102/D5
Matador, Sask. 181/D5
Matador, Texas (79244) 303/D3
Matagalpa, Nicaragua 154/E4
Matagami, Québec 174/B3
Matagami (lake), Québec 174/B3
Matagorda (co.), Texas 303/H9
Matagorda, Texas (77457) 303/J9
Matagorda (bay), Texas 188/G5
Matagorda (bay), Texas 303/H9
Matagorda (isl.), Texas 303/H9
Matagorda (pen.), Texas 303/J9
Matagorda Isl. Bombing and Gunnery Range, Texas 303/H9
Matakana (isl.), N. Zealand 100/F2
Matala (dam), Angola 115/B6
Matam, Senegal 106/B5
Matamoras, Pa. (18336) 294/N3
Matamoros, Mexico 146/J7
Matamoros, Coahuila, Mexico 150/H4
Matamoros, Tamaulipas, Mexico 150/L4
Matane (co.), Québec 172/B1
Matane (county), Québec 174/D3
Matane, Québec 174/D3
Matane, Québec 172/B1
Matane (riv.), Québec 172/B1
Matane Prov. Park, Québec 172/B1
Matanuska (riv.), Alaska 196/C1
Matanza, Colombia 126/D4
Matanzas (prov.), Cuba 158/D1
Matanzas, Cuba 146/K7
Matanzas, Cuba 158/C1
Matanzas, Cuba 156/B2
Matanzas (bay), Cuba 158/D1
Matanzas (inlet), Fla. 212/E2
Mata Palacio, Dom. Rep. 158/F6
Matapalo (cape), C. Rica 154/F6
Matapan (Tainaron) (cape), Greece 45/F7
Matapédia (county), Québec 174/D3
Matapédia (co.), Québec 172/B2
Matapédia, Québec 172/B2
Matapédia (lake), Québec 172/B1
Matapédia (riv.), Québec 172/B2
Mataquito (riv.), Chile 138/A10
Matara, Sri Lanka 68/E7
Mataram, Indonesia 85/F7
Matarani, Peru 120/B4
Matarani, Peru 128/F11
Mataranka, North. Terr. 93/C3
Matarinao (bay), Philippines 82/E5
Mataró, Spain 33/H2
Matatiele, S. Africa 118/D6
Matatindoc (pt.), Philippines 82/D6
Mataura, N. Zealand 100/B7
Mataura (riv.), N. Zealand 100/B6
Mata Utu (cap.), Wallis and Futuna 87/J7
Matawai, N. Zealand 100/F3
Matawan, Minn. (†56072) 255/E7
Matawan, N.J. (07747) 273/E3
Matawin (lake), Québec 172/C3
Matawin (riv.), Québec 172/D3
Mateare, Nicaragua 154/D4
Mateguá, Bolivia 136/D3
Matehuala, Mexico 150/J5
Matelot, Trin. & Tob. 161/B10
Matera (prov.), Italy 34/F4
Matera, Italy 34/F4
Maternillos (pt.), Cuba 158/H2
Mátészalka, Hungary 41/G3
Matetsi, Zimbabwe 118/D3
Mateur, Tunisia 106/F1
Matewan, W. Va. (25678) 312/B7
Matfield Green, Kansas (66862) 232/F3
Mather, Manitoba 179/C5
Mather, Wis. (54641) 317/F7
Mather A.F.B., Calif. 204/C8
Matherville, Ill. (61263) 222/C2
Matherville, Miss. (†39360) 256/G7
Matheson, Colo. (80830) 208/M4
Matheson, Ontario 177/K5
Matheson Island, Manitoba 179/E3
Mathews, Ala. (36052) 195/F6
Mathews (lake), Calif. 204/E11
Mathews, La. (70375) 238/J7
Mathews (co.), Va. 307/R6
Mathews, Va. (23109) 307/R6
Mathias, W. Va. (26812) 312/J5
Mathinna, Tasmania 99/E3
Mathis, Texas (78368) 303/G9
Mathiston, Miss. (39752) 256/F3
Mathoura, N.S. Wales 97/C4
Mathura, India 68/D3
Mati, Philippines 85/H4
Mati, Philippines 82/F7
Matías Romero, Mexico 150/M8
Matinenda (lake), Ontario 177/B1
Matinicus, Maine (04851) 243/F8
Matinicus Rock (isl.), Maine 243/F8
Matlock, England 10/F4
Matlock, England 13/J2
Matlock, Iowa (51244) 229/A2
Matlock, Wash. (98560) 310/B3
Matoaca, Va. (23803) 307/N6
Matoaka, W. Va. (24736) 312/D8
Matochkin Shar (str.), U.S.S.R. 48/F2
Mato Grosso (state), Brazil 132/B6
Mato Grosso, Brazil 120/D4
Mato Grosso, Brazil 132/B6
Mato Grosso (plat.), Brazil 120/D4
Mato Grosso, Planalto de (plat.), Brazil 132/B6
Mato Grosso do Sul (state), Brazil 132/C7
Matopos, Zimbabwe 118/D4
Matosinhos, Portugal 33/B2
Matoury, Fr. Guiana 131/E3
Mátra (mts.), Hungary 41/E3
Matrah, Oman 54/G7
Matrah, Oman 59/G5
Matrei in Osttirol, Austria 41/B3
Matruh, Egypt 59/A3
Matsqui, Br. Col. 184/L3
Matsu (Mazu) (isl.), China 77/K6
Matsubara, Japan 81/H8
Matsue, Japan 81/F6
Matsumae, Japan 81/J3
Matsumoto, Japan 81/H5
Matsusaka, Japan 81/H6
Matsuto, Japan 81/H5
Matsuyama, Japan 81/F7
Matsuyama, Japan 54/P6
Matt, Switzerland 39/H3
Mattabesset (riv.), Conn. 210/E2
Mattagami (riv.), Ontario 175/D3
Mattagami (riv.), Ontario 177/J5
Mattamiscontis (lake), Maine 243/F4
Mattamuskeet (lake), N.C. 281/S3
Mattapan, Mass. (02126) 249/C7
Mattapoisett, Mass. (02739) 249/L6
Mattapoisett◯, Mass. (02739) 249/L6
Mattaponi, Va. (23110) 307/P5
Mattaponi (riv.), Va. 307/O5
Mattaponi Ind. Res., Va. 307/P5
Mattawa, Ont. 162/J6
Mattawa, Ontario 177/F1
Mattawa, Ontario 175/E3
Mattawa, Wash. (99344) 310/F4
Mattawamkeag◯, Maine (04459) 243/G5
Mattawamkeag (lake), Maine 243/G4
Mattawamkeag (riv.), Maine 243/G4
Mattawan, Mich. (49071) 250/D6
Mattawana, Pa. (17054) 294/G5
Mattawoman (creek), Md. 245/K6
Matterhorn (mt.), Switzerland 39/E4
Mattersburg, Austria 41/D3
Matteson, Ill. (60443) 222/B6
Matthew, Ky. (41454) 237/P5
Matthews, Georgia (30818) 217/H4
Matthews, Ind. (46957) 227/F4
Matthews, Mo. (63857) 261/N9
Matthews, N.C. (28105) 281/H4
Matthews Ridge, Guyana 131/B2
Mattice, Ontario 175/D3
Mattice, Ontario 177/J5
Mattighofen, Austria 41/B2
Mattituck, N.Y. (11952) 276/P9
Mattoon, Ill. (61938) 222/E4
Mattoon, Wis. (54450) 317/J5
Mattson, Miss. (38758) 256/C2
Matu, Venezuela 124/F4
Matucana, Peru 128/D8
Matuku (isl.), Fiji 86/Q11
Matún, Cuba 158/D2
Matura, Trin. & Tob. 161/B10
Matura (bay), Trin. & Tob. 161/B10
Maturín, Venezuela 120/C2
Maturín, Venezuela 124/G3
Matutum (mt.), Philippines 82/E7
Matutum (mt.), Philippines 85/G4
Matveyev (isl.), U.S.S.R. 52/J1
Mau, India 68/E3
Mauá, Brazil 135/C3
Maúa, Mozambique 118/F2
Maubeuge, France 28/F2
Ma-ubin, Burma 72/B3
Mauch Chunk (Jim Thorpe), Pa. (18229) 294/L4
Mauchline, Scotland 15/D5
Mauckport, Ind. (47142) 227/E8
Maud, Ala. (†35616) 195/B1
Maud, Ky. (40042) 237/L5
Maud, Miss. (†38626) 256/D1
Maud, Ohio (†45069) 284/B7
Maud, Okla. (74854) 288/N4
Maud, Scotland 15/F3
Maud, Texas (75567) 303/K4
Maude, N.S. Wales 97/C4
Maudlow, Mont. (59714) 262/E4
Mauerkirchen, Austria 41/B2
Maués, Brazil 132/B3
Maués, Brazil 120/D3
Maués-Açu (riv.), Brazil 132/B4
Maugansville, Md. (21767) 245/H2
Mauger (cay), Belize 154/D2
Maugerville, New Bruns. 170/D3
Maui (co.), Hawaii 218/J1
Maui (isl.), Hawaii 87/L3
Maui (isl.), Hawaii 188/F5
Maui (isl.), Hawaii 218/J2
Mauk, Georgia (31058) 217/D6
Mauke (isl.), Cook Is. 87/L8
Mauldin, S.C. (29662) 296/C2
Maule (reg.), Chile 138/A11
Maule (riv.), Chile 138/A11
Mauléon-Licharre, France 28/C6
Maullín, Chile 138/D4
Maullín (riv.), Chile 138/D3
Maumakeogh (mt.), Ireland 17/C3
Maumee (riv.), Ind. 227/H2
Maumee (bay), Mich. 250/F7
Maumee, Ohio (43537) 284/C2
Maumee (bay), Ohio 284/D2
Maumee (riv.), Ohio 284/A3
Maumelle (lake), Ark. 202/E4
Maumere, Indonesia 85/G7
Maumturk (mts.), Ireland 17/B5
Maun, Botswana 118/C4
Maunabo, P. Rico 161/E3
Mauna Kea (mt.), Hawaii 87/L4
Mauna Kea (mt.), Hawaii 188/G6
Mauna Kea (mt.), Hawaii 218/H4
Maunaloa, Hawaii (96770) 218/G1
Mauna Loa (mt.), Hawaii 188/G6
Mauna Loa (mt.), Hawaii 218/G6
Maunalua (bay), Hawaii 218/F2
Maunawili, Hawaii (†96744) 218/F2
Maungaturoto, N. Zealand 100/E1
Maungdaw, Burma 72/B2
Maunie, Ill. (62861) 222/E5
Maupin, Oreg. (97037) 291/F2
Maurepas, La. (70449) 238/M2
Maurepas (lake), La. 238/M2
Mauertown, Va. (22644) 307/L3
Mauriac, France 28/E5
Maurice, Iowa (51036) 229/A3
Maurice, La. (70555) 238/F6
Maurice (riv.), N.J. 273/C4
Maurice (lake), S. Australia 88/E5
Maurice (lake), S. Australia 94/B3
Mauricetown, N.J. (08325) 273/D5
Mauricio Hirsch, Argentina 143/F7
Maurine, S. Dak. (†57626) 298/E3
Mauritania 2/J4
Mauritania 102/A3
MAURITANIA 106/B5
Mauritius 2/M6
MAURITIUS 118/G5
Maury, N.C. (28554) 281/O4
Maury (co.), Tenn. 237/G9
Maury (riv.), Va. 307/K5
Maury City, Tenn. (38050) 237/C9
Mauston, Wis. (53948) 317/F8
Mautern in Steiermark, Austria 41/C3
Mauthausen, Austria 41/C2
Mauthen-Kötschach, Austria 41/B3
Mauvoisin (dam), Switzerland 39/D4
Mavaca (riv.), Venezuela 124/F6
Maverick, Ariz. (†85920) 198/F5
Maverick (co.), Texas 303/D9
Mavila, Peru 128/H8
Mavillette, Nova Scotia 168/B4
Mavinga, Angola 115/D7
Mavora (mt.), N. Zealand 100/B6
Mavqi'im, Israel 65/B4
Mawai, Malaysia 72/F5
Mawbanna, Tasmania 99/B2
Mawer, Sask. 181/E5
Mawkmai, Burma 72/C2
Mawlaik, Burma 72/B2
Mawlu, Burma 72/C1
Mawson 5/C4
Max, Minn. (56659) 255/D3
Max, Nebr. (69037) 264/C4
Max, N. Dak. (58759) 282/H4
Maxbass, N. Dak. (58760) 282/H2
Maxcanú, Mexico 150/O6
Maxeys, Georgia (30671) 217/F3
Maxie, La. (†70526) 238/F6
Maxie, Miss. (†39458) 256/F9
Máximo Gómez, Ciego de Ávila, Cuba 158/F2
Máximo Gómez, Matanzas, Cuba 158/D1
Máximo Paz, Argentina 143/F6
Maxinkuckee, Ind. (†46511) 227/E2
Maxinkuckee (lake), Ind. 227/E2
Maxixe, Mozambique 118/F4
Max Meadows, Va. (24360) 307/G6
Maxstone, Sask. 181/F6
Maxton, N.C. (28364) 281/L5
Maxville, Mont. (59858) 262/C4
Maxville, Ontario 177/K2
Maxwell, Calif. (95955) 204/C4
Maxwell, Ind. (46154) 227/F5
Maxwell, Iowa (50161) 229/G5
Maxwell, Nebr. (69151) 264/D3
Maxwell, New Bruns. 170/C3
Maxwell, N. Mex. (87728) 274/E2
Maxwell (bay), N.W. Terrs. 187/K2
Maxwell, Tenn. (†37306) 237/J10
Maxwell Air Force Base, Ala. 195/F6
Maxwelton, Queensland 88/G4
May, Idaho (83253) 220/E5
May (cape), N.J. 188/M3
May (cape), N.J. 273/C6
May, Okla. (73851) 288/G1
May, Isle of (isl.), Scotland 15/F4
May, Texas (76857) 303/F5
Maya (mts.), Belize 154/C2
Maya (riv.), U.S.S.R. 54/P4
Maya (riv.), U.S.S.R. 48/O4
Maya Beach, Belize 154/C2
Mayaguana (isl.), Bahamas 146/L7
Mayaguana (isl.), Bahamas 156/D2
Mayaguana (passage), Bahamas 156/D2
Mayagüez (dist.), P. Rico 161/B2
Mayagüez, P. Rico 161/A2
Mayagüez, P. Rico 156/F1
Mayagüez (bay), P. Rico 161/A2
Mayajigua, Cuba 158/F2
Mayals, Spain 33/G2
Mayarí, Cuba 158/J3
Mayarí Arriba, Cuba 158/J4
Mayaro, Trin. & Tob. 161/B11
Mayaro (bay), Trin. & Tob. 161/B11
Maybee, Mich. (48159) 250/F6
Maybell, Colo. (81640) 208/C2
Mayberry, Md. (†21157) 245/K2
Maybeury, W. Va. (24861) 312/D8
Maybole, Scotland 10/D3
Maybole, Scotland 15/D5
Maybrook, N.Y. (12543) 276/M8
Mayburg, Pa. (†16347) 294/D2
Maydena, Tasmania 99/C4
Mayen, W. Germany 22/B3
Mayenne (dept.), France 28/C3
Mayenne, France 28/C3
Mayenne (riv.), France 28/C4
Mayer, Ariz. (86333) 198/C4
Mayer, Chile 138/E7
Mayer, Minn. (55360) 255/E6
Mayersville, Miss. (39113) 256/B5
Mayerthorpe, Alberta 182/C3
Mayes (co.), Okla. 288/R2
Mayesville, S.C. (29104) 296/G4
Mayetta, Kansas (66509) 232/G2
Mayetta, N.J. (†08092) 273/E4
Mayfair, Sask. 181/D2
Mayfield, Georgia (31087) 217/G4
Mayfield, Kansas (67103) 232/E4
Mayfield, Ky. (42066) 237/D7
Mayfield (creek), Ky. 237/C7
Mayfield, N.Y. (12117) 276/M4
Mayfield, Ohio (44124) 284/J9
Mayfield, Okla. (73656) 288/G4
Mayfield, Pa. (18433) 294/L2
Mayfield, Scotland 15/D2
Mayfield, Utah (84643) 304/C4
Mayfield (lake), Wash. 310/C4
Mayfield Heights, Ohio (44124) 284/J9
Mayflower, Ark. (72106) 202/F4
Mayger, Oreg. (†97016) 291/D1
Mayhew, Miss. (39753) 256/G4
Mayhill, N. Mex. (88339) 274/D6
Maykop, U.S.S.R. 7/H4
Maykop, U.S.S.R. 48/D5
Maykop, U.S.S.R. 52/F6
Mayland, Tenn. (†38555) 237/L8
Maylene, Ala. (35114) 195/E4
Maymont, Sask. 181/D3
Maymyo, Burma 72/C2
Mayna, La. (†71343) 238/G4
Maynard, Ark. (72444) 202/J1
Maynard, Iowa (50655) 229/K3
Maynard◯, Mass. (01754) 249/J3
Maynard, Minn. (56260) 255/C6
Maynardville, Tenn. (37807) 237/O8
Mayne, Br. Col. 184/K3
Maynooth, Ireland 17/H5
Maynooth, Ontario 177/G2
Mayo, Canada 4/C16
Mayo, Fla. (32066) 212/C1
Mayo (co.), Ireland 17/C4
Mayo, Md. (21106) 245/M5
Mayo (riv.), Peru 128/D6
Mayo (bay), Philippines 82/F7
Mayo, S.C. (29368) 296/D1
Mayo, Yukon 187/E3
Mayo, Yukon 162/C3
Mayo (lake), Yukon 187/E3
Mayodan, N.C. (27027) 281/K2
Mayon (vol.), Philippines 82/D4
Mayor (isl.), N. Zealand 100/F2
Mayor (cape), Spain 33/E1
Mayor Martínez, Paraguay 144/C5
Mayor Pablo Lagerenza, Paraguay 144/B1
MAYOTTE 118/G2
Mayotte (isl), France 102/G6
Mayoworth, Wyo. (†82639) 319/F2
May Park, Oreg. (†97850) 291/J2
May Pen, Jamaica 158/J6
Mayport Naval Air Sta., Fla. 212/E1
Mayrhofen, Austria 41/A3
Mays, Ind. (46155) 227/G5
Maysan (gov.), Iraq 66/E5
Maysel, W. Va. (25133) 312/D5
Mays Landing, N.J. (08330) 273/D5
Mays Lick, Ky. (41055) 237/O3
Maysville, Ark. (72747) 202/A1
Maysville, Georgia (30558) 217/E2
Maysville, Iowa (†52773) 229/M5
Maysville, Ky. (41056) 237/O3
Maysville, Mo. (64469) 261/D3
Maysville, N.C. (28555) 281/P5
Maysville, Okla. (73057) 288/M5
Maysville, W. Va. (26833) 312/H4
Maytiguid (isl.), Philippines 82/B5
Maytown, Ky. (41455) 237/O5
Mayumba, Gabon 115/A4
Mayuram, India 68/D6
Mayview, Mo. (64071) 261/E4
Mayville, Mich. (48744) 250/F5
Mayville, N.Y. (14757) 276/A6
Mayville, N. Dak. (58257) 282/R4
Mayville, Oreg. (97830) 291/G2
Mayville, Wis. (53050) 317/K9
Maywood, Calif. (90201) 204/C10
Maywood, Ill. (60153) 222/B5
Maywood, Mo. (63454) 261/J3
Maywood, Nebr. (69038) 264/D4
Maywood, N.J. (07607) 273/B2
Maywood Park, Oreg. (97220) 291/B2
Maza, N. Dak. (†58324) 282/M3
Mazabuka, Zambia 115/E7
Mazabuka, Zambia 102/E6
Mazagan (El Jadida), Morocco 106/C2
Mazagão, Brazil 132/D3
Mazama, Wash. (98833) 310/E2
Mazamet, France 28/E6
Mazán, Peru 128/F4
Mazana (lake), Québec 172/C2
Mazana (riv.), Québec 172/C2
Mazandaran (prov.), Iran 66/H2
Mazangano, Uruguay 145/E3
Mazapil, Mexico 150/J4
Mazara del Vallo, Italy 34/D6
Mazar-e Sharif, Afghanistan 59/J2
Mazar-e Sharif, Afghanistan 68/B1
Mazarrón, Spain 33/F4
Mazaruni (riv.), Guyana 131/A2
Mazaruni-Potaro (dist.), Guyana 131/A2
Mazatán, Mexico 150/E2
Mazatenango, Guatemala 154/B3
Mazatlán, Mexico 146/H7
Mazatlán, Mexico 150/F5
Mazatzal (peak), Ariz. 198/D4
Mažeikiai, U.S.S.R. 53/A2
Mazenod, Sask. 181/E6
Mazeppa, Alberta 182/D4
Mazeppa, Minn. (55956) 255/F6
Mazgirt, Turkey 63/H3
Mazıdağı, Turkey 63/J4
Mazie, Okla. (74353) 288/R2
Mazinaw (lake), Ontario 177/G3
Mazirbe, U.S.S.R. 53/B2
Mazocruz, Peru 128/H11
Mazoe (riv.), Mozambique 118/E3
Mazoe, Zimbabwe 118/E3
Mazoe (riv.), Zimbabwe 118/E3
Mazomanie, Wis. (53560) 317/G9
Mazon, Ill. (60444) 222/E2
Mazra', Israel 65/C5
Mazu (Matsu) (isl.), China 77/K6
Mazzarino, Italy 34/E6
Mbabane (cap.), Swaziland 118/E5
Mbabane (cap.), Swaziland 102/F7
Mbaïki, Cent. Afr. Rep. 115/C3
Mbakou (res.), Cameroon 115/B2
Mbala, Zambia 102/F5
Mbala, Zambia 115/F5
Mbale, Uganda 115/F3
Mbale, Uganda 102/F4
Mbalmayo, Cameroon 115/B3
Mbamba Bay, Tanzania 115/G6
Mbandaka, Zaire 115/C3
Mbandaka, Zaire 102/D5
Mbanza Congo, Angola 115/B5
Mbanza-Ngungu, Zaire 102/D5
Mbanza-Ngungu, Zaire 115/C5
Mbaracayú, Cordillera de (mts.), Paraguay 144/E3
Mbarangandu (riv.), Tanzania 115/G5
Mbarara, Uganda 115/F4
Mbemkuru (riv.), Tanzania 115/G5
Mbengga (isl.), Fiji 86/Q11
Mbéré (riv.), Cameroon 115/B2
Mbéré (riv.), Cent. Afr. Rep. 115/B2
Mbéré (riv.), Chad 111/C6
Mbeya (reg.), Tanzania 115/F5
Mbeya, Tanzania 102/F5
Mbeya, Tanzania 115/F5
M'Bigou, Gabon 115/B4
Mbinda, Congo 115/B4
Mbini, Equat. Guinea 115/A3
Mbocayaty, Paraguay 144/C5
M'Bour, Senegal 106/A6
M'Bout, Mauritania 106/B5
Mbres, Cent. Afr. Rep. 115/D2
M'Bridge (riv.), Angola 115/B5
Mbuji-Mayi, Zaire 102/E5
Mbuji-Mayi, Zaire 115/D5
Mbulu, Tanzania 115/G4
Mburucuyá, Argentina 143/E2
Mbuyapey, Paraguay 144/D5
McAdam, New Bruns. 170/C3
McAdams, Miss. (39107) 256/E4
McAdoo, Pa. (18237) 294/L4
McAdoo, Texas (79243) 303/D4
McAfee, N.J. (07428) 273/D1
McAlester, Okla. 188/G4
McAlester, Okla. (74501) 288/P5
McAlester (lake), Okla. 288/P4
McAlister, N. Mex. (88427) 274/F4
McAlisterville, Pa. (17049) 294/H4
McAllaster, Kansas (†67755) 232/A3
McAllen, Texas 188/G5
McAllen, Texas (78501) 303/F11
McAllister, Mont. (59740) 262/E5
McAllister, Wis. (†54177) 317/L5
McAlpin, Fla. (32062) 212/D1
McAndrews, Ky. (41543) 237/S5
McArthur, Calif. (96056) 204/D2
McArthur, Ohio (45651) 284/F7
McArthur River, North. Terr. 88/F3
McAuley, Manitoba 179/A4
McBain, Mich. (49657) 250/D4
McBaine, Mo. (†65201) 261/H5
McBean, Georgia (†30908) 217/J4
McBee, S.C. (29101) 296/G3
McBride, Br. Col. 184/G3
McBride, Miss. (†39144) 256/C7
McBride, Mo. (63776) 261/N7
McBride, Okla. (†74441) 288/N7
McBride Lake, Sask. 181/J3
McBrides, Mich. (48852) 250/D5
McCabe, Mont. (59245) 262/M2
McCain, N.C. (28361) 281/L4
McCall, Idaho (83638) 220/C5
McCall, La. (†70346) 238/K3
McCalla, Ala. (35111) 195/E4
McCall Creek, Miss. (39647) 256/C7
McCallsburg, Iowa (50154) 229/G4
McCallum, Newf. 166/C4
McCamey, Texas (79752) 303/B6
McCammon, Idaho (83250) 220/F7
McCanna, N. Dak. (58253) 282/P3
McCarley, Miss. (38943) 256/E3
McCarr, Ky. (41544) 237/S5
McCarthy, Alaska (†99566) 196/K2
McCaskill, Ark. (71847) 202/C6
McCauley (isl.), Br. Col. 184/B3
McCaulley, Texas (79534) 303/E5
McCausland, Iowa (52758) 229/M5
McCaysville, Georgia (30555) 217/D1
McChord A.F.B., Wash. 310/C3
McClain (co.), Okla. 288/L5
McClave, Colo. (81057) 208/O6
McCleary, Wash. (98557) 310/B3
McClellan A.F.B., Calif. 204/B8
McClelland (lake), Alberta 182/E1
McClelland, Ark. (†72006) 202/H3
McClelland, Iowa (51548) 229/B6
McClellanville, S.C. (29458) 296/H5
McCloud, Calif. (96057) 204/C2
McCloud, Tenn. (†37857) 237/R8
McClure (lake), Calif. 204/E6
McClure, Ill. (62957) 222/D6
McClure, Ohio (43534) 284/C3
McClure, Pa. (17841) 294/H4
McClure, Va. (24269) 307/D6
McClusky, N. Dak. (58463) 282/K4
McColl, S.C. (29570) 296/H2
McComb, Miss. (39648) 256/D8
McComb, Ohio (45858) 284/C3
McConaughy, C. W. (lake), Nebr. 264/C3
McCondy, Miss. (38854) 256/G3
McCone (co.), Mont. 262/L3
McConnell, Ill. (61050) 222/D1
McConnell, Manitoba 179/B4
McConnell, Tenn. (†38237) 237/D8
McConnell A.F.B., Kansas 232/E4
McConnells, S.C. (29726) 296/E2
McConnellsburg, Pa. (17233) 294/F6
McConnellsville, N.Y. (13401) 276/J4
McConnelsville, Ohio (43756) 284/G6
McCook, Nebr. (69001) 264/D4
McCook (co.), S. Dak. 298/P6
McCool, Miss. (39108) 256/F4
McCool Junction, Nebr. (68401) 264/G4
McCord, Sask. 181/E6
McCordsville, Ind. (46055) 227/F5
McCorkle, W. Va. (†25564) 312/C6
McCormick (co.), S.C. 296/C4
McCormick, S.C. (29835) 296/C4
McCoy, Colo. (80463) 208/F3
McCoy (head), New Bruns. 170/E3
McCoy, Oreg. (†97338) 291/D2
McCoy (creek), Oreg. 291/J5
McCoy, Va. (24111) 307/G6
McCoy A.F.B., Fla. 212/E3
McCoysburg, Ind. (†47978) 227/C3
McCracken, Kansas (67556) 232/C3
McCracken (co.), Ky. 237/D6
McCrea, Pa. (†17241) 294/H5
McCreary (co.), Ky. 237/N7
McCreary, Manitoba 179/C4
McCrory, Ark. (72101) 202/H3
McCulloch (co.), Texas 303/E6
McCullom Lake, Ill. (†60050) 222/E1
McCullough, Ala. (36552) 195/D8
McCune, Kansas (66753) 232/G4
McCurtain (co.), Okla. 288/S6
McCurtain, Okla. (74944) 288/R4
McCutchenville, Ohio (44844) 284/D4
McDade, Texas (78650) 303/G7
McDaniel, Md. (21647) 245/N5
McDaniels, Ky. (40152) 237/J5
McDavid, Fla. (32568) 212/B5
McDermitt, Nev. (89421) 266/D1
McDermott, Ohio (45652) 284/D8
McDonald (isls.), Australia 2/N8
McDonald, Kansas (67745) 232/A2
McDonald (co.), Mo. 261/D9
McDonald (lake), Mont. 262/B2
McDonald, N. Mex. (88262) 274/F5
McDonald, N.C. (28340) 281/L5
McDonald, Ohio (44437) 284/J3
McDonald, Pa. (15057) 294/B5
McDonald, Tenn. (37353) 237/M10
McDonalds Corners, Ontario 177/H3
McDonnell, Queensland 95/B1
McDonough (lake), Conn. 210/D1
McDonough, Del. (†19709) 245/R3
McDonough, Georgia (30253) 217/D4
McDonough (co.), Ill. 222/C3
McDonough, N.Y. (13801) 276/J5
McDougal, Ark. (72441) 202/K1
McDougall (lake), New Bruns. 170/D3
McDowell, Ala. (†35450) 195/C5
McDowell, Ky. (41647) 237/R6
McDowell (co.), N.C. 281/E3
McDowell, Va. (24458) 307/J4
McDowell (co.), W. Va. 312/C8
McDowell, W. Va. (24858) 312/D8
McDuffie (co.), Georgia 217/H4
McElhattan, Pa. (17748) 294/H3
McElmo (creek), Colo. 208/B8
McElmo (creek), Utah 304/E6
McEwen, Tenn. (37101) 237/F8
McFadden, Wyo. (82080) 319/F4
McFall, Mo. (64657) 261/D2
McFarlan, N.C. (28102) 281/J5
McFarland, Calif. (93250) 204/F8
McFarland, Kansas (66501) 232/F2
McFarland, Mich. (†49880) 250/B2
McFarland, Wis. (53558) 317/H10
McFarlane (riv.), Sask. 181/L2
McGaffey, N. Mex. (†87316) 274/A3
McGaheysville, Va. (22840) 307/L4
McGee, Sask. 181/C4
McGees Mills, Pa. (15755) 294/E4
McGehee, Ark. (71654) 202/H6
McGill, Nev. (89318) 266/G3
McGivney, New Bruns. 170/D2
McGloughlin (peak), Mont. 262/C4
McGrath, Alaska 188/C5
McGrath, Alaska (99627) 196/H2
McGrath, Minn. (56350) 255/E4
McGraw, N.Y. (13101) 276/H5
McGraw Brook, New Bruns. 170/D2
McGrawsville, Ind. (†46911) 227/E3
McGregor (lake), Alberta 182/D4
McGregor, Br. Col. 184/G3
McGregor (riv.), Br. Col. 184/G3
McGregor, Iowa (52157) 229/L2
McGregor, Minn. (55760) 255/E4
McGregor (lake), Mont. 262/B3
McGregor, N. Dak. (58755) 282/D2
McGregor, Ontario 177/B5
McGregor, Texas (76657) 303/G6
McGrew, Nebr. (69353) 264/A3
McGuffey, Ohio (45859) 284/C4
McGuire (mt.), Idaho 220/D4
McGuire A.F.B., N.J. 273/D3
McHenry (co.), Ill. 222/E1
McHenry, Ill. (60050) 222/E1
McHenry, Ky. (42354) 237/H6
McHenry, Miss. (39561) 256/F9
McHenry (co.), N. Dak. 282/J3
McHenry, N. Dak. (58464) 282/N4
McHenry Shores, Ill. (†60050) 222/E1
Mchinga, Tanzania 115/H5
Mchinji, Malawi 115/F6
McIlwraith (range), Queensland 95/B2
McIndoe Falls, Vt. (05050) 268/C3
McIntire, Iowa (50455) 229/H2
McIntosh, Ala. (36553) 195/B8
McIntosh, Fla. (32664) 212/D2
McIntosh (co.), Georgia 217/K7
McIntosh, Georgia (†31320) 217/K7
McIntosh, Minn. (56556) 255/C3
McIntosh, N. Mex. (87032) 274/D4
McIntosh (co.), N. Dak. 282/L7
McIntosh (co.), Okla. 288/P4
McIntosh, Ontario 177/F4
McIntosh, Ontario 175/B3
McIntosh, S. Dak. (57641) 298/G2
McIntyre, Georgia (31054) 217/F5
McIvor, Mich. (†48748) 250/F4
McKague, Sask. 181/G3
McKamie, Ark. (†71860) 202/C7
McKay (lake), Manitoba 179/C2
McKay (res.), Oreg. 291/J2
McKean (co.), Pa. 294/E2
McKean, Pa. (16426) 294/B2
McKeand (riv.), N.W. Terrs. 187/M3
McKee (creek), Ill. 222/C4
McKee, Ky. (40447) 237/O6
McKee City, N.J. (†08232) 273/D5
McKeesport, Pa. 188/L2
McKeesport, Pa. (*15130) 294/C7
McKees Rocks, Pa. (15136) 294/B7
McKellar, Ontario 177/D2
McKendrick, New Bruns. 170/D1
McKenna, Wash. (98558) 310/C4
McKenney, Va. (23872) 307/N7
McKenzie, Ala. (36456) 195/E7
McKenzie (co.), N. Dak. 282/D4
McKenzie, N. Dak. (58553) 282/K6
McKenzie, South Fork (riv.), Oreg. 291/E3
McKenzie, Tenn. (38201) 237/E8
McKenzie Bridge, Oreg. (97401) 291/E3
McKerrow, Ontario 177/C1
McKinlay, Queensland 95/B4
McKinlay, Queensland 88/G4
McKinley, Ala. (†36743) 195/C6
McKinley (mt.), Alaska 146/C3
McKinley (mt.), Alaska 188/D5
McKinley (mt.), Alaska 196/H2
McKinley, Cuba 158/B2
McKinley, Minn. (55761) 255/F3
McKinley (co.), N. Mex. 274/A3
McKinley (mt.), U.S. 4/C17

408 McKinley

McKinley, Wyo. (†82633) 319/G3
McKinley Park, Alaska (99755) 196/J2
McKinleyville, Calif. (95521) 204/A3
McKinney (lake), Kansas 232/A3
McKinney, Ky. (40448) 237/M6
McKinney, Texas (75069) 303/H4
McKinnon, Georgia (†31545) 217/J8
McKinnon, Tenn. (†37175) 237/F8
McKinnon, Wyo. (82938) 319/C4
McKittrick, Calif. (93251) 204/F8
McKittrick, Mo. (65056) 261/J5
McLain, Miss. (39456) 256/G8
McLane, Pa. (†16426) 294/B2
McLaughlin, Alberta 182/E3
McLaughlin, S. Dak. (57642) 298/H2
McLaurin, Miss. (†39401) 256/F8
McLean (co.), Ill. 222/E3
McLean, Ill. (61754) 222/D3
McLean (co.), Ky. 237/G5
McLean, Nebr. (68747) 264/G2
McLean, N.Y. (13102) 276/H5
McLean (co.), N. Dak. 282/G4
McLean, Sask. 181/G5
McLean, Texas (79057) 303/D2
McLean, Va. (*22101) 307/S2
McLeansboro, Ill. (62859) 222/E5
McLelan (str.), Newf. 166/B1
McLemoresville, Tenn. (38235) 237/D9
McLennan, Alberta 182/B2
McLennan (co.), Texas 303/G6
McLeod (riv.), Alberta 182/B3
McLeod (co.), Minn. 255/D6
McLeod, Mont. (59052) 262/G5
McLeod, N. Dak. (58057) 282/R7
McLeod (bay), N.W. Terrs. 187/G3
McLeod (lake), W. Australia 88/A4
McLeod (lake), W. Australia 92/A4
McLeod Lake, Br. Col. 184/F2
McLeod River, Alberta 182/B3
M'Clintock, Manitoba 179/K2
M'Clintock (chan.), N.W.T. 146/H2
M'Clintock (chan.), N.W.T. 162/F1
M'Clintock (bay), N.W. Terrs. 187/K1
M'Clintock (chan.), N.W. Terrs. 187/H2
McLoud, Okla. (74851) 288/M4
McLoughlin (mt.), Oreg. 291/E5
McLoughlin House Nat'l Hist. Site, Oreg. 291/B2
McLouth, Kansas (66054) 232/G2
McLure, Br. Col. 184/H4
M'Clure (str.), Canada 4/B15
M'Clure (cape), N.W.T. 162/D1
M'Clure (str.), N.W.T. 146/F2
M'Clure (str.), N.W.T. 162/E1
M'Clure (cape), N.W. Terrs. 187/F2
M'Clure (str.), N.W. Terrs. 187/G2
McMahon, Sask. 181/D5
McMechen, W. Va. (26040) 312/E3
McMillan, Mich. (49853) 250/D2
McMillan (lake), N. Mex. 188/F4
McMillan (lake), N. Mex. 274/E6
McMillan, Okla. (73445) 288/M6
McMinn (co.), Tenn. 237/M10
McMinnville, Oreg. (97128) 291/D2
McMinnville, Tenn. (37110) 237/K9
McMorran, Sask. 181/C4
McMullen (co.), Texas 303/F9
McMunn, Manitoba 179/G5
McMurdo (sound), Ant. 2/A10
McMurdo (sound) 5/B9
McMurdo, Br. Col. 184/J4
McMurray, Wash. (†98273) 310/C2
McNab, Alberta 182/D5
McNab, Ark. (†71838) 202/C6
McNabb, Ill. (61335) 222/D2
McNair, Texas (†77520) 303/K1
McNairy (co.), Tenn. 237/D10
McNairy, Tenn. (†38315) 237/D10
McNamee, New Bruns. 170/D2
McNary, Ariz. (85930) 198/F4
McNary, La. (†71433) 238/E5
McNary, Oreg. (97858) 291/H2
McNary (dam), Oreg. 291/H2
McNary, Texas (79839) 303/B11
McNary (dam), Wash. 310/F5
McNaughton, Wis. (54543) 317/H4
McNeal, Ariz. (85617) 198/F7
McNeil, Ark. (71752) 202/D7
McNeill, Miss. (39457) 256/E9
McNulty, Oreg. (†97053) 291/E2
McNutt (isl.), Nova Scotia 168/C5
McPhadyen (riv.), Newf. 166/A3
McPhail (riv.), Manitoba 179/F2
McPherson (co.), Kansas 232/E3
McPherson, Kansas (67460) 232/E3
McPherson (co.), Nebr. 264/C3
McPherson (range), N.S. Wales 97/G1
McPherson (co.), S. Dak. 298/L2
McQuady, Ky. (40153) 237/H5
McRae, Alberta 182/E2
McRae, Ark. (72102) 202/G3
McRae, Georgia (31055) 217/G6
McRoberts, Ky. (41835) 237/R6
McShan, Ala. (35471) 195/B4
McSherrystown, Pa. (17344) 294/H6
McTaggart, Sask. 181/H6
McTavish, Manitoba 179/E5
McTavish Arm (inlet), N.W. Terrs. 187/G3
McVeigh, Ky. (41546) 237/S5
McVeytown, Pa. (17051) 294/G4
McVicar Arm (inlet), N.W. Terrs. 187/F3
McVille, N. Dak. (58254) 282/O4
McWhorter, W. Va. (26401) 312/F4
McWilliams, Ala. (36753) 195/D7
Meacham (lake), N.Y. 276/M1
Meacham, Oreg. (97859) 291/J2
Meacham, Sask. 181/F3
Mead (lake) 188/D3
Mead (lake), Ariz. 198/A2
Mead, Colo. (80542) 208/K2
Mead, Nebr. (68041) 264/H3
Mead (lake), Nev. 266/G6
Mead, Okla. (73449) 288/O7
Mead (lake), U.S. 146/G6
Mead, Wash. (99021) 310/H3
Meade (riv.), Alaska 196/G1
Meade (peak), Idaho 220/G7
Meade (co.), Kansas 232/B4
Meade, Kansas (67864) 232/B4
Meade (co.), Ky. 237/J5
Meade (co.), S. Dak. 298/D5
Meador, W. Va. (†25678) 312/B7
Meadow (creek), Idaho 220/C4
Meadow (mt.), Md. 245/B2
Meadow (lake), Sask. 181/C1
Meadow, S. Dak. (57644) 298/E2
Meadow, Texas (79345) 303/B4
Meadow, Utah (84644) 304/B5
Meadow (riv.), W. Va. 312/E6
Meadow Bluff, W. Va. (24958) 312/E7
Meadow Bridge, W. Va. (25976) 312/E7
Meadowbrook, Ill. (†62010) 222/B2
Meadowbrook, W. Va. (26404) 312/F4
Meadow Creek, W. Va. (25977) 312/E7
Meadow Grove, Nebr. (68752) 264/G2
Meadow Lake, Sask. 181/C1
Meadow Lake Prov. Park, Sask. 181/K4
Meadowlands, Minn. (55765) 255/F3
Meadow Lands, Pa. (15347) 294/B5
Meadow Portage, Manitoba 179/C3
Meadows, Idaho (†83654) 220/B5
Meadows, Ill. (†61726) 222/E3
Meadows, Md. (†20870) 245/G5
Meadows, N.H. (03587) 268/E3
Meadows, S. Australia 94/B8
Meadows of Dan, Va. (24120) 307/H7
Meadow Vale, Ky. (†40201) 237/L1
Meadow Valley, Calif. (95956) 204/D4
Meadow Valley Wash (riv.), Nev. 266/G5
Meadowview-Emory, Va. (24361) 307/D7
Meadow Vista, N. Mex. (†79901) 274/C7
Meadville, Miss. (39653) 256/C8
Meadville, Mo. (64659) 261/F3
Meadville, Pa. 188/L2
Meadville, Pa. (16335) 294/B2
Meaford, Ontario 177/D3
Meagher (co.), Mont. 262/F4
Meaghers Grant, Nova Scotia 168/E4
Meakan (mt.), Japan 81/L2
Mealhada, Portugal 33/B2
Meally, Ky. (41234) 237/R5
Mealy (lake), Newf. 166/C3
Meander, Tasmania 99/C3
Meander River, Alberta 182/A5
Meanook, Alberta 182/D2
Means, Ky. (40346) 237/O5
Meansville, Georgia (30256) 217/D4
Meares (cape), Oreg. 291/C2
Mearim (riv.), Brazil 132/E4
Mearns, Alberta 182/D3
Mears, Mich. (49436) 250/C5
Meath (co.), Ireland 17/H4
Meathas Truim, Ireland 17/G4
Meath Park, Sask. 181/F2
Meaux, France 28/E3
Mebane, N.C. (27302) 281/L2
Mecca, Calif. (92254) 204/K10
Mecca, Ind. (47860) 227/C5
Mecca (cap.), Saudi Arabia 2/M4
Mecca (cap.), Saudi Arabia 59/C5
Mecca (cap.), Saudi Arabia 54/F7
Mechanic Falls, Maine (04256) 243/C7
Mechanic Falls○, Maine (04256) 243/C7
Mechanicsburg, Ill. (62545) 222/D4
Mechanicsburg, Ind. (†47356) 227/G5
Mechanicsburg, Ohio (43044) 284/D5
Mechanicsburg, Pa. (17055) 294/H5
Mechanicsburg, Va. (†24315) 307/G6
Mechanicstown, Ohio (44651) 284/H4
Mechanicsville, Conn. (06252) 210/H1
Mechanicsville, Georgia (30040) 217/L1
Mechanicsville, Iowa (52306) 229/L5
Mechanicsville, Md. (20659) 245/M7
Mechanicsville, Va. (23111) 307/O5
Mechanicville, N.Y. (12118) 276/N5
Mechelen, Belgium 27/F6
Mecheria, Algeria 106/D2
Mechernich, W. Germany 22/B3
Mecidiye, Turkey 63/B6
Mecitözü, Turkey 63/F2
Mecklenburg (bay), E. Germany 22/D1
Mecklenburg (reg.), E. Germany 22/E2
Mecklenburg, N.Y. (14863) 276/G6
Mecklenburg (co.), N.C. 281/H4
Mecklenburg (co.), Va. 307/M7
Mecklenburg (reg.), W. Germany 22/D1
Meckling, S. Dak. (57044) 298/R8
Meconta, Mozambique 118/F3
Mecosta (co.), Mich. 250/D5
Mecosta, Mich. (49332) 250/D5
Mecoya, Bolivia 136/C8
Mecsek (mts.), Hungary 41/D3
Mecúfi, Mozambique 118/G2
Mecula, Mozambique 118/F2
Medain Salih, Saudi Arabia 59/C4
Medan, Indonesia 54/L9
Medan, Indonesia 85/B5
Médanos, Buenos Aires, Argentina 143/D4
Médanos, Entre Ríos, Argentina 143/G6
Médanos (isth.), Venezuela 124/D2
Medanosa (pt.), Argentina 143/D6
Medaryville, Ind. (47957) 227/D2
Meddybemps○, Maine (04657) 243/J5
Meddybemps (lake), Maine 243/J5
Médéa, Algeria 106/E1
Medel (mt.), Switzerland 39/D2
Medellín, Colombia 120/B2
Medellín, Colombia 126/C4
Medellín de Bravo, Mexico 150/Q2
Medemblik, Netherlands 27/G3
Médenine, Tunisia 106/F2
Méderdra, Mauritania 106/A5
Mederville, Iowa (†52043) 229/K3
Medetsiz Tepe (mt.), Turkey 63/F4
Medfield, Mass. (02052) 249/B8
Medfield○, Mass. (02052) 249/B8
Medford, Maine (†04453) 243/F5
Medford○, Maine (†04453) 243/F5
Medford, Mass. (02155) 249/C6
Medford, Minn. (55049) 255/E6
Medford, N.J. (08055) 273/D4
Medford, Okla. (73759) 288/L1
Medford, Oreg. 188/B2
Medford, Oreg. 146/F5
Medford, Oreg. (97501) 291/E5
Medford, Wis. (54451) 317/F5
Medford Center, Maine (†04453) 243/F5
Medford Lakes, N.J. (08055) 273/D4
Medgidia, Romania 45/J3
Medgun (creek), N.S. Wales 97/E1
Media, Ill. (61460) 222/C3
Media, Pa. (*19063) 294/L7
Media Agua, Argentina 143/C3
Media Luna, Cuba 158/G4
Mediapolis, Iowa (52637) 229/L6
Mediaș, Romania 45/G2
Medical Lake, Wash. (99022) 310/H3
Medical Springs, Oreg. (97860) 291/K2
Medicine (lake), Mont. 262/M2
Medicine (creek), Nebr. 264/D4
Medicine (creek), S. Dak. 298/J6
Medicine Bow (range), Colo. 208/G1
Medicine Bow, Wyo. (82329) 319/F4
Medicine Bow (range), Wyo. 319/F4
Medicine Bow (riv.), Wyo. 319/F3
Medicine Creek (dam), Nebr. 264/D4
Medicine Hat, Alberta 182/E4
Medicine Hat, Alta. 146/H4
Medicine Hat, Alta. 162/E5
Medicine Knoll (creek), S. Dak. 298/J5
Medicine Lake, Minn. (55441) 255/G5
Medicine Lake, Mont. (59247) 262/M2
Medicine Lodge (creek), Idaho 220/F5
Medicine Lodge, Kansas (67104) 232/D4
Medicine Lodge (riv.), Kansas 232/D4
Medicine Mound, Texas (†79252) 303/E3
Medicine Park, Okla. (73557) 288/J5
Medill, Mo. (†63445) 261/J2
Medina, Colombia 126/D5
Medina (Hamel), Minn. (†55340) 255/F5
Medina, N.Y. (14103) 276/D4
Medina, N. Dak. (58467) 282/M6
Medina (co.), Ohio 284/G3
Medina, Ohio (44256) 284/G3
Medina, Saudi Arabia 54/F7
Medina, Saudi Arabia 59/D5
Medina, Tenn. (38355) 237/D9
Medina (co.), Texas 303/E8
Medina, Texas (78055) 303/E8
Medina (lake), Texas 303/E8
Medina (riv.), Texas 303/J11
Medina, Wash. (98039) 310/B2
Medinaceli, Spain 33/E2
Medina del Campo, Spain 33/D2
Medina de Rioseco, Spain 33/D2
Medina-Sidonia, Spain 33/D4
Mediodía, Colombia 126/D8
Mediterranean (sea) 2/K4
Mediterranean (sea) 7/E5
Mediterranean (sea), Algeria 106/E1
Mediterranean (sea), Egypt 111/E1
Mediterranean (sea), France 28/E7
Mediterranean (sea), Italy 34/B6
Mediterranean (sea), Libya 111/C1
Mediterranean (sea), Morocco 106/D1
Mediterranean (sea), Tunisia 106/F1
Medix Run, Pa. (†15868) 294/F3
Medjerda (riv.), Algeria 106/F1
Medjerda (riv.), Tunisia 106/F1
Medley, Fla. (†33101) 212/B4
Medley, W. Va. (26734) 312/H4
Mednogorsk, U.S.S.R. 52/J4
Mednogorsk, U.S.S.R. 48/F4
Médoc (reg.), France 28/C5
Mêdog, China 77/E6
Medon, Tenn. (38356) 237/D10
Medora, Ill. (62063) 222/C4
Medora, Ind. (47260) 227/E7
Medora, Kansas (67558) 232/E3
Medora, Manitoba 179/B5
Medora, N. Dak. (58645) 282/C6
Médouneu, Gabon 115/B3
Medstead, Sask. 181/C2
Meductic, New Bruns. 170/C3
Medveditsa (riv.), U.S.S.R. 52/F4
Medvezh'yegorsk, U.S.S.R. 48/D3
Medvezh'yegorsk, U.S.S.R. 52/D2
Medway (riv.), England 13/H6
Medway○, Maine (04460) 243/G4
Medway○, Mass. (02053) 249/J4
Medway (harb.), Nova Scotia 168/D4
Medway (riv.), Nova Scotia 168/C4
Medzilaborce, Czech. 41/F2
Meeandah, Queensland 88/K2
Meehan, Miss. (†39301) 256/G6
Meekatharra, Australia 87/B8
Meekatharra, W. Australia 88/B5
Meekatharra, W. Australia 92/B4
Meeker, Colo. (81641) 208/D2
Meeker, La. (71346) 238/F4
Meeker (co.), Minn. 255/D5
Meeker, Ohio (†43302) 284/D4
Meeker, Okla. (74855) 288/N4
Meeks, Georgia (†31049) 217/G5
Meeks Bay, Calif. (†95730) 204/E5
Meelpaeg (lake), Newf. 166/C4
Meerane, E. Germany 22/E3
Meerhout, Belgium 27/G6
Meers, Okla. (73558) 288/J5
Meersburg, W. Germany 22/C5
Meerssen, Netherlands 27/H7
Meerut, India 54/J7
Meerut, India 68/D3
Meeteetse, Wyo. (82433) 319/D1
Meeting (lake), Sask. 181/D2
Meeting Creek, Alberta 182/D3
Mega, Ethiopia 111/G7
Mega (isl.), Indonesia 85/C6
Megalópolis, Greece 45/E7
Mégantic (co.), Québec 172/F3
Mégantic (lake), Québec 172/G4
Mégara, Greece 45/F6
Megargel, Ala. (36457) 195/D8
Megargel, Texas (76370) 303/F4
Meggett, S.C. (29460) 296/G6
Meghalaya (state), India 68/G3
Megiddo, Israel 65/C2
Mehama, Oreg. (97384) 291/E3
Mehan, Okla. (†74074) 288/M2
Meherrin (riv.), N.C. 281/P1
Meherrin, Va. (23954) 307/M6
Meherrin (riv.), Va. 307/M7
Mehetia (isl.), Fr. Poly. 87/M7
Mehlville, Mo. (†63129) 261/P4
Mehoopany, Pa. (18629) 294/K2
Mehran, Iran 66/E4
Mehran (riv.), Iran 59/F4
Mehran (riv.), Iran 66/J7
Mehsana, India 68/C4
Mehun-sur-Yèvre, France 28/E4
Meifa, P.D.R. Yemen 59/E7
Meiganga, Cameroon 115/B2
Meighen (isl.), N.W.T. 162/M3
Meighen (isl.), N.W. Terrs. 187/H1
Meigle, Scotland 15/E4
Meigs, Georgia (31765) 217/D8
Meigs (co.), Ohio 284/F7
Meigs (co.), Tenn. 237/M9
Meikle (riv.), Alberta 182/A1
Meiktila, Burma 72/B2
Meilen, Switzerland 39/G2
Meiners Oaks-Mira Monte, Calif. (93023) 204/F9
Meiningen, E. Germany 22/D3
Meire Grove, Minn. (†56352) 255/C5
Meiringen, Switzerland 39/F3
Meiron (mt.), Israel 65/C1
Meise, Belgium 27/E7
Meissen, E. Germany 22/E3
Mei Xian, China 77/J7
Mejillones, Chile 120/B5
Mejillones, Chile 138/A4
Mejillones del Sur (bay), Chile 138/A4
Mekambo, Gabon 115/B3
Mekerrhane, Sebkha (salt lake), Algeria 106/E3
Mekili, Libya 111/D1
Mékinac (lake), Québec 172/E2
Mekinock, N. Dak. (58258) 282/R4
Meknès, Morocco 102/B1
Meknès, Morocco 106/C2
Mekong (riv.) 54/M8
Mekong (riv.) 2/Q4
Mekong (riv.), Burma 72/D2
Mekong (riv.), Cambodia 72/E4
Mekong (Lancang Jiang) (riv.), China 77/F7
Mekong (riv.), Laos 72/D3
Mekong (riv.), Thailand 72/E3
Mekong, Mouths of the (delta), Vietnam 72/E5
Mekoryuk, Alaska (99630) 196/E2
Melaka (state), Malaysia 72/D7
Melaka, Malaysia 54/M9
Melaka, Malaysia 72/D7
Melanesia (reg.), Pacific 87/E5
Melaval, Sask. 181/E6
Melba, Idaho (83641) 220/B6
Melber, Ky. (42069) 237/D7
Melbern, Ohio (†43506) 284/A3
Melbeta, Nebr. (69355) 264/A3
Melbourne, Ark. (72556) 202/G1
Melbourne, Australia 2/R7
Melbourne, Australia 87/E9
Melbourne, Fla. 188/K5
Melbourne, Fla. (*32901) 212/F3
Melbourne, Iowa (50162) 229/G5
Melbourne, Ky. (41059) 237/T2
Melbourne, Mo. (†64642) 261/E2
Melbourne (isl.), N.W. Terrs. 187/H3
Melbourne, Ontario 177/C5
Melbourne, Québec 172/E4
Melbourne (cap.), Victoria 88/H7
Melbourne (cap.), Victoria 97/H5
Melbourne, Wash. (†98563) 310/B4
Melbourne Airport, Victoria 88/K7
Melbourne Beach, Fla. (32951) 212/F3
Melby, Minn. (56351) 255/C4
Melchor, Honduras 154/D3
Melcher, Iowa (50163) 229/G6
Melchor (isl.), Chile 138/D6
Melchor Múzquiz, Mexico 150/H3
Melchor Ocampo, Mexico 150/H4
Melchor Ocampo del Balsas, Mexico 150/H8
Melder, La. (71451) 238/E4
Meldorf, W. Germany 22/C1
Meldrim, Georgia (31318) 217/K6
Meldrum Bay, Ontario 177/A2
Meldrum Creek, Br. Col. 184/F4
Meleb, Manitoba 179/E4
Melenki, U.S.S.R. 52/F3
Meleuz, U.S.S.R. 52/J4
Mélèzes (riv.), Québec 174/C1
Melfa, Va. (23410) 307/S5
Melfi, Chad 111/C5
Melfi, Italy 34/E4
Melfort, Sask. 162/F5
Melfort, Sask. 181/G3
Melfort, Loch (inlet), Scotland 15/C4
Melgaço, Portugal 33/B1
Melgar de Fernamental, Spain 33/D1
Melide, Switzerland 39/G5
Meligalá, Greece 45/F7
Melilla, Spain 106/D1
Melilla, Spain 102/B1
Melilla, Spain 7/D5
Melimoyu (mt.), Chile 138/D5
Melinca, Chile 138/D5
Melincué, Argentina /F6
Melipilla, Chile 138/F4
Melita, Manitoba 179/A5
Melitopol', U.S.S.R. 7/H4
Melitopol', U.S.S.R. 52/D5
Melitota, Md. (†21620) 245/O4
Melk, Austria 41/C2
Melkbosstrand, S. Africa 118/E6
Melksham, England 13/E6
Melksham, England 10/E5
Mellansel, Sweden 18/L5
Melle, W. Germany 22/C2
Mellen, Wis. (54546) 317/E3
Mellerud, Sweden 18/H7
Mellette (co.), S. Dak. 298/H6
Mellette, S. Dak. (57461) 298/N3
Mellingen, Switzerland 39/F2
Mellott, Ind. (47958) 227/C4
Mellwood, Ark. (72367) 202/H5
Melmore, Ohio (44845) 284/D3
Mělník, Czech. 41/C1
Melo, Uruguay 120/D6
Melo, Uruguay 145/E3
Melocheville, Québec 172/C4
Melozitna (riv.), Alaska 196/H1
Melrhir, Chott (salt lake), Algeria 106/F2
Melrose, Conn. (06049) 210/E1
Melrose, Fla. (32666) 212/D2
Melrose, Iowa (52569) 229/G7
Melrose, La. (71452) 238/E3
Melrose, Md. (†21102) 245/L2
Melrose, Mass. (02176) 249/D6
Melrose, Minn. (56352) 255/D5
Melrose, Mont. (59743) 262/D5
Melrose, New Bruns. 170/F2
Melrose, Newf. 166/D2
Melrose, N. Mex. (88124) 274/F4
Melrose, N.S. Wales 97/D3
Melrose, Ohio (45861) 284/B3
Melrose, Oreg. (†97470) 291/D4
Melrose, Scotland 15/F5
Melrose, Scotland 10/E3
Melrose, Wis. (54642) 317/E7
Melrose Park, Fla. (†33301) 212/B4
Melrose Park, Ill. (*60160) 222/B5
Melrose Park, N.Y. (†13021) 276/G5
Melrude, Minn. (55766) 255/F3
Mels, Switzerland 39/H2
Melsetter, Zimbabwe 118/E3
Melstone, Mont. (59054) 262/H4
Melsungen, W. Germany 22/C3
Melton, Victoria 97/C5
Melton Hill (lake), Tenn. 237/N9
Melton Mowbray, England 10/F4
Melton Mowbray, England 13/G5
Meltonville, Iowa (†50472) 229/G2
Melun, France 28/E3
Melut, Sudan 111/F5
Melvaig, Scotland 15/C3
Melvern, Kansas (66510) 232/G3
Melvern (lake), Kansas 232/G3
Melvern Square, Nova Scotia 168/C3
Melvich, Scotland 15/E2
Melville (isl.), Australia 87/D7
Melville (isl.), Canada 4/B15
Melville (pen.), Canada 4/C14
Melville (bay), Greenl. 4/B13
Melville, La. (71353) 238/G5
Melville, Mont. (59055) 262/F4
Melville (pen.), N.W.T. 146/K3
Melville (pen.), N.W.T. 162/H2
Melville (isl.), N.W.T. 146/G2
Melville (isl.), N.W.T. 162/E1
Melville (lake), N.W.T. 162/L5
Melville (lake), Newf. 166/C3
Melville, N.Y. (11746) 276/O9
Melville, N. Dak. (†58421) 282/M5
Melville (isl.), N.W. Terrs. 187/G2
Melville (pen.), N.W. Terrs. 187/K3
Melville (isl.), North. Terr. 88/E2
Melville (bay), North. Terr. 88/F2
Melville (bay), North. Terr. 93/E2
Melville (isl.), North. Terr. 93/B1
Melville (cape), Queensland 88/G2
Melville (cape), Queensland 95/C2
Melville, Sask. 162/F5
Melville, Sask. 181/J5
Melville, W. Australia 92/A1
Melvin, Ala. (36913) 195/B7
Melvin, Ill. (60952) 222/E3
Melvin, Iowa (51350) 229/B2
Melvin, Lough (lake), Ireland 10/B3
Melvin (lake), Ireland 17/E3
Melvin, Mich. (48454) 250/G5
Melvin, Minn. (†56540) 255/B3
Melvin, Lough (lake), N. Ireland 10/B3
Melvin, Texas (76858) 303/E6
Melvina, Wis. (54619) 317/E8
Melvindale, Mich. (48122) 250/B7
Melvin Mills, N.H. (†03278) 268/D5
Melvin Village, N.H. (03850) 268/E4
Mélykút, Hungary 41/E3
Memaliaj, Albania 45/D5
Memba, Mozambique 118/G2
Membij, Syria 63/G4
Memel (Klaipeda), U.S.S.R. 52/B3
Memel (Klaipeda), U.S.S.R. 53/A3
Memmingen, W. Germany 22/D5
Mempawah, Indonesia 85/D5
Memphis, Ala. (†35442) 195/B4
Memphis (ruins), Egypt 111/J3
Memphis, Fla. (†33561) 212/D4
Memphis, Ind. (47143) 227/F8
Memphis, Mich. (48041) 250/G6
Memphis, Miss. (†38680) 256/D1
Memphis, Mo. (63555) 261/H2
Memphis, Nebr. (68042) 264/H3
Memphis, Tenn. 146/K6
Memphis, Tenn. 188/J3
Memphis, Tenn. (*38101) 237/B10
Memphis, Texas (79245) 303/D3
Memphis Naval Air Sta., Tenn. 237/B10
Memphremagog (lake), Québec 172/E4
Memphremagog (lake), Vt. 268/C1
Memramcook, New Bruns. 170/F2
Mena, Ark. (71953) 202/B4
Menafra, Uruguay 145/B3
Menahga, Minn. (56464) 255/C4
Menai (str.), Wales 13/C4
Menai Bridge, Wales 13/C4
Menaik, Alberta 182/D3
Ménaka, Mali 106/E5
Menan, Idaho (83434) 220/F6
Menands, N.Y. (†12201) 276/N5
Menarandra (riv.), Madagascar 118/H4
Menard (co.), Ill. 222/D3
Menard (co.), Texas 303/E7
Menard, Texas (76859) 303/E7
Menasalbas, Spain 33/D3
Menasha, Wis. (54952) 317/J7
Mencué, Argentina 143/C5
Mendak, Saudi Arabia 59/D5
Mende, France 28/E5
Mendenhall (cape), Alaska 196/E3
Mendenhall, Miss. (39114) 256/E7
Menderes, Büyük (riv.), Turkey 59/A2
Menderes, Büyük (riv.), Turkey 63/C4
Mendes, Georgia (†30427) 217/H7
Méndez, Ecuador 128/C4
Mendham, N.J. (07945) 273/D2
Mendham, Sask. 181/B5
Mendi, Ethiopia 111/G6
Mendi, Papua N.G. 85/B7
Mendip (hills), England 13/E6
Mendocino (cape), Calif. 146/F5
Mendocino (cape), Calif. 188/A2
Mendocino (co.), Calif. 204/B4
Mendocino, Calif. (95460) 204/B4
Mendocino (cape), Calif. 204/A3
Mendon, Ill. (62351) 222/B3
Mendon○, Mass. (01756) 249/H4
Mendon, Mich. (49072) 250/D7
Mendon, Mo. (64660) 261/F3
Mendon, N.Y. (14506) 276/E4
Mendon, Ohio (45862) 284/A4
Mendon, Utah (84325) 304/B2
Mendon○, Vt. (†05701) 268/B4
Mendooran, N.S. Wales 97/E2
Mendota, Calif. (93640) 204/E7
Mendota, Ill. (61342) 222/D2
Mendota, Minn. (55050) 255/G5
Mendota, Va. (24270) 307/D7
Mendota (lake), Wis. 317/H9
Mendota Heights, Minn. (†55050) 255/G6
Mendoza (prov.), Argentina 143/C4
Mendoza, Argentina 120/C6
Mendoza, Argentina 143/C3
Mendoza (riv.), Argentina 143/C3
Mendoza, Cuba 158/A2
Mendoza, Peru 128/D6
Mendoza, Uruguay 145/C5
Mendrisio, Switzerland 39/G5
Mene de Mauroa, Venezuela 124/C2
Mene Grande, Venezuela 124/C3
Menemen, Turkey 63/B3
Menemsha, Mass. (02552) 249/L7
Menen, Belgium 27/C7
Meneses, Cuba 158/F2
Menfi, Italy 34/D6
Menfro, Mo. (63765) 261/N7
Mengcheng, China 77/J5
Mengen, Turkey 63/D2
Menggala, Indonesia 85/D6
Menghai, China 77/E7
Mengla, China 77/F7
Mengshan, China 77/H7
Mengzi, China 77/F7
Menifee, Ark. (72107) 202/E3
Menifee (co.), Ky. 237/O5
Menihek, Newf. 166/A3
Menihek (lakes), Newf. 166/A3
Menin (Menen), Belgium 27/C7
Menindee, N.S. Wales 97/B3
Menindee (lake), N.S. Wales 97/B3
Meningie, S. Australia 94/F6
Menisino, Manitoba 179/F5
Menistouc (lake), Newf. 166/A3
Menlo, Georgia (30731) 217/B2
Menlo, Iowa (50164) 229/E5
Menlo, Kansas (67746) 232/B2
Menlo, Wash. (98561) 310/B4
Menlo Park, Calif. (94025) 204/J3
Menlo Park, N.J. (08837) 273/E2
Menneval, New Bruns. 170/C1
Menno, S. Dak. (57045) 298/P7
Meno, Okla. (73760) 288/K2
Menoken, N. Dak. (58558) 282/J6
Menominee, Ill. (†61025) 222/C1
Menominee (co.), Mich. 250/B3
Menominee, Mich. (49858) 250/B3
Menominee (riv.), Mich. 250/B3
Menominee (co.), Wis. 317/J5
Menominee (riv.), Wis. 317/L5
Menominee Ind. Res., Wis. 317/J5
Menomonee Falls, Wis. (53051) 317/K1
Menomonie, Wis. (54751) 317/C6
Menongue, Angola 115/C6
Menorca (Minorca) (isl.), Spain 33/J2
Mentasta (pass), Alaska 196/K2
Mentasta Lake, Alaska (†99586) 196/K2
Mentawai (isls.), Indonesia 54/L10
Mentawai (isls.), Indonesia 85/B6
Mentmore, N. Mex. (87319) 274/A3
Menton, France 28/G6
Mentone, Ala. (35984) 195/G1
Mentone, Calif. (92359) 204/H9
Mentone, Ind. (46539) 227/E2
Mentone, Texas (79754) 303/D10
Mentor, Kansas (67465) 232/E3
Mentor, Ky. (†41060) 237/N3
Mentor, Minn. (56736) 255/B3
Mentor, Ohio (44060) 284/H2
Mentor-on-the-Lake, Ohio (44060) 284/G2
Menunketesuck (riv.), Conn. 210/E3
Menye, Turkey 63/C3
Menyuan, China 77/F4
Menzel Bourguiba, Tunisia 106/F1
Menzel Temime, Tunisia 106/G1
Menzie, Manitoba 179/B4
Menzies, W. Australia 88/C5
Menzies, W. Australia 92/C5
Menzingen, Switzerland 39/G2
Menznau, Switzerland 39/E2
Meoquí, Mexico 150/G2
Meota, Sask. 181/C2
Meppel, Netherlands 27/J3
Meppen, W. Germany 22/B2
Mequineza (res.), Spain 33/F2
Mequon, Wis. (53092) 317/L1
Mera, Ecuador 128/C3
Mera (riv.), Switzerland 39/E2
Merabéllou (gulf), Greece 45/H8
Meraia (reg.), Mauritania 106/C5
Meråker, Norway 18/G5
Meramangye (lake), S. Australia 94/C3
Meramec (riv.), Mo. 261/N3
Merano, Italy 34/C1
Merasheen (isl.), Newf. 166/C2

410 Miguel Riglos

Miguel Riglos, Argentina 143/D4
Migues, Uruguay 145/C6
Mihalıççık, Turkey 63/D3
Mihara, Japan 81/F6
Mikado, Mich. (48745) 250/F4
Mikado, Sask. 181/J4
Mikana, Wis. (54857) 317/C4
Mikhaylovgrad, Bulgaria 45/F4
Mikhaylovka, U.S.S.R. 52/F4
Mikhmoret, Israel 65/B3
Miki, Japan 81/H7
Mikinai, Greece 45/F7
Mikkalo, Oreg. (97861) 291/G2
Mikkeli (prov.), Finland 18/P6
Mikkeli, Finland 18/P6
Mikkwa (riv.), Alberta 182/B5
Mikłów, Poland 47/B4
Míkonos (isl.), Greece 45/G7
Mikulov, Czech. 41/D2
Mikumi Nat'l Park, Tanzania 115/G5
Mikun', U.S.S.R. 52/H2
Mikuni, Japan 81/G5
Milaca, Minn. (56353) 255/E5
Milagro, Ecuador 120/A3
Milagro, Ecuador 128/C4
Milagros, Philippines 82/D4
Milam (co.), Texas 303/H7
Milam, Texas (75959) 303/L6
Milam, W. Va. (26838) 312/H5
Milan, Georgia (31060) 217/G6
Milan, Ill. (61264) 222/C2
Milan, Ind. (47031) 227/G6
Milan (prov.), Italy 34/B2
Milan, Italy 2/K3
Milan, Italy 7/E4
Milan, Italy 34/B2
Milan, Kansas (67105) 232/E4
Milan, Mich. (48160) 250/F6
Milan, Minn. (56262) 255/C5
Milan, Mo. (63556) 261/F2
Milan○, N.H. (03588) 268/E2
Milan, N. Mex. (87021) 274/B3
Milan, Ohio (44846) 284/E3
Milan, Québec 172/F4
Milan, Tenn. (38358) 237/D9
Milan, Wash. (†99003) 310/H3
Milan, Wis. (54453) 317/F6
Milanje, Mozambique 118/F3
Milano, Texas (76556) 303/H7
Milanville, Pa. (18443) 294/M2
Milâs, Turkey 63/B4
Milazzo, Italy 34/E5
Milbank, S. Dak. (57252) 298/R3
Milbanke (sound), Br. Col. 184/C4
Milberger, Kansas (†67665) 232/D3
Milbridge○, Maine (04658) 243/H6
Milburn, Ky. (42070) 237/D7
Milburn, Nebr. (68857) 264/E3
Milburn, Okla. (73450) 288/O6
Milden, Sask. 181/D4
Mildenhall, England 13/H5
Mildmay, Ontario 177/C3
Mildred, Kansas (66055) 232/G3
Mildred, Mont. (59341) 262/M4
Mildred, Pa. (18632) 294/K3
Mildred, Sask. 181/D2
Mildred Lake, Alberta 182/E1
Mildura, Victoria 88/G6
Mildura, Victoria 97/A4
Mile, China 77/F7
Miles, Iowa (52064) 229/N4
Miles, Queensland 88/H5
Miles, Texas (76861) 303/D6
Milesburg, Pa. (16853) 294/G4
Miles City, Mont. 188/E1
Miles City, Mont. (59301) 262/L4
Milestone, Sask. 181/G5
Milesville, S. Dak. (57553) 298/F5
Milevsko, Czech. 41/C2
Miley, S.C. (29933) 296/E6
Milfay, Okla. (74046) 288/N3
Milford, Calif. (96121) 204/E3
Milford, Conn. (06460) 210/C4
Milford (pt.), Conn. 210/C4
Milford, Del. (19963) 245/S5
Milford, Georgia (†31762) 217/C8
Milford, Ill. (60953) 222/F3
Milford, Ind. (46542) 227/F2
Milford, Ind. (†47240) 227/F6
Milford, Iowa (51351) 229/C2
Milford, Ireland 17/F1
Milford, Kansas (66514) 232/F2
Milford (lake), Kansas 232/E2
Milford, Ky. (41061) 237/N3
Milford, Maine (04461) 243/F6
Milford○, Maine (04461) 243/F6
Milford, Mass. (01757) 249/H4
Milford○, Mass. (01757) 249/H4
Milford, Mich. (48042) 250/F6
Milford, Mo. (64766) 261/D7
Milford, Nebr. (68405) 264/H4
Milford, N.H. (03055) 268/D6
Milford○, N.H. (03055) 268/D6
Milford, N.J. (08848) 273/C2
Milford, N.Y. (13807) 276/K5
Milford (sound), N. Zealand 100/A6
Milford, Ohio (45150) 284/D9
Milford, Pa. (18337) 294/N3
Milford, Texas (76670) 303/H5
Milford, Utah (84751) 304/A5
Milford, Va. (22514) 307/O4
Milford, Wis. (†53038) 317/J9
Milford Bay, Ontario 177/E2
Milford Center, Ohio (43045) 284/D5
Milford Haven, Wales 13/B6
Milford Haven, Wales 10/D5
Milford Haven (inlet), Wales 13/B6
Milford Haven (inlet), Wales 10/D5
Milford Station, Nova Scotia 168/E3
Milh, Bahr al (lake), Iraq 66/C4
Mili (atoll), Marshall Is. 87/H5
Miliana, Algeria 106/E1
Milicz, Poland 47/C3
Milieu (riv.), Québec 172/C3
Mililani Town, Hawaii (96789) 218/E2
Milingimbi, North. Terr. 93/D2
Milk (riv.) 146/H5
Milk (riv.), Alberta 182/D5
Milk (riv.), Mont. 188/D1
Milk (riv.), Mont. 262/J2
Milk, Wadi el (dry riv.), Sudan 59/A6
Milk, Wadi el (dry riv.), Sudan 111/E4
Milk River, Alberta 182/D5
Mill (creek), Calif. 204/D3
Mill (riv.), Conn. 210/D3
Mill (riv.), Conn. 210/B4
Mill (creek), Ind. 227/D5
Mill (riv.), Mass. 249/D3
Mill (riv.), Mass. 249/C3
Mill (creek), Mich. 250/G5
Mill (creek), N.J. 273/E4
Mill (isl.), N.W. Terrs. 187/L3
Mill (riv.), Vt. 268/B4
Mill (creek), W. Va. 312/C5
Milladore, Wis. (54454) 317/G6
Millard, Ky. (†41501) 237/S6
Millard, Mo. (†63501) 261/G2
Millard (co.), Utah 304/A4
Millarton, N. Dak. (58470) 282/N6
Millarville, Alberta 182/C4
Millau, France 28/E5
Millbank, Ontario 177/D4
Mill Bay, Br. Col. 184/K3
Millboro, S. Dak. (57554) 298/K7
Millboro, Va. (24460) 307/J5
Millboro Springs, Va. (24460) 307/J4
Millbourne, Pa. (†19082) 294/M6
Millbrae, Calif. (94030) 204/J2
Millbridge, Ontario 177/G3
Millbrook, Ala. (36054) 195/F6
Millbrook, Ill. (60536) 222/E2
Millbrook, Mich. (49334) 250/D5
Millbrook, N.Y. (12545) 276/N7
Millbrook, N.C. (27558) 281/M3
Millbrook, Ontario 177/F3
Millburn○, N.J. (07041) 273/E2
Millburne, Wyo. (†82933) 319/B4
Millbury○, Mass. (01527) 249/H4
Millbury, Ohio (43447) 284/D2
Mill City, Nev. (†89418) 266/D2
Mill City, Oreg. (97360) 291/E3
Mill Cove, New Bruns. 170/D3
Mill Cove, Nova Scotia 168/D4
Millcreek, Ill. (62961) 222/D6
Mill Creek, Ind. (46365) 227/D1
Millcreek, Mo. (†63645) 261/M7
Mill Creek, Okla. (74856) 288/N6
Mill Creek, Pa. (17060) 294/G5
Mill Creek, W. Va. (26280) 312/G5
Milldale, Conn. (06467) 210/D2
Millecoquins (lake), Mich. 250/D2
Milledgeville, Georgia (31061) 217/F4
Milledgeville, Ill. (61051) 222/D1
Milledgeville, Ohio (43142) 284/C6
Milledgeville, Tenn. (38359) 237/E10
Mille Îles (riv.), Québec 172/H4
Mille Lac Ind. Res., Minn. 255/E4
Mille Lacs (co.), Minn. 255/E5
Mille Lacs (lake), Minn. 188/H1
Mille Lacs (lake), Minn. 255/E4
Mille Lacs (lake), Ontario 177/G5
Mille Lacs (lake), Ontario 175/B3
Millen, Georgia (30442) 217/J5
Miller (peak), Ariz. 198/E7
Miller (co.), Ark. 202/C7
Miller (co.), Georgia 217/C8
Miller, Iowa (50438) 229/F2
Miller, Kansas (†66868) 232/F3
Miller, Miss. (†38654) 256/E1
Miller (co.), Mo. 261/H6
Miller, Mo. (65707) 261/E8
Miller, Nebr. (68858) 264/E4
Miller, Ohio (†45623) 284/F8
Miller (creek), Oreg. 291/F5
Miller, S. Dak. (57362) 298/L4
Miller City, Ohio (45864) 284/B3
Miller Dam Flowage (res.), Wis. 317/E5
Miller House, Alaska (99730) 196/J1
Millerovo, U.S.S.R. 48/E5
Millerovo, U.S.S.R. 52/F5
Millers, Md. (21107) 245/L2
Millers (riv.), Mass. 249/E2
Millersburg, Ind. (46543) 227/F1
Millersburg, Iowa (52308) 229/J5
Millersburg, Ky. (40348) 237/N4
Millersburg, Mich. (49759) 250/F3
Millersburg, Ohio (44654) 284/F4
Millersburg, Oreg. (†97321) 291/E3
Millersburg, Pa. (17061) 294/J4
Millers Falls, Mass. (01349) 249/E2
Millers Ferry, Ala. (36760) 195/D6
Millers Ferry, Fla. (†32437) 212/C6
Millersport, Ohio (43046) 284/E6
Millerstown, Ky. (†42754) 237/J6
Millerstown, Pa. (17062) 294/H4
Millersview, Texas (76862) 303/E6
Millersville, Md. (21108) 245/M4
Millersville, Ohio (43448) 284/D3
Millersville, Pa. (17551) 294/K6
Millerton (lake), Calif. 204/F6
Millerton, Iowa (50165) 229/G7
Millerton, New Bruns. 170/E2
Millerton, N.Y. (12546) 276/O7
Millerton, Okla. (74750) 288/S7
Millerton, Pa. (16936) 294/J2
Millertown, Newf. 166/C4
Millerville, Ala. (36267) 195/G4
Millerville, Minn. (†56315) 255/C4
Millet, Alberta 182/D3
Millett, S.C. (†29836) 296/D5
Millett, Texas (†78014) 303/E9
Millgrove, Ind. (†47348) 227/G4
Mill Grove, Mo. (†64673) 261/E2
Mill Hall, Pa. (17751) 294/G3
Millhaven, Georgia (†30467) 217/J5
Millheim, Pa. (16854) 294/G4
Millhousen, Ind. (47261) 227/G6
Millican, Oreg. (†97701) 291/F4
Millicent, Alberta 182/E4
Millicent, S. Australia 88/F7
Millicent, S. Australia 94/F7
Milligan, Fla. (32537) 212/C6
Milligan, Ind. (†47856) 227/C5
Milligan, Nebr. (68406) 264/G4
Milligan College, Tenn. (37682) 237/S8
Milliken, Colo. (80543) 208/K2
Millikin, La. (†71254) 238/H1
Millingen aan den Rijn, Netherlands 27/J5
Millington, Conn. (†06423) 210/F3
Millington, Ill. (60537) 222/E2
Millington, Md. (21651) 245/P3
Millington, Mich. (48746) 250/F5
Millington, N.J. (07946) 273/D2
Millington, Tenn. (38053) 237/B10
Millinocket○, Maine (04462) 243/F4
Millinocket (lake), Maine 243/F4
Millinocket (lake), Maine 243/F3
Mill Iron, Mont. (59342) 262/M5
Millis○, Mass. (02054) 249/A8
Millis-Clicquot, Mass. (02054) 249/A8
Millisle, N. Ireland 17/K2
Millmerran, Queensland 95/D5
Millmont, Pa. (17845) 294/H4
Mill Neck, N.Y. (11765) 276/R6
Millom, England 13/D3
Mill Plain, Conn. (†06810) 210/A3
Mill Point, W. Va. (24959) 312/F6
Millport, Ala. (35576) 195/B3
Millport, N.Y. (14864) 276/G6
Millport, Pa. (16739) 294/F2
Millport, Scotland 15/A2
Millport, Scotland 10/A1
Millrift, Pa. (18340) 294/N3
Mill River, Mass. (01244) 249/A4
Mill Road, Nova Scotia 168/D4
Millrose, W. Australia 92/C4
Mill Run, Pa. (15464) 294/C6
Millry, Ala. (36558) 195/B7
Mills (co.), Iowa 229/B6
Mills, Ky. (40970) 237/O7
Mills, Nebr. (68753) 264/E2
Mills, N. Mex. (87730) 274/E2
Mills (lake), N.W. Terrs. 187/G3
Mills, Pa. (16937) 294/G2
Mills (co.), Texas 303/F6
Mills, Utah (†84639) 304/B4
Mills, Wyo. (82644) 319/F3
Millsap, Texas (76066) 303/G5
Millsboro, Del. (19966) 245/S6
Millsboro, Pa. (15348) 294/B6
Mill Shoals, Ill. (62862) 222/E5
Mill Spring, Mo. (63952) 261/L8
Mill Springs, Ky. (42632) 237/M7
Millstadt, Ill. (62260) 222/B3
Millston, Wis. (54643) 317/E7
Millstone, Ky. (41838) 237/R6
Millstone, N.J. (†08876) 273/D2
Millstone (riv.), N.J. 273/D3
Millstone, W. Va. (25261) 312/D5
Millstream Station, W. Australia 92/B3
Millstreet, Ireland 17/D7
Millthorpe, N.S. Wales 97/E5
Milltown, Ala. (†36855) 195/H4
Milltown, Ind. (47145) 227/E8
Milltown, Ireland 17/A7
Milltown, Ky. (42761) 237/L6
Milltown, Mont. (59851) 262/C4
Milltown, Newf. 166/C4
Milltown, N.J. (08850) 273/E3
Milltown, S. Dak. (†57366) 298/O7
Milltown, Wis. (54858) 317/B4
Millungera, Queensland 95/B3
Millvale, Pa. (15209) 294/B7
Mill Valley, Calif. (94941) 204/H2
Mill Village, Nova Scotia 168/D4
Mill Village, Pa. (16427) 294/C2
Millville, Del. (19967) 245/T6
Millville, Ind. (†47362) 227/G5
Millville, Iowa (†52052) 229/L3
Millville○, Mass. (01529) 249/H4
Millville, Minn. (55957) 255/F6
Millville, New Bruns. 170/C2
Millville, N.J. (08332) 273/C5
Millville, Ohio (†45011) 284/A7
Millville, Pa. (17846) 294/J3
Millville, Utah (84326) 304/C2
Millwood (lake), Ark. 202/C6
Millwood, Georgia (31552) 217/G8
Millwood, Ky. (42762) 237/J6
Millwood, Manitoba 179/A4
Millwood, Ohio (†43014) 284/F5
Millwood, Va. (22646) 307/N2
Millwood, Wash. (†99210) 310/H3
Millwood, W. Va. (25262) 312/C5
Milly Milly, W. Australia 92/B4
Milmay, N.J. (08340) 273/D5
Milmine, Ill. (61855) 222/E4
Milmont Park, Pa. (19033) 294/M7
Milnathort, Scotland 15/E4
Milne (inlet), N.W. Terrs. 187/K2
Milne (bay), Papua N.G. 85/C8
Milner, Colo. (80477) 208/F2
Milner, Georgia (30257) 217/D4
Milner Ridge, Manitoba 179/F4
Milnerton, S. Africa 118/F6
Milnesand, N. Mex. (88125) 274/F5
Milnes Landing, Br. Col. 184/J4
Milngavie, Scotland 10/B1
Milngavie, Scotland 15/B1
Milnor, N. Dak. (58060) 282/R7
Milo, Alberta 182/D4
Milo (riv.), Guinea 106/C7
Milo, Iowa (50166) 229/G6
Milo, Ky. (41235) 237/R5
Milo, Maine (04463) 243/F5
Milo○, Maine (04463) 243/F5
Milo, Mo. (64767) 261/D7
Milo, Okla. (73451) 288/M6
Milo, Oreg. (†97417) 291/E5
Milo, Tenn. (†37381) 237/L9
Milolii, Hawaii (†96704) 218/G6
Milos, Greece 45/G7
Milos (isl.), Greece 45/G7
Milot, Québec 172/F1
Milpa, N.S. Wales 97/B2
Milparinka, N.S. Wales 97/A1
Milperra, N.S. Wales 97/H4
Milpitas, Calif. (95035) 204/L3
Milroy, Ind. (46156) 227/F6
Milroy, Minn. (56263) 255/C6
Milroy, Pa. (17063) 294/G4
Milstead, Ala. (†36075) 195/G6
Milstead, Georgia (30207) 217/D3
Milton (res.), Colo. 208/K2
Milton, Conn. (†06759) 210/C1
Milton, Del. (19968) 245/S5
Milton, Fla. (32570) 212/B6
Milton, Ill. (62352) 222/C4
Milton, Ind. (47357) 227/G5
Milton, Iowa (52570) 229/J7
Milton, Kansas (67106) 232/E4
Milton, Ky. (40045) 237/L3
Milton, La. (70558) 238/F6
Milton○, Mass. (02186) 249/D7
Milton, Newf. 166/C2
Milton○, N.H. (03851) 268/F5
Milton, N.J. (07438) 273/D1
Milton, N.S. Wales 97/F4
Milton, N.Y. (12547) 276/M7
Milton, N.Y. (†12020) 276/N4
Milton, N. Zealand 100/B7
Milton, N.C. (27305) 281/L1
Milton, N. Dak. (58260) 282/O2
Milton, Nova Scotia 168/D4
Milton, Okla. (†74944) 288/S4
Milton, Ontario 177/E4
Milton, Pa. (17847) 294/J3
Milton, Tenn. (37118) 237/J9
Milton, Vt. (05468) 268/A2
Milton○, Vt. (05468) 268/A2
Milton, Wash. (98354) 310/C3
Milton, W. Va. (25541) 312/B6
Milton, Wis. (53563) 317/J10
Miltona, Minn. (56354) 255/C4
Miltona (lake), Minn. 255/C4
Milton Center, Ohio (43541) 284/C3
Milton-Freewater, Oreg. (97862) 291/J2
Milton Keynes, England 13/F5
Milton Mills, N.H. (03852) 268/F4
Miltonsburg, Ohio (†43793) 284/H6
Miltonvale, Kansas (67466) 232/E2
Miltown-Malbay, Ireland 17/C6
Milverton, Ontario 177/D4
Milwaukee, N.C. (27854) 281/P2
Milwaukee, Wis. 146/K5
Milwaukee, Wis. 188/J2
Milwaukee (co.), Wis. 317/L9
Milwaukee, Wis. (*53201) 317/M1
Milwaukie, Oreg. (97222) 291/B2
Mima, Ky. (41456) 237/P5
Mimbres, N. Mex. (88049) 274/B6
Mimbres (mts.), N. Mex. 274/B6
Mimbres (riv.), N. Mex. 274/B6
Mimінegash, Pr. Edward I. 168/D2
Mimizan, France 28/C5
Mimoň, Czech. 41/C1
Mimongo, Gabon 115/B4
Mimosa Park, La. (†70070) 238/N4
Mimoso do Sul, Brazil 135/F2
Mims, Fla. (32754) 212/F3
Mina, Nev. (89422) 266/C4
Mina, S. Dak. (57462) 298/M3
Mina al Ahmadi, Kuwait 59/E4
Mina al Fahal, Oman 59/G5
Minab, Iran 59/G2
Minab, Iran 66/K7
Minaki, Ontario 177/F4
Minaki, Ontario 175/A3
Minam, Oreg. (†97827) 291/K2
Minamata, Japan 81/E7
Minami Iwo (isl.), Japan 87/D3
Minami Iwo (isl.), Japan 81/M5
Minapasuk, Philippines 82/D5
Minard, Ireland 17/A7
Minas, Cuba 158/G2
Minas (mts.), Guatemala 154/C3
Minas (basin), Nova Scotia 168/D3
Minas (chan.), Nova Scotia 168/D3
Minas, Uruguay 145/D5
Mina Saud, Kuwait 59/E4
Mina Sa'ud, Saudi Arabia 59/E4
Minas-Cué, Paraguay 144/C3
Minas de Corrales, Uruguay 145/D2
Minas de Matahambre, Cuba 158/A1
Minas de Riotinto, Spain 33/C4
Minas Gerais (state), Brazil 135/D2
Minas Gerais (state), Brazil 132/E7
Minas Novas, Brazil 132/F7
Minatare, Nebr. (69356) 264/A3
Minatare (lake), Nebr. 264/A3
Minatitlán, Mexico 150/M8
Minbu, Burma 72/B2
Minburn, Alberta 182/E3
Minburn, Iowa (50167) 229/E5
Minbya, Burma 72/B2
Mincha, Chile 138/A8
Minchinmávida (vol.), Chile 138/E4
Mincio (riv.), Italy 34/C2
Minco, Okla. (73059) 288/L4
Mindanao (isl.), Philippines 54/O9
Mindanao (isl.), Philippines 2/R5
Mindanao (isl.), Philippines 85/H4
Mindanao (isl.), Philippines 82/D7
Mindanao (riv.), Philippines 82/E7
Mindanao (sea), Philippines 85/G4
Mindanao (sea), Philippines 82/D7
Mindelheim, W. Germany 22/D4
Mindelo, C. Verde 106/A7
Mindemoya, Ontario 177/B2
Mindemoya (lake), Ontario 177/B2
Minden, Iowa (51553) 229/C6
Minden, La. (71055) 238/D1
Minden, Nebr. (68959) 264/E4
Minden, Nev. (89423) 266/B4
Minden, Ontario 177/F3
Minden, Texas (75680) 303/K5
Minden, W. Germany 22/C2
Minden, W. Va. (25879) 312/D7
Minden City, Mich. (48456) 250/G5
Mindenmines, Mo. (64769) 261/C8
Mindiptana, Indonesia 85/L7
Mindoro (isl.), Philippines 54/N8
Mindoro (isl.), Philippines 85/G3
Mindoro (isl.), Philippines 82/C4
Mindoro (str.), Philippines 85/F3
Mindoro (str.), Philippines 82/C4
Mindoro, Wis. (54644) 317/D7
Mindouli, Congo 115/B4
Mindszent, Hungary 41/F3
Mine (head), Ireland 17/F8
Mine Centre, Ontario 177/G5
Mine Centre, Ontario 175/B3
Minehead, England 13/D6
Minehead, England 10/E5
Mine Hill○, N.J. (†07801) 273/D2
Mineiros, Brazil 132/C7
Mineiros, Brazil 120/D4
Mine La Motte, Mo. (63659) 261/M7
Mineola, Iowa (51554) 229/B6
Mineola, Mo. (†63361) 261/J5
Mineola, N.Y. (11501) 276/R7
Mineola, Texas (75773) 303/J5
Miner, Mo. (†63801) 261/N9
Miner, Mont. (†59027) 262/E5
Miner (co.), S. Dak. 298/O5
Mineral, Calif. (96063) 204/D3
Mineral (co.), Colo. 208/F7
Mineral, Ill. (61344) 222/D2
Mineral (co.), Mont. 262/B3
Mineral (co.), Nev. 266/C4
Mineral, Ohio (†45766) 284/F7
Mineral, Texas (78125) 303/G9
Mineral (mts.), Utah 304/B5
Mineral, Va. (23117) 307/N4
Mineral, Wash. (98355) 310/C4
Mineral (co.), W. Va. 312/J4
Mineral Bluff, Georgia (30559) 217/D1
Mineral Center, Minn. (†55605) 255/G2
Mineral City, Ohio (44656) 284/H4
Mineral del Monte, Mexico 150/K6
Mineral Hills, Mich. (†49935) 250/G2
Mineral'nye Vody, U.S.S.R. 52/F6
Mineral Point, Mo. (63660) 261/L7
Mineral Point, Wis. (53565) 317/F10
Mineral Springs, Ark. (71851) 202/C6
Mineral Springs, N.C. (28108) 281/H5
Mineral Wells, Miss. (38648) 256/E1
Mineral Wells, Texas (76067) 303/F5
Mineralwells, W. Va. (26150) 312/C4
Minersville, Ohio (45769) 284/G7
Minersville, Pa. (17954) 294/K4
Minersville, Utah (84752) 304/A5
Mine Run, Va. (22568) 307/N4
Minerva, Ky. (41062) 237/O3
Minerva, N.Y. (12851) 276/N3
Minerva, Ohio (44657) 284/H4
Minerva (reefs), Tonga 87/H8
Minerva Park, Ohio (†43201) 284/E5
Minetto, N.Y. (13115) 276/H4
Mineville-Witherbee, N.Y. (12956) 276/O2
Minfeng (Niya), China 77/B4
Minford, Ohio (45653) 284/E8
Mingan, Que. 162/K5
Mingan, Québec 174/E2
Mingan (Jacques-Cartier) (pass), Québec 174/E3
Mingechaur, U.S.S.R. 52/G6
Mingenew, W. Australia 88/B5
Mingenew, W. Australia 92/A5
Minginish (dist.), Scotland 15/B3
Minglanilla, Spain 33/F3
Mingo, Iowa (50168) 229/G5
Mingo, Kansas (†67701) 232/B2
Mingo (lake), N.W. Terrs. 187/L3
Mingo, Ohio (43047) 284/C5
Mingo (co.), W. Va. 312/B7
Mingo, W. Va. (26281) 312/F5
Mingo Junction, Ohio (43938) 284/J5
Mingshui, Gansu, China 77/E3
Mingshui, Heilongjiang, China 77/L2
Mingulay (isl.), Scotland 15/A4
Mingus, Texas (76463) 303/F5
Mingwal (lake), W. Australia 88/C5
Minhla, Burma 72/B3
Minho (riv.), Jamaica 158/J6
Minho (riv.), Portugal 33/B2
Minicoy (isl.), India 68/C7
Minidoka (co.), Idaho 220/E7
Minidoka, Idaho (83343) 220/E7
Minier, Ill. (61759) 222/D3
Minigwal (lake), W. Australia 92/C5
Minilya, W. Australia 92/A4
Miniota, Manitoba 179/B4
Minipi (lake), Newf. 166/B3
Minipi (riv.), Newf. 166/B3
Ministikwan (lake), Sask. 181/B1
Ministre (pt.), St. Lucia 161/G7
Minitonas, Manitoba 179/B2
Min Jiang (riv.), China 77/J6
Minlaton, S. Australia 94/E6
Minle, China 77/F4
Minna, Nigeria 106/F7
Minneapolis, Kansas (67467) 232/E2
Minneapolis, Minn. 146/J5
Minneapolis, Minn. 188/H1
Minneapolis, Minn. (*55401) 255/G5
Minneapolis, U.S. 2/E3
Minneapolis-Saint Paul Airport, Minn. 255/G5
Minnechaduza (creek), S. Dak. 298/H7
Minnedosa, Manitoba 179/B4
Minnedosa (riv.), Manitoba 179/B4
Minnehaha (co.), S. Dak. 298/R6
Minnehaha Springs, W. Va. (24960) 312/G6
Minneiska, Minn. (55958) 255/G6
Minneola, Fla. (32755) 212/E3
Minneola, Kansas (67865) 232/C4
Minneota, Minn. (56264) 255/C6
Minnesota 188/H1
MINNESOTA 255
Minnesota (riv.), Minn. 188/G2
Minnesota (riv.), Minn. 255/E6
Minnesota (riv.), S. Dak. 298/S3
Minnesota (state), U.S. 146/J5
Minnesota City, Minn. (55959) 255/G6
Minnesota Lake, Minn. (56068) 255/E7
Minnesott Beach, N.C. (†28510) 281/R5
Minnetonka, Minn. (55343) 255/G5
Minnetonka (lake), Minn. 255/F5
Minnetrista, Minn. (†55364) 255/F5
Minnewaska (lake), Minn. 255/C5
Minnewaukan, N. Dak. (58351) 282/M3
Minnigaff, Scotland 15/D6
Minnipa, S. Australia 88/F6
Minnipa, S. Australia 94/D5
Minnitaki (lake), Ontario 177/G4
Minnith, Mo. (†63673) 261/M7
Minnora, W. Va. (25263) 312/D5
Miño (riv.), Spain 7/D4
Miño (riv.), Spain 33/B1
Minoa, N.Y. (13116) 276/H4
Minobu, Japan 81/J6
Minocqua, Wis. (54548) 317/G4
Minong, Wis. (54859) 317/C3
Minonk, Ill. (61760) 222/D3
Minoo, Japan 81/J7
Minooka, Ill. (60447) 222/E2
Minorca (isl.), Spain 7/E4
Minorca (isl.), Spain 33/J2
Minor Hill, Tenn. (38473) 237/G10
Minor Lane Heights, Ky. (†40201) 237/K4
Minortown, Conn. (†06798) 210/C2
Minot, Maine (04258) 243/C7
Minot○, Maine (04258) 243/C7
Minot, Mass. (02055) 249/F8
Minot, N. Dak. 188/F1
Minot, N. Dak. 146/H5
Minot, N. Dak. (58701) 282/H3
Minot A.F.B., N. Dak. 282/H3
Minotola, N.J. (08341) 273/D4
Minqin, China 77/F4
Minsk, U.S.S.R. 7/G3
Minsk, U.S.S.R. 2/L3
Minsk, U.S.S.R. 48/C4
Minsk, U.S.S.R. 52/C4
Mińsk Mazowiecki, Poland 47/E2
Minster, Ohio (45865) 284/B5
Minstrel Island, Br. Col. 184/D5
Minter, Ala. (36761) 195/D6
Minter City, Miss. (38944) 256/D3
Mint Hill, N.C. (28212) 281/H4
Mintlaw, Scotland 15/F3
Minto, Alaska (99758) 196/J2
Minto, Manitoba 179/B5
Minto, New Bruns. 170/D2
Minto, N. Dak. (58261) 282/R3
Minto (inlet), N.W. Terrs. 187/G2
Minto (lake), Que. 162/J4
Minto (lake), Québec 174/E2
Minto, Yukon 187/E3
Minton, Sask. 181/G6
Minturn, Ark. (72445) 202/H2
Minturn, Colo. (81645) 208/G3
Minturn, Maine (04659) 243/G7
Minturn, S.C. (29573) 296/J2
Minturno, Italy 34/D4
Minûf, Egypt 111/J3
Minusinsk, U.S.S.R. 48/K4
Minusio, Switzerland 39/G4
Minute Man Nat'l Hist. Park, Mass. 249/B6
Minvoul, Gabon 115/B3
Min Xian, China 77/F5
Minyip, Victoria 97/B5
Mio, Mich. (48647) 250/E4
Miocene, Br. Col. 184/G4
Miquan, China 77/C3
Miquelon (isl.), 166/C4
Miquihuana, Mexico 150/J5
Miquillo (pt.), P. Rico 161/F1
Mira (riv.), Colombia 126/A7
Mira (riv.), Ecuador 128/C2
Mira, La. (71059) 238/C1
Mira (bay), Nova Scotia 168/J2
Mira (riv.), Nova Scotia 168/H3
Mira, Portugal 33/B2
Mira (riv.), Portugal 33/B4
Mirabad, Afghanistan 68/A2
Mirabad, Afghanistan 59/H3
Mirabel, Québec 172/H4
Mirabile, Mo. (†64671) 261/D3
Miracema, Brazil 135/E2
Miracema, Brazil 132/F8
Mirador, Brazil 132/E4
Mirador Nacional (mt.), Uruguay 145/D5
Miraflores, Boyacá, Colombia 126/D5
Miraflores, Vaupés, Colombia 126/D7
Miragoâne, Haiti 158/B6
Miragoâne, Haiti 156/D3
Miraj, India 68/D5
Miraje, Salar del (salt dep.), Chile 138/B3
Mira Loma, Calif. (91752) 204/E10
Miramar, Argentina 143/E4
Miramar, C. Rica 154/E5
Miramar, Fla. (33023) 212/B4
Miramar, Panama 154/H6
Miramichi (bay), New Bruns. 170/E1
Miram Shah, Pakistan 68/C2
Miranda, Brazil 132/C8
Miranda (riv.), Brazil 132/B8
Miranda, Colombia 126/B6
Miranda, S. Dak. (57463) 298/M4
Miranda (state), Venezuela 124/E2
Miranda de Ebro, Spain 33/E1
Miranda do Corvo, Portugal 33/B2
Miranda do Douro, Portugal 33/C2
Mirande, France 28/D6
Mirandela, Portugal 33/C2
Mirando City, Texas (78369) 303/E10
Mirandola, Italy 34/C2
Mira Por Vos (cays), Bahamas 156/C2
Mira Road, Nova Scotia 168/H2
Mirassol, Brazil 135/B2
Mira Taglio, Italy 34/D2
Mirebalais, Haiti 156/D3
Mirebalais, Haiti 158/C6
Mirecourt, France 28/G3
Mirgorod, U.S.S.R. 52/D5
Miri (hills), India 68/G3
Miri, Malaysia 85/E5
Mirik (Timiris) (cape), Mauritania 106/A5
Mirim (lake) 120/D6
Mirim (lag.), Brazil 132/C11
Mirimire, Venezuela 124/D2
Mirina, Greece 45/G6
Miritiparaná (riv.), Colombia 126/E8
Mirjaveh, Iran 59/H4
Mirjaveh, Iran 66/M6

Monomoy 411

Mirjaveh, Pakistan 59/H4
Mirnyy 5/C5
Mirnyy, U.S.S.R. 54/N3
Mirnyy, U.S.S.R. 48/M3
Mirpur, Pakistan 68/C2
Mirpur Khas, Pakistan 68/B3
Mirror, Alberta 182/D3
Mirror Lake, N.H. (03853) 268/E4
Mirtöön (sea), Greece 45/F7
Miryang, S. Korea 81/D6
Mirzapur-cum-Vindhyachal, India 68/E4
Misamis Occidental (prov.), Philippines 82/D6
Misamis Oriental (prov.), Philippines 82/E6
Misantla, Mexico 150/P1
Misawa, Japan 81/K3
Miscou (isl.), New Bruns. 170/F1
Miscou (pt.), New Bruns. 170/F1
Miscou Centre, New Bruns. 170/F1
Miscouche, Pr. Edward I. 168/D2
Miscou Harbour, New Bruns. 170/F1
Misenheimer, N.C. (28109) 281/J4
Misery (bay), Mich. 250/G1
Misery (riv.), Mich. 250/G1
Misery (mt.), St. Chris.-Nevis 161/C10
Misgar, Pakistan 68/C1
Misha'ab, Ras (cape), Saudi Arabia 59/E4
Mishagua, Peru 128/F8
Mishan, China 77/M2
Mishaum (pt.), Mass. 249/L6
Mishawaka, Ind. (46544) 227/E1
Misheguk (mt.), Alaska 196/F1
Mishicot, Wis. (54228) 317/L7
Mishmar Hanegev, Israel 65/B5
Mishmar Hayarden, Israel 65/D1
Mishmi (hills), India 68/H3
Misima (isl.), Papua N.G. 85/C8
Misiones (prov.), Argentina 143/F2
Misiones (dept.), Paraguay 144/D5
Miskitos (cays), Nicaragua 154/F3
Miskolc, Hungary 41/F2
Miskolc, Hungary 7/G4
Misool (isl.), Indonesia 85/J6
Mispec, New Bruns. 170/E3
Mispillion (riv.), Del. 245/S5
Misquah (hills), Minn. 255/F2
Missanabie, Ontario 177/J5
Missanabie, Ontario 175/D3
Missaukee (co.), Mich. 250/D4
Missi Falls, Manitoba 179/J2
Missinaibi (riv.), Ont. 162/H6
Missinaibi (lake), Ontario 175/D3
Missinaibi (riv.), Ontario 177/J5
Missinaibi (riv.), Ontario 175/D2
Mission, Br. Col. 184/L3
Mission, Kansas (66205) 232/H2
Mission (range), Mont. 262/C3
Mission, S. Dak. (57555) 298/H7
Mission, Texas (78572) 303/F11
Mission Beach, Alberta 182/C3
Mission City, Br. Col. 184/L3
Mission Hill, S. Dak. (57046) 298/P8
Mission Ridge, S. Dak. (57557) 298/H4
Mission Viejo, Calif. (92691) 204/D11
Missisa (lake), Ontario 175/D2
Missisquoi (co.), Québec 172/D4
Missisquoi (riv.), Vt. 268/B2
Mississagi (riv.), Ontario 177/A1
Mississagi (str.), Ontario 177/A2
Mississauga, Ontario 177/J4
Mississinewa (lake), Ind. 227/F3
Mississinewa (riv.), Ind. 227/F3
Mississippi 188/J4
MISSISSIPPI 256
Mississippi (riv.) 188/H4
Mississippi (sound), Ala. 195/B10
Mississippi (co.), Ark. 202/K2
Mississippi (riv.), Ark. 202/H7
Mississippi (riv.), Ill. 222/C5
Mississippi (riv.), Iowa 229/L7
Mississippi (riv.), Ky. 237/A10
Mississippi (delta), La. 146/K7
Mississippi (delta), La. 188/J5
Mississippi (delta), La. 238/M8
Mississippi (riv.), La. 238/H3
Mississippi (sound), La. 238/M6
Mississippi (riv.), Minn. 255/D4
Mississippi (riv.), Miss. 256/A8
Mississippi (sound), Miss. 256/G10
Mississippi (co.), Mo. 261/O9
Mississippi (riv.), Mo. 261/L4
Mississippi (lake), Ontario 177/H2
Mississippi (riv.), Tenn. 237/A10
Mississippi (state), U.S. 146/K6
Mississippi (riv.), U.S. 2/E4
Mississippi (riv.), U.S. 146/J6
Mississippi (riv.), Wis. 317/D10
Mississippi River Gulf Outlet (canal), La. 238/L7
Mississippi State, Miss. (39762) 256/G4
Missoula, Mont. 146/G5
Missoula, Mont. 188/D1
Missoula (co.), Mont. 262/C3
Missoula, Mont. (*59801) 262/C4
Missouri 188/H3
MISSOURI 261
Missouri (riv.) 188/H3
Missouri (riv.), Iowa 229/A4
Missouri (riv.), Kansas 232/G1
Missouri (riv.), Mo. 261/H5
Missouri (riv.), Mont. 262/L3
Missouri (riv.), Nebr. 264/H3
Missouri (riv.), N. Dak. 282/H5
Missouri (riv.), S. Dak. 298/P8
Missouri (state), U.S. 146/J6
Missouri (riv.), U.S. 2/D3
Missouri (riv.), U.S. 146/J5
Missouri Branch, W. Va. (†25511) 312/A7
Missouri City, Mo. (64072) 261/R5
Missouri City, Texas (77459) 303/J2
Missouri Coteau (hills), Sask. 181/F5
Missouri Valley, Iowa (51555) 229/B5
Mist, Ark. (†71646) 202/G7
Mist, Oreg. (97016) 291/D1
Mistake (bay), N.W. Terrs. 187/J3
Mistake Creek, North. Terr. 93/A4
Mistaken (pt.), Newf. 166/D2
Mistassibi (riv.), Que. 162/J5
Mistassibi (riv.), Québec 174/C3
Mistassini (lake), Que. 162/J5
Mistassini (lake), Que. 146/L4
Mistassini (terr.), Québec 174/B2
Mistassini, Québec 172/E1
Mistassini, Québec 174/C3
Mistassini (Baie-du-Poste), Québec 174/C2
Mistassini (lake), Québec 174/C2
Mistastin (lake), Newf. 166/B2
Mistastin (riv.), Newf. 166/B2
Mistatim, Sask. 181/H3
Mistehae (lake), Alberta 182/C2
Mistelbach an der Zaya, Austria 41/D2
Misteriosa (bank), Cayman Is. 156/A3
Misti, El (mt.), Peru 120/B4
Misti, El (mt.), Peru 128/G11
Mistinippi (lake), Newf. 166/B3
Miston, Tenn. (38056) 237/B8
Mistretta, Italy 34/E6
Misty Fjords Nat'l Mon., Alaska 196/N2
Misurata, Libya 102/D1
Misurata, Libya 111/C1
Mita (pt.), Mexico 150/G6
Mitaka, Japan 81/O2
Mitcham, S. Australia 88/D8
Mitcham, S. Australia 94/B8
Mitchell (lake), Ala. 188/J4
Mitchell (dam), Ala. 195/E5
Mitchell (lake), Ala. 195/F5
Mitchell, Ark. (†72583) 202/G1
Mitchell (co.), Georgia 217/D8
Mitchell, Georgia (30820) 217/G4
Mitchell, Ind. (47446) 227/E7
Mitchell (co.), Iowa 229/H2
Mitchell, Iowa (†50461) 229/H2
Mitchell (co.), Kansas 232/D2
Mitchell, La. (71453) 238/C3
Mitchell, Nebr. (69357) 264/A3
Mitchell (co.), N.C. 281/E2
Mitchell (mt.), N.C. 188/K3
Mitchell (mt.), N.C. 281/E3
Mitchell, Ontario 177/C4
Mitchell, Oreg. (97750) 291/G3
Mitchell, Queensland 88/H5
Mitchell, Queensland 95/C5
Mitchell (riv.), Queensland 88/G3
Mitchell (riv.), Queensland 95/B2
Mitchell, S. Dak. 188/G2
Mitchell, S. Dak. (57301) 298/N6
Mitchell (creek), S. Dak. 298/G5
Mitchell (co.), Texas 303/D5
Mitchell (riv.), Victoria 97/D5
Mitchell Bay, Ontario 177/B5
Mitchell Heights, W. Va. (†25601) 312/B7
Mitchells, Va. (22729) 307/N4
Mitchellsburg, Ky. (40452) 237/M5
Mitchellsville, Ill. (†62946) 222/E6
Mitchellton, Sask. 181/F6
Mitchellville, Ark. (†71639) 202/H6
Mitchellville, Iowa (50169) 229/G5
Mitchellville, Tenn. (37119) 237/J7
Mitchelstown, Ireland 10/B4
Mitchelstown, Ireland 17/E7
Mitchelton, Queensland 88/J2
Mitchelton, Queensland 95/D2
Mitchinamécus (res.), Québec 172/C2
Mithi, Pakistan 68/C4
Mithimna, Greece 45/G6
Mitiaro, Cook Is. 87/L7
Mitilíni, Greece 45/H6
Mitkof (isl.), Alaska 196/N2
Mitla (ruin), Mexico 150/M8
Mito, Japan 81/K5
Mitrofania (isl.), Alaska 196/G3
Mitsamiouli, Comoros 118/G2
Mitsinjo, Madagascar 118/H3
Mitsue, Alberta 182/C2
Mitsukaido, Japan 81/P2
Mittagong, N.S. Wales 97/F4
Mitta Mitta (riv.), Victoria 97/D5
Mittenwald, W. Germany 22/D5
Mittersill, Austria 41/B3
Mittie, La. (70654) 238/E5
Mittweida, E. Germany 22/E3
Mitú, Colombia 126/E7
Mitú, Colombia 120/B2
Mituas, Colombia 126/F6
Mitwaba, Zaire 115/E5
Mitzic, Gabon 115/B3
Miura, Japan 81/O3
Miura (pen.), Japan 81/O3
Mivtahim, Israel 65/A5
Mix, La. (†70760) 238/G5
Miyagi (pref.), Japan 81/K4
Miyako, Japan 81/L4
Miyako (isl.), Japan 81/L7
Miyako (isls.), Japan 81/L7
Miyakonojo, Japan 81/E8
Miyazaki (pref.), Japan 81/E8
Miyazaki, Japan 81/E8
Miyazu, Japan 81/G6
Miyoshi, Japan 81/F6
Mizan Teferi, Ethiopia 111/G6
Mizda, Libya 111/B1
Mize, Georgia (†30577) 217/F2
Mize, Miss. (39116) 256/E7
Mizen (head), Ireland 10/A5
Mizen (head), Ireland 17/B9
Mizen (head), Ireland 17/K6
Mizhi, China 77/H4
Mizil, Romania 45/H3
Mizo (hill), India 68/G4
Mizoram (terr.), India 68/G4
Mizpah, Minn. (56660) 255/D3
Mizpah, N.J. (08342) 273/D5
Mizpe Ramon, Israel 65/D5
Mizque, Bolivia 136/C5
Mizque (riv.), Bolivia 136/C6
Mizusawa, Japan 81/K4
Mjölby, Sweden 18/J7
Mkokotoni, Tanzania 115/G5
Mkushi, Zambia 115/E6
Mladá Boleslav, Czech. 41/C1
Mladá Vožice, Czech. 41/C2
Mława, Poland 47/E2
Mljet (isl.), Yugoslavia 45/C4
Mmabatho (cap.), Bophuthatswana, S. Africa 102/E7
Mmabatho, S. Africa 118/D5
Mnichovo Hradiště, Czech. 41/C1
Mo, Norway 7/F2
Mo, Norway 18/J3
Moa, Cuba 158/K3
Moa (riv.), Guinea 106/B7
Moa (isl.), Indonesia 85/H7
Moa (riv.), S. Leone 106/B7
Moab, Utah (84532) 304/E5
Moak Lake, Manitoba 179/J2
Moala (isl.), Fiji 86/Q11
Moama, N.S. Wales 97/C5
Moamba, Mozambique 118/E5
Moanalua (stream), Hawaii 218/B3
Moanda, Gabon 115/B4
Moanda, Zaire 115/B5
Moapa, Nev. (89025) 266/G6
Moapa River Ind. Res., Nev. 266/G6
Moar (lake), Manitoba 179/G2
Moark, Ark. (†72422) 202/J1
Moate, Ireland 17/F5
Moatsville, W. Va. (26405) 312/G4
Mobara, Japan 81/K6
Mobaye, Cent. Afr. Rep. 115/D3
Mobayi-Mbongo, Zaire 115/D3
Mobayi-Mbongo, Zaire 102/E4
Mobeetie, Texas (79061) 303/D2
Moberly, Br. Col. 184/J4
Moberly (lake), Br. Col. 184/F2
Moberly, Mo. (65270) 261/G4
Moberly, Mo. 188/H3
Moberly Lake, Br. Col. 184/G2
Mobile, Ala. 146/K6
Mobile, Ala. 188/J4
Mobile (bay), Ala. 188/J5
Mobile (co.), Ala. 195/B9
Mobile, Ala. (*36601) 195/B9
Mobile (bay), Ala. 195/B10
Mobile (pt.), Ala. 195/B10
Mobile (riv.), Ala. 195/C9
Mobile, Ariz. (†85239) 198/C5
Mobile, Newf. 166/D2
Mobile Big (pond), Newf. 166/D2
Mobjack, Va. (23118) 307/R6
Mobjack (bay), Va. 307/R6
Mobridge, S. Dak. (57601) 298/J2
Mobuto Sese Seko (lake) 102/F4
Mobuto Sese Seko (lake), Uganda 115/F3
Mobuto Sese Seko (lake), Zaire 115/F3
Moca, Dom. Rep. 156/D3
Moca, Dom. Rep. 158/D5
Moca, P. Rico 161/A1
Mocajuba, Brazil 132/D3
Moçambique, Mozambique 118/G3
Moçambique, Mozambique 102/F6
Moçâmedes (dist.), Angola 115/B7
Moçâmedes, Angola 102/D6
Moçâmedes, Angola 115/B7
Mocanaqua, Pa. (18655) 294/K3
Moccasin, Ariz. (†86022) 198/C2
Moccasin, Mont. (59462) 262/F3
Mocha (isl.), Chile 138/B2
Mocha, Yemen Arab Rep. 59/D7
Moc Hoa, Vietnam 72/E5
Mochudi, Botswana 118/D4
Mochudi, Botswana 102/E7
Mocímboa da Praia, Mozambique 118/G2
Mociu, Romania 45/G2
Mocksville, N.C. (27028) 281/H3
Moclips, Wash. (98562) 310/A3
Moco (mt.), Angola 115/C6
Mocoa, Colombia 126/B7
Mococa, Brazil 135/C2
Mocodome (cape), Nova Scotia 168/G3
Mocomoco, Bolivia 136/A4
Mocoretá, Argentina 143/G5
Mocorito, Mexico 150/F4
Moctezuma, San Luis Potosí, Mexico 150/J5
Moctezuma, Sonora, Mexico 150/E2
Moctezuma (riv.), Mexico 150/K6
Mocuba, Mozambique 118/F3
Modale, Iowa (51556) 229/B5
Modane, France 28/G5
Modasa, India 68/C4
Modderfontein, S. Africa 118/H6
Mode, Ill. (62444) 222/E4
Model, Colo. (81059) 208/L8
Modena (prov.), Italy 34/C2
Modena, Italy 7/E4
Modena, Italy 34/C2
Modena, Utah (84753) 304/A6
Modena, Wis. (†54755) 317/C7
Modeste, La. (70376) 238/K3
Modesto, Calif. 188/B3
Modesto, Calif. (*95350) 204/D6
Modesto, Ill. (62667) 222/D4
Modest Town, Va. (23412) 307/T5
Modica, Italy 34/E6
Mödling, Austria 41/D2
Modoc (co.), Calif. 204/E2
Modoc, Georgia (†30401) 217/H5
Modoc, Ill. (62261) 222/C5
Modoc, Ind. (47358) 227/G4
Modoc, Kansas (67866) 232/A3
Modoc, S.C. (29838) 296/C4
Modoc Point, Oreg. (†97624) 291/F5
Modra, Czech. 41/D2
Modriča, Yugoslavia 45/D3
Modrý Kameň, Czech. 41/E2
Mo Duc, Vietnam 72/F4
Moe, Victoria 88/H7
Moe, Victoria 97/D6
Moen (isl.), Micronesia 87/F5
Moencopi (plat.), Ariz. 198/D3
Moengo, Suriname 131/D3
Moenkopi, Ariz. (†86045) 198/D2
Moenkopi Wash (dry riv.), Ariz. 198/D2
Moerai, Fr. Poly. 87/L8
Moerdijk, Netherlands 27/F5
Moerewa, N. Zealand 100/E1
Moësa (riv.), Switzerland 39/H4
Moeskroen (Mouscron), Belgium 27/C7
Moffat (co.), Colo. 208/C1
Moffat, Colo. (81143) 208/H6
Moffat, Scotland 15/E5
Moffat, Scotland 10/E3
Moffet (peak), N. Zealand 100/B6
Moffett, Okla. (74946) 288/S4
Moffett Nav. Air Sta., Calif. 204/K3
Moffit, N. Dak. (58560) 282/K6
Mogadiscio (prov.), Somalia 115/J3
Mogadishu (cap.), Somalia 2/M5
Mogadishu (cap.), Somalia 102/G4
Mogadishu (cap.), Somalia 115/J3
Mogador (Essaouira), Morocco 106/B2
Mogadore, Ohio (44260) 284/H3
Mogadouro, Portugal 33/C2
Mogami (riv.), Japan 81/K4
Mogaung, Burma 72/C1
Møgeltønder, Denmark 21/B8
Mogi das Cruzes, Brazil 132/E9
Mogi das Cruzes, Brazil 135/C3
Mogi Guaçu (riv.), Brazil 135/C2
Mogi-Guaçu, Brazil 135/C3
Mogilev, U.S.S.R. 7/G3
Mogilev, U.S.S.R. 52/C4
Mogilev, U.S.S.R. 48/D4
Mogilev-Podol'skiy, U.S.S.R. 52/C5
Mogil Mogil, N.S. Wales 97/E1
Mogilno, Poland 47/C2
Mogi-Mirim, Brazil 135/C3
Mogincual, Mozambique 118/G3
Mogocha, U.S.S.R. 48/N4
Mogok, Burma 72/C2
Mogollon (plat.), Ariz. 198/D4
Mogollon, N. Mex. (†88039) 274/A5
Mogollon (mts.), N. Mex. 274/A5
Mogollon Baldy (peak), N. Mex. 274/A5
Mogollon Rim (cliffs), Ariz. 198/D4
Mogororo, Chad 111/D5
Mogotes (pt.), Argentina 143/E4
Moguer, Spain 33/C4
Mohács, Hungary 41/E4
Mohaka (riv.), N. Zealand 100/F3
Mohaleshoek, Lesotho 118/D6
Mohall, N. Dak. (58761) 282/G2
Mohammadia, Algeria 106/D1
Mohammedia, Morocco 106/C2
Mohave (co.), Ariz. 198/A3
Mohave (lake), Ariz. 198/A3
Mohave (mts.), Ariz. 198/A4
Mohave (lake), Nev. 266/G7
Mohawk (mts.), Ariz. 198/B6
Mohawk (mt.), Conn. 210/B1
Mohawk, Ind. (†46140) 227/F5
Mohawk, Mich. (49950) 250/A1
Mohawk (riv.), N.H. 268/E2
Mohawk (lake), N.J. 273/D1
Mohawk, N.Y. (13407) 276/L4
Mohawk (riv.), N.Y. 276/L5
Mohawk, Oreg. (†97477) 291/E3
Mohawk, Tenn. (37810) 237/P8
Mohawk, W. Va. (24862) 312/C7
Mohe, China 77/K1
Mohegan, Conn. (†06382) 210/G3
Mohéli (isl.), Comoros 102/G6
Mohéli (isl.), Comoros 118/G2
Mohelnice, Czech. 41/D2
Mohenjo Daro (ruins), Pakistan 68/B3
Moher (cliffs), Ireland 17/B6
Mohican (cape), Alaska 196/E2
Mohican (riv.), Ohio 284/F4
Mohill, Ireland 17/F4
Mohler, Wash. (99154) 310/G3
Möhlin, Switzerland 39/E1
Mohn, Kapp (cape), Norway 18/E1
Mohnton, Pa. (19540) 294/L5
Mohnyin, Burma 72/C1
Moho, Peru 128/H10
Mohoro, Tanzania 115/G5
Mohrsville, Pa. (19541) 294/K5
Moi, Norway 18/E7
Moidart (dist.), Scotland 15/C4
Moiese, Mont. (59824) 262/B3
Moiliili, Hawaii (96828) 218/C4
Moineşti, Romania 45/H2
Moingona, Iowa (†50036) 229/F4
Moira, N.Y. (12957) 276/M1
Moíraí, Greece 45/G8
Moirones, Uruguay 145/E2
Mõisaküla, U.S.S.R. 53/C1
Moise (riv.), Que. 146/M4
Moisés Ville, Argentina 143/E5
Moisie (riv.), Que. 162/K5
Moisie, Québec 174/D2
Moisie (riv.), Québec 174/D2
Moissac, France 28/D5
Moïssala, Chad 111/C6
Moitaco, Venezuela 124/F4
Mojácar, Spain 33/F4
Mojave, Calif. (93501) 204/G8
Mojave (des.), Calif. 204/H9
Mojave (riv.), Calif. 204/J9
Mojo, Bolivia 136/C7
Mojocoya, Bolivia 136/C6
Mojokerto, Indonesia 85/K2
Mokane, Mo. (65059) 261/J5
Mokapu, Hawaii (†96734) 218/F2
Mokapu (pen.), Hawaii 218/F2
Mokau (riv.), N. Zealand 100/E3
Mokelumne (riv.), Calif. 204/C9
Mokelumne Hill, Calif. (95245) 204/E5
Mokena, Ill. (60448) 222/B6
Mokil (atoll), Micronesia 87/G5
Moknine, Tunisia 106/G1
Mokohinau (isl.), N. Zealand 100/E1
Mokokchung, India 68/G3
Mokolo, Cameroon 115/B1
Mokp'o, S. Korea 81/C6
Moksha (riv.), U.S.S.R. 52/F4
Mokuaula (isl.), Hawaii 218/E1
Mokuaweoweo (crater), Hawaii 218/H6
Mokuhooniki (isl.), Hawaii 218/J1
Mokuleia, Hawaii (†96791) 218/D1
Mol, Belgium 27/G6
Mola di Bari, Italy 34/F4
Molalla, Oreg. (97038) 291/B3
Molalla (riv.), Oreg. 291/B3
Moland, Minn. (†55946) 255/E6
Molanosa, Sask. 181/M4
Moldoi, Greece 45/F7
Molare (peak), Switzerland 39/G3
Mold, Wales 13/G2
Moldau (Vltava) (riv.), Czech. 41/C2
Moldava nad Bodvou, Czech. 41/F2
Moldavian S.S.R., U.S.S.R. 7/G4
Moldavian S.S.R., U.S.S.R. 52/C5
Moldavian S.S.R., U.S.S.R. 48/C5
Molde, Norway 18/E5
Moldova Nouă, Romania 45/E3
Moldoveanul (mt.), Romania 45/G3
Mole (riv.), England 13/H8
Môle (cape), Haiti 158/B5
Mole Creek, Tasmania 99/C3
Molega (lake), Nova Scotia 168/D4
Molena, Georgia (30258) 217/D4
Molenbeek-Saint-Jean, Belgium 27/B9
Molepolole, Botswana 118/C4
Molepolole, Botswana 102/E7
Môle Saint Nicolas, Haiti 158/B5
Molfetta, Italy 34/F4
Molina, Chile 138/A10
Molina, Colo. (81646) 208/D4
Molina, Spain 33/F2
Molinas, Argentina 143/C2
Moline, Ill. 188/J2
Moline, Ill. (61265) 222/C2
Moline, Kansas (67353) 232/F4
Moline, Manitoba 179/B4
Moline, Mich. (49335) 250/D6
Moline Acres, Mo. (†63101) 261/R2
Molinicos, Spain 33/E3
Molinière (pt.), Grenada 161/C8
Molino, Fla. (32577) 212/B6
Molinos (pt.), P. Rico 161/G1
Moliro, Zaire 115/E5
Molise (reg.), Italy 34/E4
Mollebjerg (mt.), Denmark 21/C6
Mollendo, Peru 120/B4
Mollendo, Peru 128/F11
Mollerusa, Spain 33/G2
Molles (pt.), Chile 138/A9
Mollis, Switzerland 39/H2
Mölln, W. Germany 22/D2
Mollusk, Va. (22517) 307/P5
Mollys Falls (pond), Vt. 268/C3
Mölndal, Sweden 18/H8
Moloaa, Hawaii (†96703) 218/D1
Molodechno, U.S.S.R. 48/C4
Molodechno, U.S.S.R. 52/C4
Molokai (isl.), Hawaii 87/L3
Molokai (isl.), Hawaii 188/F5
Molokai (isl.), Hawaii 218/G1
Molokini (isl.), Hawaii 218/J2
Molong, N.S. Wales 97/E3
Molopo (riv.), Botswana 118/C5
Molopo (riv.), S. Africa 118/C5
Molotov (Perm'), U.S.S.R. 52/J3
Moloundou, Cameroon 115/C3
Molson (lake), Manitoba 179/J3
Molson, Wash. (†98844) 310/F2
Molt, Mont. (59057) 262/H5
Molteno, S. Africa 118/D6
Molucca (isls.), Indonesia 54/O10
Molucca (sea), Indonesia 54/O10
Molucca (sea), Indonesia 85/H6
Moluccas (isls.), Indonesia 85/H6
Molunkus (lake), Maine 243/G4
Moma, Mozambique 118/F3
Mombasa, Kenya 115/G4
Mombasa, Kenya 102/G5
Mombetsu, Japan 81/L1
Mombo, Tanzania 115/G4
Momchilgrad, Bulgaria 45/G5
Momence, Ill. (60954) 222/F2
Momeyer, N.C. (†27856) 281/N3
Momignies, Belgium 27/E8
Momostenango, Guatemala 154/B3
Mompog (passage), Philippines 82/D4
Mompós, Colombia 126/C3
Mon (state), Burma 72/C3
Mon (riv.), Burma 72/B2
Møn (isl.), Denmark 21/F8
Møn (isl.), Denmark 18/H9
Mona (passage) 146/M8
Mona, Cyprus 63/E5
Mona (passage), Dom. Rep. 156/E3
Mona (passage), Dom. Rep. 158/F6
Mona (isl.), P. Rico 156/E3
Mona (passage), P. Rico 156/E3
Mona (passage), P. Rico 161/A2
Mona, Utah (84645) 304/C4
Mona (res.), Utah 304/C4
Monaca, Pa. (15061) 294/B4
Monach (isls.), Scotland 15/A3
Monach (sound), Scotland 15/A3
Monaco 7/E4
MONACO 28/G6
Monadhliath (mts.), Scotland 15/D3
Monadnock (mt.), N.H. 268/C6
Monagas (state), Venezuela 124/G3
Monaghan (co.), Ireland 17/H3
Monaghan, Ireland 10/C3
Monaghan, Ireland 17/G3
Monahans, Texas (79756) 303/B6
Monango, N. Dak. (58471) 282/N7
Monapo, Mozambique 118/G2
Monar, Loch (lake), Scotland 15/C3
Monarch, Alberta 182/D5
Monarch, Mont. (59463) 262/F3
Monarch Mills, S.C. (†29379) 296/D2
Monarda, Maine (†04776) 243/G4
Monaro (range), N.S. Wales 97/E5
Monashee (mts.), Br. Col. 184/H4
Monasterevan, Ireland 17/H5
Monastery, Nova Scotia 168/G3
Monastir, Tunisia 106/G1
Monatélé, Cameroon 115/B3
Mona Vale, N.S. Wales 88/L3
Mona Vale, N.S. Wales 97/K2
Monaville, W. Va. (25636) 312/B7
Monavullagh (mts.), Ireland 17/F7
Monbetsu, Japan 81/L2
Moncalieri, Italy 34/A2
Monçao, Portugal 33/B1
Moncayo (mt.), Spain 33/F2
Moncayo, Sierra de (range), Spain 33/F2
Monchegorsk, U.S.S.R. 7/H2
Monchegorsk, U.S.S.R. 48/C3
Monchegorsk, U.S.S.R. 52/D1
Mönchengladbach, W. Germany 22/B3
Monches, Wis. (†53029) 317/J1
Monchique, Portugal 33/B4
Monchique, Serra de (mts.), Portugal 33/B4
Monción, Dom. Rep. 158/D5
Moncks Corner, S.C. (29461) 296/G5
Monclo, W. Va. (†25183) 312/C7
Monclova, Mexico 146/H7
Monclova, Mexico 150/J3
Monclova, Ohio (43542) 284/C2
Moncouche (lake), Québec 172/G1
Moncton, N. Br. 146/M5
Moncton, N. Br. 162/K6
Moncton, New Bruns. 170/F2
Moncure, N.C. (27559) 281/L3
Mondamin, Iowa (51557) 229/B5
Monday (riv.), Paraguay 144/E4
Mondego (cape), Portugal 33/B2
Mondego (riv.), Portugal 33/B2
Mondéjar, Spain 33/E2
Mondonac (lake), Québec 172/D2
Mondoñedo, Spain 33/C1
Mondovi, Wis. (54755) 317/C6
Mondovì Breo, Italy 34/A2
Mondragon, Philippines 85/H3
Mondragon, Philippines 82/E4
Mondsee, Austria 41/B3
Moneague, Jamaica 158/J6
Monee, Ill. (60449) 222/F2
Monero, N. Mex. (†87547) 274/C2
Monessen, Pa. (15062) 294/C5
Monesterio, Spain 33/C3
Moneta, Iowa (51352) 229/C2
Moneta, Va. (24121) 307/J6
Moneta, Wyo. (†82601) 319/E2
Monett, Mo. (65708) 261/E9
Monetta, S.C. (29105) 296/D4
Monette, Ark. (72447) 202/K2
Money (isl.), China 85/E2
Money, Miss. (38945) 256/D3
Moneygall, Ireland 17/F6
Moneymore, N. Ireland 17/H2
Monfalcone, Italy 34/D2
Monforte, Portugal 33/C3
Monforte, Spain 33/C1
Monga, Zaire 115/D3
Mongalla, Sudan 111/F6
Mong Cai, Vietnam 72/E2
Möng Hsat, Burma 72/C2
Monghyr, India 68/F3
Möng Maü, Burma 72/C3
Möng Mit, Burma 72/C2
Mongo, Chad 111/C5
Mongo, Chad 102/D3
Mongo, Ind. (46771) 227/G1
Mongolia 2/P3
Mongolia 54/M5
Mongoumba, Cent. Afr. Rep. 115/C3
Möng Pan, Burma 72/C2
Möng Si, Burma 72/C2
Möng Tön, Burma 72/C2
Möng Tung, Burma 72/C2
Mongu, Zambia 102/E6
Mongu, Zambia 115/D7
Monhegan○, Maine (04852) 243/E8
Monhegan (isl.), Maine 243/E8
Mönhhaan, Mongolia 77/H2
Moniac, Georgia (†31646) 217/H9
Moniaive, Scotland 10/D3
Moniaive, Scotland 15/E5
Monica, Ill. (†61559) 222/D3
Monico, Wis. (54549) 317/H4
Monida, Mont. (†59739) 262/D6
Monie, Md. (†21853) 245/P8
Monifieth, Scotland 15/F4
Moniquirá, Colombia 126/D5
Moniteau (co.), Mo. 261/G5
Monitor, Alberta 182/E4
Monitor, Ind. (†47901) 227/D4
Monitor (range), Nev. 266/E4
Monitor, Oreg. (†97072) 291/B3
Monitor, Wash. (98836) 310/E3
Monivea, Ireland 17/D5
Monkayo, Philippines 82/E7
Monkey (pt.), Nicaragua 154/F5
Monkey (hill), St. Chris.-Nevis 161/C10
Monkey River Town, Belize 154/C2
Mońki, Poland 47/F2
Monkoto, Zaire 115/D4
Monkton, Md. (21111) 245/M2
Monkton, Ontario 177/C4
Monkton○, Vt. (05469) 268/A3
Monkton Ridge, Vt. (†05473) 268/A3
Monmouth, Ill. (61462) 222/C3
Monmouth, Ind. (†46733) 227/H3
Monmouth, Iowa (52309) 229/M4
Monmouth, Maine (04259) 243/D7
Monmouth○, Maine (04259) 243/D7
Monmouth (co.), N.J. 273/E3
Monmouth, Oreg. (97361) 291/D3
Monmouth, Wales 13/E6
Monmouth, Wales 10/E5
Monmouth Beach, N.J. (07750) 273/F3
Monmouth Junction, N.J. (08852) 273/D3
Monnickendam, Netherlands 27/C4
Mono (riv.), Benin 106/E7
Mono (lake), Calif. 188/C3
Mono (co.), Calif. 204/F5
Mono (lake), Calif. 204/G5
Mono (riv.), Togo 106/E7
Monocacy (riv.), Md. 245/J3
Monocacy Nat'l Battlefield, Md. 245/J3
Mono Lake, Calif. (†93541) 204/F5
Monolith, Calif. (†93561) 204/G8
Monólithos, Greece 45/H7
Monomonac (lake), Mass. 249/G2
Monomoy (isl.), Mass. 249/O6

414 Mount Washington

Mount Washington○, Mass. (†12517) 249/A4
Mount Wellington, N. Zealand 100/C1
Mount Willing, Ala. (†36012) 195/E6
Mount Wolf, Pa. (17347) 294/J5
Mount Zion, Georgia (30150) 217/B3
Mount Zion, Ill. (62549) 222/E4
Mount Zion, Ind. (†46792) 227/G3
Mount Zion, Iowa (†52565) 229/K7
Mount Zion, W. Va. (26151) 312/D5
Moura, Portugal 33/C3
Moura, Queensland 95/D5
Moura, Queensland 88/J4
Mourão, Portugal 33/C3
Mourdi (depr.), Chad 111/D4
Mourne (Newry and Mourne) (dist.), N. Ireland17/J3
Mourne (mts.), N. Ireland 17/J3
Mourne (riv.), N. Ireland 17/G2
Mouscron, Belgium 27/C7
Moussoro, Chad 111/C5
Mouthcard, Ky. (41548) 237/S6
Mouth of Wilson, Va. (24363) 307/F7
Moutier, Switzerland 39/D2
Moûtiers, France 28/G5
Mouton (isl.), Nova Scotia 168/D5
Mouydir (mts.), Algeria 106/E3
Moville, Iowa (51039) 229/A4
Moville, Ireland 17/G1
Mowbray, Manitoba 179/D5
Mowdok Mual (mt.), Bangladesh 68/G4
Moweaqua, Ill. (62550) 222/E4
Mower (co.), Minn. 255/F7
Mowming (Maoming), China 77/H7
Mowrystown, Ohio (45155) 284/C7
Moxahala, Ohio (43761) 284/F6
Moxee City, Wash. (98936) 310/E4
Moxico (dist.), Angola 115/D6
Moxie (lake), Maine 243/D5
Moxley, Georgia (†30477) 217/H5
Moy (riv.), Ireland 17/C3
Moy, N. Ireland 17/H3
Moyale, Ethiopia 111/G7
Moyale, Kenya 115/G3
Moyamba, S. Leone 106/B7
Moycullen, Ireland 17/C5
Moyers, Okla. (74557) 288/P6
Moyers, W. Va. (26813) 312/H6
Moyeuvre-Grande, France 28/G3
Moygashel, N. Ireland 17/H3
Moyie, Br. Col. 184/K5
Moyie (riv.), Idaho 220/B1
Moyie Springs, Idaho (83845) 220/B1
Moyle (dist.), N. Ireland 17/J1
Moynalty, Ireland 17/H4
Moyo, Uganda 115/F3
Moyobamba, Peru 120/B3
Moyobamba, Peru 128/D6
Moyock, N.C. (27958) 281/S1
Moyogalpa, Nicaragua 154/E5
Moyu (Karakax), China 77/A4
Moza Illit, Israel 65/C4
Mozambique 2/L6
Mozambique 102/F6
Mozambique (chan.) 2/L7
Mozambique (chan.) 102/G6
Mozambique (pt.), La. 238/M7
Mozambique (chan.), Madagascar 118/G3
MOZAMBIQUE 118/E4
Mozambique (chan.), Mozambique 118/G3
Mozart, Sask. 181/G4
Mozer, W. Va. (†26866) 312/H5
Mozhaysk, U.S.S.R. 52/E3
Mozhga, U.S.S.R. 52/H3
Mozier, Ill. (62070) 222/C4
Mozyr', U.S.S.R. 48/C4
Mozyr', U.S.S.R. 52/C4
Mpanda, Tanzania 115/F5
Mpika, Zambia 115/F6
Mporokoso, Zambia 115/F5
M'Pouya, Congo 115/C4
Mpraeso, Ghana 106/D7
Mpulungu, Zambia 115/F5
Mpwapwa, Tanzania 115/G5
Mrągowo, Poland 47/E2
Msaken, Tunisia 106/G1
M'Sila, Algeria 106/E1
Msta (riv.), U.S.S.R. 52/D3
Mtakuja, Tanzania 115/F5
Mtsensk, U.S.S.R. 52/E4
Mtwara (reg.), Tanzania 115/G5
Mtwara-Mikindani, Tanzania 102/G6
Mtwara-Mikindani, Tanzania 115/H6
Mu (riv.), Burma 72/B2
Mualama, Mozambique 118/F3
Muang Hinboun, Laos 72/E3
Muang Kènthao, Laos 72/D3
Muang Khammouan, Laos 72/E3
Muang Không, Laos 72/E4
Muang Khôngxédôn, Laos 72/E4
Muang Khoua, Laos 72/D2
Muang May, Laos 72/E4
Muang Ou Tai, Laos 72/D2
Muang Pak-Lay, Laos 72/D3
Muang Paktha, Laos 72/D2
Muang Pakxan, Laos 72/D2
Muang Phin, Laos 72/E3
Muang Sing, Laos 72/D2
Muang Tahoi, Laos 72/E3
Muang Vangviang, Laos 72/D3
Muang Vapi, Laos 72/E4
Muang Xaignabouri (Sayaboury), Laos 72/D3
Muang Xay, Laos 72/D3
Muang Xépôn, Laos 72/E3
Muang Xon, Laos 72/D2
Muar, Malaysia 72/D7
Muarabungo, Indonesia 85/C6
Muarasiberut, Indonesia 85/B6
Muaratewe, Indonesia 85/F6
Muari, Ras (cape), Pakistan 68/B4
Muari, Ras (cape), Pakistan 59/J5
Mubarraz, Saudi Arabia 59/E4
Mubende, Uganda 115/F3
Mubi, Nigeria 106/G6
Muchanes, Bolivia 136/B4
Mücheln, E. Germany 22/D3
Muck (isl.), Scotland 10/C2
Muck (isl.), Scotland 15/B4
Muckamore, N. Ireland 17/J2
Muckle Flugga (isl.), Scotland 15/G2
Muckleshoot Ind. Res., Wash. 310/C3
Muckno (lake), Ireland 17/H3
Muco (riv.), Colombia 126/E5
Mucojo, Mozambique 118/G2
Mucope, Angola 115/B7
Mucuchachí, Venezuela 124/C3
Mucuchíes, Venezuela 124/C3
Mucugê, Brazil 132/F6
Mucur, Turkey 63/F3
Mucurapo, Trin. & Tob. 161/A10
Mucuri, Brazil 132/G7
Mucuripe (pt.), Brazil 132/G3
Mucusso, Angola 115/D7
Mud (lake), Idaho 220/F6
Mud (riv.), Ky. 237/H7
Mud (lake), La. 238/D7
Mud (lake), Minn. 255/C2
Mud (lake), Minn. 255/B5
Mud (riv.), Minn. 255/C2
Mud (isl.), Nova Scotia 168/B5
Mud (creek), Okla. 288/L6
Mud (creek), Oreg. 291/K2
Mud (creek), S. Dak. 298/N3
Mud (lake), S. Dak. 298/R2
Mud, W. Va. (†25565) 312/C6
Mud (riv.), W. Va. 312/B6
Mudanjiang (Mutankiang), China 77/M3
Mudanjiang, China54/O5
Mudan Jiang (riv.), China 77/L3
Mudanya, Turkey 63/C2
Mudauwara, Jordan 59/C4
Mud Bay, Br. Col. 184/H2
Mud Butte, S. Dak. (57758) 298/D4
Muddy (creek), Colo. 208/E4
Muddy (brook), Conn. 210/H1
Muddy (pond), Conn. 210/G1
Muddy (riv.), Conn. 210/D3
Muddy, Ill. (62965) 222/E6
Muddy (mts.), Nev. 266/G6
Muddy (creek), N. Dak. 282/G6
Muddy (pt.), St. Chris.-Nevis 161/C10
Muddy (lake), Sask. 181/B3
Muddy (creek), Utah 304/A2
Muddy (creek), Utah 304/C4
Muddy (creek), Wyo. 319/F3
Muddy (creek), Wyo. 319/D2
Muddy (mt.), Wyo. 319/F3
Muddy Boggy (creek), Okla. 288/O5
Mudge (pond), Conn. 210/B1
Mudgee, N.S. Wales 88/J6
Mudgee, N.S. Wales 97/E3
Mudhnib, Saudi Arabia 59/D4
Mudjatik (riv.), Sask. 181/L3
Mud Lake, Idaho (†83450) 220/F6
Mud Lake, Newf. 166/B3
Mud Lake (res.), S. Dak. 298/N2
Mud Mountain (lake), Wash. 310/D3
Mudon, Burma 72/C3
Mudug (prov.), Somalia 115/J2
Mudurnu, Turkey 63/D2
Muecate, Mozambique 118/F2
Mueda, Mozambique 118/F2
Muenster, Sask. 181/F3
Muenster, Texas (76252) 303/G4
Muerto, Mar (lag.), Mexico 150/N9
Muezerskiy, U.S.S.R. 52/D2
Muff, Ireland 17/G1
Mufulira, Zambia 115/E6
Mufulira, Zambia 102/E6
Muge, Portugal 33/B3
Mugford (cape), Newf. 166/B2
Mughar, Israel 65/C2
Muğla (prov.), Turkey 63/C4
Muğla, Turkey 59/A2
Muğla, Turkey 63/C4
Muglad, Sudan 111/E5
Muhammad, Ras (cape), Egypt 59/B4
Muhammad, Ras (cape), Egypt 111/F2
Muhammad Qol, Sudan 59/C5
Muhammad Qol, Sudan 111/G3
Muharraq, Bahrain 59/F4
Mühldorf am Inn, W. Germany 22/E4
Muhlenberg (co.), Ky. 237/G6
Mühlhausen (Thomas-Müntzer-Stadt), E. Germany 22/D3
Mühlviertel (reg.), Austria 41/C2
Muhu (isl.), U.S.S.R. 53/B1
Mui Bai Bung (pt.), Vietnam 54/M9
Muiden, Netherlands 27/G4
Muinebeag, Ireland 17/H6
Muir (glac.), Alaska 196/M1
Muir, Mich. (48860) 250/D5
Muir, Pa. (17957) 294/J4
Muirkirk, Md. (†20705) 245/L4
Muirkirk, Scotland 15/E5
Muir of Ord, Scotland 15/D3
Muiron (isls.), W. Australia 88/A4
Muiron (isls.), W. Australia 92/A3
Muir Woods Nat'l Mon., Calif. 204/H2
Muizenberg, S. Africa 118/E7
Muju, S. Korea 81/C6
Mukachevo, U.S.S.R. 52/B5
Mukah, Malaysia 85/E5
Mukalla, P.D.R. Yemen 54/F8
Mukalla, P.D.R. Yemen 59/E7
Mukdahan, Thailand 72/E3
Mukden, Bolivia 136/A2
Mukden (Shenyang), China 77/K3
Mukilteo, Wash. (98275) 310/C3
Mukinbudin, W. Australia 92/B5
Muko, Japan 81/J7
Muko (isl.), Japan 81/M3
Muko (riv.), Japan 81/H7
Mukutawa (lake), Manitoba 179/G2
Mukutawa (riv.), Manitoba 179/E1
Mukwonago, Wis. (53149) 317/J2
Mula, Spain 33/F3
Mulaló, Ecuador 128/C3
Mulanje (mt.), Malawi 102/F6
Mulanje (mts.), Malawi 115/G7
Mulatos, Colombia 126/B3
Mulberry (creek), Ala. 195/E5
Mulberry, Ark. (72947) 202/B2
Mulberry (riv.), Ark. 202/C2
Mulberry, Calif. (†95926) 204/D4
Mulberry, Fla. (33860) 212/E4
Mulberry, Ind. (46058) 227/D4
Mulberry, Kansas (66756) 232/H4
Mulberry, Ohio (†45150) 284/B7
Mulberry, Tenn. (37359) 237/H10
Mulberry Fork (riv.), Ala. 195/E3
Mulberry Grove, Ill. (62262) 222/D5
Mulchatna (riv.), Alaska 196/G2
Mulchén, Chile 138/E1
Mulde (riv.), E. Germany 22/E3
Muldon, Miss. (†39730) 256/G3
Muldoon, Texas (78949) 303/G8
Muldraugh, Ky. (40155) 237/J5
Muldrow, Okla. (74948) 288/S4
Mule (mts.), Ariz. 198/E7
Mule (creek), Kansas 232/C4
Mule Creek, N. Mex. (88051) 274/A5
Mule Creek, Wyo. (†57735) 319/H2
Muleculus, Nicaragua 154/E4
Mulegé, Mexico 150/C3
Mulegns, Switzerland 39/J3
Muleshoe, Texas (79347) 303/B3
Mulgrave, Nova Scotia 168/G3
Mulgrave (lake), Nova Scotia 168/F3
Mulhacén (mt.), Spain 33/E4
Mulhall, Okla. (73063) 288/M2
Mülheim an der Ruhr, W. Germany 22/B3
Mulhouse, France 7/E4
Mulhouse, France 28/G4
Mulhurst, Alberta 182/D3
Muli, China 77/F6
Muli (str.), Indonesia 85/K7
Mulino, Oreg. (97042) 291/B2
Mulinu'u (cape), W. Samoa 86/L8
Mulkear (riv.), Ireland 17/E6
Mull (head), Scotland 15/F2
Mull (head), Scotland 15/F1
Mull (isl.), Scotland 10/D2
Mull (isl.), Scotland 15/C4
Mull (sound), Scotland 15/C4
Mullagh, Ireland 17/H4
Mullaghareirk (mts.), Ireland 17/C7
Mullaghearn (mt.), N. Ireland 17/G2
Mullaghmore, Ireland 17/D3
Mullaittivu, Sri Lanka 68/E7
Mullaley, N.S. Wales 97/E2
Mullan, Idaho (83846) 220/C2
Mullardoch, Loch (lake), Scotland 15/C3
Mullen, Nebr. (69152) 264/C2
Mullens, W. Va. (25882) 312/D7
Müller (mts.), Indonesia 85/E5
Mullet (key), Fla. 212/D4
Mullett (lake), Mich. 250/E3
Mullett Lake, Mich. (49761) 250/E3
Mullewa, W. Australia 88/B5
Mullewa, W. Australia 92/A5
Müllheim, Switzerland 39/G1
Müllheim, W. Germany 22/B5
Mullica (riv.), N.J. 273/D4
Mullica Hill, N.J. (08062) 273/C4
Mulliken, Mich. (48861) 250/E6
Mullin, Texas (76864) 303/F6
Mullinahone, Ireland 17/F7
Mullinavat, Ireland 17/G7
Mullingar, Ireland 10/C4
Mullingar, Ireland 17/G4
Mullingar, Sask. 181/D2
Mullins, S.C. (29574) 296/J3
Mullinville, Kansas (67109) 232/C4
Mullion, England 13/B7
Mull of Galloway (prom.), Scotland 15/D6
Mull of Kintyre (prom.), Scotland 15/C5
Mull of Oa (prom.), Scotland 15/B5
Mullumbimby, N.S. Wales 97/G1
Mulobezi, Zambia 115/E7
Mulongo, Zaire 115/E5
Mulroy (bay), Ireland 17/F1
Multan, Pakistan 54/J6
Multan, Pakistan 68/C2
Multan, Pakistan 59/K3
Multnomah (co.), Oreg. 291/E2
Mulund, India 68/B6
Mulungushi (dam), Zambia 115/E6
Mulvane, Kansas (67110) 232/E4
Mulvihill, Manitoba 179/D4
Mulwala, N.S. Wales 97/D4
Mumbwa, Zambia 115/E6
Mumford, N.Y. (14511) 276/E4
Mümliswil-Ramiswil, Switzerland 39/E2
Mumra, U.S.S.R. 52/G5
Mun, Mae Nam (riv.), Thailand 72/D4
Muna (isl.), Indonesia 85/G7
Muna, Mexico 150/P6
Munbura, Queensland 95/C2
Munbura, Queensland 88/G2
Müncheberg, E. Germany 22/F2
München (Munich), W. Germany 22/D4
Münchenbuchsee, Switzerland 39/E2
Muncho Lake, Br. Col. 184/L2
Muncho Lake Prov. Park, Br. Col. 184/L2
Muncie, Ill. (61857) 222/F3
Muncie, Ind. 188/J2
Muncie, Ind. (*47302) 227/G4
Muncy, Pa. (17756) 294/J3
Muncy Valley, Pa. (17758) 294/J3
Munda, Solomon Is. 86/D3
Mundabullangana, W. Australia 92/B3
Mundare, Alberta 182/D3
Mundaring (res.), W. Australia 88/B2
Munday, Texas (76371) 303/E4
Mundelein, Ill. (60060) 222/A4
Munden, Kansas (66959) 232/E2
Münden, W. Germany 22/C3
Mundesley, England 13/J5
Mundijong, W. Australia 88/B3
Mundijong, W. Australia 92/A2
Mundiwindi, W. Australia 92/B3
Mundo Novo, Brazil 132/F5
Mundrabilla, W. Australia 92/E5
Mundubbera, Queensland 88/J5
Munera, Spain 33/E3
Munford, Ala. (36268) 195/F3
Munford, Tenn. (38058) 237/B10
Munfordville, Ky. (42765) 237/J6
Mungbere, Zaire 115/E3
Munger, Mich. (48747) 250/F5
Mungindi, N.S. Wales 97/E1
Mungindi, Queensland 95/D6
Munguba, Brazil 132/C2
Munhall, Pa. (15120) 294/C7
Munhango, Angola 115/C6
Munich, N. Dak. (58352) 282/N2
Munich, W. Germany 7/F4
Munich, W. Germany 22/D4
Munising, Mich. (49862) 250/C2
Munith, Mich. (49259) 250/E6
Munjor, Kansas (†67601) 232/C3
Munku-Sardyk (mt.), Mongolia 77/F1
Munnerlyn, Georgia (†30830) 217/H5
Munning (pt.), N. Zealand 100/E7
Munnsville, N.Y. (13409) 276/J4
Muñoz Gamero (pen.), Chile 138/D10
Munro (mt.), Tasmania 99/E2
Munroe Falls, Ohio (44262) 284/H3
Münsingen, Switzerland 39/E3
Munson, Alberta 182/D4
Munson, Fla. (†32570) 212/B5
Munson, Pa. (16860) 294/F4
Munsonville, N.H. (03457) 268/C5
Munster, Ind. (46321) 227/B1
Munster (prov.), Ireland 17/D7
Munster (trad. prov.), Ireland 17
Munster, Ontario 177/J2
Münster, Switzerland 39/F4
Münster, W. Germany 22/B3
Munsungan (lake), Maine 243/E3
Muntendam, Netherlands 27/K2
Muntok, Indonesia 85/D6
Munuscong (lake), Mich. 250/E2
Muojärvi (lake), Finland 18/R4
Muong Khuong, Vietnam 72/E2
Muonio (riv.) 7/G2
Muonio, Finland 18/O3
Muonio (riv.), Finland 18/M2
Muonioälv (riv.), Sweden 18/M2
Muota (riv.), Switzerland 39/G3
Muotathal, Switzerland 39/G3
Muqaddam, Wadi (dry riv.), Sudan 111/F4
Muqdadiyah, Iraq 66/D4
Muqdisho (Mogadishu) (cap.), Somalia 115/J3
Muqdisho (Mogadishu) (cap.), Somalia 102/G4
Muqeible, Israel 65/C2
Muqui, Brazil 132/F8
Mur (riv.), Austria 41/C3
Mur (riv.), Yugoslavia 45/B2
Mura (riv.), Hungary 41/D3
Muradiye, Turkey 63/K3
Murakami, Japan 81/J4
Murallón, Cerro (mt.), Argentina 143/B6
Murallón, Cerro (mt.), Chile 138/D8
Murarrie, Queensland 88/K2
Murashi, U.S.S.R. 52/G3
Murat, France 28/E5
Murat (riv.), Turkey 59/C2
Murat (riv.), Turkey 63/H3
Murat Dağı (mt.), Turkey 63/C3
Murau, Austria 41/C3
Murbat, Oman 59/G6
Murchison, N. Zealand 100/D4
Murchison (range), North. Terr. 93/D6
Murchison (falls), Uganda 115/F3
Murchison (riv.), W. Australia 88/B5
Murchison (mt.), W. Australia 92/B4
Murchison (riv.), W. Australia 92/B4
Murchison Downs, W. Australia 88/B5
Murcia (prov.), Spain 33/F4
Murcia, Spain 7/D5
Murcia, Spain 33/F4
Murcia (reg.), Spain 33/F3
Murderers (creek), Oreg. 291/H3
Murderkill (riv.), Del. 245/R5
Murdo, S. Dak. (57559) 298/H6
Murdochville, Québec 172/C1
Murdock, Fla. (33938) 212/D4
Murdock, Ill. (61941) 222/E4
Murdock, Kansas (67111) 232/E4
Murdock, Minn. (56271) 255/C5
Murdock, Nebr. (68407) 264/H4
Muren (Mörön), Mongolia 77/F2
Mureş (riv.), Romania 45/E2
Muret, France 28/D6
Muretto (pass), Switzerland 39/J4
Murfreesboro, Ark. (71958) 202/C5
Murfreesboro, N.C. (27855) 281/R2
Murfreesboro, Tenn. (37130) 237/J9
Murg (riv.), Switzerland 39/G1
Murgab, U.S.S.R. 48/H6
Murgab (riv.), U.S.S.R. 48/G6
Murghab (riv.), Afghanistan 59/H2
Murgon, Queensland 88/J5
Murgon, Queensland 95/D5
Murgoo, W. Australia 92/B4
Muri, Switzerland 39/F2
Muriaé, Brazil 135/E2
Muriaé, Brazil 132/F8
Murias de Paredes, Spain 33/C1
Muri bei Bern, Switzerland 39/E3
Muriel (lake), Alberta 182/E2
Murindó, Colombia 126/B4
Müritzsee (lake), E. Germany 22/E2
Murjek, Sweden 18/M3
Murl, Ky. (†42633) 237/M7
Murle, Ethiopia 111/G6
Murmansk, U.S.S.R. 7/H2
Murmansk, U.S.S.R. 2/L2
Murmansk, U.S.S.R. 4/C8
Murmansk, U.S.S.R. 48/D3
Murmansk, U.S.S.R. 52/D1
Murnau, W. Germany 22/D5
Murnpeowie, S. Australia 94/F3
Murom, U.S.S.R. 52/F3
Murongo, Tanzania 115/F4
Muroran, Japan 81/K2
Muros, Spain 33/B1
Muroto, Japan 81/G7
Muroto (pt.), Japan 81/G7
Murphy, Idaho (83650) 220/B6
Murphy, Miss. (†38748) 256/C4
Murphy, Mo. (†63088) 261/O4
Murphy, N.C. (28906) 281/B4
Murphy, Oreg. (97533) 291/D5
Murphy (isl.), S.C. 296/J5
Murphy, Texas (†75074) 303/H1
Murphys, Calif. (95247) 204/E5
Murphysboro, Ill. (62966) 222/D6
Murphytown, W. Va. (†26142) 312/D4
Murra Murra, Queensland 95/C6
Murray (riv.) 88/G6
Murray (river), Australia 87/E9
Murray (riv.), Br. Col. 184/G3
Murray (co.), Georgia 217/C1
Murray, Idaho (83874) 220/C2
Murray, Ind. (†46714) 227/G3
Murray, Iowa (50174) 229/F6
Murray, Ky. (42071) 237/E7
Murray (co.), Minn. 255/C6
Murray, Nebr. (68409) 264/J4
Murray (riv.), N.S. Wales 97/A4
Murray (co.), Okla. 288/M6
Murray (lake), Okla. 288/M6
Murray (lake), Papua N.G. 85/B7
Murray (riv.), S. Australia 94/F6
Murray (lake), S.C. 188/K4
Murray (lake), S.C. 296/D4
Murray, Utah (84107) 304/C3
Murray, Utah 188/D2
Murray (riv.), Victoria 97/A4
Murray (bay), Victoria 88/H7
Murray (riv.), W. Australia 92/A2
Murray Bridge, S. Australia 88/F7
Murray Bridge, S. Australia 94/F6
Murray City, Ohio (43144) 284/F6
Murray Corner, New Bruns. 170/G2
Murray Downs, North. Terr. 93/D6
Murray Harbour, Pr. Edward I. 168/F2
Murray Lake Hills, Tenn. (37416) 237/L10
Murray River, Pr. Edward I. 168/F2
Murraysville, W. Va. (26153) 312/C4
Murrayville, Georgia (30564) 217/E2
Murrayville, Ill. (62668) 222/C4
Murrayville, Victoria 97/A4
Murree, Pakistan 68/C2
Murrells Inlet, S.C. (29576) 296/K4
Mürren, Switzerland 39/E3
Murrieta, Calif. (92362) 204/H10
Murringo, N.S. Wales 97/E4
Murrumbidgee (riv.), N. S. Wales 88/H6
Murrumbidgee (riv.), N.S. Wales 97/C4
Murrumburrah, N.S. Wales 97/E4
Murrupula, Mozambique 118/F3
Murrurundi, N.S. Wales 97/F3
Murrysville, Pa. (15668) 294/C5
Murska Sobota, Yugoslavia 45/C2
Murtaröl (peak), Switzerland 39/K3
Murtaugh, Idaho (83344) 220/D7
Murten, Switzerland 39/D3
Murtle (lake), Br. Col. 184/H4
Murtoa, Victoria 97/B5
Murud, India 68/C5
Murupara, N. Zealand 100/F3
Mururoa (isl.), Fr. Poly. 87/M8
Murwara, India 68/E4
Murwillumbah, N. S. Wales 88/J5
Murwillumbah, N.S. Wales 97/G1
Muryo (mt.), Indonesia 85/J2
Mürz (riv.), Austria 41/C3
Murzuk, Libya 102/D2
Murzuk, Libya 111/B2
Mürzzuschlag, Austria 41/C3
Muş (prov.), Turkey 63/J3
Muş, Turkey 63/J3
Muş, Turkey 59/D2
Musa Khel Bazar, Pakistan 59/K3
Musa Khel Bazar, Pakistan 68/B2
Musala (mt.), Bulgaria 45/F4
Musan, N. Korea 81/D2
Musandam, Ras (cape), Oman 59/G4
Musashino, Japan 81/O2
Muscadine, Ala. (36269) 195/H3
Muscat (cap.), Oman 54/G7
Muscat (cap.), Oman 2/M4
Muscat (cap.), Oman 59/G5
Muscatatuck (riv.), Ind. 227/E7
Muscatine (co.), Iowa 229/L5
Muscatine, Iowa 188/H2
Muscatine, Iowa (52761) 229/L6
Muscle Shoals, Ala. (35660) 195/C1
Muscoda, Wis. (53573) 317/F9
Muscogee (co.), Georgia 217/C6
Musconetcong (beach), N.J. 273/C2
Muscongus (bay), Maine 243/E8
Muscotah, Kansas (66058) 232/G2
Muscoy, Calif. (92405) 204/E10
Muse, Okla. (74949) 288/S5
Musella, Georgia (31066) 217/E5
Musgrave (ranges), Australia 87/D8
Musgrave, Queensland 95/B2
Musgrave (range), S. Australia 88/E5
Musgrave (ranges), S. Australia 94/B2
Musgrave Harbour, Newf. 166/D4
Musgravetown, Newf. 166/C2
Mushaboom, Nova Scotia 168/F4
Mushandike Nat'l Park, Zimbabwe 118/D4
Mushie, Zaire 102/D5
Mushie, Zaire 115/C4
Musi (riv.), Indonesia 85/C6
Musidora, Alberta 182/E3
Muskeg (bay), Manitoba 179/G6
Muskeg (bay), Minn. 255/C2
Muskeget (chan.), Mass. 249/N7
Muskeget (isl.), Mass. 249/N7
Muskego, Wis. (53150) 317/K2
Muskegon (co.), Mich. 250/C5
Muskegon, Mich. 188/J2
Muskegon, Mich. (*49440) 250/C5
Muskegon (riv.), Mich. 250/C5
Muskegon Heights, Mich. (49444) 250/C5
Muskeg River, Alberta 182/A3
Muskingum (co.), Ohio 284/G5
Muskingum (riv.), Ohio 284/G6
Muskogee, Okla. 188/H3
Muskogee (co.), Okla. 288/R3
Muskogee, Okla. (74401) 288/R3
Muskoka (dist. munic.), Ontario 177/E3
Muskoka (lake), Ontario 177/E2
Muskrat (creek), Wyo. 319/E2
Muskwa (lake), Alberta 182/C1
Muskwa (riv.), Alberta 182/C1
Muskwa (riv.), Br. Col. 184/M2
Muslimiya, Syria 63/G4
Musmar, Sudan 111/G4
Musoma, Tanzania 115/F4
Musoma, Tanzania 102/F5
Musquacook (lakes), Maine 243/E2
Musquash (harb.), New Bruns. 170/D3
Musquodoboit (riv.), Nova Scotia 168/E4
Musquodoboit Harbour, Nova Scotia 168/E4
Mussau (isl.), Papua N.G. 86/B1
Musselburgh, Scotland 15/D2
Musselburgh, Scotland 10/C1
Musselshell (riv.), Mont. 188/E1
Musselshell (co.), Mont. 262/H4
Musselshell, Mont. (59059) 262/H4
Musselshell (riv.), Mont. 262/J3
Mustafakemalpaşa, Turkey 63/C3
Mustahil, Ethiopia 111/H6
Müstair, Switzerland 39/K3
Mustang, Nepal 68/E3
Mustang, Okla. (73064) 288/L4
Mustang (creek), Texas 303/A1
Mustang (isl.), Texas 303/G10
Mustang Draw (dry riv.), Texas 303/B5
Musters (lake), Argentina 143/C6
Mustinka (riv.), Minn. 255/B5
Mustoe, Va. (24468) 307/J4
Mustvee, U.S.S.R. 53/D1
Muswellbrook, N. S. Wales 88/J6
Muswellbrook, N.S. Wales 97/F3
Mût, Egypt 111/E2
Mût, Egypt 59/A4
Mût, Egypt 102/E2
Mut, Turkey 63/E4
Mutankiang (Mudanjiang), China 77/M3
Mutarara (Dona Ana), Mozambique 118/F3
Mutare (Umtali), Zimbabwe 118/E3
Muthanna (gov.), Iraq 66/D5
Muthill, Scotland 15/E4
Muting, Indonesia 85/K7
Mutki, Turkey 63/J3
Mutrie, Sask. 181/H5
Mutsamudu, Comoros 118/G2
Mutshatsha, Zaire 115/D6
Mutsu, Japan 81/K3
Mutsu (bay), Japan 81/K3
Muttaburra, Queensland 95/C4
Muttalip, Turkey 63/D3
Muttenz, Switzerland 39/E1
Muttler (mt.), Switzerland 39/K3
Mutton (isl.), Ireland 17/B6
Mutton Bird (isl.), N.S. Wales 97/J2
Muttonville, Mich. (†48062) 250/G6
Mutual, Ohio (†43078) 284/C5
Mutual, Okla. (73853) 288/H2
Mutum, Brazil 135/F1
Mu Us Shamo (des.), China 77/G4
Muwailih, Saudi Arabia 59/C4
Muwale, Tanzania 115/F5
Muxima, Angola 115/B5
Muy Muy, Nicaragua 154/E4
Muy Muy Viejo, Nicaragua 154/E4
Muynak, U.S.S.R. 48/F5
Muyumba, Zaire 115/E5
Muzaffarabad, Pakistan 68/C2
Muzaffarnagar, India 68/D3
Muzaffarpur, India 68/E3
Muzambinho, Brazil 135/C2
Muzo, Colombia 126/D5
Muzon (cape), Alaska 196/M2
Muztag (mt.), China 77/B4
Muztagata (mt.), China 77/A4
Mvadhi-Ousyé, Gabon 115/B3
M'Vouti, Congo 115/B4
Mwadingusha, Zaire 115/E6
Mwadui, Tanzania 115/F4
Mwanza, Malawi 115/F7
Mwanza (reg.), Tanzania 115/F4
Mwanza, Tanzania 115/F4
Mwanza, Tanzania 102/F5
Mwanza, Zaire 115/E5
Mwaya, Tanzania 115/F5
Mweelrea (mt.), Ireland 17/B4
Mweenish (isl.), Ireland 17/B5
Mweka, Zaire 115/D4
Mwene-Ditu, Zaire 115/D5
Mwenga, Zaire 115/E4
Mweru (lake) 102/E5
Mweru (lake), Zaire 115/E5
Mweru (lake), Zambia 115/E5
Mwesi, Tanzania 115/F5
Mwinilunga, Zambia 115/D6
Mya, Wadi (dry riv.), Algeria 106/E2
Myakka (riv.), Fla. 212/D4
Myakka City, Fla. (33551) 212/D4
Myall (lake), N.S. Wales 97/G3
Myanaung, Burma 72/B3
Myaungmya, Burma 72/B3
Myebon, Burma 72/B2
Myers, Ky. (†40311) 237/O4
Myers, Mont. (†59038) 262/J4
Myerstown, Pa. (17067) 294/K5
Myersville, Md. (21773) 245/H3
Myingyan, Burma 72/B2
Myitkyina, Burma 54/L7
Myitkyina, Burma 72/C1
Myitnge, Burma 72/C2
Myitnge (riv.), Burma 72/C2
Myjava, Czech. 41/D2
Mylo, N. Dak. (†58157) 282/L2
Mymensingh (Nasirabad), Bangladesh 68/G4
Mynyddislwyn, Wales 13/B6
Myohaung, Burma 72/B2
Myohyang (mt.), N. Korea 81/C3
Myŏngch'ŏn, N. Korea 81/D3

Naturaliste 415

Myra, Texas (76253) 303/G4
Myra, W. Va. (25544) 312/B6
Myricks, Mass. (†02780) 249/K5
Myrnam, Alberta 182/E3
Myrtle, Idaho (†83540) 220/B3
Myrtle, Manitoba 179/E5
Myrtle, Minn. (56070) 255/E7
Myrtle, Miss. (38650) 256/F1
Myrtle, Mo. (65778) 261/K9
Myrtle (lake), N. Dak. 282/L5
Myrtle Beach, S.C. (29577) 296/K4
Myrtle Beach A.F.B., S.C. 296/K4
Myrtle Creek, Oreg. (97457) 291/D4
Myrtleford, Victoria 97/D5
Myrtle Grove, Fla. (32506) 212/B6
Myrtle Grove, La. (†70083) 238/K7
Myrtle Point, Oreg. (97458) 291/C4
Myrtlewood, Ala. (36763) 195/C6
Mysen, Norway 18/G7
Myślenice, Poland 47/E4
Myślibórz, Poland 47/B2
Mysłowice, Poland 47/C4
Mysore, India 68/D6
Mysore, India 54/J8
Mys Shmidta, U.S.S.R. 4/C1
Mys Shmidta, U.S.S.R. 48/T3
Mystery Lake, Manitoba 179/J2
Mystic, Conn. (06355) 210/H3
Mystic (riv.), Conn. 210/H3
Mystic, Georgia (31769) 217/F7
Mystic, Iowa (52574) 229/H7
Mystic (lake), Mass. 249/C6
Mystic (riv.), Mass. 249/C6
Mystic, S. Dak. (†57778) 298/B5
Mystic Islands, N.J. (08087) 273/E4
Myszków, Poland 47/D3
My Tho, Vietnam 72/E5
Mytishchi, U.S.S.R. 52/E3
Myton, Utah (84052) 304/D3
M'zab (oasis), Algeria 106/E2
Mže (riv.), Czech. 41/B2
Mzimba, Malawi 115/F6
Mzimba, Malawi 102/F6

N

Naab (riv.), W. Germany 22/E4
Naafkopf (mt.), Switzerland 39/J2
Naaldwijk, Netherlands 27/E4
Naalehu, Hawaii (96772) 218/H7
Naalehu, Hawaii 188/G6
Naantali, Finland 18/M6
Naarden, Netherlands 27/G4
Naas, Ireland 10/C4
Naas, Ireland 17/H5
Naba, Burma 72/B1
Nababeep, S. Africa 118/B5
Nabari, Kiribati 87/J6
Nabb, Ind. (47147) 227/F7
Nabburg, W. Germany 22/E4
Naberezhnye Chelny, U.S.S.R. 52/H3
Nabesna, Alaska (†99764) 196/K2
Nabeul, Tunisia 106/G1
Nabiac, N.S. Wales 97/G3
Nabire, Indonesia 85/K6
Nablus (Nabulus), West Bank 65/C3
Nabnasset, Mass. (01861) 249/J2
Nabua, Philippines 82/D4
Nacala, Mozambique 118/G2
Nacala, Mozambique 102/G6
Nacaome, Honduras 154/D4
Naches, Wash. (98937) 310/E4
Naches (pass), Wash. 310/D3
Naches (riv.), Wash. 310/E4
Nachikatsuura, Japan 81/H7
Nachingwea, Tanzania 115/G6
Náchod, Czech. 41/D1
Nachusa, Ill. (61057) 222/D2
Nachvak (fjord), Newf. 166/B2
Nacimiento (riv.), Calif. 204/D8
Nacimiento, Chile 138/D1
Nacimiento (mts.), N. Mex. 274/C3
Nacimiento (peak), N. Mex. 274/C2
Nacka, Sweden 18/H1
Nackawic, New Bruns. 170/C2
Nacmine, Alberta 182/D4
Naco, Ariz. (85620) 198/E7
Naco, Mexico 150/D1
Nacogdoches (co.), Texas 303/K6
Nacogdoches, Texas (75961) 303/J6
Nacozari, Mexico 150/E1
Ñacunday, Paraguay 144/E5
Nadadores, Mexico 150/H3
Nadawah, Ala. (†36726) 195/D7
Nadeau, Mich. (49863) 250/B3
Nadi, Fiji 86/P10
Nadi, Fiji 87/H7
Nadiad, India 68/C4
Nădlac, Romania 45/E2
Nador, Morocco 106/D1
Nádudvar, Hungary 41/F3
Nadvoitsy, U.S.S.R. 52/D2
Nadym, U.S.S.R. 48/H3
Nadym (riv.), U.S.S.R. 48/H3
Naestved, Denmark 21/E7
Naestved, Denmark 18/G9
Naf, Idaho (83342) 220/E7
Näfels, Switzerland 39/H2
Nafenen, Switzerland 39/H3
Naft-e Shah, Iran 66/D4
Naft Kaneh, Iraq 66/D3
Naga, Philippines 85/G3
Naga, Philippines 54/O8
Naga, Philippines 82/D4
Nagahama, Ehime, Japan 81/F7
Nagahama, Shiga, Japan 81/H6
Nagai (isl.), Alaska 196/F4
Nagaland (state), India 68/G3
Nagambie, Victoria 97/C5
Nagano (pref.), Japan 81/J5
Nagano, Japan 81/J5
Nagaoka, Kyoto, Japan 81/J7
Nagaoka, Niigata, Japan 81/J5
Nagaokakyo, Japan 81/J7
Nagapattinam, India 68/E6
Nagar, Pakistan 68/D1
Nagarote, Nicaragua 154/D4
Nagar Parkar, Pakistan 68/C4
Nagarzê, China 77/C6
Nagasaki (pref.), Japan 81/D7
Nagasaki, Japan 54/O6
Nagasaki, Japan 81/D7
Nagato, Japan 81/E6
Nagaur, India 68/C3
Nagawicka (lake), Wis. 317/J1
Nagele, Netherlands 27/H3
Nagercoil, India 68/D7
Nagina, India 68/D3
Nagishot, Sudan 111/F7
Nagles (mts.), Ireland 17/E7
Nago, Japan 81/N6
Nagold, W. Germany 22/C4
Nagorno-Karabakh Aut. Obl., U.S.S.R. 48/E5
Nagorno-Karabakh Aut. Obl., U.S.S.R. 52/G7
Nagornyy, U.S.S.R. 48/N4
Nagoya, Japan 81/H6
Nagoya, Japan 2/R4
Nagoya, Japan 54/P6
Nagpur, India 54/J7
Nagpur, India 68/D4
Nagqu, China 77/D5
Nags Head, N.C. (27959) 281/T3
Nagua, Dom. Rep. 158/E5
Naguabo, P. Rico 161/F2
Naguabo, P. Rico 156/G1
Nagyatád, Hungary 41/D3
Nagybajom, Hungary 41/D3
Nagyecsed, Hungary 41/G3
Nagyhalász, Hungary 41/F2
Nagykálló, Hungary 41/F3
Nagykanizsa, Hungary 41/D3
Nagykáta, Hungary 41/E3
Nagykőrös, Hungary 41/E3
Nagyszénás, Hungary 41/F3
Naha, Japan 54/O7
Naha, Japan 81/N6
Nahan, India 68/D2
Nahang (riv.), Iran 66/N7
Nahanni Butte, N.W. Terrs. 187/F3
Nahanni Nat'l Park, N.W.T. 162/D3
Nahanni Nat'l Park, N.W. Terrs. 187/F3
Nahant○, Mass. (01908) 249/E6
Nahant (bay), Mass. 249/E6
Nahariyya, Israel 65/C1
Nahavand, Iran 59/E3
Nahavand, Iran 66/F3
Nahcotta, Wash. (98537) 310/A4
Nahhalin, West Bank 65/C4
Nahiku, Hawaii (†96713) 218/K2
Nahma, Mich. (49864) 250/C3
Nahmakanta (lake), Maine 243/E4
Nahuel Huapi (lake), Argentina 120/B7
Nahuel Huapi (lake), Argentina 143/B5
Nahuel Huapi Nat'l Park, Argentina 143/B5
Nahunta, Georgia (31553) 217/H8
Naica, Mexico 150/G2
Naicam, Sask. 181/G3
Naihati, India 68/F1
Nailsworth, England 13/E6
Naiman, China 77/K3
Na'in, Iran 66/H4
Na'in, Iran 59/F3
Nain, Jamaica 158/H6
Nain, Newf. 166/B2
Nain, Newf. 162/K4
Naini Tal, India 68/D3
Nainpur, India 68/E4
Naipo (isl.), Colombia 126/F6
Nairn, La. (†70082) 238/L8
Nairn, Ontario 177/C1
Nairn, Scotland 15/E3
Nairn, Scotland 10/E2
Nairn (trad. co.), Scotland 15/B5
Nairn (riv.), Scotland 15/D3
Nairne, S. Australia 94/C8
Nairobi, Kenya 115/G4
Nairobi (cap.), Kenya 2/L6
Nairobi (cap.), Kenya 115/G4
Nairobi (cap.), Kenya 102/F5
Naivasha, Kenya 115/G4
Najafabad, Iran 59/F3
Najafabad, Iran 66/G4
Najayo Abajo, Dom. Rep. 158/E6
Najin, N. Korea 81/E2
Najran (Aba as Sa'ud), Saudi Arabia 59/D6
Naka (riv.), Japan 81/K5
Nakalele (pt.), Hawaii 218/J1
Nakaminato, Japan 81/K5
Nakamti, Ethiopia 102/F4
Nakamti, Ethiopia 111/G6
Nakamura, Japan 81/F7
Nakasato, Japan 81/K3
Nakatane, Japan 81/E8
Nakatsu, Japan 81/E7
Na Keal, Loch (inlet), Scotland 15/B4
Naked (isl.), Alaska 196/D1
Nakfa, Ethiopia 111/G4
Nakhichevan', U.S.S.R. 7/J5
Nakhichevan', U.S.S.R. 48/E6
Nakhichevan', U.S.S.R. 52/F7
Nakhichevan' A.S.S.R., U.S.S.R. 52/F7
Nakhichevan' A.S.S.R., U.S.S.R. 48/E6
Nakhodka, U.S.S.R. 54/P5
Nakhodka, U.S.S.R. 48/O5
Nakhon Nayok, Thailand 72/D4
Nakhon Pathom, Thailand 72/C4
Nakhon Phanom, Thailand 72/D3
Nakhon Ratchasima, Thailand 72/D4
Nakhon Ratchasima, Thailand 54/M8
Nakhon Sawan, Thailand 72/D4
Nakhon Si Thammarat, Thailand 54/M9
Nakhon Si Thammarat, Thailand 72/D5
Nakina, N.C. (28455) 281/M6
Nakina, Ont. 162/H5
Nakina, Ontario 177/H4
Nakina, Ontario 175/C2
Nakło nad Notecia, Poland 47/C2
Naknek, Alaska (99633) 196/G3
Naknek (lake), Alaska 196/G3
Nakonde, Zambia 115/F5
Nakop, Namibia 118/B5
Nakskov, Denmark 21/E8
Nakskov, Denmark 18/G9
Naktong (riv.), S. Korea 81/D6
Nakuru, Kenya 102/F5
Nakuru, Kenya 115/G4
Nakusp, Br. Col. 184/J5
Nal, Pakistan 59/J4
Nal, Pakistan 68/B3
Nal (riv.), Pakistan 59/J4
Nal (riv.), Pakistan 68/B3
Nalate, Turkey 63/G4
Nalayh (Nalaikha), Mongolia 77/G2
Nalcayec (isl.), Chile 138/D6
Nal'chik, U.S.S.R. 7/J4
Nal'chik, U.S.S.R. 48/E5
Nal'chik, U.S.S.R. 52/F6
Nalgonda, India 68/D5
Nallen, W. Va. (26680) 312/E6
Nallıhan, Turkey 63/D2
Nalut, Libya 111/B1
Namacurra, Mozambique 118/F3
Namak, Daryacheh-ye (salt lake), Iran 59/F3
Namak, Daryacheh-ye (salt lake), Iran 66/G3
Namaka, Alberta 182/D4
Namaksar (salt lake), Afghanistan 59/H3
Namaksar (salt lake), Afghanistan 68/A2
Namaksar (lake), Iran 66/M4
Namaksar (salt lake), Iran 59/H3
Namakzar-e Shahdad (salt lake), Iran 59/G3
Namakzar-e Shahdad (salt lake), Iran 66/L5
Namanga, Kenya 115/G4
Namangan, U.S.S.R. 48/H5
N'amaniya, Iraq 66/D4
Namapa, Mozambique 118/F2
Namaqualand (reg.), S. Africa 118/B5
Namarrói, Mozambique 118/F3
Namasagali, Uganda 115/F3
Namasigüe, Honduras 154/D4
Namatanai, Papua N.G. 87/F6
Namatanai, Papua N.G. 86/C1
Nambe, N. Mex. (†87501) 274/D3
Nambour, Queensland 88/J5
Nambour, Queensland 95/E5
Nambucca Heads, N.S. Wales 97/G2
Nam Co (lake), China 77/D5
Nam Dinh, Vietnam 72/E2
Namekagon (lake), Wis. 317/D3
Namekagon (riv.), Wis. 317/C3
Namen (Namur), Belgium 27/F8
Námestovo, Czech. 41/E2
Nametil, Mozambique 118/F3
Namhkam, Burma 72/C2
Namib (des.), Namibia 118/A3
Namibia 2/K7
Namibia 102/D7
Namibia (des.) 102/D6
NAMIBIA (SOUTH-WEST AFRICA) 118/B3
Naminga, U.S.S.R. 48/M4
Namiquipa, Mexico 150/F2
Namlan, Burma 72/C2
Namlea, Indonesia 85/H6
Namoi (riv.), N. S. Wales 88/H6
Namoi (riv.), N.S. Wales 97/E2
Namonuito (atoll), Micronesia 87/E5
Namorik (atoll), Marshall Is. 87/G5
Nampa, Alberta 182/B1
Nampa, Idaho 146/G5
Nampa, Idaho (83651) 220/B6
Nampa, Idaho 188/C2
Nampala, Mali 106/C5
Namp'o, N. Korea 81/B4
Nampo-Shoto (isls.), Japan 81/M3
Nampula (prov.), Mozambique 118/F2
Nampula, Mozambique 118/F3
Nampula, Mozambique 102/F6
Namsen (riv.), Norway 18/H4
Namsos, Norway 7/F2
Namsos, Norway 18/G4
Nam Tram, Mui (cape), Vietnam 72/F4
Namtu, Burma 72/C2
Namu, Br. Col. 184/D4
Namuac, Philippines 82/C1
Namuli, Serra (mt.), Mozambique 118/F3
Namuno, Mozambique 118/F2
Namur (lake), Alberta 182/D1
Namur (prov.), Belgium 27/F8
Namur, Belgium 27/F8
Namur, Québec 172/C4
Namutoni, Namibia 118/B3
Namwala, Zambia 115/E7
Namwŏn, S. Korea 81/C6
Namysłów, Poland 47/C3
Namzha Parwa (mt.), China 77/E6
Nan, Thailand 72/D3
Nan, Mae Nam (riv.), Thailand 72/D3
Nanacamilpa, Mexico 150/M1
Nana Candundo, Angola 115/D6
Nanafalia, Ala. (36764) 195/B6
Nanaimo, Br. Col. 146/F5
Nanaimo, Br. Col. 162/D6
Nanaimo, Br. Col. 184/J3
Nanakuli, Hawaii (96792) 218/D2
Nanao, Japan 81/H5
Nanay (riv.), Peru 128/E4
Nancagua, Chile 138/F6
Nance (co.), Nebr. 264/F3
Nanchang, China 77/J6
Nanchang, China 54/N7
Nancheng, China 77/J6
Nanchong (Nanchung), China 77/G5
Nanchong, China 54/M6
nan Clar, Loch (lake), Scotland 15/D2
Nancowry (isl.), India 68/G7
Nancy, France 28/G3
Nancy, France 7/E4
Nancy, Ky. (42544) 237/M6
Nanda Devi (mt.), India 68/D2
Nandaime, Nicaragua 154/E5
Nander, India 68/D5
Nandi (Nadi), Fiji 87/H7
Nando, Uruguay 145/F3
Nandurbar, India 68/C4
Nandyal, India 68/D5
Nanga-Eboko, Cameroon 115/B3
Nanga Parbat (mt.), Pakistan 68/D1
Nangapinoh, Indonesia 85/E6
Nangatayap, Indonesia 85/E6
Nangnim-sanmaek (range), N. Korea 81/C3
Nangong, China 77/H4
Nangqên, China 77/E5
Nang Rong, Thailand 72/D4
Nangwarry, S. Australia 94/G7
Nang Xian, China 77/D6
Nanika (dam), Br. Col. 184/D3
Nanika (lake), Br. Col. 184/D3
Nanisivik, N.W. Terrs. /K2
Nanjemoy, Md. (20662) 245/K7
Nanjing (Nanking), China 77/J5
Nanjing, China 2/Q4
Nanjing, China 54/N6
Nanking (Nanjing), China 77/J5
Nankoku, Japan 81/F7
Nan Ling (mts.), China 77/H6
Nannine, W. Australia 92/B4
Nanning, China 77/G7
Nanning, China 54/M7
Nannup, W. Australia 92/B6
Nanoose Bay, Br. Col. 184/J3
Nanortalik, Greenl. 4/D12
Nanpan Jiang (riv.), China 77/F7
Nanping, China 77/J6
Nansei Shoto (Ryukyu) (isls.), Japan 81/M6
Nansen (sound), N.W. Terrs. 187/J1
Nanson, N. Dak. (58354) 282/L2
Nantahala, N.C. (†28702) 281/B4
Nantahala (lake), N.C. 281/B4
Nantai (mt.), Japan 81/J5
Nantasket Beach, Mass. (†02045) 249/E7
Nanterre, France 28/A1
Nantes, France 28/C4
Nantes, France 7/D4
Nantes, Québec 172/F4
Nanticoke (riv.), Del. 245/R6
Nanticoke, Md. (21840) 245/P7
Nanticoke (riv.), Md. 245/P7
Nanticoke, Ontario 177/E5
Nanticoke, Pa. (18634) 294/E7
Nanton, Alberta 182/D4
Nantong, China 77/K5
Nantua, France 28/F4
Nantucket (co.), Mass. 249/O7
Nantucket, Mass. (02554) 249/O7
Nantucket○, Mass. (02554) 249/O7
Nantucket (isl.), Mass. 188/N2
Nantucket (isl.), Mass. 249/O8
Nantucket (sound), Mass. 249/N6
Nanty Glo, Pa. (15943) 294/E5
Nantyglo and Blaina, Wales 13/B6
Nanuet, N.Y. (10954) 276/K8
Nanuktok (isls.), Newf. 166/C2
Nanuku (passage), Fiji 86/R10
Nanumea (atoll), Tuvalu 87/H6
Nanuque, Brazil 132/F7
Nanuque, Brazil 120/E4
Nanxiong, China 77/H6
Nanyang, China 77/H5
Nanyuki, Kenya 115/G3
Nanzhang, China 77/H5
Nanzhao, China 77/H5
Nao (cape), Spain 33/G3
Naococane (lake), Québec 174/C2
Naolinco de Victoria, Mexico 150/P1
Naomi, Ky. (†42544) 237/M6
Náousa, Greece 45/F5
Napa, Calif. 188/B3
Napa (co.), Calif. 204/C5
Napa, Calif. (94558) 204/C5
Napadogan, New Bruns. 170/D2
Napa Junction, Calif. (†94590) 204/J1
Napakiak, Alaska (99634) 196/F2
Napaktok (bay), Newf. 166/B2
Napanee, Ontario 177/G3
Napanoch, N.Y. (12458) 276/M7
Napaskiak, Alaska (99559) 196/F2
Napata (ruins), Sudan 111/F4
Napavine, Wash. (98565) 310/C4
Napè, Laos 72/E3
Naper, Nebr. (68755) 264/E2
Naperville, Ill. (60540) 222/A6
Napf (mt.), Switzerland 39/E3
Napier, Ky. (†40851) 237/P7
Napier, N. Zealand 100/F3
Napier, N. Zealand 87/H9
Napier (mt.), North Terr. 93/A4
Napier, W. Va. (26631) 312/E5
Napier Field, Ala. (36303) 195/H8
Napierville (co.), Québec 172/D4
Napierville, Québec 172/D4
Napili-Honokowai, Hawaii (†96761) 218/H1
Napinka, Manitoba 179/B5
Naplate, Ill. (†61350) 222/E2
Naples, Fla. (*33940) 212/E5
Naples, Idaho (83847) 220/B1
Naples, Ill. (62669) 222/C4
Naples (prov.), Italy 34/E4
Naples, Italy 7/F4
Naples, Italy 34/E4
Naples○, Maine (04055) 243/B8
Naples, N.Y. (14512) 276/F5
Naples, S. Dak. (†57271) 298/O4
Naples, Texas (75568) 303/K4
Naples Park, Fla. (†33940) 212/E5
Napo (riv.) 120/B3
Napo, China 77/G7
Napo (prov.), Ecuador 128/D3
Napo (riv.), Ecuador 128/D3
Napo (riv.), Peru 128/F4
Napoleon, Ind. (47034) 227/G6
Napoleon, Mich. (49261) 250/E6
Napoleon, Mo. (64074) 261/E4
Napoleon, N. Dak. (58561) 282/L6
Napoleon, Ohio (43545) 284/B3
Naponee, Nebr. (68960) 264/E4
Nappa Merri, Queensland 95/B5
Nappan, Nova Scotia 168/D3
Nappanee, Ind. (46550) 227/F2
Napperby, North. Terr. 93/C7
Napton, Mo. (65346) 261/F4
Naqa (ruins), Sudan 111/F4
Nara (pref.), Japan 81/J8
Nara, Japan 81/J8
Nara, Mali 106/C5
Naracoopa, Tasmania 99/B1
Naracoorte, S. Australia 88/F7
Naracoorte, S. Australia 94/G7
Naradhan, N.S. Wales 97/D3
Naramata, Br. Col. 184/H5
Naranja, Fla. (33032) 212/F6
Naranjal (riv.), Ecuador 128/C4
Naranjito, Honduras 154/C3
Naranjito, P. Rico 161/D1
Naranjos, Mexico 150/L6
Naraq, Iran 66/G3
Narashino, Japan 81/P2
Narathiwat, Thailand 72/D6
Nara Visa, N. Mex. (88430) 274/F3
Narayanganj, Bangladesh 68/G4
Narayanpet, India 68/D5
Narberth, Pa. (19072) 294/M6
Narberth, Wales 13/C6
Narbonne, France 28/E6
Narcissa, Okla. (†74354) 288/S1
Narcisse, Manitoba 179/E4
Narcondam (isl.), India 68/G6
Narcoossee, Fla. (†32769) 212/E3
Nardin, Okla. (74646) 288/M1
Nardò, Italy 34/F4
Naré, Argentina 143/F5
Nare, Colombia 126/C4
Narellan, N.S. Wales 97/F3
Nares (str.) 146/L2
Nares (str.), N.W.T. 162/N3
Nares (str.), N.W. Terrs. 187/L2
Narew (riv.), Poland 47/E2
Naricual, Venezuela 124/F2
Narinda, Madagascar 118/H3
Nariño (dept.), Colombia 126/B7
Nariva (swamp), Trin. & Tob. 161/B10
Narka, Kansas (66960) 232/E2
Narmada (riv.), India 54/J7
Narmada (riv.), India 68/D4
Narman, Turkey 63/J2
Narnaul, India 68/D3
Narni, Italy 34/D3
Naro, Italy 34/D6
Narodnaya (mt.), U.S.S.R. 7/K2
Narodnaya (mt.), U.S.S.R. 48/G3
Narodnaya (mt.), U.S.S.R. 52/J1
Narok, Kenya 115/G4
Narooma, N.S. Wales 97/F5
Narrabeen, N. S. Wales 88/L3
Narrabeen, N.S. Wales 97/K3
Narrabri, N. S. Wales 88/J6
Narrabri, N.S. Wales 97/E2
Narragansett, R.I. (02882) 249/J7
Narragansett○, R.I. (02882) 249/J7
Narragansett (bay), R.I. 249/J6
Narran (lake), N.S. Wales 97/D1
Narran (riv.), N.S. Wales 97/D1
Narrandera, N. S. Wales 88/H6
Narrandera, N.S. Wales 97/D4
Narre Warren North, Victoria 97/K5
Narrogin, W. Australia 88/B6
Narrogin, W. Australia 92/B2
Narromine, N. S. Wales 88/H6
Narromine, N.S. Wales 97/E3
Narrows, Ky. (42358) 237/H5
Narrows, Oreg. (†97721) 291/H4
Narrows, The (str.), St. Chris.-Nevis 161/D11
Narrows, The (str.), Virgin Is. (Br.) 161/C4
Narrows, The (str.), Virgin Is. (U.S.) 161/C4
Narrows, Va. (24124) 307/G6
Narrowsburg, N.Y. (12764) 276/L7
Narrows Park-La Vale, Md. (†21502) 245/C2
Narsimhapur, India 68/D4
Narsinghgarh, India 68/D4
Narssaq, Greenl. 4/C12
Naruna, Va. (24576) 307/L6
Narva, U.S.S.R. 52/C3
Narva, U.S.S.R. 53/E1
Narva (res.), U.S.S.R. 53/D1
Narvik, Norway 4/C9
Narvik, Norway 7/F2
Narvik, Norway 18/K2
Nary, Minn. (†56601) 255/D3
Nar'yan-Mar, U.S.S.R. 4/C7
Nar'yan-Mar, U.S.S.R. 7/K2
Nar'yan-Mar, U.S.S.R. 48/F3
Nar'yan-Mar, U.S.S.R. 52/H1
Naryn, U.S.S.R. 48/H5
Nasarawa, Nigeria 106/F7
Năsăud, Romania 45/G2
Naseby, N. Zealand 100/C6
Naseby, Sask. 181/C3
Naselle, Wash. (98638) 310/B4
Naselle (riv.), Wash. 310/B4
Nash (stream), N.H. 268/E2
Nash (co.), N.C. 281/O2
Nash, N. Dak. (58264) 282/P3
Nash, Okla. (73761) 288/K1
Nash, Texas (75569) 303/K4
Nashawena (isl.), Mass. 249/L7
Nash Creek, New Bruns. 170/D1
Nashoba, Okla. (74558) 288/R6
Nashotah, Wis. (53058) 317/J1
Nashport, Ohio (43830) 284/F5
Nashua, Iowa (50658) 229/J3
Nashua (riv.), Mass. 249/H3
Nashua, Minn. (56565) 255/B4
Nashua, Mont. (59248) 262/K2
Nashua, N.H. 188/M2
Nashua, N.H. (03060) 268/D6
Nashville, Ark. (71852) 202/C6
Nashville, Georgia (31639) 217/F8
Nashville, Ill. (62263) 222/D5
Nashville, Ind. (47448) 227/E6
Nashville, Kansas (67112) 232/D4
Nashville, Mich. (49073) 250/D6
Nashville, Mo. (†64855) 261/D8
Nashville, N.C. (27856) 281/O3
Nashville, Ohio (44661) 284/F4
Nashville, Oreg. (†97370) 291/D3
Nashville (cap.), Tenn. 146/K6
Nashville (cap.), Tenn. 188/J3
Nashville (cap.), Tenn. (*37201) 237/H8
Nashwaak (riv.), New Bruns. 170/D2
Nashwaak Bridge, New Bruns. 170/D2
Nashwaak Village, New Bruns. 170/D2
Nashwauk, Minn. (55769) 255/E3
Našice, Yugoslavia 45/C3
Nasielsk, Poland 47/E2
Näsijärvi (lake), Finland 18/O6
Nasik, India 68/C5
Nasik, India 54/J8
Nasir, Sudan 111/F6
Nasirabad, Bangladesh 68/G4
Nasirabad, India 68/C3
Naskaupi (riv.), Newf. 166/B3
Naso (pt.), Philippines 82/C5
Nason, Ill. (†62816) 222/D5
Nasonville, R.I. (†02830) 249/H5
Nasratabad (Zabol), Iran 59/H3
Nasratabad (Zabol), Iran 66/M5
Nass (riv.), Br. Col. 184/C2
Nassau (cap.), Bahamas 146/L7
Nassau (cap.), Bahamas 156/C1
Nassau (bay), Chile 120/C8
Nassau (bay), Chile 138/F11
Nassau (isl.), Cook Is. 87/K7
Nassau, Del. (19969) 245/T6
Nassau (co.), Fla. 212/E1
Nassau (riv.), Fla. 212/E1
Nassau (sound), Fla. 212/E1
Nassau, Minn. (56272) 255/B5
Nassau (co.), N.Y. 276/N9
Nassau, N.Y. (12123) 276/N5
Nassau Bay, Texas (†77598) 303/K2
Nassawadox, Va. (23413) 307/S6
Nassawango (creek), Md. 245/S8
Nasser (lake), Egypt 102/F2
Nasser (lake), Egypt 111/F3
Nasser (lake), Egypt 59/F3
Nassereith, Austria 41/A3
Nässjö, Sweden 18/J8
Nassogne, Belgium 27/G8
Nasty (creek), S. Dak. 298/C2
Nasu (mt.), Japan 81/J5
Nata, Botswana 118/D4
Natá, Panama 154/G6
Natagaima, Colombia 126/C6
Natal, Brazil 2/H6
Natal, Brazil 132/H4
Natal, Brazil 120/F3
Natal, Br. Col. 184/K5
Natal (prov.), S. Africa 102/F7
Natal (prov.), S. Africa 118/E5
Natalbany, La. (70451) 238/N1
Natalia, Texas (78059) 303/J11
Natalicio Talavera, Paraguay 144/D4
Natanz, Iran 59/F3
Natanz, Iran 66/H4
Natashquan (riv.) 162/K5
Natashquan (riv.), Newf. 166/B3
Natashquan, Québec 174/E3
Natashquan (riv.), Québec 174/E2
Natashquan-Est (riv.), Newf. 166/B3
Natchaug (riv.), Conn. 210/G1
Natchez, Ala. (†36425) 195/D7
Natchez, La. (71456) 238/D3
Natchez, Miss. 188/H4
Natchez, Miss. (39120) 256/B7
Natchitoches (par.), La. 238/D3
Natchitoches, La. (71457) 238/D3
Naters, Switzerland 39/E4
Natewa (bay), Fiji 86/Q10
Nathalia, Victoria 97/C5
Nathalie, Va. (24577) 307/L7
Nathan, Mich. (†49821) 250/B3
Nathrop, Colo. (81236) 208/H5
Natick○, Mass. (01760) 249/A7
Natick, R.I. (†02887) 249/H6
Natimuk, Victoria 97/A5
Nation (riv.), Br. Col. 184/F2
National Agricultural Research Center, Md. 245/G3
National Capital Region (Manila) (prov.), Philippines 82/C3
National City, Calif. (92050) 204/J11
National City, Mich. (48748) 250/F4
National Gardens, Fla. (†32074) 212/E2
National Mills, Manitoba 179/A2
National Mine, Mich. (49865) 250/B2
National Park, N.J. (08063) 273/B3
National Park, Switzerland 39/K3
National Reactor Testing Sta. (U.S.A.E.C), Idaho 220/F6
National Stock Yards, Ill. (62071) 222/A2
Natitingou, Benin 106/E6
Natividade, Brazil 132/E5
Natmauk, Burma 72/B2
Natoma, Kansas (67651) 232/D2
Natron (lake), Kenya 115/G4
Natron (lake), Tanzania 115/G4
Natrona (co.), Wyo. 319/F3
Natrona, Wyo. (82646) 319/F2
Natrona Heights, Pa. (15065) 294/C4
Nattavaara, Sweden 18/M3
Natuna (isls.), Indonesia 54/M9
Natuna (isls.), Indonesia 85/D5
Natural Bridge, Ala. (35577) 195/C2
Natural Bridge, N.Y. (13665) 276/K2
Natural Bridge, Va. (24578) 307/J5
Natural Bridges Nat'l Mon., Utah 304/E6
Natural Bridge Station, Va. (24579) 307/K5
Natural Dam, N.Y. (†13642) 276/J2
Naturaliste (cape), Tasmania 99/E2
Naturaliste (cape), W. Australia 88/A6
Naturaliste (chan.), W. Australia 88/A5
Naturaliste (cape), W. Australia 92/A6

416 Naturaliste

Naturaliste (chan.), W. Australia 92/A4
Natural Steps, Ark. (†72135) 202/F4
Naturita, Colo. (81422) 208/B6
Naubinway, Mich. (49762) 250/D2
Naucalpan de Juárez, Mexico 150/L1
Nauders, Austria 41/A3
Nauen, E. Germany 22/E2
Naugatuck, Conn. (06770) 210/C3
Naugatuck (riv.), Conn. 210/C3
Naugatuck, W. Va. (25685) 312/B7
Nauhcampatépetl (mt.), Mexico 150/O1
Naujan (lake), Philippines 82/C4
Naujoji-Akmene, U.S.S.R. 53/B2
Naumburg, E. Germany 22/D3
Na'ur, Jordan 65/D4
Nauru 2/T6
Nauru 87/G6
Naushon (isl.), Mass. 249/L7
Naustdal, Norway 18/E6
Nauta, Peru 128/F5
Nautla, Mexico 150/L6
Nauvoo, Ala. (35578) 195/D3
Nauvoo, Ill. (62354) 222/B3
Nauwigewauk, New Bruns. 170/E3
Nava, Mexico 150/J2
Nava del Rey, Spain 33/D2
Navajo (co.), Ariz. 198/E3
Navajo, Ariz. (86509) 198/F3
Navajo (creek), Ariz. 198/D2
Navajo (peak), Colo. 208/F8
Navajo (res.), Colo. 208/E8
Navajo, Mont. (†59222) 262/M2
Navajo, N. Mex. (87328) 274/A3
Navajo (dam), N. Mex. 274/B2
Navajo (res.), N. Mex. 274/B2
Navajo (mt.), Utah 304/D6
Navajo Ind. Res., Ariz. 198/D2
Navajo Ind. Res., N. Mex. 274/A2
Navajo Ind. Res., Utah 304/D7
Navajo Nat'l Mon., Ariz. 198/E2
Navajo Ord. Depot, Ariz. 198/D3
Naval Academy, U.S., Md. 245/N5
Naval Air Sta., La. 238/O4
Naval Air Station, Calif. 204/J2
Naval Air Station, Va. 307/R7
Naval Base, S.C. 296/H6
Navalcarnero, Spain 33/F4
Naval Medical Center, Md. 245/E4
Navalmoral de la Mata, Spain 33/D3
Naval Submarine Base, Conn. 210/G3
Naval Support Ctr., Wash. 310/B1
Naval Weapons Center, Md. 245/F3
Naval Yard, D.C. 245/F5
Navan (An Uaimh), Ireland 17/H4
Navan, Ontario 177/J2
Navarin (cape), U.S.S.R. 4/C18
Navarin (cape), U.S.S.R. 48/T3
Navarino (isl.), Chile 138/F11
Navarino, Wis. (54108) 317/J6
Navarra (prov.), Spain 33/F1
Navarre, Kansas (67469) 232/E3
Navarre, Ohio (44662) 284/H4
Navarro, Argentina 143/G7
Navarro, Calif. (95463) 204/B4
Navarro (riv.), Calif. 204/B4
Navarro (co.), Texas 303/H5
Navasota, Texas (77868) 303/J7
Navasota (riv.), Texas 303/H7
Navassa, N.C. (†28404) 281/O6
Navassa (isl.), Virgin Is. (U.S.) 156/C3
Naver, Loch (lake), Scotland 15/D2
Naver (riv.), Scotland 15/D2
Navesink, N.J. (07752) 273/E3
Navesink (riv.), N.J. 273/E3
Navia (riv.), Spain 33/C1
Navidad, Chile 138/A10
Navidad (riv.), Texas 303/H8
Navin, Manitoba 179/F5
Navoi, U.S.S.R. 48/G6
Navojoa, Mexico 150/E3
Navolato, Mexico 150/E4
Návpaktos, Greece 45/F6
Návplion, Greece 45/F7
Navrongo, Ghana 106/D6
Navsari, India 68/C4
Navy Board (inlet), N.W. Terrs. 187/K2
Navy Yard City, Wash. (†98310) 310/A2
Nawabganj, Bangladesh 68/F4
Nawabshah, Pakistan 68/B3
Nawabshah, Pakistan 59/J4
Nawiliwili (bay), Hawaii 218/D2
Naxera, Va. (23122) 307/R6
Náxos, Greece 45/G7
Náxos (isl.), Greece 45/G7
Naya, Colombia 126/B6
Nayarit (state), Mexico 150/G6
Nayarit, Sierra (mts.), Mexico 150/G5
Nay Band, Iran 59/F4
Nay Band, Iran 59/G3
Nay Band, Bushehr, Iran 66/H7
Nay Band, Khorasan, Iran 66/K4
Naylor, Georgia (31641) 217/F9
Naylor, Mo. (63953) 261/L9
Nayoro, Japan 81/L1
Naytahwaush, Minn. (56566) 255/C3
Nazaré, Brazil 132/G6
Nazaré, Portugal 33/B3
Nazareth, Belgium 27/D7
Nazareth, Israel 65/C2
Nazareth, Pa. (18064) 294/M4
Nazareth, Texas (79063) 303/B3
Nazarovo, U.S.S.R. 48/K4
Nazas, Mexico 150/G4
Nazas (riv.), Mexico 150/G4
Nazca, Peru 128/E10
Naze, The (prom.), England 13/J6
Naze, Japan 81/O5
Nazerat 'Illit, Israel 65/C2
Nazilli, Turkey 63/C4
Nazko, Br. Col. 184/F3
Nazret, Ethiopia 111/G6
Nazret, Ethiopia 102/F4
Nazyvayevsk, U.S.S.R. 48/H4
Ncheu (Ntcheu), Malawi 115/F6
Ndalatando, Angola 115/B5
Ndele, Cent. Afr. Rep. 115/D2
N'Dendé, Gabon 115/B4
Ndeni (isl.), Solomon Is. 87/G7
N'Djamena (cap.), Chad 111/C5
N'Djamena (cap.), Chad 2/K5
N'Djamena (cap.), Chad 102/D3
N'Djolé, Gabon 115/B4
N'Dogo (lag.), Gabon 115/B4
Ndola, Zambia 115/E6
Ndola, Zambia 102/E6
Nead, Ind. (†46970) 227/E3
Neagh (lake), N. Ireland 17/J2
Neagh, Lough (lake), N. Ireland 10/C3
Neah Bay, Wash. (98357) 310/A2
Neal, Kansas (66863) 232/F4
Neale (lake), North. Terr. 88/D4
Neale (lake), North. Terr. 93/A8
Neales, The (riv.), S. Australia 94/E3
Neales, The (riv.), S. Australia 88/F5
Neápolis, Greece 45/F7
Neapolis, Ohio (43547) 284/C3
Near (isls.), Alaska 196/H3
Neath, Wales 10/E5
Neath, Wales 13/D6
Neavitt, Md. (21652) 245/N6
Nebikon, Switzerland 39/F2
Nebish, Minn. (†56667) 255/D3
Nebit-Dag, U.S.S.R. 48/F6
Neblina, Pico da (peak), Brazil 132/G8
Neblina (Phelps) (peak), Venezuela 124/E7
Nebo (mt.), Ark. 202/D3
Nebo, Ill. (62355) 222/C4
Nebo (mt.), Jordan 65/D4
Nebo, Ky. (42441) 237/F6
Nebo, La. (†71342) 238/F3
Nebo, Mo. (65471) 261/H7
Nebo (mt.), Utah 304/C4
Nebo, W. Va. (25141) 312/D5
Nebraska 188/F2
NEBRASKA 264
Nebraska, Ind. (47262) 227/F6
Nebraska (state), U.S. 146/J5
Nebraska City, Nebr. (68410) 264/J4
Necedah, Wis. (54646) 317/F7
Nechako (riv.), Br. Col. 184/E3
Neche, N. Dak. (58265) 282/P2
Neches, Texas (75779) 303/J6
Neches (riv.), Texas 303/K6
Nechí (riv.), Colombia 126/C4
Neckar (riv.), W. Germany 22/C4
Neckarsulm, W. Germany 22/C4
Neck City, Mo. (†64755) 261/C8
Necker (isl.), Hawaii 87/K3
Necker (isl.), Hawaii 188/F6
Necker (isl.), Hawaii 218/D6
Necochea, Argentina 143/E4
Necochea, Argentina 120/D6
Nectar, Ala. (†35049) 195/E3
Necum Teuch (harb.), Nova Scotia 168/F4
Ned, Ky. (41355) 237/P6
Neded, Czech. 41/D2
Nederland, Colo. (80466) 208/H3
Nederland, Texas (77627) 303/K8
Nedgera (creek), N.S. Wales 97/E2
Nedlands, W. Australia 88/B2
Nedlands, W. Australia 92/A1
Neeb, Sask. 181/C1
Neebish (isl.), Mich. 250/E2
Neede, Netherlands 27/K4
Needham, Ala. (36915) 195/B7
Needham, Ind. (46162) 227/E5
Needham○, Mass. (02192) 249/B7
Needham Heights, Mass. (02194) 249/B7
Needle (mt.), Wyo. 319/C1
Needles, Calif. 188/C4
Needles, Calif. (92363) 204/L9
Needles (pt.), N. Zealand 100/E2
Needmore, Ind. (†47421) 227/E7
Needmore, N.C. (†28713) 281/B4
Needmore, Pa. (17238) 294/F6
Needmore, W. Va. (†26801) 312/J4
Needville, Texas (77461) 303/J8
Neelin, Manitoba 179/C5
Neely, Miss. (39461) 256/G8
Neely Henry (lake), Ala. 195/F3
Neelys Landing, Mo. (†63755) 261/O7
Neelyton, Pa. (17239) 294/G5
Neelyville, Mo. (63954) 261/M9
Ñeembucú (dept.), Paraguay 144/C-D5
Neenah, Wis. (54956) 317/J7
Neepawa, Manitoba 179/C4
Neerlandia, Alberta 182/C2
Neerpelt, Belgium 27/G6
Neeses, S.C. (29107) 296/E4
Nee Soon, Singapore 72/F6
Nee so Pah (res.), Colo. 208/D6
Neffs, Ohio (43940) 284/J5
Neffs Mills, Pa. (†16669) 294/G4
Nefta, Tunisia 106/F2
Neftekamsk, U.S.S.R. 52/J3
Nefteyugansk, U.S.S.R. 48/H3
Nefud (des.), Saudi Arabia 54/F7
Nefud (des.), Saudi Arabia 59/D4
Nefud Dahi (des.), Saudi Arabia 59/D5
Nefusa, Jebel (mts.), Libya 111/B1
Nefyn, Wales 13/C5
Negara, Indonesia 85/E7
Negaunee, Mich. (49866) 250/B2
Negba, Israel 65/B4
Negelli, Ethiopia 111/G6
Negeri Sembilan (state), Malaysia 72/D7
Negev (reg.), Israel 65/D5
Negley, Ohio (44441) 284/J4
Negomane, Mozambique 118/F2
Negombo, Sri Lanka 68/D7
Negotin, Yugoslavia 45/F3
Negra, Cordillera (mts.), Peru 128/D7
Negra (pt.), Peru 128/B6
Negra (pt.), P. Rico 161/G2
Negra (lag.), Uruguay 145/F5
Negra (range), Uruguay 145/D2
Negrais (cape), Burma 72/B3
Negreet, La. (71460) 238/C4
Negreiros, Chile 138/B2
Negreşti, Romania 45/H2
Negril, Jamaica 158/G6
Negrillos, Bolivia 136/A6
Negritos, Peru 128/B5
Negro (riv.) 2/F5
Negro (cape), Angola 115/B7
Negro (riv.), Argentina 120/C6
Negro (riv.), Argentina 143/D4
Negro (riv.), Bolivia 136/D4
Negro (riv.), Brazil 120/C3
Negro (riv.), Brazil 132/H9
Negro (riv.), Colombia 126/G7
Negro (riv.), Paraguay 144/C4
Negro (bay), Somalia 115/J2
Negro (riv.), Uruguay 120/D6
Negro, Arroyo (riv.), Uruguay 145/B3
Negro (riv.), Uruguay 145/B4
Negro (riv.), Venezuela 124/E7
Negro Bay, Virgin Is. (U.S.) 161/E4
Negros (isl.), Philippines 54/O9
Negros (isl.), Philippines 85/G4
Negros (isl.), Philippines 82/D6
Negros Occidental (prov.), Philippines 82/D6
Negros Oriental (prov.), Philippines 82/D6
Neguac, New Bruns. 170/E1
Nehalem, Oreg. (97131) 291/D2
Nehalem (riv.), Oreg. 291/D2
Nehawka, Nebr. (68413) 264/H4
Nehbandan, Iran 59/G3
Nehbandan, Iran 66/L5
Nehe, China 77/L2
Neheim-Hüsten, W. Germany 22/C3
Neiafu, Tonga 87/J7
Neiba, Dom. Rep. 158/D6
Neiba, Dom. Rep. 156/D3
Neiba (bay), Dom. Rep. 158/D6
Neiba, Sierra de (mts.), Dom. Rep. 158/D6
Neiber, Wyo. (†82401) 319/D2
Neidpath, Sask. 181/D5
Neiges (lake), Québec 172/F2
Neigette, Québec 172/J1
Neihart, Mont. (59465) 262/F4
Neijiang (Neikiang), China 77/G6
Neilburg, Sask. 181/B3
Neillsville, Wis. (54456) 317/E6
Neil's Harbour, Nova Scotia 168/H2
Neilston, Scotland 15/B2
Neilton, Wash. (98566) 310/B3
Nei Monggol (Inner Mongolian Aut. Reg.), China 77/H3
Neis Beach, Sask. 181/E2
Neisse (riv.), E. Germany 22/F3
Neisse (Nysa), Poland 47/C3
Neisse (riv.), Poland 47/B3
Neiva, Colombia 120/B2
Neiva, Colombia 126/C6
Nejanilini (lake), Manitoba 179/J1
Nejd (reg.), Saudi Arabia 59/D4
Nejdek, Czech. 41/B1
Nejo, Ethiopia 111/G6
Nekoma, Kansas (67559) 232/C3
Nekoma, N. Dak. (58355) 282/O2
Nekoosa, Wis. (54457) 317/G7
Neksø, Denmark 18/J9
Neksø, Denmark 21/F9
Nelagoney, Okla. (†74056) 288/O1
Nelas, Portugal 33/C2
Nelchina, Alaska (†99588) 196/C1
Nelidovo, U.S.S.R. 52/D3
Neligh, Nebr. (68756) 264/G2
Nel'kan, U.S.S.R. 48/O4
Nellie, Ohio (†43844) 284/F5
Nellis, W. Va. (25142) 312/C6
Nellis A.F.B., Nev. 266/F6
Nellis Air Force Range and AEC Nuclear Testing Sit, Nev. 266/E5
Nelliston, N.Y. (13410) 276/L5
Nellore, India 54/K8
Nellore, India 68/E6
Nellysford, Va. (22958) 307/L5
Nelma, Wis. (†49935) 317/J3
Nelse, Ky. (41550) 237/R6
Nelson (isl.), Alaska 196/E2
Nelson, Argentina 143/F5
Nelson, Ariz. (†86434) 198/B3
Nelson, Br. Col. 162/E6
Nelson, Br. Col. 184/J5
Nelson (str.), Chile 138/D9
Nelson, England 13/H1
Nelson, England 10/G1
Nelson, Georgia (30151) 217/D2
Nelson, Ill. (61058) 222/D2
Nelson (co.), Ky. 237/K5
Nelson, Ky. (†42330) 237/G6
Nelson (riv.), Man. 146/J4
Nelson (riv.), Man. 162/G4
Nelson (riv.), Manitoba 179/J2
Nelson, Minn. (56355) 255/C5
Nelson, Mo. (65347) 261/F4
Nelson (res.), Mont. 262/J2
Nelson, Nebr. (68961) 264/F4
Nelson, Nev. (†89046) 266/G7
Nelson (creek), Nev. 266/G2
Nelson○, N.H. (†03457) 268/C5
Nelson, N. Zealand 87/H10
Nelson, N. Zealand 100/D4
Nelson (co.), N. Dak. 282/O4
Nelson, Pa. (16940) 294/H2
Nelson (cape), Victoria 97/A6
Nelson (co.), Va. 307/L5
Nelson, Wis. (54756) 317/C7
Nelson Forks, Br. Col. 184/M2
Nelson Head (prom.), N.W. Terrs. 187/F2
Nelson House, Manitoba 179/J2
Nelson Lagoon, Alaska (†99571) 196/F3
Nelson-Miramichi, New Bruns. 170/E2
Nelsonville, Ark. (†72569) 202/H1
Nelsonville, Ky. (†40051) 237/K5
Nelsonville, N.Y. (10516) 276/N8
Nelsonville, Ohio (45764) 284/F7
Nelsonville, Wis. (54458) 317/H7
Nelspruit, S. Africa 118/E5
Néma, Mauritania 106/C5
Néma, Mauritania 102/B3
Nemacolin, Pa. (15351) 294/B6
Nemadji (riv.), Minn. 255/F4
Nemaha, Iowa (50567) 229/C3
Nemaha (co.), Kansas 232/F2
Nemaha (riv.), Kansas 232/G1
Nemaha (co.), Nebr. 264/J4
Nemaha, Nebr. (68414) 264/J4
Neméa, Greece 45/F7
Nemi, Italy 34/F7
Nemiskam, Alberta 182/E5
Nemo, S. Dak. (57759) 298/B5
Nemours, France 28/E3
Nemrut Dağı (mt.), Turkey 63/J3
Nemunas (Niemen) (riv.), U.S.S.R. 53/A3
Nemuro, Japan 81/M2
Nemuro (str.), Japan 81/M1
Nen (riv.), China 54/O5
Nenagh, Ireland 10/B4
Nenagh, Ireland 17/E6
Nenagh (riv.), Ireland 17/E6
Nenana, Alaska (99760) 196/J2
Nendaz, Switzerland 39/D4
Nene (riv.), England 10/F4
Nene (riv.), England 13/H5
Nenets Aut. Okr., U.S.S.R. 48/F3
Nenets Aut. Okr., U.S.S.R. 52/H1
Nenjiang, China 77/L2
Nen Jiang (riv.), China 77/K2
Nenzel, Nebr. (69219) 264/C2
Neodesha, Kansas (66757) 232/G4
Neoga, Ill. (62447) 222/E4
Neola, Iowa (51559) 229/B6
Neola, Utah (84053) 304/D3
Neola, W. Va. (24961) 312/F7
Neon-Fleming, Ky. (41840) 237/R6
Néon Karlóvasi, Greece 45/H7
Neopit, Wis. (54150) 317/J6
Neópolis, Brazil 132/G5
Neosho (riv.) 188/G3
Neosho (co.), Kansas 232/G4
Neosho (riv.), Kansas 232/G4
Neosho, Mo. (64850) 261/D9
Neosho (riv.), Okla. 288/R1
Neosho, Wis. (53059) 317/J9
Neosho Falls, Kansas (66758) 232/G3
Neosho Rapids, Kansas (66864) 232/F3
Neotsu, Oreg. (97364) 291/C2
Nepa, U.S.S.R. 48/L4
Nepal 2/P4
Nepal 54/K7
NEPAL 68/E3
Nepalganj, Nepal 68/E3
Nepaug (res.), Conn. 210/D1
Nepaug (riv.), Conn. 210/C1
Nepean (isl.), Norfolk I. 88/L6
Nephi, Utah (84648) 304/C4
Nephin (mt.), Ireland 17/C3
Nephin Beg (mt.), Ireland 17/B3
Nephton, Ontario 177/G3
Nepisiguit (bay), New Bruns. 170/E1
Nepisiguit (lakes), New Bruns. 170/D1
Nepisiguit (riv.), New Bruns. 170/D1
Nepomuk, Czech. 41/B2
Neponset, Ill. (61345) 222/D2
Neponset, Mass. (†02122) 249/D7
Neponset (riv.), Mass. 249/C8
Nepton, Ky. (†41039) 237/O4
Neptune○, N.J. (07753) 273/E3
Neptune, Ohio (†45822) 284/A4
Neptune (isls.), S. Australia 94/D6
Neptune Beach, Fla. (32233) 212/E1
Neptune City, N.J. (07753) 273/E3
Nera (riv.), Italy 34/D3
Nérac, France 28/D5
Nerekhta, U.S.S.R. 52/F3
Nerepis (riv.), New Bruns. 170/D3
Neresheim, W. Germany 22/D4
Nereta, U.S.S.R. 53/C2
Neretva (riv.), Yugoslavia 45/D4
Neriquinha, Angola 115/D7
Nerja, Spain 33/E4
Nerka (lake), Alaska 196/G3
Ñermete (pt.), Peru 128/B5
Nerpio, Spain 33/E3
Nerstrand, Minn. (55053) 255/E6
Nerva, Spain 33/C4
Neryungri, U.S.S.R. 48/N4
Nes (Neskaupstadhur), Iceland 21/D1
Nes, Netherlands 27/H2
Nesbit, Miss. (38651) 256/D1
Nesbitt, Manitoba 179/C5
Nescopeck, Pa. (18635) 294/K3
Nesebŭr, Bulgaria 45/H4
Neshanic Station, N.J. (†08853) 273/D3
Nesher, Israel 65/C2
Neshkoro, Wis. (54960) 317/H8
Neshoba (co.), Miss. 256/F5
Neshoba, Miss. (39365) 256/F5
Neskaupstadhur, Iceland 7/C2
Neskaupstadhur, Iceland 21/D1
Neskowin, Oreg. (97149) 291/D2
Nesmith, S.C. (29580) 296/H4
Nespelem, Wash. (99155) 310/G2
Nesquehoning, Pa. (18240) 294/L4
Ness (co.), Kansas 232/C3
Ness, Loch (lake), Scotland 15/D3
Ness, Loch (lake), Scotland 10/D2
Ness (riv.), Scotland 15/D3
Ness City, Kansas (67560) 232/C3
Nesselrode (mt.), Alaska 196/N1
Nesselwang, W. Germany 22/D5
Nesslau, Switzerland 39/H2
Neston, England 13/G2
Neston, England 10/F2
Nestor, Trin. & Tob. 161/B10
Nestor Falls, Ontario 177/F5
Nestor Falls, Ontario 175/B3
Nestoria, Mich. (†49861) 250/A2
Nestórion, Greece 45/E5
Nestorville, W. Va. (†26380) 312/G4
Néstos (riv.), Greece 45/G5
Nestow, Alberta 182/D2
Nesttun, Norway 18/D6
Nestucca (riv.), Oreg. 291/D2
Nesvady, Czech. 41/E3
Nes Ziyyona, Israel 65/B4
Net (riv.), Mich. 250/G2
Netanya, Israel 65/B3
Netarts, Oreg. (97143) 291/C2
Netawaka, Kansas (66516) 232/G2
Netcong, N.J. (07857) 273/D2
Nethe (riv.), Belgium 27/F6
Netherhill, Sask. 181/C4
Netherlands 2/K3
Netherlands 7/E3
NETHERLANDS 27/G4
Netherlands Antilles 120/C1
Netherlands Antilles 146/M8
NETHERLANDS ANTILLES 161
NETHERLANDS ANTILLES 156/E4
Nethy Bridge, Scotland 15/E3
Netivot, Israel 65/B5
Netolice, Czech. 41/C2
Netstal, Switzerland 39/H2
Nett (lake), Minn. 255/E2
Nettie, W. Va. (26681) 312/E6
Nettilling (lake), Canada 4/C13
Nettilling (fjord), N.W. Terrs. 187/M3
Nettilling (lake), N.W. Terrs. 187/L3
Nett Lake, Minn. (55772) 255/E2
Nett Lake Ind. Res., Minn. 255/E2
Nettleham, England 13/G4
Nettleton, Miss. (38858) 256/G2
Nettuno, Italy 34/D4
Netzahualcóyotl, Mexico 150/L1
Neuanlage, Sask. 181/E3
Neuberg an der Mürz, Austria 41/C3
Neubert, Tenn. (†37901) 237/O9
Neubois, Québec 172/G4
Neubrandenburg (dist.), E. Germany 22/E2
Neubrandenburg, E. Germany 22/E2
Neuburg an der Donau, W. Germany 22/D4
Neuchâtel (canton), Switzerland 39/C3
Neuchâtel, Switzerland 39/C3
Neuchâtel (lake), Switzerland 39/C3
Neudorf, Sask. 181/J5
Neuenegg, Switzerland 39/D3
Neuenhagen bei Berlin, E. Germany 22/F4
Neufchâteau, Belgium 27/G9
Neufchâteau, France 28/F3
Neufchâtel-en-Bray, France 28/D3
Neugersdorf, E. Germany 22/F3
Neuhausen am Rheinfall, Switzerland 39/G1
Neuhorst, Sask. 181/E3
Neuilly-sur-Seine, France 28/A1
Neu-Isenburg, W. Germany 22/C3
Neumarkt am Wallersee, Austria 41/B3
Neumarkt in der Oberpfalz, W. Germany 22/D4
Neumarkt in Steiermark, Austria 41/C3
Neumünster, W. Germany 22/C1
Neunkirch, Switzerland 39/F1
Neunkirchen, Austria 41/C3
Neunkirchen, W. Germany 22/B4
Neuquén (prov.), Argentina 143/C4
Neuquén, Argentina 143/C4
Neuquén, Argentina 120/C6
Neuquén (riv.), Argentina 143/C4
Neuruppin, E. Germany 22/E2
Neuse, N.C. (27561) 281/M3
Neuse (riv.), N.C. 281/R5
Neusiedl am See, Austria 41/D3
Neusiedler See (lake), Austria 41/D3
Neusiedler See (lake), Hungary 41/D3
Neuss, W. Germany 22/B3
Neustadt, E. Germany 22/D3
Neustadt, Ontario 177/D3
Neustadt (Titisee-Neustadt), W. Germany 22/C5
Neustadt an der Aisch, W. Germany 22/D4
Neustadt an der Weinstrasse, W. Germany 22/B4
Neustadt bei Coburg, W. Germany 22/D3
Neustadt-Glewe, E. Germany 22/D2
Neustadt in Holstein, W. Germany 22/D1
Neustift im Stubaital, Austria 41/A3
Neustrelitz, E. Germany 22/E2
NEUTRAL ZONE 59/E4
Neutral Zone 54/F7
Neu-Ulm, W. Germany 22/D4
Neuville, Québec 172/F3
Neuwerk (isl.), W. Germany 22/C2
Neuwied, W. Germany 22/B3
Neva, Tenn. (†37689) 237/T8
Nevada 188/C3
NEVADA 266
Nevada (co.), Ark. 202/D6
Nevada (co.), Calif. 204/E4
Nevada, Sierra (mts.), Calif. 204/E4
Nevada, Iowa (50201) 229/G5
Nevada, Mo. (64772) 261/D7
Nevada, Ohio (44849) 284/D4
Nevada, Sierra (mts.), Spain 33/E4
Nevada (state), U.S. 146/G6
Nevada City, Calif. (95959) 204/D4
Nevatim, Israel 65/B5
Nevel', U.S.S.R. 52/D3
Nevele, Belgium 27/D6
Nevel'sk, U.S.S.R. 48/P5
Nevers, France 28/E4
Neversink (res.), N.Y. 276/L7
Nevertire, N.S. Wales 97/D2
Nevesinje, Yugoslavia 45/D4
Neville, Ohio (45156) 284/B8
Neville, Sask. 181/D6
Nevils, Georgia (†30458) 217/J6
Nevinnomyssk, U.S.S.R. 52/F6
Nevinville, Iowa (50856) 229/D6
Nevis, Alberta 182/D3
Nevis, Minn. (56467) 255/D4
Nevis (isl.), St. Chris.-Nevis 161/D11
Nevis (isl.), St. Chris.-Nevis 156/F3
Nevis (peak), St. Chris.-Nevis 161/D11
Nevis, Loch (inlet), Scotland 15/C3
Nevisdale, Ky. (40754) 237/N7
Nevşehir (prov.), Turkey 63/F3
Nevşehir, Turkey 59/B2
Nevşehir, Turkey 63/F3
New (riv.), Belize 154/C2
New (riv.), Calif. 204/K11
New (for.), England 13/F6
New (riv.), Fla. 212/D1
New (riv.), Fla. 212/B1
New (riv.), Guyana 131/C4
New, South Fork (riv.), N.C. 281/G2
New (riv.), N.C. 281/O5
New (riv.), S.C. 296/E6
New (inlet), Va. 307/S6
New (riv.), Va. 307/F8
New (riv.), W. Va. 312/E7
New Abbey, Scotland 15/E6
New Agat, Guam 86/K7
Newagen, Maine (04552) 243/D8
Newala, Tanzania 115/G6
New Albany, Ind. 188/J3
New Albany, Ind. (47150) 227/F8
New Albany, Kansas (66759) 232/G4
New Albany, Miss. (38652) 256/G2
New Albany, Ohio (43054) 284/E5
New Albany, Pa. (18833) 294/J2
New Albin, Iowa (52160) 229/L2
Newald, Wis. (54551) 317/J4
New Alexandria, Ohio (†43938) 284/J5
New Alexandria, Pa. (15670) 294/C5
Newalla, Okla. (74857) 288/M4
New Alluwe, Okla. (74049) 288/R1
New Almaden, Calif. (95042) 204/L4
New Almelo, Kansas (67652) 232/B2
New Amsterdam, Guyana 120/D2
New Amsterdam, Guyana 131/B2
New Amsterdam, Ind. (†47110) 227/E8
New Amsterdam, Wis. (†54636) 317/C8
New Angledool, N.S. Wales 97/E1
Newark, Ark. (72562) 202/H2
Newark, Calif. (94560) 204/K3
Newark, Del. (19711) 245/P2
Newark, England 13/G4
Newark, England 10/F4
Newark, Ill. (60541) 222/E2
Newark, Md. (21841) 245/S7
Newark, Mo. (63458) 261/H2
Newark, N.J. 188/L2
Newark, N.J. (*07101) 273/B2
Newark (bay), N.J. 273/B2
Newark, N.Y. (14513) 276/G4
Newark, Ohio (43055) 284/F5
Newark, S. Dak. (†57453) 298/O2
Newark, Texas (76071) 303/E1
Newark○, Vt. (†05871) 268/D2
Newark, W. Va. (†26143) 312/D4
Newark Int'l Airport, N.J. 273/B2
Newark Valley, N.Y. (13811) 276/H6
Newarthill, Scotland 15/C2
New Athens, Ill. (62264) 222/D5
New Athens, Ohio (43981) 284/H5
New Auburn, Minn. (55366) 255/D6
New Auburn, Wis. (54757) 317/D5
New Augusta, Miss. (39462) 256/F8
Newaygo (co.), Mich. 250/D5
Newaygo, Mich. (49337) 250/D5
New Baden, Ill. (62265) 222/D5
New Baltimore, Mich. (48047) 250/G6
New Baltimore, N.Y. (12124) 276/N6
New Baltimore, Pa. (15553) 294/E6
New Baltimore, Va. (†22186) 307/N3
New Bavaria, Ohio (43548) 284/B3
New Beaver, Pa. (†16141) 294/B4
New Bedford, Ill. (61346) 222/D2
New Bedford, Mass. 188/N2
New Bedford, Mass. (*02740) 249/K6
New Bedford, Ohio (†43824) 284/G5
New Bedford, Pa. (16140) 294/A3
New Bellsville, Ind. (†47448) 227/E6
Newberg, Oreg. (97132) 291/A2
New Berlin, Ill. (62670) 222/D4
New Berlin, N.Y. (13411) 276/K5
New Berlin, Pa. (17855) 294/J4
New Berlin, Wis. (53151) 317/K2
Newbern, Ala. (36765) 195/C5
Newbern, Ind. (†47201) 227/F6
New Bern, N.C. 188/L4
New Bern, N.C. (28560) 281/P4
Newbern, Tenn. (38059) 237/C8
Newberne, W. Va. (26409) 312/E4
Newberry, Fla. (32669) 212/D2
Newberry, Ind. (47449) 227/C7
Newberry, Mich. (49868) 250/D2
Newberry (co.), S.C. 296/D3
Newberry, S.C. (29108) 296/D3
Newberry Springs, Calif. (92365) 204/J9
New Bethlehem, Pa. (16242) 294/D3
Newbiggin-by-the-Sea, England 13/F2
New Blaine, Ark. (72851) 202/D3
Newbliss, Ireland 17/G3
New Bloomfield, Mo. (65063) 261/J5
New Bloomfield, Pa. (17068) 294/H5
New Bloomington, Ohio (43341) 284/D4
New Bonaventure, Newf. 166/D2
Newborn, Georgia (30262) 217/E3
Newboro, Ontario 177/H3
New Boston, Ill. (61272) 222/B2
New Boston, Mich. (48164) 250/F6
New Boston, Mo. (63557) 261/G3
New Boston○, N.H. (03070) 268/D6
New Boston, Ohio (45662) 284/E8
New Boston, Texas (75570) 303/K4
New Bothwell, Manitoba 179/F5
New Braintree○, Mass. (01531) 249/F3
New Braunfels, Texas (78130) 303/K10
New Bremen, N.Y. (13412) 276/K3
New Bremen, Ohio (45869) 284/B5
Newbridge (Droichead Nua), Ireland 17/H5
New Bridge, Oreg. (†97870) 291/K3
New Brigden, Alberta 182/E4
New Brighton, Minn. (55112) 255/G5
New Brighton, Pa. (15066) 294/B4
New Britain, Conn. (*06050) 210/E2
New Britain (isl.), Papua N.G. 87/F6
New Britain (isl.), Papua N.G. 85/C7
New Britain (isl.), Papua N.G. 86/B2

N'Gounié 417

New Britain, Pa. (18901) 294/M5
New Brockton, Ala. (36351) 195/G8
Newbrook, Alberta 182/D2
New Brunswick (prov.) 162/K6
New Brunswick (prov.), Canada 146/M5
NEW BRUNSWICK 170
New Brunswick, N.J. (*08901) 273/E3
New Buena Vista, Pa. (†15550) 294/E5
New Buffalo, Mich. (49117) 250/C7
New Buffalo, Pa. (17069) 294/H5
Newburg, Ark. (72556) 202/G1
Newburg, Iowa (†50135) 229/H5
Newburg, Md. (20664) 245/L7
Newburg, Mo. (65550) 261/J7
Newburg, N. Dak. (58762) 282/J2
Newburg, Pa. (17240) 294/G5
Newburg (La Jose), Pa. (†15753) 294/E4
Newburg, W. Va. (26410) 312/G4
Newburg, Wis. (53060) 317/K9
Newburgh, Ind. (47630) 227/C9
Newburgh○, Maine (†04445) 243/F6
Newburgh, N.Y. 188/M2
Newburgh, N.Y. (12550) 276/M7
Newburgh, Ontario 177/H3
Newburgh, Scotland 10/E2
Newburgh, Grampian, Scotland 15/G3
Newburgh, Fife, Scotland 15/E4
Newburgh Heights, Ohio (†44101) 284/H9
New Burlington, Ind. (†47302) 227/G4
New Burlington, Ohio (†45201) 284/B9
New Burnside, Ill. (62967) 222/E6
Newbury, England 13/F6
Newbury, England 10/F5
Newbury○, Mass. (01950) 249/L1
Newbury○, N.H. (03255) 268/C5
Newbury, Ohio (44065) 284/H3
Newbury, Ontario 177/C5
Newbury, Vt. (05051) 268/C3
Newbury○, Vt. (05051) 268/C3
Newburyport, Mass. (01950) 249/L1
New Bussa, Nigeria 106/E6
New Caledonia (isl.) 2/T7
NEW CALEDONIA 86
New Caledonia 87/G8
New Caledonia (isl.), New Caled. 87/G8
New Caledonia (isl.), New Caled. 86/G4
New Cambria, Kansas (67470) 232/E3
New Cambria, Mo (63558) 261/G3
New Canaan○, Conn. (06840) 210/B4
New Canton, Ill. (62356) 222/B4
New Canton, Va. (23123) 307/M5
New Carlisle, Ind. (46552) 227/E1
New Carlisle, Ohio (45344) 284/C6
New Carlisle, Québec 172/D2
New Carlisle, Québec 174/E3
New Carrollton, Md. (20784) 245/G4
New Castile (reg.), Spain 33/E3
Newcastle, Australia 2/S7
Newcastle, Calif. (95658) 204/C8
New Castle, Colo. (81647) 208/E3
New Castle (co.), Del. 245/R2
New Castle, Del. (19720) 245/R2
New Castle, Ind. (47362) 227/G5
Newcastle, Ireland 10/B4
Newcastle, Ireland 17/D7
New Castle, Ky. (40050) 237/L4
Newcastle○, Maine (04553) 243/D7
Newcastle, N. Br. 162/K6
Newcastle, N. S. Wales 88/J6
Newcastle, Nebr. (68757) 264/H2
Newcastle, New Bruns. 170/E2
New Castle○, N.H. (03854) 268/F5
Newcastle, N.S. Wales 97/F3
Newcastle, N. Ireland 10/D3
Newcastle, N. Ireland 17/J3
Newcastle (creek), North. Terr. 93/C4
New Castle, Ohio (†43843) 284/F5
Newcastle, Okla. (73065) 288/L4
Newcastle, Ontario 177/F4
New Castle, Pa. 188/K2
New Castle, Pa. (*16101) 294/B3
Newcastle, St. Chris.-Nevis 161/D11
Newcastle, S. Africa 118/E5
Newcastle, Texas (76372) 303/F4
Newcastle, Utah (84756) 304/A6
New Castle, Va. (24127) 307/H5
Newcastle, Wyo. (82701) 319/H2
Newcastle Creek, New Bruns. 170/D2
Newcastle-Damariscotta, Maine (04553) 243/E7
Newcastle Emlyn, Wales 13/C5
Newcastleton, Scotland 15/F5
Newcastle-under-Lyme, England 13/E4
Newcastle-under-Lyme, England 10/E4
Newcastle upon Tyne, England 7/D3
Newcastle upon Tyne, England 10/E3
Newcastle upon Tyne, England 13/H3
Newcastle Waters, North. Terr. 93/C4
New Centerville, Pa. (†15557) 294/D6
New Chelsea, Newf. 166/D2
New Chicago, Ind. (†46342) 227/C1
New Church, Va. (23415) 307/S5
New Cinema, Br. Col. 184/F3
New City, N.Y. (10956) 276/K8
New Columbia, Pa. (17856) 294/H3
New Columbus, Pa. (†17878) 294/K3
Newcomb, N. Mex. (†87325) 274/A2
Newcomb, N.Y. (12852) 276/M3
Newcomb, Tenn. (37819) 237/N7
Newcomerstown, Ohio (43832) 284/G5
New Concord, Ky. (42076) 237/E7
New Concord, Ohio (43762) 284/G6
New Cordell (Cordell), Okla. (†73632) 288/H4
New Corydon, Ind. (†47326) 227/H3
New Court, Mo. (†63452) 261/J2
New Creek, W. Va. (26743) 312/J4
New Cumberland, Pa. (17070) 294/J5
New Cumberland, W. Va. (26047) 312/E2
New Cumnock, Scotland 15/D5
Newdale, Idaho (83436) 220/G6
Newdale, Manitoba 179/B4
New Dayton, Alberta 182/D5
New Deal, Texas (79350) 303/C4
New Deer, Scotland 15/F3
Newdegate, W. Australia 92/B6
New Delhi (cap.), India 2/N4
New Delhi, India 54/J7
New Delhi (cap.), India 68/D3
New Denmark, New Bruns. 170/C1
New Denver, Br. Col. 184/J5
New Diggings, Wis. (†61075) 317/F10
New Douglas, Ill. (62074) 222/D5
New Dover, Ohio (†43040) 284/D5
New Durham○, N.H. (03855) 268/E5
New Eagle, Pa. (15067) 294/B5
New Edinburg, Ark. (71660) 202/F6
New Effington, S. Dak. (57255) 298/R2
New Egypt, N.J. (08533) 273/E3
Newell, Ala. (36270) 195/H4
Newell (lake), Alberta 182/E4
Newell, Iowa (50568) 229/D3
Newell, S. Dak. (57760) 298/C4
Newell, W. Va. (26050) 312/E1
New Ellenton, S.C. (29809) 296/D5
Newellton, La. (71357) 238/H2
Newellton, Nova Scotia 168/C5
New England (range), N.S. Wales 97/F1
New England, N. Dak. (58647) 282/E6
New England, W. Va. (26154) 312/C4
Newenham (cape), Alaska 196/F3
New Enterprise, Pa. (16664) 294/F5
New Era, La. (†71354) 238/G4
New Era, Mich. (49446) 250/C5
New Era, Oreg. (†97013) 291/B2
Newe Yam, Israel 65/B2
Newe Zohar, Israel 65/C5
New Fairfield○, Conn. (06810) 210/B3
Newfane, N.Y. (14108) 276/C4
Newfane, Vt. (05345) 268/B6
Newfane○, Vt. (05345) 268/B6
Newfield, Maine (04056) 243/B8
Newfield○, Maine (04056) 243/B8
Newfield, N.J. (08344) 273/D4
Newfield, N.Y. (14867) 276/G6
Newfields○, N.H. (03856) 268/F5
New Fish Creek, Alberta 182/B2
New Florence, Mo. (63363) 261/K5
New Florence, Pa. (15944) 294/D5
Newfolden, Minn. (56738) 255/B2
New Fork (lakes), Wyo. 319/C2
Newfound (lake), N.H. 268/D4
Newfoundland (prov.) 162/L5
Newfoundland (isl.) 162/L6
Newfoundland (prov.), Canada 146/M4
Newfoundland (isl.), Canada 2/G3
Newfoundland, Ky. (41162) 237/P4
NEWFOUNDLAND 166
Newfoundland (isl.), Newf. 166/C4
Newfoundland (isl.), Newf. 146/N5
Newfoundland, N.J. (07435) 273/D1
Newfoundland, Pa. (18445) 294/M3
Newfoundland (mts.), Utah 304/A2
New Franken, Wis. (54229) 317/L6
New Frankfort, Mo. (†65349) 261/F4
New Franklin, Mo. (65274) 261/G4
New Freedom, Pa. (17349) 294/J6
New Freeport, Pa. (15352) 294/B6
New Galilee, Pa. (16141) 294/A4
New Galloway, Scotland 10/D3
New Galloway, Scotland 15/D5
Newgate, Br. Col. 184/K5
New Georgia (isl.), Solomon Is. 87/F6
New Georgia (isl.), Solomon Is. 86/D3
New Germantown, Pa. (17071) 294/G5
New Germany, Minn. (55367) 255/E6
New Germany, Nova Scotia 168/D4
New Glarus, Wis. (53574) 317/G10
New Glasgow, Nova Scotia 168/F3
New Glasgow, Québec 172/D4
New Gloucester, Maine (04260) 243/C8
New Gloucester○, Maine (04260) 243/C8
New Goshen, Ind. (47863) 227/B5
New Gretna, N.J. (08224) 273/E4
New Guinea (isl.) 2/S6
New Guinea (isl.) 54/P10
New Guinea (isl.) 87/E6
New Guinea (isl.), Papua N.G. 86/B2
Newgulf, Texas (77462) 303/J8
Newhalem, Wash. (†98283) 310/D2
Newhalen, Alaska (†99606) 196/H3
Newhall, Calif. (91321) 204/G9
Newhall, Iowa (52315) 229/K5
Newhall, W. Va. (24866) 312/C8
Newham, England 13/H8
Newham, England 10/B5
New Hamburg, Mo. (†63736) 261/O8
New Hamburg, Ontario 177/D4
New Hampshire 188/M2
NEW HAMPSHIRE 268
New Hampshire, Ohio (45870) 284/C4
New Hampshire (state), U.S. 146/L5
New Hampton, Iowa (50659) 229/J2
New Hampton, Mo. (64471) 261/D2
New Hampton○, N.H. (03256) 268/D4
New Hampton, N.J. (†08827) 273/D2
New Hanover (co.), N.C. 281/O6
New Hanover (Lavongai) (isl.), Papua N.G. 87/F6
New Hanover (isl.), Papua N.G. 86/B1
New Harbor, Maine (04554) 243/E8
New Harbour, Newf. 166/C4
New Harbour, Newf. 166/D2
New Harbour, Nova Scotia 168/G3
New Harmony, Ind. (47631) 227/B8
New Harmony, Utah (84757) 304/A6
New Hartford, Conn. (06057) 210/C1
New Hartford○, Conn. (06057) 210/C1
New Hartford, Iowa (50660) 229/H3
New Hartford, Mo. (63364) 261/K4
New Hartford, N.Y. (13413) 276/K4
New Haven, Conn. 188/M2
New Haven (co.), Conn. 210/D3
New Haven, Conn. (*06501) 210/D3
New Haven (harb.), Conn. 210/D3
Newhaven, England 10/F5
Newhaven, England 13/H7
New Haven, Ill. (62867) 222/E6
New Haven, Ind. (46774) 227/H2
New Haven, Ky. (40051) 237/K5
New Haven, Mich. (48048) 250/G6
New Haven, Mo. (63068) 261/K5
New Haven, N.Y. (13121) 276/H4
New Haven, Nova Scotia 168/H2
New Haven, Ohio (44850) 284/E3
New Haven○, Vt. (05472) 268/A3
New Haven, W. Va. (25265) 312/C5
New Haven, Wyo. (†82720) 319/H1
New Hazelton, Br. Col. 184/D2
New Hebrides (Vanuatu) 87/G7
Newhebron, Miss. (39140) 256/D7
New Hill, N.C. (27562) 281/M3
New Holland, Georgia (†30501) 217/E2
New Holland, Ill. (62671) 222/D3
New Holland, N.C. (27885) 281/S4
New Holland, Ohio (43145) 284/D6
New Holland, Pa. (17557) 294/K5
New Holland, S. Dak. (57364) 298/M7
New Holstein, Wis. (53061) 317/K8
New Home, Texas (79383) 303/C4
New Hope, Ala. (35760) 195/F1
Newhope, Ark. (71959) 202/C5
New Hope, Ky. (40052) 237/L5
New Hope, Minn. (†55428) 255/G5
New Hope, Ohio (†45320) 284/A6
New Hope, Pa. (18938) 294/N5
New Hope, Tenn. (†37380) 237/K11
New Hope, Va. (24469) 307/L4
New Horse Springs, N. Mex. (†87821) 274/A5
New Houlka (Houlka), Miss. (38850) 256/G2
New Hradec, N. Dak. (58648) 282/E5
New Hyde Park, N.Y. (11040) 276/P7
New Iberia, La. (70560) 238/G6
Newington○, Conn. (06111) 210/E2
Newington, Georgia (30446) 217/J5
Newington○, N.H. (†03801) 268/F5
Newington, Ontario 177/K2
Newington, Va. (22122) 307/S3
New Ipswich○, N.H. (03071) 268/D6
New Ireland (isl.), Papua N.G. 87/F6
New Ireland (isl.), Papua N.G. 86/B1
New Jersey 188/M3
NEW JERSEY 273
New Jersey, New Bruns. 170/E1
New Jersey (state), U.S. 146/L5
New Johnsonville, Tenn. (37134) 237/E8
New Kensington, Pa. (15068) 294/C4
New Kent (co.), Va. 307/P5
New Kent, Va. (23124) 307/P5
Newkirk, N. Mex. (88431) 274/E3
Newkirk, Okla. (74647) 288/N1
New Knoxville, Ohio (45871) 284/B5
New Laguna, N. Mex. (87038) 274/B4
New Lancaster, Kansas (†66040) 232/H3
Newland, Ind. (†47978) 227/C2
Newland, N.C. (28657) 281/F2
New Lebanon, Ind. (47864) 227/C6
New Lebanon, N.Y. (12125) 276/O6
New Lebanon, Ohio (45345) 284/B6
New Lebanon, Pa. (†16145) 294/B3
New Leipzig, N. Dak. (58562) 282/G7
New Lenox, Ill. (60451) 222/B6
New Lexington, Ohio (43764) 284/F6
New Liberty, Iowa (52765) 229/M5
New Liberty, Ky. (40355) 237/M3
New Lima, Okla. (74884) 288/O4
New Limerick○, Maine (04761) 243/G3
Newlin, Texas (†79245) 303/D3
New Lisbon, Ind. (47366) 227/G5
New Lisbon, N.J. (08064) 273/D4
New Lisbon, Wis. (53950) 317/F8
New Liskeard, Ont. 162/H6
New Liskeard, Ontario 177/K5
New Liskeard, Ontario 175/E3
Newllano, La. (71461) 238/D4
New London, Ark. (†71765) 202/F7
New London, Conn. 188/M2
New London (co.), Conn. 210/G2
New London, Conn. (06320) 210/G3
New London, Ind. (†46979) 227/E4
New London, Iowa (52645) 229/L7
New London, Minn. (56273) 255/C5
New London, Mo. (63459) 261/K3
New London, N.H. (03257) 268/D5
New London○, N.H. (03257) 268/D5
New London, N.C. (28127) 281/J4
New London, Ohio (44851) 284/F3
New London (bay), Pr. Edward I. 168/E2
New London, Texas (75682) 303/K5
New London, Wis. (54961) 317/J7
New Lothrop, Mich. (48460) 250/F5
New Lowell, Ontario 177/E3
New Lyme, Ohio (44066) 284/J2
New Lynn, N. Zealand 100/B1
New Madison, Ohio (45346) 284/A6
New Madrid (co.), Mo. 261/N9
New Madrid, Mo. (63869) 261/O9
Newmains, Scotland 15/C2
Newman, Calif. (95360) 204/D6
Newman, Ill. (61942) 222/B6
Newman, Ky. (†42301) 237/G5
Newman (sound), Newf. 166/D2
Newman, W. Australia 88/C4
Newman (lake), Wash. 310/H3
Newman, W. Australia 92/B3
New Manchester, W. Va. (26056) 312/E1
Newman Grove, Nebr. (68758) 264/G3
Newman Lake, Wash. (99025) 310/J3
Newmans Cove, Newf. 166/D2
New Marion, Ind. (†47023) 227/G6
New Market, Ala. (35761) 195/F1
Newmarket, England 13/H5
Newmarket, England 10/G4
New Market, Ind. (47965) 227/D5
New Market, Iowa (51646) 229/D7
Newmarket, Ireland 10/B4
Newmarket, Ireland 17/C7
Newmarket, Jamaica 158/H6
New Market, Md. (21774) 245/J3
New Market, Minn. (55054) 255/E6
New Market, Mo. (†64439) 261/C4
New Market, New Bruns. 170/D3
Newmarket, N.H. (03857) 268/F5
Newmarket○, N.H. (03857) 268/F5
New Market, Ohio (†45133) 284/C7
Newmarket, Ontario 177/E3
Newmarket, Queensland 88/K2
Newmarket, Queensland 95/D2
Newmarket, Scotland 15/B2
New Market, Tenn. (37820) 237/O8
New Market, Va. (22844) 307/L3
Newmarket-on-Fergus, Ireland 17/D6
New Marlborough○, Mass. (†01230) 249/B4
New Martinsburg, Ohio (†43160) 284/D7
New Martinsville, W. Va. (26155) 312/E3
New Maryland, New Bruns. 170/D3
New Matamoras, Ohio (45767) 284/J6
New Meadows, Idaho (83654) 220/B4
New Melle, Mo. (63365) 261/L5
New Memphis, Ill. (62266) 222/D5
Newmerella, Victoria 97/E5
New Mexico 188/E4
NEW MEXICO 274
New Mexico (state), U.S. 146/H6
New Miami, Ohio (45011) 284/A7
New Middleton, Tenn. (†38563) 237/J8
New Middletown, Ind. (47160) 227/E8
New Middletown, Ohio (44442) 284/J4
New Milford, Conn. (06776) 210/B2
New Milford○, Conn. (06776) 210/B2
New Milford, N.J. (07646) 273/B1
New Milford, Ohio (†44272) 284/H3
New Milford, Pa. (18834) 294/L2
Newmill, Scotland 15/E3
New Mills, England 13/J2
New Mills, England 10/G2
Newmilns and Greenholm, Scotland 15/D5
New Milton, W. Va. (26411) 312/E4
New Minas, Nova Scotia 168/D3
New Minden, Ill. (†62263) 222/D5
New Mount Pleasant, Ind. (†47371) 227/G4
New Munich, Minn. (56356) 255/D5
Newnan, Georgia (30263) 217/C4
Newnans (lake), Fla. 212/D2
New Norcia, W. Australia 92/A5
New Norfolk, Tasmania 88/H8
New Norfolk, Tasmania 99/C4
New Norway, Alberta 182/D3
New Offenburg, Mo. (63661) 261/M7
New Orleans, La. 188/H5
New Orleans, La. 146/K7
New Orleans, La. (*70101) 238/O4
New Orleans, U.S. 2/E4
New Osgoode, Sask. 181/H3
New Oxford, Pa. (17350) 294/H6
New Palestine, Ind. (46163) 227/F5
New Pallas, Ireland 17/E6
New Paltz, N.Y. (12561) 276/M7
New Paris, Ind. (46553) 227/F2
New Paris, Ohio (45347) 284/A6
New Paris, Pa. (15554) 294/E5
New Pass (range), Nev. 266/D3
New Pekin, Ind. (†47165) 227/F7
New Perlican, Newf. 166/D2
New Petersburg, Ohio (†45123) 284/D7
New Philadelphia, Ill. (†61459) 222/C3
New Philadelphia, Ind. (†47167) 227/F7
New Philadelphia, Ohio (44663) 284/G5
New Philadelphia, Pa. (17959) 294/K4
New Pine Creek, Oreg. (97635) 291/G5
New Pitsligo, Scotland 15/F3
New Pittsburg, Ohio (†44691) 284/F4
New Plymouth, Idaho (83655) 220/B6
New Plymouth, N. Zealand 100/D3
New Plymouth, Ohio (45654) 284/F7
New Point, Ind. (47263) 227/G6
New Point, Mo. (64473) 261/B2
Newport, Ark. (72112) 202/H2
Newport, Del. (19804) 245/R2
Newport, England 13/F7
Newport, England 13/E5
Newport, England 10/F5
Newport, Ind. (47966) 227/C5
Newport, Mayo, Ireland 17/C4
Newport, Tipperary, Ireland 17/E6
Newport, Ky. (*41071) 237/S2
Newport, Ky. 188/K3
Newport, Maine (04953) 243/E6
Newport○, Maine (04953) 243/E6
Newport, Md. (†20622) 245/L7
Newport, Minn. (55055) 255/F6
Newport, Miss. (†38641) 256/D1
Newport, Nebr. (68759) 264/E2
New Port, Neth. Ant. 161/G9
Newport, N.H. (03773) 268/C5
Newport○, N.H. (03773) 268/C5
Newport, N.J. (08345) 273/C5
Newport, N.Y. (13416) 276/K4
Newport, N.C. (28570) 281/R5
Newport, Nova Scotia 168/E3
Newport, Ohio (†43140) 284/C6
Newport, Ohio (45768) 284/H7
Newport, Oreg. (97365) 291/C3
Newport, Pa. (17074) 294/H5
Newport, Québec 172/D2
Newport, R.I. 188/M2
Newport (co.), R.I. 249/K6
Newport, R.I. (02840) 249/J7
Newport, Tenn. (37821) 237/P9
Newport, Texas (76254) 303/F4
Newport, Vt. (05855) 268/C2
Newport○, Vt. (05855) 268/C2
Newport, Va. (24128) 307/H6
Newport, Wales 10/E5
Newport, Dyfed, Wales 13/C5
Newport, Gwent, Wales 13/B6
Newport, Wash. (99156) 310/H2
Newport Beach, Calif. (*92660) 204/D11
Newport Center, Vt. (05857) 268/C2
New Portland, Maine (04954) 243/C6
New Portland○, Maine (04954) 243/C6
Newport News, Va. 188/L3
Newport News (I.C.), Va. (*23601) 307/P6
Newport-on-Tay, Scotland 15/F4
Newport Pagnell, England 13/G5
New Port Richey, Fla. (*33552) 212/D3
New Prague, Minn. (56071) 255/E6
New Preston, Conn. (06777) 210/B2
New Providence (isl.), Bahamas 156/C1
New Providence (Borden), Ind. (†47106) 227/F8
New Providence, Iowa (50206) 229/G4
New Providence, N.J. (07974) 273/E2
New Providence, Pa. (17560) 294/K6
New Prue (Prue), Okla. (†74060) 288/O2
Newquay, England 10/D5
Newquay, England 13/B7
New Quay, Wales 10/D4
New Quay, Wales 13/C5
New Raymer, Colo. (80742) 208/M1
New Richland, Minn. (56072) 255/E7
New Richmond, Ind. (47967) 227/D4
New Richmond, Ohio (45157) 284/B8
New Richmond, Québec 172/C2
New Richmond, Wis. (54017) 317/A5
New Riegel, Ohio (44853) 284/D3
New River, N.C. (28540) 281/O5
New River (inlet), N.C. 281/P6
New River, Tenn. (†37755) 237/M8
New River, Va. (24129) 307/G6
New River Beach, New Bruns. 170/D3
New Road, Nova Scotia 168/E4
New Roads, La. (70760) 238/G5
New Rochelle, N.Y. (*10801) 276/P7
New Rockford, N. Dak. (58356) 282/N4
New Romney, England 13/J7
New Ross, Ind. (47968) 227/D5
New Ross, Ireland 10/C4
New Ross, Ireland 17/H7
New Ross, Nova Scotia 168/D4
Newry, Maine (04261) 243/B6
Newry○, Maine (04261) 243/B6
Newry, N. Ireland 17/J3
Newry, N. Ireland 10/C3
Newry, North. Terr. 93/A3
Newry, Pa. (16665) 294/F5
Newry, S.C. (29665) 296/B2
New Salem, Ill. (62357) 222/C4
New Salem, Ind. (†46173) 227/G5
New Salem, Kansas (†67156) 232/F4
New Salem○, Mass. (01355) 249/E2
New Salem, N. Dak. (58563) 282/G6
New Salem, Nova Scotia 168/D3
New Salem, Ohio (†43148) 284/E6
New Salem, Pa. (15468) 294/C6
New Salem (Delmont), Pa. (†15626) 294/D5
New Salisbury, Ind. (47161) 227/E8
New Sarepta, Alberta 182/D3
New Sarpy, La. (70078) 238/N4
New Schwabenland (reg.) 5/B1
New Scone, Scotland 15/E4
New Sharon, Iowa (50207) 229/H6
New Sharon○, Maine (04955) 243/C6
New Sharon, N.J. (†08691) 273/D3
New Shoreham (Block Island)○, R.I. (†02807) 249/H8
New Siberian (isls.), U.S.S.R. 54/R2
New Siberian (isls.), U.S.S.R. 4/B2
New Siberian (isls.), U.S.S.R. 2/S2
New Siberian (isls.), U.S.S.R. 48/P2
New Site, Ala. (†35010) 195/G4
New Site, Miss. (38859) 256/H1
New Smyrna Beach, Fla. (32069) 212/F2
Newsoms, Va. (23874) 307/O7
New South Wales, /H6
New South Wales (state), Australia 87/E9
NEW SOUTH WALES 97
New Spadra, Ark. (†72830) 202/C3
New Square, N.Y. (†10901) 276/K8
New Stanton, Pa. (15672) 294/C5
New Straitsville, Ohio (43766) 284/F6
New Strawn (Strawn), Kansas (66839) 232/G3
New Stuyahok, Alaska (99636) 196/G3
New Sweden, Maine (04762) 243/G2
New Sweden○, Maine (04762) 243/G2
New Tazewell, Tenn. (37825) 237/O8
Newtok, Alaska (99681) 196/F2
Newton, Ala. (36352) 195/G8
Newton (co.), Ark. 202/D2
Newton (co.), Georgia 217/E3
Newton, Georgia (31770) 217/D8
Newton, Ill. (62448) 222/E5
Newton (co.), Ind. 227/C3
Newton, Iowa 188/H2
Newton, Iowa (50208) 229/H5
Newton, Kansas (67114) 232/E3
Newton, Mass. (†02158) 249/C7
Newton (co.), Miss. 256/F6
Newton, Miss. (39345) 256/F6
Newton (co.), Mo. 261/D9
Newton○, N.H. (03858) 268/E6
Newton, N.J. (07860) 273/D1
Newton, N.C. (28658) 281/G3
Newton, Québec 172/C4
Newton, Scotland 15/E5
Newton (co.), Texas 303/L7
Newton, Texas (75966) 303/L7
Newton, Utah (84327) 304/C2
Newton, W. Va. (25266) 312/D5
Newton Abbot, England 13/D7
Newton Abbot, England 10/E5
Newton Center, Mass. (02159) 249/C7
Newton Falls, N.Y. (13666) 276/K2
Newton Falls, Ohio (44444) 284/J3
Newtongrange, Scotland 15/D2
Newton Grove, N.C. (28366) 281/N4
Newton Hamilton, Pa. (17075) 294/G5
Newton Highlands, Mass. (02161) 249/C7
Newtonia, Mo. (64853) 261/D9
Newton Junction, N.H. (03859) 268/E6
Newton-le-Willows, England 13/F2
Newton Lower Falls, Mass. (†02162) 249/B7
Newton Mearns, Scotland 15/B2
Newton Mills, Nova Scotia 168/F3
Newtonmore, Scotland 15/D3
Newton Siding, Manitoba 179/D5
Newton Stewart, Scotland 10/D3
Newton Stewart, Scotland 15/D6
Newtonsville, Ohio (45158) 284/B7
Newton Upper Falls, Mass. (†02164) 249/C7
Newtonville, Ind. (47632) 227I)D8
Newtonville, Mass. (02160) 249/C7
Newtonville, N.J. (08346) 273/D4
Newtown, Conn. (06470) 210/B3
Newtown○, Conn. (06470) 210/B3
Newtown, Ind. (47969) 227/C4
Newtown, Ky. (†40324) 237/N4
Newtown, Mo. (64667) 261/F2
Newtown, New Bruns. 170/E3
Newtown, Newf. 166/D4
Newtown, N.S. Wales 97/C6
New Town, N. Dak. (58763) 282/F4
Newtown, Ohio (45244) 284/C10
Newtown, Pa. (18940) 294/N5
New Town, S.C. (†29536) 296/J3
Newtown, Victoria 97/C6
Newtown, Wales 13/D5
Newtown, Wales 10/E4
Newtownabbey (dist.), N. Ireland 17/J2
Newtownabbey, N. Ireland 17/K2
Newtownards, N. Ireland 17/K2
Newtownbutler, N. Ireland 17/G3
Newtown Forbes, Ireland 17/F4
Newtownhamilton, N. Ireland 17/H3
Newtownmountkennedy, Ireland 17/J5
Newtown Saint Boswells, Scotland 15/F5
Newtownsandes, Ireland 17/C6
Newtown Square○, Pa. (19073) 294/L6
Newtownstewart, N. Ireland 17/G2
New Trenton, Ind. (47035) 227/H6
New Trier, Minn. (†55031) 255/F6
New Tripoli, Pa. (18066) 294/L4
New Troy, Mich. (49119) 250/C7
New Tulsa, Okla. (†74080) 288/P2
Newtyle, Scotland 15/E4
New Ulm, Minn. (56073) 255/D6
New Ulm, Texas (78950) 303/H8
New Underwood, S. Dak. (57761) 298/D5
New Vernon, N.J. (07976) 273/D2
New Victoria, Nova Scotia 168/H2
New Vienna, Iowa (52065) 229/L3
New Vienna, Ohio (45159) 284/C7
Newville, Ala. (36353) 195/H8
Newville, Ind. (†46721) 227/H2
Newville, Pa. (17241) 294/H5
Newville, W. Va. (26632) 312/E5
New Vineyard○, Maine (04956) 243/C6
New Virginia, Iowa (50210) 229/F6
New Washington, Ind. (47162) 227/F7
New Washington, Ohio (44854) 284/E4
New Washington, Philippines 82/D5
New Waterford, Nova Scotia 168/J2
New Waterford, Ohio (44445) 284/J4
New Waverly, Ind. (46961) 227/E3
New Waverly, Texas (77358) 303/J7
New Westminster, Br. Col. 162/D6
New Westminster, Br. Col. 184/K3
New Weston, Ohio (45348) 284/A5
New Whiteland, Ind. (46184) 227/E5
New Wilmington, Pa. (16142) 294/B3
New Winchester, Ind. (†46122) 227/D5
New Winchester, Ohio (†44820) 284/D4
New Windsor, England 13/G8
New Windsor, England 10/F5
New Windsor, Ill. (61465) 222/C2
New Windsor, Md. (21776) 245/K2
New Windsor, N.Y. (12550) 276/N8
New Witten, S. Dak. (†57584) 298/K7
New Woodstock, N.Y. (13122) 276/J5
New World (isl.), Newf. 166/C4
New York 188/L2
NEW YORK 276
New York, N.Y. 146/L5
New York, N.Y. 188/M2
New York (co.), N.Y. 276/M9
New York, N.Y. (*10001) 276/M9
New York (state), U.S. 146/L5
New York, U.S. 2/F3
New York Mills, Minn. (56567) 255/C4
New York Mills, N.Y. (13417) 276/K4
New York State Barge (canal), N.Y. 276/C4
New Zealand 2/T8
New Zealand 87/G9
NEW ZEALAND 100
New Zion, New Bruns. 170/D2
New Zion, S.C. (29111) 296/H4
Ney, Ohio (43549) 284/B3
Neyagawa, Japan 81/J7
Neyland, Wales 13/B6
Neyriz, Iran 66/J6
Neyshabur, Iran 59/G2
Neyshabur, Iran 66/L2
Nezhin, U.S.S.R. 52/D4
Nez Perce (co.), Idaho 220/B3
Nezperce, Idaho (83543) 220/B3
Nez Perce Nat'l Hist. Park, Idaho 220/B-C3
Nezwar (mt.), Iran 66/H3
Ngabang, Indonesia 85/D5
N'gage, Angola 115/C5
Ngage, Angola 102/D5
Ngahere, N. Zealand 100/C5
Ngami (lake), Botswana 118/C4
Ngamiland (reg.), Botswana 118/C3
Ngamring, China 77/C6
Ngangla Ringco (lake), China 77/B5
Ngangzê Co (lake), China 77/C5
Ngao, Thailand 72/D3
Ngaoundéré, Cameroon 115/B2
Ngaoundéré, Cameroon 102/D4
Ngapara, N. Zealand 100/C6
Ngara, Tanzania 115/F4
Ngaruawahia, N. Zealand 100/E2
Ngatapa, N. Zealand 100/F3
Ngatik (atoll), Micronesia 87/F5
Ngau (isl.), Fiji 86/Q10
Ngauruhoe (mt.), N. Zealand 100/E3
Ngawi, Indonesia 85/K2
Nghia Lo, Vietnam 72/D2
Ngiva, Angola 102/D6
Ngiva, Angola 115/C7
Ngoc Linh (mt.), Vietnam 72/E4
Ngom Qu (riv.), China 77/E5
Ngong, Kenya 115/G4
Ngoring Hu (lake), China 77/E4
Ngorongoro (crater), Tanzania 115/F4
N'Gounié (riv.), Congo 115/B4

418 N'Gounié

N'Gounié (riv.), Gabon 115/B4
Ngourou, Cent. Afr. Rep. 115/D2
N'Guigmi, Niger 106/G6
Ngulu (atoll), Micronesia 87/D5
Ngunju (cape), Indonesia 85/F8
Ngunza, Angola 102/D6
Ngunza, Angola 115/B6
Nguru, Nigeria 102/D3
Nguru, Nigeria 106/G6
Nhâmundá (riv.), Brazil 120/D3
Nhamundá (riv.), Brazil 132/B3
Nharêa, Angola 115/C6
Nharêa, Angola 102/D6
Nha Trang, Vietnam 72/F4
Nha Trang, Vietnam 54/M8
Nhava-Sheva, India 68/B7
Nhill, Victoria 88/G7
Nhill, Victoria 97/A5
Nhulunbuy, North. Terr. 88/F2
Nhulunbuy, North. Terr. 93/E2
Ni (riv.), Va. 307/N4
Niafunké, Mali 106/D5
Niagara (co.), N.Y. 276/C4
Niagara (riv.), N.Y. 276/B4
Niagara, N. Dak. (58266) 282/P4
Niagara (reg. munic.), Ontario 177/E4
Niagara (riv.), Ontario 177/E4
Niagara, Wis. (54151) 317/K4
Niagara Falls, N.Y. 188/K2
Niagara Falls, N.Y. (*14301) 276/C4
Niagara Falls, Ont. 162/J7
Niagara Falls, Ontario 177/E4
Niagara-on-the-Lake, Ontario 177/E4
Niamey (cap.), Niger 2/K5
Niamey (cap.), Niger 102/C3
Niamey (cap.), Niger 106/E6
Niangara, Zaire 115/E3
Niangua, Mo. (65713) 261/G8
Niantic, Conn. (06357) 210/G3
Niantic (riv.), Conn. 210/G3
Niantic, Ill. (62551) 222/D4
Niarada, Mont. (59852) 262/B3
Niari (riv.), Congo 115/B4
Nias (isl.), Indonesia 54/L9
Nias (isl.), Indonesia 85/B5
Niassa (prov.), Mozambique 118/F2
Nibbe, Mont. (†59088) 262/H4
Nibe, Denmark 21/C4
Nibe, Denmark 18/F8
Nibley, Utah (†84321) 304/C2
Nicaragua 2/E5
Nicaragua 146/K8
Nicaragua (lake), Nic. 146/K8
NICARAGUA 154/E4
Nicaragua (lake), Nicaragua 154/E5
Nicaro, Cuba 158/J3
Nicasio, Calif. (94946) 204/H1
Nicastro, Italy 34/F5
Nicatous (lake), Maine 243/G5
Nice, France 7/E4
Nice, France 28/G6
Niceville, Fla. (32578) 212/C6
Nichinan, Japan 81/E8
Nichol (isl.), Nova Scotia 168/F4
Nicholas (chan.), Cuba 156/B2
Nicholas (chan.), Cuba 158/E1
Nicholas (co.), Ky. 237/N4
Nicholas (co.), W. Va. 312/E6
Nicholas Denys, New Bruns. 170/D1
Nicholasville, Ky. (40356) 237/N5
Nicholls, Georgia (31554) 217/G7
Nichols, Conn. (†06611) 210/C4
Nichols, Fla. (33863) 212/E4
Nichols, Iowa (52766) 229/L6
Nichols, Minn. (†56431) 255/E4
Nichols, N.Y. (13812) 276/H6
Nichols, S.C. (29581) 296/J3
Nichols, Wis. (54152) 317/K6
Nichols Hills, Okla. (†73116) 288/L3
Nicholson (riv.) 88/F3
Nicholson, Br. Col. 184/J4
Nicholson, Georgia (30565) 217/F2
Nicholson, Miss. (39463) 256/E10
Nicholson, Port (inlet), N. Zealand 100/B3
Nicholson (riv.), North. Terr. 93/E5
Nicholson, Pa. (18446) 294/L2
Nicholson (riv.), Queensland 95/A3
Nicholson, W. Australia 92/E2
Nicholsville, Ala. (†36784) 195/C6
Nicholville, N.Y. (12965) 276/L1
Nickel Centre, Ontario 175/D3
Nickel Centre, Ontario 177/D1
Nickelsville, Va. (24271) 307/D7
Nickerie (dist.), Suriname 131/C3
Nickerie (riv.), Suriname 131/C3
Nickerson, Kansas (67561) 232/D3
Nickerson, Minn. (†55797) 255/F4
Nickerson, Nebr. (68044) 264/H3
Nicobar (isls.), India 54/L9
Nicobar (isls.), India 68/G7
Nicodemus, Kansas (†67625) 232/C2
Nicola, Br. Col. 184/G5
Nicolaus, Calif. (95659) 204/B8
Nicolet (co.), Québec 172/E3
Nicolet, Québec 172/E3
Nicolet (lake), Québec 172/F4
Nicolet (riv.), Québec 172/E3
Nicollet (co.), Minn. 255/D6
Nicollet, Minn. (56074) 255/D6
Nicoma Park, Okla. (73066) 288/M4
Nicomen Island, Br. Col. 184/L3
Nico Pérez, Uruguay 145/D4
Nicosia (cap.), Cyprus 63/E5
Nicosia (cap.), Cyprus 59/B2
Nicosia (cap.), Cyprus 54/E6
Nicosia, Italy 34/E6
Nicoya, C. Rica 154/E5
Nicoya (gulf), C. Rica 154/E6
Nicoya (pen.), C. Rica 154/E6
Nictau, New Bruns. 170/C1
Nictaux, Nova Scotia 168/D4
Nidau, Switzerland 39/D2
Nidd (riv.), England 10/F3
Nidwalden (canton), Switzerland 39/F3
Nidzica, Poland 47/E2
Niebüll, W. Germany 22/C1
Niederbipp, Switzerland 39/E2
Niedere Tauern (range), Austria 41/B3
Niederurnen, Switzerland 39/G2
Nielsville, Minn. (56568) 255/B3
Niemba, Zaire 115/E5
Niemen (riv.), U.S.S.R. 7/G3
Niemen (riv.), U.S.S.R. 52/B4
Niemen (riv.), U.S.S.R. 53/A3
Nienburg, W. Germany 22/C2
Nieuport (Nieuwpoort), Belgium 27/B6
Nieuw-Amsterdam, Suriname 131/D2
Nieuw-Buinen, Netherlands 27/K3
Nieuwegein, Netherlands 27/G4
Nieuwendam, Netherlands 27/C4
Nieuwe-Pekela, Netherlands 27/L2
Nieuweschans, Netherlands 27/L2
Nieuwkoop, Netherlands 27/F4
Nieuw-Nickerie, Suriname 120/D2
Nieuw-Nickerie, Suriname 131/C2
Nieuwpoort, Belgium 27/B6
Nieuw-Schoonebeek, Netherlands 27/L3
Nieuwveld (range), S. Africa 118/C6
Nieves, Mexico 150/H5
Nièvre (dept.), France 28/E4
Nigadoo, New Bruns. 170/E1
Niğde (prov.), Turkey 63/F4
Niğde, Turkey 59/B2
Niğde, Turkey 63/F4
Nigel, S. Africa 118/J7
Niger 2/K5
Niger 102/C3
Niger (riv.) 2/K5
Niger (riv.) 102/C4
Niger (riv.), Benin 106/E6
Niger (riv.), Guinea 106/C6
Niger (riv.), Mali 106/D5
NIGER 106/F5
Niger (riv.), Niger 106/E6
Niger (state), Nigeria 106/F7
Niger (delta), Nigeria 106/F8
Niger (riv.), Nigeria 106/F7
Nigeria 2/K5
Nigeria 102/C4
NIGERIA 106/F6
Nightcaps, N. Zealand 100/B6
Nighthawk, Wash. (†98855) 310/F2
Nightingale, Alberta 182/D4
Nightingale (mts.), Nev. 266/B2
Nightingale (Bach Long Vi) (isl.), Vietnam 72/F2
Nightmute, Alaska (99690) 196/F2
Nigrita, Greece 45/F5
Nigua (riv.), P. Rico 161/D2
Nihoa (isl.), Hawaii 87/K3
Nihoa (isl.), Hawaii 188/F6
Nihoa (isl.), Hawaii 218/D6
Nii (isl.), Japan 81/J6
Niigata (pref.), Japan 81/J5
Niigata, Japan 54/P6
Niigata, Japan 81/J5
Niihama, Japan 81/F6
Niihau (isl.), Hawaii 87/K3
Niihau (isl.), Hawaii 188/E5
Niihau (isl.), Hawaii 218/A2
Niimi, Japan 81/F6
Niitsu, Japan 81/J5
Níjar, Spain 33/E4
Nijkerk, Netherlands 27/H4
Nijmegen, Netherlands 27/H5
Nijvel (Nivelles), Belgium 27/E7
Nijverdal, Netherlands 27/J4
Nikel', U.S.S.R. 52/C1
Nikep, Md. (21546) 245/C2
Nikki, Benin 106/E7
Nikko National Park, Japan 81/J5
Nikolai, Alaska (99691) 196/H2
Nikolayev, U.S.S.R. 7/H4
Nikolayev, U.S.S.R. 48/D5
Nikolayev, U.S.S.R. 52/D5
Nikolayevsk, U.S.S.R. 2/S3
Nikolayevsk, U.S.S.R. 4/D2
Nikolayevsk, U.S.S.R. 54/P4
Nikolayevsk, U.S.S.R. 52/G4
Nikolayevsk-na-Amure, U.S.S.R. 48/P4
Nikol'sk, U.S.S.R. 52/G3
Nikol'sk, U.S.S.R. 52/G4
Nikolski, Alaska (99638) 196/E4
Nikol'skoye, U.S.S.R. 48/R4
Nikopol, Bulgaria 45/G4
Nikopol', U.S.S.R. 52/D5
Niksar, Turkey 63/G2
Nikshahr, Iran 59/H4
Nikshahr, Iran 66/L7
Nikšić, Yugoslavia 45/D4
Nikumaroro (Gardner) (isl.), Kiribati 87/J6
Nila (isl.), Indonesia 85/H7
Nilahue, Chile 138/E6
Niland, Calif. (92257) 204/K10
Nilaveli, Sri Lanka 68/E7
Nile (riv.) 2/L5
Nile (riv.) 102/F2
Nile (riv.), Egypt 111/F2
Nile (riv.), Egypt 59/B4
Nile (prov.), Sudan 111/F4
Nile (riv.), Sudan 59/B6
Nile (riv.), Sudan 111/F4
Niles, Ill. (60648) 222/B5
Niles, Kansas (†67480) 232/E2
Niles, Mich. (49120) 250/C7
Niles, Ohio (44446) 284/J3
Ni'lin, West Bank 65/C4
Nilópolis, Brazil 135/E3
Nilwood, Ill. (62672) 222/D4
Nimach, India 68/D4
Nimba (lag.), Guinea 106/C7
Nimba (lag.), Ivory Coast 106/C7
Nimba (lag.), Liberia 106/C7
Nîmes, France 28/F6
Nîmes, France 7/E4
Nimmitabel, N.S. Wales 97/E5
Nimmons, Ark. (72461) 202/K1
Nimnyrskiy, U.S.S.R. 48/N4
Nimrod, Ark. (†72126) 202/D4
Nimrod (lake), Ark. 202/D4
Nimrod, Minn. (56478) 255/D4
Nimule, Sudan 111/F7
Nin (bay), Philippines 82/D4
Nin, Yugoslavia 45/B3
Ninaview, Colo. (†81054) 208/N7
Ninawa (gov.), Iraq 66/B3
Nine Degree (chan.), India 68/C7
Ninemile (pt.), Mich. 250/E3
Nine Mile (creek), Utah 304/D4
Nine Mile Falls, Wash. (99026) 310/H3
Nine Mile River, Nova Scotia 168/E3
Ninepipe (res.), Mont. 262/C3
Nine Times, S.C. (†29685) 296/B2
Ninette, Manitoba 179/C5
Ninety Mile (beach), N. Zealand 100/D1
Ninety Mile (beach), Victoria 97/D6
Ninety Six, S.C. (29666) 296/C3
Ninety Six Nat'l Hist. Site, S.C. 296/C3
Nineveh (ruins), Iraq 66/C2
Nineveh, N.Y. (13813) 276/J6
Nineveh, Pa. (15353) 294/B6
Ninfas (pt.), Argentina 143/D5
Ninga, Manitoba 179/C5
Ning'an, China 77/L3
Ningbo (Ningpo), China 77/K6
Ningbo, China 54/O7
Ningde, China 77/K6
Ningdu, China 77/J6
Ninghua, China 77/J6
Ningpo (Ningbo), China 77/K6
Ningsia (Yinchuan, Yinchwan), China 77/G4
Ningsia Hui Aut. Reg. (Ningxia Huizu), China 77/F3
Ningwu, China 77/H4
Ningxia Huizu (Ningsia Hui Aut. Reg.), China 77/F3
Ning Xian, China 77/G4
Ninh Binh, Vietnam 72/E3
Ninigo Group (isls.), Papua N.G. 87/E6
Ninilchik, Alaska (99639) 196/B1
Ninini (pt.), Hawaii 218/D2
Ninnekah, Okla. (73067) 288/L5
Ninnescah (riv.), Kansas 232/E4
Ninnis Glacier Tongue, Ant. 5/C8
Ninole, Hawaii (96773) 218/J4
Ninove, Belgium 27/D7
Nioaque, Brazil 132/C8
Niobe, N.Y. (14758) 276/B6
Niobe, N. Dak. (†58746) 282/F2
Niobrara (riv.), Nebr. 188/F2
Niobrara, Nebr. (68760) 264/G2
Niobrara (riv.), Nebr. 264/E2
Niobrara (co.), Wyo. 319/H2
Niobrara (riv.), Wyo. 319/J3
Niono, Mali 106/C6
Nioro, Mali 106/C5
Nioro, Mali 102/B3
Nioro-du-Rip, Senegal 106/A6
Niort, France 28/C4
Niota, Ill. (62358) 222/B3
Niota, Tenn. (37826) 237/M9
Niotaze, Kansas (67355) 232/F4
Nipani, India 68/C5
Nipawin, Sask. 181/H2
Nipawin Prov. Park, Sask. 181/G1
Nipe (bay), Cuba 158/J3
Nipigon, Ont. 162/H6
Nipigon (lake), Ont. 146/K5
Nipigon (lake), Ont. 162/H6
Nipigon, Ontario 177/H5
Nipigon, Ontario 175/C3
Nipigon (lake), Ontario 175/C3
Nipigon (lake), Ontario 177/H5
Nipinnawasee, Calif. (†93601) 204/F6
Nipishish (lake), Newf. 166/B3
Nipissing (terr. dist.), Ontario 177/F2
Nipissing (terr. dist.), Ontario 175/E3
Nipissing, Ontario 177/E1
Nipissing (lake), Ontario 177/E1
Nipissing (lake), Ontario 175/E3
Nipomo, Calif. (93444) 204/E8
Nippers Harbour, Newf. 166/C4
Nipton, Calif. (92364) 204/K8
Niquelândia, Brazil 132/D6
Ñiquén, Chile 138/E1
Niquero, Cuba 158/G4
Niquero, Cuba 156/C2
Niquivil, Argentina 143/C3
Nirgua, Venezuela 124/D2
Nirmal, India 68/D5
Nirvana, Mich. (†49642) 250/D5
Nir Yitzhaq, Israel 65/A5
Niš, Yugoslavia 7/G4
Niš, Yugoslavia 45/F4
Nisa, Portugal 33/C3
Nisab, P.D.R. Yemen 59/E7
Nisab, Saudi Arabia 59/D4
Nisbet, Pa. (17759) 294/H3
Niscemi, Italy 34/E6
Nishapur (Neyshabur), Iran 66/L2
Nishino (isl.), Japan 81/M3
Nishinomiya, Japan 81/H8
Nishinoomote, Japan 81/E8
Nísiros (isl.), Greece 45/H7
Niskayuna, N.Y. (†12301) 276/N5
Nisko, Poland 47/E3
Nisku, Alberta 182/D3
Nisland, S. Dak. (57762) 298/C4
Nisqually, Wash. (†98501) 310/C3
Nisqually (riv.), Wash. 310/C4
Nisqually Ind. Res., Wash. 310/C4
Nissan (isl.), Papua N.G. 86/C2
Nissum (fjord), Denmark 21/A5
Nisswa, Minn. (56468) 255/D4
Niterói, Brazil 132/F8
Niterói, Brazil 120/E5
Niterói, Brazil 135/E3
Nith (riv.), Scotland 15/E5
Nith (riv.), Scotland 10/E3
Nitil, Jordan 65/D4
Nitinat, Br. Col. 184/H3
Nitinat (lake), Br. Col. 184/H3
Niton Junction, Alberta 182/C3
Nitra, Czech. 41/E2
Nitra (riv.), Czech. 41/E2
Nitro, W. Va. (25143) 312/C6
Nitta Yuma, Miss. (38763) 256/C4
Nittedal, Norway 18/D3
Niuafo'ou (isl.), Tonga 87/J7
Niuatoputapu (isl.), Tonga 87/J7
Niue (isl.) 87/K7
Niue (isl.), N. Zealand 2/A6
Niutao (atoll), Tuvalu 87/H6
Nivala, Finland 18/O5
Nive (riv.), Tasmania 99/C4
Nivelles, Belgium 27/E7
Nivernais (trad. prov.), France 29
Niverville, Manitoba 179/F5
Niwot, Colo. (80544) 208/J2
Nixa, Mo. (65714) 261/F8
Nixburg, Ala. (36058) 195/F5
Nixon, Nev. (89424) 266/B3
Nixon, N.J. (08817) 273/E2
Nixon, Texas (78140) 303/G8
Nixonville, S.C. (†29526) 296/K4
Niya (Minfeng), China 77/B4
Nizamabad, India 68/D5
Nizao, Dom. Rep. 158/E6
Nizhnekamsk, U.S.S.R. 7/K3
Nizhnekamsk, U.S.S.R. 52/H3
Nizhneudinsk, U.S.S.R. 48/K4
Nizhnevartovsk, U.S.S.R. 48/H3
Nizhneyansk, U.S.S.R. 48/O3
Nizhniy Lomov, U.S.S.R. 52/F4
Nizhniy Novgorod (Gor'kiy), U.S.S.R. 52/F3
Nizhniy Tagil, U.S.S.R. 54/H4
Nizhniy Tagil, U.S.S.R. 48/G4
Nizhnyaya Pesha, U.S.S.R. 52/G1
Nizina, Alaska (†99566) 196/K2
Nizip, Turkey 63/G4
Nizwa, Oman 59/G5
Nizza Monferrato, Italy 34/B2
Nizzanim, Israel 65/B4
Njombe, Tanzania 115/F5
Njombe (riv.), Tanzania 115/F5
Nkambe, Cameroon 115/B2
Nkayi, Congo 115/B4
Nkhata Bay, Malawi 115/F6
Nkhotakota, Malawi 115/F6
N'Komi (lag.), Gabon 115/A4
Nkongsamba, Cameroon 115/B3
Nkongsamba, Cameroon 102/D4
Nmai (riv.), Burma 72/C1
Nnewi, Nigeria 106/F7
Noah, Tenn. (†37355) 237/J9
Noakhali, Bangladesh 68/G4
Noank, Conn. (06340) 210/G3
Noatak, Alaska (99761) 196/F1
Noatak (riv.), Alaska 196/F1
Noatak Nat'l Preserve, Alaska 196/F1
Nobel, Ontario 177/D2
Nobeoka, Japan 81/E7
Noble, Georgia (†30728) 217/B1
Noble, Ill. (62868) 222/E5
Noble (co.), Ind. 227/G2
Noble, Iowa (†52641) 229/K6
Noble, La. (71462) 238/C3
Noble, Mo. (65715) 261/G9
Noble (co.), Ohio 284/G6
Noble (co.), Okla. 288/M2
Noble, Okla. (73068) 288/M4
Nobleboro○, Maine (04555) 243/D7
Nobleford, Alberta 182/D5
Noble Lake, Ark. (†71601) 202/G5
Nobles (co.), Minn. 255/C7
Noblesville, Ind. (46060) 227/F4
Nobleton, Fla. (33554) 212/D3
Nobleton, Ontario 177/J3
Noboribetsu, Japan 81/K2
Nocatee, Fla. (33864) 212/E4
Noccundra, Queensland 95/B5
Nocera Inferiore, Italy 34/E4
Nochistlán, Mexico 150/H6
Nocona, Texas (76255) 303/G4
Noctor, Ky. (41357) 237/P5
Noda, Japan 81/P2
Nodaway, Iowa (50857) 229/D7
Nodaway (riv.), Iowa 229/D7
Nodaway (co.), Mo. 261/C2
Nodaway, Mo. (†64421) 261/C3
Node, Wyo. (82228) 319/H3
Nodine, Minn. (†55925) 255/G7
Noel, Mo. (64854) 261/D9
Noel, Nova Scotia 168/E3
Noel Road, Nova Scotia 168/E3
Noelville, Ontario 177/D1
Nogal, N. Mex. (88341) 274/D5
Nogal (reg.), Somalia 115/J2
Nogales, Ariz. 188/D4
Nogales, Ariz. (85621) 198/E7
Nogales, Chile 138/F2
Nogales, Mexico 150/P2
Nogamut, Alaska (†99668) 196/G2
Nogata, Japan 81/E7
Nogent-le-Rotrou, France 28/D3
Nogent-sur-Seine, France 28/E3
Nogoa (riv.), Queensland 88/H4
Nogoa (riv.), Queensland 95/C5
Nogoyá, Argentina 143/F6
Nógrád (co.), Hungary 41/E3
Nohili (pt.), Hawaii 218/B1
Nohkú (pt.), Mexico 150/Q7
Noinville, New Bruns. 170/E2
Noir (isl.), Chile 138/E11
Noires (mts.), Dom. Rep. 158/C5
Noires (mts.), Haiti 158/C5
Noirmont (mt.), Switzerland 39/B4
Noirmoutier (isl.), France 28/B4
Noisy-le-Sec, France 28/B1
Nojima (cape), Japan 81/K6
Nokesville, Va. (22123) 307/N3
Nokhowch, Kuh-e (mt.), Iran 66/M7
Nokia, Finland 18/N6
Nok Kundi, Pakistan 68/A3
Nok Kundi, Pakistan 59/H4
Nokomis, Ala. (†36502) 195/D8
Nokomis, Fla. (33555) 212/D4
Nokomis, Ill. (62075) 222/D4
Nokomis, Sask. 181/F4
Nokou, Chad 111/B5
Nola, Ark. (†72838) 202/C4
Nola, Cent. Afr. Rep. 115/C3
Nola, Miss. (†39665) 256/D7
Nolan (co.), Texas 303/D5
Nolan, W. Va. (25687) 312/B7
Nolichucky (riv.), N.C. 281/E2
Nolichucky (riv.), Tenn. 237/R8
Nolin, Ky. (†42776) 237/K5
Nolin (lake), Ky. 237/K6
Nolin (riv.), Ky. 237/J6
Nolinsk, U.S.S.R. 52/H3
Nollesemic (lake), Maine 243/F4
Noma, Fla. (32452) 212/C5
Nomans Land (isl.), Mass. 249/L7
Nombre de Dios, Mexico 150/G5
Nome, Alaska 146/B3
Nome, Alaska (99762) 196/E2
Nome, Alaska 188/C5
Nome, Alaska 2/A2
Nome, N. Dak. (58062) 282/P6
Nome, U.S. 4/C18
Nomgon, Mongolia 77/G3
Nominingue, Québec 172/B3
Nominingue (lake), Québec 172/B3
Nomoi (isls.), Micronesia 87/F5
Nonacho (lake), N.W.T. 162/F3
Nonacho (lake), N.W. Terrs. 187/H3
Nonamesset (isl.), Mass. 249/M6
Nondalton, Alaska (99640) 196/G2
Nong Het, Laos 72/E3
Nong Khai, Thailand 72/D3
Nong Lahan (lake), Thailand 72/D3
Nonoava, Mexico 150/F3
Nonouti (atoll), Kiribati 87/H6
Nonquitt, Mass. (02748) 249/L6
Nonsan, S. Korea 81/C5
Nontron, France 28/D5
Nooksack, Wash. (98276) 310/C2
Nooksack (riv.), Wash. 310/C2
Noonan, N. Dak. (58765) 282/D2
Noord (pt.), Neth. Ant. 161/F8
Noord (pt.), Neth. Ant. 161/D8
Noord di Salinja, Neth. Ant. 161/E8
Noordwijk, Netherlands 27/E4
Noorvik, Alaska (99763) 196/F1
Nootka, Br. Col. 184/D5
Nootka (isl.), Br. Col. 184/D5
Nootka (sound), Br. Col. 184/D5
Nopalucan de la Granja, Mexico 150/O1
Nopeming, Minn. (†55810) 255/F4
Nopiming Prov. Park, Manitoba 179/G4
Nóqui, Angola 115/B5
Noquochoke P.O. (Westport), Mass. (02790) 249/K6
Nora, Ill. (61059) 222/D1
Nora, Nebr. (68962) 264/G4
Nora, Sask. 181/H3
Nora, S. Dak. (†57001) 298/R8
Nora, Sweden 18/J7
Nora, Va. (24272) 307/D6
Noranda, Que. 162/J6
Noranda, Québec 174/B3
Noranside, Queensland 95/A4
Nora Springs, Iowa (50458) 229/H2
Norbeck, S. Dak. (†57480) 298/L3
Norberg, Sweden 18/K6
Norberto de la Riestra, Argentina 143/G7
Norbertville, Québec 172/F3
Norborne, Mo. (64668) 261/E4
Norcatur, Kansas (67653) 232/B2
Norco, Calif. (91760) 204/E11
Norco, La. (70079) 238/N3
Norcross, Georgia (*30071) 217/D3
Norcross, Maine (†04462) 243/F4
Norcross, Minn. (56274) 255/B5
Nord (dept.), France 28/E2
Nord, Greenl. 4/A10
Nord (pt.), Guadeloupe 161/B7
Nord (dept.), Haiti 158/C5
Nord (riv.), Québec 172/C4
Nordaustlandet (isl.), Norway 18/D1
Nordborg, Denmark 21/C7
Nordby, Århus, Denmark 21/D5
Nordby, Ribe, Denmark 21/B7
Norddeich, W. Germany 22/B2
Nordegg, Alberta 182/B3
Nordegg (riv.), Alberta 182/C3
Norden, Nebr. (†68778) 264/D2
Norden, W. Germany 22/B2
Nordenham, W. Germany 22/C2
Norderney, W. Germany 22/B2
Norderney (isl.), W. Germany 22/B2
Norderstedt, W. Germany 22/D2
Nord-Est (bay), Guadeloupe 161/B6
Nordfjord (fjord), Norway 18/E6
Nordhausen, E. Germany 22/D3
Nordheim, Texas (78141) 303/G9
Nordhorn, W. Germany 22/B2
Nordin, New Bruns. 170/E1
Nordjylland (co.), Denmark 21/D4
Nordkapp (cape), Norway 7/G1
Nordkapp (pt.), Norway 18/C1
Nordkinn (headland), Norway 18/Q1
Nordkinn (pen.), Norway 18/P1
Nordland (co.), Norway 18/J3
Nordland, Wash. (98358) 310/C2
Nordli, Norway 18/H4
Nördlingen, W. Germany 22/D4
Nordmaling, Sweden 18/L5
Nordman, Idaho (83848) 220/B1
Nord-Ostsee (canal), W. Germany 22/C1
Nord-Ouest (dept.), Haiti 158/B5
Nordstrand (isl.), W. Germany 22/C1
Nord-Trøndelag (co.), Norway 18/H4
Nordvik-Ugol'naya, U.S.S.R. 4/B4
Nordvik-Ugol'naya, U.S.S.R. 48/M2
Nore (riv.), Ireland 10/C4
Nore (riv.), Ireland 17/G7
Norene, Tenn. (37136) 237/J8
Norfield, Miss. (†39629) 256/C8
Norfolk (isl.), Australia 2/T7
Norfolk○, Conn. (06058) 210/C1
Norfolk (co.), England 13/H5
Norfolk (co.), Mass. 249/K4
Norfolk○, Mass. (02056) 249/J4
Norfolk, Nebr. 188/G2
Norfolk, Nebr. (68701) 264/G2
Norfolk, N.Y. (13667) 276/K1
Norfolk (bay), Tasmania 99/D4
Norfolk, Va. 188/L3
Norfolk, Va. 146/L6
Norfolk (I.C.), Va. (*23501) 307/R7
Norfolk Island, /L5
Norfolk Island (terr.), Australia 87/G8
Norfork, Ark. (72658) 202/F1
Norfork (lake), Ark. 202/F1
Norfork (lake), Mo. 261/H10
Norg, Netherlands 27/J2
Norge, Okla. (†73018) 288/K4
Norge, Va. (23127) 307/P6
Norglenwold, Alberta 182/C3
Noril'sk, U.S.S.R. 2/P2
Noril'sk, U.S.S.R. 54/L3
Noril'sk, U.S.S.R. 4/B5
Noril'sk, U.S.S.R. 48/J3
Norland, Fla. (†33169) 212/B4
Norland, Ontario 177/F3
Norlina, N.C. (27563) 281/N2
Norma, N.J. (08347) 273/C4
Norma, N. Dak. (58766) 282/G2
Norma, Tenn. (†37827) 237/N8
Normal, Ill. (61761) 222/E3
Normalville, Pa. (15469) 294/D5
Norman, Ark. (71960) 202/C5
Norman, Ind. (47264) 227/E7
Norman (co.), Minn. 255/B3
Norman, Nebr. (68963) 264/F4
Norman (cape), Newf. 166/C3
Norman, N.C. (28367) 281/K4
Norman (lake), N.C. 281/H3
Norman, Okla. (*73069) 288/M4
Norman (riv.), Queensland 88/G3
Norman (creek), Queensland 95/D3
Norman (riv.), Queensland 95/B3
Norman (isl.), Virgin Is. (Br.) 161/D4
Normanby, Queensland 88/K2
Normand (lake), Québec 172/D2
Normandale, Ontario 177/D5
Normandin, Québec 172/E1
Normandy (trad. prov.), France 29
Normandy, Mo. (63121) 261/R2
Normandy (riv.), Queensland 95/C2
Normandy, Tenn. (37360) 237/J10
Normandy, Texas (78852) 303/D9
Normandy Beach, N.J. (08739) 273/E3
Normandy Park, Wash. (†98100) 310/A2
Normangee, Texas (77871) 303/H6
Norman Park, Georgia (31771) 217/E8
Norman's Cove, Newf. 166/D2
Normanton, Australia 87/E7
Normanton, Queensland 95/B3
Normanton, Queensland 88/G3
Normantown, Georgia (†30474) 217/H6
Normantown, W. Va. (25267) 312/E5
Norman Wells, Canada 4/C16
Norman Wells, N.W.T. 146/F3
Norman Wells, N.W.T. 162/D2
Norman Wells, N.W. Terrs. 187/F3
Normétal, Québec 174/B3
Noroton, Conn. (†06820) 210/B4
Noroton Heights, Conn. (†06820) 210/B4
Norphlet, Ark. (71759) 202/E7
Norquay, Sask. 181/J4
Ñorquincó, Argentina 143/B5
Norrbotten (co.), Sweden 18/L3
Nørre Åby, Denmark 21/C7
Nørre Alslev, Denmark 21/E8
Nørre Broby, Denmark 21/D7
Nørre Nebel, Denmark 21/B6
Nørre Snede, Denmark 21/C6
Nørre Vorupør, Denmark 21/B4
Norridge, Ill. (†60656) 222/B5
Norridgewock, Maine (04957) 243/D6
Norridgewock○, Maine (04957) 243/D6
Norrie, Wis. (†54414) 317/H6
Norris, Ill. (61553) 222/C3
Norris, Miss. (†39074) 256/F6
Norris, Mont. (59745) 262/E5
Norris, S.C. (29667) 296/B2
Norris, S. Dak. (57560) 298/G7
Norris (lake), Tenn. 188/K3
Norris, Tenn. (37828) 237/N8
Norris (dam), Tenn. 237/N8
Norris (lake), Tenn. 237/O8
Norris, Wyo. (†82190) 319/B1
Norris Arm, Newf. 166/C4
Norris City, Ill. (62869) 222/E6
Norris Point, Newf. 166/C4
Norristown, Ark. (†72801) 202/D3
Norristown, Georgia (30447) 217/H5
Norristown, Ind. (†47234) 227/F6
Norristown, Pa. (*19401) 294/M5
Norrisville, Md. (†21161) 245/N2
Norrköping, Sweden 7/F3
Norrköping, Sweden 18/K7
Norrsundet, Sweden 18/K6
Norrtälje, Sweden 18/L7
Norseland, Minn. (†56082) 255/D6
Norseman, W. Australia 88/C6
Norseman, W. Australia 92/C6
Norsjö, Sweden 18/L4
Norte (pt.), Argentina 143/D5
Norte (chan.), Brazil 120/E2
Norte (chan.), Brazil 132/D2
Norte, Serra do (range), Brazil 132/B5
Norte del Cabo San Antonio (pt.), Argentina 143/E4
Norte de Santander (dept.), Colombia 126/D3
North (sea) 2/K3
North (sea) 7/E3
North (cape), Alaska 196/L4
North (pt.), Barbados 161/B8
North (sea), Belgium 27/D4
North (rocks), Bermuda 156/H2
North (sea), Denmark 21/B9
North (sea), England 13/J4
North (sea), France 28/E1
North (cape), Ice. 4/C11
North (Horn) (cape), Iceland 21/B1
North (sound), Ireland 17/B5
North (isls.), La. 238/M7
North (pass), La. 238/N8
North (pt.), La. 238/M7
North (pt.), Md. 245/N4

Northwood 419

North (riv.), Mass. 249/D2
North (riv.), Mass. 249/L4
North (chan.), Mich. 250/F2
North (pt.), Mich. 250/F3
North (lake), Minn. 255/F1
North (sea), Netherlands 27/E3
North (lake), New Bruns. 170/C3
North (riv.), Newf. 166/C3
North (riv.), Newf. 166/B2
North (isl.), N. Zealand 87/H9
North (cape), N. Zealand 87/H9
North (cape), N. Zealand 100/D1
North (isl.), N. Zealand 100/F1
North (lake), N. Dak. 282/J3
North (chan.), N. Ireland 10/D3
North (chan.), N. Ireland 17/K1
North (Nordkapp) (cape), Norway 7/G1
North (cape), Norway 4/B8
North (cape), N.S. 162/K6
North (cape), Nova Scotia 168/H1
North (mt.), Nova Scotia 168/D3
North (chan.), Ontario 177/A1
North (chan.), Ontario 175/D3
North (mt.), Pa. 294/K3
North (pt.), Pr. Edward I. 168/E1
North (chan.), Scotland 10/D3
North (chan.), Scotland 15/C5
North (sound), Scotland 15/G4
North (sound), Scotland 15/F1
North (isl.), Seychelles 118/H5
North, S.C. (29112) 296/E4
North (inlet), S.C. 296/J5
North (isl.), S.C. 296/J5
North (pt.), Tasmania 99/E1
North (creek), Utah 304/C6
North (lake), Utah 304/B2
North (riv.), Wash. 310/B4
North (sea), W. Germany 22/B2
North (riv.), W. Va. 312/J4
North (lake), Wis. 317/J1
North Abington, Mass. (02351) 249/L4
North Acton, Mass. (†01720) 249/J2
North Adams, Mass. (01247) 249/B2
North Adams, Mich. (49262) 250/E7
Northallerton, England 10/F3
Northallerton, England 13/F3
Northam, England 13/C6
Northam, W. Australia 88/B6
Northam, W. Australia 92/B1
NORTH AMERICA 146
North America 2/C4
North Amherst, Mass. (01059) 249/E3
North Amity, Maine (04465) 243/H4
Northampton, England 13/F5
Northampton, England 10/F4
Northampton, Mass. (01060) 249/D3
Northampton (co.), N.C. 281/P2
Northampton (co.), Pa. 294/M4
Northampton, Pa. (18067) 294/M4
Northampton (co.), Va. 307/S6
Northampton, W. Australia 88/A5
Northampton, W. Australia 92/A5
Northamptonshire (co.), England 13/G5
North Andaman (isl.), India 68/G6
North Andover○, Mass. (01845) 249/K2
North Anna (riv.), Va. 307/M4
North Anson, Maine (04958) 243/D6
North Apollo, Pa. (15673) 294/D4
North Arlington, N.J. (07032) 273/B2
North Arm (inlet), N.W. Terrs. 187/G3
North Asheboro, N.C. (†27203) 281/K3
North Ashford, Conn. (†06282) 210/G1
North Aspy (riv.), Nova Scotia 168/H2
North Atlantic Ocean 2/H3
North Attleboro○, Mass. (*02760) 249/J5
North Augusta, Ontario 177/J3
North Augusta, S.C. (29841) 296/C5
North Aulatsivik (isl.), Newf. 166/B2
North Aurora, Ill. (60542) 222/E2
North Avondale, Colo. (†81022) 208/L6
North Ballachulish, Scotland 15/C4
North Baltimore, Ohio (45872) 284/C3
North Bangor, N.Y. (12966) 276/M1
North Barrington, Ill. (†60010) 222/A5
North Bass (isl.), Ohio 284/E2
North Battleford, Sask. 146/H4
North Battleford, Sask. 162/F5
North Battleford, Sask. 181/C3
North Bay, N.Y. (13123) 276/J4
North Bay, Ont. 146/L5
North Bay, Ont. 162/J6
North Bay, Ontario 177/E1
North Bay, Ontario 175/E3
North Bay, Wis. (†53401) 317/M3
North Bay Ingonish (bay), Nova Scotia 168/H2
North Bay Village, Fla. (33141) 212/B4
North Beach, Md. (20831) 245/N6
North Belgrade, Maine (†04963) 243/D7
North Bellingham, Mass. (†02019) 249/J4
North Bend, Br. Col. 184/G5
North Bend, Nebr. (68649) 264/H3
North Bend, Ohio (45052) 284/B9
North Bend, Oreg. (97459) 291/C4
North Bend, Pa. (17760) 294/G3
North Bend, Wash. (98045) 310/D3
North Bend, Wis. (†54642) 317/D7
North Bennington, Vt. (05257) 268/A6
North Bergen○, N.J. (07047) 273/B2
North Berwick, Maine (03906) 243/B9
North Berwick○, Maine (03906) 243/B9
North Berwick, Scotland 15/F4
North Berwick, Scotland 10/E2
North Beveland (isl.), Netherlands 27/D5
North Billerica, Mass. (01862) 249/J2
North Bloomfield, Conn. (†06002) 210/E1
North Bloomfield, Ohio (44450) 284/J3
North Bonneville, Wash. (98639) 310/C5
North Borneo (Sabah) (state), Malaysia 85/F3
Northboro, Iowa (51647) 229/C7
Northborough, Mass. (01532) 249/H3
Northborough○, Mass. (01532) 249/H3
North Boston, N.Y. (14110) 276/C5
North Bourke, N.S. Wales 97/C2
North Brabant (prov.), Netherlands 27/F5
North Braddock, Pa. (15104) 294/C7
North Bradford, Maine (†04410) 243/F5
North Bradley, Mich. (†48618) 250/E5
Northbranch, Kansas (†66936) 232/D2
North Branch, Md. (†21502) 245/D2
North Branch, Mich. (48461) 250/F5
North Branch, Minn. (55056) 255/F5
North Branch, N.H. (†03440) 268/D5
North Branch, N.J. (08876) 273/D2
North Branch Oromocto (riv.), New Bruns. 170/D3
North Branford○, Conn. (06471) 210/E3
North Brentwood, Md. (†20722) 245/F4
Northbridge○, Mass. (01534) 249/H4
North Bridgton, Maine (04057) 243/B7
Northbrook, Ill. (60062) 222/B5
North Brook, Ontario 177/G3
North Brookfield, Mass. (01535) 249/F3
North Brookfield○, Mass. (01535) 249/F3
North Brooksville, Maine (†04617) 243/F7
North Brunswick○, N.J. (08902) 273/D3
North Bruny (isl.), Tasmania 99/D5
North Buena Vista, Iowa (52066) 229/L3
North Calais, Vt. (†05648) 268/C3
North Caldwell, N.J. (†07006) 273/B2
North Calling Lake, Alberta 182/D2
North Canadian (riv.) 188/G3
North Canadian (riv.), Okla. 288/K3
North Canton, Conn. (06059) 210/D1
North Canton, Georgia (†30114) 217/C2
North Canton, Ohio (44720) 284/H4
North Cape (Nordkapp) (pt.), Norway 18/P1
North Cape May, N.J. (08204) 273/C6
North Caribou (lake), Ontario 175/B2
North Carolina 188/L3
NORTH CAROLINA 281
North Carolina (state), U.S. 146/K6
North Carrizo (creek), Colo. 208/N8
North Carrizo (riv.), Okla. 288/A1
North Carrollton, Miss. (38947) 256/E3
North Carter (mt.), N.H. 268/E3
North Carver, Mass. (02355) 249/L5
North Cascades Nat'l Park, Wash. 310/D2
North Catasauqua, Pa. (†18032) 294/L4
North Charleston, S.C. (29406) 296/G6
North Charlestown, N.H. (†03603) 268/C5
North Chatham, Mass. (02650) 249/O6
North Chatham, N.H. (†04058) 268/E3
North Chelmsford, Mass. (01863) 249/J2
North Chesterville, Maine (†04938) 243/C6
North Chicago, Ill. (60064) 222/B4
North Chichester, N.H. (†03263) 268/E5
North Chili, N.Y. (14514) 276/E4
North City (Coello), Ill. (†62825) 222/E5
North Clarendon, Vt. (05759) 268/B4
Northcliffe, W. Australia 92/B6
North Cohasset, Mass. (†02025) 249/F7
North Colebrook, Conn. (†06021) 210/C1
North College Hill, Ohio (45239) 284/B9
North Collins, N.Y. (14111) 276/C5
North Concho (riv.), Texas 303/C6
North Concord, Vt. (05858) 268/D3
North Conway, N.H. (03860) 268/E3
North Cooking Lake, Alberta 182/D3
North Cotabato (prov.), Philippines 82/E7
Northcote, Minn. (†56728) 255/A2
Northcote, N. Zealand 100/B1
Northcote, Victoria 88/L7
Northcote, Victoria 97/J5
North Cove, N.C. (†28752) 281/F3
North Cove, Wash. (†98590) 310/A4
North Cowichan, Br. Col. 184/J3
North Creek, N.Y. (15853) 276/M3
North Crossett, Ark. (71635) 202/G7
North Cutler, Maine (†04626) 243/J6
North Dakota 188/F1
NORTH DAKOTA 282
North Dakota (state), U.S. 146/H5
North Dandalup, W. Australia 88/B3
North Danger (reef), Philippines 85/E3
North Danville, Vt. (†05819) 268/C3
North Dartmouth, Mass. (02747) 249/K6
North Dexter, Maine (†04930) 243/E5
North Dighton, Mass. (02764) 249/K5
North Dixmont, Maine (†04932) 243/E6
North Down (dist.), N. Ireland 17/K2
North Downs (hills), England 13/G6
North Eagle Butte, S. Dak. (†57625) 298/G3
Northeast (cape), Alaska 196/E2
North East (pt.), Jamaica 158/K6
Northeast (pass), La. 238/M8
North East, Md. (21901) 245/P2
North East, Pa. (16428) 294/C1
North East Breakers, Bermuda 156/H2
North East Cape Fear (riv.), N.C. 281/O4
North East Carry, Maine (†04441) 243/D4
North-Eastern (prov.), Kenya 115/G3
Northeast Foreland (pen.), Greenl. 4/A10
North Eastham, Mass. (02651) 249/O5
Northeast Harbor, Maine (04662) 243/G7
Northeast Land (isl.), Norway 4/B8
North East Margaree (riv.), Nova Scotia 168/H2
North Easton, Mass. (02356) 249/K4
North East Polder, Netherlands 27/H3
North East Providence (chan.), Bahamas 156/C1
North Edisto (riv.), S.C. 296/G6
North Edwards, Calif. (93523) 204/H8
North Egremont, Mass. (01252) 249/A4
Northeim, W. Germany 22/C3
North English, Iowa (52316) 229/J5
North Enid, Okla. (†73701) 288/L2
Northern (dist.), Israel 65/C2
Northern (head), New Bruns. 170/D4
Northern (prov.), Sudan 111/E3
Northern Cheyenne Ind. Res., Mont. 262/K5
Northern Dvina (riv.), U.S.S.R. 52/F2
Northern Dvina (riv.), U.S.S.R. 48/E3
Northern Indian (lake), Manitoba 179/J2
NORTHERN IRELAND 17
NORTHERN IRELAND 10/C3
Nottoway (riv.), Va. 307/O7
Notukeu (creek), Sask. 181/D6
Notus, Idaho (83656) 220/B6
Nouadhibou, Mauritania 106/A4
Nouadhibou, Mauritania 102/A2
Nouakchott (cap.), Mauritania 106/A5
Nouakchott (cap.), Mauritania 102/A3
Nouakchott (cap.), Mauritania 2/J5
Nouméa (cap.), New Caled. 87/G8
Nouméa (cap.), New Caledonia 2/T7
Nouméa (cap.), New Caled. 86/H5
Nounan, Idaho (†83254) 220/G7
Noup (head), Scotland 15/E1
Noupoort, S. Africa 118/C6
Nouveau-Comptoir, Québec 174/B2
Northern Ireland, U.K. 7/D3
Northern Marianas 87/E4
Northern Marianas, U.S. 2/S5
Northern Peninsula Aboriginal Reserve, Queensland 88/G2
Northern Peninsula Aboriginal Res., Queensland 95/B1
Northern Samar (prov.), Philippines 82/E4
Northern Sporades (isls.), Greece 45/F6
Northern Territory, 88/E3
NORTHERN TERRITORY 93
Northern Territory (terr.), Australia 87/D7
North Esk (riv.), Scotland 15/F4
North Esk (riv.), Tasmania 99/D3
North Fairfield, Ohio (44855) 284/E3
North Falmouth, Mass. (02556) 249/M6
North Ferrisburg, Vt. (05473) 268/A3
Northfield, Conn. (06778) 210/C2
Northfield, Ill. (60093) 222/B5
Northfield, Ky. (†40201) 237/K1
Northfield○, Maine (†04654) 243/H6
Northfield, Mass. (01360) 249/E2
Northfield○, Mass. (01360) 249/E2
Northfield, Minn. (55057) 255/E6
Northfield○, N.H. (†03276) 268/D5
Northfield, N.J. (08225) 273/D5
Northfield, Ohio (44067) 284/J10
Northfield, Texas (79246) 303/D3
Northfield, Vt. (05663) 268/B3
Northfield○, Vt. (05663) 268/B3
Northfield, Wis. (†54635) 317/D7
Northfield Falls, Vt. (05664) 268/B3
Northfield Farms, Mass. (†01360) 249/E2
Northfield-Tilton, N.H. (†03276) 268/D5
Northfleet, England 10/C5
Northfleet, England 13/J8
North Fond du Lac, Wis. (†54935) 317/J8
Northford, Conn. (06472) 210/D3
North Foreland (prom.), England 10/G5
North Foreland (prom.), England 13/J6
North Fork, Calif. (93643) 204/F6
North Fork, Frenchman (creek), Colo. 208/O1
North Fork, Gunnison (riv.), Colo. 208/D5
North Fork, Smoky Hill (riv.), Colo. 208/P4
North Fork, Idaho (83466) 220/D4
North Fork (riv.), Idaho 220/B7
North Fork, Flathead (riv.), Mont. 262/B2
North Fork, Little Humboldt (riv.), Nev. 266/D1
North Fork, Grand (riv.), N. Dak. 282/E8
Northfork, W. Va. (24868) 312/D8
North Fork, Powder (riv.), Wyo. 319/F2
North Fork, Shoshone (riv.), Wyo. 319/C1
North Fork, Wind (riv.), Wyo. 319/C2
North Fort Myers, Fla. (33903) 212/E5
North Foster, R.I. (†02857) 249/H5
North Fourchu, Nova Scotia 168/H3
North Fox (isl.), Mich. 250/D3
North Franklin, Conn. (06254) 210/G2
North Freedom, Wis. (53951) 317/G9
North Friars (bay), St. Chris.-Nevis 161/D10
North Friesland (reg.), W. Germany 22/C1
North Frisian (isls.), Denmark 21/B7
North Frisian (isls.), W. Germany 22/B1
North Fryeburg, Maine (04058) 243/B7
North Galiano, Br. Col. 184/K3
North Garden, Va. (22959) 307/L5
Northgate, N. Dak. (58767) 282/F2
Northgate, Sask. 181/J6
Northglenn, Colo. (80233) 208/K3
North Gorham, Maine (†04075) 243/B8
North Gosforth, England 13/J3
North Gower, Ontario 177/J2
North Grafton, Mass. (01536) 249/H4
North Granby, Conn. (06060) 210/D1
North Grant, Nova Scotia 168/G3
North Grosvenor Dale, Conn. (06255) 210/H1
North Groton, N.H. (†03266) 268/D4
North Grove, Ind. (†46911) 227/F3
North Guilford, Conn. (†06437) 210/E3
North Hadley, Mass. (†01035) 249/D3
North Haledon, N.J. (07508) 273/B1
North Hampton○, N.H. (03862) 268/F6
North Hampton, Ohio (45349) 284/C5
North Hanover, Mass. (†02339) 249/L4
North Hansel (mts.), Utah 304/B2
North Harbour, Newf. 166/D2
North Harlowe, N.C. (†28532) 281/R5
North Hartland, Vt. (05052) 268/C4
North Hartsville, S.C. (†29550) 296/G3
North Harwich, Mass. (†02645) 249/O6
North Hatfield, Mass. (01066) 249/D3
North Hatley, Québec 172/F4
North Haven○, Conn. (06473) 210/D3
North Haven, Maine (04853) 243/F7
North Haven○, Maine (04853) 243/F7
North Haverhill, N.H. (03774) 268/D3
North Havre, Mont. (†59501) 262/G2
North Hayden, Ind. (†46356) 227/B2
North Head, New Bruns. 170/D4
North Henderson, Ill. (61466) 222/C2
North Hero, Vt. (05474) 268/A2
North Highlands, Calif. (95660) 204/B8
North High Shoals, Georgia (†30645) 217/F3
North Hills, W. Va. (†26101) 312/D4
North Hodge, La. (†71247) 238/E2
North Holland (prov.), Netherlands 27/F3
North Holland (canal), Netherlands 27/C4
North Hollywood, Calif. (*91601) 204/B10
North Hornell, N.Y. (†14843) 276/E6
North Horr, Kenya 115/G3
North Hudson, N.Y. (12855) 276/N3
North Hudson, Wis. (†54016) 317/A5
North Hyde Park, Vt. (05665) 268/B2
North Hykeham, England 13/G4
North Industry, Ohio (44707) 284/H4
North Inishkea (isl.), Ireland 17/A3
North Java, N.Y. (14113) 276/D5
North Jay, Maine (04262) 243/C6
North Johns, Ala. (35086) 195/D4
North Judson, Ind. (46366) 227/D2
North Kansas City, Mo. (64116) 261/P5
North Kedgwick (riv.), New Bruns. 170/C1
North Kent, Conn. (†06757) 210/B1
North Kent (isl.), N.W. Terrs. 187/J2
North Kingstown○, R.I. (02852) 249/J6
North Kingsville, Ohio (44068) 284/J2
North Knife (lake), Manitoba 179/J2
North Knife Lake, Manitoba 179/J2
North Korea 54/O5
North La Junta, Colo. (†81050) 208/N7
Northlake, Ill. (60164) 222/B5
Northlake, Texas (75238) 303/F1
North Lake, Wis. (53064) 317/J1
North Lakhimpur, India 68/G3
Northland, Mich. (49869) 250/B2
Northland, Wis. (†54945) 317/H6
North Landgrove, Vt. (†05148) 268/B5
North Laramie (riv.), Wyo. 319/G3
North Las Vegas, Nev. (89030) 266/F6
North Lauderdale, Fla. (†33063) 212/B3
North Lawrence, N.Y. (12967) 276/L1
North Lawrence, Ohio (44666) 284/G4
North Leeds, Maine (04263) 243/C7
North Lewisburg, Ohio (43060) 284/C5
North Liberty, Ind. (46554) 227/E1
North Liberty, Iowa (52317) 229/K5
North Lima, Ohio (44452) 284/J4
North Limington, Maine (†04049) 243/B8
North Little Rock, Ark. (*72114) 202/F4
North Livermore, Maine (†04254) 243/C7
North Loup, Nebr. (68859) 264/F3
North Loup (riv.), Nebr. 264/E3
North Lovell, Maine (†04231) 243/B7
North Lubec, Maine (†04652) 243/J6
North Luconia (shoals), Philippines 85/E4
North Madison, Conn. (†06443) 210/E3
North Madison, Ohio (†44057) 284/H2
North Magnetic Pole (dist.) 162/F1
North Magnetic Pole, Canada 4/B15
North Magnetic Pole, N.W. Terrs. 187/H2
North Manchester, Ind. (46962) 227/F3
North Manitou, Mich. (†49654) 250/C3
North Manitou (isl.), Mich. 250/C3
North Mankato, Minn. (56001) 255/D6
North Marshfield, Mass. (02059) 249/M4
North Merritt (isl.), Fla. 212/F3
North Miami, Fla. (33161) 212/B4
North Miami, Okla. (74358) 288/R1
North Miami Beach, Fla. (33161) 212/C4
North Middleboro, Mass. (02346) 249/L5
North Middletown, Ky. (40357) 237/N4
North Minch (sound), Scotland 10/D1
North Minch (sound), Scotland 15/B3
North Montpelier, Vt. (05666) 268/C3
Northmoor, Mo. (†64152) 261/P5
North Motton, Tasmania 99/C3
North Mountain, W. Va. (†25427) 312/K3
North Muskegon, Mich. (49445) 250/C5
North Myrtle Beach, S.C. (29582) 296/K4
North Naples, Fla. (33940) 212/E5
North Natuna (isl.), Indonesia 85/D4
North Negril (pt.), Jamaica 158/G6
North Newport, N.H. (†03773) 268/C5
North New Portland, Maine (04961) 243/C6
North New River (canal), Fla. 212/F5
North Newry, Maine (†04261) 243/B6
North Newton, Kansas (67117) 232/E3
North Oaks, Minn. (†55101) 255/G5
North Ogden, Utah (†84404) 304/C2
North Olmsted, Ohio (44070) 284/G9
Northome, Minn. (56661) 255/D3
North Ossetian A.S.S.R., U.S.S.R. 48/E5
North Ossetian A.S.S.R., U.S.S.R. 52/F6
North Oxford, Mass. (01537) 249/G4
North Pacific (ocean) 87/F4
North Pacific Ocean 2/B5
North Pacific Ocean 2/T4
North Pagai (isl.), Indonesia 85/C6
North Palm Beach, Fla. (33403) 212/F5
North Park, Ill. (†61111) 222/D1
North Parsonfield, Maine (†04047) 243/A8
North Pease (riv.), Texas 303/D3
North Pekin, Ill. (†61554) 222/D3
North Pembroke, Mass. (02358) 249/M4
North Pender Island, Br. Col. 184/K3
North Penobscot, Maine (†04476) 243/F7
North Perry, Maine (†04667) 243/J5
North Perry, Ohio (†44081) 284/H2
North Petherton, England 13/D6
North Pine, Br. Col. 184/G2
North Plain, Conn. (†06371) 210/F3
North Plainfield, N.J. (07060) 273/E2
North Plains, Oreg. (97133) 291/A2
North Platte (riv.) 188/F2
North Platte (riv.), Colo. 208/G1
North Platte, Nebr. 188/F2
North Platte, Nebr. (69101) 264/D3
North Platte (riv.), Nebr. 264/B3
North Platte (riv.), U.S. 146/H5
North Platte (riv.), Wyo. 319/H3
North Plymouth, Mass. (02360) 249/L5
North Pole 4/A1
North Pole 2/F1
North Pole, Alaska (99705) 196/J2
North Pole (brook), New Bruns. 170/D1
North Pomfret, Vt. (05053) 268/B4
Northport, Ala. (35476) 195/C4
North Port, Fla. (33595) 212/D4
Northport○, Maine (†04849) 243/E7
Northport, Mich. (49670) 250/D3
Northport, Nebr. (†69336) 264/B3
Northport, N.Y. (11768) 276/O9
Northport, Nova Scotia 168/E3
Northport, Wash. (99157) 310/H2
North Portal, Sask. 181/J6
North Potomac, Md. (†20857) 245/K4
North Powder, Oreg. (97867) 291/K2
North Pownal, Vt. (05260) 268/A6
North Prairie, Wis. (53153) 317/J2
North Providence○, R.I. (02908) 249/J5
North Pulaski, Va. (†24301) 307/G6
North Randall, Ohio (†44101) 284/H9
North Randolph, Vt. (†05061) 268/B4
North Raymond, Maine (†04274) 243/C8
North Reading○, Mass. (01864) 249/C5
North Redington Beach, Fla. (†33708) 212/B3
North Redwood, Minn. (56275) 255/D6
North Renous (riv.), New Bruns. 170/D2
North Rhine-Westphalia (state), W. Germany 22/B3
North Richland Hills, Texas (76118) 303/F2
Northridge, Ohio (45414) 284/B6
North Ridgeville, Ohio (44039) 284/F3
North Rim, Ariz. (86052) 198/C2
North River, Newf. 166/D2
North River, N.Y. (12856) 276/M3
North River, N. Dak. (†58102) 282/S6
North River, Nova Scotia 168/D4
North Riverside, Ill. (60546) 222/B5
North Robinson, Ohio (44856) 284/E4
North Ronaldsay (firth), Scotland 15/F1
North Ronaldsay (isl.), Scotland 15/F1
North Ronaldsay (isl.), Scotland 10/E1
Northrop, Minn. (56075) 255/D7
North Rose, N.Y. (14516) 276/G4
North Roxboro, N.C. (†27573) 281/L2
North Royalton, Ohio (44133) 284/H10
North Rustico, Pr. Edward I. 168/E2
North Saanich, Br. Col. 184/K3
North Saint Paul, Minn. (55109) 255/G5
North Salem, Ind. (46165) 227/D5
North Salem, N.H. (03073) 268/E6
North Salt Lake, Utah (†84010) 304/C3
North Sandwich, N.H. (03259) 268/E4
North San Juan, Calif. (95960) 204/E4
North Santiam (riv.), Oreg. 291/E3
North Saskatchewan (riv.) (dist.) 162/E5
North Saskatchewan (riv.), Alberta 182/E3
North Saskatchewan (riv.), Canada 146/G4
North Saskatchewan (riv.), Sask. 181/D3
North Scituate, Mass. (02060) 249/F8
North Scituate, R.I. (02857) 249/H5
North Sea (canal), Netherlands 27/F4
North Seal (riv.), Manitoba 179/H2
North Searsmont, Maine (†04973) 243/E7
North Sentinel (isl.), India 68/G6
North Sevogle (riv.), New Bruns. 170/D1
North Shapleigh, Maine (04060) 243/B8
North Shoal (lake), Manitoba 179/E4
North Shore, Wis. 317/M1
Northside, N.C. (27564) 281/M2
Northside, Sask. 181/F2
North Sioux City, S. Dak. (57049) 298/R8
North Skunk (riv.), Iowa 229/H5
North Somercotes, England 10/G4
North Somercotes, England 13/H4
North Somers, Conn. (†06071) 210/F1
North Spectacle (lake), Conn. 210/B2
North Spirit Lake, Ontario 175/B2
North Springfield, Pa. (16430) 294/A1
North Springfield, Vt. (05150) 268/B5
North Springfield, Va. (22151) 307/S3
North Star, Alberta 182/B1
North Star, Mich. (48862) 250/E5
North Star, Ohio (45350) 284/A5
North Stonington○, Conn. (06359) 210/H3
North Stratford, N.H. (03590) 268/D2
North Sunderland, England 13/F2
North Sutton, N.H. (03260) 268/D5
North Swansea, Mass. (†02777) 249/K5
North Sydney, N. S. Wales 88/L4
North Sydney, N.S. Wales 97/J3
North Sydney, Nova Scotia 168/H2
North Syracuse, N.Y. (13212) 276/H4
North Taranaki (bight), N. Zealand 100/D3
North Tarrytown, N.Y. (10591) 276/O6
North Terre Haute, Ind. (47805) 227/C5
North Thetford, Vt. (05054) 268/C4
North Thompson (riv.), Br. Col. 184/G4
North Tidworth, England 13/F6
North Tiverton, R.I. (†02722) 249/K6
North Tolsta, Scotland 15/B2
Northton, Scotland 15/B3
North Tonawanda, N.Y. (14120) 276/C4
North Trap (isl.), N. Zealand 100/B7
North Troy, Vt. (05859) 268/C2
North Truchas (peak), N. Mex. 274/D3
North Truro, Mass. (02652) 249/O4
North Tunbridge, Vt. (†05077) 268/C4
North Turner, Maine (04266) 243/C7
North Twin (mt.), N.H. 268/D3
North Tyne (riv.), England 13/E2
North Uist (isl.), Scotland 15/A3
North Uist (isl.), Scotland 10/C2
Northumberland (co.), England 13/E2
Northumberland (co.), New Bruns. 170/D2
Northumberland (str.), New Bruns. 170/F2
Northumberland○, N.H. (†03582) 268/D2
Northumberland (str.), Nova Scotia 168/E2
Northumberland (county), Ontario 177/G3
Northumberland (co.), Pa. 294/J4
Northumberland, Pa. (17857) 294/J4
Northumberland (str.), Pr. Edward I. 168/D2
Northumberland (isls.), Queensland 95/D4
Northumberland (cape), S. Australia 94/F8
Northumberland (co.), Va. 307/R5
Northumberland National Park, England 13/E2
North Umpqua (riv.), Oreg. 291/E4
North Ural (mts.), U.S.S.R. 52/K1
North Utica (Utica), Ill. (†61373) 222/E2
North Uxbridge, Mass. (01538) 249/H4
Northvale, N.J. (07647) 273/F1
North Vancouver, Br. Col. 162/D6
North Vancouver, Br. Col. 184/K3
North Vassalboro, Maine (04962) 243/D7
North Vernon, Ind. (47265) 227/F6
Northview, Mo. (†65706) 261/G8
Northville, Conn. (†06776) 210/B2
Northville, Mich. (48167) 250/F6
Northville, N.Y. (12134) 276/M4
Northville, S. Dak. (57465) 298/M3
North Wabasca (lake), Alberta 182/D1
North Wakefield, N.H. (†03872) 268/E4
North Waldoboro, Maine (†04572) 243/E7
North Wales, Pa. (19454) 294/M5
North Walpole, N.H. (†03608) 268/C5
North Walsham, England 13/J5
North Walsham, England 10/G4
North Waltham, Mass. (02154) 249/B6
North Warren, Pa. (†16365) 294/D2
North Washington, Iowa (50661) 229/J2
North Waterboro, Maine (04061) 243/B8
North Waterford, Maine (04267) 243/B7
Northway, Alaska (99764) 196/K2
North Wayne, Maine (†04284) 243/C7
North Weare, N.H. (†03281) 268/D5
North Webster, Ind. (46555) 227/F2
Northwest (pt.), Fla. 212/E6
North West (dist.), Guyana 131/A2
North West (pt.), Jamaica 158/G5
North West (cape), Australia 87/B8
North West (cape), W. Australia 88/A4
North West (cape), W. Australia 92/A3
North-West Aboriginal Reserve, S. Australia 88/E5
North-West Aboriginal Res., W. Australia 92/E4
North West Arm (inlet), Newf. 166/D2
North West Brook, Newf. 166/C2
North West Brook (riv.), Newf. 166/D2
North Westchester, Conn. (06474) 210/F2
Northwestern (sen. dist.), Alaska 196/E2
North-West Frontier (prov.), Pakistan 68/C2
North West Gander (riv.), Newf. 166/C4
North Westminster, Vt. (†05101) 268/B5
Northwest Miramichi (riv.), New Bruns. 170/D1
Northwest Oromocto (riv.), New Bruns. 170/D3
North Westport, Mass. (02790) 249/K6
North West Providence (chan.), Bahamas 156/B1
North West River, Newf. 166/B3
Northwest Territories 162/E2
Northwest Territories (prov.), Canada 146/G3
NORTHWEST TERRITORIES 187
Northwest Upsalquitch (riv.), New Bruns. 170/D1
North Weymouth, Mass. (02191) 249/D8
North Whitefield, Maine (04353) 243/D7
Northwich, England 13/H2
Northwich, England 10/G2
North Wilbraham, Mass. (†01095) 249/E4
North Wildwood, N.J. (08260) 273/D6
North Wilkesboro, N.C. (28659) 281/G2
North Williston, Vt. (†05495) 268/A3
North Wilton, Conn. (†06897) 210/B4
North Windham, Conn. (06256) 210/G1
North Windham, Maine (04062) 243/C8
North Wolcott, Vt. (†05680) 268/C2
Northwood, Iowa (50459) 229/G2
Northwood○, N.H. (03261) 268/E5
Northwood, N. Dak. (58267) 282/P4

Olduvai Gorge 421

Oak River, Manitoba 179/D4
Oaks, Mo. (†64116) 261/P5
Oaks, Okla. (74359) 288/S2
Oakshela, Sask. 181/J5
Oakton, Ky. (42077) 237/C7
Oakton, Va. (22124) 307/R3
Oaktown, Ind. (47561) 227/C7
Oak Vale, Miss. (39656) 256/E8
Oakvale, W. Va. (24739) 312/D8
Oak Valley, Kansas (†67352) 232/G4
Oak View, Calif. (93022) 204/F9
Oakview, Manitoba 179/D3
Oakview, Mo. (†64116) 261/P5
Oakville, Conn. (06779) 210/C2
Oakville, Ind. (47367) 227/G4
Oakville, Iowa (52646) 229/L6
Oakville, Ky. (42263) 237/H7
Oakville, Manitoba 179/D5
Oakville, Ontario 177/E4
Oakville, Pa. (†17257) 294/H5
Oakville, Texas (78060) 303/G9
Oakville, Wash. (98568) 310/B4
Oakway, S.C. (†29694) 296/A2
Oakwood, Georgia (30566) 217/E2
Oakwood, Ill. (61858) 222/F3
Oakwood, Mo. (63401) 261/P5
Oakwood, N. Dak. (†58237) 282/R3
Oakwood, Ohio (†44146) 284/H9
Oakwood, Ohio (†45419) 284/B6
Oakwood, Ohio (45873) 284/B3
Oakwood, Okla. (73658) 288/J3
Oakwood, Ontario 177/F3
Oakwood, Texas (75855) 303/J6
Oakwood, Va. (24631) 307/E6
Oakwood Heights, Ill. (†62095) 222/B2
Oakwood Manor, Mo. (†64101) 261/P5
Oakwood Park, Mo. (†64116) 261/P5
Oamaru, N. Zealand 100/C6
Oani (riv.), Japan 81/K3
Oasis, Nev. (†89830) 266/G1
Oasis, Utah (84650) 304/B4
Oates Coast (reg.) 5/B8
Oatlands, Tasmania 99/D4
Oatman, Ariz. (86433) 198/A3
Oatsville, Ind. (†47567) 227/C8
Oaxaca (state), Mexico 150/L8
Oaxaca, Mexico 146/J8
Oaxaca de Juárez, Mexico 150/L8
Ob' (riv.), U.S.S.R. 2/N2
Ob' (riv.), U.S.S.R. 54/H3
Ob' (gulf), U.S.S.R. 54/J3
Ob' (gulf), U.S.S.R. 4/B6
Ob' (riv.), U.S.S.R. 4/C6
Ob' (gulf), U.S.S.R. 48/H3
Ob' (riv.), U.S.S.R. 48/G3
Oba, Ont. 162/H6
Oba, Ontario 177/J5
Oba, Ontario 175/D3
Obama, Japan 81/G6
Oban (Half Moon Bay), N. Zealand 100/B7
Oban, Sask. 181/C3
Oban, Scotland 15/C4
Oban, Scotland 10/D2
Obbia, Somalia 115/J2
Obed, Alberta 182/B3
Obed (riv.), Tenn. 237/M8
Ober, Ind. (†46534) 227/D2
Oberá, Argentina 143/F2
Oberägeri, Switzerland 39/G2
Oberalp (pass), Switzerland 39/G3
Oberalpstock (mt.), Switzerland 39/G3
Oberammergau, W. Germany 22/D5
Oberburg, Switzerland 39/E2
Oberdiessbach, Switzerland 39/E3
Oberdorf, Switzerland 39/E2
Ober Grafendorf, Austria 41/C2
Oberhausen, W. Germany 22/B3
Oberhof, E. Germany 22/D3
Oberlin, Kansas (67749) 232/B2
Oberlin, La. (70655) 238/E5
Oberlin, Mich. (†48624) 250/E4
Oberlin, Ohio (44074) 284/F3
Oberndorf bei Salzburg, Austria 41/B3
Oberon, Manitoba 179/C4
Oberon, N.S. Wales 97/E3
Oberon, N. Dak. (58357) 282/M4
Oberpfälzer Wald (for.), W. Germany 22/E4
Oberriet, Switzerland 39/J2
Obersaxen, Switzerland 39/H3
Obersiggenthal, Switzerland 39/F1
Oberstammheim, Switzerland 39/G1
Oberstdorf, W. Germany 22/D5
Obert, Nebr. (68762) 264/G2
Oberursel, W. Germany 22/C3
Obervellach, Austria 41/B3
Oberwald, Switzerland 39/F3
Oberwart, Austria 41/D3
Oberwil, Switzerland 39/D3
Oberwölz, Austria 41/C3
Oberzwil, Switzerland 39/H2
Obetz, Ohio (†43201) 284/E6
Obi (isl.), Indonesia 85/H6
Obi (isls.), Indonesia 85/H6
Óbidos, Brazil 120/D3
Óbidos, Brazil 132/C3
Óbidos, Portugal 33/B3
Obihiro, Japan 81/L2
Obion (creek), Ky. 237/C7
Obion (co.), Tenn. 237/C8
Obion, Tenn. (38240) 237/C8
Obion, Middle Fork (riv.), Tenn. 237/D8
Obion, North Fork (riv.), Tenn. 237/D8
Obion, South Fork (riv.), Tenn. 237/D8
Obion (riv.), Tenn. 237/C8
Obispos, Venezuela 124/D3
Obitsu (riv.), Japan 81/P3
Oblong, Ill. (62449) 222/F5
Obluch'ye, U.S.S.R. 48/N5
Obninsk, U.S.S.R. 52/E3
Obo, Cent. Afr. Rep. 115/E2
Obock, Djibouti 111/H5
Oborniki, Poland 47/C2
Oboyan', U.S.S.R. 52/E4
Obozerskiy, U.S.S.R. 52/E2
O'Brien, Fla. (32071) 212/D1
O'Brien (co.), Iowa 229/B2
O'Brien, Oreg. (97534) 291/D5
O'Brien, Texas (79539) 303/E4
O'Briensbridge-Montpelier, Ireland 17/D6
Observatory (inlet), Br. Col. 184/C2
Obsidian, Idaho (†83278) 220/D6
Obuasi, Ghana 106/D7
Obukowin (lake), Manitoba 179/G3
Obwalden (canton), Switzerland 39/F3
Ocala, Fla. (*32670) 212/D2
Ocamo (riv.), Venezuela 124/F6
Ocampo, Chihuahua, Mexico 150/E2
Ocampo, Coahuila, Mexico 150/H3
Ocampo, Tamaulipas, Mexico 150/K5
Ocaña, Colombia 126/D3
Ocaña, Spain 33/E3
Ocate, N. Mex. (87734) 274/E2
Ocate (creek), N. Mex. 274/E2
Occidental, Cordillera (range), Bolivia 136/A6
Occidental, Cordillera (range), Colombia 126/B5
Occidental, Cordillera (range), Peru 128/F10
Occidental Mindoro (prov.), Philippines 82/C4
Occoquan, Va. (22125) 307/O3
Occum, Conn. (†06360) 210/G2
Ocean (cape), Alaska 196/K3
Ocean (pond), Fla. 212/D1
Ocean (Banaba) (isl.), Kiribati 87/G6
Ocean (co.), N.J. 273/E4
Ocean (lake), Nova Scotia 168/G3
Ocean (lake), Wyo. 319/D2
Oceana (co.), Mich. 250/C5
Oceana, W. Va. (24870) 312/C7
Oceana N.A.S., Va. 307/S7
Ocean Beach, N.Y. (11770) 276/O9
Ocean Bluff-Brant Rock, Mass. (02065) 249/M4
Ocean Breeze Park, Fla. (†33457) 212/F4
Ocean City, Md. (21842) 245/T7
Ocean City, N.J. (08226) 273/D5
Ocean City, Wash. (98569) 310/A3
Ocean Falls, Br. Col. 184/D4
Ocean Gate, N.J. (08740) 273/E4
Ocean Grove, Mass. (02777) 249/K6
Ocean Grove, N.J. (07756) 273/F3
Ocean Isle Beach, N.C. (28459) 281/N7
Oceano, Calif. (93445) 204/E8
Oceanographic Office, Md. 245/F5
Ocean Park, Maine (04063) 243/C9
Ocean Park, Wash. (98640) 310/A4
Oceanport, N.J. (07757) 273/F3
Ocean Ridge, Fla. (33444) 212/F5
Ocean Shores, Wash. (98551) 310/A3
Oceanside, Calif. (92054) 204/H10
Oceanside, N.Y. (11572) 276/R7
Oceanside, Oreg. (97134) 291/C2
Ocean Springs, Miss. (39564) 256/G10
Ocean View, Del. (19970) 245/T6
Ocean View, N.J. (08230) 273/D5
Oceanville, N.J. (08231) 273/D5
Oceola, Ohio (44860) 284/D4
Ochamchira, U.S.S.R. 52/F6
Ochelata, Okla. (74051) 288/P1
Ocheyedan, Iowa (51354) 229/B2
Ochil (hills), Scotland 15/E4
Ochiltree (co.), Texas 303/D1
Ochlocknee, Georgia (31773) 217/E9
Ochlockonee (riv.), Fla. 212/B1
Ochlockonee (riv.), Georgia 217/C10
Ochoco (creek), Oreg. 291/G3
Ochopee, Fla. (33943) 212/E6
Ocho Rios, Jamaica 158/J6
Ochre River, Manitoba 179/C3
Ochsen (mt.), Switzerland 39/D3
Ochsenfurt, W. Germany 22/D4
Ochsenkopf (mt.), Liecht. 39/J2
Ocie, Mo. (65719) 261/G9
Ocilla, Georgia (31774) 217/F7
Ockelbo, Sweden 18/K6
Ocklawaha (lake), Fla. 212/E2
Ockley, Ind. (†46923) 227/D4
Ocmulgee (riv.), Georgia 217/E5
Ocmulgee Nat'l Mon., Georgia 217/F5
Ocna Mureş, Romania 45/G2
Ocoa, Chile 138/G2
Ocoa (bay), Dom. Rep. 158/D6
Ocoee, Fla. (32761) 212/E3
Ocoee (riv.), Tenn. 237/M10
Ocoña, Peru 128/F11
Ocoña (riv.), Peru 128/F11
Oconee (co.), Georgia 217/F3
Oconee, Georgia (31067) 217/G5
Oconee (riv.), Georgia 217/F5
Oconee, Ill. (62553) 222/D4
Oconee (co.), S.C. 296/A2
Oconomowoc, Wis. (53066) 317/H1
Oconomowoc (lake), Wis. 317/H1
Oconomowoc Lake, Wis. (†53066) 317/H1
Oconto, Nebr. (68860) 264/E3
Oconto (co.), Wis. 317/K6
Oconto, Wis. (54153) 317/L6
Oconto (riv.), Wis. 317/K5
Oconto Falls, Wis. (54154) 317/K6
Ocós, Guatemala 154/A3
Ocosingo, Mexico 150/O8
Ocosta, Wash. (†98520) 310/B4
Ocotal, Segovia, Nicaragua 154/D4
Ocotal, Zelaya, Nicaragua 154/E4
Ocotlán, Mexico 150/H6
Ocotlán de Morelos, Mexico 150/L8
Ocqueoc, Mich. (†49759) 250/F3
Ocracoke, N.C. (27960) 281/T4
Ocracoke (inlet), N.C. 281/T5
Ocracoke (isl.), N.C. 281/T4
Ocre, Ala. (†36274) 195/H4
Ocros, Peru 128/D8
Octa, Mo. (†63876) 261/M10
Octa, Ohio (†43160) 284/C6
Octagon, Ala. (†36748) 195/C6
Octavia, Nebr. (68650) 264/G3
Octavia, Okla. (74958) 288/S5
October Revolution (isl.), U.S.S.R. 54/K2
October Revolution (isl.), U.S.S.R. 4/B5
October Revolution (isl.), U.S.S.R. 48/L2
Ocú, Panama 154/G7
Ocumare de la Costa, Venezuela 124/E2
Ocumare del Tuy, Venezuela 124/E2
Ocurí, Bolivia 136/C6
Oda, Ghana 106/D7
Oda, Japan 81/F6
Oda, Jebel (mt.), Sudan 59/C5
Oda, Jebel (mt.), Sudan 111/G3
Odanah, Wis. (54861) 317/E2
Odate, Japan 81/K3
Odawara, Japan 81/J6
Odd, W. Va. (25902) 312/D7
Odda, Norway 18/E6
Odder, Denmark 21/D6
Oddur, Somalia 115/H3
Odebolt, Iowa (51458) 229/C4
Odell, Ill. (60460) 222/E2
Odell, Ind. (†47992) 227/C4
Odell, Nebr. (68415) 264/H4
Odell, Oreg. (97044) 291/F2
Odell (lake), Oreg. 291/E4
Odell, Texas (79247) 303/E3
Odell River, New Bruns. 170/C2
Odemira, Portugal 33/B4
Ödemiş, Turkey 63/C3
Oden, Ark. (71961) 202/C4
Odenburg, La. (†71369) 238/G5
Odendaalsrus, S. Africa 118/D5
Odense, Denmark 7/F3
Odense, Denmark 18/G9
Odense, Denmark 21/D7
Odense (fjord), Denmark 21/D7
Odenton, Md. (21113) 245/M4
Odenville, Ala. (35120) 195/F3
Odenwald (for.), W. Germany 22/C4
Oder (riv.) 7/F3
Oder (Odra) (riv.), Czech. 41/D2
Oder (riv.), E. Germany 22/F2
Oder (riv.), Poland 47/B2
Oder-Haff (mts.), E. Germany 22/F2
Oder-Haff (lag.), Poland 47/B2
Odessa, Del. (19730) 245/R3
Odessa, Fla. (33556) 212/D3
Odessa, Minn. (56276) 255/B5
Odessa, Mo. (64076) 261/E5
Odessa, Nebr. (68861) 264/E4
Odessa, N.Y. (14869) 276/G6
Odessa, Ontario 177/H3
Odessa, Sask. 181/H5
Odessa, Tex. 188/F4
Odessa, Texas 146/H6
Odessa, Texas (79760) 303/B6
Odessa, U.S.S.R. 2/L3
Odessa, U.S.S.R. 7/H4
Odessa, U.S.S.R. 48/D5
Odessa, U.S.S.R. 52/D5
Odessa, Wash. (99159) 310/G3
Odessadale, Georgia (†30222) 217/C5
Odgen, Utah 188/D2
Odgensburg, N.Y. 188/M2
Odiel (riv.), Spain 33/C4
Odienné, Ivory Coast 106/C7
Odin, Ill. (62870) 222/D5
Odin, Kansas (67562) 232/D3
Odin, Minn. (56160) 255/D7
Odiongan, Philippines 82/C4
Odivelas, Portugal 33/A1
Odobeşti, Romania 45/H3
Odon, Ind. (47562) 227/C7
Odongk, Cambodia 72/E5
O'Donnell, Texas (79351) 303/C5
O'Donnells, Newf. 166/D2
Odoorn, Netherlands 27/K3
Odorheiu Secuiesc, Romania 45/G2
Odra (Oder) (riv.), Poland 47/B2
Odry, Czech. 41/D2
Odum, Georgia (31555) 217/H7
Odweina, Somalia 115/J2
Oebisfelde, E. Germany 22/D2
Oeiras, Brazil 132/F4
Oeiras, Portugal 33/B3
Oelemari (riv.), Suriname 131/D4
Oella, Md. (†21228) 245/L3
Oelrichs, S. Dak. (57763) 298/C7
Oelsnitz, E. Germany 22/E3
Oelsnitz im Erzgebirge, E. Germany 22/E3
Oelwein, Iowa (50662) 229/K3
Oeno (isl.), Pitcairn Is. 87/O8
Oenpelli, North. Terr. 93/C2
Oensingen, Switzerland 39/E2
Of, Turkey 63/J2
Ofahoma, Miss. (39141) 256/E5
O'Fallon, Ill. (62269) 222/B2
O'Fallon, Mo. (63366) 261/L5
O'Fallon (creek), Mont. 262/L4
Ofanto (riv.), Italy 34/E4
Ofaqim, Israel 65/B5
Ofen (pass), Switzerland 39/K3
Ofenhorn (mt.), Switzerland 39/F4
Offa, Nigeria 106/E7
Offaly (co.), Ireland 17/F5
Offenbach am Main, W. Germany 22/C3
Offenburg, W. Germany 22/B4
Offerle, Kansas (67563) 232/C4
Offerman, Georgia (31556) 217/H8
Offutt, Ky. (41237) 237/R5
Offutt A.F.B., Nebr. 264/J3
Ofotfjorden (fjord), Norway 18/K2
Ofqui (isth.), Chile 138/D6
Oftringen, Switzerland 39/E2
Ofunato, Japan 81/K4
Oga, Japan 81/J4
Oga (pen.), Japan 81/J4
Ogaden (reg.), Ethiopia 102/G4
Ogaden (reg.), Ethiopia 111/H6
Ogaki, Japan 81/H6
Ogallah, Kansas (67656) 232/C3
Ogallala, Nebr. (69153) 264/C3
Ogasawara-gunto (Bonin) (isls.), Japan 81/M3
Ogbomosho, Nigeria 102/C4
Ogbomosho, Nigeria 106/E7
Ogden, Ark. (71853) 202/B6
Ogden, Ill. (61859) 222/F3
Ogden, Iowa (50212) 229/E4
Ogden, Kansas (66517) 232/F2
Ogden (bay), N.W. Terrs. 187/H3
Ogden, Utah 146/G6
Ogden, Utah (*84401) 304/C2
Ogden Dunes, Ind. (†46401) 227/C1
Ogdensburg, N.J. (07439) 273/D1
Ogdensburg, N.Y. (13669) 276/K1
Ogdensburg, Wis. (54962) 317/J7
Ogeechee (riv.), Georgia 217/J5
Ogema, Minn. (56569) 255/C3
Ogema, Sask. 181/G6
Ogema, Wis. (54459) 317/F5
Ogemaw, Ark. (†71764) 202/E7
Ogemaw (co.), Mich. 250/E4
Ogi, Japan 81/J5
Ogidaki (mt.), Ontario 175/D3
Ogidaki (mt.), Ontario 177/J5
Ogilvie, Manitoba 179/D4
Ogilvie, Minn. (56358) 255/E5
Ogilvie (mts.), Yukon 187/E3
Ogilvie (riv.), Yukon 187/E3
Oglala, S. Dak. (57764) 298/D7
Ogle (co.), Ill. 222/D1
Ogle, Ky. (40971) 237/O6
Oglesby, Ill. (61348) 222/D2
Oglesby, Texas (76561) 303/G6
Oglethorpe (co.), Georgia 217/F3
Oglethorpe, Georgia (31406) 217/D6
Oglio (riv.), Italy 34/C2
Ogmore, Queensland 88/J4
Ogmore and Garw, Wales 13/A6
Ogoja, Nigeria 106/F7
Ogoki (riv.), Ont. 162/H5
Ogoki (riv.), Ontario 175/C2
Ogooué (riv.), Congo 115/A4
Ogooué (riv.), Gabon 115/A4
Ogre, U.S.S.R. 53/C2
Ogulin, Yugoslavia 45/B3
Ogun (state), Nigeria 106/E7
Ogunquit, Maine (03907) 243/B9
Oğuzeli, Turkey 63/G4
Ohai, N. Zealand 100/A6
Ohakune, N. Zealand 100/E3
O'Hare Field-Chicago International Airport, Ill. 222/B5
Ohariu (stream), N. Zealand 100/B2
Ohata, Japan 81/K3
Ohatchee, Ala. (36271) 195/G3
Ohaton, Alberta 182/D3
Ohau (lake), N. Zealand 100/B6
Ohaupo, N. Zealand 100/E2
Ohey, Belgium 27/G8
O'Higgins (lake), Chile 138/D7
Ohio 188/K2
OHIO 284
Ohio (riv.) 188/J3
Ohio, Colo. (81237) 208/F5
Ohio, Ill. (61349) 222/D2
Ohio (riv.), Ill. 222/E6
Ohio (co.), Ind. 227/H7
Ohio (riv.), Ind. 227/B9
Ohio (co.), Ky. 237/H6
Ohio (riv.), Ky. 237/F5
Ohio, Nova Scotia 168/F3
Ohio (riv.), Nova Scotia 168/D4
Ohio (riv.), Ohio 284/B8
Ohio (riv.), Pa. 294/A4
Ohio (state), U.S. 146/K5
Ohio (riv.), U.S. 146/K6
Ohio (riv.), U.S. 2/E4
Ohio (co.), W. Va. 312/E2
Ohio (riv.), W. Va. 312/B5
Ohio Brush (creek), Ohio 284/D8
Ohio City, Ohio (45874) 284/A4
Ohiopyle, Pa. (15470) 294/D6
Ohioville, Pa. (†15059) 294/B4
Ohiowa, Nebr. (68416) 264/G4
Ohley, W. Va. (25147) 312/D6
Ohlman, Ill. (62076) 222/D4
Ohoopee, Georgia (†30436) 217/H6
Ohopoho, Namibia 118/A3
Ohře (riv.), Czech. 41/B1
Ohrid (lake), Albania 45/E5
Ohrid, Yugoslavia 45/E5
Ohrid (lake), Yugoslavia 45/E5
Ohura, N. Zealand 100/E3
Oiapoque (Oyapock) (riv.), Brazil 132/C2
Oich, Loch (lake), Scotland 15/D3
Oich (riv.), Scotland 15/D3
Oies (isl.), Québec 172/G2
Oil (creek), Pa. 294/C2
Oil Center, N. Mex. (88266) 274/F6
Oil City, La. (71061) 238/C1
Oil City, Ontario 177/B5
Oil City, Pa. 188/L2
Oil City, Pa. (16301) 294/F8
Oildale, Calif. (93308) 204/F8
Oilmont, Mont. (59466) 262/E2
Oil Spring Ind. Res., N.Y. 276/D6
Oil Springs, Ky. (41238) 237/P5
Oil Springs, Ontario 177/B5
Oilton, Okla. (74052) 288/N2
Oilton, Texas (78371) 303/F10
Oil Trough, Ark. (72564) 202/G2
Oinóï, Greece 45/F6
Oise (dept.), France 28/E3
Oise (riv.), France 28/E3
Oiseau (lake), Manitoba 179/G4
Oiseau (riv.), Manitoba 179/G4
Oisterwijk, Netherlands 27/G5
Oistins, Barbados 161/B9
Oistins (bay), Barbados 161/B9
Oita (pref.), Japan 81/E7
Oita, Japan 81/E7
Ojai, Calif. (93023) 204/F9
Ojibwa, Wis. (54862) 317/D4
Ojinaga, Mexico 150/G2
Ojiya, Japan 81/J5
Ojocaliente, Mexico 150/H5
Ojo Caliente, N. Mex. (87549) 274/D2
Ojo del Toro (mt.), Cuba 158/G4
Ojo Feliz, N. Mex. (87735) 274/E2
Ojo Sarco, N. Mex. (87550) 274/D2
Ojos del Salado (mt.) 120/C5
Ojos del Salado, Cerro (mt.), Argentina 143/C2
Ojos del Salado, Nevado (mt.), Chile 138/B6
Ojos Negros, Spain 33/F2
Ojus, Fla. (33163) 212/B4
Oka, Québec 172/C4
Oka (riv.), U.S.S.R. 7/J3
Oka (riv.), U.S.S.R. 48/L4
Oka (riv.), U.S.S.R. 52/F4
Okaba, Indonesia 85/K7
Okabena, Minn. (56161) 255/C7
Okahandja, Namibia 102/D7
Okahandja, Namibia 118/B4
Okahumpka, Fla. (32762) 212/D3
Okak (bay), Newf. 166/B2
Okak (isls.), Newf. 166/B2
Okaloacoochee Slough (swamp), Fla. 212/E5
Okaloosa (co.), Fla. 212/C6
Okamanpeedan (lake), Iowa 229/D2
Okanagan (lake), Br. Col. 162/D6
Okanagan (lake), Br. Col. 184/H5
Okanagan Centre, Br. Col. 184/H5
Okanagan Falls, Br. Col. 184/H5
Okanagan Landing, Br. Col. 184/H5
Okanagan Mission, Br. Col. 184/H5
Okanagan Mtn. Prov. Park, Br. Col. 184/G5
Okanogan (riv.), Br. Col. 184/H6
Okanogan (co.), Wash. 310/F2
Okanogan, Wash. (98840) 310/F2
Okanogan (riv.), Wash. 310/F2
Okarche, Okla. (73762) 288/L3
Okatibbee (creek), Miss. 256/G5
Okatibbee (lake), Miss. 256/G5
Okato, N. Zealand 100/D3
Okaton, S. Dak. (57562) 298/H6
Okauchee, Wis. (53069) 317/J1
Okauchee (lake), Wis. 317/J1
Okaukuejo, Namibia 118/B3
Okawa, Japan 81/E7
Okawville, Ill. (62271) 222/D5
Okay, Okla. (74446) 288/R3
Okaya, Japan 81/H5
Okayama (pref.), Japan 81/F6
Okayama, Japan 81/F6
Okazaki, Japan 81/H6
O'Kean, Ark. (72449) 202/J1
Okeana, Ohio (45053) 284/A7
Okee, Wis. (†53555) 317/H9
Okeechobee (lake), Fla. 188/K5
Okeechobee (co.), Fla. 212/F4
Okeechobee, Fla. (33472) 212/F4
Okeechobee (lake), Fla. 212/F5
O'Keeffe Nat'l Hist. Site, N. Mex. 274/C2
Okeene, Okla. (73763) 288/K2
Okefenokee (swamp), Fla. 212/D1
Okefenokee (swamp), Georgia 217/H9
Okehampton, England 13/D7
Okehampton, England 10/D5
Okemah, Okla. (74859) 288/O4
Okemo (Ludlow) (mt.), Vt. 268/B5
Okemos, Mich. (48864) 250/E6
Okene, Nigeria 106/F7
Oker (riv.), W. Germany 22/D2
Okesa, Okla. (†74003) 288/O1
Oketo, Kansas (66518) 232/F2
Okfuskee (co.), Okla. 288/O3
Okha, U.S.S.R. 54/R4
Okha, U.S.S.R. 48/P4
Okha Port, India 68/B4
Okhotsk (sea) 2/S3
Okhotsk (sea), Japan 81/M1
Okhotsk, U.S.S.R. 54/R4
Okhotsk (sea), U.S.S.R. 54/R4
Okhotsk, U.S.S.R. 48/P4
Okhotsk (sea), U.S.S.R. 48/P4
Oki (isls.), Japan 81/F5
Okiep, S. Africa 118/B5
Okinawa (pref.), Japan 81/N6
Okinawa (isls.), Japan 54/O7
Okinawa (isl.), Japan 81/N6
Okinawa (isls.), Japan 81/N6
Okinoerabu (isl.), Japan 81/N5
Okkan, Burma 72/B3
Okla, Sask. 181/H3
Oklahoma 188/G3
Oklahoma (co.), Okla. 288/M3
OKLAHOMA 288
Oklahoma (state), U.S. 146/J6
Oklahoma City (cap.), Okla. 146/J6
Oklahoma City (cap.), Okla. 188/G3
Oklahoma City (cap.), Okla. (*73101) 288/L4
Oklaunion, Texas (76373) 303/F3
Oklawaha, Fla. (32679) 212/E2
Oklawaha (riv.), Fla. 212/E2
Oklee, Minn. (56742) 255/C3
Okmulgee, Okla. 188/G3
Okmulgee (co.), Okla. 288/P3
Okmulgee, Okla. (74447) 288/O3
Okoboji, Iowa (51355) 229/C2
Okobojo (creek), S. Dak. 298/J4
Okolona, Ark. (71962) 202/D5
Okolona, Ky. (40219) 237/K4
Okolona, Miss. (38860) 256/G2
Okolona, Ohio (43550) 284/B3
Okondja, Gabon 115/B4
Okotoks, Alberta 182/C4
Okovango (riv.) 102/D6
Okovango (riv.), Botswana 118/C3
Okovango (swamps), Botswana 118/C3
Okovango (riv.), Namibia 118/C3
Okoyo, Congo 115/C4
Okpo, Burma 72/C3
Okreek, S. Dak. (57563) 298/J7
Oksino, U.S.S.R. 52/H1
Oktaha, Okla. (74450) 288/R3
Oktibbeha (co.), Miss. 256/G4
Oktyabr'sk, U.S.S.R. 52/G4
Oktyabr'skiy, U.S.S.R. 52/H4
Okulovka, U.S.S.R. 52/D3
Okushiri (isl.), Japan 81/J2
Ola, Ark. (72853) 202/D3
Ola, Georgia (†30253) 217/E4
Ola, Idaho (83657) 220/B5
Olá, Panama 154/G6
Ólafsfjördhur, Iceland 21/C1
Ola Grande (pt.), P. Rico 161/D3
Olalla, Br. Col. 184/H5
Olalla, Wash. (98359) 310/A2
Olamon, Maine (04467) 243/F5
Olancha, Calif. (93549) 204/H7
Olanchito, Honduras 154/D3
Öland (isl.), Sweden 7/F3
Öland (isl.), Sweden 18/K8
Olanta, Pa. (16863) 294/F4
Olanta, S.C. (29114) 296/H4
Olar, S.C. (29843) 296/E5
Olary, S. Australia 94/G5
Olathe, Colo. (81425) 208/D5
Olathe, Kansas (66061) 232/H3
Olathe Nav. Air Sta., Kansas 232/H3
Olavarría, Argentina 143/D4
Olavarría, Argentina 120/C6
Oława, Poland 47/C3
Olberg, Ariz. (†85247) 198/D5
Olbernhau, E. Germany 22/E3
Olbia, Italy 34/B4
Olcott, N.Y. (14126) 276/C4
Old (riv.), Calif. 204/L1
Old (riv.), La. 238/G5
Old (stream), Maine 243/H6
Oldany (isl.), Scotland 15/C2
Old Appleton, Mo. (63770) 261/N7
Old Bahama (chan.), Bahamas 156/B2
Old Bahama (chan.), Cuba 158/G1
Old Bahama (chan.), Cuba 156/B2
Old Bar, N.S. Wales 97/G2
Old Barkerville, Br. Col. 184/G3
Old Bennington, Vt. (†05201) 268/A6
Old Bonaventure, Newf. 166/D2
Old Bridge, N.J. (08857) 273/E3
Old Castile (reg.), Spain 33/D2
Oldcastle, Ireland 10/C4
Oldcastle, Ireland 17/G4
Old Crow, Yukon 187/E3
Oldemarkt, Netherlands 27/J3
Olden, Mo. (†65789) 261/J9
Olden, Norway 18/E6
Olden, Texas (76466) 303/F5
Oldenburg, Ind. (47036) 227/G6
Oldenburg, Miss. (†39661) 256/C7
Oldenburg, W. Germany 22/C2
Oldenburg in Holstein, W. Germany 22/D1
Old England, Jamaica 158/H6
Old Entrance, Alberta 182/B3
Oldenzaal, Netherlands 27/K4
Old Faithful, Wyo. (82190) 319/B1
Oldfield, La. (†70754) 238/L1
Old Fields, W. Va. (26845) 312/J4
Old Forge, N.Y. (13420) 276/L3
Old Forge, Pa. (18518) 294/F7
Old Fort, N.C. (28762) 281/E3
Old Fort, Ohio (44861) 284/D3
Oldfort, Tenn. (37362) 237/M10
Old Glory, Texas (79540) 303/D4
Old Greenwich, Conn. (06870) 210/A4
Oldham, England 13/H2
Oldham, England 10/G2
Oldham (co.), Ky. 237/L4
Oldham, S. Dak. (57051) 298/P5
Oldham (co.), Texas 303/B2
Old Harbor, Alaska (99643) 196/H3
Old Harbour, Jamaica 158/J6
Old Harbour (bay), Jamaica 158/J6
Old Harbour Bay, Jamaica 158/J6
Old Hickory (dam), Tenn. 237/H8
Old Hickory (lake), Tenn. 237/J8
Old Kilpatrick, Scotland 15/B2
Old Landing, Ky. (41358) 237/O5
Old Leighlin, Ireland 17/G6
Old Lodge (creek), S. Dak. 298/K6
Old Lyme○, Conn. (06371) 210/F3
Old Main Centre, Sask. 181/D5
Oldman (riv.), Alberta 182/D5
Oldman (riv.), Sask. 181/L2
Oldmans (creek), N.J. 273/C4
Old Marsh Bed, North. Terr. 93/B6
Oldmeldrum, Scotland 15/F3
Oldmeldrum, Scotland 10/E2
Old Mill Creek, Ill. (†60083) 222/B4
Old Mission, Mich. (49673) 250/D4
Old Monroe, Mo. (63369) 261/L5
Old Mystic, Conn. (06372) 210/H3
Old Orchard Beach, Maine (04064) 243/C9
Old Orchard Beach○, Maine (04064) 243/C9
Old Perlican, Newf. 166/D2
Old Rhine (riv.), Netherlands 27/E4
Old Rhodes (key), Fla. 212/F6
Old Ripley, Ill. (†62275) 222/D5
Old Road, Ant. & Bar. 161/D11
Old Road Town, St. Chris.-Nevis 161/C10
Olds, Alberta 182/D4
Olds, Iowa (52647) 229/K6
Old Saybrook, Conn. (06475) 210/F3
Old Saybrook○, Conn. (06475) 210/F3
Old Shawneetown, Ill. (†62984) 222/E6
Oldsmar, Fla. (33557) 212/B2
Old Spring Hill, Ala. (†36742) 195/C6
Old Sturbridge Village, Mass. (†01566) 249/F4
Old Tampa (bay), Fla. 212/B3
Old Tappan, N.J. (07675) 273/C1
Old Town, Fla. (32680) 212/C2
Oldtown, Idaho (†99156) 220/A1
Oldtown, Ky. (41163) 237/R4
Old Town, Maine (04468) 243/F6
Oldtown, Md. (21555) 245/D2
Old Trap, N.C. (†27974) 281/T2
Olduvai Gorge (canyon), Tanzania 115/G4

Owyhee 423

Orlando, Okla. (73073) 288/M2
Orlando, W. Va. (26412) 312/E5
Orland Park, Ill. (60462) 222/B6
Orleães, Brazil 132/D10
Orléanais (trad. prov.) France 29
Orleans, Calif. (95556) 204/B2
Orléans, France 7/E4
Orléans, France28/D3
Orleans, Ind. (47452) 227/D7
Orleans, Iowa, (†51360) 229/C2
Orleans, (par.), La. 238/L6
Orleans, Mass. (02653) 249/O5
Orleans○, Mass. (02653) 249/O5
Orleans, Minn. (56743) 255/B2
Orleans, Nebr.(68966) 264/E4
Orleans (co.), N.Y. 276/D4
Orleans Ontario 177/J2
Orléans (isl.) Québec 172/F3
Orleans (co.), Vt. 268/C2
Orleans, Vt. (05860) 268/C2
Orleans Cross Roads, W. Va. (†25422) 312/K3
Orléansville (El Asnam), Algeria 106/E1
Orlice (riv.), Czech. 41/D1
Orlická (res.), Czech. 41/C2
Orlinda, Tenn. (37141) 237/H7
Orlová, Czech. 41/E2
Orly, France 28/B2
Orma, W. Va. (25268) 312/D5
Ormara, Pakistan 59/J4
Ormara, Pakistan 68/A3
Orme, Tenn. (35740) 237/K10
Ormea, Italy 34/A2
Ormiston, Sask. 181/F6
Ormoc, Philippines 82/E5
Ormoc (bay), Philippines 82/E5
Ormond Beach, Fla. (32074) 212/E2
Ormond-by-the-Sea, Fla. (32074) 212/E2
Ormont-Dessus, Switzerland 39/D4
Ormsby, Minn. (56162) 255/D7
Ormsby, Pa. (16741) 294/E2
Ormskirk, England 10/F2
Ormskirk, England 13/G2
Ormstown, Québec 172/D4
Orne (dept.), France 28/C3
Orne (riv.), France 28/C3
Orneta, Poland 47/E1
Ornö (isl.), Sweden 18/J2
Örnsköldsvik, Sweden 18/L5
Orobayaya, Bolivia 136/D3
Orocovis, P. Rico 161/C2
Orocué, Colombia 126/E5
Orofino, Idaho (83544) 220/B3
Orofino (creek), Idaho 220/C3
Oro Grande, Calif. (92368) 204/H9
Orogrande, Idaho (†83525) 220/C4
Orogrande, N. Mex. (88342) 274/D6
Orohena (mt.), Fr. Poly. 86/T13
Oro Ingenio, Bolivia 136/C7
Oroluk (atoll), Micronesia 87/F5
Oromocto, New Bruns. 170/D3
Oromocto (lake), New Bruns. 170/C3
Oromocto (riv.), New Bruns. 170/D3
Oron, Israel 65/C6
Oron, Nigeria 106/F8
Orona (Hull) (isl.), Kiribati 87/J6
Orondo, Wash. (98843) 310/E3
Orongorongo (riv.), N. Zealand 100/B3
Oron-la-Ville, Switzerland 39/C3
Orono, Maine (04473) 243/F6
Orono○, Maine (04473) 243/F6
Orono, Minn. (†55323) 255/F5
Oronoco, Minn. (55960) 255/F6
Oronogo, Mo. (64855) 261/D8
Oronsay (isl.), Scotland 15/B4
Orontes (riv.), Syria 59/C2
Orontes (riv.), Syria 63/G5
Oropesa, Spain 33/D3
Oropuche (riv.), Trin. & Tob. 161/B10
Oroqen, China 77/K1
Oroquieta, Philippines 85/G4
Oroquieta, Philippines 82/D6
Orosei (gulf), Italy 34/B4
Orosháza, Hungary 41/F3
Orosi, Calif. (93647) 204/F7
Oroszlány, Hungary 41/E3
Orote (pen.), Guam 86/K7
Orotina, C. Rica 154/E6
Orotukan, U.S.S.R. 48/Q3
Orovada, Nev. (89425) 266/D1
Oro Valley, Ariz. (†85704) 198/E6
Oroville, Calif. (95965) 204/D4
Oroville (lake), Calif. 204/D4
Oroville, Wash. (98844) 310/F2
Orozco, Cuba 158/B1
Orpha, Wyo. (†82633) 319/G3
Orr, Minn. (55771) 255/F2
Orr, N. Dak. (†58244) 282/P3
Orr, Okla. (†73456) 288/M6
Orrefors, Sweden 18/J8
Orrick, Mo. (64077) 261/D4
Orrin, N. Dak. (58359) 282/K3
Orrin (riv.), Scotland 15/D3
Orrington, Maine (04474) 243/F6
Orrington○, Maine (04474) 243/F6
Orroroo, S. Australia 94/F5
Orrs Island, Maine (04066) 243/D8
Orrstown, Pa. (17244) 294/G5
Orrtanna, Pa. (17353) 294/H6
Orrum, N.C. (28369) 281/L6
Orrville, Ala. (36767) 195/D6
Orrville, Ohio (44667) 284/G4
Orrville, Ontario 177/E2
Orsa, Sweden 18/J6
Orsainville, Québec 172/H3
Orsha, U.S.S.R. 7/G3
Orsha, U.S.S.R. 52/C4
Orsières, Switzerland 39/D4
Orsk, U.S.S.R. 7/K3
Orsk, U.S.S.R. 48/F4
Orsk, U.S.S.R. 52/J4
Orson, Pa. (18449) 294/M2
Orsonnens, Switzerland 39/D3
Orşova, Romania 45/F3
Ørsted, Denmark 21/D5
Orta, Turkey 63/E2
Ortaca, Turkey 63/C4
Ortakaraviran, Turkey 63/E4
Ortaköy, Çorum, Turkey 63/F2
Ortaköy, Niğde, Turkey 63/F3
Ortega, Colombia 126/C6
Ortegal (cape), Spain 33/B1
Orteguaza (riv.), Colombia 126/C7
Orthez, France 28/C6
Ortigueira, Spain 33/C1
Orting, Wash. (98360) 310/C3
Ortiz, Colo. (†81120) 208/H8
Ortiz, Mexico 150/D2
Ortiz, Venezuela 124/E3
Ortles (range), Italy 34/C1
Ortley, S. Dak. (57256) 298/P3
Ortoire (riv.), Trin. & Tob. 161/B11
Ortón (riv.), Bolivia 136/B2
Ortona, Italy 34/E3
Ortonville, Mich. (48462) 250/F6
Ortonville, Minn. (56278) 255/B5
Oruro (dept.), Bolivia 136/A6
Oruro, Bolivia 120/C4
Oruro, Bolivia 136/B5
Oruzgan (Hazar Qadam), Afghanistan 68/B2
Orvieto, Italy 34/D3
Orville, Ky. (40057) 237/M4
Orviston, Pa. (16864) 294/G3
Orwell, N.Y. (13426) 276/J3
Orwell, Ohio (44076) 284/J2
Orwell○, Vt. (05760) 268/A4
Orwigsburg, Pa. (17961) 294/K4
Oryakhovo, Bulgaria 45/F4
Or Yehuda, Israel 65/B4
Orzesze, Poland 47/A4
Orzysz, Poland 47/E2
Osa, U.S.S.R. 52/J3
Osage (riv.) 188/H3
Osage, Ark. (†72638) 202/D1
Osage, Iowa (50461) 229/H2
Osage (co.), Kansas 232/G3
Osage, Minn. (56570) 255/C4
Osage (co.), Mo. 261/J6
Osage (riv.), Mo. 261/E6
Osage (co.), Okla. 288/O1
Osage, Okla. (74054) 288/O2
Osage, Sask. 181/H6
Osage, W. Va. (26543) 312/F3
Osage, Wyo. (82723) 319/H2
Osage Beach, Mo. (65065) 261/G6
Osage City, Kansas (66523) 232/G3
Osage Ind. Res., Okla. 288/O1
Osaka (pref.), Japan 81/J8
Osaka, Japan 2/R4
Osaka, Japan 54/P6
Osaka, Japan 81/J8
Osaka (bay), Japan 81/H8
Osakis, Minn. (56360) 255/C5
Osasco, Brazil 135/C3
Osawatomie, Kansas (66064) 232/H3
Osborn, Miss. (†39759) 256/G3
Osborn, Mo. (64474) 261/D3
Osborn, S.C. (†29426) 296/G6
Osborne (co.), Kansas 232/D2
Osborne, Kansas (67473) 232/D2
Osborne, Pa. (†15143) 294/B4
Osbornsville, N.J. (08723) 273/E3
Osburn, Idaho (83849) 220/B2
Oscar, Fr. Guiana 131/E4
Oscar, La. (70762) 238/H5
Oscar, Okla. (73561) 288/L7
Oscarville, Alaska (†99559) 196/F2
Osceola, Ark. (72370) 202/K2
Osceola (co.), Fla. 212/E3
Osceola, Ind. (46561) 227/E1
Osceola (co.), Iowa 229/B2
Osceola, Iowa (50213) 229/F6
Osceola (co.), Mich. 250/D5
Osceola, Mo. (64776) 261/E6
Osceola, Nebr. (68651) 264/G3
Osceola (mt.), N.H. 268/E3
Osceola, N.Y. (†13316) 276/J3
Osceola, Pa. (16942) 294/H2
Osceola, S. Dak. (†57353) 298/O5
Osceola, Wis. (54020) 317/A5
Osceola Mills, Pa. (16666) 294/F4
Oschatz, E. Germany 22/E3
Oschersleben, E. Germany 22/D2
Oscoda (co.), Mich. 250/E4
Oscoda, Mich. (48750) 250/F4
Oscura (mts.), N. Mex. 274/C5
Oscuro, N. Mex. (†88301) 274/C5
Ösel (Saaremaa) (isl.), U.S.S.R. 52/B3
Osgood, Ind. (47037) 227/G6
Osgood, Mo. (†63556) 261/F2
Osgood, Ohio (45351) 284/A5
Osgoode, Ontario 177/J2
Osh, U.S.S.R. 54/J5
Osh, U.S.S.R. 48/H5
Osha (peak), N. Mex. 274/C4
Oshawa, Ontario 177/F4
Oshikango, Namibia 118/A3
O-Shima (isl.), Japan 81/J6
Oshkosh, Nebr. (69154) 264/B3
Oshkosh, Wis. 188/J2
Oshkosh, Wis. (54901) 317/J8
Oshnoviyeh, Iran 66/D2
Oshogbo, Nigeria 102/C4
Oshogbo, Nigeria 106/F7
Oshoto, Wyo. (82724) 319/G1
Oshtoran Kuh (mt.), Iran 66/F4
Oshwe, Zaire 115/C4
Osierfield, Georgia (†31798) 217/F7
Osijek, Yugoslavia 7/F4
Osijek, Yugoslavia 45/D3
Osimo, Italy 34/D3
Osipenko (Berdyansk), U.S.S.R. 52/E5
Osipovichi, U.S.S.R. 52/C4
Oskaloosa, Iowa (52577) 229/H6
Oskaloosa, Iowa 188/H2
Oskaloosa, Kansas (66066) 232/G2
Oskaloosa, Mo. (†66711) 261/D7
Oskarshamn, Sweden 18/K8
Oskélanéo, Québec 174/C3
Oslavany, Czech. 41/D2
Osler, Sask. 181/E3
Oslo, Minn. (56744) 255/A2
Oslo (city), Norway 18/D3
Oslo (cap.), Norway 2/K2
Oslo (cap.), Norway 7/F2
Oslo (cap.), Norway 18/D3
Oslofjord (fjord), Norway 18/D4
Osmanabad, India 68/D5
Osmancık, Turkey 63/F2
Osmaneli, Turkey 63/D2
Osmaniye, Turkey 63/G4
Osmond, Nebr. (68765) 264/G2
Osnabrock, N. Dak. (58269) 282/O2
Osnabrück, W. Germany 22/C2
Osnaburgh House, Ontario 175/B2
Oso, Wash. (98223) 310/D2
Osogna, Switzerland 39/H4
Osorno, Chile 120/B7
Osorno, Chile 138/D3
Osorno, Spain 33/D1
Osoyoos, Br. Col. 184/H5
Osoyoos (lake), Wash. 310/F1
Ospino, Venezuela 124/D3
Osprey (reef), 95/C2
Osprey, Fla. (33559) 212/D4
Osprey (reef), Queensland 88/H2
Oss, Netherlands 27/H5
Ossa, Serra da (mts.), Portugal 33/C3
Ossa (mt.), Tasmania 88/H8
Ossa (mt.), Tasmania 99/C3
Ossabaw (isl.), Georgia 217/K7
Ossabaw (sound), Georgia 217/K7
Osse (riv.), Nigeria 106/F7
Osseo, Mich. (49266) 250/E7
Osseo, Minn. (55369) 255/G5
Osseo, Wis. (54758) 317/D6
Ossian, Ind. (46777) 227/G3
Ossian, Iowa (52161) 229/K2
Ossineke, Mich. (49766) 250/F4
Ossining, N.Y. (10562) 276/N8
Ossipee○, N.H. (03864) 268/E4
Ossipee (lake), N.H. 268/E4
Ossipee (mts.), N.H. 268/E4
Ossipee (riv.), N.H. 268/F4
Ossokmanuan (res.), Newf. 166/B3
Ostashkov, U.S.S.R. 52/D3
Oste (riv.), W. Germany 22/C2
Osteen, Fla. (32764) 212/E3
Ostend, Belgium 27/B6
Osterburg, Pa. (16667) 294/E5
Österdalälven (riv.), Sweden 18/H6
Osterdock, Iowa (†52035) 229/L3
Östergötland (co.), Sweden 18/J7
Osterholz-Scharmbeck, W. Germany 22/C2
Osterode am Harz, W. Germany 22/D3
Östersund, Sweden 7/F2
Östersund, Sweden 18/J5
Osterville, Mass. (02655) 249/N6
Øster Vrå, Denmark 21/D3
Osterwick, Manitoba 179/D5
Østfold (co.), Norway 18/G7
Östhammar, Sweden 18/L6
Ostia Antica, Italy 34/F7
Ostrander, Minn. (55961) 255/F7
Ostrander, Ohio (43061) 284/D5
Ostrava, Czech. 7/F4
Ostrava, Czech. 41/E2
Ostróda, Poland 47/D2
Ostrogozhsk, U.S.S.R. 48/D4
Ostrogozhsk, U.S.S.R. 52/E4
Ostrołęka (prov.), Poland 47/E2
Ostrołęka, Poland 47/E2
Ostrov, Czech. 41/B1
Ostrov, U.S.S.R. 52/C3
Ostrowiec Świętokrzyski, Poland 47/E3
Ostrów Mazowiecka, Poland 47/E2
Ostrów Wielkopolski, Poland 47/C3
Ostrzeszów, Poland 47/C3
Ostuni, Italy 34/F4
O'Sullivan (dam), Wash. 310/F4
Osŭm (riv.), Bulgaria 45/G4
Osumi (isls.), Japan 81/E8
Osumi (pen.), Japan 81/E8
Osumi (str.), Japan 81/E8
Osuna, Spain 33/D4
Oswaldtwistle, England 13/H1
Oswayo, Pa. (16915) 294/G2
Oswegatchie, N.Y. (13670) 276/K2
Oswegatchie (riv.), N.Y. 276/K2
Oswego, Ill. (60543) 222/E2
Oswego, Ind. (†46538) 227/F2
Oswego, Kansas (67356) 232/G4
Oswego, Mont. (59251) 262/L2
Oswego (riv.), N.J. 273/E4
Oswego, N.Y. 188/L2
Oswego (co.), N.Y. 276/H4
Oswego, N.Y. (13126) 276/G4
Oswego (riv.), N.Y. 276/H4
Oswego, S.C. (29121) 296/G3
Oswestry, England 10/E4
Oswestry, England 13/E5
Oświęcim, Poland 47/D3
Osyka, Miss. (39657) 256/D8
Ota, Japan 81/J5
Otago (harb.), N. Zealand 100/C6
Otago (pen.), N. Zealand 100/C6
Otahuhu, N. Zealand 100/C1
Otaki, N. Zealand 100/E4
Otakine (mt.), Japan 81/K5
Otaru, Japan 81/K2
Otautau, N. Zealand 100/B7
Otava (riv.), Czech. 41/B2
Otavalo, Ecuador 128/C2
Otavi, Namibia 118/B3
Otawara, Japan 81/K5
O.T. Downs, North Terr. 93/D4
Oteen, N.C. (28805) 281/E3
Otego, N.Y. (13825) 276/K6
Otematata, N. Zealand 100/B6
Otero (co.), Colo. 208/M7
Otero (co.), N. Mex. 274/D6
Othello, Wash. (99344) 310/F4
Otho, Iowa (50569) 229/E4
Oti (riv.), Ghana 106/E7
Oti (riv.), Togo 106/E7
Oti (riv.), Upper Volta 106/E7
Otira, N. Zealand 100/C5
Otis, Colo. (80743) 208/O2
Otis, Ind. (46367) 227/D1
Otis, Kansas (67565) 232/C3
Otis, La. (71466) 238/E4
Otis○, Mass. (01253) 249/B4
Otis (res.), Mass. 249/B4
Otis, N. Mex. (†88220) 274/E6
Otis, Oreg. (97368) 291/D2
Otis, Québec 172/G1
Otis A.F.B., Mass. 249/M6
Otisco, Ind. (47163) 227/F7
Otisco, Minn. (56077) 255/E7
Otisco (lake), N.Y. 276/H5
Otisfield, Maine (†04270) 243/B7
Otisfield○, Maine (†04270) 243/B7
Otish (mts.), Québec 174/C2
Otis Orchards-East Farms, Wash. (99027) 310/H3
Otisville, Mich. (48463) 250/F5
Otisville, N.Y. (10963) 276/L8
Otjiwarongo, Namibia 102/D7
Otjiwarongo, Namibia 118/B4
Otley, Iowa (50214) 229/G6
Oto, Iowa (51044) 229/B4
Otoe (co.), Nebr. 264/H4
Otoe, Nebr. (68417) 264/H4
Otofuke, Japan 81/L2
Otog, China 77/G4
Otorohanga, N. Zealand 100/E3
Otoskwin (riv.), Ontario 175/B2
Otra (riv.), Norway 18/E7
Otrabanda, Neth. Ant. 161/F9
Otradnyy, U.S.S.R. 52/H4
Otranto (str.), Albania 45/D5
Otranto, Iowa (†50472) 229/H2
Otranto, Italy 34/G4
Otranto (str.), Italy 34/G5
Otsego (co.), Mich. 250/E3
Otsego, Mich. (49078) 250/D6
Otsego (lake), Mich. 250/E4
Otsego (co.), N.Y. 276/K5
Otsego (lake), N.Y. 276/L5
Otsego, Ohio (†43762) 284/G5
Otsego Lake, Mich. (†49735) 250/E4
Otselic (riv.), N.Y. 276/J5
Otsu, Japan 81/J7
Otta, Norway 18/F6
Ottauquechee (riv.), Vt. 268/B4
Ottawa (riv.) 162/J6
Ottawa (cap.), Canada 2/F3
Ottawa (cap.), Canada 146/L5
Ottawa (cap.), Canada 162/J6
Ottawa (riv.), Canada 146/L5
Ottawa, Ill. (61350) 222/E2
Ottawa (co.), Kansas 232/E2
Ottawa, Kansas (66067) 232/G3
Ottawa (co.), Mich. 250/C6
Ottawa, Minn. (†56058) 255/E6
Ottawa (isls.), N.W.T. 146/K4
Ottawa (isls.), N.W.T. 162/H4
Ottawa (isls.), N.W. Terrs. 187/K4
Ottawa (co.), Ohio 284/D2
Ottawa, Ohio (45875) 284/B3
Ottawa (co.), Okla. 288/S1
Ottawa (cap.), Canada, Ontario 177/J2
Ottawa (riv.), Ontario 175/E3
Ottawa (riv.), Ontario 177/H2
Ottawa (riv.), Québec 172/B4
Ottawa (riv.), Québec 174/B3
Ottawa Beach, Mich. (†49423) 250/C6
Ottawa-Carleton (reg. munic.), Ontario 177/J2
Ottawa Hills, Ohio (†43601) 284/C2
Ottawa Lake, Mich. (49267) 250/F7
Otter (isl.), Alaska 196/D3
Otter (lakes), Alberta 182/B1
Otter, Mont. (59062) 262/K5
Otter (creek), Utah 304/C5
Otter (creek), Utah 304/C2
Otter (creek), Vt. 268/A3
Otterbein, Ind. (47970) 227/C4
Otterburne, Manitoba 179/E5
Otterburn Park, Québec 172/D4
Otter Creek, Fla. (32683) 212/D2
Otter Creek, Maine (04665) 243/G7
Otter Creek (res.), Utah 304/C5
Otter Lake, Mich. (48464) 250/F5
Otterlo, Netherlands 27/H4
Otterøya (isl.), Norway 18/E5
Otter River, Mass. (†01440) 249/F2
Otter Rock, Oreg. (97369) 291/C3
Otter Tail (co.), Minn. 255/C4
Ottertail, Minn. (56571) 255/C4
Otter Tail (lake), Minn. 255/C4
Otter Tail (riv.), Minn. 255/B4
Otterup, Denmark 21/D7
Otterville, Ill. (†62052) 222/C4
Otterville, Iowa (†50644) 229/K3
Otterville, Mo. (65348) 261/G5
Otterville, Ontario 177/D5
Ottery Saint Mary, England 13/D7
Ottery Saint Mary, England 10/E5
Otthon, Sask. 181/J4
Ottleys (creek), N.S. Wales 97/F1
Otto, Ind. (†47162) 227/G7
Otto, Mo. (63052) 261/M6
Otto, N.Y. (14766) 276/C6
Otto, N.C. (28763) 281/C4
Otto (fjord), N.W. Terrs. 187/K1
Otto, Wyo. (82434) 319/D1
Ottosen, Iowa (50570) 229/E3
Ottoville, Ohio (45876) 284/B4
Ottsville, Pa. (18942) 294/M5
Ottumwa, Iowa 188/H2
Ottumwa, Iowa (52501) 229/J6
Ottumwa, S. Dak. (57565) 298/G5
Otumba de Gómez Farías, Mexico 150/M1
Otuquis (riv.), Bolivia 136/F6
Otuzco, Peru 128/C6
Otway (bay), Chile 138/D10
Otway (sound), Chile 138/E10
Otway, Ohio (45657) 284/D8
Otway (cape), Victoria 97/B6
Otway (cape), Victoria 88/G7
Otwell, Ark. (†72401) 202/J2
Otwell, Ind. (47564) 227/C8
Otwock, Poland 47/E2
Ötztal Alps (mts.), Austria 41/A3
Ötztal Alps (range), Italy 34/C1
Ou, Nam (riv.), Laos 72/D2
Ouachita (riv.) 188/H4
Ouachita (co.), Ark. 202/E6
Ouachita, Ark. (†71763) 202/E6
Ouachita (lake), Ark. 202/C4
Ouachita (mts.), Ark. 202/B4
Ouachita (riv.), Ark. 202/E7
Ouachita (par.), La. 238/F2
Ouachita (riv.), La. 238/F1
Ouachita (mts.), Okla. 288/R5
Ouadane, Mauritania 106/B4
Ouadda, Cent. Afr. Rep. 115/D2
Ouagadougou (cap.), Upper Volta 106/D6
Ouagadougou (cap.), Upper Volta 102/B3
Ouahigouya, Upper Volta 106/D6
Ouahigouya, Upper Volta 102/B3
Oualata, Mauritania 106/C5
Ouallene, Algeria 106/E4
Ouanaminthe, Haiti 158/C5
Ouanary, Fr. Guiana 131/F3
Ouanda Djallé, Cent. Afr. Rep. 115/D2
Ouango, Cent. Afr. Rep. 115/D3
Ouaqui, Fr. Guiana 131/D4
Ouarane (reg.), Mauritania 106/B4
Ouareau (lake), Québec 172/D3
Ouareau (riv.), Québec 172/D3
Ouargla, Algeria 106/F2
Ouargla, Algeria 102/C1
Ouarzazate, Morocco 106/C2
Ouchy, Switzerland 39/C4
Oud-Beijerland, Netherlands 27/E5
Ouddorp, Netherlands 27/D5
Oudenaarde, Belgium 27/D7
Oudenbosch, Netherlands 27/E5
Oudenburg, Belgium 27/B6
Oude-Pekela, Netherlands 27/K2
Oudeschild, Netherlands 27/F2
Oude-Tonge, Netherlands 27/E5
Oudewater, Netherlands 27/F4
Oudtshoorn, S. Africa 102/E8
Oudtshoorn, S. Africa 118/C6
Oud-Turnhout, Belgium 27/F6
Oued Zem, Morocco 106/C2
Ouelle (riv.), Québec 172/H2
Ouellette, Maine (†04743) 243/G1
Ouémé (riv.), Benin 106/E7
Ouessant (isl.), France 28/A3
Ouesso, Congo 115/C3
Ouest (dept.), Haiti 158/C6
Ouest (pt.), Haiti 158/B4
Ouest (pt.), Haiti 158/B6
Ouezzane, Morocco 106/C2
Oughter (lake), Ireland 17/G3
Oughterard, Ireland 17/C5
Ouham (riv.), Cent. Afr. Rep. 115/C2
Ouham (riv.), Chad 111/C6
Ouidah, Benin 106/E7
Oujaf, Mauritania 106/C5
Oujda, Morocco 106/D2
Oujda, Morocco 102/B1
Oujeft, Mauritania 106/B4
Oulainen, Finland 18/O4
Ouled Djellal, Algeria 106/F2
Oullins, France 28/F5
Oulu (prov.), Finland 18/P4
Oulu, Finland 7/G2
Oulu, Finland 18/O4
Oulu (lake), Finland 7/G2
Oulujärvi (lake), Finland 18/P4
Oulujoki (riv.), Finland 18/O4
Oum Chalouba, Chad 111/D4
Oum el Asel (well), Mali 106/D4
Oum Hadjer, Chad 102/E3
Oum Hadjer, Chad 111/D5
Ounas (riv.), Finland 7/G2
Ounasjoki (riv.), Finland 18/O3
Oundle, England 13/G5
Oungre, Sask. 181/H6
Ounianga-Kébir, Chad 111/D4
Oupeye, Belgium 27/H7
Oupu, China 77/L1
Our (riv.), Luxembourg 27/J9
Our (riv.), W. Germany 22/B3
Ouray (co.), Colo. 208/D6
Ouray, Colo. (81427) 208/D6
Ouray (peak), Colo. 208/G6
Ouray, Utah (†84026) 304/E3
Ourinhos, Brazil 132/D8
Ourinhos, Brazil 135/B3
Ourique, Portugal 33/B4
Ouro Fino, Brazil 132/E8
Ouro Fino, Brazil 135/C3
Ouro Preto, Brazil 132/F8
Ouro Preto, Brazil 135/E2
Ourthe (riv.), Belgium 27/G8
Ouse (riv.), England 13/G6
Ouse (riv.), England 13/G4
Ouse, Tasmania 99/C4
Ouse (riv.), Tasmania 99/C4
Ousley, Georgia (†31601) 217/F9
Outagamie (co.), Wis. 317/K7
Outardes (riv.), Québec 174/D2
Outer (isl.), Wis. 317/F1
Outer Harbor, S. Australia 94/A7
Outer Hebrides (isls.), Scotland 15/A3
Outer Santa Barbara (passage), Calif. 204/G10
Outing, Minn. (56662) 255/E4
Outjo, Namibia 118/B4
Outjo, Namibia 102/D7
Outlook, Mont. (59252) 262/M2
Outlook, Sask. 181/E4
Outlook, Wash. (98938) 310/E4
Outokumpu, Finland 18/Q5
Outram, Sask. 181/H6
Outremont, Québec 172/H4
Ouyen, Victoria 88/G7
Ouyen, Victoria 97/B4
Ouzinkie, Alaska (99644) 196/H3
Ovacık, Çankırı, Turkey 63/E2
Ovacık, İçel, Turkey 63/E4
Ovacık, Tunceli, Turkey 63/H3
Ovalau (isl.), Fiji 86/Q10
Ovalle, Chile 120/B6
Ovalle, Chile 138/A8
Ovamboland (reg.), Namibia 118/B3
Ovando, Mont. (59854) 262/C3
Ovar, Portugal 33/B2
Ovens (riv.), Victoria 97/D5
Overall, Tenn. (†37130) 237/J9
Overbrook, Kansas (66524) 232/G3
Overbrook, Okla. (73453) 288/M6
Overflakkee (isl.), Netherlands 27/E5
Overflow (bay), Manitoba 179/A1
Overflowing (riv.), Manitoba 179/A1
Overflowing (riv.), Sask. 181/K2
Overflowing River, Manitoba 179/A1
Overgaard, Ariz. (85933) 198/E4
Overhills, N.C. (28370) 281/L4
Overijse, Belgium 27/F7
Overijssel (prov.), Netherlands 27/J4
Overisel, Mich. (†49423) 250/C6
Överkalix, Sweden 18/N3
Overland, Mo. (63114) 261/O2
Overland Park, Kansas (66204) 232/H3
Overlea, Md. (21206) 245/N3
Overloon, Netherlands 27/H5
Overly, N. Dak. (58360) 282/K2
Overpelt, Belgium 27/G6
Overstreet, Fla. (32453) 212/D6
Overton, Nebr. (68863) 264/E4
Overton, Nev. (89040) 266/G6
Overton, Pa. (†18833) 294/K2
Overton (co.), Tenn. 237/L8
Overton, Texas (75684) 303/K5
Övertorneå, Sweden 18/N3
Överum, Sweden 18/K7
Ovett, Miss. (39464) 256/F8
Ovid, Colo. (80744) 208/P1
Ovid, Idaho (83260) 220/G7
Ovid, Mich. (48866) 250/E6
Ovid, N.Y. (14521) 276/G5
Oviedo, Dom. Rep. 158/D7
Oviedo, Fla. (32765) 212/E3
Oviedo (prov.), Spain 33/C1
Oviedo, Spain 33/C1
Oviedo, Spain 7/D4
Ovilla, Texas (†76065) 303/G2
Ovoca (riv.), Ireland 17/J6
Övörhangay, Mongolia 77/F2
Øvre-Sirdal, Norway 18/E7
Ovruch, U.S.S.R. 52/C4
Ovtrup, Denmark 21/B6
Owaka, N. Zealand 100/B7
Owando, Congo 115/C4
Owando, Congo 102/D5
Owaneco, Ill. (62555) 222/D4
Owanka, S. Dak. (57767) 298/D5
Owasa, Iowa (†50627) 229/G4
Owasco, N.Y. (13130) 276/G5
Owasco (lake), N.Y. 276/G5
Owase, Japan 81/H6
Owassa, Ala. (†36401) 195/E8
Owassa (lake), N.J. 273/D1
Owasso, Okla. (74055) 288/P2
Owatonna, Minn. (55060) 255/E6
Owbeh, Afghanistan 68/A2
Owbeh, Afghanistan 59/H3
Owego, N.Y. (13827) 276/H6
Owel (lake), Ireland 17/G4
Owen (co.), Ind. 227/D6
Owen (co.), Ky. 237/M3
Owen (mt.), N. Zealand 100/D4
Owen (chan.), Ontario 177/C2
Owen (sound), Ontario 177/D3
Owen, Wis. (54460) 317/F6
Owen (lake), Wis. 317/D3
Owendale, Alberta 182/D5
Owendale, Mich. (48754) 250/F5
Owendo, Gabon 115/A3
Owen Falls (dam), Uganda 115/F3
Owenga, N. Zealand 100/E7
Owenkillew (riv.), N. Ireland 17/G2
Owenmore (riv.), Ireland 17/D3
Owenmore (riv.), Ireland 17/B3
Owens (lake), Calif. 188/C3
Owens (lake), Calif. 204/H7
Owens (peak), Calif. 204/H8
Owens (riv.), Calif. 204/G6
Owensboro, Ky. (42301) 237/G5
Owensboro, Ky. 188/J3
Owensburg, Ind. (47453) 227/D7
Owens Cross Roads, Ala. (35763) 195/E1
Owen Sound, Ont. 162/H7
Owen Sound, Ontario 177/D3
Owensville, Ark. (†72087) 202/E4
Owensville, Ind. (47665) 227/B8
Owensville, Mo. (65066) 261/K6
Owensville, Ohio (45160) 284/B7
Owenton, Ky. (40359) 237/M3
Owenton, Va. (†23077) 307/O5
Owerri, Nigeria 106/F7
Owey (isl.), Ireland 17/D1
Owia (bay), St. Vin. & Grens. 161/A8
Owikeno (lake), Br. Col. 184/D4
Owings, Md. (20836) 245/M6
Owings, S.C. (†29645) 296/C2
Owings Mills, Md. (21117) 245/L3
Owingsville, Ky. (40360) 237/O4
Owl (creek), Colo. 208/K1
Owl (riv.), Manitoba 179/K2
Owl (creek), S. Dak. 298/B4
Owl, North Fork (creek), Wyo. 319/D2
Owl Creek (mts.), Wyo. 319/D2
Owl River, Alberta 182/E2
Owlseye, Alberta 182/E2
Owls Head○, Maine (04854) 243/F7
Owo, Nigeria 106/F7
Owosso, Mich. (48867) 250/E5
Owraman, Iran 66/E3
Owsley (co.), Ky. 237/O6
Owyhee (riv.) 188/C2
Owyhee (co.), Idaho 220/B7
Owyhee (mts.), Idaho 220/B6
Owyhee, East Fork (riv.), Idaho 220/B7
Owyhee, Nev. (89832) 266/F1
Owyhee (riv.), Nev. 266/E1
Owyhee (dam), Oreg. 291/K4
Owyhee (lake), Oreg. 291/K4
Owyhee (mts.), Oreg. 291/K4
Owyhee, North Fork (riv.), Oreg. 291/K5
Owyhee (riv.), Oreg. 291/K5

Ox (Slieve Gamph) (mts.), Ireland 17/D3
Oxapampa, Peru 128/E8
Oxbow (dam), Idaho 220/B5
Oxbow○, Maine (04764) 243/G3
Oxbow, Oreg. (97840) 291/L2
Oxbow (dam), Oreg. 291/L3
Oxbow, Sask. 181/J6
Oxelösund, Sweden 18/K7
Oxford, Ala. (36203) 195/G3
Oxford, Ark. (72565) 202/G1
Oxford○, Conn. (06483) 210/C3
Oxford, England 13/F6
Oxford, England 10/F5
Oxford, Fla. (32684) 212/D3
Oxford, Georgia (30267) 217/E3
Oxford, Idaho (†83263) 220/F7
Oxford, Ind. (47971) 227/C3
Oxford, Iowa (52322) 229/K5
Oxford, Kansas (67119) 232/E4
Oxford, La. (†71052) 238/C3
Oxford (co.), Maine 243/B7
Oxford, Maine (04270) 243/B7
Oxford○, Maine (04270) 243/B7
Oxford (lake), Manitoba 179/J3
Oxford, Md. (21654) 245/O6
Oxford, Mass. (01540) 249/G4
Oxford○, Mass. (01540) 249/G4
Oxford, Mich. (48051) 250/F6
Oxford, Miss. (38655) 256/F2
Oxford, Nebr. (68967) 264/E4
Oxford, N.J. (07863) 273/C2
Oxford, N.Y. (13830) 276/J6
Oxford, N. Zealand 100/D5
Oxford, N.C. (27565) 281/M2
Oxford, Nova Scotia 168/E3
Oxford, Ohio (45056) 284/A6
Oxford, Pa. (19363) 294/K6
Oxford, W. Va. (†26456) 312/E4
Oxford, Wis. (53952) 317/H8
Oxford House, Manitoba 179/J3
Oxford Junction, Iowa (52323) 229/M4
Oxford Junction, Nova Scotia 168/E3
Oxford Mills, Iowa (†52323) 229/L5
Oxford Mills, Ontario 177/J3
Oxfordshire (co.), England 13/F6
Oxkutzcab, Mexico 150/P6
Oxley, N.S. Wales 97/C4
Oxley (creek), Queensland 95/D3
Oxly, Mo. (63955) 261/L9
Oxnard, Calif. (93030) 204/F9
Oxnard A.F.B., Calif. 204/F9
Oxon Hill, Md. (20745) 245/F6
Oxon Run (riv.), Md. 245/F5
Oxton, Scotland 15/F5
Oxtongue Lake, Ontario 177/E2
Oyabe, Japan 81/H5
Oyahue (vol.), Chile 138/C3
Oyama, Br. Col. 184/H5
Oyama, Japan 81/J5
Oyapock (riv.) 120/D2
Oyapock (riv.), Brazil 132/C2
Oyapock (riv.), Fr. Guiana 131/E4
Oyem, Gabon 102/D4
Oyem, Gabon 115/B3
Oyen, Alberta 182/E4
Oyens, Iowa (51045) 229/A3
Oykel (riv.), Scotland 15/D3
Oykel Bridge, Scotland 15/D3
Oylen, Minn. (†56481) 255/D4
Oymyakon, U.S.S.R. 4/C2
Oymyakon, U.S.S.R. 48/O3
Oyo, Congo 115/C4
Oyo (state), Nigeria 106/E7
Oyo, Nigeria 106/E7
Oyón, Peru 128/D8
Oyonnax, France 28/F4
Oyster (bay), Tasmania 88/H8
Oyster (bay), Tasmania 99/E4
Oyster, Va. (23419) 307/S6
Oyster Bay, N.Y. (11771) 276/R6
Oyster River (pt.), Conn. 210/D4
Oysterville, Wash. (98641) 310/A4
Özalp, Turkey 63/K3
Ozamiz, Philippines 82/D6
Ozan, Ark. (71855) 202/C6
Ozark (mts.) 188/H3
Ozark, Ala. (36360) 195/G8
Ozark, Ark. (72949) 202/C3
Ozark (lake), Ark. 202/C3
Ozark (plat.), Ark. 202/C1
Ozark (res.), Ark. 202/C3
Ozark, Ill. (62972) 222/E6
Ozark (co.), Mo. 261/H9
Ozark, Mo. (65721) 261/F8
Ozark (plat.), Mo. 261ŒE9
Ozark Nat'l Scenic Riverways, Mo. 261/K8
Ozarks, Lake of the (lake), Mo. 261/F6
Ozaukee (co.), Wis. 317/L9
Ozawkie, Kansas (66070) 232/G2
Ózd, Hungary 41/F2
Ozernovskiy, U.S.S.R. 48/Q4
Ozernoy (cape), U.S.S.R. 48/R4
Ozette, Wash. (†98326) 310/A2
Ozette (lake), Wash. 310/A2
Ozette Ind. Res., Wash. 310/A2
Ozieri, Italy 34/B4
Ozona, Fla. (33560) 212/D3
Ozona, Texas (76943) 303/C7
Ozone, Ark. (72854) 202/D2
Ozone, Tenn. (37842) 237/M9
Ozorków, Poland 47/D3
Ozu, Japan 81/F7
Ozuluama, Mexico 150/L6
Ozumba de Alzate, Mexico 150/M1

P

Pa-an, Burma 72/C3
Paarden (bay), Neth. Ant. 161/D10
Paarl, S. Africa 102/D8
Paarl, S. Africa 118/F6
Paauhau, Hawaii (96775) 218/H4
Paauilo, Hawaii (96776) 218/H4
Paavola, Finland 18/O4
Pabbay (isl.), Scotland 15/A4
Pabbay (isl.), Scotland 15/A3
Pabianice, Poland 47/D3
Pablo, Mont. (59855) 262/B3
Pabna, Bangladesh 68/F4
Pabos, Québec 172/D2
Pabos-Mills, Québec 172/D2
Pabrade, U.S.S.R. 53/C3
Pacajá Grande (riv.), Brazil 132/D4
Pacaraimã, Serra da (mts.), Brazil 132/H8
Pacaraima, Sierra (mts.), Venezuela 124/G5
Pacasmayo, Peru 128/C6
Pace, Fla. (32570) 212/B6
Pace, Miss. (38764) 256/C3
Pachaug, Conn. (†06351) 210/H2
Pachaug (pond), Conn. 210/H2
Pachaug (riv.), Conn. 210/H2
Pacheco, Calif. (94553) 204/K1
Pachino, Italy 34/E6
Pachitea (riv.), Peru 128/E7
Pachiza, Peru 128/D6
Pachmarhi, India 68/D4
Pacho, Colombia 126/C5
Pachuca de Soto, Mexico 150/K6
Pachuta, Miss. (39347) 256/G6
Pacific (ocean) 54/T5
Pacific (ocean) 146/E6
Pacific, Mo. (63069) 261/L5
Pacific (co.), Wash. 310/B4
Pacific, Wash. (98047) 310/C3
Pacifica, Calif. (94044) 204/H2
Pacific Beach, Calif. (92109) 204/H11
Pacific Beach, Wash. (98571) 310/A3
Pacific City, Oreg. (97135) 291/C2
Pacific Grove, Calif. (93950) 204/C7
Pacific Heights, Hawaii (†96801) 218/C4
Pacific Islands, Terr. of the 87/F5
Pacific Islands, Territory of the 2/S5
Pacific Junction, Iowa (51561) 229/B6
Pacific Palisades, Hawaii (†96782) 218/E2
Pacific Rim Nat'l Park, Br. Col. 184/E6
Pacitan, Indonesia 85/J2
Pack (riv.), Idaho 220/B1
Pack (creek), Utah 304/E5
Packanack Lake, N.J. (07470) 273/B1
Packertown, Ind. (†46510) 227/F2
Packerville, Conn. (†06331) 210/H2
Packington, Québec 172/J2
Packsville, W. Va. (25151) 312/C7
Packwaukee, Wis. (53953) 317/G8
Packwood, Iowa (52580) 229/J6
Packwood, Wash. (98361) 310/D4
Paco, Philippines 82/C2
Pacoa, Colombia 126/E7
Paço de Arcos, Portugal 33/A1
Pacoima, Calif. (91331) 204/B10
Pacolet, S.C. (29372) 296/D2
Pacolet (riv.), S.C. 296/D1
Pacolet Mills, S.C. (29373) 296/D2
Pacov, Czech. 41/C2
Pacsa, Hungary 41/D3
Pacsan (mt.), Philippines 82/C2
Pactolus, N.C. (†27834) 281/P3
Padada, Philippines 82/E7
Padang, Indonesia 54/L10
Padang, Indonesia 85/B6
Padangpanjang, Indonesia 85/B6
Padangsidempuan, Indonesia 85/B5
Padany, U.S.S.R. 52/D2
Padborg, Denmark 21/C8
Padcaya, Bolivia 136/C7
Paddle Prairie, Alberta 182/A5
Paddock Lake, Wis. (†53168) 317/K10
Paddockwood, Sask. 181/F2
Paden, Miss. (38861) 256/H1
Paden, Okla. (74860) 288/N3
Paden City, W. Va. (26159) 312/D3
Paderborn, W. Germany 22/C3
Padgett, S.C. (†29481) 296/F5
Padiham, England 13/H1
Padilla, Bolivia 136/C6
Padilla, Mexico 150/K5
Padilla (creek), N. Mex. 274/D5
Padilla (bay), Wash. 310/C2
Padloping (isl.), N.W.T. 162/K2
Padloping (isl.), N.W. Terrs. 187/M3
Padre (isl.), Texas 188/G5
Padre (isl.), Texas 303/G10
Padre Island Nat'l Seashore, Texas 303/G11
Padre Las Casas, Dom. Rep. 158/D6
Padrón, Spain 33/B1
Padroni, Colo. (80745) 208/N1
Padstow, England 10/D5
Padstow, England 13/B7
Padua (prov.), Italy 34/C2
Padua, Italy 7/F4
Padua, Italy 34/C2
Padua, Minn. (†56378) 255/C5
Paducah, Ky. (42001) 237/D6
Paducah, Ky. 146/K6
Paducah, Ky. 188/J3
Paducah, Texas (79248) 303/D4
Padul, Spain 33/E4
Paekam, N. Korea 81/D3
Paektu (mt.), N. Korea 81/C3
Paeroa, N. Zealand 100/E2
Páez, Colombia 126/C6
Pafúri, Mozambique 118/E4
Pag, Yugoslavia 45/B3
Pag (isl.), Yugoslavia 45/B3
Pagadian, Philippines 82/D7
Pagalungan, Philippines 82/E7
Pagan, Burma 72/B2
Pagan (isl.), No. Marianas 87/E4
Page, Ariz. (86040) 198/D2
Page (co.), Iowa 229/C7
Page, Nebr. (68766) 264/F2
Page, N. Dak. (58064) 282/P5
Page, Okla. (†74939) 288/S5
Page (co.), Va. 307/M3
Page, W. Va. (25152) 312/D6
Page City, Kansas (†67764) 232/A2
Pagedale, Mo. (†63101) 261/P2
Pageland, S.C. (29728) 296/G2
Pago (bay), Guam 86/K7
Pagoda (peak), Colo. 208/E2
Pago Pago (Cap.), Amer. Samoa 86/N9
Pago Pago (cap.), Amer. Samoa 87/J7
Pagosa Junction, Colo. (†81147) 208/E8
Pagosa Springs, Colo. (81147) 208/E8
Pagoua (bay), Dominica 161/F6
Paguate, N. Mex. (87040) 274/B3
Pagwa River, Ontario 177/J5
Pagwa River, Ontario 175/D3
Pahala, Hawaii 188/G6
Pahala, Hawaii (96777) 218/H6
Pahang (state), Malaysia 72/D7
Pahang, Sungai (riv.), Malaysia 72/D7
Pahaska, Wyo. (82414) 319/C1
Pahiatua, N. Zealand 100/F4
Pahlevi (Enzeli), Iran 59/E2
Pahlevi (Enzeli), Iran 66/F2
Pahoa, Hawaii (96778) 218/J5
Pahokee, Fla. (33476) 212/F5
Pahranagat (range), Nev. 266/F5
Pahrock (range), Nev. 266/F5
Pah-rum (peak), Nev. 266/B2
Pahrump, Nev. (89041) 266/E6
Pahrump (valley), Nev. 266/F6
Pahsimeroi (riv.), Idaho 220/E5
Pahute (mesa), Nev. 266/E5
Paia, Hawaii (96779) 218/J2
Paicheng (Baicheng), China 77/K2
Paicines, Calif. (95043) 204/D7
Paide, U.S.S.R. 53/C1
Paige, Texas (78659) 303/G7
Paihia, N. Zealand 100/D1
Paihuano, Chile 138/B8
Paiján, Peru 128/C6
Päijänne (lake), Finland 18/O6
Pailin, Cambodia 72/D4
Paillaco, Chile 138/D3
Pailolo (chan.), Hawaii 218/H1
Paimboeuf, France 28/C4
Paimpol, France 28/B3
Painan, Indonesia 85/C6
Paincourt, Ontario 177/B5
Paincourtville, La. (70391) 238/K3
Paine, Chile 138/G4
Paine, Cerro (mt.), Chile 138/D9
Painesdale, Mich. (49955) 250/G1
Painesville, Ohio (44077) 284/H2
Painswick, Ontario 177/E3
Paint (lake), Manitoba 179/J2
Paint (riv.), Mich. 250/A2
Paint (creek), Ohio 284/D7
Paint, Pa. (†15963) 294/E5
Paint Bank, Va. (24131) 307/H5
Paint Branch (riv.), Md. 245/F4
Painted (des.), Ariz. 198/D2
Painted Desert Section (Petrified Forest), Ariz. 198/F3
Painted Post, N.Y. (14870) 276/F6
Painted Rock (dam), Ariz. 198/C5
Painter, Ala. (†35962) 195/F2
Painter, Va. (23420) 307/S5
Painter Ridge (hills), Conn. 210/B2
Painters Hill, Fla. (†32036) 212/E2
Paintersville, Ohio (†45335) 284/C6
Paint Lick, Ky. (40461) 237/N5
Paint Lick (riv.), Ky. 237/M5
Paint Rock, Ala. (35764) 195/F1
Paint Rock (riv.), Ala. 195/F1
Paint Rock, Texas (76866) 303/E6
Paintsville, Ky. (41240) 237/R5
Paipa, Colombia 126/D5
Paipote, Chile 138/B6
Paipote, Quebrada de (riv.), Chile 138/B6
Paisley, Ontario 177/C3
Paisley, Oreg. (97636) 291/G5
Paisley, Scotland 10/A1
Paisley, Scotland 15/B2
Paita, Peru 128/B5
Paita (bay), Peru 128/B5
Paiute Ind. Res., Calif. 204/G6
Pajala, Sweden 18/N3
Paján, Ecuador 128/B3
Pajarito (creek), N. Mex. 274/A2
Pajaro, Calif. (†95076) 204/D7
Pájaros (isls.), Chile 138/A7
Pakanbaru, Indonesia 54/M9
Pakanbaru, Indonesia 85/C5
Pakaraima (mts.), Guyana 131/A3
Pakawau, N. Zealand 100/D4
Pakchan (riv.), Burma 72/C5
Pakchan (riv.), Thailand 72/C5
Pakch'ŏn, N. Korea 81/B4
Pakenham, Ontario 177/H2
Pakhoi (Beihai), China 77/G7
Pakistan 2/N4
Pakistan 54/H7
PAKISTAN 59/J4
PAKISTAN 68/B3
Pakokku, Burma 72/B2
Pakowki (lake), Alberta 182/E5
Paks, Hungary 41/E3
Pakwach, Uganda 115/F3
Pakxé, Laos 72/E4
Pala, Chad 111/B6
Palacios, Texas (77465) 303/H9
Palafrugell, Spain 33/H2
Palagruža (Pelagosa) (isl.), Yugoslavia 45/C4
Pala Ind. Res., Calif. 204/H10
Palamós, Spain 33/H2
Palana, U.S.S.R. 52/S4
Palana, U.S.S.R. 48/R4
Palanan, Philippines 82/D2
Palanan, Philippines 85/G2
Palanan (bay), Philippines 82/D2
Palanda, Ecuador 128/C5
Palanga, U.S.S.R. 53/A3
Palangkaraya, Indonesia 85/E6
Palanpur, India 68/C4
Palaoa (pt.), Hawaii 218/G2
Palapag, Philippines 82/E4
Palapye, Botswana 118/D4
Palas de Rey, Spain 33/C1
Palatine, Ill. (60067) 222/B5
Palatka, Ark. (†72422) 202/J1
Palatka, Fla. (32077) 212/E2
Palau (Belau) 87/D5
Palauli (bay), W. Samoa 86/L8
Palaumerak, Indonesia 85/G1
Palaw, Burma 72/C4
Palawan (prov.), Philippines 82/B6
Palawan (isl.), Philippines 2/Q5
Palawan (isl.), Philippines 54/N8
Palawan (isl.), Philippines 85/F4
Palawan (isl.), Philippines 82/B6
Palawan (passage), Philippines 85/F4
Palawan (passage), Philippines 82/A6
Palaya, Bolivia 136/A6
Palayan, Philippines 82/C3
Palayankottai, India 68/D7
Palazzolo Acreide, Italy 34/E6
Palca, Bolivia 136/A5
Palco, Kansas (67657) 232/C2
Paldiski, U.S.S.R. 53/B1
Paldiski, U.S.S.R. 52/B3
Paleleh, Indonesia 85/G5
Palembang, Indonesia 54/M10
Palembang, Indonesia 85/D6
Palena, Chile 138/E5
Palena (lake), Chile 138/E5
Palena (riv.), Chile 138/D5
Palencia (prov.), Spain 33/D1
Palencia, Spain 33/D2
Palenque (pt.), Dom. Rep. 158/E6
Palenque, Mexico 150/O8
Palenque (ruin), Mexico 150/O8
Palenville, N.Y. (12463) 276/M6
Palermo, Calif. (95968) 204/D4
Palermo (prov.), Italy 34/D5
Palermo, Italy 7/F5
Palermo, Italy 34/D5
Palermo○, Maine (04354) 243/E7
Palermo, N.J. (†08226) 273/D5
Palermo, N. Dak. (58769) 282/F3
Palermo, Uruguay 145/D4
Palestina, Chile 138/B4
Palestine, Ala. (†36252) 195/H3
Palestine, Ark. (72372) 202/J4
Palestine, Ill. (62451) 222/F4
Palestine, Ind. (†46508) 227/F2
Palestine, Ohio (45352) 284/A5
Palestine, Texas 188/H4
Palestine, Texas (75801) 303/J6
Palestine, W. Va. (26160) 312/D4
Palestrina, Italy 34/F7
Paletwa, Burma 72/B2
Palghat, India 68/D6
Palha, Mar da (bay), Portugal 33/A1
Pali, India 68/C3
Palidoro, Italy 34/F6
Paliocabe (Payocabe), Chile 138/F4
Palisade, Colo. (81526) 208/C4
Palisade, Minn. (56469) 255/E4
Palisade, Nebr. (69040) 264/C4
Palisade, Nev. (†89822) 266/E2
Palisades, Idaho (83437) 220/G6
Palisades (res.), Idaho 220/G6
Palisades, N.J. 273/C1
Palisades, N.Y. (10964) 276/K8
Palisades, Wash. (98845) 310/E3
Palisades (res.), Wyo. 319/A2
Palisades Park, N.J. (07650) 273/C2
Paliseul, Belgium 27/G9
Palizada, Mexico 150/O7
Palk (str.), India 68/D7
Palk (str.), Sri Lanka 68/D7
Pallamallawa, N.S. Wales 97/F1
Palling, Br. Col. 184/D3
Palliser (bay), N. Zealand 100/C3
Palliser (cape), N. Zealand 100/E4
Pall Mall, Tenn. (38577) 237/M7
Palm (beach), Neth. Ant. 161/D10
Palma (bay), Alaska 196/L1
Palma, Mozambique 118/G2
Palma, Spain 7/E5
Palma, Spain 33/H3
Palma (bay), Spain 33/H3
Palma del Río, Spain 33/D4
Palma di Montechiaro, Italy 34/D6
Palmarejo, Venezuela 124/C2
Palmares, Brazil 132/H5
Palmares, C. Rica 154/F6
Palmarito, Apure, Venezuela 124/D4
Palmarito, Guárico, Venezuela 124/F3
Palmarito, Mérida, Venezuela 124/C3
Palmarola (isl.), Italy 34/D4
Palmas (cape) 102/B4
Palmas, Brazil 132/C9
Palmas (cape), Liberia 106/C8
Palmas Altas (pt.), P. Rico 161/C1
Palma Soriano, Cuba 158/J4
Palm Bay, Fla. (32905) 212/F3
Palm Beach, Fla. 188/L5
Palm Beach (co.), Fla. 212/F5
Palm Beach, Fla. (33480) 212/G4
Palm Beach Gardens, Fla. (†33403) 212/F5
Palm Beach Shores, Fla. (†33404) 212/G5
Palm City, Fla. (33490) 212/F4
Palm Coast, Fla. (32037) 212/E2
Palmdale, Calif. (93550) 204/G9
Palmdale, Fla. (33944) 212/E5
Palm Desert, Calif. (92260) 204/J10
Palmeira, Brazil 132/D9
Palmeira, Brazil 135/B4
Palmeira das Missões, Brazil 132/C9
Palmeiras, Brazil 132/F6
Palmeirinhas (pt.), Angola 115/B5
Palmer, Alaska (99645) 196/C1
Palmer, Alaska 188/D5
Palmer (arch.) 5/C15
Palmer, Ill. (62556) 222/D4
Palmer, Ind. (†46307) 227/C2
Palmer, Iowa (50571) 229/D3
Palmer, Kansas (66962) 232/E2
Palmer, Mass. (01069) 249/E4
Palmer○, Mass. (01069) 249/E4
Palmer, Mich. (49871) 250/B2
Palmer, Nebr. (68864) 264/F3
Palmer (head), N. Zealand 100/B3
Palmer, P. Rico 161/F1
Palmer (riv.), Queensland 95/B2
Palmer, Sask. 181/E6
Palmer, Tenn. (37365) 237/K10
Palmer, Wash. (98048) 310/D3
Palmer (lake), Wash. 310/F2
Palmer Lake, Colo. (80133) 208/J4
Palmer Land (reg.), Ant. 2/F9
Palmer Land (reg.), Ant. 5/B15
Palmer Rapids, Ontario 177/G2
Palmers, Minn. (†55801) 255/G4
Palmers Crossing, Miss. (†39401) 256/F8
Palmer Station, Ant. 5/C15
Palmerston (atoll), Cook Is. 87/K7
Palmerston, N. Zealand 100/C6
Palmerston, Ontario 177/D4
Palmerston North, N. Zealand 87/H10
Palmerston North, N. Zealand 100/E4
Palmersville, Tenn. (38241) 237/D8
Palmerton, Pa. (18071) 294/L4
Palmerville, Queensland 95/B3
Palmetto, Fla. (33561) 212/D4
Palmetto, Georgia (30268) 217/C3
Palmetto, La. (71358) 238/G5
Palmetto (pt.), St. Chris.-Nevis 161/C10
Palm Harbor, Fla. (33563) 212/D3
Palmi, Italy 34/E5
Palmiet (riv.), S. Africa 118/F7
Palmilla, Chile 138/F6
Palmillas (pt.), Dom. Rep. 158/F6
Palmillas, Mexico 150/K5
Palmira, Colombia 120/B2
Palmira, Colombia 126/B6
Palmira, Cuba 158/E2
Palmitas, Uruguay 145/B4
Palmito de la Virgen (isl.), Mexico 150/F5
Palmito del Verde (isl.), Mexico 150/F5
Palm River-Clair Mel, Fla. (33619) 212/C3
Palms, Mich. (48465) 250/G5
Palms, Isle of (isl.), S.C. 296/H6
Palm Shores, Fla. (†32901) 212/F3
Palm Springs, Calif. 188/C4
Palm Springs, Calif. (92262) 204/J10
Palm Springs, Fla. (33460) 212/F5
Palmyra, Ill. (62674) 222/C4
Palmyra, Ind. (47164) 227/E8
Palmyra○, Maine (04965) 243/E6
Palmyra, Mich. (49268) 250/E7
Palmyra, Mo. (63461) 261/J3
Palmyra, Nebr. (68418) 264/H4
Palmyra, N.J. (08065) 273/B3
Palmyra, N.Y. (14522) 276/F4
Palmyra (atoll), Pacific 87/K5
Palmyra, Pa. (17078) 294/J5
Palmyra (ruin), Syria 59/C3
Palmyra (Tadmor) (ruins), Syria 63/H5
Palmyra, Tenn. (37142) 237/G8
Palmyra (isl.), U.S. 2/A5
Palmyra, Va. (22963) 307/M5
Palmyra, Wis. (53156) 317/H2
Palmyras (pt.), India 68/F4
Palnackie, Scotland 15/E6
Palni, India 68/D6
Palo, Iowa (52324) 229/K4
Palo, Mich. (48870) 250/E5
Palo, Minn. (†55705) 255/F3
Palo, Philippines 82/E5
Palo Alto, Calif. 188/B3
Palo Alto, Calif. (*94301) 204/K3
Palo Alto, Cuba 158/F3
Palo Alto (co.), Iowa 229/D2
Palo Alto (lake), Iowa 229/D2
Palo Bola, Mexico 150/D4
Palo Duro (creek), Texas 303/B2
Palo Duro (creek), Texas 303/C1
Paloemeu (riv.), Suriname 131/D4
Palolo (stream), Hawaii 218/D4
Paloma, Ill. (62359) 222/B3
Palomar (mt.), Calif. 204/J10
Palomas, Mexico 150/F1
Palomas, Uruguay 145/B4
Palombara Sabina, Italy 34/F6
Palometas, Bolivia 136/D5
Palompon, Philippines 82/E5
Palo Pinto (co.), Texas 303/F5
Palo Pinto, Texas (76072) 303/F5
Palopo, Indonesia 85/F6
Palos (cape), Spain 33/F4
Palo Santo, Argentina 143/E2
Palo Seco, P. Rico 161/D1
Palo Seco, Trin. & Tob. 161/A11
Palos Heights, Ill. (60463) 222/B6
Palos Hills, Ill. (60465) 222/B6
Palos Park, Ill. (60464) 222/B6
Palos Verdes Estates, Calif. (90274) 204/B11
Palotás, Hungary 41/E3
Palourde (lake), La. 238/H7
Palouse (riv.), Idaho 220/B3
Palouse, Wash. (99161) 310/H4
Palouse (riv.), Wash. 310/G4
Palo Verde, Ariz. (85343) 198/C5
Palo Verde, Calif. (92266) 204/L10
Palpa, Nepal 68/E3
Palpa, Peru 128/E10
Palsagua, Nicaragua 154/E4
Palsen (riv.), Manitoba 179/G2
Palu, Indonesia 85/F6
Palu, Turkey 63/H3
Paluan, Philippines 82/C4
Pama, Upper Volta 106/E6
Pamangkat, Indonesia 85/D5
Pamar, Colombia 126/E8
Pambrun, Sask. 181/D6
Pambula, N.S. Wales 97/E5
Pamekasan, Indonesia 85/L2
Pameungpeuk, Indonesia 85/H2
Pamiers, France 28/D6
Pamir (plat.) 54/J6
Pamlico (sound), N.C. 188/L3
Pamlico (co.), N.C. 281/R4
Pamlico (riv.), N.C. 281/R4
Pamlico (sound), N.C. 281/S4
Pampa, Texas 188/F3
Pampa, Texas (79065) 303/D2
Pampa Aullagas, Bolivia 136/B6
Pampachiri, Peru 128/F10
Pampacolca, Peru 128/F10
Pampa de la Salina (salt dep.), Argentina 143/C3
Pampa de las Salinas, Argentina 143/C3
Pampa de la Tres Hermanas (plain), Argentina 143/C6
Pampa del Infierno, Argentina 143/D2
Pampa Grande, Bolivia 136/D5
Pampanga (prov.), Philippines 82/C3
Pampas (plain), Argentina 120/C6
Pampas (plain), Argentina 143/D4
Pampas, Peru 128/E9
Pampas (riv.), Peru 128/E9
Pampilhosa da Serra, Portugal 33/C3
Pamplico, S.C. (29583) 296/H4
Pamplin, Va. (23958) 307/L6
Pamplona, Colombia 126/D4
Pamplona, Spain 33/F1
Pamplona, Spain 7/D4
Pamunkey (riv.), Va. 307/O5
Pamunkey Ind. Res., Va. 307/P5
Pana, Ill. (62557) 222/D4
Panabá, Mexico 150/P6
Panabo, Philippines 82/E7
Panaca, Nev. (89042) 266/G5
Panacachi, Bolivia 136/B6
Panacea, Fla. (32346) 212/B1
Panache (lake), Ontario 177/C1
Panagyurishte, Bulgaria 45/F4
Panaitan (isl.), Indonesia 85/C7
Panaji, India 68/C5
Panama 2/E5
Panama 146/K9
Panama (canal) 2/E5
Panama, Ill. (62077) 222/D4
Panama, Iowa (51562) 229/B5
Panama, Nebr. (68419) 264/H4
Panama, N.Y. (14767) 276/A6
Panama, Okla. (74951) 288/S4
Panamá (cap.), Pan. 146/L9
Panamá (canal), Pan. 146/L8
Panamá (gulf), Pan. 146/L9
PANAMA 154/G6
Panamá (cap.), Panama 154/H6
Panamá (gulf), Panama 154/H7
Panama City, Fla. 188/K4
Panama City, Fla. (*32401) 212/C6
Panama City Beach, Fla. (32407) 212/C6
Panamint (range), Calif. 204/H7
Panamint (valley), Calif. 204/H7
Panao, Peru 128/E7
Panaon (isl.), Philippines 82/E5
Panarea (isl.), Italy 34/E5
Panaro (riv.), Italy 34/C2
Panarukan, Indonesia 85/K2
Panay (isl.), Philippines 54/O8
Panay (isl.), Philippines 85/G3
Panay (isl.), Philippines 82/D5
Pancake (range), Nev. 266/F4
Pančevo, Yugoslavia 45/E3
Panchor, Malaysia 72/F5
Panchur, India 68/F2
Panciu, Romania 45/H3
Panda, Mozambique 118/E4
Pandale, Texas (76944) 303/C7
Panda-Likasi, Zaire 115/E6
Panda-Likasi, Zaire 102/E6
Pandan, Antique, Philippines 82/C5
Pandan, Catanduanes, Philippines 82/E4
Pan de Azúcar, Quebrado (riv.), Chile 138/B5
Pan de Azúcar, Uruguay 145/D5
Pandeglang, Indonesia 85/G1
Pandharpur, India 68/D5
Pandi Pandi, S. Australia 94/F2
Pando (dept.), Bolivia 136/B2
Pando, Cerro (mt.), Panama 154/F6
Pando, Uruguay 145/B6
Pando (riv.), Uruguay 145/B6
Pandora, Ohio (45877) 284/C4
Pandrup, Denmark 21/C3
Panevežys, U.S.S.R. 52/B3
Panevežys, U.S.S.R. 53/C3
Panfilov, U.S.S.R. 48/H5
Pangai, Tonga 87/J7
Pangala, Congo 115/B4
Pangalanes (canal), Madagascar 118/H4
Pangani, Tanzania 115/G5
Pangani (riv.), Tanzania 115/G4
Panganiban, Philippines 82/E4
Pangasinan (prov.), Philippines 82/C3
Pangburn, Ark. (72121) 202/G3
Pangi, Zaire 115/E4
Pangkalanberandan, Indonesia 85/B5
Pangkalanbuun, Indonesia 85/E6
Pangkalpinang, Indonesia 85/D6
Pangkor, Pulau (isl.), Malaysia 72/D6
Panglao (isl.), Philippines 82/D6
Pangman, Sask. 181/G6
Pangnirtung, Canada 4/C13
Pangnirtung, N.W.T. 162/K2
Pangnirtung, N.W. Terrs. 187/M3
Pangong Tso (lake), India 68/D2
Pangsau (pass), Burma 72/C1
Panguipulli, Chile 138/E2
Panguitch, Utah (84759) 304/B6
Panguitch (creek), Utah 304/B6
Pangutaran, Philippines 82/C7
Pangutaran (isl.), Philippines 82/C7
Pangutaran Group (isls.), Philippines 82/C7
Pangutaran Group (isls.), Philippines 85/G4
Panhandle, Texas (79068) 303/C2
Paniau (peak), Hawaii 218/A2
Panié (mt.), New Caled. 86/G4
Panihati, India 68/F1
Panipat, India 68/D3
Panjuli, Philippines 82/C3
Panj (riv.), Afghanistan 68/C1

Pátzcuaro 425

Panjab, Afghanistan 68/B2
Panjab, Afghanistan 59/J3
Panjang, Hon (Hon Tho Chau) (isl.), Vietnam 72/D5
Panjgur, Pakistan 68/A3
Panjgur, Pakistan 59/H4
Panjim, India 54/J8
Panjim (Panaji), India 68/C5
Pankow, E. Germany 22/F3
Pankshin, Nigeria 106/F7
P'anmunjŏm, N. Korea 81/C5
P'anmunjŏm, S. Korea 81/C5
Panmure (isl.), Pr. Edward I. 168/F2
Panna, India 68/E4
Pannawonica, W. Australia 92/B3
Pannonhalma, Hungary 41/D3
Panny (riv.), Alberta 182/C1
Panola, Ala. (35477) 195/B5
Panola, Ill. (†61738) 222/E3
Panola (co.), Miss. 256/E2
Panola, Okla. (74559) 288/R5
Panola (co.), Texas 303/K5
Panora, Iowa (50216) 229/E5
Panorama Park, Iowa (†52722) 229/N5
Panquehue, Chile 138/G2
Panruti, India 68/D6
Pansey, Ala. (36370) 195/H8
Pantanal (reg.), Brazil 120/D4
Pantar (isl.), Indonesia 85/G7
Pantego, N.C. (27860) 281/R3
Pantego, Texas (76013) 303/F2
Pantelleria, Italy 34/C6
Pantelleria (isl.), Italy 7/F5
Pantelleria (isl.), Italy 34/D6
Pantha, Burma 72/B2
Panther (creek), Idaho 220/D4
Panther (creek), Ky. 237/G5
Panther, W. Va. (24872) 312/C8
Panther Burn, Miss. (38765) 256/C4
Panthersville, Georgia (†30032) 217/L1
Pantin, France 28/B1
Pantoja, Peru 128/E3
Panton○, Vt. (†05491) 268/A3
Pánuco, Mexico 150/K6
Pánuco (riv.), Mexico 150/K5
Panuke (lake), Nova Scotia 168/D4
Pan Xian, China 77/G6
Panyam, Nigeria 106/F7
Panzós, Guatemala 154/C3
Pao (riv.), Venezuela 124/D3
Pao (riv.), Venezuela 124/F3
Paoki (Baoji), China 77/G5
Paola, Italy 34/E5
Paola, Kansas (66071) 232/H3
Paoli, Colo. (80746) 208/P1
Paoli, Ind. (47454) 227/E7
Paoli, Okla. (73074) 288/M5
Paoli, Pa. (19301) 294/M5
Paoli, Wis. (†53508) 317/G10
Paonia, Colo. (81428) 208/D5
Paopao (bay), Fr. Poly. 86/S13
Paoting (Baoding), China 77/J4
Paotow (Baotou), China 77/G3
Paoua, Cent. Afr. Rep. 115/C2
Paoy Pet, Cambodia 72/D4
Papa, Hawaii (†96704) 218/G6
Pápa, Hungary 41/D3
Papaaloa, Hawaii (96780) 218/J4
Papagaio (riv.), Brazil 132/B6
Papagayo (gulf), C. Rica 154/E5
Papago Ind. Res., Ariz. 198/C6
Papaikou, Hawaii 188/G6
Papaikou, Hawaii (96781) 218/J5
Papakura, N. Zealand 100/E2
Papallacta, Ecuador 128/D3
Papanoa, Mexico 150/J8
Papantla de Olarte, Mexico 150/L6
Papar, Malaysia 85/F4
Papara, Fr. Poly. 86/S13
Papa Stour (isl.), Scotland 10/G1
Papa Stour (isl.), Scotland 15/F2
Papatoetoe, N. Zealand 100/C1
Papa Westray (isl.), Scotland 15/F1
Papa Westray (isl.), Scotland 10/E1
Papeete (cap.), Fr. Polynesia 2/B6
Papeete (cap.), Fr. Poly. 86/S13
Papeete (cap.), Fr. Poly. 87/M7
Papelón, Venezuela 124/D3
Papenburg, W. Germany 22/B2
Papenoo, Fr. Poly. 86/T12
Papetoai, Fr. Poly. 86/S12
Paphos, Cyprus 63/E5
Papillion, Nebr. (68046) 264/J3
Papineau, Ill. (60956) 222/F3
Papineau (lake), Ontario 177/G2
Papineau (co.), Québec 172/B4
Papineau (lake), Québec 172/C4
Papineauville, Québec 172/C4
Paposo, Chile 138/A5
Papradno, Czech. 41/E2
Paps, The (mt.), Ireland 17/C7
Paps of Jura (mt.), Scotland 15/C5
Papua (gulf), Papua N.G. 87/E6
Papua New Guinea 2/S6
PAPUA NEW GUINEA 86/B1
PAPUA NEW GUINEA 85/B7
Papua New Guinea 87/E6
Papudo, Chile 138/A9
Papun, Burma 72/C3
Papunáua (riv.), Colombia 126/E6
Papunya, North. Terr. 93/B7
Papurí (riv.), Colombia 126/F7
Paquera, C. Rica 154/E6
Paquette, Québec 172/F4
Paquetville, New Bruns. 170/E1
Pará (state), Brazil 132/C4
Pará (Belém), Brazil 132/E3
Pará (est.), Brazil 120/E3
Pará (riv.), Brazil 132/D3
Para (dist.), Suriname 131/D3
Paraburdoo, W. Australia 88/B4
Paraburdoo, W. Australia 92/B3
Paracale, Philippines 82/D3
Paracas (pen.), Peru 128/D9
Paracatu, Brazil 132/E7
Paracatu (riv.), Brazil 132/E7
Paracel (isls.), China 85/E2
Parachilna, S. Australia 88/F6
Parachilna, S. Australia 94/F4
Parachute, Colo. 208/C4
Paraćin, Yugoslavia 45/E4
Parada Esperanza, Uruguay 145/B3
Parada Liebigs, Uruguay 145/A4
Parada Rivas, Uruguay 145/B2
Parade, S. Dak. (57647) 298/G3
Pará de Minas, Brazil 132/E7
Pará de Minas, Brazil 135/D1
Paradip, India 68/F4
Paradis, La. (70080) 238/M4
Paradise, Ariz. (†85632) 198/F7
Paradise, Calif. (95969) 204/D4
Paradise, Guyana 131/C3
Paradise, Kansas (67658) 232/D2
Paradise, Mich. (49768) 250/D2
Paradise (lake), Mich. 250/E3
Paradise, Mo. (†64089) 261/D4
Paradise, Mont. (59856) 262/B3
Paradise, Newf. 166/D2
Paradise (riv.), Newf. 166/C3
Paradise, Nova Scotia 168/C4
Paradise (lake), Nova Scotia 168/C4
Paradise, Pa. (17562) 294/K5
Paradise, Texas (76073) 303/G5
Paradise, Utah (84328) 304/C2
Paradise, W. Va. (†25124) 312/C5
Paradise Hill, Okla. (†74435) 288/R3
Paradise Hill, Sask. 181/B2
Paradise Inn, Wash. (98398) 310/D4
Paradise River, Newf. 166/C3
Paradise Valley, Alberta 182/E3
Paradise Valley, Ariz. (85253) 198/D5
Paradise Valley, Nev. (89119) 266/F6
Paradise Valley, Nev. (89426) 266/D1
Paradise Valley, Wyo. (†82601) 319/F3
Paradisino (peak), Switzerland 39/K4
Paradiso, Switzerland 39/G5
Paradox, Colo. (81429) 208/B6
Paragon, Ind. (46166) 227/D6
Paragonah, Utah (84760) 304/B6
Paragould, Ark. (72450) 202/J1
Paraguá (riv.), Bolivia 136/E4
Paragua (riv.), Venezuela 124/G4
Paraguaçu (riv.), Brazil 120/F4
Paraguaçu (riv.), Brazil 132/F6
Paraguaçu Paulista, Brazil 132/D8
Paraguai (riv.) 120/D4
Paraguai (riv.), Brazil 132/B8
Paraguaipoa, Venezuela 124/C2
Paraguaná (pen.), Venezuela 124/C1
Paraguarí (dept.), Paraguay 144/D4-5
Paraguay 2/F7
Paraguay 120/D5
PARAGUAY 144
Paraguay (riv.), Argentina 143/E1
Paraguay (riv.), Bolivia 136/F7
Paraguay (riv.), Paraguay 144/D4
Paraíba (state), Brazil 132/G4
Paraíba (riv.), Brazil 120/E5
Paraíba (riv.), Brazil 135/E2
Paraíba do Sul, Brazil 135/E3
Parainen, Finland 18/M6
Paraíso, C. Rica 154/F6
Paraíso, Dom. Rep. 158/D7
Paraíso, Mexico 150/N7
Paraíso de Chabasquén, Venezuela 124/D3
Parakou, Benin 106/E7
Parallel, Kansas (†66933) 232/F2
Paraloma, Ark. (†71846) 202/B6
Paramaribo (dist.), Suriname 131/D2
Paramaribo (cap.), Suriname 131/D2
Paramaribo (cap.), Suriname 2/G5
Paramaribo (cap.), Suriname 120/D2
Paramithía, Greece 45/E6
Paramonga, Peru 128/C8
Paramount, Calif. (90723) 204/C11
Paramus, N.J. (07652) 273/B1
Paramushir (isl.) 54/S5
Paramushir (isl.), U.S.S.R. 48/Q4
Paran (dry riv.), Israel 65/D5
Paraná (riv.) 2/G7
Paraná (riv.) 120/D5
Paraná, Argentina 143/F5
Paraná, Argentina 120/D6
Paraná (riv.), Argentina 143/E2
Paraná (state), Brazil 132/D9
Paraná (state), Brazil 135/B4
Paranã, Brazil 132/E6
Paraná (riv.), Brazil 132/C8
Paranã (riv.), Brazil 132/E6
Paranaguá, Brazil 120/E5
Paranaguá, Brazil 132/E9
Paranaguá, Brazil 135/B4
Paranaíba, Brazil 132/D7
Paranam, Suriname 131/D3
Paranapanema (riv.), Brazil 132/C8
Paranapanema (riv.), Brazil 135/B3
Paranapiacaba (range), Brazil 135/B4
Paranatinga (riv.), Brazil 120/D4
Paranatinga (riv.), Brazil 132/C6
Parang, Maguindanao, Philippines 82/E7
Parang, Sulu, Philippines 82/C8
Parao (riv.), Uruguay 145/E3
Paraparaumu, N. Zealand 100/E4
Parapetí (riv.), Bolivia 136/D6
Para Station, N.S. Wales 97/B3
Parati, Brazil 135/D3
Paratinga, Brazil 132/F6
Paray-le-Monial, France 28/F4
Parbhani, India 68/D5
Parchim, E. Germany 22/D2
Parchman, Miss. (38738) 256/D3
Parchment, Mich. (49004) 250/D6
Parczew, Poland 47/F3
Pardee (res.), Calif. 204/C9
Pardee, Va. (†24285) 307/C6
Pardeeville, Wis. (53954) 317/H8
Pardes Hanna-Karkur, Israel 65/B2
Parding, China 77/C5
Pardo (riv.), Brazil 132/D8
Pardo (riv.), Brazil 132/F6
Pardo (riv.), Brazil 135/B2
Pardo (riv.), Brazil 132/C8
Pardoe, Pa. (†16137) 294/B3
Pardoo, W. Australia 92/B3
Pardubice, Czech. 41/C1
Pare, Indonesia 85/K2
Parece Vela (isl.), Japan 54/P7
Parece Vela (isl.), Japan 87/D3
Parecis (mts.), Brazil 120/C4
Parecis, Serra dos (range), Brazil 132/B6
Paredes de Nava, Spain 33/D1
Paredones, Chile 138/A10
Parent, Québec 174/C3
Pareora, N. Zealand 100/C6
Parepare, Indonesia 85/F6
Parguera, P. Rico 161/A3
Parham, Ant. & Bar. 161/E11
Parham, Ontario 177/H3
Parhams, La. (†71343) 238/G4
Paria (gulf) 120/C1
Paria (plat.), Ariz. 198/D2
Paria (riv.), Ariz. 198/D1
Paria, Bolivia 136/B5
Paria (gulf), Trin. & Tob. 156/G5
Paria (gulf), Trin. & Tob. 161/A11
Paria (riv.), Utah 304/B6
Paria (gulf), Venezuela 124/H2
Paria (pen.), Venezuela 124/G2
Pariaguán, Venezuela 124/F3
Pariaman, Indonesia 85/B6
Paricutín (vol.), Mexico 150/H7
Parida (isl.), Panama 154/F6
Parika, Guyana 131/B2
Parikkala, Finland 18/Q6
Parima, Sierra (mts.), Venezuela 124/F6
Parinacochas (lake), Peru 128/F10
Parinacota, Cerro (mt.), Chile 138/B1
Pariñari, Peru 128/E5
Pariñas (pt.), Peru 128/B5
Parintins, Brazil 120/D3
Parintins, Brazil 132/B3
Paris, Ark. (72855) 202/C3
Paris (city) (dept.), France 28/B2
Paris (cap.), France 2/J3
Paris (cap.), France 7/E4
Paris (cap.), France 28/B2
Paris, Idaho (83261) 220/G7
Paris, Ill. (61944) 222/F4
Paris, Iowa (†52214) 229/K4
Paris, Ky. (40361) 237/N4
Paris○, Maine (04271) 243/B7
Paris, Mich. (49338) 250/D5
Paris, Miss. (38949) 256/F2
Paris, Mo. (65275) 261/J4
Paris, Ohio (44669) 284/H4
Paris, Ontario 177/D4
Paris, Tenn. (38242) 237/E8
Paris, Texas (75460) 303/J4
Paris, Texas 188/G4
Paris, Va. (22130) 307/N3
Paris Crossing, Ind. (47270) 227/F7
Parish, N.Y. (13131) 276/H4
Parish, Uruguay 145/C3
Parishville, N.Y. (13672) 276/L1
Parisville, Mich. (†48470) 250/G5
Parisville, Québec 172/F3
Parita, Panama 154/G6
Parita (bay), Panama 154/G6
Park (co.), Colo. 208/H4
Park (range), Colo. 208/F1
Park (riv.), Conn. 210/E2
Park, Kansas (67751) 232/B2
Park (co.), Mont. 262/F5
Park (riv.), N. Dak. 282/R3
Park (dist.), Scotland 15/B2
Park (co.), Wyo. 319/C1
Parkano, Finland 18/N6
Parkbeg, Sask. 181/E5
Park City, Ill. (†60085) 222/B4
Park City, Kansas (†67201) 232/E4
Park City, Ky. (42160) 237/J6
Park City, Mont. (59063) 262/H5
Park City, Utah (84060) 304/C3
Parkdale, Ark. (71661) 202/H7
Parkdale, Colo. (†81212) 208/H6
Parkdale, Oreg. (97041) 291/F2
Parkdale, Pr. Edward I. 168/E2
Parke (co.), Ind. 227/C5
Parker, Ariz. (85344) 198/A4
Parker (dam), Ariz. 198/A4
Parker, Colo. (80134) 208/K4
Parker, Fla. (32401) 212/C6
Parker, Idaho (83438) 220/G6
Parker, Kansas (66072) 232/H3
Parker, Pa. (16049) 294/C3
Parker, S. Dak. (57053) 298/P7
Parker (lake), S. Dak. 298/P3
Parker (co.), Texas 303/G5
Parker, Texas (†75069) 303/H1
Parker, Wash. (98939) 310/E4
Parker City, Ind. (47368) 227/G4
Parker Dam, Calif. (92267) 204/L9
Parkersburg, Ill. (62452) 222/F5
Parkersburg, Ind. (†47954) 227/D5
Parkersburg, Iowa (50665) 229/H3
Parkersburg, W. Va. 188/K3
Parkersburg, W. Va. (26101) 312/D4
Parkers Cove, Newf. 166/D4
Parkers Cove, Nova Scotia 168/C4
Parkers Lake, Ky. (42634) 237/M7
Parkers Prairie, Minn. (56361) 255/C4
Parkertown, N.J. (†08087) 273/E4
Parkerview, Sask. 181/H4
Parkerville, Kansas (†66846) 232/F3
Parkes, N.S. Wales 88/H6
Parkes, N.S. Wales 97/E3
Parkesburg, Pa. (19365) 294/L6
Park Falls, Wis. (54552) 317/F4
Park Forest, Ill. (60466) 222/B6
Park Forest South, Ill. (60466) 222/F2
Park Hall, Md. (20667) 245/N8
Park Hill, Okla. (74451) 288/R3
Parkhill, Ontario 177/C4
Park Hills, Ky. (†41011) 237/S2
Parkin, Ark. (72373) 202/J3
Parkland, Alberta 182/D4
Parkland, Fla. (†33441) 212/F5
Parkland, Okla. (†74824) 288/N3
Parkland, Wash. (98444) 310/C3
Parkman○, Maine (†04443) 243/D5
Parkman, Ohio (44080) 284/H3
Parkman, Sask. 181/K6
Parkman, Wyo. (82838) 319/E1
Park Place, Oreg. (†97045) 291/B2
Park Rapids, Minn. (56470) 255/D4
Park Rapids, Wash. (†99114) 310/H2
Park Ridge, Ill. (60068) 222/B5
Park Ridge, N.J. (07656) 273/B1
Park Ridge, Wis. (†54481) 317/H6
Park River, N. Dak. (58270) 282/P3
Parks, Ariz. (86018) 198/C3
Parks, Ark. (72950) 202/B4
Parks, La. (70582) 238/G6
Parks, Nebr. (69041) 264/C4
Parkside, Pa. (†19013) 294/M7
Parkside, Sask. 181/E2
Parksley, Va. (23421) 307/S5
Parkston, S. Dak. (57366) 298/O7
Parksville, Br. Col. 184/J3
Parksville, Ky. (40464) 237/M5
Parksville, N.Y. (12768) 276/L7
Parksville, S.C. (29844) 296/C4
Parkton, Md. (21120) 245/M2
Parkton, N.C. (28371) 281/M5
Park Valley, Utah (84329) 304/A2
Parkview (mt.), Colo. 208/G2
Parkville, Md. (21234) 245/M3
Parkville, Mo. (64152) 261/O5
Parkville, Pa. (†17331) 294/J6
Parkville, Victoria 97/H5
Parkway, Mo. (64130) 261/L6
Parkway Village, Ky. (†40201) 237/J2
Parkwood, N.C. (27707) 281/M3
Parlakhemundi, India 68/E5
Parlier, Calif. (93648) 204/F7
Parlin, Colo. (81239) 208/F6
Parlin (pond), Maine 243/C4
Parma, Idaho (83660) 220/B6
Parma (prov.), Italy 34/C2
Parma, Italy 7/E4
Parma, Italy 34/C2
Parma (riv.), Italy 34/C2
Parma, Mich. (49269) 250/E6
Parma, Mo. (63870) 261/N9
Parma, Ohio (44129) 284/H9
Parmachenee (lake), Maine 243/B5
Parma Heights, Ohio (†44130) 284/G9
Parmana, Venezuela 124/F4
Parmele, N.C. (27861) 281/P3
Parmelee, S. Dak. (57566) 298/G7
Parmer (co.), Texas 303/B3
Parnaguá, Brazil 132/E5
Parnaíba, Brazil 132/F3
Parnaíba, Brazil 120/E3
Parnaíba (riv.), Brazil 120/E3
Parnaíba (riv.), Brazil 132/F3
Parnamirim, Brazil 132/F4
Parnassus (mt.), Greece 45/F6
Parnassus, N. Zealand 100/D5
Parndana, S. Australia 94/E6
Parnell, Iowa (52325) 229/J5
Parnell, Mo. (64475) 261/C2
Pärnu, U.S.S.R. 7/G3
Pärnu, U.S.S.R. 53/C1
Pärnu, U.S.S.R. 52/C3
Pärnu, U.S.S.R. 48/C4
Paro, Bhutan 68/F3
Paron, Ark. (72132) 202/E4
Paroo (riv.), N. S. Wales 88/G5
Paroo (chan.), N.S. Wales 97/B2
Paroo (riv.), N.S. Wales 97/C1
Paroo (riv.), Queensland 95/C6
Paropamisus (mts.), Afghanistan 59/H3
Paropamisus (range), Afghanistan 68/A2
Páros (isl.), Greece 45/G7
Parow, S. Africa 118/F6
Parowan, Utah (84761) 304/B6
Parpan, Switzerland 39/J3
Parr, Ind. (†47978) 227/C2
Parr, S.C. (29066) 296/E3
Parral, Chile 138/A11
Parral, Mexico 150/G3
Parral, Ohio (†44622) 284/G4
Parramatta, N. S. Wales 88/K4
Parramatta (riv.), N. S. Wales 88/K4
Parramatta, N.S. Wales 97/H3
Parramatta (riv.), N.S. Wales 97/J3
Parramore (isl.), Va. 307/S5
Parran, Md. (†20639) 245/M6
Parras de la Fuente, Mexico 150/H4
Parratah, Tasmania 99/D4
Parrett (riv.), England 13/E6
Parrish, Ala. (35580) 195/D3
Parrish, Fla. (33564) 212/D4
Parrish, Wis. (†54435) 317/H5
Parris Island Marine Base, S.C. 296/F7
Parrott, Georgia (31777) 217/D7
Parrott, Va. (24132) 307/G6
Parrottsville, Tenn. (37843) 237/P8
Parrsboro, Nova Scotia 168/D3
Parry (isls.), N.W.T. 146/G2
Parry (chan.), N.W.T. 146/G2
Parry (chan.), N.W.T. 162/E-H1
Parry (bay), N.W. Terrs. 187/K3
Parry (cape), N.W. Terrs. 187/F2
Parry (chan.), N.W. Terrs. 187/G2
Parry (isls.), N.W. Terrs. 187/G2
Parry (pen.), N.W. Terrs. 187/F2
Parry (isl.), Ontario 177/D2
Parry (sound), Ontario 177/D2
Parry, Sask. 181/G6
Parry Sound, Ont. 162/J6
Parry Sound (terr. dist.), Ontario 175/E3
Parry Sound, Ontario 175/D3
Parry Sound, Ontario 177/E2
Parseierspitze (mt.), Austria 41/A3
Parshall, Colo. (80468) 208/G2
Parshall, N. Dak. (58770) 282/F4
Parsippany-Troy Hills○, N.J. (07054) 273/E2
Parsnip (riv.), Br. Col. 184/F3
Parson, Br. Col. 184/J4
Parsons, Kans. 188/G3
Parsons, Kansas (67357) 232/G4
Parsons, Tenn. (38363) 237/E9
Parsons, W. Va. (26287) 312/G4
Parsonsburg, Md. (21849) 245/R7
Parson's Pond, Newf. 166/C3
Partanna, Italy 34/D6
Partapgarh, India 68/C4
Parthenay, France 28/C4
Partinico, Italy 34/D6
Partizansk, U.S.S.R. 48/O5
Partizánske, Czech. 41/E2
Partlow, Va. (22534) 307/N4
Partridge, Kansas (67566) 232/D4
Partridge (riv.), Minn. 255/G3
Partridge (bay), Newf. 166/C3
Partridge (pt.), Newf. 166/C3
Partry (mts.), Ireland 17/C4
Paru (riv.), Brazil 132/C3
Paru de Oeste (riv.), Brazil 120/D3
Paru de Oeste (riv.), Brazil 132/B3
Paruro, Peru 128/F9
Parvatipuram, India 68/E5
Parys, S. Africa 118/D5
Pas, De (riv.), Québec 174/D1
Pasadena, Calif. 188/C4
Pasadena, Calif. (*91101) 204/C10
Pasadena, Md. (21122) 245/M4
Pasadena, Newf. 166/C4
Pasadena, Texas (*77501) 303/J2
Pasado (cape), Ecuador 128/B3
Pasaje, Ecuador 128/C4
Pa Sak, Mae Nam (riv.), Thailand 72/D4
Pasangkayu, Indonesia 85/F6
Pasargadae (ruins), Iran 66/H5
Pasatiempo, Calif. (†95060) 204/K4
Pasawng, Burma 72/C3
Pasayten (riv.), Wash. 310/E2
Pascagoula, Miss. (39567) 256/G10
Pascagoula (riv.), Miss. 256/G9
Pascalis, Québec 174/B3
Paşcani, Romania 45/H2
Paschall, N.C. (†27589) 281/N1
Pasco (co.), Fla. 212/D3
Pasco (dept.), Peru 128/E8
Pasco, Wash. (99301) 310/F4
Pascoag, R.I. (02859) 249/H5
Pascola, Mo. (63871) 261/N10
Pascua (riv.), Chile 138/D7
Pas-de-Calais (dept.), France 28/E2
Pasewalk, E. Germany 22/F2
Pasighat, India 68/G3
Pasinler, Turkey 63/J3
Pasión (riv.), Guatemala 154/B2
Paskenta, Calif. (96074) 204/C4
Pasłek, Poland 47/D1
Pasley (bay), N.W. Terrs. 187/J2
Pasni, Pakistan 68/A3
Pasni, Pakistan 54/H7
Pasni, Pakistan 59/H4
Paso Ataques, Uruguay 145/D2
Paso Barreto, Paraguay 144/D3
Paso de Andrés Pérez, Uruguay 145/B3
Paso de Indios, Argentina 143/C5
Paso de la Laguna, Salto, Uruguay 145/B2
Paso de la Laguna, Tacuarembó, Uruguay 145/D3
Paso de las Piedras, Uruguay 145/C2
Paso del Borracho, Uruguay 145/D2
Paso del Cerro, Uruguay 145/C2
Paso de León, Uruguay 145/B1
Paso del Horno, Uruguay 145/C2
Paso de Los Libres, Argentina 143/E2
Paso de los Toros, Uruguay 145/C3
Paso del Parque, Uruguay 145/B2
Paso de Ovejas, Mexico 150/Q2
Paso de Patria, Paraguay 144/C5
Paso de Ramos, Uruguay 145/C1
Paso de Uleste, Uruguay 145/B3
Paso Flores, Argentina 143/C5
Paso Hondo, Uruguay 145/B4
Paso Potrero, Uruguay 145/C2
Pasorapa, Bolivia 136/C6
Paso Real, Honduras 154/E3
Paso Robles, Calif. (93446) 204/E8
Paspébiac, Québec 172/D2
Pasqua, Sask. 181/F5
Pasque (isl.), Mass. 249/L7
Pasquia (hills), Sask. 181/J2
Pasquia (riv.), Sask. 181/K2
Pasquotank (co.), N.C. 281/S2
Pass (creek), Wyo. 319/F4
Passaconaway (mt.), N.H. 268/E4
Passadumkeag○, Maine (04475) 243/F5
Passage (isl.), Mich. 250/E1
Passage East, Ireland 17/G7
Passagem Franca, Brazil 132/E4
Passage West, Ireland 17/E8
Passage West, Ireland 10/B5
Passaic, Mo. (64777) 261/D6
Passaic (co.), N.J. 273/E1
Passaic, N.J. (07055) 273/E2
Passaic (riv.), N.J. 273/E2
Passamaquoddy (bay), Maine 243/J5
Passamaquoddy (bay), New Bruns. 170/C3
Passamaquoddy Ind. Res., Maine 243/J6
Passau, W. Germany 22/E4
Pass Christian, Miss. (39571) 256/F10
Passero (cape), Italy 7/F5
Passero (cape), Italy 34/E6
Passes (lake), Québec 172/F2
Passi, Philippines 82/D5
Passo Fundo, Brazil 120/D5
Passo Fundo, Brazil 132/D10
Passos, Brazil 132/E8
Passos, Brazil 135/C2
Passumpsic, Vt. (05861) 268/D3
Passumpsic (riv.), Vt. 268/D2
Pastaza (riv.) 120/B3
Pastaza (prov.), Ecuador 128/D3
Pastaza (riv.), Ecuador 128/D4
Pastaza (riv.), Peru 128/D5
Pasto, Colombia 120/B2
Pasto, Colombia 126/B7
Pastol (bay), Alaska 196/F2
Pastora (peak), Ariz. 198/F2
Pastos Bons, Brazil 132/E4
Pastrana, Spain 33/E2
Pastura, N. Mex. (88435) 274/E4
Pasuquin, Philippines 82/C1
Pasuruan, Indonesia 85/K2
Pasvalys, U.S.S.R. 53/C2
Pasvikelv (riv.), Norway 18/Q2
Paswegin, Sask. 181/H4
Pásztó, Hungary 41/E3
Pata, Bolivia 136/A4
Patacamaya, Bolivia 136/B5
Patagonia (reg.), Argentina 120/C7
Patagonia (reg.), Argentina 143/C5
Patagonia, Ariz. (85624) 198/E7
Pataguanset (lake), Conn. 210/G3
Pataha, Wash. (†99347) 310/H4
Pataha (creek), Wash. 310/H4
Patan, India 68/C4
Patapédia (riv.), New Bruns. 170/C1
Patapédia (riv.), Québec 172/B2
Patapsco, Md. (†21048) 245/L2
Patapsco (riv.), Md. 245/M4
Pataskala, Ohio (43062) 284/E5
Pataz, Peru 128/D6
Patchewollock, Victoria 97/A4
Patch Grove, Wis. (53817) 317/D10
Patchogue, N.Y. (11772) 276/P9
Patea, N. Zealand 100/E3
Paternion, Austria 41/B3
Paterno, Italy 34/E6
Pateros, Wash. (98846) 310/E2
Pateros (lake), Wash. 310/F2
Paterson, N.J. 188/M2
Paterson, N.J. (*07501) 273/B2
Paterson, Wash. (99345) 310/F5
Patesville, Ky. (†42364) 237/H5
Pathankot, India 68/D2
Pathfinder (res.), Wyo. 188/E2
Pathfinder (res.), Wyo. 319/F3
Pathiu, Thailand 72/C5
Pathlow, Sask. 181/G3
Pati (pt.), Guam 86/K6
Pati, Indonesia 85/J2
Patía, Colombia 126/B6
Patía (riv.), Colombia 126/B6
Patiala, India 68/D2
Patillas, P. Rico 161/E2
Patillas (lake), P. Rico 161/E2
Pativilca (riv.), Peru 128/D8
Patmos, Ark. (†71801) 202/C7
Pátmos (isl.), Greece 45/H7
Patna, India 54/K7
Patna, India 68/F3
Patna, Scotland 15/D5
Patnanongan (isl.), Philippines 82/D3
Patnos, Turkey 63/K3
Patoka, Ill. (62875) 222/D5
Patoka, Ind. (47666) 227/B8
Patoka (riv.), Ind. 227/C8
Paton, Iowa (50217) 229/E4
Patos, Brazil 120/F3
Patos, Brazil 132/G4
Patos (lake), Brazil 120/D6
Patos (lag.), Brazil 132/D10
Patos de Minas, Brazil 120/E4
Patos de Minas, Brazil 132/E7
Patoutville, La. (†70544) 238/G7
Patquía, Argentina 143/C3
Pátrai, Greece 7/G5
Pátrai, Greece 45/E6
Patricia, Alberta 182/E4
Patricia, S. Dak. (†57551) 298/G7
Patricia, Texas (79352) 303/B5
Patricio Lynch (isl.), Chile 138/D7
Patrick, Neth. Ant. 161/F8
Patrick, S.C. (29584) 296/G2
Patrick (co.), Va. 307/H7
Patrick A.F.B., Fla. 212/F3
Patricksburg, Ind. (47455) 227/D6
Patrick's Cove, Newf. 166/C2
Patrick Springs, Va. (24133) 307/H7
Patrickswell, Ireland 17/D6
Patriot, Ind. (47038) 227/H7
Patriot, Ohio (45658) 284/F8
Patrocínio, Brazil 132/E7
Patronville, Ind. (†47635) 227/C9
Patroon, Texas (75967) 303/L6
Patsaliga (creek), Ala. 195/F7
Patsburg, Ala. (†36049) 195/F7
Patta (isl.), Kenya 115/H4
Pattani, Thailand 72/D6
Patten, Maine (04765) 243/F4
Patten○, Maine (04765) 243/F4
Pattenburg, N.J. (†08802) 273/C2
Patterson, Ark. (72123) 202/H3
Patterson, Calif. (95363) 204/D6
Patterson, Georgia (31557) 217/H8
Patterson, Idaho (†83253) 220/E5
Patterson, Ill. (62078) 222/C4
Patterson, Iowa (50218) 229/F6
Patterson, La. (70392) 238/H7
Patterson (pt.), Mich. 250/D3
Patterson, Mo. (63956) 261/L8
Patterson, N.Y. (12563) 276/N7
Patterson, N.C. (28661) 281/F3
Patterson, Edward A. (lake), N. Dak. 282/E6
Patterson, Ohio (45843) 284/C4
Patterson, Va. (24633) 307/D6
Patterson (creek), W. Va. 312/J4
Patterson Creek, W. Va. (26746) 312/J3
Pattersonville, N.Y. (12137) 276/M5
Patti, Italy 34/E5
Pattison, Miss. (39144) 256/C7
Patton, Mo. (63662) 261/M8
Patton, Pa. (16668) 294/E4
Pattonsburg, Mo. (64670) 261/D2
Patuanak, Sask. 181/L3
Patuca, Honduras 154/E3
Patuca (pt.), Honduras 154/E3
Patuca (riv.), Honduras 154/E3
Patuha (mt.), Indonesia 85/H2
Pătulele, Romania 45/F3
Patutahi, N. Zealand 100/F3
Patuxent (riv.), Md. 245/M7
Patuxent River Nav. Air Test Ctr., Md. 245/N7
Patzau, Wis. (†54836) 317/B3
Pátzcuaro, Mexico 150/J7

Plainview, Ark. (72857) 202/D4
Plain View, Iowa (†52773) 229/M5
Plainview, Minn. (55964) 255/F6
Plainview, Nebr. (68769) 264/G2
Plainview, N.Y. (11803) 276/R
Plainview, S. Dak. (57771) 298/E4
Plainview, Texas (79072) 303/C3
Plainville○, Conn. (06062) 210/D2
Plainville, Georgia (30733) 217/C2
Plainville, Ill. (62365) 222/B4
Plainville, Ind. (47568) 227/C7
Plainville, Kansas (67663) 232/C2
Plainville○, Mass. (02762) 249/J4
Plainwell, Mich. (49080) 250/D6
Plaisance, Haiti 158/C5
Plaisance, Québec 172/B4
Plaisted, Maine (04767) 243/F1
Plaistow○, N.H. (03865) 268/E6
Plaju, Indonesia 85/D6
Plamondon, Alberta 182/D2
Plana (cays), Bahamas 156/D2
Planá, Czech. 41/B2
Planada, Calif. (95365) 204/E6
Planeta Rica, Colombia 126/C3
Plánice, Czech. 41/B2
Plankinton, S. Dak. (57368) 298/N6
Plano, Ill. (60545) 222/E2
Plano, Iowa (52581) 229/G7
Plano, Texas (75074) 303/G1
Plant, Tenn. (†37054) 237/F9
Plantagenet, Ontario 177/K2
Plantation, Fla. (33317) 212/B4
Plantation (key), Fla. 212/F7
Plantation, Ky. (†40201) 237/K1
Plant City, Fla. (33566) 212/D3
Plantersville, Ala. (36758) 195/E5
Plantersville, Miss. (38862) 256/G2
Plantersville, S.C. (29441) 296/J4
Plantsite, Ariz. (†85540) 198/F5
Plantsville, Conn. (06479) 210/D2
Plaquemine, La. (70764) 238/J2
Plaquemines (par.), La. 238/L8
Plasencia, Spain 33/C2
Plaster City, Calif. (92269) 204/K11
Plaster Rock, New Bruns. 170/C2
Plastun, U.S.S.R. 48/05
Plasy, Czech. 41/B2
Plat, Wis. (†53017) 317/K1
Plata (riv.) 2/G7
Plata, Río de la (est.), Argentina 143/E4
Plata (riv.), P. Rico 161/D2
Plata, La (riv.), Uruguay 145/B5
Platanal, Venezuela 124/F6
Platanilla, C. Rica 154/F6
Platea, Pa. (†16417) 294/B2
Plateau (creek), Colo. 208/C4
Plateau (state), Nigeria 106/F7
Plateau, Nova Scotia 168/H2
Plateau City, Colo. (†81624) 208/D4
Plate Cove, Newf. 166/D2
Platen, Kapp (pt.), Norway 18/D1
Platina, Calif. (96076) 204/B3
Platinum, Alaska (99651) 196/F3
Platner, Colo. (†80743) 208/N2
Plato, Colombia 126/C3
Plato, Minn. (55370) 255/D6
Plato, Mo. (65552) 261/H8
Plato, Sask. 181/C4
Platoro (res.), Colo. 208/F8
Platte (riv.), Iowa 229/D8
Platte (lake), Mich. 250/C4
Platte (co.), Mo. 261/C4
Platte (riv.), Mo. 261/C3
Platte (riv.), Nebr. 146/J5
Platte (riv.), Nebr. 188/G2
Platte (co.), Nebr. 264/G3
Platte (riv.), Nebr. 264/E4
Platte, S. Dak. (57369) 298/M7
Platte (lake), S. Dak. 298/M6
Platte (co.), Wyo. 319/H4
Platte Center, Nebr. (68653) 264/G3
Platte City, Mo. (64079) 261/C4
Plattenville, La. (70393) 238/K4
Platter, Okla. (74753) 288/07
Platteville, Colo. (80651) 208/K2
Platteville, Wis. (53818) 317/F10
Platte Woods, Mo. (†64152) 261/O5
Platt Nat'l Park, Okla. 288/N6
Plattsburg, Mo. (64477) 261/D3
Plattsburgh, N.Y. (12901) 276/O1
Plattsburgh A.F.B., N.Y. 276/N1
Plattsmouth, Nebr. (68048) 264/J3
Plattsville, Ontario 177/D4
Plau, E. Germany 22/E2
Plaucheville, La. (71362) 238/G5
Plauen, E. Germany 22/E3
Plauersee (lake), E. Germany 22/E2
Plav, Yugoslavia 45/D4
Plaviņas, U.S.S.R. 53/C2
Playa (pt.), Guyana 131/B1
Playa Azul, Mexico 150/H7
Playa Bonita, C. Rica 154/E6
Playa de Fajardo, P. Rico 161/F1
Playa de Humacao, P. Rico 161/F2
Playa Grande, Nicaragua 154/D4
Playas, Ecuador 128/B4
Playas (lake), N. Mex. 274/A7
Playón Chico, Panama 154/H6
Playón Grande, Panama 154/H6
Plaza, N. Dak. (58771) 282/G3
Plaza, Wash. (99028) 310/H3
Plaza Huincul, Argentina 143/B4
Pleasant (isl.), Alaska 196/M1
Pleasant (lake), Ariz. 198/C5
Pleasant, Ind. (†47043) 227/G7
Pleasant (lake), Maine 243/H5
Pleasant (lake), Maine 243/E3
Pleasant (lake), Maine 243/G3
Pleasant (riv.), Maine 243/H6
Pleasant (mt.), New Bruns. 170/D3
Pleasant (lake), N.Y. 276/M4
Pleasant (bay), Nova Scotia 168/H2
Pleasant Bay, Nova Scotia 168/H2
Pleasant City, Ohio (43772) 284/G6
Pleasant Dale, Nebr. (68423) 264/G4
Pleasantdale, Sask. 181/G3
Pleasant Gap, Ala. (†36272) 195/H3
Pleasant Gap, Pa. (16823) 294/G4
Pleasant Green, Mo. (†65276) 261/F5
Pleasant Grove, Ala. (35127) 195/D4
Pleasant Grove, Calif. (95668) 204/B8
Pleasant Grove, Miss. (38657) 256/D2
Pleasant Grove, N.J. (†07865) 273/D2
Pleasant Grove, Utah (84062) 304/C3
Pleasant Hill, Ala. (†36701) 195/E6
Pleasant Hill, Calif. (94523) 204/K2
Pleasant Hill, Ill. (62366) 222/C4
Pleasant Hill, La. (71065) 238/C3
Pleasant Hill, Miss. (†38651) 256/E1
Pleasant Hill, Mo. (64080) 261/D5
Pleasant Hill, N.C. (27866) 281/O1
Pleasant Hill, Ohio (45359) 284/B5
Pleasant Hill, S.C. (†29058) 296/F2
Pleasant Hill, Tenn. (38578) 237/L9
Pleasant Hills, Md. (†21087) 245/N3
Pleasant Hills, Pa. (15236) 294/B7
Pleasant Hope, Mo. (65725) 261/F8
Pleasant Island, Maine (†04964) 243/B5
Pleasant Lake, Ind. (46779) 227/H1
Pleasant Lake, Mass. (†02645) 249/O6
Pleasant Lake, Minn. (†56301) 255/D5
Pleasant Lake, N. Dak. (58364) 282/L3
Pleasant Lane, S.C. (†29824) 296/D4
Pleasant Mills, Ind. (46780) 227/H3
Pleasant Mound, Ill. (†62284) 222/D5
Pleasant Mount, Pa. (18453) 294/M2
Pleasanton, Calif. (94566) 204/L2
Pleasanton, Iowa (50224) 229/F7
Pleasanton, Kansas (66075) 232/H3
Pleasanton, Nebr. (68866) 264/E4
Pleasanton, N. Mex. (†88039) 274/A5
Pleasanton, Texas (78064) 303/F9
Pleasant Plain, Iowa (†52540) 229/K6
Pleasant Plain, Ohio (45162) 284/B7
Pleasant Plains, Ark. (72568) 202/G2
Pleasant Plains, Ill. (62677) 222/D4
Pleasant Point, N. Zealand 100/C6
Pleasant Pond, Maine (†04925) 243/D5
Pleasant Prairie, Wis. (53158) 317/L10
Pleasant Ridge, Mich. (48069) 250/B6
Pleasants (co.), W. Va. 312/D4
Pleasant Shade, Tenn. (37145) 237/K8
Pleasant Valley, Conn. (06063) 210/C1
Pleasant Valley, Md. (†21157) 245/L2
Pleasant Valley, Mo. (†64836) 261/R5
Pleasant Valley, Oreg. (†97814) 291/K3
Pleasant Valley (creek), S. Dak. 298/B6
Pleasant Valley, Va. (22848) 307/L4
Pleasant View, Colo. (81331) 208/B7
Pleasant View, Ill. (†62681) 222/C3
Pleasant View, Ky. (40769) 237/N7
Pleasant View, Tenn. (37146) 237/G8
Pleasant View, Utah (†84401) 304/B2
Pleasantville, Ind. (†47838) 227/C7
Pleasantville, Iowa (50225) 229/G6
Pleasantville, N.J. (08232) 273/D5
Pleasantville, N.Y. (10570) 276/N8
Pleasantville, Ohio (43148) 284/F6
Pleasantville (Alum Bank), Pa. (†15521) 294/E5
Pleasantville, Pa. (16341) 294/C2
Pleasantville, Tenn. (37147) 237/F9
Pleasure Beach, Conn. (†06385) 210/G3
Pleasure Ridge Park, Ky. (40258) 237/J4
Pleasureville, Ky. (40057) 237/L4
Pleiku, Vietnam 72/E4
Plenița, Romania 45/F3
Plenty (bay), N. Zealand 100/F2
Plenty, Sask. 181/C4
Plenty (riv.), Victoria 97/J4
Plenty (riv.), Victoria 88/L6
Plenty River Mine, North. Terr. 93/D7
Plentywood, Mont. (59254) 262/M2
Plesetsk, U.S.S.R. 52/F2
Plessis, N.Y. (13675) 276/J2
Plessisville, Québec 172/F3
Plessur (riv.), Switzerland 39/J3
Pleszew, Poland 47/C3
Pletcher, Ala. (†36750) 195/E5
Plétipi (lake), Que. 162/J5
Plétipi (lake), Québec 174/C2
Plettenberg (bay), S. Africa 118/C6
Plettenberg, W. Germany 22/C3
Pleven, Bulgaria 7/G4
Pleven, Bulgaria 45/G4
Plevna, Ala. (†35761) 195/F1
Plevna, Ind. (†46901) 227/E3
Plevna, Kansas (67568) 232/D4
Plevna, Mo. (63464) 261/H3
Plevna, Mont. (59344) 262/M4
Plevna, Ontario 177/H3
Pliny, W. Va. (25158) 312/B5
Pljevlja, Yugoslavia 45/D4
Ploče, Yugoslavia 45/C4
Płock (prov.), Poland 47/D2
Płock, Poland 47/D2
Plockton, Scotland 15/C3
Ploërmel, France 28/B4
Ploiești, Romania 45/H3
Ploiești, Romania 7/G4
Plomárion, Greece 45/H6
Plomb du Cantal (mt.), France 28/E5
Plombières, Belgium 27/F7
Plomer (pt.), N.S. Wales 97/G2
Plomosa (mts.), Ariz. 198/A5
Plön, W. Germany 22/D1
Płonia (riv.), Poland 47/B2
Płońsk, Poland 47/E2
Plovdiv, Bulgaria 7/G4
Plovdiv, Bulgaria 45/G4
Plover, Iowa (50573) 229/D3
Plover, Wis. (54467) 317/G7
Pluckemin, N.J. (07978) 273/D2
Plum (riv.), Ill. 222/C1
Plum (creek), Manitoba 179/B5
Plum (lake), Manitoba 179/B5
Plum (isl.), Mass. 249/L2
Plum (isl.), N.Y. 276/R8
Plum, Pa. (15239) 294/C5
Plumas (co.), Calif. 204/E4
Plumas, Manitoba 179/D4
Plumber (creek), Utah 304/C2
Plum Branch, S.C. (29845) 296/C4
Plum City, Wis. (54761) 317/B6
Plum Coulee, Manitoba 179/E5
Plumerville, Ark. (72127) 202/E3
Plummer, Idaho (83851) 220/B2
Plummer, Ind. (†47424) 227/C7
Plummer, Minn. (56748) 255/B3
Plummers Landing, Ky. (41081) 237/P4
Plum Point, Md. (†20639) 245/N6
Plum Springs, Ky. (†42101) 237/J7
Plumsteadville, Pa. (18949) 294/M5
Plum Tree, Ind. (†46792) 227/G3
Plumtree, Zimbabwe 118/D4
Plumville, Pa. (16246) 294/D4
Plumwood, Ohio (†43140) 284/D6
Plunge, U.S.S.R. 53/B3
Plunkett, Sask. 181/F4
Plunkettville, Okla. (†74963) 288/S6
Plush, Oreg. (97637) 291/H5
Plymouth (cap.), 156/F3
Plymouth, Calif. (95669) 204/C8
Plymouth○, Conn. (06782) 210/C2
Plymouth, England 7/D3
Plymouth, England 10/E5
Plymouth, England 13/C7
Plymouth (sound), England 13/C7
Plymouth, Fla. (32768) 212/E3
Plymouth, Ill. (62367) 222/C3
Plymouth, Ind. (46563) 227/E2
Plymouth (co.), Iowa 229/A3
Plymouth, Iowa (50464) 229/G2
Plymouth○, Maine (04969) 243/E6
Plymouth (co.), Mass. 249/L5
Plymouth, Mass. (02360) 249/M5
Plymouth○, Mass. (02360) 249/M5
Plymouth (bay), Mass. 249/M5
Plymouth, Mich. (*48170) 250/F6
Plymouth, Minn. (†55441) 255/G5
Plymouth, Nebr. (68424) 264/G4
Plymouth, N.H. (03264) 268/D4
Plymouth○, N.H. (03264) 268/D4
Plymouth, N.C. (27962) 281/R3
Plymouth, Ohio (44865) 284/E4
Plymouth, Pa. (18651) 294/E7
Plymouth, Utah (84330) 304/B2
Plymouth○, Vt. (05056) 268/B4
Plymouth, Wash. (99346) 310/F5
Plymouth, W. Va. (†25011) 312/C5
Plymouth, Wis. (53073) 317/L8
Plymouth Union, Vt. (†05056) 268/B4
Plympton○, Mass. (02367) 249/L5
Plympton, Nova Scotia 168/C4
Plynlimon (mt.), Wales 13/D5
Plzeň, Czech. 7/F4
Plzeň, Czech. 41/B2
Pniel, S. Africa 118/F6
Pniewy, Poland 47/C2
Po (riv.), Italy 7/E4
Po (riv.), Italy 34/C2
Po, Upper Volta 106/D6
Po (riv.), Va. 307/N4
Poá, Brazil 135/C3
Poatina, Tasmania 99/C3
Pobeda (peak), China 77/A3
Pobeda (peak), U.S.S.R. 48/J5
Población, Chile 138/F5
Pobla de Segur, Spain 33/G1
Poca, W. Va. (25159) 312/C6
Pocahontas, Alberta 182/B3
Pocahontas, Ark. (72455) 202/H1
Pocahontas, Ill. (62275) 222/D5
Pocahontas (co.), Iowa 229/D3
Pocahontas, Iowa (50574) 229/D3
Pocahontas, Miss. (39072) 256/D6
Pocahontas, Mo. (63779) 261/N8
Pocahontas, Tenn. (38061) 237/D10
Pocahontas, Va. (24635) 307/F6
Pocahontas (co.), W. Va. 312/F6
Pocasset, Mass. (02559) 249/M6
Pocasset, Okla. (73079) 288/L4
Pocatalico (riv.), W. Va. 312/C5
Pocatello, Idaho 146/G5
Pocatello, Idaho (*83201) 220/F7
Pocatello, Idaho 188/D2
Počátky, Czech. 41/C2
Pochep, U.S.S.R. 52/D4
Pöchlarn, Austria 41/C2
Pocklington, England 13/G4
Pocoata, Bolivia 136/B6
Poções, Brazil 132/F6
Pocola, Okla. (74902) 288/T4
Pocologan, New Bruns. 170/D3
Pocomoke (riv.), Md. 245/S8
Pocomoke (sound), Md. 245/P9
Pocomoke (sound), Va. 307/S5
Pocomoke City, Md. (21851) 245/R8
Pocomoonshine (lake), Maine 243/H5
Pocona, Bolivia 136/C5
Poconé, Brazil 132/B7
Pocono (mts.), Pa. 294/M3
Pocono Lake, Pa. (18347) 294/L3
Pocono Pines, Pa. (18350) 294/M3
Poços de Caldas, Brazil 120/E5
Poços de Caldas, Brazil 135/C2
Poços de Caldas, Brazil 132/E8
Pocotalago, Georgia (†30633) 217/F2
Pocotalico, W. Va. (†25301) 312/C6
Pocotaligo (riv.), S.C. 296/G4
Pocotopaug (lake), Conn. 210/E2
Pocpo, Bolivia 136/C6
Podbořany, Czech. 41/B1
Poděbrady, Czech. 41/C1
Podol'sk, U.S.S.R. 7/H3
Podol'sk, U.S.S.R. 52/E3
Podol'sk, U.S.S.R. 48/D4
Podor, Senegal 106/B5
Podporozh'ye, U.S.S.R. 52/D2
Podunk (riv.), Conn. 210/E1
Poe, Alberta 182/D3
Poe, Ind. (†46802) 227/G3
Poel (isl.), E. Germany 22/D1
Poenari Burchi, Romania 45/G3
Poge (cape), Mass. 249/N7
Poggibonsi, Italy 34/C3
Pogradec, Albania 45/E5
Pohakuloa (pt.), Hawaii 218/H2
P'ohang, S. Korea 81/D5
Pohatcong (creek), N.J. 273/C2
Pohénégamook, Québec 172/H2
Pohjois-Karjala (prov.), Finland 18/Q5
Pohořelice, Czech. 41/D2
Pohsien (Bo Xian), China 77/J5
Poiana Mare, Romania 45/F4
Poigan (lake), Québec 172/A2
Poinsett (co.), Ark. 202/J3
Poinsett (lake), Fla. 212/F3
Poinsett (lake), S. Dak. 298/P4
Point, La. (†71234) 238/F1
Point (lake), N.W. Terrs. 187/G3
Point, Texas (75472) 303/J5
Point Alexander, Ontario 177/G1
Point Arena, Calif. (95468) 204/B5
Point au Fer (isl.), La. 238/H8
Point au Fer (pt.), La. 238/H8
Point Baker, Alaska (99927) 196/M2
Point Cedar, Ark. (†71921) 202/D5
Point Clear, Ala. (36564) 195/C10
Point Comfort, Texas (77978) 303/H9
Point Cross, Nova Scotia 168/G2
Point de Bute, New Bruns. 170/F3
Point du Bois, Manitoba 179/G4
Pointe-à-la-Croix, Québec 172/C2
Pointe-à-la-Frégate, Québec 172/D1
Pointe-à-la-Garde, Québec 172/B2
Pointe a la Hache, La. (70082) 238/L7
Pointe-à-Pitre, Guadeloupe 161/B6
Pointe-à-Pitre, Guadeloupe 156/G3
Pointe à Raquette, Haiti 158/B6
Pointe au Baril Station, Ontario 177/D2
Pointe-au-Chêne, Québec 172/C4
Pointe-au-Père, Québec 172/J1
Pointe-au-Pic, Québec 172/G2
Pointe Aux Barques, Mich. (48467) 250/G4
Pointe-aux-Outardes, Québec 172/A1
Pointe Aux Pins, Mich. (49775) 250/E3
Pointe-aux-Trembles, Québec 172/J4
Pointe-Bleue, Québec 172/E1
Pointe-Calumet, Québec 172/G4
Pointe-Claire, Québec 172/H4
Pointe Coupee (par.), La. 238/G5
Pointe du Bout, Martinique 161/C6
Pointe-du-Chêne, New Bruns. 170/F2
Pointe-du-Lac, Québec 172/E3
Pointe-du-Moulin, Québec 172/H4
Point Edward, Ontario 177/B4
Pointe-Gatineau, Québec 172/B4
Pointe-Lebel, Québec 172/A1
Pointe-Noire, Congo 102/D5
Pointe-Noire, Congo 115/B4
Pointe-Noire, Guadeloupe 161/A6
Pointe-Sapin, New Bruns. 170/F2
Pointe-Verte, New Bruns. 170/E1
Point Fortin, Trin. & Tob. 161/A11
Point Harbor, N.C. (27964) 281/T2
Point Hope, Alaska 188/C5
Point Hope, Alaska (99766) 196/E1
Point Isabel, Ind. (†46928) 227/F4
Point La Haye, Newf. 166/D2
Point Lance, Newf. 166/C2
Point Lay, Alaska (†99723) 196/F1
Point Leamington, Newf. 166/C4
Point Marion, Pa. (15474) 294/C6
Point Mugu Pacific Missile Test Center, Calif. 204/F9
Point of Rocks, Md. (21777) 245/J3
Point of Rocks, Wyo. (82942) 319/D4
Point Pelee, Ontario 177/B6
Point Pelee Nat'l Park, Ontario 177/B5
Point Pleasant, Mo. (63873) 261/O10
Point Pleasant, N.J. (08742) 273/E3
Point Pleasant, Ohio (45163) 284/B8
Point Pleasant, Pa. (18950) 294/N5
Point Pleasant, W. Va. (25550) 312/B5
Point Pleasant Beach, N.J. (08742) 273/E3
Point Reyes Nat'l Seashore, Calif. 204/H1
Point Reyes Station, Calif. (94956) 204/H1
Point Roberts, Wash. (98281) 310/B2
Points, W. Va. (25437) 312/J4
Point Salvation Aboriginal Reserve, W. Australia 88/C5
Point Salvation Aboriginal Res., W. Australia 92/D5
Point Tupper, Nova Scotia 168/G3
Point Verde, Newf. 166/C2
Point Washington, Fla. (32454) 212/C6
Poipu, Hawaii (†96756) 218/C2
Poison (creek), Wyo. 319/E2
Poison Spider (creek), Wyo. 319/F3
Poisson Blanc (lake), Québec 172/B4
Poissons (riv.), Newf. 166/A3
Poitiers, France 7/E4
Poitiers, France 28/D4
Poitou (trad. prov.) France 29
Pojo, Bolivia 136/C5
Pojoaque, N. Mex. (†87501) 274/C3
Pokaran, India 68/C3
Pokataroo, N.S. Wales 97/E1
Pokegama (lake), Minn. 255/E3
Pokemouche (riv.), New Bruns. 170/E1
Pokesudie (isl.), New Bruns. 170/F1
Pokhara, Nepal 68/E3
Pokhvistnevo, U.S.S.R. 52/H4
Poko, Zaire 115/E3
Pokrovsk, U.S.S.R. 48/N3
Pola, Philippines 82/D4
Pola (Pula), Yugoslavia 45/A3
Polacca, Ariz. (86042) 198/E3
Polacca Wash (dry riv.), Ariz. 198/E3
Pola de Lena, Spain 33/C1
Pola de Siero, Spain 33/D1
Polanco del Yi, Uruguay 145/D4
Poland 2/K3
Poland 7/F3
POLAND 47
Poland (riv.), Conn. 210/C2
Poland, Ind. (47868) 227/C6
Poland, Maine (04273) 243/C7
Poland○, Maine (04273) 243/C7
Poland, N.Y. (13431) 276/L4
Poland, Ohio (44514) 284/J3
Poland Spring, Maine (04274) 243/C7
Polar, Wis. (54418) 317/H5
Polar Bear Prov. Park, Ontario 175/D2
Polaris, Mont. (59746) 262/C5
Polatlı, Turkey 63/E3
Polatlı, Turkey 59/B2
Połczyn-Zdrój, Poland 47/C2
Polebridge, Mont. (59928) 262/B2
Pol-e Khomri, Afghanistan 68/B1
Pol-e Khomri, Afghanistan 59/J2
Polgár, Hungary 41/F3
Polgárdi, Hungary 41/E3
Poli, Cameroon 115/B2
Policastro (gulf), Italy 34/E5
Police, Poland 47/B2
Polička, Czech. 41/D2
Poligny, France 28/F4
Poligus, U.S.S.R. 48/K3
Polikastron, Greece 45/F5
Polikhnitos, Greece 45/G6
Polillo, Philippines 82/D3
Polillo (isl.), Philippines 85/G3
Polillo (isl.), Philippines 82/C3
Polillo (str.), Philippines 82/C3
Polis, Cyprus 63/E5
Poliyiros, Greece 45/F5
Polk (co.), Ark. 202/B5
Polk (co.), Fla. 212/E4
Polk (co.), Georgia 217/B3
Polk (co.), Iowa 229/F5
Polk (co.), Minn. 255/B3
Polk (co.), Mo. 261/F7
Polk, Mo. (65727) 261/F7
Polk (co.), Nebr. 264/G3
Polk, Nebr. (68654) 264/G3
Polk (co.), N.C. 281/E4
Polk, Ohio (44866) 284/F4
Polk (co.), Oreg. 291/D3
Polk, Pa. (16342) 294/C3
Polk (co.), Tenn. 237/N10
Polk (co.), Texas 303/K7
Polk (co.), Wis. 317/B5
Polk City, Fla. (33868) 212/E3
Polk City, Iowa (50226) 229/F5
Polkowice, Poland 47/C3
Polkton, N.C. (28135) 281/J4
Polkville, Miss. (39118) 256/E6
Polkville, N.C. (28136) 281/F4
Pollaphuca (res.), Ireland 17/J5
Pollard, Ala. (†36441) 195/D8
Pollard, Ark. (72456) 202/K1
Pollards Point, Newf. 166/C4
Pöllau, Austria 41/C3
Pollensa, Spain 33/H3
Pollett (riv.), New Bruns. 170/E3
Pollett River, New Bruns. 170/E3
Pollock, Idaho (83547) 220/B4
Pollock, La. (71467) 238/F3
Pollock, Mo. (63560) 261/F2
Pollock, S. Dak. (57648) 298/J2
Pollock Pines, Calif. (95726) 204/E5
Pollocksville, N.C. (28573) 281/P5
Pollockville, Alberta 182/E4
Polmak, Norway 18/Q2
Polná, Czech. 41/C2
Polo, Dom. Rep. 158/D6
Polo, Ill. (61074) 222/D1
Polo, Mo. (64671) 261/D3
Polomka, Czech. 41/E2
Polonia, Chile 138/G6
Polonia, Wis. (†54423) 317/H6
Polonio, Uruguay 145/F5
Polonio (cape), Uruguay 145/F5
Polonnaruwa, Sri Lanka 68/E7
Polonnoye, U.S.S.R. 52/C4
Polotsk, U.S.S.R. 52/C3
Polperro, England 13/C7
Polson, Mont. (59860) 262/B3
Poltava, U.S.S.R. 7/H4
Poltava, U.S.S.R. 52/D5
Poltava, U.S.S.R. 48/D5
Poltimore, Québec 172/B4
Põltsamaa, U.S.S.R. 53/D1
Polvadera, N. Mex. (87828) 274/B4
Polyarnyy, U.S.S.R. 52/D1
Polyarnyy, U.S.S.R. 48/D3
Polynesia (reg.), Pacific 87/K7
Pomabamba, Peru 128/D7
Pomaire, Chile 138/F4
Pomán, Argentina 143/C2
Pomaria, S.C. (29126) 296/E3
Pombal, Brazil 132/G4
Pombal, Portugal 33/B3
Pomerania (reg.), E. Germany 22/E2
Pomeranian (bay), E. Germany 22/F1
Pomeranian (bay), Poland 47/B1
Pomerene, Ariz. (85627) 198/E6
Pomeroon (riv.), Guyana 131/B2
Pomeroy, Iowa (50575) 229/D3
Pomeroy, N. Ireland 17/H2
Pomeroy, Ohio (45769) 284/G7
Pomeroy, Wash. (99347) 310/H4
Pomezia, Italy 34/F7
Pomfret○, Conn. (06258) 210/H1
Pomfret, Md. (20675) 245/L6
Pomfret○, Vt. (†05067) 268/B4
Pomfret Center, Conn. (06259) 210/H1
Pomme de Terre (riv.), Minn. 255/C5
Pomme de Terre (lake), Mo. 261/E7
Pomona, Calif. 188/C4
Pomona, Calif. (*91766) 204/D10
Pomona, Kansas (66076) 232/G3
Pomona (lake), Kansas 232/G3
Pomona, Md. (†21620) 245/O4
Pomona, Mo. (65789) 261/J9
Pomona, N.J. (08240) 273/D5
Pomona Park, Fla. (32081) 212/E2
Pomonkey, Md. (†20640) 245/K6
Pomorie, Bulgaria 45/H4
Pomos (pt.), Cyprus 63/E5
Pompano Beach, Fla. (*33060) 212/F5
Pompanoosuc, Vt. (†05078) 268/C4
Pompéia, Brazil 135/A3
Pompeii (ruins), Italy 34/E4
Pompeii, Mich. (48874) 250/E5
Pomperaug, Conn. (†06798) 210/C2
Pomperaug (riv.), Conn. 210/C3
Pompey, N.Y. (13138) 276/J5
Pompeys Pillar, Mont. (59064) 262/J5
Pompton (lake), N.J. 273/B1
Pompton Lakes, N.J. (07442) 273/A1
Pompton Plains, N.J. (07444) 273/B1
Pomquet, Nova Scotia 168/G3
Pomy, Switzerland 39/C3
Ponape (isl.), Micronesia 87/F5
Ponass (lakes), Sask. 181/H3
Ponca, Ark. (72670) 202/D1
Ponca, Nebr. (68770) 264/H2
Ponca (creek), S. Dak. 298/L7
Ponca City, Okla. 188/G3
Ponca City, Okla. (74601) 288/M1
Ponce (dist.), P. Rico 161/C2
Ponce, P. Rico 161/C3
Ponce, P. Rico 156/F1
Ponce de Leon, Fla. (32455) 212/C6
Ponce de Leon (bay), Fla. 212/E6
Ponce Inlet, Fla. (†32019) 212/F2
Poncha Springs, Colo. (81242) 208/G6
Ponchatoula, La. (70454) 238/N2
Pond (pt.), Conn. 210/C4
Pond (riv.), Ky. 237/G6
Pond, Miss. (†39669) 256/B8
Pond, Mo. (†63038) 261/M3
Pond (inlet), N.W. Terrs. 187/L2
Pond Creek, Okla. (73766) 288/L1
Pond Eddy, Pa. (†12770) 294/N3
Pondera (co.), Mont. 262/D2
Ponderay, Idaho (83852) 220/B1
Ponderosa, N. Mex. (87044) 274/C3
Pond Fork (riv.), W. Va. 312/C6
Pondicherry (terr.), India 68/E6
Pondicherry, India 68/E6
Pond Inlet, Canada 4/B13
Pond Inlet, N.W.T. 162/J1
Pond Inlet, N.W. Terrs. 187/L2
Pondoland (reg.), S. Africa 118/D6
Pondosa, Calif. (96007) 204/D2
Ponds (isl.), Newf. 166/C3
Poneloya, Nicaragua 154/D4
Ponemah, Minn. (56666) 255/D2
Ponemah, N.H. (†03055) 268/D6
Poneto, Ind. (46781) 227/G3
Ponferrada, Spain 33/C1
Pongara (pt.), Gabon 115/A3
Ponhook (lake), Nova Scotia 168/D4
Poniatowa, Poland 47/E3
Ponnani, India 68/D6
Ponoka, Alberta 182/D3
Ponomarevka, U.S.S.R. 52/H4
Ponorogo, Indonesia 85/J2
Ponoy, U.S.S.R. 48/E3
Ponoy, U.S.S.R. 52/F1
Ponoy (riv.), U.S.S.R. 52/E1
Pons, France 28/C5
Ponset, Conn. (†06441) 210/E3
Ponsford, Minn. (56575) 255/C4
Pont-à-Celles, Belgium 27/E8
Ponta Delgada (dist.), Portugal 33/D2
Ponta Delgada, Portugal 33/C2
Ponta de Pedras, Brazil 132/D3
Ponta do Sol, Portugal 33/A2
Ponta Grossa, Brazil 120/D5
Ponta Grossa, Brazil 132/D9
Ponta Grossa, Brazil 135/B4
Pont-à-Mousson, France 28/G3
Ponta Porã, Brazil 132/C8
Ponta Porã, Paraguay 144/E3
Pontarlier, France 28/G4
Pontbriand, Québec 172/F3
Pont Canavese, Italy 34/A2
Pontchartrain (lake), La. 188/J5
Pontchartrain (lake), La. 238/O3
Pontchartrain Causeway, La. 238/O3
Pontecorvo, Italy 34/D4
Ponte de Sor, Portugal 33/C3
Ponte do Lima, Portugal 33/B2
Ponteix, Sask. 181/D6
Ponteland, England 13/H3
Ponte Nova, Brazil 132/F8
Ponte Nova, Brazil 135/E2
Pontevedra, Philippines 82/D5
Pontevedra (prov.), Spain 33/B1
Pontevedra, Spain 33/B1
Ponte Vedra Beach, Fla. (32082) 212/E1
Pontgrave, New Bruns. 170/F1
Pontiac, Ill. (61764) 222/E3
Pontiac, Mich. 188/K2
Pontiac, Mich. (*48053) 250/F6
Pontiac, Mo. (65729) 261/G9
Pontiac (co.), Québec 172/A3
Pontiac (county), Québec 174/B3
Pontiac, R.I. (†02887) 249/J6
Pontiac, S.C. (†29045) 296/F3
Pontianak, Indonesia 85/D6
Pontianak, Indonesia 54/N10
Pontian Kechil, Malaysia 72/E5
Pontic (mts.), Turkey 59/C1
Pontic (mts.), Turkey 63/H2
Pontine (isls.), Italy 34/D4
Pontinia, Italy 34/D4
Pontivy, France 28/B3
Pont-l'Abbe, France 28/A4
Pont-Lafrance, New Bruns. 170/E1
Pont-Landry, New Bruns. 170/F1
Pont-l'Évêque, France 28/D3
Ponto da Divisão, Brazil 132/B5
Pontoise, France 28/E3
Pontoon Beach, Ill. (†62040) 222/A2
Pontoosuc, Ill. (†62330) 222/B3
Pontoosuc (lake), Mass. 249/A3
Pontorson, France 28/C3
Pontotoc (co.), Miss. 256/F2
Pontotoc, Miss. (38863) 256/G2
Pontotoc (co.), Okla. 288/N5
Pontotoc, Okla. (74863) 288/N6
Pontotoc, Texas (76869) 303/E7
Pontremoli, Italy 34/B2
Pontresina, Switzerland 39/J3
Pontrilas, Sask. 181/H2
Pont-Rouge, Québec 172/F3
Pontypool, Ontario 177/F3
Pontypool, Wales 13/B6
Pontypridd, Wales 13/A6
Pontypridd, Wales 10/E5
Pony, Mont. (59747) 262/E5
Pony (creek), Okla. 288/C1

Puebla de Zaragoza 431

Potter Hill, R.I. (†02891) 249/H7
Potters Bar, England 13/H7
Potters Bar, England 10/B5
Pottersdale, Pa. (16871) 294/F3
Pottersville, Mo. (65790) 261/H9
Pottersville, N.J. (07979) 273/D2
Pottersville, N.Y. (12860) 276/N3
Potterville, Mich. (48876) 250/E6
Potts (creek), W. Va. 312/F7
Pottsboro, Texas (75076) 303/H4
Potts Camp, Miss. (38659) 256/F1
Pottstown, Pa. (19464) 294/L5
Pottsville, Ark. (72858) 202/D3
Pottsville, Pa. (17901) 294/K4
Pottsville, Texas (76565) 303/F6
Potwin, Kansas (67123) 232/F4
Pouce-Coupé, Br. Col. 184/G2
Pouch Cove, Newf. 166/D2
Poudre d'Or, Mauritius 118/G5
Poughkeepsie, Ark. (72569) 202/H1
Poughkeepsie, N.Y. (*12601) 276/N7
Pouillon, France 28/C6
Poulan, Georgia (31781) 217/E8
Poulet Cove (bay), Nova Scotia 168/H2
Poulin-de-Courval (lake), Québec 172/G1
Poulo Wai (isls.), Cambodia 72/D5
Poulsbo, Wash. (98370) 310/A1
Poultney, Vt. (05764) 268/A4
Poultney○, Vt. (05764) 268/A4
Poultney (riv.), Vt. 268/A4
Poulton le Fylde, England 10/F1
Poulton-le-Fylde, England 13/G1
Pound, Va. (24279) 307/C6
Pound, Wis. (54161) 317/L5
Pounding Mill, Va. (24637) 307/E6
Pouso Alegre, Brazil 135/D3
Pouthisat, Cambodia 72/D4
Považská Bystrica, Czech. 41/E2
Povenets, U.S.S.R. 52/E2
Poverty (isl.), Mich. 250/C3
Poverty (bay), N. Zealand 100/G3
Póvoa de Varzim, Portugal 33/B2
Povorino, U.S.S.R. 52/F4
Povungnituk, Que. 162/J3
Povungnituk, Québec 174/E1
Powassan, Ontario 177/E1
Poway, Calif. (92064) 204/J11
Powder (riv.) 188/E2
Powder (riv.), Mont. 262/L4
Powder (riv.), Oreg. 291/K3
Powder (riv.), Wyo. 319/F2
Powderhorn, Colo. (81243) 208/E6
Powderly, Ky. (42367) 237/G6
Powderly, Texas (75473) 303/J4
Powder River (co.), Mont. 262/L5
Powder River, Wyo. (82648) 319/F2
Powder Springs, Georgia (30073) 217/C3
Powder Springs, Tenn. (37848) 237/O8
Powderville, Mont. (59345) 262/L5
Powe, Mo. (†63822) 261/M9
Powell (lake) 188/D3
Powell (lake), Ariz. 198/E1
Powell (co.), Ky. 237/O5
Powell, Manitoba 179/A2
Powell (co.), Mont. 262/D4
Powell, Nebr. (†68352) 264/G4
Powell, Ohio (43065) 284/D5
Powell, Pa. (†18832) 294/J2
Powell, Tenn. (37849) 237/N8
Powell (riv.), Tenn. 237/P8
Powell (lake), U.S. 146/G6
Powell (lake), Utah 304/D6
Powell (riv.), Va. 307/B7
Powell, Wyo. (82435) 319/D1
Powell Butte, Oreg. (97753) 291/G3
Powell Creek, North. Terr. 93/C5
Powell River, Br. Col. 184/E5
Powell's Crossroads, Ala. (†35986) 195/G1
Powells Crossroads, Tenn. (†37397) 237/L10
Powells Point, N.C. (27966) 281/T2
Powellsville, N.C. (27967) 281/R2
Powellton, W. Va. (25161) 312/D6
Powellville, Md. (21852) 245/S7
Powelton, Georgia (†31059) 217/G4
Power (co.), Idaho 220/F7
Power, Mont. (59468) 262/E3
Powers (lake), Conn. 210/G3
Powers, Mich. (49874) 250/B3
Powers, Oreg. (97466) 291/D5
Powers Lake, N. Dak. (58773) 282/E2
Powersville, Georgia (31074) 217/E5
Powersville, Iowa (†50636) 229/H3
Powersville, Mo. (64672) 261/F1
Powerview, Manitoba 179/F4
Poweshiek (co.), Iowa 229/H5
Powhatan, Ark. (72458) 202/H1
Powhatan, La. (71066) 238/D3
Powhatan (co.), Va. 307/N5
Powhatan, Va. (23139) 307/N5
Powhatan, W. Va. (24877) 312/D8
Powhatan Point, Ohio (43942) 284/J6
Powhattan, Kansas (66527) 232/G2
Pownal○, Maine (04069) 243/C8
Pownal○, Vt. (05261) 268/A6
Pownal Center, Vt. (†05261) 268/A6
Powys (co.), Wales 13/D5
Poxoréo, Brazil 132/C6
Poyang (lake), China 54/N7
Poyang Hu (lake), China 77/J6
Poyen, Ark. (72128) 202/E5
Poygan (lake), Wis. 317/J7
Poynette, Wis. (53955) 317/G9
Poynor, Mo. (63959) 261/L9
Poynor, Texas (75782) 303/J5
Poysdorf, Austria 41/D2
Poy Sippi, Wis. (54967) 317/J7
Pozanti, Turkey 63/F4
Požarevac, Yugoslavia 45/E3
Poza Rica de Hidalgo, Mexico 150/L6
Poznań (prov.), Poland 47/C2
Poznań, Poland 47/C2
Poznań, Poland 7/F3
Pozo Almonte, Chile 138/B2
Pozoblanco, Spain 33/D3
Pozo Colorado, Paraguay 144/C3
Pozo Hondo, Argentina 143/D2
Pozohondo, Spain 33/F3
Pozuelo de Alarcón, Spain 33/D2
Pozuelos, Venezuela 124/F2
Pozuzo, Peru 128/E8
Pozzallo, Italy 34/E6
Pozzuoli, Italy 34/D4
Prabuty, Poland 47/D2
Prachatice, Czech. 41/B2
Prachin Buri, Thailand 72/D4
Prachuap Khiri Khan, Thailand 72/D5
Pradera, Colombia 126/B6
Prades, France 28/E6
Prado (dam), Calif. 204/E11
Praestø, Denmark 21/F7
Pragel (pass), Switzerland 39/G2
Prague (cap.), Czech. 7/F3
Prague (Praha) (cap.), Czech. 41/C1
Prague, Nebr. (68050) 264/H3
Prague, Okla. (74864) 288/N4
Praha (city), Czech. 41/C1
Prahan, Victoria 88/L7
Prahran, Victoria 97/J5
Praia (cap.), C. Verde 106/B8
Prainha, Amazonas, Brazil 132/A4
Prainha, Pará, Brazil 132/C3
Prairie, Ala. (36771) 195/D6
Prairie (co.), Ark. 202/G4
Prairie (creek), Ind. 227/C7
Prairie (riv.), Mich. 250/D7
Prairie (riv.), Minn. 255/E3
Prairie, Miss. (39756) 256/G3
Prairie (co.), Mont. 262/L4
Prairie, Queensland 95/C4
Prairie (lake), S. Dak. 298/P3
Prairieburg, Iowa (52219) 229/L4
Prairie City, Ill. (61470) 222/C3
Prairie City, Iowa (50228) 229/G5
Prairie City, Oreg. (97869) 291/J3
Prairie City, S. Dak. (57649) 298/D2
Prairie Creek, Ind. (47869) 227/C6
Prairie Dog Town Fork, Red (riv.), Okla. 288/F5
Prairie Dog Town Fork, Red (riv.), Texas 303/C3
Prairie du Chien, Wis. (53821) 317/D9
Prairie du Rocher, Ill. (62277) 222/C5
Prairie du Sac, Wis. (53578) 317/G9
Prairie Farm, Wis. (54762) 317/C5
Prairie Grove, Ark. (72753) 202/B2
Prairie Grove, Ill. (†60050) 222/E1
Prairie Home, Mo. (65068) 261/G5
Prairie Point, Miss. (39353) 256/H4
Prairie River, Sask. 181/J3
Prairies (riv.), Québec 172/H4
Prairieton, Ind. (47870) 227/B6
Prairietown, Ill. (†62097) 222/B2
Prairie View, Ark. (72859) 202/C3
Prairie View, Kansas (67664) 232/C2
Prairie View, Texas (77445) 303/J7
Prairie Village, Kansas (66208) 232/H2
Prairieville, La. (70769) 238/K2
Pran Buri, Thailand 72/D4
Prangins, Switzerland 39/B4
Prapat, Indonesia 85/B5
Praslin, St. Lucia 161/G6
Praslin (isl.), Seychelles 118/H5
Prat (isl.), Chile 138/D7
Pratas (Dongsha) (isl.), China 77/J7
Prathersville, Mo. (†64024) 261/R4
Prato, Italy 34/C3
Prato-Sornico, Switzerland 39/G4
Pratt (co.), Kansas 232/D4
Pratt, Kansas (67124) 232/D4
Pratt, Manitoba 179/D5
Pratt, Minn. (†55060) 255/E6
Pratt, W. Va. (25162) 312/D6
Pratteln, Switzerland 39/E1
Prattsburg, Georgia (†31039) 217/D5
Prattsburg○, N.Y. (14873) 276/F5
Prattsville, Ark. (72129) 202/F5
Prattsville, N.Y. (12468) 276/M6
Prattville, Ala. (36067) 195/E6
Pratum, Oreg. (†97301) 291/A3
Pravia, Spain 33/C1
Prawda, Manitoba 179/G5
Prawle (pt.), England 13/D7
Prawle (pt.), England 10/E5
Praxedis G. Guerrero, Mexico 150/G1
Pray, Mont. (59065) 262/F5
Praya, Indonesia 85/F7
Preble, Ind. (46782) 227/H3
Preble, N.Y. (13141) 276/H5
Preble (co.), Ohio 284/A6
Preeceville, Sask. 181/J4
Preemption, Ill. (61276) 222/C2
Preesall, England 13/E4
Preetz, W. Germany 22/D1
Pregarten, Austria 41/C2
Pregnall, S.C. (†29437) 296/G5
Pregonero, Venezuela 124/C3
Preiļi, U.S.S.R. 53/D2
Prek Pouthi, Cambodia 72/E5
Prelate, Sask. 181/B5
Přelouč, Czech. 41/C1
Premier, W. Va. (24878) 312/C8
Premium, Ky. (41845) 237/R6
Premont, Texas (78375) 303/F10
Prentice, Ill. (†62612) 222/C4
Prentice, Wis. (54556) 317/F4
Prentiss○, Maine (†04487) 243/G5
Prentiss (co.), Miss. 256/G1
Prentiss, Miss. (39474) 256/E7
Prentiss, N.C. (†28734) 281/C4
Prenzlau, E. Germany 22/E2
Preparis (isl.), Burma 72/B4
Preparis North (chan.), Burma 72/B4
Preparis South (chan.), Burma 72/B4
Přerov, Czech. 41/D2
Presanella (mt.), Italy 34/C1
Prescott, Ariz. 188/D4
Prescott, Ariz. (86301) 198/C4
Prescott, Ark. (71857) 202/D6
Prescott, Ind. (†46176) 227/F6
Prescott, Iowa (50859) 229/D6
Prescott, Kansas (66767) 232/H3
Prescott, Mich. (48756) 250/F4
Prescott (county), Ontario 177/K2
Prescott, Ontario 177/J3
Prescott, Oreg. (†97048) 291/D1
Prescott, Wash. (99348) 310/G4
Prescott, Wis. (54021) 317/A6
Prescott Valley, Ariz. (†86301) 198/C4
Preseli (mts.), Wales 13/C6
Preševo, Yugoslavia 45/E4
Presho, S. Dak. (57568) 298/J6
Presidencia de la Plaza, Argentina 143/D2
Presidencia R. Sáenz Peña, Argentina 120/C5
Presidencia Roque Sáenz Peña, Argentina 143/D2
President, Pa. (†16353) 294/C3
Presidente Dutra, Brazil 132/E4
Presidente Hayes, Paraguay 144/C3
Presidente Prudente, Brazil 132/D8
Presidente Prudente, Brazil 120/D5
Presidente Ríos (lake), Chile 138/D6
Presidente Venceslau, Brazil 132/D8
Presidential (range), N.H. 268/E3
Presidio, Calif. 204/J2
Presidio (co.), Texas 303/C12
Presidio, Texas (79845) 303/C12
Presidio Modelo, Cuba 158/C2
Prešov, Czech. 41/F2
Prespa (lake), Albania 45/E5
Prespa (lake), Greece 45/E5
Prespa (lake), Yugoslavia 45/E5
Presque Isle, Maine (04769) 243/H2
Presque Isle (co.), Mich. 250/F3
Presque Isle, Mich. (49777) 250/F3
Presque Isle (riv.), Mich. 250/F1
Presque Isle, Wis. (54557) 317/G3
Presque Isle A.F.B., Maine 243/G2
Presqu'île Prov. Park, Ontario 177/G4
Prestatyn, Wales 13/D4
Prestea, Ghana 106/D7
Presteigne, Wales 10/E4
Presteigne, Wales 13/D5
Přeštice, Czech. 41/B2
Presto, Bolivia 136/C6
Preston○, Conn. (†06360) 210/H2
Preston, England 10/F1
Preston, England 13/G1
Preston, Georgia (31824) 217/C6
Preston, Idaho (83263) 220/G7
Preston, Ill. (†62242) 222/D5
Preston, Iowa (52069) 229/N4
Preston, Kansas (67569) 232/D4
Preston, Ky. (40366) 237/O4
Preston, Md. (21655) 245/P6
Preston, Minn. (55965) 255/F7
Preston, Miss. (39354) 256/G5
Preston, Mo. (65732) 261/F7
Preston, Nebr. (†68355) 264/J4
Preston, Nev. (†89301) 266/G4
Preston, Okla. (74456) 288/P3
Preston, Scotland 15/F5
Preston, Victoria 88/L7
Preston, Victoria 97/J4
Preston, Wash. (98050) 310/D3
Preston (co.), W. Va. 312/G4
Preston City, Conn. (†06360) 210/H2
Preston Hollow, N.Y. (12469) 276/M6
Prestonpans, Scotland 15/D1
Prestonsburg, Ky. (41653) 237/R5
Prestonville, Ky. (†41008) 237/L3
Prestwich, England 13/H2
Prestwick, Scotland 10/D3
Prestwick, Scotland 15/D5
Prêto (riv.), Brazil 132/E5
Preto (riv.), Brazil 135/E3
Prêto (riv.), Brazil 132/A4
Pretoria (cap.), S. Africa 2/L7
Pretoria (cap.), S. Africa 102/E7
Pretoria (cap.), S. Africa 118/D5
Prettyboy (res.), Md. 245/M2
Pretty Prairie, Kansas (67570) 232/D4
Préveza, Greece 45/E6
Prévost, Québec 172/C4
Prevost, Wash. (†98250) 310/B2
Prewitt (res.), Colo. 208/N2
Prewitt, N. Mex. (87045) 274/B3
Prey Veng, Cambodia 72/E5
Pribilof (isls.), Alaska 188/C6
Pribilof (isls.), Alaska 196/D3
Pribilof (isls.), U.S. 4/D18
Priboj, Yugoslavia 45/D4
Příbor, Czech. 41/E2
Příbram, Czech. 41/B2
Price (isl.), Br. Col. 184/C4
Price, Md. (21656) 245/P4
Price, N. Dak. (†58547) 282/H5
Price, Québec 172/A1
Price, Utah (84501) 304/D4
Price, Utah 188/D3
Price (riv.), Utah 304/D4
Price (co.), Wis. 317/F4
Price, Wis. (†54741) 317/E6
Pricedale, Miss. (†39666) 256/D8
Price Hill, W. Va. (†25880) 312/D7
Priceville, Ala. (†35601) 195/E1
Priceville, Ky. (†42713) 237/K6
Priceville, Ontario 177/D3
Prichard, Ala. (36610) 195/B9
Prichard, Miss. (†38676) 256/D1
Prichard, W. Va. (25555) 312/A6
Prickly (pt.), Grenada 161/C9
Priddis, Alberta 182/C4
Priddy, Texas (76870) 303/F6
Pride, Ky. (†42404) 237/F5
Pride, La. (70770) 238/K1
Pridgen, Georgia (†31519) 217/G7
Priego, Spain 33/E2
Priego de Córdoba, Spain 33/D4
Priekule, U.S.S.R. 53/A2
Priekule, U.S.S.R. 53/A3
Prien am Chiemsee, W. Germany 22/E5
Prieska, S. Africa 118/C5
Priest (lake), Idaho 220/B1
Priest (riv.), Idaho 220/B1
Priest, J. Percy (lake), Tenn. 237/J8
Priestly (lake), Maine 243/E2
Priest Rapids (dam), Wash. 310/F4
Priest Rapids (lake), Wash. 310/E4
Priest River, Idaho (83856) 220/A1
Prievidza, Czech. 41/E2
Prijedor, Yugoslavia 45/C3
Prijepolje, Yugoslavia 45/D4
Prikumsk, U.S.S.R. 52/F6
Prikumsk, U.S.S.R. 48/E5
Prilep, Yugoslavia 45/E5
Priluki, U.S.S.R. 52/D4
Prim (pt.), Nova Scotia 168/C4
Prim (pt.), Pr. Edward I. 168/E2
Prima Porta, Italy 34/F6
Primate, Sask. 181/B3
Prime, New Bruns. 170/B1
Primero de Marzo, Paraguay 144/B4
Primero Enero, Cuba 158/F2
Primghar, Iowa (51245) 229/B2
Primm Springs, Tenn. (38476) 237/G9
Primorsk, U.S.S.R. 52/C2
Primorsko-Akhtarsk, U.S.S.R. 52/E5
Primos, Pa. (19018) 294/M7
Primrose (lake), Alberta 182/E2
Primrose, Georgia (†30222) 217/C4
Primrose, Iowa (†52625) 229/K7
Primrose, Nebr. (68655) 264/F3
Primrose (lake), Sask. 181/L3
Primrose Lake Air Weapons Range, Sask. 181/L3
Prince (co.), Pr. Edward I. 168/D2
Prince, Sask. 181/C3
Prince Albert (sound), N.W.T. 162/E1
Prince Albert (pen.), N.W.T. 162/E1
Prince Albert (pen.), N.W. Terrs. 187/G2
Prince Albert (sound), N.W. Terrs. 187/G2
Prince Albert, Sask. 162/F5
Prince Albert, Sask. 146/H4
Prince Albert, Sask. 181/F2
Prince Albert, S. Africa 118/C6
Prince Albert Nat'l Park, Sask. 162/F5
Prince Albert Nat'l Park, Sask. 181/E1
Prince Alfred (cape), N.W. Terrs. 187/F2
Prince Charles (isl.), Canada 4/C13
Prince Charles (isl.), N.W.T. 162/J2
Prince Charles (isl.), N.W. Terrs. 187/L3
Prince Edward (isls.) 5/E2
Prince Edward (county), Ontario 177/G3
Prince Edward (isls.), S. Africa 2/L8
Prince Edward (co.), Va. 307/M6
Prince Edward Island (prov.) 162/K6
Prince Edward Island (prov.), Canada 146/M5
PRINCE EDWARD ISLAND 168
Prince Edward Island Nat'l Park, Pr. Edward I. 168/E2
Prince Frederick, Md. (20678) 245/M6
Prince George, Br. Col. 146/F4
Prince George, Br. Col. 162/D5
Prince George, Br. Col. 184/F3
Prince George (co.), Va. 307/O6
Prince George, Va. (23875) 307/O6
Prince Georges (co.), Md. 245/L5
Prince Gustav Adolf (sea), N.W. Terrs. 187/H2
Prince of Wales (cape), Alaska 196/E1
Prince of Wales (isl.), Alaska 196/N2
Prince of Wales (isl.), Canada 4/B14
Prince of Wales, New Bruns. 170/D3
Prince of Wales (str.), N.W.T. 162/D1
Prince of Wales (isl.), N.W.T. 146/J2
Prince of Wales (isl.), N.W.T. 162/F1
Prince of Wales (isl.), N.W. Terrs. 187/J2
Prince of Wales (str.), N.W. Terrs. 187/G2
Prince of Wales (isl.), Queensland 88/G2
Prince of Wales (isl.), Queensland 95/B1
Prince of Wales (cape), U.S. 4/C18
Prince Olav Coast (reg.) 5/C3
Prince Patrick (isl.), Canada 4/B16
Prince Patrick (isl.), N.W.T. 146/F2
Prince Patrick (isl.), N.W.T. 162/M3
Prince Patrick (isl.), N.W. Terrs. 187/F2
Prince Regent (inlet), N.W.T. 162/G1
Prince Regent (inlet), N.W. Terrs. 187/J2
Prince Rupert, Br. Col. 162/C5
Prince Rupert, Br. Col. 146/F4
Prince Rupert, Br. Col. 184/B3
Prince Rupert (bay), Dominica 161/E5
Princes Lakes, Ind. (†46164) 227/E6
Princess Anne, Md. (21853) 245/P8
Princess Astrid Coast (reg.) 5/B1
Princess Charlotte (bay), Queensland 88/G2
Princess Charlotte (bay), Queensland 95/C2
Princess Harbour, Manitoba 179/F3
Princess Martha Coast (reg.) 5/B18
Princess Ragnhild Coast (reg.) 5/B2
Princess Royal (isl.), Br. Col. 184/C3
Princes Town, Trin. & Tob. 161/B11
Princeton, Ala. (35766) 195/F1
Princeton, Ark. (†71725) 202/E6
Princeton, Br. Col. 184/G5
Princeton, Calif. (95970) 204/C4
Princeton (mt.), Colo. 208/G5
Princeton, Fla. (33032) 212/F6
Princeton, Idaho (83857) 220/B3
Princeton, Ill. (61356) 222/D2
Princeton, Ind. (47670) 227/B8
Princeton, Iowa (52768) 229/N5
Princeton, Kansas (66078) 232/G3
Princeton, Ky. (42445) 237/F6
Princeton, La. (71067) 238/C1
Princeton○, Maine (04668) 243/H5
Princeton○, Mass. (01541) 249/G3
Princeton, Mich. (49875) 250/B2
Princeton, Minn. (55371) 255/E5
Princeton, Mo. (64673) 261/E2
Princeton, Newf. 166/D2
Princeton, N.J. (08540) 273/D3
Princeton, N.C. (27569) 281/N4
Princeton, Ontario 177/D4
Princeton, Oreg. (97721) 291/J4
Princeton, S.C. (29674) 296/C2
Princeton, W. Va. (24740) 312/D8
Princeton, Wis. (54968) 317/H8
Princeton Junction, N.J. (08550) 273/D3
Princeville, Hawaii (†96714) 218/C1
Princeville, Ill. (61559) 222/D3
Princeville, N.C. (†27886) 281/P3
Princeville, Québec 172/F3
Prince William (sound), Alaska 196/D1
Prince William, New Bruns. 170/C3
Prince William (co.), Va. 307/O3
Príncipe (chan.), Br. Col. 184/C3
Príncipe (isl.), São Tomé e Príncipe 106/F8
Principio Furnace, Md. (†21903) 245/P2
Prineville, Oreg. (97754) 291/G3
Prineville (res.), Oreg. 291/G3
Pringle, S. Dak. (57773) 298/B6
Prinkipo (Adalar) (isl.), Turkey 63/D6
Prinsburg, Minn. (56281) 255/C6
Prins Karls Forland (isl.), Norway 18/B2
Prinzapolca (riv.), Nicaragua 154/F4
Prinzapolka, Nicaragua 154/F4
Prior (cape), Spain 33/B1
Prior Lake, Minn. (55372) 255/E6
Priozersk, U.S.S.R. 52/D2
Pripet (marshes), U.S.S.R. 52/C4
Pripyat' (riv.), U.S.S.R. 7/G3
Pripyat' (riv.), U.S.S.R. 52/C4
Priština, Yugoslavia 45/E4
Pritchards (isl.), S.C. 296/G7
Pritchardville, S.C. (†29927) 296/E7
Pritchett, Colo. (81064) 208/O8
Pritzwalk, E. Germany 22/E2
Privas, France 28/F5
Privateer (pt.), Virgin Is. (U.S.) 161/D4
Priverno, Italy 34/D4
Privolzhskiy, U.S.S.R. 52/G4
Priyutnoye, U.S.S.R. 52/F5
Priyutovo, U.S.S.R. 52/H4
Prizren, Yugoslavia 45/E4
Probolinggo, Indonesia 85/K2
Procious, W. Va. (25164) 312/D5
Procter, Br. Col. 184/J5
Proctor, Ark. (72376) 202/K3
Proctor, Colo. (†80736) 208/N1
Proctor, Minn. (55810) 255/F4
Proctor, Mont. (59929) 262/B3
Proctor, Okla. (74457) 288/S3
Proctor, Pa. (†17701) 294/J3
Proctor, Texas (76468) 303/F5
Proctor○, Vt. (05765) 268/A4
Proctor, W. Va. (26055) 312/E3
Proctorsville, Vt. (05153) 268/B5
Proctorville, N.C. (28375) 281/M6
Proctorville, Ohio (45669) 284/F9
Proddatur, India 68/D6
Proença-a-Nova, Portugal 33/B3
Profesor Rafael Ramírez, Mexico 150/O1
Profondeville, Belgium 27/F8
Progreso, Mexico 150/P6
Progreso, Uruguay 145/B6
Progress, Br. Col. 184/G2
Progress, Oreg. (†97233) 291/A2
Progress, U.S.S.R. 48/O5
Progress Village, Fla. (†33619) 212/C3
Project City, Calif. (96079) 204/C3
Prokhladnyy, U.S.S.R. 52/F6
Prokop'yevsk, U.S.S.R. 54/K4
Prokop'yevsk, U.S.S.R. 48/J4
Prokuplje, Yugoslavia 45/E4
Prole, Iowa (50229) 229/F6
Prome (Pye), Burma 72/B3
Promise City, Iowa (52583) 229/G7
Promissão, Brazil 135/B2
Promontory, Utah (†84307) 304/B2
Prompton, Pa. (18456) 294/M2
Prongua, Sask. 181/C3
Prony (bay), New Caled. 86/H5
Prophet (riv.), Br. Col. 184/M2
Prophetstown, Ill. (61277) 222/D2
Propriá, Brazil 132/G5
Proserpine, Queensland 88/H4
Proserpine, Queensland 95/D4
Prosit, Minn. (†55702) 255/F4
Prosna (riv.), Poland 47/C3
Prospect, Ala. (†35578) 195/D3
Prospect○, Conn. (06712) 210/D2
Prospect, Ky. (40059) 237/K4
Prospect○, Maine (†04981) 243/F6
Prospect (res.), N. S. Wales 88/K4
Prospect (res.), N. S. Wales 97/H3
Prospect, N.Y. (13435) 276/K4
Prospect, Nova Scotia 168/E4
Prospect, Ohio (43342) 284/D5
Prospect, Oreg. (97536) 291/E5
Prospect, Pa. (16052) 294/B4
Prospect, S. Australia 88/D8
Prospect, S. Australia 94/B7
Prospect, Tenn. (38477) 237/G10
Prospect, Va. (23960) 307/L6
Prospect Harbor, Maine (04669) 243/H7
Prospect Heights, Ill. (60070) 222/B5
Prospect Hill, N.C. (27314) 281/L2
Prospect Park, N.J. (†07885) 273/B1
Prospect Park, Pa. (19076) 294/M7
Prosper, Mich. (†49632) 250/E4
Prosper, Minn. (55966) 255/G7
Prosper, N. Dak. (†58042) 282/R6
Prosper, Oreg. (†97411) 291/C4
Prosperidad, Philippines 82/F6
Prosperity, Pa. (15329) 294/B5
Prosperity, S.C. (29127) 296/D3
Prosser, Nebr. (68868) 264/F4
Prosser, Wash. (99350) 310/F4
Prostějov, Czech. 41/D2
Protection, Kansas (67127) 232/C4
Protem, Mo. (65733) 261/G9
Protivín, Czech. 41/C2
Protivin, Iowa (52163) 229/J2
Proulxville, Québec 172/E3
Prouts Neck, Maine (04074) 243/C8
Provadiya, Bulgaria 45/H4
Provencal, La. (71468) 238/D3
Provence (trad. prov.), France 29
Providence, Ala. (†36748) 195/C6
Providence (mts.), Calif. 204/K8
Providence, Fla. (†32061) 212/D2
Providence, Grenada 161/D9
Providence, Ind. (†46106) 227/E6
Providence, Ky. (42450) 237/F6
Providence (cape), N. Zealand 100/A7
Providence (cap.), R.I. 188/M2
Providence (cap.), R.I. 146/L5
Providence (co.), R.I. 249/H5
Providence (cap.), R.I. (*02901) 249/H5
Providence, Utah (84332) 304/C2
Providence Bay, Ontario 177/B2
Providence Forge, Va. (23140) 307/P6
Providencia (isl.), Colombia 126/B9
Providenciales (isl.), Turks & Caicos 156/D2
Provideniya, U.S.S.R. 4/C18
Provideniya, U.S.S.R. 48/T3
Province Lake, N.H. (†03888) 268/E4
Provincetown, Mass. (02657) 249/O4
Provincetown○, Mass. (02657) 249/O4
Provins, France 28/E3
Provo, Ark. (†71846) 202/B5
Provo, S. Dak. (57774) 298/B7
Provo, Utah 146/G6
Provo, Utah (84601) 304/C3
Provo, Utah 188/D2
Provo (peak), Utah 304/C3
Provo (riv.), Utah 304/C3
Provost, Alberta 182/E3
Prowers (co.), Colo. 208/P7
Prozor, Yugoslavia 45/C4
Pruden, Tenn. (37851) 237/O7
Prudence (isl.), R.I. 249/J6
Prudence Island, R.I. (02872) 249/J6
Prudentópolis, Brazil 132/D9
Prudenville, Mich. (48651) 250/E4
Prudhoe (bay), Alaska 146/D2
Prudhoe (bay), Alaska 196/J1
Prudhoe, England 13/H3
Prudhoe Bay, Alaska (†99723) 196/J1
Prud'homme, Sask. 181/F3
Prudnik, Poland 47/C3
Prue, Okla. (74060) 288/O2
Pruitt, Ark. (72671) 202/D1
Prüm, W. Germany 22/B3
Pruntytown, W. Va. (†26354) 312/F4
Pruszcz Gdanski, Poland 47/D1
Pruszków, Poland 47/E2
Prut (riv.) 7/G4
Prut (riv.), Romania 45/J2
Prut (riv.), U.S.S.R. 52/C5
Prydz (bay) 5/C4
Pryor, Colo. (81065) 208/K8
Pryor, Mont. (59066) 262/H5
Pryor, Okla. (74361) 288/R2
Pryorsburg, Ky. (†42066) 237/D7
Pryse, Ky. (40471) 237/O5
Przasnysz, Poland 47/E2
Przemkow, Poland 47/B2
Przemsza (riv.), Poland 47/B4
Przemyśl (prov.), Poland 47/F4
Przemyśl, Poland 7/G4
Przmyśl, Poland 47/F4
Przeworsk, Poland 47/F3
Przheval'sk, U.S.S.R. 48/H5
Psakhná, Greece 45/F6
Psará (isl.), Greece 45/G6
Psári, Greece 45/F7
Psel (riv.), U.S.S.R. 52/D4
Psevdhókavos (cape), Greece 45/G6
Pskov, U.S.S.R. 7/G3
Pskov, U.S.S.R. 48/C4
Pskov U.S.S.R. 52/C3
Pskov (lake), U.S.S.R. 53/D1
Ptolemaís, Greece 45/E5
Ptuj, Yugoslavia 45/C2
Puako, Hawaii (†96743) 218/G4
Puán, Argentina 143/D4
Puangue, Chile 138/F4
Puangue, Estero de (riv.), Chile 138/F3
Pubnico, Nova Scotia 168/C5
Pubnico (harb.), Nova Scotia 168/C5
Puca Barranca, Peru 128/E4
Pucallpa, Peru 128/E7
Pucallpa, Peru 120/B3
Pucara, Bolivia 136/C6
Pucará, Peru 128/G10
Pucarani, Bolivia 136/A5
Pucatrihue, Chile 138/D3
Pucaurco, Peru 128/G4
Puce, Ontario 177/B5
Pucheng, China 77/J6
Púchov, Czech. 41/E2
Puchuncaví, Chile 138/F2
Pucio (pt.), Philippines 82/C5
Pucioasa, Romania 45/G3
Puck, Poland 47/D1
Puckaway (lake), Wis. 317/H8
Puckett, Miss. (39151) 256/E6
Pucón, Chile 138/E2
Pucusana, Peru 128/D9
Pudahuel, Chile 138/G3
Pudasjärvi, Finland 18/P4
Pudding (riv.), Oreg. 291/A3
Pudozh, U.S.S.R. 52/E2
Puduchcheri (Pondicherry), India 68/E6
Pudukkottai, India 68/D6
Puebla (state), Mexico 150/L7
Puebla, Mexico 146/J8
Puebla de Alcocer, Spain 33/D3
Puebla de Don Fadrique, Spain 33/E4
Puebla del Caramiñal, Spain 33/B1
Puebla de Sanabria, Spain 33/C1
Puebla de Trives, Spain 33/C1
Puebla de Zaragoza, Mexico 150/N2

Reid, Md. (†21740) 245/H2
Reid (lake), S. Dak. 298/O3
Reid (rocks), Tasmania 99/B1
Reid, W. Australia 92/E5
Reiden, Switzerland 39/F2
Reids Grove, Md. (†21869) 245/P6
Reidsville, Georgia (30453) 217/H6
Reidsville, N.C. (27320) 281/K2
Reidville, S.C. (29375) 296/C2
Reigate, England 13/H8
Reigate, England 10/F5
Reile's Acres, N. Dak. (†58078) 282/S6
Reilly, Ohio (45060) 284/A7
Re'im, Israel 65/A5
Reims, France 7/E4
Reims, France 28/E3
Reina Adelaida (arch.), Chile 120/B8
Reina Adelaida (arch.), Chile 138/D9
Reinach in Aargau, Switzerland 39/F2
Reinach in Baselland, Switzerland 39/E2
Reinbeck, Iowa (50669) 229/H4
Reindeer (lake) 162/F4
Reindeer (lake), Canada 146/H4
Reindeer (isl.), Manitoba 179/E2
Reindeer (lake), Manitoba 179/H2
Reindeer (lake), Sask. 181/N3
Reindeer (riv.), Sask. 181/M3
Reinersville, Ohio (43756) 284/G6
Reinfeld, W. Germany 22/D2
Reinga (cape), N. Zealand 100/D1
Reinland, Manitoba 179/E5
Reinosa, Spain 33/D1
Reisaelv (riv.), Norway 18/M2
Reisduoddarhal'di (Haltiatunturi), Norway 18/M2
Reiss, Scotland 15/E2
Reisterstown, Md. (21136) 245/L3
Reitz, S. Africa 118/D5
Rejaf, Sudan 111/F7
Reliance, Md. (†19973) 245/P6
Reliance, N.W. Terrs. 187/H3
Reliance, S. Dak. (57569) 298/K6
Reliance, Tenn. (37369) 237/N10
Reliance, Va. (22649) 307/M3
Reliance, Wyo. (82943) 319/C4
Relief, Ky. (41463) 237/P5
Relizane, Algeria 106/E1
Reloncaví (bay), Chile 138/D4
Remada, Tunisia 106/F2
Remagen, W. Germany 22/B3
Remanso, Brazil 132/F5
Remates, Cuba 158/A2
Rembang, Indonesia 85/K2
Rembert, S.C. (29128) 296/G3
Rembrandt, Iowa (50576) 229/C3
Rembrandt, Manitoba 179/E4
Remedios, Colombia 126/C4
Remedios, Cuba 156/B2
Remedios, Cuba 158/E2
Remedios (pt.), El Salvador 154/B4
Remer, Minn. (56672) 255/E3
Remerton, Georgia (31601) 217/F9
Remich, Luxembourg 27/J9
Reminderville, Ohio (†44202) 284/J10
Remington, Ind. (47977) 227/C3
Remington, Ohio (†45202) 284/C9
Remington, Va. (22734) 307/N3
Rémire, Fr. Guiana 131/E3
Rémire (isls.), Fr. Guiana 131/F3
Remiremont, France 28/G3
Remlap, Ala. (35133) 195/E3
Remmel (mt.), Wash. 310/E2
Remo, Br. Col. 184/C3
Remolino, Colombia 126/C2
Remote, Oreg. (97468) 291/D5
Remscheid, W. Germany 22/B3
Remsen, Iowa (51050) 229/B3
Remsen, N.Y. (13438) 276/K4
Remus, Mich. (49340) 250/D5
Remus, Okla. (†74801) 288/N4
Remy, La. (†70763) 238/L3
Rena, Ark. (†72956) 202/B3
Rena, Norway 18/G6
Reñaca, Chile 138/F2
Renaix (Ronse), Belgium 27/D7
Rena Lara, Miss. (38767) 256/C2
Renan, Switzerland 39/C2
Renault, Ill. (62279) 222/C5
Renca, Chile 138/G3
Rencona, N. Mex. (†87562) 274/D3
Rencontre East, Newf. 166/C4
Rend (lake), Ill. 222/E5
Rendeux, Belgium 27/H8
Rendova (isl.), Solomon Is. 86/D3
Rendsburg, W. Germany 22/C1
Rendville, Ohio (†43730) 284/F6
Renens, Switzerland 39/C3
Renews, Newf. 166/D2
Renforth, New Bruns. 170/E3
Renfrew, Ont. 162/J6
Renfrew (county), Ontario 177/G2
Renfrew (county), Ontario 175/E3
Renfrew, Ontario 177/H2
Renfrew, Ontario 175/E3
Renfrew, Pa. (16053) 294/C4
Renfrew, Scotland 10/A1
Renfrew, Scotland 15/B2
Renfrew (trad. co.), Scotland 15/A5
Renfroe, Ala. (†35160) 195/F4
Renfroe, Georgia (†31805) 217/C6
Renfroe, Miss. (†39051) 256/F5
Renfrow, Okla. (†73759) 288/L1
Rengam, Malaysia 72/E5
Rengat, Indonesia 85/C6
Rengo, Chile 138/G5
Reni, U.S.S.R. 52/C5
Renick, Mo. (65278) 261/H4
Renick, W. Va. (24966) 312/F6
Renigunta, India 68/E6
Renish (pt.), Scotland 15/B3
Renk, Sudan 111/F5
Renkum, Netherlands 27/H5
Renmark, S. Australia 88/G6
Renmark, S. Australia 94/G5
Rennell (isl.), Solomon Is. 87/F7
Rennell (isl.), Solomon Is. 86/E3
Renner, S. Dak. (57055) 298/R6
Rennert, N.C. (†28386) 281/L5
Rennes, France 7/D4
Rennes, France 28/C3
Rennie, Manitoba 179/G5
Rennie (lake), N.W. Terrs. 187/H3
Renno, S.C. (†29325) 296/D2
Reno, Alberta 182/B2
Reno, Georgia (†31728) 217/D9
Reno, Ill. (†62086) 222/D5
Reno (co.), Kansas 232/D4
Reno (lake), Minn. 255/C5
Reno, Nev. 146/G6
Reno, Nev. 188/C3
Reno, Nev. (*89501) 266/B3
Reno, Ohio (45773) 284/H7
Reno, Texas (†76020) 303/E2
Reno Beach, Ohio (†43412) 284/D2
Renous, New Bruns. 170/E2
Renous (riv.), New Bruns. 170/D2
Renova, Miss. (†38732) 256/C3
Renovo, Pa. (17764) 294/G3
Renown, Sask. 181/F4
Rensburg, S. Africa 118/J7
Rensselaer, Ind. (47978) 227/C3
Rensselaer, Mo. (†63401) 261/J3
Rensselaer (co.), N.Y. 276/O5
Rensselaer, N.Y. (12144) 276/N5
Rensselaer Falls, N.Y. (13680) 276/K1
Rentchler, Ill. (†62220) 222/B3
Rentiesville, Okla. (74459) 288/R4
Renton, Scotland 15/A1
Renton, Wash. (98055) 310/B2
Rentz, Georgia (31075) 217/G6
Renville (co.), Minn. 255/C6
Renville, Minn. (56284) 255/C6
Renville (co.), N. Dak. 282/G2
Renwer, Manitoba 179/B2
Renwick, Iowa (50577) 229/E3
Répcelak, 41/D3
Repentigny, Québec 172/J4
Replete, W. Va. (†26222) 312/F5
Repos (lake), Québec 172/C2
Repton, Ala. (36475) 195/D8
Republic, Ala. (†35203) 195/E3
Republic (co.), Kansas 232/E2
Republic, Kansas (66964) 232/E2
Republic, Mich. (49879) 250/B2
Republic, Mo. (65738) 261/E8
Republic, Ohio (44867) 284/D3
Republic, Wash. (99166) 310/G2
República Dominicana, Cuba 158/F2
Republican (riv.) 188/F2
Republican (riv.), Colo. 208/P3
Republican (riv.), Kansas 232/E2
Republican (riv.), Nebr. 264/G5
Republican City, Nebr. (68971) 264/E4
Republican Grove, Va. (24585) 307/K7
Repulse (bay), Queensland 88/H4
Repulse Bay, Canada 4/C14
Repulse Bay, N.W.T. 162/H2
Repulse Bay, N.W. Terrs. 187/K3
Requa, Calif. (†95548) 204/A2
Requegua, Chile 138/G5
Requena, Peru 128/F5
Requena, Spain 33/F3
Requinoa, Chile 138/G5
Rera, Brazil 132/A1
Resaca, Georgia (30735) 217/C1
Reşadiye, Turkey 63/G2
Research, Victoria 97/J4
Reseda, Calif. (91335) 204/B10
Resende, Brazil 135/D3
Resende, Portugal 33/B2
Reserve, Kansas (66529) 232/G2
Reserve, La. (70084) 238/M3
Reserve, Mont. (59258) 262/M2
Reserve, N. Mex. (87830) 274/A5
Reserve, Sask. 181/J3
Reserve, Wis. (†54876) 317/D4
Reserve Mines, Nova Scotia 168/H2
Resht (Rasht), Iran 66/F2
Reshui, China 77/E4
Resistencia, Argentina 143/E2
Resistencia, Argentina 120/D5
Reşiţa, Romania 45/E3
Resolute, Canada 4/B14
Resolute Bay, N.W.T. 162/G1
Resolute Bay, N.W. Terrs. 187/J2
Resolution (isl.), N.W.T. 146/M3
Resolution (isl.), N.W.T. 162/K3
Resolution (isl.), N. Zealand 100/A6
Resolution (isl.), N.W. Terrs. 187/M3
Resolution Island, N.W. Terrs. 187/M3
Resort, Loch (inlet), Scotland 15/A2
Resource, Sask. 181/G3
Respenda de la Peña, Spain 33/D1
Restauración, Dom. Rep. 158/D5
Rest Haven, Georgia (†30518) 217/E2
Restigouche (co.), New Bruns. 170/C1
Restigouche (riv.), New Bruns. 170/C1
Restigouche, Québec 172/C2
Reston, Manitoba 179/A5
Reston, Va. (22090) 307/R2
Restoule, Ontario 177/E1
Restoule (lake), Ontario 177/E1
Restrepo, Colombia 126/D5
Reszel, Poland 47/E1
Retalhuleu, Guatemala 154/B3
Retamosa, Uruguay 145/E4
Rethel, France 28/F3
Réthimnon, Greece 45/G8
Retie, Belgium 27/G6
Retiro, Chile 138/A11
Retlaw, Alberta 182/D4
Rétság, Hungary 41/E3
Retsil, Wash. (98378) 310/A2
Retsof, N.Y. (14539) 276/E5
Retz, Austria 41/D2
Reubens, Idaho (83548) 220/B3
Réunion (isl.), (Fr.) 2/M7
RÉUNION 118/F5
Reus, Spain 33/G2
Reusel, Netherlands 27/G6
Reuss (riv.), Switzerland 39/F2
Reutlingen, W. Germany 22/C4
Reutte, Austria 41/A3
Reva, S. Dak. (57651) 298/C2
Revadim, Israel 65/B4
Reveille (peak), Nev. 266/E5
Reveille (range), Nev. 266/E4
Revel, France 28/E6
Revel (Tallinn), U.S.S.R. 52/B3
Revelo, Ky. (42638) 237/N7
Revelstoke, Br. Col. 162/E5
Revelstoke, Br. Col. 184/J5
Reventazón, Peru 128/B6
Revenue, Sask. 181/B3
Revere, Mass. (02151) 249/D6
Revere, Minn. (56166) 255/C6
Revere, Mo. (63465) 261/J2
Revere, N. Dak. (†58484) 282/O5
Revere, W. Va. (†26158) 312/E5
Reverie, Tenn. (38062) 237/A9
Revillagigedo (chan.), Alaska 196/N2
Revillagigedo (isl.), Alaska 196/N2
Revillagigedo (isls.), Mexico 146/G8
Revillagigedo (isls.), Mexico 2/D5
Revillagigedo (isls.), Mexico 150/C7
Revillo, S. Dak. (57259) 298/R3
Révin, France 28/F3
Revivim, Israel 65/D5
Revúca, Czech. 41/F2
Revuelto (creek), N. Mex. 274/F3
Rew, Pa. (16744) 294/F2
Rewa, India 68/E4
Reward, Sask. 181/B3
Rewataya (reef), Indonesia 85/F7
Rewey, Wis. (53580) 317/F10
Rex, N.C. (28378) 281/M5
Rex, Oreg. (†97132) 291/A2
Rexburg, Idaho (83440) 220/G6
Rexford, Kansas (67753) 232/B2
Rexford, Mont. (59930) 262/A2
Rexton, Mich. (†49734) 250/D2
Rexton, New Bruns. 170/F2
Rexville, Ind. (†47250) 227/G7
Rexville, N.Y. (14877) 276/E6
Rey, Iran 59/F2
Rey, Iran 66/G3
Rey (isl.), Panama 154/H6
Rey Bouba, Cameroon 115/B2
Reydell, Ark. (72133) 202/G5
Reydon, Okla. (73660) 288/G3
Reyes, Bolivia 136/B4
Reyes (pt.), Calif. 204/B6
Reyhanlı, Turkey 63/G4
Reykjanestá (cape), Iceland 7/B2
Reykjanestá (cape), Iceland 21/A2
Reykjavík (cap.), Iceland 4/C11
Reykjavík (cap.), Iceland 2/J2
Reykjavík (cap.), Iceland 21/B1
Reykjavík (cap.), Iceland 7/B2
Reynaud, Sask. 181/F3
Reyno, Ark. (72462) 202/J1
Reynolds, Georgia (31076) 217/D5
Reynolds (creek), Idaho 220/B6
Reynolds, Ill. (61279) 222/C2
Reynolds, Ind. (47980) 227/D3
Reynolds (co.), Mo. 261/L8
Reynolds, Mo. (63666) 261/K8
Reynolds, Nebr. (68429) 264/G4
Reynolds, N. Dak. (58275) 282/R4
Reynolds Bridge, Conn. (†06787) 210/C2
Reynoldsburg, Ohio (43068) 284/E6
Reynolds Station, Ky. (42368) 237/H5
Reynoldsville, Pa. (15851) 294/D3
Reynosa, Mexico 150/K3
Rezaiyeh (Urmia), Iran 66/D2
Reza'iyeh (Urmia), Iran 59/D2
Rezé, France 28/C4
Rēzekne, U.S.S.R. 52/C3
Rēzekne, U.S.S.R. 53/D2
Rhaetian Alps (range), Switzerland 39/J3
Rhame, N. Dak. (58651) 282/C7
Rhätikon (mts.), Liecht. 39/J2
Rhätikon (mts.), Switzerland 39/J2
Rhayader, Wales 13/D5
Rhea (creek), Oreg. 291/H2
Rhea (co.), Tenn. 237/M9
Rheatown, Tenn. (†37641) 237/R8
Rheda-Wiedenbrück, W. Germany 22/C3
Rheden, Netherlands 27/J4
Rheims (Reims), France 28/E4
Rhein, Sask. 181/J4
Rheinau, Switzerland 39/G1
Rheine, W. Germany 22/B2
Rheineck, Switzerland 39/J2
Rheinfeld, Sask. 181/D5
Rheinfelden, Switzerland 39/E1
Rheinfelden, W. Germany 22/B5
Rheinsberg, E. Germany 22/E2
Rheinwaldhorn (mt.), Switzerland 39/G4
Rhems, S.C. (†29440) 296/H4
Rhenen, Netherlands 27/H5
Rhéris, Wadi (dry riv.), Morocco 106/D2
Rheydt, W. Germany 22/B3
Rhine (riv.) 7/E4
Rhine (riv.), Austria 41/A3
Rhine (riv.), France 28/G3
Rhine, Georgia (31077) 217/F7
Rhine (riv.), Liecht. 39/J2
Rhine (riv.), Netherlands 27/J5
Rhine (riv.), Switzerland 39/J2
Rhine (riv.), W. Germany 22/B3
Rhinebeck, N.Y. (12572) 276/N7
Rhinecliff, N.Y. (12574) 276/N7
Rhineland, Mo. (65069) 261/J5
Rhineland, Sask. 181/D5
Rhinelander, Wis. (54501) 317/H4
Rhineland-Palatinate (state), W. Germany 22/B4
Rhinns, The (pen.), Scotland 15/C6
Rhinns (pt.), Scotland 15/B5
Rhino Camp, Uganda 115/F3
Rhir, Wadi (dry riv.), Algeria 106/F2
Rhir (cape), Morocco 106/B2
Rho, Italy 34/B2
Rhode Island 188/M2
RHODE ISLAND 249
Rhode Island (isl.), R.I. 249/J6
Rhode Island (sound), R.I. 249/J7
Rhode Island (state), U.S. 146/M5
Rhodell, W. Va. (25915) 312/D7
Rhodes (Ródhos), Greece 45/J7
Rhodes (isl.), Greece 7/G5
Rhodes (isl.), Greece 45/H7
Rhodes (peak), Idaho 220/D3
Rhodes, Iowa (50234) 229/G5
Rhodes, Mich. (48652) 250/E5
Rhodes Inyanga Nat'l Park, Zimbabwe 118/E3
Rhodes Point, Md. (21858) 245/O9
Rhodhiss, N.C. (28667) 281/F3
Rhododendron, Oreg. (97073) 291/F2
Rhodope (mts.), Bulgaria 45/G5
Rhodope (mts.), Greece 45/G5
Rhome, Texas (76078) 303/E1
Rhön (mts.), E. Germany 22/D3
Rhön (mts.), W. Germany 22/D3
Rhondda, Wales 13/A6
Rhondda, Wales 10/E5
Rhône (dept.), France 28/F5
Rhône (riv.), France 7/E4
Rhône (riv.), France 28/F5
Rhône (riv.), Switzerland 39/D4
Rhosllanerchrugog, Wales 13/D4
Rhu, Scotland 15/A1
Rhu Coigeach (cape), Scotland 15/C2
Rhyl, Wales 13/D4
Rhymney, Wales 13/A6
Rhymney (riv.), Wales 13/B6
Rhynie, Scotland 15/F3
Rhyolite (Ghost Town), Nev. (†89003) 266/E6
Riachão, Brazil 132/E4
Riachuelo, Uruguay 145/B5
Rialto, Calif. (92376) 204/E10
Riana, Tasmania 99/B3
Riaño, Spain 33/D1
Riau (arch.), Indonesia 85/C5
Riaza, Spain 33/E2
Rib (mt.), Wis. 317/G6
Ribadavia, Spain 33/B1
Ribadeo, Spain 33/C1
Ribamar, Brazil 132/F3
Ribas do Rio Pardo, Brazil 132/C8
Ribat Qila, Pakistan 68/A3
Ribat Qila, Pakistan 59/H4
Ribáuè, Mozambique 118/F3
Ribble (riv.), England 10/E4
Ribble (riv.), England 13/E4
Ribe (co.), Denmark 21/B7
Ribe, Denmark 21/B7
Ribe, Denmark 18/F9
Ribeira, Brazil 135/B4
Ribeira (riv.), Brazil 135/B4
Ribeira Brava, Portugal 33/A2
Ribeira de Iguape, Brazil 135/C4
Ribeira de Pena, Portugal 33/C2
Ribeira Grande, C. Verde 106/B7
Ribeirão Preto, Brazil 120/E5
Ribeirão Preto, Brazil 135/C2
Ribeirão Preto, Brazil 132/E8
Ribera, N. Mex. (87560) 274/D3
Ribérac, France 28/D5
Riberach an der Riss, W. Germany 22/C4
Riberalta, Bolivia 136/C2
Riberalta, Bolivia 120/C4
Rib Falls, Wis. (†54426) 317/G6
Ribla, Kuh-e (riv.), Iran 66/J6
Rib Lake, Wis. (54470) 317/F5
Ribnitz-Damgarten, E. Germany 22/E1
Ribstone, Alberta 182/E3
Říčany u Prahy, Czech. 41/C2
Ricaurte, Colombia 126/A7
Riccarton, N. Zealand 100/D5
Rice, Calif. (†92280) 204/L9
Rice (co.), Kansas 232/D3
Rice, Kansas (66965) 232/E2
Rice (co.), Minn. 255/E6
Rice, Minn. (56367) 255/D5
Rice (lake), Minn. 255/E4
Rice (mt.), N.H. 268/E2
Rice (lake), Ontario 177/F3
Rice, Texas (75155) 303/H5
Rice, Va. (23966) 307/M6
Rice, Wash. (99167) 310/G2
Riceboro, Georgia (31323) 217/K7
Rice Lake, Wis. (54868) 317/C5
Rices Landing, Pa. (15357) 294/C6
Riceton, Sask. 181/G5
Ricetown, Ky. (41364) 237/O6
Riceville, Iowa (50466) 229/H2
Riceville, Pa. (16432) 294/C2
Riceville, Tenn. (37370) 237/M10
Rich, Miss. (38662) 256/D2
Rich (cape), Ontario 177/D3
Rich (co.), Utah 304/C2
Richard, Sask. 181/D3
Richard City, Tenn. (†37380) 237/K11
Richard Collinson (inlet), N.W. Terrs. 187/G2
Richards, Iowa (†50579) 229/D4
Richards, Mo. (64778) 261/D7
Richards (isl.), N.W. Terrs. 187/E3
Richards Bay, S. Africa 118/E5
Richards Gebaur A.F.B., Mo. 261/P6
Richards Landing, Ontario 177/J5
Richardson (riv.), Alberta 182/C5
Richardson, Ky. (41253) 237/R5
Richardson (lakes), Maine 243/B6
Richardson (co.), Nebr. 264/J4
Richardson (isls.), N.W. Terrs. 187/G3
Richardson (mts.), N.W. Terrs. 187/E3
Richardson, Sask. 181/G5
Richardson, Texas (75080) 303/G2
Richardson, W. Va. (†26151) 312/D5
Richardson (mts.), Yukon 187/E3
Richardsons Landing, Tenn. (†38023) 237/B10
Richardsville, Ky. (42270) 237/J6
Richardsville, New Bruns. 170/D1
Richard Toll, Senegal 106/A5
Richardton, N. Dak. (58652) 282/F6
Richburg, N.Y. (14774) 276/D6
Richburg, S.C. (29729) 296/E2
Rich Creek, Va. (24147) 307/G6
Richdale, Alberta 182/E4
Riche (pt.), Newf. 166/C3
Richelieu, Ky. (42271) 237/H7
Richelieu (co.), Québec 172/D4
Richelieu, Québec 172/D4
Richer, Manitoba 179/F5
Richey, Mont. (59259) 262/L3
Richfield, Idaho (83349) 220/D6
Richfield, Kansas (67953) 232/A4
Richfield, Minn. (55423) 255/G6
Richfield, N.C. (28137) 281/J4
Richfield, Nova Scotia 168/C4
Richfield, Ohio (44286) 284/G3
Richfield, Pa. (17086) 294/H4
Richfield, Utah (84701) 304/B5
Richfield, Wis. (53076) 317/K1
Richfield Springs, N.Y. (13439) 276/K5
Richford, N.Y. (13835) 276/H6
Richford, Vt. (05476) 268/B2
Richford○, Vt. (05476) 268/B2
Richford, Wis. (†54930) 317/H7
Rich Fountain, Mo. (65070) 261/J6
Richgrove, Calif. (93261) 204/F8
Rich Hill, Mo. (64779) 261/D6
Richhill, N. Ireland 17/H3
Richibucto, New Bruns. 170/E2
Richibucto (harb.), New Bruns. 170/F2
Richibucto (riv.), New Bruns. 170/E2
Richibucto Village, New Bruns. 170/F2
Rich Lake, Alberta 182/E2
Richland, Fla. (†33599) 212/D3
Richland, Georgia (31825) 217/C6
Richland (co.), Ill. 222/E5
Richland, Ind. (47634) 227/C9
Richland (creek), Ind. 227/D6
Richland, Iowa (52585) 229/K6
Richland, Kansas (†66409) 232/G3
Richland (par.), La. 238/G2
Richland, Mich. (49083) 250/D6
Richland, Miss. (†39218) 256/D6
Richland, Mo. (65556) 261/H7
Richland (co.), Mont. 262/M3
Richland, Mont. (59260) 262/K2
Richland, Nebr. (68657) 264/G3
Richland, N.J. (08350) 273/D5
Richland, N.Y. (13144) 276/H3
Richland (co.), N. Dak. 282/R7
Richland (co.), Ohio 284/E4
Richland, Oreg. (97870) 291/K3
Richland, Pa. (17087) 294/K5
Richland (co.), S.C. 296/F4
Richland, S.C. (29675) 296/A2
Richland, S. Dak. (†57025) 298/R8
Richland (creek), Tenn. 237/G10
Richland, Texas (76681) 303/H6
Richland, Wash. 188/B1
Richland, Wash. (99352) 310/F4
Richland (co.), Wis. 317/F9
Richland Balsam (mt.), N.C. 281/D4
Richland Center, Wis. (53581) 317/F9
Richland Hills, Texas (76118) 303/F2
Richland-Kennewick, Wash. 310/80
Richlands, N.C. (28574) 281/O5
Richlands, Va. (24641) 307/E6
Richland Springs, Texas (76871) 303/F6
Richlandtown, Pa. (18955) 294/M5
Richlea, Sask. 181/C4
Richmond, Ala. (†36761) 195/D6
Richmond, Ark. (†71822) 202/B6
Richmond, Br. Col. 184/K3
Richmond, Calif. (*94801) 204/J1
Richmond, England 13/F3
Richmond, England 10/E3
Richmond (co.), Georgia 217/H4
Richmond, Ill. (60071) 222/E1
Richmond, Ind. (47374) 227/H5
Richmond, Iowa (52247) 229/K6
Richmond, Jamaica 158/J6
Richmond, Kansas (66080) 232/G3
Richmond, Ky. (40475) 237/N5
Richmond, La. (†71282) 238/H2
Richmond, Maine (04357) 243/D7
Richmond○, Maine (04357) 243/D7
Richmond○, Mass. (01254) 249/A3
Richmond, Mich. (48062) 250/G6
Richmond, Minn. (56368) 255/D5
Richmond, Mo. (64085) 261/D4
Richmond○, N.H. (†03470) 268/C6
Richmond (range), N.S. Wales 97/G1
Richmond (riv.), N.S. Wales 97/G1
Richmond (co.), N.Y. 276/M9
Richmond (Staten Island) (borough), N.Y. 276/M9
Richmond, N. Zealand 100/D4
Richmond (range), N. Zealand 100/D4
Richmond (co.), N.C. 281/K4
Richmond (co.), Nova Scotia 168/H3
Richmond (Grand River), Ohio (†44045) 284/H2
Richmond, Ohio (43944) 284/J5
Richmond, Ontario 177/J2
Richmond (co.), Québec 172/E4
Richmond, Québec 172/E4
Richmond, Queensland 88/G4
Richmond, Queensland 95/B4
Richmond (peak), St. Vin. & Grens. 161/A8
Richmond, S. Africa 118/C6
Richmond, Tasmania 99/D4
Richmond, Texas (77469) 303/J8
Richmond, Utah (84333) 304/C2
Richmond, Vt. (05477) 268/A3
Richmond○, Vt. (05477) 268/A3
Richmond, Victoria 88/L7
Richmond, Victoria 97/J5
Richmond (cap.), Va. 188/L3
Richmond (cap.), Va. 146/L6
Richmond (co.), Va. 307/P5
Richmond (cap.) (I.C.), Va. (*23201) 307/O5
Richmond Beach-Innis Arden, Wash. (98160) 310/A1
Richmond Corner, Maine (†04357) 243/D7
Richmond Corner, New Bruns. 170/C2
Richmond Dale, Ohio (45673) 284/E7
Richmond Furnace, Mass. (†01254) 249/A3
Richmond Heights, Fla. (†33158) 212/F6
Richmond Heights, Mo. (63117) 261/P3
Richmond Heights, Ohio (44143) 284/H9
Richmond Highlands, Wash. (†98133) 310/A1
Richmond Hill, Georgia (31324) 217/K7
Richmond Hill, Ontario 177/J4
Richmond Nat'l Battlefield Park, Va. 307/O6
Richmond upon Thames, England 10/B5
Richmond upon Thames, England 13/H8
Richmondville, N.Y. (12149) 276/M5
Richmond-Windsor, N.S. Wales 97/F3
Richmound, Sask. 181/B5
Rich Mountain, Ark. (†71953) 202/B4
Rich Square, N.C. (27869) 281/P2
Richterswil, Switzerland 39/G2
Richthofen (mt.), Colo. 208/G2
Richton, Miss. (39476) 256/G8
Richton Park, Ill. (60471) 222/B6
Richvale, Calif. (95974) 204/D4
Richvalley, Ind. (†46992) 227/F3
Richview, Ill. (62877) 222/D5
Richville, Mich. (48758) 250/F5
Richville, Minn. (56576) 255/C4
Richville, N.Y. (13681) 276/K2
Richwood, La. (†71201) 238/F2
Richwood, Minn. (56577) 255/C4
Richwood, N.J. (08074) 273/C4
Richwood, Ohio (43344) 284/D5
Richwood, W. Va. (26261) 312/F6
Richwood, Wis. (†53094) 317/J9
Richwoods, Mo. (63071) 261/L6
Rickardsville, Iowa (†52039) 229/M3
Rickenbacker Air Force Base, Ohio 284/E6
Ricketts, Iowa (51460) 229/B4
Ricketts (pt.), Victoria 97/J6
Ricketts (pt.), Victoria 88/L8
Rickman, Tenn. (38580) 237/L8
Rickmansworth, England 13/G8
Rickmansworth, England 10/A5
Rickreall, Oreg. (97371) 291/D3
Ricla, Spain 33/F2
Rico, Colo. (81332) 208/C7
Ricobayo (res.), Spain 33/D2
Ricse, Hungary 41/G2
Ridderkerk, Netherlands 27/F5
Riddle, Idaho (†89832) 220/B7
Riddle, Oreg. (97469) 291/D5
Riddlesburg, Pa. (16672) 294/F5
Riddleton, Tenn. (37151) 237/J8
Riddleville, Georgia (†31018) 217/G5
Riddon, Loch (inlet), Scotland 15/C5
Rideau (lake), Ontario 177/H3
Riderwood, Ala. (†36904) 195/B6
Ridge, Md. (20680) 245/N8
Ridge, Mont. (†59314) 262/M5
Ridgecrest, Calif. (93555) 204/H8
Ridgecrest, La. (†71334) 238/G3
Ridgedale, Mo. (65739) 261/F9
Ridgedale, Sask. 181/H2
Ridge Farm, Ill. (61870) 222/F4
Ridgefield, Conn. (06877) 210/B3
Ridgefield○, Conn. (06877) 210/B3
Ridgefield, N.J. (07657) 273/B2
Ridgefield, Wash. (98642) 310/C5
Ridgefield Park, N.J. (07660) 273/B2
Ridgeland, Miss. (39157) 256/D6
Ridgeland, S.C. (29936) 296/E7
Ridgeland, Wis. (54763) 317/B5
Ridgeley, W. Va. (26753) 312/J3
Ridgely, Md. (21660) 245/P5
Ridgely, Mo. (†64444) 261/C4
Ridgely, Tenn. (38080) 237/B8
Ridgeside, Tenn. (†37401) 237/L10
Ridge Spring, S.C. (29129) 296/D4
Ridgetop, Tenn. (37152) 237/H8
Ridgetown, Ontario 177/C5
Ridgeview, S. Dak. (57652) 298/H3
Ridgeville, Georgia (†31331) 217/K8
Ridgeville, Ind. (47380) 227/G4
Ridgeville, Manitoba 179/E5
Ridgeville, S.C. (29472) 296/G5
Ridgeville Corners, Ohio (43555) 284/B3
Ridgeway, Iowa (52165) 229/K2
Ridgeway, Minn. (†55943) 255/G7
Ridgeway, Mo. (64481) 261/D2
Ridgeway, N.C. (27570) 281/N2
Ridgeway, Ohio (43345) 284/C4
Ridgeway, S.C. (29130) 296/F3
Ridgeway, Va. (24148) 307/J7
Ridgeway, W. Va. (25440) 312/K4
Ridgeway, Wis. (53582) 317/F10
Ridgeway Branch, Toms (riv.), N.J. 273/E3
Ridgewood, N.J. (*07450) 273/B1
Ridgley, Tasmania 99/B3
Ridgway, Colo. (81432) 208/D6
Ridgway, Ill. (62979) 222/E6
Ridgway, Pa. (15853) 294/E3
Ridi, Nepal 68/E3
Riding (mt.), Manitoba 179/B4
Riding Mountain, Manitoba 179/C4
Riding Mountain Nat'l Park, Man. 162/F5
Riding Mountain Nat'l Park, Manitoba 179/B4
Ridley, Tenn. (†38474) 237/G9
Ridley Park, Pa. (19078) 294/M7
Ridott, Ill. (61067) 222/D1
Ridotto, Iowa (†50546) 229/D3
Ried im Innkreis, Austria 41/B2
Riegelsville, N.J. (†08865) 273/C2
Riegelsville, Pa. (18077) 294/M4
Riegelwood, N.C. (28456) 281/N6
Riehen, Switzerland 39/E1
Rienzi, Miss. (38865) 256/G1
Riesa, E. Germany 22/E3
Riesco (isl.), Chile 138/E10
Riesel, Texas (76682) 303/H6
Riesi, Italy 34/E6
Rietavas, U.S.S.R. 53/A3
Rietberg, W. Germany 22/C3
Rietfontein, Namibia 118/C4
Rieth, Oreg. (†97801) 291/J2
Rieti (prov.), Italy 34/D3
Rieti, Italy 34/D3
Rif, Er (range), Morocco 106/D2

Rosston 437

Rockford, Minn. (55373) 255/F5
Rockford, N.C. (27044) 281/H2
Rockford, Ohio (45882) 284/A4
Rockford, Sask. 181/J3
Rockford, Tenn. (37853) 237/O9
Rockford, Wash. (99030) 310/H3
Rock Forest, Québec 172/F4
Rock Glen, Pa. (18246) 294/K4
Rockglen, Sask. 181/F6
Rock Grove, Ill. (†61070) 222/D1
Rock Hall, Md. (21661) 245/O4
Rockham, S. Dak. (57470) 298/M4
Rockhampton, Australia 2/S7
Rockhampton, Australia 87/F8
Rockhampton, Queensland 88/H4
Rockhampton, Queensland 95/D4
Rockhampton Downs, North. Terr. 93/D5
Rockhaven, Sask. 181/B3
Rock Hill, Mo. (†63119) 261/P3
Rock Hill, S.C. 188/K4
Rock Hill, S.C. (29730) 296/E2
Rockholds, Ky. (40759) 237/N7
Rockingham, Georgia (†31510) 217/H7
Rockingham (co.), N.H. 268/E5
Rockingham (co.), N.C. 281/K4
Rockingham, N.C. (28379) 281/K5
Rockingham○, Vt. (†05101) 268/B5
Rockingham (co.), Va. 307/L4
Rockingham, W. Australia 88/B2
Rockingham, W. Australia 92/A2
Rock Island, Ill. 188/J2
Rock Island (co.), Ill. 222/C2
Rock Island, Ill. (61201) 222/C2
Rock Island, Okla. (†74932) 288/T4
Rock Island, Québec 172/E4
Rock Island, Tenn. (38581) 237/K9
Rock Island, Texas (77470) 303/H8
Rock Island, Wash. (†98801) 310/E3
Rock Island (dam), Wash. 310/E3
Rock Island Arsenal, Ill. 222/C2
Rocklake, N. Dak. (58365) 282/M2
Rockland, Conn. (†06443) 210/E3
Rockland, Del. (19732) 245/R1
Rockland, Idaho (83271) 220/F7
Rockland, Maine (04841) 243/E7
Rockland○, Mass. (02370) 249/L4
Rockland, Mich. (49960) 250/G1
Rockland (co.), N.Y. 276/M8
Rockland, Ontario 177/J2
Rockland, Texas (75970) 303/K6
Rockland, Wis. (54653) 317/D8
Rocklands (res.), Victoria 97/B5
Rockledge, Fla. (32955) 212/F3
Rockledge, Georgia (30454) 217/G6
Rockledge, Pa. (†19101) 294/M5
Rockleigh, N.J. (07647) 273/C1
Rocklin, Calif. (95677) 204/B8
Rockmart, Georgia (30153) 217/B2
Rock Mills, Ala. (36274) 195/H4
Rock Oak, W. Va. (†26756) 312/J4
Rock Point, Md. (20682) 245/L7
Rockport, Ark. (†72104) 202/E5
Rockport, Calif. (†95488) 204/B4
Rockport, Ill. (62370) 222/B4
Rockport, Ind. 227/C9
Rockport, Ky. (42369) 237/H6
Rockport, Maine (04856) 243/F7
Rockport○, Maine (04856) 243/F7
Rockport○, Mass. (01966) 249/M2
Rockport, Miss. (†39083) 256/D7
Rock Port, Mo. (64482) 261/B2
Rockport, Texas (78382) 303/H9
Rockport (lake), Utah 304/C3
Rockport, Wash. (98283) 310/D2
Rockport, W. Va. (26169) 312/C4
Rock Rapids, Iowa (51246) 229/A2
Rock River, Wyo. (82083) 319/G4
Rock Run, Ala. (†36272) 195/G2
Rocks, Md. (†21084) 245/N2
Rocks (pt.), N. Zealand 100/C4
Rock Springs, Mont. (59312) 262/K4
Rocksprings, Texas (78880) 303/D8
Rock Springs, Wis. (53961) 317/F8
Rock Springs, Wyo. 146/H5
Rock Springs, Wyo. 188/E2
Rock Springs, Wyo. (82901) 319/C4
Rockstone, Guyana 131/B2
Rockton, Ill. (61072) 222/E1
Rockvale, Colo. (81244) 208/J6
Rockvale, Mont. (†59080) 262/H5
Rockvale, Tenn. (37153) 237/J9
Rock Valley, Iowa (51247) 229/A2
Rockville, Conn. (†06066) 210/F1
Rockville, Ind. (47872) 227/C5
Rockville, Maine (†04841) 243/E7
Rockville, Md. (*20850) 245/K4
Rockville, Mass. (†02054) 249/A8
Rockville, Minn. (56369) 255/D5
Rockville, Mo. (64780) 261/D6
Rockville, Nebr. (68871) 264/F3
Rockville, Nova Scotia 168/B5
Rockville, R.I. (02873) 249/G6
Rockville, S.C. (†29487) 296/G6
Rockville, Utah (84763) 304/A6
Rockville, Va. (23146) 307/N5
Rockville, Wis. (†53820) 317/E10
Rockville Centre, N.Y. (*11570) 276/R7
Rockwall (co.), Texas 303/H5
Rockwall, Texas (75087) 303/H5
Rockwell, Iowa (50469) 229/G3
Rockwell, N.C. (28138) 281/J3
Rockwell City, Iowa (50579) 229/D4
Rockwood, Ala. (†35653) 195/C2
Rockwood, Ill. (62280) 222/D6
Rockwood, Maine (04478) 243/D4
Rockwood, Mich. (48173) 250/F6
Rockwood, Ontario 177/D4
Rockwood, Pa. (15557) 294/D6
Rockwood, Tenn. (37854) 237/M9
Rockwood, Texas (76873) 303/E6
Rocky (mts.) 162/D4
Rocky (mts.) 146/F4
Rocky (mts.) 188/E3
Rocky (mts.), Alberta 182/BC4
Rocky (mts.), Br. Col. 184/F2
Rocky (mts.), Canada 4/D16
Rocky (mts.), Colo. 208/F1
Rocky (mts.), Idaho 220/D1
Rocky (lake), Maine 243/J6
Rocky (mts.), Mont. 262/D4
Rocky (bay), Newf. 166/C3
Rocky (riv.), Newf. 166/D2
Rocky (mts.), N. Mex. 274/C1
Rocky (pt.), Norfolk I. 88/K6
Rocky (riv.), N.C. 281/H4
Rocky (riv.), Ohio 284/G9
Rocky, Okla. (73661) 288/J4
Rocky (riv.), S.C. 296/B3
Rocky (cape), Tasmania 99/B2
Rocky (mts.), Wash. 310/H2
Rocky (mts.), Wyo. 319/C1
Rocky (mts.), Yukon 187/F4
Rocky Bottom, S.C. (†29685) 296/B1
Rocky Boy, Mont. (†59521) 262/G2
Rocky Boy's Ind. Res., Mont. 262/G2
Rocky Comfort, Mo. (64861) 261/D9
Rocky Face, Georgia (30740) 217/C1
Rockyford, Alberta 182/D4
Rocky Ford, Colo. (81067) 208/M6
Rocky Ford, Georgia (30455) 217/J5
Rocky Fork (lake), Ohio 284/D7
Rocky Gap, Va. (24366) 307/F6
Rocky Gorge (res.), Md. 245/L4
Rocky Harbour, Newf. 166/C4
Rocky Hill○, Conn. (06067) 210/E2
Rocky Hill, Ky. (42163) 237/J6
Rocky Hill, N.J. (08553) 273/D3
Rocky Lane, Alberta 182/B5
Rocky Mount, Georgia (†30251) 217/C4
Rocky Mount, La. (†71064) 238/C1
Rocky Mount, Mo. (65072) 261/G6
Rocky Mount, N.C. 188/L3
Rocky Mount, N.C. (27801) 281/O3
Rocky Mount, Va. (24151) 307/J7
Rocky Mountain Arsenal, Colo. 208/K3
Rocky Mountain House, Alberta 182/C3
Rocky Mountain House, Alta. 162/E5
Rocky Mountain Nat'l Park, Colo. 208/H2
Rocky Point, N.C. (28457) 281/O6
Rocky Point, Wash. (†98626) 310/A2
Rockypoint, Wyo. (†82721) 319/G1
Rocky Rapids, Alberta 182/C3
Rocky Reach (dam), Wash. 310/E3
Rocky Ridge (mt.), Idaho 220/C3
Rocky Ridge, Ohio (43458) 284/D2
Rocky River, Ohio (44116) 284/G9
Rodanthe, N.C. (27968) 281/U3
Rodarte, N. Mex. (87561) 274/D2
Rodas, Cuba 158/E2
Rødby, Denmark 21/E8
Rødby, Denmark 18/G9
Roddickton, Newf. 166/C3
Rødding, Denmark 21/B7
Roddy, Tenn. (†37381) 237/M9
Rødekro, Denmark 21/C7
Roden, Netherlands 27/J2
Rodeo, Calif. (94572) 204/J1
Rodeo, Mexico 150/G4
Rodeo, N. Mex. (88056) 274/A7
Roderfield, W. Va. (24881) 312/C8
Roderick (isl.), Br. Col. 184/C4
Rodessa, La. (71069) 238/B1
Rodez, France 28/E5
Ródhos, Greece 45/J7
Roding (riv.), England 13/J7
Rodinga, North. Terr. 93/D8
Rødkaersbro, Denmark 21/C5
Rodman, Iowa (50580) 229/D2
Rodman, N.Y. (13682) 276/J3
Rodman, S.C. (†29706) 296/E2
Rodney, Mich. (49342) 250/D5
Rodney, Miss. (†39096) 256/B7
Rodney, Ontario 177/C5
Rodney Village, Del. (19901) 245/R4
Rodrigues, Brazil 132/F10
Rodríguez, Uruguay 145/C5
Rødvig, Denmark 21/F7
Roe, Ark. (72134) 202/H4
Roe (riv.), N. Ireland 17/H1
Roebling-Florence, N.J. (08554) 273/D3
Roebourne, W. Australia 88/B4
Roebourne, W. Australia 92/B3
Roebuck (bay), W. Australia 88/C3
Roebuck (bay), W. Australia 92/C2
Roebuck Plains, W. Australia 92/C2
Roeland Park, Kansas (†66205) 232/H2
Roer (riv.), Netherlands 27/J6
Roermond, Netherlands 27/J6
Roeselare, Belgium 27/C7
Roes Welcome (sound), N.W.T. 162/H2
Roes Welcome (sound), N.W. Terrs. 187/K3
Roff, Okla. (74865) 288/N5
Rogachev, U.S.S.R. 52/D4
Rogagua (lake), Bolivia 136/B3
Rogaguado (lake), Bolivia 136/C3
Rogaland (co.), Norway 18/E7
Rogatica, Yugoslavia 45/D4
Roger Mills (co.), Okla. 288/G3
Rogers, Ark. (72756) 202/B1
Rogers, Br. Col. 184/J4
Rogers (lake), Calif. 204/H9
Rogers, Conn. (06263) 210/H1
Rogers (lake), Conn. 210/F3
Rogers, La. (†71342) 238/F3
Rogers, Minn. (55374) 255/E5
Rogers, Nebr. (68659) 264/H3
Rogers, N. Mex. (88132) 274/F5
Rogers, N. Dak. (58479) 282/O5
Rogers, Ohio (44455) 284/J4
Rogers (co.), Okla. 288/P2
Rogers, Texas (76569) 303/G7
Rogers (mt.), Va. 307/E7
Rogers City, Mich. (49779) 250/F3
Rogerson, Idaho (83302) 220/D7
Rogers Springs, Tenn. (†38052) 237/D10
Rogersville, Ala. (35652) 195/D1
Rogersville, Mo. (65742) 261/G8
Rogersville, New Bruns. 170/E2
Rogersville, Pa. (15359) 294/B6
Rogersville, Tenn. (37857) 237/P8
Roger Williams Nat'l Mem., R.I. 249/J5
Roggen, Colo. (80652) 208/L2
Roggwil, Switzerland 39/E2
Rogliano, France 28/B6
Rogozno, Poland 47/C2
Rogue (riv.), Oreg. 291/C5
Rogue River, Oreg. (97537) 291/D5
Roha, India 68/C5
Rohnert Park, Calif. (94928) 204/C5
Rohnerville, Calif. (†95540) 204/B3
Rohrbach in Oberösterreich, Austria 41/B2
Rohrersville, Md. (21779) 245/H3
Rohri, Pakistan 68/B3
Rohtak, India 68/C5
Rohwer, Ark. (71666) 202/H6
Roi Et, Thailand 72/D4
Roja, U.S.S.R. 53/B2
Rojas, Argentina 143/F7
Rojo (cape), Mexico 150/L6
Rojo (cape), P. Rico 161/A3
Rojo (cape), P. Rico 156/F1
Rokan (riv.), Indonesia 85/C5
Rokeby, Sask. 181/J4
Rokiškis, U.S.S.R. 53/C2
Rokycany, Czech. 41/B2
Rokytnice nad Jizerou, Czech. 41/C1
Rola Co (lake), China 77/C4
Roland, Ark. (72135) 202/E4
Roland, Iowa (50236) 229/F4
Roland, Manitoba 179/D5
Roland, Okla. (74954) 288/S4
Røldal, Norway 18/E7
Roldán, Argentina 143/F6
Rolecha, Chile 138/D4
Rolesville, N.C. (27571) 281/N3
Rolette (co.), N. Dak. 282/L2
Rolette, N. Dak. (58366) 282/L2
Roleystone, W. Australia 88/B2
Rolfe, Iowa (50581) 229/D3
Roll, Ariz. (85347) 198/A6
Rolla, Ark. (†72104) 202/E5
Rolla, Br. Col. 184/G2
Rolla, Kansas (67954) 232/A4
Rolla, Mo. (65401) 261/J7
Rolla, N. Dak. (58367) 282/L2
Rollag, Minn. (†56549) 255/B4
Rolle, Switzerland 39/B4
Rollingbay, Wash. (98061) 310/A2
Rollingdam, New Bruns. 170/C3
Rolling Fields, Ky. (†40201) 237/K2
Rolling Fork (riv.), Ky. 237/L5
Rolling Fork, Miss. (39159) 256/C5
Rolling Hills, Alberta 182/E4
Rolling Hills, Calif. (90274) 204/B11
Rolling Hills, Ky. (†40201) 237/L1
Rolling Hills Estates, Calif. (90274) 204/B11
Rolling Meadows, Ill. (60008) 222/A5
Rolling Prairie, Ind. (46371) 227/D1
Rollingstone, Minn. (55969) 255/G6
Rollins, Mont. (59931) 262/B3
Rollo (bay), Pr. Edward I. 168/F2
Rolphton, Ontario 177/G1
Roma, Australia 87/E8
Roma (Rome) (cap.), Italy 34/F6
Roma, Queensland 88/H5
Roma, Queensland 95/D5
Roma, Sweden 18/L8
Romain (cape), S.C. 296/J6
Romaine (riv.), Newf. 166/B3
Romaine (riv.), Que. 162/K5
Romaine, Québec 174/E2
Romaine (riv.), Québec 174/E2
Roma-Los Saenz, Texas (78584) 303/E11
Roman, Romania 45/H2
Romance, Ark. (72136) 202/F3
Romance, Sask. 181/G3
Romance, W. Va. (25175) 312/C5
Romang, Argentina 143/F4
Romang (isl.), Indonesia 85/H7
Romania 2/L3
Romania 7/G4
ROMANIA 45/F3
Romano (cay), Cuba 158/G2
Romano (cay), Cuba 156/C2
Romano (cape), Fla. 212/E6
Romanshorn, Switzerland 39/H1
Romans-sur-Isère, France 28/F5
Romanzof (cape), Alaska 196/E2
Rombauer, Mo. (63962) 261/M9
Romblon (prov.), Philippines 82/D4
Romblon, Philippines 82/D4
Romblon (isl.), Philippines 82/D4
Rome, Ga. 188/K4
Rome, Georgia (30161) 217/B2
Rome, Ill. (61562) 222/D3
Rome, Ind. (47574) 227/D9
Rome, Iowa (52642) 229/K7
Rome (prov.), Italy 34/F6
Rome (cap.), Italy 7/F4
Rome (cap.), Italy 34/F6
Rome (cap.), Italy 2/K3
Rome○, Maine (†04957) 243/D6
Rome, Miss. (38768) 256/C3
Rome, N.Y. 188/M2
Rome, N.Y. (13440) 276/J4
Rome (Stout), Ohio (†45684) 284/D8
Rome, Ohio (44085) 284/J2
Rome, Oreg. (†97910) 291/K5
Rome, Pa. (18837) 294/K2
Rome, Wis. (†53178) 317/H1
Rome City, Ind. (46784) 227/G1
Romeo, Colo. (81148) 208/G8
Romeo, Mich. (48065) 250/F6
Romeoville, Ill. (60441) 222/B6
Romeroville, N. Mex. (†87701) 274/D3
Romeville, La. (†70723) 238/L3
Romilly-sur-Seine, France 28/F3
Romney, Ind. (47981) 227/D4
Romney, W. Va. (26757) 312/J4
Romny, U.S.S.R. 52/D4
Rømø, Denmark 21/B7
Rømø (isl.), Denmark 21/B7
Rømø (isl.), Denmark 18/F9
Romont, Switzerland 39/C3
Romorantin-Lanthenay, France 28/D4
Romsdalsfjorden (fjord), Norway 18/E5
Romsey, England 10/F5
Romsey, England 13/F6
Romulus, Mich. (48174) 250/F6
Romulus, N.Y. (14541) 276/G5
Ron, Vietnam 72/E3
Ron, Mui (cape), Vietnam 72/E3
Rona (isl.), Scotland 15/B3
Ronald, Wash. (98940) 310/E3
Ronan, Mont. (59864) 262/C3
Ronay (isl.), Scotland 15/A3
Roncador, Serra do (range), Brazil 132/D5
Roncador (cays), Colombia 126/B9
Ronceverte, W. Va. (24970) 312/F7
Ronciglione, Italy 34/C3
Ronda, N.C. (28670) 281/H2
Ronda, Spain 33/D4
Rønde, Denmark 21/D5
Ronde (isl.), Grenada 161/D7
Rondeau Prov. Park, Ontario 177/C5
Rondo, Ark. (†72355) 202/J4
Rondônia (terr.), Brazil 132/H10
Rondônia, Brazil 132/H10
Rondonópolis, Brazil 120/D4
Rondout (res.), N.Y. 276/M7
Rondu, Pakistan 68/D1
Rong, Koh (isl.), Cambodia 72/D5
Rong'an, China 77/G6
Ronge, Lac La (lake), Sask. 162/F4
Ronge, La (lake), Sask. 181/M3
Rongelap (atoll), Marshall Is. 87/G4
Rongjiang, China 77/G6
Rong Kwang, Thailand 72/D3
Rong Xian, China 77/H7
Ronju (mt.), Fr. Poly. 86/T13
Ronkonkoma, N.Y. (11779) 276/O9
Rønne, Denmark 21/F9
Rønne, Denmark 18/J9
Ronneby, Minn. (†56324) 255/E5
Ronneby, Sweden 18/J8
Ronne Entrance (inlet) 5/B15
Ronne Ice Shelf, Ant. 2/F10
Ronne Ice Shelf 5/B15
Ronse, Belgium 27/D7
Ronuro (riv.), Brazil 132/C6
Roodeport, S. Africa 118/H6
Roodhouse, Ill. (62082) 222/C4
Roof Butte (mt.), Ariz. 198/F2
Rooi, Neth. Ant. 161/E8
Rooks (co.), Kansas 232/C2
Roopville, Georgia (30170) 217/B4
Roosendaal, Netherlands 27/F5
Roosevelt (isl.), Ant. 2/A10
Roosevelt (isl.) 5/A10
Roosevelt (res.), Ariz. 188/D4
Roosevelt, Ariz. (85545) 198/D5
Roosevelt (riv.), Brazil 120/C3
Roosevelt (riv.), Brazil 132/A5
Roosevelt, La. (†71276) 238/H1
Roosevelt, Minn. (56673) 255/C2
Roosevelt (co.), Mont. 262/L2
Roosevelt, N.J. (08555) 273/E3
Roosevelt (co.), N. Mex. 274/F4
Roosevelt, N.Y. (11575) 276/R7
Roosevelt, Okla. (73564) 288/J5
Roosevelt, Texas (76874) 303/D7
Roosevelt, Utah (84066) 304/D3
Roosevelt, Wash. (99356) 310/E5
Roosevelt Campobello Int'l Park, New Bruns. 170/D4
Roosevelt City, Ala. (35020) 195/E4
Roosevelt Park, Mich. (49444) 250/C5
Roosevelt Road Naval Res., P. Rico 161/F2
Roosville, Br. Col. 184/K5
Root (riv.), Minn. 255/G7
Rootstown, Ohio (44272) 284/H3
Roper, N.C. (27970) 281/R3
Roper (riv.), North. Terr. 88/E3
Roper (riv.), North. Terr. 93/C3
Roper River, North. Terr. 93/D3
Roper River Mission, North. Terr. 88/E2
Roper Valley, North. Terr. 93/D3
Ropesville, Texas (79358) 303/B4
Roque Bluffs○, Maine (†04654) 243/H6
Roque González de Santa Cruz, Paraguay 144/B5
Roque Pérez, Argentina 143/G7
Roquetas, Spain 33/G2
Rora (head), Scotland 15/E2
Roraima (mt.) 120/C2
Roraima (terr.), Brazil 132/H8
Roraima (mt.), Guyana 131/A3
Roraima (mt.), Venezuela 124/H5
Rørby, Denmark 21/E6
Rorketon, Manitoba 179/C3
Røros, Norway 18/G5
Rorschach, Switzerland 39/H2
Rosa, Ala. (†35049) 195/E3
Rosa (cape), Ecuador 128/B10
Rosa (mt.), Italy 34/A1
Rosa, La. (71364) 238/G5
Rosa, Manitoba 179/F5
Rosa (mt.), Switzerland 39/E5
Rosaire, Québec 172/G3
Rosaireville, New Bruns. 170/E2
Rosalia, Kansas (67132) 232/F4
Rosalia, Wash. (99170) 310/H3
Rosalie, Dominica 161/F6
Rosalie, Nebr. (68055) 264/H2
Rosalina, Paraguay 144/D3
Rosalind, Alberta 182/D3
Rosamond, Calif. (93560) 204/G9
Rosamond (lake), Calif. 204/G9
Rosamond, Ill. (62083) 222/D4
Rosamorada, Mexico 150/G5
Rosapenna, Ireland 17/F1
Rosario, Argentina 143/F6
Rosario, Argentina 120/C6
Rosário, Brazil 132/F3
Rosario, Chile 138/F5
Rosario (cay), Cuba 158/C2
Rosario, Sinaloa, Mexico 150/G5
Rosario, Sonora, Mexico 150/E3
Rosario, Paraguay 144/D4
Rosario, P. Rico 161/A2
Rosario, Uruguay 145/B5
Rosario, Venezuela 124/B2
Rosario (str.), Wash. 310/C2
Rosario de la Frontera, Argentina 143/D2
Rosario de Lerma, Argentina 143/C1
Rosario del Tala, Argentina 143/G6
Rosáriodo Sul, Brazil 132/C10
Rosário Oeste, Brazil 132/C6
Rosas, Spain 33/H1
Rosas (gulf), Spain 33/H1
Rosati, Mo. (†65559) 261/J6
Rosa Zárate, Ecuador 128/C2
Rosburg, Wash. (98643) 310/B4
Rosbys Rock, W. Va. (†26041) 312/E3
Roscoe, Ill. (61073) 222/D1
Roscoe, Minn. (56371) 255/D5
Roscoe, Mo. (64781) 261/E7
Roscoe, Mont. (59071) 262/G5
Roscoe, Nebr. (†69153) 264/C3
Roscoe, N.Y. (12776) 276/L7
Roscoe, Pa. (15477) 294/C5
Roscoe, S. Dak. (57471) 298/L3
Roscoe, Texas (79545) 303/D5
Roscoff, France 28/A3
Roscommon (co.), Ireland 17/E4
Roscommon, Ireland 10/B4
Roscommon, Ireland 17/E4
Roscommon (co.), Mich. 250/E4
Roscommon, Mich. (48653) 250/E4
Roscrea, Ireland 10/B4
Roscrea, Ireland 17/F6
Rose (peak), Ariz. 198/F5
Rose (pt.), Br. Col. 184/B3
Rose (pt.), Martinique 161/D6
Rose, Nebr. (68772) 264/E2
Rose, N.Y. (14542) 276/G4
Rose (riv.), North. Terr. 93/D2
Rose, Okla. (74364) 288/R2
Roseau (cap.), Dominica 156/G4
Roseau (cap.), Dominica 161/E7
Roseau (riv.), Dominica 161/E7
Roseau (co.), Minn. 255/C2
Roseau, Minn. (56751) 255/C2
Roseau (riv.), Minn. 255/B2
Roseau (riv.), St. Lucia 161/G6
Roseau River, Manitoba 179/F5
Roseaux, Haiti 158/A6
Rosebank, Manitoba 179/D5
Roseberry, Br. Col. 184/J5
Rosebery, Tasmania 99/B3
Rose Blanche, Newf. 166/C4
Roseboom, N.Y. (13450) 276/L5
Roseboro, N.C. (28382) 281/N5
Rosebud, Alberta 182/D4
Rosebud (riv.), Alberta 182/D4
Rose Bud, Ark. (72137) 202/F3
Rosebud, Mo. (63091) 261/K6
Rosebud (co.), Mont. 262/K4
Rosebud, Mont. (59347) 262/K4
Rosebud (creek), Mont. 262/K4
Rosebud, S. Dak. (57570) 298/H7
Rosebud, Texas (76570) 303/G7
Rosebud (creek), Utah 304/A2
Rosebud Ind. Res., S. Dak. 298/H7
Roseburg, Oreg. (97470) 291/D4
Rosebush Mich. (48878) 250/E5
Rose City, Mich. (48654) 250/E4
Rose Creek, Minn. (55970) 255/F7
Rosedale, Ind. (47874) 227/C5
Rosedale, La. (70772) 238/G6
Rosedale, Md. (21237) 245/M3
Rosedale, Miss. (38769) 256/B3
Rosedale, Okla. (†74831) 288/M5
Rosedale, Tenn. (†37728) 237/N8
Rosedale, Va. (24280) 307/E7
Rosedale, W. Va. (26636) 312/E5
Rosefield, La. (†71435) 238/G3
Roseglen, N. Dak. (58775) 282/G4
Rosehearty, Scotland 15/F3
Rosehill, Ala. (†36028) 195/F8
Rose Hill, Barbados 161/B8
Rose Hill, Ill. (†62448) 222/E4
Rose Hill, Iowa (52586) 229/J6
Rose Hill, Kansas (67133) 232/E4
Rose Hill, Ky. (†40330) 237/M5
Rose Hill, Miss. (39356) 256/F6
Rose Hill, N.C. (28458) 281/N5
Rose Hill, Va. (24281) 307/B7
Roseisle, Manitoba 179/D5
Rose Lake, Br. Col. 184/E3
Roseland, Ark. (72463) 202/K2
Roseland, Fla. (32957) 212/F4
Roseland, Ind. (†46601) 227/E1
Roseland, Kansas (†66773) 232/H4
Roseland, La. (70456) 238/J5
Roseland, Minn. (†56216) 255/C6
Roseland, Nebr. (68973) 264/F4
Roseland, N.J. (07068) 273/A2
Roseland, Va. (22967) 307/K5
Roselawn, Ind. (†46310) 227/C2
Roselle, Ill. (60172) 222/A5
Roselle, N.J. (07203) 273/B2
Roselle Park, N.J. (07204) 273/A2
Rose Lodge, Oreg. (97372) 291/D3
Rose Lynn, Alberta 182/E4
Rosemark, Tenn. (38053) 237/B10
Rosemary, Alberta 182/E4
Rosemead, Calif. (91770) 204/C10
Rosemère, Québec 172/H4
Rosemont, Ill. (60018) 222/B5
Rosemont, Md. (†21758) 245/H3
Rosemont, N.J. (08556) 273/D3
Rosemont, Pa. (19010) 294/M5
Rosemount, Minn. (55068) 255/E6
Rosemount, Ohio (†45662) 284/D8
Rosen, Minn. (†56212) 255/B5
Rosenberg, Texas (77471) 303/J8
Rosendale, Minn. (†56243) 255/D5
Rosendale, Mo. (64483) 261/C2
Rosendale, N.Y. (12472) 276/M7
Rosendale, Wis. (54974) 317/J8
Rosenfeld, Manitoba 179/E5
Rosengart, Manitoba 179/E5
Rosenhayn, N.J. (08352) 273/C5
Rosenheim, W. Germany 22/D5
Rosenhof, Sask. 181/D5
Rosenlaui, Switzerland 39/F3
Rosenort, Manitoba 179/E5
Rosepine, La. (70659) 238/D5
Rose Prairie, Br. Col. 184/G2
Roseray, Sask. 181/C5
Roseto, Pa. (18013) 294/M4
Rosetown, Sask. 162/F5
Rosetown, Sask. 181/D4
Rosetta, Egypt 111/J2
Rosetta, Egypt 59/B3
Rosetta, Miss. (†39633) 256/B8
Rosette, Utah (†84329) 304/A2
Rose Valley, Pa. (†19065) 294/L7
Rose Valley, Sask. 181/H3
Roseville, Calif. (95678) 204/B8
Roseville, Ill. (61473) 222/C3
Roseville, Mich. (48066) 250/B6
Roseville, Minn. (55113) 255/G5
Roseville, Ohio (43777) 284/F6
Roseville, Pa. (†16933) 294/H2
Roseway (riv.), Nova Scotia 168/C4
Rosewood, North. Terr. 93/A4
Rosewood, Ohio (43070) 284/C5
Rosewood Heights, Ill. (†62024) 222/B2
Roseworthy, S. Australia 94/B6
Roshage (cape), Denmark 18/F8
Rosharon, Texas (77583) 303/J3
Rosh Ha 'Ayin, Israel 65/B3
Rosholt, S. Dak. (57260) 298/R2
Rosholt, Wis. (54473) 317/H6
Rosh Pinna, Israel 65/D2
Rosice, Czech. 41/D2
Rosiclare, Ill. (62982) 222/E6
Rosie, Ark. (72571) 202/G2
Rosier, Georgia (†30434) 217/H5
Rosignano Marittimo, Italy 34/C3
Rosignol, Guyana 131/C2
Rosine, Ky. (42370) 237/H6
Roşiori de Vede, Romania 45/G3
Rositsa, Bulgaria 45/H4
Roskilde (co.), Denmark 21/E6
Roskilde, Denmark 21/E6
Roskilde, Denmark 18/G9
Roslavl', U.S.S.R. 52/D4
Roslev, Denmark 21/B4
Roslin, Ontario 177/G3
Roslin, Tenn. (†38556) 237/M8
Roslyn, N.Y. (11576) 276/R6
Roslyn, S. Dak. (57261) 298/P2
Roslyn, Wash. (98941) 310/E3
Rosman, N.C. (28772) 281/D4
Rosmaninhal, Portugal 33/C3
Røsnaes (pen.), Denmark 21/D6
Rosneath, Scotland 15/A1
Rosneath, Scotland 10/A1
Ross (isl.), Ant. 2/T10
Ross (sea), Ant. 2/A10
Ross (isl.) 5/B9
Ross (sea) 5/B10
Ross, Calif. (94957) 204/H1
Ross, Iowa (†50025) 229/D5
Ross, Manitoba 179/F5
Ross (isl.), Manitoba 179/J3
Ross, Minn. (56753) 255/C2
Ross (isl.), New Bruns. 170/D4
Ross, N. Zealand 100/C5
Ross (pt.), Norfolk I. 88/L6
Ross, N. Dak. (58776) 282/E3
Ross (co.), Ohio 284/D7
Ross, Ohio (45061) 284/B9
Ross, Tasmania 99/D4
Ross (dam), Wash. 310/D2
Ross (lake), Wash. 310/D2
Rossa, Switzerland 39/H4
Rossall (pt.), England 13/D4
Rossan (pt.), Ireland 10/B3
Ross and Cromarty (trad. co.), Scotland 15/A5
Rossano, Italy 34/F5
Rossarden, Tasmania 99/D3
Ross Barnett (res.), Miss. 256/D6
Ross Bay Junction, Newf. 166/A3
Rossbear (lake), Alberta 182/C1
Rossburg, Ohio (45362) 284/A5
Rossburn, Manitoba 179/B4
Rosscarbery, Ireland 17/C8
Rosscarbery (bay), Ireland 10/B5
Rosscarbery (bay), Ireland 17/D9
Rosseau, Ontario 177/E2
Rosseau (lake), Ontario 177/E2
Rossel (isl.), Papua N.G. 85/D8
Rossendale, Manitoba 179/D5
Rosser, Manitoba 179/E4
Rosses (bay), Ireland 17/D1
Rosses Point, Ireland 17/D3
Rossford, Ohio (43460) 284/C2
Ross Fork, Mont. (†59457) 262/G3
Ross Ice Shelf, Ant. 2/A11
Ross Ice Shelf 5/A10
Rossie, Iowa (51356) 229/C2
Rossie, N.Y. (†13646) 276/J2
Rossignol (lake), Nova Scotia 168/C4
Rossing, Namibia 118/B4
Rossiter, Pa. (15772) 294/E4
Rosskeeragh (pt.), Ireland 17/D3
Ross Lake Nat'l Rec. Area, Wash. 310/E2
Rossland, Br. Col. 162/E6
Rossland, Br. Col. 184/H6
Rosslare, Ireland 10/C4
Rosslare, Ireland 17/J7
Rosslare (bay), Ireland 17/J7
Rosslare Harbour (Ballygeary), Ireland 17/J7
Rosslau, E. Germany 22/E3
Rosslyn Farms, Pa. (†15106) 294/B7
Rosslyn Village, Ontario 177/G5
Rosslyn Village, Ontario 175/C3
Rossmore, W. Va. (25643) 312/C7
Rossmoyne, Ohio (45236) 284/C9
Rosso, Mauritania 106/A5
Rosso, Mauritania 102/A3
Ross of Mull (pen.), Scotland 15/B4
Ross-on-Wye, England 10/E5
Ross-on-Wye, England 13/E6
Rossosh', U.S.S.R. 52/E4
Rossport, Ontario 177/H5
Ross River, Yukon 187/E3
Rosstock (mt.), Switzerland 39/G3
Rosston, Ark. (71858) 202/D6
Rosston, Ind. (†46077) 227/E4
Rosston, Okla. (73855) 288/G1

S

Sainte-Marguerite 439

Saas, Switzerland 39/J3
Saas Fee, Switzerland 39/E4
Saba (isl.), Neth. Ant. 156/F3
Saba (isl.), Virgin Is. (U.S.) 161/A4
Šabac, Yugoslavia 45/D3
Sabadell, Spain 7/E4
Sabadell, Spain 33/H2
Sabae, Japan 81/H5
Sabah (state), Malaysia 2/Q5
Sabah (state), Malaysia 85/F4
Sabah (reg.), Malaysia 54/N9
Sábalo, Cuba 158/A2
Sabana, Cuba 158/K4
Sabana (arch.), Cuba 158/E1
Sabana de la Mar, Dom. Rep. 156/E3
Sabana de la Mar, Dom. Rep. 158/F5
Sabana Grande, Dom. Rep. 158/E6
Sabanagrande, Honduras 154/D4
Sabana Grande, P. Rico 161/B2
Sabanalarga, Colombia 126/C2
Sabana Seca, P. Rico 161/D1
Sabancuy, Mexico 150/O7
Sabaneta, Dom. Rep. 158/D5
Sabaneta, Barinas, Venezuela 124/D3
Sabaneta, Falcón, Venezuela 124/D2
Sabang, Celebes, Indonesia 85/F5
Sabang, Weh, Indonesia 85/B4
Şabanözü, Turkey 63/E2
Sabará, Brazil 135/E1
Sabattus, Maine (04280) 243/C7
Sabattus○, Maine (04280) 243/C7
Sabaudia, Italy 34/D4
Sabaya, Bolivia 136/A6
Saberi, Hamun-e (lake), Iran 66/M5
Sabetha, Kansas (66534) 232/G2
Sabi (riv.), Zimbabwe 118/E3
Sabile, U.S.S.R. 53/B2
Sabillasville, Md. (21780) 245/J2
Sabin, Minn. (56580) 255/B4
Sabina, Ohio (45169) 284/C7
Sabinal (cay), Cuba 158/H2
Sabinal, Texas (78881) 303/E8
Sabinas, Mexico 150/J3
Sabinas (riv.), Mexico 150/J3
Sabinas Hidalgo, Mexico 150/J3
Sabine (riv.) 188/H4
Sabine (mt.) 5/B9
Sabine (par.), La. 238/C3
Sabine (lake), La. 238/C7
Sabine (passage), La. 238/C7
Sabine (riv.), La. 238/C5
Sabine (pen.), N.W. Terrs. 187/H2
Sabine (co.), Texas 303/L6
Sabine, Texas (†77640) 303/L8
Sabine (lake), Texas 303/L8
Sabine (riv.), Texas 303/L7
Sabine Pass, Texas (77655) 303/L8
Sabinópolis, Brazil 132/F7
Sabinoso, N. Mex. (†87746) 274/E3
Sabinov, Czech. 41/F2
Sabinsville, Pa. (16943) 294/G2
Sabir, Jebel (mt.), Yemen Arab Rep. 59/D7
Sabirabad, U.S.S.R. 52/G6
Sabkha, Syria 63/H5
Sablayan, Philippines 82/C4
Sable (cape), Fla. 188/K5
Sable (cape), Fla. 212/E6
Sable (cape), N.S. 146/M5
Sable (isl.), N.S. 146/N5
Sable (cape), N.S. 162/K7
Sable (isl.), N.S. 162/L7
Sable (cape), Nova Scotia 168/C5
Sable (isl.), Nova Scotia 168/J5
Sable (riv.), Ontario 177/B1
Sable (riv.), Québec 174/D1
Sable River, Nova Scotia 168/C5
Sables (lake), Québec 172/B3
Sables (lake), Québec 172/H1
Sablé-sur-Sarthe, France 28/C4
Sabougla, Miss. (†38955) 256/F3
Sabra (cape), Indonesia 85/J6
Sabratha, Libya 111/B1
Sabrina Coast (reg.) 5/C6
Sabtang, Philippines 82/B2
Sabtang (isl.), Philippines 82/B2
Sabugal, Portugal 33/C2
Sabula, Iowa (52070) 229/N4
Sabula, Mo. (†63620) 261/L8
Sabula, Pa. (†15801) 294/E3
Sabya, Saudi Arabia 59/D6
Sabzevar, Iran 54/G6
Sabzevar, Iran 59/G2
Sabzevar, Iran 66/K2
Sabzvaran, Iran 66/K6
Sabzvaran, Iran 59/G4
Sac (co.), Iowa 229/C4
Sac (riv.), Mo. 261/E7
Sacaba, Bolivia 136/C5
Sacaca, Bolivia 136/B6
Sacajawea (peak), Oreg. 291/K2
Sacajawea (lake), Wash. 310/G4
Sácama, Colombia 126/D4
Sacandaga (lake), N.Y. 276/L3
Sac and Fox Ind. Res., Iowa 229/H5
Sacapulas, Guatemala 154/B3
Sacaton, Ariz. (85247) 198/D5
Sacavém, Portugal 33/A1
Sac City, Iowa (50583) 229/C4
Sacedón, Spain 33/E2
Săcele, Romania 45/G3
Sac-Fox-Iowa Ind. Res., Kansas 232/G2
Sacheen (lake), Wash. 310/H2
Sachem (head), Conn. 210/E4
Sachem Head, Conn. (†06437) 210/E3
Sachigo (riv.), Ont. 162/G5
Sachigo (riv.), Ontario 175/B2
Sachojere, Bolivia 136/C4
Sachse, Texas (†75040) 303/H2
Sachseln, Switzerland 39/F3
Sachs Harbour, Canada 4/B16
Sachs Harbour, N.W.T. 162/D1
Sachs Harbour, N.W. Terrs. 187/F2
Sackets (harb.), N.Y. 276/H3
Sackets Harbor, N.Y. (13685) 276/H3
Säckingen, W. Germany 22/C5
Sackville, New Bruns. 170/F3
Sackville, Nova Scotia 168/E4
Saco, Ala. (†36081) 195/G7
Saco, Maine (04072) 243/C8
Saco (riv.), Maine 243/B8
Saco, Mo. (†63645) 261/M8
Saco, Mont. (59261) 262/J2
Saco (riv.), N.H. 268/E3
Sacol (isl.), Philippines 82/D7
Sacramento, Brazil 132/D7
Sacramento, Brazil 135/C1
Sacramento (cap.), Calif. 146/F6
Sacramento (cap.), Calif. 188/B3
Sacramento (riv.), Calif. 188/B3
Sacramento (co.), Calif. 204/D5
Sacramento (cap.), Calif. (*95801) 204/B8
Sacramento (riv.), Calif. 204/D5
Sacramento, Ky. (42372) 237/G6
Sacramento, N. Mex. (88347) 274/D6
Sacramento (mts.), N. Mex. 274/D6
Sacramento Army Depot, Calif. 204/B8
Sacramento Wash (dry riv.), Ariz. 198/A4
Sacratif (cape), Spain 33/E4
Sacré-Coeur-de-Saguenay, Québec 172/H1
Sacred Heart, Minn. (56285) 255/C6
Sacul, Texas (75788) 303/K6
Sádaba, Spain 33/F1
Sadani, Tanzania 115/G5
Saddle (hills), Alberta 182/A2
Saddle, Ark. (†72554) 202/G1
Saddle (mt.), Idaho 220/F6
Saddle (mt.), Idaho 220/D3
Saddle (riv.), N.J. 273/B1
Saddle (mts.), Wash. 310/E4
Saddle Brook○, N.J. (07662) 273/B1
Saddle Mountain, Okla. (†73023) 288/J5
Saddle River, N.J. (07458) 273/B1
Saddlestring, Wyo. (82840) 319/F1
Saddleworth, England 13/J2
Saddleworth, England 10/G2
Sa Dec, Vietnam 72/E5
Sadhoowa, Trin. & Tob. 161/B11
Sadieville, Ky. (40370) 237/M4
Sadij (riv.), Iran 66/L8
Sadiya, India 68/H3
Sa'diya, Iraq 66/D3
Sa'diya, Hor (lake), Iraq 66/E4
Sadlers Village, St. Chris.-Nevis 161/C10
Sadlersville, Tenn. (37154) 237/G7
Sado (isl.), Japan 81/J4
Sado (riv.), Portugal 33/B3
Sadon, Burma 72/C1
Sadorus, Ill. (61872) 222/E4
Saeby, Denmark 18/G8
Saeby, Denmark 21/D3
Saegertown, Pa. (16433) 294/B2
Saetermoen, Norway 18/L2
Saetermoen, Norway 18/L2
Safad (Zefat), Israel 65/C2
Safaniya, Ras (cape), Saudi Arabia 59/E4
Šafárikovo, Czech. 41/F2
Safata (bay), W. Samoa 86/M9
Safe, Mo. (†65559) 261/J6
Safety Harbor, Fla. (33572) 212/B2
Säffle, Sweden 18/H7
Safford, Ala. (36773) 195/D6
Safford, Ariz. (85546) 198/F6
Saffordville, Kansas (†66869) 232/F3
Saffron Walden, England 10/G4
Saffron Walden, England 13/H5
Safi, Jordan 65/E5
Safi, Morocco 102/B1
Safi, Morocco 106/C2
Safidar, Kuh-e (mt.), Iran 59/F4
Safidar, Kuh-e (mt.), Iran 66/H6
Safid Rud (riv.), Iran 66/F2
Safien, Switzerland 39/H3
Safita, Syria 63/G5
Safonovo, U.S.S.R. 52/D3
Safranbolu, Turkey 63/E2
Safut, Jordan 65/D3
Saga, China 77/B6
Saga (pref.), Japan 81/E7
Saga, Japan 81/E7
Sagadahoc (co.), Maine 243/D7
Sagaing (div.), Burma 72/B1
Sagaing, Burma 72/B2
Sagami (bay), Japan 81/O3
Sagami (riv.), Japan 81/O2
Sagami (sea), Japan 81/J6
Sagamihara, Japan 81/O2
Sagamore, Mass. (02561) 249/M5
Sagamore, Pa. (16250) 294/D4
Sagamore Hill Nat'l Hist. Site, N.Y. 276/R6
Sagamore Hills, Ohio (†44067) 284/J10
Saganaga (lake), Minn. 255/H2
Saganaga (lake), Ontario 175/B3
Sagar, India 68/D4
Sagavanirktok (riv.), Alaska 196/J1
Sagay, Camiguin, Philippines 82/E6
Sagay, Negros Occ., Philippines 82/D5
Sage, Ark. (72573) 202/G1
Sage (creek), Mont. 262/F2
Sage (mt.), Virgin Is. (Br.) 161/D4
Sage, Wyo. (†83101) 319/B4
Sagemace (bay), Manitoba 179/B3
Sagerton, Texas (79548) 303/E4
Sageville, Iowa (†52001) 229/M3
Sag Harbor, N.Y. (11963) 276/R8
Saginaw, Ala. (35137) 195/E4
Saginaw, Mich. 188/K2
Saginaw (bay), Mich. 188/K2
Saginaw (co.), Mich. 250/E5
Saginaw, Mich. (*48601) 250/F5
Saginaw (bay), Mich. 250/F5
Saginaw (riv.), Mich. 250/F5
Saginaw, Minn. (55779) 255/F4
Saginaw, Mo. (64864) 261/C8
Saginaw, Oreg. (97472) 291/E4
Saginaw, Texas (76179) 303/E2
Sagle, Idaho (83860) 220/B1
Saglek (bay), Newf. 166/B2
Saglek (fjord), Newf. 166/B2
Saglouc, Que. 162/J3
Saglouc, Québec 174/E1
Sagnay, Philippines 82/D4
Sagola, Mich. (49881) 250/B2
Saguache (co.), Colo. 208/G6
Saguache, Colo. (81149) 208/G6
Saguache (creek), Colo. 208/F6
Sagua de Tánamo, Cuba 158/K3
Sagua la Grande, Cuba 156/B2
Sagua la Grande, Cuba 158/E1
Sagua la Grande (riv.), Cuba 158/E1
Saguaro (lake), Ariz. 198/D5
Saguaro Nat'l Mon., Ariz. 198/E6
Saguenay (county), Québec 174/D2
Saguenay (co.), Québec 172/H1
Saguenay (riv.), Québec 174/C3
Saguenay (riv.), Québec 172/G1
Saguia el Hamra (dry riv.), Western Sahara 106/B3
Sagunto, Spain 33/F3
Sa'gya, China 77/C6
Sahagún, Colombia 126/C3
Sahagún, Spain 33/D1
Sahand, Kuh-e (mt.), Iran 66/E2
Sahara (desert) 2/J4
Sahara (des.) 102/C2
Sahara (des.), Algeria 106/E4
Sahara (des.), Chad 111/C3
Sahara (des.), Egypt 111/E3
Sahara (des.), Libya 111/C3
Sahara (des.), Mali 106/D4
Sahara (des.), Mauritania 106/C4
Sahara (des.), Niger 106/F4
Sahara (des.), Sudan 111/E3
Saharan Atlas (ranges), Algeria 106/E2
Saharanpur, India 68/D3
Saharsa, India 68/F3
Şahinli, Turkey 63/C6
Sahiwal, Pakistan 68/C2
Sahiwal, Pakistan 59/K3
Sahuaripa, Mexico 150/E2
Sahuarita, Ariz. (85629) 198/E7
Sahuayo de Díaz, Mexico 150/H7
Šahy, Czech. 41/E2
Saïda, Algeria 106/E2
Saida, Lebanon 63/F6
Sa'idabad, Iran 66/J6
Sa'idabad, Iran 59/G4
Saïdia, Morocco 106/D2
Saidor, Papua N.G. 85/B7
Saidu, Pakistan 68/C2
Saignelégier, Switzerland 39/D2
Saigo, Japan 81/F5
Saigon (Ho Chi Minh City), Vietnam 54/M8
Saihut, P.D.R. Yemen 54/G8
Saihut, P.D.R. Yemen 59/F6
Saikai National Park, Japan 81/D7
Saiki, Japan 81/E7
Sailes, La. (†71028) 238/D2
Sailor (creek), Idaho 220/C7
Sailor Springs, Ill. (62879) 222/E5
Saimaa (lake), Finland 18/Q6
Saimbeyli, Turkey 63/G4
Sain Alto, Mexico 150/H5
Sain-ni, N. Korea 81/B4
Saint Abbs, Scotland 15/F5
Saint Abbs (head), Scotland 15/F5
Saint-Adalbert, Québec 172/H3
Saint-Adelme, Québec 172/B1
Saint-Adelphe, Québec 172/E3
Saint Adolphe, Manitoba 179/E5
Saint-Adolphe, Québec 172/F2
Saint-Adolphe-d'Howard, Québec 172/C4
Saint-Adrien, Québec 172/F4
Saint-Affrique, France 28/E6
Saint-Agapitville, Québec 172/F3
Saint Agatha○, Maine (04772) 243/G1
Saint Agnes, England 13/B7
Saint-Aimé-des-Lacs, Québec 172/G2
Saint-Alban, Québec 172/E3
Saint Albans, England 13/H7
Saint Albans, England 10/F5
Saint Alban's (head), England 13/F7
Saint Albans○, Maine (04971) 243/E6
Saint Albans, Mo. (63073) 261/L5
Saint Alban's, Newf. 166/C4
Saint Albans, Vt. (05478) 268/A2
Saint Albans○, Vt. (05478) 268/A2
Saint Albans, W. Va. (25177) 312/C6
Saint Albans Bay, Vt. (05481) 268/A2
Saint Albert, Alberta 182/D3
Saint Albert, Ontario 177/J2
Saint-Albert, Québec 172/E3
Saint-Alexandre, Québec 172/D4
Saint-Alexandre-de-Kamouraska, Québec 172/H2
Saint-Alexis, Québec 172/D4
Saint-Alexis-de-Matapédia, Québec 172/B2
Saint-Alexis-des-Monts, Québec 172/D3
Saint Almo, New Bruns. 170/C2
Saint Alphonse, Manitoba 179/C5
Saint-Alphonse, Québec 172/D3
Saint Alphonse de Clare, Nova Scotia 168/B4
Saint-Alphonse-de-Caplan, Québec 172/C2
Saint-Amable, Québec 172/J4
Saint-Amand-Mont-Rond, France 28/E4
Saint Amant, La. (70774) 238/L2
Saint Ambroise, Manitoba 179/E4
Saint-Ambroise, Québec 172/F1
Saint-Anaclet, Québec 172/J1
Saint-André (cape), Madagascar 118/G3
Saint-André, New Bruns. 170/C1
Saint-André, Québec 172/B2
Saint-André, Réunion 118/G5
Saint-André-Avellin, Québec 172/B4
Saint-André-de-Kamouraska, Québec 172/H2
Saint-André-du-Lac-Saint-Jean, Québec 172/E1
Saint-André-Est, Québec 172/C4
Saint Andrew (pt.), Fla. 212/D6
Saint Andrew (sound), Georgia 217/K9
Saint Andrew (lake), Manitoba 179/E3
Saint Andrew (mt.), St. Vin. & Grens. 161/A9
Saint Andrews, New Bruns. 170/C3
Saint Andrew's, Newf. 166/C4
Saint Andrews, Nova Scotia 168/F3
Saint Andrews (chan.), Nova Scotia 168/H2
Saint Andrews, Scotland 15/F4
Saint Andrews, Scotland 10/E2
Saint Andrews (bay), Scotland 15/F4
Saint Andrews, S.C. (29407) 296/G6
Saint Andrews, Tenn. (37372) 237/K10
Saint-Anicet, Québec 172/C4
Saint Ann, Mo. (63074) 261/O2
Saint Anne, Chan. Is. 13/E8
Saint Anne, Ill. (60964) 222/F2
Saint Anns (bay), Nova Scotia 168/H2
Saint Anns, Ontario 177/E4
Saint Ann's Bay, Jamaica 156/C3
Saint Ann's Bay, Jamaica 158/J5
Saint-Anselme, Québec 172/F3
Saint Ansgar, Iowa (50472) 229/H2
Saint Anthony, Idaho (83445) 220/G6
Saint Anthony, Ind. (47575) 227/D8
Saint Anthony, Iowa (50239) 229/G4
Saint Anthony, Minn. (†56307) 255/D5
Saint Anthony, Minn. (55414) 255/G5
Saint Anthony, Newf. 166/C3
Saint Anthony, N. Dak. (58566) 282/H6
Saint-Antoine, New Bruns. 170/F2
Saint-Antoine, Québec 172/H4
Saint-Antoine-Abbé, Québec 172/D4
Saint-Antoine-sur-Richelieu, Québec 172/D4
Saint-Antonin, Québec 172/H2
Saint-Antonin-Noble-Val, France 28/D5
Saint Arnaud, Victoria 97/B5
Saint-Arsène, Québec 172/H2
Saint Arthur, New Bruns. 170/D1
Saint-Astier, France 28/D5
Saint-Athanase, Québec 172/H2
Saint-Aubert, Québec 172/G2
Saint Aubin, Chan. Is. 13/E8
Saint-Aubin-Sauges, Switzerland 39/C3
Saint Augustin (riv.), Newf. 166/C3
Saint-Augustin, Québec 172/G4
Saint-Augustin, Québec 174/F2
Saint-Augustin (riv.), Québec 174/F2
Saint-Augustin-de-Québec, Québec 172/E3
Saint Augustine, Fla. 188/K5
Saint Augustine, Fla. 146/K7
Saint Augustine, Fla. (32084) 212/E2
Saint Augustine, Ill. (61474) 222/C3
Saint Augustine, Md. (†21915) 245/P3
Saint Augustine Beach, Fla. (32084) 212/E2
Saint Austell (bay), England 13/C7
Saint Austell-with-Fowey, England 13/C7
Saint Austell with Fowey, England 10/D5
Saint-Barnabé, Québec 172/D4
Saint-Barthélemy (isl.), Guadeloupe 156/F3
Saint-Barthélemy, Québec 172/D3
Saint Basile, New Bruns. 170/B1
Saint-Basile-le-Grand, Québec 172/J4
Saint-Basile-Sud, Québec 172/F3
Saint Bees (head), England 13/D3
Saint Benedict, Kansas (†66538) 232/F2
Saint Benedict, La. (70457) 238/K5
Saint Benedict, Oreg. (97373) 291/B3
Saint Benedict, Pa. (15773) 294/E4
Saint Benedict, Sask. 181/F3
Saint-Benjamin, Québec 172/G3
Saint-Benoît, Réunion 118/G5
Saint-Benoît-Labre, Québec 172/G3
Saint Bernard, Ala. (35138) 195/E2
Saint Bernard (par.), La. 238/L7
Saint Bernard, La. (70085) 238/L7
Saint Bernard, Nova Scotia 168/B4
Saint Bernard, Ohio (45217) 284/B9
Saint-Bernard, Québec 172/F3
Saint Bernard, Great (pass), Switzerland 39/D5
Saint-Bernard-sur-Mer, Québec 172/G2
Saint Bernice, Ind. (47875) 227/C5
Saint Bethlehem, Tenn. (37155) 237/G7
Saint Blaise, Québec 172/E4
Saint-Blaise, Switzerland 39/D2
Saint-Bonaventure-de-Yamaska, Québec 172/E4
Saint-Boniface-de-Shawinigan, Québec 172/D3
Saint Bonifacius, Minn. (55375) 255/F5
Saint Brendan's, Newf. 166/D4
Saint Brides, Alberta 182/E2
Saint Bride's, Newf. 166/C2
Saint Brides (bay), Wales 10/D5
Saint Brides (bay), Wales 13/B6
Saint-Brieuc, France 28/B3
Saint Brieux, Sask. 181/G3
Saint-Bruno, Québec 172/F1
Saint-Bruno-de-Montarville, Québec 172/J4
Saint-Calais, France 28/D4
Saint-Calixte-de-Kilkenny, Québec 172/D4
Saint-Camille, Québec 172/F4
Saint-Camille-de-Bellechasse, Québec 172/G3
Saint-Casimir, Québec 172/E3
Saint Catharine, Mo. (64677) 261/G3
Saint Catharines, Ontario 177/E4
Saint Catherine, Fla. (†33513) 212/D3
Saint Catherine (mt.), Grenada 161/D8
Saint Catherine (lake), Vt. 268/A5
Saint Catherines (isl.), Georgia 217/K7
Saint Catherines (sound), Georgia 217/K7
Saint-Céré, France 28/D5
Saint-Cergue, Switzerland 39/B4
Saint-Césaire, Québec 172/D4
Saint-Chamond, France 28/F5
Saint Charles, Ark. (72140) 202/H5
Saint Charles, Idaho (83272) 220/G7
Saint Charles, Ill. (60174) 222/E2
Saint Charles, Iowa (50240) 229/F6
Saint Charles, Ky. (42453) 237/F6
Saint Charles (par.), La. 238/K7
Saint Charles, Mich. (48655) 250/E5
Saint Charles, Minn. (55972) 255/F7
Saint Charles (co.), Mo. 261/M2
Saint Charles, Mo. (63301) 261/N1
Saint-Charles, New Bruns. 170/F2
Saint Charles, Ontario 177/D1
Saint-Charles, Bellechasse, Québec 172/G3
Saint Charles, S.C. (29134) 296/G3
Saint Charles, S. Dak. (57571) 298/L7
Saint Charles, Va. (24282) 307/B7
Saint-Charles-de-Mandeville, Québec 172/D3
Saint-Charles-Garnier, Québec 172/J1
Saint-Charles-sur-Richelieu, Québec 172/D4
SAINT CHRISTOPHER-NEVIS 156/F3
SAINT CHRISTOPHER (SAINT KITTS)-NEVIS 161/D11
Saint Christopher (isl.), St. Chris.-Nevis 156/F3
Saint Christopher (isl.), St. Chris.-Nevis 161/D10
Saint Chrysostom, Pr. Edward I. 168/E2
Saint-Chrysostome, Québec 172/D4
Saint Clair (co.), Ala. 195/F3
Saint Clair, Ala. (36774) 195/E6
Saint Clair, Georgia (†30816) 217/H4
Saint Clair (co.), Ill. 222/D5
Saint Clair (lake), Mich. 188/K2
Saint Clair (co.), Mich. 250/G6
Saint Clair, Mich. (48079) 250/G6
Saint Clair (lake), Mich. 250/G6
Saint Clair (riv.), Mich. 250/G6
Saint Clair, Minn. (56080) 255/E6
Saint Clair (co.), Mo. 261/E6
Saint Clair, Mo. (63077) 261/K6
Saint Clair (lake), Ontario 177/B5
Saint Clair (riv.), Ontario 177/B5
Saint Clair, Pa. (17970) 294/K4
Saint Clair (lake), Tasmania 99/C4
Saint Clair Beach, Ontario 177/B5
Saint Clair Shores, Mich. (*48080) 250/B6
Saint Clair Springs, Ala. (†35146) 195/F3
Saint Clairsville, Ohio (43950) 284/J5
Saint Clairsville, Pa. (16676) 294/F5
Saint-Claude, France 28/F4
Saint-Claude, Guadeloupe 161/A7
Saint Claude, Manitoba 179/D5
Saint-Claude, Québec 172/F4
Saint Clears, Wales 13/C6
Saint-Clément, Québec 172/H2
Saint Clements, Ontario 177/D4
Saint-Cléophas, Québec 172/D3
Saint-Clet, Québec 172/C4
Saint Cloud, Fla. (32769) 212/E3
Saint-Cloud, France 28/A2
Saint Cloud, Minn. 188/H1
Saint Cloud, Minn. (56301) 255/D5
Saint Cloud, Wis. (53079) 317/K8
Saint Columb Major, England 13/B7
Saint Combs, Scotland 15/G3
Saint-Côme, Québec 172/D3
Saint-Constant, Québec 172/H4
Saint Croix (riv.) 188/H1
Saint Croix, Ind. (47576) 227/D8
Saint Croix (riv.), Maine 243/J5
Saint Croix (riv.), Minn. 255/F5
Saint Croix, New Bruns. 170/C3
Saint Croix (riv.), New Bruns. 170/C3
Saint Croix, Nova Scotia 168/E4
Saint Croix (isl.), Virgin Is. (U.S.) 156/H2
Saint Croix (isl.), Virgin Is. (U.S.) 161/G4
Saint Croix (co.), Wis. 317/B5
Saint Croix (lake), Wis. 317/A6
Saint Croix (riv.), Wis. 317/A4
Saint Croix Falls, Wis. (54024) 317/A5
Saint Croix Flowage (res.), Wis. 317/C3
Saint Croix Isl. Nat'l Mon., Maine 243/J5
Saint-Cuthbert, Québec 172/D3
Saint-Cyprien, Québec 172/J2
Saint-Cyrille, Québec 172/E4
Saint-Cyrille-de-L'Islet, Québec 172/G3
Saint Cyrus, Scotland 15/F4
Saint-Damase, Québec 172/B1
Saint-Damase-des-Aulnaies, Québec 172/C2
Saint-Damien-de-Brandon, Québec 172/D3
Saint-Damien-de-Buckland, Québec 172/G3
Saint David, Ariz. (85630) 198/E7
Saint David, Ill. (61563) 222/C3
Saint David, Maine (04773) 243/G1
Saint-David, Québec 172/J3
Saint-David-de-Falardeau, Québec 172/F1
Saint-David-d'Yamaska, Québec 172/E4
Saint Davids (isl.), Bermuda 156/H2
Saint David's, Wales 13/B6
Saint David's (head), Wales 10/D5
Saint David's (head), Wales 13/B6
Saint-Denis, France 28/B1
Saint-Denis, Québec 172/D4
Saint-Denis (cap.), Réunion 118/F5
Saint Denis, Sask. 181/F3
Saint-Denis-de-la-Bouteillerie, Québec 172/G2
Saint-Didace, Québec 172/D3
Saint-Dié, France 28/G3
Saint-Dizier, France 28/F3
Saint-Dominique, Québec 172/E4
Saint-Donat-de-Montcalm, Québec 172/C3
Saint-Donat-de-Rimouski, Québec 172/J1
Saint Donatus, Iowa (52071) 229/M4
Sainte-Adèle, Québec 172/C4
Sainte Agathe, Manitoba 179/E5
Sainte-Agathe, Québec 172/F3
Sainte-Agathe-des-Monts, Québec 172/C3
Sainte-Agnes-de-Charlevoix, Québec 172/G2
Sainte Amélie, Manitoba 179/C4
Sainte-Anastasie, Québec 172/F3
Sainte-Angèle-de-Mérici, Québec 172/J1
Sainte Anne (lake), Alberta 182/C3
Sainte-Anne, Guadeloupe 161/B6
Sainte Anne, Manitoba 179/F5
Sainte-Anne, Martinique 161/D7
Sainte-Anne, New Bruns. 170/E1
Sainte-Anne (lake), Québec 172/H2
Sainte-Anne (riv.), Québec 172/C1
Sainte-Anne (riv.), Québec 172/G2
Sainte-Anne (riv.), Québec 172/F3
Sainte Anne (isl.), Seychelles 118/H5
Sainte-Anne-de-Beaupré, Québec 172/F2
Sainte-Anne-de-Bellevue, Québec 172/H4
Sainte-Anne-de-Kent, New Bruns. 170/F2
Sainte-Anne-de-Madawaska, New Bruns. 170/B1
Sainte-Anne-des-Monts, Québec 172/C1
Sainte-Anne-des-Plaines, Québec 172/H4
Sainte-Anne-du-Lac, Québec 172/B3
Sainte-Apolline, Québec 172/G3
Sainte-Aurélie, Québec 172/G3
Sainte-Béatrix, Québec 172/D3
Sainte-Bernadette, Québec 172/G1
Sainte-Blandine, Québec 172/J1
Sainte-Brigide, Québec 172/D4
Sainte-Catherine, Québec 172/F3
Sainte-Cécile-de-Frontenac, Québec 172/G4
Sainte-Cécile-de-Masham, Québec 172/A4
Sainte-Claire, Québec 172/G3
Sainte-Clothilde-de-Horton, Québec 172/E4
Sainte-Croix, Québec 172/F3
Sainte-Croix, Switzerland 39/B3
Saint-Édouard-de-Kent, New Bruns. 170/F2
Saint-Édouard-de-Maskinongé, Québec 172/D3
Saint-Édouard-de-Napierville, Québec 172/D4
Saint Edward, Nebr. (68660) 264/G3
Saint Edward, Pr. Edward I. 168/D2
Sainte-Edwidge, Québec 172/F4
Sainte-Élisabeth, Québec 172/D3
Sainte-Émélie-de-l'Énergie, Québec 172/D3
Sainte-Eulalie, Québec 172/E3
Sainte-Euphémie, Québec 172/G3
Sainte-Famille-d'Aumond, Québec 172/B3
Sainte-Famille-d'Orléans, Québec 172/G3
Sainte-Félicité, Québec 172/B1
Sainte-Flavie, Québec 172/J1
Sainte-Florence, Québec 172/B2
Sainte-Foy, Québec 172/H3
Sainte-Françoise, Québec 172/H1
Sainte-Geneviève, Manitoba 179/F5
Sainte Genevieve (co.), Mo. 261/M7
Sainte Genevieve, Mo. (63670) 261/M6
Sainte-Geneviève, Québec 172/H4
Sainte-Geneviève-de-Batiscan, Québec 172/E3
Sainte-Hedwidge-de-Roberval, Québec 172/E1
Sainte-Hélène-de-Bagot, Québec 172/E4
Sainte-Hélène-de-Kamouraska, Québec 172/H2
Sainte-Hénédine, Québec 172/F3
Sainte-Julie-de-Verchères, Québec 172/J4
Sainte-Julienne, Québec 172/D4
Sainte-Julie-Station, Québec 172/F3
Sainte-Justine, Québec 172/G3
Sainte-Justine-de-Newton, Québec 172/C4
Saint Eleanors, Pr. Edward I. 168/E2
Saint-Éleuthère, Québec 172/H2
Saint Elias (mt.), Alaska 188/D5
Saint Elias (cape), Alaska 196/K3
Saint Elias (mt.), Alaska 196/K2
Saint Elias (mts.), Alaska 196/L2
Saint Elias (mt.), Yukon 162/B3
Saint Elias (mt.), Yukon 187/D3
Saint Elias (mts.), Yukon 187/E3
Saint-Élie, Fr. Guiana 131/E3
Saint-Élie, Québec 172/E3
Saint Elizabeth, Mo. (65075) 261/H6
Saint Elmo, Ala. (36568) 195/B10
Saint Elmo, Colo. (†81236) 208/G5
Saint Elmo, Ill. (62458) 222/E4
Saint-Éloi, Québec 172/H1
Sainte-Louise, Québec 172/G2
Sainte-Luce, Martinique 161/D7
Sainte-Luce, Québec 172/J1
Sainte-Lucie-de-Beauregard, Québec 172/H3
Sainte-Lucie-de-Doncaster, Québec 172/C3
Saint-Elzéar, Québec 172/F3
Saint-Elzéar-de-Bonaventure, Québec 172/C2
Sainte-Marguerite, Guadeloupe 161/B6
Sainte-Marguerite-de-Dorchester, Québec 172/G3
Sainte-Marguerite-Marie, Québec 172/B2
Sainte-Marguerite (riv.), Québec 172/G1
Sainte-Marguerite Nord-Est (riv.), Québec 172/H1
Sainte-Marguerite (riv.), Québec 174/D2

Sieradz 447

Sheep (creek), Utah 304/E3
Sheep Creek, Alberta 182/A2
Sheep Haven (harb.), Ireland 17/F1
Sheeps (head), Ireland 17/B8
Sheepscott, Maine (†04579) 243/D7
's Heerenberg, Netherlands 27/J5
Sheerness, Alberta 182/E4
Sheet (harb.), Nova Scotia 168/F4
Sheet Harbour, Nova Scotia 168/F4
Shefar'am, Israel 65/C2
Shefayim, Israel 65/B3
Sheffield, Ala. (35660) 195/C1
Sheffield, England 7/D3
Sheffield, England 10/F4
Sheffield, England 13/J2
Sheffield, Ill. (61361) 222/D2
Sheffield, Iowa (50475) 229/G3
Sheffield○, Mass. (01257) 249/A4
Sheffield, Mont. (†59347) 262/K4
Sheffield, New Bruns. 170/D3
Sheffield, Ohio (†44052) 284/F3
Sheffield, Pa. (16347) 294/D2
Sheffield, Tasmania 99/C3
Sheffield, Texas (79781) 303/B7
Sheffield○, Vt. (05866) 268/C2
Sheffield Lake, Ohio (44054) 284/F3
Shefford (co.), Québec 172/E4
Sheguiandah, Ontario 177/C2
Sheho, Sask. 181/H4
Shehy (mts.), Ireland 17/C8
Sheikh Sa'id, Yemen Arab Rep. 59/D7
Sheila, New Bruns. 170/F1
Sheki, U.S.S.R. 52/G6
Shelagh (riv.), Iran 66/M5
Shelagskiy (cape), U.S.S.R. 48/R2
Shelbiana, Ky. (41562) 237/R6
Shelbina, Mo. (63468) 261/H3
Shelburn, Ind. (47879) 227/C6
Shelburne, N.H. (†03581) 268/E3
Shelburne○, N.H. (†03581) 268/E3
Shelburne (co.), Nova Scotia 168/C5
Shelburne, Nova Scotia 168/C5
Shelburne, Ontario 177/D3
Shelburne○, Vt. (05482) 268/A3
Shelburne (pond), Vt. 268/A3
Shelburne Falls, Mass. (01370) 249/D2
Shelby (co.), Ala. 195/E4
Shelby, Ala. (35143) 195/E4
Shelby (co.), Ill. 222/E4
Shelby (co.), Ind. 227/F5
Shelby, Ind. (46377) 227/C2
Shelby (co.), Iowa 229/C5
Shelby, Iowa (51570) 229/C5
Shelby (co.), Ky. 237/L4
Shelby, Mich. (49455) 250/C5
Shelby, Miss. (38774) 256/C3
Shelby (co.), Mo. 261/H3
Shelby, Mont. (59474) 262/E2
Shelby, Nebr. (68662) 264/G3
Shelby, N.C. (28150) 281/G4
Shelby (co.), Ohio 284/B5
Shelby, Ohio (44875) 284/E4
Shelby (co.), Tenn. 237/B10
Shelby (co.), Texas 303/K6
Shelby Center, N.Y. (†14103) 276/D4
Shelbyville, Ill. (62565) 222/E4
Shelbyville (lake), Ill. 222/E4
Shelbyville, Ind. (46176) 227/F6
Shelbyville, Ky. (40065) 237/L4
Shelbyville, Mo. (63469) 261/H3
Shelbyville, Tenn. (37160) 237/H10
Shelbyville, Texas (75973) 303/L6
Sheldahl, Iowa (50243) 229/F5
Sheldon, Ill. (60966) 222/F3
Sheldon, Iowa (51201) 229/B2
Sheldon, Minn. (†55921) 255/G7
Sheldon, Mo. (64784) 261/D7
Sheldon, N. Dak. (58068) 282/P6
Sheldon, S.C. (29941) 296/F6
Sheldon, Texas (†77001) 303/K1
Sheldon○, Vt. (05483) 268/B2
Sheldon, Wis. (54766) 317/D5
Sheldon Junction, Vt. (†05483) 268/B2
Sheldon Point, Alaska (99666) 196/E2
Sheldon Springs, Vt. (05485) 268/A2
Sheldonville, Mass. (02070) 249/J4
Shelekhov (gulf), U.S.S.R. 54/S3
Shelekhov (gulf), U.S.S.R. 48/Q4
Shelikof (str.), Alaska 196/H3
Shell (pt.), Fla. 212/B1
Shell (riv.), Minn. 255/C4
Shell (creek), N. Dak. 282/F3
Shell, Loch (inlet), Scotland 15/B3
Shell (lake), Wis. 317/C4
Shell, Wyo. (82441) 319/E1
Shell (creek), Wyo. 319/E1
Shellbrook, Sask. 162/F5
Shellbrook, Sask. 181/E2
Shelley, Br. Col. 184/F3
Shelley, Idaho (83274) 220/F6
Shellharbour, N.S. Wales 97/F4
Shell Knob, Mo. (65747) 261/E9
Shell Lake, Sask. 181/D2
Shell Lake, Wis. (54871) 317/C4
Shellman, Georgia (31786) 217/C7
Shellmouth, Manitoba 179/A4
Shell Rock, Iowa (50670) 229/H3
Shellsburg, Iowa (52332) 229/K4
Shelltown, Md. (†21838) 245/R9
Shelly, Minn. (56581) 255/B3
Shelmerdine, N.C. (†27834) 281/P4
Shelocta, Pa. (15774) 294/D4
Shelter (isl.), N.Y. 276/R8
Shelton, Conn. (06484) 210/C3
Shelton, Nebr. (68876) 264/F4
Shelton, S.C. (†29015) 296/E3
Shelton, Wash. (98584) 310/B3
Shemakha, U.S.S.R. 52/G6
Shemogue, New Bruns. 170/F2
Shemya (isl.), Alaska 196/J3
Shemya Air Force Base, Alaska 196/J3
Shenandoah, Iowa (51601) 229/C7
Shenandoah, Pa. (17976) 294/K4
Shenandoah (co.), Va. 307/L3
Shenandoah, Va. (22849) 307/L4
Shenandoah (mt.), Va. 307/K3
Shenandoah (riv.), Va. 307/N2
Shenandoah (riv.), W. Va. 312/K4
Shenandoah Junction, W. Va. (25442) 312/L4
Shenandoah Nat'l Park, Va. 307/L3
Shenango, Pa. (†16125) 294/A3
Shenango River (lake), Pa. 294/B3
Shendam, Nigeria 106/F7
Shendi, Sudan 59/B6
Shendi, Sudan 102/F3
Shendi, Sudan 111/F4
Shëngjin, Albania 45/D5
Sheng Xian, China 77/K6
Shenipsit (lake), Conn. 210/F1
Shenkursk, U.S.S.R. 52/F2
Shenkursk, U.S.S.R. 48/E3
Shenmu, China 77/G4
Shennington, Wis. (†54618) 317/F7
Shennongjia, China 77/H5
Shensi (Shaanxi) (prov.), China 77/G5
Shenyang (Mukden), China 77/K3
Shenyang, China 54/O5
Shenyang, China 2/R3
Sheopur, India 68/D3
Shepard, Alberta 182/D4
Shepardsville, Ind. (47880) 227/B5
Shepaug (dam), Conn. 210/B3
Shepaug (riv.), Conn. 210/B2
Shepetovka, U.S.S.R. 52/C4
Shepherd, Mich. (48883) 250/E5
Shepherd, Mont. (59079) 262/H5
Shepherd (bay), N.W. Terrs. 187/J3
Shepherd, Texas (77371) 303/K7
Shepherdstown, W. Va. (25443) 312/L4
Shepherdsville, Ky. (40165) 237/K4
Shepody, New Bruns. 170/F3
Shepody (bay), New Bruns. 170/F3
Sheppard A.F.B., Texas 303/F3
Shepparton, Victoria 88/G7
Shepparton, Victoria 97/C5
Sheppey (isl.), England 13/J6
Sheppton, Pa. (18248) 294/K4
Shepshed, England 13/F5
Shepton Mallet, England 13/E6
Shepton Mallet, England 10/E5
Sheqi, China 77/H5
Sherack, Minn. (†56722) 255/B2
Sherard, Miss. (38669) 256/C2
Sherard (cape), N.W. Terrs. 187/L2
Sherborn○, Mass. (01770) 249/A8
Sherborne, England 10/E5
Sherborne, England 13/E7
Sherbro (isl.), S. Leone 106/B7
Sherbrooke, Nova Scotia 168/G3
Sherbrooke (lake), Nova Scotia 168/D4
Sherbrooke (riv.), Nova Scotia 168/D4
Sherbrooke, Que. 162/J7
Sherbrooke (co.), Québec 172/E4
Sherbrooke, Québec 172/E4
Sherburn, Minn. (56171) 255/D7
Sherburne (co.), Minn. 255/E5
Sherburne, N.Y. (13460) 276/K5
Shercock, Ireland 17/G4
Shereik, Sudan 111/F4
Sheridan, Ark. (72150) 202/F5
Sheridan, Calif. (95681) 204/D5
Sheridan, Colo. (†80110) 208/J3
Sheridan, Ill. (60551) 222/E2
Sheridan, Ind. (46069) 227/E4
Sheridan (co.), Kansas 232/B2
Sheridan, Maine (04775) 243/F2
Sheridan, Mich. (48884) 250/D5
Sheridan, Mo. (64486) 261/C1
Sheridan (co.), Mont. 262/M2
Sheridan, Mont. (59749) 262/D5
Sheridan (co.), Nebr. 264/B2
Sheridan, N.Y. (14135) 276/B5
Sheridan (co.), N. Dak. 282/K4
Sheridan, Oreg. (97378) 291/D2
Sheridan, W. Va. (†25506) 312/B6
Sheridan, Wis. (†54981) 317/H7
Sheridan, Wyo. 188/E2
Sheridan, Wyo. 146/H5
Sheridan (co.), Wyo. 319/F1
Sheridan, Wyo. (82801) 319/F1
Sheridan Lake, Colo. (81071) 208/P6
Sheringham, England 13/J5
Sheringham, England 10/G4
Sherkin (isl.), Ireland 17/C9
Sherman (mt.), Colo. 208/G4
Sherman○, Conn. (06784) 210/B2
Sherman, Ill. (62684) 222/D4
Sherman (co.), Kansas 232/A2
Sherman, Kansas (†67356) 232/H4
Sherman, Ky. (†41035) 237/M3
Sherman, Maine (†04777) 243/G4
Sherman○, Maine (†04777) 243/G4
Sherman, Mich. (†49668) 250/D4
Sherman, Miss. (38869) 256/G2
Sherman, Mo. (63078) 261/N3
Sherman (co.), Nebr. 264/F3
Sherman (res.), Nebr. 264/E3
Sherman, N. Mex. (†88057) 274/B6
Sherman, N.Y. (14781) 276/A6
Sherman (inlet), N.W. Terrs. 187/J3
Sherman (co.), Oreg. 291/G2
Sherman, S. Dak. (57060) 298/S6
Sherman (co.), Texas 303/C1
Sherman, Texas (75090) 303/H4
Sherman, Texas 188/G4
Sherman, W. Va. (26173) 312/C5
Sherman City, Mich. (†48632) 250/D5
Sherman Mills, Maine (04776) 243/G4
Shermans Dale, Pa. (17090) 294/H5
Sherman Station, Maine (04777) 243/F4
Sherrard, Ill. (61281) 222/C2
Sherrard, W. Va. (†26003) 312/E3
Sherridon, Man. 162/G4
Sherridon, Manitoba 179/H3
Sherrill, Ark. (72152) 202/F5
Sherrill, Iowa (52073) 229/M3
Sherrill, N.Y. (13461) 276/J4
Sherrington, Québec 172/D4
Sherrodsville, Ohio (44675) 284/H4
Sherry, Wis. (†54454) 317/G6
's Hertogenbosch, Netherlands 27/G5
Sherwood, Ark. (72116) 202/F4
Sherwood (pt.), Conn. 210/B4
Sherwood (for.), England 13/F4
Sherwood, Mich. (49089) 250/D6
Sherwood, N. Dak. (58782) 282/G2
Sherwood, Ohio (43556) 284/A3
Sherwood, Okla. (†74728) 288/S6
Sherwood, Oreg. (97140) 291/A2
Sherwood, Pr. Edward I. 168/E2
Sherwood, Tenn. (37376) 237/K10
Sherwood, Texas (†76941) 303/D6
Sherwood, Wis. (54169) 317/K7
Sherwood Park, Alberta 182/D3
Sheslay (riv.), Br. Col. 184/J2
Shetek (lake), Minn. 255/C6
Shetland (islands area), Scotland 15/F2
Shetland (isls.), Scotland 7/D2
Shetland (isls.), Scotland 10/G1
Shetland (isls.), Scotland 15/G2
Shetucket (riv.), Conn. 210/G2
Shevchenko, U.S.S.R. 54/G5
Shevchenko, U.S.S.R. 48/F5
Shevlin, Manitoba 179/A3
Shevlin, Minn. (56676) 255/C3
Sheyenne, N. Dak. (58374) 282/M4
Sheyenne (riv.), N. Dak. 188/G1
Sheyenne (riv.), N. Dak. 282/O6
Sheykh Sho'eyb (isl.), Iran 66/H7
Shiant (isls.), Scotland 15/B3
Shiant (sound), Scotland 15/B3
Shiawassee (co.), Mich. 250/E6
Shiawassee (riv.), Mich. 250/E5
Shibam, P.D.R. Yemen 59/E6
Shibata, Japan 81/J5
Shibetsu, Japan 81/M2
Shibin el Kom, Egypt 111/J3
Shibogama (lake), Ontario 175/C2
Shickley, Nebr. (68436) 264/G4
Shickshinny, Pa. (18655) 294/K3
Shideler, Ind. (†47338) 227/G4
Shidler, Okla. (74652) 288/N1
Shiel, Loch (lake), Scotland 10/D2
Shiel, Loch (lake), Scotland 15/C4
Shieldaig, Scotland 15/C3
Shields, Kansas (67874) 232/B3
Shields (riv.), Mont. 262/F4
Shields, N. Dak. (58569) 282/H7
Shieldsville, Minn. (†55021) 255/E6
Shifnal, England 13/E5
Shiga (pref.), Japan 81/J7
Shigatse (Xigazê), China 77/C6
Shigawake, Québec 172/D2
Shihezi (Shihhotzu), China 77/C3
Shihr, P.D.R. Yemen 59/E7
Shijak, Albania 45/D5
Shijiazhuang (Shihkiachwang), China 77/J4
Shijiazhuang, China 54/N6
Shikarpur, Pakistan 68/B3
Shikarpur, Pakistan 59/J4
Shikoku, Japan 54/P6
Shikoku (isl.), Japan 2/R4
Shikoku (isl.), Japan 81/F7
Shikotan (isl.), Japan 81/N2
Shikotsu (lake), Japan 81/K2
Shikotsu-Toya National Park, Japan 81/K2
Shilbottle, England 13/F2
Shildon, England 13/F3
Shilka (riv.), U.S.S.R. 54/N4
Shilka, U.S.S.R. 48/M4
Shillelagh, Ireland 17/J6
Shillelagh, Ireland 10/C4
Shillington, Pa. (19607) 294/K5
Shillong, India 68/G3
Shilo, Manitoba 179/C5
Shiloh, Ala. (†35979) 195/G2
Shiloh, Ala. (†36754) 195/C6
Shiloh, Georgia (31826) 217/C5
Shiloh, Ill. (†62220) 222/B3
Shiloh, N.J. (08353) 273/C5
Shiloh, Ohio (44878) 284/E4
Shiloh, S.C. (†29080) 296/G4
Shiloh, Tenn. (38376) 237/E10
Shiloh, Va. (22549) 307/O4
Shiloh Nat'l Mil. Park, Tenn. 237/E10
Shilovo, U.S.S.R. 52/F4
Shimabara, Japan 81/E7
Shimamoto, Japan 81/J7
Shimane (pref.), Japan 81/F6
Shimane (pen.), Japan 81/F6
Shimanovsk, U.S.S.R. 48/N4
Shimbir Berris (mt.), Somalia 115/J1
Shimizu, Japan 81/J6
Shimoda, Japan 81/J6
Shimoga, India 68/D6
Shimokita (pen.), Japan 81/K3
Shimonoseki, Japan 81/E6
Shin (falls), Scotland 15/D3
Shin, Loch (lake), Scotland 15/D2
Shin, Loch (lake), Scotland 10/D1
Shin (riv.), Scotland 15/D3
Shinano (riv.), Japan 81/J5
Shinas, Oman 59/G5
Shindand, Afghanistan 59/H3
Shindand, Afghanistan 68/A2
Shindler, S. Dak. (†57101) 298/R7
Shiner, Texas (77984) 303/G8
Shingbwiyang, Burma 72/B1
Shinglehouse, Pa. (16748) 294/F2
Shingler, Georgia (†31781) 217/E7
Shingle Springs, Calif. (95682) 204/C8
Shingleton, Mich. (49884) 250/C2
Shingu, Japan 81/H7
Shining Tree, Ontario 177/J5
Shinjo, Japan 81/K4
Shinko (riv.), Cent. Afr. Rep. 115/D2
Shinnecock Ind. Res., N.Y. 276/R9
Shinnston, W. Va. (26431) 312/F4
Shin Pond, Maine (†04765) 243/F3
Shinrone, Ireland 17/F5
Shinyanga (reg.), Tanzania 115/F4
Shinyanga, Tanzania 115/F4
Shinyanga, Tanzania 102/F5
Shiocton, Wis. (54170) 317/K7
Shiogama, Japan 81/K4
Shiono (cape), Japan 81/H7
Ship (isl.), Miss. 256/G10
Ship Bottom, N.J. (08008) 273/E4
Ship Harbour, Newf. 166/D2
Ship Harbour, Nova Scotia 168/F4
Shiping, China 77/F7
Shipki (pass), India 68/D2
Shipman, Ill. (62685) 222/C4
Shipman, Sask. 181/F2
Shipman, Va. (22971) 307/L5
Shippan (pt.), Conn. 210/A4
Shippegan, New Bruns. 170/F1
Shippegan (gully), New Bruns. 170/F1
Shippegan (bay), New Bruns. 170/E1
Shippensburg, Pa. (17257) 294/H5
Shippenville, Pa. (16254) 294/D3
Shiprock, N. Mex. (87420) 274/A2
Ship Rock (peak), N. Mex. 274/A2
Shipshaw (riv.), Québec 172/F1
Shipshewana, Ind. (46565) 227/F1
Ship Shoal (isl.), Va. 307/S6
Shipston on Stour, England 13/F5
Shiqian, China 77/G6
Shiqma (riv.), Israel 65/B4
Shiquan, China 77/G5
Shiquanhe, China 77/A5
Shiragami (cape), Japan 81/J3
Shirakawa, Japan 81/K5
Shirane (mt.), Japan 81/H6
Shirane (mt.), Japan 81/J5
Shiranuka, Japan 81/M2
Shiraz, Iran 54/G7
Shiraz, Iran 66/H6
Shiraz, Iran 59/F4
Shire (riv.), Malawi 115/G7
Shire (riv.), Mozambique 118/E3
Shiretoko (cape), Japan 81/M1
Shiriya (cape), Japan 81/K3
Shir Kuh (mt.), Iran 59/F3
Shir Kuh (mt.), Iran 66/J5
Shirland, Ill. (61079) 222/D1
Shirley, Ark. (72153) 202/F2
Shirley, Ill. (61772) 222/E3
Shirley, Ind. (47384) 227/F5
Shirley, Mass. (01464) 249/H2
Shirley○, Mass. (01464) 249/H2
Shirley, Mo. (†63664) 261/L7
Shirley, W. Va. (26434) 312/E4
Shirley (basin), Wyo. 319/F3
Shirley Basin, Wyo. (82615) 319/F3
Shirley Center, Mass. (01465) 249/H2
Shirley City (Woodburn), Ind. (†46797) 227/H2
Shirley Mills, Maine (04485) 243/D5
Shirley Mills○, Maine (04485) 243/D5
Shirleysburg, Pa. (17260) 294/G5
Shiro, Texas (77876) 303/J7
Shiroishi, Japan 81/K4
Shirvan, Iran 59/G2
Shirvan, Iran 66/K2
Shirvan (riv.), Iran 66/E3
Shishaldin (vol.), Alaska 196/E4
Shishmaref, Alaska (99772) 196/E1
Shithatha, Iraq 59/D3
Shithatha, Iraq 66/C4
Shitike (creek), Oreg. 291/F3
Shiukwan (Shaoyuan), China 77/H7
Shively, Calif. (†95565) 204/B3
Shively, Ky. (40216) 237/K4
Shivers, Miss. (39164) 256/E7
Shivpuri, India 68/D3
Shivwits (plat.), Ariz. 198/B2
Shivwits Ind. Res., Utah 304/A6
Shiyan, China 77/H5
Shizuishan (Shihsuishan), China 77/G4
Shizunai, Japan 81/L2
Shizuoka (pref.), Japan 81/H6
Shizuoka, Japan 54/P6
Shizuoka, Japan 81/H6
Shkodër, Albania 7/F4
Shkodër, Albania 45/D5
Shoa (prov.), Ethiopia 111/G6
Shoal (riv.), Fla. 212/C6
Shoal (creek), Ill. 222/D5
Shoal (lake), Manitoba 179/B4
Shoal (lake), Manitoba 179/G5
Shoal (riv.), Manitoba 179/B2
Shoal (bay), Newf. 166/D2
Shoal (bay), Nova Scotia 168/F4
Shoal (creek), Tenn. 237/F10
Shoal (creek), Utah 304/A6
Shoal Branch, Wading (riv.), N.J. 273/D4
Shoal Cove, Newf. 166/C3
Shoal Harbour, Newf. 166/C2
Shoalhaven (riv.), N.S. Wales 97/E4
Shoal Lake, Manitoba 179/B4
Shoals, Ind. (47581) 227/D7
Shoals (isls.), N.H. 268/F6
Shoals, N.C. (†27043) 281/J2
Shoals, W. Va. (25562) 312/B6
Shoals Junction, S.C. (29638) 296/C3
Shoalwater (bay), Queensland 88/J4
Shoalwater (cape), Wash. 310/A4
Shoalwater Ind. Res., Wash. 310/B4
Shobara, Japan 81/F6
Shobonier, Ill. (62885) 222/D5
Shock, W. Va. (26638) 312/D5
Shoemakersville, Pa. (19555) 294/K4
Shoffner, Ark. (†72112) 202/H2
Shohola, Pa. (18458) 294/N3
Sholapur, India 54/J8
Sholapur, India 68/D5
Sholes, Nebr. (†68771) 264/G2
Shona (isl.), Scotland 15/C4
Shongaloo, La. (71072) 238/D1
Shonkin, Mont. (59476) 262/F3
Shonto, Ariz. (86054) 198/E2
Shonto (plat.), Ariz. 198/E2
Shook, Mo. (63963) 261/M8
Shooting Creek, N.C. (†28904) 281/B4
Shopiere, Wis. (†53525) 317/H10
Shop Springs, Tenn. (†37184) 237/J8
Shorapur, India 68/D5
Shoreacres, Br. Col. 184/J5
Shore Acres, N.J. (†08723) 273/E3
Shore Acres, Texas (†77571) 303/K2
Shoreham, Mich. (†49085) 250/C6
Shoreham, Minn. (†56501) 255/C4
Shoreham, N.Y. (11786) 276/P8
Shoreham○, Vt. (05770) 268/A4
Shoreham-by-Sea, England 13/G7
Shoreham-by-Sea, England 10/F5
Shoreview, Minn. (†55112) 255/G5
Shorewood, Ill. (60435) 222/E2
Shorewood, Minn. (†55331) 255/F5
Shorewood, Wis. (53211) 317/M1
Shorewood Hills, Mich. (†49125) 250/C7
Shorewood Hills, Wis. (†53701) 317/G9
Short, Okla. (†72955) 288/S3
Short Beach, Conn. (†06405) 210/D3
Short Creek, Ohio (43989) 284/J5
Shortdale, Manitoba 179/A3
Shorter, Ala. (36075) 195/G6
Shorterville, Ala. (36373) 195/H7
Short Falls, N.H. (†03234) 268/E5
Short Hills, N.J. (07078) 273/E2
Shortland (isls.), Solomon Is. 86/D2
Shortleaf, Ala. (†36732) 195/C6
Shortsville, N.Y. (14548) 276/F5
Shoshone, Calif. (92384) 204/J8
Shoshone (co.), Idaho 220/B2
Shoshone, Idaho (83352) 220/D7
Shoshone (falls), Idaho 220/D7
Shoshone (mt.), Nev. 266/E6
Shoshone (mts.), Nev. 266/D3
Shoshone (range), Nev. 266/E2
Shoshone (lake), Wyo. 319/B1
Shoshone (riv.), Wyo. 319/D1
Shoshong, Botswana 118/D4
Shoshoni, Wyo. (82649) 319/D2
Shostka, U.S.S.R. 52/D4
Shotley, England 13/J6
Shotts, Scotland 15/C2
Shouldice, Alberta 182/D4
Shoultes, Wash. (†98270) 310/C2
Shouns, Tenn. (†37683) 237/T8
Shoup, Idaho (83469) 220/D4
Shoval, Israel 65/B5
Shovel Lake, Minn. (†55785) 255/E4
Showak, Sudan 111/G5
Showell, Md. (21862) 245/T7
Show Low, Ariz. (85901) 198/F4
Shoyna, U.S.S.R. 52/F1
Shpola, U.S.S.R. 52/D5
Shreve, Ohio (44676) 284/F4
Shreveport, La. 146/J6
Shreveport, La. 188/H4
Shreveport, La. (*71101) 238/C2
Shrewsbury, England 13/E5
Shrewsbury, England 10/E4
Shrewsbury○, Mass. (01545) 249/H3
Shrewsbury, Mo. (†63101) 261/P3
Shrewsbury, N.J. (07701) 273/E3
Shrewsbury, Pa. (17361) 294/J6
Shrewsbury○, Vt. (†05738) 268/B4
Shrule, Ireland 17/C4
Shuangcheng, China 77/L2
Shuangliao, China 77/K3
Shuangyashan, China 77/M2
Shubenacadie, Nova Scotia 168/E3
Shubenacadie (lake), Nova Scotia 168/E4
Shubenacadie (riv.), Nova Scotia 168/E3
Shubert, Nebr. (68437) 264/J4
Shubuta, Miss. (39360) 256/G7
Shue (creek), S. Dak. 298/N5
Shu'eib, Wadi (dry riv.), Jordan 65/D4
Shueyville, Iowa (†52401) 229/K5
Shu'fat, West Bank 65/C4
Shuicheng, China 77/G6
Shuksan (mt.), Wash. 310/D2
Shulan, China 77/L3
Shulerville, S.C. (29480) 296/H5
Shullsburg, Wis. (53586) 317/F10
Shumagin (isls.), Alaska 196/G4
Shumen, Bulgaria 45/H4
Shumerlya, U.S.S.R. 52/G3
Shumway, Ill. (62461) 222/E4
Shunat Nimrin, Jordan 65/D4
Shunchang, China 77/J6
Shungnak, Alaska (99773) 196/G1
Shungopavy (Shongopovi), Ariz. (†86043)198/E3
Shunk, Pa. (17768) 294/J2
Shunock (riv.), Conn. 210/H3
Shuo Xian, China 77/H4
Shuqaiq, Saudi Arabia 59/D6
Shuqra, P.D.R. Yemen 59/E7
Shuqualak, Miss. (39361) 256/G5
Shur (riv.), Iran 66/J7
Shusf, Iran 66/L5
Shush, Iran 66/F4
Shushan, N.Y. (12873) 276/O4
Shushenskoye, U.S.S.R. 48/K4
Shushtar, Iran 66/F4
Shushtar, Iran 59/E3
Shuswap (lake), Br. Col. 162/E5
Shuswap (lake), Br. Col. 184/H4
Shutesbury○, Mass. (01072) 249/E3
Shuttle Meadow (res.), Conn. 210/D2
Shutty Bench, Br. Col. 184/J5
Shuweika, West Bank 65/C3
Shuya, U.S.S.R. 52/F3
Shuyak (isl.), Alaska 196/H3
Shwebo, Burma 72/B2
Shwegyin, Burma 72/C3
Shweli (riv.), Burma 72/C2
Shwenyaung, Burma 72/C2
Shyok, India 68/D2
Si (riv.), China 54/N7
Siahan (mts.), Pakistan 59/H4
Siahan (range), Pakistan 68/A3
Siah Kuh (mt.), Iran 66/L3
Siak (riv.), Indonesia 85/C5
Siaksriinderapura, Indonesia 85/C5
Siakwan (Xiaguan), China 77/E6
Sialkot, Pakistan 68/C2
Sialkot, Pakistan 59/K3
Siam (Thailand) (gulf), Thailand 72/D5
Sian (Xi'an), China 77/G5
Siangtan (Xiangtan), China 77/H5
Siangtan (Xiangtan), China 77/H6
Siapa (riv.), Venezuela 124/E7
Siargao (isl.), Philippines 85/H4
Siargao (isl.), Philippines 82/F6
Siasconset, Mass. (02564) 249/P7
Siasi, Philippines 82/C8
Siasi (isl.), Philippines 82/C8
Siátista, Greece 45/E5
Siaton, Philippines 82/D6
Siaton (pt.), Philippines 82/D6
Siau (isl.), Indonesia 85/H5
Šiauliai, U.S.S.R. 7/G3
Šiauliai, U.S.S.R. 53/B3
Šiauliai, U.S.S.R. 52/B3
Šiauliai, U.S.S.R. 48/C4
Sib, Iran 66/N7
Sibalom, Philippines 82/C5
Sibanicú, Cuba 158/G3
Sibay (isl.), Philippines 82/C5
Sibay, U.S.S.R. 52/J4
Sibbald, Alberta 182/E4
Šibenik, Yugoslavia 45/C4
Siberia, Ind. (47582) 227/D8
Siberia (reg.), U.S.S.R. 4/C2
Siberia (reg.), U.S.S.R. 2/P2
Siberia (reg.), U.S.S.R. 54/M4
Siberia (reg.), U.S.S.R. 48/M3
Sibert, Ky. (†40962) 237/O6
Siberut (isl.), Indonesia 54/L10
Siberut (isl.), Indonesia 85/B6
Siberut (str.), Indonesia 85/B6
Sibi, Pakistan 68/B3
Sibi, Pakistan 59/J4
Sibiti, Congo 115/B4
Sibiu, Romania 7/G4
Sibiu, Romania 45/G3
Sibley, Ill. (61773) 222/E3
Sibley, Iowa (51249) 229/B2
Sibley, La. (71073) 238/D1
Sibley (co.), Minn. 255/D6
Sibley, Miss. (39165) 256/B8
Sibley, Mo. (64088) 261/S5
Sibley, N. Dak. (†58429) 282/P5
Sibley Prov. Park, Ontario 175/C3
Sibley Prov. Park, Ontario 177/H5
Sibolga, Indonesia 85/B5
Siboney, Cuba 158/J4
Sibsagar, India 68/H3
Sibu, Malaysia 85/E5
Sibu, Malaysia 54/N9
Sibube, C. Rica 154/F6
Sibuco, Philippines 82/C7
Sibuguey (bay), Philippines 82/D7
Sibundoy, Colombia 126/B7
Sibut, Cent. Afr. Rep. 115/C2
Sibutu (passage), Philippines 85/F4
Sibutu (passage), Philippines 82/B8
Sibutu Group (isls.), Philippines 82/B8
Sibuyan (isl.), Philippines 85/G3
Sibuyan (isl.), Philippines 82/D4
Sibuyan (sea), Philippines 82/D4
Sibuyan (sea), Philippines 85/G3
Sicamous, Br. Col. 184/H5
Sicasica, Bolivia 136/B5
Siccus (riv.), S. Australia 88/F6
Sichuan (Szechwan) (prov.), China 77/F5
Sicily (reg.), Italy 34/D6
Sicily (isl.), Italy 7/F5
Sicily (isl.), Italy 34/E6
Sicily (str.), Italy 34/D6
Sicily Island, La. (71368) 238/G3
Sicklerville, N.J. (08081) 273/D4
Sico (riv.), Honduras 154/E3
Sicuani, Peru 128/G10
Šid, Yugoslavia 45/D3
Sidamo (prov.), Ethiopia 111/G7
Siddipet, India 68/D5
Sideby, Finland 18/M5
Side Lake, Minn. (55781) 255/E3
Sidell, Ill. (61876) 222/F4
Siderno, Italy 34/F5
Sidewood, Sask. 181/C5
Sidheros (cape), Greece 45/H8
Sidhi, India 68/E4
Sidhirókastron, Greece 45/F5
Sidhpur, India 68/C4
Sidi Barrani, Egypt 111/E1
Sidi Barrani, Egypt 59/A3
Sidi Bel-Abbes, Algeria 106/D1
Sidi Bel Abbes, Algeria 102/C1
Sidi Kacem, Morocco 106/C2
Siding Springs, N.S. Wales 97/E2
Sidlaw (hills), Scotland 15/E4
Sidley (mt.) 5/B12
Sidmouth, England 13/D7
Sidmouth, England 10/E5
Sidmouth (cape), Queensland 95/C2
Sidnaw, Mich. (49961) 250/G2
Sidney, Ark. (72577) 202/G1
Sidney, Br. Col. 184/K3
Sidney, Ill. (61877) 222/E3
Sidney, Ind. (46566) 227/F2
Sidney, Iowa (51652) 229/B7
Sidney○, Maine (†04330) 243/D7
Sidney, Manitoba 179/C5
Sidney, Mich. (48885) 250/D5
Sidney, Mont. (59270) 262/M3
Sidney, Nebr. (69162) 264/B3
Sidney, N.Y. (13838) 276/K6
Sidney, Ohio (45365) 284/B5
Sidney Center, N.Y. (13839) 276/K6
Sidney Lanier (lake), Georgia 217/D2
Sidoharjo, Indonesia 85/K2
Sidon, Ark. (†72137) 202/G3
Sidon (Saida), Lebanon 63/F6
Sidon, Miss. (38954) 256/D4
Sidonia, Tenn. (†38255) 237/D8
Sidra (gulf) 102/D1
Sidra (gulf), Libya 111/C1
Siedlce (prov.), Poland 47/F2
Siedlce, Poland 47/F2
Siegas, New Bruns. 170/C1
Siegburg, W. Germany 22/B3
Siegen, W. Germany 22/C3
Siemianowice Śląskie, Poland 47/B4
Siemiatycze, Poland 47/F2
Siempang, Cambodia 72/E4
Siemreab, Cambodia 72/D4
Siena (prov.), Italy 34/C3
Siena, Italy 34/C3
Sienyang (Xianyang), China 77/G5
Sieper, La. (71472) 238/E4
Sieradz (prov.), Poland 47/D3

Songhua Hu 449

Skull Valley Ind. Res., Utah 304/B3
Skuna (riv.), Miss. 256/F2
Skungamaug (riv.), Conn. 210/F1
Skunk (riv.), Iowa 229/K6
Skuteč, Czech. 41/D2
Skutskär, Sweden 18/K6
Skwentna, Alaska (99667) 196/B1
Skwentna (riv.), Alaska 196/A1
Skwierzyna, Poland 47/B2
Skye, Isle of (isl.), Scotland 15/B3
Skye (isl.), Scotland 10/C2
Skykomish, Wash. (98288) 310/D3
Skykomish (riv.), Wash. 310/D3
Skyland, N.C. (28776) 281/D4
Skylight (mt.), N.Y. 276/M2
Skyline, Minn. (†56001) 255/D6
Skyring (bay), Chile 138/E10
Skytop, Pa. (18357) 294/M3
Sky Valley, Georgia (30525) 217/F1
Slab Fork, W. Va. (25920) 312/D7
Slade, Ky. (40376) 237/O5
Sládečkovce, Czech. 41/D2
Slag (bay), Neth. Ant. 161/D8
Slagelse, Denmark 21/E7
Slagelse, Denmark 18/G9
Slagle, La. (71475) 238/D4
Slakow, Poland 47/B4
Slamannan, Scotland 15/C2
Slamet (mt.), Indonesia 85/J2
Slana, Alaska 196/K2
Slaná (riv.), Czech. 41/F2
Slane, Ireland 17/H4
Slanesville, W. Va. (25444) 312/K4
Slaney (riv.), Ireland 17/H7
Slangerup, Denmark 21/E6
Slangkop (pt.), S. Africa 118/E7
Slănic, Romania 45/G3
Slantsy, U.S.S.R. 52/C3
Slaný, Czech. 41/C1
Slate (mt.), Ariz. 198/D3
Slate (riv.), Colo. 208/E5
Slate (creek), Idaho 220/B4
Slate (isls.), Ontario 175/C3
Slate (riv.), Va. 307/L5
Slate, W. Va. (†26143) 312/D4
Slate (creek), Wyo. 319/C3
Slatedale, Pa. (18079) 294/L4
Slater, Colo. (81653) 208/E1
Slater, Iowa (50244) 229/F5
Slater, Mo. (65349) 261/G4
Slater, Wyo. (82201) 319/H4
Slater-Marietta, S.C. (29683) 296/C1
Slatersville, R.I. (02876) 249/H4
Slate Run, Pa. (17769) 294/H3
Slaterville Springs, N.Y. (14881) 276/H6
Slate Spring, Miss. (38955) 256/F3
Slatina, Romania 45/G3
Slatington, Pa. (18080) 294/L4
Slaton, Texas (79364) 303/C4
Slaughter, La. (70777) 238/H5
Slaughter Beach, Del. (†19963) 245/S5
Slaughters, Ky. (42456) 237/F6
Slaughterville, Okla. (†73051) 288/M4
Slave (riv.) 162/E3
Slave (riv.), Alberta 182/C5
Slave (riv.), Canada 146/G3
Slave (riv.), N.W. Terrs. 187/G3
Slave Coast (reg.), Benin 106/E7
Slave Coast (reg.), Nigeria 106/E7
Slave Coast (reg.), Togo 106/E7
Slave Lake, Alberta 182/C2
Slavgorod, U.S.S.R. 48/H4
Slavkov, Czech. 41/D2
Slavonia (reg.), Yugoslavia 45/C3
Slavonska Požega, Yugoslavia 45/C3
Slavonski Brod, Yugoslavia 45/D3
Slavuta, U.S.S.R. 52/C4
Slavyansk, U.S.S.R. 52/E5
Slavyansk-na-Kubani, U.S.S.R. 52/E5
Sławno, Poland 47/C1
Slayden, Miss. (†38642) 256/F1
Slayden, Tenn. (37165) 237/G8
Slayton, Minn. (56172) 255/C7
Sleaford, England 13/G5
Sleaford, England 10/F4
Sleat (dist.), Scotland 15/C3
Sleat (pt.), Scotland 15/B4
Sleat (sound), Scotland 15/C3
Sledge, Miss. (38670) 256/D2
Sleeper, Mo. (†65536) 261/G7
Sleeping Bear Dunes Nat'l Lakeshore, Mich. 250/C4
Sleeping Deer (mt.), Idaho 220/D5
Sleepy Creek, W. Va. (†25411) 312/K3
Sleepy Eye, Minn. (56085) 255/D6
Sleepy Eye (creek), Minn. 255/C6
Sleepy Hollow, Ill. (†60118) 222/E1
Sleetmute, Alaska (99668) 196/G2
Sleeve (lake), Manitoba 179/E3
Slemish (mt.), N. Ireland 17/J2
Slemon (lake), Manitoba 179/G1
Slemp, Ky. (41763) 237/P6
Slick, Okla. (74071) 288/O3
Slickford, Ky. (†42633) 237/M7
Slickville, Pa. (15684) 294/C5
Slide (mt.), N.Y. 276/L6
Slidell, La. (70458) 238/L6
Sliedrecht, Netherlands 27/F5
Sliema, Malta 34/E7
Slieve Anierin (mt.), Ireland 17/F3
Slieve Aughty (mts.), Ireland 17/D5
Slieve Beagh (mt.), N. Ireland 17/G3
Slieve Bernagh (mt.), Ireland 17/D6
Slieve Bloom (mts.), Ireland 17/F5
Slieve Callan (mt.), Ireland 17/C6
Slieve Car (mt.), Ireland 17/B3
Slieve Donard (mt.), N. Ireland 10/D3
Slieve Donard (mt.), N. Ireland 17/K3
Slieve Elva (mt.), Ireland 17/C5
Slievefelim (mts.), Ireland 17/E6
Slieve Gamph (mts.), Ireland 17/D3
Slieve Gullion (mt.), N. Ireland 17/J3
Slieve League (mt.), Ireland 17/D2
Slieve Mishkish (mts.), Ireland 17/B8
Slievenaman (mt.), Ireland 17/F7
Sligo (co.), Ireland 17/D3
Sligo, Ireland 17/E3
Sligo, Ireland 10/B3
Sligo (bay), Ireland 10/B3
Sligo (bay), Ireland 17/D3
Sligo, La. (†71037) 238/C2
Sligo, Pa. (16255) 294/C3
Slinger, Wis. (53086) 317/K9
Slipper (isl.), N. Zealand 100/F2
Slippery Rock, Pa. (16057) 294/B3
Slite, Sweden 18/L8
Sliven, Bulgaria 45/H4
Sliven, Bulgaria 7/G4
Sloan, Iowa (51055) 229/A4
Sloan, Nev. (†89114) 266/F7
Sloan, N.Y. (†14201) 276/C5
Sloans Valley, Ky. (42555) 237/N7
Sloat, Calif. (†96103) 204/E4
Sloatsburg, N.Y. (10974) 276/M8
Slobodskoy, U.S.S.R. 48/E4
Slobodskoy, U.S.S.R. 52/H3
Slobozia, Romania 45/H3
Slocan, Br. Col. 184/J5
Slocan (lake), Br. Col. 184/J5
Slocan Park, Br. Col. 184/J5
Slochteren, Netherlands 27/K2
Slocomb, Ala. (36375) 195/G8
Slocum, R.I. (02877) 249/H6
Slocum, Texas (†75839) 303/J6
Slonim, U.S.S.R. 52/B4
Slope (co.), N. Dak. 282/C7
Slot, The (chan.), Solomon Is. 86/D3
Sloten, Friesland, Netherlands 27/H3
Sloten, North Holland, Netherlands 27/B5
Sloterdijk, Netherlands 27/B4
Slotermeer (lake), Netherlands 27/H3
Slough, England 13/G8
Sloughhouse, Calif. (95683) 204/C8
Slovak Socialist Rep., Czech. 41/E2
Slovenia (rep.), Yugoslavia 45/B2
Slovenské Rudohorie (mts.), Czech. 41/E2
Słubice, Poland 47/B2
Sluis, Netherlands 27/C6
Słupca, Poland 47/D2
Słupia (riv.), Poland 47/C1
Słupsk (prov.), Poland 47/C1
Słupsk, Poland 47/C1
Słupsk, Poland 7/F3
Slutsk, U.S.S.R. 52/C4
Slyne (head), Ireland 10/A4
Slyne (head), Ireland 17/A5
Slyudyanka, U.S.S.R. 48/L4
Smackover, Ark. (71762) 202/E7
Smale, Ark. (†72021) 202/H4
Small, Idaho (†83423) 220/F5
Small (cape), Maine 243/D8
Small Isles (isls.), Scotland 15/B4
Small Point, Maine (04567) 243/D8
Smallwood (res.), Newf. 166/B3
Smallwood (res.), Newf. 146/M4
Smallwood (res.), Newf. 162/K5
Smarr, Georgia (31086) 217/E5
Smarts (mt.), N.H. 268/C4
Smartt, Tenn. (37378) 237/K9
Smartville, Calif. (95977) 204/D4
Smeaton, Sask. 181/G2
Smederevo, Yugoslavia 45/E3
Smederevska Palanka, Yugoslavia 45/E3
Smedjebacken, Sweden 18/J6
Smela, U.S.S.R. 52/D5
Smelterville, Idaho (83868) 220/B2
Smerwick (harb.), Ireland 17/A7
Smethport, Pa. (16749) 294/F2
Smicksburg, Pa. (16256) 294/D4
Smilax, Ky. (41764) 237/P6
Smilde, Netherlands 27/K3
Smiley, Sask. 181/B4
Smiley, Texas (78159) 303/G8
Smiltene, U.S.S.R. 53/C2
Smith (bay), Alaska 196/H1
Smith, Alberta 182/D2
Smith (sound), Br. Col. 184/C4
Smith (riv.), Calif. 204/A2
Smith (creek), Idaho 220/B1
Smith (co.), Kansas 232/D2
Smith (isl.), Md. 245/O8
Smith (co.), Miss. 256/E6
Smith (riv.), Mont. 262/E3
Smith, Nev. (89430) 266/B4
Smith (sound), Newf. 166/D2
Smith (isl.), N.C. 281/O7
Smith (basin), N.W.T. 162/N3
Smith (cape), N.W.T. 162/H3
Smith (bay), N.W. Terrs. 187/L2
Smith (cape), N.W. Terrs. 187/L3
Smith (sound), N.W. Terrs. 187/L2
Smith (cape), Ontario 177/C2
Smith (riv.), Oreg. 291/D4
Smith (creek), S. Dak. 298/L6
Smith (co.), Tenn. 237/J8
Smith (co.), Texas 303/J5
Smith (isl.), Va. 307/S6
Smith (riv.), Va. 307/J7
Smith Arm (inlet), N.W. Terrs. 187/F3
Smithboro, Ill. (62284) 222/D5
Smithburg, N.J. (†07728) 273/E3
Smithburg, W. Va. (26436) 312/E4
Smith Center, Kansas (66967) 232/D2
Smith Creek (valley), Nev. 266/D3
Smith Creek, W. Va. (†26807) 312/H5
Smithdale, Miss. (39664) 256/C8
Smithers, Br. Col. 146/F4
Smithers, Br. Col. 162/D5
Smithers, Br. Col. 184/D3
Smithers, W. Va. (25186) 312/D6
Smithfield, Ill. (61477) 222/C3
Smithfield, Ky. (40068) 237/L4
Smithfield○, Maine (04978) 243/D6
Smithfield, Nebr. (68976) 264/E4
Smithfield, N.C. (27577) 281/N3
Smithfield, Ohio (43948) 284/J5
Smithfield, Ontario 177/G3
Smithfield, Pa. (15478) 294/C6
Smithfield, Texas (†76180) 303/F2
Smithfield, Utah (84335) 304/C2
Smithfield, Va. (23430) 307/P7
Smithfield, W. Va. (26437) 312/E4
Smith Hill, Manitoba 179/C5
Smithland, Iowa (51056) 229/B4
Smithland, Ky. (42081) 237/E6
Smithmill, Pa. (16680) 294/F4
Smith Mills, Ky. (42457) 237/F5
Smith Mountain (lake), Va. 307/J6
Smithonia, Georgia (†30628) 217/F2
Smithport (lake), La. 238/C2
Smith River, Calif. (95567) 204/A2
Smiths, Ala. (36877) 195/H5
Smithsburg, Md. (21783) 245/H2
Smiths Cove, Nova Scotia 168/C4
Smiths Creek, Mich. (48074) 250/G6
Smiths Creek, New Bruns. 170/E3
Smiths Falls, Ontario 177/H3
Smiths Ferry, Idaho (†83611) 220/C5
Smiths Fork (riv.), Wyo. 319/B3
Smiths Grove, Ky. (42171) 237/J6
Smithshire, Ill. (61478) 222/C3
Smiths Station, Miss. (†39066) 256/C6
Smithton, Ark. (†71743) 202/D6
Smithton, Ill. (62285) 222/C5
Smithton, Mo. (65350) 261/F5
Smithton, Pa. (15479) 294/C5
Smithton, Tasmania 99/A2
Smithton, Tasmania 88/H8
Smith Town, Ky. (†42647) 237/M7
Smithtown, N.H. (†03874) 268/F6
Smithtown, N.Y. (11787) 276/O9
Smithtown-Gladstone, N.S. Wales 97/G2
Smith Valley, Ind. (†46142) 227/E5
Smithville, Ark. (72466) 202/H1
Smithville, Georgia (31787) 217/D7
Smithville, Ind. (47458) 227/D6
Smithville, Miss. (38870) 256/H2
Smithville, Mo. (64089) 261/D4
Smithville, N.J. (†08060) 273/D4
Smithville, N.J. (08201) 273/E5
Smithville, Ohio (44677) 284/G4
Smithville, Okla. (74957) 288/S6
Smithville, Ontario 177/E4
Smithville, Tenn. (37166) 237/K9
Smithville, Texas (78957) 303/G7
Smithville, W. Va. (26178) 312/D4
Smithville Flats, N.Y. (13841) 276/J6
Smithwick, S. Dak. (57782) 298/C7
Smoaks, S.C. (29481) 296/F5
Smoke Bend, La. (†70346) 238/K3
Smoke Creek (des.), Nev. 266/B2
Smoke Hole, W. Va. (†26866) 312/H5
Smokey Burn, Sask. 181/H2
Smoky (riv.), Alberta 182/A2
Smoky (riv.), Alta. 162/E5
Smoky (mts.), Idaho 220/D6
Smoky (cape), N.S. Wales 97/G2
Smoky (lake), N. Dak. 282/K3
Smoky (cape), Nova Scotia 168/H2
Smoky Bay, S. Australia 88/E6
Smoky Bay, S. Australia 94/D5
Smoky Hill (riv.) 188/G3
Smoky Hill (riv.), Colo. 208/P5
Smoky Hill, North Fork (riv.), Kansas 232/A2
Smoky Hill (riv.), Kansas 232/C3
Smoky Junction, Tenn. (†37827) 237/N8
Smoky Lake, Alberta 182/D2
Smøla (isl.), Norway 18/E5
Smolan, Kansas (67479) 232/E3
Smolensk, U.S.S.R. 7/H3
Smolensk, U.S.S.R. 48/D4
Smolensk, U.S.S.R. 52/D4
Smolyan, Bulgaria 45/G5
Smoot, W. Va. (24977) 312/E7
Smoot, Wyo. (83126) 319/B3
Smooth Rock Falls, Ontario 177/J5
Smooth Rock Falls, Ontario 175/D3
Smugglers Notch (pass), Vt. 268/B2
Smuts, Sask. 181/F3
Smyadovo, Bulgaria 45/H4
Smyer, Ala. (†36727) 195/B7
Smyrna, Del. (19977) 245/R3
Smyrna (res.), Del. 245/R3
Smyrna, Georgia (30080) 217/K1
Smyrna, Mich. (48887) 250/D5
Smyrna, N.Y. (13464) 276/J5
Smyrna, N.C. (28579) 281/R5
Smyrna, S.C. (29743) 296/E1
Smyrna, Tenn. (37167) 237/H9
Smyrna (Izmir), Turkey 63/B3
Smyrna, Wash. (†99357) 310/F4
Smyrna Mills, Maine (04780) 243/G3
Smyrna Mills○, Maine (04780) 243/G3
Smyth (co.), Va. 307/E7
Snaefell (mt.), I. of Man 13/C3
Snaefell (mt.), I. of Man 10/D3
Snake (riv.) 188/C1
Snake (riv.), Idaho 220/A3
Snake (riv.), Minn. 255/A2
Snake (riv.), Minn. 255/E4
Snake (riv.), Nebr. 264/C2
Snake (mts.), Nev. 266/F1
Snake (range), Nev. 266/G3
Snake (riv.), Oreg. 291/K3
Snake (creek), S. Dak. 298/F4
Snake (creek), S. Dak. 298/F5
Snake (creek), S. Dak. 298/M3
Snake (riv.), U.S. 146/G5
Snake (isl.), Victoria 97/D6
Snake (riv.), Wash. 310/G4
Snake (riv.), Wyo. 319/B2
Snake Creek (canal), Fla. 212/B4
Snake Indian (riv.), Alberta 182/A3
Snake River (plain), Idaho 220/D7
Snake River (range), Idaho 220/G6
Snake River, Wash. (†99301) 310/G4
Snare (riv.), N.W. Terrs. 187/G3
Snare Lake, N.W. Terrs. 187/G3
Snares, The (isls.), N. Zealand 100/A7
Snåsa, Norway 18/H4
Snåsavatn (lake), Norway 18/H4
Snead, Ala. (35952) 195/F2
Sneads, Fla. (32460) 212/B1
Sneads Ferry, N.C. (28460) 281/P5
Snedsted, Denmark 21/B4
Sneedville, Tenn. (37869) 237/P7
Sneek, Netherlands 27/H2
Sneekermeer (lake), Netherlands 27/H2
Sneem, Ireland 17/B8
Sneeuwkop (mt.), S. Africa 118/F6
Sneffels (mt.), Colo. 208/D7
Snegamook (lake), Newf. 166/B3
Snell, Va. (22553) 307/N4
Snelling, Calif. (95369) 204/E6
Snelling, S.C. (†29812) 296/E5
Snellville, Georgia (30278) 217/D3
Snezhnogorsk, U.S.S.R. 48/J3
Śniardwy, Jezioro (lake), Poland 47/E2
Sniečkus, U.S.S.R. 53/D3
Snina, Czech. 41/G2
Snipe (lake), Alberta 182/B2
Snipe Lake, Sask. 181/B4
Snizort, Loch (inlet), Scotland 15/B3
Snohomish (co.), Wash. 310/D2
Snohomish, Wash. (98290) 310/D3
Snohomish (riv.), Wash. 310/C3
Snoqualmie, Wash. (†98065) 310/D3
Snoqualmie (pass), Wash. 310/D3
Snoqualmie (riv.), Wash. 310/D3
Snoqualmie Falls, Wash. (†98065) 310/D3
Snover, Mich. (48472) 250/G5
Snow, Okla. (74567) 288/R6
Snow (mt.), Vt. 268/B6
Snow (peak), Wash. 310/G2
Snowball, Ark. (†72650) 202/E2
Snowbird (lake), N.W. Terrs. 187/H3
Snow Camp, N.C. (27349) 281/L3
Snowden, N.C. (†27929) 281/S2
Snowden, Sask. 181/G2
Snowdon (mt.), Wales 13/D4
Snowdon (mt.), Wales 10/D4
Snowdonia Nat'l Park, Wales 13/D4
Snowdoun, Ala. (†36104) 195/F6
Snowdrift, N.W.T. 162/E3
Snowdrift, N.W. Terrs. 187/G3
Snowfield (peak), Wash. 310/D2
Snowflake, Ariz. (85937) 198/E4
Snowflake, Manitoba 179/D5
Snow Hill, Ala. (36778) 195/E7
Snow Hill, Ark. (†71751) 202/E7
Snow Hill, Md. (21863) 245/S8
Snow Hill, N.C. (28580) 281/O4
Snow Lake, Ark. (72379) 202/H5
Snow Lake, Man. 162/G5
Snow Lake, Manitoba 179/H3
Snowmass, Colo. (81654) 208/E4
Snowshoe (lake), Manitoba 179/G4
Snow Shoe, Pa. (16874) 294/G3
Snowtown, S. Australia 94/E5
Snowville, N.H. (†03849) 268/E4
Snowville, Utah (84336) 304/B2
Snow Water (lake), Nev. 266/G2
Snowy (mts.), N.S. Wales 97/E5
Snowy (riv.), N.S. Wales 97/E5
Snowy (riv.), Victoria 88/H7
Snug, Tasmania 99/D5
Snyder, Ark. (†71658) 202/G7
Snyder, Colo. (80750) 208/M2
Snyder, Mo. (†65286) 261/F3
Snyder, Nebr. (68664) 264/H3
Snyder, Okla. (73566) 288/J5
Snyder (co.), Pa. 294/H4
Snyder, Texas (79549) 303/D5
Snydertown, Pa. (17877) 294/J4
So (isl.), S. Korea 81/C6
Soalala, Madagascar 118/H3
Soalara, Madagascar 118/G4
Soanierana-Ivongo, Madagascar 118/H3
Soap (lake), Wash. 310/F3
Soap Lake, Wash. (98851) 310/F3
Soasiu, Indonesia 85/H5
Soatá, Colombia 126/D4
Soay (isl.), Scotland 15/A2
Soay (isl.), Scotland 15/B3
Sobat (riv.), Sudan 111/F6
Sober (isl.), Nova Scotia 168/F4
Soběslav, Czech. 41/C2
Sobieski, Minn. (†56345) 255/D5
Sobieski, Wis. (54171) 317/L6
Sobotka, Czech. 41/C1
Sobral, Brazil 120/E3
Sobral, Brazil 132/G3
Sobrance, Czech. 41/G2
Soca, Uruguay 145/C6
Sochaczew, Poland 47/E2
Soche (Shache), China 77/A4
Sochi, U.S.S.R. 7/H4
Sochi, U.S.S.R. 48/D5
Sochi, U.S.S.R. 52/E6
Social Circle, Georgia (30279) 217/E3
Society (isls.), Fr. Poly. 87/L7
Society Hill, Ala. (†36801) 195/H6
Society Hill, S.C. (29593) 296/H2
Socompa (vol.), Chile 138/B4
Socorro, Brazil 135/C3
Socorro, Colombia 126/D4
Socorro (isl.), Mexico 150/D7
Socorro, N. Mex. 188/E4
Socorro (co.), N. Mex. 274/C5
Socorro, N. Mex. (87801) 274/C4
Socotra (isl.), P.D.R. Yemen 54/G8
Socotra (isl.), P.D.R. Yemen 2/M5
Socotra (isl.), P.D.R. Yemen 59/F7
Socuéllamos, Spain 33/E3
Soda (lake), Calif. 204/K8
Soda (plains), India 68/D1
Soda, Jebel es (mts.), Libya 111/C2
Soda Creek, Br. Col. 184/F4
Sodankylä, Finland 18/P3
Soda Plains, Pakistan 68/D1
Soda Springs, Calif. (95728) 204/E4
Soda Springs, Idaho (83276) 220/G7
Sodaville, Oreg. (†97355) 291/E3
Soddu, Ethiopia 111/G6
Soddy-Daisy, Tenn. (37319) 237/L10
Söderhamn, Sweden 18/K6
Söderköping, Sweden 18/K7
Södermanland (co.), Sweden 18/K7
Södertälje, Sweden 18/G1
Sodiri, Sudan 111/E5
Sodus, Mich. (49126) 250/C6
Sodus, N.Y. (14551) 276/G4
Sodus Point, N.Y. (14555) 276/G4
Soe, Indonesia 85/G7
Soest, Netherlands 27/G4
Soest, W. Germany 22/C3
Soesterberg, Netherlands 27/G4
Soeurs (isl.), Québec 172/H4
Sofala (prov.), Mozambique 118/E3
Sofia (cap.), Bulgaria 7/G4
Sofia (cap.), Bulgaria 45/F4
Sofia (riv.), Madagascar 118/H3
Sofkee, Georgia (†31201) 217/E5
Soft Shell, Ky. (41853) 237/P6
Sogamoso, Colombia 126/D5
Sogamoso (riv.), Colombia 126/D4
Soğanlı (mts.), Turkey 63/H2
Soğanlı (riv.), Turkey 63/E2
Sognafjorden (fjord), Norway 18/D6
Sognefjorden (fjord), Norway 7/E2
Sogn og Fjordane (co.), Norway 18/E6
Sogod, Philippines 82/E5
Sogod (bay), Philippines 82/E5
Söğüt, Turkey 63/D3
Söğüt (lake), Turkey 63/D4
Sog Xian, China 77/D5
Soh, Iran 66/G4
Sohâg, Egypt 111/F2
Sohâg, Egypt 59/B4
Sohâg, Egypt 102/F2
Soham, N. Mex. (†87565) 274/D3
Sohar, Oman 59/G5
Söhüng, N. Korea 81/C4
Soignies, Belgium 27/D7
Sointula, Br. Col. 184/D5
Soissons, France 28/E3
Soka, Japan 81/O2
Sokch'o, S. Korea 81/D4
Söke, Turkey 63/B4
Söke, Turkey 59/A2
Sokna, Libya 111/C2
Sokodé, Togo 106/E7
Sokol, U.S.S.R. 52/F3
Sokol, U.S.S.R. 48/E4
Sokółka, Poland 47/F2
Sokolo, Mali 106/C6
Sokolov, Czech. 41/B1
Sokołów Podlaski, Poland 47/F2
Sokota, Ethiopia 111/G5
Sokoto (state), Nigeria 106/F6
Sokoto, Nigeria 102/C3
Sokoto, Nigeria 106/F6
Sokoto (riv.), Nigeria 106/F6
Sola, Cuba 158/G2
Solana Beach, Calif. (92075) 204/H11
Solander (isl.), N. Zealand 100/A7
Solano (co.), Calif. 204/D5
Solano (pt.), Colombia 126/B4
Solano, N. Mex. (87746) 274/E3
Solano, Philippines 82/C2
Solano, Venezuela 124/E6
Solbad Hall in Tirol, Austria 41/A3
Solca, Romania 45/G2
Soldado (pt.), P. Rico 161/G2
Soldier, Iowa (51572) 229/B5
Soldier, Kansas (66540) 232/G2
Soldier, Ky. (41173) 237/P4
Soldier Pond, Maine (04781) 243/F1
Soldiers Cove, Nova Scotia 168/H3
Soldiers Grove, Wis. (54655) 317/E9
Soldier Summit, Utah (†84601) 304/C4
Soldotna, Alaska (99669) 196/B1
Soledad, Argentina 143/F5
Soledad, Calif. (93960) 204/D7
Soledad, Colombia 126/C2
Soledad, Venezuela 124/G3
Soledad de Doblado, Mexico 150/Q2
Soledad Díez Gutiérrez, Mexico 150/J5
Soleduck (riv.), Wash. 310/A3
Solen, N. Dak. (58570) 282/J7
Solent (chan.), England 13/F7
Solentiname (isls.), Nicaragua 154/E5
Soleure (Solothurn) (canton), Switzerland 39/E2
Solgohachia, Ark. (72156) 202/E3
Solhan, Turkey 63/J3
Soligalich, U.S.S.R. 52/F3
Soligorsk, U.S.S.R. 52/C4
Solihull, England 13/F5
Solihull, England 10/G3
Solikamsk, U.S.S.R. 7/K3
Solikamsk, U.S.S.R. 48/F3
Solikamsk, U.S.S.R. 52/J3
Sol'-Iletsk, U.S.S.R. 52/J4
Solingen, W. Germany 22/B3
Solís, Uruguay 145/D5
Solís de Mataojo, Uruguay 145/D5
Solitary (isl.), N.S. Wales 97/G1
Sollefteå, Sweden 18/K5
Sollentuna, Sweden 18/H1
Sóller, Spain 33/H3
Søllested, Denmark 21/E8
Solna, Sweden 18/H1
Solo (Surakarta), Indonesia 85/J2
Solo, Mo. (65564) 261/J8
Sologne (reg.), France 28/E4
Solok, Indonesia 85/C6
Sololá, Guatemala 154/B3
Solomon (sea) 87/F6
Solomon, Alaska (†99762) 196/F2
Solomon, Ariz. (85551) 198/F6
Solomon, Kansas (67480) 232/E3
Solomon (riv.), Kansas 232/E2
Solomon (isls.), Pacific 87/F6
Solomon (isls.), Papua N.G. 86/C3
Solomon (sea), Papua N.G. 85/C7
Solomon (isls.), Solomon Is. 86/C3
Solomon (sea), Solomon Is. 86/D3
Solomon Islands 2/T6
SOLOMON ISLANDS 86/D2
Solomon Islands 87/G6
Solomons, Md. (20688) 245/N7
Solon, China 77/K2
Solon, Ind. (†47111) 227/F7
Solon, Iowa (52333) 229/L5
Solon○, Maine (04979) 243/D6
Solon, Ohio (44139) 284/J9
Solon Springs, Wis. (54873) 317/C3
Solor (isl.), Indonesia 85/G7
Solothurn (elec. div.), Switzerland 39/E2
Solothurn (Soleure), Switzerland 39/E2
Solovetskiye (isls.), U.S.S.R. 52/E1
Solsberry, Ind. (47459) 227/D6
Solsgirth, Manitoba 179/B4
Solsona, Philippines 82/C1
Solsona, Spain 33/G2
Solt, Hungary 41/E3
Šolta (isl.), Yugoslavia 45/C4
Soltau, W. Germany 22/C2
Soltvadkert, Hungary 41/E3
Soluk, Libya 111/D1
Solund, Norway 18/D6
Solvang, Calif. (93463) 204/E9
Solvay, N.Y. (13209) 276/H4
Sölvesborg, Sweden 18/J9
Solway (firth), England 13/D3
Solway, Minn. (56678) 255/C3
Solway (firth), Scotland 10/D3
Solway (firth), Scotland 15/E6
Solwezi, Zambia 115/E6
Soma, Japan 81/K5
Soma, Turkey 63/B3
Somabula, Zimbabwe 118/D3
Somalia 2/M5
Somalia 102/G4
SOMALIA 115/J2
Sombor, Yugoslavia 45/D3
Sombra, Ontario 177/B5
Sombrerete, Mexico 150/H5
Sombrero (chan.), India 68/G7
Sombrero (isl.), St. Chris.-Nevis 156/F3
Somerdale, N.J. (08083) 273/B4
Somers, Conn. (06071) 210/F1
Somers○, Conn. (06071) 210/F1
Somers, Iowa (50586) 229/E4
Somers, Mont. (59932) 262/B2
Somers, Wis. (53171) 317/M3
Somerset, (22972) 307/M4
Somerset (isl.), Bermuda 156/G3
Somerset (isl.), Canada 4/B14
Somerset, Colo. (81434) 208/E5
Somerset (co.), England 13/E6
Somerset, Ind. (46984) 227/F3
Somerset, Ky. (42501) 237/M6
Somerset, La. (†71357) 238/H2
Somerset (co.), Maine 243/C4
Somerset, Manitoba 179/D5
Somerset (co.), Md. 245/R8
Somerset, Md. (†20015) 245/E4
Somerset○, Mass. (02725) 249/K5
Somerset (co.), N.J. 273/D2
Somerset, N.Y. (†14012) 276/C4
Somerset (isl.), N.W.T. 146/J2
Somerset (isl.), N.W.T. 162/G1
Somerset (isl.), N.W. Terrs. 187/J2
Somerset, Nova Scotia 168/D3
Somerset, Ohio (43783) 284/F6
Somerset (co.), Pa. 294/D6
Somerset, Pa. (15501) 294/D6
Somerset, Texas (78069) 303/J11
Somerset (res.), Vt. 268/A5
Somerset, Wis. (54025) 317/A5
Somerset East, S. Africa 118/D6
Somerset West, S. Africa 118/F6
Somers Point, N.J. (08244) 273/D5
Somersville, Conn. (06072) 210/F1
Somersworth, N.H. (03878) 268/F5
Somerton, Ariz. (85350) 198/A6
Somerton, England 13/E6
Somerton, Ohio (43784) 284/H6
Somervell (co.), Texas 303/G5
Somerville, Ala. (35670) 195/E2
Somerville, Ind. (47683) 227/C8
Somerville○, Maine (†04341) 243/D7
Somerville, Mass. (02143) 249/C6
Somerville, New Bruns. 170/C2
Somerville, N.J. (08876) 273/D2
Somerville, Ohio (45064) 284/A6
Somerville, Tenn. (38068) 237/C10
Somerville, Texas (77879) 303/H7
Somes (isl.), N. Zealand 100/B2
Someş (riv.), Romania 45/F2
Somesbar, Calif. (95568) 204/B2
Somesville (Mount Desert), Maine (†04660) 243/G7
Somme (dept.), France 28/E3
Somme (riv.), France 28/D2
Somme, Sask. 181/J3
Somme-Leuze, Belgium 27/G8
Sommen (lake), Sweden 18/J8
Sömmerda, E. Germany 22/D3
Somogy (co.), Hungary 41/D3
Somonauk, Ill. (60552) 222/E2
Somotillo, Nicaragua 154/D4
Somoto, Nicaragua 154/D4
Somvix, Switzerland 39/G3
Son (riv.), India 68/E3
Son, Norway 18/D4
Son, Con (isls.), Vietnam 72/E5
Soná, Panama 154/G6
Sonaguera, Honduras 154/D3
Sönch'ŏn, N. Korea 81/B4
Sønderborg, Denmark 21/C8
Sønderborg, Denmark 18/G9
Sønderho, Denmark 21/B7
Sønderjylland (co.), Denmark 21/C7
Sønder Nissum, Denmark 21/A5
Sønder Omme, Denmark 21/B6
Sondershausen, E. Germany 22/D3
Søndersø, Denmark 21/D7
Sondheimer, La. (71276) 238/H1
Søndre Strømfjord, Greenl. 4/C12
Sondrio (prov.), Italy 34/B1
Sondrio, Italy 34/B1
Sonepur, India 68/E4
Sonestown, Pa. (17770) 294/K3
Song Ba (riv.), Vietnam 72/F4
Song Ca (riv.), Vietnam 72/E3
Song Cai (riv.), Vietnam 72/E4
Song Cau, Vietnam 72/F4
Song Da (Black) (riv.), Vietnam 72/E2
Songea, Tanzania 115/G6
Songea, Tanzania 102/F6
Song Hong (Red) (riv.), Vietnam 72/E2
Songhua (riv.), China 54/P5
Songhua Hu (lake), China 77/L3

Starogard Gdański 451

South Willington, Conn. (06265) 210/F1
South Wilmington, Ill. (60474) 222/E2
South Wilton, Conn. (†06897) 210/B4
South Windham, Conn. (06266) 210/G2
South Windham (Little Falls-South Windham), Maine (04082) 243/C8
South Windham, Vt. (†05359) 268/B5
South Windsor○, Conn. (06074) 210/E1
Southwold, England 13/J5
Southwold, England 10/G4
South Wolf (isl.), Newf. 166/C3
South Wolfeboro, N.H. (†03894) 268/E4
South Woodbury, Vt. (†05681) 268/C3
South Woodstock, Conn. (06267) 210/G1
South Woodstock, Vt. (05071) 268/B4
Southworth, Wash. (98386) 310/A2
South Worthington, Mass. (†01098) 249/C3
South Yadkin (riv.), N.C. 281/H3
South Yarmouth, Mass. (02664) 249/O6
South Yorkshire (co.), England 13/F4
South Zanesville, Ohio (43701) 284/F6
Sovata, Romania 45/G2
Sovereign, Sask. 181/D4
Sovetsk, U.S.S.R. 7/J3
Sovetsk, U.S.S.R. 52/G3
Sovetsk (Tilsit), U.S.S.R. 52/B4
Sovetskaya Gavan', U.S.S.R. 54/R5
Sovetskaya Gavan', U.S.S.R. 48/P5
SOVIET UNION (U.S.S.R.) 48
Sowerby Bridge, England 13/H1
Sowerby Bridge, England 10/G2
Soweto, S. Africa 118/H6
Soya (pt.), Japan 81/L1
Soyhières, Switzerland 39/D2
Soyo, Angola 115/B5
Soyo, Angola 102/D5
Sozopol, Bulgaria 45/H4
Spa, Belgium 27/H8
Spades, Ind. (†47041) 227/G6
Spain 2/J3
Spain 7/D4
SPAIN 33
Spalding, England 13/G5
Spalding, England 10/F4
Spalding (co.), Georgia 217/D4
Spalding, Mich. (49886) 250/B3
Spalding, Mo. (†63401) 261/J3
Spalding, Nebr. (68665) 264/F3
Spalding, Sask. 181/G3
Spaldings, Jamaica 158/H6
Spallumcheen, Br. Col. 184/H5
Spanaway, Wash. (98387) 310/C3
Spandau, W. Germany 22/E3
Spangle, Wash. (99031) 310/H3
Spangler, Pa. (15775) 294/E4
Spaniard's Bay, Newf. 166/D2
Spanish (head), I. of Man 13/C3
Spanish, Ontario 177/J5
Spanish (riv.), Ontario 177/C1
Spanishburg, W. Va. (25922) 312/D8
Spanish Fork, Utah (84660) 304/C3
Spanish Fork (riv.), Utah 304/C3
Spanish Fort, Ala. (36527) 195/C9
Spanish Fort, Texas (†76255) 303/G4
Spanish Lake, Mo. (†63138) 261/R1
Spanish Ship Bay, Nova Scotia 168/G4
Spanish Town, Jamaica 158/J6
Spanish Town, Jamaica 156/C3
Sparkill, N.Y. (10976) 276/K8
Sparkman, Ark. (71763) 202/E6
Sparks, Georgia (31647) 217/F8
Sparks, Kansas (†66035) 232/G2
Sparks, Nebr. (69220) 264/D2
Sparks, Nev. 188/C3
Sparks, Nev. (89431) 266/B3
Sparks, Okla. (74869) 288/N3
Sparks (lake), Oreg. 291/F3
Sparksville, Ky. (42778) 237/L6
Sparland, Ill. (61565) 222/D2
Sparlingville, Mich. (†48060) 250/G6
Sparr, Fla. (32690) 212/D2
Sparrow Bush, N.Y. (12780) 276/L8
Sparrows Point, Md. (21219) 245/N4
Sparta, Georgia (31087) 217/F4
Sparta, Greece 45/F7
Sparta, Ill. (62286) 222/D5
Sparta, Ky. (41086) 237/M3
Sparta, Mich. (49345) 250/D5
Sparta, Mo. (65753) 261/F9
Sparta○, N.J. (07871) 273/D1
Sparta, N.C. (28675) 281/G1
Sparta, Ohio (43350) 284/E5
Sparta, Ontario 177/C5
Sparta, Oreg. (†97870) 291/K3
Sparta, Tenn. (38583) 237/K9
Sparta, Va. (22552) 307/O4
Sparta, Wis. (54656) 317/E8
Spartanburg, Ind. (†47355) 227/H4
Spartanburg, S.C. 188/K4
Spartanburg (co.), S.C. 296/D2
Spartanburg, S.C. (*29301) 296/C1
Spartansburg, Pa. (16434) 294/C2
Spartivento (cape), Italy 34/B5
Spartivento (cape), Italy 34/F6
Sparwood, Br. Col. 184/K5
Spassk-Dal'niy, U.S.S.R. 48/O5
Spátha (cape), Greece 45/F8
Spaulding, Ill. (†62561) 222/D4
Spavinaw, Okla. (74366) 288/R2
Spavinaw (lake), Okla. 288/S2
Spean (riv.), Scotland 15/D4
Spean Bridge, Scotland 15/D4
Spear (cape), New Bruns. 170/G2
Spear (cape), Newf. 166/D2
Spearfish, S. Dak. (57783) 298/B5
Spearman, Texas (79081) 303/C1
Spearsville, Ind. (†46181) 227/E6
Spearsville, La. (71277) 238/E1
Spearville, Kansas (67876) 232/C4
Spectacle (lakes), Conn. 210/B2
Specter (range), Nev. 266/E6
Speculator, N.Y. (12164) 276/M3
Spedden, Alberta 182/E2
Spednik (lake), New Bruns. 170/C3
Speed, Ind. (47172) 227/F8
Speed, Kansas (†67639) 232/C2
Speed, N.C. (27881) 281/P3
Speedway, Ind. (46224) 227/E5
Speedwell, Tenn. (37870) 237/O8
Speedwell, Va. (24374) 307/F8
Speer (mt.), Switzerland 39/H2
Speers, Sask. 181/D3
Speightstown, Barbados 161/B8
Speightstown, Barbados 156/G4
Speigner, Ala. (†36025) 195/F5
Spelterville, Ind. (†47808) 227/C5
Spelve, Loch (inlet), Scotland 15/C4
Spenard, Alaska (99503) 196/C1
Spenborough, England 13/J1
Spence Bay, N.W. Terrs. 187/J3
Spencer (cape), Alaska 196/L1
Spencer (pt.), Alaska 196/E1
Spencer (lake), Alberta 182/E2
Spencer (gulf), Australia 87/D9
Spencer, Idaho (†83423) 220/F5
Spencer (co.), Ind. 227/C9
Spencer, Ind. (47460) 227/D6
Spencer, Iowa (51301) 229/C2
Spencer (co.), Ky. 237/L4
Spencer, La. (71278) 238/F1
Spencer (pond), Maine 243/D4
Spencer (stream), Maine 243/C5
Spencer, Mass. (01562) 249/F3
Spencer○, Mass. (01562) 249/F3
Spencer, Nebr. (68777) 264/F2
Spencer (cape), New Bruns. 170/E3
Spencer, N.Y. (14883) 276/H6
Spencer, N.C. (28159) 281/H3
Spencer, Ohio (44275) 284/F3
Spencer, Okla. (73084) 288/M3
Spencer (creek), Oreg. 291/E5
Spencer (gulf), S. Australia 88/F6
Spencer (cape), S. Australia 88/F7
Spencer (cape), S. Australia 94/E6
Spencer (gulf), S. Australia 94/E6
Spencer, S. Dak. (57374) 298/O6
Spencer, Tenn. (38585) 237/L9
Spencer, Va. (24165) 307/J7
Spencer, W. Va. (25276) 312/D5
Spencer, Wis. (54479) 317/F6
Spencerburg, Mo. (†63441) 261/K4
Spencerport, N.Y. (14559) 276/E4
Spencers Island, Nova Scotia 168/D3
Spencerville, Ind. (46788) 227/G2
Spencerville, Ohio (45887) 284/B4
Spencerville, Okla. (74760) 288/R6
Spencerville, Ontario 177/J3
Spences Bridge, Br. Col. 184/G5
Spennymoor, England 13/F3
Spennymoor, England 10/F3
Spenser (mts.), N. Zealand 100/D5
Sperling, Manitoba 179/E5
Sperrin (mts.), N. Ireland 17/G2
Sperry, Iowa (52650) 229/L7
Sperry, Okla. (74073) 288/P2
Sperryville, Va. (22740) 307/M3
Spessart (range), W. Germany 22/C4
Spétsai, Greece 45/F7
Spey (riv.), Scotland 10/E2
Spey (riv.), Scotland 15/E3
Speyer, W. Germany 22/C4
Sphinx (mt.), Mont. 262/E5
Spiceland, Ind. (47385) 227/F5
Spicer, Minn. (56288) 255/C5
Spicer (isls.), N.W. Terrs. 187/L3
Spicewood, Texas (78669) 303/F7
Spickard, Mo. (64679) 261/F2
Spiddal, Ireland 17/C5
Spider (lake), Maine 243/E3
Spider (lake), Wis. 317/D3
Spiekeroog (isl.), W. Germany 22/B2
Spies, N.C. (†27325) 281/K4
Spiez, Switzerland 39/E3
Spili, Greece 45/G8
Spillimacheen, Br. Col. 184/J5
Spillville, Iowa (52168) 229/J2
Spilsby, England 13/H4
Spin Buldak, Afghanistan 68/B2
Spin Buldak, Afghanistan 59/J3
Spindale, N.C. (28160) 281/F4
Spink (co.), S. Dak. 298/N4
Spink, S. Dak. (†57010) 298/R8
Spinnerstown, Pa. (18968) 294/M5
Spirit (lake), Idaho 220/B2
Spirit (lake), Iowa 229/C2
Spirit (lake), S. Dak. 298/O4
Spirit (lake), Wash. 310/C4
Spirit, Wis. (†54513) 317/F5
Spirit Lake, Idaho (83869) 220/A2
Spirit Lake, Iowa (51360) 229/C2
Spirit River, Alberta 182/A2
Spirit River, Alta. 162/E4
Spiritwood, N. Dak. (58481) 282/N6
Spiritwood, Sask. 181/D2
Spiro, Okla. (74959) 288/S4
Spišská Belá, Czech. 41/F2
Spišská Nová Ves, Czech. 41/F2
Spital am Pyhrn, Austria 41/C3
Spithead (chan.), England 13/F7
Spitsbergen (isl.), Norway 4/B9
Spitsbergen (isl.), Norway 18/C2
Spittal an der Drau, Austria 41/B3
Spitz, Austria 41/C2
Spivey, Kansas (67142) 232/D4
Splendora, Texas (77372) 303/J7
Split (lake), Manitoba 179/J2
Split (cape), Nova Scotia 168/D3
Split, Yugoslavia 7/F4
Split, Yugoslavia 45/C4
Split Lake, Manitoba 179/J2
Split Rock, Wis. (†54486) 317/H6
Splügen (pass), Italy 34/B1
Splügen, Switzerland 39/H3
Splügen (pass), Switzerland 39/H3
Spofford, N.H. (03462) 268/C6
Spofford, Texas (78877) 303/D8
Spokane, Mo. (65754) 261/F9
Spokane, Wash. 146/G5
Spokane, Wash. 188/C1
Spokane (co.), Wash. 310/H3
Spokane, Wash. (*99201) 310/H3
Spokane (mt.), Wash. 310/H3
Spokane (riv.), Wash. 310/H3
Spokane Ind. Res., Wash. 310/G3
Spöl (riv.), Switzerland 39/F2
Spoleto, Italy 34/D3
Spoon (riv.), Ill. 222/C3
Spooner, Wis. (54801) 317/B4
Spot (pond), Mass. 249/C6
Spotswood, N.J. (08884) 273/E3
Spotsylvania (co.), Va. 307/N4
Spotsylvania, Va. (22553) 307/N4
Spotted (range), Nev. 266/F6
Spotted Horse, Wyo. (†82831) 319/G1
Spottsville, Ky. (42458) 237/G5
Spottswood, Va. (24475) 307/K5
Spotville, Ark. (†71753) 202/D7
Spragge, Ontario 177/J5
Sprague, Ala. (36076) 195/F6
Sprague, Manitoba 179/G5
Sprague, Nebr. (68438) 264/H4
Sprague (riv.), Oreg. 291/F5
Sprague, Wash. (99032) 310/G3
Sprague (lake), Wash. 310/G3
Sprague River, Oreg. (97639) 291/F5
Spragueville, Iowa (52074) 229/N4
Spratly (isl.), Philippines 85/E4
Spratt, Mich. (†49753) 250/F3
Spray (mts.), Alberta 182/C4
Spray, Oreg. (97874) 291/H3
Spray Lakes, Alberta 182/C4
Spraytown, Ind. (†47228) 227/E6
Spread Eagle, Wis. (†54121) 317/K4
Spreckelsville, Hawaii (96779) 218/J1
Spree (riv.), E. Germany 22/F3
Spreewald (for.), E. Germany 22/F3
Spremberg, E. Germany 22/F3
Sprent, Tasmania 99/C3
Sprigg, W. Va. (25693) 312/B7
Sprimont, Belgium 27/H8
Spring (riv.), Ark. 202/H1
Spring (creek), Nev. 266/D2
Spring (mts.), Nev. 266/F6
Spring (valley), Nev. 266/G3
Spring (creek), N. Dak. 282/E5
Spring (creek), S. Dak. 298/J2
Spring (creek), S. Dak. 298/C6
Spring, Texas (*77373) 303/J7
Spring Arbor, Mich. (49283) 250/E6
Spring Bay, Ill. (†61601) 222/D3
Spring Bay, Ontario 177/B2
Springbok, S. Africa 118/B5
Springboro, Ohio (45066) 284/B6
Springboro, Pa. (16435) 294/B2
Springbrook, Iowa (52075) 229/N4
Spring Brook, N. Dak. (58850) 282/D3
Springbrook, Ontario 177/G3
Springbrook, Oreg. (†97132) 291/A2
Springbrook, Wis. (54875) 317/C4
Spring City, Mo. (†64801) 261/C9
Spring City, Pa. (19475) 294/L5
Spring City, Tenn. (37381) 237/M9
Spring City, Utah (84662) 304/C4
Spring Coulée, Alberta 182/D5
Spring Creek, Pa. (16436) 294/D2
Spring Creek, Tenn. (38378) 237/D9
Spring Creek, W. Va. (†24966) 312/F7
Springdale, Ark. (72764) 202/B1
Springdale, Iowa (†52776) 229/L5
Springdale, Mont. (59082) 262/F5
Springdale, Newf. 166/C4
Springdale, Ohio (45246) 284/B9
Springdale, Pa. (15144) 294/C6
Springdale, S.C. (†29720) 296/F2
Springdale, S.C. (29169) 296/E4
Springdale, Utah (84767) 304/B6
Springdale, Wash. (99173) 310/H2
Springe, W. Germany 22/C2
Springer (mt.), Georgia 217/D1
Springer (lake), Ill. 222/E4
Springer, N. Mex. (87747) 274/E2
Springer, Okla. (73458) 288/M6
Springerton, Ill. (62887) 222/E5
Springerville, Ariz. (85938) 198/F4
Springfield, Ark. (72157) 202/E3
Springfield, Colo. (81073) 208/O8
Springfield, Fla. (32401) 212/D6
Springfield, Georgia (31329) 217/K6
Springfield, Idaho (83277) 220/F6
Springfield (cap.), Ill. 146/J6
Springfield (cap.), Ill. 188/H3
Springfield (cap.), Ill. (*62701) 222/D4
Springfield (lake), Ill. 222/D4
Springfield, Ind. (†47638) 227/B8
Springfield, Ky. (40069) 237/L5
Springfield, La. (70462) 238/M2
Springfield○, Maine (04487) 243/G5
Springfield, Mass. 188/M2
Springfield, Mass. (*01101) 249/D4
Springfield, Mich. (49015) 250/D6
Springfield, Minn. (56087) 255/C6
Springfield, Mo. (*65801) 261/F8
Springfield, Mo. 188/H3
Springfield, Mo. 146/J6
Springfield, Nebr. (68059) 264/H3
Springfield, King's, New Bruns. 170/E3
Springfield, York, New Bruns. 170/C2
Springfield○, N.H. (†03284) 268/C4
Springfield○, N.J. (07081) 273/E2
Springfield, Nova Scotia 168/D4
Springfield, Ohio 188/K2
Springfield, Ohio (*45501) 284/C6
Springfield, Ontario 177/C5
Springfield, Oreg. (97477) 291/E3
Springfield○, Pa. (19064) 294/M7
Springfield, Queensland 88/G5
Springfield, Queensland 95/B5
Springfield, S.C. (29146) 296/E4
Springfield, S. Dak. (57062) 298/N8
Springfield, Tenn. (37172) 237/H8
Springfield, Vt. (05156) 268/B5
Springfield○, Vt. (05156) 268/B5
Springfield, Va. (*22150) 307/S3
Springfield, W. Va. (26763) 312/J4
Springfield Armory Nat'l Hist. Site, Mass. 249/D4
Springford, Ontario 177/D5
Spring Garden, Ala. (36275) 195/G3
Spring Garden, Calif. (95971) 204/D4
Spring Garden, Ill. (†62846) 222/E5
Spring Green, Wis. (53588) 317/G9
Spring Grove, Ill. (60081) 222/E1
Spring Grove, Ind. (†47374) 227/H5
Spring Grove, Minn. (55974) 255/G7
Spring Grove, Pa. (17362) 294/J6
Spring Grove, Va. (23881) 307/P6
Spring Hall, Barbados 161/B8
Springhaven, Nova Scotia 168/C5
Spring Hill, Ark. (†71801) 202/C6
Spring Hill, Iowa (†50125) 229/F6
Spring Hill, Kansas (66083) 232/H3
Springhill, La. (71075) 238/D1
Spring Hill, Minn. (†56352) 255/D5
Springhill, Nova Scotia 168/E3
Spring Hill, Tenn. (37174) 237/H9
Springhill Junction, Nova Scotia 168/D3
Springhills, Ohio (†43357) 284/C5
Springholm, Scotland 15/E5
Spring Hope, N.C. (27882) 281/N3
Springhouse, Br. Col. 184/G4
Spring Lake, Ind. (†46140) 227/F5
Spring Lake, Mich. (49456) 250/C5
Spring Lake, Minn. (†55056) 255/E5
Spring Lake, Minn. (56680) 255/E3
Spring Lake, N.J. (07762) 273/F3
Spring Lake, N.C. (28390) 281/M4
Springlake, Texas (79082) 303/B3
Spring Lake, Wis. (†54960) 317/H8
Spring Lake Heights, N.J. (†07762) 273/E3
Spring Lake Park, Minn. (†55432) 255/E5
Springlee, Ky. (†40201) 237/K2
Spring Lick, Ky. (42779) 237/H6
Spring Mills, Pa. (16875) 294/G4
Spring Mills, S.C. (†29067) 296/F2
Spring Park, Minn. (55384) 255/F5
Spring Place, Georgia (†30705) 217/C1
Springport, Ind. (47386) 227/G4
Springport, Mich. (49284) 250/E6
Spring Ridge, La. (†71047) 238/B2
Springs, S. Africa 118/J6
Springside, Sask. 181/J4
Springstein, Manitoba 179/E5
Springsure, Queensland 95/D5
Springton (res.), Pa. 294/L6
Springtown, Ark. (72767) 202/B1
Springtown, Texas (76082) 303/G5
Springvale, Georgia (31788) 217/C7
Springvale, Maine (04083) 243/B9
Springvale, Victoria 88/L7
Springvale, Victoria 97/J5
Spring Valley, Ala. (†35674) 195/C1
Spring Valley, Ill. (61362) 222/D2
Spring Valley, Minn. (55975) 255/F7
Spring Valley, N.Y. (10977) 276/K8
Spring Valley, Ohio (45370) 284/C6
Spring Valley, Sask. 181/F6
Spring Valley, Texas (†77001) 303/J1
Spring Valley, Wis. (54767) 317/B6
Springview, Nebr. (68778) 264/E2
Springville, Ala. (35146) 195/E3
Springville, Calif. (93265) 204/G7
Springville, Ind. (47462) 227/D7
Springville, Iowa (52336) 229/L4
Springville, La. (†70754) 238/L2
Springville, Miss. (†38863) 256/F2
Springville, N.Y. (14141) 276/C5
Springville, Pa. (18844) 294/L2
Springville, Tenn. (38256) 237/E8
Springville, Utah (84663) 304/C3
Springwater, N.Y. (14560) 276/E5
Springwater, Sask. 181/C4
Springwood, Va. (†24066) 307/J5
Sproat Lake, Br. Col. 184/H3
Sprott, Ala. (36779) 195/D5
Sprowston, England 13/J5
Spruce (isl.), Manitoba 179/B1
Spruce, Mich. (48762) 250/F4
Spruce (mt.), Vt. 268/C3
Spruce Creek, Pa. (16683) 294/F4
Sprucedale, Ontario 177/E2
Spruce Grove, Alberta 182/D3
Spruce Home, Sask. 181/F2
Spruce Knob (mt.), W. Va. 312/G5
Spruce Knob-Seneca Rocks Nat'l Rec. Area, W. Va. 312/H5
Spruce Lake, Sask. 181/B2
Spruce Pine, Ala. (35585) 195/C2
Spruce Pine, N.C. (28777) 281/E3
Spruce Run (res.), N.J. 273/D2
Spruce View, Alberta 182/C3
Spruce Woods, Manitoba 179/C5
Spruce Woods Prov. Park, Manitoba 179/C5
Sprule, Ky. (40986) 237/O7
Spry (harb.), Nova Scotia 168/F4
Spry Harbour, Nova Scotia 168/F4
Spur, Texas (79370) 303/D4
Spurgeon, Ind. (47584) 227/C8
Spurlockville, W. Va. (25565) 312/B6
Spurn (head), England 13/H4
Spurn (head), England 10/G4
Spurr (mt.), Alaska 196/B1
Spur Tree, Jamaica 158/H6
Spuzzum, Br. Col. 184/G5
Spy (pond), Mass. 249/C6
Spy Hill, Sask. 181/K5
Squam (lake), N.H. 268/E4
Squamish, Br. Col. 184/F5
Squa Pan, Maine (†04732) 243/G2
Squa Pan (lake), Maine 243/G2
Square (lake), Maine 243/G1
Square Butte, Mont. (†59442) 262/F3
Square Islands, Newf. 166/C3
Squatec, Québec 172/J2
Squatec (lake), Québec 172/J2
Squaw (creek), Idaho 220/B5
Squaw (peak), Idaho 220/D4
Squaw (creek), Oreg. 291/F3
Squaw (creek), S. Dak. 298/G3
Squaw Harbor, Alaska (†99661) 196/F3
Squaw Lake, Minn. (56681) 255/D3
Squaw Rapids, Sask. 181/H2
Squibnocket (pt.), Mass. 249/M7
Squillace (gulf), Italy 34/F5
Squinzano, Italy 34/G4
Squire, W. Va. (24884) 312/C8
Squires, Mo. (65755) 261/G9
Squires Mem. Park, Newf. 166/C4
Squirrel, Idaho (83447) 220/G5
Sragen, Indonesia 85/J2
Sre Ambel, Cambodia 72/D5
Srebrenica, Yugoslavia 45/D3
Srednekolymsk, U.S.S.R. 4/C2
Srednekolymsk, U.S.S.R. 48/Q3
Sre Khtum, Cambodia 72/E4
Śrem, Poland 47/C2
Sremska Mitrovica, Yugoslavia 45/D3
Srepok (riv.), Cambodia 72/E4
Sretensk, U.S.S.R. 54/N4
Sretensk, U.S.S.R. 48/M4
Srikakulam, India 68/E5
Sri Lanka 54/K9
SRI LANKA (CEYLON) 68/E7
Srinagar, India 68/D2
Srinagar, India 54/J6
Srivardhan, India 68/C5
Środa Śląska, Poland 47/C3
Środa Wielkopolska, Poland 47/C2
Staaten (riv.), Queensland 88/G3
Staaten (riv.), Queensland 95/B3
Staatsburg, N.Y. (12580) 276/N7
Stab, Ky. (42557) 237/N6
Stacks (mts.), Ireland 17/B7
Stacy, Minn. (55079) 255/E5
Stacy, N.C. (28581) 281/S5
Stacy, Va. (24616) 307/E6
Stacyville, Iowa (50476) 229/H2
Stacyville, Maine (04782) 243/F4
Stacyville○, Maine (04782) 243/F4
Stade, W. Germany 22/C2
Staden, Belgium 27/B7
Stadskanaal, Netherlands 27/L3
Stadthagen, W. Germany 22/C2
Stäfa, Switzerland 39/G2
Staffa (isl.), Scotland 15/B4
Staffelstein, W. Germany 22/D3
Staffhorst, W. Germany 22/C2
Stafford○, Conn. (06075) 210/F1
Stafford, England 10/G2
Stafford, England 13/E5
Stafford (lake), Fla. 212/D2
Stafford (co.), Kansas 232/D3
Stafford, Kansas (67578) 232/D4
Stafford, N.Y. (14143) 276/D5
Stafford, Ohio (43786) 284/H6
Stafford, Okla. (†73601) 288/H3
Stafford, Queensland 88/K2
Stafford, Queensland 95/D2
Stafford, Texas (77477) 303/J2
Stafford (co.), Va. 307/O4
Stafford, Va. (22554) 307/O4
Staffordshire (co.), England 13/E5
Stafford Springs, Conn. (06076) 210/F1
Staffordsville, Ky. (41256) 237/R5
Staffordville, Conn. (06077) 210/G1
Staffordville, N.J. (†08092) 273/E4
Staines (pen.), Chile 138/D9
Staines, England 10/B5
Staines, England 13/G8
Stainville, Tenn. (†37710) 237/N8
Staked (Llano Estacado) (plain), N. Mex. 274/F5
Staked (Llano Estacado) (plain), Texas 303/B4
Stakhanov, U.S.S.R. 52/E5
Stalden, Switzerland 39/E4
Staley, N.C. (27355) 281/K3
Stalham, England 13/J5
Stalheim, Norway 18/E6
Stalin, Albania 45/D5
Stalingrad (Volgograd), U.S.S.R. 7/J4
Stalingrad (Volgograd), U.S.S.R. 48/E5
Stalingrad (Volgograd), U.S.S.R. 52/F5
Stallings, N.C. (†28079) 281/H4
Stallo, Miss. (†39350) 256/F5
Stallworthy (cape), N.W. Terrs. 187/J1
Stalowa Wola, Poland 47/F3
Stalwart, Mich. (49789) 250/E2
Stalwart, Sask. 181/F4
Stambaugh, Mich. (49964) 250/G2
Stamford, Conn. (*06901) 210/A4
Stamford, England 13/G5
Stamford, England 10/F4
Stamford, Nebr. (68977) 264/E4
Stamford, N.Y. (12167) 276/L6
Stamford, Queensland 88/G4
Stamford, Texas (79553) 303/E5
Stamford (lake), Texas 303/E4
Stamford○, Vt. (05352) 268/A6
Stampa, Switzerland 39/J4
Stamping Ground, Ky. (40379) 237/M4
Stampriet, Namibia 118/B4
Stamps, Ark. (71860) 202/D7
Stanardsville, Va. (22973) 307/L4
Stanberry, Mo. (64489) 261/C2
Stanbridge-Est, Québec 172/D4
Stanchfield, Minn. (55080) 255/E5
Standard, Alberta 182/D4
Standard, Calif. (95373) 204/E6
Standard, Ill. (61363) 222/D2
Standard, La. (†71465) 238/F3
Standard City, Ill. (62686) 222/D4
Standerton, S. Africa 118/D5
Standfast (pt.), Ant. & Bar. 161/E11
Standing Rock, Ala. (36878) 195/H4
Standing Rock Ind. Res., N. Dak. 282/J7
Standish, Calif. (96128) 204/E3
Standish, Maine (04084) 243/B8
Standish○, Maine (04084) 243/B8
Standish, Mich. (48658) 250/F5
Standish-with-Langtree, England 13/G2
Stand Off, Alberta 182/D5
Stanfield, Ariz. (85272) 198/C6
Stanfield, N.C. (28163) 281/J4
Stanfield, Oreg. (97875) 291/H2
Stanford, Calif. (94305) 204/J3
Stanford, Ill. (61774) 222/D3
Stanford, Ind. (47463) 227/D6
Stanford, Ky. (40484) 237/M5
Stanford, Mont. (59479) 262/F3
Stanfordville, N.Y. (12581) 276/N7
Stangelville, Wis. (†54208) 317/L7
Stanger, S. Africa 118/E5
Stanhope, England 13/E3
Stanhope, Iowa (50246) 229/F4
Stanhope, N.J. (07874) 273/D2
Stanhope, Pr. Edward I. 168/E2
Stanhope, Québec 172/F4
Stanislaus (co.), Calif. 204/D6
Stanke Dimitrov, Bulgaria 45/F4
Stanley, England 13/H3
Stanley (cap.), Falk. Is. 120/D8
Stanley (cap.), Falk. Is. 143/E7
Stanley, Idaho (83278) 220/D5
Stanley, Iowa (50671) 229/K3
Stanley, Kansas (†66223) 232/H3
Stanley, Ky. (42375) 237/G5
Stanley, La. (†71049) 238/C3
Stanley, New Bruns. 170/D2
Stanley, N. Mex. (87056) 274/D3
Stanley, N.Y. (14561) 276/F5
Stanley, N.C. (28164) 281/G4
Stanley, N. Dak. (58784) 282/F3
Stanley (mt.), North. Terr. 93/B7
Stanley, Nova Scotia 168/E3
Stanley, Okla. (†74536) 288/R5
Stanley, Scotland 15/E4
Stanley (co.), S. Dak. 298/H5
Stanley, Tasmania 99/B2
Stanley (mt.), Tasmania 99/A1
Stanley, Va. (22851) 307/L3
Stanley, Wis. (54768) 317/E6
Stanley (falls), Zaire 102/E5
Stanley (falls), Zaire 115/D3
Stanley Pool (lake), Zaire 115/C4
Stanleytown, Va. (24168) 307/H7
Stanleyville, N.C. (†27045) 281/J2
Stanly (co.), N.C. 281/J4
Stanmore, Alberta 182/E4
Stannards, N.Y. (†14895) 276/E6
Stann Creek Town, Belize 154/C2
Stanovoy (range), U.S.S.R. 54/O4
Stanovoy (range), U.S.S.R. 48/N4
Stans, Switzerland 39/F3
Stanstead (co.), Québec 172/F4
Stanstead Plain, Québec 172/F4
Stanthorpe, Queensland 88/J5
Stanthorpe, Queensland 95/D6
Stanton, Ala. (36790) 195/E5
Stanton, Calif. (90680) 204/D11
Stanton, England 13/H5
Stanton, Iowa (51573) 229/C7
Stanton (co.), Kansas 232/A4
Stanton, Ky. (40380) 237/O5
Stanton, Mich. (48888) 250/D5
Stanton, Miss. (†39120) 256/B7
Stanton, Mo. (63079) 261/K6
Stanton (co.), Nebr. 264/G3
Stanton, Nebr. (68779) 264/G3
Stanton, N.J. (08885) 273/D2
Stanton, N. Dak. (58571) 282/H5
Stanton, Tenn. (38069) 237/C10
Stanton, Texas (79782) 303/C5
Stantonsburg, N.C. (27883) 281/O3
Stantonville, Tenn. (38379) 237/E10
Stanwood, Iowa (52337) 229/L5
Stanwood, Mich. (49346) 250/D5
Stanwood, Wash. (98292) 310/C2
Stanzel, Iowa (†50849) 229/E6
Staphorst, Netherlands 27/J3
Staplehurst, Nebr. (68439) 264/G4
Staples, Minn. (56479) 255/D4
Staples, Ontario 177/B5
Stapleton, Ala. (36578) 195/C9
Stapleton, Georgia (30823) 217/H4
Stapleton, Nebr. (69163) 264/D3
Stapylton (bay), N.W. Terrs. 187/G3
Star, Alberta 182/D3
Star, Idaho (83669) 220/B6
Star (lake), Minn. 255/C4
Star, Miss. (39167) 256/D6
Star, N.C. (27356) 281/K4
Star, Texas (76880) 303/F6
Starachowice, Poland 47/E3
Stará L'ubovňa, Czech. 41/F2
Staraya Russa, U.S.S.R. 52/D3
Stara Zagora, Bulgaria 7/G4
Stara Zagora, Bulgaria 45/G4
Starbuck (isl.), Kiribati 87/L6
Starbuck, Manitoba 179/E5
Starbuck, Minn. (56381) 255/C5
Starbuck, Wash. (99359) 310/G4
Star City, Ark. (71667) 202/G6
Star City, Ind. (46985) 227/D3
Star City, Sask. 181/G3
Star City, W. Va. (26505) 312/F3
Staré Město, Czech. 41/D2
Stargard Szczeciński, Poland 47/B2
Stargo, Ariz. (†85540) 198/F5
Starhill, La. (†70748) 238/H5
Stark (co.), Ill. 222/D2
Stark, Kansas (66775) 232/G4
Stark, Minn. (†55032) 255/E5
Stark, Mont. (†59846) 262/B3
Stark○, N.H. (†03582) 268/E2
Stark (co.), N. Dak. 282/E6
Stark (co.), Ohio 284/H4
Stark City, Mo. (64866) 261/D9
Starke, Fla. (32091) 212/D2
Starke (co.), Ind. 227/D2
Starkey, Oreg. (†97850) 291/J2
Star Keys (isls.), N. Zealand 100/E7
Starks, La. (70661) 238/C6
Starks○, Maine (†04980) 243/D6
Starks, Wis. (†54501) 317/H4
Starksboro○, Vt. (05487) 268/A3
Starkville, Colo. (81074) 208/L8
Starkville, Miss. (39759) 256/G4
Starkweather, N. Dak. (58377) 282/N3
Star Lake, N.Y. (13690) 276/K2
Star Lake, Wis. (54561) 317/G3
Starlight, Ind. (†47119) 227/F8
Starnberg, W. Germany 22/D4
Starnbergersee (lake), W. Germany 22/D5
Starodub, U.S.S.R. 52/D4
Starogard Gdański, Poland 47/D2

Surfside Beach 453

Strong (riv.), Miss. 256/D7
Strong City, Kansas (66869) 232/F3
Strong City, Okla. (73665) 288/G3
Strongfield, Sask. 181/E4
Stronghurst, Ill. (61480) 222/C3
Strongs, Mich. (49790) 250/E2
Strongs, Miss. (†39730) 256/G3
Strongsville, Ohio (44136) 284/G10
Stronsay (firth), Scotland 15/F1
Stronsay (isl.), Scotland 10/E1
Stronsay (isl.), Scotland 15/F1
Strontian, Scotland 15/C4
Stropkov, Czech. 41/F2
Stroud, Ala. (†36855) 195/H4
Stroud, England 13/E6
Stroud, England 10/E5
Stroud, N.S. Wales 97/G3
Stroud, Okla. (74079) 288/N3
Stroud, Ontario 177/E3
Stroudsburg, Pa. (18360) 294/M4
Struan, Sask. 181/D3
Struan, Scotland 15/B3
Struble, Iowa (51057) 229/A3
Struer, Denmark 21/B5
Struer, Denmark 18/F8
Struga, Yugoslavia 45/E5
Strum, Wis. (54770) 317/D6
Struma (riv.), Bulgaria 45/F5
Strumble (head), Wales 13/B5
Strumica, Yugoslavia 45/F5
Strunk, Ky. (42649) 237/N7
Struthers, Ohio (44471) 284/J3
Stryker, Mont. (59933) 262/B2
Stryker, Ohio (43557) 284/B3
Strykersville, N.Y. (14145) 276/C5
Strzegom, Poland 47/C3
Strzelce Krajeńskie, Poland 47/B2
Strzelce Opolskie, Poland 47/D3
Strzelecki (creek), S. Australia 88/G5
Strzelecki (creek), S. Australia 94/G3
Strzelecki (mt.), Tasmania 99/D2
Strzelin, Poland 47/C3
Strzelno, Poland 47/D2
Strzyżów, Poland 47/E4
Stuart (isl.), Alaska 196/F2
Stuart (lake), Br. Col. 184/E3
Stuart, Fla. (33494) 212/F4
Stuart, Iowa (50250) 229/E6
Stuart, Nebr. (68780) 264/E2
Stuart, Okla. (74570) 288/O5
Stuart (range), S. Australia 94/D3
Stuart, Va. (24171) 307/H7
Stuart (mt.), Wash. 310/E3
Stuartburn, Manitoba 179/F5
Stuart Island, Br. Col. 184/E5
Stuarts Draft, Va. (24477) 307/L4
Stuart Town, N.S. Wales 97/E3
Stubbekøbing, Denmark 21/F8
Stubbenkammer (pt.), E. Germany 22/E1
Stub Hill (mt.), N.H. 268/E1
Stuckey, S.C. (29554) 296/H4
Studénka, Czech. 41/D2
Studley, Kansas (67759) 232/B2
Studley, Va. (23162) 307/O5
Stukely-Sud, Québec 172/E4
Stump (lake), N. Dak. 282/O4
Stumptown, W. Va. (25280) 312/E5
Stumpy Point, N.C. (27978) 281/T3
Stupino, U.S.S.R. 52/E4
Stura (riv.), Italy 34/A2
Sturbridge, Mass. (01566) 249/F4
Sturbridge○, Mass. (01566) 249/F4
Sturdivant, Mo. (63782) 261/M8
Sturgeon (lake), Alberta 182/B2
Sturgeon (bay), Manitoba 179/E3
Sturgeon (riv.), Mich. 250/C2
Sturgeon (riv.), Minn. 255/F3
Sturgeon, Mo. (65284) 261/H4
Sturgeon (lake), Ontario 177/G5
Sturgeon, Pa. (15082) 294/B5
Sturgeon, Pr. Edward I. 168/F2
Sturgeon (riv.), Sask. 181/E2
Sturgeon Bay, Wis. (54235) 317/M6
Sturgeon Falls, Ont. 162/H6
Sturgeon Falls, Ontario 175/E3
Sturgeon Falls, Ontario 177/E1
Sturgeon Heights, Alberta 182/B2
Sturgeon Lake, Minn. (55783) 255/F4
Sturgeon Point, Ontario 177/F3
Sturgeon Weir, Sask. 181/N4
Sturgis, Ky. (42459) 237/F5
Sturgis, Mich. (49091) 250/D7
Sturgis, Miss. (39769) 256/G4
Sturgis, Sask. 181/J4
Sturgis, S. Dak. (57785) 298/B5
Štúrovo, Czech. 41/E3
Sturt (mt.), N.S. Wales 97/A1
Sturt (plain), North. Terr. 93/C4
Sturt (des.), Queensland 88/G5
Sturt (des.), Queensland 95/B3
Sturt (riv.), S. Australia 88/D8
Sturt (des.), S. Australia 94/G3
Sturt (riv.), S. Australia 94/B8
Sturt (creek), W. Australia 88/D3
Sturt (creek), W. Australia 92/D2
Sturtevant, Wis. (53177) 317/M3
Stutsman (co.), N. Dak. 282/M5
Stutterheim, S. Africa 118/D6
Stuttgart, Ark. (72160) 202/H4
Stuttgart, Kansas (67670) 232/C2
Stuttgart, W. Germany 7/E4
Stuttgart, W. Germany 22/C4
Styria (prov.), Austria 41/C3
Suai, Malaysia 85/E5
Suakin, Sudan 102/F3
Suakin, Sudan 59/C6
Suakin, Sudan 111/G4
Suakin (arch.), Sudan 111/G4
Suamico, Wis. (54173) 317/K6
Suao, China 77/K7
Suapi, Bolivia 136/B4
Suapure (riv.), Venezuela 124/E4
Suaqui, Mexico 150/E2
Suárez (riv.), Colombia 126/D4
Subang, Indonesia 85/H2
Subata, U.S.S.R. 53/D2
Subei, China 77/E4
Subeihi, Jordan 65/D3
Subh, Jebel (mt.), Saudi Arabia 59/C5
Subiaco, Ark. (72865) 202/C3
Subiaco, W. Australia 88/B2
Subi Besar (isl.), Indonesia 85/D5
Subic (bay), Philippines 82/C3
Sublett (mts.), Idaho 220/E7
Sublett, Ky. (41470) 237/P5
Sublette, Ill. (61367) 222/D2
Sublette, Kansas (67877) 232/B4
Sublette, Mo. (†63546) 261/G2
Sublette (co.), Wyo. 319/C3
Subligna, Georgia (†30747) 217/B1
Sublimity, Oreg. (97385) 291/E3
Subotica, Yugoslavia 7/F4
Subotica, Yugoslavia 45/D2
Subtle, Ky. (42129) 237/L7
Sucarnochee, Miss. (†39352) 256/H5
Sucarnoochee (creek), Miss. 256/G5
Succasunna, N.J. (07876) 273/D2
Success, Ark. (72470) 202/J1
Success, Mo. (65570) 261/H8
Success, Sask. 181/D5
Succor (creek), Oreg. 291/K4
Suceava, Romania 45/G2
Suchedniów, Poland 47/E3
Suches, Bolivia 136/A4
Suches (riv.), Bolivia 136/A4
Suches, Georgia (30572) 217/E1
Suchitoto, El Salvador 154/C4
Süchow (Xuzhou), China 77/J5
Sucia (bay), P. Rico 161/A3
Sucia (isl.), Wash. 310/C2
Sucio (riv.), Colombia 126/B4
Suck (riv.), Ireland 17/E5
Sucre (cap.), Bolivia 2/F6
Sucre (cap.), Bolivia 120/C4
Sucre (cap.), Bolivia 136/C6
Sucre (dept.), Colombia 126/C3
Sucre, Bolívar, Colombia 126/C3
Sucre, Caquetá, Colombia 126/C7
Sucre, Ecuador 128/B3
Sucre (state), Venezuela 124/G2
Sucre, Venezuela 124/D3
Sucúa, Ecuador 128/C4
Sucuriju, Brazil 132/D2
Sud (dept.), Haiti 158/A6
Sud (chan.), Haiti 158/B6
Suda (riv.), U.S.S.R. 52/E3
Sudak, U.S.S.R. 52/E6
Sudan 2/L5
Sudan 102/E3
SUDAN 111/E4
SUDAN 59/B6
Sudan (reg.) 102/D3
Sudan (reg.), Benin 106/E6
Sudan (reg.), Chad 111/C5
Sudan (reg.), Mali 106/D6
Sudan (reg.), Niger 106/F6
Sudan (reg.), Nigeria 106/F6
Sudan (reg.), Sudan 111/E5
Sudan, Texas (79371) 303/B3
Sudan (reg.), Upper Volta 106/D6
Sudbury, England 10/G4
Sudbury, England 13/H5
Sudbury○, Mass. (01776) 249/A6
Sudbury (res.), Mass. 249/H3
Sudbury (riv.), Mass. 249/A6
Sudbury, Ont. 162/H6
Sudbury, Ont. 146/K5
Sudbury (reg. munic.), Ontario 175/D3
Sudbury (terr. dist.), Ontario 175/D3
Sudbury (terr. dist.), Ontario 177/J5
Sudbury (reg. munic.), Ontario 177/K6
Sudbury, Ontario 177/K5
Sudbury, Ontario 175/D3
Sudbury○, Vt. (†05733) 268/A4
Sudd (swamp), Sudan 102/F4
Sudd (swamp), Sudan 111/F6
Suddie, Guyana 131/B2
Sudeten (mts.), Czech. 41/C1
Sudeten (range), Poland 47/B3
Sudhuroy (isl.), Denmark 21/B3
Sudirman (range), Indonesia 85/K6
Sudith, Ky. (40381) 237/O4
Sudlersville, Md. (21668) 245/P4
Sue (riv.), Sudan 111/E6
Sueca, Spain 33/F3
Suemez (isl.), Alaska 196/M2
Suez (canal) 2/L4
Suez, Egypt 111/K3
Suez, Egypt 59/B4
Suez, Egypt 102/F2
Suez (canal), Egypt 102/F1
Suez (canal), Egypt 111/K3
Suez (canal), Egypt 59/B3
Suez (gulf), Egypt 111/F2
Suez (gulf), Egypt 59/B4
Suf, Jordan 65/D3
Sufeina, Saudi Arabia 59/D5
Sufers, Switzerland 39/H3
Suffern, N.Y. (10901) 276/J8
Suffield, Alberta 182/E4
Suffield, Conn. (06078) 210/E1
Suffield○, Conn. (06078) 210/E1
Suffield, Ohio (†44260) 284/H3
Suffolk (co.), England 13/H5
Suffolk (co.), Mass. 249/K3
Suffolk, Mont. (†59451) 262/G3
Suffolk (co.), N.Y. 276/P9
Suffolk (I.C.), Va. (*23432) 307/P7
Sufian, Iran 66/E1
Sugar (creek), Ind. 227/B3
Sugar (creek), Ind. 227/F5
Sugar (creek), Ind. 227/C5
Sugar (isl.), Mich. 250/E2
Sugar (riv.), N.H. 268/C5
Sugar (creek), Pa. 294/J2
Sugar (riv.), Wis. 317/H10
Sugar Bush, Wis. (†54961) 317/J7
Sugarbush Hill (mt.), Wis. 317/J4
Sugar City, Colo. (81076) 208/M6
Sugar City, Idaho (83448) 220/G6
Sugar Creek, Mo. (64054) 261/R5
Sugarcreek, Ohio (44681) 284/G5
Sugar Creek, Pa. (†16323) 294/C3
Sugar Grove, Ark. (†72927) 202/C3
Sugar Grove, Ill. (60554) 222/E2
Sugar Grove, Ohio (43155) 284/E6
Sugargrove, Pa. (16350) 294/D1
Sugar Grove, Va. (24375) 307/E7
Sugar Grove, W. Va. (26815) 312/H5
Sugar Hill, Georgia (†30518) 217/E2
Sugar Hill○, N.H. (03585) 268/D3
Sugar Island, Mich. (†49783) 250/E2
Sugar Land, Texas (77478) 303/J8
Sugarloaf (key), Fla. 212/E7
Sugarloaf (hill), Hawaii 218/C4
Sugarloaf (mt.), Ireland 17/B8
Sugarloaf (pt.), N. S. Wales 88/J6
Sugarloaf (passage), N.S. Wales 97/J1
Sugarloaf (pt.), N.S. Wales 97/G3
Sugarloaf P.O. (Big Bear City), Calif. (92314) 204/J9
Sugar Notch, Pa. (18706) 294/E7
Sugartown, La. (70662) 238/D5
Sugar Tree, Tenn. (38380) 237/E9
Sugar Tree Ridge, Ohio (45133) 284/C7
Sugar Valley, Georgia (30746) 217/C1
Sugbai (passage), Philippines 82/C8
Sugden, Okla. (†73565) 288/L6
Suggsville, Ala. (†36482) 195/C7
Sühbaatar, Mongolia 77/H2
Sühbaatar (Sukhe Bator), Mongolia 77/G1
Sühbaatar, Mongolia 54/M5
Suheli Par (atoll), India 68/C6
Suhl (dist.), E. Germany 22/D3
Suhl, E. Germany 22/D3
Suhr, Switzerland 39/F2
Şuhut, Turkey 63/D3
Sui, Pakistan 68/B3
Suiattle (riv.), Wash. 310/D2
Suichang, China 77/J6
Suide, China 77/G4
Suifenhe, China 77/M3
Suihua, China 77/L2
Suijiang, China 77/F6
Suileng, China 77/L2
Suining, China 77/G5
Suipacha, Argentina 143/G7
Suipacha, Bolivia 136/C7
Suir (riv.), Ireland 10/C4
Suir (riv.), Ireland 17/G7
Suisun (bay), Calif. 204/K1
Suisun City, Calif. (94585) 204/K1
Suit, N.C. (28906) 281/A4
Suita, Japan 81/J7
Suitland-Silver Hill, Md. (†20746) 245/F5
Sui Xian, China 77/H5
Suizhong, China 77/K3
Sukabumi, Indonesia 85/H2
Sukadana, Indonesia 85/E6
Sukagawa, Japan 81/K5
Sukhana, U.S.S.R. 48/M3
Sukhinichi, U.S.S.R. 52/E4
Sukhona (riv.), U.S.S.R. 52/F2
Sukhothai, Thailand 72/D3
Sukhumi, U.S.S.R. 7/H4
Sukhumi, U.S.S.R. 52/F6
Sukhumi, U.S.S.R. 48/D5
Suk, Sudan 111/F5
Sukkertoppen, Greenl. 4/C12
Sukkur, Pakistan 54/H7
Sukkur, Pakistan 59/J4
Sukkur, Pakistan 68/B3
Sükösd, Hungary 41/E3
Sukumo, Japan 81/F7
Sul (chan.), Brazil 120/E2
Sul (chan.), Brazil 132/D2
Sula (isls.), Indonesia 54/O10
Sula (isls.), Indonesia 85/H6
Sula, Mont. (59871) 262/B5
Sulaco, Honduras 154/D3
Sulaco (riv.), Honduras 154/D3
Sulaiman (range), Pakistan 68/C3
Sulaimaniya (gov.), Iraq 66/D3
Sulaimaniya, Iraq 59/E2
Sulaimaniya, Iraq 66/D3
Sulaiyil, Saudi Arabia 59/E5
Sulakyurt, Turkey 63/E2
Sulanheer, Mongolia 77/G3
Sulawesi (isl.), Indonesia 85/G6
Sulechów, Poland 47/B2
Sulęcin, Poland 47/B2
Sulgen, Switzerland 39/H1
Sulina, Romania 45/J3
Sulitelma (mt.), Sweden 18/K3
Sulitjelma, Norway 18/K3
Sulitjelma (mt.), Norway 18/J3
Sullana, Peru 128/B5
Sullana, Peru 120/A3
Sulligent, Ala. (35586) 195/B3
Sullivan (lake), Alberta 182/D3
Sullivan, Ill. (61951) 222/E4
Sullivan (co.), Ind. 227/C6
Sullivan, Ind. (47882) 227/C6
Sullivan, Ky. (42460) 237/E6
Sullivan, Maine (†04689) 243/G6
Sullivan○, Maine (†04689) 243/G6
Sullivan (co.), Mo. 261/F2
Sullivan, Mo. (63080) 261/K6
Sullivan (co.), N.H. 268/C5
Sullivan○, N.H. (†03445) 268/C5
Sullivan (co.), N.Y. 276/L7
Sullivan, Ohio (44880) 284/F3
Sullivan (co.), Pa. 294/J3
Sullivan (co.), Tenn. 237/S7
Sullivan (lake), Wash. 310/H2
Sullivan, W. Va. (†25847) 312/D7
Sullivan, Wis. (53178) 317/H1
Sullivan Gardens, Tenn. (†37660) 237/R8
Sullivan Mines, Québec 174/B3
Sullivans Island, S.C. (29482) 296/H6
Sully, Iowa (50251) 229/H5
Sully, Québec 172/H2
Sully (co.), S. Dak. 298/J4
Sulmona, Italy 34/D3
Sulphide, Ontario 177/G3
Sulphur (riv.), Ark. 202/B7
Sulphur, Ind. (47174) 227/E8
Sulphur, Ky. (40070) 237/L4
Sulphur, La. (70663) 238/D6
Sulphur, Nev. (†89445) 266/C2
Sulphur, Okla. (73086) 288/N5
Sulphur (creek), S. Dak. 298/D4
Sulphur (riv.), Texas 303/J4
Sulphur City, Ark. (†72701) 202/B2
Sulphur Creek, Tasmania 99/C3
Sulphur Draw (dry riv.), Texas 303/B4
Sulphur Fork, Red (riv.), Tenn. 237/H8
Sulphur Rock, Ark. (72579) 202/H2
Sulphur Spring (valley), Ariz. 198/F6
Sulphur Spring (range), Nev. 266/E3
Sulphur Springs, Ala. (†30738) 195/G1
Sulphur Springs, Ark. (72768) 202/B1
Sulphur Springs, Ind. (47388) 227/G4
Sulphur Springs, Iowa (†50588) 229/C3
Sulphur Springs, Mo. (63083) 261/M6
Sulphur Springs, Ohio (44881) 284/E4
Sulphur Springs, Texas (75482) 303/J4
Sulphur Springs (creek), Texas 303/B4
Sulphur Well, Ky. (42129) 237/K6
Sultan, Ontario 175/D3
Sultan, Ontario 177/J5
Sultan (mts.), Turkey 63/D3
Sultan, Wash. (98294) 310/D3
Sultan (riv.), Wash. 310/D3
Sultanabad (Kashmar), Iran 66/L3
Sultandağı, Turkey 63/D3
Sultanhanı, Turkey 63/E3
Sultan Kudarat (prov.), Philippines 82/E7
Sulu (prov.), Philippines 82/C7
Sulu (arch.), Philippines 54/O9
Sulu (sea), Philippines 54/N9
Sulu (arch.), Philippines 82/B8
Sulu (arch.), Philippines 85/G4
Sulu (sea), Philippines 85/G4
Sulu (sea), Philippines 82/B6
Suluan (isl.), Philippines 82/F5
Suluova, Turkey 63/F2
Sulz, Switzerland 39/F1
Sulzbach, W. Germany 22/B4
Sulzbach-Rosenberg, W. Germany 22/D4
Sulzberger (bay) 5/B11
Sulzflüh (mt.), Switzerland 39/J2
Sumami Auma, Brazil 132/B4
Sumampa, Argentina 143/D2
Sumas, Wash. (98295) 310/C2
Sumatra, Fla. (32335) 212/B1
Sumatra (isl.), Indonesia 2/P6
Sumatra (isl.), Indonesia 54/L9
Sumatra (isl.), Indonesia 85/B5
Sumatra, Mont. (59083) 262/J4
Sumava Resorts, Ind. (46379) 227/C2
Sumba (isl.), Indonesia 54/N11
Sumba (isl.), Indonesia 85/F7
Sumba (str.), Indonesia 85/F7
Sumbawa (isl.), Indonesia 54/N11
Sumbawa (isl.), Indonesia 85/F7
Sumbawa Besar, Indonesia 85/F7
Sumbawanga, Tanzania 115/F5
Sumbay, Peru 128/G10
Sumbilca, Peru 128/D8
Sumbing (mt.), Indonesia 85/J2
Sumburgh (head), Scotland 15/G2
Sumedang, Indonesia 85/H2
Sümeg, Hungary 41/D3
Sumenep, Indonesia 85/L2
Sumgait, U.S.S.R. 7/J4
Sumgait, U.S.S.R. 52/G6
Sumidero, Cuba 158/A2
Sumiswald, Switzerland 39/E2
Sumiton, Ala. (35148) 195/D3
Summan (plat.), Saudi Arabia 59/E4
Summer (isl.), Mich. 250/C3
Summer (lake), Oreg. 188/C2
Summer (lake), Oreg. 291/G5
Summerberry, Sask. 181/J5
Summerdale, Ala. (36580) 195/C10
Summerfield, Ala. (†36701) 195/E5
Summerfield, Fla. (32691) 212/D2
Summerfield, Ill. (62289) 222/D5
Summerfield, Kansas (66541) 232/F2
Summerfield, La. (71079) 238/E1
Summerfield, Mo. (†65013) 261/J6
Summerfield, N.C. (27358) 281/K2
Summerfield, Ohio (43788) 284/H6
Summerfield, Okla. (74966) 288/S5
Summerfield, Texas (79085) 303/B3
Summerford, Newf. 166/C4
Summerford, Ohio (†43140) 284/D6
Summer Hill, Ill. (62372) 222/C4
Summerhill, Pa. (15958) 294/E5
Summer Isles (isls.), Scotland 15/C2
Summer Lake, Oreg. (97640) 291/G5
Summerland, Br. Col. 184/G5
Summerland, Calif. (93067) 204/F9
Summerland, Miss. (†39168) 256/F7
Summerland Key, Fla. (33042) 212/E7
Summers, Ark. (72769) 202/A2
Summers (co.), W. Va. 312/E7
Summerset, Iowa (†50125) 229/F6
Summer Shade, Ky. (42166) 237/K7
Summerside, Pr. Edward I. 168/E2
Summersville, Ky. (42782) 237/K6
Summersville, Mo. (65571) 261/J8
Summersville, Ohio (†43344) 284/D5
Summersville, W. Va. (26651) 312/E6
Summersville (lake), W. Va. 312/E6
Summerton, S.C. (29148) 296/G4
Summertown, Georgia (30466) 217/H5
Summertown, Tenn. (38483) 237/G10
Summerville, Georgia (30747) 217/B2
Summerville, La. (†71465) 238/F3
Summerville, Newf. 166/D2
Summerville, Oreg. (97876) 291/K2
Summerville, Pa. (15864) 294/D3
Summerville, S.C. (29483) 296/G5
Summerville Centre, Nova Scotia 168/D5
Summit, Ala. (†35031) 195/F2
Summit, Alaska (†99729) 196/J2
Summit, Ark. (72677) 202/E1
Summit (co.), Colo. 208/G3
Summit (peak), Colo. 208/F8
Summit (lake), Iowa 229/E6
Summit, Miss. (39666) 256/D8
Summit (lake), Nev. 266/C1
Summit, N.J. (07901) 273/E2
Summit (co.), Ohio 284/G3
Summit (creek), Oreg. 291/J3
Summit, Québec 172/E2
Summit, R.I. (†02827) 249/H6
Summit, S.C. (†29054) 296/E4
Summit, S. Dak. (57266) 298/P3
Summit (co.), Utah 304/D3
Summit, Utah (84772) 304/B6
Summit-Argo, Ill. (60501) 222/B6
Summit Bridge, Del. (†19709) 245/R2
Summit City, Calif. (96089) 204/C3
Summit City, Mich. (†49649) 250/D4
Summit Hill, Pa. (18250) 294/L4
Summit Lake, Wis. (54485) 317/H5
Summit Lake Ind. Res., Nev. 266/B1
Summit Point, W. Va. (25446) 312/K4
Summitville, Ind. (46070) 227/F4
Summitville, Iowa (†52632) 229/K8
Summitville, N.Y. (12781) 276/L7
Summitville, Ohio (43962) 284/J4
Summitville, Tenn. (37382) 237/K9
Summum, Ill. (†61501) 222/C3
Sumner (str.), Alaska 196/M2
Sumner, Georgia (31789) 217/E7
Sumner, Ill. (62466) 222/F5
Sumner, Iowa (50674) 229/J3
Sumner (co.), Kansas 232/E4
Sumner○, Maine (†04292) 243/C7
Sumner, Mich. (48889) 250/E5
Sumner, Miss. (38957) 256/D3
Sumner, Mo. (64681) 261/F3
Sumner, Nebr. (68878) 264/E4
Sumner (dam), N. Mex. 274/E4
Sumner (lake), N. Mex. 274/E4
Sumner (lake), N. Zealand 100/D5
Sumner, Oreg. (†97420) 291/C4
Sumner (co.), Tenn. 237/J8
Sumner, Wash. (98390) 310/C3
Sumner-East Sumner, Maine (04232) 243/C7
Sumoto, Japan 81/G6
Šumperk, Czech. 41/D1
Sumprabum, Burma 72/C1
Sumpter, Ark. (†71647) 202/F7
Sumpter, Oreg. (97877) 291/J3
Sumrall, Miss. (39482) 256/E8
Sumter (co.), Ala. 195/B5
Sumter, Ala. (†35086) 195/D4
Sumter (co.), Fla. 212/D3
Sumter (co.), Georgia 217/D6
Sumter (co.), S.C. 296/G4
Sumter, S.C. (29150) 296/G4
Sumterville, Ala. (†35460) 195/B5
Sumy, U.S.S.R. 7/H3
Sumy, U.S.S.R. 52/E4
Sumy, U.S.S.R. 48/D4
Sun, La. (70463) 238/L5
Sun (riv.), Mont. 262/D3
Sunagawa, Japan 81/K2
Sunapee○, N.H. (03782) 268/C5
Sunapee (lake), N.H. 268/C5
Sunart, Loch (inlet), Scotland 15/C4
Sunbeam, Colo. (†81640) 208/C1
Sunbeam, Idaho (†83278) 220/D5
Sunbright, Tenn. (37872) 237/M8
Sunburg, Minn. (56289) 255/C5
Sunburst, Mont. (59482) 262/E2
Sunbury, Iowa (†52778) 229/M5
Sunbury (co.), New Bruns. 170/D3
Sunbury, N.C. (27979) 281/R2
Sunbury, Ohio (43074) 284/E5
Sunbury, Pa. (17801) 294/J4
Sunbury, Victoria 97/C5
Sunbury-on-Thames, England 13/G8
Sunbury-on-Thames, England 10/B6
Sunchales, Argentina 143/F5
Suncho Corral, Argentina 143/D2
Sunch'ŏn, N. Korea 81/B4
Sunch'ŏn, S. Korea 81/C6
Sun City, Ariz. (*85351) 198/C5
Sun City, Calif. (92381) 204/F11
Sun City, Fla. (33586) 212/D4
Sun City, Kansas (67143) 232/D4
Sun City Center, Fla. (†33570) 212/C3
Suncook, N.H. (03275) 268/D5
Suncook (lakes), N.H. 268/E5
Suncook (riv.), N.H. 268/E5
Sunda (isls.), Indonesia 54/L10
Sunda (str.), Indonesia 54/M10
Sunda (str.), Indonesia 85/C7
Sundahl, Minn. (†56545) 255/B3
Sundance, Wyo. (82729) 319/H1
Sundarbans (reg.), Bangladesh 68/F4
Sundarbans (reg.), India 68/F4
Sundargarh, India 68/E4
Sunday (riv.), Maine 243/B6
Sundbyberg, Sweden 18/G1
Sunderland, England 13/J3
Sunderland, England 10/F3
Sunderland○, Mass. (01375) 249/D3
Sunderland, Ontario 177/E3
Sunderland○, Vt. (†05250) 268/A5
Sundown, Manitoba 179/F5
Sundown, Texas (79372) 303/B4
Sundra, S. Africa 118/J6
Sundre, Alberta 182/C4
Sundridge, Ontario 177/E2
Sundsvall, Sweden 18/K5
Sundsvall, Sweden 7/F2
Sunfield, Ill. (†62832) 222/D5
Sunfield, Mich. (48890) 250/D6
Sunfish Lake, Minn. (†55075) 255/E6
Sunflower, Ala. (36581) 195/B8
Sunflower (mt.), Kansas 232/A2
Sunflower (co.), Miss. 256/C3
Sunflower, Miss. (38778) 256/C3
Sunflower (riv.), Miss. 256/C5
Sungaipenuh, Indonesia 85/C6
Sungai Petani, Malaysia 72/C6
Sungurlu, Turkey 63/F2
Sunland, Calif. (91040) 204/C10
Sunland Gardens, Fla. (†33450) 212/F4
Sunman, Ind. (47041) 227/G6
Sunndalsøra, Norway 18/F5
Sunne, Sweden 18/H7
Sunnybrae, Nova Scotia 168/F3
Sunnybrook, Alberta 182/C3
Sunny Corner, New Bruns. 170/E2
Sunnydale, Wash. (†98101) 310/B2
Sunny Isles, Fla. (33160) 212/C4
Sunnymead, Calif. (92388) 204/F11
Sunnynook, Alberta 182/E4
Sunny Point Mil. Ocean Term., N.C. 281/O6
Sunnyside, Fla. (32461) 212/C6
Sunny Side, Georgia (30284) 217/D4
Sunnyside, Ill. (†60050) 222/A4
Sunnyside, New Bruns. 170/D1
Sunnyside, Newf. 166/D2
Sunnyside, Utah (84539) 304/D4
Sunnyside, Wash. (98944) 310/F4
Sunnyslope, Alberta 182/D4
Sunny South, Ala. (36780) 195/C7
Sunnyvale, Calif. (*94086) 204/K3
Sunnyvale, Texas (†75149) 303/H2
Sunny Valley, Oreg. (97478) 291/D5
Sunol, Calif. (94586) 204/L2
Sunol, Nebr. (†69149) 264/B3
Sun Prairie, Wis. (53590) 317/H9
Sunray, Texas (79086) 303/C1
Sunrise, Fla. (33313) 212/B4
Sunrise, Wyo. (†82215) 319/H3
Sunrise Beach, Mo. (65079) 261/G6
Sunrise Manor, Nev. (†89110) 266/F6
Sunrise Ridge, Ill. (†60097) 222/E1
Sunrise Valley, Br. Col. 184/G2
Sun River, Mont. (59483) 262/E3
Sunsas, Serranía de (mts.), Bolivia 136/F5
Sunset, Ark. (†72364) 202/K3
Sunset (peak), Idaho 220/E6
Sunset, La. (70584) 238/F6
Sunset, Maine (04683) 243/F7
Sunset, S.C. (29685) 296/B2
Sunset, Texas (79407) 303/G4
Sunset, Utah (†84015) 304/B2
Sunset Beach, Calif. (90742) 204/C11
Sunset Beach, Hawaii (†96712) 218/E1
Sunset Beach, N.C. (28459) 281/N7
Sunset Crater Nat'l Mon., Ariz. 198/D3
Sunset Hills, Mo. (†63101) 261/O4
Sunset Hills, Va. (22090) 307/R2
Sunset House, Alberta 182/B2
Sunset Prairie, Br. Co. 184/G2
Sunshine, La. (†70776) 238/K2
Sunshine, Maine (†04627) 243/G7
Sunshine, Victoria 88/K7
Sunshine, Victoria 97/H5
Sunspot, N. Mex. (88349) 274/D6
Suntar, U.S.S.R. 48/M3
Suntrana, Alaska (†99743) 196/J2
Sun Valley, Idaho (83353) 220/D6
Sun Valley, Nev. (†89431) 266/B3
Sun Valley, Sask. 181/F5
Sunyani, Ghana 106/D7
Sunzu (mt.), Zambia 115/F5
Suo (sea), Japan 81/E7
Suolahti, Finland 18/O5
Suomussalmi, Finland 18/Q4
Suonenjoki, Finland 18/P5
Suong, Cambodia 72/E5
Suoyarvi, U.S.S.R. 52/D2
Supai, Ariz. (86435) 198/C2
Supe, Peru 128/D8
Superb, Sask. 181/B4
Superior (lake) 162/G-H6
Superior (lake) 146/K5
Superior (lake) 188/J1
Superior, Ariz. (85273) 198/D5
Superior, Colo. (†80027) 208/J3
Superior, Iowa (51363) 229/D2
Superior (lag.), Mexico 150/M9
Superior (lake), Mich. 250/C2
Superior (lake), Minn. 255/G3
Superior, Mont. (59872) 262/B3
Superior, Nebr. (68978) 264/F4
Superior (lake), Ontario 177/H5
Superior (lake), Ontario 175/C3
Superior, Wis. 188/H1
Superior, Wis. (54880) 317/C2
Superior (lake), Wis. 317/F1
Superior, Wyo. (82945) 319/D4
Superior Village, Wis. (†54880) 317/B2
Superstition (mts.), Ariz. 198/D5
Suphan Buri, Thailand 72/C4
Süphan Dağı (mt.), Turkey 59/D2
Süphan Dağı (mt.), Turkey 63/K3
Supiori (isl.), Indonesia 85/K6
Supply, N.C. (28462) 281/N6
Supreme, La. (†70372) 238/K4
Supung (res.), N. Korea 81/B3
Suqian, China 77/J5
Suquamish, Wash. (98392) 310/A1
Sur (pt.), Calif. 204/D7
Sur, Lebanon 63/F6
Sur, Oman 59/G5
Sura, Ras (cape), Somalia 115/J1
Sura (riv.), U.S.S.R. 52/G4
Surab, Pakistan 68/B3
Surab, Pakistan 59/J4
Surabaya, Indonesia 54/N10
Surabaya, Indonesia 85/K2
Surada, India 68/E5
Surahammar, Sweden 18/J7
Surakarta, Indonesia 54/N10
Surakarta, Indonesia 85/J2
Šurany, Czech. 41/E2
Surat, India 54/J7
Surat, India 68/C4
Surat, Queensland 88/H5
Suratgarh, India 68/C3
Surat Thani, Thailand 72/C5
Sur del Cabo San Antonio (pt.), Argentina 143/E4
Surdulica, Yugoslavia 45/F4
Surendranagar, India 68/C4
Suresnes, France 28/A2
Suretka, C. Rica 154/F6
Surette Island, Nova Scotia 168/B5
Surf, Calif. (†93436) 204/E9
Surf City, N.J. (08008) 273/E4
Surf City, N.C. (28445) 281/O6
Surfside, Fla. (33154) 212/B4
Surfside Beach, S.C. (29577) 296/K4

Taurianova 455

Taichung, China 77/K7
Taichung, Taiwan 54/O7
Taieri (riv.), N. Zealand 100/C7
Taif, Saudi Arabia 54/F7
Taif, Saudi Arabia 59/D5
Taigu, China 77/H4
Taihape, N. Zealand 100/E3
Taihe, China 77/J6
Tai Hu (lake), China 77/J5
Tailem Bend, S. Australia 88/F7
Tailem Bend, S. Australia 94/F6
Tailfingen, W. Germany 22/C4
Taima, Saudi Arabia 59/C4
Tain, Scotland 15/D3
Tain, Scotland 10/D2
Tainan, China 77/J7
Tainaron (cape), Greece 7/G5
Tainaron (cape), Greece 45/F7
Taintor, Iowa (50253) 229/H6
Taipei, China 77/K7
Taipei (cap.), Rep. of China 54/O7
Taipei (cap.), Rep. of China 2/R4
Taiping, Malaysia 72/D6
Taitao (pen.), Chile 120/B7
Taitao (cape), Chile 138/D6
Taitao (pen.), Chile 138/D6
Taits Gap, Ala. (†35121) 195/F3
Taitung, China 77/K7
Taivalkoski, Finland 18/P4
Taiwan 54/N7
Taiwan 2/R4
Taiwan (str.) 54/N7
Taiwan (isl.) 54/N7
Taiwan, China 77/K7
Taiwan (Formosa) (isl.), China 77/K7
Taiwan (Formosa) (str.), China 77/J7
Taiyuan, China 77/H4
Taiyuan, China 54/N6
Taizhou (Tachen) (isls.), China 77/K6
Taizhou (Taichow), China 77/K5
Ta'izz, Yemen Arab Rep. 54/F8
Ta'izz, Yemen Arab Rep. 59/D7
Tajimi, Japan 81/H6
Tajique, N. Mex. (87057) 274/C4
Tajo (Tagus) (riv.), Spain 33/D3
Tajrish, Iran 66/G3
Tajumulco (vol.), Guatemala 154/B3
Tak, Thailand 72/C3
Takaishi, Japan 81/H8
Takaka, N. Zealand 100/D4
Takalar, Indonesia 85/F7
Takama, Guyana 131/C3
Takamatsu, Japan 81/F6
Takaoka, Japan 81/H5
Takapau, N. Zealand 100/F4
Takapuna, N. Zealand 100/B1
Takarazuka, Japan 81/H7
Takaroa (atoll), Fr. Poly. 87/M7
Takasaki, Japan 81/J5
Takatsuki, Japan 81/J7
Takayama, Japan 81/H5
Takefu, Japan 81/G6
Takeshima (isls.), Japan 81/F5
Takestan, Iran 66/F2
Takev, Cambodia 72/E5
Takhiatash, U.S.S.R. 48/F5
Takhta-Bazar, U.S.S.R. 48/G6
Takikawa, Japan 81/K2
Takingeun, Indonesia 85/B5
Takitimu (mts.), N. Zealand 100/A6
Takkaze (riv.), Ethiopia 111/G5
Takla (lake), Br. Col. 184/D2
Takla Makan (des.), China 54/K6
Takla Makan (Taklimakan Shamo) (des.), China 77/B4
Taklimakan Shamo (des.), China 77/B4
Tako, Sask. 181/B3
Takoma Park, Md. (20912) 245/F4
Takoradi, Ghana 106/D8
Takoradi-Sekondi, Ghana 102/B4
Taksimo, U.S.S.R. 48/M4
Taku (glac.), Alaska 196/N1
Taku (riv.), Alaska 196/N1
Taku (riv.), Br. Col. 184/J2
Takua Pa, Thailand 72/C5
Takutu (riv.), Guyana 131/B4
Tala, Mexico 150/H6
Tala, Uruguay 145/D5
Talab (riv.), Iran 59/H4
Talab (riv.), Iran 66/N6
Talab (riv.), Pakistan 68/A3
Talagante, Chile 138/G4
Talai (Da'an, Dalai), China 77/K2
Talak (reg.), Niger 106/E5
Talala, Okla. (74080) 288/P1
Talamanca (range), C. Rica 154/F6
Talangbetutu, Indonesia 85/C6
Talara, Peru 128/B5
Talara, Peru 120/A3
Talaud (isls.), Indonesia 54/O9
Talaud (isls.), Indonesia 85/H5
Talavera de la Reina, Spain 33/D2
Talawe (mt.), Papua N.G. 86/B2
Talbert, Ky. (41377) 237/P6
Talbingo, N.S. Wales 97/E4
Talbot, Alberta 182/E3
Talbot (isl.), Fla. 212/E1
Talbot (co.), Georgia 217/C5
Talbot, Ind. (47984) 227/C3
Talbot (co.), Md. 245/O5
Talbot (inlet), N.W. Terrs. 187/L2
Talbot (cape), W. Australia 88/D2
Talbot (cape), W. Australia 92/D1
Talbott, Tenn. (37877) 237/P8
Talbotton, Georgia (31827) 217/C5
Talca, Chile 138/A11
Talca, Chile 120/B6
Talca (pt.), Chile 138/E3
Talcahuano, Chile 138/D1
Talcahuano, Chile 120/B6
Talcán (isl.), Chile 138/D4
Talco, Texas (75487) 303/K4
Talcott (range), Conn. 210/D1
Talcott, W. Va. (24981) 312/E7
Talcottville, Conn. (†06066) 210/F1
Taldy-Kurgan, U.S.S.R. 54/J5
Taldy-Kurgan, U.S.S.R. 48/H5
Taleh, Somalia 115/J2
Talent, Oreg. (97540) 291/E5
Talgar, U.S.S.R. 48/H5
Talgarth, Wales 13/D5
Tali (Dali), China 77/E6
Taliabu (isl.), Indonesia 85/G6
Taliaferro (co.), Georgia 217/G3
Talibon, Philippines 82/E5
Talihina, Okla. (74571) 288/S5
Talina, Bolivia 136/B7
Tali Post, Sudan 111/F6
Talisayan, Philippines 82/E6
Talisheek, La. (70464) 238/L5
Talita, Uruguay 145/D4
Tal Kaif, Iraq 66/C2
Talkeetna, Alaska (99676) 196/B1
Talkeetna (mts.), Alaska 196/J2
Talkheh (riv.), Iran 66/E1
Talking Rock, Georgia (30175) 217/D1
Tallaboa, P. Rico 161/B3
Talladega (co.), Ala. 195/F4
Talladega, Ala. (35160) 195/F4
Talladega Springs, Ala. (†35150) 195/F4
Tallaght, Ireland 17/J5
Tallahaga (creek), Miss. 256/F4
Tallahala (creek), Miss. 256/F7
Tallahassee (cap.), Fla. 146/K6
Tallahassee (cap.), Fla. 188/K4
Tallahassee (cap.), Fla. (*32301) 212/B1
Tallahatchie (co.), Miss. 256/D3
Tallahatchie (riv.), Miss. 256/D3
Tallahatta Springs, Ala. (†36784) 195/C7
Tallangatta, Victoria 97/D5
Tallant, Okla. (†74002) 288/O1
Tallapoosa (co.), Ala. 195/G5
Tallapoosa (riv.), Ala. 195/G4
Tallapoosa, Georgia (30176) 217/B3
Tallapoosa, Mo. (63878) 261/N9
Tallassee, Ala. (36078) 195/G5
Tallinn, U.S.S.R. 7/G3
Tallinn (cap.), U.S.S.R. 53/C1
Tallinn, U.S.S.R. 48/C4
Tallinn, U.S.S.R. 52/B3
Tallmadge, Ohio (44278) 284/H3
Tallman, N.Y. (10982) 276/J8
Tallman, Sask. 181/E3
Tallmansville, W. Va. (26237) 312/F5
Tallow, Ireland 17/F7
Tallula, Ill. (62688) 222/D4
Tallulah, La. (71282) 238/H2
Tallulah Falls, Georgia (30573) 217/F1
Talma, Ind. (†46975) 227/E2
Talmage, Kansas (67482) 232/E2
Talmage, Nebr. (68448) 264/H4
Talmage, Sask. 181/H6
Talmage, Utah (84073) 304/D3
Talmo, Georgia (30575) 217/E2
Talmo, Kansas (†66935) 232/E2
Talmoon, Minn. (56637) 255/E3
Talodi, Sudan 111/F5
Talofofo (bay), Guam 86/K7
Taloga, Okla. (73667) 288/J2
Talon (lake), Ontario 177/E1
Taloqan, Afghanistan 68/B1
Taloqan, Afghanistan 59/J2
Talpa, Texas (76882) 303/E6
Talpa de Allende, Mexico 150/G6
Talparo, Trin. & Tob. 161/B10
Talquin (lake), Fla. 212/B1
Talsi, U.S.S.R. 53/B2
Taltal, Chile 138/A5
Taltal, Chile 120/B5
Taltal, Quebrada de (riv.), Chile 138/B5
Taltson (riv.), N.W. Terrs. 187/G3
Talvik, Norway 18/N2
Talyawalka (creek), N.S. Wales 97/B2
Talyawalka Ana Branch, Darling (riv.), N.S. Wales 97/B3
Tama (co.), Iowa 229/H4
Tama, Iowa (52339) 229/H5
Tama (riv.), Japan 81/O2
Tamaha, Okla. (†74462) 288/S4
Tamaki (str.), N. Zealand 100/C1
Tamale, Ghana 102/B4
Tamale, Ghana 106/D7
Tamalpais (mt.), Calif. 204/H1
Tamana (mt.), Trin. & Tob. 161/B10
Tamanrasset, Algeria 106/F4
Tamanrasset, Algeria 102/C2
Tamanrasset, Wadi (dry riv.), Algeria 106/E4
Tamaqua, Pa. (18252) 294/L4
Tamar (riv.), England 13/C7
Tamar (riv.), England 10/D5
Tamar (riv.), Tasmania 99/D3
Támara, Colombia 126/D5
Tamarac, Fla. (†33321) 212/B3
Tamarac (riv.), Minn. 255/A2
Tamarack, Idaho (†83654) 220/B5
Tamarack (isl.), Manitoba 179/F3
Tamarack, Minn. (55787) 255/E4
Tamarack (riv.), Minn. 255/D2
Tamarack, Pa. (†17729) 294/G3
Tamarite de Litera, Spain 33/G2
Tamaro (mt.), Switzerland 39/G4
Tamaroa, Ill. (62888) 222/D5
Tamarugal, Pampa del (plain), Chile 138/B3
Tamási, Hungary 41/E3
Tamassee, S.C. (29686) 296/A2
Tamatama, Venezuela 124/F6
Tamatave (Toamasina), Madagascar 118/H3
Tamaulipas (state), Mexico 150/K4
Tamaya, Chile 138/A8
Tamayo, Dom. Rep. 158/D6
Tamazula, Mexico 150/F4
Tamazulapan del Progreso, Mexico 150/L8
Tamazunchale, Mexico 150/K6
Tambacounda, Senegal 106/B6
Tambar Springs, N.S. Wales 97/E2
Tambelan (isls.), Indonesia 85/D5
Tamberías, Argentina 143/C3
Tambey, U.S.S.R. 48/G2
Tambo (riv.), Peru 128/G11
Tambo, Queensland 88/H4
Tambo, Queensland 95/C5
Tambo de Mora, Peru 128/D9
Tambo Grande, Peru 128/B5
Tambohorano, Madagascar 118/G3
Tambopata (riv.), Peru 128/H9
Tambores, Uruguay 145/C2
Tamboril, Dom. Rep. 158/D5
Tamboritha (mt.), Victoria 97/D5
Tambov, U.S.S.R. 7/J3
Tambov, U.S.S.R. 52/F4
Tambov, U.S.S.R. 48/E4
Tambura, Sudan 111/E6
Tamchakett, Mauritania 106/B5
Tame, Colombia 126/E4
Tame (riv.), England 10/G3
Tâmega (riv.), Portugal 33/C2
Tamentit, Algeria 106/D3
Tamiahua, Mexico 150/L6
Tamiami (canal), Fla. 212/E6
Tamil Nadu (state), India 68/D6
Tamin (gov.), Iraq 66/D3
Tamina (riv.), Switzerland 39/H3
Tamins, Switzerland 39/H3
Tamise (Temse), Belgium 27/E6
Tam Ky, Vietnam 72/F4
Tammisaari (Ekenäs), Finland 18/N6
Tamms, Ill. (62988) 222/D6
Tammun, West Bank 65/C3
Tamo, Ark. (71644) 202/G5
Tamora, Nebr. (†68434) 264/G4
Tampa, Fla. 188/K5
Tampa, Fla. 146/K7
Tampa (bay), Fla. 188/K5
Tampa, Fla. (*33601) 212/C2
Tampa (bay), Fla. 212/D4
Tampa, Kansas (67483) 232/E3
Tampere, Finland 7/G2
Tampere, Finland 18/N6
Tampico, Ill. (61283) 222/D2
Tampico, Ind. (†47220) 227/F7
Tampico, Mexico 146/J7
Tampico, Mexico 150/L5
Tampico, Mont. (†59230) 262/K2
Tampico, Wash. (†98901) 310/E4
Tampoc (riv.), Fr. Guiana 131/E4
Tam Quan, Vietnam 72/F4
Tamra, Saudi Arabia 59/E5
Tams, W. Va. (25933) 312/D7
Tamsagbulag, Mongolia 77/J2
Tamsagout, Mauritania 106/C4
Tamshiyacu, Peru 128/F5
Tamsweg, Austria 41/B3
Tamuín, Mexico 150/K6
Tamuning, Guam 86/K7
Tamworth, Australia 87/E9
Tamworth, England 13/F5
Tamworth, England 10/G3
Tamworth○, N.H. (03886) 268/E4
Tamworth, N.S. Wales 88/J6
Tamworth, N.S. Wales 97/F2
Tamworth, Ontario 177/H3
Tamyang, S. Korea 81/C6
Tana (lake), Ethiopia 102/F3
Tana (lake), Ethiopia 111/G5
Tana (riv.), Finland 18/P2
Tana (riv.), Kenya 102/G5
Tana (riv.), Kenya 115/G4
Tana, Norway 18/Q1
Tana (riv.), Norway 18/P1
Tanabe, Kyoto, Japan 81/J7
Tanabe, Wakayama, Japan 81/G7
Tanacross, Alaska (99776) 196/K2
Tanafjord (fjord), Norway 18/Q1
Tanaga (isl.), Alaska 196/K4
Tanaga (vol.), Alaska 196/K4
Tanahgrogot, Indonesia 85/F6
Tanahmerah, Indonesia 85/K7
Tanah Merah, Malaysia 72/D6
Tanamá (riv.), P. Rico 161/B1
Tanami (des.), North. Terr. 88/E3
Tanami, North. Terr. 93/A5
Tanami (des.), North. Terr. 93/C5
Tánamo, Cuba 158/J3
Tan An, Vietnam 72/E5
Tanana, Alaska 188/D5
Tanana, Alaska (99777) 196/H1
Tanana (riv.), Alaska 146/D3
Tanana (riv.), Alaska 188/D5
Tanana (riv.), Alaska 196/J2
Tananarive (Antananarivo) (cap.), Madagascar 118/H3
Tanaro (riv.), Italy 34/B2
Tanch'ŏn, N. Korea 81/D3
Tancook Island, Nova Scotia 168/D4
Tanda, India 68/E3
Tandag, Philippines 82/F6
Tandil, Argentina 143/E4
Tandil, Argentina 120/D6
Tando Adam, Pakistan 68/B3
Tando Allahyar, Pakistan 68/B3
Tandou (lake), N.S. Wales 97/A3
Tandragee, N. Ireland 17/J3
Tanega (isl.), Japan 81/E8
Taney (co.), Mo. 261/F9
Taneycomo (lake), Mo. 261/F9
Taneytown, Md. (21787) 245/K2
Taneyville, Mo. (65759) 261/F9
Tanezrouft (des.), Algeria 102/C2
Tanezrouft (des.), Algeria 106/E4
Tang, Kas (isl.), Cambodia 72/D5
Tanga (isls.), Papua N.G. 86/C1
Tanga (reg.), Tanzania 115/G5
Tanga, Tanzania 115/G4
Tanga, Tanzania 102/F5
Tangainony, Madagascar 118/H4
Tangalla, Sri Lanka 68/E7
Tanganyika (lake) 102/F5
Tanganyika (lake), Burundi 115/E5
Tanganyika (lake), Tanzania 115/E5
Tanganyika (lake), Zaire 115/E5
Tanganyika (lake), Zambia 115/E5
Tangent (pt.), Alaska 196/H1
Tangent, Alberta 182/B2
Tangent, Oreg. (97389) 291/D3
Tangerang, Indonesia 85/G1
Tangermünde, E. Germany 22/D2
Tanggula Shan (range), China 77/D5
Tangier, Ind. (47985) 227/C5
Tangier (sound), Md. 245/P8
Tangier (Tanger), Morocco 106/C1
Tangier, Morocco 102/B1
Tangier, Nova Scotia 168/F4
Tangier (riv.), Nova Scotia 168/F4
Tangier, Okla. (†73801) 288/G2
Tangier, Va. (23440) 307/R5
Tangier (isl.), Va. 307/R5
Tangier (sound), Va. 307/S5
Tangipahoa (par.), La. 238/K5
Tangipahoa, La. (70465) 238/J5
Tangipahoa (riv.), La. 238/N1
Tangra Yumco (lake), China 77/C5
Tangshan, China 77/J4
Tangshan, China 54/N5
Tangub, Philippines 82/D6
Tangyanika (lake) 2/L6
Tangyuan, China 77/L2
Tanimbar (isls.), Indonesia 54/P10
Tanimbar (isls.), Indonesia 85/J7
Tanjay, Philippines 82/D6
Tanjore (Thanjavur), India 68/D6
Tanjungbalai, Indonesia 85/C5
Tanjungkarang, Indonesia 54/M10
Tanjungkarang, Indonesia 85/C7
Tanjungpandan, Indonesia 85/D6
Tanjungpinang, Indonesia 85/C5
Tanjungpriok, Indonesia 85/H1
Tanjungpura, Indonesia 85/B5
Tanjungredeb, Indonesia 85/F5
Tanjungselor, Indonesia 85/F5
Tanna (isl.), Vanuatu 87/H7
Tanner, Ala. (35671) 195/E1
Tanner, W. Va. (26179) 312/E5
Tannersville, N.Y. (12485) 276/M6
Tannersville, Pa. (18372) 294/M3
Tannis (bay), Denmark 21/D2
Tannu-Ola (range), Mongolia 77/D1
Tannu-Ola (range), U.S.S.R. 48/K5
Tanon (str.), Philippines 82/D6
Tanout, Niger 106/F6
Tanque Verde, Ariz. (†85701) 198/E6
Tanta, Egypt 111/J3
Tanta, Egypt 59/B3
Tantallon, Sask. 181/K5
Tantalus (mt.), Hawaii 218/D4
Tan-Tan, Morocco 106/B3
Tantoyuca, Mexico 150/L6
Tantung (Dandong), China 77/K3
Tanumshede, Sweden 18/G7
Tanunda, S. Australia 94/C6
Tanzania 2/L6
Tanzania 102/F5
TANZANIA 115/F5
Tao, Ko (isl.), Thailand 72/C5
Tao'an, China 77/K2
Taole, China 77/G4
Taongi (atoll), Marshall Is. 87/G4
Taopi, Minn. (55977) 255/F7
Taormina, Italy 34/E6
Taos, Mo. (†65101) 261/H5
Taos (co.), N. Mex. 274/D2
Taos, N. Mex. (87571) 274/D2
Taos Pueblo, N. Mex. (†87571) 274/D2
Taoudenni, Mali 106/D4
Taoudenni, Mali 102/B2
Taourirt, Algeria 106/E3
Taourirt, Morocco 106/D2
Taouz, Morocco 106/D2
Taoyuan, China 77/K6
Tapa, U.S.S.R. 53/C1
Tapacarí, Bolivia 136/B5
Tapachula, Mexico 150/N9
Tapajós (riv.), Brazil 2/G6
Tapajós (riv.), Brazil 120/D3
Tapajós (riv.), Brazil 132/B4
Tapaktuan, Indonesia 85/B5
Tapalquén, Argentina 143/E4
Tapanahoni (riv.), Suriname 131/D4
Tapani (lake), Québec 172/B3
Tapanui, N. Zealand 100/B6
Tapaz, Philippines 82/D5
Tapera do Jeronimo, Brazil 132/C2
Tapeta, Liberia 106/C7
Tapi, Mae Nam (riv.), Thailand 72/C5
Tapiantana Group (isls.), Philippines 82/D7
Tapiche (riv.), Peru 128/E6
Taping (riv.), Burma 72/C1
Tápiószele, Hungary 41/E3
Tapirapecó, Sierra (mts.), Venezuela 124/F7
Tapiutan (isl.), Philippines 82/B5
Tapoco, N.C. (28780) 281/A4
Tapolca, Hungary 41/D3
Tappahannock, Va. (22560) 307/O5
Tappan (lake), N.J. 273/C1
Tappan, N.Y. (10983) 276/K8
Tappan (lake), Ohio 284/H5
Tappen, N. Dak. (58487) 282/L6
Tappi (cape), Japan 81/K3
Tapti (riv.), India 68/D4
Tapul (isl.), Philippines 82/C8
Tapul Group (isls.), Philippines 85/G4
Tapul Group (isls.), Philippines 82/C8
Taputapu (cape), Amer. Samoa 86/N9
Taquari (riv.), Brazil 132/C7
Taquaritinga, Brazil 132/D8
Taquaritinga, Brazil 135/B2
Tar (riv.), N.C. 281/O3
Tara (hill), Ireland 17/H4
Tara, Ontario 177/C3
Tara (isl.), Philippines 82/C4
Tara, Queensland 95/D5
Tara, Queensland 88/J5
Tara, U.S.S.R. 48/H4
Tara (riv.), Yugoslavia 45/D4
Tarabuco, Bolivia 136/C6
Tarabulus, Lebanon 63/F5
Tarabulus, Lebanon 59/C3
Taradale, N. Zealand 100/F3
Taraira (riv.), Colombia 126/F8
Tarairí, Bolivia 136/D7
Tarakan, Indonesia 54/N9
Tarakan, Indonesia 85/F5
Taralga, N.S. Wales 97/E4
Tarama (isl.), Japan 81/L7
Tarancón, Spain 33/E3
Tarangire Nat'l Park, Tanzania 115/G4
Taranna, Tasmania 99/D5
Taransay (isl.), Scotland 15/A3
Taranto (prov.), Italy 34/F4
Taranto, Italy 34/F4
Taranto, Italy 7/F4
Taranto (gulf), Italy 7/F5
Taranto (gulf), Italy 34/F5
Tarapacá (reg.), Chile 138/B2
Tarapacá, Chile 138/B2
Tarapacá, Colombia 126/F9
Tarapaya, Bolivia 136/B6
Tarapoto, Peru 120/B3
Tarapoto, Peru 128/D6
Tarare, France 28/F5
Tararua (range), N. Zealand 100/E4
Tarascon, France 28/F6
Tarasp, Switzerland 39/K3
Tarata, Bolivia 136/C5
Tarata, Peru 128/H11
Tarauacá, Brazil 132/G10
Tarauaca, Brazil 120/C3
Taravao (bay), Fr. Poly. 86/T13
Taravao (isth.), Fr. Poly. 86/T13
Tarawa (atoll), Kiribati 87/H5
Tarazona, Spain 33/E2
Tarazona de la Mancha, Spain 33/F3
Tarbat Ness (prom.), Scotland 15/E3
Tarbert, Ireland 17/C6
Tarbert, Strathclyde, Scotland 15/C5
Tarbert, W. Isles, Scotland 15/B3
Tarbert, East Loch (inlet), Scotland 15/B3
Tarbert, Loch (inlet), Scotland 15/B5
Tarbert, West Loch (inlet), Scotland 15/C5
Tarbert, West Loch (inlet), Scotland 15/A3
Tarbes, France 7/E4
Tarbes, France 28/D6
Tarbolton, Scotland 15/D5
Tarboro, Georgia (†31568) 217/J8
Tarboro, N.C. (27886) 281/O3
Tarbot, Nova Scotia 168/H2
Tarcoola, S. Australia 88/E6
Tarcoola, S. Australia 94/D4
Tarcutta, N.S. Wales 97/D4
Tardienta, Spain 33/F2
Tardošked, Czech. 41/E2
Taree, N. S. Wales 88/J6
Taree, N.S. Wales 97/G2
Tärendö, Sweden 18/N3
Tarentum, Pa. (15084) 294/C4
Tarfaya, Morocco 106/B3
Tarfaya, Morocco 102/A2
Tar Heel, N.C. (28392) 281/M5
Tarhuna, Libya 102/D1
Tarhuna, Libya 111/B1
Tariana, Colombia 126/F7
Táriba, Venezuela 124/B4
Tarifa, Spain 33/D4
Tariff, W. Va. (25281) 312/D5
Tariffville, Conn. (06081) 210/D1
Tarija (riv.), Argentina 143/D1
Tarija (dept.), Bolivia 136/D7
Tarija, Bolivia 120/C5
Tarija, Bolivia 136/C7
Tarija, Río Grande de (riv.), Bolivia 136/C8
Tariku (riv.), Indonesia 85/K6
Tarim (riv.), China 54/K5
Tarim, P.D.R. Yemen 59/E6
Tarim He (riv.), China 77/B3
Tarim Pendi (basin), China 77/B4
Tar Island, Alberta 182/E1
Taritatu (riv.), Indonesia 85/K6
Tarkio, Mo. (64491) 261/B2
Tarkio, Mont. (†59872) 262/B4
Tarko-Sale, U.S.S.R. 48/H3
Tarkwa, Ghana 106/D7
Tarlac (prov.), Philippines 82/C3
Tarlac, Philippines 82/C3
Tarlac, Philippines 85/G2
Tarland, Scotland 15/F3
Tarleton (lake), N.H. 268/D4
Tarlton, Ohio (43156) 284/E6
Tarlton, Tenn. (†37301) 237/K9
Tarlton Downs, North. Terr. 93/E7
Tarm, Denmark 21/B6
Tarma, Peru 128/E8
Tarn (dept.), France 28/E6
Tarn (riv.), France 28/E6
Tarna (riv.), Hungary 41/F3
Tärnaby, Sweden 18/J4
Tarnak (riv.), Afghanistan 68/B2
Tårnby, Denmark 21/F6
Tarn-et-Garonne (dept.), France 28/D5
Tarnobrzeg (prov.), Poland 47/E3
Tarnobrzeg, Poland 47/E3
Tarnopol, Sask. 181/F3
Tarnov, Nebr. (68642) 264/G3
Tarnów (prov.), Poland 47/E4
Tarnów, Poland 7/G3
Tarnów, Poland 47/E4
Tarnowskie Góry, Poland 47/A3
Tarom, Iran 66/J6
Tarom, Iran 59/G4
Taroom, Queensland 95/D5
Tarouca, Portugal 33/C2
Taroudannt, Morocco 106/C2
Taroudant, Morocco 102/A1
Tarpa, Hungary 41/G2
Tarpon Springs, Fla. (*33589) 212/D3
Tarqui, Peru 128/E3
Tarquinia, Italy 34/C3
Tarqumiya, West Bank 65/C4
Tarragona (prov.), Spain 33/G2
Tarragona, Spain 33/G2
Tarragona, Spain 7/E4
Tarraleah, Tasmania 99/C4
Tarrant (co.), Texas 303/G5
Tarrant City, Ala. (35217) 195/E3
Tarrants, Mo. (†63334) 261/K4
Tarrasa, Spain 33/G2
Tárrega, Spain 33/G2
Tarryall (creek), Colo. 208/H4
Tarrytown, Georgia (30470) 217/H6
Tarrytown, N.Y. (10591) 276/O6
Tarsney Lakes, Mo. (†64063) 261/R6
Tarsus, Turkey 59/C2
Tarsus, Turkey 63/F4
Tart, China 77/D4
Tartagal, Argentina 143/D1
Tartagal, Argentina 120/C5
Tartas, France 28/C6
Tartu, U.S.S.R. 7/G3
Tartu, U.S.S.R. 53/D1
Tartu, U.S.S.R. 48/C4
Tartu, U.S.S.R. 52/C3
Tartus (prov.), Syria 63/G5
Tartus, Syria 63/F5
Tarutung, Indonesia 85/B5
Tarver, Georgia (†31648) 217/G9
Tarzan, Texas (79783) 303/B5
Tarzana, Calif. (91356) 204/B10
Täsch, Switzerland 39/E4
Tasco, Kansas (†67740) 232/B2
Tashauz, U.S.S.R. 48/F5
Tashk (lake), Iran 59/F4
Tashk (lake), Iran 66/J6
Tashkent, U.S.S.R. 54/H5
Tashkent, U.S.S.R. 2/N3
Tashkent, U.S.S.R. 48/G5
Tasikmalaya, Indonesia 85/H2
Tasisuak (lake), Newf. 166/B2
Taşkent, Turkey 63/E4
Taşköprü, Turkey 63/F2
Taşlıçay, Turkey 63/K3
Tasman (sea) 2/S7
Tasman (sea) 87/G9
Tasman (sea) 88/J7
Tasman (sea), N.S. Wales 97/F5
Tasman (bay), N. Zealand 100/D4
Tasman (mt.), N. Zealand 100/C5
Tasman (mts.), N. Zealand 100/D4
Tasman (sea), N. Zealand 100/B4
Tasman (pen.), Tasmania 88/H8
Tasman (head), Tasmania 99/D5
Tasman (pen.), Tasmania 99/E5
Tasman (sea), Tasmania 99/E4
Tasman (sea), Victoria 97/F5
Tasmania, 87/H8
Tasmania (state), Australia 87/E10
TASMANIA 99
Tasmania (isl.), Australia 2/S8
Tăşnad, Romania 45/F2
Taşova, Turkey 63/F4
Tassili N'Ahagger (plat.), Algeria 106/E4
Tassili N'Ajjer (plat.), Algeria 106/F3
Tåstrup, Denmark 21/F6
Tasu, Br. Col. 184/A4
Taşucu (gulf), Turkey 63/E4
Taswell, Ind. (47175) 227/D8
Tata, Hungary 41/E3
Tataa (pt.), Fr. Poly. 86/S13
Tatabánya, Hungary 41/E3
Tatahouine, Tunisia 106/G2
Tatalrose, Br. Col. 184/D3
Tatamagouche, Nova Scotia 168/E3
Tatamba, Solomon Is. 86/D3
Tatamy, Pa. (18085) 294/M4
Tatar (str.), U.S.S.R. 54/R5
Tatar (str.), U.S.S.R. 48/P4
Tatar A.S.S.R., U.S.S.R. 52/G3
Tatar A.S.S.R., U.S.S.R. 48/F4
Tatarsk, U.S.S.R. 48/H4
Tate, Georgia (30177) 217/D2
Tate (co.), Miss. 256/E1
Tate, Sask. 181/G4
Tateville, Ky. (42558) 237/M7
Tateyama, Japan 81/K6
Tathlina (lake), N.W. Terrs. 187/G3
Tathlith, Saudi Arabia 59/D6
Tathra, N.S. Wales 97/F5
Tati (riv.), Botswana 118/D4
Tatitlek, Alaska (99677) 196/D1
Tatla Lake, Br. Col. 184/E4
Tatlatui (lake), Br. Col. 184/D2
Tatlayoko (lake), Br. Col. 184/E4
Tatnam (cape), Manitoba 179/K2
Tatnum (cape), Man. 162/G4
Tatoosh (isl.), Wash. 310/A2
Tatra, High (mts.), Czech. 41/E2
Tatra, High (range), Poland 47/D4
Tatta, Pakistan 59/J5
Tatta, Pakistan 68/B4
Tattnall (co.), Georgia 217/J6
Tatuí, Brazil 135/C3
Tatum, N. Mex. (88267) 274/F5
Tatum, S.C. (29594) 296/H2
Tatum, Texas (75691) 303/K5
Tatums, Okla. (73087) 288/M6
Tatung (Datong), China 77/H3
Tatura, Victoria 97/C5
Tatvan, Turkey 63/K3
Taubaté, Brazil 132/E8
Taubaté, Brazil 135/D3
Tauber (riv.), W. Germany 22/C4
Täuffelen, Switzerland 39/D2
Taumarunui, N. Zealand 100/E3
Taum Sauk (mt.), Mo. 261/L7
Taung, S. Africa 118/C5
Taungdwingyi, Burma 72/C2
Taunggyi, Burma 72/C2
Taungthonton (mt.), Burma 72/B1
Taungup, Burma 72/B3
Taunton, England 13/D6
Taunton, England 10/E5
Taunton, Mass. (02780) 249/K5
Taunton (riv.), Mass. 249/K5
Taunton, Minn. (56291) 255/B6
Taunus (range), W. Germany 22/C3
Taupo, N. Zealand 100/F3
Taupo (lake), N. Zealand 100/F3
Tauq, Iraq 66/D3
Taurage, U.S.S.R. 53/B3
Taurage, U.S.S.R. 52/B3
Tauranga, N. Zealand 100/F2
Taureau (res.), Québec 172/D3
Taurianova, Italy 34/E5

Timor 457

Thailand (gulf), Cambodia 72/D5
THAILAND (SIAM) 72
Thailand (gulf), Thailand 72/D5
Thai Nguyen, Vietnam 72/E2
Thakhek (Muang Khammouan), Laos 72/E3
Thal, Pakistan 59/K3
Thal, Switzerland 39/J2
Thalberg, Manitoba 179/F4
Thale, E. Germany 22/D3
Thale Luang (lag.), Thailand 72/D6
Thalia, Texas (79227) 303/E4
Thalmann, Georgia (†31520) 217/J8
Thalu, Ko (isls.), Thailand 72/C5
Thalwil, Switzerland 39/G2
Thame, England 13/G6
Thame (riv.), England 13/G7
Thames (riv.), Conn. 210/G3
Thames (riv.), England 10/F5
Thames (riv.), England 13/H6
Thames, N. Zealand 100/E2
Thames (firth), N. Zealand 100/E2
Thames (riv.), Ontario 177/B5
Thamesford, Ontario 177/C4
Thamesville, Conn. (†06360) 210/G2
Thamesville, Ontario 177/C5
Thana, India 68/B6
Thana (creek), India 68/B7
Thane, Alaska (†99801) 196/N1
Thangool, Queensland 95/D5
Thanh Hoa, Vietnam 72/E3
Thanh Tri, Vietnam 72/E5
Thanjavur, India 68/D6
Thann, France 28/G4
Thar (des.), Pakistan 68/C3
Thargomindah, Queensland 88/G5
Thargomindah, Queensland 95/C5
Tharrawaddy, Burma 72/C3
Tharthar, Wadi (dry riv.), Iraq 66/C3
Tharthar (res.), Iraq 66/C3
Thásos, Greece 45/G5
Thásos (isl.), Greece 45/G5
Thatch (cay), Virgin Is. (U.S.) 161/B4
Thatcham, England 13/F6
Thatcher, Ariz. (85552) 198/F6
Thatcher, Colo. (†81082) 208/L7
Thatcher, Idaho (83283) 220/G7
That Khe, Vietnam 72/E2
Thaton, Burma 72/C3
Thau (mts.), France 28/F6
Thaungdut, Burma 72/B1
Thawville, Ill. (60968) 222/E3
Thaxton, Miss. (38871) 256/F2
Thaxton, Va. (24174) 307/K6
Thaya (riv.), Austria 41/C2
Thayawthadangyi Kyun (isl.), Burma 72/C4
Thayer, Ill. (62689) 222/D4
Thayer, Ind. (46381) 227/C2
Thayer, Iowa (50254) 229/E6
Thayer, Kansas (66776) 232/G4
Thayer, Mo. (65791) 261/J9
Thayer (co.), Nebr. 264/G4
Thayer, Nebr. (†68467) 264/G4
Thayer, W. Va. (†25936) 312/E7
Thayer Junction, Wyo. (†82901) 319/D4
Thayetmyo, Burma 72/B3
Thayne, Wyo. (83127) 319/A3
Thayngen, Switzerland 39/G1
Thazi, Burma 72/C2
The Alberga (riv.), S. Australia 94/D2
Thealka, Ky. (41259) 237/R5
Theano (pt.), Ontario 177/J5
Thebarton, S. Australia 88/D8
Thebarton, S. Australia 94/A7
The Battlefords Prov. Park, Sask. 181/C2
Thebes, Ill. (62990) 222/D6
The Colony, Texas 303/G1
The Coorong (lag.), S. Australia 94/F6
The Dalles, Oreg. 188/B1
The Dalles, Oreg. (97058) 291/F2
The Dalles (dam), Oreg. 291/F2
The Dalles (dam), Wash. 310/D5
Thedford, Nebr. (69166) 264/D3
Thedford, Ontario 177/C4
The Entrance, N. S. Wales 88/J6
The Entrance, N.S. Wales 97/F3
The Gap, N.S. Wales 97/A2
The Gap, Queensland 88/J2
The Glen, N.Y. (†12885) 276/N3
The Granites, North. Terr. 93/B6
The Hamilton (riv.), S. Australia 94/D2
The Hawk, Nova Scotia 168/C5
The Heads (prom.), Oreg. 291/C5
The Hermitage, N. Zealand 100/C5
Theilman, Minn. (55978) 255/F6
Thelon (riv.), N.W.T. 146/H3
Thelon (riv.), N.W.T. 162/F3
Thelon (riv.), N.W. Terrs. 187/H3
Them, Denmark 21/C5
The Macumba (riv.), S. Australia 94/E2
The Narrows (str.), N.J. 273/E2
Thendara, N.Y. (13472) 276/K3
The Neales (riv.), S. Australia 94/E3
Theodore, Ala. (36582) 195/B9
Theodore, Queensland 95/D5
Theodore, Sask. 181/J4
Theodore Roosevelt (dam), Ariz. 198/D5
Theodore Roosevelt (lake), Ariz. 198/D5
Theodore Roosevelt Nat'l Park, N. Dak. 282/D4
Theodore Roosevelt Nat'l Park, N. Dak. 282/C5
Theodore Roosevelt Nat'l Park, N. Dak. 282/D6
Theodosia, Mo. (65761) 261/G9
The Pas, Man. 162/F5
The Pas, Manitoba 179/H3
The Plains, Ohio (45780) 284/F7
The Plains, Va. (22171) 307/N3
The Range, New Bruns. 170/E2
Theresa, N.Y. (13691) 276/J2
Theresa, Wis. (53091) 317/K8
Therien, Alberta 182/E2
Theriot, La. (70397) 238/J8
Thermaic (gulf), Greece 45/F6
Thermal, Calif. (92274) 204/J10
Thermalito, Calif. (†95965) 204/D4
Thermopolis, Wyo. (82443) 319/D2
The Rock, Georgia (30285) 217/D5
The Rock, N.S. Wales 97/D4
The Round (mt.), N.S. Wales 97/G2
Therwil, Switzerland 39/E1
The Salt (lake), N.S. Wales 97/B2
Thesiger (bay), N.W. Terrs. 187/F2
The Skaw (Skagens Odde) (cape), Denmark 21/D2
Thessalon, Ont. 162/H6
Thessalon, Ontario 177/J5
Thessalon, Ontario 175/D3
Thessaloníki, Greece 7/G4
Thessaloníki, Greece 45/F5
Thessaly (reg.), Greece 45/F6
The Stevenson (riv.), S. Australia 94/D2
Thetford, England 13/H5
Thetford, England 10/G4
Thetford○, Vt. (05074) 268/C4
Thetford Center, Vt. (05075) 268/C4
Thetford Mines, Québec 172/F3
Thetis Island, Br. Col. 184/J3
The Twins (mt.), Alberta 182/B3
Theux, Belgium 27/H8
The Village, Okla. (73120) 288/L3
The Warburton (riv.), S. Australia 94/F2
Thibault, New Bruns. 170/C1
Thibodaux, La. (70301) 238/J7
Thicket Portage, Manitoba 179/J3
Thickwood (hills), Alberta 182/D1
Thickwood (hills), Sask. 181/D2
Thida, Ark. (72165) 202/H2
Thief (lake), Minn. 255/C2
Thief (riv.), Minn. 255/B2
Thief River Falls, Minn. (56701) 255/B2
Thielsen (mt.), Oreg. 291/F4
Thiensville, Wis. (53092) 317/L1
Thiers, France 28/E5
Thiès, Senegal 106/A5
Thiès, Senegal 102/A3
Thika, Kenya 102/F5
Thika, Kenya 115/G4
Thimphu (cap.), Bhutan 54/L7
Thimphu (cap.), Bhutan 68/G3
Thio, Ethiopia 111/H5
Thio, New Caled. 86/H4
Thionville, France 28/G3
Thíra, Greece 45/G7
Thíra (isl.), Greece 45/G7
Third (lake), Maine 243/H5
Third (lake), N.H. 268/E1
Third Cataract, Sudan 111/E4
Third Cataract (dam), Sudan 102/E3
Third Cataract, Sudan 59/B6
Third Lake, Ill. (†60046) 222/B4
Thirsk, England 13/F3
Thirty Mile (creek), N. Dak. 282/F6
Thirtymile (creek), Oreg. 291/G2
Thisted, Denmark 21/B4
Thisted, Denmark 18/F8
Thistle (isl.), S. Australia 94/E6
Thistle, Utah (†84629) 304/C4
Thithia (isl.), Fiji 86/R10
Thivai, Greece 45/F6
Thiviers, France 28/D5
Thjórsá (riv.), Iceland 21/C1
Thlewiaza (riv.), N.W. Terrs. 187/J3
Thoa (riv.), N.W. Terrs. 187/H3
Tho Chau, Hon (isl.), Vietnam 72/D5
Thoen, Thailand 72/C3
Thohoyandou, S. Africa 118/E4
Thohoyandou (cap.), Venda, S. Africa 102/F7
Tholen, Netherlands 27/E5
Thomas (co.), Georgia 217/E9
Thomas (co.), Kansas 232/A2
Thomas, Md. (†21613) 245/N6
Thomas (co.), Nebr. 264/D3
Thomas, Okla. (73669) 288/J3
Thomas (creek), Oreg. 291/G5
Thomas, S. Dak. (†57242) 298/P4
Thomas (lake), Texas 303/C5
Thomas (range), Utah 304/A4
Thomas, W. Va. (26292) 312/H4
Thomasboro, Ill. (61878) 222/E3
Thomas-Müntzer-Stadt, E. Germany 22/D3
Thomas Stone Nat'l Hist. Site, Md. 245/K6
Thomaston, Ala. (36783) 195/C6
Thomaston○, Conn. (06787) 210/C2
Thomaston (res.), Conn. 210/C2
Thomaston, Georgia (30286) 217/D5
Thomaston, Maine (04861) 243/E7
Thomaston○, Maine (04861) 243/E7
Thomaston, N.Y. (†11020) 276/P7
Thomastown, Ireland 10/C4
Thomastown, Ireland 17/G7
Thomastown, La. (†71262) 238/H2
Thomastown, Miss. (39171) 256/E5
Thomastown, Victoria 97/J4
Thomasville, Ala. (36784) 195/C7
Thomasville, Ga. 188/K4
Thomasville, Georgia (31792) 217/E9
Thomasville, Miss. (†39073) 256/E6
Thomasville, Mo. (†65438) 261/J9
Thomasville, N.C. (27360) 281/J3
Thomasville, Pa. (17364) 294/J6
Thomonde, Haiti 158/C6
Thompson, Ala. (†36089) 195/G6
Thompson (riv.), Br. Col. 184/G5
Thompson○, Conn. (06277) 210/H1
Thompson (peak), Idaho 220/C5
Thompson, Iowa (50478) 229/F2
Thompson (riv.), Iowa 229/E7
Thompson, Man. 162/G4
Thompson, Man. 146/J4
Thompson, Manitoba 179/J2
Thompson (isl.), Mass. 249/D7
Thompson, Mich. (49889) 250/C3
Thompson (creek), Miss. 256/G8
Thompson, Mo. (65285) 261/J4
Thompson (peak), N. Mex. 274/D3
Thompson, N. Dak. (58278) 282/R4
Thompson, Ohio (44086) 284/H2
Thompson, Pa. (18465) 294/L2
Thompson (riv.), Queensland 95/B5
Thompson (lake), S. Dak. 298/O5
Thompson, Utah (84540) 304/E5
Thompson (mt.), Wyo. 319/B3
Thompson Falls, Mont. (59873) 262/A3
Thompsons (creek), S.C. 296/G2
Thompsons Station, Tenn. (37179) 237/H9
Thompsontown, Pa. (17094) 294/H4
Thompson Valley (res.), Oreg. 291/F5
Thompsonville, Conn. (†06082) 210/E1
Thompsonville, Ill. (62890) 222/E6
Thompsonville, Mich. (49683) 250/C4
Thomsen (riv.), N.W. Terrs. 187/G2
Thomson, Georgia (30824) 217/H4
Thomson, Ill. (61285) 222/C2
Thomson, Minn. (†56319) 255/F4
Thomson (riv.), Queensland 88/G4
Thomson's Falls, Kenya 115/G3
Thon Buri, Thailand 72/D4
Thongwa, Burma 72/C3
Thonon-les-Bains, France 28/G4
Thonotosassa, Fla. (33592) 212/D3
Thor, Iowa (50591) 229/E3
Thorburn, Nova Scotia 168/F3
Thoreau, N. Mex. (87323) 274/A3
Thoresby (mt.), Newf. 166/B2
Thorhild, Alberta 182/D2
Thorn, Miss. (†38851) 256/F3
Thornaby-on-Tees, England 10/F3
Thornaby-on-Tees, England 13/F3
Thornburg, Iowa (50255) 229/J6
Thornburg, Va. (22565) 307/N4
Thornbury, England 13/E6
Thornbury, Ontario 177/D3
Thorndale, Ontario 177/C4
Thorndale, Texas (76577) 303/G7
Thorndike○, Maine (04986) 243/E6
Thorndike, Mass. (01079) 249/E4
Thorne, England 13/F4
Thorne, N. Dak. (†58366) 282/L2
Thorne, Ontario 175/E3
Thorne Bay, Alaska (†99901) 196/M2
Thornfield, Mo. (65762) 261/G9
Thornhill, Br. Col. 184/C3
Thornhill, Ky. (†40222) 237/K1
Thornhill, Manitoba 179/D5
Thornhill, Central, Scotland 15/D4
Thornhill, Dumf. & Gall., Scotland 15/E5
Thorn Hill, Tenn. (37881) 237/P8
Thornhurst, Pa. (†18424) 294/L3
Thornley, England 13/J4
Thornloe, Ontario 175/E3
Thornloe, Ontario 177/K5
Thornton, Ark. (71766) 202/F6
Thornton, Calif. (95686) 204/B9
Thornton, Colo. (80229) 208/K3
Thornton, Idaho (†83453) 220/G6
Thornton, Ill. (60476) 222/C6
Thornton, Iowa (50479) 229/G3
Thornton, Miss. (39172) 256/D4
Thornton○, N.H. (†03285) 268/D4
Thornton, Ontario 177/E3
Thornton, Texas (76687) 303/H6
Thornton, Wash. (99176) 310/H3
Thornton, W. Va. (26440) 312/G4
Thornton Cleveleys, England 13/G1
Thornton Cleveleys, England 10/F1
Thorntown, Ind. (46071) 227/D4
Thornville, Ohio (43076) 284/F6
Thornwell, La. (†70549) 238/E6
Thornwood, W. Va. (†24920) 312/G5
Thorofare, N.J. (08086) 273/B4
Thorold, Ontario 177/E4
Thorp, Wash. (98946) 310/E3
Thorp, Wis. (54771) 317/E6
Thorpe (lake), N.C. 281/C4
Thorpe, W. Va. (24888) 312/D8
Thorp Spring, Texas (†76048) 303/F5
Thorsby, Ala. (35171) 195/E5
Thorsby, Alberta 182/C3
Thouars, France 28/C4
Thouin (pt.), W. Australia 88/B4
Thouin (pt.), W. Australia 92/B3
Thousand (isls.), N.Y. 276/H2
Thousand (isls.), Ontario 177/H3
Thousand Island Park, N.Y. (13692) 276/J2
Thousand Lake (mt.), Utah 304/C5
Thousand Oaks, Calif. (*91360) 204/G9
Thousand Palms, Calif. (92276) 204/J10
Thousand Spring (creek), Nev. 266/G1
Thousand Springs, Nev. (†89835) 266/G1
Thrace (reg.), Greece 45/G5
Thrall, Kansas (†66853) 232/F3
Thrasher, Miss. (†38829) 256/G1
Three (isls.), New Bruns. 170/D4
Three Bridges, N.J. (08887) 273/D2
Three Churches, W. Va. (26765) 312/J4
Three Creek, Idaho (†83302) 220/C7
Three Creeks, Alberta 182/B1
Three Creeks, Ark. (†71749) 202/E7
Three Forks, Mont. (59752) 262/E5
Three Guardsmen (mt.), Br. Col. 184/H1
Three Hills, Alberta 182/D4
Three Hummock (isl.), Tasmania 99/B2
Three Kings (isls.), N. Zealand 100/D1
Three Lakes, Wis. (54562) 317/H4
Three Mile Bay, N.Y. (13693) 276/H2
Three Mile Plains, Nova Scotia 168/D4
Three Notch, Ala. (†36053) 195/G6
Three Oaks, Mich. (49128) 250/C7
Three Pagodas (pass), Burma 72/C4
Three Pagodas (pass), Thailand 72/C4
Three Points (cape), Ghana 106/D8
Three Rivers, Mass. (01080) 249/E4
Three Rivers, Mich. (49093) 250/D7
Three Rivers, N. Mex. (†88352) 274/C5
Three Rivers (Trois-Rivières), Que. 172/E3
Three Rivers, Texas (78071) 303/F9
Three Rivers, W. Australia 92/B4
Three Sisters (mt.), Oreg. 291/F3
Three Springs, Pa. (17264) 294/G5
Three Springs, W. Australia 88/B5
Three Springs, W. Australia 92/A5
Throckmorton (co.), Texas 303/E4
Throckmorton, Texas (76083) 303/F4
Throne, Alberta 182/E3
Throop, Pa. (18512) 294/F7
Thrums, Br. Col. 184/J5
Thrumster, Scotland 15/E2
Thuin, Belgium 27/E8
Thule, Greenl. 4/B13
Thule, Greenland 2/F2
Thule, Greenland 146/M2
Thule A.F.B. (Dundas), Greenl. 4/B13
Thule A.F.B. (Dundas), Greenland 146/M2
Thumail, Iraq 66/C4
Thun, Switzerland 39/E3
Thunder (bay), Mich. 250/F4
Thunder (hills), Sask. 181/L4
Thunder (creek), S. Dak. 298/N4
Thunder (lake), Wis. 317/H4
Thunder Bay (riv.), Mich. 250/F3
Thunder Bay, Ont. 162/H6
Thunder Bay, Ont. 146/K5
Thunder Bay (terr. dist.), Ontario 175/C3
Thunder Bay (terr. dist.), Ontario 177/H5
Thunder Bay, Ontario 175/C3
Thunder Bay, Ontario 177/H5
Thunderbird (lake), Okla. 288/M4
Thunderbolt, Georgia (†31404) 217/K6
Thunder Butte (creek), S. Dak. 298/E3
Thunder Hawk, S. Dak. (†57638) 298/F2
Thunder Lake, Alberta 182/C2
Thunersee (lake), Switzerland 39/E3
Thunstetten, Switzerland 39/E2
Thur (riv.), Switzerland 39/G1
Thurgau (canton), Switzerland 39/H1
Thüringer Wald (for.), E. Germany 22/D3
Thuringia (reg.), E. Germany 22/D3
Thurles, Ireland 10/B4
Thurles, Ireland 17/F6
Thurloo Downs, N.S. Wales 97/B1
Thurlow (dam), Ala. 195/G6
Thurlow, Mont. (†59347) 262/K4
Thurman, Iowa (51654) 229/B7
Thurman, N.Y. (†12885) 276/M3
Thurman, Ohio (45685) 284/F8
Thurmond, W. Va. (25936) 312/D7
Thurmont, Md. (21788) 245/J2
Thurrock, England 13/J8
Thurrock, England 10/C5
Thursday Island, Queensland 88/G2
Thursday Island, Queensland 95/B1
Thurso, Québec 172/B4
Thurso, Scotland 10/E1
Thurso, Scotland 15/E2
Thurso (riv.), Scotland 15/E2
Thurston (isl.) 5/C14
Thurston (co.), Nebr. 264/H2
Thurston, Nebr. (68062) 264/H2
Thurston, Ohio (43157) 284/E6
Thurston (co.), Wash. 310/C4
Thusis, Switzerland 39/H3
Thutade (lake), Br. Col. 184/D2
Thyatira, Miss. (†38668) 256/E1
Thyborøn, Denmark 21/A4
Thyolo, Malawi 115/F7
Thyregod, Denmark 21/C6
Tia, N.S. Wales 97/F2
Tiahuanacu, Bolivia 136/A5
Tia Juana, Venezuela 124/C2
Tiandong, China 77/G7
Tianjin, China 2/Q4
Tianjin, China 54/N6
Tianjin (Tientsin), China 77/J4
Tianjun, China 77/E4
Tianlin, China 77/G7
Tian Shan (range), China 77/C3
Tianshui, China 77/F5
Tianzhu, China 77/F4
Tiaret, Algeria 106/E1
Tiatucurá, Uruguay 145/C3
Tiavea, W. Samoa 86/M8
Tiawah, Okla. (†74017) 288/P2
Tib, Ras el (Bon) (cape), Tunisia 106/G1
Tibagi, Brazil 135/A4
Tibagi (riv.), Brazil 135/A4
Tibaná, Colombia 126/D5
Tibati, Cameroon 115/B2
Tibbie, Ala. (36583) 195/B8
Tibbita, N.S. Wales 97/C4
Tiber (riv.), Italy 7/F4
Tiber (riv.), Italy 34/D3
Tiberias, Israel 65/C2
Tiberias (lake), Israel 65/D2
Tibesti (mts.) 102/D2
Tibesti, Serir (des.), Chad 111/C3
Tibesti (mts.), Chad 111/C3
Tibesti, Serir (des.), Libya 111/C3
Tibet (reg.), China 2/P4
Tibet (reg.), China 54/K6
Tibet (reg.), China 77/B5
Tibet Aut. Reg. (Xizang), China 77/B5
Tibooburra, N. S. Wales 88/G5
Tibooburra, N.S. Wales 97/B1
Tibro, Sweden 18/J7
Tibugá (gulf), Colombia 126/B5
Tiburon, Calif. (94920) 204/J2
Tiburon, Haiti 158/A6
Tiburon (cape), Haiti 156/C3
Tiburon (cape), Haiti 158/A6
Tiburón (isl.), Mexico 150/C2
Tiburón (pt.), Panama 154/J6
Ticaco, Peru 128/H11
Ticao (isl.), Philippines 82/D4
Tice, Fla. (33905) 212/E5
Ticehurst, England 13/H6
Tichfield, Sask. 181/D4
Tichigan, Wis. (†53185) 317/K2
Tichigan (lake), Wis. 317/K2
Tichitt, Mauritania 106/C5
Tichlá (well), Western Sahara 106/B4
Tichnor, Ark. (72166) 202/H5
Ticino (canton), Switzerland 39/G4
Ticino (riv.), Switzerland 39/G4
Tickfaw, La. (70466) 238/M1
Tickfaw (riv.), La. 238/M1
Tickle (bay), Newf. 166/D2
Ticonderoga, N.Y. (12883) 276/N3
Ticonic, Iowa (†51010) 229/B4
Ticul, Mexico 150/P6
Tidaholm, Sweden 18/J7
Tide Head, New Bruns. 170/D1
Tidewater, Oreg. (97390) 291/D3
Tidikelt (oasis), Algeria 106/E3
Tidioute, Pa. (16351) 294/D2
Tidjikja, Mauritania 102/A3
Tidjikja, Mauritania 106/B5
Tidnish, Nova Scotia 168/E3
Tidore (isl.), Indonesia 85/H5
Tidra (isl.), Mauritania 106/A5
Tiedemann (mt.), Br. Col. 184/E4
Tiefencastel, Switzerland 39/J3
Tiel, Netherlands 27/G5
Tieling, China 77/K3
Tielt, Belgium 27/C7
Tielt-Winge, Belgium 27/F7
Tienen, Belgium 27/F7
Tien Shan (range) 54/K5
Tienshui (Tianshui), China 77/F5
Tientsin (Tianjin), China 77/J4
Tien Yen, Vietnam 72/E2
Tie Plant, Miss. (38960) 256/E3
Tiernan, Oreg. (†97453) 291/C3
Tierp, Sweden 18/K6
Tierra Amarilla, Chile 138/A6
Tierra Amarilla, N. Mex. (87575) 274/C2
Tierra Blanca, Mexico 150/L7
Tierra Blanca (creek), N. Mex. 274/B6
Tierra Blanca (creek), Texas 303/B3
Tierra del Fuego (isl.) 2/F8
Tierra del Fuego (isl.) 120/C8
Tierra del Fuego, Antártida, e Islas del Atlántico del sur (prov.) Argentina 143/C7
Tierra del Fuego, Grande de (isl.), Argentina 143/C7
Tierra del Fuego, Grande de (isl.), Chile 138/E11
Tierralta, Colombia 126/C3
Tie Siding, Wyo. (82084) 319/G4
Tietê, Brazil 135/C3
Tietê (riv.), Brazil 120/E5
Tietê (riv.), Brazil 132/D8
Tietê (riv.), Brazil 135/B2
Tieton, Wash. (98947) 310/E4
Tieton (riv.), Wash. 310/D4
Tieyon, S. Australia 94/C2
Tiff, Mo. (63674) 261/L6
Tiffany, Colo. (†81137) 208/D8
Tiffany (mt.), Wash. 310/F2
Tiff City, Mo. (64868) 261/C9
Tiffin, Iowa (52340) 229/K5
Tiffin, Mo. (†64744) 261/E7
Tiffin, Ohio (44883) 284/D3
Tiffin (riv.), Ohio 284/B3
Tiflis (Tbilisi), U.S.S.R. 52/F6
Tift (co.), Georgia 217/E7
Tifton, Georgia (31794) 217/F8
Tiftona, Tenn. (†37401) 237/L11
Tigalda (isl.), Alaska 196/F4
Tigard, Oreg. (97223) 291/A2
Tiger, Georgia (30576) 217/F1
Tiger (falls), Guyana 131/C4
Tiger (Macan) (isls.), Indonesia 85/G7
Tiger (falls), Suriname 131/C4
Tiger, Wash. (†99180) 310/H2
Tiger Lily, Alberta 182/C2
Tigerton, Wis. (54486) 317/H6
Tigerville, S.C. (29688) 296/C1
Tighina (Bendery), U.S.S.R. 52/C5
Tigieglo, Somalia 115/H3
Tignall, Georgia (30668) 217/G3
Tignamar, Chile 138/B1
Tignéré, Cameroon 115/B2
Tignish, Pr. Edward I. 168/D2
Tigre, Argentina 143/G7
Tigre (prov.), Ethiopia 111/H5
Tigre (riv.), Peru 128/E4
Tigre (isl.), Uruguay 145/A7
Tigre (riv.), Venezuela 124/G3
Tigrett, Tenn. (38070) 237/C9
Tigris (riv.) 54/F6
Tigris (riv.), Iran 59/E3
Tigris (riv.), Iraq 59/E3
Tigris (riv.), Iraq 66/E4
Tigris (riv.), Syria 59/E3
Tigris (riv.), Syria 63/K4
Tigris (Dicle) (riv.), Turkey 63/J4
Tigris (riv.), Turkey 59/E3
Tiguentourine, Algeria 106/F3
Tihama (reg.), Saudi Arabia 59/C5
Tihama (reg.), Yemen Arab Rep. 59/C5
Tihany, Hungary 41/D3
Tihwa (Ürümqi), China 77/C3
Tijamuchi (riv.), Bolivia 136/C4
Tijeras, N. Mex. (87059) 274/C3
Tijuana, Mexico 150/A1
Tijuana, Mexico 146/G6
Tijucas, Brazil 132/D9
Tikal, Guatemala 154/C2
Tikamgarh, India 68/D4
Tikchik (lkes), Alaska 196/G2
Tikhoretsk, U.S.S.R. 52/F5
Tikhvin, U.S.S.R. 52/D3
Tiko, Cameroon 102/C4
Tiko, Cameroon 115/A3
Tikopia (isl.), Solomon Is. 87/G7
Tikrit, Iraq 59/D3
Tikrit, Iraq 66/C3
Tiksi, U.S.S.R. 4/B3
Tiksi, U.S.S.R. 54/P2
Tiksi, U.S.S.R. 48/N2
Tila, Mexico 150/N8
Tilburg, Netherlands 27/G5
Tilbury, Ontario 177/B5
Tilcara, Argentina 143/C1
Tilcha, S. Australia 94/G3
Tilden, Ill. (62292) 222/D5
Tilden, Ky. (†42409) 237/F5
Tilden, Miss. (†38843) 256/H2
Tilden, Nebr. (68781) 264/G2
Tilden, Texas (78072) 303/F9
Tilehurst, England 13/F6
Tilemsi (valley), Mali 106/E5
Tilford, S. Dak. (†57769) 298/C5
Tilghman, Md. (21671) 245/N6
Tilin, Burma 72/B2
Tiline, Ky. (42083) 237/E6
Till (riv.), Englnd 13/E2
Tillabéry, Niger 106/E6
Tillamook (co.), Oreg. 291/D2
Tillamook, Oreg. (97141) 291/D2
Tillamook (head), Oreg. 291/C2
Tillanchong (isl.), India 68/G7
Tillar, Ark. (71670) 202/H6
Tillatoba, Miss. (38961) 256/E3
Tilleda, Wis. (54978) 317/J6
Tiller, Oreg. (97484) 291/E5
Tillery, N.C. (27887) 281/O2
Tillery (lake), N.C. 281/J4
Tilley, Alberta 182/E4
Tilley, New Bruns. 170/C2
Tillicoultry, Scotland 10/B1
Tillicoultry, Scotland 15/C1
Tillicum, Wash. (98492) 310/C3
Tillman, Miss. (†39150) 256/C7
Tillman (co.), Okla. 288/J6
Tillman, S.C. (29943) 296/E7
Tillson, N.Y. (12486) 276/M7
Tillsonburg, Ontario 177/D5
Tilney, Sask. 181/F5
Tilomonte, Chile 138/B4
Tílos (isl.), Greece 45/H7
Tilpa, N.S. Wales 97/C2
Tilsit (Sovetsk), U.S.S.R. 52/B4
Tilston, Manitoba 179/A5
Tilt (riv.), Scotland 15/E4
Tiltagara, N.S. Wales 97/C2
Tiltil, Chile 138/G2
Tilting, Newf. 166/D4
Tilton, Ark. (†72347) 202/J3
Tilton, Georgia (†30720) 217/B1
Tilton, Ill. (†61832) 222/F3
Tilton○, N.H. (03276) 268/D5
Tilton-Northfield, N.H. (03276) 268/D5
Tiltonsville, Ohio (43963) 284/J5
Tim, Denmark 21/B5
Timagami, Ontario 177/K5
Timagami, Ontario 175/E3
Timagami (lake), Ontario 177/K5
Timagami (lake), Ontario 175/D3
Timan (ridge), U.S.S.R. 52/G1
Timaná, Colombia 126/C7
Timane (riv.), Paraguay 144/B2
Timaru, N. Zealand 100/C6
Timashevsk, U.S.S.R. 52/E5
Timbákion, Greece 45/G8
Timbalier (bay), La. 238/K8
Timbalier (isl.), La. 238/K8
Timbarra (riv.), N.S. Wales 97/G1
Timbédra, Mauritania 106/C5
Timber (mt.), Nev. 266/E5
Timber (mt.), Nev. 266/F4
Timber, Oreg. (97144) 291/D2
Timber Bay, Sask. 181/F1
Timber Creek, North. Terr. 88/E3
Timberlake, N.C. (27583) 281/M2
Timberlake, Ohio (†44094) 284/J8
Timber Lake, S. Dak. (57656) 298/H3
Timberlea, Nova Scotia 168/E4
Timberville, Va. (22853) 307/L3
Timbío, Colombia 126/B6
Timbiquí, Colombia 126/B6
Timblin, Pa. (15778) 294/D4
Timbo, Ark. (72680) 202/F2
Timboulaga (well), Niger 106/F5
Timbuktu (Tombouctou), Mali 106/D5
Timbuktu, Mali 102/B3
Time, Ill. (†62363) 222/C4
Times Beach, Mo. (†63025) 261/N4
Timewell, Ill. (62375) 222/C3
Timgad, Algeria 106/F1
Timia, Niger 106/F4
Timia, Niger 102/C2
Timimoun, Algeria 102/C2
Timimoun, Algeria 106/E3
Timiris (cape), Mauritania 106/A5
Timiș (riv.), Romania 45/E3
Timiskaming (lake) 162/J6
Timiskaming (terr. dist.), Ontario 177/K5
Timiskaming (terr. dist.), Ontario 175/D3
Timiskaming (lake), Ontario 175/E3
Timișoara, Romania 7/G4
Timișoara, Romania 45/E3
Timken, Kansas (67582) 232/C3
Timmendorfer Strand, W. Germany 22/D1
Timmins, Ont. 146/K5
Timmins, Ont. 162/H6
Timmins, Ontario 177/J5
Timmins, Ontario 175/D3
Timmissao (well), Algeria 106/E4
Timmonsville, S.C. (29161) 296/H3
Timms Hill (mt.), Wis. 317/F5
Timnath, Colo. (80547) 208/J2
Timok (riv.), Bulgaria 45/F3
Timok (riv.), Yugoslavia 45/F3
Timoleague, Ireland 17/D8
Timon, Brazil 132/F4
Timonium-Lutherville, Md. (21093) 245/M3
Timor (sea) 54/O11
Timor (sea) 88/D2
Timor (isl.), Indonesia 54/O10
Timor (isl.), Indonesia 2/R6

Trousdale 459

Toronto, Canada 2/F3
Toronto, Iowa (52343) 229/M5
Toronto, Kansas (66777) 232/G4
Toronto (lake), Kansas 232/F4
Toronto (res.), N.Y. 276/L7
Toronto, Ohio (43964) 284/J5
Toronto (cap.), Ont. 146/K5
Toronto (cap.), Ont. 162/H7
Toronto (metro. munic.), Ontario 177/K4
Toronto (cap.), Ontario 177/K4
Toronto, S. Dak. (57268) 298/R4
Toropalca, Bolivia 136/B7
Toropets, U.S.S.R. 52/D3
Tororo, Uganda 115/F3
Torote (riv.), Spain 33/G4
Torotoro, Bolivia 136/C6
Torpedo, Pa. (†16340) 294/D2
Torphins, Scotland 15/F3
Torpoint, England 13/C7
Torquay (Torbay), England 13/D7
Torquay, Sask. 181/H6
Torquemada, Spain 33/D1
Torr (head), N. Ireland 17/K1
Torrance, Calif. 188/C4
Torrance, Calif. (*90501) 204/C11
Torrance (co.), N. Mex. 274/D4
Torrance, Ontario 177/E3
Torrance, Pa. (15779) 294/D5
Torre, Cerro de la (mt.), Chile 138/E4
Torre Annunziata, Italy 34/E4
Torreblanca, Spain 33/G2
Torrecilla (lag.), P. Rico 161/E1
Torre del Greco, Italy 34/E4
Torre de Moncorvo, Portugal 33/C2
Torredonjimeno, Spain 33/D4
Torre Gaia, Italy 34/F6
Torrejón (res.), Spain 33/D3
Torrejoncillo, Spain 33/C3
Torrejón de Ardoz, Spain 33/G4
Torrelaguna, Spain 33/E2
Torrelavega, Spain 33/D1
Torremaggiore, Italy 34/E4
Torremolinos, Spain 33/D4
Torrens (riv.) 88/E7
Torrens (lake), Australia 87/D9
Torrens (isl.), S. Australia 88/D7
Torrens (lake), S. Australia 88/F6
Torrens (lake), S. Australia 94/E4
Torrens (riv.), S. Australia 94/C7
Torrente, Spain 33/F3
Torreón, Mexico 146/H7
Torreón, Mexico 150/H4
Torreon, N. Mex. (87061) 274/C4
Torre-Pacheco, Spain 33/F4
Torres (strait) 87/E7
Torres (str.), Papua N.G. 85/A7
Torres (str.), Queensland 88/G2
Torres (str.), Queensland 95/B1
Torres (isls.), Vanuatu 87/G7
Torres Martinez Ind. Res., Calif. 204/J10
Torres Novas, Portugal 33/B3
Torres Vedras, Portugal 33/B3
Torrevieja, Spain 33/F4
Torrey, Utah (84775) 304/C5
Torridge (riv.), England 13/C7
Torridon, Loch (inlet), Scotland 15/C3
Torriente, Cuba 158/D1
Torrijos, Philippines 82/D4
Torrijos, Spain 33/D2
Tørring, Denmark 21/C6
Torringford, Conn. (†06790) 210/C1
Torrington, Alberta 182/D4
Torrington, Conn. (06790) 210/C1
Torrington, Wyo. (82240) 319/H3
Torroella de Montgrí, Spain 33/H1
Torrowangee, N.S. Wales 97/A2
Torrox, Spain 33/E4
Torsby, Sweden 18/H6
Tors Cove, Newf. 166/D2
Torshälla, Sweden 18/K7
Tórshavn, Denmark 7/D2
Tórshavn (cap.), Faerøe Is., Denmark 21/A3
Tortilla Flat, Ariz. (85290) 198/D5
Tortola (isl.), Virgin Is. (Br.) 161/D3
Tortola (isl.), Virgin Is. (Br.) 156/H1
Tórtolas, Cerro de las (mt.), Chile 138/B8
Tortona, Italy 34/B2
Tortorici, Italy 34/E6
Tortosa, Spain 33/G2
Tortosa (cape), Spain 33/G2
Tortue (chan.), Haiti 158/C5
Tortue (Tortuga) (isl.), Haiti 156/D2
Tortue (Tortuga) (isl.), Haiti 158/C4
Tortuga (isl.), Haiti 158/C4
Tortuga (isl.), Haiti 156/D2
Tortugas (gulf), Colombia 126/B6
Tortuguero (lag.), P. Rico 161/D1
Tortuguilla (pt.), Cuba 158/K4
Tortum, Turkey 63/J2
Torud, Iran 59/F2
Torud, Iran 66/J3
Torul, Turkey 63/H2
Toruń (prov.), Poland 47/D2
Toruń, Poland 7/F3
Toruń, Poland 47/D2
Torunos, Venezuela 124/C3
Törva, U.S.S.R. 53/C1
Tory (isl.), Ireland 17/E1
Tory (isl.), Ireland 10/B3
Tory (sound), Ireland 17/E1
Torysa (riv.), Czech. 41/F2
Torzhok, U.S.S.R. 52/D3
Tosa, Japan 81/F7
Tosa (bay), Japan 81/F7
Tosashimizu, Japan 81/F7
Toson Hu (lake), China 77/E4
Töss (riv.), Switzerland 39/G1
Tostado, Argentina 143/D2
Toston, Mont. (59643) 262/E4
Tosu, Japan 81/E7
Tosya, Turkey 63/F2
Tota, Laguna de (lake), Colombia 126/D5
Totana, Spain 33/F4
Tótkomlós, Hungary 41/F3
Tot'ma, U.S.S.R. 48/E4
Tot'ma, U.S.S.R. 52/F3
Totnes, England 13/D7
Totnes, England 10/E5
Totnes, Sask. 181/C4
Totness, Suriname 131/C3
Toto, Ind. (†46534) 227/D2
Totoket, Conn. (†06405) 210/D3
Totonicapán, Guatemala 154/B3
Totora, Cochabamba, Bolivia 136/C5
Totora, Oruro, Bolivia 136/A5
Totoral, Chile 138/A6
Totoral, Quebrada (riv.), Chile 138/A6
Totoral, Uruguay 145/C3
Totowa, N.J. (07512) 273/B1
Totoya (isl.), Fiji 86/R11
Tottenham, N.S. Wales 97/D3
Tottenham, Ontario 177/E3
Tottori (pref.), Japan 81/G6
Tottori, Japan 81/G6
Touat (oasis), Algeria 106/E3
Touba, Ivory Coast 106/C7
Touba, Senegal 106/A6
Toubkal, Jebel (mt.), Morocco 102/B1
Toubkal, Jebel (mt.), Morocco 106/C2
Touchet, Wash. (99360) 310/G4
Touchet (riv.), Wash. 310/G4
Touchwood (lake), Alberta 182/E2
Touchwood (hills), Sask. 181/G4
Toufourine (well), Mali 106/C4
Tougaloo, Miss. (39174) 256/D6
Tougan, Upper Volta 106/D6
Touggourt, Algeria 106/F2
Touggourt, Algeria 102/C1
Toughkenamon, Pa. (19374) 294/L6
Tougué, Guinea 106/B6
Touila (well), Algeria 106/C3
Touila (well), Mauritania 106/C3
Toukoto, Mali 106/C6
Toul, France 28/F3
Touladi, Grand Lac (lake), Québec 172/J1
Toulnustouc (riv.), Québec 174/D2
Toulon, France 7/E4
Toulon, France 28/F6
Toulon, Ill. (61483) 222/D2
Toulouse, France 7/E4
Toulouse, France 28/D6
Toumodi, Ivory Coast 106/D7
Toungo, Nigeria 106/G7
Toungoo, Burma 72/C3
Touraine (trad. prov.), France 29
Tourakom, Laos 72/D3
Tourbis (lake), Québec 172/C2
Tourcoing, France 28/E2
Tour d'Aï (mt.), Switzerland 39/C4
Tourelle, Québec 172/C1
Tournai, Belgium 27/C7
Tournavista, Peru 128/E7
Tournon, France 28/F5
Tournus, France 28/F4
Touros, Brazil 132/H4
Touro Synagogue Nat'l Hist. Site, R.I. 249/J7
Tours, France 28/D4
Tours, France 7/E4
Tourville, Québec 172/H2
Toutes Aides, Manitoba 179/C3
Toutle, Wash. (98649) 310/C4
Toutle, North Fork (riv.), Wash. 310/C4
Toutle, South Fork (riv.), Wash. 310/C4
Toužim, Czech. 41/B1
Töv, Mongolia 77/G2
Tovar, Venezuela 124/C3
Tovey, Ill. (62570) 222/D4
Towaco, N.J. (07082) 273/E2
Towada, Japan 81/K3
Towada (lake), Japan 81/K3
Towada-Hachimantai National Park, Japan 81/K3
Towakaima, Guyana 131/B2
Towanda, Ill. (61776) 222/E3
Towanda, Kansas (67144) 232/E4
Towanda, Pa. (18848) 294/J2
Towanda (creek), Pa. 294/J2
Towaoc, Colo. (81334) 208/B8
Towcester, England 13/F5
Tower, Mich. (49792) 250/E3
Tower, Minn. (55790) 255/F3
Tower, Wyo. (†82190) 319/B1
Tower City, N. Dak. (58071) 282/P6
Tower City, Pa. (17980) 294/J4
Tower Hamlets, England 13/H8
Tower Hill, Ill. (62571) 222/E4
Tower Lakes, Ill. (†60010) 222/A4
Towers of Silence, India 68/B7
Tow Law, England 13/H4
Town (creek), Ala. 195/C1
Town (creek), Md. 245/E2
Town and Country, Mo. (†63101) 261/O3
Town and Country, Wash. (†99218) 310/H3
Town Creek, Ala. (35672) 195/D1
Towner, Colo. (81080) 208/P6
Towner (co.), N. Dak. 282/M2
Towner, N. Dak. (58788) 282/K3
Townley, Ala. (35587) 195/D3
Town of Pines, Ind. (†46360) 227/D1
Town Point, Md. (†21915) 245/P3
Towns (co.), Georgia 217/E1
Towns, Georgia (†31055) 217/G7
Townsend, Del. (19736) 245/R3
Townsend, Georgia (31331) 217/J7
Townsend, Mass. (01469) 249/H2
Townsend○, Mass. (01469) 249/H2
Townsend, Mont. (59644) 262/E4
Townsend (inlet), N.J. 273/D5
Townsend, Tenn. (37882) 237/O9
Townsend, Va. (23443) 307/R6
Townsend, Wis. (54175) 317/K5
Townsend Harbor, Mass. (†01469) 249/G2
Townsends Inlet, N.J. (†08243) 273/D5
Townshend○, Vt. (05353) 268/B5
Townsville, Australia 2/S6
Townsville, Australia 87/E7
Townsville, N.C. (27584) 281/N1
Townsville, Queensland 88/H3
Townsville, Queensland 95/C3
Townville, Pa. (16360) 294/C2
Townville, S.C. (29689) 296/B2
Towot, Sudan 111/F6
Towraghondi, Afghanistan 68/A1
Towson, Md. (21204) 245/M3
Towuti (lake), Indonesia 85/G6
Towy (riv.), Wales 13/D6
Towy (riv.), Wales 10/E5
Toxey, Ala. (36921) 195/B7
Toya (lake), Japan 81/K2
Toyah, Texas (79785) 303/D11
Toyah (creek), Texas 303/D11
Toyah (lake), Texas 303/A6
Toyahvale, Texas (79786) 303/D11
Toyama (pref.), Japan 81/H5
Toyama, Japan 81/H5
Toyama (bay), Japan 81/H5
Toyohashi, Japan 81/H6
Toyonaka, Japan 81/J7
Toyooka, Japan 81/G6
Toyota, Japan 81/H6
Tozeur, Tunisia 106/F2
Trabzon (prov.), Turkey 63/H2
Trabzon, Turkey 54/E5
Trabzon, Turkey 63/H2
Trabzon, Turkey 59/C1
Tracadie, New Bruns. 170/F1
Tracadie, Nova Scotia 168/G3
Tracadie (bay), Pr. Edward I. 168/F2
Trachselwald, Switzerland 39/E2
Tracy, Calif. (95376) 204/D6
Tracy, Conn. (†06492) 210/D2
Tracy, Iowa (50256) 229/H6
Tracy, Ky. (†42123) 237/K7
Tracy, Minn. (56175) 255/C6
Tracy, Mo. (64079) 261/C4
Tracy, New Bruns. 170/D3
Tracy, Québec 172/D3
Tracy Arm (inlet), Alaska 196/N1
Tracy City, Tenn. (37387) 237/K10
Tracyton, Wash. (98393) 310/A2
Trade, Tenn. (37691) 237/T8
Trade Lake, Wis. (†54837) 317/A4
Tradespark, Scotland 15/E3
Tradesville, S.C. (†29720) 296/F2
Tradewater (riv.), Ky. 237/F6
Trading (bay), Alaska 196/B1
Trading Post, Kansas (†66075) 232/H3
Traer, Iowa (50675) 229/J4
Traer, Kansas (†67749) 232/B2
Trafalgar, Ind. (46181) 227/E6
Trafalgar, Nova Scotia 168/F3
Trafalgar (cape), Spain 33/C4
Trafaria, Portugal 33/A1
Trafford, Ala. (35172) 195/E3
Trafford, Pa. (15085) 294/C5
Traghen, Libya 111/B2
Traiguén, Chile 138/D2
Traiguén (isl.), Chile 138/D6
Trail, Br. Col. 162/E6
Trail, Br. Col. 146/G4
Trail, Br. Col. 184/J6
Trail, Minn. (56684) 255/C3
Trail, Oreg. (97541) 291/E5
Trail City, S. Dak. (57657) 298/H3
Trail Creek, Ind. (†46360) 227/D1
Traill (isl.), Greenl. 4/B10
Traill (co.), N. Dak. 282/R5
Traîne (lake), Québec 172/D2
Trainer, Pa. (†19013) 294/L7
Traiskirchen, Austria 41/D2
Trakai, U.S.S.R. 53/C3
Tralake, Miss. (38757) 256/C4
Tralee, Ireland 10/B4
Tralee, Ireland 17/B7
Tralee (bay), Ireland 17/B7
Tramán-tepuí (mt.), Venezuela 124/G5
Tramelan, Switzerland 39/D2
Trammel, Va. (24289) 307/D6
Tramore, Ireland 10/C4
Tramore, Ireland 17/G7
Tramore (bay), Ireland 17/G7
Trampas, N. Mex. (87576) 274/D2
Tramperos (creek), N. Mex. 274/F2
Tramping (lake), Sask. 181/C3
Tramping Lake, Sask. 181/B3
Tranås, Sweden 18/J7
Trancoso, Portugal 33/C2
Tranebjerg, Denmark 21/D6
Tranebjerg (mt.), Denmark 21/C6
Tranent, Scotland 15/F5
Trang, Thailand 72/C6
Trangan (isl.), Indonesia 85/J7
Trangie, N.S. Wales 97/D3
Trani, Italy 34/F4
Tranquebar, India 68/E6
Tranqueras, Uruguay 145/D2
Tranqui (isl.), Chile 138/D4
Tranquility, N.J. (07879) 273/D2
Tranquillity, Calif. (93668) 204/E7
Transantarctic (mts.) 5/B17
Trans-Carpathian Oblast, U.S.S.R. 52/B5
Transfer, Pa. (16154) 294/A3
Transkei (aut. rep.), S. Africa 102/E8
Transkei (aut. rep.), S. Africa 118/D6
Transquaking (riv.), Md. 245/P7
Transvaal (prov.), S. Africa 102/E7
Transvaal (prov.), S. Africa 118/D4
Transylvania, La. (71286) 238/H1
Transylvania (co.), N.C. 281/D4
Transylvanian Alps (mts.), Romania 45/G3
Trapani (prov.), Italy 34/D5
Trapani, Italy 7/F5
Trapani, Italy 34/D5
Trap Falls (res.), Conn. 210/C3
Traphill, N.C. (28685) 281/H2
Trappe, Md. (21673) 245/O6
Trappers (lake), Colo. 208/E3
Traralgon, Victoria 97/D6
Traralgon, Victoria 88/H7
Trarza (reg.), Mauritania 106/A5
Trasimeno (lake), Italy 34/D3
Traskwood, Ark. (72167) 202/E5
Trat, Thailand 72/D4
Traun, Austria 41/C2
Traun (riv.), Austria 41/C2
Traun See (lake), Austria 41/B3
Traunstein, W. Germany 22/E5
Travancore (reg.), India 68/D7
Travelers Rest, S.C. (29690) 296/C2
Travellers (lake), N.S. Wales 97/B3
Travellers Rest, Ky. (†41314) 237/O6
Travemünde, W. Germany 22/D2
Travers, Alberta 182/D4
Travers (res.), Alberta 182/D4
Traverse (bay), Manitoba 179/F4
Traverse (isl.), Mich. 250/A1
Traverse (pt.), Mich. 250/A1
Traverse (co.), Minn. 255/B5
Traverse, Minn. (†56082) 255/D6
Traverse (lake), Minn. 255/B5
Traverse (lake), S. Dak. 298/R2
Traverse City, Mich. 188/K2
Traverse City, Mich. (49684) 250/D4
Tra Vinh (Phu Vinh), Vietnam 72/E5
Travis (co.), Texas 303/G7
Travis (lake), Texas 303/G7
Travis A.F.B., Calif. 204/L1
Travnik, Yugoslavia 45/C3
Trawbreaga (bay), Ireland 17/F1
Traynor, Sask. 181/C3
Traytown, Newf. 166/D1
Trbovlje, Yugoslavia 45/B2
Treadway, Tenn. (37883) 237/P8
Treasure (isl.), Fla. 212/B3
Treasure (co.), Mont. 262/J4
Treasure Island, Fla. (33740) 212/B3
Treasury (isls.), Solomon Is. 86/C2
Treaty, Ind. (†46992) 227/F3
Trebbia (riv.), Italy 34/B2
Třebíč, Czech. 41/C2
Trebinje, Yugoslavia 45/D4
Trebišov, Czech. 41/F2
Trebizond (Trabzon), Turkey 63/H2
Trebloc, Miss. (38875) 256/G3
Třeboň, Czech. 41/C2
Trece Martires, Philippines 82/C3
Tredegar, Wales 13/B6
Treece, Kansas (66778) 232/H4
Treelon, Sask. 181/C6
Trees, La. (71081) 238/B1
Treesbank, Manitoba 179/C5
Tregaron, Wales 13/D5
Tregaron, Wales 10/E4
Tregarva, Sask. 181/G5
Trego (co.), Kansas 232/C3
Trego, Mont. (59934) 262/B2
Trego, Wis. (54888) 317/C4
Treherne, Manitoba 179/D5
Treig, Loch (lake), Scotland 15/D4
Treinta y Tres (dept.), Uruguay 145/E4
Treinta y Tres, Uruguay 145/E4
Trelew, Argentina 143/C5
Trelleborg, Sweden 18/H9
Tremadoc (bay), Wales 10/D4
Tremadoc (prom.), Wales 13/C5
Tremblant (lake), Québec 172/C3
Trembleur (lake), Br. Col. 184/E3
Trementina, N. Mex. (88439) 274/E3
Tremiti (isls.), Italy 34/E3
Tremont, Ill. (61568) 222/D3
Tremont, Maine (†04653) 243/G7
Tremont○, Maine (†04653) 243/G7
Tremont, Miss. (38876) 256/H2
Tremont, Pa. (17981) 294/K4
Tremont City, Ohio (45372) 284/C5
Tremonton, Utah (84337) 304/B2
Tremp, Spain 33/G1
Trempealeau (co.), Wis. 317/D7
Trempealeau, Wis. (54661) 317/C8
Trempealeau (riv.), Wis. 317/C7
Trenary, Mich. (49891) 250/C2
Trenčín, Czech. 41/E2
Trenel, Argentina 143/D4
Trenggalek, Indonesia 85/K2
Trenque Lauquen, Argentina 143/D4
Trent (riv.), England 13/G4
Trent (riv.), England 10/F4
Trent (riv.), N.C. 281/P4
Trent, Oreg. (†97431) 291/E4
Trent, S. Dak. (57065) 298/R6
Trent, Texas (79561) 303/D5
Trente et un Milles (lake), Québec 172/B3
Trentham, Manitoba 179/F5
Trentham Cliffs, N.S. Wales 97/B4
Trentino-Alto Adige (reg.), Italy 34/C1
Trento (prov.), Italy 34/C1
Trento, Italy 34/C1
Trenton, Ala. (35774) 195/F1
Trenton, Ark. (†72374) 202/J5
Trenton, Fla. (32693) 212/D2
Trenton, Georgia (30752) 217/A1
Trenton, Ill. (62293) 222/D5
Trenton, Iowa (†52641) 229/K6
Trenton, Ky. (42286) 237/G7
Trenton, Maine (†04605) 243/G7
Trenton○, Maine (†04605) 243/G7
Trenton, Md. (†21155) 245/L2
Trenton, Mich. (48183) 250/B7
Trenton, Miss. (†39153) 256/E6
Trenton, Mo. (64683) 261/E2
Trenton, Nebr. (69044) 264/D4
Trenton (cap.), N.J. 146/L5
Trenton (cap.), N.J. 188/M2
Trenton (cap.), N.J. (*08601) 273/D3
Trenton, N.C. (28585) 281/P4
Trenton, N. Dak. (58853) 282/C3
Trenton, Nova Scotia 168/F3
Trenton, Ohio (45067) 284/B7
Trenton, Ontario 177/G3
Trenton, S.C. (29847) 296/D4
Trenton, Tenn. (38382) 237/D9
Trenton, Texas (75490) 303/H4
Trenton, Utah (84338) 304/B2
Trent Woods, N.C. (†28560) 281/P4
Trepassey, Newf. 166/D2
Treptow, E. Germany 22/F4
Tres Árboles, Uruguay 145/C3
Tres Arroyos, Argentina 143/D4
Tres Arroyos, Argentina 120/C6
Tres Bocas, Uruguay 145/B2
Tresckow, Pa. (18254) 294/K4
Tresco (isl.), England 13/A8
Três Corações, Brazil 132/E8
Três Corações, Brazil 135/D2
Tres Cruces, Nevada (mt.), Chile 138/B6
Tres Esquinas, Colombia 126/C7
Treshnish (isls.), Scotland 15/B4
Tres Islas, Uruguay 145/E3
Três Lagoas, Brazil 120/D5
Três Lagoas, Brazil 132/C8
Três Marias (res.), Brazil 120/E4
Tres Montes (cape), Chile 120/B7
Tres Montes (cape), Chile 138/C7
Tres Montes (gulf), Chile 138/D6
Tres Montes (pen.), Chile 138/C6
Tres Palmas, Colombia 126/B3
Trespassey (bay), Newf. 166/D2
Tres Picos, Cerro (mt.), Argentina 143/B5
Tres Piedras, N. Mex. (87577) 274/D2
Tres Pinos, Calif. (95075) 204/D7
Três Pontas, Brazil 135/D2
Tres Puntas (cape), Argentina 120/C7
Tres Puntas (cape), Argentina 143/D6
Tres Puntas (cape), Guatemala 154/C3
Três Rios, Brazil 135/E3
Três Rios, Brazil 132/F8
Tres Ritos, N. Mex. (†87579) 274/D2
Třešť, Czech. 41/C2
Treuchtlingen, W. Germany 22/D4
Treungen, Norway 18/F7
Treutlen (co.), Georgia 217/G6
Trevelin, Argentina 143/B5
Trevett, Maine (04571) 243/D8
Treviglio, Italy 34/B2
Treviño, Spain 33/E1
Treviso (prov.), Italy 34/D2
Treviso, Italy 34/D2
Trevlac, Ind. (†47448) 227/E6
Trevorton, Pa. (17881) 294/J4
Trevose (head), England 13/B7
Trévoux, France 28/F5
Treynor, Iowa (51575) 229/B6
Treyvaux, Switzerland 39/D3
Trezevant, Tenn. (38258) 237/D8
Trhové Sviny, Czech. 41/C2
Triabunna, Tasmania 99/D4
Triadelphia (lake), Md. 245/L4
Triadelphia, W. Va. (26059) 312/E2
Triana, Ala. (†35758) 195/E1
Triangle, Alberta 182/B2
Triangle, Va. (22172) 307/O3
Triángulo Este (isl.), Mexico 150/N6
Triángulo Oeste (isl.), Mexico 150/N6
Tribbett, Miss. (38779) 256/C4
Tribbey, Okla. (†74852) 288/M4
Triberg im Schwarzwald, W. Germany 22/C4
Tribune, Kansas (67879) 232/A3
Tribune, Sask. 181/H6
Tricase, Italy 34/G5
Trichur, India 68/D6
Trida, N.S. Wales 97/C3
Tridell, Utah (84076) 304/E3
Trident, Mont. (59752) 262/E5
Trident (peak), Nev. 266/C1
Trieben, Austria 41/C3
Trier, W. Germany 22/B4
Triesen, Liecht. 39/H2
Trieste (prov.), Italy 34/E2
Trieste, Italy 34/E2
Trieste, Italy 7/F4
Trieste (gulf), Italy 34/D2
Trigal, Bolivia 136/C6
Trigg (co.), Ky. 237/F7
Triglav (mt.), Yugoslavia 45/A2
Trigueros, Spain 33/C4
Tríkkala, Greece 45/E6
Tri Lakes, Ind. (†46725) 227/G2
Trilby, Fla. (33593) 212/D3
Trilla, Ill. (62469) 222/E4
Trillick, N. Ireland 17/G3
Trim, Ireland 17/H4
Trim, Ireland 10/C4
Trimble, Ill. (†62454) 222/F4
Trimble (co.), Ky. 237/L3
Trimble, Ky. (42559) 237/M6
Trimble, Mo. (64492) 261/D4
Trimble, Ohio (45782) 284/F7
Trimble, Tenn. (38259) 237/C8
Trim Cane (creek), Miss. 256/G4
Trimmis, Switzerland 39/J3
Trimont, Minn. (56176) 255/D7
Trin, Switzerland 39/H3
Trinchera, Colo. (81081) 208/M8
Trinchera (peak), Colo. 208/J8
Trinchera (riv.), Colo. 208/H8
Trincheras, Mexico 150/D1
Trincomalee, Sri Lanka 54/K9
Trincomalee, Sri Lanka 68/E7
Trindade, Brazil 132/D7
Třinec, Czech. 41/E2
Tring, England 13/G7
Tring, England 10/F5
Tring-Jonction, Québec 172/F3
Trinidad (isl.), Argentina 143/D4
Trinidad, Bolivia 120/C4
Trinidad, Bolivia 136/C4
Trinidad, Calif. (95570) 204/A2
Trinidad (head), Calif. 204/A2
Trinidad (gulf), Chile 138/D8
Trinidad, Colombia 126/E5
Trinidad, Colo. 146/H6
Trinidad, Colo. 188/F3
Trinidad, Colo. (81082) 208/L8
Trinidad, Cuba 158/E2
Trinidad, Cuba 156/B2
Trinidad, Honduras 154/C3
Trinidad, Paraguay 144/E5
Trinidad, Texas (75163) 303/J5
Trinidad (isl.), Trin. & Tob. 156/G5
Trinidad (isl.), Trin. & Tob. 161/A9
Trinidad, Uruguay 145/B4
Trinidad, Wash. (†98848) 310/F3
Trinidad and Tobago 2/G5
Trinidad and Tobago 146/N8
TRINIDAD and TOBAGO 161
TRINIDAD and TOBAGO 156/G5
Trinity, Ala. (35673) 195/D1
Trinity (isls.), Alaska 196/H3
Trinity (co.), Calif. 204/B3
Trinity (riv.), Calif. 204/B3
Trinity (mt.), Idaho 220/C6
Trinity, Ky. (†41179) 237/O3
Trinity (range), Nev. 266/C2
Trinity, Newf. 166/D4
Trinity, Newf. 166/D2
Trinity (bay), Newf. 166/D2
Trinity (bay), Queensland 88/H3
Trinity (bay), Queensland 95/C3
Trinity (co.), Texas 303/J6
Trinity, Texas (75862) 303/J7
Trinity (bay), Texas 303/L2
Trinity (riv.), Texas 188/G4
Trinity (riv.), Texas 303/H5
Trinity, West Fork (riv.), Texas 303/G2
Trinity Center, Calif. (96091) 204/C2
Trinity Springs, Ind. (†47581) 227/D7
Trinity Ville, Jamaica 158/K6
Trinkitat, Sudan 111/G4
Trinkitat, Sudan 59/C6
Trino, Italy 34/B2
Trinway, Ohio (43842) 284/F5
Trio, S.C. (29595) 296/H5
Trion, Georgia (30753) 217/B1
Triplet, Va. (23886) 307/N7
Triplett, Mo. (65286) 261/F4
Tripoli, Iowa (50676) 229/J3
Tripoli (Tarabulus), Lebanon 59/C3
Tripoli (Tarabulus), Lebanon 63/F5
Tripoli (cap.), Libya 2/K4
Tripoli (cap.), Libya 102/D1
Tripoli (cap.), Libya 111/B1
Tripoli, Wis. (54564) 317/G4
Trípolis, Greece 45/F7
Tripolitania (reg.), Libya 102/D1
Tripolitania (reg.), Libya 111/B1
Tripp (co.), S. Dak. 298/K7
Tripp, S. Dak. (57376) 298/N7
Tripura (state), India 68/G4
Trischen (isl.), W. Germany 22/C1
Tristan da Cunha (isl.), St. Helena 2/J7
Triste (gulf), Venezuela 124/D2
Triton (isl.), China 85/E2
Triumph, Ill. (61371) 222/E2
Triumph-Buras, La. (†70041) 238/L8
Triune, Tenn. (†37014) 237/H9
Trivandrum, India 54/J9
Trivandrum, India 68/D7
Trivoli, Ill. (61569) 222/D3
Trnava, Czech. 41/D2
Trobriand (isls.), Papua N.G. 87/F6
Trobriand (isls.), Papua N.G. 85/C7
Trochu, Alberta 182/D4
Troense, Denmark 21/D7
Trofaiach, Austria 41/C3
Trogir, Yugoslavia 45/C4
Troisdorf, W. Germany 22/B3
Trois-Pistoles, Québec 172/H1
Trois Pitons, Morne (mt.), Dominica 161/E6
Trois-Ponts, Belgium 27/H8
Trois-Rivières, Guadeloupe 161/A7
Trois-Rivières (riv.), Haiti 158/B5
Trois-Rivières, Que. 162/J6
Trois-Rivières, Que. 146/L5
Trois-Rivières, Que. 172/E3
Trois-Rivières-Ouest, Québec 172/E3
Trois-Saumons, Québec 172/G2
Troistorrents, Switzerland /C4
Troisvierges, Luxembourg 27/J9
Troitsa (lake), Br. Col. 184/D3
Troitsk, U.S.S.R. 48/G4
Troitsko-Pechorsk, U.S.S.R. 52/J2
Trojan, S. Dak. (†57754) 298/B5
Trollhättan, Sweden 18/H7
Trombay, India 68/B7
Trombetas (riv.), Brazil 132/B3
Tromie (riv.), Scotland 15/D4
Trommald, Minn. (†56455) 255/D4
Troms (co.), Norway 18/L2
Tromsø, Norway 4/B9
Tromsø, Norway 7/F2
Tromsø, Norway 18/L2
Trona, Calif. (93562) 204/H8
Tronador (mt.), Argentina 143/B5
Tronador, Cerro (mt.), Chile 138/E3
Trondheim, Norway 7/F2
Trondheim, Norway 18/F5
Trondheimsfjorden (fjord), Norway 7/F2
Trondheimsfjorden (fjord), Norway 18/G5
Troodos (mt.), Cyprus 63/E5
Troon, Scotland 10/D3
Troon, Scotland 15/D5
Tropic, Utah (84776) 304/B6
Trosa, Sweden 18/K7
Trosky, Minn. (56177) 255/B7
Trossachs, Sask. 181/G6
Trossachs, The, (valley), Scotland 15/D4
Trostan (mt.), N. Ireland 17/J1
Trotternish (dist.), Scotland 15/B3
Trotters, N. Dak. (58657) 282/C5
Trotwood, Ohio (45426) 284/B6
Trou Bonbon, Haiti 158/A6
Trou du Nord, Haiti 158/C5
Troup (co.), Georgia 217/B4
Troup (head), Scotland 15/F3
Troup, Texas (75789) 303/J5
Troupsburg, N.Y. (14885) 276/F6
Trousdale, Kansas (†67059) 232/C4
Trousdale, Okla. (†74878) 288/M4

Upper Fairmount 461

Twelvepole (creek), W. Va. 312/A6
Twentynine Palms, Calif. (92277) 204/K9
Twentynine Palms Marine Base, Calif. 204/J9
Twig, Minn. (55791) 255/F4
Twiggs (co.), Georgia 217/F5
Twila, Ky. (†40873) 237/P7
Twillingate, Newf. 166/C4
Twin (lakes), Conn. 210/B1
Twin (falls), Idaho 220/D7
Twin (lakes), Maine 243/F4
Twin (lakes), Wash. 310/G2
Twin Bridges, Mont. (59754) 262/D5
Twin Brooks, S. Dak. (57269) 298/R3
Twin City, Georgia (30471) 217/H5
Twin Falls (co.), Idaho 220/D7
Twin Falls, Idaho (83301) 220/D7
Twin Falls, Idaho 188/C2
Twin Falls, Idaho 146/G5
Twin Falls, Newf. 166/B3
Twin Hills, Alaska (†99576) 196/F3
Twining, Mich. (48766) 250/F4
Twin Lake, Mich. (49457) 250/C5
Twin Lakes, Calif. (†95060) 204/K4
Twin Lakes, Colo. (81251) 208/G4
Twin Lakes (res.), Colo. 208/G4
Twin Lakes, Minn. (56089) 255/E7
Twin Lakes, Wis. (53181) 317/K11
Twin Mountain, N.H. (03595) 268/D3
Twin Oaks, Mo. (†63088) 261/N3
Twin Peaks, Calif. (92391) 204/H9
Twin Peaks (mt.), Idaho 220/D5
Twin Rocks, Oreg. (†97136) 291/C2
Twin Rocks, Pa. (15960) 294/E4
Twinsburg, Ohio (44087) 284/J10
Twin Sisters (mt.), Wash. 310/D2
Twin Valley, Minn. (56584) 255/B3
Twisp, Wash. (98856) 310/E2
Twisp (pass), Wash. 310/E2
Twisp (riv.), Wash. 310/E2
Twitchell (res.), Calif. 204/E9
Two Arm (bay), Alaska 196/C2
Two Butte (creek), Colo. 208/N7
Two Buttes, Colo. (81084) 208/P7
Two Buttes (res.), Colo. 208/O7
Twodot, Mont. (59085) 262/F4
Twofold (bay), N.S. Wales 97/F5
Two Harbors, Minn. (55616) 255/G3
Two Hearted (riv.), Mich. 250/D2
Two Hills, Alberta 182/E3
Two Rivers (riv.), Minn. 255/A1
Two Rivers (res.), N. Mex. 274/E5
Two Rivers, Wis. (54241) 317/M7
Two Water (creek), Utah 304/E4
Twynholm, Scotland 15/D6
Tyaskin, Md. (21865) 245/P7
Tybee Island, Georgia (31328) 217/L6
Tybee Roads (chan.), S.C. 296/F7
Tychy, Poland 47/B4
Tye, Texas (79563) 303/E5
Tye River, Va. (22975) 307/L5
Tygart (lake), W. Va. 312/G4
Tygart Valley (riv.), W. Va. 312/F5
Tyger (riv.), S.C. 296/D2
Tygh Valley, Oreg. (97063) 291/F2
Tyler, Ala. (36785) 195/E6
Tyler (lake), Conn. 210/B1
Tyler, Minn. (56178) 255/B6
Tyler, Mo. (†63877) 261/N10
Tyler, N. Dak. (†58075) 282/S7
Tyler, Pa. (†15849) 294/F3
Tyler (co.), Texas 303/K7
Tyler, Texas 188/H4
Tyler, Texas (*75701) 303/J5
Tyler, Wash. (†99004) 310/H3
Tyler (co.), W. Va. 312/E4
Tylersburg, Pa. (16361) 294/D3
Tylersville, Pa. (17773) 294/G4
Tylertown, Miss. (39667) 256/D8
Tylerville, Conn. (†06438) 210/F3
Tym (riv.), U.S.S.R. 48/J3
Tymovskoye, U.S.S.R. 48/P4
Týn, Czech. 41/C2
Tynagh, Ireland 17/E5
Tynan, Texas (78391) 303/G9
Tynda, U.S.S.R. 48/N4
Tyndall, Manitoba 179/F4
Tyndall, S. Dak. (57066) 298/O8
Tyndall A.F.B., Fla. 212/C6
Tyndrum, Scotland 15/D4
Tyne (riv.), England 13/F3
Tyne (riv.), England 10/F3
Tyne (riv.), Scotland 15/F5
Tyne and Wear (co.), England 13/H3
Tynemouth, England 13/J3
Tynemouth, England 10/F3
Tyner, Ind. (46572) 227/E2
Tyner, Ky. (40486) 237/O6
Tyner, N.C. (27980) 281/R2
Tyner, Sask. 181/C4
Tyne Valley, Pr. Edward I. 168/E2
Tyngsboro○, Mass. (01879) 249/J2
Tynset, Norway 18/G5
Tyntynder South, Victoria 97/B4
Tyonek, Alaska (99682) 196/B1
Tyra (cays), Nicaragua 154/F4
Tyre (Sur), Lebanon 63/F6
Tyrifjord (lake), Norway 18/C3
Tyringham○, Mass. (01264) 249/A4
Tyrnyauz, U.S.S.R. 52/F6
Tyro, Kansas (67364) 232/G4
Tyro, Miss. (†38668) 256/E1
Tyro, Va. (22976) 307/K5
Tyrol (Tirol) (prov.), Austria 41/A3
Tyrone, Colo. (†81059) 208/L8
Tyrone, Georgia (30290) 217/C4
Tyrone, Ky. (†40342) 237/M4
Tyrone, Mo. (†65564) 261/J8
Tyrone, N. Mex. (88065) 274/A6
Tyrone, Okla. (73951) 288/D1
Tyrone, Pa. (16686) 294/F4
Tyronza, Ark. (72386) 202/K3
Tyronza (riv.), Ark. 202/K2
Tyrrell (co.), N.C. 281/S3
Tyrrell (lake), Victoria 97/B4
Tyrrellspass, Ireland 17/G5
Tyrrhenian (sea) 7/F4
Tyrrhenian (sea), Italy 34/C4
Tysnes, Norway 18/D6
Tyson, Vt. (†05149) 268/B5
Tyson Wash (dry riv.), Ariz. 198/A5
Ty Ty, Georgia (31795) 217/E8
Tyumen, U.S.S.R. 54/H4
Tyumen', U.S.S.R. 48/G4
Tyung (riv.), U.S.S.R. 48/M3
Tyvan, Sask. 181/H5
Tywyn, Wales 13/C5
Tywyn, Wales 10/D4
Tzaneen, S. Africa 118/E4
Tzekung (Zigong), China 77/F6
Tzepo (Zibo), China 77/J4
Tzucabab, Mexico 150/P7

U

Uahuka (isl.), Fr. Poly. 87/N6
Uanda, Queensland 95/C4
Uanle Uen, Somalia 115/H3
Uanle Uen, Somalia 102/G4
Uapou (isl.), Fr. Poly. 87/M6
Uatumã (riv.), Brazil 132/B3
Uaupés (riv.), Brazil 132/G9
Ub, Yugoslavia 45/E3
Ubá, Brazil 135/E2
Ubá, Brazil 132/F8
Übach-Palenberg, W. Germany 22/B3
Ubaíra, Brazil 132/G6
Ubaitaba, Brazil 132/G6
Ubaiyidh, Wadi (dry riv.), Iraq 66/B5
Ubangi (riv.) 102/D4
Ubangi (riv.), Cent. Afr. Rep. 115/C3
Ubangi (riv.), Congo 115/C3
Ubangi (riv.), Zaire 115/C3
Ubari, Libya 102/D2
Ubari, Libya 111/B2
Ubaté, Colombia 126/D5
Ubatuba, Brazil 135/D3
Ubay, Philippines 82/E5
Ube, Japan 81/E6
Úbeda, Spain 33/E3
Uberaba (lag.), Bolivia 136/G5
Uberaba, Brazil 120/E4
Uberaba, Brazil 132/D7
Uberaba, Brazil 135/C1
Uberlândia, Brazil 120/E4
Uberlândia, Brazil 132/E7
Überlingen, W. Germany 22/C5
Ubina, Bolivia 136/B7
Ubinas, Peru 128/G11
Ubly, Mich. (48475) 250/G5
Ubombo, S. Africa 118/E5
Ubon, Thailand 54/M8
Ubon, Thailand 72/E4
Ubrique, Spain 33/D4
Ubundu, Zaire 115/E4
Ucayali (dept.), Peru 128/E6
Ucayali (riv.), Peru 2/F6
Ucayali (riv.), Peru 120/B3
Ucayali (riv.), Peru 128/F5
Uccle, Belgium 27/B9
Uch, Pakistan 68/B3
Uchaly, U.S.S.R. 7/K3
Uchaly, U.S.S.R. 52/J4
Ucharonidge, North. Terr. 93/D4
Uchee, Ala. (†36858) 195/H6
Uchiura (bay), Japan 81/K2
Uchiza, Peru 128/D7
Uch Turfan (Wushi), China 77/A3
Uckange, France 28/G3
Ücker (riv.), E. Germany 22/E2
Uckfield, England 10/G5
Uckfield, England 13/H7
Ucluelet, Br. Col. 184/E6
Ucon, Idaho (83454) 220/F6
Ucross, Wyo. (†82835) 319/F1
Ucumasi, Bolivia 136/B6
Uda (riv.), U.S.S.R. 48/O4
Udaipur, India 68/C4
Udall, Kansas (67146) 232/E4
Udaypur, India 54/J7
Uddevalla, Sweden 18/G7
Uddingston, Scotland 15/B2
Uddjaur (lake), Sweden 18/L4
Udell, Iowa (52593) 229/H7
Uden, Netherlands 27/H5
Udhampur, India 68/D2
Udine (prov.), Italy 34/D1
Udine, Italy 34/D2
Udine, Italy 7/F4
Udipi, India 68/C6
Udmurt A.S.S.R., U.S.S.R. 48/F4
Udmurt A.S.S.R., U.S.S.R. 52/H3
Udon Thani, Thailand 54/M8
Udon Thani, Thailand 72/D3
Udora, Ontario 177/E3
Ueckermünde, E. Germany 22/F2
Ueda, Japan 81/J5
Uehling, Nebr. (68063) 264/H3
Uele (riv.) 102/E4
Uele (riv.), Zaire 115/E3
Uelen, U.S.S.R. 54/V3
Uelen, U.S.S.R. 4/C18
Uelen, U.S.S.R. 48/T3
Uelzen, W. Germany 22/D2
Uen (isl.), New Caled. 86/H5
Uetendorf, Switzerland 39/E3
Uetersen, W. Germany 22/C2
Ufa, U.S.S.R. 2/M3
Ufa, U.S.S.R. 7/K3
Ufa, U.S.S.R. 48/F4
Ufa, U.S.S.R. 52/J4
Ufa (riv.), U.S.S.R. 52/J3
Ugab (riv.), Namibia 118/A4
Uganda 2/L5
Uganda 102/F4
UGANDA 115/F3
Ugashik, Alaska (†99649) 196/G3
Ugashik (lakes), Alaska 196/G3
Ugie (riv.), Scotland 15/G3
Ugíjar, Spain 33/E4
Ugjoktok (bay), Newf. 166/B2
Uglegorsk, U.S.S.R. 48/P5
Uglich, U.S.S.R. 52/E3
Ugo, Japan 81/K4
Ugod, Hungary 41/D3
Uherské Hradiště, Czech. 41/D2
Uherský Brod, Czech. 41/D2
Úhlava (riv.), Czech. 41/B2
Uhlířské Janovice, Czech. 41/C2
Uhrichsville, Ohio (44683) 284/H5
Uig, Scotland 10/C2
Uig, Highland, Scotland 15/B3
Uig, W. Isles, Scotland 15/A2
Uige (dist.), Angola 115/B5
Uíge, Angola 115/C5
Uiju, N. Korea 81/B3
Uinkaret (plat.), Ariz. 198/B2
Uinta (mts.), Utah 304/D3
Uinta (riv.), Utah 304/D3
Uinta (co.), Wyo. 319/B4
Uintah (co.), Utah 304/E3
Uintah, Utah (†84401) 304/C2
Uintah and Ouray Ind. Res., Utah 304/D3
Ŭisŏng, S. Korea 81/D5
Uitenhage, S. Africa 102/E8
Uitenhage, S. Africa 118/C6
Uithoorn, Netherlands 27/F4
Uithuizen, Netherlands 27/K2
Uitkijk, Suriname 131/D3
Uivak (cape), Newf. 166/B2
Ujelang (atoll), Marshall Is. 87/F5
Újfehértó, Hungary 41/F3
Uji, Honduras 154/F3
Uji, Japan 81/J7
Ujiji (Kigoma-Ujiji), Tanz. 115/E4
Ujjain, India 68/D4
Újpest, Hungary 41/E3
Újszász, Hungary 41/F2
Ujung Pandang, Indonesia 54/N10
Ujung Pandang, Indonesia 85/F7
Ukasiksalik (isl.), Newf. 166/B2
Ukhta, U.S.S.R. 48/F3
Ukiah, Calif. (95482) 204/B4
Ukiah, Oreg. (97880) 291/J2
Ukkel (Uccle), Belgium 27/B9
Ukmerge, U.S.S.R. 53/C3
Ukmerge, U.S.S.R. 52/C3
Ukrainian S.S.R., U.S.S.R. 7/G4
Ukrainian S.S.R., U.S.S.R. 48/C5
Ukrainian S.S.R., U.S.S.R. 52/D5
Ula, Turkey 63/C4
Ulaanbaatar (Ulan Bator) (cap.), Mongolia 77/G2
Ulaanbaatar (cap.), Mongolia 54/M5
Ulaanbaatar (cap.), Mongolia 2/Q3
Ulaangom (Ulangom), Mongolia 77/D2
Ulaangom, Mongolia 54/L5
Ulah, N.C. (†27203) 281/K3
Ulak (isl.), Alaska 196/K4
Ulan, China 77/E4
Ulanhot (Horquin Youyi Qianqi), China 77/K2
Ulan-Ude, U.S.S.R. 54/M4
Ulan-Ude, U.S.S.R. 2/Q3
Ulan-Ude, U.S.S.R. 48/L4
Ulapes, Argentina 143/C3
Ulaş, Turkey 63/G3
Ulchin, S. Korea 81/D5
Ulcinj, Yugoslavia 45/D5
Uldum, Denmark 21/C6
Ulegei (Ölgiy), Mongolia 77/C2
Ulen, Ind. (†46052) 227/E4
Ulen, Minn. (56585) 255/B3
Uler, W. Va. (25282) 312/D5
Ulfborg, Denmark 21/B5
Ulhasnagar, India 68/C5
Uliastay (Jibhalanta), Mongolia 77/E2
Uliastay, Mongolia 54/L5
Ulindi (riv.), Zaire 115/E4
Ulithi (atoll), Micronesia 87/D4
Ulla (riv.), Spain 33/B1
Ulladulla, N.S. Wales 97/F4
Ullapool, Scotland 10/D2
Ullapool, Scotland 15/C3
Ulla Ulla, Bolivia 136/A4
Ulldecona, Spain 33/G2
Ullensvang, Norway 18/E6
Ullin, Ill. (62992) 222/D6
Ulloma, Bolivia 136/A5
Ullŭng (isl.), S. Korea 81/E5
Ulm, Ark. (72170) 202/H4
Ulm, Mont. (59485) 262/E3
Ulm, W. Germany 22/C4
Ulm, Wyo. (†82835) 319/F1
Ulman, Mo. (65083) 261/H6
Ulmarra, N.S. Wales 97/G1
Ulmer, Iowa (51464) 229/D4
Ulmer, S.C. (29849) 296/E5
Ulongue, Mozambique 118/E2
Ulricehamn, Sweden 18/H8
Ulrichen, Switzerland 39/F3
Ulriksfors, Sweden 18/K5
Ulrum, Netherlands 27/J2
Ulsan, S. Korea 81/D6
Ulster (part) (prov.), Ireland 17/G2
Ulster (trad. prov.), Ireland 17/K8
Ulster (co.), N.Y. 276/M7
Ulster (part) (prov.), N. Ireland 17/G2
Ulster, Pa. (18850) 294/J2
Ulster Spring, Jamaica 158/H6
Última Esperanza (sound), Chile 138/E9
Ulúa (riv.), Honduras 154/D3
Ulubat (lake), Turkey 63/C2
Ulubey, Turkey 63/C3
Uluborlu, Turkey 63/D3
Uludağ (mt.), Turkey 63/C3
Uludere, Turkey 63/K4
Ulugan (bay), Philippines 82/B5
Ulughchat (Wuqia), China 77/A4
Ulukışla, Turkey 63/F4
Ulumalu, Hawaii (†96708) 218/K2
Ulu Muztag (mt.), China 77/C4
Ulundi, S. Africa 118/E5
Ulungur He (riv.), China 77/C2
Ulungur Hu (lake), China 77/C2
Ulupalakua, Hawaii (†96790) 218/J2
Ulus, Turkey 63/E2
Ulutau (mts.), U.S.S.R. /G5
Ulu Tiram, Malaysia 72/F5
Ulva (isl.), Scotland 15/B4
Ulverston, England 13/D3
Ulverston, England 10/E3
Ulverstone, Tasmania 99/C3
Ulvik, Norway 18/E6
Ulvila, Finland 18/N6
Ul'yanovsk, U.S.S.R. 7/J3
Ul'yanovsk, U.S.S.R. 48/E4
Ul'yanovsk, U.S.S.R. 52/G4
Ulysses, Kansas (67880) 232/A4
Ulysses, Ky. (†41232) 237/R5
Ulysses, Nebr. (68669) 264/G3
Ulysses, Pa. (16948) 294/G2
Umag, Yugoslavia 45/A3
Umala, Bolivia 136/B5
Umán, Mexico 150/P6
Uman', U.S.S.R. 52/D5
Umanun (pt.), Philippines 82/F6
Umapine, Oreg. (97881) 291/J2
Umarkot, Pakistan 59/J4
Umatilla, Fla. (32784) 212/E3
Umatilla (co.), Oreg. 291/J2
Umatilla, Oreg. (97882) 291/H2
Umatilla (lake), Oreg. 291/G2
Umatilla (riv.), Oreg. 291/H2
Umatilla (lake), Wash. 310/E5
Umatilla Army Depot, Oreg. 291/H2
Umatilla Ind. Res., Oreg. 291/J2
Umba, U.S.S.R. 52/D1
Umbagog (lake), Maine 243/A6
Umbagog (lake), N.H. 268/E2
Umbakumba, North. Terr. 93/E3
Umbarger, Texas (79091) 303/B3
Umbeara, North. Terr. 93/C8
Umbertide, Italy 34/D3
Umboi (isl.), Papua N.G. 86/A2
Umbrail (peak), Switzerland 39/K3
Umbria, Colombia 126/B7
Umbria (reg.), Italy 34/D3
Umcalcus (lake), Maine 243/G3
Ume (riv.), Sweden 7/F2
Umeå, Sweden 7/F2
Umeå, Sweden 18/M5
Umeälv (riv.), Sweden 18/L4
Umiakovik (lake), Newf. 166/B2
Umiat, Alaska (†99701) 196/H1
Umikoa, Hawaii (†96776) 218/H4
Um Jauza, Jordan 65/D3
Umm al Qaiwain, U.A.E. 59/G4
Umm el Abid, Libya 111/C2
Umm el Fahm, Israel 65/C2
Umm Hajar, Ethiopia 111/G5
Umm Keddada, Sudan 111/E5
Umm Lajj, Saudi Arabia 59/C4
Umm Qasr, Iraq 66/E5
Umm Ruwaba, Sudan 111/F5
Umm Ruwaba, Sudan 102/F3
Umm Ruwaba, Sudan 59/B7
Umm Sa'id, Qatar 59/F5
Umnak (isl.), Alaska 196/E4
Umnak (passage), Alaska 196/E4
Umnak (isl.), U.S. 4/D18
Umpire, Ark. (71971) 202/B5
Umpqua, Oreg. (97486) 291/D4
Umpqua (riv.), Oreg. 291/D4
Umrer, India 68/D4
Umsaskis (lake), Maine 243/E2
Umtali, Zimbabwe 102/F6
Umtali, Zimbabwe 118/E3
Umtata, S. Africa 118/D6
Umtata (cap.), Transkei, S. Africa 102/E8
Umurbey, Turkey 63/C6
Umvukwe (range), Zimbabwe 118/E3
Umvuma, Zimbabwe 118/D3
Umzimbuvu, S. Africa 118/D6
Umzinto, S. Africa 118/E6
Una (mt.), N. Zealand 100/D5
Una (riv.), Yugoslavia 45/C3
Unadilla, Georgia (31091) 217/E6
Unadilla, Nebr. (68454) 264/H4
Unadilla, N.Y. (13849) 276/K6
Unadilla (riv.), N.Y. 276/K5
Unaí, Brazil 132/E7
Unaka, N.C. (28908) 281/A4
Unaka (mts.), N.C. 281/E2
Unaka (mts.), Tenn. 237/S8
Unalakleet, Alaska (99684) 196/G2
Unalakleet, Alaska 188/C5
Unalaska, Alaska 188/C6
Unalaska, Alaska (99685) 196/E4
Unalaska (isl.), Alaska 196/E4
Unalaska (isl.), U.S. 4/D18
Unare (riv.), Venezuela 124/F3
Uncas, Okla. (†74601) 288/M1
Uncastillo, Spain 33/F1
Uncasville, Conn. (06382) 210/G3
Uncertain, Texas (†75661) 303/K5
Uncia, Bolivia 136/B6
Uncompahgre (peak), Colo. 208/E6
Uncompahgre (plat.), Colo. 208/B5
Uncompahgre (riv.), Colo. 208/D5
Underbool, Victoria 97/A4
Underhill, Manitoba 179/B5
Underhill○, Vt. (05489) 268/B2
Underhill, Wis. (54176) 317/K6
Underhill Center, Vt. (05490) 268/B2
Underwood, Ind. (47177) 227/F7
Underwood, Iowa (51576) 229/B6
Underwood, Minn. (56586) 255/C4
Underwood, N. Dak. (58576) 282/H5
Underwood, Ontario 177/C3
Underwood, Wash. (98651) 310/D5
Undu (pt.), Fiji 86/R10
Undzha (riv.), U.S.S.R. 52/F3
Unecha, U.S.S.R. 52/D4
Uneeda, W. Va. (25205) 312/C6
Unga (isl.), Alaska 196/F3
Ungalik, Alaska (†99684) 196/F2
Ungarie, N.S. Wales 97/D3
Ungava (bay), Canada 146/M4
Ungava (bay), N.W.T. 162/K4
Ungava (bay), N.W. Terrs. 187/M4
Ungava (bay), Québec 174/F1
Ungava (pen.), Que. 146/L3
Ungava (pen.), Que. 162/J3
Ungava (pen.), Québec 174/E1
Ungeny, U.S.S.R. 52/C5
Unger, W. Va. (25447) 312/K4
Unggi, N. Korea 81/E2
União, Brazil 132/F4
União da Vitória, Brazil 132/D9
União dos Palmares, Brazil 132/H5
Unicoi (mts.), N.C. 281/A4
Unicoi (co.), Tenn. 237/S8
Unicoi, Tenn. (37692) 237/S8
Unicoi (mts.), Tenn. 237/N10
Uničov, Czech. 41/D2
Unimak (isl.), Alaska 188/C6
Unimak (bight), Alaska 196/F4
Unimak (isl.), Alaska 196/E4
Unimak (passage), Alaska 196/F4
Unimak (isl.), U.S. 4/D18
Unini, Peru 128/F8
Union, Ala. (†35462) 195/C5
Union (mt.), Ariz. 198/C4
Union (co.), Ark. 202/E7
Union, Ark. (†72576) 202/G1
Union○, Conn. (†06076) 210/G1
Union (co.), Fla. 212/D1
Union (co.), Georgia 217/E1
Union, Grenada 161/D8
Union (co.), Ill. 222/D6
Union, Ill. (60180) 222/E1
Union (co.), Ind. 227/H5
Union, Ind. (†47540) 227/C8
Union (co.), Iowa 229/E7
Union, Iowa (50258) 229/G4
Union (co.), Ky. 237/F5
Union, Ky. (41091) 237/M3
Union (par.), La. 238/F1
Union, La. (†70723) 238/L3
Union, Maine (04862) 243/E7
Union○, Maine (04862) 243/E7
Union, West Branch (riv.), Maine 243/G6
Union (co.), Miss. 256/F2
Union, Miss. (39365) 256/F5
Union, Mo. (63084) 261/L6
Union, Nebr. (68455) 264/J4
Union, N.H. (03887) 268/E5
Union (co.), N.J. 273/E2
Union○, N.J. (07083) 273/A2
Union (lake), N.J. 273/C5
Union (co.), N. Mex. 274/F2
Union (co.), N.C. 281/H4
Union, N. Dak. (58279) 282/O2
Union (co.), Ohio 284/D5
Union, Ohio (45322) 284/B6
Union, Ontario 177/C5
Union (co.), Oreg. 291/J2
Union, Oreg. (97883) 291/K2
Unión, Paraguay 144/D4
Union (co.), Pa. 294/H4
Union (isl.), St. Vin. & Grens. 156/G4
Union (co.), S.C. 296/D2
Union, S.C. (29379) 296/D2
Union (co.), S. Dak. 298/R8
Union (co.), Tenn. 237/O8
Unión, Uruguay 145/B7
Union, Wash. (98592) 310/B3
Union (lake), Wash. 310/B2
Union, W. Va. (24983) 312/E7
Union Bay, Br. Col. 184/H2
Union Beach, N.J. (07735) 273/E3
Union Bridge, Md. (21791) 245/K2
Union Center, S. Dak. (57787) 298/D4
Union Center, Wis. (53962) 317/F8
Union Church, Miss. (39668) 256/C7
Union City, Calif. (94587) 204/K2
Union City, Conn. (†06770) 210/C2
Union City, Georgia (30291) 217/J2
Union City, Ind. (47390) 227/H4
Union City, Mich. (49094) 250/D6
Union City, N.J. (07087) 273/C2
Union City, Ohio (†47390) 284/A5
Union City, Okla. (73090) 288/L4
Union City, Pa. (16438) 294/C2
Union City, Tenn. (38261) 237/C8
Union Creek, Oreg. (†97536) 291/E5
Uniondale, Ind. (46791) 227/G3
Uniondale, N.Y. (11553) 276/R7
Union Dale, Pa. (18470) 294/M2
Unión de Reyes, Cuba 158/C1
Unión de Tula, Mexico 150/G7
Union Furnace, Ohio (43158) 284/F7
Union Gap, Wash. (98903) 310/E4
Union Grove, Ala. (35175) 195/E2
Union Grove, N.C. (28689) 281/H2
Union Grove, Wis. (53182) 317/L3
Union Hall, Va. (24176) 307/J6
Unión Hidalgo, Mexico 150/M8
Union Hill, Ill. (60969) 222/E2
Union Hill, N.Y. (14563) 276/F4
Union Level, Va. (23973) 307/M7
Union Mills, Ind. (46382) 227/D2
Union Mills, Md. (†21157) 245/K2
Union Mills, N.C. (28167) 281/F3
Union of Soviet Socialist Republics 2/L2
Union of Soviet Socialist Republics 4/C2
Union of Soviet Socialist Republics 54/L3
Union of Soviet Socialist Republics 7/H2
UNION OF SOVIET SOCIALIST REPUBLICS 48
UNION OF SOVIET SOCIALIST REPUBLICS, EUROPEAN 52
Union Pier, Mich. (49129) 250/C7
Union Point, Georgia (30669) 217/F3
Unionport, Ind. (†47340) 227/G4
Unionport, Ohio (43966) 284/J5
Union Springs, Ala. (36089) 195/G6
Union Springs, N.Y. (13160) 276/G5
Union Star, Ky. (40171) 237/H5
Union Star, Mo. (64494) 261/D2
Uniontown, Ala. (36786) 195/D6
Uniontown, Ark. (72955) 202/B2
Uniontown, Ind. (†47515) 227/D
Uniontown, Kansas (66779) 232/G4
Uniontown, Ky. (42461) 237/F5
Uniontown, Md. (21157) 245/K2
Uniontown, Mo. (63783) 261/N7
Uniontown, Ohio (44685) 284/H4
Uniontown, Pa. (15401) 294/C6
Uniontown, Wash. (99179) 310/H4
Union Village, Vt. (†05075) 268/C4
Unionville, Conn. (06085) 210/D1
Unionville, Georgia (†31794) 217/F8
Unionville, Ill. (†61270) 222/E6
Unionville, Ind. (47468) 227/E6
Unionville, Iowa (52594) 229/H7
Unionville, Maine (†04622) 243/H6
Unionville, Md. (21792) 245/K3
Unionville, Mich. (48767) 250/F5
Unionville, Mo. (63565) 261/G2
Unionville, Nev. (†89418) 266/C2
Unionville, N.Y. (10988) 276/L8
Unionville, N.C. (†28110) 281/J4
Unionville, Ohio (44088) 284/J2
Unionville (Fleming), Pa. (19375) 294/G4
Unionville, Tenn. (37180) 237/H9
Unionville, Va. (22567) 307/N4
Unionville Center, Ohio (43077) 284/D5
Uniopolis, Ohio (45888) 284/B4
United, Pa. (15689) 294/D5
United Arab Emirates 2/M4
United Arab Emirates 54/G7
UNITED ARAB EMIRATES 59/F5
UNITED KINGDOM 10
United Kingdom 2/J3
United Kingdom 7/D3
United States 2/D4
United States 146/H5
United States 4/C17
UNITED STATES 188
U.S. Capitol, D.C. 245/F5
U.S.S. Arizona Memorial, Hawaii 218/B3
U.S. Nav. Air Sta., Virgin Is. (U.S.) 161/A4
U.S. Naval Base, Va. 307/R7
Unity○, Maine (04988) 243/E6
Unity, Md. (†20729) 245/K4
Unity, Mo. (64063) 261/R6
Unity○, N.H. (†03743) 268/C5
Unity, Ohio (†44413) 284/J4
Unity, Oreg. (97884) 291/J3
Unity, Sask. 181/B3
Unity, Wis. (54488) 317/F6
Unityville, Pa. (17774) 294/K3
Unityville, S. Dak. (†57058) 298/P6
Universal, Ind. (47884) 227/C5
Universal City, Texas (78148) 303/K10
University, Fla. (33620) 212/C2
University, N.C. (†27701) 281/L2
University City, Mo. (63130) 261/P3
University City, Mo. 188/H3
University Heights, Iowa (†52240) 229/K5
University Heights, Ohio (44118) 284/H9
University Park, Iowa (52595) 229/H6
University Park, Md. (†20740) 245/F4
University Park, N. Mex. (88003) 274/C6
University Park, Texas (†75205) 303/G2
Unley, S. Australia 88/D8
Unley, S. Australia 94/B8
Unnao, India 68/E3
Uno, Manitoba 179/B4
Unsan, N. Korea 81/C4
Unst (isl.), Scotland 15/G2
Unst (isl.), Scotland 10/H1
Unstrut (riv.), E. Germany 22/D3
Unterägeri, Switzerland 39/G2
Unteriberg, Switzerland 39/G2
Unterkulm, Switzerland 39/F2
Untermann (mt.), Utah 304/E3
Untersee (lake), Switzerland 39/H1
Unterseen, Switzerland 39/E3
Untervaz, Switzerland 39/H3
Unterwalden (reg.), Switzerland 39/F3
Unuk (riv.), Alaska 196/N2
Unuk (riv.), Br. Col. 184/B2
Ünye, Turkey 59/C1
Ünye, Turkey 63/G2
Unzen (mt.), Japan 81/D7
Unzen-Amakusa National Park, Japan 81/D7
Uozu, Japan 81/H5
Upalco, Utah (†84007) 304/D3
Upata, Venezuela 124/G3
Upemba (lake), Zaire 115/E5
Upemba Nat'l Park, Zaire 115/E5
Upernavik, Greenl. 4/B12
Uphall, Scotland 15/C1
Upham, New Bruns. 170/E3
Upham, N. Dak. (58789) 282/J2
Upía (riv.), Colombia 126/D5
Úpice, Czech. 41/C1
Upington, S. Africa 102/E7
Upington, S. Africa 118/C5
Upland, Calif. (91786) 204/E10
Upland, Ind. (46989) 227/F4
Upland, Kansas (†67431) 232/E2
Upland, Nebr. (68981) 264/F4
Upland, Pa. (†19013) 294/L7
Upolu (pt.), Hawaii 218/G3
Upolu (isl.), W. Samoa 87/J7
Upolu (isl.), W. Samoa 86/M8
Upolu (isl.), W. Samoa 86/M8
Upper Alkali (lake), Calif. 204/E2
Upper Amherst Cove, Newf. 166/D2
Upper Ammonoosuc (riv.), N.H. 268/E2
Upper Arlington, Ohio (43221) 284/D6
Upper Arrow (lake), Br. Col. 184/H5
Upper Austria (prov.), Austria 41/B2
Upper Black Eddy, Pa. (18972) 294/N4
Upper Blackville, New Bruns. 170/E2
Upper Buctouche, New Bruns. 170/F2
Upper Chateaugay (lake), N.Y. 276/M1
Upperco, Md. (21155) 245/L2
Upper Dam, Maine (†04293) 243/B6
Upper Darby○, Pa. (*19082) 294/M6
Upper Des Lacs (lake), N. Dak. 282/F2
Upper Engadine (valley), Switzerland 39/J4
Upper Fairmount, Md. (21867) 245/P8

V

Victoria Harbour 463

Vandenberg A.F.B., Calif. 204/E9
Vanderbijl Park, S. Africa 118/D5
Vanderbilt, Mich. (49795) 250/E3
Vanderbilt, Pa. (15486) 294/C5
Vanderbilt, Texas (77991) 303/H9
Vanderburgh (co.), Ind. 227/B8
Vandergrift, Pa. (15690) 294/D4
Vanderhoof, Br. Col. 162/D5
Vanderhoof, Br. Col. 184/E3
Vanderlin (isl.), North. Terr. 88/F3
Vanderlin (isl.), North. Terr. 93/E3
Vanderpool, Texas (78885) 303/E8
Vanderpool, Va. (†24465) 307/J4
Vandervoort, Ark. (71972) 202/B5
Van Diemen (cape), North. Terr. 88/D2
Van Diemen (cape), North. Terr. 93/A1
Van Diemen (gulf), North. Terr. 88/E2
Van Diemen (gulf), North. Terr. 93/B1
Vandiver, Ala. (35176) 195/F4
Vandiver, Mo. (†65265) 261/J4
Vandling, Pa. (18421) 294/M2
Vändra, U.S.S.R. 53/C1
Vandura, Sask. 181/K5
Vanduser, Mo. (63784) 261/N9
Vanegas, Mexico 150/J5
Vänern (lake), Sweden 7/F3
Vänern (lake), Sweden 18/H7
Vänersborg, Sweden 18/G7
Van Etten, N.Y. (14889) 276/G6
Vanga, Kenya 115/G4
Vangaindrano, Madagascar 118/H4
Vanguard, Sask. 181/D6
Vangunu (isl.), Solomon Is. 86/D3
Van Hoa, Vietnam 72/E2
Van Horn, Texas (79855) 303/C11
Van Horne, Iowa (52346) 229/J4
Van Hornesville, N.Y. (13475) 276/L5
Vanier, Ontario 177/J2
Vanier, Québec 172/J3
Vanikoro (isl.), Solomon Is. 87/G7
Vanil Noir (mt.), Switzerland 39/D3
Vanimo, Papua N.G. 87/E6
Vanimo, Papua N.G. 85/B6
Vanino, U.S.S.R. 48/P5
Vaniyambadi, India 68/D6
Vankleek Hill, Ontario 177/K2
Van Lear, Ky. (41265) 237/R5
Vanleer, Tenn. (37181) 237/G8
Vanlue, Ohio (45890) 284/C4
Van Meter, Iowa (50261) 229/E5
Vanna, Georgia (30672) 217/F2
Vännäs, Sweden 18/L5
Vanndale, Ark. (72387) 202/J3
Vannes, France 28/B4
Van Ninh, Vietnam 72/F4
Vannøy (isl.), Norway 18/L1
Van Nuys, Calif. (*91401) 204/B10
Van Orin, Ill. (61374) 222/D2
Vanoss, Okla. (†74820) 288/N5
Vanrhynsdorp, S. Africa 118/B6
Van Rook, Queensland 95/B3
Vansant, Va. (24656) 307/D6
Vansbro, Sweden 18/H6
Vanscoy, Sask. 181/D4
Vansittart (isl.), N.W. Terrs. 187/K3
Vansittart (isl.), Tasmania 99/E2
Vantage, Sask. 181/F6
Vantage, Wash. (98950) 310/E4
Van Tassell, Wyo. (82242) 319/H3
Vanua Levu (isl.), Fiji 87/H7
Vanua Levu (isl.), Fiji 86/Q10
Vanuatu 2/T6
Vanuatu 87/G7
Van Vleet, Miss. (†38851) 256/G3
Vanvoorhis, W. Va. (†26505) 312/G3
Van Wert, Georgia (†30153) 217/B3
Van Wert, Iowa (50262) 229/F7
Van Wert (co.), Ohio 284/A4
Van Wert, Ohio (45891) 284/A4
Van Wyck, S.C. (29744) 296/F2
Van Yen, Vietnam 72/E2
Vanylven, Norway 18/E5
Van Zandt (co.), Texas 303/J5
Van Zandt, Wash. (†98244) 310/C2
Vanzant, Mo. (65768) 261/H9
Var (dept.), France 28/G6
Vara, Sweden 18/H7
Vara de María, Venezuela 124/C4
Varadero, Cuba 158/D1
Varakļāni, U.S.S.R. 53/D2
Varallo Pombia, Italy 34/B2
Varamin, Iran 66/G3
Varanasi, India 54/K7
Varanasi, India 68/E3
Varangerfjorden (fjord), Norway 18/Q2
Varangerfjorden (fjord), Norway 7/H1
Varangerhalvøya (pen.), Norway 18/Q1
Varano (lake), Italy 34/F3
Varaždin, Yugoslavia 45/B2
Varazze, Italy 34/B2
Varberg, Sweden 18/G8
Vardaman, Miss. (38878) 256/F3
Vardar (riv.), Greece 45/E5
Vardar (riv.), Yugoslavia 45/E5
Varde, Denmark 18/F9
Varde, Denmark 21/B6
Varde (riv.), Denmark 21/B6
Vardø, Norway 18/R1
Varel, W. Germany 22/C2
Varella, Mui (cape), Vietnam 72/F4
Varena, U.S.S.R. 53/C3
Varennes, Québec 172/J4
Vareš, Yugoslavia 45/D3
Varese (prov.), Italy 34/B2
Varese, Italy 34/B2
Vargem Bonita, Brazil 135/E3
Varginha, Brazil 135/D2
Varginha, Brazil 132/E8
Varina, Iowa (50593) 229/D3
Varkaus, Finland 18/Q5
Värmland (co.), Sweden 18/H7
Varna, Bulgaria 7/G4
Varna, Bulgaria 45/J4
Varna, Ill. (61375) 222/D2
Varnado, La. (70467) 238/L5
Värnamo, Sweden 18/J8
Varnek, U.S.S.R. 52/J1
Varnell, Georgia (30756) 217/C1
Varner, Kansas (†67068) 232/D4
Varney, Ontario 177/D3
Varney, W. Va. (25696) 312/B7
Varnsdorf, Czech. 41/C1
Varnville, S.C. (29944) 296/E6
Várpalota, Hungary 41/E3
Vars, Ontario 177/J2
Vartholomión, Greece 45/E7
Varto, Turkey 63/J3
Varysburg, N.Y. (14167) 276/D5
Varzarin, Kuh-e (mt.), Iran 59/E3
Varzarin, Kuh-e (mt.), Iran 66/E4
Vas (co.), Hungary 41/D3
Vasa (Vaasa), Finland 18/M5
Vasa, Minn. (†55089) 255/F6
Vasa Barris (riv.), Brazil 132/G5
Vásárosnamény, Hungary 41/G2
Vascongadas (reg.), Spain 33/E1
Vashi, India 68/B7
Vashka (riv.), U.S.S.R. 52/G2
Vashon, Wash. (98070) 310/A2
Vasile Roaită, Romania 45/J3
Vasil'kov, U.S.S.R. 52/D4
Vaslui, Romania 45/H2
Vass, N.C. (28394) 281/L4
Vassalboro, Maine (04989) 243/D7
Vassalboro○, Maine (04989) 243/D7
Vassar, Kansas (66543) 232/G3
Vassar, Manitoba 179/G5
Vassar, Mich. (48768) 250/F5
Vassouras, Brazil 135/E3
Vastenjaure (lake), Sweden 18/K3
Västerås, Sweden 7/F3
Västerås, Sweden 18/K7
Västerbotten (co.), Sweden 18/K4
Västerdalälven (riv.), Sweden 18/H6
Västerhaninge, Sweden 18/H1
Västernorrland (co.), Sweden 18/K5
Västervik, Sweden 18/K8
Västmanland (co.), Sweden 18/K7
Vasto, Italy 34/E3
Vasvár, Hungary 41/D3
Vaternish (dist.), Scotland 15/B3
Vaternish (pt.), Scotland 15/B3
Vatersay (isl.), Scotland 15/A4
Vathí, Greece 45/H7
Vatican City 7/F4
VATICAN CITY 34
Vatican City, Vatican City 34/B6
Vaticano (cape), Italy 34/E5
Vatnajökull (glac.), Iceland 21/C1
Vatomandry, Madagascar 118/H3
Vatra Dornei, Romania 45/G2
Vättern (lake), Sweden 7/F3
Vättern (lake), Sweden 18/J7
Vatukoula, Fiji 86/P10
Vatulele (isl.), Fiji 86/P11
Vauclin (mt.), Martinique 161/D6
Vaucluse (dept.), France 28/F6
Vaucluse, S.C. (29850) 296/D7
Vaud (canton), Switzerland 39/B3
Vaudreuil (co.), Québec 172/C4
Vaudreuil, Québec 172/C4
Vaughan, Miss. (39179) 256/D5
Vaughan, N.C. (27586) 281/N2
Vaughan, Ontario 177/J4
Vaughan, W. Va. (†26656) 312/D6
Vaughn, Mont. (59487) 262/E3
Vaughn, N. Mex. (88353) 274/D4
Vaughn, Wash. (98394) 310/C3
Vaughnsville, Ohio (45893) 284/B4
Vaupés (comm.), Colombia 126/E7
Vaupés (riv.), Colombia 120/B2
Vaupés (riv.), Colombia 126/E7
Vauxhall, Alberta 182/D4
Vauxhall, N.J. (07088) 273/A2
Vaux-sur-Sûre, Belgium 27/H9
Vava'u Group (isls.), Tonga 87/J7
Vavenby, Br. Col. 184/H4
Vavuniya, Sri Lanka 68/E7
Vawn, Sask. 181/C2
Vaxholm, Sweden 18/J1
Växjö, Sweden 7/F3
Växjö, Sweden 18/J8
Vaygach (isl.), U.S.S.R. 4/C6
Vaygach (isl.), U.S.S.R. 52/K1
Vayland, S. Dak. (†57381) 298/M5
Važec, Czech. 41/E2
Vazhgort, U.S.S.R. 52/G2
Vaz-Obervaz, Switzerland 39/J3
Vázquez, Cuba 158/H3
Veagh (lake), Ireland 17/F1
Vealmoor, Texas (79720) 303/C5
Veazie○, Maine (04401) 243/F6
Veblen, S. Dak. (57270) 298/P2
Vechigen, Switzerland 39/E3
Vecht (riv.), Netherlands 27/F4
Vechta, W. Germany 22/C2
Vechte (riv.), Netherlands 27/J3
Vechte (riv.), W. Germany 22/B2
Vecsés, Hungary 41/E3
Vedaranniyam, India 68/E6
Vedia, Argentina 143/F7
Veedersburg, Ind. (47987) 227/C4
Veendam, Netherlands 27/K2
Veenendaal, Netherlands 27/G4
Veenhuizen, Netherlands 27/J2
Veere, Netherlands 27/D5
Veersche Meer (lake), Netherlands 27/D5
Vega (pt.), Alaska 196/J4
Vega, Alberta 182/C2
Vega (isl.), Norway 18/G4
Vega, Texas (79092) 303/B2
Vega Alta, P. Rico 161/D1
Vega Baja, P. Rico 161/D1
Vegafjorden (fjord), Norway 18/G4
Vegas Creek, Nev. (89121) 266/G6
Veghel, Netherlands 27/H5
Vegreville, Alberta 182/E3
Vegreville, Alta. 162/E5
Veguita, N. Mex. (87062) 274/C4
Vehar (lake), India 68/B7
Veinticinco (25) de Agosto, Uruguay 145/A6
Veinticinco (25) de Diciembre, Paraguay 144/D4
Veinticinco de Mayo, Argentina 143/F7
Veinticinco de Mayo, Ecuador 128/C4
Veinticinco (25) de Mayo, Uruguay 145/C5
Veintiocho de Noviembre, Argentina 143/B7
Vejen, Denmark 21/C7
Vejer de la Frontera, Spain 33/C4
Vejle (co.), Denmark 21/C6
Vejle, Denmark 21/C6
Vejle, Denmark 18/F9
Vejle (fjord), Denmark 21/C6
Vejprty, Czech. 41/B1
Vela, La (cape), Colombia 126/D1
Vela, Roca que (cay), Colombia 126/B8
Vélan (mt.), Switzerland 39/D5
Velarde, N. Mex. (87582) 274/C2
Velas (cape), C. Rica 154/D5
Velasco, Ciego de Ávila, Cuba 158/G2
Velasco, Holguín, Cuba 158/H3
Velázquez, Uruguay 145/E5
Velda, Mo. (†63101) 261/P2
Velden am Wörthersee, Austria 41/C3
Veldhoven, Netherlands 27/G6
Veldrif, S. Africa 118/B6
Velence, Hungary 41/E3
Velenje, Yugoslavia 45/B2
Vélez, Colombia 126/D4
Vélez-Blanco, Spain 33/E4
Vélez-Málaga, Spain 33/E4
Vélez-Rubio, Spain 33/E4
Velhas (riv.), Brazil 132/E7
Velika Plana, Yugoslavia 45/E3
Velikaya (riv.), U.S.S.R. 48/S3
Velikaya (riv.), U.S.S.R. 52/C3
Veliki Bečkerek (Zrenjanin), Yugoslavia 45/E3
Velikiye Luki, U.S.S.R. 7/H3
Velikiye Luki, U.S.S.R. 52/D3
Velikiye Luki, U.S.S.R. 48/D4
Velikiy Ustyug, U.S.S.R. 7/J2
Velikiy Ustyug, U.S.S.R. 48/E3
Velikiy Ustyug, U.S.S.R. 52/F2
Veliko Tŭrnovo, Bulgaria 45/G4
Velikovisochnoye, U.S.S.R. 52/H1
Velizh, U.S.S.R. 52/D3
Velká Bíteš, Czech. 41/D2
Velká Bystřice, Czech. 41/D2
Vel'ké Kapušany, Czech. 41/G2
Velké Meziříčí, Czech. 41/D2
Vel'ké Rovné, Czech. 41/E2
Vella Lavella (isl.), Solomon Is. 86/D2
Velletri, Italy 34/F7
Vellore, India 68/D6
Velluda, Sierra (mt.), Chile 138/E1
Velma, Okla. (73091) 288/L6
Velp, Netherlands 27/J5
Velpen, Ind. (47590) 227/C8
Velsen, Netherlands 27/F4
Vel'sk, U.S.S.R. 52/F2
Vel'sk, U.S.S.R. 48/E3
Velten, E. Germany 22/E2
Veluwe (reg.), Netherlands 27/H4
Velva, N. Dak. (58790) 282/J3
Velvendós, Greece 45/F5
Vemb, Denmark 21/B5
Véménd, Hungary 41/E3
Venadillo, Colombia 126/C5
Venado, Mexico 150/J5
Venado Tuerto, Argentina 143/D3
Venafro, Italy 34/E4
Venaissin (trad. prov.), France 29
Venamo (mt.), Guyana 131/A3
Venamo, Cerro (mt.), Venezuela 124/H4
Venamo (riv.), Venezuela 124/H4
Venango, Nebr. (69168) 264/C4
Venango (co.), Pa. 294/C3
Venango, Pa. (16440) 294/B2
Vena Park, Queensland 95/B3
Vence, France 28/G6
Venda (aut. rep.), S. Africa 102/F7
Venda (aut. rep.), S. Africa 118/E4
Vendas Novas, Portugal 33/B3
Vendée (dept.), France 28/C4
Vendôme, France 28/D4
Vendrell, Spain 33/G2
Venedocia, Ohio (45894) 284/B4
Venedy, Ill. (62296) 222/D5
Veneta, Oreg. (97487) 291/D3
Venetie, Alaska (99781) 196/J1
Veneto (reg.), Italy 34/D3
Venezia (Venice), Italy 34/D2
Venezuela 2/F5
Venezuela 120/C2
Venezuela, Cuba 158/F2
VENEZUELA 124
Venezuela (gulf), Venezuela 120/B1
Venezuela (gulf), Venezuela 124/C2
Vengurla, India 68/C5
Veniaminof (crater), Alaska 196/F3
Venice, Alberta 182/E2
Venice, Calif. (90291) 204/B11
Venice, Fla. (*33595) 212/D4
Venice, Ill. (62090) 222/A2
Venice (prov.), Italy 34/D2
Venice, Italy 7/F4
Venice, Italy 34/D2
Venice (gulf), Italy 34/D2
Venice, La. (70091) 238/M8
Venice, Utah (†84701) 304/C5
Vénissieux, France 28/F5
Venkatagiri, India 68/D6
Venlo, Netherlands 27/J6
Venn, Sask. 181/F4
Venosa, Italy 34/E4
Venraij, Netherlands 27/H6
Venta (riv.), U.S.S.R. 53/B2
Venterspos, S. Africa 118/G6
Ventimiglia, Italy 34/A3
Ventnor, England 10/F5
Ventnor, England 13/F7
Ventnor City, N.J. (08406) 273/E5
Ventotene (isl.), Italy 34/D4
Ventspils, U.S.S.R. 48/B4
Ventspils, U.S.S.R. 53/A2
Ventspils, U.S.S.R. 52/B3
Ventuari (riv.), Venezuela 124/E5
Ventura (co.), Calif. 204/F9
Ventura, Calif. (*93001) 204/F9
Ventura, Iowa (50482) 229/F2
Venturia, N. Dak. (58489) 282/L7
Venus, Fla. (33960) 212/E4
Venus (pt.), Fr. Poly. 86/T12
Venus, Pa. (16364) 294/C3
Venus (bay), Victoria 97/C6
Venustiano Carranza, Mexico 150/N8
Venustiano Carranza (res.), Mexico 150/J3
Ver (riv.), England 13/H7
Vera, Argentina 143/F5
Vera, Ill. (†62080) 222/D4
Vera, Okla. (74082) 288/P2
Vera (lag.), Paraguay 144/D5
Vera, Spain 33/F4
Vera, Texas (76383) 303/E4
Vera, Va. (†24522) 307/L6
Vera Cruz, Brazil 135/B3
Vera Cruz, Ind. (†46714) 227/G3
Veracruz (state), Mexico 150/L7
Veracruz, Mexico 150/Q1
Veracruz, Mexico 2/E5
Veracruz, Mexico 146/J8
Veradale, Wash. (99037) 310/H3
Veragua Abajo, Dom. Rep. 158/E5
Veras, Uruguay 145/C2
Veraval, India 68/C4
Verbania, Italy 34/B2
Verbena, Ala. (36091) 195/E5
Verboort, Oreg. (†97116) 291/A2
Vercelli (prov.), Italy 34/B2
Vercelli, Italy 34/B2
Verchères (co.), Québec 172/J4
Verchères, Québec 172/J4
Verçinin Tepesi (mt.), Turkey 63/J2
Verda, Ky. (†40828) 237/P7
Verda, La. (71481) 238/E3
Verde (riv.), Ariz. 188/D4
Verde (riv.), Ariz. 198/D5
Verde (cay), Bahamas 156/C2
Verde (riv.), Brazil 132/C7
Verde (riv.), Mexico 150/F3
Verde (riv.), Mexico 150/L8
Verde (riv.), Paraguay 144/C3
Verde (cape), Senegal 102/A3
Verde (cape), Senegal 106/A6
Verde Island (passage), Philippines 82/C4
Verdel, Nebr. (68782) 264/F2
Verden, Okla. (73092) 288/K4
Verden, W. Germany 22/C2
Verdery, S.C. (†29819) 296/C3
Verdi, Minn. (56179) 255/B6
Verdi, Nev. (89439) 266/B3
Verdigre, Nebr. (68783) 264/F2
Verdigris (riv.), Kansas 232/G5
Verdigris, Okla. (†74017) 288/P2
Verdigris (riv.), Okla. 288/P2
Verdinho (riv.), Brazil 132/D7
Verdon, Nebr. (68457) 264/J4
Verdon, S. Dak. (57478) 298/N3
Verdun, Québec 172/H4
Verdún, Uruguay 145/D5
Verdun-sur-Meuse, France 28/F3
Verdunville, W. Va. (25649) 312/B7
Vereeniging, S. Africa 102/E7
Vereeniging, S. Africa 118/D5
Veregin, Sask. 181/K4
Verendrye, N. Dak. (†58717) 282/J3
Vereshchagino, U.S.S.R. 52/H3
Verga (cape), Guinea 106/B6
Vergara, Argentina 143/H7
Vergara, Spain 33/E1
Vergara, Uruguay 145/E3
Vergas, Minn. (56587) 255/C4
Vergeletto, Switzerland 39/G4
Vergennes, Ill. (62994) 222/D6
Vergennes, Vt. (05491) 268/A3
Veribest, Texas (76886) 303/D6
Verín, Spain 33/C2
Veríssimo, Brazil 135/B1
Verkhnevilyuysk, U.S.S.R. 48/N3
Verkhnyaya Toyma, U.S.S.R. 52/G2
Verkhoyansk, U.S.S.R. 2/R2
Verkhoyansk, U.S.S.R. 4/C3
Verkhoyansk, U.S.S.R. 54/P3
Verkhoyansk, U.S.S.R. 48/N3
Verkhoyansk (range), U.S.S.R. 48/N3
Verkhoyansk (range), U.S.S.R. 4/C3
Verkhoyansk (range), U.S.S.R. 54/O3
Verkniy At-Uryakh, U.S.S.R. 48/Q3
Verlo, Sask. 181/C5
Vermejo (riv.), N. Mex. 274/E2
Vermejo Park, N. Mex. (†81091) 274/D2
Vermilion, Alberta 182/E3
Vermilion (riv.), Alberta 182/E3
Vermilion (cliffs), Ariz. 198/D2
Vermilion (co.), Ill. 222/F3
Vermilion, Ill. (61955) 222/F4
Vermilion (riv.), Ind. 227/B4
Vermilion (par.), La. 238/F7
Vermilion (bay), La. 238/F7
Vermilion (lake), Minn. 188/H1
Vermilion (lake), Minn. 255/F3
Vermilion (range), Minn. 255/F3
Vermilion (riv.), Minn. 255/F2
Vermilion, Ohio (44089) 284/F3
Vermilion (riv.), Ohio 284/F3
Vermilion (hills), Sask. 181/E5
Vermilion (cliffs), Utah 304/B6
Vermilion Bay, Ontario 177/G4
Vermilion Bay, Ontario 175/B3
Vermilion Grove, Ill. (†61870) 222/F4
Vermillion (co.), Ind. 227/C5
Vermillion, Kansas (66544) 232/F2
Vermillion, Minn. (55085) 255/F6
Vermillion, S. Dak. (57069) 298/R8
Vermillion (riv.), S. Dak. 298/P6
Vermillion (riv.), Québec 172/D2
Vermont 188/M2
Vermont, Ill. (61484) 222/C3
Vermont (state), U.S. 146/L5
VERMONT 268
Vermontville, Mich. (49096) 250/E6
Vernal, Utah (84078) 304/E3
Vernayaz, Switzerland 39/D4
Verndale, Minn. (56481) 255/C4
Verndon, Minn. (†55752) 255/E4
Verner, Ontario 177/D1
Verneuil-sur-Avre, France 28/D3
Vernon, Ala. (35592) 195/B3
Vernon, Ariz. (85940) 198/F4
Vernon, Br. Col. 162/E5
Vernon, Br. Col. 184/H5
Vernon, Colo. (80755) 208/P3
Vernon○, Conn. (06066) 210/F1
Vernon, Fla. (32462) 212/C6
Vernon, France 28/D3
Vernon, Ill. (62892) 222/D5
Vernon, Ind. (47282) 227/F7
Vernon, Ky. (†42151) 237/L7
Vernon (par.), La. 238/D4
Vernon, La. (†71228) 238/E2
Vernon (lake), La. 238/D4
Vernon, Mich. (48476) 250/F6
Vernon (co.), Mo. 261/D7
Vernon, N.J. (07462) 273/E1
Vernon, Okla. (74877) 288/P4
Vernon, Ontario 177/J2
Vernon (lake), Ontario 177/E2
Vernon, Pr. Edward I. 168/E2
Vernon, Texas (76384) 303/E3
Vernon, Utah (84080) 304/B3
Vernon○, Vt. (05354) 268/B6
Vernon (co.), Wis. 317/E8
Vernonburg, Georgia (†31401) 217/K7
Vernon Center, Conn. (†06066) 210/F1
Vernon Center, Minn. (56090) 255/D7
Vernon Fork (creek), Ind. 227/F7
Vernon Hill, Va. (24597) 307/K7
Vernon Hills, Ill. (60061) 222/B4
Vernonia, Oreg. (97064) 291/D2
Vero Beach, Fla. (32960) 212/F4
Veroli, Italy 34/D4
Verona, Ill. (60479) 222/E2
Verona (prov.), Italy 34/C2
Verona, Italy 34/C2
Verona, Italy 7/F4
Verona, Ky. (41092) 237/M3
Verona, Miss. (38879) 256/G2
Verona, Mo. (65769) 261/E9
Verona, N.J. (07044) 273/B2
Verona, N. Dak. (58490) 282/O7
Verona, Ohio (45378) 284/A6
Verona, Ontario 177/H3
Verona, Pa. (15147) 294/C6
Verona, Va. (24482) 307/K4
Verona, Wis. (53593) 317/G9
Verónica, Argentina 143/H7
Verpelét, Hungary 41/F2
Verret (lake), La. 238/H7
Verret, New Bruns. 170/B1
Verrettes, Haiti 158/C5
Vérroia, Greece 45/F5
Versailles, Conn. (06383) 210/G2
Versailles, France 28/A2
Versailles, France 7/E4
Versailles, Ill. (62378) 222/C4
Versailles, Ind. (47042) 227/G6
Versailles, Ky. (40383) 237/M4
Versailles, Mo. (65084) 261/G6
Versailles, N.Y. (14168) 276/B6
Versailles, Ohio (45380) 284/A5
Versailles, Pa. (15132) 294/C7
Versalles, Bolivia 136/D3
Vershire○, Vt. (05079) 268/C4
Versoix, Switzerland 39/B4
Verte (bay), New Bruns. 170/G2
Verte (bay), Nova Scotia 168/D2
Verte (isl.), Québec 172/H1
Vertientes, Cuba 158/G3
Vert-Pré, Martinique 161/D6
Vertus, France 28/E3
Verviers, Belgium 27/H7
Verwoerd, Hendrik (dam), S. Africa 118/D6
Verwood, Sask. 181/F6
Vesava, India 68/B7
Vesdre (riv.), Belgium 27/H7
Veseleyville, N. Dak. (†58237) 282/R3
Veseli, Minn. (55086) 255/E6
Veselí nad Lužnicí, Czech. 41/C2
Veselí nad Moravou, Czech. 41/D2
Vesoul, France 28/F4
Vesper, Kansas (†67455) 232/D2
Vesper, Sask. 181/D5
Vesper, Wis. (54489) 317/F7
Vesta, C. Rica 154/F6
Vesta, Minn. (56292) 255/C6
Vesta, Va. (24177) 307/H7
Vestaburg, Mich. (48891) 250/E5
Vest-Agder (co.), Norway 18/E7
Vestal○, N.Y. (13850) 276/H6
Vestavia Hills, Ala. (35216) 195/E4
Vesterålen (isls.), Norway 7/F2
Vesterålen (isls.), Norway 18/J2
Vester Skerninge, Denmark 21/D7
Vestervig, Denmark 21/B4
Vestfjord (fjord), Norway 18/H3
Vestfjorden (fjord), Norway 7/F2
Vestfold (co.), Norway 18/G7
Vestmannaeyjar, Iceland 7/C2
Vestmannaeyjar, Iceland 21/B2
Vestsjaelland (co.), Denmark 21/E6
Vestvågøya (isl.), Norway 18/H3
Vesuvius (vol.), Italy 34/E4
Vesuvius, Va. (24483) 307/K5
Veszprém (co.), Hungary 41/D3
Veszprém, Hungary 41/D3
Vésztő, Hungary 41/F3
Vetal, S. Dak. (57575) 298/G7
Veteran, Alberta 182/E3
Veteran, Wyo. (82243) 319/H4
Vetlanda, Sweden 18/J8
Vetluga (riv.), U.S.S.R. 52/G3
Veurne, Belgium 27/B6
Vevay, Ind. (47043) 227/G7
Vevey, Switzerland 39/C4
Vex, Switzerland 39/D4
Veyo, Utah (†84722) 304/A6
Veys, Iran 66/F5
Veytaux, Switzerland 39/C4
Vezirköprü, Turkey 63/F2
Viacha, Bolivia 120/C4
Viacha, Bolivia 136/A5
Viadana, Italy 34/C2
Viale, Argentina 143/F5
Vian, Okla. (74962) 288/S4
Viana, Brazil 132/E3
Viana del Bollo, Spain 33/C1
Viana do Alentejo, Spain 33/C3
Viana do Castelo, Portugal 33/B2
Vianden, Luxembourg 27/J9
Vianen, Netherlands 27/G5
Viangchan (Vientiane), Laos 72/D3
Viangphoukha, Laos 72/D2
Viano do Castelo (dist.), Portugal 33/B2
Viareggio, Italy 34/C3
Vibank, Sask. 181/H5
Vibbard, Mo. (†64062) 261/D4
Viborg (co.), Denmark 21/C4
Viborg, Denmark 18/F8
Viborg, Denmark 21/C5
Viborg, S. Dak. (57070) 298/P7
Vibo Valentia, Italy 34/F5
Viburnum, Mo. (65566) 261/K7
Viby, Denmark 21/F6
Vicálvaro, Spain 33/G4
Vicam, Mexico 150/D3
Vicco, Ky. (41773) 237/P6
Vicente Guerrero, Baja California, Mexico 150/A1
Vicente Guerrero, Durango, Mexico 150/G5
Vicente López, Argentina 143/G7
Vicenza (prov.), Italy 34/C2
Vicenza, Italy 34/C2
Viceroy, Sask. 181/F6
Vich, Spain 33/H2
Vichacla, Bolivia 136/C7
Vichada (comm.), Colombia 126/F5
Vichada (riv.), Colombia 126/F5
Vichadero, Uruguay 145/E2
Vichaya, Bolivia 136/A5
Viche, Ecuador 128/C2
Vichuga, U.S.S.R. 52/F3
Vichy, France 28/E4
Vichy, Mo. (65580) 261/J6
Vici, Okla. (73859) 288/H2
Vick, Ark. (†71648) 202/F7
Vick, La. (71372) 238/F4
Vickers (lake), Manitoba 179/F3
Vickery, Ohio (43464) 284/D3
Vicksburg, Ariz. (†85348) 198/B5
Vicksburg, Ind. (†47441) 227/C6
Vicksburg, Mich. (49097) 250/D6
Vicksburg, Miss. 188/H4
Vicksburg, Miss. (39180) 256/C6
Vicksburg Nat'l Mil. Park, Miss. 256/C6
Viçosa, Brazil 135/E2
Viçosa, Brazil 132/G5
Vicosoprano, Switzerland 39/J4
Vicovaro, Italy 34/F6
Victoire, Sask. 181/D2
Victor, Calif. (95253) 204/C9
Victor, Colo. (80860) 208/J5
Victor, Idaho (83455) 220/G6
Victor, Iowa (52347) 229/J5
Victor, Mont. (59875) 262/B4
Victor, N.Y. (14564) 276/F5
Victor, S. Dak. (†57260) 298/R2
Victor, W. Va. (25938) 312/D6
Victor Harbor, S. Australia 88/F7
Victor Harbor, S. Australia 94/F6
Victoria 88/G7
Victoria (lake) 2/L6
Victoria (lake) 102/F5
Victoria (Mosi-Oa-Tunya) (falls) 102/E6
Victoria, Argentina 143/F6
Victoria, Ark. (72388) 202/K2
Victoria (state), Australia 87/E9
Victoria (cap.), Br. Col. 146/F5
Victoria (cap.), Br. Col. 162/D6
Victoria (cap.), Br. Col. 184/K4
Victoria (mt.), Burma 72/B2
Victoria (Limbe), Cameroon 115/A3
Victoria (isl.), Canada 2/D2
Victoria (isl.), Canada 4/B15
Victoria, Malleco, Chile 138/D2
Victoria, Tarapacá, Chile 138/A3
Victoria, Grenada 161/D8
Victoria, Guinea 106/B6
Victoria, Ill. (61485) 222/C2
Victoria, Kansas (67671) 232/C3
Victoria (lake), Kenya 115/F4
Victoria, Malta 34/E6
Victoria, Minn. (55386) 255/F6
Victoria, Miss. (38679) 256/E1
Victoria, Mo. (†63020) 261/M6
Victoria (co.), New Bruns. 170/C1
Victoria, Newf. 166/D2
Victoria (lake), Newf. 166/C4
Victoria (lake), N.S. Wales 97/A3
Victoria (riv.), North. Terr. 88/E3
Victoria (riv.), North. Terr. 93/B3
Victoria (isl.), N.W.T. 146/G2
Victoria (isl.), N.W.T. 162/E1
Victoria (isl.), N.W. Terrs. 187/G2
Victoria (str.), N.W.T. 162/F2
Victoria (str.), N.W. Terrs. 187/H3
Victoria (co.), Nova Scotia 168/H2
Victoria (county), Ontario 177/F3
Victoria (lake), Ontario 177/F2
Victoria (peaks), Philippines 82/B6
Victoria, Pr. Edward I. 168/E2
Victoria (cap.), Seychelles 118/H5
Victoria (lake), Tanzania 115/F4
Victoria, Tenn. (†37397) 237/K10
Victoria (co.), Texas 303/H9
Victoria, Texas 188/G5
Victoria, Texas (77901) 303/H9
Victoria (lake), Uganda 115/F4
VICTORIA 97
Victoria, Va. (23974) 307/M6
Victoria (falls), Zambia 115/E7
Victoria (falls), Zimbabwe 118/C3
Victoria Beach, Manitoba 179/F4
Victoria Beach, Nova Scotia 168/C4
Victoria de las Tunas, Cuba 158/H3
Victoria Harbour, Ontario 177/E3

Wamic 465

Vordingborg, Denmark 21/E7
Vordingborg, Denmark 18/G9
Vorgod (riv.), Denmark 21/B6
Vorkuta, U.S.S.R. 4/C6
Vorkuta, U.S.S.R. 7/L2
Vorkuta, U.S.S.R. 52/K1
Vorkuta, U.S.S.R. 48/G3
Vormsi (isl.), U.S.S.R. 53/B1
Vorona (riv.), U.S.S.R. 52/F4
Voronezh, U.S.S.R. 7/H3
Voronezh, U.S.S.R. 52/E4
Voronezh, U.S.S.R. 48/E4
Voroshilovgrad, U.S.S.R. 7/H4
Voroshilovgrad, U.S.S.R. 52/E5
Voroshilovgrad, U.S.S.R. 48/E5
Vorskla (riv.), U.S.S.R. 52/E4
Vorst (Forest), Belgium 27/B9
Võrtsjärv (lake), U.S.S.R. 53/D1
Võru, U.S.S.R. 52/C2
Võru, U.S.S.R. 53/D2
Vosges (dept.), France 28/G3
Vosges (mts.), France 28/G3
Voskresensk, U.S.S.R. 52/E3
Voss, N. Dak. (58280) 282/R3
Voss, Norway 18/E6
Vossburg, Miss. (39366) 256/F7
Vostochnyy, U.S.S.R. 48/O5
Vostok (isl.), Kiribati 2/B6
Vostok (isl.), Kiribati 87/L7
Votamo (riv.), Venezuela 124/F6
Votice, Czech. 41/C2
Votkinsk, U.S.S.R. 48/F4
Votkinsk, U.S.S.R. 52/H3
Votuporanga, Brazil 135/B2
Vouvry, Switzerland 39/C4
Voúxa (cape), Greece 45/F8
Vouziers, France 28/F3
Voyageurs Nat'l Park, Minn. 255/F2
Voy-Vozh, U.S.S.R. 48/F3
Voy-Vozh, U.S.S.R. 52/H2
Vozhe (lake), U.S.S.R. 52/F2
Vozhega, U.S.S.R. 52/F2
Vozhma, U.S.S.R. 52/G3
Voznesensk, U.S.S.R. 52/D5
Vrå, Denmark 21/C3
Vráble, Czech. 41/E2
Vracov, Czech. 41/D2
Vrangelya (isl.), U.S.S.R. 54/U2
Vranje, Yugoslavia 45/F4
Vranov nad Teplou, Czech. 41/F2
Vratsa, Bulgaria 45/F4
Vrbas, Yugoslavia 45/D3
Vrbas (riv.), Yugoslavia 45/C3
Vrbno pod Pradědem, Czech. 41/D1
Vrbovce, Czech. 41/D1
Vrbové, Czech. 41/D2
Vrchlabí, Czech. 41/C1
Vrede, S. Africa 118/D5
Vredenburg, S. Africa 118/B6
Vredenburgh, Ala. (36481) 195/D7
Vredendal, S. Africa 118/B6
Vreed-en-Hoop, Guyana 131/B2
Vresse-sur-Semois, Belgium 27/F9
Vriezenveen, Netherlands 27/K4
Vrondádhes, Greece 45/G6
Vršac, Yugoslavia 45/E3
Vrútky, Czech. 41/E2
Vryburg, S. Africa 118/C5
Vryheid, S. Africa 118/E5
Vsetín, Czech. 41/D2
Vsevidof (mt.), Alaska 196/E4
Vuadens, Switzerland 39/C3
Vučitrn, Yugoslavia 45/E4
Vught, Netherlands 27/G5
Vukovar, Yugoslavia 45/D3
Vulcan, Alberta 182/D4
Vulcan, Mich. (49892) 250/B3
Vulcan, Mo. (63675) 261/L8
Vulcan, W. Va. (25697) 312/B7
Vulcano (isl.), Italy 34/E5
Vu Liet, Vietnam 72/E3
Vung Tau, Vietnam 72/E5
Vuollerim, Sweden 18/M3
Vuolvojaure (lake), Sweden 18/L3
Vuotso, Finland 18/P2
Vya, Nev. (†96104) 266/B1
Vyatka (riv.), U.S.S.R. 52/H3
Vyatskiye Polyany, U.S.S.R. 52/H3
Vyazemskiy, U.S.S.R. 48/O5
Vyaz'ma, U.S.S.R. 52/D3
Vyborg, U.S.S.R. 7/G2
Vyborg, U.S.S.R. 52/C2
Vyborg, U.S.S.R. 48/C3
Vychegda (riv.), U.S.S.R. 52/G2
Východočeský (reg.), Czech. 41/C1
Východoslovenský (reg.), Czech. 41/F2
Vyg (lake), U.S.S.R. 52/E2
Vyksa, U.S.S.R. 52/F3
Vym' (riv.), U.S.S.R. 52/H2
Vyshniy Volochek, U.S.S.R. 7/H2
Vyshniy Volochek, U.S.S.R. 52/D3
Vyshniy Volochek, U.S.S.R. 48/D4
Vyškov, Czech. 41/D2
Vysoké Mýto, Czech. 41/D2
Vysoké Tatry, Czech. 41/F2
Vyšší Brod, Czech. 41/C2
Vytegra, U.S.S.R. 52/E2

W

Wa, Ghana 106/D6
Waal (riv.), Netherlands 27/G5
Waalre, Netherlands 27/G6
Waalwijk, Netherlands 27/F5
Waarschoot, Belgium 27/D6
Waas (mt.), Utah 304/E5
Waasis, New Bruns. 170/D3
Wabamun, Alberta 182/C3
Waban, Mass. (†02168) 249/B7
Wabana, Newf. 166/D2
Wabaningo, Mich. (49463) 250/C5
Wabasca, Alberta 182/D2
Wabasca (riv.), Alberta 182/C1
Wabasca (riv.), Alta. 162/E4
Wabash (riv.) 188/J3
Wabash, Ark. (72389) 202/J5
Wabash (co.), Ill. 222/F5
Wabash (riv.), Ill. 222/F5
Wabash (co.), Ind. 227/F3
Wabash, Ind. (46992) 227/F3
Wabash (riv.), Ind. 227/B7
Wabash, Ohio (†45822) 284/A4
Wabash (riv.), Ohio 284/A5
Wabasha (co.), Minn. 255/F6
Wabasha, Minn. (55981) 255/G6
Wabasso, Fla. (32970) 212/F4
Wabasso, Ontario 177/D2
Wabasso, Minn. (56293) 255/C6
Wabatawangang (lake), Minn. 255/D3
Wabaunsee (co.), Kansas 232/F3
Wabaunsee, Kansas (†66547) 232/F2
Wabbaseka, Ark. (72175) 202/G5
Wabeno, Wis. (54566) 317/J5
Wabi (riv.), Ethiopia 111/H6
Wabigoon, Ontario 175/B3
Wabigoon, Ontario 177/G5
Wabi Shebelle (riv.) 102/G4
Wabi Shebelle (riv.), Ethiopia 111/H6
Wabowden, Manitoba 179/J3
Wąbrzeźno, Poland 47/D2
Wabuk (pt.), Ontario 175/D1
Wabush, Newf. 166/A3
Wabush, Newf. 162/K5
Wabuska, Nev. (†89447) 266/B3
Waccamaw (lake), N.C. 281/N6
Waccamaw (riv.), N.C. 281/M7
Waccamaw (riv.), S.C. 296/J5
Waccasassa (bay), Fla. 212/D2
Waccasassa (riv.), Fla. 212/D2
Wachapreague, Va. (23480) 307/S5
Wachapreague (inlet), Va. 307/T6
Wachtebeke, Belgium 27/D6
Wachusett (mt.), Mass. 249/G3
Wachusett (res.), Mass. 249/G3
Wacissa, Fla. (32361) 212/B1
Waco, Georgia (30182) 217/B3
Waco, Ky. (40385) 237/N5
Waco, Mo. (63869) 261/C8
Waco, Nebr. (68460) 264/G4
Waco, N.C. (28169) 281/G4
Waco, Texas 188/G4
Waco, Texas 146/J6
Waco, Texas (*76701) 303/G6
Waconda (lake), Kansas 232/D2
Waconia, Minn. (55387) 255/E6
Wadai (reg.), Chad 111/D5
Waddamana, Tasmania 99/C4
Waddan, Libya 102/D2
Waddan, Libya 111/C2
Waddell, Ariz. (85355) 198/C5
Waddenzee (sound), Netherlands 27/G2
Waddington (mt.), Br. Col. 162/D5
Waddington (mt.), Br. Col. 184/E4
Waddington, N.Y. (13694) 276/K1
Waddy, Ky. (40076) 237/L4
Wade, Miss. (†39567) 256/G9
Wade (lake), Newf. 166/A3
Wade, N.C. (28395) 281/M4
Wade, Okla. (†74723) 288/O7
Wadebridge, England 13/C7
Wade-Hampton, S.C. (†29607) 296/C2
Wadena, Ind. (†47944) 227/C3
Wadena, Iowa (52169) 229/K3
Wadena (co.), Minn. 255/D4
Wadena, Minn. (56482) 255/C4
Wadena, Sask. 181/H4
Wädenswil, Switzerland 39/G2
Wadesboro, La. (†70454) 238/M2
Wadesboro, N.C. (28170) 281/J5
Wadestown, W. Va. (26589) 312/F3
Wadesville, Ind. (47638) 227/B8
Wadeville, N.C. (†27306) 281/J4
Wadhams, N.Y. (12990) 276/N2
Wadi Dra, Morocco 102/B2
Wadi es Sir, Jordan 65/D4
Wadi Halfa, Sudan 111/F3
Wadi Musa, Jordan 65/E5
Wading (riv.), N.J. 273/D4
Wading River, N.Y. (11792) 276/P9
Wadley, Ala. (36276) 195/G4
Wadley, Georgia (30477) 217/H5
Wadmalaw (isl.), S.C. 296/G6
Wad Medani, Sudan 111/F5
Wad Medani, Sudan 59/B7
Wad Medani, Sudan 102/F3
Wadowice, Poland 47/D4
Wadsworth, Ala. (†36022) 195/E5
Wadsworth, Ill. (60083) 222/B4
Wadsworth, Nev. (89442) 266/B3
Wadsworth, Ohio (44281) 284/G3
Wadsworth, Texas (77483) 303/J9
Waelder, Texas (78959) 303/G8
Wagait Aboriginal Res., North. Terr. 93/B2
Wagarville, Ala. (36585) 195/B8
Wagener, S.C. (29164) 296/E4
Wageningen, Netherlands 27/H5
Wageningen, Suriname 131/C3
Wager (bay), N.W.T. 146/J3
Wager (bay), N.W.T. 162/G2
Wager (bay), N.W. Terrs. 187/K3
Wagga Wagga, Australia 87/E9
Wagga Wagga, N. S. Wales 88/H7
Wagga Wagga, N.S. Wales 97/D4
Waggoner, Ill. (62572) 222/D4
Waggrakine, W. Australia 92/A5
Wagin, W. Australia 88/B6
Wagin, W. Australia 92/B2
Wagner, Alberta 182/C2
Wagner, Mont. (59543) 262/H2
Wagner, S. Dak. (57380) 298/N7
Wagoner (co.), Okla. 288/P3
Wagoner, Okla. (74467) 288/R3
Wagon Mound, N. Mex. (87752) 274/E2
Wagontire, Oreg. (†97720) 291/H4
Wagon Wheel Gap, Colo. (†81130) 208/F7
Wagram, N.C. (28396) 281/L5
Wągrowiec, Poland 47/C2
Wah, Pakistan 68/C2
Wahai, Indonesia 85/H6
Wahalak, Miss. (†39358) 256/G5
Wahiawa, Hawaii (96786) 218/E2
Wahiawa, Hawaii 188/F5
Wahkiacus, Wash. (98670) 310/D5
Wahkiakum (co.), Wash. 310/B4
Wahkon, Minn. (56386) 255/E4
Wahlern, Switzerland 39/D3
Wahoo, Nebr. (68066) 264/H3
Wahpeton, Iowa (†51360) 229/C2
Wahpeton, N. Dak. 188/G1
Wahpeton, N. Dak. (58075) 282/S7
Wahsatch, Utah (†82930) 304/C2
Wah Wah (mts.), Utah 304/A5
Wahwashkesh (lake), Ontario 177/D2
Wahweap (creek), Utah 304/C6
Wai, Poulo (isls.), Vietnam 72/E4
Waiakoa, Hawaii (†96788) 218/J2
Waialae, Hawaii (96816) 218/D4
Waialeale (mt.), Hawaii 218/C1
Waialee, Hawaii (†96731) 218/E1
Waialua, Hawaii 188/F5
Waialua, Molokai, Hawaii (†96748) 218/H1
Waialua, Oahu, Hawaii (96791) 218/E1
Waianae, Hawaii (96792) 218/D2
Waiau, N. Zealand 100/D5
Waiau (riv.), N. Zealand 100/A6
Waidhofen an der Thaya, Austria 41/C2
Waidhofen an der Ybbs, Austria 41/C3
Waidsboro, Va. (†24088) 307/J7
Waigama, Indonesia 85/H6
Waigeo (isl.), Indonesia 85/J5
Waihee, Hawaii (†96793) 218/J2
Waiheke (isl.), N. Zealand 100/E2
Waihi, N. Zealand 100/E2
Waikabubak, Indonesia 85/F7
Waikanae, N. Zealand 100/E4
Waikane, Hawaii (†96744) 218/F2
Waikapu, Hawaii (†96793) 218/J2
Waikaremoana (lake), N. Zealand 100/F3
Waikari, N. Zealand 100/D5
Waikato (riv.), N. Zealand 100/E2
Waikawa, N. Zealand 100/B7
Waikerie, S. Australia 94/F6
Waikii, Hawaii (†96743) 218/H4
Waikiki (canton), Hawaii (96815) 218/C4
Waikiki (beach), Hawaii 218/C4
Waikouaiti, N. Zealand 100/C6
Wailau, Hawaii (†96748) 218/H1
Wailea, Hawaii (†96710) 218/J4
Wailea, Maui, Hawaii (†96790) 218/J2
Wailua, Hawaii (†96746) 218/D2
Wailuku, Hawaii (96793) 218/J2
Wailuku, Hawaii 188/F5
Wailuku (riv.), Hawaii 218/J5
Waimakariri (riv.), N. Zealand 100/D5
Waimalu, Hawaii (†96701) 218/B3
Waimanalo, Hawaii (96795) 218/F2
Waimanalo Bch., Hawaii (†96795) 218/F2
Waimangaroa, N. Zealand 100/C4
Waimate, N. Zealand 100/C6
Waimea (Kamuela), Hawaii, (†96743) 218/G3
Waimea, Kauai, Hawaii (96796) 218/B2
Waimea, Oahu, Hawaii (†96712) 218/E1
Waimea (bay), Hawaii 218/B2
Waimea (riv.), Hawaii 218/C2
Waimes, Belgium 27/J8
Wainaku, Hawaii (†96720) 218/J5
Wainfleet, Ontario 177/E4
Wainfleet All Saints, England 13/H4
Waingapu, Indonesia 85/G7
Waini (riv.), Guyana 131/B2
Wainiha, Hawaii (†96714) 218/C1
Wainiha (riv.), Hawaii 218/C1
Wainuiomata, N. Zealand 100/B3
Wainui-o-mata (riv.), N. Zealand 100/B3
Wainwright, Alaska (99782) 196/F1
Wainwright, Alberta 182/E3
Wainwright, Ohio (44686) 284/G5
Wainwright, Okla. (74468) 288/R3
Wainwright, U.S. 4/B18
Waiohinu, Hawaii (†96772) 218/G7
Waipa (riv.), N. Zealand 100/E2
Waipahu, Hawaii 188/F5
Waipahu, Hawaii (96797) 218/A3
Waipara, N. Zealand 100/D5
Waipawa, N. Zealand 100/F3
Waipio, Hawaii (†96758) 218/H3
Waipio (bay), Hawaii 218/H3
Waipio (pen.), Hawaii 218/A3
Waipio (pt.), Hawaii 218/A4
Waipio Acres, Hawaii (†96786) 218/E2
Waipiro Bay, N. Zealand 100/G3
Waipukurau, N. Zealand 100/F4
Wairau (riv.), N. Zealand 100/D4
Wairoa, N. Zealand 100/F3
Wairoa (riv.), N. Zealand 100/E1
Waitakere, N. Zealand 100/B1
Waitakere (range), N. Zealand 100/A1
Waitaki (riv.), N. Zealand 100/C6
Waitangi, N. Zealand 100/D7
Waitara, N. Zealand 100/E3
Waite○, Maine (04492) 243/H5
Waite Hill, Ohio (†44094) 284/H2
Waitemata (harb.), N. Zealand 100/B1
Waite Park, Minn. (56387) 255/D5
Waiteville, W. Va. (24984) 312/F8
Waitotara, N. Zealand 100/E3
Waits (riv.), Vt. 268/C3
Waitsburg, Wash. (99361) 310/G4
Waitsfield○, Vt. (05673) 268/B3
Waits River, Vt. (†05076) 268/C3
Waitville, Sask. 181/F3
Waiuku, N. Zealand 100/E2
Waiyevu, Fiji 86/R10
Wajabula, Indonesia 85/H5
Wajima, Japan 81/H5
Wajir, Kenya 115/H3
Wajir, Kenya 102/F4
Waka, Ethiopia 111/G6
Waka, Texas (79093) 303/D1
Waka, Zaire 115/D3
Wakarusa, Ind. (46573) 227/F1
Wakarusa, Kansas (66546) 232/G3
Wakasa, Japan 81/G6
Wakasa (bay), Japan 81/G6
Wakatipu (lake), N. Zealand 100/B6
Wakaw, Sask. 181/F3
Wakaw Lake, Sask. 181/F3
Wakayama (pref.), Japan 81/G6
Wakayama, Japan 54/P6
Wakayama, Japan 81/G6
Wakde (isl.), Indonesia 85/K6
Wake (co.), N.C. 281/M3
Wake (isl.), Pacific 87/G4
WaKeeney, Kansas (67672) 232/C2
Wakefield, England 10/F4
Wakefield, England 13/J2
Wakefield, Kansas (67487) 232/E2
Wakefield, La. (70784) 238/H5
Wakefield○, Mass. (01880) 249/C5
Wakefield, Mich. (49968) 250/F2
Wakefield, Nebr. (68784) 264/H2
Wakefield○, N.H. (†03872) 268/F4
Wakefield, Ohio (45687) 284/E8
Wakefield, Va. (23888) 307/O7
Wakefield-Peace Dale, R.I. (*02879) 249/J7
Wake Forest, N.C. (27587) 281/M3
Wakema, Burma 72/B3
Wakeman, Ohio (44889) 284/F3
Wakenda, Mo. (64687) 261/F4
Wake Village, Texas (75501) 303/K4
Wakita, Okla. (73771) 288/L1
Wakkanai, Japan 81/K1
Wakonda, S. Dak. (57073) 298/P7
Wakool, N.S. Wales 97/C4
Wakopa, Manitoba 179/C5
Wakpala, S. Dak. (57658) 298/H2
Wakulla (co.), Fla. 212/B1
Wakulla, Fla. (†32327) 212/B1
Wakwekobi (lake), Ontario 177/A1
Wala, Kuh-i- (mt.), Afghanistan 59/H3
Walbridge, Ohio (43465) 284/C2
Wałbrzych (prov.), Poland 47/C3
Wałbrzych, Poland 47/C3
Walcha, N.S. Wales 97/F2
Walchensee (lake), W. Germany 22/D5
Walcheren (isl.), Netherlands 27/C5
Walcott, Ark. (72474) 202/J1
Walcott, Br. Col. 184/D3
Walcott (lake), Idaho 220/E7
Walcott, Iowa (52773) 229/M5
Walcott, N. Dak. (58077) 282/R6
Walcott, Wyo. (82335) 319/F4
Walcourt, Belgium 27/F8
Wałcz, Poland 47/C2
Wald, Switzerland 39/G2
Waldeck, Sask. 181/D5
Walden, Colo. (80480) 208/G1
Walden, Georgia (†31201) 217/E5
Walden, Ky. (40768) 237/N7
Walden (pond), Mass. 249/A6
Walden, N.Y. (12586) 276/M7
Walden, Ontario 175/D3
Walden, Ontario 177/J5
Walden, Tenn. (†37377) 237/L10
Walden○, Vt. (†05873) 268/C3
Waldenburg, Ark. (72475) 202/J2
Waldenburg (Wałbrzych), Poland 47/C3
Waldenburg, Switzerland 39/E2
Walden Heights, Vt. (†05873) 268/C3
Waldersee, Manitoba 179/D4
Waldheim, E. Germany 22/E3
Waldheim, La. (†70433) 238/L5
Waldheim, Sask. 181/E3
Waldia, Ethiopia 111/G5
Waldkirch, Switzerland 39/H2
Waldkirch, W. Germany 22/B4
Waldkraiburg, W. Germany 22/E4
Waldo, Ala. (†35150) 195/F4
Waldo, Ark. (71770) 202/D7
Waldo, Br. Col. 184/K5
Waldo, Fla. (32694) 212/D2
Waldo, Kansas (67673) 232/D2
Waldo (co.), Maine 243/E6
Waldo○, Maine (†04915) 243/E7
Waldo, Ohio (43356) 284/D5
Waldo (lake), Oreg. 291/E4
Waldo, Wis. (53093) 317/L8
Waldoboro, Maine (04572) 243/E7
Waldoboro○, Maine (04572) 243/E7
Waldorf, Md. (20601) 245/L6
Waldorf, Minn. (56091) 255/E7
Waldport, Oreg. (97394) 291/C3
Waldron, Ark. (72958) 202/B4
Waldron, Ind. (46182) 227/F6
Waldron, Kansas (67150) 232/D4
Waldron, Mich. (49288) 250/E7
Waldron, Mo. (64092) 261/O5
Waldron, Sask. 181/J5
Waldron, Wash. (98297) 310/B2
Waldrup, Miss. (†39422) 256/F7
Waldsassen, W. Germany 22/E3
Waldshut-Tiengen, W. Germany 22/C5
Waldwick, N.J. (07463) 273/B1
Waldwick, Wis. (†53565) 317/G10
Walensee (lake), Switzerland 39/H2
Walenstadt, Switzerland 39/H2
Wales, Alaska (99783) 196/E1
Wales, Alaska 188/C5
Wales○, Mass. (01081) 249/F4
Wales, Minn. (†55616) 255/G3
Wales, N. Dak. (58281) 282/N2
Wales (isl.), N.W. Terrs. 187/K3
Wales, Tenn. (†38478) 237/G10
Wales, U.K. 7/D3
Wales, Utah (84667) 304/C4
WALES 13
WALES, Wales 10/E4
Wales, Wis. (53183) 317/J1
Walesboro, Ind. (†47201) 227/F6
Waleska, Georgia (30183) 217/D2
Walford, Iowa (52351) 229/K5
Walford, Ontario 177/B1
Walgett, N. S. Wales 88/H6
Walgett, N.S. Wales 97/E2
Walgreen Coast (reg.) 5/B13
Walhachin, Br. Col. 184/G5
Walhalla, Mich. (49458) 250/C5
Walhalla, N. Dak. (58282) 282/P2
Walhalla, S.C. (29691) 296/A2
Walhonding, Ohio (43843) 284/F5
Walikale, Zaire 115/E4
Walker (co.), Ala. 195/D3
Walker (creek), Ariz. 198/F2
Walker (mt.), Ark. 202/E2
Walker (co.), Georgia 217/B1
Walker, Iowa (52352) 229/K4
Walker, Kansas (67674) 232/C3
Walker, Ky. (40997) 237/O7
Walker, La. (70785) 238/L1
Walker, Mich. (49504) 250/D6
Walker, Minn. (56484) 255/D3
Walker, Mo. (64790) 261/D7
Walker (lake), Nev. 188/C3
Walker (lake), Nev. 266/C4
Walker (riv.), Nev. 266/C3
Walker, N.Y. (†14468) 276/E4
Walker (bay), N.W. Terrs. 187/G2
Walker, Oreg. (†97426) 291/D4
Walker, S. Dak. (57659) 298/G2
Walker (isl.), Tasmania 99/B2
Walker (co.), Texas 303/J7
Walker (creek), Va. 307/F6
Walker, W. Va. (26180) 312/D4
Walkerburn, Scotland 15/F5
Walker Mill, Md. (†20023) 245/F5
Walker River Ind. Res., Nev. 266/C3
Walker Springs, Ala. (36586) 195/C7
Walkerston, Queensland 88/H4
Walkerston, Queensland 95/D4
Walkersville, Md. (21793) 245/J3
Walkersville, W. Va. (26447) 312/F5
Walkerton, Ind. (46574) 227/E2
Walkerton, Ontario 177/C3
Walkerton, Va. (23177) 307/O5
Walkertown, N.C. (27051) 281/J2
Walkerville, Mich. (49459) 250/C5
Walkerville, Mont. (59701) 262/D4
Walkerville, S. Australia 88/E8
Wall○, N.J. (07719) 273/E3
Wall, Pa. (†15148) 294/C5
Wall, S. Dak. (57790) 298/E6
Wall, Texas (76957) 303/D6
Wallace, Ala. (†36426) 195/D8
Wallace (mt.), Alberta 182/C2
Wallace, Calif. (95254) 204/C9
Wallace, Idaho (83873) 220/C2
Wallace, Ind. (47988) 227/C5
Wallace (co.), Kansas 232/A3
Wallace, Kansas (67761) 232/A3
Wallace, La. (†70049) 238/M3
Wallace (lake), La. 238/C2
Wallace, Mich. (49893) 250/B3
Wallace, Nebr. (69169) 264/C4
Wallace, N.Y. (14890) 276/E6
Wallace, N.C. (28466) 281/N5
Wallace, Nova Scotia 168/E3
Wallace (harb.), Nova Scotia 168/E3
Wallace, S.C. (29596) 296/H2
Wallace, S. Dak. (57272) 298/P3
Wallace, W. Va. (26448) 312/E4
Wallaceburg, Ontario 177/B5
Wallace Lake, Manitoba 179/G3
Wallaceton, Pa. (16876) 294/F4
Wallacetown, Ontario 177/C5
Wallaga (prov.), Ethiopia 111/G6
Wallal Station, W. Australia 92/C2
Walland, Tenn. (37886) 237/O9
Wallaroo, S. Australia 94/E5
Wallasey, England 13/G2
Wallasey, England 10/F2
Walla Walla, N.S. Wales 97/D4
Walla Walla (riv.), Oreg. 291/J1
Walla Walla, Wash. 188/C1
Walla Walla, Wash. (99362) 310/G4
Walla Walla (co.), Wash. 310/G4
Walla Walla (riv.), Wash. 310/G4
Wallback, W. Va. (25285) 312/D5
Wallburg, N.C. (27373) 281/J3
Walldürn, W. Germany 22/C4
Walled Lake, Mich. (48088) 250/F6
Wallen, Ind. (†46802) 227/G2
Wallendbeen, N.S. Wales 97/E4
Wallenpaupack (lake), Pa. 294/M3
Waller (co.), Texas 303/J8
Wallerawang, N.S. Wales 97/F3
Wallerville, Miss. (†38652) 256/G2
Wallibu, St. Vin. & Grens. 161/A8
Walling, Tenn. (38587) 237/K9
Wallingford, Conn. (06492) 210/D3
Wallingford○, Conn. (06492) 210/D3
Wallingford, England 13/F6
Wallingford, Iowa (51365) 229/D2
Wallingford, Ky. (41093) 237/O4
Wallingford, Pa. (19086) 294/L7
Wallingford, Vt. (05773) 268/B5
Wallingford○, Vt. (05773) 268/B5
Wallington, N.J. (07057) 273/B2
Wallins Creek, Ky. (40873) 237/O7
Wallis (lake), N.S. Wales 97/G3
Wallis, Texas (77485) 303/H8
Wallis (isls.), Wallis and Futuna 87/J7
Wallis and Futuna 87/J7
Wallisellen, Switzerland 39/G2
Wallisville, Texas (77597) 303/L1
Wallkill (riv.), N.J. 273/D1
Wallkill, N.Y. (12589) 276/M7
Wallkill (riv.), N.Y. 276/L8
Wall Lake, Iowa (51466) 229/C4
Wallo (prov.), Ethiopia 111/H5
Wallonia, Ky. (†42405) 237/F7
Walloon (lake), Mich. 250/E3
Walloon Lake, Mich. (49796) 250/E3
Wallops (isl.), Va. 307/T5
Wallowa (co.), Oreg. 291/K2
Wallowa, Oreg. (97885) 291/K2
Wallowa (mts.), Oreg. 291/K2
Wallowa (riv.), Oreg. 291/K2
Wallpack Center, N.J. (07881) 273/D1
Walls, Miss. (38680) 256/D1
Walls, Scotland 15/G2
Wallsburg, Utah (84082) 304/C3
Wallsend, England 13/J3
Wallula (lake), Oreg. 291/H1
Wallula, Wash. (99363) 310/G4
Wallula (lake), Wash. 310/F4
Walney, Isle of (isl.), England 13/D3
Walney, Isle of (isl.), England 10/E3
Walnut, Calif. (91789) 204/D10
Walnut (creek), Calif. 204/K1
Walnut, Ill. (61376) 222/D2
Walnut, Iowa (51577) 229/C6
Walnut, Kansas (66780) 232/G4
Walnut (creek), Kansas 232/B3
Walnut (riv.), Kansas 232/E4
Walnut, Miss. (38683) 256/G1
Walnut, N.C. (28753) 281/D3
Walnut, Pa. (†17082) 294/G4
Walnut (creek), Texas 303/F3
Walnut Bottom, Pa. (17266) 294/H5
Walnut Canyon Nat'l Mon., Ariz. 198/D3
Walnut Cove, N.C. (27052) 281/J2
Walnut Creek, Calif. (*94595) 204/K2
Walnut Creek, N.C. (†27530) 281/O4
Walnut Creek, Ohio (44687) 284/G4
Walnut Grove, Ala. (35990) 195/F2
Walnut Grove, Calif. (95690) 204/B9
Walnut Grove, Georgia (†30209) 217/E3
Walnut Grove, Ill. (†61470) 222/C3
Walnut Grove, Ky. (42563) 237/M6
Walnut Grove, Minn. (56180) 255/C6
Walnut Grove, Miss. (39189) 256/F5
Walnut Grove, Mo. (65770) 261/E8
Walnut Hill, Ark. (†71826) 202/C7
Walnut Hill, Fla. (32568) 212/B5
Walnut Hill, Ill. (62893) 222/E5
Walnut Hill, Maine (†04021) 243/C8
Walnutport, Pa. (18088) 294/L4
Walnut Ridge, Ark. (72476) 202/J1
Walnut Springs, Texas (76690) 303/G5
Walpole, Mass. (02081) 249/B8
Walpole○, Mass. (02081) 249/B8
Walpole○, N.H. (03608) 268/C5
Walpole (isl.), Ontario 177/B5
Walpole, Sask. 181/K6
Walpole, W. Australia 92/B6
Walrus (isl.), Alaska 196/E3
Walrus (isls.), Alaska 196/F3
Walsall, England 10/G3
Walsall, England 13/E5
Walsenburg, Colo. (81089) 208/K7
Walsh, Alberta 182/E5
Walsh, Colo. (81090) 208/P8
Walsh (co.), N. Dak. 282/P3
Walsh, Queensland 95/B3
Walshville, Ill. (62091) 222/D4
Walsingham, England 13/H5
Walsingham (cape), N.W.T. 162/K2
Walsingham (cape), N.W. Terrs. 187/M3
Walsrode, W. Germany 22/C2
Walston, Pa. (15781) 294/D4
Walstonburg, N.C. (27888) 281/O3
Walterboro, S.C. (29488) 296/F6
Walter F. George (dam), Ala. 195/H7
Walter F. George (res.), Ala. 195/H7
Walter F. George (dam), Georgia 217/B7
Walter F. George (res.), Georgia 217/B7
Walterhill, Tenn. (†37130) 237/J9
Walter Reed Army Med. Ctr., D.C. 245/E4
Walter Reed Army Med. Ctr. Annex, Md. 245/E4
Walters, La. (71374) 238/G3
Walters, Minn. (56092) 255/E7
Walters, Okla. (73572) 288/K6
Walters Falls, Ontario 177/D3
Waltershausen, E. Germany 22/D3
Waltersville, Ky. (†40312) 237/N5
Waltersville, Miss. (†39180) 256/C6
Walterville, Oreg. (97489) 291/E3
Walthall (co.), Miss. 256/D8
Walthall, Miss. (39771) 256/F3
Waltham○, Maine (†04605) 243/G6
Waltham, Mass. (02154) 249/B6
Waltham, Minn. (55982) 255/F7
Waltham○, Vt. (†05491) 268/A3
Waltham Forest, England 13/H8
Waltham Forest, England 10/B5
Waltham Holy Cross, England 13/H7
Waltham Holy Cross, England 10/B5
Walthill, Nebr. (68067) 264/H2
Walthourville, Georgia (31333) 217/J7
Waltman, Wyo. (†82648) 319/E2
Walton (co.), Fla. 212/C6
Walton, Fla. (†33457) 212/F4
Walton (co.), Georgia 217/E3
Walton, Ind. (46994) 227/E3
Walton, Kansas (67151) 232/E3
Walton, Ky. (41094) 237/M3
Walton, Nebr. (68461) 264/H4
Walton, N.Y. (13856) 276/K6
Walton, Nova Scotia 168/E3
Walton, Ontario 177/C4
Walton, Oreg. (97490) 291/D3
Walton, W. Va. (25286) 312/D5
Walton and Weybridge, England 13/G8
Walton and Weybridge, England 10/B6
Walton Hills, Ohio (†44146) 284/J10
Walton-le-Dale, England 13/G1
Walton-le-Dale, England 10/F1
Waltonville, Ill. (62894) 222/D5
Waltreak, Ark. (†72833) 202/C4
Waltz, Mich. (†48164) 250/F6
Walum, N. Dak. (†58448) 282/O5
Walupt (lake), Wash. 310/D4
Walvis (bay), S. Africa 118/A4
Walvis Bay, S. Africa 2/K7
Walvis Bay, S. Africa 102/D7
Walvis Bay, S. Africa 118/A4
Walworth, N.Y. (14568) 276/F4
Walworth (co.), S. Dak. 298/J3
Walworth (co.), Wis. 317/J10
Walworth, Wis. (53184) 317/J10
Walzenhausen, Switzerland 39/J2
Wamac, Ill. (†62801) 222/D5
Wamba, Kenya 115/G3
Wamba, Nigeria 106/F7
Wamba, Zaire 115/E3
Wamego, Kansas (66547) 232/F2
Wamel, Netherlands 27/H5
Wamena, Indonesia 85/K6
Wamgumbaug (lake), Conn. 210/F1
Wami (riv.), Tanzania 115/G5
Wamic, Oreg. (97063) 291/F2

466 Wampee

Wampee, S.C. (†29582) 296/K4
Wampsville, N.Y. (13163) 276/J4
Wampum, Manitoba 179/G5
Wampum, Pa. (16157) 294/B4
Wamsutter, Wyo. (82336) 319/E4
Wana, Pakistan 68/C2
Wana, Pakistan 59/J3
Wana, W. Va. (26590) 312/F3
Wanaaring, N.S. Wales 97/B1
Wanaka, N. Zealand 100/B6
Wanaka (lake), N. Zealand 100/B6
Wanakah, N.Y. (†14075) 276/C5
Wanakena, N.Y. (13695) 276/K2
Wanamassa, N.J. (†07712) 273/E3
Wanamingo, Minn. (55983) 255/F6
Wan'an, China 77/H6
Wanapitei (riv.), Ontario 177/D1
Wanapum (dam), Wash. 310/E4
Wanapum (lake), Wash. 310/E3
Wanaque, N.J. (07465) 273/B1
Wanaque (res.), N.J. 273/E1
Wanatah, Ind. (46390) 227/D2
Wanblee, S. Dak. (57577) 298/F6
Wanchese, N.C. (27981) 281/T3
Wanda, Minn. (56294) 255/C6
Wandel (sea), Greenl. 4/A10
Wandering, W. Australia 92/B2
Wandering River, Alberta 182/D2
Wanderoos, Wis. (†54001) 317/B5
Wandfluhhorn (mt.), Switzerland 39/G4
Wando, S.C. (29492) 296/H6
Wando (riv.), S.C. 296/H6
Wandoan, Queensland 95/D5
Wandsworth, England 13/H8
Wandsworth, England 10/B5
Wanette, Okla. (74878) 288/M5
Wang, Mae Nam (riv.), Thailand 72/C3
Wanganella, N.S. Wales 97/C4
Wanganui, N. Zealand 87/H9
Wanganui, N. Zealand 100/E3
Wanganui (riv.), N. Zealand 100/E3
Wangaratta, Victoria 88/H7
Wangaratta, Victoria 97/D5
Wangen an der Aare, Switzerland 39/E2
Wangen im Allgäu, W. Germany 22/C5
Wangerooge (isl.), W. Germany 22/B2
Wängi, Switzerland 39/H1
Wangi-Rathmines, N.S. Wales 97/F3
Wangiwangi (isl.), Indonesia 85/G7
Wangqing, China 77/M3
Wangum (lake), Conn. 210/B1
Wanham, Alberta 182/A2
Wanhsien (Wanxian), China 77/G5
Wanilla, S. Australia 94/D6
Wanipigow, Manitoba 179/F3
Wanipigow (riv.), Manitoba 179/G3
Wankai, Sudan 111/E6
Wankie, Zimbabwe 118/D3
Wankie, Zimbabwe 102/E6
Wanks (Coco) (riv.), Honduras 154/E3
Wanks (Coco) (riv.), Nicaragua 154/E3
Wanless, Manitoba 179/H3
Wann, Okla. (74083) 288/P1
Wanna (lakes), W. Australia 92/E5
Wannaska, Minn. (56761) 255/C2
Wanne-Eickel, W. Germany 22/B3
Wanneroo, W. Australia 88/B2
Wanneroo, W. Australia 92/A1
Wanning, China 77/H8
Wanship, Utah (†84017) 304/C3
Wantage, England 13/F6
Wantage, England 10/F5
Wantagh, N.Y. (11793) 276/R7
Wanxian (Wanhsien), China 77/G5
Wanzai, China 77/H6
Wao, Philippines 82/E7
Wapakoneta, Ohio (45895) 284/B4
Wapanucka, Okla. (73461) 288/N6
Wapato, Wash. (98951) 310/E4
Wapawekka (hills), Sask. 181/M4
Wapella, Ill. (61777) 222/E3
Wapella, Sask. 181/K5
Wapello (co.), Iowa 229/J6
Wapello, Iowa (52653) 229/L6
Wapinitia, Oreg. (†97037) 291/F2
Wapiti (riv.), Alberta 182/A2
Wapiti (riv.), Br. Col. 184/H3
Wapiti, Wyo. (82450) 319/C1
Wappapello, Mo. (63966) 261/M9
Wappapello (lake), Mo. 261/L8
Wappau (lake), Alberta 182/E2
Wappingers Falls, N.Y. (12590) 276/N7
Wapsipinicon (riv.), Iowa 229/J3
Wapske, New Bruns. 170/C2
Wapwallopen, Pa. (18660) 294/K3
Waqqas, Jordan 65/D2
Waquoit, Mass. (02536) 249/M6
War, W. Va. (24892) 312/C8
Warabi, Japan 81/O2
Waramaug (lake), Conn. 210/B2
Waranga (res.), Victoria 97/C5
Warangal, India 54/J8
Warangal, India 68/D5
Waratah, Tasmania 99/B3
Waratah (bay), Victoria 97/C6
Warba, Minn. (55743) 255/E3
Warburg, Alberta 182/C3
Warburg, W. Germany 22/C3
Warburton, The (riv.), S. Australia 94/F2
Warburton, The (riv.), S. Australia 88/F5
Warburton, Victoria 97/C5
Warburton Aboriginal Reserve, W. Australia 88/D5
Warburton Aboriginal Res., W. Australia 92/D4
Ward, Ala. (36922) 195/B6
Ward, Ark. (72176) 202/F3
Ward, Colo. (80481) 208/H2
Ward (peak), Mont. 262/A3
Ward, N. Zealand 100/E4
Ward (co.), N. Dak. 282/G3
Ward, S.C. (29166) 296/D4
Ward, S. Dak. (57074) 298/R5
Ward (co.), Texas 303/A6
Ward, W. Va. (†25039) 312/D6
Ward Cove, Alaska (99928) 196/N2
Wardell, Mo. (63879) 261/N10
Warden, La. (71289) 238/H1
Warden, Québec 172/E4
Warden, Wash. (98857) 310/F4
Wardensville, W. Va. (26851) 312/J4
Wardere, Ethiopia 111/J6
Wardha, India 68/D4
Wardha (riv.), India 68/D4
Wardlow, Alberta 182/E4
Wardner, Br. Col. 184/K5
Wardner, Idaho (†83837) 220/B2
Ward Ridge, Fla. (†32456) 212/D6
Wardsboro○, Vt. (05355) 268/B5
Ward Springs, Minn. (†56336) 255/D5
Wardsville, Mo. (†65101) 261/H6
Wardsville, Ontario 177/C5
Wardville, La. (†71301) 238/F4
Wardville, Okla. (74576) 288/P5
Ware, Br. Col. 184/E1
Ware, England 13/H7
Ware, England 10/F5
Ware (co.), Georgia 217/H8
Ware, Mass. (01082) 249/E3
Ware○, Mass. (01082) 249/E3
Ware (riv.), Mass. 249/F3
War Eagle, Ark. (†72756) 202/C1
War Eagle, W. Va. (†24862) 312/C7
Waregem, Belgium 27/C7
Wareham, England 13/E7
Wareham, England 10/E5
Wareham, Mass. (02571) 249/L5
Wareham○, Mass. (02571) 249/L5
Wareham Center, Mass. (02571) 249/L5
Warehouse Point, Conn. (06088) 210/E1
Waremme, Belgium 27/G7
Waren, E. Germany 22/E2
Waren, Indonesia 85/K6
Warenda, Queensland 95/B4
Warendorf, W. Germany 22/B3
Ware Neck, Va. (23178) 307/R6
Waresboro, Georgia (31564) 217/H8
Ware Shoals, S.C. (29692) 296/C3
Waretown, N.J. (08758) 273/E4
Warfield, Br. Col. 184/J5
Warfield, Ky. (41267) 237/S5
Warfield, Va. (23889) 307/N7
Warfordsburg, Pa. (17267) 294/F6
Warialda, N.S. Wales 97/F1
Warin Chamrap, Thailand 72/E4
Waring (mts.), Alaska 196/G1
Waring, Texas (78074) 303/F8
Warka, Poland 47/E3
Warkworth, N. Zealand 100/E2
Warkworth, Ontario 177/G3
Warley, England 13/E5
Warley, England 10/G3
Warm (creek), Utah 304/C6
Warman, Sask. 181/E3
Warmbad, Namibia 118/B5
Warmbad, S. Africa 118/D5
Warm Beach, Wash. (†98292) 310/C2
Warmenhuizen, Netherlands 27/F3
Warmia (reg.), Poland 47/D1
Warminster, England 10/E5
Warminster, England 13/E6
Warm Lake, Idaho (83611) 220/C5
Warm River, Idaho (†83420) 220/G5
Warm Springs, Ark. (72478) 202/H1
Warm Springs, Georgia (31830) 217/C5
Warmsprings, Mont. (59756) 262/D4
Warm Springs, Oreg. (97761) 291/F3
Warm Springs (res.), Oreg. 291/J4
Warm Springs, Va. (24484) 307/J4
Warm Springs Ind. Res., Oreg. 291/F3
Warne, N.C. (28909) 281/B5
Warner, Alberta 182/D5
Warner○, N.H. (03278) 268/D5
Warner (riv.), N.H. 268/D5
Warner, Ohio (45785) 284/H6
Warner, Okla. (74469) 288/R4
Warner, S. Dak. (57479) 298/M3
Warner Robins, Georgia (31093) 217/E5
Warners, N.Y. (13164) 276/H4
Warnerton, La. (†70438) 238/K5
Warnes, Bolivia 136/D5
Warnow (riv.), E. Germany 22/D2
Waroona, W. Australia 92/A2
Warrabri, North. Terr. 93/D6
Warrabri Aboriginal Reserve, North. Terr. 88/E4
Warracknabeal, Victoria 97/B5
Warracknabeal, Victoria 88/G7
Warr Acres, Okla. (73132) 288/L3
Warragamba, N.S. Wales 97/F3
Warragul, Victoria 97/D6
Warrandyte, Victoria 97/J4
Warrandyte, Victoria 88/M6
Warrego (riv.), N.S. Wales 97/C1
Warrego, North. Terr. 93/C5
Warrego (range), Queensland 88/H5
Warrego (range), Queensland 95/C5
Warrego (riv.), Queensland 88/H5
Warrego (riv.), Queensland 95/C5
Warren, Ark. (71671) 202/F6
Warren○, Conn. (06754) 210/B2
Warren (co.), Georgia 217/G4
Warren, Idaho (83671) 220/C4
Warren (co.), Ill. 222/C3
Warren, Ill. (61087) 222/C1
Warren (co.), Ind. 227/C4
Warren, Ind. (46792) 227/G3
Warren (co.), Iowa 229/F6
Warren (co.), Ky. 237/H6
Warren, Maine (04864) 243/E7
Warren○, Maine (04864) 243/E7
Warren, Manitoba 179/E4
Warren, Mass. (01083) 249/F4
Warren○, Mass. (01083) 249/F4
Warren, Mich. (*48089) 250/B6
Warren, Minn. (56762) 255/B2
Warren (co.), Miss. 256/C6
Warren (co.), Mo. 261/K5
Warren, Mo. (†63456) 261/J3
Warren○, N.H. (03279) 268/D4
Warren (co.), N.J. 273/C2
Warren○, N.J. (†07060) 273/D2
Warren, N.S. Wales 88/H6
Warren, N.S. Wales 97/D2
Warren (co.), N.Y. 276/N3
Warren (co.), N.C. 281/N2
Warren, Nova Scotia 168/D3
Warren (co.), Ohio 284/B7
Warren, Ohio (*44481) 284/J3
Warren, Ontario 177/D1
Warren, Oreg. (97053) 291/E2
Warren (co.), Pa. 294/D2
Warren, Pa. (16365) 294/D2
Warren○, R.I. (02885) 249/J6
Warren (res.), S. Australia 94/C7
Warren (co.), Tenn. 237/K9
Warren○, Vt. (05674) 268/B3
Warren (co.), Va. 307/M3
Warren Center, Pa. (18851) 294/K2
Warrenpoint, N. Ireland 17/J3
Warrens, Wis. (54666) 317/E7
Warrensburg, Ill. (62573) 222/D4
Warrensburg, Mo. (64093) 261/E5
Warrensburg, N.Y. (12885) 276/N3
Warrensville, Alberta 182/B1
Warrensville, N.C. (28693) 281/F2
Warrensville, Pa. (†17701) 294/J3
Warrensville Heights, Ohio (44128) 284/H9
Warrenton, Georgia (30828) 217/G4
Warrenton, Ind. (†47539) 227/B8
Warrenton, Mo. (63383) 261/K5
Warrenton, N.C. (27589) 281/N2
Warrenton, Oreg. (97146) 291/C1
Warrenton, S. Africa 118/C5
Warrenton, Va. (22186) 307/N3
Warrenville, Conn. (†06278) 210/G1
Warrenville, Ill. (60555) 222/A6
Warrenville, S.C. (29851) 296/D4
Warri, Nigeria 106/F7
Warrick (co.), Ind. 227/C8
Warrick, Mont. (†59520) 262/G2
Warrina, S. Australia 94/D3
Warringah, N.S. Wales 97/K3
Warrington, England 13/G2
Warrington, England 10/F2
Warrington, Fla. (32507) 212/B6
Warrington, Ind. (†46186) 227/F5
Warrior, Ala. (35180) 195/E3
Warrior (dam), Ala. 195/C5
Warrior Run, Pa. (18706) 294/E7
Warriors Mark, Pa. (16877) 294/F4
Warrnambool, Australia 87/D9
Warrnambool, Victoria 97/B6
Warrnambool, Victoria 88/G7
Warroad, Minn. (56763) 255/C2
Warrumbungle (range), N. S. Wales 88/H6
Warsaw, Ill. (62379) 222/B3
Warsaw, Ind. (46580) 227/F2
Warsaw, Ky. (41095) 237/M3
Warsaw, Minn. (55087) 255/E6
Warsaw, Mo. (65355) 261/F6
Warsaw, N.Y. (14569) 276/D5
Warsaw, N.C. (28398) 281/N4
Warsaw, N. Dak. (†58261) 282/R3
Warsaw, Ohio (43844) 284/G5
Warsaw, Ontario 177/F3
Warsaw (city), Poland 47/E2
Warsaw (prov.), Poland 47/E2
Warsaw (cap.), Poland 7/G3
Warsaw (cap.), Poland 2/L3
Warsaw (Warszawa) (cap.), Poland 47/E2
Warsaw, Va. (22572) 307/P5
Warson Woods, Mo. (†63101) 261/O3
Warsop, England 13/F4
Warspite, Alberta 182/D2
Warta (riv.), Poland 7/F3
Warta (riv.), Poland 47/B2
Wartau, Switzerland 39/H2
Wartburg, Tenn. (37887) 237/M8
Warthen, Georgia (31094) 217/G4
Wartime, Sask. 181/C4
Wartrace, Tenn. (37183) 237/J9
Warwick, Alberta 182/D3
Warwick, England 10/F4
Warwick, England 13/F5
Warwick, Georgia (31796) 217/E7
Warwick, Md. (21912) 245/P3
Warwick○, Mass. (†01364) 249/E2
Warwick, N.Y. (10990) 276/M8
Warwick, N. Dak. (58381) 282/N4
Warwick (chan.), North. Terr. 93/E3
Warwick, Okla. (†74834) 288/M3
Warwick, Québec 172/F4
Warwick, Queensland 88/J5
Warwick, Queensland 95/D6
Warwick, R.I. (*02886) 249/J6
Warwickshire (co.), England 13/F5
Wasa, Br. Col. 184/K5
Wasaga Beach, Ontario 177/D3
Wasagaming, Manitoba 179/C4
Wasatch (range), Idaho 220/G7
Wasatch (co.), Utah 304/C3
Wasatch (plat.), Utah 304/C4
Wasatch (range), Utah 304/C3
Wasco, Calif. (93280) 204/F8
Wasco (co.), Oreg. 291/F2
Wasco, Oreg. (97065) 291/G2
Wascott, Wis. (54890) 317/C3
Waseca (co.), Minn. 255/E6
Waseca, Minn. (56093) 255/E6
Waseca, Sask. 181/B2
Wasen, Switzerland 39/E2
Wash, The (bay), England 13/H5
Wash, The (bay), England 10/G4
Washademoak (lake), New Bruns. 170/E3
Washago, Ontario 177/E3
Washakie (co.), Wyo. 319/E2
Washakie Ind. Res., Utah 304/B2
Washburn, Ark. (†72936) 202/B3
Washburn, Ill. (61570) 222/D3
Washburn, Iowa (50706) 229/J4
Washburn, Maine (04786) 243/G2
Washburn○, Maine (04786) 243/G2
Washburn, Mo. (65772) 261/E9
Washburn, N. Dak. (58577) 282/J5
Washburn (co.), Pakistan 317/C4
Washburn, Tenn. (37888) 237/O8
Washburn, W. Va. (†26362) 312/D4
Washburn, Wis. (54891) 317/D2
Washburn (mt.), Wyo. 319/B1
Washdyke, N. Zealand 100/C6
Washington 188/B1
WASHINGTON 310
Washington (co.), Ala. 195/B8
Washington (co.), Ark. 202/B2
Washington, Ark. (71862) 202/C6
Washington (co.), Colo. 208/N3
Washington○, Conn. (06793) 210/B2
Washington, England 13/J3
Washington (co.), Fla. 212/C6
Washington (lake), Fla. 212/F3
Washington (co.), Georgia 217/G4
Washington, Georgia (30673) 217/G3
Washington (co.), Idaho 220/B5
Washington (co.), Ill. 222/D5
Washington, Ill. (61571) 222/D3
Washington (co.), Ind. 227/E7
Washington, Ind. (47501) 227/C7
Washington (co.), Iowa 229/K6
Washington, Iowa (52353) 229/K6
Washington (co.), Kansas 232/E2
Washington, Kansas (66968) 232/F2
Washington (co.), Ky. 237/L5
Washington, Ky. (41096) 237/O3
Washington (isl.), Kiribati 87/L5
Washington (par.), La. 238/K5
Washington, La. (70589) 238/G5
Washington (co.), Maine 243/H6
Washington○, Maine (04574) 243/E7
Washington (co.), Md. 245/G2
Washington○, Mass. (†01223) 249/B3
Washington (co.), Minn. 255/F5
Washington (co.), Miss. 256/C4
Washington, Miss. (39190) 256/B7
Washington (co.), Mo. 261/L7
Washington, Mo. (63090) 261/K5
Washington (co.), Nebr. 264/H3
Washington, Nebr. (68068) 264/H3
Washington○, N.H. (03280) 268/C5
Washington (mt.), N.H. 268/E3
Washington, N.J. (07882) 273/D2
Washington (co.), N.Y. 276/O4
Washington (co.), N.C. 281/R3
Washington, N.C. (27889) 281/R3
Washington (co.), Ohio 284/H7
Washington (Old Washington), Ohio (†43768) 284/H5
Washington (co.), Okla. 288/P1
Washington, Okla. (73093) 288/L4
Washington (co.), Oreg. 291/D2
Washington (co.), Pa. 294/B5
Washington, Pa. (15301) 294/B5
Washington (co.), R.I. 249/H7
Washington (Coventry), R.I. (†02816) 249/H6
Washington (co.), Tenn. 237/R8
Washington (co.), Texas 303/H7
Washington, Texas (77880) 303/J7
Washington (state), U.S. 146/F5
Washington, D.C. (cap.), U.S. 146/L6
Washington, D.C. (cap.), U.S. 188/L3
Washington, D.C. (cap.), U.S., (*20001) 245/F5
Washington (cap.), U.S. 2/F4
Washington (co.), Utah 304/A6
Washington, Utah (84780) 304/A6
Washington (co.), Vt. 268/B3
Washington○, Vt. (05675) 268/C3
Washington (co.), Va. 307/D7
Washington, Va. (22747) 307/M3
Washington (lake), Wash. 310/B2
Washington, W. Va. (26181) 312/C4
Washington (co.), Wis. 317/K9
Washington (isl.), Wis. 317/M5
Washington Court House, Ohio (43160) 284/D6
Washington Crossing, N.J. (†08560) 273/D3
Washington Crossing, Pa. (18977) 294/N5
Washington Depot, Conn. (06794) 210/B2
Washington Grove, Md. (20880) 245/K4
Washington Island, Wis. (54246) 317/M5
Washington Lands, W. Va. (†26041) 312/E3
Washington Park, Ill. (62204) 222/B2
Washington Park, N.C. (†27889) 281/R3
Washington Terrace, Utah (†84403) 304/B2
Washingtonville, N.Y. (10992) 276/M8
Washingtonville, Ohio (44490) 284/J4
Washingtonville, Pa. (17884) 294/J3
Washita, Ark. (†71957) 202/C4
Washita (co.), Okla. 288/J4
Washita, Okla. (73094) 288/K
Washita (riv.), Okla. 288/M5
Washita (riv.), Texas 303/D2
Washoe, Mont. (†59007) 262/G5
Washoe (co.), Nev. 266/B2
Washoe (lake), Nev. 266/B3
Washougal, Wash. (98671) 310/C5
Washow (bay), Manitoba 179/F3
Washta, Iowa (51061) 229/B3
Washtenaw (co.), Mich. 250/F6
Washtucna, Wash. (99371) 310/G4
Washunga, Okla. (†74641) 288/N1
Wasilkow, Poland 47/F2
Wasilla, Alaska (99687) 196/B1
Wasior, Indonesia 85/K6
Wasit (gov.), Iraq 66/D4
Waskada, Manitoba 179/B5
Waskana (creek), Sask. 181/G5
Waskatenau, Alberta 182/D2
Waskesiu (lake), Sask. 181/E2
Waskesiu Lake, Sask. 181/E2
Waskigomog (lake), Ontario 177/F2
Waskish, Minn. (56685) 255/D2
Waskom, Texas (75692) 303/L5
Waspán, Nicaragua 154/E3
Waspuk (riv.), Nicaragua 154/E3
Wassataquoik (stream), Maine 243/F4
Wassaw (sound), Georgia 217/L7
Wassen, Switzerland 39/G3
Wasser, Namibia 118/B5
Wasserbillig, Luxembourg 27/J9
Wasserburg am Inn, W. Germany 22/E4
Wasserkuppe (mt.), W. Germany 22/C3
Wasson, Ill. (†62930) 222/E6
Wassuk (range), Nev. 266/C4
Wassy, France 28/F3
Wasta, S. Dak. (57791) 298/D5
Wataga, Ill. (61488) 222/C2
Watampone, Indonesia 85/G6
Watauga (co.), N.C. 281/F2
Watauga, S. Dak. (57660) 298/F2
Watauga, Tenn. (37694) 237/S8
Watauga (lake), Tenn. 237/T8
Watauga, Texas (76248) 303/F2
Watauga Valley, Tenn. (†37643) 237/S8
Watchet, England 13/D6
Watch Hill, R.I. (02891) 249/G7
Watch Hill (pt.), R.I. 249/G7
Watchman (isl.), Newf. 166/B2
Watchung, N.J. (07060) 273/E2
Watchusk (lake), Alberta 182/E1
Water (isl.), Virgin Is. (U.S.) 161/A4
Waterberg, Namibia 118/B4
Waterboro, Maine (04087) 243/B8
Waterboro○, Maine (04087) 243/B8
Waterbury, Conn. 188/M2
Waterbury, Conn. (*06701) 210/C2
Waterbury, Nebr. (68785) 264/H2
Waterbury, Vt. (05676) 268/B3
Waterbury○, Vt. (05676) 268/B3
Waterbury (res.), Vt. 268/B3
Waterbury Center, Vt. (05677) 268/B3
Waterdown, Ontario 177/D4
Wateree, S.C. (†29044) 296/F4
Wateree (lake), S.C. 296/F3
Wateree (riv.), S.C. 296/F3
Waterflow, N. Mex. (87421) 274/A2
Waterford, Calif. (95386) 204/E6
Waterford, Conn. (06385) 210/G3
Waterford○, Conn. (06385) 210/G3
Waterford (co.), Ireland 17/F7
Waterford, Ireland 17/G7
Waterford, Ireland 10/C4
Waterford (harb.), Ireland 10/C4
Waterford (harb.), Ireland 17/G7
Waterford, Maine (04088) 243/B7
Waterford○, Maine (04088) 243/B7
Waterford, Miss. (38685) 256/E1
Waterford, New Bruns. 170/E3
Waterford, N.Y. (12188) 276/N5
Waterford, Ohio (45786) 284/G6
Waterford, Pa. (16441) 294/B2
Waterford, Va. (22190) 307/N2
Waterford, Wis. (53185) 317/K3
Waterford Works, N.J. (08089) 273/D4
Watergap, Ky. (41665) 237/R5
Waterhen (lake), Manitoba 179/C2
Waterhouse (isl.), Tasmania 99/D2
Waterloo, Ala. (35677) 195/B1
Waterloo, Ark. (†71858) 202/D6
Waterloo, Belgium 27/E7
Waterloo, Ill. (62298) 222/C5
Waterloo, Ind. (46793) 227/G2
Waterloo, Iowa 188/H2
Waterloo, Iowa 146/J5
Waterloo, Iowa (*50701) 229/J4
Waterloo, Kansas (†67111) 232/E4
Waterloo, Mont. (†59759) 262/D5
Waterloo, Nebr. (68069) 264/H3
Waterloo, N.Y. (13165) 276/G5
Waterloo, North. Terr. 93/A4
Waterloo, Ohio (45688) 284/F8
Waterloo (reg. munic.), Ontario 177/D4
Waterloo, Ontario 177/D4
Waterloo, Oreg. (†97355) 291/E3
Waterloo, Québec 172/E4
Waterloo, S.C. (29384) 296/C3
Waterloo, Trin. & Tob. 161/A10
Waterloo, Wis. (53594) 317/J9
Watermaal-Bosvoorde (Watermael-Boitsfort), Belgium 27/C9
Watermael-Boitsfort, Belgium 27/C9
Waterman, Ill. (60556) 222/E2
Waterman, Ind. (†47952) 227/C5
Waterpocket Fold (butte), Utah 304/D6
Waterport, N.Y. (14571) 276/D4
Waterproof, La. (71375) 238/H3
Waters, Mich. (49797) 250/E4
Watersmeet, Mich. (49969) 250/G2
Waterton-Glacier Int'l Peace Park, Alberta 182/C5
Waterton-Glacier International Peace Park, Alta. 162/E6
Waterton-Glacier Int'l Peace Park, Mont. 262/C2
Waterton Lakes Nat'l Park, Alberta 182/C5
Waterton Park, Alberta 182/D5
Watertown○, Conn. (06795) 210/C2
Watertown, Fla. (†32055) 212/D1
Watertown○, Mass. (02172) 249/C6
Watertown, Minn. (55388) 255/E6
Watertown, N.Y. 188/M2
Watertown, N.Y. (13601) 276/J3
Watertown, Ohio (45787) 284/G7
Watertown, S. Dak. 188/G1
Watertown, S. Dak. (57201) 298/P4
Watertown, Tenn. (37184) 237/J8
Watertown, Wis. (53094) 317/J9
Waterval-Bo, S. Africa 118/D5
Water Valley, Ala. (†36908) 195/B7
Water Valley, Alberta 182/C4
Water Valley, Ky. (42085) 237/D7
Water Valley, Miss. (38965) 256/E2
Water Valley, Texas (76958) 303/C6
Waterview, Ky. (42786) 237/L7
Waterview, Md. (†21840) 245/P8
Water View, Va. (23180) 307/P5
Waterville, Iowa (52170) 229/L2
Waterville, Ireland 17/A8
Waterville, Kansas (66548) 232/F2
Waterville, Maine 188/N2
Waterville, Maine (04901) 243/D6
Waterville, Mass. (†01475) 249/F2
Waterville, Minn. (56096) 255/E6
Waterville, New Bruns. 170/C2
Waterville, N.Y. (13480) 276/K5
Waterville, Nova Scotia 168/D3
Waterville, Ohio (43566) 284/C3
Waterville, Québec 172/F4
Waterville○, Vt. (05492) 268/B2
Waterville, Wash. (98858) 310/E3
Waterville Valley○, N.H. (03223) 268/D4
Watervliet, Mich. (49098) 250/C6
Watervliet, N.Y. (12189) 276/N5
Waterways, Alberta 182/E1
Watford, England 10/B5
Watford, England 13/H7
Watford City, N. Dak. (58854) 282/D4
Watford, Ontario 177/C5
Watha, N.C. (28471) 281/O5
Wathaman (riv.), Sask. 181/M3
Wathena, Kansas (66090) 232/H2
Watheroo, W. Australia 92/A5
Watino, Alberta 182/B2
Watkins, Iowa (52354) 229/J5
Watkins, Minn. (55389) 255/D5
Watkins Glen, N.Y. (14891) 276/G6
Watkinsville, Georgia (30677) 217/E3
Watling (San Salvador) (isl.), Bahamas 156/C1
Watonga, Okla. (73772) 288/K3
Watonwan (co.), Minn. 255/D7
Watova, Okla. (†74048) 288/P1
Watrous, N. Mex. (87753) 274/D3
Watrous, Sask. 162/F5
Watrous, Sask. 181/F4
Watsa, Zaire 115/E3
Watseka, Ill. (60970) 222/F3
Watson, Ark. (71674) 202/H6
Watson, Ill. (62473) 222/E4
Watson, Ind. (†47130) 227/F8
Watson, La. (70786) 238/L1
Watson, Minn. (56295) 255/C5
Watson, Mo. (64496) 261/A1
Watson, Okla. (74963) 288/S6
Watson, Sask. 181/G3
Watson (mt.), Utah 304/C3
Watson Lake, Yukon 187/F3
Watson Lake, Yukon 162/D3
Watsontown, Pa. (17777) 294/J3
Watsonville, Calif. (95076) 204/D7
Watten, Scotland 15/E2
Watten, Loch (lake), Scotland 15/E2
Wattensaw (bayou), Ark. 202/G4
Watton, England 13/H5
Watton, Mich. (49970) 250/G2
Watts, Okla. (74964) 288/S2
Watts Bar (dam), Tenn. 237/M9
Watts Bar (lake), Tenn. 237/M9
Watts Bar Dam, Tenn. (37395) 237/M9
Wattsburg, Pa. (16442) 294/C1
Watt Section Sheet Harbour, Nova Scotia 168/F4
Watts Mills, S.C. (†29360) 296/D2
Wattsview, Manitoba 179/A4
Wattsville, Ala. (35182) 195/F3
Wattwil, Switzerland 39/H2
Watubela (isls.), Indonesia 85/J6
Watuppa (pond), Mass. 249/K6
Watzmann (mt.), W. Germany 22/E5
Wau, Papua N.G. 85/B7
Wau, Papua N.G. 87/E6
Wau, Sudan 111/E6
Wau, Sudan 102/E4
Waubamik, Ontario 177/E2
Waubaushene, Ontario 177/E3
Waubay, S. Dak. (57273) 298/P3
Waubay (lake), S. Dak. 298/O3
Waubeek, Iowa (†52214) 229/K4
Waubeka, Wis. (53021) 317/L9
Waubun, Minn. (56589) 255/C3
Waucedah, Mich. (†49892) 250/B3
Wauchope, N.S. Wales 97/G2
Wauchope, Sask. 181/K6
Wauchula, Fla. (33873) 212/E4
Waucoma, Iowa (52171) 229/J2
Wauconda, Ill. (60084) 222/A4
Wauconda, Wash. (98859) 310/F2
Wau el Kebir, Libya 111/C2
Waugh, Ala. (†36104) 195/F6
Waugh (mt.), Idaho 220/D4
Waugh, Manitoba 179/G5
Waukarlyearly (lake), W. Australia 88/C4
Waukee, Iowa (50263) 229/F5
Waukeenah, Fla. (†32344) 212/C1
Waukegan, Ill. (60085) 222/B4
Waukesha (co.), Wis. 317/K9
Waukesha, Wis. (53186) 317/K1
Waukomis, Okla. (73773) 288/K2
Waukon, Iowa (52172) 229/L2
Waukon, Wash. (†99008) 310/H3
Waukon Junction, Iowa (†52146) 229/L2
Waumandee, Wis. (†54622) 317/C7
Waumbek (mt.), N.H. 268/E3
Wauna, Oreg. (†97016) 291/D1
Wauna, Wash. (98395) 310/C3
Waunakee, Wis. (53597) 317/G9
Wauneta, Kansas (†67024) 232/F4
Wauneta, Nebr. (69045) 264/C4
Waupaca (co.), Wis. 317/J6
Waupaca, Wis. (54981) 317/H7
Waupun, Wis. (53963) 317/J8
Wauregan, Conn. (06387) 210/H2
Waurika, Okla. (73573) 288/L6
Waurika (lake), Okla. 288/K6
Wausa, Nebr. (68786) 264/G2
Wausau, Fla. (32463) 212/D6
Wausau, Wis. 188/J2
Wausau, Wis. (54401) 317/G6
Wausau○, Wis. 317/80
Wausaukee, Wis. (54177) 317/K5
Wauseon, Ohio (43567) 284/B2
Waushara (co.), Wis. 317/H7
Wautoma, Wis. (54982) 317/H7
Wauwatosa, Wis. (53226) 317/L1
Wauzeka, Wis. (53826) 317/E9
Wave Hill, North. Terr. 88/E3
Wave Hill, North. Terr. 93/B4
Waveland, Ark. (72867) 202/C3
Waveland, Ind. (47989) 227/D5
Waveland, Miss. (39576) 256/F10

Westernport 467

Waver (Wavre), Belgium 27/F7
Waverley, Mass. (02179) 249/B6
Waverley, N. S. Wales 88/L4
Waverley, N. S. Wales 97/K3
Waverley, N. Zealand 100/E3
Waverley, Nova Scotia 168/E4
Waverley, Ontario 177/E3
Waverley, Victoria 97/J5
Waverley, Victoria 88/L7
Waverley Downs, N.S. Wales 97/B1
Waverly, Ala. (36879) 195/G5
Waverly, Fla. (33877) 212/E4
Waverly, Georgia (31565) 217/J8
Waverly, Ill. (62692) 222/D4
Waverly, Iowa (50677) 229/J3
Waverly, Kansas (66871) 232/G3
Waverly, Ky. (42462) 237/F5
Waverly, La. (71232) 238/H2
Waverly, Minn. (55390) 255/E5
Waverly, Mo. (64096) 261/E4
Waverly, Nebr. (68462) 264/H4
Waverly, N.Y. (14892) 276/G7
Waverly, Ohio (45690) 284/D7
Waverly, S. Dak. (57202) 298/R3
Waverly, Tenn. (37185) 237/F8
Waverly, Va. (23890) 307/O6
Waverly, Wash. (99039) 310/H3
Waverly, W. Va. (26184) 312/D4
Waverly Hall, Georgia (31831) 217/C5
Waves, N.C. (27982) 281/U3
Wavre, Belgium 27/F7
Wawa (riv.), Nicaragua 154/E3
Wawa, Ontario 175/C3
Wawa, Ontario 177/J5
Wawaka, Ind. (46794) 227/F2
Wawanesa, Manitoba 179/C5
Wawasee, Ind. (†46567) 227/F2
Wawasee (lake), Ind. 227/F2
Wawayanda (lake), N.J. 273/E1
Waweig, New Bruns. 170/C3
Wawina, Minn. (55794) 255/E3
Wawota, Sask. 181/J6
Wawpecong, Ind. (†46901) 227/F3
Wax, Ky. (42787) 237/J6
Waxahachie, Texas (75165) 303/H5
Waxhaw, N.C. (28173) 281/H5
Way, Miss. (†39046) 256/E5
Way (lake), W. Australia 88/C5
Way (lake), W. Australia 92/C4
Wayagamac (lake), Québec 172/E2
Wayan, Idaho (83285) 220/G7
Wayatinah, Tasmania 99/C4
Waycross, Ga. 188/K4
Waycross, Georgia (31501) 217/H8
Wayerton, New Bruns. 170/E1
Wayland, Iowa (52654) 229/K6
Wayland, Ky. (41666) 237/R6
Wayland○, Mass. (01778) 249/A7
Wayland, Mich. (49348) 250/D6
Wayland, Mo. (63472) 261/J2
Wayland, N.Y. (14572) 276/E5
Wayland, Ohio (44285) 284/H3
Waymansville, Ind. (†47201) 227/E6
Waymart, Pa. (18472) 294/M2
Wayne, Ala. (†36763) 195/C6
Wayne, Alberta 182/D4
Wayne (co.), Georgia 217/J7
Wayne (co.), Ill. 222/E5
Wayne, Ill. (60184) 222/E2
Wayne (co.), Ind. 227/G5
Wayne (co.), Iowa 229/G7
Wayne, Kansas (†66930) 232/E2
Wayne (co.), Ky. 237/M7
Wayne, Maine (04284) 243/D7
Wayne○, Maine (04284) 243/D7
Wayne (co.), Mich. 250/F6
Wayne, Mich. (48184) 250/F6
Wayne (co.), Miss. 256/G7
Wayne (co.), Mo. 261/L8
Wayne (co.), Nebr. 264/G2
Wayne, Nebr. (68787) 264/G2
Wayne○, N.J. (07470) 273/A1
Wayne (co.), N.Y. 276/F4
Wayne, N.Y. (14893) 276/F6
Wayne (co.), N.C. 281/N4
Wayne (co.), Ohio 284/G4
Wayne, Ohio (43466) 284/C3
Wayne, Okla. (73095) 288/M5
Wayne (co.), Pa. 294/M2
Wayne, Pa. (19087) 294/M6
Wayne (co.), Tenn. 237/F10
Wayne (co.), Utah 304/C5
Wayne (co.), W. Va. 312/B6
Wayne, W. Va. (25570) 312/B6
Wayne City, Ill. (62895) 222/E5
Waynesboro, Georgia (30830) 217/J4
Waynesboro, Miss. (39367) 256/G7
Waynesboro, Pa. (17268) 294/G6
Waynesboro, Tenn. (38485) 237/F10
Waynesboro (I.C.), Va. (22980) 307/K4
Waynesburg, Ky. (40489) 237/M6
Waynesburg, Ohio (44688) 284/H4
Waynesburg, Pa. (15370) 294/B6
Waynesfield, Ohio (45896) 284/C4
Waynesville, Georgia (31566) 217/J8
Waynesville, Ill. (61778) 222/D3
Waynesville, Ind. (†47201) 227/F6
Waynesville, Mo. (65583) 261/H7
Waynesville, N.C. (28786) 281/D4
Waynesville, Ohio (45068) 284/B6
Waynetown, Ind. (47990) 227/C4
Waynoka, Okla. (73860) 288/J1
Wayside, Georgia (†31032) 217/E4
Wayside, Kansas (†67301) 232/G4
Wayside, Miss. (38780) 256/C4
Wayside, Texas (79094) 303/C3
Wayside, Wis. (†54126) 317/L7
Wayzata, Minn. (55391) 255/G5
Wazirabad, Pakistan 59/K3
We (isl.), Indonesia 85/B4
Wé, New Caled. 86/H4
Weagamow Lake, Ontario 175/B2
Weakley (co.), Tenn. 237/D8
Weald, The (reg.), England 13/H6
Wear (riv.), England 13/F3
Wear (riv.), England 10/F3
Weare○, N.H. (03281) 268/D5
Weare P.O. (North Weare), N.H. (03281) 268/D5
Weatherby, Mo. (64497) 261/D3
Weatherby Lake, Mo. (†64152) 261/O5
Weatherford, Okla. (73096) 288/J4
Weatherford, Texas (76086) 303/G5
Weatherly, Pa. (18255) 294/L4
Weathers, Okla. (†74560) 288/P5
Weathersby, Miss. (†39114) 256/E7
Weatogue, Conn. (06089) 210/D1
Weaubleau, Mo. (65774) 261/F7
Weaver, Ala. (36277) 195/G3
Weaver (riv.), England 13/G2
Weaver (lake), Manitoba 179/F2
Weaver, Minn. (†55958) 255/G6
Weaver, New Bruns. 170/E2
Weaver, N. Dak. (†58352) 282/N2
Weaverville, Calif. (96093) 204/B3
Weaverville, N.C. (28787) 281/D3
Webb, Ala. (36376) 195/H8
Webb, Iowa (51366) 229/D3
Webb (lake), Maine 243/C6
Webb, Miss. (38966) 256/D3
Webb (bay), Newf. 166/B2
Webb, Sask. 181/C5
Webb (co.), Texas 303/E10
Webb, Texas (†76010) 303/F3
Webb City, Ark. (†72949) 202/C3
Webb City, Mo. (64870) 261/C8
Webb City, Okla. (74654) 288/N1
Webber, Kansas (66970) 232/D2
Webbers Falls, Okla. (74470) 288/R3
Webbers Falls (res.), Okla. 288/R3
Webberville, Mich. (48892) 250/E6
Webb Lake, Wis. (54892) 317/B3
Webbs Cross Roads, Ky. (42652) 237/L6
Webbville, Ky. (41180) 237/R4
Webbwood, Ontario 177/C1
Webequie, Ontario 175/C2
Weber (co.), Utah 304/B2
Weber (riv.), Utah 304/C3
Weber City, Va. (24251) 307/C7
Webi Shabelle (riv.), Somalia 115/H3
Webster, Fla. (33597) 212/D3
Webster (co.), Georgia 217/C6
Webster, Ind. (47392) 227/H5
Webster (co.), Iowa 229/E4
Webster, Iowa (52355) 229/J6
Webster (res.), Kansas 232/C2
Webster (co.), Ky. 237/F5
Webster, Ky. (40176) 237/J5
Webster (par.), La. 238/D1
Webster (brook), Maine 243/E3
Webster, Mass. (01570) 249/G4
Webster○, Mass. (01570) 249/G4
Webster (lake), Mass. 249/G4
Webster, Minn. (55088) 255/E6
Webster (co.), Miss. 256/F3
Webster (co.), Mo. 261/G8
Webster (co.), Nebr. 264/F4
Webster○, N.H. (†03301) 268/D5
Webster, N.Y. (14580) 276/F4
Webster, N.C. (28788) 281/C4
Webster, N. Dak. (58382) 282/N3
Webster, Pa. (15087) 294/C5
Webster, S. Dak. (57274) 298/P3
Webster, Texas (77598) 303/K2
Webster (co.), W. Va. 312/F6
Webster, Wis. (54893) 317/B4
Webster City, Iowa (50595) 229/F4
Webster Groves, Mo. (63119) 261/P3
Webster Mills, Pa. (†17233) 294/F6
Webster Springs, W. Va. (26288) 312/F6
Websterville, Vt. (05678) 268/B3
Wecota, S. Dak. (57480) 298/L3
Weda, Indonesia 85/H5
Wedau, Papua N.G. 85/C7
Weddel (isl.), 143/D7
Weddell (sea), Ant. 2/H10
Weddell (sea) 5/C16
Wedderburn, Oreg. (97491) 291/C5
Wedderburn, Victoria 97/B5
Weddington, Ark. (†72701) 202/B1
Wedel, W. Germany 22/C2
Wedgefield, S.C. (29168) 296/F4
Wedgeport, Nova Scotia 168/C5
Wedgeworth, Ala. (†36776) 195/C5
Wedowee, Ala. (36278) 195/H4
Weed, Calif. (96094) 204/C2
Weed, N. Mex. (88354) 274/D6
Weed (hills), Sask. 181/J5
Weed Heights, Nev. (89443) 266/B4
Weedon-Centre, Québec 172/F4
Weedsport, N.Y. (13166) 276/G4
Weedville, Pa. (15868) 294/F3
Weehawken○, N.J. (07087) 273/C2
Week (isls.), Chile 138/D10
Weekapaug, R.I. (02891) 249/G7
Weekes, Sask. 181/J3
Weeki Wachee, Fla. (†33512) 212/D3
Weeks, La. (†70569) 238/G7
Weeks, Nev. (†89447) 266/B3
Weeks (isl.), N. Zealand 100/B1
Weeksbury, Ky. (41667) 237/R6
Weeks Mills, Maine (04361) 243/E7
Weeksville, N.C. (27909) 281/S2
Weems, Va. (22576) 307/P5
Weeping Water, Nebr. (68463) 264/J4
Weert, Netherlands 27/H6
Weesatche, Texas (77993) 303/G9
Weesen, Switzerland 39/H2
Weesp, Netherlands 27/C5
Weethalle, N.S. Wales 97/D3
Wee Waa, N.S. Wales 97/E2
Wegdahl, Minn. (†56265) 255/C6
Weggis, Switzerland 39/F2
Węgorzewo, Poland 47/E1
Wegra-Flat Creek, Ala. (†35129) 195/D3
Węgrów, Poland 47/E2
Weichang, China 77/J3
Weida, E. Germany 22/D3
Weiden in der Oberpfalz, W. Germany 22/D4
Weidman, Mich. (48893) 250/D5
Weifang, China 77/J4
Weihai (Weihaiwei), China 77/K4
Wei He (riv.), China 77/G5
Weilburg, W. Germany 22/C3
Weilheim im Oberbayern, W. Germany 22/D5
Weimar, E. Germany 22/D3
Weimar, Texas (78962) 303/H8
Weinan, China 77/H5
Weiner, Ark. (72479) 202/J2
Weinert, Texas (76388) 303/E4
Weinfelden, Switzerland 39/H1
Weingarten, W. Germany 22/C5
Weinheim, W. Germany 22/C4
Weining, China 77/F6
Weinsberg, W. Germany 22/C4
Weipa, Queensland 88/G1
Weipa, Queensland 95/B2
Weippe, Idaho (83553) 220/C3
Weir (lake), Fla. 212/E2
Weir, Kansas (66781) 232/H4
Weir, Miss. (39772) 256/F4
Weirdale, Sask. 181/F3
Weirgor, Wis. (†54835) 317/D4
Weir River, Manitoba 179/J2
Weirsdale, Fla. (32695) 212/D3
Weirton, W. Va. (26062) 312/E2
Weirwood, Va. (23484) 307/S6
Weisburg, Ind. (†47041) 227/H6
Weiser, Idaho (83672) 220/B5
Weiser (riv.), Idaho 220/B5
Weishan, China 77/F6
Weismes (Waimes), Belgium 27/J8
Weiss (lake), Ala. 195/G2
Weiss (lake), Georgia 217/A2
Weissenburg im Bayern, W. Germany 22/D4
Weissenfels, E. Germany 22/D3
Weisswasser, E. Germany 22/F3
Weissenstein (mts.), Switzerland 39/D2
Weisserstein (mt.), Belgium 27/J8
Weissert, Nebr. (68880) 264/E3
Weisshorn (mt.), Switzerland 39/J3
Weisshorn (mt.), Switzerland 39/E4
Weissmies (mt.), Switzerland 39/F4
Weisswasser, E. Germany 22/F3
Weitchpec, Calif. (†95546) 204/B2
Weitensfeld-Flattnitz, Austria 41/B3
Weitra, Austria 41/C2
Weixi, China 77/E6
Weixin, China 77/F6
Weiz, Austria 41/C3
Wejh, Saudi Arabia 59/C4
Wejh, Saudi Arabia 54/E7
Wejherowo, Poland 47/D1
Welaka, Fla. (32093) 212/E2
Welbekend, S. Africa 118/J6
Welch, Okla. (74369) 288/R1
Welch, Texas (79377) 303/B5
Welch, W. Va. (24801) 312/C8
Welches, Oreg. (†97067) 291/E2
Welchman Hall, Barbados 161/B8
Welchville, Maine (†04270) 243/C7
Welcome, La. (†70086) 238/L3
Welcome, Md. (20693) 245/K7
Welcome, Minn. (56181) 255/D7
Welcome, N.C. (27374) 281/J3
Welcome, Ontario 177/F4
Welcome All, Georgia (†30304) 217/J2
Weld (co.), Colo. 208/L1
Weld○, Maine (04285) 243/C6
Weld (range), W. Australia 92/B4
Welda, Kansas (66091) 232/G3
Weldon, Ark. (72177) 202/H3
Weldon, Calif. (93283) 204/G8
Weldon, Ill. (61882) 222/E3
Weldon, Iowa (50264) 229/F7
Weldon, New Bruns. 170/F3
Weldon, N.C. (27890) 281/O2
Weldon, Sask. 181/F2
Weldon, Texas (75863) 303/J6
Weldona, Colo. (80653) 208/M2
Weldon Spring Heights, Mo. (†63301) 261/M2
Weleetka, Okla. (74880) 288/O4
Welford, Queensland 95/C5
Welkom, S. Africa 102/E7
Welkom, S. Africa 118/D5
Welland (riv.), England 13/G5
Welland (riv.), England 10/F4
Welland, Ontario 177/E5
Welland (canal), Ontario 177/E5
Wellandport, Ontario 177/E4
Wellborn, Fla. (32094) 212/D1
Wellersburg, Pa. (15564) 294/E6
Wellesley (isls.), Australia 87/D7
Wellesley○, Mass. (02181) 249/B7
Wellesley, Ontario 177/D4
Wellesley (isls.), Queensland 88/F3
Wellesley (isls.), Queensland 95/A3
Wellesley Hills, Mass. (02181) 249/B7
Wellfleet○, Mass. (02667) 249/O5
Wellfleet (harb.), Mass. 249/O5
Wellfleet, Nebr. (69170) 264/D4
Wellford, S.C. (29385) 296/C2
Wellin, Belgium 27/G8
Welling, Alberta 182/D5
Welling, Okla. (74471) 288/S3
Wellingborough, England 13/G5
Wellingborough, England 10/F4
Wellington, Ala. (36279) 195/G3
Wellington (isl.), Chile 120/B7
Wellington (isl.), Chile 138/D8
Wellington, Colo. (80549) 208/K1
Wellington, England 13/D7
Wellington, England 10/E5
Wellington, Ill. (60973) 222/F3
Wellington, Kansas (67152) 232/E4
Wellington, Ky. (†40201) 237/K2
Wellington, Ky. (40387) 237/O5
Wellington○, Maine (04990) 243/D5
Wellington, Mo. (64097) 261/E4
Wellington, Nev. (89444) 266/B4
Wellington, N.S. Wales 97/E3
Wellington (cap.), N. Zealand 2/T8
Wellington (cap.), N. Zealand 87/H10
Wellington (cap.), N. Zealand 100/A3
Wellington (bay), N.W. Terrs. 187/H3
Wellington (chan.), N.W.T. 162/G1
Wellington (chan.), N.W. Terrs. 187/J2
Wellington, Nova Scotia 168/E4
Wellington, Ohio (44090) 284/F3
Wellington (county), Ontario 177/D4
Wellington, Ontario 177/G4
Wellington, Pr. Edward I. 168/D2
Wellington, S. Africa 118/B6
Wellington, Texas (79095) 303/D3
Wellington, Utah (84542) 304/D4
Wellington (lake), Victoria 97/D6
Wellington, Va. (†22308) 307/T3
Wellman, Iowa (52356) 229/K6
Wellman (lake), Manitoba 179/B3
Wellman, Texas (79378) 303/B5
Wellpinit, Wash. (99040) 310/G3
Wells, Br. Col. 184/G3
Wells, England 13/E6
Wells, England 10/E5
Wells (co.), Ind. 227/G3
Wells, Kansas (67488) 232/E2
Wells, Maine (04090) 243/B9
Wells○, Maine (04090) 243/B9
Wells, Mich. (49894) 250/B3
Wells, Minn. (56097) 255/E7
Wells, Nev. (89835) 266/G1
Wells, N.Y. (12190) 276/M4
Wells (co.), N. Dak. 282/L4
Wells, Texas (75976) 303/J6
Wells○, Vt. (05774) 268/A5
Wells (riv.), Vt. 268/C3
Wells (dam), Wash. 310/F3
Wells (lake), W. Australia 88/C5
Wells (lake), W. Australia 92/C4
Wells Beach, Maine (04090) 243/B9
Wellsboro, Ind. (†46382) 227/D1
Wellsboro, Pa. (16901) 294/H2
Wells Bridge, N.Y. (13859) 276/K6
Wellsburg, Iowa (50680) 229/H4
Wellsburg, N.Y. (14894) 276/G6
Wellsburg, N. Dak. (†58341) 282/L4
Wellsburg, W. Va. (26070) 312/E2
Wellsford, N. Zealand 100/E2
Wells Gray Prov. Park, Br. Col. 184/H4
Wells-next-the-Sea, England 13/H5
Wells-next-the-Sea, England 10/G4
Wells River, Vt. (05081) 268/C3
Wellston, Mich. (49689) 250/D4
Wellston, Mo. (63112) 261/R2
Wellston, Ohio (45692) 284/F7
Wellston, Okla. (74881) 288/M3
Wellsville, Kansas (66092) 232/G3
Wellsville, Mo. (63384) 261/K4
Wellsville, N.Y. (14895) 276/E6
Wellsville, Ohio (43968) 284/J4
Wellsville, Pa. (17365) 294/J5
Wellsville, Utah (84339) 304/C2
Wellton, Ariz. (85356) 198/A6
Wellwood, Manitoba 179/C4
Wels, Austria 41/C2
Welsford, New Bruns. 170/D3
Welsford, Nova Scotia 168/E3
Welsh, La. (70591) 238/E6
Welshfield, Ohio (†44021) 284/H3
Welshpool, New Bruns. 170/D4
Welshpool, Wales 10/E4
Welshpool, Wales 13/D5
Welton, Iowa (52774) 229/M5
Welty, Okla. (74882) 288/O3
Welwyn, England 13/H7
Welwyn, England 10/F5
Welwyn, Sask. 181/K5
Wem, England 13/E5
Wembere (riv.), Tanzania 115/F4
Wembley, Alberta 182/A2
Wemmel, Belgium 27/B9
Wemyss Bay, Scotland 15/A2
Wenamu (riv.), Guyana 131/A2
Wenas (creek), Wash. 310/E4
Wenasoga, Miss. (†38834) 256/G1
Wenatchee, Wash. 188/B1
Wenatchee, Wash. (98801) 310/E3
Wenatchee (lake), Wash. 310/E3
Wenatchee (mts.), Wash. 310/E3
Wenatchee (riv.), Wash. 310/E3
Wenchi, Ghana 106/D7
Wenchow (Wenzhou), China 77/J6
Wendel, Calif. (96136) 204/E3
Wendel, W. Va. (26450) 312/F4
Wendell, Idaho (83355) 220/D7
Wendell○, Mass. (01379) 249/E2
Wendell, Minn. (56590) 255/B4
Wendell, N.H. (03783) 268/C5
Wendell, N.C. (27591) 281/N3
Wendell Depot, Mass. (01380) 249/E2
Wenden, Ariz. (85357) 198/B5
Wendeng, China 77/K4
Wendover, England 13/G7
Wendover, Ontario 177/J2
Wendover, Utah (84083) 304/A3
Wendover, Wyo. (†82214) 319/H3
Wendron, England 13/B7
Wendte, S. Dak. (†57532) 298/H5
Wenham○, Mass. (01984) 249/L2
Wenling, China 77/K6
Wenlock (riv.), Queensland 88/G2
Wenman (isl.), Ecuador 128/B8
Wenona, Georgia (†31015) 217/E7
Wenona, Ill. (61377) 222/E2
Wenona, Md. (21870) 245/P8
Wenona, N.C. (†27860) 281/R3
Wenonah, Ill. (†62075) 222/D4
Wenonah, N.J. (08090) 273/C4
Wenquan, Qinghai, China 77/D5
Wenquan, Xinjiang Uygur, China 77/B3
Wenshan, China 77/F7
Wensum (riv.), England 13/J5
Wentworth, Mo. (64873) 261/D8
Wentworth○, N.H. (03282) 268/D4
Wentworth (lake), N.H. 268/E4
Wentworth, N.S. Wales 97/B4
Wentworth, N.C. (27375) 281/K2
Wentworth, Nova Scotia 168/E3
Wentworth, S. Dak. (57075) 298/R6
Wentworth, Wis. (54894) 317/C2
Wentworths Location○, N.H. (†03579) 268/E2
Wentzville, Mo. (63385) 261/L5
Wen Xian, China 77/G5
Wenzhou (Wenchow), China 77/J6
Wenzhou, China 54/N7
Weogufka, Ala. (35183) 195/F4
Weohyakapka (lake), Fla. 212/E4
Weott, Calif. (95571) 204/A3
Wepawaug (riv.), Conn. 210/C3
Wequetequock, Conn. (†02891) 210/H3
Werdau, E. Germany 22/E3
Werder, E. Germany 22/E2
Werner Lake, Ontario 175/A2
Wernersville, Pa. (19565) 294/K5
Wernigerode, E. Germany 22/D3
Werra (riv.), E. Germany 22/D3
Werra (riv.), W. Germany 22/D3
Werribee, Victoria 88/G7
Werrimull, Victoria 97/A4
Werris Creek, N.S. Wales 97/F2
Wertheim, W. Germany 22/C4
Wervik, Belgium 27/B7
Wesco, Mo. (65586) 261/K7
Wesel, W. Germany 22/B3
Weser (riv.), Germany 7/E3
Weser (riv.), W. Germany 22/C2
Weskan, Kansas (67762) 232/A3
Weslaco, Texas (78596) 303/F11
Weslemkoon (lake), Ontario 177/G2
Wesley, Ark. (72773) 202/C1
Wesley, Dominica 161/F5
Wesley, Georgia (†30401) 217/H6
Wesley, Iowa (50483) 229/E2
Wesley, Maine (04686) 243/H6
Wesley○, Maine (04686) 243/H6
Wesley Vale, Tasmania 99/C3
Wesleyville, Newf. 166/D4
Wesleyville, Pa. (16510) 294/C1
Wes-Rand, S. Africa 118/G6
Wessel (isls.), Australia 87/D7
Wessel (cape), North. Terr. 88/F2
Wessel (cape), North. Terr. 93/E1
Wessel (isls.), North. Terr. 88/F2
Wessel (isls.), North. Terr. 93/E1
Wessington, S. Dak. (57381) 298/M5
Wessington Springs, S. Dak. (57382) 298/M5
Wesson, Ark. (†71749) 202/E7
Wesson, Miss. (39191) 256/D7
West (riv.), Conn. 210/D3
West (riv.), Conn. 210/E3
West, Iowa (52357) 229/J5
West (bay), La. 238/M8
West (isl.), Mass. 249/L6
West (riv.), Mass. 249/H4
West, Miss. (39192) 256/E4
West (isls.), New Bruns. 170/D4
West (cape), N. Zealand 100/A6
West (bay), Nova Scotia 168/G3
West (pt.), Nova Scotia 168/H5
West (riv.), Nova Scotia 168/F3
West (pt.), Pr. Edward I. 168/D2
West (pt.), Tasmania 99/A2
West, Texas (76691) 303/G6
West (bay), Texas 303/K3
West (riv.), Vt. 268/B5
West Acton, Mass. (01720) 249/H3
West Alexander, Pa. (15376) 294/B5
West Alexandria, Ohio (45381) 284/A6
West Allis, Wis. (53214) 317/L1
West Alton, Mo. (63386) 261/M5
West Alton, N.H. (†03246) 268/E4
West Amboy, N.Y. (†13643) 276/J4
West Arichat, Nova Scotia 168/G3
West Ashford, Conn. (†06251) 210/G1
West Aspetuck (riv.), Conn. 210/C1
West Athens, Maine (†04912) 243/D6
West Augusta, Va. (24485) 307/K4
West Avon, Conn. (†06001) 210/D1
West Baden Springs, Ind. (47469) 227/D7
West Baines (riv.), North. Terr. 93/A4
West Baldwin, Maine (04091) 243/B8
Westbank, Br. Col. 184/H5
WEST BANK 59/C3
WEST BANK 65/C3
West Bank (reg.), 65/C3
West Baraboo, Wis. (†53913) 317/G9
West Barnet, Vt. (05870) 268/C3
West Barns, Scotland 15/F5
West Barnstable, Mass. (02668) 249/N6
West Barrington, R.I. (†02806) 249/J5
West Bath○, Maine (†04530) 243/D8
West Baton Rouge (par.), La. 238/H6
West Bay, Fla. (32407) 212/C6
West Bay, Nova Scotia 168/G3
West Bay Road, Nova Scotia 168/G3
West Bend, Iowa (50597) 229/D3
Westbend, Ky. (40388) 237/N5
West Bend, Sask. 181/H4
West Bend, Wis. (53095) 317/K9
West Bengal (state), India 68/F4
West Berkshire, Vt. (†05450) 268/B2
West Berlin, Mass. (†01503) 249/H3
West Berlin, N.J. (08091) 273/D4
West Bethel, Maine (04286) 243/B7
West Blocton, Ala. (35184) 195/D4
West Bloomfield, Wis. (†54983) 317/J7
Westboro, Mo. (64498) 261/B1
Westboro, Ohio (†45148) 284/C7
Westboro, Wis. (54490) 317/F5
Westborough, Mass. (01581) 249/H3
Westborough○, Mass. (01581) 249/H3
West Bountiful, Utah (†84087) 304/B3
Westbourne, Manitoba 179/D4
Westbourne, Tenn. (†37766) 237/O7
West Boxford, Mass. (01885) 249/K2
West Boylston○, Mass. (01583) 249/G3
West Braintree, Vt. (†05669) 268/B4
West Branch (res.), Conn. 210/C1
West Branch, Iowa (52358) 229/L5
West Branch, Farmington (riv.), Mass. 249/B4
West Branch, Mich. (48661) 250/E4
West Branch, Rocky (riv.), Ohio 284/G10
West Brattleboro, Vt. (05301) 268/B6
West Brentwood, N.H. (†03848) 268/E6
West Brewster, Mass. (†02631) 249/O5
Westbridge, Br. Col. 184/H5
West Bridgewater○, Mass. (02379) 249/K4
West Bridgewater, Vt. (†05034) 268/B4
West Bridgford, England 13/F5
West Bromwich, England 13/F5
West Bromwich, England 10/G3
Westbrook, Conn. (06498) 210/F3
Westbrook○, Conn. (06498) 210/F3
Westbrook, Maine (04092) 243/C8
Westbrook, Minn. (56183) 255/C6
West Brook, Nova Scotia 168/D3
Westbrook, Texas (79565) 303/C5
West Brookfield, Mass. (01585) 249/F4
West Brookfield○, Mass. (01585) 249/F4
West Brooklyn, Ill. (61378) 222/D2
West Brooksville, Maine (†04617) 243/F7
West Brownsville, Pa. (15417) 294/C5
West Buechel, Ky. (†40218) 237/K2
West Burke, Vt. (05871) 268/C2
West Burlington, Iowa (52655) 229/L7
West Burra (isl.), Scotland 15/G2
Westbury, England 10/E5
Westbury, England 13/E6
Westbury, N.Y. (11590) 276/R7
Westbury, Tasmania 99/C3
West Buxton, Maine (04093) 243/B8
Westby, Mont. (59275) 262/M2
Westby, Wis. (54667) 317/E8
West Calder, Scotland 15/C2
West Caldwell, N.J. (07006) 273/A2
West Campton, N.H. (03228) 268/D4
West Canaan, N.H. (03741) 268/C4
West Cape May, N.J. (†08204) 273/D6
West Carroll (par.), La. 238/H1
West Carrollton, Ohio (45449) 284/B6
West Carthage, N.Y. (†13619) 276/J3
West Charleston, Vt. (05872) 268/C2
West Chatham, Mass. (02669) 249/O6
West Chazy, N.Y. (12992) 276/N1
West Chelmsford, Mass. (†01824) 249/J2
Westchester, Conn. (†06474) 210/F2
Westchester, Ill. (60153) 222/B5
West Chester, Iowa (52359) 229/K6
Westchester (co.), N.Y. 276/N8
West Chester, Ohio (45069) 284/C9
West Chester, Pa. (19380) 294/L6
West Chesterfield, Mass. (01084) 249/C3
Westchester Station, Nova Scotia 168/E3
West Chicago, Ill. (60185) 222/A5
West Chop (pt.), Mass. 249/M7
West City, Ill. (†62812) 222/E5
Westcliffe, Colo. (81252) 208/H6
West College Corner, Ind. (†47353) 227/H5
West Columbia, S.C. (29169) 296/E4
West Columbia, Texas (77486) 303/J8
West Columbia, W. Va. (25287) 312/B5
West Concord, Mass. (†01742) 249/A6
West Concord, Minn. (55985) 255/F6
West Corinth, Vt. (†05039) 268/C3
West Cornwall, Conn. (06796) 210/B1
West Cornwall, Vt. (†05753) 268/A4
West Cote Blanche (bay), La. 238/G7
Westcott, Alberta 182/C4
Westcott Cove (bay), Conn. 210/A4
West Covina, Calif. (*91790) 204/D10
Westcreek, Colo. (†80135) 208/J4
West Creek, N.J. (08092) 273/E4
West Crossett, Ark. (†71635) 202/F7
West Cummington, Mass. (†01026) 249/B3
West Danville, Vt. (05873) 268/C3
West Dean, England 13/E6
West Demerara-Essequibo Coast (dist.), Guyana 131/B2
West Dennis, Mass. (02670) 249/O6
West Deptford○, N.J. (†08086) 273/B3
West Des Moines, Iowa (50318) 229/F5
West Dover, Nova Scotia 168/E4
West Dover, Vt. (05356) 268/B6
West Dublin, Nova Scotia 168/D4
West Dudley, Mass. (†01550) 249/F4
West Dummerston, Vt. (05357) 268/B6
West Dundee (Dundee), Ill. (†60118) 222/E1
West Eau Gallie, Fla. (32935) 212/F3
West Elizabeth, Pa. (15088) 294/C5
West Elkton, Ohio (45070) 284/A6
West Elmira, N.Y. (†14901) 276/G6
West Eminence, Mo. (†65466) 261/J8
Westend, Calif. (†93562) 204/H8
West End, N.C. (27376) 281/K4
West End, Sask. 181/J5
West End, Virgin Is. (Br.) 161/C4
West End-Cobb Town, Ala. (†36201) 195/G3
Westend Saltpond (lag.), Virgin Is. (U.S.) 161/E4
West Enfield, Maine (04493) 243/F5
West Epping, N.H. (†03042) 268/E5
Wester Eems (chan.), Netherlands 27/K1
Westerland, W. Germany 22/C1
Westerlo, Belgium 27/F6
Westerlo, N.Y. (12193) 276/M6
Westerly, R.I. (02891) 249/G7
Westerly○, R.I. (02891) 249/G7
Western (prov.), Kenya 115/G3
Western, Nebr. (68464) 264/G4
Western (head), Nova Scotia 168/D5
Western Australia 88/B5
WESTERN AUSTRALIA 92
Western Australia (state), Australia 87/C8
Western Bay, Newf. 166/D2
Western Channel (str.), Japan 81/D6
Western Dvina (riv.), U.S.S.R. 53/C2
Western Dvina (riv.), U.S.S.R. 52/C3
Western Dvina (riv.), U.S.S.R. 48/C4
Western Ghats (mts.), India 68/C5
Western Grove, Ark. (72685) 202/D1
Western Institute, Tenn. (38074) 237/C10
Western Isles (islands area), Scotland 15/A3
Westernport, Md. (21562) 245/B3

Willow Springs 469

White City, Sask. 181/G5
Whiteclay, Nebr. (69365) 264/B2
White Cliffs, N.S. Wales 97/B2
White Cloud, Ind. (†47112) 227/E8
White Cloud, Kansas (66094) 232/G2
White Cloud, Mich. (49349) 250/D5
White Coomb (mt.), Scotland 15/E5
White Cottage, Ohio (43791) 284/F6
Whitecourt, Alberta 182/C2
White Deer, Pa. (17887) 294/J3
White Deer, Texas (79097) 303/C2
White Earth, Minn. (56591) 255/C3
White Earth, N. Dak. (58794) 282/E3
White Earth (riv.), N. Dak. 282/E3
White Earth Ind. Res., Minn. 255/C3
White Elster (riv.), E. Germany 22/E3
Whiteface (riv.), Minn. 255/F3
Whiteface, N.H. (†03259) 268/E4
Whiteface (mt.), N.H. 268/E4
Whiteface (mt.), N.Y. 276/N2
Whiteface, Texas (79379) 303/B4
White Face (mt.), Vt. 268/B2
Whitefield, Maine (04362) 243/D7
Whitefield○, Maine (04362) 243/D7
Whitefield, N.H. (03598) 268/D3
Whitefield○, N.H. (03598) 268/D3
Whitefield, Okla. (74472) 288/R4
Whitefish (bay), Mich. 250/E2
Whitefish (pt.), Mich. 250/E2
Whitefish (riv.), Mich. 250/C2
Whitefish (lake), Minn. 255/D4
Whitefish, Mont. (59937) 262/B2
Whitefish (lake), Mont. 262/B2
Whitefish Falls, Ontario 177/C1
Whitefish Point, Mich. (†49768) 250/E2
Whiteflat, Texas (†79234) 303/D3
Whiteford, Md. (21160) 245/N2
White Fox, Sask. 181/H2
White Fox (riv.), Sask. 181/G2
Whitegate, Ireland 17/E8
White Gull (creek), Sask. 181/G2
White Hall, Ala. (†36040) 195/E6
Whitehall, Ark. (†72432) 202/J3
White Hall, Ark. (71602) 202/F5
White Hall, Georgia (†30601) 217/F3
White Hall, Ill. (62092) 222/C4
Whitehall, Ind. (†47401) 227/D6
Whitehall, La. (†70462) 238/M2
White Hall, Md. (21161) 245/M2
Whitehall, Mich. (49461) 250/C5
Whitehall, Mont. (59759) 262/D5
Whitehall, N.Y. (12887) 276/O3
Whitehall, Ohio (43213) 284/E6
Whitehall, Pa. (†15234) 294/B7
Whitehall, Scotland 15/F1
White Hall, S.C. (†29945) 296/F6
White Hall, Va. (22987) 307/L4
Whitehall, Wis. (54773) 317/D7
White Handkerchief (cape), Newf. 166/B2
Whitehaven, England 13/D3
Whitehaven, England 10/E3
Whitehaven, Md. (21873) 245/P7
Whitehaven (harb.), Nova Scotia 168/G3
White Haven, Pa. (18661) 294/L3
White Head, New Bruns. 170/D4
White Head (isl.), New Bruns. 170/D4
Whitehead, N. Ireland 17/K2
Whitehead, Nova Scotia 168/G3
White Heath, Ill. (61884) 222/E3
Whitehills, Scotland 15/F3
White Horn, Tenn. (†37711) 237/R8
Whitehorse, Canada 4/C16
Whitehorse, Canada 2/C3
Whitehorse, S. Dak. (57661) 298/H3
Whitehorse (cap.), Yukon 187/E3
Whitehorse (cap.), Yukon 162/C3
Whitehorse (cap.), Yukon 146/E3
White Horse Lake, N. Mex. (87073) 274/B3
Whitehouse, Ky. (41269) 237/R5
Whitehouse, N.J. (08888) 273/D2
Whitehouse, Ohio (43571) 284/C2
White House, Tenn. (37188) 237/H8
White House Station, N.J. (08889) 273/D2
White Iron (lake), Minn. 255/G3
White Knob (mts.), Idaho 220/E6
White Lake, N.C. (28337) 281/M5
White Lake, Ontario 177/H2
White Lake, S. Dak. (57383) 298/M6
White Lake, Wis. (54491) 317/J5
Whiteland, Ind. (46184) 227/E5
Whitelaw, Alberta 182/A1
Whitelaw, Wis. (54247) 317/L7
Whiteman A.F.B., Mo. 261/E5
Whitemark, Tasmania 99/D2
White Marsh, Md. (21162) 245/N3
White Meadow Lake, N.J. (†07866) 273/D2
White Mills, Ky. (42788) 237/J5
White Mills, Pa. (18473) 294/M2
White Mountain, Alaska (99784) 196/F2
White Mountains Nat'l Rec. Area, Alaska 196/J1
Whitemouth, Manitoba 179/G5
Whitemouth (lake), Manitoba 179/G5
Whitemouth (riv.), Manitoba 179/G5
Whitemud (riv.), Alberta 182/A1
Whiten (head), Scotland 15/D2
White Nile (riv.) 2/L5
White Nile (riv.) 102/F4
White Nile (prov.), Sudan 111/F5
White Nile (riv.), Sudan 111/F5
White Nile (riv.), Sudan 59/B7
White Oak (lake), Ark. 202/D6
White Oak, Georgia (31568) 217/J8
White Oak, Md. (†20901) 245/F3
Whiteoak, Mo. (63880) 261/M10
White Oak, N.C. (28399) 281/M5
Whiteoak (swamp), N.C. 281/P5
Whiteoak (creek), Ohio 284/C7
White Oak, Okla. (†74301) 288/R1
White Oak, Pa. (15131) 294/C7
White Oak, S.C. (29176) 296/E3
Whiteoak (creek), Tenn. 237/F8
White Oak, Texas (75693) 303/K5
White Oaks, Conn. (†06488) 210/C2
White Oaks, N. Mex. (†88301) 274/D5
White Owl, S. Dak. (57792) 298/E4
White Partridge (lake), Ontario 177/G2
White Pass, Wash. (†98937) 310/D4
White Pigeon, Mich. (49099) 250/D7
White Pine, Mich. (49971) 250/F1
Whitepine, Mont. (†59874) 262/A3
White Pine (co.), Nev. 266/F3
White Pine (range), Nev. 266/F3
White Pine, Tenn. (37890) 237/P8
White Pines, Calif. (†95223) 204/E5
White Plains, Ala. (†36862) 195/G3
White Plains, Georgia (30678) 217/F4
White Plains, Ky. (42464) 237/G6
White Plains, Md. (20695) 245/L6
White Plains, N.Y. (*10601) 276/P6
White Plains, N.C. (27031) 281/H2
White Plains, Va. (23893) 307/N7
White Pond, S.C. (29854) 296/D5
White Post, Va. (22663) 307/M2
White Quartz Hill, North. Terr. 93/D7
White Rapids, New Bruns. 170/E2
Whiteriver, Ariz. (85941) 198/E5
White River, Ont. 162/H6
White River, Ontario 175/C3
White River, Ontario 177/J5
White River, S. Dak. (57579) 298/H6
White River (lake), Texas 303/C4
White River Junction, Vt. (05001) 268/C4
White Rock, Br. Col. 184/K3
White Rock (creek), Kansas 232/D2
White Rock, N. Mex. (87544) 274/C3
Whiterock, N.C. (†28753) 281/D3
White Rock, S.C. (29177) 296/E3
White Rock, S. Dak. (†57260) 298/R2
White Rock (creek), Texas 303/G2
Whiterocks, Utah (84085) 304/E3
White Russian S.S.R., U.S.S.R. 7/G3
White Russian S.S.R., U.S.S.R. 52/C4
White Russian S.S.R., U.S.S.R. 48/C4
Whites, Wash. (†98541) 310/B3
Whitesail (lake), Br. Col. 184/D3
White Salmon, Wash. (98672) 310/D5
White Salmon (riv.), Wash. 310/D4
White Sands (des.), N. Mex. 274/C5
White Sands Missile Range, N. Mex. (88002) 274/C6
White Sands Missile Range, N. Mex. 274/C5
White Sands Nat'l Mon., N. Mex. 274/C6
Whitesbog, N.J. (†08015) 273/E4
Whitesboro, N.J. (08252) 273/D5
Whitesboro, N.Y. (13492) 276/K4
Whitesboro, Okla. (74577) 288/S5
Whitesboro, Texas (76273) 303/H4
Whitesburg, Georgia (30185) 217/B4
Whitesburg, Ky. (41858) 237/R6
Whitesburg, Tenn. (37891) 237/P8
Whites Chapel, Ala. (†35094) 195/F3
Whites City, N. Mex. (88268) 274/E6
Whites Creek, W. Va. (†25530) 312/A6
White Settlement, Texas (76108) 303/E2
Whiteshell Prov. Park, Manitoba 179/G4
White Shield, N. Dak. (†58534) 282/G4
Whiteshore (lake), Sask. 181/C3
Whiteside (chan.), Chile 138/E10
Whiteside (co.), Ill. 222/D2
Whiteside, Mo. (63387) 261/K4
Whiteside, Tenn. (37396) 237/K10
Whites Lake, Nova Scotia 168/E4
Whiteson, Oreg. (†97128) 291/D2
White Springs, Fla. (32096) 212/D1
Whitestone, Georgia (30186) 217/C1
White Stone, Va. (22578) 307/R5
Whitestown, Ind. (46075) 227/E5
White Sulphur Springs, Georgia (†31822) 217/C5
White Sulphur Springs, La. (†71371) 238/F3
White Sulphur Springs, Mont. (59645) 262/E4
White Sulphur Springs, W. Va. (24986) 312/F7
Whitesville, Georgia (†31833) 217/C5
Whitesville, Ky. (42378) 237/H5
Whitesville, Mo. (†64480) 261/C2
Whitesville, N.J. (†08701) 273/E3
Whitesville, N.Y. (14897) 276/E6
Whitesville, W. Va. (25209) 312/C6
Whiteswan (lakes), Sask. 181/F1
White Swan, Wash. (98952) 310/E4
Whitetail, Mont. (59276) 262/L2
Whitetop, Va. (24292) 307/E7
Whiteville, La. (71376) 238/F5
Whiteville, N.C. (28472) 281/M6
Whiteville, Tenn. (38075) 237/C10
White Volta (riv.) 102/B4
White Volta (riv.), Ghana 106/D6
White Volta (riv.), Upper Volta 106/D6
Whitewater, Colo. (81527) 208/C5
Whitewater (bay), Fla. 212/F6
Whitewater, Ind. (†47374) 227/H5
Whitewater (riv.), Ind. 227/H6
Whitewater, Kansas (67154) 232/E4
Whitewater, Manitoba 179/B5
Whitewater (lake), Manitoba 179/B5
Whitewater, Mo. (63785) 261/N8
Whitewater, Mont. (59544) 262/J2
Whitewater, Wis. (53190) 317/J10
Whitewater Baldy (mt.), N. Mex. 274/A5
Whitewood, Sask. 181/J5
Whitewood, S. Dak. (57793) 298/B5
Whitewood (creek), S. Dak. 298/B4
Whitewood, Va. (24657) 307/E6
Whitewright, Texas (75491) 303/H4
Whitfield, Ala. (†36925) 195/B6
Whitfield (co.), Georgia 217/B1
Whitfield, Miss. (39193) 256/E6
Whitford, Alberta 182/D3
Whitharral, Texas (79380) 303/B4
Whithorn, Scotland 10/D3
Whithorn, Scotland 15/D6
Whitianga, N. Zealand 100/E2
Whiting, Ind. (46394) 227/C1
Whiting, Iowa (51063) 229/A4
Whiting, Kansas (66552) 232/G2
Whiting○, Maine (04691) 243/J6
Whiting, Mo. (†63845) 261/O9
Whiting, N.J. (08759) 273/E4
Whiting○, Vt. (05778) 268/A4
Whiting, Wis. (†54481) 317/H7
Whiting Bay, Scotland 15/C5
Whiting Field Naval Air Sta., Fla. 212/B6
Whitingham○, Vt. (05361) 268/B6
Whitinsville, Mass. (01588) 249/H4
Whitkow, Sask. 181/D3
Whitla, Alberta 182/E5
Whitlash, Mont. (59545) 262/E2
Whitley (co.), Ind. 227/F2
Whitley (co.), Ky. 237/N7
Whitley Bay, England 13/J3
Whitley City, Ky. (42653) 237/N7
Whitleyville, Tenn. (38588) 237/K8
Whitlock, Tenn. (†38242) 237/E8
Whitman○, Mass. (02382) 249/L4
Whitman (riv.), Mass. 249/G2
Whitman, Nebr. (69366) 264/C2
Whitman, N. Dak. (58283) 282/O3
Whitman (co.), Wash. 310/H4
Whitman Mission Nat'l Hist. Site, Wash. 310/G4
Whitmer, W. Va. (26296) 312/G5
Whitmire, S.C. (29178) 296/D3
Whitmore, Calif. (96096) 204/D3
Whitmore Lake, Mich. (48189) 250/F6
Whitmore Village, Hawaii (†96786) 218/E1
Whitnel, N.C. (28645) 281/F3
Whitney (mt.), Calif. 188/C3
Whitney (mt.), Calif. 204/G7
Whitney (lake), Conn. 210/D3
Whitney, Nebr. (69367) 264/A2
Whitney, New Bruns. 170/E2
Whitney, Ontario 177/F2
Whitney, Pa. (15693) 294/D5
Whitney, S.C. (29303) 296/D1
Whitney, Texas (76692) 303/G6
Whitney Point, N.Y. (13862) 276/J6
Whitney Point (lake), N.Y. 276/J6
Whitneyville, Conn. (06517) 210/D3
Whitneyville○, Maine (04692) 243/H6
Whitsett, Texas (78075) 303/F9
Whitsunday (isl.), Queensland 88/H4
Whitsunday (isl.), Queensland 95/D4
Whitt, Texas (76090) 303/G5
Whittaker, Mich. (48190) 250/F6
Whittemore, Iowa (50598) 229/E2
Whittemore, Mich. (48770) 250/F4
Whitten, Iowa (50269) 229/H4
Whittier, Alaska (99693) 196/C1
Whittier, Calif. (*90601) 204/D11
Whittier, Iowa (52360) 229/K4
Whittier, N.C. (28789) 281/C4
Whittle (cape), Québec 174/F2
Whittlesea, Victoria 97/C5
Whittlesey, England 13/G5
Whittlesey, Wis. (†54451) 317/F5
Whitton, N.S. Wales 97/D4
Whitwell, Tenn. (37397) 237/K10
Wholdaia (lake), N.W. Terrs. 187/H3
Why, Ariz. (85321) 198/C6
Whyalla, Australia 87/D9
Whyalla, S. Australia 94/E5
Whycocomagh, Nova Scotia 168/G3
Whyjonta, N.S. Wales 97/B1
Wiarton, Ontario 177/C3
Wiau (lake), Alberta 182/E2
Wiawso, Ghana 106/D7
Wiay (isl.), Scotland 15/A3
Wibaux (co.), Mont. 262/M4
Wibaux, Mont. (59353) 262/M3
Wichabai, Guyana 131/B4
Wichita, Kans. 188/G3
Wichita (co.), Kansas 232/A3
Wichita, Kansas 146/J6
Wichita, Kansas (*67201) 232/E4
Wichita (mts.), Okla. 288/J5
Wichita (co.), Texas 303/F3
Wichita (riv.), Texas 303/F4
Wichita Falls, Texas 146/H6
Wichita Falls, Texas (*76301) 303/F4
Wichita Falls, Texas 188/G4
Wick, Iowa (†50240) 229/F6
Wick, Scotland 10/E1
Wick, Scotland 15/E2
Wick (riv.), Scotland 15/E2
Wick, W. Va. (26185) 312/E4
Wickahoney (creek), Idaho 220/C7
Wickatunk, N.J. (07765) 273/E3
Wicked (pt.), Manitoba 179/D2
Wickenburg, Ariz. (85358) 198/C5
Wickepin, W. Australia 92/B2
Wickersham, Wash. (†98284) 310/C2
Wickes, Ark. (71973) 202/B5
Wickes, Mont. (†59638) 262/D4
Wickett, Texas (79788) 303/A6
Wickham, New Bruns. 170/D3
Wickham, Québec 172/E4
Wickham (cape), Tasmania 99/A1
Wickham, W. Australia 92/B3
Wickiup (res.), Oreg. 291/F4
Wickliffe, Ky. (42087) 237/C7
Wickliffe, Ohio (44092) 284/J9
Wicklow (co.), Ireland 17/J5
Wicklow, Ireland 10/C4
Wicklow, Ireland 17/K6
Wicklow (head), Ireland 17/K6
Wicklow (head), Ireland 10/D4
Wicklow (mts.), Ireland 17/J6
Wicklow, New Bruns. 170/C2
Wicksburg, Ala. (†36352) 195/G8
Wicomico (co.), Md. 245/R7
Wicomico, Md. (†20611) 245/L7
Wicomico (riv.), Md. 245/R7
Wicomico (riv.), Md. 245/L7
Wicomico Church, Va. (22579) 307/R5
Wiconisco, Pa. (17097) 294/J4
Wide (chan.), Chile 138/D8
Wide (bay), Papua N.G. 86/C2
Wide (bay), Queensland 95/E5
Wideman, Ark. (72585) 202/G1
Widemouth, W. Va. (†24736) 312/D8
Widen, W. Va. (25211) 312/E6
Widener, Ark. (72394) 202/J3
Widewater, Alberta 182/C2
Widgiemooltha, W. Australia 88/C6
Widgiemooltha, W. Australia 92/C5
Widnes, England 10/F2
Widnes, England 13/G2
Widnoon, Pa. (16261) 294/D4
Więcbork, Poland 47/C2
Wiederkehr Village, Ark. 202/C3
Wiehl, W. Germany 22/B3
Wiek, E. Germany 22/E1
Wieliczka, Poland 47/E3
Wieluń, Poland 47/D3
Wien (Vienna) (cap.), Austria 41/D2
Wiener Neustadt, Austria 41/D3
Wieprz (riv.), Poland 47/F3
Wierden, Netherlands 27/K4
Wieringermeer Polder, Netherlands 27/G3
Wierum, Netherlands 27/H2
Wieruszów, Poland 47/D3
Wiesbaden, W. Germany 7/E3
Wiesbaden, W. Germany 22/B3
Wiese (isl.), U.S.S.R. 4/B6
Wiese (isl.), U.S.S.R. 48/H2
Wiesmoor, W. Germany 22/B2
Wigan, England 13/G2
Wigan, England 10/G2
Wiggins, Colo. (80654) 208/L2
Wiggins, Miss. (39577) 256/F9
Wiggins, S.C. (†29446) 296/F6
Wight (isl.), England 13/F7
Wight (isl.), England 10/F5
Wigston, England 13/F5
Wigton, England 13/D3
Wigtown, Scotland 10/D3
Wigtown, Scotland 15/D6
Wigtown (trad. co.), Scot. 15/A5
Wigtown (bay), Scotland 10/D3
Wigtown (bay), Scotland 15/D6
Wijhe, Netherlands 27/J4
Wijk bij Duurstede, Netherlands 27/G5
Wijk en Aalburg, Netherlands 27/F5
Wikel, W. Va. (†24945) 312/E7
Wikieup, Ariz. (85360) 198/B4
Wikwemikong, Ontario 177/C2
Wil, Switzerland 39/H2
Wilawana, Pa. (†18840) 294/J2
Wilbarger (co.), Texas 303/E3
Wilber, Nebr. (68465) 264/G4
Wilberforce, Ontario 177/F3
Wilbert, Minn. (†56031) 255/D7
Wilbraham, Mass. (01095) 249/E4
Wilbraham○, Mass. (01095) 249/E4
Wilbur, Ind. (†46151) 227/D5
Wilbur, Ky. (†41124) 237/R5
Wilbur, Oreg. (97494) 291/D4
Wilbur, Wash. (99185) 310/G3
Wilbur, W. Va. (26459) 312/E4
Wilbur Park, Mo. (†63101) 261/P3
Wilburton, Kansas (†67950) 232/A4
Wilburton, Okla. (74578) 288/R5
Wilcannia, N. S. Wales 88/G6
Wilcannia, N.S. Wales 97/B2
Wilchingen, Switzerland 39/F1
Wilcox (co.), Ala. 195/D7
Wilcox, Fla. (†32693) 212/D2
Wilcox (co.), Georgia 217/F7
Wilcox, Mo. (†64468) 261/C2
Wilcox, Nebr. (68982) 264/E4
Wilcox, Pa. (15870) 294/E2
Wilcox, Sask. 181/G5
Wilczek Land (isl.), U.S.S.R. 4/B6
Wilczek Land (isl.), U.S.S.R. 48/G1
Wild Ammonoosuc (riv.), N.H. 268/D3
Wildbad im Schwarzwald, W. Germany 22/C4
Wildcat (creek), Ind. 227/E4
Wild Cat, Ky. (40998) 237/O6
Wild Cherry, Ark. (†72576) 202/F1
Wild Cove, Newf. 166/C3
Wilder, Idaho (83676) 220/A6
Wilder, Minn. (56184) 255/C7
Wilder (dam), N.H. 268/C4
Wilder, Tenn. (38589) 237/L8
Wilder, Vt. (05088) 268/C4
Wilder (dam), Vt. 268/C4
Wilderness, Va. (†22553) 307/N4
Wilders, Ky. (†41071) 237/S2
Wildersville, Tenn. (38388) 237/E9
Wilderswil, Switzerland 39/E3
Wildervank, Netherlands 27/K2
Wilderville, Oreg. (97543) 291/D5
Wildeshausen, W. Germany 22/C2
Wild Goose, Manitoba 179/D2
Wild Goose, Ontario 177/H5
Wild Goose, Ontario 175/C3
Wildhaus, Switzerland 39/H2
Wildhay (riv.), Alberta 182/B3
Wildhorn (mt.), Switzerland 39/D4
Wild Horse, Colo. (80862) 208/N5
Wild Horse (res.), Nev. 266/E1
Wildhorse (creek), Okla. 288/L5
Wildie, Ky. (40492) 237/N6
Wildomar, Calif. (92395) 204/H10
Wildon, Austria 41/C3
Wildorado, Texas (79098) 303/B2
Wild Rice (lake), Minn. 255/F4
Wild Rice (riv.), Minn. 255/B3
Wild Rice, N. Dak. (†58047) 282/S6
Wild Rice (riv.), N. Dak. 282/R7
Wildrose, N. Dak. (58795) 282/D2
Wild Rose, Wis. (54984) 317/H7
Wildspitze (mt.), Austria 41/A3
Wildstrubel (mt.), Switzerland 39/E4
Wildsville, La. (71377) 238/G3
Wildwood, Alberta 182/C3
Wildwood, Fla. (32785) 212/D3
Wildwood, Minn. (†56643) 255/E3
Wildwood, N.J. (08260) 273/D6
Wildwood Crest, N.J. (08260) 273/D6
Wileville, Nova Scotia 168/D4
Wiley, Colo. (81092) 208/O6
Wiley, Georgia (30581) 217/F1
Wiley (creek), Oreg. 291/E3
Wiley City, Wash. (98906) 310/E4
Wiley Ford, W. Va. (26767) 312/J3
Wileyville, W. Va. (26186) 312/E3
Wilfred, Ind. (†47879) 227/C6
Wilhelm (mt.), Papua N.G. 85/B7
Wilhelm II Coast (reg.) 5/C5
Wilhelmina (canal), Netherlands 27/G6
Wilhelmina (mts.), Suriname 131/C4
Wilhelm-Pieck-Stadt, E. Germany 22/F3
Wilhelmsburg, Austria 41/C2
Wilhelmshaven, W. Germany 22/B2
Wilkes (co.), Georgia 217/G3
Wilkes (co.), N.C. 281/G2
Wilkes (lake), Ontario 177/F1
Wilkes-Barre, Pa. 188/L2
Wilkes-Barre, Pa. (*18701) 294/F7
Wilkesboro, N.C. (28697) 281/G2
Wilkes Land (reg.), Ant. 2/R10
Wilkes Land (reg.) 5/B7
Wilkeson, Wash. (98396) 310/D3
Wilkesville, Ohio (45695) 284/F7
Wilke, Sask. 181/C3
Wilkin (co.), Minn. 255/B4
Wilkins, Nev. (†89835) 266/G1
Wilkinsburg, Pa. (15221) 294/C7
Wilkinson (co.), Georgia 217/F5
Wilkinson, Ind. (46186) 227/F5
Wilkinson, Minn. (†56633) 255/D3
Wilkinson (co.), Miss. 256/B8
Wilkinson, Miss. (†39669) 256/B8
Wilkinson (lakes), S. Australia 94/C3
Wilkinson, W. Va. (25653) 312/B7
Wilkinsonville, Mass. (01590) 249/G4
Will (co.), Ill. 222/F2
Willacoochee, Georgia (31650) 217/G8
Willacy (co.), Texas 303/G11
Willamette (riv.), Oreg. 291/A3
Willamette, Middle Fork (riv.), Oreg. 291/E4
Willamina, Oreg. (97396) 291/D2
Willandra Billabong (creek), N.S. Wales 97/C3
Willapa, Wash. (†98577) 310/B4
Willapa (bay), Wash. 310/A4
Willard, Kansas (†66601) 232/G2
Willard, Mich. (†48611) 250/E5
Willard, Mo. (65781) 261/F8
Willard, Mont. (59354) 262/M4
Willard, N. Mex. (87063) 274/D4
Willard, N.Y. (14588) 276/G5
Willard, N.C. (28478) 281/O5
Willard, Ohio (44890) 284/E3
Willard, Utah (84340) 304/C2
Willard, Wis. (54493) 317/E6
Willards, Md. (21874) 245/S7
Willaumez (pen.), Papua N.G. 86/B2
Willaura, Victoria 97/B5
Willcox, Ariz. (85643) 198/F6
Willebroek, Belgium 27/E6
Willems (canal), Netherlands 27/G5
Willemstad, Netherlands 27/F5
Willemstad (cap.), Neth. Ant. 161/F9
Willemstad (cap.), Neth. Ant. 156/E4
Willen, Manitoba 179/A4
Willernie, Minn. (55090) 255/G5
Willeroo, North. Terr. 93/B3
Willette, Tenn. (†37150) 237/K8
Willey, Iowa (†51401) 229/D5
Willey House, N.H. (†03812) 268/E3
William (riv.), Sask. 181/L2
William Creek, S. Australia 94/E3
William H. Taft Nat'l Hist. Site, Ohio 284/C10
William L. Springer (lake), Ill. 222/E4
Williams, Ariz. (86046) 198/C3
Williams, Calif. (95987) 204/C4
Williams, Ind. (47470) 227/D7
Williams, Iowa (50271) 229/F3
Williams, Minn. (56686) 255/D2
Williams (co.), N. Dak. 282/C3
Williams (co.), Ohio 284/A2
Williams, Okla. (†74932) 288/T4
Williams, Oreg. (97544) 291/D5
Williams, S.C. (29493) 296/F5
Williams, W. Australia 92/B2
Williams (riv.), W. Va. 312/F6
Williams A.F.B., Ariz. 198/D5
Williams Bay, Wis. (53191) 317/J10
Williamsboro, N.C. (†27536) 281/M2
Williamsburg, Colo. (†81226) 208/J6
Williamsburg, Iowa (52361) 229/J5
Williamsburg, Kansas (66095) 232/G3
Williamsburg, Ky. (40769) 237/N7
Williamsburg, Md. (21674) 245/P6
Williamsburg○, Mass. (01096) 249/C3
Williamsburg, Mich. (49690) 250/D4
Williamsburg, Mo. (63388) 261/J5
Williamsburg, New Bruns. 170/D2
Williamsburg, N. Mex. (87942) 274/B5
Williamsburg, Ohio (45176) 284/B7
Williamsburg, Ontario 177/J3
Williamsburg, Pa. (16693) 294/F5
Williamsburg (co.), S.C. 296/H4
Williamsburg (I.C.), Va. (23185) 307/P6
Williamsburg, W. Va. (24991) 312/F7
Williamsfield, Ill. (61489) 222/C3
Williamsfield, Jamaica 158/H6
Williamsfield, Ohio (44093) 284/J2
Williamsford, Ontario 177/D3
Williamsford, Tasmania 99/B3
Williams Fork, Colorado (riv.), Colo. 208/G3
Williams Fork, Yampa (riv.), Colo. 208/E2
Williams Harbour, Newf. 166/C3
Williams Lake, Br. Col. 162/D5
Williams Lake, Br. Col. 184/F4
Williamson, Georgia (30292) 217/D4
Williamson (co.), Ill. 222/E6
Williamson, Ill. (†62088) 222/D5
Williamson, Iowa (50272) 229/G6
Williamson, N.Y. (14589) 276/F4
Williamson (riv.), Oreg. 291/F5
Williamson (co.), Tenn. 237/H9
Williamson (co.), Texas 303/G7
Williamson, W. Va. (25661) 312/B7
Williamsport, Ind. (47993) 227/C4
Williamsport, Ky. (41271) 237/R5
Williamsport, Md. (21795) 245/G2
Williamsport, Newf. 166/C3
Williamsport, Ohio (43164) 284/D6
Williamsport, Pa. 188/L2
Williamsport, Pa. (17701) 294/H3
Williamsport, Tenn. (38487) 237/G9
Williamston, Mich. (48895) 250/E6
Williamston, N.C. (27892) 281/R3
Williamston, S.C. (29697) 296/B2
Williamstown, Kansas (†66073) 232/G2
Williamstown, Ky. (41097) 237/M3
Williamstown, Mass. (01267) 249/B2
Williamstown○, Mass. (01267) 249/B2
Williamstown, Mo. (63473) 261/J2
Williamstown, New Bruns. 170/C2
Williamstown, N.J. (08094) 273/D4
Williamstown, N.Y. (13493) 276/J4
Williamstown, Ontario 177/K2
Williamstown, Pa. (17098) 294/J4
Williamstown, S. Australia 94/C7
Williamstown○, Vt. (05679) 268/B3
Williamstown, Victoria 97/H5
Williamstown, Victoria 88/K7
Williamstown, W. Va. (26187) 312/C4
Williamsville, Ill. (62693) 222/D4
Williamsville, Miss. (†39090) 256/F4
Williamsville, Mo. (63977) 261/L9
Williamsville, N.Y. (14221) 276/C5
Williamsville, Vt. (05362) 268/B6
Williamsville, Va. (24487) 307/J4
Willies (range), Queensland 95/C6
Williford, Ark. (72482) 202/H1
Willimantic, Conn. (06226) 210/G2
Willimantic (riv.), Conn. 210/F1
Willimantic, Maine (†04443) 243/E5
Willimantic○, Maine (†04443) 243/E5
Willingboro○, N.J. (08046) 273/D3
Willingdon, Alberta 182/E3
Willington○, Conn. (†06279) 210/F1
Willington, S.C. (29852) 296/C4
Willis (islets), Australia 87/F7
Willis (isls.), Coral Sea Is. Terr. 88/J3
Willis, Kansas (66435) 232/G2
Willis, Mich. (48191) 250/F6
Willis, Okla. (†73439) 288/N7
Willis, Texas (77378) 303/J7
Willis, Va. (24380) 307/H7
Willis (riv.), Va. 307/M5
Willisau, Switzerland 39/F2
Willisburg, Ky. (40078) 237/L5
Williston (lake), Br. Col. 162/D4
Williston (lake), Br. Col. 184/F2
Williston, Fla. (32696) 212/D2
Williston, N. Dak. 188/F1
Williston, N. Dak. (58801) 282/C3
Williston, S.C. (29853) 296/E5
Williston, Tenn. (38076) 237/C10
Williston○, Vt. (05495) 268/A3
Williston Park, N.Y. (11596) 276/R7
Willisville, Ark. (71864) 202/D6
Willisville, Ill. (62997) 222/D6
Willisville, Ontario 177/C1
Willis Wharf, Va. (23486) 307/S5
Williton, England 13/D6
Willits, Calif. (95490) 204/B4
Willmar, Minn. (56201) 255/C5
Willmar, Sask. 181/J6
Willmathsville, Mo. (†63546) 261/G2
Willmore Wilderness Prov. Park, Alberta 182/A3
Willoughby (bay), Ant. & Bar. 161/E11
Willoughby, N. S. Wales 88/K3
Willoughby, N.S. Wales 97/J3
Willoughby, Ohio (44094) 284/J8
Willoughby, Vt. (†05822) 268/C2
Willoughby (lake), Vt. 268/D2
Willoughby Hills, Ohio (†44094) 284/J9
Willow, Alaska (99688) 196/B1
Willow, Ark. (†72084) 202/E5
Willow (creek), Calif. 204/E3
Willow (creek), Idaho 220/G6
Willow (riv.), Minn. 255/E4
Willow (creek), Mont. 262/E2
Willow, Okla. (73673) 288/G4
Willow (creek), Oreg. 291/H2
Willow (creek), Oreg. 291/K3
Willow (creek), S. Dak. 298/C4
Willow (creek), Utah 304/E4
Willow (res.), Wis. 317/F4
Willow (creek), Wyo. 319/F2
Willow (lake), Wyo. 319/C2
Willow Bend, W. Va. (24992) 312/F7
Willow Branch, Ind. (46187) 227/F5
Willowbrook, Ill. (†60521) 222/B6
Willowbrook, Kansas (†67501) 232/D3
Willowbrook, Sask. 181/J4
Willow Bunch, Sask. 181/F6
Willow Bunch (lake), Sask. 181/F6
Willow City, N. Dak. (58384) 282/K2
Willow City, Texas (78675) 303/F7
Willow Creek, Calif. (95573) 204/B3
Willow Creek, Mont. (59760) 262/E5
Willow Creek (res.), Mont. 262/D3
Willowcreek, Oreg. (†97918) 291/K3
Willow Creek, Sask. 181/B6
Willowdale, Oreg. (†97741) 291/G3
Willow Grove, Del. (†19934) 245/R4
Willow Grove, New Bruns. 170/E3
Willow Grove, Pa. (19090) 294/M5
Willow Hill, Ill. (62480) 222/E5
Willow Hill, Pa. (17271) 294/G5
Willowick, Ohio (44094) 284/J8
Willow Island, Nebr. (69171) 264/D4
Willowlake (riv.), N.W. Terr. 187/F3
Willow Lake, S. Dak. (57278) 298/O4
Willowmore, S. Africa 118/C6
Willowra, North. Terr. 93/C6
Willow Ranch, Calif. (96108) 204/E2
Willow River, Br. Col. 184/F3
Willow River, Minn. (55795) 255/F4
Willows, Calif. (95988) 204/C4
Willows, Md. (†20732) 245/M6
Willows, Sask. 181/F6
Willow Springs, Ill. (60480) 222/B6

Zzyzx 473

Yura, Bolivia 136/B7
Yuraguanal, Cuba 158/G2
Yurga, U.S.S.R. 48/J4
Yurimaguas, Peru 128/E5
Yuruá (riv.), Peru 128/F7
Yuruari (riv.), Venezuela 124/H4
Yurungkax He (riv.), China 77/A4
Yur'yevets, U.S.S.R. 52/F3
Yuscarán, Honduras 154/D4
Yushan (isls.), China 77/K6
Yü Shan (mt.), China 77/K7
Yushu, Jilin, China 77/L3
Yushu, Qinghai, China 77/E5
Yusufeli, Turkey 63/J2
Yutan, Nebr. (68073) 264/H3
Yutian, Hebei, China 77/J4
Yutian, Xinjiang Uygur, China 77/B4
Yuty, Paraguay 144/D5
Yütze (Yuci), China 77/H4
Yuxi, China 77/F7
Yu Xian, China 77/H4
Yuzawa, Japan 81/K4
Yuzhno-Kuril'sk, U.S.S.R. 48/P5
Yuzhno-Sakhalinsk, U.S.S.R. 54/R5
Yuzhno-Sakhalinsk, U.S.S.R. 48/P5
Yvelines (dept.), France 28/D3
Yverdon, Switzerland 39/C3
Yvetot, France 28/D3
Yvoir, Belgium 27/F8
Yvonand, Switzerland 39/C3
Ywathit, Burma 72/C3

Z

Zaachila, Mexico 150/L8
Zaandam (Zaanstad), Netherlands 27/B4
Zaandijk, Netherlands 27/B4
Zabaykal'sk, U.S.S.R. 48/M5
Zabid, Yemen Arab Rep. 59/D7
Ząbki, Poland 47/E2
Ząbkowice, Poland 47/B3
Ząbkowice Śląskie, Poland 47/C3
Žabljak, Yugoslavia 45/D4
Zabol, Iran 59/H3
Zabol, Iran 66/M5
Zabré, Upper Volta 106/D6
Zábřeh, Czech. 41/D2
Zabrze, Poland 7/F3
Zabrze, Poland 47/A4
Zacapa, Guatemala 154/C3
Zacapoaxtla, Mexico 150/O1
Zacapu, Mexico 150/J7
Zacatecas (state), Mexico 150/H5
Zacatecas, Mexico 150/H5
Zacatecoluca, El Salvador 154/C4
Zacatelco, Mexico 150/N1
Zacatepec, Mexico 150/L2
Zacatlán, Mexico 150/N1
Zach, Tenn. (†38320) 237/E8
Zachariah, Ky. (41396) 237/O5
Zachary, La. (70791) 238/K1
Zachow, Wis. (54182) 317/K6
Zacoalco de Torres, Mexico 150/H6
Zadar, Yugoslavia 45/B3
Zadetkyi Kyun (isl.), Burma 72/C5
Zadi, Burma 72/C4
Zadoi, China 77/E5
Zafra, Spain 33/C3
Żagań, Poland 47/B3
Žagare, U.S.S.R. 53/B2
Zagarolo, Italy 34/F7
Zagazig, Egypt 59/B3
Zagazig, Egypt 111/K3
Zagheh, Iran 66/F4
Zagora, Morocco 106/C2
Zagorsk, U.S.S.R. 7/H3
Zagorsk, U.S.S.R. 52/E3
Zagreb, Yugoslavia 7/F4
Zagreb, Yugoslavia 45/C3
Zagros (mts.), Iran 59/E3
Zagros (mts.), Iran 66/E4
Zagyva (riv.), Hungary 41/F3
Zahedan, Iran 59/H4
Zahedan, Iran 66/M6
Zahedan, Iran 54/G7
Zahl, N. Dak. (58856) 282/C2
Zahle, Lebanon 63/F6
Záhony, Hungary 41/G2
Zahran, Saudi Arabia 59/D6
Zaidín, Spain 33/G2
Zaire 2/K6
Zaire 102/E5
ZAIRE 115/D4
Zaire (Congo) (riv.) 102/E4
Zaire (dist.), Angola 115/B5
Zaire (Congo) (riv.), Zaire 115/C4
Zaječar, Yugoslavia 45/E4
Zakamensk, U.S.S.R. 48/L4
Zakho, Iraq 66/C2
Zákinthos, Greece 45/E7
Zákinthos (Zante) (isl.), Greece 45/E7
Zako, Cent. Afr. Rep. 115/D2
Zakopane, Poland 47/D4
Zala (co.), Hungary 41/D3
Zala (riv.), Hungary 41/D3
Zalaegerszeg, Hungary 41/D3
Zalamea de la Serena, Spain 33/D3
Zalamea la Real, Spain 33/C4
Zalaszentgrót, Hungary 41/D3
Zalău, Romania 45/F2
Zaleski, Ohio (45698) 284/F7
Zalim, Saudi Arabia 59/D5
Zalingei, Sudan 111/D5
Zalma, Mo. (63787) 261/N8
Zaltbommel, Netherlands 27/G5
Zalun, Burma 72/B3
Zama (lake), Alberta 182/A5
Zama, Miss. (†39090) 256/F5
Zambales (prov.), Philippines 82/C3
Žamberk, Czech. 41/D1
Zambezi (riv.) 2/L6
Zambezi (riv.) 102/E6
Zambezi (riv.), Angola 115/D6
Zambezi (riv.), Mozambique 118/E3
Zambezi (riv.), Namibia 118/C3
Zambezi, Zambia 115/D6
Zambezi (riv.), Zambia 115/D7
Zambezi (riv.), Zimbabwe 118/E3
Zambézia (prov.), Mozambique 118/F3
Zambia 2/L6
Zambia 102/E6
ZAMBIA 115/E7
Zamboanga, Philippines 85/G4
Zamboanga, Philippines 82/C7
Zamboanga, Philippines 54/N9
Zamboanga del Norte (prov.), Philippines 82/D6
Zamboanga del Sur (prov.), Philippines 82/D7
Zambrów, Poland 47/E2
Zamora, Calif. (95698) 204/C5
Zamora, Ecuador 128/C5
Zamora (riv.), Ecuador 128/B4
Zamora (prov.), Spain 33/D2
Zamora, Spain 33/D2
Zamora-Chinchipe (prov.), Ecuador 128/C5
Zamora de Hidalgo, Mexico 150/H7
Zamość (prov.), Poland 47/F3
Zamość, Poland 47/F3
Zams, Austria 41/A3
Zamtang, China 77/F5
Zanaga, Congo 115/B4
Zanda, China 77/A5
Zanderij, Suriname 131/D3
Zanderij, Suriname 120/D2
Zandvoort, Netherlands 27/E4
Zanesfield, Ohio (43360) 284/C5
Zanesville, Ind. (46799) 227/G3
Zanesville, Ohio 188/K3
Zanesville, Ohio (43701) 284/G6
Zanja de Lira, Venezuela 124/E3
Zanjan (governorate), Iran 66/F2
Zanjan, Iran 59/E2
Zanjan, Iran 66/K5
Zanjan (riv.), Iran 66/F2
Zanoni, Mo. (65784) 261/H9
Zante (Zákinthos), Greece 45/E7
Zanthus, W. Australia 92/C5
Zanzibar, Tanzania 102/F5
Zanzibar, Tanzania 115/G5
Zanzibar (isl.), Tanzania 2/M6
Zanzibar (isl.), Tanzania 102/F5
Zanzibar (isl.), Tanzania 115/G5
Zanzibar Mjini (reg.), Tanzania 115/G5
Zanzibar Shambani North (reg.), Tanzania 115/G5
Zanzibar Shambani South (reg.), Tanzania 115/G5
Zao (mt.), Japan 81/K5
Zaouiet Kounta, Algeria 106/D3
Zaoyang, China 77/H5
Zaozernyy, U.S.S.R. 48/K4
Zaozhuang, China 77/J5
Zap, N. Dak. (58580) 282/G5
Západočeský (reg.), Austria 41/B2
Západoslovenský (reg.), Austria 41/D2
Zapala, Argentina 143/B4
Zapala, Argentina 120/B6
Zapaleri, Cerro (mt.), Argentina 143/C1
Zapaleri, Cerro (mt.), Bolivia 136/B8
Zapaleri, Cerro (mt.), Chile 138/C4
Zapallar, Chile 138/A9
Zapata (pen.), Cuba 158/C2
Zapata (co.), Texas 303/E11
Zapata, Texas (78076) 303/E11
Zapata Occidental (swamp), Cuba 158/D2
Zapata Oriental (swamp), Cuba 158/D2
Zapatera (isl.), Nicaragua 154/E5
Zapatoca, Colombia 126/D4
Zapatosa, Ciénaga de (swamp), Colombia 126/D3
Zapicán, Uruguay 145/E4
Zapiga, Chile 138/B2
Zapolyarnyy, U.S.S.R. 52/D1
Zaporozh'ye, U.S.S.R. 7/H4
Zaporozh'ye, U.S.S.R. 48/D5
Zaporozh'ye, U.S.S.R. 52/E5
Zapotillo, Ecuador 128/B5
Zapucay, Uruguay 145/D2
Zapug, China 77/B5
Za Qu (riv.), China 77/E5
Zara, Turkey 59/C1
Zara, Turkey 63/G3
Zara (Zadar), Yugoslavia 45/B3
Zarafshan, 48/G5
Zaragoza, Colombia 126/C4
Zaragoza, Chihuahua, Mexico 150/F1
Zaragoza, Coahuila, Mexico 150/J2
Zaragoza, Puebla, Mexico 150/O1
Zaragoza (prov.), Spain 33/F2
Zaragoza (Saragossa), Spain 33/F2
Zarand, Iran 59/G3
Zarand, Iran 66/H6
Zaranj, Afghanistan 68/A2
Zaranj, Afghanistan 59/H3
Zarasai, U.S.S.R. 53/C3
Zárate, Argentina 143/G6
Zaraza, Venezuela 124/F3
Zard Kuh (mt.), Iran 66/F4
Zarembo (isl.), Alaska 196/N2
Zarephath, N.J. (08890) 273/D2
Zaria, Nigeria 106/F6
Zaria, Nigeria 102/C3
Zarineh (riv.), Iran 66/E2
Zărnești, Romania 45/G3
Zarqa' (riv.), Jordan 65/D3
Zarqam, Iran 66/H6
Zaruma, Ecuador 128/C4
Zarumilla, Peru 128/B4
Zary, Poland 47/B3
Zarzal, Colombia 126/B5
Zarza la Mayor, Spain 33/C3
Zarzis, Tunisia 106/G2
Zarzis, Tunisia 102/D1
Zaskar (mts.), India 68/D2
Zastron, S. Africa 118/D6
Žatec, Czech. 41/B1
Zavala (co.), Texas 303/E9
Zavalla, Argentina 143/F6
Zavalla, Texas (75980) 303/K6
Zavdi'el, Israel 65/B4
Zaventem, Belgium 27/C9
Zavitinsk, U.S.S.R. 48/O4
Zawi, Zimbabwe 118/D3
Zawia, Libya 102/D1
Zawia, Libya 111/B1
Zawiercie, Poland 47/D3
Zayandeh (riv.), Iran 66/H4
Zayar, China 77/B3
Zaysan, U.S.S.R. 48/J5
Zaysan (lake), U.S.S.R. 54/K5
Zaysan (lake), U.S.S.R. 48/J5
Zayü, China 77/E6
Zaza del Medio, Cuba 158/F2
Zázrivá, Czech. 41/E2
Zbąszyń, Poland 47/B2
Zbiroh, Czech. 41/B2
Zborov, Czech. 41/F2
Žďár nad Sázavou, Czech. 41/C2
Zduńska Wola, Poland 47/D3
Zealand (Sjaelland) (isl.), Den. 21/E6
Zealand, New Bruns. 170/D2
Zealandia, Sask. 181/D4
Zearing, Iowa (50278) 229/G4
Zeballos, Br. Col. 184/D5
Zebdani, Syria 63/G6
Zebirget (isl.), Egypt 59/C5
Zebulon, Georgia (30295) 217/D4
Zebulon, Ky. (†41501) 237/S5
Zebulon, N.C. (27597) 281/N3
Zedelgem, Belgium 27/C6
Zeebrugge, Belgium 27/C6
Zeehan, Tasmania 99/B3
Zeeland, Mich. (49464) 250/D6
Zeeland (prov.), Netherlands 27/D6
Zeeland, N. Dak. (58581) 282/L8
Ze'elim, Israel 65/A5
Zeerust, S. Africa 118/D5
Zeewolde, Netherlands 27/G4
Zefat, Israel 65/C2
Zegharta, Lebanon 63/G5
Zegrzyńskie (lake), Poland 47/E2
Zehdenick, E. Germany 22/E2
Zehner, Sask. 181/G5
Zeigler, Ill. (62999) 222/D6
Zeila, Somalia 115/H1
Zeil am Main, W. Germany 22/D4
Zeist, Netherlands 27/G4
Zeitz, E. Germany 22/E3
Zekiah Swamp (riv.), Md. 245/L7
Zêkog, China 77/F5
Zele, Belgium 27/E6
Zelenoborskiy, U.S.S.R. 52/D1
Zelenodol'sk, U.S.S.R. 52/G3
Zelenokumsk, U.S.S.R. 52/F6
Zelienople, Pa. (16063) 294/B4
Želiezovce, Czech. 41/E2
Zell, S. Dak. (57483) 298/M4
Zell, Luzern, Switzerland 39/E2
Zell, Zürich, Switzerland 39/G2
Zell, W. Germany 22/B4
Zella, Libya 102/D2
Zella, Libya 111/C2
Zella-Mehlis, E. Germany 22/D3
Zell am See, Austria 41/B3
Zell am Ziller, Austria 41/A3
Zellersee (lake), Switzerland 39/G1
Zellwood, Fla. (32798) 212/E3
Zelma, Sask. 181/F4
Zelow, Poland 47/D3
Zelten, Jebel (mts.), Libya 111/D2
Zeltweg, Austria 41/C3
Zelzate, Belgium 27/D6
Zemio, Cent. Afr. Rep. 115/D2
Zemongo, Cent. Afr. Rep. 115/E2
Zemple, Minn. (†56636) 255/E3
Zempoala, Mexico 150/Q1
Zemst, Belgium 27/E7
Zenas, Ind. (†47223) 227/G6
Zenda, Kansas (67159) 232/D4
Zeneta, Sask. 181/J5
Zenia, Calif. (95495) 204/B3
Zenica, Yugoslavia 45/C3
Zenith, Ill. (†62899) 222/E5
Zenith, Kansas (†67578) 232/D4
Zenith, W. Va. (†24951) 312/F7
Zenith-Saltwater, Wash. (†98101) 310/C3
Zenjan (Zanjan), Iran 66/F2
Zenobia (peak), Colo. 208/B1
Zenon Park, Sask. 181/H2
Zenoria, La. (†71371) 238/F3
Zent, Ark. (†72021) 202/H4
Zenta (Senta), Yugo. 45/D3
Zeona, S. Dak. (57795) 298/D3
Žepče, Yugoslavia 45/D3
Zepernick, E. Germany 22/F3
Zephyr, Ontario 177/E3
Zephyr, Texas (76890) 303/F6
Zephyr Cove, Nev. (89448) 266/A3
Zephyrhills, Fla. (33599) 212/D3
Zepp, Va. (†22654) 307/L3
Zerbst, E. Germany 22/E3
Zereh, Gowd-e (depr.), Afghanistan 68/A3
Zermatt, Switzerland 39/E4
Zernez, Switzerland 39/K3
Zernograd, U.S.S.R. 52/F5
Zessfontein, Namibia 118/A3
Zêtang, China 77/D6
Zetland (trad. co.), Scot. 15/B4
Zeulenroda, E. Germany 22/D3
Zeven, W. Germany 22/C2
Zevenaar, Netherlands 27/J5
Zevenbergen, Netherlands 27/E5
Zeya, U.S.S.R. 48/N4
Zeya (riv.), U.S.S.R. 48/N4
Zeytinburnu, Turkey 63/D6
Zeytindağ, Turkey 63/B3
Zgierz, Poland 47/D3
Zgorzelec, Poland 47/B3
Zhanang, China 77/D6
Zhanghei, China 77/J3
Zhangjiakou (Kalgan), China 77/J3
Zhangjiakou, China 54/N5
Zhangping, China 77/J6
Zhangye (Changyeh), China 77/F4
Zhangye, China 54/M6
Zhangzhou (Changchow), China 77/J7
Zhanjiang (Chankiang), China 77/H7
Zhanjiang, China 54/N7
Zhanyi, China 77/F6
Zhaodong, China 77/K2
Zhaojue, China 77/F6
Zhaoqing, China 77/H7
Zhaosu, China 77/B3
Zhaotong (Chaotung), China 77/F6
Zhari Namco (lake), China 77/C5
Zhashui, China 77/G5
Zhatay, U.S.S.R. 48/O3
Zhaxi Co (lake), China 77/C5
Zhdanov, U.S.S.R. 7/H4
Zhdanov, U.S.S.R. 48/D5
Zhdanov, U.S.S.R. 52/E5
Zhejiang (Chekiang) (prov.), China 77/K6
Zhelaniye (cape), U.S.S.R. 48/H2
Zheleznodorozhnyy, U.S.S.R. 52/H2
Zheleznogorsk, U.S.S.R. 52/E4
Zheleznogorsk-Ilimskiy, U.S.S.R. 48/L4
Zhenba, China 77/G5
Zheng'an, China 77/G6
Zhenglan, China 77/J3
Zhengzhou (Chengchow), China 77/H5
Zhengzhou, China 54/N6
Zhenjiang (Chinkiang), China 77/J5
Zhenxiong, China 77/F6
Zhenyuan, China 77/G6
Zhido, China 77/E5
Zhigalovo, U.S.S.R. 48/L4
Zhigansk, U.S.S.R. 4/C3
Zhigansk, U.S.S.R. 54/N3
Zhigansk, U.S.S.R. 48/N3
Zhigulevsk, U.S.S.R. 52/G4
Zhi Qu (Tongtian He) (riv.), China 77/E5
Zhirnovsk, U.S.S.R. 52/G4
Zhitomir, U.S.S.R. 7/G3
Zhitomir, U.S.S.R. 48/C4
Zhitomir, U.S.S.R. 52/C4
Zhlobin, U.S.S.R. 52/D4
Zhmerinka, U.S.S.R. 52/C5
Zhob (riv.), Pakistan 59/J3
Zhob (riv.), Pakistan 68/B2
Zhodino, U.S.S.R. 52/C4
Zhongba, China 77/B6
Zhongdian, China 77/F6
Zhongning, China 77/G4
Zhongshan (Chungshan), China 77/H7
Zhongwei, China 77/F4
Zhoushan (arch.), China 77/K5
Zhovtnevoye, U.S.S.R. 52/D5
Zhuanghe, China 77/K4
Zhucheng, China 77/J4
Zhukovka, U.S.S.R. 52/D4
Zhumadian (Chumatien), China 77/H5
Zhushan, China 77/G5
Zhuzhou (Chuchow), China 77/H6
Zhuzhou, China 54/N7
Zia Pueblo, N. Mex. (†87053) 274/C3
Žiar nad Hronom, Czech. 41/E2
Zibak, Afghanistan 59/K2
Zibak, Afghanistan 68/C1
Zibo (Tzepo), China 77/J4
Zibo, China 54/N6
Zichang, China 77/G4
Židlochovice, Czech. 41/D2
Ziebach (co.), S. Dak. 298/F4
Ziębice, Poland 47/C3
Ziel (mt.), North. Terr. 88/E4
Ziel (mt.), North. Terr. 93/C7
Zielona Góra (prov.), Poland 47/B3
Zielona Góra, Poland 47/B3
Zierikzee, Netherlands 27/D5
Zifta, Egypt 111/J3
Zigong (Tzekung), China 77/F6
Ziguei, Chad 111/C5
Zigui, China 77/H5
Ziguinchor, Senegal 106/A6
Ziguinchor, Senegal 102/A3
Zihuatanejo, Mexico 150/J8
Zikhron Ya'aqov, Israel 65/B2
Zilbir (riv.), Iran 66/D1
Zile, Turkey 59/C1
Zile, Turkey 63/G2
Zilfi, Saudi Arabia 59/E4
Žilina, Czech. 41/E2
Zillah, Wash. (98953) 310/E4
Zillis-Reischen, Switzerland 39/H3
Zilupe, U.S.S.R. 53/D2
Zilwaukee, Mich. (†48601) 250/F5
Zim, Minn. (55799) 255/F3
Zima, U.S.S.R. 48/L4
Zimatlán de Álvarez, Mexico 150/L8
Zimbabwe 2/L6
Zimbabwe 102/E6
ZIMBABWE 118/D4
Zimbabwe Nat'l Park, Zimbabwe 118/E4
Zimmerdale, Kansas (†67117) 232/E3
Zimmerman, La. (†71409) 238/E4
Zimmerman, Minn. (55398) 255/E5
Zimnicea, Romania 45/G4
Zimnitsa, Bulgaria 45/H4
Zinal, Switzerland 39/E4
Zinc, Ark. (†72601) 202/E1
Zinder, Niger 106/F6
Zinder, Niger 102/C3
Zingren, China 77/G6
Zingst, E. Germany 22/E1
Zinhui, China 77/H7
Zinjibar, P.D.R. Yemen 59/E7
Zinnik (Soignies), Belgium 27/D7
Zion, Ark. (72589) 202/G1
Zion, Ill. (60099) 222/F1
Zion, Md. (†21901) 245/P2
Zion, Mo. (†63645) 261/M8
Zion, N.J. (†08853) 273/D3
Zion, S.C. (†29574) 296/J3
Zion Hill, St. Chris.-Nevis 161/D11
Zion National Park, Utah (84767) 304/B6
Zion Nat'l Park, Utah 304/A6
Zionsville, Ind. (46077) 227/E5
Zionville, N.C. (28698) 281/F2
Zipaquirá, Colombia 126/D5
Zippori, Israel 65/C2
Zirc, Hungary 41/D3
Žirje (isl.), Yugoslavia 45/B4
Zirkel (mt.), Colo. 208/F1
Zirko (isl.), U.A.E. 59/F5
Zirl, Austria 41/A3
Zirndorf, W. Germany 22/D4
Zistersdorf, Austria 41/D2
Zitácuaro, Mexico 150/J7
Zittau, E. Germany 22/F3
Zitterwald (plat.), Belgium 27/J8
Zıvarık, Turkey 63/E3
Ziwa Magharibi (West Lake) (reg.), Tanzania 115/F4
Ziyang, China 77/F5
Ziz, Wadi (dry riv.), Morocco 106/D2
Zizers, Switzerland 39/J3
Zlaté Moravce, Czech. 41/E2
Zlatograd, Bulgaria 45/G5
Zlatoust, U.S.S.R. 54/G4
Zlatoust, U.S.S.R. 48/F4
Zlín (Gottwaldov), Czech. 41/D2
Zliten, Libya 111/C1
Złocieniec, Poland 47/C2
Złotoryja, Poland 47/C3
Złotów, Poland 47/C2
Žlutice, Czech. 41/B1
Znamenka, U.S.S.R. 52/D5
Żnin, Poland 47/C2
Znojmo, Czech. 41/C2
Zoar (lake), Conn. 210/C3
Zoar, Ohio (44697) 284/H4
Zoarville, Ohio (44698) 284/H4
Zofingen, Switzerland 39/F2
Zogang, China 77/E5
Zohreh (riv.), Iran 66/F5
Zoigê, China 77/F5
Zolfo Springs, Fla. (33890) 212/E4
Zollikofen, Switzerland 39/E3
Zollikon, Switzerland 39/G2
Zolotonosha, U.S.S.R. 52/D5
Zomba, Malawi 115/G7
Zomba, Malawi 102/F6
Zonderend (riv.), S. Africa 118/G6
Zongo, Bolivia 136/B5
Zongo, Zaire 115/C3
Zongolica, Mexico 150/P2
Zonguldak (prov.), Turkey 63/D2
Zonguldak, Turkey 63/D2
Zonguldak, Turkey 59/B1
Zonhoven, Belgium 27/G6
Zoo Baba (well), Niger 106/G5
Zook, Kansas (†67550) 232/C3
Zorbatiya, Iraq 66/D4
Zorita, Spain 33/D3
Zorritos, Peru 128/B4
Zortman, Mont. (59546) 262/H3
Zottegem, Belgium 27/D7
Zouar, Chad 111/C3
Zouîrât, Mauritania 106/B4
Zoutkamp, Netherlands 27/J2
Zrenjanin, Yugoslavia 45/E3
Zuata, Venezuela 124/F3
Zuata (riv.), Venezuela 124/F3
Zububa, West Bank 65/C2
Zucchero (mt.), Switzerland 39/G4
Zudáñez, Bolivia 136/C6
Zug (canton), Switzerland 39/G2
Zug, Switzerland 39/G2
Zugdidi, U.S.S.R. 52/F6
Zugersee (lake), Switzerland 39/F2
Zugspitze (mt.), Austria 41/A3
Zugspitze (mt.), W. Germany 22/D5
Zuidelijke IJsselmeerpolders (prov.), Netherlands 27/H4
Zuienkerke, Belgium 27/C6
Zuila, Libya 111/C2
Zújar, Spain 33/E4
Zújar (res.), Spain 33/D3
Zula, Ethiopia 111/G4
Zula, Ethiopia 59/C6
Zula, Ky. (†42603) 237/M7
Zulia (state), Venezuela 124/B2
Zulia (riv.), Venezuela 124/B3
Zülpich, W. Germany 22/B3
Zulu, Ind. (†46773) 227/H2
Zulueta, Cuba 158/E2
Zululand (reg.), S. Africa 118/E5
Zumba, Ecuador 128/C5
Zumbo, Mozambique 118/E3
Zumbro (riv.), Minn. 255/F6
Zumbro Falls, Minn. (55991) 255/F6
Zumbrota, Minn. (55992) 255/F6
Zumpango del Río, Mexico 150/J8
Zumpango de Ocampo, Mexico 150/L1
Zundert, Netherlands 27/F6
Zungeru, Nigeria 106/F7
Zunhua, China 77/J3
Zuni (riv.), Ariz. 198/F4
Zuni, N. Mex. (87327) 274/A3
Zuni (mts.), N. Mex. 274/A3
Zuni (riv.), N. Mex. 274/A3
Zuni, Va. (23898) 307/P7
Zuni Ind. Res., N. Mex. 274/A3
Zunyi (Tsunyi), China 77/G6
Zunyi, China 54/M7
Zuoz, Switzerland 39/J3
Zuqar (isl.), Yemen Arab Rep. 59/D7
Zurabad, Iran 66/M3
Zurich, Kansas (67676) 232/C2
Zurich, Mont. (59547) 262/G2
Zurich, Ontario 177/C4
Zürich (canton), Switzerland 39/G2
Zürich, Switzerland 39/G2
Zürich, Switzerland 7/E4
Zürichsee (lake), Switzerland 39/G2
Zuromin, Poland 47/E2
Zurzach, Switzerland 39/F1
Zushi, Japan 81/O3
Zutphen, Netherlands 27/J4
Zuweiza, Jordan 65/D4
Zuyevka, U.S.S.R. 52/H3
Zvolen, Czech. 41/E2
Zvornik, Yugoslavia 45/D3
Zwai (lake), Ethiopia 111/G6
Zwanenburg, Netherlands 27/A4
Zwara, Libya 111/B1
Zwart (riv.), S. Africa 118/G7
Zwartsluis, Netherlands 27/H3
Zweibrücken, W. Germany 22/B4
Zweisimmen, Switzerland 39/D3
Zwelitsha, S. Africa 118/D6
Zwenkau, E. Germany 22/E3
Zwettl-Niederösterreich, Austria 41/C2
Zwickau, E. Germany 22/E3
Zwijndrecht, Netherlands 27/E5
Zwingle, Iowa (52079) 229/M4
Zwischenahn, W. Germany 22/B2
Zwoleń, Poland 47/E3
Zwolle, La. (71486) 238/C3
Zwolle, Netherlands 27/J3
Zychlin, Poland 47/D2
Żyrardów, Poland 47/E2
Zyryanka, U.S.S.R. 4/C2
Zyryanka, U.S.S.R. 54/S3
Zyryanka, U.S.S.R. 48/Q3
Zyryanovsk, U.S.S.R. 48/J5
Żywiec, Poland 47/D4
Zzyzx, Calif. (†92309) 204/J8

GEOGRAPHICAL TERMS

A. = Arabic Burm. = Burmese Camb. = Cambodian Ch. = Chinese Czech. = Czechoslovakian Dan. = Danish Du. = Dutch Finn. = Finnish Fr. = French Ger. = German Ice. = Icelandic It. = Italian Jap. = Japanese Mong. = Mongol Nor. = Norwegian Per. = Persian Port. = Portuguese Russ. = Russian Sp. = Spanish Sw. = Swedish Turk. = Turkish

Å	Nor., Sw.	Stream
Aas	Dan., Nor.	Hills
Abajo	Sp.	Lower
Ada, Adasi	Turk.	Island
Altipiano	It.	Plateau
Altiplano	Sp.	Plateau
Alv, Alf, Elf	Sw.	River
Arrecife	Sp.	Reef
Asa	Nor., Sw.	Hill
Asaga	Turk.	Lower
Austral	Sp.	Southern
Baai	Du.	Bay
Bab	Arabic	Gate or Strait
Bahia	Sp.	Bay
Bahr	Arabic	Marsh, Lake, Sea, River
Baia	Port.	Bay
Baie	Fr.	Bay, Gulf
Baizo	Port.	Low
Bakke	Dan.	Hill
Bana	Jap.	Cape
Bañados	Sp.	Marshes
Band	Per.	Mt. Range
Bandao	Ch.	Peninsula
Bandar	Per.	Harbor
Barra	Sp.	Reef
Bel	Turk.	Pass
Belt	Ger.	Strait
Ben	Gaelic	Mountain
Bera	Du.	Mountain
Berg	Ger., Du.	Mountain
Bir	Arabic	Well
Boca	Sp.	Gulf, Inlet
Boğhaz	Turk.	Strait
Bolshoi, Bolshaya	Russ.	Big
Bolson	Sp.	Depression
Bong	Korean	Mountain
Boreal	Sp.	Northern
Breen	Nor.	Glacier
Bro	Dan., Nor., Sw.	Bridge
Bucht	Ger.	Bay
Bugt	Dan.	Bay
Bukhta	Russ.	Bay
Bukit	Malay	Hill, Mountain
Bukt	Nor., Sw.	Bay, Gulf
Burnu, Burun	Turk.	Cape, Point
By	Dan., Nor., Sw.	Town
Cabo	Port., Sp.	Cape
Campos	Port.	Plains
Canal	Port., Sp.	Channel
Cap, Capo	Fr., It.	Cape
Cataratas	Sp.	Falls
Catena	It.	Mt. Range
Catingas	Port.	Open Woodlands
Cayos	Sp.	Islands
Central, Centrale	Fr., It.	Middle
Cerrito, Cerro	Sp.	Hill
Cerros	Sp.	Hills, Mountains
Chai	Turk.	River
Chott	Arabic	Salt Lake
Ciénaga	Sp.	Swamp
Ciudad	Sp.	City
Col	Fr.	Pass
Cordillera	Sp.	Mt. Range, Mts.
Côte	Fr.	Coast
Csatoria	Magyar	Canal
Cuchilla	Sp.	Mt. Range
Curiche	Sp.	Swamp
Dağ, Daği	Turk.	Mountain, Peak
Dağlari	Turk.	Mt. Range
Dal	Nor., Sw.	Valley
Dar	Arabic	Land
Dar'ya	Russ.	River
Daryacheh	Per.	Marshy Lake
Dasht	Per.	Desert, Plain
Deniz, Denizi	Turk.	Sea, Lake
Desierto	Sp.	Desert
Détroit	Fr.	Strait
Djeziret	Arabic, Turk.	Island
Do	Korean	Island
Doi	Thai	Mountain
Eiland	Du.	Island
Elv	Dan., Nor.	River
Embalse	Sp.	Reservoir
Emi	Berber	Mountain
Erg	Arabic	Dune, Desert
Eski	Turk.	Old
Est, Este	Fr., Port., Sp.	East
Estero	Sp.	Estuary, Creek
Estrecho, Estreito	Sp., Port.	Strait
Etang	Fr.	Pond, Lagoon, Lake
Feng	Ch.	Mountain
Fiume	It.	River
Fjäll	Sw.	Mountain
Fjeld, Fjell	Nor.	Hills, Mountain
Fjord	Dan., Nor., Sw.	Fiord
Fleuve	Fr.	River
Fljót	Ice.	Stream
Fluss	Ger.	River
Fors	Sw.	Waterfall
Fos, Foss	Dan., Nor.	Waterfall
Gamla	Nor.	Old
Gamle	Dan.	Old
Gata	Jap.	Lake
Gawa	Jap.	River
Gebel	Arabic	Mountain
Gebergte	Du.	Mt. Range
Gebirge	Ger.	Mt. Range
Gobi	Mongol	Desert
Goe	Jap.	Pass
Gol	Mongol, Turk.	Lake, Stream
Golf	Ger., Du.	Gulf
Golfe	Fr.	Gulf
Golfo	Sp., It., Port.	Gulf
Gölü	Turk.	Lake
Gora	Russ.	Mountain
Grand, Grande	Fr., Sp.	Big
Groot	Du.	Big
Gross	Ger.	Big
Grosso	It., Port.	Big
Guba	Russ.	Bay, Gulf
Gunto	Jap.	Archipelago
Gunung	Malay	Mountain
Hai	Ch.	Sea
Haixia	Ch.	Strait
Halbinsel	Ger.	Peninsula
Hamáda, Hammada	Arabic	Rocky Plateau
Hamn	Sw.	Harbor
Hamún	Per.	Marsh
Hanto	Jap.	Peninsula
Has, Hassi	Arabic	Well
Hav	Dan., Nor., Sw.	Sea, Ocean
Havet	Nor.	Bay
Havn	Dan., Nor.	Harbor
Havre	Fr.	Harbor
He	Ch.	River, Stream
Higashi, Higasi	Jap.	East
Hochebene	Ger.	Plateau
Hoek	Du.	Cape
Hoku	Jap.	North
Holm	Dan., Nor., Sw.	Island
Hory	Czech.	Mountains
Hoved	Dan., Nor.	Cape, Promontory
Hu	Ch.	Lake
Huang	Ch.	Yellow
Huk	Dan., Nor., Sw.	Point
Hus, Huus	Dan., Nor., Sw.	House
Idehan	Arabic	Desert
Ile	Fr.	Island
Ilet	Fr.	Islet
Ilot	Fr.	Islet
Indre	Dan., Nor.	Inner
Inferieur, Inferiore	Fr., It.	Lower
Inner, Inre	Sw.	Inner
Insel	Ger.	Island
Irmak	Turk.	River
Isla	Sp.	Island
Isola	It.	Island
Jabal, Jebel	Arabic	Mountains
Järvi	Finn.	Lake
Jaure	Sw.	Lake
Jiang	Ch.	River, Stream
Jima	Jap.	Island
Joki	Finn.	River
Kaap	Du.	Cape
Kabir, Kebir	Arabic	Big
Kai	Jap.	Sea
Kaikyo	Jap.	Strait
Kami	Turk.	Upper
Kanaal	Du.	Canal
Kanal	Russ., Ger.	Canal, Channel
Kao	Thai	Mountain
Kap, Kapp	Nor., Sw., Ice.	Cape
Kaupunki	Finn.	Town
Kawa	Jap.	River
Khao	Thai	Mountain
Khrebet	Russ.	Mt. Range
Kita	Jap.	North
Klein	Du., Ger.	Small
Klint	Dan.	Promontory
Kō	Jap.	Lake
Ko	Thai	Island
Koh	Camb., Khmer	Island
Kop	Du.	Peak, Head
Köping	Sw.	Market, Borough
Körfez, Körfezi	Turk.	Gulf
Kosa	Russ.	Spit
Kosui	Jap.	Lake
Kraal	Du.	Native Village
Kuchuk	Turk.	Small
Kuh, Kuhha	Per.	Mt. Range, Mts.
Kul	Sinkiang Turki	Lake
Kum	Turk.	Desert
Kuro	Jap.	Black
Laag	Du.	Low
Lac	Fr.	Lake
Lago	Port., Sp., It.	Lake
Lagoa	Port.	Lagoon
Laguna	Sp.	Lagoon
Lagune	Fr.	Lagoon
Lahti	Finn.	Bay, Bight
Län	Sw.	County
Liedao	Ch.	Islands, Archipelago
Lilla	Sw.	Small
Lille	Dan., Nor.	Small
Ling	Ch.	Mountain
Llanos	Sp.	Plains
Mae Nam	Thai	River
Mali, Malaya	Russ.	Small
Man	Korean	Bay
Mar	Sp., Port.	Sea
Mare	It.	Sea
Medio	Sp.	Middle
Meer	Du.	Lake
Meer	Ger.	Sea
Mer	Fr.	Sea
Meridionale	It.	Southern
Meseta	Sp.	Plateau
Middelst, Midden	Du.	Middle
Minami	Jap.	Southern
Mis	Russ.	Cape
Misaki	Jap.	Cape
Mittel	Ger.	Middle
Mont	Fr.	Mountain
Montagne	Fr.	Mountain
Montaña	Sp.	Mountains
Monte	Sp., It., Port.	Mountain
More	Russ.	Sea
Mörön	Mong.	Stream
Morro	Port., Sp.	Mountain, Promontory
Morue	Fr.	Hill
Moyen	Fr.	Middle
Muang	Siamese	Town
Mui	Vietnamese	Cape, Point
Mys	Russ.	Cape
Nada	Jap.	Sea
Naka	Jap.	Middle
Nam	Burm., Lao	River
Namakzar	Per.	Salt Waste
Nan	Jap.	South
Nes	Nor.	Cape, Point
Nevado	Sp.	Snow-covered Peak
Nieder	Ger.	Lower
Nishi, Nisi	Jap.	West
Nizhni, Nizhnyaya	Russ.	Lower
Njarga	Finn.	Peninsula, Promontory
Nong	Thai	Lake
Noord	Du.	North
Nord	Fr., Ger.	North
Norte	Sp., It., Port.	North
Nos	Russ.	Cape
Novi, Novaya	Russ.	New
Nur, Nuur	Ch., Mong.	Lake
Nuruu	Mong.	Mountains
Nusa	Malay	Island
Ny, Nya	Nor., Sw.	New
O	Jap.	Big
Ö	Nor., Sw.	Island
Ober	Ger.	Upper
Occidental, Occidentale	Sp., It.	Western
Odde	Dan.	Point
Oeste	Port.	West
Ooster	Du.	Eastern
Opper, Over	Du.	Upper
Oriental	Sp., Fr.	Eastern
Orientale	It.	Eastern
Orta	Turk.	Middle
Ost	Ger.	East
Ostrov	Russ.	Island
Ouest	Fr.	West
öy	Nor.	Island
Ozero	Russ.	Lake
Pampa	Sp.	Plain
Pas	Fr.	Channel, Strait
Paso	Sp.	Pass
Passo	It., Port.	Pass
Peña	Sp.	Rock, Mountain
Pendi	Ch.	Basin
Penisola	It.	Peninsula
Pequeño	Sp.	Small
Pereval	Russ.	Pass
Peski	Russ.	Desert
Petit, Petite	Fr.	Small
Phu	Lao, Annamese	Mtn.
Pic	Fr.	Mountain
Piccolo	It.	Small
Pico	Port., Sp.	Mountain, Peak
Pik	Russ.	Mountain, Peak
Piton	Fr.	Mountain, Peak
Planalto	Port.	Plateau
Plato	Russ.	Plateau
Pointe	Fr.	Point
Poluostrov	Russ.	Peninsula
Ponta	Port.	Point
Presa	Sp.	Reservoir
Presqu'île	Fr.	Peninsula
Proliv	Russ.	Strait
Pulou, Pulo	Malay	Island
Punt	Du.	Point
Punta	Sp., It., Port.	Point
Qiryat	Hebrew	City, Settlement
Qum	Turk.	Desert
Qundao	Ch.	Islands
Rada	Sp.	Inlet
Rade	Fr.	Bay, Inlet
Ras	Arabic	Cape
Reka	Russ.	River
Retto	Jap.	Archipelago
Ria	Sp.	Estuary
Río	Sp.	River
Rivier, Rivière	Du., Fr.	River
Rud	Per.	River
Sai	Jap.	West
Saki	Jap.	Cape
Salar, Salina	Sp.	Salt Deposit
Salto	Sp., Port.	Falls
San	Jap., Korean	Hill
Sanmaek	Korean	Mt. Range
Schiereiland	Du.	Peninsula
Se	Camb., Khmer	River
See	Ger.	Sea, Lake
Selvas	Sp., Port.	Woods, Forest
Seno	Sp.	Bay, Gulf
Serra	Port.	Mts.
Serranía	Sp.	Mts.
Seto	Jap.	Strait
Settentrionale	It.	Northern
Severni, Severnaya	Russ.	North
Shamo	Ch.	Desert
Shan	Ch., Jap.	Hill, Mts.
Shankou	Ch.	Pass
Shatt	Arabic	River
Shima	Jap.	Island
Shimo	Jap.	Lower
Shin	Jap.	Land
Shiro	Jap.	White
Shoto	Jap.	Islands
Si	Ch.	West
Sierra	Sp.	Mt. Range, Mts.
Sjö	Nor., Sw.	Lake, Sea
Sok, Suk, Souk	Arabic	Market
Song	Annamese	River
Sopka	Russ.	Volcano
Spitze	Ger.	Mt. Peak
Sredni, Srednyaya	Russ.	Middle
Stad	Dan., Nor., Sw.	City
Stari, Staraya	Russ.	Old
Step	Russ.	Treeless Plain
Straat	Du.	Strait
Strasse	Ger.	Strait
Stretto	It.	Strait
Ström	Dan., Nor., Sw.	Sound
Stung	Camb., Khmer	River
Su	Turk.	River
Sud, Süd	Sp., Fr., Ger.	South
Suido	Jap.	Strait, Channel
Sul	Port.	South
Sund	Dan., Nor., Sw.	Sound
Sungei	Malay	River
Supérieur	Fr.	Upper
Superior, Superiore	Sp., It.	Upper
Sur	Sp.	South
Suyu	Turk.	River
Ta	Ch.	Big
Tafelland	Du.	Plateau
Tagh	Turk.	Mt. Range
Take	Jap.	Peak, Ridge
Takht	Arabic	Lower
Tal	Ger.	Valley
Tanjung	Malay	Cape, Point
Tell	Arabic	Hill
Thale	Thai	Sea, Lake
Tind	Nor.	Peak
Tō	Jap.	East
To	Jap.	Island
Toge	Jap.	Pass
Trask	Finn.	Lake
Tugh	Somali	Dry River
Ujung	Malay	Point
Umi	Jap.	Bay
Unter	Ger.	Lower
Ura	Jap.	Inlet
Uul	Mong.	Mountain
Val	Fr.	Valley
Vatn	Nor.	Lake
Vecchio	It.	Old
Veld	Du.	Plain, Field
Velho	Port.	Old
Verkhni	Russ.	Upper
Vesi	Finn.	Lake
Viejo	Sp.	Old
Vik	Nor., Sw.	Bay
Vishni, Vishnyaya	Russ.	High
Vodokhranilishche	Russ.	Reservoir
Volcán	Sp.	Volcano
Vostochni, Vostochnaya	Russ.	East, Eastern
Wadi	Arabic	Dry River
Wald	Ger.	Forest
Wan	Jap.	Bay
Westersch	Du.	Western
Wüste	Ger.	Desert
Yama	Jap.	Mountain
Yug, Yuzhni, Yuzhnaya	Russ.	South, Southern
Zaki	Jap.	Cape
Zaliv	Russ.	Bay, Gulf
Zangbo	Tibetan	River, Stream
Zapadni, Zapadnaya	Russ.	Western
Zee	Du.	Sea
Zemlya	Russ.	Land
Zizhiqu	Ch.	Autonomous Region
Zuid	Du.	South

MAP PROJECTIONS

by Erwin Raisz

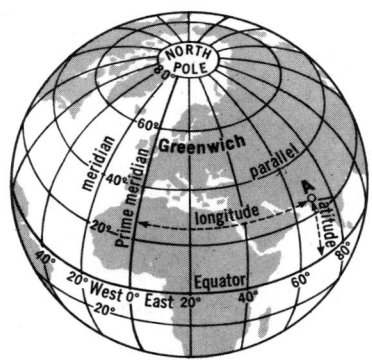

Our earth is rotating around its *axis* once a day. The two end points of its axis are the *poles;* the line circling the earth midway between the poles is the *equator.* The arc from either of the poles to the equator is divided into 90 *degrees.* The distance, expressed in degrees, from the equator to any point is its *latitude* and circles of equal latitude are the *parallels.* On maps it is customary to show parallels of evenly-spaced degrees such as every fifth or every tenth.

The equator is divided into 360 degrees. Lines circling from pole to pole through the degree points on the equator are called *meridians.* They are all equal in length but by international agreement the meridian passing through the Greenwich Observatory in London has been chosen as *prime meridian.* The distance, expressed in degrees, from the prime meridian to any point is its *longitude.* While meridians are all equal in length, parallels become shorter and shorter as they approach the poles. Whereas one degree of latitude represents everywhere approximately 69 miles, one degree of longitude varies from 69 miles at the equator to nothing at the poles.

Each degree is divided into 60 minutes and each minute into 60 seconds. One minute of latitude equals a nautical mile.

The map is flat but the earth is nearly spherical. Neither a rubber ball nor any part of a rubber ball may be flattened without stretching or tearing unless the part is very small. To present the curved surface of the earth on a flat map is not difficult as long as the areas under consideration are small, but the mapping of countries, continents, or the whole earth requires some kind of *projection.* Any regular set of parallels and meridians upon which a map can be drawn makes a map projection. Many systems are used.

In any projection only the parallels or the meridians or some other set of lines can be *true* (the same length as on the globe of corresponding scale); all other lines are too long or too short. Only on a globe is it possible to have both the parallels and the meridians true. The scale given on a flat map cannot be true everywhere. The construction of the various projections begins usually with laying out the parallels or meridians which have true lengths.

Rectangular Projection

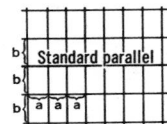

RECTANGULAR PROJECTION — This is a set of evenly-placed meridians and horizontal parallels. The central or *standard parallel* and all meridians are true. All other parallels are either too long or too short. The projection is used for simple maps of small areas, as city plans, etc.

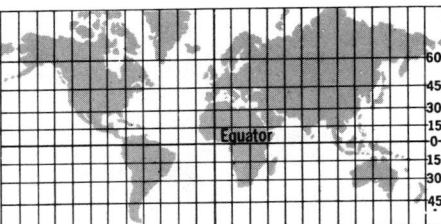

Mercator Projection

MERCATOR PROJECTION — In this projection the meridians are evenly-spaced vertical lines. The parallels are horizontal, spaced so that their length has the same relation to the meridians as on a globe. As the meridians converge at higher latitudes on the globe, while on the map they do not, the parallels have to be drawn also farther and farther apart to maintain the correct relationship. When every very small area has the same shape as on a globe we call the projection *conformal.* The most interesting quality of this projection is that all *compass directions* appear as straight lines. For this reason it is generally used for marine charts. It is also frequently used for world maps in spite of the fact that the high latitudes are very much exaggerated in size. Only the equator is true to scale; all other parallels and meridians are too long. The Mercator projection did *not* derive from projecting a globe upon a cylinder.

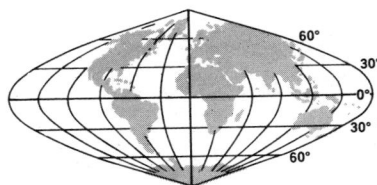

Sinusoidal Projection

SINUSOIDAL PROJECTION — The parallels are truly-spaced horizontal lines. They are divided truly and the connecting curves make the meridians. It does not make a good world map because the outer regions are distorted, but the

central portion is good and this part is often used for maps of Africa and South America. Every part of the map has the same area as the corresponding area on the globe. It is an *equal-area* projection.

MOLLWEIDE PROJECTION — The meridians are equally-spaced ellipses; the parallels are horizontal lines spaced so that every belt of latitude should have the same area as on a globe. This projection is popular for world maps, especially in European atlases.

GOODE'S INTERRUPTED PROJECTIONS—Only the good central part of the Mollweide or sinusoidal (or both) projection is used and the oceans are cut. This makes an equal-area map with little distortion of shape. It is commonly used for world maps.

ECKERT PROJECTIONS — These are similar to the sinusoidal or the Mollweide projections, but the poles are shown as lines half the length of the equator. There are several variants; the meridians are either sine curves or ellipses; the parallels are horizontal and spaced either evenly or so as to make the projection equal area. Their use for world maps is increasing. The figure shows the elliptical equal-area variant.

CONIC PROJECTION — The original idea of the conic projection is that of capping the globe by a cone upon which both the parallels and meridians are projected from the center of the globe. The cone is then cut open and laid flat. A cone can be made tangent to any chosen *standard parallel*.

The actually-used conic projection is a modification of this idea. The radius of the standard parallel is obtained as above. The meridians are straight radiating lines spaced truly on the standard parallel. The parallels are concentric circles spaced at true distances. All parallels except the standard are too long. The projection is used for maps of countries in middle latitudes, as it presents good shapes with small scale error.

There are several variants: The use of *two standard parallels*, one near the top, the other near the bottom of the map, reduces the scale error. In the *Albers projection* the parallels are spaced unevenly, to make the projection equal-area. This is a good projection for the United States. In the *Lambert conformal conic projection* the parallels are spaced so that any small quadrangle of the grid should have the same shape as on the globe. This is the best projection for air-navigation charts as it has relatively straight azimuths.

An *azimuth* is a great-circle direction reckoned clockwise from north. A *great-circle direction* points to a place along the shortest line on the earth's surface. This is not the same as compass direction. The center of a great circle is the center of the globe.

BONNE PROJECTION — The parallels are laid out exactly as in the conic projection. All parallels are divided truly and the connecting curves make the meridians. It is an equal-area projection. It is used for maps of the northern continents, as Asia, Europe, and North America.

POLYCONIC PROJECTION — The central meridian is divided truly. The parallels are non-concentric circles, the radii of which are obtained by drawing tangents to the globe as though the globe were covered by several cones rather than by only one. Each parallel is divided truly and the connecting curves make the meridians. All meridians except the central one are too long. This projection is used for large-scale topographic sheets — less often for countries or continents.

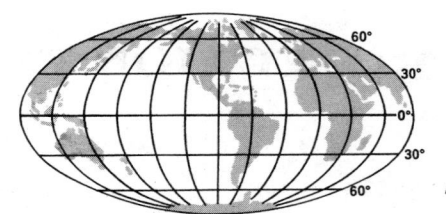

Mollweide Projection

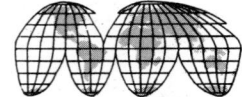

Goode's Interrupted Projection

Eckert Projection

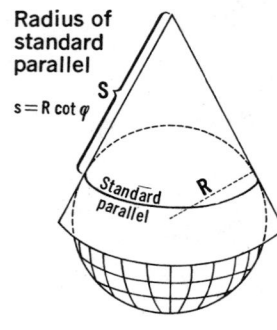

Radius of standard parallel

$s = R \cot \varphi$

Conic Projection

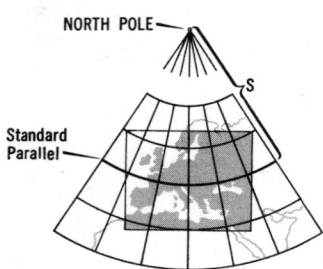

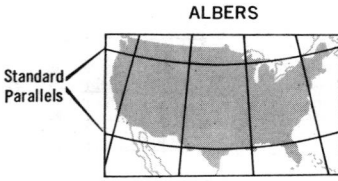

Albers Projection

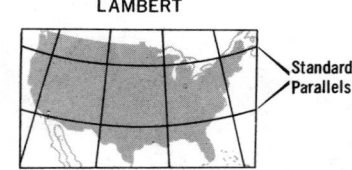

Lambert Conformal Conic Projection

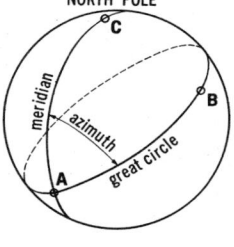

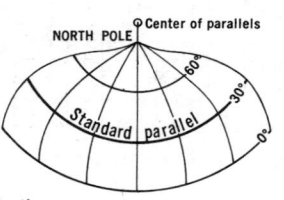

Bonne Projection

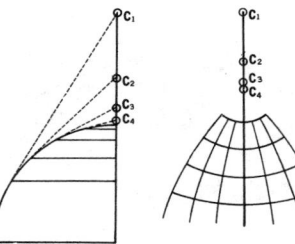

Polyconic Projection

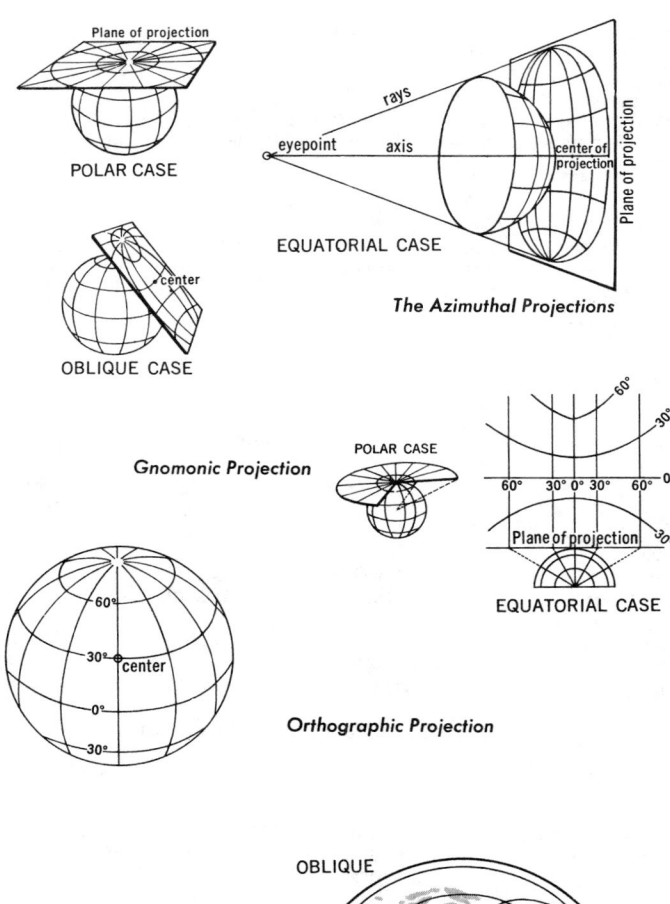

POLAR CASE

Plane of projection

EQUATORIAL CASE

eyepoint · rays · axis · center of projection · Plane of projection

OBLIQUE CASE · center

The Azimuthal Projections

Gnomonic Projection

POLAR CASE

EQUATORIAL CASE

Plane of projection

Orthographic Projection

center

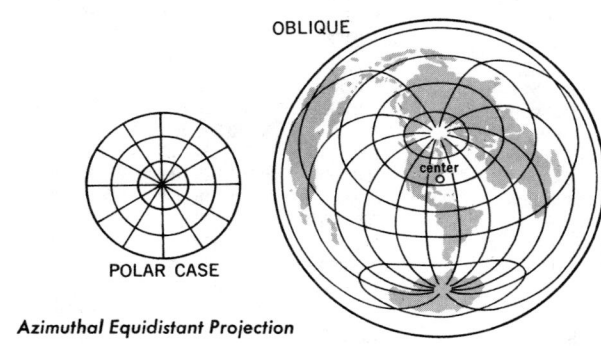

OBLIQUE

POLAR CASE

center

Azimuthal Equidistant Projection

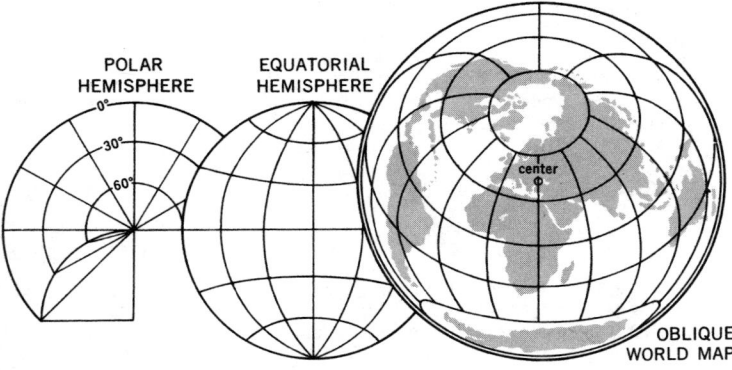

POLAR HEMISPHERE · EQUATORIAL HEMISPHERE

center

OBLIQUE WORLD MAP

Lambert Azimuthal Equal-Area Projection

THE AZIMUTHAL PROJECTIONS — In this group a part of the globe is projected from an eyepoint onto a plane. The eyepoint can be at different distances, making different projections. The plane of projection can be tangent at the equator, at a pole, or at any other point on which we want to focus attention. The most important quality of all azimuthal projections is that they show every point at its true direction (azimuth) from the center point, and all points equally distant from the center point will be equally distant on the map also.

GNOMONIC PROJECTION — This projection has the eyepoint at the center of the globe Only the central part is good; the outer regions are badly distorted. Yet the projection has one important quality, all great circles being shown as straight lines. For this reason it is used for laying out the routes for long range flying or trans-oceanic navigation.

ORTHOGRAPHIC PROJECTION — This projection has the eyepoint at infinite distance and the projecting rays are parallel. The polar or equatorial varieties are rare but the oblique case became very popular on account of its visual quality. It looks like a picture of a globe. Although the distortion on the peripheries is extreme, we see it correctly because the eye perceives it not as a map but as a picture of a three-dimensional globe. Obviously only a hemisphere (half globe) can be shown.

Some azimuthal projections do not derive from the actual process of projecting from an eyepoint, but are arrived at by other means:

AZIMUTHAL EQUIDISTANT PROJECTION — This is the only projection in which every point is shown both at true great-circle direction and at true distance from the center point, but all other directions and distances are distorted. The principle of the projection can best be understood from the polar case. Most polar maps are in this projection. The oblique case is used for radio direction finding, for earthquake research, and in long-distance flying. A separate map has to be constructed for each central point selected.

LAMBERT AZIMUTHAL EQUAL-AREA PROJECTION—The construction of this projection can best be understood from the polar case. All three cases are widely used. It makes a good polar map and it is often extended to include the southern continents. It is the most common projection used for maps of the Eastern and Western Hemispheres, and it is a good projection for continents as it shows correct areas with relatively little distortion of shape. Most of the continent maps in this atlas are in this projection.

IN THIS ATLAS, on almost all maps, parallels and meridians have been marked because they are useful for the following:

(a) They show the north-south and east-west directions which appear on many maps at oblique angles especially near the margins.

(b) With the help of parallels and meridians every place can be exactly located; for instance, New York City is at 41° N and 74° W on any map.

(c) They help to measure distances even in the distorted parts of the map. The scale given on each map is true only along certain lines which are specified in the foregoing discussion for each projection. One degree of latitude equals nearly 69 statute miles or 60 nautical miles. The length of one degree of longitude varies (1° long. = 1° lat. × cos lat.).

WORLD STATISTICAL TABLES

Elements of the Solar System

	Mean Distance from Sun:		Period of Revolution around Sun	Period of Rotation on Axis	Equatorial Diameter:		Surface Gravity (Earth = 1)	Mass (Earth = 1)	Mean Density (Water = 1)	Number of Satellites
	in Miles	in Kilometers			in Miles	in Kilometers				
MERCURY	35,990,000	57,900,000	87.97 days	59 days	3,032	4,880	0.38	0.055	5.5	0
VENUS	67,240,000	108,200,000	224.70 days	243 days†	7,523	12,106	0.90	0.815	5.25	0
EARTH	93,000,000	149,700,000	365.26 days	23h 56m	7,926	12,755	1.00	1.00	5.5	1
MARS	141,730,000	228,100,000	687.00 days	24h 37m	4,220	6,790	0.38	0.107	4.0	2
JUPITER	483,880,000	778,700,000	11.86 years	9h 50m	88,750	142,800	2.87	317.9	1.3	16
SATURN	887,130,000	1,427,700,000	29.46 years	10h 14m	74,580	120,020	1.32	95.2	0.7	17
URANUS	1,783,700,000	2,870,500,000	84.01 years	10h 49m†	31,600	50,900	0.93	14.6	1.3	5
NEPTUNE	2,795,500,000	4,498,800,000	164.79 years	15h 48m	30,200	48,600	1.23	17.2	1.8	3
PLUTO	3,667,900,000	5,902,800,000	247.70 years	6.39 days (?)	1,500	2,400	0.03 (?)	0.01 (?)	0.7 (?)	1

†Retrograde motion

Facts About the Sun

Equatorial diameter	865,000 miles	1,392,000 kilometers
Period of rotation on axis	25-35 days*	
Orbit of galaxy	every 225 million years	
Surface gravity (Earth = 1)	27.8	
Mass (Earth = 1)	333,000	
Density (Water = 1)	1.4	
Mean distance from Earth	93,000,000 miles	149,700,000 kilometers

*Rotation of 25 days at Equator, decreasing to about 35 days at the poles.

Facts About the Moon

Equatorial diameter	2,160 miles	3,476 kilometers
Period of rotation on axis	27 days, 7 hours, 43 minutes	
Period of revolution around Earth (sidereal month)	27 days, 7 hours, 43 minutes	
Phase period between new moons (synodic month)	29 days, 12 hours, 44 minutes	
Surface gravity (Earth = 1)	0.16	
Mass (Earth = 1)	0.0123	
Density (Water = 1)	3.34	
Maximum distance from Earth	252,710 miles	406,690 kilometers
Minimum distance from Earth	221,460 miles	356,400 kilometers
Mean distance from Earth	238,860 miles	384,400 kilometers

Dimensions of the Earth

	Area in Sq. Miles	Sq. Kilometers
Superficial area	197,751,000	512,175,090
Land surface	57,970,000	150,142,300
Water surface	139,781,000	362,032,790

	Miles	Kilometers
Equatorial circumference	24,902	40,075
Polar circumference	24,860	40,007
Equatorial diameter	7,926.68	12,756.4
Polar diameter	7,899.99	12,713.4
Equatorial radius	3,963.34	6,378.2
Polar radius	3,949.99	6,356.7

Volume of the Earth	2.6×10^{11} cubic miles	10.84×10^{11} cubic kilometers
Mass or weight	6.6×10^{21} short tons	6.0×10^{21} metric tons
Maximum distance from Sun	94,600,000 miles	152,000,000 kilometers
Minimum distance from Sun	91,300,000 miles	147,000,000 kilometers

The Continents

	Area in:		Percent of World's Land
	Sq. Miles	Sq. Km.	
Asia	17,128,500	44,362,815	29.5
Africa	11,707,000	30,321,130	20.2
North America	9,363,000	24,250,170	16.2
South America	6,875,000	17,806,250	11.8
Antarctica	5,500,000	14,245,000	9.5
Europe	4,057,000	10,507,630	7.0
Australia	2,966,136	7,682,300	5.1

Oceans and Major Seas

	Area in:		Greatest Depth in:	
	Sq. Miles	Sq. Km.	Feet	Meters
Pacific Ocean	64,186,000	166,241,700	36,198	11,033
Atlantic Ocean	31,862,000	82,522,600	28,374	8,648
Indian Ocean	28,350,000	73,426,500	25,344	7,725
Arctic Ocean	5,427,000	14,056,000	17,880	5,450
Caribbean Sea	970,000	2,512,300	24,720	7,535
Mediterranean Sea	969,000	2,509,700	16,896	5,150
Bering Sea	875,000	2,266,250	15,800	4,800
Gulf of Mexico	600,000	1,554,000	12,300	3,750
Sea of Okhotsk	590,000	1,528,100	11,070	3,370
East China Sea	482,000	1,248,400	9,500	2,900
Sea of Japan	389,000	1,007,500	12,280	3,740
Hudson Bay	317,500	822,300	846	258
North Sea	222,000	575,000	2,200	670
Black Sea	185,000	479,150	7,365	2,245
Red Sea	169,000	437,700	7,200	2,195
Baltic Sea	163,000	422,170	1,506	459

Major Ship Canals

	Length in:		Minimum Depth in:	Depth in:
	Miles	Kms.	Feet	Meters
Volga-Baltic, U.S.S.R.	225	362	—	—
Baltic-White Sea, U.S.S.R.	140	225	16	5
Suez, Egypt	100.76	162	42	13
Albert, Belgium	80	129	16.5	5
Moscow-Volga, U.S.S.R.	80	129	18	6
Volga-Don, U.S.S.R.	62	100	—	—
Göta, Sweden	54	87	10	3
Kiel (Nord-Ostsee), W. Ger.	53.2	86	38	12
Panama Canal, Panama	50.72	82	41.6	13
Houston Ship, U.S.A.	50	81	36	11

Largest Islands

	Area in:			Area in:			Area in:	
	Sq. Mi.	Sq. Km.		Sq. Mi.	Sq. Km.		Sq. Mi.	Sq. Km.
Greenland	840,000	2,175,600	South I., New Zealand	58,393	151,238	Hokkaido, Japan	28,983	75,066
New Guinea	305,000	789,950	Java, Indonesia	48,842	126,501	Banks, Canada	27,038	70,028
Borneo	290,000	751,100	North I., New Zealand	44,187	114,444	Ceylon, Sri Lanka	25,332	65,610
Madagascar	226,400	586,376	Newfoundland, Canada	42,031	108,860	Tasmania, Australia	24,600	63,710
Baffin, Canada	195,928	507,454	Cuba	40,533	104,981	Svalbard, Norway	23,957	62,049
Sumatra, Indonesia	164,000	424,760	Luzon, Philippines	40,420	104,688	Devon, Canada	21,331	55,247
Honshu, Japan	88,000	227,920	Iceland	39,768	103,000	Novaya Zemlya (north isl.), U.S.S.R.	18,600	48,200
Great Britain	84,400	218,896	Mindanao, Philippines	36,537	94,631	Marajó, Brazil	17,991	46,597
Victoria, Canada	83,896	217,290	Ireland	31,743	82,214	Tierra del Fuego, Chile & Argentina	17,900	46,360
Ellesmere, Canada	75,767	196,236	Sakhalin, U.S.S.R.	29,500	76,405	Alexander, Antarctica	16,700	43,250
Celebes, Indonesia	72,986	189,034	Hispaniola, Haiti & Dom. Rep.	29,399	76,143			

Principal Mountains of the World

	Feet	Meters		Feet	Meters		Feet	Meters
Everest, Nepal-China	29,028	8,848	Pissis, Argentina	22,241	6,779	Kazbek, U.S.S.R.	16,512	5,033
Godwin Austen (K2), Pakistan-China	28,250	8,611	Mercedario, Argentina	22,211	6,770	Puncak Jaya, Indonesia	16,503	5,030
Kanchenjunga, Nepal-India	28,208	8,598	Huascarán, Peru	22,205	6,768	Tyree, Antarctica	16,289	4,965
Lhotse, Nepal-China	27,923	8,511	Llullaillaco, Chile-Argentina	22,057	6,723	Blanc, France	15,771	4,807
Makalu, Nepal-China	27,824	8,481	Nevada Ancohuma, Bolivia	21,489	6,550	Klyuchevskaya Sopka, U.S.S.R.	15,584	4,750
Dhaulagiri, Nepal	26,810	8,172	Illampu, Bolivia	21,276	6,485	Fairweather (Br. Col., Canada)	15,300	4,663
Nanga Parbat, Pakistan	26,660	8,126	Chimborazo, Ecuador	20,561	6,267	Dufourspitze (Mte. Rosa), Italy-Switzerland	15,203	4,634
Annapurna, Nepal	26,504	8,078	McKinley, Alaska	20,320	6,194	Ras Dashan, Ethiopia	15,157	4,620
Gasherbrum, Pakistan-China	26,740	8,068	Logan, Canada (Yukon)	19,524	5,951	Matterhorn, Switzerland	14,691	4,478
Nanda Devi, India	25,645	7,817	Cotopaxi, Ecuador	19,347	5,897	Whitney, California, U.S.A.	14,494	4,418
Rakaposhi, Pakistan	25,550	7,788	Kilimanjaro, Tanzania	19,340	5,895	Elbert, Colorado, U.S.A.	14,433	4,399
Kamet, India	25,447	7,756	El Misti, Peru	19,101	5,822	Rainier, Washington, U.S.A.	14,410	4,392
Gurla Mandhada, China	25,355	7,728	Pico Cristóbal Colón, Colombia	19,029	5,800	Shasta, California, U.S.A.	14,162	4,350
Kongur Shan, China	25,325	7,719	Huila, Colombia	18,865	5,750	Pikes Peak, Colorado, U.S.A.	14,110	4,301
Tirich Mir, Pakistan	25,230	7,690	Citlaltépetl (Orizaba), Mexico	18,855	5,747	Finsteraarhorn, Switzerland	14,022	4,274
Gongga Shan, China	24,790	7,556	El'brus, U.S.S.R.	18,510	5,642	Mauna Kea, Hawaii, U.S.A.	13,796	4,205
Muztagata, China	24,757	7,546	Damavand, Iran	18,376	5,601	Mauna Loa, Hawaii, U.S.A.	13,677	4,169
Communism Peak, U.S.S.R.	24,599	7,498	St. Elias, Alaska-Canada (Yukon)	18,008	5,489	Jungfrau, Switzerland	13,642	4,158
Pobeda Peak, U.S.S.R.	24,406	7,439	Vilcanota, Peru	17,999	5,486	Cameroon, Cameroon	13,350	4,069
Chomo Lhari, Bhutan-China	23,997	7,314	Popocatépetl, Mexico	17,887	5,452	Grossglockner, Austria	12,457	3,797
Muztag, China	23,891	7,282	Dykhtau, U.S.S.R.	17,070	5,203	Fuji, Japan	12,389	3,776
Cerro Aconcagua, Argentina	22,831	6,959	Kenya, Kenya	17,058	5,199	Cook, New Zealand	12,349	3,764
Ojos del Salado, Chile-Argentina	22,572	6,880	Ararat, Turkey	16,946	5,165	Etna, Italy	11,053	3,369
Bonete, Chile-Argentina	22,541	6,870	Vinson Massif, Antarctica	16,864	5,140	Kosciusko, Australia	7,310	2,228
Tupungato, Chile-Argentina	22,310	6,800	Margherita (Ruwenzori), Africa	16,795	5,119	Mitchell, North Carolina, U.S.A.	6,684	2,037

Longest Rivers of the World

	Miles	Kms.		Miles	Kms.		Miles	Kms.
Nile, Africa	4,145	6,671	São Francisco, Brazil	1,811	2,914	Ohio-Allegheny, U.S.A.	1,306	2,102
Amazon, S. Amer.	3,915	6,300	Indus, Asia	1,800	2,897	Kama, U.S.S.R.	1,262	2,031
Chang Jiang (Yangtze), China	3,900	6,276	Danube, Europe	1,775	2,857	Red, U.S.A.	1,222	1,966
Mississippi-Missouri-Red Rock, U.S.A.	3,741	6,019	Salween, Asia	1,770	2,849	Don, U.S.S.R.	1,222	1,967
Ob'Irtysh-Black Irtysh, U.S.S.R.	3,362	5,411	Brahmaputra, Asia	1,700	2,736	Columbia, U.S.A.-Canada	1,214	1,953
Yenisey-Angara, U.S.S.R.	3,100	4,989	Euphrates, Asia	1,700	2,736	Saskatchewan, Canada	1,205	1,939
Huang He (Yellow), China	2,877	4,630	Tocantins, Brazil	1,677	2,699	Peace-Finlay, Canada	1,195	1,923
Amur-Shilka-Onon, Asia	2,744	4,416	Xi (Si), China	1,650	2,655	Tigris, Asia	1,181	1,901
Lena, U.S.S.R.	2,734	4,400	Amudar'ya, Asia	1,616	2,601	Darling, Australia	1,160	1,867
Congo (Zaire), Africa	2,718	4,374	Nelson-Saskatchewan, Canada	1,600	2,575	Angara, U.S.S.R.	1,135	1,827
Mackenzie-Peace-Finlay, Canada	2,635	4,241	Orinoco, S. Amer.	1,600	2,575	Sungari, Asia	1,130	1,819
Mekong, Asia	2,610	4,200	Zambezi, Africa	1,600	2,575	Pechora, U.S.S.R.	1,124	1,809
Missouri-Red Rock, U.S.A.	2,564	4,125	Paraguay, S. Amer.	1,584	2,549	Snake, U.S.A.	1,000	1,609
Niger, Africa	2,548	4,101	Kolyma, U.S.S.R.	1,562	2,514	Churchill, Canada	1,000	1,609
Paraná-La Plata, S. Amer.	2,450	3,943	Ganges, Asia	1,550	2,494	Pilcomayo, S. Amer.	1,000	1,609
Mississippi, U.S.A.	2,348	3,778	Ural, U.S.S.R.	1,509	2,428	Magdalena, Colombia	1,000	1,609
Murray-Darling, Australia	2,310	3,718	Japurá, S. Amer.	1,500	2,414	Uruguay, S. Amer.	994	1,600
Volga, U.S.S.R.	2,194	3,531	Arkansas, U.S.A.	1,450	2,334	Platte-N. Platte, U.S.A.	990	1,593
Madeira, S. Amer.	2,013	3,240	Colorado, U.S.A.-Mexico	1,450	2,334	Ohio, U.S.A.	981	1,578
Purus, S. Amer.	1,995	3,211	Negro, S. Amer.	1,400	2,253	Pecos, U.S.A.	926	1,490
Yukon, Alaska-Canada	1,979	3,185	Dnieper, U.S.S.R.	1,368	2,202	Oka, U.S.S.R.	918	1,477
St. Lawrence, Canada-U.S.A.	1,900	3,058	Orange, Africa	1,350	2,173	Canadian, U.S.A.	906	1,458
Rio Grande, Mexico-U.S.A.	1,885	3,034	Irrawaddy, Burma	1,325	2,132	Colorado, Texas, U.S.A.	894	1,439
Syrdar'ya-Naryn, U.S.S.R.	1,859	2,992	Brazos, U.S.A.	1,309	2,107	Dniester, U.S.S.R.	876	1,410

Principal Natural Lakes

	Sq. Miles	Sq. Km.	Feet	Meters		Sq. Miles	Sq. Km.	Feet	Meters
Caspian Sea, U.S.S.R.-Iran	143,243	370,999	3,264	995	Lake Eyre, Australia	3,500-0	9,000-0	—	—
Lake Superior, U.S.A.-Canada	31,820	82,414	1,329	405	Lake Titicaca, Peru-Bolivia	3,200	8,288	1,000	305
Lake Victoria, Africa	26,724	69,215	270	82	Lake Nicaragua, Nicaragua	3,100	8,029	230	70
Aral Sea, U.S.S.R.	25,676	66,501	256	78	Lake Athabasca, Canada	3,064	7,936	400	122
Lake Huron, U.S.A.-Canada	23,010	59,596	748	228	Reindeer Lake, Canada	2,568	6,651	—	—
Lake Michigan, U.S.A.	22,400	58,016	923	281	Lake Turkana (Rudolf), Africa	2,463	6,379	240	73
Lake Tanganyika, Africa	12,650	32,764	4,700	1,433	Issyk-Kul', U.S.S.R.	2,425	6,281	2,303	702
Lake Baykal, U.S.S.R.	12,162	31,500	5,316	1,620	Lake Torrens, Australia	2,230	5,776	—	—
Great Bear Lake, Canada	12,096	31,328	1,356	413	Vänern, Sweden	2,156	5,584	328	100
Lake Nyasa (Malawi), Africa	11,555	29,928	2,320	707	Nettilling Lake, Canada	2,140	5,543	—	—
Great Slave Lake, Canada	11,031	28,570	2,015	614	Lake Winnipegosis, Canada	2,075	5,374	38	12
Lake Erie, U.S.A.-Canada	9,940	25,745	210	64	Lake Mobutu Sese Seko (Albert), Africa	2,075	5,374	160	49
Lake Winnipeg, Canada	9,417	24,390	60	18	Kariba Lake, Zambia-Zimbabwe	2,050	5,310	295	90
Lake Ontario, U.S.A.-Canada	7,540	19,529	775	244	Lake Nipigon, Canada	1,872	4,848	540	165
Lake Ladoga, U.S.S.R.	7,104	18,399	738	225	Lake Mweru, Zaire-Zambia	1,800	4,662	60	18
Lake Balkhash, U.S.S.R.	7,027	18,200	87	27	Lake Manitoba, Canada	1,799	4,659	12	4
Lake Maracaibo, Venezuela	5,120	13,261	100	31	Lake Taymyr, U.S.S.R.	1,737	4,499	85	26
Lake Chad, Africa	4,000-10,000	10,360-25,900	25	8	Lake Khanka, China-U.S.S.R.	1,700	4,403	33	10
Lake Onega, U.S.S.R.	3,710	9,609	377	115	Lake Kioga, Uganda	1,700	4,403	25	8

Foreign City Weather

Two figures are given for each of the months, thus 88/73. The first figure is the average daily high temperature (°F) and the second is the average daily low temperature (°F) for the month. The boldface figures indicate the average number of days with rain for each month.

City	January	February	March	April	May	June	July	August	September	October	November	December
ABIDJAN, Ivory Coast	88/73 **3**	90/75 **4**	90/75 **6**	90/75 **9**	88/75 **16**	85/73 **18**	83/73 **8**	82/71 **7**	83/73 **8**	85/74 **13**	87/74 **13**	88/74 **6**
ACAPULCO, Mexico	85/70 **0**	87/70 **0**	87/70 **0**	87/71 **1**	89/74 **4**	89/76 **15**	89/75 **11**	89/75 **14**	88/75 **18**	88/74 **12**	88/72 **4**	87/70 **1**
ACCRA, Ghana	87/73 **1**	88/75 **1**	88/76 **4**	88/76 **6**	87/75 **9**	84/74 **10**	81/73 **4**	80/71 **3**	81/73 **4**	85/74 **6**	87/75 **3**	88/75 **2**
ADDIS ABABA, Ethiopia	75/43 **2**	76/47 **5**	77/49 **8**	77/50 **10**	77/50 **10**	74/49 **20**	69/50 **28**	69/50 **27**	72/49 **21**	75/45 **3**	73/43 **2**	73/41 **2**
ALGIERS, Algeria	59/49 **11**	61/49 **9**	63/52 **9**	68/55 **5**	73/59 **5**	78/65 **2**	83/70 **1**	85/71 **1**	81/69 **4**	74/63 **7**	66/56 **11**	60/51 **12**
AMSTERDAM, Netherlands	40/34 **19**	41/34 **15**	46/37 **13**	52/43 **14**	60/50 **12**	65/55 **12**	69/59 **14**	68/59 **14**	64/56 **15**	56/48 **18**	47/41 **19**	41/35 **19**
ANKARA, Turkey	39/24 **8**	42/26 **8**	51/31 **7**	63/40 **7**	73/49 **7**	78/53 **5**	86/59 **2**	87/59 **1**	78/52 **3**	69/44 **5**	57/37 **6**	43/29 **9**
APIA, Western Samoa	86/75 **22**	85/76 **19**	86/74 **19**	86/75 **14**	85/74 **12**	85/74 **7**	85/74 **9**	84/75 **9**	84/74 **11**	85/75 **14**	86/74 **16**	85/74 **19**
ATHENS, Greece	54/42 **7**	55/43 **6**	60/46 **5**	67/52 **3**	77/60 **3**	85/67 **2**	90/72 **1**	90/72 **1**	83/66 **2**	74/60 **4**	64/52 **6**	57/46 **7**
BAGHDAD, Iraq	60/39 **4**	64/42 **3**	71/48 **4**	85/57 **3**	97/67 **1**	105/73 **0**	110/76 **1**	110/76 **0**	104/70 **0**	92/61 **1**	77/51 **3**	64/42 **5**
BALI, Indonesia	88/74 **19**	88/74 **14**	88/74 **13**	88/74 **7**	88/73 **5**	87/71 **3**	87/70 **1**	87/70 **0**	89/71 **1**	90/73 **2**	90/75 **6**	88/74 **14**
BANGKOK, Thailand	89/68 **1**	91/72 **1**	93/75 **3**	95/77 **3**	93/77 **9**	91/76 **10**	90/76 **13**	90/76 **13**	89/76 **15**	88/75 **14**	87/72 **5**	87/68 **1**
BARCELONA, Spain	56/42 **5**	57/44 **7**	61/47 **7**	64/51 **8**	71/57 **8**	77/63 **5**	81/69 **4**	82/69 **5**	78/65 **7**	71/58 **8**	62/50 **7**	57/44 **6**
BEIRUT, Lebanon	62/51 **15**	63/51 **12**	66/54 **9**	72/58 **5**	78/64 **2**	84/74 **12**	83/73 **11**	84/74 **11**	84/74 **9**	85/74 **9**	85/73 **12**	85/73 **15**
BELFAST, Northern Ireland	45/34 **22**	47/34 **18**	49/35 **20**	53/39 **18**	59/43 **17**	64/49 **10**	66/51 **18**	65/51 **20**	62/48 **17**	55/42 **19**	50/37 **21**	46/35 **25**
BELGRADE, Yugoslavia	37/27 **8**	41/27 **7**	53/35 **7**	64/45 **9**	74/53 **9**	79/58 **9**	84/61 **6**	83/60 **7**	76/55 **6**	65/47 **8**	52/39 **7**	40/30 **9**
BERLIN, Germany	35/26 **10**	38/27 **8**	46/32 **9**	55/38 **9**	65/46 **8**	70/51 **9**	74/55 **10**	72/54 **10**	66/48 **8**	55/41 **8**	43/33 **8**	37/29 **11**
BIARRITZ, France	54/40 **10**	52/38 **11**	63/43 **11**	63/44 **11**	69/53 **11**	72/56 **10**	80/66 **7**	77/61 **7**	77/58 **9**	74/55 **11**	58/44 **12**	53/41 **14**
BOGOTA, Colombia	67/48 **6**	68/49 **7**	67/50 **13**	67/51 **20**	66/51 **16**	65/51 **16**	64/50 **18**	65/50 **16**	66/49 **13**	66/50 **20**	66/50 **16**	66/49 **15**
BOMBAY, India	83/67 **1**	83/67 **1**	86/72 **1**	89/76 **1**	91/80 **1**	89/79 **14**	85/76 **19**	85/76 **19**	85/76 **13**	89/76 **3**	89/73 **1**	87/69 **1**
BONN, West Germany	39/30 **7**	37/26 **6**	50/35 **7**	58/39 **14**	67/46 **13**	69/52 **19**	73/56 **16**	72/55 **17**	67/50 **16**	58/45 **16**	47/37 **15**	44/36 **15**
BRASILIA, Brazil	80/65 **17**	81/64 **20**	82/64 **7**	82/62 **10**	79/56 **5**	77/52 **0**	78/51 **2**	82/55 **0**	87/60 **2**	82/64 **16**	82/66 **17**	78/64 **16**
BRINDISI, Italy	55/43 **10**	57/43 **6**	60/45 **5**	65/50 **5**	73/57 **3**	80/64 **2**	84/68 **1**	84/69 **3**	80/65 **4**	70/58 **8**	64/52 **10**	58/46 **8**
BUCHAREST, Romania	33/20 **6**	38/24 **5**	51/33 **6**	64/41 **8**	74/51 **8**	81/58 **9**	86/61 **7**	86/60 **6**	80/53 **5**	65/44 **5**	49/35 **9**	37/26 **6**
BUDAPEST, Hungary	35/29 **9**	40/28 **7**	51/36 **7**	62/44 **8**	72/52 **9**	78/57 **8**	82/61 **7**	81/59 **6**	74/53 **7**	61/45 **8**	47/37 **8**	38/31 **9**
BUENOS AIRES, Argentina	85/63 **7**	83/63 **6**	79/60 **7**	72/53 **8**	64/47 **7**	57/41 **7**	57/42 **8**	60/43 **9**	64/46 **8**	69/50 **9**	76/56 **9**	82/61 **8**
CAIRO, Egypt	65/47 **1**	69/48 **1**	75/52 **1**	83/57 **1**	91/63 **0**	95/68 **0**	96/70 **0**	95/71 **0**	90/68 **0**	86/65 **1**	78/58 **1**	68/50 **1**
CALCUTTA, India	80/55 **1**	84/59 **2**	93/69 **3**	97/75 **3**	96/77 **7**	92/79 **13**	89/79 **18**	89/78 **18**	90/78 **13**	89/74 **6**	84/64 **1**	79/55 **1**
CAPE TOWN, South Africa	78/60 **3**	79/60 **2**	77/58 **3**	72/53 **6**	67/49 **9**	64/46 **9**	63/45 **10**	64/46 **9**	65/49 **7**	70/52 **6**	73/55 **3**	76/58 **3**
CARACAS, Venezuela	75/56 **6**	79/60 **2**	79/58 **3**	81/60 **4**	80/62 **9**	78/62 **14**	78/61 **15**	79/61 **15**	80/61 **13**	79/61 **12**	78/58 **10**	78/58 **10**
CHARLOTTE AMALIE, Virgin Islands	82/73 **18**	81/72 **13**	82/73 **12**	83/74 **13**	85/76 **15**	86/77 **18**	87/78 **16**	88/78 **19**	87/78 **17**	87/77 **18**	85/76 **19**	83/74 **18**
COLOMBO, Sri Lanka	86/72 **7**	87/72 **6**	88/74 **8**	88/76 **14**	87/78 **19**	85/77 **18**	85/77 **12**	85/77 **11**	85/77 **13**	85/75 **19**	85/73 **16**	85/72 **10**
COPENHAGEN, Denmark	36/29 **9**	36/28 **7**	41/31 **8**	50/37 **9**	61/44 **8**	67/51 **8**	72/55 **9**	69/54 **12**	63/49 **8**	53/42 **9**	43/35 **10**	38/32 **11**
DARWIN, Australia	90/77 **20**	90/77 **18**	91/77 **17**	92/76 **6**	91/73 **1**	88/69 **1**	87/67 **0**	89/70 **1**	91/74 **2**	93/77 **5**	94/78 **10**	92/78 **15**
DJAKARTA, Indonesia	84/74 **18**	84/74 **17**	86/74 **15**	87/75 **11**	87/75 **9**	87/74 **7**	87/73 **5**	87/73 **4**	88/74 **5**	87/74 **8**	86/74 **12**	85/74 **14**
DUBLIN, Ireland	47/35 **13**	47/35 **11**	51/36 **10**	54/38 **11**	59/42 **11**	65/48 **11**	67/51 **13**	67/51 **13**	63/47 **12**	57/43 **12**	51/38 **12**	47/36 **13**
EDINBURGH, Scotland	43/35 **18**	43/35 **15**	47/36 **15**	50/39 **16**	55/43 **15**	62/48 **15**	65/52 **17**	64/52 **17**	60/48 **16**	53/44 **18**	47/39 **18**	44/36 **17**
FLORENCE, Italy	49/35 **9**	53/36 **9**	60/40 **7**	68/46 **7**	75/53 **9**	84/58 **5**	89/63 **4**	88/62 **4**	81/58 **6**	69/51 **9**	58/42 **10**	50/37 **9**
GENEVA, Switzerland	39/29 **10**	43/30 **9**	51/35 **10**	58/41 **11**	66/48 **12**	73/55 **11**	77/58 **9**	76/57 **10**	69/52 **10**	58/44 **11**	47/37 **11**	40/31 **10**
GUAYAQUIL, Ecuador	88/70 **20**	87/71 **25**	88/72 **24**	89/71 **14**	88/68 **9**	87/68 **4**	84/67 **2**	86/65 **0**	87/66 **2**	86/68 **3**	88/68 **3**	88/70 **10**
HAMBURG, West Germany	35/28 **12**	37/30 **10**	42/33 **10**	51/39 **11**	60/47 **9**	67/53 **10**	69/56 **12**	67/55 **13**	63/51 **10**	53/44 **11**	44/36 **11**	38/31 **12**
HAMILTON, Bermuda	68/58 **14**	68/57 **13**	68/57 **12**	71/59 **11**	76/64 **9**	81/69 **9**	85/73 **10**	86/74 **13**	84/72 **10**	79/69 **12**	74/63 **13**	70/60 **15**
HAVANA, Cuba	79/65 **6**	79/65 **4**	81/67 **4**	84/69 **4**	86/72 **7**	88/74 **10**	89/75 **9**	89/75 **10**	88/75 **11**	85/73 **11**	81/69 **7**	79/67 **6**
HELSINKI, Finland	27/17 **11**	26/15 **8**	32/22 **8**	43/31 **8**	55/41 **8**	63/49 **9**	71/57 **8**	66/55 **12**	57/46 **11**	45/37 **12**	37/30 **11**	31/22 **11**
HONG KONG	64/56 **4**	63/55 **5**	67/60 **7**	75/67 **8**	82/74 **13**	85/78 **18**	87/78 **17**	87/78 **15**	85/77 **12**	81/73 **6**	74/65 **2**	68/59 **3**
JERUSALEM, Israel	55/41 **9**	56/42 **11**	65/46 **3**	73/50 **3**	81/57 **1**	85/60 **0**	87/63 **0**	87/64 **0**	85/62 **1**	81/59 **1**	70/53 **4**	59/45 **7**
JOHANNESBURG, South Africa	78/58 **12**	77/58 **9**	75/55 **9**	72/50 **4**	66/43 **3**	62/39 **1**	63/39 **1**	68/43 **1**	73/48 **2**	77/53 **7**	77/55 **10**	78/57 **11**
KARACHI, Pakistan	77/55 **1**	79/58 **1**	85/67 **1**	90/73 **1**	93/79 **1**	93/82 **1**	91/81 **2**	88/79 **2**	88/77 **1**	91/72 **1**	87/64 **1**	80/57 **1**
KINGSTON, Jamaica	86/67 **3**	86/67 **3**	86/68 **2**	87/70 **3**	87/72 **4**	89/74 **5**	90/73 **4**	90/73 **7**	89/73 **6**	88/73 **8**	87/71 **5**	87/69 **4**
LAGOS, Nigeria	88/74 **2**	89/77 **3**	89/78 **7**	89/77 **10**	87/76 **16**	85/74 **20**	83/74 **16**	82/73 **10**	83/74 **14**	85/74 **16**	88/75 **7**	88/75 **2**
LA PAZ, Bolivia	63/43 **21**	63/43 **18**	64/42 **16**	65/40 **9**	64/37 **5**	62/34 **2**	62/33 **2**	63/35 **4**	64/38 **9**	66/40 **9**	67/42 **11**	65/42 **18**

Foreign City Weather

	January	February	March	April	May	June	July	August	September	October	November	December
LAS PALMAS, Canary Is.	70/58 8	71/58 5	71/59 5	71/61 3	73/62 1	75/65 1	77/67 1	79/70 1	79/69 1	79/67 5	76/64 7	72/60 8
LENINGRAD, USSR	23/12 17	24/12 15	33/18 13	45/31 11	58/42 12	66/51 12	71/57 13	66/53 15	57/45 14	45/37 15	34/27 17	26/18 18
LIMA, Peru	82/66 1	83/67 1	83/66 1	80/63 1	74/60 1	68/58 1	67/57 1	66/56 2	68/57 1	71/58 1	74/60 1	78/62 1
LISBON, Portugal	56/46 9	58/47 8	61/49 10	64/52 7	69/56 6	75/60 2	79/63 1	80/64 1	76/62 4	69/57 7	62/52 10	57/47 10
LIVERPOOL, England	44/36 18	44/36 13	48/38 13	52/41 14	58/46 14	63/51 13	66/55 15	65/55 16	61/51 15	55/46 17	48/41 17	45/37 18
LONDON, England	44/35 17	45/35 13	51/47 11	56/40 14	63/45 13	69/51 11	73/55 13	72/54 13	67/51 13	58/44 14	49/39 16	45/36 16
MADRID, Spain	47/33 9	51/35 9	57/40 11	64/44 9	71/50 9	80/57 6	87/62 3	86/62 2	77/56 6	66/48 8	54/40 10	48/35 9
MANILA, Philippines	86/69 6	88/69 3	91/71 4	93/73 4	93/75 12	91/75 17	88/75 24	87/75 23	88/75 22	88/74 19	87/72 14	86/70 11
MARACAIBO, Venezuela	90/73 1	90/73 1	91/74 1	92/76 1	92/77 6	93/77 6	94/76 5	94/77 7	94/77 6	92/76 7	91/76 8	91/75 2
MARSEILLE, France	53/38 10	52/37 9	55/38 8	59/41 10	65/46 10	72/52 9	78/58 6	83/61 6	83/61 5	76/57 7	67/50 10	59/43 11
MELBOURNE, Australia	78/57 9	78/57 8	75/55 9	68/51 13	62/47 14	57/44 16	56/42 17	59/43 17	63/46 15	67/48 14	71/51 13	75/54 11
MEXICO CITY, Mexico	66/42 4	69/43 5	75/47 9	77/51 14	78/54 17	76/55 21	73/53 27	73/54 27	74/53 23	70/50 13	68/46 6	66/43 4
MILAN, Italy	40/29 7	47/33 6	56/38 6	66/46 6	72/54 9	80/61 6	84/64 6	82/63 6	76/58 6	64/49 7	51/39 7	42/33 7
MONTEVIDEO, Uruguay	83/62 6	82/61 5	78/59 5	71/53 6	64/48 8	59/43 5	58/43 6	58/43 6	63/46 6	68/49 7	74/54 6	79/59 7
MOSCOW, USSR	21/ 9 11	23/10 10	32/17 8	47/31 9	65/44 9	73/51 10	76/55 12	72/52 12	61/43 9	46/34 11	31/23 10	23/13 9
MUNICH, West Germany	33/23 10	37/25 9	45/31 10	54/37 13	63/45 13	69/51 14	72/54 14	71/53 13	64/48 11	53/40 10	42/31 9	36/26 11
NAIROBI, Kenya	77/54 5	79/55 6	77/57 11	75/58 16	72/56 17	70/53 9	69/51 6	70/52 7	75/52 6	76/55 8	74/56 15	74/55 11
NAPLES, Italy	54/42 11	55/43 11	60/46 6	67/50 6	73/56 6	81/62 3	86/67 1	86/67 3	81/63 6	72/56 9	63/49 11	57/45 11
NASSAU, Bahamas	77/65 4	77/64 5	79/66 5	81/69 6	84/71 7	87/74 12	88/75 14	89/76 14	88/75 15	85/73 13	81/70 9	79/67 6
NEW DELHI, India	70/44 2	75/49 2	87/58 1	97/68 4	105/79 2	102/83 3	96/81 8	93/79 6	93/75 4	93/65 9	84/52 1	73/46 1
NICE, France	56/40 8	56/41 8	59/45 8	64/49 7	69/56 8	76/62 5	81/66 2	81/66 5	77/62 6	70/55 9	62/48 7	58/43 8
NOUMEA, New Caledonia	86/72 10	85/73 12	85/72 16	83/70 13	79/66 15	77/64 13	76/62 13	76/61 12	78/63 8	80/65 7	83/68 7	86/70 6
ODESSA, USSR	28/22 7	31/26 4	39/32 5	52/41 6	67/55 6	74/62 7	79/65 6	78/65 5	68/56 4	57/47 5	43/35 5	33/27 6
OSLO, Norway	30/20 8	32/20 7	40/25 7	50/34 7	62/43 7	69/51 8	73/56 10	69/53 11	60/45 8	49/37 9	37/29 9	31/24 10
PALERMO, Sicily, Italy	58/47 14	60/47 10	62/49 7	67/53 5	83/59 5	82/66 1	86/71 1	87/72 1	83/69 4	75/62 10	67/55 9	61/50 11
PALMA, Majorca, Spain	57/42 8	59/43 8	62/45 8	66/49 5	73/55 5	80/61 3	84/66 1	86/67 2	81/64 6	74/57 8	65/50 9	59/44 10
PAPEETE, Tahiti	89/72 16	89/72 16	89/72 17	89/72 10	87/70 10	86/69 8	86/68 5	86/68 6	86/69 9	87/70 9	88/71 13	88/72 14
PARIS, France	42/32 15	45/33 13	52/36 15	60/41 14	67/47 13	67/52 11	76/55 12	75/55 12	69/50 11	59/44 14	49/38 15	43/33 17
PEKING, China	35/15 3	41/20 3	53/30 3	68/44 4	80/56 6	88/65 9	89/75 13	87/69 11	80/58 7	69/44 4	50/30 2	37/19 2
PHNOM PENH, Cambodia	87/70 1	90/72 1	93/74 3	94/76 6	92/76 14	91/76 15	89/75 16	89/76 17	88/76 19	87/76 17	86/74 7	86/71 4
PORT-AU-PRINCE, Haiti	87/68 3	88/68 5	89/69 7	89/71 11	90/72 13	92/73 8	94/74 7	93/73 11	91/73 12	90/72 12	88/71 7	87/69 3
PORT OF SPAIN, Trinidad	85/67 14	86/67 8	87/67 8	88/69 7	89/70 10	88/75 13	87/70 20	87/71 21	88/71 18	88/71 16	87/70 17	86/69 16
PRAGUE, Czechoslovakia	34/25 12	38/28 11	45/33 13	55/40 12	65/49 13	72/55 14	74/58 14	73/57 12	65/52 11	54/44 11	41/35 12	34/29 13
RANGOON, Burma	89/65 1	92/67 1	96/71 1	97/76 2	92/77 14	86/76 23	85/76 26	85/76 25	86/76 20	88/76 10	88/73 3	88/67 1
RIO DE JANEIRO, Brazil	84/73 13	85/73 11	83/72 12	80/69 10	77/66 10	76/64 7	75/63 7	76/64 7	75/65 11	77/66 13	79/68 13	82/71 14
ROME, Italy	54/39 8	56/39 11	62/42 5	68/46 6	74/55 6	82/60 3	88/64 2	88/64 3	83/61 6	73/53 9	63/46 8	56/41 9
SAIGON (HO CHI MINH CITY), Vietnam	89/70 2	91/71 1	93/74 2	95/76 4	92/76 16	89/75 21	88/75 23	88/75 21	88/74 21	88/74 20	87/73 11	87/71 7
SAN JUAN, Puerto Rico	80/70 20	80/70 15	81/70 15	82/72 14	84/74 14	85/75 17	85/75 19	85/76 20	86/75 18	85/75 13	84/73 19	81/72 21
SANTIAGO, Chile	85/53 0	84/52 0	80/49 1	74/45 1	65/41 5	58/37 6	59/37 6	62/39 5	66/42 3	72/45 3	78/48 1	83/51 0
SAO PAULO, Brazil	81/63 19	82/64 17	81/62 15	78/58 10	73/54 10	71/51 8	71/49 6	73/51 8	74/54 11	76/57 13	79/59 14	80/61 13
SEOUL, South Korea	32/15 8	37/20 6	47/29 7	62/41 8	72/51 10	80/61 10	84/70 16	87/71 13	78/59 9	67/45 7	51/32 9	37/20 6
SEVILLE, Spain	59/41 8	62/44 9	67/48 9	73/51 8	80/57 9	82/67 11	96/67 1	97/68 1	89/64 3	78/57 4	67/49 9	60/44 8
SHANGHAI, China	46/33 6	47/34 9	55/40 9	66/50 9	77/59 9	88/75 13	90/74 9	90/74 9	82/66 11	74/57 7	63/45 6	53/36 6
SINGAPORE, Singapore	86/73 17	88/73 11	88/75 14	88/75 15	89/75 15	88/75 13	88/75 13	87/75 14	87/75 14	87/74 16	87/74 18	87/74 19
SOFIA, Bulgaria	34/22 6	39/25 7	51/32 8	62/41 8	70/49 11	76/54 9	82/57 7	82/56 6	74/50 6	63/42 7	50/35 7	37/26 7
STOCKHOLM, Sweden	31/23 9	31/22 7	37/26 7	45/32 6	57/41 8	65/49 7	70/55 9	66/53 10	58/46 8	48/39 8	38/31 9	33/26 9
SYDNEY, Australia	78/65 14	78/65 13	76/63 14	71/58 14	66/52 13	61/48 12	60/46 12	63/48 11	67/51 12	71/56 12	74/60 12	77/63 13
TAIPEI, Taiwan, China	66/54 9	65/53 13	70/57 12	77/63 14	83/69 12	89/73 13	92/76 10	91/75 12	88/73 10	81/67 9	75/62 7	69/57 8
TEHRAN, Iran	45/27 4	50/32 4	59/39 5	71/49 3	82/58 2	93/66 1	99/72 1	97/71 1	90/64 1	76/53 1	63/43 3	51/33 4
TEL AVIV, Israel	47/29 5	65/48 8	67/50 9	74/54 2	81/60 1	84/65 0	87/69 0	87/70 0	86/68 1	84/64 2	77/59 7	66/52 11
TOKYO, Japan	72/56 7	72/56 9	70/54 1	67/52 1	71/57 8	76/63 12	83/70 10	86/72 9	79/66 12	69/55 11	60/43 7	71/54 1
VALPARAISO, Chile	43/33 6	46/35 5	54/41 6	63/49 5	63/50 5	60/48 7	60/47 7	61/47 5	62/48 2	65/50 2	54/43 3	46/37 7
VENICE, Italy	34/26 8	38/28 7	47/34 7	57/41 9	71/57 8	78/64 8	82/67 8	82/67 5	78/62 5	65/52 5	44/36 8	37/30 9
VIENNA, Austria	69/56 10	69/56 9	67/54 11	63/51 13	66/50 9	71/56 9	75/59 9	73/58 10	66/52 7	55/44 8	63/50 13	67/54 12
WELLINGTON, New Zealand	69/56 10	69/56 9	67/54 11	63/51 13	58/47 16	55/44 17	53/42 18	54/43 17	57/46 15	60/48 14	63/50 13	67/54 12
ZURICH, Switzerland	48/14 11	52/15 11	62/22 14	70/32 14	77/39 14	83/47 15	86/51 15	84/49 14	78/42 11	68/32 14	57/25 12	49/16 13

U.S. City Weather

City	Record Temperature High (F°)	Record Temperature Low (F°)	Annual Average: Precip. (Water equiv.) (in.)	Annual Average: Snow and Sleet (in.)	Wind Speed (mph)	First Freeze Date 32 F° or less Average	First Freeze Date 32 F° or less Earliest on record	Last Freeze Date 32 F° or less Average	Last Freeze Date 32 F° or less Latest on record	Elevation of Station (feet)
Albany	104	—28	36.46	65.7	8.8	Oct. 13	Sept. 23	Apr. 27	May 20	292
Albuquerque	105	—17	8.33	10.7	9.0	Oct. 29	Oct. 11	Apr. 16	May 18	5,314
Atlanta	103	— 9	48.66	1.5	9.1	Nov. 12	Oct. 24	Mar. 24	Apr. 15	1,034
Baltimore	107	— 7	41.62	21.9	9.5	Oct. 26	Oct. 8	Apr. 15	May 11	155
Birmingham	107	—10	53.46	1.2	7.4	Nov. 10	Oct. 17	Mar. 17	Apr. 21	630
Bismarck	114	—45	16.15	38.4	10.6	Sept. 22	Sept. 6	May 11	May 30	1,660
Boise	111	—23	11.97	21.7	9.0	Oct. 12	Sept. 9	May 6	May 31	2,868
Boston	104	—18	41.55	41.9	12.6	Nov. 7	Oct. 5	Apr. 8	May 3	29
Buffalo	99	—21	35.19	88.6	12.3	Oct. 25	Sept. 23	Apr. 30	May 24	706
Burlington, Vt.	101	—30	32.54	78.4	8.8	Oct. 3	Sept. 13	May 10	May 24	340
Charleston, W. Va.	108	—24	43.66	28.8	6.5	Oct. 28	Sept. 29	Apr. 18	May 11	951
Charlotte	104	— 5	45.00	5.6	7.6	Nov. 4	Oct. 15	Apr. 2	Apr. 16	769
Cheyenne	100	—38	14.48	52.0	13.3	Sept. 27	Aug. 25	May 18	June 18	6,141
Chicago	105	—23	33.47	40.7	10.3	Oct. 26	Sept. 25	Apr. 20	May 14	623
Cincinnati	102	—19	40.40	23.2	9.1	Oct. 25	Sept. 28	Apr. 15	May 25	877
Cleveland	103	—19	34.15	51.5	10.8	Nov. 2	Sept. 29	Apr. 21	May 14	805
Columbia, S.C.	107	— 2	45.23	1.8	6.9	Nov. 3	Oct. 4	Mar. 30	Apr. 21	225
Columbus, Ohio	106	—20	36.98	27.7	8.7	Oct. 31	Oct. 7	Apr. 16	May 9	833
Concord, N.H.	102	—37	38.13	64.1	6.7	Sept. 24	Sept. 13	May 17	June 6	346
Dallas-Ft. Worth, Tex.	112	— 8	32.11	2.7	11.1	Nov. 21	Oct. 27	Mar. 16	Apr. 13	596
Denver	105	—30	14.60	60.1	9.0	Oct. 14	Sept. 16	May 2	May 28	5,332
Des Moines	110	—30	31.49	33.2	11.1	Oct. 10	Sept. 28	Apr. 20	May 11	963
Detroit	105	—24	31.49	31.7	10.2	Oct. 21	Sept. 23	Apr. 23	May 12	626
El Paso	109	— 8	8.47	4.4	9.6	Nov. 11	Oct. 31	Mar. 13	Apr. 11	3,916
Great Falls	107	—49	14.83	57.7	13.1	Sept. 26	Sept. 7	May 14	June 8	3,657
Hartford	102	—26	43.00	53.1	9.0	Oct. 15	Sept. 27	Apr. 22	May 10	179
Houston	108	5	47.07	0.4	7.6	Dec. 11	Oct. 25	Feb. 5	Mar. 27	108
Indianapolis	107	—25	39.98	21.3	9.7	Oct. 22	Sept. 27	Apr. 23	May 27	808
Jackson	107	— 5	50.96	0.8	7.7	Nov. 8	Oct. 9	Mar. 18	Apr. 25	331
Jacksonville	105	10	51.75	Trace	8.6	Dec. 16	Nov. 3	Feb. 6	Mar. 31	31
Juneau	90	—22	53.95	109.1	8.5	Oct. 21	Sept. 9	Apr. 22	June 8	24
Kansas City, Mo.	113	—22	36.66	19.7	10.2	Oct. 26	Sept. 30	Apr. 7	May 6	1,025
Little Rock	110	—13	48.17	5.3	8.2	Nov. 15	Oct. 23	Mar. 16	Apr. 13	265
Los Angeles	110	23	11.94	Trace	7.4	—	Dec. 9	—	Jan. 21	104
Louisville	107	—20	42.94	17.3	8.4	Oct. 25	Oct. 15	Apr. 10	Apr. 19	488
Memphis	106	—13	48.74	5.7	9.2	Nov. 5	Oct. 17	Mar. 20	Apr. 15	284
Miami	100	26	59.21	—	9.1	—	—	—	Feb. 6	12
Milwaukee	105	—25	30.18	45.2	11.8	Oct. 23	Sept. 20	Apr. 25	May 27	693
Minneapolis-St. Paul	108	—34	26.62	45.8	10.6	Oct. 13	Sept. 3	Apr. 29	May 24	838
Mobile	104	— 1	63.26	0.4	9.3	Dec. 12	Nov. 15	Feb. 17	Mar. 20	221
Nashville	107	—15	46.61	10.9	7.9	Oct. 31	Oct. 7	Apr. 3	Apr. 24	605
New Orleans	102	7	58.93	0.2	8.4	Dec. 3	Nov. 11	Feb. 15	Apr. 8	30
New York City	106	—15	43.56	29.1	9.4	Nov. 12	Oct. 19	Apr. 7	Apr. 24	87
Norfolk	105	2	45.22	7.2	10.6	Nov. 21	Nov. 7	Mar. 22	Apr. 14	30
Oklahoma City	113	—17	31.71	9.2	12.9	Nov. 7	Oct. 7	Apr. 1	May 3	1,304
Omaha	114	—32	28.48	32.5	10.9	Oct. 20	Sept. 24	Apr. 14	May 11	982
Philadelphia	106	—11	41.18	20.3	9.6	Nov. 17	Oct. 19	Mar. 30	Apr. 20	28
Phoenix	118	16	7.41	Trace	6.1	Dec. 11	Nov. 4	Jan. 27	Mar. 3	1,107
Pittsburgh	103	—20	36.21	45.5	9.4	Oct. 20	Oct. 10	Apr. 21	May 4	1,225
Portland, Me.	103	—39	42.15	74.3	8.8	Sept. 27	Sept. 17	May 12	May 31	63
Portland, Ore.	107	— 3	37.98	7.5	7.8	Dec. 1	Oct. 26	Feb. 25	May 4	39
Providence	104	—17	40.90	37.8	10.8	Oct. 26	Oct. 3	Apr. 14	Apr. 24	62
Reno	106	—19	7.65	26.8	6.4	Oct. 2	Aug. 30	May 14	June 25	4,400
Richmond	107	—12	43.77	14.3	7.6	Nov. 8	Oct. 5	Apr. 2	May 11	177
Sacramento	115	17	17.33	Trace	8.3	Dec. 11	Nov. 4	Jan. 24	Mar. 14	25
St. Louis	115	—23	36.70	17.8	9.5	Oct. 20	Sept. 28	Apr. 15	May 10	564
Salt Lake City	107	—30	15.63	58.1	8.7	Nov. 1	Sept. 25	Apr. 12	Apr. 30	4,227
San Francisco	106	20	18.88	Trace	10.5	—	Dec. 11	—	Jan. 21	18
Seattle	100	0	40.30	15.2	9.3	Dec. 1	Oct. 19	Feb. 23	Apr. 3	450
Spokane	108	—30	16.19	54.0	8.7	Oct. 12	Sept. 13	Apr. 20	May 16	2,365
Washington, D.C.	106	—15	40.00	16.8	9.2	Nov. 10	Oct. 2	Mar. 29	May 12	65
Wichita	114	—22	30.06	16.3	12.6	Nov. 1	Sept. 27	Apr. 5	Apr. 21	1,340
Wilmington, Del.	107	—15	43.63	20.1	9.1	Oct. 26	Sept. 27	Apr. 18	May 9	80

SOURCE: National Climatic Center

U.S. City Weather

City	Jan.	Feb.	Mar.	April	May	June	July	Aug.	Sept.	Oct.	Nov.	Dec.	ANNUAL
													AVERAGE MONTHLY TEMPERATURES (in °F)
Albany	23.0°	23.7°	33.5°	46.5°	58.4°	67.7°	72.5°	70.2°	62.7°	51.4°	39.7°	27.7°	48.1°
Albuquerque	34.5	39.5	46.3	54.8	63.8	73.3	77.1	75.1	68.4	56.8	43.9	35.1	55.7
Atlanta	43.5	45.6	52.6	61.3	69.6	76.4	78.5	77.8	73.1	62.9	52.0	44.7	61.5
Baltimore	33.2	35.0	42.6	53.6	63.1	72.1	76.8	75.3	68.5	57.3	46.0	36.4	55.0
Birmingham	45.6	47.1	55.0	62.9	70.7	77.8	79.9	79.6	75.2	64.6	53.4	46.3	63.2
Bismarck	8.1	12.2	25.3	42.9	54.6	64.1	70.6	68.5	57.9	45.7	28.6	15.4	41.1
Boise	29.9	35.5	42.3	49.6	57.8	65.4	74.5	72.5	62.7	52.3	40.6	32.1	51.3
Boston	28.9	29.1	36.9	46.9	57.7	67.0	72.6	70.7	64.0	54.2	43.5	32.6	50.3
Buffalo	25.1	24.5	32.3	43.3	54.6	64.7	70.3	68.9	62.6	51.8	40.0	29.5	47.3
Burlington, Vt.	18.0	18.4	29.3	42.6	55.2	64.8	69.7	67.3	59.6	48.8	36.6	23.3	44.5
Charleston, W. Va.	36.6	38.0	46.0	56.0	64.8	72.3	76.0	74.8	69.3	58.0	46.7	38.2	56.4
Charlotte	42.0	43.9	51.0	60.0	68.9	76.0	78.7	77.4	72.2	61.6	50.9	43.1	60.5
Cheyenne	26.1	27.7	32.4	41.4	51.0	61.0	67.7	66.4	57.3	46.4	35.2	28.6	45.1
Chicago	24.7	27.1	36.4	47.8	58.2	68.4	73.8	72.5	65.6	54.5	40.4	29.4	49.9
Cincinnati	30.8	33.6	41.7	53.5	63.3	71.9	75.5	74.2	67.3	56.3	43.6	34.4	53.9
Cleveland	27.5	27.8	35.9	47.0	58.3	67.9	72.2	70.6	64.6	53.8	41.6	31.3	49.9
Columbia, S.C.	46.6	48.1	55.1	63.5	71.9	78.5	80.8	79.9	75.1	64.5	54.4	47.2	63.8
Columbus, Ohio	29.4	30.8	40.0	51.1	61.9	70.9	74.8	72.9	66.6	55.0	42.3	32.4	52.3
Concord, N.H.	21.3	22.8	31.9	44.4	56.2	64.9	70.0	67.3	59.7	49.2	37.5	25.6	45.9
Dallas-Ft. Worth, Tex.	45.6	48.8	56.9	65.2	72.7	80.9	84.5	84.6	77.8	67.8	56.1	47.7	65.7
Denver	30.1	32.8	38.7	47.4	56.7	66.6	72.6	71.3	62.6	51.6	39.6	32.3	50.2
Des Moines	20.8	24.7	36.3	50.4	61.5	71.1	76.1	73.7	65.3	54.2	38.5	26.1	49.9
Detroit	25.3	25.8	34.5	46.7	58.1	68.2	73.0	71.1	64.2	53.1	40.1	29.5	49.2
El Paso	44.7	49.3	55.6	63.8	72.2	80.8	81.9	80.2	74.8	64.7	52.5	45.2	63.8
Great Falls	21.2	26.1	31.4	43.3	53.3	60.9	69.7	67.9	57.6	48.3	34.8	27.1	45.1
Hartford	27.1	27.7	36.9	47.9	59.0	67.9	73.1	70.9	63.7	53.3	42.1	30.4	50.0
Houston	53.2	54.6	62.0	67.9	74.3	79.8	82.4	81.3	77.5	70.2	59.6	55.5	68.2
Indianapolis	28.5	30.8	40.1	52.0	62.5	71.8	75.7	73.7	66.9	55.5	42.0	31.9	52.6
Jackson	48.4	50.9	57.3	65.3	72.6	79.6	81.8	81.5	76.9	66.5	55.7	49.5	65.5
Jacksonville	55.0	56.6	61.8	67.5	73.7	78.5	80.4	80.1	77.1	68.9	60.6	54.9	67.9
Juneau	22.2	27.3	31.2	38.4	46.4	52.8	55.5	54.1	49.0	41.5	32.0	26.9	39.8
Kansas City, Mo.	29.7	33.1	43.2	55.5	65.3	74.7	79.5	78.0	70.0	59.1	44.7	33.6	55.6
Little Rock	41.7	44.8	52.9	62.5	70.1	78.2	81.3	80.5	74.1	63.8	51.9	43.8	62.1
Los Angeles	54.6	55.9	56.9	59.3	62.1	64.9	68.3	69.5	68.5	65.2	60.4	56.4	61.8
Louisville	34.7	36.8	45.6	56.3	66.0	74.6	78.3	76.8	70.4	58.9	46.4	37.2	56.9
Memphis	41.3	44.1	52.2	62.1	70.5	78.2	81.2	80.0	74.1	63.5	51.6	43.6	61.9
Miami	67.5	68.0	71.3	74.9	78.0	80.9	82.2	82.7	81.6	77.8	72.3	68.5	75.5
Milwaukee	20.9	23.2	32.6	44.3	54.3	64.5	70.7	69.7	62.5	51.5	37.7	26.1	46.5
Minneapolis-St. Paul	13.2	16.7	29.6	45.7	57.9	67.8	73.1	70.7	61.5	50.0	33.0	19.5	44.9
Mobile	51.9	54.4	60.1	67.1	74.3	80.3	81.8	81.5	78.1	68.9	58.9	53.1	67.6
Nashville	39.1	41.0	49.5	59.5	68.2	76.3	79.4	78.3	72.2	61.1	48.9	41.1	59.6
New Orleans	54.3	56.5	61.7	68.9	75.4	80.8	82.2	82.0	78.8	70.7	60.7	55.6	69.0
New York City	32.3	32.7	40.6	51.1	61.9	70.9	76.1	74.6	68.0	58.0	46.7	35.7	54.1
Norfolk	41.6	42.3	48.8	57.4	66.7	74.7	78.6	77.5	72.4	62.2	52.1	43.6	59.8
Oklahoma City	37.2	40.8	49.8	60.2	68.2	77.0	81.4	81.1	73.7	62.7	49.4	39.9	60.1
Omaha	22.0	26.5	37.5	51.7	62.7	72.3	77.4	75.1	66.3	55.0	39.3	27.5	51.1
Philadelphia	33.1	33.8	41.6	52.2	63.0	71.8	76.6	74.7	68.4	57.5	46.2	36.2	54.6
Phoenix	51.6	55.4	60.5	67.7	76.0	85.2	90.8	89.0	83.6	71.7	59.8	52.4	70.3
Pittsburgh	30.7	31.3	39.9	51.1	62.0	70.6	74.6	72.8	66.6	55.2	43.2	33.6	52.7
Portland, Me.	22.4	23.4	32.3	42.8	53.2	62.4	68.2	66.6	59.6	49.6	38.6	26.9	45.5
Portland, Ore.	38.5	43.0	45.9	50.6	57.0	60.2	65.8	65.3	62.7	54.0	45.7	41.1	52.5
Providence	29.4	29.3	37.6	47.5	57.8	66.9	72.7	71.0	63.9	54.0	43.4	32.6	50.5
Reno	31.8	36.6	41.2	47.4	54.9	62.5	70.2	68.5	60.7	50.9	41.0	33.4	49.9
Richmond	38.0	39.4	46.9	56.9	66.1	74.0	77.6	76.1	69.9	58.9	48.7	39.7	57.7
Sacramento	44.9	49.8	53.1	58.1	64.5	70.8	75.4	74.3	71.6	63.4	52.9	45.7	60.4
St. Louis	31.7	34.8	44.3	56.1	65.9	75.1	79.3	77.5	70.1	59.0	45.3	35.3	56.2
Salt Lake City	28.0	33.2	40.7	49.0	58.3	68.1	77.2	75.4	65.1	53.1	40.5	31.4	51.7
San Francisco	48.0	50.9	52.9	54.6	57.3	60.3	61.5	62.0	62.9	60.0	54.3	49.3	56.2
Seattle	38.2	42.2	43.9	48.1	55.0	59.9	64.4	63.8	59.6	51.8	44.6	40.5	51.0
Spokane	26.8	31.7	39.4	47.6	55.8	62.5	70.2	68.7	59.5	48.7	37.0	30.4	48.2
Washington, D.C.	36.1	37.7	45.7	56.1	65.8	74.3	78.4	76.9	70.3	59.6	48.4	38.4	57.3
Wichita	31.6	35.2	44.7	56.3	65.4	75.3	80.3	79.3	70.9	59.6	45.2	35.0	56.5
Wilmington, Del.	32.6	33.1	41.9	52.2	62.7	71.4	76.0	74.1	67.9	56.8	45.7	35.2	54.2

SOURCE: National Climatic Center (data based on normals for 1936-1975)

TABLES OF AIRLINE DISTANCES

All Distances in Statute Miles

Between Principal Cities of the World

FROM/TO	Azores	Bagdad	Berlin	Bombay	Buenos Aires	Callao	Cairo	Cape Town	Chicago	Istanbul	Guam	Honolulu	Juneau	London	Los Angeles
Azores	....	3906	2148	5930	5385	4825	3325	5670	3305	2880	8985	7421	4715	1562	5034
Bagdad	3906	....	2040	2022	8215	8618	785	4923	6490	1085	6380	8445	6180	2568	7695
Berlin	2148	2040	....	3947	7411	6937	1823	5949	4458	1068	7158	7384	4638	575	5849
Bombay	5930	2022	3947	....	9380	10530	2698	5133	8144	3043	4831	8172	6992	4526	8810
Buenos Aires	5385	8215	7411	9380	....	1982	7428	4332	5598	7638	10516	7653	7964	6919	6148
Callao	4825	8618	6937	10530	1982	....	7870	6195	3765	7666	9760	5993	5806	6376	4155
Cairo	3325	785	1823	2698	7428	7870	....	4476	6231	780	7175	8925	6352	2218	7675
Cape Town	5670	4923	5949	5133	4332	6195	4476	....	8551	5210	8918	11655	10382	5975	10165
Chicago	3305	6490	4458	8144	5598	3765	6231	8551	....	5530	7510	4315	2310	4015	1741
Istanbul	2880	1085	1068	3043	7638	7666	780	5210	5530	....	7015	8200	5665	1540	6895
Guam	8985	6380	7158	4831	10516	9760	7175	8918	7510	7015	....	3896	5225	7605	6255
Honolulu	7421	8445	7384	8172	7653	5993	8925	11655	4315	8200	3896	....	2825	7320	2620
Juneau	4715	6180	4638	6992	7964	5806	6352	10382	2310	5665	5225	2825	....	4496	1835
London	1562	2568	575	4526	6919	6376	2218	5975	4015	1540	7605	7320	4496	....	5496
Los Angeles	5034	7695	5849	8810	6148	4155	7675	10165	1741	6895	6255	2620	1835	5496	....
Melbourne	12190	8150	9992	6140	7336	8196	8720	6510	9837	9189	3497	5581	8162	10590	8098
Mexico City	4584	8155	6119	9818	4609	2619	7807	8620	1690	7160	7690	3846	3210	5605	1445
Montreal	2548	5814	3776	7582	5619	3954	5502	7975	750	4825	7840	4992	2647	3370	2468
New Orleans	3718	7212	5182	8952	4902	2990	6862	8390	827	6220	7895	4305	2860	4656	1695
New York	2604	6066	4026	7875	5295	3633	5701	7845	727	5060	8115	5051	2874	3500	2466
Panama	3918	7807	5902	9832	3319	1450	7230	7090	2320	6797	9220	5347	4456	5310	3025
Paris	1617	2385	540	4391	6891	6455	2020	5762	4219	1390	7675	7525	4700	210	5711
Rio de Janeiro	4312	7012	6246	8438	1230	2400	6242	3850	5320	6420	11710	8400	7611	5747	6330
San Francisco	5114	7521	5744	8523	6487	4500	7554	10340	1875	6770	5952	2407	1530	5440	345
Santiago	5718	8876	7842	10127	731	1548	8100	5080	5325	8230	9946	6935	7320	7275	5595
Seattle	4720	6848	5121	7830	6956	4964	6915	10305	1753	6124	5785	2707	870	4850	961
Shanghai	7324	4468	5323	3219	12295	10760	5290	8179	7155	5084	1945	5009	4968	5841	6598
Singapore	8338	4443	6226	2425	9940	11700	5152	6025	9475	5440	2990	6874	7375	6818	8955
Tokyo	7370	5242	5623	4247	11601	9740	6005	9234	6410	5649	1596	3940	4117	6050	5600
Wellington	11475	9782	11384	7752	6341	6696	10360	7149	8465	10790	4206	4676	7501	11790	6806

FROM/TO	Melbourne	Mexico City	Montreal	New Orleans	New York	Panama	Paris	Rio de Janeiro	San Francisco	Santiago	Seattle	Shanghai	Singapore	Tokyo	Wellington
Azores	12190	4584	2548	3718	2604	3918	1617	4312	5114	5718	4720	7324	8338	7370	11475
Bagdad	8150	8155	5814	7212	6066	7807	2385	7012	7521	8876	6848	4468	4443	5242	9782
Berlin	9992	6119	3776	5182	4026	5902	540	6246	5744	7842	5121	5323	6226	5623	11384
Bombay	6140	9818	7582	8952	7875	9832	4391	8438	8523	10127	7830	3219	2425	4247	7752
Buenos Aires	7336	4609	5619	4902	5295	3319	6891	1230	6487	731	6956	12295	9940	11601	6341
Callao	8196	2619	3954	2990	3633	1450	6455	2400	4500	1548	4964	10760	11700	9740	6696
Cairo	8720	7807	5502	6862	5701	7230	2020	6242	7554	8100	6915	5290	5152	6005	10360
Cape Town	6510	8620	7975	8390	7845	7090	5732	3850	10340	5080	10305	8179	6025	9234	7149
Chicago	9837	1690	750	827	727	2320	4219	5320	1875	5325	1753	7155	9475	6410	8465
Istanbul	9189	7160	4825	6220	5060	6797	1390	6420	6770	8230	6124	5084	5440	5649	10790
Guam	3497	7690	7840	7895	8115	9220	7675	11710	5952	9946	5785	1945	2990	1596	4206
Honolulu	5581	3846	4992	4305	5051	5347	7525	8400	2407	6935	2707	5009	6874	3940	4676
Juneau	8162	3210	2647	2860	2874	4456	4700	7611	1530	7320	870	4968	7375	4117	7501
London	10590	5605	3370	4656	3500	5310	210	5747	5440	7275	4850	5841	6818	6050	11790
Los Angeles	8098	1445	2468	1695	2466	3025	5711	6330	345	5595	961	6598	8955	5600	6806
Melbourne	....	8599	10553	9455	10541	9211	10500	8340	7970	7130	8330	4967	3768	5172	1655
Mexico City	8599	....	2247	940	2110	1532	5800	4810	1870	4122	2339	8120	10495	7190	7003
Montreal	10553	2247	....	1390	340	2545	3490	5110	2557	5461	2309	7141	9280	6546	9206
New Orleans	9455	940	1390	....	1161	1600	4846	4798	1960	4553	2137	7830	10255	6993	7950
New York	10541	2110	340	1161	....	2211	3600	4810	2606	5134	2440	7460	9617	6846	9067
Panama	9211	1532	2545	1600	2211	....	5440	3311	3349	3000	3680	9430	11800	8560	7580
Paris	10500	5800	3490	4846	3600	5440	....	5710	5680	7300	5080	5855	6730	6132	11865
Rio de Janeiro	8340	4810	5110	4798	4810	3311	5710	....	6655	1852	6945	11510	9875	11600	7510
San Francisco	7970	1870	2557	1960	2606	3349	5680	6655	....	5960	692	6245	8440	5250	6800
Santiago	7130	4122	5461	4553	5134	3000	7300	1852	5960	....	6466	11850	10270	10850	5925
Seattle	8330	2339	2309	2137	2440	3680	5080	6945	692	6466	....	5780	8200	4863	7310
Shanghai	4967	8120	7141	7830	7460	9430	5855	11510	6245	11850	5780	....	2395	1095	6080
Singapore	3768	10495	9280	10255	9617	11800	6730	9875	8440	10270	8200	2395	....	3350	5360
Tokyo	5172	7190	6546	6993	6846	8560	6132	11600	5250	10850	4863	1095	3350	....	5730
Wellington	1655	7003	9206	7950	9067	7580	11865	7510	6800	5925	7310	6080	5360	5730	......

Between Principal Cities of Europe

	Amsterdam	Athens	Baku	Barcelona	Belgrade	Berlin	Brussels	Bucharest	Budapest	Cologne	Copenhagen	Istanbul	Dresden	Dublin	Frankfort
Amsterdam	....	1340	2218	770	875	365	105	1100	710	128	381	1360	385	468	228
Athens	1340	....	1395	1160	500	1112	1292	460	698	1200	1320	350	1022	1765	1113
Baku	2218	1395	....	2427	1487	1867	2240	1220	1562	2127	1980	1070	1837	2490	2055
Barcelona	770	1160	2427	....	998	925	658	1210	924	692	1085	1380	860	919	665
Belgrade	875	500	1487	998	....	618	850	295	205	750	840	502	530	1327	652
Berlin	365	1112	1867	925	618	....	401	798	425	300	225	1068	95	815	268
Brussels	105	1292	2240	658	850	401	....	1110	700	110	475	1345	407	480	198
Bucharest	1100	460	1220	1210	295	798	1110	....	295	982	970	272	725	1560	890
Budapest	710	698	1562	924	205	425	700	295	....	590	629	650	345	1176	504
Cologne	128	1200	2127	692	750	300	110	982	590	....	400	1240	292	585	93
Copenhagen	381	1320	1960	1085	840	225	475	970	629	400	....	1240	315	768	412
Istanbul	1360	350	1070	1380	502	1068	1345	272	650	1240	1240	....	995	1830	1150
Dresden	385	1022	1837	860	530	95	407	725	345	292	315	995	....	852	236
Dublin	468	1765	2490	919	1327	815	480	1560	1176	585	768	1830	852	....	671
Frankfort	228	1113	2055	665	652	268	198	890	504	93	412	1150	236	671	....
Hamburg	232	1250	2020	910	760	165	301	950	572	228	180	1222	238	668	250
Leningrad	1090	1535	1570	1740	1165	815	1175	1080	965	1090	708	1292	885	1440	1075
Lisbon	1140	1770	3050	610	1555	1410	998	1842	1515	1126	1520	2005	1380	1015	1160
London	220	1476	2435	707	1040	575	202	1285	900	308	590	1540	592	300	392
Lyon	458	1100	2238	327	752	601	352	1025	680	370	760	1238	540	720	350
Madrid	912	1463	2742	316	1235	1149	807	1518	1214	875	1272	1690	1100	902	888
Marseilles	627	1025	2238	211	750	730	521	1020	718	528	906	1205	655	875	492
Milan	517	900	2028	450	540	570	435	819	476	390	720	1030	435	880	323
Moscow	1325	1388	1175	1852	1160	995	1392	920	965	1285	970	1180	1200	1728	1240
Munich	415	925	1912	648	475	310	372	725	350	282	520	975	227	855	193
Oslo	568	1610	2118	1330	1112	520	672	1245	920	635	303	1505	620	786	675
Paris	257	1300	2335	518	890	540	170	1152	770	250	634	1390	523	480	295
Riga	820	1310	1590	1440	855	520	900	870	685	805	453	1115	585	1210	780
Rome	808	650	1900	530	440	730	730	700	500	675	948	840	630	1175	698
Sofia	1073	335	1360	1072	231	810	945	194	395	945	1010	315	730	1525	860
Stockholm	695	1495	1862	1410	1005	503	793	1080	820	722	330	1340	598	1010	730
Toulouse	625	1215	2425	156	930	815	515	1210	883	875	962	1400	762	761	560
Warsaw	673	990	1555	1150	510	320	720	580	342	602	415	852	325	1130	550
Vienna	580	795	1700	830	300	322	568	520	128	460	538	790	235	1040	370
Zurich	375	1000	2050	513	590	410	312	855	498	259	595	1090	342	768	193

	Hamburg	Leningrad	Lisbon	London	Lyon	Madrid	Marseilles	Milan	Moscow	Munich	Oslo	Paris	Riga	Rome	Sofia	Stockholm	Toulouse	Warsaw	Vienna	Zurich
Amsterdam	232	1090	1140	220	458	912	627	517	1325	415	568	257	820	808	1073	695	625	673	580	375
Athens	1250	1535	1770	1476	1100	1463	1025	900	1388	925	1610	1300	1310	650	335	1495	1215	990	795	1000
Baku	2020	1570	3050	2435	2238	2742	2238	2028	1175	1912	2118	2335	1590	1900	1360	1862	2425	1555	1700	2050
Barcelona	910	1740	610	707	327	316	211	450	1852	648	1330	518	1440	530	1072	1410	156	1150	830	513
Belgrade	760	1165	1555	1040	752	1235	750	540	1160	475	1112	890	855	440	231	1005	930	510	300	590
Berlin	165	815	1410	575	601	1149	730	570	995	310	520	540	520	730	810	503	815	320	322	410
Brussels	301	1175	998	202	352	807	521	435	1392	372	672	170	900	730	945	793	515	720	568	312
Bucharest	950	1080	1842	1285	1025	1518	1020	819	920	725	1245	1152	870	700	194	1080	1210	580	520	855
Budapest	572	965	1515	900	680	1214	718	476	965	350	920	770	685	500	395	820	883	342	128	498
Cologne	228	1090	1126	308	370	875	528	390	1285	282	635	250	805	675	945	722	875	602	460	259
Copenhagen	180	708	1520	590	760	1272	906	720	970	520	303	634	453	948	1010	330	962	415	538	595
Istanbul	1222	1292	2005	1540	1238	1690	1205	1030	1180	975	1505	1390	1115	840	315	1340	1400	852	790	1090
Dresden	238	885	1380	592	540	1100	655	435	1200	227	620	523	585	630	730	598	762	325	235	342
Dublin	668	1440	1015	300	720	902	875	880	1728	855	786	480	1210	1175	1525	1010	761	1130	1040	768
Frankfort	250	1075	1160	392	350	888	492	323	1240	193	675	295	780	698	860	730	560	550	370	193
Hamburg	....	880	1301	448	580	1098	730	570	1100	378	445	459	600	810	954	502	780	462	460	432
Leningrad	880	....	2235	1300	1420	1980	1540	1315	391	1100	670	1335	300	1440	1218	435	1635	640	975	1225
Lisbon	1301	2235	....	975	850	313	810	1350	430	1208	1690	890	1940	1150	1685	1848	640	1700	1415	1058
London	448	1300	975	....	455	777	620	595	1540	526	720	210	1035	890	1235	885	550	890	762	480
Lyon	580	1420	850	455	....	577	170	210	1560	352	1005	248	1122	462	928	1080	228	850	562	206
Madrid	1098	1980	313	777	557	....	394	728	2120	910	1474	645	1670	840	1385	1598	344	1410	1110	765
Marseilles	730	1540	810	620	170	394	....	238	1642	445	1165	410	1238	372	895	1225	196	950	620	318
Milan	570	1315	1350	595	210	728	238	....	1408	215	1000	400	1010	295	715	1020	400	705	385	137
Moscow	1100	391	430	1540	1560	2120	1642	1408	....	1220	1030	1538	520	1462	1100	770	1770	710	1028	1350
Munich	378	1100	1208	526	352	910	445	215	1220	....	810	425	800	430	672	811	570	500	222	158
Oslo	445	670	1690	720	1005	1474	1165	1000	1030	810	....	830	531	1242	1295	267	1140	653	835	869
Paris	459	1335	890	210	248	645	410	400	1538	425	830	....	1050	690	1080	950	431	845	770	295
Riga	600	300	1940	1035	1122	1670	1238	1010	520	800	531	1050	....	1155	985	276	1335	350	685	930
Rome	810	1440	1150	890	462	840	372	295	1462	430	1242	690	1155	....	545	1220	569	810	470	421
Sofia	954	1218	1685	1235	928	1385	895	715	1100	672	1295	1080	985	545	....	1170	1080	662	500	780
Stockholm	502	435	1848	885	1080	1598	1225	1020	770	811	267	950	276	1220	1170	....	1281	500	770	908
Toulouse	780	1635	640	550	228	344	196	400	1770	570	1140	431	1335	569	1080	1281	....	1062	725	425
Warsaw	462	640	1700	890	850	1410	950	705	710	500	653	845	350	810	662	500	1062	....	345	640
Vienna	460	975	1415	762	562	1110	620	385	1028	222	835	770	685	470	500	770	725	345	....	365
Zurich	432	1225	1058	480	206	765	318	137	1350	158	869	295	930	421	780	908	425	640	365	....

Atlas of the Bible Lands

Edited by HARRY THOMAS FRANK

Professor of Religion
Oberlin College

HAMMOND INCORPORATED   MAPLEWOOD, NEW JERSEY

Title page illustration:
Aerial view of Jerusalem from the east.
Buildings in foreground are on the Mount
of Olives. Beyond is the Dome of the Rock.

Wall painting from tomb at Beni-hasan
depicts Asian people, probably Amorites,
entering Egypt about 1900 B.C.

ATLAS OF THE BIBLE LANDS, New Edition
*Entire contents © Copyright 1977, 1984
by* HAMMOND INCORPORATED
*All rights reserved. No part of this book may
be reproduced or utilized in any form or by any
means, electronic or mechanical including photo-
copying, recording or by any information storage
and retrieval system, without permission in writing
from the publisher.*

*The maps "Routes in Palestine" and "Economy of
Palestine" on pages 5 and 7 were prepared especially for
Abingdon Press and published in* The Interpreter's
Dictionary of the Bible, Supplementary Volume. *They are
reproduced here with Abingdon's permission.*

Library of Congress Cataloging in Publication Data

Hammond Incorporated.
    Atlas of the Bible lands.

    Includes index.
    1. Bible—Geography—Maps.   I. Frank, Harry Thomas.
II. Title.   III. Title: Atlas of the Bible lands.
G2230.H3   1984   912'.33   83-675795
ISBN 0-8437-7056-2 case bound edition
ISBN 0-8437-7055-4 soft cover edition
Printed in the United States of America

Contents

Preface

THE BIBLE is a universal book, restricted neither by time nor place. Over the centuries on all continents its words have carried a message of hope, solace and salvation for the believer, and on the authority of the Holy Word, societies have been shaped and great events set afoot. Moreover, for the individual person of faith, now as in the past, the Bible is both an indispensable guide and a fundamental point of reference.

Yet the events spoken of in the Bible took place at certain times and in definite places. It is, in fact, basic to a Biblical understanding of revelation that its timeless message was given in historical events, through real persons and at places which can be visited by you and by me. The Bible is thus neither a speculative nor a philosophical book. Rather, it is concrete. It offers no essays on the goodness or the near presence of God, but speaks, for instance, of his being with Abraham as he leaves Ur to journey with many adventures and at God's beckoning to Haran, Shechem and Egypt before returning to settle in Beer-sheba (Genesis 11:28-22:19). It was through Moses in "the Wilderness of Sinai" that Israel received the Ten Commandments (Exodus 19-20). God, says the Bible, was present in the struggles of Deborah and her followers ". . . at Taanach, by the waters of Megiddo" (Judges 5:19). And he was revealing himself in the actions of Joseph, who "went up from Galilee, from the city of Nazareth, to Judea, to the city of David, which is called Bethlehem, because he was of the house and lineage of David, to be enrolled with Mary, his betrothed, who was with child" (Luke 2:4-5).

Where are Ur, Haran, Shechem, Egypt, Beer-sheba, the Wilderness of Sinai, Taanach, Megiddo, Galilee, Nazareth, Judea and Bethlehem? Even the casual reader of the Bible will be struck by the frequency and importance of places in the narrative, and no serious student of the Bible can long afford to be without detailed and accurate knowledge of the lands of the Bible. Indeed, from Haran in the north of Syria to Beer-sheba in the south of Israel, Biblical memories haunt almost every ancient site, and once you pass below the towering Lebanon Mountains and the majestic heights of Hermon there is virtually no town or city, no valley, mountain pass or plain which was not the location of some Biblical event.

Consider Paul as he walked northward from Jerusalem, making his way slowly toward Damascus and his startling conversion to Christianity. What places did he pass, and what memories did they hold? We do not know his exact route, but whatever way he went from the Holy City, Biblical memories lay all about him and whispered to him from the soil of the great deeds of God. If Paul went straight north along the mountain ridge, he passed Gibeah within the hour — Gibeah, the home of Saul, first king of Israel — and shortly passed Ramah and Mizpah, both hallowed by Samuel. The next day Paul would ascend slowly as he neared the desolate site of Bethel, which once echoed to Amos' ringing denunciations. Thus along the road through Samaria, following the course of the great Biblical cities that trace that route: Shiloh, Shechem, Samaria, Dothan — and then into and across the Great Plain where Deborah won an astounding victory with the aid of ". . . the onrushing torrent, the torrent Kishon." As the road winds up into the Galilee hills Nazareth lies nestled to the west, and to the east there are the brooding heights of Gilboa on which Saul and Jonathan ". . . swifter than eagles, stronger than lions . . ." had fallen before the Philistines. And so eventually past the Sea of Galilee with all of its associations with Jesus, and up to the Syrian Heights (The Golan) and into Damascus.

Obviously geography alone cannot convey the Biblical message. But geography, history and religion are inseparably bound together in the Bible. Full understanding and a more complete appreciation of the Bible's unique historical revelation depend upon a certain level of knowledge of its physical setting.

With the aid of this completely new edition of *Hammond's Atlas of the Bible Lands,* sites mentioned in the text of both the Old and New Testaments can quickly be located. Journeys — from that of Abraham to those of the early Christian missionaries — can be easily traced, understood and learned. Fresh, up-to-date maps have been combined with evocative photographs and graphic city plans to serve as a readily usable and convenient companion to the study of the Scriptures. Not only does the user of this Atlas gain a sense of the land itself, but because of the large number of concise, uncluttered, historically-oriented maps each Biblical period comes alive. This historical orientation of the maps is aided by the Time Charts which show parallel events at a glance. These charts help the student of the Bible place Biblical events in their larger historical context.

> ". . . the land which you are going over to possess is a land
> of hills and valleys, which drinks water by the rain from
> heaven, a land which the Lord your God cares for; the eyes
> of the Lord your God are always upon it, from the beginning
> of the year to the end of the year."
> — Deuteronomy 11:11-12

HARRY THOMAS FRANK

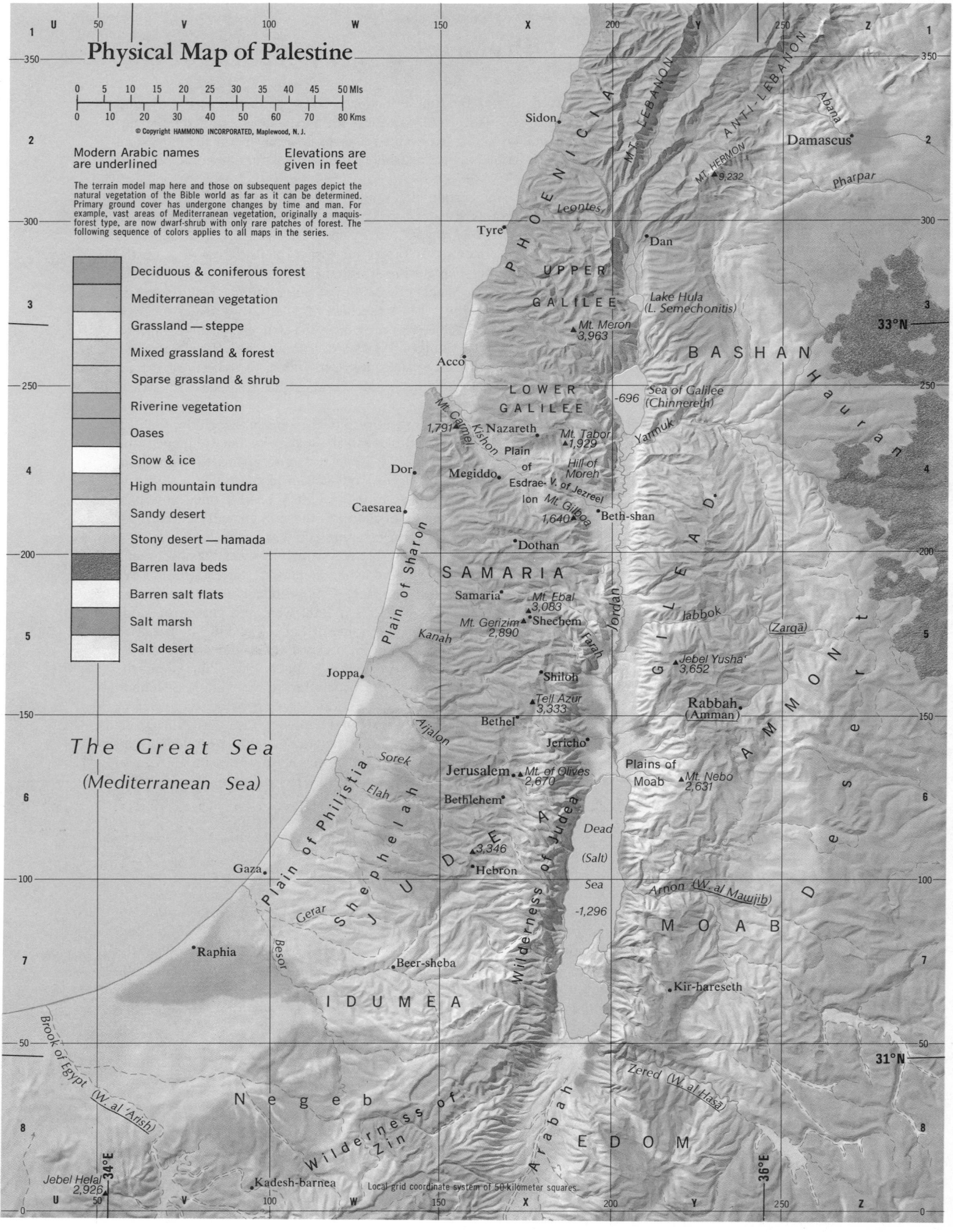

Physical Map of Palestine

0 5 10 15 20 25 30 35 40 45 50 Mls
0 10 20 30 40 50 60 70 80 Kms

© Copyright HAMMOND INCORPORATED, Maplewood, N. J.

Modern Arabic names
are underlined

Elevations are
given in feet

The terrain model map here and those on subsequent pages depict the
natural vegetation of the Bible world as far as it can be determined.
Primary ground cover has undergone changes by time and man. For
example, vast areas of Mediterranean vegetation, originally a maquis-
forest type, are now dwarf-shrub with only rare patches of forest. The
following sequence of colors applies to all maps in the series.

Deciduous & coniferous forest

Mediterranean vegetation

Grassland — steppe

Mixed grassland & forest

Sparse grassland & shrub

Riverine vegetation

Oases

Snow & ice

High mountain tundra

Sandy desert

Stony desert — hamada

Barren lava beds

Barren salt flats

Salt marsh

Salt desert

The Great Sea
(Mediterranean Sea)

PHOENICIA

Sidon

Leontes

Tyre

Dan

UPPER
GALILEE

Lake Hula
(L. Semechonitis)

Mt. Meron
3,963

MT. LEBANON

ANTI-LEBANON

MT. HERMON
9,232

Damascus

Abana

Pharpar

33°N

BASHAN

Hauran

LOWER
GALILEE

Sea of Galilee
(Chinnereth)

-696

Acco

Mt. Carmel
1,791

Kishon

Nazareth

Mt. Tabor
1,929

Plain
of
Esdrae-
lon

Hill of
Moreh

V. of Jezreel

Mt. Gilboa
1,640

Beth-shan

Yarmuk

Dor

Megiddo

Caesarea

Plain of Sharon

Dothan

SAMARIA

Samaria

Mt. Ebal
3,083

Mt. Gerizim
2,890

Shechem

Kanah

Farah

Jordan

GILEAD

Jabbok

Zarqa

Jebel Yusha'
3,652

AMMON

Joppa

Shiloh

Tell Azur
3,333

Aijalon

Bethel

Sorek

Jericho

Jerusalem

Mt. of Olives
2,670

Plains of
Moab

Mt. Nebo
2,631

Rabbah
(Amman)

Bethlehem

Elah

Shephelah

JUDEA

Wilderness of Judea

Dead
(Salt)
Sea

-1,296

Gaza

3,346

Hebron

Gerar

Besor

Raphia

Beer-sheba

IDUMEA

Arnon (W. al Mawjib)

MOAB

Kir-hareseth

Arabah

EDOM

Brook of Egypt (W. al 'Arish)

Negeb

Wilderness of Zin

31°N

Zered (W. al Hasa)

Jebel Helal
2,926

Kadesh-barnea

Local grid coordinate system of 50-kilometer squares.

34°E

36°E

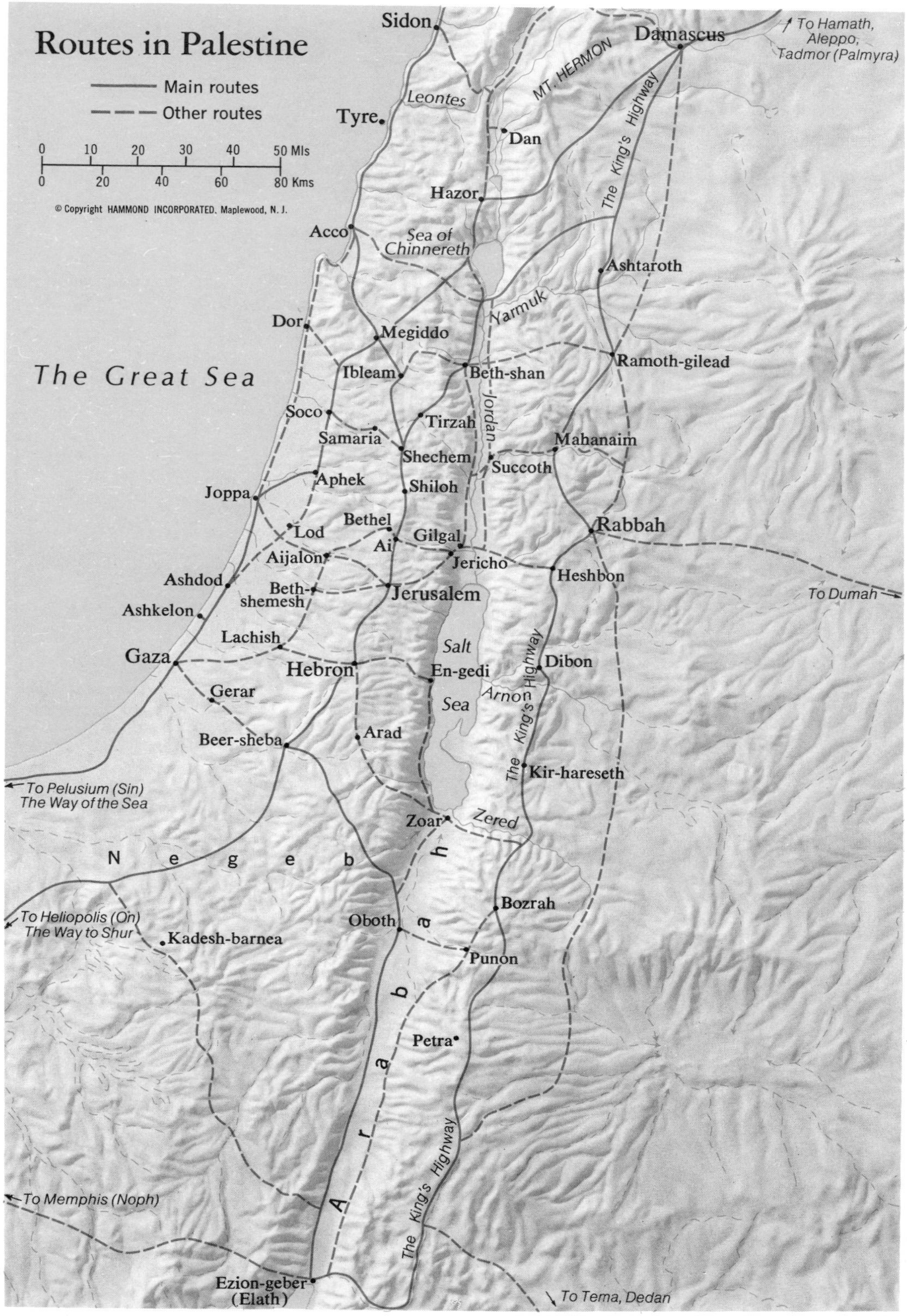

The Plain of Esdraelon looking north toward Mount Tabor.

Routes in Palestine

— Main routes
-- Other routes

0 10 20 30 40 50 Mls
0   20   40   60   80 Kms

© Copyright HAMMOND INCORPORATED. Maplewood, N. J.

The Great Sea

Sidon
Damascus
To Hamath, Aleppo, Tadmor (Palmyra)
MT HERMON
Leontes
Tyre
Dan
The King's Highway
Hazor
Acco
Sea of Chinnereth
Ashtaroth
Dor
Megiddo
Yarmuk
Jordan
Ibleam
Beth-shan
Ramoth-gilead
Soco
Tirzah
Samaria
Shechem
Mahanaim
Aphek
Shiloh
Succoth
Joppa
Bethel
Lod
Ai
Gilgal
Rabbah
Aijalon
Jericho
Heshbon
Ashdod
Beth-shemesh
Jerusalem
To Dumah
Ashkelon
Lachish
Salt
Dibon
Gaza
Hebron
En-gedi
Sea
Arnon
The King's Highway
Gerar
Arad
Kir-hareseth
Beer-sheba
To Pelusium (Sin) The Way of the Sea
Zoar
Zered
N e g e b
Bozrah
To Heliopolis (On) The Way to Shur
Oboth
Kadesh-barnea
Punon
A r a b a h
Petra
The King's Highway
To Memphis (Noph)
Ezion-geber (Elath)
To Tema, Dedan

Goats graze in the forbidding central Samaria hills, where the invading Hebrews found a home for their flocks in Biblical times.

Today children frolic in the cool waters beneath the waterfalls of En-gedi, celebrated in the Song of Songs.

The placid Dead Sea looking eastward toward the hills of Transjordan. Wind erosion at this lowest spot on earth produces an eerie, lunar landscape along the western shore.

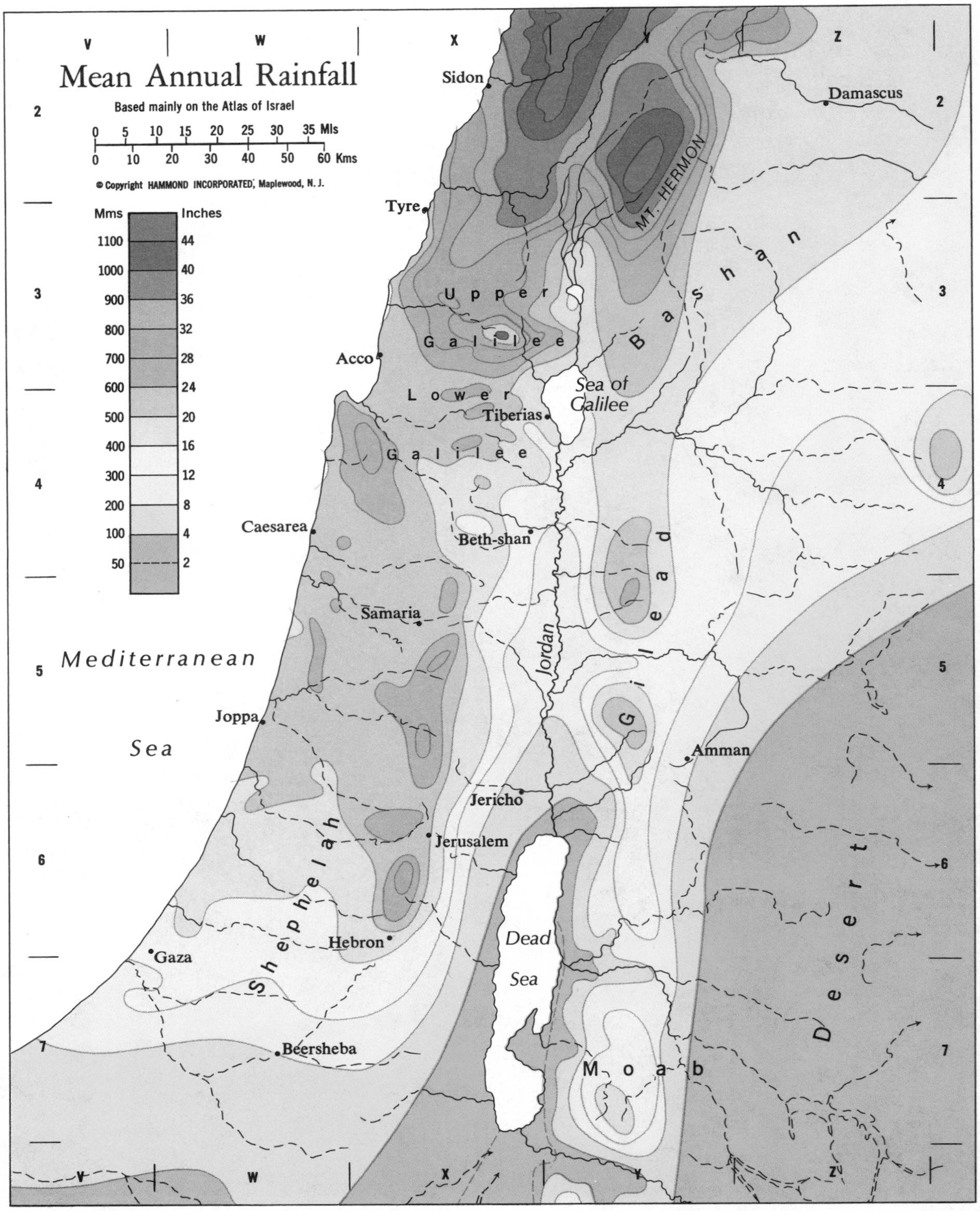

Mean Annual Rainfall

Based mainly on the Atlas of Israel

0 5 10 15 20 25 30 35 Mls
0   10   20   30   40   50   60 Kms

© Copyright HAMMOND INCORPORATED, Maplewood, N. J.

Mms		Inches
1100		44
1000		40
900		36
800		32
700		28
600		24
500		20
400		16
300		12
200		8
100		4
50		2

Sidon

Damascus

Tyre

MT. HERMON

Upper Galilee

Bashan

Acco

Sea of Galilee

Lower

Tiberias

Galilee

Caesarea

Beth-shan

Gilead

Samaria

Mediterranean

Jordan

Sea

Gilead

Joppa

Amman

Jericho

Jerusalem

Shephelah

Dead Sea

Desert

Hebron

Gaza

Beersheba

Moab

Temperature, rainfall,
and relative humidity
for selected stations

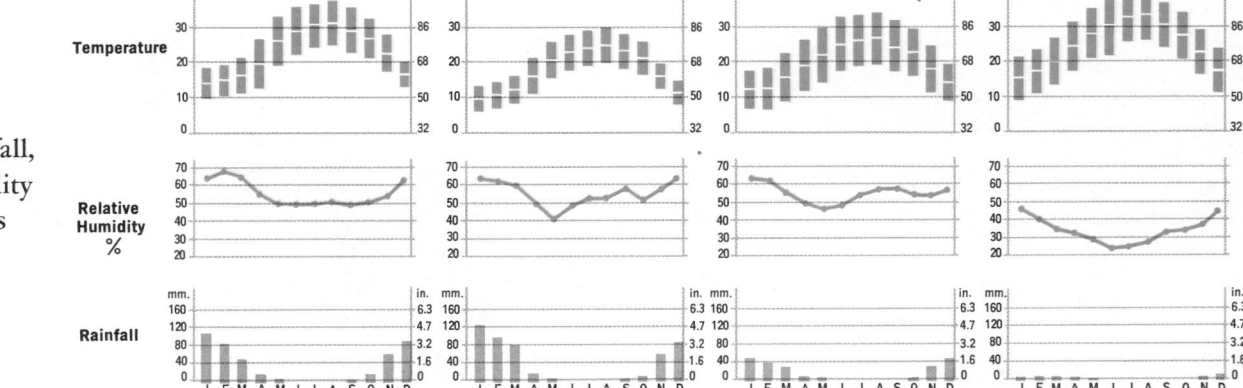

Temperature

Relative Humidity %

Rainfall

Tiberias   Jerusalem   Beersheba   Elath

© Copyright HAMMOND INC., Maplewood, N. J.

Sources: World Climatic Data, 1972; Statistical Abstract of Israel, 1969

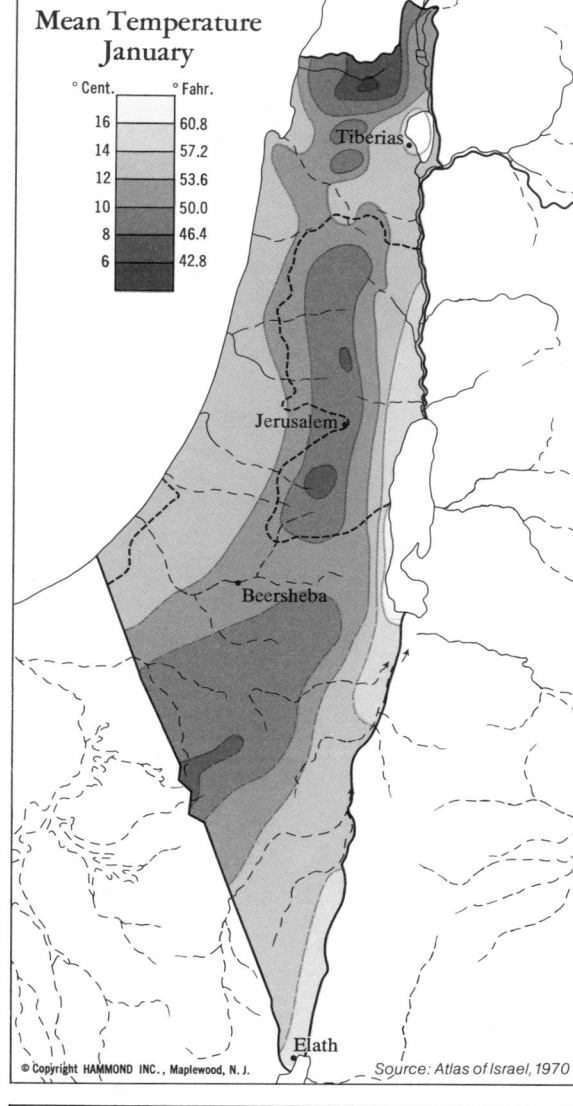

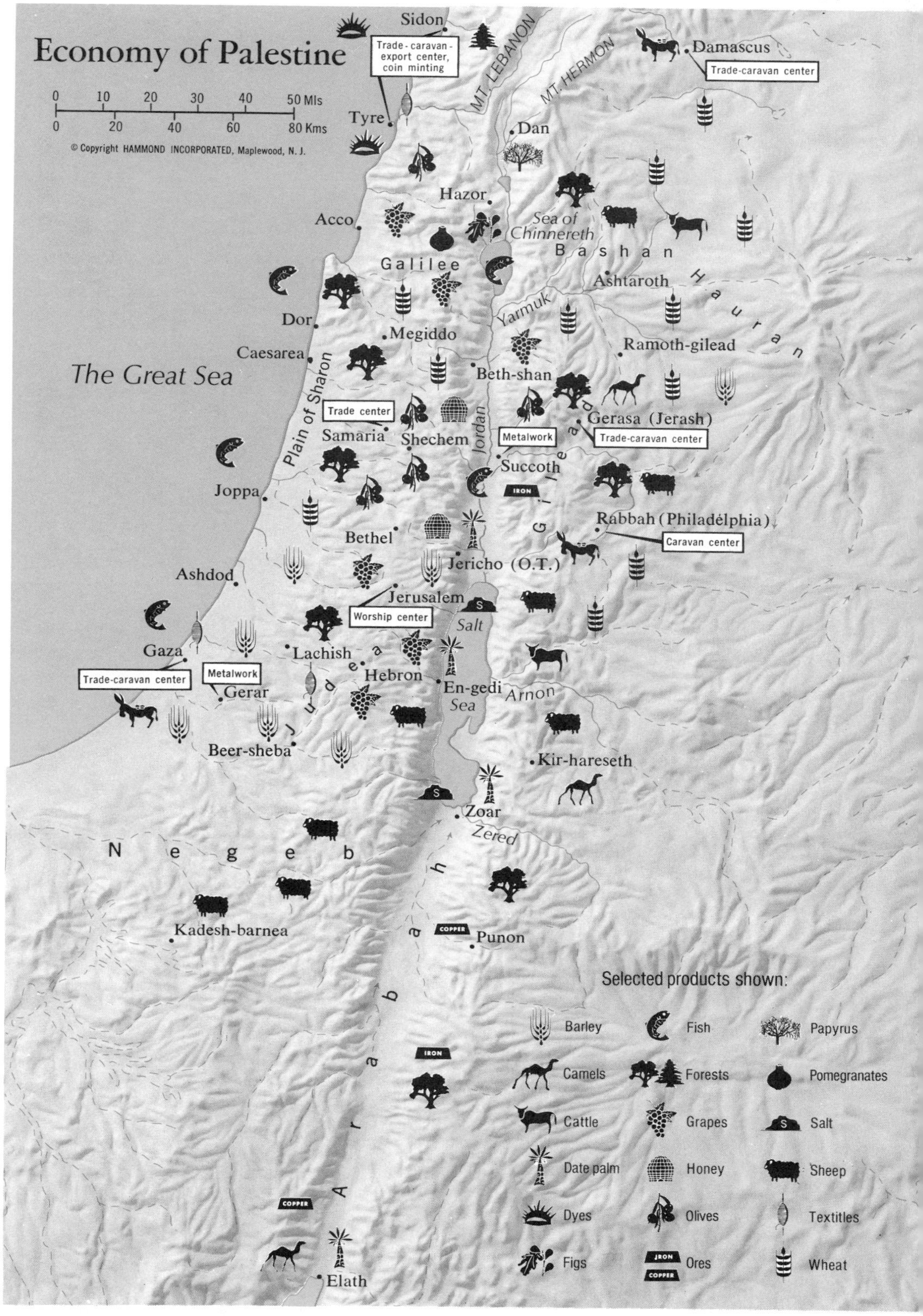

Mean Temperature January

°Cent.	°Fahr.
16	60.8
14	57.2
12	53.6
10	50.0
8	46.4
6	42.8

Tiberias

Jerusalem

Beersheba

Elath

© Copyright HAMMOND INC., Maplewood, N.J.   *Source: Atlas of Israel, 1970*

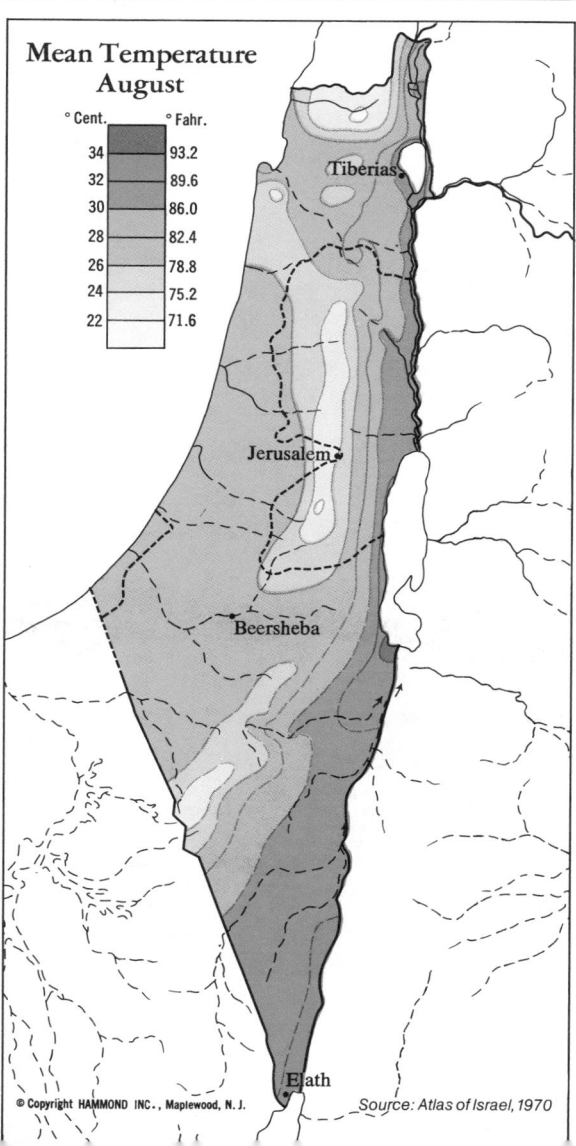

Mean Temperature August

°Cent.	°Fahr.
34	93.2
32	89.6
30	86.0
28	82.4
26	78.8
24	75.2
22	71.6

Tiberias

Jerusalem

Beersheba

Elath

© Copyright HAMMOND INC., Maplewood, N.J.   *Source: Atlas of Israel, 1970*

Economy of Palestine

0	10	20	30	40	50 Mls
0	20	40	60	80 Kms	

© Copyright HAMMOND INCORPORATED, Maplewood, N.J.

Sidon

Trade - caravan - export center, coin minting

MT. LEBANON   MT HERMON   Damascus

Trade-caravan center

Tyre   Dan

Hazor   Sea of Chinnereth   B a s h a n

Acco   Galilee   Ashtaroth   Hauran

Dor   Megiddo   Yarmuk   Ramoth-gilead

Caesarea   Beth-shan

The Great Sea   Plain of Sharon   Trade center   Gerasa (Jerash)

Samaria   Shechem   Jordan   Metalwork   Trade-caravan center

Joppa   Succoth   IRON

Bethel   Rabbah (Philadélphia)

Ashdod   Jericho (O.T.)   Caravan center

Jerusalem   S

Worship center   Salt

Gaza   Lachish   Judaea

Trade-caravan center   Metalwork   Hebron   En-gedi   Arnon

Gerar   Sea

Beer-sheba   Kir-hareseth

S

Zoar   Zered

N e g e b

Kadesh-barnea   COPPER   Punon

Selected products shown:

Barley		Fish		Papyrus	
Camels		Forests		Pomegranates	
Cattle		Grapes		Salt	
Date palm		Honey		Sheep	
Dyes		Olives		Textitles	
Figs		Ores		Wheat	

IRON

COPPER

Elath

Grapes being weighed in a manner reminiscent of a period when both kings and prophets in Israel were concerned with honest measure.

A cluster of dates suggests the richness and plenty of well-watered date palm plantations such as those at Jericho.

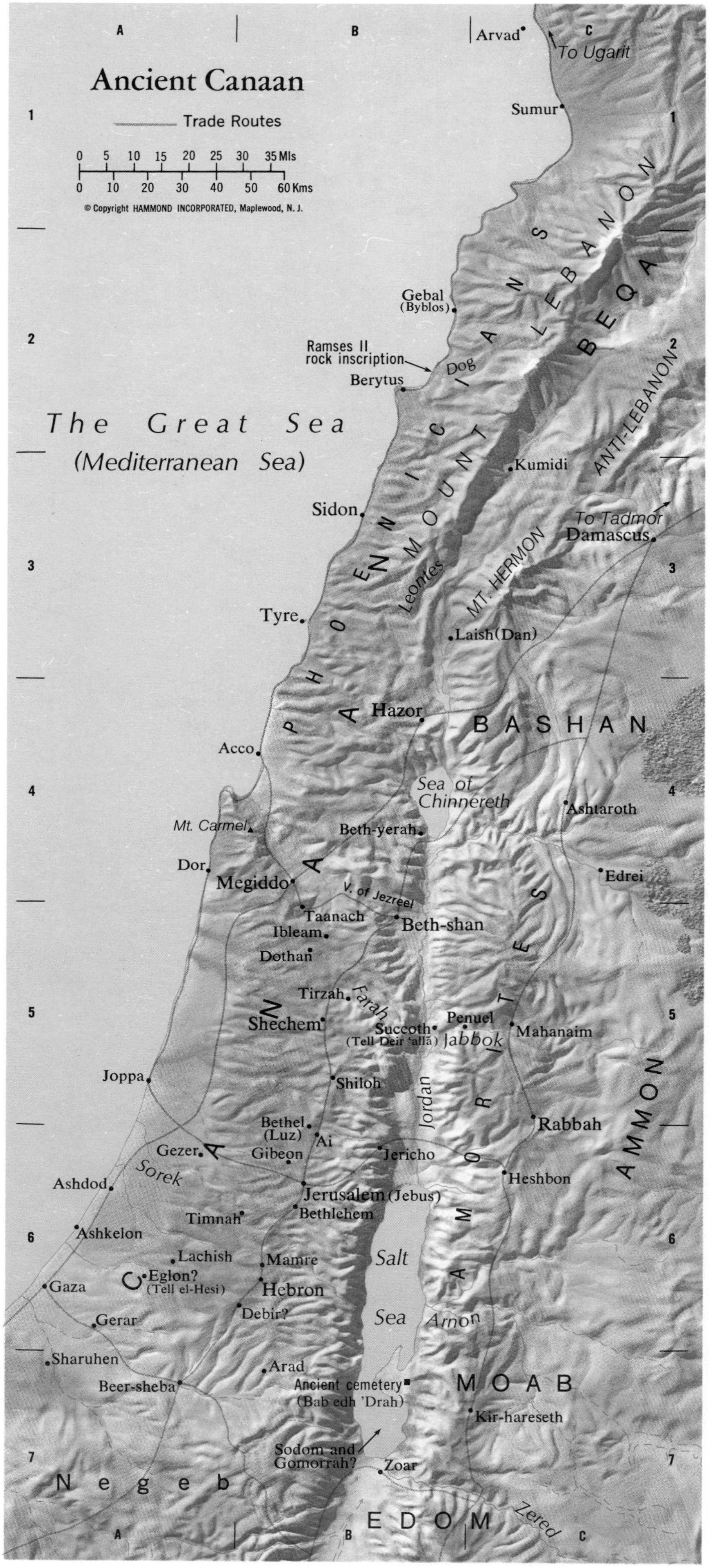

Ancient Canaan

———— Trade Routes

0 5 10 15 20 25 30 35 Mls
0 10 20 30 40 50 60 Kms

© Copyright HAMMOND INCORPORATED, Maplewood, N.J.

Arvad •
To Ugarit

Sumur •

The Great Sea
(Mediterranean Sea)

Gebal •
(Byblos)

Ramses II
rock inscription → Dog

Berytus •

Kumidi •

Sidon •

To Tadmor
Damascus •

Tyre •

Laish (Dan) •

Hazor •

B A S H A N

Acco •

Ashtaroth •

Mt. Carmel ▲

Sea of
Chinnereth

Beth-yerah •

Dor •

Megiddo •

Edrei •

V. of Jezreel

Taanach •

Beth-shan •

Ibleam •

Dothan •

Tirzah •

Penuel •

Shechem •

Succoth • *Jabbok* Mahanaim •
(Tell Deir 'alla)

Joppa •

Shiloh •

A M M O N

Bethel •
(Luz)   Ai •

Rabbah •

Gezer •

Gibeon •   Jericho •

Ashdod •

Sorek

Heshbon •

Jerusalem (Jebus) •
Bethlehem •

Timnah •

Ashkelon •

Salt

Lachish •

Mamre •

Gaza •   Eglon? •
(Tell el-Hesi)   Hebron •

Sea   *Arnon*

Gerar •

Debir? •

Sharuhen •

Arad •

Beer-sheba •   Ancient cemetery ■
(Bab edh 'Drah)   M O A B

Kir-haresheth •

Sodom and
Gomorrah? → Zoar •

N e g e b

E D O M   *Zered*

B l a c

Troy •

A S S U W A

Hermes

▲ Karabel

Maeander   • Beycesulta

A R Z A W A

L U K K A

M I N O A N D O M A I N

Rhodes

Cnossus •

C A P H T O R   M Y C E N A E A N
(Crete)

Mediterranean   Se

(Great   or   Upper   Sea)

L i b y a n

Ava
(Zo

L o w e r
E g y p t
On

Memphis •
(Noph)

Heracleopolis •

Hermop

Akhetaton •
(Tell el-Amarna)   *Nile*

U p p

Abydo •

E g

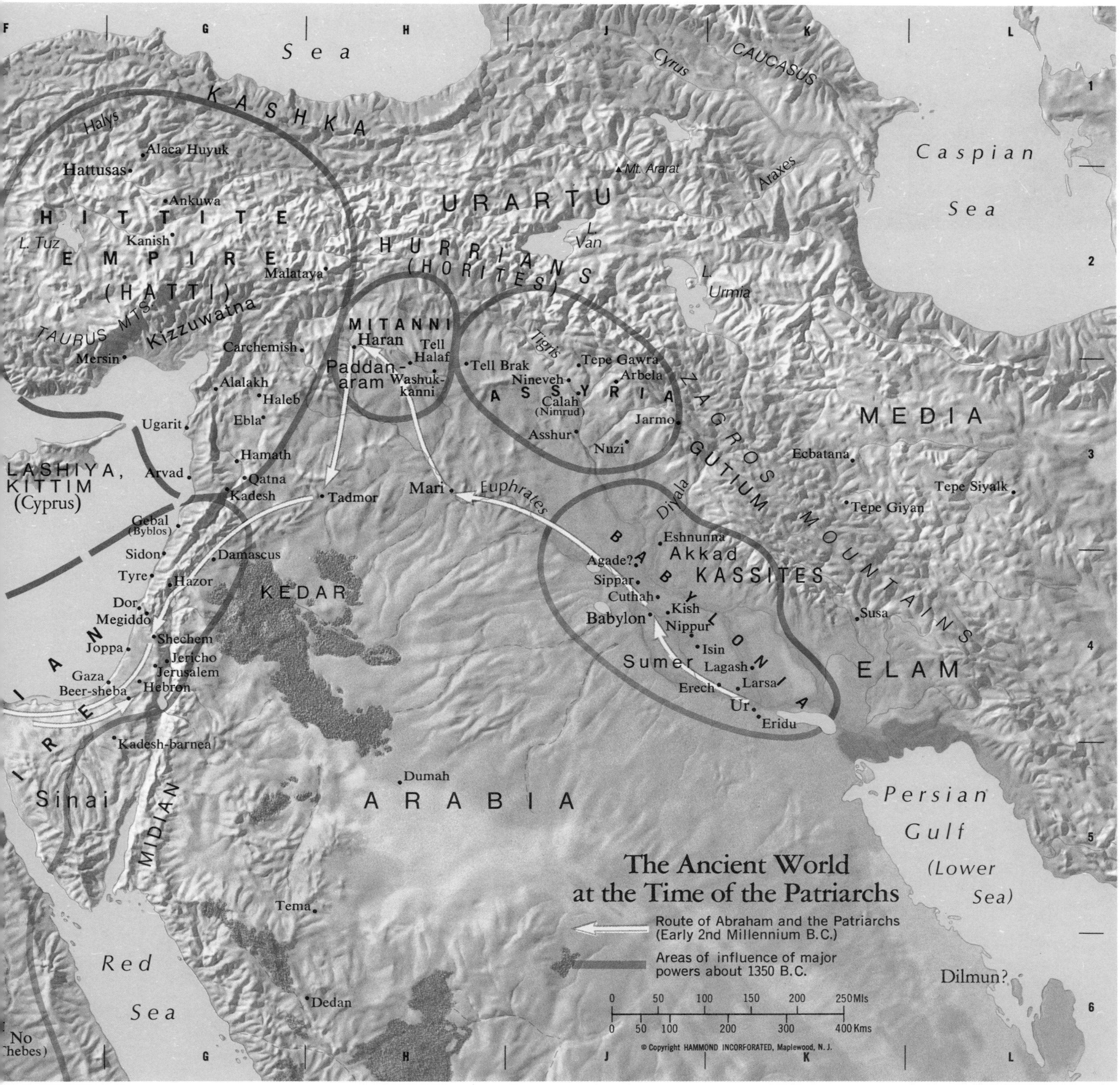

Map Labels

Sea
KASHKA
Halys
Alaca Huyuk
Hattusas
Ankuwa
HITTITE
L. Tuz
Kanish
EMPIRE
(HATTI)
Malataya
TAURUS MTS.
Kizzuwatna
Mersin
Carchemish
MITANNI
Haran
Tell Halaf
Paddan-aram
Washuk-kanni
Alalakh
Haleb
Ebla
Ugarit
Hamath
LASHIYA,
KITTIM
(Cyprus)
Arvad
Qatna
Kadesh
Gebal
(Byblos)
Tadmor
Mari
Euphrates
Sidon
Damascus
Tyre
Hazor
KEDAR
Dor
Megiddo
Joppa
Shechem
Jericho
Gaza
Jerusalem
Beer-sheba
Hebron

URARTU
Mt. Ararat
HURRIANS
(HORITES)
Van
L. Urmia
Tell Brak
Nineveh
Tepe Gawra
Arbela
ASSYRIA
Calah
(Nimrud)
Asshur
Nuzi
Jarmo
ZAGROS
GUTIUM
MOUNTAINS
Eshnunna
Agade?
Akkad
KASSITES
Sippar
Cuthah
Kish
Babylon
Nippur
BABYLONIA
Isin
Sumer
Lagash
Erech
Larsa
Ur
Eridu
ELAM
Susa
Diyala

Caucasus
Cyrus
Araxes
Caspian
Sea
MEDIA
Ecbatana
Tepe Siyalk
Tepe Giyan

Kadesh-barnea
MIDIAN
Sinai
Dumah
ARABIA
Tema
Red
Sea
Dedan
(No
Thebes)

Persian
Gulf
(Lower
Sea)
Dilmun?

The Ancient World at the Time of the Patriarchs

→ Route of Abraham and the Patriarchs
(Early 2nd Millennium B.C.)

━━ Areas of influence of major
powers about 1350 B.C.

0 50 100 150 200 250Mls
0 50 100 200 300 400Kms

© Copyright HAMMOND INCORPORATED, Maplewood, N.J.

Discoveries in the royal tombs at Ur
have made it possible to reconstruct
this magnificent sounding box of a lyre
The bull's head is of gold, silver and
lapis lazuli. Below the head are panels
of shell inlay.

The Canaanite altar for burnt
offerings at Megiddo. This
splendid "high place" was
built in the Early Bronze Age
and continued in use as late as
the 19th century B.C., the time
of the Hebrew Patriarchs.

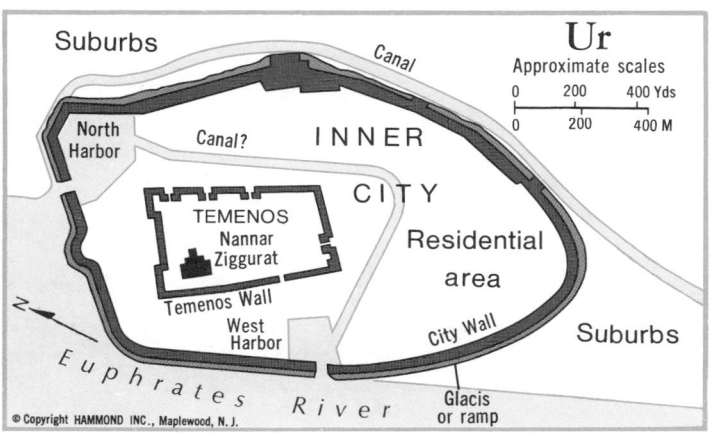

Ur
Approximate scales
0 200 400 Yds
0 200 400 M

Suburbs
Canal
North
Harbor
Canal?
INNER
CITY
TEMENOS
Nannar
Ziggurat
Residential
area
Temenos Wall
West
Harbor
City Wall
Suburbs
Euphrates River
Glacis
or ramp

© Copyright HAMMOND INC., Maplewood, N.J.

In a timeless scene the pyramids dominate the sandy Egyptian horizon beyond the fertile fields of the Nile River plain.

A wall painting from the reign of Thutmoses III (15th century B.C.) shows the various stages of brickmaking.

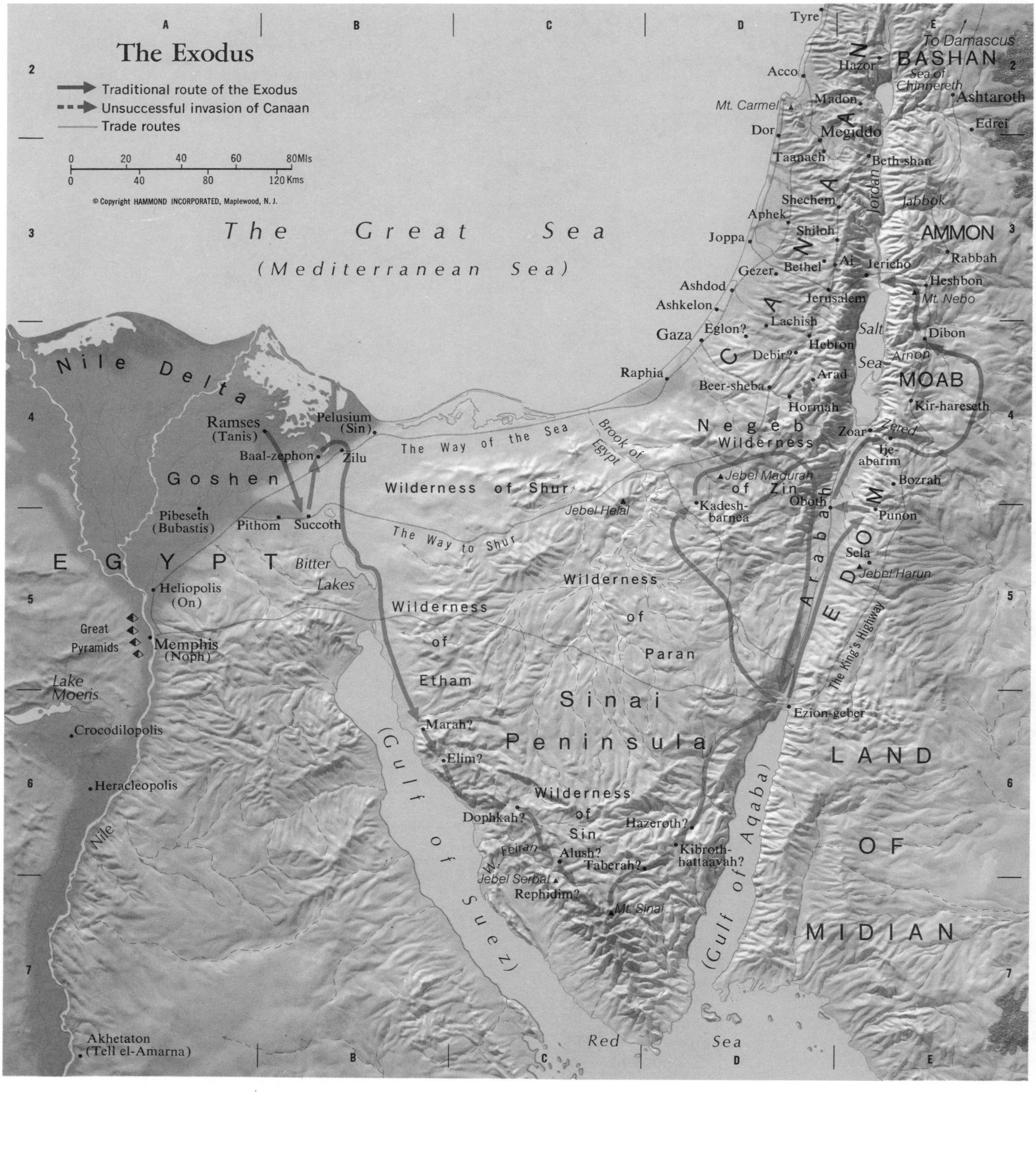

The Exodus

→ Traditional route of the Exodus
⇢ Unsuccessful invasion of Canaan
— Trade routes

0 20 40 60 80 Mls
0   40   80   120 Kms

© Copyright HAMMOND INCORPORATED, Maplewood, N.J.

The Great Sea
(Mediterranean Sea)

Tyre
To Damascus
BASHAN
Acco
Hazor
Sea of Chinnereth
Ashtaroth
Mt. Carmel
Madon
Edrei
Dor
Megiddo
Taanach
Beth-shan
Shechem
Aphek
Shiloh
AMMON
Joppa
Jordan
Jabbok
Gezer
Bethel
Ai
Jericho
Rabbah
Ashdod
Jerusalem
Heshbon
Ashkelon
Mt. Nebo
Eglon?
Lachish
Salt
Gaza
Hebron
Dibon
Debir?
Sea
Raphia
Arad
Arnon
MOAB
Beer-sheba
Kir-hareseth
Hormah
Zoar
Zered
Negeb
Wilderness
Ije-abarim

Nile Delta

Ramses (Tanis)
Pelusium (Sin)
Baal-zephon
Zilu
The Way of the Sea
Brook of Egypt
Bozrah
Goshen
Jebel Madurah
of Zin
Punon
Pibeseth (Bubastis)
Pithom
Succoth
The Way to Shur
Wilderness of Shur
Jebel Helal
Kadesh-barnea
Oboth
EGYPT
Bitter Lakes
Sela
Heliopolis (On)
Wilderness
Jebel Harun
Wilderness
of
Great Pyramids
Etham
of
Paran
Memphis (Noph)
Sinai
Lake Moeris
Marah?
Peninsula
Crocodilopolis
Elim?
Ezion-geber
The King's Highway
Heracleopolis
Wilderness
LAND
of
Nile
Dophkah?
Sin
Hazeroth?
Feiran
Alush?
Kibroth-hattaavah?
OF
Jebel Serbal
Taberah?
Rephidim?
Mt. Sinai
MIDIAN
Akhetaton (Tell el-Amarna)

Red   Sea

N
A
A
N
C
A
N
A
E D O M
Arabah

Gulf of Suez
Gulf of Aqaba

Mount Tabor, where the forces of Deborah gathered to give battle to the army of Sisera (Judges 4:6f.). A torrent turned the Esdraelon Plain (in the foreground) into a quagmire, rendering Sisera's Canaanite chariots ineffective.

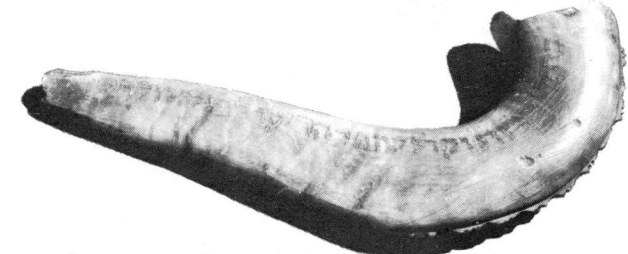

A *shofar,* a type of trumpet used extensively in ancient Israel for special religious purposes in both war and peace.

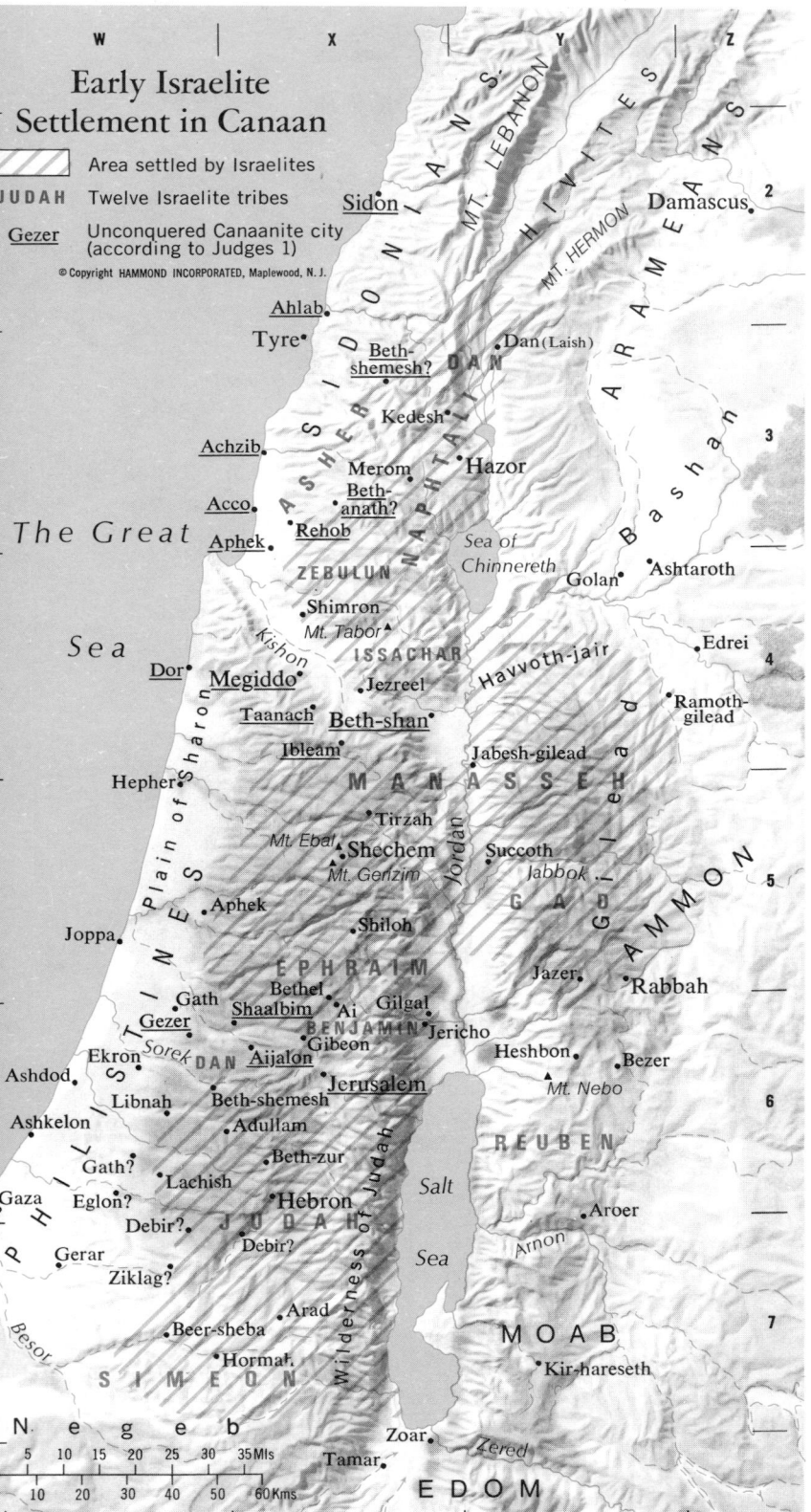

Early Israelite Settlement in Canaan

Area settled by Israelites

JUDAH Twelve Israelite tribes

Gezer Unconquered Canaanite city (according to Judges 1)

© Copyright HAMMOND INCORPORATED, Maplewood, N. J.

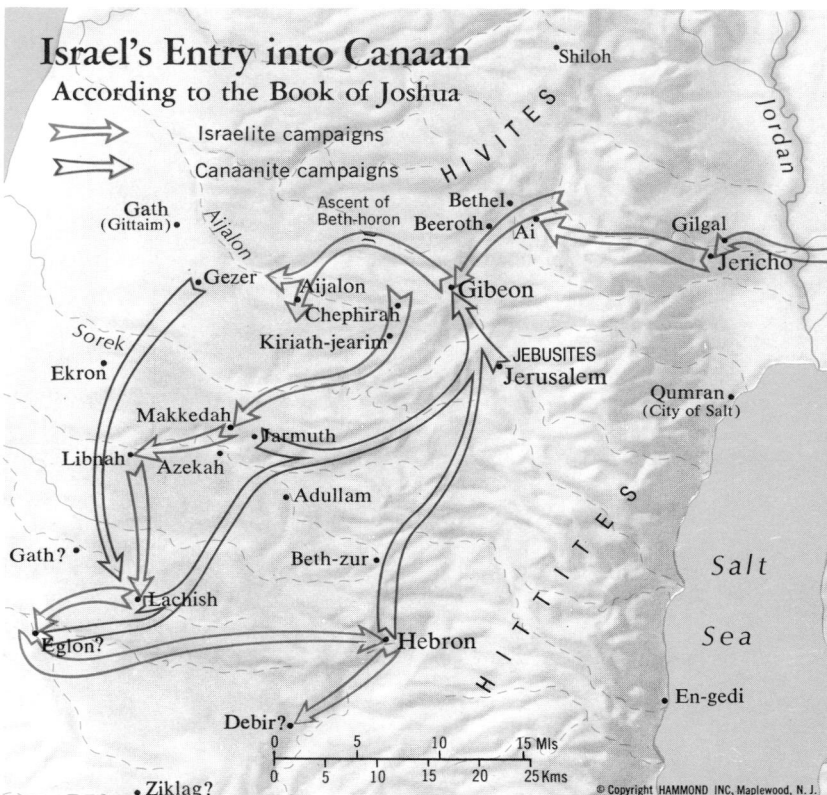

Israel's Entry into Canaan
According to the Book of Joshua

Israelite campaigns

Canaanite campaigns

© Copyright HAMMOND INC, Maplewood, N. J.

The fortress-temple of Baal-berith, probably the scene of Joshua's covenant (Joshua 24:1-28), was built at Shechem around 1650 B.C. and with modifications continued in use throughout the Period of the Judges.

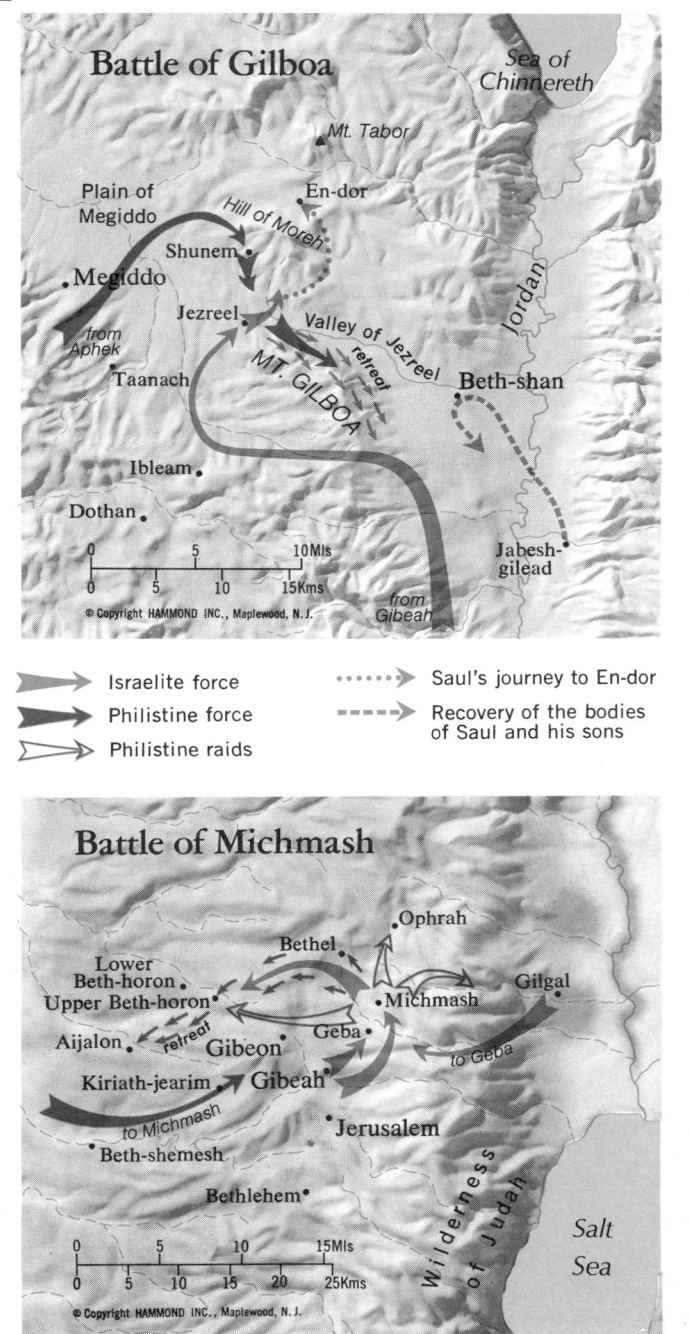

Battle of Gilboa

Sea of Chinnereth

Mt. Tabor

Plain of Megiddo

En-dor

Hill of Moreh

Shunem

Megiddo

Jezreel

from Aphek

Valley of Jezreel

retreat

Taanach

MT. GILBOA

Beth-shan

Jordan

Ibleam

Dothan

Jabesh-gilead

from Gibeah

0 5 10 Mls
0 5 10 15 Kms
© Copyright HAMMOND INC., Maplewood, N.J.

→ Israelite force
→ Philistine force
▷ Philistine raids
···▷ Saul's journey to En-dor
---▷ Recovery of the bodies of Saul and his sons

Battle of Michmash

Ophrah

Bethel

Lower Beth-horon

Upper Beth-horon

Michmash

Gilgal

Aijalon

retreat

Geba

to Geba

Gibeon

Kiriath-jearim

Gibeah

to Michmash

Beth-shemesh

Jerusalem

Bethlehem

Wilderness of Judah

Salt Sea

0 5 10 15Mls
0 5 10 15 20 25Kms
© Copyright HAMMOND INC., Maplewood, N.J.

The Kingdom of Saul

━━ Approximate limits of the Kingdom of Saul

0 5 10 15 20 25 30 35 Mls
0 10 20 30 40 50 60 Kms
© Copyright HAMMOND INCORPORATED, Maplewood, N.J.

W   X   Y   Z

Sidon

BETH-REHOB

MT. HERMON   Damascus

Ijon

Tyre

Abel-beth-maachah   Dan

MAACHAH

ASHER

Kedesh

Achzib

Merom   Hazor

GESHUR

Bashan

Acco

Chinnereth

Aphek   Sea of Chinnereth   Golan   Ashtaroth

Hammath   TOB

The Great

Shimron

Edrei

Sea

Kishon   Mt. Tabor

Dor   Megiddo   Jezreel   MT. GILBOA

Taanach   Beth-shan   Ramoth-gilead

Ibleam

Hepher   Thebez   Bezek   Jabesh-gilead

Plain of Sharon   Tirzah

Mt. Ebal   Shechem   Succoth   Mahanaim

Mt. Gerizim   Jabbok

Aphek   EPHRAIM   AMMON

Joppa   Shiloh

Ramah

Bethel   Jazer   Rabbah

Gath   Gibeon   Gilgal

Gezer   BENJAMIN   Michmash   Heshbon

Sorek   Kiriath-jearim   Gibeah

Ekron

Ashdod   Jerusalem   Medeba

Beth-shemesh   Bethlehem

Ashkelon   Socoh   Adullam

Gath?   Beth-zur   Salt

Eglon?   Lachish   Hebron   Sea

Gaza   Debir?   En-gedi   Aroer

Gerar   JUDAH   Arnon

Ziklag?   Wilderness of Judah

Beer-sheba   Arad   MOAB

Hormah   Kir-hareseth

Negeb

Tamar   Zoar   Zered

W   X   Y

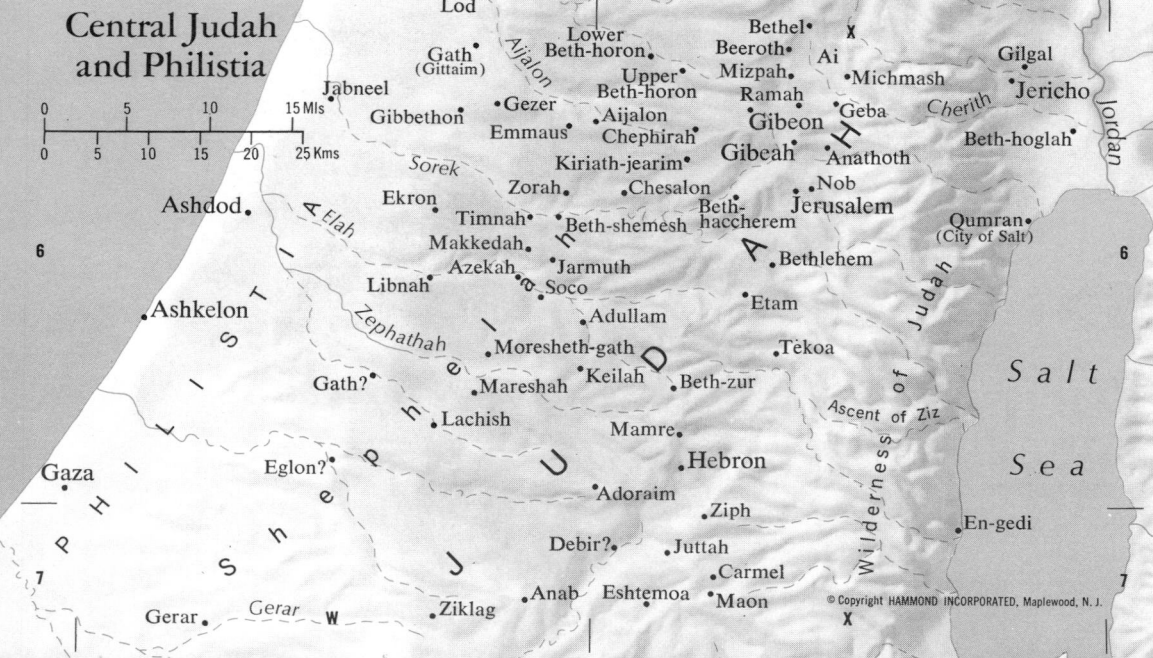

Central Judah and Philistia

0 5 10 15 Mls
0 5 10 15 20 25 Kms

Lod

Bethel

Lower Beth-horon   Beeroth   Ai   Gilgal

Gath (Gittaim)   Aijalon   Mizpah   Michmash   Jericho

Jabneel   Upper Beth-horon   Ramah   Geba

Gibbethon   Gezer   Aijalon   Chephirah   Gibeon   Cherith

Emmaus   Kiriath-jearim   Gibeah   Beth-hoglah

Sorek   Zorah   Chesalon   Anathoth

Ashdod   Ekron   Nob

Timnah   Beth-shemesh   Beth-haccherem   Jerusalem

Makkedah   Qumran (City of Salt)

Ashkelon   Azekah   Jarmuth   Soco   Bethlehem

Libnah   Etam   Salt

Zephathah   Adullam

Moresheth-gath   Tekoa

Gath?   Keilah   Ascent of Ziz   Sea

Mareshah   Beth-zur

Lachish   Mamre

Gaza   Hebron

Eglon?   Adoraim

Ziph

Debir?   Juttah   En-gedi

Gerar   Gerar   Ziklag   Anab   Eshtemoa   Maon   Carmel

© Copyright HAMMOND INCORPORATED, Maplewood, N.J.

At Gibeah the remains of Saul's fortress-palace (background) are surrounded by later construction (foregound). The rude simplicity of Saul's capital contrasted sharply with Solomon's magnificent buildings constructed four miles away in Jerusalem only a few years later.

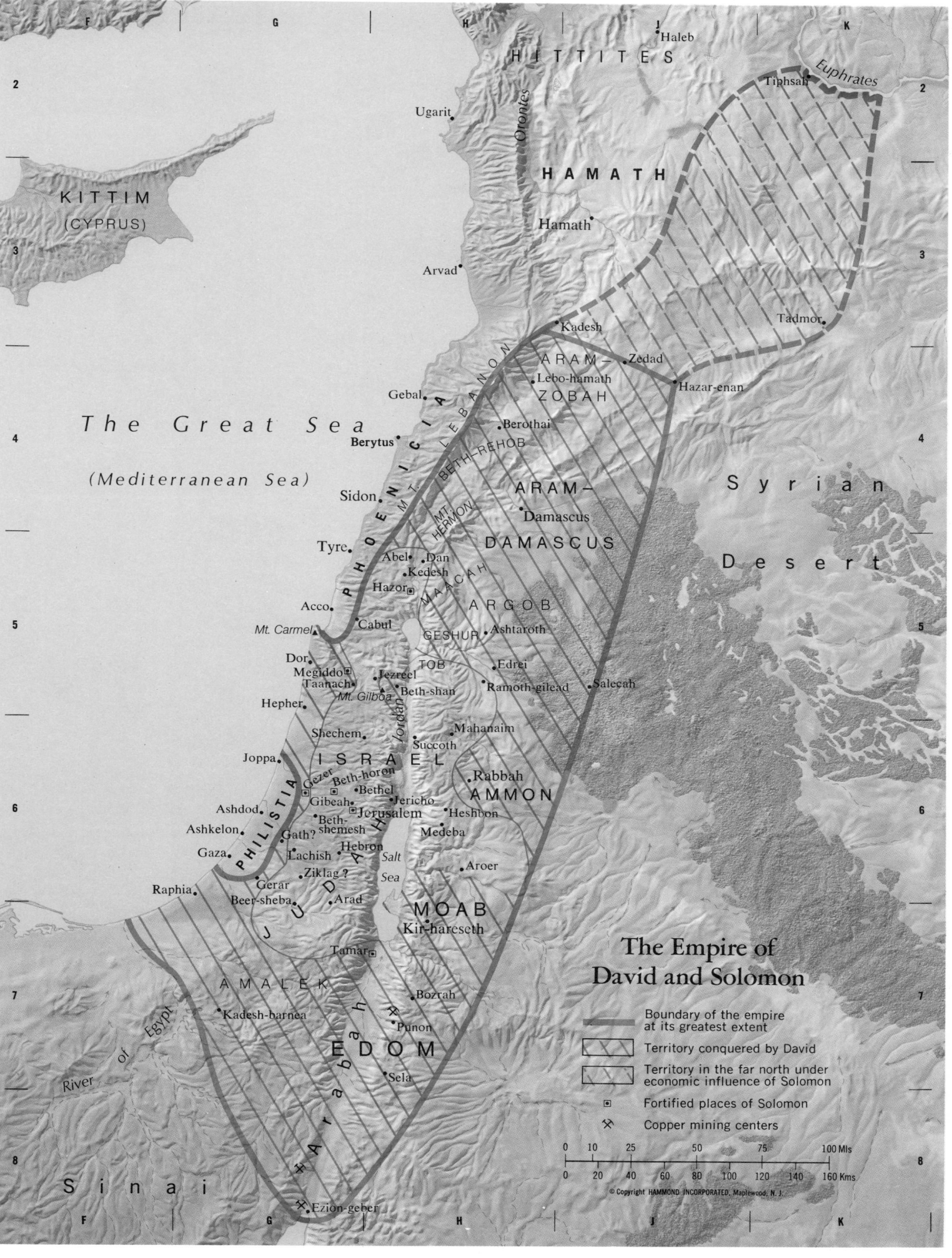

HITTITES

Haleb

Euphrates

Ugarit

Tiphsah

HAMATH

Hamath

Arvad

Oronies

Tadmor

The Great Sea

Kadesh

Gebal

Zedad

ARAM –

Lebo-hamath

ZOBAH

Hazar-enan

(Mediterranean Sea)

Berothai

Berytus

BETH-REHOB

S y r i a n

Sidon

ARAM –

Damascus

D e s e r t

Tyre

DAMASCUS

Abel   Dan

Kedesh

Hazor

MAACAH

ARGOB

Acco

Ashtaroth

Mt. Carmel   Cabul

GESHUR

Dor

TOB

Edrei

Megiddo   Jezreel

Ramoth-gilead

Salecah

Taanach   Beth-shan

Mt. Gilboa

Hepher

Mahanaim

Shechem

Succoth

Joppa

ISRAEL

Gezer   Beth-horon

Rabbah

Bethel

AMMON

Ashdod

Gibeah   Jericho

Jerusalem

Heshbon

Ashkelon

Beth-

shemesh

Medeba

Gath?

Gaza

Hebron

Lachish

Salt

Gerar   Ziklag?

Sea

Aroer

Raphia

Arad

Beer-sheba

MOAB

JUDAH

Kir-hareseth

Tamar

The Empire of

AMALEK

David and Solomon

Bozrah

Kadesh-barnea

Punon

Boundary of the empire
at its greatest extent

EDOM

Territory conquered by David

Territory in the far north under
economic influence of Solomon

Sela

Fortified places of Solomon

Copper mining centers

0	10	25	50	75	100 Mls

0	20	40	60	80	100	120	140	160 Kms.

River

of

Egypt

S i n a i

Ezion-geber

© Copyright HAMMOND INCORPORATED, Maplewood, N. J.

PHOENICIA

MT. LEBANON

MT. HERMON

Jordan

PHILISTIA

Arabah

The Israelite gate at Gezer is one of the finest Solomonic structures yet found. Its design of two outer towers and six flanking guardrooms is virtually identical to Solomon's fortification gates at Megiddo and Hazor.

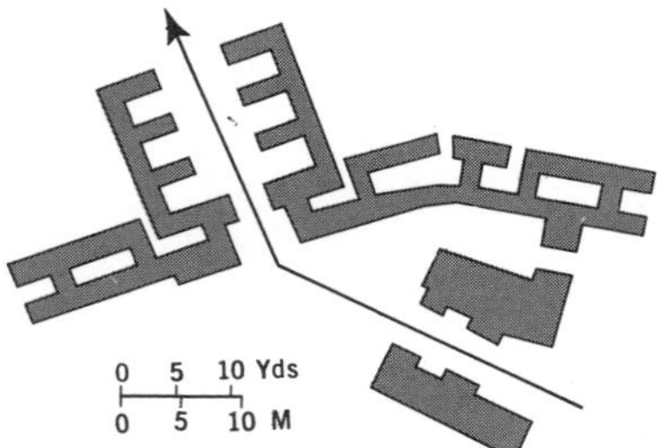

0 5 10 Yds
0 5 10 M

Solomonic Gate at Gezer

A proto-Ionic capital of the type that graced the gates of the royal cities and palaces of Israel and Judah: Samaria, Megiddo, Hazor, Ramat Rahel and most likely Jerusalem and Gezer.

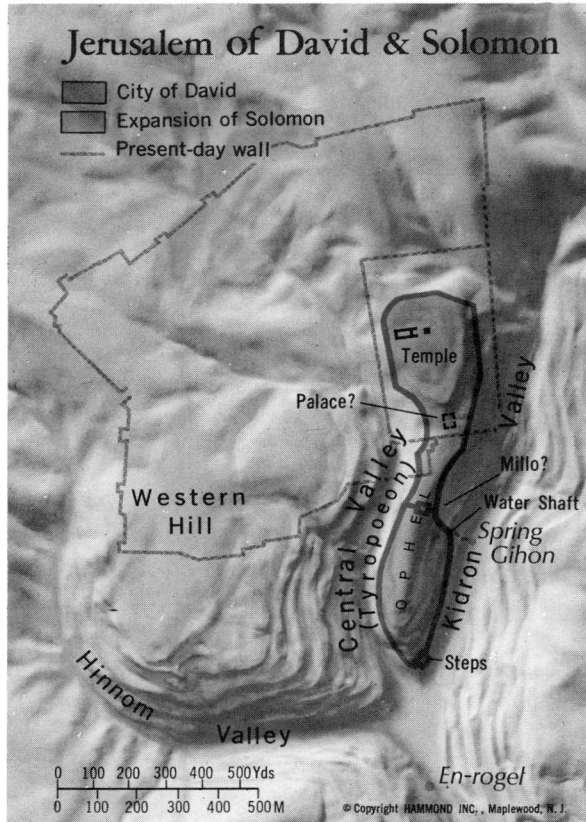

Jerusalem of David & Solomon

- City of David
- Expansion of Solomon
- Present-day wall

Temple
Palace?
Millo?
Water Shaft
Spring Gihon
Steps

Western Hill

Central Valley (Tyropoeon)

OPHEL

Kidron Valley

Hinnom Valley

En-rogel

0 100 200 300 400 500 Yds
0 100 200 300 400 500 M

© Copyright HAMMOND INC., Maplewood, N.J.

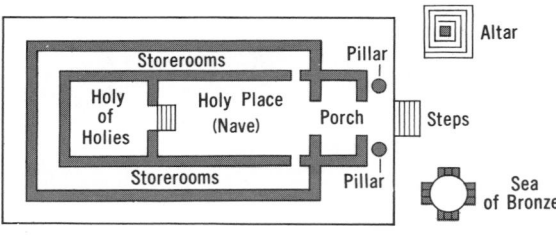

Storerooms
Pillar
Holy of Holies
Holy Place (Nave)
Porch
Storerooms
Pillar

Altar
Steps
Sea of Bronze

Temple of Solomon

0 10 20 30 Cubits
0 5 10 15 M

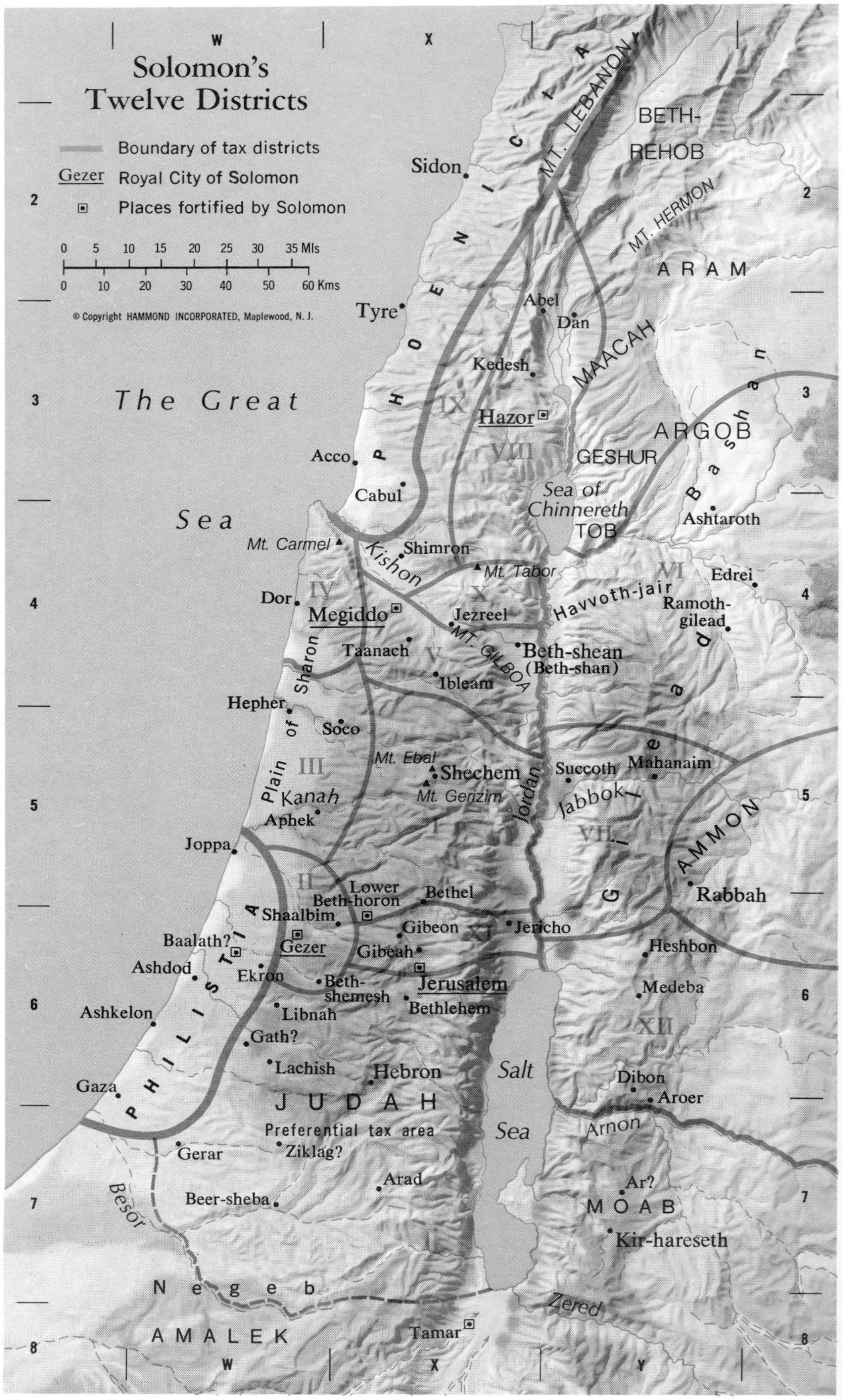

Solomon's Twelve Districts

— Boundary of tax districts
Gezer   Royal City of Solomon
⊡   Places fortified by Solomon

0 5 10 15 20 25 30 35 Mls
0 10 20 30 40 50 60 Kms

© Copyright HAMMOND INCORPORATED, Maplewood, N.J.

W   X

BETH-REHOB

Sidon

MT. LEBANON

MT. HERMON

ARAM

Tyre

Abel
Dan

PHOENICIA

Kedesh

MAACAH

Hazor ⊡

ARGOB

IX

VIII

GESHUR

Acco

Cabul

Sea of Chinnereth

TOB

Ashtaroth

Bashan

The Great

Sea

Mt. Carmel

Kishon

Shimron

Mt. Tabor

Havvoth-jair

VI

Edrei

Dor

IV

Megiddo ⊡

Jezreel

Ramoth-gilead

Taanach

V

MT. GILBOA

Beth-shean (Beth-shan)

Ibleam

Plain of Sharon

Hepher

Soco

Mt. Ebal

Shechem

Mt. Gerizim

Succoth

Mahanaim

Kanah

Jordan

Jabbok

VII

Aphek

Joppa

AMMON

II

Lower Beth-horon

Bethel

Rabbah

Shaalbim

Gibeon

Jericho

Baalath?

Gibeah

Heshbon

Gezer

Jerusalem

Medeba

Ashdod

Ekron

Beth-shemesh

Bethlehem

XII

Ashkelon

Libnah

Gath?

Salt

Dibon

Gaza

Lachish

Hebron

Sea

Aroer

JUDAH

Arnon

Preferential tax area

Gerar

Ziklag?

Atad

Ar?

Beer-sheba

MOAB

Besor

Kir-hareseth

Negeb

Zered

AMALEK

Tamar ⊡

W   X   Y

The Kingdoms of Israel and Judah

ISRAEL — — — Approximate frontiers
AMMON — Hebrew kingdoms
— Foreign kingdoms

0 5 10 15 20 25 30 35 40 45 50 Mls
0 10 20 30 40 50 60 70 80 Kms

© Copyright HAMMOND INCORPORATED, Maplewood, N.J.

SYRIA (ARAM)

Damascus

PHOENICIA

Sidon

MT. HERMON

Leontes

Ijon

Tyre

Abel-beth-maachah

Dan

Kedesh

Hazor

BASHAN

Merom

Galilee

Acco

Chinnereth

Cabul

Sea of Chinnereth

Karnaim

Ashtaroth

Rumah

Hammath

Gath-hepher

Aphek

Mt. Carmel

Kishon

Mt. Tabor

Plain of Esdraelon

Yarmuk

Havvoth-jair

Edrei

Dor

Megiddo

Shunem

Jezreel

Mt. Gilboa

Taanach

Beth-shan

Ramoth-gilead

Beth-haggan

Abel-meholah

Plain of Sharon

Dothan

Ibleam

Jabesh-gilead

Tishbe

Socoh

ISRAEL

Tirzah

Gilead

Samaria

Mt. Ebal

Penuel

Mahanaim

Shechem

Mt. Gerizim

Succoth

Jabbok

AMMON

Kanah

Aphek

Shiloh

The Great Sea
(Mediterranean Sea)

Joppa

Zeredah

Jordan

Jazer

Rabbah

Lod

Bethel

Zemaraim

Gath

Gilgal

Gibeon

Gezer

Mizpah

Geba

Jericho

Shittim?

Heshbon

Jabneel

Ramah

Gibbethon

Aijalon

Mt. Nebo

Ekron

Zorah

Jerusalem

Medeba

Jahaz

Ashdod

Beth-shemesh

Bethlehem

Ashkelon

Socoh

Adullam

Etam

Tekoa

Mareshah

Beth-zur

Wilderness of Judah

Ataroth

Lachish

JUDAH

Salt Sea

Dibon

Gaza

Adoraim

Hebron

En-gedi

Aroer

Debir?

Ziph

Arnon

PHILISTIA

Gerar

Ziklag?

Arad

Ar

Raphia

Sharuhen

MOAB

Besor

Beer-sheba

Kir-hareseth

Zoar

Ziph

Tamar

Zered

Negeb

Ascent of Akrabbim

Arabah

EDOM

Bozrah

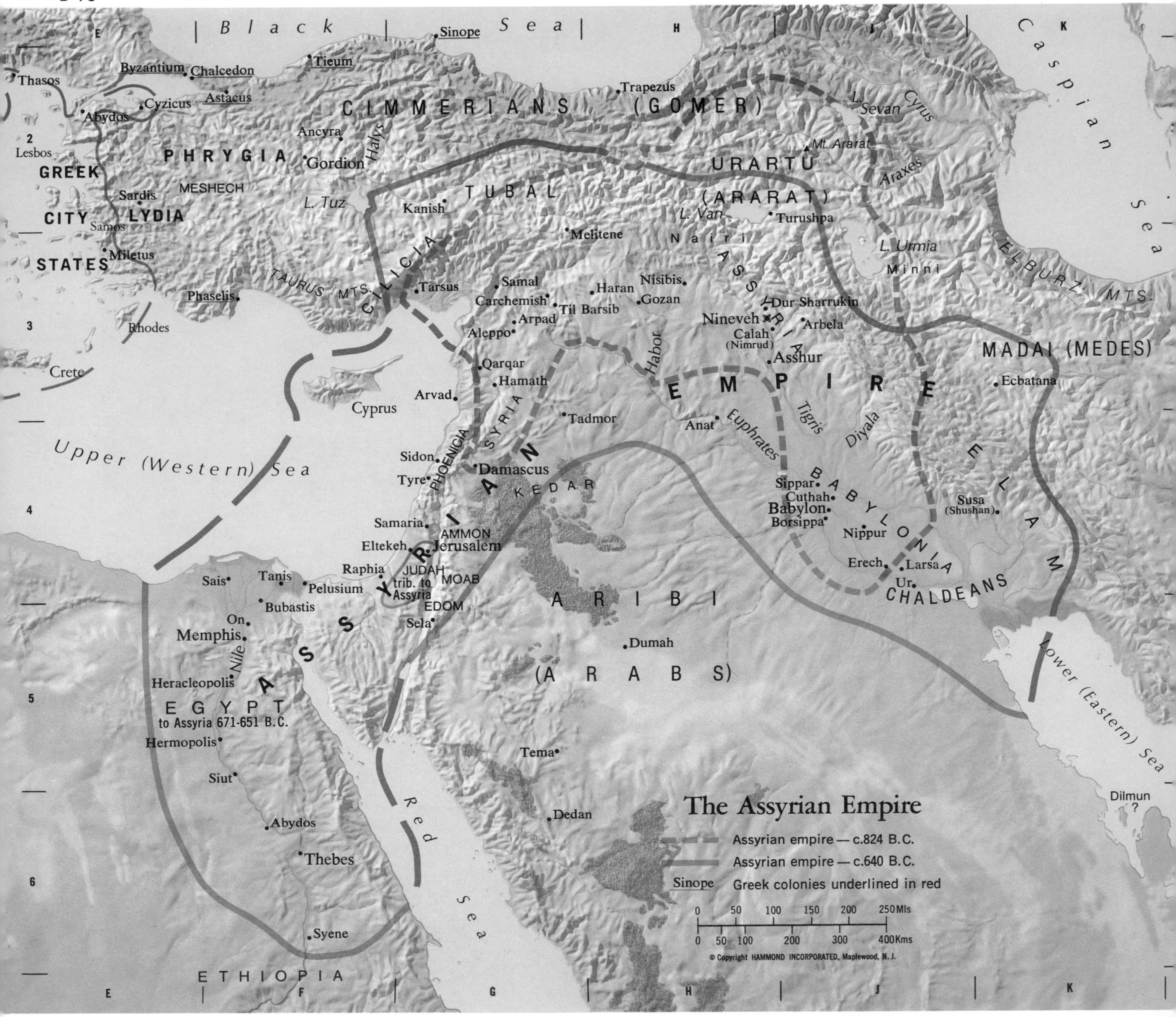

Black Sea

Thasos
Byzantium • Chalcedon
• Tieum
Sinope
Trapezus
L. Sevan
Cyrus

CIMMERIANS (GOMER)

Cyzicus • Astacus
Abydos •
Lesbos •
GREEK
PHRYGIA • Gordion
Ancyra
Halys
L. Tuz
Kanish
• Melitene
Nairi
URARTU
(ARARAT)
Mt. Ararat
L. Van • Turushpa
Araxes
ELBURZ MTS.

CITY
Sardis
MESHECH
TUBAL
L. Urmia
Minni

LYDIA
Samos •
Miletus •
STATES

Caspian Sea

Phaselis
TAURUS MTS.
CILICIA
Tarsus •
Samal •
Carchemish •
Arpad •
Aleppo •
Haran • Nisibis •
Til Barsib •
Gozan
Dur Sharrukin •
Nineveh • Arbela •
Calah
(Nimrud)
Asshur •
ASSYRIA
MADAI (MEDES)

Rhodes •

Crete •

Cyprus
Arvad •
Qarqar •
Hamath •
SYRIA
EMPIRE
Euphrates
Tigris
Diyala
Ecbatana •
ELAM

Upper (Western) Sea
Tadmor •
Anat •
Sippar •
Cuthah •
Babylon •
Borsippa •
BABYLONIA
Nippur •
Susa
(Shushan) •

Sidon •
Tyre •
PHOENICIA
Damascus •
KEDAR
ASSYRIAN

Samaria •
Eltekeh •
AMMON
Jerusalem •
Erech •
Larsa •
Ur •
CHALDEANS

Raphia •
JUDAH
trib. to
Assyria
MOAB
Sais •
Tanis •
Pelusium •
Bubastis •
EDOM
Sela •

On •
Memphis •
ASSYRIAN
ARIBI

Heracleopolis •
EGYPT
to Assyria 671-651 B.C.
Dumah •
(ARABS)

Hermopolis •
Nile
Lower (Eastern) Sea

Siut •
Tema •
Dilmun ?

Abydos •
Dedan •

Thebes •
Red Sea

The Assyrian Empire

Assyrian empire — c.824 B.C.
Assyrian empire — c.640 B.C.
Sinope   Greek colonies underlined in red

0   50   100   150   200   250 Mls
0   50 100   200   300   400 Kms

© Copyright HAMMOND INCORPORATED, Maplewood, N.J.

Syene •

ETHIOPIA

Tiglath-pileser III extended the
Assyrian Empire in the 8th
century B.C. and caused political
chaos in Israel.

The only contemporary picture of a Hebrew
monarch occurs on the Black Obelisk, an
Assyrian monument from Nimrud. It shows
Jehu on his knees before Shalmaneser III.

Assyrian wall relief from the throne room of
Sennacherib shows Hebrews fleeing the doomed
city of Lachish in southwest Judah when it was
under Assyrian siege in 701 B.C.

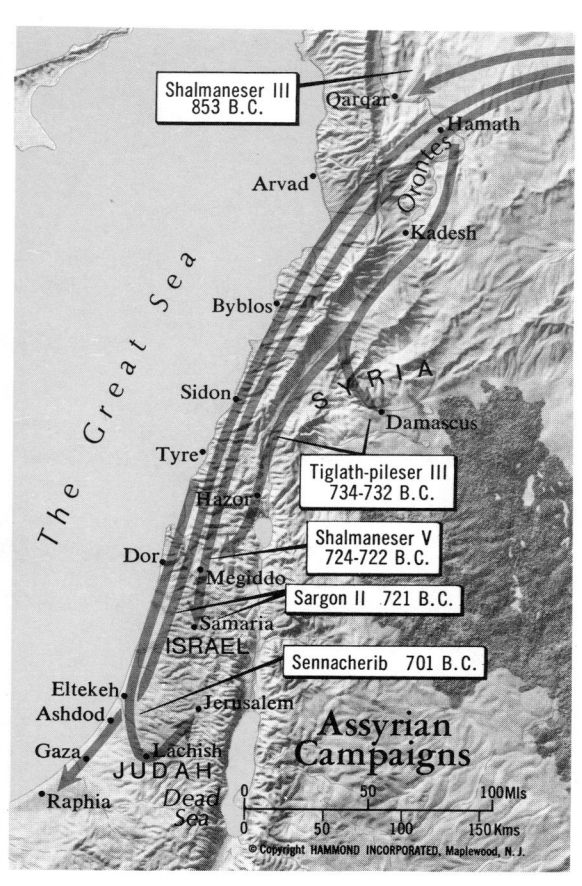

Assyrian Campaigns

Shalmaneser III 853 B.C.

Tiglath-pileser III 734-732 B.C.

Shalmaneser V 724-722 B.C.

Sargon II 721 B.C.

Sennacherib 701 B.C.

© Copyright HAMMOND INCORPORATED, Maplewood, N.J.

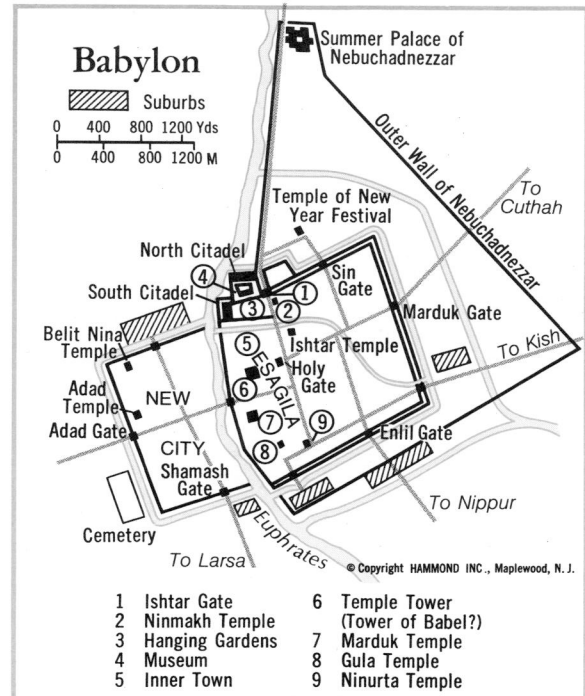

Babylon

Suburbs

0	400	800	1200 Yds
0	400	800	1200 M

Summer Palace of Nebuchadnezzar

Temple of New Year Festival

North Citadel

South Citadel

Belit Nina Temple

Adad Temple

Adad Gate

NEW

CITY

Cemetery

Shamash Gate

Sin Gate

Marduk Gate

Ishtar Temple

ESAGILA

Holy Gate

Enlil Gate

Outer Wall of Nebuchadnezzar

To Cuthah

To Kish

To Nippur

To Larsa

Euphrates

© Copyright HAMMOND INC., Maplewood, N.J.

1 Ishtar Gate
2 Ninmakh Temple
3 Hanging Gardens
4 Museum
5 Inner Town
6 Temple Tower (Tower of Babel?)
7 Marduk Temple
8 Gula Temple
9 Ninurta Temple

A reconstruction of the Ishtar Gate at Babylon, with the famous "hanging gardens" in the right background. The king entering the gate is Nebuchadnezzar II (605-562 B.C.), who destroyed Jerusalem.

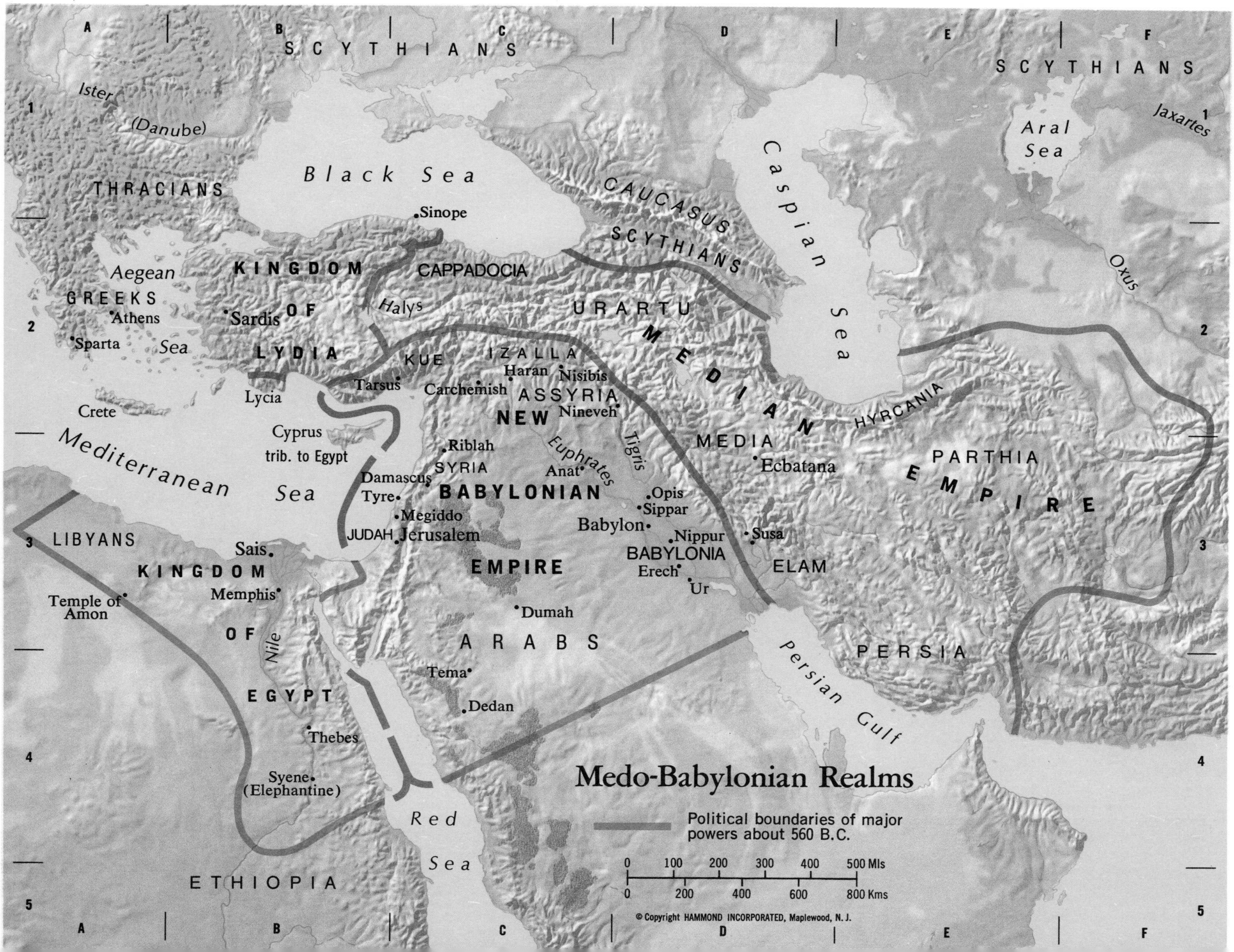

Medo-Babylonian Realms

Political boundaries of major powers about 560 B.C.

0	100	200	300	400	500 Mls
0	200	400	600	800 Kms	

© Copyright HAMMOND INCORPORATED, Maplewood, N.J.

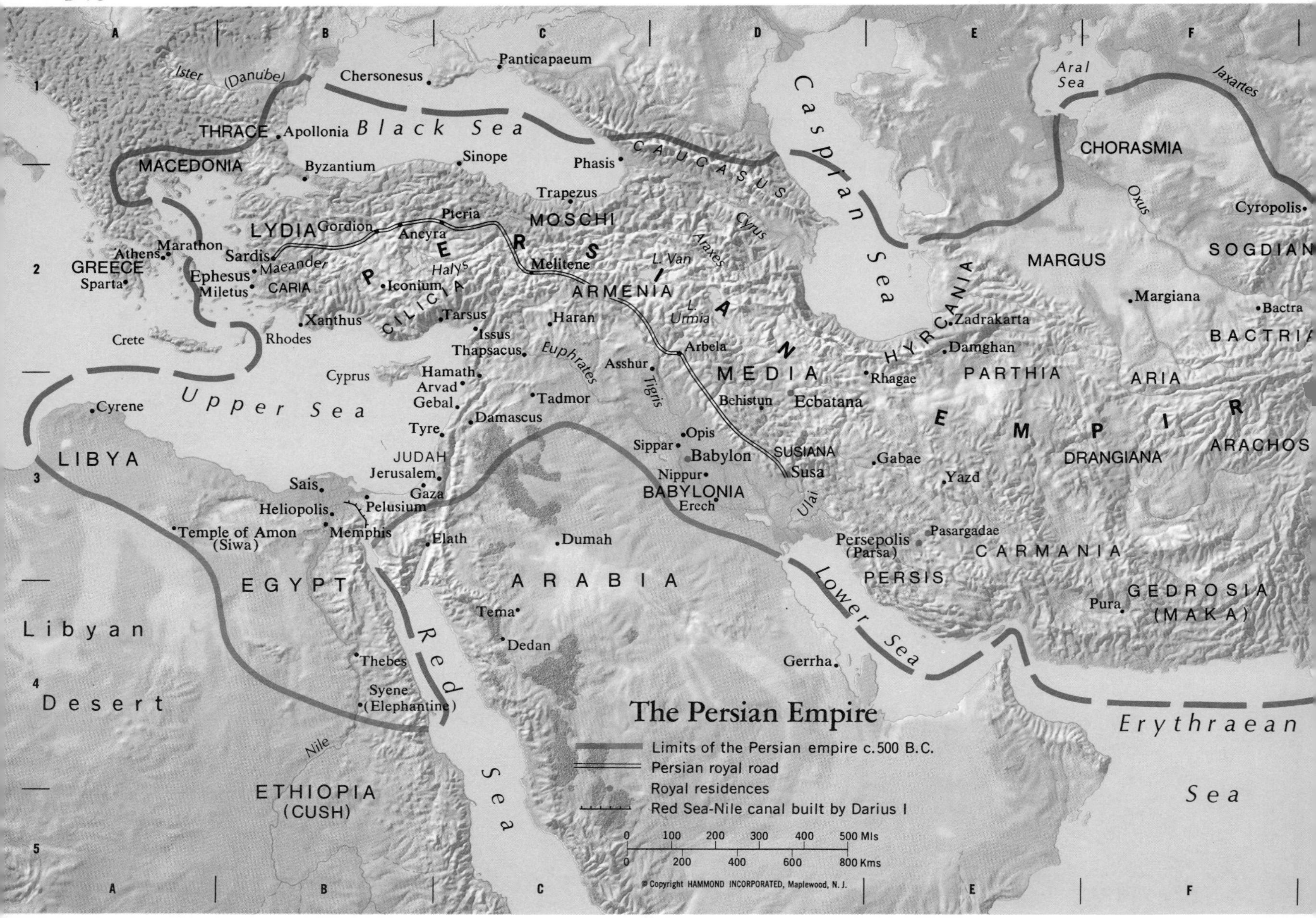

The Map

A 1 Ister (Danube)
THRACE • Apollonia *Black Sea*
MACEDONIA • Byzantium • Sinope
• Chersonesus • Panticapaeum
• Phasis
CAUCASUS
LYDIA • Gordion • Ancyra • Trapezus
Athens • Marathon • Pieria MOSCHI
GREECE • Sardis • Maeander • Melitene
Sparta • Ephesus • Iconium • Halys L. Van ARMENIA
• Miletus CARIA • Urmia
Crete • Xanthus • Tarsus L. Urmia
Rhodes CILICIA • Issus Euphrates • Arbela MEDIA
Cyprus • Thapsacus • Asshur Tigris • Rhagae PARTHIA
• Hamath • Behistun Ecbatana
Upper Sea Arvad • Damascus • Opis • Gabae
• Cyrene Gebal • Tadmor Sippar • Babylon SUSIANA
LIBYA Tyre • Susa
JUDAH BABYLONIA Ulai • Yazd
Jerusalem • Nippur Persepolis Pasargadae
Sais • Gaza Erech (Parsa) CARMANIA
Heliopolis • Pelusium PERSIS • Pura GEDROSIA
Temple of Amon • Memphis • Elath • Dumah (MAKA)
(Siwa)
EGYPT ARABIA Lower Sea
Libyan • Tema
Desert • Dedan • Gerrha *Erythraean*
• Thebes *Sea*
Syene
•(Elephantine) Nile
ETHIOPIA
(CUSH)

The Persian Empire

— Limits of the Persian empire c. 500 B.C.
— Persian royal road
— Royal residences
···· Red Sea-Nile canal built by Darius I

0 100 200 300 400 500 Mls
0 200 400 600 800 Kms

© Copyright HAMMOND INCORPORATED, Maplewood, N.J.

On this clay cylinder of 538 B.C., Cyrus provides royal authorization for the rebuilding of temples "beyond the Euphrates."

Tomb of Cyrus the Great at Pasargadae, Iran. When he conquered Babylon, Cyrus allowed the Jews to return to Jerusalem and rebuild their temple.

The earliest coin used in the Holy Land is this 4th-century silver Persian piece. The obverse has a falcon with the inscription "Yahud." The reverse has a lily with no inscription.

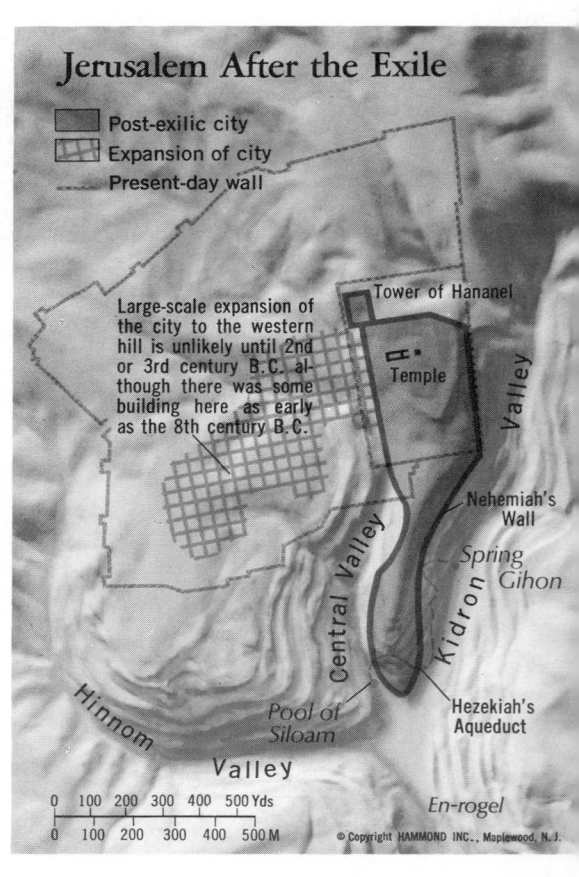

Jerusalem After the Exile

■ Post-exilic city
▨ Expansion of city
--- Present-day wall

Large-scale expansion of the city to the western hill is unlikely until 2nd or 3rd century B.C. although there was some building here as early as the 8th century B.C.

Tower of Hananel
Temple
Kidron Valley
Nehemiah's Wall
Spring Gihon
Central Valley
Hinnom Valley
Pool of Siloam
Hezekiah's Aqueduct
En-rogel

0 100 200 300 400 500 Yds
0 100 200 300 400 500 M

© Copyright HAMMOND INC., Maplewood, N.J.

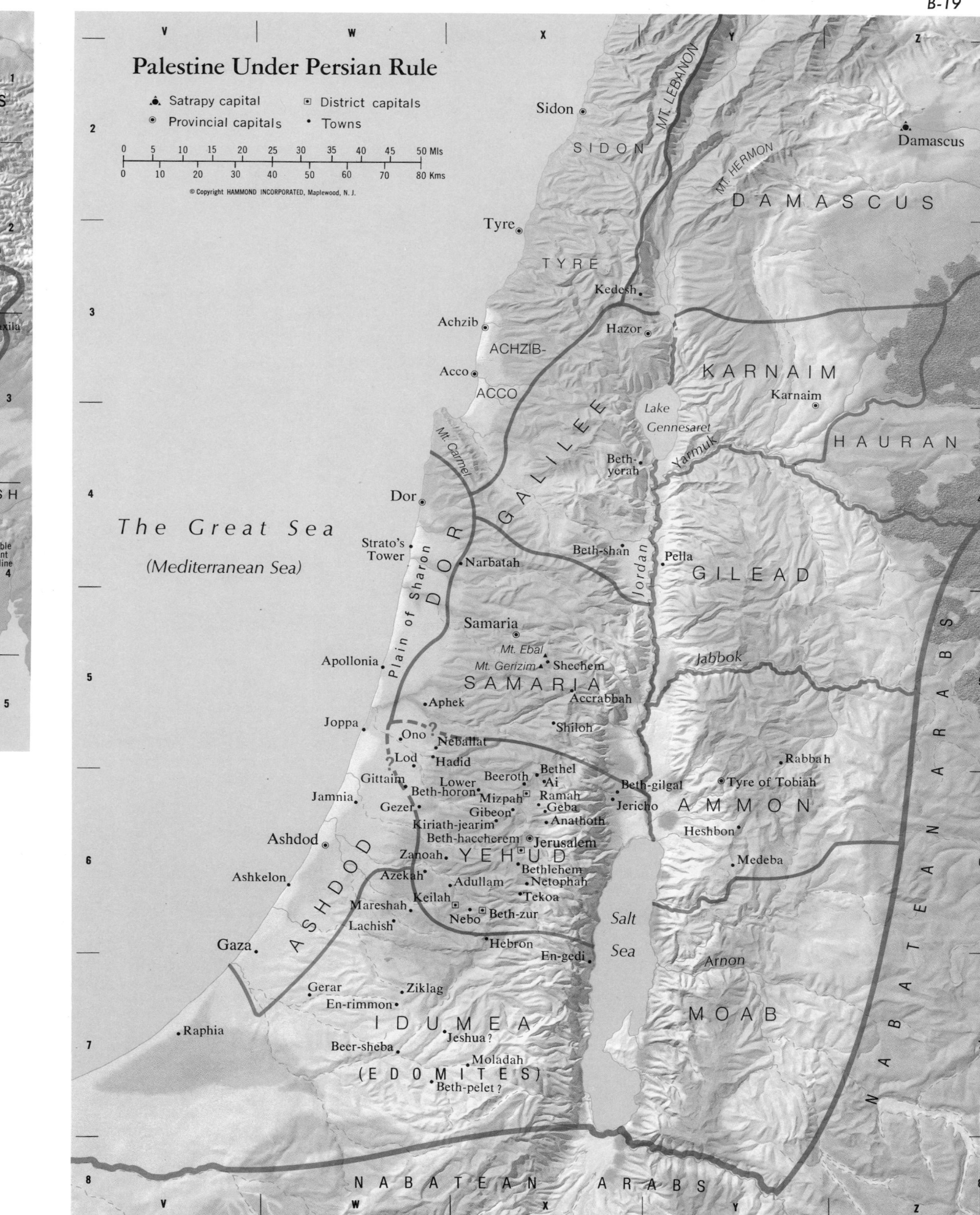

Palestine Under Persian Rule

- 🔺 Satrapy capital
- ⦿ Provincial capitals
- ◻ District capitals
- • Towns

```
0   5   10  15  20  25  30  35  40  45  50 Mis
0    10    20    30    40    50    60    70    80 Kms
```
© Copyright HAMMOND INCORPORATED, Maplewood, N.J.

SCYTHIANS
(SAKA)

HINDU KUSH

Cophen
(Kabul)
GANDARA
•Taxila

Indus

HINDUSH
(INDIA)

•Pattala

Probable
ancient
coastline

Sidon

SIDON

MT. LEBANON

MT. HERMON

Damascus

DAMASCUS

Tyre

TYRE

Kedesh

Achzib
ACHZIB-

Hazor

KARNAIM

Acco
ACCO

Karnaim

HAURAN

Mt. Carmel

GALILEE

Lake
Gennesaret

Dor

DOR

Beth-
yerah

Yarmuk

Jordan

The Great Sea

Strato's
Tower

Narbatah

Beth-shan

Pella

GILEAD

(Mediterranean Sea)

Plain of Sharon

Samaria

Mt. Ebal
Mt. Gerizim ▲ •Shechem

Jabbok

Apollonia

SAMARIA

Accrabbah

•Aphek

Shiloh

Joppa

Ono
•Neballat

Lod
•Hadid

Bethel
Beeroth •Ai

Beth-gilgal

•Tyre of Tobiah

•Rabbah

Gittaim
Lower
Beth-horon• Mizpah

Ramah
Geba

Jericho

AMMON

Jamnia

Gezer

Gibeon•
•Anathoth

Heshbon

Kiriath-jearim

Ashdod

Beth-haccherem ◻Jerusalem

YEHUD

Zanoah

Bethlehem

Medeba

Ashkelon

Azekah

•Adullam
Keilah

Netophah
•Tekoa

Mareshah

◻Nebo ◻Beth-zur

Salt

ASHDOD

Lachish

Sea

Gaza

•Hebron

En-gedi

Arnon

Gerar

Ziklag

En-rimmon

MOAB

•Raphia

IDUMEA

Jeshua?

Beer-sheba

Moladah

(EDOMITES)

Beth-pelet?

NABATEAN ARABS

NABATEAN ARABS

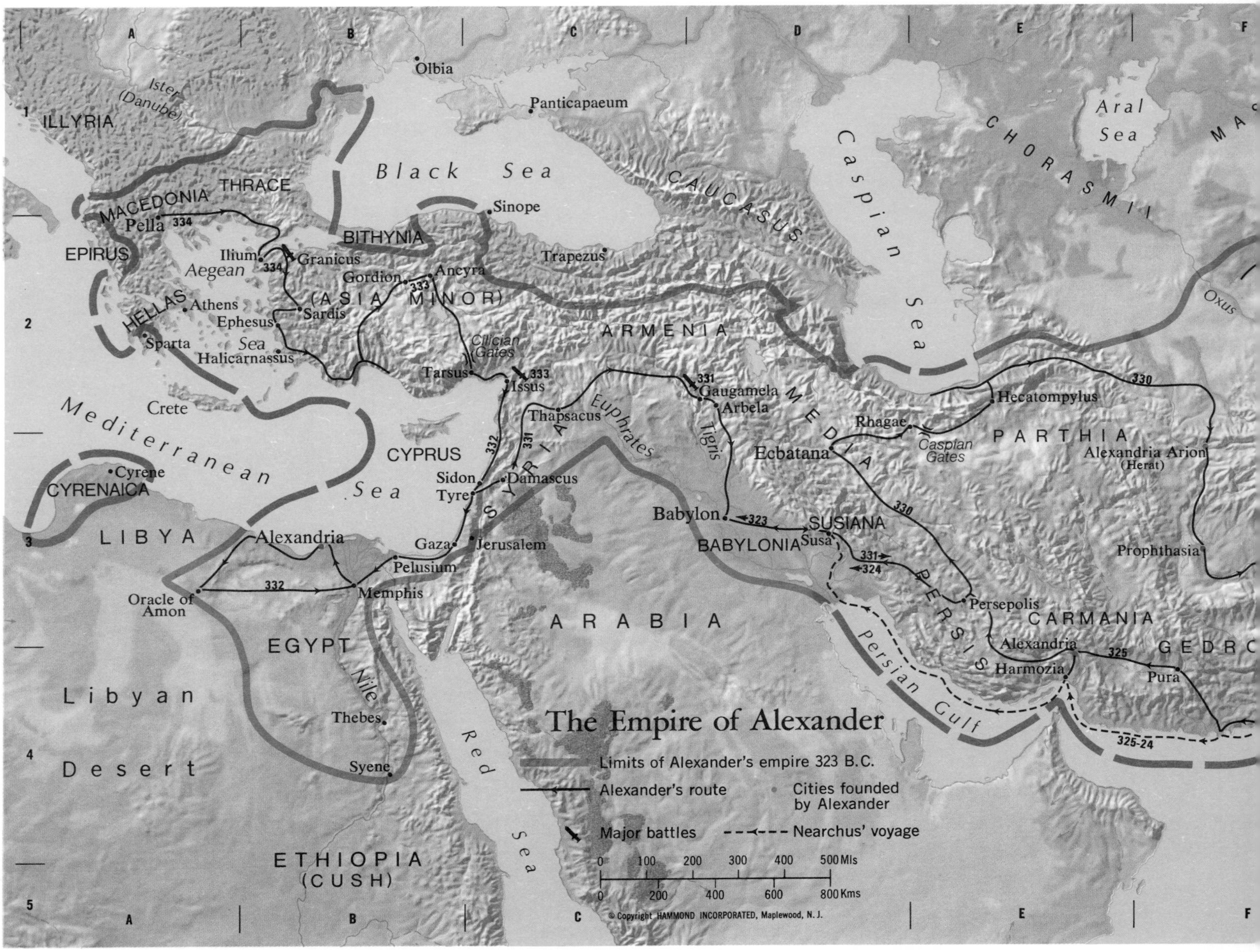

The Empire of Alexander

ILLYRIA

Ister (Danube)

Olbia

Panticapaeum

Black Sea

Aral Sea

CHORASMII

MACEDONIA
THRACE
Pella · 334

EPIRUS

Ilium
Aegean · 334
Granicus
Gordion
Ancyra · 333
BITHYNIA

Sinope

Trapezus

CAUCASUS

Caspian Sea

HELLAS
Athens
Ephesus
Sparta
Halicarnassus

Sardis
(ASIA MINOR)

Cilician Gates

Tarsus
Issus · 333

ARMENIA

MEDIA

Hecatompylus · 330

Oxus

Crete

Mediterranean Sea

CYPRUS

Thapsacus · 331
Euphrates
Tigris

Gaugamela · 331
Arbela

Rhagae
Caspian Gates

PARTHIA

Alexandria Arion
(Herat)

Cyrene
CYRENAICA

Sidon
Tyre · 332
Damascus · 331

Ecbatana

330

Prophthasia

LIBYA
Alexandria

Gaza
Jerusalem · 332

Pelusium

Babylon ← 323
SUSIANA
BABYLONIA
Susa · 331 →
← 324

Persepolis

CARMANIA

Oracle of Amon · 332 →
Memphis

ARABIA

PERSIS

Alexandria · 325
Harmozia

GEDRO
Pura

EGYPT

Nile

Libyan Desert

Thebes ·

Syene ·

Red Sea

Persian Gulf

325-24

ETHIOPIA
(CUSH)

The Empire of Alexander

—— Limits of Alexander's empire 323 B.C.

—— Alexander's route

· Cities founded by Alexander

✈ Major battles

- - -◄- - - Nearchus' voyage

| 0 | 100 | 200 | 300 | 400 | 500 Mls |
| 0 | 200 | 400 | 600 | 800 Kms |

© Copyright HAMMOND INCORPORATED, Maplewood, N.J.

Alexander the Great at the Battle of Issus, where he defeated the Persians. This Roman mosaic from Pompeii shows the determination of this brilliant soldier who established an empire at age thirty.

Silver tetradrachm of Ptolemy I struck in Egypt shows Alexander wearing an elephant head-dress. Reverse: the goddess Athena.

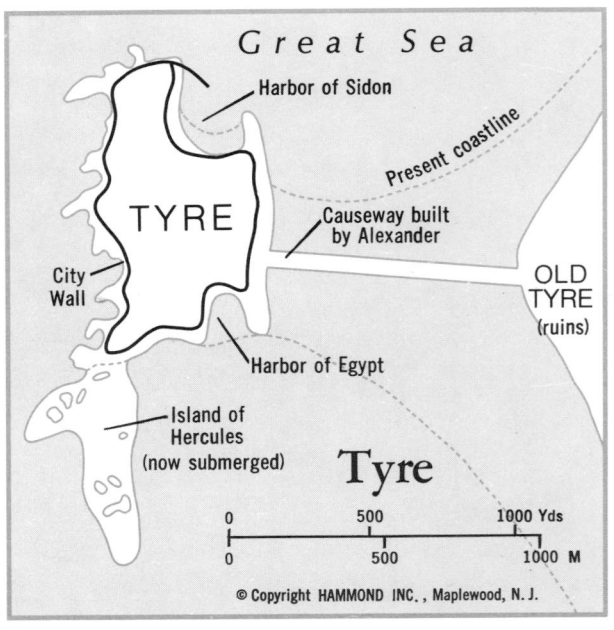

Great Sea

Harbor of Sidon

Present coastline

TYRE

Causeway built by Alexander

OLD TYRE
(ruins)

City Wall

Harbor of Egypt

Island of Hercules
(now submerged)

Tyre

| 0 | 500 | 1000 Yds |
| 0 | 500 | 1000 M |

© Copyright HAMMOND INC., Maplewood, N.J.

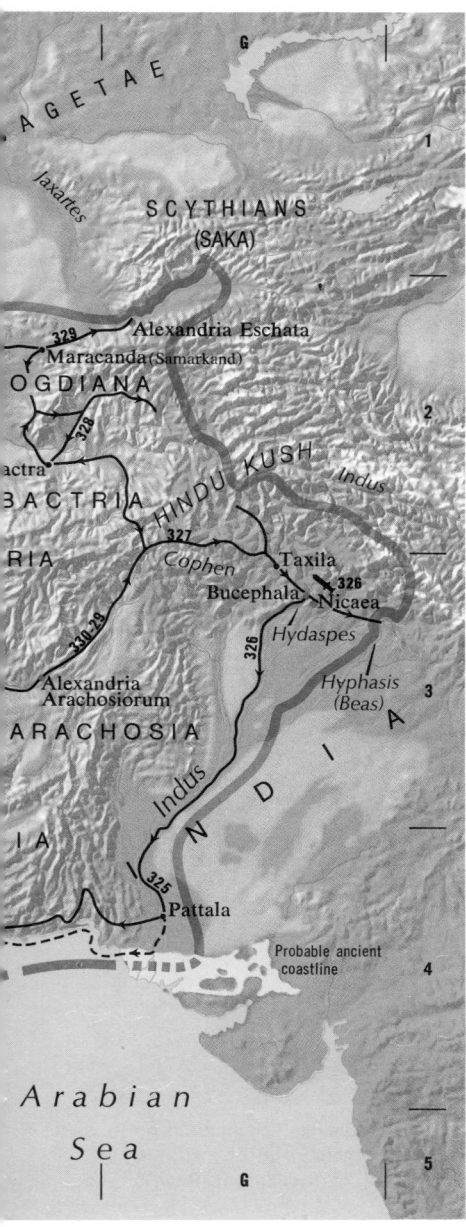

Massive round towers such as this one were set into Israelite walls at Samaria by Alexander's military engineers. Samaria, once capital of Israel, became one of the most Hellenized cities of Palestine.

Seleucus I, "Nicator," continued Alexander's Hellenizing policies.

Ptolemy I, "Soter," turned Egypt into his personal domain.

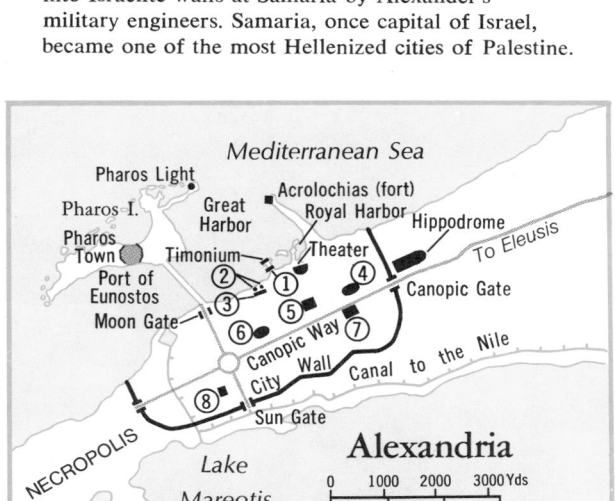

Alexandria

Mediterranean Sea

Pharos Light
Pharos I.
Pharos Town
Port of Eunostos
Moon Gate
Timonium
Great Harbor
Acrolochias (fort)
Royal Harbor
Theater
Hippodrome
To Eleusis
Canopic Gate
Canopic Way
City Wall
Canal to the Nile
Sun Gate
NECROPOLIS
Lake Mareotis

② ① ④ ⑤ ③ ⑥ ⑦ ⑧

| 0 | 1000 | 2000 | 3000 Yds |
| 0 | 1000 | 2000 | 3000 M |

© Copyright HAMMOND INC., Maplewood, N.J.

1 Poseidium
2 Obelisks (later Cleopatra's Needles)
3 Caesarium
4 Stadium
5 Library and Museum
6 Amphitheater
7 Sports Grounds
8 Serapeion

Terracotta statuette of a war elephant with driver and tower.

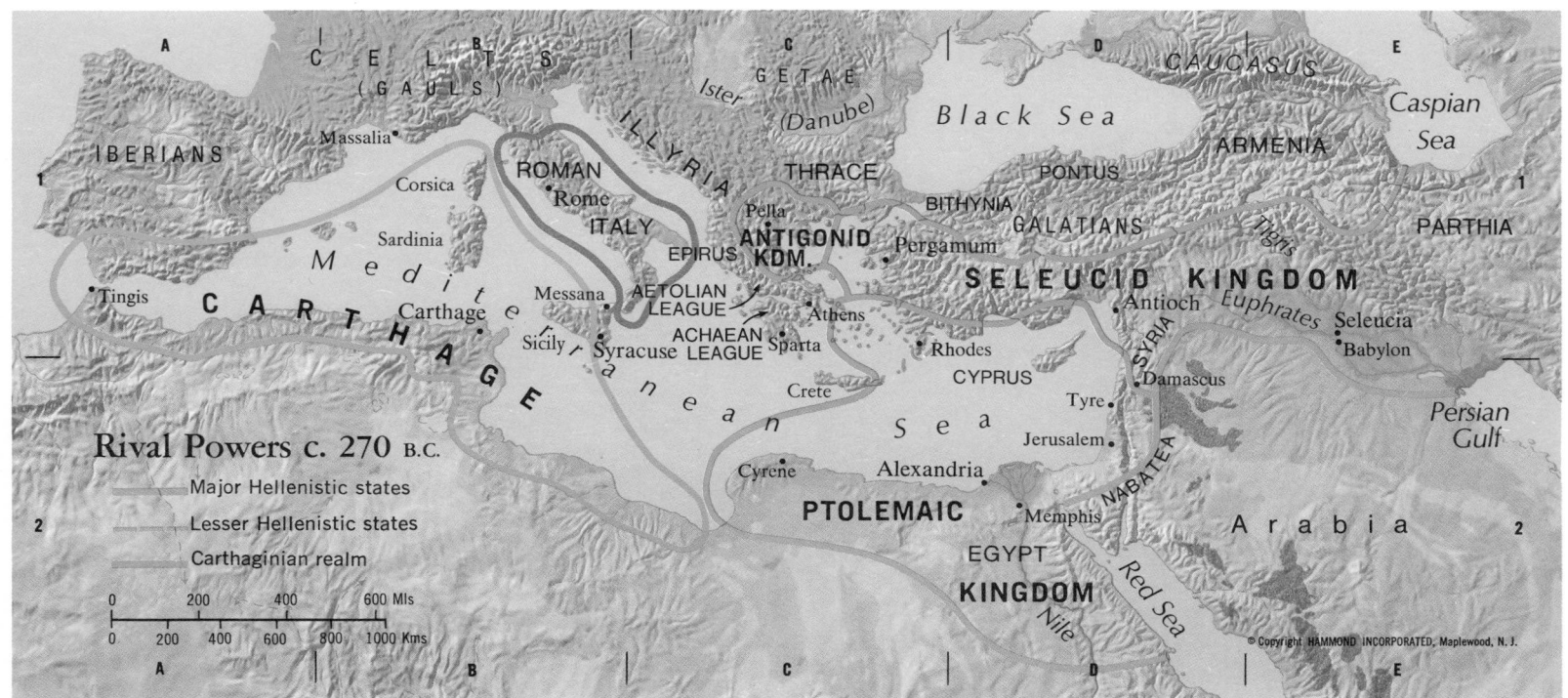

Rival Powers c. 270 B.C.

— Major Hellenistic states
— Lesser Hellenistic states
— Carthaginian realm

| 0 | 200 | 400 | 600 Mls |
| 0 | 200 | 400 | 600 | 800 | 1000 Kms |

CELTS (GAULS)
IBERIANS
Massalia
Corsica
Sardinia
Tingis
CARTHAGE
Carthage
Sicily
Messana
ROMAN
Rome
ITALY
ILLYRIA
Ister (Danube)
GETAE
THRACE
EPIRUS
ANTIGONID KDM.
Pella
Pergamum
AETOLIAN LEAGUE
ACHAEAN LEAGUE
Syracuse
Athens
Sparta
Rhodes
Crete
Mediterranean Sea
CYPRUS
BITHYNIA
PONTUS
GALATIANS
CAUCASUS
Black Sea
ARMENIA
Caspian Sea
PARTHIA
SELEUCID KINGDOM
Antioch
Euphrates
Seleucia
Babylon
Tigris
Damascus
SYRIA
Tyre
Jerusalem
NABATEA
Cyrene
Alexandria
Memphis
PTOLEMAIC
EGYPT
KINGDOM
Red Sea
Nile
Persian Gulf
Arabia

© Copyright HAMMOND INCORPORATED, Maplewood, N.J.

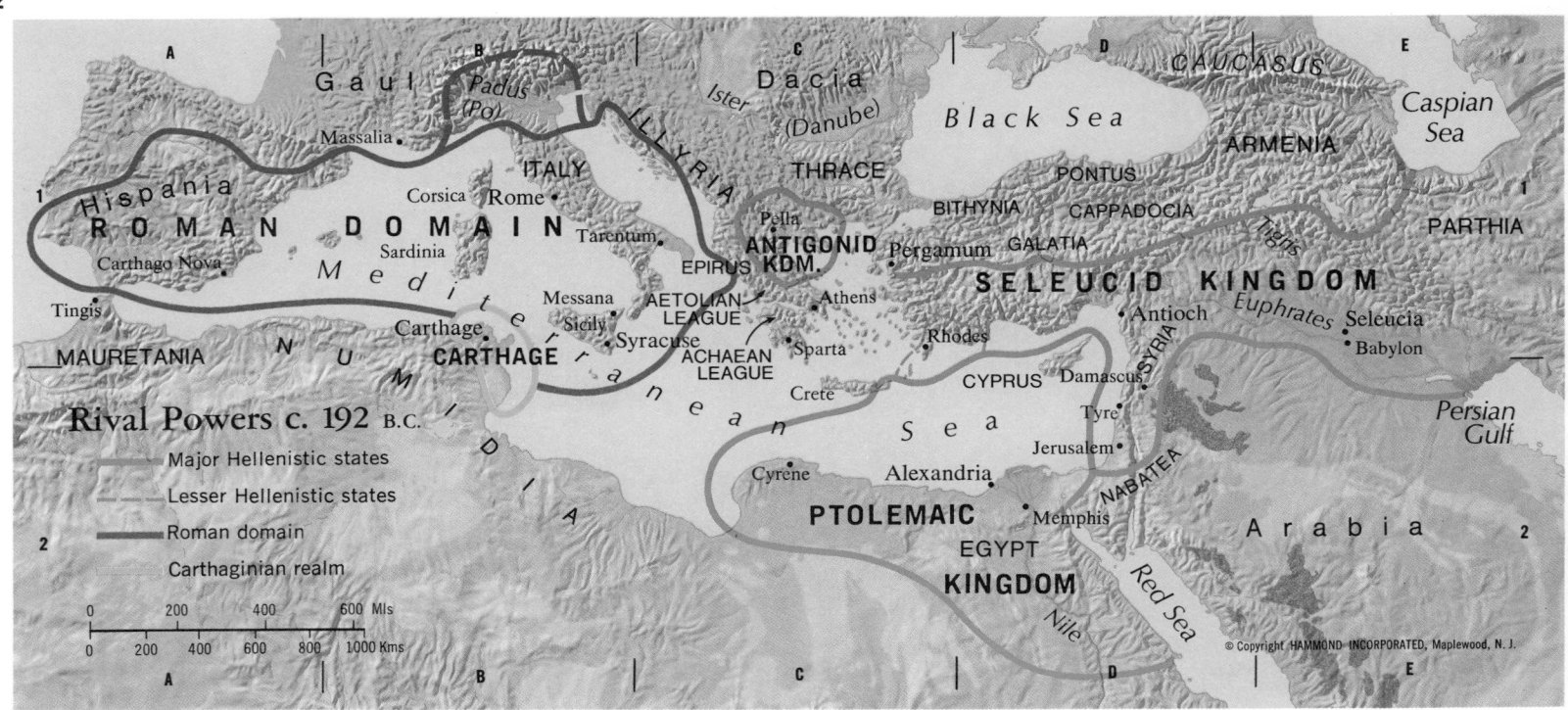

Rival Powers c. 192 B.C.

— Major Hellenistic states
-- Lesser Hellenistic states
— Roman domain
— Carthaginian realm

© Copyright HAMMOND INCORPORATED, Maplewood, N.J.

Antiochus III, "The Great," who took Palestine from the Ptolemies at the Battle of Panias in 197 B.C.

Naked Greek youths participating in athletic contests are pictured on this 6th-century B.C. Greek vase. Such practices introduced into Jerusalem were a cause of the Maccabean Revolt.

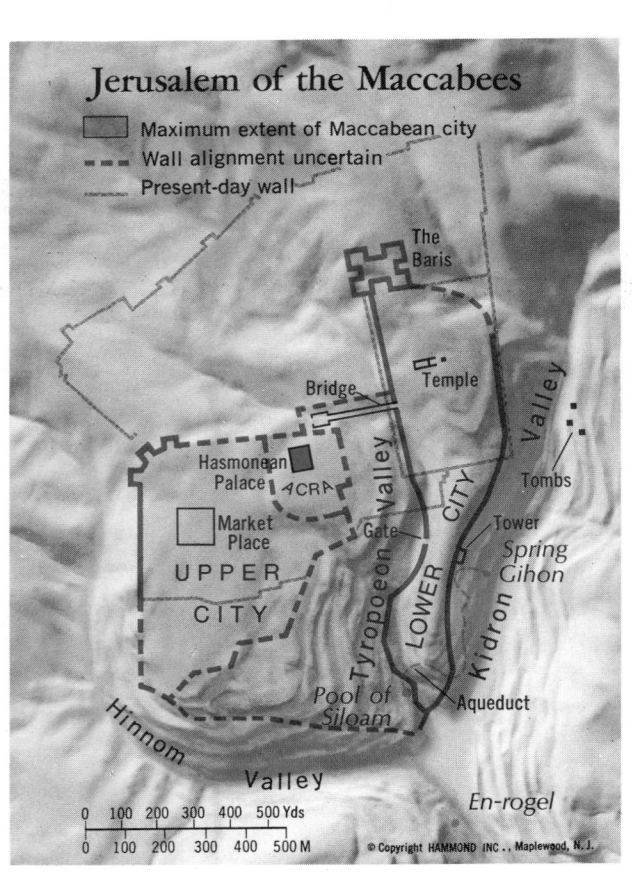

Jerusalem of the Maccabees

▭ Maximum extent of Maccabean city
--- Wall alignment uncertain
— Present-day wall

The Baris
Bridge
Temple
Hasmonean Palace
ACRA
Market Place
Tombs
Gate
Tower
Spring Gihon
UPPER CITY
Tyropoeon Valley
LOWER CITY
Kidron Valley
Valley
Pool of Siloam
Aqueduct
Hinnom Valley
En-rogel

© Copyright HAMMOND INC., Maplewood, N.J.

Antiochus IV, "Epiphanes," tried to Hellenize the Jews, which led to the Maccabean War in 166 B.C.

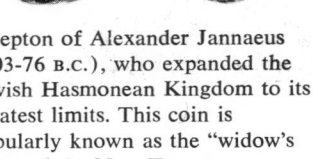

A lepton of Alexander Jannaeus (103-76 B.C.), who expanded the Jewish Hasmonean Kingdom to its greatest limits. This coin is popularly known as the "widow's mite" of the New Testament. (Mark 12:42, Luke 21:2).

A Jewish "slipper lamp" from the time of the Hasmonean Kingdom.

Antigonus II (40-37 B.C.), the last of the Hasmonean rulers, issued debased coinage, but did show the Menorah on some coins such as this perutah. He lost his throne to Herod the Great.

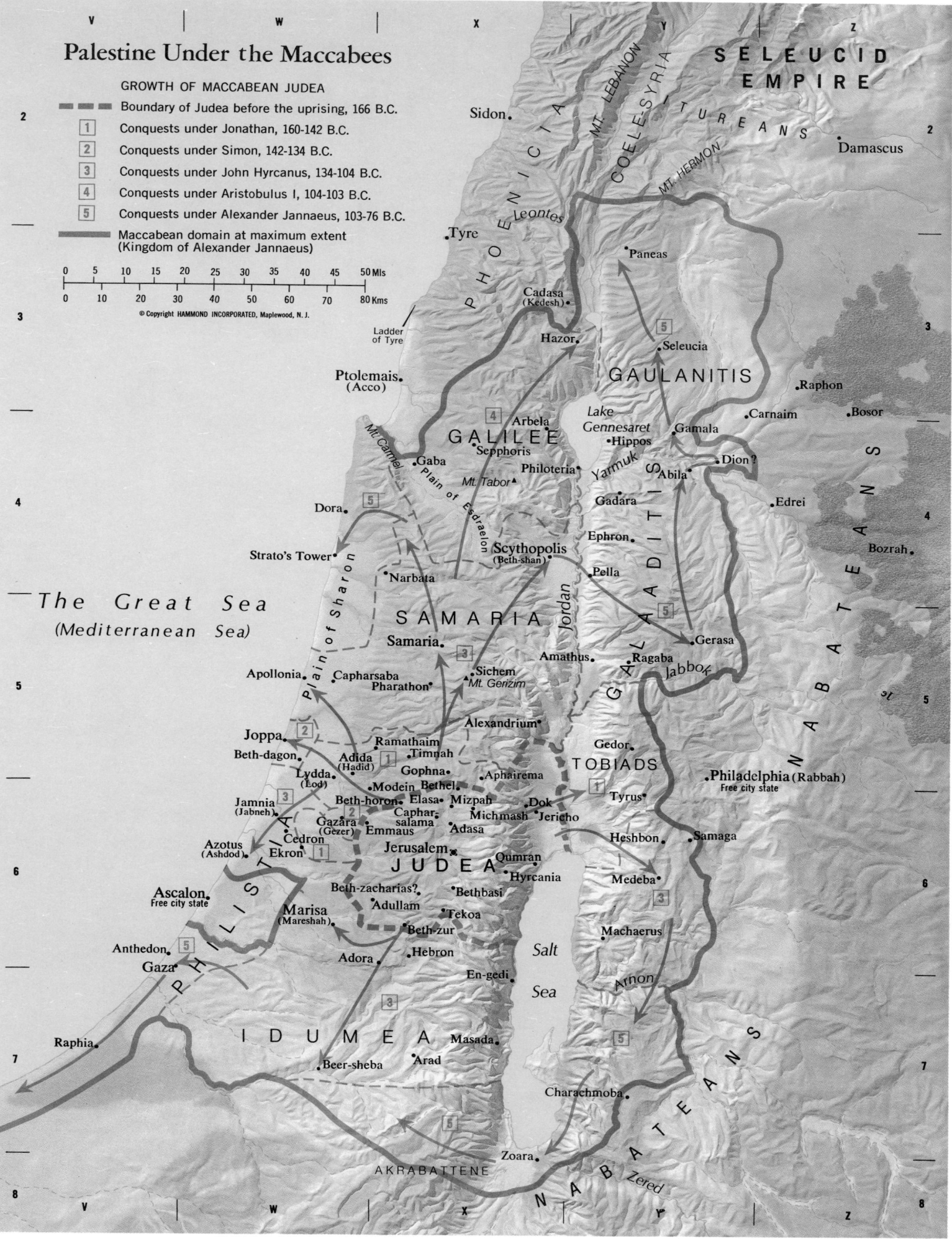

Palestine Under the Maccabees

GROWTH OF MACCABEAN JUDEA

‑ ‑ ‑ Boundary of Judea before the uprising, 166 B.C.

[1] Conquests under Jonathan, 160-142 B.C.

[2] Conquests under Simon, 142-134 B.C.

[3] Conquests under John Hyrcanus, 134-104 B.C.

[4] Conquests under Aristobulus I, 104-103 B.C.

[5] Conquests under Alexander Jannaeus, 103-76 B.C.

Maccabean domain at maximum extent
(Kingdom of Alexander Jannaeus)

0 5 10 15 20 25 30 35 40 45 50 Mls
0 10 20 30 40 50 60 70 80 Kms

© Copyright HAMMOND INCORPORATED, Maplewood, N.J.

SELEUCID EMPIRE

Sidon

PHOENICIA

MT. LEBANON

COELE-SYRIA

ITUREANS

Damascus

MT. HERMON

Tyre

Leontes

Paneas

Cadasa (Kedesh)

Ladder of Tyre

Hazor

Seleucia

GAULANITIS

Ptolemais (Acco)

Raphon

Mt. Carmel

Arbela

Lake Gennesaret

Gamala

Carnaim

Bosor

GALILEE

Sephphoris

Hippos

Dion ?

Gaba

Philoteria

Abila

Plain of Esdraelon

Mt. Tabor

Yarmuk

Edrei

Dora

Gadara

Strato's Tower

Ephron

Bozrah

Scythopolis (Beth-shan)

Pella

GALAADITIS

Narbata

Jordan

NABATEANS

The Great Sea
(Mediterranean Sea)

SAMARIA

Amathus

Ragaba

Jabbok

Samaria

Gerasa

Apollonia

Capharsaba

Sichem

Pharathon

Mt. Gerizim

NABATEANS

Alexandrium

Gedor

TOBIADS

Joppa

Ramathaim

Timnah

Philadelphia (Rabbah)
Free city state

Beth-dagon

Adida (Hadid)

Gophna

Aphairema

Tyrus

Lydda (Lod)

Modein

Bethel

Jamnia (Jabneh)

Beth-horon

Elasa

Mizpah

Dok

Gazara (Gezer)

Caphar-salama

Michmash

Jericho

Heshbon

Samaga

Azotus (Ashdod)

Emmaus

Adasa

Cedron

Ekron

Jerusalem

JUDEA

Qumran

Medeba

Ascalon
Free city state

Hyrcania

Beth-zacharias?

Bethbasi

Adullam

Tekoa

Marisa (Mareshah)

Beth-zur

Salt Sea

Machaerus

Anthedon

Adora

Hebron

En-gedi

Arnon

Gaza

PHILISTIA

I D U M E A

Masada

Raphia

Beer-sheba

Arad

Charachmoba

Zered

Zoara

AKRABATTENE

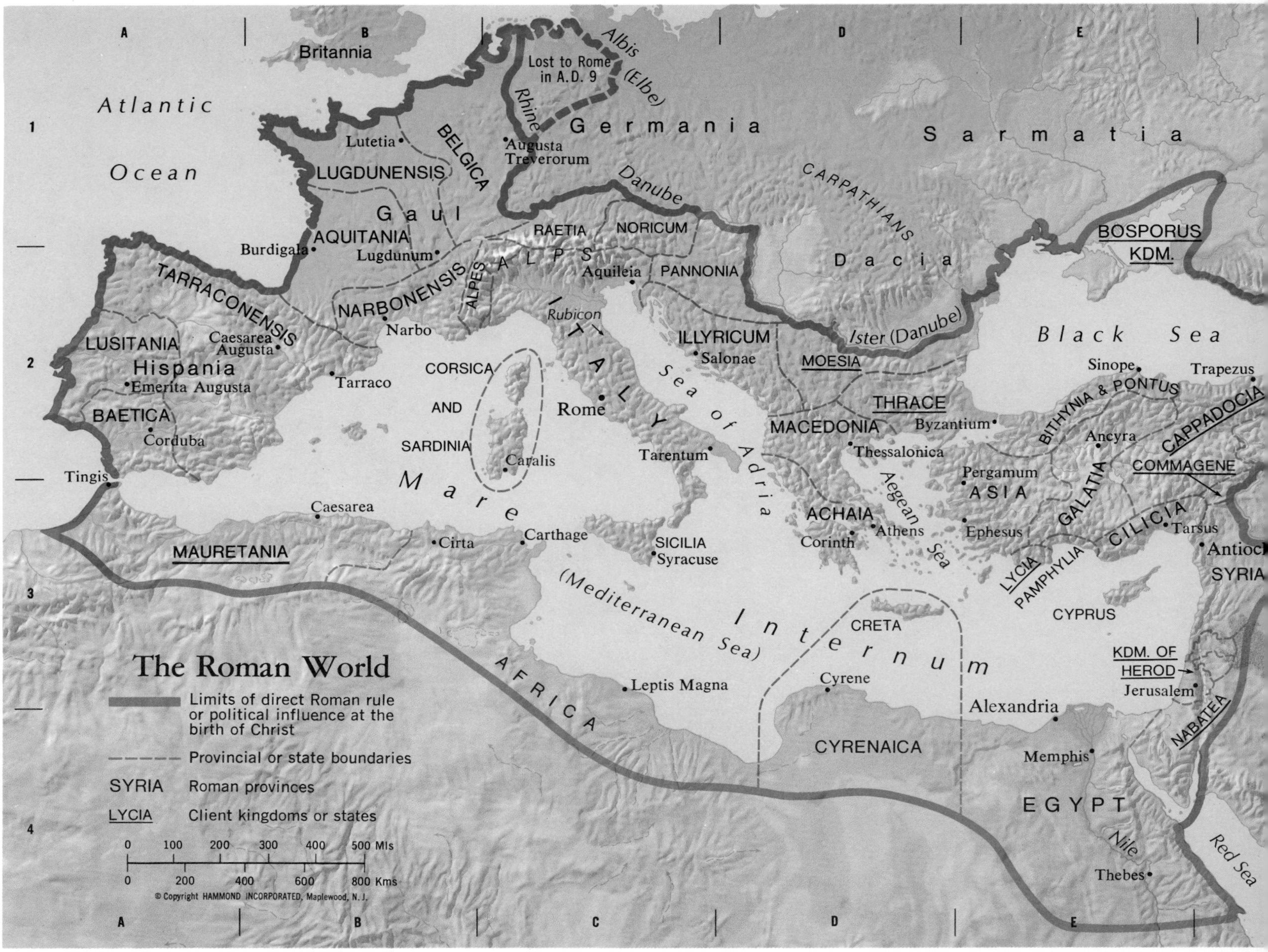

The Roman World

A | B
1
Britannia
Atlantic
Ocean
Lutetia •
BELGICA
• Augusta Treverorum
Germania
Lost to Rome in A.D. 9
Albis (Elbe)
Rhine
Sarmatia
LUGDUNENSIS
Gaul
Danube
CARPATHIANS
D | E
AQUITANIA
Burdigala •
Lugdunum •
RAETIA
NORICUM
Aquileia •
Dacia
BOSPORUS KDM.
Caesarea Augusta •
TARRACONENSIS
NARBONENSIS
ALPES
ALPS
Narbo •
Rubicon
PANNONIA
ILLYRICUM
Salonae •
ITALY
Ister (Danube)
MOESIA
Black Sea
Sinope •
Trapezus •
2
LUSITANIA
Hispania
Emerita Augusta •
Tarraco •
CORSICA
AND
SARDINIA
Sea of Adria
Rome •
THRACE
Byzantium •
MACEDONIA
Thessalonica •
BITHYNIA & PONTUS
Pergamum •
ASIA
Ancyra •
GALATIA
CAPPADOCIA
COMMAGENE
BAETICA
Corduba •
Caralis •
Tarentum •
ACHAIA
Corinth •
Athens •
Aegean Sea
Ephesus •
LYCIA
PAMPHYLIA
CILICIA
Tarsus •
Antioch
SYRIA
Tingis •
Mare
Caesarea •
• Cirta
Carthage •
SICILIA
Syracuse •
Internum
(Mediterranean Sea)
CYPRUS
CRETA
KDM. OF HEROD →
Jerusalem •
3
MAURETANIA
AFRICA
Leptis Magna •
Cyrene •
Alexandria •
NABATEA

The Roman World
━━━ Limits of direct Roman rule or political influence at the birth of Christ
--- Provincial or state boundaries
SYRIA   Roman provinces
LYCIA   Client kingdoms or states

CYRENAICA
Memphis •
EGYPT
Nile
Red Sea
Thebes •

0 100 200 300 400 500 Mls
0   200   400   600   800 Kms
© Copyright HAMMOND INCORPORATED, Maplewood, N.J.

4

Senate House in the Imperial Forum.

Octavian (Caesar Augustus).

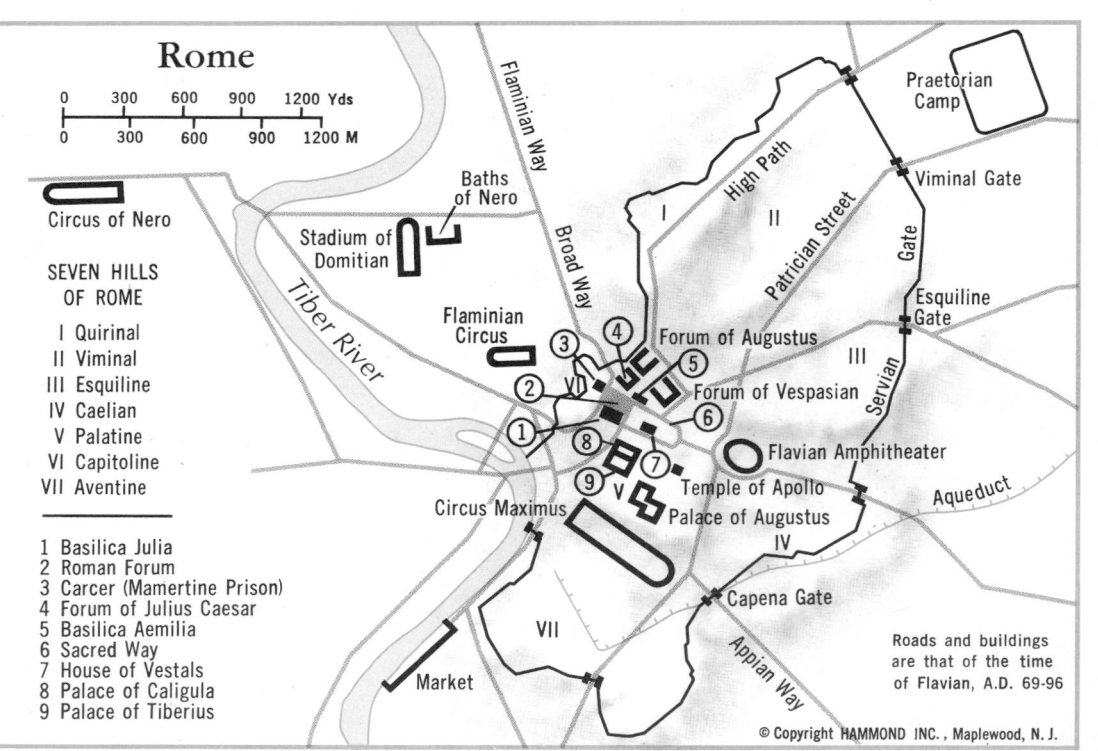

Rome

0 300 600 900 1200 Yds
0 300 600 900 1200 M

Circus of Nero

SEVEN HILLS OF ROME
I Quirinal
II Viminal
III Esquiline
IV Caelian
V Palatine
VI Capitoline
VII Aventine

1 Basilica Julia
2 Roman Forum
3 Carcer (Mamertine Prison)
4 Forum of Julius Caesar
5 Basilica Aemilia
6 Sacred Way
7 House of Vestals
8 Palace of Caligula
9 Palace of Tiberius

Flaminian Way
Praetorian Camp
Baths of Nero
Stadium of Domitian
High Path
Viminal Gate
Broad Way
Patrician Street
Gate
Tiber River
Flaminian Circus
Forum of Augustus
Esquiline Gate
Forum of Vespasian
Servian
Flavian Amphitheater
Temple of Apollo
Aqueduct
Circus Maximus
Palace of Augustus
Capena Gate
Market
Appian Way

Roads and buildings are that of the time of Flavian, A.D. 69-96

© Copyright HAMMOND INC., Maplewood, N.J.

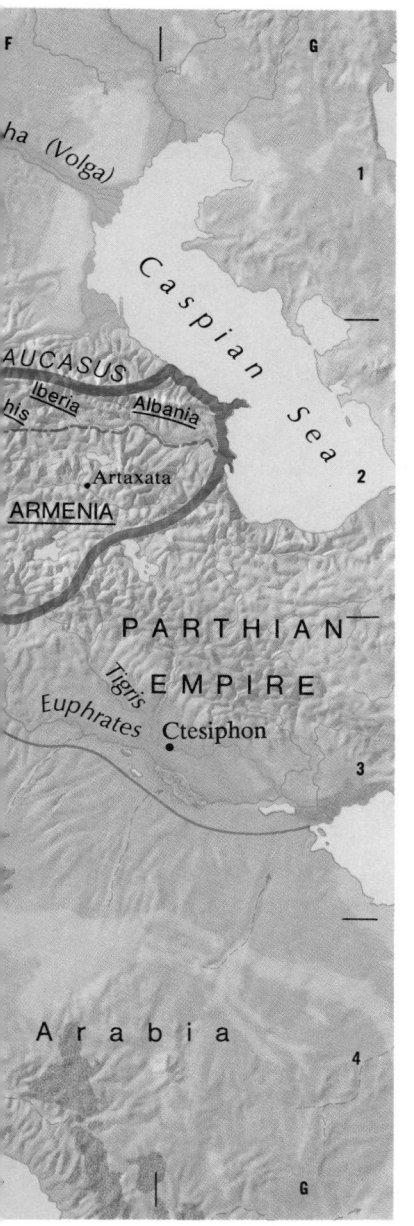

The Kingdom of Herod the Great

Boundary of Herod's kingdom
Other boundaries
⊡ Cities of the Decapolis
⋈ Fortresses

0 5 10 15 20 25 30 35 40 45 50 Mls
0 10 20 30 40 50 60 70 80 Kms

© Copyright HAMMOND INCORPORATED, Maplewood, N.J.

ha (Volga)

Caspian Sea

AUCASUS
Iberia   Albania
his
ARMENIA
Artaxata

PARTHIAN
EMPIRE
Tigris
Euphrates
Ctesiphon

Arabia

Mediterranean

Sea

Chalcis
ABILENE
Abila
Sidon
Iturea   Damascus ⊡
SYRIA
MT. LEBANON
Leontes   Paneas
Tyre   Paneas
Ulatha
Cadasa   Gaulanitis   Trachonitis
Gischala   Batanea
Ptolemais   Bethsaida   Raphana ⊡
GALILEE   Sea of Galilee   Auranitis
Taricheae   Hippos ⊡   Dion ? ⊡
(Magdala)
Mt. Carmel ▲   Gabae ⋈   Sepphoris   Abila ⊡
Nazareth   Gadara ⊡
Dora   Bostra ⊡
Caesarea
(Strato's Tower)   Scythopolis ⊡   Pella ⊡   DECAPOLIS
Narbata
SAMARIA   Jordan   Gerasa ⊡
Sebaste   Amathus ⋈
(Samaria)   Jabbok
Mt. Gerizim ▲
Apollonia   Gadara ⋈   Philadelphia ⊡
Antipatris   Alexandrium ⋈   PEREA
Joppa   Phasaelis
Lydda   Gophna   Betharamphtha
Jamnia   Jericho   Esbus ⋈
Emmaus   Cyprus ⋈
Azotus   Jerusalem   Bethany   Qumran   Medeba
Ascalon   Bethlehem   Hyrcania ⋈
(free city)   Herodium ⋈   Callirrhoe ⋈
JUDEA   Machaerus ⋈
Agrippias
(Anthedon)   Hebron   Engaddi   Arnon
Gaza   Adora
IDUMEA   Masada ⋈
Bersabe
Malatha ⋈
Elusa   Khirbet Tannur
Nabatean sanctuary
NABATEA
Nessana

Plain of Sharon

Lake
Asphaltitis
(Dead Sea)

Jerusalem in Herod's Time

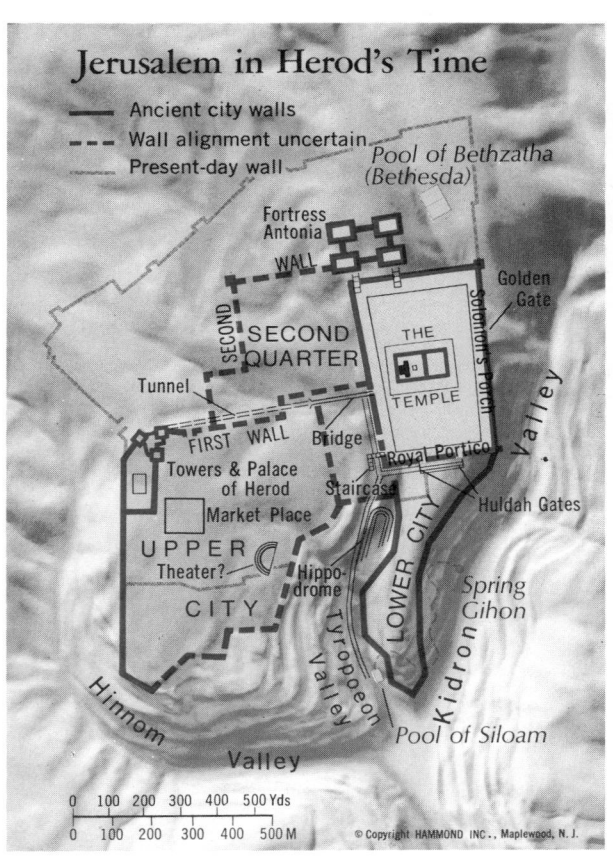

— Ancient city walls
-- Wall alignment uncertain
··· Present-day wall

Pool of Bethzatha
(Bethesda)
Fortress
Antonia
WALL   Golden
Gate
SECOND
SECOND
QUARTER   THE   Solomon's Porch
Tunnel   TEMPLE
FIRST WALL   Bridge
Royal Portico
Towers & Palace   Staircase
of Herod   Huldah Gates
Market Place
UPPER   Hippo-
Theater?   drome
CITY   Spring
LOWER   Gihon
Tyropoeon
Hinnom   CITY
Valley   Valley
Pool of Siloam   Kidron
Valley

© Copyright HAMMOND INC., Maplewood, N.J.

Temple of Herod

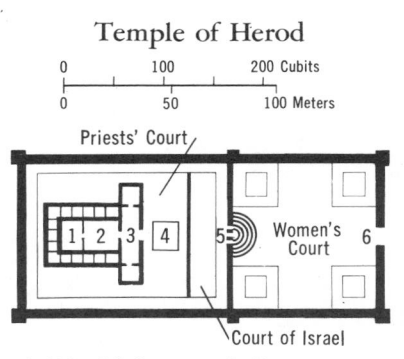

0   100   200 Cubits
0   50   100 Meters

Priests' Court

1 2 3 4 5 ⊙ 6   Women's
Court

Court of Israel

1 Holy of Holies   4 Altar
2 Holy Place (Nave)   5 Nicanor Gate
3 Porch   6 Beautiful Gate?

Model of Herod's Temple, with surrounding
courts and Royal Portico in the background.

Palestine in New Testament Times

Political boundaries A.D. 6-44
Major roads
Other roads
⊡ Cities of the Decapolis
⋈ Fortresses

0   10   20   30   40 Mls
0   20   40   60 Kms
© Copyright HAMMOND INCORPORATED, Maplewood, N.J.

ABILENE
Abila
Sidon
Iturea
Damascus
SYRIA
Sarepta
Paneas
MT. LEBANON
MT. HERMON
Leontes
Caesarea Philippi
(Paneas)
Tyre
Ulatha
Ladder
of Tyre
Ecdippa
Cadasa
Trachonitis
Gischala
Batanea
Ptolemais
Chorazin
Bethsaida-Julias
Raphana
GALILEE
Capernaum
Cana Magdala
Sea
of
Galilee
Bosor
Mt. Carmel
Asochis
Tiberias
Hippos
Dion?
Auranitis
Sepphoris
Mediterranean
Gabae
Nazareth Philoteria
Yarmuk
Abila
Plain
Mt. Tabor
Gadara
Capitolias
Sea
Dora
of
Nain
Agrippina
Crocodilon
Esdraelon
Arbela
Bostra
Caesarea
Scythopolis
DECAPOLIS
Narbata Ginae
Pella
Apollonia
SAMARIA
Salim
Aenon
Sebaste
(Samaria)
Mt. Ebal
Jordan
Gerasa
Antipatris
Mt. Gerizim Sychar
Amathus
Jabbok
Joppa
Arimathea?
Phasaelis
Gadara
PEREA
Philadelphia
Gophna Ephraim
Lydda
Archelais
Jamnia
Jericho
Betharamphtha
(Livias, Julias)
Emmaus
(Nicopolis)
Emmaus?
Cyprus
Esbus
Azotus
Jerusalem Bethany
Qumran
Medeba
Bethlehem
Essene community
JUDEA
Hyrcania
Ascalon
Marisa
Herodium
Callirrhoe
Bethsura
Machaerus
Agrippias
Hebron
Gaza
Engaddi
Arnon
Raphia
Masada
IDUMEA
Areopolis
Bersabe
Malatha
Charachmoba
Elusa
NABATEA
Plain of Sharon
Phoenicia
Gaulanitis
Lake Asphaltitis
(Dead Sea)

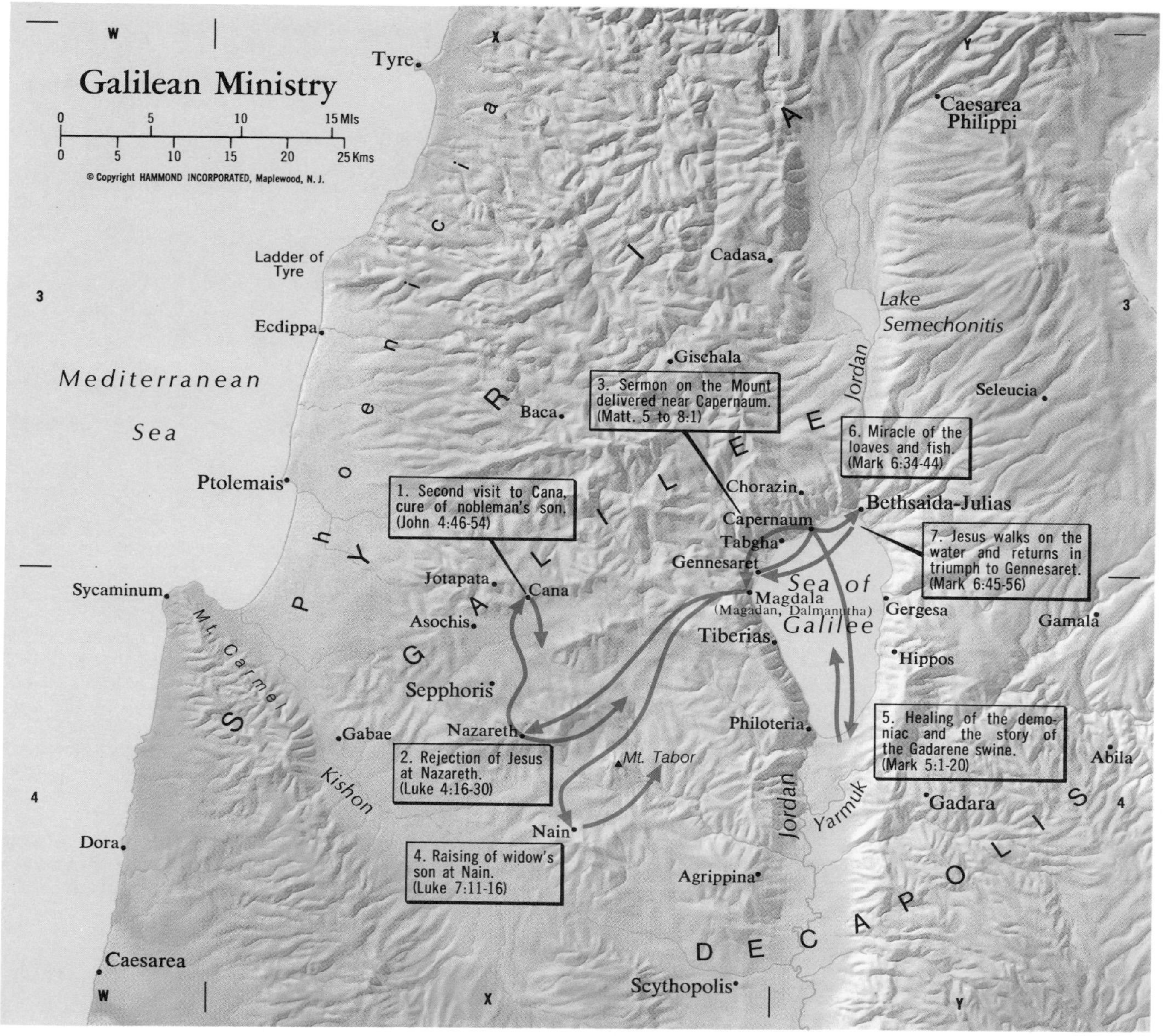

Galilean Ministry

0   5   10   15 Mls
0 5 10 15 20 25 Kms
© Copyright HAMMOND INCORPORATED, Maplewood, N.J.

W

Mediterranean Sea

Tyre.

Ladder of Tyre

Ecdippa.

3

Cadasa.

Caesarea Philippi

Lake Semechonitis

.Gischala

Seleucia.

Baca.

3. Sermon on the Mount delivered near Capernaum. (Matt. 5 to 8:1)

6. Miracle of the loaves and fish. (Mark 6:34-44)

Ptolemais•

1. Second visit to Cana, cure of nobleman's son. (John 4:46-54)

Chorazin•

Bethsaida-Julias

Capernaum•
Tabgha•
Gennesaret

7. Jesus walks on the water and returns in triumph to Gennesaret. (Mark 6:45-56)

Sycaminum.

Jotapata•

Cana•

Sea of Galilee

Magdala
(Magadan, Dalmanutha)

Gergesa•

Gamala•

Asochis•

Tiberias•

Mt. Carmel

Sepphoris•

Nazareth•

•Hippos

•Gabae

Philoteria•

5. Healing of the demoniac and the story of the Gadarene swine. (Mark 5:1-20)

Abila•

Kishon

2. Rejection of Jesus at Nazareth. (Luke 4:16-30)

Mt. Tabor

•Gadara

4

4

Dora•

Nain•

Jordan

Yarmuk

4. Raising of widow's son at Nain. (Luke 7:11-16)

•Caesarea

Agrippina•

D E C A P O L I S

Scythopolis•

Above the waters of the Sea of Galilee the Church of the Beatitudes dominates the hill where tradition says Jesus preached the Sermon on the Mount.

The excavated synagogue at Capernaum (right) is later than the time of Jesus, but recalls that the Galilean Ministry was based in Capernaum, where Jesus spent much time teaching and healing in the synagogue.

The traditional site of Jesus' baptism is here at the Jordan River.

Machaerus, where John the Baptist was put to death on orders of Herod Antipas.

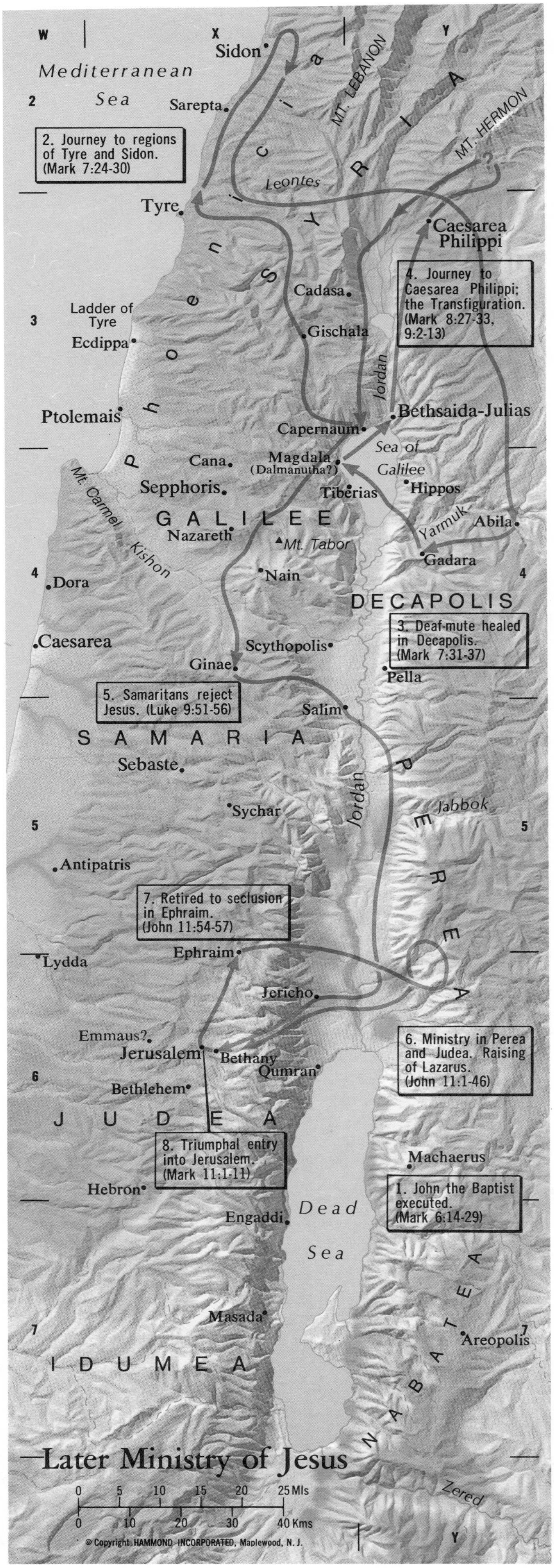

Later Ministry of Jesus

W X Y

Mediterranean
Sea

Sidon

Sarepta.

2. Journey to regions
of Tyre and Sidon.
(Mark 7:24-30)

Tyre.

Caesarea
Philippi

4. Journey to
Caesarea Philippi;
the Transfiguration.
(Mark 8:27-33,
9:2-13)

Cadasa.

Ladder of
Tyre

Ecdippa.

Gischala

Ptolemais.

Capernaum. Bethsaida-Julias

Cana. Magdala
(Dalmanutha?)

Sea of
Galilee

Sepphoris.

Tiberias. Hippos

GALILEE

Nazareth Yarmuk Abila.

Mt. Tabor

Nain. Gadara

Dora.

DECAPOLIS

Caesarea

Scythopolis.

Ginae. Pella

3. Deaf-mute healed
in Decapolis.
(Mark 7:31-37)

5. Samaritans reject
Jesus. (Luke 9:51-56)

Salim.

S A M A R I A

Sebaste.

Sychar.

Antipatris.

7. Retired to seclusion
in Ephraim.
(John 11:54-57)

Jabbok

Lydda.

Ephraim.

Jericho.

Emmaus?.

Jerusalem Bethany

Qumran.

Bethlehem.

6. Ministry in Perea
and Judea. Raising
of Lazarus.
(John 11:1-46)

J U D E A

8. Triumphal entry
into Jerusalem
(Mark 11:1-11)

Hebron.

Machaerus.

Dead
Sea

Engaddi.

Masada.

Areopolis.

I D U M E A

1. John the Baptist
executed.
(Mark 6:14-29)

0 5 10 15 20 25 Mls
0 10 20 30 40 Kms

© Copyright HAMMOND INCORPORATED, Maplewood, N.J.

The Events of Passion Week
(According to the Synoptic Gospels)

	MATT.	MARK	LUKE
SUNDAY (Palm Sunday)			
Triumphal entry into Jerusalem	21:1-9	11:1-10	19:28-44
Visit to Temple and return to Bethany	21:10-17	11:11	19:45-46
MONDAY			
On the way to Jerusalem Jesus curses an unfruitful fig tree	21:18-19	11:12-14	
The Temple court cleansed		11:15-19	19:45-48
TUESDAY			
Returning to Jerusalem, Jesus explains the withering of the fig tree	21:20-22	11:20-26	
Jesus' authority is questioned	21:23-27	11:27-33	20:1-8
Teachings in the Temple	21:28-46; 22	12:1-37a	20:9-44
Condemnation of scribes and Pharisees	23:1-36	12:37b-40	20:45-47
Jesus in Temple treasury calls attention to widow's gift		12:41-44	21:1-4
Prediction of destruction of the Temple and the end of the World	24:1-44	13:1-37	21:5-38
WEDNESDAY			
Conspiracy against Jesus	26:1-5	14:1-2	22:1-2
Anointing at Bethany	26:6-13	14:1-9	
Judas agrees to betray Jesus	26:14-16	14:10-11	22:3-6
THURSDAY (Maundy Thursday)			
Jesus prepares to celebrate Passover	26:17-19	14:12-16	22:7-13
The Last Supper	26:20-29	14:17-25	22:14-38
Withdrawal to Gethsemane	26:30-46	14:26-42	22:39-46
Betrayal and arrest of Jesus	26:47-56	14:43-52	22:47-53
Jesus before Caiaphas and members of the Sanhedrin; Peter's denial	26:57-75	14:53-72	22:54-71
FRIDAY (Good Friday)			
Trial before Pilate; Judas' suicide	27:1-2	15:1-5	23:1-5
Jesus sent to Herod			23:6-16
Pilate imposes sentence of death	27:15-26	15:6-15	23:17-25
Jesus scourged and led to Golgotha	27:27-32	15:15-21	
Jesus' crucifixion and death	27:33-56	15:22-41	23:33-49
Jesus is buried	27:57-61	15:42-47	23:50-56
SATURDAY			
The guarded tomb	27:62-66		
SUNDAY (Easter)			
The empty tomb and the risen Christ	28:1-10	16:1-8	24:1-12

A modern church at ancient Bethany marks the traditional place where Jesus raised Lazarus from the dead (John 11:1-44).

Silver denarius of Tiberius, "tribute money" of Luke 20:21-26.

At Caesarea, residence of the Roman governors, archaeologists found this dedication stone with the only known inscriptional reference to Pontius Pilate.

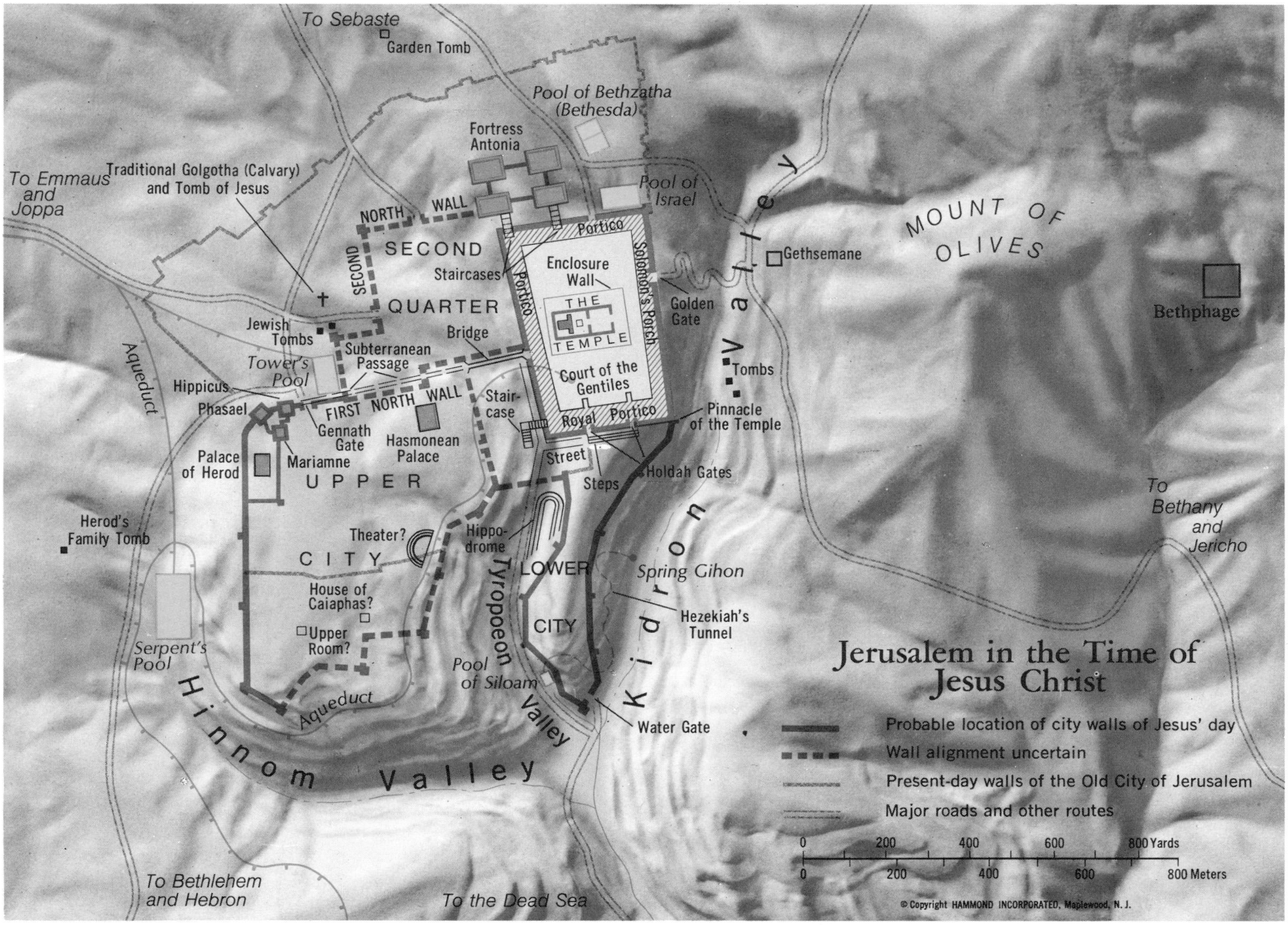

Jerusalem in the Time of Jesus Christ

To Sebaste
Garden Tomb

Pool of Bethzatha
(Bethesda)

Fortress
Antonia

Traditional Golgotha (Calvary)
and Tomb of Jesus

To Emmaus
and
Joppa

Pool of
Israel

NORTH   WALL

Portico

SECOND

Staircases

Enclosure
Wall

MOUNT OF
OLIVES

Gethsemane

QUARTER

Portico

THE
TEMPLE

Solomon's Porch

Golden
Gate

Bethphage

Jewish
Tombs

Bridge

Subterranean
Passage

Court of the
Gentiles

Tower's
Pool

Hippicus

Tombs

Phasael

FIRST NORTH WALL

Staircase

Royal   Portico

Pinnacle
of the Temple

Gennath
Gate

Hasmonean
Palace

Palace
of Herod

Mariamne

Street

Steps   Holdah Gates

UPPER

To
Bethany
and
Jericho

Herod's
Family Tomb

CITY

Theater?

Hippo-
drome

LOWER

Spring Gihon

House of
Caiaphas?

Upper
Room?

CITY

Hezekiah's
Tunnel

Serpent's
Pool

Pool
of Siloam

Water Gate

Aqueduct

Jerusalem in the Time of
Jesus Christ

Probable location of city walls of Jesus' day

Wall alignment uncertain

Present-day walls of the Old City of Jerusalem

Major roads and other routes

0   200   400   600   800 Yards
0   200   400   600   800 Meters

© Copyright HAMMOND INCORPORATED, Maplewood, N.J.

To Bethlehem
and Hebron

To the Dead Sea

Today a mosque, the magnificent Dome of the Rock, occupies the platform where Herod's Temple stood in Jesus' day.

Judas' 30 pieces of silver may have been Tyrian shekels of this type.

A model of Jerusalem shows the Temple platform and four towers of Fortress Antonia. The Pool of Bethzatha where Jesus healed the crippled man is the square-shaped building with reddish roof in the foreground.

The Garden Tomb, a rock-cut tomb of the type in which Jesus was buried. North of Jerusalem, this quiet spot just outside the present north wall is a rival to the traditional site of the crucifixion and burial.

"The Pavement" (courtyard) of the Fortress Antonia was possibly the place where Jesus was tried by Pilate. Today it is the crypt of a church and convent.

Theodotus synagogue inscription found on Mount Zion in Jerusalem. Some think this dedicatory inscription refers to the "Synagogue of the Freedmen" mentioned in Acts 6:9.

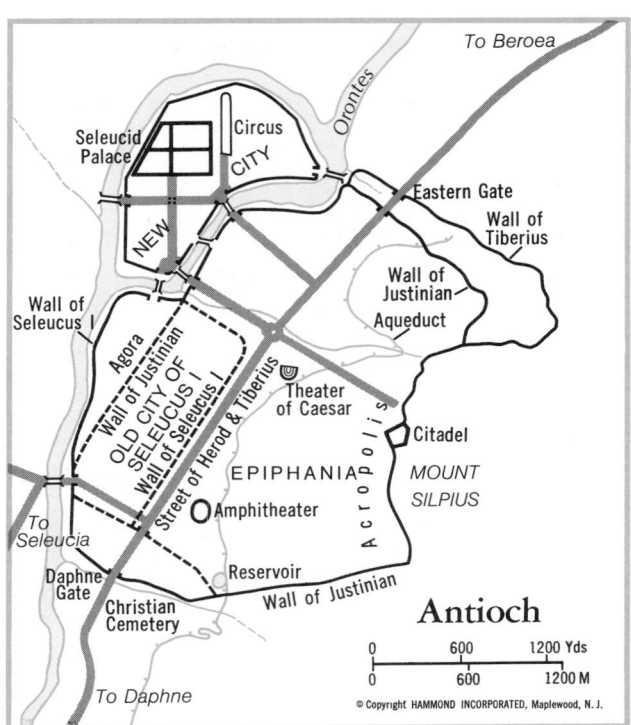

Antioch

The Lion Gate in Jerusalem's east wall. Medieval Christian tradition locates the martyrdom of Stephen (Acts 7:58-60) nearby. Therefore Christians call this "St. Stephen's Gate."

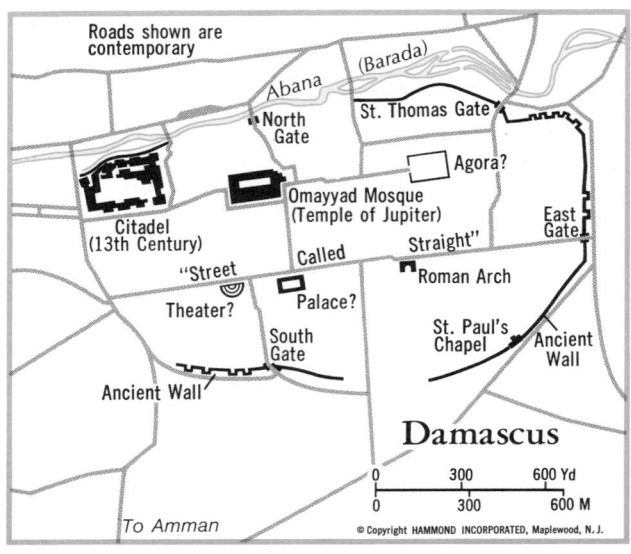

Damascus

St. Paul's Chapel, Damascus. This is the traditional location of Paul's escape over the city wall (Acts 9:25).

The theater by the sea at Caesarea where in 10 B.C. Herod dedicated his splendid new city. Now restored, it is used for concerts.

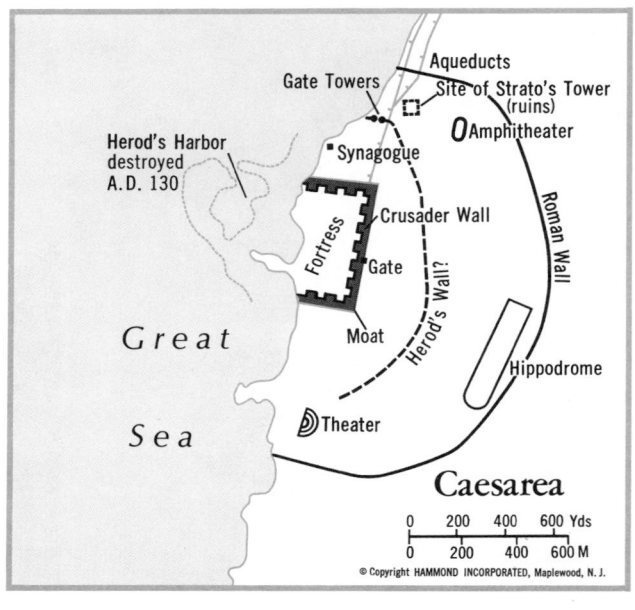

Caesarea

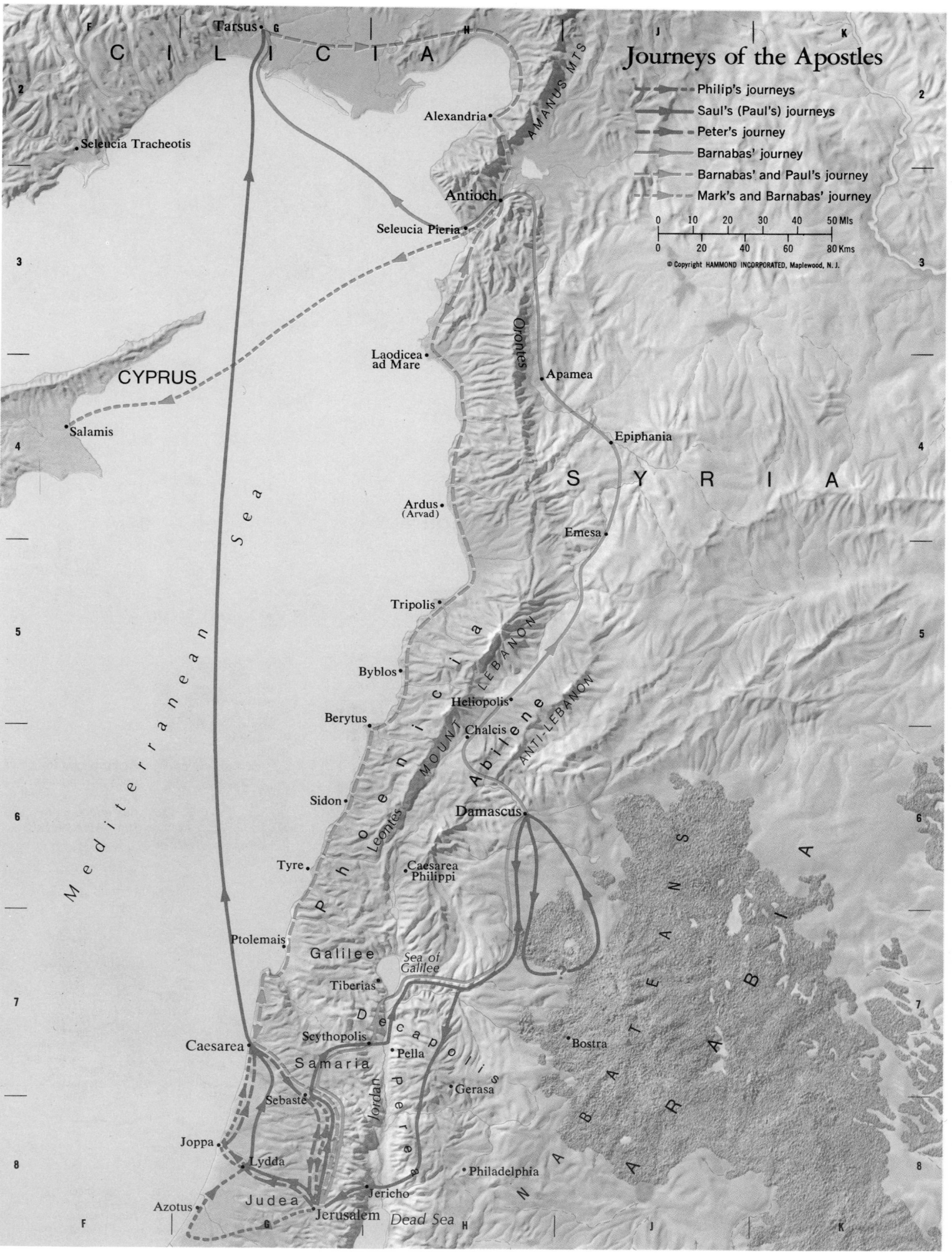

Tarsus

CILICIA

Alexandria

Seleucia Tracheotis

Antioch

Seleucia Pieria

CYPRUS

Salamis

Mediterranean Sea

Laodicea
ad Mare

Apamea

Orontes

Epiphania

SYRIA

Ardus
(Arvad)

Emesa

Tripolis

Byblos

Heliopolis

Berytus

Chalcis

Damascus

Sidon

Caesarea
Philippi

Tyre

MOUNT LEBANON

ANTI-LEBANON

Abilene

Leontes

Ptolemais

Galilee

Sea of
Galilee

Tiberias

Caesarea

Scythopolis

Decapolis

Bostra

Samaria

Pella

Sebaste

Gerasa

Joppa

Jordan

Perea

Lydda

Philadelphia

Azotus

Judea

Jericho

NABATEAN ARABIA

Jerusalem

Dead Sea

Journeys of the Apostles

- ▸ Philip's journeys
- ▸ Saul's (Paul's) journeys
- ▸ Peter's journey
- ── Barnabas' journey
- ▸ Barnabas' and Paul's journey
- ▸ Mark's and Barnabas' journey

```
0    10   20   30   40   50 MIs
0   20    40    60    80 Kms
```

© Copyright HAMMOND INCORPORATED, Maplewood, N. J.

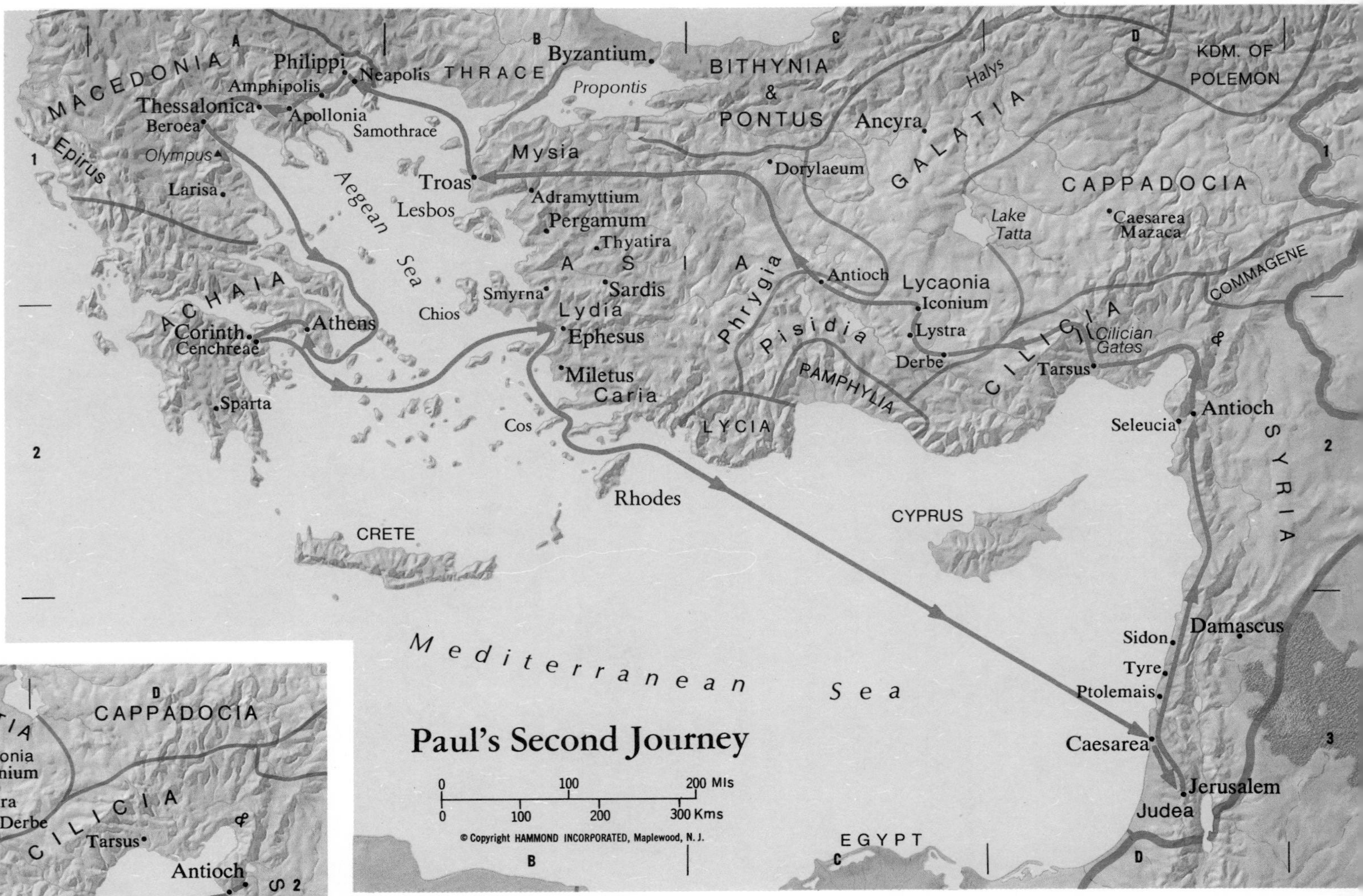

Paul's Second Journey

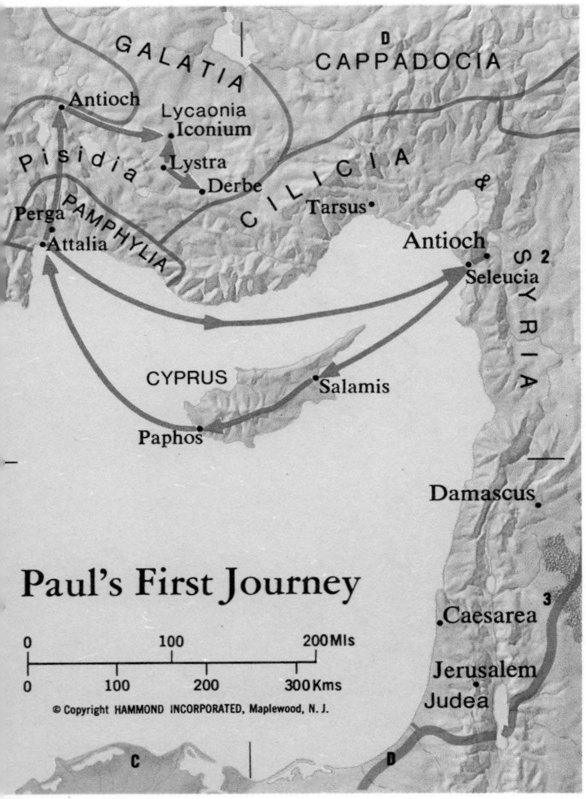

0   100   200 Mls
0   100   200   300 Kms
© Copyright HAMMOND INCORPORATED, Maplewood, N.J.

Paul's First Journey

0   100   200 Mls
0   100   200   300 Kms
© Copyright HAMMOND INCORPORATED, Maplewood, N.J.

Temple of Apollo, Corinth.
Only 7 of the 38 columns seen
by Paul are now standing.

Artemis was the chief
deity of Ephesus. Paul's
attack on the worship of
this goddess provoked a
riot (Acts 19:23f.).

The Acropolis rises behind the Areopagus
(foreground) where Paul was mocked by the
Athenian elders (Acts 17:32).

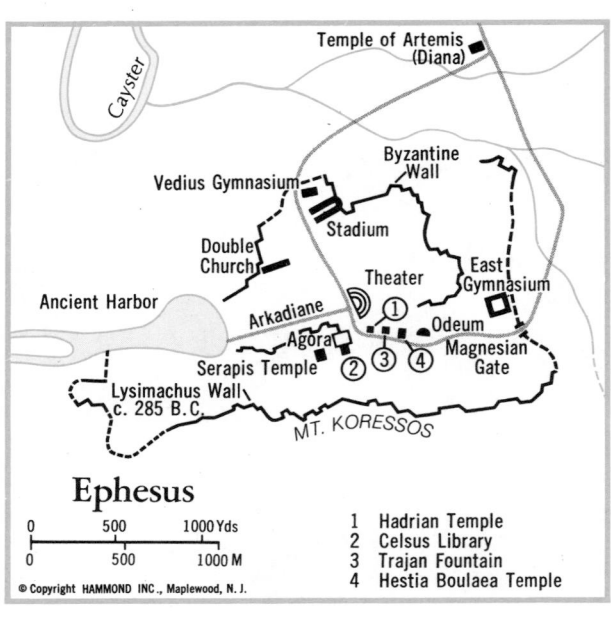

Ephesus

0   500   1000 Yds
0   500   1000 M
© Copyright HAMMOND INC., Maplewood, N.J.

1 Hadrian Temple
2 Celsus Library
3 Trajan Fountain
4 Hestia Boulaea Temple

Paul's Third Journey

MACEDONIA
Philippi
Amphipolis · Neapolis THRACE · Byzantium
Thessalonica · Apollonia
Beroea
Epirus *Olympus* ▲
Larisa
ACHAIA
Corinth
Athens
Sparta
Aegean Sea
Lesbos
Mitylene
Chios
Samos
Cos
Rhodes
Samothrace
Mysia
Troas · Adramyttium
Assos
Pergamum
Smyrna
Sardis
Lydia
Ephesus
Miletus
Caria
ASIA
Phrygia
Pisidia
PAMPHYLIA
LYCIA
Patara
Propontis
BITHYNIA & PONTUS
Ancyra
GALATIA
Antioch
Lycaonia
Iconium
Halys
Lake Tatta
CAPPADOCIA
Caesarea Mazaca
COMMAGENE &
CILICIA
Cilician Gates
Tarsus
KDM. OF POLEMON
CYPRUS
Seleucia · Antioch
SYRIA
Sidon · Damascus
Tyre
Ptolemais
Caesarea
Jerusalem
Judea
EGYPT

Mediterranean Sea

Scale
0 — 100 — 200 Mis
0 — 100 — 200 — 300 Kms
© Copyright HAMMOND INCORPORATED, Maplewood, N.J.

Paul's Voyage to Rome

Rome
Three Taverns
Forum of Appius
Puteoli
ITALY
SICILY
Rhegium
Syracuse
Malta (Melita)
Adriatic
Apollonia
Dyrrhachium
MACEDONIA
Thessalonica
Philippi
THRACE
ACHAIA
Athens
Corinth
Aegean Sea
Byzantium
BITHYNIA & PONTUS
Adramyttium
ASIA
Ephesus
Colossae
Cnidus
LYCIA
Myra
Rhodes
CRETE
Phoenix
Cauda
Lasea
Fair Havens
C. Salmone
CYPRUS
GALATIA
CAPPADOCIA
Tarsus
CILICIA
Antioch
& SYRIA
Sidon
Caesarea
Jerusalem
Alexandria
Black Sea
CYRENAICA (LIBYA)
EGYPT

Mediterranean Sea

Boundary of the Roman Empire
Provincial boundary

0 — 100 — 200 — 300 Mis
0 — 100 — 200 — 300 — 400 — 500 Kms

A Roman eagle on an altar in Jerusalem.

Masada from the north showing the archaeologically recovered fortress of Herod. Behind the imperial apartments is a bathhouse surrounded by storerooms.

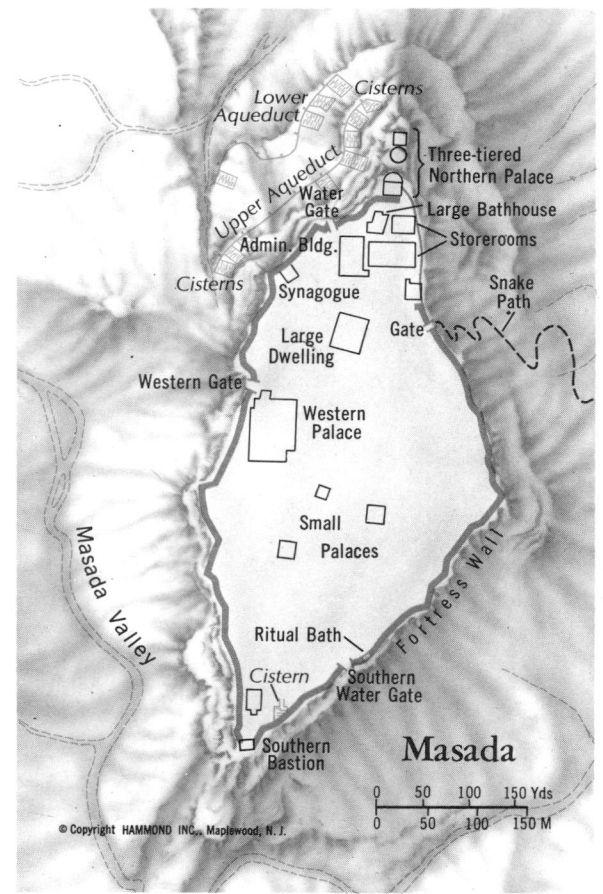

Masada

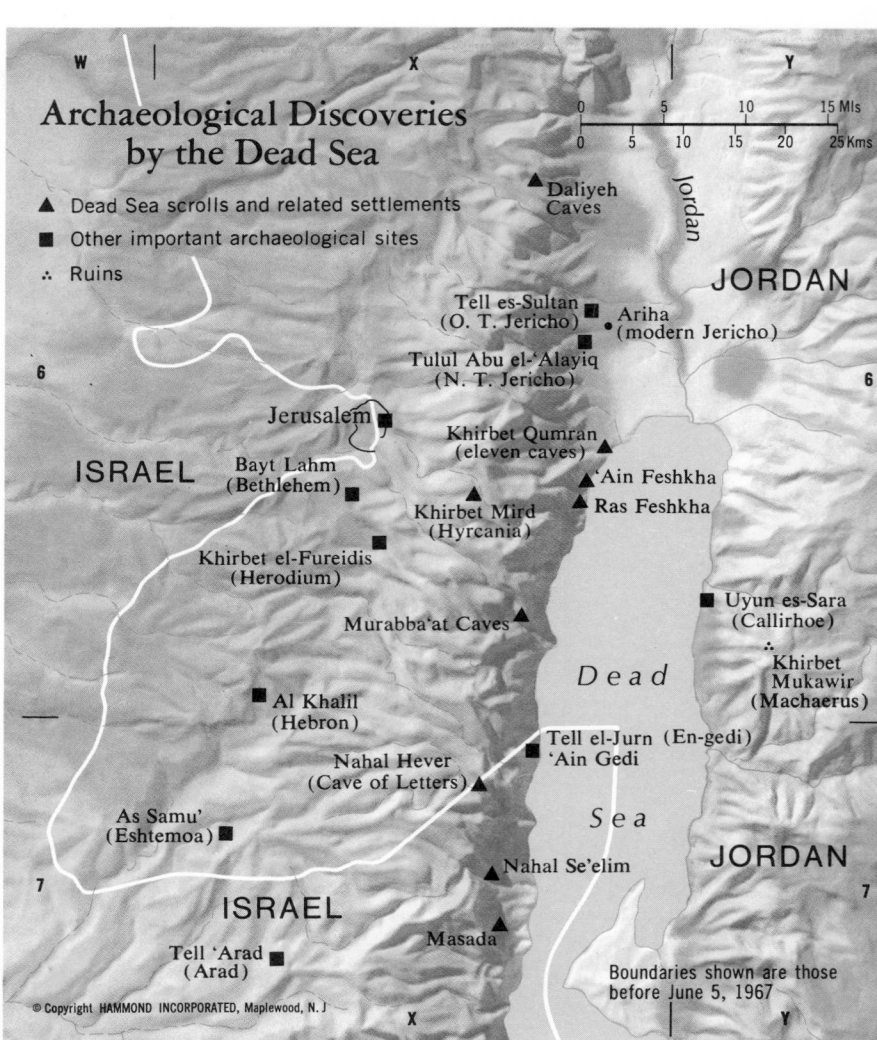

Archaeological Discoveries by the Dead Sea

▲ Dead Sea scrolls and related settlements
■ Other important archaeological sites
∴ Ruins

JORDAN

Daliyeh Caves

Tell es-Sultan (O. T. Jericho) Ariha (modern Jericho)
Tulul Abu el-'Alayiq (N. T. Jericho)

Jerusalem

ISRAEL   Bayt Lahm (Bethlehem)
Khirbet Qumran (eleven caves) 'Ain Feshkha
Khirbet Mird (Hyrcania) Ras Feshkha
Khirbet el-Fureidis (Herodium)

Uyun es-Sara (Callirhoe)
Murabba'at Caves
Khirbet Mukawir (Machaerus)

Dead

Al Khalil (Hebron)

Tell el-Jurn (En-gedi) 'Ain Gedi
Nahal Hever (Cave of Letters)

As Samu' (Eshtemoa)

Sea

JORDAN

Nahal Se'elim

ISRAEL

Masada

Tell 'Arad (Arad)

Boundaries shown are those before June 5, 1967

© Copyright HAMMOND INCORPORATED, Maplewood, N.J.

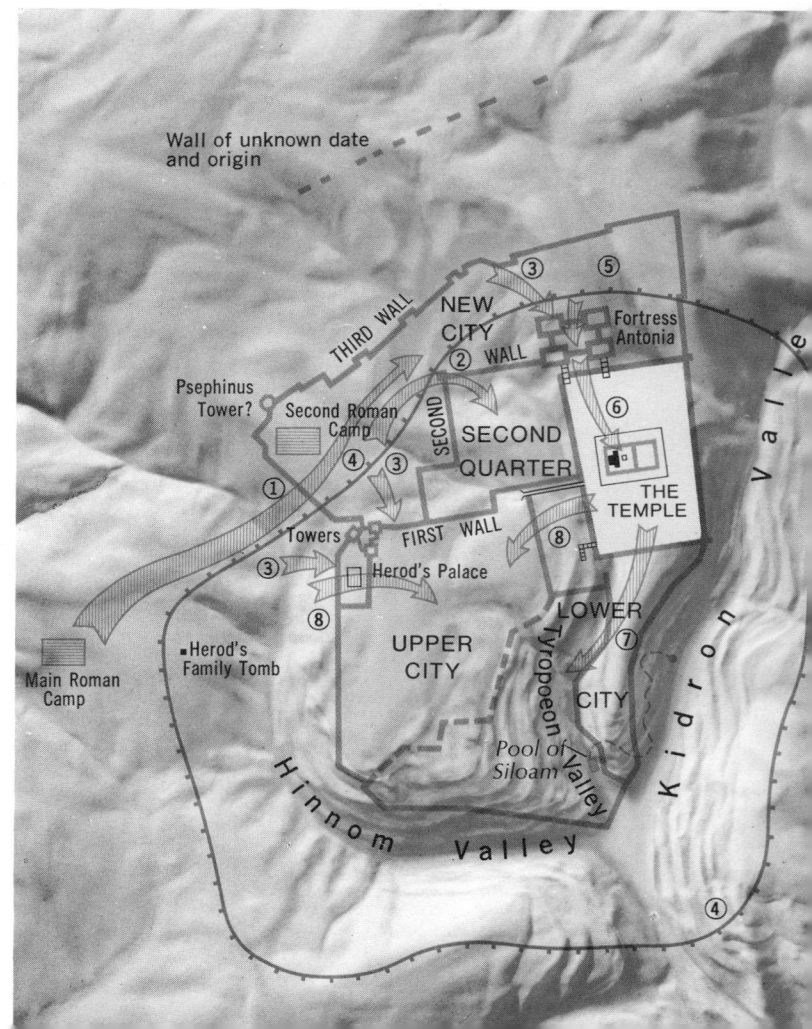

Wall of unknown date and origin

Psephinus Tower?   Second Roman Camp
THIRD WALL   NEW CITY   Fortress Antonia
SECOND   SECOND QUARTER   THE TEMPLE
Towers   FIRST WALL
Herod's Palace   LOWER CITY
Herod's Family Tomb   UPPER CITY   Tyropoeon Valley
Main Roman Camp   Pool of Siloam
Hinnom Valley   Kidron Valley

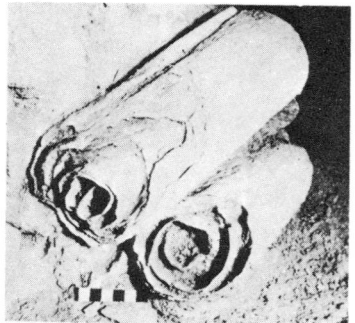

Copper Scrolls found at Qumran.

Cave Four at Qumran (center) in which a wealth of precious scrolls were found.

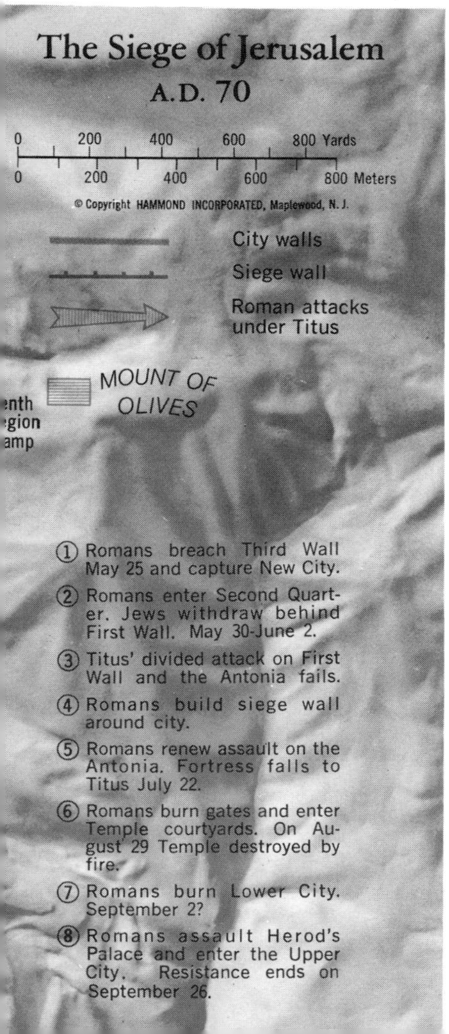

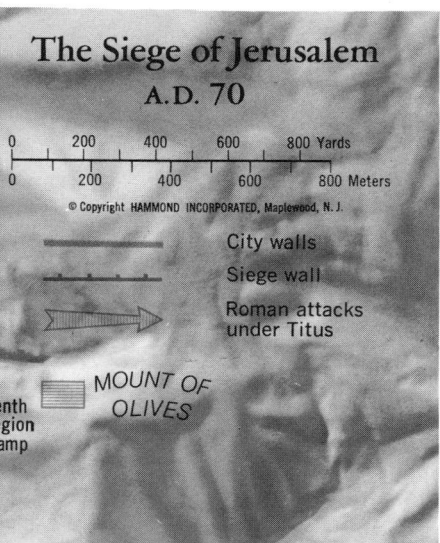

The Siege of Jerusalem
A.D. 70

| 0 | 200 | 400 | 600 | 800 Yards |
| 0 | 200 | 400 | 600 | 800 Meters |

© Copyright HAMMOND INCORPORATED, Maplewood, N.J.

————————— City walls

············· Siege wall

⟩⟩⟩⟩⟩ Roman attacks under Titus

▨ MOUNT OF OLIVES

enth
egion
amp

① Romans breach Third Wall May 25 and capture New City.

② Romans enter Second Quarter. Jews withdraw behind First Wall. May 30-June 2.

③ Titus' divided attack on First Wall and the Antonia fails.

④ Romans build siege wall around city.

⑤ Romans renew assault on the Antonia. Fortress falls to Titus July 22.

⑥ Romans burn gates and enter Temple courtyards. On August 29 Temple destroyed by fire.

⑦ Romans burn Lower City. September 2?

⑧ Romans assault Herod's Palace and enter the Upper City. Resistance ends on September 26.

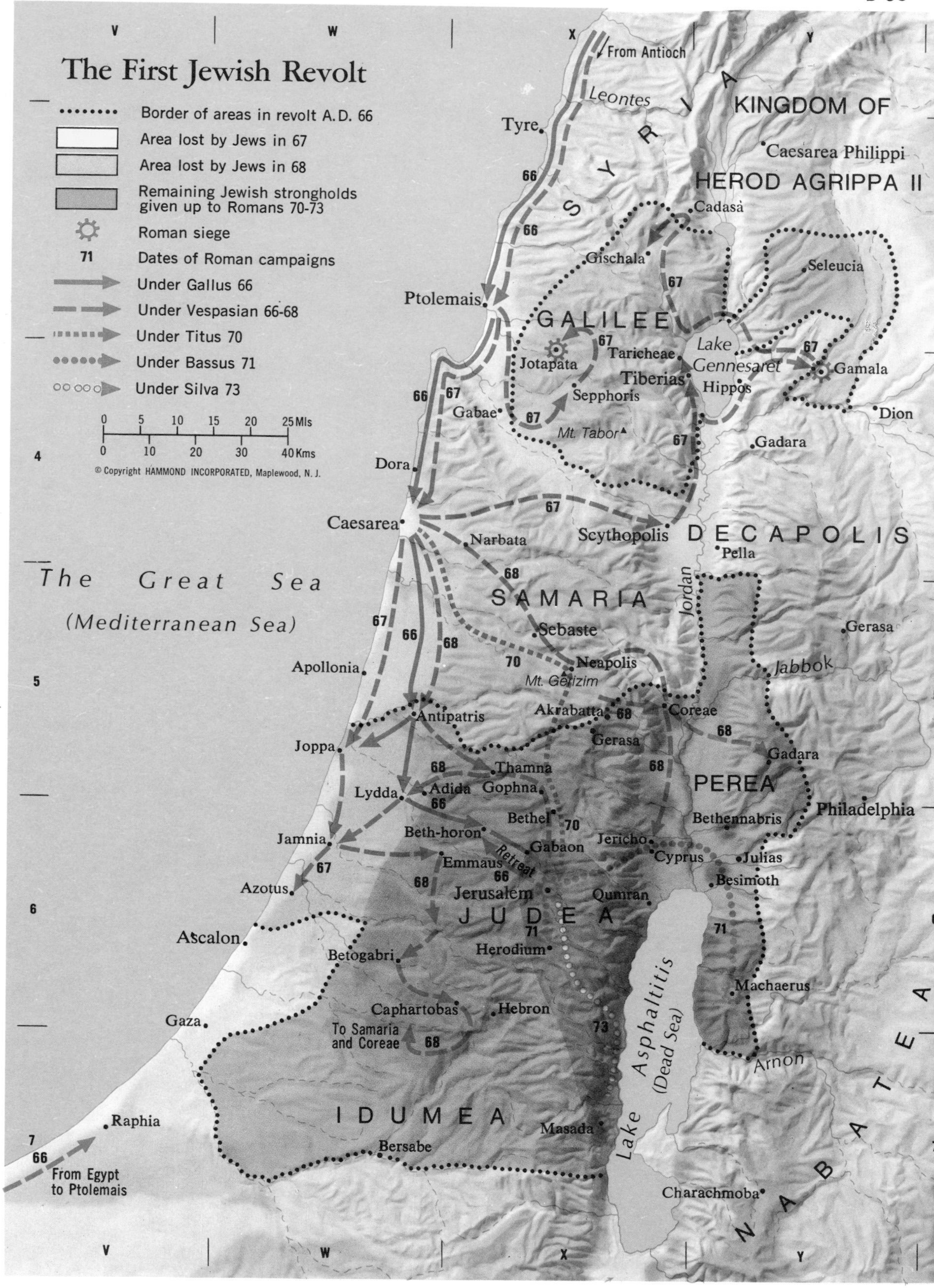

The First Jewish Revolt

·········· Border of areas in revolt A.D. 66
▢ Area lost by Jews in 67
▢ Area lost by Jews in 68
▨ Remaining Jewish strongholds given up to Romans 70-73
✿ Roman siege
71 Dates of Roman campaigns
➤ Under Gallus 66
➤ Under Vespasian 66-68
➤ Under Titus 70
➤ Under Bassus 71
➤ Under Silva 73

| 0 | 5 | 10 | 15 | 20 | 25 Mls |
| 0 | 10 | 20 | 30 | 40 Kms |

© Copyright HAMMOND INCORPORATED, Maplewood, N.J.

The Great Sea
(Mediterranean Sea)

KINGDOM OF
HEROD AGRIPPA II
Caesarea Philippi
From Antioch
Leontes
Tyre
Cadasa
Gischala
Seleucia
Ptolemais
GALILEE
Lake Gennesaret
Gamala
Jotapata
Taricheae
Tiberias
Hippos
Dion
Gabae
Sepphoris
Mt. Tabor
Gadara
Dora
Scythopolis
DECAPOLIS
Caesarea
Narbata
Pella
SAMARIA
Jordan
Gerasa
Sebaste
Jabbok
Apollonia
Neapolis
Mt. Gerizim
Akrabatta
Coreae
Antipatris
Gerasa
Gadara
Joppa
Thamna
PEREA
Lydda
Adida
Gophna
Philadelphia
Jamnia
Beth-horon
Bethel
Bethennabris
Gabaon
Jericho
Emmaus
Retreat
Cyprus
Julias
Azotus
Jerusalem
Qumran
Besimoth
Ascalon
JUDEA
Herodium
Betogabri
Lake Asphaltitis (Dead Sea)
Machaerus
Caphartobas
Hebron
Gaza
To Samaria and Coreae
Raphia
IDUMEA
Masada
Arnon
From Egypt to Ptolemais
Bersabe
Charachmoba
NABATEA
SYRIA

Silver shekel from the "year three," the third year of the Revolt (A.D. 68).

Roman "Judaea Capta" coins. Above are Vespasian and Titus. Sestertius, right, shows a captive Jewess.

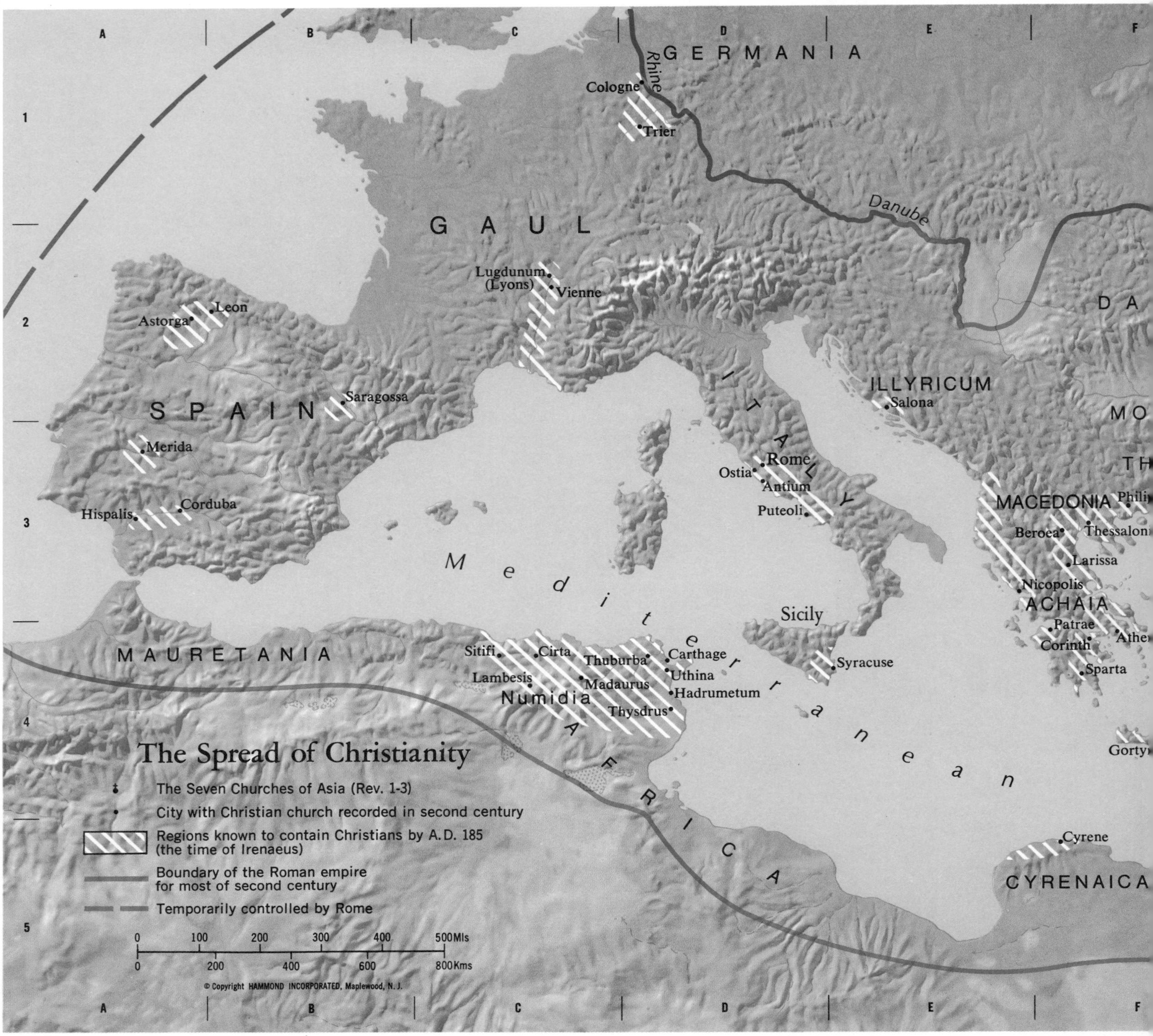
The Spread of Christianity
The Seven Churches of Asia (Rev. 1-3)
City with Christian church recorded in second century
Regions known to contain Christians by A.D. 185 (the time of Irenaeus)
Boundary of the Roman empire for most of second century
Temporarily controlled by Rome
0 100 200 300 400 500Mls
0 200 400 600 800Kms
© Copyright HAMMOND INCORPORATED, Maplewood, N. J.
A
B
C
D
E
F
1
2
3
4
5
GERMANIA
Rhine
Cologne
Trier
Danube
GAUL
Lugdunum (Lyons)
Vienne
DA
Astorga
Leon
SPAIN
Saragossa
Merida
Hispalis
Corduba
ITALY
ILLYRICUM
Salona
MO
TH
Ostia
Rome
Antium
Puteoli
MACEDONIA
Phili
Beroea
Thessalon
Larissa
Nicopolis
ACHAIA
Patrae
Corinth
Athe
Sparta
Mediterranean
Sicily
Syracuse
MAURETANIA
Sitifi
Cirta
Thuburba
Carthage
Uthina
Lambesis
Madaurus
Hadrumetum
Numidia
Thysdrus
AFRICA
Gorty
Cyrene
CYRENAICA

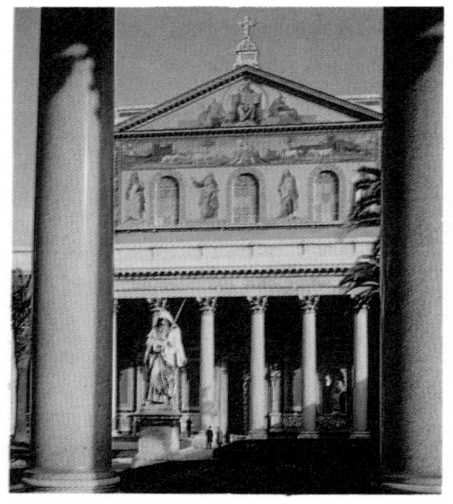

St. Paul's-Outside-the-Walls, Rome, traditional site of the tomb of Paul.

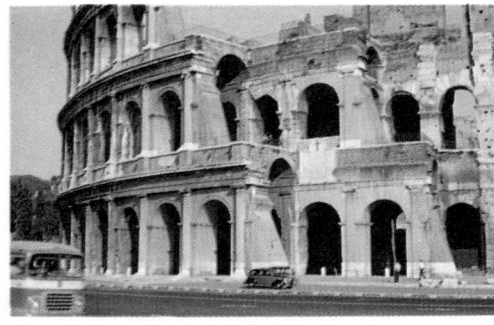

The Flavian Amphitheater (Colosseum) in Rome, where many Christians were martyred.

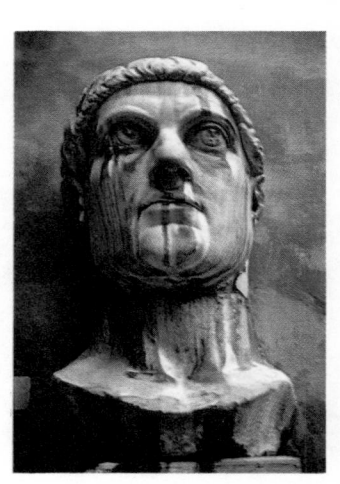

Constantine made Christianity a "legal religion" in A.D. 311.

Limestone statuette of Coptic Christian woman with cross, from 4th-century A.D. Egypt.

The map shows the following labeled locations:

Caspian Sea

Black Sea

Anchialus
Ionopolis
Debeltum
Amastris
PONTUS
Sinope
Amisus
ARMENIA
Byzantium
BITHYNIA
Nicomedia
Mysia
Ancyra
PARTHIA
Troas
Phrygia
GALATIA
Caesarea
Melitene
Pergamum
CAPPADOCIA
Beit Zabde
Nisibis
Thyatira
Sardis
Antioch
Samosata
Edessa
Smyrna
Philadelphia
Iconium
Tigris
Ephesus
Laodicea
Lystra
Derbe
Tarsus
MESOPOTAMIA
Miletus
Colossae
Perga
CILICIA
Rhossus
Antioch
Euphrates
Seleucia
SYRIA
Patmos
Myra
Laodicea
Apamea
Dura-Europos
Cyprus
Salamis
Tripolis
Cnossus
Paphos
Crete
Sidon
Damascus
Sea
Tyre
Caesarea
Pella
Joppa
Jerusalem
ARABIA
Alexandria
Naucratis
Memphis
Nile
EGYPT

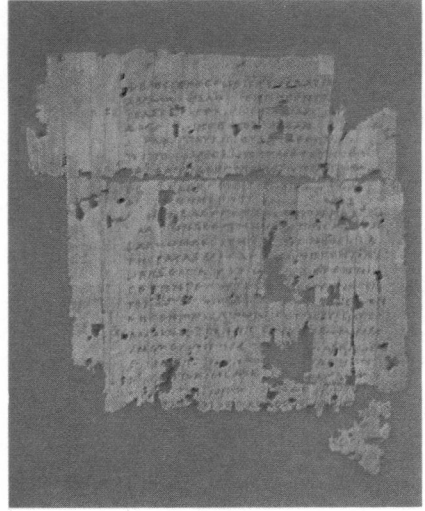

Papyrus fragment of the Gospel of Matthew from Qxyrhynchus, Egypt.

Patmos, where The Revelation to St. John the Divine, the last book in the New Testament, was written.

Chalice of Antioch shows Christ and apostles. It dates from 4th or 5th century A.D.

Lid of Philistine anthropoid coffin
from Beth-shan.

The Moabite Stone, found in 1868
at Mesha's capital. Carved about
840-820 B.C., it tells of the events of
2 Kings 3:4-27 and their aftermath
from a Moabite point of view.

The mound of Tell el-Hesi. One of
the first sites to be excavated in
Palestine, it is thought to be
Biblical Eglon, a Canaanite royal
city taken by Joshua (Joshua 10).

Archaeological Sites in Israel and Jordan

- ◖ Prehistoric cave sites
- ■ Major excavated sites
- ▪ Other important excavations

0   5   10   15   20   25 Mls
0   10   20   30   40 Kms

© Copyright HAMMOND INCORPORATED, Maplewood, N.J.

Mediterranean

Sea

LEB.

SYRIA

Tyre
Dan
Tell Anafa
Achzib
Kafr Bir'im
Nahariyah
HAZOR
Nabratein
Meiron
Acco—
Ptolemais
Chorazin
Capernaum
Shikmona
Tabgha
Sea of Galilee
Tell Abu Hawan
Irbid
Sepphoris
Tiberias
Hippos
'Atlit
Beth Yerah
Beth Shearim
Wadi el-Mughara
Dor
MEGIDDO
Taanach
Beth-Alfa
BETH-SHAN—SCYTHOPOLIS
Caesarea
Pella
Tell Zeror
Dothan
TIRZAH
Tell es-Saidiyeh
(Zarethan?)
Jerash
SAMARIA—SEBASTE
SHECHEM
Aphek—Antipatris
Tell Deir 'allā
(Succoth?)
Tell el-Qasileh
Izbet Sarta
JORDAN
Shiloh
Joppa
Amman
Mesad Hashavyahu
BETHEL
Kh. el-Mefjir
(Gilgal?)
Araq el-Emir
Tell en-Nasbeh
(Mizpah?)
Ai
GEZER
JERICHO
Tel Mor
Gibeon
Gibeah
Heshbon
ISRAEL
'Ain Karim
JERUSALEM
Teleilat el-Ghassul
Ashdod
BETH-SHEMESH
Ramat Rahel
Qumran
Bethlehem
'Ain Feshkha
Madaba
Azekah
Herodium
Hyrcania
Tell es-Safi
Ascalon
Tell ej-Judeideh
Beth-zur
Tell el-'Areini
Murabba'at Caves
LACHISH
Mareshah
Dead
Hebron
Gaza
Tell el-Hesi
(Eglon?)
'Ain Gedi
Dibon
TELL AJJUL
TELL BEIT MIRSIM
Sea
Khirbet 'Ar'ir
Khirbet Rabûd
(Debir?)
Tell Jemmeh
Tell el-Far'a
Tell 'Arad
Masada
Bab edh 'Drah
Tell Abu Matar
Tell es-Seba
Khirbet el-Kerak
Khirbet el-Mishash
Tell el-Milh
Khalasa
Numeira
Karnub
Zoar
Khirbet et-Tannur
Auja el-Hafir
Isbeita
Avdat
EGYPT
Kadesh-barnea

This four-spouted lamp is
from Patriarchal times.

A footed lamp from the
period of the Hebrew kings.

Jesus knew this type of
Herodian lamp.

Time Chart of Bible History

DATE	PALESTINE	EGYPT	MESOPOTAMIA & PERSIA	ANATOLIA & SYRIA	GREECE & ROME
4000 BC	Neolithic culture (Jericho) Ghassulian culture c.3500 The Canaanites, a Semitic people, were ancestral to the Phoenicians Early Bronze urban culture c.3300 Amorite invasions c.2500-2300	— First use of metal: copper and bronze — Hieroglyphic writing developed **Archaic Period** Menes unifies Egypt **Old Kingdom** The Great Pyramids at Gizeh c.2550 Old Kingdom falls	Halaf culture Cuneiform writing developed Sumerian city states c.2800-2360 **Akkadian Empire** Sargon I 2360-2305 Gutian kings Ur dominance	Early Bronze cities Byblos, Troy, Ugarit Syria under Akkadian Empire Hittites enter Anatolia	Beginning of Minoan civilization on Crete Greeks invade Balkan peninsula
2000 BC	Egypt controls Canaan Abraham — oral tradition Israelite sojourn in Egypt Battle of Megiddo 1468 Amarna letters c.1370-1353 The Exodus c.1290 Israelite invasion Philistine penetration Kdm. of Saul c.1020-1000	**Middle Kingdom** Hyksos invaders from Asia c.1720-1550 **New Kingdom** Akhenaton 1370-1353 Tutankhamen 1353-1344 Ramses II 1290-1224 Ramses III defeats Sea Peoples c.1170 **Late Dynastic Period**	Ur falls c.1950 **Isin-Larsa Period** **Old Babylonian Empire** Hammurabi 1728-1686 **Kassite Period** Hittites sack Babylon 1531 Mitanni Kdm. **Rise of Assyria** Shalmaneser I Tiglath-pileser I 1115-1078	Amorite invasions Hittites intro. Iron Labarnas I c.1600 **Old Hittite Kingdom** Mursilis I c.1540 Suppilullumas **Hittite Empire** Battle of Kedesh 1296 Sack of Troy 1192	**Minoan Sea Empire** Mycenae shaft graves Cretan palaces destroyed c.1400 Dorians invade Greece Trojan War c.1200
1000 BC	**United Kingdom** David c.1000-961 Solomon c.961-922 First Temple completed c.950 **Divided Kingdom** Rehoboam & Jeroboam I Omri dynasty 876-842 Samaria founded c.875 Jehu dynasty 842-745	Period of decline Shishak c.935-914 Libyan dynasties 950-710	**Assyrian Empire** Asshurnasirpal II 883-859 Shalmaneser III 859-824 Adad-nirari III 807-782	Arameans flood into Syria Hiram of Tyre 969-936 Damascus city state Ben-hadad II Battle of Qarqar 853 Phoenicians found Carthage 814	Decline of Aegean Bronze Age civilization Latins settle in central Italy
800 BC 600 BC	Israel resurgence under Jeroboam II 786-746 Amos, Hosea Fall of Samaria and exile of Israel 722/721 Hezekiah of Judah 715-687/6 Isaiah Micah Judah resurgence under Josiah 640-609 Jeremiah	Nubian dynasties 715-663 Egypt under Assyrian rule 671-652 Thebes sacked 663 Neco II 609-593	Tiglath-pileser III 745-727 Sargon II 722-705 Sennacherib 705-681 Asshurbanapal 669-633 Rise of Babylon under Nabopolassar Fall of Nineveh to Medes and Babylonians 612	Phrygian Kdm. Midas c.715 Lydian Kdm. Gyges of Lydia 680-652	First Olympics 776 Legendary founding of Rome 753 Etruscan period Homer Draco codifies Athenian law 621

Kings of Judah and Israel

JUDAH	ISRAEL	JUDAH	ISRAEL
Rehoboam 922-915	922-901 Jeroboam I	Jotham 750-735	746-745 Zechariah
Abijah 915-913	901-900 Nadab		745 Shallum
Asa 913-873	900-877 Baasha		745-738 Menahem
	877-876 Elah		738-737 Pekahiah
	876 Zimri	Ahaz 735-715	737-732 Pekah
Jehoshaphat 873-849	876-869 Omri		732-724 Hoshea
	869-850 Ahab	Hezekiah 715-687/6	
	850-849 Ahaziah	Manasseh 687/6-642	
Jehoram 849-842	849-842 Jehoram	Amon 642-640	
Ahaziah 842	842-815 Jehu	Josiah 640-609	
Athaliah 842-837		Jehoahaz 609	
Joash 837-800	815-801 Jehoahaz	Jehoaikim 609-598	
Amaziah 800-783	801-786 Jehoash	Jehoiachin 598-597	
Uzziah 783-742	786-746 Jeroboam II	Zedekiah 597-587	

DATE	PALESTINE	EGYPT	MESOPOTAMIA & PERSIA	ANATOLIA & SYRIA	GREECE & ROME
600 BC	Destruction of Jerusalem and exile of Judah 587 Ezekiel **Babylonian Captivity** Edict of Cyrus allows return of Jews 538 Zerubbabel Temple rebuilt 520-515 **Persian Period** Ezra's mission 458?? Nehemiah comes to Judah 445 (440?)	Egypt under Persian rule 525-401 Unsuccessful revolt Return to native rule	**New Babylonian Empire** Nebuchadnezzar II 605-562 **Persian Empire** Cyrus 550-530 Babylon falls 539 Cambyses 530-522 Darius I 522-486 Xerxes I 486-465 Artaxerxes I Darius II 433-404	Syria and Anatolia under Persian rule Phoenicians provide fleet for Persian attacks on Greece	Solon's judicial reforms c. 590 Rome ruled by Etruscan kings Roman Republic established 509 Persian Wars 499-479 Thermopylae-Salamis 480 Pericles 461-429 Herodotus
400 BC	Ezra's mission 398? Palestine passes under Alexander's rule and Hellenization begins 332 Ptolemaic Egyptian rule 312	Persian rule 342-332 Alexander conquers Egypt 332 Ptolemy I 323-284 **Ptolemaic Kingdom** Alexandrian Jews translate Pentateuch into Greek Ptolemy V 203-181	Artaxerxes III 358-338 Alexander invades Persia 331 Seleucid rule Parthians and Bactrians gain independence c. 250	Alexander takes Tyre 332 Seleucid rule Seleucus I 312-280 **Seleucid Empire** Antiochus I 280-261 Seleucus II 246-226 Antiochus III (The Great) 223-187	Socrates' death Sack of Rome by Gauls Philip II of Macedon Alexander the Great 336-323 **Alexander's Empire** Wars of the Diodochi 1st and 2nd Punic Wars Hannibal in Italy 218
200 BC	Palestine comes under Seleucid Syrian control 198 **Maccabean Period** Judas Maccabeus leads revolt of Jews 166-160 Temple rededicated 164 Jonathan 160-142 Simon 142-134 John Hyrcanus I 134-104 Aristobulus I 104-103	Ptolemy VI 181-146 Antiochus IV campaigns in Egypt Ptolemy VII 146-116	**Parthian Empire** Mithridates I 171-138 Mithridates II 124-88	Battle of Magnesia 190 Antiochus IV (Epiphanes) 175-163 Antiochus V 163-162 Demetrius I 162-150 Demetrius II 145-139 Tyre independent	Spain annexed by Rome **Empire of the Roman Republic** 3rd Punic War Romans destroy Carthage and Corinth 146 Reforms of the Gracchi
100 BC 50 BC	Alexander Jannaeus 103-76 Alexandra 76-67 Aristobulus II 67-63 Pompey takes Jerusalem for Rome 63 Hyrcanus II, high priest 63-40 Antipater governor 55	Ptolemy VIII 116-81 Ptolemy XI 80-81 Cleopatra VII 51-30	Tigranes of Armenia Phrates III 70-57 Orodes I 57-38 War with Rome 55-38 Crassus defeated	Mithridatic Wars Antiochus XIII 68-67 Anatolia and Syria under Roman control	Sulla dictator 82-79 1st Triumvirate Pompey's campaigns in Asia 66-63 Caesar's Gallic Wars 58-51

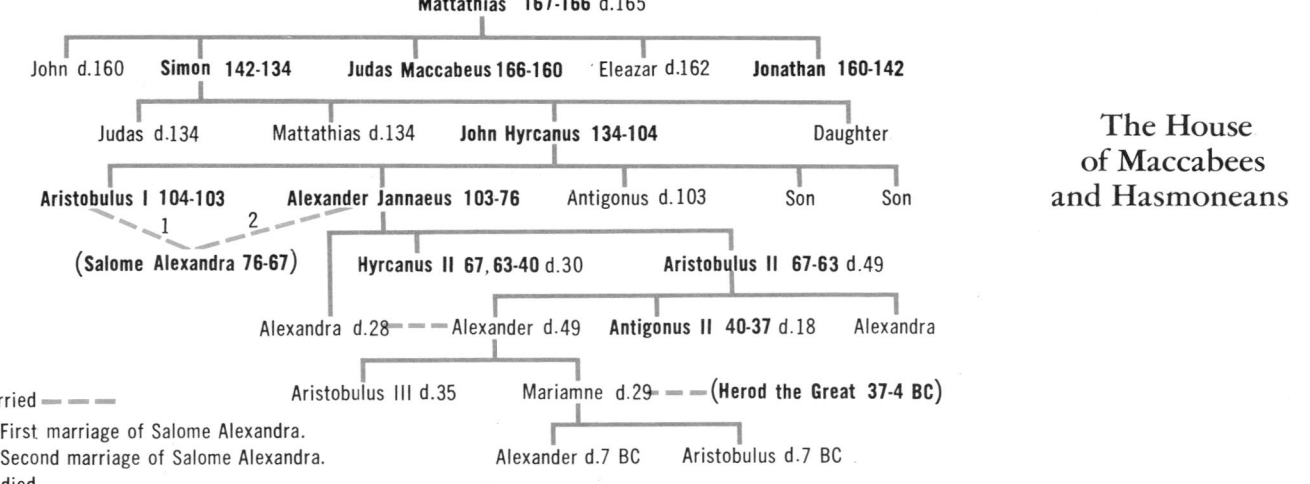

The House of Maccabees and Hasmoneans

Mattathias 167-166 d.165

John d.160   **Simon 142-134**   **Judas Maccabeus 166-160**   Eleazar d.162   **Jonathan 160-142**

Judas d.134   Mattathias d.134   **John Hyrcanus 134-104**   Daughter

Aristobulus I 104-103   **Alexander Jannaeus 103-76**   Antigonus d.103   Son   Son

1   2

(Salome Alexandra 76-67)

Hyrcanus II 67, 63-40 d.30   **Aristobulus II 67-63 d.49**

Alexandra d.28 — — Alexander d.49   **Antigonus II 40-37 d.18**   Alexandra

Aristobulus III d.35   Mariamne d.29 — — (Herod the Great 37-4 BC)

Alexander d.7 BC   Aristobulus d.7 BC

Married — — —
1. First marriage of Salome Alexandra.
2. Second marriage of Salome Alexandra.
d. died

Time Chart of Bible History, Continued

DATE	PALESTINE	THE WEST	THE EAST
50 BC	**Roman Rule** Caesar in Judea 47 Parthian invasion 40 Antigonus 40-37 Herod the Great 37-4 BC Herod's Temple begun 18 Birth of Christ c.4 BC Archelaus 4 BC-AD 6	Death of Pompey 48 Death of Caesar 44 2nd Triumvirate Battle of Philippi 42 Battle of Actium 31 Augustus — First emperor 27 BC-AD 14 **Roman Empire**	**Parthian Empire** Phraates 37-32 Parthians defeat Antony 36
0	Roman governors 6-41 Pontius Pilate 27-37 Death of Christ c.29 Herod Agrippa I 41-44 Paul's 1st journey, Council at Jerusalem 46/47	Varus defeated in Germany 9 Tiberius 14-37 Gaius (Caligula) 37-41 Claudius 41-54 Conquest of Britain begun 43	Artabanus II 10-40
50 AD	Antonius Felix 52-60 Imprisonment of Paul 58 Porcius Festus 60-62 Paul sent to Rome 60 Gessius Florus 64-66 First Jewish Revolt 66-73 Destruction of Jerusalem 70 Fall of Masada 73 Jewish center at Jamnia	Nero 54-68 1st Persecution of Christians 64 Galba, Otho, Vitellius 68/69 Vespasian 69-79 Titus 79-81 Domitian 81-96 Nerva 96-98 Trajan 98-117	Vologases I 51-80 Parthian War with Rome 53-63 Osroes (Chosroes) 89-128
100 AD **135 AD**	Jewish uprisings in Palestine, Egypt, Mesopotamia 116-117 Bar-Kochba Revolt 132-135 Jerusalem razed, Aelia Capitolina built on site	Campaigns in Dacia 101-107 Hadrian 117-138	Conquest of Nabateans by Romans Trajan invades Parthia 114 Territory lost to Romans regained 118

Herod and His Descendants

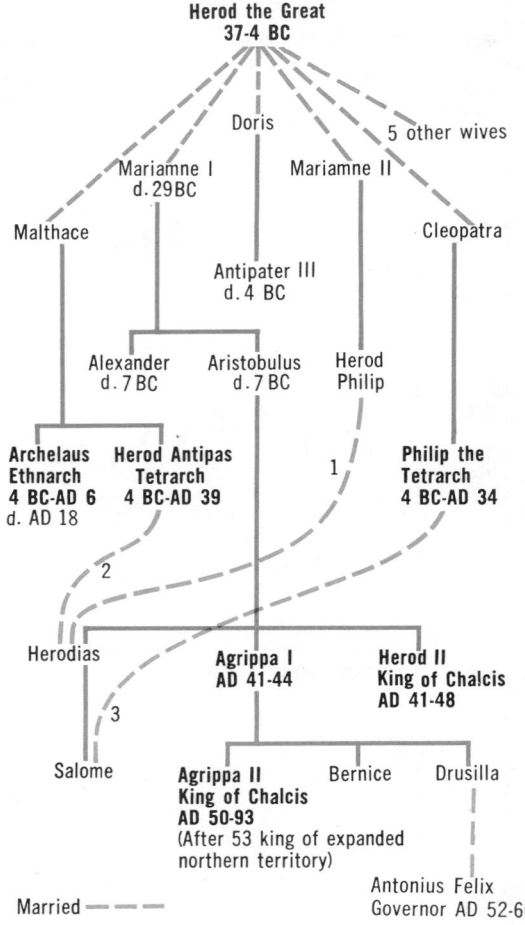

Married - - - - -

1. First marriage of Herodias.
2. Second marriage of Herodias.
3. Salome, daughter of Herodias and Herod (sometimes referred to as Philip), danced before Herod Antipas for John the Baptist's head. She married her great-uncle Philip the Tetrarch.

d. died

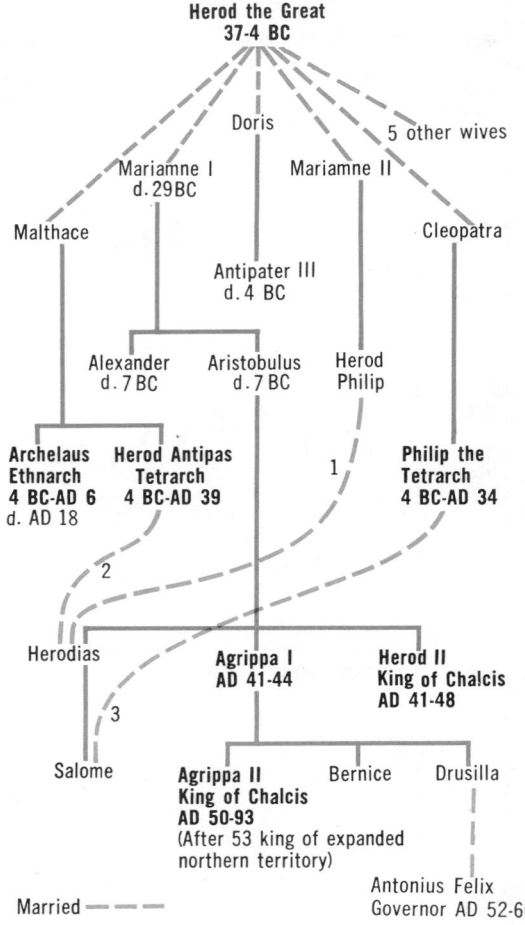

Roman catapult. A type of artillery used effectively by both Romans and Jews in the battle for Jerusalem, A.D. 69-70.

Gazetteer-Index

This Gazetteer-Index is an alphabetical listing of all geographical names found on the maps of this volume. The spelling of Biblical names used on maps and index is that found in the Revised Standard Version (RSV). Alternative Biblical or other ancient names are given in parentheses. Wherever possible, the modern equivalent (Arabic, Hebrew, Turkish, etc.) of an ancient name is given in italic type. A question mark after the identification of a site indicates that the location is possible or probable but not yet certain. The page numbers of the maps on which the name appears are listed in sequence. The key or grid reference (a letter-figure combination) following the page number(s) refers to the letters and figures at the margins of the maps. For example, Azotus (Ashdod in Old Testament times) [Arabic *Isdud,* Hebrew *Tel Ashdod*] can be found on the maps on pages 23, 25, 26 and 35 at key reference W6 and on page 31 at G8. Entries for locations within or near Jerusalem give the page numbers only for the appropriate Jerusalem maps.

ABBREVIATIONS

T. = Tell, Tel (mound)
Kh. = Khirbet (ruin)
H. = Horvat (ruin)
J. = Jebel (hill or mount)
W. = Wadi (seasonal stream)

A

Abana, *Nahr Barada,* river. 4:Z2
Abel, (Abel-beth-maachah), *T. Abil.* 12, 14, 15:Y3; 13:H5
Abel-meholah, *Kh. el-Maqlub.* 15:Y4
Abila, *T. Abil,* in Decapolis. 23, 25, 26, 27, 28:Y4
Abila, *T. Abila,* in Abilene. 25, 26:Z2
Abilene, region. 25, 26:X2; 31:H6
Abū Rudays. 39:C6
Abū Zanimah. 39:C6
Abydos, *Arabet el-Madfuneh,* in Egypt. 9, 16:F6
Abydos, *Canakkale,* in Asia Minor. 16:E2
Accaron, *see* Ekron
Acco, (Ptolemais, Acre), *'Akko, T. el-Fukhkhar.* 4, 11, 12, 14, 15, 19, 23, 38:X3; 8:B4; 10:D2; 13:G5
Accrabbah, (Akrabatta), *'Aqraba.* 19:X5
Achaean League. 21, 22:C1
Achaia, Roman province. 32, 33:A1; 36:F3
Achmetha, *see* Ecbatana
Achzib, (Ecdippa), *es-Zib.* 11, 12, 19, 38:X3
Achzib-Acco, region. 19:X3
Acra, in Jerusalem. 22
Adasa, *Kh. 'Addasa.* 23:X6
Adida, (Hadid), *el-Haditheh.* 23, 35:W5
Adora, (Adoraim), *Dura.* 23, 25:W6
Adoraim, (Adora), *Dura.* 12, 15:W6
Adramyttium, *Edremit.* 32, 33:B1; 33:C4
Adria, (Adriatic Sea). 33:A4
Adullam, *T. esh-Sheikh Madhkur.* 11, 12, 15, 19, 23:X6
Aegean Sea. 17, 20, 32, 33:A1
Aenon, spring north of *Kh. Umm el-'Umdan* (?). 26:X5
Aetolian League. 21, 22:C1
Africa, Roman province. 36:C4
'Afula. 39:D3
Agade, *Abu Ghubar* (?). 9:J4
Agrippias, (Anthedon), *el-Blahiyeh.* 25,26:V6
Agrippina, *Kaukab el-Hawa.* 26, 27:X4
Ahlab, *Kh. el-Mahalib.* 11:X2
Ai, *et-Tell.* 8:B6; 10:E3; 11, 12, 19, 38:X6
Aijalon, *Yalo.* 11, 12, 15:X6
Aijalon, Valley of, *W. Selman.* 4, 11, 12:W6
'Ain Feshkha, spring. 34, 38:X6

'Ain Gedi, (En-gedi). 34, 38:X7
'Ain Karim, (Beth-haccherem). 38:X6
'Ajlūn. 39:E3
Akhetaton, *Tell el-Amarna.* 8:E5; 10:A7
Akkad, region. 9:J4
'Akko, (Acco, Ptolemais). 39:D2
Akrabatta, (Accrabbah), *'Aqraba.* 35:X5
Akrabattene, region. 23:X8
Akrabbim, Ascent of, *Naqb es-Safa.* 15:X8
Alaca Huyuk. 9:G1
Alalakh. 9:G3
Al 'Aqabah. 39:D5
Al 'Arīsh. 39:C4
Alashiya, (Cyprus). 9:F3
Aleppo, (Haleb), *Halab.* 16:G3
Alexandria, *Alexandretta,* in Syria. 31:H2
Alexandria, *Gulashkird,* in Carmania. 20:E4
Alexandria, *Iskandariyeh,* in Egypt. 20:B3; 21, 22:D2; 33:66; 37:G5; *see also city plan p. 21*
Alexandria Arachosiorum, *Ghazni.* 20:F3
Alexandria Arion, *Herat.* 20:F3
Alexandria Eschata, *Khodzent.* 21:G2
Alexandrium, *Qarn Sartabeh.* 23, 25, 26:X5
Al Fayyūm. 39:A6
Al Firdān. 39:B4
Al Harmal. 39:E1
Al Karak. 39:E4
Al Khalil, (Hebron). 34:X6
Al Khuraybah. 39:D7
Al Kuntillah. 39:D5
Al Mafraq. 39:E3
Al Mahallah al Kubra. 39:A4
Al Manṣūrāh. 39:A4
Al Minyā. 39:A7
Al Mudawwarah. 39:E6
Al Qāhirah, (Cairo). 39:A5
Al Qantarah. 39:B4
Al Qatrānah. 39:E4
Al Qunaytirah. 39:E2
Al Qusaymah. 39:D4
Alush, *Wadi el-Esh* (?). 10:C6
Amalek, Amalekites, people. 12:X6; 13:G7; 14:W8
Amanus Mts. 31:H2
Amarna, Tell el-, (Akhetaton). 10, 39:A7
Amastris. 37:G3
Amathus, *T. 'Ammata.* 23, 25, 26:Y5
Amisus. 37:H3
Amman, (Rabba, Philadelphia). 38:Y5; 39:E3
Ammon, region. 4, 11, 12, 14, 15, 19:Z5; 8:C5; 10:E3; 13:H6; 16:G4

Amon, Temple of, *Siwa.* 18, 20:A3
Amorites, people. 8:B6
Amphipolis, *Neochori.* 32, 33:A1
Anab, *Kh. 'Anab es-Saghireh.* 12:W6
Anat, *'Anah.* 16:H4; 17:C3
Anathoth, *Ras el-Kharrubeh.* 12, 19:X6
Anchialus. 37:G3
Ancyra, *Ankara.* 16:F2; 18, 20:B2; 32, 33:C1; 37:G3
Ankuwa, *Alisar Huyuk.* 9:G2
An Nakhl. 39:C5
Anthedon, (Agrippias), *el-Blahiyeh.* 23, 25:V6
Anti-Lebanon, mts. 4:Y2; 8:C2; 31:J5
Antioch, *Antakya,* in Syria. 22:D1; 31:H3; 32, 33:D2; 37:H4; *see also city plan p. 30*
Antioch, *Yalvac,* in Pisidia. 32:C1; 32:C2; 37:G3
Antipatris, (Aphek), *Ras el-'Ain.* 25, 26, 28, 35, 38:W5
Antium, *Anzio.* 36:D3
Antonia Fortress, in Jerusalem. 25, 29, 34
Apamea, *Qal'at el-Mudiq.* 31, 37:H4
Aphairema, (Ephraim, Ophrah), *et-Taiyibeh* (?). 23:X5
Aphek, (Antipatris), *Ras el-'Ain.* 10:D3; 11, 12, 14, 15, 38:X5
Aphek, *Fiq,* in Transjordan. 15:Y4
Aphek, *T. Kurdaneh,* in Asher. 11, 12:X3
Apollonia, *Arsuf,* in Palestine. 19, 23, 25, 26, 35:W5
Apollonia, *Pollinia,* in Macedonia. 32, 33:A1
Apollonia, *Sozopol,* on Black Sea. 18:B1
Appius, Forum of, (Appi Forum). 33:A4
Aqaba, Gulf of. 10, 39:D6
Ar, *el-Misna'.* 14, 15:Y7
Arabah, *el- Ghor, Wadi al 'Arabah.* 4, 15:X8; 10:D5; 13:H8; 39:E4
Arabia, region. 9:H5; 18, 20:C3; 21, 22:E2; 37:J5
Arabian Sea. 21:F4
Arabs, people. 16:H5; 17:C3
Arachosia, region. 18, 20:F3
Arad, *T. 'Arad.* 8:B7; 10:D4; 11, 12, 14, 15, 23, 34:X7; 13:G6; 39:D3
Aral Sea. 17, 18, 20:E1
Aram, (Syria), region. 14, 15:Y2
Aram-Damascus, region. 13:H4
Arameans, people. 11:Y2
Aram-zobah, region. 13:J4
Araq, el-Emir, (Tyrus). 38:Y6

Ararat, (Urartu), region. 16:H2
Ararat, Mt., *Buyuk Agri Dagi.* 9, 16:J2
Araxes, river. 9:K2; 16:J2; 18:D1
Arbela, *Erbil,* in Assyria. 9, 16:J3; 18, 20:D2
Arbela, *Irbid,* in Decapolis. 26:Y4
Arbela, *Kh. Irbid,* in Galilee. 23:X4
Archelais, *Kh. 'Auja et-Tahta.* 26:X5
Ardus, (Arvad), *Erwad, Ruwad.* 31:H4
Areopolis, (Rabbath-moab), *Kh. er-Rabba.* 26, 28:Y7
Argob, region. 13:H5; 14:Y3
Aria, region. 18, 21:F3
Aribi, (Arabs), people. 16:H4
Ariha, (Jericho). 34:X6
Arimathea, (Ramathaim), *Rentis.* 26:X5
'Arish, Wadi al-, (River of Egypt). 4:V8; 39:C5
Armenia, region. 18, 20:C2; 21, 22:E1; 37:J3
Arnon, *W. al-Mawjib,* river. 4, 11, 12, 14, 15, 19, 23, 25, 26, 35:Y7; 8:B6; 10:E4
Aroer, *'Ara'ir,* in Moab. 11, 12:Y6; 13:H6
Arpad, *T. Erfad.* 16:G3
Arvad, (Ardus), *Erwad, Ruwad.* 9, 16:G3; 13:H3; 18:C3; 31:H4
Arzawa, region. 8:E2
Ascalon, (Ashkelon), *'Ashqelon.* 23, 25, 26, 35, 38:W6
Ashdod, (Azotus), *Isdud, T. Ashdod.* 8:A6; 11, 12, 14, 15, 19, 23, 38:W6; 10, 39:D3
Ashdod, region. 19:W6
Asher, tribe. 11, 12:X3
Ashkelon, (Ascalon), *'Ashqelon.* 8:A6; 10:D3; 11, 12, 14, 15, 19, 23:W6; 13:G6
'Ashqelon. 39:D3
Ashtaroth, *T. 'Ashtarah.* 8:C4; 10:E2; 11, 12, 14, 15:Y4; 13:H5
Asia, Roman province. 32, 33:B1; 33:C5; 37:G3
Asia Minor, region. 20:B2
Asochis, *Kh. el-Lon.* 26, 27:X4
Asphaltitis, Lake, (Dead Sea). 25, 26, 35:X6
As Salṭ. 39:E3
As Samu', (Eshtemoa). 34:X7
Asshur, *Qal'at Sherqat.* 9:J3; 16:J3; 18:C2
Assuwa, region. 8:E1
Assyria, region. 9:J3; 16:H3; 17:C2
Assyrian Empire. 16:G4
Astacus. 16:F2
Astorga. 36:A2
Ataroth, *Kh. Attarus.* 15:Y6

Picture Credits

The editor and publisher wish to express their thanks and appreciation to the following for supplying illustrations:

The American Numismatic Society, New York: pages 20 (bottom), 21 (top right), 22 (center left), 28 (bottom right), 29 (bottom left), 35 (bottom). Henry Angelo-Castrillon: page 32 (top right), 36 (right). The Bettmann Archive, New York: page 42. The Trustees of the British Museum: pages 16 (all three photos), 18 (top). The Brooklyn Museum, Charles Edwin Wilbour Fund: page 37 (top right). Ernest J. Dupuy: pages 32 (top left), 36 (center), 37 (center). GAF Pana-Vue Slides: pages 24 (top), 28 (top). Hebrew University, Jerusalem, Department of Archaeology: page 22 (bottom right). Iran National Tourist Office, New York: page 18 (left). Israel Government Tourist Office, New York: title page, pages 5 (bottom left), 11 (two photos at top), 27 (left), 29 (top left), 30 (second from top), 34 (center left), 35 (center left). The Israel Museum, Jerusalem: pages 14 (top right), 18 (bottom right), 28 (bottom left). Istanbul Museum: page 30 (top). Italian Government Travel Office: page 36 (left). Nancy L. Lapp: page 12. From Lepsius, *Denkmaeler:* page 10 (right). Herbert G. May: page 27 (bottom right). The Metropolitan Museum of Art: pages 2, 22 (top left and top right), 37 (bottom right). Museo Nazionale, Naples: pages 20 (top), 21 (center right). Museum of Fine Arts, Boston: page 24 (bottom). Notre Dame de Sion, Jerusalem: page 29 (center bottom). The Oriental Institute, University of Chicago: pages 17, 38 (center). William L. Reed, courtesy American Schools of Oriental Research: page 35 (top). The University Museum, University of Pennsylvania: pages 9, 37 (left). Wide World Photos: page 30 (third from top).

Photographs from collection of Professor Harry Thomas Frank: pages 5 (three photos at right), 7 (both), 8, 10 (left), 11 (bottom), 14 (top left), 21 (top left), 22 (center right and bottom left), 25, 27 (center and top right), 29 (center top and right), 30 (bottom), 32 (bottom), 34 (top), 38 (top and four bottom photos).

WORLD HISTORY ATLAS

A collection of maps illustrating geographically the most significant periods and events in the history of civilization.

EUROPE·
PHYSICAL

Copyright by C. S. HAMMOND & Co., N. Y.

TABLE OF CONTENTS

Published by

HAMMOND
INCORPORATED

MAPLEWOOD, NEW JERSEY

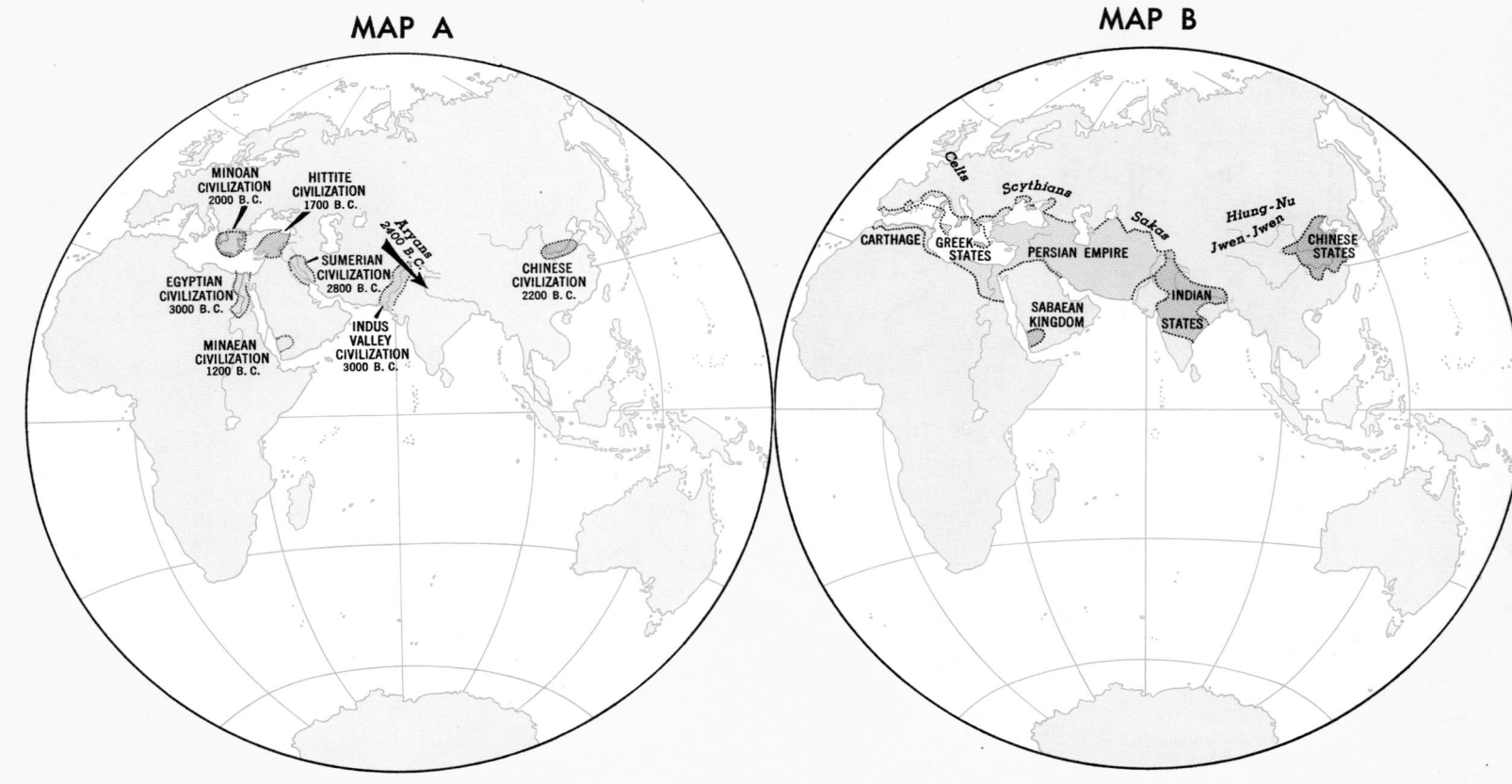

MAP A

MINOAN
CIVILIZATION
2000 B.C.

HITTITE
CIVILIZATION
1700 B.C.

Aryans
2000 B.C.

EGYPTIAN
CIVILIZATION
3000 B.C.

SUMERIAN
CIVILIZATION
2800 B.C.

CHINESE
CIVILIZATION
2200 B.C.

MINAEAN
CIVILIZATION
1200 B.C.

INDUS
VALLEY
CIVILIZATION
3000 B.C.

The Cradles of Civilization
3000-1000 B.C.

MAP B

Celts

Scythians

Sakas

Hiung-Nu
Jwen-Jwen

CARTHAGE

GREEK
STATES

PERSIAN EMPIRE

CHINESE
STATES

SABAEAN
KINGDOM

INDIAN
STATES

Major States and Empires
in 500 B.C.

MAP C

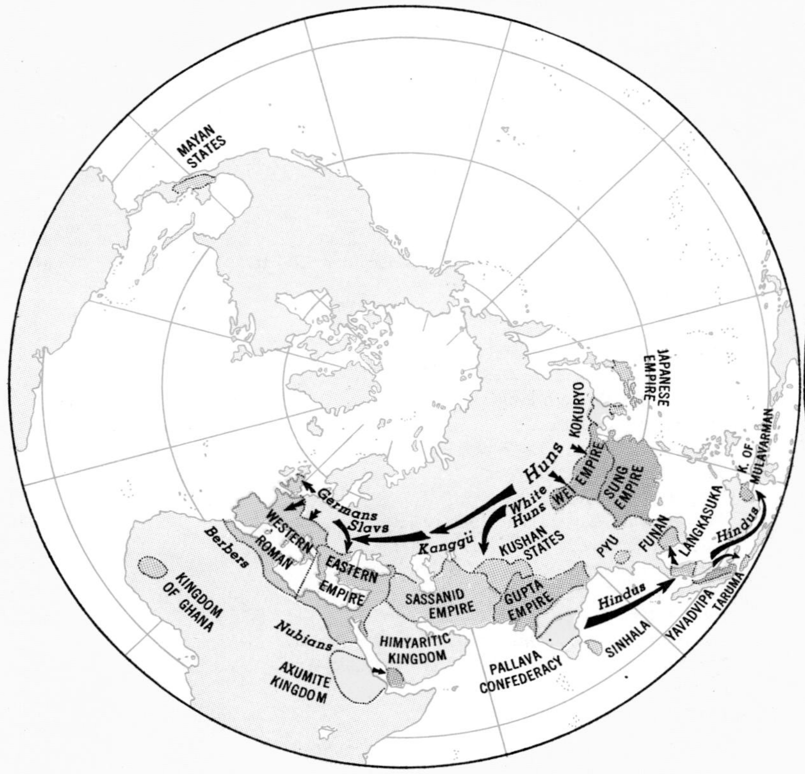

MAYAN
STATES

JAPANESE
EMPIRE

KOKURYO

Huns

WEI EMPIRE

Germans
Slavs

White
Huns

WEI

SUING
EMPIRE

Kanggü

Berbers

WESTERN
ROMAN

EASTERN
EMPIRE

KUSHAN
STATES

PYU

FUNAN

K. OF
MULAVARMAN

KINGDOM
OF GHANA

SASSANID
EMPIRE

GUPTA
EMPIRE

Hindus

LANGKASUKA

Hindus

Nubians

HIMYARITIC
KINGDOM

PALLAVA
CONFEDERACY

SINHALA

YAVADVIPA

TARUMA

AXUMITE
KINGDOM

Major States and Empires
in 400 A.D.

MAP D

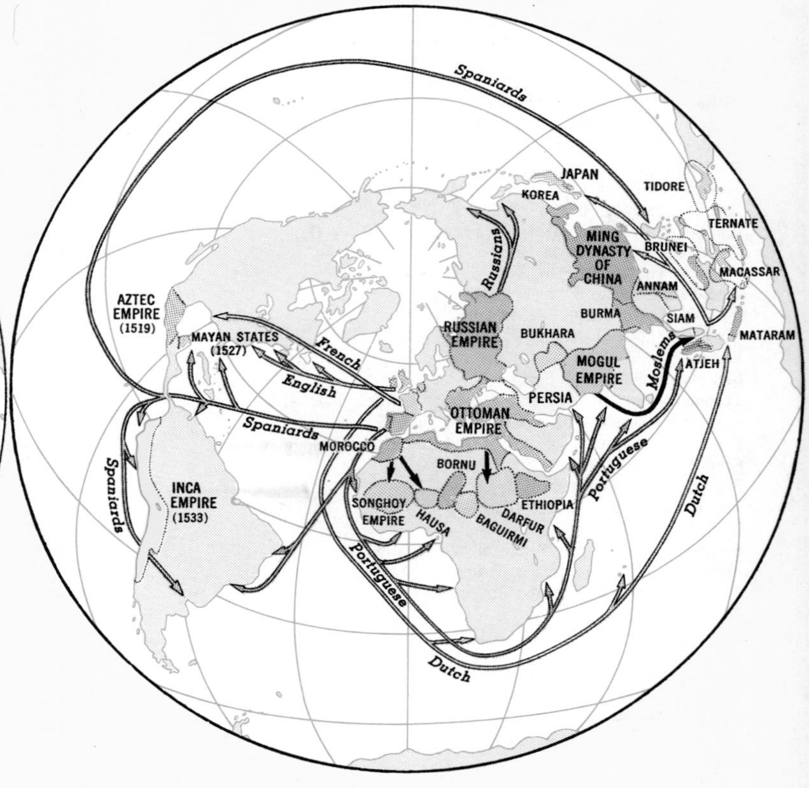

Spaniards

JAPAN

KOREA

TIDORE

MING
DYNASTY
OF
CHINA

BRUNEI

TERNATE

AZTEC
EMPIRE
(1519)

MAYAN STATES
(1527)

French

Russians

BUKHARA

ANNAM

MACASSAR

English

RUSSIAN
EMPIRE

BURMA

SIAM

MATARAM

Spaniards

Moslems

ATJEH

MOGUL
EMPIRE

OTTOMAN
EMPIRE

PERSIA

Portuguese

Dutch

Spaniards

INCA
EMPIRE
(1533)

MOROCCO

BORNU

SONGHOY
EMPIRE

HAUSA

DARFUR

BAGUIRMI

ETHIOPIA

Portuguese

Dutch

The Expansion
of Western Civilization
1600 A.D.

Copyright by C. S. HAMMOND & Co., N. Y.

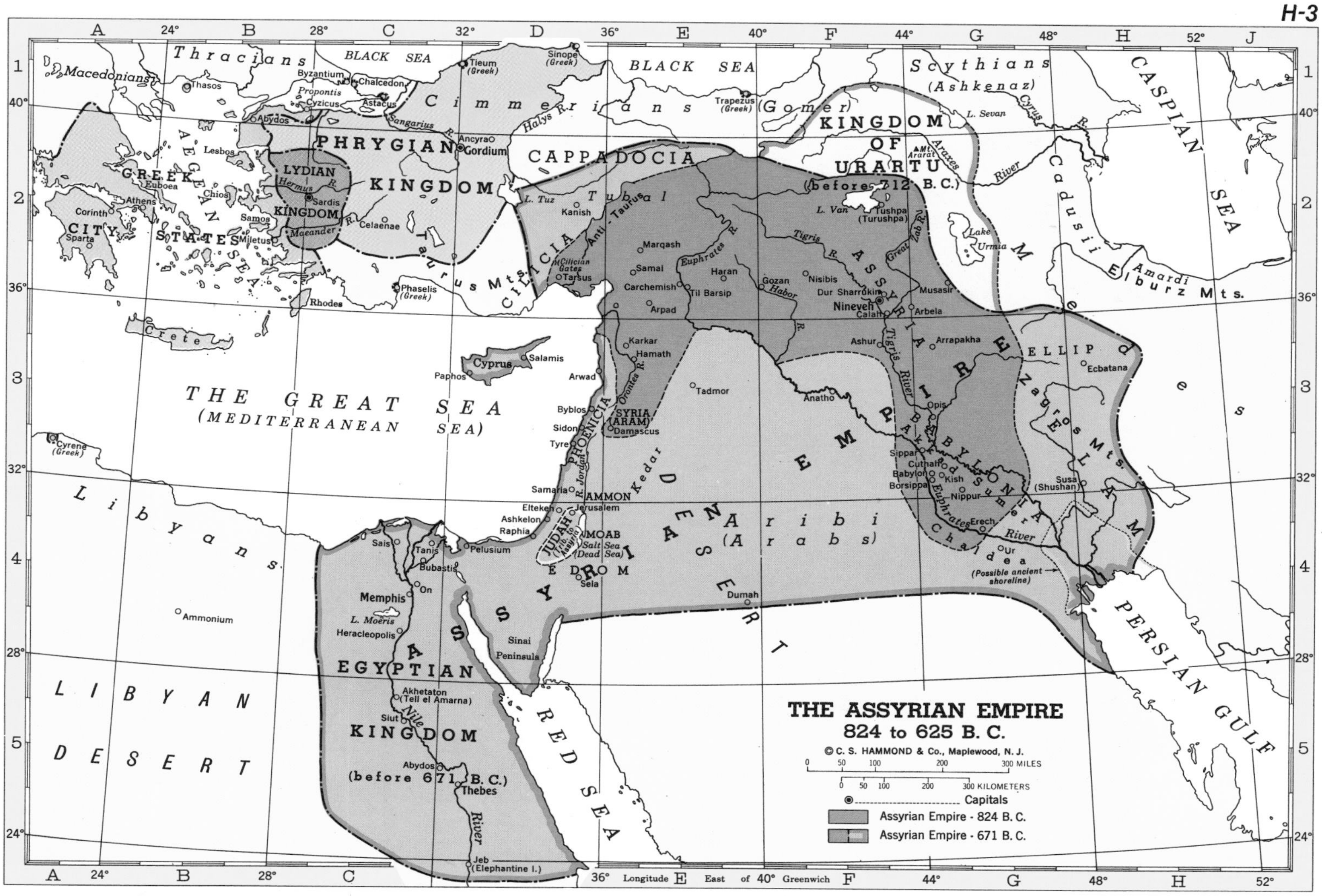

THE ASSYRIAN EMPIRE
824 to 625 B.C.

© C. S. HAMMOND & Co., Maplewood, N.J.

0 50 100 200 300 MILES
0 50 100 200 300 KILOMETERS

Capitals
Assyrian Empire - 824 B.C.
Assyrian Empire - 671 B.C.

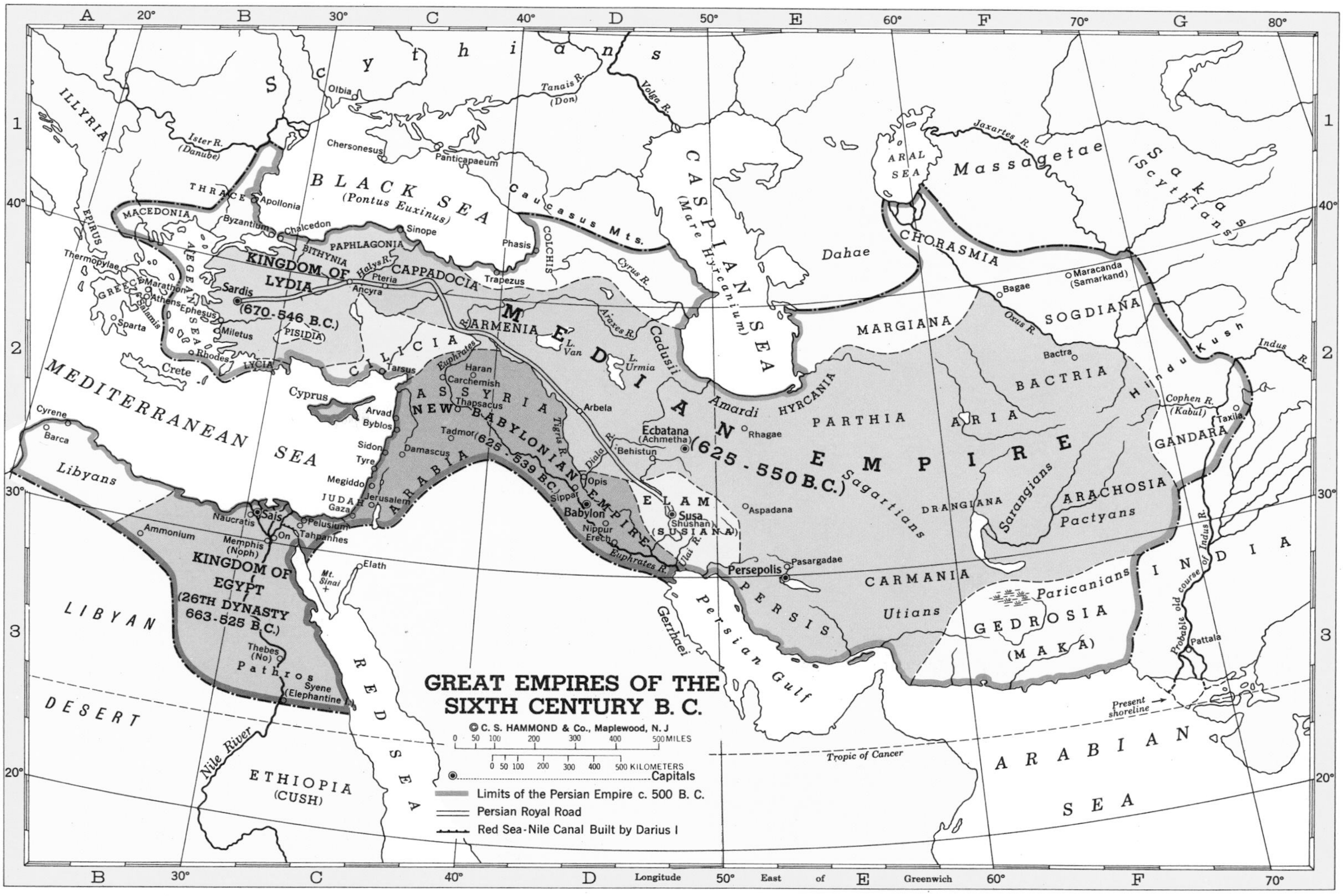

Longitude East of 40° Greenwich

Macedonians
Thracians
BLACK SEA
Thasos
Byzantium
Chalcedon
Propontis
Cyzicus
Astacus
Abydos
Tieum (Greek)
Sinope (Greek)
BLACK SEA
Trapezus (Greek)
Gomer
Scythians (Ashkenaz)
CASPIAN SEA
PHRYGIAN KINGDOM
Ancyra
Gordium
CAPPADOCIA
KINGDOM OF URARTU
(before 712 B.C.)
L. Sevan
Cimmerians
Halys R.
Tushpa (Turushpa)
L. Van
Ararat
Araxes River
Cadusii
Elburz Mts.
Amardi
LYDIAN KINGDOM
Hermus R.
Sardis
Celaenae
L. Tuz
Kanish
Tubal
Marqash
Samal
Carchemish
Arpad
Tigris R.
Gozan
Habor
Nisibis
Dur Sharrokin
Musasir
Lake Urmia
GREEK CITY STATES
Lesbos
Chios
Euboea
Samos
Miletus
Maeander R.
Taurus Mts.
CILICIA
Cilician Gates
Tarsus
Anti-Taurus
Haran
Til Barsip
Nineveh
Calah
Ashur
Arbela
Arrapakha
ELLIPI
Ecbatana
Athens
Corinth
Sparta
AEGEAN SEA
Rhodes
Phaselis (Greek)
Karkar
Hamath
Cyprus
Salamis
Paphos
Arwad
ASSYRIAN EMPIRE
Opis
BABYLONIA
Zagros Mts.
ELAM
THE GREAT SEA (MEDITERRANEAN SEA)
Tadmor
Anatho
Sippar
Cutha
Agade
Babylon
Kish
Borsippa
Nippur
Erech
Susa (Shushan)
Byblos
Sidon
Tyre
PHOENICIA
SYRIA (ARAM)
Damascus
Kedar
Chaldea
Ur
Euphrates River
(Possible ancient shoreline)
Samaria
Elteken
Ashkelon
Raphia
AMMON
Jerusalem
JUDAH
MOAB
Salt Sea (Dead)
EDOM
Sela
IDUMAEA
ARIBI (Arabs)
Dumah
ASSYRIAN DESERT
PERSIAN GULF
Libyans
Sais
Tanis
Bubastis
Pelusium
Sinai Peninsula
Memphis
On
Ammonium
L. Moeris
Heracleopolis
EGYPTIAN KINGDOM
Akhetaton (Tell el Amarna)
Siut
Nile River
RED SEA
Abydos
Thebes
(before 671 B.C.)
Jeb (Elephantine I.)
LIBYAN DESERT
Cyrene (Greek)
Crete

GREAT EMPIRES OF THE SIXTH CENTURY B.C.

© C. S. HAMMOND & Co., Maplewood, N.J

0 50 100 200 300 400 500 MILES
0 50 100 200 300 400 500 KILOMETERS

Capitals
Limits of the Persian Empire c. 500 B.C.
Persian Royal Road
Red Sea-Nile Canal Built by Darius I

Longitude East of Greenwich

ILLYRIA
Scythians
Ister R. (Danube)
Olbia
Tanais R. (Don)
Volga R.
Massagetae
Sakas (Scythians)
THRACE
Apollonia
Chersonesus
Panticapaeum
BLACK SEA (Pontus Euxinus)
Byzantium
Chalcedon
Sinope
Caucasus Mts.
Phasis
COLCHIS
ARAL SEA
Jaxartes R.
CHORASMIA
MACEDONIA
Thermopylae
Marathon
Athens
Ephesus
Sparta
Miletus
Rhodes
Crete
Sardis
KINGDOM OF LYDIA (670-546 B.C.)
PAPHLAGONIA
BITHYNIA
Pteria
CAPPADOCIA
Ancyra
Halys R.
Trapezus
ARMENIA
L. Van
L. Urmia
Cyrus R.
CASPIAN SEA (Mare Hyrcanium)
Dahae
Maracanda (Samarkand)
Bagae
SOGDIANA
MARGIANA
Oxus R.
Hindu Kush
BACTRIA
Bactra
ARIA
Cophen R. (Kabul)
Taxila
GANDARA
PISIDIA
LYCIA
CILICIA
Tarsus
Cyprus
Arvad
Byblos
Sidon
Tyre
ASSYRIA
Haran
Carchemish
Thapsacus
Arbela
MEDIAN EMPIRE (625-550 B.C.)
Ecbatana (Achmetha) (625-550 B.C.)
Behistun
Rhagae
HYRCANIA
PARTHIA
Amardi
Cadusii
Araxes R.
Aspadana
DRANGIANA
Sagartians
Sarangians
ARACHOSIA
Pactyans
INDIA
Indus R.
MEDITERRANEAN SEA
Libyans
Cyrene
Barca
NEW BABYLONIAN EMPIRE (625-539 B.C.)
Tadmor
Damascus
Megiddo
Jerusalem
Gaza
JUDAH
ARABIA
Opis
Sippar
Babylon
Nippur
Erech
Ur
Euphrates R.
Tigris R.
ELAM
Susa (Shushan) (SUSIANA)
PERSIS
Persepolis
Pasargadae
CARMANIA
Utians
Paricanians
GEDROSIA (MAKA)
Pattala
Probable old course of Indus R.
Ammonium
Naucratis
Sais
Memphis (Noph)
On
Pelusium
Tahpanhes
Elath
Mt. Sinai
KINGDOM OF EGYPT (26TH DYNASTY 663-525 B.C.)
Pathros
Thebes (No)
Syene
Elephantine
Nile River
RED SEA
Gerrhaei
Persian Gulf
ARABIAN SEA
LIBYAN DESERT
ETHIOPIA (CUSH)
Tropic of Cancer
Present shoreline

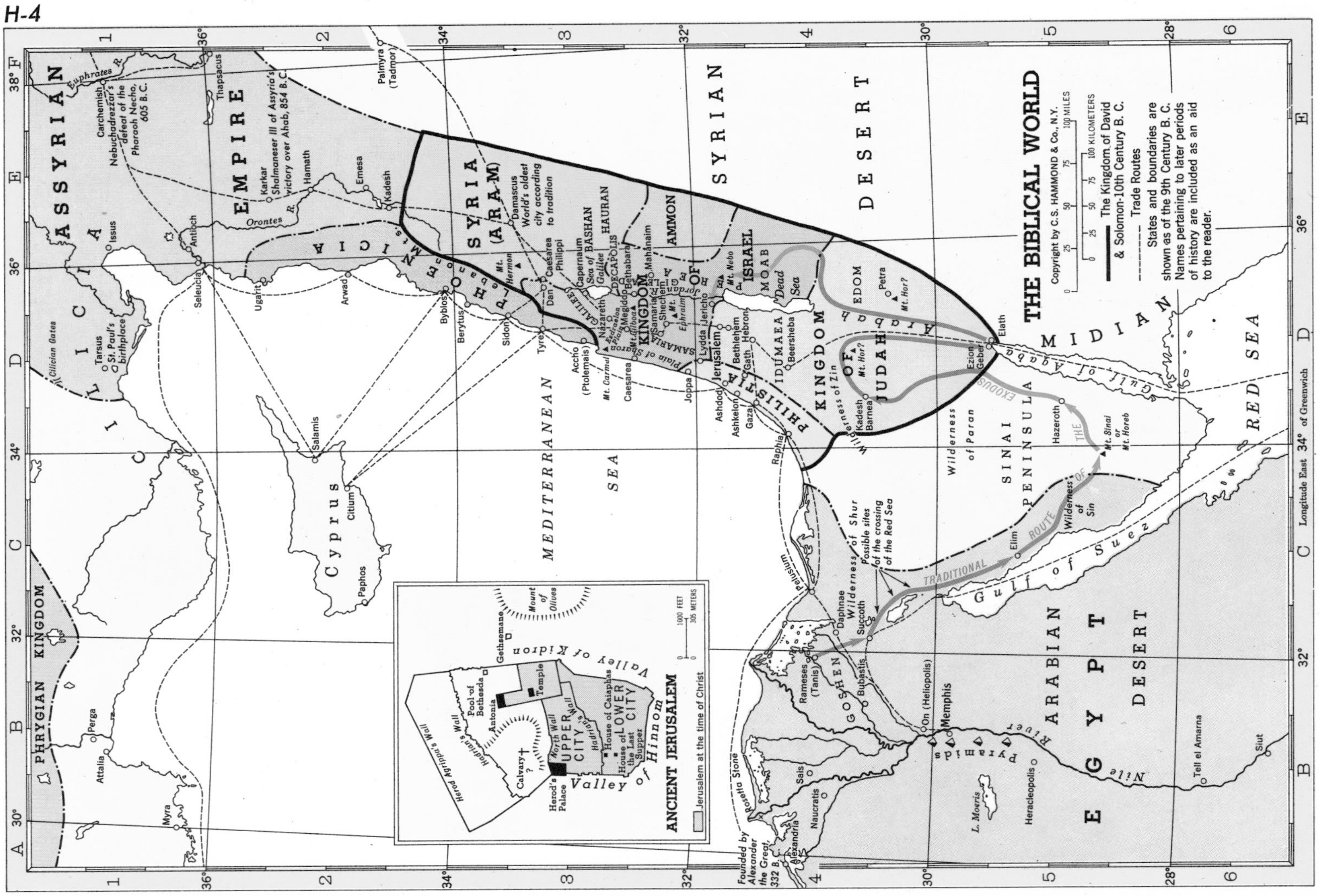

THE BIBLICAL WORLD

Copyright by C.S. HAMMOND & Co. N.Y.

0 25 50 75 100 MILES
0 25 50 75 100 KILOMETERS

— The Kingdom of David & Solomon-10th Century B.C.
--- Trade Routes

States and boundaries are shown as of the 9th Century B.C. Names pertaining to later periods of history are included as an aid to the reader.

ASSYRIAN EMPIRE

CILICIA

PHRYGIAN KINGDOM

SYRIA (ARAM)

PHOENICIA

SYRIAN DESERT

KINGDOM OF ISRAEL

KINGDOM OF JUDAH

PHILISTIA

AMMON

MOAB

EDOM

IDUMAEA

MIDIAN

MEDITERRANEAN SEA

CYPRUS

SINAI PENINSULA

ARABIAN DESERT

EGYPT

GOSHEN

RED SEA

Gulf of Suez

Gulf of Aqabah

Dead Sea

Euphrates

Orontes R.

Nile River

Carchemish, Nebuchadnezzar's defeat of the Pharaoh Necho, 605 B.C.

Palmyra (Tadmor)

Damascus World's oldest city according to tradition

Antioch

Tarsus, St. Paul's birthplace

Cilician Gates

Issus

Seleucia

Salamis

Paphos

Citium

Byblos

Berytus

Sidon

Tyre

Accho (Ptolemais)

Mt. Carmel

Caesarea

Joppa

Ashdod

Ashkelon

Gaza

Raphia

Jerusalem

Bethlehem

Hebron

Beersheba

Kadesh Barnea

Mt. Hor?

Petra

Elath

Ezion Geber

EXODUS

THE ROUTE

TRADITIONAL ROUTE

Wilderness of Paran

Wilderness of Zin

Wilderness of Shur

Wilderness of Sin

Possible sites of the crossing of the Red Sea

Mt. Sinai

Mt. Horeb

Hazeroth

Elim

Succoth

Daphnae

Rameses (Tanis)

Bubastis

On (Heliopolis)

Memphis

Sais

Naucratis

Alexandria

Founded by Alexander the Great, 332 B.C.

L. Moeris

Heracleopolis

Tell el Amarna

Siut

Pyramids

ANCIENT JERUSALEM

1000 FEET
305 METERS

Mount of Olives

Valley of Kidron

Temple

Gethsemane

Pool of Bethesda

Antonia

UPPER CITY

LOWER CITY

House of Caiaphas

House of the Last Supper

Herod's Palace

Calvary?

Hinnom Valley

North Wall

Second Wall

Herod Agrippa's Wall

Jerusalem at the time of Christ

ANCIENT GREECE

Copyright by C.S. HAMMOND & Co., N.Y.

0 20 40 60 MILES
0 20 40 60 KILOMETERS

Dorians   Ionians   Aeolians

ILLYRIS

MACEDONIA

EPIRUS

THESSALY

THRACE

PROPONTIS (Sea of Marmora)

CHALCIDICE

MAGNESIA

AETOLIA

ACARNANIA

DORIS

LOCRIS

BOEOTIA

ATTICA

ACHAIA

ARCADIA

ELIS

ARGOLIS

LACONIA

MESSENIA

PELOPONNESUS

EUBOEA

PHRYGIA

TROAS

LYDIA

CARIA

IONIAN SEA

THRACIAN SEA

AEGEAN SEA

MYRTOUM SEA

Antipatria

Lake Bigorritis

Aegae (Edessa)

Pella

Therma (Thessalonica)

Amphipolis

Abdera

Bisanthe

Aenus

Thasos

Samothrace

Imbros

Lemnos

Antigonia

Beroea (Berrhoea)

Pydna

Stagirus (Stagira)

Olynthus

Acanthus

Xerxes' Canal

Potidaea (Cassandra)

Mt. Athos

Mt. Olympus

Phila

Corcyra

Dodona

Ephyra

Gyrton

Mt. Ossa

Larissa

Crannon

Pherae

Iolcus

Demetrias

Pharsalus

Thebae

Neae

Scyrus

Lampsacus

Cyzicus

Sestus

Abydos

Ilium (Troy)

Sigeum

Tenedos

Lesbos

Mitilene

Pergamum

Nicopolis

Actium

Anactorium

Stratus

Leucas

Cephallenia

Ithaca

Same

Patrae

Dyme

Aegium

Thermum

Amphissa

Naupactus

Delphi

Mt. Parnassus

Chaeronea

Coronea

Orchomenus

Thespiae

Plataea

Thebes

Aulis

Chalcis

Eretria

Oreus

Artemisium Prom.

Psyra

Chios

Phocaea

Cyme

Smyrna nova

Clazomenae

Teos

Colophon

Ephesus

Sardis

Hermus R.

Maeander R.

Magnesia

Priene

Miletus

Halicarnassus

Elis

Pylus

Olympia

Lepreum

Megalopolis

Strophades I.

Zacynthos

Mantinea

Tegea

Mycenae

Argos

Tiryns

Midea

Corinth

Nemea

Cleonae

Sicyon

Pellene

Aegira

Megara

Salamis

Eleusis

Athens

Piraeus

Aegina

Marathon

Decelea

Styra

Carystus

Andros

Tenos

Delos

Ceos

Cythnus

Syros

Seriphus

Siphnus

Paros

Naxos

Icaria

Samos

Ios

Amorgos

Melos

Thera

Astypalaea

Cos

Telus

Rhodes

Megalopolis

Sparta (Lacedaemon)

Amyclae

Messene

Pherae

Thuria

Pylus

Methone

Gythium

Boeae

Cythera

Taenarum Prom.

Thyrea

Troezen

CYCLADES

SPORADES

ANCIENT ATHENS

INNER CERAMICUS

AGORA

Pnyx

Acropolis

NEW ATHENS

Theater of Dionysus

Olympieum

Stadium

COELE

North Long Wall

Middle Long Wall

Ilissus R.

CRETE

Polyrrhenia

Eleuthernae

Cnossus

Gortyn

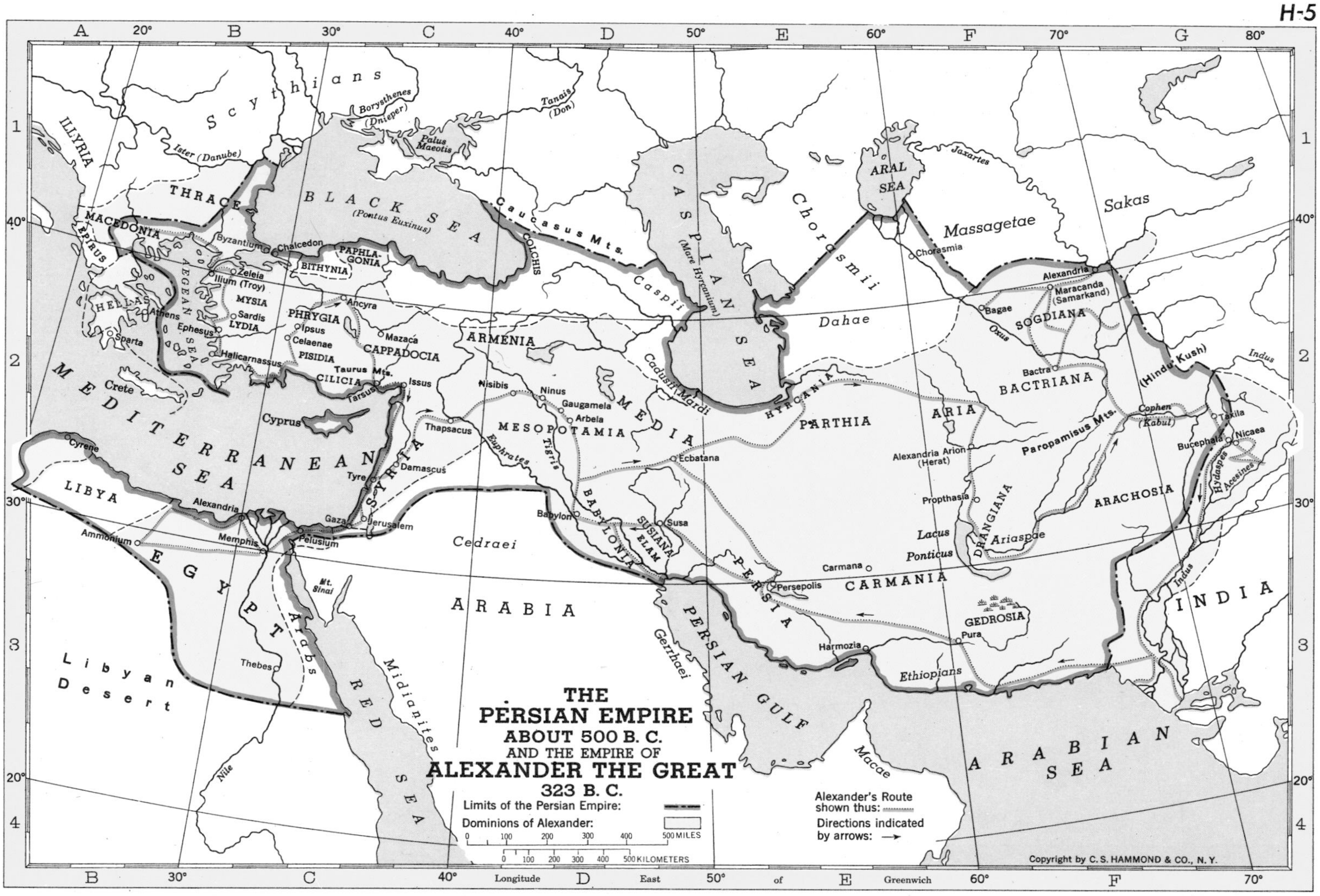
Scythians
ILLYRIA
Ister (Danube)
Borysthenes (Dnieper)
Tanais (Don)
Palus Maeotis
THRACE
MACEDONIA
EPIRUS
BLACK SEA (Pontus Euxinus)
Caucasus Mts.
CASPIAN SEA (Mare Hyrcanium)
ARAL SEA
Jaxartes
Chorasmii
Massagetae
Sakas
Byzantium
Chalcedon
PAPHLAGONIA
BITHYNIA
COLCHIS
Zeleia
Ilium (Troy)
MYSIA
AEGEAN SEA
HELLAS
Athens
Sardis
LYDIA
Ephesus
Sparta
PHRYGIA
Ipsus
Celaenae
PISIDIA
Halicarnassus
Ancyra
Mazaca
CAPPADOCIA
ARMENIA
Caspii
Chorasmia
Alexandria
Maracanda (Samarkand)
Bagae
SOGDIANA
Oxus
Dahae
Taurus Mts.
CILICIA
Tarsus
Issus
Crete
MEDITERRANEAN SEA
Cyprus
Nisibis
Ninus
Gaugamela
Arbela
MESOPOTAMIA
MEDIA
Cadusii
Mardi
HYRCANIA
PARTHIA
ARIA
Bactra
BACTRIANA
(Hindu Kush)
Indus
Cophen (Kabul)
Taxila
Nicaea
Bucephala
Hydaspes
Acesines
Paropamisus Mts.
Alexandria Arion (Herat)
Thapsacus
Euphrates
Tigris
SYRIA
Damascus
Tyre
Cyrene
LIBYA
Alexandria
Gaza
Jerusalem
Ammonium
Memphis
Pelusium
Ecbatana
Babylon
BABYLONIA
SUSIANA ELAM
Susa
Propthasia
DRANGIANA
Ariaspae
ARACHOSIA
Lacus Ponticus
Cedraei
EGYPT
Mt. Sinai
Arabs
ARABIA
Carmana
Persepolis
PERSIA
CARMANIA
GEDROSIA
Pura
INDIA
Harmozia
Ethiopians
Thebes
Libyan Desert
RED SEA
Midianites
Gerrhaei
PERSIAN GULF
Macae
ARABIAN SEA
Nile
Limits of the Persian Empire:
Dominions of Alexander:
0 100 200 300 400 500 MILES
0 100 200 300 400 500 KILOMETERS
Alexander's Route shown thus:
Directions indicated by arrows:
Copyright by C. S. HAMMOND & CO., N. Y.
Longitude East of Greenwich

THE
PERSIAN EMPIRE
ABOUT 500 B. C.
AND THE EMPIRE OF
ALEXANDER THE GREAT
323 B. C.

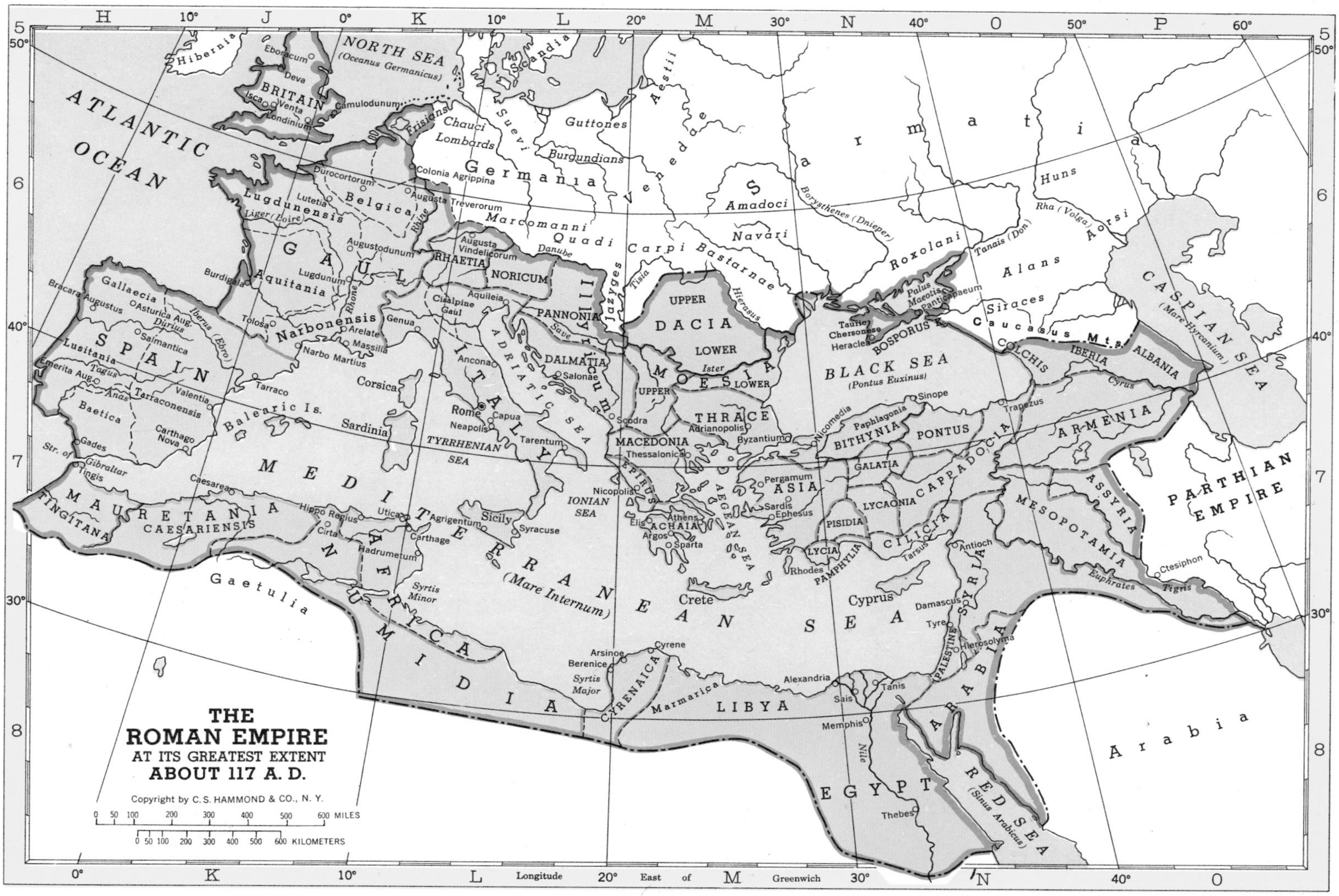
Hibernia
Eboracum
NORTH SEA (Oceanus Germanicus)
Scandia
Deva
BRITAIN
Isca
Venta
Londinium
Camulodunum
ATLANTIC OCEAN
Frisians
Chauci
Lombards
Suevi
Guttones
Aestii
Venedae
Burgundians
Germania
Colonia Agrippina
Durocortorum
Lutetia
Belgica
Augusta Treverorum
Lugdunensis
Liger (Loire)
Marcomanni
Quadi
Sarmatia
Amadoci
Navari
Borysthenes (Dnieper)
Huns
Rha (Volga)
Tanais (Don)
Aorsi
Alans
Roxolani
Augusta Vindelicorum
RHAETIA
NORICUM
Danube
Augustodunum
GAUL
Aquitania
Lugdunum
Burdigala
Carpi
Bastarnae
Jazyges
Tisia
Hierasus
UPPER DACIA LOWER
Palus Maeotis
Panticapaeum
Siraces
Caucasus Mts.
CASPIAN SEA (Mare Hyrcanium)
Gallaecia
Bracara Augustus
Asturica Aug.
Iberus (Ebro)
Durius
Rhone
Cisalpine Gaul
Aquileia
PANNONIA
Save
ILLYRICUM
Tauric Chersonese
Heraclea
BOSPORUS
COLCHIS
IBERIA
ALBANIA
Cyrus
SPAIN
Salmantica
Tolosa
Narbonensis
Arelate
Massilia
Narbo Martius
Genua
Ancona
DALMATIA
Salonae
UPPER MOESIA LOWER
Ister
BLACK SEA (Pontus Euxinus)
Lusitania
Emerita Aug.
Tagus
Valentia
Anas
Tarraco
Tarraconensis
Corsica
ADRIATIC SEA
ITALY
Rome
Capua
Neapolis
THRACE
Adrianopolis
Sinope
Paphlagonia
Nicomedia
Trapezus
BITHYNIA
PONTUS
ARMENIA
Baetica
Carthago Nova
Balearic Is.
Sardinia
TYRRHENIAN SEA
Tarentum
Scodra
MACEDONIA
Thessalonica
Byzantium
GALATIA
CAPPADOCIA
ASSYRIA
PARTHIAN EMPIRE
Gades
Str. of Gibraltar
Tingis
Caesarea
MEDITERRANEAN SEA (Mare Internum)
EPIRUS
Nicopolis
AEGEAN SEA
Pergamum
ASIA
Sardis
Ephesus
LYCAONIA
MESOPOTAMIA
MAURETANIA TINGITANA
MAURETANIA CAESARIENSIS
Hippo Regius
Cirta
Utica
Carthage
Agrigentum
Sicily
Syracuse
IONIAN SEA
Athens
Elis
Argos
ACHAIA
Sparta
PISIDIA
LYCIA
PAMPHYLIA
CILICIA
Tarsus
Antioch
Rhodes
Ctesiphon
Euphrates
Tigris
Hadrumetum
AFRICA
Gaetulia
Syrtis Minor
Crete
Cyprus
Damascus
Tyre
SYRIA
PALESTINE
Hierosolyma
NUMIDIA
Arsinoe
Cyrene
Berenice
Syrtis Major
CYRENAICA
Marmarica
LIBYA
Alexandria
Sais
Tanis
Memphis
Nile
ARABIA
Arabia
EGYPT
Thebes
RED SEA (Sinus Arabicus)
Copyright by C. S. HAMMOND & CO., N. Y.
0 50 100 200 300 400 500 600 MILES
0 50 100 200 300 400 500 600 KILOMETERS
Longitude East of Greenwich

THE
ROMAN EMPIRE
AT ITS GREATEST EXTENT
ABOUT 117 A. D.

ANCIENT ITALY
ITALIA, LIGURIA, VENETIA, GALLIA-CISALPINA, HISTRIA, SICILIA & CORSICA

Before the time of Augustus

Copyright by C.S. HAMMOND & CO., N.Y.

Roman Colonies, thus: — — — — Ostia
Greek Colonies, thus: — — — SYRACUSAE (G)
Carthaginian Colonies, thus: _ _ _ _ Eryx (C)
Dotted lines show the Modern shore line

THE FORUM CAPITOLIUM and PALATIUM

1. Templum Saturni
2. Templum Concordiae
3. Sealae Gemoniae
4. Carcer (Tullianum)
5. Senaculum
6. Graecostasis
7. Rostra
8. Templum Jani

IMPERIAL FORA

1. Scalae Gemoniae
2. Templum Vespasiani
3. Porticus Deorum Consentium
4. Equus Caesaris
5. T. Castoris et Pollucis
6. Templum Divi Julii
7. Arcus Augusti
8. Arcus Titi
9. Templum Antonini et Faustinae

ROME
Under the Emperors

1. Templum Jovis Capitolini
2. Arx
3. Forum Romanum
4. Templum Aesculapii
5. Forum Trajani
6. Forum Augusti
7. Porta Carmentalis
8. Arcus Septimii Severi
9. Arcus Constantini
10. Arcus Titi
11. Arcus Claudii
12. Arcus Tiberii
13. Arcus Gallieni
14. Arcus Marci Aurelii
15. Arcus Diocletiani
16. Porta Flumentara
17. Templum Mercurii
18. Theatrum Marcelli

REGIONES AUGUSTI
I. Porta Capena
II. Caelimontium
III. Isis et Serapis
IV. Templum Pacis
V. Esquiliae
VI. Alta Semita
VII. Via Lata
VIII. Forum Romanum
IX. Circus Flaminius
X. Palatium
XI. Circus Maximus
XII. Piscina Publica
XIII. Aventinus
XIV. Trans Tiberim

ROME
In the time of the Republic

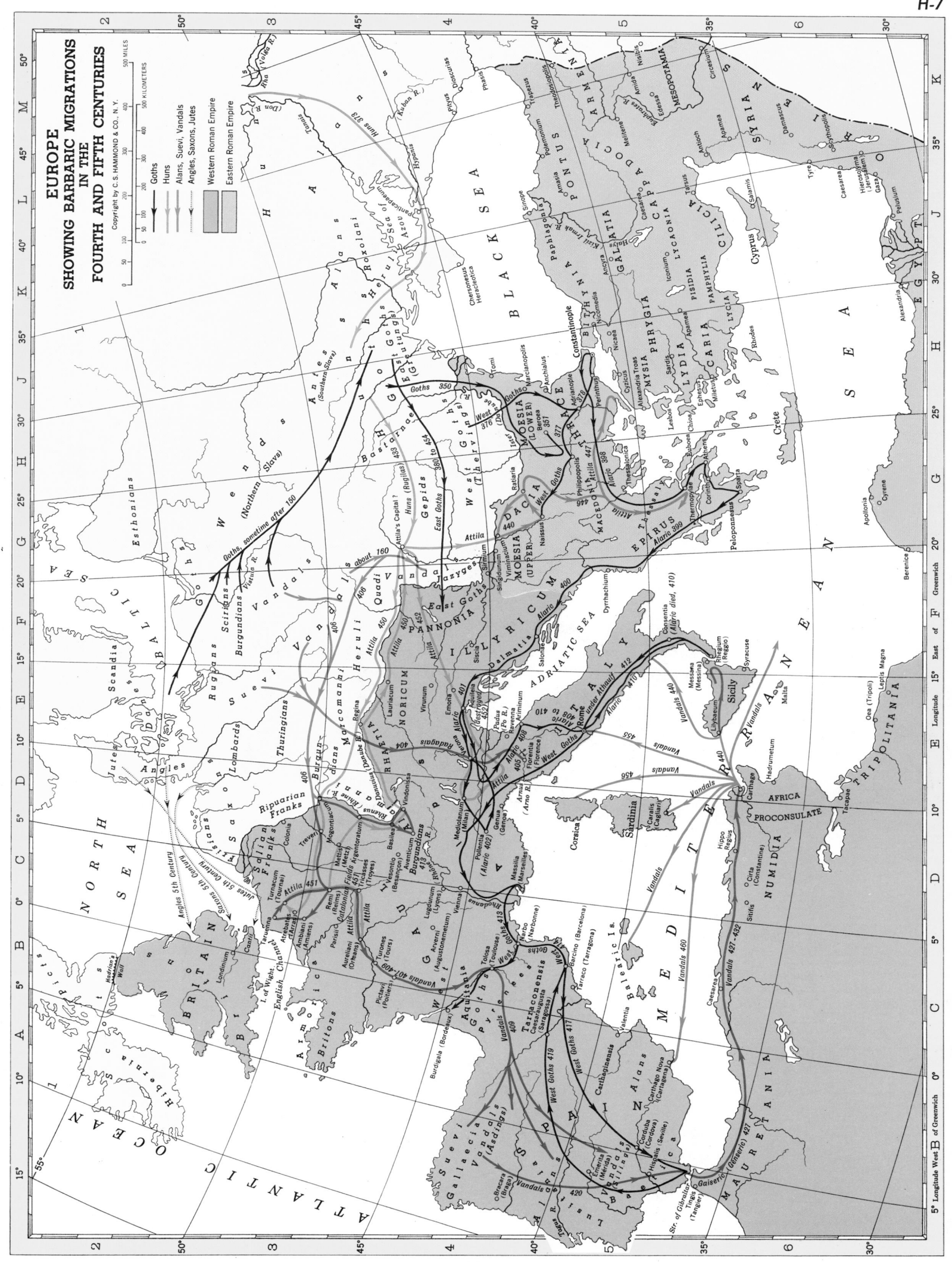

EUROPE
SHOWING BARBARIC MIGRATIONS
IN THE
FOURTH AND FIFTH CENTURIES

Copyright by C.S. HAMMOND & CO., N.Y.

Goths
Huns
Alans, Suevi, Vandals
Angles, Saxons, Jutes
Western Roman Empire
Eastern Roman Empire

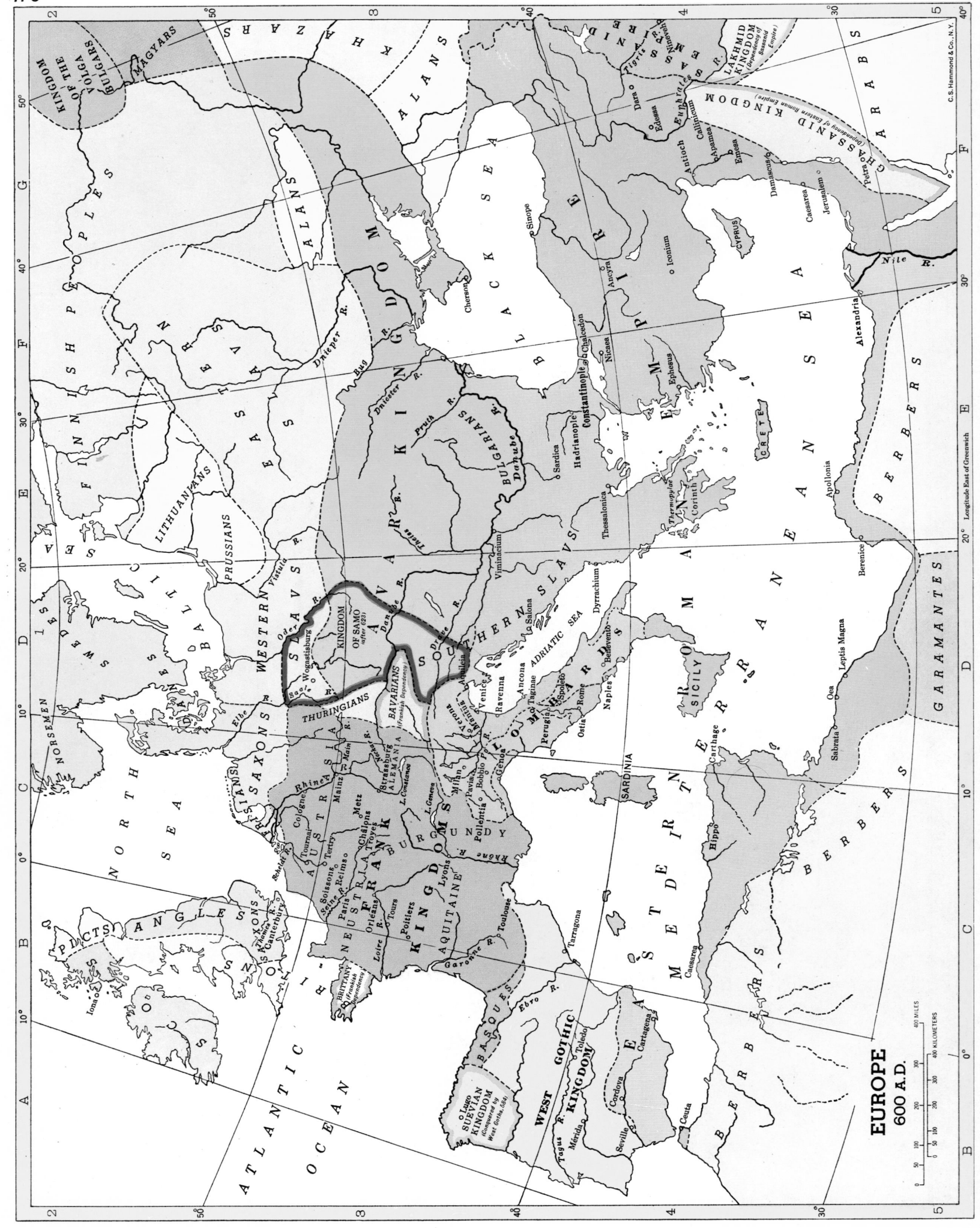

EUROPE
600 A.D.

KINGDOM OF THE VOLGA BULGARS

MAGYARS

KHAZARS

ALANS

FINNISH PEOPLES

SLAVES

EASTERN SLAVS

LITHUANIANS

PRUSSIANS

WESTERN SLAVS

AVAR KINGDOM

BULGARIANS

SOUTHERN SLAVS

GRASSANID KINGDOM (dependency of Eastern Roman Empire)

LAKHMID KINGDOM (dependency of Sassanid Empire)

ARABS

BERBERS

GARAMANTES

SWEDES

NORSEMEN

DANES

BALTIC SEA

NORTH SEA

FRISIANS

SAXONS

THURINGIANS

BAVARIANS (Frankish Dependency)

KINGDOM OF SAMO (after 623)

Wogastisburg

Oder R.

Elbe R.

Saale R.

Main R.

Rhine R.

AUSTRASIA

Cologne

Mainz

Metz

Strassburg

ALEMANIA

L. Constance

BURGUNDY

FRANKISH KINGDOMS

NEUSTRIA

Paris

Soissons

Reims

Chalons

Troyes

Tournai

Seine R.

Tours

Orleans

Poitiers

Loire R.

AQUITAINE

Lyons

Rhône R.

Garonne R.

Toulouse

BASQUES

Ebro R.

WEST GOTHIC KINGDOM

SUEVIAN KINGDOM (conquered by West Goths 584)

Tagus R.

Mérida

Toledo

Cordova

Seville

Cartagena

Tarragona

Ceuta

PICTS

ANGLES

SAXONS

JUTES

Iona

York

London

Canterbury

Thames R.

BRITTANY (Frankish Dependency)

ATLANTIC OCEAN

MEDITERRANEAN SEA

Hippo

Carthage

Caesarea

Sabrata

Oea

Leptis Magna

SARDINIA

SICILY

Naples

Rome

Ostia

Perugia

Spoleto

Benevento

LOMBARDS

Ravenna

Ancona

Bobbio

Pavia

Milan

Genoa

Verona

Venice

Aquileia

Pola

ADRIATIC SEA

La Salona

Dyrrachium

Apollonia

Berenice

Thessalonica

Corinth

Thermopylae

CRETE

Ephesus

Nicaea

Constantinople

Chalcedon

Hadrianople

Sardica

Viminacium

Danube R.

Theiss R.

Pruth R.

Dniester R.

Bug R.

Dnieper R.

Chersonesus

Sinope

Ancyra

Iconium

BLACK SEA

EASTERN ROMAN EMPIRE

CYPRUS

Antioch

Apamea

Emesa

Damascus

Caesarea

Jerusalem

Petra

Nile R.

Alexandria

Dara

Edessa

Nineveh

Tigris R.

Euphrates R.

Callinicum

Nisibis

Nile R.

C.S. Hammond & Co., N.Y.

400 MILES

KILOMETERS

Longitude East of Greenwich

Longitude West of Greenwich

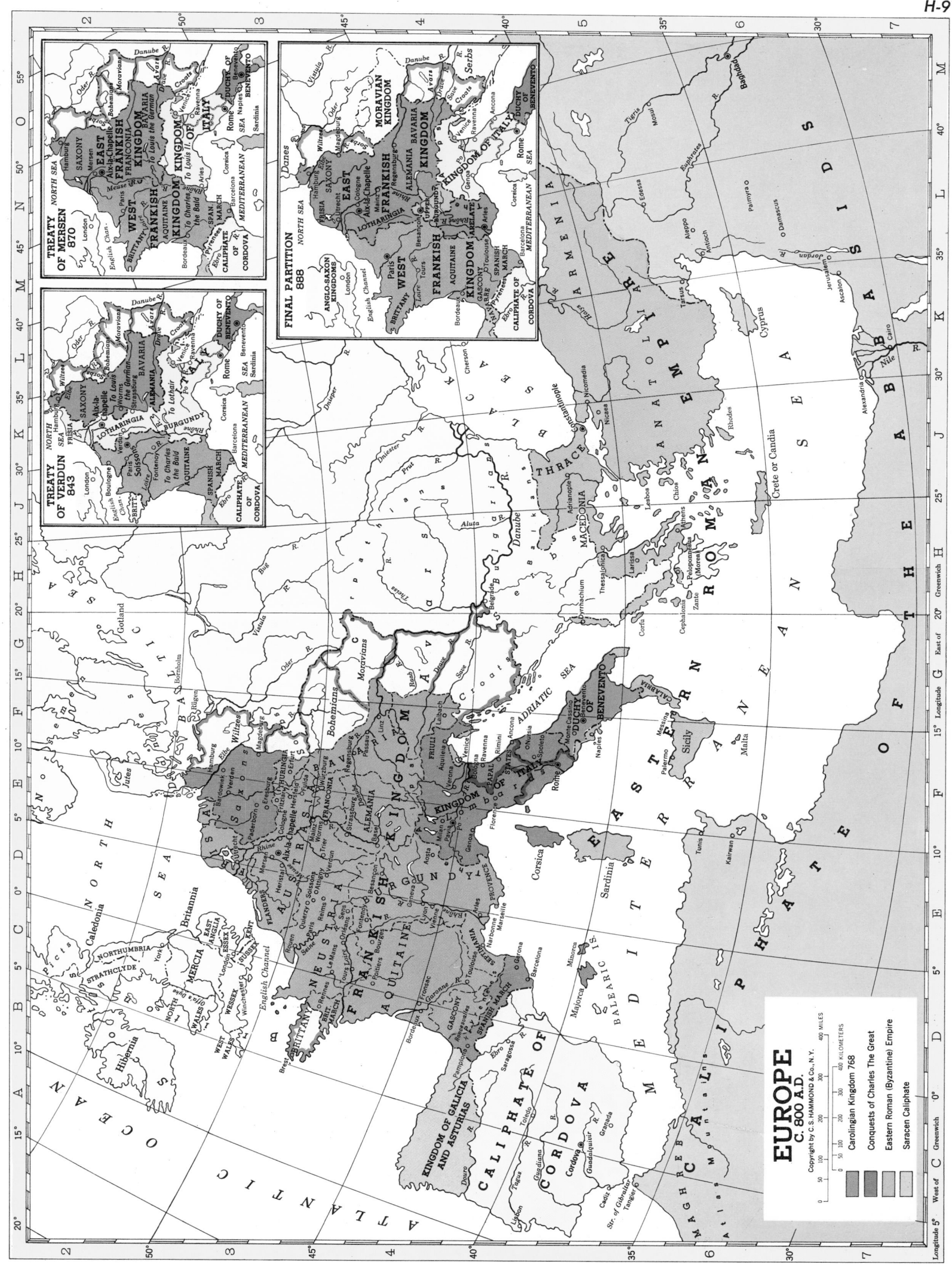

EUROPE
C. 800 A.D.

Copyright by C. S. HAMMOND & Co., N.Y.

Carolingian Kingdom 768
Conquests of Charles The Great
Eastern Roman (Byzantine) Empire
Saracen Caliphate

TREATY OF MERSEN 870

TREATY OF VERDUN 843

FINAL PARTITION 888

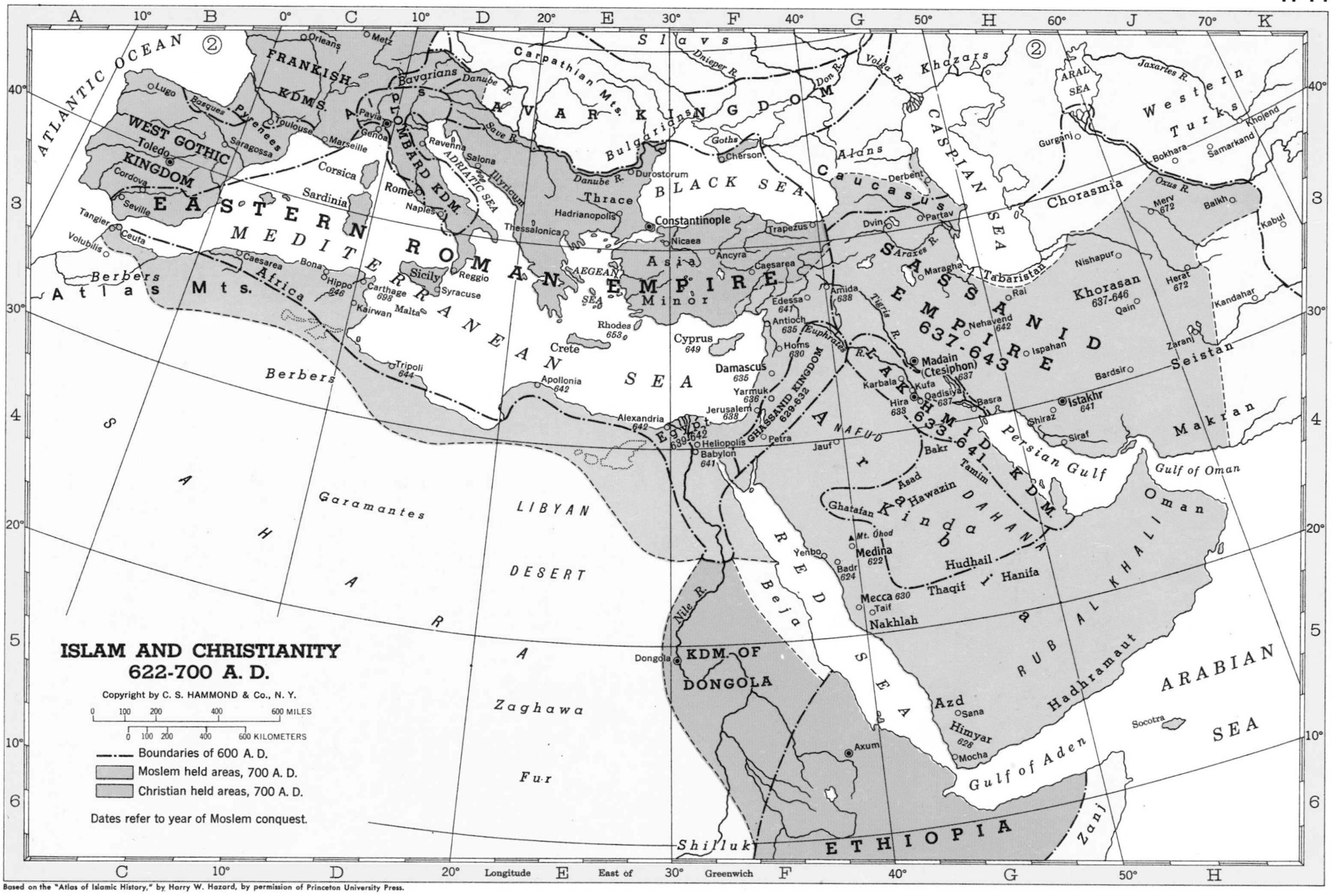

Map 1

ATLANTIC OCEAN

Orleans · Metz · Carpathian Mts. · Slavs · Dnieper R. · Khazars · ②

FRANKISH KDMS. · Lugo · Bordeaux · Pavia · Bavarians · Danube R. · AVAR KINGDOM · Don R. · Volga R. · Western Turks

WEST GOTHIC KINGDOM · Toledo · Pyrenees · Marseille · Genoa · LOMBARD KDM. · Ravenna · Save R. · Illyricum · Bulgarians · Goths · Cherson · ARAL SEA · Jaxartes R.

Saragossa · Corsica · ADRIATIC SEA · Thrace · CAUCASUS · CASPIAN SEA · Chorasmia · Kholend

Cordova · Seville · Sardinia · Rome · Naples · Hadrianopolis · Durostorum · BLACK SEA · Partav · Dvin · Maragha · Tabaristan · Nishapur · Bokhara · Samarkand · Balkh

EASTERN ROMAN EMPIRE · Thessalonica · Constantinople · Nicaea · Trapezus · Araxes R. · SASSANID EMPIRE 637-643 · Khorasan 637-646 · Herat 672 · Kabul

Tangier · Ceuta · Volubilis · Caesarea · Bona · Hippo · Carthage 698 · Sicily · Reggio · Syracuse · Malta · Asia Minor · Caesarea · Ancyra · Amida 638 · Edessa 641 · Nehavend 642 · Rai · Ispahan · Bardsir · Zaranj · Seistan

Berbers · Atlas Mts. · Africa · MEDITERRANEAN SEA · Crete · Rhodes 653 · Cyprus 649 · Antioch 635 · Homs 636 · Damascus 635 · Madain (Ctesiphon) 637 · Istakhr 641 · Makran

Tripoli 644 · Apollonia 642 · Alexandria 642 · Heliopolis 640 · Babylon 641 · Jerusalem 637 · Yarmuk 636 · Hira 633 · Qadisiya 637 · Kufa · Karbala · Basra · Shiraz · Siraf · Persian Gulf · Gulf of Oman

S A H A R A · Garamantes · LIBYAN DESERT · EGYPT · GHASSAND KINGDOM 629-632 · Petra · Bakr · Tamim · Asad · Ghatafan · Hawazin · Kinda · DAHANA · Gulf of Oman · Oman

Zaghawa · Fur · Dongola · KDM. OF DONGOLA · Beja · RED SEA · Yenbo · Badr 624 · Medina 622 · Mecca 630 · Taif · Nakhlah · Hudhail · Hanifa · Thaqif · RUB AL KHALI · Hadhramaut · ARABIAN SEA

Azd · Sana · Himyar 628 · Mocha · Axum · Gulf of Aden · Socotra

Shilluk · ETHIOPIA · Zanj

ISLAM AND CHRISTIANITY 622-700 A.D.

Copyright by C. S. HAMMOND & Co., N. Y.

100 200 400 600 MILES
100 200 400 600 KILOMETERS

– · – · Boundaries of 600 A. D.
▨ Moslem held areas, 700 A. D.
▨ Christian held areas, 700 A. D.

Dates refer to year of Moslem conquest.

Based on the "Atlas of Islamic History," by Harry W. Hazard, by permission of Princeton University Press.

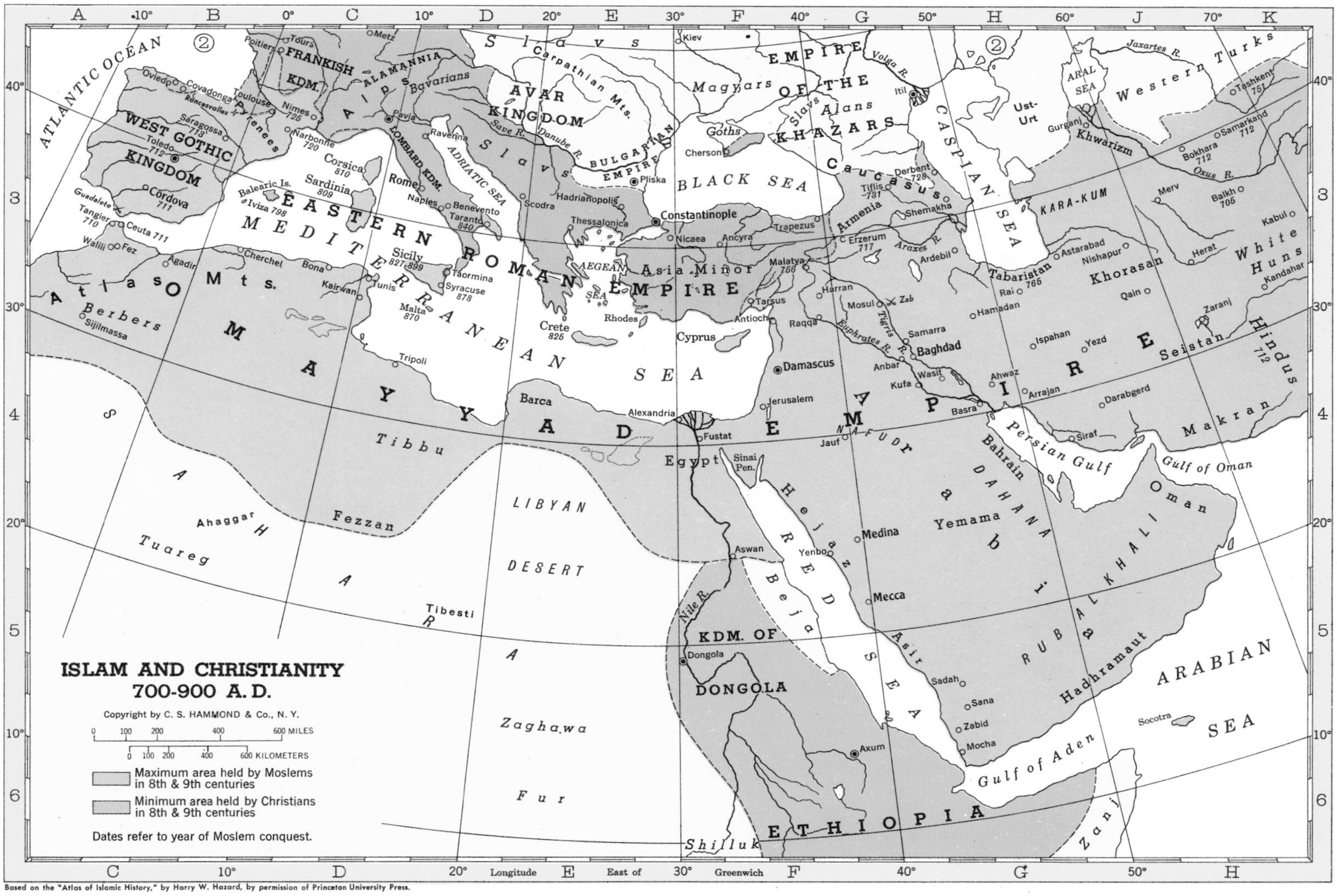

Longitude East of Greenwich

Map 2

ATLANTIC OCEAN

Poitiers · Tours · Metz · Slavs · Carpathian Mts. · Kiev · EMPIRE OF THE · ②

FRANKISH KDM. · ALAMANNIA · Bavarians · AVAR KINGDOM · Magyars · KHAZARS · Volga R. · Itil · Western Turks · Tashkent 751

WEST GOTHIC KINGDOM · Toledo 712 · Oviedo · Covadonga · Toulouse · Pyrenees · Narbonne 720 · LOMBARD KDM. · Ravenna · Save R. · Danube R. · BULGARIAN EMPIRE · Goths · Alans · Cherson · ARAL SEA · Jaxartes R.

Cordova 711 · Saragossa · Nimes 725 · Corsica 810 · Sardinia 810 · Rome · Pliska · Caucasus · Derbent · CASPIAN SEA · Khwarizm · Bokhara 712 · Samarkand 712

Guadalete · Tangier 710 · Ceuta 711 · Balearic Is. · Iviza 798 · Naples · Benevento · Taranto 840 · Hadrianopolis · Thessalonica · Constantinople · Nicaea · Ancyra · Trapezus · Armenia · Tiflis 737 · Shemakha · KARA-KUM · Merv · Balkh 705 · Oxus R.

Walili 710 · Fez · Agadir · Cherchel · Bona · Tunis · Kairwan · Sicily 827-896 · Taormina · Syracuse 878 · Malta 870 · AEGEAN SEA · Asia Minor · Tarsus · Malatya 760 · Erzerum · Araxes R. · Ardebil 728 · Rai 766 · Tabaristan · Astarabad · Nishapur · Khorasan · Herat · WHITE HUNS

Berbers · Sijilmassa · Atlas Mts. · MEDITERRANEAN SEA · Crete 825 · Rhodes · Cyprus · Antioch · Harran · Mosul · Zab · Tigris · Hamadan · Ispahan · Yezd · Qain · Zaranj · Seistan · Kabul · Kandahar · Hindus 712

S O M A Y Y A D · Tripoli · Barca · Alexandria · Damascus · Jerusalem · Fustat · EGYPT · Raqqa · Euphrates · Samarra · Baghdad · Anbar · Kufa · Wasit · Basra · Ahwaz · Arrajan · Darabgerd · Makran

Tibbu · LIBYAN DESERT · Sinai Pen. · NAFUD · Jauf · Bahrain · Persian Gulf · Siraf · Gulf of Oman

Ahaggar · Fezzan · Tibesti R. · A D · E M P I R E · Hejaz · RED SEA · Beja · Yenbo · Medina · Mecca · Asir · Yemama · DAHANA · Oman · RUB AL KHALI · Hadhramaut · ARABIAN SEA

Tuareg · Zaghawa · Fur · Dongola · KDM. OF DONGOLA · Sadah · Sana · Zabid · Mocha · Axum · Socotra

Shilluk · ETHIOPIA · Gulf of Aden · Zanj

ISLAM AND CHRISTIANITY 700-900 A.D.

Copyright by C. S. HAMMOND & Co., N. Y.

100 200 400 600 MILES
100 200 400 600 KILOMETERS

▨ Maximum area held by Moslems in 8th & 9th centuries
▨ Minimum area held by Christians in 8th & 9th centuries

Dates refer to year of Moslem conquest.

Based on the "Atlas of Islamic History," by Harry W. Hazard, by permission of Princeton University Press.

Longitude East of Greenwich

EUROPE
and the
BYZANTINE EMPIRE
ABOUT 1000

Copyright by C.S. HAMMOND & CO., N.Y.

Co. = County   Kdm. = Kingdom
D. = Duchy   Th. = Theme

—————— Boundary of the Holy Roman Empire
·············· Route of the Varangians

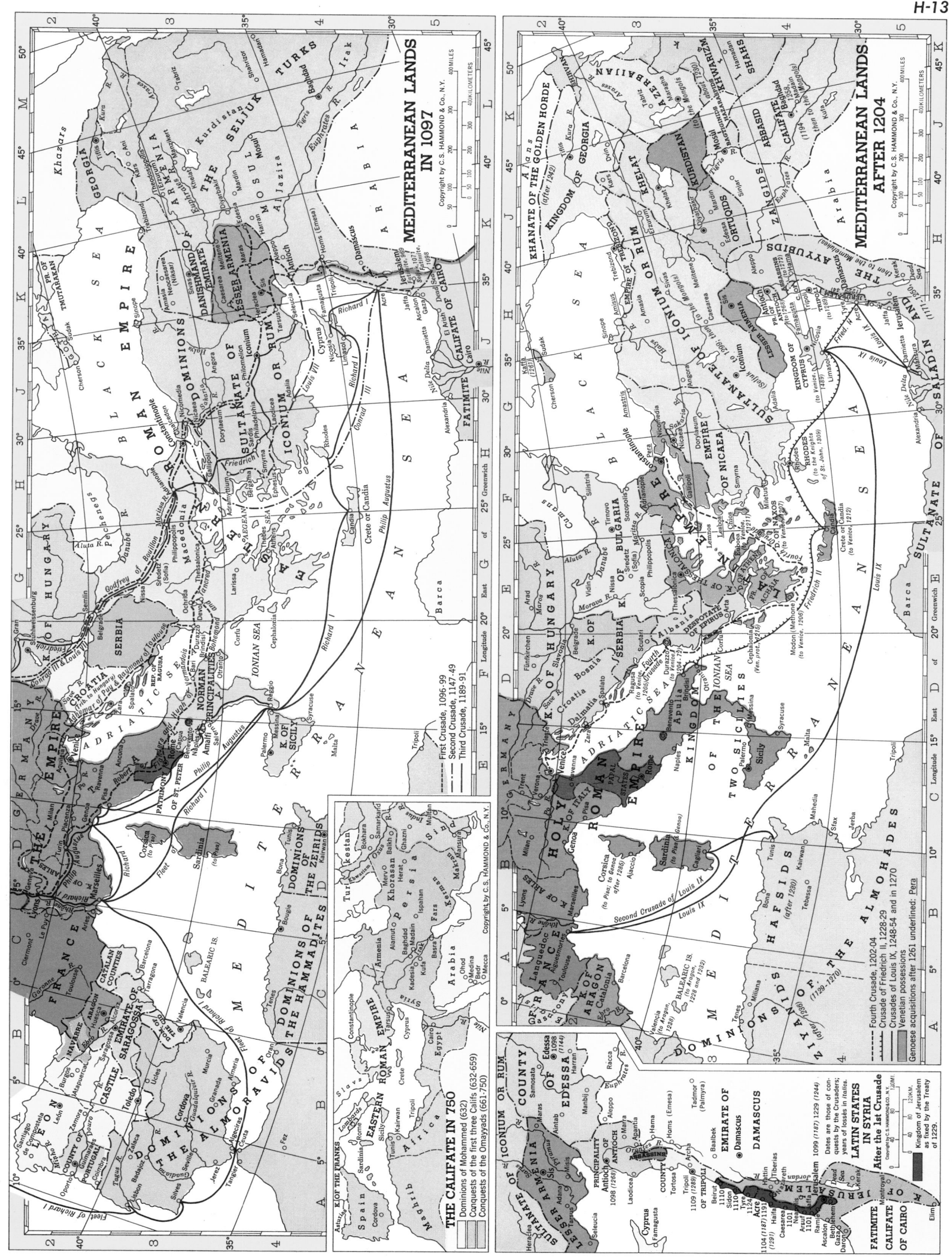

MEDITERRANEAN LANDS IN 1097

Copyright by C. S. HAMMOND & Co., N.Y.

First Crusade, 1096-99
Second Crusade, 1147-49
Third Crusade, 1189-91

THE CALIFATE IN 750

Dominions of Mohammed (632)
Conquests of the first three Califs (632-659)
Conquests of the Ommayads (661-750)

Copyright by C. S. HAMMOND & Co., N.Y.

MEDITERRANEAN LANDS AFTER 1204

Copyright by C. S. HAMMOND & Co., N.Y.

Fourth Crusade, 1202-04
Crusade of Friedrich II, 1228-29
Crusades of Louis IX, 1248-54 and in 1270
Venetian possessions
Genoese acquisitions after 1261 underlined: Pera

LATIN STATES IN SYRIA
After the 1st Crusade

Dates are those of conquests by the Crusaders; years of losses in italics.
Kingdom of Jerusalem as fixed by the Treaty of 1229.

Copyright by C. S. HAMMOND & Co., N.Y.

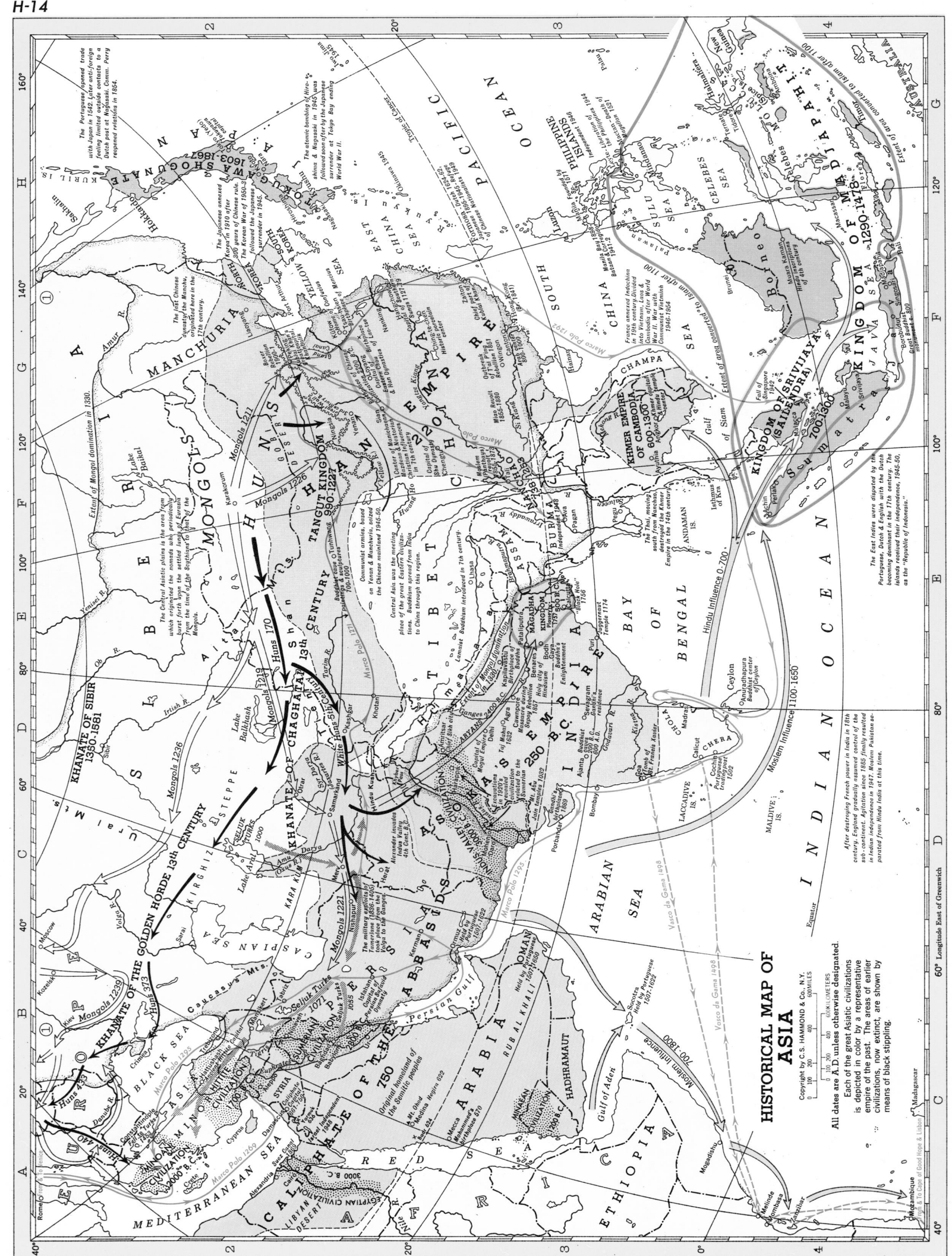

HISTORICAL MAP OF ASIA

Copyright by C.S. HAMMOND & CO. N.Y.

All dates are A.D. unless otherwise designated.

Each of the great Asiatic civilizations is depicted in color by a representative empire of the past. The areas of earlier civilizations, now extinct, are shown by means of black stippling.

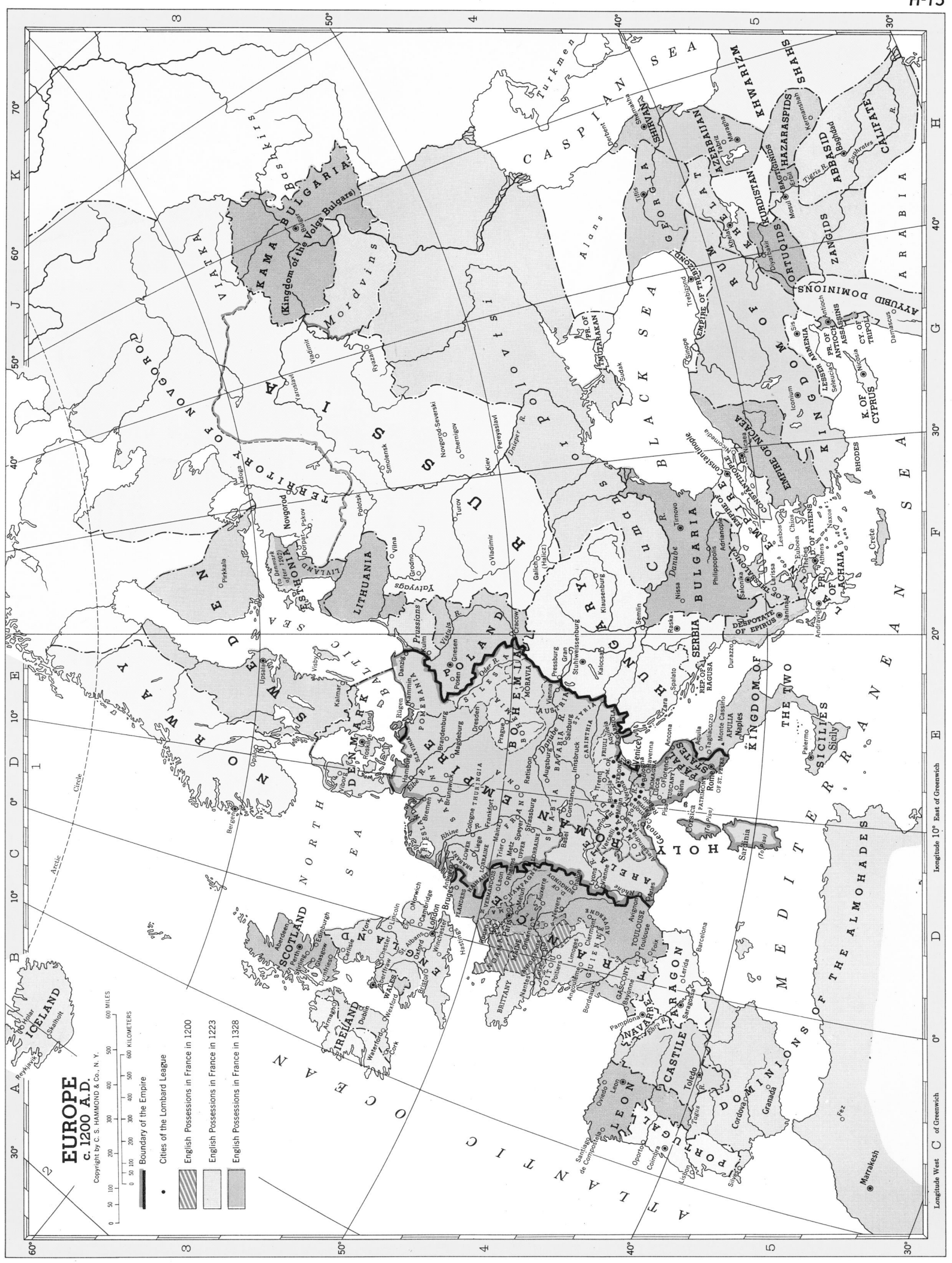

EUROPE
c. 1200 A.D.

Copyright by C. S. HAMMOND & Co., N. Y.

Boundary of the Empire

Cities of the Lombard League

English Possessions in France in 1200

English Possessions in France in 1223

English Possessions in France in 1328

MILES

KILOMETERS

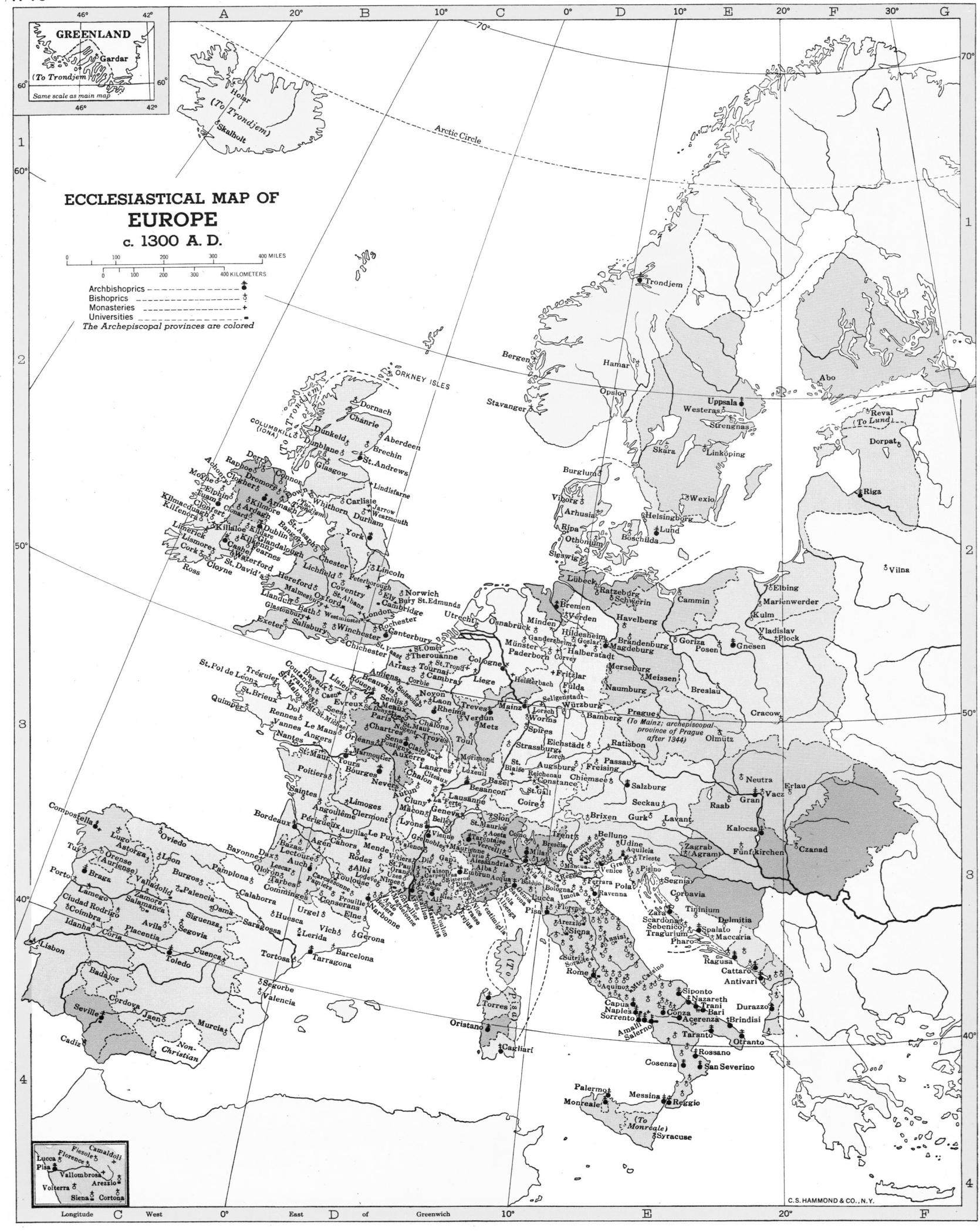

GREENLAND

Gardar

(To Trondjem)

Same scale as main map

ECCLESIASTICAL MAP OF
EUROPE
c. 1300 A. D.

100   200   300   400 MILES

100   200   300   400 KILOMETERS

Archbishoprics
Bishoprics
Monasteries
Universities

The Archepiscopal provinces are colored

Camaldoli
Fiesole
Florence
Lucca
Pisa   Vallombrosa
Volterra   Arezzio
        Siena   Cortona

Longitude   West   0°   East   of   Greenwich

C. S. HAMMOND & CO., N.Y.

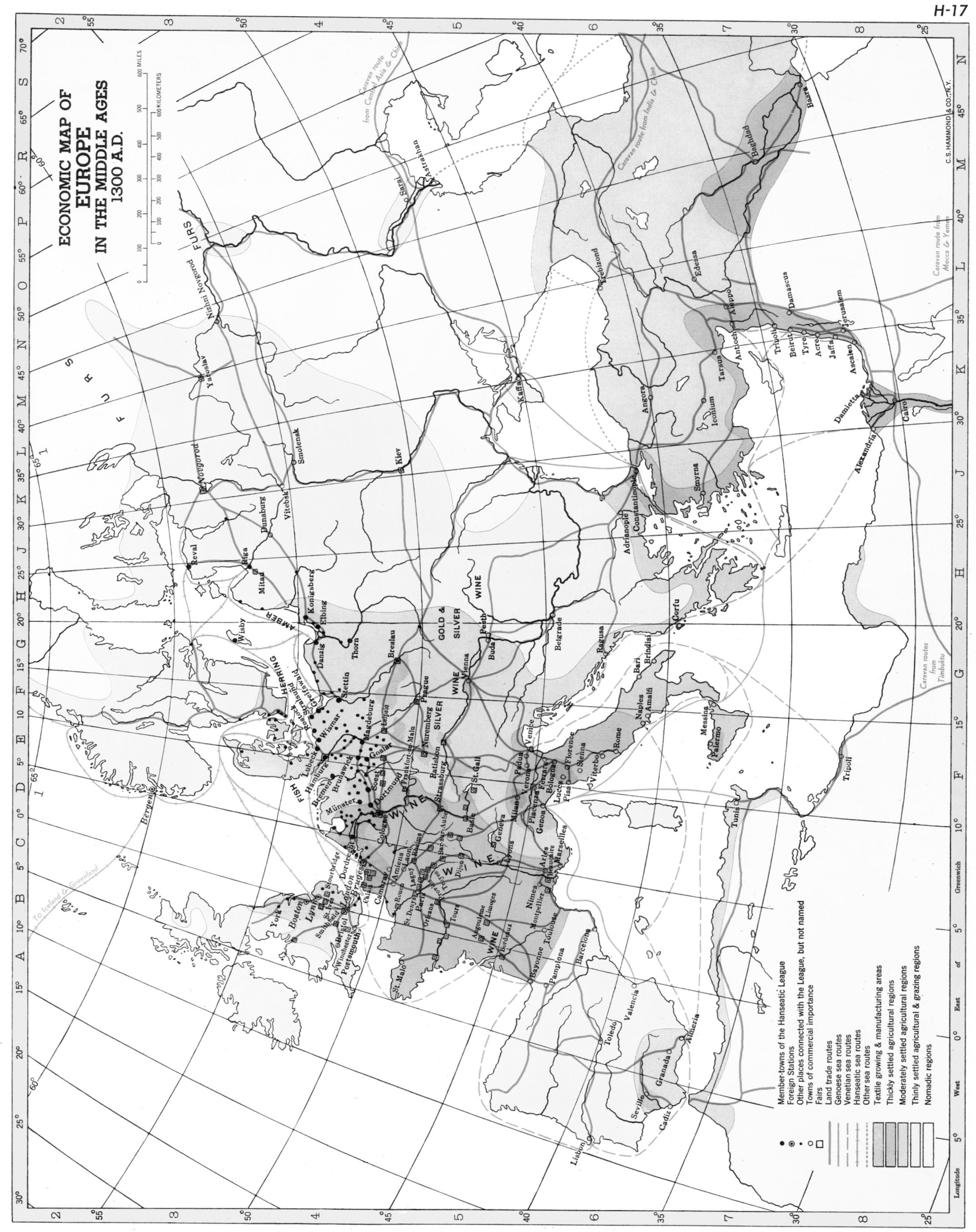

ECONOMIC MAP OF
EUROPE
IN THE MIDDLE AGES
1300 A.D.

MILES
KILOMETERS

C.S. HAMMOND & CO., N.Y.

Member-towns of the Hanseatic League
Foreign Stations
Other places connected with the League, but not named
Towns of commercial importance
Fairs
Land trade routes
Genoese sea routes
Venetian sea routes
Hanseatic sea routes
Other sea routes
Textile growing & manufacturing areas
Thickly settled agricultural regions
Moderately settled agricultural regions
Thinly settled agricultural & grazing regions
Nomadic regions

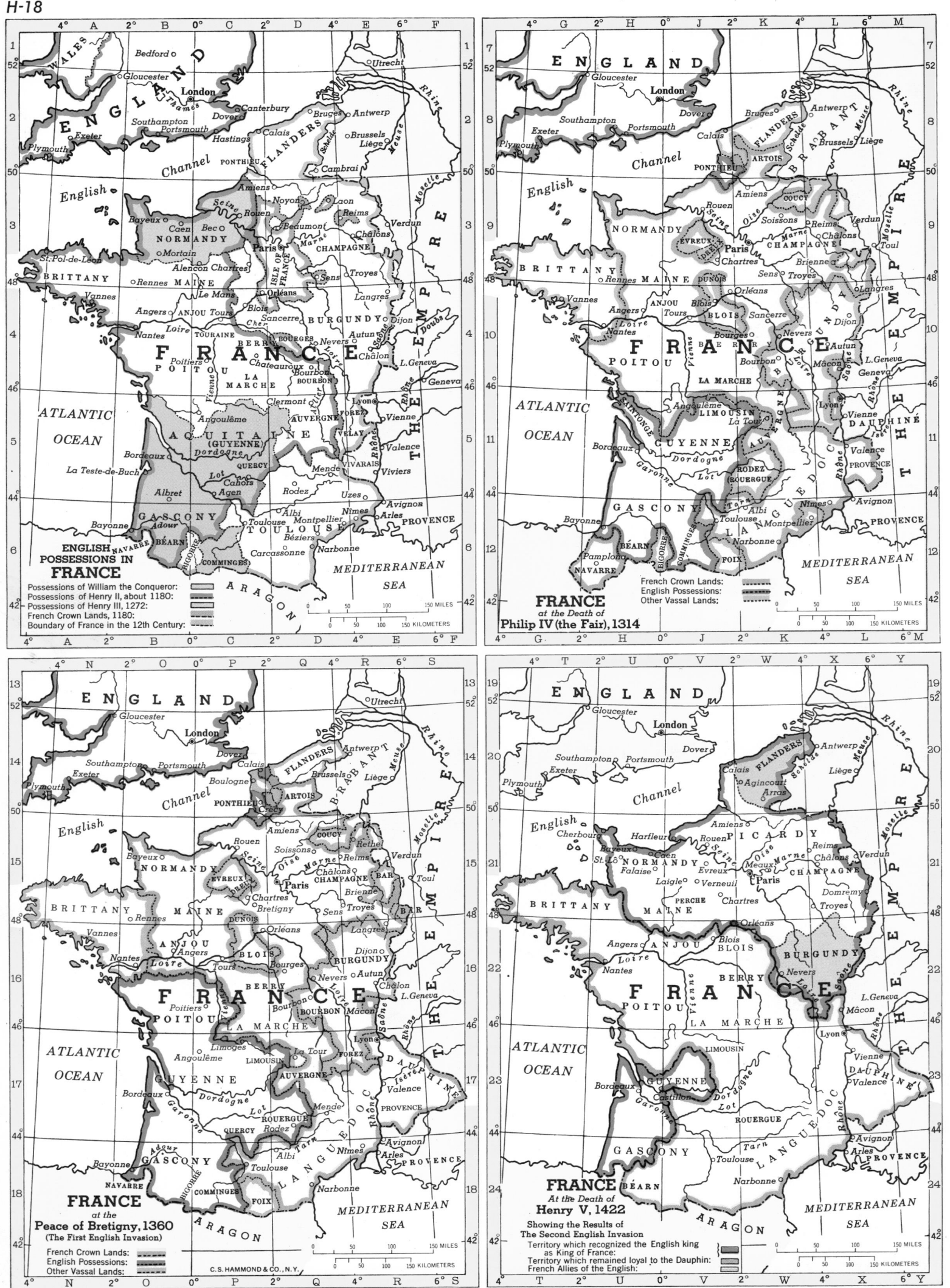

ENGLISH POSSESSIONS IN FRANCE

Possessions of William the Conqueror:
Possessions of Henry II, about 1180:
Possessions of Henry III, 1272:
French Crown Lands, 1180:
Boundary of France in the 12th Century:

FRANCE
at the Death of
Philip IV (the Fair), 1314

French Crown Lands:
English Possessions:
Other Vassal Lands:

FRANCE
at the
Peace of Bretigny, 1360
(The First English Invasion)

French Crown Lands:
English Possessions:
Other Vassal Lands:

C. S. HAMMOND & CO., N.Y.

FRANCE
At the Death of
Henry V, 1422
Showing the Results of
The Second English Invasion

Territory which recognized the English king
as King of France:
Territory which remained loyal to the Dauphin:
French Allies of the English:

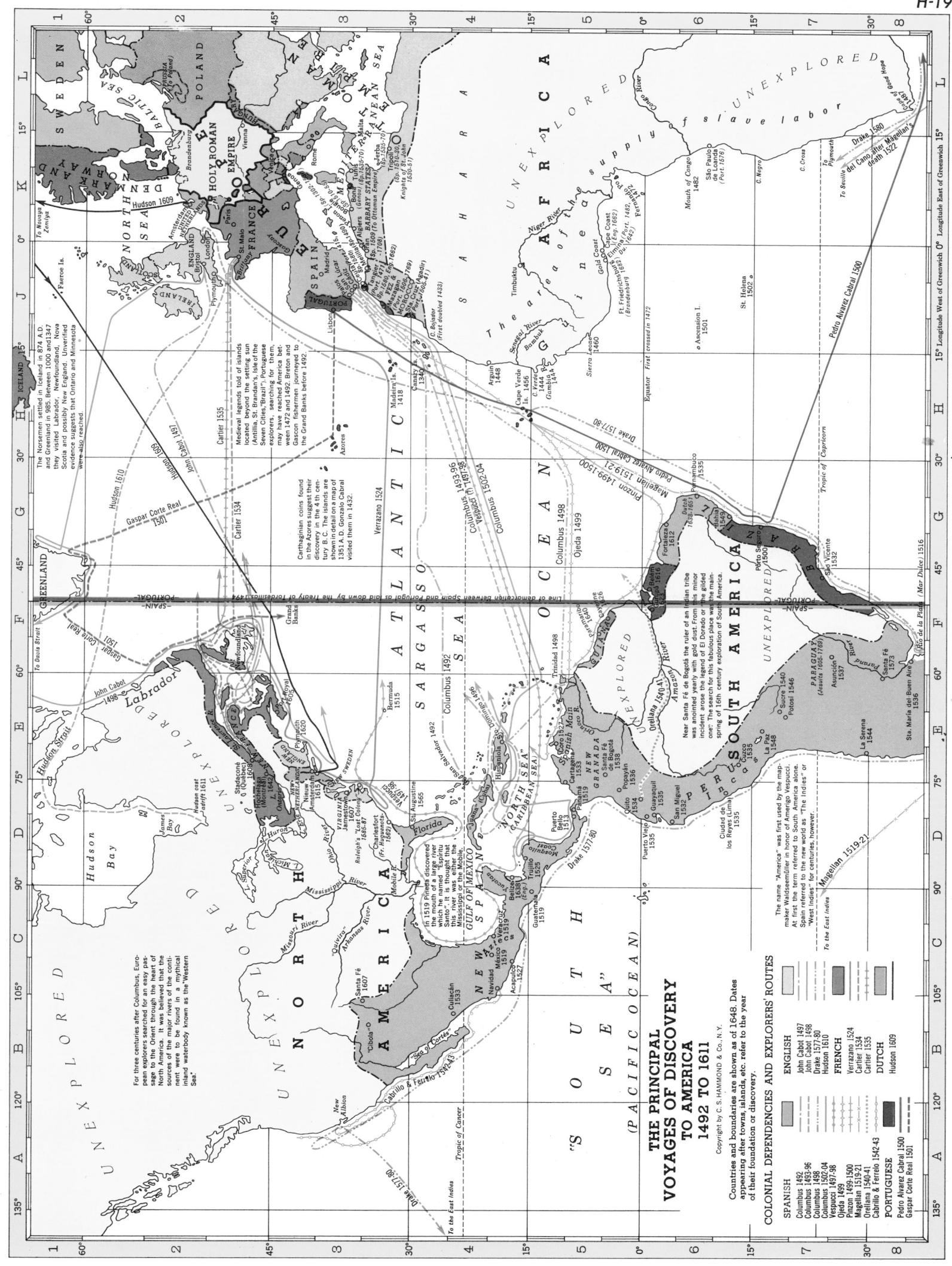

THE PRINCIPAL VOYAGES OF DISCOVERY TO AMERICA 1492 TO 1611

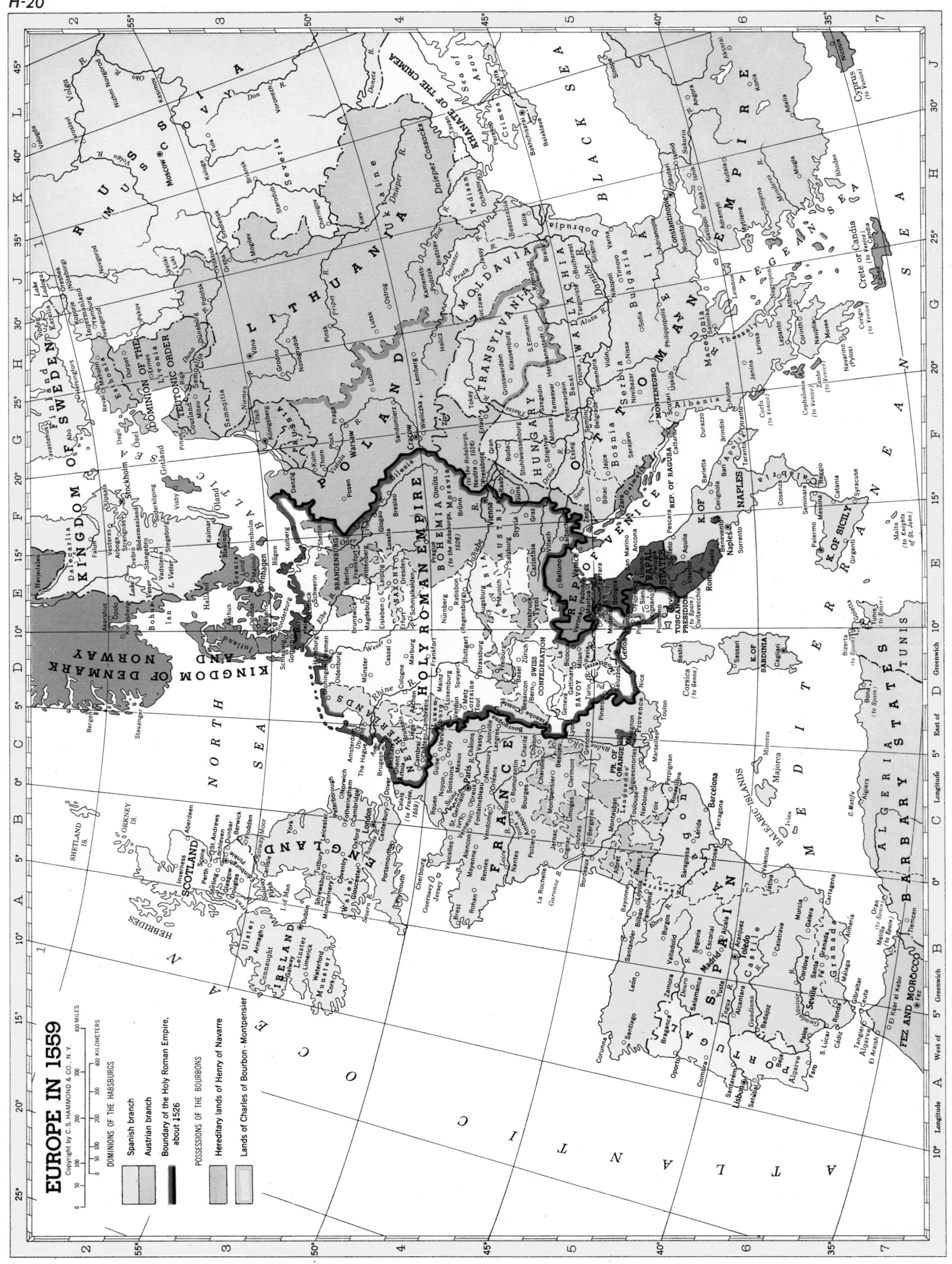

EUROPE IN 1559

Copyright by C.S. HAMMOND & CO., N.Y.

DOMINIONS OF THE HABSBURGS

Spanish branch

Austrian branch

Boundary of the Holy Roman Empire, about 1526

POSSESSIONS OF THE BOURBONS

Hereditary lands of Henry of Navarre

Lands of Charles of Bourbon-Montpensier

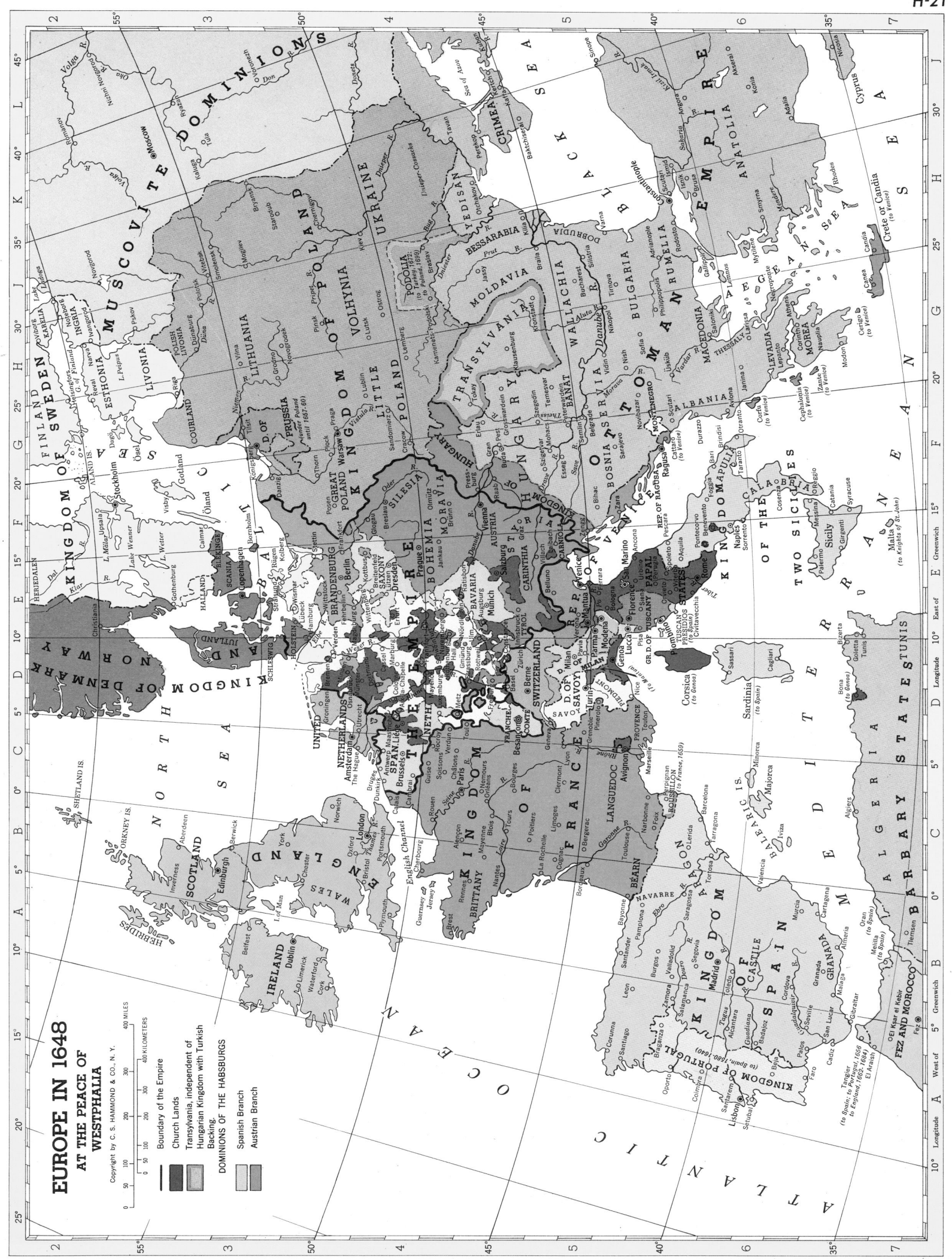

EUROPE IN 1648
AT THE PEACE OF
WESTPHALIA

Copyright by C. S. HAMMOND & CO., N. Y.

- Boundary of the Empire
- Church Lands
- Transylvania, independent of Hungarian Kingdom with Turkish Backing.
DOMINIONS OF THE HABSBURGS
- Spanish Branch
- Austrian Branch

400 MILES
400 KILOMETERS
0 50 100 200 300

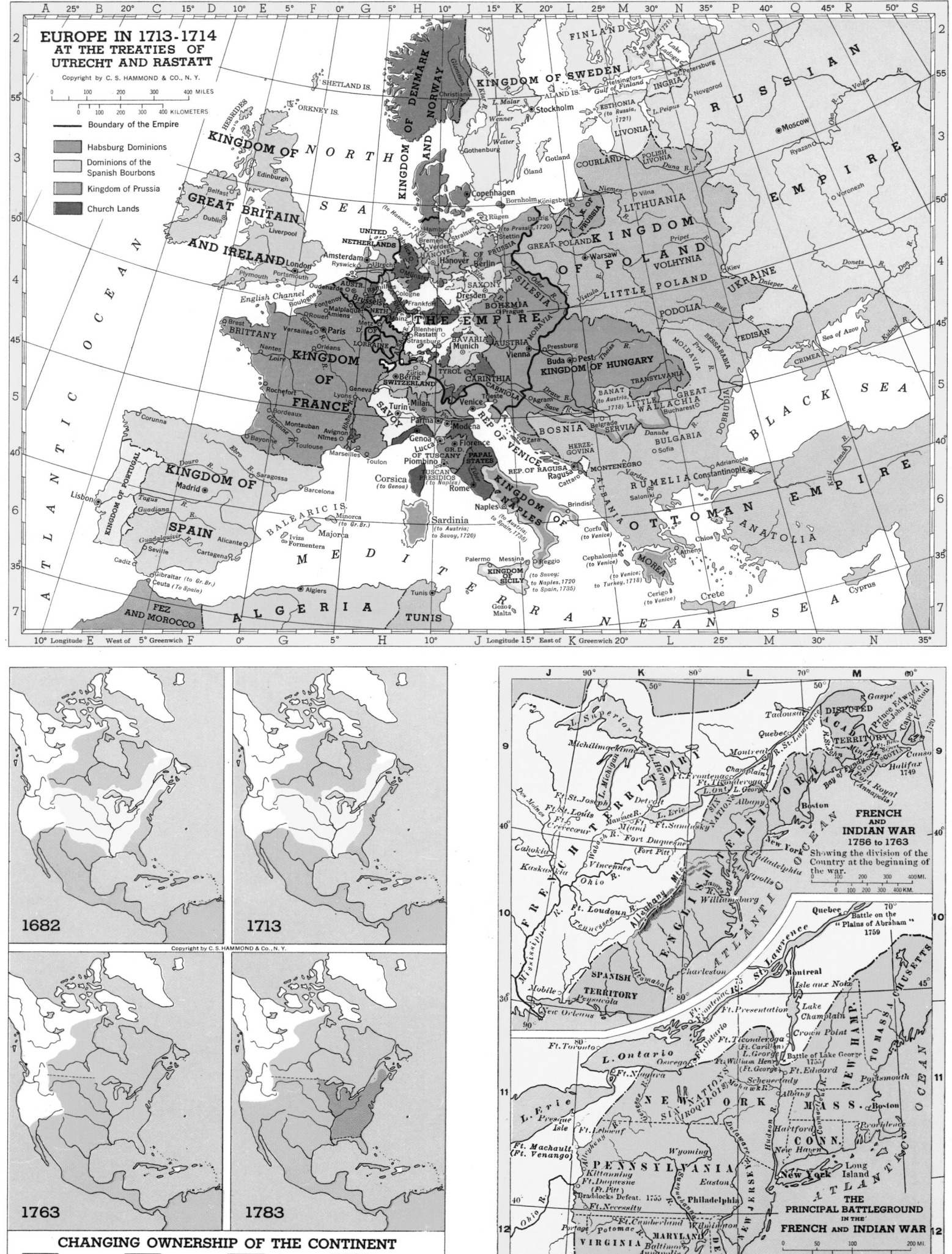

EUROPE IN 1713-1714 AT THE TREATIES OF UTRECHT AND RASTATT

Copyright by C. S. HAMMOND & CO., N.Y.

Boundary of the Empire

Habsburg Dominions

Dominions of the Spanish Bourbons

Kingdom of Prussia

Church Lands

CHANGING OWNERSHIP OF THE CONTINENT

1682   1713   1763   1783

ENGLISH   FRENCH   SPANISH   INDEPENDENT

FRENCH AND INDIAN WAR
1756 to 1763
Showing the division of the Country at the beginning of the war.

Battle on the "Plains of Abraham" 1759

THE PRINCIPAL BATTLEGROUND IN THE FRENCH AND INDIAN WAR

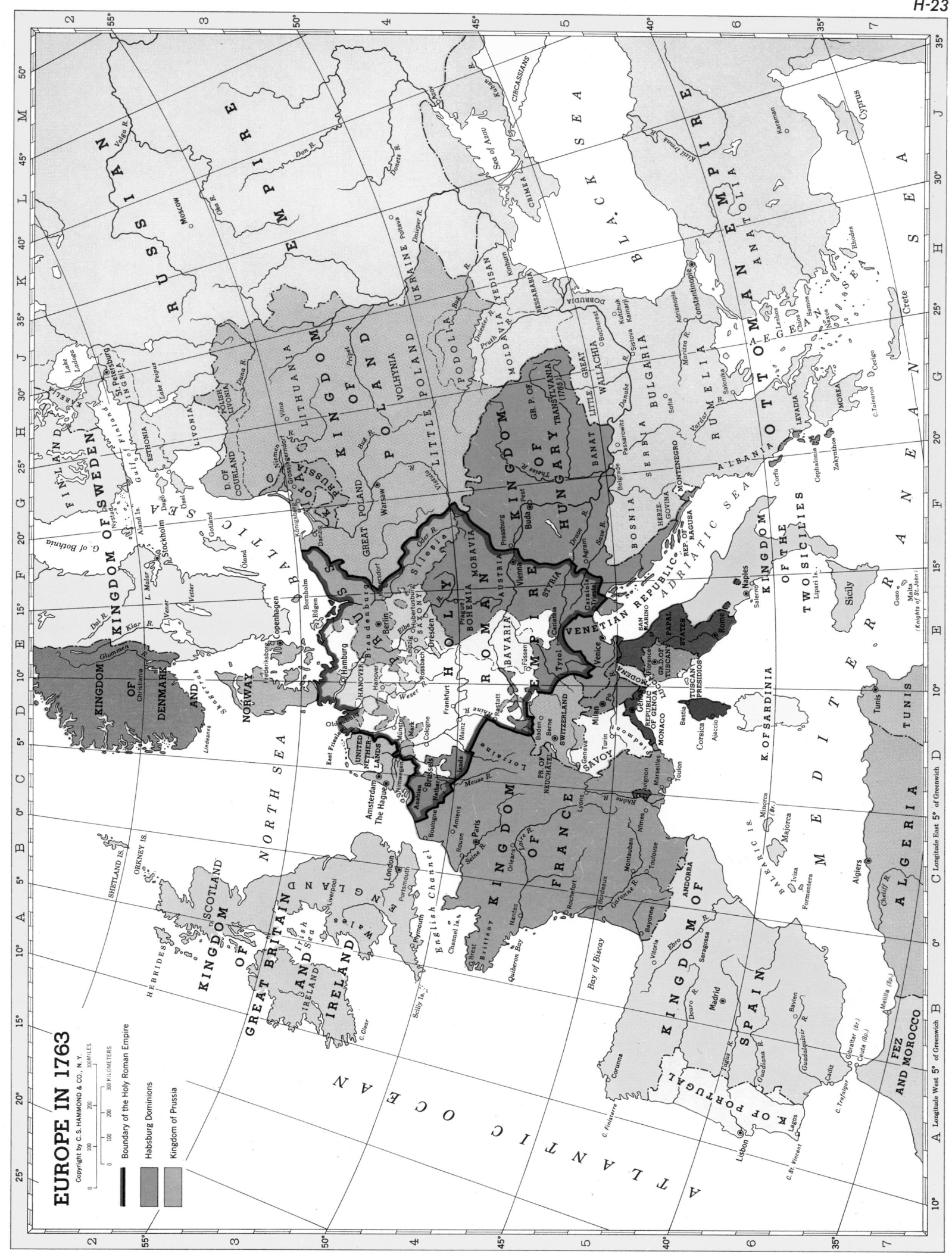

EUROPE IN 1763

Copyright by C.S. HAMMOND & CO., N.Y.

Boundary of the Holy Roman Empire

Habsburg Dominions

Kingdom of Prussia

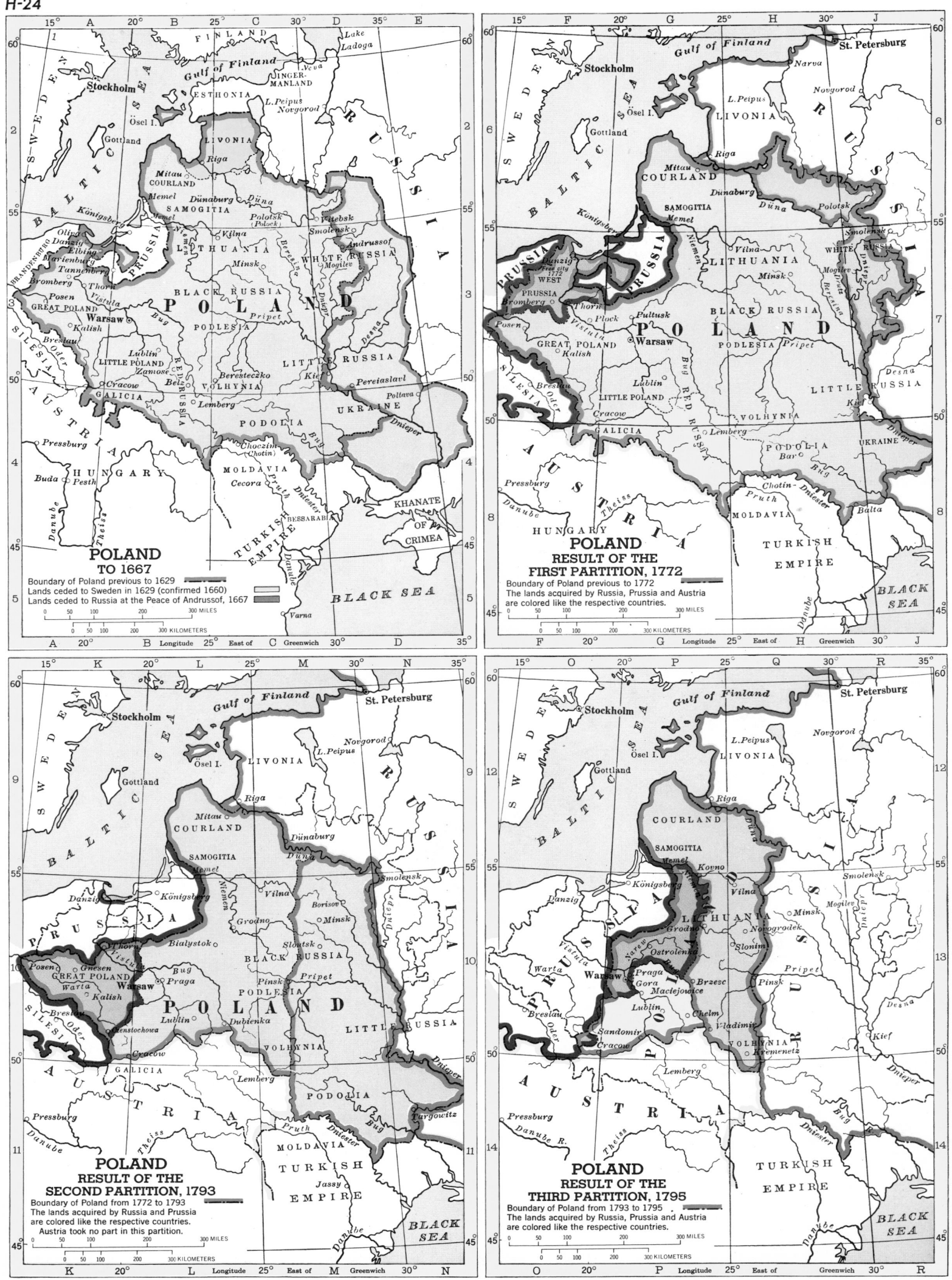

POLAND
TO 1667

Boundary of Poland previous to 1629 ▬▬▬
Lands ceded to Sweden in 1629 (confirmed 1660) ▢
Lands ceded to Russia at the Peace of Andrussof, 1667 ▢

0 50 100 200 300 MILES
0 50 100 200 300 KILOMETERS

POLAND
RESULT OF THE
FIRST PARTITION, 1772

Boundary of Poland previous to 1772 ▬▬▬
The lands acquired by Russia, Prussia and Austria
are colored like the respective countries.

0 50 100 200 300 MILES
0 50 100 200 300 KILOMETERS

POLAND
RESULT OF THE
SECOND PARTITION, 1793

Boundary of Poland from 1772 to 1793 ▬▬▬
The lands acquired by Russia and Prussia
are colored like the respective countries.
Austria took no part in this partition.

0 50 100 200 300 MILES
0 50 100 200 300 KILOMETERS

POLAND
RESULT OF THE
THIRD PARTITION, 1795

Boundary of Poland from 1793 to 1795 ▬▬▬
The lands acquired by Russia, Prussia and Austria
are colored like the respective countries.

0 50 100 200 300 MILES
0 50 100 200 300 KILOMETERS

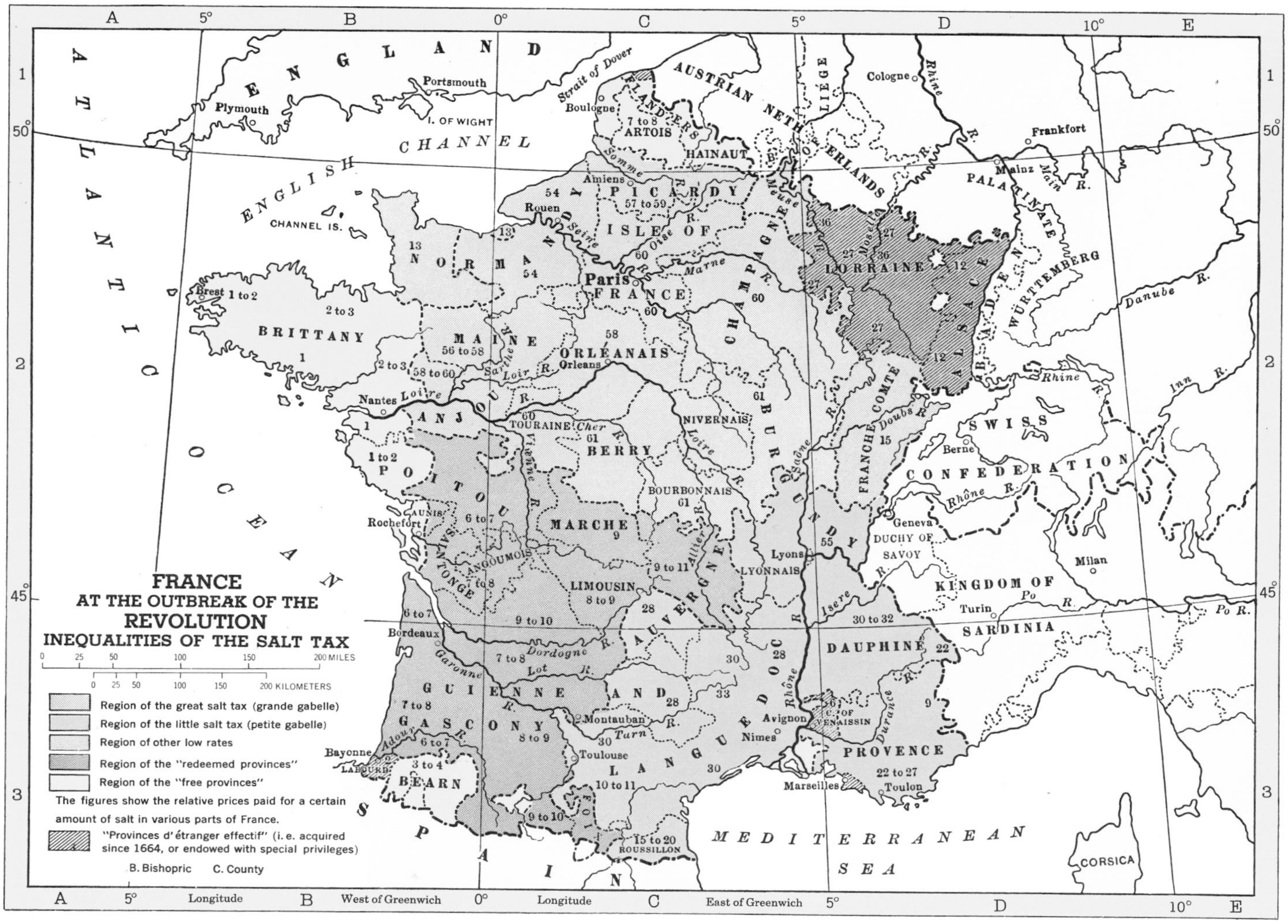

FRANCE
AT THE OUTBREAK OF THE REVOLUTION
INEQUALITIES OF THE SALT TAX

ATLANTIC OCEAN

ENGLAND
Plymouth
Portsmouth
I. OF WIGHT
ENGLISH CHANNEL
CHANNEL IS.
Strait of Dover
Boulogne
AUSTRIAN NETHERLANDS
LIÈGE
Cologne
Rhine R.
Frankfort
Mainz
Main R.
PALATINATE

FLANDERS
7 to 8
ARTOIS
HAINAUT
Amiens
PICARDY
57 to 59
54
Rouen
Seine R.
ISLE OF
Oise R.
FRANCE
Paris
Marne R.
CHAMPAGNE
LORRAINE
12
BADEN
WÜRTTEMBERG
Danube R.

NORMANDY
13
54
MAINE
56 to 58
58 to 60
ORLÉANAIS
58
Orleans
Loire R.
60
BURGUNDY
60
Doubs R.
FRANCHE COMTÉ
15
Rhine
SWISS CONFEDERATION
Berne

BRITTANY
2 to 3
1
Nantes
Loire R.
ANJOU
2 to 3
TOURAINE
60
Cher R.
Vienne R.
BERRY
61
NIVERNAIS
Allier R.
BOURBONNAIS
61
Saône R.
Rhône R.
DUCHY OF SAVOY
55
Geneva
Milan

POITOU
1 to 2
Rochefort
AUNIS
6 to 7
MARCHE
9
LIMOUSIN
8 to 9
AUVERGNE
28
Lyons
LYONNAIS
9 to 11
Isère R.
KINGDOM OF SARDINIA
Turin
Po R.

Brest 1 to 2

Bordeaux
6 to 7
Garonne R.
Dordogne R.
9 to 10
7 to 8
Lot R.
GUIENNE AND GASCONY
7 to 8
8 to 9
Montauban
Toulouse
Tarn R.
30
LANGUEDOC
33
28
30
Rhône R.
28
30 to 32
DAUPHINE
22
Durance R.
9
PROVENCE
22 to 27
Avignon
C. OF VENAISSIN
Nîmes
Marseilles
Toulon

Bayonne
6 to 7
LABOURD
3 to 4
BÉARN
9 to 10
15 to 20
ROUSSILLON

SPAIN

MEDITERRANEAN SEA

CORSICA

Scale: 0 25 50 100 150 200 MILES / 0 25 50 100 150 200 KILOMETERS

Legend:
- Region of the great salt tax (grande gabelle)
- Region of the little salt tax (petite gabelle)
- Region of other low rates
- Region of the "redeemed provinces"
- Region of the "free provinces"

The figures show the relative prices paid for a certain amount of salt in various parts of France.

"Provinces d'étranger effectif" (i.e. acquired since 1664, or endowed with special privileges)

B. Bishopric   C. County

Longitude West of Greenwich   Longitude East of Greenwich

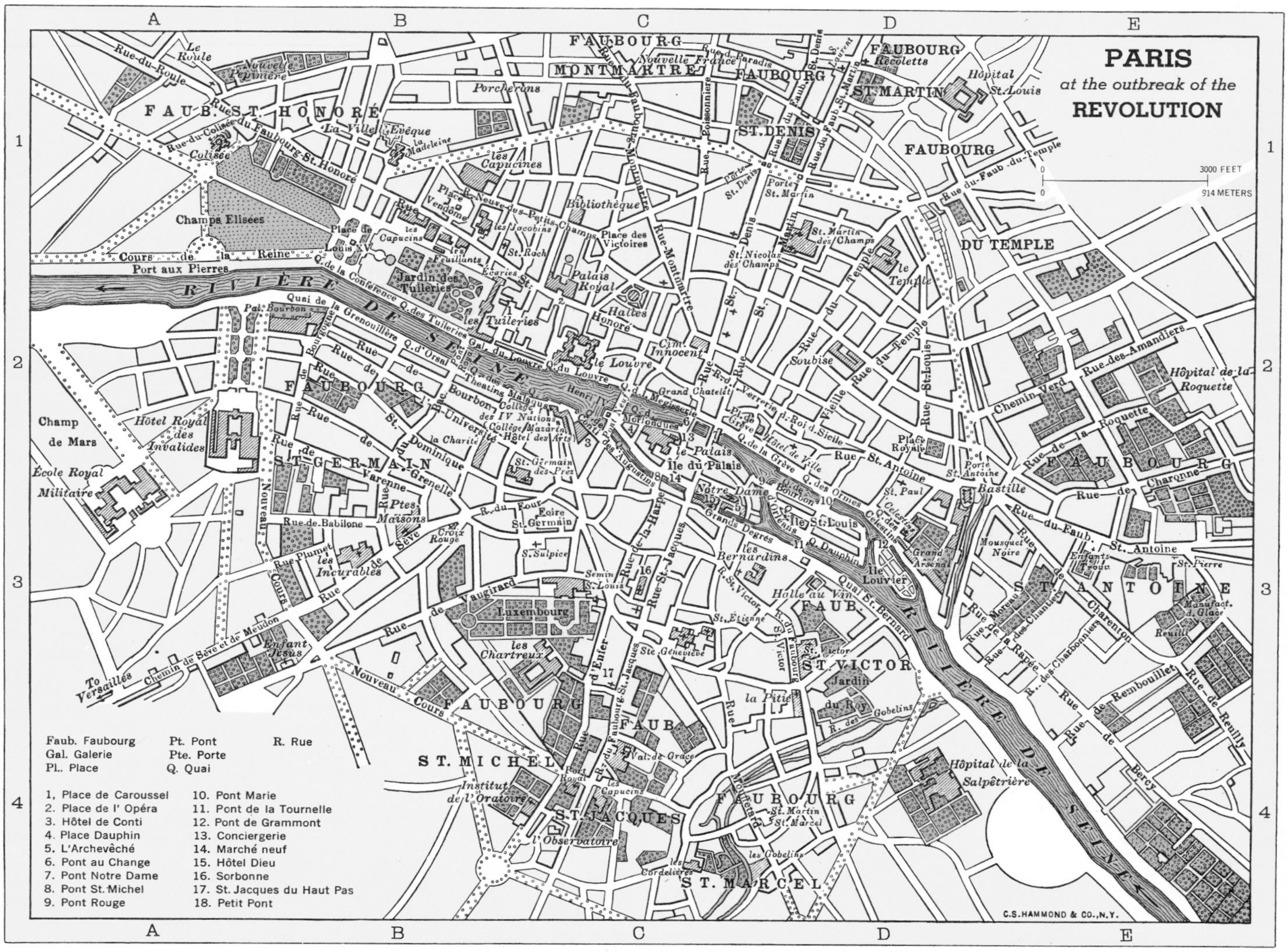

PARIS
at the outbreak of the
REVOLUTION

Le Roule
Rue du Roule
Nouvelle France
La Pepinière
FAUB. ST. HONORÉ
Rue du Faubourg St. Honoré
La Ville l'Evêque
La Madeleine
Porcherons
FAUBOURG MONTMARTRE
FAUBOURG
Nouvelle France
Paradis
Recollets
FAUBOURG ST. MARTIN
Hôpital St. Louis

Champs Elisées
Colisée
les Capucines
Pl. Vendôme
ST. DENIS
FAUBOURG
Porte St. Martin
DU TEMPLE

Cours de la Reine
Port aux Pierres
RIVIÈRE DE SEINE
Jardin des Tuileries
Palais Royal
Halles
St. Nicolas des Champs
St. Martin des Champs
Rue du Faub. du Temple

Champ de Mars
École Royal Militaire
Hôtel Royal des Invalides
ST. GERMAIN
FAUBOURG
Rue de Grenelle
Rue de Varenne
Les Incurables
Enfant Jésus
Rue de Babilone
Sèvre
St. Sulpice
Croix Rouge
Ptes Maisons
le Louvre
Grand Chatelet
Ile du Palais
Notre Dame
Hôtel de Ville
Place de Grève
St. Antoine
Bastille
Rue St. Antoine
FAUBOURG
Rue de Charonne
Hôpital de la Roquette
Rue de la Roquette
Chemin Vert
Rue des Amandiers
Hôpital de la Roquette

Luxembourg
les Chartreux
St. Étienne
Ste. Geneviève
Sorbonne
les Bernardins
Hôtel au Vin
Quai St. Bernard
ST. VICTOR
Jardin du Roy
ST. ANTOINE
Mousquetaires Noirs
Arsenal
Grand Arsenal
Ile Louvier

To Versailles
Nouveau Cours
FAUBOURG ST. MICHEL
Institut de l'Oratoire
Observatoire
ST. JACQUES
Cordeliers
Val de Grace
les Gobelins
ST. MARCEL
FAUBOURG
St. Marcel
Hôpital de la Salpêtrière
Rue de Bercy
Rue de Reuilly
Rue de Rambouillet

Scale: 0 3000 FEET / 914 METERS

Abbreviations:
Faub. Faubourg   Pt. Pont   R. Rue
Gal. Galerie   Pte. Porte
Pl. Place   Q. Quai

1. Place de Caroussel
2. Place de l'Opéra
3. Hôtel de Conti
4. Place Dauphin
5. L'Archevêché
6. Pont au Change
7. Pont Notre Dame
8. Pont St. Michel
9. Pont Rouge
10. Pont Marie
11. Pont de la Tournelle
12. Pont de Grammont
13. Conciergerie
14. Marché neuf
15. Hôtel Dieu
16. Sorbonne
17. St. Jacques du Haut Pas
18. Petit Pont

C.S. HAMMOND & CO., N.Y.

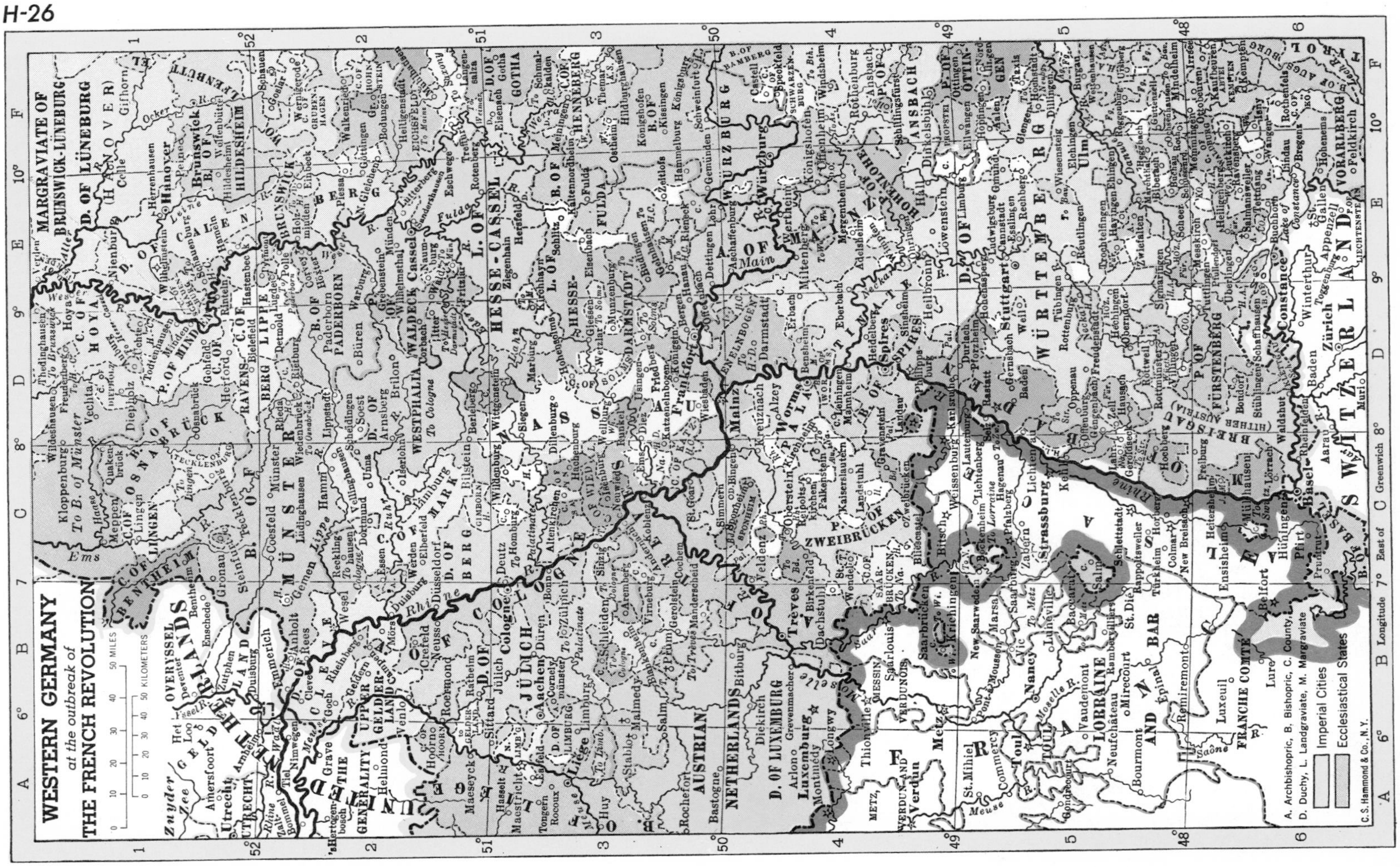

WESTERN GERMANY
at the outbreak of
THE FRENCH REVOLUTION

MILES
KILOMETERS

MARGRAVIATE OF BRUNSWICK-LÜNEBURG
D. OF LÜNEBURG (HANOVER)

UNITED NETHERLANDS
GENERALITY LANDS
OVERYSSEL
UPPER GELDER

C. OF BENTHEIM
B. OF MÜNSTER
C. OF OSNABRÜCK
C. OF RAVENSBERG
BERG
C. OF LIPPE
WALDECK
PADERBORN
HESSE-CASSEL
L.-CASSEL
HESSE
WESTPHALIA
BERG
JÜLICH
D. OF COLOGNE
COLOGNE
NASSAU
HESSE-DARMSTADT
FRANKFURT
WÜRZBURG
P. OF ANSBACH
WÜRTTEMBERG
BADEN
BREISGAU (HITHER AUSTRIA)
SWITZERLAND
VORARLBERG
TYROL

AUSTRIAN NETHERLANDS
D. OF LUXEMBURG
Luxemburg
TREVES
P. OF ZWEIBRÜCKEN
ALSACE
LORRAINE
BAR
FRANCHE COMTE
Strassburg
Metz
Verdun
Toul
Nancy
Nantes

A. Archbishopric, B. Bishopric, C. County.
D. Duchy, L. Landgraviate, M. Margraviate
Imperial Cities
Ecclesiastical States

C. S. Hammond & Co., N.Y.

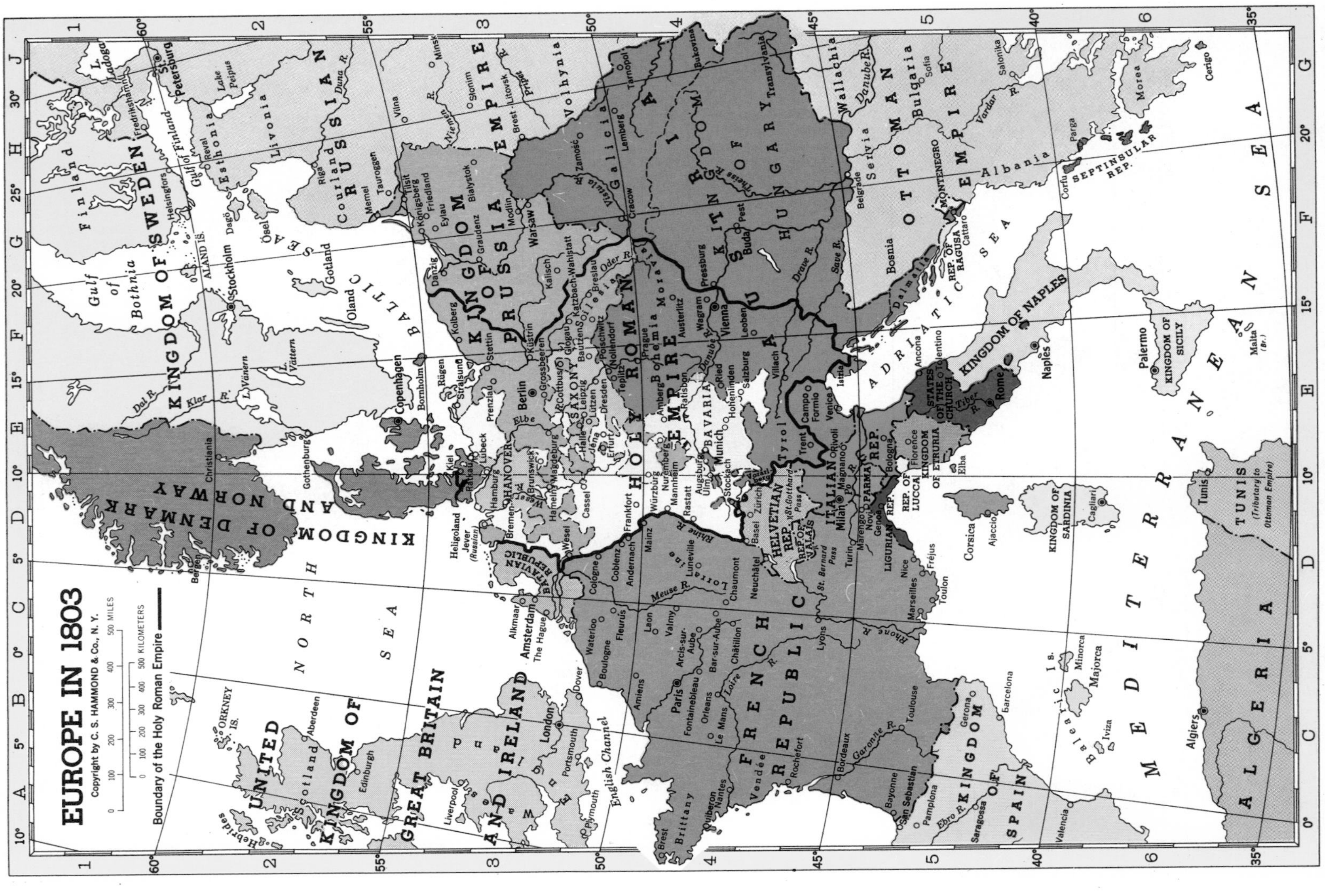

EUROPE IN 1803

Copyright by C. S. Hammond & Co., N.Y.

MILES
KILOMETERS
Boundary of the Holy Roman Empire

UNITED KINGDOM OF GREAT BRITAIN AND IRELAND
London

KINGDOM OF DENMARK AND NORWAY
KINGDOM OF SWEDEN

NORTH SEA
BALTIC SEA

Gulf of Bothnia
Gulf of Finland
Finland
L. Ladoga
St. Petersburg

RUSSIAN EMPIRE
Livonia
Estonia
Courland
Volhynia

KINGDOM OF PRUSSIA
Berlin
Warsaw
Galicia

HANOVER
SAXONY
HOLY ROMAN EMPIRE
BAVARIA
Munich
Vienna
AUSTRIA
HUNGARY
KINGDOM OF HUNGARY
Transylvania
Bohemia
Moravia

BATAVIAN REPUBLIC
Amsterdam
The Hague

FRENCH REPUBLIC
Paris

HELVETIAN REP.
VALAIS
ITALIAN REP.
Milan
LIGURIAN REP.
Genoa
PARMA
KINGDOM OF ETRURIA
LUCCA
STATES OF THE CHURCH
Rome
Florence

KINGDOM OF SARDINIA
Corsica

KINGDOM OF NAPLES
Naples
KINGDOM OF SICILY
Palermo
Malta (Br.)

ADRIATIC SEA
Bosnia
Serbia
OTTOMAN EMPIRE
Bulgaria
Sofia
Montenegro
Albania
Wallachia
Danube R.
SEPTINSULAR REP.

MEDITERRANEAN SEA

SPAIN
Barcelona

ALGERIA
Algiers
TUNIS (Tributary to Ottoman Empire)
Tunis

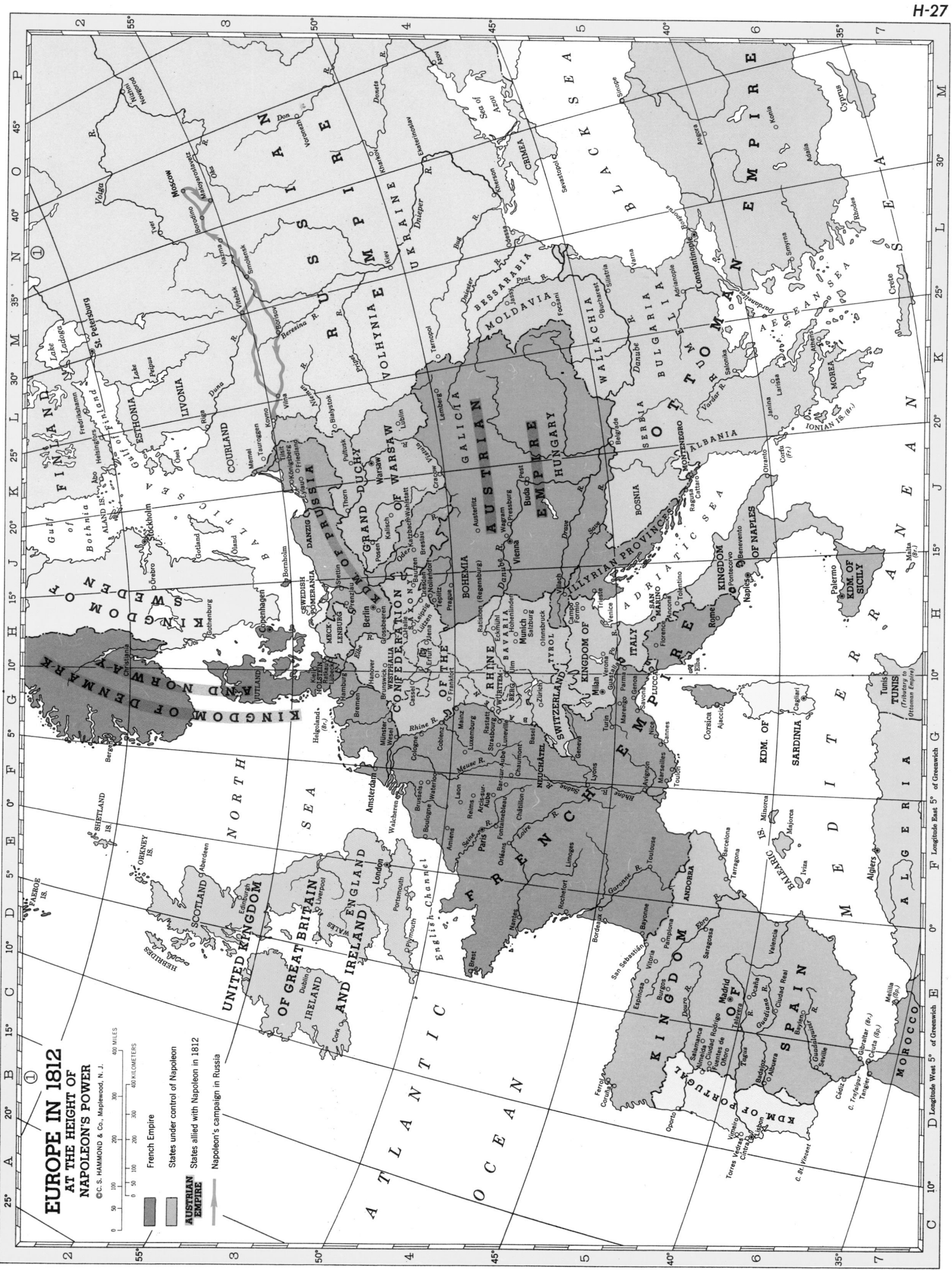

EUROPE IN 1812
AT THE HEIGHT OF NAPOLEON'S POWER
©C. S. HAMMOND & Co., Maplewood, N. J.

French Empire

States under control of Napoleon

States allied with Napoleon in 1812

Napoleon's campaign in Russia

AUSTRIAN EMPIRE

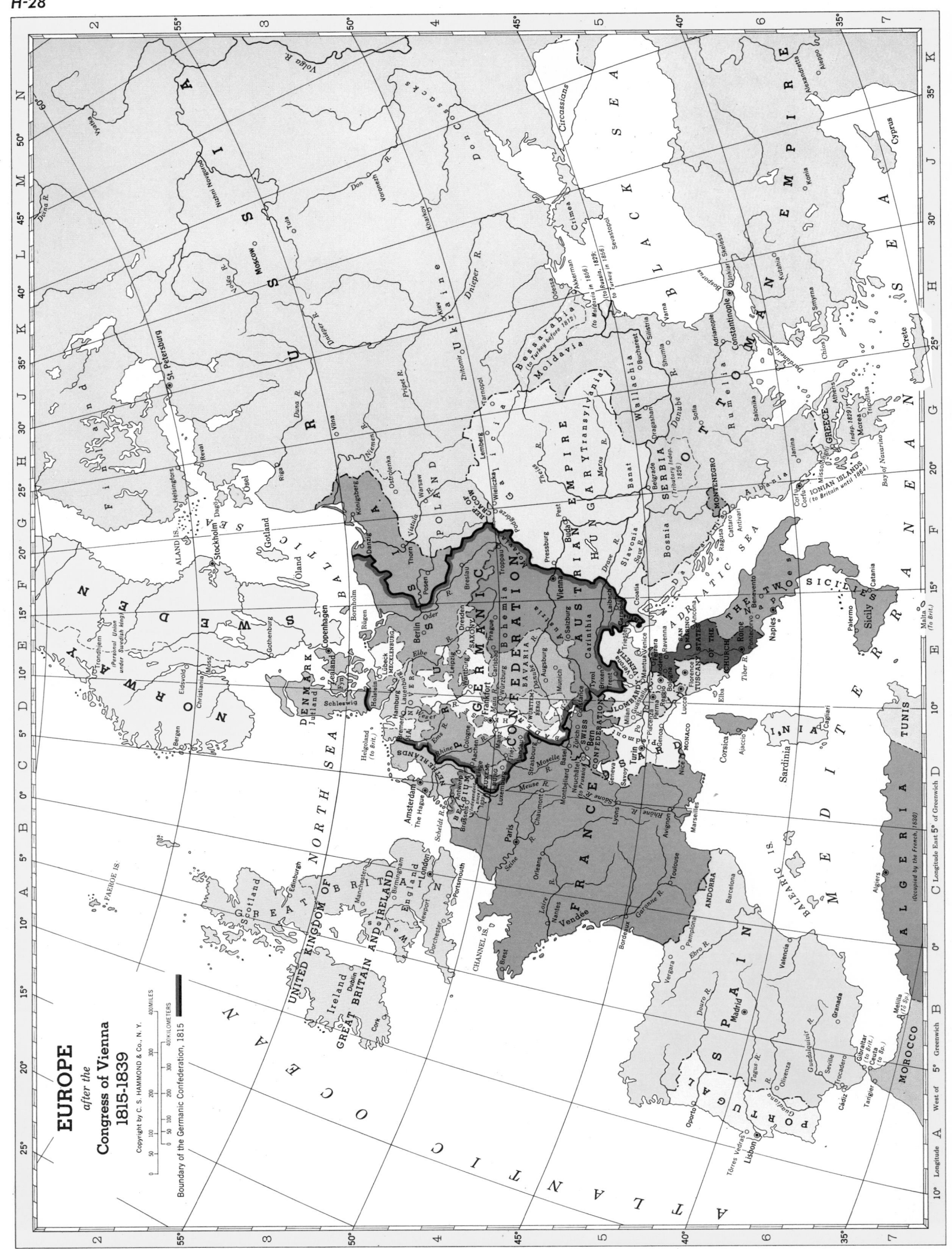

EUROPE
after the
Congress of Vienna
1815-1839

Copyright by C. S. HAMMOND & CO., N.Y.

▬ Boundary of the Germanic Confederation, 1815

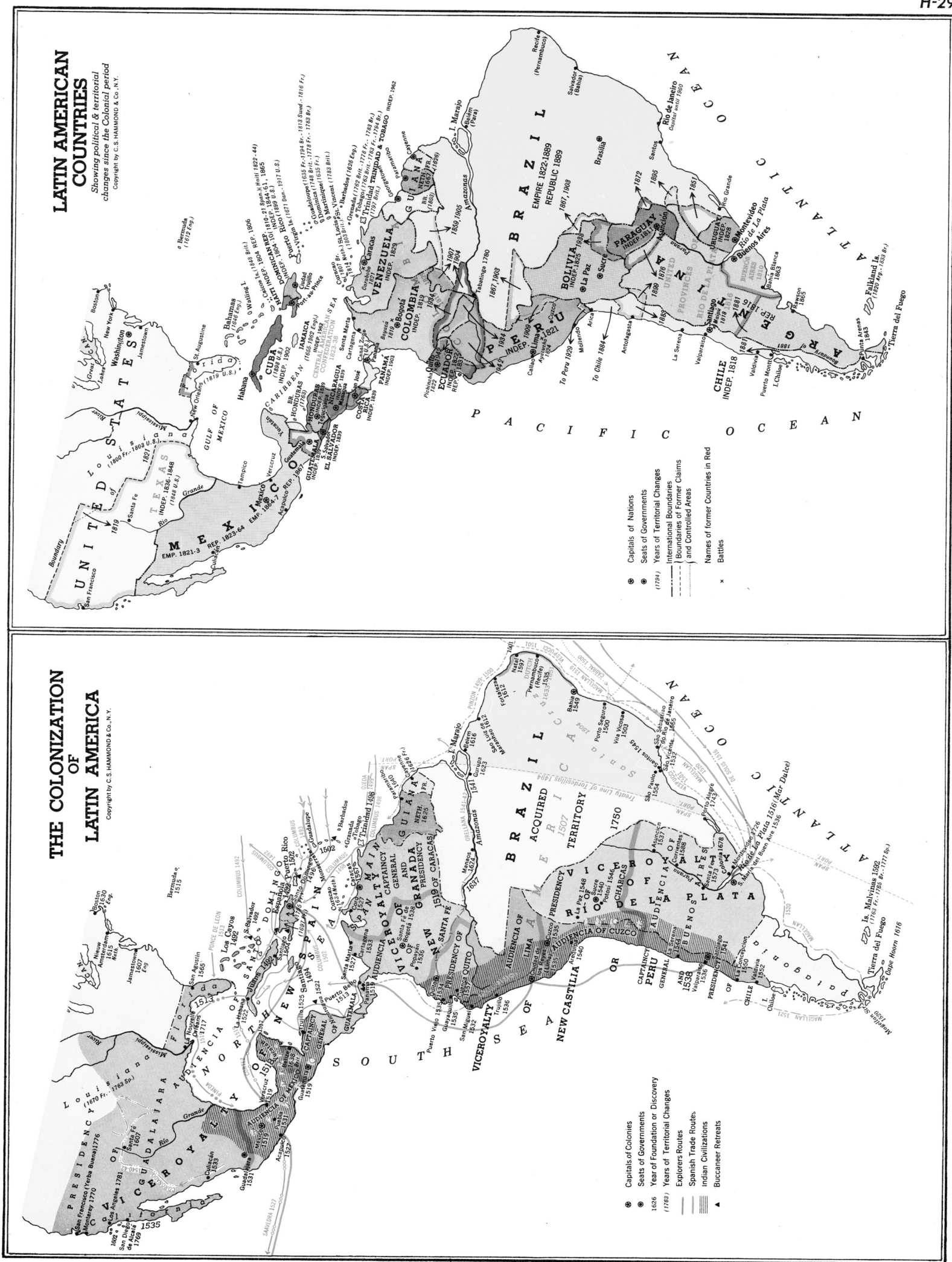

LATIN AMERICAN COUNTRIES

Showing political & territorial
changes since the Colonial period

Copyright by C. S. HAMMOND & Co., N.Y.

Capitals of Nations
Seats of Governments
(1794) Years of Territorial Changes
International Boundaries
Boundaries of Former Claims
and Controlled Areas
Names of former Countries in Red
Battles

THE COLONIZATION
OF
LATIN AMERICA

Copyright by C. S. HAMMOND & Co., N.Y.

Capitals of Colonies
Seats of Governments
1626 Year of Foundation or Discovery
(1763) Years of Territorial Changes
Explorers Routes
Spanish Trade Routes
Indian Civilizations
Buccaneer Retreats

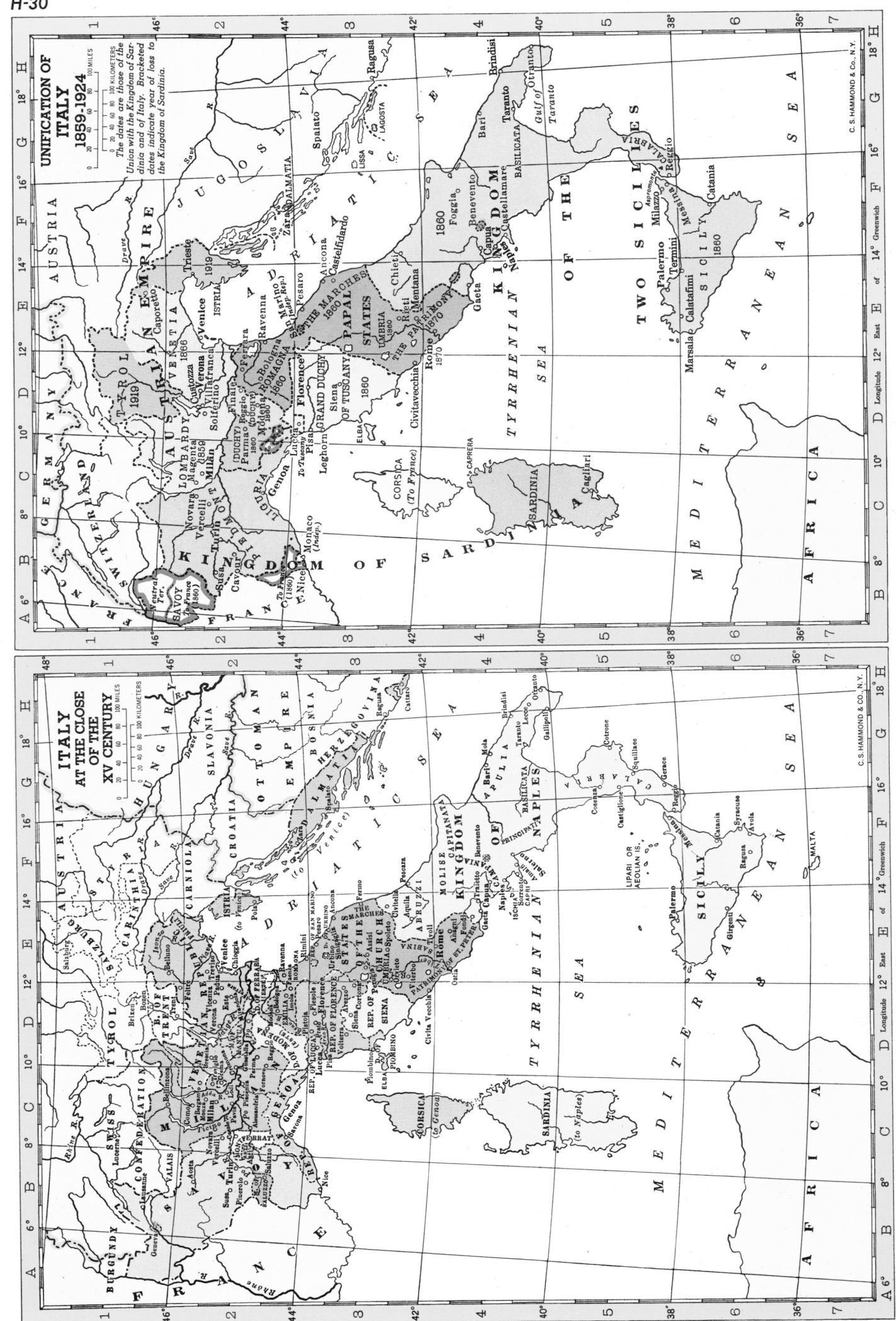

UNIFICATION OF ITALY
1859-1924

The dates are those of the Union with the Kingdom of Sardinia and of Italy. Bracketed dates indicate year of loss to the Kingdom of Sardinia.

ITALY
AT THE CLOSE OF THE
XV CENTURY

C. S. HAMMOND & CO., N.Y.

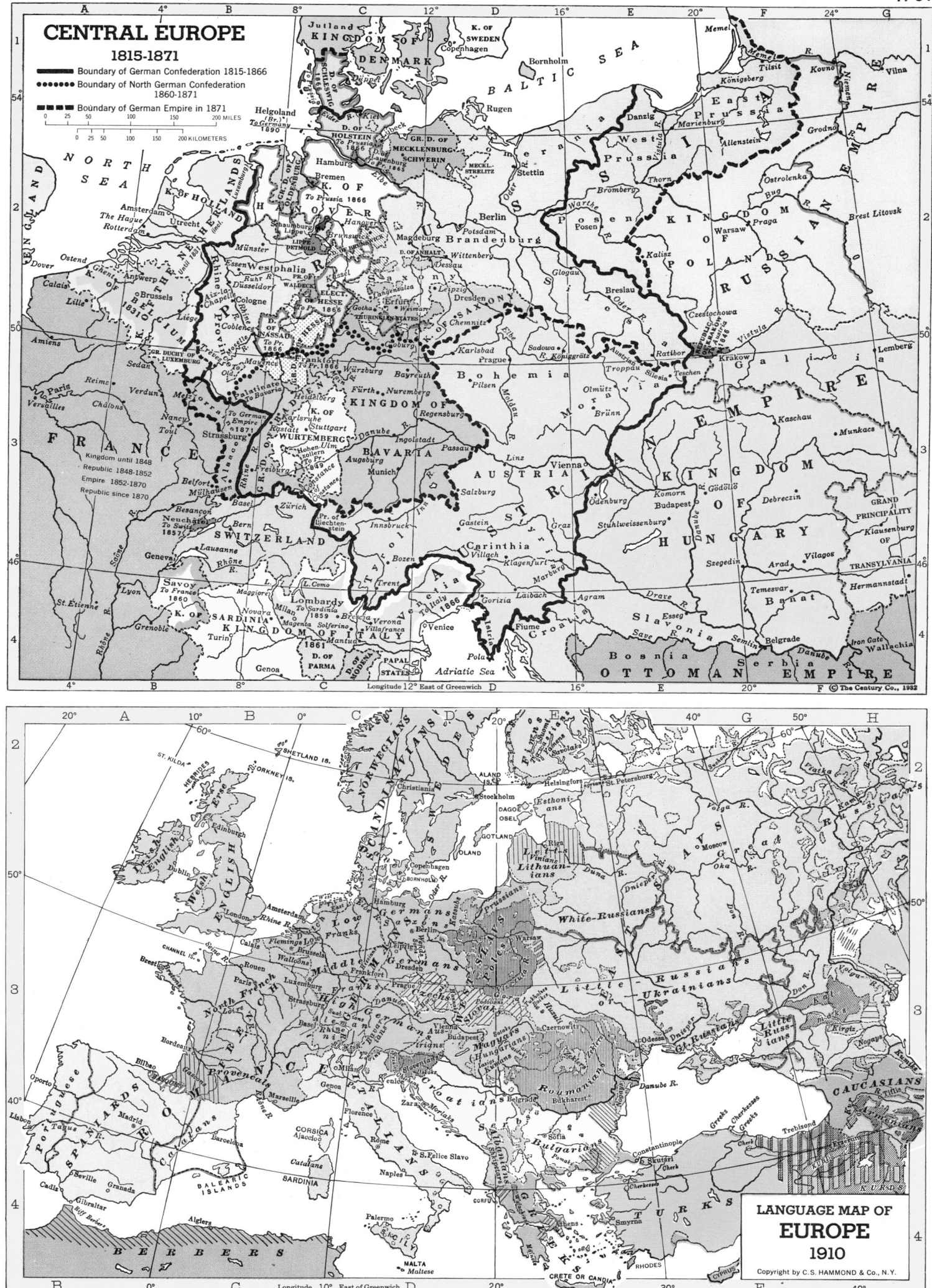

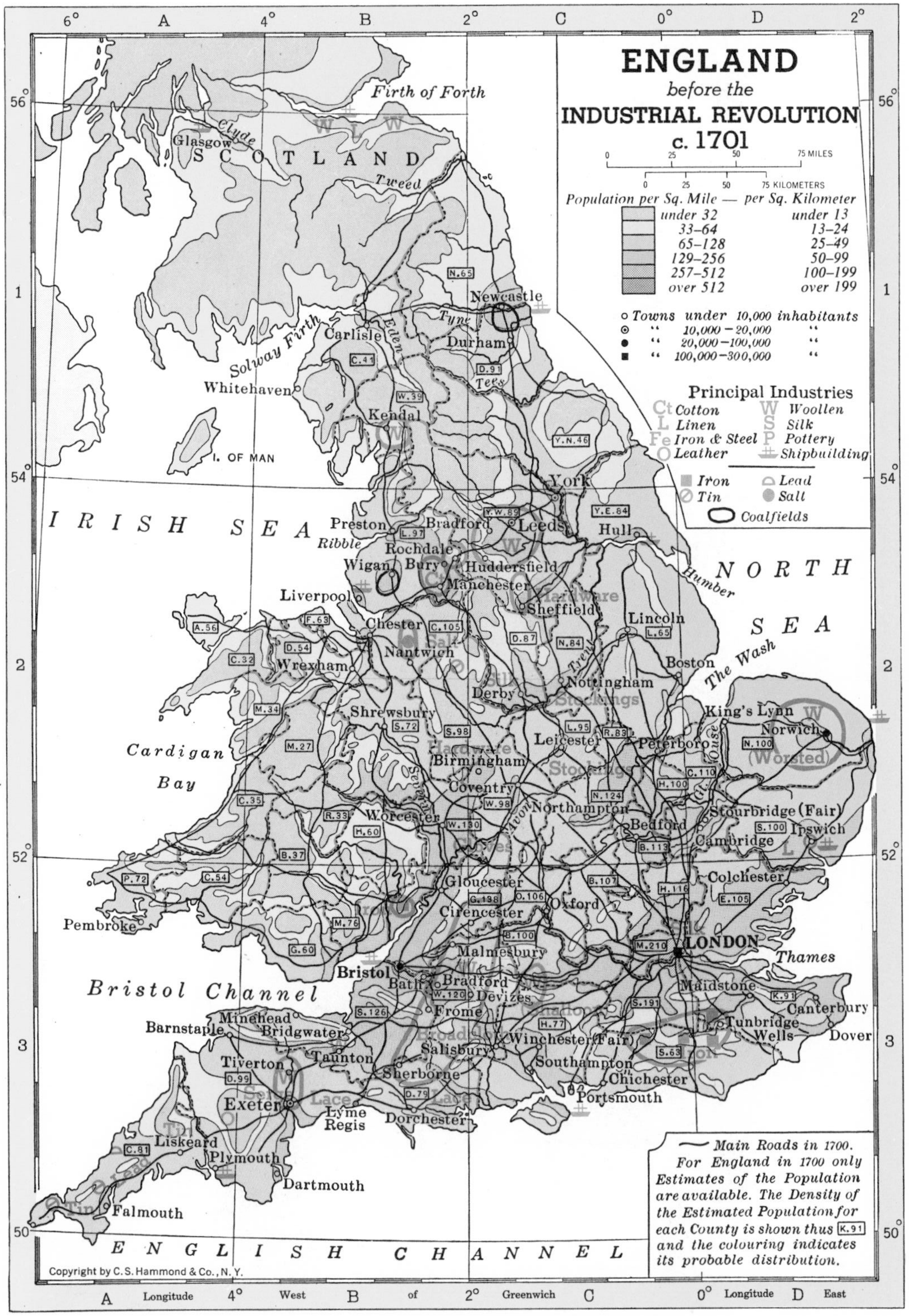

Right map

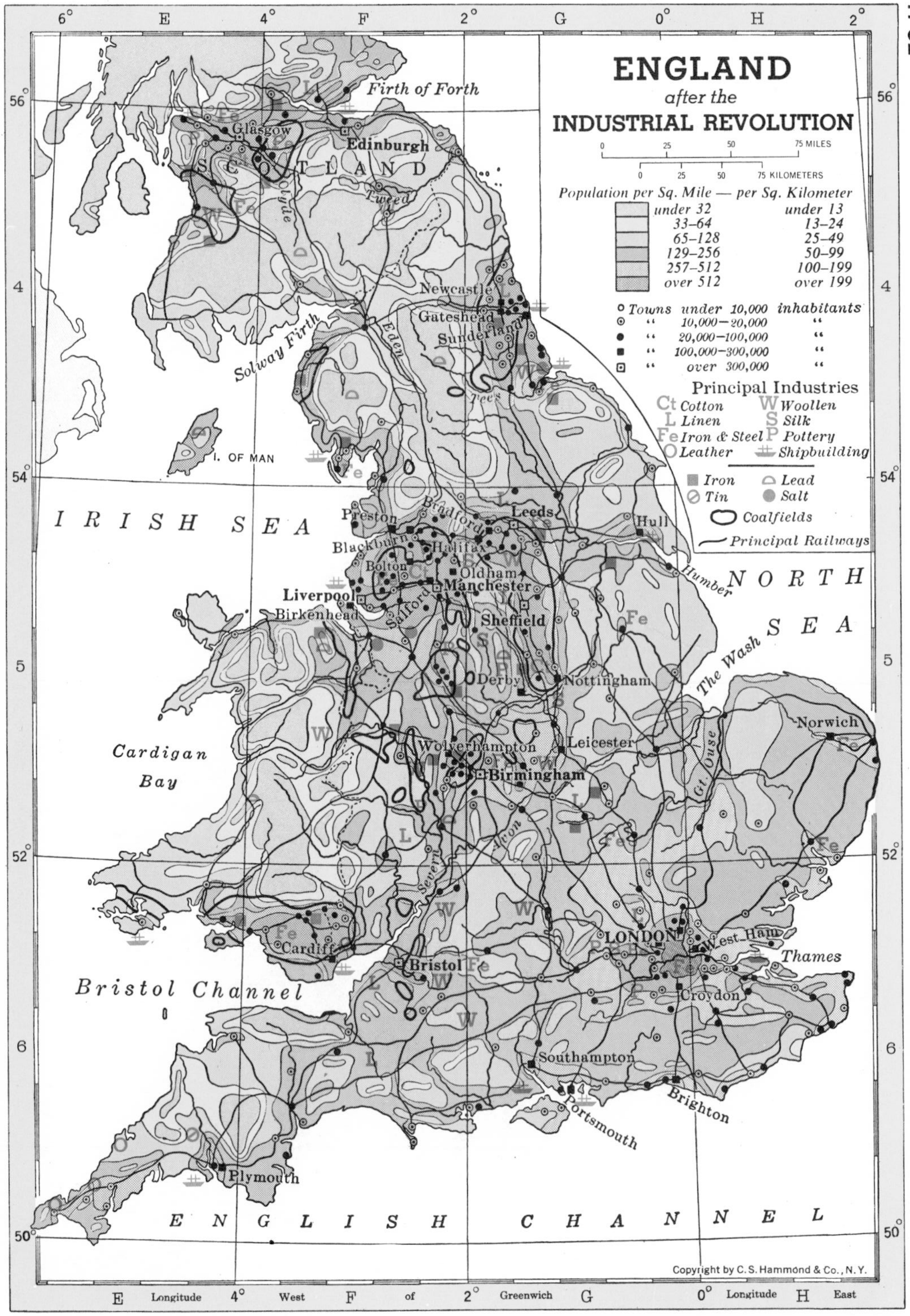

ENGLAND
after the
INDUSTRIAL REVOLUTION

75 KILOMETERS
0   25   50   75
0   25   50   75 MILES

Population per Sq. Mile — per Sq. Kilometer

under 32	under 13
33–64	13–24
65–128	25–49
129–256	50–99
257–512	100–199
over 512	over 199

○ Towns under 10,000 inhabitants
⊙   10,000–20,000
⦿   20,000–100,000
■   100,000–300,000
▣   over 300,000

Principal Industries
Ct Cotton   W Woollen   S Silk
L Linen   P Pottery
Fe Iron & Steel   ⚓ Shipbuilding
○ Leather

△ Iron   △ Lead   ● Salt
⊘ Tin   ● Coalfields
⌒ Principal Railways

Copyright by C. S. Hammond & Co., N.Y.

SCOTLAND
Firth of Forth
Edinburgh
Glasgow
Clyde
Solway Firth
Eden
Tyne
Newcastle
Gateshead
Sunderland
I. OF MAN
IRISH SEA
Preston
Blackburn
Liverpool
Birkenhead
Manchester
Oldham
Bradford
Leeds
Halifax
Sheffield
Hull
NORTH SEA
Norwich
Gt. Ouse
The Wash
Humber
Nottingham
Derby
Leicester
Birmingham
Cardiff
Bristol
Cardigan Bay
Bristol Channel
Plymouth
ENGLISH CHANNEL
Southampton
Portsmouth
Brighton
LONDON
Thames
Croydon
E. Ham
Dover

Left map

ENGLAND
before the
INDUSTRIAL REVOLUTION
c. 1701

75 KILOMETERS
0   25   50   75
0   25   50   75 MILES

Population per Sq. Mile — per Sq. Kilometer

under 32	under 13
33–64	13–24
65–128	25–49
129–256	50–99
257–512	100–199
over 512	over 199

○ Towns under 10,000 inhabitants
⊙   10,000–20,000
⦿   20,000–100,000
■   100,000–300,000

Principal Industries
Ct Cotton   W Woollen   S Silk
L Linen   P Pottery
Fe Iron & Steel   ⚓ Shipbuilding
○ Leather

△ Iron   △ Lead   ● Salt
⊘ Tin   ● Coalfields

— Main Roads in 1700 only
For England in 1700 only
Estimates of the Population
are available. The Density of
the Estimated Population for
each County is shown thus
and the colouring indicates
its probable distribution.

Copyright by C. S. Hammond & Co., N.Y.

SCOTLAND
Firth of Forth
Glasgow
Clyde
Tweed
Solway Firth
Whitehaven
Carlisle
Eden
Newcastle
Durham
Tees
York
I. OF MAN
IRISH SEA
Ribble
Preston
Kendal
Liverpool
Wigan
Bury
Rochdale
Huddersfield
Bradford
Leeds
Manchester
Chester
Nantwich
Wrexham
Shrewsbury
Sheffield
Derby
Nottingham
Leicester
Coventry
Birmingham
Stourbridge
Worcester
Gloucester
Bristol
Bath
Frome
Devizes
Salisbury
Sherborne
Dorchester
Lyme Regis
Dartmouth
Exeter
Tiverton
Taunton
Bridgewater
Minehead
Barnstaple
Liskeard
Plymouth
Falmouth
Pembroke
Cardigan Bay
Bristol Channel
ENGLISH CHANNEL
NORTH SEA
The Wash
Humber
Boston
Lincoln
Hull
King's Lynn
Norwich (Worsted)
Cambridge (Fair)
Ipswich
Colchester
Northampton
Oxford
Banbury
Malmesbury
Winchester
Southampton
Portsmouth
Chichester
Maidstone
Canterbury
Tunbridge Wells
Dover
LONDON
Thames
Greenwich

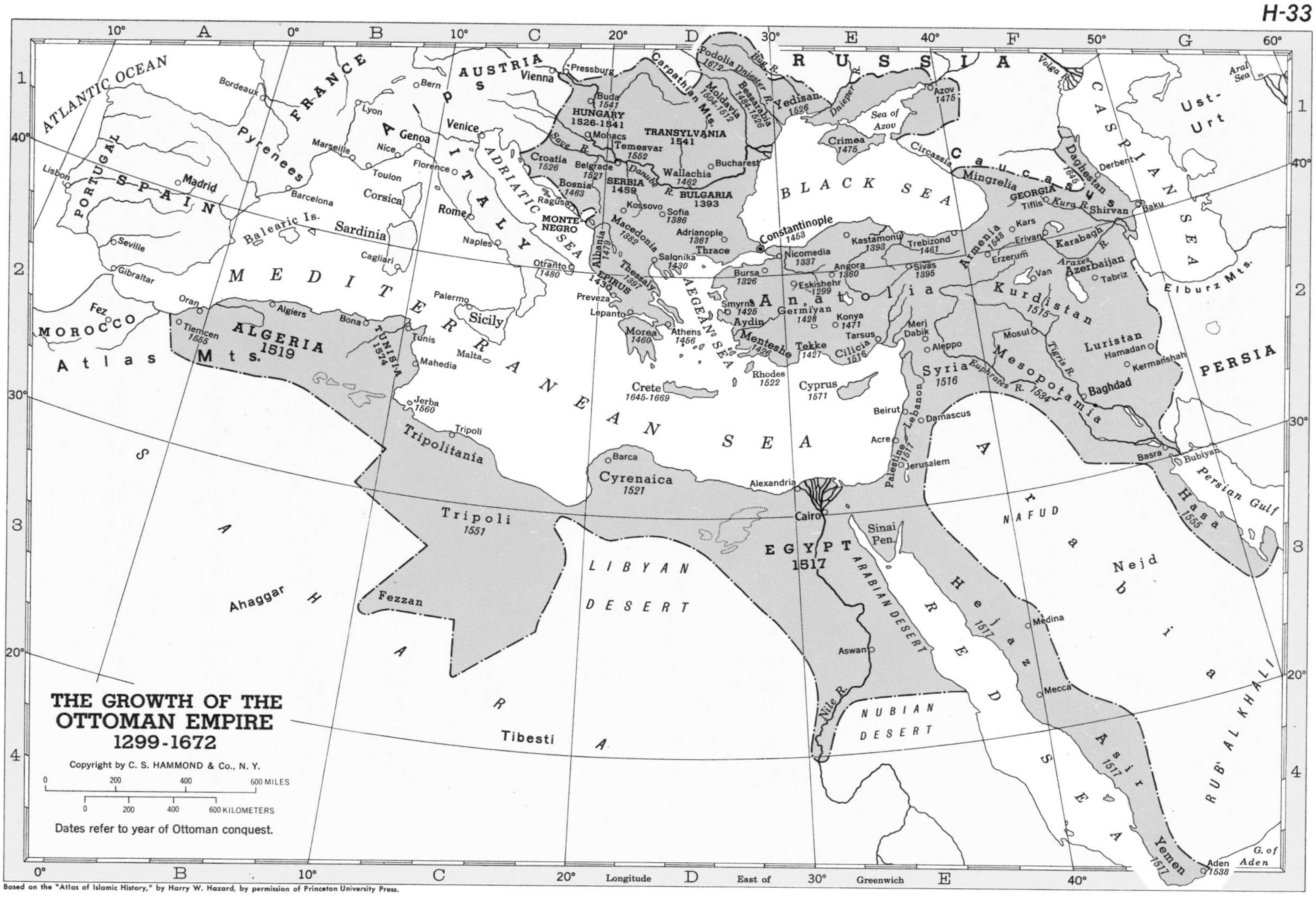

ATLANTIC OCEAN
FRANCE
SPAIN
PORTUGAL
AUSTRIA
RUSSIA
HUNGARY 1526-1541
TRANSYLVANIA 1541
Wallachia 1462
Moldavia
SERBIA 1459
BULGARIA 1393
Bosnia 1463
Croatia 1526
MONTE-NEGRO
Albania 1479
Macedonia 1382
Thessaly 1391
EPIRUS 1430
Crimea 1475
Yedisan 1526
Azov 1475
Podolia 1672
BLACK SEA
Constantinople 1453
CASPIAN SEA
GEORGIA
Mingrelia
Daghestan
Shirvan
Armenia
Karabagh
Azerbaijan
Kurdistan 1515
Luristan
PERSIA
Mesopotamia 1534
Baghdad
Syria 1516
Cyprus 1571
Crete 1645-1669
Rhodes 1522
Anatolia
Rome
Naples
Sicily
Sardinia
Corsica
Balearic Is.
MEDITERRANEAN SEA
ALGERIA 1519
TUNISIA 1574
MOROCCO
Atlas Mts.
Tripolitania
Tripoli 1551
Cyrenaica 1521
Fezzan
LIBYAN DESERT
EGYPT 1517
Cairo
Alexandria
Sinai Pen.
ARABIAN DESERT
NUBIAN DESERT
SAHARA
Ahaggar
Tibesti
RED SEA
Hejaz 1517
Medina
Mecca
Asir 1517
Yemen 1517
Aden 1538
G. of Aden
Arabia
NAFUD
Nejd
RUB' AL KHALI
Hasa 1555
Persian Gulf
Basra
Longitude East of Greenwich

THE GROWTH OF THE OTTOMAN EMPIRE 1299-1672

Copyright by C. S. HAMMOND & Co., N. Y.

0 200 400 600 MILES
0 200 400 600 KILOMETERS

Dates refer to year of Ottoman conquest.

Based on the "Atlas of Islamic History," by Harry W. Hazard, by permission of Princeton University Press.

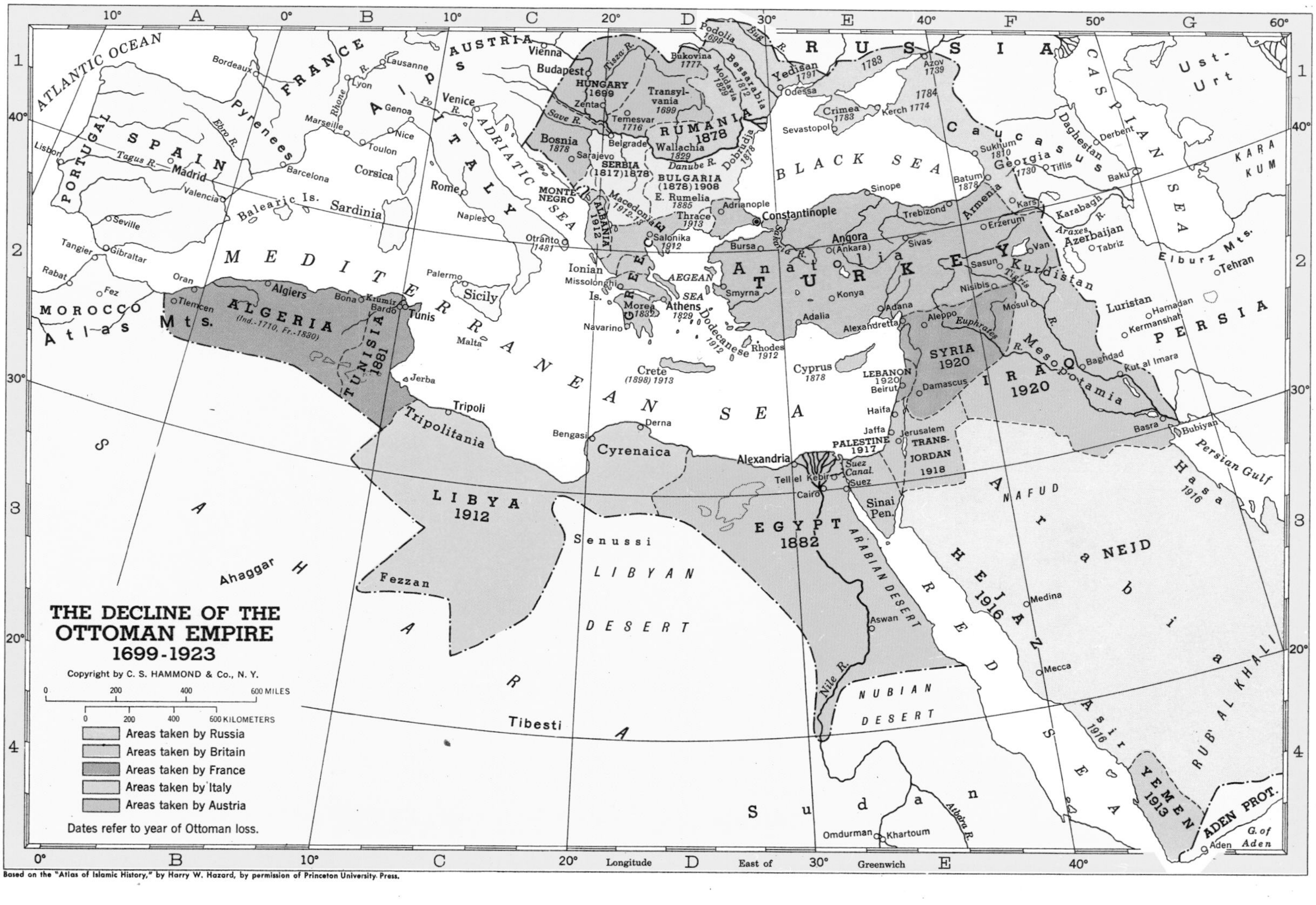

ATLANTIC OCEAN
FRANCE
SPAIN
PORTUGAL
AUSTRIA
RUSSIA
HUNGARY 1699
Transylvania 1699
RUMANIA 1878
Wallachia 1829
Bukovina 1777
Bessarabia 1812
Bosnia 1878
SERBIA (1817) 1878
BULGARIA (1878) 1908
E. Rumelia 1885
Thrace 1913
MONTE-NEGRO
ALBANIA 1912
Macedonia 1912-13
GREECE
Morea 1832
Athens 1829
Crimea 1783
Yedisan 1791
Azov 1739
BLACK SEA
Constantinople
Angora (Ankara)
TURKEY
Caucasus
Georgia 1730
Batum 1878
Kars
CASPIAN SEA
PERSIA
Kurdistan
SYRIA 1920
IRAQ 1920
LEBANON 1920
PALESTINE 1917
TRANS-JORDAN 1918
Cyprus 1878
Crete (1898) 1913
Dodecanese 1912
Rhodes 1912
MEDITERRANEAN SEA
ALGERIA (Ind.-1710, Fr.-1830)
TUNISIA 1881
MOROCCO
LIBYA 1912
Cyrenaica
Tripolitania
Senussi
EGYPT 1882
Suez Canal
LIBYAN DESERT
NUBIAN DESERT
Sudan
Khartoum
Omdurman
HEJAZ 1916
NEJD
Asir 1916
YEMEN 1913
ADEN PROT.
Hasa 1916
RUB' AL KHALI
Longitude East of Greenwich

THE DECLINE OF THE OTTOMAN EMPIRE 1699-1923

Copyright by C. S. HAMMOND & Co., N. Y.

0 200 400 600 MILES
0 200 400 600 KILOMETERS

- Areas taken by Russia
- Areas taken by Britain
- Areas taken by France
- Areas taken by Italy
- Areas taken by Austria

Dates refer to year of Ottoman loss.

Based on the "Atlas of Islamic History," by Harry W. Hazard, by permission of Princeton University Press.

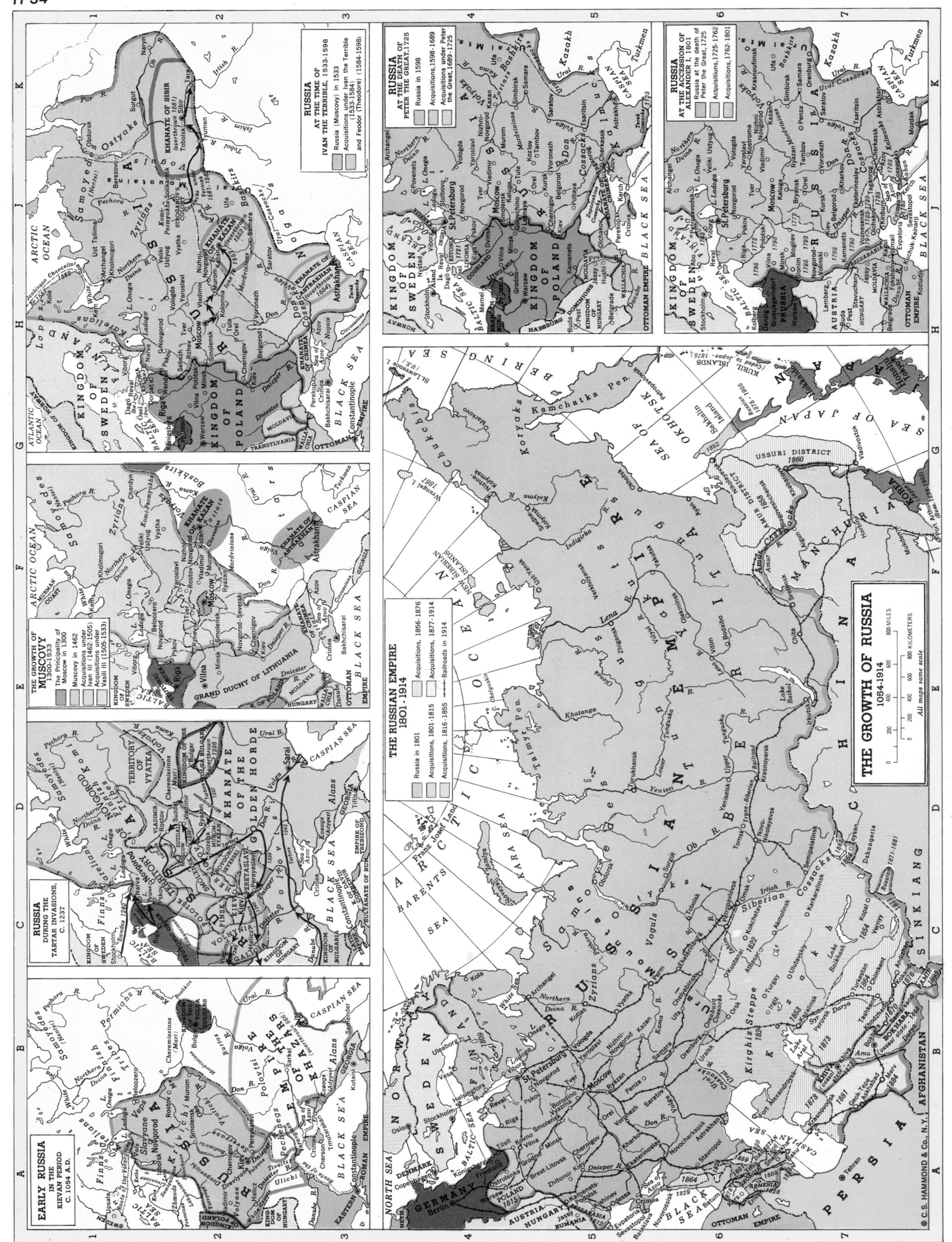

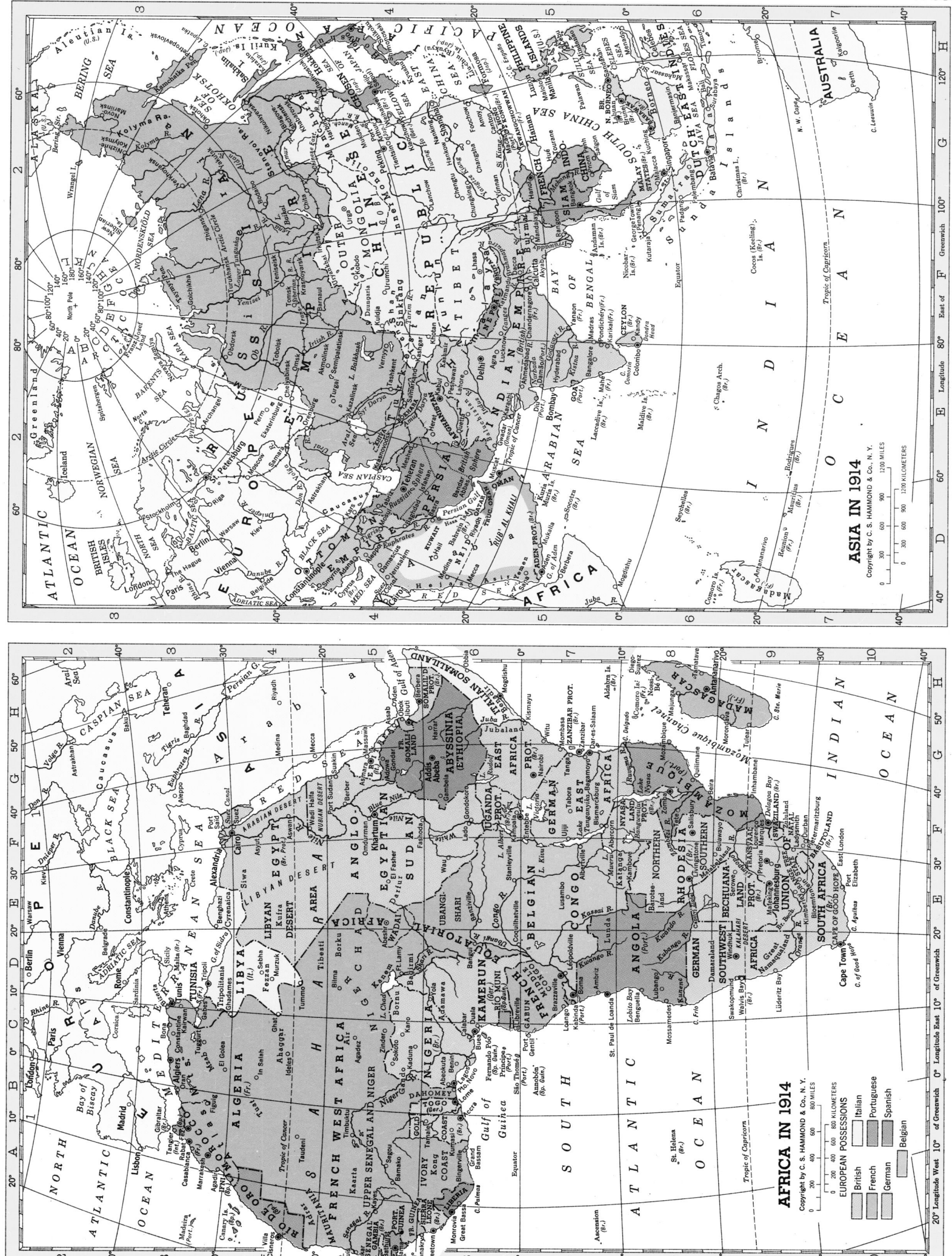

ASIA IN 1914

Copyright by C. S. HAMMOND & Co., N. Y.

AFRICA IN 1914

Copyright by C. S. HAMMOND & Co., N. Y.

EUROPEAN POSSESSIONS
British
French
German
Italian
Portuguese
Spanish
Belgian

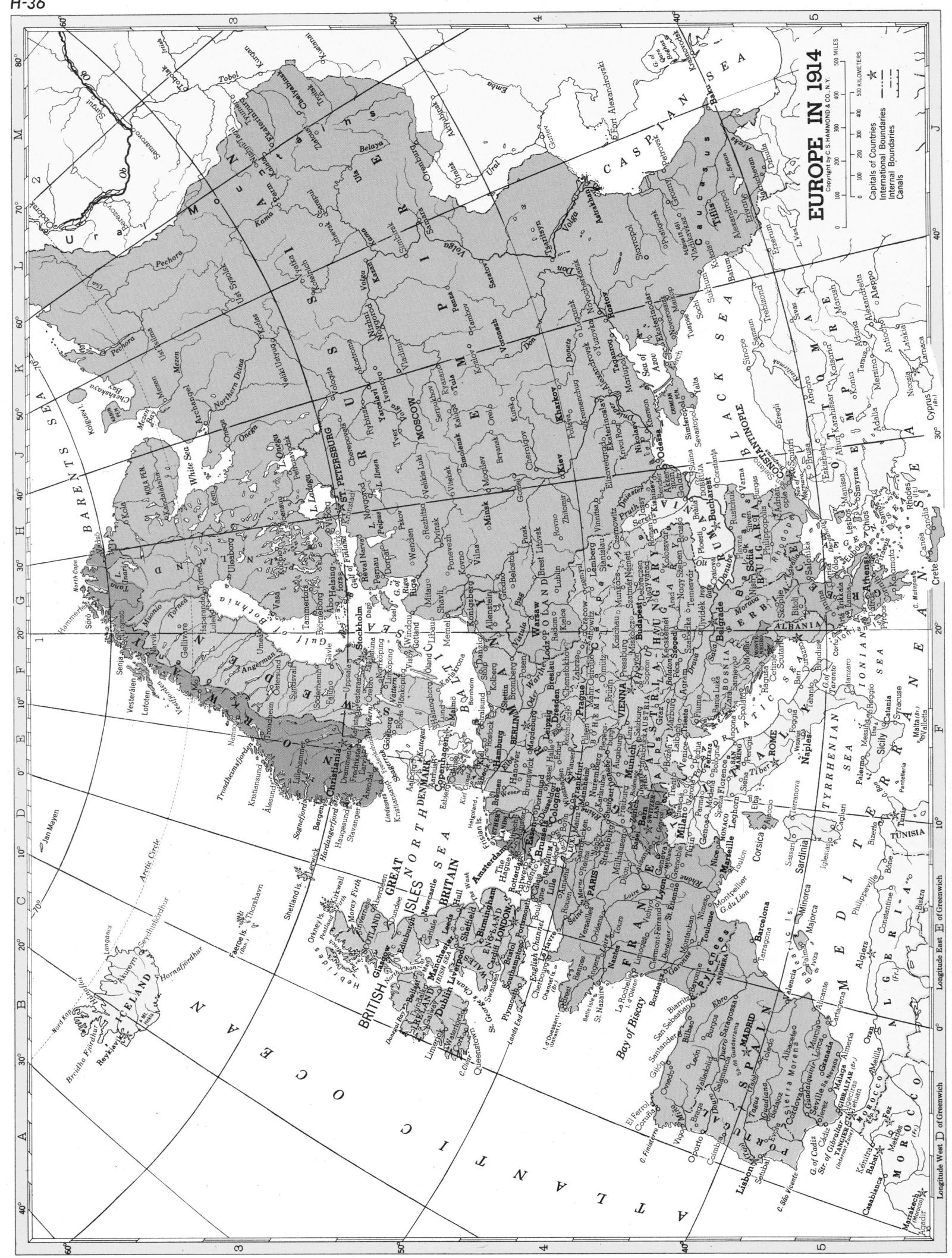

EUROPE IN 1914

Copyright by C. S. HAMMOND & CO., N.Y.

Capitals of Countries
International Boundaries
Internal Boundaries
Canals

100   200   300   400   500 KILOMETERS
100   200   300   400   500 MILES

EUROPE AND THE NEAR EAST

0	100	200	300	400	500 MILES
0	100	200	300	400	500 KILOMETERS

— — — Stabilized Line on the Western Front, 1914-1917

— — — Eastern Front on the Eve of the Russian Revolution, Oct. 1917

·········· Limit of Allied Advances in the East

Area Occupied by the Central Powers after Brest Litovsk Treaty, 1918

THE FIRST WORLD WAR
1914-1918

© C. S. HAMMOND & Co., Maplewood, N.J.

The Allies

Neutral States

The Central Powers

Areas Occupied by the Central Powers

→ Advances of the Allies

→ Advances of the Central Powers

THE WESTERN FRONT

0	20	40	60	80 MILES
0	20	40	60	80 KILOMETERS

——— Limit of German Advance, 1914

——— Limit of Trench Warfare, 1914-1917

– – – Hindenburg Line, 1917

— · — Limit of Final German Advance, 1918

—··—··— Armistice Line, November 11, 1918

——— Limit of Allied Occupation Zone

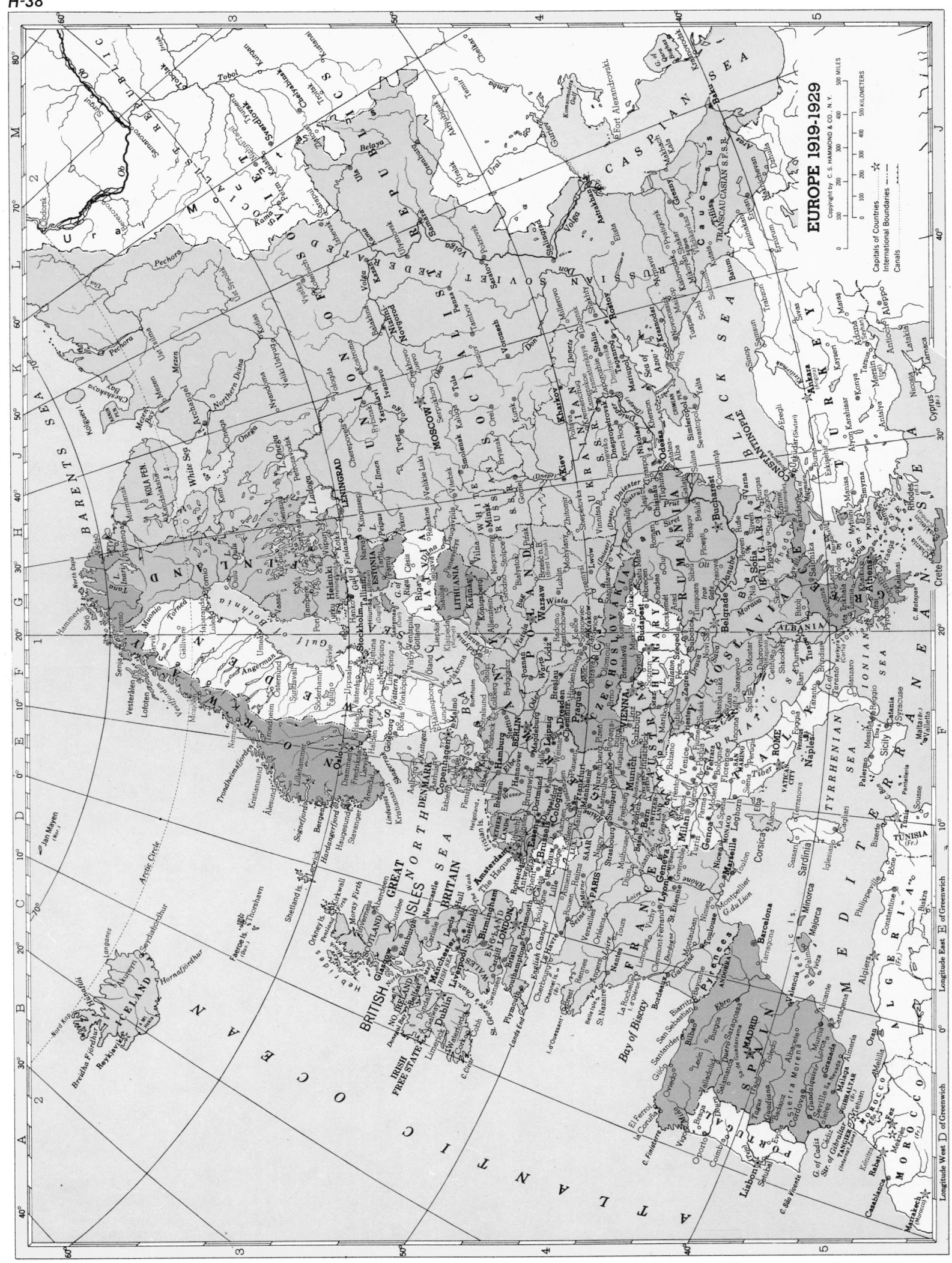

EUROPE 1919-1929

Copyright by C. S. HAMMOND & CO., N.Y.

Capitals of Countries ☆
International Boundaries _____
Canals _____

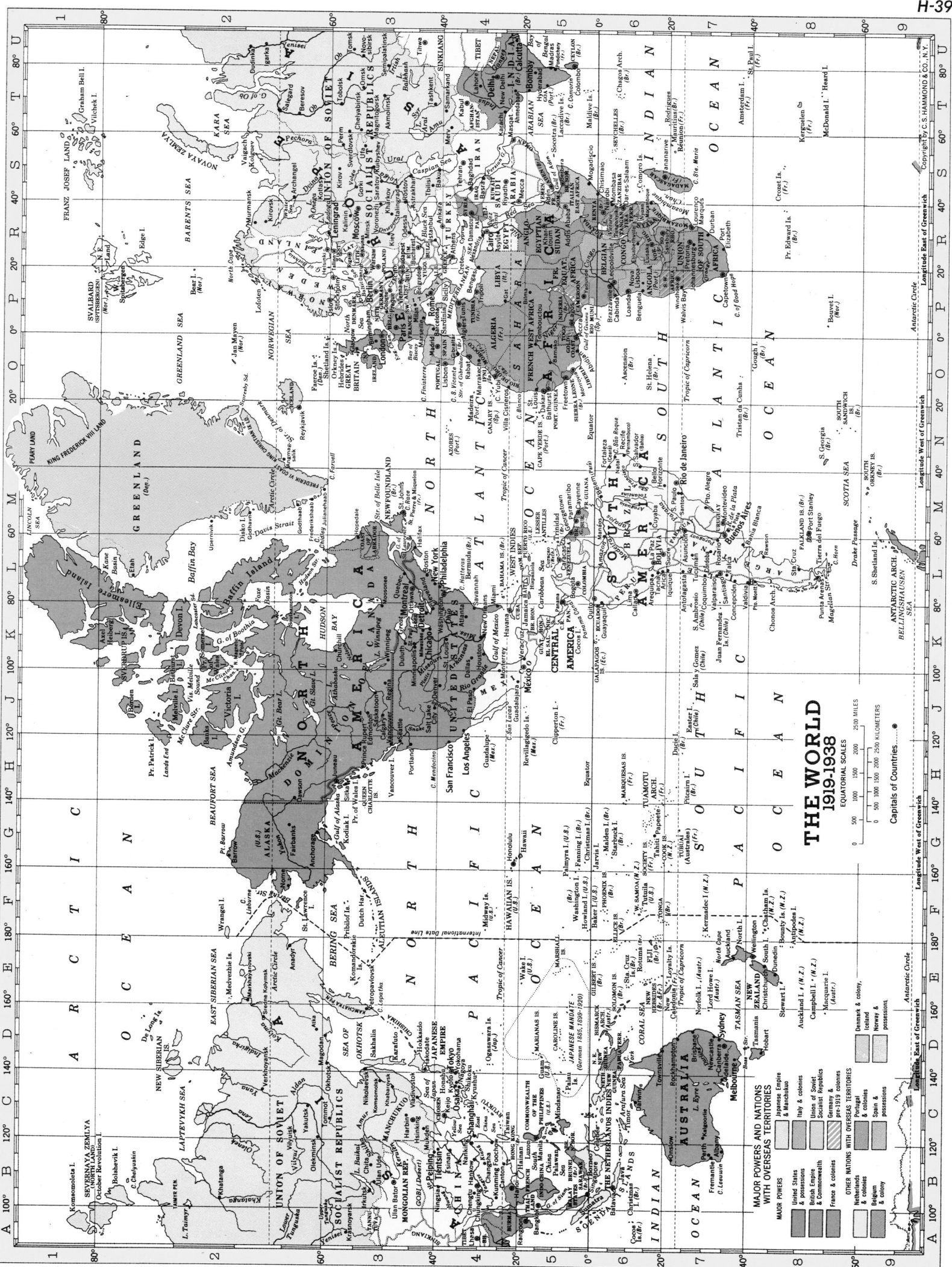

THE WORLD
1919-1938

EQUATORIAL SCALES

Capitals of Countries.......●

MAJOR POWERS AND NATIONS WITH OVERSEAS TERRITORIES

MAJOR POWERS

- United States & possessions
- British Empire & Commonwealth
- France & colonies
- Japanese Empire & Manchukuo
- Italy & colonies
- Union of Soviet Socialist Republics
- Germany & pre-1919 colonies

OTHER NATIONS WITH OVERSEAS TERRITORIES

- Netherlands & colonies
- Belgium & colony
- Portugal & colonies
- Spain & possessions
- Denmark & colony, Iceland
- Norway & possessions

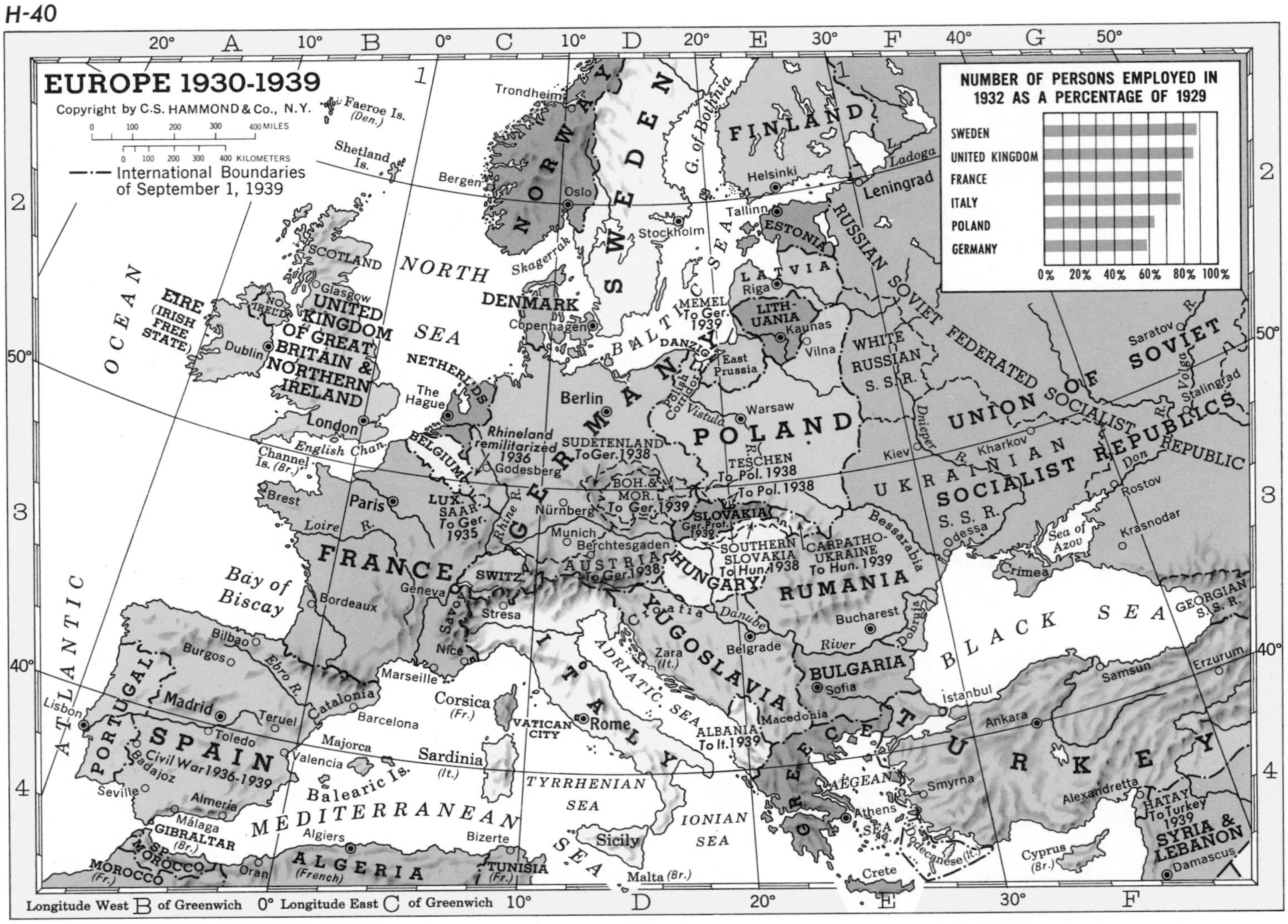

EUROPE 1930-1939

Copyright by C.S. HAMMOND & Co., N.Y.

0 100 200 300 400 MILES
0 100 200 300 400 KILOMETERS

— — — International Boundaries of September 1, 1939

NUMBER OF PERSONS EMPLOYED IN 1932 AS A PERCENTAGE OF 1929

SWEDEN
UNITED KINGDOM
FRANCE
ITALY
POLAND
GERMANY

0% 20% 40% 60% 80% 100%

ATLANTIC OCEAN

NORTH SEA

Faeroe Is. (Den.)
Shetland Is.
Trondheim
Bergen
Oslo
NORWAY
SWEDEN
Stockholm
Skagerrak
Skager
G. of Bothnia
FINLAND
Helsinki
Leningrad
L. Ladoga

SCOTLAND
Glasgow
NO. IRELAND
EIRE (IRISH FREE STATE)
Dublin
UNITED KINGDOM OF GREAT BRITAIN & NORTHERN IRELAND
London
English Chan.
Channel Is. (Br.)
Brest

DENMARK
Copenhagen
BALTIC SEA
Tallinn
ESTONIA
Riga
LATVIA
MEMEL To Ger. 1939
LITH-UANIA
Kaunas
Vilna
WHITE RUSSIAN S.S.R.
RUSSIAN SOVIET FEDERATED SOCIALIST

Saratov
SOVIET UNION OF SOCIALIST REPUBLICS
Stalingrad
Volga R.

NETHERLDS.
The Hague
BELGIUM
Berlin
DANZIG
East Prussia
Vistula
Warsaw
POLAND
Corridor
Kiev
UKRAINIAN SOCIALIST REPUBLICS S.S.R.
Kharkov
Don R.
Rostov
Krasnodar

Rhineland remilitarized 1936
Godesberg
GERMANY
SUDETENLAND To Ger. 1938
TESCHEN To Pol. 1938
BOH. & MOR. To Ger. 1939
To Pol. 1938
LUX.
SAAR To Ger. 1935
Nürnberg
Munich
Berchtesgaden
SLOVAKIA Ger. Prot. 1939
SOUTHERN SLOVAKIA To Hun. 1938
CARPATHO-UKRAINE To Hun. 1939
Bessarabia

Paris
Loire R.
FRANCE
Rhine R.
SWITZ.
Geneva
Savoy
AUSTRIA To Ger. 1938
HUNGARY
Danube
RUMANIA
Odessa
Sea of Azov
Crimea

Bay of Biscay
Bordeaux
Stresa
Nice
Croatia
Belgrade
River
Bucharest
BLACK SEA
Georgian S.S.R.

Bilbao
Burgos
Ebro R.
Marseille
Corsica (Fr.)
ITALY
Zara (It.)
ADRIATIC SEA
YUGOSLAVIA
Macedonia
BULGARIA
Sofia
Istanbul
Ankara
Samsun
Erzurum
TURKEY

Lisbon
Madrid
Toledo
Teruel
SPAIN
Civil War 1936-1939
Valencia
Barcelona
Catalonia
Majorca
Balearic Is.
Sardinia (It.)
Rome
VATICAN CITY
ALBANIA To It. 1939
GREECE
AEGEAN SEA
Athens
Smyrna
Alexandretta
HATAY To Turkey 1939
SYRIA & LEBANON
Damascus

PORTUGAL
Badajoz
Seville
Almeria
Málaga
GIBRALTAR (Br.)
MOROCCO (Fr.)
Algiers
Oran
MEDITERRANEAN SEA
ALGERIA (French)
TUNISIA (Fr.)
Bizerte
Sicily
TYRRHENIAN SEA
IONIAN SEA
Malta (Br.)
Crete
Dodecanese (It.)
Cyprus (Br.)

Longitude West B of Greenwich   0° Longitude East C of Greenwich   10°   D   20°   E   30°   F

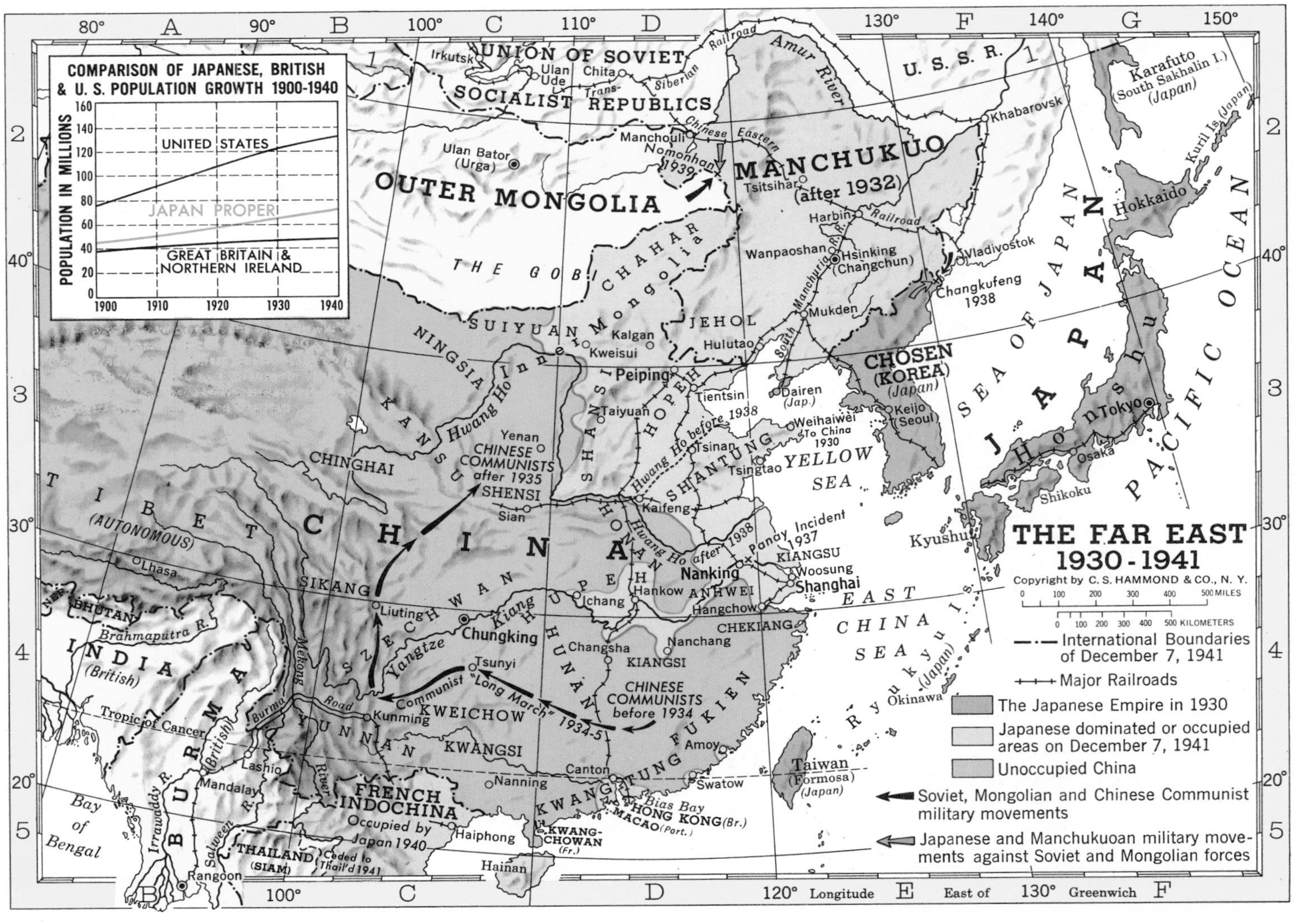

THE FAR EAST 1930-1941

Copyright by C.S. HAMMOND & CO., N.Y.

0 100 200 300 400 500 MILES
0 100 200 300 400 500 KILOMETERS

— — — International Boundaries of December 7, 1941
+ + + Major Railroads

The Japanese Empire in 1930
Japanese dominated or occupied areas on December 7, 1941
Unoccupied China

← Soviet, Mongolian and Chinese Communist military movements
← Japanese and Manchukuoan military movements against Soviet and Mongolian forces

COMPARISON OF JAPANESE, BRITISH & U.S. POPULATION GROWTH 1900-1940

POPULATION IN MILLIONS

160
140
120
100
80
60
40
20

UNITED STATES
JAPAN PROPER
GREAT BRITAIN & NORTHERN IRELAND

1900 1910 1920 1930 1940

UNION OF SOVIET SOCIALIST REPUBLICS

Irkutsk
Ulan Ude
Chita
Trans-Siberian Railroad
Amur River
U.S.S.R.
Khabarovsk
Karafuto (South Sakhalin I.) (Japan)

Ulan Bator (Urga)
OUTER MONGOLIA
Manchouli
Nomonhan 1939
Chinese Eastern Railroad
MANCHUKUO (after 1932)
Tsitsihar
Kuril Is. (Japan)

THE GOBI
CHAHAR
Inner Mongolia
Harbin
Railroad
Hsinking (Changchun)
Wanpaoshan
Vladivostok
Hokkaido

NINGSIA
SUIYUAN
Kalgan
Kweisui
JEHOL
Hulutao
Mukden
Changkufeng 1938
SEA OF JAPAN

KANSU
Hwang Ho
Yenan
CHINESE COMMUNISTS after 1935
SHENSI
Peiping
HOPEH
Tientsin
Dairen (Jap.)
CHÖSEN (KOREA) (Japan)
Keijo Seoul
Weihaiwei To China 1930

CHINGHAI
Sian
SHANSI
Taiyuan
Tsinan
Tsingtao (Jap.)
SHANTUNG
YELLOW SEA
Osaka
PACIFIC OCEAN

TIBET (AUTONOMOUS)
Lhasa
HONAN
Kaifeng
Hwang Ho before 1938
Hwang Ho after 1938
JAPAN
Tokyo
HONSHU

BHUTAN
Brahmaputra R.
CHINA
Liuting
SZECHWAN
Chungking
Hwang Ho
HUPEH
Ichang
Hankow
ANHWEI
Nanking
Panay Incident 1937
KIANGSU
Woosung
Shanghai
Hangchow
CHEKIANG
Shikoku
Kyushu

INDIA (British)
SIKANG
Tsunyi
Yangtze
Kiang
HUNAN
Changsha
Nanchang
KIANGSI
EAST CHINA SEA
Kyushu

Tropic of Cancer
Mekong
Communist "Long March" 1934-5
KWEICHOW
Kunming
YUNNAN
CHINESE COMMUNISTS before 1934
FUKIEN
Amoy
Ryukyu Is. (Japan)
Okinawa
Taiwan (Formosa) (Japan)

BURMA (British)
Lashio
Mandalay
Burma Road
KWANGSI
Nanning
KWANGTUNG
Canton
Swatow
Bias Bay
HONG KONG (Br.)
MACAO (Port.)

Bay of Bengal
Irrawaddy R.
Salween R.
Rangoon
THAILAND (SIAM)
FRENCH INDOCHINA
Occupied by Japan 1940
Haiphong
KWANG-CHOWAN (Fr.)
Hainan
Ceded to Thail. 1941

80° A 90° B 100° C 110° D 120° Longitude E 130° East of Greenwich F G 140° 150°

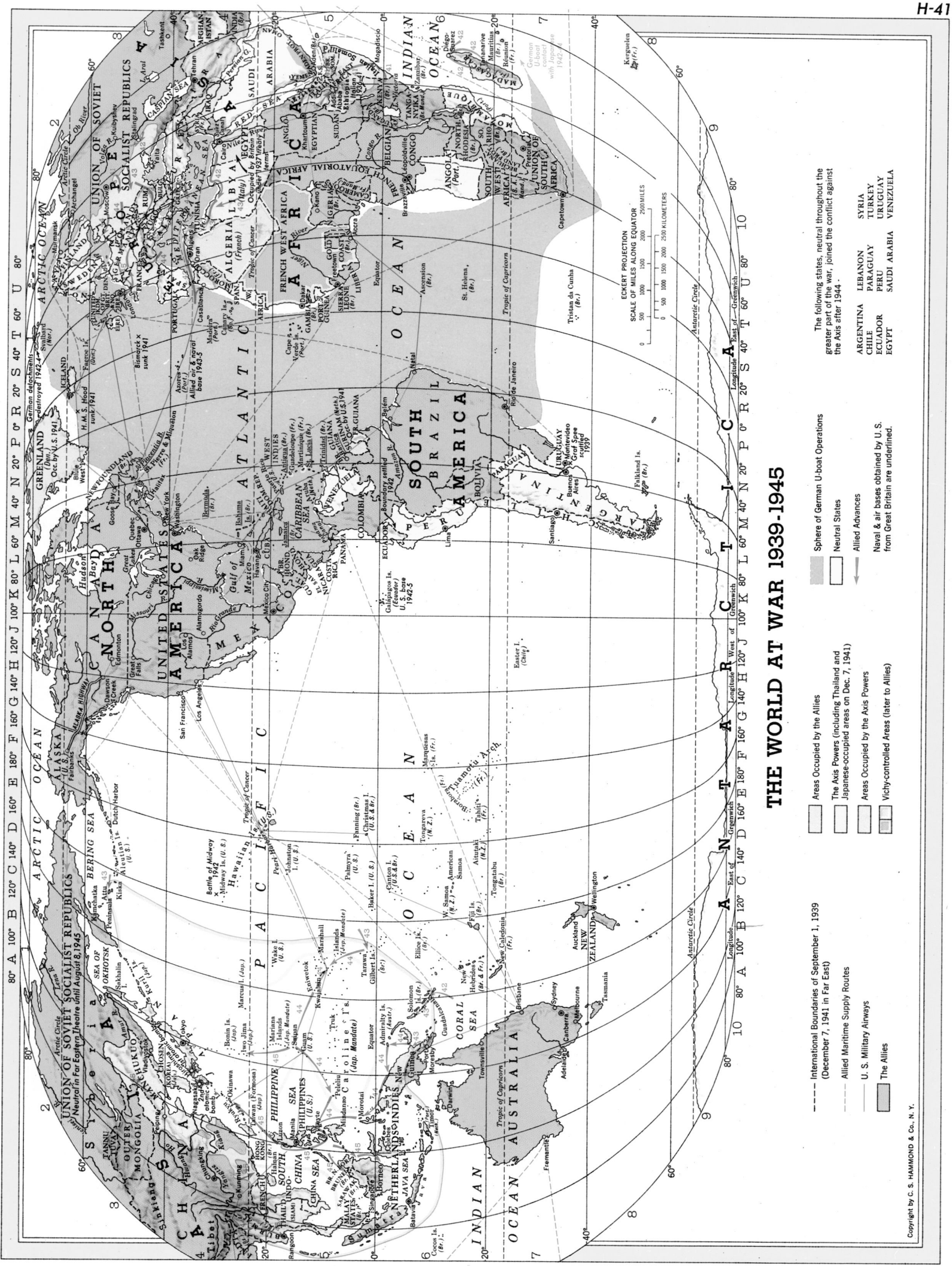

THE WORLD AT WAR 1939-1945

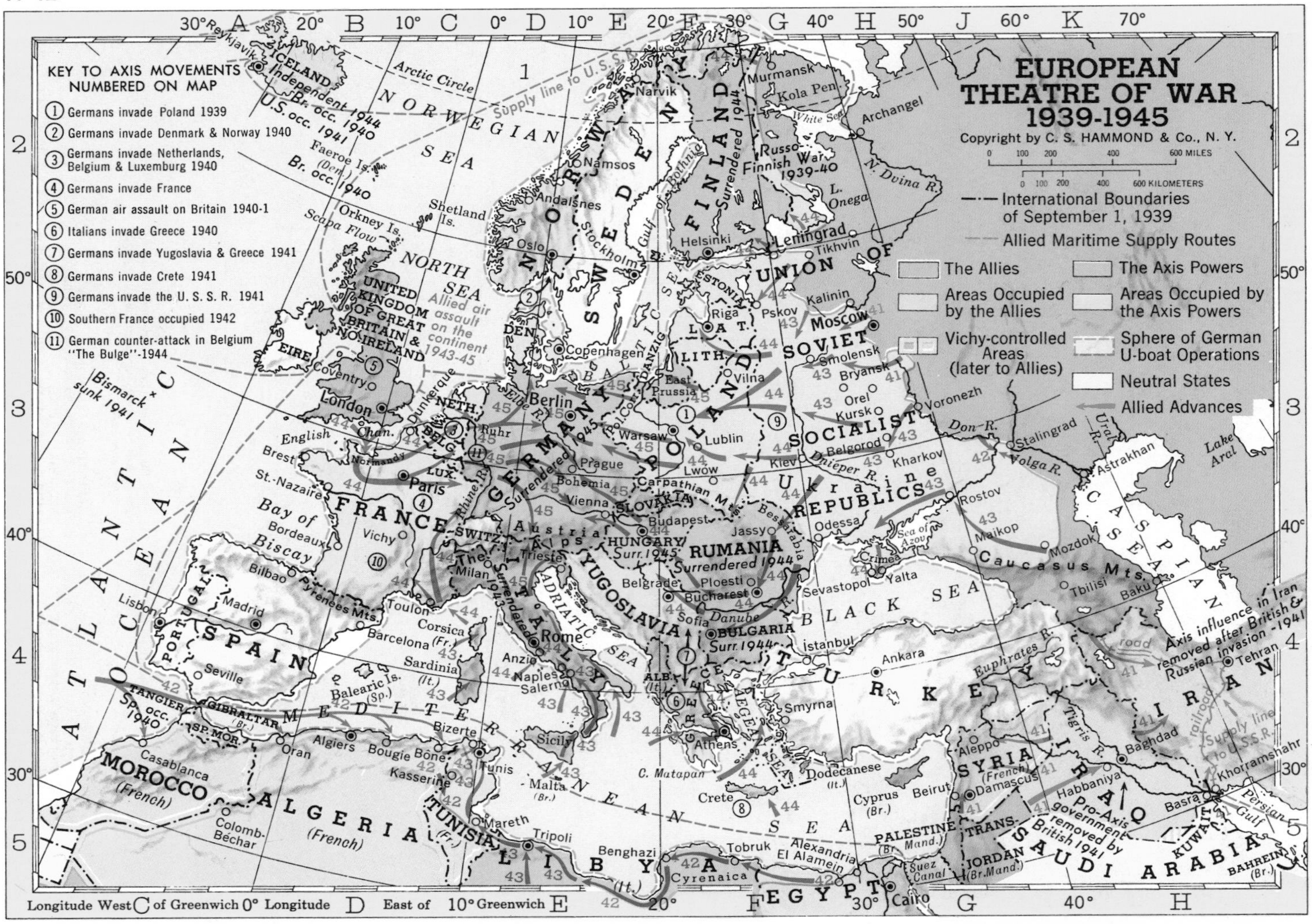

EUROPEAN THEATRE OF WAR 1939-1945
Copyright by C. S. HAMMOND & Co., N.Y.

KEY TO AXIS MOVEMENTS NUMBERED ON MAP

1. Germans invade Poland 1939
2. Germans invade Denmark & Norway 1940
3. Germans invade Netherlands, Belgium & Luxemburg 1940
4. Germans invade France 1940
5. German air assault on Britain 1940-1
6. Italians invade Greece 1940
7. Germans invade Yugoslavia & Greece 1941
8. Germans invade Crete 1941
9. Germans invade the U.S.S.R. 1941
10. Southern France occupied 1942
11. German counter-attack in Belgium "The Bulge"-1944

Scale: 0 100 200 400 600 MILES
0 100 200 400 600 KILOMETERS

— · — International Boundaries of September 1, 1939
— — — Allied Maritime Supply Routes

The Allies
The Axis Powers
Areas Occupied by the Allies
Areas Occupied by the Axis Powers
Vichy-controlled Areas (later to Allies)
Sphere of German U-boat Operations
Neutral States
Allied Advances

Longitude West of Greenwich 0° Longitude   East of 10° Greenwich

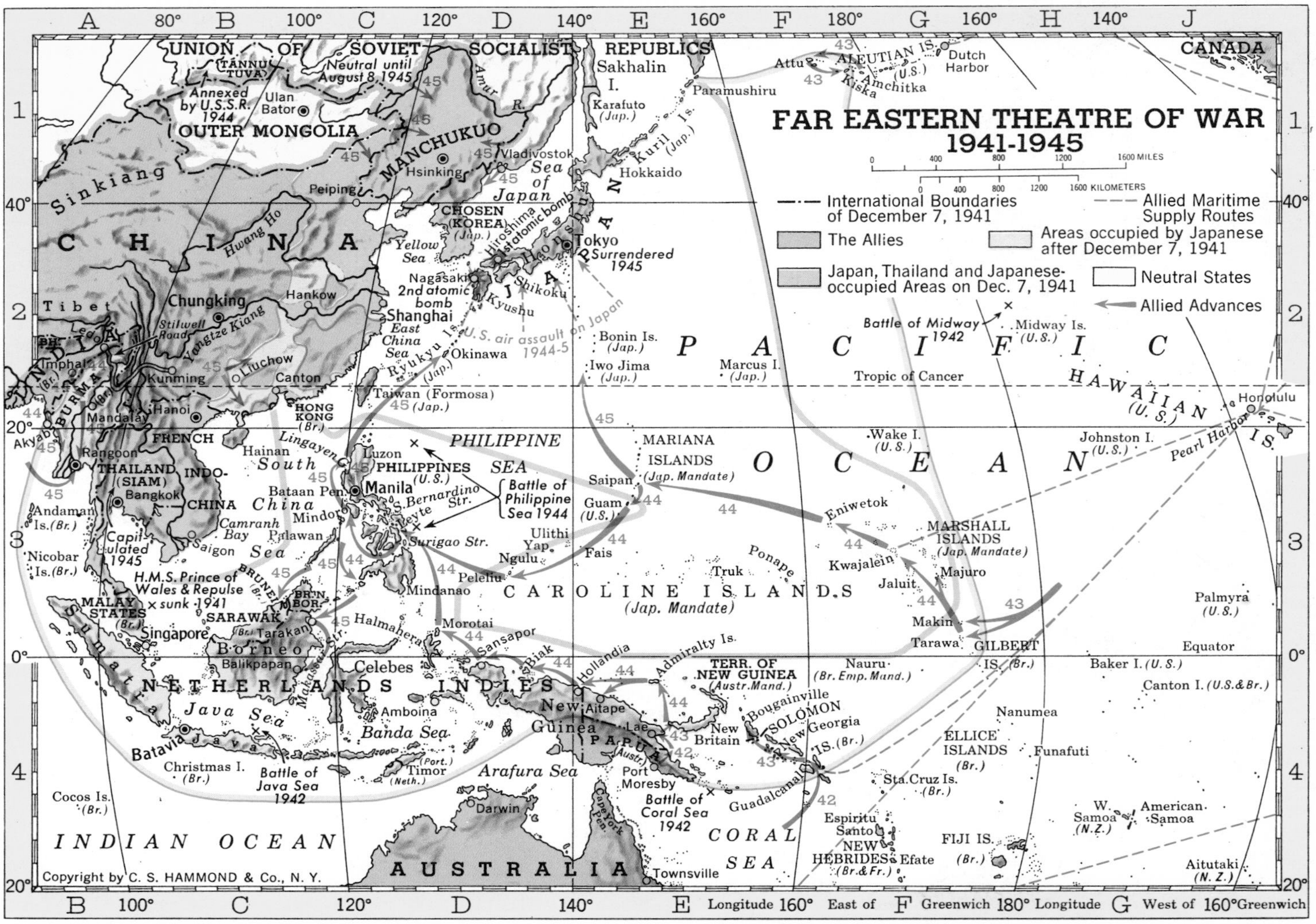

FAR EASTERN THEATRE OF WAR 1941-1945

Scale: 0 400 800 1200 1600 MILES
0 400 800 1200 1600 KILOMETERS

— · — International Boundaries of December 7, 1941
— — — Allied Maritime Supply Routes

The Allies
Areas occupied by Japanese after December 7, 1941
Japan, Thailand and Japanese-occupied Areas on Dec. 7, 1941
Neutral States
→ Allied Advances

Copyright by C. S. HAMMOND & Co., N.Y.

Longitude 160° East of Greenwich 180° Longitude West of 160° Greenwich

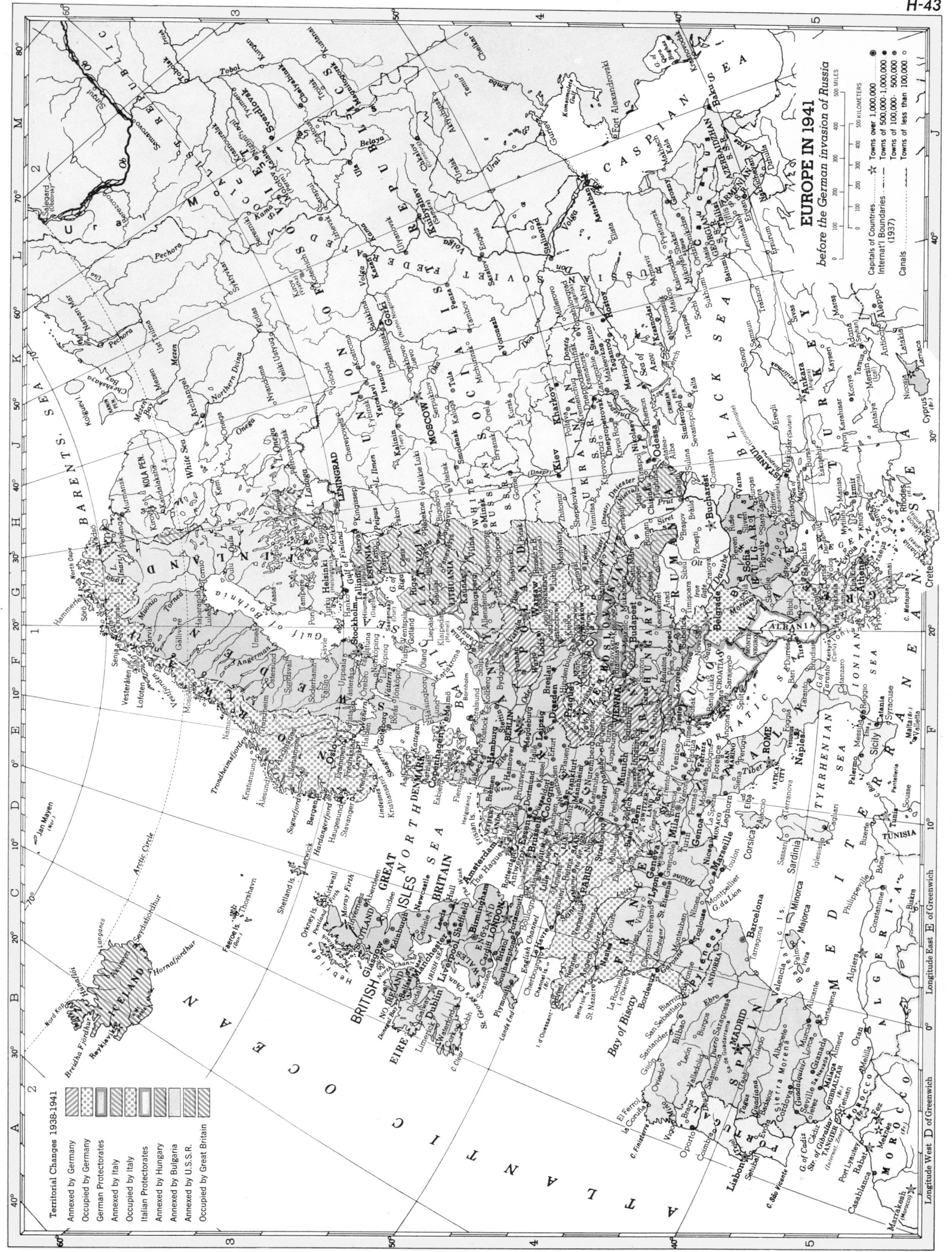

EUROPE IN 1941

before the German invasion of Russia

Capitals of Countries ☆
Internat'l Boundaries (1937) ····
Canals

Towns over 1,000,000 ●
Towns of 500,000–1,000,000 ●
Towns of 100,000–500,000 ■
Towns of less than 100,000 ○

Territorial Changes 1938–1941

Annexed by Germany
Occupied by Germany
German Protectorates
Annexed by Italy
Occupied by Italy
Italian Protectorates
Annexed by Hungary
Annexed by Bulgaria
Annexed by U.S.S.R.
Occupied by Great Britain

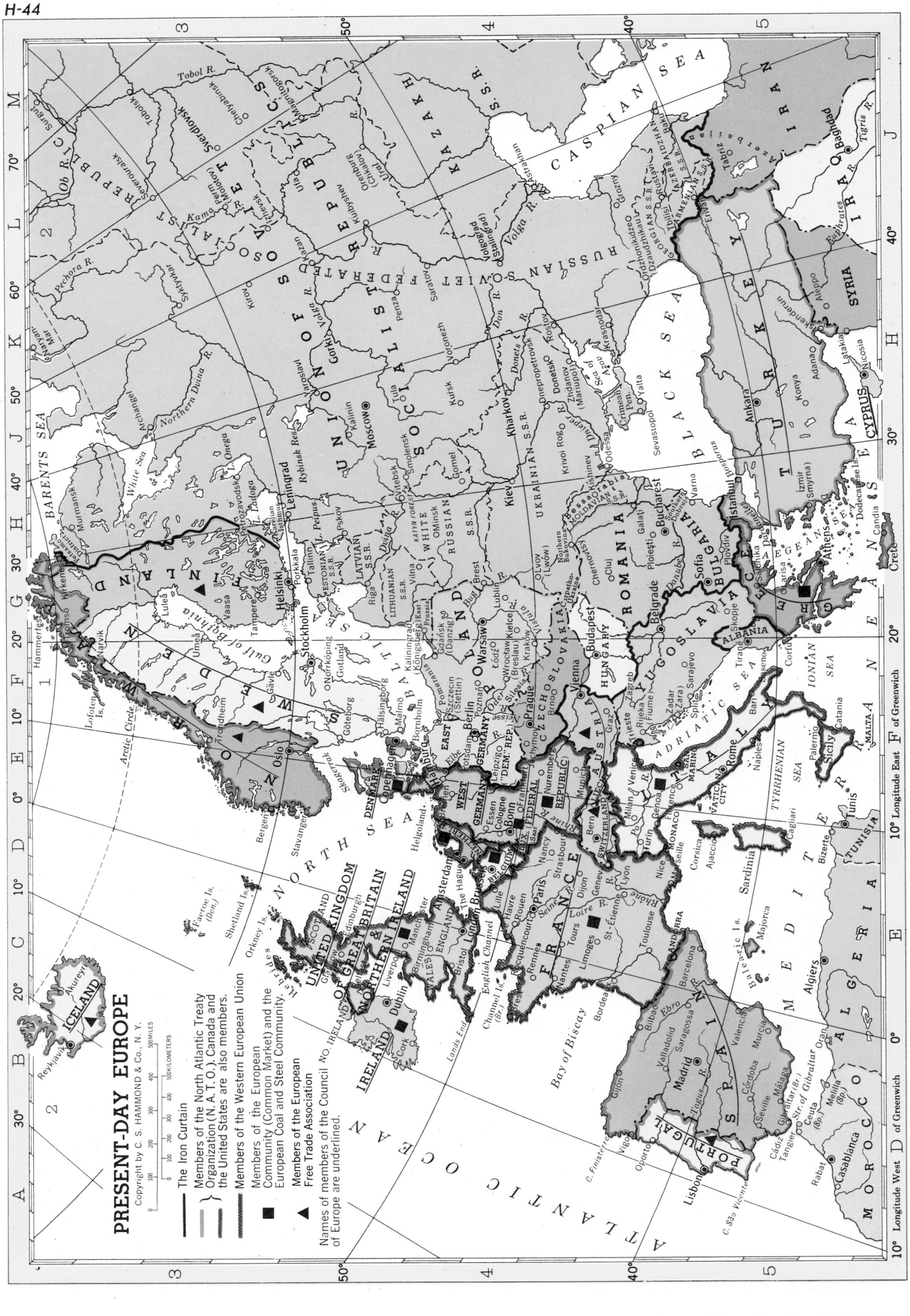

PRESENT-DAY EUROPE

Copyright by C. S. HAMMOND & Co., N.Y.

Legend:

— The Iron Curtain

Members of the North Atlantic Treaty Organization (N.A.T.O.) Canada and the United States are also members.

Members of the Western European Union

Members of the European Community (Common Market) and the European Coal and Steel Community.

Members of the European Free Trade Association

Names of members of the Council of Europe are underlined.

SCALE

0 100 200 300 400 500 MILES
0 100 200 300 400 500 KILOMETERS

(Map labels — seas, countries and cities)

ATLANTIC OCEAN

BARENTS SEA

WHITE SEA

NORTH SEA

BALTIC SEA

BLACK SEA

CASPIAN SEA

MEDITERRANEAN SEA

ADRIATIC SEA

TYRRHENIAN SEA

IONIAN SEA

AEGEAN SEA

Bay of Biscay

Gulf of Bothnia

ICELAND — Reykjavik, Akureyri

IRELAND — Dublin, Cork

UNITED KINGDOM OF GREAT BRITAIN & NORTHERN IRELAND — London, Edinburgh, Glasgow, Belfast, Manchester, Liverpool, Birmingham, Bristol, Cardiff

NORWAY — Oslo, Bergen, Trondheim, Narvik, Tromsö, Hammerfest, Stavanger

SWEDEN — Stockholm, Göteborg, Malmö, Göteborg, Luleå, Umeå, Gävle

FINLAND — Helsinki, Tampere, Vaasa

DENMARK — Copenhagen

WEST GERMANY (FEDERAL REPUBLIC) — Bonn, Berlin, Hamburg, Cologne, Essen, Frankfurt, Nuremberg, Munich

EAST GERMANY (DEM. REP.) — Leipzig

NETHERLANDS — Amsterdam, The Hague, Rotterdam

BELGIUM — Brussels, Antwerp

LUX.

FRANCE — Paris, Marseille, Lyon, Bordeaux, Toulouse, Nantes, Strasbourg, Nice, Rennes, Le Havre, Lille, Nancy, Dijon, Limoges, Tours, St.-Étienne

SWITZERLAND — Bern, Geneva, Zürich

AUSTRIA — Vienna, Graz

ITALY — Rome, Milan, Venice, Genoa, Turin, Naples, Florence, Palermo, Catania, Cagliari

VATICAN CITY, SAN MARINO, MONACO, ANDORRA

SPAIN — Madrid, Barcelona, Valencia, Seville, Bilbao, Valladolid, Saragossa, Málaga, Murcia, Córdoba, Granada

PORTUGAL — Lisbon, Oporto

POLAND — Warsaw, Gdańsk (Danzig), Poznań, Wrocław (Breslau), Kraków, Łódź, Szczecin (Stettin), Lublin, Kielce

CZECHOSLOVAKIA — Prague, Brno, Bratislava

HUNGARY — Budapest

ROMANIA — Bucharest, Galați, Ploiești, Cluj

YUGOSLAVIA — Belgrade, Zagreb, Sarajevo, Rijeka (Fiume), Split, Skopje

BULGARIA — Sofia, Plovdiv, Varna

ALBANIA — Tirana

GREECE — Athens, Salonika

TURKEY — Ankara, Istanbul, İzmir (Smyrna), Adana, Konya

CYPRUS — Nicosia

SYRIA — Aleppo, Latakia

IRAN — Tabriz, Tehran

IRAQ — Baghdad

MALTA

CRETE (Candia)

UNION OF SOVIET SOCIALIST REPUBLICS

RUSSIAN SOVIET FEDERATED SOCIALIST REPUBLIC — Moscow, Leningrad, Gorki, Kazan, Kuibyshev, Saratov, Volgograd (Stalingrad), Rostov, Voronezh, Kirov, Sverdlovsk, Chelyabinsk, Magnitogorsk, Archangel, Murmansk, Tula, Kalinin, Penza, Ufa, Krasnodar

KAZAKH S.S.R.

UKRAINIAN S.S.R. — Kiev, Kharkov, Odessa, Dnepropetrovsk, Donetsk, Lvov (Lwów), Krivoi Rog, Zhdanov (Mariupol)

WHITE RUSSIAN S.S.R. — Minsk, Gomel, Vitebsk

LITHUANIAN S.S.R. — Vilna, Kaunas

LATVIAN S.S.R. — Riga

ESTONIAN S.S.R. — Tallinn

MOLDAVIAN S.S.R. — Kishinev

GEORGIAN S.S.R. — Tbilisi

ARMENIAN S.S.R. — Erevan

AZERBAIDZHAN S.S.R. — Baku

MOROCCO — Casablanca, Rabat, Tangier

ALGERIA — Algiers, Oran

TUNISIA — Tunis, Bizerte

Gibraltar (Br.), Ceuta (Sp.), Melilla (Sp.)

Arctic Circle

Tobol R., Ob R., Pechora R., Kama R., Volga R., Don R., Donets R., Dnieper R., Loire R., Rhône R., Tigris R., Euphrates R., Northern Dvina R.

Longitude West of Greenwich / Longitude East of Greenwich

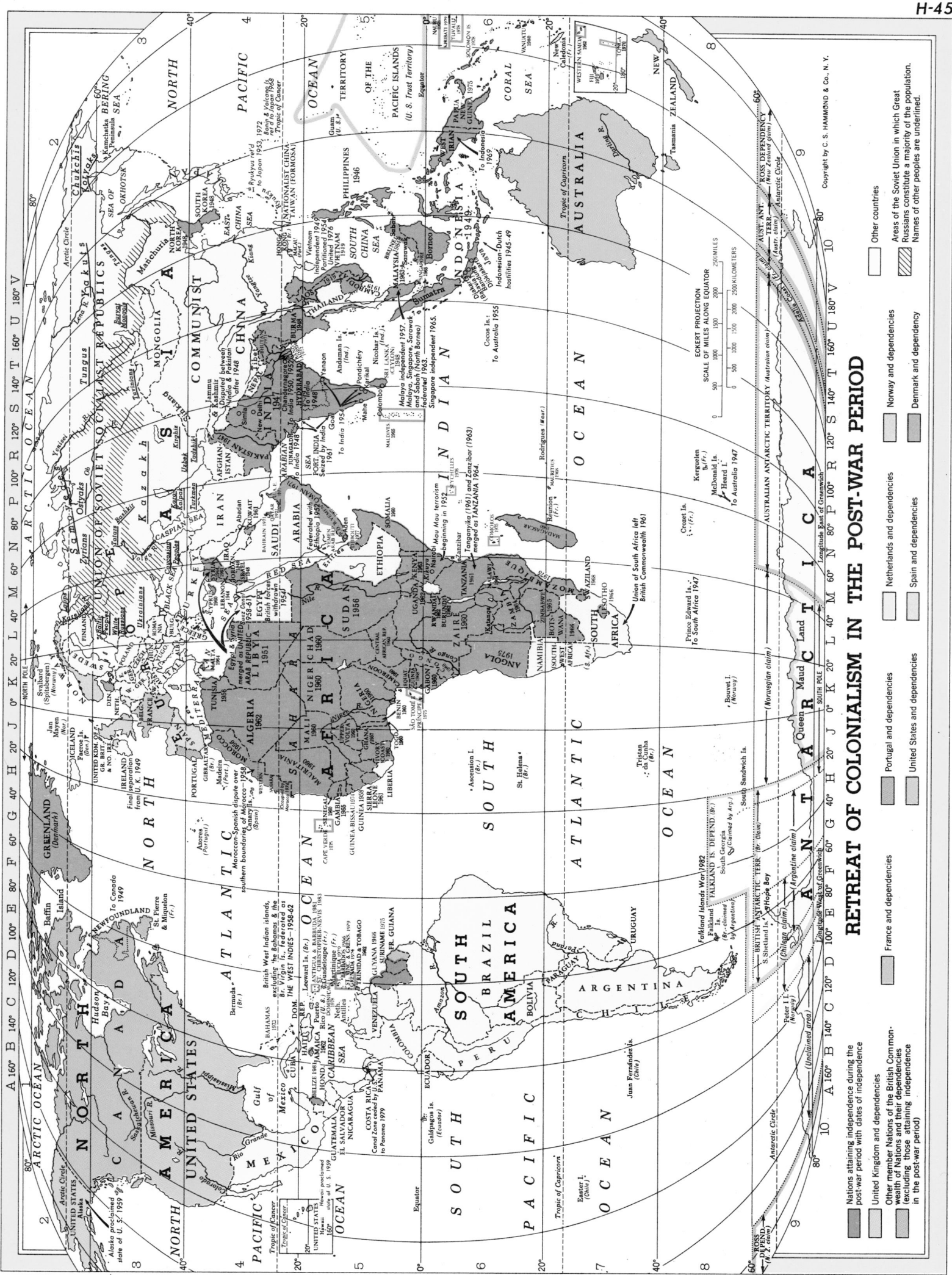

RETREAT OF COLONIALISM IN THE POST-WAR PERIOD

ECKERT PROJECTION
SCALE OF MILES ALONG EQUATOR

Copyright by C. S. HAMMOND & Co., N. Y.

Areas of the Soviet Union in which Great
Russians constitute a majority of the population.
Names of other peoples are underlined.

Other countries

Nations attaining independence during the
post-war period with dates of independence

United Kingdom and dependencies

Other member Nations of the British Commonwealth of Nations and their dependencies
(excluding those attaining independence
in the post-war period)

France and dependencies

Portugal and dependencies

United States and dependencies

Netherlands and dependencies

Spain and dependencies

Norway and dependencies

Denmark and dependency

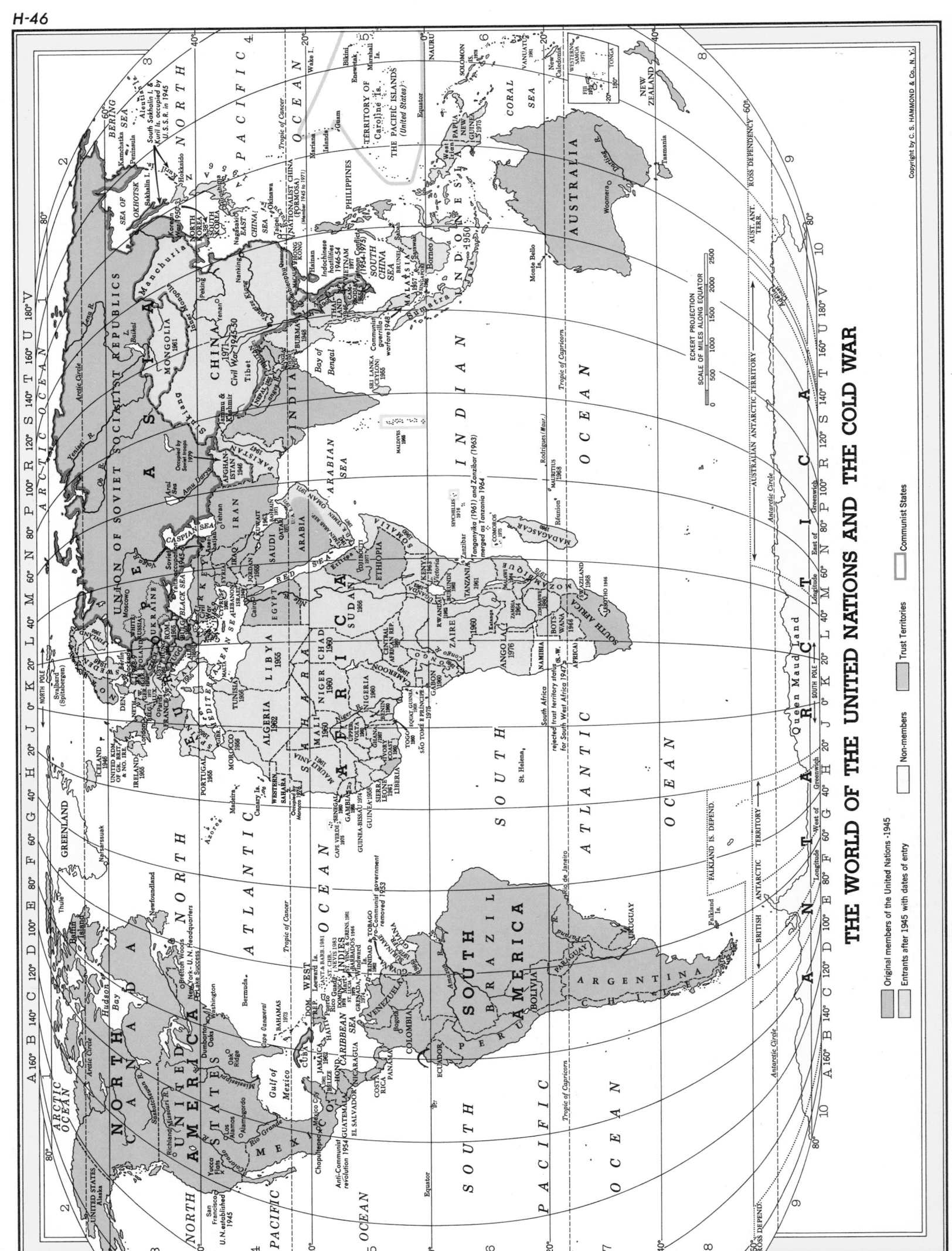

THE WORLD OF THE UNITED NATIONS AND THE COLD WAR

Original members of the United Nations -1945

Entrants after 1945 with dates of entry

Non-members

Trust Territories

Communist States

ECKERT PROJECTION
SCALE OF MILES ALONG EQUATOR
0   500   1000   1500   2000   2500

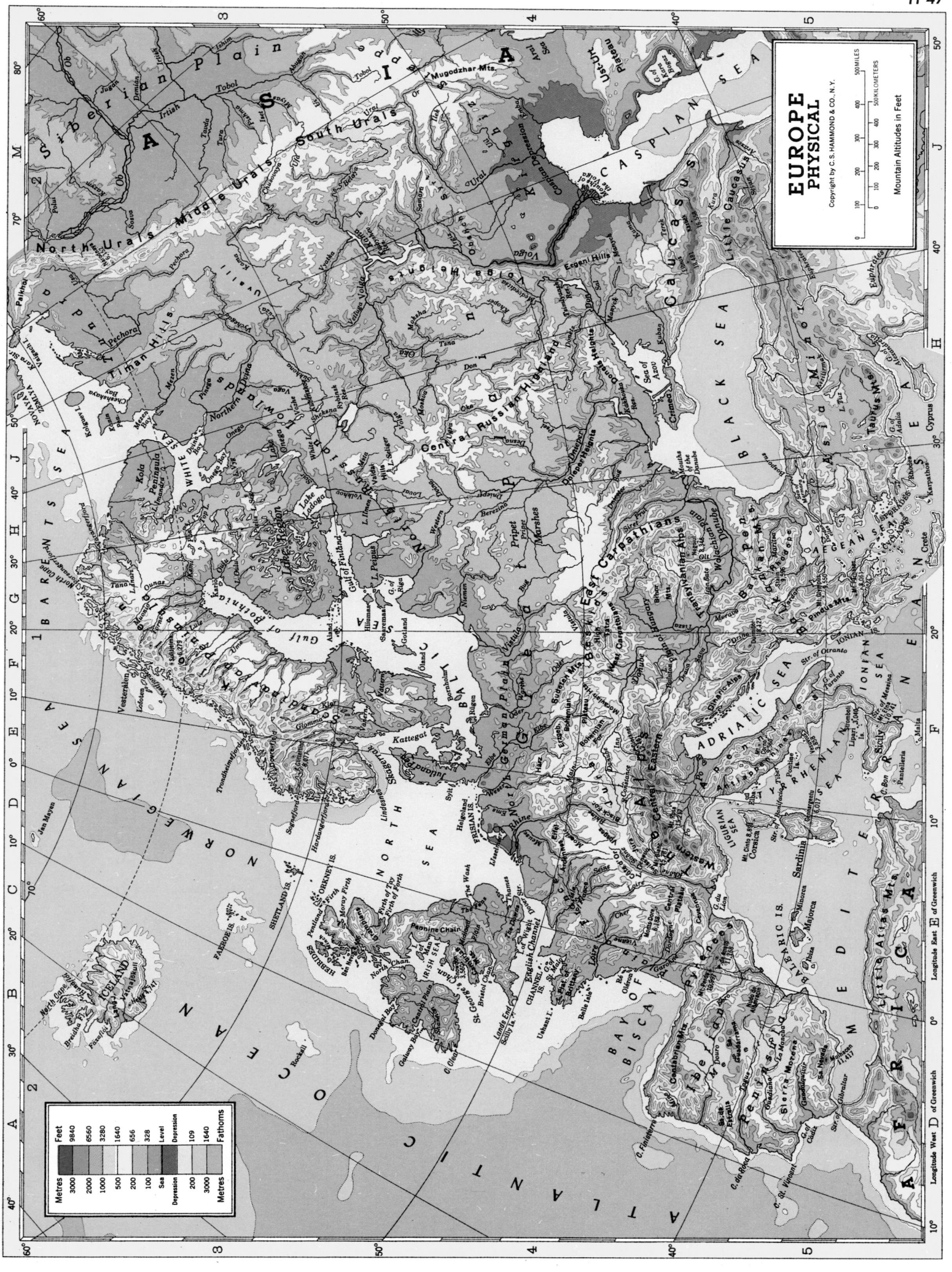

EUROPE
PHYSICAL

Copyright by C.S. HAMMOND & CO., N.Y.

Mountain Altitudes in Feet

50 MILES

50 KILOMETERS

Metres	Feet
3000	9840
2000	6560
1000	3280
500	1640
200	656
100	328
Sea	Level
Depression	Depression
109	
1640	
3000	
Metres	Fathoms

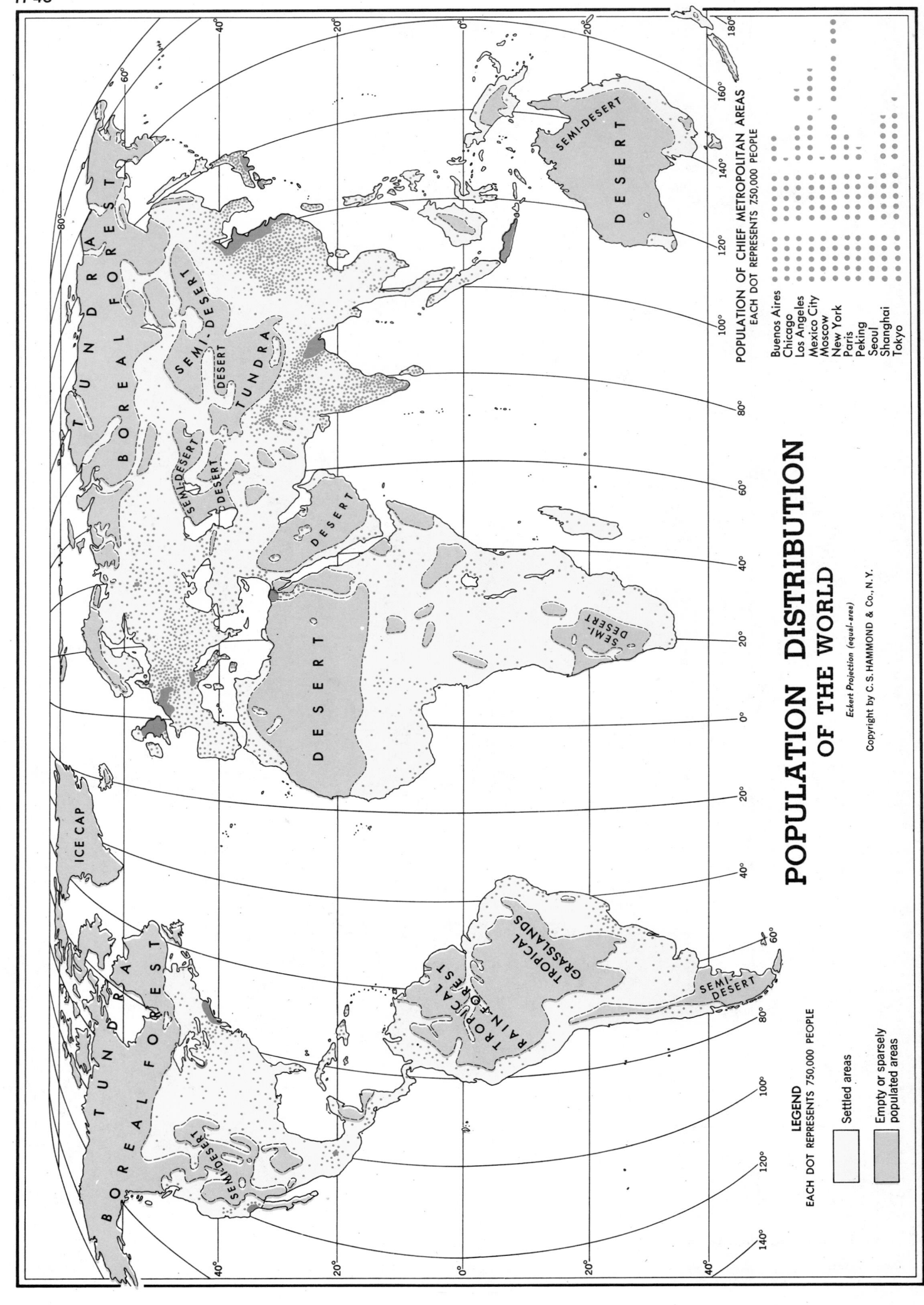

POPULATION OF CHIEF METROPOLITAN AREAS
EACH DOT REPRESENTS 750,000 PEOPLE

Buenos Aires
Chicago
Los Angeles
Mexico City
Moscow
New York
Paris
Peking
Seoul
Shanghai
Tokyo

POPULATION DISTRIBUTION
OF THE WORLD

Eckert Projection (equal-area)

Copyright by C. S. HAMMOND & Co., N.Y.

LEGEND
EACH DOT REPRESENTS 750,000 PEOPLE

Settled areas

Empty or sparsely
populated areas

United States
History
Atlas

HAMMOND®
INCORPORATED
MAPLEWOOD, NEW JERSEY 07040

Introduction

The *United States History Atlas* was developed to help the student discover the geographic patterns underlying much of our nation's history. Using the maps and diagrams of this atlas, the student will develop a feeling of involvement in the great territorial, geopolitical and economic questions that constitute the American story. Such involvement should motivate the student to inquire on his own, into the geographic factors that underlie 400 years of political, economic and social life on this continent.

It will be noted that the contents of this atlas consist of far more than simple political maps merely showing political boundaries and towns at various dates. Instead, the maps and diagrams bring out the economic, social, demographic and ecological factors that have molded American history. For example, the maps of *Colonial America in 1770* on pages 12 and 13 present not only the boundaries of the thirteen colonies but, also, cartographic representation of colonial settlement patterns at three different dates, distribution maps showing the colonial economy, and an ethnic map illustrating the cultural diversity of the Atlantic seaboard area in the eighteenth century. Many other maps and graphs in the atlas bring out the socio-geographic elements of various periods in our history.

The sequence of maps in the atlas is broadly chronological, beginning with maps portraying the major Indian tribes and families and ending with maps and diagrams depicting current urban problems, economic data and election results. However, many topical maps, covering long periods of time, appear throughout the work. Thus the map of *Expansion of the United States* on page 16 shows the territorial growth of our nation from 1783 to 1898 — a single topic through 116 years of time. The maps entitled *Growth of Industry and Cities* on pages 34 and 35 cover modern industrial and urban development from its beginning at the time of the Civil War to the present decade. At the end of the atlas is a useful index locating specific place names important in American history.

The publishers of this wholly new teaching tool have succeeded in producing maps and graphs that are notable for their conciseness, legibility and scholarship. The type faces used for place names on the maps are distinguished for their clarity and large size. Colors have been selected to delineate clearly one geographic area from another. Confusing detail and overcrowding have been avoided by creating several maps for each topic and period of American history. Many of the maps indicate terrain by a shaded relief technique, so that the student will be made aware of the influence of topography on the events and movements of history. The result is a historical atlas that is both eye-pleasing and authoritative.

Contents

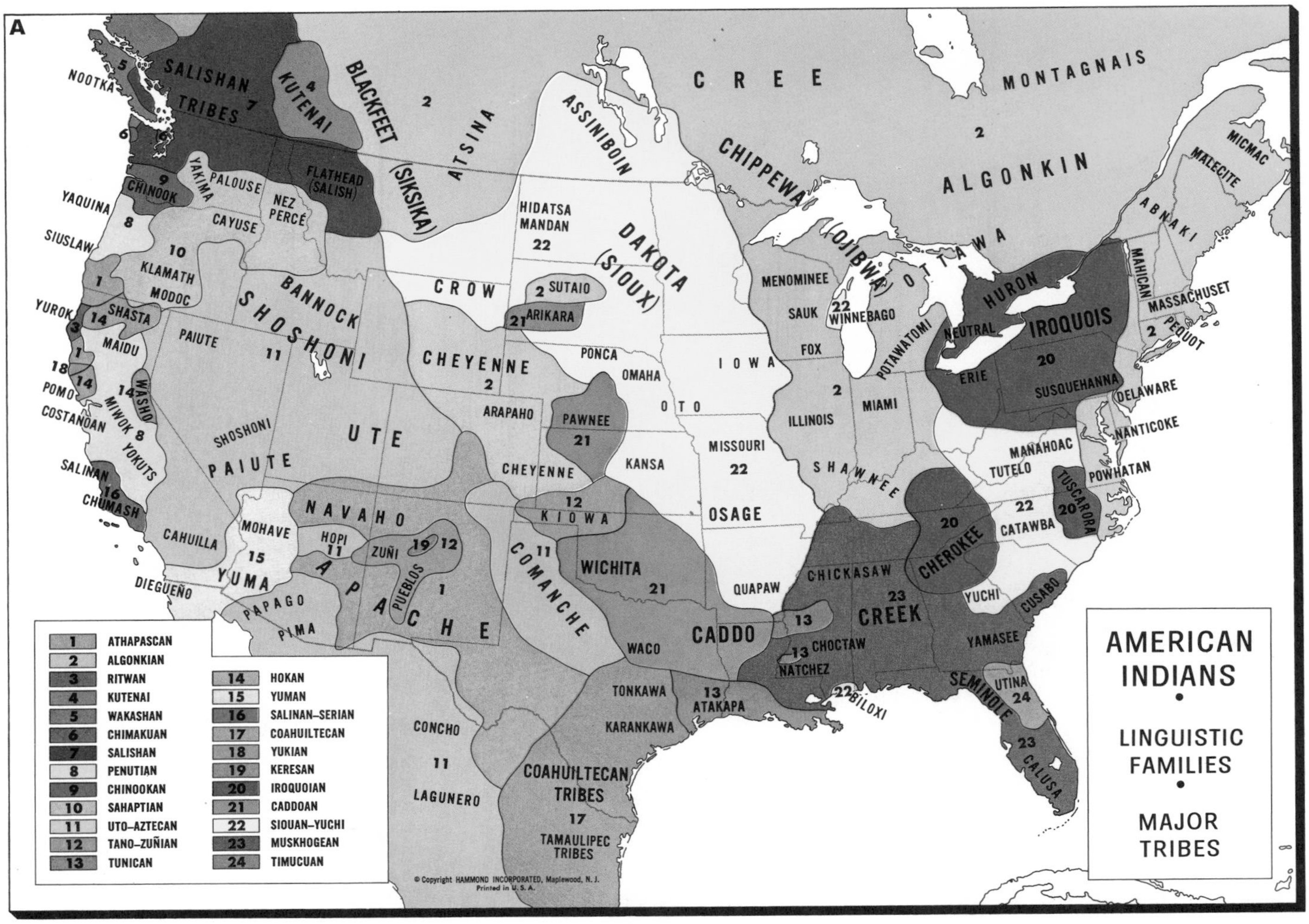

A

SALISHAN TRIBES
NOOTKA
KUTENAI
BLACKFEET
2
C R E E
MONTAGNAIS
ATSINA
ASSINIBOIN
CHIPPEWA
2
A L G O N K I N
MICMAC
MALECITE
YAKIMA PALOUSE
CHINOOK
NEZ PERCÉ
FLATHEAD (SALISH)
HIDATSA MANDAN 22
DAKOTA (SIOUX)
(OJIBWA) OTTAWA
ABNAKI
YAQUINA
CAYUSE
CROW
HURON
MASSACHUSET
SIUSLAW
KLAMATH MODOC
BANNOCK
SUTAIO 2
ARIKARA 21
MENOMINEE
SAUK
WINNEBAGO 22
IROQUOIS 20
NEUTRAL ERIE
PEQUOT 2
YUROK
SHASTA
SHOSHONI
CHEYENNE
PONCA
FOX
SUSQUEHANNA
DELAWARE
MAIDU
PAIUTE
OMAHA
IOWA
ILLINOIS
MIAMI
2
POTAWATOMI
MANAHOAC
NANTICOKE
POMO
WASHO
OTO
MISSOURI 22
SHAWNEE
TUTELO
POWHATAN
COSTANOAN
MIWOK
YOKUTS
SHOSHONI
UTE
ARAPAHO
PAWNEE 21
KANSA
OSAGE
TUSCARORA 20
SALINAN 16
CHUMASH
PAIUTE
CHEYENNE 2
KIOWA 12
CHEYENNE
WICHITA
QUAPAW
CHICKASAW
CHEROKEE 20
CATAWBA 22
YUCHI
CUSABO
CAHUILLA
MOHAVE
NAVAHO
HOPI 11
ZUÑI
19 12
PUEBLOS 1
COMANCHE 11
21
CADDO
13
CREEK 23
YAMASEE
DIEGUEÑO
YUMA
PAPAGO
PIMA
A P A C H E
WACO
CHOCTAW 13
NATCHEZ
SEMINOLE
UTINA 24
CONCHO
11
TONKAWA
ATAKAPA 13
BILOXI 22
CALUSA 23
LAGUNERO
COAHUILTECAN TRIBES 17
KARANKAWA
TAMAULIPEC TRIBES

1	ATHAPASCAN
2	ALGONKIAN
3	RITWAN
4	KUTENAI
5	WAKASHAN
6	CHIMAKUAN
7	SALISHAN
8	PENUTIAN
9	CHINOOKAN
10	SAHAPTIAN
11	UTO–AZTECAN
12	TANO–ZUÑIAN
13	TUNICAN
14	HOKAN
15	YUMAN
16	SALINAN–SERIAN
17	COAHUILTECAN
18	YUKIAN
19	KERESAN
20	IROQUOIAN
21	CADDOAN
22	SIOUAN–YUCHI
23	MUSKHOGEAN
24	TIMUCUAN

© Copyright HAMMOND INCORPORATED, Maplewood, N.J.
Printed in U.S.A.

AMERICAN INDIANS
•
LINGUISTIC FAMILIES
•
MAJOR TRIBES

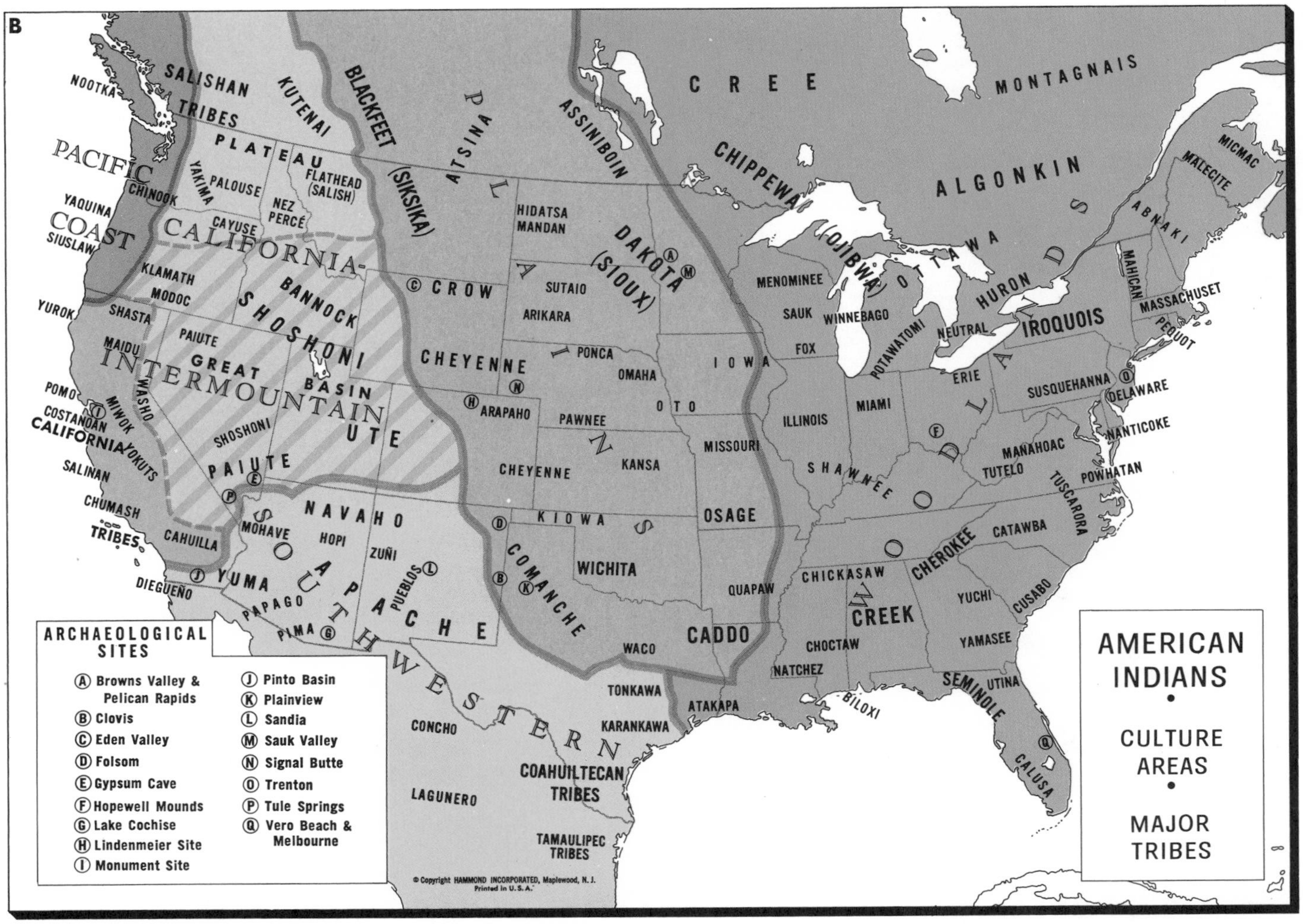

B

SALISHAN TRIBES
NOOTKA
KUTENAI
BLACKFEET
C R E E
MONTAGNAIS
PACIFIC
PLATEAU
ATSINA
P L A I
ASSINIBOIN
CHIPPEWA
A L G O N K I N
MICMAC
MALECITE
YAKIMA PALOUSE
CHINOOK
NEZ PERCÉ
FLATHEAD (SALISH)
(SIKSIKA)
HIDATSA MANDAN
DAKOTA (SIOUX)
(OJIBWA) OTTAWA
ABNAKI
YAQUINA
CAYUSE
CALIFORNIA–
CROW ©C
HURON
IROQUOIS
MASSACHUSET
COAST
SIUSLAW
KLAMATH MODOC
BANNOCK
SUTAIO
ARIKARA
MENOMINEE
SAUK
WINNEBAGO
NEUTRAL ERIE
PEQUOT
YUROK
SHASTA
SHOSHONI
GREAT BASIN
CHEYENNE
PONCA
FOX
SUSQUEHANNA
DELAWARE
MAIDU
PAIUTE
©H ARAPAHO
©N
OMAHA
IOWA
ILLINOIS
MIAMI
POTAWATOMI
NANTICOKE
POMO
WASHO
INTERMOUNTAIN
UTE
OTO
MISSOURI
©F
MANAHOAC
CALIFORNIA
COSTANOAN
MIWOK
YOKUTS
SHOSHONI
PAWNEE
KANSA
SHAWNEE
TUTELO
POWHATAN
SALINAN
PAIUTE
©E
CHEYENNE
KIOWA ©D
OSAGE
TUSCARORA
CHUMASH
TRIBES
CAHUILLA
MOHAVE
NAVAHO
HOPI
ZUÑI
PUEBLOS ©L
WICHITA
QUAPAW
CHICKASAW
CHEROKEE
CATAWBA
YUCHI CUSABO
DIEGUEÑO
©J YUMA
PAPAGO
PIMA ©G
A P A C H E
©P
©B
COMANCHE ©K
CADDO
CREEK
YAMASEE
S O U T H W E S T E R N
WACO
CHOCTAW
NATCHEZ
SEMINOLE
UTINA
CONCHO
TONKAWA
ATAKAPA
BILOXI
CALUSA ©Q
LAGUNERO
COAHUILTECAN TRIBES
KARANKAWA
TAMAULIPEC TRIBES

ARCHAEOLOGICAL SITES

Ⓐ Browns Valley & Pelican Rapids	Ⓙ Pinto Basin
Ⓑ Clovis	Ⓚ Plainview
Ⓒ Eden Valley	Ⓛ Sandia
Ⓓ Folsom	Ⓜ Sauk Valley
Ⓔ Gypsum Cave	Ⓝ Signal Butte
Ⓕ Hopewell Mounds	Ⓞ Trenton
Ⓖ Lake Cochise	Ⓟ Tule Springs
Ⓗ Lindenmeier Site	Ⓠ Vero Beach & Melbourne
Ⓘ Monument Site	

© Copyright HAMMOND INCORPORATED, Maplewood, N.J.
Printed in U.S.A.

AMERICAN INDIANS
•
CULTURE AREAS
•
MAJOR TRIBES

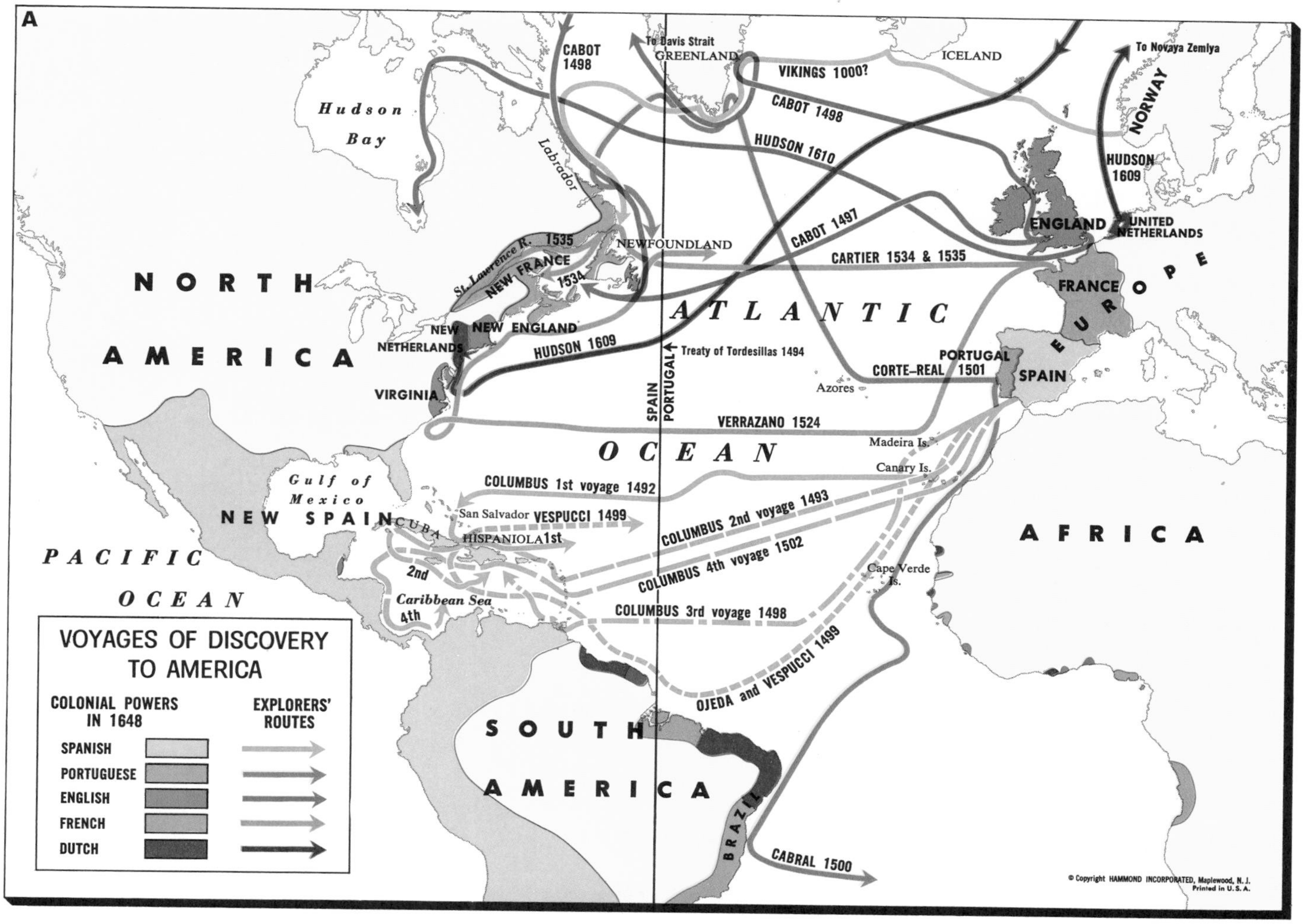

A

To Davis Strait

CABOT 1498

GREENLAND

VIKINGS 1000?

ICELAND

To Novaya Zemlya

CABOT 1498

NORWAY

HUDSON 1610

Hudson Bay

HUDSON 1609

ENGLAND

UNITED NETHERLANDS

HUDSON 1609

CABOT 1497

Labrador

St. Lawrence R. 1535

NEW FRANCE

NEWFOUNDLAND

1534

CARTIER 1534 & 1535

N O R T H

A M E R I C A

A T L A N T I C

FRANCE

E U R O P E

NEW NETHERLANDS

NEW NEW ENGLAND

HUDSON 1609

PORTUGAL

Treaty of Tordesillas 1494

CORTE-REAL 1501

PORTUGAL

SPAIN

VIRGINIA

Azores

SPAIN PORTUGAL

VERRAZANO 1524

O C E A N

Madeira Is.

Canary Is.

Gulf of Mexico

COLUMBUS 1st voyage 1492

NEW SPAIN

CUBA

San Salvador VESPUCCI 1499

HISPANIOLA 1st

COLUMBUS 2nd voyage 1493

A F R I C A

PACIFIC

OCEAN

2nd

Caribbean Sea

COLUMBUS 4th voyage 1502

Cape Verde Is.

4th

COLUMBUS 3rd voyage 1498

OJEDA and VESPUCCI 1499

VOYAGES OF DISCOVERY TO AMERICA

SOUTH

AMERICA

COLONIAL POWERS IN 1648

EXPLORERS' ROUTES

SPANISH

PORTUGUESE

ENGLISH

FRENCH

DUTCH

BRAZIL

CABRAL 1500

© Copyright HAMMOND INCORPORATED, Maplewood, N.J.
Printed in U.S.A.

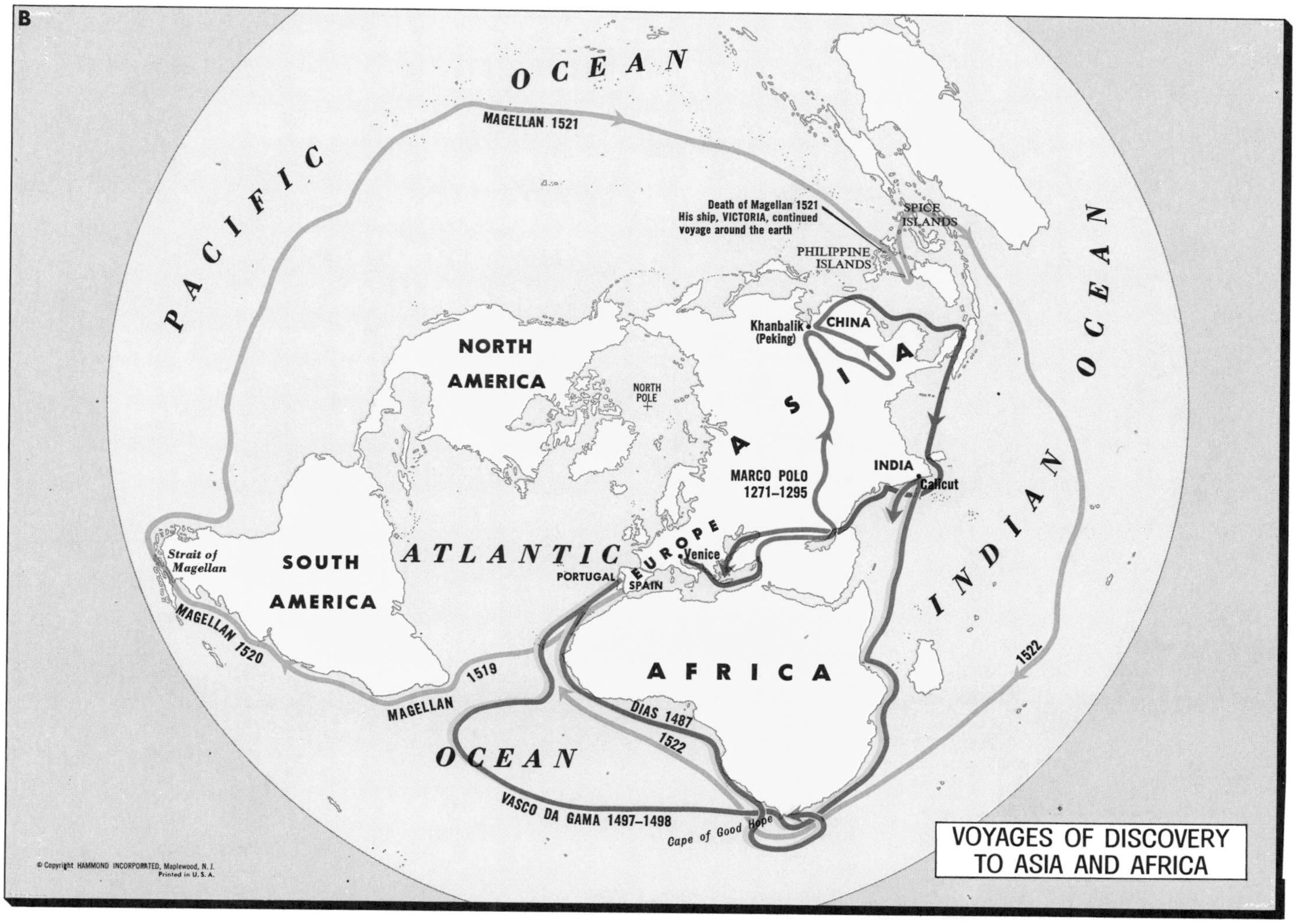

B

O C E A N

MAGELLAN 1521

PACIFIC

Death of Magellan 1521
His ship, VICTORIA, continued voyage around the earth

SPICE ISLANDS

PHILIPPINE ISLANDS

Khanbalik (Peking)

CHINA

NORTH AMERICA

NORTH POLE

A S I A

MARCO POLO 1271-1295

INDIA

Calicut

Strait of Magellan

ATLANTIC

Venice

E U R O P E

I N D I A N   O C E A N

SOUTH AMERICA

PORTUGAL SPAIN

MAGELLAN 1520

1519

MAGELLAN

AFRICA

DIAS 1487

1522

1522

OCEAN

VASCO DA GAMA 1497-1498

Cape of Good Hope

VOYAGES OF DISCOVERY TO ASIA AND AFRICA

© Copyright HAMMOND INCORPORATED, Maplewood, N.J.
Printed in U.S.A.

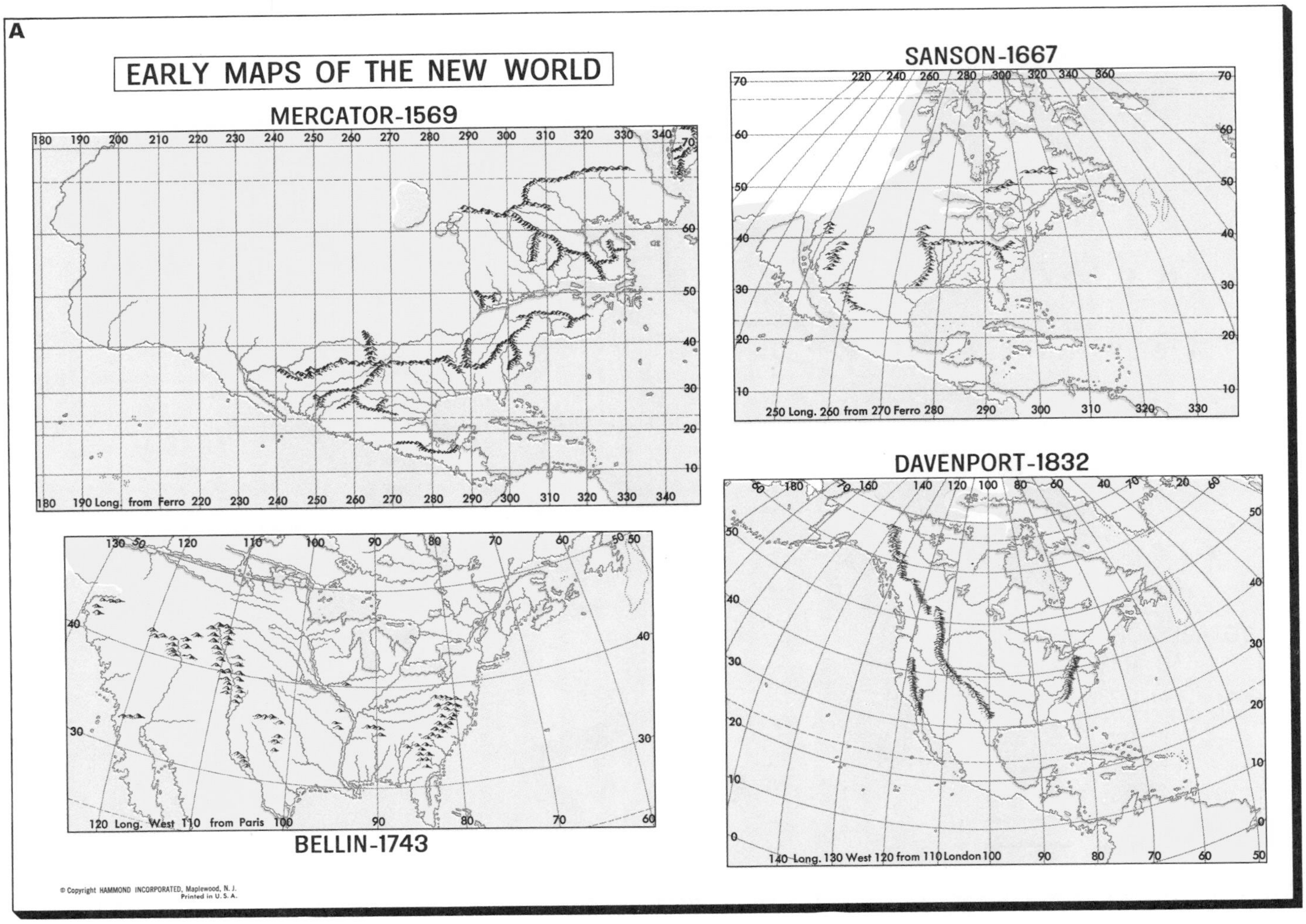

A

EARLY MAPS OF THE NEW WORLD

MERCATOR-1569

SANSON-1667

DAVENPORT-1832

BELLIN-1743

© Copyright HAMMOND INCORPORATED, Maplewood, N.J.
Printed in U.S.A.

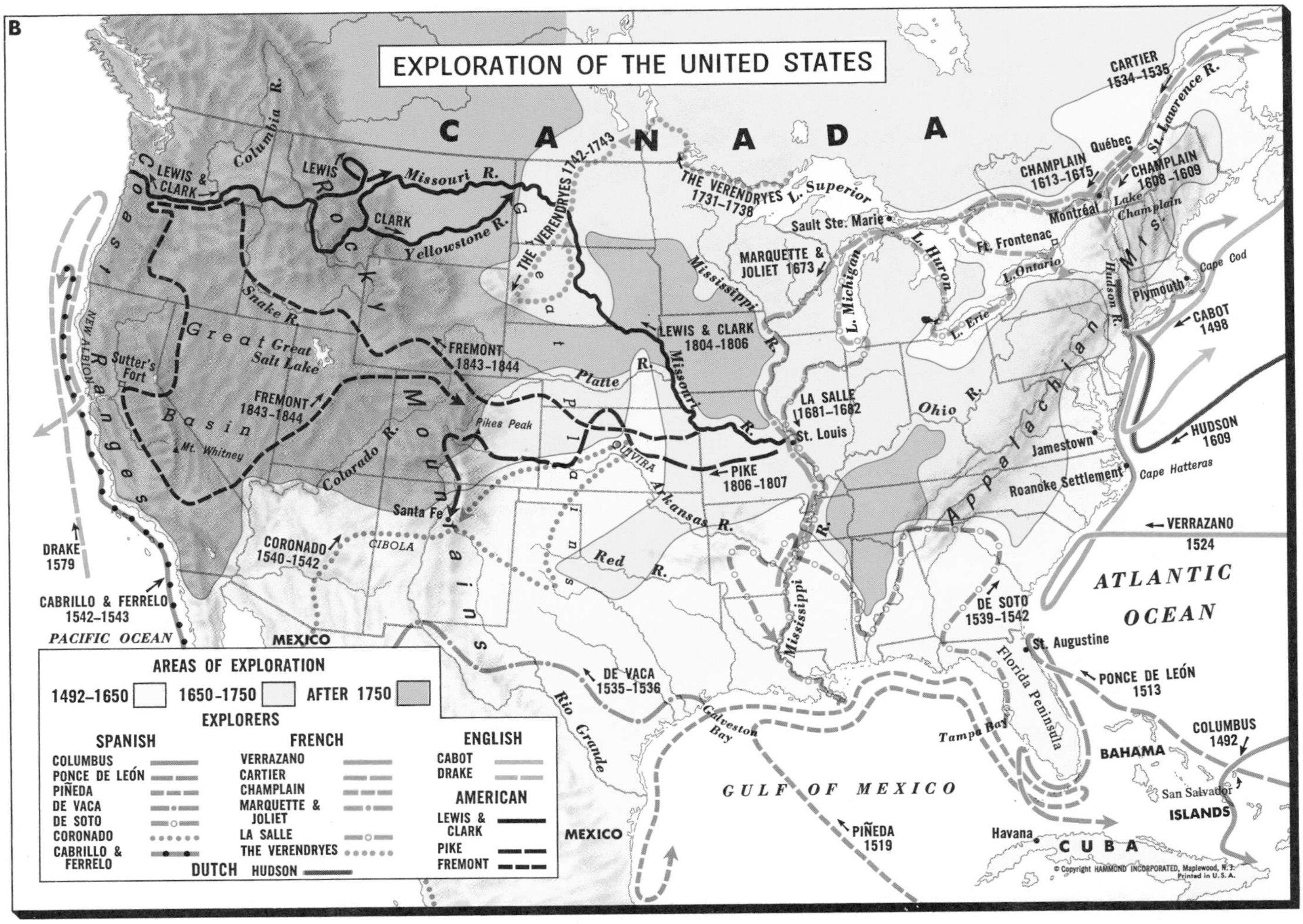

B

EXPLORATION OF THE UNITED STATES

CARTIER 1534-1535

CANADA

LEWIS & CLARK

Columbia R.

Missouri R.

THE VERENDRYES 1742-1743

THE VERENDRYES 1731-1738

L. Superior

MARQUETTE & JOLIET 1673

CHAMPLAIN 1613-1615

Québec

St. Lawrence R.

CHAMPLAIN 1608-1609

Montréal

Lake Champlain

Sault Ste. Marie

Ft. Frontenac

L. Michigan

L. Huron

L. Ontario

Hudson R.

Cape Cod

Plymouth

CABOT 1498

CLARK

Yellowstone R.

Snake R.

Great Great Salt Lake

Basin

FREMONT 1843-1844

Platte R.

LEWIS & CLARK 1804-1806

Mississippi R.

LA SALLE 1681-1682

Ohio R.

St. Louis

L. Erie

Jamestown

HUDSON 1609

Sutter's Fort

FREMONT 1843-1844

Pikes Peak

Platte R.

Missouri R.

PIKE 1806-1807

Appalachian Mts.

Roanoke Settlement

Cape Hatteras

Mt. Whitney

Colorado R.

QUIVIRA

Arkansas R.

New Albion

Santa Fe

VERRAZANO 1524

DRAKE 1579

CORONADO 1540-1542

CIBOLA

Red R.

ATLANTIC OCEAN

CABRILLO & FERRELO 1542-1543

Mississippi R.

DE SOTO 1539-1542

St. Augustine

PACIFIC OCEAN

MEXICO

DE VACA 1535-1536

Florida Peninsula

PONCE DE LEÓN 1513

Rio Grande

Galveston Bay

Tampa Bay

COLUMBUS 1492

BAHAMA

AREAS OF EXPLORATION

| 1492-1650 | 1650-1750 | AFTER 1750 |

EXPLORERS

SPANISH
COLUMBUS
PONCE DE LEÓN
PIÑEDA
DE VACA
DE SOTO
CORONADO
CABRILLO & FERRELO

FRENCH
VERRAZANO
CARTIER
CHAMPLAIN
MARQUETTE & JOLIET
LA SALLE
THE VERENDRYES

DUTCH   HUDSON

ENGLISH
CABOT
DRAKE

AMERICAN
LEWIS & CLARK
PIKE
FREMONT

PIÑEDA 1519

Havana

MEXICO

GULF OF MEXICO

San Salvador

CUBA

ISLANDS

© Copyright HAMMOND INCORPORATED, Maplewood, N.J.
Printed in U.S.A.

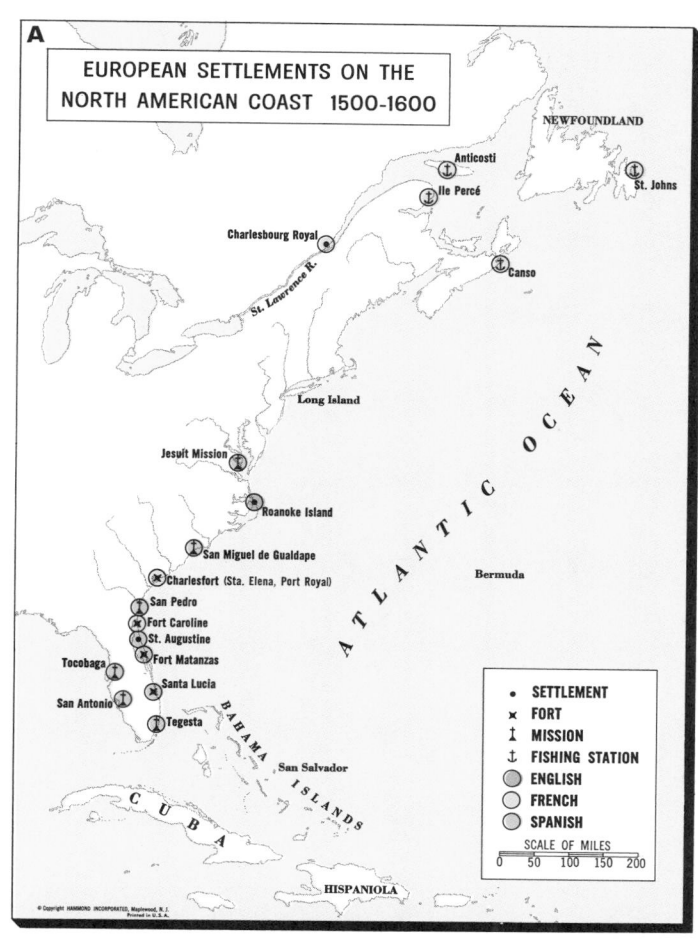

A EUROPEAN SETTLEMENTS ON THE NORTH AMERICAN COAST 1500-1600

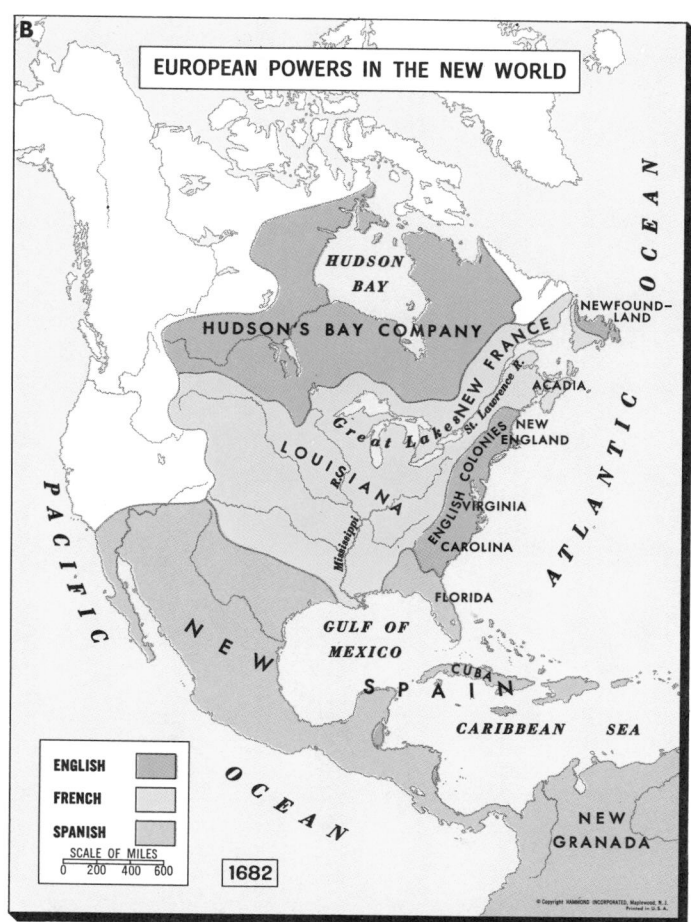

B EUROPEAN POWERS IN THE NEW WORLD

1682

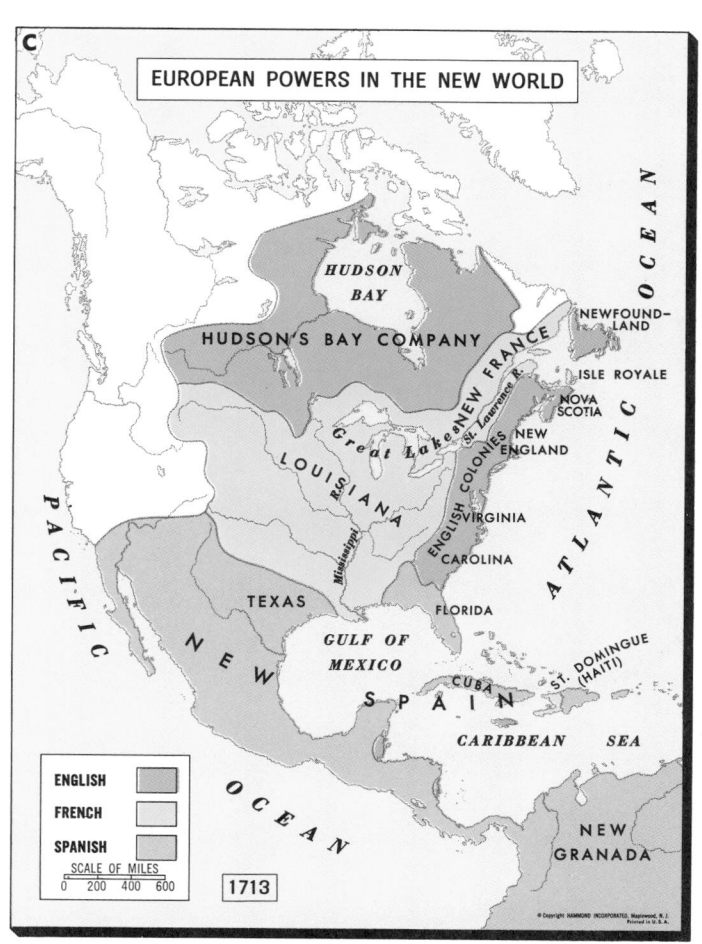

C EUROPEAN POWERS IN THE NEW WORLD

1713

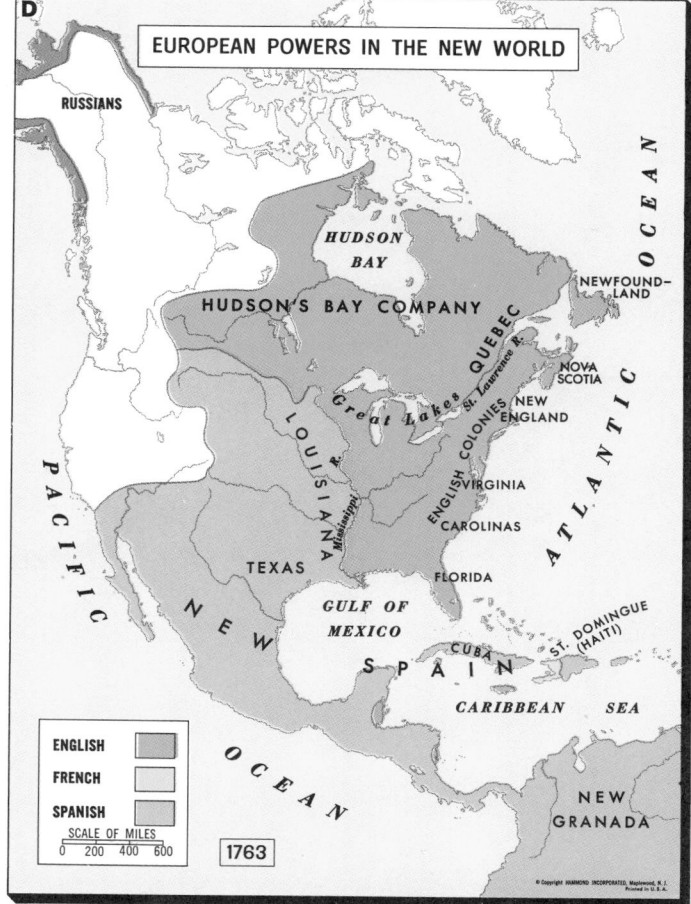

D EUROPEAN POWERS IN THE NEW WORLD

1763

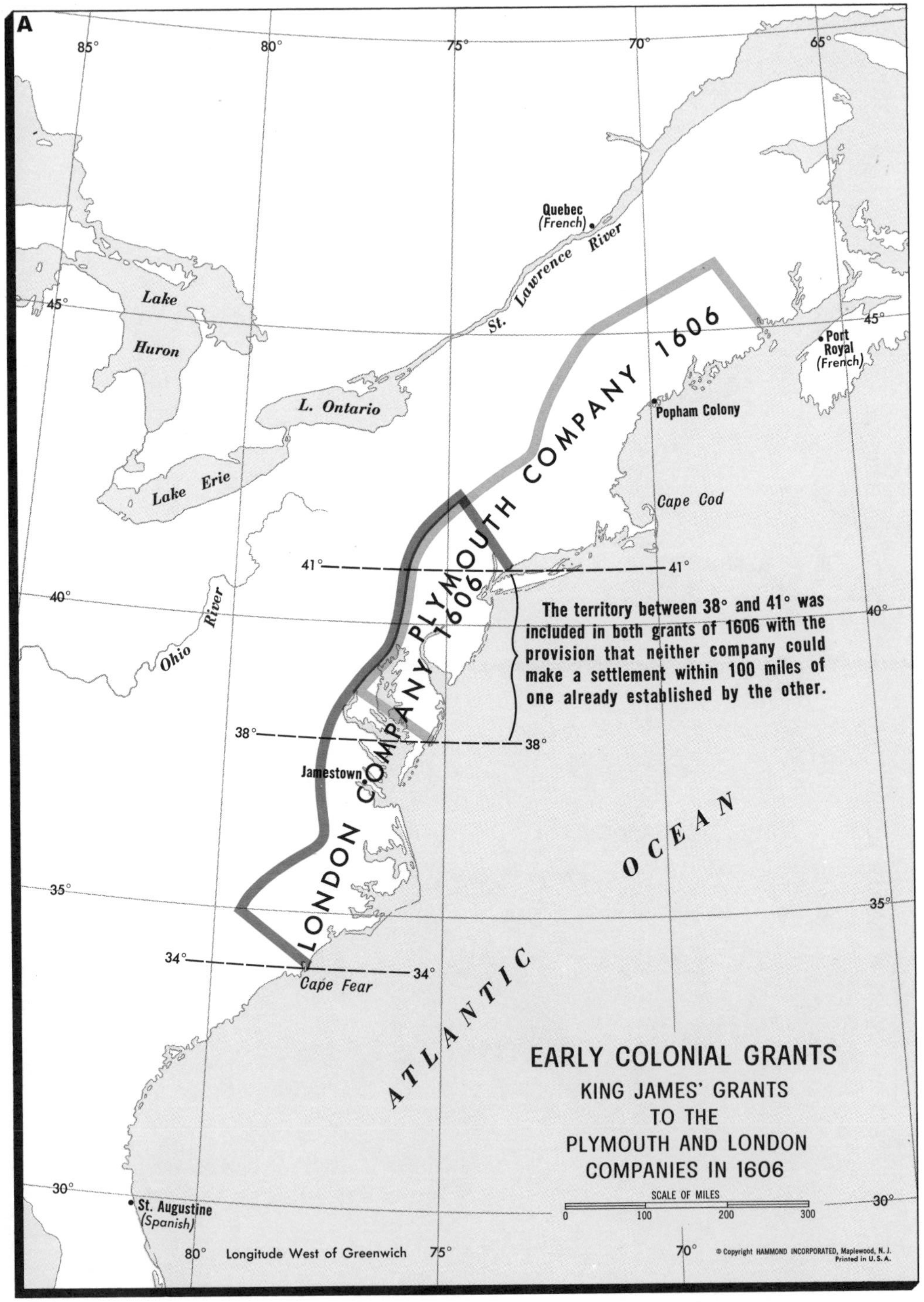

EARLY COLONIAL GRANTS
GRANTS TO THE VIRGINIA
COMPANY OF LONDON 1609
AND THE PLYMOUTH COUNCIL
FOR NEW ENGLAND 1620

PLYMOUTH COUNCIL
FOR NEW ENGLAND
1620

VIRGINIA COMPANY
OF
LONDON
1609

"from sea to sea"

"from sea to sea"

Port Royal (French)

Quebec (French)

St. Lawrence River

Cape Cod

Plymouth

L. Ontario

Lake Erie

Lake Huron

Lake

Ohio River

Jamestown

Point Comfort

Cape Fear

St. Augustine (Spanish)

ATLANTIC

OCEAN

Longitude West of Greenwich

SCALE OF MILES
0 100 200 300

© Copyright HAMMOND INCORPORATED, Maplewood, N.J.
Printed in U.S.A.

EARLY COLONIAL GRANTS
KING JAMES' GRANTS
TO THE
PLYMOUTH AND LONDON
COMPANIES IN 1606

PLYMOUTH COMPANY 1606

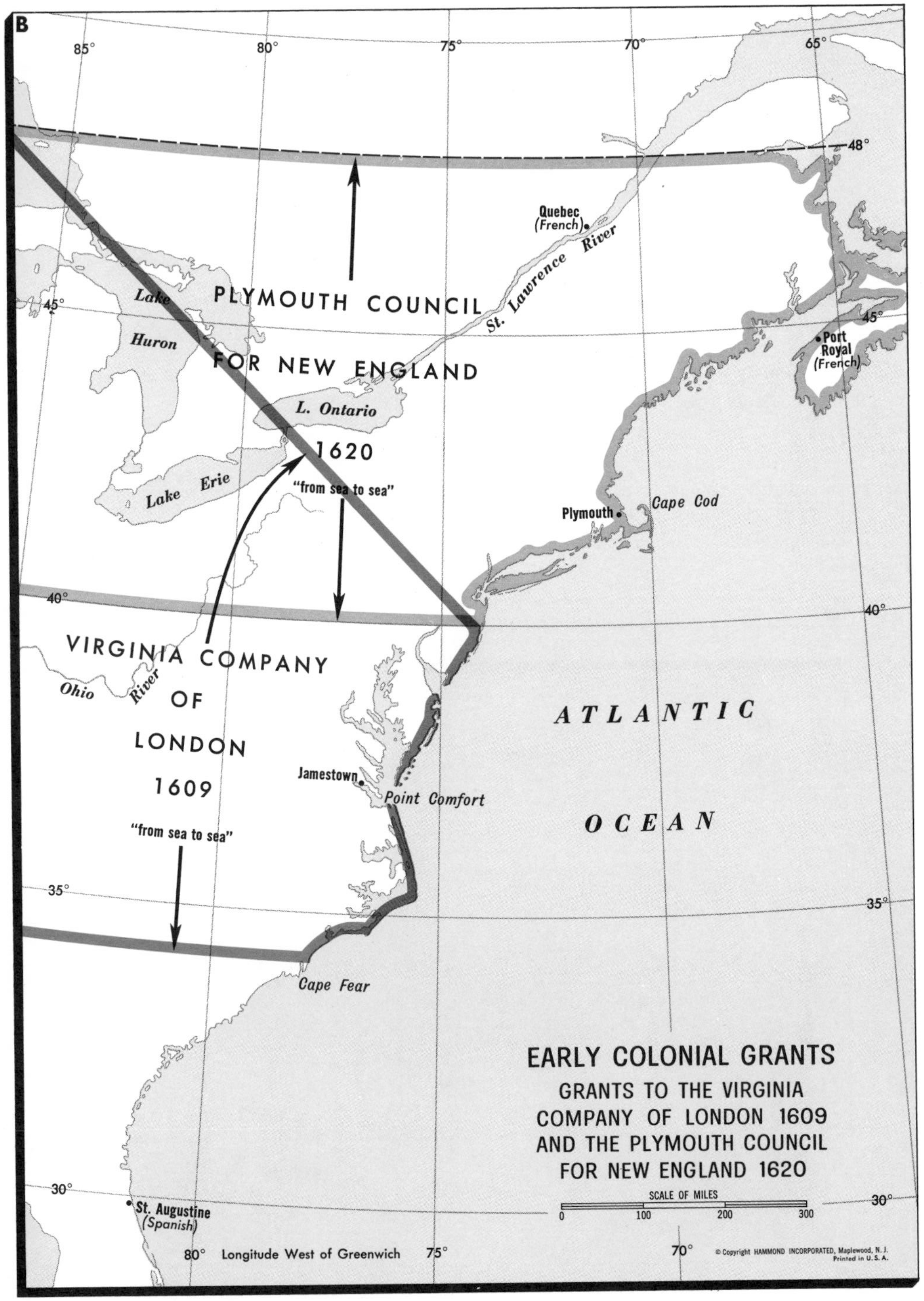

LONDON COMPANY 1606

The territory between 38° and 41° was
included in both grants of 1606 with the
provision that neither company could
make a settlement within 100 miles of
one already established by the other.

Port Royal (French)

Quebec (French)

St. Lawrence River

Popham Colony

Cape Cod

L. Ontario

Lake Erie

Lake Huron

Lake

Ohio River

Jamestown

Cape Fear

St. Augustine (Spanish)

ATLANTIC

OCEAN

41°

41°

38°

38°

34°

34°

Longitude West of Greenwich

SCALE OF MILES
0 100 200 300

© Copyright HAMMOND INCORPORATED, Maplewood, N.J.
Printed in U.S.A.

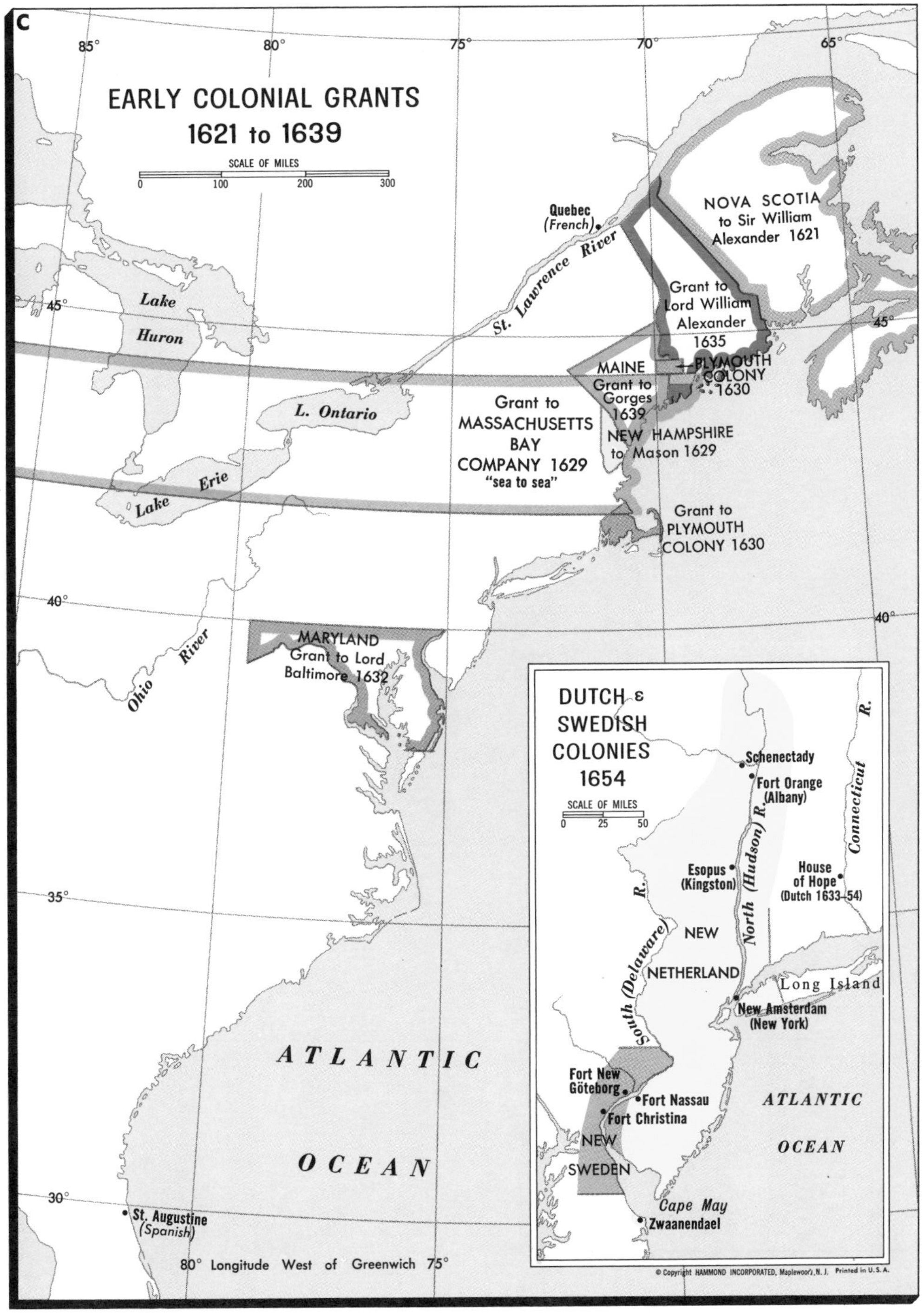

Map D — EARLY COLONIAL GRANTS 1662 to 1732

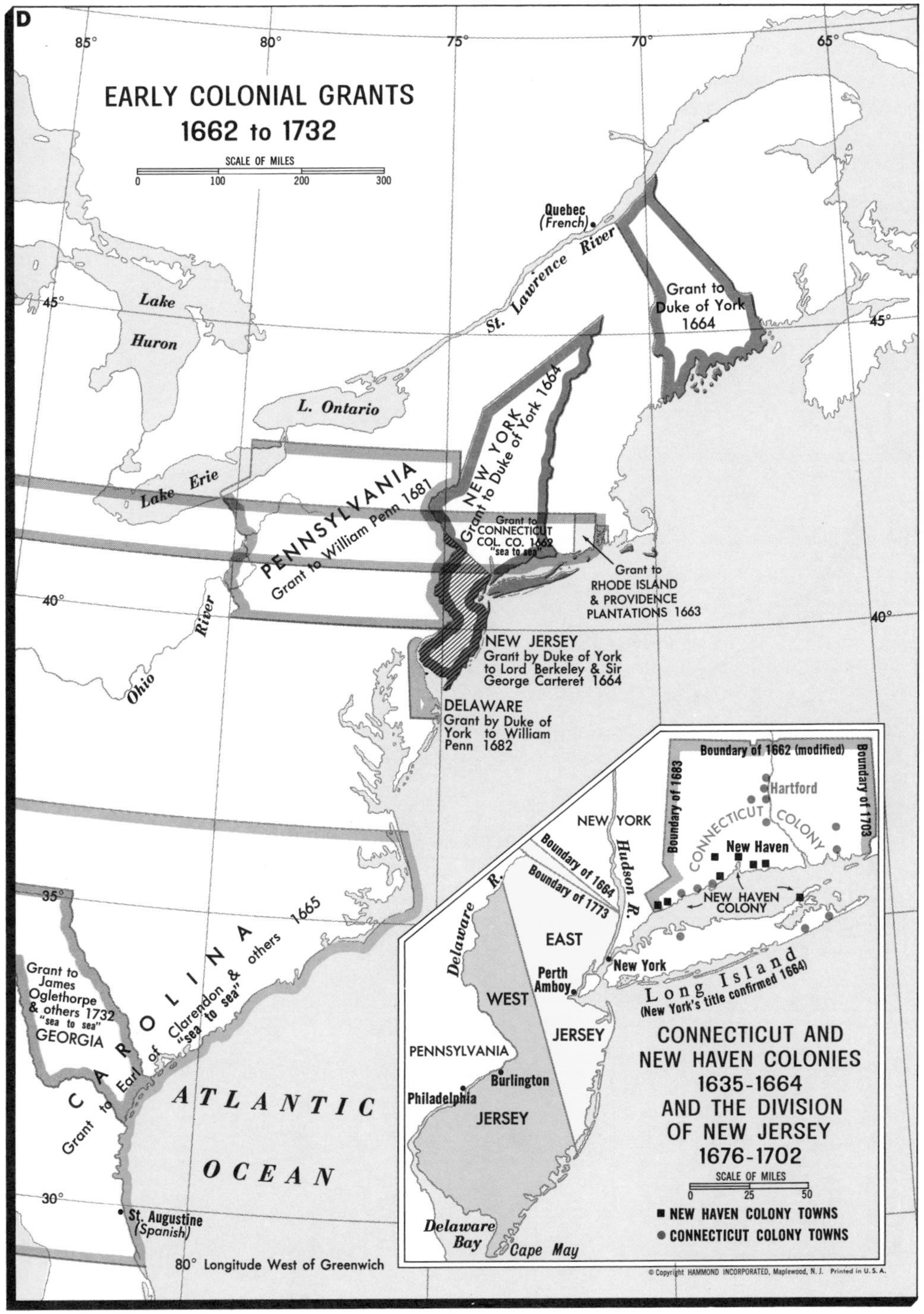

SCALE OF MILES
0 100 200 300

65°
45°
Quebec (French)
St. Lawrence River
Grant to Duke of York 1664
70°
L. Ontario
Lake Erie
Lake Huron
NEW YORK Grant to Duke of York 1664
Grant to CONNECTICUT COL. 1662 "sea to sea"
75°
PENNSYLVANIA Grant to William Penn 1681
Ohio River
Grant to RHODE ISLAND & PROVIDENCE PLANTATIONS 1663
NEW JERSEY Grant by Duke of York to Lord Berkeley & Sir George Carteret 1664
DELAWARE Grant by Duke of York to William Penn 1682
80°
85°
CAROLINA
Grant of Clarendon "sea to sea" & others 1665
GEORGIA Grant to James Oglethorpe & others 1732 "sea to sea"
35°
ATLANTIC OCEAN
30°
St. Augustine (Spanish)
80° Longitude West of Greenwich

Inset — CONNECTICUT AND NEW HAVEN COLONIES 1635-1664 AND THE DIVISION OF NEW JERSEY 1676-1702

Boundary of 1703
Boundary of 1662 (modified)
Hartford
Boundary of 1683 (New York's title confirmed 1680)
CONNECTICUT COLONY
New Haven
NEW HAVEN COLONY
Long Island
Boundary of 1664
Boundary of 1773
NEW YORK
Hudson R.
New York
Perth Amboy
EAST JERSEY
WEST JERSEY
Burlington
Delaware R.
PENNSYLVANIA
Philadelphia
Delaware Bay
Cape May

■ NEW HAVEN COLONY TOWNS
● CONNECTICUT COLONY TOWNS

SCALE OF MILES
0 25 50

© Copyright HAMMOND INCORPORATED, Maplewood, N.J. Printed in U.S.A.

D

Map C — EARLY COLONIAL GRANTS 1621 to 1639

SCALE OF MILES
0 100 200 300

65°
45°
40°
Quebec (French)
St. Lawrence River
NOVA SCOTIA to Sir William Alexander 1621
Grant to Lord William Alexander 1635
PLYMOUTH COLONY 1630
MAINE Grant to Gorges 1639
NEW HAMPSHIRE to Mason 1629
70°
Grant to MASSACHUSETTS BAY COMPANY 1629 "sea to sea"
Grant to PLYMOUTH COLONY 1630
L. Ontario
Lake Erie
Lake Huron
75°
Ohio River
MARYLAND Grant to Lord Baltimore 1632
80°
85°
ATLANTIC OCEAN
35°
30°
St. Augustine (Spanish)
80° Longitude West of Greenwich 75°

Inset — DUTCH & SWEDISH COLONIES 1654

Connecticut R.
Schenectady
Fort Orange (Albany)
House of Hope (Dutch 1633-54)
Esopus (Kingston)
North (Hudson) R.
NEW NETHERLAND
New Amsterdam (New York)
Long Island
ATLANTIC OCEAN
South (Delaware) R.
Fort Nassau
Fort New Göteborg
Fort Christina
NEW SWEDEN
Cape May
Zwaanendael

SCALE OF MILES
0 25 50

© Copyright HAMMOND INCORPORATED, Maplewood, N.J. Printed in U.S.A.

C

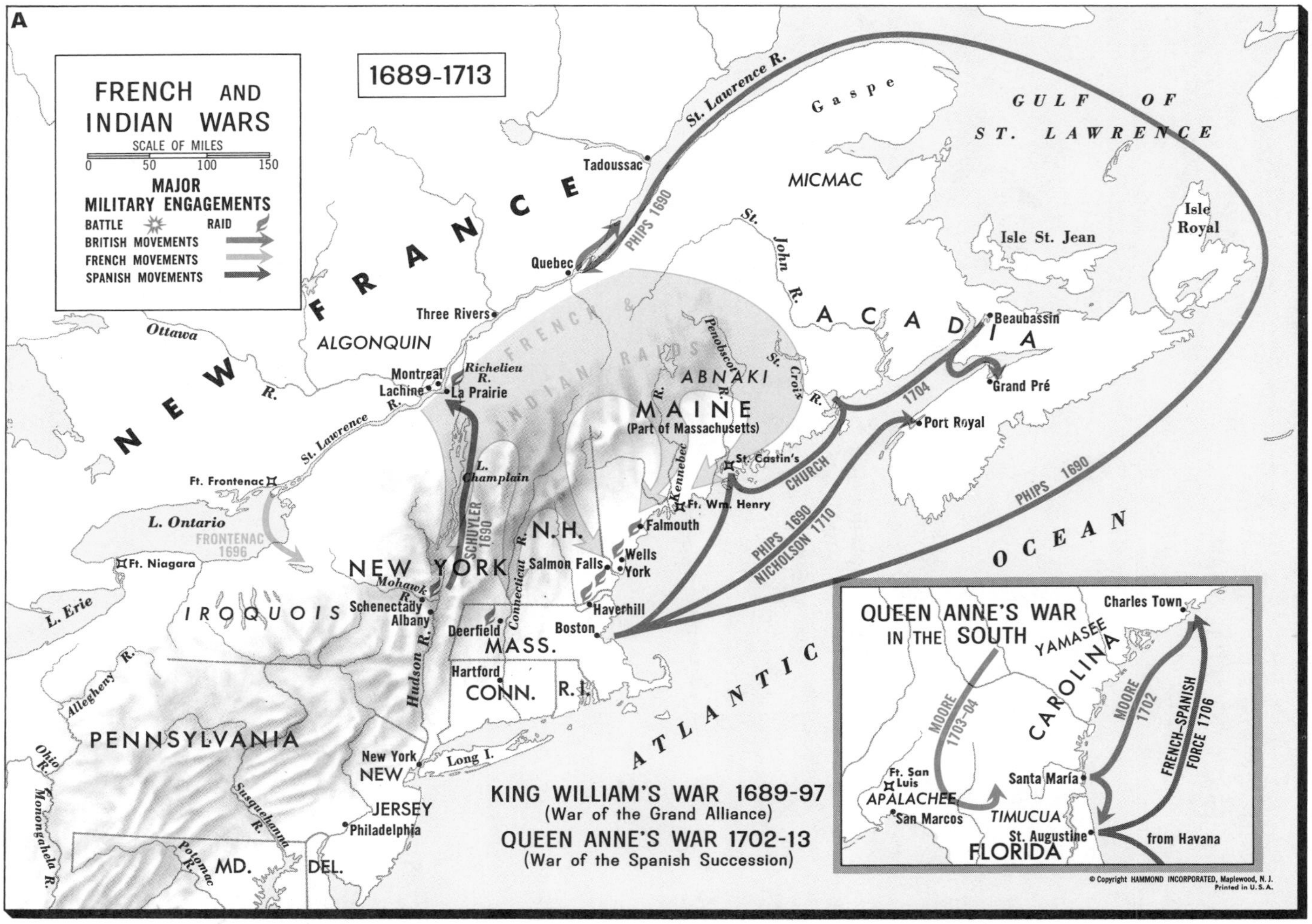

A

FRENCH AND INDIAN WARS

1689-1713

SCALE OF MILES
0   50   100   150

MAJOR MILITARY ENGAGEMENTS
BATTLE   RAID
BRITISH MOVEMENTS
FRENCH MOVEMENTS
SPANISH MOVEMENTS

NEW FRANCE

GULF OF ST. LAWRENCE

St. Lawrence R.
Gaspe
MICMAC
Tadoussac
Quebec
PHIPS 1690
Three Rivers
ALGONQUIN
Ottawa R.
Montreal
Lachine
Richelieu R.
La Prairie
Ft. Frontenac
FRONTENAC 1696
L. Ontario
Ft. Niagara
L. Erie
IROQUOIS
SCHUYLER 1690
L. Champlain
Mohawk R.
Schenectady
Albany
Deerfield
Hartford
CONN.
R.I.
PENNSYLVANIA
Allegheny R.
Ohio R.
Monongahela R.
Susquehanna R.
Potomac R.
MD.   DEL.
Philadelphia
JERSEY
NEW
New York
Long I.
NEW YORK
N.H.
Salmon Falls
Wells
York
Haverhill
Boston
MASS.
Falmouth
Ft. Wm. Henry
St. Castin's
Kennebec R.
ABNAKI
MAINE (Part of Massachusetts)
FRENCH RAIDS
St. John R.
St. Croix R.
Penobscot R.
ACADIA
Beaubassin
Grand Pré
Port Royal
1704
CHURCH
PHIPS 1690
NICHOLSON 1710
Isle St. Jean
Isle Royal
PHIPS 1690
ATLANTIC OCEAN

KING WILLIAM'S WAR 1689-97
(War of the Grand Alliance)
QUEEN ANNE'S WAR 1702-13
(War of the Spanish Succession)

QUEEN ANNE'S WAR IN THE SOUTH
Charles Town
YAMASEE
CAROLINA
MOORE 1703-04
MOORE 1702
FRENCH-SPANISH FORCE 1706
Ft. San Luis
APALACHEE
San Marcos
Santa María
TIMUCUA
St. Augustine
FLORIDA
from Havana

© Copyright HAMMOND INCORPORATED, Maplewood, N.J.
Printed in U.S.A.

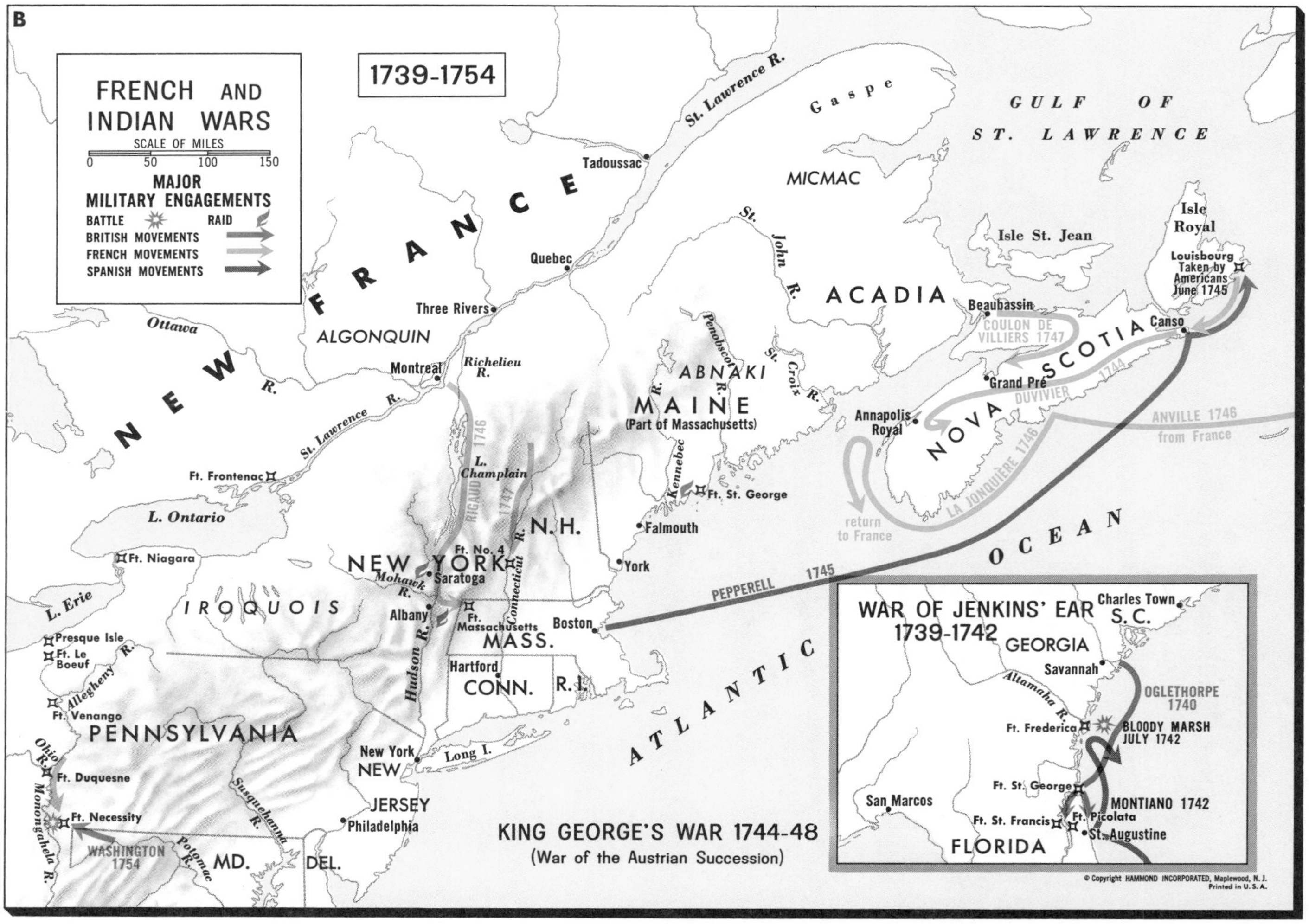

B

FRENCH AND INDIAN WARS

1739-1754

SCALE OF MILES
0   50   100   150

MAJOR MILITARY ENGAGEMENTS
BATTLE   RAID
BRITISH MOVEMENTS
FRENCH MOVEMENTS
SPANISH MOVEMENTS

NEW FRANCE

GULF OF ST. LAWRENCE

St. Lawrence R.
Gaspe
MICMAC
Tadoussac
Quebec
Three Rivers
ALGONQUIN
Ottawa R.
Montreal
Richelieu R.
Ft. Frontenac
L. Ontario
Ft. Niagara
L. Erie
Presque Isle
Ft. Le Boeuf
Allegheny R.
Ft. Venango
IROQUOIS
L. Champlain
RIGAUD 1747
Mohawk R.
Saratoga
Albany
Ft. No. 4
Hudson R.
Massachusetts Ft.
Hartford
CONN.
R.I.
NEW YORK
N.H.
Ft. St. George
Falmouth
York
Kennebec R.
ABNAKI
MAINE (Part of Massachusetts)
St. John R.
St. Croix R.
Penobscot R.
ACADIA
Beaubassin
Grand Pré
Annapolis Royal
NOVA SCOTIA
Canso
COULON DE VILLIERS 1747
DUVIVIER 1744
LA JONQUIÈRE 1746
ANVILLE 1746 from France
return to France
Louisbourg Taken by Americans June 1745
Isle St. Jean
Isle Royal
PEPPERELL 1745
Boston
MASS.
1746
Ohio R.
Monongahela R.
Ft. Duquesne
Ft. Necessity
WASHINGTON 1754
PENNSYLVANIA
Susquehanna R.
Potomac R.
MD.   DEL.
Philadelphia
JERSEY
NEW
New York
Long I.
ATLANTIC OCEAN

KING GEORGE'S WAR 1744-48
(War of the Austrian Succession)

WAR OF JENKINS' EAR 1739-1742
Charles Town S.C.
GEORGIA
Savannah
Altamaha R.
OGLETHORPE 1740
Ft. Frederica
BLOODY MARSH JULY 1742
Ft. St. George
Ft. St. Francis
Ft. Picolata
St. Augustine
MONTIANO 1742
San Marcos
FLORIDA

© Copyright HAMMOND INCORPORATED, Maplewood, N.J.
Printed in U.S.A.

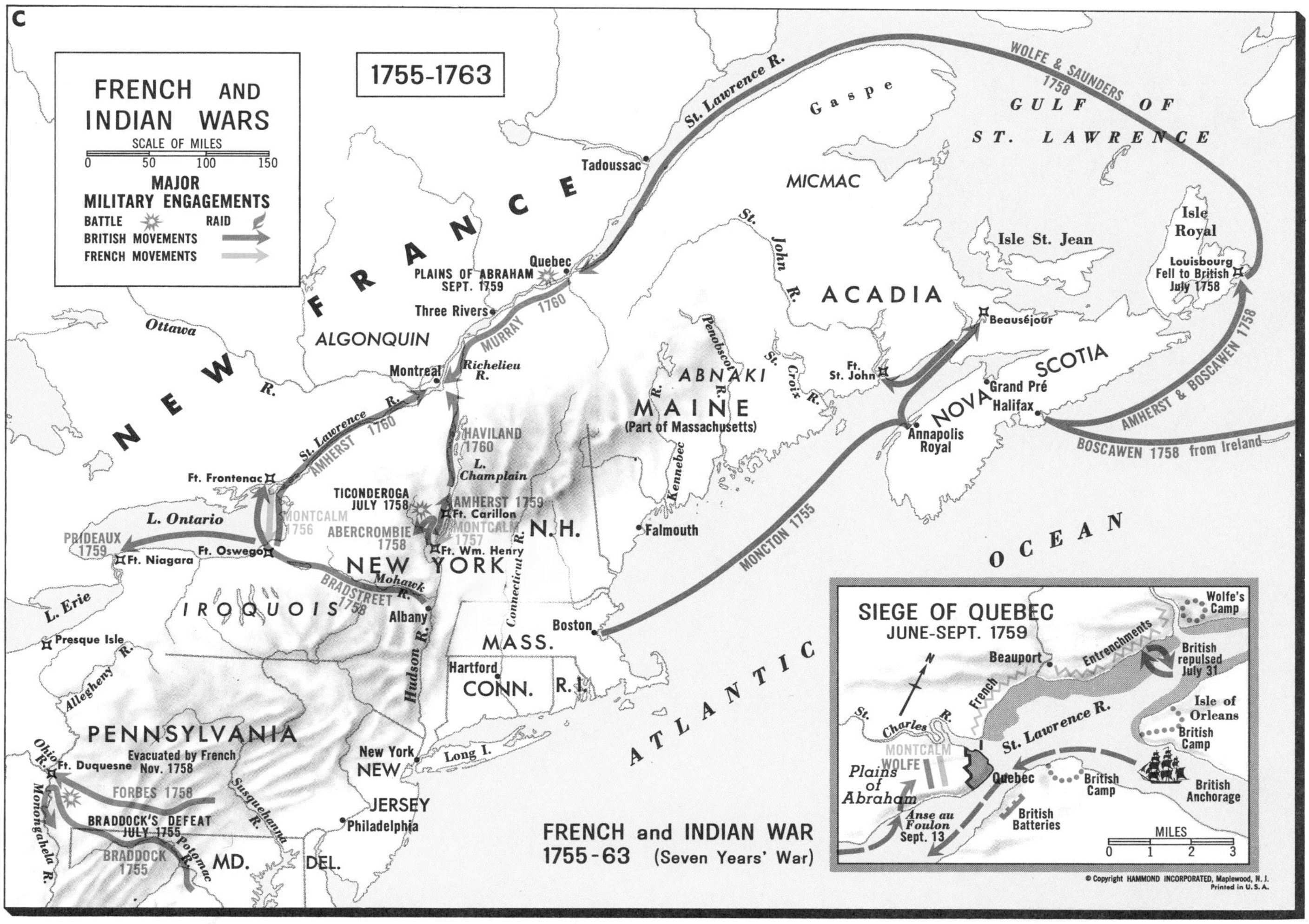

Map C

1755-1763

FRENCH AND INDIAN WARS

SCALE OF MILES
0 50 100 150

MAJOR MILITARY ENGAGEMENTS
BATTLE ☼   RAID ➴
BRITISH MOVEMENTS →
FRENCH MOVEMENTS →

NEW FRANCE

Ottawa R.
ALGONQUIN
Montreal
Richelieu R.
St. Lawrence R.
AMHERST 1760
Ft. Frontenac
PRIDEAUX 1759
Ft. Niagara
L. Ontario
MONTCALM 1756
Ft. Oswego
ABERCROMBIE 1758
BRADSTREET 1758
L. Erie
Presque Isle
IROQUOIS
Allegheny R.
PENNSYLVANIA
Ohio R.
Ft. Duquesne — Evacuated by French Nov. 1758
FORBES 1758
Monongahela R.
BRADDOCK'S DEFEAT JULY 1755
BRADDOCK 1755
MD.   DEL.
Susquehanna R.
Potomac R.
Philadelphia
NEW JERSEY
New York
Long I.
NEW YORK
Hudson R.
Albany
Mohawk R.
MURRAY 1760
TICONDEROGA JULY 1758
MONTCALM 1757
Ft. Carillon
Ft. Wm. Henry
AMHERST 1759
HAVILAND 1760
L. Champlain
N.H.
Connecticut R.
MASS.
Boston
Hartford
CONN.   R.I.

PLAINS OF ABRAHAM SEPT. 1759
Quebec
Three Rivers
Tadoussac
St. Lawrence R.
Gaspe
MICMAC
ABNAKI
MAINE (Part of Massachusetts)
Penobscot R.
Kennebec R.
St. Croix R.
St. John R.
Falmouth
Ft. St. John
Beauséjour
MONCTON 1755
Grand Pré
Annapolis Royal
Halifax
NOVA SCOTIA
Isle St. Jean
Isle Royal
Louisbourg Fell to British July 1758
GULF OF ST. LAWRENCE
WOLFE & SAUNDERS 1758
AMHERST & BOSCAWEN 1758
BOSCAWEN 1758 from Ireland
ATLANTIC OCEAN

SIEGE OF QUEBEC JUNE-SEPT. 1759
Wolfe's Camp
Beauport
Entrenchments
British repulsed July 31
Isle of Orleans
British Camp
St. Charles R.
French R.
St. Lawrence R.
MONTCALM
WOLFE
Plains of Abraham
Quebec
Anse au Foulon Sept. 13
British Batteries
British Camp
British Anchorage
MILES 0 1 2 3

FRENCH and INDIAN WAR 1755-63 (Seven Years' War)
© Copyright HAMMOND INCORPORATED, Maplewood, N.J. Printed in U.S.A.

Map D

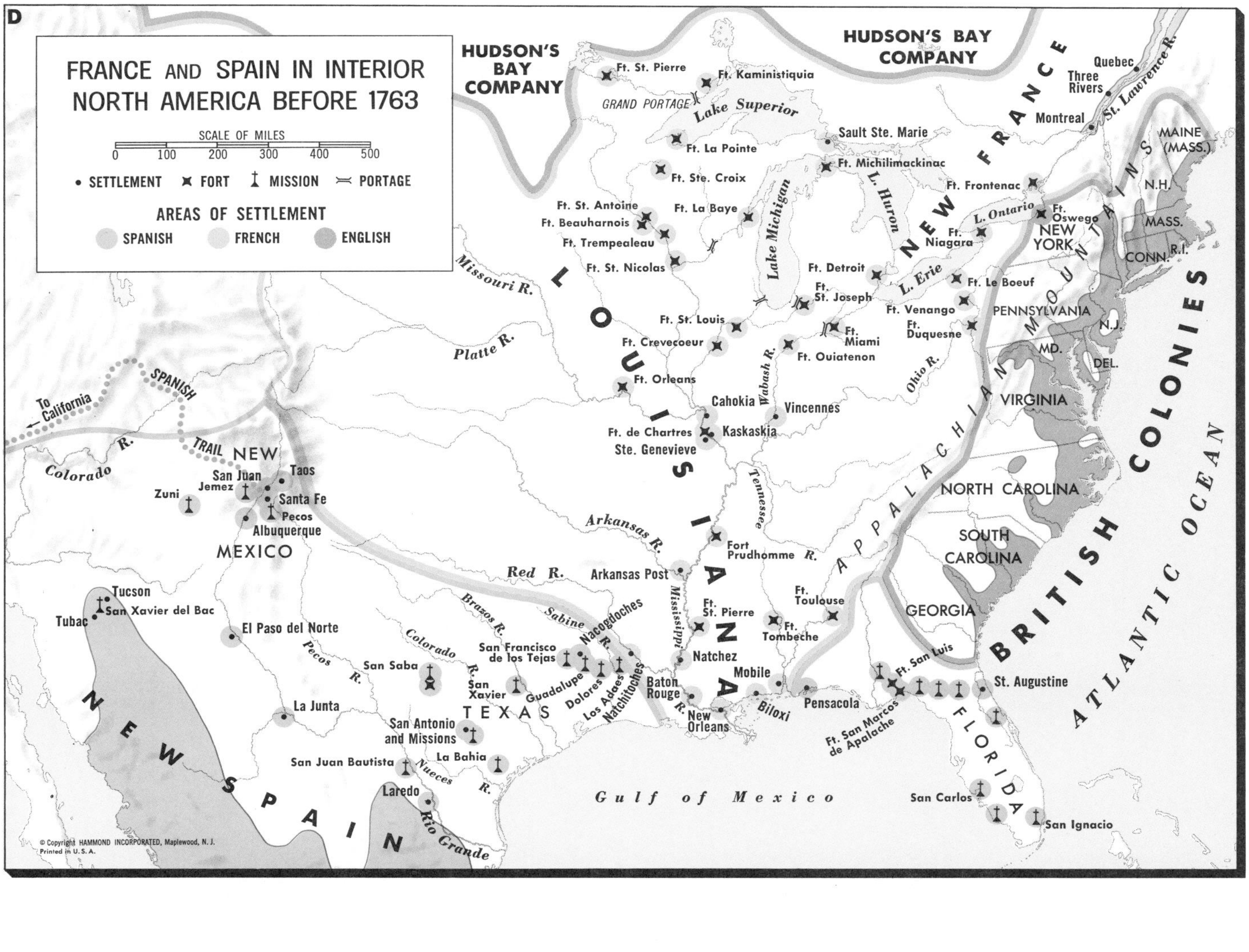

FRANCE AND SPAIN IN INTERIOR NORTH AMERICA BEFORE 1763

SCALE OF MILES
0 100 200 300 400 500

• SETTLEMENT   ✕ FORT   ⊥ MISSION   ⋈ PORTAGE

AREAS OF SETTLEMENT
● SPANISH   ● FRENCH   ● ENGLISH

HUDSON'S BAY COMPANY
Ft. St. Pierre
Ft. Kaministiquia
GRAND PORTAGE
Lake Superior
Sault Ste. Marie
Ft. La Pointe
Ft. Ste. Croix
Ft. St. Antoine
Ft. Beauharnois
Ft. Trempealeau
Ft. St. Nicolas
Ft. La Baye
Ft. Michilimackinac
Lake Michigan
L. Huron
Ft. St. Louis
Ft. Crevecoeur
Ft. St. Joseph
Ft. Detroit
Ft. Miami
Ft. Ouiatenon
Ft. Orleans
Cahokia
Vincennes
Wabash R.
Ft. de Chartres
Ste. Genevieve
Kaskaskia
Missouri R.
Platte R.
LOUISIANA
Ft. Le Boeuf
Ft. Venango
Ft. Duquesne
L. Erie
L. Ontario
Ft. Niagara
Oswego
NEW YORK
NEW FRANCE
Quebec
Three Rivers
Montreal
St. Lawrence R.
MAINE (MASS.)
N.H.
MASS.
CONN. R.I.
PENNSYLVANIA
N.J.
MD. DEL.
VIRGINIA
NORTH CAROLINA
SOUTH CAROLINA
GEORGIA
APPALACHIAN MOUNTAINS
BRITISH COLONIES
ATLANTIC OCEAN
Ohio R.
Tennessee R.
Arkansas R.
Fort Prudhomme
Arkansas Post
Red R.
Ft. St. Pierre
Ft. Toulouse
Ft. Tombeche
Natchez
Mobile
Biloxi
New Orleans
Baton Rouge
Pensacola
Ft. San Marcos de Apalache
St. Augustine
FLORIDA
San Carlos
San Ignacio
To California
SPANISH TRAIL
Colorado R.
NEW MEXICO
Zuni
Taos
San Juan
Jemez
Santa Fe
Pecos
Albuquerque
MEXICO
Tucson
San Xavier del Bac
Tubac
El Paso del Norte
Pecos R.
San Saba
La Junta
Colorado R.
Brazos R.
Sabine R.
Nacogdoches
San Francisco de los Tejas
San Xavier
Guadalupe
Dolores
Los Adaes
Natchitoches
TEXAS
San Antonio and Missions
La Bahia
San Juan Bautista
Nueces R.
Laredo
Rio Grande
NEW SPAIN
Gulf of Mexico
Ft. San Luis

© Copyright HAMMOND INCORPORATED, Maplewood, N.J. Printed in U.S.A.

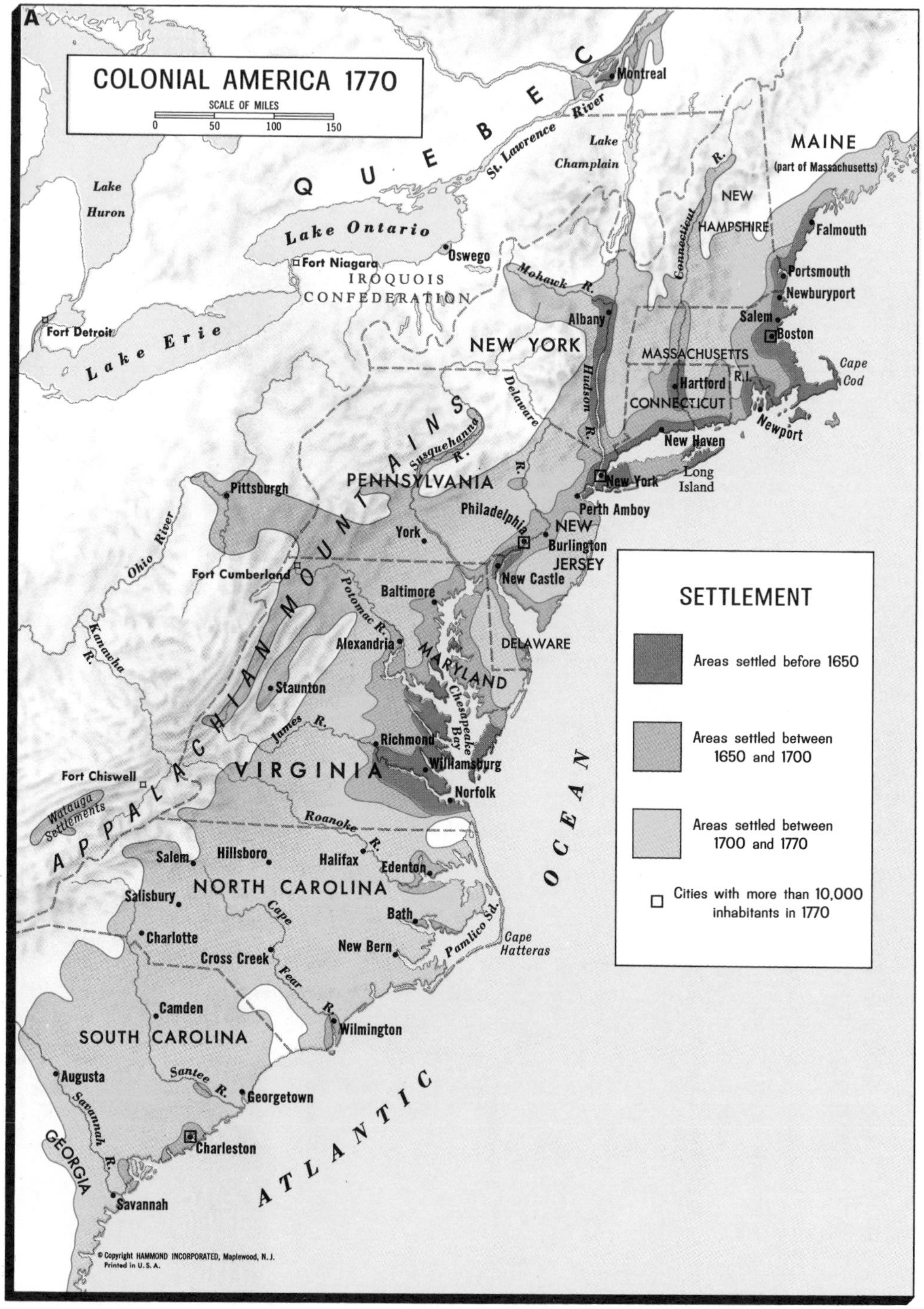

COLONIAL AMERICA 1770

ECONOMY AND ROADS

General Farming: Grain and Livestock
Tobacco
Rice and Indigo
Naval Stores and Timber
Iron Works
Main Roads

AN EXAMPLE OF A TRIANGULAR TRADE ROUTE

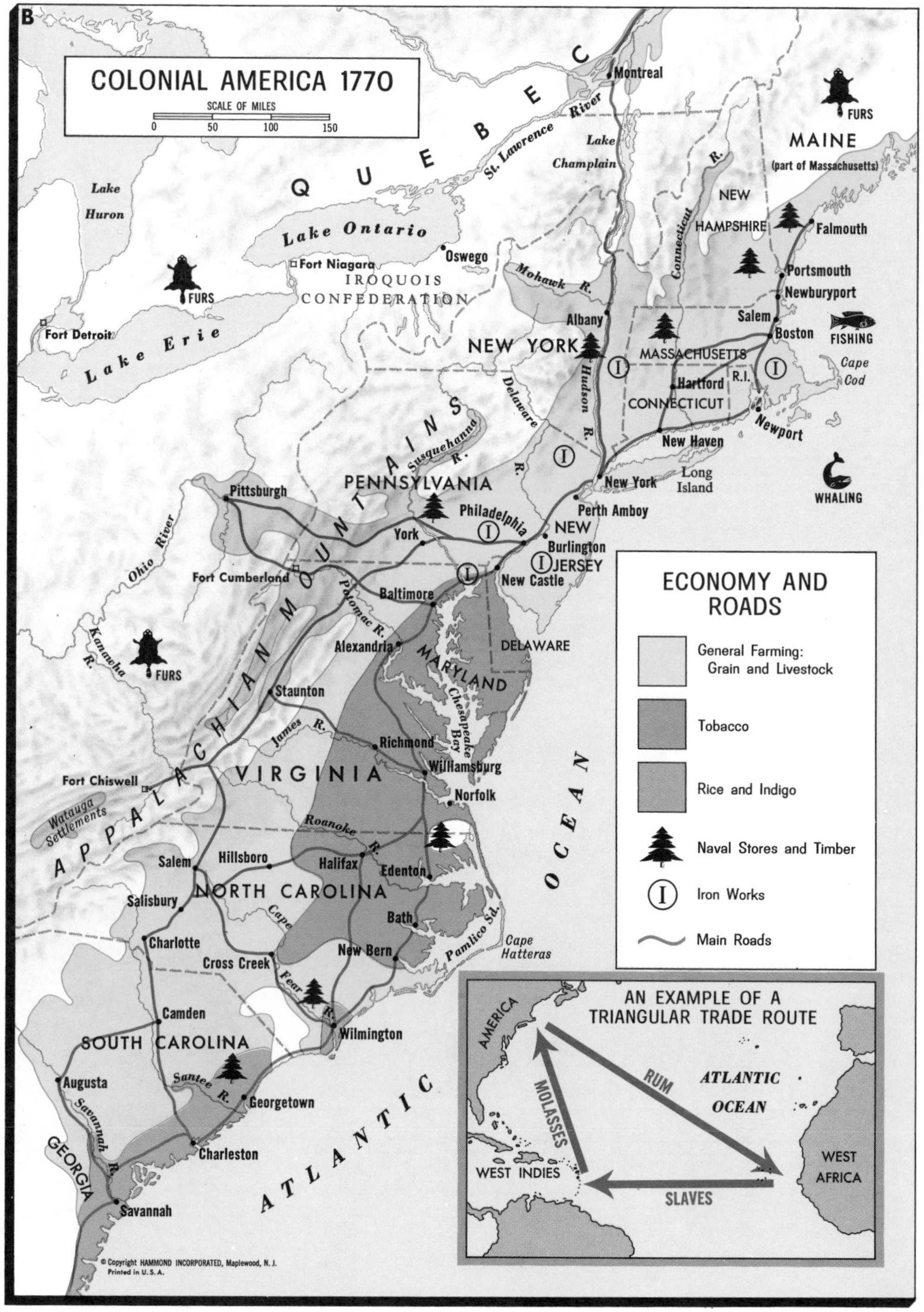

COLONIAL AMERICA 1770

SETTLEMENT

Areas settled before 1650
Areas settled between 1650 and 1700
Areas settled between 1700 and 1770
Cities with more than 10,000 inhabitants in 1770

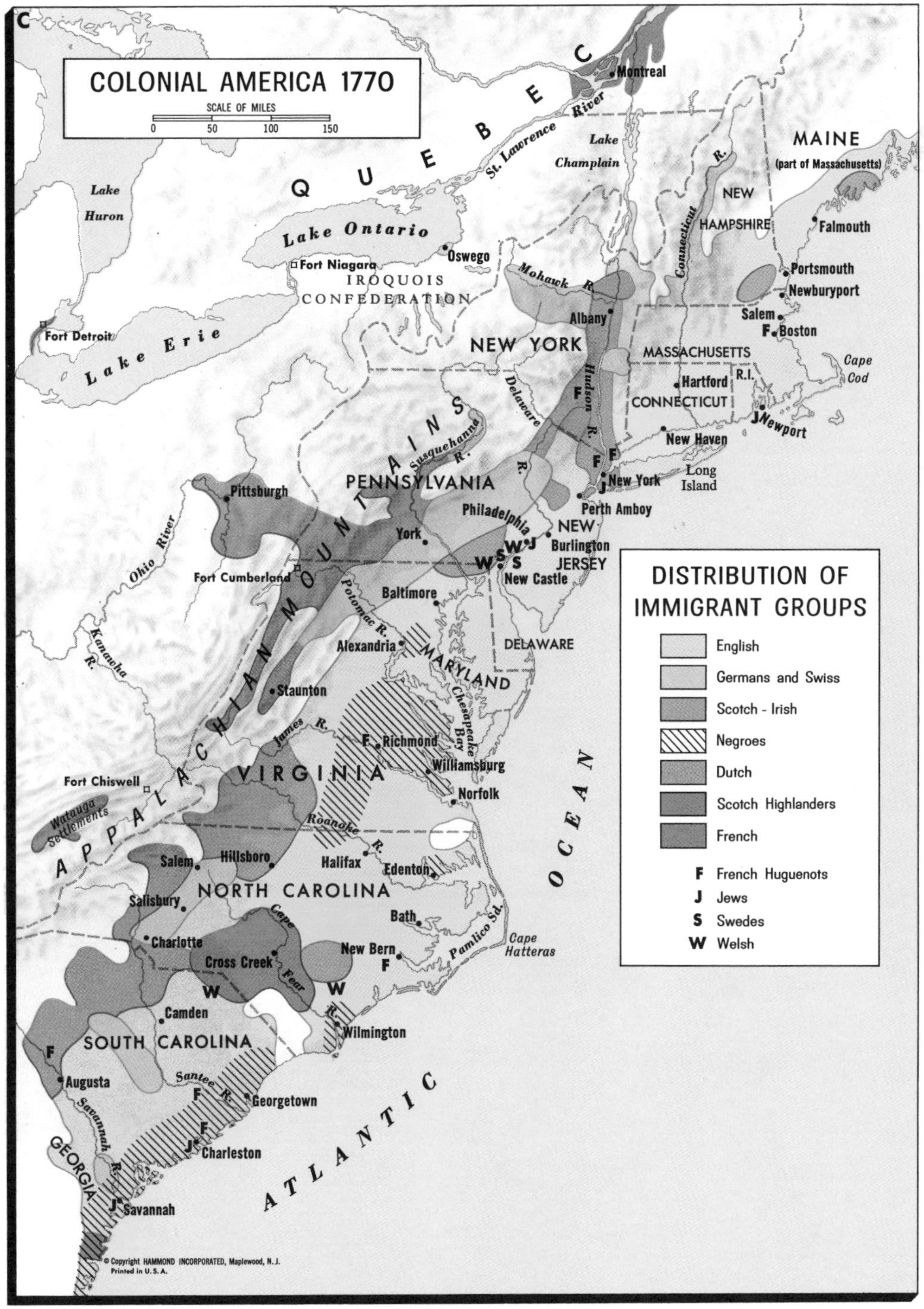

COLONIAL CALIFORNIA

SCALE OF MILES
0   25   50   75   100

D

S I E R R A   N E V A D A

Sacramento R.

San Joaquin R.

Mojave Desert

SPANISH TRAIL

Cajon Pass

EL CAMINO REAL

C O A S T   R A N G E S

Fort Ross (Russian)

San Francisco Solano 1823
San Rafael 1817
San Francisco de Asis 1776
San Francisco
Santa Clara 1777
San José 1797
San José
Santa Cruz 1791
Monterey
San Carlos Borromeo 1770
San Juan Bautista 1797
Soledad 1791
Salinas R.
San Antonio de Padua 1771
San Miguel Arcángel 1797
San Luis Obispo 1772
La Purísima 1787
Santa Inés 1804
Santa Bárbara 1786
Santa Barbara
San Buenaventura 1782
San Fernando 1797
San Gabriel 1771
Los Angeles
San Juan Capistrano 1776
San Luis Rey 1798
San Diego
San Diego de Alcalá 1769

S A N T A   B A R B A R A   I S L A N D S

P A C I F I C   O C E A N

Settlement (Civic Pueblo)
Mission
Presidio or Fort
Areas settled by 1823

© Copyright HAMMOND INCORPORATED, Maplewood, N.J.
Printed in U.S.A.

COLONIAL AMERICA 1770

SCALE OF MILES
0   50   100   150

C

Lake Huron
Lake Erie
Lake Ontario
Lake Champlain
St. Lawrence River

Q U E B E C

Fort Detroit
Fort Chiswell
Fort Niagara
Oswego
Montreal

IROQUOIS CONFEDERATION

MAINE (part of Massachusetts)
Falmouth
Portsmouth
Newburyport
Salem
Boston
Newport
NEW HAMPSHIRE
Connecticut R.
MASSACHUSETTS
R.I.
Hartford
CONNECTICUT
New Haven
New York
Long Island
Perth Amboy
NEW JERSEY
Burlington
New Castle
Albany
Mohawk R.
Hudson R.
NEW YORK
Delaware R.
PENNSYLVANIA
Philadelphia
Pittsburgh
Fort Cumberland
Ohio River
Kanawha R.
York
Susquehanna R.
DELAWARE
MARYLAND
Baltimore
Potomac R.
Alexandria
Chesapeake Bay
Williamsburg
Richmond
Norfolk
VIRGINIA
Staunton
Roanoke R.
Edenton
Bath
New Bern
Halifax
Hillsboro
Cape Fear
NORTH CAROLINA
Wilmington
Salisbury
Salem
Charlotte
Cross Creek
Camden
Cape Cod
Cape Hatteras
Pamlico Sd.
SOUTH CAROLINA
Georgetown
Charleston
Santee R.
Augusta
Savannah
GEORGIA
Savannah R.

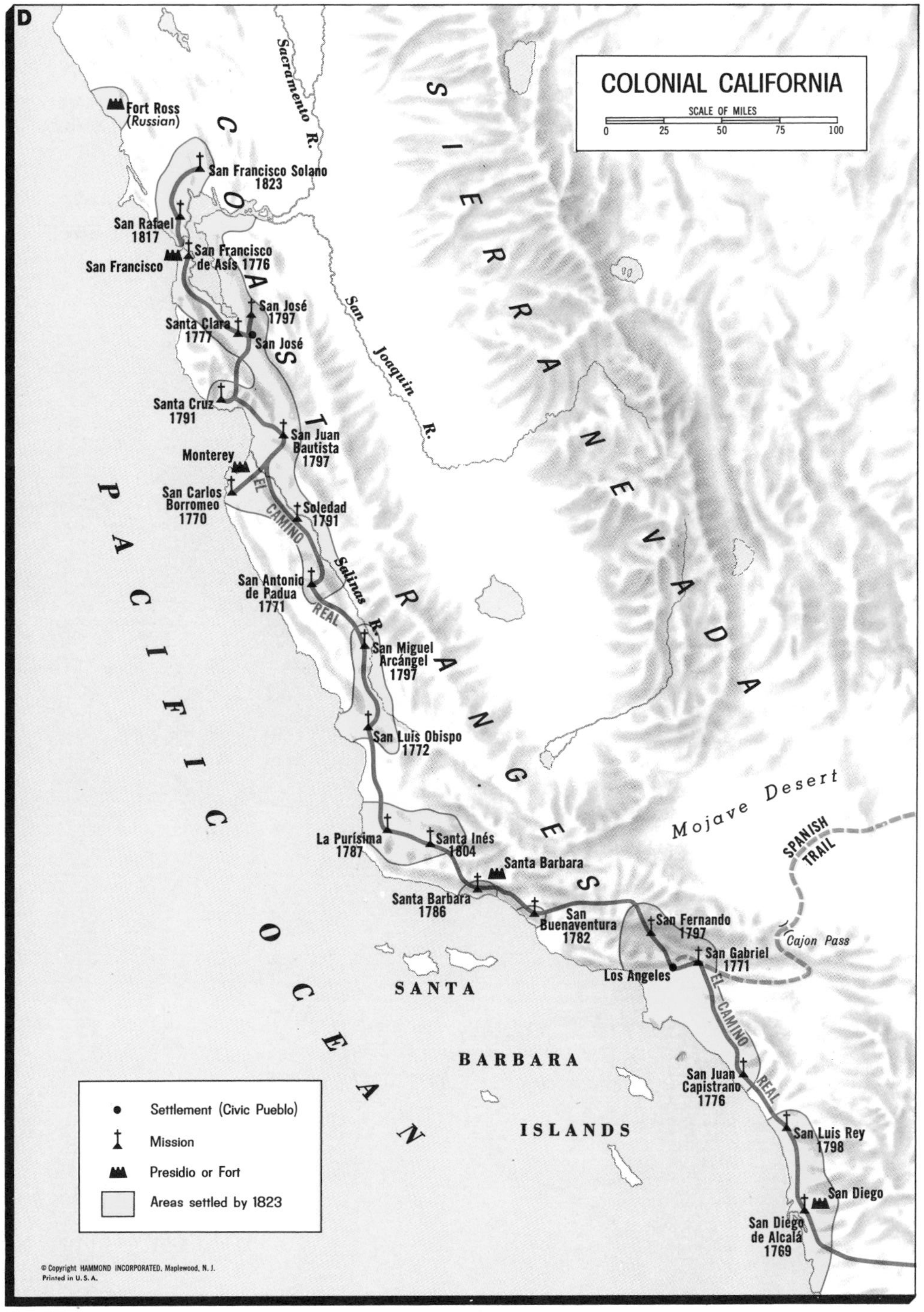

A P P A L A C H I A N   M O U N T A I N S

A T L A N T I C   O C E A N

DISTRIBUTION OF IMMIGRANT GROUPS

English
Germans and Swiss
Scotch - Irish
Negroes
Dutch
Scotch Highlanders
French

F   French Huguenots
J   Jews
S   Swedes
W   Welsh

© Copyright HAMMOND INCORPORATED, Maplewood, N.J.
Printed in U.S.A.

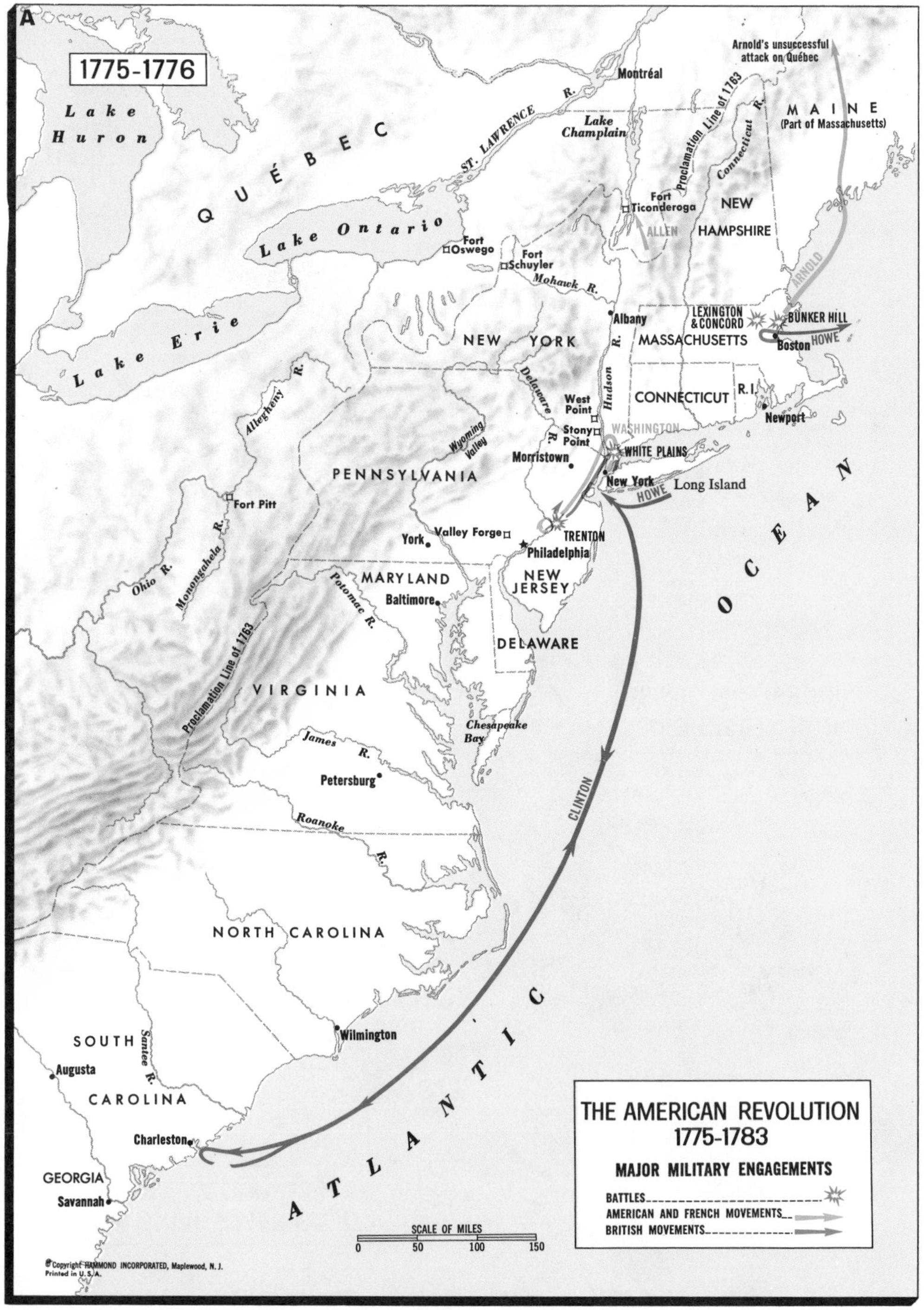

Map B (1777-1778)

B

1777-1778

THE AMERICAN REVOLUTION
1775-1783

MAJOR MILITARY ENGAGEMENTS

BATTLES
AMERICAN AND FRENCH MOVEMENTS
BRITISH MOVEMENTS

SCALE OF MILES
0   50   100   150

Inset:
THE BRITISH PLAN TO SPLIT THE COLONIES

Montréal · St. LAWRENCE R. · QUÉBEC · Lake Champlain · Proclamation Line of 1763 · BURGOYNE · Mohawk R. · ST. LEGER · Hudson R. · HOWE · Albany · New York · NEW YORK · NEW JERSEY · PENNSYLVANIA · Delaware

Map B labels:
M A I N E (Part of Massachusetts) · Boston · Newport · R.I. · NEW HAMPSHIRE · Connecticut R. · Proclamation Line of 1763 · Fort Ticonderoga · STARK · BENNINGTON · MASSACHUSETTS · CONNECTICUT · Long Island · New York · Monmouth C.H. · BURGOYNE · Montréal · St. LAWRENCE R. · Lake Champlain · SARATOGA · GATES · ARNOLD · Albany · Hudson R. · West Point · Stony Point · Morristown · Philadelphia · NEW JERSEY · DELAWARE · HOWE · Fort Schuyler · Mohawk R. · Fort Oswego · ST. LEGER · NEW YORK · Delaware R. · Paoli · Germantown · Valley Forge · BRANDYWINE · WASHINGTON · York · PENNSYLVANIA · MARYLAND · Baltimore · Chesapeake Bay · Q U É B E C · Lake Ontario · Lake Erie · L a k e H u r o n · Allegheny R. · Fort Pitt · Monongahela R. · Ohio R. · CLARK · George Rogers Clark to Kaskaskia and Vincennes · Proclamation Line of 1763 · VIRGINIA · Potomac R. · James R. · Petersburg · Roanoke R. · NORTH CAROLINA · Wilmington · SOUTH CAROLINA · Santee R. · Charleston · Augusta · GEORGIA · Savannah · CAMPBELL · A T L A N T I C O C E A N

© Copyright HAMMOND, INCORPORATED, Maplewood, N.J.
Printed in U.S.A.

Map A (1775-1776)

A

1775-1776

THE AMERICAN REVOLUTION
1775-1783

MAJOR MILITARY ENGAGEMENTS

BATTLES
AMERICAN AND FRENCH MOVEMENTS
BRITISH MOVEMENTS

SCALE OF MILES
0   50   100   150

Map A labels:
M A I N E (Part of Massachusetts) · Arnold's unsuccessful attack on Québec · ARNOLD · BUNKER HILL · Boston · HOWE · Newport · R.I. · NEW HAMPSHIRE · Connecticut R. · Proclamation Line of 1763 · LEXINGTON & CONCORD · MASSACHUSETTS · CONNECTICUT · Long Island · New York · WHITE PLAINS · HOWE · Montréal · Fort Ticonderoga · ALLEN · Lake Champlain · St. LAWRENCE R. · Albany · Hudson R. · WASHINGTON · West Point · Stony Point · TRENTON · Morristown · Philadelphia · NEW JERSEY · DELAWARE · Fort Schuyler · Mohawk R. · Fort Oswego · NEW YORK · Delaware R. · Paoli · Valley Forge · Germantown · York · PENNSYLVANIA · MARYLAND · Baltimore · Chesapeake Bay · CLINTON · Q U É B E C · Lake Ontario · Lake Erie · L a k e H u r o n · Allegheny R. · Fort Pitt · Monongahela R. · Ohio R. · Proclamation Line of 1763 · VIRGINIA · Potomac R. · James R. · Petersburg · Roanoke R. · NORTH CAROLINA · Wilmington · SOUTH CAROLINA · Santee R. · Charleston · Augusta · GEORGIA · Savannah · A T L A N T I C O C E A N

© Copyright HAMMOND, INCORPORATED, Maplewood, N.J.
Printed in U.S.A.

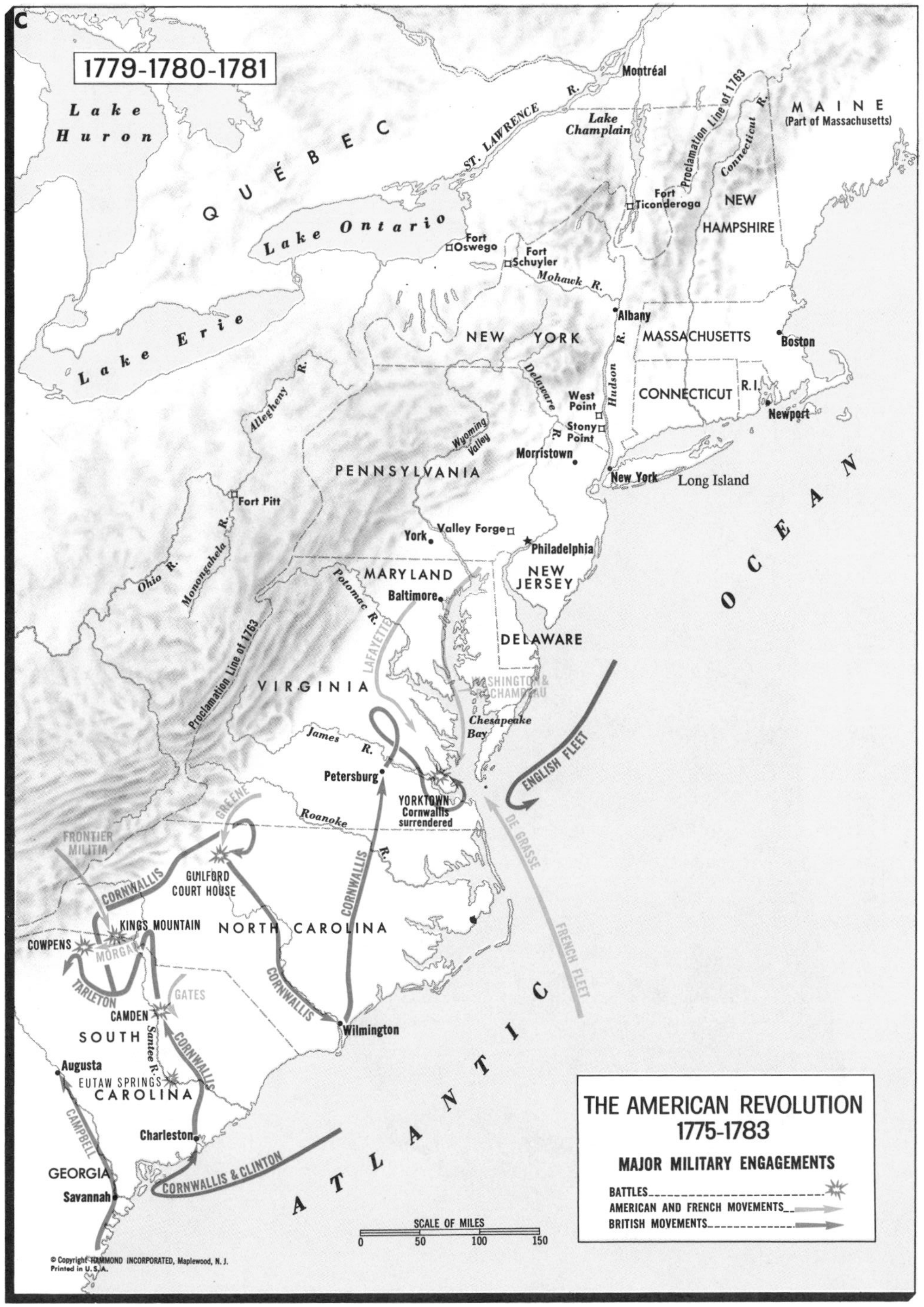

ENGAGEMENTS NEAR BOSTON
1775-1776

SCALE OF MILES

0 1 2 3 4

AMERICAN LINES

PAUL REVERE'S RIDE

DAWES' ROUTE

PRESCOTT'S ROUTE

© Copyright HAMMOND INCORPORATED, Maplewood, N.J. Printed in U.S.A.

Smith and Percy retreat to Boston

Bunker Hill

Breeds Hill

GAGE

North Church

HOWE to Halifax

Boston Harbor

Dorchester Heights

Boston

Charlestown

Roxbury

Percy to Lexington to support British retreat toward Boston

Brookline

Medford

Mystic R.

SMITH

DAWES

Cambridge

Watertown

Charles R.

Arlington (Menotomy)

Dawes joins Revere

Revere captured, Dawes turns back ×

MINUTEMEN

Lexington

LEXINGTON

Prescott joins Revere and Dawes

MINUTEMEN

PRESCOTT

MASSACHUSETTS

Weston

Waltham

Lincoln

Sudbury R.

MINUTEMEN

North Bridge

Concord

CONCORD

British retreat toward Boston

D

THE AMERICAN REVOLUTION
1775-1783

MAJOR MILITARY ENGAGEMENTS

BATTLES

AMERICAN MOVEMENTS

BRITISH MOVEMENTS

THE WESTERN CAMPAIGNS
1778-1781

SCALE OF MILES

0 50 100 150

Ft. Pitt

Redstone Old Fort

Proclamation Line of 1763

Ft. Henry

Lake Erie

Ohio R.

CLARK

Detroit

Maumee R.

HAMILTON

X Blue Licks (Indian Battle)

Boonesboro

Falls of the Ohio

Harrodstown

Cumberland R.

Lake Michigan

Ft. St. Joseph

Wabash R.

Kankakee R.

Vincennes

CLARK

VINCENNES

Ohio R.

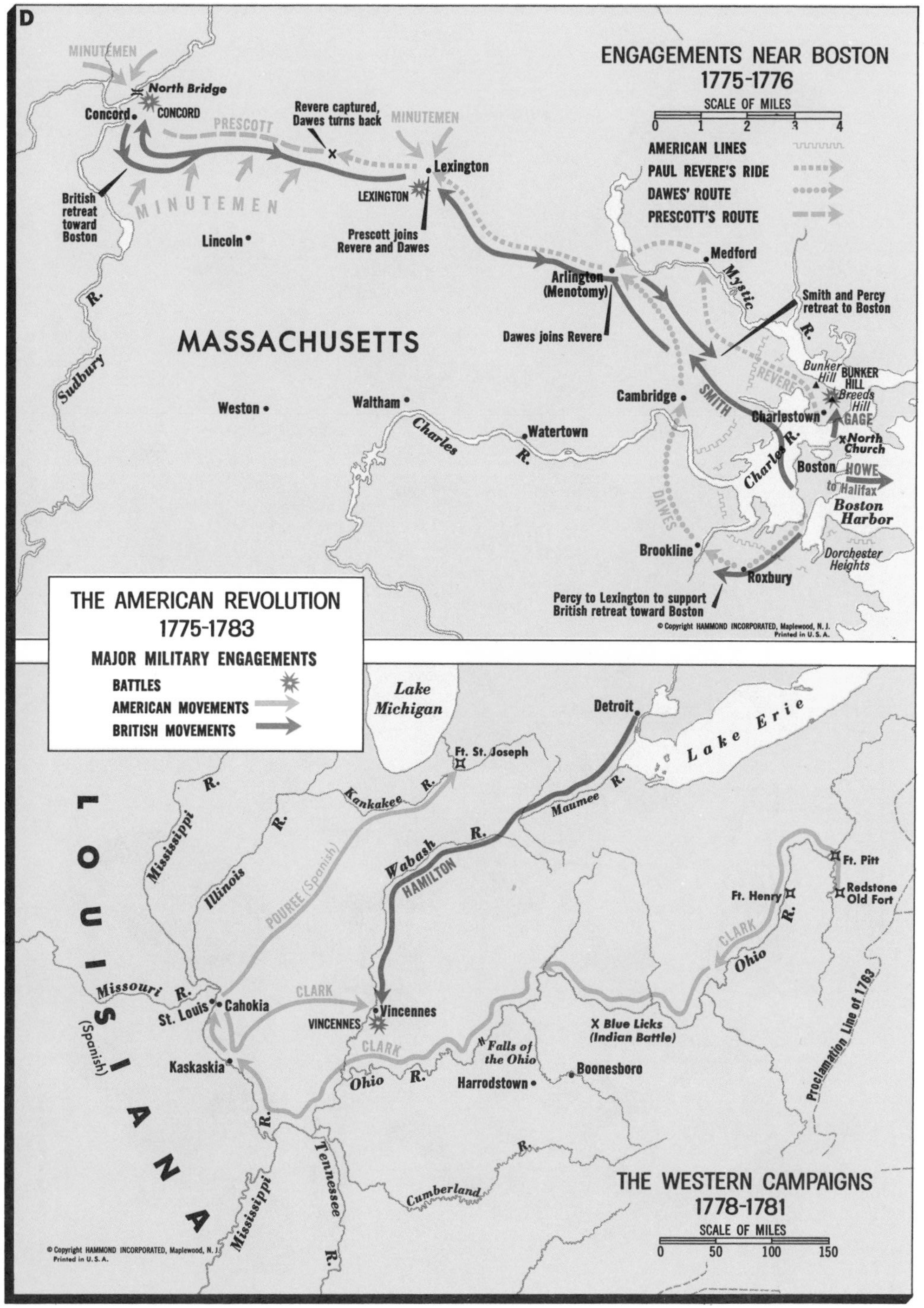

Tennessee R.

POURÉE (Spanish)

Illinois R.

St. Louis

Cahokia

Kaskaskia

Missouri R.

Mississippi R.

L O U I S I A N A

(Spanish)

© Copyright HAMMOND INCORPORATED, Maplewood, N.J. Printed in U.S.A.

1779-1780-1781

M A I N E
(Part of Massachusetts)

Boston

Newport

NEW HAMPSHIRE

Connecticut R.

Proclamation Line of 1763

Montréal

Fort Ticonderoga

Lake Champlain

St. Lawrence R.

Q U É B E C

Lake Huron

Lake Ontario

Lake Erie

Fort Oswego

Albany

NEW YORK

Hudson R.

West Point

Stony Point

Morristown

Delaware R.

Mohawk R.

Fort Schuyler

NEW YORK

New York

Long Island

CONNECTICUT

R.I.

MASSACHUSETTS

O C E A N

PENNSYLVANIA

Valley Forge

Philadelphia

NEW JERSEY

DELAWARE

York

Baltimore

MARYLAND

Fort Pitt

Allegheny R.

Monongahela R.

Juniata R.

Susquehanna R.

WASHINGTON & ROCHAMBEAU

Chesapeake Bay

Potomac R.

VIRGINIA

Proclamation Line of 1763

Petersburg

James R.

Roanoke R.

LAFAYETTE

YORKTOWN Cornwallis surrendered

DE GRASSE

ENGLISH FLEET

FRENCH FLEET

A T L A N T I C

CORNWALLIS

Wilmington

NORTH CAROLINA

GUILFORD COURT HOUSE

GREENE

CORNWALLIS

KINGS MOUNTAIN

GATES

FRONTIER MILITIA

COWPENS

TARLETON

CAMDEN

Santee R.

MORGAN

CORNWALLIS & CLINTON

Charleston

SOUTH CAROLINA

EUTAW SPRINGS

Augusta

CAMPBELL

GEORGIA

Savannah

THE AMERICAN REVOLUTION
1775-1783

MAJOR MILITARY ENGAGEMENTS

BATTLES

AMERICAN AND FRENCH MOVEMENTS

BRITISH MOVEMENTS

SCALE OF MILES

0 50 100 150

© Copyright HAMMOND INCORPORATED, Maplewood, N.J. Printed in U.S.A.

C

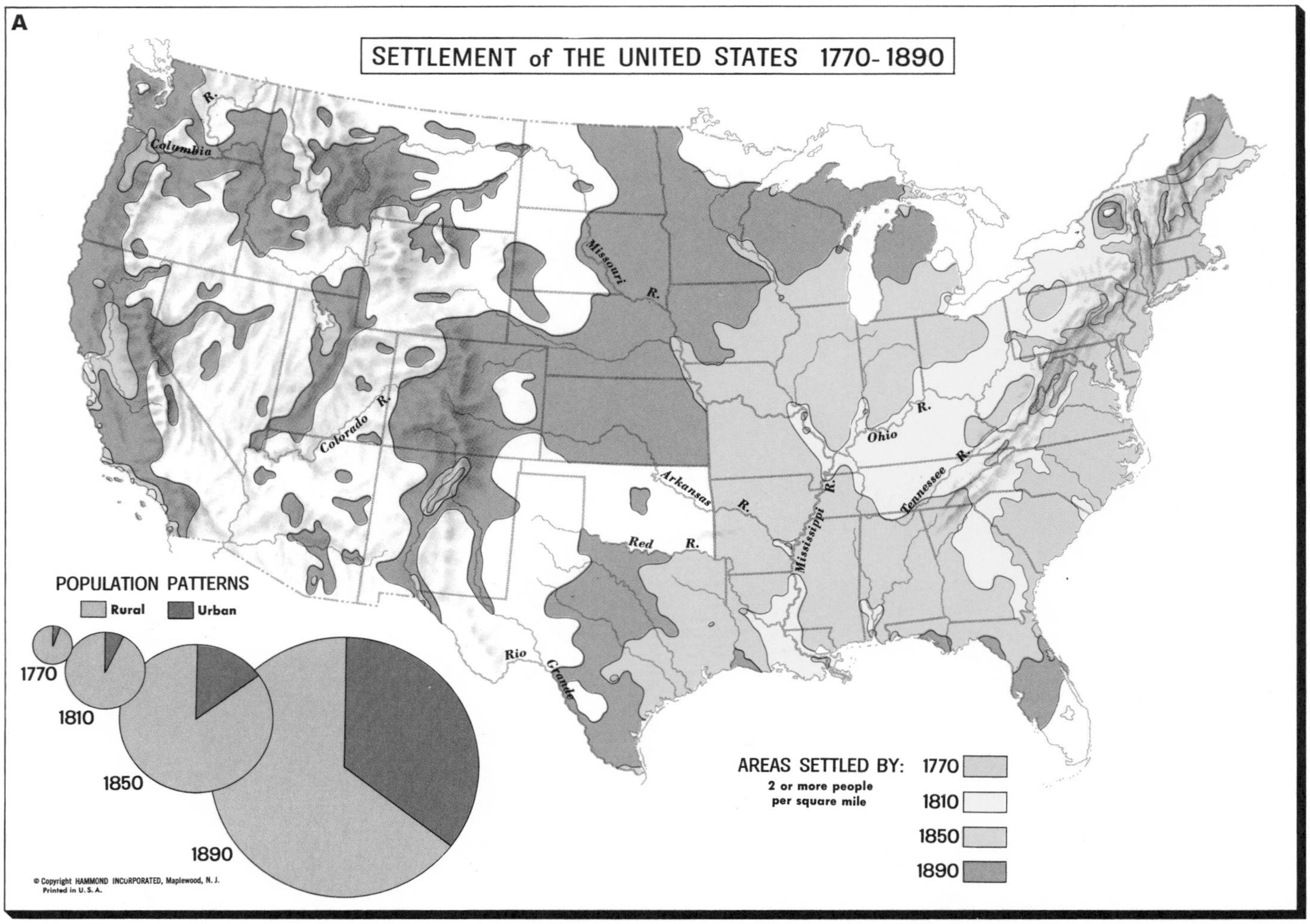
A
SETTLEMENT of THE UNITED STATES 1770-1890
Columbia R.
Missouri R.
Colorado R.
Arkansas R.
Red R.
Rio Grande
Mississippi R.
Ohio R.
Tennessee R.
POPULATION PATTERNS
Rural
Urban
1770
1810
1850
1890
AREAS SETTLED BY:
2 or more people per square mile
1770
1810
1850
1890
© Copyright HAMMOND INCORPORATED, Maplewood, N. J.
Printed in U. S. A.

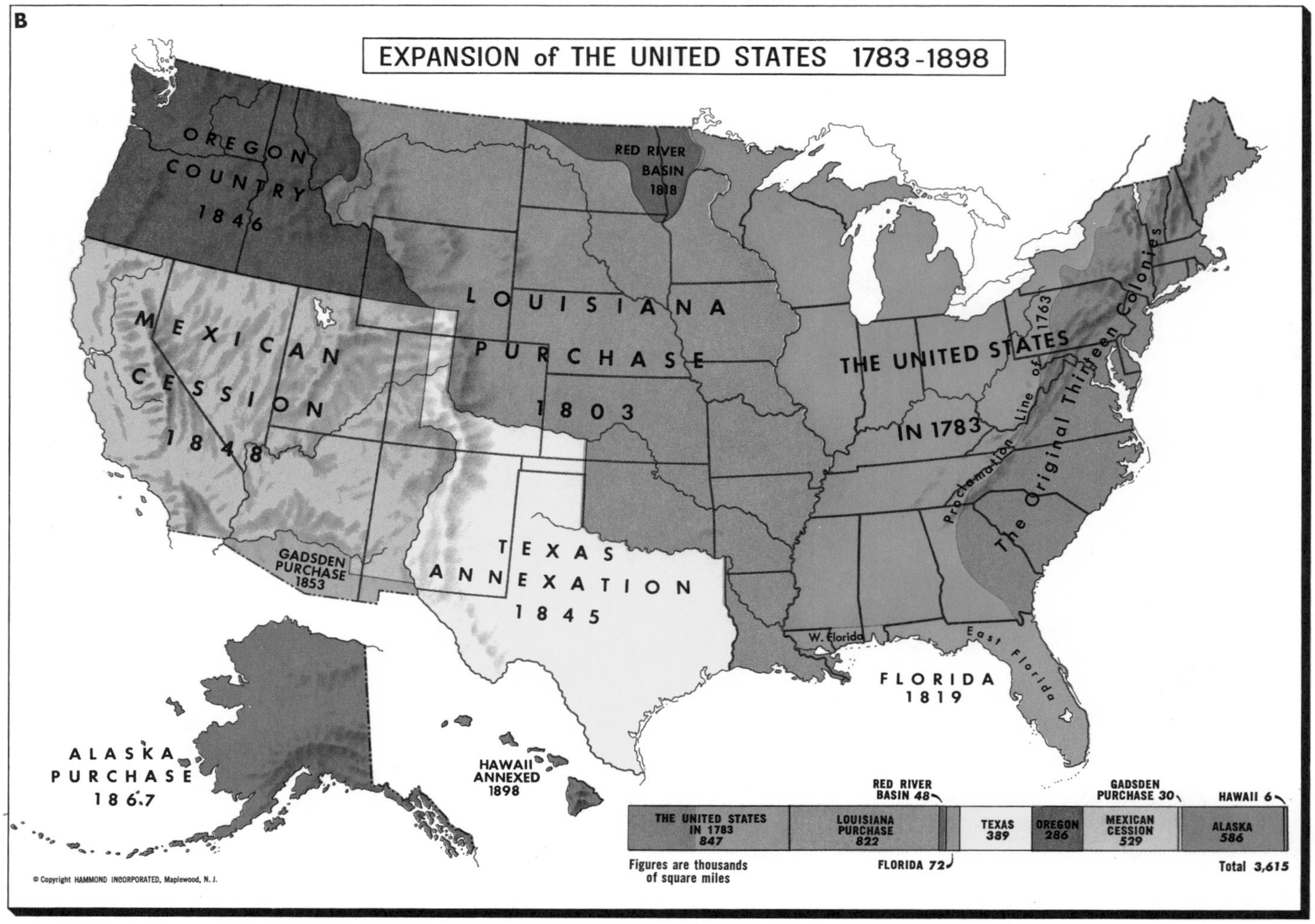
B
EXPANSION of THE UNITED STATES 1783-1898
OREGON COUNTRY 1846
RED RIVER BASIN 1818
LOUISIANA PURCHASE 1803
MEXICAN CESSION 1848
THE UNITED STATES IN 1783
Proclamation Line of 1763
The Original Thirteen Colonies
GADSDEN PURCHASE 1853
TEXAS ANNEXATION 1845
W. Florida
East Florida
FLORIDA 1819
ALASKA PURCHASE 1867
HAWAII ANNEXED 1898
RED RIVER BASIN 48
GADSDEN PURCHASE 30
HAWAII 6
THE UNITED STATES IN 1783 847
LOUISIANA PURCHASE 822
TEXAS 389
OREGON 286
MEXICAN CESSION 529
ALASKA 586
Figures are thousands of square miles
FLORIDA 72
Total 3,615
© Copyright HAMMOND INCORPORATED, Maplewood, N. J.

CONFLICTING CLAIMS TO THE WEST
AFTER THE TREATY OF 1783

BRITISH POSSESSIONS

CANADA

Boundary in dispute

Lake Superior

Ft. Michilimackinac

L. Huron

L. Michigan

St. Lawrence R.

Maine

Vermont claimed by N.H., Mass., & N.Y.

Pte.-au-Fer

Oswegatchie

VIRGINIA

LOUISIANA

Mississippi R.

MASSACHUSETTS CLAIM

Detroit

L. Erie

Ft. Miami

Western Reserve

CONNECTICUT CLAIM

L. Ontario

Oswego

Ft. Niagara

MASS. CLAIM

CONNECTICUT CLAIM

Vermont

N.H.

MASSACHUSETTS

NEW YORK

CONN.

R.I.

NEW YORK CLAIM

Ohio R.

Kentucky

PENNSYLVANIA

MARYLAND

NEW JERSEY

DELAWARE

VIRGINIA

(Spanish)

NORTH CAROLINA CLAIM

Tennessee

Franklin

NORTH CAROLINA

ATLANTIC

GEORGIA CLAIM

Mississippi R.

SOUTH CAROLINA

Savannah R.

GEORGIA

OCEAN

SOUTH CAROLINA claimed a 12 mile-wide strip extending west to the Mississippi between the headwaters of the Savannah and the North Carolina boundary. Since the Savannah headwaters began in North Carolina, the strip did not exist in reality.

Claimed by Spain, United States & Georgia

FLORIDA

(Spanish)

GULF OF MEXICO

BAHAMA

ISLANDS (British)

Boundary undefinite

⊠• Posts in U.S. Territory held by British until 1796

SCALE OF MILES
0   100   200   300

© Copyright HAMMOND INCORPORATED, Maplewood, N.J. Printed in U.S.A.

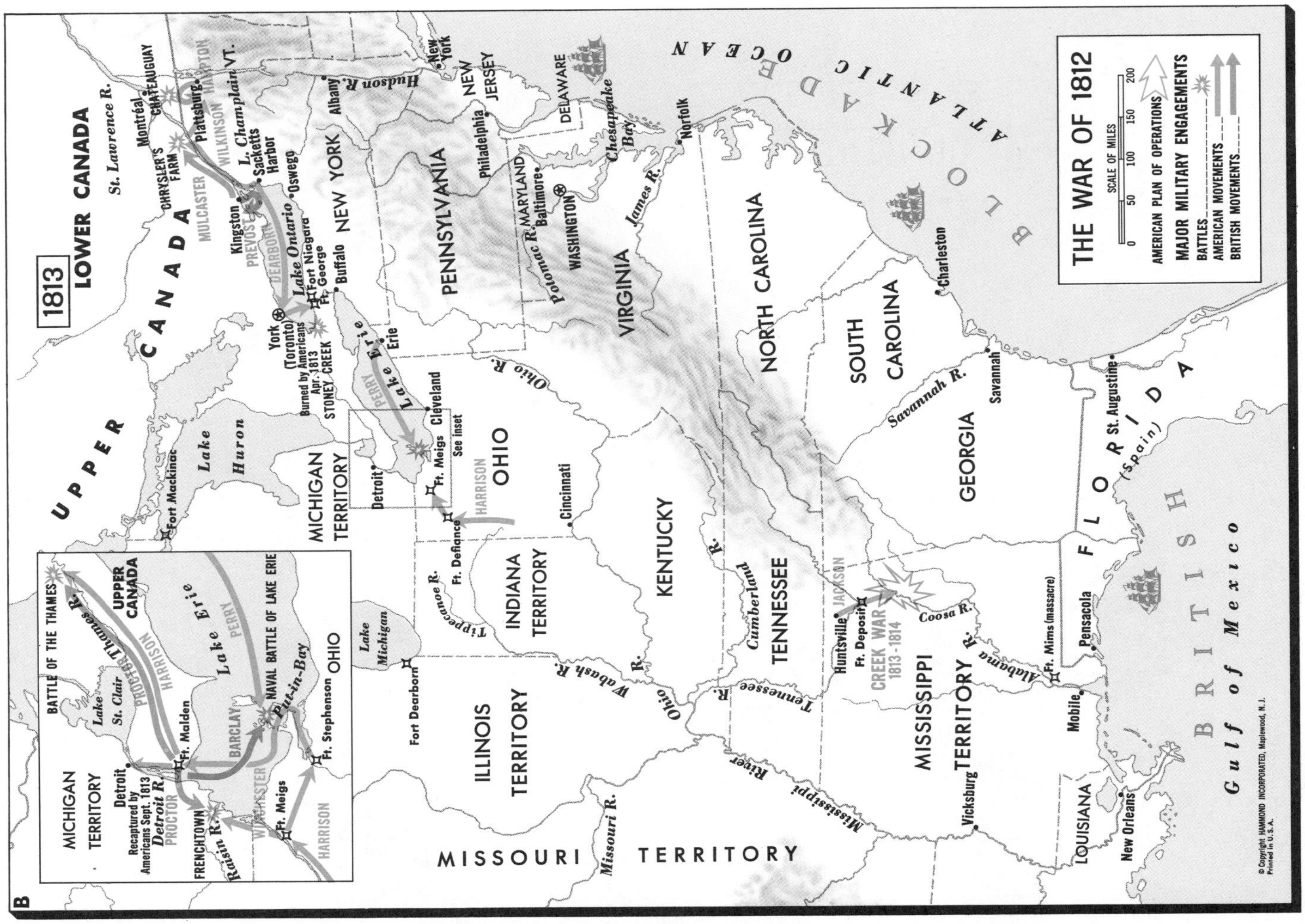

THE WAR OF 1812

SCALE OF MILES

0 50 100 150 200

AMERICAN PLAN OF OPERATIONS

MAJOR MILITARY ENGAGEMENTS

BATTLES

AMERICAN MOVEMENTS

BRITISH MOVEMENTS

B — 1813

LOWER CANADA

UPPER CANADA

Inset: BATTLE OF THE THAMES

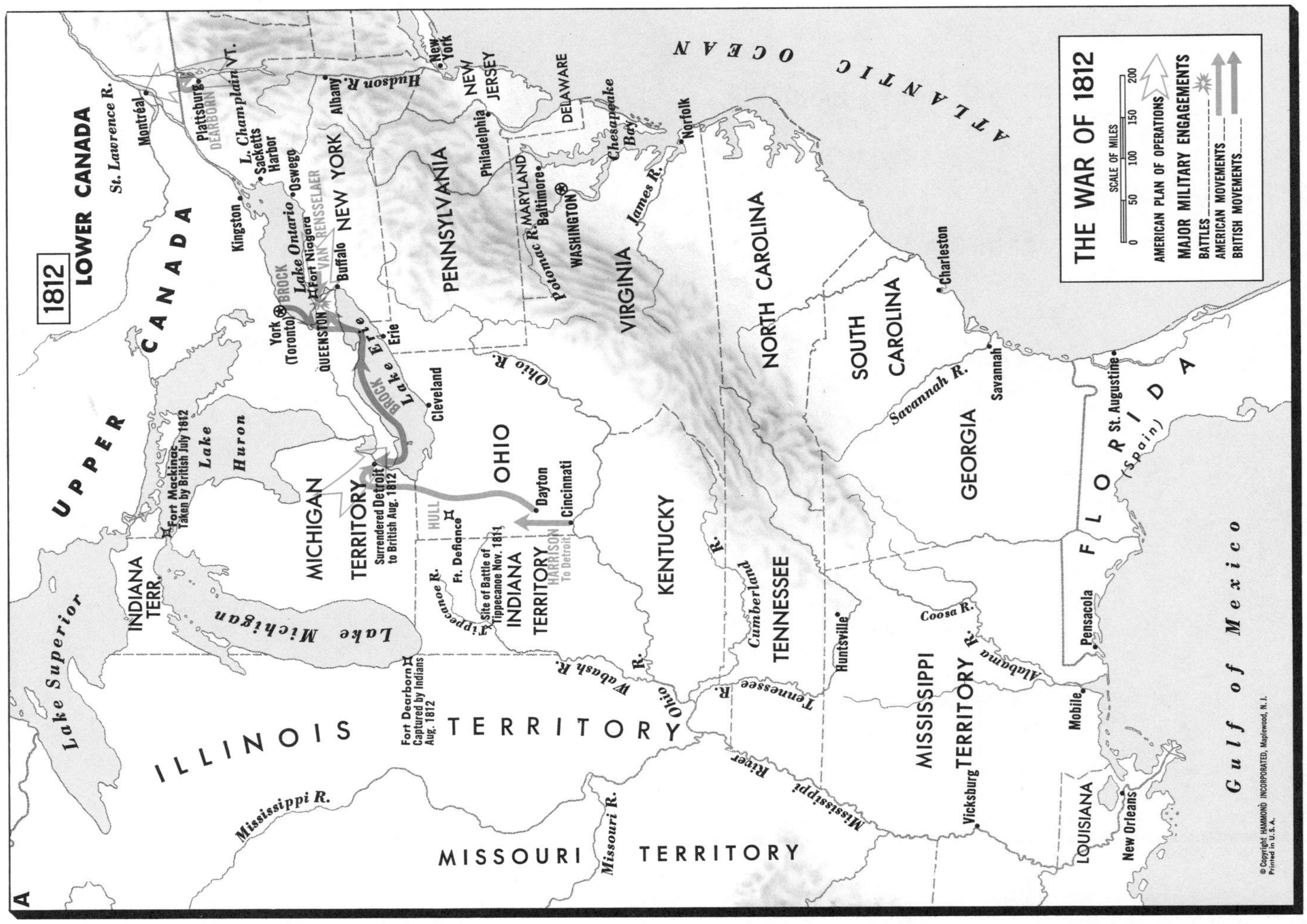

A — 1812

LOWER CANADA

UPPER CANADA

THE WAR OF 1812

SCALE OF MILES

0 50 100 150 200

AMERICAN PLAN OF OPERATIONS

MAJOR MILITARY ENGAGEMENTS

BATTLES

AMERICAN MOVEMENTS

BRITISH MOVEMENTS

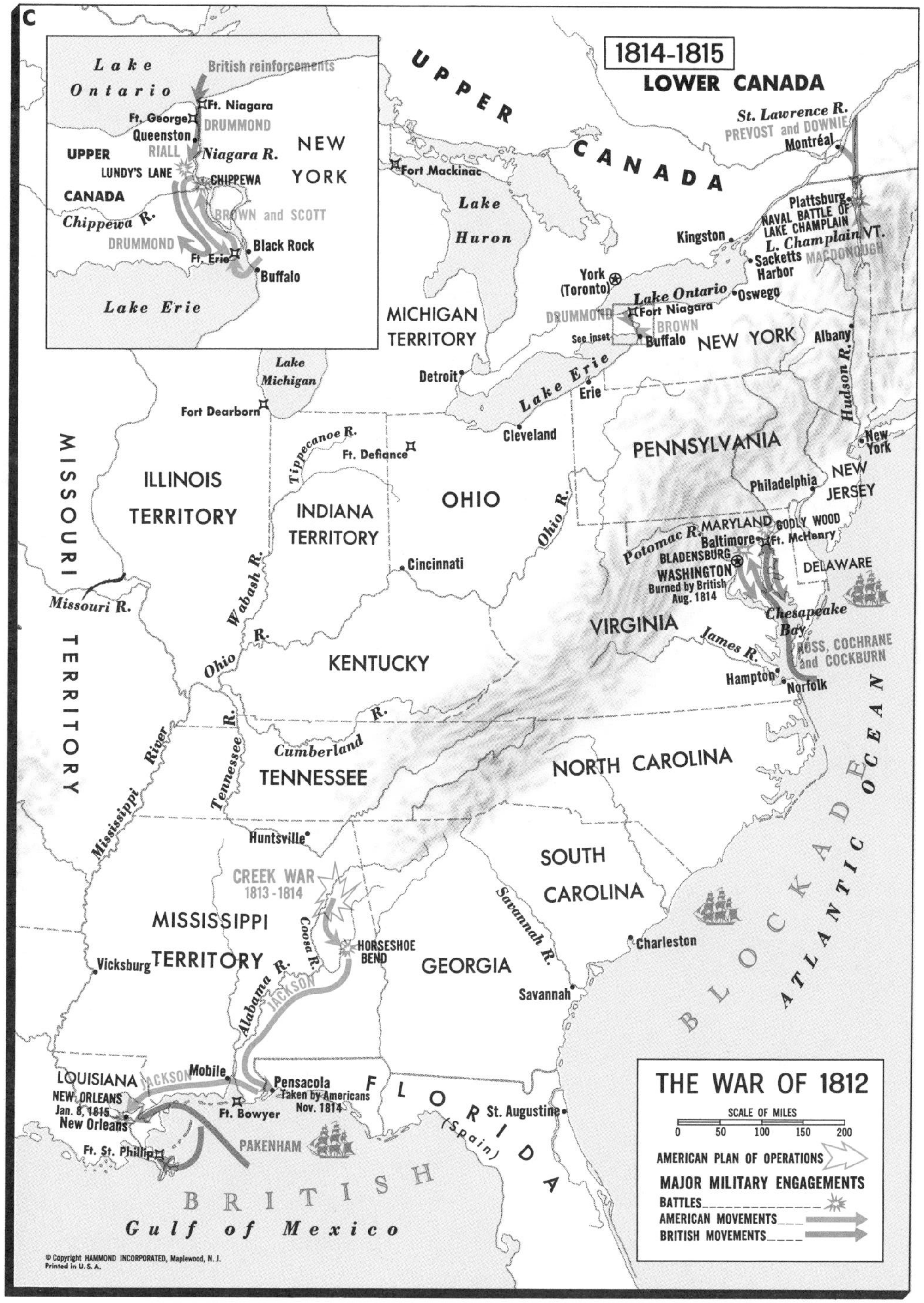

Map D — NAVAL BATTLES 1777-1815 / AMERICAN REVOLUTION / WAR WITH FRANCE / WAR OF 1812

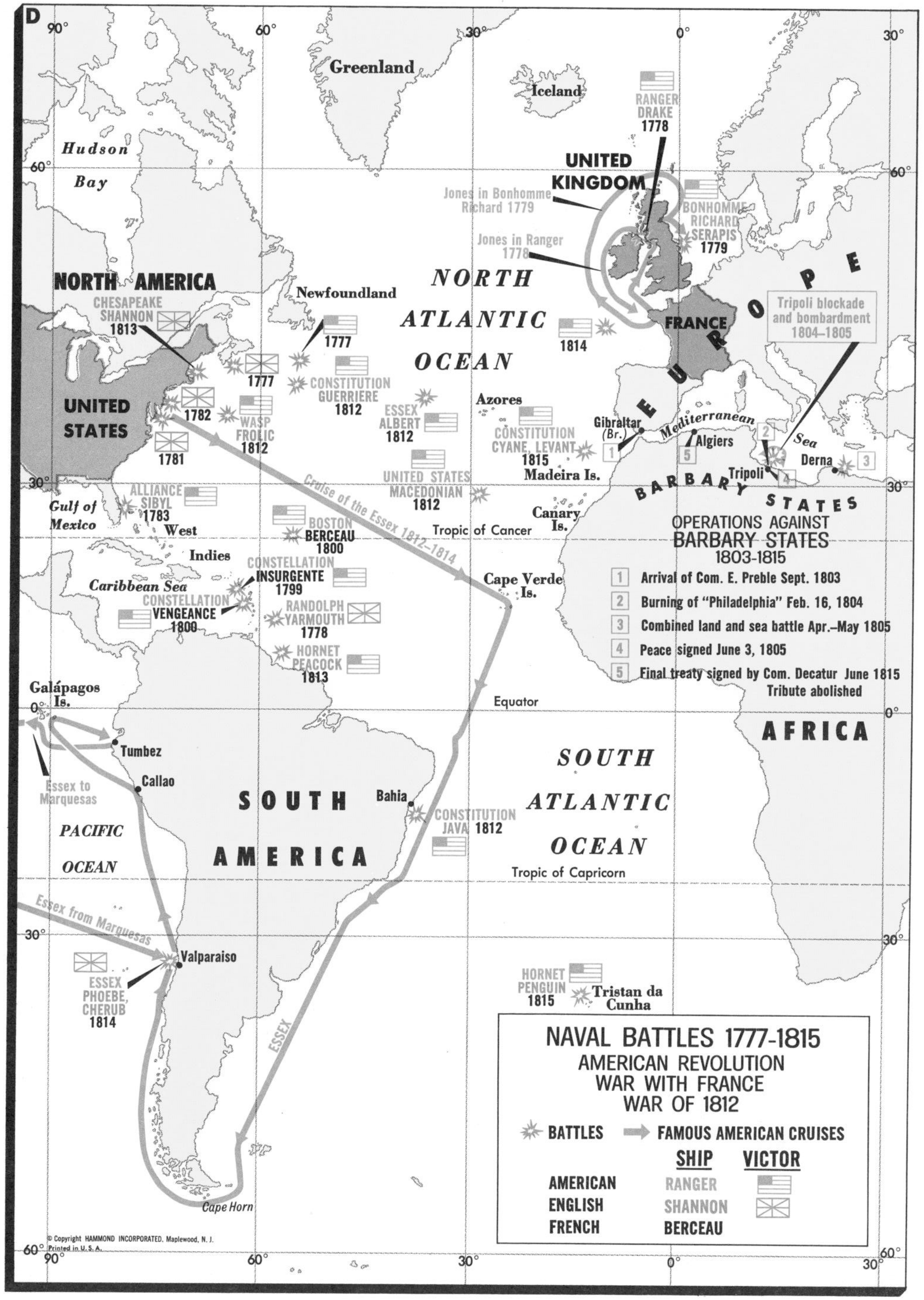

EUROPE

AFRICA

UNITED KINGDOM

FRANCE

Iceland

Greenland

NORTH AMERICA

UNITED STATES

NORTH ATLANTIC OCEAN

SOUTH ATLANTIC OCEAN

SOUTH AMERICA

PACIFIC OCEAN

Hudson Bay

Gulf of Mexico

Caribbean Sea

West Indies

Newfoundland

Azores

Madeira Is.

Canary Is.

Cape Verde Is.

Gibraltar (Br.)

Mediterranean Sea

BARBARY STATES

Algiers

Tripoli

Derna

Tristan da Cunha

Bahia

Valparaiso

Callao

Tumbez

Galápagos Is.

Cape Horn

Tropic of Cancer

Equator

Tropic of Capricorn

Essex to Marquesas

Cruise of the Essex 1812-1814

ESSEX

Essex from Marquesas

BONHOMME RICHARD SERAPIS 1779
Jones in Bonhomme Richard 1779
Jones in Ranger 1778

RANGER DRAKE 1778

1814

CONSTITUTION CYANE LEVANT 1815

CONSTITUTION GUERRIERE 1812

ESSEX ALBERT 1812

UNITED STATES MACEDONIAN 1812

CONSTITUTION JAVA 1812

BOSTON BERCEAU 1800

CONSTELLATION INSURGENTE 1799

CONSTELLATION VENGEANCE 1800

RANDOLPH YARMOUTH 1778

HORNET PEACOCK 1813

CHESAPEAKE SHANNON 1813

ALLIANCE SIBYL 1783

WASP FROLIC 1812

ESSEX PHOEBE CHERUB 1814

HORNET PENGUIN 1815

1777 · 1777 · 1782 · 1781

Tripoli blockade and bombardment 1804-1805

OPERATIONS AGAINST BARBARY STATES 1803-1815
1. Arrival of Com. E. Preble Sept. 1803
2. Burning of "Philadelphia" Feb. 16, 1804
3. Combined land and sea battle Apr.–May 1805
4. Peace signed June 3, 1805
5. Final treaty signed by Com. Decatur June 1815 Tribute abolished

LEGEND
BATTLES — FAMOUS AMERICAN CRUISES
SHIP / VICTOR
AMERICAN · ENGLISH · FRENCH
RANGER · SHANNON · BERCEAU

© Copyright HAMMOND INCORPORATED, Maplewood, N.J. Printed in U.S.A.

Map C — THE WAR OF 1812 1814-1815 LOWER CANADA

UPPER CANADA

LOWER CANADA

St. Lawrence R.

PREVOST and DOWNIE

Montreal

Plattsburg

NAVAL BATTLE OF LAKE CHAMPLAIN

L. Champlain VT.

Sacketts Harbor

Oswego

Kingston

Lake Ontario

Fort Niagara

BROWN

Buffalo

York (Toronto)

DRUMMOND

Sea Inset

Lake Erie

NEW YORK

Albany

Hudson R.

NEW JERSEY

PENNSYLVANIA

Philadelphia

DELAWARE

MARYLAND

Sodus Wood

Baltimore

McHenry

WASHINGTON Burned by British Aug. 1814

BLADENSBURG

Potomac R.

ROSS, COCHRANE and COCKBURN

Chesapeake Bay

James R.

Hampton

Norfolk

VIRGINIA

NORTH CAROLINA

SOUTH CAROLINA

Charleston

GEORGIA

Savannah R.

Savannah

FLORIDA (Spain)

St. Augustine

ATLANTIC OCEAN

BLOCKADE

Ohio R.

Cleveland

Detroit

Fort Mackinac

Lake Huron

Lake Michigan

Fort Dearborn

MICHIGAN TERRITORY

OHIO

Cincinnati

Ft. Defiance

Tippecanoe R.

INDIANA TERRITORY

ILLINOIS TERRITORY

KENTUCKY

TENNESSEE

Huntsville

Cumberland R.

CREEK WAR 1813-1814

HORSESHOE BEND

Coosa R.

Alabama R.

Tombigbee R.

JACKSON

Pensacola Taken by Americans Nov. 1814

Ft. Bowyer

Mobile

MISSISSIPPI TERRITORY

LOUISIANA

NEW ORLEANS Jan. 8, 1815

PAKENHAM

Ft. St. Philip

Mississippi River

Vicksburg

Gulf of Mexico

BRITISH

MISSOURI TERRITORY

Missouri R.

Wabash R.

Tennessee R.

THE WAR OF 1812
SCALE OF MILES
0 50 100 150 200

AMERICAN PLAN OF OPERATIONS
MAJOR MILITARY ENGAGEMENTS
BATTLES
AMERICAN MOVEMENTS
BRITISH MOVEMENTS

Inset:
Lake Ontario
Upper Canada
UPPER CANADA
NEW YORK
Ft. Niagara
British reinforcements
DRUMMOND
RIALL
Queenston
Ft. George
Niagara R.
CHIPPEWA
LUNDY'S LANE
Chippewa R.
DRUMMOND
BROWN and SCOTT
Black Rock
Buffalo
Ft. Erie
Lake Erie

© Copyright HAMMOND INCORPORATED, Maplewood, N.J. Printed in U.S.A.

C

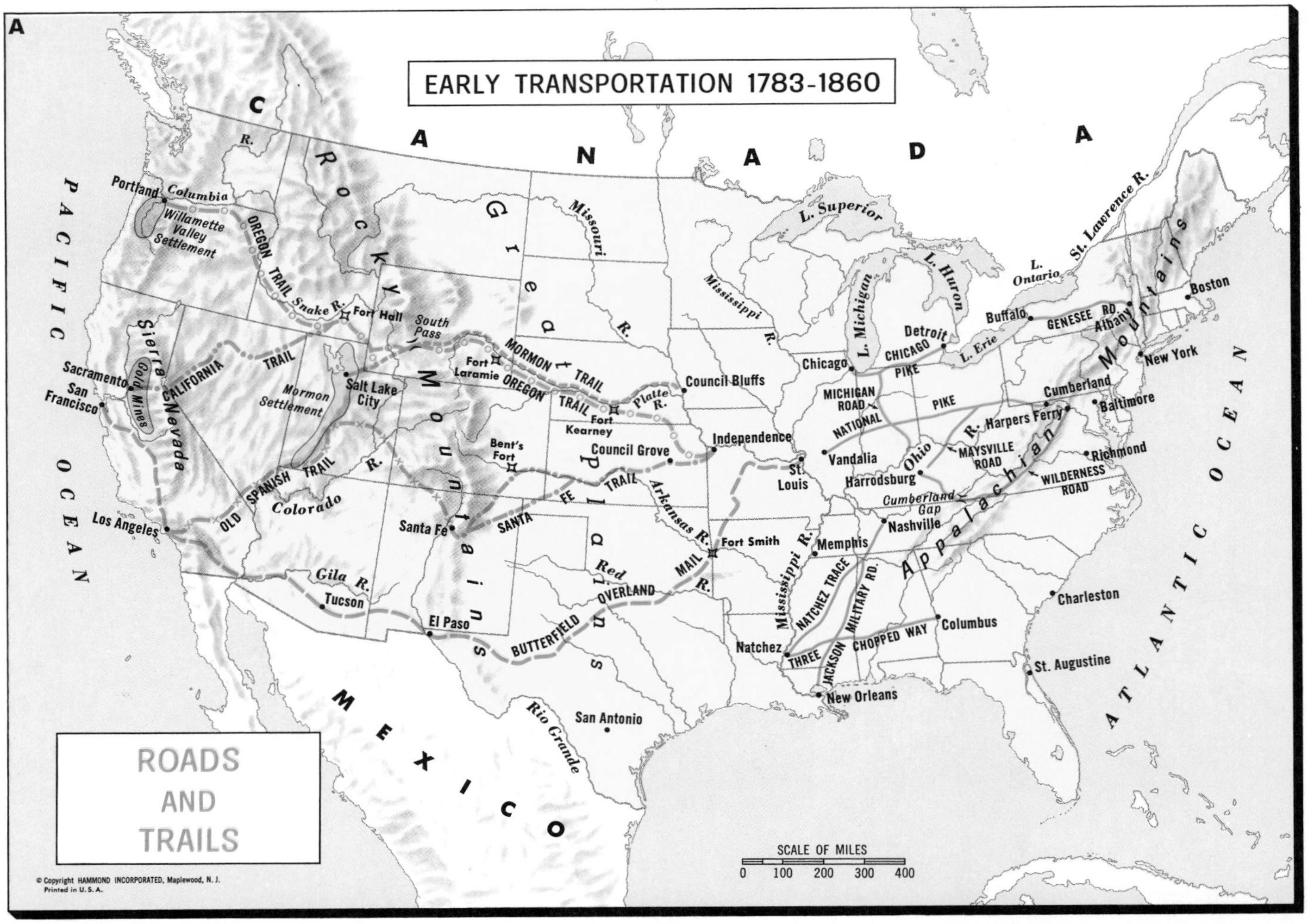
A
EARLY TRANSPORTATION 1783-1860
ROADS AND TRAILS
C A N A D A
PACIFIC OCEAN
ATLANTIC OCEAN
MEXICO
Rocky Mountains
Great Plains
Appalachian Mountains
Sierra Nevada
Columbia R.
Willamette Valley Settlement
OREGON TRAIL
Snake R.
Fort Hall
South Pass
MORMON TRAIL
Fort Laramie
OREGON TRAIL
Fort Kearney
Platte R.
Council Bluffs
CALIFORNIA TRAIL
Gold Mines
Mormon Settlement
Salt Lake City
Portland
Sacramento
San Francisco
Los Angeles
OLD SPANISH TRAIL
Colorado R.
Bent's Fort
Council Grove
Independence
SANTA FE TRAIL
Santa Fe
Arkansas R.
Fort Smith
Gila R.
Tucson
El Paso
BUTTERFIELD OVERLAND MAIL
Red R.
Rio Grande
San Antonio
Missouri R.
Mississippi R.
L. Superior
L. Michigan
L. Huron
L. Erie
L. Ontario
St. Lawrence R.
Chicago
Detroit
CHICAGO PIKE
MICHIGAN ROAD
NATIONAL PIKE
Vandalia
St. Louis
Ohio R.
Harrodsburg
MAYSVILLE ROAD
Harpers Ferry
Cumberland
Baltimore
Richmond
WILDERNESS ROAD
Cumberland Gap
Nashville
Memphis
NATCHEZ TRACE
MILITARY RD.
JACKSON
THREE CHOPPED WAY
Natchez
Columbus
New Orleans
Charleston
St. Augustine
Buffalo
GENESEE RD.
Albany
Boston
New York
SCALE OF MILES
0 100 200 300 400
© Copyright HAMMOND INCORPORATED, Maplewood, N. J.
Printed in U. S. A.

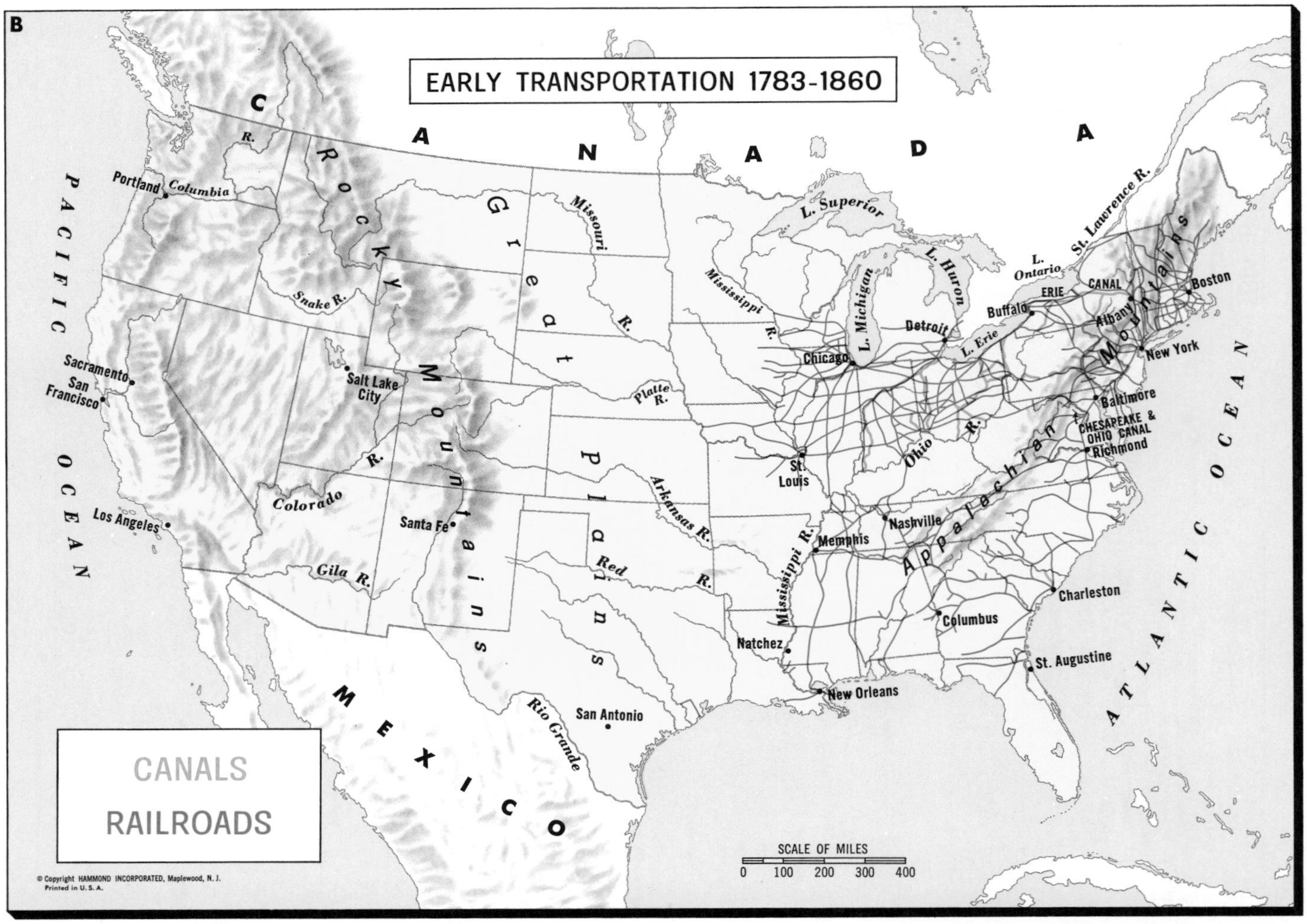
B
EARLY TRANSPORTATION 1783-1860
CANALS
RAILROADS
C A N A D A
PACIFIC OCEAN
ATLANTIC OCEAN
MEXICO
Rocky Mountains
Great Plains
Appalachian Mountains
Portland
Columbia R.
Snake R.
Sacramento
San Francisco
Salt Lake City
Los Angeles
Colorado R.
Santa Fe
Gila R.
Platte R.
Arkansas R.
Red R.
Rio Grande
San Antonio
Missouri R.
Mississippi R.
L. Superior
L. Michigan
L. Huron
L. Erie
L. Ontario
St. Lawrence R.
ERIE CANAL
Buffalo
Albany
Boston
New York
Detroit
Chicago
St. Louis
Ohio R.
Baltimore
CHESAPEAKE & OHIO CANAL
Richmond
Nashville
Memphis
Natchez
Columbus
Charleston
St. Augustine
New Orleans
SCALE OF MILES
0 100 200 300 400
© Copyright HAMMOND INCORPORATED, Maplewood, N. J.
Printed in U. S. A.

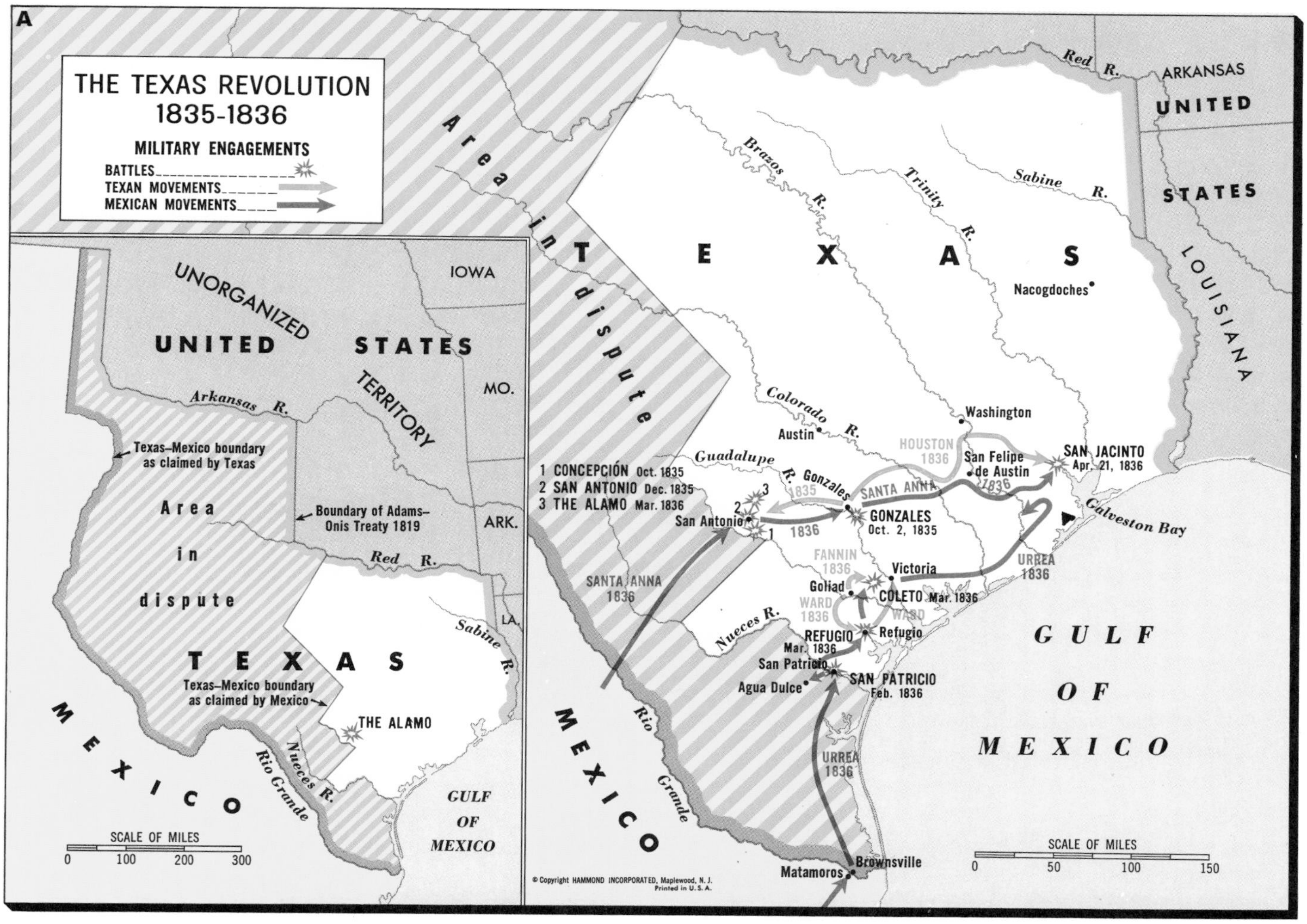

A

THE TEXAS REVOLUTION 1835-1836

MILITARY ENGAGEMENTS
BATTLES
TEXAN MOVEMENTS
MEXICAN MOVEMENTS

IOWA

MO.

UNORGANIZED UNITED STATES TERRITORY

Arkansas R.

Texas–Mexico boundary as claimed by Texas

Area in dispute

Boundary of Adams–Onis Treaty 1819

ARK.

Red R.

Sabine R.

LA.

TEXAS

Texas–Mexico boundary as claimed by Mexico

THE ALAMO

MEXICO

Nueces R.

Rio Grande

GULF OF MEXICO

SCALE OF MILES
0   100   200   300

T E X A S

Area in dispute

Red R.

Brazos R.

Trinity R.

Sabine R.

ARKANSAS

UNITED

STATES

LOUISIANA

Nacogdoches

1 CONCEPCIÓN Oct. 1835
2 SAN ANTONIO Dec. 1835
3 THE ALAMO Mar. 1836

Guadalupe R.

Washington

Austin

Colorado R.

Gonzales

HOUSTON 1836

San Felipe de Austin 1836

San Antonio

SANTA ANNA 1836

GONZALES Oct. 2, 1835

SAN JACINTO Apr. 21, 1836

Galveston Bay

SANTA ANNA 1836

FANNIN 1836

Victoria

URREA 1836

SANTA ANNA 1836

Goliad

COLETO Mar. 1836

Nueces R.

WARD 1836

WARD

REFUGIO Mar. 1836

Refugio

San Patricio

SAN PATRICIO Feb. 1836

Agua Dulce

Rio Grande

URREA 1836

GULF OF MEXICO

MEXICO

Matamoros

Brownsville

SCALE OF MILES
0   50   100   150

© Copyright HAMMOND INCORPORATED, Maplewood, N.J.
Printed in U.S.A.

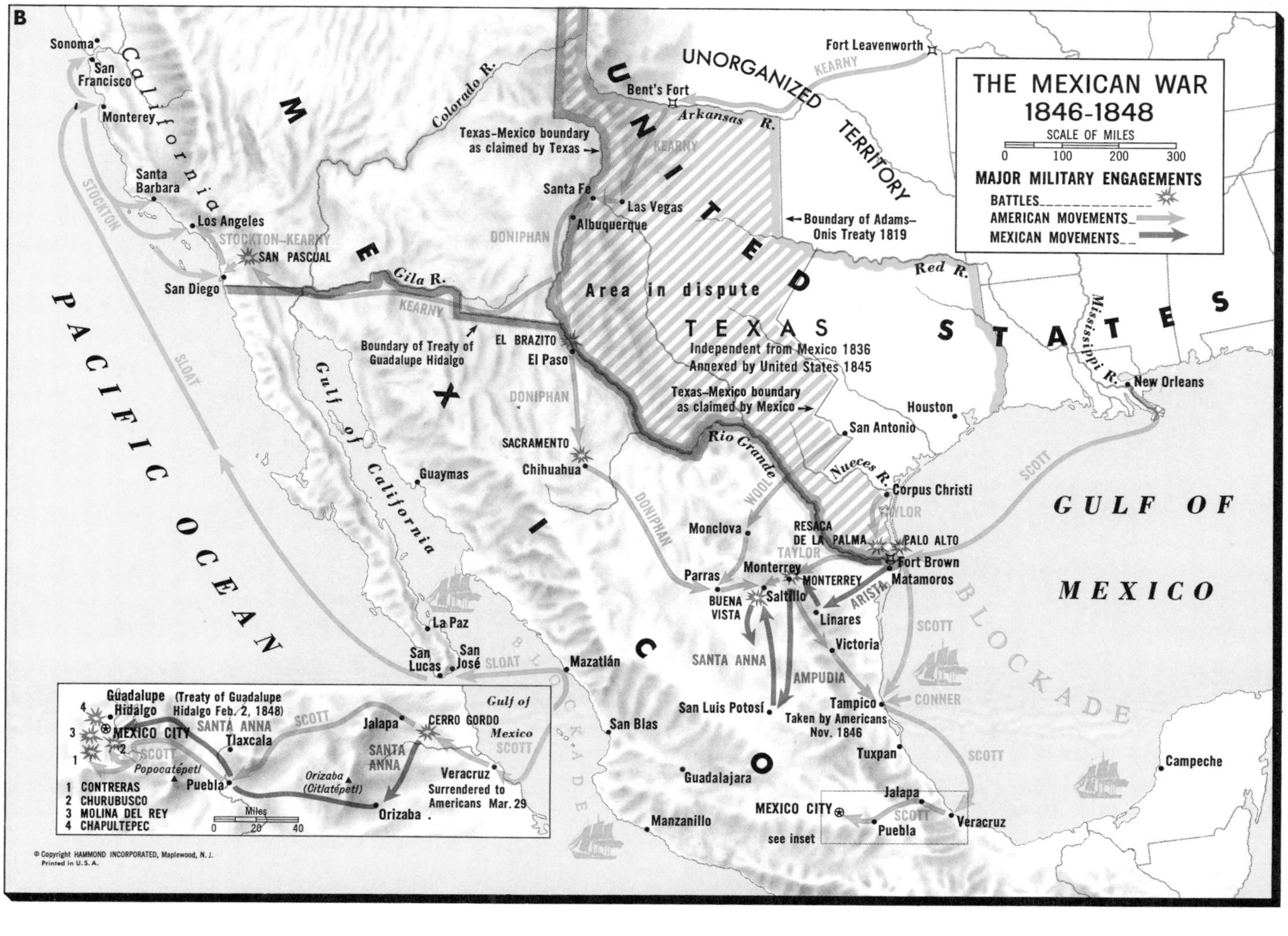

B

Sonoma

San Francisco

California

Colorado R.

UNORGANIZED

Fort Leavenworth

KEARNY

Monterey

M E X

Bent's Fort

KEARNY

Arkansas R.

CALIFORNIA TERRITORY

THE MEXICAN WAR 1846-1848

SCALE OF MILES
0   100   200   300

MAJOR MILITARY ENGAGEMENTS
BATTLES
AMERICAN MOVEMENTS
MEXICAN MOVEMENTS

Santa Barbara

Los Angeles

STOCKTON

Texas–Mexico boundary as claimed by Texas

Santa Fé

Las Vegas

DONIPHAN

Albuquerque

Boundary of Adams–Onis Treaty 1819

STOCKTON-KEARNY

SAN PASCUAL

Gila R.

KEARNY

Area in dispute

UNITED STATES

Red R.

San Diego

Boundary of Treaty of Guadalupe Hidalgo

EL BRAZITO

El Paso

DONIPHAN

T E X A S

Independent from Mexico 1836
Annexed by United States 1845

Mississippi R.

New Orleans

Gulf of California

SACRAMENTO

Chihuahua

Texas–Mexico boundary as claimed by Mexico

Houston

PACIFIC OCEAN

Guaymas

DONIPHAN

Rio Grande

San Antonio

Nueces R.

Corpus Christi

GULF OF MEXICO

Monclova

RESACA DE LA PALMA

PALO ALTO

TAYLOR

Fort Brown

Parras

Monterrey

MONTERREY

Matamoros

La Paz

San Lucas   San José

SLOAT

BLOCKADE

Mazatlán

Saltillo

ARISTA

BUENA VISTA

Linares

SANTA ANNA

Victoria

SCOTT

San Blas

M E X I C O

San Luis Potosí

AMPUDIA

Tampico

CONNER

Guadalajara

Taken by Americans Nov. 1846

Tuxpan

Manzanillo

MEXICO CITY
see inset

Jalapa

Puebla

Veracruz

Campeche

BLOCKADE

Inset:

Guadalupe Hidalgo   (Treaty of Guadalupe Hidalgo Feb. 2, 1848)

SANTA ANNA

SCOTT

MEXICO CITY

Tlaxcala

Popocatépetl

Puebla

1 CONTRERAS
2 CHURUBUSCO
3 MOLINA DEL REY
4 CHAPULTEPEC

Jalapa

CERRO GORDO

SANTA ANNA

Orizaba (Citlaltépetl)

Gulf of Mexico

SCOTT

Veracruz
Surrendered to Americans Mar. 29

Orizaba

Miles
0   20   40

© Copyright HAMMOND INCORPORATED, Maplewood, N.J.
Printed in U.S.A.

A

FREE AND SLAVE AREAS 1821

1. Free by Missouri Compromise—1820

Free by Northwest Ordinance—1787

MAINE 1820

VT. N.H.

NEW YORK

MASS. CONN. R.I.

PENNSYLVANIA

N.J.

ILLINOIS INDIANA OHIO

MD. DEL.

MISSOURI 1821

VIRGINIA

KENTUCKY

36° 30'

NORTH CAROLINA

TERRITORY ARKANSAS

TENNESSEE

SOUTH CAROLINA

MISSISSIPPI ALABAMA GEORGIA

LOUISIANA

FREE STATES AND TERRITORIES

SLAVE STATES AND TERRITORIES

© Copyright HAMMOND INCORPORATED, Maplewood, N.J.
Printed in U.S.A.

B

FREE AND SLAVE AREAS 1850

OREGON TERRITORY 1848

1. Free by Missouri Compromise—1820

Free by Northwest Ordinance—1787

MINNESOTA TERRITORY 1849

MICHIGAN 1837

MAINE 1820

WISCONSIN 1848

VT. N.H.

NEW YORK

MASS. CONN. R.I.

CALIFORNIA 1850

UTAH TERRITORY

IOWA 1846

PENNSYLVANIA

N.J.

ILLINOIS INDIANA OHIO

MD. DEL.

MISSOURI 1821

VIRGINIA

KENTUCKY

NEW MEXICO TERRITORY

36° 30'

NORTH CAROLINA

UNORGANIZED TERRITORY

ARKANSAS 1836

TENNESSEE

SOUTH CAROLINA

MISSISSIPPI ALABAMA GEORGIA

TEXAS 1845

LOUISIANA

FLORIDA 1845

FREE STATES AND TERRITORIES

SLAVE STATES AND TERRITORIES

AREAS AT FIRST FREE, LATER OPEN TO SLAVERY

© Copyright HAMMOND INCORPORATED, Maplewood, N.J.
Printed in U.S.A.

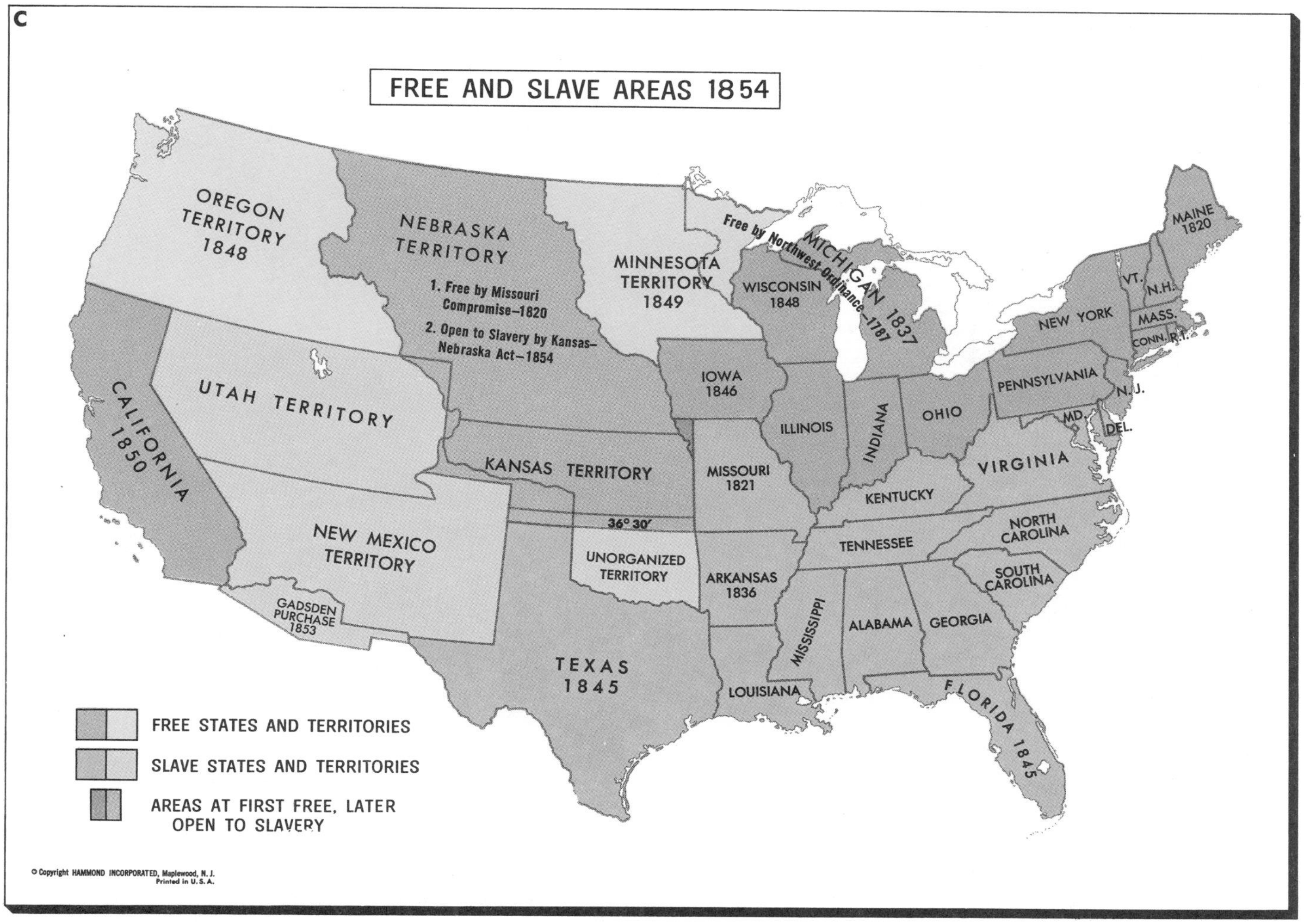

C

FREE AND SLAVE AREAS 1854

OREGON TERRITORY 1848

NEBRASKA TERRITORY
1. Free by Missouri Compromise—1820
2. Open to Slavery by Kansas–Nebraska Act—1854

MINNESOTA TERRITORY 1849

Free by Northwest Ordinance—1787

MICHIGAN 1837

WISCONSIN 1848

MAINE 1820

VT.

N.H.

NEW YORK

MASS.

CONN. R.I.

UTAH TERRITORY

IOWA 1846

ILLINOIS

INDIANA

OHIO

PENNSYLVANIA

N.J.

MD.

DEL.

CALIFORNIA 1850

KANSAS TERRITORY

MISSOURI 1821

KENTUCKY

VIRGINIA

NEW MEXICO TERRITORY

36° 30'

UNORGANIZED TERRITORY

TENNESSEE

NORTH CAROLINA

GADSDEN PURCHASE 1853

ARKANSAS 1836

SOUTH CAROLINA

MISSISSIPPI

ALABAMA

GEORGIA

TEXAS 1845

LOUISIANA

FLORIDA 1845

FREE STATES AND TERRITORIES

SLAVE STATES AND TERRITORIES

AREAS AT FIRST FREE, LATER OPEN TO SLAVERY

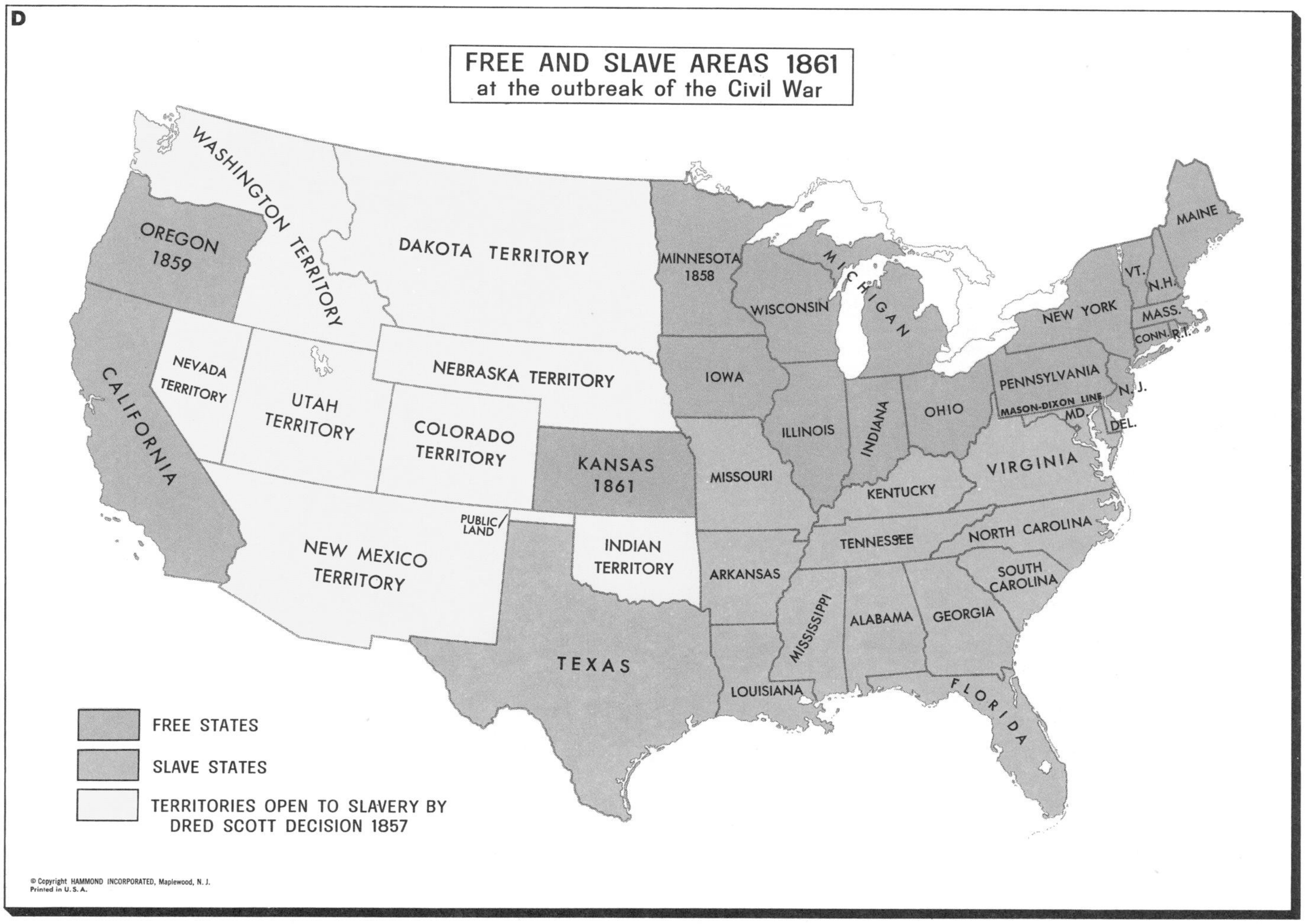

D

FREE AND SLAVE AREAS 1861
at the outbreak of the Civil War

WASHINGTON TERRITORY

OREGON 1859

DAKOTA TERRITORY

MINNESOTA 1858

MICHIGAN

MAINE

WISCONSIN

VT.

N.H.

NEW YORK

MASS.

CONN. R.I.

NEVADA TERRITORY

UTAH TERRITORY

NEBRASKA TERRITORY

IOWA

PENNSYLVANIA

N.J.

MASON-DIXON LINE

MD.

DEL.

CALIFORNIA

COLORADO TERRITORY

KANSAS 1861

ILLINOIS

INDIANA

OHIO

MISSOURI

KENTUCKY

VIRGINIA

PUBLIC LAND

NEW MEXICO TERRITORY

INDIAN TERRITORY

TENNESSEE

NORTH CAROLINA

ARKANSAS

SOUTH CAROLINA

MISSISSIPPI

ALABAMA

GEORGIA

TEXAS

LOUISIANA

FLORIDA

FREE STATES

SLAVE STATES

TERRITORIES OPEN TO SLAVERY BY DRED SCOTT DECISION 1857

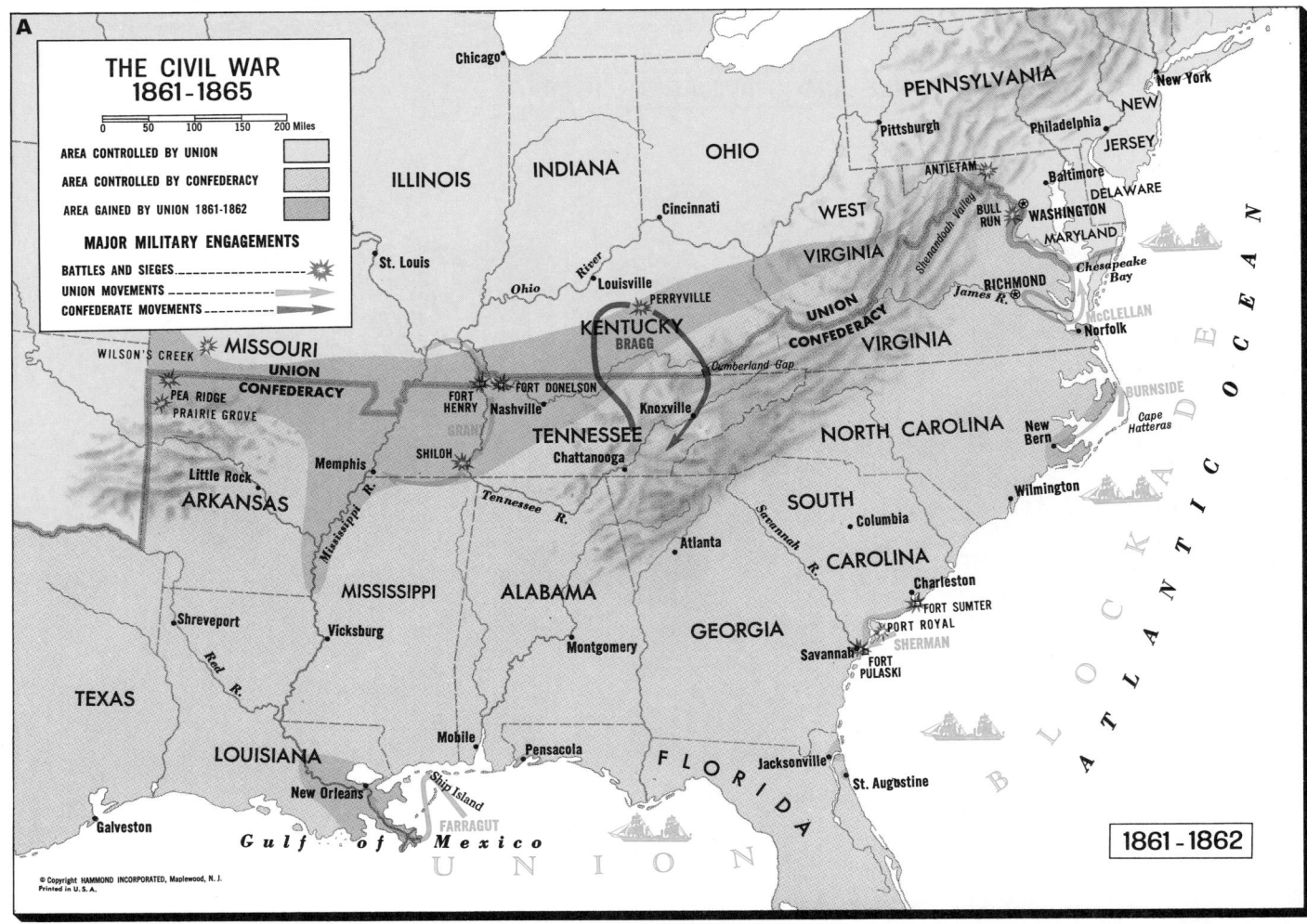

A
THE CIVIL WAR
1861-1865
0 50 100 150 200 Miles
AREA CONTROLLED BY UNION
AREA CONTROLLED BY CONFEDERACY
AREA GAINED BY UNION 1861-1862
MAJOR MILITARY ENGAGEMENTS
BATTLES AND SIEGES
UNION MOVEMENTS
CONFEDERATE MOVEMENTS
Chicago
PENNSYLVANIA
New York
NEW
JERSEY
Pittsburgh
Philadelphia
ILLINOIS
INDIANA
OHIO
ANTIETAM
Baltimore
DELAWARE
Cincinnati
WEST
BULL RUN
WASHINGTON
MARYLAND
St. Louis
VIRGINIA
Shenandoah Valley
Chesapeake Bay
Ohio
River
Louisville
RICHMOND
James R.
PERRYVILLE
UNION
McCLELLAN
KENTUCKY
BRAGG
CONFEDERACY
VIRGINIA
Norfolk
WILSON'S CREEK
MISSOURI
UNION
Cumberland Gap
CONFEDERACY
FORT HENRY
FORT DONELSON
BURNSIDE
PEA RIDGE
PRAIRIE GROVE
Nashville
Knoxville
NORTH CAROLINA
New Bern
Cape Hatteras
GRANT
TENNESSEE
SHILOH
Chattanooga
Memphis
Little Rock
ARKANSAS
Tennessee R.
Wilmington
Mississippi R.
SOUTH
Columbia
Savannah R.
Atlanta
CAROLINA
Charleston
MISSISSIPPI
ALABAMA
FORT SUMTER
Shreveport
Vicksburg
PORT ROYAL
GEORGIA
Montgomery
SHERMAN
Savannah
FORT PULASKI
Red R.
TEXAS
Mobile
Pensacola
LOUISIANA
FLORIDA
Jacksonville
St. Augustine
New Orleans
Ship Island
Galveston
FARRAGUT
Gulf of Mexico
ATLANTIC OCEAN
UNION BLOCKADE
1861-1862
© Copyright HAMMOND INCORPORATED, Maplewood, N. J.
Printed in U. S. A.

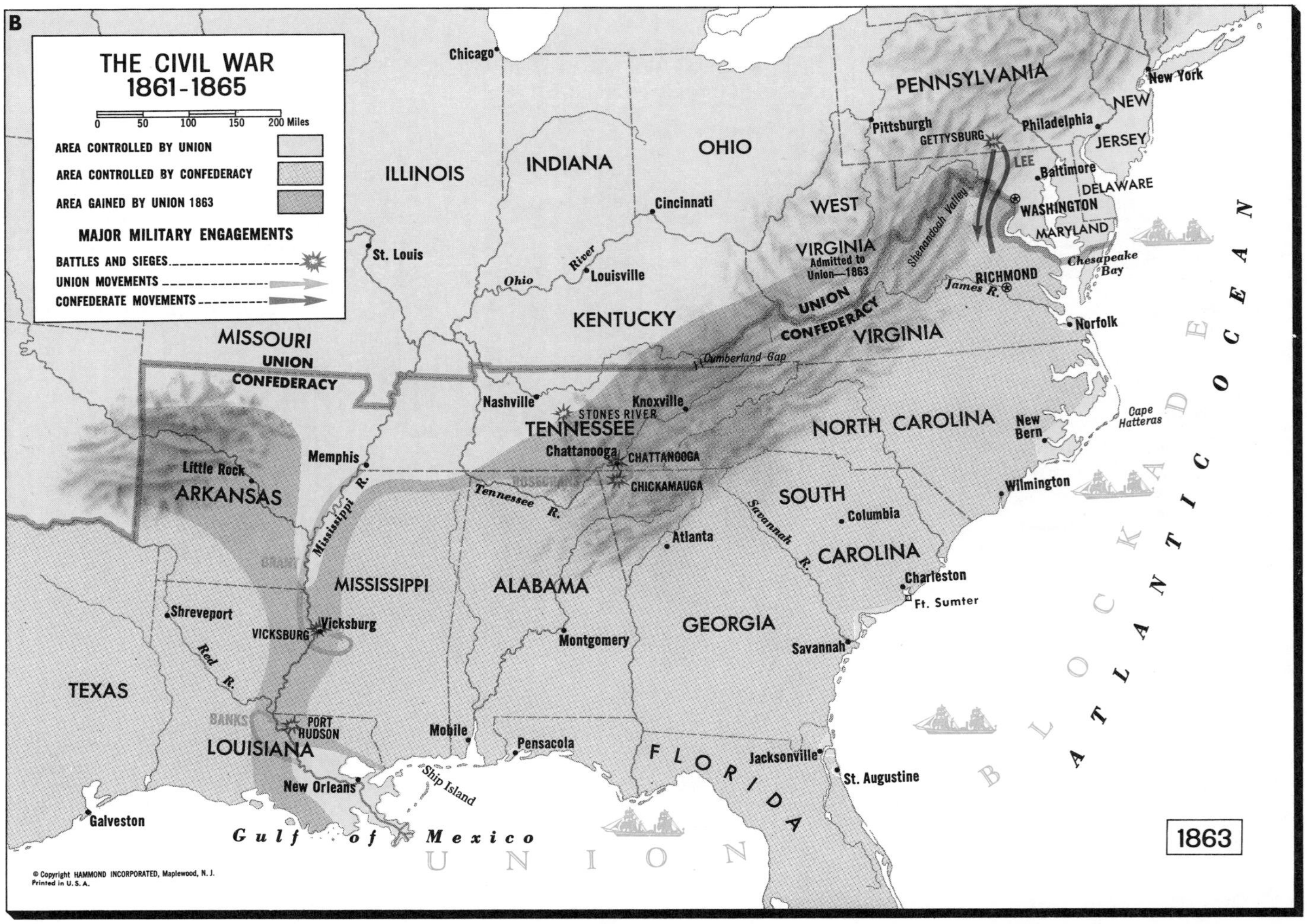

B
THE CIVIL WAR
1861-1865
0 50 100 150 200 Miles
AREA CONTROLLED BY UNION
AREA CONTROLLED BY CONFEDERACY
AREA GAINED BY UNION 1863
MAJOR MILITARY ENGAGEMENTS
BATTLES AND SIEGES
UNION MOVEMENTS
CONFEDERATE MOVEMENTS
Chicago
PENNSYLVANIA
New York
NEW
JERSEY
Pittsburgh
GETTYSBURG
Philadelphia
ILLINOIS
INDIANA
OHIO
LEE
Baltimore
DELAWARE
Cincinnati
WEST
WASHINGTON
MARYLAND
St. Louis
VIRGINIA
Admitted to Union—1863
Shenandoah Valley
Chesapeake Bay
Ohio
River
Louisville
RICHMOND
James R.
KENTUCKY
UNION
CONFEDERACY
VIRGINIA
Norfolk
MISSOURI
UNION
Cumberland Gap
CONFEDERACY
Nashville
STONES RIVER
Knoxville
TENNESSEE
NORTH CAROLINA
New Bern
Cape Hatteras
Chattanooga
CHATTANOOGA
CHICKAMAUGA
ROSECRANS
Memphis
Little Rock
ARKANSAS
Tennessee R.
Wilmington
Mississippi R.
SOUTH
Columbia
Savannah R.
Atlanta
CAROLINA
GRANT
Charleston
MISSISSIPPI
ALABAMA
Ft. Sumter
Shreveport
VICKSBURG
Vicksburg
GEORGIA
Montgomery
Savannah
Red R.
TEXAS
BANKS
PORT HUDSON
Mobile
Pensacola
LOUISIANA
FLORIDA
Jacksonville
St. Augustine
New Orleans
Ship Island
Galveston
Gulf of Mexico
ATLANTIC OCEAN
UNION BLOCKADE
1863
© Copyright HAMMOND INCORPORATED, Maplewood, N. J.
Printed in U. S. A.

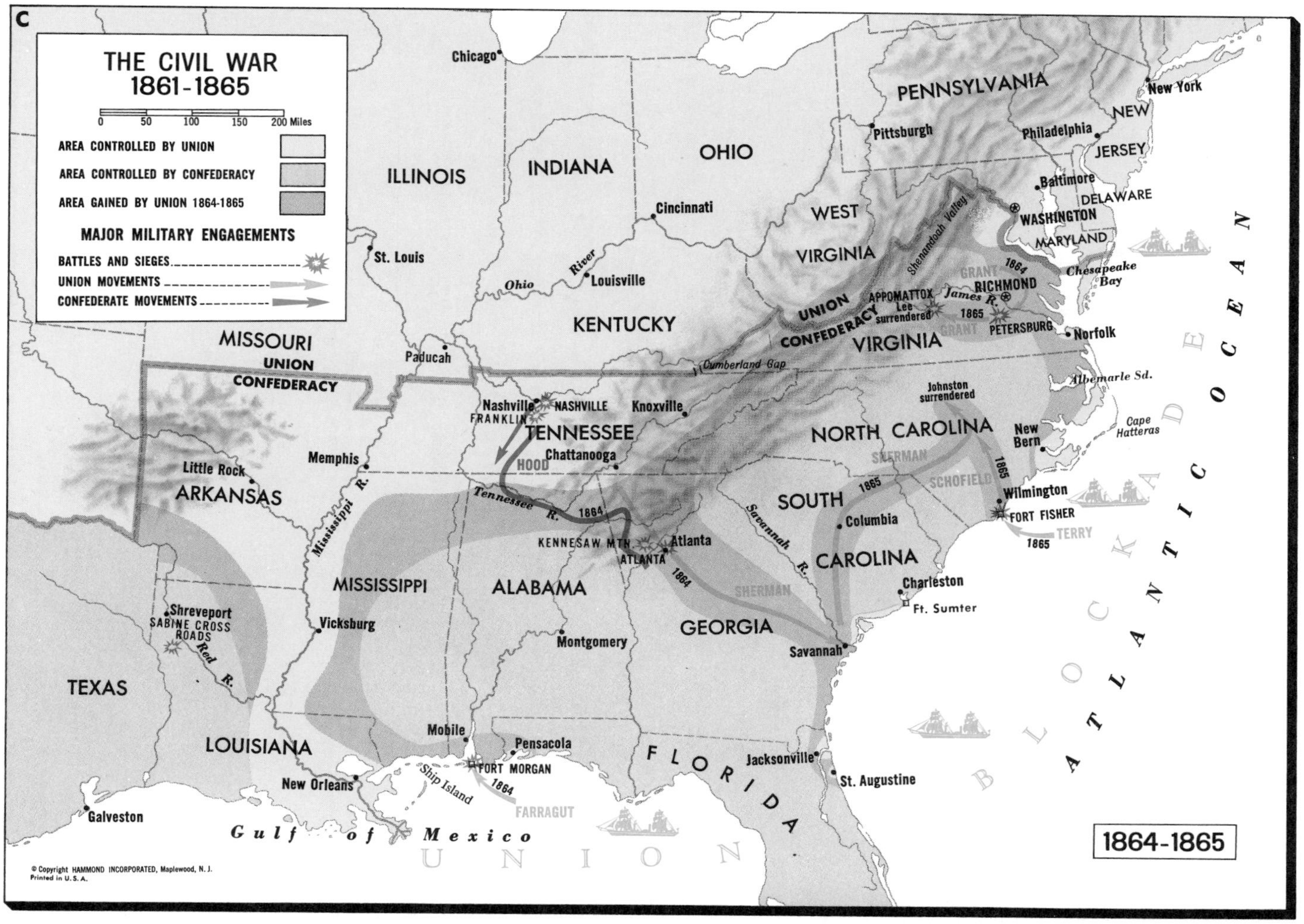

C

THE CIVIL WAR
1861-1865

0   50   100   150   200 Miles

AREA CONTROLLED BY UNION

AREA CONTROLLED BY CONFEDERACY

AREA GAINED BY UNION 1864-1865

MAJOR MILITARY ENGAGEMENTS

BATTLES AND SIEGES
UNION MOVEMENTS
CONFEDERATE MOVEMENTS

Chicago

ILLINOIS   INDIANA   OHIO   PENNSYLVANIA   New York

Pittsburgh   Philadelphia   NEW JERSEY

St. Louis   Cincinnati   WEST VIRGINIA   Baltimore   DELAWARE   MARYLAND   WASHINGTON

Ohio River   Louisville   KENTUCKY   Shenandoah Valley   GRANT 1864   Chesapeake Bay

MISSOURI   UNION   CONFEDERACY   Paducah   Cumberland Gap   UNION CONFEDERACY   VIRGINIA   APPOMATTOX Lee surrendered   RICHMOND   James R.   GRANT 1865   PETERSBURG   Norfolk   Albemarle Sd.

Nashville NASHVILLE   Knoxville   Johnston surrendered   NORTH CAROLINA   New Bern   Cape Hatteras

Memphis   FRANKLIN   TENNESSEE   Chattanooga   SHERMAN   SCHOFIELD   1865

Little Rock   Mississippi R.   HOOD   Tennessee R. 1864   SOUTH   1865   Wilmington FORT FISHER   TERRY 1865

ARKANSAS   KENNESAW MTN.   Atlanta   Columbia   CAROLINA   Savannah R.

MISSISSIPPI   ALABAMA   ATLANTA   1864   SHERMAN   Charleston   Ft. Sumter

Shreveport   Vicksburg   GEORGIA   Savannah

SABINE CROSS ROADS   Red R.   Montgomery

TEXAS   LOUISIANA   Mobile   Pensacola   Jacksonville

New Orleans   Ship Island   FORT MORGAN 1864   FLORIDA   St. Augustine

Galveston   Gulf of Mexico   FARRAGUT   UNION

ATLANTIC OCEAN

BLOCKADE

1864-1865

© Copyright HAMMOND INCORPORATED, Maplewood, N.J.
Printed in U.S.A.

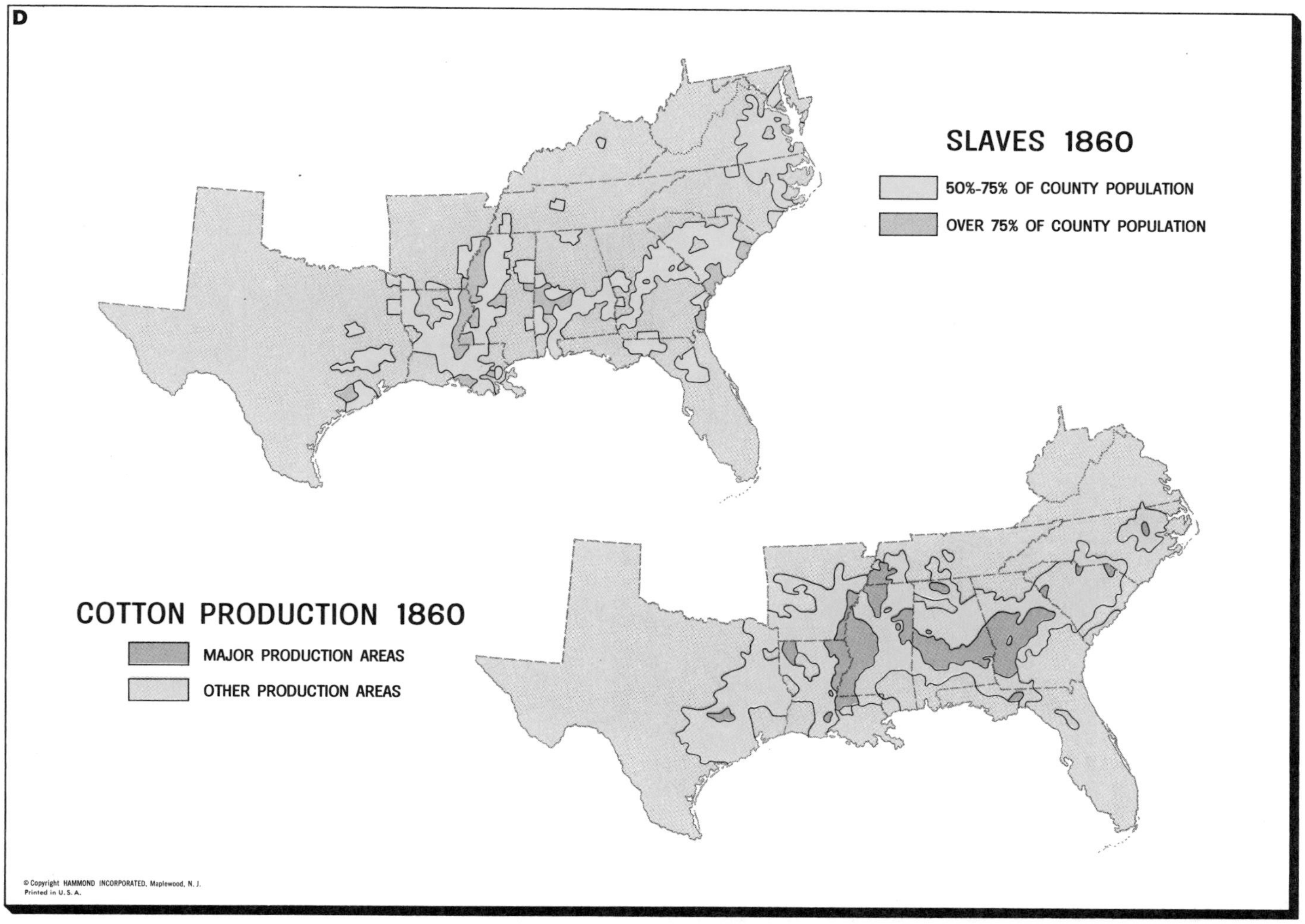

D

SLAVES 1860

50%-75% OF COUNTY POPULATION

OVER 75% OF COUNTY POPULATION

COTTON PRODUCTION 1860

MAJOR PRODUCTION AREAS

OTHER PRODUCTION AREAS

© Copyright HAMMOND INCORPORATED, Maplewood, N.J.
Printed in U.S.A.

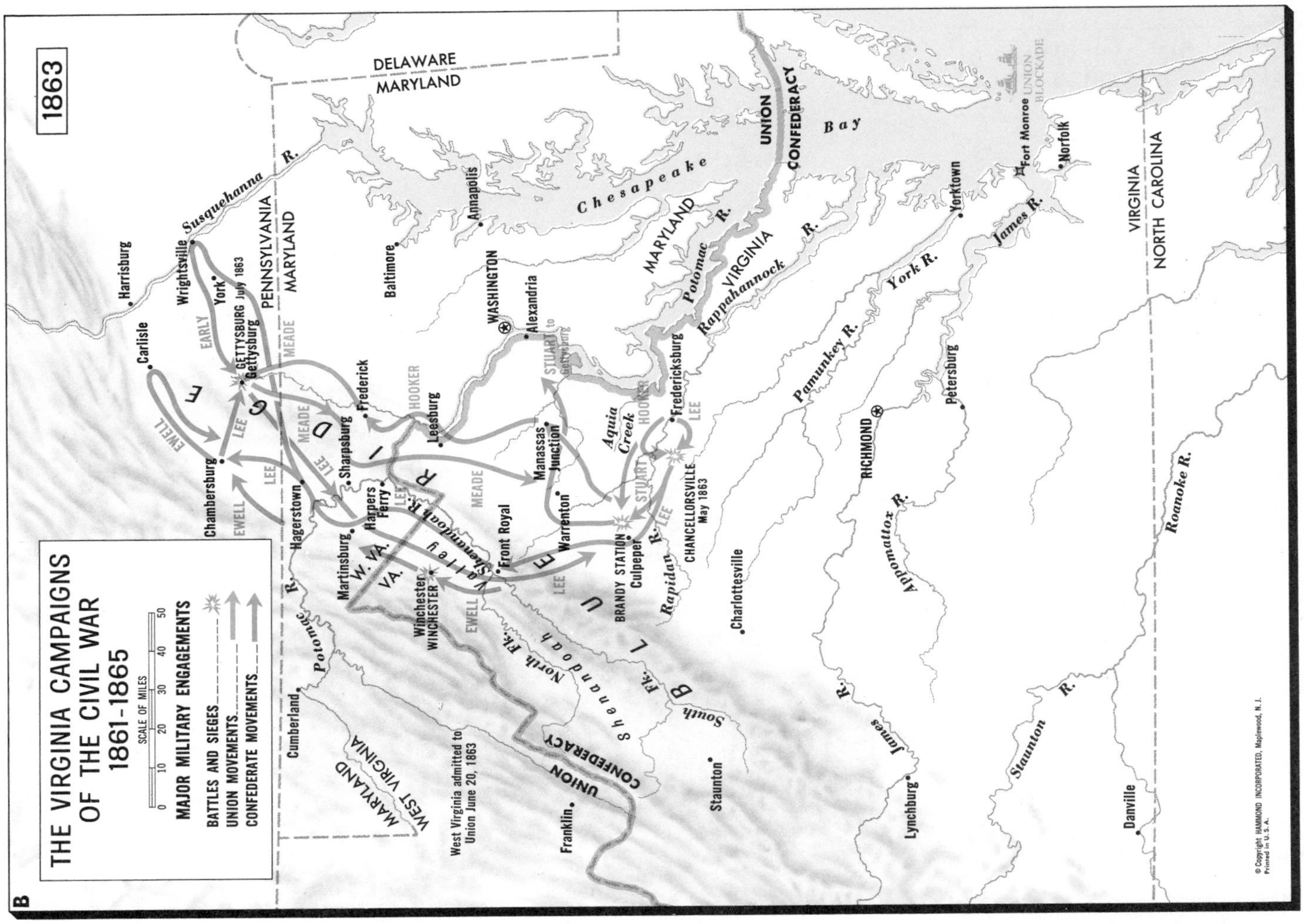

1863

B

THE VIRGINIA CAMPAIGNS
OF THE CIVIL WAR
1861-1865

SCALE OF MILES
0 10 20 30 40 50

MAJOR MILITARY ENGAGEMENTS

BATTLES AND SIEGES
UNION MOVEMENTS
CONFEDERATE MOVEMENTS

West Virginia admitted to
Union June 20, 1863

DELAWARE
MARYLAND

PENNSYLVANIA
MARYLAND

Chesapeake

Bay

UNION
CONFEDERACY

UNION
BLOCKADE

Harrisburg
Carlisle
Wrightsville
York
Susquehanna R.
GETTYSBURG July 1863
Gettysburg
Chambersburg
Hagerstown
Sharpsburg
Frederick
Leesburg
Martinsburg
W. VA.
VA.
Harpers Ferry
Winchester
Front Royal
Warrenton
Manassas Junction
WASHINGTON
Alexandria
Annapolis
Baltimore
Brandy Station
Culpeper
CHANCELLORSVILLE May 1863
Fredericksburg
Aquia Creek
Rapidan R.
Charlottesville
RICHMOND
Petersburg
Staunton
Franklin
Cumberland
MARYLAND
WEST VIRGINIA
UNION
CONFEDERACY
Lynchburg
Danville
VIRGINIA
NORTH CAROLINA
Fort Monroe
Norfolk
Yorktown
James R.
York R.
Pamunkey R.
Appomattox R.
Roanoke R.
James R.
Staunton R.
Potomac R.
Rappahannock R.
Shenandoah R.
North Fk.
South Fk.
Shenandoah
Valley
EARLY
EWELL
MEADE
LEE
HOOKER
STUART
MEADE

© Copyright HAMMOND INCORPORATED, Maplewood, N.J.
Printed in U.S.A.

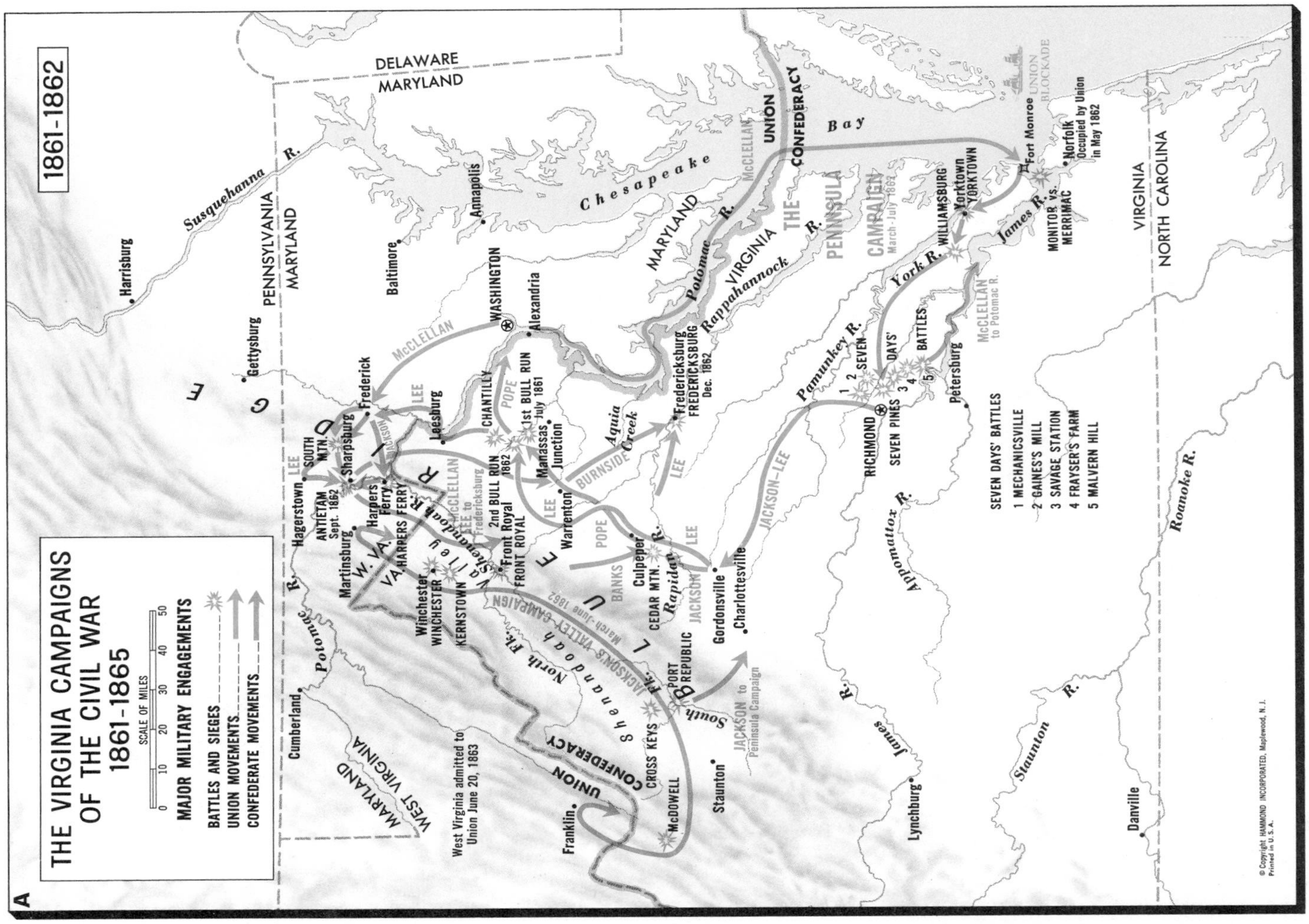

1861-1862

A

THE VIRGINIA CAMPAIGNS
OF THE CIVIL WAR
1861-1865

SCALE OF MILES
0 10 20 30 40 50

MAJOR MILITARY ENGAGEMENTS

BATTLES AND SIEGES
UNION MOVEMENTS
CONFEDERATE MOVEMENTS

West Virginia admitted to
Union June 20, 1863

SEVEN DAYS' BATTLES
1 MECHANICSVILLE
2 GAINES'S MILL
3 SAVAGE STATION
4 FRAYSER'S FARM
5 MALVERN HILL

DELAWARE
MARYLAND

PENNSYLVANIA
MARYLAND

Chesapeake

Bay

UNION
CONFEDERACY

THE PENINSULA CAMPAIGN
March-July 1862

UNION
BLOCKADE

Harrisburg
Gettysburg
Hagerstown
ANTIETAM Sept. 1862
Sharpsburg
SOUTH MTN.
Frederick
Leesburg
CHANTILLY
1st BULL RUN 1861
2nd BULL RUN 1862
Manassas Junction
Martinsburg
W. VA.
VA.
Harpers Ferry
Winchester
KERNSTOWN
Front Royal
CEDAR MTN.
Warrenton
Culpeper
Rapidan R.
Gordonsville
Charlottesville
CROSS KEYS
PORT REPUBLIC
McDOWELL
Franklin
Staunton
WASHINGTON
Alexandria
Annapolis
Baltimore
Fredericksburg
FREDERICKSBURG Dec. 1862
Aquia Creek
RICHMOND
SEVEN PINES
SEVEN DAYS' BATTLES
Petersburg
WILLIAMSBURG
YORKTOWN
Yorktown
MONITOR VS. MERRIMAC
Fort Monroe
Norfolk Occupied by Union in May 1862
James R.
York R.
Pamunkey R.
Appomattox R.
Roanoke R.
Lynchburg
Danville
Cumberland
MARYLAND
WEST VIRGINIA
UNION
CONFEDERACY
VIRGINIA
NORTH CAROLINA
Potomac R.
Rappahannock R.
Shenandoah R.
North Fk.
South Fk.
Shenandoah Valley
JACKSON'S VALLEY CAMPAIGN March-June 1862
JACKSON to Peninsula Campaign
McCLELLAN
POPE
BURNSIDE
LEE
JACKSON
BANKS
JACKSON-LEE
James R.
Staunton R.

© Copyright HAMMOND INCORPORATED, Maplewood, N.J.
Printed in U.S.A.

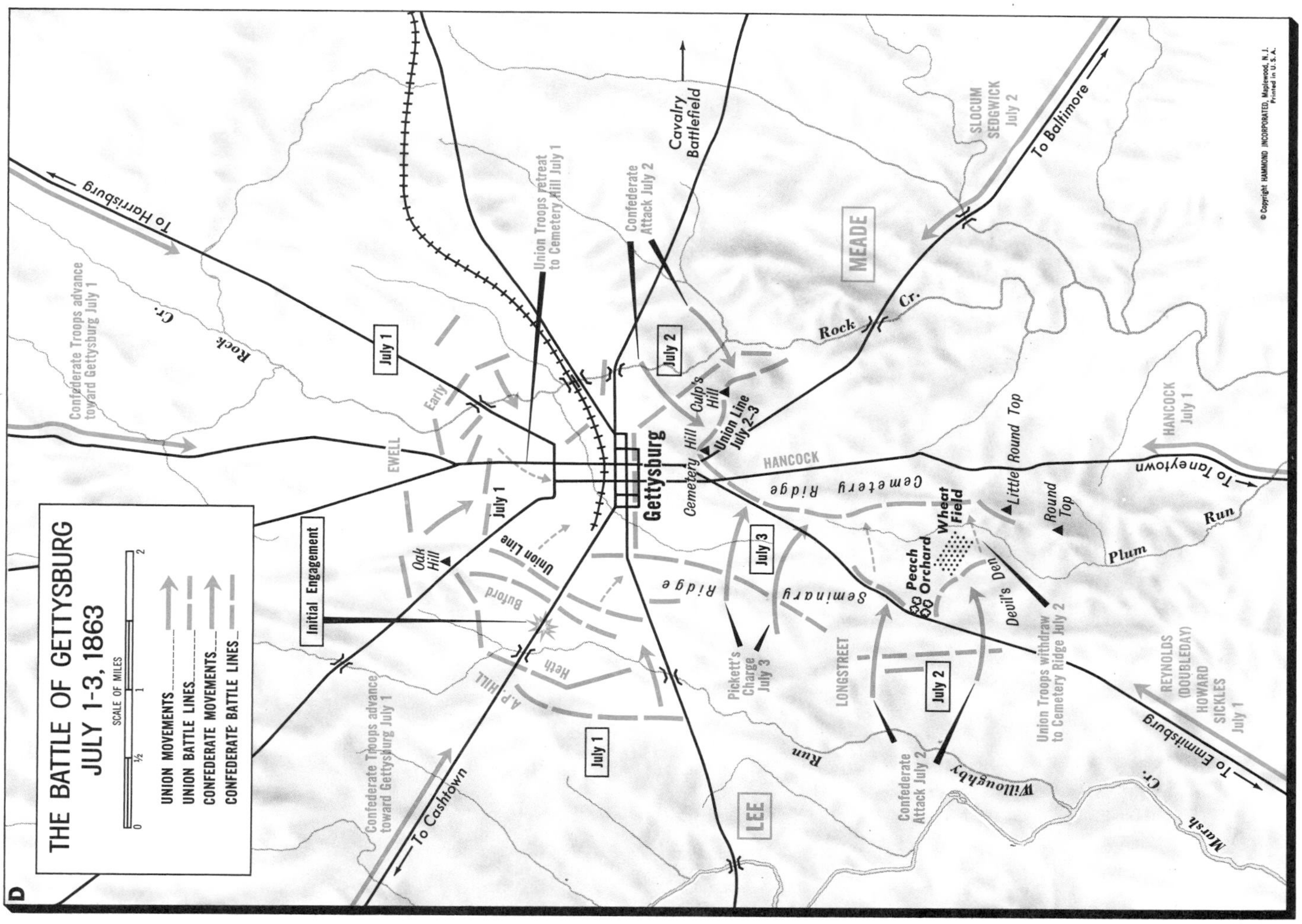

Map D — THE BATTLE OF GETTYSBURG JULY 1-3, 1863

THE BATTLE OF GETTYSBURG JULY 1-3, 1863

SCALE OF MILES

0   ½   1   2

Initial Engagement

UNION MOVEMENTS
UNION BATTLE LINES
CONFEDERATE MOVEMENTS
CONFEDERATE BATTLE LINES

To Harrisburg

Confederate Troops advance toward Gettysburg July 1

Rock Cr.

EWELL

Early

July 1

Union Troops retreat to Cemetery Hill July 1

Confederate Attack July 2

Cavalry Battlefield

SLOCUM
SEDGWICK July 2

To Baltimore

MEADE

Rock Cr.

July 2

Culp's Hill

Union Line July 2-3

HANCOCK

Gettysburg

Cemetery Hill

Cemetery Ridge

Little Round Top

HANCOCK July 1

To Taneytown

Run

Plum

Round Top

Wheat Field

Devil's Den

Peach Orchard

Seminary Ridge

July 3

Pickett's Charge July 3

A.P. HILL

Heth

Buford

Union Line

July 1

Oak Hill

Ridge

LEE

LONGSTREET

July 2

Union Troops withdraw to Cemetery Ridge July 2

Confederate Attack July 2

Willoughby Run

REYNOLDS (DOUBLEDAY)
HOWARD
SICKLES July 1

To Emmitsburg

Marsh Cr.

Run

LEE

Confederate Troops advance toward Gettysburg July 1

To Cashtown

© Copyright HAMMOND INCORPORATED, Maplewood, N.J.
Printed in U.S.A.

D

Map C — THE VIRGINIA CAMPAIGNS OF THE CIVIL WAR 1861-1865

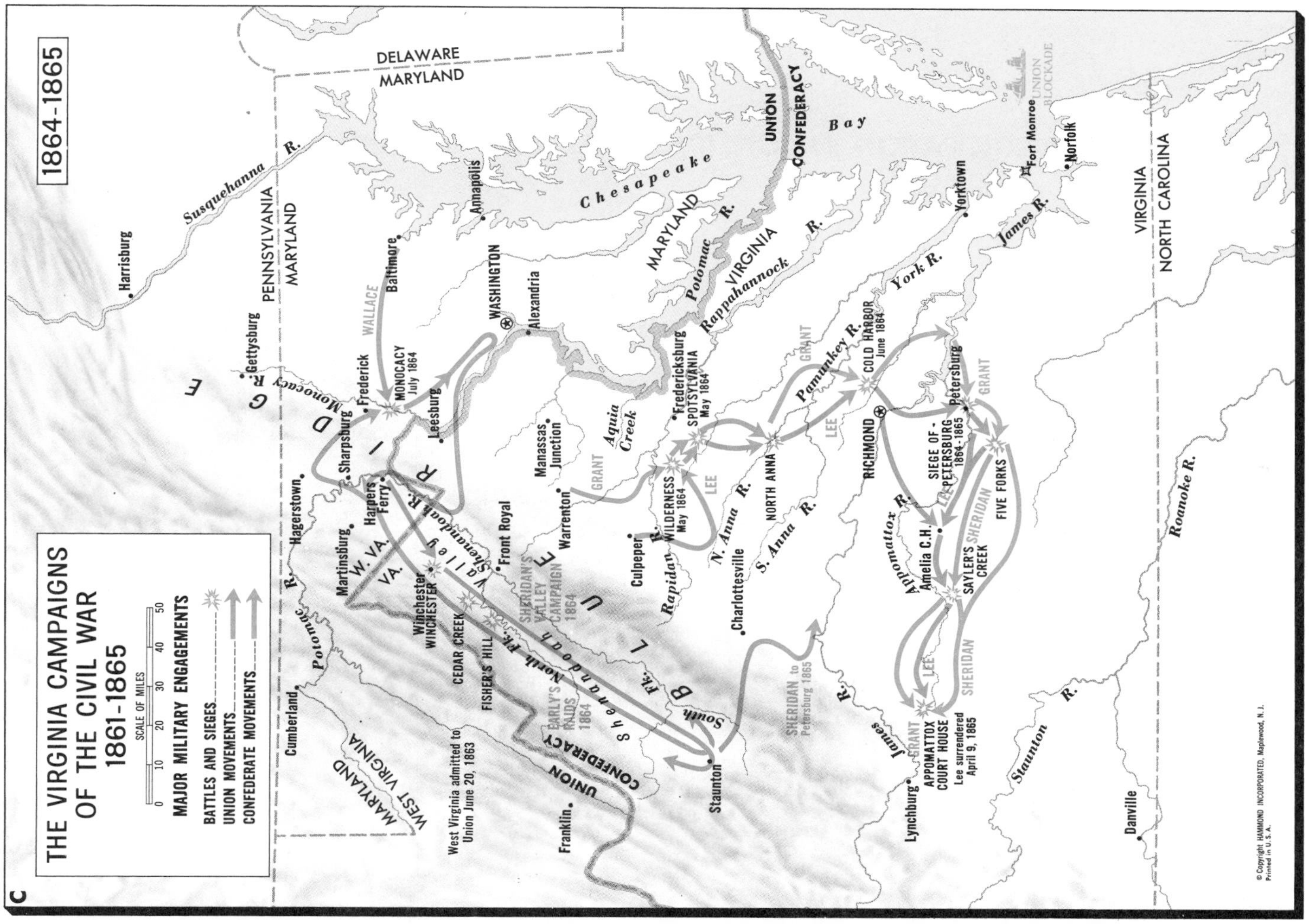

THE VIRGINIA CAMPAIGNS OF THE CIVIL WAR 1861-1865

SCALE OF MILES

0 10 20 30 40 50

MAJOR MILITARY ENGAGEMENTS

BATTLES AND SIEGES
UNION MOVEMENTS
CONFEDERATE MOVEMENTS

1864-1865

DELAWARE
MARYLAND

UNION

CONFEDERACY

Chesapeake Bay

UNION BLOCKADE

Fort Monroe

Norfolk

VIRGINIA

NORTH CAROLINA

Roanoke R.

James R.

Yorktown

York R.

Pamunkey R.

COLD HARBOR June 1864

GRANT

Petersburg

SIEGE OF PETERSBURG 1864-1865

RICHMOND

FIVE FORKS

SHERIDAN

Appomattox R.

Amelia C.H.

SAYLER'S CREEK

LEE

SHERIDAN

James R.

APPOMATTOX COURT HOUSE
Lee surrendered April 9, 1865

GRANT

Lynchburg

SHERIDAN to Petersburg 1865

Staunton

Danville

Charlottesville

S. Anna R.

N. Anna R.

NORTH ANNA

Aquia Creek

Fredericksburg May 1864

SPOTSYLVANIA

Rappahannock R.

LEE

WILDERNESS May 1864

Rapidan R.

GRANT

Culpeper

Front Royal

Warrenton

Manassas Junction

Alexandria

WASHINGTON

Annapolis

Potomac R.

MARYLAND

VIRGINIA

SHERIDAN'S VALLEY CAMPAIGN 1864

Winchester

WINCHESTER

CEDAR CREEK

FISHER'S HILL

EARLY'S RAIDS 1864

North Fork Shenandoah R.

South Fork Shenandoah R.

Shenandoah Valley

Martinsburg

Harper's Ferry

Hagerstown

W. VA.
VA.

Cumberland

Potomac R.

MARYLAND

WEST VIRGINIA

West Virginia admitted to Union June 20, 1863

Franklin

Sharpsburg

Leesburg

Frederick

MONOCACY July 1864

WALLACE

Monocacy R.

Gettysburg

Baltimore

PENNSYLVANIA
MARYLAND

Harrisburg

Susquehanna R.

E D G I R

Potomac R.

© Copyright HAMMOND INCORPORATED, Maplewood, N.J.
Printed in U.S.A.

C

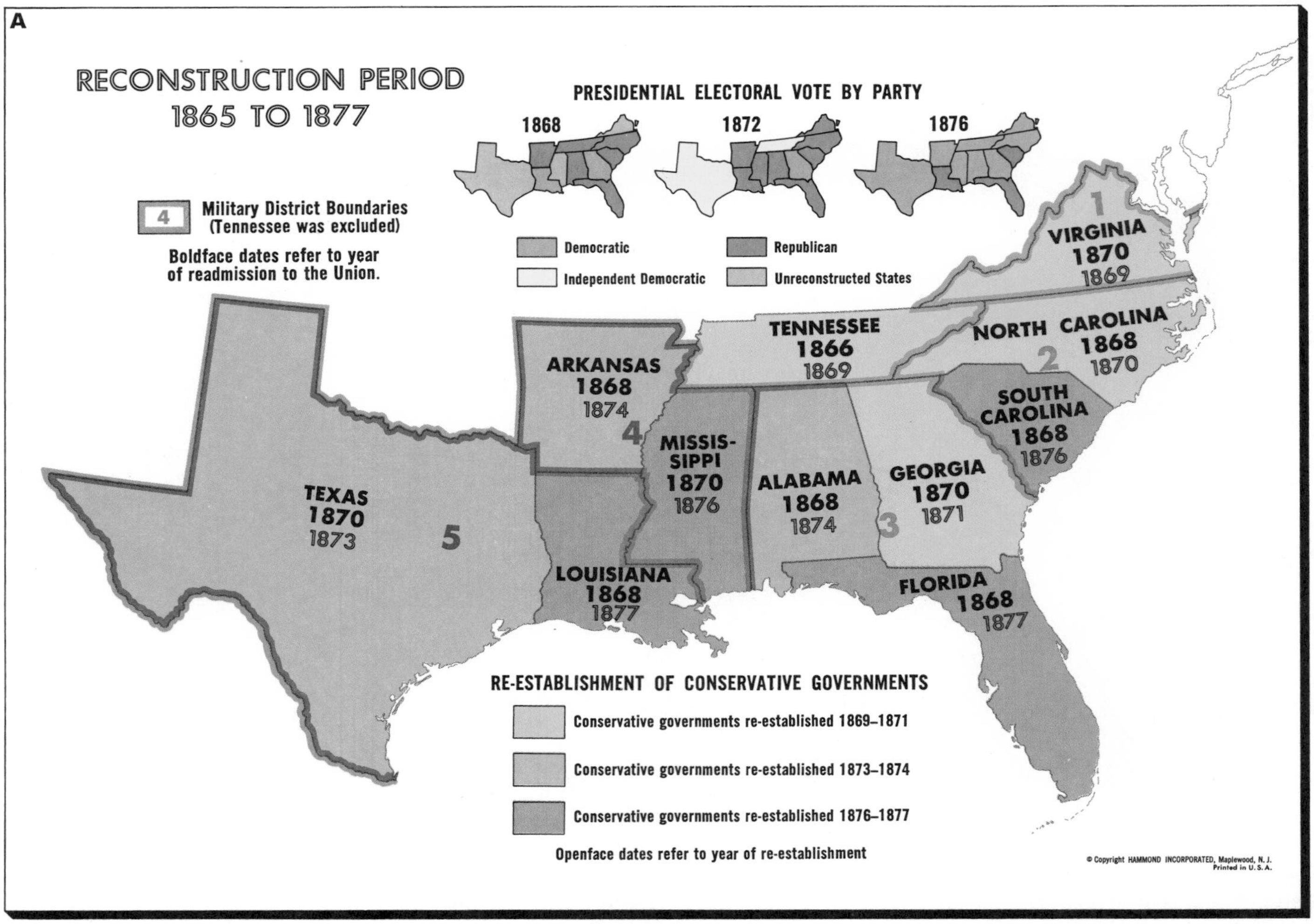

A

RECONSTRUCTION PERIOD 1865 TO 1877

PRESIDENTIAL ELECTORAL VOTE BY PARTY

1868   1872   1876

4   Military District Boundaries
(Tennessee was excluded)

Boldface dates refer to year
of readmission to the Union.

Democratic   Republican
Independent Democratic   Unreconstructed States

VIRGINIA
1870
1869

TENNESSEE
1866
1869

NORTH CAROLINA
1868
1870

ARKANSAS
1868
1874

SOUTH
CAROLINA
1868
1876

MISSIS-
SIPPI
1870
1876

ALABAMA
1868
1874

GEORGIA
1870
1871

TEXAS
1870
1873

LOUISIANA
1868
1877

FLORIDA
1868
1877

RE-ESTABLISHMENT OF CONSERVATIVE GOVERNMENTS

Conservative governments re-established 1869–1871

Conservative governments re-established 1873–1874

Conservative governments re-established 1876–1877

Openface dates refer to year of re-establishment

© Copyright HAMMOND INCORPORATED, Maplewood, N.J.
Printed in U.S.A.

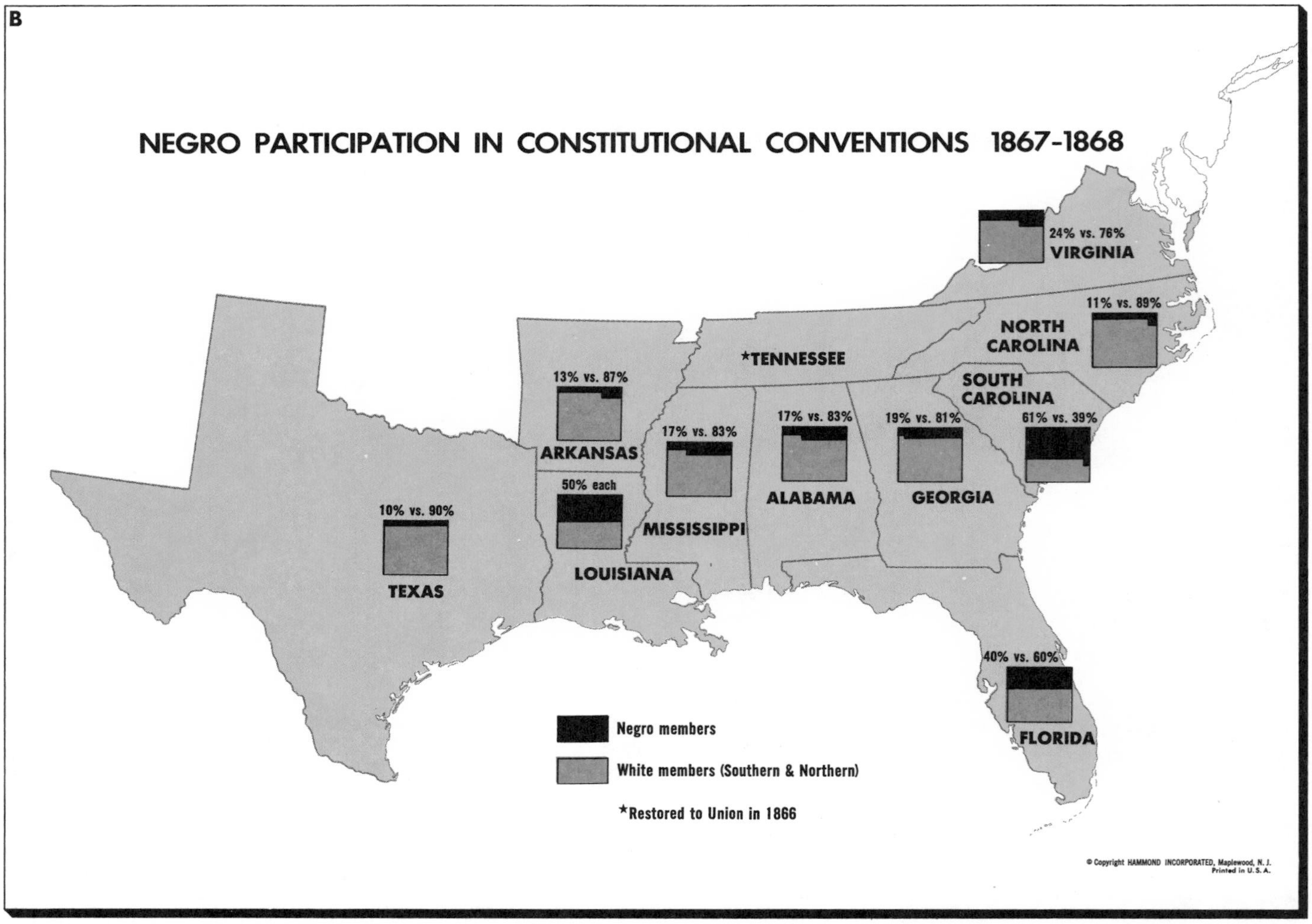

B

NEGRO PARTICIPATION IN CONSTITUTIONAL CONVENTIONS 1867-1868

24% vs. 76%
VIRGINIA

11% vs. 89%
NORTH
CAROLINA

*TENNESSEE

SOUTH
CAROLINA

13% vs. 87%
ARKANSAS

17% vs. 83%
MISSISSIPPI

17% vs. 83%
ALABAMA

19% vs. 81%
GEORGIA

61% vs. 39%

50% each

10% vs. 90%
TEXAS

LOUISIANA

40% vs. 60%
FLORIDA

Negro members

White members (Southern & Northern)

*Restored to Union in 1866

© Copyright HAMMOND INCORPORATED, Maplewood, N.J.
Printed in U.S.A.

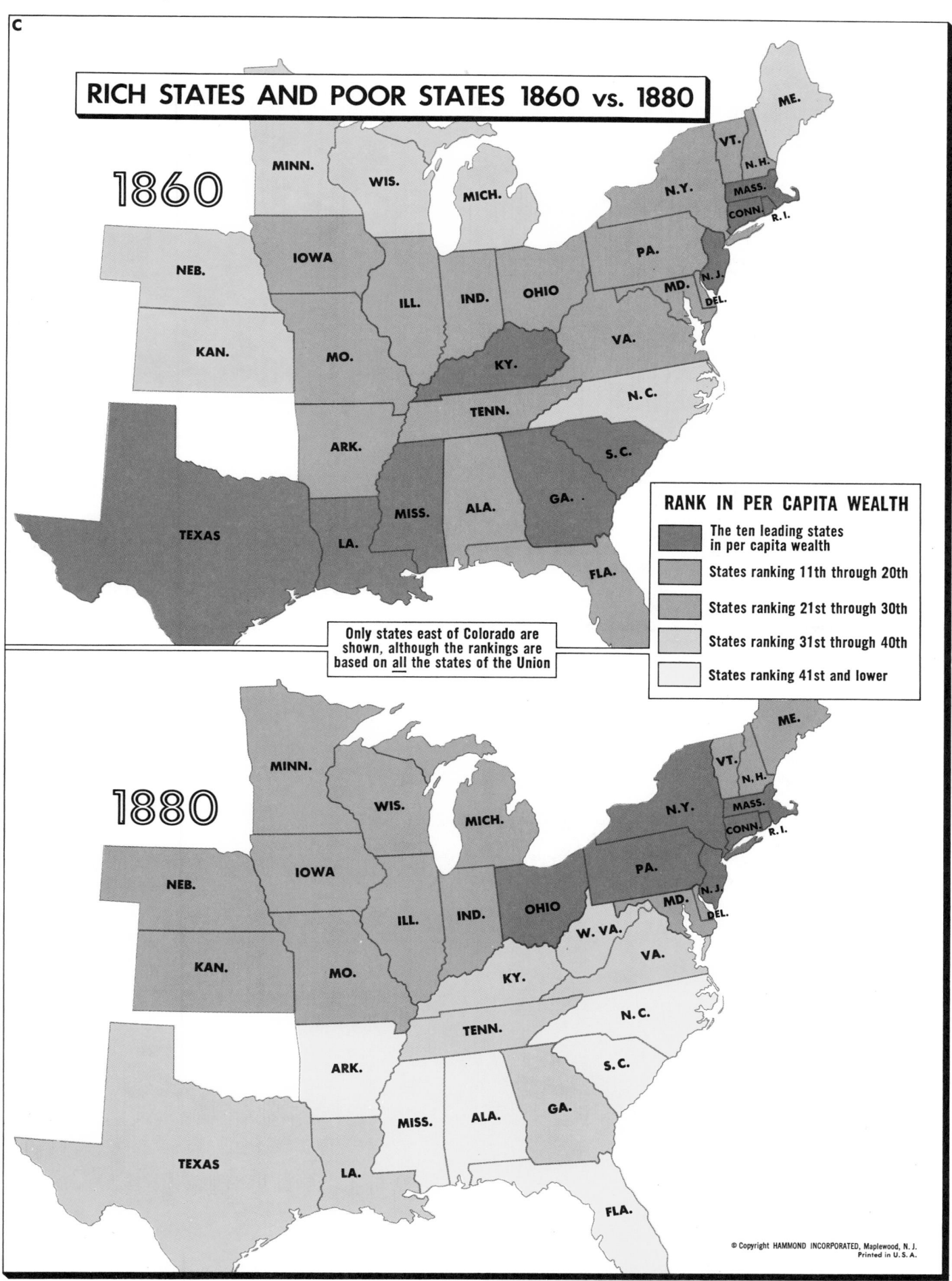

RICH STATES AND POOR STATES 1860 vs. 1880

1860

ME.
VT.
N.H.
MINN.
WIS.
MICH.
N.Y.
MASS.
CONN.
R.I.
IOWA
PA.
NEB.
MD.
N.J.
ILL.
IND.
OHIO
DEL.
KAN.
MO.
KY.
VA.
TENN.
N.C.
ARK.
S.C.
GA.
MISS.
ALA.
TEXAS
LA.
FLA.

Only states east of Colorado are shown, although the rankings are based on <u>all</u> the states of the Union

RANK IN PER CAPITA WEALTH

The ten leading states in per capita wealth

States ranking 11th through 20th

States ranking 21st through 30th

States ranking 31st through 40th

States ranking 41st and lower

1880

ME.
VT.
N.H.
MINN.
WIS.
MICH.
N.Y.
MASS.
CONN.
R.I.
IOWA
PA.
NEB.
MD.
N.J.
ILL.
IND.
OHIO
DEL.
KAN.
MO.
W. VA.
VA.
KY.
TENN.
N.C.
ARK.
S.C.
MISS.
ALA.
GA.
TEXAS
LA.
FLA.

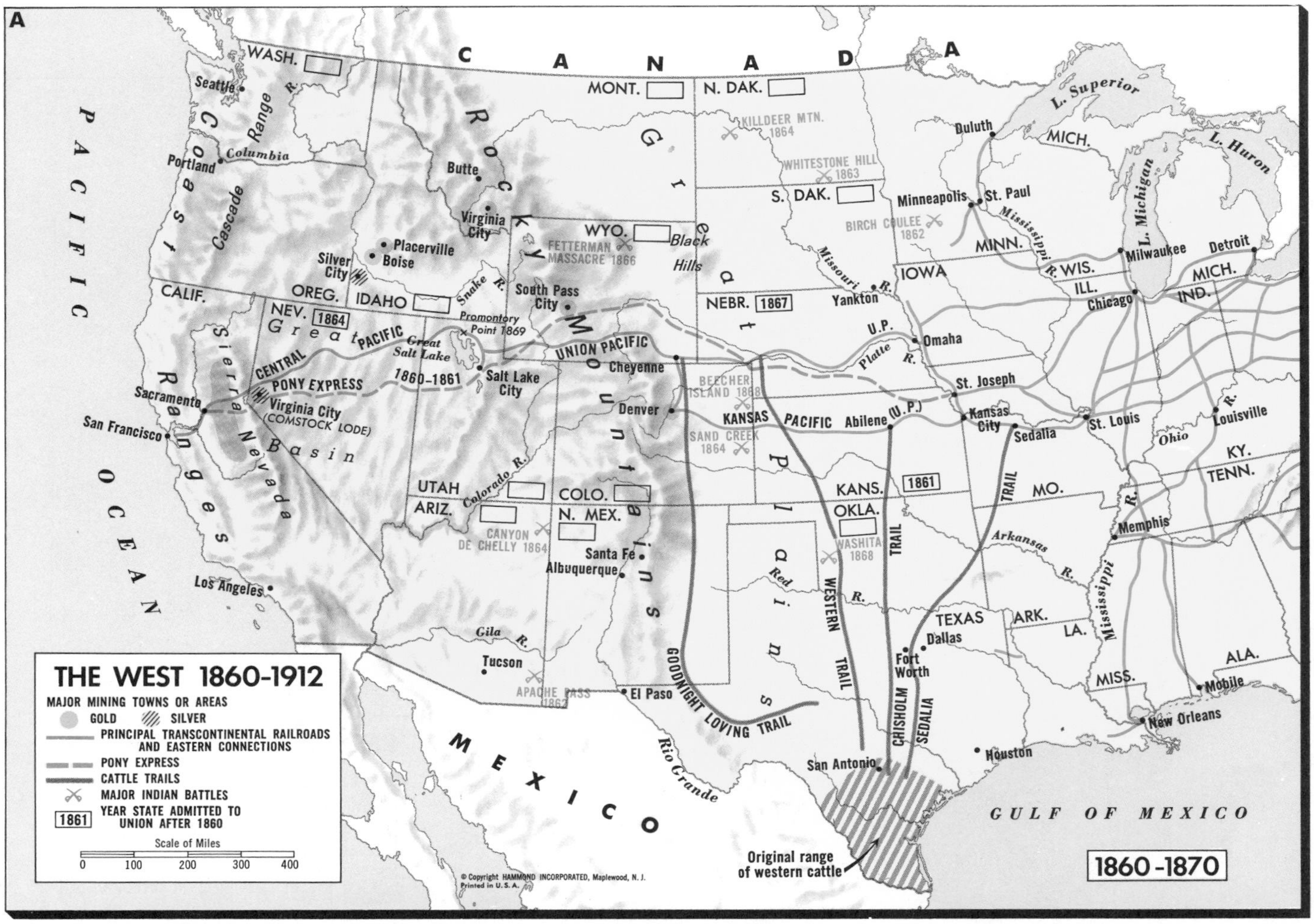

A

CANADA

WASH.

MONT.   N. DAK.

L. Superior

Seattle

Portland

Columbia R.

Butte

Virginia City

Placerville
Boise

Silver City

CALIF.   OREG.   IDAHO

NEV. 1864

Sacramento

San Francisco

Los Angeles

PACIFIC OCEAN

Coast Range

Cascade Range

Sierra Nevada Ranges

CENTRAL PACIFIC
PONY EXPRESS
Virginia City (COMSTOCK LODE)

Great Salt Lake

Great Basin

UTAH   ARIZ.

Colorado R.

CANYON DE CHELLY 1864

Gila R.

Tucson

APACHE PASS 1862

El Paso

Rio Grande

MEXICO

KILLDEER MTN. 1864
WHITESTONE HILL 1863

S. DAK.

Minneapolis   St. Paul

BIRCH COULEE 1862

MINN.   WIS.

Duluth   L. Michigan   L. Huron

MICH.

Milwaukee   Detroit

MICH.

ILL.   IND.

Rocky Mountains

South Pass City
Promontory Point 1869

Salt Lake City

WYO.   Black Hills

FETTERMAN MASSACRE 1866

Snake R.

Cheyenne

Denver

COLO.   N. MEX.

Santa Fe
Albuquerque

Great Plains

NEBR. 1867

Yankton

Missouri R.

IOWA

Chicago

U.P.
Omaha   Platte R.

BEECHER ISLAND 1868

KANSAS PACIFIC   Abilene (U.P.)

SAND CREEK 1864

KANS. 1861   OKLA.

WASHITA 1868

Red R.

WESTERN TRAIL

TRAIL

TEXAS   Dallas

Fort Worth

GOODNIGHT LOVING TRAIL

CHISHOLM   SEDALIA

San Antonio

Original range of western cattle

St. Joseph   St. Louis   Louisville

Kansas City   Sedalia

MO.   KY.   TENN.

Arkansas R.   Memphis

ARK.   LA.   Mississippi R.

MISS.   ALA.   Mobile

Houston

New Orleans

GULF OF MEXICO

THE WEST 1860-1912

MAJOR MINING TOWNS OR AREAS
GOLD   SILVER

PRINCIPAL TRANSCONTINENTAL RAILROADS AND EASTERN CONNECTIONS

PONY EXPRESS

CATTLE TRAILS

MAJOR INDIAN BATTLES

1861   YEAR STATE ADMITTED TO UNION AFTER 1860

Scale of Miles
0   100   200   300   400

© Copyright HAMMOND INCORPORATED, Maplewood, N.J.
Printed in U.S.A.

1860-1870

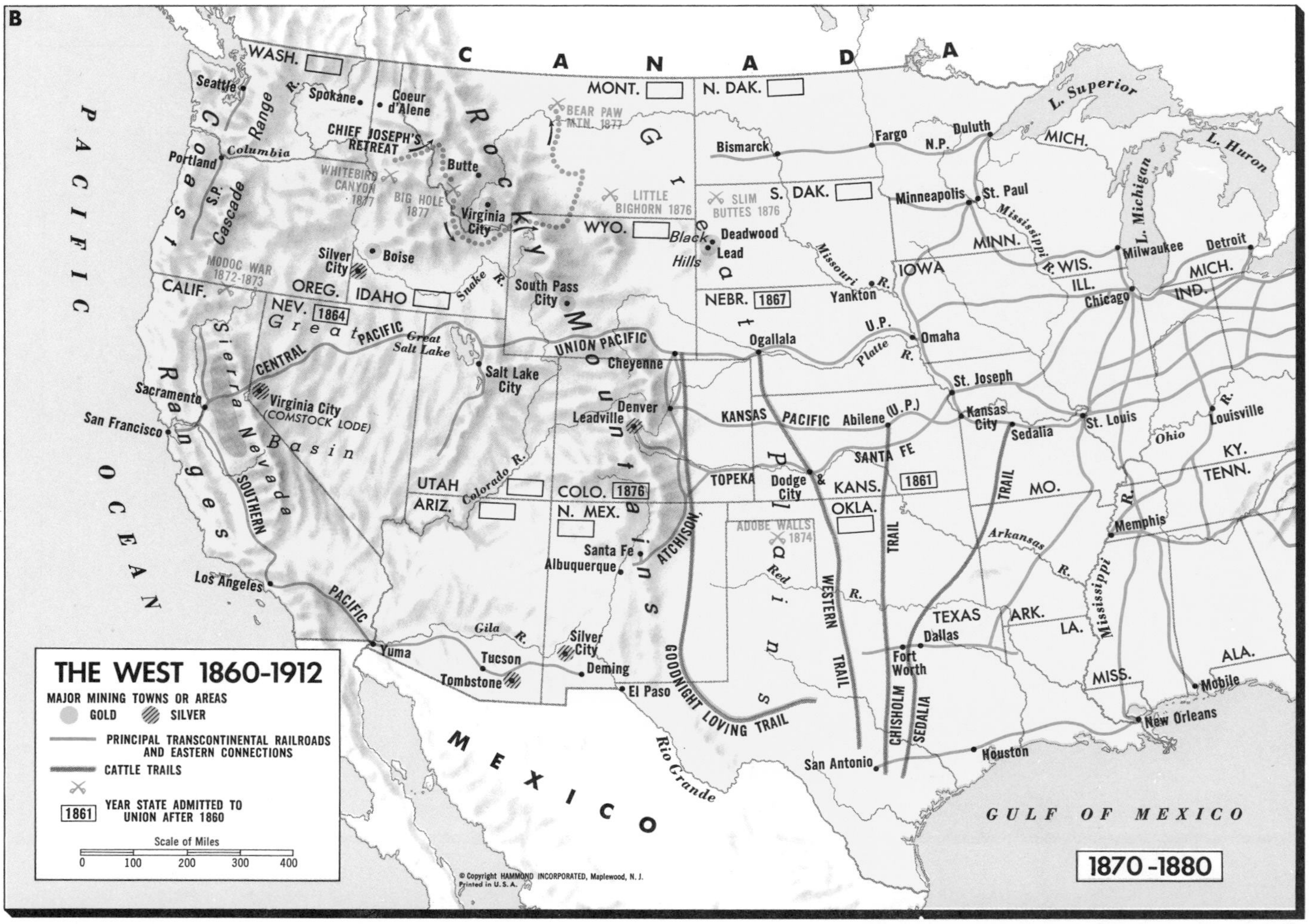

B

CANADA

WASH.   MONT.   N. DAK.

L. Superior

Seattle
Spokane   Coeur d'Alene

Portland

Columbia R.

CHIEF JOSEPH'S RETREAT

WHITEBIRD CANYON 1877

Butte

BIG HOLE 1877

Virginia City

BEAR PAW MTN. 1877

Bismarck   Fargo

N.P.   Duluth

MICH.   L. Huron

S.P.

Cascade Range

Coast Range

MODOC WAR 1872-1873

Silver City   Boise

CALIF.   OREG.   IDAHO

NEV. 1864

Sacramento

San Francisco

Los Angeles

PACIFIC OCEAN

Sierra Nevada Ranges

SOUTHERN PACIFIC

CENTRAL PACIFIC

Virginia City (COMSTOCK LODE)

Great Salt Lake

Great Basin

UTAH   ARIZ.

Colorado R.

Yuma

Gila R.

Tucson
Tombstone

Silver City   Deming

El Paso

Rio Grande

MEXICO

LITTLE BIGHORN 1876

SLIM BUTTES 1876

S. DAK.

Minneapolis   St. Paul

Rocky Mountains

South Pass City

Salt Lake City

WYO.   Black Hills

Deadwood
Lead

UNION PACIFIC

Snake R.

Cheyenne

Denver
Leadville

COLO. 1876   N. MEX.

Santa Fe
Albuquerque

ADOBE WALLS 1874

Ogallala

U.P.
Omaha   Platte R.

KANSAS PACIFIC   Abilene (U.P.)

TOPEKA   Dodge City

ATCHISON

KANS. 1861   OKLA.

SANTA FE

Red R.

WESTERN TRAIL

TRAIL

TEXAS   Dallas

Fort Worth

GOODNIGHT LOVING TRAIL

CHISHOLM   SEDALIA

San Antonio

NEBR. 1867

Yankton

Missouri R.

IOWA

MINN.   WIS.

Chicago   L. Michigan

MICH.

Milwaukee   Detroit

ILL.   IND.

St. Joseph   St. Louis   Louisville

Kansas City   Sedalia

MO.   KY.   TENN.

Arkansas R.   Memphis

ARK.   LA.   Mississippi R.

MISS.   ALA.   Mobile

Houston

New Orleans

GULF OF MEXICO

THE WEST 1860-1912

MAJOR MINING TOWNS OR AREAS
GOLD   SILVER

PRINCIPAL TRANSCONTINENTAL RAILROADS AND EASTERN CONNECTIONS

CATTLE TRAILS

YEAR STATE ADMITTED TO UNION AFTER 1860

1861

Scale of Miles
0   100   200   300   400

© Copyright HAMMOND INCORPORATED, Maplewood, N.J.
Printed in U.S.A.

1870-1880

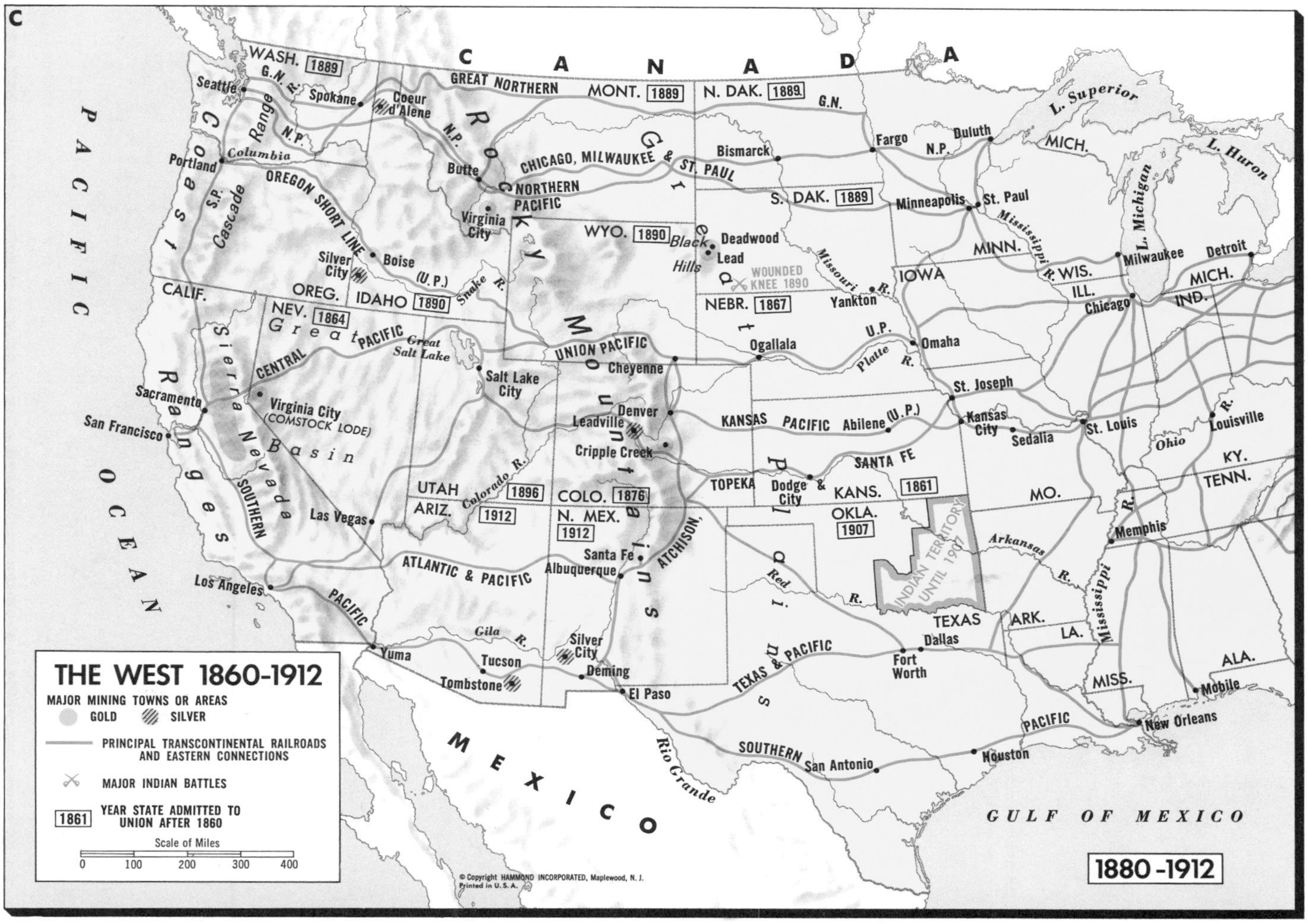

C

THE WEST 1860-1912

MAJOR MINING TOWNS OR AREAS
GOLD   SILVER

PRINCIPAL TRANSCONTINENTAL RAILROADS
AND EASTERN CONNECTIONS

MAJOR INDIAN BATTLES

1861 YEAR STATE ADMITTED TO
UNION AFTER 1860

Scale of Miles
0   100   200   300   400

© Copyright HAMMOND INCORPORATED, Maplewood, N.J.
Printed in U.S.A.

1880-1912

CANADA

PACIFIC OCEAN

MEXICO

GULF OF MEXICO

WASH. 1889
Seattle
Spokane
G.N.R.
GREAT NORTHERN
Coeur d'Alene
Columbia
N.P.
Portland
Coast Range
Cascade
OREGON SHORT LINE
Butte
Virginia City
N.P.
CHICAGO, MILWAUKEE & ST. PAUL
NORTHERN PACIFIC
MONT. 1889
N. DAK. 1889
G.N.
Bismarck
Fargo
N.P.
Duluth
L. Superior
MICH.
L. Huron
Silver City
Boise (U.P.)
IDAHO 1890
Snake R.
WYO. 1890
Black Hills
Deadwood
Lead
WOUNDED KNEE 1890
S. DAK. 1889
Minneapolis
St. Paul
Mississippi R.
WIS.
Milwaukee
Detroit
MICH.
CALIF.
NEV. 1864
Great
Salt Lake
Salt Lake City
UNION PACIFIC
Cheyenne
NEBR. 1867
Yankton
Ogallala
U.P.
Omaha
Platte R.
IOWA
Chicago
ILL.
IND.
Sierra Nevada
Basin
Great
Virginia City (COMSTOCK LODE)
Leadville
Denver
KANSAS PACIFIC
Abilene (U.P.)
St. Joseph
Kansas City
Sedalia
St. Louis
Louisville
KY.
TENN.
Sacramento
San Francisco
Southern
Las Vegas
Colorado R.
UTAH 1896
ARIZ. 1912
COLO. 1876
Cripple Creek
N. MEX. 1912
TOPEKA
Dodge City
SANTA FE
KANS. 1861
OKLA. 1907
INDIAN TERRITORY UNTIL 1907
MO.
Ohio R.
Memphis
ALA.
Los Angeles
PACIFIC
ATLANTIC & PACIFIC
Santa Fe
Albuquerque
ATCHISON
ARK.
LA.
MISS.
Mobile
Yuma
Gila R.
Tucson
Silver City
Deming
El Paso
Red R.
TEXAS & PACIFIC
TEXAS
Dallas
Fort Worth
PACIFIC
New Orleans
Tombstone
SOUTHERN
San Antonio
Houston
Rio Grande
ROCKY MOUNTAINS

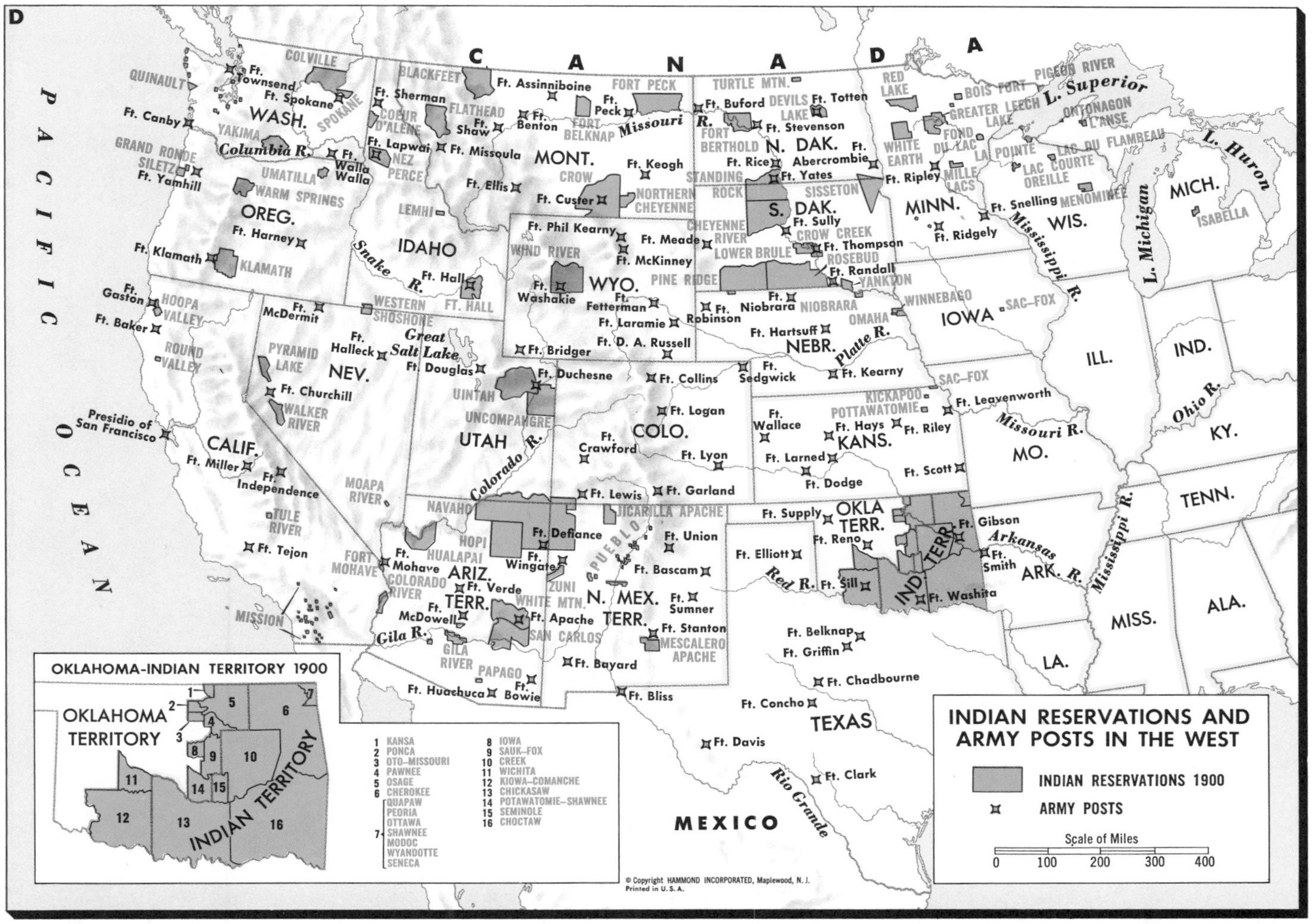

D

**INDIAN RESERVATIONS AND
ARMY POSTS IN THE WEST**

INDIAN RESERVATIONS 1900

ARMY POSTS

Scale of Miles
0   100   200   300   400

© Copyright HAMMOND INCORPORATED, Maplewood, N.J.
Printed in U.S.A.

CANADA

PACIFIC OCEAN

MEXICO

OKLAHOMA-INDIAN TERRITORY 1900

OKLAHOMA
TERRITORY

INDIAN TERRITORY

1 KANSA
2 PONCA
3 OTO-MISSOURI
4 PAWNEE
5 OSAGE
6 CHEROKEE
7 QUAPAW
PEORIA
OTTAWA
SHAWNEE
MODOC
WYANDOTTE
SENECA
8 IOWA
9 SAUK-FOX
10 CREEK
11 WICHITA
12 KIOWA-COMANCHE
13 CHICKASAW
14 POTAWATOMIE-SHAWNEE
15 SEMINOLE
16 CHOCTAW

QUINAULT
COLVILLE
Ft. Townsend
Ft. Spokane
BLACKFEET
FORT PECK
TURTLE MTN.
RED LAKE
BOIS FORT
PIGEON RIVER
L. Superior
Ft. Canby
YAKIMA
WASH.
SPOKANE
COEUR D'ALENE
Ft. Sherman
Ft. Shaw
Ft. Assinniboine
Ft. Peck
Ft. Buford
DEVILS LAKE
Ft. Totten
GREATER LEECH LAKE
ONTONAGON
L'ANSE
FOND DU LAC
L. Huron
GRAND RONDE
SILETZ
Columbia R.
FLATHEAD
Ft. Benton
FORT BELKNAP
Missouri R.
FORT BERTHOLD
N. DAK.
Ft. Stevenson
Ft. Rice
WHITE EARTH
Ft. Ripley
LA POINTE
LAC COURTE OREILLE
LAC DU FLAMBEAU
Ft. Lapwai
NEZ PERCE
Ft. Missoula
MONT.
Ft. Keogh
STANDING ROCK
Ft. Yates
MILLE LACS
Ft. Snelling
MENOMINEE
MICH.
WARM SPRINGS
UMATILLA
YAMHILL
OREG.
Ft. Ellis
CROW
Ft. Custer
NORTHERN CHEYENNE
CHEYENNE RIVER
S. DAK.
Ft. Sully
MINN.
Ft. Ridgely
WIS.
ISABELLA
Ft. Harney
LEMHI
Ft. Phil Kearny
Ft. Meade
CROW CREEK
Ft. Thompson
Ft. Klamath
KLAMATH
IDAHO
Snake R.
WIND RIVER
Ft. McKinney
LOWER BRULE
ROSEBUD
Ft. Randall
YANKTON
Ft. Hall
Ft. Washakie
WYO.
PINE RIDGE
Ft. Niobrara
NIOBRARA
WINNEBAGO
IOWA
SAC-FOX
HOOPA VALLEY
Ft. Gaston
Ft. Baker
WESTERN SHOSHONE
FT. HALL
Ft. Fetterman
Ft. Laramie
Ft. Robinson
OMAHA
Ft. Hartsuff
NEBR.
Platte R.
SAC-FOX
ILL.
IND.
Ft. McDermit
Great Salt Lake
Ft. Bridger
Ft. D. A. Russell
Ft. Miller
ROUND VALLEY
Ft. Halleck
Ft. Douglas
Ft. Collins
Ft. Sedgwick
Ft. Kearny
Ft. Leavenworth
Ohio R.
KY.
PYRAMID LAKE
NEV.
Ft. Churchill
UINTAH
Ft. Duchesne
Ft. Logan
Ft. Wallace
KICKAPOO
POTTAWATOMIE
Ft. Hays
Ft. Riley
MO.
Presidio of San Francisco
WALKER RIVER
UNCOMPAHGRE
UTAH
Colorado R.
COLO.
Ft. Crawford
KANS.
Ft. Larned
MISSOURI R.
TENN.
CALIF.
Ft. Independence
MOAPA RIVER
Ft. Lyon
Ft. Garland
Ft. Dodge
Ft. Scott
ARK. R.
Ft. Tejon
TULE RIVER
NAVAHO
HOPI
Ft. Lewis
JICARILLA APACHE
Ft. Supply
OKLA TERR.
Ft. Reno
Ft. Gibson
IND. TERR.
Arkansas R.
Ft. Mohave
HUALAPAI
Wingate
Ft. Defiance
Ft. Union
Ft. Elliott
Ft. Smith
ARK.
FORT MOHAVE
COLORADO RIVER
ARIZ. TERR.
ZUNI
PUEBLO
N. MEX. TERR.
Ft. Bascam
Red R.
Ft. Sill
Ft. Washita
MISS.
MISSION
McDowell
WHITE MTN.
SAN CARLOS
Ft. Apache
Ft. Sumner
ALA.
Gila R.
PAPAGO
Ft. Bayard
Ft. Stanton
MESCALERO APACHE
LA.
GILA RIVER
Ft. Huachuca
Ft. Bowie
Ft. Bliss
Ft. Belknap
Ft. Griffin
Ft. Chadbourne
Ft. Concho
TEXAS
Ft. Davis
Ft. Clark
Rio Grande

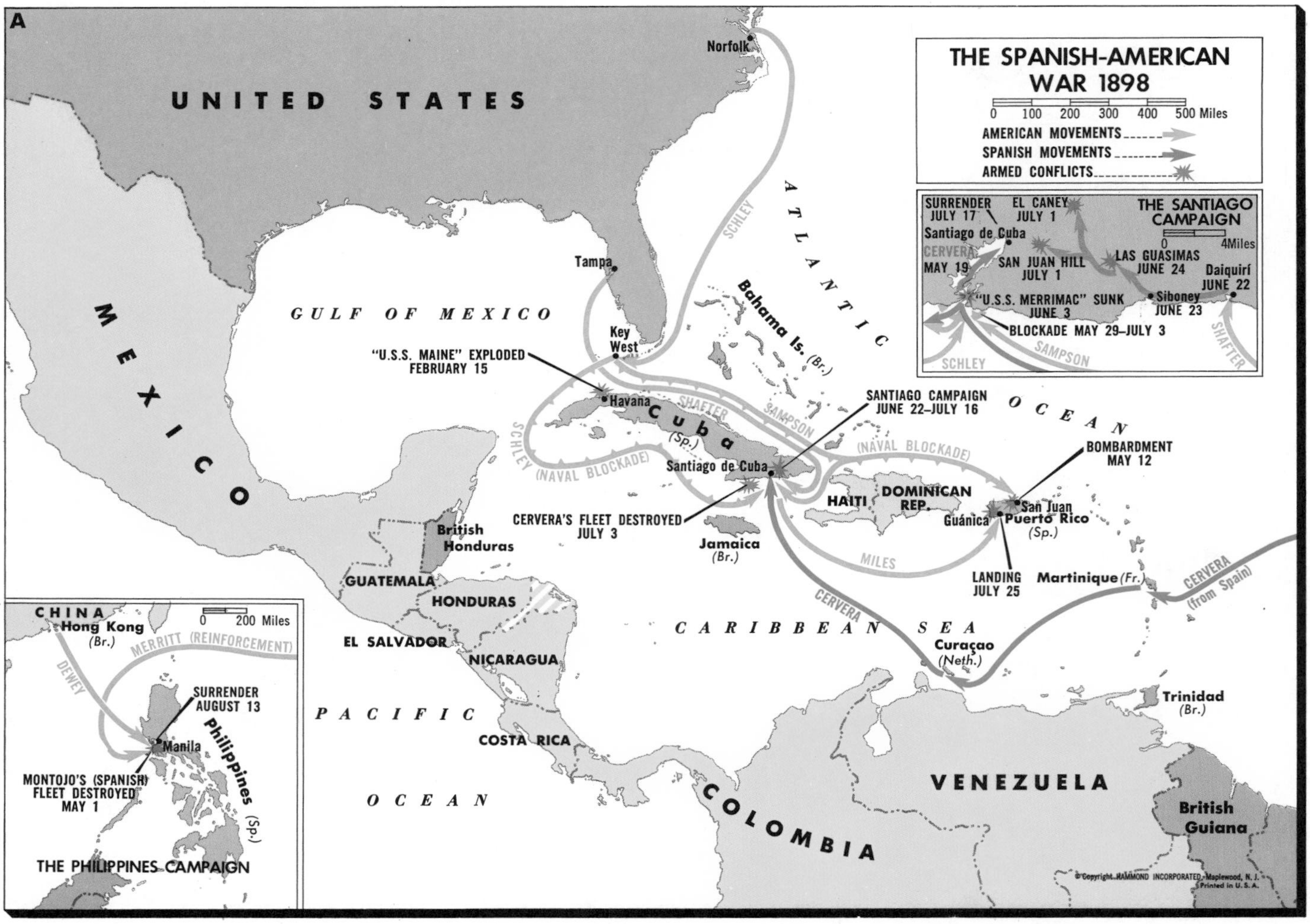

A

UNITED STATES

Norfolk

THE SPANISH-AMERICAN
WAR 1898

0 100 200 300 400 500 Miles

AMERICAN MOVEMENTS
SPANISH MOVEMENTS
ARMED CONFLICTS

ATLANTIC

Tampa

GULF OF MEXICO

Bahama Is. (Br.)

Key West

SURRENDER
JULY 17   EL CANEY
JULY 1   THE SANTIAGO
CAMPAIGN
Santiago de Cuba
CERVERA
MAY 19   SAN JUAN HILL
JULY 1   LAS GUASIMAS
JUNE 24   0   4 Miles
Daiquirí
JUNE 22
"U.S.S. MERRIMAC" SUNK
JUNE 3   Siboney
JUNE 23
BLOCKADE MAY 29–JULY 3

"U.S.S. MAINE" EXPLODED
FEBRUARY 15

Havana

SHAFTER

SAMPSON

SCHLEY

OCEAN

SANTIAGO CAMPAIGN
JUNE 22–JULY 16

SCHLEY (NAVAL BLOCKADE)

SAMPSON

Cuba (Sp.)

(NAVAL BLOCKADE)

BOMBARDMENT
MAY 12

Santiago de Cuba

CERVERA'S FLEET DESTROYED
JULY 3

HAITI   DOMINICAN
REP.   Guánica   San Juan
Puerto Rico
(Sp.)

Jamaica
(Br.)

MILES

LANDING
JULY 25   Martinique (Fr.)

CERVERA
(from Spain)

British
Honduras

GUATEMALA

HONDURAS

EL SALVADOR

NICARAGUA

CARIBBEAN   SEA

Curaçao
(Neth.)

Trinidad
(Br.)

CHINA
Hong Kong
(Br.)   0   200 Miles

MERRITT (REINFORCEMENT)

DEWEY

SURRENDER
AUGUST 13

Manila

Philippines (Sp.)

MONTOJO'S (SPANISH)
FLEET DESTROYED
MAY 1

PACIFIC

COSTA RICA

OCEAN

VENEZUELA

COLOMBIA

British
Guiana

THE PHILIPPINES CAMPAIGN

© Copyright HAMMOND INCORPORATED—Maplewood, N.J.
Printed in U.S.A.

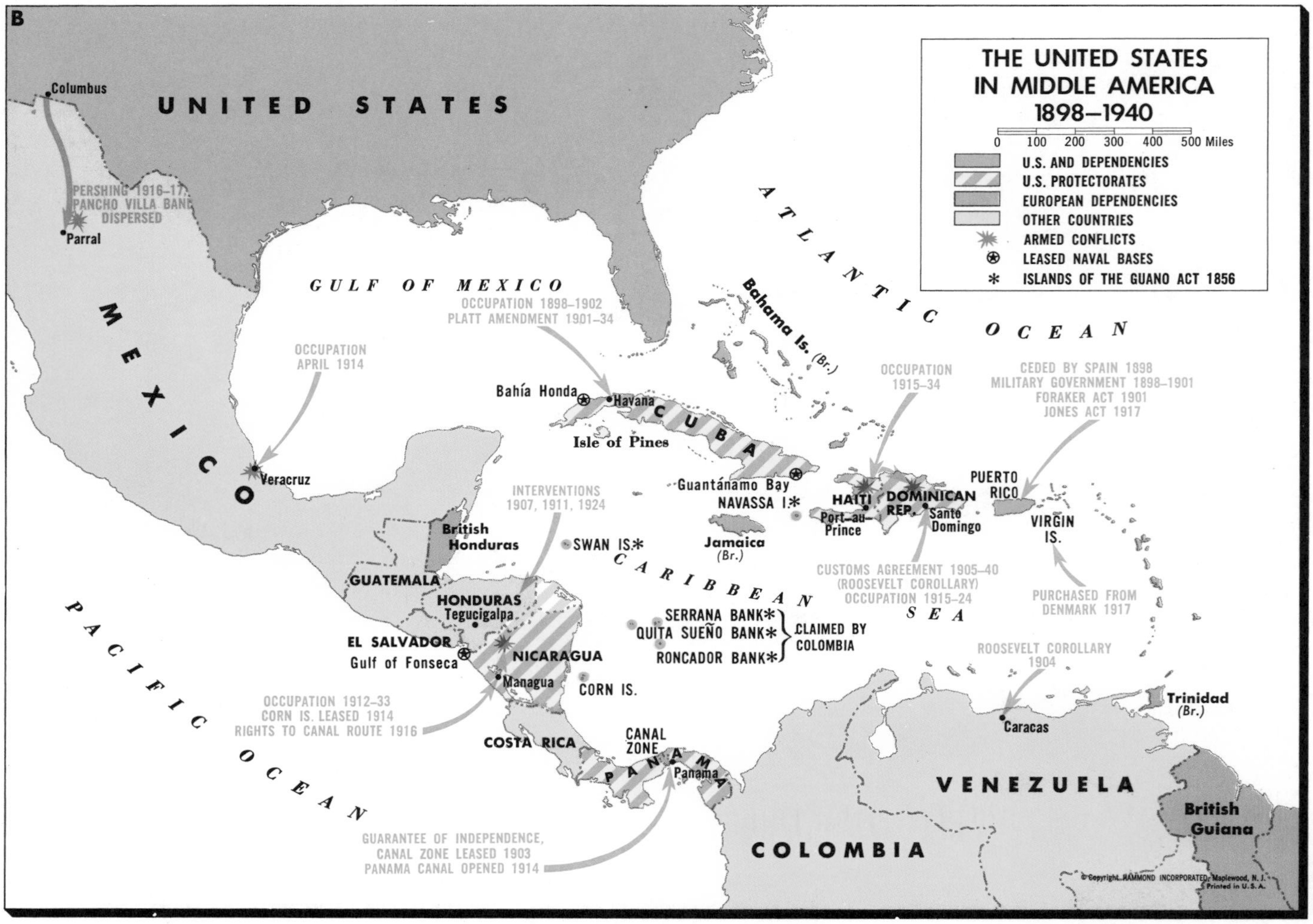

B

Columbus

UNITED   STATES

THE UNITED STATES
IN MIDDLE AMERICA
1898–1940

0 100 200 300 400 500 Miles

U.S. AND DEPENDENCIES
U.S. PROTECTORATES
EUROPEAN DEPENDENCIES
OTHER COUNTRIES
ARMED CONFLICTS
LEASED NAVAL BASES
ISLANDS OF THE GUANO ACT 1856

PERSHING 1916–17,
PANCHO VILLA BAND
DISPERSED

Parral

ATLANTIC

GULF OF MEXICO

OCCUPATION 1898–1902
PLATT AMENDMENT 1901–34

Bahama Is. (Br.)

OCCUPATION
APRIL 1914

Bahía Honda   Havana

OCCUPATION
1915–34

CEDED BY SPAIN 1898
MILITARY GOVERNMENT 1898–1901
FORAKER ACT 1901
JONES ACT 1917

Veracruz

Isle of Pines

CUBA

PUERTO
RICO

Guantánamo Bay
NAVASSA I.*   HAITI   DOMINICAN
REP.   Santo
Domingo   VIRGIN
IS.

Port-au-
Prince

MEXICO

INTERVENTIONS
1907, 1911, 1924

SWAN IS.*

Jamaica
(Br.)

PURCHASED FROM
DENMARK 1917

British
Honduras

GUATEMALA

HONDURAS
Tegucigalpa

EL SALVADOR
Gulf of Fonseca

NICARAGUA
Managua

SERRANA BANK*
QUITA SUEÑO BANK*
RONCADOR BANK*

CUSTOMS AGREEMENT 1905–40
(ROOSEVELT COROLLARY)
OCCUPATION 1915–24

CARIBBEAN   SEA

CLAIMED BY
COLOMBIA

ROOSEVELT COROLLARY
1904

PACIFIC

CORN IS.

OCCUPATION 1912–33
CORN IS. LEASED 1914
RIGHTS TO CANAL ROUTE 1916

COSTA RICA

CANAL
ZONE
PANAMA   Panama

Trinidad
(Br.)

Caracas

OCEAN

VENEZUELA

British
Guiana

GUARANTEE OF INDEPENDENCE,
CANAL ZONE LEASED 1903
PANAMA CANAL OPENED 1914

COLOMBIA

© Copyright HAMMOND INCORPORATED—Maplewood, N.J.
Printed in U.S.A.

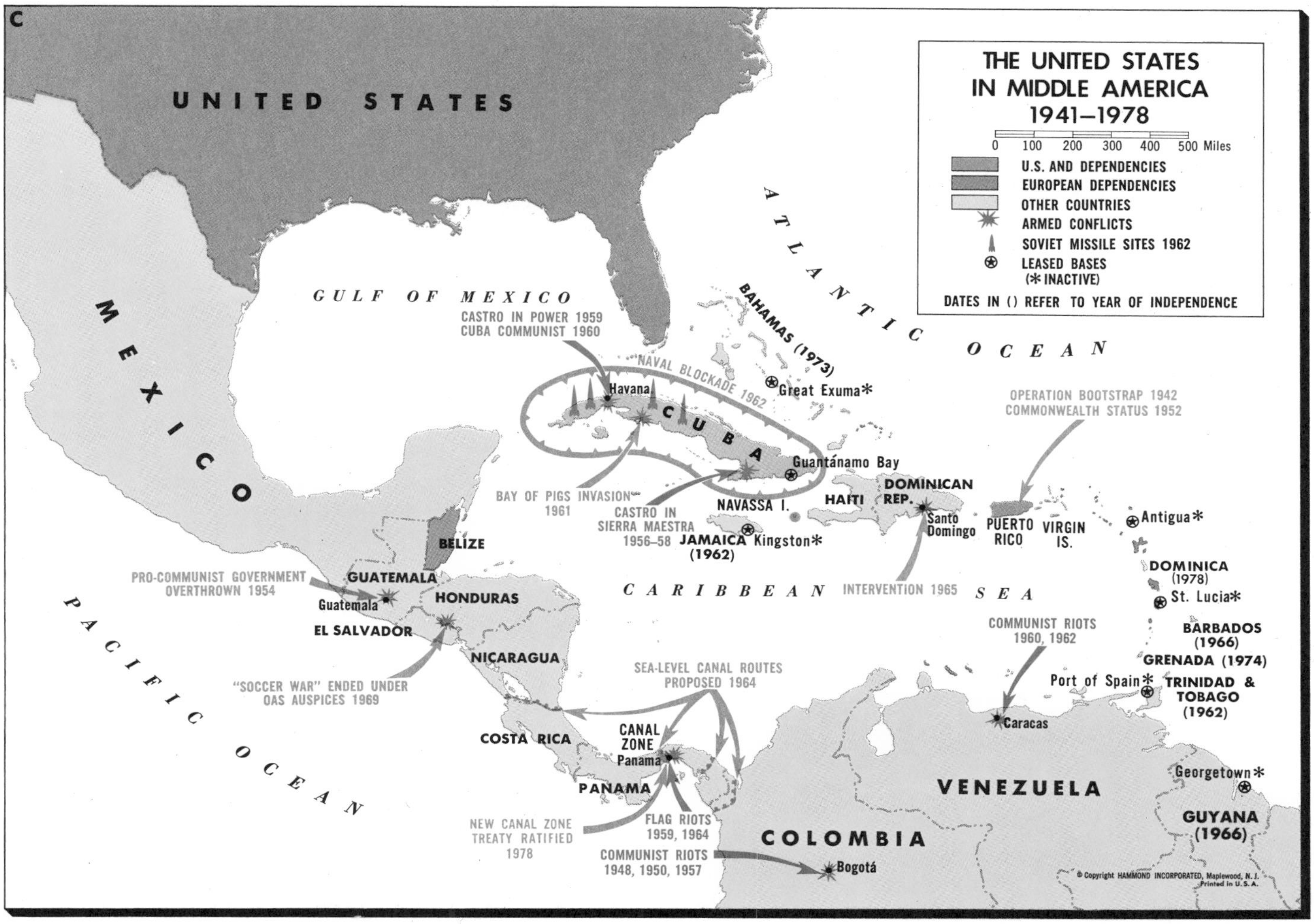

THE UNITED STATES IN MIDDLE AMERICA 1941–1978

0 100 200 300 400 500 Miles

- U.S. AND DEPENDENCIES
- EUROPEAN DEPENDENCIES
- OTHER COUNTRIES
- ✳ ARMED CONFLICTS
- ⚓ SOVIET MISSILE SITES 1962
- ⊛ LEASED BASES (✳ INACTIVE)

DATES IN ( ) REFER TO YEAR OF INDEPENDENCE

UNITED STATES

GULF OF MEXICO

MEXICO

PACIFIC OCEAN

ATLANTIC OCEAN

BAHAMAS (1973)

CASTRO IN POWER 1959
CUBA COMMUNIST 1960

NAVAL BLOCKADE 1962

Havana

CUBA

⊛ Great Exuma ✳

OPERATION BOOTSTRAP 1942
COMMONWEALTH STATUS 1952

Guantánamo Bay

BAY OF PIGS INVASION 1961

CASTRO IN SIERRA MAESTRA 1956–58

NAVASSA I.

HAITI

JAMAICA Kingston ✳
(1962)

DOMINICAN REP.

Santo Domingo

PUERTO RICO

VIRGIN IS.

⊛ Antigua ✳

DOMINICA (1978)

⊛ St. Lucia ✳

CARIBBEAN SEA

INTERVENTION 1965

COMMUNIST RIOTS 1960, 1962

BARBADOS (1966)

GRENADA (1974)

Port of Spain ✳ TRINIDAD & TOBAGO (1962)

BELIZE

PRO-COMMUNIST GOVERNMENT OVERTHROWN 1954

GUATEMALA

Guatemala

HONDURAS

EL SALVADOR

NICARAGUA

"SOCCER WAR" ENDED UNDER OAS AUSPICES 1969

COSTA RICA

SEA-LEVEL CANAL ROUTES PROPOSED 1964

CANAL ZONE

Panama

PANAMA

NEW CANAL ZONE TREATY RATIFIED 1978

FLAG RIOTS 1959, 1964

COMMUNIST RIOTS 1948, 1950, 1957

COLOMBIA

✳ Bogotá

VENEZUELA

✳ Caracas

Georgetown ✳

GUYANA (1966)

© Copyright HAMMOND INCORPORATED, Maplewood, N. J.
Printed in U.S.A.

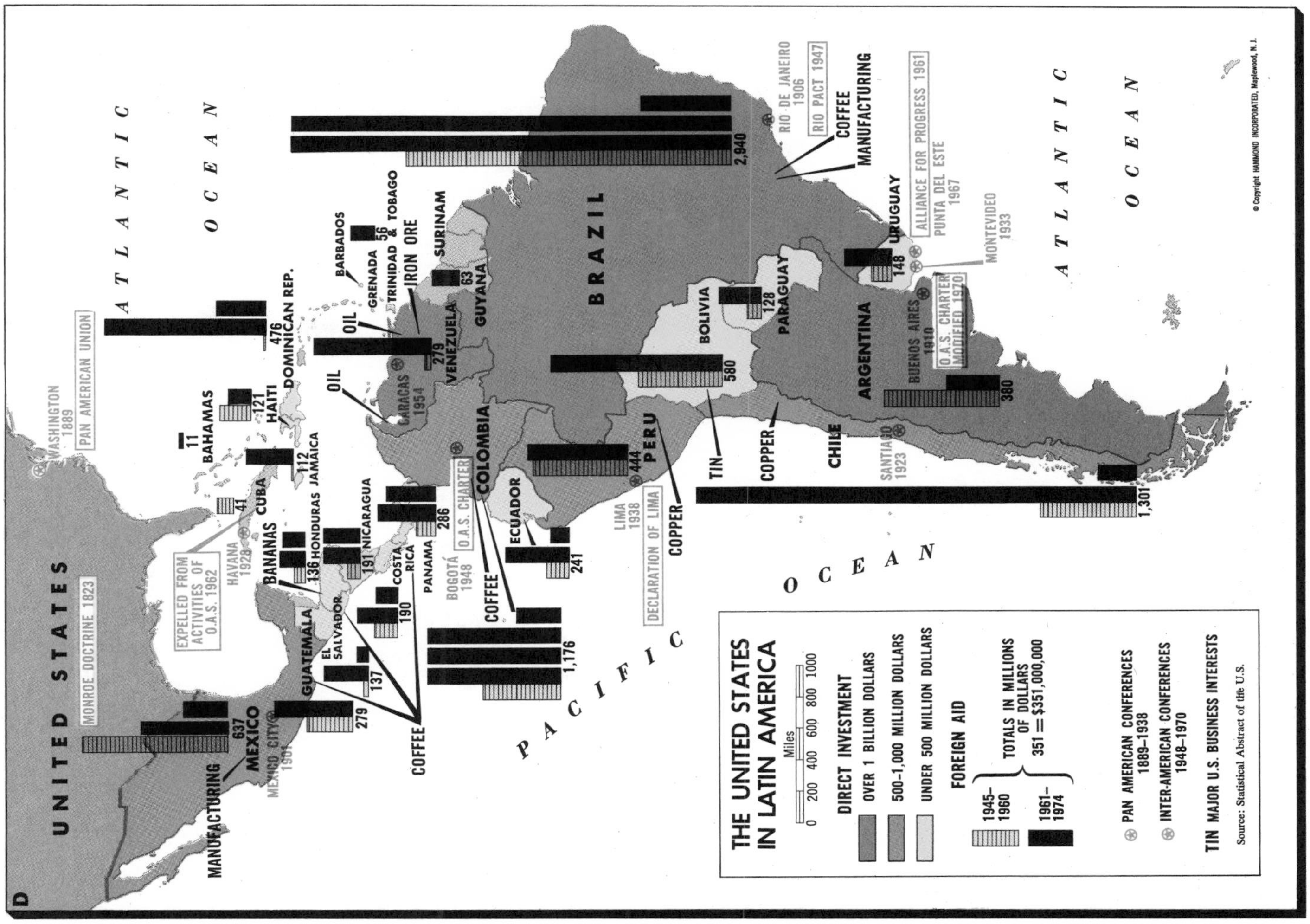

THE UNITED STATES IN LATIN AMERICA

Miles
0 200 400 600 800 1000

DIRECT INVESTMENT
- OVER 1 BILLION DOLLARS
- 500–1,000 MILLION DOLLARS
- UNDER 500 MILLION DOLLARS

FOREIGN AID
- 1945–1960
- 1961–1974

TOTALS IN MILLIONS OF DOLLARS
351 = $351,000,000

⊛ PAN AMERICAN CONFERENCES 1889–1938
⊛ INTER-AMERICAN CONFERENCES 1948–1970

TIN MAJOR U.S. BUSINESS INTERESTS

Source: Statistical Abstract of the U.S.

UNITED STATES

MANUFACTURING

MEXICO CITY 1901

MONROE DOCTRINE 1823

PAN AMERICAN UNION

WASHINGTON 1889

ATLANTIC OCEAN

EXPELLED FROM ACTIVITIES OF O.A.S. 1962

HAVANA 1928

BANANAS

MEXICO 637

GUATEMALA 279

EL SALVADOR 137

COFFEE

BAHAMAS 11

HAITI 121

DOMINICAN REP. 476

CUBA 41

JAMAICA 112

HONDURAS 136

NICARAGUA 191

COSTA RICA 190

PANAMA 1,176

BOGOTÁ 1948

O.A.S. CHARTER

COLOMBIA 286

COFFEE

ECUADOR 241

OIL

VENEZUELA 279

Caracas 1954

IRON ORE

GUYANA 63

SURINAM

BARBADOS

GRENADA 56

TRINIDAD & TOBAGO

BRAZIL 2,940

COFFEE
MANUFACTURING

RIO DE JANEIRO 1906

RIO PACT 1947

ALLIANCE FOR PROGRESS 1961

PUNTA DEL ESTE 1967

URUGUAY 148

MONTEVIDEO 1933

O.A.S. CHARTER MODIFIED 1970

BUENOS AIRES 1910

ARGENTINA 380

PARAGUAY 128

BOLIVIA 580

TIN

PERU 444

LIMA 1938

DECLARATION OF LIMA

COPPER

CHILE 1,301

COPPER

SANTIAGO 1923

ATLANTIC OCEAN

PACIFIC OCEAN

© Copyright HAMMOND INCORPORATED, Maplewood, N.J.

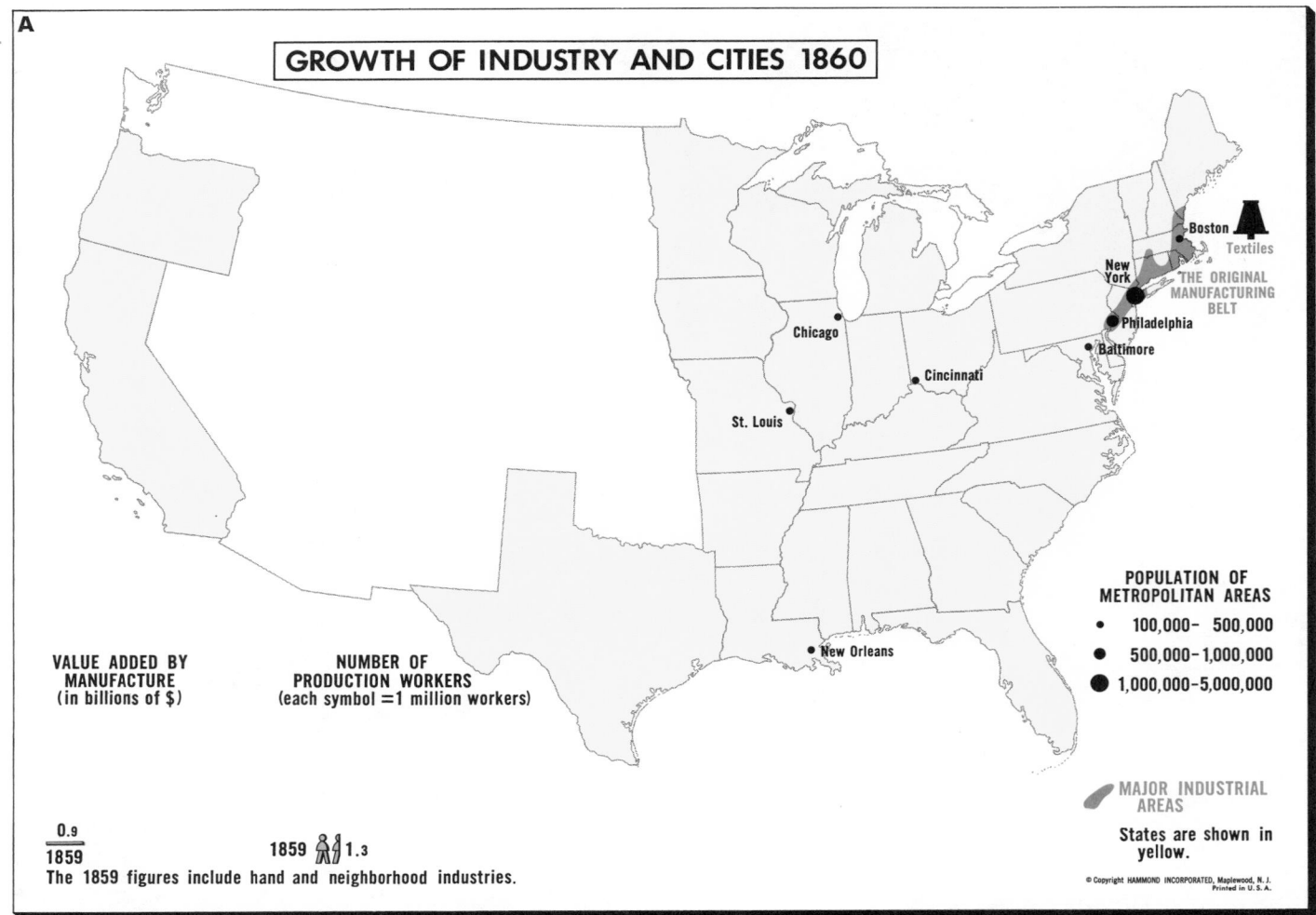

A

GROWTH OF INDUSTRY AND CITIES 1860

Boston
Textiles
New York
THE ORIGINAL MANUFACTURING BELT
Philadelphia
Baltimore
Chicago
Cincinnati
St. Louis
New Orleans

POPULATION OF METROPOLITAN AREAS

- • 100,000- 500,000
- • 500,000-1,000,000
- ● 1,000,000-5,000,000

MAJOR INDUSTRIAL AREAS

States are shown in yellow.

VALUE ADDED BY MANUFACTURE (in billions of $)

NUMBER OF PRODUCTION WORKERS (each symbol =1 million workers)

0.9
1859

1859 1.3

The 1859 figures include hand and neighborhood industries.

© Copyright HAMMOND INCORPORATED, Maplewood, N.J.
Printed in U.S.A.

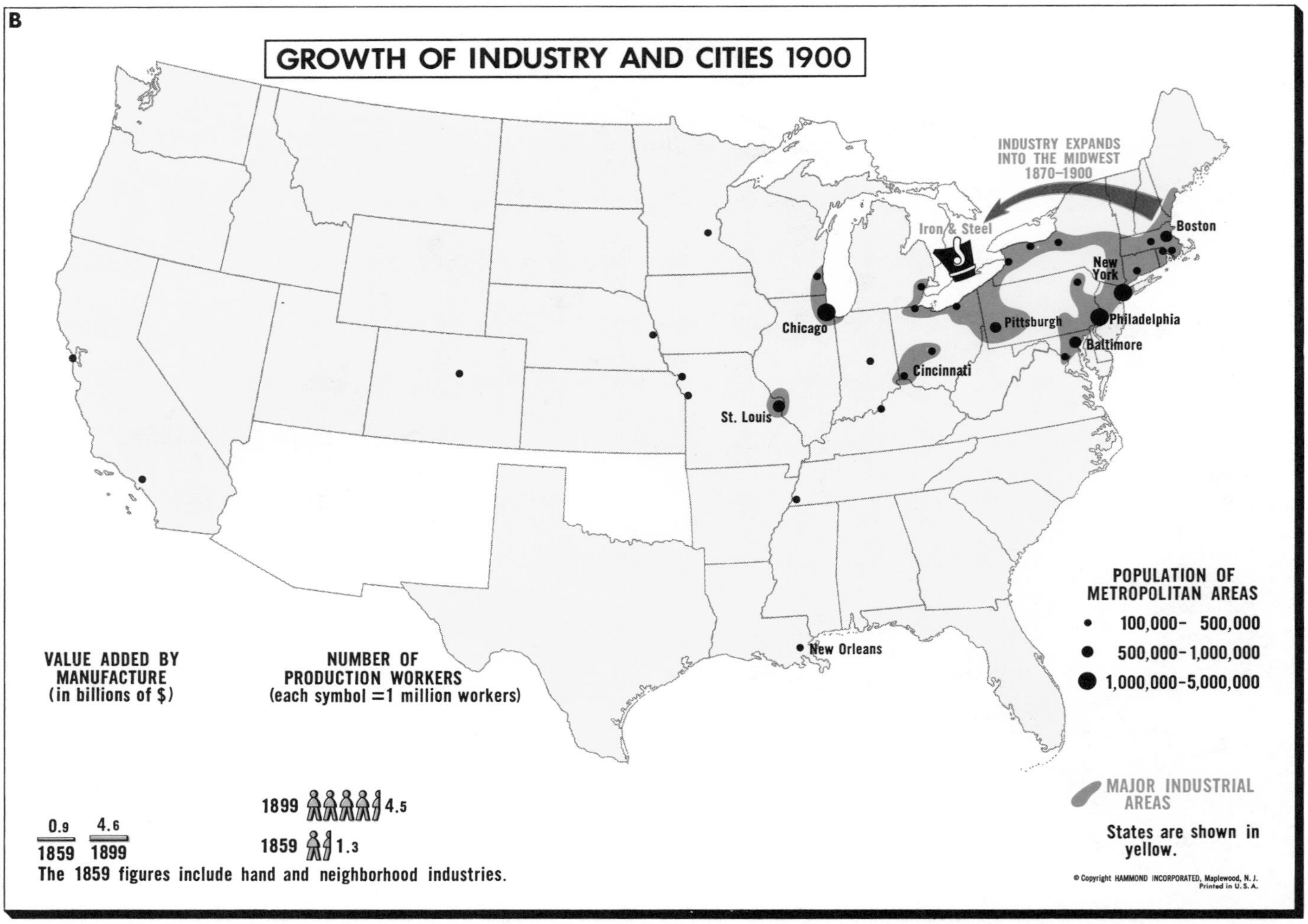

B

GROWTH OF INDUSTRY AND CITIES 1900

INDUSTRY EXPANDS INTO THE MIDWEST 1870-1900
Iron & Steel
Boston
New York
Chicago
Pittsburgh
Philadelphia
Baltimore
Cincinnati
St. Louis
New Orleans

POPULATION OF METROPOLITAN AREAS

- • 100,000- 500,000
- • 500,000-1,000,000
- ● 1,000,000-5,000,000

MAJOR INDUSTRIAL AREAS

States are shown in yellow.

VALUE ADDED BY MANUFACTURE (in billions of $)

NUMBER OF PRODUCTION WORKERS (each symbol =1 million workers)

1899 4.5

0.9   4.6
1859   1899

1859 1.3

The 1859 figures include hand and neighborhood industries.

© Copyright HAMMOND INCORPORATED, Maplewood, N.J.
Printed in U.S.A.

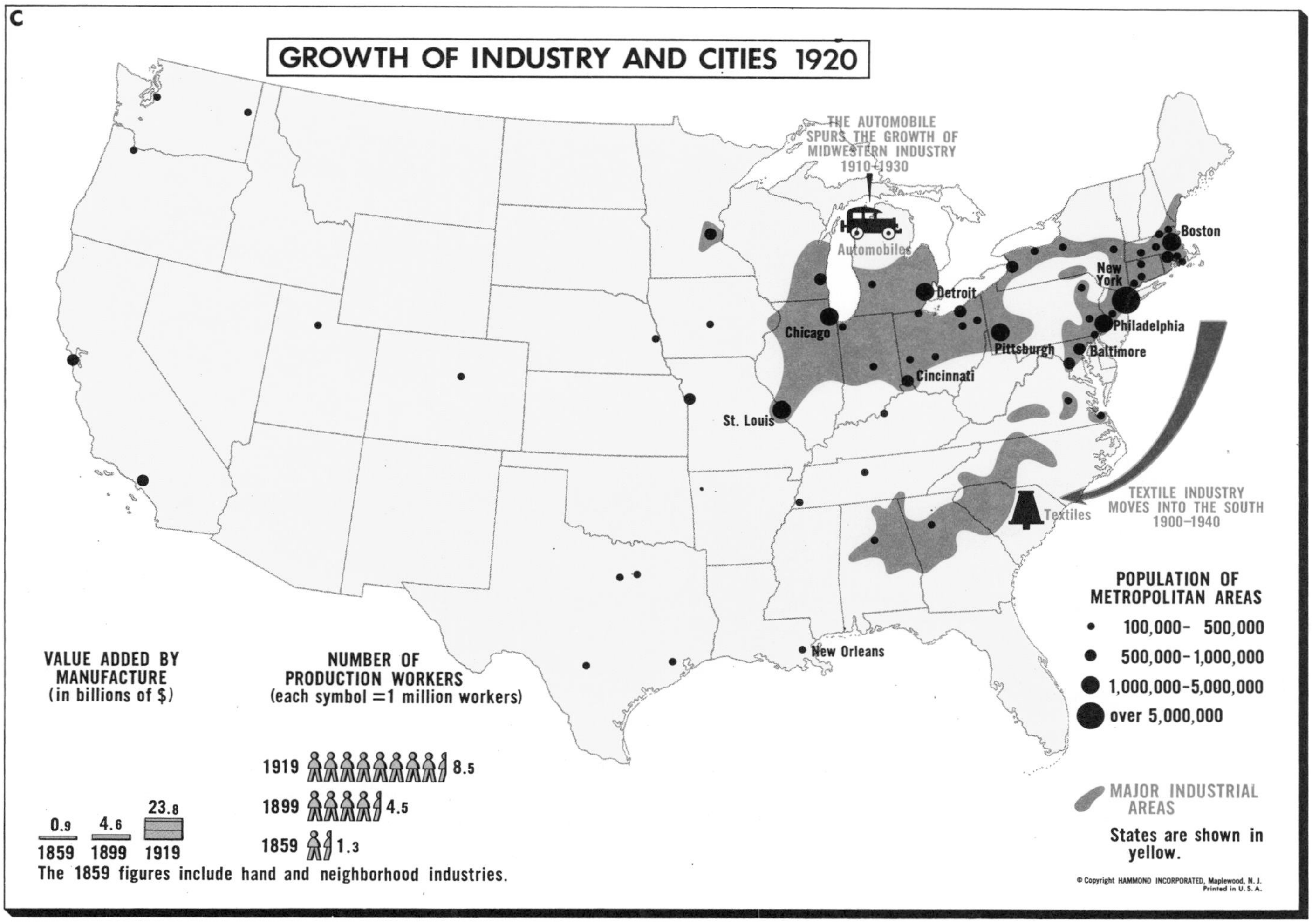

C

GROWTH OF INDUSTRY AND CITIES 1920

THE AUTOMOBILE SPURS THE GROWTH OF MIDWESTERN INDUSTRY 1910–1930

Automobiles

Boston
New York
Detroit
Chicago
Philadelphia
Pittsburgh
Baltimore
Cincinnati
St. Louis

Textiles

TEXTILE INDUSTRY MOVES INTO THE SOUTH 1900–1940

New Orleans

POPULATION OF METROPOLITAN AREAS

- 100,000– 500,000
- 500,000–1,000,000
- 1,000,000–5,000,000
- over 5,000,000

MAJOR INDUSTRIAL AREAS

States are shown in yellow.

© Copyright HAMMOND INCORPORATED, Maplewood, N.J.
Printed in U.S.A.

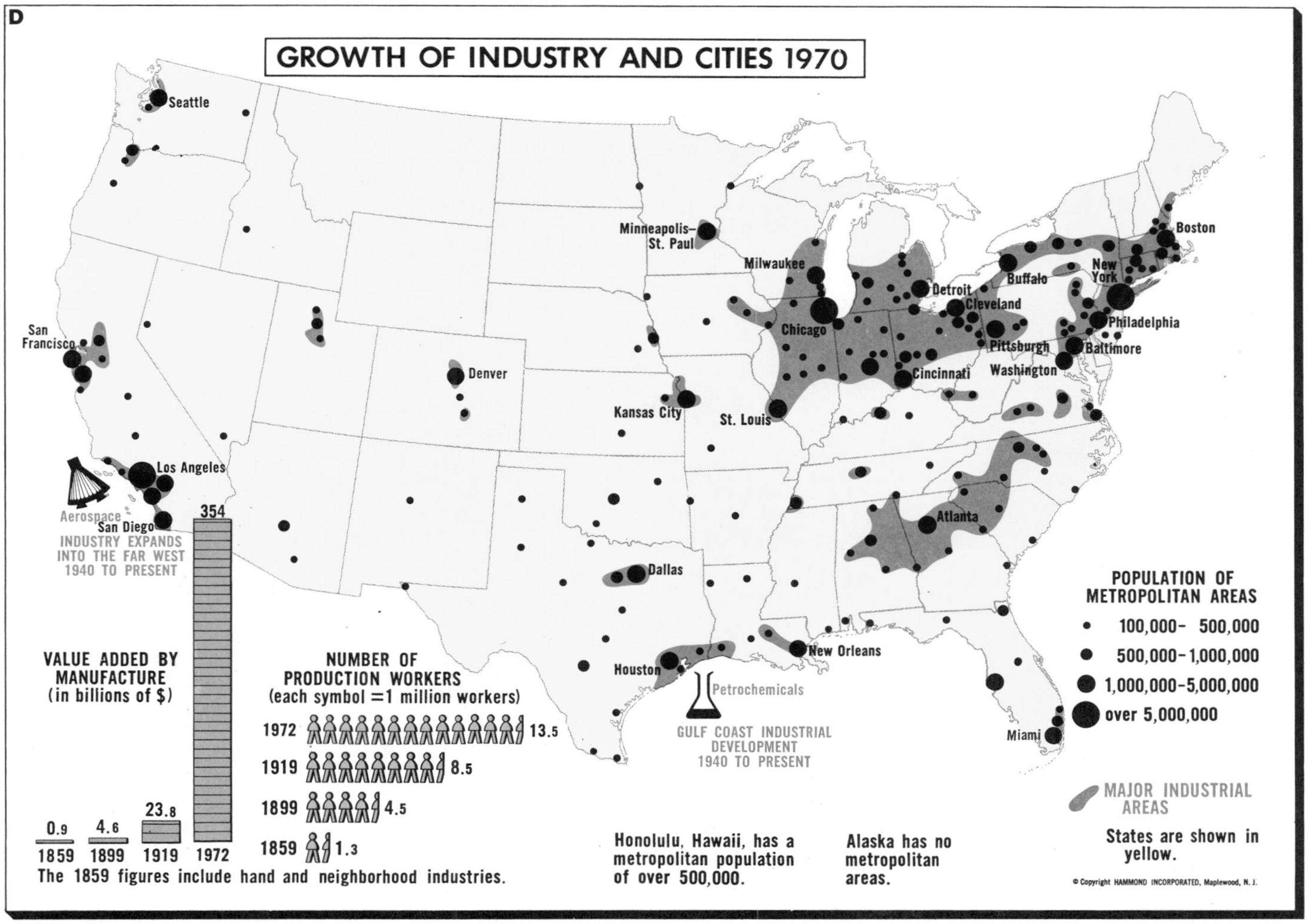

VALUE ADDED BY MANUFACTURE
(in billions of $)

NUMBER OF PRODUCTION WORKERS
(each symbol = 1 million workers)

1919 8.5
1899 4.5
1859 1.3

0.9   4.6   23.8
1859 1899 1919

The 1859 figures include hand and neighborhood industries.

D

GROWTH OF INDUSTRY AND CITIES 1970

Seattle

Minneapolis–St. Paul
Milwaukee
Buffalo
Boston
Detroit
New York
Cleveland
San Francisco
Chicago
Philadelphia
Pittsburgh
Baltimore
Denver
Cincinnati
Washington
Kansas City
St. Louis
Los Angeles

Aerospace
San Diego
INDUSTRY EXPANDS INTO THE FAR WEST 1940 TO PRESENT

Atlanta

Dallas

Houston
New Orleans
Petrochemicals
GULF COAST INDUSTRIAL DEVELOPMENT 1940 TO PRESENT

Miami

POPULATION OF METROPOLITAN AREAS

- 100,000– 500,000
- 500,000–1,000,000
- 1,000,000–5,000,000
- over 5,000,000

MAJOR INDUSTRIAL AREAS

States are shown in yellow.

© Copyright HAMMOND INCORPORATED, Maplewood, N.J.

VALUE ADDED BY MANUFACTURE
(in billions of $)

354

NUMBER OF PRODUCTION WORKERS
(each symbol = 1 million workers)

1972 13.5
1919 8.5
1899 4.5
1859 1.3

0.9   4.6   23.8
1859 1899 1919 1972

The 1859 figures include hand and neighborhood industries.

Honolulu, Hawaii, has a metropolitan population of over 500,000.

Alaska has no metropolitan areas.

A

TARIFF RATES ON DUTIABLE IMPORTS 1821–1974
RATIO OF DUTIES TO VALUE OF DUTIABLE IMPORTS

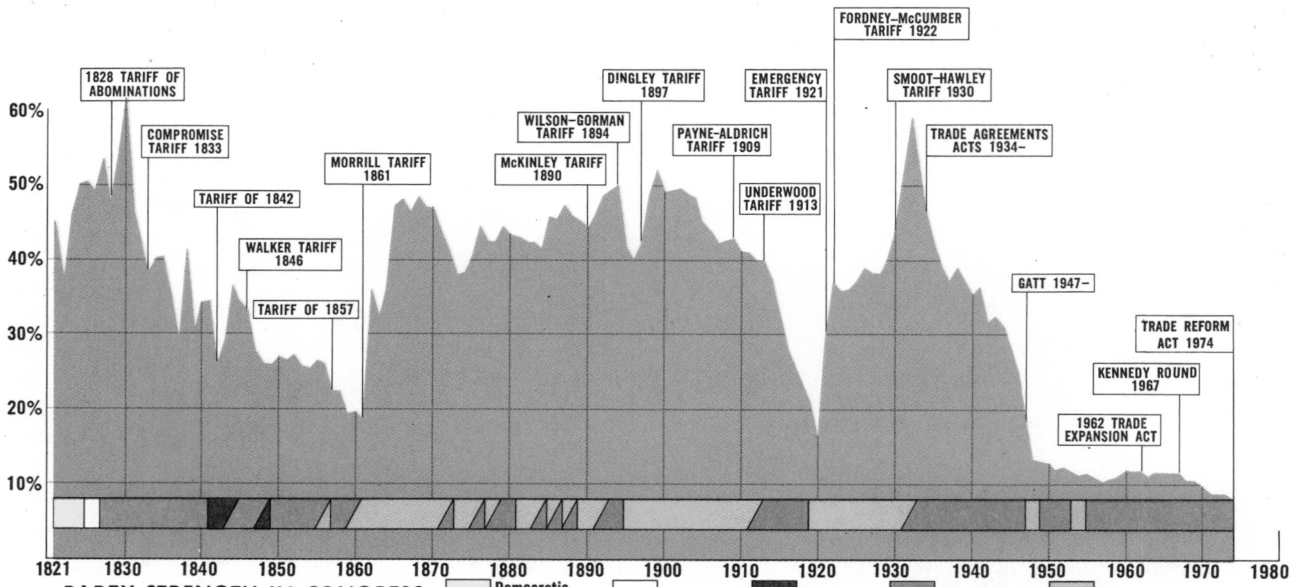

FORDNEY–McCUMBER
TARIFF 1922

1828 TARIFF OF
ABOMINATIONS

DINGLEY TARIFF
1897

EMERGENCY
TARIFF 1921

SMOOT–HAWLEY
TARIFF 1930

COMPROMISE
TARIFF 1833

WILSON–GORMAN
TARIFF 1894

TRADE AGREEMENTS
ACTS 1934–

TARIFF OF 1842

MORRILL TARIFF
1861

McKINLEY TARIFF
1890

PAYNE–ALDRICH
TARIFF 1909

WALKER TARIFF
1846

UNDERWOOD
TARIFF 1913

GATT 1947–

TARIFF OF 1857

TRADE REFORM
ACT 1974

KENNEDY ROUND
1967

1962 TRADE
EXPANSION ACT

60%

50%

40%

30%

20%

10%

1821 1830 1840 1850 1860 1870 1880 1890 1900 1910 1920 1930 1940 1950 1960 1970 1980

PARTY STRENGTH IN CONGRESS   Democratic-Republican   No Party   Whig   Democratic   Republican

© Copyright HAMMOND INCORPORATED, Maplewood, N.J.

Source: *Historical Statistics of the United States*

B

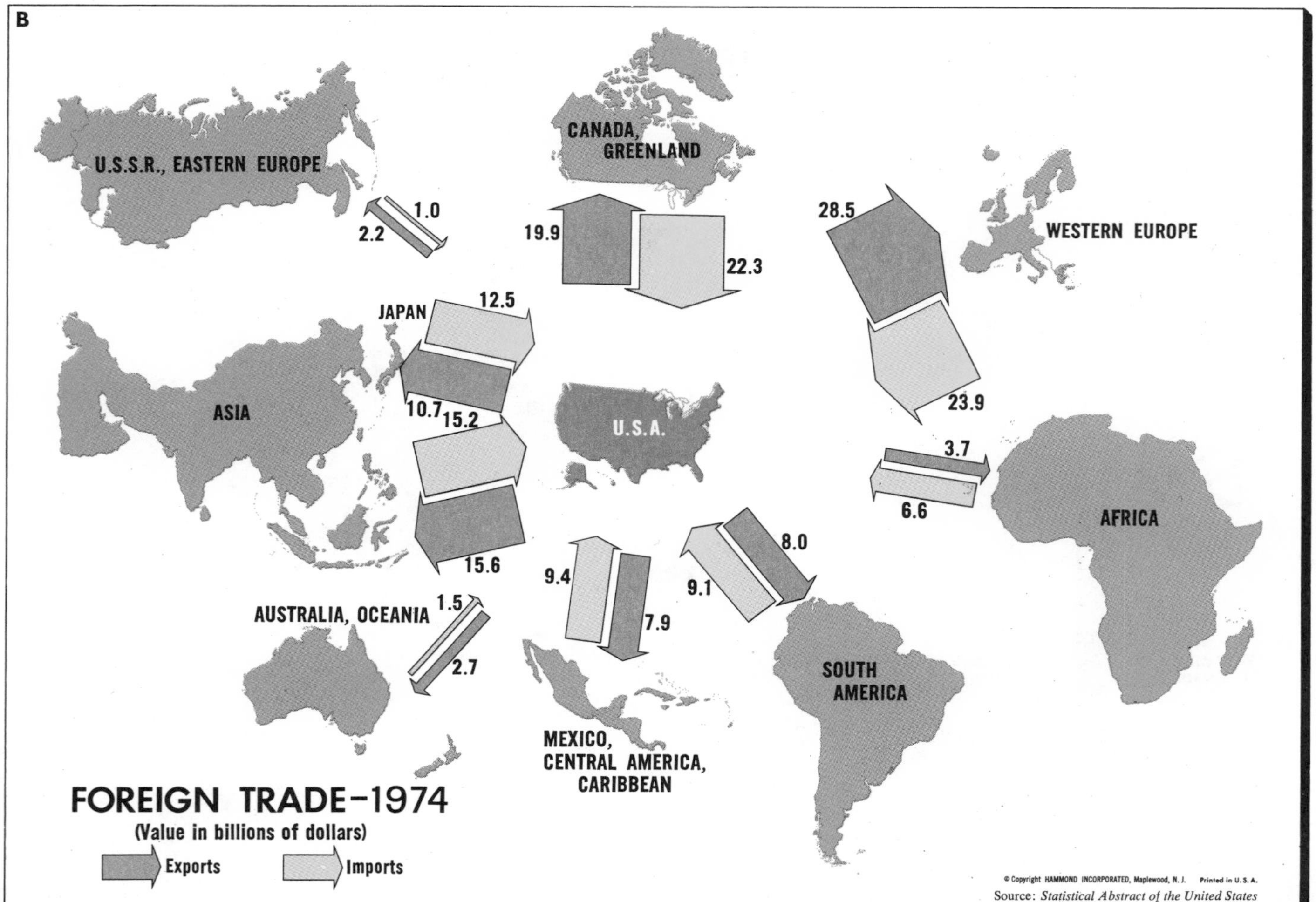

U.S.S.R., EASTERN EUROPE

CANADA,
GREENLAND

WESTERN EUROPE

1.0
2.2

19.9   22.3

28.5

JAPAN   12.5

ASIA

10.7 15.2

U.S.A.

23.9

3.7
6.6

AFRICA

15.6

8.0

9.4   9.1

AUSTRALIA, OCEANIA   1.5

7.9

SOUTH
AMERICA

2.7

MEXICO,
CENTRAL AMERICA,
CARIBBEAN

FOREIGN TRADE–1974
(Value in billions of dollars)

Exports   Imports

© Copyright HAMMOND INCORPORATED, Maplewood, N.J.   Printed in U.S.A.

Source: *Statistical Abstract of the United States*

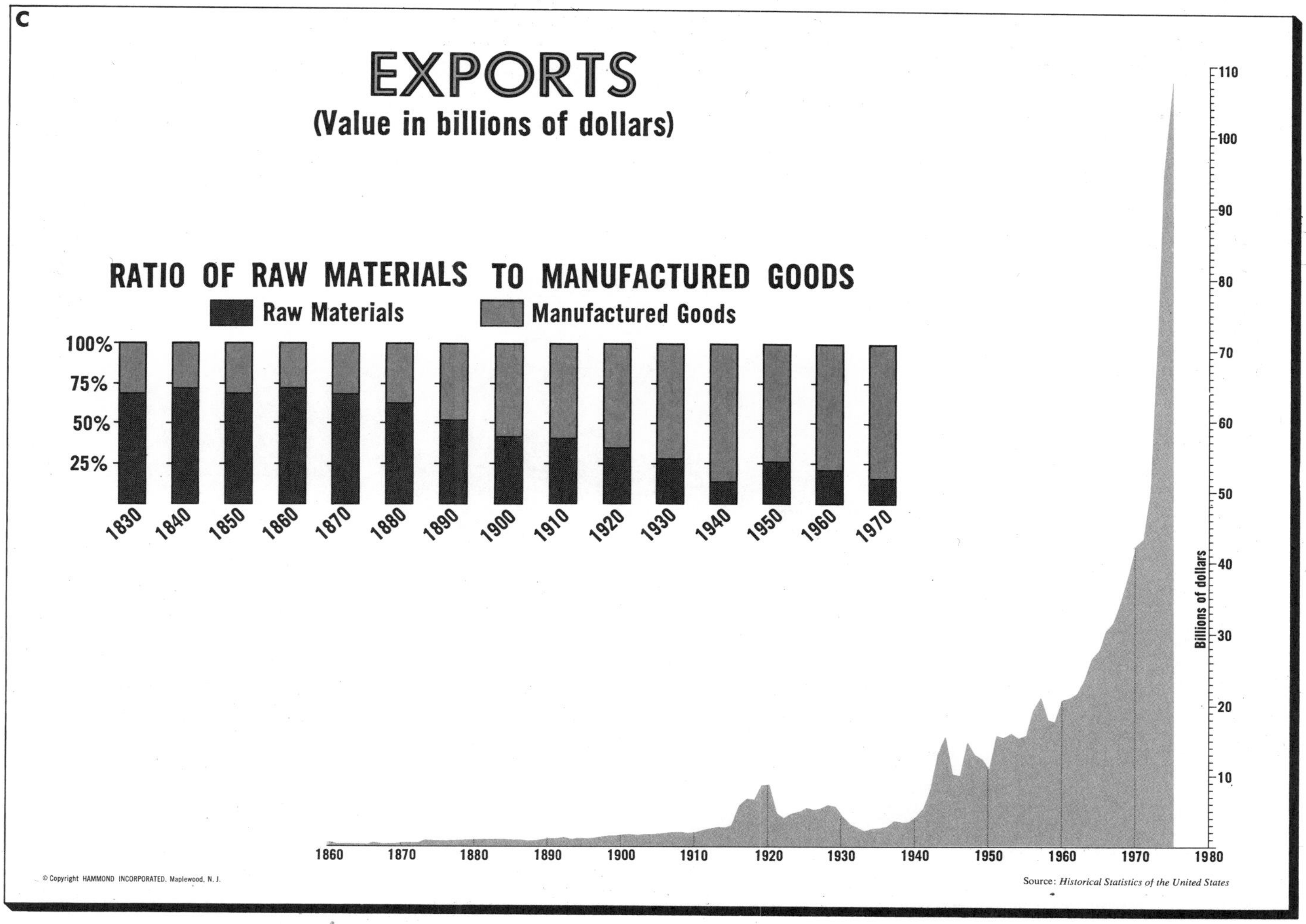

C

EXPORTS
(Value in billions of dollars)

RATIO OF RAW MATERIALS TO MANUFACTURED GOODS

■ Raw Materials   ▨ Manufactured Goods

100%
75%
50%
25%

1830 1840 1850 1860 1870 1880 1890 1900 1910 1920 1930 1940 1950 1960 1970

Billions of dollars

110 100 90 80 70 60 50 40 30 20 10

1860 1870 1880 1890 1900 1910 1920 1930 1940 1950 1960 1970 1980

Source: *Historical Statistics of the United States*

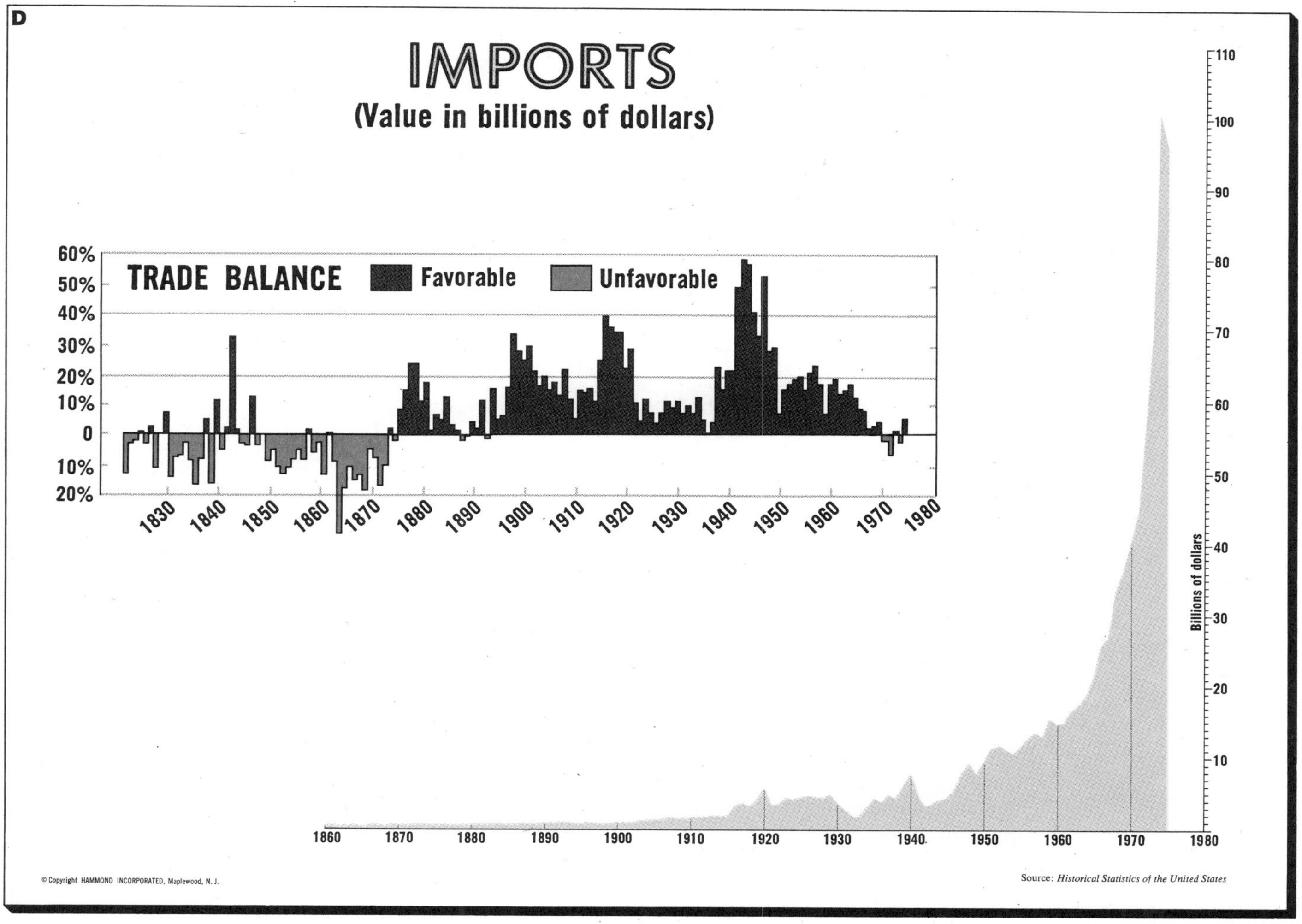

D

IMPORTS
(Value in billions of dollars)

TRADE BALANCE   ■ Favorable   ▨ Unfavorable

60%
50%
40%
30%
20%
10%
0
10%
20%

1830 1840 1850 1860 1870 1880 1890 1900 1910 1920 1930 1940 1950 1960 1970 1980

Billions of dollars

110 100 90 80 70 60 50 40 30 20 10

1860 1870 1880 1890 1900 1910 1920 1930 1940 1950 1960 1970 1980

Source: *Historical Statistics of the United States*

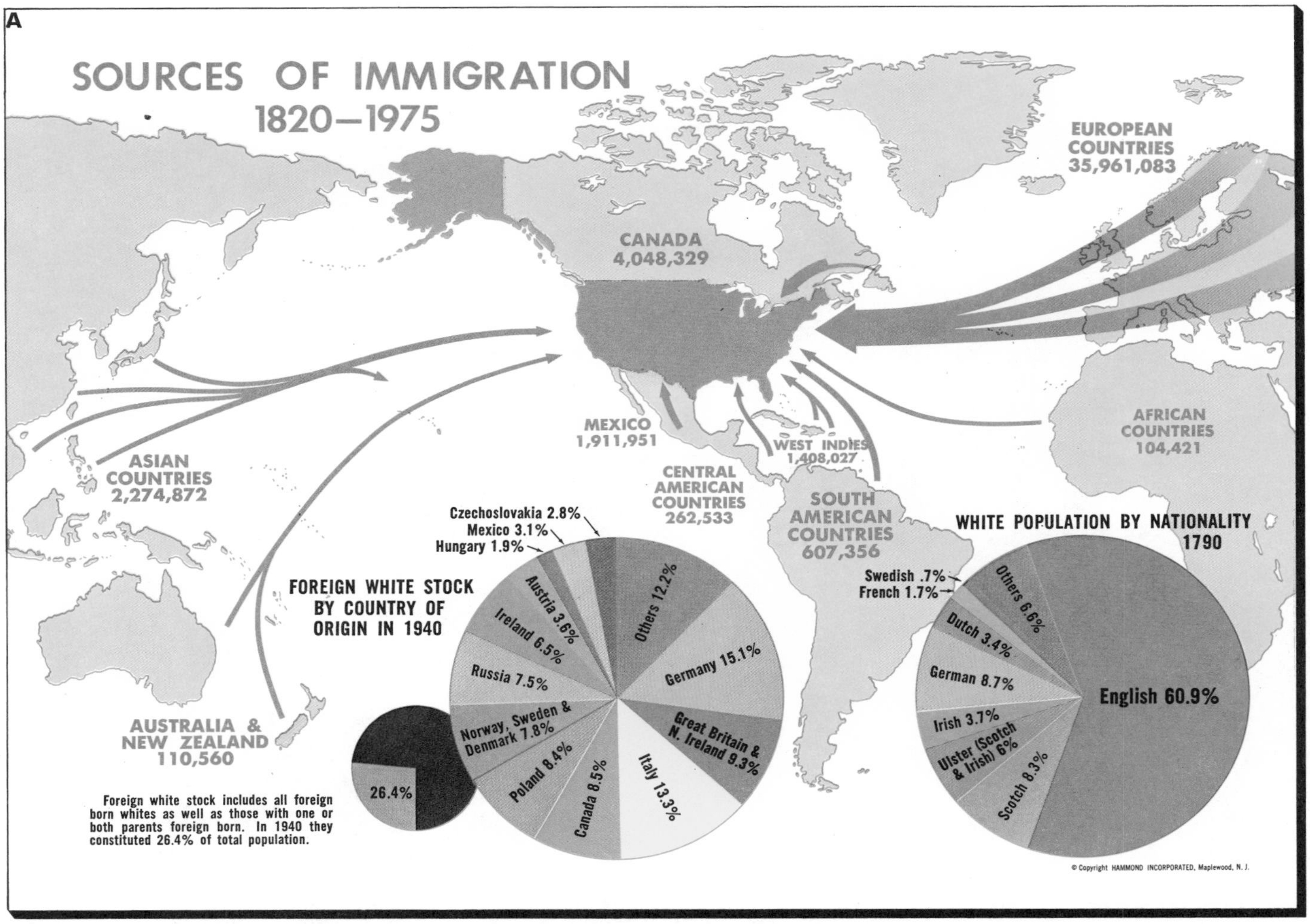
A
SOURCES OF IMMIGRATION
1820—1975
EUROPEAN COUNTRIES 35,961,083
CANADA 4,048,329
MEXICO 1,911,951
WEST INDIES 1,408,027
AFRICAN COUNTRIES 104,421
ASIAN COUNTRIES 2,274,872
CENTRAL AMERICAN COUNTRIES 262,533
SOUTH AMERICAN COUNTRIES 607,356
AUSTRALIA & NEW ZEALAND 110,560
FOREIGN WHITE STOCK BY COUNTRY OF ORIGIN IN 1940
Czechoslovakia 2.8%
Mexico 3.1%
Hungary 1.9%
Austria 3.6%
Ireland 6.5%
Russia 7.5%
Norway, Sweden & Denmark 7.8%
Poland 8.4%
Canada 8.5%
Italy 13.3%
Great Britain & N. Ireland 9.3%
Germany 15.1%
Others 12.2%
26.4%
Foreign white stock includes all foreign born whites as well as those with one or both parents foreign born. In 1940 they constituted 26.4% of total population.
WHITE POPULATION BY NATIONALITY 1790
Swedish .7%
French 1.7%
Others 6.6%
Dutch 3.4%
German 8.7%
Irish 3.7%
Ulster (Scotch & Irish) 6%
Scotch 8.3%
English 60.9%
© Copyright HAMMOND INCORPORATED, Maplewood, N. J.

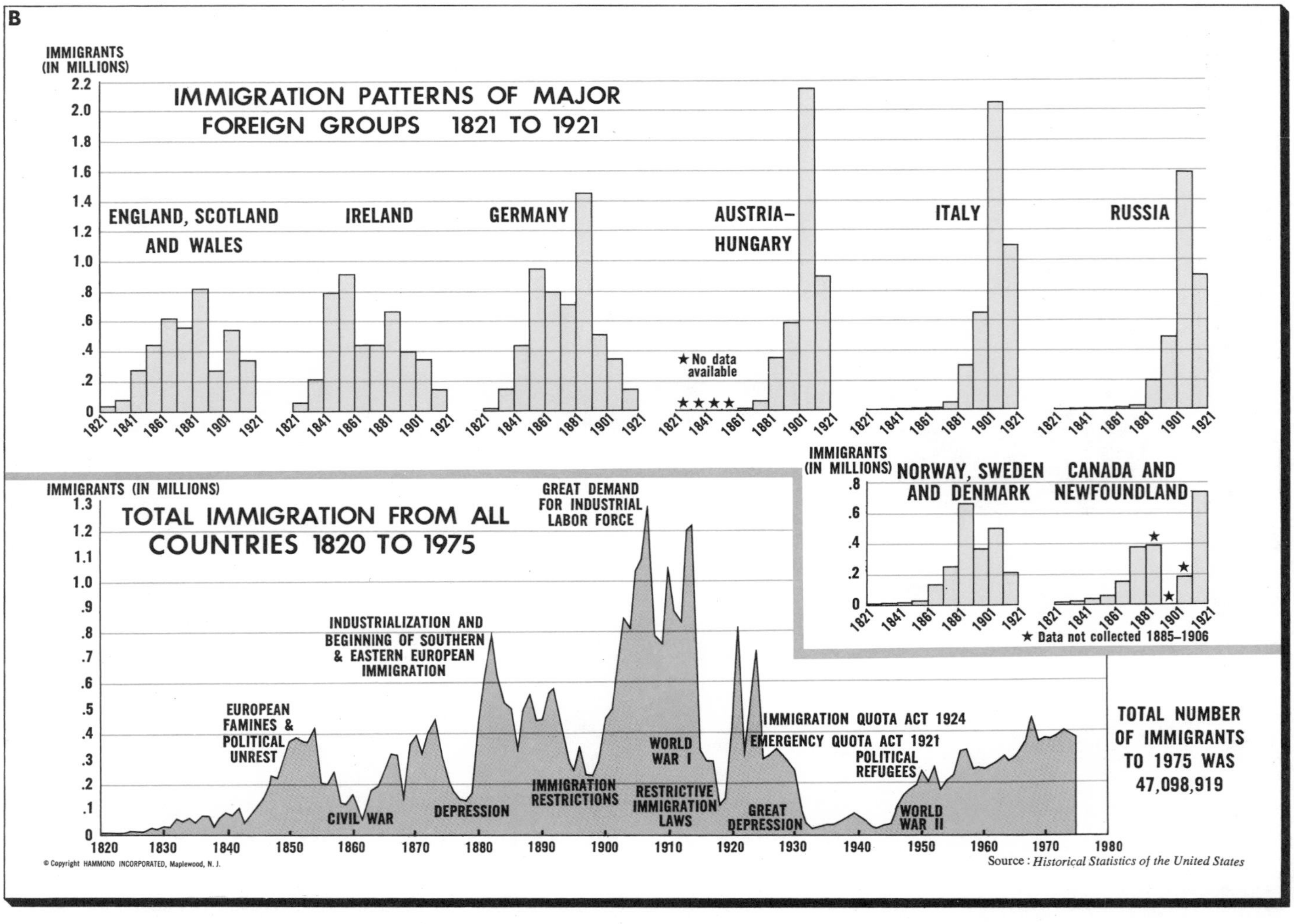
B
IMMIGRANTS (IN MILLIONS)
IMMIGRATION PATTERNS OF MAJOR FOREIGN GROUPS 1821 TO 1921
ENGLAND, SCOTLAND AND WALES
IRELAND
GERMANY
AUSTRIA-HUNGARY
ITALY
RUSSIA
★ No data available
NORWAY, SWEDEN AND DENMARK
CANADA AND NEWFOUNDLAND
★ Data not collected 1885–1906
IMMIGRANTS (IN MILLIONS)
TOTAL IMMIGRATION FROM ALL COUNTRIES 1820 TO 1975
GREAT DEMAND FOR INDUSTRIAL LABOR FORCE
INDUSTRIALIZATION AND BEGINNING OF SOUTHERN & EASTERN EUROPEAN IMMIGRATION
EUROPEAN FAMINES & POLITICAL UNREST
CIVIL WAR
DEPRESSION
IMMIGRATION RESTRICTIONS
WORLD WAR I
RESTRICTIVE IMMIGRATION LAWS
IMMIGRATION QUOTA ACT 1924
EMERGENCY QUOTA ACT 1921
GREAT DEPRESSION
POLITICAL REFUGEES
WORLD WAR II
TOTAL NUMBER OF IMMIGRANTS TO 1975 WAS 47,098,919
© Copyright HAMMOND INCORPORATED, Maplewood, N. J.
Source: Historical Statistics of the United States

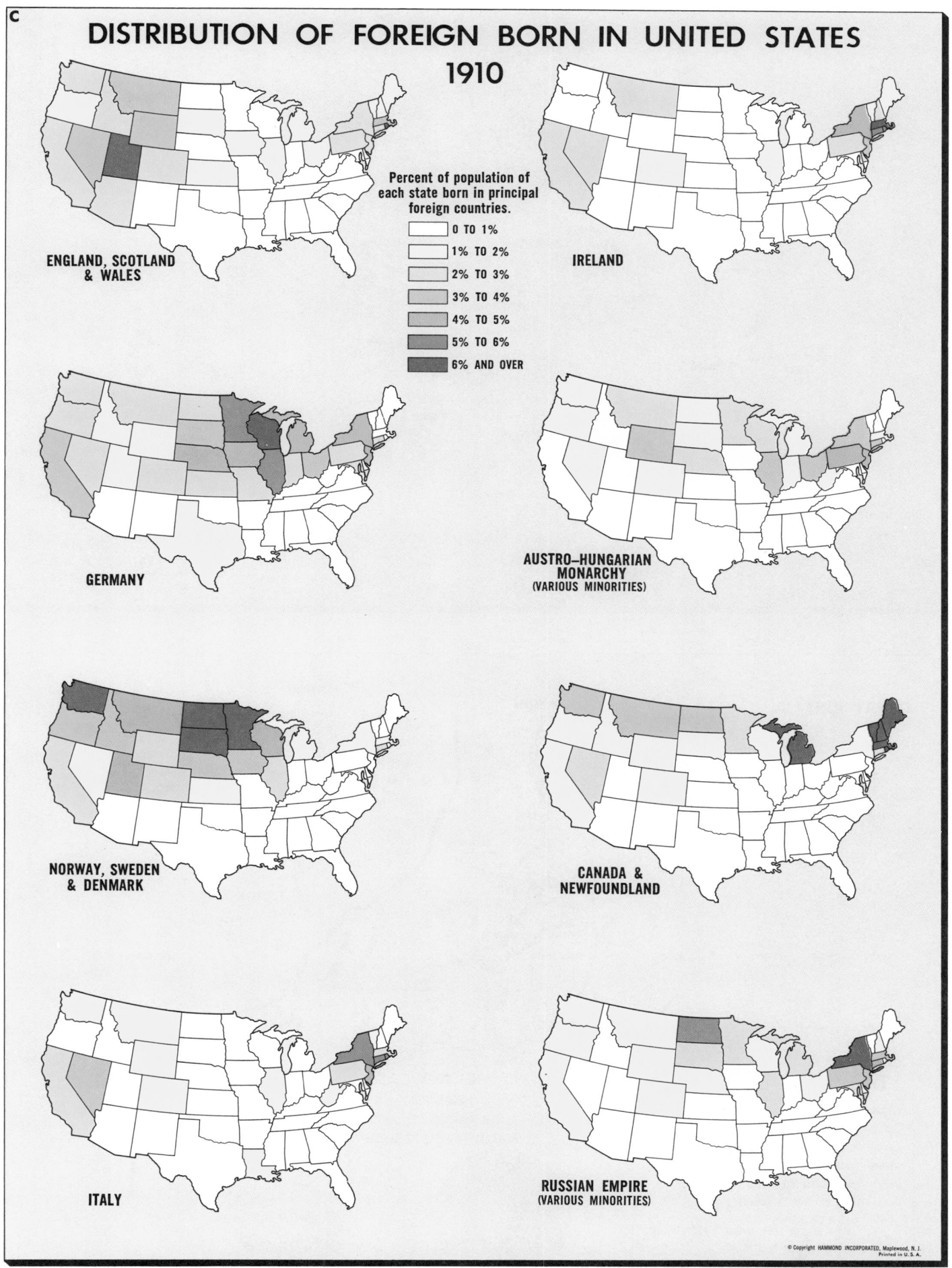

DISTRIBUTION OF FOREIGN BORN IN UNITED STATES
1910

ENGLAND, SCOTLAND & WALES

IRELAND

Percent of population of each state born in principal foreign countries.

- 0 TO 1%
- 1% TO 2%
- 2% TO 3%
- 3% TO 4%
- 4% TO 5%
- 5% TO 6%
- 6% AND OVER

GERMANY

AUSTRO—HUNGARIAN MONARCHY
(VARIOUS MINORITIES)

NORWAY, SWEDEN & DENMARK

CANADA & NEWFOUNDLAND

ITALY

RUSSIAN EMPIRE
(VARIOUS MINORITIES)

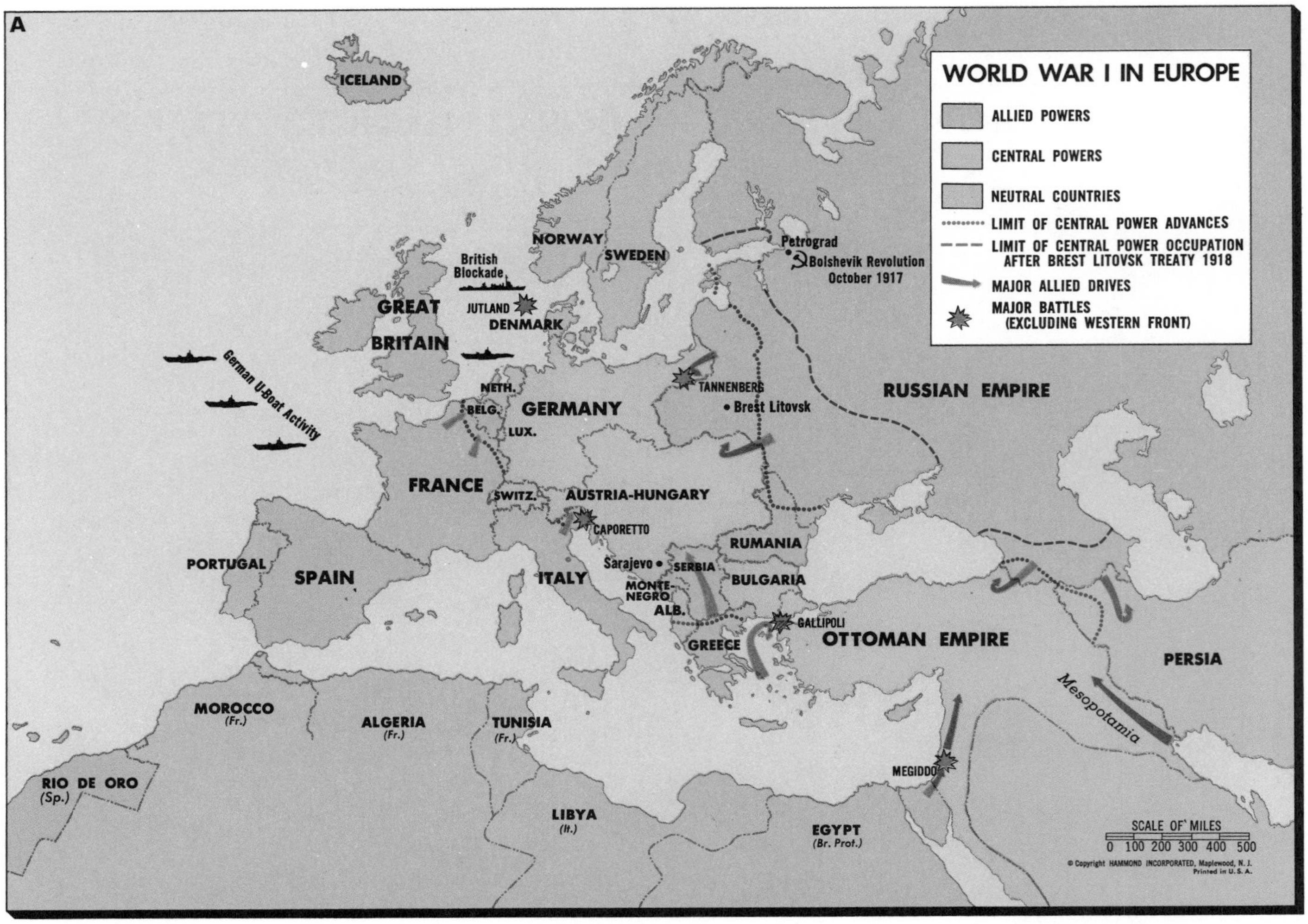

A

WORLD WAR I IN EUROPE

- ALLIED POWERS
- CENTRAL POWERS
- NEUTRAL COUNTRIES
- ···· LIMIT OF CENTRAL POWER ADVANCES
- --- LIMIT OF CENTRAL POWER OCCUPATION AFTER BREST LITOVSK TREATY 1918
- ➡ MAJOR ALLIED DRIVES
- ✸ MAJOR BATTLES (EXCLUDING WESTERN FRONT)

ICELAND

NORWAY
SWEDEN

British Blockade
JUTLAND ✸
DENMARK

GREAT BRITAIN

German U-Boat Activity

NETH.
BELG.
LUX.

GERMANY

Petrograd
Bolshevik Revolution
October 1917

TANNENBERG ✸
Brest Litovsk

RUSSIAN EMPIRE

FRANCE

SWITZ.

AUSTRIA-HUNGARY

CAPORETTO ✸

PORTUGAL

SPAIN

ITALY

Sarajevo •
SERBIA
MONTE-
NEGRO
ALB.

RUMANIA

BULGARIA

GALLIPOLI ✸

GREECE

OTTOMAN EMPIRE

PERSIA

MOROCCO
(Fr.)

ALGERIA
(Fr.)

TUNISIA
(Fr.)

Mesopotamia

RIO DE ORO
(Sp.)

LIBYA
(It.)

EGYPT
(Br. Prot.)

MEGIDDO ✸

SCALE OF MILES
0 100 200 300 400 500

© Copyright HAMMOND INCORPORATED, Maplewood, N.J.
Printed in U.S.A.

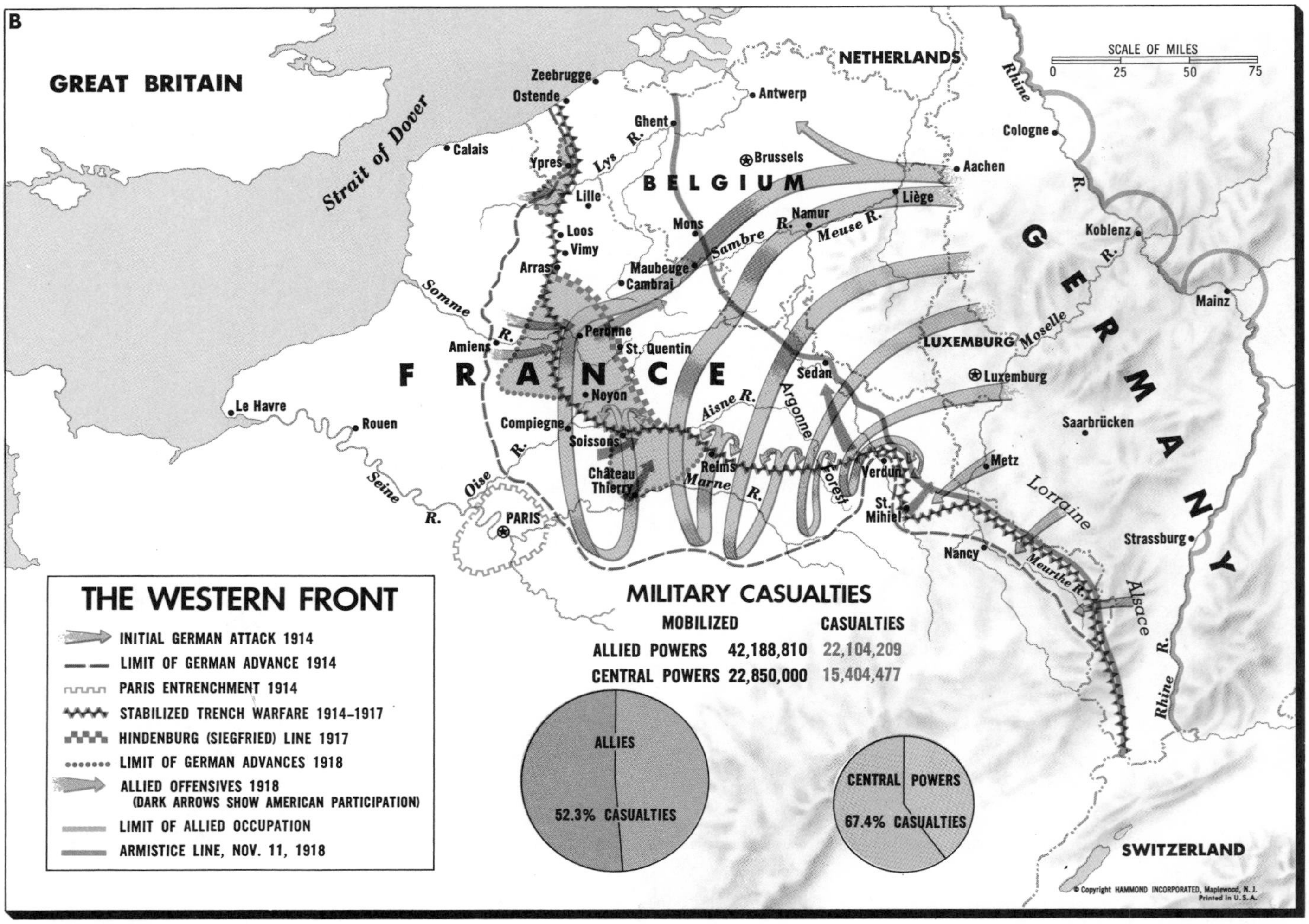

B

GREAT BRITAIN

NETHERLANDS

SCALE OF MILES
0 25 50 75

Zeebrugge
Ostende
Ghent
Antwerp
Rhine
Calais
Ypres
Lys R.
Cologne
BELGIUM
Brussels
Aachen
Lille
Loos
Mons
Namur
Liège
Vimy
Sambre R.
Meuse R.
Arras
Maubeuge
Cambrai
Koblenz
Somme
Péronne
St. Quentin
Amiens
R.
LUXEMBURG
Moselle
Mainz
FRANCE
Noyon
Sedan
Luxemburg
GERMANY
Le Havre
Rouen
Compiègne
Aisne R.
Argonne Forest
Metz
Oise R.
Soissons
Reims
Verdun
Saarbrücken
Seine R.
Château Thierry
Marne R.
St. Mihiel
Lorraine
PARIS
Strassburg
Nancy
Meurthe R.
Alsace
Rhine R.

THE WESTERN FRONT

- ➡ INITIAL GERMAN ATTACK 1914
- --- LIMIT OF GERMAN ADVANCE 1914
- 〰 PARIS ENTRENCHMENT 1914
- ⋏⋏⋏ STABILIZED TRENCH WARFARE 1914–1917
- ⋈⋈⋈ HINDENBURG (SIEGFRIED) LINE 1917
- ···· LIMIT OF GERMAN ADVANCES 1918
- ➡ ALLIED OFFENSIVES 1918 (DARK ARROWS SHOW AMERICAN PARTICIPATION)
- ▌ LIMIT OF ALLIED OCCUPATION
- ▬ ARMISTICE LINE, NOV. 11, 1918

MILITARY CASUALTIES

	MOBILIZED	CASUALTIES
ALLIED POWERS	42,188,810	22,104,209
CENTRAL POWERS	22,850,000	15,404,477

ALLIES
52.3% CASUALTIES

CENTRAL POWERS
67.4% CASUALTIES

SWITZERLAND

© Copyright HAMMOND INCORPORATED, Maplewood, N.J.
Printed in U.S.A.

C

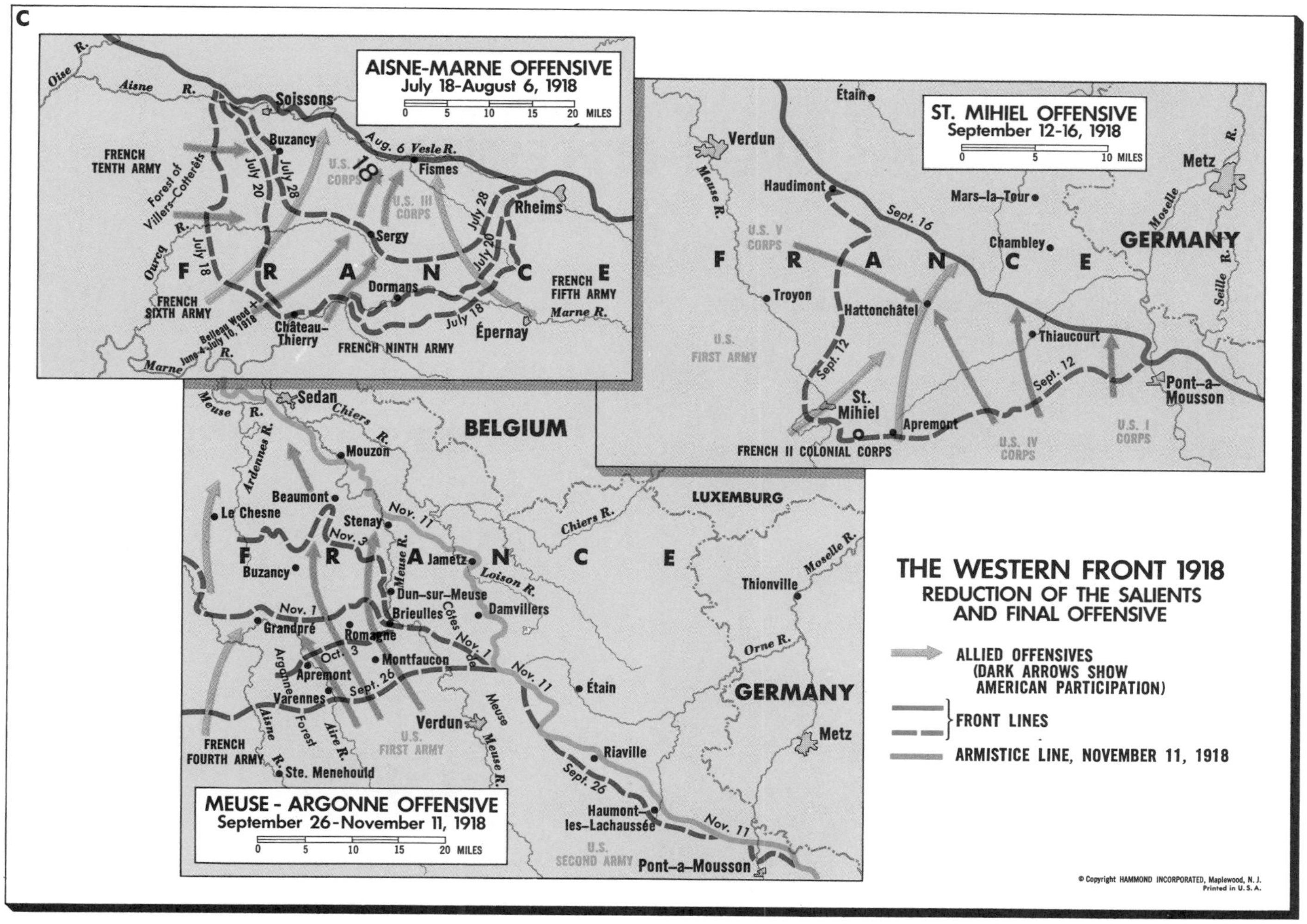

AISNE-MARNE OFFENSIVE
July 18-August 6, 1918
0 5 10 15 20 MILES

Oise R.
Aisne R.
Soissons
Buzancy
Aug. 6 Vesle R.
FRENCH TENTH ARMY
July 28
Fismes
Forest of Villers-Cotterêts
July 20
U.S. III CORPS
July 28
Rheims
Ourcq R.
July 18
Sergy
July 20
F R A N C E
FRENCH FIFTH ARMY
FRENCH SIXTH ARMY
Dormans
Château-Thierry
Belleau Wood June 6-July 10, 1918
July 18
Épernay
Marne R.
FRENCH NINTH ARMY
Marne R.

ST. MIHIEL OFFENSIVE
September 12-16, 1918
0 5 10 MILES

Étain
Verdun
Haudimont
Mars-la-Tour
Metz
Moselle R.
Sept. 16
U.S. V CORPS
Chambley
GERMANY
F R A N C E
Troyon
Hattonchâtel
Thiaucourt
Seille R.
U.S. FIRST ARMY
Sept. 12
St. Mihiel
Apremont
Sept. 12
Pont-a-Mousson
FRENCH II COLONIAL CORPS
U.S. IV CORPS
U.S. I CORPS

Meuse R.
Sedan
Chiers R.
BELGIUM
LUXEMBURG
Mouzon
Beaumont
Le Chesne
Stenay
Nov. 11
Ardennes R.
Nov. 3
Meuse R.
Jametz
Chiers R.
Buzancy
Nov. 11
Loison R.
Dun-sur-Meuse
Brieulles
Damvillers
Thionville
Moselle R.
F R A N C E
Nov. 1
Grandpré
Romagne
Côtes de Meuse
Nov. 1
Montfaucon
Nov. 11
Orne R.
Oct. 3
Apremont
Sept. 26
Étain
GERMANY
Argonne Forest
Varennes
Aire R.
Meuse R.
Metz
Verdun
FRENCH FOURTH ARMY
U.S. FIRST ARMY
Riaville
Ste. Menehould
Sept. 26
Haumont-les-Lachaussée
Nov. 11
U.S. SECOND ARMY
Pont-a-Mousson

MEUSE-ARGONNE OFFENSIVE
September 26-November 11, 1918
0 5 10 15 20 MILES

THE WESTERN FRONT 1918
REDUCTION OF THE SALIENTS AND FINAL OFFENSIVE

➤ ALLIED OFFENSIVES (DARK ARROWS SHOW AMERICAN PARTICIPATION)

FRONT LINES

ARMISTICE LINE, NOVEMBER 11, 1918

D

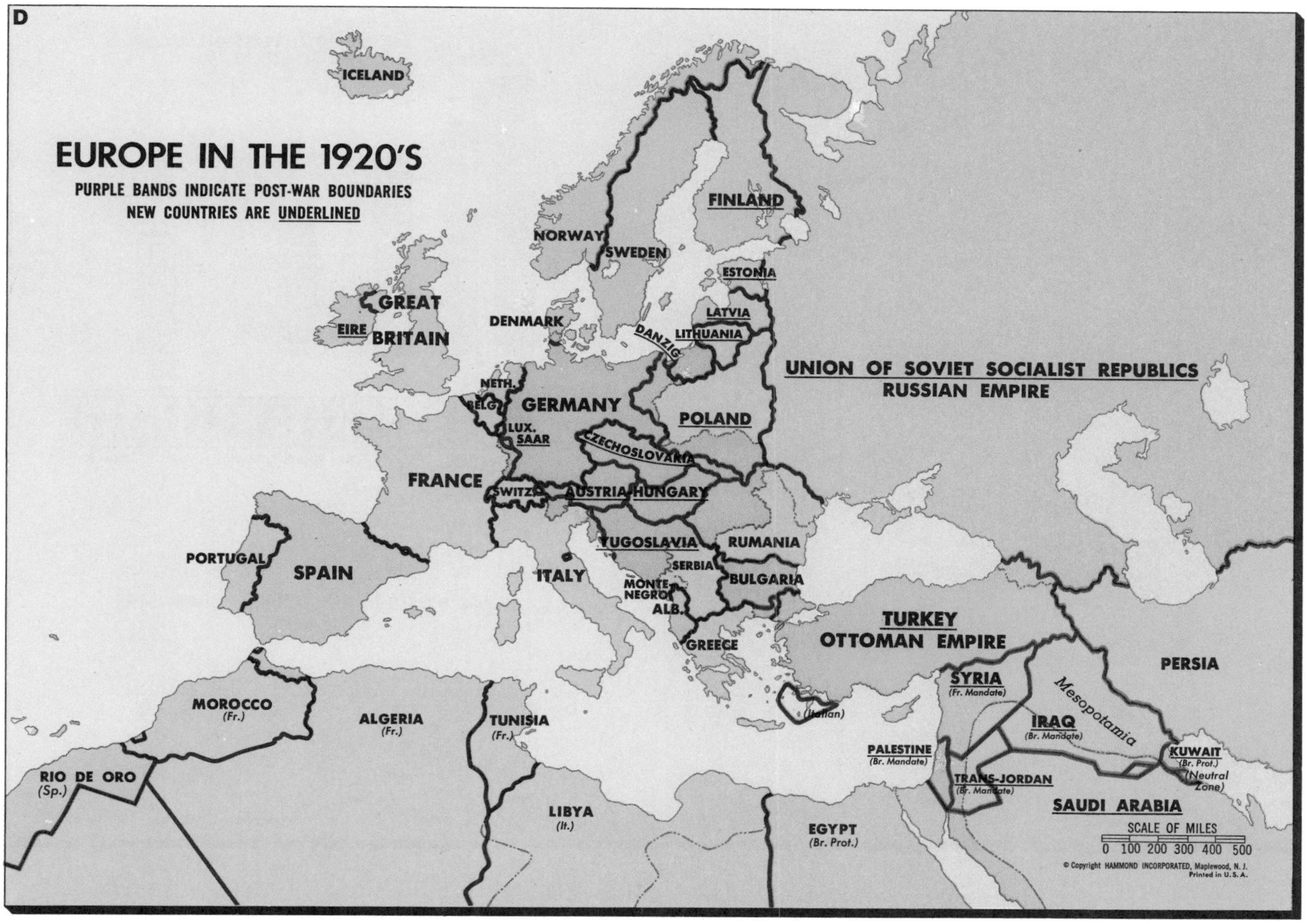

EUROPE IN THE 1920'S

PURPLE BANDS INDICATE POST-WAR BOUNDARIES
NEW COUNTRIES ARE UNDERLINED

ICELAND
FINLAND
NORWAY
SWEDEN
ESTONIA
GREAT BRITAIN
EIRE
DENMARK
LATVIA
DANZIG
LITHUANIA
UNION OF SOVIET SOCIALIST REPUBLICS
RUSSIAN EMPIRE
NETH.
BELG.
GERMANY
POLAND
LUX.
SAAR
CZECHOSLOVAKIA
FRANCE
SWITZ.
AUSTRIA HUNGARY
YUGOSLAVIA
RUMANIA
PORTUGAL
SPAIN
ITALY
SERBIA
BULGARIA
MONTE NEGRO
ALB.
TURKEY
OTTOMAN EMPIRE
GREECE
PERSIA
MOROCCO
(Fr.)
ALGERIA
(Fr.)
TUNISIA
(Fr.)
SYRIA
(Fr. Mandate)
Mesopotamia
IRAQ
(Br. Mandate)
KUWAIT
(Br. Prot.)
(Neutral Zone)
RIO DE ORO
(Sp.)
LIBYA
(It.)
EGYPT
(Br. Prot.)
PALESTINE
(Br. Mandate)
TRANS-JORDAN
(Br. Mandate)
SAUDI ARABIA

SCALE OF MILES
0 100 200 300 400 500

A

THE GREAT DEPRESSION

THE DECLINE AND RECOVERY OF THE NATIONAL ECONOMY

IN BILLIONS OF DOLLARS

TOTAL GROSS NATIONAL PRODUCT

PERSONAL INCOME

THE GREAT DEPRESSION

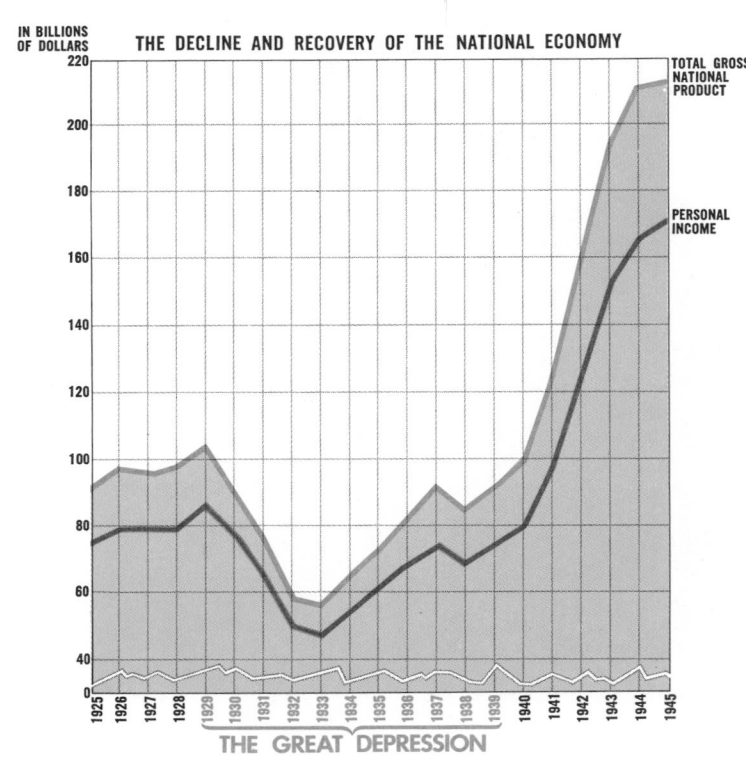

NUMBER OF BANK SUSPENSIONS 1919–1933

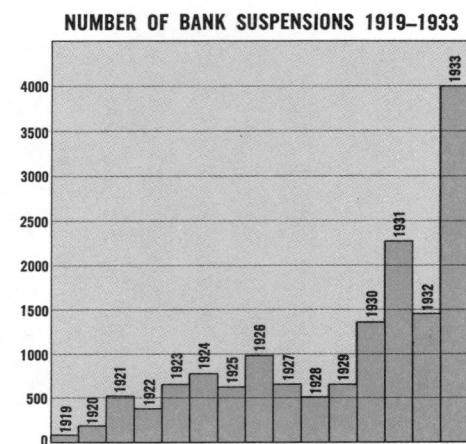

HOW U.S. TOTAL PERSONAL INCOME WAS DIVIDED IN 1929

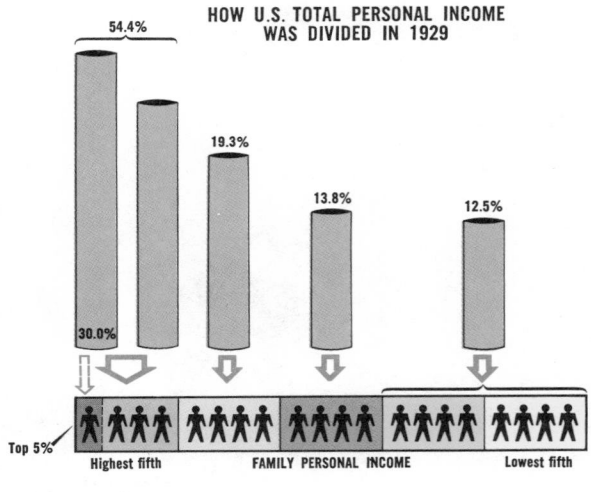

54.4%

19.3%

13.8%

12.5%

30.0%

Top 5%

Highest fifth

FAMILY PERSONAL INCOME

Lowest fifth

UNEMPLOYMENT

THE UNEMPLOYED AS A PERCENT OF THE CIVILIAN LABOR FORCE

PERCENT

THE GREAT DEPRESSION

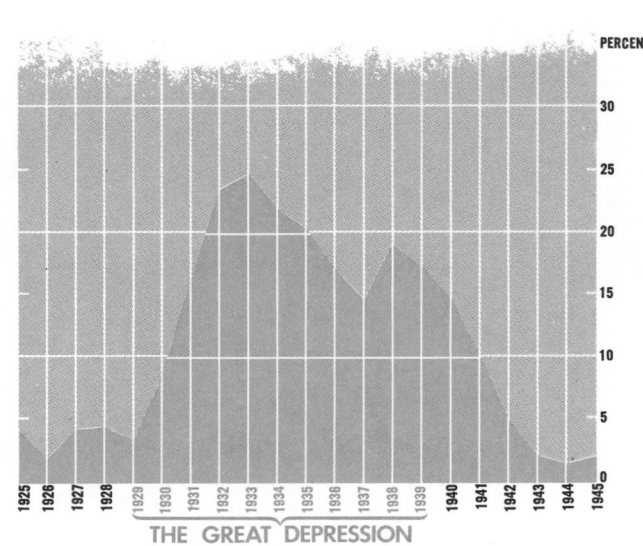

HOURS WORKED IN MANUFACTURING (1925–1945)
(WEEKLY AVERAGE)

HOURS

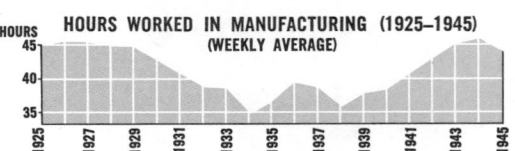

Source: *Historical Statistics of the United States*

THE GREAT DEPRESSION
SPECULATION IN THE STOCK MARKET

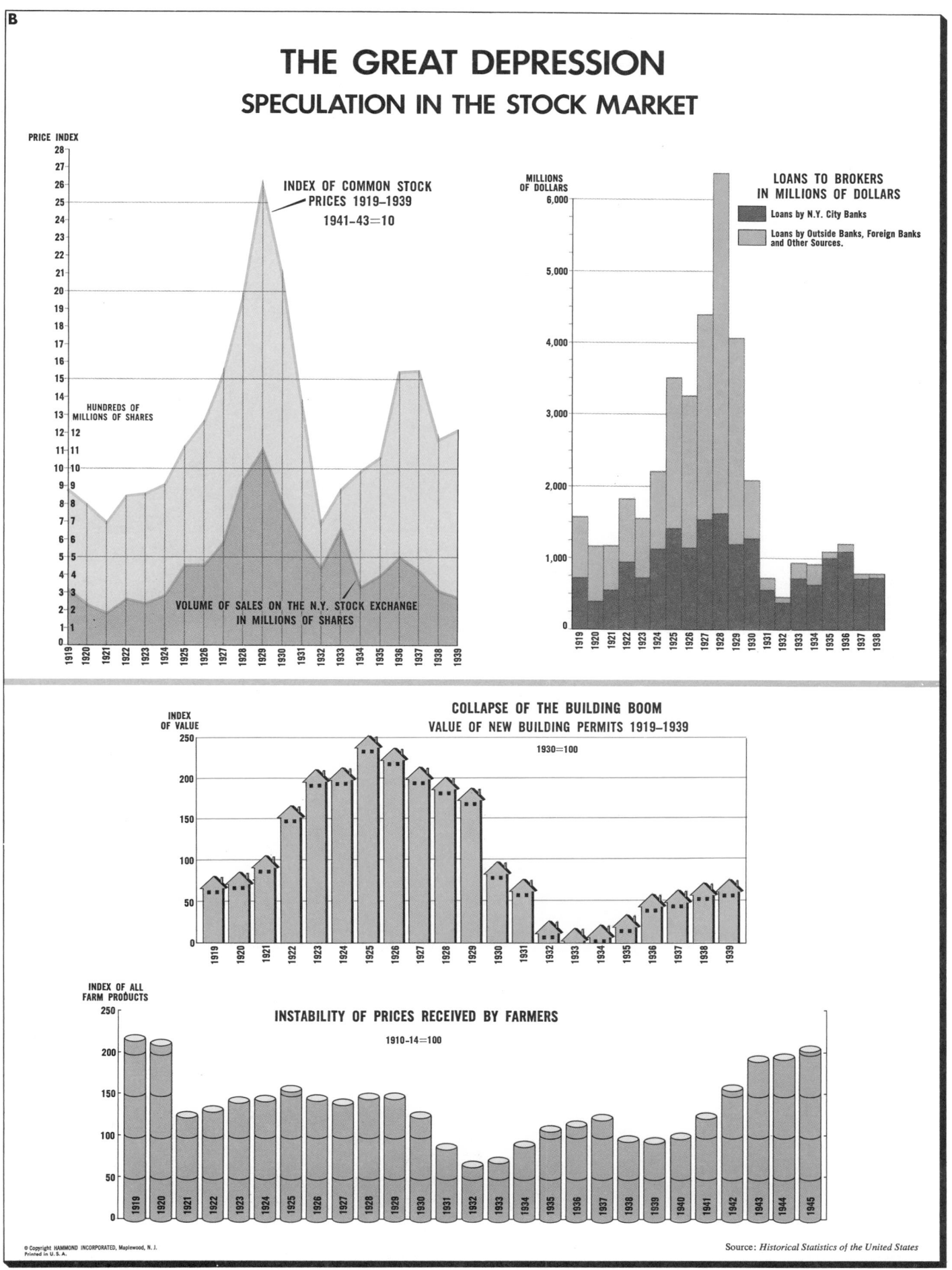

PRICE INDEX

INDEX OF COMMON STOCK
PRICES 1919–1939

1941–43=10

HUNDREDS OF
MILLIONS OF SHARES

VOLUME OF SALES ON THE N.Y. STOCK EXCHANGE
IN MILLIONS OF SHARES

MILLIONS
OF DOLLARS

LOANS TO BROKERS
IN MILLIONS OF DOLLARS

Loans by N.Y. City Banks

Loans by Outside Banks, Foreign Banks
and Other Sources.

COLLAPSE OF THE BUILDING BOOM
VALUE OF NEW BUILDING PERMITS 1919–1939

INDEX
OF VALUE

1930=100

INDEX OF ALL
FARM PRODUCTS

INSTABILITY OF PRICES RECEIVED BY FARMERS

1910–14=100

Source: *Historical Statistics of the United States*

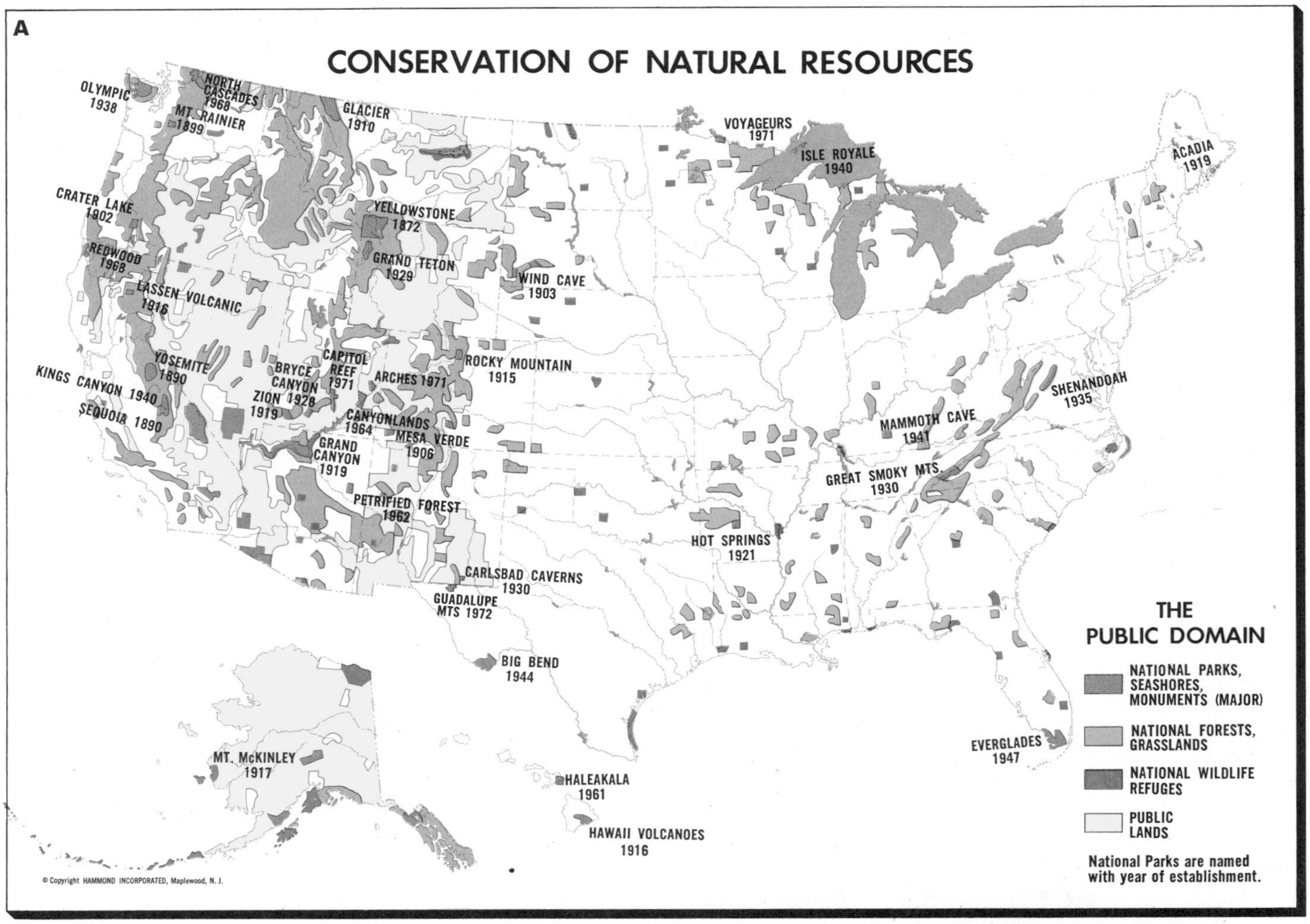

A

CONSERVATION OF NATURAL RESOURCES

OLYMPIC 1938
NORTH CASCADES 1968
MT. RAINIER 1899
GLACIER 1910
VOYAGEURS 1971
ISLE ROYALE 1940
ACADIA 1919
CRATER LAKE 1902
YELLOWSTONE 1872
REDWOOD 1968
GRAND TETON 1929
WIND CAVE 1903
LASSEN VOLCANIC 1916
YOSEMITE 1890
CAPITOL REEF 1971
BRYCE CANYON 1928
ARCHES 1971
ROCKY MOUNTAIN 1915
SHENANDOAH 1935
KINGS CANYON 1940
ZION 1919
CANYONLANDS 1964
MESA VERDE 1906
MAMMOTH CAVE 1941
SEQUOIA 1890
GRAND CANYON 1919
GREAT SMOKY MTS. 1930
PETRIFIED FOREST 1962
CARLSBAD CAVERNS 1930
HOT SPRINGS 1921
GUADALUPE MTS 1972
BIG BEND 1944
MT. McKINLEY 1917
EVERGLADES 1947
HALEAKALA 1961
HAWAII VOLCANOES 1916

© Copyright HAMMOND INCORPORATED, Maplewood, N. J.

THE PUBLIC DOMAIN

- NATIONAL PARKS, SEASHORES, MONUMENTS (MAJOR)
- NATIONAL FORESTS, GRASSLANDS
- NATIONAL WILDLIFE REFUGES
- PUBLIC LANDS

National Parks are named with year of establishment.

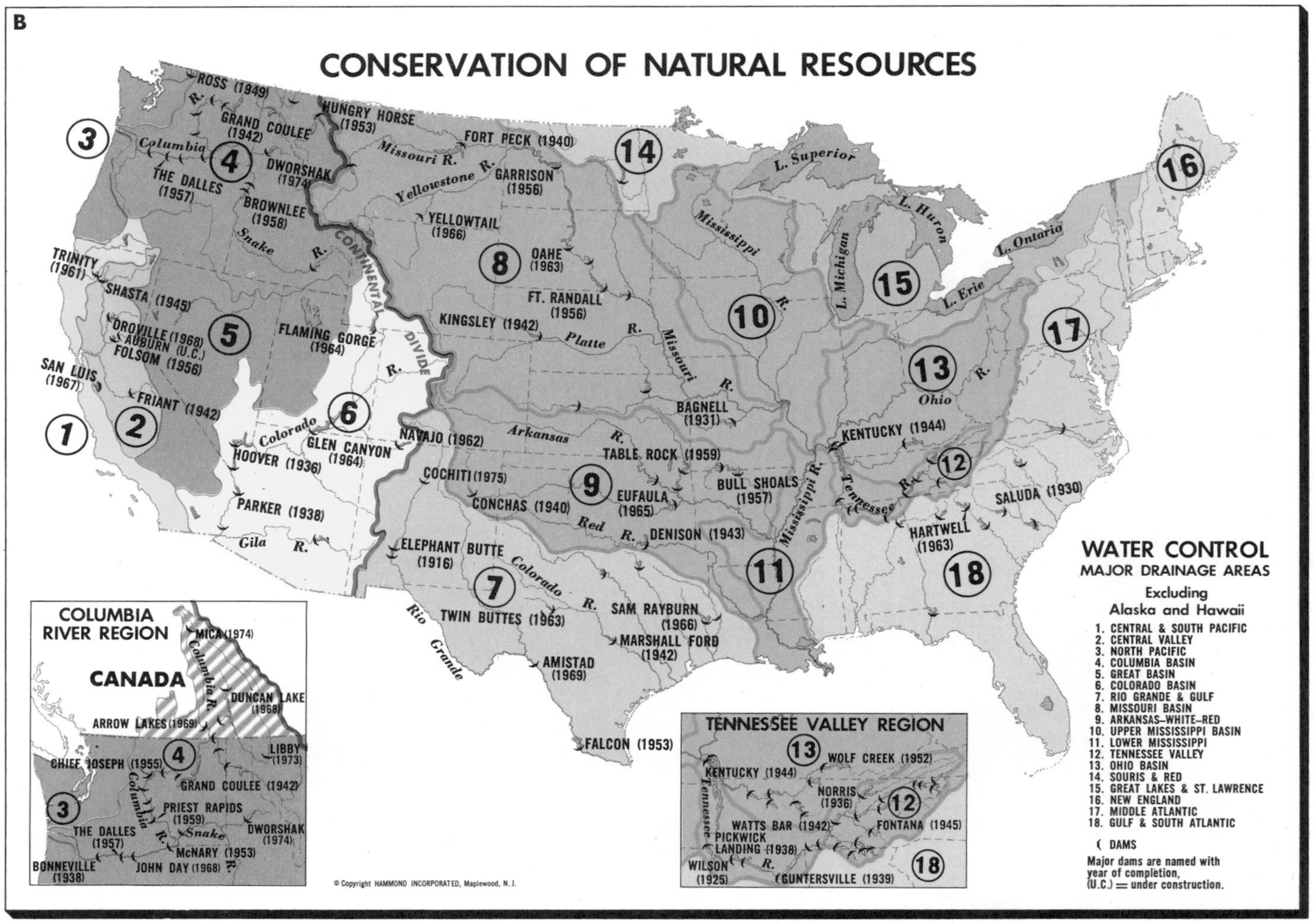

B

CONSERVATION OF NATURAL RESOURCES

ROSS (1949)
GRAND COULEE (1942)
HUNGRY HORSE (1953)
FORT PECK (1940)
Columbia
THE DALLES (1957)
DWORSHAK (1974)
Missouri R.
GARRISON (1956)
L. Superior
Yellowstone R.
YELLOWTAIL (1966)
BROWNLEE (1958)
Snake R.
CONTINENTAL DIVIDE
OAHE (1963)
Mississippi
L. Huron
TRINITY (1961)
FT. RANDALL (1956)
L. Michigan
L. Ontario
SHASTA (1945)
KINGSLEY (1942)
Platte R.
Missouri R.
L. Erie
OROVILLE (1968)
FLAMING GORGE (1964)
AUBURN (U.C.)
FOLSOM (1956)
SAN LUIS (1967)
FRIANT (1942)
Colorado R.
NAVAJO (1962)
Arkansas R.
BAGNELL (1931)
Ohio R.
KENTUCKY (1944)
GLEN CANYON (1964)
TABLE ROCK (1959)
Tennessee R.
HOOVER (1936)
COCHITI (1975)
EUFAULA (1965)
BULL SHOALS (1957)
SALUDA (1930)
PARKER (1938)
CONCHAS (1940)
Red R.
DENISON (1943)
HARTWELL (1963)
Gila R.
ELEPHANT BUTTE (1916)
Colorado R.
SAM RAYBURN (1966)
TWIN BUTTES (1963)
MARSHALL FORD (1942)
Rio Grande
AMISTAD (1969)
FALCON (1953)

COLUMBIA RIVER REGION
MICA (1974)
CANADA
Columbia R.
DUNCAN LAKE (1968)
ARROW LAKES (1969)
LIBBY (1973)
CHIEF JOSEPH (1955)
GRAND COULEE (1942)
PRIEST RAPIDS (1959)
DWORSHAK (1974)
THE DALLES (1957)
Snake R.
BONNEVILLE (1938)
McNARY (1953)
JOHN DAY (1968)

© Copyright HAMMOND INCORPORATED, Maplewood, N. J.

TENNESSEE VALLEY REGION
Tennessee R.
WOLF CREEK (1952)
KENTUCKY (1944)
NORRIS (1936)
FONTANA (1945)
WATTS BAR (1942)
PICKWICK LANDING (1938)
WILSON (1925)
GUNTERSVILLE (1939)

WATER CONTROL
MAJOR DRAINAGE AREAS

Excluding Alaska and Hawaii

1. CENTRAL & SOUTH PACIFIC
2. CENTRAL VALLEY
3. NORTH PACIFIC
4. COLUMBIA BASIN
5. GREAT BASIN
6. COLORADO BASIN
7. RIO GRANDE & GULF
8. MISSOURI BASIN
9. ARKANSAS–WHITE–RED
10. UPPER MISSISSIPPI BASIN
11. LOWER MISSISSIPPI
12. TENNESSEE VALLEY
13. OHIO BASIN
14. SOURIS & RED
15. GREAT LAKES & ST. LAWRENCE
16. NEW ENGLAND
17. MIDDLE ATLANTIC
18. GULF & SOUTH ATLANTIC

DAMS

Major dams are named with year of completion, (U.C.) = under construction.

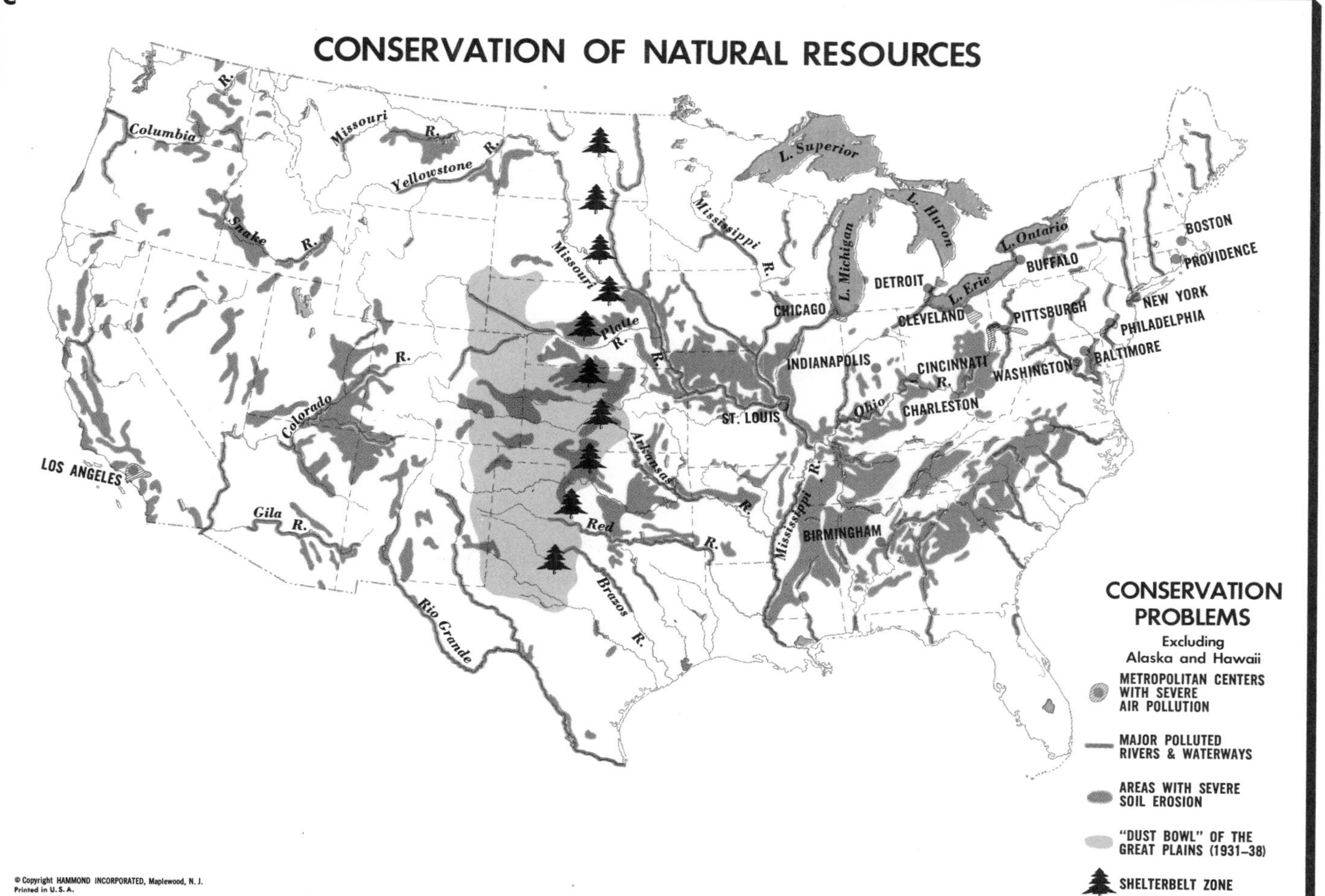

CONSERVATION OF NATURAL RESOURCES

Columbia R.
Missouri R.
Yellowstone R.
Snake R.
Missouri R.
L. Superior
L. Huron
L. Michigan
L. Ontario
L. Erie
Mississippi R.
BOSTON
PROVIDENCE
DETROIT
BUFFALO
CHICAGO
CLEVELAND
PITTSBURGH
NEW YORK
PHILADELPHIA
Colorado R.
Platte R.
INDIANAPOLIS
CINCINNATI R.
WASHINGTON
BALTIMORE
LOS ANGELES
ST. LOUIS
Ohio
CHARLESTON
Gila R.
Arkansas R.
Red R.
Mississippi R.
BIRMINGHAM
Rio Grande
Brazos R.

CONSERVATION PROBLEMS

Excluding
Alaska and Hawaii

METROPOLITAN CENTERS WITH SEVERE AIR POLLUTION

MAJOR POLLUTED RIVERS & WATERWAYS

AREAS WITH SEVERE SOIL EROSION

"DUST BOWL" OF THE GREAT PLAINS (1931–38)

SHELTERBELT ZONE

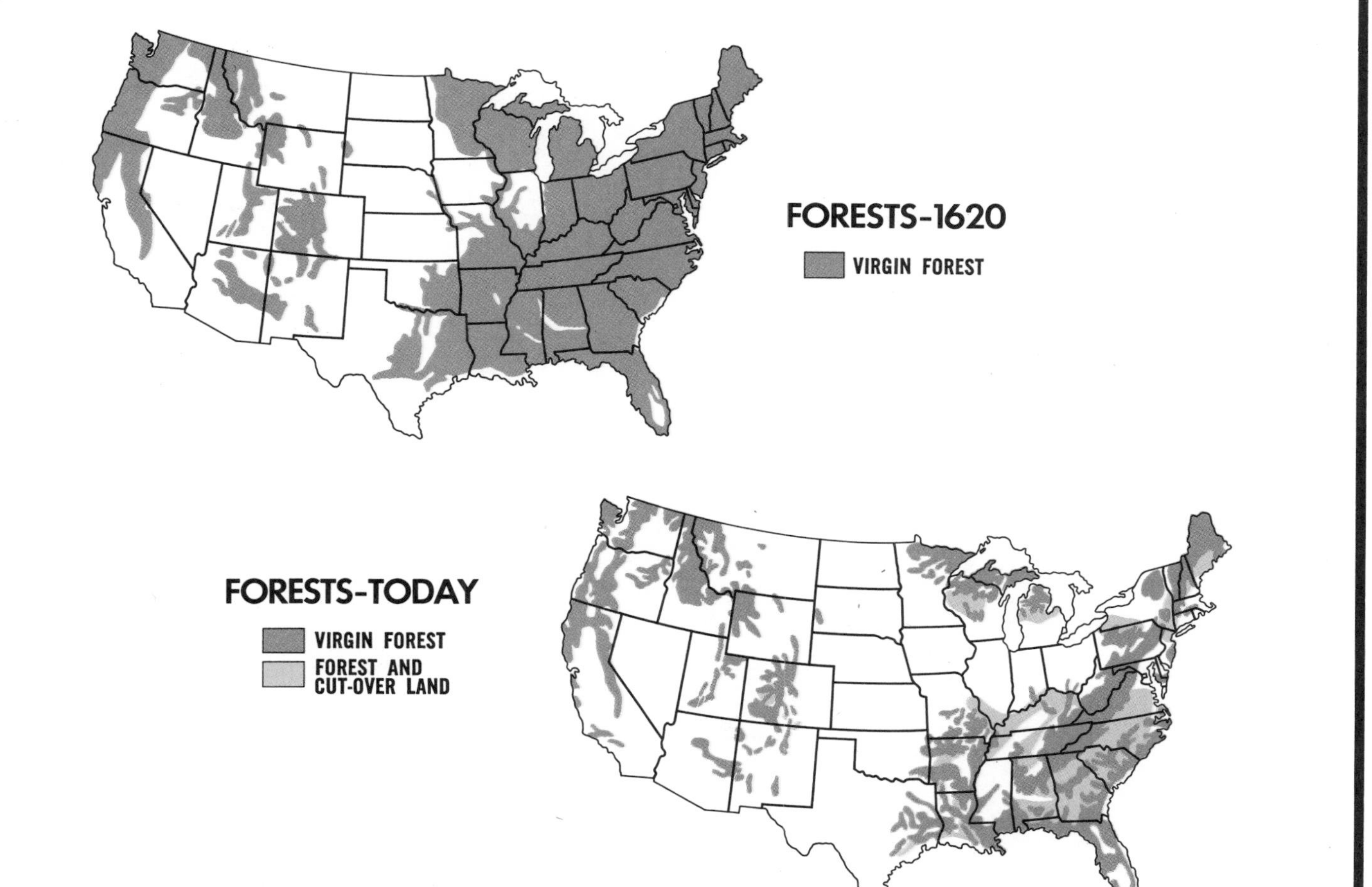

FORESTS–1620

VIRGIN FOREST

FORESTS–TODAY

VIRGIN FOREST

FOREST AND CUT-OVER LAND

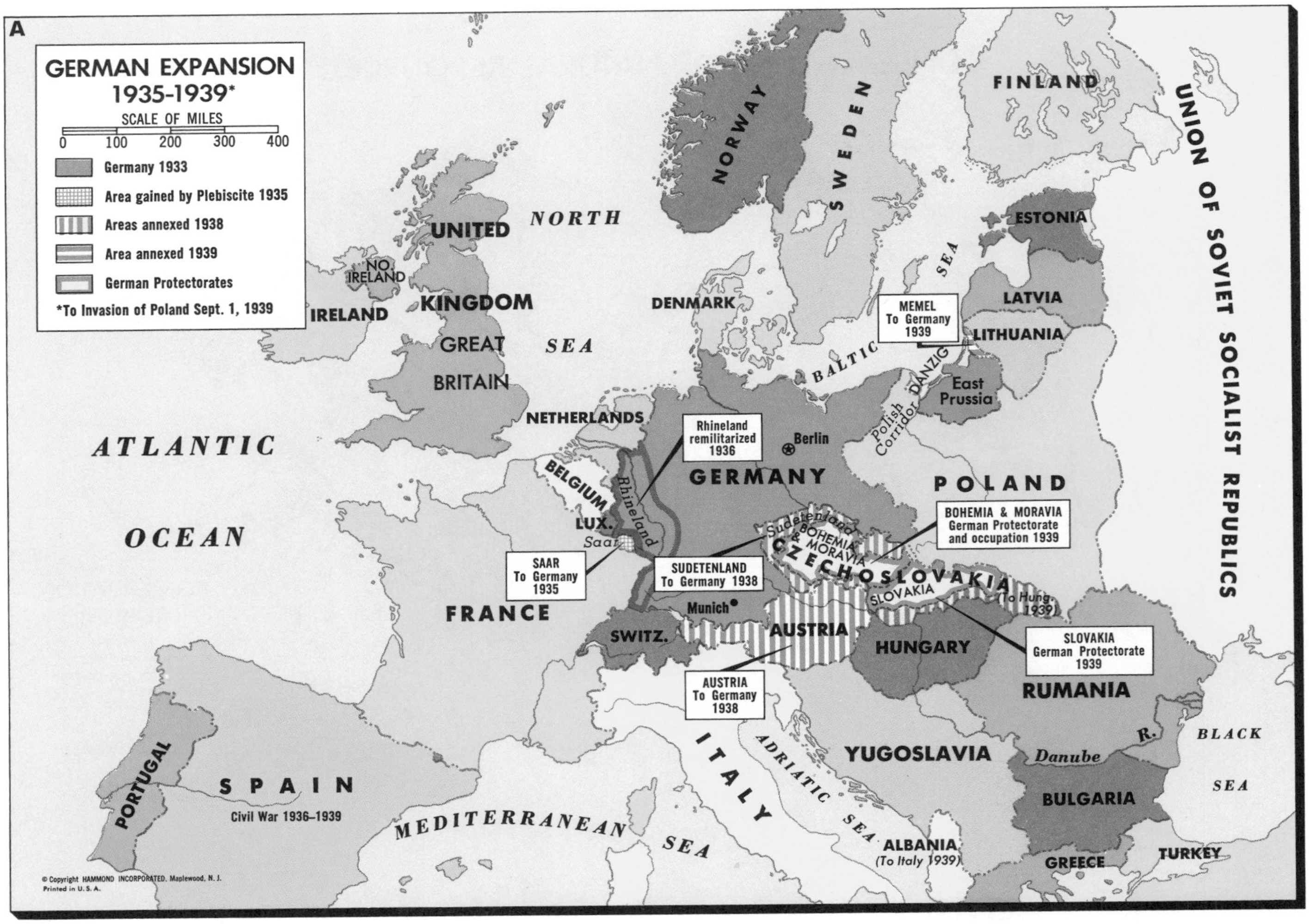

A

GERMAN EXPANSION 1935-1939*

SCALE OF MILES

0   100   200   300   400

Germany 1933
Area gained by Plebiscite 1935
Areas annexed 1938
Area annexed 1939
German Protectorates

*To Invasion of Poland Sept. 1, 1939

NORWAY
SWEDEN
FINLAND
NORTH SEA
ESTONIA
UNITED KINGDOM
DENMARK
LATVIA
MEMEL To Germany 1939
LITHUANIA
IRELAND
NO. IRELAND
GREAT BRITAIN
BALTIC SEA
DANZIG
East Prussia
Polish Corridor
ATLANTIC OCEAN
NETHERLANDS
Rhineland remilitarized 1936
Berlin
GERMANY
POLAND
UNION OF SOVIET SOCIALIST REPUBLICS
BELGIUM
Rhineland
LUX.
Saar
BOHEMIA MORAVIA
BOHEMIA & MORAVIA German Protectorate and occupation 1939
SAAR To Germany 1935
SUDETENLAND To Germany 1938
Sudetenland
CZECHOSLOVAKIA
SLOVAKIA
(To Hung. 1939)
FRANCE
Munich
AUSTRIA
SLOVAKIA German Protectorate 1939
HUNGARY
SWITZ.
AUSTRIA To Germany 1938
RUMANIA
SPAIN
Civil War 1936-1939
PORTUGAL
ITALY
ADRIATIC SEA
YUGOSLAVIA
Danube
R.
BLACK SEA
BULGARIA
MEDITERRANEAN SEA
ALBANIA (To Italy 1939)
GREECE
TURKEY

© Copyright HAMMOND INCORPORATED. Maplewood, N.J.
Printed in U.S.A.

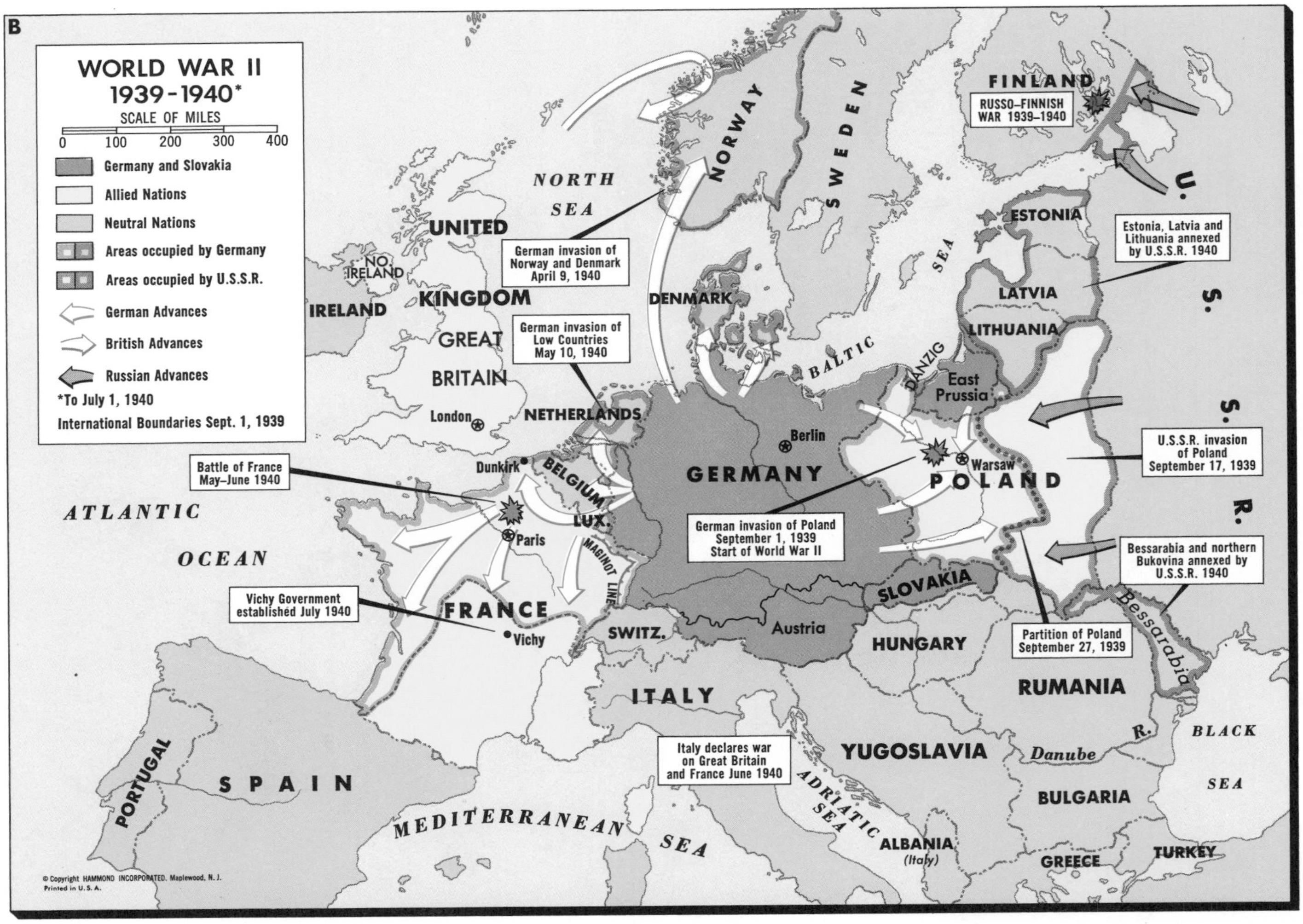

B

WORLD WAR II 1939-1940*

SCALE OF MILES

0   100   200   300   400

Germany and Slovakia
Allied Nations
Neutral Nations
Areas occupied by Germany
Areas occupied by U.S.S.R.
German Advances
British Advances
Russian Advances

*To July 1, 1940

International Boundaries Sept. 1, 1939

NORWAY
SWEDEN
FINLAND
RUSSO-FINNISH WAR 1939-1940
NORTH SEA
UNITED KINGDOM
DENMARK
ESTONIA
Estonia, Latvia and Lithuania annexed by U.S.S.R. 1940
NO. IRELAND
IRELAND
German invasion of Norway and Denmark April 9, 1940
U.
LATVIA
BALTIC SEA
LITHUANIA
GREAT BRITAIN
DANZIG
East Prussia
S.
German invasion of Low Countries May 10, 1940
London
NETHERLANDS
Berlin
Warsaw
U.S.S.R. invasion of Poland September 17, 1939
S.
Battle of France May-June 1940
Dunkirk
BELGIUM
GERMANY
POLAND
ATLANTIC OCEAN
LUX.
Paris
R.
MAGINOT LINE
German invasion of Poland September 1, 1939 Start of World War II
Bessarabia and northern Bukovina annexed by U.S.S.R. 1940
Vichy Government established July 1940
FRANCE
Vichy
SLOVAKIA
Partition of Poland September 27, 1939
SWITZ.
Austria
HUNGARY
Bessarabia
RUMANIA
SPAIN
ITALY
Italy declares war on Great Britain and France June 1940
YUGOSLAVIA
Danube
R.
BLACK SEA
PORTUGAL
ADRIATIC SEA
BULGARIA
MEDITERRANEAN SEA
ALBANIA (Italy)
GREECE
TURKEY

© Copyright HAMMOND INCORPORATED. Maplewood, N.J.
Printed in U.S.A.

C

WORLD WAR II EUROPEAN THEATER 1940-1942

Allied Nations and Allied controlled Nations

Axis Powers and Axis controlled Nations

Neutral Nations

Vichy France; Vichy controlled Areas (later to Allies)

Areas occupied by Axis

German Air Strikes

Famous Battles or Sieges

German Advances

Allied Advances

Western Front

Eastern Front

British occupation 1940 U.S. occupation 1941 Independent 1944

ICELAND

SUPPLY ROUTE FROM U.S. & BRITISH COMMONWEALTH

NORWEGIAN SEA

NORWAY

SWEDEN

FINLAND

Murmansk

NORTH SEA

EST.

Leningrad

LATVIA LITH.

1941

Moscow

UNITED KINGDOM

IRELAND

DENMARK

UNION OF SOVIET SOCIALIST REPUBLICS

SUPPLY ROUTE FROM U.S.

London

NETH.

BELG.

Berlin

GERMANY

POLAND

Ukraine

1941

1942

Stalingrad

German U-boat Blockade

LUX.

Paris

SWITZ.

Austria

HUNGARY

RUMANIA

1941

CASPIAN SEA

VICHY FRANCE

SLOVAKIA

ATLANTIC OCEAN

PORTUGAL

SPAIN

ITALY

YUGOSLAVIA

BULGARIA

BLACK SEA

Axis influence removed after British and Russian invasion 1941

IRAN

Corsica

Rome

Sardinia

ALB. (It.)

GREECE

TURKEY Neutral until Feb. 1945

ALLIED SUPPLY ROUTE

IRAN

Gibraltar (Br.)

MEDITERRANEAN

Sicily

Malta (Br.)

Crete

Cyprus (Br.)

SYRIA (Fr.)

IRAQ

Canary Is. (Sp.)

SP. MOR.

Casablanca

Oran

Algiers

Tunis

SEA

PALESTINE (Br. Mandate)

TRANS-JORDAN (Br. Mandate)

Persian Gulf

Pro-Axis government removed by British 1941

MOROCCO (Fr.)

ALGERIA (Fr.)

TUNISIA (Fr.)

Tripoli

El Alamein

Cairo

EGYPT

SAUDI ARABIA Neutral until Mar. 1945

RIO DE ORO (Sp.)

LIBYA (It.)

1941

1942

1940

1942

SCALE OF MILES
0 100 200 300 400 500

Copyright HAMMOND INCORPORATED, Maplewood, N.J. Printed in U.S.A.

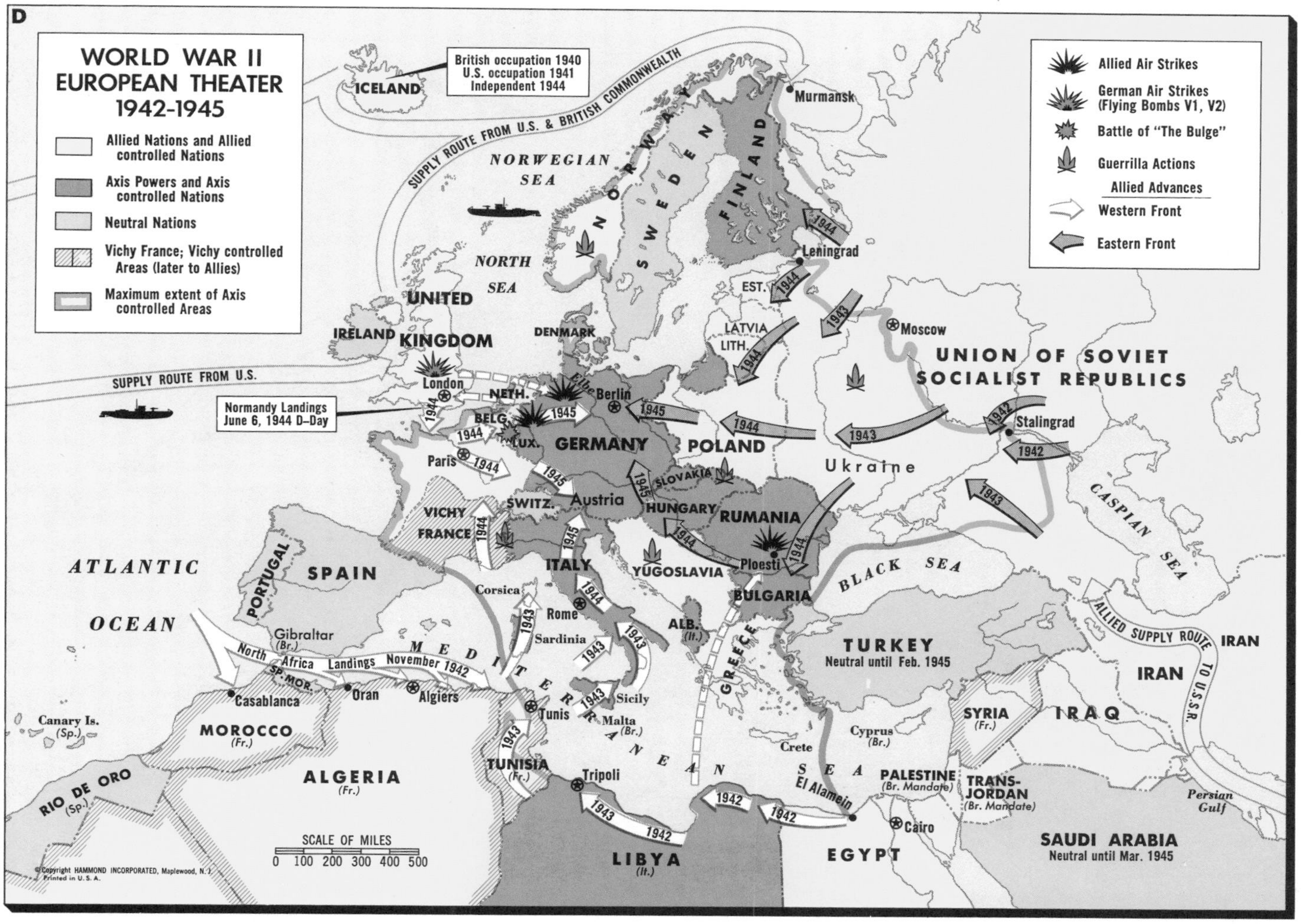

D

WORLD WAR II EUROPEAN THEATER 1942-1945

Allied Nations and Allied controlled Nations

Axis Powers and Axis controlled Nations

Neutral Nations

Vichy France; Vichy controlled Areas (later to Allies)

Maximum extent of Axis controlled Areas

Allied Air Strikes

German Air Strikes (Flying Bombs V1, V2)

Battle of "The Bulge"

Guerrilla Actions

Allied Advances

Western Front

Eastern Front

British occupation 1940 U.S. occupation 1941 Independent 1944

ICELAND

SUPPLY ROUTE FROM U.S. & BRITISH COMMONWEALTH

NORWEGIAN SEA

NORWAY

SWEDEN

FINLAND

Murmansk

NORTH SEA

1944

Leningrad

EST.

1944

LATVIA LITH.

1943

Moscow

UNITED KINGDOM

IRELAND

DENMARK

UNION OF SOVIET SOCIALIST REPUBLICS

SUPPLY ROUTE FROM U.S.

London

NETH.

Elbe

Berlin

1945

1945

1944

Stalingrad

1942

Normandy Landings June 6, 1944 D-Day

BELG.

LUX.

1944

GERMANY

POLAND

1943

Ukraine

1943

Paris

1944

1945

SWITZ.

Austria

1945

SLOVAKIA

HUNGARY

RUMANIA

1944

CASPIAN SEA

VICHY FRANCE

1944

ATLANTIC OCEAN

PORTUGAL

SPAIN

ITALY

1941

YUGOSLAVIA

Ploesti

1944

BULGARIA

BLACK SEA

Corsica

Rome

Sardinia

1943

1943

ALB. (It.)

GREECE

TURKEY Neutral until Feb. 1945

ALLIED SUPPLY ROUTE

IRAN

Gibraltar (Br.)

North Africa Landings November 1942

SP. MOR.

Casablanca

Oran

Algiers

MEDITERRANEAN

Tunis

1943

Sicily

Malta (Br.)

Crete

Cyprus (Br.)

SYRIA (Fr.)

IRAQ

IRAN

Canary Is. (Sp.)

MOROCCO (Fr.)

ALGERIA (Fr.)

TUNISIA (Fr.)

Tripoli

SEA

El Alamein

PALESTINE (Br. Mandate)

TRANS-JORDAN (Br. Mandate)

Persian Gulf

RIO DE ORO (Sp.)

LIBYA (It.)

1943

1942

1942

1942

Cairo

EGYPT

SAUDI ARABIA Neutral until Mar. 1945

SCALE OF MILES
0 100 200 300 400 500

Copyright HAMMOND INCORPORATED, Maplewood, N.J. Printed in U.S.A.

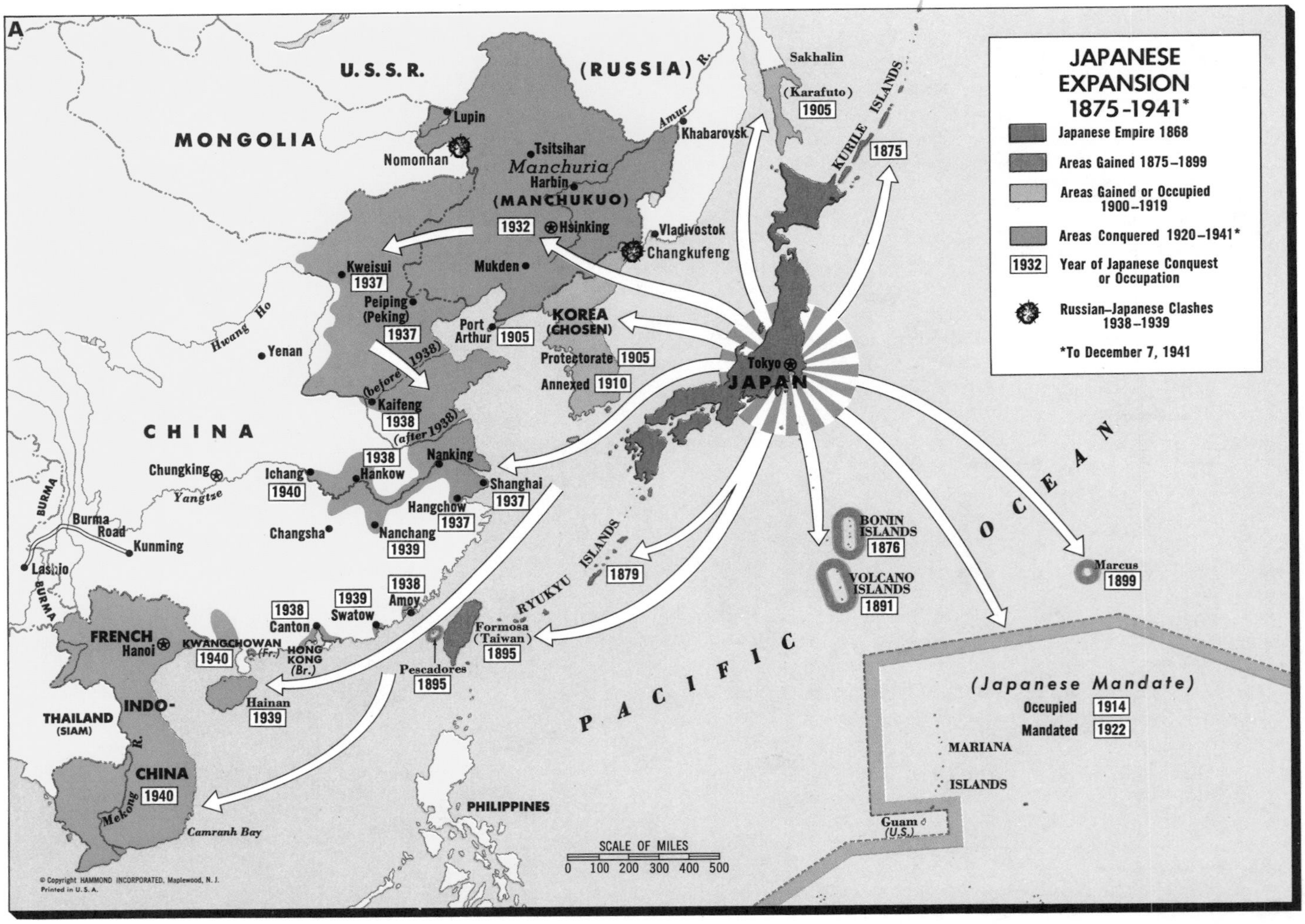

A

JAPANESE EXPANSION 1875-1941*

■	Japanese Empire 1868
■	Areas Gained 1875-1899
▨	Areas Gained or Occupied 1900-1919
▨	Areas Conquered 1920-1941*
1932	Year of Japanese Conquest or Occupation
❂	Russian-Japanese Clashes 1938-1939

*To December 7, 1941

U.S.S.R. (RUSSIA)

MONGOLIA

Lupin
Nomonhan
Tsitsihar
Harbin
Manchuria (MANCHUKUO)
1932
Hsinking
Khabarovsk
Amur R.
Sakhalin (Karafuto) 1905
KURILE ISLANDS
1875

Kweisui 1937
Mukden
Vladivostok
Changkufeng
Port Arthur 1905
KOREA (CHOSEN)
Protectorate 1905
Annexed 1910

Peiping (Peking) 1937
Hwang Ho R.
Yenan

CHINA

Kaifeng (before 1938) 1938
(after 1938)
Nanking 1938
Shanghai 1937

Chungking
Ichang 1940
Hankow 1938
Yangtze
Changsha
Nanchang 1939
Hangchow 1937

Burma Road
Kunming
Lashio
BURMA

Swatow 1939
Canton 1938
Amoy 1938
Kwangchowan (Fr.) 1940
HONG KONG (Br.)

FRENCH
Hanoi
INDO-CHINA 1940
THAILAND (SIAM)
Hainan 1939
Mekong R.
Camranh Bay

RYUKYU ISLANDS 1879
Formosa (Taiwan) 1895
Pescadores 1895

PHILIPPINES

Tokyo
JAPAN

PACIFIC OCEAN

BONIN ISLANDS 1876
VOLCANO ISLANDS 1891
Marcus 1899

(Japanese Mandate)
Occupied 1914
Mandated 1922

MARIANA ISLANDS
Guam (U.S.)

SCALE OF MILES
0 100 200 300 400 500

© Copyright HAMMOND INCORPORATED, Maplewood, N.J.
Printed in U.S.A.

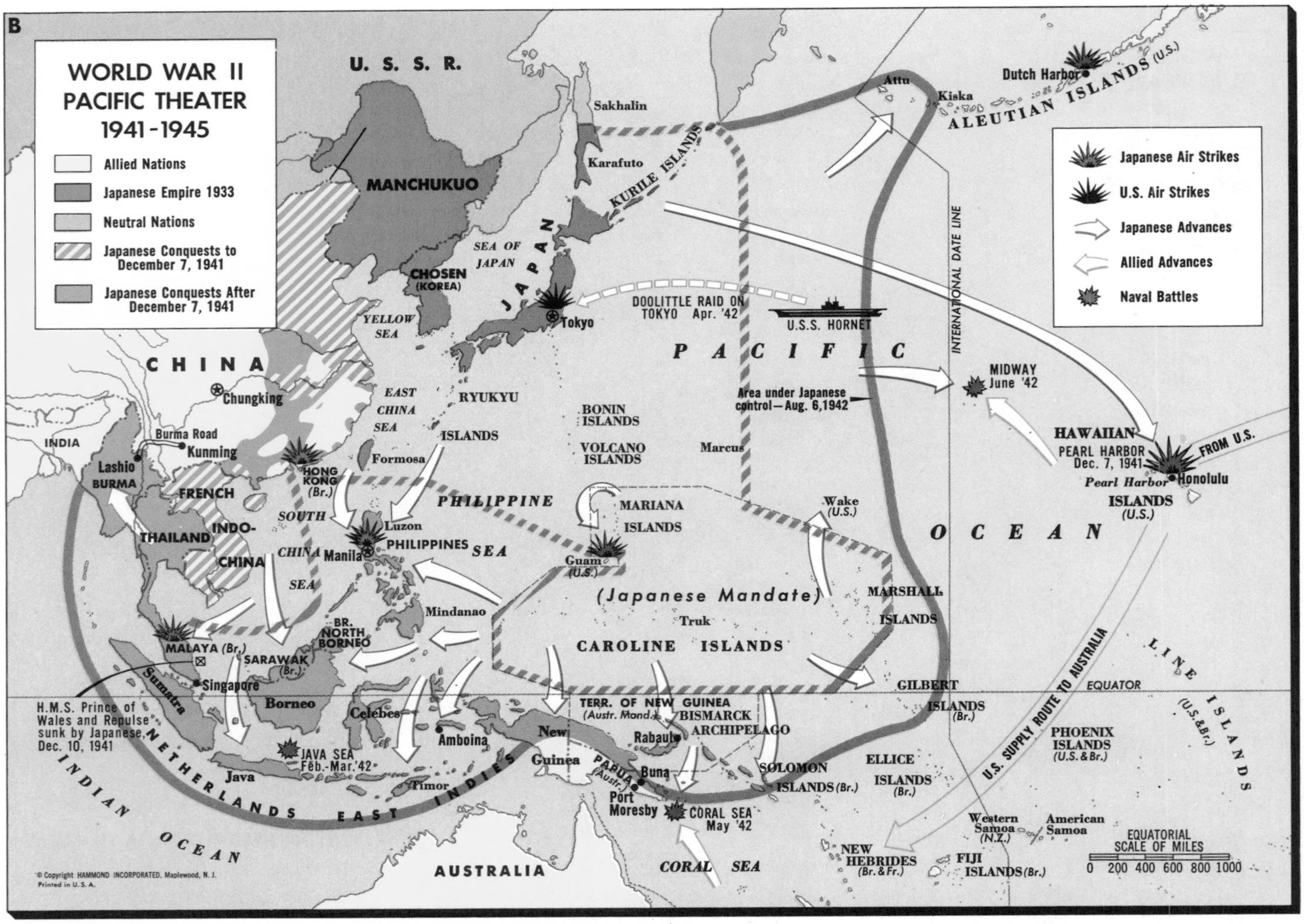

B

WORLD WAR II PACIFIC THEATER 1941-1945

□	Allied Nations
■	Japanese Empire 1933
▨	Neutral Nations
▨	Japanese Conquests to December 7, 1941
■	Japanese Conquests After December 7, 1941

U.S.S.R.

MANCHUKUO
CHOSEN (KOREA)
Sakhalin
Karafuto
KURILE ISLANDS
SEA OF JAPAN
JAPAN
Tokyo
DOOLITTLE RAID ON TOKYO Apr. '42
U.S.S. HORNET

CHINA
Chungking
YELLOW SEA
EAST CHINA SEA
RYUKYU ISLANDS
Formosa
BONIN ISLANDS
VOLCANO ISLANDS
Marcus

Attu
Kiska
Dutch Harbor (U.S.)
ALEUTIAN ISLANDS (U.S.)

INDIA
Burma Road
Kunming
Lashio
BURMA
FRENCH
THAILAND
INDO-CHINA

HONG KONG (Br.)
Luzon
Manila
PHILIPPINES
SOUTH CHINA SEA
Mindanao

Area under Japanese control—Aug. 6, 1942
MIDWAY June '42

INTERNATIONAL DATE LINE

HAWAIIAN
PEARL HARBOR Dec. 7, 1941
Pearl Harbor FROM U.S.
Honolulu
ISLANDS (U.S.)

PHILIPPINE SEA
MARIANA ISLANDS
Guam (U.S.)
Wake (U.S.)

(Japanese Mandate)
Truk
CAROLINE ISLANDS

MARSHALL ISLANDS

PACIFIC OCEAN

MALAYA (Br.)
SARAWAK (Br.)
BR. NORTH BORNEO
Singapore
Sumatra
Borneo

H.M.S. Prince of Wales and Repulse sunk by Japanese Dec. 10, 1941

NETHERLANDS EAST INDIES

Celebes
Java
JAVA SEA Feb.-Mar. '42
Timor
Amboina

New Guinea
PAPUA (Aust.)
Port Moresby
Buna

TERR. OF NEW GUINEA (Austr. Mand.)
BISMARCK ARCHIPELAGO
Rabaul

SOLOMON ISLANDS (Br.)
CORAL SEA May '42

GILBERT ISLANDS (Br.)
ELLICE ISLANDS (Br.)

U.S. SUPPLY ROUTE TO AUSTRALIA
EQUATOR

PHOENIX ISLANDS (U.S. & Br.)

LINE ISLANDS (U.S. & Br.)

INDIAN OCEAN

AUSTRALIA

CORAL SEA

NEW HEBRIDES (Br. & Fr.)
FIJI ISLANDS (Br.)
Western Samoa (N.Z.)
American Samoa

EQUATORIAL SCALE OF MILES
0 200 400 600 800 1000

✹	Japanese Air Strikes
✹	U.S. Air Strikes
⇨	Japanese Advances
⇦	Allied Advances
✸	Naval Battles

© Copyright HAMMOND INCORPORATED, Maplewood, N.J.
Printed in U.S.A.

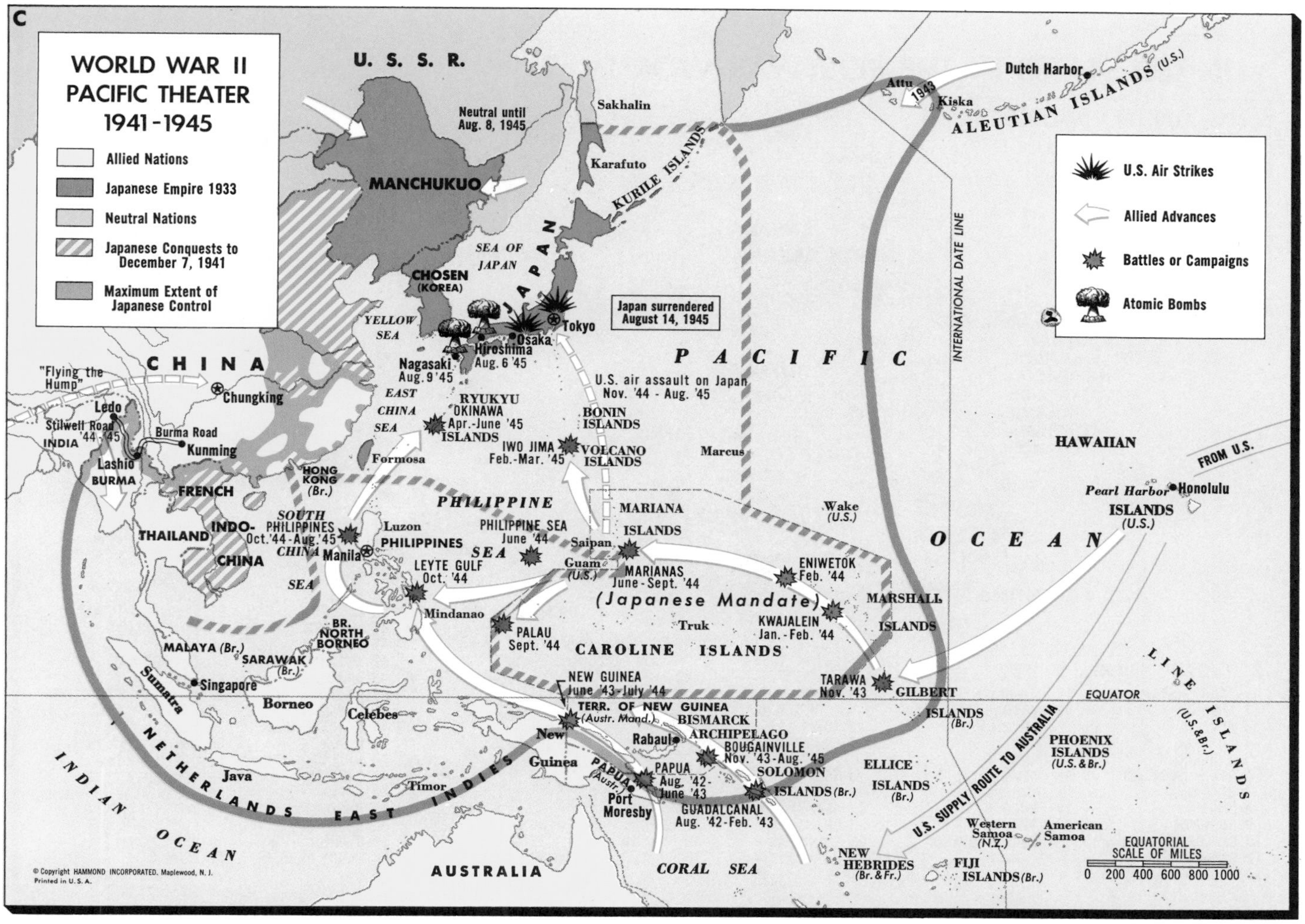

C

WORLD WAR II PACIFIC THEATER 1941-1945

Allied Nations
Japanese Empire 1933
Neutral Nations
Japanese Conquests to December 7, 1941
Maximum Extent of Japanese Control

U.S. Air Strikes
Allied Advances
Battles or Campaigns
Atomic Bombs

U. S. S. R.

Sakhalin
Neutral until Aug. 8, 1945
Karafuto
MANCHUKUO
KURILE ISLANDS

Attu 1943
Kiska
Dutch Harbor
ALEUTIAN ISLANDS (U.S.)

SEA OF JAPAN
JAPAN
CHOSEN (KOREA)

YELLOW SEA
Tokyo
Japan surrendered August 14, 1945

CHINA
"Flying the Hump"
Stilwell Road
Ledo '44-'45
INDIA
Burma Road
Kunming
Lashio
BURMA
FRENCH INDO-CHINA
THAILAND

Chungking

Osaka Aug.6 '45
Nagasaki Aug.9 '45
Hiroshima

U.S. air assault on Japan Nov. '44 - Aug. '45

EAST CHINA SEA
RYUKYU
OKINAWA Apr.-June '45 ISLANDS
IWO JIMA Feb.-Mar. '45
Formosa
HONG KONG (Br.)

BONIN ISLANDS
VOLCANO ISLANDS
Marcus

PACIFIC

HAWAIIAN

INTERNATIONAL DATE LINE

FROM U.S.

SOUTH CHINA SEA
PHILIPPINES Oct.'44-Aug.'45
Luzon
PHILIPPINES
Manila
LEYTE GULF Oct. '44
PHILIPPINE SEA June '44

MARIANA ISLANDS
Saipan
Guam (U.S.)
MARIANAS June-Sept. '44
(Japanese Mandate)

Wake (U.S.)

Pearl Harbor
Honolulu
ISLANDS (U.S.)

OCEAN

MALAYA (Br.)
SARAWAK (Br.)
BR. NORTH BORNEO
Mindanao
PALAU Sept. '44
Truk
CAROLINE ISLANDS
KWAJALEIN Jan.-Feb. '44
ENIWETOK Feb. '44
MARSHALL ISLANDS

LINE ISLANDS (U.S.)

EQUATOR

Singapore
Sumatra
Borneo
Celebes
Java
Timor
NETHERLANDS EAST INDIES

New Guinea
NEW GUINEA June '43-July '44
TERR. OF NEW GUINEA (Austr. Mand.)
PAPUA (Austr.)
PAPUA Aug. '42 June '43
Port Moresby
Rabaul
BISMARCK ARCHIPELAGO
BOUGAINVILLE Nov. '43-Aug.'45
SOLOMON ISLANDS (Br.)
GUADALCANAL Aug. '42-Feb. '43

TARAWA Nov. '43
GILBERT ISLANDS (Br.)

ELLICE ISLANDS (Br.)

PHOENIX ISLANDS (U.S.&Br.)

U.S. SUPPLY ROUTE TO AUSTRALIA

INDIAN OCEAN

AUSTRALIA

CORAL SEA

NEW HEBRIDES (Br.&Fr.)
FIJI ISLANDS (Br.)

Western Samoa (N.Z.)
American Samoa

EQUATORIAL SCALE OF MILES
0 200 400 600 800 1000

© Copyright HAMMOND INCORPORATED. Maplewood, N.J.
Printed in U.S.A.

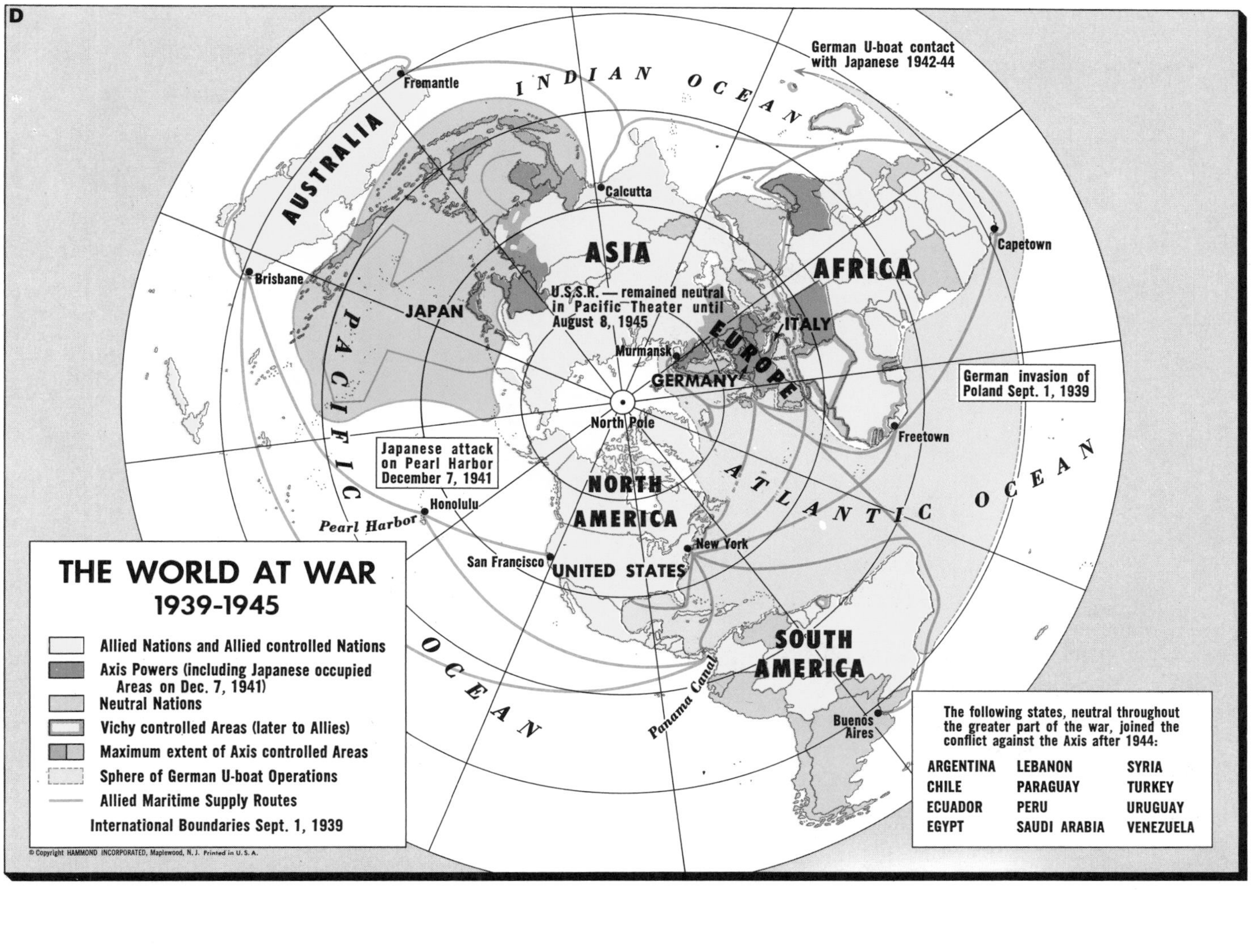

D

German U-boat contact with Japanese 1942-44

Fremantle
INDIAN OCEAN
Calcutta
Capetown

AUSTRALIA
PACIFIC
ASIA
AFRICA
JAPAN
U.S.S.R. — remained neutral in Pacific Theater until August 8, 1945
ITALY
EUROPE
GERMANY
Murmansk
Brisbane

German invasion of Poland Sept. 1, 1939

Japanese attack on Pearl Harbor December 7, 1941

North Pole

Freetown

Honolulu
Pearl Harbor
NORTH AMERICA
San Francisco
UNITED STATES
New York
ATLANTIC OCEAN

OCEAN
Panama Canal
SOUTH AMERICA

Buenos Aires

THE WORLD AT WAR 1939-1945

Allied Nations and Allied controlled Nations
Axis Powers (including Japanese occupied Areas on Dec. 7, 1941)
Neutral Nations
Vichy controlled Areas (later to Allies)
Maximum extent of Axis controlled Areas
Sphere of German U-boat Operations
Allied Maritime Supply Routes
International Boundaries Sept. 1, 1939

© Copyright HAMMOND INCORPORATED, Maplewood, N.J. Printed in U.S.A.

The following states, neutral throughout the greater part of the war, joined the conflict against the Axis after 1944:

ARGENTINA	LEBANON	SYRIA
CHILE	PARAGUAY	TURKEY
ECUADOR	PERU	URUGUAY
EGYPT	SAUDI ARABIA	VENEZUELA

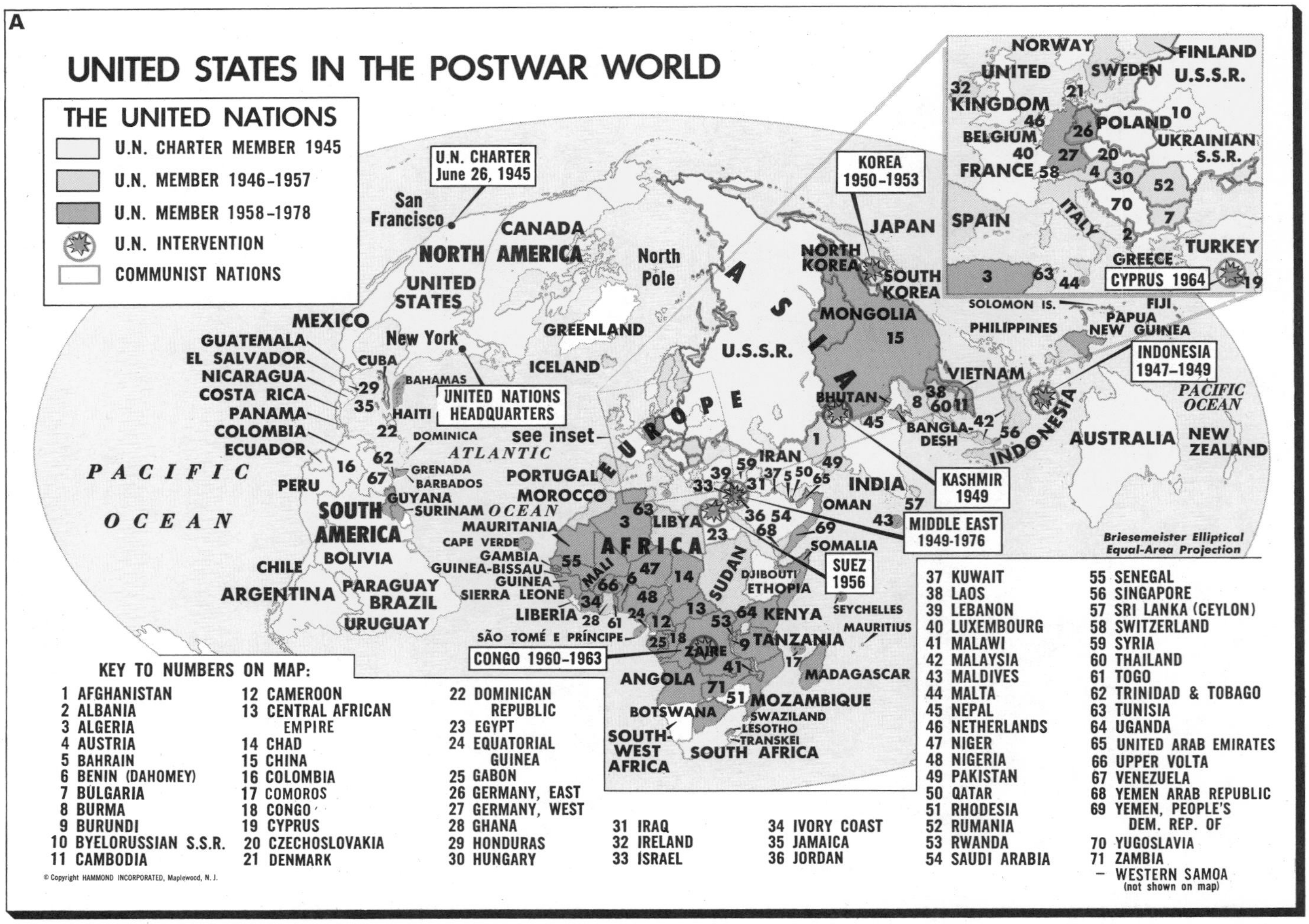

A

UNITED STATES IN THE POSTWAR WORLD

THE UNITED NATIONS

- U.N. CHARTER MEMBER 1945
- U.N. MEMBER 1946–1957
- U.N. MEMBER 1958–1978
- ⊛ U.N. INTERVENTION
- COMMUNIST NATIONS

U.N. CHARTER June 26, 1945

San Francisco

KOREA 1950–1953

CANADA
NORTH AMERICA
UNITED STATES
North Pole
GREENLAND
ICELAND

JAPAN
NORTH KOREA
SOUTH KOREA
MONGOLIA 15
U.S.S.R.
VIETNAM
BHUTAN
BANGLA-DESH

MEXICO
New York
GUATEMALA
EL SALVADOR
NICARAGUA
COSTA RICA
PANAMA
COLOMBIA
ECUADOR
CUBA
BAHAMAS
HAITI
DOMINICA
UNITED NATIONS HEADQUARTERS
see inset

INDONESIA 1947–1949
PACIFIC OCEAN
AUSTRALIA
NEW ZEALAND

SOLOMON IS.
PHILIPPINES
PAPUA NEW GUINEA
FIJI

PERU
PACIFIC OCEAN
SOUTH AMERICA
GRENADA
BARBADOS
GUYANA
SURINAM
PORTUGAL
MOROCCO
ATLANTIC OCEAN
MAURITANIA
CAPE VERDE
GAMBIA
GUINEA-BISSAU
GUINEA
SIERRA LEONE
LIBERIA
SÃO TOMÉ E PRÍNCIPE

IRAN
INDIA
OMAN
KASHMIR 1949
MIDDLE EAST 1949–1976

LIBYA
AFRICA
SUDAN
MALI
DJIBOUTI
ETHIOPIA
KENYA
SOMALIA
SEYCHELLES
MAURITIUS
TANZANIA
MADAGASCAR

SUEZ 1956

CONGO 1960–1963

ANGOLA
BOTSWANA
SOUTH-WEST AFRICA
SOUTH AFRICA
SWAZILAND
LESOTHO
TRANSKEI
ZAIRE
MOZAMBIQUE

CHILE
BOLIVIA
PARAGUAY
ARGENTINA
BRAZIL
URUGUAY

Briesemeister Elliptical Equal-Area Projection

Inset:
NORWAY
SWEDEN
FINLAND
UNITED KINGDOM 32
21
U.S.S.R.
POLAND 10
BELGIUM 40
46
26
UKRAINIAN S.S.R.
FRANCE 58
27
4
30
52
SPAIN
20
70
7
GREECE
ITALY
3
63
44
TURKEY
CYPRUS 1964
19

KEY TO NUMBERS ON MAP:

1 AFGHANISTAN	12 CAMEROON	22 DOMINICAN REPUBLIC
2 ALBANIA	13 CENTRAL AFRICAN EMPIRE	23 EGYPT
3 ALGERIA	14 CHAD	24 EQUATORIAL GUINEA
4 AUSTRIA	15 CHINA	25 GABON
5 BAHRAIN	16 COLOMBIA	26 GERMANY, EAST
6 BENIN (DAHOMEY)	17 COMOROS	27 GERMANY, WEST
7 BULGARIA	18 CONGO	28 GHANA
8 BURMA	19 CYPRUS	29 HONDURAS
9 BURUNDI	20 CZECHOSLOVAKIA	30 HUNGARY
10 BYELORUSSIAN S.S.R.	21 DENMARK	
11 CAMBODIA		

31 IRAQ	34 IVORY COAST
32 IRELAND	35 JAMAICA
33 ISRAEL	36 JORDAN

37 KUWAIT	55 SENEGAL
38 LAOS	56 SINGAPORE
39 LEBANON	57 SRI LANKA (CEYLON)
40 LUXEMBOURG	58 SWITZERLAND
41 MALAWI	59 SYRIA
42 MALAYSIA	60 THAILAND
43 MALDIVES	61 TOGO
44 MALTA	62 TRINIDAD & TOBAGO
45 NEPAL	63 TUNISIA
46 NETHERLANDS	64 UGANDA
47 NIGER	65 UNITED ARAB EMIRATES
48 NIGERIA	66 UPPER VOLTA
49 PAKISTAN	67 VENEZUELA
50 QATAR	68 YEMEN ARAB REPUBLIC
51 RHODESIA	69 YEMEN, PEOPLE'S DEM. REP. OF
52 RUMANIA	70 YUGOSLAVIA
53 RWANDA	71 ZAMBIA
54 SAUDI ARABIA	— WESTERN SAMOA (not shown on map)

© Copyright HAMMOND INCORPORATED, Maplewood, N.J.

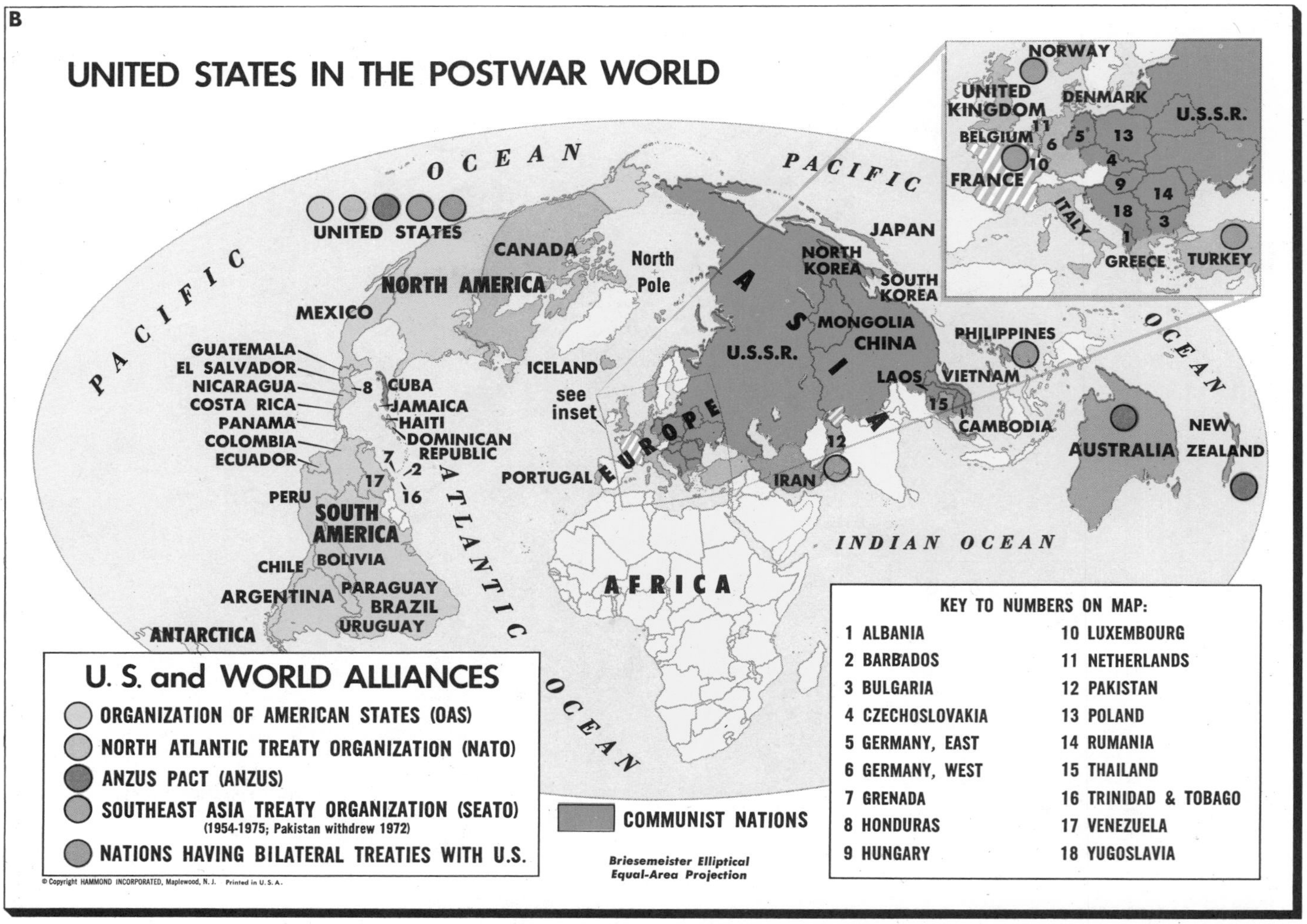

B

UNITED STATES IN THE POSTWAR WORLD

PACIFIC OCEAN
UNITED STATES
CANADA
NORTH AMERICA
North Pole
ICELAND
see inset
MEXICO

PACIFIC OCEAN
JAPAN
NORTH KOREA
SOUTH KOREA
MONGOLIA
CHINA
U.S.S.R.
LAOS
VIETNAM
CAMBODIA
PHILIPPINES
AUSTRALIA
NEW ZEALAND

GUATEMALA
EL SALVADOR
NICARAGUA
COSTA RICA
PANAMA
COLOMBIA
ECUADOR
CUBA
JAMAICA
HAITI
DOMINICAN REPUBLIC

PERU
SOUTH AMERICA
ATLANTIC OCEAN
PORTUGAL
EUROPE
ASIA
IRAN
AFRICA
INDIAN OCEAN

CHILE
BOLIVIA
ARGENTINA
PARAGUAY
BRAZIL
URUGUAY
ANTARCTICA

Inset:
NORWAY
UNITED KINGDOM
DENMARK
U.S.S.R.
BELGIUM 11
6 5 13
FRANCE 10
4
9 14
ITALY
18 3
1
GREECE
TURKEY

U. S. and WORLD ALLIANCES

- ORGANIZATION OF AMERICAN STATES (OAS)
- NORTH ATLANTIC TREATY ORGANIZATION (NATO)
- ANZUS PACT (ANZUS)
- SOUTHEAST ASIA TREATY ORGANIZATION (SEATO) (1954–1975; Pakistan withdrew 1972)
- NATIONS HAVING BILATERAL TREATIES WITH U.S.

COMMUNIST NATIONS

KEY TO NUMBERS ON MAP:

1 ALBANIA	10 LUXEMBOURG
2 BARBADOS	11 NETHERLANDS
3 BULGARIA	12 PAKISTAN
4 CZECHOSLOVAKIA	13 POLAND
5 GERMANY, EAST	14 RUMANIA
6 GERMANY, WEST	15 THAILAND
7 GRENADA	16 TRINIDAD & TOBAGO
8 HONDURAS	17 VENEZUELA
9 HUNGARY	18 YUGOSLAVIA

Briesemeister Elliptical Equal-Area Projection

© Copyright HAMMOND INCORPORATED, Maplewood, N.J.   Printed in U.S.A.

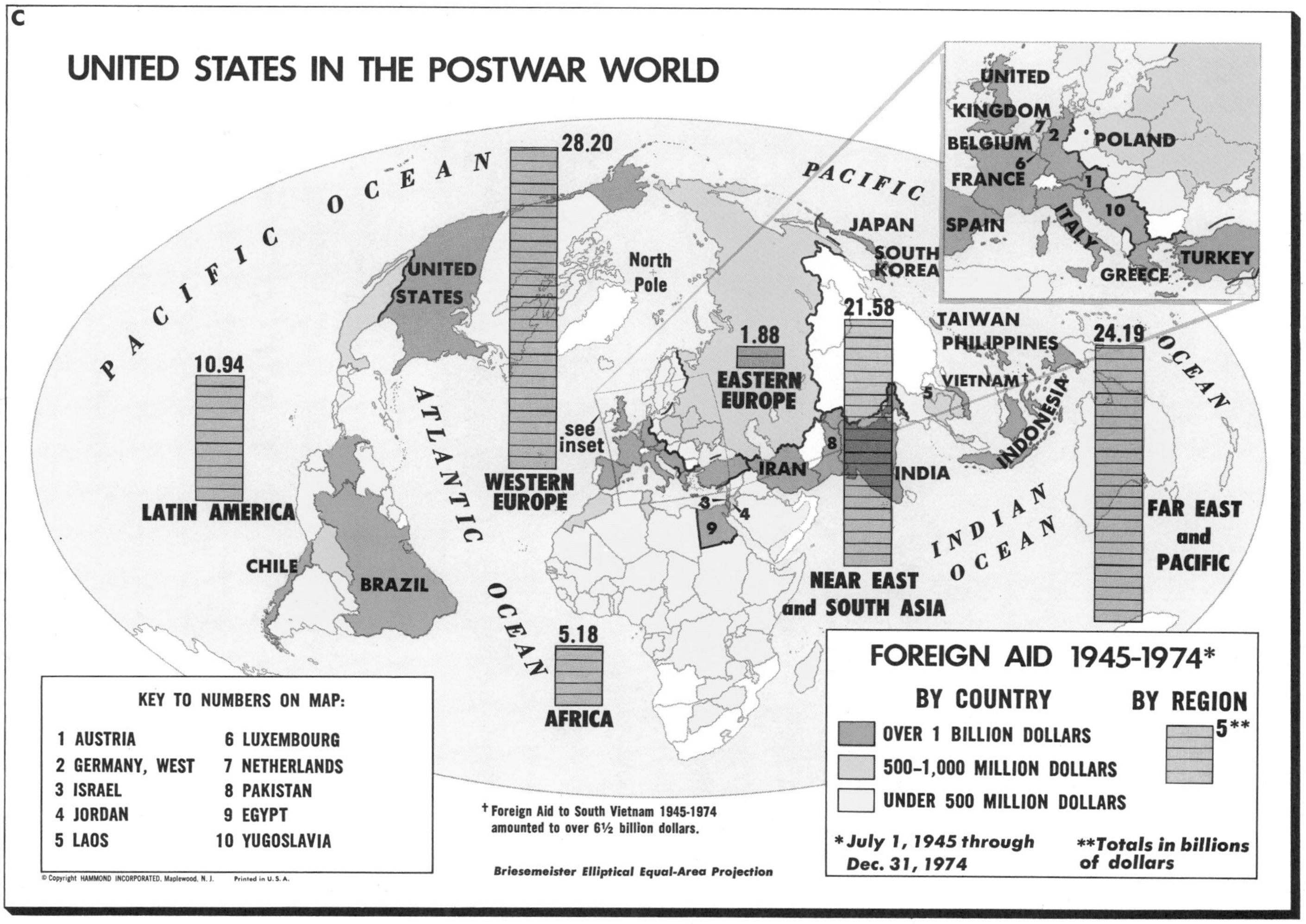

C

UNITED STATES IN THE POSTWAR WORLD

Inset labels:
UNITED KINGDOM
BELGIUM 7 2 POLAND
FRANCE 6 1
SPAIN 10
ITALY
GREECE TURKEY

PACIFIC OCEAN

ATLANTIC OCEAN

INDIAN OCEAN

28.20
UNITED STATES
North Pole

10.94
LATIN AMERICA
CHILE
BRAZIL

1.88
EASTERN EUROPE

see inset

WESTERN EUROPE

21.58

JAPAN
SOUTH KOREA
TAIWAN
PHILIPPINES
VIETNAM† 5
INDONESIA

IRAN
8
INDIA
3 4
9

24.19
FAR EAST and PACIFIC

NEAR EAST and SOUTH ASIA

5.18
AFRICA

KEY TO NUMBERS ON MAP:

1	AUSTRIA	6	LUXEMBOURG
2	GERMANY, WEST	7	NETHERLANDS
3	ISRAEL	8	PAKISTAN
4	JORDAN	9	EGYPT
5	LAOS	10	YUGOSLAVIA

© Copyright HAMMOND INCORPORATED, Maplewood, N.J.   Printed in U.S.A.

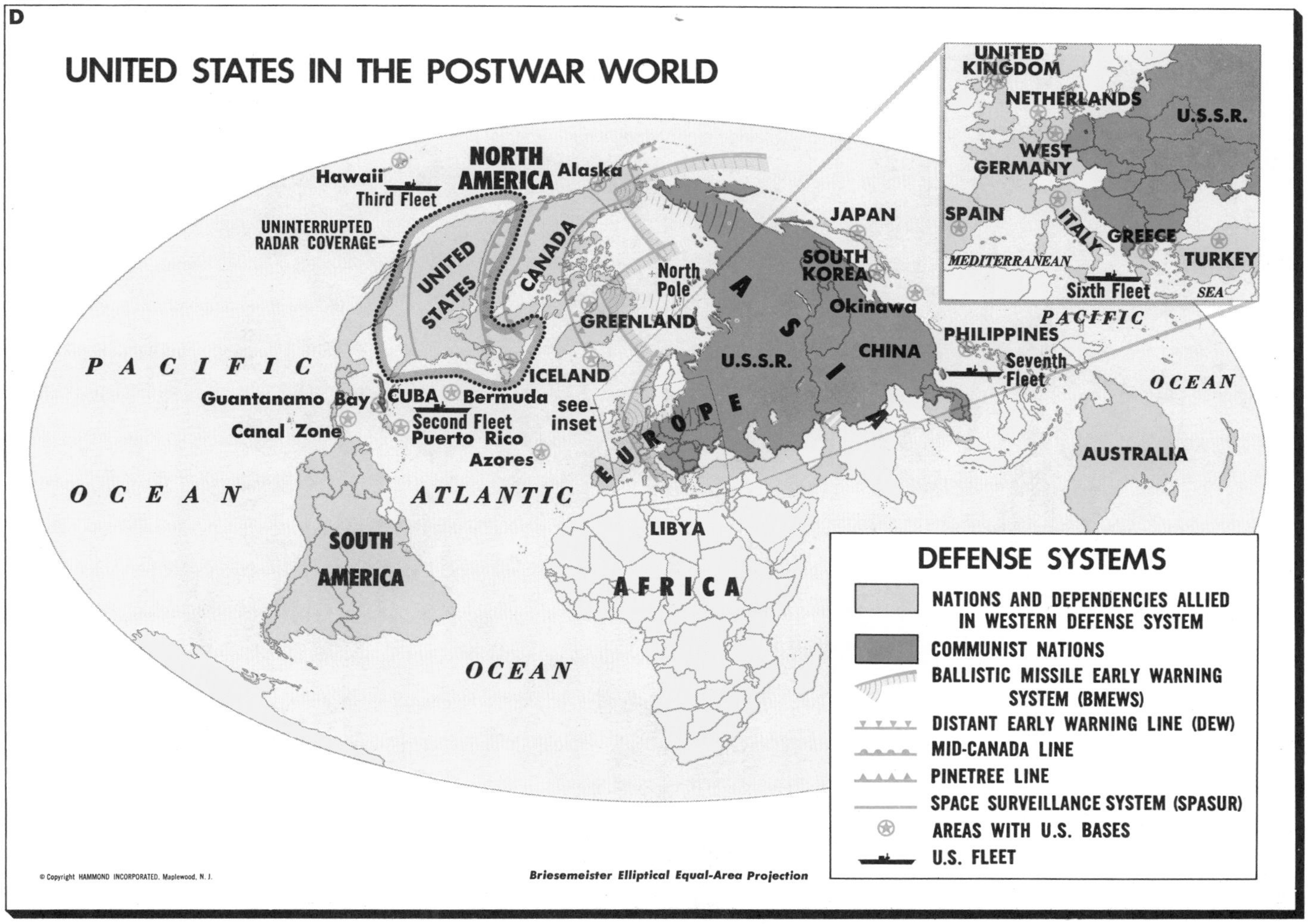

† Foreign Aid to South Vietnam 1945-1974 amounted to over 6½ billion dollars.

Briesemeister Elliptical Equal-Area Projection

FOREIGN AID 1945-1974*

BY COUNTRY
- OVER 1 BILLION DOLLARS
- 500–1,000 MILLION DOLLARS
- UNDER 500 MILLION DOLLARS

BY REGION
- 5**

*July 1, 1945 through Dec. 31, 1974

**Totals in billions of dollars

D

UNITED STATES IN THE POSTWAR WORLD

Inset labels:
UNITED KINGDOM
NETHERLANDS
U.S.S.R.
WEST GERMANY
SPAIN
ITALY
GREECE
TURKEY
MEDITERRANEAN
Sixth Fleet
SEA
PACIFIC

Hawaii
Third Fleet
NORTH AMERICA
Alaska

UNINTERRUPTED RADAR COVERAGE

UNITED STATES
CANADA
GREENLAND
North Pole

ASIA

JAPAN
SOUTH KOREA
Okinawa
CHINA
PHILIPPINES
Seventh Fleet

U.S.S.R.

ICELAND
CUBA Bermuda
see inset
Guantanamo Bay
Second Fleet
Canal Zone
Puerto Rico
Azores

EUROPE

PACIFIC OCEAN

ATLANTIC

SOUTH AMERICA

LIBYA
AFRICA

OCEAN

AUSTRALIA

OCEAN

DEFENSE SYSTEMS

- NATIONS AND DEPENDENCIES ALLIED IN WESTERN DEFENSE SYSTEM
- COMMUNIST NATIONS
- BALLISTIC MISSILE EARLY WARNING SYSTEM (BMEWS)
- DISTANT EARLY WARNING LINE (DEW)
- MID-CANADA LINE
- PINETREE LINE
- SPACE SURVEILLANCE SYSTEM (SPASUR)
- AREAS WITH U.S. BASES
- U.S. FLEET

© Copyright HAMMOND INCORPORATED, Maplewood, N.J.

Briesemeister Elliptical Equal-Area Projection

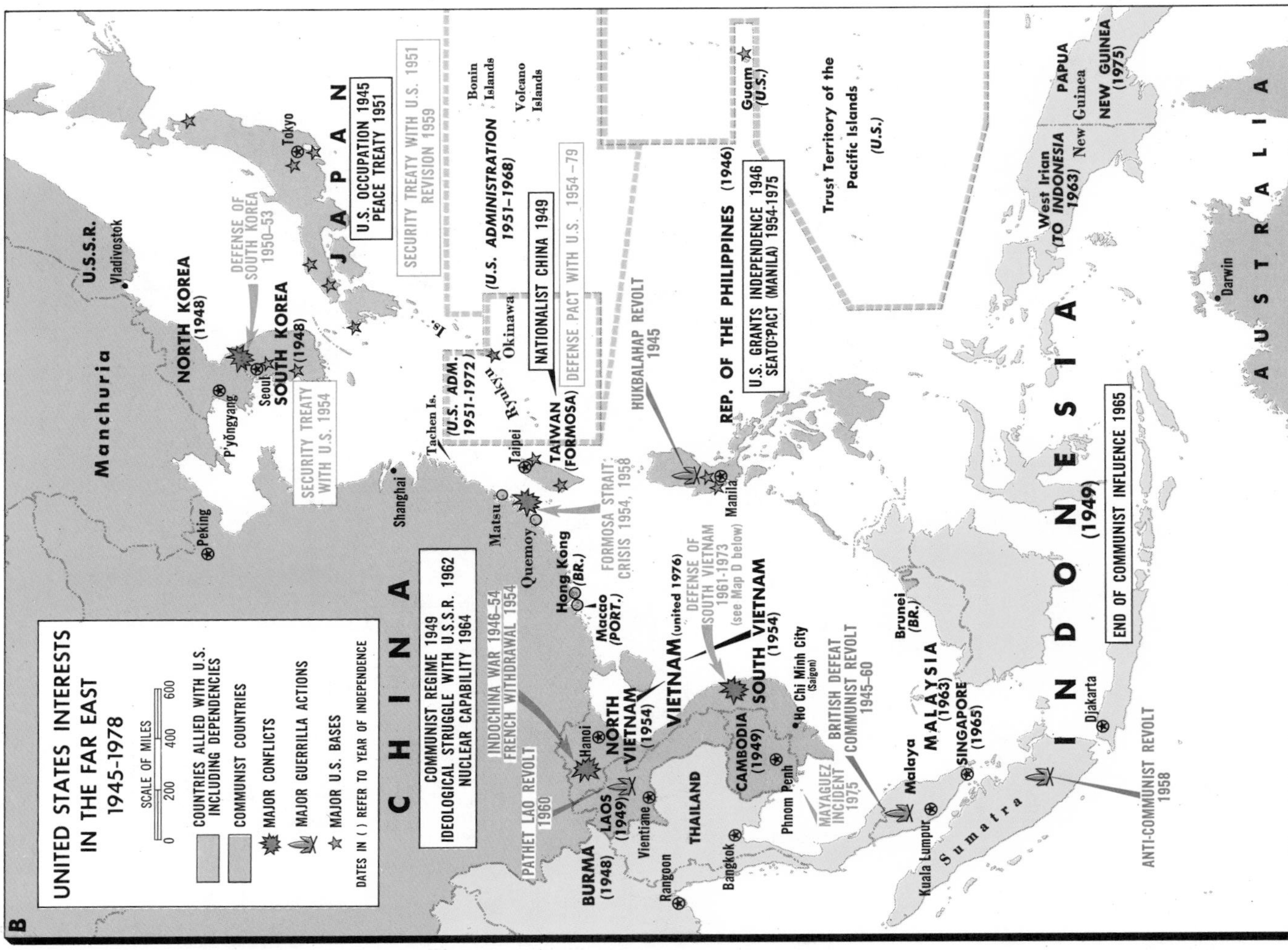

B. UNITED STATES INTERESTS IN THE FAR EAST 1945-1978

SCALE OF MILES
0 200 400 600

Legend:
- COUNTRIES ALLIED WITH U.S. INCLUDING DEPENDENCIES
- COMMUNIST COUNTRIES
- MAJOR CONFLICTS
- MAJOR GUERRILLA ACTIONS
- MAJOR U.S. BASES
- DATES IN ( ) REFER TO YEAR OF INDEPENDENCE

U.S.S.R. — Vladivostok
Manchuria
Peking
NORTH KOREA (1948) — Pyongyang
SOUTH KOREA (1948) — Seoul
SECURITY TREATY WITH U.S. 1954
DEFENSE OF SOUTH KOREA 1950-53
JAPAN — Tokyo
U.S. OCCUPATION 1945 PEACE TREATY 1951
SECURITY TREATY WITH U.S. 1951 REVISION 1959
Bonin Islands
Volcano Islands
(U.S. ADMINISTRATION 1951-1968)
Okinawa (U.S. ADM. 1951-1972)
NATIONALIST CHINA 1949
DEFENSE PACT WITH U.S. 1954-79
TAIWAN (FORMOSA) — Taipei
Tachen Is.
Shanghai
Matsu
Quemoy
FORMOSA STRAIT CRISIS 1954, 1958
CHINA
COMMUNIST REGIME 1949
IDEOLOGICAL STRUGGLE WITH U.S.S.R. 1962
NUCLEAR CAPABILITY 1964
Hong Kong (BR.)
Macao (PORT.)
INDOCHINA WAR 1946-54 FRENCH WITHDRAWAL 1954
PATHET LAO REVOLT 1960
NORTH VIETNAM (1954) — Hanoi
LAOS (1949) — Vientiane
VIETNAM (united 1976)
DEFENSE OF SOUTH VIETNAM 1961-1973 (see Map D below)
SOUTH VIETNAM (1954)
Ho Chi Minh City (Saigon)
BURMA (1948) — Rangoon
THAILAND — Bangkok
CAMBODIA (1949) — Phnom Penh
MAYAGUEZ INCIDENT 1975
BRITISH DEFEAT COMMUNIST REVOLT 1945-60
Brunei (BR.)
MALAYSIA (1963)
Malaya
Kuala Lumpur
SINGAPORE (1965)
Sumatra
ANTI-COMMUNIST REVOLT 1958
INDONESIA (1949)
Djakarta
END OF COMMUNIST INFLUENCE 1965
REP. OF THE PHILIPPINES (1946)
HUKBALAHAP REVOLT 1945
Manila
U.S. GRANTS INDEPENDENCE 1946 SEATO-PACT (MANILA) 1954-1975
Guam (U.S.)
Trust Territory of the Pacific Islands (U.S.)
West Irian (TO INDONESIA 1963) New Guinea
PAPUA NEW GUINEA (1975)
AUSTRALIA — Darwin

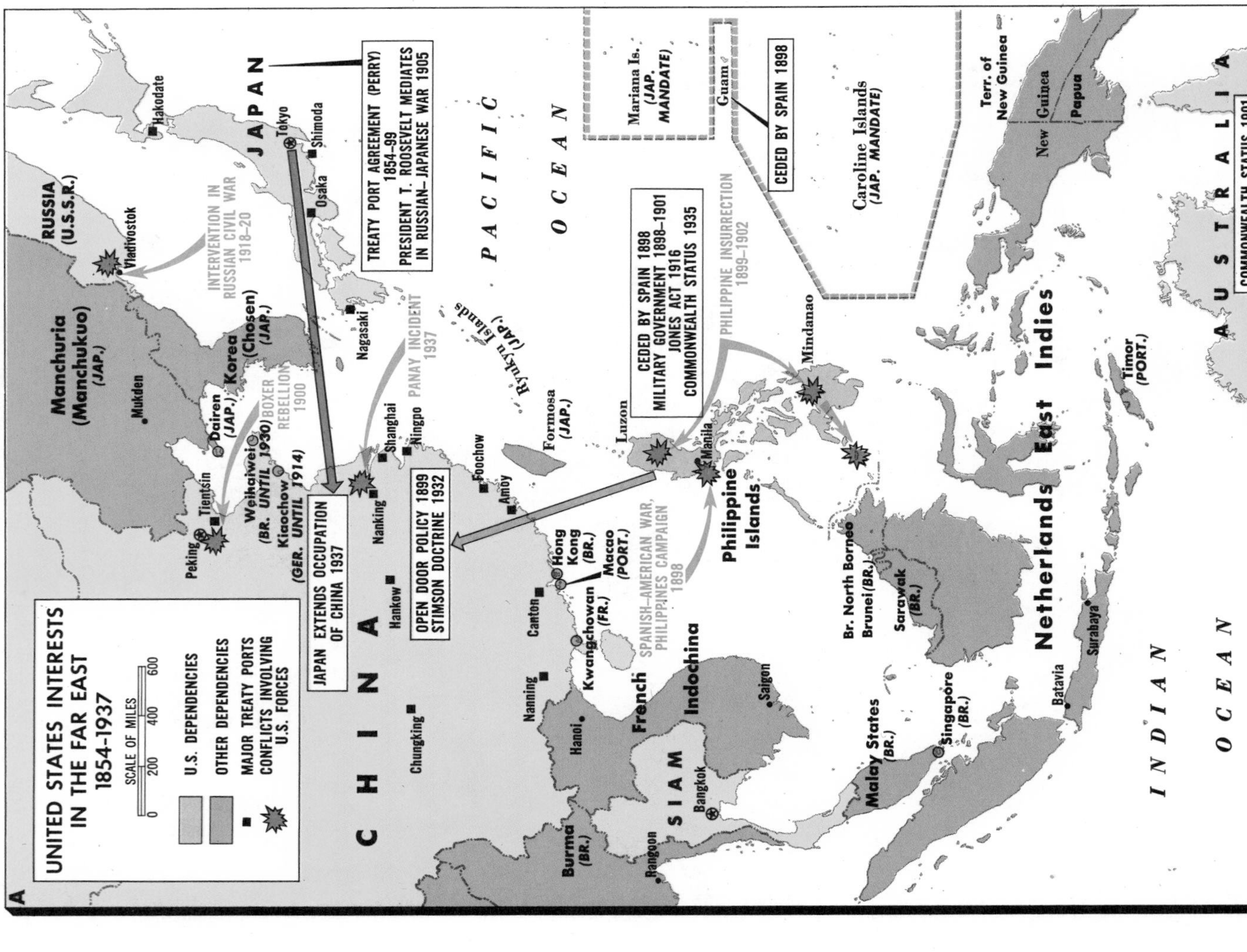

A. UNITED STATES INTERESTS IN THE FAR EAST 1854-1937

SCALE OF MILES
0 200 400 600

Legend:
- U.S. DEPENDENCIES
- OTHER DEPENDENCIES
- MAJOR TREATY PORTS
- CONFLICTS INVOLVING U.S. FORCES

RUSSIA (U.S.S.R.) — Vladivostok
INTERVENTION IN RUSSIAN CIVIL WAR 1918-20
Manchuria (Manchukuo) (JAP.)
Mukden
Korea (Chosen) (JAP.)
Hakodate
JAPAN — Tokyo — Shimoda
Osaka
Nagasaki
TREATY PORT AGREEMENT (PERRY) 1854-99
PRESIDENT T. ROOSEVELT MEDIATES IN RUSSIAN-JAPANESE WAR 1905
Ryukyu Islands (JAP.)
Peking
Tientsin
Weihaiwei (BR. UNTIL 1930)
Kiaochow (GER. UNTIL 1914)
Dairen (JAP.)
BOXER REBELLION 1900
JAPAN EXTENDS OCCUPATION OF CHINA 1937
CHINA
Nanking
Shanghai
Ningpo
Hankow
Foochow
Amoy
Formosa (JAP.)
PANAY INCIDENT 1937
OPEN DOOR POLICY 1899 STIMSON DOCTRINE 1932
Chungking
Nanning
Canton
Hong Kong (BR.)
Macao (PORT.)
Kwangchowan (FR.)
BURMA (BR.) — Rangoon
SIAM — Bangkok
Hanoi
French Indochina
Saigon
Malay States (BR.)
Singapore (BR.)
Philippine Islands
Luzon
Manila
SPANISH-AMERICAN WAR, PHILIPPINES CAMPAIGN 1898
CEDED BY SPAIN 1898 MILITARY GOVERNMENT 1898-1901 JONES ACT 1916 COMMONWEALTH STATUS 1935
PHILIPPINE INSURRECTION 1899-1902
Mindanao
Br. North Borneo (BR.)
Brunei (BR.)
Sarawak (BR.)
Netherlands East Indies
Batavia
Surabaya
Timor (PORT.)
Mariana Is. (JAP. MANDATE)
Guam
CEDED BY SPAIN 1898
Caroline Islands (JAP. MANDATE)
PACIFIC OCEAN
INDIAN OCEAN
Terr. of New Guinea
New Guinea — Papua
AUSTRALIA
COMMONWEALTH STATUS 1901

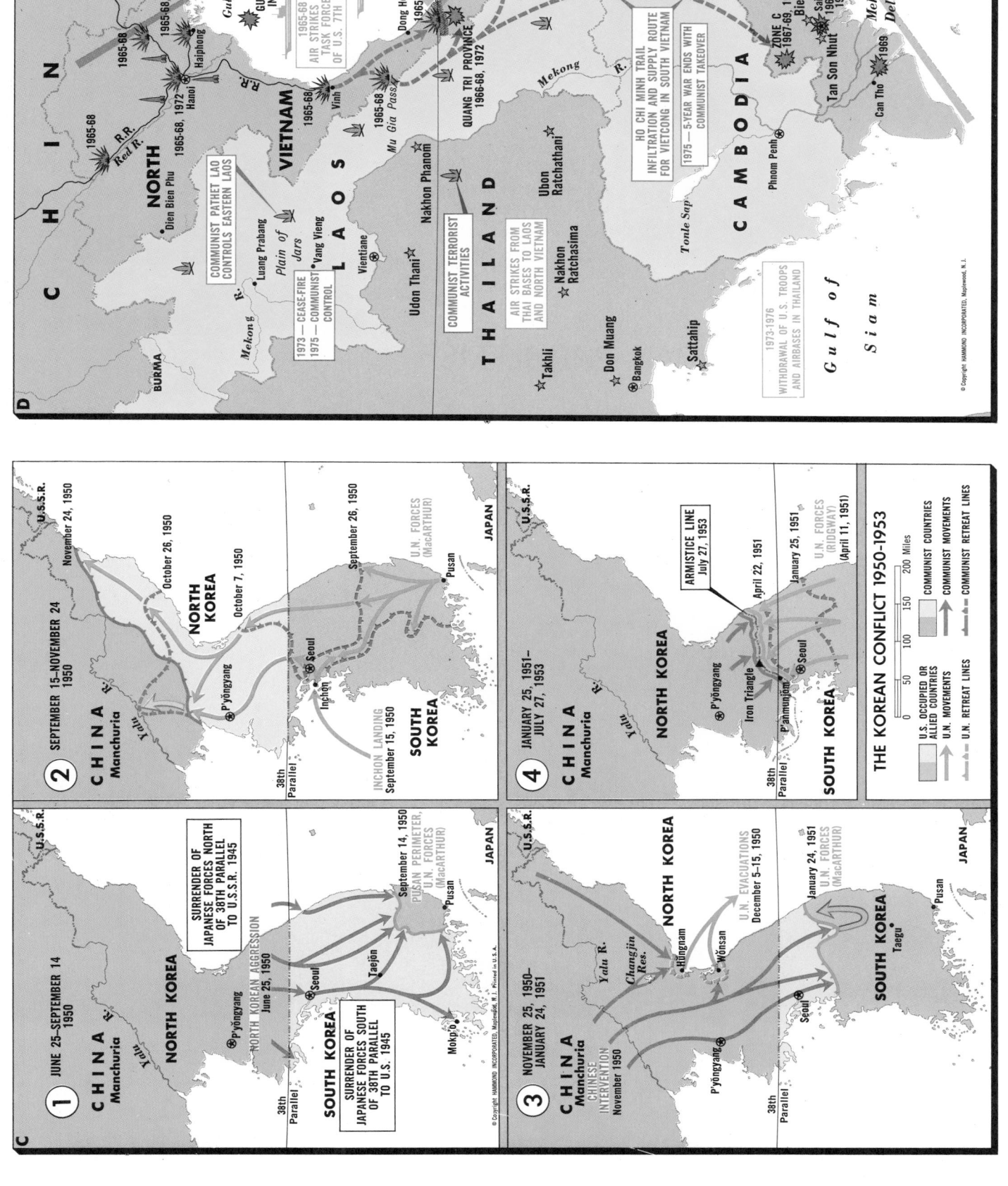

A

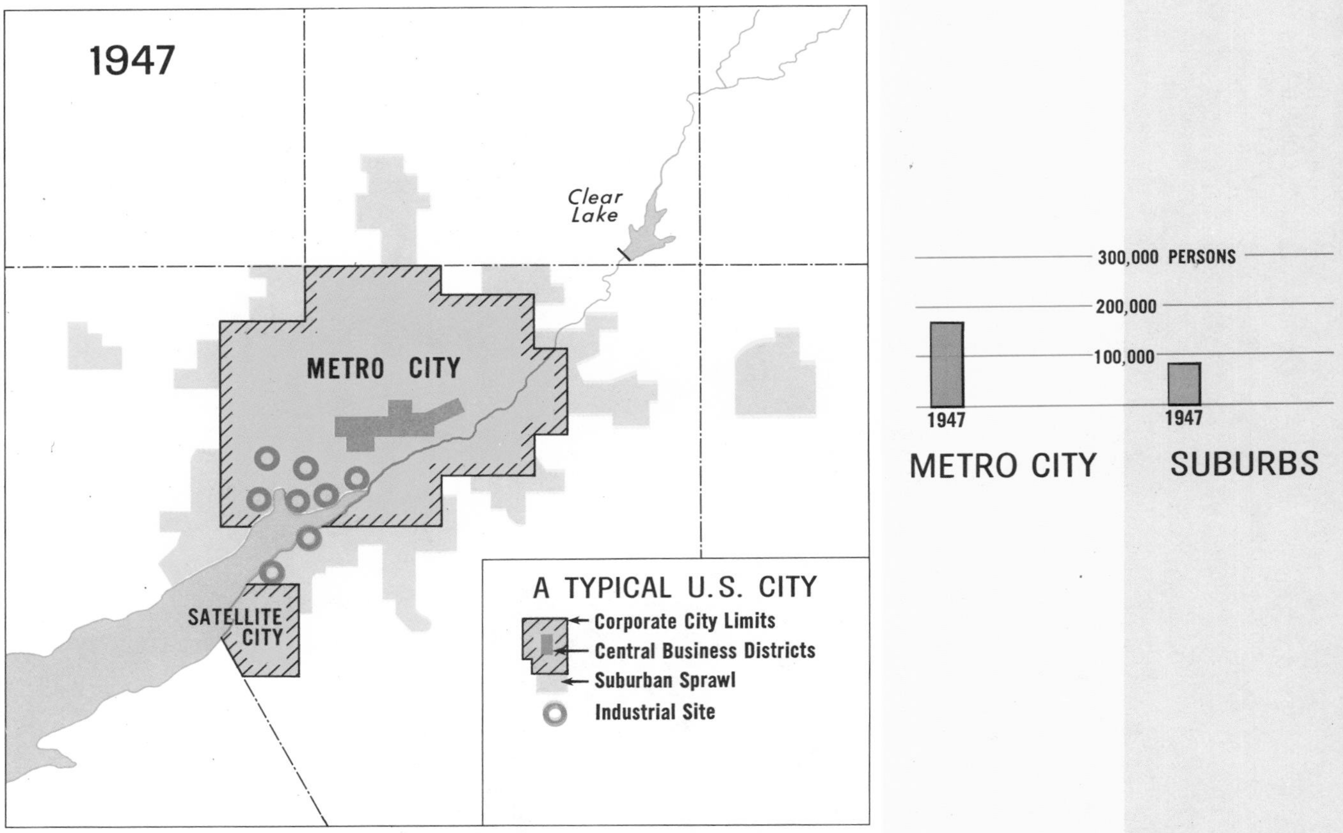

1947

Clear
Lake

METRO CITY

SATELLITE
CITY

A TYPICAL U.S. CITY
← Corporate City Limits
← Central Business Districts
← Suburban Sprawl
○ Industrial Site

300,000 PERSONS
200,000
100,000

1947   1947
METRO CITY   SUBURBS

MODERN URBAN PROBLEMS

© Copyright HAMMOND INCORPORATED, Maplewood, N. J.

B

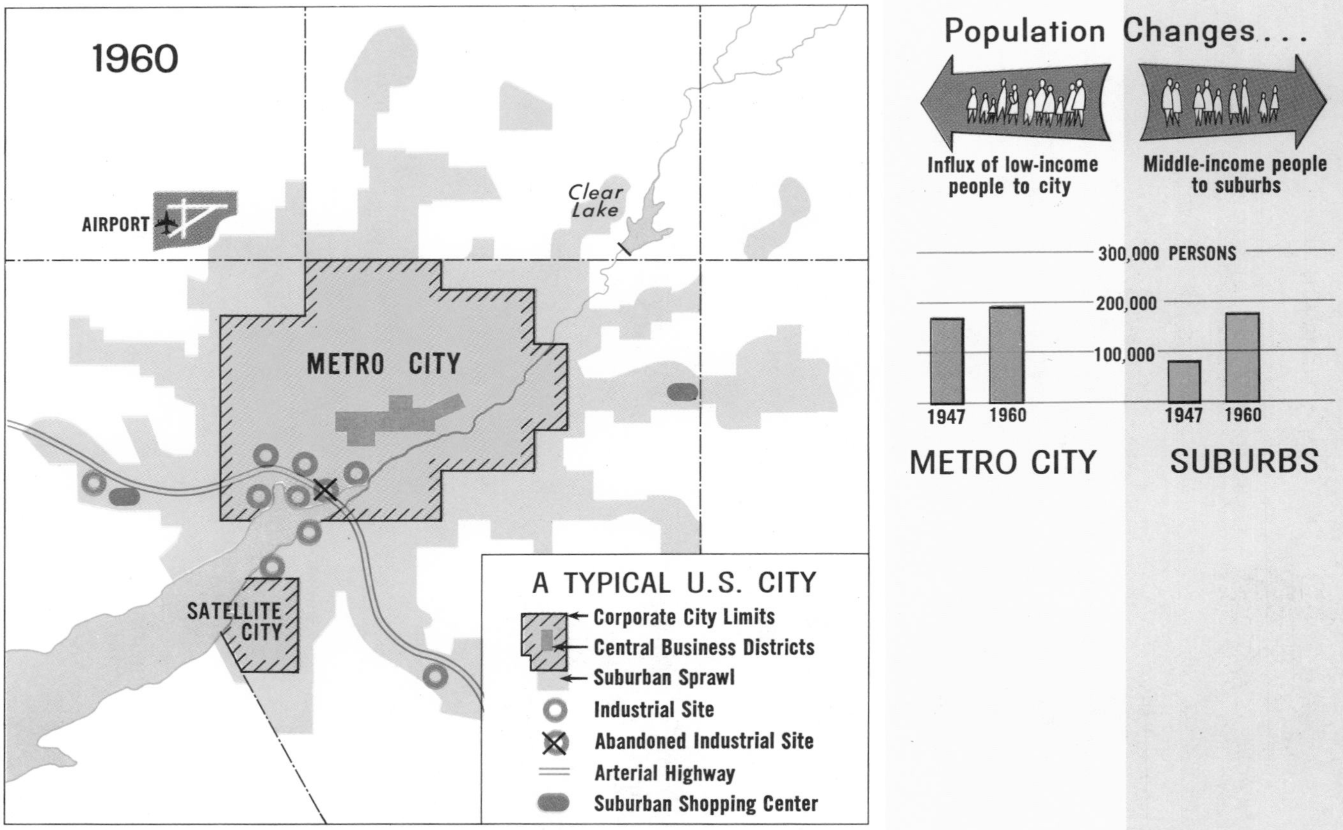

1960

AIRPORT

Clear
Lake

METRO CITY

SATELLITE
CITY

A TYPICAL U.S. CITY
← Corporate City Limits
← Central Business Districts
← Suburban Sprawl
○ Industrial Site
✕ Abandoned Industrial Site
═ Arterial Highway
◼ Suburban Shopping Center

Population Changes...

Influx of low-income
people to city

Middle-income people
to suburbs

300,000 PERSONS
200,000
100,000

1947 1960   1947 1960
METRO CITY   SUBURBS

MODERN URBAN PROBLEMS

© Copyright HAMMOND INCORPORATED, Maplewood, N. J.

C

1975

RESERVOIR

CLEAR LAKE PARK

Clear Lake

AIRPORT

METRO CITY

SATELLITE CITY

A TYPICAL U.S. CITY
- Corporate City Limits
- Central Business Districts
- Suburban Sprawl
- ○ Industrial Site
- ⊗ Abandoned Industrial Site
- Arterial Highway
- Suburban Shopping Center

MODERN URBAN PROBLEMS

© Copyright HAMMOND INCORPORATED, Maplewood, N.J.

Population Changes...

Influx of low-income people to city

Middle-income people to suburbs

300,000 PERSONS
200,000
100,000

1947 1960 1975   1947 1960 1975

METRO CITY   **SUBURBS**

...Physical Changes

Residential Blight | New Housing Developments

Obsolete Industrial Plants | New Industrial Plants

Declining Downtown Stores | New Shopping Centers

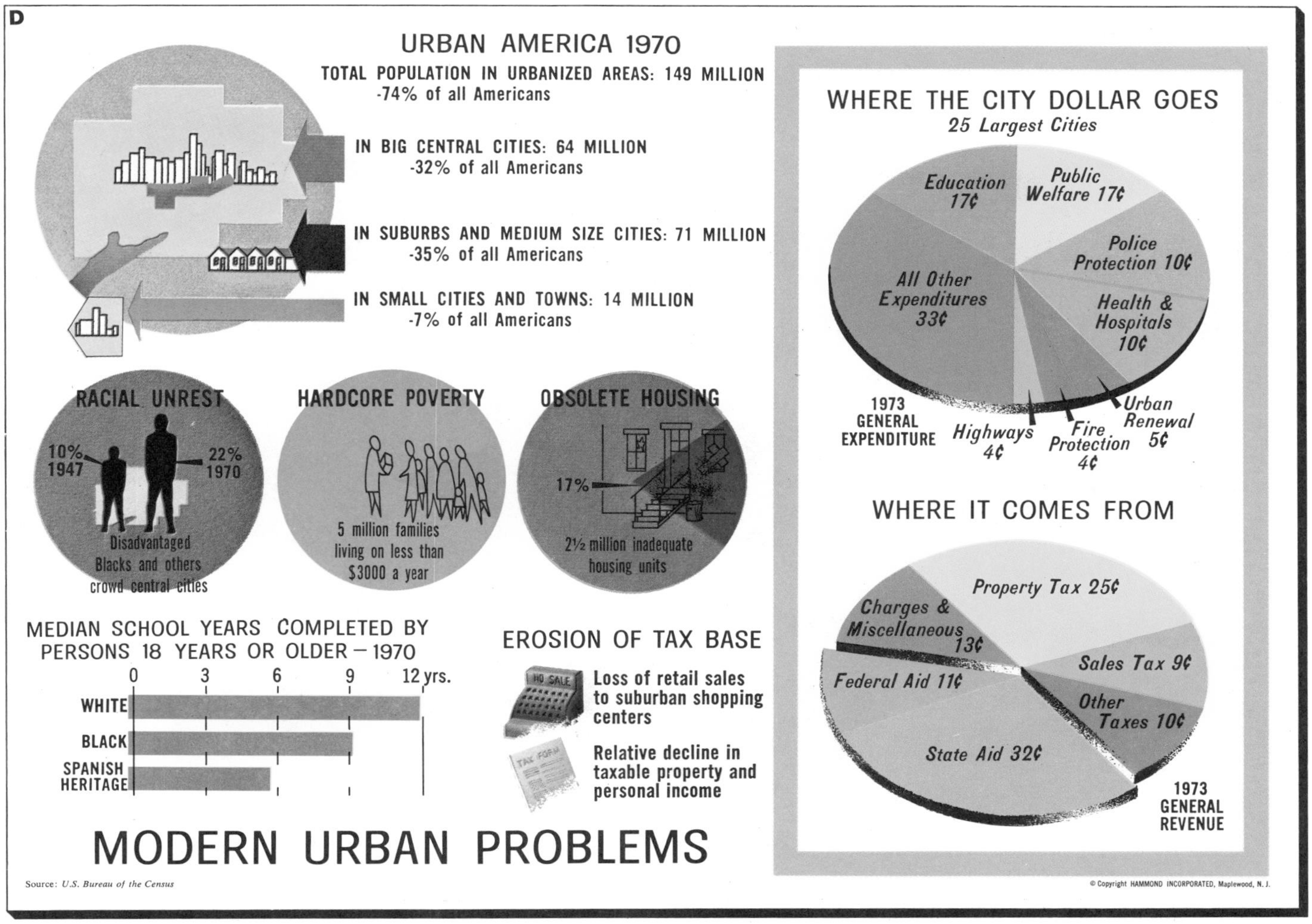

D

URBAN AMERICA 1970
TOTAL POPULATION IN URBANIZED AREAS: 149 MILLION
-74% of all Americans

IN BIG CENTRAL CITIES: 64 MILLION
-32% of all Americans

IN SUBURBS AND MEDIUM SIZE CITIES: 71 MILLION
-35% of all Americans

IN SMALL CITIES AND TOWNS: 14 MILLION
-7% of all Americans

RACIAL UNREST
10% 1947   22% 1970
Disadvantaged Blacks and others crowd central cities

HARDCORE POVERTY
5 million families living on less than $3000 a year

OBSOLETE HOUSING
17%
2½ million inadequate housing units

MEDIAN SCHOOL YEARS COMPLETED BY PERSONS 18 YEARS OR OLDER—1970
0 3 6 9 12 yrs.
WHITE
BLACK
SPANISH HERITAGE

EROSION OF TAX BASE
Loss of retail sales to suburban shopping centers

Relative decline in taxable property and personal income

WHERE THE CITY DOLLAR GOES
25 Largest Cities
Education 17¢
Public Welfare 17¢
Police Protection 10¢
All Other Expenditures 33¢
Health & Hospitals 10¢
Highways 4¢
Fire Protection 4¢
Urban Renewal 5¢
1973 GENERAL EXPENDITURE

WHERE IT COMES FROM
Property Tax 25¢
Charges & Miscellaneous 13¢
Sales Tax 9¢
Federal Aid 11¢
Other Taxes 10¢
State Aid 32¢
1973 GENERAL REVENUE

MODERN URBAN PROBLEMS

Source: *U.S. Bureau of the Census*

© Copyright HAMMOND INCORPORATED, Maplewood, N.J.

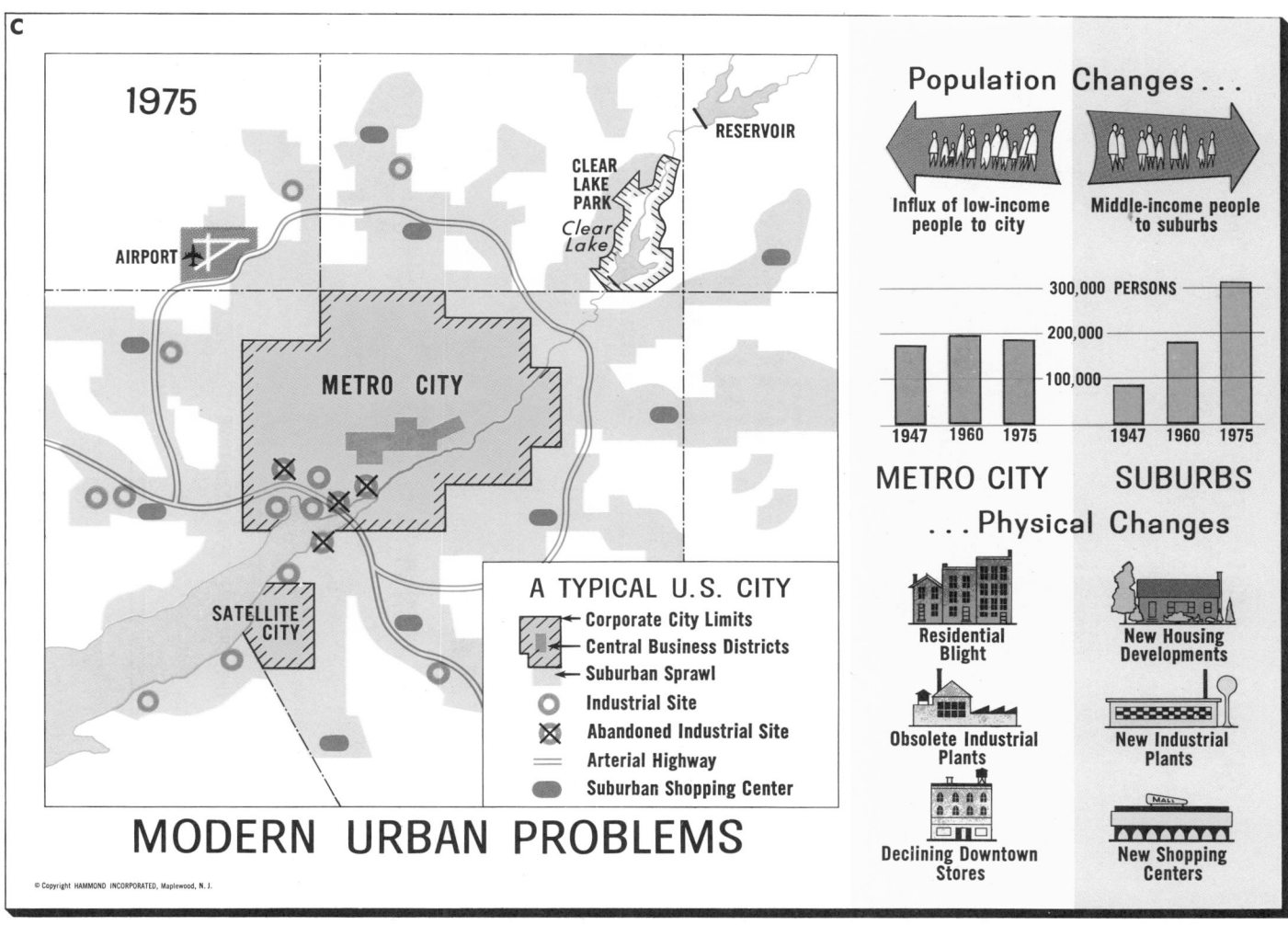

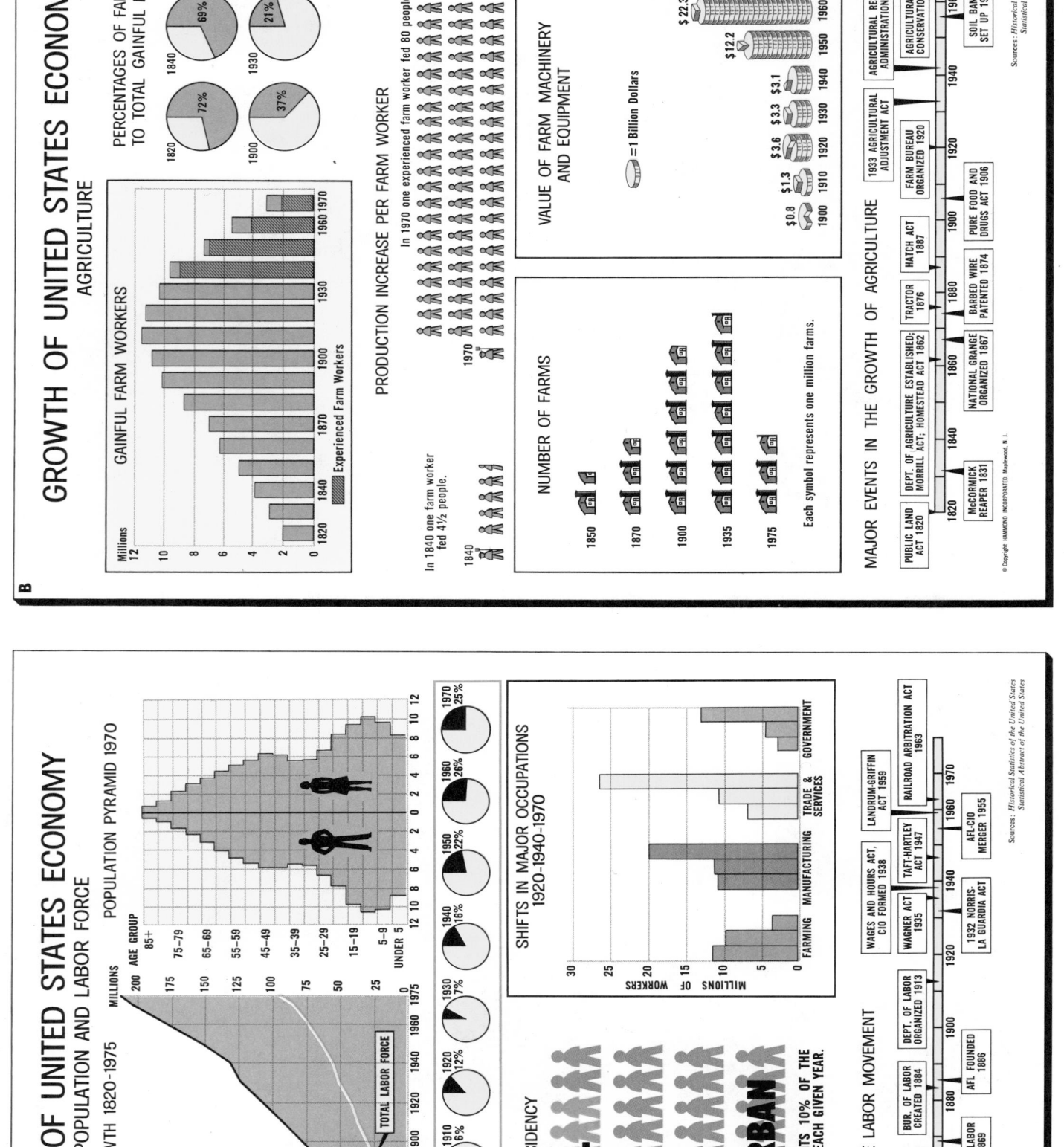

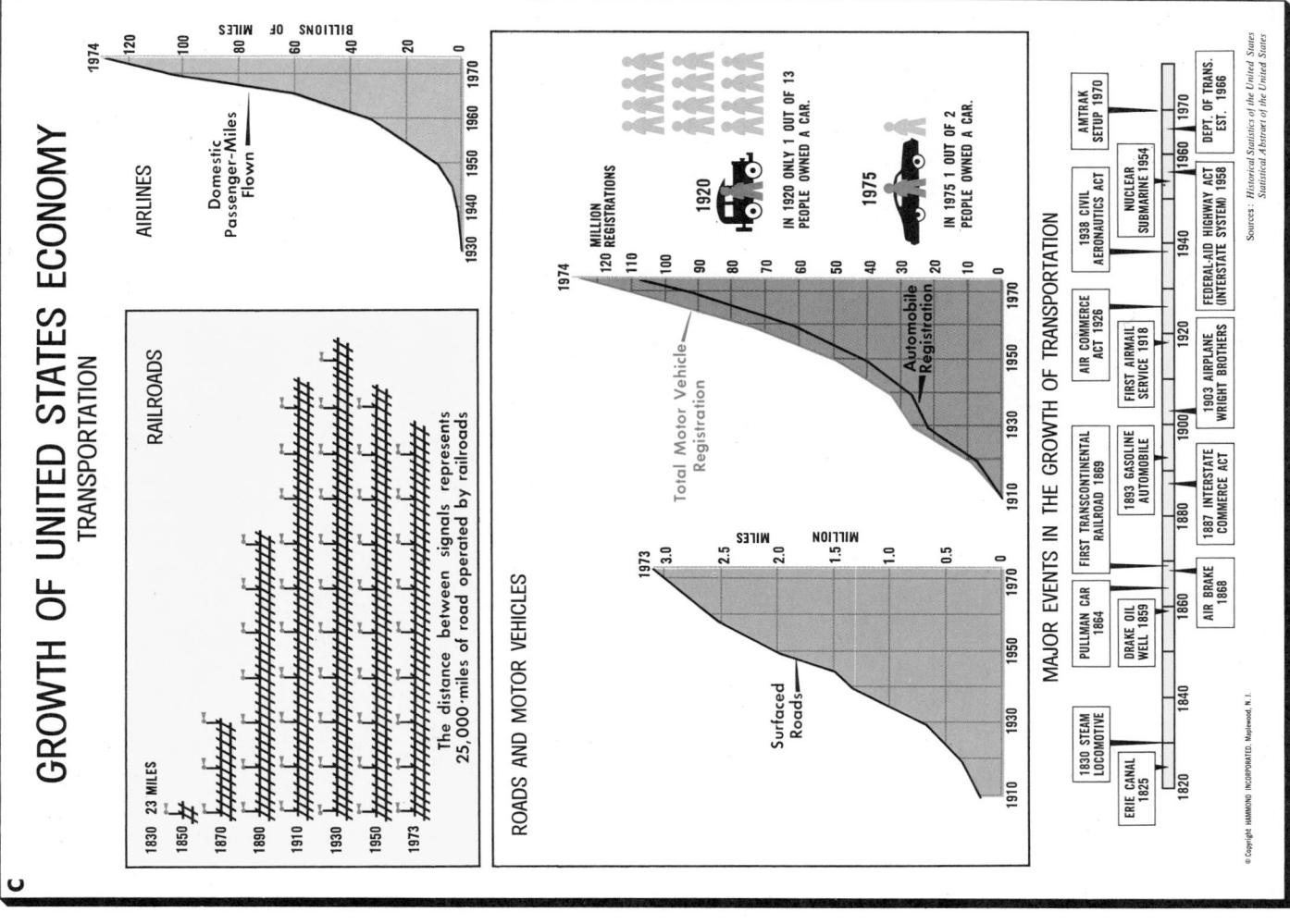

GROWTH OF UNITED STATES ECONOMY
NATIONAL PRODUCT AND INCOME

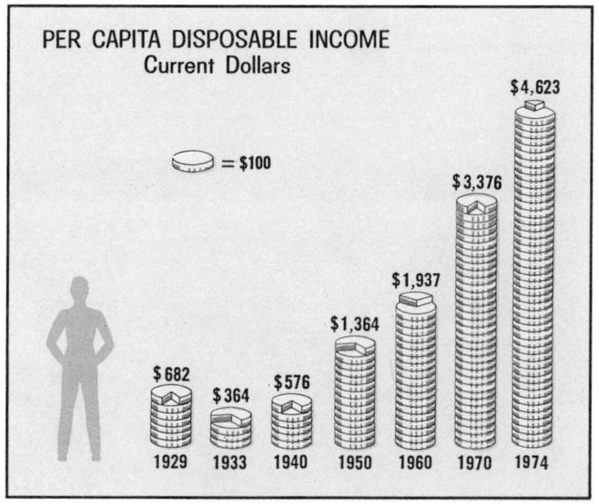

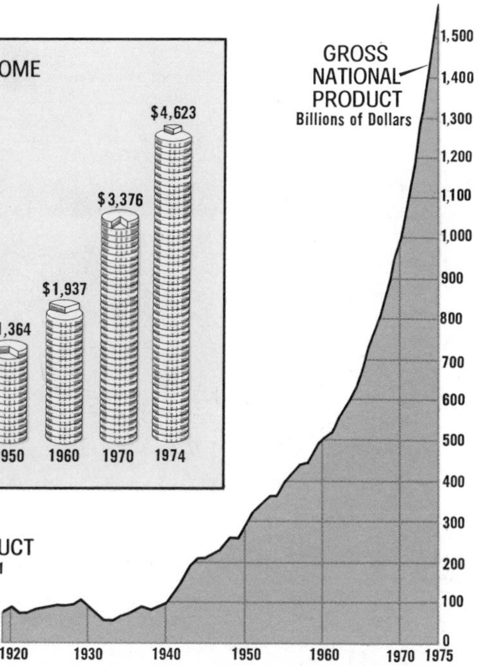

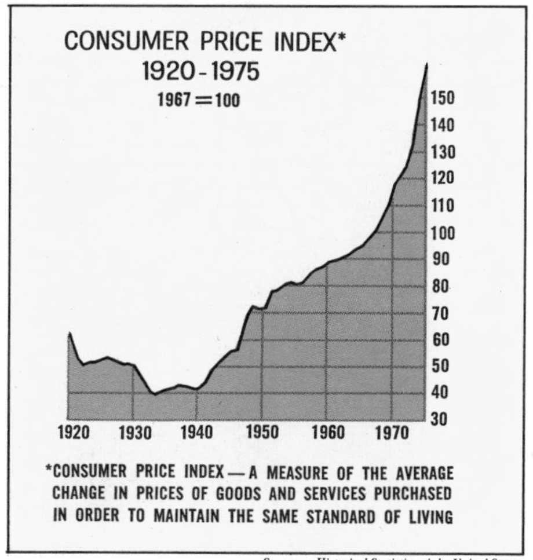

D

GROSS NATIONAL PRODUCT
Billions of Dollars

1,500
1,400
1,300
1,200
1,100
1,000
900
800
700
600
500
400
300
200
100
0

1920 1930 1940 1950 1960 1970 1975

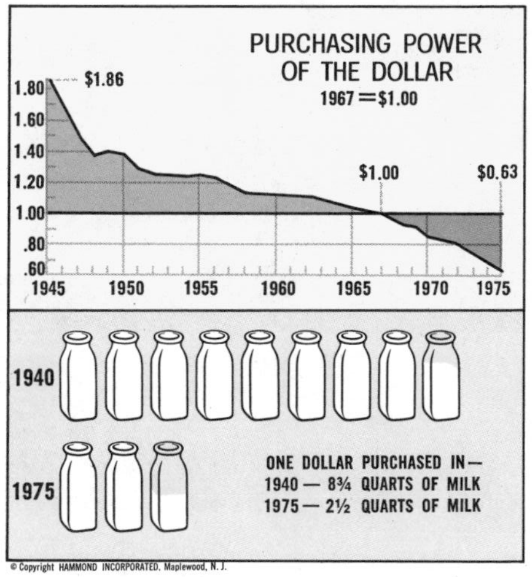

PER CAPITA DISPOSABLE INCOME
Current Dollars

= $100

$4,623 — 1974
$3,376 — 1970
$1,937 — 1960
$1,364 — 1950
$576 — 1940
$364 — 1933
$682 — 1929

GROSS NATIONAL PRODUCT
FIVE YEAR AVERAGES 1892-1921

1892 1900 1910 1920 1921

CONSUMER PRICE INDEX*
1920 - 1975
1967 = 100

150 140 130 120 110 100 90 80 70 60 50 40 30

1920 1930 1940 1950 1960 1970

*CONSUMER PRICE INDEX — A MEASURE OF THE AVERAGE CHANGE IN PRICES OF GOODS AND SERVICES PURCHASED IN ORDER TO MAINTAIN THE SAME STANDARD OF LIVING

PURCHASING POWER OF THE DOLLAR
1967 = $1.00

1.80 1.60 1.40 1.20 1.00 .80 .60

$1.86
$1.00
$0.63

1945 1950 1955 1960 1965 1970 1975

ONE DOLLAR PURCHASED IN—
1940 — 8¾ QUARTS OF MILK
1975 — 2½ QUARTS OF MILK

1940
1975

© Copyright HAMMOND INCORPORATED, Maplewood, N.J.

Sources: Historical Statistics of the United States
Statistical Abstract of the United States

GROWTH OF UNITED STATES ECONOMY
TRANSPORTATION

C

AIRLINES

BILLIONS OF MILES

120 100 80 60 40 20 0

Domestic Passenger-Miles Flown

1930 1940 1950 1960 1970 1974

RAILROADS

1830 23 MILES
1850
1870
1890
1910
1930
1950
1973

The distance between signals represents 25,000-miles of road operated by railroads

ROADS AND MOTOR VEHICLES

MILLION REGISTRATIONS

120 110 100 90 80 70 60 50 40 30 20 10 0

1910 1930 1950 1970 1974

1920 — IN 1920 ONLY 1 OUT OF 13 PEOPLE OWNED A CAR.
1975 — IN 1975 1 OUT OF 2 PEOPLE OWNED A CAR.

Automobile Registration

Total Motor Vehicle Registration

MILES (MILLION)

3.0 2.5 2.0 1.5 1.0 0.5 0

Surfaced Roads

1910 1930 1950 1970 1973

MAJOR EVENTS IN THE GROWTH OF TRANSPORTATION

ERIE CANAL 1825
1830 STEAM LOCOMOTIVE
DRAKE OIL WELL 1859
AIR BRAKE 1868
PULLMAN CAR 1864
FIRST TRANSCONTINENTAL RAILROAD 1869
1887 INTERSTATE COMMERCE ACT
1893 GASOLINE AUTOMOBILE
1903 AIRPLANE WRIGHT BROTHERS
FIRST AIRMAIL SERVICE 1918
AIR COMMERCE ACT 1926
1938 CIVIL AERONAUTICS ACT
NUCLEAR SUBMARINE 1954
FEDERAL-AID HIGHWAY ACT (INTERSTATE SYSTEM) 1958
AMTRAK SETUP 1970
DEPT. OF TRANS. EST. 1966

1820 1840 1860 1880 1900 1920 1940 1960 1970

© Copyright HAMMOND INCORPORATED, Maplewood, N.J.

Sources: Historical Statistics of the United States
Statistical Abstract of the United States

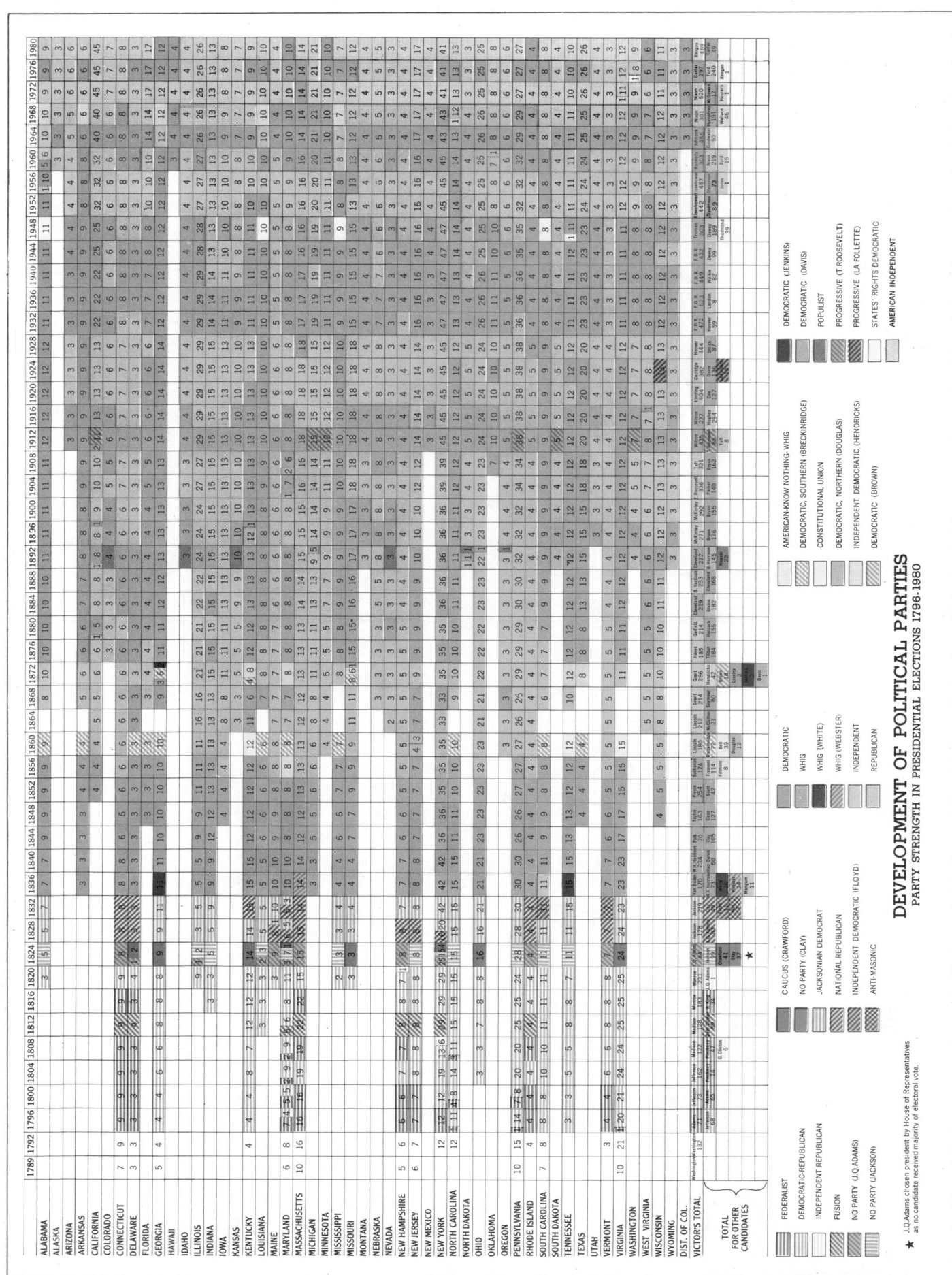

DEVELOPMENT OF POLITICAL PARTIES
PARTY STRENGTH IN PRESIDENTIAL ELECTIONS 1796-1980

★ J.Q.Adams chosen president by House of Representatives as no candidate received majority of electoral vote.

POLITICAL SECTIONALISM 1796-1868
PRESIDENTIAL ELECTORAL VOTE BY STATES AND PARTIES

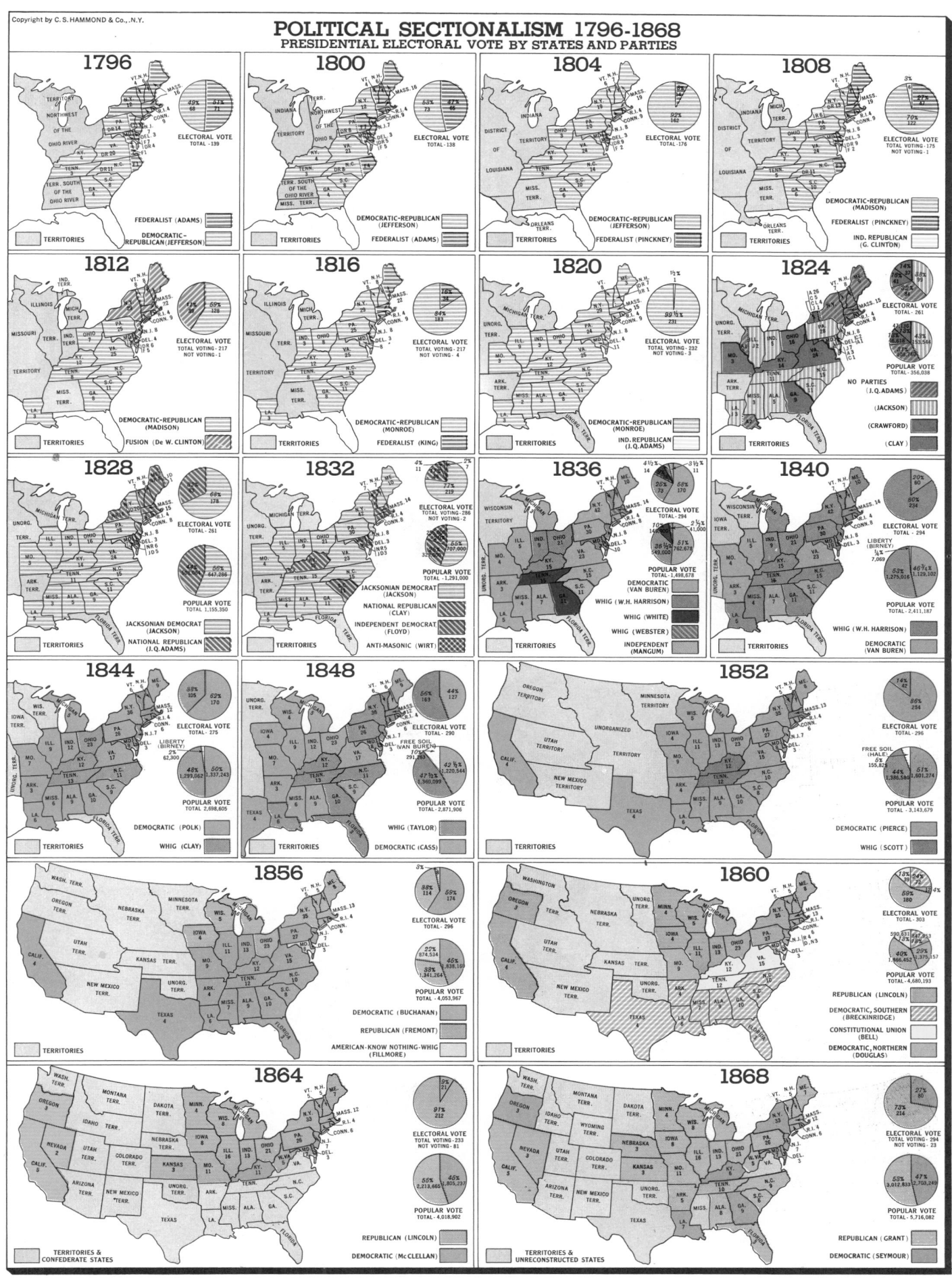

POLITICAL SECTIONALISM 1872-1916
PRESIDENTIAL ELECTORAL VOTE BY STATES AND PARTIES

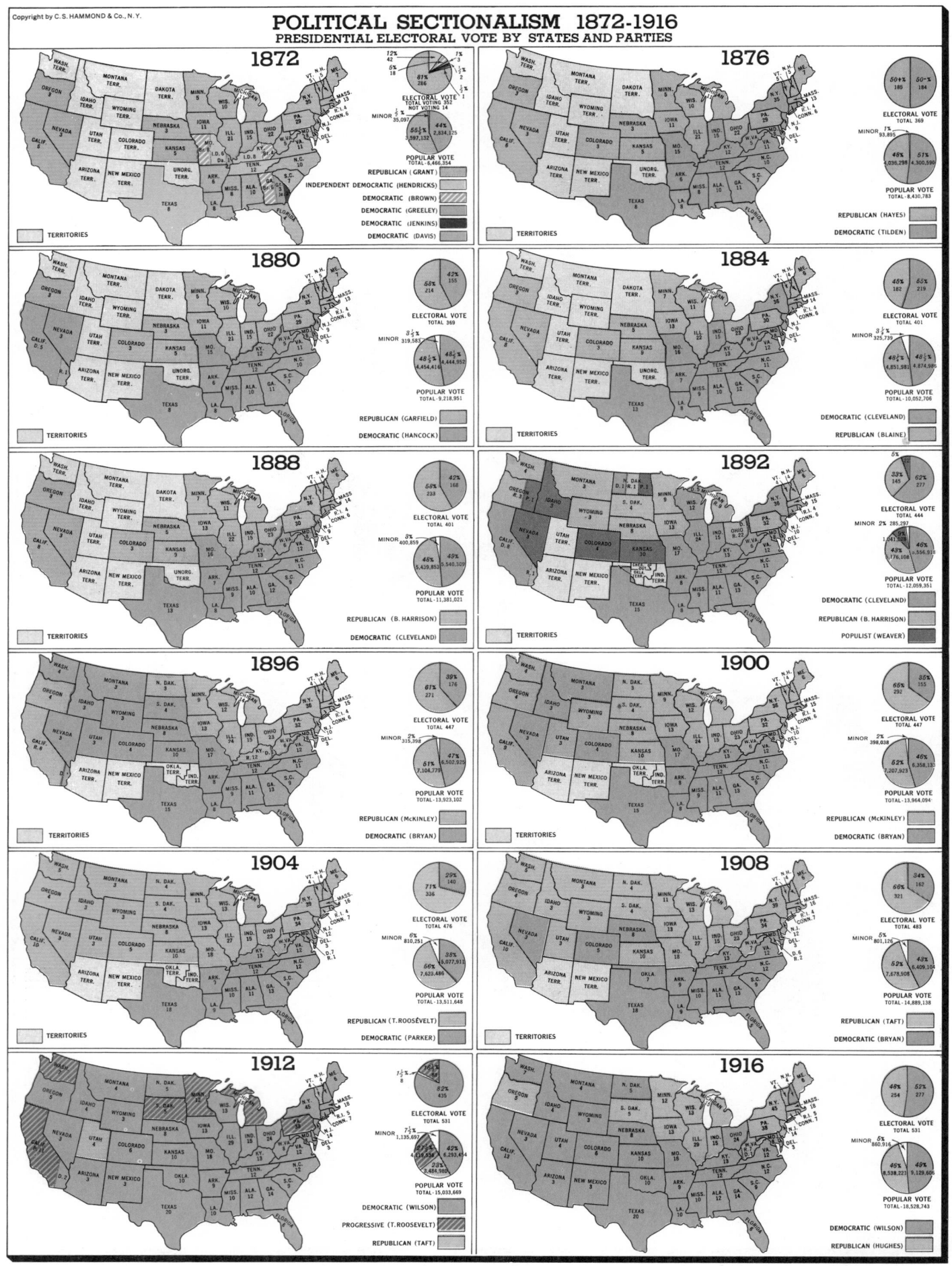

POLITICAL SECTIONALISM 1920-1964
PRESIDENTIAL ELECTORAL VOTE BY STATES AND PARTIES

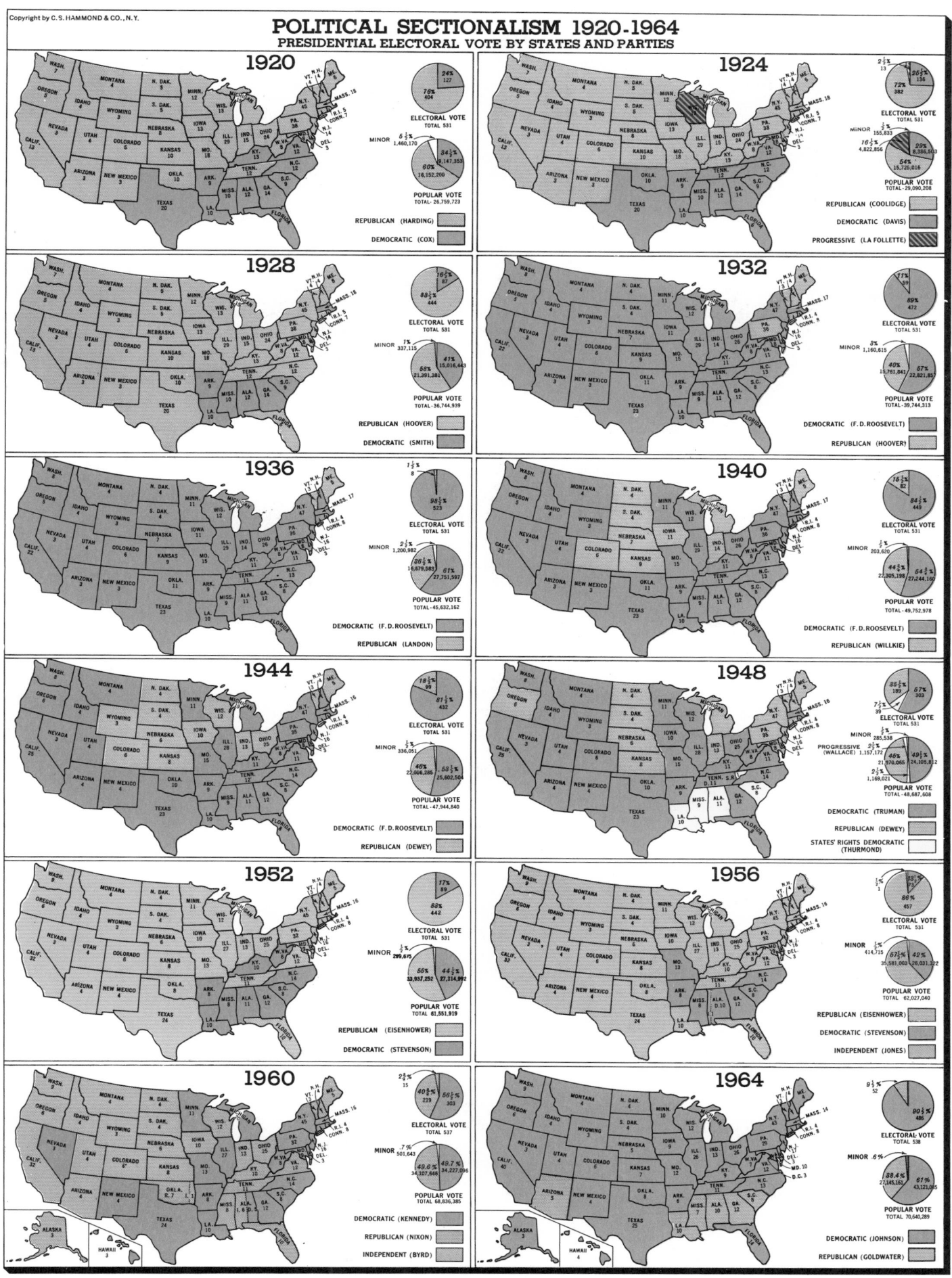

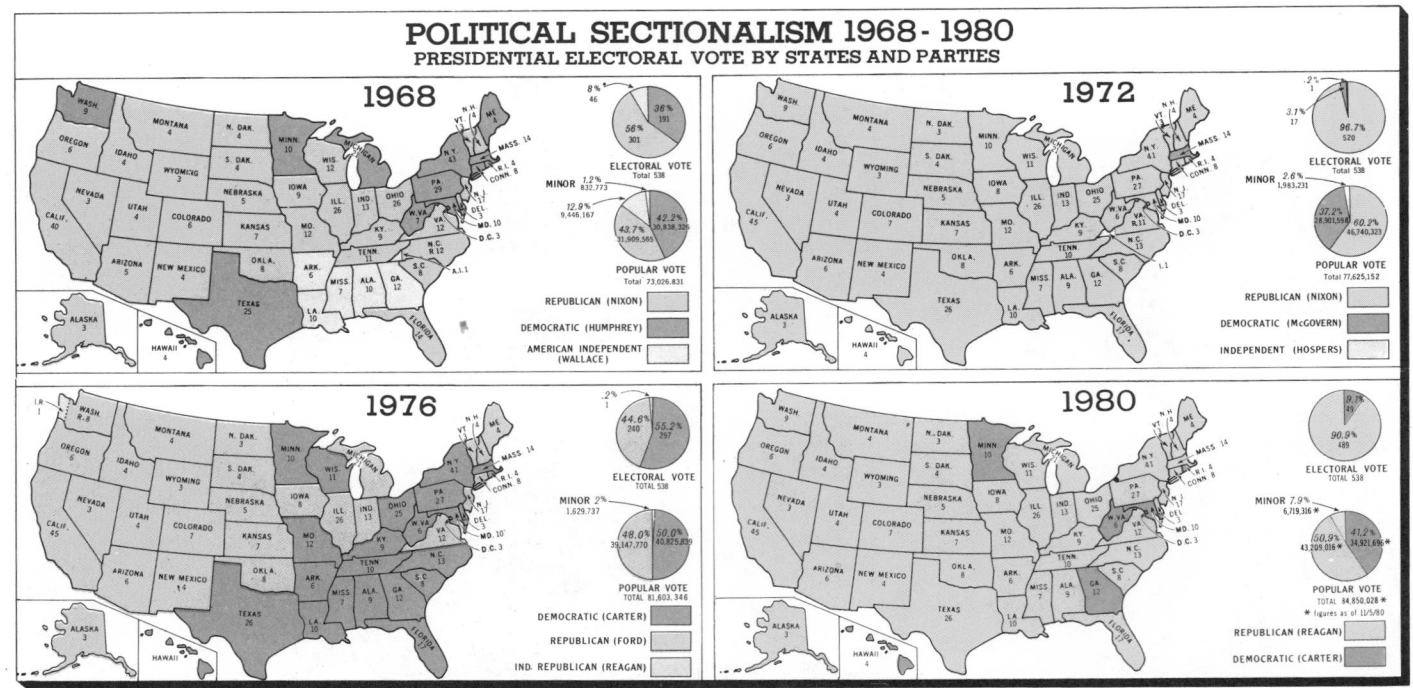

POLITICAL SECTIONALISM 1968-1980
PRESIDENTIAL ELECTORAL VOTE BY STATES AND PARTIES

PRESIDENTS OF THE UNITED STATES

No.	Name	Politics	Native State	Age at Inauguration	Age at Death
1	George Washington	Federalist	Va.	57	67
2	John Adams	Federalist	Mass.	61	90
3	Thomas Jefferson	Rep.-Dem.	Va.	57	83
4	James Madison	Rep.-Dem.	Va.	57	85
5	James Monroe	Rep.-Dem.	Va.	58	73
6	John Quincy Adams	Rep.-Dem.	Mass.	57	80
7	Andrew Jackson	Democrat	S.C.	61	78
8	Martin Van Buren	Democrat	N.Y.	54	79
9	William Henry Harrison	Whig	Va.	68	68
10	John Tyler	Whig	Va.	51	71
11	James Knox Polk	Democrat	N.C.	49	53
12	Zachary Taylor	Whig	Va.	64	65
13	Millard Fillmore	Whig	N.Y.	50	74
14	Franklin Pierce	Democrat	N.H.	48	64
15	James Buchanan	Democrat	Pa.	65	77
16	Abraham Lincoln	Republican	Ky.	52	56
17	Andrew Johnson	Democrat	N.C.	56	66
18	Ulysses Simpson Grant	Republican	Ohio	46	63
19	Rutherford B. Hayes	Republican	Ohio	54	70
20	James Abram Garfield	Republican	Ohio	49	49
21	Chester Alan Arthur	Republican	Vt.	50	56
22	Grover Cleveland	Democrat	N.J.	47	71
23	Benjamin Harrison	Republican	Ohio	55	67
24	Grover Cleveland	Democrat	N.J.	55	71
25	William McKinley	Republican	Ohio	54	58
26	Theodore Roosevelt	Republican	N.Y.	42	60
27	William Howard Taft	Republican	Ohio	51	72
28	Woodrow Wilson	Democrat	Va.	56	67
29	Warren G. Harding	Republican	Ohio	55	57
30	Calvin Coolidge	Republican	Vt.	51	60
31	Herbert Clark Hoover	Republican	Iowa	54	90
32	Franklin D. Roosevelt	Democrat	N.Y.	51	63
33	Harry S. Truman	Democrat	Mo.	60	88
34	Dwight D. Eisenhower	Republican	Texas	62	78
35	John F. Kennedy	Democrat	Mass.	43	46
36	Lyndon B. Johnson	Democrat	Texas	55	64
37	Richard M. Nixon	Republican	Calif.	56	....
38	Gerald R. Ford	Republican	Mich.	61	....
39	James E. Carter, Jr.	Democrat	Ga.	52	....
40	Ronald W. Reagan	Republican	Ill.	69	....

Index

This index lists historically important places, areas, events and geographical features appearing on the maps of the United States History Atlas. Each entry is followed by the page number on which the name appears. The letters following the page number designate a particular map on pages containing more than one map. Names that appear on more than one map are indexed to the map or maps portraying the place at its most historically significant period.